I0605473

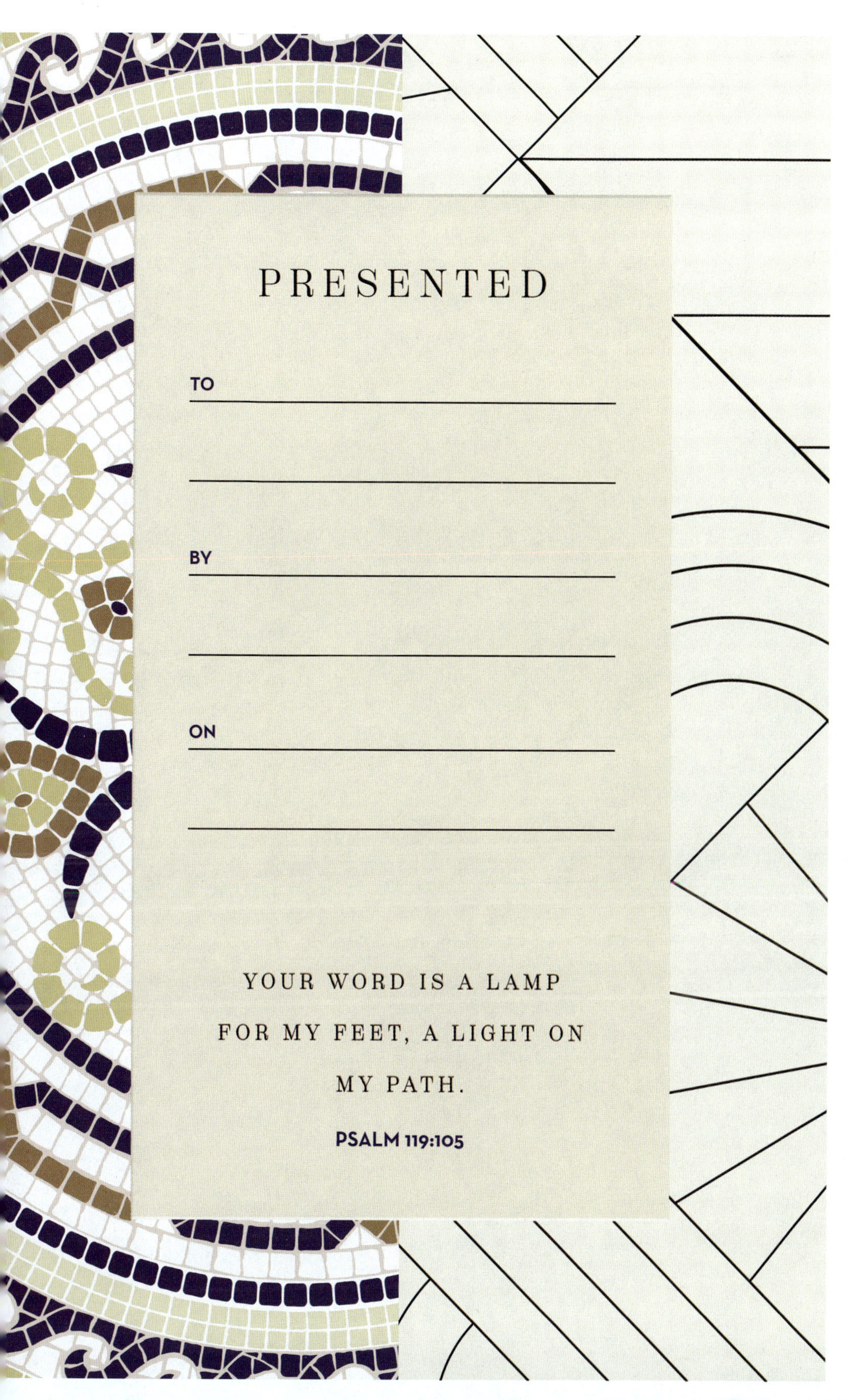
PRESENTED
TO
BY
ON
YOUR WORD IS A LAMP FOR MY FEET, A LIGHT ON MY PATH.
PSALM 119:105

NEW INTERNATIONAL VERSION

NIV
APPLICATION
BIBLE

NEW INTERNATIONAL VERSION

NIV APPLICATION BIBLE

ZONDERVAN®

NIV Application Bible
Published by Zondervan, 2025
3950 Sparks Drive SE, Suite 101, Grand Rapids, Michigan 49546, USA
www.Zondervan.com

This Bible was set in the Zondervan NIV Typeface, created at the 2K/DENMARK type foundry.

Library of Congress Catalog Card Number 2024939522

HarperCollins Publishers, Macken House, 39/40 Mayor Street Upper, Dublin 1, D01 C9W8, Ireland (https://www.harpercollins.com)

Printed in China

---

26 27 28 29 30 31 32 33 34 35 /DSC/ 20 19 18 17 16 15 14 13 12 11 10 9 8 7 6 5 4

A portion of the purchase price of your NIV® Bible is provided to Biblica so together we support the mission of Transforming Lives Through God's Word. Biblica provides God's Word to people through translation, publishing, and Bible engagement in Africa, Asia Pacific, Europe, Latin America, Middle East, and North America. Through its worldwide reach, Biblica engages people with God's Word so that their lives are transformed through a relationship with Jesus Christ.

Contents

Old Testament

New Testament

NIV Application Bible Preface

Welcome to the *NIV Application Bible*, a comprehensive resource designed to enhance your understanding and application of the Word of God. This unique edition has been meticulously crafted to provide both faithful interpretation of God's Word and a practical guide for everyday living.

The Bible's enduring relevance lies in its inspired account of the relationship between God and his people, exploring the human condition and addressing themes such as love, faith, suffering, justice, and redemption. From the creation narrative in Genesis to the prophetic visions of Revelation, the Bible offers insights that resonate across the ancient world and distant locations of the Bible. God has generously provided his Word to speak to the human heart and mind; yet understanding how these ancient texts apply to modern living can be challenging.

The Bible was written in vastly different cultural and historical contexts than the one we live in today, and its original audiences had different worldviews and life experiences. Understanding these contexts is essential for interpreting the text accurately. The study notes in the *NIV Application Bible* have been designed to serve as a bridge from the past to the present, helping readers navigate the cultural and historical gap between the biblical world and the world of today.

In addition, the Bible has always been meant to be read, discussed, and lived out within the context of the larger global community of faith. The study tools in this Bible can serve as a valuable resource for group studies, biblical studies courses, and other settings. These were among the original goals of the NIV Application Commentary series, from which the notes of this study Bible have been derived (for further information, see the Introduction, p. x).

The NIV Application Commentary Resource Series

The *NIV Application Bible* has been designed as part of a wider body of resources, all of which have been crafted to bring the teachings of the Bible to life in today's world. These resources are all based upon the 44-volume NIV Application Commentary series. The *NIV Application Commentary on the Bible, One-Volume Edition* and other Bible study, reference, and devotional resources are part of this wider church-engagement initiative. As you enjoy your new study Bible, the valuable resources in this line are available to augment and deepen your application of God's Word to your life.

A Bible for Deeper Understanding and Connection

Whether you are seeking encouragement, wisdom, or a deeper connection with God, we pray that the *NIV Application Bible* will become an invaluable companion for every season of life.

In his service,
The Zondervan Bibles Publisher
and Editorial Team

NIV Application Bible Introduction

Like the NIV Application Commentary series on which it is based, the *NIV Application Bible* is unique. Most commentaries and study Bibles help us make the journey from the twenty-first century back to the first century. They enable us to cross the barriers of time, culture, language, and geography that separate us from the biblical world. Yet they only offer a one-way ticket to the past and assume that we can somehow make the return journey on our own.

The primary goal of the *NIV Application Bible* is to help you with the vital task of bringing an ancient message into a modern context. It features a comprehensive study system designed to bridge the enduring truths of the Bible in their original biblical, historical contexts with the practical realities of contemporary life. These notes accompany the text of the New International Version of the Bible; they have been carefully curated from the *NIV Application Commentary on the Bible*, which was curated from the larger, bestselling NIV Application Commentary series. Paired with these extensive study notes are many other helpful study features.

The *NIV Application Bible* and the NIV Application Commentary Series

The history of the note structure for this Bible begins in the mid-1990s. That's when the Zondervan Academic team launched a concept for a new resource that would bring the ancient text of the Bible into a modern context in a new way. This massive project was intended to help pastors, teachers, and small-group leaders communicate to others the deeper meanings behind the words of Scripture in a way that would be accessible to all.

Since its release, which spanned over 25 years from the first volume to the last, the NIV Application Commentary series carefully followed a three-part process to help anyone communicate and apply biblical texts effectively in a contemporary context.

To bring the ancient messages of the Bible into today's world, each passage in the commentary series was addressed in three sections: (1) *Original Meaning*: Concise exegesis helped readers understand the original meaning of the biblical text in its historical, literary, and cultural context. (2) *Bridging Contexts*: Writers built a bridge between the world of the Bible and the world of today by discerning what was timeless in the timely pages of the Bible. (3) *Contemporary Significance*: This section identified comparable situations to those faced in the Bible and explored relevant application of the biblical messages.

This unique, award-winning commentary in 44 volumes was curated down to a single volume (see its Introduction, p. xxi), and from that single volume the Zondervan editorial team carefully crafted the study notes of the *NIV Application Bible*. The notes and features of this title were gathered with a view toward giving readers the tools, ideas, and insights they would need to better understand and communicate God's Word with the same powerful impact it had when it was first written.

Features of the *NIV Application Bible*

The NIV Translation: The complete text of the accurate, readable, and clear New International Version (NIV) is the centerpiece of this Bible. The NIV translation team is united by their conviction that the Bible is God's inspired Word. That, along with their individual expertise and career-spanning years spent studying biblical languages, helps the members of this team as they continually review the translation. While updates to the translation are only released periodically, the work of this committee continues as global understanding and use of the English language changes (for more on the committee's process, see the NIV Preface, p. xvii).

The NIV translation has been carefully and thoughtfully designed to provide the best reading experience possible. The goal of the translators is always to convey the meaning of the original documents so that the teachings of the Bible are expressed in a way that is easily accessible to a global English-speaking audience.

A few notes about the NIV translation itself as it appears in the *NIV Application Bible*:

NIV Text Notes/Footnotes: NIV textual notes appear at the bottom of the Bible text in the right-hand column, above the line separating Scripture from study notes. They are indicated in the text by raised italic letters following the words or phrases they explain. An important part of the NIV Committee on Bible Translation's translation process, NIV footnotes examine such things as alternative translations, meanings of Hebrew and Greek terms, and OT quotations and variant readings in ancient biblical manuscripts. There are also some explanatory notes.

The NIV Cross-Reference System: This robust cross-reference system resembles a series of interlocking chains with many links. Within the NIV text, cross references are indicated by raised letters. This system "links" you to other verses that relate to the same topic as that addressed in the verse with the raised letter. Following these links allows readers to deepen their study as they examine related texts in the NIV.

The cross references themselves appear in a center column on the text page. When necessary, they continue at the bottom of the Scripture portion of the page, below the NIV text notes.

The lists of references are in biblical order with one exception: If reference is made to a verse within the same chapter, that verse (indicated by "ver") is listed first. If an OT verse is quoted in the NT, the NT reference is marked with an asterisk (*). When a single word is addressed by both NIV text notes and NIV cross references, the NIV text note letter comes first (again, these are set in italics).

Parallel Passages: When two or more passages of Scripture are nearly identical or deal with the same event, this "parallel" is noted at the sectional headings for those passages, indicated with "//". Such passages are especially common in the books of 1, 2 Samuel; 1, 2 Kings; and 1, 2 Chronicles, as well as in the Gospels of Matthew, Mark, Luke, and John. Identical or nearly identical passages are noted with "pp." Similar passages—those not dealing with the same event—are noted with "Ref."

Each of the study features in the *NIV Application Bible* represent the four pillars of Bible study that we've tried diligently to build into the notes of these study resources: (1) *discovery*, (2) *study*, (3) *connection*, and (4) *application*, represented by this symbol ✜. The design of the Bible has been crafted to remind readers of these four pillars as they see them represented repeatedly on the text pages.

Book Introductions. Located at the start of each Bible book, these 66 introductions are designed to provide perspective and application for every book of the Bible. In these features readers will find unique insights that provide a background for deeper study. Also included in each of these introductions are historical timelines, reading guides, and more.

Author: Moses
Audience: God's chosen people, the Israelites
Date: Between 1446 and 1406 BC

Theme: Genesis is a book of beginnings that introduces central themes of the Bible such as creation and redemption.

PERSPECTIVE

When we think of God, we typically want to jump immediately to what God can do for us. God saves us, we remember. We are grateful. But is this self-centered starting point really the most effective way of thinking about God? Reading Genesis leads one to question whether the above assertion is the best starting point. It certainly wasn't the starting point for Abram and his family. Or better, perhaps, it wasn't the starting point for God as he revealed himself in the book of Genesis.

In Genesis, the starting point was revelation. Especially after the tower of Babel it became evident that people had forgotten who God was. They needed reminding. The moves God made were essentially concerned with putting himself in front of the world's peoples. He covenanted with Abram and his family for them to represent God by the way they lived according to the law they embraced. This covenant is about revelation (what God wants for us), not salvation (what we get from God). God wanted to remind his creation that he was still around: Then you will know that I am Yahweh.

Forgetfulness of God is still a problem. Today it may take a little different form; instead of asking *who* God is, we are more likely to ask *whether* God is. But we are still fixed too narrowly on salvation—what we can get—instead of first opening ourselves to revelation. Because of this we suffer various losses.

The first thing lost is a sense of the distinction between Creator (God) and created (us). Revelation is about God making himself known through creation, through the Holy Spirit, through the mighty acts we celebrate in worship. At the heart of all these "revelations" is

Reading Genesis

Genesis divides into two main sections. Chapters 1-11 describe the origin of the world and God's dealings with the human race in general. Chapters 12-50 describe God's dealings with one particular family: Abraham and his descendants. This book contains the familiar stories of Adam and Eve, Cain and Abel, Noah, Abraham, Isaac, Jacob, and Joseph.

1

Maps and Charts. Helpful, full-color maps and charts have been designed to organize information and give readers the opportunity to envision many different concepts in the Bible. Placed in the Bible specifically where this information will be most relevant to readers, these 46 maps and 52 charts provide detailed overviews of the Bible's people, places, and teachings.

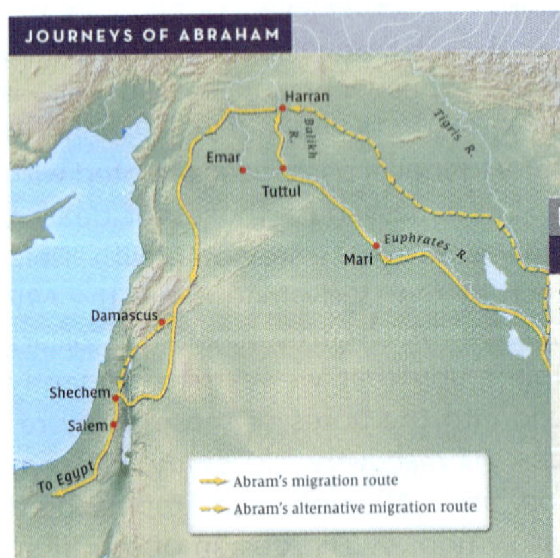

KEY POINTS IN ABRAHAM'S LIFE

EVENT	REFERENCE
God calls Abraham from Haran; Abraham moves his family to Canaan at the age of 75.	Ge 12:1-5
The Altar Narratives—Abraham builds altars to the Lord in several locations: Moreh; between Bethel and Ai; the terebinth trees of Mamre.	Ge 12:7; 12:8; 13:18
The Promise Narratives—God promises Abraham that he will be the father of many nations. Abraham believes God, and his faith is counted to him as righteousness.	Ge 12:2, 7; 13:16; 15:1-6; 17:1-5; 18:9-10; 22:15-17
Abraham journeys to Egypt, risking Sarah's security and compromising his integrity.	Ge 12
Abraham and Lot separate.	Ge 13:7-11
Abraham is blessed by Melchizedek.	Ge 14:18-20
Abraham heeds Sarah's advice, producing Ishmael from his union with Hagar.	Ge 16
The Lord establishes the covenant of circumcision.	Ge 17:9-14
Abraham negotiates for the people of Sodom.	Ge 18:16-33
As before in Egypt, Abraham endangers Sarah to secure his own safety, lying to Abimelech.	Ge 20
Abraham and Sarah have Isaac in their old age.	Ge 21
God tests Abraham's faith, ordering him to sacrifice Isaac as a burnt offering.	Ge 22
Sarah, Abraham's wife and companion, dies.	Ge 23
Abraham ensures that Isaac will find an appropriate mate.	Ge 24
Abraham remarries; he and Keturah have six sons; at 175 years old, Abraham dies.	Ge 25:1-7

Each map and chart has been designed to deepen the reader's understanding. Additionally, 16 pages of full-color maps placed in the back of this Bible provide a helpful visual backdrop for the stories of the Bible.

Original Meaning Notes. The thousands of notes that appear at the bottom of the text pages are designed to help readers understand the meaning of each passage in its context. They have been carefully written and edited by a wide range of faithful evangelical scholars, each of whom added their expertise to one or more volumes of the NIV Application Commentary series. (For a listing of the authors who contributed to the series, see p. 2165.) These notes walk through each passage to illuminate the narrative or reasoning that the biblical author had in mind for that section.

6:14–16 The dimensions of the ark are easy enough to determine, and the general shape of it is therefore discernible. Based on 1 cubit equaling 18 inches, Noah's ark is 450 feet long, 75 feet wide, and 45 feet deep. It is evident that Noah's ark was not designed to be navigated. Consequently, the fate of the company aboard was left in the hands of God.
6:17 The Hebrew word for Noah's flood is used twelve times in Ge 6–11. Broader cultural usage suggests that the word may have had broader currency as a cosmic water weapon wielded by a deity.
6:19–20; 7:2–3 While the initial instructions indicate that pairs of all living creatures are to be taken into the ark, when more specific instructions are given, one pair each of unclean animals and seven pairs each of clean animals are to be taken. The distinction between clean and unclean animals was not an innovation established at Sinai but is seen here as early as Noah.

Application Notes. These notes, placed alongside the Original Meaning Notes in highlighted boxes and marked with the application symbol (✜), are what make the *NIV Application Bible* unique from other study Bibles. Based on the meaning of the passage explored through the Original Meaning notes, these notes bring real-time application designed to help readers connect the changeless truths of Scripture with their daily experiences.

These notes offer practical insights that encourage readers to reflect on how the teachings of the Bible can inform their actions, decisions, and relationships. By providing concrete examples and contemporary analogies, these application notes make the Bible's messages more accessible and actionable so that God's Word can penetrate deep into readers' hearts and minds.

✜ **13:1—15:21** When God doesn't perform his operations in nanoseconds, our impatience begins to show as our expectations go unfulfilled. There is a certain tension between expectations and relationship.

Relationships operate in the here and now, while expectations are always looking to the future. Parents who cherish each stage of development and focus on the present tolerate whatever drawbacks accompany each stage so that they can enjoy their child. This is the focus on *present relationship* rather than *future expectation.* If we are to achieve the goal of putting relationships ahead of expectations, we must learn to see relationships as of greater consequence than expectations.

Questions for Growth. Nearly 1200 application questions can be found in smaller boxes toward the top of the text pages. These small notes, accompanying every chapter in the Bible, have been designed to help readers reflect on how they can better apply Scripture to life. They include suggestions for prayer, reflection, and action, helping readers integrate the lessons learned into their daily decisions and routines. Each of these has been designed to foster a deeper connection with God through the nurture of one's personal spiritual growth.

Ge 5:21–24 ✜ Enoch is a mysterious figure. He walked faithfully with God, and "God took him away" (v. 24). What does walking faithfully with God mean for us today?

People to Know Articles. Through over 150 articles, readers will be able to learn lessons for their own lives based on the lives of Bible characters. These brief studies show how God accomplished his purposes through the people in the Bible, giving us encouragement and insight into ways we can live a faithful life before God.

Through studying the lives of these men and women of the Bible, readers will gain a sense of God's care and concern for the individual; of his daily oversight and gentle leading in the lives of those who have followed in his way—or who perhaps haven't. The application sections (marked with ✣) of these features can help us see and understand how to integrate these life lessons into our daily experiences. For an index listing all of these articles, see p. 2161.

PEOPLE TO KNOW // **ADAM**

GENESIS 2:7–9: Adam is the first human named in the Bible. God formed him out of the dust of the earth; Adam's name can be translated "from the ground." God placed Adam in a special garden called Eden to care for God's beautiful creation (Ge 2:15).

God also created a woman, Eve, and she and Adam together cared for the garden. At first everything was wonderful. Adam and Eve lived free from all sin and shame. They could walk and talk with God himself.

One day, however, the serpent tempted them to eat from the one tree God had forbidden them to eat of: the tree of the knowledge of good and evil. Deceived by the serpent, Eve took some fruit and shared it with Adam. Suddenly, sin entered creation, as did the shameful reality of its consequences. God was merciful and covered their shame. But God punished Adam and Eve for disobeying his specific commands. They were exiled from the garden. For this first couple, the ground itself came under a curse (Ge 3:17).

Adam's grief was not over. Adam and Eve had two sons: Cain and Abel. In the course of time, Cain's envy and anger led him to kill his brother. The effects of Adam's sin rippled outward. And we still feel them today.

APPLICATION ✣ Adam sinned by trying to put himself in God's place. The serpent told him and Eve that if they ate the forbidden fruit, they would be like God. By giving in to that temptation, Adam and Eve also showed that he wanted to remove God as the ultimate autho

The temptat
In his mercy, h
came to show
rection. Thoug
can be free of t

CHARACTER OF GOD // **GOD IS CREATOR**

Genesis 1:1: In the beginning God created the heavens and the earth.

At the beginning of the Bible, God is introduced as the great Creator. God spoke the universe into being and ordered it according to his plan. God created humankind in his image and gave them a privileged place in his creation (Ge 1:26–30). Everything that God created was good.

Since God created everything, all creation testifies to his greatness. Psalm 19:1 says that the heavens declare God's glory and the skies proclaim his handiwork. Everything around us—all that microscopes and telescopes reveal, all that science discovers—witnesses to God's creative majesty.

God created not only all that is visible but also everything invisible. The heavenly host of angels is no less God's creation than the earth and humans. Everything that is not God himself was created by God—an act of selfless love. God is self-sufficient and did not need to create anything in order to be complete, but out of love he created everything (see Ac 17:25).

Even after humanity's fall into sin, God's creation remained good, though it now suffers under the weight of a curse (Ro 8:22). First Timothy 4:4 teaches that everything God created is good and no part of it should be rejected if it is received with thanksgiving. After all, each new tree, sunset, and human baby is a creation of God. The Lord is not finished creating!

APPLICATION ✣ Understanding God as the great Creator should give us respect and love for the world around us. Creation continues to point us to God, and the beauty of the world should lift our hearts toward praise and gratitude, since it is a large portion of his witness to the world (Ro 1:18–20). Furthermore, God's creative nature is passed to humans as his image bearers in the world: Humans can glorify God by cultivating our own capacity to create.

Character of God Articles. These 52 articles explore aspects of God's character and what they mean for our lives as believers. Designed to give readers a glimpse into many different facets of who God is, how he sees us, and what he has done in the world, these articles also include application sections (marked with ✣) specifically designed to give readers insight into how a better understanding of God's character can change our lives today. For an index listing all of these articles, see p. 2161.

Other Helpful Study Tools

- *Chart Your Course* includes topical, annual, and three-year reading plans to help readers study at their own pace. Designed to appeal to readers who enjoy a consistent approach to Bible reading, these reading plans allow students of the Bible the opportunity to choose the plan that best fits their interests and schedule (see p. 2167).
- *The NIV Dictionary-Concordance* is a reference tool that both defines terms and helps readers find Bible stories, teachings, and characters within the text. By looking up key words, students of the Bible can find verses for which they remember a word or two but not their location. This helpful study tool essentially provides an overview and a glossary of the Bible's key teachings and events (see p. 2181).
- *Indexes* for the maps, charts, and the Character of God and People to Know articles help readers to quickly and easily find information on topics that suit their study interests (see p. 2161).

As you embark on your journey through your new *NIV Application Bible*, the authors and editors of this volume invite you to allow the ancient words to speak to you in new and profound ways, and let the study tools provided guide you in applying these unshakable truths to your everyday life.

Free Digital Access to the *NIV Application Bible*

As an owner of the *NIV Application Bible*, you now have complimentary digital access to all its invaluable study notes and resources through the free NIV Bible app. In the NIV Bible app, you can keep the *NIV Application Bible* in your pocket via your mobile device and take it with you everywhere you go.

Here's what you'll find in the app:

- Free access to the NIV, plus bonus access to the New International Reader's Version (NIrV) and the Spanish translation, Nueva Versión Internacional (NVI).
- All the content in the *NIV Application Bible*, including study notes, book introductions, articles, maps, and more
- New ways to connect digitally with the *NIV Application Bible*. You'll be able to:
  - Create a custom reading plan
  - Easily search for any key word or phrase
  - Make study personal by taking verse notes, saving Bible verses, and highlighting Scripture passages using over 100 colors
  - And much more

To get started, use your camera app to scan the QR code, which will provide further instructions to access the NIV Bible app and unlock your digital *NIV Application Bible* content.

Scan here to unlock your complimentary digital access

NIV Preface

The goal of the New International Version (NIV) is to enable English-speaking people from around the world to read and hear God's eternal Word in their own language. Our work as translators is motivated by our conviction that the Bible is God's Word in written form. We believe that the Bible contains the divine answer to the deepest needs of humanity, sheds unique light on our path in a dark world and sets forth the way to our eternal well-being. Out of these deep convictions, we have sought to recreate as far as possible the experience of the original audience—blending transparency to the original text with accessibility for the millions of English speakers around the world. We have prioritized accuracy, clarity and literary quality with the goal of creating a translation suitable for public and private reading, evangelism, teaching, preaching, memorizing and liturgical use. We have also sought to preserve a measure of continuity with the long tradition of translating the Scriptures into English.

The complete NIV Bible was first published in 1978. It was a completely new translation made by over a hundred scholars working directly from the best available Hebrew, Aramaic and Greek texts. The translators came from the United States, Great Britain, Canada, Australia and New Zealand, giving the translation an international scope. They were from many denominations and churches—including Anglican, Assemblies of God, Baptist, Brethren, Christian Reformed, Church of Christ, Evangelical Covenant, Evangelical Free, Lutheran, Mennonite, Methodist, Nazarene, Presbyterian, Wesleyan and others. This breadth of denominational and theological perspective helped to safeguard the translation from sectarian bias. For these reasons, and by the grace of God, the NIV has gained a wide readership in all parts of the English-speaking world.

The work of translating the Bible is never finished. As good as they are, English translations must be regularly updated so that they will continue to communicate accurately the meaning of God's Word. Updates are needed in order to reflect the latest developments in our understanding of the biblical world and its languages and to keep pace with changes in English usage. Recognizing, then, that the NIV would retain its ability to communicate God's Word accurately only if it were regularly updated, the original translators established the Committee on Bible Translation (CBT). The Committee is a self-perpetuating group of biblical scholars charged with keeping abreast of advances in biblical scholarship and changes in English and issuing periodic updates to the NIV. The CBT is an independent, self-governing body and has sole responsibility for the NIV text. The Committee mirrors the original group of translators in its diverse international and denominational makeup and in its unifying commitment to the Bible as God's inspired Word.

In obedience to its mandate, the Committee has issued periodic updates to the NIV. An initial revision was released in 1984. A more thorough revision process was completed in 2005, resulting in the separately published TNIV. The updated NIV you now have in your hands builds on both the original NIV and the TNIV and represents the latest effort of the Committee to articulate God's unchanging Word in the way the original authors might have said it had they been speaking in English to the global English-speaking audience today.

Translation Philosophy

The Committee's translating work has been governed by three widely accepted principles about the way people use words and about the way we understand them.

First, the meaning of words is determined by the way that users of the language actually use them at any given time. For the biblical languages, therefore, the Committee utilizes the best and most recent scholarship on the way Hebrew, Aramaic and Greek words were being used in biblical times. At the same time, the Committee carefully studies the state of modern English. Good translation is like good communication: one must know the target audience so that the appropriate choices can be made about which English words to use to represent the original words of Scripture. From its inception, the NIV has had as its target the general English-speaking population all over the world, the "International" in its title reflecting this concern. The aim of the Committee is to put the Scriptures into natural English that will communicate effectively with the broadest possible audience of English speakers.

Modern technology has enhanced the Committee's ability to choose the right English words to convey the meaning of the original text. The field of computational linguistics harnesses the power of computers to provide broadly applicable and current data about the state of the language. Translators can now access huge databases of modern English to better understand the current meaning and usage of key words. The Committee utilized this resource in preparing the 2011 edition of the NIV. An area of especially rapid and significant change in English is the way certain nouns and pronouns are used to refer to human beings. The Committee therefore requested experts in computational linguistics at Collins Dictionaries to pose some key questions about this usage to its database of English—the largest in the world, with over 4.4 billion words, gathered from several English-speaking countries and including both spoken and written English. (The Collins Study, called "The Development and Use of Gender Language in Contemporary English," can be accessed at *http://www.thenivbible.com/about-the-niv/about-the-2011-edition/*.) The study revealed that the most popular words to describe the human race in modern U.S. English were "humanity," "man" and "mankind." The Committee then used this data in the updated NIV, choosing from among these three words (and occasionally others also) depending on the context.

A related issue creates a larger problem for modern translations: the move away from using the third-person masculine singular pronouns—"he/him/his"—to refer to men and women equally. This usage does persist in some forms of English, and this revision therefore occasionally uses these pronouns in a generic sense. But the tendency, recognized in day-to-day usage and confirmed by the Collins study, is away from the generic use of "he," "him" and "his." In recognition of this shift in language and in an effort to translate into the natural English that people are actually using, this revision of the NIV generally uses other constructions when the biblical text is plainly addressed to men and women equally. The reader will encounter especially frequently a "they," "their" or "them" to express a generic singular idea. Thus, for instance, Mark 8:36 reads: "What good is it for someone to gain the whole world, yet forfeit their soul?" This generic use of the "distributive" or "singular" "they/them/their" has been used for many centuries by respected writers of English and has now become established as standard English, spoken and written, all over the world.

A second linguistic principle that feeds into the Committee's translation work is that meaning is found not in individual words, as vital as they are, but in larger clusters: phrases, clauses, sentences, discourses. Translation is not, as many people think, a matter of word substitution: English word *x* in place of Hebrew word *y*. Translators must first determine the meaning of the words of the biblical languages in the context of the passage and then select English words that accurately communicate that meaning to modern listeners and readers. This means that accurate translation will not always reflect the exact structure of the original language. To be sure, there is debate over the degree to which translators should try to preserve the "form" of the original text in English. From the beginning, the NIV has taken a mediating position on this issue. The manual produced when the translation that became the NIV was first being planned states: "If the Greek or Hebrew syntax has a good parallel in modern English, it should be used. But if there is no good parallel, the English syntax appropriate to the meaning of the original is to be chosen." It is fine, in other words, to carry over the form of the biblical languages into English—but not at the expense of natural expression. The principle that meaning resides in larger clusters of words means that the Committee has not insisted on a "word-for-word" approach to translation. We certainly believe that every word of Scripture is inspired by God and therefore to be carefully studied to determine what God is saying to us. It is for this reason that the Committee labors over every single word of the original texts, working hard to determine how each of those words contributes to what the text is saying. Ultimately, however, it is how these individual words function in combination with other words that determines meaning.

A third linguistic principle guiding the Committee in its translation work is the recognition that words have a spectrum of meaning. It is popular to define a word by using another word, or "gloss," to substitute for it. This substitute word is then sometimes called the "literal" meaning of a word. In fact, however, words have a range of possible meanings. Those meanings will vary depending on the context, and words in one language will usually not occupy the same semantic range as words in another language. The Committee therefore studies each original word of Scripture in its context to identify its meaning in a particular verse and then chooses an appropriate English word (or phrase) to represent it. It is impossible, then, to translate any given Hebrew, Aramaic or Greek word with the same English word all the time. The Committee does try to translate related occurrences of a word in the original languages with the same English word in order to preserve the connection for the English reader. But the Committee generally privileges clear natural meaning over a concern with consistency in rendering particular words.

Textual Basis

For the Old Testament the standard Hebrew text, the Masoretic Text as published in the latest edition of *Biblia Hebraica*, has been used throughout. The Masoretic Text tradition contains marginal notations that offer variant readings. These have sometimes been followed instead of the text itself. Because such instances involve variants within the Masoretic tradition, they have not been indicated in the textual notes. In a few cases, words in the basic consonantal text have been divided differently than in the Masoretic Text. Such cases are usually indicated in the textual footnotes. The Dead Sea Scrolls contain biblical texts that represent an earlier stage of the transmission of the Hebrew text. They have been consulted, as have been the Samaritan Pentateuch and the ancient scribal traditions concerning deliberate textual changes. The translators also consulted the more important early versions. Readings from these versions, the Dead Sea Scrolls and the scribal traditions were occasionally followed where the Masoretic Text seemed doubtful and where accepted principles of textual criticism showed that one or more of these textual witnesses appeared to provide the correct reading. In rare cases, the translators have emended the Hebrew text where it appears to have become corrupted at an even earlier stage of its transmission. These departures from the Masoretic Text are also indicated in the textual footnotes. Sometimes the vowel indicators (which are later additions to the basic consonantal text) found in the Masoretic Text did not, in the judgment of the translators, represent the correct vowels for the original text. Accordingly, some words have been read with a different set of vowels. These instances are usually not indicated in the footnotes.

The Greek text used in translating the New Testament has been an eclectic one,

editorial counterparts for Zondervan Academic. We set out with specific guidelines when it came to the abridgment, namely, significantly reducing book introductions and outlines; removing the Bridging Contexts sections; avoiding footnotes and internal notes unless otherwise necessary; updating NIV quotations and references to the NIV 2011; and revising, when necessary, content in the Contemporary Application section. The format of each book with its commentary includes the following: Introduction, Book Outline, Original Meaning, and Application.

Abridgment did not fall on our plates exclusively. When it became clear that our editorial plates were too full to make significant progress on the project, we chose the abridging assistance of our esteemed friend, pastor, and co-laborer, Adam T. Barr. After Adam finished his work, Nancy and Chris reviewed every line, making changes and updates as we deemed necessary and regularly referring to the original published volumes.

Like the initial purpose of the multivolume NIVAC set, we hope that the one-volume commentary finds its way into the hands of the church. May it be an ever-rich resource pointing to the reading and study of Scripture.

Nancy L. Erickson
Old Testament editor

Christopher A. Beetham,
New Testament editor

Old Testament Chronology

?	?	?	?

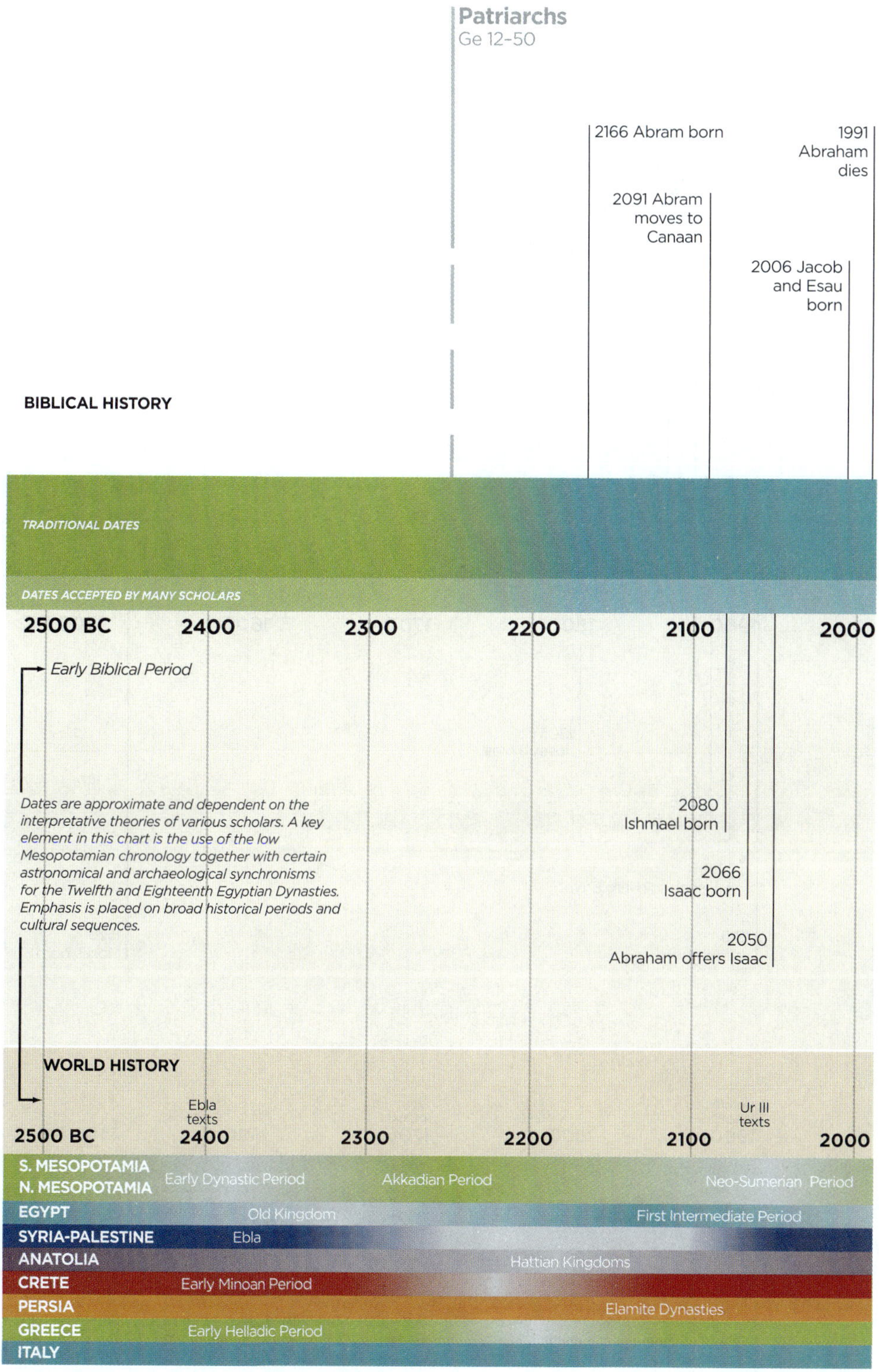

Patriarchs
Ge 12–50

2166 Abram born

1991 Abraham dies

2091 Abram moves to Canaan

2006 Jacob and Esau born

BIBLICAL HISTORY

TRADITIONAL DATES

DATES ACCEPTED BY MANY SCHOLARS

2500 BC **2400** **2300** **2200** **2100** **2000**

Early Biblical Period

Dates are approximate and dependent on the interpretative theories of various scholars. A key element in this chart is the use of the low Mesopotamian chronology together with certain astronomical and archaeological synchronisms for the Twelfth and Eighteenth Egyptian Dynasties. Emphasis is placed on broad historical periods and cultural sequences.

2080 Ishmael born

2066 Isaac born

2050 Abraham offers Isaac

WORLD HISTORY

Ebla texts

Ur III texts

2500 BC **2400** **2300** **2200** **2100** **2000**

S. MESOPOTAMIA
N. MESOPOTAMIA Early Dynastic Period; Akkadian Period; Neo-Sumerian Period

EGYPT Old Kingdom; First Intermediate Period

SYRIA-PALESTINE Ebla

ANATOLIA Hattian Kingdoms

CRETE Early Minoan Period

PERSIA Elamite Dynasties

GREECE Early Helladic Period

ITALY

1929 Jacob flees to Harran

1876 Jacob and family settle in Egypt

1859 Jacob dies

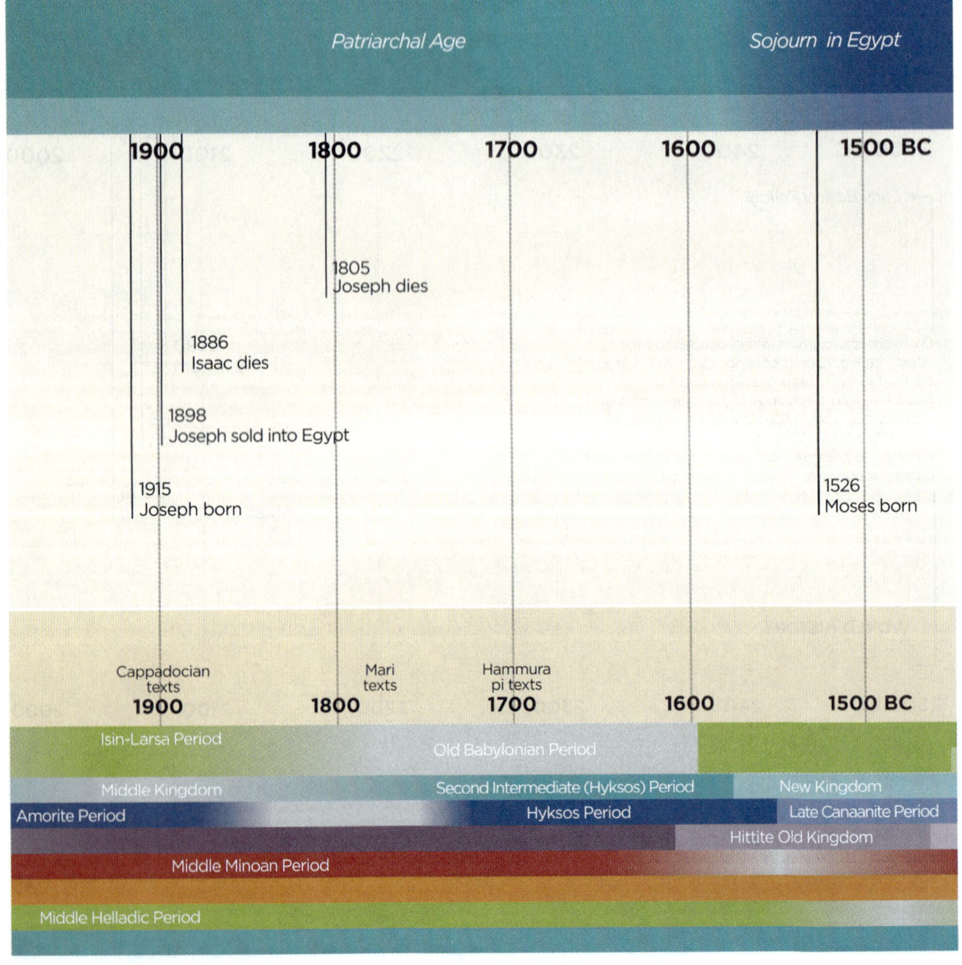

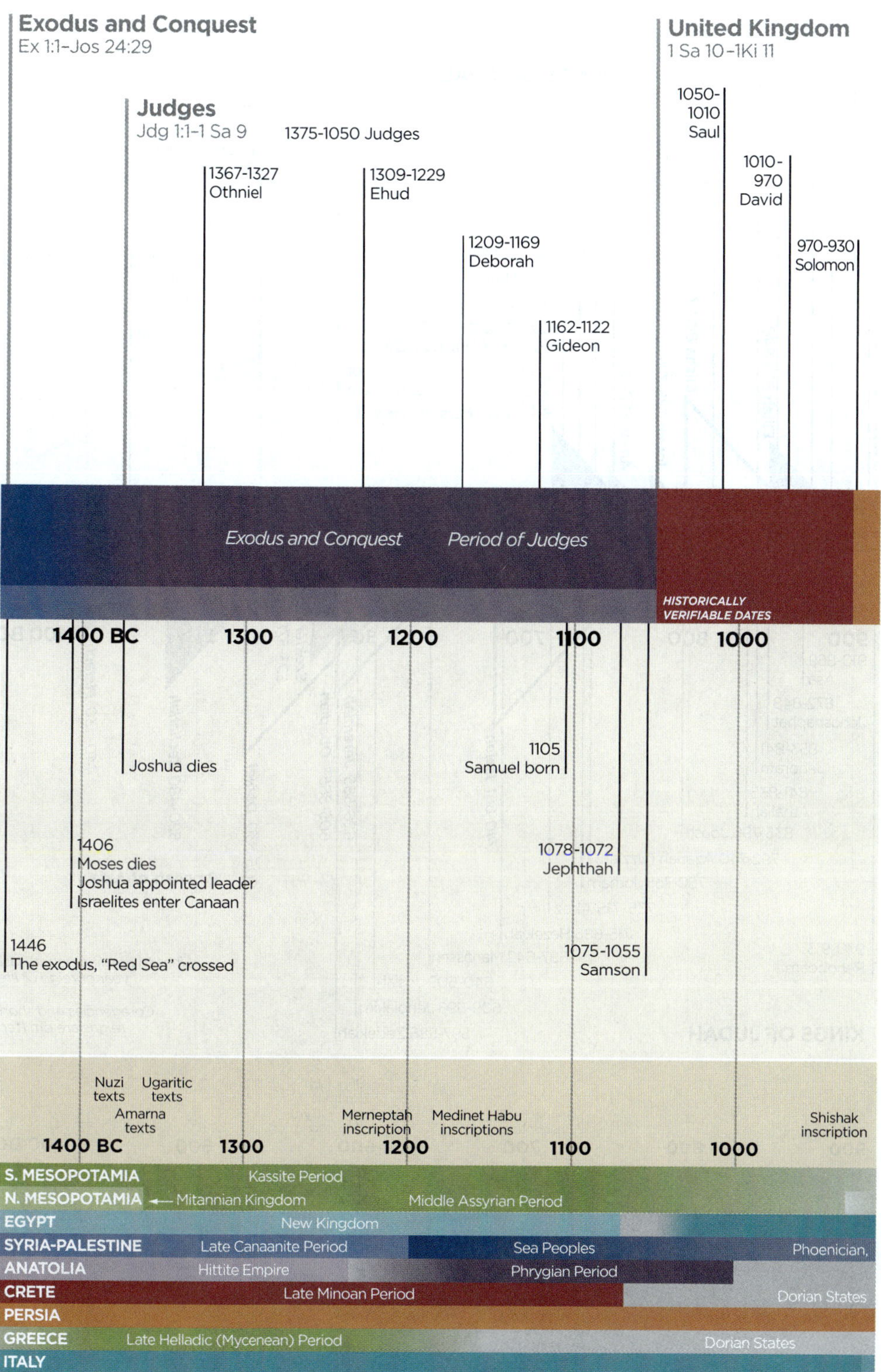
Exodus and Conquest
Ex 1:1–Jos 24:29
Judges
Jdg 1:1–1 Sa 9
1375-1050 Judges
1367-1327 Othniel
1309-1229 Ehud
1209-1169 Deborah
1162-1122 Gideon
United Kingdom
1 Sa 10–1Ki 11
1050-1010 Saul
1010-970 David
970-930 Solomon
Exodus and Conquest
Period of Judges
HISTORICALLY VERIFIABLE DATES
1400 BC
1300
1200
1100
1000
Joshua dies
1105 Samuel born
1406 Moses dies Joshua appointed leader Israelites enter Canaan
1078-1072 Jephthah
1446 The exodus, "Red Sea" crossed
1075-1055 Samson
Nuzi texts
Ugaritic texts
Amarna texts
Merneptah inscription
Medinet Habu inscriptions
Shishak inscription
1400 BC
1300
1200
1100
1000
S. MESOPOTAMIA
Kassite Period
N. MESOPOTAMIA
Mitannian Kingdom
Middle Assyrian Period
EGYPT
New Kingdom
SYRIA-PALESTINE
Late Canaanite Period
Sea Peoples
Phoenician,
ANATOLIA
Hittite Empire
Phrygian Period
CRETE
Late Minoan Period
Dorian States
PERSIA
GREECE
Late Helladic (Mycenean) Period
Dorian States
ITALY

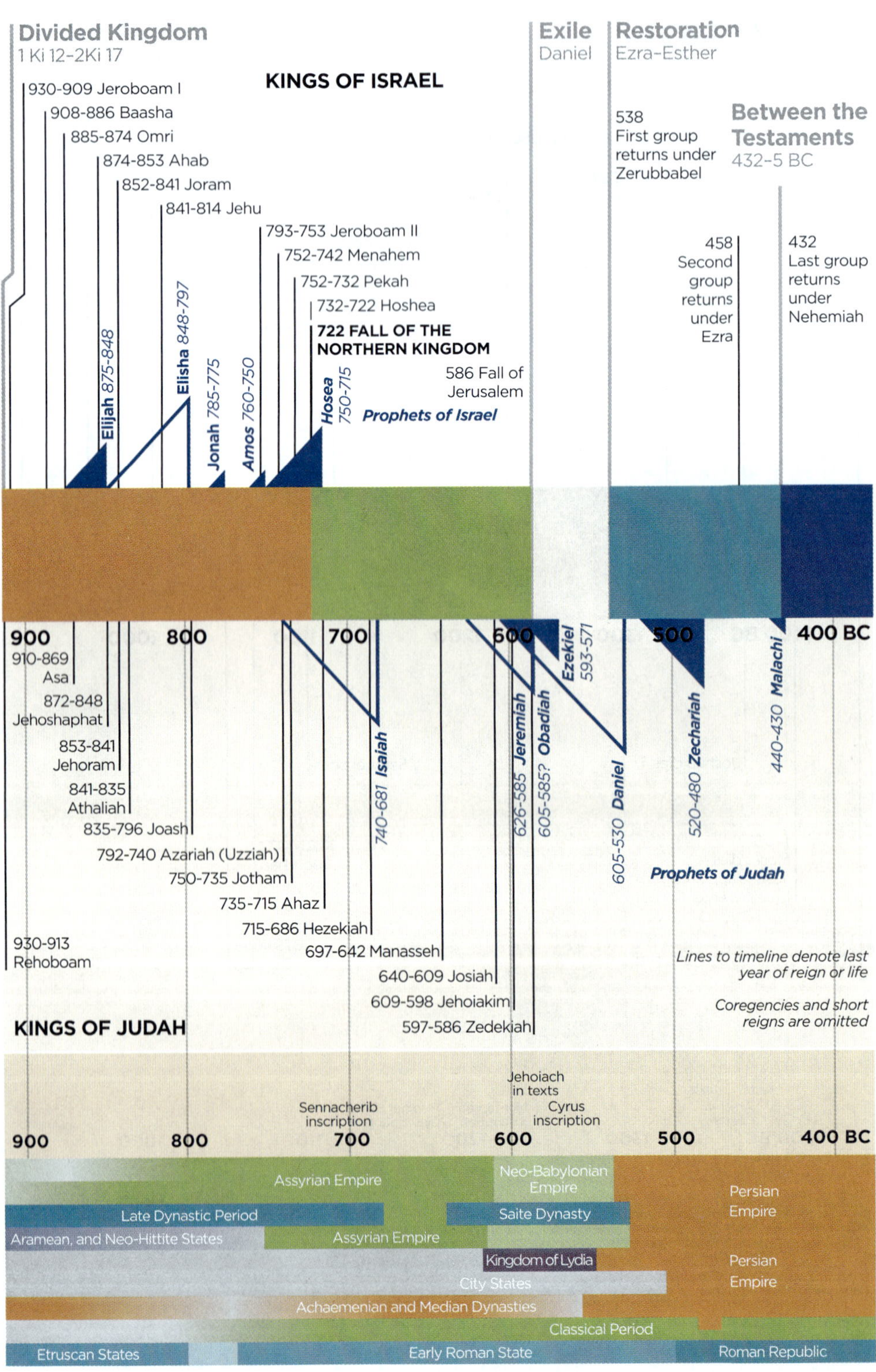

Divided Kingdom
1 Ki 12–2Ki 17
Exile
Daniel
Restoration
Ezra–Esther
KINGS OF ISRAEL
930-909 Jeroboam I
908-886 Baasha
885-874 Omri
874-853 Ahab
852-841 Joram
841-814 Jehu
793-753 Jeroboam II
752-742 Menahem
752-732 Pekah
732-722 Hoshea
722 FALL OF THE NORTHERN KINGDOM
586 Fall of Jerusalem
538 First group returns under Zerubbabel
Between the Testaments
432–5 BC
458 Second group returns under Ezra
432 Last group returns under Nehemiah
Elijah 875-848
Elisha 848-797
Jonah 785-775
Amos 760-750
Hosea 750-715
Prophets of Israel
900
800
700
600
500
400 BC
910-869 Asa
872-848 Jehoshaphat
853-841 Jehoram
841-835 Athaliah
835-796 Joash
792-740 Azariah (Uzziah)
750-735 Jotham
735-715 Ahaz
715-686 Hezekiah
697-642 Manasseh
640-609 Josiah
609-598 Jehoiakim
597-586 Zedekiah
930-913 Rehoboam
KINGS OF JUDAH
740-681 Isaiah
626-585 Jeremiah
605-585? Obadiah
Ezekiel 593-571
605-530 Daniel
520-480 Zechariah
440-430 Malachi
Prophets of Judah
Lines to timeline denote last year of reign or life
Coregencies and short reigns are omitted
Sennacherib inscription
Jehoiach in texts
Cyrus inscription
900
800
700
600
500
400 BC
Assyrian Empire
Neo-Babylonian Empire
Persian Empire
Late Dynastic Period
Saite Dynasty
Aramean, and Neo-Hittite States
Assyrian Empire
Kingdom of Lydia
Persian Empire
City States
Achaemenian and Median Dynasties
Classical Period
Etruscan States
Early Roman State
Roman Republic

THE OLD TESTAMENT

Genesis

Author: Moses

Audience: God's chosen people, the Israelites

Date: Between 1446 and 1406 BC

Theme: Genesis is a book of beginnings that introduces central themes of the Bible such as creation and redemption.

PERSPECTIVE

When we think of God, we typically want to jump immediately to what God can do for us. God saves us, we remember. We are grateful. But is this self-centered starting point really the most effective way of thinking about God? Reading Genesis leads one to question whether the above assertion is the best starting point. It certainly wasn't the starting point for Abram and his family. Or better, perhaps, it wasn't the starting point for God as he revealed himself in the book of Genesis.

In Genesis, the starting point was revelation. Especially after the tower of Babel it became evident that people had forgotten who God was. They needed reminding. The moves God made were essentially concerned with putting himself in front of the world's peoples. He covenanted with Abram and his family for them to represent God by the way they lived according to the law they embraced. This covenant is about revelation (what God wants for us), not salvation (what we get from God). God wanted to remind his creation that he was still around: Then you will know that I am Yahweh.

Forgetfulness of God is still a problem. Today it may take a little different form; instead of asking *who* God is, we are more likely to ask *whether* God is. But we are still fixed too narrowly on salvation—what we can get—instead of first opening ourselves to revelation. Because of this we suffer various losses.

The first thing lost is a sense of the distinction between Creator (God) and created (us). Revelation is about God making himself known through creation, through the Holy Spirit, through the mighty acts we celebrate in worship. At the heart of all these "revelations" is

Reading Genesis

Genesis divides into two main sections. Chapters 1–11 describe the origin of the world and God's dealings with the human race in general. Chapters 12–50 describe God's dealings with one particular family: Abraham and his descendants. This book contains the familiar stories of Adam and Eve, Cain and Abel, Noah, Abraham, Isaac, Jacob, and Joseph.

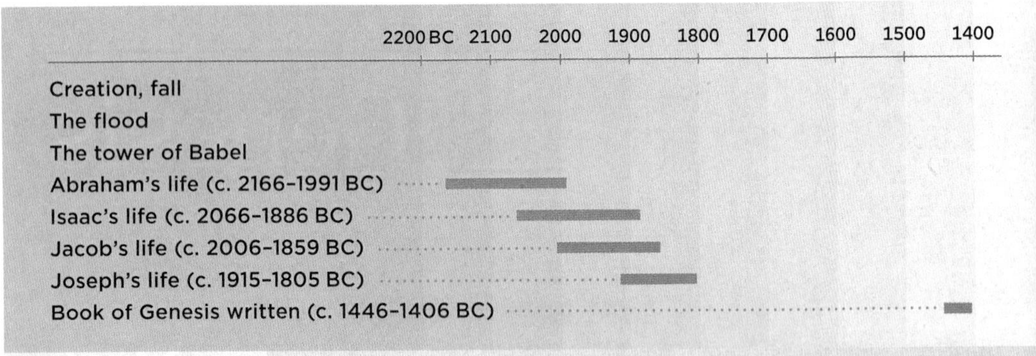

2200 BC 2100 2000 1900 1800 1700 1600 1500 1400

Creation, fall
The flood
The tower of Babel
Abraham's life (c. 2166–1991 BC)
Isaac's life (c. 2066–1886 BC)
Jacob's life (c. 2006–1859 BC)
Joseph's life (c. 1915–1805 BC)
Book of Genesis written (c. 1446–1406 BC)

Key Verse

In the beginning God created the heavens and the earth.

—Genesis 1:1

a Revealer; recognizing that reminds us that we are creations of that Creator God—mini-revelations ourselves.

The second thing lost is a proper sense of harmony between community and individual. Salvation, in focusing on the fates of both "communities" and "individuals," tempts us to overemphasize one or the other. Revelation, on the other hand, shifts the focus away from both onto God and insists that both the community and the individual find their true meaning only when in relationship with God.

The third thing lost is the realization that both faith and action are necessary in the Spirit-led life. The treasure may be lost in the field, John Calvin wrote, and it is a point of faith to recognize that God put it there. But once we realize it is there, it is up to us to act, to go find it. Revelation insists that the treasure, the only treasure, is the one God put in the field.

Finally, an emphasis on salvation to the exclusion of revelation paradoxically leads us to forget the mystery of salvation. We live in a society that worships the problem-solving approach to life. In such a climate, it is easy to reduce the process of salvation to a problem-solving technique that humans can master. Salvation is not achieved through a technique. Salvation is a miracle. Salvation is a mystery. Salvation is a gift of God.

A proper reading of Genesis reminds us of who God is and what God did. Only when we get those two things straight can we faithfully embrace what God does for us.

TAKING THE NEXT STEPS

Genesis, traditionally understood as a work of Moses, is a book of beginnings that introduces us to the general outline of the Bible: Creation-Fall-Redemption. At the center of the book is God, who made the world and upholds and rules all things. The human race, made in God's image and instructed to obey him, fell into sin. But God loved Adam and Eve and their descendants so much that, in his grace, he promised them a Savior and gave them another chance to serve him. In fact, with Abraham and his descendants, God formed a special relationship highlighted by a covenant; the rest of Bible history is the story of God's covenant people.

Genesis is like a mirror in which we can see our own lives. (1) We too are infected with sin. Like Adam and Eve, we have disobeyed God's will; like Jacob, we are out to get our own way, regardless of whom we hurt along the way. (2) But God freely offers us his forgiving grace, just as he did to our first parents in the Garden of Eden. He took away our guilt and defeated the power of Satan when he sent his Son, Jesus, to die on the cross. He promises to be with us, as he promised Jacob at Bethel. (3) Just as God called Abraham to believe in the promise that God would revive the dead womb of Sarah and give them a son, so God wants us to put our faith in the crucified and risen Christ. (4) We can be confident of God's protecting care in our lives, trusting that even when bad things happen to us as they did to Joseph, God can and will make good come out of them.

WHAT TO LOOK FOR IN GENESIS

- Creation (chs. 1–2)
- Adam and Eve and their family (chs. 2–4)
- The fall into sin (ch. 3)
- Noah and the flood (chs. 6–9)
- The tower of Babel (ch. 11)
- The life of Abraham (chs. 12–25)
- Stories of Hagar and Ishmael (chs. 16; 21)
- Sodom and Gomorrah (chs. 18–19)
- Abraham's test to sacrifice Isaac (ch. 22)
- The life of Isaac (chs. 21–22; 24–26)
- The life of Jacob (chs. 25; 27–35; 48–49)
- Jacob gets the blessing intended for Esau (chs. 31–33)
- Jacob works for Laban (chs. 29–30)
- Jacob returns home and meets Esau (chs. 31–33)
- Joseph sold into Egypt (ch. 37)
- Joseph in Potiphar's house and in prison (chs. 39–40)
- Joseph becomes governor of Egypt (ch. 41)
- Joseph and his brothers (chs. 42–45; 50)

The Beginning

1 In the beginning[a] God created
the heavens and the earth.[b] 2 Now
the earth was formless and empty,[c] darkness was over the surface
of the deep, and the Spirit of God[d]
was hovering over the waters.
3 And God said,[e] "Let there be light," and
there was light.[f] 4 God saw that the
light was good, and he separated the
light from the darkness. 5 God called
the light "day," and the darkness he
called "night."[g] And there was evening, and there was morning — the
first day.

1:1 [a] Jn 1:1-2 [b] Job 38:4; Ps 90:2; Isa 42:5; 44:24; 45:12, 18; Ac 17:24; Heb 11:3; Rev 4:11
1:2 [c] Jer 4:23 [d] Ps 104:30
1:3 [e] Ps 33:6,9; 148:5; Heb 11:3 [f] 2Co 4:6*
1:5 [g] Ps 74:16

1:1 "In the beginning." It sounds so simple, yet the moment we begin to ponder the phrase, its cloudlike simplicity dissipates to reveal rugged mountain peaks. Does it refer to some creative activity that preceded the seven days, or does it introduce and summarize the activity of the seven days? There are two evidences for the second option: (1) The book of Genesis operates literarily by introducing sections with a summary statement. (2) Even more persuasive is that the account of the six days closes with the comment that "the heavens and the earth" were completed (2:1).

In discussing creation, the author's concerns were much like others in the ancient Near East, where the greatest exercise of the power of the gods was demonstrated in the fixing of destinies. Israel's God demonstrates his power by assigning roles and functions, an affirmation of his exclusive sovereignty.

1:2 There is a clear establishment of order from disorder. That disorder is described in v. 2. The terms indicate that the cosmos was empty of purpose, meaning, and function—a place that had no order or intelligibility; a desertlike wasteland. While both darkness and the watery deep are elements of chaos, there is nothing sinister or menacing about this chaos in Genesis; it is simply the indication that God has not yet done his work.

Regarding the Spirit, the Hebrew uses the same word for "wind" or "spirit." Here, it represents an extension of God's power, like his hand or his breath.

1:3–4 Day one does not concern itself with the creation of "light" as a physical entity with physical properties. On day one, God created *time*. This is the first of the functions God will use to bring order to the chaos of the cosmos: the orderly and regular sequence of time.

1:5 Why is evening listed first? The coming of evening and then of morning marked the first series of transitions and completed the cycle, showing that what God had set up had now taken effect. In the rest of the narrative, God's activity will take place during the daylight hours, after which the established transitions, represented by evening and morning, will again take place.

CHARACTER OF GOD // GOD IS CREATOR

Genesis 1:1: In the beginning God created the heavens and the earth.

At the beginning of the Bible, God is introduced as the great Creator. God spoke the universe into being and ordered it according to his plan. God created humankind in his image and gave them a privileged place in his creation (Ge 1:26–30). Everything that God created was good.

Since God created everything, all creation testifies to his greatness. Psalm 19:1 says that the heavens declare God's glory and the skies proclaim his handiwork. Everything around us—all that microscopes and telescopes reveal, all that science discovers—witnesses to God's creative majesty.

God created not only all that is visible but also everything invisible. The heavenly host of angels is no less God's creation than the earth and humans. Everything that is not God himself was created by God—an act of selfless love. God is self-sufficient and did not need to create anything in order to be complete, but out of love he created everything (see Ac 17:25).

Even after humanity's fall into sin, God's creation remained good, though it now suffers under the weight of a curse (Ro 8:22). First Timothy 4:4 teaches that everything God created is good and no part of it should be rejected if it is received with thanksgiving. After all, each new tree, sunset, and human baby is a creation of God. The Lord is not finished creating!

APPLICATION ✚ Understanding God as the great Creator should give us respect and love for the world around us. Creation continues to point us to God, and the beauty of the world should lift our hearts toward praise and gratitude, since it is a large portion of his witness to the world (Ro 1:18–20). Furthermore, God's creative nature is passed to humans as his image bearers in the world: Humans can glorify God by cultivating our own capacity to create.

6 And God said, "Let there be a vault[h] between the waters to separate water
from water." 7 So God made the vault
and separated the water under the
vault from the water above it.[i] And
it was so. 8 God called the vault "sky."
And there was evening, and there
was morning — the second day.
9 And God said, "Let the water under
the sky be gathered to one place,[j]

1:6 [h] Jer 10:12
1:7 [i] Job 38:8-11, 16; Ps 148:4
1:9 [j] Job 38:8-11; Ps 104:6-9; Pr 8:29; Jer 5:22; 2Pe 3:5

The word translated "day" could mean (1) the daylight hours, (2) a twenty-four-hour day, (3) special days (e.g., day of his death), and (4) a plural use that can refer to a few days or even a year. Furthermore, (5) the definite article can be added to make it mean "today," or (6) a preposition can be tacked on the front and a demonstrative pronoun associated with it to say "in that day" or simply "when." Though "day" sometimes refers to an extended period, that usage is limited to certain expressions.

It is difficult to conclude that anything other than a twenty-four-hour day was intended. It is not the text that causes people to think otherwise but the demands of trying to harmonize the text with modern science.

APPLICATION ✚ 1:1–5 If we see the world in terms of science and nature on one side and God on another, we are going to end up with a worldview problem. God will be a God of the gaps, filling in only where science cannot. We will end up as practical deists. But there is no nature apart from God. Science, when it accurately portrays nature, is describing the work of God. Sometimes, undoubtedly, nature was his agent. But he is not limited to the use of a single agent, and whatever he did through other agencies, science has no way of detecting.

More than ever we need a theology that recognizes God's role in holding in check the chaos of our world as he sustains the cosmos moment by moment. What would change in our outlook on life if we took this issue seriously? Instead of saying that "the cosmos was created by God" (using past tense as if the job is done), we should say, "The Cosmos is God's creation." In this way, we claim the dynamic role of God in a perpetual act of creation.

1:6–8 Day two describes the setting up of the "vault," perceived by the original readers of Genesis as a solid dome. Its function was to regulate the weather, as is evident from the description of the waters above it. The author has apparently used the cosmological language available to him to describe weather. The intention of the text is not to convey structure but function.

1:9–13 Day three has two elements attached to it: the separation of water and dry land, and the production of vegetation. The two elements

and let dry ground appear." And it
was so. 10God called the dry ground
"land," and the gathered waters he
called "seas." And God saw that it
was good.
11Then God said, "Let the land
produce vegetation:[k] seed-bearing
plants and trees on the land that
bear fruit with seed in it, according to their various kinds." And it
was so. 12The land produced vegetation: plants bearing seed according
to their kinds and trees bearing fruit
with seed in it according to their
kinds. And God saw that it was good.
13And there was evening, and there
was morning — the third day.
14 And God said, "Let there be lights[l] in
the vault of the sky to separate the
day from the night, and let them
serve as signs[m] to mark sacred
times,[n] and days and years, 15and
let them be lights in the vault of
the sky to give light on the earth."
And it was so. 16God made two great
lights — the greater light to govern[o] the day and the lesser light
to govern[p] the night. He also made
the stars.[q] 17God set them in the
vault of the sky to give light on the
earth, 18to govern the day and the
night,[r] and to separate light from
darkness. And God saw that it was
good. 19And there was evening, and
there was morning — the fourth
day.
20 And God said, "Let the water teem with
living creatures, and let birds fly
above the earth across the vault of
the sky." 21So God created the great
creatures of the sea and every living
thing with which the water teems
and that moves about in it,[s] according to their kinds, and every winged
bird according to its kind. And God
saw that it was good. 22God blessed
them and said, "Be fruitful and increase in number and fill the water
in the seas, and let the birds increase
on the earth."[t] 23And there was evening, and there was morning — the
fifth day.
24 And God said, "Let the land produce
living creatures according to their
kinds: the livestock, the creatures
that move along the ground, and
the wild animals, each according
to its kind." And it was so. 25God
made the wild animals[u] according
to their kinds, the livestock according to their kinds, and all the creatures that move along the ground
according to their kinds. And God
saw that it was good.
26Then God said, "Let us[v] make
mankind in our image,[w] in our likeness, so that they may rule[x] over
the fish in the sea and the birds

1:11 [k] Ps 65:9-13; 104:14
1:14 [l] Ps 74:16 [m] Jer 10:2 [n] Ps 104:19
1:16 [o] Ps 136:8 [p] Ps 136:9 [q] Job 38:7, 31-32; Ps 8:3; Isa 40:26
1:18 [r] Jer 33:20, 25
1:21 [s] Ps 104:25-26
1:22 [t] ver 28; Ge 8:17
1:25 [u] Jer 27:5
1:26 [v] Ps 100:3 [w] Ge 9:6; Jas 3:9 [x] Ps 8:6-8

---

are intrinsically related in a functional approach, brought together on the third day to provide for vegetation and agriculture.

1:6–13 Time, weather/climate, and agriculture are the three functions of the cosmos of most significance to us. They are beyond our control, yet they define our existence. When God drew order out of chaos and made the world functional, he created coherence and established meaning for the cosmos and for each life. We can only discover who we are as we come to understand who God is. He is utterly and eternally coherent.

1:14–19 Signs function theologically in the OT as indicators through which God conveys knowledge and reveals himself. The celestial bodies serve for identifying the related festivals and religious feast days of the liturgical calendar.

In v. 16 we read, "God made two great lights." The text does not address how or when the bodies originated; rather, the assignment of function is described. The report of the fourth day concludes with the presentation of other functions of the heavenly bodies: giving light and dividing and ruling over the day and night.

1:20–23 While we may be inclined to identify some of these creatures as whales, sharks, and the like, that is not what the Hebrew word communicated to its audience. Other uses of this word associate it with the chaos monsters that were believed to inhabit the cosmic waters. These creatures are not antagonists but creatures that have been given functions just like any other.

In v. 20 is the first occurrence of the designation "living creatures." The same designation is used for land animals in v. 24 and includes some sea creatures and birds in v. 28; in 2:7 it indicates what Adam became when God breathed into him. Though people will be differentiated from the animal world by the image of God, they hold in common with all creatures the quality of life.

1:24–25 The categories are divided into domesticated animals, wild herd animals that often serve as prey, and wild, predatory animals. In keeping with the functional emphasis, this describes not a biological process but a functional relationship.

1:26–27 The use of the plural pronouns has occasioned vigorous discussion among the commentators. In the OT the heavenly court

Ge 1:26–30 ❖ What special status and vocation did God give humankind in creation? How might this status shape everything we do?

in the sky, over the livestock and
all the wild animals,[a] and over all
the creatures that move along the
ground."

27 So God created mankind in his own
image,[y]
in the image of God he created
them;
male and female[z] he created
them.

28 God blessed them and said to
them, "Be fruitful and increase in
number; fill the earth[a] and subdue
it. Rule over the fish in the sea and
the birds in the sky and over every
living creature that moves on the
ground."
29 Then God said, "I give you every seed-bearing plant on the face
of the whole earth and every tree
that has fruit with seed in it. They
will be yours for food.[b] 30 And to all
the beasts of the earth and all the
birds in the sky and all the creatures
that move along the ground — everything that has the breath of life
in it — I give every green plant for
food.[c]" And it was so.
31 God saw all that he had made,[d]
and it was very good.[e] And there was
evening, and there was morning —
the sixth day.

2 Thus the heavens and the earth
were completed in all their vast array.

2 By the seventh day God had finished
the work he had been doing; so on
the seventh day he rested from all
his work.[f] 3 Then God blessed the
seventh day and made it holy,[g] because on it he rested from all the
work of creating that he had done.

Adam and Eve

4 This is the account of the heavens
and the earth when they were created,
when the LORD God made the earth and
the heavens.

5 Now no shrub had yet appeared on
the earth[b] and no plant had yet sprung
up,[h] for the LORD God had not sent rain
on the earth[i] and there was no one to
work the ground, 6 but streams[c] came up
from the earth and watered the whole
surface of the ground. 7 Then the LORD
God formed a man[d] from the dust[j] of the
ground[k] and breathed into his nostrils

1:27 [y] 1Co 11:7 [z] Ge 5:2; Mt 19:4*; Mk 10:6* 1:28 [a] Ge 9:1,7; Lev 26:9 1:29 [b] Ps 104:14 1:30 [c] Ps 104:14, 27; 145:15 1:31 [d] Ps 104:24 [e] 1Ti 4:4 2:2 [f] Ex 20:11; 31:17; Heb 4:4* 2:3 [g] Lev 23:3; Isa 58:13 2:5 [h] Ge 1:11 [i] Ps 65:9-10 2:7 [j] Ge 3:19 [k] Ps 103:14

[a] *26* Probable reading of the original Hebrew text (see Syriac); Masoretic Text *the earth* [b] *5* Or *land*; also in verse 6 [c] *6* Or *mist* [d] *7* The Hebrew for *man (adam)* sounds like and may be related to the Hebrew for *ground (adamah)*; it is also the name *Adam* (see verse 20).

---

is made up of angels or, more specifically, the "sons of God."

1:27–28 The governing work of God is seen in Genesis to be accomplished by people. Information from other contexts that can be gleaned about the image includes that (1) the image of God is not lost at the fall (9:6) and (2) it does differentiate people from animals (9:6), though that does not mean that anything that differentiates humans from animals is part of the image. Perhaps most significant, the image of God in people provides them with the capacity to be and act like him.

While the image of God defines a role for humanity, the blessing indicates the functions that people will have because of that role. "Subdue" is associated with the prior verb, "fill" (v. 28), and has the earth as its focus. "Rule" is directed toward the animals and implies domestication or some other level of use or control. Of course, this does not legitimize slaughter, abuse, or neglect.

2:1–3 The seventh day is marked by God's ceasing the work of the previous six days and by his settling into the stability of the cosmos he created, perhaps experiencing refreshment as he did so. By blessing it, he extends his favor to it.

✣ **1:14—2:3** Being made in the image of God confers on us *dignity*, entrusts us with *responsibility*, and implants in us a certain potential—namely, the *capacity* to mirror our Creator. As Christians, our redemption has greatly enhanced this capacity and, in the process, has made us more sensitive to the responsibility we have and the dignity shared by all humankind.

2:4–7 The point made by v. 5 is that there is no food growing in uncultivated areas and there is no cultivation for the farmable land.

2:5–6 This passage in an interpretive paraphrase is: "No shrubs or plants were yet growing wild (for food) because God had not yet sent rain, and people were not yet around to work the ground (for irrigation), so the regular floods saturated the ground indiscriminately (thus no food was being grown)."

2:7 "Dust" represents what people return to when they die; God breathes the "breath of life" into every person who is born.

PEOPLE TO KNOW // ADAM

GENESIS 2:7-9: Adam is the first human named in the Bible. God formed him out of the dust of the earth; Adam's name can be translated "from the ground." God placed Adam in a special garden called Eden to care for God's beautiful creation (Ge 2:15).

God also created a woman, Eve, and she and Adam together cared for the garden. At first everything was wonderful. Adam and Eve lived free from all sin and shame. They could walk and talk with God himself.

One day, however, the serpent tempted them to eat from the one tree God had forbidden them to eat of: the tree of the knowledge of good and evil. Deceived by the serpent, Eve took some fruit and shared it with Adam. Suddenly, sin entered creation, as did the shameful reality of its consequences. God was merciful and covered their shame. But God punished Adam and Eve for disobeying his specific commands. They were exiled from the garden. For this first couple, the ground itself came under a curse (Ge 3:17).

Adam's grief was not over. Adam and Eve had two sons: Cain and Abel. In the course of time, Cain's envy and anger led him to kill his brother. The effects of Adam's sin rippled outward. And we still feel them today.

APPLICATION ✥ Adam sinned by trying to put himself in God's place. The serpent told him and Eve that if they ate the forbidden fruit, they would be like God. By giving in to that temptation, Adam and Eve also showed that he wanted to remove God as the ultimate authority. He wanted to make his own rules.

The temptation to remove God from our lives and choose our own way is still strong. In his mercy, however, God provided a second Adam, Jesus Christ (1Co 15:22). Jesus came to show us God's love and to break the power of sin through his death and resurrection. Though we still carry the effects of sin from the first Adam, by God's grace we can be free of that sin nature and walk the new path opened to us by the second Adam.

the breath[l] of life,[m] and the man became
a living being.[n]
8Now the LORD God had planted a garden in the east, in Eden;[o] and there he
put the man he had formed. 9The LORD
God made all kinds of trees grow out of
the ground—trees that were pleasing to
the eye and good for food. In the middle of the garden were the tree of life[p]
and the tree of the knowledge of good
and evil.[q]
10A river watering the garden flowed
from Eden; from there it was separated
into four headwaters. 11The name of the
first is the Pishon; it winds through the
entire land of Havilah, where there is
gold. 12(The gold of that land is good;
aromatic resin[a] and onyx are also there.)
13The name of the second river is the
Gihon; it winds through the entire land
of Cush.[b] 14The name of the third river
is the Tigris;[r] it runs along the east side
of Ashur. And the fourth river is the Euphrates.
15The LORD God took the man and put
him in the Garden of Eden to work it
and take care of it. 16And the LORD God
commanded the man, "You are free to
eat from any tree in the garden; 17but
you must not eat from the tree of the
knowledge of good and evil, for when
you eat from it you will certainly die."[s]

2:7 [l] Job 33:4 [m] Ac 17:25 [n] 1Co 15:45*
2:8 [o] Ge 3:23, 24; Isa 51:3
2:9 [p] Ge 3:22, 24; Rev 2:7; 22:2,14,19 [q] Eze 47:12
2:14 [r] Da 10:4
2:17 [s] Dt 30:15, 19; Ro 5:12; 6:23; Jas 1:15

[a] 12 Or *good; pearls* [b] 13 Possibly southeast Mesopotamia

2:8-17 Gardens of this variety were a common feature in palace complexes in the ancient world. The produce of these temple gardens was used in offerings to the deity. The picture presented is of a mighty spring that is channeled through the garden for irrigation.

The geography used here for the location of the garden is not land-based but cosmic, given so that its strategic role can be appreciated. All fertility derives from the presence of God.

We should view the "tree of life" as having fruit that extends life rather than instantly grants immortality. Understanding the second tree depends on the meaning of the phrase "knowledge of good and evil" (vv. 9, 17). Knowing good and evil is characteristic of God (3:22) but not of children (Dt 1:39), the elderly (2Sa 19:35), or the inexperienced (1Ki 3:9); when people gain the knowledge by eating the fruit, they can legitimately be described as being like God.

2:15-17 The tasks given to Adam are priestly: caring for sacred space. In ancient thinking, this made one a participant with God in the ongoing task of sustaining the equilibrium God had established in the cosmos. A paraphrase of v. 17 is "When

Ge 2:18–25 ❖ How does this story form the basis of human relationships and marriage? How do the words of Jesus (Mt 19:4–6) and Paul (Eph 5:31–32) expand our understanding of this passage?

18The LORD God said, "It is not good
for the man to be alone. I will make a
helper suitable for him."[t]
19Now the LORD God had formed out
of the ground all the wild animals[u] and
all the birds in the sky. He brought them
to the man to see what he would name
them; and whatever the man called each
living creature,[v] that was its name. 20So
the man gave names to all the livestock,
the birds in the sky and all the wild animals.

But for Adam[a] no suitable helper was
found. 21So the LORD God caused the man
to fall into a deep sleep; and while he
was sleeping, he took one of the man's
ribs[b] and then closed up the place with
flesh. 22Then the LORD God made a woman from the rib[c][w] he had taken out of the
man, and he brought her to the man.
23The man said,

"This is now bone of my bones
and flesh of my flesh;[x]
she shall be called 'woman,'
for she was taken out of man."

24That is why a man leaves his father
and mother and is united[y] to his wife,
and they become one flesh.[z]
25Adam and his wife were both naked,[a]
and they felt no shame.

2:18 [t]1Co 11:9
2:19 [u]Ps 8:7 [v]Ge 1:24
2:22 [w]1Co 11:8, 9,12
2:23 [x]Ge 29:14; Eph 5:28-30
2:24 [y]Mal 2:15 [z]Mt 19:5*; Mk 10:7-8*; 1Co 6:16*; Eph 5:31*
2:25 [a]Ge 3:7, 10-11
3:1 [b]2Co 11:3; Rev 12:9; 20:2
3:4 [c]Jn 8:44; 2Co 11:3
3:5 [d]Isa 14:14; Eze 28:2
3:6 [e]Jas 1:14-15; 1Jn 2:16 [f]1Ti 2:14

The Fall

3 Now the serpent[b] was more crafty
than any of the wild animals the LORD
God had made. He said to the woman,
"Did God really say, 'You must not eat
from any tree in the garden'?"
2The woman said to the serpent, "We
may eat fruit from the trees in the garden, 3but God did say, 'You must not eat
fruit from the tree that is in the middle
of the garden, and you must not touch
it, or you will die.'"
4"You will not certainly die," the serpent said to the woman.[c] 5"For God
knows that when you eat from it your
eyes will be opened, and you will be like
God,[d] knowing good and evil."
6When the woman saw that the fruit of
the tree was good for food and pleasing
to the eye, and also desirable[e] for gaining
wisdom, she took some and ate it. She
also gave some to her husband, who was
with her, and he ate it.[f] 7Then the eyes
of both of them were opened, and they
realized they were naked; so they sewed
fig leaves together and made coverings
for themselves.

[a] *20* Or *the man* [b] *21* Or *took part of the man's side* [c] *22* Or *part*

---

you eat of it, you will be sentenced to death and therefore doomed to die."

2:18–25 Nothing in the phrase "suitable helper" suggests a subservient status of the one helping; in fact, the opposite is more likely. Another translation could be "partner" or "counterpart."

2:21–22 The text portrays God as taking a handful of bone and flesh out of Adam's side to use in the construction of Eve. "Then the LORD God built up the side he had taken from the man for (the purpose of making) a woman" (alternate translation, v. 22).

2:23–24 We would be mistaken to think that Adam names Eve here. He rather indicates in what category she belongs. Verse 24 does not speak exclusively of sexual desire. Conceiving children (being fruitful) is the idea.

2:25 Their nakedness indicates a level of naivete. It will be contrasted to the picture in 3:7.

2:4–25 Regardless of what conclusions can be drawn about the issue as a whole once NT texts are considered, this text is concerned with human roles, not gender roles. Man and woman serve together.

3:1 The serpent is classified as one of the wild animals. This classification diminishes any speculation concerning an Israelite understanding of a hidden identity of the serpent. It comes with nothing out of the ordinary that would alert the woman's suspicions.

3:1b–5 According to the serpent, it was never God's intention to put them to death. In effect, the serpent does not contradict God; he only suggests there is nothing to worry about.

3:6 All the verbs in this section are plural. Why does Adam not correct Eve's statement? The text offers no explanation.

3:7 They were not ashamed when they were unaware of their nakedness; when they become aware, they feel shame.

3:1–7 God offered Adam and Eve the privilege of freedom and the joy of dependence. Our society treats this as an oxymoron. In rejecting dependence on God, people choose a far more costly dependency—on themselves and their own resources. In seeking autonomy, freedom, and power, they only forge new chains.

[8]Then the man and his wife heard the
sound of the LORD God as he was walking[g] in the garden in the cool of the day,
and they hid[h] from the LORD God among
the trees of the garden. [9]But the LORD
God called to the man, "Where are you?"
[10]He answered, "I heard you in the
garden, and I was afraid because I was
naked; so I hid."
[11]And he said, "Who told you that you
were naked? Have you eaten from the tree
that I commanded you not to eat from?"
[12]The man said, "The woman you put
here with me—she gave me some fruit
from the tree, and I ate it."
[13]Then the LORD God said to the woman, "What is this you have done?"
The woman said, "The serpent deceived me,[i] and I ate."
[14]So the LORD God said to the serpent,
"Because you have done this,

"Cursed[j] are you above all livestock
and all wild animals!
You will crawl on your belly
and you will eat dust[k]
all the days of your life.
15 And I will put enmity
between you and the woman,
and between your offspring[a][l] and
hers;[m]
he will crush[b] your head,[n]
and you will strike his heel."

[16]To the woman he said,

"I will make your pains in
childbearing very severe;
with painful labor you will give
birth to children.
Your desire will be for your
husband,
and he will rule over you.[o]"

3:8 [g] Dt 23:14 [h] Job 31:33; Ps 139:7-12; Jer 23:24
3:13 [i] 2Co 11:3; 1Ti 2:14
3:14 [j] Dt 28:15-20 [k] Isa 65:25; Mic 7:17
3:15 [l] Jn 8:44; Ac 13:10; 1Jn 3:8 [m] Isa 7:14; Mt 1:23; Rev 12:17 [n] Ro 16:20; Heb 2:14
3:16 [o] 1Co 11:3; Eph 5:22
3:17 [p] Ge 5:29; Ro 8:20-22 [q] Job 5:7; 14:1; Ecc 2:23
3:18 [r] Ps 104:14
3:19 [s] 2Th 3:10 [t] Ge 2:7; Ps 90:3; 104:29; Ecc 12:7

Ge 3:4–5 ❖ How did the serpent plant doubt about God's words? What voices threaten to sow doubt about God's truth in the world around us today?

Ge 3:15 ❖ Many Christians have said this verse contains the first glimpse of the gospel in the Bible. What hope for the future does this verse point toward, and how does it impact the way we live?

[17]To Adam he said, "Because you listened to your wife and ate fruit from the
tree about which I commanded you, 'You
must not eat from it,'

"Cursed[p] is the ground because of
you;
through painful toil you will eat
food from it
all the days of your life.[q]
18 It will produce thorns and thistles
for you,
and you will eat the plants of the
field.[r]
19 By the sweat of your brow
you will eat your food[s]
until you return to the ground,
since from it you were taken;
for dust you are
and to dust you will return."[t]

[20]Adam[c] named his wife Eve,[d] because
she would become the mother of all the
living.
[21]The LORD God made garments of skin
for Adam and his wife and clothed them.
[22]And the LORD God said, "The man has
now become like one of us, knowing
good and evil. He must not be allowed

[a] *15* Or *seed* [b] *15* Or *strike* [c] *20* Or *The man* [d] *20* *Eve* probably means *living*.

3:8–13 We could translate v. 8 in this way: "They heard the roar of the LORD moving about in the garden in the wind of the storm." The context makes this new rendering a possibility, but one that can only be held tentatively.
3:14 The curse on the serpent can be understood as wishing upon it a status associated with docility (crawling on belly) and death (eating dust).
3:15 Throughout the history of the church, this has been read as the first foreshadowing of Christ's defeat of Satan. Given the repetition of the verb and the potentially mortal nature of both attacks, the verse is depicting a continual, unresolved conflict between humans and the representatives of evil.
3:16 The first half of this verse is referring to the anxiety that a woman will experience through the whole process from conception to birth. If reproduction is going to be so fraught with anguish, why do it? The answer is found in the woman's instinct: her desire to have children.
3:17–19 The ground is removed from God's favor, protection, and blessing. The impact of this curse is that, though food is still made available to people, it will be much harder to produce.
3:20–21 It is a serious error to read sacrifice between the lines of v. 21. The institution of sacrifice is far too significant an occurrence to leave it entirely to inference. This provision should probably be seen as an act of grace by God, preparing them for the more difficult environment and providing a remedy for their newly developed shame.
3:22–24 Banishment from the garden and

to reach out his hand and take also from
the tree of life[u] and eat, and live forever."
23So the LORD God banished him from
the Garden of Eden[v] to work the ground[w]
from which he had been taken. 24After he
drove the man out, he placed on the east
side[a] of the Garden of Eden cherubim[x]
and a flaming sword[y] flashing back and
forth to guard the way to the tree of life.[z]

3:22 [u] Rev 22:14
3:23 [v] Ge 2:8 [w] Ge 4:2
3:24 [x] Ex 25:18-22 [y] Ps 104:4 [z] Ge 2:9
4:2 [a] Lk 11:51

Cain and Abel

4 Adam[b] made love to his wife Eve,
and she became pregnant and gave
birth to Cain.[c] She said, "With the help of
the LORD I have brought forth[d] a man."
2Later she gave birth to his brother Abel.[a]
Now Abel kept flocks, and Cain worked
the soil. 3In the course of time Cain
brought some of the fruits of the soil as
an offering to the LORD.[b] 4And Abel also
brought an offering — fat portions[c] from
some of the firstborn of his flock.[d] The
LORD looked with favor on Abel and his
offering,[e] 5but on Cain and his offering
he did not look with favor. So Cain was
very angry, and his face was downcast.
6Then the LORD said to Cain, "Why are
you angry? Why is your face downcast?
7If you do what is right, will you not be

4:3 [b] Nu 18:12
4:4 [c] Lev 3:16 [d] Ex 13:2,12 [e] Heb 11:4

Ge 4:4 ❖ Abel brought God the best of what he had as an offering. How can we give our "best" to God? What does that mean in your own life?

[a] *24* Or *placed in front* [b] *1* Or *The man*
[c] *1* *Cain* sounds like the Hebrew for *brought forth* or *acquired.* [d] *1* Or *have acquired*

---

removal of access to the tree of life are the means by which the death penalty is carried out. The cherubim guard the way to the tree of life, now forbidden property of God.

❖ **3:8–24** As always, the serpent is most successful in contexts in which what is true or right can be twisted around to create an obstacle. The fact is that we can defend with integrity certain beliefs without insulting or criticizing those who have come to different conclusions.

4:3–5 The problem with Cain's sacrifice does not have anything to do with the absence of blood. The only thing the text makes clear is that Cain, in some way, does not "do what is right" (v. 7). The text is more interested in his response to God's reaction than it is in outlining the details.

4:6–7 "Desires" is best understood as a basic instinct

PEOPLE TO KNOW // EVE

GENESIS 4:1–2: God placed Adam in the Garden of Eden and gave him the task of caring for it. But God knew it was not good for Adam to be alone (Ge 2:18). God put Adam into a deep sleep and formed a suitable partner for him out of Adam's side. She was Eve, "the mother of all the living" (Ge 3:20).

Eve lived with Adam in Eden in complete harmony; they were naked and unashamed. They fellowshipped with God himself in the garden. Yet soon their actions would cause their paradise to fall apart.

The serpent tempted Eve to eat of the tree of the knowledge of good and evil, which God had forbidden them to eat from (Ge 2:17). The serpent promised Eve if she ate the fruit, she would be like God. Eve took some of the fruit and shared it with Adam, who was with her. They suddenly felt shame. Adam and Eve tried to cover their bodies and hide from God (Ge 3:21–24).

Paradise was lost, yet Eve received a hopeful promise when God cursed the serpent. God promised that a descendant from the woman would crush the head of the serpent and destroy the power of evil (Ge 3:15). No sooner had humanity fallen into sin than God promised Eve's descendant would be a Savior; that Savior was Jesus Christ.

APPLICATION ❖ On one hand, Eve's story is a sad illustration of the human condition. None of us can help but to fall into sin (Ro 3:23). We each fail in the face of certain temptations. Yet there is hope in Eve's story, which comes through God's promise. Jesus Christ came into the world as God-made-flesh to right the wrong of human sin and to bring God's ultimate victory over evil. Eve's story not only shows us who we are but also points to the good news of who God is, the one who destroys evil and saves his children through Jesus Christ.

accepted? But if you do not do what is
right, sin is crouching at your door;[f] it
desires to have you, but you must rule
over it.[g]"
8Now Cain said to his brother Abel,
"Let's go out to the field."[a] While they
were in the field, Cain attacked his brother Abel and killed him.[h]
9Then the LORD said to Cain, "Where
is your brother Abel?"
"I don't know," he replied. "Am I my
brother's keeper?"
10The LORD said, "What have you done?
Listen! Your brother's blood cries out to
me from the ground.[i] 11Now you are under a curse and driven from the ground,
which opened its mouth to receive your
brother's blood from your hand. 12When
you work the ground, it will no longer
yield its crops for you. You will be a restless wanderer on the earth."
13Cain said to the LORD, "My punishment is more than I can bear. 14Today
you are driving me from the land, and I
will be hidden from your presence;[j] I will
be a restless wanderer on the earth, and
whoever finds me will kill me."[k]
15But the LORD said to him, "Not so[b];
anyone who kills Cain[l] will suffer vengeance seven times over.[m]" Then the
LORD put a mark on Cain so that no one
who found him would kill him. 16So Cain
went out from the LORD's presence and
lived in the land of Nod,[c] east of Eden.[n]
17Cain made love to his wife, and she
became pregnant and gave birth to
Enoch. Cain was then building a city, and
he named it after his son[o] Enoch. 18To
Enoch was born Irad, and Irad was the
father of Mehujael, and Mehujael was the
father of Methushael, and Methushael
was the father of Lamech.
19Lamech married two women, one
named Adah and the other Zillah. 20Adah
gave birth to Jabal; he was the father of
those who live in tents and raise livestock. 21His brother's name was Jubal; he
was the father of all who play stringed
instruments and pipes. 22Zillah also had
a son, Tubal-Cain, who forged all kinds
of tools out of[d] bronze and iron. Tubal-
Cain's sister was Naamah.
23Lamech said to his wives,

"Adah and Zillah, listen to me;
wives of Lamech, hear my words.
I have killed[p] a man for
wounding me,
a young man for injuring me.
24If Cain is avenged[q] seven times,[r]
then Lamech seventy-seven
times."

25Adam made love to his wife again,
and she gave birth to a son and named
him Seth,[e][s] saying, "God has granted me

4:7 [f] Nu 32:23 [g] Ro 6:16
4:8 [h] Mt 23:35; 1Jn 3:12
4:10 [i] Ge 9:5; Nu 35:33; Heb 12:24; Rev 6:9-10
4:14 [j] 2Ki 17:18; Ps 51:11; 139:7-12; Jer 7:15; 52:3 [k] Ge 9:6; Nu 35:19, 21, 27, 33
4:15 [l] Eze 9:4, 6 [m] ver 24; Ps 79:12
4:16 [n] Ge 2:8
4:17 [o] Ps 49:11
4:23 [p] Ex 20:13; Lev 19:18
4:24 [q] Dt 32:35 [r] ver 15
4:25 [s] Ge 5:3

[a] *8* Samaritan Pentateuch, Septuagint, Vulgate and Syriac; Masoretic Text does not have *"Let's go out to the field."* [b] *15* Septuagint, Vulgate and Syriac; Hebrew *Very well* [c] *16* *Nod* means *wandering* (see verses 12 and 14). [d] *22* *Or who instructed all who work in* [e] *25* *Seth* probably means *granted.*

(here the instinct would be to deprave). "Sin" is personified as a crouching demon waiting to strike.
4:8–16 God's question is avoided by deflecting blame to others. Cain's response is simply a lie (v. 9) followed by an evasive denial of responsibility.
4:10–12 As 3:13 introduced the pronouncement with a statement that assigned guilt, so 4:10 introduces Yahweh's pronouncement with essentially the same statement. Becoming a "restless wanderer" (v. 12) is a consequence of the land not providing his food; rather, he will be forced to wander to get food.
4:13–14 Who does Cain think is out there to kill him, and what is the mark affixed by Yahweh? It is difficult to determine how sin came to all humanity unless all humans are descendants of Adam and Eve. This theological inference cannot be elaborated since the text offers no further information.
4:15 The "mark" placed on Cain plays a parallel role in this narrative to the garments provided for Adam and Eve in 3:21.

4:1–16 When we refuse to take responsibility for our sin, to accept blame for the consequences of our actions, and to be held accountable for what we do and say, we burn down the bridges of reconciliation. The only way back to reconciliation, forgiveness, and God has as its first step a recognition of the problem and repentant desire to do something about it.

4:17–22 Because Cain and his family were forced into an extreme situation, they could only survive by means of human advancement. There is nothing to reflect rebellion here, only an indication that even Cain's line continues to enjoy the blessing by subduing and ruling.
4:23–24 The most notable member of Cain's descendants is boastful Lamech. The words of his speech constitute what is often considered an example of earliest poetry. The parallelism makes it clear that a single incident of combat is the subject of the triumphant declaration, so that the "man" and the "young man" (v. 23) are one and the same. The text has moved from unrepentant Cain to defiant Lamech. The human situation is degenerating.
4:25–26 The line of Seth is associated with religious

another child in place of Abel, since Cain killed him."[t] 26 Seth also had a son, and he named him Enosh.

At that time people began to call on[a] the name of the LORD.[u]

From Adam to Noah

5 This is the written account of Adam's family line.

When God created mankind, he made them in the likeness of God.[v] 2 He created them male and female[w] and blessed them. And he named them "Mankind"[b] when they were created.

3 When Adam had lived 130 years, he had a son in his own likeness, in his own image;[x] and he named him Seth. 4 After Seth was born, Adam lived 800 years and had other sons and daughters. 5 Altogether, Adam lived a total of 930 years, and then he died.[y]

6 When Seth had lived 105 years, he became the father[c] of Enosh. 7 After he became the father of Enosh, Seth lived 807 years and had other sons and daughters. 8 Altogether, Seth lived a total of 912 years, and then he died.

9 When Enosh had lived 90 years, he became the father of Kenan. 10 After he became the father of Kenan, Enosh lived 815 years and had other sons and daughters. 11 Altogether, Enosh lived a total of 905 years, and then he died.

12 When Kenan had lived 70 years, he became the father of Mahalalel. 13 After he became the father of Mahalalel, Kenan lived 840 years and had other sons and daughters. 14 Altogether, Kenan lived a total of 910 years, and then he died.

15 When Mahalalel had lived 65 years, he became the father of Jared. 16 After he became the father of Jared, Mahalalel lived 830 years and had other sons and daughters. 17 Altogether, Mahalalel lived a total of 895 years, and then he died.

18 When Jared had lived 162 years, he became the father of Enoch.[z] 19 After he became the father of Enoch, Jared lived 800 years and had other sons and daughters. 20 Altogether, Jared lived a total of 962 years, and then he died.

21 When Enoch had lived 65 years, he became the father of Methuselah. 22 After he became the father of Methuselah, Enoch walked faithfully with God[a] 300 years and had other sons and daughters. 23 Altogether, Enoch lived a total of 365 years. 24 Enoch walked faithfully with God;[b] then he was no more, because God took him away.[c]

25 When Methuselah had lived 187 years, he became the father of Lamech. 26 After he became the father of Lamech, Methuselah lived 782 years and had other sons and daughters. 27 Altogether, Methuselah lived a total of 969 years, and then he died.

28 When Lamech had lived 182 years, he had a son. 29 He named him Noah[d] and said, "He will comfort us in the labor and painful toil of our hands caused by the ground the LORD has cursed.[d]" 30 After Noah was born, Lamech lived 595 years and had other sons and daughters. 31 Altogether, Lamech lived a total of 777 years, and then he died.

4:25 [t] ver 8
4:26 [u] Ge 12:8; 1Ki 18:24; Ps 116:17; Joel 2:32; Zep 3:9; Ac 2:21; 1Co 1:2
5:1 [v] Ge 1:27; Eph 4:24; Col 3:10
5:2 [w] Ge 1:27; Mt 19:4; Mk 10:6; Gal 3:28
5:3 [x] Ge 1:26; 1Co 15:49
5:5 [y] Ge 3:19
5:18 [z] Jude 14
5:22 [a] ver 24; Ge 6:9; 17:1; 48:15; Mic 6:8; Mal 2:6
5:24 [b] ver 22 [c] 2Ki 2:1,11; Heb 11:5
5:29 [d] Ge 3:17; Ro 8:20

Ge 5:21-24 ❖ Enoch is a mysterious figure. He walked faithfully with God, and "God took him away" (v. 24). What does walking faithfully with God mean for us today?

[a] 26 Or *to proclaim* [b] 2 Hebrew *adam*
[c] 6 *Father* may mean *ancestor*; also in verses 7-26.
[d] 29 *Noah* sounds like the Hebrew for *comfort.*

---

practice. When people "call on the name of the LORD" (v. 26), this constitutes a designation and recognition of Yahweh as God. This is the beginning of worship and shows that the development of civilization did not bring a total abandonment of the Lord.

5:1-32 Anyone even casually familiar with the Bible has noticed how many Israelite names end in *-iah* or *-el* or start with *Jeho-* or *El-*. All of these represent Israel's God. This type of name affirms the nature of the deity, proclaims the attributes of the deity, or requests the blessing of the deity.

If we accept the biblical account at face value, there are reasons we might expect long lives in the shadow of Eden. Whether we would speculate that the long lives testify to the gradual penetration of sin (and death) or to the enduring effect of Adam and Eve's temporary (pre-fall) diet from the tree of life, the accuracy of these numbers can be defended.

5:21-24 The text does not say where Enoch was taken, a possible indication that the author did not profess to know. The text stops short of saying he went to heaven or to be with God.

5:28-31 It may have been Lamech's hope that Noah would somehow bring about the reversal of the curse, but the flood's destruction and Noah's survival does not accomplish this end.

32After Noah was 500 years old, he became the father of Shem, Ham and Japheth.

Wickedness in the World

6 When human beings began to increase in number on the earth[e] and daughters were born to them, 2the sons of God saw that the daughters of humans were beautiful, and they married any of them they chose. 3Then the LORD said, "My Spirit will not contend with[a] humans forever,[f] for they are mortal[b];[g] their days will be a hundred and twenty years."

4The Nephilim[h] were on the earth in those days—and also afterward—when the sons of God went to the daughters of humans and had children by them. They were the heroes of old, men of renown.

5The LORD saw how great the wickedness of the human race had become on the earth, and that every inclination of the thoughts of the human heart was only evil all the time.[i] 6The LORD regretted[j] that he had made human beings on the earth, and his heart was deeply troubled. 7So the LORD said, "I will wipe from the face of the earth the human race I have created—and with them the animals, the birds and the creatures that move along the ground—for I regret that I have made them." 8But Noah found favor in the eyes of the LORD.[k]

6:1 [e] Ge 1:28
6:3 [f] Isa 57:16 [g] Ps 78:39
6:4 [h] Nu 13:33
6:5 [i] Ge 8:21; Ps 14:1-3
6:6 [j] 1Sa 15:11, 35; Isa 63:10

Ge 6:9-22 ❖ Noah lived in an extremely wicked time, yet he remained righteous. What must it have been like for Noah to remain faithful to God despite the evil influences around him? How can we follow Noah's example?

Noah and the Flood

9This is the account of Noah and his family.

Noah was a righteous man, blameless among the people of his time,[l] and he walked faithfully with God.[m] 10Noah had three sons: Shem, Ham and Japheth.[n]

11Now the earth was corrupt in God's sight and was full of violence.[o] 12God saw how corrupt the earth had become, for all the people on earth had corrupted their ways.[p] 13So God said to Noah, "I am going to put an end to all people, for the earth

6:8 [k] Ge 19:19; Ex 33:12,13,17; Lk 1:30; Ac 7:46
6:9 [l] Ge 7:1; Eze 14:14, 20; Heb 11:7; 2Pe 2:5 [m] Ge 5:22
6:10 [n] Ge 5:32
6:11 [o] Eze 7:23; 8:17
6:12 [p] Ps 14:1-3

[a] 3 Or *My spirit will not remain in*
[b] 3 Or *corrupt*

❖ **4:17—5:32** These chapters illustrate how, from nearly the beginning, the conditions existed for good and evil to flourish in one another's company. This is how God works in a fallen world. Since he has chosen not to destroy a fallen race but to redeem it, he does his work in an imperfect context. Until the final blow is struck, evil will always find ways to pervert that which has the potential to do good and will prosper under the umbrella of protection created by the aura of that which is good.

6:1-4 The "Nephilim" (v. 4) are referred to only in this passage and in Nu 13:33, where the spies speak of the descendants of Anak, who were of considerable size. The descendants are associated with the Nephilim in that passage, so some consider the Nephilim giants.

In both passages the Nephilim appear as renowned warrior heroes. Verse 4 may indicate that the actions of the sons of God took place during the heroic age, though perhaps they were also seen as the offspring of these unions.

❖ **6:1-4** What happens when oppression becomes institutionalized? In Ge 1–11 the institutionalization of oppression is the last step that develops into the condition described in 6:5. If rulers and leaders are oppressive or corrupt, there is either a *double standard* (by which the population is held accountable to a level of behavior from which the rulers are exempt) or an erosion of the moral fiber as the population follows the example of its leaders. Violence breeds violence. Corruption breeds corruption. Racism breeds racism. Sexual misconduct breeds sexual misconduct. Lies breed lies.

6:5, 11-13 The text makes it clear that the problem leading to the flood was simply the wickedness of the human heart and the behavior that resulted. Sin has reached critical mass and divine response is now inevitable.

6:7 Passages using terminology such as God's being sorry, repenting, or changing his mind have been the source of theological confusion, consternation, and debate. It may be that "regret" can be best understood in accounting terms. If the books get out of balance, something must be adjusted. Whenever transactions are made, entries must be made accordingly, keeping personal, national, or cosmic "ledgers" in balance.

When God has set a course for punishment, it can at times be counterbalanced by an act of grace that revokes that punishment and brings the "ledger" back into balance (Jer 26:13). God is disturbed when people have sinned and been warned of the coming consequences of the imbalance represented by their wickedness, but they refuse to balance their ledgers with repentance (Jer 8:6).

6:9 Noah's righteousness and blamelessness is in comparison to the people of his time.

PEOPLE TO KNOW // NOAH

GENESIS 6:9–22: When Noah's father named him, he declared his son would be a bringer of comfort and rest, which is the meaning of his name (Ge 5:29). The world in Noah's lifetime was exceedingly wicked. People's hearts were bent only on evil, and God resolved to wipe out humanity for their sin and start over. Noah alone found favor in God's eyes, being righteous within his generation. He "walked faithfully with God" (Ge 6:9).

Warning Noah of his intention to destroy evil humanity, God directed him to build an ark for himself, his family, and an enormous menagerie of animals. Noah obeyed and built this massive vessel despite the mocking scorn of those who watched. When Noah was six hundred years old, God told him to enter the ark. Then rains fell and springs from the deep burst open, causing a flood that covered the earth. All humans and land animals not on the ark perished.

When the waters receded and Noah left the ark, God established a covenant with him and all living creatures (Ge 9:8–11). God promised to never again destroy all life in a flood and gave the rainbow as a sign of his promise.

APPLICATION ✣ Imagine being the only righteous person in a completely wicked society. That person would be mocked and scorned, judged by everyone around them. Noah's neighbors must have thought he was insane, yet he persisted in his calling and was eventually vindicated. If Noah had caved in to pressure and blended into the community around him, he would have been destroyed as they were. Noah's story reminds us that no matter what others around us are doing, we need to stand firm in our obedience to God.

is filled with violence because of them.
I am surely going to destroy both them
and the earth.[q] 14So make yourself an ark
of cypress[a] wood;[r] make rooms in it and
coat it with pitch[s] inside and out. 15This
is how you are to build it: The ark is to
be three hundred cubits long, fifty cubits wide and thirty cubits high.[b] 16Make
a roof for it, leaving below the roof an
opening one cubit[c] high all around.[d] Put
a door in the side of the ark and make
lower, middle and upper decks. 17I am
going to bring floodwaters on the earth
to destroy all life under the heavens, every creature that has the breath of life
in it. Everything on earth will perish.[t]
18But I will establish my covenant with
you,[u] and you will enter the ark[v]—you
and your sons and your wife and your
sons' wives with you. 19You are to bring
into the ark two of all living creatures,
male and female, to keep them alive with
you. 20Two[w] of every kind of bird, of every kind of animal and of every kind of
creature that moves along the ground
will come to you to be kept alive. 21You
are to take every kind of food that is to
be eaten and store it away as food for
you and for them."
22Noah did everything just as God
commanded him.[x]

7 The LORD then said to Noah, "Go into
the ark, you and your whole family,[y]
because I have found you righteous[z] in
this generation. 2Take with you seven
pairs of every kind of clean[a] animal, a
male and its mate, and one pair of every
kind of unclean animal, a male and its
mate, 3and also seven pairs of every kind

6:13 [q] ver 17; Eze 7:2-3
6:14 [r] Heb 11:7; 1Pe 3:20 [s] Ex 2:3
6:17 [t] Ge 7:4, 21-23; 2Pe 2:5
6:18 [u] Ge 9:9-16 [v] Ge 7:1,7,13
6:20 [w] Ge 7:15
6:22 [x] Ge 7:5, 9,16
7:1 [y] Mt 24:38 [z] Ge 6:9; Eze 14:14
7:2 [a] ver 8; Ge 8:20; Lev 10:10; 11:1-47

[a] *14* The meaning of the Hebrew for this word is uncertain. [b] *15* That is, about 450 feet long, 75 feet wide and 45 feet high or about 135 meters long, 23 meters wide and 14 meters high [c] *16* That is, about 18 inches or about 45 centimeters [d] *16* The meaning of the Hebrew for this clause is uncertain.

6:14–16 The dimensions of the ark are easy enough to determine, and the general shape of it is therefore discernible. Based on 1 cubit equaling 18 inches, Noah's ark is 450 feet long, 75 feet wide, and 45 feet deep. It is evident that Noah's ark was not designed to be navigated. Consequently, the fate of the company aboard was left in the hands of God.
6:17 The Hebrew word for Noah's flood is used twelve times in Ge 6–11. Broader cultural usage suggests that the word may have had broader currency as a cosmic water weapon wielded by a deity.
6:19–20; 7:2–3 While the initial instructions indicate that pairs of all living creatures are to be taken into the ark, when more specific instructions are given, one pair each of unclean animals and seven pairs each of clean animals are to be taken. The distinction between clean and unclean animals was not an innovation established at Sinai but is seen here as early as Noah.

Ge 7:11–12 ❖ God's judgment on human sin through the flood was devastating. How does this chapter give us new appreciation for the grace of God in Christ, who takes away the sins of the world (see Jn 1:29)?

of bird, male and female, to keep their
various kinds alive throughout the earth.
4Seven days from now I will send rain on
the earth for forty days and forty nights,
and I will wipe from the face of the earth
every living creature I have made."
5And Noah did all that the LORD commanded him.[b]
6Noah was six hundred years old when
the floodwaters came on the earth. 7And
Noah and his sons and his wife and his
sons' wives entered the ark to escape
the waters of the flood. 8Pairs of clean
and unclean animals, of birds and of all
creatures that move along the ground,
9male and female, came to Noah and
entered the ark, as God had commanded Noah. 10And after the seven days the
floodwaters came on the earth.
11In the six hundredth year of Noah's
life, on the seventeenth day of the second month — on that day all the springs
of the great deep[c] burst forth, and the
floodgates of the heavens[d] were opened.
12And rain fell on the earth forty days
and forty nights.[e]
13On that very day Noah and his sons,
Shem, Ham and Japheth, together with
his wife and the wives of his three sons,
entered the ark. 14They had with them
every wild animal according to its kind,
all livestock according to their kinds,
every creature that moves along the
ground according to its kind and every
bird according to its kind, everything
with wings. 15Pairs of all creatures that
have the breath of life in them came to
Noah and entered the ark.[f] 16The animals
going in were male and female of every
living thing, as God had commanded
Noah. Then the LORD shut him in.
17For forty days[g] the flood kept coming
on the earth, and as the waters increased
they lifted the ark high above the earth.
18The waters rose and increased greatly
on the earth, and the ark floated on the
surface of the water. 19They rose greatly
on the earth, and all the high mountains
under the entire heavens were covered.[h]
20The waters rose and covered the mountains to a depth of more than fifteen cubits.[a,b] 21Every living thing that moved
on land perished — birds, livestock, wild
animals, all the creatures that swarm
over the earth, and all mankind.[i] 22Ev-
erything on dry land that had the breath
of life[j] in its nostrils died. 23Every living
thing on the face of the earth was wiped
out; people and animals and the creatures that move along the ground and
the birds were wiped from the earth.[k]
Only Noah was left, and those with him
in the ark.[l]
24The waters flooded the earth for a
hundred and fifty days.[m]

8 But God remembered[n] Noah and all
the wild animals and the livestock
that were with him in the ark, and he
sent a wind over the earth,[o] and the waters receded. 2Now the springs of the
deep and the floodgates of the heavens[p] had been closed, and the rain had
stopped falling from the sky. 3The water
receded steadily from the earth. At the
end of the hundred and fifty days the
water had gone down, 4and on the seventeenth day of the seventh month the
ark came to rest on the mountains of
Ararat. 5The waters continued to recede
until the tenth month, and on the first
day of the tenth month the tops of the
mountains became visible.
6After forty days Noah opened a window he had made in the ark 7and sent
out a raven, and it kept flying back and
forth until the water had dried up from
the earth. 8Then he sent out a dove to
see if the water had receded from the
surface of the ground. 9But the dove
could find nowhere to perch because
there was water over all the surface of
the earth; so it returned to Noah in the

[a] 20 That is, about 23 feet or about 6.8 meters
[b] 20 *Or rose more than fifteen cubits, and the mountains were covered*

7:5 [b] Ge 6:22
7:11 [c] Eze 26:19 [d] Ge 8:2
7:12 [e] ver 4
7:15 [f] Ge 6:19
7:17 [g] ver 4
7:19 [h] Ps 104:6
7:21 [i] Ge 6:7,13
7:22 [j] Ge 1:30
7:23 [k] Mt 24:39; Lk 17:27; 1Pe 3:20; 2Pe 2:5 [l] Heb 11:7
7:24 [m] Ge 8:3
8:1 [n] Ge 9:15; 19:29; Ex 2:24; 1Sa 1:11,19 [o] Ex 14:21
8:2 [p] Ge 7:11

7:4 The biblical text sets the period of rain at forty days and nights. The one hundred fifty days that the water prevails (v. 24) and the additional one hundred fifty that it recedes (8:5), added to several periods of waiting (7:10; 8:6, 10, 12), amount to just over a year spent on the ark.

8:4 The mountains of Ararat are located in the Lake Van region of eastern Turkey in the area of Armenia.
8:6–12 Ancient navigators used birds to find land, but Noah's use of the birds is not to find direction but to determine the readiness of the land for habitation.

ark. He reached out his hand and took
the dove and brought it back to himself
in the ark. 10He waited seven more days
and again sent out the dove from the ark.
11When the dove returned to him in the
evening, there in its beak was a freshly
plucked olive leaf! Then Noah knew that
the water had receded from the earth.
12He waited seven more days and sent
the dove out again, but this time it did
not return to him.
13By the first day of the first month of
Noah's six hundred and first year, the water had dried up from the earth. Noah then
removed the covering from the ark and
saw that the surface of the ground was dry.
14By the twenty-seventh day of the second
month the earth was completely dry.
15Then God said to Noah, 16"Come out
of the ark, you and your wife and your
sons and their wives.[q] 17Bring out every kind of living creature that is with
you — the birds, the animals, and all the
creatures that move along the ground —
so they can multiply on the earth and be
fruitful and increase in number on it."[r]
18So Noah came out, together with his
sons and his wife and his sons' wives.
19All the animals and all the creatures
that move along the ground and all
the birds — everything that moves on
land — came out of the ark, one kind
after another.
20Then Noah built an altar to the LORD[s]
and, taking some of all the clean animals
and clean[t] birds, he sacrificed burnt offerings[u] on it. 21The LORD smelled the pleasing aroma[v] and said in his heart: "Never
again will I curse the ground[w] because of
humans, even though[a] every inclination
of the human heart is evil from childhood.[x] And never again will I destroy all
living creatures,[y] as I have done.

22"As long as the earth endures,
seedtime and harvest,
cold and heat,
summer and winter,
day and night
will never cease."[z]

Ge 8:21–22 ❖ How does God's promise demonstrate his amazing grace even in the face of human failure? How does this gracious promise impact the way we live our lives today?

8:16 [q] Ge 7:13
8:17 [r] Ge 1:22
8:20 [s] Ge 12:7-8; 13:18; 22:9 [t] Ge 7:8; Lev 11:1-47 [u] Ge 22:2,13; Ex 10:25
8:21 [v] Lev 1:9, 13; 2Co 2:15 [w] Ge 3:17
[x] Ge 6:5; Ps 51:5; Jer 17:9 [y] Ge 9:11,15; Isa 54:9
8:22 [z] Ge 1:14; Jer 33:20,25
9:1 [a] Ge 1:22
9:3 [b] Ge 1:29
9:4 [c] Lev 3:17; 17:10-14; Dt 12:16,23-25; 1Sa 14:33
9:5 [d] Ex 21:28-32 [e] Ge 4:10
9:6 [f] Ge 4:14; Ex 21:12,14; Lev 24:17; Mt 26:52

God's Covenant With Noah

9 Then God blessed Noah and his sons,
saying to them, "Be fruitful and increase in number and fill the earth.[a] 2The
fear and dread of you will fall on all the
beasts of the earth, and on all the birds
in the sky, on every creature that moves
along the ground, and on all the fish in
the sea; they are given into your hands.
3Everything that lives and moves about
will be food for you.[b] Just as I gave you
the green plants, I now give you everything.
4"But you must not eat meat that has
its lifeblood still in it.[c] 5And for your lifeblood I will surely demand an accounting. I will demand an accounting from
every animal.[d] And from each human
being, too, I will demand an accounting
for the life of another human being.[e]

6"Whoever sheds human blood,
by humans shall their blood be
shed;[f]

[a] 21 Or *humans, for*

8:20–21 The purpose of Noah's sacrifice is not stated. The burnt offerings that Moses' audience were familiar with are usually associated with petitions or appeals set before God. Noah's purpose is likely to request God's favor and blessing.

✣ **6:5—8:22** We can see from the flood narrative that God is able to bring restoration where he has brought destruction. The re-creation theme in the flood narrative shows God's starting again with humanity.

Noah and his family are saved; the world and human civilization are salvaged. Salvaging involves retrieving that which is valuable from the wreckage. We can find God's salvage work in individual lives. It is this quality of God that finds, amid Saul's destructive, skeptic zeal, Paul's apostolic vision for the church. The same God finds and nurtures in each one of us that which transforms our lives from sinful rubble to useful ministry. God is in the business of re-creating, and our lives testify to that grace. We are saved from our sin and its condemnation; we are salvaged for ministry and its service to God.

9:1–7 After the fall, the ground would not be cooperative. Obtaining food will continue to be a challenge. It is likely that permission to use animals for food should be seen as a concession of grace. Human life, because of the image of God, remains under the protection of God. Accountability to God for preserving human life is put into humanity's hands.

for in the image of God[g]
has God made mankind.

7As for you, be fruitful and increase in
number; multiply on the earth and increase upon it."[h]
8Then God said to Noah and to his sons
with him: 9"I now establish my covenant
with you[i] and with your descendants after you 10and with every living creature
that was with you — the birds, the livestock and all the wild animals, all those
that came out of the ark with you — every living creature on earth. 11I establish
my covenant[j] with you: Never again will
all life be destroyed by the waters of a
flood; never again will there be a flood
to destroy the earth.[k]"
12And God said, "This is the sign of the
covenant[l] I am making between me and
you and every living creature with you, a
covenant for all generations to come: 13I
have set my rainbow in the clouds, and it
will be the sign of the covenant between
me and the earth. 14Whenever I bring
clouds over the earth and the rainbow
appears in the clouds, 15I will remember
my covenant[m] between me and you and
all living creatures of every kind. Never
again will the waters become a flood to
destroy all life. 16Whenever the rainbow
appears in the clouds, I will see it and
remember the everlasting covenant[n]
between God and all living creatures of
every kind on the earth."

9:6 [g] Ge 1:26
9:7 [h] Ge 1:22
9:9 [i] Ge 6:18
9:11 [j] ver 16; Isa 24:5 [k] Ge 8:21; Isa 54:9
9:12 [l] ver 17; Ge 17:11
9:15 [m] Ex 2:24; Lev 26:42, 45; Dt 7:9; Eze 16:60
9:16 [n] ver 11; Ge 17:7, 13, 19; 2Sa 7:13; 23:5

Ge 9:12–16 ❖ God gave the rainbow as a sign to remind himself of his covenant promises to creation. Is there an object or sign in your life that reminds you of the promises you have made to God?

17So God said to Noah, "This is the sign
of the covenant[o] I have established between me and all life on the earth."

The Sons of Noah

18The sons of Noah who came out of
the ark were Shem, Ham and Japheth.
(Ham was the father of Canaan.)[p] 19These
were the three sons of Noah, and from
them came the people who were scattered over the whole earth.[q]
20Noah, a man of the soil, proceeded[a]
to plant a vineyard. 21When he drank
some of its wine, he became drunk and
lay uncovered inside his tent. 22Ham, the
father of Canaan, saw his father naked
and told his two brothers outside. 23But
Shem and Japheth took a garment and
laid it across their shoulders; then they
walked in backward and covered their
father's naked body. Their faces were
turned the other way so that they would
not see their father naked.
24When Noah awoke from his wine and
found out what his youngest son had
done to him, 25he said,

9:17 [o] ver 12; Ge 17:11
9:18 [p] ver 25-27; Ge 10:6, 15
9:19 [q] Ge 10:32

[a] 20 Or *soil, was the first*

9:8–17 Perhaps the closest concept to a covenant in our society is a legal contract. Here the covenant is used as a means for God to formalize a pledge that he will not undo the blessing again.

Since the Hebrew word for "rainbow" is the same as the one used for the bow weapon, this offers an interesting image. It is a deeply meaningful image to have God hanging up his bow.

9:18–23 The phrase "man of the soil" (v. 20) probably connotes more than simply "farmer." Noah is mortal and must continue to struggle with the curse. At the same time, Noah finds himself again on dry soil, with a second chance for humanity.

The text does not explain, excuse, or condemn Noah's drunkenness. This does not mean that there is no explanation, no excuse, or no condemnation—it simply indicates that the text is not willing to be deterred from its purpose. The parallel to the fall is in Ham's action, not in Noah's condition.

If Ham's offense is parallel to the fall, then we should look for the common denominator of the parallels for clues. Both Eve and Ham are betrayed by their eyes. Eve *saw* that the fruit was desirable, and Ham *saw* his father's nakedness. Moreover, both Eve and Ham seek to entice others to join them in the offensive act.

9:24–29 Many have wondered why Canaan is cursed when apparently Ham committed the offense. This question can be resolved when we recognize the nature of Noah's statements. Verses 25–27 fit into the category of "patriarchal pronouncement." These pronouncements concern fertility of the family and ground and the question of who will dominate whom. Such pronouncements often include both negative and positive statements and are often given by a father on his deathbed, but they need not be limited to that situation.

As to the details of the pronouncement, the Hebrew reads literally: "May God extend Japheth and may *he* dwell in the tents of Shem" (alternate translation). Since there is no question concerning the slave status assigned to Canaan, any situation in which Canaan is under someone else's power qualifies.

As to the function of the pronouncement, the author is more interested in Canaan than he is in Ham. He implies that the Canaanites got off on the wrong foot from the beginning; thus, it is no surprise that by the time of Moses and his audience, they have earned the wrath and punishment of God.

MAJOR COVENANTS IN THE OLD TESTAMENT

COVENANTS	REFERENCE	TYPE	PARTICIPANT	DESCRIPTION
Noahic	Ge 9:8-17	Royal Grant	Made with righteous (6:9) Noah (and his descendants and every living thing on earth—all life that is subject to human jurisdiction)	An unconditional divine promise never to destroy all earthly life with some natural catastrophe, the covenant "sign" (9:13, 17) being the rainbow in the storm cloud
Abrahamic A	Ge 15:6-21	Royal (land) Grant	Made with "righteous" (his faith was "credited … to him as righteousness," v. 6) Abram (and his descendants, v. 16)	An unconditional divine promise to fulfill the grant of the land; a self-maledictory oath symbolically enacted it (v. 17; see note)
Abrahamic B	Ge 17	Suzerain-vassal	Made with Abraham as patriarchal head of his household	A conditional divine pledge to be Abraham's God and the God of his descendants (cf. "as for me," v. 4; "as for you," v. 9); the condition: total consecration to the Lord as symbolized by circumcision
Sinaitic	Ex 19-24	Suzerain-vassal	Made with Israel as the descendants of Abraham, Isaac and Jacob and as the people the Lord had redeemed from bondage to an earthly power	A conditional divine pledge to be Israel's God (as her protector and the guarantor of her blessed destiny); the condition: Israel's total consecration to the Lord as his people (his kingdom) who live by his rule and serve his purposes in history
Phinehas	Nu 25:10-13	Royal Grant	Made with the zealous priest Phinehas	An unconditional divine promise to maintain the family of Phinehas in a "lasting priesthood" (v. 13; implicitly a pledge to Israel to provide her forever with a faithful priesthood)
Davidic	2Sa 7:5-16	Royal Grant	Made with faithful King David after his devotion to God as Israel's king and the Lord's anointed vassal had come to special expression (v. 2)	An unconditional divine promise to establish and maintain the Davidic dynasty on the throne of Israel (implicitly a pledge to Israel to provide her forever with a godly king like David and through that dynasty to do for her what he had done through David—bring her into rest in the promised land [1Ki 4:20-21; 5:3-4])
New	Jer 31:31-34	Royal Grant	Promised to rebellious Israel as they are about to be expelled from the promised land in actualization of the most severe covenant curse (Lev 26:27-39; Dt 28:36-37, 45-68)	An unconditional divine promise to unfaithful Israel to forgive their sins and establish his relationship with them on a new basis by writing his law "on their hearts" (v. 33)—a covenant of pure grace

"Cursed be Canaan![r]
The lowest of slaves
will he be to his brothers.[s]"

26He also said,

"Praise be to the LORD, the God of Shem!
May Canaan be the slave of Shem.
27May God extend Japheth's[a] territory;
may Japheth live in the tents of Shem,
and may Canaan be the slave of Japheth."

28After the flood Noah lived 350 years.
29Noah lived a total of 950 years, and
then he died.

The Table of Nations

10 This is the account[t] of Shem, Ham and Japheth, Noah's sons, who themselves had sons after the flood.

The Japhethites
10:2–5pp // 1Ch 1:5–7

2The sons[b] of Japheth:
Gomer,[u] Magog,[v] Madai, Javan, Tubal,[w] Meshek and Tiras.
3The sons of Gomer:
Ashkenaz,[x] Riphath and Togarmah.[y]
4The sons of Javan:
Elishah, Tarshish,[z] the Kittites and the Rodanites.[c]
5(From these the maritime peoples spread out into their territories by their clans within their nations, each with its own language.)

The Hamites
10:6–20pp // 1Ch 1:8–16

6The sons of Ham:
Cush, Egypt, Put and Canaan.[a]
7The sons of Cush:
Seba, Havilah, Sabtah, Raamah and Sabteka.
The sons of Raamah:
Sheba and Dedan.

9:25 [r] ver 18 [s] Ge 25:23; Jos 9:23
10:1 [t] Ge 2:4
10:2 [u] Eze 38:6 [v] Eze 38:2; Rev 20:8 [w] Isa 66:19
10:3 [x] Jer 51:27 [y] Eze 27:14; 38:6
10:4 [z] Eze 27:12, 25; Jnh 1:3
10:6 [a] ver 15; Ge 9:18

Ge 10:1 ❖ This genealogy traces the lineage of Noah's sons. Each of these was father to a nation. How can we understand our influence in light of future generations? Are we reaching out to others to leave a legacy for Christ?

8Cush was the father[d] of Nimrod, who
became a mighty warrior on the earth.
9He was a mighty hunter before the
LORD; that is why it is said, "Like Nimrod, a mighty hunter before the LORD."
10The first centers of his kingdom were
Babylon,[b] Uruk, Akkad and Kalneh, in[e]
Shinar.[f][c] 11From that land he went to
Assyria,[d] where he built Nineveh,[e] Rehoboth Ir,[g] Calah 12and Resen, which is
between Nineveh and Calah—which is
the great city.

13Egypt was the father of
the Ludites, Anamites, Lehabites, Naphtuhites, 14Pathrusites, Kasluhites (from whom the Philistines[f] came) and Caphtorites.
15Canaan[g] was the father of
Sidon[h] his firstborn,[h] and of the Hittites,[i] 16Jebusites,[j] Amorites, Girgashites, 17Hivites, Arkites, Sinites, 18Arvadites, Zemarites and Hamathites.

Later the Canaanite[k] clans scattered
19and the borders of Canaan[l] reached
from Sidon[m] toward Gerar as far as Gaza,
and then toward Sodom, Gomorrah, Admah and Zeboyim, as far as Lasha.
20These are the sons of Ham by their

10:10 [b] Ge 11:9 [c] Ge 11:2
10:11 [d] Ps 83:8; Mic 5:6 [e] Jnh 1:2; 4:11; Na 1:1
10:14 [f] Ge 21:32, 34; 26:1,8
10:15 [g] ver 6; Ge 9:18 [h] Eze 28:21 [i] Ge 23:3,20
10:16 [j] 1Ch 11:4
10:18 [k] Ge 12:6; Ex 13:11
10:19 [l] Ge 11:31; 13:12; 17:8 [m] ver 15

[a] 27 *Japheth* sounds like the Hebrew for *extend.* [b] 2 *Sons* may mean *descendants* or *successors* or *nations*; also in verses 3, 4, 6, 7, 20-23, 29 and 31. [c] 4 Some manuscripts of the Masoretic Text and Samaritan Pentateuch (see also Septuagint and 1 Chron. 1:7); most manuscripts of the Masoretic Text *Dodanites* [d] 8 *Father* may mean *ancestor* or *predecessor* or *founder*; also in verses 13, 15, 24 and 26. [e] 10 Or *Uruk and Akkad—all of them in* [f] 10 That is, Babylonia [g] 11 Or *Nineveh with its city squares* [h] 15 Or *of the Sidonians, the foremost*

❖ **9:1-29** God has pledged that he will not bring the return of chaos through his actions. But that does not mean he will prevent us from bringing ecological doom on ourselves. The security we may derive from God's commitment should not make us so comfortable that we consider ourselves invulnerable to ecological catastrophe, with license to be as reckless as our indulgences demand.

10:1-32 The organization of the list of nations in ch. 10 is somewhat genealogical, but genealogy is not its purpose. Japheth is first. Ham's line is addressed in vv. 6–20. Shem's descendants are outlined in vv. 21–31.

clans and languages, in their territories
and nations.

The Semites

10:21–31pp // Ge 11:10–27; 1Ch 1:17–27

21Sons were also born to Shem, whose
older brother was[a] Japheth; Shem was
the ancestor of all the sons of Eber.[n]

22The sons of Shem:
Elam,[o] Ashur, Arphaxad,[p] Lud and
Aram.
23The sons of Aram:
Uz,[q] Hul, Gether and Meshek.[b]
24Arphaxad was the father of[c] Shelah,
and Shelah the father of Eber.[r]
25Two sons were born to Eber:
One was named Peleg,[d] because
in his time the earth was divided;
his brother was named Joktan.
26Joktan was the father of
Almodad, Sheleph, Hazarmaveth,
Jerah, 27Hadoram, Uzal, Diklah,
28Obal, Abimael, Sheba, 29Ophir,
Havilah and Jobab. All these were
sons of Joktan.

30The region where they lived stretched
from Mesha toward Sephar, in the eastern hill country.
31These are the sons of Shem by their
clans and languages, in their territories
and nations.

32These are the clans of Noah's sons,[s]
according to their lines of descent, within their nations. From these the nations
spread out over the earth[t] after the flood.

The Tower of Babel

11 Now the whole world had one language and a common speech. 2As
people moved eastward,[e] they found a
plain in Shinar[f][u] and settled there.
3They said to each other, "Come, let's
make bricks[v] and bake them thoroughly." They used brick instead of stone, and
tar[w] for mortar. 4Then they said, "Come,
let us build ourselves a city, with a tower
that reaches to the heavens,[x] so that we
may make a name[y] for ourselves; otherwise we will be scattered over the face of
the whole earth."[z]
5But the LORD came down[a] to see the
city and the tower the people were building. 6The LORD said, "If as one people
speaking the same language they have
begun to do this, then nothing they plan
to do will be impossible for them. 7Come,
let us[b] go down and confuse their language so they will not understand each
other."[c]
8So the LORD scattered them from
there over all the earth,[d] and they
stopped building the city. 9That is why
it was called Babel[g][e] — because there
the LORD confused the language of the
whole world. From there the LORD scattered them over the face of the whole
earth.

Ge 11:4 ❖ The people pridefully wanted to make a glorious tower and a name for themselves. In a world of viral media and quick fame, how can Christians avoid falling into the alluring sin of pride?

From Shem to Abram

11:10–27pp // Ge 10:21–31; 1Ch 1:17–27

10This is the account of Shem's family line.

10:21 [n]ver 24; Nu 24:24
10:22 [o]Jer 49:34 [p]Lk 3:36
10:23 [q]Job 1:1
10:24 [r]ver 21
10:32 [s]ver 1 [t]Ge 9:19
11:2 [u]Ge 10:10
11:3 [v]Ex 1:14 [w]Ge 14:10
11:4 [x]Dt 1:28; 9:1 [y]Ge 6:4 [z]Dt 4:27
11:5 [a]ver 7; Ge 18:21; Ex 3:8; 19:11, 18, 20
11:7 [b]Ge 1:26 [c]Ge 42:23
11:8 [d]Ge 9:19; Lk 1:51
11:9 [e]Ge 10:10

[a] 21 Or *Shem, the older brother of* [b] 23 See Septuagint and 1 Chron. 1:17; Hebrew *Mash.* [c] 24 Hebrew; Septuagint *father of Cainan, and Cainan was the father of* [d] 25 *Peleg* means *division.* [e] 2 Or *from the east*; or *in the east* [f] 2 That is, Babylonia [g] 9 That is, Babylon; *Babel* sounds like the Hebrew for *confused.*

11:1–9 In the early stages of urbanization, the city was comprised of public buildings such as administrative buildings and granaries, which were mostly connected with the temple. Most interpreters have identified the tower of Babel as a ziggurat.

The ziggurat was built to support a stairway, a visual representation of the passage believed to be used by the gods to travel from one realm to another. At the top of the ziggurat was the gate of the gods, the entrance into their heavenly abode.

The needs and nature of the deities who would make use of a ziggurat stairway reflect the weakness and distortion of deity brought about by the Babylonians assigning humanlike attributes to the gods. The offense in this passage went beyond mere idolatry; it degraded the nature of God by portraying him as having needs.

Yahweh views this as a first step with inevitable results—human beings have crossed a significant threshold from which there will be no turning back. This is expressed in his observation that now "nothing they plan to do will be impossible" (v. 6). The inhibitions that may prevent them from further corruption have been overcome.

11:10–26 Here the intention is to trace the genealogical line from Noah to Abram as a means of establishing continuity from the blessed line of Shem to the forefather of the Hebrews.

TABLE OF NATIONS

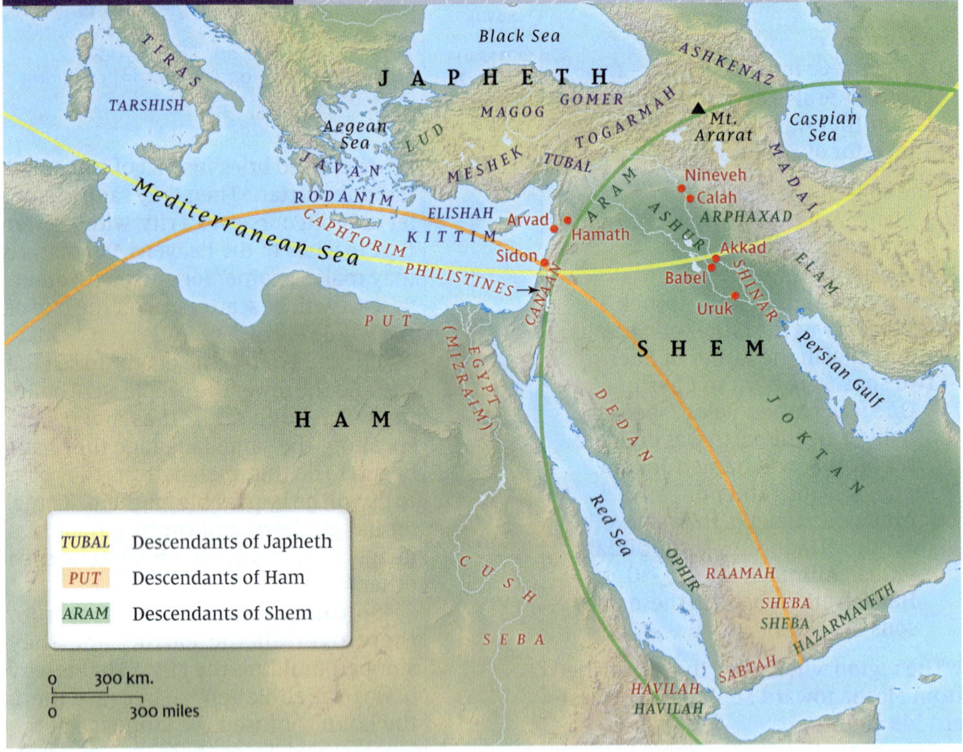

TUBAL Descendants of Japheth
PUT Descendants of Ham
ARAM Descendants of Shem

Two years after the flood, when Shem
was 100 years old, he became the father[a]
of Arphaxad. 11And after he became the
father of Arphaxad, Shem lived 500 years
and had other sons and daughters.
12When Arphaxad had lived 35 years,
he became the father of Shelah.[f] 13And
after he became the father of Shelah,
Arphaxad lived 403 years and had other
sons and daughters.[b]
14When Shelah had lived 30 years, he
became the father of Eber. 15And after
he became the father of Eber, Shelah
lived 403 years and had other sons and
daughters.
16When Eber had lived 34 years, he
became the father of Peleg. 17And after he became the father of Peleg, Eber
lived 430 years and had other sons and
daughters.
18When Peleg had lived 30 years, he
became the father of Reu. 19And after he
became the father of Reu, Peleg lived 209
years and had other sons and daughters.
20When Reu had lived 32 years, he became the father of Serug.[g] 21And after he
became the father of Serug, Reu lived 207
years and had other sons and daughters.
22When Serug had lived 30 years, he
became the father of Nahor. 23And after
he became the father of Nahor, Serug
lived 200 years and had other sons and
daughters.

11:12 [f] Lk 3:35
11:20 [g] Lk 3:35

[a] 10 *Father* may mean *ancestor*; also in verses 11-25. [b] 12,13 Hebrew; Septuagint (see also Luke 3:35,36 and note at Gen. 10:24) *35 years, he became the father of Cainan. 13And after he became the father of Cainan, Arphaxad lived 430 years and had other sons and daughters, and then he died. When Cainan had lived 130 years, he became the father of Shelah. And after he became the father of Shelah, Cainan lived 330 years and had other sons and daughters*

10:1—11:26 God's power is an awesome thing. We dilute his power when we try to tap into it in order to redirect it for our own purpose or benefit. We are called to be the channel of that power. This becomes a problem when, instead of letting God's power work through us or in us to carry out his plans, we want him to do our bidding. We are often delighted for God's power to work wonders in our lives but reluctant to allow his power to purify us.

24When Nahor had lived 29 years, he became the father of Terah.[h] 25And after he became the father of Terah, Nahor lived 119 years and had other sons and daughters.

26After Terah had lived 70 years, he became the father of Abram,[i] Nahor[j] and Haran.

Abram's Family

27This is the account of Terah's family line.

Terah became the father of Abram, Nahor and Haran. And Haran became the father of Lot.[k] 28While his father Terah was still alive, Haran died in Ur of the Chaldeans,[l] in the land of his birth. 29Abram and Nahor both married. The name of Abram's wife was Sarai,[m] and the name of Nahor's wife was Milkah;[n] she was the daughter of Haran, the father of both Milkah and Iskah. 30Now Sarai was childless because she was not able to conceive.[o]

31Terah took his son Abram, his grandson Lot son of Haran, and his daughter-in-law Sarai, the wife of his son Abram, and together they set out from Ur of the Chaldeans[p] to go to Canaan.[q] But when they came to Harran, they settled there.

32Terah lived 205 years, and he died in Harran.

The Call of Abram

12 The LORD had said to Abram, "Go from your country, your people and your father's household to the land I will show you.[r]

2"I will make you into a great nation,[s]
and I will bless you;[t]
I will make your name great,
and you will be a blessing.[a]
3I will bless those who bless you,
and whoever curses you I will curse;[u]
and all peoples on earth
will be blessed through you.[v]"[b]

> Ge 12:1-3 ❖ In light of Jesus' work on the cross, how do these words increase our understanding of God's faithfulness?

4So Abram went, as the LORD had told him; and Lot went with him. Abram was seventy-five years old when he set out from Harran.[w] 5He took his wife Sarai, his nephew Lot, all the possessions they had accumulated and the people[x] they had acquired in Harran, and they set out for the land of Canaan, and they arrived there.

6Abram traveled through the land[y] as far as the site of the great tree of Moreh[z] at Shechem. At that time the Canaanites[a] were in the land. 7The LORD appeared to Abram[b] and said, "To your offspring[c] I will give this land."[c] So he built an altar there to the LORD,[d] who had appeared to him.

8From there he went on toward the hills east of Bethel[e] and pitched his tent, with Bethel on the west and Ai on the east. There he built an altar to the LORD and called on the name of the LORD.

9Then Abram set out and continued toward the Negev.[f]

Abram in Egypt

12:10–20Ref // Ge 20:1–18; 26:1–11

10Now there was a famine in the land, and Abram went down to Egypt to live there for a while because the famine was severe. 11As he was about to enter Egypt,

11:24 [h] Lk 3:34
11:26 [i] Lk 3:34 [j] Jos 24:2
11:27 [k] ver 31; Ge 12:4; 14:12; 19:1; 2Pe 2:7
11:28 [l] ver 31; Ge 15:7
11:29 [m] Ge 17:15 [n] Ge 22:20
11:30 [o] Ge 16:1; 18:11
11:31 [p] Ge 15:7; Ne 9:7; Ac 7:4 [q] Ge 10:19
12:1 [r] Ac 7:3*; Heb 11:8
12:2 [s] Ge 15:5; 17:2,4; 18:18; 22:17; Dt 26:5 [t] Ge 24:1,35
12:3 [u] Ge 27:29; Ex 23:22; Nu 24:9 [v] Ge 18:18; 22:18; 26:4; Ac 3:25; Gal 3:8*
12:4 [w] Ge 11:31
12:5 [x] Ge 14:14; 17:23
12:6 [y] Heb 11:9 [z] Ge 35:4; Dt 11:30 [a] Ge 10:18
12:7 [b] Ge 17:1; 18:1; Ex 6:3 [c] Ge 13:15,17; 15:18; 17:8; Ps 105:9-11 [d] Ge 13:4
12:8 [e] Ge 13:3
12:9 [f] Ge 13:1,3

[a] 2 Or *be seen as blessed* [b] 3 Or *earth / will use your name in blessings* (see 48:20) [c] 7 Or *seed*

11:27–30, 32 Abram's entry into Canaan can be plausibly placed somewhere between 2100 and 1875 BC.
11:31 A quick check of the maps at the back of most Bibles confirms a consensus in popular circles concerning the identification of Abram's hometown, Ur of the Chaldeans. Though it makes for a convenient identification and there is no other archaeological site that carries the ancient name of Ur, the identification is uncertain.
12:1–3 Yahweh makes the covenant initiative offer to Abram. Abram must trust Yahweh to deliver what he has offered so that he can receive what God has promised.
12:4–9 The trip from Haran to Canaan is about five hundred miles and takes the better part of a month even if Abram travels at normal caravan pace (about twenty miles per day). Shechem and Bethel become major sacred sites in later Israelite history. Abram builds an altar at each location.
12:10–18 Modern archaeologists and geologists have found evidence of a massive three-hundred-year drought cycle that occurred during one of the time periods to which Abram is dated. There is a built-in theological question here when Abram goes to Egypt. The famine raises questions about the ability of God to take care of his followers. The temporary solution to the food problem creates a family problem.
12:11–13 This is the first of three narratives in which a patriarch attempts to identify his wife as his sister

PEOPLE TO KNOW // ABRAHAM

GENESIS 12:1-9: God's covenant with Abraham (Abram) begins the story of God's relationship with a people that he would use to bless the entire world. God chose Abraham and his descendants to be that channel of blessing for all nations (Ge 12:1-3), redeeming creation from the curse of sin. There was just one problem: Abraham's wife Sarah could not have children. Where were all these descendants supposed to come from?

Abraham's first solution was to pass his inheritance on to his servant, Eliezer (Ge 15:2-3). When God specifically promised Abraham a son of his own flesh and descendants as numerous as the stars, Abraham believed God, and God "credited it to him as righteousness" (Ge 15:6). God made a covenant with Abraham, promising his descendants the land of Canaan.

Sarah suggested Abraham have a child with her Egyptian slave, Hagar, in order to have a son. Abraham slept with Hagar, and she bore Ishmael. Yet God told Abraham that Sarah herself would have a son. Abraham and Sarah both laughed at this promise due to Sarah's age and barrenness, but in the course of time Sarah had a son they named Isaac. God had fulfilled his promise.

God later tested Abraham's commitment by telling him to offer Isaac as a burnt sacrifice (Ge 22:2). Abraham obeyed, but God stopped him at the last moment, saving Isaac's life and then providing a ram for Abraham to sacrifice instead (Ge 22:13). In this story we see a foreshadowing of God's sacrifice of his own Son in Jesus.

Abraham's descendants through Isaac became the Israelite people. From his line came Jesus Christ, the Savior of the world, through whom all peoples are blessed.

APPLICATION Abraham is a hero of the faith, obeying God's commands and trusting God's unbelievable promises. His descendants through Isaac—a child born by a miracle—became God's treasured inheritance and a channel of blessing to the world. Through Jesus, the Son of God born in a miraculous way, the church extends the mission of Israel into the world (Gal 3:29), bringing God's hope and blessing to all peoples. By faith, every believer is a child of Abraham and an agent of God's grand redemption story.

he said to his wife Sarai, "I know what
a beautiful woman you are. 12When the
Egyptians see you, they will say, 'This is
his wife.' Then they will kill me but will
let you live. 13Say you are my sister,[g] so
that I will be treated well for your sake
and my life will be spared because of you."
14When Abram came to Egypt, the
Egyptians saw that Sarai was a very beautiful woman. 15And when Pharaoh's officials saw her, they praised her to Phar-
aoh, and she was taken into his palace.
16He treated Abram well for her sake, and
Abram acquired sheep and cattle, male
and female donkeys, male and female
servants, and camels.
17But the LORD inflicted serious diseases on Pharaoh and his household[h]
because of Abram's wife Sarai. 18So Pharaoh summoned Abram. "What have you
done to me?"[i] he said. "Why didn't you
tell me she was your wife? 19Why did you
say, 'She is my sister,' so that I took her
to be my wife? Now then, here is your
wife. Take her and go!" 20Then Pharaoh
gave orders about Abram to his men, and
they sent him on his way, with his wife
and everything he had.

12:13 [g] Ge 20:2; 26:7
12:17 [h] 1Ch 16:21
12:18 [i] Ge 20:9; 26:10

---

to avoid problems with the power establishment of the region (chs. 12; 20; 26). The original Israelite audience undoubtedly knew what advantage was to be gained from the deception, so there was no need for the author to explain it. For our part, we accomplish nothing by welcoming or devising solutions designed to either vindicate Abram or to accuse him of doing something wrong.

12:14 We need not assume that Sarai has miraculously retained the stunning beauty of youth. Her dignity, her bearing, her countenance, and her outfitting may all contribute to the impression that she is a striking woman.

12:17 A sudden onslaught of disease would naturally lead to an investigation of activities that may have upset the gods. Pharaoh's reprimand of Abram is not a judgment of Abram's ethics, but a chastening for putting Pharaoh in jeopardy.

11:27—12:20 Genesis gives us a chance to explore the brightly shining stars in the dawn of the theology of grace. What shines brighter than anything else is the grace shown by God as he reveals himself to and through his people. And though we are not wrong to be in constant awe of the grace of our salvation, we cannot afford to lose our awe of the grace of revelation.

Abram and Lot Separate

13 So Abram went up from Egypt to
the Negev,[j] with his wife and everything he had, and Lot went with him.
2Abram had become very wealthy in livestock and in silver and gold.
3From the Negev he went from place
to place until he came to Bethel,[k] to the
place between Bethel and Ai where his
tent had been earlier 4and where he had
first built an altar.[l] There Abram called
on the name of the LORD.
5Now Lot, who was moving about with
Abram, also had flocks and herds and
tents. 6But the land could not support
them while they stayed together, for their
possessions were so great that they were
not able to stay together.[m] 7And quarreling[n] arose between Abram's herders and
Lot's. The Canaanites and Perizzites were
also living in the land[o] at that time.

13:1 [j] Ge 12:9
13:3 [k] Ge 12:8
13:4 [l] Ge 12:7
13:6 [m] Ge 36:7
13:7 [n] Ge 26:20, 21 [o] Ge 12:6

Ge 13:8-13 ❖ In light of Lot being a potential rival for land and resources, what is inspiring about Abram's example?

8So Abram said to Lot, "Let's not have
any quarreling between you and me,[p]
or between your herders and mine, for
we are close relatives.[q] 9Is not the whole
land before you? Let's part company. If
you go to the left, I'll go to the right; if
you go to the right, I'll go to the left."
10Lot looked around and saw that the
whole plain of the Jordan toward Zoar[r]
was well watered, like the garden of the
LORD,[s] like the land of Egypt. (This was
before the LORD destroyed Sodom and
Gomorrah.)[t] 11So Lot chose for himself
the whole plain of the Jordan and set
out toward the east. The two men parted

13:8 [p] Pr 15:18; 20:3 [q] Ps 133:1
13:10 [r] Ge 19:22, 30 [s] Ge 2:8-10; Isa 51:3 [t] Ge 14:8; 19:17-29

In grace, God has communicated to us about what pleases him and what angers him. We don't have to guess. He has opened to us his character, his attributes, his heart. How sad it is that the reality of revelation has become so commonplace to us. What a tragedy that we take it for granted. Though we have every reason to revel in the thrill of our eternal destiny, we would be terribly careless if we failed to realize that greater than the privilege of living forever is that of knowing God. In the end, our faith is about God, not about us.

13:1-18 The land of Canaan had limited water and grazing. The needs of Abram and Lot soon outgrew the available resources. Competing needs lead to conflict, and Abram and Lot decide they must go their separate ways.

13:11 By moving to the vicinity of the cities of the

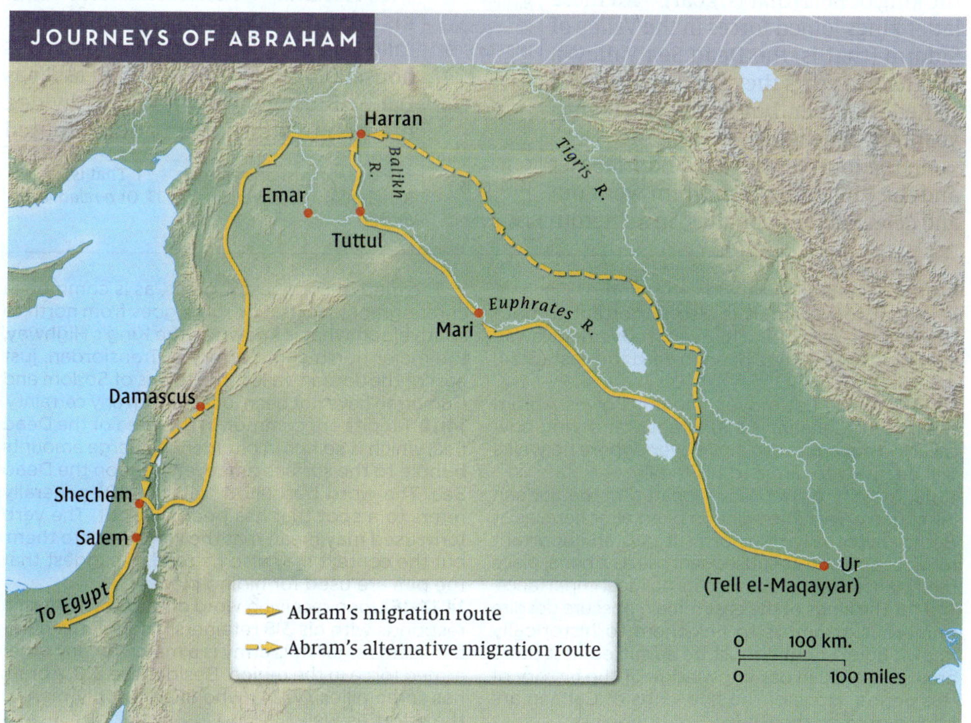

company: 12Abram lived in the land of Canaan, while Lot lived among the cities of the plain[u] and pitched his tents near Sodom.[v] 13Now the people of Sodom were wicked and were sinning greatly against the LORD.[w]

14The LORD said to Abram after Lot had parted from him, "Look around from where you are, to the north and south, to the east and west.[x] 15All the land that you see I will give to you and your offspring[*a*] forever.[y] 16I will make your offspring like the dust of the earth, so that if anyone could count the dust, then your offspring could be counted. 17Go, walk through the length and breadth of the land,[z] for I am giving it to you."

18So Abram went to live near the great trees of Mamre[a] at Hebron,[b] where he pitched his tents. There he built an altar to the LORD.[c]

Abram Rescues Lot

14 At the time when Amraphel was king of Shinar,[*b*][d] Arioch king of Ellasar, Kedorlaomer king of Elam and Tidal king of Goyim, 2these kings went to war against Bera king of Sodom, Birsha king of Gomorrah, Shinab king of Admah, Shemeber king of Zeboyim,[e] and the king of Bela (that is, Zoar).[f] 3All these latter kings joined forces in the Valley of Siddim (that is, the Dead Sea Valley[g]). 4For twelve years they had been subject to Kedorlaomer, but in the thirteenth year they rebelled.

5In the fourteenth year, Kedorlaomer and the kings allied with him went out and defeated the Rephaites[h] in Ashteroth Karnaim, the Zuzites in Ham, the Emites[i] in Shaveh Kiriathaim 6and the Horites[j] in the hill country of Seir,[k] as far as El Paran[l] near the desert. 7Then they turned back and went to En Mishpat (that is, Kadesh), and they conquered the whole territory of the Amalekites, as well as the Amorites who were living in Hazezon Tamar.[m]

8Then the king of Sodom, the king of Gomorrah,[n] the king of Admah, the king of Zeboyim[o] and the king of Bela (that is, Zoar) marched out and drew up their battle lines in the Valley of Siddim 9against Kedorlaomer king of Elam, Tidal king of Goyim, Amraphel king of Shinar and Arioch king of Ellasar — four kings against five. 10Now the Valley of Siddim was full of tar pits, and when the kings of Sodom and Gomorrah fled, some of the men fell into them and the rest fled to the hills.[p] 11The four kings seized all the goods of Sodom and Gomorrah and all their food; then they went away. 12They also carried off Abram's nephew Lot and his possessions, since he was living in Sodom.

13A man who had escaped came and reported this to Abram the Hebrew. Now Abram was living near the great trees of Mamre[q] the Amorite, a brother[*c*] of Eshkol and Aner, all of whom were allied with Abram. 14When Abram heard that his relative had been taken captive, he called out the 318 trained men born in his household[r] and went in pursuit as far as Dan.[s] 15During the night Abram divided his men to attack them and he routed

13:12 [u] Ge 19:17, 25,29 [v] Ge 14:12
13:13 [w] Ge 18:20; Eze 16:49-50; 2Pe 2:8
13:14 [x] Ge 28:14; Dt 3:27
13:15 [y] Ge 12:7; Gal 3:16*
13:17 [z] ver 15; Nu 13:17-25
13:18 [a] Ge 14:13, 24; 18:1 [b] Ge 35:27 [c] Ge 8:20
14:1 [d] Ge 10:10
14:2 [e] Ge 10:19 [f] Ge 13:10
14:3 [g] Nu 34:3, 12; Dt 3:17; Jos 3:16; 15:2,5
14:5 [h] Ge 15:20; Dt 2:11,20 [i] Dt 2:10
14:6 [j] Dt 2:12, 22 [k] Dt 2:1,5, 22 [l] Ge 21:21; Nu 10:12
14:7 [m] 2Ch 20:2
14:8 [n] Ge 13:10; 19:17-29 [o] Dt 29:23
14:10 [p] Ge 19:17, 30
14:13 [q] ver 24; Ge 13:18
14:14 [r] Ge 15:3 [s] Dt 34:1; Jdg 18:29

a 15 Or *seed*; also in verse 16 *b* 1 That is, Babylonia; also in verse 9 *c* 13 Or *a relative*; or *an ally*

---

plain, Lot has gone outside the land of Canaan, leaving it to Abram. It is also important to note "toward the east" in v. 11. Every movement away from God thus far has been toward the east (3:24; 4:16; 11:2).

13:14–17 Once Lot moves, the Lord gives Abram the land of Canaan. His itinerant wandering now takes on new purpose since everywhere he walks will be given to him and his family.

13:18 The city of Hebron is located in the Judean hill country. The construction of an altar here, as at Bethel, eventually transforms it into an important religious site, and its subsequent use as a burial place for the ancestors established its political importance.

14:1–16 The kings of the east remain obscure despite numerous attempts to link them to historically known figures, but it must be admitted that there are many gaps in our knowledge of the history of this period. None of the five kings of Canaan are known outside the Bible. The map of conquest is given, as is common in chronographic texts. The route goes from north to south along what is known as the King's Highway, the major north-south artery in Transjordan, just east of the Jordan Valley. The towns of Sodom and Gomorrah have not been located with any certainty.

14:10 Tar pits are common in this area of the Dead Sea, which is so rich in bitumen that large amounts bubble to the surface and even float on the Dead Sea. The word translated "pits" (v. 10) generally refers to a spot that has been dug out. The verb form used may mean that the kings fall into them, but the context may also be read to suggest that the pits are used for hiding places.

14:13–16 Upon receiving word of the attack, Abram responds with his 318 retainers. Though the number seems small, this army is a match for any other armed force in the region. Besides the 318, Abram has three allies (v. 24) who likely supply men to the effort as well.

them, pursuing them as far as Hobah,
north of Damascus. 16He recovered all
the goods and brought back his relative
Lot and his possessions, together with
the women and the other people.
17After Abram returned from defeating
Kedorlaomer and the kings allied with
him, the king of Sodom came out to meet
him in the Valley of Shaveh (that is, the
King's Valley).[t]
18Then Melchizedek[u] king of Salem[v]
brought out bread and wine. He was
priest of God Most High, 19and he blessed
Abram,[w] saying,

"Blessed be Abram by God Most High,
Creator of heaven and earth.[x]
20And praise be to God Most High,[y]
who delivered your enemies into
your hand."

Then Abram gave him a tenth of everything.[z]
21The king of Sodom said to Abram,
"Give me the people and keep the goods
for yourself."
22But Abram said to the king of Sodom,
"With raised hand[a] I have sworn an oath
to the LORD, God Most High, Creator of
heaven and earth,[b] 23that I will accept
nothing belonging to you,[c] not even a
thread or the strap of a sandal, so that
you will never be able to say, 'I made
Abram rich.' 24I will accept nothing but
what my men have eaten and the share
that belongs to the men who went with
me — to Aner, Eshkol and Mamre. Let
them have their share."

14:17 [t]2Sa 18:18
14:18 [u]Ps 110:4; Heb 5:6 [v]Ps 76:2; Heb 7:2
14:19 [w]Heb 7:6 [x]ver 22
14:20 [y]Ge 24:27 [z]Ge 28:22; Dt 26:12; Heb 7:4
14:22 [a]Ex 6:8; Da 12:7; Rev 10:5-6 [b]ver 19
14:23 [c]2Ki 5:16

15:1 [d]Da 10:1 [e]Ge 21:17; 26:24; 46:3; 2Ki 6:16; Ps 27:1; Isa 41:10, 13-14 [f]Dt 33:29; 2Sa 22:3,31; Ps 3:3
15:2 [g]Ac 7:5
15:3 [h]Ge 24:2, 34
15:4 [i]Gal 4:28
15:5 [j]Ps 147:4; Jer 33:22 [k]Ge 12:2; 22:17; Ex 32:13; Ro 4:18*; Heb 11:12
15:6 [l]Ps 106:31; Ro 4:3*,20-24*; Gal 3:6*; Jas 2:23*

Ge 14:18–20 ❖ Early Christians connected Melchizedek to Jesus (see Heb 7). In what ways does Melchizedek point to Christ, and what does that mean for our understanding of the OT?

Ge 15:6 ❖ Abram believed God against all odds, and God credited it to him as righteousness. How is God calling us to put bold trust and faith in him?

The LORD's Covenant With Abram

15 After this, the word of the LORD
came to Abram[d] in a vision:

"Do not be afraid,[e] Abram.
I am your shield,[a][f]
your very great reward.[b]"

2But Abram said, "Sovereign LORD, what
can you give me since I remain childless[g]
and the one who will inherit[c] my estate is
Eliezer of Damascus?" 3And Abram said,
"You have given me no children; so a servant[h]
in my household will be my heir."
4Then the word of the LORD came to
him: "This man will not be your heir, but
a son who is your own flesh and blood
will be your heir.[i]" 5He took him outside
and said, "Look up at the sky and count
the stars[j] — if indeed you can count
them." Then he said to him, "So shall
your offspring[d] be."[k]
6Abram believed the LORD, and he
credited it to him as righteousness.[l]

[a] *1 Or sovereign* [b] *1 Or shield; / your reward will be very great* [c] 2 The meaning of the Hebrew for this phrase is uncertain. [d] *5 Or seed*

14:17–24 Melchizedek is introduced as the "king of Salem" (v. 18) and is portrayed as the principal king of the region in that he receives a portion of the plunder. Salem is generally considered to be Jerusalem (based on Ps 76:2). The Hebrew name of God that he uses to bless Abram associates the common title Elyon with the name of El. Since El Elyon could represent the designation of a Canaanite god, we have no reason to think of Melchizedek as a worshiper of Yahweh or even as monotheistic. His joint role as king and priest is common in the ancient Near East.

The communal meal Abram and Melchizedek share indicates a peaceful agreement. Melchizedek is anxious to make peace with such a proven military force, and Abram submits to the chief king of the region by paying a tithe, thereby acknowledging Melchizedek's status.

14:21–24 The other king involved is the "king of Sodom." He acknowledges that Abram has a right to the plunder but asks that the people be returned to him. Abram refuses any share due him with the explanation that he is under oath to El Elyon (whom he identifies in Hebrew as Yahweh) not to profit from his military action.

15:1–21 This is the only chapter where God's communication with Abram takes place through a vision (v. 1). The first topic for discussion concerns an heir. All of God's promises are dependent on Abram's having a son. It was common practice in the ancient world for childless couples to adopt a son to care for them in their old age and receive the inheritance when they died. It appears that Eliezer currently has that role.

15:4–8 Yahweh's response is to assure Abram that the heir will be his biological son. God shows Abram the stars and indicates that his offspring will be equally innumerable. Abram accepts this confirmation regarding family, but he still has questions regarding possession of the land.

Abram's belief has nothing to do with salvation and nothing to do with a faith system. He simply believed that God could make his offspring as numerous as the stars of the sky.

How does taking God at his word become "credited . . . to him as righteousness" (v. 6b)? If

7He also said to him, "I am the LORD,
who brought you out of Ur of the Chaldeans to give you this land to take possession of it."
8But Abram said, "Sovereign LORD,
how can I know[m] that I will gain possession of it?"
9So the LORD said to him, "Bring me
a heifer, a goat and a ram, each three
years old, along with a dove and a young
pigeon."
10Abram brought all these to him, cut
them in two and arranged the halves opposite each other;[n] the birds, however, he
did not cut in half.[o] 11Then birds of prey
came down on the carcasses, but Abram
drove them away.
12As the sun was setting, Abram fell
into a deep sleep,[p] and a thick and dreadful darkness came over him. 13Then the
LORD said to him, "Know for certain that
for four hundred years[q] your descendants will be strangers in a country not
their own and that they will be enslaved[r]
and mistreated there. 14But I will punish
the nation they serve as slaves, and afterward they will come out[s] with great
possessions.[t] 15You, however, will go to
your ancestors in peace and be buried at
a good old age.[u] 16In the fourth generation your descendants will come back
here, for the sin of the Amorites[v] has not
yet reached its full measure."
17When the sun had set and darkness
had fallen, a smoking firepot with a
blazing torch appeared and passed between the pieces.[w] 18On that day the LORD
made a covenant with Abram and said,
"To your descendants I give this land,[x]
from the Wadi[a] of Egypt[y] to the great
river, the Euphrates — 19the land of the
Kenites, Kenizzites, Kadmonites, 20Hit-
tites, Perizzites, Rephaites, 21Amorites,
Canaanites, Girgashites and Jebusites."

15:8 [m] Lk 1:18
15:10 [n] ver 17; Jer 34:18
[o] Lev 1:17
15:12 [p] Ge 2:21
15:13 [q] ver 16; Ex 12:40; Ac 7:6,17
[r] Ex 1:11
15:14 [s] Ac 7:7*
[t] Ex 12:32-38
15:15 [u] Ge 25:8
15:16 [v] 1Ki 21:26
15:17 [w] ver 10
15:18 [x] Ge 12:7
[y] Nu 34:5
16:1 [z] Ge 11:30; Gal 4:24-25
[a] Ge 21:9

Hagar and Ishmael

16 Now Sarai, Abram's wife, had borne
him no children.[z] But she had an
Egyptian slave[a] named Hagar; 2so she said

[a] 18 Or *river*

Abram's belief has nothing to do with his salvation, it would follow that neither does his righteousness. The verse cannot therefore refer to the righteousness that modern theologians associate with justification. The righteousness that is credited to him creates a legacy (in this case, a covenant).

In summary, v. 6 should be seen as the premise on which the covenant is approved. Because Abram takes God at his word, God credits him with a legacy on the basis of the "rightness" of his faith. Recognized righteousness becomes the basis for blessing.

15:8–11 When God speaks of giving him the land, Abram seems skeptical (v. 8). Why the difference between the two responses? The difference is that the first will come about in his lifetime (he will have a son), while the second will not. God shows no frustration or disappointment at Abram's request for assurance.

The ritual of dividing a series of animals in half and in some way passing between the halves is not widely attested. Texts from Mari and Alalakh feature the killing of animals as part of the ceremony of making a treaty. In these texts, walking through this sacrificial pathway can be seen as a symbolic action enacting the treaty as well as a curse on the one who violates the promise. This sort of explanation is less satisfactory in this chapter because it is unclear what significance a self-curse can possibly have for God. Abram's driving away the birds of prey is identified as symbolic of future protection from Israel's enemies that is provided by Abram's faith.

15:17–21 In v. 17 a "smoking firepot" and a "blazing torch" make their appearance. The firepot functions as an oven for baking, including the baking of grain offerings (Lev 2:4). The torch can be used to provide light, but it is also used in military contexts or to speak of God's judgment (Zec 12:6).

13:1—15:21 When God doesn't perform his operations in nanoseconds, our impatience begins to show as our expectations go unfulfilled. There is a certain tension between expectations and relationship.

Relationships operate in the here and now, while expectations are always looking to the future. Parents who cherish each stage of development and focus on the present tolerate whatever drawbacks accompany each stage so that they can enjoy their child. This is the focus on *present relationship* rather than *future expectation*. If we are to achieve the goal of putting relationships ahead of expectations, we must learn to see relationships as of greater consequence than expectations.

16:1–16 Sarai suggests a way that Abram can have a son as the Lord has promised. In the context of the ancient world, this was not only appropriate but at times contractually required.

Hagar's spite and feeling of superiority come from her confidence that a deity has blessed her and that Abram is now dependent on her since she carries the heir to the family in her womb. Sarai's accusation against Abram is that he has neglected the necessary steps that would keep Hagar remembering her appropriate place within the household. When Abram puts the matter in Sarai's hands, Sarai's mistreatment of the girl drives Hagar to desertion.

This situation now represents triple jeopardy. (1) The covenant promises are in jeopardy because of the absence of the true heir. (2) An attempt at resolution of the initial jeopardy creates the second

to Abram, "The LORD has kept me from
having children. Go, sleep with my slave;
perhaps I can build a family through her."[b]
Abram agreed to what Sarai said. 3So
after Abram had been living in Canaan[c]
ten years, Sarai his wife took her Egyptian slave Hagar and gave her to her husband to be his wife. 4He slept with Hagar,
and she conceived.
When she knew she was pregnant, she
began to despise her mistress. 5Then Sarai
said to Abram, "You are responsible for
the wrong I am suffering. I put my slave
in your arms, and now that she knows
she is pregnant, she despises me. May
the LORD judge between you and me."[d]
6"Your slave is in your hands," Abram
said. "Do with her whatever you think
best." Then Sarai mistreated Hagar; so
she fled from her.
7The angel of the LORD[e] found Hagar
near a spring in the desert; it was the
spring that is beside the road to Shur.[f]
8And he said, "Hagar, slave of Sarai,
where have you come from, and where
are you going?"
"I'm running away from my mistress
Sarai," she answered.
9Then the angel of the LORD told her,
"Go back to your mistress and submit to
her." 10The angel added, "I will increase
your descendants so much that they will
be too numerous to count."[g]
11The angel of the LORD also said to her:

"You are now pregnant
and you will give birth to a son.
You shall name him Ishmael,[a]
for the LORD has heard of your
misery.[h]
12He will be a wild donkey of a man;
his hand will be against everyone
and everyone's hand against him,
and he will live in hostility
toward[b] all his brothers.[i]"

> **Ge 16:13** ❖ Hagar described God with a name based on his kindness to her. What descriptive name would you give God based on his faithfulness in your life, and why?

13She gave this name to the LORD who
spoke to her: "You are the God who sees
me," for she said, "I have now seen[c] the
One who sees me."[j] 14That is why the well
was called Beer Lahai Roi[d]; it is still there,
between Kadesh and Bered.
15So Hagar bore Abram a son,[k] and
Abram gave the name Ishmael to the son
she had borne. 16Abram was eighty-six
years old when Hagar bore him Ishmael.

The Covenant of Circumcision

17 When Abram was ninety-nine years
old, the LORD appeared to him and
said, "I am God Almighty[e];[l] walk before
me faithfully and be blameless.[m] 2Then
I will make my covenant between me
and you[n] and will greatly increase your
numbers."
3Abram fell facedown, and God said
to him, 4"As for me, this is my covenant
with you:[o] You will be the father of many
nations.[p] 5No longer will you be called
Abram[f]; your name will be Abraham,[g][q]

16:2 [b] Ge 30:3-4,9-10
16:3 [c] Ge 12:5
16:5 [d] Ge 31:53
16:7 [e] Ge 21:17; 22:11,15; 31:11 [f] Ge 20:1
16:10 [g] Ge 13:16; 17:20
16:11 [h] Ex 2:24; 3:7,9
16:12 [i] Ge 25:18
16:13 [j] Ge 32:30
16:15 [k] Gal 4:22
17:1 [l] Ge 28:3; Ex 6:3 [m] Dt 18:13
17:2 [n] Ge 15:18
17:4 [o] Ge 15:18 [p] ver 16; Ge 12:2; 35:11; 48:19
17:5 [q] ver 15; Ne 9:7

[a] 11 *Ishmael* means *God hears.* [b] 12 Or *live to the east / of* [c] 13 Or *seen the back of* [d] 14 *Beer Lahai Roi* means *well of the Living One who sees me.* [e] 1 Hebrew *El-Shaddai* [f] 5 *Abram* means *exalted father.* [g] 5 *Abraham* probably means *father of many.*

---

jeopardy of a son who will be a competing heir. (3) The makeshift heir is now in jeopardy of being lost to Abram and Sarai before he is even born.

16:7 The "angel of the LORD" makes his first appearance in Genesis in v. 7. The message of the angel shows distinct covenantal overtones in making reference to a large family. Hagar is going to be fruitful and multiply.

16:11–13 The pronouncement here starts with a birth pronouncement. The name is given as a reminder of God's response to her suffering at the hands of Sarai. Verse 12 does not sound at all positive.

Hagar may well believe that the messenger was a deity, but we would expect little in terms of spiritual insight or discerning subtleties from an Egyptian slave girl. Most likely Hagar is expressing surprise that she has encountered in such an unlikely place a deity inclined to show favor to her. The narrator identifies the deity (16:13) as "the LORD" (i.e., Yahweh) but gives no indication that Hagar knows the deity is Yahweh.

17:1–8 One of the first elements in this partnership is God's assignment of new names to Abram and Sarai. The names themselves indicate an expansion of the covenant. In ch. 12 it was promised that God would make Abram a great nation. The new name "Abraham" indicates that he will be "a father of many nations" (v. 5).

It is true that naming is an act of authority, but we must also recognize it, as Abram undoubtedly did, as constituting a great privilege. Up until now, God has been interacting with Abram and directing him, but this is more like taking him into the household.

In 9:16 the covenant with Noah was identified as an "everlasting" covenant; that same terminology is used here (17:7, 13, 19). Additionally, the land

for I have made you a father of many
nations.[r] 6I will make you very fruitful;[s]
I will make nations of you, and kings
will come from you.[t] 7I will establish my
covenant as an everlasting covenant between me and you and your descendants
after you for the generations to come,
to be your God[u] and the God of your descendants after you.[v] 8The whole land
of Canaan,[w] where you now reside as a
foreigner,[x] I will give as an everlasting
possession to you and your descendants
after you;[y] and I will be their God."

9Then God said to Abraham, "As for
you, you must keep my covenant, you
and your descendants after you for the
generations to come. 10This is my covenant with you and your descendants
after you, the covenant you are to keep:
Every male among you shall be circumcised.[z] 11You are to undergo circumcision,[a]
and it will be the sign of the covenant[b]
between me and you. 12For the generations to come every male among you who
is eight days old must be circumcised,[c]
including those born in your household
or bought with money from a foreigner—those who are not your offspring.
13Whether born in your household or
bought with your money, they must be
circumcised. My covenant in your flesh is
to be an everlasting covenant. 14Any uncircumcised male, who has not been circumcised in the flesh, will be cut off from
his people;[d] he has broken my covenant."

15God also said to Abraham, "As for Sarai your wife, you are no longer to call
her Sarai; her name will be Sarah. 16I will
bless her and will surely give you a son
by her.[e] I will bless her so that she will be
the mother of nations;[f] kings of peoples
will come from her."

17Abraham fell facedown; he laughed[g]
and said to himself, "Will a son be born

17:5 [r] Ro 4:17*
17:6 [s] Ge 35:11 [t] Mt 1:6
17:7 [u] Ex 29:45, 46 [v] Ro 9:8; Gal 3:16
17:8 [w] Ps 105:9, 11 [x] Ge 23:4; 28:4; Ex 6:4 [y] Ge 12:7
17:10 [z] ver 23; Ge 21:4; Jn 7:22; Ac 7:8; Ro 4:11
17:11 [a] Ex 12:48; Dt 10:16 [b] Ro 4:11
17:12 [c] Lev 12:3; Lk 2:21
17:14 [d] Ex 4:24-26
17:16 [e] Ge 18:10 [f] Ge 35:11; Gal 4:31
17:17 [g] Ge 18:12; 21:6

---

is identified as an "everlasting" possession (v. 8), correlating to 13:15, where God promised to give it to Abram's offspring "forever."

17:9–14 Circumcision was practiced widely in the ancient Near East as a rite of puberty or marriage. The Israelite reader was well aware of this fact. It was obvious enough to them that God was adopting a well-known sociological practice and adapting it for a unique theological function.

17:16–17 It has taken twenty-five years for Abraham to receive complete information. First God was going to make a great nation of him (12:2), then it was clarified that his heir would be his biological son (15:4), and now it is stated that the heir will also be Sarah's biological son (17:16). Abraham's puzzled wonder about Sarah's bearing a son is practically cut off in midstream as the wider implications sink in: Where does this leave Ishmael?

CHARACTER OF GOD // GOD IS OMNIPOTENT

Genesis 17:1: "I am God Almighty; walk before me faithfully and be blameless."

God appeared to Abraham and announced, "I am *El Shaddai*," translated "God Almighty" (Ge 17:1). God's all-powerful might is called his "omnipotence." Nothing is impossible for God (Jer 32:27). Indeed, he spoke the universe itself into existence.

When God announced himself this way to Abraham, Abraham was certainly in need of a God who was Almighty. God had promised to make Abraham a great nation, but Abraham had no children, and his wife was unable to conceive. Abraham and Sarah attempted a workaround for God's promise: Abraham had a child with Sarah's Egyptian slave, Hagar. God told Abraham, however, that Hagar's son was not the child God had promised. Sarah herself, though beyond childbearing age, would conceive a son. Only an Almighty God could do that.

God's omnipotence means nothing can stand against his plans. God will not be tossed about by the winds of fate or by the forces of evil. God stands beyond and above all powers and authorities. The Bible shows that kingdoms rise and fall according to God's will. Nothing in all creation can compete with or challenge God's authority. After all, he is the creator of it all.

APPLICATION ✣ God's omnipotence means we do not have to fear the powers of evil or darkness in this world. No evil force can upset God's plans. Though the enemy may wreak havoc for a little while, evil will never reach beyond God's control. God's omnipotence also reminds us that God's promises are guaranteed. God's plan of salvation and redemption is not a vague hope or ambition. It is an absolute certainty, sealed in the precious blood of Christ.

PEOPLE TO KNOW // ISHMAEL

GENESIS 17:20: Ishmael was the son of Abraham and Sarah's slave, Hagar. Sarah told Abraham to sleep with Hagar in order to have an heir, since Sarah was unable to conceive. When Hagar became pregnant, however, conflict arose between the two women.

Sarah mistreated Hagar, who fled from her into the wilderness. An angel appeared to Hagar and told her to name her unborn son Ishmael. The angel said Ishmael would be "a wild donkey of a man" (Ge 16:12), at odds with those around him. The angel told Hagar to return to Abraham and Sarah.

After Hagar returned, she gave birth to Ishmael. Ishmael was circumcised and given a place within Abraham's household. However, when Sarah's son, Isaac, was born, tensions once again arose. Seeing Ishmael's mocking, Sarah had Abraham send Hagar and Ishmael away. In the wilderness, Hagar thought Ishmael would die of thirst. Too heartbroken to watch, she laid him under a bush, walked a short distance away, and wept (Ge 21:16).

An angel came to Hagar again. He opened her eyes to see a spring of water and told her once again that God would make her son, Ishmael, into a great nation (Ge 21:18). Ishmael grew up in the wilderness and settled away from his family, but he later helped his half-brother Isaac bury their father (Ge 25:9).

APPLICATION ✜ God declared Ishmael would have a contentious relationship with those around him, and indeed he and his descendants continued to have strained relationships with the Israelites. Even so, God bestowed his promise and blessing upon Ishmael.

It is difficult to understand the complexities of God's plan within the branches of Abraham's family. Both Ishmael and Isaac received God's gracious blessing, and yet God foresaw that there would be strife. If Abraham and Sarah had trusted God's plan instead of trying to take matters into their own hands, the situation would have been different. But God's plan cannot be derailed by human sin. He brought blessings to humanity from the line of Abraham through his son with Sarah. Yet Ishmael also had a place in God's plan and received a blessing from the Lord.

to a man a hundred years old? Will Sarah
bear a child at the age of ninety?" 18And
Abraham said to God, "If only Ishmael
might live under your blessing!"
19Then God said, "Yes, but your wife
Sarah will bear you a son,[h] and you will
call him Isaac.[a] I will establish my covenant with him[i] as an everlasting covenant for his descendants after him.
20And as for Ishmael, I have heard you:
I will surely bless him; I will make him
fruitful and will greatly increase his
numbers.[j] He will be the father of twelve
rulers,[k] and I will make him into a great
nation.[l] 21But my covenant I will establish with Isaac, whom Sarah will bear to
you by this time next year."[m] 22When he
had finished speaking with Abraham,
God went up from him.
23On that very day Abraham took his
son Ishmael and all those born in his
household or bought with his money,
every male in his household, and circumcised them, as God told him. 24Abra-
ham was ninety-nine years old when he
was circumcised,[n] 25and his son Ishmael was thirteen; 26Abraham and his son
Ishmael were both circumcised on that
very day. 27And every male in Abraham's
household, including those born in his
household or bought from a foreigner,
was circumcised with him.

17:19 [h] Ge 18:14; 21:2 [i] Ge 26:3
17:20 [j] Ge 16:10 [k] Ge 25:12-16 [l] Ge 21:18
17:21 [m] Ge 21:2
17:24 [n] Ro 4:11
18:1 [o] Ge 13:18; 14:13

Ge 17:17 ✜ Have you ever wanted to laugh because God's promises seemed unrealistic? What encouragement does Abraham's story provide for Christians today?

The Three Visitors

18 The LORD appeared to Abraham
near the great trees of Mamre[o]

[a] 19 *Isaac* means *he laughs.*

The poignancy of this question is lost if we fail to realize that for the last thirteen years, Abraham has lived in the belief that Ishmael is the promised son and that God's covenant will be carried out through him. Abraham has not been anxiously awaiting the arrival of another son. In response to Abraham's expression of concern, God extends certain of the covenant benefits to Ishmael, but he also makes it clear that the covenant program is going to proceed through Isaac.

18:1–15 The text treats the visit of the three men as a theophany: God appearing in visible form. Abraham's

while he was sitting at the entrance to
his tent in the heat of the day. 2Abraham
looked up and saw three men[p] standing
nearby. When he saw them, he hurried
from the entrance of his tent to meet
them and bowed low to the ground.
3He said, "If I have found favor in your
eyes, my lord,[a] do not pass your servant
by. 4Let a little water be brought, and
then you may all wash your feet[q] and rest
under this tree. 5Let me get you something to eat,[r] so you can be refreshed and
then go on your way — now that you have
come to your servant."
"Very well," they answered, "do as you
say."
6So Abraham hurried into the tent to
Sarah. "Quick," he said, "get three seahs[b]
of the finest flour and knead it and bake
some bread."
7Then he ran to the herd and selected a choice, tender calf and gave it to a
servant, who hurried to prepare it. 8He
then brought some curds and milk and
the calf that had been prepared, and set
these before them.[s] While they ate, he
stood near them under a tree.
9"Where is your wife Sarah?" they
asked him.
"There, in the tent," he said.
10Then one of them said, "I will surely
return to you about this time next year,
and Sarah your wife will have a son."[t]
Now Sarah was listening at the entrance to the tent, which was behind him.
11Abraham and Sarah were already very
old,[u] and Sarah was past the age of childbearing.[v] 12So Sarah laughed[w] to herself as
she thought, "After I am worn out and my
lord[x] is old, will I now have this pleasure?"
13Then the LORD said to Abraham,
"Why did Sarah laugh and say, 'Will I
really have a child, now that I am old?'
14Is anything too hard for the LORD?[y] I
will return to you at the appointed time
next year, and Sarah will have a son."
15Sarah was afraid, so she lied and said,
"I did not laugh."
But he said, "Yes, you did laugh."

18:2 [p] ver 16, 22; Ge 32:24; Jos 5:13; Jdg 13:6-11; Heb 13:2
18:4 [q] Ge 19:2; 43:24
18:5 [r] Jdg 13:15
18:8 [s] Ge 19:3
18:10 [t] Ro 9:9*
18:11 [u] Ge 17:17 [v] Ro 4:19
18:12 [w] Ge 17:17; 21:6 [x] 1Pe 3:6
18:14 [y] Jer 32:17, 27; Zec 8:6; Mt 19:26; Lk 1:37; Ro 4:21

Ge 18:1-8 ❖ When have you doubted God's word in your life? Have you ever, like Sarah, been surprised by God's graciousness despite your disbelief?

Abraham Pleads for Sodom

16When the men got up to leave, they
looked down toward Sodom, and Abraham walked along with them to see them

[a] 3 Or *eyes, Lord* [b] 6 That is, probably about 36 pounds or about 16 kilograms

treatment of the men includes nothing to indicate whether he recognizes their supernatural nature.

18:6–10a The question in v. 9 is designed to ask for an explanation. Perhaps the question is prompted by the fact that Abraham is waiting on them rather than Sarah. In those times, menstruation was a common reason for a woman to be confined in her house or tent.

In v. 6 Abraham asked Sarah to bake some bread, an activity often forbidden to menstruating women in Abraham's time, so at that point her period had not begun. Yet she would not be confined to her tent unless she actually had her period. If this is the issue, then she presumably experienced the onset of her period as dinner was being served. If this is the case, it would have constituted a remarkable sign of the resumption of her fertility.

18:10b–15 Sarah's laughter is often a topic of conversation when this text is studied. Abraham's incredulous laughter is immediately followed by a statement that shows he accepts the pronouncement regardless of how unbelievable it is. In contrast, Sarah's question is left hanging in the air and begging for a response.

The question about why Sarah laughs is simply the lead into the more important statement of v. 14. The word translated "hard" here refers to that which goes beyond what human workmanship can attain. The sense of the word goes beyond "wonderful" or "astonishing" to something more like "mystical" or "supernatural." Here we see a clear statement of what the text is teaching about God.

16:1—18:15 We need not think of times of waiting as failures or as unproductive. God does not waste our experiences. He is shaping us for his service. Perhaps we too often think of God's plan for our lives as a perfectly straight track leading to his perfect will. It is more helpful to think of our lives in terms of a complicated model train set with inside tracks, outside tracks, and many crisscrossing tracks. It doesn't matter whether we are on the inside or the outside track or cutting across. Our goal is not to "get somewhere" but to serve. We must remember that we are on the rails and God is at the switch. What is most important about our faith is not where we are going but what we are becoming.

18:16–33 Verses 20–21 portrays the Lord again on a fact-finding mission. Statements as these should not be viewed as calling into question characteristics of God such as his omnipresence or omniscience, but as reinforcing attributes such as justice.

It is the "outcry" (v. 20) that has motivated God's response (vv. 20–21; 19:13). Innocent bloodshed cries out to the Lord for vengeance (cf. 4:10).

Sodom and Gomorrah have stood throughout history as an example of wickedness and divine judgment. How strange it is, then, that there is

on their way. 17 Then the LORD said, "Shall
I hide from Abraham[z] what I am about
to do?[a] 18 Abraham will surely become a
great and powerful nation,[b] and all nations on earth will be blessed through
him.[a] 19 For I have chosen him, so that he
will direct his children[c] and his household after him to keep the way of the
LORD[d] by doing what is right and just, so
that the LORD will bring about for Abraham what he has promised him."
20 Then the LORD said, "The outcry
against Sodom and Gomorrah is so great
and their sin so grievous 21 that I will go
down[e] and see if what they have done
is as bad as the outcry that has reached
me. If not, I will know."
22 The men turned away and went toward Sodom,[f] but Abraham remained
standing before the LORD.[b] 23 Then Abraham approached him and said: "Will you
sweep away the righteous with the wicked?[g] 24 What if there are fifty righteous
people in the city? Will you really sweep
it away and not spare[c] the place for the
sake of the fifty righteous people in it?[h]
25 Far be it from you to do such a thing—
to kill the righteous with the wicked,
treating the righteous and the wicked
alike. Far be it from you! Will not the
Judge of all the earth do right?"[i]
26 The LORD said, "If I find fifty righteous people in the city of Sodom, I will
spare the whole place for their sake.[j]"
27 Then Abraham spoke up again: "Now
that I have been so bold as to speak to
the Lord, though I am nothing but dust
and ashes,[k] 28 what if the number of the
righteous is five less than fifty? Will you
destroy the whole city for lack of five
people?"
"If I find forty-five there," he said, "I
will not destroy it."
29 Once again he spoke to him, "What
if only forty are found there?"
He said, "For the sake of forty, I will
not do it."
30 Then he said, "May the Lord not be
angry, but let me speak. What if only thirty can be found there?"
He answered, "I will not do it if I find
thirty there."
31 Abraham said, "Now that I have been
so bold as to speak to the Lord, what if
only twenty can be found there?"
He said, "For the sake of twenty, I will
not destroy it."
32 Then he said, "May the Lord not be
angry, but let me speak just once more.[l]
What if only ten can be found there?"
He answered, "For the sake of ten,[m] I
will not destroy it."
33 When the LORD had finished speaking with Abraham, he left, and Abraham
returned home.

Sodom and Gomorrah Destroyed

19 The two angels arrived at Sodom[n]
in the evening, and Lot was sitting
in the gateway of the city.[o] When he saw
them, he got up to meet them and bowed
down with his face to the ground. 2 "My
lords," he said, "please turn aside to your
servant's house. You can wash your feet[p]
and spend the night and then go on your
way early in the morning."
"No," they answered, "we will spend
the night in the square."
3 But he insisted so strongly that they
did go with him and entered his house.
He prepared a meal for them, baking
bread without yeast, and they ate.[q] 4 Before they had gone to bed, all the men
from every part of the city of Sodom—
both young and old—surrounded the
house. 5 They called to Lot, "Where are
the men who came to you tonight? Bring
them out to us so that we can have sex
with them."[r]
6 Lot went outside to meet them[s] and
shut the door behind him 7 and said,
"No, my friends. Don't do this wicked
thing. 8 Look, I have two daughters who
have never slept with a man. Let me
bring them out to you, and you can do
what you like with them. But don't do

18:17 [z] Am 3:7 [a] Ge 19:24
18:18 [b] Gal 3:8*
18:19 [c] Dt 4:9-10; 6:7 [d] Jos 24:15; Eph 6:4
18:21 [e] Ge 11:5
18:22 [f] Ge 19:1
18:23 [g] Nu 16:22
18:24 [h] Jer 5:1
18:25 [i] Job 8:3, 20; Ps 58:11; 94:2; Isa 3:10-11; Ro 3:6
18:26 [j] Jer 5:1
18:27 [k] Ge 2:7; 3:19; Job 30:19; 42:6
18:32 [l] Jdg 6:39 [m] Jer 5:1
19:1 [n] Ge 18:22 [o] Ge 18:1
19:2 [p] Ge 18:4; Lk 7:44
19:3 [q] Ge 18:6
19:5 [r] Jdg 19:22; Isa 3:9; Ro 1:24-27
19:6 [s] Jdg 19:23

[a] 18 Or *will use his name in blessings* (see 48:20)
[b] 22 Masoretic Text; an ancient Hebrew scribal tradition *but the LORD remained standing before Abraham*
[c] 24 Or *forgive*; also in verse 26

little recollection of the location of these "cities of the plain" (13:12). Their association with Zoar and the tar pits in "the Valley of Siddim" (14:10) both point to the southern end of the Dead Sea.

19:1–14 The sin of the Sodomites is self-evident and multileveled, blatant and unambiguous. The text also makes it clear that the wicked behavior is not isolated (v. 4).

19:8 Lot's response to the demand of the men in is startling. Is Lot truly offering his daughters to be gang-raped and probably murdered? An alternative is that his suggestion implies a more subtle statement: "I would as soon have you violate my family members as violate those whom I have taken in and offered hospitality." Such a comment is not suggesting that they will really do that. If this is the

PEOPLE TO KNOW // LOT

GENESIS 19:1–11: Lot was the nephew of Abraham. They and their families traveled together to Canaan from Harran. In Canaan, a conflict arose between the two men's shepherds, and they decided to separate. Abraham let Lot choose which land he wanted, and Lot selected the lush-looking Jordan plain (Ge 13:10–13). He settled in the town of Sodom, where its people were known for their sinfulness.

Lot was later captured in a skirmish between local kings. Word reached Abraham, and he set out to save Lot and his family. Defeating the forces of Kedorlaomer, Abraham rescued Lot (Ge 14:8–16). Lot then returned to Sodom.

God later resolved to destroy Sodom for its evil. God sent two angels who looked like men to the city. The angels told Lot and his family to flee and not look back, and when they hesitated, the angels forced them (Ge 19:16). God rained fire and sulfur on Sodom and the surrounding towns, destroying them. When Lot's wife looked back, she became a pillar of salt (Ge 19:23–26). Lot and his daughters lived in a cave in the mountains. With no men around to be their husbands, Lot's daughters made Lot drunk and slept with him. They each bore a son. These sons were the ancestors of the Moabites and Ammonites (Ge 19:30–38), who were persistent enemies of God's people, the Israelites.

APPLICATION ✜ The community you choose is important. Lot chose to live in Sodom, a city known for its sinfulness, and he hesitated to leave even when the angels warned him destruction was coming. When we are continually surrounded by those who live sinful lifestyles, we can become numb to God's instructions. Lot's life shows that God is serious about dealing with sin and serious about removing his children from sinful influences.

anything to these men, for they have
come under the protection of my roof."[t]
9"Get out of our way," they replied.
"This fellow came here as a foreigner,
and now he wants to play the judge![u]
We'll treat you worse than them." They
kept bringing pressure on Lot and moved
forward to break down the door.
10But the men inside reached out and
pulled Lot back into the house and shut
the door. 11Then they struck the men who
were at the door of the house, young and
old, with blindness[v] so that they could
not find the door.
12The two men said to Lot, "Do you
have anyone else here — sons-in-law,
sons or daughters, or anyone else in the
city who belongs to you?[w] Get them out
of here, 13because we are going to destroy
this place. The outcry to the LORD against
its people is so great that he has sent us
to destroy it."[x]

14So Lot went out and spoke to his
sons-in-law, who were pledged to marry[a] his daughters. He said, "Hurry and
get out of this place, because the LORD is
about to destroy the city![y]" But his sons-
in-law thought he was joking.[z]
15With the coming of dawn, the angels
urged Lot, saying, "Hurry! Take your wife
and your two daughters who are here, or
you will be swept away[a] when the city is
punished.[b]"
16When he hesitated, the men grasped
his hand and the hands of his wife and
of his two daughters and led them safely
out of the city, for the LORD was merciful
to them. 17As soon as they had brought
them out, one of them said, "Flee for
your lives![c] Don't look back,[d] and don't
stop anywhere in the plain! Flee to the
mountains or you will be swept away!"

19:8 [t]Jdg 19:24
19:9 [u]Ex 2:14; Ac 7:27
19:11 [v]Dt 28:28-29; 2Ki 6:18; Ac 13:11
19:12 [w]Ge 7:1
19:13 [x]1Ch 21:15
19:14 [y]Nu 16:21 [z]Ex 9:21; Lk 17:28
19:15 [a]Nu 16:26 [b]Rev 18:4
19:17 [c]Jer 48:6 [d]ver 26

[a] 14 Or *were married to*

correct way to read v. 8, Lot's offer of his daughters is intended to awaken the conscience of the mob.
19:10–11 Lot is beyond any power to enforce the law or punish violators. It is the divine messengers who come to his rescue as they strike the mob with blindness.
19:14 Lot now seeks to influence those who have other reasons to respect him. Here he lobbies his sons-in-law. Their assessment of Lot's warning leads them not to take him seriously.
19:15–26 The angel's prohibition does not concern looking at the destruction. After all, people standing on the city walls of Zoar would have been able to watch the carnage take place. Rather, it is constructive to see the three commands as forming a sequence: (1) Get out of here; (2) don't turn back; and (3) don't stop before reaching your destination. This means that the verb used in 19:17 and 26 ("looked") must have idiomatic value that goes beyond looking. In this interpretation the command of the angel is broken not by glancing over one's shoulder and seeing what should not be seen but in directing attention back and returning to the city.

18But Lot said to them, "No, my lords,[a] please! 19Your[b] servant has found favor in your[b] eyes, and you[b] have shown great kindness to me in sparing my life. But I can't flee to the mountains; this disaster will overtake me, and I'll die. 20Look, here is a town near enough to run to, and it is small. Let me flee to it — it is very small, isn't it? Then my life will be spared."

21He said to him, "Very well, I will grant this request too; I will not overthrow the town you speak of. 22But flee there quickly, because I cannot do anything until you reach it." (That is why the town was called Zoar.[c])

23By the time Lot reached Zoar, the sun had risen over the land. 24Then the LORD rained down burning sulfur on Sodom and Gomorrah[e] — from the LORD out of the heavens.[f] 25Thus he overthrew those cities and the entire plain, destroying all those living in the cities — and also the vegetation in the land.[g] 26But Lot's wife looked back,[h] and she became a pillar of salt.[i]

27Early the next morning Abraham got up and returned to the place where he had stood before the LORD.[j] 28He looked down toward Sodom and Gomorrah, toward all the land of the plain, and he saw dense smoke rising from the land, like smoke from a furnace.[k]

29So when God destroyed the cities of the plain, he remembered Abraham, and he brought Lot out of the catastrophe[l] that overthrew the cities where Lot had lived.

Lot and His Daughters

30Lot and his two daughters left Zoar and settled in the mountains,[m] for he was afraid to stay in Zoar. He and his two daughters lived in a cave. 31One day the older daughter said to the younger, "Our father is old, and there is no man around here to give us children — as is the custom all over the earth. 32Let's get our father to drink wine and then sleep with him and preserve our family line through our father."

33That night they got their father to drink wine, and the older daughter went in and slept with him. He was not aware of it when she lay down or when she got up.

34The next day the older daughter said to the younger, "Last night I slept with my father. Let's get him to drink wine again tonight, and you go in and sleep with him so we can preserve our family line through our father." 35So they got their father to drink wine that night also, and the younger daughter went in and slept with him. Again he was not aware of it when she lay down or when she got up.

36So both of Lot's daughters became pregnant by their father. 37The older daughter had a son, and she named him Moab[d]; he is the father of the Moabites[n] of today. 38The younger daughter also had a

> **Ge 19:24-26** ❖ How does the destruction of Sodom and Gomorrah provide a warning, especially given Jesus' words that those who don't welcome him are in an even worse state (see Mt 11:23-24)?

19:24 [e] Dt 29:23; Isa 1:9; 13:19 [f] Lk 17:29; 2Pe 2:6; Jude 7
19:25 [g] Ps 107:34; Eze 16:48
19:26 [h] ver 17 [i] Lk 17:32
19:27 [j] Ge 18:22
19:28 [k] Rev 9:2; 18:9
19:29 [l] 2Pe 2:7
19:30 [m] ver 19
19:37 [n] Dt 2:9

[a] 18 Or *No, Lord;* or *No, my lord* [b] 19 The Hebrew is singular. [c] 22 *Zoar* means *small.* [d] 37 *Moab* sounds like the Hebrew for *from father.*

19:24-26 The result that Lot's wife becomes a pillar of salt need not be seen as an arbitrary and instantaneous transformation. The destruction is described in terms of sulfur (brimstone) and fire raining down (v. 24) on the cities. The scene is one of divine retribution, and the use of brimstone appears here and elsewhere as an agent of purification and divine wrath on the wicked.

19:27-38 The five cities of the plain are the only cities in the region. With the destruction of those cities, it most likely seems to them that they are the last people on earth. This may be the reason behind the plot of Lot's daughters to become pregnant by their father.

Lot is exonerated in that the daughters realize they have to get him drunk in order to carry out their intentions. This implies that he would not have agreed to the course of action they propose. Their judgment concerning how to resolve a difficult situation is as unacceptable as their father's.

> ✣ **18:16—19:38** Righteous people have always been and will always be a minority. Still, individually and as the corporate church, God expects us to have an impact for righteousness in the world. Examples of such individuals abound. From the apostle Paul to Martin Luther to Mother Teresa, there are those who have refused to think they were too insignificant for God to use. Their impact came not because they were full of self-importance and thought themselves capable of big things, but because they humbly did what needed to be done.
>
> Often, making an impact for righteousness in a fallen world entails a good deal of plodding. It may take time for the church to have an impact on the world. We can only be faithful to the call of Christ and do what needs to be done. The harvest is his and will come as his will determines.

son, and she named him Ben-Ammi[a]; he
is the father of the Ammonites[b][o] of today.

Abraham and Abimelek

20:1–18Ref // Ge 12:10–20; 26:1–11

20 Now Abraham moved on from
there[p] into the region of the Negev and lived between Kadesh and Shur.
For a while he stayed in Gerar,[q] 2and
there Abraham said of his wife Sarah,
“She is my sister.[r]” Then Abimelek king
of Gerar sent for Sarah and took her.[s]
3But God came to Abimelek in a dream[t]
one night and said to him, “You are as
good as dead because of the woman you
have taken; she is a married woman.”[u]
4Now Abimelek had not gone near her,
so he said, “Lord, will you destroy an innocent nation?[v] 5Did he not say to me,
‘She is my sister,’ and didn’t she also say,
‘He is my brother’? I have done this with
a clear conscience and clean hands.”
6Then God said to him in the dream,
“Yes, I know you did this with a clear
conscience, and so I have kept[w] you from
sinning against me. That is why I did not
let you touch her. 7Now return the man’s
wife, for he is a prophet, and he will pray
for you[x] and you will live. But if you do
not return her, you may be sure that you
and all who belong to you will die.”
8Early the next morning Abimelek
summoned all his officials, and when
he told them all that had happened, they
were very much afraid. 9Then Abimelek
called Abraham in and said, “What have
you done to us? How have I wronged you
that you have brought such great guilt
upon me and my kingdom? You have
done things to me that should never be
done.[y]” 10And Abimelek asked Abraham,
“What was your reason for doing this?”
11Abraham replied, “I said to myself,

Ge 20:11 ❖ Why might knowing another person has a relationship with God make us more comfortable with their potential behavior?

‘There is surely no fear of God[z] in this
place, and they will kill me because of my
wife.’[a] 12Besides, she really is my sister, the
daughter of my father though not of my
mother; and she became my wife. 13And
when God had me wander from my father’s household, I said to her, ‘This is how
you can show your love to me: Everywhere
we go, say of me, “He is my brother.”’”
14Then Abimelek brought sheep and
cattle and male and female slaves and
gave them to Abraham,[b] and he returned
Sarah his wife to him. 15And Abimelek
said, “My land is before you; live wherever you like.”[c]
16To Sarah he said, “I am giving your
brother a thousand shekels[c] of silver.
This is to cover the offense against you
before all who are with you; you are completely vindicated.”
17Then Abraham prayed to God,[d] and
God healed Abimelek, his wife and his
female slaves so they could have children
again, 18for the LORD had kept all the wom-
en in Abimelek’s household from conceiving because of Abraham’s wife Sarah.[e]

The Birth of Isaac

21 Now the LORD was gracious to Sarah[f] as he had said, and the LORD
did for Sarah what he had promised.[g]
2Sarah became pregnant and bore a son[h]
to Abraham in his old age,[i] at the very
time God had promised him. 3Abraham

19:38 [o] Dt 2:19
20:1 [p] Ge 18:1 [q] Ge 26:1, 6, 17
20:2 [r] ver 12; Ge 12:13; 26:7 [s] Ge 12:15
20:3 [t] Job 33:15; Mt 27:19 [u] Ps 105:14
20:4 [v] Ge 18:25
20:6 [w] 1Sa 25:26, 34
20:7 [x] ver 17; 1Sa 7:5; Job 42:8
20:9 [y] Ge 12:18; 26:10; 34:7
20:11 [z] Ge 42:18; Ps 36:1 [a] Ge 12:12; 26:7
20:14 [b] Ge 12:16
20:15 [c] Ge 13:9
20:17 [d] Job 42:9
20:18 [e] Ge 12:17
21:1 [f] 1Sa 2:21 [g] Ge 8:1; 17:16, 21; Gal 4:23
21:2 [h] Ge 17:19 [i] Gal 4:22; Heb 11:11

[a] *38 Ben-Ammi* means *son of my father’s people.*
[b] *38* Hebrew *Bene-Ammon*
[c] *16* That is, about 25 pounds or about 12 kilograms

20:1-18 This is the second time that the text records Abraham’s identifying Sarah as his sister, but it is not unlikely that this is their regular custom when they are in unfamiliar places (20:13).

20:16-17 God informs Abimelek of his offense in a dream. Here the accusation concerns the potential of adultery. Hittite laws, Middle Assyrian Laws, and the Laws of Hammurabi all contain legislation against adultery.

20:17 Verse 7 contains the first occurrence of the term “prophet” in the OT. God identifies Abraham as one who is capable of intercession on Abimelek’s behalf. Generally, the prophet offered a message from the deity, but here Abraham is praying for healing. This reflects the broader view of a prophet as one who has powerful connections to the deity, such that he can initiate or remove curses.

20:18 It is clear that the plague on Abimelek’s house has something to do with barrenness or, more likely, with sexual dysfunction since Abimelek also requires healing. Anything that prevented childbirth could be described as “closing the womb.”

Abimelek responds generously (vv. 14–16), probably as an act of appeasement to Abraham’s God. Abimelek gives Abraham unspecified numbers of cattle and slaves, grants freedom to move about the land, and gives 1,000 shekels of silver—more than a common worker could expect to make in a lifetime.

21:1-21 The scene has been well set for the name Isaac (“laughter,” see 17:17; 18:12–15), but there is an ill turn on the name in 21:9 (“mocking”). In 21:10 the text is not clear whether Ishmael has done something that warrants the drastic response of Sarah.

PEOPLE TO KNOW // HAGAR

GENESIS 21:8–21: Hagar was an Egyptian slave of Abraham's wife, Sarah. God had promised Abraham descendants as numerous as the stars (Ge 15:5), but Sarah was unable to have children. Because of this, she suggested Abraham sleep with Hagar in order to produce an heir.

When Hagar became pregnant, conflict arose between the two women and Sarah blamed Abraham. Instead of protecting Hagar, Abraham responded that Sarah could do with Hagar whatever she wanted. Sarah mistreated Hagar to the point that Hagar ran away. Abraham and Sarah spoke of Hagar as though she were a mere object, not even using her name (Ge 16:5–6).

When God's angel came to Hagar in the wilderness, however, the first word the angel spoke was "Hagar" (Ge 16:8). The angel promised Hagar that the child in her womb, Ishmael, would become a great nation. In response to the angel, Hagar called God *El Roi*: "the God who sees me" (Ge 16:13). Returning to Abraham and Sarah at the angel's instruction, Hagar bore Ishmael.

APPLICATION ✚ Hagar's story shows us God's amazing grace. God calls her by name, and she even gives God a new name. God promised that her son would become a great nation. In all these ways, Hagar's story in Genesis beautifully illustrates God's love and care for the downtrodden. Hagar's name can mean "forsaken," but she was not forsaken by God.

gave the name Isaac[a][j] to the son Sarah
bore him. 4When his son Isaac was eight
days old, Abraham circumcised him,[k] as
God commanded him. 5Abraham was a
hundred years old when his son Isaac
was born to him.

6Sarah said, "God has brought me
laughter,[l] and everyone who hears about
this will laugh with me." 7And she added,
"Who would have said to Abraham that
Sarah would nurse children? Yet I have
borne him a son in his old age."

Hagar and Ishmael Sent Away

8The child grew and was weaned, and
on the day Isaac was weaned Abraham
held a great feast. 9But Sarah saw that the
son whom Hagar the Egyptian had borne
to Abraham[m] was mocking,[n] 10and she
said to Abraham, "Get rid of that slave
woman and her son, for that woman's
son will never share in the inheritance
with my son Isaac."[o]

11The matter distressed Abraham
greatly because it concerned his son.[p]
12But God said to him, "Do not be so
distressed about the boy and your slave
woman. Listen to whatever Sarah tells
you, because it is through Isaac that
your offspring[b] will be reckoned.[q] 13I will
make the son of the slave into a nation[r]
also, because he is your offspring."

14Early the next morning Abraham
took some food and a skin of water and
gave them to Hagar. He set them on her
shoulders and then sent her off with the
boy. She went on her way and wandered
in the Desert of Beersheba.[s]

15When the water in the skin was gone,
she put the boy under one of the bushes.
16Then she went off and sat down about a
bowshot away, for she thought, "I cannot
watch the boy die." And as she sat there,
she[c] began to sob.

17God heard the boy crying,[t] and the
angel of God called to Hagar from heav-
en and said to her, "What is the matter,
Hagar? Do not be afraid; God has heard
the boy crying as he lies there. 18Lift the
boy up and take him by the hand, for
I will make him into a great nation.[u]"

19Then God opened her eyes[v] and she
saw a well of water. So she went and filled
the skin with water and gave the boy a
drink.

20God was with the boy[w] as he grew
up. He lived in the desert and became
an archer. 21While he was living in the

Ge 21:17 ❖ When have you felt God's loving presence in the midst of a painful or confusing time?

21:3 [j] Ge 17:19
21:4 [k] Ge 17:10, 12; Ac 7:8
21:6 [l] Ge 17:17; Isa 54:1
21:9 [m] Ge 16:15 [n] Gal 4:29
21:10 [o] Gal 4:30*
21:11 [p] Ge 17:18
21:12 [q] Ro 9:7*; Heb 11:18*
21:13 [r] ver 18
21:14 [s] ver 31, 32
21:17 [t] Ex 3:7
21:18 [u] ver 13
21:19 [v] Nu 22:31
21:20 [w] Ge 26:3, 24; 28:15; 39:2, 21, 23

[a] 3 *Isaac* means *he laughs.* [b] 12 Or *seed*
[c] 16 Hebrew; Septuagint *the child*

For a second time (see 16:10–13) Hagar receives a visitation from God. He not only comforts her with a promise (21:18) but provides for her immediate needs (v. 19).

Desert of Paran, his mother got a wife
for him[x] from Egypt.

The Treaty at Beersheba

22At that time Abimelek and Phicol the
commander of his forces said to Abraham, "God is with you in everything you
do. 23Now swear[y] to me here before God
that you will not deal falsely with me or
my children or my descendants. Show
to me and the country where you now
reside as a foreigner the same kindness
I have shown to you."
24Abraham said, "I swear it."
25Then Abraham complained to Abimelek about a well of water that Abimelek's
servants had seized.[z] 26But Abimelek
said, "I don't know who has done this.
You did not tell me, and I heard about
it only today."
27So Abraham brought sheep and cattle
and gave them to Abimelek, and the two
men made a treaty.[a] 28Abraham set apart
seven ewe lambs from the flock, 29and
Abimelek asked Abraham, "What is the
meaning of these seven ewe lambs you
have set apart by themselves?"
30He replied, "Accept these seven
lambs from my hand as a witness[b] that
I dug this well."
31So that place was called Beersheba,[a][c] because the two men swore an
oath there.
32After the treaty had been made at Beersheba, Abimelek and Phicol the commander of his forces returned to the land
of the Philistines. 33Abraham planted a
tamarisk tree in Beersheba, and there
he called on the name of the LORD,[d] the
Eternal God.[e] 34And Abraham stayed in
the land of the Philistines for a long time.

Abraham Tested

22 Some time later God tested[f] Abraham. He said to him, "Abraham!"
"Here I am," he replied.
2Then God said, "Take your son[g], your
only son, whom you love — Isaac — and
go to the region of Moriah.[h] Sacrifice him
there as a burnt offering on a mountain
I will show you."
3Early the next morning Abraham
got up and loaded his donkey. He took
with him two of his servants and his son

21:21 [x] Ge 24:4, 38
21:23 [y] ver 31; Jos 2:12
21:25 [z] Ge 26:15, 18, 20-22
21:27 [a] Ge 26:28, 31
21:30 [b] Ge 31:44, 47, 48, 50, 52
21:31 [c] Ge 26:33
21:33 [d] Ge 4:26 [e] Dt 33:27
22:1 [f] Dt 8:2, 16; Heb 11:17; Jas 1:12-13
22:2 [g] ver 12, 16; Jn 3:16; Heb 11:17; 1Jn 4:9 [h] 2Ch 3:1

[a] 31 *Beersheba* can mean *well of seven* and *well of the oath.*

21:22–34 In a land of seasonally confined rainfall, wells are extremely important to the welfare of the human population and their herds and flocks. Abimelek excuses himself as not knowing about the offense. Abraham gives sheep, cattle, and "seven ewe lambs" to Abimelek as a testimony that the well belongs to Abraham.
21:31 The designation of significance to a name is not necessarily a suggestion that the name originated at that time. The ancients were less concerned with the origin of a name than they were with the significance the name acquired.
21:33–34 Abraham's worship is expressed in several ways. (1) He plants a tamarisk tree, which was at times connected with cosmic stability. In this sense, planting a tree can have as much significance as building an altar. (2) Abraham "called on the name of the LORD." That seems to be the case here in that the epithet "Eternal God" is attached to explain how Abraham designates God. In Isaiah the epithet is part of the prophet's presentation of Yahweh as the God who holds history, the nations, and Israel's destiny in his hands. (3) Abraham's dwelling is identified as "the land of the Philistines" (21:34). The first-known mention of the Philistines outside the Bible is in the records of Pharaoh Ramesses III (1182–1151 BC). As part of the invading Sea Peoples, they settled in five city-states along the southern coast of Canaan and were employed by the Egyptians as mercenaries and trading partners.

✣ **20:1—21:34** Does the fact that God can open the womb mean that women who cannot bear children ought to pray for God to give them the ability to bear children, as Hannah did (see 1Sa 1:1—2:10)? Such petitions are on the same level as prayers for healing from those who are sick. We pray because we know that God is able, but we must also be ready to hear a "no" answer. If God chooses not to grant fertility, we can only accept his wisdom and seek to honor him as we are. God's decisions will be designed to serve his purposes.

It is counterproductive to our service of God to allow bitterness to infect our spirits, whatever our complaints against him may be. When Christ was questioned about the offense that caused a man to be born blind (Jn 9:1–5), his answer is instructive. He did not answer the question in terms of cause but in terms of purpose. It is immaterial what caused the man's condition—what is important is that God be honored through it. We cannot determine cause; we cannot assume disfavor. We can only turn our attention away from the past and look toward the future, seeking to honor God in whatever situation he places us in.

22:1 When God tests, he tests some value, quality, or attribute by stretching it to its limits. In most cases he is testing the faith and faithfulness of individuals or of Israel by expecting them to obey in difficult circumstances.
22:3–12 The command to sacrifice his son would not have been as shocking to Abraham as it is to us. In the Canaanite worldview, the god who provided fertility (El) was also entitled to demand a

PEOPLE TO KNOW // ISAAC

GENESIS 22:1–19: Isaac was the miracle child of Abraham and Sarah—miraculous because Sarah was over ninety years old when she gave birth, and she had always been infertile. God told Abraham to name his son Isaac, which means "laughter," because Abraham laughed when God told him Sarah would have a son (Ge 17:17–21).

When Isaac was young, God tested Abraham by telling him to sacrifice Isaac as a burnt offering (Ge 22:2). At the last moment God stopped Abraham, seeing that Abraham fully trusted him. God provided a ram for Abraham to sacrifice instead of his son. The site of this sacrifice later became the site of God's temple.

When Isaac was old enough for marriage, Abraham sent his servant back to his homeland to find a wife for Isaac from among his own people. His servant returned with Rebekah, whom Isaac then married (Ge 24:67). Rebekah, like Sarah, was unable to have children, and as with Sarah, God performed a miracle. Rebekah became pregnant with twins whom God said would become two nations, the older serving the younger (Ge 25:23). Isaac favored the older twin, Esau; Rebekah favored Jacob.

Isaac was chosen by God, yet he sometimes allowed sin to rule his choices. Like his father Abraham, he lied out of fear and said his wife was his sister (Ge 26:7). He intended to give his best blessing to Esau, even though God had told Rebekah that her older child would serve the younger. In this instance, he allowed his preferences to rule his decisions. Yet God confirmed his covenant to Isaac, and Isaac built an altar and worshiped God (Ge 26:24–25).

APPLICATION ✣ Isaac's life is a testimony to the amazing power of God's promises. Isaac was born to Sarah in her extreme old age. He had been promised to Abraham by God, and God's promises will never fail.

From the account of Isaac's life, it seems he was more a passive person. Events seemed to happen to him rather than his directing events. Even though Isaac is not known for the same dramatic faith of his father Abraham, he did end up making his own choices, resulting in faith that was visible to others. May we also live our lives in a way that people will say, "We saw clearly that the LORD was with you" (Ge 26:28).

Isaac. When he had cut enough wood
for the burnt offering, he set out for the
place God had told him about. 4On the
third day Abraham looked up and saw
the place in the distance. 5He said to his
servants, "Stay here with the donkey
while I and the boy go over there. We
will worship and then we will come back
to you."
6Abraham took the wood for the burnt
offering and placed it on his son Isaac,[i]
and he himself carried the fire and the
knife. As the two of them went on together, 7Isaac spoke up and said to his
father Abraham, "Father?"
"Yes, my son?" Abraham replied.
"The fire and wood are here," Isaac
said, "but where is the lamb[j] for the
burnt offering?"
8Abraham answered, "God himself will
provide the lamb for the burnt offering,
my son." And the two of them went on
together.

22:6 [i] Jn 19:17
22:7 [j] Lev 1:10
22:9 [k] Heb 11:17-19; Jas 2:21
22:12 [l] 1Sa 15:22; Jas 2:21-22 [m] ver 2; Jn 3:16

Ge 22:8 ❖ Abraham's trust during this situation was exemplary; he trusted God in the face of a seemingly impossible situation. How does Abraham's statement point to Christ?

9When they reached the place God
had told him about, Abraham built an
altar there and arranged the wood on
it. He bound his son Isaac and laid him
on the altar,[k] on top of the wood. 10Then
he reached out his hand and took the
knife to slay his son. 11But the angel of
the LORD called out to him from heaven,
"Abraham! Abraham!"
"Here I am," he replied.
12"Do not lay a hand on the boy," he
said. "Do not do anything to him. Now
I know that you fear God,[l] because you
have not withheld from me your son,
your only son.[m]"
13Abraham looked up and there in a

portion of what had been produced. Abraham's willingness to move ahead with the task, as much as it reflects the power of his faith, also suggests that human sacrifice is familiar to his conceptual worldview.

22:13–14 The verb translated "provide" in vv. 8 and

thicket he saw a ram[a] caught by its horns.
He went over and took the ram and sacrificed it as a burnt offering instead of
his son.[n] 14So Abraham called that place
The LORD Will Provide. And to this day
it is said, "On the mountain of the LORD
it will be provided.[o]"
15The angel of the LORD called to Abraham from heaven a second time 16and
said, "I swear by myself,[p] declares the
LORD, that because you have done this and
have not withheld your son, your only son,
17I will surely bless you and make your
descendants[q] as numerous as the stars in
the sky[r] and as the sand on the seashore.[s]
Your descendants will take possession of
the cities of their enemies,[t] 18and through
your offspring[b] all nations on earth will be
blessed,[c][u] because you have obeyed me."[v]
19Then Abraham returned to his servants, and they set off together for Beersheba. And Abraham stayed in Beersheba.

Nahor's Sons

20Some time later Abraham was told,
"Milkah is also a mother; she has borne
sons to your brother Nahor:[w] 21Uz the firstborn, Buz his brother, Kemuel (the father
of Aram), 22Kesed, Hazo, Pildash, Jidlaph
and Bethuel." 23Bethuel became the father
of Rebekah.[x] Milkah bore these eight sons
to Abraham's brother Nahor. 24His concubine, whose name was Reumah, also had
sons: Tebah, Gaham, Tahash and Maakah.

The Death of Sarah

23 Sarah lived to be a hundred and
twenty-seven years old. 2She died
at Kiriath Arba[y] (that is, Hebron)[z] in the
land of Canaan, and Abraham went to
mourn for Sarah and to weep over her.
3Then Abraham rose from beside his
dead wife and spoke to the Hittites.[d] He
said, 4"I am a foreigner and stranger[a]
among you. Sell me some property for
a burial site here so I can bury my dead."
5The Hittites replied to Abraham, 6"Sir,
listen to us. You are a mighty prince[b]
among us. Bury your dead in the choicest
of our tombs. None of us will refuse you
his tomb for burying your dead."
7Then Abraham rose and bowed down
before the people of the land, the Hittites. 8He said to them, "If you are willing
to let me bury my dead, then listen to me
and intercede with Ephron son of Zohar[c]
on my behalf 9so he will sell me the cave
of Machpelah, which belongs to him and
is at the end of his field. Ask him to sell
it to me for the full price as a burial site
among you."
10Ephron the Hittite was sitting among
his people and he replied to Abraham in

22:13 [n] Ro 8:32
22:14 [o] ver 8
22:16 [p] Lk 1:73; Heb 6:13
22:17 [q] Heb 6:14* [r] Ge 15:5 [s] Ge 26:24; 32:12 [t] Ge 24:60
22:18 [u] Ge 12:2, 3; Ac 3:25*; Gal 3:8* [v] ver 10
22:20 [w] Ge 11:29
22:23 [x] Ge 24:15
23:2 [y] Jos 14:15 [z] ver 19; Ge 13:18
23:4 [a] Ge 17:8; 1Ch 29:15; Ps 105:12; Heb 11:9,13
23:6 [b] Ge 14:14-16; 24:35
23:8 [c] Ge 25:9

Ge 23:5–9 ❖ Given God's promise to Abraham in Genesis 12:1-3, why was it important for Abraham to buy a cave to bury Sarah rather than to lay her in one of the tombs of the Hittites?

[a] *13* Many manuscripts of the Masoretic Text, Samaritan Pentateuch, Septuagint and Syriac; most manuscripts of the Masoretic Text *a ram behind him* [b] *18* Or *seed* [c] *18* Or *and all nations on earth will use the name of your offspring in blessings* (see 48:20) [d] *3* Or *the descendants of Heth*; also in verses 5, 7, 10, 16, 18 and 20

---

14 is the verb "to see." This usage approximates one of the uses of the verb "to see" that we also have in English to convey that the details will be taken care of. Abraham is convinced that the Lord will work out all of the details (v. 8).

The only two other mountains that are ever referred to as "the mountain of the LORD" are Jerusalem and Sinai. Both places are locations where God took care of details—the law at Mount Sinai and sacrifice at the temple in Jerusalem.

22:15–24 The reiteration of the covenant contains several elements worthy of note. (1) Yahweh swears an oath in his own name (v. 16). When the rest of the OT mentions the land God swore to Abraham, it is referring specifically back to this passage. (2) This reiteration is also an advance because it explicitly promises that Abraham's descendants "will take possession of the cities of their enemies" (v. 17). This is the first indication of a conquest. As a result of conquest, the nations will want to bring themselves under Israel's blessing. (3) Finally, note that the oath and covenant agreement are here cited as a consequence of Abraham's obedience (v. 18). This identifies his obedience as having served as a stimulus for this advance.

✚ **22:1–24** When we are not in control, it is easy to become anxious and fearful. We may feel that we are free-falling through life, but we are held by God, who is in absolute control. Having faith that our situation is never out of God's control can calm our fears.

23:1–3 It is difficult to determine whether the Hittites mentioned here are related to those of the Hittite Empire known from Anatolia a few centuries later.

Farmable land was so precious in the ancient world that owners usually refrained from selling it to anyone outside the kinship group. But Abraham is not trying to buy farmland, only property for a burial site. Most often a family tomb was used by several generations.

23:4–16 Four hundred shekels of silver is equivalent to about 7.25 pounds of silver. Abraham is

the hearing of all the Hittites who had
come to the gate[d] of his city. 11“No, my
lord,” he said. “Listen to me; I give[a][e] you
the field, and I give[a] you the cave that is
in it. I give[a] it to you in the presence of
my people. Bury your dead.”
12Again Abraham bowed down before
the people of the land 13and he said to
Ephron in their hearing, “Listen to me, if
you will. I will pay the price of the field.
Accept it from me so I can bury my dead
there.”
14Ephron answered Abraham, 15“Listen
to me, my lord; the land is worth four hundred shekels[b] of silver,[f] but what is that
between you and me? Bury your dead.”
16Abraham agreed to Ephron’s terms
and weighed out for him the price he had
named in the hearing of the Hittites: four
hundred shekels of silver,[g] according to
the weight current among the merchants.
17So Ephron’s field in Machpelah near
Mamre[h]—both the field and the cave in
it, and all the trees within the borders of
the field—was deeded 18to Abraham as
his property in the presence of all the
Hittites who had come to the gate of
the city. 19Afterward Abraham buried
his wife Sarah in the cave in the field
of Machpelah near Mamre (which is at
Hebron) in the land of Canaan. 20So the
field and the cave in it were deeded[i] to
Abraham by the Hittites as a burial site.

Isaac and Rebekah

24 Abraham was now very old, and
the LORD had blessed him in ev-
ery way.[j] 2He said to the senior servant
in his household, the one in charge of all
that he had,[k] “Put your hand under my
thigh.[l] 3I want you to swear by the LORD,
the God of heaven and the God of earth,[m]
that you will not get a wife for my son[n]
from the daughters of the Canaanites,[o]
among whom I am living, 4but will go to
my country and my own relatives[p] and
get a wife for my son Isaac.”
5The servant asked him, “What if the
woman is unwilling to come back with
me to this land? Shall I then take your
son back to the country you came from?”
6“Make sure that you do not take my
son back there,” Abraham said. 7“The
LORD, the God of heaven, who brought
me out of my father’s household and my
native land and who spoke to me and
promised me on oath, saying, ‘To your
offspring[c][q] I will give this land’[r]—he
will send his angel before you[s] so that
you can get a wife for my son from there.
8If the woman is unwilling to come back
with you, then you will be released from
this oath of mine. Only do not take my
son back there.” 9So the servant put his
hand under the thigh[t] of his master Abraham and swore an oath to him concerning this matter.
10Then the servant left, taking with him
ten of his master’s camels loaded with all
kinds of good things from his master. He
set out for Aram Naharaim[d] and made his
way to the town of Nahor. 11He had the
camels kneel down near the well[u] outside
the town; it was toward evening, the time
the women go out to draw water.[v]
12Then he prayed, “LORD, God of my
master Abraham,[w] make me successful
today, and show kindness to my master
Abraham. 13See, I am standing beside
this spring, and the daughters of the
townspeople are coming out to draw water. 14May it be that when I say to a young

23:10 [d] Ge 34:20-24; Ru 4:4
23:11 [e] 2Sa 24:23
23:15 [f] Eze 45:12
23:16 [g] Jer 32:9; Zec 11:12
23:17 [h] Ge 25:9; 49:30-32; 50:13; Ac 7:16
23:20 [i] Jer 32:10
24:1 [j] ver 35
24:2 [k] Ge 39:4-6 [l] ver 9; Ge 47:29
24:3 [m] Ge 14:19 [n] Ge 28:1; Dt 7:3 [o] Ge 10:15-19
24:4 [p] Ge 12:1; 28:2
24:7 [q] Gal 3:16* [r] Ge 12:7; 13:15 [s] Ex 23:20,23
24:9 [t] ver 2
24:11 [u] Ex 2:15 [v] ver 13; 1Sa 9:11
24:12 [w] ver 27, 42,48; Ge 26:24; Ex 3:6,15,16

[a] *11* Or *sell* [b] *15* That is, about 10 pounds or about 4.6 kilograms [c] *7* Or *seed* [d] *10* That is, Northwest Mesopotamia

likely willing to pay full price because a discounted price could be later connected to family debt problems and also allow the heirs of Ephron to reclaim the land.

23:17–20 Mamre is about two miles north of Hebron. Excavations indicate a wall around an ancient terebinth already there in the Second Temple period.

24:1–9 Abraham’s insistence that Isaac’s wife be chosen from among family rather than from the people of the land (24:3) is a covenant matter. Intermarriage with the people of the land would risk integration with pagan belief and practices and thus jeopardize the covenant promises of the land to Abraham’s descendants.

The servant takes the oath with the symbolic gesture of placing his hand in the vicinity of the genitals. The oath concerned not just Isaac but ultimately all of Abraham’s offspring.

24:10–21 Aram Naharaim (“Aram of the Two Rivers”), includes the general area between the Euphrates River and the Habur River triangle in northern Mesopotamia. Trips to a well were generally made during the cooler hours of the day. It was normal protocol for a stranger to ask permission to use a town’s well and for the people of the town to offer a drink.

24:12–14 The prayer of Abraham’s servant uses a testing approach for identifying Isaac’s bride-to-be. The yes/no question he poses reveals whether the girl he approaches is the right wife for Isaac. His test is based on a question: Will she give him a drink? The expected answer to that question would be yes, so that the only logical unique answer

Ge 24:14–15 ❖ Remember and describe a time you experienced a clear and timely answer to a prayer.

woman, 'Please let down your jar that I
may have a drink,' and she says, 'Drink,
and I'll water your camels too' — let her
be the one you have chosen for your servant Isaac. By this I will know[x] that you
have shown kindness to my master."
15Before he had finished praying,[y]
Rebekah[z] came out with her jar on her
shoulder. She was the daughter of Bethuel son of Milkah,[a] who was the wife of
Abraham's brother Nahor.[b] 16The woman
was very beautiful,[c] a virgin; no man had
ever slept with her. She went down to the
spring, filled her jar and came up again.
17The servant hurried to meet her and
said, "Please give me a little water from
your jar."
18"Drink,[d] my lord," she said, and
quickly lowered the jar to her hands and
gave him a drink.
19After she had given him a drink, she
said, "I'll draw water for your camels too,[e]
until they have had enough to drink."
20So she quickly emptied her jar into the
trough, ran back to the well to draw more
water, and drew enough for all his camels.
21Without saying a word, the man watched
her closely to learn whether or not the
LORD had made his journey successful.[f]
22When the camels had finished drinking, the man took out a gold nose ring[g]
weighing a beka[a] and two gold bracelets
weighing ten shekels.[b] 23Then he asked,
"Whose daughter are you? Please tell me,
is there room in your father's house for
us to spend the night?"
24She answered him, "I am the daughter of Bethuel, the son that Milkah bore
to Nahor.[h]" 25And she added, "We have
plenty of straw and fodder, as well as
room for you to spend the night."
26Then the man bowed down and worshiped the LORD,[i] 27saying, "Praise be to
the LORD,[j] the God of my master Abraham,
who has not abandoned his kindness and
faithfulness[k] to my master. As for me, the
LORD has led me on the journey[l] to the
house of my master's relatives."[m]
28The young woman ran and told her
mother's household about these things.
29Now Rebekah had a brother named Laban,[n] and he hurried out to the man at
the spring. 30As soon as he had seen the
nose ring, and the bracelets on his sister's
arms, and had heard Rebekah tell what
the man said to her, he went out to the
man and found him standing by the camels near the spring. 31"Come, you who are
blessed by the LORD,"[o] he said. "Why are
you standing out here? I have prepared
the house and a place for the camels."
32So the man went to the house, and
the camels were unloaded. Straw and
fodder were brought for the camels, and
water for him and his men to wash their
feet.[p] 33Then food was set before him, but
he said, "I will not eat until I have told
you what I have to say."
"Then tell us," Laban said.
34So he said, "I am Abraham's servant.
35The LORD has blessed my master abundantly,[q] and he has become wealthy. He
has given him sheep and cattle, silver
and gold, male and female servants, and
camels and donkeys.[r] 36My master's wife
Sarah has borne him a son in her old
age,[s] and he has given him everything
he owns.[t] 37And my master made me
swear an oath, and said, 'You must not
get a wife for my son from the daughters
of the Canaanites, in whose land I live,[u]

24:14 [x] Jdg 6:17, 37
24:15 [y] ver 45 [z] Ge 22:23 [a] Ge 22:20 [b] Ge 11:29
24:16 [c] Ge 26:7
24:18 [d] ver 14
24:19 [e] ver 14
24:21 [f] ver 12
24:22 [g] ver 47
24:24 [h] ver 15
24:26 [i] ver 48, 52; Ex 4:31
24:27 [j] Ex 18:10; Ru 4:14; 1Sa 25:32 [k] ver 49; Ge 32:10; Ps 98:3 [l] ver 21 [m] ver 12, 48
24:29 [n] ver 4; Ge 29:5, 12, 13
24:31 [o] Ge 26:29; Ru 3:10; Ps 115:15
24:32 [p] Ge 43:24; Jdg 19:21
24:35 [q] ver 1 [r] Ge 13:2
24:36 [s] Ge 21:2, 10 [t] Ge 25:5
24:37 [u] ver 3

[a] *22* That is, about 1/5 ounce or about 5.7 grams
[b] *22* That is, about 4 ounces or about 115 grams

---

would be no. Thus, for the alternative the servant must choose something far out of the range of expectation—such as the girl's volunteering to water all his camels.

24:15–18 A camel that has gone a few days without water can drink as much as twenty-five gallons. Ancient jars used for drawing water usually held no more than three gallons. In other words, this offer involves perhaps eighty to a hundred drawings from the well. Such an unbelievable proposal would indicate that God is working to override human nature in specified ways. Rebekah passes the test of Abraham's servant.

24:22–54 The giving of gifts serves several functions. On the most basic level it can be thought of as an exorbitant payment for exorbitant service. The gifts give evidence of his master's wealth and serve as motivation for the eventual proposal to be taken seriously. Finally, they serve as a down payment on a bride price.

Bracelets were bands worn around the wrist as bangles. They were popular items and are often found on the arms and wrists of females in tombs. These extremely costly gifts from Abraham would have undoubtedly caused a stir of great excitement.

Laban eagerly takes the servant in, and the bulk of the chapter contains the repetition of the story. The retelling of the story is significant because of the evidence that it offers that this marriage is divinely sanctioned (esp. vv. 40, 48, 50).

38but go to my father's family and to my own clan, and get a wife for my son.'[v]

39"Then I asked my master, 'What if the woman will not come back with me?'[w]

40"He replied, 'The LORD, before whom I have walked faithfully, will send his angel with you[x] and make your journey a success, so that you can get a wife for my son from my own clan and from my father's family. 41You will be released from my oath if, when you go to my clan, they refuse to give her to you — then you will be released from my oath.'[y]

42"When I came to the spring today, I said, 'LORD, God of my master Abraham, if you will, please grant success[z] to the journey on which I have come. 43See, I am standing beside this spring.[a] If a young woman comes out to draw water and I say to her, "Please let me drink a little water from your jar,"[b] 44and if she says to me, "Drink, and I'll draw water for your camels too," let her be the one the LORD has chosen for my master's son.'

45"Before I finished praying in my heart,[c] Rebekah came out, with her jar on her shoulder.[d] She went down to the spring and drew water, and I said to her, 'Please give me a drink.'[e]

46"She quickly lowered her jar from her shoulder and said, 'Drink, and I'll water your camels too.'[f] So I drank, and she watered the camels also.

47"I asked her, 'Whose daughter are you?'[g]

"She said, 'The daughter of Bethuel son of Nahor, whom Milkah bore to him.'[h]

"Then I put the ring in her nose and the bracelets on her arms,[i] 48and I bowed down and worshiped the LORD.[j] I praised the LORD, the God of my master Abraham, who had led me on the right road to get the granddaughter of my master's brother for his son.[k] 49Now if you will show kindness and faithfulness[l] to my master, tell me; and if not, tell me, so I may know which way to turn."

50Laban and Bethuel answered, "This is from the LORD;[m] we can say nothing to you one way or the other.[n] 51Here is Rebekah; take her and go, and let her become the wife of your master's son, as the LORD has directed."

52When Abraham's servant heard what they said, he bowed down to the ground before the LORD.[o] 53Then the servant brought out gold and silver jewelry and articles of clothing and gave them to Rebekah; he also gave costly gifts[p] to her brother and to her mother. 54Then he and the men who were with him ate and drank and spent the night there.

When they got up the next morning, he said, "Send me on my way[q] to my master."

55But her brother and her mother replied, "Let the young woman remain with us ten days or so; then you[a] may go."

56But he said to them, "Do not detain me, now that the LORD has granted success to my journey. Send me on my way so I may go to my master."

57Then they said, "Let's call the young woman and ask her about it." 58So they called Rebekah and asked her, "Will you go with this man?"

"I will go," she said.

59So they sent their sister Rebekah on her way, along with her nurse[r] and Abraham's servant and his men. 60And they blessed Rebekah and said to her,

"Our sister, may you increase
  to thousands upon thousands;[s]
may your offspring possess
  the cities of their enemies."[t]

61Then Rebekah and her attendants got ready and mounted the camels and went back with the man. So the servant took Rebekah and left.

62Now Isaac had come from Beer Lahai Roi,[u] for he was living in the Negev.[v] 63He went out to the field one evening to meditate,[b][w] and as he looked up, he

24:38 [v] ver 4
24:39 [w] ver 5
24:40 [x] ver 7
24:41 [y] ver 8
24:42 [z] ver 12
24:43 [a] ver 13 [b] ver 14
24:45 [c] 1Sa 1:13 [d] ver 15 [e] ver 17
24:46 [f] ver 18-19
24:47 [g] ver 23 [h] ver 24 [i] Eze 16:11-12
24:48 [j] ver 26 [k] ver 27
24:49 [l] Ge 47:29; Jos 2:14
24:50 [m] Ps 118:23 [n] Ge 31:7,24, 29,42
24:52 [o] ver 26
24:53 [p] ver 10, 22
24:54 [q] ver 56, 59
24:59 [r] Ge 35:8
24:60 [s] Ge 17:16 [t] Ge 22:17
24:62 [u] Ge 16:14; 25:11 [v] Ge 20:1
24:63 [w] Ps 1:2; 77:12; 119:15, 27,48,97,148; 143:5; 145:5

[a] 55 Or *she* [b] 63 The meaning of the Hebrew for this word is uncertain.

24:55–67 For a marriage to be arranged, the groom's family must provide a bride price while the bride's family provides a dowry. It was unusual in the ancient world for the woman to have any part in major decisions, but when the servant asks to leave right away, the men look to Rebekah for consent. She is probably consulted because of the substantial risk involved in leaving family protection under such unusual circumstances.
24:60 With Rebekah leaving home, the family recites a blessing that reiterates some of the elements that have by now been identified firmly within the covenant benefits. The increase of descendants goes back to Ge 1, but the possession of enemy cities was not included until Ge 22.
24:62–67 When the group arrives in Beer Lahai Roi, Abraham's servant identifies Isaac in the fields, and Rebekah dons her veil. She is probably now indicating that she is Isaac's bride. By taking Rebekah into his mother's tent, Isaac demonstrates that she is now the mistress of the household.

saw camels approaching. 64 Rebekah also
looked up and saw Isaac. She got down
from her camel 65 and asked the servant,
"Who is that man in the field coming to
meet us?"
"He is my master," the servant answered. So she took her veil and covered
herself.
66 Then the servant told Isaac all he
had done. 67 Isaac brought her into the
tent of his mother Sarah, and he married
Rebekah.[x] So she became his wife, and
he loved her;[y] and Isaac was comforted
after his mother's death.[z]

The Death of Abraham

25:1–4pp // 1Ch 1:32–33

25 Abraham had taken another
wife, whose name was Keturah.
2 She bore him Zimran, Jokshan, Medan,
Midian, Ishbak and Shuah.[a] 3 Jokshan
was the father of Sheba and Dedan; the
descendants of Dedan were the Ashur-
ites, the Letushites and the Leummites.
4 The sons of Midian were Ephah, Epher,
Hanok, Abida and Eldaah. All these were
descendants of Keturah.
5 Abraham left everything he owned to
Isaac.[b] 6 But while he was still living, he
gave gifts to the sons of his concubines[c]
and sent them away from his son Isaac[d]
to the land of the east.
7 Abraham lived a hundred and seventy-five years. 8 Then Abraham breathed
his last and died at a good old age,[e] an
old man and full of years; and he was
gathered to his people.[f] 9 His sons Isaac
and Ishmael buried him[g] in the cave of
Machpelah near Mamre, in the field of
Ephron son of Zohar the Hittite,[h] 10 the
field Abraham had bought from the Hittites.[a][i] There Abraham was buried with
his wife Sarah. 11 After Abraham's death,
God blessed his son Isaac, who then lived
near Beer Lahai Roi.[j]

Ishmael's Sons

25:12–16pp // 1Ch 1:29–31

12 This is the account of the family line
of Abraham's son Ishmael, whom Sarah's slave, Hagar[k] the Egyptian, bore to
Abraham.[l]

13 These are the names of the sons of
Ishmael, listed in the order of their birth:
Nebaioth the firstborn of Ishmael, Kedar, Adbeel, Mibsam, 14 Mishma, Dumah,
Massa, 15 Hadad, Tema, Jetur, Naphish
and Kedemah. 16 These were the sons of
Ishmael, and these are the names of the
twelve tribal rulers[m] according to their
settlements and camps. 17 Ishmael lived
a hundred and thirty-seven years. He
breathed his last and died, and he was
gathered to his people.[n] 18 His descendants settled in the area from Havilah to
Shur, near the eastern border of Egypt,
as you go toward Ashur. And they lived
in hostility toward[b] all the tribes related
to them.[o]

Jacob and Esau

19 This is the account of the family line
of Abraham's son Isaac.

24:67 [x] Ge 25:20 [y] Ge 29:18,20 [z] Ge 23:1-2
25:2 [a] 1Ch 1:32,33
25:5 [b] Ge 24:36
25:6 [c] Ge 22:24 [d] Ge 21:10,14
25:8 [e] Ge 15:15 [f] ver 17; Ge 35:29; 49:29,33
25:9 [g] Ge 35:29 [h] Ge 50:13
25:10 [i] Ge 23:16
25:11 [j] Ge 16:14
25:12 [k] Ge 16:1 [l] Ge 16:15
25:16 [m] Ge 17:20
25:17 [n] ver 8
25:18 [o] Ge 16:12

[a] 10 Or *the descendants of Heth* [b] 18 Or *lived to the east of*

25:1–11 The use of the plural "concubines" in v. 6 and the lack of any time-related clause stating clearly that Keturah came on the scene after Sarah's death suggest that Keturah may have entered the family at an earlier period (between Ishmael and Isaac). The author does not always relate everything in chronological order.

Of the children of Keturah, Midian is the most familiar to the modern Bible reading audience. In the Pentateuch the Midianites initially have neutral standing as the traders who transport Joseph to Egypt, then a favorable standing because Moses marries into the family of the priest of Midian, Jethro. By the end of the period, however, they are in collusion with the Moabites.

25:12–18 This is another case of the narrator pursuing the unimportant line and drawing it to conclusion before coming back and discussing the line he is interested in following. Thus, Ishmael's descendants are listed before Isaac's descendants. In 21:18 the angel told Hagar that Ishmael would become a great nation. In 25:13-16 the text indicates the fulfillment of that statement.

✣ **23:1—25:18** In the process of discerning God's will in our lives, there are aspects that are our responsibility and others that are God's responsibility. We should ask him to help us think clearly about the decision. If we faithfully do our part, it is then his job to guide us to the right decision. He can do this through abnormal circumstances, but more frequently he will do it through closed and open doors, through our own thinking process, and through his Spirit working within us.

25:19–28 Though the barrenness we saw in the Abraham story recurs in this generation, the text does not dwell on it. Instead, the focus is that once Rebekah conceives, she is troubled by a problem pregnancy. The terminology "to inquire of the LORD" (v. 22) usually indicates the asking of an oracle.

PEOPLE TO KNOW // REBEKAH

GENESIS 25:21-26: Rebekah was the sister of Laban. She married Abraham and Sarah's son, Isaac. Abraham sent his servant to Harran to find a wife for Isaac from his own people. Abraham's servant prayed for God to make clear who the wife should be, and God answered his prayer by having him meet Rebekah (Ge 24:15).

Rebekah returned with Abraham's servant, and she married Isaac. Like Sarah, she was unable to conceive, but when Isaac prayed to God for her, God blessed her and Isaac with twin sons. God told Rebekah the older would serve the younger and they would both become fathers of nations (Ge 25:23). The older twin, Esau, was a hunter and outdoorsman; Isaac favored him. The younger twin, Jacob, liked to stay inside, and Rebekah loved Jacob more.

When Isaac was old and blind, he intended to bless his favorite, Esau—a binding blessing that would determine the path of his future. Rebekah wanted the blessing for her favorite child. So she helped Jacob fool Isaac so that Jacob would receive the blessing instead. The plan worked: Isaac was fooled, Jacob received the blessing, and what the Lord had said to Rebekah before the twins were born was proven true.

APPLICATION Despite Rebekah's deceptive ways, God used her to continue his redemptive plan and his blessing through the line of Jacob. Rebekah's life demonstrates the sovereignty of God, who is always working things together for his "higher story" no matter how chaotic things may appear in the "lower story" of our lives. We need to trust that human foibles, failures and deceit cannot undermine God's good plan to redeem and restore creation and to bring about God's kingdom. In the chaos, there is hope.

Abraham became the father of Isaac,
20and Isaac was forty years old[p] when he
married Rebekah[q] daughter of Bethuel
the Aramean from Paddan Aram[a] and
sister of Laban[r] the Aramean.
21Isaac prayed to the LORD on behalf of
his wife, because she was childless. The
LORD answered his prayer,[s] and his wife
Rebekah became pregnant. 22The babies
jostled each other within her, and she
said, "Why is this happening to me?" So
she went to inquire of the LORD.[t]
23The LORD said to her,

"Two nations[u] are in your womb,
and two peoples from within you
will be separated;
one people will be stronger than the
other,
and the older will serve the
younger.[v]"

24When the time came for her to give
birth, there were twin boys in her womb.
25The first to come out was red, and his
whole body was like a hairy garment;[w] so
they named him Esau.[b] 26After this, his
brother came out, with his hand grasping
Esau's heel;[x] so he was named Jacob.[c][y]
Isaac was sixty years old when Rebekah
gave birth to them.
27The boys grew up, and Esau became a
skillful hunter, a man of the open country,[z] while Jacob was content to stay at
home among the tents. 28Isaac, who had
a taste for wild game,[a] loved Esau, but
Rebekah loved Jacob.[b]
29Once when Jacob was cooking
some stew, Esau came in from the open

25:20 [p] ver 26; Ge 26:34 [q] Ge 24:67 [r] Ge 24:29
25:21 [s] 1Ch 5:20; 2Ch 33:13; Ezr 8:23; Ps 127:3; Ro 9:10
25:22 [t] 1Sa 9:9; 10:22
25:23 [u] Ge 17:4 [v] Ge 27:29, 40; Mal 1:3; Ro 9:11-12*
25:25 [w] Ge 27:11
25:26 [x] Hos 12:3 [y] Ge 27:36
25:27 [z] Ge 27:3,5
25:28 [a] Ge 27:19 [b] Ge 27:6

[a] *20* That is, Northwest Mesopotamia
[b] *25* *Esau* may mean *hairy.*
[c] *26* *Jacob* means *he grasps the heel,* a Hebrew idiom for *he deceives.*

25:22–23 Rebekah is carrying twins, and there will be conflict between them, with the younger prevailing. It is this conflict and reversal (the younger prevailing) that define the dominant obstacles for the new generation.

25:24–28 The contrast between the two continues in their preferred lifestyles, and the conflict between them is energized by the favoritism shown by the parents. The verb translated "loved" (v. 28) is indicative of favor, choice, and preference. Rebekah undoubtedly loves both her children, but Jacob is her favorite and receives preferential treatment from her.

The qualities that endear Jacob to Rebekah are summarized in v. 27. The description of Jacob likely has to do with being an organized, administrative type of person. The second description of him, staying "among the tents," identifies him as engaged in seminomadic livestock herding and breeding rather than being a hunter like Esau.

25:29–34 The birthright was the oldest son's share of the material estate of the family. In the ancient world the firstborn typically received a double share of the inheritance. Esau would receive two-thirds—twice what Jacob would receive. The

KEY POINTS IN ABRAHAM'S LIFE

EVENT	REFERENCE
God calls Abraham from Haran; Abraham moves his family to Canaan at the age of 75.	Ge 12:1-5
The Altar Narratives—Abraham builds altars to the Lord in several locations: Moreh; between Bethel and Ai; the terebinth trees of Mamre.	Ge 12:7; 12:8; 13:18
The Promise Narratives—God promises Abraham that he will be the father of many nations. Abraham believes God, and his faith is counted to him as righteousness.	Ge 12:2, 7; 13:16; 15:1-6; 17:1-5; 18:9-10; 22:15-17
Abraham journeys to Egypt, risking Sarah's security and compromising his integrity.	Ge 12
Abraham and Lot separate.	Ge 13:7-11
Abraham is blessed by Melchizedek.	Ge 14:18-20
Abraham heeds Sarah's advice, producing Ishmael from his union with Hagar.	Ge 16
The Lord establishes the covenant of circumcision.	Ge 17:9-14
Abraham negotiates for the people of Sodom.	Ge 18:16-33
As before in Egypt, Abraham endangers Sarah to secure his own safety, lying to Abimelech.	Ge 20
Abraham and Sarah have Isaac in their old age.	Ge 21
God tests Abraham's faith, ordering him to sacrifice Isaac as a burnt offering.	Ge 22
Sarah, Abraham's wife and companion, dies.	Ge 23
Abraham ensures that Isaac will find an appropriate mate.	Ge 24
Abraham remarries; he and Keturah have six sons; at 175 years old, Abraham dies.	Ge 25:1-7

country, famished. 30He said to Jacob,
"Quick, let me have some of that red
stew! I'm famished!" (That is why he
was also called Edom.[a])
31Jacob replied, "First sell me your
birthright."
32"Look, I am about to die," Esau said.
"What good is the birthright to me?"
33But Jacob said, "Swear to me first."
So he swore an oath to him, selling his
birthright[c] to Jacob.
34Then Jacob gave Esau some bread
and some lentil stew. He ate and drank,
and then got up and left.
So Esau despised his birthright.

25:33 [c] Ge 27:36; Heb 12:16

Ge 25:30-33 ❖ Esau didn't value his birthright and gave it away because of hunger. How can we protect ourselves from moments of weakness and temptation? How can we make sure we prioritize what's most important?

[a] 30 *Edom* means *red.*

---

sense of injustice would be substantially increased when the second born was a twin. Thus, it is easy to understand the sort of bitterness and jealousy that could result from such inequity.

Jacob is cooking stew. In a large household such as Isaac's, one would expect servants to do this sort of work. The most logical solution is that the setting is not at their home base but at a shepherd camp. Jacob is in charge of one of the groups of herders at a grazing site.

Giving Esau the benefit of the doubt, we may accept that he believes that hunger threatens his life. The original audience would react to Esau's blunt statement ("What good is the birthright to me?" v. 32) with horror, regardless of his extreme hunger. The only evaluation the text offers appears in the last verb of v. 34: "Esau despised his birthright." This verb does not reflect Esau's feelings about the birthright but comments on his valuation of it.

Isaac and Abimelek

26:1–11Ref // Ge 12:10–20; 20:1–18

26 Now there was a famine in the
land[d] — besides the previous famine in Abraham's time — and Isaac went
to Abimelek king of the Philistines in
Gerar.[e] 2The LORD appeared[f] to Isaac and
said, "Do not go down to Egypt; live in
the land where I tell you to live.[g] 3Stay in
this land for a while,[h] and I will be with
you and will bless you.[i] For to you and
your descendants I will give all these
lands[j] and will confirm the oath I swore
to your father Abraham. 4I will make
your descendants as numerous as the
stars in the sky[k] and will give them all
these lands, and through your offspring[a]
all nations on earth will be blessed,[b][l] 5be-
cause Abraham obeyed me[m] and did everything I required of him, keeping my
commands, my decrees and my instructions." 6So Isaac stayed in Gerar.

7When the men of that place asked
him about his wife, he said, "She is my
sister,[n]" because he was afraid to say,
"She is my wife." He thought, "The men
of this place might kill me on account
of Rebekah, because she is beautiful."

8When Isaac had been there a long
time, Abimelek king of the Philistines
looked down from a window and saw
Isaac caressing his wife Rebekah. 9So
Abimelek summoned Isaac and said,
"She is really your wife! Why did you
say, 'She is my sister'?"

Isaac answered him, "Because I
thought I might lose my life on account
of her."

10Then Abimelek said, "What is this
you have done to us?[o] One of the men
might well have slept with your wife, and
you would have brought guilt upon us."

11So Abimelek gave orders to all the
people: "Anyone who harms[p] this man
or his wife shall surely be put to death."

12Isaac planted crops in that land and
the same year reaped a hundredfold, because the LORD blessed him.[q] 13The man
became rich, and his wealth continued to

26:1 [d] Ge 12:10 [e] Ge 20:1
26:2 [f] Ge 12:7; 17:1; 18:1 [g] Ge 12:1
26:3 [h] Ge 20:1; 28:15 [i] Ge 12:2; 22:16-18 [j] Ge 12:7; 13:15; 15:18
26:4 [k] Ge 15:5; 22:17; Ex 32:13 [l] Ge 12:3; 22:18; Gal 3:8
26:5 [m] Ge 22:16
26:7 [n] Ge 12:13; 20:2,12; Pr 29:25
26:10 [o] Ge 20:9
26:11 [p] Ps 105:15
26:12 [q] ver 3; Job 42:12
26:13 [r] Pr 10:22
26:14 [s] Ge 24:36 [t] Ge 37:11
26:15 [u] Ge 21:30 [v] Ge 21:25
26:16 [w] Ex 1:9
26:18 [x] Ge 21:30
26:20 [y] Ge 21:25
26:22 [z] Ge 17:6; Ex 1:7
26:24 [a] Ge 24:12; Ex 3:6 [b] Ge 15:1 [c] ver 4 [d] Ge 17:7

Ge 26:7 ❖ Isaac repeated the foolish behavior of his father, Abraham. How does generational sin impact us? How can we break bad patterns?

grow until he became very wealthy.[r] 14He
had so many flocks and herds and servants[s] that the Philistines envied him.[t]
15So all the wells[u] that his father's servants had dug in the time of his father
Abraham, the Philistines stopped up,[v]
filling them with earth.

16Then Abimelek said to Isaac, "Move
away from us; you have become too powerful for us.[w]"

17So Isaac moved away from there and
encamped in the Valley of Gerar, where
he settled. 18Isaac reopened the wells[x]
that had been dug in the time of his father Abraham, which the Philistines had
stopped up after Abraham died, and he
gave them the same names his father
had given them.

19Isaac's servants dug in the valley and
discovered a well of fresh water there.
20But the herders of Gerar quarreled
with those of Isaac and said, "The water
is ours!"[y] So he named the well Esek,[c]
because they disputed with him. 21Then
they dug another well, but they quarreled over that one also; so he named it
Sitnah.[d] 22He moved on from there and
dug another well, and no one quarreled
over it. He named it Rehoboth,[e] saying,
"Now the LORD has given us room and
we will flourish[z] in the land."

23From there he went up to Beersheba.
24That night the LORD appeared to him
and said, "I am the God of your father
Abraham.[a] Do not be afraid,[b] for I am
with you; I will bless you and will increase the number of your descendants[c]
for the sake of my servant Abraham."[d]

[a] 4 Or *seed* [b] 4 Or *and all nations on earth will use the name of your offspring in blessings* (see 48:20) [c] 20 *Esek* means *dispute.* [d] 21 *Sitnah* means *opposition.* [e] 22 *Rehoboth* means *room.*

26:1–35 What are the obligations, decrees, and instructions that the patriarchs live by? An example of a "command/obligation" is when Abraham was told to sacrifice Isaac. An example of a "decree/ regulation" is the ordinance of circumcision. An example of a "law/ instruction" is that circumcision should be done on the eighth day.

26:7 Isaac's rationale for the deception is the same as Abraham's, but Rebekah is not actually taken by the ruler as Sarah had been on both occasions. We can note, therefore, a decreasing danger in the accounts.

26:15 Perhaps most important to the author, the men of Gerar recognize God's blessing on Isaac and, as the covenant has suggested, seek to join themselves to him.

25Isaac built an altar[e] there and called
on the name of the LORD. There he
pitched his tent, and there his servants
dug a well.
26Meanwhile, Abimelek had come to
him from Gerar, with Ahuzzath his personal adviser and Phicol the commander
of his forces.[f] 27Isaac asked them, "Why
have you come to me, since you were
hostile to me and sent me away?[g]"
28They answered, "We saw clearly
that the LORD was with you;[h] so we said,
'There ought to be a sworn agreement
between us'—between us and you. Let
us make a treaty with you 29that you will
do us no harm, just as we did not harm
you but always treated you well and sent
you away peacefully. And now you are
blessed by the LORD."[i]
30Isaac then made a feast[j] for them,
and they ate and drank. 31Early the next
morning the men swore an oath[k] to each
other. Then Isaac sent them on their way,
and they went away peacefully.
32That day Isaac's servants came and
told him about the well they had dug.
They said, "We've found water!" 33He
called it Shibah,[a] and to this day the
name of the town has been Beersheba.[b][l]

Jacob Takes Esau's Blessing

34When Esau was forty years old,[m] he
married Judith daughter of Beeri the
Hittite, and also Basemath daughter of
Elon the Hittite.[n] 35They were a source
of grief to Isaac and Rebekah.[o]
27 When Isaac was old and his eyes
were so weak that he could no lon-
ger see,[p] he called for Esau his older son[q]
and said to him, "My son."
"Here I am," he answered.
2Isaac said, "I am now an old man and
don't know the day of my death.[r] 3Now
then, get your equipment—your quiver and bow—and go out to the open
country[s] to hunt some wild game for
me. 4Prepare me the kind of tasty food
I like and bring it to me to eat, so that I
may give you my blessing[t] before I die."
5Now Rebekah was listening as Isaac
spoke to his son Esau. When Esau left
for the open country to hunt game and
bring it back, 6Rebekah said to her son
Jacob,[u] "Look, I overheard your father
say to your brother Esau, 7'Bring me
some game and prepare me some tasty
food to eat, so that I may give you my
blessing in the presence of the LORD before I die.' 8Now, my son, listen carefully
and do what I tell you:[v] 9Go out to the
flock and bring me two choice young
goats, so I can prepare some tasty food
for your father, just the way he likes it.
10Then take it to your father to eat, so
that he may give you his blessing before he dies."
11Jacob said to Rebekah his mother,
"But my brother Esau is a hairy man[w]
while I have smooth skin. 12What if my
father touches me?[x] I would appear to
be tricking him and would bring down a
curse on myself rather than a blessing."
13His mother said to him, "My son, let
the curse fall on me.[y] Just do what I say;[z]
go and get them for me."
14So he went and got them and brought
them to his mother, and she prepared
some tasty food, just the way his father
liked it. 15Then Rebekah took the best
clothes[a] of Esau her older son, which she
had in the house, and put them on her

26:25 [e] Ge 12:7, 8; 13:4,18; Ps 116:17
26:26 [f] Ge 21:22
26:27 [g] ver 16
26:28 [h] Ge 21:22
26:29 [i] Ge 24:31; Ps 115:15
26:30 [j] Ge 19:3
26:31 [k] Ge 21:31
26:33 [l] Ge 21:14
26:34 [m] Ge 25:20 [n] Ge 28:9; 36:2
26:35 [o] Ge 27:46
27:1 [p] Ge 48:10; 1Sa 3:2 [q] Ge 25:25
27:2 [r] Ge 47:29
27:3 [s] Ge 25:27
27:4 [t] ver 10,25, 31; Ge 49:28; Dt 33:1; Heb 11:20
27:6 [u] Ge 25:28
27:8 [v] ver 13,43
27:11 [w] Ge 25:25
27:12 [x] ver 22
27:13 [y] Mt 27:25 [z] ver 8
27:15 [a] ver 27

[a] 33 *Shibah* can mean *oath* or *seven.*
[b] 33 *Beersheba* can mean *well of the oath* and *well of seven.*

27:1–46 Isaac desires to put his house in order by giving a blessing to Esau. The occasion of the giving of the blessing is obviously celebratory.

Isaac is planning to give the patriarchal blessing, which must be distinguished from the material inheritance (birthright) discussed at the end of ch. 25. These pronouncements can be viewed from three different perspectives: social, theological, and canonical.

From the *social* perspective, there is no question that these pronouncements are taken with the utmost gravity. The power of the pronouncement is vested in its being spoken. That is why Isaac cannot take it back after he learns he has been tricked.

Theologically these pronouncements are not presented as prophetic messages from the Lord. They simply represent the hopes and wishes of a father for his son(s). There is no intrinsic authority vested in the blessing.

When we look at the situation from a *canonical* perspective, however, we must admit that their inclusion by the narrator indicates a sense that the pronouncement also enjoys God's seal of approval.

27:5–12 What first strikes one as Rebekah's scheme unfolds is the sheer improbability that this can possibly work. We must conclude that beyond being blind, all of Isaac's senses are dulled—not only his five senses but his common sense and his sense of reason as well. Jacob is thus again exploiting the vulnerability of his relatives.

27:13 A second unusual twist is Rebekah's offer to take the curse on herself if Jacob is discovered. Rebekah is likely referring to the consequences of the curse rather than to the curse itself.

younger son Jacob. 16She also covered his
hands and the smooth part of his neck
with the goatskins. 17Then she handed
to her son Jacob the tasty food and the
bread she had made.
18He went to his father and said, "My
father."
"Yes, my son," he answered. "Who
is it?"
19Jacob said to his father, "I am Esau
your firstborn. I have done as you told
me. Please sit up and eat some of my
game, so that you may give me your
blessing."[b]
20Isaac asked his son, "How did you
find it so quickly, my son?"
"The LORD your God gave me success,[c]"
he replied.
21Then Isaac said to Jacob, "Come near
so I can touch you,[d] my son, to know
whether you really are my son Esau or
not."
22Jacob went close to his father Isaac,
who touched him and said, "The voice is
the voice of Jacob, but the hands are the
hands of Esau." 23He did not recognize
him, for his hands were hairy like those
of his brother Esau;[e] so he proceeded
to bless him. 24"Are you really my son
Esau?" he asked.
"I am," he replied.
25Then he said, "My son, bring me
some of your game to eat, so that I may
give you my blessing."[f]
Jacob brought it to him and he ate;
and he brought some wine and he
drank. 26Then his father Isaac said to
him, "Come here, my son, and kiss me."
27So he went to him and kissed him[g].
When Isaac caught the smell of his
clothes,[h] he blessed him and said,

"Ah, the smell of my son
is like the smell of a field
that the LORD has blessed.[i]
28May God give you heaven's dew[j]
and earth's richness[k]—
an abundance of grain and new
wine.[l]

27:19 [b]ver 4
27:20 [c]Ge 24:12
27:21 [d]ver 12
27:23 [e]ver 16
27:25 [f]ver 4
27:27 [g]Heb 11:20 [h]SS 4:11 [i]Ps 65:9-13
27:28 [j]Dt 33:13 [k]ver 39 [l]Ge 45:18; Nu 18:12; Dt 33:28
27:29 [m]Isa 45:14, 23; 49:7,23 [n]Ge 9:25; 25:23; 37:7 [o]Ge 12:3; Nu 24:9; Zep 2:8
27:31 [p]ver 4
27:32 [q]ver 18
27:33 [r]ver 29; Ge 28:3,4; Ro 11:29
27:34 [s]Heb 12:17
27:35 [t]Jer 9:4; 12:6
27:36 [u]Ge 25:26 [v]Ge 25:33

Ge 27:21-24 ❖ In light of God's will for his life, was Jacob's deception justifiable? Why or why not?

29May nations serve you
and peoples bow down to you.[m]
Be lord over your brothers,
and may the sons of your mother
bow down to you.[n]
May those who curse you be cursed
and those who bless you be
blessed.[o]"

30After Isaac finished blessing him,
and Jacob had scarcely left his father's
presence, his brother Esau came in from
hunting. 31He too prepared some tasty
food and brought it to his father. Then
he said to him, "My father, please sit up
and eat some of my game, so that you
may give me your blessing."[p]
32His father Isaac asked him, "Who
are you?"[q]
"I am your son," he answered, "your
firstborn, Esau."
33Isaac trembled violently and said,
"Who was it, then, that hunted game and
brought it to me? I ate it just before you
came and I blessed him—and indeed
he will be blessed![r]"
34When Esau heard his father's words,
he burst out with a loud and bitter cry[s]
and said to his father, "Bless me—me
too, my father!"
35But he said, "Your brother came deceitfully[t] and took your blessing."
36Esau said, "Isn't he rightly named Jacob[a]?[u] This is the second time he has tak-
en advantage of me: He took my birthright,[v] and now he's taken my blessing!"
Then he asked, "Haven't you reserved
any blessing for me?"
37Isaac answered Esau, "I have made
him lord over you and have made all his
relatives his servants, and I have sustained

[a] 36 *Jacob* means *he grasps the heel*, a Hebrew idiom for *he takes advantage of* or *he deceives.*

27:20-29 Isaac conducts five tests concerning the identity of his son: logic (v. 20), touch (vv. 21-22), sound (v. 22), his word (v. 24), and scent (v. 27). Isaac proceeds with the blessing: fertility of the land and authority over others (v. 29).

27:30-36 The suspense continues as Esau arrives right on the heels of Jacob. As the deception is revealed, Jacob's name is seen to reflect the reality of his character.

27:37-40 Esau's desperation creates a dilemma for Isaac, who would like to accommodate his son's request but has little to offer. The resulting blessing is far from ideal. The first part uses the same words he has just spoken to Jacob but to the opposite effect. In the second part of the blessing, all Isaac can do is to indicate that Esau's descendants will eventually be able to break free from Jacob's.

him with grain and new wine.[w] So what
can I possibly do for you, my son?"
38Esau said to his father, "Do you have
only one blessing, my father? Bless me
too, my father!" Then Esau wept aloud.[x]
39His father Isaac answered him,

"Your dwelling will be
away from the earth's richness,
away from the dew[y] of heaven
above.
40You will live by the sword
and you will serve[z] your brother.[a]
But when you grow restless,
you will throw his yoke
from off your neck.[b]"

41Esau held a grudge[c] against Jacob[d]
because of the blessing his father had
given him. He said to himself, "The days
of mourning[e] for my father are near;
then I will kill my brother Jacob."[f]
42When Rebekah was told what her
older son Esau had said, she sent for her
younger son Jacob and said to him, "Your
brother Esau is planning to avenge himself by killing you. 43Now then, my son,
do what I say:[g] Flee at once to my brother
Laban[h] in Harran.[i] 44Stay with him for a
while[j] until your brother's fury subsides.
45When your brother is no longer angry
with you and forgets what you did to
him,[k] I'll send word for you to come back
from there. Why should I lose both of
you in one day?"
46Then Rebekah said to Isaac, "I'm
disgusted with living because of these
Hittite women. If Jacob takes a wife from
among the women of this land, from Hittite women like these, my life will not be
worth living."[l]

28 So Isaac called for Jacob and
blessed him. Then he commanded
him: "Do not marry a Canaanite woman.[m] 2Go at once to Paddan Aram,[a] to the
house of your mother's father Bethuel.[n] Take a wife for yourself there, from
among the daughters of Laban, your
mother's brother. 3May God Almighty[b][o]
bless you and make you fruitful[p] and increase your numbers until you become
a community of peoples. 4May he give
you and your descendants the blessing
given to Abraham,[q] so that you may take
possession of the land where you now
reside as a foreigner,[r] the land God gave
to Abraham." 5Then Isaac sent Jacob on
his way, and he went to Paddan Aram,[s]
to Laban son of Bethuel the Aramean,
the brother of Rebekah,[t] who was the
mother of Jacob and Esau.
6Now Esau learned that Isaac had
blessed Jacob and had sent him to Paddan Aram to take a wife from there,
and that when he blessed him he commanded him, "Do not marry a Canaanite
woman,"[u] 7and that Jacob had obeyed
his father and mother and had gone to
Paddan Aram. 8Esau then realized how
displeasing the Canaanite women[v] were
to his father Isaac;[w] 9so he went to Ishmael and married Mahalath, the sister of
Nebaioth[x] and daughter of Ishmael son
of Abraham, in addition to the wives he
already had.[y]

27:37 [w] ver 28
27:38 [x] Heb 12:17
27:39 [y] ver 28
27:40 [z] 2Sa 8:14 [a] Ge 25:23 [b] 2Ki 8:20-22
27:41 [c] Ge 37:4 [d] Ge 32:11 [e] Ge 50:4,10 [f] Ob 10
27:43 [g] ver 8 [h] Ge 24:29 [i] Ge 11:31
27:44 [j] Ge 31:38, 41
27:45 [k] ver 35
27:46 [l] Ge 26:35
28:1 [m] Ge 24:3
28:2 [n] Ge 25:20
28:3 [o] Ge 17:1 [p] Ge 17:6
28:4 [q] Ge 12:2,3 [r] Ge 17:8
28:5 [s] Hos 12:12 [t] Ge 24:29
28:6 [u] ver 1
28:8 [v] Ge 24:3 [w] Ge 26:35
28:9 [x] Ge 25:13 [y] Ge 26:34

[a] 2 That is, Northwest Mesopotamia; also in verses 5, 6 and 7 [b] 3 Hebrew *El-Shaddai*

27:41–46 The narrative now moves rapidly to the unsurprising results: escalated tensions and greater conflict. Rebekah shares in this consequence as she is forced to send her favorite away. In this sense, the resulting curse is on her. The jeopardy to the covenant is encapsulated in Rebekah's expression of her worst fear (v. 45). The covenant again hangs by a thread with the frighteningly realistic prospect that both Isaac and Jacob could be lost in a twinkling.

25:19—27:46 It is particularly painful when a son or daughter shows no concern for the rich heritage and solid upbringing they have received. In the famous parable (see Lk 15), though the prodigal son did not fail to appreciate his inheritance, he did reject the value system of his father. Just as Esau is painted as one who did not adopt the value system of his family, many today turn aside from their family's values and in the process forfeit God's blessing in missed opportunities.

What can we expect from God when we show ourselves unworthy of his blessing by despising the values that are the foundation of our spiritual heritage? Christians who have grown up in difficult family situations may often fantasize about growing up in a loving, nurturing Christian environment. But the Bible and history are replete with examples of those who have grown up in the homes of great spiritual leaders but have found the pathway less than smooth. Enough stories are available about prodigal kids of preachers or missionaries for all to be aware of the problems.

28:1–9 Jacob is already seventy-seven years old. The marriage instructions are similar to those given by Abraham to his servant almost one hundred years earlier when Isaac was ready to marry. In addition to the instructions, Jacob is sent away with the covenant blessing (vv. 3–4).

PEOPLE TO KNOW // JACOB

GENESIS 28:10–22: Jacob was Esau's younger twin. His name fittingly means "he grasps the heel" or "he deceives." Jacob tricked Esau out of his birthright for a bowl of stew (Ge 25:29–34). Jacob later tricked his father, Isaac, into giving him the blessing Isaac had intended for Esau (Ge 27:1–41). Esau's fury sent Jacob fleeing.

Jacob moved to Paddan Aram. On the way, God appeared to Jacob in a dream, promising him numerous descendants who would bless all peoples (Ge 28:14). In Paddan Aram, Jacob lived with his uncle Laban. He married two of Laban's daughters, Rachel and Leah. Through Leah, Jacob had many children, but Rachel was infertile. Still, Jacob loved Rachel more than he loved Leah. Eventually God blessed Rachel with a baby: Joseph.

When Jacob left Laban, he was afraid of the reception he would receive from Esau. He sent a generous gift of livestock ahead for his brother. Before the fateful reunion, Jacob wrestled with God, demanding a blessing. God gave Jacob the new name Israel and blessed him (Ge 32:22–32).

Jacob's reunion with Esau was sweet but short. The two soon went separate ways. Rachel later had another son, Benjamin, but died in the process of childbirth (Ge 35:18). Jacob favored his son Joseph above the others because he was Rachel's son, so Joseph's jealous brothers sold him into slavery. Jacob thought Joseph had been killed, but in fact he was taken to Egypt where he ascended to a high position. Famine in Canaan later brought the family back together, and Jacob died at an old age in Egypt (Ge 49:33).

APPLICATION ✣ God told Rebekah before her twins were born that the older would serve the younger, and God later said through the prophet Malachi that he loved Jacob and not Esau (Mal 1:2–3). It seems strange that God would choose to bless a trickster like Jacob. This story reminds us, however, that God's love is not based on our actions. God's love comes only through grace. God promised Jacob that his descendants would be a nation of blessing, and indeed the Israelites were Jacob's descendants through his twelve sons. God promised to bless all other nations through them, a promise fulfilled in the Savior of the world, Jesus Christ.

Ge 28:10–15 ❖ God appeared to Jacob when he was on the run from Esau. When and how has God given you strength and reassurance in a time of need?

Jacob's Dream at Bethel

10Jacob left Beersheba and set out for
Harran.[z] 11When he reached a certain
place, he stopped for the night because
the sun had set. Taking one of the stones
there, he put it under his head and lay
down to sleep. 12He had a dream[a] in
which he saw a stairway resting on the
earth, with its top reaching to heaven,
and the angels of God were ascending
and descending on it.[b] 13There above it[a]
stood the LORD,[c] and he said: "I am the
LORD, the God of your father Abraham
and the God of Isaac.[d] I will give you and
your descendants the land[e] on which
you are lying. 14Your descendants will be
like the dust of the earth, and you[f] will
spread out to the west and to the east, to
the north and to the south.[g] All peoples
on earth will be blessed through you and
your offspring.[bh] 15I am with you[i] and will
watch over you[j] wherever you go, and I
will bring you back to this land. I will not

28:10 [z] Ge 11:31
28:12 [a] Ge 20:3 [b] Jn 1:51
28:13 [c] Ge 12:7; 35:7,9; 48:3 [d] Ge 26:24 [e] Ge 13:15; 35:12
28:14 [f] Ge 26:4 [g] Ge 13:14 [h] Ge 12:3; 18:18; 22:18; Gal 3:8
28:15 [i] Ge 26:3; 48:21 [j] Nu 6:24; Ps 121:5,7-8

[a] 13 Or *There beside him* [b] 14 Or *will use your name and the name of your offspring in blessings* (see 48:20)

28:10–22 The 550-mile trip from Beersheba to Haran would have taken Jacob over a month. It probably takes several days to get as far as Bethel, 60 miles from Beersheba. What Jacob is dreaming is the same stairway that is architecturally depicted in the famous ziggurats in Mesopotamian cities (see notes on 11:1–9).

In ch. 28 the messengers of God are using this stairway to travel between realms. Angels (messengers) descended to embark on their errands throughout the earth and ascended when returning with reports.

The important part of all of this is the content of the message conveyed by it. This is Jacob's first theophany, and it parallels the "Yahweh theophany" that Abraham received in ch. 15. The main thrust of the message is that Yahweh will bring Jacob back to the land. Jacob is virtually the same age as Abraham was when God asked him to leave his home and travel to a new land (12:1–4).

leave you[k] until I have done what I have
promised you."[l]
16When Jacob awoke from his sleep,
he thought, "Surely the LORD is in this
place, and I was not aware of it." 17He
was afraid and said, "How awesome is
this place![m] This is none other than the
house of God; this is the gate of heaven."
18Early the next morning Jacob took
the stone he had placed under his head
and set it up as a pillar[n] and poured oil on
top of it.[o] 19He called that place Bethel,[a]
though the city used to be called Luz.[p]
20Then Jacob made a vow,[q] saying, "If
God will be with me and will watch over
me[r] on this journey I am taking and will
give me food to eat and clothes to wear
21so that I return safely[s] to my father's
household, then the LORD[b] will be my
God[t] 22and[c] this stone that I have set up
as a pillar will be God's house,[u] and of all
that you give me I will give you a tenth.[v]"

Jacob Arrives in Paddan Aram

29 Then Jacob continued on his journey and came to the land of the
eastern peoples.[w] 2There he saw a well
in the open country, with three flocks
of sheep lying near it because the flocks
were watered from that well. The stone
over the mouth of the well was large.
3When all the flocks were gathered there,
the shepherds would roll the stone away
from the well's mouth and water the
sheep. Then they would return the stone
to its place over the mouth of the well.
4Jacob asked the shepherds, "My
brothers, where are you from?"
"We're from Harran,[x]" they replied.
5He said to them, "Do you know Laban,
Nahor's grandson?"
"Yes, we know him," they answered.
6Then Jacob asked them, "Is he well?"
"Yes, he is," they said, "and here comes
his daughter Rachel with the sheep."
7"Look," he said, "the sun is still high; it
is not time for the flocks to be gathered.
Water the sheep and take them back to
pasture."
8"We can't," they replied, "until all the
flocks are gathered and the stone has
been rolled away from the mouth of the
well. Then we will water the sheep."
9While he was still talking with them,
Rachel came with her father's sheep,[y] for
she was a shepherd. 10When Jacob saw
Rachel daughter of his uncle Laban, and
Laban's sheep, he went over and rolled
the stone away from the mouth of the
well and watered his uncle's sheep.[z]
11Then Jacob kissed Rachel and began to
weep aloud.[a] 12He had told Rachel that he
was a relative[b] of her father and a son of
Rebekah. So she ran and told her father.[c]

28:15 [k] Dt 31:6,8 [l] Nu 23:19
28:17 [m] Ex 3:5; Jos 5:15
28:18 [n] Ge 35:14 [o] Lev 8:11
28:19 [p] Jdg 1:23, 26
28:20 [q] Ge 31:13; Jdg 11:30; 2Sa 15:8 [r] ver 15
28:21 [s] Jdg 11:31 [t] Dt 26:17
28:22 [u] Ge 35:7, 14 [v] Ge 14:20; Lev 27:30
29:1 [w] Jdg 6:3, 33
29:4 [x] Ge 28:10
29:9 [y] Ex 2:16
29:10 [z] Ex 2:17
29:11 [a] Ge 33:4
29:12 [b] Ge 13:8; 14:14,16 [c] Ge 24:28

[a] *19 Bethel* means *house of God.* [b] *20,21* Or *Since God . . . father's household, the LORD* [c] *21,22* Or *household, and the LORD will be my God, 22then*

28:16–19 When Jacob awakes, he has two responses. First, he recognizes the nature of the place. Since Jacob has seen a portal here, he identifies the space as sacred space—a house of God. Jacob sets up the stone as a pillar. Sacred pillars and standing stones are familiar in the religious environment of the ancient world. Anointing the pillar constitutes its dedication. Jacob names the place Bethel, meaning "house of God" (28:19), which formalizes his new information about the place.
28:20–22 The second response is a personal one from Jacob that comes in terms of a vow. Vows are promises made (almost always to God) with conditions attached. Here the conditions include provision and protection from God that will result in Jacob's return as Yahweh promised in the dream theophany. The tangible element of Jacob's gift is a tithe of all he receives from the hand of God.

Jacob most likely anticipates that any wealth coming to him will be in the form of flocks and herds. In such a case the tithe will be represented in sacrifices at Bethel. There was also a more intangible element to Jacob's promises. If Providence smiles on him and returns Jacob to this land, Jacob will recognize that Yahweh is behind that Providence and is guiding his destiny. Since ch. 35 records Jacob's fulfillment of his vow, he carries out this part by setting aside other gods (35:2).

✤ **28:1–22** Dare we dictate to God the terms of our commitment or suggest that our service will only be rendered when he proves himself worthy? That is what Jacob is doing when he makes his vow. God has unlimited grace, yet in our attitudes we can presume upon his grace and tire him with our self-serving requests. Perhaps God would be pleased if more of our requests focused on spiritual gain. These are the sort of requests that never presume upon his grace. They will achieve his purpose of helping us come to an understanding of our true nature and of our dependence on him.

29:1–14 Jacob's warm welcome of Rachel and her resulting excitement is understandable given that there may have been no news of Rebekah since she left with Abraham's servant nearly a century earlier. We have a hint of what is to come when Laban comments that Jacob is his own flesh and blood (v. 14). This is, of course, an innocent statement on Laban's part, but the reader has already gotten a taste of Jacob's nature, and in Laban we will encounter one "cut from the same cloth."

13As soon as Laban[d] heard the news about Jacob, his sister's son, he hurried to meet him. He embraced him and kissed him and brought him to his home, and there Jacob told him all these things. 14Then Laban said to him, "You are my own flesh and blood."[e]

Jacob Marries Leah and Rachel

After Jacob had stayed with him for a whole month, 15Laban said to him, "Just because you are a relative of mine, should you work for me for nothing? Tell me what your wages should be."

16Now Laban had two daughters; the name of the older was Leah, and the name of the younger was Rachel. 17Leah had weak[a] eyes, but Rachel had a lovely figure and was beautiful. 18Jacob was in love with Rachel and said, "I'll work for you seven years in return for your younger daughter Rachel."[f]

19Laban said, "It's better that I give her to you than to some other man. Stay here with me." 20So Jacob served seven years to get Rachel, but they seemed like only a few days to him because of his love for her.[g]

21Then Jacob said to Laban, "Give me my wife. My time is completed, and I want to make love to her.[h]"

22So Laban brought together all the people of the place and gave a feast.[i] 23But when evening came, he took his daughter Leah and brought her to Jacob, and Jacob made love to her. 24And Laban gave his servant Zilpah to his daughter as her attendant.

25When morning came, there was Leah! So Jacob said to Laban, "What is this you have done to me?[j] I served you for Rachel, didn't I? Why have you deceived me?[k]"

26Laban replied, "It is not our custom here to give the younger daughter in marriage before the older one. 27Finish this daughter's bridal week;[l] then we will give you the younger one also, in return for another seven years of work."

28And Jacob did so. He finished the week with Leah, and then Laban gave him his daughter Rachel to be his wife. 29Laban gave his servant Bilhah[m] to his daughter Rachel as her attendant.[n] 30Jacob made love to Rachel also, and his love for Rachel was greater than his love for Leah.[o] And he worked for Laban another seven years.[p]

Jacob's Children

31When the LORD saw that Leah was not loved,[q] he enabled her to conceive,[r] but Rachel remained childless. 32Leah became pregnant and gave birth to a son. She named him Reuben,[b] for she said, "It is because the LORD has seen my misery.[s] Surely my husband will love me now."

33She conceived again, and when she gave birth to a son she said, "Because the LORD heard that I am not loved, he gave me this one too." So she named him Simeon.[c][t]

34Again she conceived, and when she gave birth to a son she said, "Now at last my husband will become attached to me,[u] because I have borne him three sons." So he was named Levi.[d][v]

Ge 29:31-34 ❖ Leah's sorrow over Jacob's favoritism for Rachel is painful to read. Where have we seen the bitter effects of unfair favoritism? How does God view those circumstances?

29:13 [d] Ge 24:29
29:14 [e] Ge 2:23; Jdg 9:2; 2Sa 19:12-13
29:18 [f] Hos 12:12
29:20 [g] SS 8:7; Hos 12:12
29:21 [h] Jdg 15:1
29:22 [i] Jdg 14:10; Jn 2:1-2
29:25 [j] Ge 12:18 [k] Ge 27:36
29:27 [l] Jdg 14:12
29:29 [m] Ge 30:3 [n] Ge 16:1
29:30 [o] ver 16 [p] Ge 31:41
29:31 [q] Dt 21:15-17 [r] Ge 11:30; 30:1; Ps 127:3
29:32 [s] Ge 16:11; 31:42; Ex 4:31; Dt 26:7; Ps 25:18
29:33 [t] Ge 34:25; 49:5
29:34 [u] Ge 30:20; 1Sa 1:2-4 [v] Ge 49:5-7

[a] 17 Or *delicate* [b] 32 *Reuben* sounds like the Hebrew for *he has seen my misery;* the name means *see, a son.* [c] 33 *Simeon* probably means *one who hears.* [d] 34 *Levi* sounds like and may be derived from the Hebrew for *attached.*

29:15–21 Jacob is impressed by Rachel's appearance. Leah pales in comparison to Rachel's overall beauty. The agreement between Laban and Jacob is intended to provide for the bride price. This was a payment made from the groom or his family to the family of the bride. Its function was to serve as a trust fund of sorts to provide for the support of the wife should the husband divorce her or die.
29:22–25 The traditional feast is held. A bride was veiled during these public festivities, and it was not uncommon for the celebratory mood to lead to drunkenness. Though we have no indication that Jacob is drunk, that is one way to account for his inability to recognize the substitution of Leah for Rachel.
29:26–30 Jacob ends up obliging himself to seven more years of work, though he is allowed to marry Rachel in short order. The scene is also set for the favoritism that will be a significant factor in the next generation (v. 30).
29:31—30:24 As God begins to provide a family for Jacob, we see a new twist on an old theme of the unloved and the firstborn. Now it is the unloved wife, Leah, who produces the firstborn child. It is clear from the names given to her sons that Leah is haunted by her inability to elicit favor and affection from Jacob, though providing four

PEOPLE TO KNOW // LEAH

GENESIS 29:31–32: Leah was the heartbroken, unloved wife of Jacob. Reduced to being a pawn in the drama of her family of origin, she was part of a setup by her father Laban, who substituted her for her sister Rachel on Rachel and Jacob's wedding day. Jacob was justifiably upset with this arrangement and confronted the girls' father, who gave him Rachel as well. Genesis tells us, "his love for Rachel was greater than his love for Leah" (Ge 29:30), which made for a miserable family situation.

Why was Leah unloved? The text only tells us that "Leah had weak eyes, but Rachel had a lovely figure and was beautiful" (Ge 29:17). We further find that after the unforgettable humiliation of that sham wedding and the immediate intrusion of Rachel into the marriage, "the LORD saw that Leah was not loved" (Ge 29:31) and allowed her to start having children.

Not so with Rachel, Leah's sister and competitor. The battle between these two sisters for their husband's attention rages throughout Genesis chapters 29 and 30. About Leah we read these desperate words: "Leah became pregnant and gave birth to a son. She named him Reuben, for she said, 'It is because the LORD has seen my misery. Surely my husband will love me now'" (Ge 29:32). The narrator of Genesis records Leah's despairing words every time a new baby is born. Despite her palpable heartache over her family situation, the Bible credits Leah with bearing (or helping to bear, through her surrogates) seven of the patriarchs of the twelve tribes of Israel.

APPLICATION ✣ Struggles are part of all our lives, but it's hard when we have done nothing to cause the trouble and we can do nothing to change the situation. Leah was born into a family where her father saw her as a bargaining chip to get what he wanted and into a culture that didn't give women opportunities to make choices for themselves. But in spite of the helpless and hopeless parts of her life, Leah found blessings. As the years went by, she found joy in the births of her children and thanked God for them. And God used Leah in his plans. In the book of Ruth, Leah is mentioned with words of honor. As Boaz takes Ruth in, the elders of the town proclaim, "May the LORD make the woman who is coming into your home like Rachel and Leah, who together built up the family of Israel" (Ruth 4:11).

35 She conceived again, and when she gave birth to a son she said, "This time I will praise the LORD." So she named him Judah.[a][w] Then she stopped having children.

30

When Rachel saw that she was not bearing Jacob any children,[x] she became jealous of her sister.[y] So she said to Jacob, "Give me children, or I'll die!"

2 Jacob became angry with her and said, "Am I in the place of God, who has kept you from having children?"[z]

3 Then she said, "Here is Bilhah, my servant. Sleep with her so that she can bear children for me and I too can build a family through her."[a]

4 So she gave him her servant Bilhah as a wife.[b] Jacob slept with her,[c] 5 and she became pregnant and bore him a son.

29:35 [w] Ge 49:8; Mt 1:2-3
30:1 [x] Ge 29:31; 1Sa 1:5-6 [y] Lev 18:18
30:2 [z] Ge 16:2; 20:18; 29:31
30:3 [a] Ge 16:2
30:4 [b] ver 9,18 [c] Ge 16:3-4
30:6 [d] Ps 35:24; 43:1; La 3:59 [e] Ge 49:16-17
30:8 [f] Hos 12:3-4 [g] Ge 49:21

Ge 30:1–24 ✣ The rivalry for children between Rachel and Leah was bitter. How can God's children avoid such ugly jealousies and division?

6 Then Rachel said, "God has vindicated me;[d] he has listened to my plea and given me a son." Because of this she named him Dan.[b][e]

7 Rachel's servant Bilhah conceived again and bore Jacob a second son. 8 Then Rachel said, "I have had a great struggle with my sister, and I have won."[f] So she named him Naphtali.[c][g]

9 When Leah saw that she had stopped

[a] *35 Judah* sounds like and may be derived from the Hebrew for *praise.* [b] *6 Dan* here means *he has vindicated.* [c] *8 Naphtali* means *my struggle.*

---

sons would be expected to gain her some standing in his eyes.

30:1–6 Rachel's condition occasions angry frustration (v. 2). Consequently, Rachel encourages Jacob to resort to her handmaid to provide a child to their marriage through a surrogate. Rachel's naming of the son Dan ("vindication") indicates that she feels vindicated; her infertility would bring at least the tacit accusation that she is undoubtedly suffering punishment for secret sins.

30:9–21 The family continues to grow. Leah goes through her own period of infertility, likely curbing

having children, she took her servant Zilpah and gave her to Jacob as a wife.[h] 10 Leah's servant Zilpah bore Jacob a son. 11 Then Leah said, "What good fortune!"[a] So she named him Gad.[b][i]

12 Leah's servant Zilpah bore Jacob a second son. 13 Then Leah said, "How happy I am! The women will call me[j] happy."[k] So she named him Asher.[c][l]

14 During wheat harvest, Reuben went out into the fields and found some mandrake plants,[m] which he brought to his mother Leah. Rachel said to Leah, "Please give me some of your son's mandrakes."

15 But she said to her, "Wasn't it enough[n] that you took away my husband? Will you take my son's mandrakes too?"

"Very well," Rachel said, "he can sleep with you tonight in return for your son's mandrakes."

16 So when Jacob came in from the fields that evening, Leah went out to meet him. "You must sleep with me," she said. "I have hired you with my son's mandrakes." So he slept with her that night.

17 God listened to Leah,[o] and she became pregnant and bore Jacob a fifth son. 18 Then Leah said, "God has rewarded me for giving my servant to my husband." So she named him Issachar.[d][p]

19 Leah conceived again and bore Jacob a sixth son. 20 Then Leah said, "God has presented me with a precious gift. This time my husband will treat me with honor, because I have borne him six sons." So she named him Zebulun.[e][q]

21 Some time later she gave birth to a daughter and named her Dinah.

22 Then God remembered Rachel;[r] he listened to her and enabled her to conceive.[s] 23 She became pregnant and gave birth to a son[t] and said, "God has taken away my disgrace."[u] 24 She named him Joseph,[f][v] and said, "May the LORD add to me another son."[w]

Jacob's Flocks Increase

25 After Rachel gave birth to Joseph, Jacob said to Laban, "Send me on my way[x] so I can go back to my own homeland. 26 Give me my wives and children, for whom I have served you,[y] and I will be on my way. You know how much work I've done for you."

27 But Laban said to him, "If I have found favor in your eyes, please stay. I have learned by divination that the LORD has blessed me because of you."[z] 28 He added, "Name your wages,[a] and I will pay them."

29 Jacob said to him, "You know how I have worked for you[b] and how your livestock has fared under my care.[c] 30 The little you had before I came has increased greatly, and the LORD has blessed you wherever I have been. But now, when may I do something for my own household?[d]"

30:9 [h] ver 4
30:11 [i] Ge 49:19
30:13 [j] Ps 127:3 [k] Pr 31:28; Lk 1:48 [l] Ge 49:20
30:14 [m] SS 7:13
30:15 [n] Nu 16:9, 13
30:17 [o] Ge 25:21
30:18 [p] Ge 49:14
30:20 [q] Ge 35:23; 49:13; Mt 4:13
30:22 [r] Ge 8:1; 1Sa 1:19-20 [s] Ge 29:31
30:23 [t] ver 6 [u] Isa 4:1; Lk 1:25
30:24 [v] Ge 35:24; 37:2; 39:1; 49:22-26 [w] Ge 35:17
30:25 [x] Ge 24:54
30:26 [y] Ge 29:20, 30; Hos 12:12
30:27 [z] Ge 26:24; 39:3,5
30:28 [a] Ge 29:15
30:29 [b] Ge 31:6 [c] Ge 31:38-40
30:30 [d] 1Ti 5:8

[a] *11* Or *"A troop is coming!"* [b] *11* *Gad* can mean *good fortune* or *a troop.* [c] *13* *Asher* means *happy.* [d] *18* *Issachar* sounds like the Hebrew for *reward.* [e] *20* *Zebulun* probably means *honor.* [f] *24* *Joseph* means *may he add.*

---

her scorn of Rachel, and the handmaids continue to have their role in producing children. The children's names by and large reflect the tension in the family. Yet Rachel is still without children. When Leah's son Reuben finds some mandrakes, Rachel thinks they may help her. The mandrake has narcotic and purgative properties, which explain its medicinal use. Its shape and pungent fragrance may be the origin of its use in fertility rites and as an aphrodisiac.

The exchange between the women concerning the mandrakes again illustrates the bitter conflict and rivalry between Leah and Rachel. Ironically, the night with Jacob that Rachel trades for the mandrakes brings renewed fertility to Leah rather than a child to Rachel.

30:22–24 Rachel's barrenness is resolved as God opens her womb. Finally getting pregnant herself completes the process of erasing her public disgrace (v. 23). The end to this portion of the family history does not come when all the children have been born, but when Rachel is no longer barren. This suggests that Rachel's barrenness is not an obstacle to the covenant from a family standpoint but only to the audience, who is well aware of the importance of Joseph.

30:25–26 It is not coincidental that Jacob requests permission to take his leave of Laban only after Joseph is born (v. 25). If a woman has not borne children, she can easily be discarded or demoted. Prior to Joseph's birth, a request to leave would have been inappropriate from Jacob's standpoint and risky from Rachel's, for it would rob Rachel of her protection.

30:27–28 Though Laban is relieved of his concern for Rachel's well-being, economic issues lead him to negotiate for Jacob to stay. There are few indications of Laban's religious practices, but here we see him engaged in divination. Laban claims that his divination has led him to conclude that Yahweh has blessed him because of Jacob.

30:29–36 Laban's offer results in an agreement to give Jacob part ownership of the herd and the potential to increase his interest as time goes on. The passage suggests Laban has the better end of the deal.

31"What shall I give you?" he asked.
"Don't give me anything," Jacob replied. "But if you will do this one thing
for me, I will go on tending your flocks
and watching over them: 32Let me go
through all your flocks today and remove
from them every speckled or spotted
sheep, every dark-colored lamb and every spotted or speckled goat.[e] They will
be my wages. 33And my honesty will testify for me in the future, whenever you
check on the wages you have paid me.
Any goat in my possession that is not
speckled or spotted, or any lamb that
is not dark-colored, will be considered
stolen."
34"Agreed," said Laban. "Let it be as you
have said." 35That same day he removed
all the male goats that were streaked or
spotted, and all the speckled or spotted female goats (all that had white on
them) and all the dark-colored lambs,
and he placed them in the care of his
sons.[f] 36Then he put a three-day journey between himself and Jacob, while
Jacob continued to tend the rest of Laban's flocks.
37Jacob, however, took fresh-cut
branches from poplar, almond and plane
trees and made white stripes on them
by peeling the bark and exposing the
white inner wood of the branches. 38Then
he placed the peeled branches in all the
watering troughs, so that they would be
directly in front of the flocks when they
came to drink. When the flocks were in
heat and came to drink, 39they mated
in front of the branches. And they bore
young that were streaked or speckled or
spotted. 40Jacob set apart the young of
the flock by themselves, but made the
rest face the streaked and dark-colored
animals that belonged to Laban. Thus
he made separate flocks for himself and
did not put them with Laban's animals.
41Whenever the stronger females were
in heat, Jacob would place the branches
in the troughs in front of the animals so
they would mate near the branches, 42but
if the animals were weak, he would not
place them there. So the weak animals
went to Laban and the strong ones to Jacob. 43In this way the man grew exceedingly prosperous and came to own large
flocks, and female and male servants,
and camels and donkeys.[g]

30:32 [e] Ge 31:8, 12
30:35 [f] Ge 31:1
30:43 [g] ver 30; Ge 12:16; 13:2; 24:35; 26:13-14
31:3 [h] ver 13; Ge 32:9 [i] Ge 21:22; 26:3; 28:15
31:5 [j] Ge 21:22; 26:3
31:6 [k] Ge 30:29
31:7 [l] ver 41; Job 19:3 [m] ver 52; Ps 37:28; 105:14
31:8 [n] Ge 30:32
31:9 [o] ver 1,16; Ge 30:42
31:11 [p] Ge 16:7; 48:16

Ge 31:6-7 ❖ How do we respond when faced with unfair treatment in the workplace? How can we rest in God's presence in such situations?

Jacob Flees From Laban

31 Jacob heard that Laban's sons were
saying, "Jacob has taken everything
our father owned and has gained all this
wealth from what belonged to our father."
2And Jacob noticed that Laban's attitude
toward him was not what it had been.
3Then the LORD said to Jacob, "Go
back[h] to the land of your fathers and to
your relatives, and I will be with you."[i]
4So Jacob sent word to Rachel and
Leah to come out to the fields where his
flocks were. 5He said to them, "I see that
your father's attitude toward me is not
what it was before, but the God of my father has been with me.[j] 6You know that
I've worked for your father with all my
strength,[k] 7yet your father has cheated me
by changing my wages ten times.[l] However, God has not allowed him to harm
me.[m] 8If he said, 'The speckled ones will
be your wages,' then all the flocks gave
birth to speckled young; and if he said,
'The streaked ones will be your wages,'[n]
then all the flocks bore streaked young.
9So God has taken away your father's livestock and has given them to me.[o]
10"In breeding season I once had a
dream in which I looked up and saw that
the male goats mating with the flock
were streaked, speckled or spotted. 11The
angel of God[p] said to me in the dream,
'Jacob.' I answered, 'Here I am.' 12And he

30:37–43 Jacob applies the science of his day to compensate for Laban's shrewd strategy. Any shepherd knows that strong parents breed strong lambs and kids. Jacob therefore engages in common sense selective breeding as a means to produce strong, healthy offspring (v. 41). This strategy is combined with folk traditions that conditions during breeding, such as what is in the animals' visual field, may have an impact on the offspring. Whatever level of success Jacob enjoys while using this procedure is attributable only to God, regardless of the conclusions Jacob may have drawn.

31:1–21 Jacob's decision to return to Canaan is a combination of his awareness of the hostility of Laban's sons toward him and of the direction from God. The willingness of Leah and Rachel to leave is premised on an accusation against their father concerning his handling of their inheritance. The equivalent of Jacob's wages should have been set aside for the women. Apparently, that was never done. Jacob's labor has benefited

said, 'Look up and see that all the male
goats mating with the flock are streaked,
speckled or spotted, for I have seen all
that Laban has been doing to you.[q] 13I am
the God of Bethel,[r] where you anointed a
pillar and where you made a vow to me.
Now leave this land at once and go back
to your native land.[s]' "
14Then Rachel and Leah replied, "Do we
still have any share in the inheritance of
our father's estate? 15Does he not regard
us as foreigners? Not only has he sold us,
but he has used up what was paid for us.[t]
16Surely all the wealth that God took away
from our father belongs to us and our children. So do whatever God has told you."
17Then Jacob put his children and his
wives on camels, 18and he drove all his
livestock ahead of him, along with all
the goods he had accumulated in Paddan
Aram,[a] to go to his father Isaac[u] in the
land of Canaan.[v]
19When Laban had gone to shear his
sheep, Rachel stole her father's household gods.[w] 20Moreover, Jacob deceived[x]
Laban the Aramean by not telling him he
was running away.[y] 21So he fled with all
he had, crossed the Euphrates River, and
headed for the hill country of Gilead.[z]

Laban Pursues Jacob

22On the third day Laban was told that
Jacob had fled. 23Taking his relatives
with him, he pursued Jacob for seven
days and caught up with him in the hill
country of Gilead. 24Then God came to
Laban the Aramean in a dream at night
and said to him,[a] "Be careful not to say
anything to Jacob, either good or bad."[b]

31:12 [q] Ex 3:7
31:13 [r] Ge 28:10-22 [s] ver 3; Ge 32:9
31:15 [t] Ge 29:20
31:18 [u] Ge 35:27 [v] Ge 10:19
31:19 [w] ver 30, 32, 34-35; Ge 35:2; Jdg 17:5; 1Sa 19:13; Hos 3:4
31:20 [x] Ge 27:36 [y] ver 27
31:21 [z] Ge 37:25
31:24 [a] Ge 20:3; Job 33:15 [b] Ge 24:50

[a] *18* That is, Northwest Mesopotamia

Laban, not the women; thus, it is as if he has "sold" them to Jacob.
31:14–19 They choose sheep-shearing time to make their escape because they know that Laban will be away and preoccupied. The text also includes Rachel's theft of the household gods. They were believed to bring prosperity and protection. Given how Rachel is able to conceal them, these must be very small.
31:22–55 The site of Mizpah (where Laban catches up to Jacob) is not known, but from Haran to the northern end of the hill country of Gilead is approximately three hundred miles. When Laban and Jacob finally meet face-to-face, there is a major confrontation between them.

PEOPLE TO KNOW // LABAN

GENESIS 31:22–29: When Abraham sent his servant to find Isaac a wife from among his own people, the servant found Rebekah and her brother Laban. The first mention of Laban hints at his character: he immediately noticed the rich gifts Abraham sent. He treated Abraham's servant kindly after his eyes settled on the gold (Ge 24:29–31).

Much later, when Rebekah's sons grew up, she sent Jacob to Laban in order for her son to escape Esau's wrath (Ge 27:43–44). Laban warmly welcomed Jacob into his home. While there, Jacob fell in love with Laban's daughter Rachel and agreed to work seven years to marry her. When the seven years were complete, however, Laban tricked Jacob by giving him his older daughter Leah in marriage instead. Jacob worked another seven years for Rachel.

Later, Jacob desired to return to his homeland. Laban asked Jacob what he could give him for wages, but Jacob asked for nothing but goats of a certain coloration from Laban's flocks. Jacob then craftily ensured that more of those goats were produced (Ge 30:31–43). When Laban saw Jacob's flock increasing far beyond his own, his anger turned against Jacob.

Jacob fled with his wives and all he had. Unbeknownst to him, Rachel had stolen her father's household idols. Laban chased Jacob down, but God warned Laban not to harm Jacob. Jacob denied stealing Laban's idols, which Rachel kept hidden. Jacob also accused Laban of mistreating him during his 20 years of work (Ge 31:38–42). In the end, the two men made a wary covenant and went their separate ways.

APPLICATION Laban was a man motivated by increasing his wealth. He allowed his desire to get *more* affect his relationships. In his focus on gaining more things, he lost the most important things in his life: his relationships with his daughters and their families. In today's world we are surrounded by alluring advertisements and new trends, and the desire for *more* is something we face every day. Greed, however, is a dangerous trap. It pulls our hearts away from loving God and others, leading us to lose the things that are much more important than material possessions.

25 Jacob had pitched his tent in the hill
country of Gilead when Laban overtook
him, and Laban and his relatives camped
there too. 26 Then Laban said to Jacob,
"What have you done? You've deceived
me,[c] and you've carried off my daughters like captives in war.[d] 27 Why did you
run off secretly and deceive me? Why
didn't you tell me, so I could send you
away with joy and singing to the music of
timbrels[e] and harps?[f] 28 You didn't even
let me kiss my grandchildren and my
daughters goodbye.[g] You have done a
foolish thing. 29 I have the power to harm
you;[h] but last night the God of your father[i] said to me, 'Be careful not to say
anything to Jacob, either good or bad.'
30 Now you have gone off because you
longed to return to your father's household. But why did you steal my gods?[j]"
31 Jacob answered Laban, "I was afraid,
because I thought you would take your
daughters away from me by force. 32 But if
you find anyone who has your gods, that
person shall not live.[k] In the presence
of our relatives, see for yourself whether there is anything of yours here with
me; and if so, take it." Now Jacob did not
know that Rachel had stolen the gods.
33 So Laban went into Jacob's tent and
into Leah's tent and into the tent of the
two female servants, but he found nothing. After he came out of Leah's tent, he
entered Rachel's tent. 34 Now Rachel had
taken the household gods and put them
inside her camel's saddle and was sitting
on them. Laban searched[l] through everything in the tent but found nothing.
35 Rachel said to her father, "Don't be
angry, my lord, that I cannot stand up in
your presence;[m] I'm having my period."
So he searched but could not find the
household gods.

31:26 [c] Ge 27:36 [d] 1Sa 30:2-3
31:27 [e] Ex 15:20 [f] Ge 4:21
31:28 [g] ver 55
31:29 [h] ver 7 [i] ver 53
31:30 [j] ver 19; Jdg 18:24
31:32 [k] Ge 44:9
31:34 [l] ver 37; Ge 44:12
31:35 [m] Ex 20:12; Lev 19:3,32

36 Jacob was angry and took Laban to
task. "What is my crime?" he asked Laban. "How have I wronged you that you
hunt me down? 37 Now that you have
searched through all my goods, what
have you found that belongs to your
household? Put it here in front of your
relatives[n] and mine, and let them judge
between the two of us.
38 "I have been with you for twenty
years now. Your sheep and goats have
not miscarried, nor have I eaten rams
from your flocks. 39 I did not bring you
animals torn by wild beasts; I bore the
loss myself. And you demanded payment from me for whatever was stolen
by day or night.[o] 40 This was my situation:
The heat consumed me in the daytime
and the cold at night, and sleep fled
from my eyes. 41 It was like this for the
twenty years I was in your household. I
worked for you fourteen years for your
two daughters[p] and six years for your
flocks, and you changed my wages ten
times.[q] 42 If the God of my father,[r] the God
of Abraham and the Fear of Isaac,[s] had
not been with me,[t] you would surely have
sent me away empty-handed. But God
has seen my hardship and the toil of my
hands,[u] and last night he rebuked you."
43 Laban answered Jacob, "The women
are my daughters, the children are my
children, and the flocks are my flocks.
All you see is mine. Yet what can I do
today about these daughters of mine,
or about the children they have borne?
44 Come now, let's make a covenant,[v] you
and I, and let it serve as a witness between us."[w]
45 So Jacob took a stone and set it up as
a pillar.[x] 46 He said to his relatives, "Gather some stones." So they took stones and
piled them in a heap, and they ate there

31:37 [n] ver 23
31:39 [o] Ex 22:13
31:41 [p] Ge 29:30 [q] ver 7
31:42 [r] ver 5; Ex 3:15; 1Ch 12:17 [s] ver 53; Isa 8:13 [t] Ps 124:1-2 [u] Ge 29:32
31:44 [v] Ge 21:27; 26:28 [w] Jos 24:27
31:45 [x] Ge 28:18

31:25-32 Laban's complaints focus first on Jacob's secret flight, turn to the stolen gods, and climax in the claim that all of Jacob's prosperity has been at his expense. Jacob's grievances begin with Laban's general untrustworthiness. The only thing both agree on is that Jacob's God has protected him and prospered him. Rachel's deception is added to her theft as she lies about her condition as an excuse to prevent Laban from finding the stolen images. **31:45-50** The covenant Laban and Jacob make is designed to protect each one against hostility or ill-treatment at the hands of the other. The use of a heap of stones as a boundary marker, a memorial to an event, or a witness to a covenant appears several places in the biblical text. The fact that both Jacob and Laban erect a "pillar" (v. 45) here and give each a name suggests an invoking ritual in which the god(s) of each party are called to witness the treaty-making ceremony and to enforce its stipulations.

✣ **29:1—31:55** We live in a society that has taught us to "look out for number one." This means taking whatever steps are necessary to assure ourselves of success and to achieve our goals or ambitions. Many Christians can compete with Jacob as master manipulators, making their own way through life and taking their destiny into their own hands. But that is not God's way. God wants to be recognized as

by the heap. 47 Laban called it Jegar Sahadutha, and Jacob called it Galeed.[a]
48 Laban said, "This heap is a witness
between you and me today." That is why
it was called Galeed. 49 It was also called
Mizpah,[b][y] because he said, "May the LORD
keep watch between you and me when
we are away from each other. 50 If you
mistreat my daughters or if you take
any wives besides my daughters, even
though no one is with us, remember that
God is a witness[z] between you and me."
51 Laban also said to Jacob, "Here is this
heap, and here is this pillar[a] I have set
up between you and me. 52 This heap is
a witness, and this pillar is a witness,[b]
that I will not go past this heap to your
side to harm you and that you will not
go past this heap and pillar to my side to
harm me.[c] 53 May the God of Abraham[d]
and the God of Nahor, the God of their
father, judge between us."[e]
So Jacob took an oath[f] in the name of
the Fear of his father Isaac.[g] 54 He offered
a sacrifice there in the hill country and
invited his relatives to a meal. After they
had eaten, they spent the night there.
55 Early the next morning Laban kissed
his grandchildren and his daughters[h]
and blessed them. Then he left and returned home.[c][i]

Jacob Prepares to Meet Esau

32 [d] Jacob also went on his way, and
the angels of God[j] met him.
2 When Jacob saw them, he said, "This
is the camp of God!"[k] So he named that
place Mahanaim.[e][l]
3 Jacob sent messengers ahead of him
to his brother Esau[m] in the land of Seir,
the country of Edom.[n] 4 He instructed
them: "This is what you are to say to
my lord Esau: 'Your servant Jacob says,
I have been staying with Laban and have
remained there till now. 5 I have cattle
and donkeys, sheep and goats, male and
female servants.[o] Now I am sending this
message to my lord, that I may find favor
in your eyes.[p]' "
6 When the messengers returned to Jacob, they said, "We went to your brother
Esau, and now he is coming to meet you,
and four hundred men are with him."[q]
7 In great fear[r] and distress Jacob divided the people who were with him into
two groups,[f] and the flocks and herds
and camels as well. 8 He thought, "If
Esau comes and attacks one group,[g] the
group[g] that is left may escape."
9 Then Jacob prayed, "O God of my father Abraham, God of my father Isaac,[s]
LORD, you who said to me, 'Go back to
your country and your relatives, and I
will make you prosper,'[t] 10 I am unworthy of all the kindness and faithfulness[u]
you have shown your servant. I had only
my staff when I crossed this Jordan, but
now I have become two camps. 11 Save
me, I pray, from the hand of my brother
Esau, for I am afraid he will come and
attack me,[v] and also the mothers with
their children.[w] 12 But you have said, 'I

31:49 [y] Jdg 11:29; 1Sa 7:5-6
31:50 [z] Jer 29:23; 42:5
31:51 [a] Ge 28:18
31:52 [b] Ge 21:30 [c] ver 7; Ge 26:29
31:53 [d] Ge 28:13 [e] Ge 16:5 [f] Ge 21:23,27 [g] ver 42
31:55 [h] ver 28 [i] Ge 18:33; 30:25
32:1 [j] Ge 16:11; 2Ki 6:16-17; Ps 34:7; 91:11; Heb 1:14
32:2 [k] Ge 28:17 [l] 2Sa 2:8,29
32:3 [m] Ge 27:41-42 [n] Ge 25:30; 36:8,9
32:5 [o] Ge 12:16; 30:43 [p] Ge 33:8,10,15
32:6 [q] Ge 33:1
32:7 [r] ver 11
32:9 [s] Ge 28:13; 31:42 [t] Ge 31:13
32:10 [u] Ge 24:27
32:11 [v] Ps 59:2 [w] Ge 27:41

[a] 47 The Aramaic *Jegar Sahadutha* and the Hebrew *Galeed* both mean *witness heap.*
[b] 49 *Mizpah* means *watchtower.*
[c] 55 In Hebrew texts this verse (31:55) is numbered 32:1.
[d] In Hebrew texts 32:1-32 is numbered 32:2-33.
[e] 2 *Mahanaim* means *two camps.*
[f] 7 Or *camps*
[g] 8 Or *camp*

---

the source of our success. Shrewd or cunning strategies, especially when they involve a level of dishonesty, are counterproductive to God's work in our lives. Just as God negated Jacob's attempts to succeed in order to replace them with his own blessings, God sometimes uses failure in our lives to draw us to depend on him.

This is not to say we should never plan or strategize. But it does point out the need to acknowledge God as the source of our prosperity and to give him credit for all that works out well in our lives.

32:1–2 The chapter opens with another indication that God is directing the events of Jacob's return. Just as his dream twenty years earlier had led him to name a place Bethel, so this second encounter with God's messengers produces the name Mahanaim ("Two Camps").

32:3–5 Jacob decides that it is best to inform Esau of his return. He probably assumes that his father has died by now. If his father has died, Esau may have come into the entire inheritance, Jacob's status or whereabouts being undetermined.

32:9–12 In these difficult straits we finally find Jacob resorting to prayer. Jacob does not yet call him "Yahweh, my God." The prayer is further compromised as he sounds as if he is collecting on a debt and that God needs to be held to his word.

Jacob is at his best in v. 10 as he acknowledges his unworthiness and God's faithfulness. That leads into his actual petition in v. 11: He wants deliverance for himself and his family. Unfortunately, v. 12 finds him again sounding as if he has to hold something over God's head to persuade him to act on his behalf. At least he realizes something that will eventually put him where God can do something with him: He cannot rely on his own skills to assure the safety of his family.

will surely make you prosper and will
make your descendants like the sand[x]
of the sea, which cannot be counted.[y]' "
13He spent the night there, and from
what he had with him he selected a gift[z]
for his brother Esau: 14two hundred female goats and twenty male goats, two
hundred ewes and twenty rams, 15thirty
female camels with their young, forty
cows and ten bulls, and twenty female
donkeys and ten male donkeys. 16He put
them in the care of his servants, each
herd by itself, and said to his servants,
"Go ahead of me, and keep some space
between the herds."
17He instructed the one in the lead:
"When my brother Esau meets you and
asks, 'Who do you belong to, and where
are you going, and who owns all these
animals in front of you?' 18then you are
to say, 'They belong to your servant[a] Jacob. They are a gift sent to my lord Esau,
and he is coming behind us.' "
19He also instructed the second, the
third and all the others who followed the
herds: "You are to say the same thing to
Esau when you meet him. 20And be sure
to say, 'Your servant Jacob is coming behind us.' " For he thought, "I will pacify
him with these gifts I am sending on
ahead; later, when I see him, perhaps he
will receive me."[b] 21So Jacob's gifts went
on ahead of him, but he himself spent
the night in the camp.

Jacob Wrestles With God

22That night Jacob got up and took his
two wives, his two female servants and
his eleven sons and crossed the ford of
the Jabbok.[c] 23After he had sent them
across the stream, he sent over all his
possessions. 24So Jacob was left alone,
and a man[d] wrestled with him till daybreak. 25When the man saw that he
could not overpower him, he touched
the socket of Jacob's hip[e] so that his hip
was wrenched as he wrestled with the
man. 26Then the man said, "Let me go,
for it is daybreak."
But Jacob replied, "I will not let you
go unless you bless me."[f]
27The man asked him, "What is your
name?"
"Jacob," he answered.
28Then the man said, "Your name will
no longer be Jacob, but Israel,[a][g] because
you have struggled with God and with
humans and have overcome."
29Jacob said, "Please tell me your
name."[h]

32:12 [x] Ge 22:17 [y] Ge 28:13-15; Hos 1:10; Ro 9:27
32:13 [z] Ge 43:11, 15,25,26; Pr 18:16
32:18 [a] Ge 18:3
32:20 [b] Ge 33:10; Pr 21:14
32:22 [c] Dt 2:37; 3:16; Jos 12:2
32:24 [d] Ge 18:2
32:25 [e] ver 32
32:26 [f] Hos 12:4
32:28 [g] Ge 17:5; 35:10; 1Ki 18:31
32:29 [h] Jdg 13:17

[a] 28 *Israel* probably means *he struggles with God.*

32:13–21 This realization, however, does not prevent him from doing all of the strategic planning we have come to expect from Jacob. In this passage he selects the gifts he sends to Esau. This gift is larger than towns were likely to pay in tribute to foreign kings. In addition to seeking Esau's favor as a response to his generosity, Jacob plans three strategic advantages. (1) If they were planning an ambush, Esau's band would have to set it up each time a group arrives. After five times it is unlikely that they are as alert for combat as they may have been at first. (2) As the gifts arrive, Esau becomes more and more encumbered in his travel. (3) As Jacob's servants bring the gifts, they join the march of Esau's band. How can he cope with members of Jacob's household mixed in among his own retinue of soldiers?

These tactics—along with the divisions of his camp using the river as strategically as possible—exhaust all of Jacob's reserve, yet he still feels vulnerable to Esau's attack. This is precisely where God wants him—feeling in need with no recourse left but to rely on God. Now the real struggle begins.

32:22–32 Who is this stranger? The narrator refers to him throughout the episode as "a man," which is as noncommittal as our referring to "an individual" who wrestles with Jacob. At the end of the episode, Jacob designates the individual as a supernatural being. The clearest statement comes in Hos 12:4, where the prophet indicates that Jacob struggled with an angel.

What implications attach to this story in the context of the ancient Near East? Crossings were understood as gateways guarded by the gods or their servants, so the concept of struggling with a deity upon entrance to his territory would have been familiar. Another common motif is asking a detained deity to secure a blessing. To the Israelite audience this episode may not have seemed as unusual as it does to us.

32:22–25 When the text tells us that Jacob's opponent cannot overcome him, it is not suggesting that Jacob is physically besting the man. The ease with which he inflicts physical damage on Jacob (v. 25) indicates that any inability must be in the spiritual arena. If the wrestler is unable to overcome Jacob spiritually, it is because Jacob is not willing to yield. Only when the man threatens to go without offering assurances of God's help does Jacob show his willingness to negotiate in the critical issues.

32:26 The turning point comes when Jacob informs the stranger that he will not release him unless he receives such assurances (i.e., a blessing). This likely indicates Jacob's willingness to submit himself to God's demands on him. He is ready to do whatever it takes.

32:27–28 The blessing comes in the form of a name change. This is significant for Jacob since his name

But he replied, "Why do you ask my name?"[i] Then he blessed[j] him there.

[30]So Jacob called the place Peniel,[a] saying, "It is because I saw God face to face,[k] and yet my life was spared."

[31]The sun rose above him as he passed Peniel,[b] and he was limping because of his hip. [32]Therefore to this day the Israelites do not eat the tendon attached to the socket of the hip, because the socket of Jacob's hip was touched near the tendon.

Jacob Meets Esau

33 Jacob looked up and there was Esau, coming with his four hundred men;[l] so he divided the children among Leah, Rachel and the two female servants. [2]He put the female servants and their children in front, Leah and her children next, and Rachel and Joseph in the rear. [3]He himself went on ahead and bowed down to the ground[m] seven times as he approached his brother.

[4]But Esau ran to meet Jacob and embraced him; he threw his arms around his neck and kissed him. And they wept.[n] [5]Then Esau looked up and saw the women and children. "Who are these with you?" he asked.

Jacob answered, "They are the children God has graciously given your servant.[o]"

[6]Then the female servants and their children approached and bowed down. [7]Next, Leah and her children came and bowed down. Last of all came Joseph and Rachel, and they too bowed down.

[8]Esau asked, "What's the meaning of all these flocks and herds I met?"[p]

"To find favor in your eyes, my lord,"[q] he said.

[9]But Esau said, "I already have plenty, my brother. Keep what you have for yourself."

[10]"No, please!" said Jacob. "If I have found favor in your eyes, accept this gift from me. For to see your face is like seeing the face of God,[r] now that you have received me favorably.[s] [11]Please accept the present[t] that was brought to you, for God has been gracious to me[u] and I have all I need." And because Jacob insisted, Esau accepted it.

[12]Then Esau said, "Let us be on our way; I'll accompany you."

[13]But Jacob said to him, "My lord knows that the children are tender and that I must care for the ewes and cows that are nursing their young. If they are driven hard just one day, all the animals will die. [14]So let my lord go on ahead of his servant, while I move along slowly at the pace of the flocks and herds before me and the pace of the children, until I come to my lord in Seir.[v]"

[15]Esau said, "Then let me leave some of my men with you."

"But why do that?" Jacob asked. "Just let me find favor in the eyes of my lord."[w]

[16]So that day Esau started on his way back to Seir. [17]Jacob, however, went to Sukkoth,[x] where he built a place for himself and made shelters for his livestock. That is why the place is called Sukkoth.[c]

[18]After Jacob came from Paddan

[a] 30 *Peniel* means *face of God.* [b] 31 Hebrew *Penuel,* a variant of *Peniel* [c] 17 *Sukkoth* means *shelters.*

32:29 [i]Jdg 13:18 [j]Ge 35:9
32:30 [k]Ge 16:13; Ex 24:11; Nu 12:8; Jdg 6:22; 13:22
33:1 [l]Ge 32:6
33:3 [m]Ge 18:2; 42:6
33:4 [n]Ge 45:14-15
33:5 [o]Ge 48:9; Ps 127:3; Isa 8:18
33:8 [p]Ge 32:14-16 [q]Ge 24:9; 32:5
33:10 [r]Ge 16:13 [s]Ge 32:20
33:11 [t]1Sa 25:27 [u]Ge 30:43
33:14 [v]Ge 32:3
33:15 [w]Ge 34:11; 47:25; Ru 2:13
33:17 [x]Jos 13:27; Jdg 8:5,6,8, 14-16; Ps 60:6

Ge 32:28 ❖ God gave Jacob the name "Israel" because he "struggled with God and humans." When have we wrestled with God's plan and purpose in our lives?

Ge 33:4 ❖ Has God's grace ever made an unlikely reconciliation occur in our lives? How have we seen God soften grudges?

---

has embodied his character throughout the narrative. A name change therefore signifies a character change. The name "Israel" is now introduced (v. 28). It is theophoric, making a statement about God, El.

The last element in the narrative to deal with is Jacob's "hip" (v. 25). Whatever this part is, it is most logical that this is the part that is injured. The text says that in the morning he is limping—it does not say that he has a limp the rest of his life.

33:1–11 When the dreaded meeting finally takes place, Jacob is as humble and submissive as possible. For his part, Esau is sentimental and interested in catching up on family news. Esau is flattered by Jacob's generous gifts and tries to return them, but Jacob will not hear of it. This is a family reunion of the sort where dysfunctions have, for the moment, faded into the background.

33:12–20 Esau offers several options to accompany Jacob or to provide protection for him, but Jacob declines them, and the two part company.

33:18–20 Sometime later Jacob and his family move to Shechem, about thirty-five miles north of Jerusalem. Its strategic location at the crossroads of major transportation arteries attracted frequent settlers.

In addition to a land purchase, Jacob builds his first altar here and so identifies with the religious practices of his forefathers. This is the first

Aram,[a][y] he arrived safely at the city of
Shechem[z] in Canaan and camped within
sight of the city. 19For a hundred pieces
of silver,[b] he bought from the sons of
Hamor, the father of Shechem,[a] the plot
of ground[b] where he pitched his tent.
20There he set up an altar and called it
El Elohe Israel.[c]

33:18 [y]Ge 25:20; 28:2 [z]Jos 24:1; Jdg 9:1
33:19 [a]Jos 24:32 [b]Jn 4:5
34:1 [c]Ge 30:21
34:6 [d]Jdg 14:2-5

Dinah and the Shechemites

34 Now Dinah,[c] the daughter Leah
had borne to Jacob, went out to
visit the women of the land. 2When Shechem son of Hamor the Hivite, the ruler
of that area, saw her, he took her and
raped her. 3His heart was drawn to Dinah
daughter of Jacob; he loved the young
woman and spoke tenderly to her. 4And
Shechem said to his father Hamor, "Get
me this girl as my wife."
5When Jacob heard that his daughter
Dinah had been defiled, his sons were
in the fields with his livestock; so he did
nothing about it until they came home.
6Then Shechem's father Hamor went
out to talk with Jacob.[d] 7Meanwhile, Jacob's sons had come in from the fields

[a] *18* That is, Northwest Mesopotamia
[b] *19* Hebrew *hundred kesitahs;* a kesitah was a unit of money of unknown weight and value.
[c] *20* *El Elohe Israel* can mean *El is the God of Israel* or *mighty is the God of Israel.*

---

instance, however, in which an altar was named. The name shows at last a personal appropriation of the God of Jacob's fathers. The transformation of Jacob's character is largely complete; it only has to be formalized in ch. 35.

32:1–33:20 God has the power to transform us. The problem is that most of us are not motivated to change. We must see there is a problem and be given a reason to change before we submit, just as we must be persuaded that something is drastically wrong with our bodies before we willingly put ourselves under the surgeon's knife.

The first step is trusting the surgeon. God can transform us. God can resolve the conflict that is the result of character flaws. Sometimes our response to conflict is a prayer that God will work on the other person to produce harmony. Perhaps we need to be more willing to pray that God will change us—take away our bitterness, overcome our habits, help us step back from our expectations, and weaken our pride.

34:1–24 The focus of the account is not the relationship between Dinah and Shechem. That is just a set-up for the violence of Simeon and Levi, which is the author's real focus.

34:7 It is intriguing that Dinah's brothers are outraged because such "an outrageous thing [is not done] in Israel." There was no territory named Israel. This stands as a good example of the author's use of anachronism. A number of law collections from the ancient Near East that predate Sinai contain prescriptions against illicit or violent sexual relationships.

PEOPLE TO KNOW // ESAU

GENESIS 33:1–4: Esau, son of Isaac and Rebekah, was the older twin brother of Jacob. Before Esau's birth, God said the twins in Rebekah's womb would become two nations and the older would serve the younger (Ge 25:23). Esau and Jacob present one of many examples in Genesis where a younger brother is shown favor over the older.

Esau was ever the target of his clever brother, Jacob. On one occasion, Jacob tricked Esau out of his birthright in exchange for a bowl of stew. When Isaac was old and blind, he sought to bestow his blessing on Esau, his firstborn. Jacob (with Rebekah's help) used trickery to steal Esau's blessing (Ge 27). Esau was furious and intended to kill Jacob, but Jacob ran away.

Esau married Hittite women, a source of anguish for his parents. Esau's descendants were the Edomites, with whom the Israelites had frequent conflicts.

The prophet Malachi contrasted Esau with Jacob in order to illustrate God's love and election (Mal 1:2–3).

APPLICATION Esau was impatient and vengeful, though it is hard not to feel that he was unfairly victimized by his scheming younger brother, Jacob. Esau's loving welcome toward Jacob after his absence shows that transformation and forgiveness are always possible (Ge 33:1–16). Esau's story also illustrates the principle of God's election. Why God chose Jacob over Esau, we do not know. Paul writes that it was not based on works but rather on God's sovereign will (Ro 9:11–12). While we cannot understand God's reasons, our hope rests on the certainty that God's choices are merciful and just (Ro 9:14–16).

as soon as they heard what had happened. They were shocked and furious,
because Shechem had done an outrageous thing in[a] Israel[e] by sleeping with
Jacob's daughter—a thing that should
not be done.[f]
8But Hamor said to them, "My son Shechem has his heart set on your daughter.
Please give her to him as his wife. 9In-
termarry with us; give us your daughters
and take our daughters for yourselves.
10You can settle among us;[g] the land is
open to you.[h] Live in it, trade[b] in it,[i] and
acquire property in it."
11Then Shechem said to Dinah's father
and brothers, "Let me find favor in your
eyes, and I will give you whatever you
ask. 12Make the price for the bride[j] and
the gift I am to bring as great as you like,
and I'll pay whatever you ask me. Only
give me the young woman as my wife."
13Because their sister Dinah had been
defiled, Jacob's sons replied deceitfully
as they spoke to Shechem and his father
Hamor. 14They said to them, "We can't
do such a thing; we can't give our sister
to a man who is not circumcised.[k] That
would be a disgrace to us. 15We will enter into an agreement with you on one
condition only: that you become like us
by circumcising all your males.[l] 16Then
we will give you our daughters and take
your daughters for ourselves. We'll settle
among you and become one people with
you. 17But if you will not agree to be circumcised, we'll take our sister and go."
18Their proposal seemed good to Hamor and his son Shechem. 19The young
man, who was the most honored of all
his father's family, lost no time in doing
what they said, because he was delighted
with Jacob's daughter.[m] 20So Hamor and
his son Shechem went to the gate of their
city[n] to speak to the men of their city.
21"These men are friendly toward us,"
they said. "Let them live in our land and
trade in it; the land has plenty of room
for them. We can marry their daughters
and they can marry ours. 22But the men
will agree to live with us as one people
only on the condition that our males
be circumcised, as they themselves are.
23Won't their livestock, their property
and all their other animals become ours?
So let us agree to their terms, and they
will settle among us."
24All the men who went out of the city
gate[o] agreed with Hamor and his son
Shechem, and every male in the city was
circumcised.
25Three days later, while all of them
were still in pain, two of Jacob's sons,
Simeon and Levi, Dinah's brothers, took
their swords[p] and attacked the unsuspecting city, killing every male.[q] 26They
put Hamor and his son Shechem to the
sword and took Dinah from Shechem's
house and left. 27The sons of Jacob came
upon the dead bodies and looted the city
where[c] their sister had been defiled.
28They seized their flocks and herds and
donkeys and everything else of theirs
in the city and out in the fields. 29They
carried off all their wealth and all their
women and children, taking as plunder
everything in the houses.
30Then Jacob said to Simeon and Levi,
"You have brought trouble on me by
making me obnoxious[r] to the Canaanites
and Perizzites, the people living in this
land.[s] We are few in number,[t] and if they
join forces against me and attack me, I
and my household will be destroyed."

34:7 [e] Dt 22:21; Jdg 20:6; 2Sa 13:12 [f] Jos 7:15
34:10 [g] Ge 47:6, 27 [h] Ge 13:9; 20:15 [i] Ge 42:34
34:12 [j] Ex 22:16; Dt 22:29; 1Sa 18:25
34:14 [k] Ge 17:14; Jdg 14:3
34:15 [l] Ex 12:48
34:19 [m] ver 3
34:20 [n] Ru 4:1; 2Sa 15:2
34:24 [o] Ge 23:10
34:25 [p] Ge 49:5 [q] Ge 49:7
34:30 [r] Ex 5:21; 1Sa 13:4 [s] Ge 13:7 [t] Ge 46:27; 1Ch 16:19; Ps 105:12

[a] 7 Or *against* [b] 10 Or *move about freely;* also in verse 21 [c] 27 Or *because*

Ge 34:30-31 ❖ Jacob was angry at Simeon and Levi for their actions. Evaluate their actions in the light of God's statement in Dt 32:35.

34:8-23 Jacob's sons are motivated by the prospect for revenge in the name of the family honor. Shechem himself is motivated by infatuation (vv. 11-12, 19), while his father and the rest of the town are motivated by economic prospects (vv. 21-23). The situation is ripe for deceit, and it is attributed to Jacob's sons rather than to Jacob.
34:24 The decision by the men of Shechem takes place at the city gate. This was the common place of assembly for legal and business transactions or public meetings to occur.
34:25-31 Archaeological excavations have identified Shechem as having been resettled in about 1900 BC. The gate suggests sufficient size that it seems implausible that two men could wipe out all of the male population by themselves. We may assume that Simeon and Levi recruited a band of servants to go with them.

Beyond the slaughter of the entire male population, the brothers take all the women and children as well as all the goods in the city as plunder. Presumably the brothers rationalize their conduct. Nevertheless, the level of brutality far exceeds any justifiable retribution.

31 But they replied, "Should he have treated our sister like a prostitute?"

Jacob Returns to Bethel

35 Then God said to Jacob, "Go up to Bethel[u] and settle there, and build an altar there to God, who appeared to you when you were fleeing from your brother Esau."[v]

2 So Jacob said to his household[w] and to all who were with him, "Get rid of the foreign gods[x] you have with you, and purify yourselves and change your clothes.[y] 3 Then come, let us go up to Bethel, where I will build an altar to God, who answered me in the day of my distress[z] and who has been with me wherever I have gone.[a]" 4 So they gave Jacob all the foreign gods they had and the rings in their ears, and Jacob buried them under the oak at Shechem.[b] 5 Then they set out, and the terror of God[c] fell on the towns all around them so that no one pursued them.

6 Jacob and all the people with him came to Luz[d] (that is, Bethel) in the land of Canaan. 7 There he built an altar, and he called the place El Bethel,[a] because it was there that God revealed himself to him[e] when he was fleeing from his brother.

8 Now Deborah, Rebekah's nurse,[f] died and was buried under the oak outside Bethel. So it was named Allon Bakuth.[b]

9 After Jacob returned from Paddan Aram,[c] God appeared to him again and blessed him.[g] 10 God said to him, "Your name is Jacob,[d] but you will no longer be called Jacob; your name will be Israel.[e]"[h] So he named him Israel.

11 And God said to him, "I am God Almighty[f];[i] be fruitful and increase in number. A nation[j] and a community of nations will come from you, and kings will be among your descendants.[k] 12 The land I gave to Abraham and Isaac I also give to you, and I will give this land to your descendants after you.[l]"[m] 13 Then God went up from him[n] at the place where he had talked with him.

14 Jacob set up a stone pillar at the place where God had talked with him, and he poured out a drink offering on it; he also poured oil on it.[o] 15 Jacob called the place where God had talked with him Bethel.[g][p]

> **Ge 35:2** ❖ What would it look like for us to purify our lives for God's glory?

The Deaths of Rachel and Isaac

35:23–26pp // 1Ch 2:1–2

16 Then they moved on from Bethel. While they were still some distance from Ephrath, Rachel began to give birth and had great difficulty. 17 And as she was having great difficulty in childbirth, the midwife said to her, "Don't despair, for you have another son."[q] 18 As she breathed her last — for she was dying — she named her son Ben-Oni.[h] But his father named him Benjamin.[i]

19 So Rachel died and was buried on the way to Ephrath (that is, Bethlehem[r]). 20 Over her tomb Jacob set up a pillar, and to this day that pillar marks Rachel's tomb.[s]

21 Israel moved on again and pitched his tent beyond Migdal Eder. 22 While Israel was living in that region, Reuben went in and slept with his father's concubine[t] Bilhah,[u] and Israel heard of it.

35:1 [u] Ge 28:19 [v] Ge 27:43
35:2 [w] Ge 18:19; Jos 24:15 [x] Ge 31:19 [y] Ex 19:10,14
35:3 [z] Ge 32:7 [a] Ge 28:15,20-22; 31:3,42
35:4 [b] Jos 24:25-26
35:5 [c] Ex 15:16; 23:27; Jos 2:9
35:6 [d] Ge 28:19; 48:3
35:7 [e] Ge 28:13
35:8 [f] Ge 24:59
35:9 [g] Ge 32:29
35:10 [h] Ge 17:5
35:11 [i] Ge 17:1; Ex 6:3 [j] Ge 28:3; 48:4 [k] Ge 17:6
35:12 [l] Ge 13:15; 28:13 [m] Ge 12:7; 26:3
35:13 [n] Ge 17:22
35:14 [o] Ge 28:18
35:15 [p] Ge 28:19
35:17 [q] Ge 30:24
35:19 [r] Ge 48:7; Ru 1:1,19; Mic 5:2; Mt 2:16
35:20 [s] 1Sa 10:2
35:22 [t] Ge 49:4; 1Ch 5:1 [u] Ge 29:29; Lev 18:8

[a] 7 *El Bethel* means *God of Bethel.* [b] 8 *Allon Bakuth* means *oak of weeping.* [c] 9 That is, Northwest Mesopotamia; also in verse 26 [d] 10 *Jacob* means *he grasps the heel*, a Hebrew idiom for *he deceives.* [e] 10 *Israel* probably means *he struggles with God.* [f] 11 Hebrew *El-Shaddai* [g] 15 *Bethel* means *house of God.* [h] 18 *Ben-Oni* means *son of my trouble.* [i] 18 *Benjamin* means *son of my right hand.*

35:1–15 When Jacob originally made his vow (28:20–22), he included three promises: acknowledging Yahweh as his God, setting up a shrine, and paying a tithe. Before Jacob proceeds to Bethel, he engages his entire household in a purification ritual.

35:4–8 Burying idols (v. 4) is not the same as destroying them. When the family of Jacob arrives at Bethel, Rebekah's nurse, Deborah, is also buried under a tree (v. 8). Perhaps more important in the author's communication to his audience is this first instance of disposing of other gods. There has been little discussion thus far in Genesis about the issue of other gods and no clear call to monotheistic belief or practice. But here a statement is made in the actions of Jacob.

35:11–12 This chapter has another theophany for Jacob. It is the El Shaddai theophany, meaning "God Almighty" (v. 11). These theophanies are watersheds in the developing relationship between God and his people and in his ongoing revelation of himself to them.

35:16–29 The chapter closes with a short narrative and a summary that completes the family history for Jacob. Rachel's death in childbirth was not an uncommon occurrence in the ancient world.

PEOPLE TO KNOW // RACHEL

GENESIS 35:16–18: Rachel, daughter of Laban, was the younger sister of Leah. When Jacob went to work for Laban, he fell in love with Rachel and agreed to work seven years in order to marry her (Ge 29:18). At the wedding, however, Laban tricked Jacob by giving him Leah instead. The next day when Jacob realized what Laban had done, Laban said it was their custom to marry off the older daughter before the younger. Jacob worked another seven years to marry Rachel (Ge 29:23–30).

While Leah began having children with Jacob, Rachel remained childless, yet Jacob loved Rachel more than he loved Leah. Rachel was grieved by her childless state. But after a long time, Rachel was finally able to conceive, and she and Jacob had a son named Joseph.

When Jacob left Laban to return to his homeland, Rachel stole Laban's household gods. When Laban caught up with Jacob and accused him of the theft, Jacob denied any wrongdoing and let Laban search his possessions. Rachel lied to conceal the stolen gods (Ge 31:35). Deception was a family trait.

Some time later, Rachel became pregnant again, but she had great difficulty in the delivery. She named her newborn son Ben-Oni, "son of my trouble," and then she breathed her last (Ge 35:18). Jacob renamed the child Benjamin, "son of my right hand." Rachel's two sons were Jacob's favorites among his twelve sons.

APPLICATION ✜ Rachel lived during a time and in a culture where she had few choices. As a daughter, she was obligated to abide by her father's choices for her. When her father determined that her sister Leah be given to her finance, Jacob, Rachel had no choice but to try to deal with the difficult situation that followed. It's no wonder she was angry at her father and resented him to the point where she stole his gods and willingly moved away from him.

Sometimes we have to deal with the consequences of other people's choices. It's not fair, but to make the best of a bad situation, we have to decide what actions we will take in response. When we have to deal with hardship, disfunction or pain, we must remember that God sees our tears, he hears our cries for help, and he can begin to heal our hearts of the trauma over time and with prayer.

Jacob had twelve sons:
23 The sons of Leah:
Reuben the firstborn[v] of Jacob,
Simeon, Levi, Judah,[w] Issachar
and Zebulun.[x]
24 The sons of Rachel:
Joseph[y] and Benjamin.[z]
25 The sons of Rachel's servant Bilhah:
Dan and Naphtali.[a]
26 The sons of Leah's servant Zilpah:
Gad[b] and Asher.[c]
These were the sons of Jacob, who
were born to him in Paddan Aram.

27 Jacob came home to his father Isaac
in Mamre,[d] near Kiriath Arba[e] (that is,
Hebron), where Abraham and Isaac
had stayed. 28 Isaac lived a hundred and
eighty years.[f] 29 Then he breathed his last
and died and was gathered to his people,[g]
old and full of years.[h] And his sons Esau
and Jacob buried him.[i]

35:23 [v] Ge 46:8 [w] Ge 29:35 [x] Ge 30:20
35:24 [y] Ge 30:24 [z] ver 18
35:25 [a] Ge 30:8
35:26 [b] Ge 30:11 [c] Ge 30:13
35:27 [d] Ge 13:18; 18:1 [e] Jos 14:15
35:28 [f] Ge 25:7, 20
35:29 [g] Ge 25:8; 49:33 [h] Ge 15:15 [i] Ge 25:9
36:1 [j] Ge 25:30
36:2 [k] Ge 28:8-9 [l] Ge 26:34 [m] ver 25
36:4 [n] 1Ch 1:35

Esau's Descendants

36:10–14pp // 1Ch 1:35–37
36:20–28pp // 1Ch 1:38–42

36 This is the account of the family
line of Esau (that is, Edom).[j]

2 Esau took his wives from the
women of Canaan:[k] Adah daughter
of Elon the Hittite,[l] and Oholibamah
daughter of Anah[m] and granddaughter of Zibeon the Hivite — 3 also Basemath daughter of Ishmael and sister of Nebaioth.
4 Adah bore Eliphaz to Esau, Basemath bore Reuel,[n] 5 and Oholibamah bore Jeush, Jalam and Korah.
These were the sons of Esau, who
were born to him in Canaan.

36:1–43 With the summary of Jacob's family (35:23–26) and the death of Isaac (35:27–29), the Jacob story comes to an end. Before proceeding, the text first disposes of Esau, following the procedure that the line that is of less interest is addressed first.

As in the table of nations in ch. 10, many of these names are presented as clan names connected to chieftains rather than as individual names. Moreover, the text includes a section that appears to have been added later, listing the kings of Edom "before any Israelite king reigned" (36:31). Another notable name is Uz (v. 28), which is the home of Job.

6Esau took his wives and sons and
daughters and all the members of
his household, as well as his livestock and all his other animals and
all the goods he had acquired in Canaan,[o] and moved to a land some
distance from his brother Jacob.
7Their possessions were too great for
them to remain together; the land
where they were staying could not
support them both because of their
livestock.[p] 8So Esau[q] (that is, Edom)
settled in the hill country of Seir.[r]

9This is the account of the family line of Esau the father of the Edomites in the hill country of Seir.

10These are the names of Esau's sons:
Eliphaz, the son of Esau's wife Adah, and Reuel, the son of Esau's wife Basemath.
11The sons of Eliphaz:[s]
Teman,[t] Omar, Zepho, Gatam and Kenaz.
12Esau's son Eliphaz also had a concubine named Timna, who bore him Amalek.[u] These were grandsons of Esau's wife Adah.[v]
13The sons of Reuel:
Nahath, Zerah, Shammah and Mizzah. These were grandsons of Esau's wife Basemath.
14The sons of Esau's wife Oholibamah daughter of Anah and granddaughter of Zibeon, whom she bore to Esau:
Jeush, Jalam and Korah.

15These were the chiefs[w] among Esau's descendants:
The sons of Eliphaz the firstborn of Esau:
Chiefs Teman,[x] Omar, Zepho, Kenaz,
16Korah,[a] Gatam and Amalek. These were the chiefs descended from Eliphaz in Edom; they were grandsons of Adah.[y]
17The sons of Esau's son Reuel:[z]
Chiefs Nahath, Zerah, Shammah and Mizzah. These were the chiefs descended from Reuel in Edom; they were grandsons of Esau's wife Basemath.
18The sons of Esau's wife Oholibamah:
Chiefs Jeush, Jalam and Korah. These were the chiefs descended from Esau's wife Oholibamah daughter of Anah.
19These were the sons of Esau (that is, Edom),[a] and these were their chiefs.

20These were the sons of Seir the Horite,[b] who were living in the region:
Lotan, Shobal, Zibeon, Anah,
21Dishon, Ezer and Dishan. These sons of Seir in Edom were Horite chiefs.
22The sons of Lotan:
Hori and Homam.[b] Timna was Lotan's sister.
23The sons of Shobal:
Alvan, Manahath, Ebal, Shepho and Onam.
24The sons of Zibeon:
Aiah and Anah. This is the Anah who discovered the hot springs[c] in the desert while he was grazing the donkeys of his father Zibeon.
25The children of Anah:
Dishon and Oholibamah daughter of Anah.
26The sons of Dishon[d]:
Hemdan, Eshban, Ithran and Keran.
27The sons of Ezer:
Bilhan, Zaavan and Akan.
28The sons of Dishan:
Uz and Aran.
29These were the Horite chiefs:
Lotan, Shobal, Zibeon, Anah,

36:6 [o] Ge 12:5
36:7 [p] Ge 13:6; 17:8; 28:4
36:8 [q] Dt 2:4 [r] Ge 32:3
36:11 [s] ver 15-16; Job 2:11 [t] Am 1:12; Hab 3:3
36:12 [u] Ex 17:8, 16; Nu 24:20; 1Sa 15:2 [v] ver 16
36:15 [w] Ex 15:15 [x] Job 2:11
36:16 [y] ver 12
36:17 [z] 1Ch 1:37
36:19 [a] Ge 25:30
36:20 [b] Ge 14:6; Dt 2:12, 22; 1Ch 1:38

[a] *16* Masoretic Text; Samaritan Pentateuch (also verse 11 and 1 Chron. 1:36) does not have *Korah.*
[b] *22* Hebrew *Hemam,* a variant of *Homam* (see 1 Chron. 1:39)
[c] *24* Vulgate; Syriac *discovered water;* the meaning of the Hebrew for this word is uncertain.
[d] *26* Hebrew *Dishan,* a variant of *Dishon*

34:1—36:43 God's patient work in Jacob's life offers a lesson as we assess how God can bring us each along step by step in the process of spiritual maturity. We may at times look at where we are in our spiritual walk and feel as if we haven't gotten anywhere. We can feel overwhelmed by our failures and our inability to master the Christian life. Those are the times when we need to pause and look back so that we can gain an appreciation of how far God has brought us. As is evident in his dealings with Jacob, God does not demand instant perfection, but he leads us little by little, making inroads into our self-centeredness and doing his work in our lives one step at a time.

[30]Dishon, Ezer and Dishan. These were the Horite chiefs, according to their divisions, in the land of Seir.

The Rulers of Edom

36:31–43pp // 1Ch 1:43–54

[31]These were the kings who reigned in Edom before any Israelite king[c] reigned:

[32]Bela son of Beor became king of Edom. His city was named Dinhabah.

[33]When Bela died, Jobab son of Zerah from Bozrah[d] succeeded him as king.

[34]When Jobab died, Husham from the land of the Temanites[e] succeeded him as king.

[35]When Husham died, Hadad son of Bedad, who defeated Midian in the country of Moab,[f] succeeded him as king. His city was named Avith.

[36]When Hadad died, Samlah from Masrekah succeeded him as king.

[37]When Samlah died, Shaul from Rehoboth on the river succeeded him as king.

[38]When Shaul died, Baal-Hanan son of Akbor succeeded him as king.

[39]When Baal-Hanan son of Akbor died, Hadad[a] succeeded him as king. His city was named Pau, and his wife's name was Mehetabel daughter of Matred, the daughter of Me-Zahab.

[40]These were the chiefs descended from Esau, by name, according to their clans and regions:

Timna, Alvah, Jetheth, [41]Oholibamah, Elah, Pinon, [42]Kenaz, Teman, Mibzar, [43]Magdiel and Iram. These were the chiefs of Edom, according to their settlements in the land they occupied.

This is the family line of Esau, the father of the Edomites.

36:31 [c]Ge 17:6; 1Ch 1:43
36:33 [d]Jer 49:13,22
36:34 [e]Eze 25:13
36:35 [f]Ge 19:37; Nu 22:1; Dt 1:5; Ru 1:1,6

Ge 36:40 ❖ Even though Esau was not the son who continued the line of the Abrahamic blessing, God blessed his descendants and made them rulers. Where have we seen God bring blessing in unexpected places?

Ge 37:4 ❖ How can God help us resolve real, deep, emotional family conflict such as we see here?

Joseph's Dreams

37 Jacob lived in the land where his father had stayed,[g] the land of Canaan.[h]

[2]This is the account of Jacob's family line.

Joseph, a young man of seventeen, was tending the flocks[i] with his brothers, the sons of Bilhah[j] and the sons of Zilpah,[k] his father's wives, and he brought their father a bad report[l] about them.

[3]Now Israel loved Joseph more than any of his other sons,[m] because he had been born to him in his old age;[n] and he made an ornate[b] robe[o] for him. [4]When his brothers saw that their father loved him more than any of them, they hated him[p] and could not speak a kind word to him.

[5]Joseph had a dream,[q] and when he told it to his brothers, they hated him all the more. [6]He said to them, "Listen to this dream I had: [7]We were binding sheaves of grain out in the field when suddenly my sheaf rose and stood upright, while your sheaves gathered around mine and bowed down to it."[r]

[8]His brothers said to him, "Do you intend to reign over us? Will you actually rule us?"[s] And they hated him all the more because of his dream and what he had said.

37:1 [g]Ge 17:8 [h]Ge 10:19
37:2 [i]Ps 78:71 [j]Ge 35:25 [k]Ge 35:26 [l]1Sa 2:24
37:3 [m]Ge 25:28 [n]Ge 44:20 [o]2Sa 13:18-19
37:4 [p]Ge 27:41; 49:22-23; Ac 7:9
37:5 [q]Ge 20:3; 28:12
37:7 [r]Ge 42:6, 9; 43:26, 28; 44:14; 50:18
37:8 [s]Ge 49:26

[a] *39* Many manuscripts of the Masoretic Text, Samaritan Pentateuch and Syriac (see also 1 Chron. 1:50); most manuscripts of the Masoretic Text *Hadar* [b] *3* The meaning of the Hebrew for this word is uncertain; also in verses 23 and 32.

37:1–4 The favoritism that Jacob felt for Rachel has apparently transferred to her older son, Joseph, for Jacob bestows special status on Joseph. Most scholars acknowledge that status, not just favor, is what the special coat represents. Most commentators favor something along the line of a full-length coat or a long-sleeved coat, either of which would indicate that Joseph is management, not labor.

37:5–11 Dreams of a rise to power like the ones Joseph had are known in the ancient Near East. There is nothing in Joseph's dream that leads them to consider that Joseph's eventual prominence will extend beyond the confines of the family. It is only his family members who bow down to him. It would not have occurred to any of them that Joseph would rise to the position of second-in-command of a dominant world power.

9Then he had another dream, and he
told it to his brothers. "Listen," he said,
"I had another dream, and this time the
sun and moon and eleven stars were
bowing down to me."
10When he told his father as well as
his brothers,[t] his father rebuked him
and said, "What is this dream you had?
Will your mother and I and your brothers actually come and bow down to the
ground before you?"[u] 11His brothers were
jealous of him,[v] but his father kept the
matter in mind.[w]

Joseph Sold by His Brothers

12Now his brothers had gone to graze
their father's flocks near Shechem, 13and
Israel said to Joseph, "As you know, your
brothers are grazing the flocks near Shechem. Come, I am going to send you to
them."
"Very well," he replied.
14So he said to him, "Go and see if all
is well with your brothers and with the
flocks, and bring word back to me." Then
he sent him off from the Valley of Hebron.[x]
When Joseph arrived at Shechem, 15a
man found him wandering around in
the fields and asked him, "What are you
looking for?"
16He replied, "I'm looking for my
brothers. Can you tell me where they
are grazing their flocks?"
17"They have moved on from here," the
man answered. "I heard them say, 'Let's
go to Dothan.'[y]"
So Joseph went after his brothers and
found them near Dothan. 18But they
saw him in the distance, and before he
reached them, they plotted to kill him.[z]
19"Here comes that dreamer!" they said
to each other. 20"Come now, let's kill him
and throw him into one of these cisterns[a]
and say that a ferocious animal devoured
him. Then we'll see what comes of his
dreams."[b]
21When Reuben heard this, he tried
to rescue him from their hands. "Let's
not take his life," he said.[c] 22"Don't shed
any blood. Throw him into this cistern
here in the wilderness, but don't lay a
hand on him." Reuben said this to rescue him from them and take him back
to his father.
23So when Joseph came to his brothers, they stripped him of his robe — the
ornate robe he was wearing — 24and
they took him and threw him into the
cistern.[d] The cistern was empty; there
was no water in it.
25As they sat down to eat their meal,
they looked up and saw a caravan of
Ishmaelites coming from Gilead. Their
camels were loaded with spices, balm
and myrrh,[e] and they were on their way
to take them down to Egypt.[f]
26Judah said to his brothers, "What
will we gain if we kill our brother and
cover up his blood?[g] 27Come, let's sell
him to the Ishmaelites and not lay our
hands on him; after all, he is our brother,[h] our own flesh and blood." His brothers agreed.

37:10 [t] ver 5 [u] ver 7; Ge 27:29
37:11 [v] Ac 7:9 [w] Lk 2:19,51
37:14 [x] Ge 13:18; 35:27
37:17 [y] 2Ki 6:13
37:18 [z] 1Sa 19:1; Mk 14:1; Ac 23:12
37:20 [a] Jer 38:6, 9 [b] Ge 50:20
37:21 [c] Ge 42:22
37:24 [d] Jer 41:7
37:25 [e] Ge 43:11 [f] ver 28
37:26 [g] ver 20; Ge 4:10
37:27 [h] Ge 42:21

37:9–10 A curious feature of the second dream is the inclusion of his parents, because the dream does not just suggest that Joseph will be first among his brothers. It suggests Joseph's eventual prominence in the ancestral line, superseding even his parents in significance.
37:12–17 Joseph fails to find his brothers at Shechem and receives direction from a stranger.
37:18–22 Joseph's brothers see him coming and begin to formulate a plan. The text refrains from indicating which brother or brothers make the initial suggestion and in so doing implies that it represents something of a consensus. Reuben is the only objector as he adopts part of their suggestion (the cistern) but seeks to avoid violence.

Cisterns were either hollowed out of limestone bedrock or dug in the ground and lined with plaster. Since most of Israel's rainfall is confined to three or four months of the year, these cisterns collected the rainwater and made it available during the dry period.
37:25–28 Dothan is on the normal caravan route from Gilead to Egypt. It is no surprise that a caravan should pass, but the timing is providential. This caravan is made up of Midianites and Ishmaelites (vv. 25, 28). Midianites are descendants of Abraham through Keturah (25:2), while the Ishmaelites descended from Abraham through Hagar, so these are relatives; therefore, these traders are second or third cousins to Joseph and his brothers.

Judah is the one who offers the idea of selling Joseph rather than killing him. This is the first appearance of a number of significant actions by Judah. It is probably significant that in all three of the narrative contexts of the Joseph story where Judah plays a role, he successfully persuades others to do as he suggests.
37:26–28 While Reuben's motives are clarified by the text (v. 22), Judah's are not elaborated. Is he trying to save Joseph or just get rid of him conveniently? From his statement it appears as if he has inhibitions against killing relatives but has no concern for Joseph's welfare. The twenty-shekel sale price is typical for slaves in this period and represents about two years' wages for a common shepherd.

28So when the Midianite[i] merchants
came by, his brothers pulled Joseph up
out of the cistern and sold him for twenty shekels[a] of silver to the Ishmaelites,
who took him to Egypt.[j]
29When Reuben returned to the cistern
and saw that Joseph was not there, he
tore his clothes.[k] 30He went back to his
brothers and said, "The boy isn't there!
Where can I turn now?"[l]
31Then they got Joseph's robe,[m] slaughtered a goat and dipped the robe in the
blood. 32They took the ornate robe back
to their father and said, "We found this.
Examine it to see whether it is your son's
robe."
33He recognized it and said, "It is my
son's robe! Some ferocious animal[n] has
devoured him. Joseph has surely been
torn to pieces."[o]
34Then Jacob tore his clothes,[p] put
on sackcloth[q] and mourned for his son
many days.[r] 35All his sons and daughters
came to comfort him, but he refused to
be comforted. "No," he said, "I will continue to mourn until I join my son in
the grave.[s]" So his father wept for him.
36Meanwhile, the Midianites[b] sold Joseph in Egypt to Potiphar, one of Pharaoh's officials, the captain of the guard.[t]

Judah and Tamar

38 At that time, Judah left his brothers and went down to stay with a
man of Adullam named Hirah. 2There
Judah met the daughter of a Canaanite
man named Shua.[u] He married her and
made love to her; 3she became pregnant
and gave birth to a son, who was named
Er.[v] 4She conceived again and gave birth
to a son and named him Onan. 5She gave
birth to still another son and named him
Shelah. It was at Kezib that she gave birth
to him.
6Judah got a wife for Er, his firstborn,
and her name was Tamar. 7But Er, Judah's
firstborn, was wicked in the LORD's sight;
so the LORD put him to death.[w]
8Then Judah said to Onan, "Sleep with
your brother's wife and fulfill your duty
to her as a brother-in-law to raise up
offspring for your brother."[x] 9But Onan
knew that the child would not be his;
so whenever he slept with his brother's
wife, he spilled his semen on the ground
to keep from providing offspring for his
brother. 10What he did was wicked in
the LORD's sight; so the LORD put him
to death also.[y]
11Judah then said to his daughter-in-
law Tamar, "Live as a widow in your father's household until my son Shelah
grows up."[z] For he thought, "He may die
too, just like his brothers." So Tamar went
to live in her father's household.
12After a long time Judah's wife, the

37:28 [i]Ge 25:2; Jdg 6:1-3 [j]Ge 45:4-5; Ps 105:17; Ac 7:9
37:29 [k]ver 34; Ge 44:13; Job 1:20
37:30 [l]ver 22; Ge 42:13,36
37:31 [m]ver 3,23
37:33 [n]ver 20 [o]Ge 44:20,28
37:34 [p]ver 29 [q]2Sa 3:31 [r]Ge 50:3,10,11
37:35 [s]Ge 42:38; 44:22,29,31
37:36 [t]Ge 39:1
38:2 [u]1Ch 2:3
38:3 [v]ver 6; Ge 46:12; Nu 26:19
38:7 [w]ver 10; Ge 46:12; 1Ch 2:3
38:8 [x]Dt 25:5-6; Mt 22:24-28
38:10 [y]Ge 46:12; Dt 25:7-10
38:11 [z]Ru 1:13

[a] *28* That is, about 8 ounces or about 230 grams
[b] *36* Samaritan Pentateuch, Septuagint, Vulgate and Syriac (see also verse 28); Masoretic Text *Medanites*

37:12–36 When Reuben returns, his dismay reflects his sense that, as the oldest, he is the one ultimately held responsible for Joseph's safety—so much for regaining Jacob's favor. We are not told which brother comes up with this plot to deceive Jacob about Joseph's fate. Jacob is allowed to draw his own conclusions and is literally inconsolable.

38:1–11 Levirate marriage laws required that if a woman's husband died without offspring having been produced, it was the duty of his brother to bear a child by her in order to continue his dead brother's line. This custom is established as legislation in the Mosaic law (Dt 25:5–10). When Onan refuses to do his duty by Tamar, he is punished by God and likewise expires.

Judah, like his father before him, is being treated in the same way that he has treated others, especially Joseph. Recognition that the deaths of his sons may well be punishment for his treatment of Joseph gives plausibility to his fear that his last son, Shelah, will meet the same fate as his brothers (v. 11).

38:12–23 The formulation of the Hittite law regarding levirate marriage stipulates that when a widow marries her late husband's brother, if he dies, she is then to marry his father (i.e., her father-in-law). This is not how the later Israelite legislation reads, but it appears to be the procedure that Tamar is following. She carries out her scheme by means of yet another masquerade as Jacob's deception continues to echo through the family history.

38:12–18 Judah's encounter with Tamar takes place around sheep-shearing time. Judah's guarantee of payment for his act of prostitution is his seal, cord, and staff. The seal is most likely a stamp seal engraved with a design that would uniquely identify Judah. It would be used by him for any transaction or correspondence much as we use a signature today. Taking this as a pledge for payment ensures a quick response on Judah's part because seals were used with some frequency. Seals were often worn around the neck on a cord, so that is probably the cord referred to here. His staff is a walking stick but may have been a symbol of authority in his clan. If so, Tamar holds in her possession symbols of his individual and corporate identity—in modern terms, items akin

daughter of Shua, died. When Judah had recovered from his grief, he went up to Timnah,[a] to the men who were shearing his sheep, and his friend Hirah the Adullamite went with him.

13When Tamar was told, "Your father-in-law is on his way to Timnah to shear his sheep," 14she took off her widow's clothes, covered herself with a veil to disguise herself, and then sat down at the entrance to Enaim, which is on the road to Timnah. For she saw that, though Shelah[b] had now grown up, she had not been given to him as his wife.

15When Judah saw her, he thought she was a prostitute, for she had covered her face. 16Not realizing that she was his daughter-in-law,[c] he went over to her by the roadside and said, "Come now, let me sleep with you."

"And what will you give me to sleep with you?" she asked.

17"I'll send you a young goat[d] from my flock," he said.

"Will you give me something as a pledge[e] until you send it?" she asked.

18He said, "What pledge should I give you?"

"Your seal[f] and its cord, and the staff in your hand," she answered. So he gave them to her and slept with her, and she became pregnant by him. 19After she left, she took off her veil and put on her widow's clothes[g] again.

20Meanwhile Judah sent the young goat by his friend the Adullamite in order to get his pledge back from the woman, but he did not find her. 21He asked the men who lived there, "Where is the shrine prostitute[h] who was beside the road at Enaim?"

"There hasn't been any shrine prostitute here," they said.

22So he went back to Judah and said, "I didn't find her. Besides, the men who lived there said, 'There hasn't been any shrine prostitute here.'"

38:12 [a] ver 14; Jos 15:10, 57
38:14 [b] ver 11
38:16 [c] Lev 18:15; 20:12
38:17 [d] Eze 16:33 [e] ver 20
38:18 [f] ver 25
38:19 [g] ver 14
38:21 [h] Lev 19:29; Hos 4:14

Ge 38:26 ❖ When have we seen an unlikely person provide an example of righteousness in our lives?

23Then Judah said, "Let her keep what she has, or we will become a laughingstock. After all, I did send her this young goat, but you didn't find her."

24About three months later Judah was told, "Your daughter-in-law Tamar is guilty of prostitution, and as a result she is now pregnant."

Judah said, "Bring her out and have her burned to death!"[i]

25As she was being brought out, she sent a message to her father-in-law. "I am pregnant by the man who owns these," she said. And she added, "See if you recognize whose seal and cord and staff these are."[j]

26Judah recognized them and said, "She is more righteous than I,[k] since I wouldn't give her to my son Shelah.[l]" And he did not sleep with her again.

27When the time came for her to give birth, there were twin boys in her womb.[m] 28As she was giving birth, one of them put out his hand; so the midwife took a scarlet thread and tied it on his wrist and said, "This one came out first." 29But when he drew back his hand, his brother came out, and she said, "So this is how you have broken out!" And he was named Perez.[a][n] 30Then his brother, who had the scarlet thread on his wrist, came out. And he was named Zerah.[b][o]

Joseph and Potiphar's Wife

39 Now Joseph had been taken down to Egypt. Potiphar, an Egyptian who was one of Pharaoh's officials, the captain of the guard,[p] bought him from the Ishmaelites who had taken him there.[q]

38:24 [i] Lev 21:9; Dt 22:21, 22
38:25 [j] ver 18
38:26 [k] 1Sa 24:17 [l] ver 11
38:27 [m] Ge 25:24
38:29 [n] Ge 46:12; Nu 26:20, 21; Ru 4:12, 18; 1Ch 2:4; Mt 1:3
38:30 [o] 1Ch 2:4
39:1 [p] Ge 37:36 [q] Ge 37:25; Ps 105:17

[a] *29 Perez* means *breaking out.* [b] *30 Zerah* can mean *scarlet* or *brightness.*

---

to someone's driver's license or other important form of identification.

38:24–30 When Tamar's pregnancy gives evidence of her behavior, Judah is at first harsh in his criticism. He would be happy for the excuse to get rid of her and bring this long, unfortunate chapter of his life to a close. But he is made aware of his own participation and guilt when he is shown the things he left as a pledge and is forced to identify them.

38:24–26 In a brief two verses, Judah moves from demands that Tamar be burned (v. 24) to the declaration that she is more righteous than he (v. 26)—that is to say, that her actions are more justifiable than his. This is the first hint of a change taking place in Judah as he admits to moral failure. This stands in stark contrast to Joseph's moral resilience in the next chapter and is the first step that leads eventually to the transformed Judah in 44:18–34.

39:1 Potiphar was an important official in Pharaoh's court. His name, meaning "he whom Re gives," occurs occasionally in Egyptian inscriptions, generally between the seventh and third

2The LORD was with Joseph[r] so that he
prospered, and he lived in the house of
his Egyptian master. 3When his master
saw that the LORD was with him[s] and
that the LORD gave him success in everything he did,[t] 4Joseph found favor in his
eyes and became his attendant. Potiphar
put him in charge of his household, and
he entrusted to his care everything he
owned.[u] 5From the time he put him in
charge of his household and of all that he
owned, the LORD blessed the household
of the Egyptian because of Joseph.[v] The
blessing of the LORD was on everything
Potiphar had, both in the house and in
the field. 6So Potiphar left everything
he had in Joseph's care; with Joseph in
charge, he did not concern himself with
anything except the food he ate.

Now Joseph was well-built and handsome,[w] 7and after a while his master's
wife took notice of Joseph and said,
"Come to bed with me!"[x]

8But he refused.[y] "With me in charge,"
he told her, "my master does not concern
himself with anything in the house; everything he owns he has entrusted to
my care. 9No one is greater in this house
than I am.[z] My master has withheld nothing from me except you, because you
are his wife. How then could I do such
a wicked thing and sin against God?"[a]
10And though she spoke to Joseph day
after day, he refused to go to bed with
her or even be with her.

11One day he went into the house to at-

Ge 39:10 ❖ How can we stand firm against sexual temptation as Joseph did?

tend to his duties, and none of the household servants was inside. 12She caught
him by his cloak[b] and said, "Come to bed
with me!" But he left his cloak in her
hand and ran out of the house.

13When she saw that he had left his
cloak in her hand and had run out of
the house, 14she called her household
servants. "Look," she said to them, "this
Hebrew has been brought to us to make
sport of us! He came in here to sleep with
me, but I screamed.[c] 15When he heard me
scream for help, he left his cloak beside
me and ran out of the house."

16She kept his cloak beside her until
his master came home. 17Then she told
him this story:[d] "That Hebrew slave you
brought us came to me to make sport of
me. 18But as soon as I screamed for help,
he left his cloak beside me and ran out
of the house."

19When his master heard the story
his wife told him, saying, "This is how
your slave treated me," he burned with
anger.[e] 20Joseph's master took him and
put him in prison,[f] the place where the
king's prisoners were confined.

But while Joseph was there in the prison, 21the LORD was with him; he showed
him kindness and granted him favor in
the eyes of the prison warden.[g] 22So the

39:2 [r] Ge 21:20, 22; Ac 7:9
39:3 [s] Ge 21:22; 26:28 [t] Ps 1:3
39:4 [u] ver 8, 22; Ge 24:2
39:5 [v] Ge 26:24; 30:27
39:6 [w] 1Sa 16:12
39:7 [x] 2Sa 13:11; Pr 7:15-18
39:8 [y] Pr 6:23-24
39:9 [z] Ge 41:33, 40 [a] Ge 20:6; 42:18; 2Sa 12:13
39:12 [b] Pr 7:13
39:14 [c] Dt 22:24, 27
39:17 [d] Ex 23:1, 7; Ps 101:5
39:19 [e] Pr 6:34
39:20 [f] Ge 40:3; Ps 105:18
39:21 [g] Ex 3:21

---

century BC, but as early as the eleventh century BC. The two titles given to him, "one of Pharaoh's officials" and "captain of the guard" (v. 1), are both fairly general in nature.

39:2–6a In contrast to the detail in the last chapter that God put Judah's sons to death, here the Lord is with Joseph, and he prospers. As Laban recognized that the Lord's favor was with Jacob (30:27), Potiphar sees the same in Joseph and trusts him with responsibility. As a result, the blessing side of the covenant continues to be realized on a small scale as Potiphar and his house are blessed through Joseph (39:5–6). But his success is short-lived.

39:6b–12 The account of the attempted seduction of Joseph shows him in a positive light. The details are given in such a way as to confirm Joseph's unquestionable innocence. He does not lead on Potiphar's wife or allow himself to enjoy her company at any level. He is compromised only by a desperate and spiteful act, supported by shameless lies that none can contest but the accused.

39:13–16 Note that once again Joseph is being identified by his cloak that has been taken from him. Here it is supposed to incriminate Joseph, just as the sign of Judah's identity incriminated him of sexual wrongdoing in the last chapter. The difference is, of course, that Joseph is being falsely accused.

39:17–23 Potiphar responds by "burn[ing] with anger" (v. 19). Given his wife's slander of his own motives, the proven trustworthiness of Joseph, and his knowledge of his wife's character or lack of it, Potiphar's anger arguably burns at his wife, not at Joseph. This is further suggested by the fact that Joseph is only put in the king's prison. If Potiphar believed his wife and was truly angry with Joseph, Joseph would probably have been executed on the spot, no questions asked. In contrast, the king's prison was a place for political prisoners and would hardly have been expected to accommodate foreign slaves guilty of crimes against their masters. The action he takes against Joseph is as minimal as it can be while still retaining his family's honor.

It also appears that the prison is on Potiphar's premises, for 40:3 identifies it as "in the house of the captain of the guard," using the same title previously given to Potiphar (39:1).

ANCIENT EGYPT

warden put Joseph in charge of all those held in the prison, and he was made responsible for all that was done there.[h] 23The warden paid no attention to anything under Joseph's care, because the LORD was with Joseph and gave him success in whatever he did.[i]

The Cupbearer and the Baker

40 Some time later, the cupbearer[j] and the baker of the king of Egypt offended their master, the king of Egypt. 2Pharaoh was angry[k] with his two officials, the chief cupbearer and the chief baker, 3and put them in custody in the house of the captain of the guard,[l] in the same prison where Joseph was confined. 4The captain of the guard assigned them to Joseph,[m] and he attended them.

After they had been in custody for some time, 5each of the two men — the cupbearer and the baker of the king of Egypt, who were being held in prison — had a dream the same night, and each dream had a meaning of its own.[n]

6When Joseph came to them the next morning, he saw that they were dejected. 7So he asked Pharaoh's officials who were in custody with him in his master's house, "Why do you look so sad today?"[o]

8"We both had dreams," they answered, "but there is no one to interpret them."[p]

Then Joseph said to them, "Do not interpretations belong to God?[q] Tell me your dreams."

9So the chief cupbearer told Joseph his dream. He said to him, "In my dream I saw a vine in front of me, 10and on the vine were three branches. As soon as it budded, it blossomed, and its clusters ripened into grapes. 11Pharaoh's cup was in my hand, and I took the grapes, squeezed them into Pharaoh's cup and put the cup in his hand."

12"This is what it means,[r]" Joseph said to him. "The three branches are three days. 13Within three days Pharaoh will lift up your head and restore you to your position, and you will put Pharaoh's cup in his hand, just as you used to do when you were his cupbearer. 14But when all goes well with you, remember me[s] and show me kindness;[t] mention me to Pharaoh and get me out of this prison. 15I was forcibly carried off from the land of the Hebrews,[u] and even here I have done nothing to deserve being put in a dungeon."

16When the chief baker saw that Joseph had given a favorable interpretation, he said to Joseph, "I too had a dream: On my head were three baskets of bread.[a] 17In the top basket were all kinds of baked goods for Pharaoh, but the birds were eating them out of the basket on my head."

18"This is what it means," Joseph said. "The three baskets are three days.[v] 19Within three days Pharaoh will lift off your head[w] and impale your body on a pole. And the birds will eat away your flesh."

20Now the third day was Pharaoh's birthday,[x] and he gave a feast for all his

39:22 [h] ver 4
39:23 [i] ver 3
40:1 [j] Ne 1:11
40:2 [k] Pr 16:14, 15
40:3 [l] Ge 39:20
40:4 [m] Ge 39:4
40:5 [n] Ge 41:11
40:7 [o] Ne 2:2
40:8 [p] Ge 41:8, 15 [q] Ge 41:16; Da 2:22, 28, 47
40:12 [r] Ge 41:12, 15, 25; Da 2:36; 4:19
40:14 [s] Lk 23:42 [t] Jos 2:12; 1Sa 20:14, 42; 1Ki 2:7
40:15 [u] Ge 37:26-28
40:18 [v] ver 12
40:19 [w] ver 13
40:20 [x] Mt 14:6-10

Ge 40:8 ❖ Consider a time you were able to point someone toward God's power. What are ways you could do so more often in the future?

[a] 16 Or *three wicker baskets*

40:1–4 Joseph spends eleven years in Potiphar's house and in prison, though there is no indication how that time period divides. The officers whom Joseph encounters in prison are high-ranking members of the court. They are responsible for safeguarding two of the ways that a potential assassin could strike the king.

Chapter 40 gives no hint what sequence of events has landed these officials under Joseph's care. Whether these officials are suspected of involvement in a conspiracy or just guilty of displeasing the king in the administration of their duties is impossible to tell.

40:5–8a In the ancient Near East, dream interpretations were sought from experts. Both the Egyptians and Babylonians compiled what are called "dream books," which contain sample dreams along with a key to their interpretation. The dream books preserved the empirical data concerning past dreams and interpretations and therefore offered the security of scientific documentation. It was believed that the gods revealed the meanings of dreams by giving wisdom in the expert's research.

40:8b–11 Joseph was not familiar with any of the "scientific" literature, so he consulted God. Regardless, his interpretation follows the way the dream literature interpreted comparable symbols. Joseph draws a time indication from a number featured in the dream.

40:12–19 The operative difference between the interpretations given for the two men turns on the phrase, "Pharaoh will lift up/off your head" (40:13, 19). In Hebrew the phrase is exactly the same, but the surrounding context gives each a different meaning.

40:20–23 The third day, Pharaoh's birthday, brings

officials.[y] He lifted up the heads of the chief cupbearer and the chief baker in the presence of his officials: 21He restored the chief cupbearer to his position, so that he once again put the cup into Pharaoh's hand[z] — 22but he impaled the chief baker,[a] just as Joseph had said to them in his interpretation.[b]

23The chief cupbearer, however, did not remember Joseph; he forgot him.[c]

Pharaoh's Dreams

41 When two full years had passed, Pharaoh had a dream:[d] He was standing by the Nile, 2when out of the river there came up seven cows, sleek and fat,[e] and they grazed among the reeds.[f] 3After them, seven other cows, ugly and gaunt, came up out of the Nile and stood beside those on the riverbank. 4And the cows that were ugly and gaunt ate up the seven sleek, fat cows. Then Pharaoh woke up.

5He fell asleep again and had a second dream: Seven heads of grain, healthy and good, were growing on a single stalk. 6After them, seven other heads of grain sprouted — thin and scorched by the east wind. 7The thin heads of grain swallowed up the seven healthy, full heads. Then Pharaoh woke up; it had been a dream.

8In the morning his mind was troubled,[g] so he sent for all the magicians[h] and wise men of Egypt. Pharaoh told them his dreams, but no one could interpret them for him.

9Then the chief cupbearer said to Pharaoh, "Today I am reminded of my shortcomings. 10Pharaoh was once angry with his servants,[i] and he imprisoned me and the chief baker in the house of the captain of the guard.[j] 11Each of us had a dream the same night, and each dream had a meaning of its own.[k] 12Now a young Hebrew was there with us, a servant of the captain of the guard. We told him our dreams, and he interpreted them for us, giving each man the interpretation of his dream.[l] 13And things turned out exactly as he interpreted them to us: I was restored to my position, and the other man was impaled.[m]"

14So Pharaoh sent for Joseph, and he was quickly brought from the dungeon.[n] When he had shaved and changed his clothes, he came before Pharaoh.

15Pharaoh said to Joseph, "I had a dream, and no one can interpret it. But I have heard it said of you that when you hear a dream you can interpret it."[o]

16"I cannot do it," Joseph replied to Pharaoh, "but God will give Pharaoh the answer he desires."[p]

17Then Pharaoh said to Joseph, "In my dream I was standing on the bank of the Nile, 18when out of the river there came up seven cows, fat and sleek, and they grazed among the reeds. 19After them, seven other cows came up — scrawny and very ugly and lean. I had never seen such ugly cows in all the land of Egypt. 20The lean, ugly cows ate up the seven fat cows that came up first. 21But even after they ate them, no one could tell that they had done so; they looked just as ugly as before. Then I woke up.

22"In my dream I saw seven heads of grain, full and good, growing on a single stalk. 23After them, seven other heads sprouted — withered and thin and scorched by the east wind. 24The thin heads of grain swallowed up the seven good heads. I told this to the magicians, but none of them could explain it to me.[q]"

25Then Joseph said to Pharaoh, "The

40:20 [y] Mk 6:21
40:21 [z] ver 13
40:22 [a] ver 19 [b] Ps 105:19
40:23 [c] Job 19:14; Ecc 9:15
41:1 [d] Ge 20:3
41:2 [e] ver 26 [f] Isa 19:6
41:8 [g] Da 2:1,3; 4:5,19 [h] Ex 7:11, 22; Da 1:20; 2:2, 27; 4:7
41:10 [i] Ge 40:2 [j] Ge 39:20
41:11 [k] Ge 40:5
41:12 [l] Ge 40:12
41:13 [m] Ge 40:22
41:14 [n] Ps 105:20; Da 2:25
41:15 [o] Da 5:16
41:16 [p] Ge 40:8; Da 2:30; Ac 3:12; 2Co 3:5
41:24 [q] ver 8

Ge 41:7 ❖ How can God's people be a source of blessing and nourishment to a hungry world? How can we contribute to that blessing?

---

about exactly the result that Joseph's interpretation has indicated. The cupbearer's good fortune, however, goes for nothing because in his joy at being restored, he forgets (for the time being) his debt to Joseph.

41:1–38 In the ancient Near East, dreams sometimes received special emphasis when they were repeated or came in a set of two (cf. v. 32). Here the pharaoh has two visions that warn of the coming famine in Egypt.

41:8 Since the pharaoh was considered divine, it would be unusual for him to seek out an interpreter for his dreams. The Hebrew word used to describe the specialists whom the pharaoh sends for (NIV "magicians") is from a technical Egyptian term used to describe the famous official Imhotep in a late inscription (second century BC), where he is portrayed giving advice to Pharaoh concerning a seven-year famine.

41:14–16 When Joseph is finally brought before Pharaoh, he is careful to deny that he is a trained expert in dream interpretation. Whatever success he has, he insists, comes from God. He assures Pharaoh that God will give him the "answer he desires" (v. 16).

41:25–32 As Joseph presents the interpretation,

dreams of Pharaoh are one and the
same. God has revealed to Pharaoh what
he is about to do.[r] 26The seven good
cows[s] are seven years, and the seven
good heads of grain are seven years; it
is one and the same dream. 27The seven
lean, ugly cows that came up afterward
are seven years, and so are the seven
worthless heads of grain scorched by
the east wind: They are seven years of
famine.[t]

28"It is just as I said to Pharaoh: God
has shown Pharaoh what he is about to
do. 29Seven years of great abundance[u] are
coming throughout the land of Egypt,
30but seven years of famine[v] will follow
them. Then all the abundance in Egypt
will be forgotten, and the famine will
ravage the land.[w] 31The abundance in
the land will not be remembered, because the famine that follows it will be
so severe. 32The reason the dream was
given to Pharaoh in two forms is that
the matter has been firmly decided[x] by
God, and God will do it soon.

33"And now let Pharaoh look for a discerning and wise man[y] and put him in
charge of the land of Egypt. 34Let Pharaoh appoint commissioners over the
land to take a fifth[z] of the harvest of
Egypt during the seven years of abundance.[a] 35They should collect all the food
of these good years that are coming and
store up the grain under the authority of
Pharaoh, to be kept in the cities for food.[b]
36This food should be held in reserve for
the country, to be used during the sev-
en years of famine that will come upon
Egypt,[c] so that the country may not be
ruined by the famine."

37The plan seemed good to Pharaoh
and to all his officials.[d] 38So Pharaoh
asked them, "Can we find anyone like
this man, one in whom is the spirit of
God[a]?"[e]

39Then Pharaoh said to Joseph, "Since
God has made all this known to you,
there is no one so discerning and wise
as you. 40You shall be in charge of my
palace, and all my people are to submit
to your orders.[f] Only with respect to the
throne will I be greater than you."

41:25 [r] Da 2:45
41:26 [s] ver 2
41:27 [t] Ge 12:10; 2Ki 8:1
41:29 [u] ver 47
41:30 [v] ver 54; Ge 47:13 [w] ver 56
41:32 [x] Nu 23:19; Isa 46:10-11
41:33 [y] ver 39
41:34 [z] 1Sa 8:15 [a] ver 48
41:35 [b] ver 48
41:36 [c] ver 56
41:37 [d] Ge 45:16
41:38 [e] Nu 27:18; Job 32:8; Da 4:8-9,18; 5:11,14
41:40 [f] Ps 105:21-22; Ac 7:10

[a] 38 Or *of the gods*

---

he also treats the dream as a message from God (41:25). He does not specifically identify the God Yahweh as the deity who has sent the message. He uses generic terminology, and Pharaoh is left to draw his own conclusion about which deity is responsible. Certainly, any deity who could inflict such a severe famine on Egypt must be a powerful one. The gods connected to the Nile and its annual flooding were considered to be powerful gods who would have to be restrained in some way (or angered by some offense) for the annual flooding to fail for seven years.

No cause is offered for the coming famine. It would appear odd for a dream to carry prospects of both tremendous prosperity and devastating tragedy. What could possibly be motivating any deity to offer such mutually exclusive determinations? Joseph is clearly no complainer conspiring to speak ill of the throne, nor is he a flatterer trying to get on Pharaoh's good side by offering joyous news of divine favor. It is not surprising, then, that Pharaoh decides that Joseph is both credible and trustworthy.

41:33–36 In addition to offering an interpretation, Joseph shows himself quick on his feet as he promotes a plan for action. This includes a team of administrators exacting a twenty percent tax in kind (v. 34) to be stored in savings and doled out later. What he proposes is also attractive from the government's standpoint. Not only does it provide a strategy by which the country and its people will be able to survive but it also does so in a way that is economically advantageous. It procures the excess food through taxation and then sells it back to the very people who have contributed it. When finally the people have no money left to buy food, the government can take their land.

41:37–38 It is no surprise that Pharaoh is open to such a profitable course of action. His assessment of Joseph is that he is one who possesses the "spirit of God" (v. 38). Pharaoh is acknowledging that in his estimation the deity is indeed the source of Joseph's wisdom.

41:39–57 The text goes into significant detail concerning the elevation of Joseph to high office. The ring was necessary for Joseph to do business in Pharaoh's name since it was used to seal official documents. The linen robes and the gold chain are part of the outward symbols that signify his rank, status, and office. Chariots were the limousines of the day, so it is arranged that Joseph will ride in style. The men going before him clearing the way are the equivalent of the Secret Service protection that is offered to important dignitaries and officers in the United States.

Placing Joseph second-in-command may mean several different things. The second-in-command in all administrative matters in ancient Egypt was the Grand Vizier. It is not impossible that Joseph is given that position, but there are other posts that could make the claim of being second-in-command in the area of their responsibility. This is similar to a company today that has a president/CEO and a staff of vice presidents. Each of these individuals can legitimately claim to be second-in-command in his or her particular area.

Joseph in Charge of Egypt

41So Pharaoh said to Joseph, "I hereby
put you in charge of the whole land of
Egypt."[g] 42Then Pharaoh took his signet
ring[h] from his finger and put it on Joseph's finger. He dressed him in robes of
fine linen and put a gold chain around
his neck.[i] 43He had him ride in a chariot
as his second-in-command,[a] and people
shouted before him, "Make way[b]!"[j] Thus
he put him in charge of the whole land
of Egypt.

44Then Pharaoh said to Joseph, "I am
Pharaoh, but without your word no one
will lift hand or foot in all Egypt."[k] 45Phar-
aoh gave Joseph the name Zaphenath-
Paneah and gave him Asenath daughter
of Potiphera, priest of On,[c] to be his wife.[l]
And Joseph went throughout the land
of Egypt.

46Joseph was thirty years old[m] when he
entered the service[n] of Pharaoh king of
Egypt. And Joseph went out from Pharaoh's presence and traveled throughout Egypt. 47During the seven years of
abundance the land produced plentifully.
48Joseph collected all the food produced
in those seven years of abundance in
Egypt and stored it in the cities. In each
city he put the food grown in the fields
surrounding it. 49Joseph stored up huge
quantities of grain, like the sand of the
sea; it was so much that he stopped
keeping records because it was beyond
measure.

50Before the years of famine came, two
sons were born to Joseph by Asenath
daughter of Potiphera, priest of On.[o] 51Jo-
seph named his firstborn[p] Manasseh[d]
and said, "It is because God has made me
forget all my trouble and all my father's
household." 52The second son he named
Ephraim[e][q] and said, "It is because God
has made me fruitful[r] in the land of my
suffering."

53The seven years of abundance in
Egypt came to an end, 54and the seven
years of famine began,[s] just as Joseph
had said. There was famine in all the other lands, but in the whole land of Egypt
there was food. 55When all Egypt began
to feel the famine,[t] the people cried to
Pharaoh for food. Then Pharaoh told all
the Egyptians, "Go to Joseph and do what
he tells you."[u]

56When the famine had spread over
the whole country, Joseph opened all
the storehouses and sold grain to the
Egyptians, for the famine[v] was severe
throughout Egypt. 57And all the world
came to Egypt to buy grain from Joseph,[w] because the famine was severe
everywhere.

Joseph's Brothers Go to Egypt

42 When Jacob learned that there was
grain in Egypt,[x] he said to his sons,
"Why do you just keep looking at each
other?" 2He continued, "I have heard that
there is grain in Egypt. Go down there
and buy some for us, so that we may live
and not die."[y]

3Then ten of Joseph's brothers went
down to buy grain from Egypt. 4But
Jacob did not send Benjamin, Joseph's
brother, with the others, because he was
afraid that harm might come to him.[z]
5So Israel's sons were among those who
went to buy grain,[a] for there was famine
in the land of Canaan also.[b]

6Now Joseph was the governor of the
land,[c] the person who sold grain to all
its people. So when Joseph's brothers
arrived, they bowed down to him with

41:41 [g] Ge 42:6; Da 6:3
41:42 [h] Est 3:10 [i] Da 5:7,16,29
41:43 [j] Est 6:9
41:44 [k] Ps 105:22
41:45 [l] ver 50; Ge 46:20,27
41:46 [m] Ge 37:2 [n] 1Sa 16:21; Da 1:19
41:50 [o] Ge 46:20; 48:5
41:51 [p] Ge 48:14,18,20
41:52 [q] Ge 48:1,5; 50:23 [r] Ge 17:6; 28:3; 49:22
41:54 [s] ver 30; Ps 105:11; Ac 7:11
41:55 [t] Dt 32:24 [u] ver 41
41:56 [v] Ge 12:10
41:57 [w] Ge 42:5; 47:15
42:1 [x] Ac 7:12
42:2 [y] Ge 43:8
42:4 [z] ver 38
42:5 [a] Ge 41:57 [b] Ge 12:10; Ac 7:11
42:6 [c] Ge 41:41

[a] 43 Or *in the chariot of his second-in-command;* or *in his second chariot* [b] 43 Or *Bow down* [c] 45 That is, Heliopolis; also in verse 50 [d] 51 *Manasseh* sounds like and may be derived from the Hebrew for *forget.* [e] 52 *Ephraim* sounds like the Hebrew for *twice fruitful.*

41:44–45 The meaning of Joseph's Egyptian name is uncertain but may be "the God has spoken and he will live" or "the one who knows." An example of renaming a Semite official elevated to high office with an Egyptian name is also found in the reign of Pharaoh Merneptah (1224–1208 BC). The marriage arranged for Joseph places him within the circle of one of the most powerful priestly families in Egypt.

41:46–57 The last section of Ge 41 confirms that everything works out exactly as Joseph has said and that his policies are successful in dealing with the crisis. In this passage we discover that the famine not only affects Egypt but all the countries nearby as well. Thus, the covenant blessing echoes through the passage with all the nations of the earth being blessed by Abraham's family, now represented in Joseph, ruler in Egypt.

42:1–5 The impact of Joseph's disappearance remains evident in Jacob's protectiveness of Benjamin (v. 4).

42:6–13 The text moves in a rapid manner to the initial meeting between Joseph and his brothers. Again, a masquerade figures in the plot (v. 7). There is also reversal as Joseph treats his brothers harshly. Joseph accuses them of being spies; the situation

their faces to the ground.[d] 7As soon as
Joseph saw his brothers, he recognized
them, but he pretended to be a stranger
and spoke harshly to them.[e] "Where do
you come from?" he asked.
"From the land of Canaan," they replied, "to buy food."
8Although Joseph recognized his
brothers, they did not recognize him.[f]
9Then he remembered his dreams[g] about
them and said to them, "You are spies!
You have come to see where our land is
unprotected."
10"No, my lord," they answered. "Your
servants have come to buy food. 11We are
all the sons of one man. Your servants
are honest men, not spies."
12"No!" he said to them. "You have
come to see where our land is unprotected."
13But they replied, "Your servants
were twelve brothers, the sons of one
man, who lives in the land of Canaan.
The youngest is now with our father, and
one is no more."[h]
14Joseph said to them, "It is just as I
told you: You are spies! 15And this is how
you will be tested: As surely as Pharaoh
lives,[i] you will not leave this place unless your youngest brother comes here.
16Send one of your number to get your
brother; the rest of you will be kept in
prison, so that your words may be tested
to see if you are telling the truth.[j] If you
are not, then as surely as Pharaoh lives,
you are spies!" 17And he put them all in
custody[k] for three days.
18On the third day, Joseph said to
them, "Do this and you will live, for I
fear God:[l] 19If you are honest men, let

42:6 [d] Ge 37:7-10
42:7 [e] ver 30
42:8 [f] Ge 37:2
42:9 [g] Ge 37:7
42:13 [h] Ge 37:30,33; 44:20
42:15 [i] 1Sa 17:55
42:16 [j] ver 11
42:17 [k] Ge 40:4
42:18 [l] Ge 20:11; Lev 25:43
42:20 [m] ver 15, 34; Ge 43:5; 44:23
42:21 [n] Ge 37:26-28 [o] Hos 5:15
42:22 [p] Ge 37:21-22 [q] Ge 9:5 [r] 1Ki 2:32; 2Ch 24:22; Ps 9:12
42:24 [s] ver 13; Ge 43:14,23; 45:14-15
42:25 [t] Ge 43:2 [u] Ge 44:1,8 [v] Ro 12:17,20-21

Ge 42:8-9 ❖ Why did Joseph treat his brothers so severely? Imagine what their experience was like, then think about it from Joseph's perspective. What insights come to mind?

one of your brothers stay here in prison,
while the rest of you go and take grain
back for your starving households. 20But
you must bring your youngest brother
to me,[m] so that your words may be verified and that you may not die." This they
proceeded to do.
21They said to one another, "Surely
we are being punished because of our
brother.[n] We saw how distressed he was
when he pleaded with us for his life, but
we would not listen; that's why this distress[o] has come on us."
22Reuben replied, "Didn't I tell you not
to sin against the boy?[p] But you wouldn't
listen! Now we must give an accounting[q]
for his blood."[r] 23They did not realize that
Joseph could understand them, since he
was using an interpreter.
24He turned away from them and began to weep, but then came back and
spoke to them again. He had Simeon tak-
en from them and bound before their
eyes.[s]
25Joseph gave orders to fill their bags
with grain,[t] to put each man's silver back
in his sack,[u] and to give them provisions
for their journey.[v] After this was done for
them, 26they loaded their grain on their
donkeys and left.
27At the place where they stopped for
the night one of them opened his sack
to get feed for his donkey, and he saw his

---

is heavy with irony and becomes almost laughable as the brothers protest their honesty (v. 11), though it takes on a sad tone as they remark about their brother who "is no more" (v. 13).

42:14–20 As Joseph's plan unfolds, he is indeed testing his brothers as he says (v. 15), but not concerning whether they are spies. The purpose of Joseph's test is to determine whether his brothers have reformed.

42:21–23 Here we discover that in the thirteen intervening years the guilt experienced by Joseph's brothers has imprisoned them no less than Joseph's chains had done to him. They clearly recognize their guilt and acknowledge that punishment is therefore due. They confess to hard-heartedness (v. 21) and bloodguilt (v. 22). Though their confessions bring an emotional response from Joseph, he is determined to see the test through to the end to test the spirit of his brothers' remorse.

42:24 Putting his brothers in prison continues the line of reversal, but the test has two important elements in it that go well beyond revenge. (1) By keeping Simeon (v. 24) he gives them the chance to abandon one of their brothers to prison and slavery as they previously did to him. The test will be most effective if there is no strong motivation to bring the brothers back except their own sense of mercy (if they have found any). (2) Joseph needs to also have Benjamin there for the test he has in mind to discover whether his full brother is being treated in the same way he was.

42:27–36 When the brothers discover they still have their silver, they continue to attribute their misfortune to punishment from the hand of God (v. 28). Jacob is less specific as he laments, "Everything is against me!" (42:36). Being unaware of the sins of his sons, he has no point of connection to make between crime and punishment.

silver in the mouth of his sack.[w] 28“My silver has been returned,” he said to his brothers. “Here it is in my sack.”

Their hearts sank and they turned to each other trembling and said, “What is this that God has done to us?”[x]

29When they came to their father Jacob in the land of Canaan, they told him all that had happened to them. They said, 30“The man who is lord over the land spoke harshly to us[y] and treated us as though we were spying on the land. 31But we said to him, ‘We are honest men; we are not spies.[z] 32We were twelve brothers, sons of one father. One is no more, and the youngest is now with our father in Canaan.’

33“Then the man who is lord over the land said to us, ‘This is how I will know whether you are honest men: Leave one of your brothers here with me, and take food for your starving households and go.[a] 34But bring your youngest brother to me so I will know that you are not spies but honest men. Then I will give your brother back to you, and you can trade[a] in the land.[b]’ ”

35As they were emptying their sacks, there in each man’s sack was his pouch of silver! When they and their father saw the money pouches, they were frightened.[c] 36Their father Jacob said to them, “You have deprived me of my children. Joseph is no more and Simeon is no more, and now you want to take Benjamin.[d] Everything is against me!”

37Then Reuben said to his father, “You may put both of my sons to death if I do not bring him back to you. Entrust him to my care, and I will bring him back.”

38But Jacob said, “My son will not go down there with you; his brother is dead[e] and he is the only one left. If harm comes to him[f] on the journey you are taking, you will bring my gray head down to the grave[g] in sorrow.[h]”

The Second Journey to Egypt

43 Now the famine was still severe in the land.[i] 2So when they had eaten all the grain they had brought from Egypt, their father said to them, “Go back and buy us a little more food.”

3But Judah said to him, “The man warned us solemnly, ‘You will not see my face again unless your brother is with you.’[j] 4If you will send our brother along with us, we will go down and buy food for you. 5But if you will not send him, we will not go down, because the man said to us, ‘You will not see my face again unless your brother is with you.[k]’ ”

6Israel asked, “Why did you bring this trouble on me by telling the man you had another brother?”

7They replied, “The man questioned us closely about ourselves and our family. ‘Is your father still living?’[l] he asked us. ‘Do you have another brother?’[m] We simply answered his questions. How were we to know he would say, ‘Bring your brother down here’?”

8Then Judah said to Israel his father, “Send the boy along with me and we will go at once, so that we and you and our children may live and not die.[n] 9I myself will guarantee his safety; you can hold me personally responsible for him. If I do not bring him back to you and set him here before you, I will bear the blame before you all my life.[o] 10As it is, if we had not delayed, we could have gone and returned twice.”

11Then their father Israel said to them, “If it must be, then do this: Put some of the best products of the land in your bags and take them down to the man as a gift[p] — a little balm[q] and a little honey, some spices[r] and myrrh, some pistachio nuts and almonds. 12Take double the amount of silver with you, for you must return the silver that was put back into the mouths of your sacks.[s] Perhaps it was a mistake. 13Take your brother also and go back to the man at once. 14And may God Almighty[b][t] grant you mercy before the man so that he will let your other brother and Benjamin come back

a 34 Or *move about freely* *b* 14 Hebrew *El-Shaddai*

42:27 w Ge 43:21-22
42:28 x Ge 43:23
42:30 y ver 7
42:31 z ver 11
42:33 a ver 19, 20
42:34 b Ge 34:10
42:35 c Ge 43:12, 15,18
42:36 d Ge 43:14
42:38 e Ge 37:33 f ver 4 g Ge 37:35 h Ge 44:29,34
43:1 i Ge 12:10; 41:56-57
43:3 j Ge 42:15; 44:23
43:5 k Ge 42:15; 2Sa 3:13
43:7 l ver 27 m Ge 42:13
43:8 n Ge 42:2; Ps 33:18-19
43:9 o Ge 42:37; 44:32; Phm 18-19
43:11 p Ge 32:20; Pr 18:16 q Ge 37:25; Jer 8:22 r 1Ki 10:2
43:12 s Ge 42:25
43:14 t Ge 17:1; 28:3; 35:11

42:37–38 Reuben and Judah continue to be the only active brothers in the drama. In each case Reuben’s efforts are ineffective while Judah’s, for good or ill, accomplish their goal. The audience of Genesis in this way sees Judah’s tribal leadership begin to emerge.

43:1–34 Just as Rebekah told Jacob that she would bear the brunt of Isaac’s curse (27:13), now Judah asserts that he will bear the blame if Benjamin does not return. With no alternatives, Jacob sends Benjamin with them again, having taken every precaution (43:11–12; cf. 32:13–21), praying for God’s mercy (43:14; cf. 32:9–12), and then fatalistically settling down to await the outcome (43:14; cf. 32:7–8, 22).

PEOPLE TO KNOW // JUDAH

GENESIS 43:8–9: Judah was Jacob's fourth son. He led his brothers in selling his brother Joseph, whom they all despised, into slavery (Ge 37:26–27). The brothers then deceived their father Jacob into believing Joseph had been killed by a wild animal by showing him Joseph's robe dipped in animal blood.

Judah's dishonorable actions with his daughter-in-law Tamar did not keep him from being in the line of Jesus. He had failed to care for Tamar after her husband died, not once but twice. Tamar disguised herself as a prostitute and slept with Judah. When Judah learned that Tamar was pregnant, he demanded her death. Then she revealed to him that he was the father of her twins. Realizing he had wronged her, he confessed, "She is more righteous than I" (Ge 38:26).

When famine struck Jacob's family, he sent his sons (except for Benjamin) to get food in Egypt. Joseph himself was the Egyptian official in charge of food distribution, but his brothers did not recognize him. Joseph had his brother Simeon imprisoned and sent the rest home with food, telling them not to return without Benjamin.

The food from Egypt eventually ran out, but Jacob resisted sending his sons with Benjamin to get more—after all, they had now twice returned home one brother short. Finally, Judah promised Jacob that he himself would be held responsible for Benjamin's life (Ge 43:8–9), a promise he reiterated later (Ge 44:33). Moved to weeping, Joseph finally revealed his identity to his brothers, and they were reunited fully.

Judah's willingness to sacrifice himself restored the family. Many generations later, a descendent of Judah willingly sacrificed himself in order to restore sinful humanity to the family of God: Jesus Christ.

APPLICATION Judah learned to say the words "I was wrong." He learned that in how he treated his brothers; he learned it when he found out that Tamar was pregnant; he learned it when he had to tell his aged father the news that another of his sons was lost to him. Judah allowed these realizations to transform him. The same person who sold a brother into slavery later laid down his life for a brother. How did he do this? With humility, he allowed the Lord to work in his heart and bring about repentance, leading him to become a changed man. Judah's life shows that God is all about transformation. Despite Judah's failures, his family line was honored above all the others when David, and then Jesus, descended from it (Mt 1:1–3).

with you.[u] As for me, if I am bereaved, I
am bereaved."[v]
15So the men took the gifts and double the amount of silver, and Benjamin
also. They hurried[w] down to Egypt and
presented themselves[x] to Joseph. 16When
Joseph saw Benjamin with them, he said
to the steward of his house,[y] "Take these
men to my house, slaughter an animal
and prepare a meal;[z] they are to eat with
me at noon."
17The man did as Joseph told him and
took the men to Joseph's house. 18Now
the men were frightened[a] when they
were taken to his house. They thought,
"We were brought here because of the
silver that was put back into our sacks
the first time. He wants to attack us and
overpower us and seize us as slaves and
take our donkeys."
19So they went up to Joseph's steward and spoke to him at the entrance to
the house. 20"We beg your pardon, our
lord," they said, "we came down here
the first time to buy food.[b] 21But at the
place where we stopped for the night we
opened our sacks and each of us found
his silver — the exact weight — in the
mouth of his sack. So we have brought
it back with us.[c] 22We have also brought
additional silver with us to buy food.
We don't know who put our silver in
our sacks."
23"It's all right," he said. "Don't be
afraid. Your God, the God of your father,
has given you treasure in your sacks;[d] I

43:14 [u] Ge 42:24 [v] Est 4:16
43:15 [w] Ge 45:9, 13 [x] Ge 47:2,7
43:16 [y] Ge 44:1, 4,12 [z] ver 31; Lk 15:23
43:18 [a] Ge 42:35
43:20 [b] Ge 42:3
43:21 [c] ver 15; Ge 42:27,35
43:23 [d] Ge 42:28

43:17–28 The first shock comes when they are invited guests at a feast in the home of this important man. They can only imagine the worst of intentions (v. 18). The reply to their hurried explanations about the silver is met with a second shocking occurrence as the steward interprets their good fortune theologically: "Your God, the God of your father, has given you treasure in your sacks" (v. 23). This cryptic statement is exactly the opposite of their own interpretation—that God was punishing them (v. 28).

received your silver." Then he brought Simeon out to them.[e]

24The steward took the men into Joseph's house,[f] gave them water to wash their feet[g] and provided fodder for their donkeys. 25They prepared their gifts for Joseph's arrival at noon, because they had heard that they were to eat there.

26When Joseph came home, they presented to him the gifts[h] they had brought into the house, and they bowed down before him to the ground.[i] 27He asked them how they were, and then he said, "How is your aged father you told me about? Is he still living?"[j]

28They replied, "Your servant our father is still alive and well." And they bowed down, prostrating themselves before him.[k]

29As he looked about and saw his brother Benjamin, his own mother's son, he asked, "Is this your youngest brother, the one you told me about?"[l] And he said, "God be gracious to you,[m] my son." 30Deeply moved[n] at the sight of his brother, Joseph hurried out and looked for a place to weep. He went into his private room and wept[o] there.

31After he had washed his face, he came out and, controlling himself,[p] said, "Serve the food."

32They served him by himself, the brothers by themselves, and the Egyptians who ate with him by themselves, because Egyptians could not eat with Hebrews,[q] for that is detestable to Egyptians.[r] 33The men had been seated before him in the order of their ages, from the firstborn to the youngest; and they looked at each other in astonishment. 34When portions were served to them from Joseph's table, Benjamin's portion was five times as much as anyone else's.[s] So they feasted and drank freely with him.

43:23 [e] Ge 42:24
43:24 [f] ver 16 [g] Ge 18:4; 24:32
43:26 [h] Mt 2:11 [i] Ge 37:7,10
43:27 [j] ver 7
43:28 [k] Ge 37:7
43:29 [l] Ge 42:13 [m] Nu 6:25; Ps 67:1
43:30 [n] Jn 11:33, 38 [o] Ge 42:24; 45:2,14,15; 46:29
43:31 [p] Ge 45:1
43:32 [q] Gal 2:12 [r] Ge 46:34; Ex 8:26
43:34 [s] Ge 37:3; 45:22

Ge 43:30 ❖ Should Joseph have revealed his true identity earlier than he did? Why or why not? What good and bad things happened because he didn't reveal who he was?

A Silver Cup in a Sack

44 Now Joseph gave these instructions to the steward of his house: "Fill the men's sacks with as much food as they can carry, and put each man's silver in the mouth of his sack.[t] 2Then put my cup, the silver one, in the mouth of the youngest one's sack, along with the silver for his grain." And he did as Joseph said.

3As morning dawned, the men were sent on their way with their donkeys. 4They had not gone far from the city when Joseph said to his steward, "Go after those men at once, and when you catch up with them, say to them, 'Why have you repaid good with evil?[u] 5Isn't this the cup my master drinks from and also uses for divination?[v] This is a wicked thing you have done.'"

6When he caught up with them, he repeated these words to them. 7But they said to him, "Why does my lord say such things? Far be it from your servants to do anything like that! 8We even brought back to you from the land of Canaan the silver we found inside the mouths of our sacks.[w] So why would we steal silver or gold from your master's house? 9If any of your servants is found to have it, he will die;[x] and the rest of us will become my lord's slaves."

10"Very well, then," he said, "let it be as you say. Whoever is found to have it will become my slave; the rest of you will be free from blame."

11Each of them quickly lowered his sack to the ground and opened it. 12Then the steward proceeded to search,

44:1 [t] Ge 42:25
44:4 [u] Ps 35:12
44:5 [v] Ge 30:27; Dt 18:10-14
44:8 [w] Ge 42:25; 43:21
44:9 [x] Ge 31:32

43:29–34 In Joseph's home the care for their needs is meticulous. The special treatment of Benjamin is important, for it repeats the special treatment Joseph himself had received in the special coat that had stimulated the jealousy of his brothers. As in his own case, the brothers' needs are well cared for, but one is singled out for preferential treatment. Will they respond with jealousy toward Benjamin just as they had toward him?

44:1–5 The test of the silver cup is designed to see if the brothers are still inclined to abandon one of Rachel's sons who receives preferential treatment.

44:6–9 When Joseph's servant catches up to the brothers and sets forth the accusation, they are so sure of their innocence that they invoke the death penalty on anyone who is found with the treasured cup. The finding of the silver cup offers yet another example of the steward's comment of the day before that God put treasure in their sacks.

44:10–13 The grief of the brothers upon the discovery of the cup in Benjamin's sack gives an early indication that they are indeed changed men. But the charade must be played out to the very last scene, and they all shuffle back to Egypt.

beginning with the oldest and ending with the youngest. And the cup was found in Benjamin's sack.[y] 13At this, they tore their clothes.[z] Then they all loaded their donkeys and returned to the city.

14Joseph was still in the house when Judah and his brothers came in, and they threw themselves to the ground before him.[a] 15Joseph said to them, "What is this you have done? Don't you know that a man like me can find things out by divination?[b]"

16"What can we say to my lord?" Judah replied. "What can we say? How can we prove our innocence? God has uncovered your servants' guilt. We are now my lord's slaves[c] — we ourselves and the one who was found to have the cup.[d]"

17But Joseph said, "Far be it from me to do such a thing! Only the man who was found to have the cup will become my slave. The rest of you, go back to your father in peace."

18Then Judah went up to him and said: "Pardon your servant, my lord, let me speak a word to my lord. Do not be angry[e] with your servant, though you are equal to Pharaoh himself. 19My lord asked his servants, 'Do you have a father or a brother?'[f] 20And we answered, 'We have an aged father, and there is a young son born to him in his old age.[g] His brother is dead,[h] and he is the only one of his mother's sons left, and his father loves him.'[i]

21"Then you said to your servants, 'Bring him down to me so I can see him for myself.'[j] 22And we said to my lord, 'The boy cannot leave his father; if he leaves him, his father will die.'[k] 23But you told your servants, 'Unless your youngest brother comes down with you, you will not see my face again.'[l] 24When we went back to your servant my father, we told him what my lord had said.

25"Then our father said, 'Go back and buy a little more food.'[m] 26But we said, 'We cannot go down. Only if our youngest brother is with us will we go. We cannot see the man's face unless our youngest brother is with us.'

27"Your servant my father said to us, 'You know that my wife bore me two sons.[n] 28One of them went away from me, and I said, "He has surely been torn to pieces."[o] And I have not seen him since. 29If you take this one from me too and harm comes to him, you will bring my gray head down to the grave in misery.'[p]

30"So now, if the boy is not with us when I go back to your servant my father, and if my father, whose life is closely bound up with the boy's life,[q] 31sees that the boy isn't there, he will die. Your servants will bring the gray head of our father down to the grave in sorrow. 32Your servant guaranteed the boy's safety to my father. I said, 'If I do not bring him back to you, I will bear the blame before you, my father, all my life!'[r]

33"Now then, please let your servant remain here as my lord's slave[s] in place of the boy,[t] and let the boy return with his brothers. 34How can I go back to my father if the boy is not with me? No! Do not let me see the misery that would come on my father."[u]

44:12 [y] ver 2
44:13 [z] Ge 37:29; Nu 14:6; 2Sa 1:11
44:14 [a] Ge 37:7, 10
44:15 [b] ver 5; Ge 30:27
44:16 [c] ver 9; Ge 43:18 [d] ver 2
44:18 [e] Ge 18:30; Ex 32:22
44:19 [f] Ge 43:7
44:20 [g] Ge 37:3 [h] Ge 37:33 [i] Ge 42:13
44:21 [j] Ge 42:15
44:22 [k] Ge 37:35
44:23 [l] Ge 43:5
44:25 [m] Ge 43:2
44:27 [n] Ge 46:19
44:28 [o] Ge 37:33
44:29 [p] Ge 42:38
44:30 [q] 1Sa 18:1
44:32 [r] Ge 43:9
44:33 [s] Ge 43:18 [t] Jn 15:13
44:34 [u] Est 8:6

Ge 44:33-34 ❖ Judah put himself on the line for his brother. What testimony do we show the world when we sacrifice for others?

44:14-15 Joseph's statement when they are again before him is another of the cryptic statements woven through the narrative: "Don't you know that a man like me can find things out by divination?" (v. 15). Divination in Egypt was generally only accessible to people of high status.

But it is possible that Joseph insinuates more than this. Joseph has begun to see God's plan. In the larger scheme of things, his early dreams had indicated the destiny that he has now fulfilled, and he is beginning to understand what God is doing through him.

44:16-17 The scene rushes to its conclusion. The brothers admit their communal guilt and desire to establish their innocence. He gives them one last chance to repeat their crime as he sets the opportunity for them to escape at Benjamin's expense (v. 17). This is the pivot point of this section of the Joseph narrative.

44:18-34 Judah's speech reveals important information that is critical to Joseph's test. It becomes clear that the brothers have a new sensitivity to their father's feelings. Judah even subtly tries to make Joseph feel guilty about the part he will have in Jacob's death from grief (v. 31).

Moreover, Joseph discovers what Jacob has believed about his fate all these years (v. 28). He thus is made aware that his father actually believes him to be dead. Most important, it becomes clear that Judah has become noble. He would rather bear slavery than blame. This transformation of the brothers represented in Judah is every bit as miraculous as the transformation in the status of Joseph.

Joseph Makes Himself Known

45 Then Joseph could no longer control himself[v] before all his attendants, and he cried out, "Have everyone leave my presence!" So there was no
one with Joseph when he made himself
known to his brothers. 2And he wept[w]
so loudly that the Egyptians heard him,
and Pharaoh's household heard about it.[x]
3Joseph said to his brothers, "I am Joseph! Is my father still living?"[y] But his
brothers were not able to answer him,[z]
because they were terrified at his presence.
4Then Joseph said to his brothers,
"Come close to me." When they had done
so, he said, "I am your brother Joseph,
the one you sold into Egypt![a] 5And now,
do not be distressed[b] and do not be angry with yourselves for selling me here,[c]
because it was to save lives that God sent
me ahead of you.[d] 6For two years now
there has been famine in the land, and
for the next five years there will be no
plowing and reaping. 7But God sent me
ahead of you to preserve for you a remnant[e] on earth and to save your lives by
a great deliverance.[a][f]
8"So then, it was not you who sent me
here, but God. He made me father[g] to
Pharaoh, lord of his entire household
and ruler of all Egypt.[h] 9Now hurry back
to my father and say to him, 'This is what
your son Joseph says: God has made me
lord of all Egypt. Come down to me; don't
delay.[i] 10You shall live in the region of
Goshen[j] and be near me—you, your children and grandchildren, your flocks and
herds, and all you have. 11I will provide
for you there,[k] because five years of famine are still to come. Otherwise you and
your household and all who belong to
you will become destitute.'
12"You can see for yourselves, and so
can my brother Benjamin, that it is really
I who am speaking to you. 13Tell my father
about all the honor accorded me in Egypt
and about everything you have seen. And
bring my father down here quickly.[l]"
14Then he threw his arms around his
brother Benjamin and wept, and Benjamin embraced him, weeping. 15And he
kissed[m] all his brothers and wept over
them. Afterward his brothers talked with
him.[n]
16When the news reached Phar-
aoh's palace that Joseph's brothers had
come,[o] Pharaoh and all his officials were
pleased. 17Pharaoh said to Joseph, "Tell
your brothers, 'Do this: Load your animals and return to the land of Canaan,
18and bring your father and your families
back to me. I will give you the best of the
land of Egypt[p] and you can enjoy the fat
of the land.'[q]
19"You are also directed to tell them,
'Do this: Take some carts[r] from Egypt
for your children and your wives, and
get your father and come. 20Never mind
about your belongings, because the best
of all Egypt will be yours.'"
21So the sons of Israel did this. Joseph
gave them carts, as Pharaoh had commanded, and he also gave them provisions for their journey.[s] 22To each of them

45:1 [v]Ge 43:31
45:2 [w]Ge 29:11 [x]ver 16; Ge 46:29
45:3 [y]Ac 7:13 [z]ver 15
45:4 [a]Ge 37:28
45:5 [b]Ge 42:21 [c]Ge 42:22 [d]ver 7-8; Ge 50:20; Ps 105:17
45:7 [e]2Ki 19:4, 30, 31; Isa 10:20, 21; Mic 4:7; Zep 2:7 [f]Ex 15:2; Est 4:14; Isa 25:9
45:8 [g]Jdg 17:10 [h]Ge 41:41
45:9 [i]Ge 43:10
45:10 [j]Ge 46:28, 34; 47:1
45:11 [k]Ge 47:12
45:13 [l]Ac 7:14
45:15 [m]Lk 15:20 [n]ver 3
45:16 [o]Ac 7:13
45:18 [p]Ge 27:28; 46:34; 47:6, 11, 27; Nu 18:12, 29 [q]Ps 37:19
45:19 [r]Ge 46:5
45:21 [s]Ge 42:25

Ge 45:15 ❖ God gave his people a ministry of reconciliation (see 2Co 5:18). How can we be agents of reconciliation for God?

[a] 7 Or *save you as a great band of survivors*

45:1-3 When Joseph finally is convinced of the transformation that has taken place in his brothers, he reveals himself to them. The first statement he makes, "I am Joseph," is logical enough, but the next one seems odd: "Is my father still living?" (v. 3). The brothers have been speaking all along of the actions and statements of Jacob. It is likely that the Hebrew for "living" is the equivalent of our question, "Is my father well?" Up until now the communications have been given to him as an outsider. He wants more intimate and detailed news of his father.

45:4-8 Meanwhile, the brothers are understandably stunned into speechlessness. As they cower in fear and shock, Joseph seeks to calm their fears by voicing the theology that is the centerpiece of the Joseph story: God has sovereignly directed the sequence of events in order to accomplish his purposes. It serves as a transition to the third segment of the story, which involves the resettlement of the covenant family in the land of Egypt.

45:9-28 The first suggestion of this plan comes from Joseph in vv. 9-11. The argument to support this major departure from patriarchal policy is, first of all, that God has clearly sanctioned Joseph's leadership and judgment. Next is the fact that their very existence requires this move to be made. Joseph's suggestion is reiterated in a generous offering from Pharaoh to provide the best for them while they are in Egypt—another sign of God's blessing. This will incidentally give the Israelites of the exodus generation a far more complimentary picture of Pharaoh than they have seen in their lifetimes.

he gave new clothing, but to Benjamin he
gave three hundred shekels[a] of silver and
five sets of clothes.[t] 23And this is what he
sent to his father: ten donkeys loaded
with the best things of Egypt, and ten
female donkeys loaded with grain and
bread and other provisions for his journey. 24Then he sent his brothers away,
and as they were leaving he said to them,
"Don't quarrel on the way!"[u]
25So they went up out of Egypt and
came to their father Jacob in the land
of Canaan. 26They told him, "Joseph is
still alive! In fact, he is ruler of all Egypt."
Jacob was stunned; he did not believe
them.[v] 27But when they told him everything Joseph had said to them, and when
he saw the carts[w] Joseph had sent to carry him back, the spirit of their father
Jacob revived. 28And Israel said, "I'm
convinced! My son Joseph is still alive. I
will go and see him before I die."

Jacob Goes to Egypt

46 So Israel set out with all that was
his, and when he reached Beersheba,[x] he offered sacrifices to the God
of his father Isaac.[y]
2And God spoke to Israel in a vision at
night[z] and said, "Jacob! Jacob!"
"Here I am,"[a] he replied.
3"I am God, the God of your father,"[b]
he said. "Do not be afraid to go down to
Egypt, for I will make you into a great
nation[c] there.[d] 4I will go down to Egypt
with you, and I will surely bring you back
again.[e] And Joseph's own hand will close
your eyes.[f]"
5Then Jacob left Beersheba, and Israel's
sons took their father Jacob and their
children and their wives in the carts[g] that
Pharaoh had sent to transport him. 6So
Jacob and all his offspring went to Egypt,[h]
taking with them their livestock and the
possessions they had acquired in Canaan.
7Jacob brought with him to Egypt his

45:22 [t] Ge 37:3; 43:34
45:24 [u] Ge 42:21-22
45:26 [v] Ge 44:28
45:27 [w] ver 19
46:1 [x] Ge 21:14; 28:10 [y] Ge 26:24; 28:13; 31:42
46:2 [z] Ge 15:1; Job 33:14-15 [a] Ge 22:1; 31:11
46:3 [b] Ge 28:13 [c] Ge 12:2; Dt 26:5 [d] Ex 1:7
46:4 [e] Ge 28:15; 48:21; Ex 3:8 [f] Ge 50:1,24
46:5 [g] Ge 45:19
46:6 [h] Dt 26:5; Jos 24:4; Ps 105:23; Isa 52:4; Ac 7:15
46:7 [i] Ge 45:10
46:8 [j] Ex 1:1; Nu 26:4
46:9 [k] 1Ch 5:3
46:10 [l] Ge 29:33; Nu 26:14 [m] Ex 6:15
46:11 [n] Ge 29:34; Nu 3:17
46:12 [o] Ge 29:35 [p] 1Ch 2:5; Mt 1:3
46:13 [q] Ge 30:18 [r] 1Ch 7:1
46:14 [s] Ge 30:20
46:16 [t] Ge 30:11 [u] Nu 26:15

> **Ge 46:3** ❖ How has God assured us of his love during seasons of change?

sons and grandsons and his daughters
and granddaughters — all his offspring.[i]
8These are the names of the sons of
Israel[j] (Jacob and his descendants) who
went to Egypt:

Reuben the firstborn of Jacob.
9The sons of Reuben:[k]
Hanok, Pallu, Hezron and Karmi.
10The sons of Simeon:[l]
Jemuel,[m] Jamin, Ohad, Jakin,
Zohar and Shaul the son of a Canaanite woman.
11The sons of Levi:[n]
Gershon, Kohath and Merari.
12The sons of Judah:[o]
Er, Onan, Shelah, Perez and Zerah
(but Er and Onan had died in the
land of Canaan).
The sons of Perez:[p]
Hezron and Hamul.
13The sons of Issachar:[q]
Tola, Puah,[b][r] Jashub[c] and Shimron.
14The sons of Zebulun:[s]
Sered, Elon and Jahleel.
15These were the sons Leah bore to Jacob in Paddan Aram,[d] besides his daughter Dinah. These sons and daughters of
his were thirty-three in all.
16The sons of Gad:[t]
Zephon,[e][u] Haggi, Shuni, Ezbon,
Eri, Arodi and Areli.

[a] *22* That is, about 7 1/2 pounds or about 3.5 kilograms [b] *13* Samaritan Pentateuch and Syriac (see also 1 Chron. 7:1); Masoretic Text *Puvah* [c] *13* Samaritan Pentateuch and some Septuagint manuscripts (see also Num. 26:24 and 1 Chron. 7:1); Masoretic Text *Iob* [d] *15* That is, Northwest Mesopotamia [e] *16* Samaritan Pentateuch and Septuagint (see also Num. 26:15); Masoretic Text *Ziphion*

46:1–4 Jacob's movements in and out of the land have been marked by angels and theophanies. Thus, it is no surprise that his preparation to leave the land and settle in Egypt is marked by a vision. This theophany is briefer and makes only passing reference to the two covenant benefits.

46:5–7 Jacob and his family ignore Pharaoh's advice to leave their belongings behind (45:20) as they pack everything up for the journey (46:6). The text makes a point of saying that all Jacob's offspring go to Egypt (vv. 6–7) to make it clear that no part of the family is left behind to hold the fort and preserve the family holdings while the main part leaves. In that sense this is a complete act of faith.

46:8–27 It may be best to consider the list in ch. 46 as a document listing those who are considered charter members of the Goshen settlement rather than something like a flight manifest or a census document. That this is the case is indicated somewhat in the text itself as it notes that the number does not include the sons' wives (v. 26). They would have physically participated in the journey and resettlement, but their charter status is represented in their husbands.

17The sons of Asher:[v]
Imnah, Ishvah, Ishvi and Beriah.
Their sister was Serah.
The sons of Beriah:
Heber and Malkiel.
18These were the children born to Ja-
cob by Zilpah,[w] whom Laban had given
to his daughter Leah[x] — sixteen in all.

19The sons of Jacob's wife Rachel:
Joseph and Benjamin.[y] 20In Egypt,
Manasseh[z] and Ephraim[a] were
born to Joseph by Asenath daughter of Potiphera, priest of On.[a]
21The sons of Benjamin:[b]
Bela, Beker, Ashbel, Gera, Naaman,
Ehi, Rosh, Muppim, Huppim and
Ard.
22These were the sons of Rachel who
were born to Jacob — fourteen in all.

23The son of Dan:
Hushim.
24The sons of Naphtali:
Jahziel, Guni, Jezer and Shillem.
25These were the sons born to Jacob
by Bilhah,[c] whom Laban had given to his
daughter Rachel[d] — seven in all.

26All those who went to Egypt with Jacob — those who were his direct descendants, not counting his sons' wives —
numbered sixty-six persons.[e] 27With the
two sons[b] who had been born to Joseph
in Egypt, the members of Jacob's family, which went to Egypt, were seventy[c]
in all.[f]

28Now Jacob sent Judah ahead of him
to Joseph to get directions to Goshen.[g]
When they arrived in the region of Goshen, 29Joseph had his chariot made
ready and went to Goshen to meet his
father Israel. As soon as Joseph appeared
before him, he threw his arms around his
father[d] and wept for a long time.[h]
30Israel said to Joseph, "Now I am
ready to die, since I have seen for myself that you are still alive."
31Then Joseph said to his brothers and
to his father's household, "I will go up
and speak to Pharaoh and will say to him,
'My brothers and my father's household,
who were living in the land of Canaan,
have come to me.[i] 32The men are shepherds; they tend livestock, and they have
brought along their flocks and herds and
everything they own.' 33When Pharaoh
calls you in and asks, 'What is your occupation?'[j] 34you should answer, 'Your
servants have tended livestock from our
boyhood on, just as our fathers did.' Then
you will be allowed to settle in the region
of Goshen,[k] for all shepherds are detestable to the Egyptians.[l]"

47 Joseph went and told Pharaoh,
"My father and brothers, with
their flocks and herds and everything
they own, have come from the land of
Canaan and are now in Goshen."[m] 2He
chose five of his brothers and presented
them before Pharaoh.
3Pharaoh asked the brothers, "What is
your occupation?"[n]
"Your servants are shepherds," they
replied to Pharaoh, "just as our fathers
were." 4They also said to him, "We have
come to live here for a while,[o] because
the famine is severe in Canaan[p] and
your servants' flocks have no pasture.

46:17 [v] Ge 30:13; 1Ch 7:30-31
46:18 [w] Ge 30:10 [x] Ge 29:24
46:19 [y] Ge 44:27
46:20 [z] Ge 41:51 [a] Ge 41:52
46:21 [b] Nu 26:38-41; 1Ch 7:6-12; 8:1
46:25 [c] Ge 30:8 [d] Ge 29:29
46:26 [e] ver 5-7; Ex 1:5; Dt 10:22
46:27 [f] Ac 7:14
46:28 [g] Ge 45:10
46:29 [h] Ge 45:14-15; Lk 15:20
46:31 [i] Ge 47:1
46:33 [j] Ge 47:3
46:34 [k] Ge 45:10 [l] Ge 43:32; Ex 8:26
47:1 [m] Ge 46:31
47:3 [n] Ge 46:33
47:4 [o] Ge 15:13; Dt 26:5 [p] Ge 43:1

[a] *20* That is, Heliopolis [b] *27* Hebrew; Septuagint *the nine children* [c] *27* Hebrew (see also Exodus 1:5 and note); Septuagint (see also Acts 7:14) *seventy-five* [d] *29* Hebrew *around him*

46:28–30 In v. 28 the emergence of Judah takes its next step forward as he is given a role of responsibility by being sent ahead to Joseph for the family. This role is going to be finalized in the blessings of ch. 49 and, of course, is represented in the reality of the exodus generation and eventually in the kingship of the Davidic dynasty.

"Goshen" is a Semitic term most likely referring to the delta region of Lower (northern) Egypt in the area of the Wadi Tumilat. Egyptian texts from the Hyksos period (c. 1750–1550 BC) refer to Semites in this region, and it is an area that provides excellent pasturage for herds, which is what Jacob and his sons need. Joseph meets Jacob there for their emotional reunion.

46:31–34 Joseph's instructions to his brothers concerning their occupation and their subsequent conversation with Pharaoh (47:1–4) highlight the low opinion of shepherds in Egypt (46:34). "Shepherds" may be ambiguous, referring not only to a vocation that was legitimate and acceptable (since there is no indication of dishonor attached to the profession in Egypt), but also to a group of people who were already infiltrating the land and, as a group, were despised. Joseph would want to ensure that his family was classified in the former category rather than the latter.

47:1–12 The meeting with Pharaoh is successful in procuring permission for Jacob's family to settle in Goshen. But it reaches its climax in the conversation between Pharaoh and Jacob. Both at the beginning of the conversation (v. 7) and at the end (v. 10) Jacob blesses Pharaoh, adding another illustration of the covenant promise that "all peoples on earth will be blessed through you" (12:3).

So now, please let your servants settle
in Goshen."[q]
5Pharaoh said to Joseph, "Your father
and your brothers have come to you,
6and the land of Egypt is before you;
settle your father and your brothers in
the best part of the land.[r] Let them live in
Goshen. And if you know of any among
them with special ability,[s] put them in
charge of my own livestock."
7Then Joseph brought his father Jacob
in and presented him before Pharaoh.
After Jacob blessed[a] Pharaoh,[t] 8Pharaoh
asked him, "How old are you?"
9And Jacob said to Pharaoh, "The years
of my pilgrimage are a hundred and thirty.[u] My years have been few and difficult,[v]
and they do not equal the years of the
pilgrimage of my fathers.[w]" 10Then Jacob
blessed[b] Pharaoh[x] and went out from
his presence.
11So Joseph settled his father and his
brothers in Egypt and gave them property
in the best part of the land, the district of
Rameses,[y] as Pharaoh directed. 12Joseph
also provided his father and his brothers
and all his father's household with food,
according to the number of their children.[z]

Joseph and the Famine

13There was no food, however, in the
whole region because the famine was severe; both Egypt and Canaan wasted away
because of the famine.[a] 14Joseph collected
all the money that was to be found in
Egypt and Canaan in payment for the
grain they were buying, and he brought
it to Pharaoh's palace.[b] 15When the money
of the people of Egypt and Canaan was
gone, all Egypt came to Joseph and said,
"Give us food. Why should we die before
your eyes?[c] Our money is all gone."
16"Then bring your livestock," said Joseph. "I will sell you food in exchange
for your livestock, since your money is
gone." 17So they brought their livestock
to Joseph, and he gave them food in exchange for their horses,[d] their sheep and
goats, their cattle and donkeys. And he
brought them through that year with
food in exchange for all their livestock.
18When that year was over, they came to
him the following year and said, "We cannot hide from our lord the fact that since
our money is gone and our livestock belongs to you, there is nothing left for our
lord except our bodies and our land. 19Why
should we perish before your eyes—we
and our land as well? Buy us and our land
in exchange for food, and we with our land
will be in bondage to Pharaoh. Give us
seed so that we may live and not die, and
that the land may not become desolate."
20So Joseph bought all the land in
Egypt for Pharaoh. The Egyptians, one
and all, sold their fields, because the famine was too severe for them. The land
became Pharaoh's, 21and Joseph reduced
the people to servitude,[c] from one end
of Egypt to the other. 22However, he did
not buy the land of the priests, because
they received a regular allotment from
Pharaoh and had food enough from the
allotment[e] Pharaoh gave them. That is
why they did not sell their land.
23Joseph said to the people, "Now that I
have bought you and your land today for
Pharaoh, here is seed for you so you can
plant the ground. 24But when the crop
comes in, give a fifth[f] of it to Pharaoh. The

47:4 [q] Ge 46:34
47:6 [r] Ge 45:18 [s] Ex 18:21,25
47:7 [t] ver 10; 2Sa 14:22
47:9 [u] Ge 25:7 [v] Heb 11:9,13 [w] Ge 35:28
47:10 [x] ver 7
47:11 [y] Ex 1:11; 12:37
47:12 [z] Ge 45:11
47:13 [a] Ge 41:30; Ac 7:11
47:14 [b] Ge 41:56
47:15 [c] ver 19; Ex 16:3
47:17 [d] Ex 14:9
47:22 [e] Dt 14:28-29; Ezr 7:24
47:24 [f] Ge 41:34

[a] 7 Or *greeted* [b] 10 Or *said farewell to*
[c] 21 Samaritan Pentateuch and Septuagint (see also Vulgate); Masoretic Text *and he moved the people into the cities*

47:13–26 The text documents the sequence of how the people were impoverished by the famine. First, they spent all their money buying food (vv. 14–15), then they traded away their livestock (vv. 16–17), and finally, they gave up their land and worked as tenant farmers (vv. 18–20). This turned Egypt into a state in which all the wealth was centralized in the government. The priests shared in the centralization of wealth since they were subsidized by the government. This was the common practice in Egypt and led to significant wealth (and therefore political power) being attached to long-standing priestly families.

Despite the personal hardship and servitude that resulted, the people are grateful for their lives (v. 25). Once more, then, the point is made that through Joseph, the representative of Abraham's family, people are experiencing deliverance and blessing.

37:1—47:26 One cannot pretend to offer any language that resolves all the problems of reconciling God's sovereignty with the presence of evil in the world. It should be noted, however, that the Bible's own attempt to reconcile these issues is not represented by detailed and technical philosophical treatises. Instead, the important theology is clarified by illustration because, as we all know, where language may fail, illustration can succeed. The story of Joseph, therefore, can stand as a living treatise on the theology of God's sovereignty.

other four-fifths you may keep as seed for the fields and as food for yourselves and your households and your children."

25"You have saved our lives," they said. "May we find favor in the eyes of our lord;[g] we will be in bondage to Pharaoh."

26So Joseph established it as a law concerning land in Egypt — still in force today — that a fifth of the produce belongs to Pharaoh. It was only the land of the priests that did not become Pharaoh's.[h]

27Now the Israelites settled in Egypt in the region of Goshen. They acquired property there and were fruitful and increased greatly in number.[i]

28Jacob lived in Egypt[j] seventeen years, and the years of his life were a hundred and forty-seven. 29When the time drew near for Israel to die,[k] he called for his son Joseph and said to him, "If I have found favor in your eyes, put your hand under my thigh[l] and promise that you will show me kindness and faithfulness.[m] Do not bury me in Egypt, 30but when I rest with my fathers, carry me out of Egypt and bury me where they are buried."[n]

"I will do as you say," he said.

31"Swear to me,"[o] he said. Then Joseph swore to him,[p] and Israel worshiped as he leaned on the top of his staff.[a][q]

Manasseh and Ephraim

48 Some time later Joseph was told, "Your father is ill." So he took his two sons Manasseh and Ephraim[r] along with him. 2When Jacob was told, "Your son Joseph has come to you," Israel rallied his strength and sat up on the bed.

3Jacob said to Joseph, "God Almighty[b] appeared to me at Luz[s] in the land of Canaan, and there he blessed me[t] 4and said to me, 'I am going to make you fruitful and increase your numbers.[u] I will make you a community of peoples, and I will give this land as an everlasting possession to your descendants after you.'

5"Now then, your two sons born to you in Egypt[v] before I came to you here will be reckoned as mine; Ephraim and Manasseh will be mine,[w] just as Reuben and Simeon are mine. 6Any children born to you after them will be yours; in the territory they inherit they will be reckoned under the names of their brothers. 7As I was returning from Paddan,[c] to my sorrow Rachel died in the land of Canaan while we were still on the way, a little distance from Ephrath. So I buried her there beside the road to Ephrath" (that is, Bethlehem).[x]

8When Israel saw the sons of Joseph, he asked, "Who are these?"

Ge 47:27 ❖ How has God provided beautiful blessings in unexpected places? Explain.

47:25 [g] Ge 32:5
47:26 [h] ver 22
47:27 [i] Ge 17:6; 46:3; Ex 1:7
47:28 [j] Ps 105:23
47:29 [k] Dt 31:14 [l] Ge 24:2 [m] Ge 24:49
47:30 [n] Ge 49:29-32; 50:5,13; Ac 7:15-16
47:31 [o] Ge 21:23 [p] Ge 24:3 [q] Heb 11:21 fn; 1Ki 1:47
48:1 [r] Ge 41:52
48:3 [s] Ge 28:19 [t] Ge 28:13; 35:9-12
48:4 [u] Ge 17:6
48:5 [v] Ge 41:50-52; 46:20 [w] 1Ch 5:1; Jos 14:4
48:7 [x] Ge 35:19

[a] 31 Or *Israel bowed down at the head of his bed*
[b] 3 Hebrew *El-Shaddai*
[c] 7 That is, Northwest Mesopotamia

47:27–28 We must not miss the strong covenant language in the opening verses of this section. The Israelites have acquired property, albeit in Egypt (v. 27). Moreover, the Israelites have become fruitful and multiplied. In other words, God has granted them covenant-type blessings in Egypt in a mini-fulfillment of the promises that will eventually come to full fruition only in the return to Canaan. The time in Egypt is not an interruption of the covenant but an incubation of the covenant people.

47:29–30 Jacob's use of deferential language when addressing Joseph may simply be a reflection of Joseph's office, but as the narrative develops it seems rather to indicate a new status for Joseph as the head of the clan—a fulfillment of the dreams in ch. 37.

47:31 The idea that there is a transfer of status here also helps explain this verse. Jacob's bowing at the head of his bed is an acknowledgement of divine care that has allowed him to pass clan leadership successfully to his son Joseph.

48:1–22 In this second transition segment Jacob adopts Ephraim and Manasseh as replacements for Reuben and Simeon. That is, they become the firstborn sons of Jacob. This, in effect, provides the double portion of the firstborn's inheritance to Joseph, though in a roundabout way. At the same time, it is still possible that Judah receives the double portion, though 48:22 suggests that Joseph has that role (cf. 1Ch 5:1–2).

48:3–7 Jacob begins his speech by summarizing the covenant promises (vv. 3–4). The connection of this to the adoption proceedings is unclear until the discussion turns to the inheritance of property at the end of v. 6. The land was given to him, and this adoption dictates how he will allocate it. Likewise, v. 7 may seem like pointless rambling until we make the connection that Jacob legitimates the adoption of Ephraim and Manasseh on the basis of the premature death of Rachel. Just as a man who dies without children can have his line perpetuated by his surviving widow's production of descendants that become legally his, so Jacob sees Rachel's line, prematurely cut short, as perpetuated by her survivor, Joseph. Jacob thus considers Joseph's two sons as legally his. He lost Rachel during his wandering years (v. 7), and Ephraim and Manasseh were born before his wandering came to a conclusion in Egypt (v. 5).

48:8–14 The ceremony begins in v. 8 with the

9"They are the sons God has given me here,"[y] Joseph said to his father.

Then Israel said, "Bring them to me so I may bless[z] them."

10Now Israel's eyes were failing because of old age, and he could hardly see.[a] So Joseph brought his sons close to him, and his father kissed them[b] and embraced them.

11Israel said to Joseph, "I never expected to see your face again, and now God has allowed me to see your children too."[c]

12Then Joseph removed them from Israel's knees and bowed down with his face to the ground. 13And Joseph took both of them, Ephraim on his right toward Israel's left hand and Manasseh on his left toward Israel's right hand,[d] and brought them close to him. 14But Israel reached out his right hand and put it on Ephraim's head, though he was the younger, and crossing his arms, he put his left hand on Manasseh's head, even though Manasseh was the firstborn.[e]

15Then he blessed[f] Joseph and said,

"May the God before whom my fathers
Abraham and Isaac walked faithfully,
the God who has been my shepherd[g]
all my life to this day,
16the Angel who has delivered me from all harm
—may he bless these boys.[h]
May they be called by my name
and the names of my fathers Abraham and Isaac,[i]
and may they increase greatly
on the earth."

17When Joseph saw his father placing his right hand on Ephraim's head[j] he was displeased; so he took hold of his father's hand to move it from Ephraim's head to Manasseh's head. 18Joseph said to him, "No, my father, this one is the firstborn; put your right hand on his head."

19But his father refused and said, "I know, my son, I know. He too will become a people, and he too will become great.[k] Nevertheless, his younger brother will be greater than he,[l] and his descendants will become a group of nations." 20He blessed them that day and said,

"In your[a] name will Israel
pronounce this blessing:
'May God make you like Ephraim[m]
and Manasseh.[n]' "

So he put Ephraim ahead of Manasseh.

21Then Israel said to Joseph, "I am about to die, but God will be with you[b][o] and take you[b] back to the land of your[b] fathers.[p] 22And to you I give one more ridge of land[c][q] than to your brothers,[r] the ridge I took from the Amorites with my sword and my bow."

48:9 [y] Ge 33:5 [z] Ge 27:4
48:10 [a] Ge 27:1 [b] Ge 27:27
48:11 [c] Ge 50:23; Ps 128:6
48:13 [d] Ps 110:1
48:14 [e] Ge 41:51
48:15 [f] Ge 17:1 [g] Ge 49:24
48:16 [h] Heb 11:21 [i] Ge 28:13
48:17 [j] ver 14
48:19 [k] Ge 17:20 [l] Ge 25:23
48:20 [m] Nu 2:18 [n] Nu 2:20; Ru 4:11
48:21 [o] Ge 26:3; 46:4 [p] Ge 28:13; 50:24
48:22 [q] Jos 24:32; Jn 4:5 [r] Ge 37:8
49:1 [s] Nu 24:14; Jer 23:20
49:2 [t] Ps 34:11

Ge 48:21 ❖ Reflect on the legacy that an older family member or mentor has had on your life. How have they pointed you toward God's faithfulness?

Jacob Blesses His Sons

49:1–28Ref // Dt 33:1–29

49 Then Jacob called for his sons and said: "Gather around so I can tell you what will happen to you in days to come.[s]

2"Assemble and listen, sons of Jacob;
listen to your father Israel.[t]

[a] *20* The Hebrew is singular. [b] *21* The Hebrew is plural. [c] *22* The Hebrew for *ridge of land* is identical with the place name Shechem.

---

question, "Who are these?" This question is not an indication of Jacob's blindness but of the initiation of the ceremony—just as in modern-day weddings when, near the beginning, the minister may ask, "Who gives this woman to be married to this man?" The ceremony continues without delay or surprise until Jacob insists on favoring the younger Ephraim over his older brother.

48:15–16, 20 The actual blessing occurs here. The only real oddity in the blessing is the reference to the angel (v. 16a). The grammatical parallel indicates that the angel need not be a title for deity but may simply be positioned parallel to God. In other words, Jacob is blessing Ephraim and Manasseh by putting them under the care of God, who shepherds, and under his angel, who delivers.

48:22 That a blessing on Joseph is also specifically included can be seen in this verse, which has, like 47:31, been consistently elusive to translators. Historically, this must refer to the conquest of Shechem (or should we call it the slaughter of the Shechemites?) by Simeon and Levi. Jacob did not approve of this act and was not proud of it, but it was irreversible and undeniable. The land is therefore his to give since it was taken in his name and by his clan.

49:1–28 In this last and most extensive example of patriarchal pronouncement, we must again observe that the patriarch's words are not fashioned as a

3 "Reuben, you are my firstborn,[u]
my might, the first sign of my strength,[v]
excelling in honor, excelling in power.
4 Turbulent as the waters,[w] you will no longer excel,
for you went up onto your father's bed,
onto my couch and defiled it.[x]

5 "Simeon and Levi are brothers—
their swords[a] are weapons of violence.[y]
6 Let me not enter their council,
let me not join their assembly,[z]
for they have killed men in their anger[a]
and hamstrung oxen as they pleased.
7 Cursed be their anger, so fierce,
and their fury, so cruel!
I will scatter them in Jacob
and disperse them in Israel.[b]

8 "Judah,[b] your brothers will praise you;
your hand will be on the neck of your enemies;
your father's sons will bow down to you.[c]
9 You are a lion's[d] cub, Judah;[e]
you return from the prey, my son.

49:3 [u] Ge 29:32 [v] Dt 21:17; Ps 78:51
49:4 [w] Isa 57:20 [x] Ge 35:22; Dt 27:20
49:5 [y] Ge 34:25; Pr 4:17
49:6 [z] Pr 1:15; Eph 5:11 [a] Ge 34:26
49:7 [b] Jos 19:1, 9; 21:1-42
49:8 [c] Dt 33:7; 1Ch 5:2
49:9 [d] Nu 24:9; Eze 19:5; Mic 5:8 [e] Rev 5:5
49:10 [f] Nu 24:17, 19; Ps 60:7 [g] Ps 2:9; Isa 42:1, 4
49:13 [h] Ge 30:20; Dt 33:18-19; Jos 19:10-11

Ge 49:8-12 ❖ How does Judah's blessing point forward toward to Christ?

Like a lion he crouches and lies down,
like a lioness—who dares to rouse him?
10 The scepter will not depart from Judah,[f]
nor the ruler's staff from between his feet,[c]
until he to whom it belongs[d] shall come
and the obedience of the nations shall be his.[g]
11 He will tether his donkey to a vine,
his colt to the choicest branch;
he will wash his garments in wine,
his robes in the blood of grapes.
12 His eyes will be darker than wine,
his teeth whiter than milk.[e]

13 "Zebulun[h] will live by the seashore
and become a haven for ships;
his border will extend toward Sidon.

[a] 5 The meaning of the Hebrew for this word is uncertain. [b] 8 *Judah* sounds like and may be derived from the Hebrew for *praise.* [c] 10 Or *from his descendants* [d] 10 Or *to whom tribute belongs*; the meaning of the Hebrew for this phrase is uncertain. [e] 12 Or *will be dull from wine, / his teeth white from milk*

---

prophetic message from God. It would not have been viewed as prediction as much as a determination of individual and tribal destiny. Just as the giving of a name was believed to have some role in determining the destiny of an individual, so these pronouncements were taken seriously.

49:3-7 These sections focus on the past and function as indictments. The only reference to their resulting destiny is that at least Simeon and Levi will be dispersed (v. 7) in Israel. As tribal history goes, Simeon's claim is to villages scattered in Judah's territory, and Levi has no claim as the Levites are distributed among the tribes to serve their priestly functions.

In the saying connected to Simeon and Levi, the word translated "swords" (v. 5) occurs only here in the OT and is highly disputed. It can also be read as a noun form from the verb "to cut," a verb occasionally used for circumcision (e.g., Ex 4:25). In this reading their "cutters/knives" (used for the circumcision of the men of Shechem) became weapons of violence.

"Hamstrung oxen" (49:6) may also mean "they castrated oxen." This in turn may be understood metaphorically to refer to "princes." Thus, we understand the statement to mean "they mutilated the genitals of a prince," alluding to the Shechem incident.

49:8-12 Here the focus turns away from the past to the future. At the same time, the blessing now adopts the use of animal metaphors, which become characteristic of many of the remaining sayings.

49:8-10 Judah assumes the role of the younger son who is emerging to a place of leadership. The indication that his father's sons will bow down to him (v. 8) puts him on a par with Joseph.

The most important item for the understanding of this verse is related to the conjunction universally translated "until" (v. 10). Even those who interpret the verse either in a Davidic or messianic way are troubled by this because in neither case did the scepter depart from Judah. David/Messiah is a representative of Judah, not a replacement for him.

This saying, in effect, points to Judah as the primary channel of blessing to all the nations of the earth in the future, even though Joseph filled that role in the context of Jacob's immediate family. Again, we can see the emphasis on the blessing clause of the covenant in this section of Genesis and Judah's emergence as the tribe destined for leadership.

49:13 The territory allotted to Zebulun after the conquest was the area of Western Lower Galilee. At no point does this territory reach the sea. The area along the sea north of the Carmel promontory was assigned to Asher. There is no known period when Zebulun controlled the coastal regions. This

14 "Issachar[i] is a rawboned[a] donkey
lying down among the sheep
pens.[b]
15 When he sees how good is his
resting place
and how pleasant is his land,
he will bend his shoulder to the
burden
and submit to forced labor.

16 "Dan[c][j] will provide justice for his
people
as one of the tribes of Israel.
17 Dan[k] will be a snake by the roadside,
a viper along the path,
that bites the horse's heels
so that its rider tumbles backward.

18 "I look for your deliverance, LORD.[l]

19 "Gad[d][m] will be attacked by a band of
raiders,
but he will attack them at their
heels.

20 "Asher's[n] food will be rich;
he will provide delicacies fit for a
king.

21 "Naphtali[o] is a doe set free
that bears beautiful fawns.[e]

22 "Joseph[p] is a fruitful vine,
a fruitful vine near a spring,
whose branches climb over a
wall.[f]
23 With bitterness archers attacked him;
they shot at him with hostility.[q]
24 But his bow remained steady,
his strong arms[r] stayed[g] limber,
because of the hand of the Mighty
One of Jacob,[s]
because of the Shepherd, the Rock
of Israel,[t]
25 because of your father's God,[u] who
helps you,
because of the Almighty,[h] who
blesses you
with blessings of the skies above,
blessings of the deep springs
below,[v]
blessings of the breast and womb.
26 Your father's blessings are greater
than the blessings of the ancient
mountains,
than[i] the bounty of the age-old
hills.

49:14 [i] Ge 30:18
49:16 [j] Ge 30:6; Dt 33:22; Jdg 18:26-27
49:17 [k] Jdg 18:27
49:18 [l] Ps 119:166, 174
49:19 [m] Ge 30:11; Dt 33:20; 1Ch 5:18
49:20 [n] Ge 30:13; Dt 33:24
49:21 [o] Ge 30:8; Dt 33:23
49:22 [p] Ge 30:24; Dt 33:13-17
49:23 [q] Ge 37:24
49:24 [r] Ps 18:34 [s] Ps 132:2, 5; Isa 1:24; 41:10 [t] Isa 28:16
49:25 [u] Ge 28:13 [v] Ge 27:28

[a] 14 Or *strong* [b] 14 Or *the campfires*; or *the saddlebags* [c] 16 *Dan* here means *he provides justice.* [d] 19 *Gad* sounds like the Hebrew for *attack* and also for *band of raiders.* [e] 21 Or *free; / he utters beautiful words* [f] 22 Or *Joseph is a wild colt, / a wild colt near a spring, / a wild donkey on a terraced hill* [g] 23,24 Or *archers will attack . . . will shoot . . . will remain . . . will stay* [h] 25 Hebrew *Shaddai* [i] 26 Or *of my progenitors, / as great as*

---

is problematic and makes interpretation of this saying difficult.

49:14–15 Issachar was allotted most of the Jezreel Valley when Israel came into the land. In fact, the idea of lying down between sheep pens can describe the way in which Issachar's territory jutted south between the Carmel range and the Gilboa range. The main highway from Egypt to Babylon passed through the Jezreel Valley so that any country trying to control the trade routes would seek to take control of that region. It is therefore understandable that the one inhabiting that region would be subject to forced labor.

49:16–17 The saying associated with Dan has nothing to do with territory. The saying focuses on the characteristics and function of the tribe, not its location. What is the role and identity of "his people" in v. 16? If the saying refers to the tribe, then "his people" must logically refer to some group outside the tribe. An intriguing alternative is to understand "his people" as the subject of the verb rather than the object. The fact that the verb "to provide justice" is a play on the name Dan justifies this kind of statement being made. An alternative that suits the context a little better is to take the verb here as "to be strong," rather than "to judge." This also resolves the obscurity of the second line comparing Dan to one of the tribes of Israel. The resulting translation is: "Dan—his people will be strong like one of the tribes of Israel." It suggests that Dan will eventually take its proper place among the tribes.

49:19–20 There is little light that can be shed on Gad and Asher. The statements about them are rich in wordplay with little to offer about the patriarch or tribe's situations.

49:21 Finally, the main controversy surrounding the Naphtali statement concerns what animal metaphor is being used. The alternative to the traditional doe with fawns is a reference to a lambing ewe with lambs. The issue is difficult and technical with no resolution resulting.

49:22–27 All major translations present the initial metaphor as a plant metaphor ("fruitful vine," v. 22), but the technicalities of this translation are too complex to discuss here since it would take us far beyond the scope of these notes. Regardless of the extent that kingship implications may or may not be involved for Joseph, there is a clear distinction articulated between Joseph and his brothers in the last line of the saying. Joseph's ruling position has also been established in the surrounding narrative context. But Joseph's ruling role is in the present; there is nothing to compare or compete with the role given to the tribe of Judah for the long term.

The saying concerning Benjamin is straightforward enough as far as translation goes, but as with the sayings associated with the other minor tribes, it has little obvious connection to what we know of Benjamin as a person or of the tribal history.

Let all these rest on the head of
Joseph,
on the brow of the prince among[a]
his brothers.[w]

27 "Benjamin[x] is a ravenous wolf;
in the morning he devours the
prey,
in the evening he divides the
plunder."

28 All these are the twelve tribes of Israel, and this is what their father said to
them when he blessed them, giving each
the blessing appropriate to him.

The Death of Jacob

29 Then he gave them these instructions:[y] "I am about to be gathered to my
people.[z] Bury me with my fathers[a] in the
cave in the field of Ephron the Hittite,
30 the cave in the field of Machpelah,[b]
near Mamre in Canaan, which Abraham
bought along with the field[c] as a burial
place from Ephron the Hittite. 31 There
Abraham[d] and his wife Sarah[e] were buried, there Isaac and his wife Rebekah[f]
were buried, and there I buried Leah.
32 The field and the cave in it were bought
from the Hittites.[b]"

33 When Jacob had finished giving instructions to his sons, he drew his feet
up into the bed, breathed his last and
was gathered to his people.[g]

50 Joseph threw himself on his father and wept over him and kissed
him.[h] 2 Then Joseph directed the physicians in his service to embalm his father Israel. So the physicians embalmed
him,[i] 3 taking a full forty days, for that
was the time required for embalming.
And the Egyptians mourned for him
seventy days.[j]

4 When the days of mourning had
passed, Joseph said to Pharaoh's court,
"If I have found favor in your eyes, speak
to Pharaoh for me. Tell him, 5 'My father
made me swear an oath[k] and said, "I am
about to die; bury me in the tomb I dug
for myself[l] in the land of Canaan."[m] Now
let me go up and bury my father; then
I will return.' "

6 Pharaoh said, "Go up and bury your
father, as he made you swear to do."

7 So Joseph went up to bury his father.
All Pharaoh's officials accompanied
him — the dignitaries of his court and
all the dignitaries of Egypt — 8 besides all
the members of Joseph's household and
his brothers and those belonging to his
father's household. Only their children
and their flocks and herds were left in Goshen. 9 Chariots and horsemen[c] also went
up with him. It was a very large company.

10 When they reached the threshing
floor of Atad, near the Jordan, they lamented loudly and bitterly;[n] and there
Joseph observed a seven-day period[o] of
mourning for his father. 11 When the Canaanites who lived there saw the mourning at the threshing floor of Atad, they
said, "The Egyptians are holding a solemn ceremony of mourning." That is
why that place near the Jordan is called
Abel Mizraim.[d]

12 So Jacob's sons did as he had commanded them: 13 They carried him to
the land of Canaan and buried him in
the cave in the field of Machpelah, near
Mamre, which Abraham had bought
along with the field[p] as a burial place

[a] 26 Or *of the one separated from* [b] 32 Or *the descendants of Heth* [c] 9 Or *charioteers* [d] 11 *Abel Mizraim* means *mourning of the Egyptians.*

49:26 [w] Dt 33:15-16
49:27 [x] Ge 35:18; Jdg 20:12-13
49:29 [y] Ge 50:16 [z] Ge 25:8 [a] Ge 15:15; 47:30; 50:13
49:30 [b] Ge 23:9 [c] Ge 23:20
49:31 [d] Ge 25:9 [e] Ge 23:19 [f] Ge 35:29
49:33 [g] ver 29; Ge 25:8; Ac 7:15
50:1 [h] Ge 46:4
50:2 [i] ver 26; 2Ch 16:14
50:3 [j] Ge 37:34; Nu 20:29; Dt 34:8
50:5 [k] Ge 47:31 [l] 2Ch 16:14; Isa 22:16 [m] Ge 47:31
50:10 [n] 2Sa 1:17; Ac 8:2 [o] 1Sa 31:13; Job 2:13
50:13 [p] Ge 23:20; Ac 7:16

49:28 In case there is any remaining doubt, this verse shows that the emphasis is on tribes, not just sons.

49:29–33 The phrase "gathered to my people" (v. 29) may reflect not only burial in the family tomb, as evident in the next sentence, but also the contemporary perspective on the afterlife. The Israelites had as yet no revelation that offered them a hope of heaven, but perhaps we can speak of an ancestral village in the netherworld where the spirit of the individual who has died rejoins the spirits of the ancestors. Caution is necessary here, however, and we should be reluctant to draw firm philosophical conclusions from stock phrases.

50:1–3 Embalming of Israelites is found only in this chapter. The fact that the bodies of Jacob and Joseph are embalmed may suggest the desire of the Israelites to soothe the feelings of the Egyptians, but it also serves the purpose of preserving their bodies for later burial in Canaan. The seventy-day period of mourning for Jacob (v. 3) may include the forty days required to embalm the body plus the traditional thirty-day mourning period (see Dt 34:8).

50:4–14 The accompaniment by Egyptian dignitaries and a military escort reflects the importance of Joseph and the dignity that is thereby accorded to Jacob. It also serves a theological purpose, showing how far this little family of Abraham's has progressed. God promised to make Abraham's name great and to bless him. Now all of Egypt stops and pays attention with great pomp and circumstance at the passing of his grandson.

PEOPLE TO KNOW // JOSEPH, SON OF JACOB AND RACHEL

GENESIS 50:19–21: Joseph was the son of Jacob's beloved wife, Rachel. He and his younger brother, Benjamin, were the youngest of Jacob's sons. Jacob favored Joseph above Joseph's older brothers. He gave Joseph a beautiful robe, and Joseph's brothers were understandably jealous and angry at this visible sign of favoritism (Ge 37:3–4). Their anger at Joseph only increased when he recounted to them his dreams in which they all served him. In their hatred they sold Joseph into slavery and deceived Jacob, leading him to believe Joseph had been killed by wild animals.

Joseph was taken to Egypt and imprisoned on false charges, but God was with him (Ge 39:21). God gave Joseph power to interpret Pharaoh's dream, and Pharaoh raised Joseph to second in command over all Egypt. Joseph oversaw the storage and distribution of food.

When famine struck in the land of Joseph's family, his father Jacob sent Joseph's older brothers to Egypt to get food. They did not recognize Joseph, who treated them harshly and kept Simeon as prisoner when he sent the other nine back home. He told them not to return without their youngest brother, Benjamin. Jacob was distraught, but eventually had no choice but to send the brothers back along with Benjamin. Joseph tested the brothers again, and when Judah traded his life for the life of his brother Benjamin (Ge 44:33–34), Joseph revealed his true identity, and the brothers were reunited. They brought Jacob to Egypt, where he lived out his days. Joseph's statement about his brothers' evil and God's intentions stands as a shining example of trust in God to control the circumstances of life to his divine ends (Ge 50:20).

APPLICATION ✣ God can use even the messiest family dysfunction and wrong motives to accomplish his will. God's providence moves through all human actions. Even something as horrible as selling a brother into slavery led to the saving of many lives. Surely there were long periods of darkness and despair for Joseph, but in the end God's plan was good, and Joseph recognized that when he looked back at his past hardships. When we find ourselves in times of uncertainty, Joseph's story reminds us that God is always in control.

from Ephron the Hittite. 14After burying his father, Joseph returned to Egypt,
together with his brothers and all the
others who had gone with him to bury
his father.

Joseph Reassures His Brothers

15When Joseph's brothers saw that
their father was dead, they said, "What
if Joseph holds a grudge against us and
pays us back for all the wrongs we did
to him?"[q] 16So they sent word to Joseph,
saying, "Your father left these instructions before he died: 17'This is what you
are to say to Joseph: I ask you to forgive
your brothers the sins and the wrongs
they committed in treating you so badly.'
Now please forgive the sins of the servants of the God of your father." When
their message came to him, Joseph wept.
18His brothers then came and threw

50:15 [q]Ge 37:28; 42:21-22
50:18 [r]Ge 37:7 [s]Ge 43:18
50:19 [t]Ro 12:19; Heb 10:30
50:20 [u]Ge 37:20 [v]Mic 4:11-12 [w]Ro 8:28 [x]Ge 45:5
50:21 [y]Ge 45:11; 47:12

Ge 50:20 ❖ Where have we seen God bring good from situations that looked bad, both in the stories of the Bible and in our real lives?

themselves down before him.[r] "We are
your slaves,"[s] they said.
19But Joseph said to them, "Don't be
afraid. Am I in the place of God?[t] 20You
intended to harm me,[u] but God intended[v] it for good[w] to accomplish what is
now being done, the saving of many
lives.[x] 21So then, don't be afraid. I will
provide for you and your children.[y]" And
he reassured them and spoke kindly to
them.

The Death of Joseph

22Joseph stayed in Egypt, along with
all his father's family. He lived a hundred

50:15–21 These verses show that Joseph's brothers have not fully absorbed his forgiveness.
50:22–26 The indirect repentance of the brothers, the forgiveness extended by Joseph, and the theological statement concerning God's purposes contain the climax to the Joseph story and, in some ways, to the message of both this story and the entire book.

and ten years[z] 23and saw the third generation[a] of Ephraim's children. Also the
children of Makir[b] son of Manasseh were
placed at birth on Joseph's knees.[a]
24Then Joseph said to his brothers,
"I am about to die.[c] But God will surely
come to your aid[d] and take you up out
of this land to the land[e] he promised
on oath to Abraham, Isaac and Jacob."[f]
25And Joseph made the Israelites swear
an oath and said, "God will surely come
to your aid, and then you must carry my
bones up from this place."[g]
26So Joseph died at the age of a hundred and ten. And after they embalmed
him,[h] he was placed in a coffin in Egypt.

50:22 [z] Ge 25:7; Jos 24:29
50:23 [a] Job 42:16 [b] Nu 32:39,40
50:24 [c] Ge 48:21 [d] Ex 3:16-17 [e] Ge 15:14 [f] Ge 12:7; 26:3; 28:13; 35:12
50:25 [g] Ge 47:29-30; Ex 13:19; Jos 24:32; Heb 11:22
50:26 [h] ver 2

[a] *23* That is, were counted as his

47:27—50:26 God's solution to the plight of humankind is self-revelation. By showing us what he is like, he gives us something to which we can aspire.

Life can break us because we live in a fallen world. God can use such circumstances, for he intends them for good. Moreover, God can break us if we choose to live like the fallen world. But he has given us the revelation of himself in the Bible so that we may not drown in self but learn to swim toward him stroke by stroke and finally, diving in, be totally submerged in him as we submit to his will and yield our lives to his mastery.

But as committed as we may be to attain this end result, we must acknowledge that whatever path we take, the separation from self and sin cannot be painless—the surgeon must cut to heal, and the builder must demolish to rebuild.

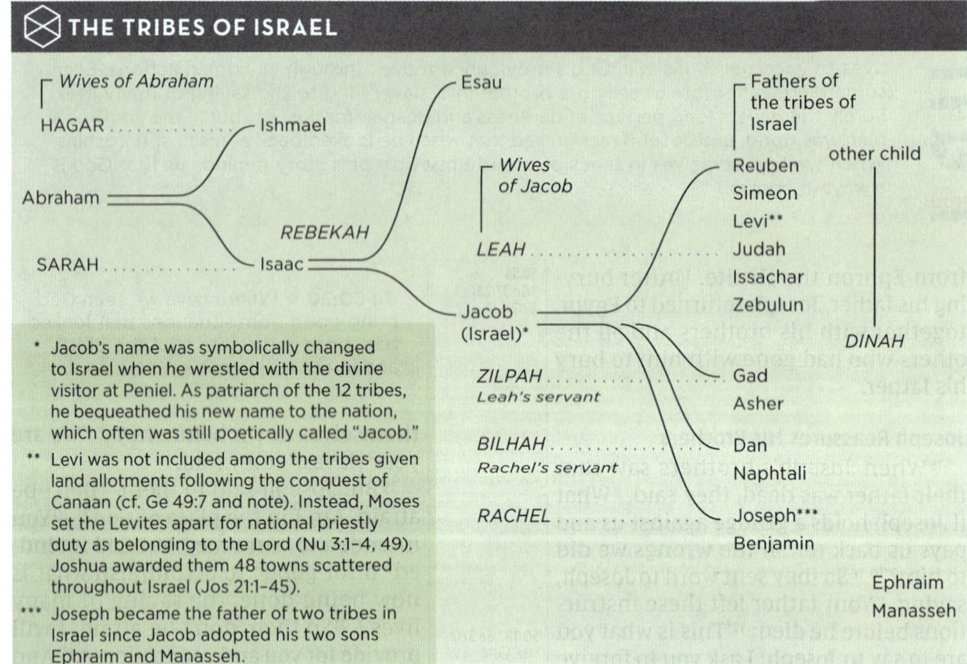

* Jacob's name was symbolically changed to Israel when he wrestled with the divine visitor at Peniel. As patriarch of the 12 tribes, he bequeathed his new name to the nation, which often was still poetically called "Jacob."

** Levi was not included among the tribes given land allotments following the conquest of Canaan (cf. Ge 49:7 and note). Instead, Moses set the Levites apart for national priestly duty as belonging to the Lord (Nu 3:1-4, 49). Joshua awarded them 48 towns scattered throughout Israel (Jos 21:1-45).

*** Joseph became the father of two tribes in Israel since Jacob adopted his two sons Ephraim and Manasseh.

Author: Moses
Audience: God's chosen people, the Israelites
Date: Between 1446 and 1406 BC

Theme: God reveals himself to his people and delivers them from slavery in Egypt to establish a covenant with them in the desert.

PERSPECTIVE

Exodus makes great theater.

- An exciting plot: a dramatic escape by thousands of people from an abusive despot
- Special effects: a flight accompanied by miracles galore
- Great actors: Moses, a charismatic leader, negotiating the release of God's people

It is a gripping story.

It is a story made even more enthralling because its underlying theme—leaving an unacceptable situation in search of a better one—is one to which we can all relate. Indeed, one might say that life itself is precisely such a journey. We undertake countless journeys, large and small, in search of abundant life.

These countless, private exoduses are anything but certain as to their outcome. When we first undertake them and as we undergo them, we do not know if we will succeed. Sometimes we know the destination, but often we don't. Sometimes we know the route, but often we are reduced to aimless wandering. We exit from a known evil in search of an unknown good.

Is it any wonder that under such nebulous circumstances, we frequently wonder about the meaning of our exoduses? How can we possibly understand why evil befell us in the first place (the Job question)? How can we hope for guidance in the deserts of our journeys (the psalmists' question)? How in the world will we know when we have arrived at the correct destination (the __________ question)? In

Reading Exodus

Exodus divides into two main sections. Chapters 1–18 outline the history of the oppression of the Israelites in Egypt, their miraculous escape under the leadership of Moses, and their journey through the wilderness to Mount Sinai. Chapters 19–40 describe the events that occurred at Mount Sinai, including the laws by which God wanted his people to live.

	2200 BC	2100	2000	1900	1800	1700	1600	1500	1400
Moses' birth (c. 1526 BC)								♦	
The plagues; the Passover (c. 1446 BC)									♦
The exodus (c. 1446 BC)									♦
Desert wanderings (c. 1446–1406 BC)									▬
The Ten Commandments (c. 1445 BC)									♦
Book of Exodus written (c. 1440 BC)									♦
Moses dies; Joshua becomes leader (c. 1406 BC)									♦
Israelites enter Canaan (c. 1406 BC)									♦

Key Verse

"Therefore, say to the Israelites: 'I am the LORD, and I will bring you out from under the yoke of the Egyptians. I will free you from being slaves to them, and I will redeem you with an outstretched arm and with mighty acts of judgment.'"

—Exodus 6:6

the midst of these massive uncertainties, don't we need an anchor, a hermeneutical certainty to orient us?

In the book of Exodus, we have an answer: "Yes, we need such an anchor, and yes, we have such an anchor. The anchor is Jesus Christ—the story of Jesus Christ contained in the NT." But since the story of Jesus Christ occurred hundreds of years after the exodus, the meaning we seek in the exodus and in our exoduses has special features.

First, life is dynamic. We are meant to move. Or, more accurately perhaps, we are not meant to stay rooted in our sufferings. God does not require either that we seek suffering or that we passively endure it if and when it comes. The exodus is not a one-time historical oddity but part of the Christian lifestyle.

Second, our exodus is uncertain—at least in the details. We move not knowing everything about the reasons, the journey, or the destination. The details of Moses' exodus only became clear in the light of the life of Jesus Christ hundreds of years later. The details of our exoduses may only become clear in the future, in the events of the move itself or even later. If we wait until we know all the details, we will probably never go. True exodus requires faith.

Third, because of our faith, we can be sure there is meaning in our moving even when it is not entirely clear to us. Part of that meaning is a confidence that our lives are of a single piece. Often our reluctance is rooted in an exodus's strangeness. It doesn't seem to fit the trajectory of our life. But that is often part of what we cannot see—how it does fit. Exodus leads to more life, not less; more exodus means more meaning.

The most important events of Moses' exodus occurred on the journey. The discovery of God's will at every step of the way was provided on a need-to-know basis. Moses never reached the Promised Land, but his trip was still a success—for him and for his people.

Exodus is more than a gripping story. It is the nature of our life together in Christ.

TAKING THE NEXT STEPS

Exodus begins with the remarkable story of how God protected a little baby named Moses, had him brought up in Pharoah's palace, and then called him eighty years later to lead the Israelites to freedom from slavery in Egypt. In delivering the Israelites, God did many miracles through Moses and Aaron: great signs and wonders that brought judgment against their oppressors. In the second half of the book God established his covenant with the Israelites at Mount Sinai, a covenant that centered around the law. At the same time, God formally organized the worship of his people by having the tabernacle built, by instituting a system of sacrifices, and by setting priests apart as holy to the Lord.

This book contains some remarkable teachings about God. (1) God is a powerful God, who is willing and able to deliver us from our enemies, even when all the odds are against us. He defeated our greatest enemy, the devil, through the death and resurrection of Jesus Christ. (2) God is a caring God, whose heart bleeds when he sees us being treated in an inhumane manner and who takes the appropriate means to bring us relief. (3) God is an awesome God, who we ought to revere because of his glory and majesty. (4) God is a forgiving God, who continues to offer us his grace and mercy, even when we run after other gods. (5) God is an orderly God, who is not pleased with haphazard worship; he is a passionately loving God who scorns apathetic ritual and delights in the exuberant and expressive adoration of his people.

WHAT TO LOOK FOR IN EXODUS

- Oppression of Israelites (chs. 1; 5)
- Life and call of Moses (chs. 2–6)
- The ten plagues (chs. 7–12)
- The Passover and exodus from Egypt (chs. 12–13)
- Crossing the Red Sea (ch. 14)
- Trip to Sinai (chs. 15–18)
- The Ten Commandments (ch. 20)
- The golden calf (chs. 32–33)
- The building of the tabernacle (chs. 25–31; 35–40)

The Israelites Oppressed

1 These are the names of the sons of
Israel[a] who went to Egypt with Jacob,
each with his family: 2Reuben, Simeon,
Levi and Judah; 3Issachar, Zebulun and
Benjamin; 4Dan and Naphtali; Gad and
Asher. 5The descendants of Jacob numbered seventy[a] in all;[b] Joseph was already in Egypt.
6Now Joseph and all his brothers and
all that generation died,[c] 7but the Israelites were exceedingly fruitful; they multiplied greatly, increased in numbers[d]
and became so numerous that the land
was filled with them.
8Then a new king, to whom Joseph
meant nothing, came to power in Egypt.
9"Look," he said to his people, "the Israelites have become far too numerous[e] for
us. 10Come, we must deal shrewdly[f] with
them or they will become even more numerous and, if war breaks out, will join
our enemies, fight against us and leave
the country."[g]
11So they put slave masters[h] over
them to oppress them with forced
labor,[i] and they built Pithom and

1:1 [a]Ge 46:8
1:5 [b]Ge 46:26
1:6 [c]Ge 50:26
1:7 [d]Ge 46:3; Dt 26:5; Ac 7:17
1:9 [e]Ps 105:24-25
1:10 [f]Ps 83:3 [g]Ac 7:17-19
1:11 [h]Ex 3:7 [i]Ge 15:13; Ex 2:11; 5:4; 6:6-7

[a] 5 Masoretic Text (see also Gen. 46:27); Dead Sea Scrolls and Septuagint (see also Acts 7:14 and note at Gen. 46:27) *seventy-five*

1:1 The Hebrew text shows that v. 1 begins with the harmless word "and," joining the book of Exodus to what has come before.

1:7 The Hebrew of v. 7 can also be translated more emphatically: "The Israelites became fruitful and swarmed; they increased in number and became exceedingly strong" (alternate translation). "Swarm," also used in Ge 1:21 and 8:17, is another description of what God's created beings do.

1:9-14 Pharaoh is not at all happy with what he sees. What troubles him is the increasing number of Israelites (v. 9). Pharaoh represents not only a force hostile to God's people by enslaving them (vv. 11–14) but a force hostile to God himself, who wills that his people multiply.

PEOPLE TO KNOW // SHIPHRAH AND PUAH

EXODUS 1:1–21: After Joseph and his brothers settled in Egypt, their families grew and became numerous. This started to worry the new king of Egypt, who had no connection to or affection for Joseph or his descendants.

The king of Egypt subjected the Hebrews in his kingdom to harsh labor, forcing them to build storage cities for him. Yet despite their oppression, they continued to be fruitful. The Egyptians feared the growing numbers of Israelites in their midst.

Devising an evil plan, the king of Egypt conscripted Shiphrah and Puah, Hebrew midwives, to kill all the Hebrew baby boys they delivered (Ex 1:16). This frightful order was given directly by the most powerful man in their world. What could they do?

What they did was remarkable. Shiphrah and Puah "feared God" (Ex 1:17), and they righteously and boldly ignored the king's command. When the king confronted them about why they had not killed all the Hebrew baby boys, the women lied, saying Hebrew women always gave birth before the midwives arrived.

God blessed Shiphrah and Puah for their courage in the face of the tyrant king. For their obedience to him and their bravery in opposing the evil command, God gave Shiphrah and Puah families of their own.

APPLICATION Shiphrah and Puah were heroic women. It is hard to imagine how much inner strength it took for them to blatantly disobey the king's orders. He held the power of life and death in his hands; however, these two women trusted in God alone. Their courage is an ongoing testimony for readers today. Our trust and obedience should always be oriented toward God, no matter how imposing or powerful the forces of this world appear.

Rameses[j] as store cities[k] for Pharaoh.
12But the more they were oppressed, the
more they multiplied and spread; so the
Egyptians came to dread the Israelites
13and worked them ruthlessly.[l] 14They
made their lives bitter with harsh labor in brick and mortar and with all kinds of work in the fields; in all their harsh labor the Egyptians worked them ruthlessly.[m]
15The king of Egypt said to the Hebrew
midwives, whose names were Shiphrah
and Puah, 16"When you are helping the
Hebrew women during childbirth on the delivery stool, if you see that the baby is a boy, kill him; but if it is a girl, let her
live." 17The midwives, however, feared[n]
God and did not do what the king of Egypt had told them to do;[o] they let the
boys live. 18Then the king of Egypt summoned the midwives and asked them,

1:11 [j] Ge 47:11 [k] 1Ki 9:19; 2Ch 8:4
1:13 [l] Dt 4:20
1:14 [m] Ex 2:23; 6:9; Nu 20:15; Ps 81:6; Ac 7:19
1:17 [n] ver 21; Pr 16:6 [o] Da 3:16-18; Ac 4:18-20; 5:29
1:19 [p] Jos 2:4-6; 2Sa 17:20
1:20 [q] ver 12; Pr 11:18; Isa 3:10
1:21 [r] 1Sa 2:35; 2Sa 7:11,27-29; 1Ki 11:38
1:22 [s] Ac 7:19

Ex 1:17 What are some ways we feel the influence of evil and unjust powers today? How can we stand against them, in big and small ways?

"Why have you done this? Why have you let the boys live?"
19The midwives answered Pharaoh,
"Hebrew women are not like Egyptian women; they are vigorous and give birth before the midwives arrive."[p]
20So God was kind to the midwives[q]
and the people increased and became even more numerous.
21And because the
midwives feared God, he gave them families[r] of their own.
22Then Pharaoh gave this order to all
his people: "Every Hebrew boy that is born you must throw into the Nile, but let every girl live."[s]

1:22 Pharaoh's final solution is the murder of all male infants by throwing them into the Nile. The text does not give us information regarding the sweeping ramifications of this decree. All we are told is that one special child escaped Pharaoh's evil intention.

APPLICATION 1:1–22 Why does God let this slaughter happen? Doesn't he see what's happening? Doesn't being a Christian mean always feeling God's presence? God's people through all time have struggled with his apparent disinterest in their personal affairs. Neither our present circumstances nor our perceptions of God's absence determine reality. When we cry out to the Lord, he hears us.

The Birth of Moses

2 Now a man of the tribe of Levi married a Levite woman,[t] 2and she became pregnant and gave birth to a son.
When she saw that he was a fine child,
she hid him for three months.[u] 3But
when she could hide him no longer, she
got a papyrus basket[a] for him and coated
it with tar and pitch. Then she placed the
child in it and put it among the reeds
along the bank of the Nile. 4His sister[v]
stood at a distance to see what would
happen to him.
5Then Pharaoh's daughter went down
to the Nile to bathe, and her attendants
were walking along the riverbank.[w] She
saw the basket among the reeds and sent
her female slave to get it. 6She opened
it and saw the baby. He was crying, and
she felt sorry for him. "This is one of the
Hebrew babies," she said.
7Then his sister asked Pharaoh's daughter, "Shall I go and get one of the Hebrew
women to nurse the baby for you?"
8"Yes, go," she answered. So the girl
went and got the baby's mother. 9Phar-
aoh's daughter said to her, "Take this
baby and nurse him for me, and I will
pay you." So the woman took the baby
and nursed him. 10When the child grew
older, she took him to Pharaoh's daughter and he became her son. She named
him Moses,[b] saying, "I drew him out of
the water."

Moses Flees to Midian

11One day, after Moses had grown up,
he went out to where his own people[x]
were and watched them at their hard
labor. He saw an Egyptian beating a Hebrew, one of his own people. 12Looking
this way and that and seeing no one, he
killed the Egyptian and hid him in the
sand. 13The next day he went out and saw
two Hebrews fighting. He asked the one
in the wrong, "Why are you hitting your
fellow Hebrew?"[y]
14The man said, "Who made you ruler
and judge over us?[z] Are you thinking of
killing me as you killed the Egyptian?"
Then Moses was afraid and thought,
"What I did must have become known."
15When Pharaoh heard of this, he tried
to kill Moses, but Moses fled from Pharaoh and went to live in Midian,[a] where
he sat down by a well. 16Now a priest of
Midian[b] had seven daughters, and they
came to draw water[c] and fill the troughs
to water their father's flock. 17Some shepherds came along and drove them away,
but Moses got up and came to their rescue and watered their flock.[d]
18When the girls returned to Reuel[e]
their father, he asked them, "Why have
you returned so early today?"
19They answered, "An Egyptian rescued us from the shepherds. He even
drew water for us and watered the flock."
20"And where is he?" Reuel asked his
daughters. "Why did you leave him? Invite him to have something to eat."[f]
21Moses agreed to stay with the man,
who gave his daughter Zipporah[g] to Moses in marriage. 22Zipporah gave birth to
a son, and Moses named him Gershom,[c]
saying, "I have become a foreigner[h] in a
foreign land."
23During that long period,[i] the king

2:1 [t] Ex 6:20; Nu 26:59
2:2 [u] Ac 7:20; Heb 11:23
2:4 [v] Ex 15:20; Nu 26:59
2:5 [w] Ex 7:15; 8:20
2:11 [x] Ac 7:23; Heb 11:24-26
2:13 [y] Ac 7:26
2:14 [z] Ac 7:27*
2:15 [a] Ac 7:29; Heb 11:27
2:16 [b] Ex 3:1 [c] Ge 24:11
2:17 [d] Ge 29:10
2:18 [e] Nu 10:29
2:20 [f] Ge 31:54
2:21 [g] Ex 18:2
2:22 [h] Ex 18:3-4; Heb 11:13
2:23 [i] Ac 7:30

[a] *3* The Hebrew can also mean *ark*, as in Gen. 6:14. [b] *10* *Moses* sounds like the Hebrew for *draw out.* [c] *22* *Gershom* sounds like the Hebrew for *a foreigner there.*

2:2–4 When Moses' mother looked at the child after his birth, she saw that he was "fine" or "good" (v. 2). The boy is set in an "ark" (v. 3), a term that provides a clear connection to Genesis. In all of the OT, this Hebrew word is found only here and in the flood story (Ge 6:14—9:18). Big sister watches her little brother float along and sees the vessel retrieved by the handmaidens of Pharaoh's daughter.

2:7–9 The sister seizes the moment and offers as a nurse a Hebrew woman she just happens to know (vv. 7-8). Pharaoh's daughter agrees to this arrangement and even pays the nurse for her efforts (v. 9).

2:1-10 Did Moses grow up resenting his new mother because she was not an Israelite? Or is it more likely that he came to rely on her, look up to her, depend on her—love her? We should not be surprised if in the process of growing us into spiritual maturity, the Lord uses unexpected people to change us.

2:11–12 Moses has apparently grown to be a man, as the following narrative makes clear. It is not certain whether he at this point has already consciously identified himself with his true countrymen. Moses is incensed enough at what he sees to kill the Egyptian, thus severing his ties with the Egyptian aristocracy.

2:13–15 This incident serves to introduce two interconnected themes that recur throughout the Pentateuch: Israel's rebellion and the rejection of Moses. Moses' departure from Egypt into the Sinai desert foreshadows the exodus itself.

2:23–25 The Israelites "groaned" and "cried out." God responds because he remembers (vv. 23-24).

of Egypt died. The Israelites groaned in
their slavery and cried out, and their cry[j]
for help because of their slavery went
up to God. 24God heard their groaning
and he remembered his covenant[k] with
Abraham, with Isaac and with Jacob. 25So
God looked on the Israelites and was concerned[l] about them.

Moses and the Burning Bush

3 Now Moses was tending the flock of
Jethro[m] his father-in-law, the priest
of Midian, and he led the flock to the far
side of the wilderness and came to Horeb,[n] the mountain[o] of God. 2There the
angel of the LORD[p] appeared to him in
flames of fire from within a bush.[q] Moses
saw that though the bush was on fire it
did not burn up. 3So Moses thought, "I
will go over and see this strange sight —
why the bush does not burn up."
4When the LORD saw that he had gone
over to look, God called to him from
within the bush, "Moses! Moses!"
And Moses said, "Here I am."
5"Do not come any closer," God said.
"Take off your sandals, for the place
where you are standing is holy ground."[r]
6Then he said, "I am the God of your father,[a] the God of Abraham, the God of
Isaac and the God of Jacob."[s] At this, Moses hid his face, because he was afraid to
look at God.
7The LORD said, "I have indeed seen
the misery of my people in Egypt. I have
heard them crying out because of their
slave drivers, and I am concerned[t] about
their suffering. 8So I have come down[u] to
rescue them from the hand of the Egyptians and to bring them up out of that
land into a good and spacious land, a

2:23 [j] Ex 3:7,9; Dt 26:7; Jas 5:4
2:24 [k] Ex 6:5; Ps 105:10,42
2:25 [l] Ex 3:7; 4:31
3:1 [m] Ex 2:18 [n] 1Ki 19:8 [o] Ex 18:5
3:2 [p] Ge 16:7 [q] Dt 33:16; Mk 12:26; Ac 7:30
3:5 [r] Ge 28:17; Jos 5:15; Ac 7:33*
3:6 [s] Ex 4:5; Mt 22:32*; Mk 12:26*; Lk 20:37*; Ac 7:32*
3:7 [t] Ex 2:25
3:8 [u] Ge 50:24

Ex 2:24-25 ❖ What does this statement demonstrate about God's concern and love for the oppressed? How can this encourage us today?

Ex 3:2 ❖ How and when has God entered your life in surprising ways?

land flowing with milk and honey[v] — the
home of the Canaanites, Hittites, Amorites, Perizzites, Hivites and Jebusites.[w]
9And now the cry of the Israelites has
reached me, and I have seen the way the
Egyptians are oppressing[x] them. 10So now,
go. I am sending you to Pharaoh to bring
my people the Israelites out of Egypt."[y]
11But Moses said to God, "Who am I[z]
that I should go to Pharaoh and bring
the Israelites out of Egypt?"
12And God said, "I will be with you.[a]
And this will be the sign to you that it
is I who have sent you: When you have
brought the people out of Egypt, you[b]
will worship God on this mountain."
13Moses said to God, "Suppose I go to
the Israelites and say to them, 'The God
of your fathers has sent me to you,' and
they ask me, 'What is his name?' Then
what shall I tell them?"
14God said to Moses, "I AM WHO I AM.[c]
This is what you are to say to the Israelites: 'I AM[b] has sent me to you.'"
15God also said to Moses, "Say to the
Israelites, 'The LORD,[d] the God of your
fathers — the God of Abraham, the God
of Isaac and the God of Jacob — has sent
me to you.'

[v] ver 17; Ex 13:5; Dt 1:25 [w] Ge 15:18-21
3:9 [x] Ex 1:14; 2:23
3:10 [y] Mic 6:4
3:11 [z] Ex 6:12,30; 1Sa 18:18
3:12 [a] Ge 31:3; Jos 1:5; Ro 8:31
3:14 [b] Ex 6:2-3; Jn 8:58; Heb 13:8

[a] *6* Masoretic Text; Samaritan Pentateuch (see Acts 7:32) *fathers* [b] *12* The Hebrew is plural. [c] *14* Or *I WILL BE WHAT I WILL BE* [d] *15* The Hebrew for *LORD* sounds like and may be related to the Hebrew for *I AM* in verse 14.

✣ **2:11-25** Humility is a central quality that defines the Christian. There are times, however, when humility is not something we choose but is thrust upon us. Moses chose to help his Hebrew brother; he never intended to flee his home as a result. Christians often find themselves in a state of enforced humility simply by virtue of their Christian witness. We who are Christ's ambassadors can expect nothing less than that which our Lord himself endured.

3:1-10 In the context of the ancient Near East, messengers normally spoke for the sender. The angel of the Lord remains a mysterious but prominent figure in the context of God's self-revelation to his people, and his role is ultimately fulfilled in Christ. Moses removes his sandals, a sign of reverence common in the ancient Near East.

3:7-8 Yahweh knows what his people have been enduring under Egyptian oppression. Israel is "my people." He will "bring them up" from one land and into another: from the land of Egypt—which meant captivity and slavery—and into "a land flowing with milk and honey."

3:11-12 Moses' assertion that *he* cannot do this task is correct but entirely beside the point. He is not doing the saving. Moses says, "I cannot do this." Yahweh responds, "You're not; I am."

3:13-22 The purpose of vv. 14-15 is not to introduce a new name but to underscore the precise identity of the God who is now addressing Moses. God is saying to him: "I am Yahweh, the 'I AM,' the God of the patriarchs. The one you have heard about is the one speaking with you now."

"This is my name[c] forever,
the name you shall call me
from generation to generation.

16"Go, assemble the elders[d] of Israel and say to them, 'The LORD, the God of your fathers — the God of Abraham, Isaac and Jacob — appeared to me and said: I have watched over you and have seen what has been done to you in Egypt. 17And I have promised to bring you up out of your misery in Egypt[e] into the land of the Canaanites, Hittites, Amorites, Perizzites, Hivites and Jebusites — a land flowing with milk and honey.'

18"The elders of Israel will listen[f] to you. Then you and the elders are to go to the king of Egypt and say to him, 'The LORD, the God of the Hebrews, has met with us. Let us take a three-day journey into the wilderness to offer sacrifices[g] to the LORD our God.' 19But I know that the king of Egypt will not let you go unless a mighty hand[h] compels him. 20So I will stretch out my hand[i] and strike the Egyptians with all the wonders[j] that I will perform among them. After that, he will let you go.[k]

21"And I will make the Egyptians favorably disposed[l] toward this people, so that when you leave you will not go empty-handed.[m] 22Every woman is to ask her neighbor and any woman living in her house for articles of silver and gold[n] and for clothing, which you will put on your sons and daughters. And so you will plunder[o] the Egyptians."

Signs for Moses

4 Moses answered, "What if they do not believe me or listen[p] to me and say, 'The LORD did not appear to you'?"

2Then the LORD said to him, "What is that in your hand?"

"A staff,"[q] he replied.

3The LORD said, "Throw it on the ground."

3:15 [c] Ps 135:13; Hos 12:5
3:16 [d] Ex 4:29
3:17 [e] Ge 15:16; Jos 24:11
3:18 [f] Ex 4:1, 8, 31 [g] Ex 5:1, 3
3:19 [h] Ex 4:21; 5:2
3:20 [i] Ex 6:1, 6; 9:15 [j] Dt 6:22; Ne 9:10; Ac 7:36 [k] Ex 12:31-33
3:21 [l] Ex 12:36 [m] Ps 105:37
3:22 [n] Ex 11:2 [o] Eze 39:10
4:1 [p] Ex 3:18; 6:30
4:2 [q] ver 17, 20
4:5 [r] Ex 19:9
4:6 [s] Nu 12:10; 2Ki 5:1, 27
4:7 [t] Nu 12:13-15; Dt 32:39; 2Ki 5:14; Mt 8:3
4:9 [u] Ex 7:17-21
4:10 [v] Ex 6:12; Jer 1:6
4:11 [w] Ps 94:9; Mt 11:5
4:12 [x] Isa 50:4; Jer 1:9; Mt 10:19-20; Mk 13:11; Lk 12:12; 21:14-15

Ex 4:10–12 ❖ What kinds of excuses have caused us to resist God using us for his purposes?

Moses threw it on the ground and it became a snake, and he ran from it. 4Then the LORD said to him, "Reach out your hand and take it by the tail." So Moses reached out and took hold of the snake and it turned back into a staff in his hand. 5"This," said the LORD, "is so that they may believe[r] that the LORD, the God of their fathers — the God of Abraham, the God of Isaac and the God of Jacob — has appeared to you."

6Then the LORD said, "Put your hand inside your cloak." So Moses put his hand into his cloak, and when he took it out, the skin was leprous[a] — it had become as white as snow.[s]

7"Now put it back into your cloak," he said. So Moses put his hand back into his cloak, and when he took it out, it was restored,[t] like the rest of his flesh.

8Then the LORD said, "If they do not believe you or pay attention to the first sign, they may believe the second. 9But if they do not believe these two signs or listen to you, take some water from the Nile and pour it on the dry ground. The water you take from the river will become blood[u] on the ground."

10Moses said to the LORD, "Pardon your servant, Lord. I have never been eloquent, neither in the past nor since you have spoken to your servant. I am slow of speech and tongue."[v]

11The LORD said to him, "Who gave human beings their mouths? Who makes them deaf or mute? Who gives them sight or makes them blind?[w] Is it not I, the LORD? 12Now go; I will help you speak and will teach you what to say."[x]

[a] 6 The Hebrew word for *leprous* was used for various diseases affecting the skin.

3:18 Most commentators suggest that "three-day journey" simply indicates the amount of time needed to get to where they need to go for their celebration without necessarily implying a return trip.

3:19 Pharaoh will not listen to reasoned persuasion. Only a "mighty hand" will compel him.

4:1–9 Moses is concerned not with whether Pharaoh will recognize his authority but whether Israel will. God answers Moses' objection by providing him with three signs.

4:10–12 Moses' fourth objection focuses on another reason why he might not be received by his countrymen. The precise nature of Moses' problem is difficult to identify. Whatever the problem, legitimate or illegitimate, it is not enough to deflect God from his path of action. The significance of God's answer in vv. 11–12 is that God is in control not only of the elements and of the Egyptian government, but he is also in control over the messenger.

13 But Moses said, "Pardon your servant, Lord. Please send someone else."
14 Then the LORD's anger burned
against Moses and he said, "What about
your brother, Aaron the Levite? I know
he can speak well. He is already on his
way to meet[y] you, and he will be glad to
see you. 15 You shall speak to him and put
words in his mouth;[z] I will help both of
you speak and will teach you what to do.
16 He will speak to the people for you, and
it will be as if he were your mouth[a] and
as if you were God to him. 17 But take this
staff[b] in your hand so you can perform
the signs[c] with it."

Moses Returns to Egypt

18 Then Moses went back to Jethro his
father-in-law and said to him, "Let me
return to my own people in Egypt to see
if any of them are still alive."
Jethro said, "Go, and I wish you well."
19 Now the LORD had said to Moses in
Midian, "Go back to Egypt, for all those
who wanted to kill[d] you are dead.[e]" 20 So
Moses took his wife and sons, put them
on a donkey and started back to Egypt.
And he took the staff[f] of God in his hand.
21 The LORD said to Moses, "When you
return to Egypt, see that you perform
before Pharaoh all the wonders[g] I have
given you the power to do. But I will
harden his heart[h] so that he will not let
the people go. 22 Then say to Pharaoh,
'This is what the LORD says: Israel is my
firstborn son,[i] 23 and I told you, "Let my
son go,[j] so he may worship me." But you
refused to let him go; so I will kill your
firstborn son.'"[k]
24 At a lodging place on the way, the
LORD met Moses[a] and was about to kill[l]
him. 25 But Zipporah took a flint knife,
cut off her son's foreskin[m] and touched
Moses' feet with it.[b] "Surely you are a
bridegroom of blood to me," she said.
26 So the LORD let him alone. (At that time
she said "bridegroom of blood," referring
to circumcision.)
27 The LORD said to Aaron, "Go into
the wilderness to meet Moses." So he
met Moses at the mountain[n] of God and
kissed[o] him. 28 Then Moses told Aaron
everything the LORD had sent him to
say,[p] and also about all the signs he had
commanded him to perform.
29 Moses and Aaron brought together all
the elders[q] of the Israelites, 30 and Aaron
told them everything the LORD had said
to Moses. He also performed the signs before the people, 31 and they believed.[r] And
when they heard that the LORD was concerned[s] about them and had seen their
misery, they bowed down and worshiped.

4:14 [y] ver 27
4:15 [z] Nu 23:5, 12,16
4:16 [a] Ex 7:1-2
4:17 [b] ver 2 [c] Ex 7:9-21
4:19 [d] Ex 2:15 [e] Ex 2:23
4:20 [f] Ex 17:9; Nu 20:8-9,11
4:21 [g] Ex 3:19, 20 [h] Ex 7:3,13; 9:12,35; 14:4, 8; Dt 2:30; Isa 63:17; Jn 12:40; Ro 9:18
4:22 [i] Isa 63:16; 64:8; Jer 31:9; Hos 11:1; Ro 9:4
4:23 [j] Ex 5:1; 7:16 [k] Ex 11:5; 12:12,29
4:24 [l] Nu 22:22
4:25 [m] Ge 17:14; Jos 5:2,3
4:27 [n] Ex 3:1 [o] ver 14
4:28 [p] ver 8-9, 16
4:29 [q] Ex 3:16
4:31 [r] ver 8; Ex 3:18 [s] Ex 2:25

[a] *24* Hebrew *him* [b] *25* The meaning of the Hebrew for this clause is uncertain.

4:13–14 Moses' last objection is not based on some legitimate circumstance; Moses just doesn't want to do it. Hence, the Lord becomes angry with him for the first time (v. 14).

4:15–17 Apparently, what concerns Moses is his speech difficulty. Aaron will be Moses' mouth, but Moses will be like Aaron's God (v. 16). The dialogue between Moses and God ends somewhat abruptly: "Don't forget your staff, Moses." The staff is to become a conspicuous player in the plague narratives.

> ✣ **3:1–4:17** Although doubts will certainly arise with God's call, the Father imparts the very spirit of Christ to us in that call. God is not *with* us but *in* us—and we are *in* Christ. This intimacy is greater than what Moses experienced.

4:18–21 Verse 19 is an announcement to Moses that the first installment of the exodus has commenced. Those who enslaved the Israelites are dead—the process has begun.

The purpose of v. 21 is not to introduce some abstract philosophical notion of God's sovereignty. Rather, it is further confirmation of what we have seen earlier in ch. 4—that God is with Moses and with Israel.

4:22–23 These verses conclude the Lord's final talk with Moses before his mission begins. God's demand for Israel's release is not simply for Israel to be free *from* service to Egypt but for Israel *to* serve the Lord.

4:24–26 We must remember that circumcision as a sign of God's covenant was commanded of the patriarch Abraham (Ge 17:1–27). This connection to the patriarchs also imposes a covenant obligation on Moses and the Israelites.

4:27–31 That Aaron and Moses meet on the "mountain of God" is significant. As God had earlier commissioned Moses on Mount Horeb, Moses now inaugurates Aaron before they meet with the elders of Israel.

> ✣ **4:18–31** For Christians, our guilt for not doing what we ought to do needs to be tempered by a knowledge that we are God's children and that he is our Father. If children do something wrong, parents want them to feel guilty, but they do not want them to be paralyzed with guilt. Nor do they want them to feel guilty about silly things. They need to learn which things are worthy of guilt and which are not. However gracious we are to our children, we know that the God of the exodus is, in Christ, more gracious still with us.

Bricks Without Straw

5 Afterward Moses and Aaron went to
Pharaoh and said, "This is what the
LORD, the God of Israel, says: 'Let my people go, so that they may hold a festival[t]
to me in the wilderness.'"
2Pharaoh said, "Who is the LORD,[u] that
I should obey him and let Israel go? I
do not know the LORD and I will not let
Israel go."[v]
3Then they said, "The God of the Hebrews has met with us. Now let us take
a three-day journey into the wilderness
to offer sacrifices to the LORD our God, or
he may strike us with plagues[w] or with
the sword."
4But the king of Egypt said, "Moses and
Aaron, why are you taking the people away
from their labor?[x] Get back to your work!"
5Then Pharaoh said, "Look, the people of
the land are now numerous,[y] and you are
stopping them from working."
6That same day Pharaoh gave this order to the slave drivers and overseers in
charge of the people: 7"You are no longer
to supply the people with straw for making bricks; let them go and gather their
own straw. 8But require them to make
the same number of bricks as before;
don't reduce the quota. They are lazy;
that is why they are crying out, 'Let us go
and sacrifice to our God.' 9Make the work
harder for the people so that they keep
working and pay no attention to lies."
10Then the slave drivers and the overseers went out and said to the people,
"This is what Pharaoh says: 'I will not give
you any more straw. 11Go and get your
own straw wherever you can find it, but
your work will not be reduced at all.'"
12So the people scattered all over Egypt to
gather stubble to use for straw. 13The slave
drivers kept pressing them, saying, "Complete the work required of you for each
day, just as when you had straw." 14And
Pharaoh's slave drivers beat the Israelite
overseers they had appointed,[z] demanding, "Why haven't you met your quota
of bricks yesterday or today, as before?"
15Then the Israelite overseers went and
appealed to Pharaoh: "Why have you treated your servants this way? 16Your servants
are given no straw, yet we are told, 'Make
bricks!' Your servants are being beaten,
but the fault is with your own people."
17Pharaoh said, "Lazy, that's what you
are — lazy![a] That is why you keep saying, 'Let us go and sacrifice to the LORD.'
18Now get to work. You will not be given
any straw, yet you must produce your full
quota of bricks."
19The Israelite overseers realized they
were in trouble when they were told,
"You are not to reduce the number of
bricks required of you for each day."
20When they left Pharaoh, they found
Moses and Aaron waiting to meet them,
21and they said, "May the LORD look on
you and judge you! You have made us obnoxious[b] to Pharaoh and his officials and
have put a sword in their hand to kill us."[c]

God Promises Deliverance

22Moses returned to the LORD and
said, "Why, Lord, why have you brought
trouble on this people?[d] Is this why you

5:1 [t] Ex 3:18
5:2 [u] 2Ki 18:35; Job 21:15 [v] Ex 3:19
5:3 [w] Ex 3:18
5:4 [x] Ex 1:11
5:5 [y] Ex 1:7, 9
5:14 [z] Isa 10:24
5:17 [a] ver 8
5:21 [b] Ge 34:30 [c] Ex 14:11
5:22 [d] Nu 11:11

5:1-3 Perhaps nowhere is Pharaoh's hardness of heart demonstrated more clearly than in the first words he utters (v. 2). The true battle in Exodus is between the God of Israel and Pharaoh, whose ultimate purpose is to oppose God. Verse 3 is not a cowering response on Moses' part, who, after Pharaoh's rebuff, is willing to settle for the next best thing. Moses says: "Read my lips; perhaps I didn't make myself clear. It is *God* who met with us. *He* came to us with this message. *God* is speaking to you now, not two old men."

5:6-9 Pharaoh's godless claim on the lives of this growing population is made explicit beginning in 5:6. Pharaoh says he wants to make their "work harder" (v. 9). The irony, of course, is that as Pharaoh punishes Israel by making the people work "hard," his own heart is "hardened," which results in his punishment.

5:10-14 The slave drivers and foremen preface their message by saying, "This is what Pharaoh says," a deliberate echo of 4:22 and 5:1. Verses 13-14 then tell us that the Israelite foremen are beaten by their Egyptian slave drivers.

5:17-18 Pharaoh refuses to heed their cry and mocks them (v. 17). He turns a deaf ear and borders on the irrational, simply telling them to get back to work (v. 18).

5:19-23 For now, Pharaoh's strategy of disparaging Moses' reputation among the people has worked. The foremen see Moses and Aaron, turn on them and pronounce a curse on them (v. 21).

> **5:1-21** What enables Moses to march into Pharaoh's court is the boldness that comes from knowing and being known by God. As was true with Moses, when God assigns us a mission, the message we preach to unbelievers is not our own.

5:22—6:12 In effect, Moses is calling into question God's character, concluding that God is actually bringing trouble on them. God's response to Moses

sent me? 23Ever since I went to Pharaoh to speak in your name, he has brought trouble on this people, and you have not rescued[e] your people at all."

6 Then the LORD said to Moses, "Now you will see what I will do to Pharaoh: Because of my mighty hand[f] he will let them go;[g] because of my mighty hand he will drive them out of his country."[h]

2God also said to Moses, "I am the LORD. 3I appeared to Abraham, to Isaac and to Jacob as God Almighty,[a][i] but by my name[j] the LORD[b][k] I did not make myself fully known to them. 4I also established my covenant[l] with them to give them the land of Canaan, where they resided as foreigners.[m] 5Moreover, I have heard the groaning[n] of the Israelites, whom the Egyptians are enslaving, and I have remembered my covenant.

6"Therefore, say to the Israelites: 'I am the LORD, and I will bring you out from under the yoke of the Egyptians. I will free you from being slaves to them, and I will redeem[o] you with an outstretched arm[p] and with mighty acts of judgment. 7I will take you as my own people, and I will be your God.[q] Then you will know[r] that I am the LORD your God, who brought you out from under the yoke of the Egyptians. 8And I will bring you to the land[s] I swore with uplifted hand[t] to give to Abraham, to Isaac and to Jacob.[u] I will give it to you as a possession. I am the LORD.'"

9Moses reported this to the Israelites, but they did not listen to him because of their discouragement and harsh labor.

10Then the LORD said to Moses, 11"Go, tell Pharaoh king of Egypt to let the Israelites go out of his country."

12But Moses said to the LORD, "If the Israelites will not listen to me, why would Pharaoh listen to me, since I speak with faltering lips[c]?"[v]

Family Record of Moses and Aaron

13Now the LORD spoke to Moses and Aaron about the Israelites and Pharaoh king of Egypt, and he commanded them to bring the Israelites out of Egypt.

14These were the heads of their families[d]:[w]

The sons of Reuben the firstborn son of Israel were Hanok and Pallu, Hezron and Karmi. These were the clans of Reuben.

15The sons of Simeon[x] were Jemuel, Jamin, Ohad, Jakin, Zohar and Shaul the son of a Canaanite woman. These were the clans of Simeon.

16These were the names of the sons of Levi according to their records: Gershon,[y] Kohath and Merari.[z] Levi lived 137 years.

17The sons of Gershon, by clans, were Libni and Shimei.[a]

18The sons of Kohath were Amram, Izhar, Hebron and Uzziel.[b] Kohath lived 133 years.

19The sons of Merari were Mahli and Mushi.[c]

These were the clans of Levi according to their records.

20Amram married his father's sister Jochebed, who bore him Aaron and Moses.[d] Amram lived 137 years.

21The sons of Izhar[e] were Korah, Nepheg and Zikri.

22The sons of Uzziel were Mishael, Elzaphan[f] and Sithri.

23Aaron married Elisheba, daugh-

5:23 [e] Jer 4:10
6:1 [f] Ex 3:19 [g] Ex 3:20 [h] Ex 12:31,33,39
6:3 [i] Ge 17:1 [j] Ps 68:4; 83:18; Isa 52:6 [k] Ex 3:14
6:4 [l] Ge 15:18 [m] Ge 28:4,13
6:5 [n] Ex 2:23
6:6 [o] Dt 7:8; 1Ch 17:21 [p] Dt 26:8
6:7 [q] Dt 4:20; 2Sa 7:24 [r] Ex 16:12; Isa 41:20
6:8 [s] Ge 15:18; 26:3 [t] Ge 14:22 [u] Ps 136:21-22
6:12 [v] ver 30; Ex 4:10; Jer 1:6
6:14 [w] Ge 46:9
6:15 [x] Ge 46:10; 1Ch 4:24
6:16 [y] Ge 46:11 [z] Nu 3:17
6:17 [a] 1Ch 6:17
6:18 [b] 1Ch 6:2,18
6:19 [c] Nu 3:20, 33; 1Ch 6:19; 23:21
6:20 [d] Ex 2:1-2; Nu 26:59
6:21 [e] 1Ch 6:38
6:22 [f] Lev 10:4; Nu 3:30

Ex 5:22 ❖ Have you ever doubted God's call on your life? What tough questions can we bring to God in prayer?

Ex 6:9 ❖ How can difficult life situations dull our senses to God's Good News? What can we do to increase our sensitivity to God's presence and work?

a 3 Hebrew *El-Shaddai* *b* 3 See note at 3:15. *c* 12 Hebrew *I am uncircumcised of lips*; also in verse 30 *d* 14 The Hebrew for *families* here and in verse 25 refers to units larger than clans.

is, "Let's try it again, but this time listen closely. This is who I am; I am Yahweh [5:2]. I made a promise to the patriarchs that I have every intention of keeping [5:3–4]. I know what is happening, and I am now poised to do something about it [5:5]. Stand back and watch."

6:3–10 Verse 3 does not say that God is now giving a new name but that God's name is now going to be fully known; that is, the significance of the name is going to be understood at this most pivotal time in Israel's history. Armed, then, with this reaffirmation of God's character, Moses is again sent back (v. 10).

6:13–27 Verses 10–12 and 28–30 surround the genealogy. This repetition shows that the insertion of the genealogy here is purposeful. It establishes the pedigree of Moses and Aaron—both are of the tribe of Levi.

ter of Amminadab[g] and sister of
Nahshon, and she bore him Nadab
and Abihu,[h] Eleazar[i] and Ithamar.[j]
24The sons of Korah[k] were Assir,
Elkanah and Abiasaph. These were
the Korahite clans.
25Eleazar son of Aaron married
one of the daughters of Putiel, and
she bore him Phinehas.[l]

These were the heads of the Levite
families, clan by clan.

26It was this Aaron and Moses to whom
the LORD said, "Bring the Israelites out of
Egypt by their divisions."[m] 27They were
the ones who spoke to Pharaoh king of
Egypt about bringing the Israelites out
of Egypt — this same Moses and Aaron.

Aaron to Speak for Moses

28Now when the LORD spoke to Moses in Egypt, 29he said to him, "I am the
LORD.[n] Tell Pharaoh king of Egypt everything I tell you."
30But Moses said to the LORD, "Since
I speak with faltering lips,[o] why would
Pharaoh listen to me?"
7 Then the LORD said to Moses, "See,
I have made you like God[p] to Pharaoh, and your brother Aaron will be your
prophet. 2You are to say everything I
command you, and your brother Aaron is
to tell Pharaoh to let the Israelites go out
of his country. 3But I will harden Pharaoh's heart,[q] and though I multiply my
signs and wonders in Egypt, 4he will not
listen[r] to you. Then I will lay my hand on
Egypt and with mighty acts of judgment[s]
I will bring out my divisions, my people

6:23 [g] Ru 4:19, 20 [h] Lev 10:1 [i] Nu 3:2,32 [j] Nu 26:60
6:24 [k] Nu 26:11
6:25 [l] Nu 25:7, 11; Jos 24:33; Ps 106:30
6:26 [m] Ex 7:4; 12:17,41,51
6:29 [n] ver 11; Ex 7:2
6:30 [o] ver 12; Ex 4:10
7:1 [p] Ex 4:16
7:3 [q] Ex 4:21; 11:9
7:4 [r] Ex 11:9 [s] Ex 3:20; 6:6
7:5 [t] ver 17; Ex 8:19,22 [u] Ex 3:20
7:6 [v] ver 2
7:7 [w] Dt 31:2; 34:7; Ac 7:23,30
7:9 [x] Isa 7:11; Jn 2:18 [y] Ex 4:2-5
7:11 [z] Ge 41:8; 2Ti 3:8 [a] ver 22; Ex 8:7,18
7:13 [b] Ex 4:21
7:14 [c] Ex 8:15, 32; 10:1,20,27

> **Ex 7:3-4** ❖ How should we react to God's hardening Pharaoh's heart? How can we reconcile this with God's love and God's desire for all to repent (see 2Pe 3:9)?

the Israelites. 5And the Egyptians will
know that I am the LORD[t] when I stretch
out my hand[u] against Egypt and bring
the Israelites out of it."
6Moses and Aaron did just as the LORD
commanded[v] them. 7Moses was eighty
years old[w] and Aaron eighty-three when
they spoke to Pharaoh.

Aaron's Staff Becomes a Snake

8The LORD said to Moses and Aaron,
9"When Pharaoh says to you, 'Perform a
miracle,[x]' then say to Aaron, 'Take your
staff and throw it down before Pharaoh,'
and it will become a snake."[y]
10So Moses and Aaron went to Pharaoh
and did just as the LORD commanded.
Aaron threw his staff down in front of
Pharaoh and his officials, and it became
a snake. 11Pharaoh then summoned wise
men and sorcerers, and the Egyptian
magicians[z] also did the same things
by their secret arts:[a] 12Each one threw
down his staff and it became a snake. But
Aaron's staff swallowed up their staffs.
13Yet Pharaoh's heart[b] became hard and
he would not listen to them, just as the
LORD had said.

The Plague of Blood

14Then the LORD said to Moses, "Pharaoh's heart is unyielding;[c] he refuses
to let the people go. 15Go to Pharaoh in

6:28–7:7 In their first conversation on Mount Horeb, God tells Moses that he will be God to *Aaron*. Here the roles played by Moses and Aaron are presented differently: Moses is to be God directly to Pharaoh (7:1). That is, Moses will be an authority figure to Pharaoh rather than just to Aaron. We may think of this as an extra dose of power that God bestows on Moses for the purpose of confronting the king of Egypt.

> ✥ **5:22–7:7** Although not yet fully the case, we truly reflect the image-bearing status that was marred in the garden but that will, for believers, once again be fully perfected in eternity. Such knowledge ought to have an effect on how we live from day to day. We are known by God. He gives us a new start, a fresh beginning, but that high reality does not always translate well in our contact with the world in which we live.

7:8–13 In vv. 8–13 Aaron and Moses confront Pharaoh with God's power. The overarching point is clear: This encounter is an initial sparring between rival gods. This brief incident embodies the main elements of the ten plagues that follow—God shows his power, and Pharaoh resists the obvious conclusion that he is no match for the God of Israel.
7:14–25 Egypt was wholly dependent on the life-giving waters of the Nile. An attack on the Nile was nothing less than an attack on Egypt itself. The Nile was personified and worshiped as a god in Egypt. If the previous sign (staff to a snake) served as a preview of the ensuing plagues, the plague on the Nile was the first toll of the bell that signaled Egypt's demise. Judgment had come. The plagues and the Red Sea incident were nothing less than a series of creation reversals. God unleashed his creative forces on Egypt for punishment but employed those same forces for Israel's benefit.

the morning as he goes out to the river. Confront him on the bank of the Nile, and take in your hand the staff that was changed into a snake. 16Then say to him, 'The LORD, the God of the Hebrews, has sent me to say to you: Let my people go, so that they may worship[d] me in the wilderness. But until now you have not listened. 17This is what the LORD says: By this you will know that I am the LORD:[e] With the staff that is in my hand I will strike the water of the Nile, and it will be changed into blood.[f] 18The fish in the Nile will die, and the river will stink; the Egyptians will not be able to drink its water.' "[g]

19The LORD said to Moses, "Tell Aaron, 'Take your staff and stretch out your hand[h] over the waters of Egypt — over the streams and canals, over the ponds and all the reservoirs — and they will turn to blood.' Blood will be everywhere in Egypt, even in vessels[a] of wood and stone."

20Moses and Aaron did just as the LORD had commanded. He raised his staff in the presence of Pharaoh and his officials and struck the water of the Nile,[i] and all the water was changed into blood.[j] 21The fish in the Nile died, and the river smelled so bad that the Egyptians could not drink its water. Blood was everywhere in Egypt.

22But the Egyptian magicians did the same things by their secret arts,[k] and Pharaoh's heart became hard; he would not listen to Moses and Aaron, just as the LORD had said. 23Instead, he turned and went into his palace, and did not take even this to heart. 24And all the Egyptians dug along the Nile to get drinking water, because they could not drink the water of the river.

The Plague of Frogs

25Seven days passed after the LORD

8[b] struck the Nile. 1Then the LORD said to Moses, "Go to Pharaoh and say to him, 'This is what the LORD says: Let my people go, so that they may worship[l] me. 2If you refuse to let them go, I will send a plague of frogs on your whole country. 3The Nile will teem with frogs. They will come up into your palace and your bedroom and onto your bed, into the houses of your officials and on your people,[m] and into your ovens and kneading troughs. 4The frogs will come up on you and your people and all your officials.' "

5Then the LORD said to Moses, "Tell Aaron, 'Stretch out your hand with your staff[n] over the streams and canals and ponds, and make frogs come up on the land of Egypt.' "

6So Aaron stretched out his hand over the waters of Egypt, and the frogs[o] came up and covered the land. 7But the magicians did the same things by their secret arts;[p] they also made frogs come up on the land of Egypt.

8Pharaoh summoned Moses and Aaron and said, "Pray[q] to the LORD to take the frogs away from me and my people, and I will let your people go to offer sacrifices[r] to the LORD."

9Moses said to Pharaoh, "I leave to you the honor of setting the time for me to pray for you and your officials and your people that you and your houses may be rid of the frogs, except for those that remain in the Nile."

10"Tomorrow," Pharaoh said.

Moses replied, "It will be as you say, so that you may know there is no one like the LORD our God.[s] 11The frogs will leave you and your houses, your officials and your people; they will remain only in the Nile."

12After Moses and Aaron left Pharaoh, Moses cried out to the LORD about the frogs he had brought on Pharaoh. 13And the LORD did what Moses asked. The frogs died in the houses, in the courtyards and in the fields. 14They were piled into heaps, and the land reeked of them. 15But when Pharaoh saw that there was relief, he hardened his heart[t] and would not listen to Moses and Aaron, just as the LORD had said.

7:16 [d] Ex 3:18; 5:1,3
7:17 [e] Ex 5:2 [f] Ex 4:9; Rev 11:6; 16:4
7:18 [g] ver 21,24
7:19 [h] Ex 8:5-6, 16; 9:22; 10:12, 21; 14:21
7:20 [i] Ex 17:5 [j] Ps 78:44; 105:29
7:22 [k] ver 11
8:1 [l] Ex 3:12,18; 4:23
8:3 [m] Ex 10:6
8:5 [n] Ex 7:19
8:6 [o] Ps 78:45; 105:30
8:7 [p] Ex 7:11
8:8 [q] ver 28; Ex 9:28; 10:17 [r] ver 25
8:10 [s] Ex 9:14; Dt 4:35; 33:26; 2Sa 7:22; 1Ch 17:20; Ps 86:8; Isa 46:9; Jer 10:6
8:15 [t] Ex 7:14

[a] 19 Or *even on their idols* [b] In Hebrew texts 8:1-4 is numbered 7:26-29, and 8:5-32 is numbered 8:1-28.

8:1–15 Heqet, a goddess of childbirth, is depicted in Egyptian art with the head of a frog. A plague of frogs can be understood as an attack on the Egyptian fertility goddess for the Egyptians' previous attempt at eradicating the Israelites' male infant population (ch. 1). In light of this, it is, like the first plague, a pointed theological statement: Yahweh is bigger than the gods of Egypt and will unleash the forces of creation to drive this point home.

As soon as the plague is out of sight, it is also out of mind. Yahweh's second display of his control over creation is not enough to convince the king of Egypt that he is no match for God.

The Plague of Gnats

16Then the LORD said to Moses, "Tell
Aaron, 'Stretch out your staff and strike
the dust of the ground,' and throughout
the land of Egypt the dust will become
gnats." 17They did this, and when Aaron stretched out his hand with the staff
and struck the dust of the ground, gnats[u]
came on people and animals. All the dust
throughout the land of Egypt became
gnats. 18But when the magicians[v] tried
to produce gnats by their secret arts,[w]
they could not.
Since the gnats were on people and animals everywhere, 19the magicians said to
Pharaoh, "This is the finger[x] of God." But
Pharaoh's heart was hard and he would
not listen, just as the LORD had said.

The Plague of Flies

20Then the LORD said to Moses, "Get
up early in the morning[y] and confront
Pharaoh as he goes to the river and say
to him, 'This is what the LORD says: Let
my people go, so that they may worship[z]
me. 21If you do not let my people go, I
will send swarms of flies on you and your
officials, on your people and into your
houses. The houses of the Egyptians will
be full of flies; even the ground will be
covered with them.
22" 'But on that day I will deal differently with the land of Goshen, where my
people live;[a] no swarms of flies will be
there, so that you will know[b] that I, the
LORD, am in this land. 23I will make a distinction[a] between my people and your
people. This sign will occur tomorrow.' "
24And the LORD did this. Dense swarms
of flies poured into Pharaoh's palace and
into the houses of his officials; throughout Egypt the land was ruined by the
flies.[c]

8:17 [u] Ps 105:31
8:18 [v] Ex 9:11; Da 5:8 [w] Ex 7:11
8:19 [x] Ex 7:5; 10:7; Ps 8:3; Lk 11:20
8:20 [y] Ex 7:15; 9:13 [z] ver 1; Ex 3:18
8:22 [a] Ex 9:4, 6, 26; 10:23; 11:7 [b] Ex 7:5; 9:29
8:24 [c] Ps 78:45; 105:31
8:25 [d] ver 8; Ex 9:27
8:26 [e] Ge 43:32; 46:34
8:27 [f] Ex 3:18
8:28 [g] ver 8; Ex 9:28; 1Ki 13:6
8:29 [h] ver 15
8:30 [i] ver 12
8:32 [j] ver 8, 15; Ex 4:21
9:1 [k] Ex 8:1

Ex 8:22 ❖ Think of a time when you witnessed God's miraculous protection, and tell someone about it.

25Then Pharaoh summoned[d] Moses
and Aaron and said, "Go, sacrifice to your
God here in the land."
26But Moses said, "That would not be
right. The sacrifices we offer the LORD
our God would be detestable to the Egyptians.[e] And if we offer sacrifices that are
detestable in their eyes, will they not
stone us? 27We must take a three-day journey into the wilderness to offer sacrifices[f]
to the LORD our God, as he commands us."
28Pharaoh said, "I will let you go to
offer sacrifices to the LORD your God in
the wilderness, but you must not go very
far. Now pray[g] for me."
29Moses answered, "As soon as I leave
you, I will pray to the LORD, and tomorrow the flies will leave Pharaoh and his
officials and his people. Only let Pharaoh
be sure that he does not act deceitfully[h]
again by not letting the people go to offer
sacrifices to the LORD."
30Then Moses left Pharaoh and prayed
to the LORD,[i] 31and the LORD did what
Moses asked. The flies left Pharaoh and
his officials and his people; not a fly remained. 32But this time also Pharaoh
hardened his heart[j] and would not let
the people go.

The Plague on Livestock

9 Then the LORD said to Moses, "Go to
Pharaoh and say to him, 'This is what
the LORD, the God of the Hebrews, says:
"Let my people go, so that they may worship[k] me." 2If you refuse to let them go

[a] 23 Septuagint and Vulgate; Hebrew *will put a deliverance*

8:16–19 The plague of gnats receives the shortest account. The first two plagues concern the water, which is the life and power of Egypt, politically, economically, and religiously. The gnats, however, come from the dust of the earth, which is not the Egyptian "power source." The magicians' secret arts are empowered by the Nile, but with the third plague the magicians are out of their element.

The God of Israel is the God of all nature. The magicians recognize that they are in over their heads by confessing, "This is the finger of God" (v. 19). Here they may simply be saying, "This is too big for us," or, "This is no trick."

8:20–32 The identity of the creatures employed by God in this plague is not entirely clear, but a fly of some sort is nearly universally accepted. This is the first plague to make a distinction between God's people and the people of Pharaoh. This distinction is maintained throughout the remainder of the plagues (except for the locust plague), either explicitly or implicitly. It culminates in the tenth plague, where the "destroyer" sees the blood of the Passover lamb on the doorframes of the Israelites and passes them by.

The hardness of Pharaoh's heart can be seen: "*I* will let you go to offer sacrifices" (v. 28, emphasis added). But Pharaoh's repentance is only on the surface.

9:1–7 The precise nature of the fifth plague itself is not specified, but that is not important. The

and continue to hold them back, 3the hand[l] of the LORD will bring a terrible plague on your livestock in the field — on your horses, donkeys and camels and on your cattle, sheep and goats. 4But the LORD will make a distinction between the livestock of Israel and that of Egypt,[m] so that no animal belonging to the Israelites will die.' "

5The LORD set a time and said, "Tomorrow the LORD will do this in the land." 6And the next day the LORD did it: All the livestock[n] of the Egyptians died,[o] but not one animal belonging to the Israelites died. 7Pharaoh investigated and found that not even one of the animals of the Israelites had died. Yet his heart was unyielding and he would not let the people go.[p]

The Plague of Boils

8Then the LORD said to Moses and Aaron, "Take handfuls of soot from a furnace and have Moses toss it into the air in the presence of Pharaoh. 9It will become fine dust over the whole land of Egypt, and festering boils[q] will break out on people and animals throughout the land."

10So they took soot from a furnace and stood before Pharaoh. Moses tossed it into the air, and festering boils broke out on people and animals. 11The magicians[r] could not stand before Moses because of the boils that were on them and on all the Egyptians. 12But the LORD hardened Pharaoh's heart[s] and he would not listen to Moses and Aaron, just as the LORD had said to Moses.

The Plague of Hail

13Then the LORD said to Moses, "Get up early in the morning, confront Pharaoh and say to him, 'This is what the LORD, the God of the Hebrews, says: Let my people go, so that they may worship[t] me, 14or this time I will send the full force of my plagues against you and against your officials and your people, so you may know[u] that there is no one like[v] me in all the earth. 15For by now I could have stretched out my hand and struck you and your people[w] with a plague that would have wiped you off the earth. 16But I have raised you up[a] for this very purpose,[x] that I might show you my power[y] and that my name might be proclaimed in all the earth. 17You still set yourself against my people and will not let them go. 18Therefore, at this time tomorrow I will send the worst hailstorm[z] that has ever fallen on Egypt, from the day it was founded till now.[a] 19Give an order now to bring your livestock and everything you have in the field to a place of shelter, because the hail will fall on every person and animal that has not been brought in and is still out in the field, and they will die.' "

20Those officials of Pharaoh who feared[b] the word of the LORD hurried to bring their slaves and their livestock inside. 21But those who ignored the word of the LORD left their slaves and livestock in the field.

22Then the LORD said to Moses, "Stretch out your hand toward the sky so that hail will fall all over Egypt — on people and animals and on everything growing in the fields of Egypt." 23When Moses stretched out his staff toward the sky, the LORD sent thunder[c] and hail,[d] and lightning flashed down to the ground. So the LORD rained hail on the land of Egypt; 24hail fell and lightning flashed back and forth. It was the worst storm

9:3 [l] Ex 7:4
9:4 [m] ver 26; Ex 8:22
9:6 [n] ver 19-21; Ex 11:5 [o] Ps 78:48-50
9:7 [p] Ex 7:14; 8:32
9:9 [q] Dt 28:27, 35; Rev 16:2
9:11 [r] Ex 8:18
9:12 [s] Ex 4:21
9:13 [t] Ex 8:20
9:14 [u] Ex 8:10 [v] 2Sa 7:22; 1Ch 17:20; Ps 86:8; Isa 46:9; Jer 10:6
9:15 [w] Ex 3:20
9:16 [x] Pr 16:4 [y] Ro 9:17*
9:18 [z] ver 23 [a] ver 24
9:20 [b] Pr 13:13
9:23 [c] Ps 18:13 [d] Jos 10:11; Ps 78:47; 105:32; Isa 30:30; Eze 38:22; Rev 8:7; 16:21

[a] 16 Or *have spared you*

---

narrative's focus is clearly on what was afflicted: Egypt's livestock. Perhaps this is a polemic against Egyptian religion, since Hathor, the mother and sky goddess, was depicted as a cow. In this case we see another psychological blow to Pharaoh's perceived source of strength.

9:8–12 This is the first real demonstration to the Egyptians that their lives are in danger. Heretofore it has been pesky frogs and insects or plagues on livestock. Now humans bear the brunt of God's judgment. This plague represents a concrete step toward the ultimate, irrevocable outcome: the death of the firstborn and of the Egyptian army in the sea. Taking soot from the kiln is poetic justice for the kiln-baked bricks the Israelites had to make as Pharaoh's slaves.

9:13–35 Hail is often associated with an act of judgment on God's part (Jos 10:11; Ps 18:12; Isa 28:2, 17; 30:30; Eze 13:11–13; 38:22). In fact, weather disturbances of a variety of sorts often represent theophanic language—that is, not just that God is judging but also that God is present. The hail hurts not only human beings and animals but "everything growing in the fields of Egypt" (9:22).

Verse 27 brings us to the point we have been expecting—what appears as a truly heartfelt capitulation by Pharaoh. However authentic this repentance seems to be at first blush, it is certainly short-lived. As we have seen (vv. 12, 16), Pharaoh's stubbornness is by God's design.

Ex 9:27–28 ❖ How can we tell the difference between true repentance and a fleeting "foxhole prayer" like Pharaoh's?

in all the land of Egypt since it had become a nation. 25Throughout Egypt hail
struck everything in the fields — both
people and animals; it beat down everything growing in the fields and stripped
every tree.[e] 26The only place it did not
hail was the land of Goshen,[f] where the
Israelites were.[g]
27Then Pharaoh summoned Moses and
Aaron. "This time I have sinned,"[h] he said
to them. "The LORD is in the right,[i] and I
and my people are in the wrong. 28Pray[j]
to the LORD, for we have had enough
thunder and hail. I will let you go;[k] you
don't have to stay any longer."
29Moses replied, "When I have gone
out of the city, I will spread out my
hands[l] in prayer to the LORD. The thunder will stop and there will be no more
hail, so you may know that the earth[m]
is the LORD's. 30But I know that you and
your officials still do not fear the LORD
God."
31(The flax and barley[n] were destroyed,
since the barley had headed and the flax
was in bloom. 32The wheat and spelt,
however, were not destroyed, because
they ripen later.)
33Then Moses left Pharaoh and went
out of the city. He spread out his hands
toward the LORD; the thunder and hail
stopped, and the rain no longer poured
down on the land. 34When Pharaoh saw
that the rain and hail and thunder had
stopped, he sinned again: He and his officials hardened their hearts. 35So Pharaoh's heart[o] was hard and he would not
let the Israelites go, just as the LORD had
said through Moses.

The Plague of Locusts

10 Then the LORD said to Moses, "Go
to Pharaoh, for I have hardened
his heart[p] and the hearts of his officials
so that I may perform these signs[q] of
mine among them 2that you may tell
your children[r] and grandchildren how
I dealt harshly with the Egyptians and
how I performed my signs among them,
and that you may know that I am the
LORD."
3So Moses and Aaron went to Pharaoh
and said to him, "This is what the LORD,
the God of the Hebrews, says: 'How long
will you refuse to humble[s] yourself before me? Let my people go, so that they
may worship me. 4If you refuse to let
them go, I will bring locusts[t] into your
country tomorrow. 5They will cover the
face of the ground so that it cannot be
seen. They will devour what little you
have left[u] after the hail, including every
tree that is growing in your fields. 6They
will fill your houses and those of all your
officials and all the Egyptians — something neither your parents nor your ancestors have ever seen from the day they
settled in this land till now.'" Then Moses
turned and left Pharaoh.
7Pharaoh's officials said to him, "How
long will this man be a snare[v] to us? Let
the people go, so that they may worship
the LORD their God. Do you not yet realize
that Egypt is ruined?"[w]
8Then Moses and Aaron were brought
back to Pharaoh. "Go, worship[x] the LORD
your God," he said. "But tell me who will
be going."
9Moses answered, "We will go with our
young and our old, with our sons and
our daughters, and with our flocks and
herds, because we are to celebrate a festival to the LORD."
10Pharaoh said, "The LORD be with
you — if I let you go, along with your
women and children! Clearly you are
bent on evil.[a] 11No! Have only the men go
and worship the LORD, since that's what
you have been asking for." Then Moses
and Aaron were driven out of Pharaoh's
presence.
12And the LORD said to Moses, "Stretch
out your hand[y] over Egypt so that locusts swarm over the land and devour

9:25 [e] Ps 105:32-33
9:26 [f] ver 4 [g] Ex 8:22; 10:23; 11:7; 12:13
9:27 [h] Ex 10:16 [i] 2Ch 12:6; Ps 129:4; La 1:18
9:28 [j] Ex 10:17 [k] Ex 8:8
9:29 [l] 1Ki 8:22, 38; Ps 143:6; Isa 1:15 [m] Ex 19:5; Ps 24:1; 1Co 10:26
9:31 [n] Ru 1:22; 2:23
9:35 [o] Ex 4:21
10:1 [p] Ex 4:21 [q] Ex 7:3
10:2 [r] Ex 12:26-27; 13:8,14; Dt 4:9; Ps 44:1; 78:4,5; Joel 1:3
10:3 [s] 1Ki 21:29; Jas 4:10; 1Pe 5:6
10:4 [t] Rev 9:3
10:5 [u] Ex 9:32; Joel 1:4
10:7 [v] Ex 23:33; Jos 23:13; 1Sa 18:21; Ecc 7:26 [w] Ex 8:19
10:8 [x] Ex 8:8
10:12 [y] Ex 7:19

[a] 10 Or *Be careful, trouble is in store for you!*

10:1–20 The time for discussion is over. God has hardened Pharaoh's heart. His magicians abandoned him long ago (8:19); now his court officials ask, "How long?" a clear echo of the words Moses and Aaron are told to bring to Pharaoh in 10:3. The confrontation between the true God and the false one is now beginning to draw to a climax.

This unprecedented event of a locust plague brings Pharaoh to his knees. He quickly calls for Moses and Aaron and confesses, once again, that he has sinned (vv. 16–17). When the locusts are gone, God again hardens Pharaoh's heart.

everything growing in the fields, everything left by the hail."
13So Moses stretched out his staff over
Egypt, and the LORD made an east wind
blow across the land all that day and all
that night. By morning the wind had
brought the locusts;[z] 14they invaded all
Egypt and settled down in every area
of the country in great numbers. Never before had there been such a plague
of locusts,[a] nor will there ever be again.
15They covered all the ground until it
was black. They devoured[b] all that was
left after the hail—everything growing
in the fields and the fruit on the trees.
Nothing green remained on tree or plant
in all the land of Egypt.
16Pharaoh quickly summoned Mo-
ses and Aaron and said, "I have sinned[c]
against the LORD your God and against
you. 17Now forgive my sin once more and
pray[d] to the LORD your God to take this
deadly plague away from me."
18Moses then left Pharaoh and prayed
to the LORD.[e] 19And the LORD changed the
wind to a very strong west wind, which
caught up the locusts and carried them
into the Red Sea.[a] Not a locust was left
anywhere in Egypt. 20But the LORD hardened Pharaoh's heart,[f] and he would not
let the Israelites go.

The Plague of Darkness

21Then the LORD said to Moses, "Stretch
out your hand toward the sky so that
darkness[g] spreads over Egypt—darkness
that can be felt." 22So Moses stretched
out his hand toward the sky, and total
darkness[h] covered all Egypt for three
days. 23No one could see anyone else or
move about for three days. Yet all the
Israelites had light in the places where
they lived.[i]
24Then Pharaoh summoned Moses
and said, "Go, worship the LORD. Even
your women and children[j] may go with
you; only leave your flocks and herds
behind."
25But Moses said, "You must allow us
to have sacrifices and burnt offerings to
present to the LORD our God. 26Our livestock too must go with us; not a hoof is
to be left behind. We have to use some
of them in worshiping the LORD our God,
and until we get there we will not know
what we are to use to worship the LORD."
27But the LORD hardened Pharaoh's
heart,[k] and he was not willing to let them
go. 28Pharaoh said to Moses, "Get out of
my sight! Make sure you do not appear
before me again! The day you see my
face you will die."
29"Just as you say," Moses replied. "I
will never appear[l] before you again."

10:13 [z] Ps 105:34
10:14 [a] Ps 78:46; Joel 2:1-11, 25
10:15 [b] ver 5; Ps 105:34-35
10:16 [c] Ex 9:27
10:17 [d] Ex 8:8
10:18 [e] Ex 8:30
10:20 [f] Ex 4:21; 11:10
10:21 [g] Dt 28:29
10:22 [h] Ps 105:28; Rev 16:10
10:23 [i] Ex 8:22
10:24 [j] ver 8-10
10:27 [k] ver 20; Ex 4:21
10:29 [l] Heb 11:27

> **Ex 10:21** ❖ God showed his authority over the Egyptian sun god by blotting out the sun. What do people worship today that God will one day put to shame?

[a] 19 Or *the Sea of Reeds*

10:21–29 A plague of darkness is almost certainly intended to be understood as a polemic against an Egyptian solar deity, possibly Re (Ra), a common sun god throughout Egypt's history. Egyptian kings were sometimes referred to as the son of Re. Once again, creation does not work against the Israelites but for them.

Pharaoh once again seems to capitulate, but this time with one seemingly inconsequential stipulation: They are to leave the animals behind. This is likely a ploy by Pharaoh to get the people to return.

God is bringing this contest between himself and Egypt's king to a speedy resolution. Ironically, Pharaoh now cuts off the only means of salvation he has by banishing Moses from his presence forever.

> ✣ **7:8—10:29** The point of the plagues for today is not so much in what we do with it but in having our hearts and minds opened to what God has done and thereby understanding him better. In the final analysis, the story of the plagues is not about what God does to save you, or perhaps even so much a story of how he saved Israel. It is about God, period; for when all is said and done, we all need to be reminded of him now and then. The question, then, to ask of our passage is not, "What does this have to do with me?" We must at least first ask, "What does this tell me about who God is?"

Perhaps the application is, in a word, doxological. We praise, that is, worship God for his fearful might and great love, both of which he has employed for the sake of his beloved children. Praising God is not a lesser form of application. Rather, it is what so much of the Bible is driving us toward. It is the goal of redemption itself—not to feel self-important by being part of God's club but to turn ourselves away from our sinful inclination toward self-centeredness and toward God. This, one may suggest, is how the ancient Israelites properly "applied" the plagues. They saw what God had done for them, and they fell back in awe—and they remembered.

The Plague on the Firstborn

11 Now the LORD had said to Moses, "I will bring one more plague on Pharaoh and on Egypt. After that, he will let you go from here, and when he does, he will drive you out completely. 2 Tell the people that men and women alike are to ask their neighbors for articles of silver and gold."[m] 3 (The LORD made the Egyptians favorably disposed toward the people, and Moses himself was highly regarded[n] in Egypt by Pharaoh's officials and by the people.)

4 So Moses said, "This is what the LORD says: 'About midnight[o] I will go throughout Egypt. 5 Every firstborn[p] son in Egypt will die, from the firstborn son of Pharaoh, who sits on the throne, to the firstborn son of the female slave, who is at her hand mill, and all the firstborn of the cattle as well. 6 There will be loud wailing[q] throughout Egypt—worse than there has ever been or ever will be again. 7 But among the Israelites not a dog will bark at any person or animal.' Then you will know that the LORD makes a distinction[r] between Egypt and Israel. 8 All these officials of yours will come to me, bowing down before me and saying, 'Go,[s] you and all the people who follow you!' After that I will leave." Then Moses, hot with anger, left Pharaoh.

9 The LORD had said to Moses, "Pharaoh will refuse to listen[t] to you—so that my wonders may be multiplied in Egypt." 10 Moses and Aaron performed all these wonders before Pharaoh, but the LORD hardened Pharaoh's heart,[u] and he would not let the Israelites go out of his country.

The Passover and the Festival of Unleavened Bread

12:14–20pp // Lev 23:4–8; Nu 28:16–25; Dt 16:1–8

12 The LORD said to Moses and Aaron in Egypt, 2 "This month is to be for you the first month,[v] the first month of your year. 3 Tell the whole community of Israel that on the tenth day of this month each man is to take a lamb[a] for his family, one for each household. 4 If any household is too small for a whole lamb, they must share one with their nearest neighbor, having taken into account the number of people there are. You are to determine the amount of lamb needed in accordance with what each person will eat. 5 The animals you choose must be year-old males without defect,[w] and you may take them from the sheep or the goats. 6 Take care of them until the fourteenth day of the month,[x] when all the members of the community of Israel must slaughter them at twilight.[y] 7 Then they are to take some of the blood and put it on the sides and tops of the doorframes of the houses where they eat the lambs. 8 That same night[z] they are to eat the meat roasted[a] over the fire, along with bitter herbs,[b] and bread made without yeast.[c] 9 Do not eat the meat raw or boiled in water, but roast it over a fire—with the head, legs and internal organs. 10 Do not leave any of it till morning;[d] if some is left till morning, you must burn it. 11 This is how you are to eat it: with your cloak tucked into your belt, your sandals on your feet and your staff in your hand. Eat it in haste;[e] it is the LORD's Passover.[f]

12 "On that same night I will pass through[g] Egypt and strike down every firstborn of both people and animals,

11:2 [m] Ex 3:21,22
11:3 [n] Dt 34:11
11:4 [o] Ex 12:29
11:5 [p] Ex 4:23; Ps 78:51
11:6 [q] Ex 12:30
11:7 [r] Ex 8:22
11:8 [s] Ex 12:31-33
11:9 [t] Ex 7:4
11:10 [u] Ex 4:21; 10:20,27
12:2 [v] Ex 13:4; Dt 16:1
12:5 [w] Lev 22:18-21; Heb 9:14
12:6 [x] Lev 23:5; Nu 9:1-3,5, 11 [y] Ex 16:12; Dt 16:4,6
12:8 [z] Ex 34:25; Nu 9:12 [a] Dt 16:7 [b] Nu 9:11 [c] Dt 16:3-4; 1Co 5:8
12:10 [d] Ex 23:18; 34:25
12:11 [e] Dt 16:3 [f] ver 13,21,27, 43; Dt 16:1
12:12 [g] Ex 11:4; Am 5:17

Ex 11:9 ❖ God can use anyone to display his wonders. How can God's wonders be put on display in our lives?

Ex 12:13 ❖ How does the protective blood placed on doorframes during Passover deepen our understanding of the power of Christ's blood shed on the cross?

[a] *3* The Hebrew word can mean *lamb* or *kid*; also in verse 4.

11:1-10 The conversation between Moses and Pharaoh that follows is a continuation of the conversation of 10:24-29. It is as if, while leaving, Moses turns to Pharaoh and says, "Oh yes, one more thing before I go."

The significance of this plague may be seen in part that Pharaoh is considered a son of the sun god Re in Egyptian religion—a fact that lends some continuity between the ninth and tenth plagues. This plague can be construed as an attack on Pharaoh's power. This is clearly retribution for Pharaoh's attempt to kill the male children of Israel in ch. 1.

12:1-28 There is more to the exodus than simply delivering slaves from Egypt. The deliverance from Egypt is a new beginning for Israel; from now on, every glance at the calendar will remind them of this fact. It also provides a connection to Genesis and creation. At the exodus, God's people are being "re-created"; they are starting over with a fresh slate.

and I will bring judgment on all the gods[h]
of Egypt. I am the LORD.[i] 13The blood will
be a sign for you on the houses where
you are, and when I see the blood, I will
pass over you. No destructive plague will
touch you when I strike Egypt.
14"This is a day you are to commemorate;[j] for the generations to come you
shall celebrate it as a festival to the
LORD—a lasting ordinance.[k] 15For seven
days you are to eat bread made without
yeast.[l] On the first day remove the yeast
from your houses, for whoever eats anything with yeast in it from the first day
through the seventh must be cut off[m]
from Israel. 16On the first day hold a sacred assembly, and another one on the
seventh day. Do no work at all on these

12:12 [h]Nu 33:4 [i]Ex 6:2
12:14 [j]Ex 13:9 [k]ver 17,24; Ex 13:5,10; 2Ki 23:21
12:15 [l]Ex 13:6-7; 23:15; 34:18; Lev 23:6; Dt 16:3 [m]Ge 17:14; Nu 9:13

The Israelites are instructed to "roast" the meat and eat it with "bitter herbs" (v. 8) and "bread made without yeast" (v. 15). The significance of bitter herbs is not made explicit, although it is tempting to see in them a reminder of the "bitter" service of the Israelites. The focus of this section of Exodus is not simply on the regulations. This celebration is to be a lasting, eternal ordinance.

HEBREW CALENDAR AND SELECTED EVENTS

NUMBER OF MONTH		HEBREW NAME	MODERN EQUIVALENT	BIBLICAL REFERENCES	AGRICULTURE	FESTIVALS**
1 Sacred sequence begins	7	**Aviv; Nisan**	March-April	Ex 12:2; 13:4; 23:15; 34:18; Dt 16:1; Ne 2:1; Est 3:7	Spring (latter) rains; barley and flax harvest begins	Passover; Unleavened Bread; Firstfruits
2	8	**Ziv (Iyyar)***	April-May	1Ki 6:1, 37	Barley harvest; dry season begins	
3	9	**Sivan**	May-June	Est 8:9	Wheat harvest	Pentecost (Weeks)
4	10	**(Tammuz)***	June-July		Tending vines	
5	11	**(Av)***	July-August		Ripening of grapes, figs and olives	
6	12	**Elul**	August-September	Ne 6:15	Processing grapes, figs and olives	
7	1 Civil sequence begins	**Ethanim (Tishri)***	September-October	1Ki 8:2	Autumn (early) rains begin; plowing	Trumpets; Day of Atonement; Tabernacles (Booths)
8	2	**Bul (Marcheshvan)***	October-November	1Ki 6:38	Sowing of wheat and barley	
9	3	**Kislev**	November-December	Ne 1:1; Zec 7:1	Winter rains begin (snow in some areas)	Hanukkah ("Dedication")
10	4	**Tebeth**	December-January	Est 2:16		
11	5	**Shebat**	January-February	Zec 1:7		
12	6	**Adar**	February-March	Ezr 6:15; Est 3:7,13; 8:12; 9:1, 15, 17, 19, 21	Almond trees bloom; citrus fruit harvest	Purim
		(Adar Sheni)*—Second Adar	This intercalary month was added about every three years so the lunar calendar would correspond to the solar year.			

*Names of months in parentheses are not in the Bible **For more information on the festivals, see chart, pp. 196-197.

PEOPLE TO KNOW // PHARAOH OF EGYPT

EXODUS 12:31–36: When Moses and Aaron came before Pharaoh with God's message to let the enslaved Israelites go, Pharaoh resisted. This set in motion a chain of events in which God demonstrated his power, and Pharaoh was soundly defeated. God declared that he hardened Pharaoh's heart in order to display his signs and wonders, so that Egypt would know God's authority (Ex 7:3–5).

Pharaoh's own magicians were able to match God's signs at first. They made a staff turn into a snake (Ex 7:11–12), turned water into blood (Ex 7:22), and produced frogs (Ex 8:7). After that, however, God's plagues were beyond their ability to copy (Ex 8:18). The magicians told Pharaoh that what was happening was from the hand of God, but Pharaoh's heart remained hard.

As God continued to send plagues upon Egypt, Pharaoh vacillated between penitent and obstinate. He told Moses the Israelites could leave if God stopped the plagues. When God did so, Pharaoh changed his mind. Pharaoh's own officials pleaded with him to let the Israelites go (Ex 10:7). Only when God struck the firstborn son of everyone in Egypt did Pharaoh tell Moses to leave with all the Israelites and their livestock (Ex 12:31–32).

But Pharaoh changed his mind yet again as the Israelites left Egypt. He pursued them with his chariots and cornered them by the sea. God then divided the waters for Israel to cross on dry land, but when the Egyptians pursued them, the waters crashed down upon them. Pharaoh's entire army was destroyed.

APPLICATION ✜ Pharaoh's story is difficult, since the Bible says God hardened Pharaoh's heart. Can Pharaoh be blamed for his sin? It is important to understand that God can use human evil to accomplish his plans, as when God used Nebuchadnezzar to punish Judah's sins. Pharaoh's sin was his own; God merely used him to display his own power in Egypt. Pharaoh's story shows that even the strongest human rulers are really directed by God's hands.

How does hardening one's heart happen today? Are we hardened against a friend or family member who has ideas that don't comply with ours? Are we hardened against the plight of people who are less fortunate? Are our hearts hardened to the gentle calling of the Spirit to move in a particular direction? Jesus had plenty to say about the Jewish leaders whose hearts were hardened against his message (see Mt 12:34; 23:33). Let's examine our own attitudes and actions to ensure that they comply with the rule to love God and love others above all (Mt 22:37–40).

days, except to prepare food for everyone
to eat; that is all you may do.
17"Celebrate the Festival of Unleavened Bread, because it was on this very
day that I brought your divisions out of
Egypt.[n] Celebrate this day as a lasting
ordinance for the generations to come.
18In the first month[o] you are to eat bread
made without yeast, from the evening of
the fourteenth day until the evening of
the twenty-first day. 19For seven days no
yeast is to be found in your houses. And
anyone, whether foreigner or native-
born, who eats anything with yeast in
it must be cut off from the community
of Israel. 20Eat nothing made with yeast.
Wherever you live, you must eat unleavened bread."
21Then Moses summoned all the elders
of Israel and said to them, "Go at once
and select the animals for your families and slaughter the Passover[p] lamb.

12:17 [n]ver 41; Ex 13:3
12:18 [o]ver 2; Lev 23:5-8; Nu 28:16-25
12:21 [p]ver 11; Mk 14:12-16
12:22 [q]ver 7; Heb 11:28
12:23 [r]Rev 7:3 [s]ver 13 [t]1Co 10:10; Heb 11:28
12:26 [u]Ex 10:2; 13:8,14-15; Jos 4:6
12:27 [v]ver 11

22Take a bunch of hyssop, dip it into the
blood in the basin and put some of the
blood[q] on the top and on both sides of
the doorframe. None of you shall go out
of the door of your house until morning. 23When the LORD goes through the
land to strike down the Egyptians, he
will see the blood[r] on the top and sides
of the doorframe and will pass over[s] that
doorway, and he will not permit the destroyer[t] to enter your houses and strike
you down.
24"Obey these instructions as a lasting ordinance for you and your descendants. 25When you enter the land that
the LORD will give you as he promised,
observe this ceremony. 26And when
your children[u] ask you, 'What does
this ceremony mean to you?' 27then tell
them, 'It is the Passover[v] sacrifice to the
LORD, who passed over the houses of
the Israelites in Egypt and spared our

JOURNEY OF ISRAEL FROM EGYPT TO CANAAN

homes when he struck down the Egyptians.'" Then the people bowed down
and worshiped.[w] 28The Israelites did
just what the LORD commanded Moses
and Aaron.

29At midnight[x] the LORD struck down
all the firstborn[y] in Egypt, from the firstborn of Pharaoh, who sat on the throne,
to the firstborn of the prisoner, who was
in the dungeon, and the firstborn of all
the livestock[z] as well. 30Pharaoh and all
his officials and all the Egyptians got
up during the night, and there was loud
wailing[a] in Egypt, for there was not a
house without someone dead.

12:27 [w] Ex 4:31
12:29 [x] Ex 11:4 [y] Ex 4:23; Ps 78:51 [z] Ex 9:6
12:30 [a] Ex 11:6
12:31 [b] Ex 8:8
12:32 [c] Ex 10:9, 26
12:33 [d] Ps 105:38

The Exodus

31During the night Pharaoh summoned
Moses and Aaron and said, "Up! Leave
my people, you and the Israelites! Go,
worship[b] the LORD as you have requested. 32Take your flocks and herds,[c] as you
have said, and go. And also bless me."

33The Egyptians urged the people to
hurry and leave[d] the country. "For otherwise," they said, "we will all die!" 34So
the people took their dough before the
yeast was added, and carried it on their
shoulders in kneading troughs wrapped
in clothing. 35The Israelites did as Moses
instructed and asked the Egyptians for

12:29–42 God's threat is made good (vv. 29–30). Loud wailing is heard throughout Egypt. This prompts Pharaoh, once again, to call for Israel's release (vv. 31–32). He has done so before (9:27–28; 10:16), but here there is a new sense of urgency, for he calls to them at night, right then and there, without a moment to lose, saying as it were: "Just get out! Take what you want, but just get out!" Even the people "urge" the Israelites to leave at once (12:33), which they do, but not before they plunder the Egyptians.

We are told that "six hundred thousand men" leave, not including women and children (12:37). Most commentators mention that such a large number would require a total population of roughly two million, a number that the archaeological data do not support.

articles of silver and gold[e] and for clothing. 36 The LORD had made the Egyptians
favorably disposed toward the people,
and they gave them what they asked for;
so they plundered[f] the Egyptians.
37 The Israelites journeyed from Rameses to Sukkoth.[g] There were about six
hundred thousand men[h] on foot, besides women and children. 38 Many other people[i] went up with them, and also
large droves of livestock, both flocks and
herds. 39 With the dough the Israelites
had brought from Egypt, they baked
loaves of unleavened bread. The dough
was without yeast because they had been
driven out[j] of Egypt and did not have
time to prepare food for themselves.
40 Now the length of time the Israelite
people lived in Egypt[a] was 430 years.[k]
41 At the end of the 430 years, to the very
day, all the LORD's divisions[l] left Egypt.[m]
42 Because the LORD kept vigil that night
to bring them out of Egypt, on this night
all the Israelites are to keep vigil to honor
the LORD for the generations to come.[n]

Passover Restrictions

43 The LORD said to Moses and Aaron,
"These are the regulations for the Passover meal:[o]
"No foreigner[p] may eat it. 44 Any slave
you have bought may eat it after you
have circumcised[q] him, 45 but a temporary resident or a hired worker[r] may not
eat it.
46 "It must be eaten inside the house;
take none of the meat outside the house.
Do not break any of the bones.[s] 47 The
whole community of Israel must celebrate it.
48 "A foreigner residing among you who
wants to celebrate the LORD's Passover
must have all the males in his household
circumcised; then he may take part like
one born in the land.[t] No uncircumcised
male may eat it. 49 The same law applies
both to the native-born and to the foreigner[u] residing among you."
50 All the Israelites did just what the
LORD had commanded Moses and Aaron.
51 And on that very day the LORD brought
the Israelites out of Egypt by their divisions.[v]

Consecration of the Firstborn

13 The LORD said to Moses, 2 "Consecrate to me every firstborn male.[w]
The first offspring of every womb among
the Israelites belongs to me, whether
human or animal."
3 Then Moses said to the people, "Commemorate this day, the day you came out
of Egypt, out of the land of slavery, because the LORD brought you out of it with
a mighty hand.[x] Eat nothing containing
yeast.[y] 4 Today, in the month of Aviv,[z] you
are leaving. 5 When the LORD brings you
into the land of the Canaanites, Hittites,
Amorites, Hivites and Jebusites[a] — the
land he swore to your ancestors to give
you, a land flowing with milk and honey — you are to observe this ceremony[b]
in this month: 6 For seven days eat bread
made without yeast and on the seventh
day hold a festival[c] to the LORD. 7 Eat
unleavened bread during those seven
days; nothing with yeast in it is to be
seen among you, nor shall any yeast be
seen anywhere within your borders. 8 On
that day tell your son,[d] 'I do this because
of what the LORD did for me when I came
out of Egypt.' 9 This observance will be
for you like a sign on your hand and a
reminder on your forehead[e] that this
law of the LORD is to be on your lips. For
the LORD brought you out of Egypt with
his mighty hand. 10 You must keep this
ordinance[f] at the appointed time year
after year.

12:35 [e] Ex 3:22
12:36 [f] Ex 3:22
12:37 [g] Nu 33:3-5 [h] Ex 38:26; Nu 1:46; 11:13, 21
12:38 [i] Nu 11:4
12:39 [j] ver 31-33; Ex 6:1; 11:1
12:40 [k] Ge 15:13; Ac 7:6; Gal 3:17
12:41 [l] ver 17; Ex 6:26 [m] Ex 3:10
12:42 [n] Ex 13:10; Dt 16:1, 6
12:43 [o] ver 11 [p] ver 48; Nu 9:14
12:44 [q] Ge 17:12-13
12:45 [r] Lev 22:10
12:46 [s] Nu 9:12; Jn 19:36*
12:48 [t] Nu 9:14
12:49 [u] Nu 15:15-16, 29; Gal 3:28
12:51 [v] ver 41; Ex 6:26
13:2 [w] ver 12, 13, 15; Ex 22:29; Nu 3:13; Dt 15:19; Lk 2:23*
13:3 [x] Ex 3:20; 6:1 [y] Ex 12:19
13:4 [z] Ex 12:2
13:5 [a] Ex 3:8 [b] Ex 12:25-26
13:6 [c] Ex 12:15-20
13:8 [d] ver 14; Ex 10:2; Ps 78:5-6
13:9 [e] ver 16; Dt 6:8; 11:18
13:10 [f] Ex 12:24-25

[a] 40 Masoretic Text; Samaritan Pentateuch and Septuagint *Egypt and Canaan*

12:43–51 In vv. 43–49 we are given additional Passover regulations. The regulations concerning foreigners seem to reflect the fact that non-Israelites left Egypt along with the Israelites (see v. 38). We have here an attractive mixture of exclusivism and, ultimately, universalism. Although God has throughout made a distinction between the Israelites and the Egyptians, those who are willing may nevertheless partake of this holy celebration. The appeal to circumcision emphasizes that, although the meal is to be celebrated inside the home, it is more properly considered a community affair. Like so much of this chapter, these regulations are future oriented.

13:1–10 This passage reiterates and expands on the regulations concerning the Festival of Unleavened Bread (vv. 3–10) and the future consecration of the firstborn (vv. 11–16). However redundant such repetition may seem to us, these regulations form the heart of the exodus story. The Festival of Unleavened Bread is to be scrupulously observed, and its meaning is to be impressed on the children from generation to generation. Israel's identity is a function of what God has done for them.

11“After the LORD brings you into the
land of the Canaanites and gives it to
you, as he promised on oath to you and
your ancestors, 12you are to give over
to the LORD the first offspring of every
womb. All the firstborn males of your
livestock belong to the LORD.[g] 13Redeem
with a lamb every firstborn donkey, but
if you do not redeem it, break its neck.[h]
Redeem every firstborn among your
sons.[i]
14“In days to come, when your son[j] asks
you, ‘What does this mean?’ say to him,
‘With a mighty hand the LORD brought us
out of Egypt, out of the land of slavery.[k]
15When Pharaoh stubbornly refused to
let us go, the LORD killed the firstborn of
both people and animals in Egypt. This is
why I sacrifice to the LORD the first male
offspring of every womb and redeem
each of my firstborn sons.’[l] 16And it will
be like a sign on your hand and a symbol
on your forehead[m] that the LORD brought
us out of Egypt with his mighty hand.”

Crossing the Sea

17When Pharaoh let the people go, God
did not lead them on the road through
the Philistine country, though that was
shorter. For God said, “If they face war,
they might change their minds and return to Egypt.”[n] 18So God led[o] the people
around by the desert road toward the
Red Sea.[a] The Israelites went up out of
Egypt ready for battle.[p]
19Moses took the bones of Joseph[q] with
him because Joseph had made the Israelites swear an oath. He had said, “God
will surely come to your aid, and then
you must carry my bones up with you
from this place.”[b][r]
20After leaving Sukkoth they camped
at Etham on the edge of the desert.[s] 21By
day the LORD went ahead of them in a
pillar of cloud[t] to guide them on their
way and by night in a pillar of fire to give
them light, so that they could travel by
day or night. 22Neither the pillar of cloud
by day nor the pillar of fire by night left
its place in front of the people.
14 Then the LORD said to Moses, 2“Tell
the Israelites to turn back and encamp near Pi Hahiroth, between Migdol[u] and the sea. They are to encamp by
the sea, directly opposite Baal Zephon.
3Pharaoh will think, ‘The Israelites are

13:12 [g] Lev 27:26; Lk 2:23*
13:13 [h] Ex 34:20 [i] Nu 18:15
13:14 [j] Ex 10:2; 12:26-27; Dt 6:20 [k] ver 3,9
13:15 [l] Ex 12:29
13:16 [m] ver 9
13:17 [n] Ex 14:11; Nu 14:1-4; Dt 17:16
13:18 [o] Ps 136:16 [p] Jos 1:14
13:19 [q] Jos 24:32; Ac 7:16 [r] Ge 50:24-25
13:20 [s] Nu 33:6
13:21 [t] Ex 14:19, 24; 33:9-10; Nu 9:16; Dt 1:33; Ne 9:12,19; Ps 78:14; 99:7; 105:39; Isa 4:5; 1Co 10:1
14:2 [u] Nu 33:7; Jer 44:1

Ex 13:21-22 ❖ How does God guide us through unknown and threatening circumstances?

[a] 18 *Or the Sea of Reeds* [b] 19 See Gen. 50:25.

13:11-16 Likewise, after they enter the land they must be careful to consecrate to God the firstborn of every womb in Israel, whether human or animal, a point made plain later in 22:29-30. We should understand this ritual in light of the tenth plague itself: Israel as God's son (see 4:22) was redeemed (delivered from Egypt) by the death of Egypt's firstborn sons.

We see, then, a hint of what becomes clearer almost fifteen hundred years later on a cross near Jerusalem: Life comes from death, or better, life can only come from death. The tenth plague is the implementation of a redemptive pattern, one that requires death as a means to fuller life. The consecration of the firstborn, therefore, is a foreshadowing of the once-for-all substitutionary death of the beloved firstborn Son who is to come.

✜ **11:1—13:16** The most obvious point of application of the Passover is the regular celebration of the Lord's Supper. In the Lord's Supper, we are celebrating redemption through Christ and the glory that awaits us. But we should also remember that the Lord's Supper is itself a fulfillment of that Israelite meal at an earlier stage of God's redemptive work. By partaking in Communion, we are participating in the effects of God's redemptive work that he began to execute in Israel's day and that came to completion on Easter Sunday. It seems, then, that we, like the Israelites, in celebrating the Lord's Supper, are not merely remembering what God has done. By partaking of the body and blood of Christ, we are, in some mysterious sense, participating in his death and resurrection.

13:17-18 God leads the Israelites on the longer route rather than the shorter. The reason stated is that the shorter route will bring them into military conflict with the Philistines. Yahweh does not want the Israelites to become discouraged and change their minds, so he has them avoid this region entirely. The Hebrew word translated as "ready for battle" (v. 18) has posed problems for interpreters and translators throughout history, and its meaning is still uncertain.

13:19-22 The reference to Joseph's bones is a reminder of the past; so too is the mention of the pillars of cloud and of fire. Although this is the first time we encounter these phenomena, we have had a hint of them in 3:2 with the account of the burning bush.

14:1 God is not finished with the Egyptians yet. He devises what by common military standards is a foolish strategy—march the Israelites toward the sea, leaving them no escape route. Then entice Pharaoh to follow the Israelites.

wandering around the land in confusion, hemmed in by the desert.’ 4 And I will harden Pharaoh’s heart,[v] and he will pursue them. But I will gain glory[w] for myself through Pharaoh and all his army, and the Egyptians will know that I am the LORD.”[x] So the Israelites did this.

5 When the king of Egypt was told that the people had fled, Pharaoh and his officials changed their minds about them and said, “What have we done? We have let the Israelites go and have lost their services!” 6 So he had his chariot made ready and took his army with him. 7 He took six hundred of the best chariots, along with all the other chariots of Egypt, with officers over all of them. 8 The LORD hardened the heart[y] of Pharaoh king of Egypt, so that he pursued the Israelites, who were marching out boldly.[z] 9 The Egyptians — all Pharaoh’s horses and chariots, horsemen[a] and troops — pursued the Israelites and overtook[a] them as they camped by the sea near Pi Hahiroth, opposite Baal Zephon.

10 As Pharaoh approached, the Israelites looked up, and there were the Egyptians, marching after them. They were terrified and cried[b] out to the LORD. 11 They said to Moses, “Was it because there were no graves in Egypt that you brought us to the desert to die?[c] What have you done to us by bringing us out of Egypt? 12 Didn’t we say to you in Egypt, ‘Leave us alone; let us serve the Egyptians’? It would have been better for us to serve the Egyptians than to die in the desert!”

13 Moses answered the people, “Do not be afraid.[d] Stand firm and you will see[e] the deliverance the LORD will bring you today. The Egyptians you see today you will never see[f] again. 14 The LORD will fight[g] for you; you need only to be still.”[h]

15 Then the LORD said to Moses, “Why are you crying out to me? Tell the Israelites to move on. 16 Raise your staff[i] and stretch out your hand over the sea to divide the water[j] so that the Israelites can go through the sea on dry ground. 17 I will harden the hearts of the Egyptians so that they will go in after them.[k] And I will gain glory through Pharaoh and all his army, through his chariots and his horsemen. 18 The Egyptians will know that I am the LORD when I gain glory through Pharaoh, his chariots and his horsemen.”

19 Then the angel of God, who had been traveling in front of Israel’s army, withdrew and went behind them. The pillar of cloud[l] also moved from in front and stood behind them, 20 coming between the armies of Egypt and Israel. Throughout the night the cloud brought darkness to the one side and light to the other side; so neither went near the other all night long.

21 Then Moses stretched out his hand over the sea, and all that night the LORD drove the sea back with a strong east wind[m] and turned it into dry land. The waters were divided,[n] 22 and the Israelites went through the sea on dry ground,[o] with a wall of water on their right and on their left.

Ex 14:10-14 ❖ Even with God’s leading presence, the Israelites panicked when they saw trouble. How can we trust, “be still,” and “stand firm” in the face of fear?

14:4 [v] Ex 4:21 [w] Ro 9:17,22-23 [x] Ex 7:5
14:8 [y] ver 4; Ex 11:10 [z] Nu 33:3; Ac 13:17
14:9 [a] Ex 15:9
14:10 [b] Jos 24:7; Ne 9:9; Ps 34:17
14:11 [c] Ps 106:7-8
14:13 [d] Ge 15:1 [e] 2Ch 20:17; Isa 41:10,13-14
[f] ver 30
14:14 [g] ver 25; Ex 15:3; Dt 1:30; 3:22; 2Ch 20:29 [h] Ps 37:7; 46:10; Isa 30:15
14:16 [i] Ex 4:17; Nu 20:8-9,11 [j] Isa 10:26
14:17 [k] ver 4
14:19 [l] Ex 13:21
14:21 [m] Ex 15:8 [n] Ps 74:13; 114:5; Isa 63:12
14:22 [o] Ex 15:19; Ne 9:11; Ps 66:6; Heb 11:29

[a] 9 Or *charioteers*; also in verses 17, 18, 23, 26 and 28

14:5-9 The thought that the Israelites will not come back is too much for Pharaoh, so he chases them (v. 7). The irony, of course, is that Pharaoh has gone to fight Israel’s God, the God of the plagues, with mere chariots, horsemen, and troops (v. 9).

14:10-12 In one sense one can hardly blame the Israelites for reacting the way they do (v. 10). Still, their cry, so soon after they have witnessed God’s mighty acts in the plagues, is nothing less than capitulation to the appearance of their immediate circumstances—of which the events of the previous thirteen chapters should have cured them.

14:14-15 We should understand v. 14 in the context of the Israelites’ faithlessness in light of what God has done. Why is it, after the Israelites cry out in v. 14 and Moses rebukes them for their lack of faith, that Moses is reprimanded by God for crying out? There is a close identification between Moses and the people he is leading. He is the mediator who connects the people to God (e.g., 32:9-14). Their guilt becomes his.

14:19 Here we meet “the angel of God.” He is a concrete manifestation of God’s presence with his people.

14:21 In v. 16 Moses is told to raise his staff to divide the water. Verse 21 begins, “Moses stretched out his hand,” but then we read that the Lord is the one who does the parting. Who, then, is responsible? As the mediator between the people and God, Moses takes on characteristics of both.

23The Egyptians pursued them, and all
Pharaoh's horses and chariots and horsemen followed them into the sea. 24Dur-
ing the last watch of the night the LORD
looked down from the pillar of fire and
cloud[p] at the Egyptian army and threw it
into confusion. 25He jammed[a] the wheels
of their chariots so that they had difficulty driving. And the Egyptians said, "Let's
get away from the Israelites! The LORD is
fighting[q] for them against Egypt."
26Then the LORD said to Moses,
"Stretch out your hand over the sea so
that the waters may flow back over the
Egyptians and their chariots and horsemen." 27Moses stretched out his hand
over the sea, and at daybreak the sea
went back to its place.[r] The Egyptians
were fleeing toward[b] it, and the LORD
swept them into the sea.[s] 28The water
flowed back and covered the chariots and
horsemen — the entire army of Pharaoh
that had followed the Israelites into the
sea. Not one of them survived.
29But the Israelites went through the
sea on dry ground,[t] with a wall of water
on their right and on their left. 30That day
the LORD saved[u] Israel from the hands of
the Egyptians, and Israel saw the Egyptians lying dead on the shore. 31And when
the Israelites saw the mighty hand of the
LORD displayed against the Egyptians,
the people feared the LORD and put their
trust[v] in him and in Moses his servant.

The Song of Moses and Miriam

15 Then Moses and the Israelites sang
this song[w] to the LORD:

"I will sing[x] to the LORD,
for he is highly exalted.

> **Ex 15:1** ❖ Why is it so important to praise God's mighty acts through singing and worship?

Both horse and driver
he has hurled into the sea.

2"The LORD is my strength[y] and my
defense[c];
he has become my salvation.[z]
He is my God,[a] and I will praise him,
my father's God, and I will exalt[b]
him.
3The LORD is a warrior;[c]
the LORD is his name.[d]
4Pharaoh's chariots and his army[e]
he has hurled into the sea.
The best of Pharaoh's officers
are drowned in the Red Sea.[d]
5The deep waters have covered
them;
they sank to the depths like a
stone.[f]
6Your right hand,[g] LORD,
was majestic in power.
Your right hand, LORD,
shattered the enemy.

7"In the greatness of your majesty
you threw down those who
opposed you.
You unleashed your burning anger;[h]
it consumed them like stubble.
8By the blast of your nostrils[i]
the waters piled up.[j]
The surging waters stood up like a
wall;[k]

14:24 [p] Ex 13:21
14:25 [q] ver 14
14:27 [r] Jos 4:18 [s] Ex 15:1,21; Ps 78:53; 106:11
14:29 [t] ver 22
14:30 [u] Ps 106:8, 10,21
14:31 [v] Ps 106:12; Jn 2:11
15:1 [w] Rev 15:3 [x] Ps 106:12
15:2 [y] Ps 59:17 [z] Ps 18:2, 46; Isa 12:2; Hab 3:18 [a] Ge 28:21 [b] Ex 3:6,15-16; Isa 25:1
15:3 [c] Ex 14:14; Ps 24:8; Rev 19:11 [d] Ex 6:2-3,7-8; Ps 83:18
15:4 [e] Ex 14:6-7
15:5 [f] ver 10; Ne 9:11
15:6 [g] Ps 118:15
15:7 [h] Ps 78:49-50
15:8 [i] Ex 14:21 [j] Ps 78:13 [k] Ex 14:22

[a] *25* See Samaritan Pentateuch, Septuagint and Syriac; Masoretic Text *removed* [b] *27* Or *from* [c] *2* Or *song* [d] *4* Or *the Sea of Reeds*; also in verse 22

14:23–25 The sea is parted and the Egyptians follow in pursuit. But they finally grasp that all hope is lost, for God throws the Egyptians "into confusion" (v. 24). This is a terrifying confusion, and it takes the form of wheel trouble (v. 25)—most likely either that their wheels come off or that they get stuck in the muddy road that once was the bottom of the Red Sea.

> ✣ **13:17—14:31** As Christians we have crossed over from our slavery to sin and death to a new beginning as God's people, in subjection to him. We who are in Christ have moved out of one country and into another (or more accurately, we are moving toward another country), which itself is a preview of our entrance to the heavenly country that awaits us. The application of the exodus theme to our lives could not be more central.

15:1–13 This song is a poetic rendering of the narrative of the death of Egypt's army described toward the end of ch. 14. Verses 1–12 recount the destruction of the Egyptians. Verse 13 introduces the purpose for which the Israelites have been permitted to escape the doomed Egyptian army: God "redeemed" his people in order to lead them to his "holy dwelling." What is the identity of this dwelling? We can say that God is bringing his people out of Egypt in order that he might be present with them, and that presence will be manifest in "sacred space." God's self-revelation at Sinai is, although itself a frighteningly powerful reality, a prelude to the permanence of his presence in the land and the temple.

the deep waters congealed in the
heart of the sea.
9 The enemy boasted,
'I will pursue,[l] I will overtake
them.
I will divide the spoils;[m]
I will gorge myself on them.
I will draw my sword
and my hand will destroy them.'
10 But you blew with your breath,
and the sea covered them.
They sank like lead
in the mighty waters.[n]
11 Who among the gods
is like you,[o] LORD?
Who is like you —
majestic in holiness,[p]
awesome in glory,[q]
working wonders?

12 "You stretch out your right hand,
and the earth swallows your
enemies.
13 In your unfailing love you will lead[r]
the people you have redeemed.
In your strength you will guide them
to your holy dwelling.[s]
14 The nations will hear and tremble;[t]
anguish will grip the people of
Philistia.
15 The chiefs[u] of Edom will be terrified,
the leaders of Moab will be seized
with trembling,[v]
the people[a] of Canaan will melt[w]
away;
16 terror[x] and dread will fall on
them.
By the power of your arm
they will be as still as a stone[y] —
until your people pass by, LORD,
until the people you bought[bz]
pass by.

15:9 [l] Ex 14:5-9 [m] Jdg 5:30; Isa 53:12
15:10 [n] ver 5; Ex 14:27-28
15:11 [o] Ex 8:10; Dt 3:24; Ps 77:13 [p] Isa 6:3; Rev 4:8 [q] Ps 8:1
15:13 [r] Ne 9:12; Ps 77:20 [s] Ps 78:54
15:14 [t] Dt 2:25
15:15 [u] Ge 36:15 [v] Nu 22:3 [w] Jos 5:1
15:16 [x] Ex 23:27; Jos 2:9 [y] 1Sa 25:37 [z] Ps 74:2
15:17 [a] Ps 44:2 [b] Ps 78:54, 68
15:19 [c] Ex 14:28 [d] Ex 14:22
15:20 [e] Nu 26:59 [f] Jdg 4:4 [g] Jdg 11:34; 1Sa 18:6; Ps 30:11; 150:4
15:21 [h] ver 1; Ex 14:27
15:23 [i] Nu 33:8
15:24 [j] Ex 14:12; 16:2
15:25 [k] Ex 14:10

17 You will bring them in and plant[a]
them
on the mountain[b] of your
inheritance —
the place, LORD, you made for your
dwelling,
the sanctuary, Lord, your hands
established.

18 "The LORD reigns
for ever and ever."

19 When Pharaoh's horses, chariots and
horsemen[c] went into the sea,[c] the LORD
brought the waters of the sea back over
them, but the Israelites walked through
the sea on dry ground.[d] 20 Then Miriam[e]
the prophet,[f] Aaron's sister, took a timbrel in her hand, and all the women followed her, with timbrels and dancing.[g]
21 Miriam sang to them:

"Sing to the LORD,
for he is highly exalted.
Both horse and driver
he has hurled into the sea."[h]

The Waters of Marah and Elim

22 Then Moses led Israel from the Red
Sea and they went into the Desert of
Shur. For three days they traveled in the
desert without finding water. 23 When
they came to Marah, they could not drink
its water because it was bitter. (That is
why the place is called Marah.[di]) 24 So the
people grumbled[j] against Moses, saying,
"What are we to drink?"
25 Then Moses cried out[k] to the LORD,
and the LORD showed him a piece of
wood. He threw it into the water, and
the water became fit to drink.

[a] 15 Or *rulers* [b] 16 Or *created* [c] 19 Or *charioteers* [d] 23 *Marah* means *bitter.*

15:18–21 The song concludes in a most fitting way (v. 18). The rule of God is eternal, and if the Israelites are to learn anything from the death of the Egyptians, it is that the exodus story is about more than the exodus. The exodus is about God and who he is. The focus of the song is not on what happens to the Israelites or to the Egyptians, but on God, who "reigns for ever and ever."

15:1–21 The songs of the OT were models for worship. They were written down precisely so that they could be pondered, studied, and reflected on—not only for ancient Israelites but also for those who live in the light of the resurrection of God's Son. They are not trophies on a mantel but inspired examples—not so much because they have to be followed word for word, but because they give us a glimpse of who God is and, therefore, what our proper stance toward him should be.

15:22–27 In 15:22—17:7 we find three stories that should be taken together. These three rapid-fire stories of rebellion in the desert stagger the imagination. This first story concerns the provision of water at Marah.

Moses responds in a manner familiar to us; he "cries out" (v. 25). God, in turn, responds in a manner reminiscent of the plagues and the exodus: He performs another water miracle.

What do the "commands" and "decrees" mentioned in v. 26 refer to? What God is telling his

There the LORD issued a ruling and instruction for them and put them to the
test.[l] 26He said, "If you listen carefully to
the LORD your God and do what is right
in his eyes, if you pay attention to his
commands and keep all his decrees,[m] I
will not bring on you any of the diseases[n]
I brought on the Egyptians, for I am the
LORD, who heals[o] you."
27Then they came to Elim, where there
were twelve springs and seventy palm
trees, and they camped[p] there near the
water.

Manna and Quail

16 The whole Israelite community
set out from Elim and came to the
Desert of Sin,[q] which is between Elim
and Sinai, on the fifteenth day of the
second month after they had come out

15:25 [l] Jdg 3:4
15:26 [m] Dt 7:12 [n] Dt 28:27,58-60 [o] Ex 23:25-26
15:27 [p] Nu 33:9
16:1 [q] Nu 33:11,12
16:2 [r] Ex 14:11; 15:24; 1Co 10:10
16:3 [s] Ex 17:3 [t] Nu 11:4,34
16:4 [u] Dt 8:3; Jn 6:31*

Ex 16:3 ❖ When has our vision been too narrow to see the good things God is doing for us?

of Egypt. 2In the desert the whole community grumbled[r] against Moses and
Aaron. 3The Israelites said to them, "If
only we had died by the LORD's hand in
Egypt![s] There we sat around pots of meat
and ate all the food[t] we wanted, but you
have brought us out into this desert to
starve this entire assembly to death."
4Then the LORD said to Moses, "I will
rain down bread from heaven[u] for you.
The people are to go out each day and
gather enough for that day. In this way I
will test them and see whether they will
follow my instructions. 5On the sixth day
they are to prepare what they bring in,

---

people at this crucial juncture in their young life as a people is: "Stick to me and you will never relive the horrors of Egypt again. If you ignore my law, although you will not return to Egypt physically, you will be treated as they were."

16:1–36 Surely, having just seen again God's care for them, rebellion is now out of the question, right? Wrong. A mere month has passed since the departure from Egypt. Is their memory so short?

16:3 Only the most calloused heart or the most cynical mind could conceive of such a ridiculous charge.

16:4 God provides for his people again but with one minor provision. This is a test to see if they will follow God's instructions. That the Israelites will "know" God is another echo of the departure narrative. God is not yet finished teaching his people who he is. In fact, he has hardly begun.

PEOPLE TO KNOW // MIRIAM

EXODUS 15:20–21: Miriam was the sister of Moses and Aaron. Though Miriam is not mentioned by name in Exodus 2, she is likely the sister who watched over Moses when their mother placed him in a basket in the reeds, where he was found by Pharaoh's daughter. This sister volunteered to find a Hebrew woman to nurse the baby, so Moses was in the care of his own mother until he was returned to Pharaoh's daughter (Ex 2:7–8).

When the Israelites crossed the Red Sea on dry land, Miriam, called a prophet, led the women in a song of praise to God (Ex 15:20–21). Later, Miriam and Aaron grumbled against Moses because of his Cushite wife (Nu 12:1). They questioned Moses' authority, noting that God spoke through them as well. God's anger burned against them, and Miriam's skin became leprous. Moses prayed on her behalf, and after seven days she was healed.

Miriam died during Israel's years in the wilderness. Immediately after her death, Israel suffered a water shortage and for the second time God helped Moses bring water out of a rock (Nu 20:1–2). The fact that this happened immediately after Miriam's death gave rise to a Jewish tradition that "Miriam's Rock" had traveled with the Israelites and supplied them water in the wilderness; and that when she died it stopped yielding water, necessitating the second instance of water from a rock. While the Torah does not say this, in 1 Corinthians 10:4 Paul refers to a rock traveling with Israel in the wilderness, which provided them water.

APPLICATION ✚ Miriam's legacy is mixed. On one hand she demonstrated faith and bravery, ensuring her baby brother's safety and praising God after the miraculous crossing of the sea. She also had the honor of being named one of the few female prophets in the OT. However, she also let envy and judgment get the better of her when she and Aaron opposed Moses. Even those of us with the most courageous faith sometimes falter and question God's plans. It's easy to let envy get the better of us. The good news is that just as Miriam did, we can experience forgiveness for those moments when we fail.

CHARACTER OF GOD // GOD IS A HEALER

Exodus 15:26: "I am the LORD, who heals you."

Throughout the Bible, God heals. Healing does not only mean curing diseases, though God certainly does that. Jesus had an active healing ministry. He healed people of disease, paralysis and bleeding. He gave sight to the blind and helped people to walk again. However, the physical healings he performed were not the most important part of Christ's ministry to these individuals. While it was happy news for the paralyzed man when Jesus told him to get up and walk, it was better news still when Jesus told him, "Son, your sins are forgiven" (Mk 2:5). Being healed from a physical condition is not as important as being healed spiritually.

The Bible also says that God heals psychological and emotional hurts: "He heals the brokenhearted and binds up their wounds" (Ps 147:3). God is compassionate towards those who suffer and are in distress. God showed this through his kindness to Hannah when she was distraught, praying earnestly that God would bless her with a son (1Sa 1:1–20). He ministered to Elijah when Elijah became discouraged and depressed after receiving death threats from the king and queen of the land.

APPLICATION The healing power of God is good news, but sometimes it is difficult to wait for healing. We can each name plenty of situations when a person was not healed, even when fervent and sincere prayers for healing were offered to God. Physical and emotional healings are not the norm, even in the Bible. When they do occur, it is for the purpose of showing God's power to the world. Our greater hope is in the spiritual healing God offers, which brings us something far better than good health today. God's spiritual healing promises us eternal life with Christ.

and that is to be twice[v] as much as they
gather on the other days."
6So Moses and Aaron said to all the
Israelites, "In the evening you will know
that it was the LORD who brought you out
of Egypt,[w] 7and in the morning you will
see the glory[x] of the LORD, because he has
heard your grumbling[y] against him. Who
are we, that you should grumble against
us?"[z] 8Moses also said, "You will know
that it was the LORD when he gives you
meat to eat in the evening and all the
bread you want in the morning, because
he has heard your grumbling against
him. Who are we? You are not grumbling
against us, but against the LORD."[a]
9Then Moses told Aaron, "Say to the entire Israelite community, 'Come before the
LORD, for he has heard your grumbling.'"
10While Aaron was speaking to the
whole Israelite community, they looked
toward the desert, and there was the glory[b] of the LORD appearing in the cloud.[c]
11The LORD said to Moses, 12"I have
heard the grumbling[d] of the Israelites.
Tell them, 'At twilight you will eat meat,
and in the morning you will be filled
with bread. Then you will know that I
am the LORD your God.'"
13That evening quail[e] came and covered the camp, and in the morning there
was a layer of dew[f] around the camp.
14When the dew was gone, thin flakes
like frost[g] on the ground appeared on
the desert floor. 15When the Israelites
saw it, they said to each other, "What is
it?" For they did not know what it was.
Moses said to them, "It is the bread[h]
the LORD has given you to eat. 16This is
what the LORD has commanded: 'Everyone is to gather as much as they need.
Take an omer[a][i] for each person you have
in your tent.'"
17The Israelites did as they were told;
some gathered much, some little. 18And
when they measured it by the omer, the
one who gathered much did not have too
much, and the one who gathered little
did not have too little.[j] Everyone had
gathered just as much as they needed.
19Then Moses said to them, "No one is
to keep any of it until morning."[k]

16:5 [v] ver 22
16:6 [w] Ex 6:6
16:7 [x] ver 10; Isa 35:2; 40:5 [y] ver 12; Nu 14:2, 27,28 [z] Nu 16:11
16:8 [a] 1Sa 8:7; Ro 13:2
16:10 [b] ver 7; Nu 16:19 [c] Ex 13:21; 1Ki 8:10
16:12 [d] ver 7
16:13 [e] Nu 11:31; Ps 78:27-28; 105:40 [f] Nu 11:9
16:14 [g] ver 31; Nu 11:7-9; Ps 105:40
16:15 [h] ver 4; Jn 6:31
16:16 [i] ver 32,36
16:18 [j] 2Co 8:15*
16:19 [k] ver 23; Ex 12:10; 23:18

[a] *16* That is, possibly about 3 pounds or about 1.4 kilograms; also in verses 18, 32, 33 and 36

16:16 God provides bread in the morning and quail at night. This gracious provision of food is not to be hoarded. God is to be trusted anew every day, a lesson the Israelites will have to learn for their long trek in the desert and their life as a nation thereafter.

20However, some of them paid no attention to Moses; they kept part of it until morning, but it was full of maggots
and began to smell. So Moses was angry
with them.
21Each morning everyone gathered as
much as they needed, and when the sun
grew hot, it melted away. 22On the sixth
day, they gathered twice[l] as much — two
omers[a] for each person — and the leaders
of the community[m] came and reported
this to Moses. 23He said to them, "This
is what the LORD commanded: 'Tomorrow is to be a day of sabbath rest, a holy
sabbath[n] to the LORD. So bake what you
want to bake and boil what you want to
boil. Save whatever is left and keep it
until morning.'"
24So they saved it until morning, as
Moses commanded, and it did not stink
or get maggots in it. 25"Eat it today," Moses said, "because today is a sabbath to
the LORD. You will not find any of it on
the ground today. 26Six days you are to
gather it, but on the seventh day, the
Sabbath,[o] there will not be any."
27Nevertheless, some of the people
went out on the seventh day to gather it, but they found none. 28Then the
LORD said to Moses, "How long will you[b]
refuse to keep my commands[p] and my
instructions? 29Bear in mind that the
LORD has given you the Sabbath; that is
why on the sixth day he gives you bread
for two days. Everyone is to stay where
they are on the seventh day; no one is
to go out." 30So the people rested on the
seventh day.
31The people of Israel called the bread
manna.[c][q] It was white like coriander seed
and tasted like wafers made with honey.
32Moses said, "This is what the LORD has
commanded: 'Take an omer of manna
and keep it for the generations to come,
so they can see the bread I gave you to
eat in the wilderness when I brought you
out of Egypt.'"
33So Moses said to Aaron, "Take a jar
and put an omer of manna[r] in it. Then
place it before the LORD to be kept for
the generations to come."
34As the LORD commanded Moses,
Aaron put the manna with the tablets
of the covenant law,[s] so that it might be
preserved. 35The Israelites ate manna[t]
forty years,[u] until they came to a land
that was settled; they ate manna until
they reached the border of Canaan.[v]
36(An omer is one-tenth of an ephah.)

Water From the Rock

17 The whole Israelite community set
out from the Desert of Sin,[w] traveling from place to place as the LORD
commanded. They camped at Rephidim,
but there was no water[x] for the people to
drink. 2So they quarreled with Moses and
said, "Give us water[y] to drink."
Moses replied, "Why do you quarrel
with me? Why do you put the LORD to
the test?"[z]
3But the people were thirsty for water
there, and they grumbled[a] against Moses.
They said, "Why did you bring us up out
of Egypt to make us and our children and
livestock die of thirst?"
4Then Moses cried out to the LORD,
"What am I to do with these people? They
are almost ready to stone[b] me."
5The LORD answered Moses, "Go out in

16:22 [l] ver 5 [m] Ex 34:31
16:23 [n] Ge 2:3; Ex 20:8; 23:12; Lev 23:3
16:26 [o] Ex 20:9-10
16:28 [p] 2Ki 17:14; Ps 78:10; 106:13
16:31 [q] Nu 11:7-9
16:33 [r] Heb 9:4
16:34 [s] Ex 25:16, 21,22; 40:20; Nu 17:4,10
16:35 [t] Jn 6:31, 49 [u] Ne 9:21 [v] Jos 5:12
17:1 [w] Ex 16:1 [x] Nu 33:14
17:2 [y] Nu 20:2 [z] Dt 6:16; Ps 78:18,41; 1Co 10:9
17:3 [a] Ex 15:24; 16:2-3
17:4 [b] Nu 14:10; 1Sa 30:6

[a] *22* That is, possibly about 6 pounds or about 2.8 kilograms [b] *28* The Hebrew is plural.
[c] *31* *Manna* sounds like the Hebrew for *What is it?* (see verse 15).

16:20 As might be expected, some of the Israelites do not see the necessity of obeying the God who has saved them, and they go out on the Sabbath anyway. A second act of disobedience is met with a stunning rebuke by God (v. 28).

16:33–36 The manna seems to be a foretaste (literally) of the blessings of Canaan. The point here is not simply to fill their stomachs but to teach his people something that will be passed on for generations.

17:1–7 The third rebellion episode is the famous incident at Rephidim, and here the Israelites again complain to God about the lack of water. To have two similar episodes so close to each other in the narrative points out the absurdity of Israel's lack of trust in God. Moses responds by reminding the people that a complaint against him is really a complaint against God.

✢ **15:22—17:7** We are in a privileged position of living in the age in which the kingdom of God has indeed already come in Christ, although we still await its final implementation at his second coming. Still, grumbling and complaining as our Israelite ancestors did remains a live option for us. And thus we must make every effort to guard against this in view of the clearer vision we have of God's goodness that is ours by virtue of the Spirit who dwells in us. Indeed, it is precisely because of the Spirit's indwelling that we are able to resist an attitude of discontent.

front of the people. Take with you some
of the elders of Israel and take in your
hand the staff with which you struck the
Nile,[c] and go. 6I will stand there before
you by the rock at Horeb. Strike the rock,
and water[d] will come out of it for the
people to drink." So Moses did this in
the sight of the elders of Israel. 7And he
called the place Massah[a] and Meribah[be]
because the Israelites quarreled and because they tested the LORD saying, "Is the
LORD among us or not?"

The Amalekites Defeated

8The Amalekites[f] came and attacked
the Israelites at Rephidim. 9Moses said
to Joshua, "Choose some of our men and
go out to fight the Amalekites. Tomorrow I will stand on top of the hill with
the staff[g] of God in my hands."
10So Joshua fought the Amalekites as
Moses had ordered, and Moses, Aaron
and Hur[h] went to the top of the hill. 11As
long as Moses held up his hands, the
Israelites were winning,[i] but whenever
he lowered his hands, the Amalekites
were winning. 12When Moses' hands
grew tired, they took a stone and put it
under him and he sat on it. Aaron and
Hur held his hands up — one on one side,
one on the other — so that his hands
remained steady till sunset. 13So Joshua overcame the Amalekite army with
the sword.
14Then the LORD said to Moses, "Write[j]
this on a scroll as something to be remembered and make sure that Joshua
hears it, because I will completely blot
out the name of Amalek[k] from under
heaven."

17:5 [c] Ex 7:20
17:6 [d] Nu 20:11; Ps 114:8; 1Co 10:4
17:7 [e] Nu 20:13, 24; Ps 81:7
17:8 [f] Ge 36:12; Dt 25:17-19
17:9 [g] Ex 4:17
17:10 [h] Ex 24:14
17:11 [i] Jas 5:16
17:14 [j] Ex 24:4; 34:27; Nu 33:2 [k] 1Sa 15:3; 30:17-18

Ex 17:6 ❖ If God can bring water out of a rock in the desert, what can he accomplish in our lives? Hint: It's more than we think (see Eph 3:20).

15Moses built an altar and called it
The LORD is my Banner. 16He said, "Because hands were lifted up against[c] the
throne of the LORD,[d] the LORD will be at
war against the Amalekites from generation to generation."

Jethro Visits Moses

18 Now Jethro, the priest of Midian[l]
and father-in-law of Moses, heard
of everything God had done for Moses
and for his people Israel, and how the
LORD had brought Israel out of Egypt.
2After Moses had sent away his wife
Zipporah,[m] his father-in-law Jethro received her 3and her two sons.[n] One son
was named Gershom,[e] for Moses said,
"I have become a foreigner in a foreign
land";[o] 4and the other was named Eliezer,[fp] for he said, "My father's God was
my helper; he saved me from the sword
of Pharaoh."
5Jethro, Moses' father-in-law, together
with Moses' sons and wife, came to him
in the wilderness, where he was camped
near the mountain[q] of God. 6Jethro had
sent word to him, "I, your father-in-law
Jethro, am coming to you with your wife
and her two sons."

18:1 [l] Ex 2:16; 3:1
18:2 [m] Ex 2:21; 4:25
18:3 [n] Ex 4:20; Ac 7:29 [o] Ex 2:22
18:4 [p] 1Ch 23:15
18:5 [q] Ex 3:1

[a] 7 *Massah* means *testing.* [b] 7 *Meribah* means *quarreling.* [c] 16 Or *to* [d] 16 The meaning of the Hebrew for this clause is uncertain.
[e] 3 *Gershom* sounds like the Hebrew for *a foreigner there.* [f] 4 *Eliezer* means *my God is helper.*

17:8–10 The Amalekites are a mysterious people. In Ex 17, we only learn of their apparently unprovoked attack on the Israelites. The struggles of the Israelites with the Amalekites do not end after crossing the Jordan. Joshua's name appears four times in this brief passage. Joshua will be leading the Israelites into the promised land, and it is only fitting that he be prominently displayed here. In v. 10 we see that Joshua's obedience makes him a fitting successor to Moses.
17:11–13 In another foreshadowing of the coming division of labor in ch. 18, Hur and Aaron assist Moses.
17:14 It seems best to understand the reference to blotting out the Amalekites as God's promise of what he will eventually do through Saul and David.
17:15 The purpose of the altar here is not for sacrifice but a means by which Israel will remember what God has done for them in the desert.

✜ **17:8–16** The defeat of the Amalekites is an early manifestation of a grander and more basic battle, one that comes to a head on the cross and in the empty tomb. This is the proper perspective from which to apply the defeat of the Amalekites to our lives. The true identity of the enemies of God's people has finally been unmasked. They are not tribes or nations, kings or princes. They are a spiritual entity, and they have been defeated already.

18:1–12 The word of Yahweh's victory over Egypt has spread so as to reach Jethro's ears. We meet again Gershom, who is a reminder not only that Moses was a foreigner in Midian (2:22) but that the Israelites experienced a similar alienation in Egypt. And here we meet Eliezer (18:4), meaning "my God is helper." He is a reminder of deliverance not only for Moses but for Israel.

7 So Moses went out to meet his father-
in-law and bowed down[r] and kissed[s] him.
They greeted each other and then went
into the tent. 8 Moses told his father-in-
law about everything the LORD had done
to Pharaoh and the Egyptians for Israel's
sake and about all the hardships they had
met along the way and how the LORD had
saved[t] them.
9 Jethro was delighted to hear about all
the good things the LORD had done for
Israel in rescuing them from the hand
of the Egyptians. 10 He said, "Praise be
to the LORD,[u] who rescued you from the
hand of the Egyptians and of Pharaoh,
and who rescued the people from the
hand of the Egyptians. 11 Now I know that
the LORD is greater than all other gods,[v]
for he did this to those who had treated
Israel arrogantly."[w] 12 Then Jethro, Moses'
father-in-law, brought a burnt offering
and other sacrifices to God, and Aaron
came with all the elders of Israel to eat
a meal with Moses' father-in-law in the
presence[x] of God.
13 The next day Moses took his seat to
serve as judge for the people, and they
stood around him from morning till evening. 14 When his father-in-law saw all
that Moses was doing for the people, he
said, "What is this you are doing for the
people? Why do you alone sit as judge,
while all these people stand around you
from morning till evening?"
15 Moses answered him, "Because the
people come to me to seek God's will.[y]
16 Whenever they have a dispute, it is
brought to me, and I decide between
the parties and inform them of God's
decrees and instructions."[z]

18:7 [r] Ge 43:28 [s] Ge 29:13
18:8 [t] Ex 15:6, 16; Ps 81:7
18:10 [u] Ge 14:20; Ps 68:19-20
18:11 [v] Ex 12:12; 15:11; 2Ch 2:5 [w] Lk 1:51
18:12 [x] Dt 12:7
18:15 [y] Nu 9:6, 8; Dt 17:8-13
18:16 [z] Lev 24:12

18:7–9 Moses kisses his father-in-law, just as earlier he kissed Aaron. Exodus 4:28 parallels somewhat 18:8–9. In both places, Moses recounts "everything" God has done or said.
18:11–12 Jethro, the Midianite, has learned the lesson of the exodus: "The LORD is greater than all other gods." This can be viewed as the central theological point of this chapter. The "burnt offering and other sacrifices" (v. 12) presumably takes place in "the tent" (v. 7; likely Moses' tent) "in the presence of God." The meal provides a hint of what is to come in 24:11.
18:13–27 These verses record the second topic of this chapter—Jethro's advice to Moses to divide the labor of judging the people's disputes. Moses is said to "judge" (v. 13), which in context means arbitrating legal issues between parties based on the standard of "God's decrees and instructions" (v. 16). Jethro's advice (vv. 17–23) is detailed and may indicate that he had experience in these matters, being a priest.

PEOPLE TO KNOW // JETHRO (REUEL)

EXODUS 18:17–26: Jethro (also called Reuel) was a priest of Midian. Jethro became the father-in-law of Moses after Moses fled from Egypt upon being found out for killing an Egyptian man (Ex 2:11–15). In Midian, Moses helped Jethro's seven daughters when some local shepherds harassed them. When Jethro learned what Moses had done, he invited Moses to stay with him. Moses married Jethro's daughter, Zipporah.

For forty years Moses stayed with Jethro until God called Moses from within a burning bush and sent him to deliver the Israelites from slavery in Egypt. After the Israelites left Egypt, Jethro came to the Israelite camp to meet with Moses (Ex 18:1–12). Hearing what God had done for the Israelites, Jethro praised God's name and offered a sacrifice, declaring the Lord to be greater than all other gods.

Jethro then offered Moses some leadership advice. He learned Moses was handling every individual dispute among the people and getting worn out. Jethro told Moses to focus on being the people's representative before God and to teach them God's decrees. Then he needed to delegate smaller leadership tasks to trusted helpers. Jethro helped Moses lead in a more efficient way. After this, Jethro returned to Midian. The early church would later use this model of leadership as the apostles selected deacons to help with the daily needs of the believers (Ac 6:1–7), allowing the apostles to focus on other responsibilities.

APPLICATION Jethro was a priest and follower of God. He led others to praise the Lord after God delivered the Israelites from Egypt, and he offered sacrifices to God in thanksgiving. Jethro also showed hospitality and gratitude when he welcomed Moses to stay with him after Moses had helped his daughters. His generosity of spirit and openness to God are a lasting witness for Bible readers today. We should also be open to God's Spirit and ready to give wise counsel to others.

17 Moses' father-in-law replied, "What you are doing is not good. 18 You and these people who come to you will only wear yourselves out. The work is too heavy for you; you cannot handle it alone.[a] 19 Listen now to me and I will give you some advice, and may God be with you.[b] You must be the people's representative before God and bring their disputes[c] to him. 20 Teach them his decrees and instructions,[d] and show them the way they are to live[e] and how they are to behave.[f] 21 But select capable men[g] from all the people — men who fear God, trustworthy men who hate dishonest gain[h] — and appoint them as officials[i] over thousands, hundreds, fifties and tens. 22 Have them serve as judges for the people at all times, but have them bring every difficult case[j] to you; the simple cases they can decide themselves. That will make your load lighter, because they will share[k] it with you. 23 If you do this and God so commands, you will be able to stand the strain, and all these people will go home satisfied."

24 Moses listened to his father-in-law and did everything he said. 25 He chose capable men from all Israel and made them leaders of the people, officials over thousands, hundreds, fifties and tens.[l] 26 They served as judges for the people at all times. The difficult cases they brought to Moses, but the simple ones they decided themselves.[m]

27 Then Moses sent his father-in-law on his way, and Jethro returned to his own country.[n]

At Mount Sinai

19 On the first day of the third month after the Israelites left Egypt — on that very day — they came to the Desert of Sinai. 2 After they set out from Rephidim,[o] they entered the Desert of Sinai, and Israel camped there in the desert in front of the mountain.[p]

3 Then Moses went up to God, and the LORD called[q] to him from the mountain and said, "This is what you are to say to the descendants of Jacob and what you are to tell the people of Israel: 4 'You yourselves have seen what I did to Egypt,[r] and how I carried you on eagles' wings[s] and brought you to myself. 5 Now if you obey me fully[t] and keep my covenant,[u] then out of all nations you will be my treasured possession.[v] Although the whole earth[w] is mine, 6 you[a] will be for me a kingdom of priests[x] and a holy nation.'[y] These are the words you are to speak to the Israelites."

7 So Moses went back and summoned the elders of the people and set before them all the words the LORD had commanded him to speak. 8 The people all responded together, "We will do everything the LORD has said."[z] So Moses brought their answer back to the LORD.

9 The LORD said to Moses, "I am going to come to you in a dense cloud,[a] so that the people will hear me speaking[b] with you and will always put their trust in you." Then Moses told the LORD what the people had said.

10 And the LORD said to Moses, "Go to the people and consecrate[c] them today and tomorrow. Have them wash their

[a] 5,6 Or *possession, for the whole earth is mine.* [6] *You*

18:18 [a] Nu 11:11, 14,17
18:19 [b] Ex 3:12 [c] Nu 27:5
18:20 [d] Dt 5:1 [e] Ps 143:8 [f] Dt 1:18
18:21 [g] Ac 6:3 [h] Dt 16:19; Ps 15:5; Eze 18:8 [i] Dt 1:13,15; 2Ch 19:5-10
18:22 [j] Dt 1:17-18 [k] Nu 11:17
18:25 [l] Dt 1:13-15
18:26 [m] ver 22
18:27 [n] Nu 10:29-30
19:2 [o] Ex 17:1 [p] Ex 3:1
19:3 [q] Ex 3:4; Ac 7:38
19:4 [r] Dt 29:2 [s] Isa 63:9
19:5 [t] Ex 15:26 [u] Dt 5:2 [v] Dt 14:2; Ps 135:4 [w] Ex 9:29; Dt 10:14
19:6 [x] 1Pe 2:5 [y] Dt 7:6; 26:19; Isa 62:12
19:8 [z] Ex 24:3,7; Dt 5:27
19:9 [a] ver 16; Ex 24:15-16 [b] Dt 4:12,36
19:10 [c] Lev 11:44; Heb 10:22

Ex 18:24 ❖ How can we rely on wise advice from others in difficult situations?

Ex 19:6 ❖ What does it mean to be "a kingdom of priests"? How can the church live in this calling (see 1Pe 2:9)?

18:24–26 Moses listens to his father-in-law and puts the plan into operation. It seems that the reason why Moses obeys Jethro is not to be polite or to try it to see if it works. Jethro's advice is also God's command.

18:27 Jethro and Moses part company. Presumably Moses' family remains behind since Gershom's descendants serve as priests (Jdg 18:30).

✣ **18:1–27** As Ex 18 shows us, the nations are part of God's plan. This is no less true today. The dividing wall of hostility between the Jews and Gentiles has been broken down because of the resurrection of Christ (Eph 2:14–18). The gospel now goes freely to the whole world.

19:1–6 God's first speech to Israel is a simple message—remember. Not only are the Israelites to remember what God has done but that memory is to motivate them to obey (v. 5). Note especially the three consequences of Israel's obedience (vv. 5–6): Israel will be a treasured possession, a kingdom of priests, and a holy nation.

19:7–8 Moses descends the mountain for the first time and tells the elders what is required of them. They respond with an unqualified "yes." We will see, however, that much of Israel's subsequent history falls far short of this enthusiastic and perhaps well-intentioned assent.

19:10–13 The Israelites are to prepare themselves to approach the mountain and meet their God. They

clothes[d] 11and be ready by the third day,[e]
because on that day the LORD will come
down on Mount Sinai in the sight of all
the people. 12Put limits for the people
around the mountain and tell them, 'Be
careful that you do not approach the
mountain or touch the foot of it. Whoever touches the mountain is to be put
to death. 13They are to be stoned[f] or shot
with arrows; not a hand is to be laid on
them. No person or animal shall be permitted to live.' Only when the ram's horn
sounds a long blast may they approach
the mountain."

14After Moses had gone down the
mountain to the people, he consecrated them, and they washed their clothes.
15Then he said to the people, "Prepare
yourselves for the third day. Abstain
from sexual relations."

16On the morning of the third day
there was thunder and lightning, with
a thick cloud over the mountain, and a
very loud trumpet blast.[g] Everyone in
the camp trembled.[h] 17Then Moses led
the people out of the camp to meet with
God, and they stood at the foot of the
mountain. 18Mount Sinai was covered
with smoke,[i] because the LORD descended on it in fire.[j] The smoke billowed up
from it like smoke from a furnace,[k] and
the whole mountain[a] trembled[l] violently. 19As the sound of the trumpet grew
louder and louder, Moses spoke and the
voice[m] of God answered[n] him.[b]

20The LORD descended to the top of
Mount Sinai and called Moses to the top
of the mountain. So Moses went up 21and
the LORD said to him, "Go down and warn
the people so they do not force their way
through to see[o] the LORD and many of
them perish. 22Even the priests, who
approach[p] the LORD, must consecrate
themselves, or the LORD will break out
against them."[q]

23Moses said to the LORD, "The people
cannot come up Mount Sinai, because
you yourself warned us, 'Put limits[r]
around the mountain and set it apart
as holy.' "

24The LORD replied, "Go down and
bring Aaron[s] up with you. But the priests
and the people must not force their way
through to come up to the LORD, or he
will break out against them."

25So Moses went down to the people
and told them.

The Ten Commandments

20:1–17pp // Dt 5:6–21

20 And God spoke all these words:

2"I am the LORD your God, who
brought you out of Egypt, out
of the land of slavery.[t]

3"You shall have no other gods before[c] me.[u]

4"You shall not make for yourself
an image[v] in the form of anything in heaven above or on the

19:10 [d] Ge 35:2
19:11 [e] ver 16
19:13 [f] Heb 12:20*
19:16 [g] Heb 12:18-19; Rev 4:1 [h] Heb 12:21
19:18 [i] Ps 104:32 [j] Ex 3:2; 24:17; Dt 4:11; 2Ch 7:1; Ps 18:8; Heb 12:18 [k] Ge 19:28 [l] Jdg 5:5; Ps 68:8; Jer 4:24
19:19 [m] Ne 9:13 [n] Ps 81:7
19:21 [o] Ex 3:5; 1Sa 6:19
19:22 [p] Lev 10:3 [q] 2Sa 6:7
19:23 [r] ver 12
19:24 [s] Ex 24:1,9
20:2 [t] Ex 13:3
20:3 [u] Dt 6:14; Jer 35:15
20:4 [v] Lev 26:1; Dt 4:15-19, 23; 27:15

[a] 18 Most Hebrew manuscripts; a few Hebrew manuscripts and Septuagint *and all the people*
[b] 19 Or *and God answered him with thunder*
[c] 3 Or *besides*

are about to do something that no other nation has ever done—to meet their heavenly King and listen to his voice. The fact that limits are placed around the mountain accents the holiness of God's dwelling. Having been consecrated, the people are now ready to meet God.

19:16–17 Not only are they surrounded by thunder, lightning, and thick clouds (standard theophany language) but also by a loud trumpet blast. The climax of the scene comes when Moses and God converse.

19:20–25 God repeats essentially the same warning three times (vv. 12–13, 21–22, 24). Verse 25 reports Moses' third descent down the mountain. He again reports to the people what God has said. These events have prepared them to listen to the words of God and to hear the laws their holy God requires of them, which will further define them as servants of God, both now and for generations to come.

19:1–25 First Peter 2:4-12 makes a connection between Israel and the church. The church as the new Israel is to exhibit impeccable behavior, which is what OT Israel essentially failed to do. The intention of God to reconcile the world to himself through a select and holy people—a plan first announced in Ge 12:1-3 and more clearly defined in Ex 19:5-6, which will come to a climax in the death and resurrection of Christ—is something God is still working out. As instruments of God's plan, we are to live holy lives before God and humanity. This is a just summary of the path that all Christians are to walk. Both elements are crucial.

20:1–2 Verse 2 reminds Israel who God is and what he has done. The relationship between them has already been established. The law, in other words, is connected to grace.

20:3 This first commandment is the basis from which the other nine derive their meaning. Yahweh alone is God, and he is speaking to the people who belong to him.

20:4–6 God is jealous for his people to remain truly faithful to him.

CHARACTER OF GOD // GOD IS JEALOUS

Exodus 20:5: "You shall not bow down to them or worship them; for I, the LORD your God, am a jealous God."

It may sound strange to read that God is jealous. Aren't we jealous of people who have more than we do? And who could ever have more than God? However, it is important to distinguish between being jealous and being envious. Envy is when we are miserable that someone else is better off than we are. Saul, for example, envied David's popularity (1Sa 18:8). Jealousy, on the other hand, means wanting what is rightfully ours. For example, a spouse is jealous for their partner's love and will be offended if they see their partner flirting with someone else.

This is the metaphor God uses so often in the OT. Israel often worships other gods, prostituting themselves (e.g., Jdg 2:17). This metaphor shows the intensity of God's passion for Israel. God warns his people against worshiping other gods because he is jealous for their full love and devotion. When they direct their worship away from him, God describes their sin the way a spouse describes an unfaithful partner.

Israel's existence was a miraculous gift of God. Abraham and Sarah would never have had a child without God's intervention. Later, God delivered his people from slavery and brought them into a spacious land. He provided godly leadership through Moses and Joshua and asked the people to worship only him in the promised land. To fail in this would, and did, arouse God's righteous jealousy.

APPLICATION God rightfully deserves all our worship and devotion. He made us, and we are his (Ps 100:3). The Bible tells us to offer our lives as a living sacrifice to God, which is our true and proper worship (Ro 12:1). We are to love the Lord with all our heart, soul, mind and strength (Mk 12:30)—that leaves no room for worshiping anything else.

earth beneath or in the waters
below. 5You shall not bow down
to them or worship[w] them; for
I, the LORD your God, am a jealous God,[x] punishing the children for the sin of the parents
to the third and fourth generation[y] of those who hate me,
6but showing love to a thousand[z] generations of those who love me and keep my commandments.
7"You shall not misuse the name of the LORD your God, for the LORD will not hold anyone guiltless who misuses his name.[a]
8"Remember the Sabbath[b] day by keeping it holy.
9Six days you shall labor and do all your work,[c]
10but the seventh day is a sabbath to the LORD your God. On it you shall not do any work, neither you, nor your son or daughter, nor your male or female servant, nor your animals, nor any foreigner residing in your towns.
11For in six days the LORD made the heavens and the earth, the sea, and all that is in them, but he rested[d] on the seventh day. Therefore the LORD blessed the Sabbath day and made it holy.
12"Honor your father and your mother,[e] so that you may live long in the land the LORD your God is giving you.
13"You shall not murder.[f]
14"You shall not commit adultery.[g]
15"You shall not steal.[h]

20:5 [w] Isa 44:15, 17,19 [x] Ex 34:14; Dt 4:24 [y] Nu 14:18; Jer 32:18
20:6 [z] Dt 7:9
20:7 [a] Lev 19:12; Mt 5:33
20:8 [b] Ex 31:13-16; Lev 26:2
20:9 [c] Ex 34:21; Lk 13:14
20:11 [d] Ge 2:2
20:12 [e] Mt 15:4*; Mk 7:10*; Eph 6:2
20:13 [f] Mt 5:21*; Ro 13:9*
20:14 [g] Mt 19:18*
20:15 [h] Lev 19:11, 13; Mt 19:18*

20:7 Even today, many Jews make no attempt to use or even pronounce the name of God.
20:8–11 The Israelites are told to "remember" (v. 8) the Sabbath day. "Keeping it holy" (v. 8) should be understood as the result of remembering.
20:12 Honoring one's parents means long life in the land.
20:13 The Hebrew word translated "murder" is a restricted term, generally referring to the killing of someone who is not an "enemy" of the people. It is not used in contexts of war or just punishment for a crime.
20:14 Maintaining the physical sanctity of marriage is a central element in the maintenance of social cohesion and is an earthly symbol of the intimacy between God and his people.
20:15 Clearly the Israelites have some notion of ownership and rightful property for such a command to make sense.

the money and the dead animal equally.
36However, if it was known that the bull
had the habit of goring, yet the owner
did not keep it penned up, the owner
must pay, animal for animal, and take
the dead animal in exchange.

Protection of Property

22[a] "Whoever steals an ox or a sheep
and slaughters it or sells it must
pay back[p] five head of cattle for the ox
and four sheep for the sheep.
2"If a thief is caught breaking in[q] at
night and is struck a fatal blow, the defender is not guilty of bloodshed;[r] 3but
if it happens after sunrise, the defender
is guilty of bloodshed.
"Anyone who steals must certainly
make restitution, but if they have nothing,
they must be sold[s] to pay for their theft.
4If the stolen animal is found alive in their
possession — whether ox or donkey or
sheep — they must pay back double.[t]
5"If anyone grazes their livestock in
a field or vineyard and lets them stray
and they graze in someone else's field,
the offender must make restitution from
the best of their own field or vineyard.
6"If a fire breaks out and spreads into
thornbushes so that it burns shocks of
grain or standing grain or the whole
field, the one who started the fire must
make restitution.
7"If anyone gives a neighbor silver or
goods for safekeeping and they are stolen from the neighbor's house, the thief,
if caught, must pay back double.[u] 8But if
the thief is not found, the owner of the
house must appear before the judges,[v]
and they must[b] determine whether the
owner of the house has laid hands on the
other person's property. 9In all cases of
illegal possession of an ox, a donkey, a
sheep, a garment, or any other lost property about which somebody says, 'This
is mine,' both parties are to bring their
cases before the judges.[c][w] The one whom
the judges declare[d] guilty must pay back
double to the other.
10"If anyone gives a donkey, an ox, a
sheep or any other animal to their neighbor for safekeeping and it dies or is injured or is taken away while no one is
looking, 11the issue between them will be
settled by the taking of an oath[x] before
the LORD that the neighbor did not lay
hands on the other person's property.
The owner is to accept this, and no restitution is required. 12But if the animal
was stolen from the neighbor, restitution must be made to the owner. 13If it
was torn to pieces by a wild animal, the
neighbor shall bring in the remains as
evidence and shall not be required to
pay for the torn animal.[y]
14"If anyone borrows an animal from
their neighbor and it is injured or dies
while the owner is not present, they
must make restitution. 15But if the owner
is with the animal, the borrower will not
have to pay. If the animal was hired, the
money paid for the hire covers the loss.

Social Responsibility

16"If a man seduces a virgin[z] who is
not pledged to be married and sleeps
with her, he must pay the bride-price,
and she shall be his wife. 17If her father
absolutely refuses to give her to him, he
must still pay the bride-price for virgins.
18"Do not allow a sorceress[a] to live.
19"Anyone who has sexual relations
with an animal[b] is to be put to death.
20"Whoever sacrifices to any god other
than the LORD must be destroyed.[e][c]
21"Do not mistreat or oppress a foreigner,[d] for you were foreigners[e] in Egypt.

22:1 [p] 2Sa 12:6; Pr 6:31; Lk 19:8
22:2 [q] Mt 6:19-20; 24:43 [r] Nu 35:27
22:3 [s] Ex 21:2; Mt 18:25
22:4 [t] Ge 43:12
22:7 [u] ver 4
22:8 [v] Ex 21:6; Dt 17:8-9; 19:17
22:9 [w] ver 28; Dt 25:1
22:11 [x] Heb 6:16
22:13 [y] Ge 31:39
22:16 [z] Dt 22:28
22:18 [a] Lev 20:27; Dt 18:11; 1Sa 28:3
22:19 [b] Lev 18:23; Dt 27:21
22:20 [c] Dt 17:2-5
22:21 [d] Lev 19:33 [e] Dt 10:19

[a] In Hebrew texts 22:1 is numbered 21:37, and 22:2-31 is numbered 22:1-30. [b] 8 Or *before God, and he will* [c] 9 Or *before God* [d] 9 Or *whom God declares* [e] 20 The Hebrew term refers to the irrevocable giving over of things or persons to the LORD, often by totally destroying them.

22:1–17 A virgin who is not pledged to be married and who is seduced by a man shall become that man's wife (this is not called rape, hence some consent on the part of the woman is implied). It is important to understand this law from the point of view of the wronged party. It is not the virgin who suffers a loss in such a situation but her father. This law falls under the category of "property damage," not "social responsibility." That is why the man who seduced her will have to make restitution to her father, not to her (v. 17). Marriage, which would help the daughter save face, is something the father can refuse, but the bride-price must be paid to him nonetheless.

22:18–20 These three laws are brief. Of the three, the third law relates most specifically to religious practice: sacrificing to other gods is punishable by death.

22:21–28 These three laws highlight what we have seen throughout the book of Exodus. God loves his people dearly. He is protective of them against any abuse, including abuse at the hands of fellow Israelites. God's people must not show any sign that they are becoming like the Egyptians who oppressed them.

22“Do not take advantage of the widow or the fatherless.[f] 23If you do and they cry out[g] to me, I will certainly hear their cry.[h] 24My anger will be aroused, and I will kill you with the sword; your wives will become widows and your children fatherless.[i]

25“If you lend money to one of my people among you who is needy, do not treat it like a business deal; charge no interest.[j] 26If you take your neighbor’s cloak as a pledge,[k] return it by sunset, 27because that cloak is the only covering your neighbor has. What else can they sleep in? When they cry out to me, I will hear, for I am compassionate.[l]

28“Do not blaspheme God[a][m] or curse the ruler of your people.[n]

29“Do not hold back offerings[o] from your granaries or your vats.[b]

“You must give me the firstborn of your sons.[p] 30Do the same with your cattle and your sheep.[q] Let them stay with their mothers for seven days, but give them to me on the eighth day.[r]

31“You are to be my holy people.[s] So do not eat the meat of an animal torn by wild beasts;[t] throw it to the dogs.

Laws of Justice and Mercy

23 “Do not spread false reports.[u] Do not help a guilty person by being a malicious witness.[v]

2“Do not follow the crowd in doing wrong. When you give testimony in a lawsuit, do not pervert justice[w] by siding with the crowd, 3and do not show favoritism to a poor person in a lawsuit.

4“If you come across your enemy’s ox or donkey wandering off, be sure to return it.[x] 5If you see the donkey[y] of someone who hates you fallen down under its load, do not leave it there; be sure you help them with it.

6“Do not deny justice[z] to your poor people in their lawsuits. 7Have nothing to do with a false charge[a] and do not put an innocent or honest person to death, for I will not acquit the guilty.

8“Do not accept a bribe,[b] for a bribe blinds those who see and twists the words of the innocent.

9“Do not oppress a foreigner;[c] you yourselves know how it feels to be foreigners, because you were foreigners in Egypt.

Sabbath Laws

10“For six years you are to sow your fields and harvest the crops, 11but during the seventh year let the land lie unplowed and unused. Then the poor among your people may get food from it, and the wild animals may eat what is left. Do the same with your vineyard and your olive grove.

12“Six days do your work,[d] but on the seventh day do not work, so that your ox and your donkey may rest, and so that the slave born in your household and the foreigner living among you may be refreshed.

22:22 f Dt 24:6, 10,12,17
22:23 g Lk 18:7 h Dt 15:9; Ps 18:6
22:24 i Ps 69:24; 109:9
22:25 j Lev 25:35-37; Dt 23:20; Ps 15:5
22:26 k Dt 24:6
22:27 l Ex 34:6
22:28 m Lev 24:11, 16 n Ecc 10:20; Ac 23:5*
22:29 o Ex 23:15, 16,19 p Ex 13:2
22:30 q Ex 13:12; Dt 15:19 r Lev 22:27
22:31 s Lev 19:2 t Eze 4:14
23:1 u Ex 20:16; Ps 101:5 v Ps 35:11; Ac 6:11
23:2 w Dt 16:19
23:4 x Dt 22:1-3
23:5 y Dt 22:4
23:6 z ver 2
23:7 a Eph 4:25
23:8 b Dt 10:17; 16:19; Pr 15:27
23:9 c Ex 22:21
23:12 d Ex 20:9

Ex 22:21 ❖ How does our own experience make us more compassionate toward others going through difficult times?

Ex 23:12 ❖ How might we practice Sabbath in our lives? Consider both the personal and social aspects within the Sabbath instructions.

[a] *28* Or *Do not revile the judges* [b] *29* The meaning of the Hebrew for this phrase is uncertain.

22:29–31 The Israelites are reminded here that their best belongs to God. Of course, a human firstborn was to be redeemed by substituting a lamb or a firstborn donkey for the child (13:12–13). Verse 31 contains another reminder—that Israel is to be God’s “holy people.”
23:1–9 The final cycle of laws pertaining to social responsibility focuses mainly on matters of legal justice. God’s people are called upon to do what *is* right, not what *feels* right.
23:3 This verse emphasizes the rights of the poor, but here the Israelites are warned not to take this to the extreme. No one should assume that the rights of the poor are emphasized to the point that favoritism can be shown them.
23:4–9 These verses are case laws. They envision situations in which one Israelite should go out of his way to help another. Israelites are to deal fairly and lovingly with everyone in their midst—fellow countrymen, whether poor or rich (vv. 1–3, 6–8); enemies (vv. 4–5); and even non-Israelites, the foreigners (v. 9). As a kingdom of priests, they are not to oppress those to whom they are to reflect the glory of God.
23:10–13 The book of the covenant ends with a number of regulations concerning worship. The Sabbath year is an extension of the fourth commandment. Note that the Israelites “keep it holy” (see Ex 20:8) not by offering the produce of the seventh year to God in the form of a religious offering but by leaving it for the poor (v. 11).

13“Be careful[e] to do everything I have
said to you. Do not invoke the names of
other gods; do not let them be heard on
your lips.

The Three Annual Festivals

14“Three times[f] a year you are to celebrate a festival to me.
15“Celebrate the Festival of Unleavened
Bread;[g] for seven days eat bread made
without yeast, as I commanded you. Do
this at the appointed time in the month
of Aviv, for in that month you came out
of Egypt.
“No one is to appear before me empty-
handed.[h]
16“Celebrate the Festival of Harvest
with the firstfruits[i] of the crops you sow
in your field.
“Celebrate the Festival of Ingathering
at the end of the year, when you gather
in your crops from the field.[j]
17“Three times[k] a year all the men are
to appear before the Sovereign LORD.
18“Do not offer the blood of a sacrifice
to me along with anything containing
yeast.[l]
“The fat of my festival offerings must
not be kept until morning.[m]
19“Bring the best of the firstfruits[n] of
your soil to the house of the LORD your
God.
“Do not cook a young goat in its mother’s milk.[o]

23:13 [e] 1Ti 4:16
23:14 [f] Ex 34:23, 24
23:15 [g] Ex 12:17 [h] Ex 34:20
23:16 [i] Ex 34:22 [j] Dt 16:13
23:17 [k] Dt 16:16
23:18 [l] Ex 34:25 [m] Dt 16:4
23:19 [n] Ex 22:29; Dt 26:2,10 [o] Dt 14:21
23:20 [p] Ex 14:19; 32:34 [q] Ex 15:17
23:21 [r] Nu 14:11; Dt 18:19 [s] Ps 78:8,40,56
23:22 [t] Ge 12:3; Dt 30:7
23:23 [u] ver 20; Jos 24:8,11
23:24 [v] Ex 20:5 [w] Dt 12:30-31 [x] Ex 34:13; Nu 33:52
23:25 [y] Dt 6:13; Mt 4:10 [z] Dt 7:12-15; 28:1-14 [a] Ex 15:26
23:26 [b] Dt 7:14; Mal 3:11 [c] Job 5:26
23:27 [d] Ex 15:14; Dt 2:25 [e] Dt 7:23
23:28 [f] Dt 7:20; Jos 24:12
23:29 [g] Dt 7:22

God’s Angel to Prepare the Way

20“See, I am sending an angel[p] ahead
of you to guard you along the way and to
bring you to the place I have prepared.[q]
21Pay attention to him and listen[r] to
what he says. Do not rebel against him;
he will not forgive your rebellion,[s] since
my Name is in him. 22If you listen carefully to what he says and do all that I say,
I will be an enemy[t] to your enemies and
will oppose those who oppose you. 23My
angel will go ahead of you and bring you
into the land of the Amorites, Hittites,
Perizzites, Canaanites, Hivites and Jebusites,[u] and I will wipe them out. 24Do
not bow down before their gods or worship[v] them or follow their practices.[w] You
must demolish[x] them and break their
sacred stones to pieces. 25Worship the
LORD your God,[y] and his blessing[z] will be
on your food and water. I will take away
sickness[a] from among you, 26and none
will miscarry or be barren[b] in your land.
I will give you a full life span.[c]
27“I will send my terror[d] ahead of you
and throw into confusion[e] every nation
you encounter. I will make all your enemies turn their backs and run. 28I will
send the hornet[f] ahead of you to drive
the Hivites, Canaanites and Hittites out
of your way. 29But I will not drive them
out in a single year, because the land
would become desolate and the wild animals[g] too numerous for you. 30Little by

---

23:14–19 Verse 13 serves as a sort of transition to the religious practice matters of vv. 14–19. It serves to introduce the topic of faithfulness to God.

The Festival of Unleavened Bread is to be understood in conjunction with the Passover night described in Ex 12. This ceremony is a yearly commemoration of that deliverance. The Festival of Harvest, also referred to as the Festival of Weeks (34:22), entails offering to God the firstfruits of one’s produce and symbolizes the harvest that is to come. The Festival of Ingathering is celebrated at the end of the agricultural year. The land’s ability to produce is a gift from God.

20:22—23:19 The book of the covenant is not meant to be mined today for those laws that seem applicable. The law reflects the nature of God, but it does so in a historical context. The book of the covenant is God’s law, but it reveals God to a people living at a particular point in time and for whom he has a particular purpose. Christians are supposed to glean an understanding of the nature of God and what he requires of his people—what Jesus summarized as loving God and treating your neighbor as you would want to be treated.

23:20–26 These verses fall into two parts, each with a command followed by consequences of either obeying or disobeying the command. Listening to the angel will result in the nations being driven out of Canaan (vv. 20–23). By worshiping Yahweh alone, Israel is promised well-being, long life, and offspring (vv. 24–26).

What is somewhat striking here is the warning that the angel will not forgive Israel if they rebel. Hyperbole is not unknown in the OT, and this is what we may be dealing with here. A warning must be made in no uncertain terms.

23:27–30 The conquest will take place little by little. The “terror” is the report that Canaan will hear of Yahweh’s dealings with the Egyptians.

23:9–30 Canaan supports a much larger population than the Israelites who will be displacing them. Simply annihilating or chasing off the inhabitants will leave the land to be overrun by wild animals. Its farmable land cannot be cultivated without enough workers and will become desolate. Hence, the conquest will take place little by little, in stages.

little I will drive them out before you, until you have increased enough to take possession of the land.

31 “I will establish your borders from the Red Sea[a] to the Mediterranean Sea,[b] and from the desert to the Euphrates River.[h] I will give into your hands the people who live in the land, and you will drive them out[i] before you. 32 Do not make a covenant[j] with them or with their gods. 33 Do not let them live in your land or they will cause you to sin against me, because the worship of their gods will certainly be a snare[k] to you.”

The Covenant Confirmed

24 Then the LORD said to Moses, “Come up to the LORD, you and Aaron, Nadab and Abihu,[l] and seventy of the elders[m] of Israel. You are to worship at a distance, 2 but Moses alone is to approach the LORD; the others must not come near. And the people may not come up with him.”

3 When Moses went and told the people all the LORD’s words and laws, they responded with one voice, “Everything the LORD has said we will do.”[n] 4 Moses then wrote[o] down everything the LORD had said.

He got up early the next morning and built an altar at the foot of the mountain and set up twelve stone pillars[p] representing the twelve tribes of Israel. 5 Then he sent young Israelite men, and they offered burnt offerings and sacrificed young bulls as fellowship offerings to the LORD. 6 Moses took half of the blood[q] and put it in bowls, and the other half he splashed against the altar. 7 Then he took the Book of the Covenant[r] and read it to the people. They responded, “We will do everything the LORD has said; we will obey.”

8 Moses then took the blood, sprinkled it on the people and said, “This is the blood of the covenant[s] that the LORD has made with you in accordance with all these words.”

9 Moses and Aaron, Nadab and Abihu, and the seventy elders[t] of Israel went up 10 and saw[u] the God of Israel. Under his feet was something like a pavement made of lapis lazuli,[v] as bright blue as the sky.[w] 11 But God did not raise his hand against these leaders of the Israelites; they saw[x] God, and they ate and drank.

12 The LORD said to Moses, “Come up to me on the mountain and stay here, and I will give you the tablets of stone[y]

23:31 [h] Ge 15:18 [i] Jos 21:44; 24:12,18
23:32 [j] Ex 34:12; Dt 7:2
23:33 [k] Dt 7:16; Ps 106:36
24:1 [l] Ex 6:23; Lev 10:1-2 [m] Nu 11:16
24:3 [n] Ex 19:8; Dt 5:27
24:4 [o] Dt 31:9 [p] Ge 28:18
24:6 [q] Heb 9:18
24:7 [r] Heb 9:19
24:8 [s] Heb 9:20*; 1Pe 1:2
24:9 [t] ver 1
24:10 [u] Mt 17:2; Jn 1:18; 6:46 [v] Eze 1:26 [w] Rev 4:3
24:11 [x] Ge 32:30; Ex 19:21
24:12 [y] Ex 32:15-16

Ex 24:12 ❖ Learning from God involves drawing close to him. How can we more effectively draw near to God (See Jn 17)?

[a] *31* Or *the Sea of Reeds* [b] *31* Hebrew *to the Sea of the Philistines*

23:31-33 The general borders God intends for Israel’s possession are given. Verses 32-33 remind the Israelites once again about worshiping other gods. What anchors the message of this entire section is Yahweh’s repeated teaching to his people that they belong to him and him alone.

✣ **23:20-33** The “angel” is more deeply felt now than ever before. The spirit of the risen Christ, the Holy Spirit, is always with us. This is Jesus’ final statement to his disciples (Mt 28:20). Christ does for us what the angel did for the Israelites. He is truly with us at every step in our journey. He was there at our redemption calling us into his presence. And having called us, he guards us and guides us home.

24:1-4 Likely “words” and “laws” are a shorthand reference to the Ten Commandments and the Book of the Covenant. Burnt offerings are typically made for atonement for sin and to show commitment to God. Fellowship offerings celebrate fellowship with God. One half of the blood sacrificed was sprinkled on the altar while the other half was sprinkled on the people (v. 8). The former represents sin atonement (burnt offerings), the latter fellowship.

24:9-10 The covenant stipulations have just been given and the covenant confirmed by the sprinkling of blood. By showing himself to the leaders, God is giving them an added dose of his presence to solemnize what has just happened and to prepare them for what is to come.

Even the vision of the ground under his feet is too much for words. The best the writer can do is to say it is “something like a pavement” (v. 10). The company on the mountain eat and drink a covenant meal (v. 11; cf. 18:12).

24:12-18 As Moses ascends the mountain, he has left things in what he no doubt thinks are trustworthy hands: his older brother Aaron, whom God appointed as his partner, and Hur, a respected member of the community. The anger he shows later is an appropriate response (32:19-20).

✣ **24:1-18** The Lord’s Supper is a continual reminder both of what God has done in Christ and of the final eschatological meal to be shared by the universal church in the presence of God at the end of the present world order.

with the law and commandments I have
written for their instruction."
13Then Moses set out with Joshua[z] his
aide, and Moses went up on the mountain[a] of God. 14He said to the elders,
"Wait here for us until we come back to
you. Aaron and Hur are with you, and
anyone involved in a dispute can go to
them."
15When Moses went up on the mountain, the cloud[b] covered it, 16and the glory[c] of the LORD settled on Mount Sinai.
For six days the cloud covered the mountain, and on the seventh day the LORD
called to Moses from within the cloud.[d]
17To the Israelites the glory of the LORD
looked like a consuming fire[e] on top of
the mountain. 18Then Moses entered the
cloud as he went on up the mountain.
And he stayed on the mountain forty[f]
days and forty nights.[g]

Offerings for the Tabernacle

25:1–7pp // Ex 35:4–9

25 The LORD said to Moses, 2"Tell the
Israelites to bring me an offering.
You are to receive the offering for me
from everyone whose heart prompts[h]
them to give. 3These are the offerings
you are to receive from them: gold, silver and bronze; 4blue, purple and scarlet
yarn and fine linen; goat hair; 5ram skins
dyed red and another type of durable
leather[a]; acacia wood; 6olive oil[i] for the
light; spices for the anointing oil and for
the fragrant incense; 7and onyx stones
and other gems to be mounted on the
ephod[j] and breastpiece.[k]

24:13 [z] Ex 17:9 [a] Ex 3:1
24:15 [b] Ex 19:9
24:16 [c] Ex 16:10 [d] Ps 99:7
24:17 [e] Ex 3:2; Dt 4:36; Heb 12:18,29
24:18 [f] Dt 9:9 [g] Ex 34:28
25:2 [h] Ex 35:21; 1Ch 29:5,7, 9; Ezr 2:68; 2Co 8:11-12; 9:7
25:6 [i] Ex 27:20; 30:22-32
25:7 [j] Ex 28:4, 6-14 [k] Ex 28:15-30
25:8 [l] Ex 36:1-5; Heb 9:1-2 [m] Ex 29:45; 1Ki 6:13; 2Co 6:16; Rev 21:3
25:9 [n] ver 40; Ac 7:44; Heb 8:5
25:10 [o] Dt 10:1-5; Heb 9:4
25:15 [p] 1Ki 8:8
25:16 [q] Dt 31:26; Heb 9:4
25:17 [r] Ro 3:25

Ex 25:2 ❖ In view of God's love and mercy, what offering does our heart prompt us to give to God?

8"Then have them make a sanctuary[l]
for me, and I will dwell[m] among them.
9Make this tabernacle and all its furnishings exactly like the pattern[n] I will
show you.

The Ark

25:10–20pp // Ex 37:1–9

10"Have them make an ark[b][o] of acacia
wood — two and a half cubits long, a cubit and a half wide, and a cubit and a half
high.[c] 11Overlay it with pure gold, both
inside and out, and make a gold molding around it. 12Cast four gold rings for
it and fasten them to its four feet, with
two rings on one side and two rings on
the other. 13Then make poles of acacia
wood and overlay them with gold. 14In-
sert the poles into the rings on the sides
of the ark to carry it. 15The poles are to
remain in the rings of this ark; they are
not to be removed.[p] 16Then put in the ark
the tablets of the covenant law,[q] which I
will give you.
17"Make an atonement cover[r] of pure
gold — two and a half cubits long and a
cubit and a half wide. 18And make two
cherubim out of hammered gold at the

[a] *5* Possibly the hides of large aquatic mammals
[b] *10* That is, a chest [c] *10* That is, about 3 3/4 feet long and 2 1/4 feet wide and high or about 1.1 meters long and 68 centimeters wide and high; similarly in verse 17

25:1—31:18; 35:1—40:33 The matter of the tabernacle spans thirteen of the remaining sixteen chapters of Exodus. Chapters 35-40 essentially repeat the content of chs. 25-31 with only insignificant and minor additions and/or deletions. These parallel sections have been grouped under one heading.

25:1-9; 35:4-9 The reader is provided with a list of the materials that are to be brought before God for the purpose of building the tabernacle and related items—precious metals, expensive yarns and linen, acacia wood, olive oil, spices, precious stones, and gems. The only possible source of these items that can be inferred from the text is the Egyptians, whom the Israelites plundered (12:36).

The suitable abode for God is one that reflects the "pattern" given to Moses. This is an early indication that the tabernacle is an earthly symbol of a greater, heavenly reality. The phrase "the LORD said to Moses" occurs seven times in chs. 25-31. The first six concern the building of the tabernacle, while the final introduces the Sabbath command (31:12). The purpose of this arrangement is to aid the reader in making the connection between the building of the tabernacle and the seven days of creation, both of which involve six creative acts culminating in a seventh-day rest.

25:10-22; 37:1-9 The writer stresses the importance of the ark. By placing the ark first, the reader's attention is drawn to the central concern of the tabernacle narrative. The ark is the focus of God's presence with his people, the central point of contact between heaven and the tabernacle, the earthly symbol of heaven.

The presence of the cherubim emphasizes the holiness of the ark. Over the ark, which measures approximately 3 feet and 9 inches long by 2 feet and 4 inches wide and high, is the "atonement cover." From above this cover, between the cherubim, God will meet with his people and speak with them (25:22). The fact that the law, God's supreme self-revelation to his people, is kept inside the ark also indicates that the ark is the center of gravity of God's presence with his people.

THE TABERNACLE

The new religious observances taught by Moses in the wilderness centered on rituals connected with the tabernacle and amplified Israel's sense of separateness, purity and oneness under the lordship of Yahweh.

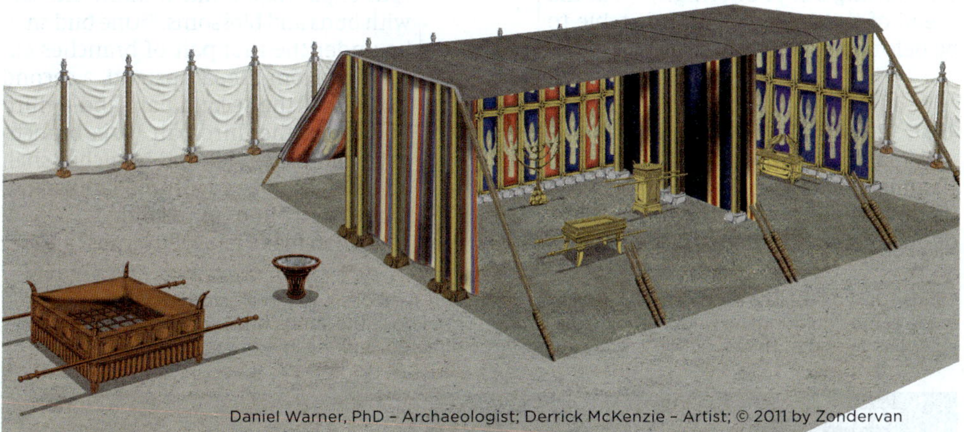

Daniel Warner, PhD - Archaeologist; Derrick McKenzie - Artist; © 2011 by Zondervan

A few desert shrines have been found in Sinai (notably at Serabit el-Khadem) and at Timnah in the Negev. They show marked Egyptian influence.

Specific cultural antecedents to portable shrines carried on poles and covered with thin sheets of gold can be found in ancient Egypt as early as the Old Kingdom (2800-2250 BC), but they were especially prominent in the Eighteenth and Nineteenth Dynasties (1570-1180). The best examples come from the fabulous tomb of Tutankhamun, c. 1300 BC.

Comparisons of construction details in the text of Ex 25-40 with the frames, shrines, poles, sheathing, draped fabric covers, gilt rosettes and winged protective figures from the shrine of Tutankhamun are instructive. The period, the Late Bronze Age, is equivalent in all dating systems to the era of Moses and the exodus.

ends of the cover. 19Make one cherub on
one end and the second cherub on the
other; make the cherubim of one piece
with the cover, at the two ends. 20The
cherubim are to have their wings spread
upward, overshadowing[s] the cover with
them. The cherubim are to face each other, looking toward the cover. 21Place the
cover on top of the ark[t] and put in the
ark the tablets of the covenant law[u] that
I will give you. 22There, above the cover
between the two cherubim[v] that are over
the ark of the covenant law, I will meet[w]
with you and give you all my commands
for the Israelites.

25:20 [s]1Ki 8:7; 1Ch 28:18; Heb 9:5
25:21 [t]Ex 26:34 [u]ver 16
25:22 [v]Nu 7:89; 1Sa 4:4; 2Sa 6:2; 2Ki 19:15; Ps 80:1; Isa 37:16 [w]Ex 29:42-43
25:23 [x]Heb 9:2

The Table

25:23–29pp // Ex 37:10–16

23"Make a table[x] of acacia wood—two
cubits long, a cubit wide and a cubit
and a half high.[a] 24Overlay it with pure
gold and make a gold molding around
it. 25Also make around it a rim a handbreadth[b] wide and put a gold molding
on the rim. 26Make four gold rings for

[a] *23* That is, about 3 feet long, 1 1/2 feet wide and 2 1/4 feet high or about 90 centimeters long, 45 centimeters wide and 68 centimeters high
[b] *25* That is, about 3 inches or about 7.5 centimeters

25:23-30; 37:10-16 The table is constructed for holding "the bread of the Presence" (25:30). Its dimensions are 3 feet long by 1 foot and 6 inches wide and 2 feet and 3 inches high.

No explanation is given here for "the bread of the Presence." It is an ambiguous term, which may simply mean "bread that is in the presence [of God]." As to any further significance of the bread we are given little information. Perhaps the bread of the Presence along with the drink offering implied in 25:29 are elements in another covenant meal between God and Israel's leaders.

the table and fasten them to the four
corners, where the four legs are. 27The
rings are to be close to the rim to hold the
poles used in carrying the table. 28Make
the poles of acacia wood, overlay them
with gold and carry the table with them.
29And make its plates and dishes of pure
gold, as well as its pitchers and bowls for
the pouring out of offerings.[y] 30Put the
bread of the Presence[z] on this table to
be before me at all times.

The Lampstand

25:31–39pp // Ex 37:17–24

31"Make a lampstand[a] of pure gold.
Hammer out its base and shaft, and make
its flowerlike cups, buds and blossoms
of one piece with them. 32Six branches
are to extend from the sides of the lampstand — three on one side and three on
the other. 33Three cups shaped like almond flowers with buds and blossoms
are to be on one branch, three on the
next branch, and the same for all six
branches extending from the lampstand.
34And on the lampstand there are to be
four cups shaped like almond flowers
with buds and blossoms. 35One bud shall
be under the first pair of branches extending from the lampstand, a second
bud under the second pair, and a third
bud under the third pair — six branches in all. 36The buds and branches shall
all be of one piece with the lampstand,
hammered out of pure gold.
37"Then make its seven lamps[b] and set

25:29 [y] Nu 4:7
25:30 [z] Lev 24:5-9
25:31 [a] 1Ki 7:49; Zec 4:2; Heb 9:2; Rev 1:12
25:37 [b] Ex 27:21; Lev 24:3-4; Nu 8:2

25:31–40; 37:17–24 The lampstand and its lamps are made of pure gold with no wood. Tending the lamps is serious business. Their function is likely ritualistic and symbolic, though precisely in what way we do not know. The lampstand is to be made as God has directed, and the light is to be kept burning.

TABERNACLE FURNISHINGS

The symbolism of God's redemptive covenant was preserved in the tabernacle, making each element an object lesson for the worshiper. Likely reconstructions of the furnishings are based on the detailed descriptions and precise measurements recorded in Exodus 25–40. (The bronze basin is not shown here, but see photo, p. 133.)

1 ARK OF THE COVENANT
The ark of the covenant compares with the roughly contemporary shrine and funerary furniture of Tutankhamun (c. 1300 BC), which, along with the Nimrud and Samaria ivories from a later period, have been used to guide the graphic interpretation of the text. Both sources show the conventional way of depicting extreme reverence, with facing winged guardians shielding a sacred place.

2 INCENSE ALTAR

3 LAMPSTAND
The traditional form of the lampstand is not attested archaeologically until much later.

4 TABLE
The table holding the bread of the Presence was made of wood overlaid with thin sheets of gold. All of the objects were portable and were fitted with rings and carrying poles, practices typical of Egyptian ritual processions as early as the Old Kingdom period (c. 2715–2640 BC).

5 BRONZE ALTAR
The altar of burnt offering was made of wood overlaid with bronze. The size, five cubits square and three cubits high, matches that of an altar found at Arad from the time of Solomon.

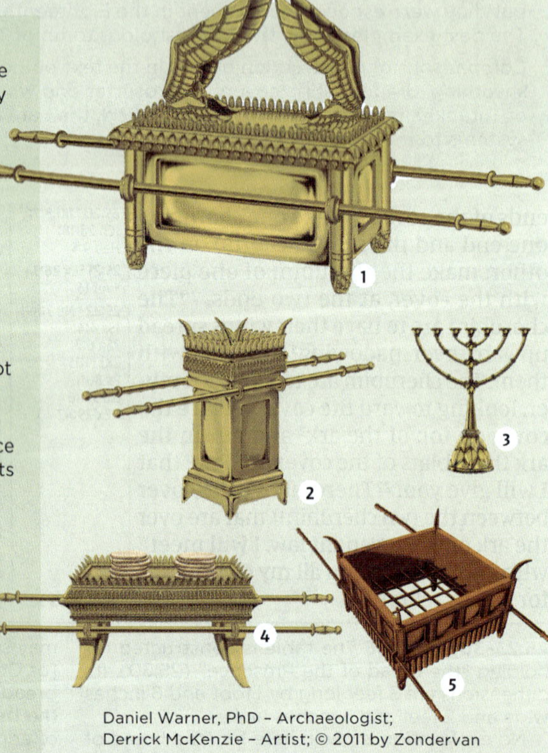

Daniel Warner, PhD - Archaeologist;
Derrick McKenzie - Artist; © 2011 by Zondervan

them up on it so that they light the space
in front of it. 38Its wick trimmers and
trays are to be of pure gold. 39A talent[a]
of pure gold is to be used for the lampstand and all these accessories. 40See that
you make them according to the pattern[c]
shown you on the mountain.

The Tabernacle

26:1–37pp // Ex 36:8–38

26 "Make the tabernacle with ten
curtains of finely twisted linen
and blue, purple and scarlet yarn, with
cherubim woven into them by a skilled
worker. 2All the curtains are to be the
same size — twenty-eight cubits long and
four cubits wide.[b] 3Join five of the curtains together, and do the same with the
other five. 4Make loops of blue material
along the edge of the end curtain in one
set, and do the same with the end curtain
in the other set. 5Make fifty loops on one
curtain and fifty loops on the end curtain
of the other set, with the loops opposite
each other. 6Then make fifty gold clasps
and use them to fasten the curtains together so that the tabernacle is a unit.
7"Make curtains of goat hair for the
tent over the tabernacle — eleven altogether. 8All eleven curtains are to be the
same size — thirty cubits long and four
cubits wide.[c] 9Join five of the curtains
together into one set and the other six
into another set. Fold the sixth curtain
double at the front of the tent. 10Make
fifty loops along the edge of the end curtain in one set and also along the edge of
the end curtain in the other set. 11Then
make fifty bronze clasps and put them
in the loops to fasten the tent together
as a unit. 12As for the additional length
of the tent curtains, the half curtain that
is left over is to hang down at the rear of
the tabernacle. 13The tent curtains will
be a cubit[d] longer on both sides; what is
left will hang over the sides of the tabernacle so as to cover it. 14Make for the
tent a covering of ram skins dyed red,
and over that a covering of the other durable leather.[e][d]
15"Make upright frames of acacia wood
for the tabernacle. 16Each frame is to be
ten cubits long and a cubit and a half
wide,[f] 17with two projections set parallel
to each other. Make all the frames of the
tabernacle in this way. 18Make twenty
frames for the south side of the tabernacle 19and make forty silver bases to go
under them — two bases for each frame,
one under each projection. 20For the other side, the north side of the tabernacle,

25:40 [c]Ex 26:30; Nu 8:4; Ac 7:44; Heb 8:5*

26:14 [d]Ex 36:19; Nu 4:25

Ex 26 ❖ The tabernacle was ornately designed to be the place of God's presence. How can our lives and bodies be set apart to hold God's presence with equal care (see 1Co 6:19)?

[a] *39* That is, about 75 pounds or about 34 kilograms [b] *2* That is, about 42 feet long and 6 feet wide or about 13 meters long and 1.8 meters wide [c] *8* That is, about 45 feet long and 6 feet wide or about 13.5 meters long and 1.8 meters wide [d] *13* That is, about 18 inches or about 45 centimeters [e] *14* Possibly the hides of large aquatic mammals (see 25:5) [f] *16* That is, about 15 feet long and 2 1/4 feet wide or about 4.5 meters long and 68 centimeters wide

26:1-37; 36:8-38 The tabernacle is basically a series of curtains and frames. The curtains covering the entire structure are to be made of fine linen and colored yarn. Cherubim are to be worked into them, an ever-present reminder that the tabernacle is an earthly representation of the heavenly tabernacle. This first layer of curtains must be covered on the outside by a second layer made of goat hair, most likely to protect the inner curtains from the elements. There are apparently two further layers of ram skins and hides of sea cows covering the layer of goat hair (26:14). These curtains are to be kept together by a system of bronze clasps and loops.

The Lord reminds Moses to adhere strictly to this plan (26:30). Exodus 26:31 commences with instructions concerning the curtain to separate the Holy Place from the Most Holy Place. Another similarly constructed curtain is to be placed at the entrance of the tent (i.e., between the Holy Place and the outer court). This curtain has no cherubim worked into it since this is one step removed from the Most Holy Place.

The entire structure measured 150 feet on the north and south sides and 75 feet on the east and west, thus forming a rectangle made up of two squares 75 feet by 75 feet. One square constituted the outer court. Inside the other square was the Holy Place, a rectangle the same proportions as the tabernacle as a whole. The adjoining Most Holy Place measured a perfect 15-foot square.

The tabernacle seems to represent a microcosm of creation itself. The splendor and beauty of the materials used—fine fabrics, precious metals, and stones—affirm the goodness of the created world. The precise and perfect dimensions of the tabernacle indicate a sense of order amid chaos.

The tabernacle is laden with redemptive significance, not just because of the sacrifices and offerings within its walls but simply because of what it is—a piece of holy ground in a world that has lost its way.

make twenty frames 21 and forty silver bases — two under each frame. 22 Make six frames for the far end, that is, the west end of the tabernacle, 23 and make two frames for the corners at the far end. 24 At these two corners they must be double from the bottom all the way to the top and fitted into a single ring; both shall be like that. 25 So there will be eight frames and sixteen silver bases — two under each frame.

26 "Also make crossbars of acacia wood: five for the frames on one side of the tabernacle, 27 five for those on the other side, and five for the frames on the west, at the far end of the tabernacle. 28 The center crossbar is to extend from end to end at the middle of the frames. 29 Overlay the frames with gold and make gold rings to hold the crossbars. Also overlay the crossbars with gold.

30 "Set up the tabernacle according to the plan[e] shown you on the mountain.

31 "Make a curtain[f] of blue, purple and scarlet yarn and finely twisted linen, with cherubim[g] woven into it by a skilled worker. 32 Hang it with gold hooks on four posts of acacia wood overlaid with gold and standing on four silver bases. 33 Hang the curtain from the clasps and place the ark of the covenant law behind the curtain.[h] The curtain will separate the Holy Place from the Most Holy Place.[i] 34 Put the atonement cover[j] on the ark of the covenant law in the Most Holy Place. 35 Place the table[k] outside the curtain on the north side of the tabernacle and put the lampstand[l] opposite it on the south side.

36 "For the entrance to the tent make a curtain of blue, purple and scarlet yarn and finely twisted linen — the work of an embroiderer. 37 Make gold hooks for this curtain and five posts of acacia wood overlaid with gold. And cast five bronze bases for them.

The Altar of Burnt Offering

27:1–8pp // Ex 38:1–7

27 "Build an altar[m] of acacia wood, three cubits[a] high; it is to be square, five cubits long and five cubits wide.[b] 2 Make a horn[n] at each of the four corners, so that the horns and the altar are of one piece, and overlay the altar with bronze. 3 Make all its utensils of bronze — its pots to remove the ashes, and its shovels, sprinkling bowls, meat forks and firepans. 4 Make a grating for it, a bronze network, and make a bronze ring at each of the four corners of the network. 5 Put it under the ledge of the altar so that it is halfway up the altar. 6 Make poles of acacia wood for the altar and overlay them with bronze. 7 The poles are to be inserted into the rings so they will be on two sides of the altar when it is carried. 8 Make the altar hollow, out of boards. It is to be made just as you were shown[o] on the mountain.

The Courtyard

27:9–19pp // Ex 38:9–20

9 "Make a courtyard for the tabernacle. The south side shall be a hundred cubits[c] long and is to have curtains of finely twisted linen, 10 with twenty posts and twenty bronze bases and with silver hooks and bands on the posts. 11 The north side shall also be a hundred cubits long and is to have curtains, with twenty posts and twenty bronze bases and with silver hooks and bands on the posts.

12 "The west end of the courtyard shall be fifty cubits[d] wide and have curtains, with ten posts and ten bases. 13 On the east end, toward the sunrise, the courtyard shall also be fifty cubits wide. 14 Curtains fifteen cubits[e] long are to be on one side of the entrance, with three posts and three bases, 15 and curtains fifteen cubits long are to be on the other side, with three posts and three bases.

16 "For the entrance to the courtyard,

26:30 [e] Ex 25:9, 40; Ac 7:44; Heb 8:5
26:31 [f] 2Ch 3:14; Mt 27:51; Heb 9:3 [g] Ex 36:35
26:33 [h] Ex 40:3, 21; Lev 16:2 [i] Heb 9:2-3
26:34 [j] Ex 25:21; 40:20; Heb 9:5
26:35 [k] Heb 9:2 [l] Ex 40:22, 24
27:1 [m] Eze 43:13
27:2 [n] Ps 118:27
27:8 [o] Ex 25:9, 40

[a] *1* That is, about 4 1/2 feet or about 1.4 meters
[b] *1* That is, about 7 1/2 feet or about 2.3 meters long and wide
[c] *9* That is, about 150 feet or about 45 meters; also in verse 11
[d] *12* That is, about 75 feet or about 23 meters; also in verse 13
[e] *14* That is, about 23 feet or about 6.8 meters; also in verse 15

27:1-8; 38:1-7 The altar measures 7 feet by 6 inches square and is 4 feet by 6 inches tall; it is to be located in the outer court. This altar is for offering burnt offerings. Details of this sacrifice are presented in Lev 1:1–17.

One of its curious characteristics is a horn at each of its four corners. We read in 29:12 that blood is to be put on the horns, thus suggesting some type of redemptive symbolism. The presence of horned altars in antiquity is well established, which lends credence to the historicity of the altar described here.

27:9–19; 38:9–20 The courtyard is the entire enclosure, not to be confused with the outer court.

provide a curtain twenty cubits[a] long, of
blue, purple and scarlet yarn and finely
twisted linen — the work of an embroiderer — with four posts and four bases. 17 All the posts around the courtyard
are to have silver bands and hooks, and
bronze bases. 18 The courtyard shall be
a hundred cubits long and fifty cubits
wide,[b] with curtains of finely twisted
linen five cubits[c] high, and with bronze
bases. 19 All the other articles used in the
service of the tabernacle, whatever their
function, including all the tent pegs for
it and those for the courtyard, are to be
of bronze.

Oil for the Lampstand

27:20–21pp // Lev 24:1–3

20 "Command the Israelites to bring
you clear oil of pressed olives for the
light so that the lamps may be kept burning. 21 In the tent of meeting,[p] outside
the curtain that shields the ark of the
covenant law,[q] Aaron and his sons are
to keep the lamps[r] burning before the
LORD from evening till morning. This
is to be a lasting ordinance[s] among the
Israelites for the generations to come.

The Priestly Garments

28 "Have Aaron[t] your brother brought
to you from among the Israelites,
along with his sons Nadab and Abihu, Eleazar and Ithamar, so they may serve me
as priests.[u] 2 Make sacred garments[v] for
your brother Aaron to give him dignity
and honor. 3 Tell all the skilled workers[w]
to whom I have given wisdom[x] in such
matters that they are to make garments
for Aaron, for his consecration, so he may
serve me as priest. 4 These are the garments they are to make: a breastpiece,[y]
an ephod, a robe,[z] a woven tunic,[a] a turban and a sash. They are to make these
sacred garments for your brother Aaron
and his sons, so they may serve me as
priests. 5 Have them use gold, and blue,
purple and scarlet yarn, and fine linen.

27:21 [p] Ex 28:43 [q] Ex 26:31, 33 [r] Ex 25:37; 30:8; 1Sa 3:3; 2Ch 13:11 [s] Ex 29:9; Lev 3:17; 16:34; Nu 18:23; 19:21
28:1 [t] Heb 5:4 [u] Nu 18:1-7; Heb 5:1
28:2 [v] Ex 29:5, 29; 31:10; 39:1; Lev 8:7-9, 30
28:3 [w] Ex 31:6; 36:1 [x] Ex 31:3
28:4 [y] ver 15-30 [z] ver 31-35 [a] ver 39

Ex 27:21 ❖ The lamp never went out in God's tabernacle. How can we celebrate and trust in God's unrelenting presence in our lives, no matter how dark it seems?

The Ephod

28:6–14pp // Ex 39:2–7

6 "Make the ephod of gold, and of blue,
purple and scarlet yarn, and of finely twisted linen — the work of skilled
hands. 7 It is to have two shoulder pieces
attached to two of its corners, so it can
be fastened. 8 Its skillfully woven waistband is to be like it — of one piece with
the ephod and made with gold, and with
blue, purple and scarlet yarn, and with
finely twisted linen.
9 "Take two onyx stones and engrave
on them the names of the sons of Israel
10 in the order of their birth — six names
on one stone and the remaining six on
the other. 11 Engrave the names of the
sons of Israel on the two stones the way
a gem cutter engraves a seal. Then mount
the stones in gold filigree settings 12 and
fasten them on the shoulder pieces of
the ephod as memorial stones for the

[a] *16* That is, about 30 feet or about 9 meters
[b] *18* That is, about 150 feet long and 75 feet wide or about 45 meters long and 23 meters wide
[c] *18* That is, about 7 1/2 feet or about 2.3 meters

27:20–21 Clear olive oil is to be used, as it produces little smoke and gives off better light.

28:1–43; 39:1–31 This lengthy section treats the garments that Aaron (28:1-39) and his sons (28:40-43) are to wear when ministering in the tabernacle. The garments are to give Aaron "dignity and honor," and they are to be prepared in advance of his consecration (28:3).

These materials are not just costly but they also parallel the materials used to make the tabernacle: gold, blue, purple, and scarlet yarn; fine linen; onyx, and other precious stones. By being dressed similarly to the tabernacle itself, the high priest in his service becomes the focus of God's presence for the people of God—a mini-tabernacle, as it were.

The ephod is likely an apron-like garment. Over the ephod is a "breastpiece for making decisions" (28:15). This garment sports four rows of three stones, each of which is engraved with the name of one of the tribes of Israel. Also placed in the breastpiece are the Urim and Thummim (28:30). The people must have known what they were and how they were to be used since they simply appear here in Ex 28 without any explanation (see also Lev 8:8; Nu 27:21; Dt 33:8).

Next we read of the plate of pure gold on the front of the turban, on which is engraved: "HOLY TO THE LORD" (28:36). The words on Aaron's forehead are a reminder to God that the offerings Aaron is bringing are "acceptable to the LORD."

The final garments mentioned are tunics, sashes, headbands, and undergarments. What is conspicuously absent from the list is shoes, perhaps because of what has already been suggested in 3:5. The priests stand in God's presence and must conduct themselves appropriately.

sons of Israel. Aaron is to bear the names on his shoulders as a memorial before the LORD. 13Make gold filigree settings 14and two braided chains of pure gold, like a rope, and attach the chains to the settings.

The Breastpiece

28:15–28pp // Ex 39:8–21

15"Fashion a breastpiece for making decisions — the work of skilled hands. Make it like the ephod: of gold, and of blue, purple and scarlet yarn, and of finely twisted linen. 16It is to be square — a span[a] long and a span wide — and folded double. 17Then mount four rows of precious stones on it. The first row shall be carnelian, chrysolite and beryl; 18the second row shall be turquoise, lapis lazuli and emerald; 19the third row shall be jacinth, agate and amethyst; 20the fourth row shall be topaz, onyx and jasper.[b] Mount them in gold filigree settings. 21There are to be twelve stones, one for each of the names of the sons of Israel, each engraved like a seal with the name of one of the twelve tribes.

22"For the breastpiece make braided chains of pure gold, like a rope. 23Make two gold rings for it and fasten them to two corners of the breastpiece. 24Fasten the two gold chains to the rings at the corners of the breastpiece, 25and the other ends of the chains to the two settings, attaching them to the shoulder pieces of the ephod at the front. 26Make two gold rings and attach them to the other two corners of the breastpiece on the inside edge next to the ephod. 27Make two more gold rings and attach them to the bottom of the shoulder pieces on the front of the ephod, close to the seam just above the waistband of the ephod. 28The rings of the breastpiece are to be tied to the rings of the ephod with blue cord, connecting it to the waistband, so that the breastpiece will not swing out from the ephod.

29"Whenever Aaron enters the Holy Place,[b] he will bear the names of the sons of Israel over his heart on the breastpiece of decision as a continuing memorial before the LORD. 30Also put the Urim and the Thummim[c] in the breastpiece, so they may be over Aaron's heart whenever he enters the presence of the LORD. Thus Aaron will always bear the means of making decisions for the Israelites over his heart before the LORD.

28:29 [b]ver 12
28:30 [c]Lev 8:8; Nu 27:21; Dt 33:8; Ezr 2:63; Ne 7:65

Ex 28:29 ❖ How might we better bear the names and lives of others on our hearts as we come to God in prayer?

Other Priestly Garments

28:31–43pp // Ex 39:22–31

31"Make the robe of the ephod entirely of blue cloth, 32with an opening for the head in its center. There shall be a woven edge like a collar[c] around this opening, so that it will not tear. 33Make pomegranates of blue, purple and scarlet yarn around the hem of the robe, with gold bells between them. 34The gold bells and the pomegranates are to alternate around the hem of the robe. 35Aaron must wear it when he ministers. The sound of the bells will be heard when he enters the Holy Place before the LORD and when he comes out, so that he will not die.

36"Make a plate of pure gold and engrave on it as on a seal: HOLY TO THE LORD.[d] 37Fasten a blue cord to it to attach it to the turban; it is to be on the front of the turban. 38It will be on Aaron's forehead, and he will bear the guilt[e] involved in the sacred gifts the Israelites consecrate, whatever their gifts may be. It will be on Aaron's forehead continually so that they will be acceptable to the LORD.

39"Weave the tunic of fine linen and make the turban of fine linen. The sash is to be the work of an embroiderer. 40Make tunics, sashes and caps for Aaron's sons[f] to give them dignity and honor. 41After you put these clothes on your brother Aaron and his sons, anoint[g] and ordain them. Consecrate them so they may serve me as priests.[h]

42"Make linen undergarments[i] as a covering for the body, reaching from the waist to the thigh. 43Aaron and his sons must wear them whenever they enter the tent of meeting[j] or approach the altar to minister in the Holy Place, so that they will not incur guilt and die.[k]

"This is to be a lasting ordinance[l] for Aaron and his descendants.

28:36 [d]Zec 14:20
28:38 [e]Lev 10:17; 22:9, 16; Nu 18:1; Heb 9:28; 1Pe 2:24
28:40 [f]ver 4; Ex 39:41
28:41 [g]Ex 29:7; Lev 10:7 [h]Ex 29:7-9; 30:30; 40:15; Lev 8:1-36; Heb 7:28
28:42 [i]Lev 6:10; 16:4, 23; Eze 44:18
28:43 [j]Ex 27:21 [k]Ex 20:26 [l]Lev 17:7

[a] *16* That is, about 9 inches or about 23 centimeters [b] *20* The precise identification of some of these precious stones is uncertain. [c] *32* The meaning of the Hebrew for this word is uncertain.

Consecration of the Priests

29:1–37pp // Lev 8:1–36

29 “This is what you are to do to consecrate them, so they may serve
me as priests: Take a young bull and two
rams without defect. 2And from the finest wheat flour make round loaves without yeast, thick loaves without yeast and
with olive oil mixed in, and thin loaves
without yeast and brushed with olive
oil.[m] 3Put them in a basket and present
them along with the bull and the two
rams. 4Then bring Aaron and his sons to
the entrance to the tent of meeting and
wash them with water.[n] 5Take the garments[o] and dress Aaron with the tunic,
the robe of the ephod, the ephod itself
and the breastpiece. Fasten the ephod on
him by its skillfully woven waistband.[p]
6Put the turban on his head and attach
the sacred emblem[q] to the turban. 7Take
the anointing oil[r] and anoint him by
pouring it on his head. 8Bring his sons
and dress them in tunics 9and fasten caps
on them. Then tie sashes on Aaron and
his sons.[a][s] The priesthood is theirs by a
lasting ordinance.[t]

“Then you shall ordain Aaron and his
sons.

10“Bring the bull to the front of the
tent of meeting, and Aaron and his
sons shall lay their hands on its head.
11Slaughter it in the LORD’s presence
at the entrance to the tent of meeting.
12Take some of the bull’s blood and put

29:2 [m] Lev 2:1, 4; 6:19-23
29:4 [n] Ex 40:12; Heb 10:22
29:5 [o] Ex 28:2; Lev 8:7
[p] Ex 28:8
29:6 [q] Lev 8:9
29:7 [r] Ex 30:25, 30,31; Lev 8:12; 21:10; Nu 35:25; Ps 133:2
29:9 [s] Ex 28:40 [t] Ex 40:15; Nu 3:10; 18:7; 25:13; Dt 18:5

[a] 9 Hebrew; Septuagint *on them*

29:1-46 Chapter 29 is devoted to the sacrifices involved in the consecration of the priests. Aaron and his sons are to be consecrated by a series of sacrifices and offerings, an anointing with oil, and the donning of the tunics, headbands, and sashes. The entire ceremony is neatly summarized in vv. 1-9.

29:10-37 The sacrifices are of three types: a bull for a sin offering, a ram for a burnt offering, and another ram for a wave offering. This sequence is significant. The sin offering cleanses the priests from sin. Next, the burnt offering is an expression of devotion and commitment on the part of the worshiper. The second ram, along with a loaf of bread, a cake made with oil, and a wafer, is to be a wave offering.

It is not clear what a wave offering is, but according to Lev 7:28-36, a wave offering is a type of fellowship offering, the purpose of which concerns the establishing of communion between God and his people. This is the expected finale to the consecration ceremony.

PEOPLE TO KNOW // AARON

EXODUS 29:9: Aaron was the brother of Moses and Miriam. One of the first things God says about Aaron is that he could speak well (Ex 4:14); indeed, one of Aaron’s chief roles was to speak the words that God gave Moses. When Moses faced off against Pharaoh, telling him to let God’s people go free from slavery, Aaron was there by his side as Moses’ mouthpiece, which indicates he was an important helper for Moses. As Levites, Aaron and his sons were called to be priests (Ex 28). They carried out important duties in the tabernacle, such as offering sacrifices to God on behalf of Israel. As high priest, Aaron was able to enter the Most Holy Place on the Day of Atonement to atone for the sins of the people. God specifically chose Aaron and his descendants for this sacred role.

Unfortunately, Aaron made some big mistakes. The most well-known is the incident of the golden calf in Exodus 32. While Moses was on Mount Sinai, the Israelites convinced Aaron to make an idol for them. Aaron collected their gold jewelry and fashioned an idol in the shape of a calf. The people worshiped it, and their idolatry led to the deaths of many in the Israelite camp. Aaron was also implicated along with Moses in the sin of striking the rock to get water for the people (Nu 20:1-13); God chastised them both for failing to fully trust and honor him.

APPLICATION As high priest, Aaron had the weighty task of representing God to the people and also of interceding for the people’s sins before God. His ministry pointed to the mission of Jesus Christ, who is called our “great high priest” in Hebrews 4:14-15. Jesus offered a one-time sacrifice—his own blood shed on the cross—for the sins of the world.

The NT says that all Christians are a “royal priesthood” (1Pe 2:9). Christians carry on the priestly ministry, pioneered by Aaron and his descendants, of representing God to the world around them. This holy calling is for each one of us.

it on the horns[u] of the altar with your finger, and pour out the rest of it at the base of the altar. 13 Then take all the fat[v] on the internal organs, the long lobe of the liver, and both kidneys with the fat on them, and burn them on the altar. 14 But burn the bull's flesh and its hide and its intestines outside the camp.[w] It is a sin offering.[a]

15 "Take one of the rams, and Aaron and his sons shall lay their hands on its head. 16 Slaughter it and take the blood and splash it against the sides of the altar. 17 Cut the ram into pieces and wash the internal organs and the legs, putting them with the head and the other pieces. 18 Then burn the entire ram on the altar. It is a burnt offering to the LORD, a pleasing aroma,[x] a food offering presented to the LORD.

19 "Take the other ram,[y] and Aaron and his sons shall lay their hands on its head. 20 Slaughter it, take some of its blood and put it on the lobes of the right ears of Aaron and his sons, on the thumbs of their right hands, and on the big toes of their right feet. Then splash blood against the sides of the altar. 21 And take some blood[z] from the altar and some of the anointing oil[a] and sprinkle it on Aaron and his garments and on his sons and their garments. Then he and his sons and their garments will be consecrated.[b]

22 "Take from this ram the fat, the fat tail, the fat on the internal organs, the long lobe of the liver, both kidneys with the fat on them, and the right thigh. (This is the ram for the ordination.) 23 From the basket of bread made without yeast, which is before the LORD, take one round loaf, one thick loaf with olive oil mixed in, and one thin loaf. 24 Put all these in the hands of Aaron and his sons and have them wave them before the LORD as a wave offering.[c] 25 Then take them from their hands and burn them on the altar along with the burnt offering for a pleasing aroma to the LORD, a food offering presented to the LORD. 26 After you take the breast of the ram for Aaron's ordination, wave it before the LORD as a wave offering, and it will be your share.[d]

27 "Consecrate those parts of the ordination ram that belong to Aaron and his sons:[e] the breast that was waved and the thigh that was presented. 28 This is always to be the perpetual share from the Israelites for Aaron and his sons. It is the contribution the Israelites are to make to the LORD from their fellowship offerings.[f]

29 "Aaron's sacred garments will belong to his descendants so that they can be anointed and ordained in them.[g] 30 The son[h] who succeeds him as priest and comes to the tent of meeting to minister in the Holy Place is to wear them seven days.

31 "Take the ram for the ordination and cook the meat in a sacred place. 32 At the entrance to the tent of meeting, Aaron and his sons are to eat the meat of the ram and the bread[i] that is in the basket. 33 They are to eat these offerings by which atonement was made for their ordination and consecration. But no one else may eat[j] them, because they are sacred. 34 And if any of the meat of the ordination ram or any bread is left over till morning,[k] burn it up. It must not be eaten, because it is sacred.

35 "Do for Aaron and his sons everything I have commanded you, taking seven days to ordain them. 36 Sacrifice a bull each day[l] as a sin offering to make atonement. Purify the altar by making atonement for it, and anoint it to consecrate[m] it. 37 For seven days make atonement for the altar and consecrate it. Then the altar will be most holy, and whatever touches it will be holy.[n]

38 "This is what you are to offer on the altar regularly each day:[o] two lambs a year old. 39 Offer one in the morning and the other at twilight.[p] 40 With the first lamb offer a tenth of an ephah[b] of the finest flour mixed with a quarter of a hin[c] of oil from pressed olives, and a quarter of a hin of wine as a drink offering. 41 Sacrifice the other lamb at twilight with the same grain offering and its drink offering as in the morning — a

29:12 [u] Ex 27:2
29:13 [v] Lev 3:3, 5,9
29:14 [w] Lev 4:11-12,21; Heb 13:11
29:18 [x] Ge 8:21
29:19 [y] ver 3
29:21 [z] Heb 9:22 [a] Ex 30:25,31 [b] ver 1
29:24 [c] Lev 7:30
29:26 [d] Lev 7:31-34
29:27 [e] Lev 7:31, 34; Dt 18:3
29:28 [f] Lev 10:15
29:29 [g] Nu 20:26,28
29:30 [h] Nu 20:28
29:32 [i] Mt 12:4
29:33 [j] Lev 10:14; 22:10,13
29:34 [k] Ex 12:10
29:36 [l] Heb 10:11 [m] Ex 40:10
29:37 [n] Ex 30:28-29; 40:10; Mt 23:19
29:38 [o] Nu 28:3-8; 1Ch 16:40; Da 12:11
29:39 [p] Eze 46:13-15

[a] *14* Or *purification offering*; also in verse 36
[b] *40* That is, probably about 3 1/2 pounds or about 1.6 kilograms
[c] *40* That is, probably about 1 quart or about 1 liter

29:38–43 These verses describe the institution of the regular morning and evening sacrifices "for the generations to come" (v. 42). Here we have apparently left the topic of the consecration of the priests.

pleasing aroma, a food offering presented to the LORD.

42"For the generations to come[q] this burnt offering is to be made regularly at the entrance to the tent of meeting, before the LORD. There I will meet you and speak to you;[r] 43there also I will meet with the Israelites, and the place will be consecrated by my glory.[s]

44"So I will consecrate the tent of meeting and the altar and will consecrate Aaron and his sons to serve me as priests.[t] 45Then I will dwell[u] among the Israelites and be their God.[v] 46They will know that I am the LORD their God, who brought them out of Egypt so that I might dwell among them. I am the LORD their God.[w]

The Altar of Incense

30:1–5pp // Ex 37:25–28

30 "Make an altar[x] of acacia wood for burning incense.[y] 2It is to be square, a cubit long and a cubit wide, and two cubits high[a]—its horns[z] of one piece with it. 3Overlay the top and all the sides and the horns with pure gold, and make a gold molding around it. 4Make two gold rings for the altar below the molding—two on each of the opposite sides—to hold the poles used to carry it. 5Make the poles of acacia wood and overlay them with gold. 6Put the altar in front of the curtain that shields the ark of the covenant law—before the atonement cover[a] that is over the tablets of the covenant law—where I will meet with you.

7"Aaron must burn fragrant incense[b] on the altar every morning when he tends the lamps. 8He must burn incense again when he lights the lamps at twilight so incense will burn regularly before the LORD for the generations to come. 9Do not offer on this altar any other incense[c] or any burnt offering or grain offering, and do not pour a drink offering on it. 10Once a year Aaron shall make atonement[d] on its horns. This annual atonement must be made with the blood of the atoning sin offering[b] for the generations to come. It is most holy to the LORD."

29:42 [q] Ex 30:8 [r] Ex 25:22
29:43 [s] 1Ki 8:11
29:44 [t] Lev 21:15
29:45 [u] Ex 25:8; Lev 26:12; Zec 2:10; Jn 14:17 [v] 2Co 6:16; Rev 21:3
29:46 [w] Ex 20:2
30:1 [x] Ex 37:25 [y] Rev 8:3
30:2 [z] Ex 27:2
30:6 [a] Ex 25:22; 26:34
30:7 [b] ver 34-35; Ex 27:21; 1Sa 2:28
30:9 [c] Lev 10:1
30:10 [d] Lev 16:18-19,30
30:12 [e] Ex 38:25; Nu 1:2,49; 2Sa 24:1 [f] Nu 31:50; Mt 20:28 [g] 2Sa 24:13
30:13 [h] Nu 3:47; Mt 17:24
30:15 [i] Pr 22:2; Eph 6:9

Ex 29:45 ❖ God wants to dwell among his people (see Jn 1:14). How can we welcome God's presence more fully into our lives?

Ex 30:10 ❖ How does Hebrews 11:10–14 expand our understanding of the role of the atonement sacrifice?

Atonement Money

11Then the LORD said to Moses, 12"When you take a census[e] of the Israelites to count them, each one must pay the LORD a ransom[f] for his life at the time he is counted. Then no plague[g] will come on them when you number them. 13Each one who crosses over to those already counted is to give a half shekel,[c] according to the sanctuary shekel,[h] which weighs twenty gerahs. This half shekel is an offering to the LORD. 14All who cross over, those twenty years old or more, are to give an offering to the LORD. 15The rich are not to give more than a half shekel and the poor are not to give less[i] when you make the offering to the LORD to atone for your lives. 16Receive

[a] *2* That is, about 1 1/2 feet long and wide and 3 feet high or about 45 centimeters long and wide and 90 centimeters high [b] *10* Or *purification offering* [c] *13* That is, about 1/5 ounce or about 5.8 grams; also in verse 15

29:42–46 These verses reiterate a number of themes treated elsewhere. The tabernacle is the place where God's glory dwells and where he has chosen to meet with his people. It is God's presence, his glory, that actually consecrates the tabernacle (v. 43; cf. v. 44: "I will consecrate"). There is nothing magical or manipulative on the part of the people to make it happen. It is God's tabernacle, his priesthood, his people. He will prepare his people to be a suitable dwelling for himself.

30:1–10; 37:25–28 This altar measures about 1 foot by 6 inches square and 3 feet tall. It is to be placed in the Holy Place (30:6) and therefore must be constructed of gold. A question left unanswered is the symbolism of the incense. What is its purpose? It has been suggested that the placement of the altar immediately between the priest and the Most Holy Place indicates that the incense performs a protective function: Its smoke conceals the atonement cover from the priest so he will not die (cf. Lev 16:12–13).

30:11–16 We find here the assumption that a census will be taken from time to time and some provision is necessary in order to avoid calamity. It may be that the ransom is a reminder to Israel not to rely on her own strength. The money is to be used for "the service of the tent of meeting." It is a reminder to the Israelites that atonement has been made for their lives. It seems that the human penchant for assessing self-worth is something God will "tax" for the good of the tabernacle and as a prodding reminder to the people of who really has worth.

the atonement money from the Israelites and use it for the service of the tent
of meeting.[j] It will be a memorial for
the Israelites before the LORD, making
atonement for your lives."

Basin for Washing

17Then the LORD said to Moses, 18"Make
a bronze basin,[k] with its bronze stand,
for washing. Place it between the tent
of meeting and the altar, and put water
in it. 19Aaron and his sons are to wash
their hands and feet[l] with water[m] from it.
20Whenever they enter the tent of meeting, they shall wash with water so that
they will not die. Also, when they approach the altar to minister by presenting a food offering to the LORD, 21they
shall wash their hands and feet so that
they will not die. This is to be a lasting ordinance[n] for Aaron and his descendants
for the generations to come."

Anointing Oil

22Then the LORD said to Moses, 23"Take
the following fine spices: 500 shekels[a] of
liquid myrrh,[o] half as much (that is, 250
shekels) of fragrant cinnamon, 250 shekels[b] of fragrant calamus, 24500 shekels of
cassia[p] — all according to the sanctuary
shekel — and a hin[c] of olive oil. 25Make
these into a sacred anointing oil, a fragrant blend, the work of a perfumer.[q] It
will be the sacred anointing oil.[r] 26Then
use it to anoint[s] the tent of meeting, the
ark of the covenant law, 27the table and
all its articles, the lampstand and its accessories, the altar of incense, 28the altar
of burnt offering and all its utensils, and
the basin with its stand. 29You shall consecrate them so they will be most holy,
and whatever touches them will be holy.[t]

30"Anoint Aaron and his sons and consecrate[u] them so they may serve me as
priests. 31Say to the Israelites, 'This is
to be my sacred anointing oil for the
generations to come. 32Do not pour it
on anyone else's body and do not make
any other oil using the same formula. It
is sacred, and you are to consider it sacred.[v] 33Whoever makes perfume like it
and puts it on anyone other than a priest
must be cut off[w] from their people.' "

Incense

34Then the LORD said to Moses, "Take
fragrant spices — gum resin, onycha and
galbanum — and pure frankincense, all
in equal amounts, 35and make a fragrant
blend of incense, the work of a perfumer.[x] It is to be salted and pure and sacred.
36Grind some of it to powder and place
it in front of the ark of the covenant law
in the tent of meeting, where I will meet
with you. It shall be most holy[y] to you.
37Do not make any incense with this formula for yourselves; consider it holy[z] to
the LORD. 38Whoever makes incense like
it to enjoy its fragrance must be cut off[a]
from their people."

Bezalel and Oholiab

31:2–6pp // Ex 35:30–35

31 Then the LORD said to Moses, 2"See,
I have chosen Bezalel[b] son of Uri,
the son of Hur, of the tribe of Judah, 3and
I have filled him with the Spirit of God,
with wisdom, with understanding, with
knowledge and with all kinds of skills[c] —
4to make artistic designs for work in

30:16 [j] Ex 38:25-28
30:18 [k] Ex 38:8; 40:7,30
30:19 [l] Ex 40:31-32; Isa 52:11 [m] Ps 26:6
30:21 [n] Ex 27:21; 28:43
30:23 [o] Ge 37:25
30:24 [p] Ps 45:8
30:25 [q] Ex 37:29 [r] Ex 40:9
30:26 [s] Ex 40:9; Lev 8:10; Nu 7:1
30:29 [t] Ex 29:37
30:30 [u] Ex 29:7; Lev 8:2,12,30
30:32 [v] ver 25, 37
30:33 [w] ver 38; Ge 17:14
30:35 [x] ver 25
30:36 [y] ver 32; Ex 29:37; Lev 2:3
30:37 [z] ver 32
30:38 [a] ver 33
31:2 [b] Ex 36:1,2; 1Ch 2:20
31:3 [c] 1Ki 7:14

[a] *23* That is, about 12 1/2 pounds or about 5.8 kilograms; also in verse 24 [b] *23* That is, about 6 1/4 pounds or about 2.9 kilograms [c] *24* That is, probably about 1 gallon or about 3.8 liters

---

30:17–21; 38:8 The basin for washing is to be placed in the courtyard between the curtain to the Holy Place and the altar of burnt offering. The priests are to use it to wash themselves before entering the Holy Place. This washing likely has a practical as well as a ceremonial function. The slaughter that takes place at the altar will certainly leave the priests bloody.

Exodus 38:8 offers a piece of information not found in 30:17–21: The bronze basin and stand are to be made from "the mirrors of the women who served at the entrance to the tent of meeting." Mirrors in the ancient world were not made of glass but of polished bronze.

30:22–38; 37:29 The recipe for the oil is about 16 pounds of cinnamon and spices and 1 gallon of olive oil—an expensive and even extravagant recipe. The purpose of the oil is to anoint the tabernacle and the furnishings, thereby consecrating them (as was the high priest, 29:7). Both are to be set apart for a holy purpose.

31:1–11; 35:30—36:7 Two men, Bezalel and Oholiab, are singled out for the task of putting all the information together and building the tabernacle with all its furnishings and other elements (the list in 31:7–11 is quite complete). To do so they are filled with the spirit of God (31:3, perhaps the same spirit of God that was present at creation in Ge 1:2). Bezalel probably means "in the shadow/protection of El [a name for God]." Oholiab can mean either "father is my tent" or perhaps "father is a tent." Thus, the names themselves may be an allusion to the tabernacle.

gold, silver and bronze, 5to cut and set
stones, to work in wood, and to engage
in all kinds of crafts. 6Moreover, I have
appointed Oholiab son of Ahisamak, of
the tribe of Dan, to help him. Also I have
given ability to all the skilled workers
to make everything I have commanded
you: 7the tent of meeting,[d] the ark of the
covenant law[e] with the atonement cover[f]
on it, and all the other furnishings of the
tent— 8the table[g] and its articles, the
pure gold lampstand[h] and all its accessories, the altar of incense, 9the altar of
burnt offering and all its utensils, the basin with its stand— 10and also the woven
garments[i], both the sacred garments for
Aaron the priest and the garments for his
sons when they serve as priests, 11and the
anointing oil[j] and fragrant incense for
the Holy Place. They are to make them
just as I commanded you."

The Sabbath

12Then the LORD said to Moses, 13"Say
to the Israelites, 'You must observe my
Sabbaths.[k] This will be a sign[l] between
me and you for the generations to come,
so you may know that I am the LORD,
who makes you holy.[m]

14" 'Observe the Sabbath, because it is
holy to you. Anyone who desecrates it is to
be put to death;[n] those who do any work
on that day must be cut off from their

31:7 [d] Ex 36:8-38 [e] Ex 37:1-5 [f] Ex 37:6
31:8 [g] Ex 37:10-16 [h] Ex 37:17-24
31:10 [i] Ex 28:2; 39:1,41
31:11 [j] Ex 30:22-32
31:13 [k] Ex 20:8; Lev 19:3,30 [l] Eze 20:12,20 [m] Lev 11:44
31:14 [n] Nu 15:32-36
31:15 [o] Ex 20:8-11 [p] Ge 2:3; Ex 16:23
31:17 [q] ver 13 [r] Ge 2:2-3
31:18 [s] Ex 24:12 [t] Ex 32:15-16; 34:1,28; Dt 4:13; 5:22
32:1 [u] Ex 24:18; Dt 9:9-12 [v] Ac 7:40*
32:2 [w] Ex 35:22

Ex 31:2-5 ❖ What special skills has God given you that you can use to bring him glory?

people. 15For six days work[o] is to be done,
but the seventh day is a day of sabbath
rest,[p] holy to the LORD. Whoever does any
work on the Sabbath day is to be put to
death. 16The Israelites are to observe the
Sabbath, celebrating it for the generations
to come as a lasting covenant. 17It will
be a sign[q] between me and the Israelites
forever, for in six days the LORD made the
heavens and the earth, and on the seventh day he rested and was refreshed.[r]' "

18When the LORD finished speaking
to Moses on Mount Sinai, he gave him
the two tablets of the covenant law, the
tablets of stone[s] inscribed by the finger
of God.[t]

The Golden Calf

32 When the people saw that Moses
was so long in coming down from
the mountain,[u] they gathered around
Aaron and said, "Come, make us gods[a]
who will go before us. As for this fellow
Moses who brought us up out of Egypt, we
don't know what has happened to him."[v]

2Aaron answered them, "Take off the
gold earrings[w] that your wives, your

[a] 1 Or *a god*; also in verses 23 and 31

31:12–18; 35:1–3 The instructions concerning the building of the tabernacle end with the command to keep the Sabbath. The Sabbath is a sign of the covenant God has made with Israel. God's conduct toward Israel in bringing them out of Egypt and establishing them as his people—an event that culminates here in the construction of the tabernacle and the institution of Israel's religious system—is tied to creation in 31:17.

31:13 The purpose of the Sabbath is "so you may know that I am the LORD, who makes you holy." It is, in other words, a reminder of who God is and what his intentions are for his people. We also see here what Jesus meant when he said, "The Sabbath was made for man, not man for the Sabbath" (Mk 2:27).

31:14 Failure to keep the Sabbath ("desecrates it"), therefore, is to be met with severe punishment, death—or, as with the oil and incense, being "cut off from their people."

31:15–18 Finally, the reference to the Sabbath at the end of the first part of the tabernacle section has further significance beyond that of continuing the connection of exodus to creation. The building of the tabernacle is a microcosm of the created world—heavenly order amid earthly chaos. It is a true sanctuary where Israel continually experiences connection to their God who brought them out of Egypt. The tabernacle is like no other place on earth. It is built according to a divine plan to reflect a heavenly reality. It is a piece of holy ground.

✣ **25:1—31:18** See application section at the end of 35:1—40:33.

32:1–4 Suddenly we find ourselves caught up in an event that could threaten to unravel God's entire plan. The people approach Aaron and refer to Moses as "this fellow Moses," a phrase that communicates a sense of derision and contempt. We have already seen such contempt in Exodus and will see it again later in the Pentateuch. However we explain their motives, God will later punish the Israelites for what they are about to do.

Aaron tells the people to take off their gold earrings, which he will then use to form an idol in the shape of a calf. The people want what the tabernacle was intended to provide—a concrete point of contact between the people and God.

The calf was a common idol image in the ancient Near East. The ancients did not equate an idol with the god, but it was some sort of earthly

sons and your daughters are wearing,
and bring them to me." 3So all the people
took off their earrings and brought them
to Aaron. 4He took what they handed him
and made it into an idol cast in the shape
of a calf,[x] fashioning it with a tool. Then
they said, "These are your gods,[a] Israel,
who brought you up out of Egypt."
5When Aaron saw this, he built an altar in front of the calf and announced,
"Tomorrow there will be a festival[y] to
the LORD." 6So the next day the people
rose early and sacrificed burnt offerings
and presented fellowship offerings.[z] Afterward they sat down to eat and drink
and got up to indulge in revelry.[a]
7Then the LORD said to Moses, "Go
down, because your people, whom you
brought up out of Egypt,[b] have become
corrupt.[c] 8They have been quick to turn
away from what I commanded them and
have made themselves an idol[d] cast in
the shape of a calf. They have bowed
down to it and sacrificed[e] to it and have
said, 'These are your gods, Israel, who
brought you up out of Egypt.'[f]
9"I have seen these people," the
LORD said to Moses, "and they are a
stiff-necked[g] people. 10Now leave me
alone so that my anger may burn against
them and that I may destroy them. Then
I will make you into a great nation."[h]

32:4 [x] Dt 9:16; Ne 9:18; Ps 106:19; Ac 7:41
32:5 [y] Lev 23:2, 37; 2Ki 10:20
32:6 [z] Nu 25:2; Ac 7:41 [a] ver 17-19; 1Co 10:7*
32:7 [b] ver 4, 11 [c] Ge 6:11-12; Dt 9:12
32:8 [d] Ex 20:4 [e] Ex 22:20 [f] 1Ki 12:28
32:9 [g] Ex 33:3,5; 34:9; Isa 48:4; Ac 7:51
32:10 [h] Nu 14:12; Dt 9:14
32:11 [i] Dt 9:18 [j] Dt 9:26
32:12 [k] Nu 14:13-16; Dt 9:28
32:13 [l] Ex 2:24 [m] Ge 22:16; Heb 6:13 [n] Ge 15:5; 26:4 [o] Ge 12:7
32:14 [p] 2Sa 24:16; Ps 106:45
32:15 [q] Ex 31:18 [r] Dt 9:15
32:16 [s] Ex 31:18

11But Moses sought the favor[i] of the
LORD his God. "LORD," he said, "why
should your anger burn against your
people, whom you brought out of Egypt
with great power and a mighty hand?[j]
12Why should the Egyptians say, 'It was
with evil intent that he brought them
out, to kill them in the mountains and
to wipe them off the face of the earth'?[k]
Turn from your fierce anger; relent and
do not bring disaster on your people.
13Remember[l] your servants Abraham,
Isaac and Israel, to whom you swore by
your own self:[m] 'I will make your descendants as numerous as the stars[n] in the
sky and I will give your descendants all
this land[o] I promised them, and it will
be their inheritance forever.'" 14Then the
LORD relented[p] and did not bring on his
people the disaster he had threatened.
15Moses turned and went down the
mountain with the two tablets of the
covenant law[q] in his hands.[r] They were
inscribed on both sides, front and back.
16The tablets were the work of God; the
writing was the writing of God, engraved
on the tablets.[s]
17When Joshua heard the noise of the
people shouting, he said to Moses, "There
is the sound of war in the camp."

[a] 4 Or *This is your god*; also in verse 8

---

representation of that god. Specifically, it was thought that calves or bulls functioned as pedestals for the gods seated or standing over them. It is unlikely that the calf *itself* is being declared "god" by the Israelites.

32:5–6 In v. 5 Aaron builds an altar, a parallel to the altar that will be built for the tabernacle. He proclaims that there will be a "festival to the LORD" the next day (cf. 10:9; 12:14; 13:6).

In 24:4–5 Moses rises early and sacrifices burnt and fellowship offerings. The similar wording in 32:6 suggests that the festival here is a reversal—indeed, a perversion—of the true celebration of ch. 24. The same goes for the eating and drinking mentioned at the end of v. 6. Remember that this is what the leaders of Israel did in 24:11 after they were given a brief glimpse of God himself.

32:7–10 God refers to the Israelites as "your people" (i.e., Moses' people), an ominous hint of what is to come. Israel is no longer "*my* [God's] people" (4:22). In 32:9 God continues to use derisive language to speak of Israel, referring to them as "*these* people," a phrase that brings to mind the Israelites' reference to Moses as "*this* fellow" (v. 1, emphasis added). God's solution is to have his "anger . . . burn against them" (v. 10) and start over with Moses.

32:11–14 Rebellion is followed by mediation. Moses reminds God of the very things that God himself regularly enjoins the Israelites to remember—that God delivered Israel out of Egypt with "great power and a mighty hand" (v. 11). He also reminds the Lord that his own honor is at stake. Had he not just finished dismantling the Egyptian army and their gods? Will he now turn around and give these very same enemies a reason to rejoice in Yahweh's defeat? Never! Moses bases his argument ultimately on the very element that God seems to have discounted in the previous verses: the promise to the patriarchs (v. 13). God turns from his anger and does not bring about the threatened disaster (v. 14).

How can God's sovereignty be reconciled to the fact that he here changes his mind? We should likely look at this in the broadest context possible. The Bible gives us a varied portrait of the nature of God. At times we seem to be peering into heaven itself. At other times, the Bible presents God in human pictures. The dialogue of vv. 11–14 is more in keeping with the latter category than the former. The reason for the inclusion here seems to be that the writer is focusing his attention on Moses' role as intercessor, not on the inner workings of God's psyche.

32:17–18 Joshua is unaware of what is happening in the camp below. He surmises on the basis of the sounds he hears that there must be war in the camp. Moses informs Joshua of what is actually happening (v. 18).

18 Moses replied:

"It is not the sound of victory,
it is not the sound of defeat;
it is the sound of singing that I
hear."

19 When Moses approached the camp
and saw the calf[t] and the dancing, his
anger burned and he threw the tablets
out of his hands, breaking them to pieces[u] at the foot of the mountain. 20 And he
took the calf the people had made and
burned it in the fire; then he ground it
to powder, scattered it on the water[v] and
made the Israelites drink it.
21 He said to Aaron, "What did these
people do to you, that you led them into
such great sin?"
22 "Do not be angry, my lord," Aaron answered. "You know how prone these people are to evil.[w] 23 They said to me, 'Make
us gods who will go before us. As for this
fellow Moses who brought us up out of
Egypt, we don't know what has happened
to him.'[x] 24 So I told them, 'Whoever has
any gold jewelry, take it off.' Then they
gave me the gold, and I threw it into the
fire, and out came this calf!"[y]
25 Moses saw that the people were running wild and that Aaron had let them
get out of control and so become a laughingstock to their enemies. 26 So he stood
at the entrance to the camp and said,
"Whoever is for the LORD, come to me."
And all the Levites rallied to him.
27 Then he said to them, "This is what
the LORD, the God of Israel, says: 'Each
man strap a sword to his side. Go back
and forth through the camp from one
end to the other, each killing his brother
and friend and neighbor.' "[z] 28 The Levites
did as Moses commanded, and that day
about three thousand of the people died.
29 Then Moses said, "You have been set
apart to the LORD today, for you were
against your own sons and brothers, and
he has blessed you this day."
30 The next day Moses said to the people, "You have committed a great sin.[a]
But now I will go up to the LORD; perhaps
I can make atonement[b] for your sin."
31 So Moses went back to the LORD and
said, "Oh, what a great sin these people
have committed![c] They have made themselves gods of gold.[d] 32 But now, please
forgive their sin—but if not, then blot
me[e] out of the book[f] you have written."
33 The LORD replied to Moses, "Whoever
has sinned against me I will blot out[g] of
my book. 34 Now go, lead the people to
the place[h] I spoke of, and my angel[i] will
go before you. However, when the time
comes for me to punish,[j] I will punish
them for their sin."
35 And the LORD struck the people with
a plague because of what they did with
the calf[k] Aaron had made.

33 Then the LORD said to Moses,
"Leave this place, you and the people you brought up out of Egypt, and
go up to the land I promised on oath to
Abraham, Isaac and Jacob, saying, 'I will
give it to your descendants.'[l] 2 I will send
an angel[m] before you and drive out the
Canaanites, Amorites, Hittites, Perizzites,

32:19 [t] Dt 9:16 [u] Dt 9:17
32:20 [v] Dt 9:21
32:22 [w] Dt 9:24
32:23 [x] ver 1
32:24 [y] ver 4
32:27 [z] Nu 25:3, 5; Dt 33:9
32:30 [a] 1Sa 12:20 [b] Lev 1:4; Nu 25:13
32:31 [c] Dt 9:18 [d] Ex 20:23
32:32 [e] Ro 9:3 [f] Ps 69:28; Da 12:1; Php 4:3; Rev 3:5; 21:27
32:33 [g] Dt 29:20; Ps 9:5
32:34 [h] Ex 3:17 [i] Ex 23:20 [j] Dt 32:35; Ps 99:8; Ro 2:5 6
32:35 [k] ver 4
33:1 [l] Ge 12:7
33:2 [m] Ex 32:34

Ex 32:30 ❖ What prayers of interces-sion can we bring to God on behalf of the sins of the world around us?

32:19–20 The breaking of the tablets is symbolic. By smashing the tablets on which is written the law—by God's finger, no less—the law is symbolically undone. Moses' act says to the Israelites that if they are not prepared to obey the law, they do not deserve to have it. The smashing of the tablets, with one resounding crash, tells the Israelites below that their attempt to create a religion of their own design has failed.

32:21–24 The confrontation between Moses and Aaron appears somewhat pathetic and almost comical on the surface. Aaron's answer is so ridiculous that Moses gives no response, as if he will not even dignify it with an answer.

32:26 The fact that all the Levites come forward indicates that God's house is still in order.

32:30–35 The text implies two levels of guilt in the making of the golden calf. The "more guilty" parties have been put to death by the Levites. The rest of the Israelites are apparently also guilty in some sense, otherwise atonement would not have to be made.

In his attempt to make atonement by pleading for the life of his people, Moses' argument essentially amounts to "take me instead." The Lord rejects Moses' offer (v. 33). Sinners, not the guiltless, will be blotted out—for now at least.

33:1–6 God announces that he himself will not be going with them (v. 3). The whole purpose of the exodus was for God and his people to be together. The events of the previous thirty-one chapters are being undone.

The reason God gives for not going with them is twofold: They are a stiff-necked, stubborn people, and God is afraid he "might destroy [them] on the way." The writer is not concerned to reveal to us the absolute, abstract essence of God but rather God in the context of his dealings with his people.

Hivites and Jebusites.[n] 3Go up to the
land flowing with milk and honey.[o] But
I will not go with you, because you are a
stiff-necked[p] people and I might destroy[q]
you on the way."
4When the people heard these distressing words, they began to mourn[r] and
no one put on any ornaments. 5For the
LORD had said to Moses, "Tell the Israelites, 'You are a stiff-necked people. If I
were to go with you even for a moment,
I might destroy you. Now take off your
ornaments and I will decide what to do
with you.'" 6So the Israelites stripped off
their ornaments at Mount Horeb.

The Tent of Meeting

7Now Moses used to take a tent and
pitch it outside the camp some distance
away, calling it the "tent of meeting."[s]
Anyone inquiring of the LORD would
go to the tent of meeting outside the
camp. 8And whenever Moses went out
to the tent, all the people rose and stood
at the entrances to their tents,[t] watching Moses until he entered the tent. 9As
Moses went into the tent, the pillar of
cloud[u] would come down and stay at the
entrance, while the LORD spoke[v] with
Moses. 10Whenever the people saw the
pillar of cloud standing at the entrance
to the tent, they all stood and worshiped,
each at the entrance to their tent. 11The
LORD would speak to Moses face to face,[w]
as one speaks to a friend. Then Moses
would return to the camp, but his young
aide Joshua son of Nun did not leave
the tent.

33:2 [n] Ex 23:27-31; Jos 24:11
33:3 [o] Ex 3:8 [p] Ex 32:9 [q] Ex 32:10
33:4 [r] Nu 14:39
33:7 [s] Ex 29:42-43
33:8 [t] Nu 16:27
33:9 [u] Ex 13:21 [v] Ex 31:18; Ps 99:7
33:11 [w] Nu 12:8; Dt 34:10

Ex 33:18–23 ❖ When have you vividly witnessed or experienced God's glory?

Moses and the Glory of the LORD

12Moses said to the LORD, "You have
been telling me, 'Lead these people,'[x]
but you have not let me know whom you
will send with me. You have said, 'I know
you by name[y] and you have found favor
with me.' 13If you are pleased with me,
teach me your ways[z] so I may know you
and continue to find favor with you. Remember that this nation is your people."[a]
14The LORD replied, "My Presence[b] will
go with you, and I will give you rest."[c]
15Then Moses said to him, "If your
Presence does not go with us, do not
send us up from here. 16How will anyone know that you are pleased with me
and with your people unless you go with
us?[d] What else will distinguish me and
your people from all the other people on
the face of the earth?"[e]
17And the LORD said to Moses, "I will do
the very thing you have asked, because
I am pleased with you and I know you
by name."
18Then Moses said, "Now show me your
glory."
19And the LORD said, "I will cause all
my goodness to pass in front of you, and I
will proclaim my name, the LORD, in your
presence. I will have mercy on whom I
will have mercy, and I will have compassion on whom I will have compassion.[f]
20But," he said, "you cannot see my face,
for no one may see[g] me and live."

33:12 [x] Ex 3:10 [y] ver 17; Jn 10:14-15; 2Ti 2:19
33:13 [z] Ps 25:4; 86:11; 119:33 [a] Ex 34:9; Dt 9:26,29
33:14 [b] Isa 63:9 [c] Jos 21:44; 22:4
33:16 [d] Nu 14:14 [e] Ex 34:10
33:19 [f] Ro 9:15*
33:20 [g] Ge 32:30; Isa 6:5

33:7–11 It is the events of ch. 32 that prompt the action of 33:7–11. The fact that a temporary tent of meeting is set up and that God meets with Moses as a representative of the people signals to the reader that God has not entirely abandoned Israel. This so-called tent of meeting (v. 7) will soon give way to the splendor of the tabernacle: the true Tent of Meeting. The cloud will soon descend to guide the entire camp.
33:12–13 Moses may also be asking, "I know you want me to lead, but which people are going out with me?" In other words, Moses wants to know who will be left after the purge of 33:5. Moses does not want to make the journey alone. He sees no honor in being the only one to reach Canaan. He reminds God in v. 13, "Remember that this nation is your people."
33:14 God's response can be seen as somewhat of a veiled denial to Moses' pleading: "My Presence will go with *you*, and I will give *you* rest" (emphasis added). Rest should not be understood psychologically, as if God is promising that Moses' mind will be put to ease. God seems to be saying to Moses, albeit subtly, "Don't worry Moses. I'll be with you."
33:15–17 The argument of vv. 12–16 serves the singular purpose of ensuring that the people will not be left behind. The clincher for Moses is v. 16, which, like vv. 11–14, is an appeal to God's reputation among the people of the world. God promises to do as Moses asked (v. 17). Once again, Moses has succeeded in moving God to compassion.
33:18–23 Moses asks to see God's glory. This is not simply to satisfy his curiosity or some deep spiritual longing. He is in effect asking God for some demonstration of the promise he has just made.

Verse 23 is a captivating image. God is "there" in some tangible form, passing by in front of Moses. The anthropomorphism is apparent, but we should not conclude, on the basis that God does not have a body, that Moses does not see anything. If we dwell on what precisely Moses sees, we lose sight of the point of the story as a whole. God's appearance is a mystery—a mystery that even Moses himself is able to see only partially.

21Then the LORD said, "There is a place
near me where you may stand on a rock.
22When my glory passes by, I will put you
in a cleft in the rock and cover you with
my hand[h] until I have passed by. 23Then
I will remove my hand and you will see
my back; but my face must not be seen."

The New Stone Tablets

34 The LORD said to Moses, "Chisel
out two stone tablets like the first
ones, and I will write on them the words
that were on the first tablets,[i] which you
broke.[j] 2Be ready in the morning, and
then come up on Mount Sinai.[k] Present
yourself to me there on top of the mountain. 3No one is to come with you or be
seen anywhere on the mountain;[l] not
even the flocks and herds may graze in
front of the mountain."
4So Moses chiseled out two stone tablets like the first ones and went up Mount
Sinai early in the morning, as the LORD
had commanded him; and he carried the
two stone tablets in his hands. 5Then the
LORD came down in the cloud and stood
there with him and proclaimed his name,
the LORD.[m] 6And he passed in front of
Moses, proclaiming, "The LORD, the
LORD, the compassionate[n] and gracious
God, slow to anger,[o] abounding in love[p]
and faithfulness,[q] 7maintaining love to
thousands,[r] and forgiving wickedness,
rebellion and sin.[s] Yet he does not leave
the guilty unpunished;[t] he punishes the
children and their children for the sin
of the parents to the third and fourth
generation."
8Moses bowed to the ground at once
and worshiped. 9"Lord," he said, "if I
have found favor in your eyes, then let
the Lord go with us.[u] Although this is a
stiff-necked people, forgive our wickedness and our sin, and take us as your
inheritance."[v]
10Then the LORD said: "I am making
a covenant[w] with you. Before all your

33:22 [h]Ps 91:4
34:1 [i]Dt 10:2, 4 [j]Ex 32:19
34:2 [k]Ex 19:11
34:3 [l]Ex 19:12-13, 21
34:5 [m]Ex 33:19
34:6 [n]Ps 86:15 [o]Nu 14:18; Ro 2:4 [p]Ne 9:17; Ps 103:8; Joel 2:13 [q]Ps 108:4
34:7 [r]Ex 20:6 [s]Ps 103:3; 130:4, 8; Da 9:9; 1Jn 1:9 [t]Job 10:14; Na 1:3
34:9 [u]Ex 33:15 [v]Ps 33:12
34:10 [w]Dt 5:2-3

Ex 34:6-7 ❖ How can God's description of his character encourage and comfort us?

34:1-5 The beginning of ch. 34 reinforces that the covenant between God and Israel is reestablished after the golden calf incident.

34:6-7 This list of attributes is true not only of God's behavior in ch. 34 but throughout Exodus.

34:8-10 Moses wants some added evidence or

CHARACTER OF GOD // GOD IS MERCIFUL

Exodus 34:6: "The LORD, the LORD, the compassionate and gracious God, slow to anger, abounding in love and faithfulness."

When God describes his own nature to Moses, God calls himself "compassionate and gracious." This self-description comes only two chapters after the golden calf incident, when the Israelites plunged themselves into idolatry (Ex 32). God acted swiftly to cause a plague on the people as punishment for their sin. Yet he also promised Moses that he would be with Moses (Ex 33:14). Psalm 103:10 promises that God does not treat us as our sins deserve. While God does hold the guilty accountable, God's mercy is ever more abundant. And that mercy never runs dry (La 3:22).

God showed his mercy almost immediately after humanity fell into sin. God provided animal skins to cover Adam and Eve in their nakedness and shame. Furthermore, God promised in his words to the serpent that an offspring from the woman would crush the head of the snake (Ge 3:15). This promise is called the *protoevangelium* (from the Greek word transliterated *protoeuangelion*), the first glimpse in the Bible of the Good News about Jesus Christ. From the moment humans sinned, God showed he had a merciful plan of salvation.

God displayed his mercy most fully through Christ, who came as God incarnate to take away the sins of the world. On the cross, God the Son offered himself as a sacrifice to accomplish God the Father's plan of salvation. What greater mercy can there be than this: God himself accepted the just punishment for human sin.

APPLICATION ✚ Understanding God's mercy should fill us with joy and gratitude. We do not get what we deserve; instead, God extends to us the invitation to be saved through Jesus Christ. Though we were dead in our transgressions, God mercifully made us alive in Christ (Eph 2:5). Thanks be to God!

people I will do wonders never before
done in any nation in all the world.[x] The
people you live among will see how awesome is the work that I, the LORD, will
do for you. 11 Obey what I command you
today. I will drive out before you the Amorites, Canaanites, Hittites, Perizzites,
Hivites and Jebusites.[y] 12 Be careful not
to make a treaty with those who live in
the land where you are going, or they
will be a snare[z] among you. 13 Break down
their altars, smash their sacred stones
and cut down their Asherah poles.[a][a] 14 Do
not worship any other god,[b] for the LORD,
whose name is Jealous, is a jealous God.[c]
15 "Be careful not to make a treaty with
those who live in the land; for when they
prostitute[d] themselves to their gods and
sacrifice to them, they will invite you and
you will eat their sacrifices.[e] 16 And when
you choose some of their daughters as
wives[f] for your sons and those daughters
prostitute themselves to their gods,[g] they
will lead your sons to do the same.
17 "Do not make any idols.[h]
18 "Celebrate the Festival of Unleavened
Bread.[i] For seven days eat bread made
without yeast,[j] as I commanded you. Do
this at the appointed time in the month
of Aviv,[k] for in that month you came out
of Egypt.
19 "The first offspring[l] of every womb
belongs to me, including all the firstborn
males of your livestock, whether from
herd or flock. 20 Redeem the firstborn
donkey with a lamb, but if you do not
redeem it, break its neck.[m] Redeem all
your firstborn sons.
"No one is to appear before me empty-
handed.[n]
21 "Six days you shall labor, but on the
seventh day you shall rest;[o] even during the plowing season and harvest you
must rest.
22 "Celebrate the Festival of Weeks with
the firstfruits of the wheat harvest, and
the Festival of Ingathering[p] at the turn of
the year.[b] 23 Three times[q] a year all your
men are to appear before the Sovereign
LORD, the God of Israel. 24 I will drive out
nations[r] before you and enlarge your territory, and no one will covet your land
when you go up three times each year to
appear before the LORD your God.
25 "Do not offer the blood of a sacrifice
to me along with anything containing
yeast,[s] and do not let any of the sacrifice from the Passover Festival remain
until morning.[t]
26 "Bring the best of the firstfruits of
your soil to the house of the LORD your
God.
"Do not cook a young goat in its mother's milk."[u]
27 Then the LORD said to Moses, "Write[v]
down these words, for in accordance with
these words I have made a covenant
with you and with Israel." 28 Moses was
there with the LORD forty days and forty
nights[w] without eating bread or drinking
water. And he wrote on the tablets[x] the
words of the covenant — the Ten Commandments.[y]

The Radiant Face of Moses

29 When Moses came down from Mount
Sinai with the two tablets of the covenant
law in his hands,[z] he was not aware that
his face was radiant[a] because he had spoken with the LORD. 30 When Aaron and
all the Israelites saw Moses, his face was
radiant, and they were afraid to come
near him. 31 But Moses called to them;
so Aaron and all the leaders of the community came back to him, and he spoke
to them. 32 Afterward all the Israelites
came near him, and he gave them all the
commands[b] the LORD had given him on
Mount Sinai.
33 When Moses finished speaking to
them, he put a veil[c] over his face. 34 But
whenever he entered the LORD's presence
to speak with him, he removed the veil

[a] *13* That is, wooden symbols of the goddess Asherah [b] *22* That is, in the autumn

34:10 [x] Ex 33:16; Dt 4:32
34:11 [y] Ex 33:2
34:12 [z] Ex 23:32-33
34:13 [a] Ex 23:24; Dt 12:3; 2Ki 18:4
34:14 [b] Ex 20:3 [c] Ex 20:5; Dt 4:24
34:15 [d] Jdg 2:17 [e] Nu 25:2; 1Co 8:4
34:16 [f] Dt 7:3 [g] 1Ki 11:4
34:17 [h] Ex 32:8
34:18 [i] Ex 12:17 [j] Ex 12:15 [k] Ex 12:2
34:19 [l] Ex 13:2
34:20 [m] Ex 13:13, 15 [n] Ex 23:15; Dt 16:16
34:21 [o] Ex 20:9; Lk 13:14
34:22 [p] Ex 23:16
34:23 [q] Ex 23:14
34:24 [r] Ex 23:28; 33:2; Ps 78:55
34:25 [s] Ex 23:18 [t] Ex 12:8,10
34:26 [u] Ex 23:19
34:27 [v] Ex 17:14; 24:4
34:28 [w] Ge 7:4; Ex 24:18; Mt 4:2 [x] ver 1; Ex 31:18 [y] Dt 4:13; 10:4
34:29 [z] Ex 32:15 [a] Ps 34:5; Mt 17:2; 2Co 3:7,13
34:32 [b] Ex 24:3
34:33 [c] 2Co 3:13

proof that God will go with his people. God will make "a covenant" with the people (v. 10). To put it more accurately, he will renew the covenant.
34:11–30 This section is essentially a repetition of a number of things seen in previous sections of Exodus. Such repetition forces the reader to understand what is happening as a renewal of the covenant. After receiving the synopsis of the law, Moses writes it on the tablets he chiseled and makes his way back down the mountain. This time, however, he is not greeted with the sound of "singing." Instead, the people are afraid. Why? Because Moses' face has become radiant (v. 30). Although the reason why Moses' face shines is not made explicit in the text, it is probably to impress on the people that God's authority and presence rest unequivocally with Moses.
34:34 Within the broader context of Exodus, we may think of Moses' veil functioning in a similar way to the veil or curtain in the tabernacle.

until he came out. And when he came out and told the Israelites what he had been commanded, 35 they saw that his face was radiant. Then Moses would put the veil back over his face until he went in to speak with the LORD.

Sabbath Regulations

35 Moses assembled the whole Israelite community and said to them, "These are the things the LORD has commanded[d] you to do: 2 For six days, work is to be done, but the seventh day shall be your holy day, a day of sabbath[e] rest to the LORD. Whoever does any work on it is to be put to death. 3 Do not light a fire in any of your dwellings on the Sabbath day.[f]"

Materials for the Tabernacle

35:4–9pp // Ex 25:1–7
35:10–19pp // Ex 39:32–41

4 Moses said to the whole Israelite community, "This is what the LORD has commanded: 5 From what you have, take an offering for the LORD. Everyone who is willing is to bring to the LORD an offering of gold, silver and bronze; 6 blue, purple and scarlet yarn and fine linen; goat hair; 7 ram skins dyed red and another type of durable leather[a]; acacia wood; 8 olive oil for the light; spices for the anointing oil and for the fragrant incense; 9 and onyx stones and other gems to be mounted on the ephod and breastpiece.

10 "All who are skilled among you are to come and make everything the LORD has commanded:[g] 11 the tabernacle[h] with its tent and its covering, clasps, frames, crossbars, posts and bases; 12 the ark[i] with its poles and the atonement cover and the curtain that shields it; 13 the table[j] with its poles and all its articles and the bread of the Presence; 14 the lampstand[k] that is for light with its accessories, lamps and oil for the light; 15 the altar[l] of incense with its poles, the anointing oil[m] and the fragrant incense;[n] the curtain for the doorway at the entrance to the tabernacle; 16 the altar[o] of burnt offering with its bronze grating, its poles and all its utensils; the bronze basin with its stand; 17 the curtains of the courtyard with its posts and bases, and the curtain for the entrance to the courtyard;[p] 18 the tent pegs for the tabernacle and for the courtyard, and their ropes; 19 the woven garments worn for ministering in the sanctuary—both the sacred garments[q] for Aaron the priest and the garments for his sons when they serve as priests."

20 Then the whole Israelite community withdrew from Moses' presence, 21 and everyone who was willing and whose heart moved them came and brought an offering to the LORD for the work on the tent of meeting, for all its service, and for the sacred garments. 22 All who were willing, men and women alike, came and brought gold jewelry of all kinds: brooches, earrings, rings and ornaments. They all presented their gold as a wave offering to the LORD. 23 Everyone who had blue, purple or scarlet yarn[r] or fine linen, or goat hair, ram skins dyed red or the other durable leather brought them. 24 Those presenting an offering of silver or bronze brought it as an offering to the LORD, and everyone who

35:1 [d] Ex 34:32
35:2 [e] Ex 20:9-10; 34:21; Lev 23:3
35:3 [f] Ex 16:23
35:10 [g] Ex 31:6
35:11 [h] Ex 26:1-37
35:12 [i] Ex 25:10-22
35:13 [j] Ex 25:23-30; Lev 24:5-6
35:14 [k] Ex 25:31
35:15 [l] Ex 30:1-6 [m] Ex 30:25 [n] Ex 30:34-38
35:16 [o] Ex 27:1-8
35:17 [p] Ex 27:9
35:19 [q] Ex 28:2; 31:10; 39:1
35:23 [r] 1Ch 29:8

[a] 7 Possibly the hides of large aquatic mammals; also in verse 23

Ex 35:10 ❖ What opportunities exist in our lives to work alongside other Christians as we obey God's commands together? What can we do today to engage in such work?

32:1—34:35 Israel's sin at the foot of Mount Sinai occurs before there is any official means of sin atonement. The tabernacle has not yet been built, and the priestly system has not yet been inaugurated. At this point these things have only been planned for. This is why Moses himself needs to step in and say, "I will go up to the LORD; perhaps I can make atonement for your sin" (32:30). For Israel, the official means of atoning for sin is still in the future. For the church, the final, complete, once-for-all atonement for sin has happened. The means of atonement Moses offered, substituting himself for his people, which God did not accept, is what Christ was able to do.

35:1-3 See notes on 31:12-18.
35:4-9 See notes on 25:1-9.
35:10-29 Verses 10-19 review what the Israelites are to build—the tabernacle, its furnishings, and the priestly garments. Verses 20-29 recount the actual collecting of the materials necessary to do the work. The emphasis here seems to be on the willingness of the Israelite men and women to participate and give. Women are particularly singled out by the writer as spinners of yarn and goat hair (35:25-26).

had acacia wood for any part of the work
brought it. 25 Every skilled woman[s] spun
with her hands and brought what she
had spun — blue, purple or scarlet yarn
or fine linen. 26 And all the women who
were willing and had the skill spun the
goat hair. 27 The leaders[t] brought onyx
stones and other gems to be mounted
on the ephod and breastpiece. 28 They
also brought spices and olive oil for the
light and for the anointing oil and for the
fragrant incense.[u] 29 All the Israelite men
and women who were willing[v] brought
to the LORD freewill offerings[w] for all
the work the LORD through Moses had
commanded them to do.

Bezalel and Oholiab

35:30–35pp // Ex 31:2–6

30 Then Moses said to the Israelites,
"See, the LORD has chosen Bezalel son of
Uri, the son of Hur, of the tribe of Judah,
31 and he has filled him with the Spirit
of God, with wisdom, with understanding, with knowledge and with all kinds
of skills[x] — 32 to make artistic designs
for work in gold, silver and bronze, 33 to
cut and set stones, to work in wood and
to engage in all kinds of artistic crafts.
34 And he has given both him and Oholiab[y] son of Ahisamak, of the tribe of Dan,
the ability to teach[z] others. 35 He has filled
them with skill to do all kinds of work[a]
as engravers, designers, embroiderers
in blue, purple and scarlet yarn and fine
linen, and weavers — all of them skilled

36 workers and designers. 1 So Bezalel, Oholiab and every skilled person[b] to whom the LORD has given skill
and ability to know how to carry out all
the work of constructing the sanctuary[c]
are to do the work just as the LORD has
commanded."

2 Then Moses summoned Bezalel[d]
and Oholiab[e] and every skilled person
to whom the LORD had given ability
and who was willing[f] to come and do
the work. 3 They received from Moses all
the offerings[g] the Israelites had brought
to carry out the work of constructing the
sanctuary. And the people continued to
bring freewill offerings morning after
morning. 4 So all the skilled workers who
were doing all the work on the sanctuary
left what they were doing 5 and said to
Moses, "The people are bringing more

35:25 [s] Ex 28:3
35:27 [t] 1Ch 29:6; Ezr 2:68
35:28 [u] Ex 25:6
35:29 [v] ver 21; 1Ch 29:9 [w] ver 4-9; Ex 25:1-7; 36:3; 2Ki 12:4
35:31 [x] ver 35; 2Ch 2:7,14
35:34 [y] Ex 31:6
[z] 2Ch 2:14
35:35 [a] ver 31; Ex 31:3,6; 1Ki 7:14
36:1 [b] Ex 28:3 [c] Ex 25:8
36:2 [d] Ex 31:2 [e] Ex 31:6 [f] Ex 25:2; 35:21, 26; 1Ch 29:5
36:3 [g] Ex 35:29

Ex 36:2 ❖ Serving God is not just about ability—it's also about willingness. How can we be more willing and ready to wholeheartedly serve God?

35:30—36:7 See notes on 31:1-11.

PEOPLE TO KNOW // BEZALEL AND OHOLIAB

EXODUS 35:30-35: When God gave Moses extensive and detailed instructions for fashioning the tabernacle and all that went with it, it's reasonable to imagine Moses had some trepidation about who could possibly carry out this task according to God's design. It must have come as a huge relief to Moses, therefore, when God mentioned Bezalel and Oholiab (Ex 31:1-6).

God described Bezalel as being filled with the Spirit of God, with wisdom and understanding of all kinds of skills. Those skills included the ability to work with gold, silver and bronze, the ability to cut fine stones, and the ability to work with wood. To assist Bezalel, God appointed Oholiab—every great craftsperson needs a skilled assistant.

Bezalel and Oholiab went on to lead all the skilled artisans in the community to craft and build God's tabernacle exactly as God desired. They followed God's instructions down to the finest details of curtain threads and metal clasps. Bezalel himself built the ark of the covenant out of acacia wood and overlaid it with solid gold, even sculpting the gold cherubim that stood atop the atonement cover (Ex 37:1-9).

APPLICATION ✤ Imagine being the person who hand made the ark of God, where God's very presence lived in the tabernacle. While none of us will ever have that amazing experience, Bezalel and Oholiab show us the beautiful fact that God gives people artistic skills to be used for his glory. God grants us amazing abilities of artistic expression—design, music, dance, writing, painting, building—and so many more. As we read the story of Bezalel and Oholiab, we can be inspired to use all our talents to glorify God.

than enough[h] for doing the work the
LORD commanded to be done."
6 Then Moses gave an order and they
sent this word throughout the camp: "No
man or woman is to make anything else
as an offering for the sanctuary." And so
the people were restrained from bringing
more, 7 because what they already had
was more[i] than enough to do all the work.

36:5 [h] 2Ch 24:14; 31:10; 2Co 8:2-3
36:7 [i] 1Ki 7:47
36:13 [j] ver 18
36:18 [k] ver 13

The Tabernacle

36:8–38pp // Ex 26:1–37

8 All those who were skilled among the
workers made the tabernacle with ten
curtains of finely twisted linen and blue,
purple and scarlet yarn, with cherubim
woven into them by expert hands. 9 All
the curtains were the same size — twenty-
eight cubits long and four cubits wide.[a]
10 They joined five of the curtains together and did the same with the other five.
11 Then they made loops of blue material
along the edge of the end curtain in one
set, and the same was done with the end
curtain in the other set. 12 They also made
fifty loops on one curtain and fifty loops
on the end curtain of the other set, with
the loops opposite each other. 13 Then they
made fifty gold clasps and used them to
fasten the two sets of curtains together
so that the tabernacle was a unit.[j]
14 They made curtains of goat hair for
the tent over the tabernacle — eleven
altogether. 15 All eleven curtains were the
same size — thirty cubits long and four
cubits wide.[b] 16 They joined five of the
curtains into one set and the other six
into another set. 17 Then they made fifty
loops along the edge of the end curtain
in one set and also along the edge of the
end curtain in the other set. 18 They made
fifty bronze clasps to fasten the tent together as a unit.[k] 19 Then they made for
the tent a covering of ram skins dyed
red, and over that a covering of the other
durable leather.[c]
20 They made upright frames of acacia
wood for the tabernacle. 21 Each frame
was ten cubits long and a cubit and a half
wide,[d] 22 with two projections set parallel
to each other. They made all the frames
of the tabernacle in this way. 23 They
made twenty frames for the south side
of the tabernacle 24 and made forty silver
bases to go under them — two bases for
each frame, one under each projection.
25 For the other side, the north side of the
tabernacle, they made twenty frames
26 and forty silver bases — two under each
frame. 27 They made six frames for the far
end, that is, the west end of the tabernacle, 28 and two frames were made for the
corners of the tabernacle at the far end.
29 At these two corners the frames were
double from the bottom all the way to
the top and fitted into a single ring; both
were made alike. 30 So there were eight
frames and sixteen silver bases — two
under each frame.
31 They also made crossbars of acacia
wood: five for the frames on one side of
the tabernacle, 32 five for those on the
other side, and five for the frames on
the west, at the far end of the tabernacle. 33 They made the center crossbar so
that it extended from end to end at the
middle of the frames. 34 They overlaid the
frames with gold and made gold rings to
hold the crossbars. They also overlaid the
crossbars with gold.
35 They made the curtain[l] of blue, purple and scarlet yarn and finely twisted
linen, with cherubim woven into it by a
skilled worker. 36 They made four posts of
acacia wood for it and overlaid them with
gold. They made gold hooks for them
and cast their four silver bases. 37 For the
entrance to the tent they made a curtain
of blue, purple and scarlet yarn and finely twisted linen — the work of an embroiderer;[m] 38 and they made five posts with
hooks for them. They overlaid the tops of
the posts and their bands with gold and
made their five bases of bronze.

The Ark

37:1–9pp // Ex 25:10–20

37 Bezalel[n] made the ark[o] of acacia
wood — two and a half cubits long,
a cubit and a half wide, and a cubit and
a half high.[e] 2 He overlaid it with pure
gold,[p] both inside and out, and made

36:35 [l] Ex 39:38; Mt 27:51; Lk 23:45; Heb 9:3
36:37 [m] Ex 27:16
37:1 [n] Ex 31:2 [o] Ex 30:6; 39:35; Dt 10:3
37:2 [p] ver 11, 26

[a] *9* That is, about 42 feet long and 6 feet wide or about 13 meters long and 1.8 meters wide
[b] *15* That is, about 45 feet long and 6 feet wide or about 14 meters long and 1.8 meters wide
[c] *19* Possibly the hides of large aquatic mammals (see 35:7)
[d] *21* That is, about 15 feet long and 2 1/4 feet wide or about 4.5 meters long and 68 centimeters wide
[e] *1* That is, about 3 3/4 feet long and 2 1/4 feet wide and high or about 1.1 meters long and 68 centimeters wide and high; similarly in verse 6

36:8–38 See notes on 26:1-37.

37:1–9 See notes on 25:10-22.

a gold molding around it. 3He cast four gold rings for it and fastened them to its four feet, with two rings on one side and two rings on the other. 4Then he made poles of acacia wood and overlaid them with gold. 5And he inserted the poles into the rings on the sides of the ark to carry it.

6He made the atonement cover[q] of pure gold—two and a half cubits long and a cubit and a half wide. 7Then he made two cherubim[r] out of hammered gold at the ends of the cover. 8He made one cherub on one end and the second cherub on the other; at the two ends he made them of one piece with the cover. 9The cherubim had their wings spread upward, overshadowing[s] the cover with them. The cherubim faced each other, looking toward the cover.[t]

The Table

37:10–16pp // Ex 25:23–29

10They[a] made the table[u] of acacia wood—two cubits long, a cubit wide and a cubit and a half high.[b] 11Then they overlaid it with pure gold[v] and made a gold molding around it. 12They also made around it a rim a handbreadth[c] wide and put a gold molding on the rim. 13They cast four gold rings for the table and fastened them to the four corners, where the four legs were. 14The rings[w] were put close to the rim to hold the poles used in carrying the table. 15The poles for carrying the table were made of acacia wood and were overlaid with gold. 16And they made from pure gold the articles for the table—its plates and dishes and bowls and its pitchers for the pouring out of drink offerings.

The Lampstand

37:17–24pp // Ex 25:31–39

17They made the lampstand[x] of pure gold. They hammered out its base and shaft, and made its flowerlike cups, buds and blossoms of one piece with them. 18Six branches extended from the sides of the lampstand—three on one side and three on the other. 19Three cups shaped like almond flowers with buds and blossoms were on one branch, three on the next branch and the same for all six branches extending from the lampstand. 20And on the lampstand were four cups shaped like almond flowers with buds and blossoms. 21One bud was under the first pair of branches extending from the lampstand, a second bud under the second pair, and a third bud under the third pair—six branches in all. 22The buds and the branches were all of one piece with the lampstand, hammered out of pure gold.[y]

23They made its seven lamps,[z] as well as its wick trimmers and trays, of pure gold. 24They made the lampstand and all its accessories from one talent[d] of pure gold.

The Altar of Incense

37:25–28pp // Ex 30:1–5

25They made the altar of incense[a] out of acacia wood. It was square, a cubit long and a cubit wide and two cubits high[e]—its horns[b] of one piece with it. 26They overlaid the top and all the sides and the horns with pure gold, and made a gold molding around it. 27They made two gold rings[c] below the molding—two on each of the opposite sides—to hold the poles used to carry it. 28They made the poles of acacia wood and overlaid them with gold.[d]

29They also made the sacred anointing oil[e] and the pure, fragrant incense[f]—the work of a perfumer.

Ex 37 ❖ Only the purest gold was used in the temple furnishings. What does this show about how God should be worshiped?

37:6 [q] Ex 26:34; 31:7; Heb 9:5
37:7 [r] Eze 41:18
37:9 [s] Heb 9:5 [t] Dt 10:3
37:10 [u] Heb 9:2
37:11 [v] ver 2
37:14 [w] ver 27
37:17 [x] Heb 9:2; Rev 1:12
37:22 [y] ver 17; Nu 8:4
37:23 [z] Ex 40:4, 25
37:25 [a] Ex 30:34-36; Lk 1:11; Heb 9:4; Rev 8:3 [b] Ex 27:2; Rev 9:13
37:27 [c] ver 14
37:28 [d] Ex 25:13
37:29 [e] Ex 31:11 [f] Ex 30:1, 25; 39:38

[a] *10* Or *He;* also in verses 11-29 [b] *10* That is, about 3 feet long, 1 1/2 feet wide and 2 1/4 feet high or about 90 centimeters long, 45 centimeters wide and 68 centimeters high [c] *12* That is, about 3 inches or about 7.5 centimeters [d] *24* That is, about 75 pounds or about 34 kilograms [e] *25* That is, about 1 1/2 feet long and wide and 3 feet high or about 45 centimeters long and wide and 90 centimeters high

37:10-16 See notes on 25:23-30.
37:17-24 See notes on 25:31-40.
37:25-28 See notes on 30:1-10.
37:29 See notes on 30:22-38.
38:1-7 See notes on 27:1-8.
38:8 See notes on 30:17-21.
38:9-20 See notes on 27:9-19.
38:21-31 We have here a list not only of the materials used but also of their weights. The approximate weights of the material listed, in today's measures, are as follows: 2,193.25 pounds (994.8 kg) of gold; 7,544.38 pounds (3422 kg) of silver; 5,310 pounds

The Altar of Burnt Offering
38:1–7pp // Ex 27:1–8

38 They[a] built the altar of burnt offering of acacia wood, three cubits[b]
high; it was square, five cubits long and
five cubits wide.[c] 2They made a horn
at each of the four corners, so that the
horns and the altar were of one piece,
and they overlaid the altar with bronze.[g]
3They made all its utensils[h] of bronze —
its pots, shovels, sprinkling bowls, meat
forks and firepans. 4They made a grating
for the altar, a bronze network, to be under its ledge, halfway up the altar. 5They
cast bronze rings to hold the poles for
the four corners of the bronze grating.
6They made the poles of acacia wood and
overlaid them with bronze. 7They inserted the poles into the rings so they would
be on the sides of the altar for carrying
it. They made it hollow, out of boards.

The Basin for Washing

8They made the bronze basin[i] and its
bronze stand from the mirrors of the
women[j] who served at the entrance to
the tent of meeting.

The Courtyard
38:9–20pp // Ex 27:9–19

9Next they made the courtyard. The
south side was a hundred cubits[d] long
and had curtains of finely twisted linen,
10with twenty posts and twenty bronze
bases, and with silver hooks and bands
on the posts. 11The north side was also
a hundred cubits long and had twenty
posts and twenty bronze bases, with sil
ver hooks and bands on the posts.
12The west end was fifty cubits[e] wide
and had curtains, with ten posts and ten
bases, with silver hooks and bands on the
posts. 13The east end, toward the sunrise, was also fifty cubits wide. 14Curtains
fifteen cubits[f] long were on one side of
the entrance, with three posts and three
bases, 15and curtains fifteen cubits long
were on the other side of the entrance
to the courtyard, with three posts and
three bases. 16All the curtains around the
courtyard were of finely twisted linen.
17The bases for the posts were bronze.
The hooks and bands on the posts were
silver, and their tops were overlaid with
silver; so all the posts of the courtyard
had silver bands.
18The curtain for the entrance to the
courtyard was made of blue, purple and
scarlet yarn and finely twisted linen —
the work of an embroiderer. It was twenty cubits[g] long and, like the curtains of
the courtyard, five cubits[h] high, 19with
four posts and four bronze bases. Their
hooks and bands were silver, and their
tops were overlaid with silver. 20All the
tent pegs[k] of the tabernacle and of the
surrounding courtyard were bronze.

The Materials Used

21These are the amounts of the materials used for the tabernacle, the tabernacle
of the covenant law,[l] which were recorded
at Moses' command by the Levites under
the direction of Ithamar[m] son of Aaron,
the priest. 22(Bezalel[n] son of Uri, the son
of Hur, of the tribe of Judah, made everything the LORD commanded Moses; 23with
him was Oholiab[o] son of Ahisamak, of the
tribe of Dan — an engraver and designer,
and an embroiderer in blue, purple and
scarlet yarn and fine linen.) 24The total
amount of the gold from the wave offering used for all the work on the sanctuary[p]
was 29 talents and 730 shekels,[i] according
to the sanctuary shekel.[q]
25The silver obtained from those of the
community who were counted in the cen-
sus[r] was 100 talents[j] and 1,775 shekels,[k] according to the sanctuary shekel — 26one

Ex 38:25–26 ❖ Everyone contributed to the work of funding God's tabernacle. How can we contribute—and help others contribute—to the Christian community we are part of?

38:2 [g] 2Ch 1:5
38:3 [h] Ex 31:9
38:8 [i] Ex 30:18; 40:7 [j] Dt 23:17; 1Sa 2:22; 1Ki 14:24
38:20 [k] Ex 35:18
38:21 [l] Nu 1:50, 53; 8:24; 9:15; 10:11; 17:7; 1Ch 23:32; 2Ch 24:6; Ac 7:44; Rev 15:5 [m] Nu 4:28,33
38:22 [n] Ex 31:2
38:23 [o] Ex 31:6
38:24 [p] Ex 30:16 [q] Ex 30:13; Lev 27:25; Nu 3:47; 18:16
38:25 [r] Ex 30:12

[a] *1* Or *He*; also in verses 2-9 [b] *1* That is, about 4 1/2 feet or about 1.4 meters [c] *1* That is, about 7 1/2 feet or about 2.3 meters long and wide [d] *9* That is, about 150 feet or about 45 meters [e] *12* That is, about 75 feet or about 23 meters [f] *14* That is, about 22 feet or about 6.8 meters [g] *18* That is, about 30 feet or about 9 meters [h] *18* That is, about 7 1/2 feet or about 2.3 meters [i] *24* The weight of the gold was a little over a ton or about 1 metric ton. [j] *25* That is, about 3 3/4 tons or about 3.4 metric tons; also in verse 27 [k] *25* That is, about 44 pounds or about 20 kilograms; also in verse 28

(2408.5 kg) of bronze. To put it in perspective, the total weight in precious metals the Israelites carried out of Egypt was about 15,000 pounds (6804 kg). This may seem like an excessively heavy amount in the abstract, but it comes to approximately .025 pounds (.01 kg) for every adult male Israelite—pocket change.

beka per person,[s] that is, half a shekel,[a] according to the sanctuary shekel,[t] from everyone who had crossed over to those counted, twenty years old or more,[u] a total of 603,550 men.[v] 27The 100 talents of silver were used to cast the bases[w] for the sanctuary and for the curtain — 100 bases from the 100 talents, one talent for each base. 28They used the 1,775 shekels to make the hooks for the posts, to overlay the tops of the posts, and to make their bands.

29The bronze from the wave offering was 70 talents and 2,400 shekels.[b] 30They used it to make the bases for the entrance to the tent of meeting, the bronze altar with its bronze grating and all its utensils, 31the bases for the surrounding courtyard and those for its entrance and all the tent pegs for the tabernacle and those for the surrounding courtyard.

The Priestly Garments

39 From the blue, purple and scarlet yarn[x] they made woven garments for ministering in the sanctuary.[y] They also made sacred garments[z] for Aaron, as the LORD commanded Moses.

The Ephod

39:2–7pp // Ex 28:6–14

2They[c] made the ephod of gold, and of blue, purple and scarlet yarn, and of finely twisted linen. 3They hammered out thin sheets of gold and cut strands to be worked into the blue, purple and scarlet yarn and fine linen — the work of skilled hands. 4They made shoulder pieces for the ephod, which were attached to two of its corners, so it could be fastened. 5Its skillfully woven waistband was like it — of one piece with the ephod and made with gold, and with blue, purple and scarlet yarn, and with finely twisted linen, as the LORD commanded Moses.

6They mounted the onyx stones in gold filigree settings and engraved them like a seal with the names of the sons of Israel. 7Then they fastened them on the shoulder pieces of the ephod as memorial[a] stones for the sons of Israel, as the LORD commanded Moses.

The Breastpiece

39:8–21pp // Ex 28:15–28

8They fashioned the breastpiece[b] — the work of a skilled craftsman. They made it like the ephod: of gold, and of blue, purple and scarlet yarn, and of finely twisted linen. 9It was square — a span[d] long and a span wide — and folded double. 10Then they mounted four rows of precious stones on it. The first row was carnelian, chrysolite and beryl; 11the second row was turquoise, lapis lazuli and emerald; 12the third row was jacinth, agate and amethyst; 13the fourth row was topaz, onyx and jasper.[e] They were mounted in gold filigree settings. 14There were twelve stones, one for each of the names of the sons of Israel, each engraved like a seal with the name of one of the twelve tribes.[c]

15For the breastpiece they made braided chains of pure gold, like a rope. 16They made two gold filigree settings and two gold rings, and fastened the rings to two of the corners of the breastpiece. 17They fastened the two gold chains to the rings at the corners of the breastpiece, 18and the other ends of the chains to the two settings, attaching them to the shoulder pieces of the ephod at the front. 19They made two gold rings and attached them to the other two corners of the breastpiece on the inside edge next to the ephod. 20Then they made two more gold rings and attached them to the bottom of the shoulder pieces on the front of the ephod, close to the seam just above the waistband of the ephod. 21They tied the rings of the breastpiece to the rings of the ephod with blue cord, connecting it to the waistband so that the breastpiece would not swing out from the ephod — as the LORD commanded Moses.

Other Priestly Garments

39:22–31pp // Ex 28:31–43

22They made the robe of the ephod entirely of blue cloth — the work of a weaver — 23with an opening in the center of the robe like the opening of a collar,[f] and a band around this opening, so that it would not tear. 24They made

38:26 [s] Ex 30:12 [t] Ex 30:13 [u] Ex 30:14 [v] Ex 12:37; Nu 1:46
38:27 [w] Ex 26:19
39:1 [x] Ex 35:23 [y] Ex 35:19 [z] ver 41; Ex 28:2
39:7 [a] Lev 24:7; Jos 4:7
39:8 [b] Lev 8:8
39:14 [c] Rev 21:12

[a] *26* That is, about 1/5 ounce or about 5.7 grams
[b] *29* The weight of the bronze was about 2 1/2 tons or about 2.4 metric tons.
[c] *2* Or *He;* also in verses 7, 8 and 22
[d] *9* That is, about 9 inches or about 23 centimeters
[e] *13* The precise identification of some of these precious stones is uncertain.
[f] *23* The meaning of the Hebrew for this word is uncertain.

39:1-31 See notes on 28:1-43.

pomegranates of blue, purple and scarlet
yarn and finely twisted linen around the
hem of the robe. 25And they made bells
of pure gold and attached them around
the hem between the pomegranates.
26The bells and pomegranates alternated around the hem of the robe to be worn
for ministering, as the LORD commanded
Moses.

27For Aaron and his sons, they made
tunics of fine linen[d] — the work of a
weaver — 28and the turban[e] of fine linen,
the linen caps and the undergarments
of finely twisted linen. 29The sash was
made of finely twisted linen and blue,
purple and scarlet yarn — the work of an
embroiderer — as the LORD commanded
Moses.

30They made the plate, the sacred emblem, out of pure gold and engraved on
it, like an inscription on a seal: HOLY TO
THE LORD. 31Then they fastened a blue
cord to it to attach it to the turban, as
the LORD commanded Moses.

Moses Inspects the Tabernacle

39:32–41pp // Ex 35:10–19

32So all the work on the tabernacle,
the tent of meeting, was completed. The
Israelites did everything just as the LORD
commanded Moses.[f] 33Then they brought
the tabernacle to Moses: the tent and all
its furnishings, its clasps, frames, crossbars, posts and bases; 34the covering of
ram skins dyed red and the covering of
another durable leather[a] and the shielding curtain; 35the ark of the covenant
law[g] with its poles and the atonement
cover; 36the table with all its articles and
the bread of the Presence; 37the pure gold
lampstand[h] with its row of lamps and
all its accessories, and the olive oil for
the light; 38the gold altar,[i] the anointing
oil, the fragrant incense, and the curtain[j] for the entrance to the tent; 39the
bronze altar with its bronze grating, its
poles and all its utensils; the basin with
its stand; 40the curtains of the courtyard
with its posts and bases, and the curtain
for the entrance to the courtyard;[k] the
ropes and tent pegs for the courtyard;
all the furnishings for the tabernacle,
the tent of meeting; 41and the woven
garments worn for ministering in the
sanctuary, both the sacred garments for
Aaron the priest and the garments for his
sons when serving as priests.

42The Israelites had done all the work
just as the LORD had commanded Moses.[l]
43Moses inspected the work and saw that
they had done it just as the LORD had
commanded. So Moses blessed[m] them.

39:27 [d] Lev 6:10
39:28 [e] Ex 28:4
39:32 [f] ver 42-43; Ex 25:9
39:35 [g] Ex 30:6
39:37 [h] Ex 25:31
39:38 [i] Ex 30:1-10 [j] Ex 36:35
39:40 [k] Ex 27:9-19
39:42 [l] Ex 25:9
39:43 [m] Lev 9:22,23; Nu 6:23-27; 2Sa 6:18; 1Ki 8:14,55; 2Ch 30:27
40:2 [n] Nu 1:1 [o] ver 17; Ex 12:2
40:3 [p] ver 21; Nu 4:5; Ex 26:33
40:4 [q] Ex 25:30 [r] ver 22-25; Ex 26:35
40:5 [s] ver 26; Ex 30:1
40:7 [t] ver 30; Ex 30:18
40:9 [u] Ex 30:26; Lev 8:10
40:10 [v] Ex 29:36
40:12 [w] Lev 8:1-13
40:13 [x] Ex 28:41

Ex 39:30 ❖ The priests wore a headpiece emblazoned with the words HOLY TO THE LORD. How do our lives display that we, too, are set apart for God's glory?

Setting Up the Tabernacle

40 Then the LORD said to Moses:
2"Set up the tabernacle, the tent
of meeting,[n] on the first day of the first
month.[o] 3Place the ark[p] of the covenant
law in it and shield the ark with the curtain. 4Bring in the table and set out what
belongs on it.[q] Then bring in the lampstand[r] and set up its lamps. 5Place the
gold altar[s] of incense in front of the ark
of the covenant law and put the curtain
at the entrance to the tabernacle.

6"Place the altar of burnt offering in
front of the entrance to the tabernacle,
the tent of meeting; 7place the basin[t] between the tent of meeting and the altar
and put water in it. 8Set up the courtyard
around it and put the curtain at the entrance to the courtyard.

9"Take the anointing oil and anoint[u]
the tabernacle and everything in it; consecrate it and all its furnishings, and it
will be holy. 10Then anoint the altar of
burnt offering and all its utensils; consecrate[v] the altar, and it will be most holy.
11Anoint the basin and its stand and consecrate them.

12"Bring Aaron and his sons to the entrance to the tent of meeting and wash
them with water.[w] 13Then dress Aaron in
the sacred garments,[x] anoint him and

[a] *34* Possibly the hides of large aquatic mammals

39:32–43 This passage recounts Israel's obedience, provides a summary of what is made, and outlines Moses' inspection. Verse 32 explicitly equates the tabernacle and the Tent of Meeting.

40:1–33 The narrative of the tabernacle concludes, appropriately, by recounting how it is set up. Verses 1–11 are the detailed commands given by God to Moses concerning what needs to be done. Verses 12–15 follow with the commands concerning the anointing of the priests. After the summary acknowledgment that Moses obeys God fully (v. 16), the details of the set-up are described (vv. 17–33).

consecrate[y] him so he may serve me as
priest. 14 Bring his sons and dress them in
tunics. 15 Anoint them just as you anointed their father, so they may serve me
as priests. Their anointing will be to a
priesthood that will continue throughout
their generations.[z]" 16 Moses did everything just as the LORD commanded him.

17 So the tabernacle[a] was set up on the
first day of the first month[b] in the second
year. 18 When Moses set up the tabernacle, he put the bases in place, erected the
frames, inserted the crossbars and set up
the posts. 19 Then he spread the tent over
the tabernacle and put the covering over
the tent, as the LORD commanded him.

20 He took the tablets of the covenant
law[c] and placed them in the ark, attached
the poles to the ark and put the atonement cover over it. 21 Then he brought
the ark into the tabernacle and hung the
shielding curtain[d] and shielded the ark
of the covenant law, as the LORD commanded him.

40:13 [y] Lev 8:12
40:15 [z] Ex 29:9; Nu 25:13
40:17 [a] Nu 7:1 [b] ver 2
40:20 [c] Ex 16:34; 25:16; Dt 10:5; 1Ki 8:9; Heb 9:4
40:21 [d] Ex 26:33

There is also creation language here. In fact, this section ends (v. 33) by repeating almost verbatim the language of Ge 2:2. Moses' overseeing the construction of the tabernacle is like God building the universe.

40:17 We also see that the tabernacle is set up "on the first day of the first month in the second year" (40:17). As we saw in 12:2, the exodus inaugurated a new calendar in Israelite life: The month in which the exodus took place would be the first month of the year. It is no surprise, therefore, that the tabernacle, itself a microcosm of creation, is also set up one year later on the first day of the first month. It, too, is a new creation.

40:18-33 The uncompromising attention to specific details is another indication that the tabernacle is an act of creation—it reflects the order that God originally created in the universe. There is no room for human disorder or for chaos to invade this holy space. Everything must be exactly as God has commanded. The order of the tabernacle reflects God's very nature, a nature that creation itself reflects.

25:1—31:18; 35:1—40:33 We have noted repeatedly that the tabernacle is a microcosm of creation. In it we see the God of all creation dwelling on earth in a structure intended to reflect the perfect created order—a piece of heaven on earth. Then, at the climactic stage in redemptive history, God took up residence in Christ, the temple who "tabernacled" among his people (Jn 1:1-5, 9-14). He is not a building constructed to reflect heavenly glory. He himself is from heaven and is therefore the concrete manifestation of what the tabernacle symbolized. And finally, inexplicably, the God of creation has built us up to be his house so he can take up residence in us. He has fashioned us with material far more precious than gold or silver, dyed yarn, or fine linen. We are created in the very image of the risen Christ so that even we reflect a piece of heaven. We are worthy of the Spirit's indwelling because we have been re-created by the power of God into heavenly beings.

What does this mean? The paths to understanding and applying this profound mystery are endless. But following are two implications for how we, as tabernacles, should reflect the order of God amid the chaos around us: how we worship and how we live. (1) The tabernacle was a place of worship, a place of giving God praise and acknowledging that he alone is worthy. It was a place for connecting with God. (2) When we think of our bodies as the temple of God, it puts sinning in a different perspective. This is really Paul's point in 1Co 6:18–20 where he equates individual Christians at Corinth with the temple. Some in Corinth were engaging in sexual immorality. Paul's rebuke essentially amounts to this: "How can you possibly think of doing anything like this? Don't you know God himself resides in you?"

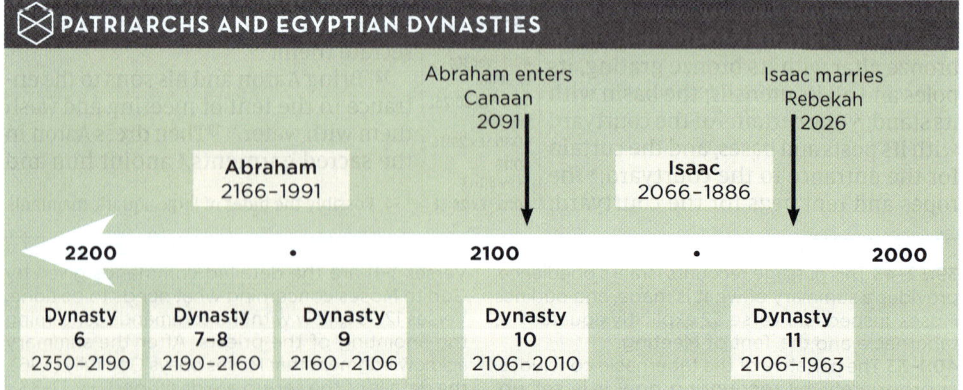

22Moses placed the table[e] in the tent
of meeting on the north side of the tabernacle outside the curtain 23and set out
the bread[f] on it before the LORD, as the
LORD commanded him.
24He placed the lampstand[g] in the
tent of meeting opposite the table on
the south side of the tabernacle 25and
set up the lamps[h] before the LORD, as
the LORD commanded him.
26Moses placed the gold altar[i] in the
tent of meeting in front of the curtain
27and burned fragrant incense on it, as
the LORD commanded[j] him.
28Then he put up the curtain[k] at the
entrance to the tabernacle. 29He set the
altar of burnt offering near the entrance
to the tabernacle, the tent of meeting,
and offered on it burnt offerings and
grain offerings,[l] as the LORD commanded him.
30He placed the basin[m] between the
tent of meeting and the altar and put
water in it for washing, 31and Moses and
Aaron and his sons used it to wash their
hands and feet. 32They washed whenever they entered the tent of meeting
or approached the altar,[n] as the LORD
commanded Moses.

40:22 [e] Ex 26:35
40:23 [f] ver 4
40:24 [g] Ex 26:35
40:25 [h] ver 4; Ex 25:37
40:26 [i] ver 5; Ex 30:6
40:27 [j] Ex 30:7
40:28 [k] Ex 26:36
40:29 [l] ver 6; Ex 29:38-42
40:30 [m] ver 7
40:32 [n] Ex 30:20
40:33 [o] Ex 27:9 [p] ver 8
40:34 [q] Nu 9:15-23; 1Ki 8:12
40:35 [r] 1Ki 8:11; 2Ch 5:13-14
40:36 [s] Nu 9:17-23; 10:13; Ne 9:19
40:38 [t] Ex 13:21; Nu 9:15; 1Co 10:1

Ex 40:34 ❖ Just as God's presence filled the tabernacle, it should fill each believer (Eph 3:19). What does it mean to be filled with the fullness of God?

33Then Moses set up the courtyard[o]
around the tabernacle and altar and put
up the curtain[p] at the entrance to the
courtyard. And so Moses finished the
work.

The Glory of the LORD

34Then the cloud[q] covered the tent of
meeting, and the glory of the LORD filled
the tabernacle. 35Moses could not enter
the tent of meeting because the cloud
had settled on it, and the glory of the
LORD filled the tabernacle.[r]
36In all the travels of the Israelites,
whenever the cloud lifted from above
the tabernacle, they would set out;[s] 37but
if the cloud did not lift, they did not set
out — until the day it lifted. 38So the
cloud[t] of the LORD was over the tabernacle by day, and fire was in the cloud
by night, in the sight of all the Israelites
during all their travels.

40:34-38 The reappearance of the cloud in particular attracts our attention. The recurring appearance of this symbol ties various parts of the book together and communicates loud and clear that the God of the exodus is still with his people.

40:36-38 These verses prepare us for what will become a dominant element in the books of Numbers and Deuteronomy—the relentless push toward the land of Canaan. The purpose of these closing verses of Exodus is to explain how this will happen. When God moves, the people move. This is a lesson the Israelites, unfortunately, will be slow to learn.

Thus, the first phase of Israel's story comes to an end. One chapter of this grand story is closing and another is beginning, so our gaze is directed forward to the next phase in Israel's journey.

✣ **40:34-38** We, too, have been delivered and are waiting to arrive at the final destination. We, like the Israelites, are poised to reach our rest. Admittedly, there is no cloud overhead, but we have the Spirit of Christ dwelling in us. God is present with his people wherever they go, for he still leads and guides them, not to Canaan, but to a "better country—a heavenly one" (Heb 11:16).

Leviticus

Author: Moses
Audience: God's chosen people, the Israelites
Date: Probably between 1446 and 1406 BC

Theme: God judges his rebellious people but reaffirms his intent to bring them into the promised land.

Reading Leviticus

Most of Leviticus is a collection of laws, such as the laws concerning proper sacrifices (chs. 1-7), rules for Aaron as high priest (chs. 8-10; 21), and regulations on what is clean and unclean (chs. 11-15).

PERSPECTIVE

One of the major weaknesses of modern culture is our loss of morality. We misunderstand the nature of laws and rules and commandments, calling them legalisms; then, based on this misunderstanding, we reject them. We think legalism and morality are the same thing. We don't like either one and begin to squirm when the subject of morality comes up.

Actually, many of us begin to squirm as well when the subject of the biblical books of Leviticus and Numbers comes up—and for much the same reasons: our discomfort with morality. We don't like reading what appear to be the outdated dictates of a grouchy God who seems to have gotten up on the wrong side of bed. What is the point?

One of the primary emphases of the commentary on these books is that Levitical laws are not legalistic and outdated. By carefully and thoroughly reviewing each chapter and verse, we discover that we can learn from other people's morality, even when their culture is radically different from ours.

The point is this: If you read Leviticus and Numbers faithfully, your squeamishness about morality itself will begin to disappear. In order to explain this lesson, two ideas emerge from reading this authoritative material. (1) The laws of Leviticus are effective because they are created for and implemented in a community of people. They describe the dynamic worship system of ancient Israel, a system that has theological meaning. These are not laws for individuals.

These are laws that are only secondarily about safety and health and order and good manners. They are about the worship of God, which is the precondition, the setting, of all the Levitical laws. Why

	2200 BC	2100	2000	1900	1800	1700	1600	1500	1400
Moses' birth (c. 1526 BC)								♦	
The plagues; the Passover (c. 1446 BC)									♦
The exodus (c. 1446 BC)									♦
Desert wanderings (c. 1446–1406 BC)									▬
The Ten Commandments (c. 1445 BC)									♦
Book of Leviticus written (c. 1440 BC)									♦
Moses dies; Joshua becomes leader (c. 1406 BC)									♦
Israelites enter Canaan (c. 1406 BC)									♦

are we to love our neighbor (17:9)? Because we cannot worship God unless we love our neighbor as ourselves. Once this is established, we discover that loving our neighbor creates good, safe, healthy, intercommunal relationships.

We live in a culture where we tend to understand laws and rules and commandments primarily as they relate to us as individuals. Because we live in an individualistic age, it takes deliberate effort to realize that individual morality is rooted in communal morality. In the Bible, this is not made as explicit as it could be because in biblical times it was assumed that the values of the community precede those of the individual. Today the order is reversed, and understanding the Levitical laws demands that we include in our interpretation an acknowledgment of the Bible's priorities.

(2) The laws of Leviticus only make sense to us if we are able to transpose their meaning from a cultural context three millennia in time and half a world in distance from our own. The content of the laws of Leviticus can seem strange. The questions on mildew in chapter 13, for example, can best be understood by those who live in a humid environment where this is still a problem. The community implications of this law are manifest. Any destructive force that has the potential to spread throughout the body of Christ is something we should all be concerned with corralling.

Is it any wonder, given these two ideas, that the NT so often refers to the laws of Leviticus to explain the morality of the people of the kingdom of God? They are laws sent to us by God through Moses. That means they are important. They are laws that ordered the lives of a holy, tribal community centered in the divine presence. Since that is what we long to happen in the church (and churches) of today, we could do worse than try to live the lifestyle created by these laws.

God's call to holiness is not a call to be embraced by hermits. It is a call that is always lived out in relation to a community, a group of people centered in the worship of God—a group of people situated in a wider world of decentered, sometimes immoral, sometimes amoral cultural groups. It turns out that in many ways we are not so different from this tribe wandering in the deserts of Sinai after all.

Key Verse

"You are to be holy to me because I, the LORD, am holy, and I have set you apart from the nations to be my own."

—Leviticus 20:26

TAKING THE NEXT STEPS

In Leviticus, Moses wrote down the numerous laws that God revealed to him. These laws regulated both the worship of God and the everyday affairs of Israelite life. God's motive was not to make their lives miserable through legalistic observance of the law, but to show them the high priority he placed on holiness.

Much of the book of Leviticus may strike us as irrelevant and dull. But it contains principles that are valid yet today. (1) Most important, God wants us to live holy lives in dedicated service to him. Any sin is an attack on and an offense to his holiness. (2) By stressing the need for perfect sacrifices, God reminds us that he expects the very best. (3) Worship of a holy God is a serious business that requires careful, sincere preparation on the part of both the worship leader and the worshiper. (4) The shedding of blood is an absolute requirement for the forgiveness of sins; thus the book of Leviticus directs our attention to Jesus Christ, who spilled his blood for us on the cross of Calvary.

WHAT TO LOOK FOR IN LEVITICUS

- The Day of Atonement (ch. 16)
- Laws similar to the Ten Commandments (ch. 19)
- The seven feasts of Israel (ch. 23)
- The Year of Jubilee (ch. 25)
- Rewards and punishments (ch. 26)

The Burnt Offering

1 The LORD called to Moses[a] and spoke
to him from the tent of meeting.[b] He
said, 2"Speak to the Israelites and say to
them: 'When anyone among you brings
an offering to the LORD, bring as your
offering an animal from either the herd
or the flock.[c]
3" 'If the offering is a burnt offering
from the herd, you are to offer a male
without defect.[d] You must present it at
the entrance to the tent[e] of meeting so
that it will be acceptable to the LORD.
4You are to lay your hand on the head[f] of
the burnt offering, and it will be accepted
on your behalf to make atonement[g] for
you. 5You are to slaughter[h] the young
bull before the LORD, and then Aaron's
sons the priests shall bring the blood and
splash it against the sides of the altar[i]
at the entrance to the tent of meeting.
6You are to skin[j] the burnt offering and
cut it into pieces. 7The sons of Aaron the
priest are to put fire on the altar and arrange wood[k] on the fire. 8Then Aaron's
sons the priests shall arrange the pieces,
including the head and the fat,[l] on the
wood that is burning on the altar. 9You
are to wash the internal organs and the
legs with water, and the priest is to burn
all of it on the altar.[m] It is a burnt offering, a food offering, an aroma pleasing
to the LORD.[n]
10" 'If the offering is a burnt offering
from the flock, from either the sheep
or the goats,[o] you are to offer a male

Lev 1:4 ❖ Why is it important to have a sacrifice presented on our behalf?

1:1 [a] Ex 19:3; 25:22 [b] Nu 7:89
1:2 [c] Lev 22:18-19
1:3 [d] Ex 12:5; Dt 15:21; Heb 9:14; 1Pe 1:19 [e] Lev 17:9
1:4 [f] Ex 29:10, 15; Lev 3:2 [g] 2Ch 29:23-24
1:5 [h] Lev 3:2, 8 [i] Heb 12:24; 1Pe 1:2
1:6 [j] Lev 7:8
1:7 [k] Lev 6:12
1:8 [l] ver 12
1:9 [m] Ex 29:18 [n] ver 13; Ge 8:21; Nu 15:8-10; Eph 5:2
1:10 [o] ver 3; Ex 12:5

1:1–17 Leviticus picks up where Exodus ends. While the physical structure of the sanctuary was crucial, the resident presence of God made the place powerful. This is where Leviticus comes in. Here at the heart of the Torah, the focus is on the way God's people are to interact with divine holiness.

When the Lord calls to Moses from the "tent of meeting" (v. 1) he wastes no time launching into a series of commands regarding the heart of worship: sacrifice. Given that animal sacrifices are foreign and even repulsive to us, how do we begin to understand the divine message and get something out of it? Where is the meaning in a ritual?

A ritual is a system of activities. Through rituals the Israelites could enjoy limited *interaction* with God. They could come to the sanctuary, the "tent of meeting" (vv. 1, 3, 5, etc.), and give something tangible to him to express their devotion, thanks, or desire to receive forgiveness. In the case of the burnt offering, they could give him a token food gift (v. 9) and receive his gracious response of expiation, that is, removal of evil ("make atonement"; v. 4).

without defect. 11You are to slaughter it at the north side of the altar before the LORD, and Aaron's sons the priests shall splash its blood against the sides of the altar.[p] 12You are to cut it into pieces, and the priest shall arrange them, including the head and the fat, on the wood that is burning on the altar. 13You are to wash the internal organs and the legs with water, and the priest is to bring all of them and burn them on the altar. It is a burnt offering, a food offering, an aroma pleasing to the LORD.

14" 'If the offering to the LORD is a burnt offering of birds, you are to offer a dove or a young pigeon.[q] 15The priest shall bring it to the altar, wring off the head and burn it on the altar; its blood shall be drained out on the side of the altar.[r] 16He is to remove the crop and the feathers[a] and throw them down east of the altar where the ashes[s] are. 17He shall tear it open by the wings, not dividing it completely,[t] and then the priest shall burn it on the wood[u] that is burning on the altar. It is a burnt offering, a food offering, an aroma pleasing to the LORD.

1:11 [p] ver 5
1:14 [q] Ge 15:9; Lev 5:7; Lk 2:24
1:15 [r] Lev 5:9
1:16 [s] Lev 6:10
1:17 [t] Ge 15:10 [u] Lev 5:8
2:1 [v] Lev 6:14-18 [w] Nu 15:4
2:2 [x] Lev 5:11 [y] Lev 6:15; Isa 66:3 [z] ver 9, 16; Lev 5:12; 6:15; 24:7; Ac 10:4

The Grain Offering

2 " 'When anyone brings a grain offering[v] to the LORD, their offering is to be of the finest flour. They are to pour olive oil[w] on it, put incense on it 2and take it to Aaron's sons the priests. The priest shall take a handful of the flour[x] and oil, together with all the incense,[y] and burn this as a memorial[b] portion[z]

[a] 16 Or *crop with its contents*; the meaning of the Hebrew for this word is uncertain. [b] 2 Or *representative*; also in verses 9 and 16

APPLICATION ✣ 1:1-17 Rituals, including Christian rituals of baptism and the Lord's Supper/Communion, transcend the boundary between the seen and unseen realms. So does prayer. We are not completely cut off from God. Through prayer and ritual, it is as though we can reach out and touch him. When Jesus came, people could touch him because he came without a "bubble" to isolate him from the moral and physical disease of the fallen human race. His death and resurrection make it possible for us to be restored to face-to-face communion with God so that rituals will no longer be needed (cf. Rev 21:22).

2:1-3 The grain offering handed over to the priest was to be semolina/grits of wheat. Although this was not the "finest flour" (v. 1) in terms of texture, it was fine in the sense that it was choice food rather than ordinary flour. The oil helped the offering burn on the altar, and the incense enhanced the pleasing aroma (v. 2). Both oil and incense are associated with joy (Pr 27:9).

KEY HEBREW TERMS IN LEVITICUS

WORD	MEANING	USAGE
olah	whole burnt offering ascend, go up	Lev 1:9 "[T]he priest is to burn all of it on the altar. It is a burnt offering, a food offering, an aroma pleasing to the LORD."
qorban	offering oblation	Lev 1:2 "Speak to the Israelites and say to them: 'When anyone among you brings an offering to the LORD, bring as your offering an animal from either the herd or the flock.' "
kâpar	make an atonement, make reconciliation, purge	Lev 1:4 "You are to lay your hand on the head of the burnt offering, and it will be accepted on your behalf to make atonement for you."
dam	blood	Lev 1:5 "You are to slaughter the young bull before the LORD, and then Aaron's sons the priests shall bring the blood and splash it against the sides of the altar at the entrance to the tent of meeting."
hata	to miss, go wrong, sin	Lev 4:22-23 "When a leader sins unintentionally and does what is forbidden in any of the commands of the LORD his God, when he realizes his guilt and the sin he has committed becomes known, he must bring as his offering a male goat without defect."

on the altar, a food offering, an aroma
pleasing to the LORD. 3 The rest of the
grain offering belongs to Aaron and his
sons;[a] it is a most holy part of the food
offerings presented to the LORD.
4 “ ‘If you bring a grain offering baked
in an oven, it is to consist of the finest
flour: either thick loaves made without
yeast and with olive oil mixed in or thin
loaves made without yeast and brushed
with olive oil.[b] 5 If your grain offering is
prepared on a griddle, it is to be made
of the finest flour mixed with oil, and
without yeast. 6 Crumble it and pour oil
on it; it is a grain offering. 7 If your grain
offering is cooked in a pan,[c] it is to be
made of the finest flour and some olive
oil. 8 Bring the grain offering made of
these things to the LORD; present it to
the priest, who shall take it to the altar.
9 He shall take out the memorial portion[d]
from the grain offering and burn it on
the altar as a food offering, an aroma
pleasing to the LORD.[e] 10 The rest of the
grain offering belongs to Aaron and his
sons;[f] it is a most holy part of the food
offerings presented to the LORD.
11 “ ‘Every grain offering you bring to
the LORD must be made without yeast,[g]
for you are not to burn any yeast or honey
in a food offering presented to the LORD.
12 You may bring them to the LORD as an
offering of the firstfruits,[h] but they are
not to be offered on the altar as a pleasing aroma. 13 Season all your grain offerings with salt. Do not leave the salt of the
covenant[i] of your God out of your grain
offerings; add salt to all your offerings.

2:3 [a] ver 10; Lev 6:16; 10:12,13
2:4 [b] Ex 29:2
2:7 [c] Lev 7:9
2:9 [d] ver 2 [e] Ex 29:18; Lev 6:15
2:10 [f] ver 3
2:11 [g] Ex 23:18; 34:25; Lev 6:16
2:12 [h] Lev 7:13; 23:10
2:13 [i] Nu 18:19; Eze 43:24
2:14 [j] Lev 23:10
2:16 [k] ver 2
3:1 [l] Lev 7:11-34 [m] Lev 1:3; 22:21
3:2 [n] Ex 29:10,15 [o] Lev 1:5
3:3 [p] Ex 29:13
3:5 [q] Lev 7:29-34 [r] Ex 29:13, 38-42

Lev 2:9 ❖ How can our lives offer a pleasing aroma to God (see 2Co 2:15)?

Lev 3:1 ❖ Why does God expect offerings without defect? How does this relate to Christians today?

14 “ ‘If you bring a grain offering of firstfruits[j] to the LORD, offer crushed heads
of new grain roasted in the fire. 15 Put
oil and incense on it; it is a grain offering. 16 The priest shall burn the memorial
portion[k] of the crushed grain and the oil,
together with all the incense, as a food
offering presented to the LORD.

The Fellowship Offering

3 “ ‘If your offering is a fellowship offering,[l] and you offer an animal from
the herd, whether male or female, you
are to present before the LORD an animal without defect.[m] 2 You are to lay your
hand on the head[n] of your offering and
slaughter it[o] at the entrance to the tent
of meeting. Then Aaron’s sons the priests
shall splash the blood against the sides of
the altar. 3 From the fellowship offering
you are to bring a food offering to the
LORD: the internal organs and all the fat[p]
that is connected to them, 4 both kidneys
with the fat on them near the loins, and
the long lobe of the liver, which you will
remove with the kidneys. 5 Then Aaron’s
sons[q] are to burn it on the altar on top of
the burnt offering[r] that is lying on the
burning wood; it is a food offering, an
aroma pleasing to the LORD.
6 “ ‘If you offer an animal from the flock

A grain offering involved no butchering, blood, or hide to serve as a priest’s commission, so the priest kept the remainder of the grain offering after he scooped a handful from it and burned that part as a token portion for the Lord on the altar (v. 2).

2:11–13 The first rule is a prohibition against yeast. The second general rule is positive: The “salt of the covenant” must be included with all grain offerings (v. 13).

2:14–16 This section resumes the series of subcases within the overall category of cooked grain offerings.

✣ **2:1–16** Bloodless Israelite sacrifices of grain have helped us to understand that we can offer a “living sacrifice” and “be transformed by the renewing” of our minds rather than conforming “to the pattern of this world” (Ro 12:1–2). “Through Jesus, therefore, let us continually offer to God a sacrifice of praise—the fruit of lips that openly profess his name. And do not forget to do good and to share with others, for with such sacrifices God is pleased” (Heb 13:15–16).

3:1–16a The “fellowship offering” can be translated “well-being offering” (so-called peace or fellowship offering). This sacrifice is offered for happy circumstances. This category differs from burnt and purification offerings in that those who offer *these* sacrifices eat the meat, thereby materially benefiting from their own sacrifices. While well-being offering animals, like burnt offerings, must be without physical defect, there are two differences. (1) Birds are not used for well-being offerings. (2) A well-being offering can be either male or female (vv. 1, 6).

The offeror’s portion is sacrificial meat from an animal that has been dedicated to God. Because the meat is holy and therefore must not be brought into contact with ritual impurity, the offeror must be ritually pure in order to eat it (7:19–21).

as a fellowship offering[s] to the LORD, you
are to offer a male or female without defect. 7If you offer a lamb, you are to present it before the LORD,[t] 8lay your hand on
its head and slaughter it[u] in front of the
tent of meeting. Then Aaron's sons shall
splash its blood against the sides of the
altar. 9From the fellowship offering you
are to bring a food offering to the LORD:
its fat, the entire fat tail cut off close to
the backbone, the internal organs and all
the fat that is connected to them, 10both
kidneys with the fat on them near the
loins, and the long lobe of the liver, which
you will remove with the kidneys. 11The
priest shall burn them on the altar[v] as
a food offering[w] presented to the LORD.
12" 'If your offering is a goat, you are
to present it before the LORD, 13lay your
hand on its head and slaughter it in front
of the tent of meeting. Then Aaron's sons
shall splash[x] its blood against the sides of
the altar. 14From what you offer you are
to present this food offering to the LORD:
the internal organs and all the fat that is
connected to them, 15both kidneys with
the fat on them near the loins, and the
long lobe of the liver, which you will remove with the kidneys. 16The priest shall
burn them on the altar as a food offering,
a pleasing aroma. All the fat is the LORD's.[y]
17" 'This is a lasting ordinance for the
generations to come,[z] wherever you live:
You must not eat any fat or any blood.[a]' "

The Sin Offering

4 The LORD said to Moses, 2"Say to the
Israelites: 'When anyone sins unintentionally[b] and does what is forbidden
in any of the LORD's commands —

3" 'If the anointed priest sins, bringing
guilt on the people, he must bring to the
LORD a young bull[c] without defect as a
sin offering[a][d] for the sin he has committed. 4He is to present the bull at the entrance to the tent of meeting before the
LORD.[e] He is to lay his hand on its head
and slaughter it there before the LORD.
5Then the anointed priest shall take some
of the bull's blood[f] and carry it into the
tent of meeting. 6He is to dip his finger
into the blood and sprinkle some of it
seven times before the LORD, in front of
the curtain of the sanctuary. 7The priest
shall then put some of the blood on the
horns of the altar of fragrant incense that
is before the LORD in the tent of meeting. The rest of the bull's blood he shall
pour out at the base of the altar[g] of burnt
offering[h] at the entrance to the tent of
meeting. 8He shall remove all the fat[i]
from the bull of the sin offering — all
the fat that is connected to the internal
organs, 9both kidneys with the fat on
them near the loins, and the long lobe of
the liver, which he will remove with the
kidneys[j] — 10just as the fat is removed
from the ox[b] sacrificed as a fellowship
offering. Then the priest shall burn them
on the altar of burnt offering. 11But the
hide of the bull and all its flesh, as well
as the head and legs, the internal organs
and the intestines[k] — 12that is, all the
rest of the bull — he must take outside
the camp[l] to a place ceremonially clean,[m]
where the ashes are thrown, and burn
it there in a wood fire on the ash heap.

13" 'If the whole Israelite community sins unintentionally[n] and does
what is forbidden in any of the LORD's

3:6 [s] ver 1
3:7 [t] Lev 17:8-9
3:8 [u] ver 2; Lev 1:5
3:11 [v] ver 5 [w] ver 16; Lev 21:6,17
3:13 [x] Ex 24:6
3:16 [y] 1Sa 2:16
3:17 [z] Lev 6:18; 17:7 [a] Ge 9:4; Lev 7:25-26; 17:10-16; Dt 12:16; Ac 15:20
4:2 [b] Lev 5:15-18; Ps 19:12; Heb 9:7
4:3 [c] ver 14; Ps 66:15 [d] Lev 9:2-22; Heb 9:13-14
4:4 [e] Lev 1:3
4:5 [f] Lev 16:14
4:7 [g] ver 34; Lev 8:15 [h] ver 18, 30; Lev 5:9; 9:9; 16:18
4:8 [i] Lev 3:3-5
4:9 [j] Lev 3:4
4:11 [k] Ex 29:14; Lev 9:11; Nu 19:5
4:12 [l] Heb 13:11 [m] Lev 6:11
4:13 [n] ver 2; Lev 5:2-4,17; Nu 15:24-26

[a] 3 Or *purification offering*; here and throughout this chapter [b] 10 The Hebrew word can refer to either male or female.

Lev 4:13-14 ❖ How might Christians make restitution for the communal sins of their past?

3:16b–17 These verses state general sacrificial rules regarding suet/fat and blood that are especially relevant to the well-being offering because its fat is removed for the Lord and the flesh is consumed by the offeror.

✣ **3:1–17** Like ancient Israelites, we can joyfully express thanks to God in all kinds of ways. We can also fulfill vows of commitment, resources, or service, and we can simply express love and devotion to him anytime we wish. In these ways we can learn to live in God's presence.

4:1–2 The purification offerings prescribed in Lev 4 are required to remedy inadvertent violations of any of the Lord's commands (v. 2) once the sinner realizes what they have done. Leviticus teaches us about the nature of sin and about what God thinks of it. While an inadvertent fault is not as serious as an attitude of rebellion, it still must be taken seriously and properly remedied. Regarding these offerings, we can distinguish between what can be called "outer sanctum" (vv. 3–21) and "outer altar" (vv. 22–35) purification offerings.

4:3–12 Notice that the high priest performs two applications of blood in the outer sanctum. Then, he goes out to the courtyard and disposes of the remaining blood by pouring it at the base of the outer altar (vv. 7b, 18b).

OLD TESTAMENT SACRIFICES

SACRIFICE	OT REFERENCES	ELEMENTS	PURPOSE
Burnt Offering	Lev 1; 6:8-13; 8:18-21; 16:24	Bull, ram or male bird (dove or young pigeon for the poor); wholly consumed; no defect	Voluntary act of worship; atonement for unintentional sin in general; expression of devotion, commitment and complete surrender to God
Grain Offering	Lev 2; 6:14-23	Grain, finest flour, olive oil, incense, baked bread (cakes or wafers), salt; no yeast or honey; accompanied burnt offering and fellowship offering (along with drink offering)	Voluntary act of worship; recognition of God's goodness and provisions; devotion to God
Fellowship Offering	Lev 3; 7:11-34	Any animal without defect from herd or flock; variety of breads	Voluntary act of worship; thanksgiving and fellowship (it included a communal meal)
Sin Offering	Lev 4:1–5:13; 6:24-30; 8:14-17; 16:3-22	1. Young bull: for high priest and congregation 2. Male goat: for leader 3. Female goat or lamb: for common person 4. Dove or pigeon: for the poor 5. Tenth of an ephah of finest flour: for the very poor	Mandatory atonement for specific unintentional sin; confession of sin; forgiveness of sin; cleansing from defilement
Guilt Offering	Lev 5:14–6:7; 7:1-6	Ram	Mandatory atonement for unintentional sin requiring restitution; cleansing from defilement; making restitution; paying 20% fine

When more than one kind of offering was presented (as in Nu 7:13-17), the procedure was usually as follows: (1) sin offering or guilt offering, (2) burnt offering and grain offering, (3) fellowship offering and grain offering (along with a drink offering). This sequence furnishes part of the spiritual significance of the sacrificial system. First, sin had to be dealt with (sin offering or guilt offering). Second, the worshipers committed themselves completely to God (burnt offering and grain offering). Third, fellowship or communion between the Lord, the priest and the worshiper (fellowship offering) was established. To state it another way, there were sacrifices of atonement (sin offerings and guilt offerings), consecration (burnt offerings and grain offerings) and communion (fellowship offerings—these included vow offerings, thank offerings and freewill offerings).

commands, even though the community is unaware of the matter, when they
realize their guilt 14and the sin they committed becomes known, the assembly
must bring a young bull[o] as a sin offering[p] and present it before the tent of
meeting. 15The elders of the community
are to lay their hands on the bull's head[q]
before the LORD, and the bull shall be
slaughtered before the LORD. 16Then the
anointed priest is to take some of the
bull's blood[r] into the tent of meeting.
17He shall dip his finger into the blood
and sprinkle it before the LORD[s] seven

4:14 [o]ver 3 [p]ver 23,28
4:15 [q]Lev 1:4; 8:14,22; Nu 8:10
4:16 [r]ver 5
4:17 [s]ver 6
4:18 [t]ver 7
4:19 [u]ver 8
4:20 [v]Heb 10:10-12 [w]Nu 15:25

times in front of the curtain. 18He is to
put some of the blood on the horns of
the altar that is before the LORD[t] in the
tent of meeting. The rest of the blood
he shall pour out at the base of the altar
of burnt offering at the entrance to the
tent of meeting. 19He shall remove all
the fat[u] from it and burn it on the altar,
20and do with this bull just as he did
with the bull for the sin offering. In this
way the priest will make atonement[v] for
the community, and they will be forgiv-
en.[w] 21Then he shall take the bull outside
the camp and burn it as he burned the

first bull. This is the sin offering for the
community.[x]

22"'When a leader[y] sins unintentionally[z] and does what is forbidden in any
of the commands of the LORD his God,
when he realizes his guilt 23and the sin
he has committed becomes known, he
must bring as his offering a male goat
without defect. 24He is to lay his hand on
the goat's head and slaughter it at the
place where the burnt offering is slaughtered before the LORD. It is a sin offering.
25Then the priest shall take some of the
blood of the sin offering with his finger
and put it on the horns of the altar of
burnt offering and pour out the rest of
the blood at the base of the altar.[a] 26He
shall burn all the fat on the altar as he
burned the fat of the fellowship offering.
In this way the priest will make atonement for the leader's sin, and he will be
forgiven.[b]

27"'If any member of the community sins unintentionally[c] and does what
is forbidden in any of the LORD's commands, when they realize their guilt
28and the sin they have committed becomes known, they must bring as their
offering[d] for the sin they committed a
female goat[e] without defect. 29They are
to lay their hand on the head[f] of the sin
offering[g] and slaughter it at the place of
the burnt offering. 30Then the priest is
to take some of the blood with his finger
and put it on the horns of the altar of
burnt offering[h] and pour out the rest of
the blood at the base of the altar. 31They
shall remove all the fat, just as the fat is
removed from the fellowship offering,
and the priest shall burn it on the altar
as an aroma pleasing to the LORD.[i] In this
way the priest will make atonement for
them, and they will be forgiven.

32"'If someone brings a lamb as their
sin offering, they are to bring a female
without defect.[j] 33They are to lay their
hand on its head and slaughter it for
a sin offering at the place where the
burnt offering is slaughtered.[k] 34Then
the priest shall take some of the blood
of the sin offering with his finger and
put it on the horns of the altar of burnt
offering and pour out the rest of the
blood at the base of the altar.[l] 35They
shall remove all the fat, just as the fat
is removed from the lamb of the fellowship offering, and the priest shall
burn it on the altar[m] on top of the food
offerings presented to the LORD. In this
way the priest will make atonement for
them for the sin they have committed,
and they will be forgiven.

5 "'If anyone sins because they do not
speak up when they hear a public
charge to testify[n] regarding something
they have seen or learned about, they
will be held responsible.[o]

2"'If anyone becomes aware that they
are guilty—if they unwittingly touch
anything ceremonially unclean (whether
the carcass of an unclean animal, wild or
domestic, or of any unclean creature that
moves along the ground)[p] and they are
unaware that they have become unclean,
but then they come to realize their guilt;
3or if they touch human uncleanness[q]
(anything that would make them unclean) even though they are unaware of
it, but then they learn of it and realize
their guilt; 4or if anyone thoughtlessly
takes an oath[r] to do anything, whether
good or evil (in any matter one might
carelessly swear about) even though they
are unaware of it, but then they learn of
it and realize their guilt— 5when anyone becomes aware that they are guilty
in any of these matters, they must confess[s] in what way they have sinned. 6As a
penalty for the sin they have committed,
they must bring to the LORD a female

4:21 [x] Lev 16:5, 15
4:22 [y] Nu 31:13 [z] ver 2
4:25 [a] ver 7, 18, 30, 34; Lev 9:9
4:26 [b] Lev 5:10
4:27 [c] ver 2; Nu 15:27
4:28 [d] ver 23 [e] ver 3
4:29 [f] ver 4, 24 [g] Lev 1:4
4:30 [h] ver 7
4:31 [i] Ge 8:21
4:32 [j] ver 28
4:33 [k] ver 29
4:34 [l] ver 7
4:35 [m] ver 26, 31
5:1 [n] Pr 29:24 [o] ver 17
5:2 [p] Lev 11:11, 24-40; Dt 14:8
5:3 [q] Nu 19:11-16
5:4 [r] Nu 30:6, 8
5:5 [s] Lev 16:21; 26:40; Nu 5:7; Pr 28:13

4:22–35 The outline of activities belonging to the "outer altar" purification offering appears three times to allow for variations concerning the offeror and the animal victim. A chieftain is required to bring a male goat (vv. 22–26), but a commoner offers a female flock animal, whether a goat (vv. 27–31) or a sheep (vv. 32–35).

4:1–35 To for*give* means to *give* up something. True forgiveness is tough. It is not automatic, and it has a cost, even for God—who absorbs the cost in the sacrifice of his Son. We should have a forgiving attitude as Jesus did when he was being crucified (Lk 23:34).

5:1–10 Gradations of sacrificial victims/materials are presented in order of descending value. The rituals in vv. 1–13 comprise a related but distinct subcategory of purification offerings.

A bird cannot be offered by itself as a purification offering, presumably because it is too small a victim, so it is accompanied by another bird for

lamb or goat from the flock as a sin offering[a];[t] and the priest shall make atonement for them for their sin.

7 "'Anyone who cannot afford[u] a lamb is to bring two doves or two young pigeons to the LORD as a penalty for their sin—one for a sin offering and the other for a burnt offering. 8 They are to bring them to the priest, who shall first offer the one for the sin offering. He is to wring its head from its neck,[v] not dividing it completely,[w] 9 and is to splash some of the blood of the sin offering against the side of the altar; the rest of the blood must be drained out at the base of the altar.[x] It is a sin offering. 10 The priest shall then offer the other as a burnt offering in the prescribed way[y] and make atonement for them for the sin they have committed, and they will be forgiven.[z]

11 "'If, however, they cannot afford two doves or two young pigeons, they are to bring as an offering for their sin a tenth of an ephah[b] of the finest flour[a] for a sin offering. They must not put olive oil or incense on it, because it is a sin offering. 12 They are to bring it to the priest, who shall take a handful of it as a memorial[c] portion and burn it on the altar on top of the food offerings presented to the LORD. It is a sin offering. 13 In this way the priest will make atonement[b] for them for any of these sins they have committed, and they will be forgiven. The rest of the offering will belong to the priest,[c] as in the case of the grain offering.'"

The Guilt Offering

14 The LORD said to Moses: 15 "When anyone is unfaithful to the LORD by sinning unintentionally in regard to any of the LORD's holy things, they are to bring to the LORD as a penalty[d] a ram[e] from the flock, one without defect and of the proper value in silver, according to the sanctuary shekel.[d][f] It is a guilt offering. 16 They must make restitution[g] for what they have failed to do in regard to the holy things, pay an additional penalty of a fifth of its value[h] and give it all to the priest. The priest will make atonement for them with the ram as a guilt offering, and they will be forgiven.

17 "If anyone sins and does what is forbidden in any of the LORD's commands, even though they do not know it,[i] they are guilty and will be held responsible. 18 They are to bring to the priest as a guilt offering a ram from the flock, one without defect and of the proper value. In this way the priest will make atonement for them for the wrong they have committed unintentionally, and they will be forgiven.[j] 19 It is a guilt offering; they have been guilty of[e] wrongdoing against the LORD."

6 [f] The LORD said to Moses: 2 "If anyone sins and is unfaithful to the LORD[k] by deceiving a neighbor[l] about

Lev 5:17 ❖ Is it fair that someone who sins in ignorance is still counted guilty? Why or why not?

5:6 [t] Lev 4:28
5:7 [u] Lev 12:8; 14:21
5:8 [v] Lev 1:15 [w] Lev 1:17
5:9 [x] Lev 4:7,18
5:10 [y] Lev 1:14-17 [z] Lev 4:26
5:11 [a] Lev 2:1
5:13 [b] Lev 4:26 [c] Lev 2:3
5:15 [d] Lev 22:14 [e] Nu 5:8 [f] Ex 30:13
5:16 [g] Lev 6:4 [h] Lev 22:14; Nu 5:7
5:17 [i] ver 15; Lev 4:2
5:18 [j] ver 15
6:2 [k] Nu 5:6; Ac 5:4; Col 3:9 [l] Pr 24:28

[a] *6* Or *purification offering;* here and throughout this chapter [b] *11* That is, probably about 3 1/2 pounds or about 1.6 kilograms [c] *12* Or *representative* [d] *15* That is, about 2/5 ounce or about 12 grams [e] *19* Or *offering; atonement has been made for their* [f] In Hebrew texts 6:1-7 is numbered 5:20-26, and 6:8-30 is numbered 6:1-23.

---

a burnt offering (vv. 7–10). That the bird rituals are a unit is shown by the fact that the penance formula is stated only once, covering both rituals as a single complex (v. 10).

5:11–13 The purification offering of grain is like the uncooked semolina offering in 2:1–3.

5:1–13 If mercy and justice are crucial components of God's love, we should think about how to implement them *together in a balanced way*. Mercy and justice are principles to be implemented as decisions; they are not simply emotions. Justice is the standard/rule governing a given situation, which serves as an anchor as we extend mercy.

5:14–19 There are two subcases. In the first subcase an Israelite inadvertently misappropriates something that belongs to the Lord for his or her own purpose. An example could be eating produce that has been dedicated as tithe or firstfruits. The second subcase (vv. 17–19) is inadvertent violation of any of the Lord's prohibitive commandments ("You shall not") without knowing it *and continuing to not know about it.*

6:1–7 A sinner who has wronged both a human being and God must remedy the offense by making compensation to the wronged human party (including a twenty percent penalty) and by giving a ram as an offering to the Lord (vv. 5–6).

5:14—6:7 Unresolved guilt is one among many causes of anxiety disorder, and unidentified guilt erodes assurance and gives birth to depression. But Lev 5:17–19 supplied God's people with a solution: They could be freed from worry by giving the burden of *suspected* guilt over to God.

Lev 6:1–7 ❖ Does the one-time sacrifice of Christ erase our need to make restitution for the wrong we do to others? Why or why not?

something entrusted to them or left in
their care[m] or about something stolen,
or if they cheat their neighbor, 3or if
they find lost property and lie about it,[n]
or if they swear falsely about any such
sin that people may commit— 4when
they sin in any of these ways and realize their guilt, they must return[o] what
they have stolen or taken by extortion,
or what was entrusted to them, or the
lost property they found, 5or whatever
it was they swore falsely about. They
must make restitution[p] in full, add a
fifth of the value to it and give it all to
the owner on the day they present their
guilt offering.[q] 6And as a penalty they
must bring to the priest, that is, to the
LORD, their guilt offering,[r] a ram from
the flock, one without defect and of the
proper value. 7In this way the priest will
make atonement[s] for them before the
LORD, and they will be forgiven for any
of the things they did that made them
guilty."

The Burnt Offering

8The LORD said to Moses: 9"Give Aaron
and his sons this command: 'These are
the regulations for the burnt offering:
The burnt offering is to remain on the
altar hearth throughout the night, till
morning, and the fire must be kept burning on the altar. 10The priest shall then
put on his linen clothes, with linen undergarments next to his body,[t] and shall
remove the ashes of the burnt offering
that the fire has consumed on the altar
and place them beside the altar. 11Then
he is to take off these clothes and put
on others, and carry the ashes outside
the camp to a place that is ceremonially clean.[u] 12The fire on the altar must be
kept burning; it must not go out. Every
morning the priest is to add firewood
and arrange the burnt offering on the
fire and burn the fat of the fellowship
offerings on it. 13The fire must be kept
burning on the altar continuously; it
must not go out.

The Grain Offering

14" 'These are the regulations for the
grain offering:[v] Aaron's sons are to bring
it before the LORD, in front of the altar.
15The priest is to take a handful of the
finest flour and some olive oil, together
with all the incense on the grain offering,[w] and burn the memorial[a] portion[x]
on the altar as an aroma pleasing to the
LORD. 16Aaron and his sons[y] shall eat the
rest[z] of it, but it is to be eaten without
yeast[a] in the sanctuary area;[b] they are
to eat it in the courtyard of the tent of
meeting. 17It must not be baked with
yeast; I have given it as their share of
the food offerings presented to me. Like
the sin offering[b] and the guilt offering, it
is most holy.[c] 18Any male descendant of
Aaron may eat it.[d] For all generations to
come it is his perpetual share of the food
offerings presented to the LORD. Whatever touches them will become holy.[c][e]' "

19The LORD also said to Moses, 20"This
is the offering Aaron and his sons are
to bring to the LORD on the day he[d] is
anointed: a tenth of an ephah[e][f] of the finest flour as a regular grain offering,[g] half
of it in the morning and half in the evening. 21It must be prepared with oil on a
griddle;[h] bring it well-mixed and present
the grain offering broken[f] in pieces as an
aroma pleasing to the LORD. 22The son
who is to succeed him as anointed priest
shall prepare it. It is the LORD's perpetual
share and is to be burned completely.
23Every grain offering of a priest shall
be burned completely; it must not be
eaten."

6:2 [m] Ex 22:7
6:3 [n] Dt 22:1-3
6:4 [o] Lk 19:8
6:5 [p] Nu 5:7 [q] Lev 5:15
6:6 [r] Lev 5:15
6:7 [s] Lev 4:26
6:10 [t] Ex 28:39-42,43; 39:28
6:11 [u] Lev 4:12
6:14 [v] Lev 2:1; 15:4
6:15 [w] Lev 2:9 [x] Lev 2:2
6:16 [y] Lev 2:3 [z] Eze 44:29 [a] Lev 2:11 [b] Lev 10:13
6:17 [c] ver 29; Ex 40:10; Nu 18:9,10
6:18 [d] ver 29; Nu 18:9-10 [e] ver 27
6:20 [f] Ex 16:36 [g] Ex 29:2
6:21 [h] Lev 2:5

[a] 15 Or *representative* [b] 17 Or *purification offering*; also in verses 25 and 30 [c] 18 Or *Whoever touches them must be holy*; similarly in verse 27 [d] 20 Or *each* [e] 20 That is, probably about 3 1/2 pounds or about 1.6 kilograms [f] 21 The meaning of the Hebrew for this word is uncertain.

6:8–13 Keeping the altar fire going is of paramount importance (vv. 9, 12, 13). Leviticus 9:24 tells us why: The Lord himself lit it! So, when the altar fire consumes a sacrifice, it is the Lord consuming it by fire.

6:8–23 These verses are subdivided into two parts. The first specifies the way priests must eat their portions of grain offerings (vv. 14–18). The second gives directions for grain offerings brought by priests (vv. 19–23). Because the high priest sacrifices his special grain offering on his own behalf, it must be wholly burned up (v. 22), with no portion serving as an agent's commission.

The Sin Offering

24 The LORD said to Moses, 25 "Say to
Aaron and his sons: 'These are the regulations for the sin offering: The sin offering is to be slaughtered before the
LORD[i] in the place[j] the burnt offering is
slaughtered; it is most holy. 26 The priest
who offers it shall eat it; it is to be eaten
in the sanctuary area,[k] in the courtyard[l]
of the tent of meeting. 27 Whatever touches any of the flesh will become holy,[m]
and if any of the blood is spattered on a
garment, you must wash it in the sanctuary area. 28 The clay pot[n] the meat is
cooked in must be broken; but if it is
cooked in a bronze pot, the pot is to be
scoured and rinsed with water. 29 Any
male in a priest's family may eat it;[o] it is
most holy.[p] 30 But any sin offering whose
blood is brought into the tent of meeting
to make atonement in the Holy Place[q]
must not be eaten; it must be burned up.[r]

The Guilt Offering

7 " 'These are the regulations for the
guilt offering,[s] which is most holy:
2 The guilt offering is to be slaughtered
in the place where the burnt offering
is slaughtered, and its blood is to be
splashed against the sides of the altar.
3 All its fat[t] shall be offered: the fat tail
and the fat that covers the internal organs, 4 both kidneys with the fat on them
near the loins, and the long lobe of the
liver, which is to be removed with the
kidneys. 5 The priest shall burn them on
the altar as a food offering presented
to the LORD. It is a guilt offering. 6 Any
male in a priest's family may eat it,[u] but
it must be eaten in the sanctuary area;
it is most holy.[v]

6:25 [i] Lev 1:3 [j] Lev 1:5,11
6:26 [k] ver 16 [l] Lev 10:17-18
6:27 [m] Ex 29:37
6:28 [n] Lev 11:33; 15:12
6:29 [o] ver 18 [p] ver 17
6:30 [q] Lev 4:18 [r] Lev 4:12
7:1 [s] Lev 5:14-6:7
7:3 [t] Ex 29:13; Lev 3:4,9
7:6 [u] Lev 6:18; Nu 18:9-10 [v] Lev 2:3

Lev 7:12 ❖ What might a "thank offering" look like in our lives?

7 " 'The same law applies to both the
sin offering[a] and the guilt offering: They
belong to the priest[w] who makes atonement with them. 8 The priest who offers
a burnt offering for anyone may keep
its hide for himself. 9 Every grain offering baked in an oven or cooked in a pan
or on a griddle[x] belongs to the priest
who offers it, 10 and every grain offering, whether mixed with olive oil or dry,
belongs equally to all the sons of Aaron.

The Fellowship Offering

11 " 'These are the regulations for the
fellowship offering anyone may present
to the LORD:
12 " 'If they offer it as an expression of
thankfulness, then along with this thank
offering[y] they are to offer thick loaves
made without yeast and with olive oil
mixed in, thin loaves[z] made without
yeast and brushed with oil, and thick
loaves of the finest flour well-knead-
ed and with oil mixed in. 13 Along with
their fellowship offering of thanksgiving they are to present an offering with
thick loaves of bread made with yeast.[a]
14 They are to bring one of each kind as
an offering, a contribution to the LORD;
it belongs to the priest who splashes the
blood of the fellowship offering against
the altar. 15 The meat of their fellowship
offering of thanksgiving must be eaten
on the day it is offered; they must leave
none of it till morning.[b]

7:7 [w] Lev 6:17, 26; 1Co 9:13
7:9 [x] Lev 2:5
7:12 [y] ver 13, 15 [z] Lev 2:4; Nu 6:15
7:13 [a] Lev 23:17; Am 4:5
7:15 [b] Lev 22:30

[a] 7 Or *purification offering*; also in verse 37

6:24–30 Because the meat is "most holy" (v. 29), it carries restrictions: The priest must eat it in the courtyard and can share it only with males among priestly family members.

7:1–10 As with the purification offering, the meat of a most sacred reparation offering must be eaten by a male of the priests in the sacred areas of the tabernacle (vv. 6–7). The following verses (vv. 8–10) summarize priestly perquisites for most holy sacrifices.

✤ 6:8—7:10 At the center of ancient Israelite worship was holy fire. At its core, the religion of God's people was an ongoing encounter with the divine. For this experience to continue, the "pilot light" had to remain lit.

As in OT times, God's ministers of the twenty-first century AD are to be keepers of the flame and teachers of instruction (Torah) from the Lord, not lighters of the fire and inventors of their own doctrines. Rather than presuming to preach and teach our own thoughts in the interest of polishing our popular image, we are obliged to allow God's Word, illuminated by his Spirit, to kindle inspiration.

7:12–13 Along with a "thanksgiving " (v. 13) offering a person must offer special grain. After giving one of each kind of cake or wafer, the offeror can eat the rest.

7:15–17 While thank offerings must be eaten on the day they are offered, the rule for votive and freewill offerings is more flexible; however, anything left over on the third day must be incinerated (v. 17).

16“ ‘If, however, their offering is the result of a vow or is a freewill offering, the sacrifice shall be eaten on the day they offer it, but anything left over may be eaten on the next day.[c] 17Any meat of the sacrifice left over till the third day must be burned up. 18If any meat of the fellowship offering is eaten on the third day, the one who offered it will not be accepted.[d] It will not be reckoned[e] to their credit, for it has become impure; the person who eats any of it will be held responsible.

19“ ‘Meat that touches anything ceremonially unclean must not be eaten; it must be burned up. As for other meat, anyone ceremonially clean may eat it. 20But if anyone who is unclean eats any meat of the fellowship offering belonging to the LORD, they must be cut off from their people.[f] 21Anyone who touches something unclean[g] —whether human uncleanness or an unclean animal or any unclean creature that moves along the ground[a] —and then eats any of the meat of the fellowship offering belonging to the LORD must be cut off from their people.’ ”

Eating Fat and Blood Forbidden

22The LORD said to Moses, 23“Say to the Israelites: ‘Do not eat any of the fat of cattle, sheep or goats.[h] 24The fat of an animal found dead or torn by wild animals[i] may be used for any other purpose, but you must not eat it. 25Anyone who eats the fat of an animal from which a food offering may be[b] presented to the LORD must be cut off from their people. 26And wherever you live, you must not eat the blood[j] of any bird or animal. 27Anyone who eats blood[k] must be cut off from their people.’ ”

The Priests’ Share

28The LORD said to Moses, 29“Say to the Israelites: ‘Anyone who brings a fellowship offering to the LORD is to bring part of it as their sacrifice to the LORD. 30With their own hands they are to present the food offering to the LORD; they are to bring the fat, together with the breast, and wave the breast before the LORD as a wave offering.[l] 31The priest shall burn the fat on the altar, but the breast belongs to Aaron and his sons.[m] 32You are to give the right thigh of your fellowship offerings to the priest as a contribution.[n] 33The son of Aaron who offers the blood and the fat of the fellowship offering shall have the right thigh as his share. 34From the fellowship offerings of the Israelites, I have taken the breast that is waved and the thigh[o] that is presented and have given them to Aaron the priest and his sons[p] as their perpetual share from the Israelites.’ ”

35This is the portion of the food offerings presented to the LORD that were allotted to Aaron and his sons on the day they were presented to serve the LORD as priests. 36On the day they were anointed,[q] the LORD commanded that the Israelites give this to them as their perpetual share for the generations to come.

37These, then, are the regulations for the burnt offering,[r] the grain offering,[s] the sin offering, the guilt offering, the ordination offering[t] and the fellowship offering, 38which the LORD gave Moses at Mount Sinai in the Desert of Sinai on the day he commanded the Israelites to bring their offerings to the LORD.[u]

The Ordination of Aaron and His Sons

8:1–36pp // Ex 29:1–37

8 The LORD said to Moses, 2“Bring Aaron and his sons, their garments, the anointing oil,[v] the bull for the sin

7:16 [c] Lev 19:5-8
7:18 [d] Lev 19:7 [e] Nu 18:27
7:20 [f] Lev 22:3-7
7:21 [g] Lev 5:2; 11:24,28
7:23 [h] Lev 3:17; 17:13-14
7:24 [i] Ex 22:31
7:26 [j] Ge 9:4
7:27 [k] Lev 17:10-24; Ac 15:20,29
7:30 [l] Ex 29:24; Nu 6:20
7:31 [m] ver 34
7:32 [n] ver 34; Lev 9:21; Nu 6:20
7:34 [o] Lev 10:15 [p] Ex 29:27; Nu 18:18-19
7:36 [q] Ex 40:13, 15; Lev 8:12,30
7:37 [r] Lev 6:9 [s] Lev 6:14 [t] ver 1,11
7:38 [u] Lev 1:2
8:2 [v] Ex 30:23-25,30

[a] 21 A few Hebrew manuscripts, Samaritan Pentateuch, Syriac and Targum (see 5:2); most Hebrew manuscripts *any unclean, detestable thing* [b] 25 Or *offering is*

7:22–27 All fat of animals that can be sacrificed belongs to God. The prohibition of eating blood—that is, meat from which the blood is not drained out at the time of slaughter—has its roots much earlier than the Israelite sacrificial system. The command began in the instructions that God gave to Noah after the flood (Ge 9:3–4).

7:30–38 The priestly portions of a well-being offering consist of the breast (v. 30) and the right thigh (vv. 32, 34). Verses 37–38 conclude the first major portion of the book of Leviticus—chs. 1–7, which provide strict rules governing how sacrifices are to be performed.

✣ **7:11–38** Our ability to effectively express joy in worship is dependent on Christ and his sacrifice. We need Christ for joyful worship because all of our communication with heaven is dependent on him. As the divine “Word” who “became flesh” (Jn 1:1–5, 14), he serves as Jacob’s ladder, a highway of interaction

offering,[a] the two rams and the basket
containing bread made without yeast,[w]
3and gather the entire assembly[x] at the
entrance to the tent of meeting." 4Moses
did as the LORD commanded him, and
the assembly gathered at the entrance
to the tent of meeting.
5Moses said to the assembly, "This is
what the LORD has commanded to be
done." 6Then Moses brought Aaron and
his sons forward and washed them with
water.[y] 7He put the tunic on Aaron, tied
the sash around him, clothed him with
the robe and put the ephod on him. He
also fastened the ephod with a decora-
tive waistband, which he tied around
him.[z] 8He placed the breastpiece on him
and put the Urim and Thummim[a] in the
breastpiece. 9Then he placed the turban
on Aaron's head and set the gold plate,
the sacred emblem,[b] on the front of it,
as the LORD commanded Moses.
10Then Moses took the anointing oil[c]
and anointed[d] the tabernacle and everything in it, and so consecrated them. 11He
sprinkled some of the oil on the altar
seven times, anointing the altar and all
its utensils and the basin with its stand,
to consecrate them.[e] 12He poured some
of the anointing oil on Aaron's head and
anointed[f] him to consecrate him.[g] 13Then
he brought Aaron's sons forward, put tunics on them, tied sashes around them
and fastened caps on them, as the LORD
commanded Moses.
14He then presented the bull[h] for the
sin offering,[i] and Aaron and his sons
laid their hands on its head. 15Moses
slaughtered the bull and took some of
the blood, and with his finger he put it
on all the horns of the altar[j] to purify
the altar.[k] He poured out the rest of the
blood at the base of the altar. So he consecrated it to make atonement for it.[l]

8:2 [w] Ex 29:2-3
8:3 [x] Nu 8:9
8:6 [y] Ex 29:4; 30:19; Ps 26:6; Ac 22:16; 1Co 6:11; Eph 5:26
8:7 [z] Ex 28:4
8:8 [a] Ex 28:30
8:9 [b] Ex 28:36
8:10 [c] ver 2 [d] Ex 30:26
8:11 [e] Ex 30:29
8:12 [f] Lev 21:10, 12 [g] Ex 30:30
8:14 [h] Lev 4:3 [i] Ps 66:15; Eze 43:19
8:15 [j] Lev 4:7 [k] Heb 9:22 [l] Eze 43:20
8:17 [m] Lev 4:11 [n] Lev 4:12
8:18 [o] ver 2
8:22 [p] ver 2
8:24 [q] Heb 9:18-22

Lev 8:12 ❖ What ministry or task has God anointed us for (see 2Co 1:21–22)?

16Moses also took all the fat around the
internal organs, the long lobe of the liver, and both kidneys and their fat, and
burned it on the altar. 17But the bull with
its hide and its flesh and its intestines[m]
he burned up outside the camp,[n] as the
LORD commanded Moses.
18He then presented the ram[o] for the
burnt offering, and Aaron and his sons
laid their hands on its head. 19Then Moses slaughtered the ram and splashed the
blood against the sides of the altar. 20He
cut the ram into pieces and burned the
head, the pieces and the fat. 21He washed
the internal organs and the legs with
water and burned the whole ram on the
altar. It was a burnt offering, a pleasing
aroma, a food offering presented to the
LORD, as the LORD commanded Moses.
22He then presented the other ram,
the ram for the ordination,[p] and Aaron and his sons laid their hands on its
head. 23Moses slaughtered the ram and
took some of its blood and put it on the
lobe of Aaron's right ear, on the thumb
of his right hand and on the big toe of
his right foot. 24Moses also brought Aaron's sons forward and put some of the
blood on the lobes of their right ears, on
the thumbs of their right hands and on
the big toes of their right feet. Then he
splashed blood against the sides of the
altar.[q] 25After that, he took the fat, the
fat tail, all the fat around the internal
organs, the long lobe of the liver, both
kidneys and their fat and the right thigh.
26And from the basket of bread made

[a] 2 Or *purification offering*; also in verse 14

between heaven and earth (Jn 1:51; cf. Ge 28:12). Without him and the priestly mediation bought by his sacrifice, we would have no access to God.

8:1–4 Chapter 8 describes the ceremonies by which the sanctuary and its priesthood were consecrated and the priests ordained.

8:5–13 Before dressing Aaron's sons, Moses consecrated the tabernacle, the altar, and Aaron's head.

8:14–17 At the heart of the ritual complex were three sacrifices on behalf of the priests. The first sacrifice had the primary goal of purifying and consecrating the outer altar (v. 15). The remainder of the "outer altar" purification offering was incinerated outside the camp rather than eaten by Moses as an agent's commission (v. 17). Although Moses officiated on this occasion, he was not an Aaronic priest qualified to partake of the most holy sacrifices.

8:18–32 The third sacrifice was unique to the ordination event. Aside from the fact that it was a "pleasing aroma," a food gift to the Lord (v. 28), Moses elevated the breast and kept it as his portion for officiating (v. 29). Furthermore, the offerors ate the remaining meat (vv. 31–32), and the sacrifice involved special grain items like the thank offering (v. 26).

without yeast, which was before the
LORD, he took one thick loaf, one thick
loaf with olive oil mixed in, and one thin
loaf, and he put these on the fat portions
and on the right thigh. 27He put all these
in the hands of Aaron and his sons, and
they waved them before the LORD as a
wave offering. 28Then Moses took them
from their hands and burned them on
the altar on top of the burnt offering as
an ordination offering, a pleasing aroma,
a food offering presented to the LORD.
29Moses also took the breast, which was
his share of the ordination ram,[r] and
waved it before the LORD as a wave offering, as the LORD commanded Moses.

30Then Moses took some of the anointing oil and some of the blood from the
altar and sprinkled them on Aaron and
his garments[s] and on his sons and their
garments. So he consecrated[t] Aaron and
his garments and his sons and their garments.

31Moses then said to Aaron and his
sons, "Cook the meat at the entrance to
the tent of meeting and eat it there with
the bread from the basket of ordination
offerings, as I was commanded: 'Aaron
and his sons are to eat it.' 32Then burn
up the rest of the meat and the bread.
33Do not leave the entrance to the tent of
meeting for seven days, until the days of
your ordination are completed, for your
ordination will last seven days. 34What
has been done today was commanded by
the LORD[u] to make atonement for you.
35You must stay at the entrance to the
tent of meeting day and night for seven
days and do what the LORD requires,[v] so
you will not die; for that is what I have
been commanded."

36So Aaron and his sons did everything
the LORD commanded through Moses.

The Priests Begin Their Ministry

9 On the eighth day[w] Moses summoned
Aaron and his sons and the elders of
Israel. 2He said to Aaron, "Take a bull calf
for your sin offering[a] and a ram for your
burnt offering, both without defect, and
present them before the LORD. 3Then say
to the Israelites: 'Take a male goat for a
sin offering, a calf and a lamb — both
a year old and without defect — for a
burnt offering, 4and an ox[b] and a ram
for a fellowship offering to sacrifice before the LORD, together with a grain offering mixed with olive oil. For today the
LORD will appear to you.[x]' "

5They took the things Moses commanded to the front of the tent of meeting, and the entire assembly came near
and stood before the LORD. 6Then Moses
said, "This is what the LORD has commanded you to do, so that the glory of
the LORD[y] may appear to you."

7Moses said to Aaron, "Come to the
altar and sacrifice your sin offering and
your burnt offering and make atonement for yourself and the people; sacrifice the offering that is for the people
and make atonement for them, as the
LORD has commanded.[z]"

8So Aaron came to the altar and
slaughtered the calf as a sin offering[a]
for himself. 9His sons brought the blood
to him,[b] and he dipped his finger into
the blood and put it on the horns of the
altar; the rest of the blood he poured out
at the base of the altar.[c] 10On the altar he
burned the fat, the kidneys and the long
lobe of the liver from the sin offering, as
the LORD commanded Moses; 11the flesh
and the hide[d] he burned up outside the
camp.[e]

12Then he slaughtered the burnt offering. His sons handed him the blood,
and he splashed it against the sides of
the altar. 13They handed him the burnt
offering piece by piece, including the

8:29 [r]Lev 7:31-34
8:30 [s]Ex 28:2 [t]Nu 3:3
8:34 [u]Heb 7:16
8:35 [v]Nu 3:7; 9:19; Dt 11:1; 1Ki 2:3; Eze 48:11
9:1 [w]Eze 43:27
9:4 [x]Ex 29:43
9:6 [y]ver 23; Ex 24:16
9:7 [z]Heb 5:1, 3; 7:27
9:8 [a]Lev 4:1-12
9:9 [b]ver 12,18 [c]Lev 4:7
9:11 [d]Lev 4:11 [e]Lev 4:12; 8:17

[a] 2 Or *purification offering*; here and throughout this chapter [b] 4 The Hebrew word can refer to either male or female; also in verses 18 and 19.

8:33-35 Completion of the priests' "rite of passage" required completion of a seven-day period. During the week, a purification offering was to be performed each day to purify the outer altar.

✣ **8:1-36** It is the Spirit who empowers for leadership and the authority that goes with it, just as he distributes all other spiritual gifts (1Co 12). Christians are called and consecrated to go out into the world to praise God for transformation from darkness to light that has been wrought by Christ.

9:1-21 Aaron and his sons performed a complex of sacrifices as their first work on the eighth day. Every major kind of sacrifice prescribed in Lev 1-7 is represented except for the reparation offering, which never appears as a public sacrifice, presumably because its specialized role involves certain or suspected sacrilege.

head, and he burned them on the altar.[f]
14He washed the internal organs and the
legs and burned them on top of the burnt
offering on the altar.
15Aaron then brought the offering that
was for the people.[g] He took the goat for
the people's sin offering and slaughtered
it and offered it for a sin offering as he
did with the first one.
16He brought the burnt offering and
offered it in the prescribed way.[h] 17He
also brought the grain offering, took a
handful of it and burned it on the altar in addition to the morning's burnt
offering.[i]
18He slaughtered the ox and the ram
as the fellowship offering for the people.[j]
His sons handed him the blood, and he
splashed it against the sides of the altar.
19But the fat portions of the ox and the
ram — the fat tail, the layer of fat, the
kidneys and the long lobe of the liver —
20these they laid on the breasts, and then
Aaron burned the fat on the altar. 21Aar-
on waved the breasts and the right thigh
before the LORD as a wave offering,[k] as
Moses commanded.
22Then Aaron lifted his hands toward
the people and blessed them.[l] And having sacrificed the sin offering, the burnt
offering and the fellowship offering, he
stepped down.
23Moses and Aaron then went into the
tent of meeting. When they came out,
they blessed the people; and the glory
of the LORD[m] appeared to all the people.
24Fire[n] came out from the presence of the
LORD and consumed the burnt offering
and the fat portions on the altar. And
when all the people saw it, they shouted
for joy and fell facedown.[o]

9:13 [f] Lev 1:8
9:15 [g] Lev 4:27-31
9:16 [h] Lev 1:1-13
9:17 [i] Lev 2:1-2; 3:5
9:18 [j] Lev 3:1-11
9:21 [k] Ex 29:24, 26; Lev 7:30-34
9:22 [l] Nu 6:23; Dt 21:5; Lk 24:50
9:23 [m] ver 6
9:24 [n] Jdg 6:21; 2Ch 7:1 [o] 1Ki 18:39

10:1 [p] Ex 24:1; Nu 3:2-4; 26:61 [q] Lev 16:12 [r] Ex 30:9
10:2 [s] Nu 3:4; 16:35; 26:61
10:3 [t] Ex 19:22 [u] Ex 30:29; Lev 21:6; Eze 28:22 [v] Isa 49:3
10:4 [w] Ex 6:22 [x] Ex 6:18 [y] Ac 5:6,9,10
10:5 [z] Lev 8:13
10:6 [a] Lev 21:10 [b] Nu 1:53; 16:22; Jos 7:1; 22:18; 2Sa 24:1

Lev 9:23 ❖ When have God's servants been a blessing and shown us the glory of God?

Lev 10:1-2 ❖ Where have we seen people add improper elements to worshiping God? Why is this sometimes tempting?

The Death of Nadab and Abihu

10 Aaron's sons Nadab and Abihu[p]
took their censers, put fire in
them[q] and added incense; and they offered unauthorized fire before the LORD,
contrary to his command.[r] 2So fire came
out from the presence of the LORD and
consumed them,[s] and they died before
the LORD. 3Moses then said to Aaron,
"This is what the LORD spoke of when
he said:

"'Among those who approach me[t]
I will be proved holy;[u]
in the sight of all the people
I will be honored.[v]'"

Aaron remained silent.
4Moses summoned Mishael and Elzaphan,[w] sons of Aaron's uncle Uzziel,[x]
and said to them, "Come here; carry your
cousins outside the camp,[y] away from the
front of the sanctuary." 5So they came
and carried them, still in their tunics,[z]
outside the camp, as Moses ordered.
6Then Moses said to Aaron and his
sons Eleazar and Ithamar, "Do not let
your hair become unkempt[aa] and do not
tear your clothes, or you will die and the
LORD will be angry with the whole community.[b] But your relatives, all the Israelites, may mourn for those the LORD

[a] 6 Or *Do not uncover your heads*

9:21–24 The fire that consumed the inaugural sacrifices and thereby legitimized the Aaronic priesthood was to be kept continually burning on the altar to preserve the miracle of divine acceptance.

✣ **9:1–24** Christ appears "for us in God's presence" (Heb 9:24) as our advocate/mediator (1Jn 2:1). John saw him in heaven symbolically depicted as a Lamb that had just been slaughtered (Rev 5:6). The point is that Christ continually carries the altar/cross event with him *as if it were happening right now* in order to drive home the evidence that gives us peace with God (Ro 5:1). Even if we have no earthly mediator to speak up for us and nobody here below is praying for our need, we can be certain that Jesus is interceding for us.

10:1–2 These men burned incense to the Lord with unauthorized fire. This fire must have consisted of live coals from a source other than the authorized sacred fire on the outer altar that God himself had lit.

10:3 In response to the death of his nephews, Moses conveyed the Lord's interpretation of the event to Aaron, their father.

10:4–6 Outside the camp is where sacred ashes from the altar and incinerated remains of sacrifices were disposed. To prevent further misrepresentation of God and loss of life, the Lord commanded Aaron and his surviving sons to abstain from mourning (v. 6). By virtue of their consecration, the priests and their vestments belonged to the sacred sphere that was to be dissociated from death and corpse contamination.

has destroyed by fire. 7Do not leave the
entrance to the tent of meeting or you
will die, because the LORD's anointing
oil[c] is on you." So they did as Moses said.
8Then the LORD said to Aaron, 9"You
and your sons are not to drink wine[d] or
other fermented drink[e] whenever you
go into the tent of meeting, or you will
die. This is a lasting ordinance for the
generations to come, 10so that you can
distinguish between the holy and the
common, between the unclean and the
clean,[f] 11and so you can teach[g] the Israelites all the decrees the LORD has given
them through Moses.[h]"
12Moses said to Aaron and his remaining sons, Eleazar and Ithamar, "Take the
grain offering left over from the food
offerings prepared without yeast and
presented to the LORD and eat it beside
the altar,[i] for it is most holy. 13Eat it in the
sanctuary area, because it is your share
and your sons' share of the food offerings
presented to the LORD; for so I have been
commanded. 14But you and your sons
and your daughters may eat the breast
that was waved and the thigh that was
presented. Eat them in a ceremonially clean place;[j] they have been given to
you and your children as your share of
the Israelites' fellowship offerings. 15The
thigh[k] that was presented and the breast
that was waved must be brought with the
fat portions of the food offerings, to be
waved before the LORD as a wave offering. This will be the perpetual share for
you and your children, as the LORD has
commanded."
16When Moses inquired about the goat
of the sin offering[a][l] and found that it
had been burned up, he was angry with
Eleazar and Ithamar, Aaron's remaining
sons, and asked, 17"Why didn't you eat
the sin offering[m] in the sanctuary area?
It is most holy; it was given to you to
take away the guilt of the community
by making atonement for them before
the LORD. 18Since its blood was not tak-
en into the Holy Place,[n] you should have
eaten the goat in the sanctuary area, as
I commanded."
19Aaron replied to Moses, "Today they
sacrificed their sin offering and their
burnt offering[o] before the LORD, but
such things as this have happened to
me. Would the LORD have been pleased
if I had eaten the sin offering today?"
20When Moses heard this, he was satisfied.

10:7 [c] Ex 28:41; Lev 21:12
10:9 [d] Hos 4:11 [e] Pr 20:1; Isa 28:7; Eze 44:21; Lk 1:15; Eph 5:18; 1Ti 3:3; Titus 1:7
10:10 [f] Lev 11:47; 20:25; Eze 22:26
10:11 [g] Mal 2:7 [h] Dt 24:8
10:12 [i] Lev 6:14-18; 21:22
10:14 [j] Ex 29:24, 26-27; Lev 7:31, 34; Nu 18:11
10:15 [k] Lev 7:34
10:16 [l] Lev 9:3
10:17 [m] Lev 6:24-30
10:18 [n] Lev 6:26, 30
10:19 [o] Lev 9:12
11:2 [p] Ac 10:12-14
11:7 [q] Isa 65:4; 66:3,17
11:8 [r] Isa 52:11; Heb 9:10

Clean and Unclean Food

11:1–23pp // Dt 14:3–20

11 The LORD said to Moses and Aaron,
2"Say to the Israelites: 'Of all the animals that live on land, these are the ones
you may eat:[p] 3You may eat any animal
that has a divided hoof and that chews
the cud.
4" 'There are some that only chew the
cud or only have a divided hoof, but you
must not eat them. The camel, though
it chews the cud, does not have a divided hoof; it is ceremonially unclean for
you. 5The hyrax, though it chews the
cud, does not have a divided hoof; it is
unclean for you. 6The rabbit, though it
chews the cud, does not have a divided hoof; it is unclean for you. 7And the
pig,[q] though it has a divided hoof, does
not chew the cud; it is unclean for you.
8You must not eat their meat or touch
their carcasses; they are unclean for you.[r]
9" 'Of all the creatures living in the water of the seas and the streams you may
eat any that have fins and scales. 10But
all creatures in the seas or streams that
do not have fins and scales—whether

[a] 16 Or *purification offering*; also in verses 17 and 19

10:12–18 When Moses discovered that the priests had incinerated the remainder of the purification offering (9:11), he "hit the roof" (see 10:16). Undoubtedly, he suspected that Eleazar and Ithamar were reckless like their dead brothers.

10:19–20 Aaron's abstaining from the meat was not a careless ritual mistake but a choice based on his family's unworthiness to bear the culpability of others on the very day that their family had fallen under divine condemnation.

✣ **10:1–20** By serving others and by interceding for them in prayer, we have the privilege of assisting Christ in his priestly ministry. Like Aaron, we must sometimes carry on in spite of private pain. When other people's struggles become our own, we truly "carry each other's burdens" (Gal 6:2).

11:1 The reason for observing the Lord's dietary distinctions is to imitate the Lord's holiness, which is opposed to impurity (vv. 44–45). When the Lord created the animals, he pronounced them all "good" (Ge 1:21, 25), but Lev 11 has to do with the matter of eating animals that were not intended to be eaten.

CLEAN AND UNCLEAN ANIMALS

CLASSES	CLEAN	UNCLEAN
Mammals	Two qualifications: 1. Cloven hoofs 2. Chewing of the cud *Lev 11:3-7; Dt 14:6-8*	Carnivores and those not meeting both "clean" qualifications
Birds	Those not specifically listed as forbidden	Birds of prey or scavengers *Lev 11:13-19; Dt 14:11-20*
Reptiles	None	All *Lev 11:29-30*
Water Animals	Two qualifications: 1. Fins 2. Scales *Lev 11:9-12; Dt 14:9-10*	Those not meeting both "clean" qualifications
Insects	Those in the grasshopper family *Lev 11:20-23*	Winged quadrupeds

Tom Watson, *Chronological and Background Charts of the Old Testament*, rev. and exp. ed. (Grand Rapids: Zondervan, 1994), 23.

among all the swarming things or among all the other living creatures in the water—you are to regard as unclean.[s] 11And since you are to regard them as unclean, you must not eat their meat; you must regard their carcasses as unclean. 12Anything living in the water that does not have fins and scales is to be regarded as unclean by you.

13" 'These are the birds you are to regard as unclean and not eat because they are unclean: the eagle,[a] the vulture, the black vulture, 14the red kite, any kind of black kite, 15any kind of raven, 16the horned owl, the screech owl, the gull, any kind of hawk, 17the little owl, the cormorant, the great owl, 18the white owl, the desert owl, the osprey, 19the stork, any kind of heron, the hoopoe and the bat.

20" 'All flying insects that walk on all fours are to be regarded as unclean by you.[t] 21There are, however, some flying insects that walk on all fours that you may eat: those that have jointed legs for hopping on the ground. 22Of these you may eat any kind of locust,[u] katydid, cricket or grasshopper. 23But all other flying insects that have four legs you are to regard as unclean.

24" 'You will make yourselves unclean by these; whoever touches their carcasses will be unclean till evening. 25Whoever picks up one of their carcasses must wash their clothes,[v] and they will be unclean till evening.[w]

26" 'Every animal that does not have a divided hoof or that does not chew the cud is unclean for you; whoever touches the carcass of any of them will be unclean. 27Of all the animals that walk on all fours, those that walk on their paws are unclean for you; whoever touches their carcasses will be unclean till evening. 28Anyone who picks up their carcasses must wash their clothes, and they will be unclean till evening. These animals are unclean for you.

29" 'Of the animals that move along the ground, these are unclean for you: the weasel, the rat,[x] any kind of great lizard, 30the gecko, the monitor lizard, the wall lizard, the skink and the chameleon. 31Of all those that move along the ground, these are unclean for you. Whoever touches them when they are dead will be unclean till evening. 32When one of them dies and falls on something, that article, whatever its use, will be unclean, whether it is made of wood, cloth, hide or sackcloth.[y] Put it in water; it will be unclean till evening, and then it will be clean. 33If one of them falls into a clay pot, everything in it will be unclean, and you must break the pot.[z] 34Any food you are allowed to eat that has come into contact with water from any such pot is unclean, and any liquid that is drunk from such a pot is unclean. 35Anything that one of their carcasses falls on becomes

11:10 [s] Lev 7:18
11:20 [t] Ac 10:14
11:22 [u] Mt 3:4; Mk 1:6
11:25 [v] Lev 14:8, 47; 15:5 [w] ver 40; Nu 31:24
11:29 [x] Isa 66:17
11:32 [y] Lev 15:12
11:33 [z] Lev 6:28; 15:12

[a] *13* The precise identification of some of the birds, insects and animals in this chapter is uncertain.

unclean; an oven or cooking pot must be
broken up. They are unclean, and you are
to regard them as unclean. 36 A spring,
however, or a cistern for collecting water
remains clean, but anyone who touches
one of these carcasses is unclean. 37 If a
carcass falls on any seeds that are to be
planted, they remain clean. 38 But if water
has been put on the seed and a carcass
falls on it, it is unclean for you.
39 " 'If an animal that you are allowed to
eat dies, anyone who touches its carcass
will be unclean till evening. 40 Anyone
who eats some of its carcass must wash
their clothes, and they will be unclean
till evening.[a] Anyone who picks up the
carcass must wash their clothes, and they
will be unclean till evening.
41 " 'Every creature that moves along
the ground is to be regarded as unclean;
it is not to be eaten. 42 You are not to
eat any creature that moves along the
ground, whether it moves on its belly
or walks on all fours or on many feet;
it is unclean. 43 Do not defile yourselves
by any of these creatures.[b] Do not make
yourselves unclean by means of them
or be made unclean by them. 44 I am the
LORD your God;[c] consecrate yourselves[d]
and be holy,[e] because I am holy.[f] Do not
make yourselves unclean by any creature
that moves along the ground. 45 I am the

11:40 [a] Lev 17:15; 22:8; Eze 44:31
11:43 [b] Lev 20:25
11:44 [c] Ex 6:2, 7; Isa 43:3; 51:15 [d] Lev 20:7 [e] Ex 19:6 [f] Lev 19:2; Ps 99:3; Eph 1:4; 1Th 4:7; 1Pe 1:15, 16*

11:43–45 The conclusion emphasizes the most important point of the chapter: Observing the Lord's dietary regulations has the purpose of imitating the Lord's holiness, which is antithetical to impurity. Living according to the dietary distinctions is vital for the Israelites to maintain the health of the divine-human relationship.

✣ **11:1–47** While the Bible cannot deal with every detail of our lives, some of which were not known when it was written (e.g., smoking), it covers all the major bases to the extent that we can apply those principles to particulars that crop up. The Bible rightly places our well-being within the context of our covenant connection with God, whose grace alone can give us ultimate health as a gift, not because we earn it.

CHARACTER OF GOD // GOD IS HOLY

Leviticus 11:44: "I am the LORD your God; consecrate yourselves and be holy, because I am holy."

Much of Leviticus centers on the topic of holiness. Specifically, the instructions in Leviticus address how common humans can have communion with a holy God.

God's holiness means that he is completely set apart and completely pure. There is nothing unrighteous or sinful in God. Because God's holiness was so intense, God gave the Israelites precautions for interacting with his presence. He established priests as the ones to perform duties before him on behalf of the people. He sanctioned a system of sacrifices and ceremonies to remind the people how to reflect their holy status.

God's expectation was not only that the people honor his holiness. God wanted them to reflect their holy status (Lev 19:2). God designated Israel as a holy nation, a nation of priests (Ex 19:6) and by doing so identified them with himself. The covenant brought them into the divine realm. Just as the Levites functioned as priests for the Israelites, so God wanted all the Israelites to have a priestly function for all the other nations. God wanted them to display his holiness in their conduct so that the other nations would see what God is like.

Unfortunately, the story of OT Israel is riddled with failures in living out the call to holiness. More often than not, Israel looked more like the nations around them than like a kingdom of priests or a holy nation. But God had a plan.

Christ, the Son of God, came to fulfill the mission of Israel as a light to the nations. Christ sent his followers to go into all the world, baptizing and teaching everyone about God. The Holy Spirit filled Christ's followers at Pentecost, leading them in the way of Christ and sanctifying them for mission. The word *sanctify* attaches us to the very nature of God: *to sanctify* means "make holy."

APPLICATION ✣ Through the Holy Spirit within us, we can live out the calling of Leviticus 19:2, to be holy people as God is holy. The Spirit within us and the Bible are our guides for holy living. Despite our sins, if we are in Christ, the Spirit continues to move us into repentance and righteousness. Our task is to walk in step with the Spirit that Christ imparted to us, dying to our old sinful natures and living as new creations in Jesus Christ, our holy Lord (2Co 5:17).

LORD, who brought you up out of Egypt[g] to be your God;[h] therefore be holy, because I am holy.[i]

46 "'These are the regulations concerning animals, birds, every living thing that moves about in the water and every creature that moves along the ground. 47 You must distinguish between the unclean and the clean, between living creatures that may be eaten and those that may not be eaten.[j]'"

Purification After Childbirth

12 The LORD said to Moses, 2 "Say to the Israelites: 'A woman who becomes pregnant and gives birth to a son will be ceremonially unclean for seven days, just as she is unclean during her monthly period.[k] 3 On the eighth day the boy is to be circumcised.[l] 4 Then the woman must wait thirty-three days to be purified from her bleeding. She must not touch anything sacred or go to the sanctuary until the days of her purification are over. 5 If she gives birth to a daughter, for two weeks the woman will be unclean, as during her period. Then she must wait sixty-six days to be purified from her bleeding.

6 "'When the days of her purification for a son or daughter are over,[m] she is to bring to the priest at the entrance to the tent of meeting a year-old lamb[n] for a burnt offering and a young pigeon or a dove for a sin offering.[a][o] 7 He shall offer them before the LORD to make atonement for her, and then she will be ceremonially clean from her flow of blood.

"'These are the regulations for the woman who gives birth to a boy or a girl. 8 But if she cannot afford a lamb, she is to bring two doves or two young pigeons,[p] one for a burnt offering and the other for a sin offering.[q] In this way the priest will make atonement for her, and she will be clean.[r]'"

Regulations About Defiling Skin Diseases

13 The LORD said to Moses and Aaron, 2 "When anyone has a swelling[s] or a rash or a shiny spot[t] on their skin that may be a defiling skin disease,[b][u] they must be brought to Aaron the priest[v] or to one of his sons[c] who is a priest. 3 The priest is to examine the sore on the skin, and if the hair in the sore has turned white and the sore appears to be more than skin deep, it is a defiling skin disease. When the priest examines that person, he shall pronounce them ceremonially unclean.[w] 4 If the shiny spot[x] on the skin is white but does not appear to be more than skin deep and the hair in it has not turned white, the priest is to isolate the affected person for seven

11:45 [g] Lev 25:38, 55; Ex 6:7; 20:2 [h] Ge 17:7 [i] Ex 19:6; 1Pe 1:16*
11:47 [j] Lev 10:10
12:2 [k] Lev 15:19; 18:19
12:3 [l] Ge 17:12; Lk 1:59; 2:21
12:6 [m] Lk 2:22 [n] Ex 29:38; Lev 23:12; Nu 6:12,14; 7:15 [o] Lev 5:7
12:8 [p] Ge 15:9; Lev 14:22 [q] Lev 5:7; Lk 2:22-24* [r] Lev 4:26
13:2 [s] ver 10,19, 28,43 [t] ver 4, 38,39; Lev 14:56 [u] ver 3,9, 15; Ex 4:6; Lev 14:3,32; Nu 5:2; Dt 24:8 [v] Dt 24:8
13:3 [w] ver 8,11, 20,30; Lev 21:1; Nu 9:6
13:4 [x] ver 2

[a] 6 Or *purification offering*; also in verse 8
[b] 2 The Hebrew word for *defiling skin disease*, traditionally translated "leprosy," was used for various diseases affecting the skin; here and throughout verses 3-46. [c] 2 Or *descendants*

Lev 11:45 ❖ How can we live out a holiness that mirrors God's holiness?

Lev 12:8 ❖ How does this provision demonstrate God's love for the poor? See also Lk 2:24.

12:1-5 The first week or two of a child's life is treated like the regular ritual impurity of a menstrual period (vv. 2, 5).

12:6-8 When the period of impurity is over, the mother must bring a pair of sacrifices. The goal of the ritual is to remove physical ritual impurity, not moral fault. Why does ritual impurity last twice as long if she has a girl? Interpreters have suggested since some vaginal bleeding can occur on the part of a newborn girl, the doubled time could be based on the actual and potential discharge of both females.

✣ **12:1-8** The effects of sin are present at birth, pervading our being. It is no accident that Christ gave forgiveness with healing during his earthly ministry. This is a foretaste of the gift provided by his sacrifice, the ultimate purification offering. We think of this as a sacrifice for sin, and so it was (Jn 1:29). However, by overlooking the fact that purification offerings addressed not only *acts* of sin but also the state of *mortality* that results from sin, Christians have sometimes missed a magnificent truth.

13:1 The common translation "leprosy" applies to a complex of conditions, including some that resemble psoriasis and vitiligo and could have at least included an ancient form of the disease we label "leprosy" (now known as Hansen's disease).

Here is an outline of the diagnoses and other instructions in Lev 13:

- vv. 2–44: Impure skin disease on persons
- vv. 45–46: Prescribed behavior of skin-diseased persons
- vv. 47–59: Impure spoiling = mold in fabrics

13:2-44 The diagnostic procedure is logical. Apparently as a result of a two-week quarantine for suspected skin disease, the person has incurred minor impurity that requires laundering his or her clothes (vv. 6, 34).

days.[y] 5 On the seventh day[z] the priest is to examine them,[a] and if he sees that the sore is unchanged and has not spread in the skin, he is to isolate them for another seven days. 6 On the seventh day the priest is to examine them again, and if the sore has faded and has not spread in the skin, the priest shall pronounce them clean;[b] it is only a rash. They must wash their clothes,[c] and they will be clean.[d] 7 But if the rash does spread in their skin after they have shown themselves to the priest to be pronounced clean, they must appear before the priest again.[e] 8 The priest is to examine that person, and if the rash has spread in the skin, he shall pronounce them unclean; it is a defiling skin disease.

9 "When anyone has a defiling skin disease, they must be brought to the priest. 10 The priest is to examine them, and if there is a white swelling in the skin that has turned the hair white and if there is raw flesh in the swelling, 11 it is a chronic skin disease[f] and the priest shall pronounce them unclean. He is not to isolate them, because they are already unclean.

12 "If the disease breaks out all over their skin and, so far as the priest can see, it covers all the skin of the affected person from head to foot, 13 the priest is to examine them, and if the disease has covered their whole body, he shall pronounce them clean. Since it has all turned white, they are clean. 14 But whenever raw flesh appears on them, they will be unclean. 15 When the priest sees the raw flesh, he shall pronounce them unclean. The raw flesh is unclean; they have a defiling disease.[g] 16 If the raw flesh changes and turns white, they must go to the priest. 17 The priest is to examine them, and if the sores have turned white, the priest shall pronounce the affected person clean;[h] then they will be clean.

18 "When someone has a boil[i] on their skin and it heals, 19 and in the place where the boil was, a white swelling or reddish-white[j] spot[k] appears, they must present themselves to the priest. 20 The priest is to examine it, and if it appears to be more than skin deep and the hair in it has turned white, the priest shall pronounce that person unclean. It is a defiling skin disease[l] that has broken out where the boil was. 21 But if, when the priest examines it, there is no white hair in it and it is not more than skin deep and has faded, then the priest is to isolate them for seven days. 22 If it is spreading in the skin, the priest shall pronounce them unclean; it is a defiling disease. 23 But if the spot is unchanged and has not spread, it is only a scar from the boil, and the priest shall pronounce them clean.[m]

24 "When someone has a burn on their skin and a reddish-white or white spot appears in the raw flesh of the burn, 25 the priest is to examine the spot, and if the hair in it has turned white, and it appears to be more than skin deep, it is a defiling disease that has broken out in the burn. The priest shall pronounce them unclean; it is a defiling skin disease.[n] 26 But if the priest examines it and there is no white hair in the spot and if it is not more than skin deep and has faded, then the priest is to isolate them for seven days.[o] 27 On the seventh day the priest is to examine that person,[p] and if it is spreading in the skin, the priest shall pronounce them unclean; it is a defiling skin disease. 28 If, however, the spot is unchanged and has not spread in the skin but has faded, it is a swelling from the burn, and the priest shall pronounce them clean; it is only a scar from the burn.[q]

29 "If a man or woman has a sore on their head[r] or chin, 30 the priest is to examine the sore, and if it appears to be more than skin deep and the hair in it is yellow and thin, the priest shall pronounce them unclean; it is a defiling skin disease on the head or chin. 31 But if, when the priest examines the sore, it does not seem to be more than skin deep and there is no black hair in it, then the priest is to isolate the affected person for seven days.[s] 32 On the seventh day the priest is to examine the sore,[t] and if it has not spread and there is no yellow hair in it and it does not appear to be more than skin deep, 33 then the man or woman must shave themselves, except for the affected area, and the priest is to keep them isolated another seven days. 34 On the seventh day the priest is to examine the sore,[u] and if it has not spread in the skin and appears to be no more than skin deep, the priest shall pronounce them clean. They must wash their clothes, and they will be clean.[v] 35 But if the sore does spread in the skin

13:4 [y] ver 5, 21, 26, 33, 46; Lev 14:38; Nu 12:14, 15; Dt 24:9
13:5 [z] Lev 14:9 [a] ver 27, 32, 34, 51
13:6 [b] ver 13, 17, 23, 28, 34; Mt 8:3; Lk 5:12-14 [c] Lev 11:25 [d] Lev 11:25; 14:8, 9, 20, 48; 15:8; Nu 8:7
13:7 [e] Lk 5:14
13:11 [f] Ex 4:6; Lev 14:8; Nu 12:10; Mt 8:2
13:15 [g] ver 2
13:17 [h] ver 6
13:18 [i] Ex 9:9
13:19 [j] ver 24, 42; Lev 14:37 [k] ver 2
13:20 [l] ver 2
13:23 [m] ver 6
13:25 [n] ver 11
13:26 [o] ver 4
13:27 [p] ver 5
13:28 [q] ver 2
13:29 [r] ver 43, 44
13:31 [s] ver 4
13:32 [t] ver 5
13:34 [u] ver 5 [v] Lev 11:25

after they are pronounced clean, 36the priest is to examine them, and if he finds that the sore has spread in the skin, he does not need to look for yellow hair; they are unclean.[w] 37If, however, the sore is unchanged so far as the priest can see, and if black hair has grown in it, the affected person is healed. They are clean, and the priest shall pronounce them clean.

38"When a man or woman has white spots on the skin, 39the priest is to examine them, and if the spots are dull white, it is a harmless rash that has broken out on the skin; they are clean.

40"A man who has lost his hair and is bald[x] is clean. 41If he has lost his hair from the front of his scalp and has a bald forehead, he is clean. 42But if he has a reddish-white sore on his bald head or forehead, it is a defiling disease breaking out on his head or forehead. 43The priest is to examine him, and if the swollen sore on his head or forehead is reddish-white like a defiling skin disease, 44the man is diseased and is unclean. The priest shall pronounce him unclean because of the sore on his head.

45"Anyone with such a defiling disease must wear torn clothes,[y] let their hair be unkempt,[a] cover the lower part of their face[z] and cry out, 'Unclean! Unclean!'[a] 46As long as they have the disease they remain unclean. They must live alone; they must live outside the camp.[b]

Regulations About Defiling Molds

47"As for any fabric that is spoiled with a defiling mold—any woolen or linen clothing, 48any woven or knitted material of linen or wool, any leather or anything made of leather— 49if the affected area in the fabric, the leather, the woven or knitted material, or any leather article, is greenish or reddish, it is a defiling mold and must be shown to the priest.[c] 50The priest is to examine the affected area[d] and isolate the article for seven days. 51On the seventh day he is to examine it,[e] and if the mold has spread in the fabric, the woven or knitted material, or the leather, whatever its use, it is a persistent defiling mold; the article is unclean.[f] 52He must burn the fabric, the woven or knitted material of wool or linen, or any leather article that has been spoiled; because the defiling mold is persistent, the article must be burned.[g]

53"But if, when the priest examines it, the mold has not spread in the fabric, the woven or knitted material, or the leather article, 54he shall order that the spoiled article be washed. Then he is to isolate it for another seven days. 55After the article has been washed, the priest is to examine it again, and if the mold has not changed its appearance, even though it has not spread, it is unclean. Burn it, no matter which side of the fabric has been spoiled. 56If, when the priest examines it, the mold has faded after the article has been washed, he is to tear the spoiled part out of the fabric, the leather, or the woven or knitted material. 57But if it reappears in the fabric, in the woven or knitted material, or in the leather article, it is a spreading mold; whatever has the mold must be burned. 58Any fabric, woven or knitted material, or any leather article that has been washed and is rid of the mold, must be washed again. Then it will be clean."

59These are the regulations concerning defiling molds in woolen or linen clothing, woven or knitted material, or any leather article, for pronouncing them clean or unclean.

13:36 [w] ver 30
13:40 [x] Lev 21:5; 2Ki 2:23; Isa 3:24; 15:2; 22:12; Eze 27:31; 29:18; Am 8:10; Mic 1:16
13:45 [y] Lev 10:6 [z] Eze 24:17, 22; Mic 3:7 [a] Lev 5:2; La 4:15; Lk 17:12
13:46 [b] Nu 5:1-4; 12:14; 2Ki 7:3; 15:5; Lk 17:12
13:49 [c] Mk 1:44
13:50 [d] Eze 44:23
13:51 [e] ver 5 [f] Lev 14:44
13:52 [g] ver 55,57

[a] 45 Or *clothes, uncover their head*

Lev 13:46 ❖ Why was this regulation necessary? How did Jesus respond to people in this condition (see Mt 8:3)?

13:47–59 A parallel procedure of priestly examination at one-week intervals is applied to fabrics affected by mold or mildew, with the following differences: (1) The priest does not pronounce a fabric impure without quarantining it for at least a week. (2) The affected material is washed before a second week of quarantine if it is necessary. (3) If the abnormal condition fades after the fabric has been washed and quarantined for a second week, the priest tears/cuts out the affected area. (4) An impure fabric is destroyed by fire.

13:1–59 The instructions in Lev 13–14 are obsolete in terms of our obligation to observe them. However, from them we learn about the human condition. This impure affliction is a powerful metaphor for the human state induced by sin.

Cleansing From Defiling Skin Diseases

14 The LORD said to Moses, 2"These
are the regulations for any diseased
person at the time of their ceremonial
cleansing, when they are brought to the
priest:[h] 3The priest is to go outside the
camp and examine them.[i] If they have
been healed of their defiling skin disease,[a] 4the priest shall order that two live
clean birds and some cedar wood, scarlet
yarn and hyssop be brought for the person to be cleansed.[j] 5Then the priest shall
order that one of the birds be killed over
fresh water in a clay pot. 6He is then to
take the live bird and dip it, together with
the cedar wood, the scarlet yarn and the
hyssop, into the blood of the bird that
was killed over the fresh water.[k] 7Sev-
en times he shall sprinkle[l] the one to be
cleansed of the defiling disease, and then
pronounce them clean. After that, he is
to release the live bird in the open fields.

8"The person to be cleansed must wash
their clothes,[m] shave off all their hair
and bathe with water;[n] then they will
be ceremonially clean.[o] After this they
may come into the camp,[p] but they must
stay outside their tent for seven days.
9On the seventh day they must shave
off all their hair; they must shave their
head, their beard, their eyebrows and
the rest of their hair. They must wash
their clothes and bathe themselves with
water, and they will be clean.

10"On the eighth day[q] they must bring
two male lambs and one ewe lamb a
year old, each without defect, along
with three-tenths of an ephah[b] of the
finest flour mixed with olive oil for a
grain offering,[r] and one log[c] of oil.[s] 11The
priest who pronounces them clean shall
present both the one to be cleansed and
their offerings before the LORD at the
entrance to the tent of meeting.

12"Then the priest is to take one of
the male lambs and offer it as a guilt
offering,[t] along with the log of oil; he
shall wave them before the LORD as a
wave offering.[u] 13He is to slaughter the
lamb in the sanctuary area[v] where the
sin offering[d] and the burnt offering are
slaughtered. Like the sin offering, the
guilt offering belongs to the priest;[w] it is
most holy. 14The priest is to take some of
the blood of the guilt offering and put it
on the lobe of the right ear of the one to
be cleansed, on the thumb of their right
hand and on the big toe of their right
foot.[x] 15The priest shall then take some
of the log of oil, pour it in the palm of
his own left hand, 16dip his right forefinger into the oil in his palm, and with
his finger sprinkle some of it before the
LORD seven times. 17The priest is to put
some of the oil remaining in his palm
on the lobe of the right ear of the one
to be cleansed, on the thumb of their
right hand and on the big toe of their
right foot, on top of the blood of the guilt
offering. 18The rest of the oil in his palm
the priest shall put on the head of the
one to be cleansed and make atonement
for them before the LORD.

19"Then the priest is to sacrifice the
sin offering and make atonement for the
one to be cleansed from their uncleanness. After that, the priest shall slaughter
the burnt offering 20and offer it on the
altar, together with the grain offering,
and make atonement for them, and they
will be clean.[y]

21"If, however, they are poor[z] and cannot afford these,[a] they must take one
male lamb as a guilt offering to be waved
to make atonement for them, together
with a tenth of an ephah[e] of the finest

14:2 [h] Mt 8:2-4; Mk 1:40-44; Lk 5:12-14; 17:14
14:3 [i] Lev 13:46
14:4 [j] ver 6, 49, 51, 52; Nu 19:6; Ps 51:7
14:6 [k] ver 4
14:7 [l] 2Ki 5:10, 14; Isa 52:15; Eze 36:25
14:8 [m] Lev 11:25; 13:6 [n] ver 9 [o] ver 20 [p] Nu 5:2, 3; 12:14, 15; 2Ch 26:21
14:10 [q] Mt 8:4; Mk 1:44; Lk 5:14 [r] Lev 2:1 [s] ver 12, 15, 21, 24
14:12 [t] Lev 5:18; 6:6-7 [u] Ex 29:24
14:13 [v] Ex 29:11 [w] Lev 6:24-30; 7:7
14:14 [x] Ex 29:20; Lev 8:23
14:20 [y] ver 8
14:21 [z] Lev 5:7; 12:8 [a] ver 22, 32

[a] *3* The Hebrew word for *defiling skin disease*, traditionally translated "leprosy," was used for various diseases affecting the skin; also in verses 7, 32, 54 and 57. [b] *10* That is, probably about 11 pounds or about 5 kilograms [c] *10* That is, about 1/3 quart or about 0.3 liter; also in verses 12, 15, 21 and 24 [d] *13* Or *purification offering*; also in verses 19, 22 and 31 [e] *21* That is, probably about 3 1/2 pounds or about 1.6 kilograms

---

14:1–32 A person healed from skin disease undergoes an elaborate purification process in phases that occur on the first, seventh, and eighth days. Each of these phases progressively moves the individual toward full purity status so that he or she can be reinstated into the society of the Lord's people, who dwell within the bounds of the camp where God's sanctuary is located.

- vv. 4–7: Bird ritual
- vv. 4–8: First-day procedures
- v. 8: Shaving and cleansings
- v. 9: Seventh-day shaving and cleansings
- vv. 10–20: Eighth-day sacrifices

14:4–7 When the priest confirms that the skin disease is gone, he presides over a nonsacrificial elimination ritual that involves two birds. The ritual impurity is transferred from the person to the living bird via the blood of the slain bird, and the living bird carries the impurity away into oblivion.
14:10–20 The final stage on the eighth day requires the Israelite to offer a group of sacrifices at the sanctuary.

flour mixed with olive oil for a grain offering, a log of oil, 22and two doves or two young pigeons,[b] such as they can afford, one for a sin offering and the other for a burnt offering.

23"On the eighth day they must bring them for their cleansing to the priest at the entrance to the tent of meeting, before the LORD.[c] 24The priest is to take the lamb for the guilt offering,[d] together with the log of oil,[e] and wave them before the LORD as a wave offering.[f] 25He shall slaughter the lamb for the guilt offering and take some of its blood and put it on the lobe of the right ear of the one to be cleansed, on the thumb of their right hand and on the big toe of their right foot.[g] 26The priest is to pour some of the oil into the palm of his own left hand,[h] 27and with his right forefinger sprinkle some of the oil from his palm seven times before the LORD. 28Some of the oil in his palm he is to put on the same places he put the blood of the guilt offering — on the lobe of the right ear of the one to be cleansed, on the thumb of their right hand and on the big toe of their right foot. 29The rest of the oil in his palm the priest shall put on the head of the one to be cleansed, to make atonement for them before the LORD.[i] 30Then he shall sacrifice the doves or the young pigeons, such as the person can afford,[j] 31one as a sin offering and the other as a burnt offering,[k] together with the grain offering. In this way the priest will make atonement before the LORD on behalf of the one to be cleansed.[l]"

32These are the regulations for anyone who has a defiling skin disease[m] and who cannot afford the regular offerings[n] for their cleansing.

Cleansing From Defiling Molds

33The LORD said to Moses and Aaron, 34"When you enter the land of Canaan,[o] which I am giving you as your possession,[p] and I put a spreading mold in a house in that land, 35the owner of the house must go and tell the priest, 'I have seen something that looks like a defiling mold in my house.' 36The priest is to order the house to be emptied before he goes in to examine the mold, so that nothing in the house will be pronounced unclean. After this the priest is to go in and inspect the house. 37He is to examine the mold on the walls, and if it has greenish or reddish[q] depressions that appear to be deeper than the surface of the wall, 38the priest shall go out the doorway of the house and close it up for seven days.[r] 39On the seventh day[s] the priest shall return to inspect the house. If the mold has spread on the walls, 40he is to order that the contaminated stones be torn out and thrown into an unclean place outside the town.[t] 41He must have all the inside walls of the house scraped and the material that is scraped off dumped into an unclean place outside the town. 42Then they are to take other stones to replace these and take new clay and plaster the house.

43"If the defiling mold reappears in the house after the stones have been torn out and the house scraped and plastered, 44the priest is to go and examine it and, if the mold has spread in the house, it is a persistent defiling mold; the house is unclean.[u] 45It must be torn down — its stones, timbers and all the plaster — and taken out of the town to an unclean place.

46"Anyone who goes into the house while it is closed up will be unclean till evening.[v] 47Anyone who sleeps or eats in the house must wash their clothes.[w]

48"But if the priest comes to examine it and the mold has not spread after the house has been plastered, he shall pronounce the house clean,[x] because the defiling mold is gone. 49To purify the house he is to take two birds and

14:22 [b] Lev 5:7
14:23 [c] ver 10,11
14:24 [d] Nu 6:14 [e] ver 10 [f] ver 12
14:25 [g] ver 14; Ex 29:20
14:26 [h] ver 15
14:29 [i] ver 18
14:30 [j] Lev 5:7
14:31 [k] ver 22; Lev 5:7; 15:15,30 [l] ver 18,19
14:32 [m] Lev 13:2 [n] ver 21
14:34 [o] Ge 12:5; Ex 6:4; Nu 13:2 [p] Ge 17:8; 48:4; Nu 27:12; 32:22; Dt 3:27; 7:1; 32:49
14:37 [q] Lev 13:19
14:38 [r] Lev 13:4
14:39 [s] Lev 13:5
14:40 [t] ver 45
14:44 [u] Lev 13:51
14:46 [v] Lev 11:24
14:47 [w] Lev 11:25
14:48 [x] Lev 13:6

14:33–53 The diagnostic procedure for a house (vv. 35–45) largely resembles that of ch. 13 with regard to persons and garments.

14:43–53 If after its repair the house suffers a relapse of fungous infection, it is "unclean" and must be demolished. By contrast, if priestly inspection reveals that replacement of the infected material has solved the problem, he pronounces the house "clean" because the infection is gone (v. 48). To decontaminate (v. 49) the house and pronounce it "clean," the priest performs an elimination ritual.

14:46–47 A quarantined house makes any person who even enters it unclean until evening, and the residential activities of lying down or eating there require laundering of clothes as well.

The Israelite priest's declaration of quarantine carries legal force. Obviously this is not the way medical science works. If you come in contact with an individual carrying a contagious disease before examination by a physician, you are no less at risk than if your contact was after the exam.

some cedar wood, scarlet yarn and hyssop.[y] 50He shall kill one of the birds over
fresh water in a clay pot.[z] 51Then he is
to take the cedar wood, the hyssop,[a] the
scarlet yarn and the live bird, dip them
into the blood of the dead bird and the
fresh water, and sprinkle the house seven
times.[b] 52He shall purify the house with
the bird's blood, the fresh water, the live
bird, the cedar wood, the hyssop and the
scarlet yarn. 53Then he is to release the
live bird in the open fields[c] outside the
town. In this way he will make atonement for the house, and it will be clean.[d]"
54These are the regulations for any
defiling skin disease,[e] for a sore, 55for
defiling molds[f] in fabric or in a house,
56and for a swelling, a rash or a shiny
spot,[g] 57to determine when something
is clean or unclean.

These are the regulations for defiling
skin diseases and defiling molds.[h]

Discharges Causing Uncleanness

15 The LORD said to Moses and Aaron,
2"Speak to the Israelites and say
to them: 'When any man has an unusual bodily discharge,[i] such a discharge is
unclean. 3Whether it continues flowing
from his body or is blocked, it will make
him unclean. This is how his discharge
will bring about uncleanness:
4" 'Any bed the man with a discharge
lies on will be unclean, and anything
he sits on will be unclean. 5Anyone who
touches his bed must wash their clothes[j]
and bathe with water,[k] and they will be
unclean till evening.[l] 6Whoever sits on
anything that the man with a discharge
sat on must wash their clothes and bathe
with water, and they will be unclean till
evening.

14:49 [y] ver 4; 1Ki 4:33; ver 4
14:50 [z] ver 5
14:51 [a] ver 6; Ps 51:7 [b] ver 4,7
14:53 [c] ver 7 [d] ver 20
14:54 [e] Lev 13:2, 30
14:55 [f] Lev 13:47-52
14:56 [g] Lev 13:2
14:57 [h] Lev 10:10
15:2 [i] ver 16, 32; Lev 22:4; Nu 5:2; 2Sa 3:29; Mt 9:20
15:5 [j] Lev 11:25 [k] Lev 14:8 [l] Lev 11:24
15:7 [m] ver 19; Lev 22:5 [n] ver 16; Lev 22:4
15:8 [o] Nu 12:14
15:10 [p] Nu 19:10
15:12 [q] Lev 6:28 [r] Lev 11:32
15:13 [s] Lev 8:33 [t] ver 5
15:14 [u] Lev 14:22
15:15 [v] Lev 5:7

Lev 14:50 ❖ Sacrifices had to be made to atone for sin, but why did God demand a sacrifice to cleanse a house from mold?

7" 'Whoever touches the man[m] who has
a discharge[n] must wash their clothes and
bathe with water, and they will be unclean till evening.
8" 'If the man with the discharge spits[o]
on anyone who is clean, they must wash
their clothes and bathe with water, and
they will be unclean till evening.
9" 'Everything the man sits on when
riding will be unclean, 10and whoever touches any of the things that were
under him will be unclean till evening;
whoever picks up those things[p] must
wash their clothes and bathe with water,
and they will be unclean till evening.
11" 'Anyone the man with a discharge
touches without rinsing his hands with
water must wash their clothes and bathe
with water, and they will be unclean till
evening.
12" 'A clay pot[q] that the man touches
must be broken, and any wooden article[r]
is to be rinsed with water.
13" 'When a man is cleansed from his
discharge, he is to count off seven days[s]
for his ceremonial cleansing; he must
wash his clothes and bathe himself with
fresh water, and he will be clean.[t] 14On
the eighth day he must take two doves
or two young pigeons[u] and come before
the LORD to the entrance to the tent of
meeting and give them to the priest.
15The priest is to sacrifice them, the one
for a sin offering[a][v] and the other for a

[a] 15 Or *purification offering*; also in verse 30

14:1–57 In our age of instant gratification, we want leaps rather than steps. But most human progress happens in steps. A reason for steps is to understand and/or teach how a process is accomplished. In addition to providing comprehension, steps are encouraging because they show measurable progress that would not register if shown in leaps.

This is true in many areas of the physical world; it can also be true in the spiritual realm as believers rely on the Spirit to lead them into sanctification and becoming more Christlike. Paul talks about this process in Ro 15:14–16 in relation to the Gentiles, yet he himself had to go through a process of justification first, then sanctification (see Ac 9:1–31).

15:1–3 Discharges from genital organs are private matters. Thus, in Lev 15, determination of ritual impurities from these sources requires no examination by priests (contrast chs. 13–14).

15:4–18 Because seminal emissions are of short duration, they give rise to light impurities that only require a man to bathe, launder any fabric or leather with semen on it, and wait until evening (vv. 16–18) for restoration to purity, which allows contact with holy things. In the case of intercourse, these rules also apply to the woman (v. 18). Just as a woman shares equally in the light impurity of a man with whom she has intercourse (v. 18), a man who has intercourse with a menstruating woman shares her seven-day impurity.

burnt offering.[w] In this way he will make atonement before the LORD for the man because of his discharge.[x]

16 " 'When a man has an emission of semen,[y] he must bathe his whole body with water, and he will be unclean till evening.[z] 17 Any clothing or leather that has semen on it must be washed with water, and it will be unclean till evening. 18 When a man has sexual relations with a woman and there is an emission of semen,[a] both of them must bathe with water, and they will be unclean till evening.

19 " 'When a woman has her regular flow of blood, the impurity of her monthly period[b] will last seven days, and anyone who touches her will be unclean till evening.

20 " 'Anything she lies on during her period will be unclean, and anything she sits on will be unclean. 21 Anyone who touches her bed will be unclean; they must wash their clothes and bathe with water, and they will be unclean till evening.[c] 22 Anyone who touches anything she sits on will be unclean; they must wash their clothes and bathe with water, and they will be unclean till evening. 23 Whether it is the bed or anything she was sitting on, when anyone touches it, they will be unclean till evening.

24 " 'If a man has sexual relations with her and her monthly flow[d] touches him, he will be unclean for seven days; any bed he lies on will be unclean.

25 " 'When a woman has a discharge of blood for many days at a time other than her monthly period[e] or has a discharge that continues beyond her period, she will be unclean as long as she has the discharge, just as in the days of her period. 26 Any bed she lies on while her discharge continues will be unclean, as is her bed during her monthly period, and anything she sits on will be unclean, as during her period. 27 Anyone who touches them will be unclean; they must wash their clothes and bathe with water, and they will be unclean till evening.

28 " 'When she is cleansed from her discharge, she must count off seven days, and after that she will be ceremonially clean. 29 On the eighth day she must take two doves or two young pigeons[f] and bring them to the priest at the entrance to the tent of meeting. 30 The priest is to sacrifice one for a sin offering and the other for a burnt offering. In this way he will make atonement for her before the LORD for the uncleanness of her discharge.[g]

31 " 'You must keep the Israelites separate from things that make them unclean, so they will not die in their uncleanness for defiling my dwelling place,[a][h] which is among them.' "

32 These are the regulations for a man with a discharge, for anyone made unclean by an emission of semen,[i] 33 for a woman in her monthly period, for a man or a woman with a discharge, and for a man who has sexual relations with a woman who is ceremonially unclean.[j]

Lev 15:25–27 ❖ How does Jesus' treatment of the bleeding woman (see Lk 8:43–48) offer hope to the hopeless?

15:15 [w] Lev 14:31 [x] Lev 14:18,19
15:16 [y] ver 2; Lev 22:4; Dt 23:10 [z] ver 5; Dt 23:11
15:18 [a] 1Sa 21:4
15:19 [b] ver 24; Lev 12:2
15:21 [c] ver 27
15:24 [d] ver 19; Lev 12:2; 18:19; 20:18; Eze 18:6
15:25 [e] Mt 9:20; Mk 5:25; Lk 8:43
15:29 [f] Lev 14:22
15:30 [g] Lev 5:10; 14:20,31; 18:19; 2Sa 11:4; Mk 5:25; Lk 8:43
15:31 [h] Lev 20:3; Nu 5:3; 19:13, 20; 2Sa 15:25; 2Ki 21:7; Ps 33:14; 74:7; 76:2; Eze 5:11; 23:38
15:32 [i] ver 2
15:33 [j] ver 19, 24,25

[a] 31 Or *my tabernacle*

15:19–30 Menstruation is a fairly severe impurity, lasting seven days. But because it is normal and regular, purification calls for no sacrifices. While monthly menstruation was undoubtedly inconvenient, an ancient Israelite woman was not ritually impure and therefore barred from participation in worship at the sanctuary as often as we might suppose. During much of her childbearing phase of life, a woman was in a state of pregnancy, which interrupts menstruation, or breastfeeding, which can suppress it.

15:31–33 Verse 31 puts serious teeth into the legislation. Here at the end of the section of the book regulating physical ritual impurities, the Lord warns Moses and Aaron. The implication is that anyone in the camp could defile the sanctuary simply by being illegitimately impure; that is, without undergoing proper purification. The Israelite camp was simply a larger unit of defined space, within which severe enough impurity defiled that which was most sensitive to it: the sacred domain of the sanctuary (cf. Nu 5:1–4).

✥ **15:1–33** In ancient Israel the concept of mortality could spread like a virus through the influence of physical contact or location within a defined space. It was crucial that this contagious influence not reach and infect sacred things. Such contact would misrepresent the nature of God to the Israelites.

Erosion of respect for God's immortal nature, which contrasts with human mortality, inevitably leads human beings to underestimate their accountability to him. While we are no longer required to literally observe the rules of

The Day of Atonement

16:2–34pp // Lev 23:26–32; Nu 29:7–11

16 The LORD spoke to Moses after
the death of the two sons of Aaron who died when they approached the
LORD.[k] 2The LORD said to Moses: "Tell
your brother Aaron that he is not to come
whenever he chooses[l] into the Most Holy
Place[m] behind the curtain in front of the
atonement cover on the ark, or else he
will die. For I will appear[n] in the cloud[o]
over the atonement cover.
3"This is how Aaron is to enter the Most
Holy Place:[p] He must first bring a young
bull for a sin offering[a] and a ram for a
burnt offering. 4He is to put on the sacred
linen tunic, with linen undergarments
next to his body; he is to tie the linen
sash around him and put on the linen
turban.[q] These are sacred garments;[r] so
he must bathe himself with water[s] before he puts them on. 5From the Israelite community[t] he is to take two male
goats[u] for a sin offering and a ram for a
burnt offering.
6"Aaron is to offer the bull for his own
sin offering to make atonement for himself and his household.[v] 7Then he is to
take the two goats and present them before the LORD at the entrance to the tent
of meeting. 8He is to cast lots for the two
goats—one lot for the LORD and the other for the scapegoat.[b] 9Aaron shall bring
the goat whose lot falls to the LORD and
sacrifice it for a sin offering. 10But the
goat chosen by lot as the scapegoat shall
be presented alive before the LORD to be
used for making atonement[w] by sending
it into the wilderness as a scapegoat.
11"Aaron shall bring the bull for his
own sin offering to make atonement
for himself and his household,[x] and he
is to slaughter the bull for his own sin

> **Lev 16** ❖ How does the work of Christ echo and fulfill the Day of Atonement (see Heb 10:12)?

offering. 12He is to take a censer full of
burning coals[y] from the altar before the
LORD and two handfuls of finely ground
fragrant incense[z] and take them behind
the curtain. 13He is to put the incense on
the fire before the LORD, and the smoke
of the incense will conceal the atonement cover above the tablets of the covenant law, so that he will not die.[a] 14He is
to take some of the bull's blood[b] and with
his finger sprinkle it on the front of the
atonement cover; then he shall sprinkle
some of it with his finger seven times
before the atonement cover.[c]
15"He shall then slaughter the goat for
the sin offering for the people[d] and take
its blood behind the curtain[e] and do with
it as he did with the bull's blood: He shall
sprinkle it on the atonement cover and
in front of it. 16In this way he will make
atonement[f] for the Most Holy Place because of the uncleanness and rebellion
of the Israelites, whatever their sins have
been. He is to do the same for the tent
of meeting, which is among them in the
midst of their uncleanness. 17No one is
to be in the tent of meeting from the
time Aaron goes in to make atonement
in the Most Holy Place until he comes
out, having made atonement for himself,
his household and the whole community of Israel.
18"Then he shall come out to the altar[g] that is before the LORD and make
atonement for it. He shall take some of

[a] 3 Or *purification offering;* here and throughout this chapter [b] 8 The meaning of the Hebrew for this word is uncertain; also in verses 10 and 26.

16:1 [k] Lev 10:1
16:2 [l] Ex 30:10; Heb 9:7 [m] Heb 9:25; 10:19 [n] Ex 25:22 [o] Ex 40:34
16:3 [p] Heb 9:24, 25
16:4 [q] Ex 28:39 [r] Ex 28:42 [s] ver 24; Heb 10:22
16:5 [t] Lev 4:13-21 [u] 2Ch 29:23
16:6 [v] Lev 9:7; Heb 5:3; 7:27; 9:7,12
16:10 [w] Isa 53:4-10; Ro 3:25; 1Jn 2:2
16:11 [x] Heb 7:27; 9:7
16:12 [y] Lev 10:1 [z] Ex 30:34-38
16:13 [a] Ex 28:43; Lev 22:9
16:14 [b] Lev 4:5; Heb 9:7,13,25 [c] Lev 4:6
16:15 [d] Heb 9:7, 12 [e] Heb 9:3
16:16 [f] Ex 29:36
16:18 [g] Lev 4:7

> Leviticus governing ritual impurities, reverence for God's holiness is as important as ever. How do we portray God's nature and character? This question applies on a number of levels, including our individual and family lives, our church communities, and our nation.

16:1–10 To prepare for the inner sanctum, the high priest bathed his entire body. Then he put on sacred linen garments reserved for this occasion (v. 4). Once the high priest was ready and the required animals were assembled in the courtyard of the sanctuary, he performed a unique preparatory casting of lots to determine the respective ritual roles of two goats provided by the people.

16:11–19 After the purification offering, the high priest was to deposit a censer in the inner sanctum ("the Most Holy Place") to provide a cloud of incense smoke (vv. 12–13) to shield him from God's lethally glorious presence. By sprinkling the blood, the priest would avoid touching the cover (the so-called mercy seat or atonement cover). By this sprinkling, the high priest removed ritual impurities and two kinds of moral faults—transgressions and sins.

The high priest sprinkled the altar itself seven times (v. 19b) because the Israelites had brought their sins and impurities to it throughout the year.

the bull's blood and some of the goat's
blood and put it on all the horns of the
altar.[h] 19He shall sprinkle some of the
blood on it with his finger seven times
to cleanse it and to consecrate it from the
uncleanness of the Israelites.[i]
20"When Aaron has finished making
atonement for the Most Holy Place, the
tent of meeting and the altar, he shall
bring forward the live goat. 21He is to
lay both hands on the head of the live
goat and confess[j] over it all the wickedness and rebellion of the Israelites — all
their sins — and put them on the goat's
head. He shall send the goat away into
the wilderness in the care of someone
appointed for the task. 22The goat will
carry on itself all their sins[k] to a remote
place; and the man shall release it in the
wilderness.
23"Then Aaron is to go into the tent
of meeting and take off the linen garments he put on before he entered the
Most Holy Place, and he is to leave them
there.[l] 24He shall bathe himself with water in the sanctuary area and put on his
regular garments.[m] Then he shall come
out and sacrifice the burnt offering for
himself and the burnt offering for the
people, to make atonement for himself
and for the people. 25He shall also burn
the fat of the sin offering on the altar.
26"The man who releases the goat as
a scapegoat must wash his clothes[n] and
bathe himself with water; afterward
he may come into the camp. 27The bull
and the goat for the sin offerings, whose
blood was brought into the Most Holy
Place to make atonement, must be tak-
en outside the camp;[o] their hides, flesh
and intestines are to be burned up. 28The
man who burns them must wash his
clothes and bathe himself with water;
afterward he may come into the camp.
29"This is to be a lasting ordinance
for you: On the tenth day of the seventh
month you must deny yourselves[a][p] and
not do any work — whether native-born
or a foreigner residing among you —
30because on this day atonement will
be made for you, to cleanse you. Then,
before the LORD, you will be clean from
all your sins.[q] 31It is a day of sabbath rest,
and you must deny yourselves;[r] it is a
lasting ordinance. 32The priest who is
anointed and ordained to succeed his
father as high priest is to make atonement. He is to put on the sacred linen
garments[s] 33and make atonement for the
Most Holy Place, for the tent of meeting
and the altar, and for the priests and all
the members of the community.[t]
34"This is to be a lasting ordinance for
you: Atonement is to be made once a
year[u] for all the sins of the Israelites."
And it was done, as the LORD commanded Moses.

Eating Blood Forbidden

17 The LORD said to Moses, 2"Speak to
Aaron and his sons and to all the
Israelites and say to them: 'This is what
the LORD has commanded: 3Any Israelite
who sacrifices an ox,[b] a lamb or a goat
in the camp or outside of it 4instead of
bringing it to the entrance to the tent

16:18 [h] Lev 4:25
16:19 [i] Eze 43:20
16:21 [j] Lev 5:5
16:22 [k] Isa 53:12
16:23 [l] Eze 42:14; 44:19
16:24 [m] ver 3-5
16:26 [n] Lev 11:25
16:27 [o] Lev 4:12, 21; Heb 13:11
16:29 [p] Lev 23:27, 32; Nu 29:7; Isa 58:3
16:30 [q] Jer 33:8; Eph 5:26
16:31 [r] Isa 58:3,5
16:32 [s] ver 4; Nu 20:26,28
16:33 [t] ver 11, 16-18
16:34 [u] Heb 9:7, 25

[a] 29 Or *must fast;* also in verse 31 [b] 3 The Hebrew word can refer to either male or female.

16:20–22 The nonsacrificial procedure with the live goat is an elimination ritual that transfers evils away from people and disposes of them by abandonment. From the sanctuary the priest removed *physical ritual impurities*, rebellious sins that could not be atoned for, and pardonable sins (v. 16), but on the live goat he placed *culpabilities*, unpardonable rebellious sins, and pardonable sins (v. 21).
16:23–25 Having completed the dangerous process of expelling moral evil from the sanctuary and camp, the high priest was to bathe again before dressing himself in his ornate garments and performing the required burnt offerings for the priests and non-priests at the outer altar (vv. 23–24). The core of the Day of Atonement ritual procedure began with the purification offerings (vv. 11–19) and ended with them (v. 25).
16:26–28 Contact with these animals defiles each person involved in carrying them outside the camp and incinerating them. Purification of an assistant is like that of the live goat's handler: they are required to launder their clothes and bathe (v. 28).
16:29–34 These verses wrap up instructions for the Day of Atonement by commanding the Israelites to practice self-denial and refrain from work (vv. 29–31).

✣ **16:1–34** Purging the ancient Israelite sanctuary once a year signified the clearing of God's reputation with regard to his treatment of people who had made different kinds of choices regarding him. Christ's better sacrifice has this function at the beginning of his priestly ministry.

17:1–9 The fact that some Israelites were sacrificing away from the sanctuary and its altar (vv. 5, 7) indicates that they regarded these "goat idols" as supernatural beings. That the Lord did not immediately strike dead the Israelites sacrificing to "goat

of meeting to present it as an offering
to the LORD in front of the tabernacle
of the LORD[v] — that person shall be considered guilty of bloodshed; they have
shed blood and must be cut off from
their people.[w] 5This is so the Israelites
will bring to the LORD the sacrifices they
are now making in the open fields. They
must bring them to the priest, that is, to
the LORD, at the entrance to the tent of
meeting and sacrifice them as fellowship offerings. 6The priest is to splash
the blood against the altar of the LORD[x] at
the entrance to the tent of meeting and
burn the fat as an aroma pleasing to the
LORD.[y] 7They must no longer offer any
of their sacrifices to the goat idols[a][z] to
whom they prostitute themselves.[a] This
is to be a lasting ordinance for them and
for the generations to come.'

8"Say to them: 'Any Israelite or any foreigner residing among them who offers
a burnt offering or sacrifice 9and does
not bring it to the entrance to the tent
of meeting[b] to sacrifice it to the LORD
must be cut off from the people of Israel.

10" 'I will set my face against any Israelite or any foreigner residing among them
who eats blood,[c] and I will cut them off
from the people. 11For the life of a creature is in the blood,[d] and I have given it
to you to make atonement for yourselves
on the altar; it is the blood that makes
atonement for one's life.[b][e] 12Therefore I
say to the Israelites, "None of you may
eat blood, nor may any foreigner residing
among you eat blood."

13" 'Any Israelite or any foreigner residing among you who hunts any animal
or bird that may be eaten must drain
out the blood and cover it with earth,[f]
14because the life of every creature is its
blood. That is why I have said to the Is-

17:4 [v]Dt 12:5-21 [w]Ge 17:14
17:6 [x]Lev 3:2 [y]Nu 18:17
17:7 [z]Ex 22:20; 2Ch 11:15 [a]Ex 32:8; 34:15; Dt 32:17; 1Co 10:20
17:9 [b]ver 4
17:10 [c]Ge 9:4; Lev 3:17; Dt 12:16, 23; 1Sa 14:33
17:11 [d]ver 14; Ge 9:4 [e]Heb 9:22
17:13 [f]Lev 7:26; Dt 12:16
17:14 [g]ver 11; Ge 9:4
17:15 [h]Ex 22:31; Dt 14:21
18:2 [i]Ex 6:7; Lev 11:44; Eze 20:5
18:3 [j]ver 24-30; Ex 23:24; Lev 20:23
18:4 [k]ver 2
18:5 [l]Eze 20:11; Ro 10:5*; Gal 3:12*
18:7 [m]Lev 20:11 [n]Eze 22:10

Lev 17:11 ❖ How does Mt 26:28 deepen our understanding of the connection between blood and atonement?

Lev 18:3 ❖ How can we keep from yielding to the sexual sins and temptations of the world around us? Why is this important to God?

raelites, "You must not eat the blood of
any creature, because the life of every
creature is its blood; anyone who eats it
must be cut off."[g]

15" 'Anyone, whether native-born or
foreigner, who eats anything found dead
or torn by wild animals[h] must wash their
clothes and bathe with water, and they
will be ceremonially unclean till evening;
then they will be clean. 16But if they do
not wash their clothes and bathe themselves, they will be held responsible.' "

Unlawful Sexual Relations

18 The LORD said to Moses, 2"Speak
to the Israelites and say to them:
'I am the LORD your God.[i] 3You must not
do as they do in Egypt, where you used
to live, and you must not do as they do
in the land of Canaan, where I am bringing you. Do not follow their practices.[j]
4You must obey my laws and be careful to follow my decrees. I am the LORD
your God.[k] 5Keep my decrees and laws,
for the person who obeys them will live
by them.[l] I am the LORD.

6" 'No one is to approach any close
relative to have sexual relations. I am
the LORD.

7" 'Do not dishonor your father[m] by having sexual relations with your mother.[n]

[a] *7* Or *the demons* [b] *11* Or *atonement by the life in the blood*

idols" implies that he mercifully recognized that they did not understand the full implications of what they were doing.

17:10–14 The life is in the blood, which is why God has assigned it the function of ransoming the lives of offerors on the altar (v. 11).

17:15–16 The law applies only to non-priests. A later law holds priests to a higher standard of purity, as befits their holiness, by prohibiting them from eating such animals altogether (22:8).

17:1–16 How do biblical laws, including those of Lev 17, speak to us today? They do not comprehensively specify every detail of the ways we should act and think. Rather, they provide illustrations that reveal the character and values of the divine Lawgiver, thereby establishing the constitution/charter of covenant life with him. Can we summarize a single, simple rule of thumb to determine whether the Bible intends for Christians to keep a given OT law? Here is an attempt: *A law should be kept to the extent that its principle can be applied unless the NT removes the reason for its application.*

18:1–5 Incest is here defined more broadly than our modern understanding in that relatives by marriage, to whom a man would have easy access within the household, are off limits in addition to blood relatives.

She is your mother; do not have relations
with her.
8“ ‘Do not have sexual relations with
your father’s wife;[o] that would dishonor
your father.[p]
9“ ‘Do not have sexual relations with
your sister,[q] either your father’s daughter
or your mother’s daughter, whether she
was born in the same home or elsewhere.
10“ ‘Do not have sexual relations with
your son’s daughter or your daughter’s
daughter; that would dishonor you.
11“ ‘Do not have sexual relations with
the daughter of your father’s wife, born
to your father; she is your sister.
12“ ‘Do not have sexual relations with
your father’s sister;[r] she is your father’s
close relative.
13“ ‘Do not have sexual relations with
your mother’s sister, because she is your
mother’s close relative.
14“ ‘Do not dishonor your father’s
brother by approaching his wife to have
sexual relations; she is your aunt.[s]
15“ ‘Do not have sexual relations with
your daughter-in-law.[t] She is your son’s
wife; do not have relations with her.
16“ ‘Do not have sexual relations with
your brother’s wife;[u] that would dishonor
your brother.
17“ ‘Do not have sexual relations with
both a woman and her daughter.[v] Do
not have sexual relations with either
her son’s daughter or her daughter’s
daughter; they are her close relatives.
That is wickedness.
18“ ‘Do not take your wife’s sister as a
rival wife and have sexual relations with
her while your wife is living.
19“ ‘Do not approach a woman to have
sexual relations during the uncleanness
of her monthly period.[w]
20“ ‘Do not have sexual relations with
your neighbor’s wife[x] and defile yourself
with her.
21“ ‘Do not give any of your children[y]
to be sacrificed to Molek,[z] for you must
not profane the name of your God.[a] I am
the LORD.
22“ ‘Do not have sexual relations with
a man as one does with a woman;[b] that
is detestable.
23“ ‘Do not have sexual relations with
an animal and defile yourself with it. A
woman must not present herself to an
animal to have sexual relations with it;
that is a perversion.[c]
24“ ‘Do not defile yourselves in any
of these ways, because this is how the
nations that I am going to drive out before you[d] became defiled.[e] 25Even the
land was defiled; so I punished it for its
sin,[f] and the land vomited out its inhabitants.[g] 26But you must keep my decrees
and my laws. The native-born and the
foreigners residing among you must not
do any of these detestable things, 27for
all these things were done by the people
who lived in the land before you, and the
land became defiled. 28And if you defile
the land, it will vomit you out as it vomited out the nations that were before you.

18:8 [o] 1Co 5:1 [p] Lev 20:11
18:9 [q] Lev 20:17
18:12 [r] Lev 20:19
18:14 [s] Lev 20:20
18:15 [t] Lev 20:12
18:16 [u] Lev 20:21
18:17 [v] Lev 20:14
18:19 [w] Lev 15:24; 20:18
18:20 [x] Ex 20:14; Lev 20:10; Mt 5:27, 28; 1Co 6:9; Heb 13:4
18:21 [y] Dt 12:31 [z] Lev 20:2-5 [a] Lev 19:12; 21:6; Eze 36:20
18:22 [b] Lev 20:13; Dt 23:18; Ro 1:27
18:23 [c] Ex 22:19; Lev 20:15; Dt 27:21
18:24 [d] ver 3, 27, 30 [e] Dt 18:12
18:25 [f] Lev 20:23; Dt 9:5; 18:12 [g] ver 28; Lev 20:22

18:8-16 Forbidden relatives who marry into one’s family include a wife of one’s father (v. 8), aunt by marriage (v. 14), daughter-in-law (v. 15), and sister-in-law (v. 16). However, Dt 25:5–6 recognizes the notable exception of levirate marriage.

18:17-18 Leviticus prohibits a man from sexual unions with two women who are blood relatives of each other: a woman and her daughter or granddaughter (v. 17) or a woman and her sister while the first is alive (v. 18).

18:19-21 Intercourse with a menstruating woman is absolutely forbidden in v. 19, and the consequence is being “cut off from their people” (v. 29). Leviticus 15:24 covers situations of accidental violation.

At the center of the final group of five laws is a prohibition against sacrificing children to the god Molek (18:21), who was worshiped especially by the Ammonites (cf. 2Ki 16:3; 23:10). Molek worship parallels adultery: Both violate covenant relationships by disloyally giving precious “seed” to parties forbidden to receive it.

18:22 This verse is devastatingly untechnical, leaving no room for ambiguity. Notice, however, that Leviticus does not condemn persons who have same-sex attraction tendencies as long as they do not act on them.

18:23 The last law in ch. 18 prohibits bestiality, whether by a man or a woman. Leviticus 20 mandates capital punishment for both the humans and animals involved (20:15–16).

18:24-30 The conclusion of Lev 18 provides powerful incentives to follow the Lord’s directives.

18:1-30 While the church has no biblical license to sanction the practice of homosexuality in any form, Christ’s approach demands that the church be a haven of support to help precious people—including people who are gay, lesbian, bisexual, or who struggle with identity—in their often painful and traumatic journeys of recovery from all kinds of lifestyles. The same is true for all who walk in the doors of the local church, whatever their struggles with sin may be (Ro 3:23). To restore the church as the trusted friend rather than the enemy of sinners requires a major shift of attitude on our part.

29“ ‘Everyone who does any of these
detestable things — such persons must
be cut off from their people. 30Keep my
requirements[h] and do not follow any of
the detestable customs that were practiced before you came and do not defile
yourselves with them. I am the LORD
your God.[i]’ ”

Various Laws

19 The LORD said to Moses, 2“Speak to
the entire assembly of Israel and
say to them: ‘Be holy because I, the LORD
your God, am holy.[j]
3“ ‘Each of you must respect your mother and father,[k] and you must observe my
Sabbaths. I am the LORD your God.[l]
4“ ‘Do not turn to idols or make metal gods for yourselves.[m] I am the LORD
your God.
5“ ‘When you sacrifice a fellowship offering to the LORD, sacrifice it in such a
way that it will be accepted on your behalf. 6It shall be eaten on the day you sacrifice it or on the next day; anything left
over until the third day must be burned
up. 7If any of it is eaten on the third day,
it is impure and will not be accepted.
8Whoever eats it will be held responsible because they have desecrated what
is holy to the LORD; they must be cut off
from their people.
9“ ‘When you reap the harvest of your
land, do not reap to the very edges of
your field or gather the gleanings of your
harvest.[n] 10Do not go over your vineyard
a second time or pick up the grapes that
have fallen. Leave them for the poor and
the foreigner. I am the LORD your God.
11“ ‘Do not steal.[o]
“ ‘Do not lie.[p]
“ ‘Do not deceive one another.

18:30 [h] Dt 11:1 [i] ver 2
19:2 [j] 1Pe 1:16*; Lev 11:44
19:3 [k] Ex 20:12 [l] Lev 11:44
19:4 [m] Ex 20:4, 23; 34:17; Lev 26:1; Ps 96:5; 115:4-7
19:9 [n] Lev 23:10, 22; Dt 24:19-22
19:11 [o] Ex 20:15 [p] Eph 4:25
19:12 [q] Ex 20:7; Mt 5:33
19:13 [r] Ex 22:15, 25-27 [s] Dt 24:15; Jas 5:4
19:14 [t] Dt 27:18
19:15 [u] Ex 23:2, 6 [v] Dt 1:17
19:16 [w] Ps 15:3; Eze 22:9 [x] Ex 23:7
19:17 [y] 1Jn 2:9; 3:15 [z] Mt 18:15; Lk 17:3
19:18 [a] Ro 12:19 [b] Ps 103:9 [c] Mt 5:43*; 19:16*; 22:39*; Mk 12:31*; Lk 10:27*; Jn 13:34; Ro 13:9*; Gal 5:14*; Jas 2:8*
19:19 [d] Dt 22:9 [e] Dt 22:11

Lev 19:9-10 ❖ What can we do to show mercy and generosity to the poor and the foreigner?

12“ ‘Do not swear falsely by my name[q]
and so profane the name of your God. I
am the LORD.
13“ ‘Do not defraud or rob your neighbor.[r]
“ ‘Do not hold back the wages of a hired
worker overnight.[s]
14“ ‘Do not curse the deaf or put a stumbling block in front of the blind,[t] but fear
your God. I am the LORD.
15“ ‘Do not pervert justice;[u] do not show
partiality[v] to the poor or favoritism to
the great, but judge your neighbor fairly.
16“ ‘Do not go about spreading slander[w]
among your people.
“ ‘Do not do anything that endangers
your neighbor’s life.[x] I am the LORD.
17“ ‘Do not hate a fellow Israelite in
your heart.[y] Rebuke your neighbor frankly[z] so you will not share in their guilt.
18“ ‘Do not seek revenge[a] or bear a
grudge[b] against anyone among your
people, but love your neighbor as yourself.[c] I am the LORD.
19“ ‘Keep my decrees.
“ ‘Do not mate different kinds of animals.
“ ‘Do not plant your field with two
kinds of seed.[d]
“ ‘Do not wear clothing woven of two
kinds of material.[e]
20“ ‘If a man sleeps with a female slave
who is promised to another man but
who has not been ransomed or given
her freedom, there must be due punishment.[a] Yet they are not to be put to

[a] 20 Or *be an inquiry*

19:1-3 Following the overall command to be holy because the Lord is holy, these verses reiterate several of the Ten Commandments.
19:5-8 These verses repeat the ritual instructions governing acceptable consumption of the offeror’s portion of the well-being offering (7:16-18).
19:9-15 These verses safeguard the disadvantaged in society. Verse 14 prohibits treating a person who is physically challenged disrespectfully or harmfully.
19:16-18 These verses address damaging behaviors and the underlying attitudes toward other people that cause or prevent them. By starting malicious rumors, it is possible to hurt or even destroy a person and, in the process, gain advantage. Verse 17 strikes at the root of antagonistic behavior. By rebuking rather than hating, a person avoids bearing blame/culpability with regard to someone else.
19:19 These laws do not state their rationale and appear strange to modern readers who wear clothes made of all kinds of mixtures. The cherubim remind us that in ancient Near Eastern art and literature, mixed beings belong to the supernatural realm of the gods. The laws regarding mixtures seem intended to protect the distinction between the ordinary domain of laypersons and the sacred sphere of the sanctuary.
19:20-22 Although violation of a designated slave woman is not a capital offense, it is immoral activity that is offensive to God, violating the spirit of the seventh commandment of the Ten Commandments, which prohibits adultery. Thus, a man who commits this wrong must sacrifice a reparation offering to the Lord.

death, because she had not been freed.
21 The man, however, must bring a ram
to the entrance to the tent of meeting
for a guilt offering to the LORD.[f] 22 With
the ram of the guilt offering the priest is
to make atonement for him before the
LORD for the sin he has committed, and
his sin will be forgiven.
23 " 'When you enter the land and
plant any kind of fruit tree, regard its
fruit as forbidden.[a] For three years you
are to consider it forbidden[a]; it must
not be eaten. 24 In the fourth year all its
fruit will be holy,[g] an offering of praise
to the LORD. 25 But in the fifth year you
may eat its fruit. In this way your harvest will be increased. I am the LORD
your God.
26 " 'Do not eat any meat with the blood
still in it.[h]
" 'Do not practice divination or seek
omens.[i]
27 " 'Do not cut the hair at the sides of
your head or clip off the edges of your
beard.[j]
28 " 'Do not cut your bodies for the dead
or put tattoo marks on yourselves. I am
the LORD.
29 " 'Do not degrade your daughter by
making her a prostitute,[k] or the land will
turn to prostitution and be filled with
wickedness.
30 " 'Observe my Sabbaths and have reverence for my sanctuary. I am the LORD.[l]
31 " 'Do not turn to mediums or seek
out spiritists,[m] for you will be defiled by
them. I am the LORD your God.
32 " 'Stand up in the presence of the
aged, show respect for the elderly[n] and
revere your God. I am the LORD.
33 " 'When a foreigner resides among
you in your land, do not mistreat them.
34 The foreigner residing among you
must be treated as your native-born.[o]
Love them as yourself, for you were foreigners in Egypt.[p] I am the LORD your
God.
35 " 'Do not use dishonest standards
when measuring length, weight or
quantity. 36 Use honest scales and honest weights, an honest ephah[b] and an
honest hin.[c][q] I am the LORD your God,
who brought you out of Egypt.
37 " 'Keep all my decrees and all my laws
and follow them. I am the LORD.' "

19:21 [f] Lev 5:15
19:24 [g] Pr 3:9
19:26 [h] Lev 17:10 [i] Dt 18:10
19:27 [j] Lev 21:5
19:29 [k] Dt 23:18
19:30 [l] Lev 26:2
19:31 [m] Lev 20:6; Isa 8:19
19:32 [n] 1Ti 5:1
19:34 [o] Ex 12:48 [p] Dt 10:19
19:36 [q] Dt 25:13-15
20:3 [r] Lev 15:31 [s] Lev 18:21
20:4 [t] Dt 17:2-5

Punishments for Sin

20 The LORD said to Moses, 2 "Say to
the Israelites: 'Any Israelite or any
foreigner residing in Israel who sacrifices
any of his children to Molek is to be put
to death. The members of the community are to stone him. 3 I myself will set
my face against him and will cut him
off from his people; for by sacrificing
his children to Molek, he has defiled my
sanctuary[r] and profaned my holy name.[s]
4 If the members of the community close
their eyes when that man sacrifices one
of his children to Molek and if they fail
to put him to death,[t] 5 I myself will set my
face against him and his family and will
cut them off from their people together
with all who follow him in prostituting
themselves to Molek.
6 " 'I will set my face against anyone
who turns to mediums and spiritists

[a] 23 Hebrew *uncircumcised* [b] 36 An ephah was a dry measure having the capacity of about 3/5 of a bushel or about 22 liters. [c] 36 A hin was a liquid measure having the capacity of about 1 gallon or about 3.8 liters.

19:23–25 The Lord commands the Israelites to regard the fruit of trees that they plant for food as "uncircumcised" (see NIV text note; i.e., "forbidden" to eat) for the first three years. In the fourth year the first fruit considered edible is holy. God's promise that the yield of the tree would eventually increase encourages obedience (v. 25).

19:26 Israelites are prohibited from eating on/over the blood. Eating over the blood may involve occult consultation of ancestral spirits.

19:29–36 Leviticus revisits various areas of ethical or religious life touched on by the earlier laws.

19:1–37 The nature of the love in view in Lev 19:18 is clarified by its antithesis: taking revenge or bearing a grudge. This is not romantic or easy love but tough love that faces a challenge and is linked to action. In an imperfect world and society, people inevitably have differences among themselves, but they must get along in spite of those differences.

20:1–21 Whereas 18:21 simply outlaws giving any children to Molek and thus profaning God's name, 20:2–5 adds several elements: (1) The law also applies to resident aliens (v. 2). (2) The people living in the land are to stone a violator to death (v. 2). (3) A Molek worshiper, whether an Israelite or a resident alien in God's holy land, not only profanes his holy name; he also defiles his sanctuary (v. 3). (4) Anyone who fails to carry out the death penalty is condemned to the same divine punishment (vv. 4–5). (5) In 18:21, Molek worship is spiritual prostitution/promiscuity.

to prostitute themselves by following
them, and I will cut them off from their
people.[u]
7 "'Consecrate yourselves and be holy,[v]
because I am the LORD your God. 8 Keep
my decrees and follow them. I am the
LORD, who makes you holy.[w]
9 "'Anyone who curses their father or
mother[x] is to be put to death.[y] Because
they have cursed their father or mother,
their blood will be on their own head.[z]
10 "'If a man commits adultery with
another man's wife[a]—with the wife of
his neighbor—both the adulterer and
the adulteress are to be put to death.
11 "'If a man has sexual relations with
his father's wife, he has dishonored his
father.[b] Both the man and the woman
are to be put to death; their blood will
be on their own heads.
12 "'If a man has sexual relations with
his daughter-in-law,[c] both of them are to
be put to death. What they have done is
a perversion; their blood will be on their
own heads.
13 "'If a man has sexual relations with
a man as one does with a woman, both
of them have done what is detestable.[d]
They are to be put to death; their blood
will be on their own heads.
14 "'If a man marries both a woman
and her mother,[e] it is wicked. Both he
and they must be burned in the fire, so
that no wickedness will be among you.[f]
15 "'If a man has sexual relations with
an animal,[g] he is to be put to death, and
you must kill the animal.
16 "'If a woman approaches an animal
to have sexual relations with it, kill both
the woman and the animal. They are to
be put to death; their blood will be on
their own heads.
17 "'If a man marries his sister[h], the
daughter of either his father or his mother, and they have sexual relations, it is
a disgrace. They are to be publicly removed from their people. He has dishonored his sister and will be held responsible.

20:6 [u] Lev 19:31
20:7 [v] Eph 1:4; 1Pe 1:16*
20:8 [w] Ex 31:13
20:9 [x] Dt 27:16 [y] Ex 21:17; Mt 15:4*; Mk 7:10* [z] ver 11; 2Sa 1:16
20:10 [a] Ex 20:14; Dt 5:18; 22:22
20:11 [b] Lev 18:7; Dt 27:23
20:12 [c] Lev 18:15
20:13 [d] Lev 18:22
20:14 [e] Lev 18:17 [f] Dt 27:23
20:15 [g] Lev 18:23
20:17 [h] Lev 18:9
20:18 [i] Lev 15:24; 18:19
20:19 [j] Lev 18:12-13
20:20 [k] Lev 18:14
20:21 [l] Lev 18:16
20:22 [m] Lev 18:25-28
20:23 [n] Lev 18:3 [o] Lev 18:24, 27,30
20:24 [p] Ex 3:8; 13:5; 33:3 [q] Ex 33:16
20:25 [r] Lev 11:1-47; Dt 14:3-21
20:26 [s] Lev 19:2
20:27 [t] Lev 19:31

Lev 20:26 ❖ What does it look like to be holy to the Lord in the time after Christ? Do all the same rules apply? Why or why not?

18 "'If a man has sexual relations with
a woman during her monthly period,[i]
he has exposed the source of her flow,
and she has also uncovered it. Both of
them are to be cut off from their people.
19 "'Do not have sexual relations with
the sister of either your mother or your
father,[j] for that would dishonor a close
relative; both of you would be held responsible.
20 "'If a man has sexual relations with
his aunt,[k] he has dishonored his uncle.
They will be held responsible; they will
die childless.
21 "'If a man marries his brother's wife,[l]
it is an act of impurity; he has dishonored his brother. They will be childless.
22 "'Keep all my decrees and laws and
follow them, so that the land[m] where I
am bringing you to live may not vomit
you out. 23 You must not live according to
the customs of the nations[n] I am going to
drive out before you.[o] Because they did
all these things, I abhorred them. 24 But I
said to you, "You will possess their land;
I will give it to you as an inheritance, a
land flowing with milk and honey."[p] I
am the LORD your God, who has set you
apart from the nations.[q]
25 "'You must therefore make a distinction between clean and unclean animals
and between unclean and clean birds.[r]
Do not defile yourselves by any animal
or bird or anything that moves along the
ground—those that I have set apart as
unclean for you. 26 You are to be holy to
me because I, the LORD, am holy,[s] and I
have set you apart from the nations to
be my own.
27 "'A man or woman who is a medium
or spiritist among you must be put to
death.[t] You are to stone them; their blood
will be on their own heads.'"

20:25–26 The closing exhortation recapitulates 11:43–47, where the Israelites are commanded to be holy as God is holy by abstaining from defilement through impure animals.

✣ **20:1–27** These days, pictures of thousands of missing children are posted on public flyers, the internet, and television. Children are found, dead or alive, molested or not, but hundreds each year are never recovered. It appears that some are exploited for pornography, pedophilia, and/or prostitution, then disposed of. This is not far from Molek worship: Sacrifice of a child for personal gain is similarly detestable.

Rules for Priests

21 The LORD said to Moses, "Speak to the priests, the sons of Aaron, and say to them: 'A priest must not make himself ceremonially unclean for any of his people who die,[u] 2 except for a close relative, such as his mother or father, his son or daughter, his brother, 3 or an unmarried sister who is dependent on him since she has no husband — for her he may make himself unclean. 4 He must not make himself unclean for people related to him by marriage,[a] and so defile himself.

5 " 'Priests must not shave their heads or shave off the edges of their beards[v] or cut their bodies.[w] 6 They must be holy to their God and must not profane the name of their God.[x] Because they present the food offerings to the LORD,[y] the food of their God, they are to be holy.

7 " 'They must not marry women defiled by prostitution or divorced from their husbands,[z] because priests are holy to their God.[a] 8 Regard them as holy,[b] because they offer up the food of your God. Consider them holy, because I the LORD am holy — I who make you holy.

9 " 'If a priest's daughter defiles herself by becoming a prostitute, she disgraces her father; she must be burned in the fire.[c]

10 " 'The high priest, the one among his brothers who has had the anointing oil poured on his head and who has been ordained to wear the priestly garments,[d] must not let his hair become unkempt[b] or tear his clothes.[e] 11 He must not enter a place where there is a dead body.[f] He must not make himself unclean,[g] even for his father or mother, 12 nor leave the sanctuary of his God or desecrate it, because he has been dedicated by the anointing oil[h] of his God. I am the LORD.

13 " 'The woman he marries must be a virgin.[i] 14 He must not marry a widow, a divorced woman, or a woman defiled by prostitution, but only a virgin from his own people, 15 so that he will not defile his offspring among his people. I am the LORD, who makes him holy.' "

16 The LORD said to Moses, 17 "Say to Aaron: 'For the generations to come none of your descendants who has a defect may come near to offer the food of his God.[j] 18 No man who has any defect[k] may come near: no man who is blind or lame, disfigured or deformed; 19 no man with a crippled foot or hand, 20 or who is a hunchback or a dwarf, or who has any eye defect, or who has festering or running sores or damaged testicles.[l] 21 No descendant of Aaron the priest who has any defect is to come near to present the food offerings to the LORD. He has a defect; he must not come near to offer the food of his God. 22 He may eat the most holy food of his God,[m] as well as the holy food; 23 yet because of his defect, he must not go near the curtain or approach the altar, and so desecrate my sanctuary. I am the LORD, who makes them holy.' "

24 So Moses told this to Aaron and his sons and to all the Israelites.

21:1 [u] Eze 44:25
21:5 [v] Eze 44:20 [w] Lev 19:28; Dt 14:1
21:6 [x] Lev 18:21 [y] Lev 3:11
21:7 [z] ver 13,14 [a] Eze 44:22
21:8 [b] ver 6
21:9 [c] Ge 38:24; Lev 19:29
21:10 [d] Lev 16:32 [e] Lev 10:6
21:11 [f] Nu 19:11, 13,14 [g] Lev 19:28
21:12 [h] Ex 29:6-7; Lev 10:7
21:13 [i] Eze 44:22
21:17 [j] ver 6
21:18 [k] Lev 22:19-25
21:20 [l] Dt 23:1; Isa 56:3
21:22 [m] 1Co 9:13

[a] 4 Or *unclean as a leader among his people*
[b] 10 Or *not uncover his head*

Lev 21:8 ❖ How should believers regard and respect those in ordained ministry?

21:1-7 Priests in general must guard their holiness in several ways. (1) They must not incur corpse contamination (vv. 1-4). (2) Priests may not practice the pagan mourning customs (v. 5). (3) A priest's holiness prevents him from marrying certain women (v. 7).
21:8-9 Israelites must treat the priest as holy. A priest's family members participate in his holiness. A priest's daughter enjoys an elevated status of holiness, but this privilege carries moral responsibility.
21:10-15 The high priest is consecrated for intimate access to God on behalf of all Israelites. Correspondingly, he must live by the strictest rules of all.
21:16-23 Although those in the priestly family who have physical defects in that they are blind, lame, disfigured, and so on may eat most holy and holy sacrificial food, they are forbidden to desecrate the sanctuary by engaging in priestly service.

✣ **21:1-24** Although the NT has no earthly mediatorial priesthood, as spiritual leaders in the community of faith, Christian ministers and their families carry some of the same burdens that were laid on the ancient priests and their close relatives. The reason is essentially the same—to rightly present the Lord's character to the people. We know that ministers are imperfect, but it is devastating when they fall in a serious way.

A ministry is a terrible thing to waste, but it is also a wonderful thing to nurture. Rather than exhausting valuable creative energies in contention and criticism, congregations benefit themselves, their communities, and the cause of God by focusing their energies on upholding dedicated leaders and walking with them on the path of holiness.

22 The LORD said to Moses, 2"Tell
Aaron and his sons to treat with
respect the sacred offerings the Israelites consecrate to me, so they will not
profane my holy name. I am the LORD.
3"Say to them: 'For the generations to
come, if any of your descendants is ceremonially unclean and yet comes near the
sacred offerings that the Israelites consecrate to the LORD, that person must be
cut off from my presence.[n] I am the LORD.
4" 'If a descendant of Aaron has a defiling skin disease[a] or a bodily discharge,[o]
he may not eat the sacred offerings
until he is cleansed. He will also be unclean if he touches something defiled
by a corpse[p] or by anyone who has an
emission of semen, 5or if he touches any
crawling thing[q] that makes him unclean,
or any person[r] who makes him unclean,
whatever the uncleanness may be. 6The
one who touches any such thing will be
unclean till evening. He must not eat
any of the sacred offerings unless he has
bathed himself with water. 7When the
sun goes down, he will be clean, and after that he may eat the sacred offerings,
for they are his food.[s] 8He must not eat
anything found dead[t] or torn by wild animals,[u] and so become unclean[v] through
it. I am the LORD.
9" 'The priests are to perform my service in such a way that they do not become guilty and die[w] for treating it with
contempt. I am the LORD, who makes
them holy.
10" 'No one outside a priest's family
may eat the sacred offering, nor may
the guest of a priest or his hired worker
eat it. 11But if a priest buys a slave with
money, or if slaves are born in his household, they may eat his food.[x] 12If a priest's
daughter marries anyone other than a
priest, she may not eat any of the sacred
contributions. 13But if a priest's daughter
becomes a widow or is divorced, yet has
no children, and she returns to live in
her father's household as in her youth,
she may eat her father's food. No unauthorized person, however, may eat it.
14" 'Anyone who eats a sacred offering by mistake must make restitution
to the priest for the offering and add a
fifth of the value[y] to it. 15The priests must
not desecrate the sacred offerings the
Israelites present to the LORD[z] 16by allowing them to eat the sacred offerings
and so bring upon them guilt requiring
payment.[a] I am the LORD, who makes
them holy.' "

Unacceptable Sacrifices

17The LORD said to Moses, 18"Speak to
Aaron and his sons and to all the Israelites and say to them: 'If any of you —
whether an Israelite or a foreigner residing in Israel — presents a gift[b] for a
burnt offering to the LORD, either to fulfill a vow or as a freewill offering, 19you
must present a male without defect[c]
from the cattle, sheep or goats in order
that it may be accepted on your behalf.
20Do not bring anything with a defect,[d]
because it will not be accepted on your
behalf. 21When anyone brings from the
herd or flock a fellowship offering[e] to
the LORD to fulfill a special vow or as a
freewill offering, it must be without defect or blemish to be acceptable. 22Do not
offer to the LORD the blind, the injured or
the maimed, or anything with warts or
festering or running sores. Do not place
any of these on the altar as a food offering presented to the LORD. 23You may,
however, present as a freewill offering
an ox[b] or a sheep that is deformed or
stunted, but it will not be accepted in
fulfillment of a vow. 24You must not offer
to the LORD an animal whose testicles are
bruised, crushed, torn or cut.[f] You must
not do this in your own land, 25and you
must not accept such animals from the

[a] 4 The Hebrew word for *defiling skin disease*, traditionally translated "leprosy," was used for various diseases affecting the skin. [b] 23 The Hebrew word can refer to either male or female.

22:3 [n] Lev 7:20, 21; Nu 19:13
22:4 [o] Lev 14:1-32; 15:2-15 [p] Lev 11:24-28,39
22:5 [q] Lev 11:24-28,43 [r] Lev 15:7
22:7 [s] Nu 18:11
22:8 [t] Lev 11:39 [u] Ex 22:31; Lev 17:15 [v] Lev 11:40
22:9 [w] ver 16; Ex 28:43
22:11 [x] Ge 17:13; Ex 12:44
22:14 [y] Lev 5:15
22:15 [z] Nu 18:32
22:16 [a] ver 9
22:18 [b] Lev 1:2
22:19 [c] Lev 1:3
22:20 [d] Dt 15:21; 17:1; Mal 1:8, 14; Heb 9:14; 1Pe 1:19
22:21 [e] Lev 3:6; Nu 15:3,8
22:24 [f] Lev 21:20

22:1–7 Moses deals with *temporary* disqualification of non-defective priests from serving. Impurity that represents human mortality may not contact the pure, immortal sphere of God.

22:8–14 Verse 8 prohibits priests from eating animals that die naturally or are killed by animals, not those slaughtered by humans. While *most holy* sacrificial portions must be eaten in the sacred precincts, *holy* portions may be shared with other family members as part of their livelihood. If an unauthorized person inadvertently eats a holy thing, he or she must make reparation (v. 14).

22:15–16 If the priests desecrate the sacred things that laypersons dedicate to the Lord, they will cause the Israelites to bear blame that requires restitution (v. 16).

22:17–25 From earlier regulations we know a sacrifice had to be free from defect (vv. 18–21). Verses 22–24 specify the kinds of defects that render animals unfit.

hand of a foreigner and offer them as
the food of your God.[g] They will not be
accepted on your behalf, because they
are deformed and have defects.'"
26The LORD said to Moses, 27"When a
calf, a lamb or a goat is born, it is to remain with its mother for seven days.[h]
From the eighth day on, it will be acceptable as a food offering presented to
the LORD. 28Do not slaughter a cow or a
sheep and its young on the same day.[i]
29"When you sacrifice a thank offering[j]
to the LORD, sacrifice it in such a way
that it will be accepted on your behalf.
30It must be eaten that same day; leave
none of it till morning.[k] I am the LORD.
31"Keep[l] my commands and follow
them. I am the LORD. 32Do not profane
my holy name,[m] for I must be acknowledged as holy by the Israelites.[n] I am the
LORD, who made you holy 33and who
brought you out of Egypt to be your God.[o]
I am the LORD."

The Appointed Festivals

23 The LORD said to Moses, 2"Speak
to the Israelites and say to them:
'These are my appointed festivals,[p] the
appointed festivals of the LORD, which
you are to proclaim as sacred assemblies.[q]

The Sabbath

3"'There are six days when you may
work,[r] but the seventh day is a day of
sabbath rest,[s] a day of sacred assembly.
You are not to do any work; wherever you
live, it is a sabbath to the LORD.

22:25 [g] Lev 21:6
22:27 [h] Ex 22:30
22:28 [i] Dt 22:6,7
22:29 [j] Lev 7:12; Ps 107:22
22:30 [k] Lev 7:15
22:31 [l] Dt 4:2, 40; Ps 105:45
22:32 [m] Lev 18:21 [n] Lev 10:3
22:33 [o] Lev 11:45
23:2 [p] ver 4, 37, 44; Nu 29:39 [q] ver 21,27
23:3 [r] Ex 20:9 [s] Ex 20:10; 31:13-17; Lev 19:3; Dt 5:13; Heb 4:9,10
23:5 [t] Ex 12:18-19; Nu 28:16-17; Dt 16:1-8
23:7 [u] ver 3,8
23:10 [v] Ex 23:16, 19; 34:26
23:11 [w] Ex 29:24

Lev 22:32 ❖ What does it mean to profane God's name? What actions might profane God's glory today?

Lev 23:2 ❖ How might we practice a rhythm of life that routinely draws us back to God's mercy and redemption?

The Passover and the Festival of Unleavened Bread

23:4–8pp // Ex 12:14–20; Nu 28:16–25; Dt 16:1–8

4"'These are the LORD's appointed festivals, the sacred assemblies you are to
proclaim at their appointed times: 5The
LORD's Passover begins at twilight on
the fourteenth day of the first month.[t]
6On the fifteenth day of that month the
LORD's Festival of Unleavened Bread begins; for seven days you must eat bread
made without yeast. 7On the first day
hold a sacred assembly[u] and do no regular work. 8For seven days present a food
offering to the LORD. And on the seventh
day hold a sacred assembly and do no
regular work.'"

Offering the Firstfruits

9The LORD said to Moses, 10"Speak to
the Israelites and say to them: 'When
you enter the land I am going to give
you and you reap its harvest, bring to
the priest a sheaf[v] of the first grain you
harvest. 11He is to wave the sheaf before
the LORD[w] so it will be accepted on your
behalf; the priest is to wave it on the day

22:26–30 Out of respect for life, a baby animal may not be taken from its mother as a sacrifice during the first seven days of its life (v. 27), and an animal and its young are not to be sacrificed on the same day (v. 28).
22:31–33 A concluding decree contains elements that parallel ingredients of exhortations in chs. 18–21.

22:1–33 Do we devote our best to God in terms of time, energy, and other resources? Or do we condescendingly give him leftovers? Do we ever "sacrifice" anything from our abundance for anyone else?

Although Paul encouraged his readers to "pray in the Spirit on all occasions with all kinds of prayers and requests" (Eph 6:18), one misappropriation of prayer is to ask God to do for us things we can and ought to do for ourselves. When we ask him to bless us in spite of the fact that we violate the cause-and-effect principles through which his blessing comes, we are being unreasonable. When God appears harsh, unfeeling, or unresponsive, sometimes it is because he is unwilling to support our addiction to sin. Just as family members of those addicted to destructive drugs, alcohol, illicit sex, or gambling need to learn redemptive "tough love" by refusing to bear responsibility that is not theirs, so also God reinforces our willpower by teaching us the nature, consequences, and power of our own choices.

23:1–3 The Creator established this pause from work as the way to enact holiness in the dimension of time (Ge 2:2–3).
23:9–21 Two observances, fifty days apart, celebrate and implicitly thank God for the beginnings of the barley and wheat harvests, respectively.
23:11–12 The Israelites are to bring to the sanctuary the first sheaf of grain that they harvest in the spring, which is undoubtedly barley. By giving the Lord a token portion before eating any of the new harvest, they acknowledge that the harvest is from him.

after the Sabbath. 12 On the day you wave
the sheaf, you must sacrifice as a burnt
offering to the LORD a lamb a year old
without defect, 13 together with its grain
offering[x] of two-tenths of an ephah[a] of
the finest flour mixed with olive oil — a
food offering presented to the LORD, a
pleasing aroma — and its drink offering of a quarter of a hin[b] of wine. 14 You
must not eat any bread, or roasted or
new grain, until the very day you bring
this offering to your God.[y] This is to be
a lasting ordinance for the generations
to come,[z] wherever you live.

The Festival of Weeks
23:15–22pp // Nu 28:26–31; Dt 16:9–12

15 " 'From the day after the Sabbath, the
day you brought the sheaf of the wave
offering, count off seven full weeks.
16 Count off fifty days up to the day after
the seventh Sabbath,[a] and then present
an offering of new grain to the LORD.
17 From wherever you live, bring two
loaves made of two-tenths of an ephah
of the finest flour, baked with yeast,
as a wave offering of firstfruits[b] to the
LORD. 18 Present with this bread seven
male lambs, each a year old and without
defect, one young bull and two rams.
They will be a burnt offering to the LORD,
together with their grain offerings and
drink offerings — a food offering, an aroma pleasing to the LORD. 19 Then sacrifice
one male goat for a sin offering[c] and two
lambs, each a year old, for a fellowship
offering. 20 The priest is to wave the two
lambs before the LORD as a wave offering,
together with the bread of the firstfruits.
They are a sacred offering to the LORD for
the priest. 21 On that same day you are
to proclaim a sacred assembly[c] and do
no regular work.[d] This is to be a lasting
ordinance for the generations to come,
wherever you live.

22 " 'When you reap the harvest[e] of your
land, do not reap to the very edges of
your field or gather the gleanings of your
harvest.[f] Leave them for the poor and for
the foreigner residing among you. I am
the LORD your God.' "

The Festival of Trumpets
23:23–25pp // Nu 29:1–6

23 The LORD said to Moses, 24 "Say to the
Israelites: 'On the first day of the seventh
month you are to have a day of sabbath
rest, a sacred assembly commemorated
with trumpet blasts.[g] 25 Do no regular
work,[h] but present a food offering to the
LORD.' "

The Day of Atonement
23:26–32pp // Lev 16:2–34; Nu 29:7–11

26 The LORD said to Moses, 27 "The
tenth day of this seventh month[i] is
the Day of Atonement.[j] Hold a sacred
assembly[k] and deny yourselves,[d] and
present a food offering to the LORD.
28 Do not do any work on that day, because it is the Day of Atonement, when
atonement is made for you before the
LORD your God. 29 Those who do not
deny themselves on that day must be
cut off from their people.[l] 30 I will destroy from among their people[m] anyone
who does any work on that day. 31 You
shall do no work at all. This is to be a
lasting ordinance for the generations
to come, wherever you live. 32 It is a day
of sabbath rest for you, and you must
deny yourselves. From the evening of
the ninth day of the month until the
following evening you are to observe
your sabbath."

23:13 [x] Lev 2:14-16; 6:20
23:14 [y] Ex 34:26 [z] Nu 15:21
23:16 [a] Nu 28:26; Ac 2:1
23:17 [b] Ex 34:22; Lev 2:12
23:21 [c] ver 2 [d] ver 3
23:22 [e] Lev 19:9 [f] Lev 19:10; Dt 24:19-21; Ru 2:15
23:24 [g] Lev 25:9; Nu 10:9,10; 29:1
23:25 [h] ver 21
23:27 [i] Lev 16:29 [j] Ex 30:10 [k] Nu 29:7
23:29 [l] Ge 17:14; Nu 5:2
23:30 [m] Lev 20:3

[a] 13 That is, probably about 7 pounds or about 3.2 kilograms; also in verse 17 [b] 13 That is, about 1 quart or about 1 liter [c] 19 Or *purification offering* [d] 27 Or *and fast*; similarly in verses 29 and 32

23:16–20 The wheat was to be baked in two loaves of *leavened* bread and presented along with a group of animal sacrifices. Like the earlier barley sheaf, the two loaves constituted a wave offering (v. 17). Through acknowledging God as the One who sustains the lives of his creatures by giving them food, the Israelites honored him as their Creator.

23:1–22 Ironically, one of the greatest blessings of the commandment to abstain from work on the Sabbath is the very fact that the Bible presents it as an absolute requirement. A goal-oriented, driven, "Type A" workaholic needs it to be a command from the Lord himself, or they will restlessly continue to work and thereby risk physical and emotional burnout. It is an immense relief to stop work for twenty-four peaceful hours in order to enjoy God through church, family, and walks in the woods or by a lake without feeling the slightest twinge of guilt for doing so!

23:23–25 This is ten days before the Day of Atonement, when the Lord affirms his relationship with those who show loyalty but rejects those who neglect to do so.

The Festival of Tabernacles

23:33–43pp // Nu 29:12–39; Dt 16:13–17

33The LORD said to Moses, 34"Say to the Israelites: 'On the fifteenth day of the seventh month the LORD's Festival of Tabernacles[n] begins, and it lasts for seven days. 35The first day is a sacred assembly; do no regular work. 36For seven days present food offerings to the LORD, and on the eighth day hold a sacred assembly[o] and present a food offering to the LORD. It is the closing special assembly; do no regular work.

37(" 'These are the LORD's appointed festivals, which you are to proclaim as sacred assemblies for bringing food offerings to the LORD—the burnt offerings and grain offerings, sacrifices and drink offerings[p] required for each day. 38These offerings are in addition to those for the LORD's Sabbaths[q] and[a] in addition to your gifts and whatever you have vowed and all the freewill offerings you give to the LORD.)

39" 'So beginning with the fifteenth day of the seventh month, after you have gathered the crops of the land, celebrate the festival to the LORD for seven days;[r] the first day is a day of sabbath rest, and the eighth day also is a day of sabbath rest. 40On the first day you are to take branches from luxuriant trees—from palms, willows and other leafy trees[s]—and rejoice before the LORD your God for seven days. 41Celebrate this as a festival to the LORD for seven days each year. This is to be a lasting ordinance for the generations to come; celebrate it in the seventh month. 42Live in temporary shelters[t] for seven days: All native-born Israelites are to live in such shelters 43so your descendants will know[u] that I had the Israelites live in temporary shelters when I brought them out of Egypt. I am the LORD your God.' "

23:34 [n] Ex 23:16; Dt 16:13; Ezr 3:4; Ne 8:14; Zec 14:16; Jn 7:2
23:36 [o] 2Ch 7:9; Ne 8:18; Jn 7:37
23:37 [p] ver 2, 4
23:38 [q] Eze 45:17
23:39 [r] Ex 23:16; Dt 16:13
23:40 [s] Ne 8:14-17
23:42 [t] Ne 8:14-16
23:43 [u] Dt 31:13; Ps 78:5

Lev 24:2–4 ❖ Why did God want the lamps in his house to be lit continually? How might this have been a source of hope and comfort to the community?

44So Moses announced to the Israelites the appointed festivals of the LORD.

Olive Oil and Bread Set Before the LORD

24:1–3pp // Ex 27:20–21

24 The LORD said to Moses, 2"Command the Israelites to bring you clear oil of pressed olives for the light so that the lamps may be kept burning continually. 3Outside the curtain that shields the ark of the covenant law in the tent of meeting, Aaron is to tend the lamps before the LORD from evening till morning, continually. This is to be a lasting ordinance for the generations to come. 4The lamps on the pure gold lampstand[v] before the LORD must be tended continually.

5"Take the finest flour and bake twelve loaves of bread,[w] using two-tenths of an ephah[b] for each loaf. 6Arrange them in two stacks, six in each stack, on the table of pure gold[x] before the LORD. 7By each stack put some pure incense as a memorial[c] portion[y] to represent the bread and to be a food offering presented to the LORD. 8This bread is to be set out before the LORD regularly,[z] Sabbath after Sabbath,[a] on behalf of the Israelites, as a lasting covenant. 9It belongs to Aaron and his sons,[b] who are to eat it in the sanctuary area, because it is a most holy part of their perpetual share of the food offerings presented to the LORD."

24:4 [v] Ex 25:31; 31:8
24:5 [w] Ex 25:30
24:6 [x] Ex 25:23-30; 1Ki 7:48
24:7 [y] Lev 2:2
24:8 [z] Nu 4:7; 1Ch 9:32; 2Ch 2:4 [a] Mt 12:5
24:9 [b] Lev 8:31; Mt 12:4; Mk 2:26; Lk 6:4

[a] 38 Or *These festivals are in addition to the LORD's Sabbaths, and these offerings are*
[b] 5 That is, probably about 7 pounds or about 3.2 kilograms
[c] 7 Or *representative*

23:33–43 The Festival of Tabernacles runs for seven days (v. 34); plus, a connected but distinct solemn assembly is on the eighth day (v. 36).

23:23–44 Christians who accept salvation and receive forgiveness must continue in their faith (Col 1:23), just as the ancient Israelites were to maintain their loyalty. Believing in Christ does not exempt us from judgment. Speaking to Christians, Paul wrote: "For we will all stand before God's judgment seat" (Ro 14:10). However, there are two pieces of good news. For those who are forgiven and remain reconciled to God, judgment reaffirms assurance; it does not take it away. When Christ comes in glory, he will know which individuals are really his.

24:2–4 By burning through the night, the lamps parallel the evening regular burnt offering on the outer altar (6:12).

24:8–9 Another regular (v. 8) priestly ritual duty in the outer sanctum was to renew the "bread" of the Presence each Sabbath on the golden table (vv. 5–9).

A Blasphemer Put to Death

10Now the son of an Israelite mother
and an Egyptian father went out among
the Israelites, and a fight broke out in the
camp between him and an Israelite. 11The
son of the Israelite woman blasphemed
the Name[c] with a curse; so they brought
him to Moses. (His mother's name was
Shelomith, the daughter of Dibri the
Danite.) 12They put him in custody until the will of the LORD should be made
clear to them.[d]
13Then the LORD said to Moses: 14"Take
the blasphemer outside the camp. All
those who heard him are to lay their
hands on his head, and the entire assembly is to stone him.[e] 15Say to the Israelites: 'Anyone who curses their God[f]
will be held responsible; 16anyone who
blasphemes the name of the LORD is to
be put to death.[g] The entire assembly
must stone them. Whether foreigner or
native-born, when they blaspheme the
Name they are to be put to death.
17" 'Anyone who takes the life of a human being is to be put to death.[h] 18Any-
one who takes the life of someone's animal must make restitution[i]—life for
life. 19Anyone who injures their neighbor
is to be injured in the same manner:
20fracture for fracture, eye for eye, tooth
for tooth.[j] The one who has inflicted
the injury must suffer the same injury.
21Whoever kills an animal must make
restitution, but whoever kills a human
being is to be put to death.[k] 22You are
to have the same law for the foreigner[l] and the native-born.[m] I am the LORD
your God.' "
23Then Moses spoke to the Israelites,
and they took the blasphemer outside
the camp and stoned him. The Israelites did as the LORD commanded Moses.

The Sabbath Year

25 The LORD said to Moses at Mount
Sinai, 2"Speak to the Israelites and
say to them: 'When you enter the land
I am going to give you, the land itself
must observe a sabbath to the LORD.
3For six years sow your fields, and for
six years prune your vineyards and gather their crops.[n] 4But in the seventh year
the land is to have a year of sabbath rest,
a sabbath to the LORD. Do not sow your
fields or prune your vineyards. 5Do not
reap what grows of itself or harvest the
grapes of your untended vines. The land
is to have a year of rest. 6Whatever the
land yields during the sabbath year[o]
will be food for you—for yourself, your
male and female servants, and the hired
worker and temporary resident who live
among you, 7as well as for your livestock
and the wild animals in your land. Whatever the land produces may be eaten.

The Year of Jubilee

25:8–38Ref // Dt 15:1–11
25:39–55Ref // Ex 21:2–11; Dt 15:12–18

8" 'Count off seven sabbath years—
seven times seven years—so that the
seven sabbath years amount to a period of forty-nine years. 9Then have the

24:11 [c] Ex 3:15
24:12 [d] Ex 18:16; Nu 15:34
24:14 [e] Lev 20:27; Dt 13:9; 17:5,7; 21:21
24:15 [f] Ex 22:28
24:16 [g] 1Ki 21:10, 13; Mt 26:66
24:17 [h] Ge 9:6; Ex 21:12; Nu 35:30-31; Dt 27:24
24:18 [i] ver 21
24:20 [j] Ex 21:24; Mt 5:38*
24:21 [k] ver 17
24:22 [l] Ex 12:49 [m] Nu 9:14; 15:16
25:3 [n] Ex 23:10
25:6 [o] ver 20

24:10–16 The circumstances involved in 24:10–14 generate the ensuing legislation regarding blasphemy and physical assault (vv. 15–22). In fact, the laws are framed by the divine sentence of death on the blasphemer (v. 14) and the report of his execution (v. 23).

Saying God's name could be permissible in OT times (e.g., Ru 2:4). However, the half-Israelite does not simply take God's name in vain as a construction worker might when he accidentally whacks his thumbnail; he curses (Lev 24:11). He assaults the Lord by cursing *him* personally, as shown by the way the following legislation begins (vv. 15–16). This reiterates the command of Ex 22:28.

24:17–22 The following legislation lays down a series of penalties for various kinds of violence related to the case at hand by logical extension (*lex talionis*), including murder, assault, and killing animals belonging to others.

✣ **24:1–23** While the *lex talionis* made good sense for ancient Israel from the viewpoints of justice, theology, and practicality, it could be viewed as "cruel and unusual punishment" today, even for those who perpetrate cruel and unusually painful and damaging crimes. Nevertheless, Leviticus teaches us the importance of respecting the sanctity of another person's body, facing the full consequences of one's physical violence, treating everyone equally before the law, and protecting the rights of victims.

25:2–3 After seven sabbatical years totaling forty-nine years, the Jubilee year is the fiftieth year, beginning the Day of Atonement. The relationship between sabbatical and Jubilee years in Lev 25 parallels the relationship between seven weekly Sabbaths and the Festival of Weeks on the fiftieth day (23:15–16).

25:4–6 Letting the land revert to its natural state carried religious significance. The question arises: "What will we eat in the seventh year?" (v. 20). God answers (vv. 21–22): The harvest in the sixth year had to last over a fallow sabbatical year.

OLD TESTAMENT FESTIVALS AND OTHER SACRED DAYS

NAME	OLD TESTAMENT REFERENCES	OLD TESTAMENT TIME	MODERN EQUIVALENT
Sabbath	Ex 20:8-11; 31:12-17; Lev 23:3; Dt 5:12-15	7th day	Same
Sabbath Year	Ex 23:10-11; Lev 25:1-7	7th year	Same
Year of Jubilee	Lev 25:8-55; 27:17-24; Nu 36:4	50th year; Nisan	Same
Passover	Ex 12:1-14; Lev 23:5; Nu 9:1-14; 28:16; Dt 16:1-3a, 4b-7	1st month (Aviv; Nisan) 14	March-April
Unleavened Bread	Ex 12:15-20; 13:3-10; 23:15; 34:18; Lev 23:6-8; Nu 28:17-25; Dt 16:3b, 4a, 8	1st month (Aviv; Nisan) 15-21	March-April
Firstfruits	Lev 23:9-14	1st month (Aviv; Nisan) 16	March-April
Weeks (Pentecost) (Harvest)	Ex 23:16a; 34:22a; Lev 23:15-21; Nu 28:26-31; Dt 16:9-12	3rd month (Sivan) 6	May-June
Trumpets (later: Rosh Hashanah-New Year's Day)	Lev 23:23-25; Nu 29:1-6	7th month (Tishri; Ethanim) 1	September-October
Day of Atonement (Yom Kippur)	Lev 16; 23:26-32; Nu 29:7-11	7th month (Tishri; Ethanim) 10	September-October
Tabernacles (Booths) (Ingathering)	Ex 23:16b; 34:22b; Lev 23:33-36a, 39-43; Nu 29:12-34; Dt 16:13-15; Zec 14:16-19	7th month (Tishri; Ethanim) 15-21	September-October
Sacred Assembly	Lev 23:36b; Nu 29:35-38	7th month (Tishri; Ethanim) 22	September-October
Purim	Est 9:18-32	12th month (Adar) 14, 15	February-March

On Kislev 25 (mid-December), Hanukkah, the Festival of Dedication or Festival of Lights, commemorated the purification of the temple and altar in the Maccabean period (165/4 BC). This festival is mentioned in Jn 10:22.

DESCRIPTION	PURPOSE	NEW TESTAMENT REFERENCES
Day of rest; no work	Provide rest for people and animals	Mt 12:1-14; 28:1; Lk 4:16; Jn 5:9-10; Ac 13:42; Col 2:16; Heb 4:1-11
Year of rest; fallow fields	Provide rest for land	
Canceled debts; liberation of slaves and indentured servants; land returned to original family owners	Give help to the poor; stabilize society	Lk 4:18-19
Slaying and eating a lamb, together with bitter herbs and bread made without yeast, in every household	Remember Israel's deliverance from Egypt	Mt 26:17; Mk 14:12-26; Jn 2:13; 11:55; 1Co 5:7; Heb 11:28
Eating bread made without yeast; holding several assemblies; making designated offerings	Remember how the Lord brought the Israelites out of Egypt in haste	Mk 14:1; Ac 12:3; 1Co 5:6-8
Presenting a sheaf of the first of the barley harvest as a wave offering; making a burnt offering and a grain offering	Recognize the Lord's bounty in the land	Ro 8:23; 1Co 15:20-23
A festival of joy; mandatory and voluntary offerings, including the firstfruits of the wheat harvest	Show joy and thankfulness for the Lord's blessing of harvest	Ac 2:1-4; 20:16; 1Co 16:8
An assembly on a day of rest commemorated with trumpet blasts and sacrifices	Present Israel before the Lord for his favor	
A day of rest, fasting, and sacrifices of atonement for priests and people and atonement for the tabernacle and altar	Atone for the sins of priests and people and purify the Most Holy Place	Ro 3:24-26; Heb 9:7; 10:3, 19-22
A week of celebration for the harvest; living in booths (temporary shelters) and offering sacrifices	Memorialize the journey from Egypt to Canaan; give thanks for the productivity of Canaan	Jn 7:2, 37
A day of convocation, rest and offering sacrifices	Commemorate the closing of the cycle of festivals	
A day of joy and feasting and giving presents	Remind the Israelites of their national deliverance in the time of Esther	

In addition, New Moon feasts were prescribed (see Nu 28:11-15; 1Sa 20:5; Isa 1:14; see also 1Ch 23:31; Ezr 3:5; Ne 10:33; Ps 81:3; Hos 5:7; Am 8:5; Col 2:16).

trumpet[p] sounded everywhere on the
tenth day of the seventh month; on the
Day of Atonement sound the trumpet
throughout your land. 10Consecrate
the fiftieth year and proclaim liberty[q]
throughout the land to all its inhabitants. It shall be a jubilee[r] for you; each
of you is to return to your family property and to your own clan. 11The fiftieth
year shall be a jubilee for you; do not sow
and do not reap what grows of itself or
harvest the untended vines. 12For it is a
jubilee and is to be holy for you; eat only
what is taken directly from the fields.
13" 'In this Year of Jubilee[s] everyone is
to return to their own property.
14" 'If you sell land to any of your own
people or buy land from them, do not
take advantage of each other.[t] 15You are
to buy from your own people on the basis
of the number of years[u] since the Jubilee.
And they are to sell to you on the basis
of the number of years left for harvesting crops. 16When the years are many,
you are to increase the price, and when
the years are few, you are to decrease
the price,[v] because what is really being
sold to you is the number of crops. 17Do
not take advantage of each other,[w] but
fear your God.[x] I am the LORD your God.[y]
18" 'Follow my decrees and be careful
to obey my laws, and you will live safely
in the land.[z] 19Then the land will yield its
fruit,[a] and you will eat your fill and live
there in safety. 20You may ask, "What
will we eat in the seventh year[b] if we do
not plant or harvest our crops?" 21I will
send you such a blessing[c] in the sixth
year that the land will yield enough for
three years. 22While you plant during
the eighth year, you will eat from the old
crop and will continue to eat from it until
the harvest of the ninth year comes in.[d]
23" 'The land must not be sold perma-

25:9 [p] Lev 23:24
25:10 [q] Isa 61:1; Jer 34:8,15, 17; Lk 4:19 [r] Nu 36:4
25:13 [s] ver 10
25:14 [t] Lev 19:13; 1Sa 12:3,4
25:15 [u] Lev 27:18,23
25:16 [v] ver 27, 51,52
25:17 [w] Pr 22:22; Jer 7:5, 6; 1Th 4:6 [x] Lev 19:14 [y] Lev 19:32
25:18 [z] Lev 26:4, 5; Dt 12:10; Ps 4:8; Jer 23:6
25:19 [a] Lev 26:4
25:20 [b] ver 4
25:21 [c] Dt 28:8, 12; Hag 2:19; Mal 3:10
25:22 [d] Lev 26:10
25:23 [e] Ex 19:5 [f] Ge 23:4; 1Ch 29:15; Ps 39:12; Heb 11:13; 1Pe 2:11
25:25 [g] Ru 2:20; Jer 32:7 [h] Lev 27:13,19, 31; Ru 4:4
25:28 [i] ver 10

Lev 25:8-55 ❖ What might practicing Jubilee look like in the world today? How might believers point to God's grace through radical forgiveness and liberation?

nently, because the land is mine[e] and
you reside in my land as foreigners[f] and
strangers. 24Throughout the land that
you hold as a possession, you must provide for the redemption of the land.
25" 'If one of your fellow Israelites becomes poor and sells some of their property, their nearest relative[g] is to come
and redeem[h] what they have sold. 26If,
however, there is no one to redeem it
for them but later on they prosper and
acquire sufficient means to redeem it
themselves, 27they are to determine the
value for the years since they sold it and
refund the balance to the one to whom
they sold it; they can then go back to
their own property. 28But if they do not
acquire the means to repay, what was
sold will remain in the possession of the
buyer until the Year of Jubilee. It will be
returned in the Jubilee, and they can
then go back to their property.[i]
29" 'Anyone who sells a house in a
walled city retains the right of redemption a full year after its sale. During that
time the seller may redeem it. 30If it is
not redeemed before a full year has
passed, the house in the walled city shall
belong permanently to the buyer and the
buyer's descendants. It is not to be returned in the Jubilee. 31But houses in villages without walls around them are to
be considered as belonging to the open
country. They can be redeemed, and they
are to be returned in the Jubilee.
32" 'The Levites always have the right
to redeem their houses in the Levitical

25:10 The Israelites as privileged servants of the Lord were to recover their landed property and independence after a succession of seven sabbatical years, during which there were no crops.

25:23-24 The starting point for consideration of Israelite ownership of the land is that it was all "crown property" in the sense that it belonged to the divine King. To protect this distribution, the Lord decreed that *nobody* outside the clan to which a given property was attached could hold more than a temporary interest in it.

25:29-31 If a person became poor and sold part of his land, his kinsman should buy it back. If he had no redeemer but his situation later improved, he could redeem the property himself (vv. 26-27). Failing the above options, the land would revert to the original owner at the Jubilee (v. 28).

25:32-33 Real estate belonging to Levites was unique. Their pastures could not be sold at all.

✚ **25:1-55** Our good management is the first phase of a ministry of sharing. By taking good care of the blessings God gives us and passing them on, we acknowledge that they are not simply our own. Even with all our efforts, we would have nothing without the ability that God has given us (Dt 8:17-18). We can't take it all with us anyway.

towns,[j] which they possess. 33So the
property of the Levites is redeemable —
that is, a house sold in any town they
hold — and is to be returned in the Jubilee, because the houses in the towns
of the Levites are their property among
the Israelites. 34But the pastureland belonging to their towns must not be sold;
it is their permanent possession.[k]
35" 'If any of your fellow Israelites become poor[l] and are unable to support
themselves among you, help them[m] as
you would a foreigner and stranger, so
they can continue to live among you.
36Do not take interest[n] or any profit from
them, but fear your God, so that they
may continue to live among you. 37You
must not lend them money at interest
or sell them food at a profit. 38I am the
LORD your God, who brought you out of
Egypt to give you the land of Canaan and
to be your God.[o]
39" 'If any of your fellow Israelites become poor and sell themselves to you, do
not make them work as slaves.[p] 40They
are to be treated as hired workers or temporary residents among you; they are
to work for you until the Year of Jubilee. 41Then they and their children are
to be released, and they will go back to
their own clans and to the property[q] of
their ancestors. 42Because the Israelites
are my servants, whom I brought out of
Egypt, they must not be sold as slaves.
43Do not rule over them ruthlessly,[r] but
fear your God.
44" 'Your male and female slaves are
to come from the nations around you;
from them you may buy slaves. 45You
may also buy some of the temporary residents living among you and members
of their clans born in your country, and
they will become your property. 46You
can bequeath them to your children as
inherited property and can make them
slaves for life, but you must not rule over
your fellow Israelites ruthlessly.
47" 'If a foreigner residing among you
becomes rich and any of your fellow

25:32 [j] Nu 35:1-8; Jos 21:2
25:34 [k] Nu 35:2-5
25:35 [l] Dt 24:14, 15 [m] Dt 15:8; Ps 37:21,26; Lk 6:35
25:36 [n] Ex 22:25; Dt 23:19-20
25:38 [o] Ge 17:7; Lev 11:45
25:39 [p] Ex 21:2; Dt 15:12; 1Ki 9:22
25:41 [q] ver 28
25:43 [r] Ex 1:13; Eze 34:4; Col 4:1

Lev 26:3-4 ❖ How have you experienced the blessings that follow true obedience to God?

Israelites become poor and sell themselves to the foreigner or to a member
of the foreigner's clan, 48they retain the
right of redemption after they have sold
themselves. One of their relatives[s] may
redeem them: 49An uncle or a cousin or
any blood relative in their clan may redeem them. Or if they prosper,[t] they may
redeem themselves. 50They and their
buyer are to count the time from the
year they sold themselves up to the Year
of Jubilee. The price for their release is
to be based on the rate paid to a hired
worker[u] for that number of years. 51If
many years remain, they must pay for
their redemption a larger share of the
price paid for them. 52If only a few years
remain until the Year of Jubilee, they
are to compute that and pay for their
redemption accordingly. 53They are to
be treated as workers hired from year
to year; you must see to it that those to
whom they owe service do not rule over
them ruthlessly.
54" 'Even if someone is not redeemed
in any of these ways, they and their children are to be released in the Year of
Jubilee, 55for the Israelites belong to me
as servants. They are my servants, whom
I brought out of Egypt. I am the LORD
your God.

Reward for Obedience

26 " 'Do not make idols[v] or set up an
image or a sacred stone[w] for yourselves, and do not place a carved stone[x]
in your land to bow down before it. I am
the LORD your God.
2" 'Observe my Sabbaths and have reverence for my sanctuary.[y] I am the LORD.
3" 'If you follow my decrees and are
careful to obey[z] my commands, 4I will
send you rain[a] in its season, and the
ground will yield its crops and the trees

25:48 [s] Ne 5:5
25:49 [t] ver 26
25:50 [u] Job 7:1; Isa 16:14; 21:16
26:1 [v] Ex 20:4; Lev 19:4; Dt 5:8 [w] Ex 23:24 [x] Nu 33:52
26:2 [y] Lev 19:30
26:3 [z] Dt 7:12; 11:13,22; 28:1,9
26:4 [a] Dt 11:14

While it is important that the church not try to take over functions of the state, the church is not exempt from addressing social problems, such as poverty and equality or ecological concerns, just because the state is working on the same problems. Leviticus 25 teaches us that for believers, faith and ethics impact the larger context of our lives.

26:1-2 Staying away from idolatry, keeping Sabbath, and reverencing the Lord's sanctuary are basic ways that the Israelites can show loyalty to him.

26:3-16 The blessings in vv. 3-13 touch the major aspects of life that are dear to an ancient Israelite.

their fruit.[b] 5 Your threshing will continue until grape harvest and the grape harvest will continue until planting, and you will eat all the food you want[c] and live in safety in your land.[d]

6 " 'I will grant peace in the land,[e] and you will lie down[f] and no one will make you afraid.[g] I will remove wild beasts[h] from the land, and the sword will not pass through your country. 7 You will pursue your enemies, and they will fall by the sword before you. 8 Five of you will chase a hundred, and a hundred of you will chase ten thousand, and your enemies will fall by the sword before you.[i]

9 " 'I will look on you with favor and make you fruitful and increase your numbers,[j] and I will keep my covenant[k] with you. 10 You will still be eating last year's harvest when you will have to move it out to make room for the new.[l] 11 I will put my dwelling place[a][m] among you, and I will not abhor you. 12 I will walk[n] among you and be your God, and you will be my people.[o] 13 I am the LORD your God, who brought you out of Egypt so that you would no longer be slaves to the Egyptians; I broke the bars of your yoke[p] and enabled you to walk with heads held high.

Punishment for Disobedience

14 " 'But if you will not listen to me and carry out all these commands,[q] 15 and if you reject my decrees and abhor my laws and fail to carry out all my commands and so violate my covenant, 16 then I will do this to you: I will bring on you sudden terror, wasting diseases and fever[r] that will destroy your sight and sap your strength.[s] You will plant seed in vain, because your enemies will eat it.[t] 17 I will set my face[u] against you so that you will be defeated by your enemies; those who hate you will rule over you,[v] and you will flee even when no one is pursuing you.[w]

18 " 'If after all this you will not listen to me, I will punish you for your sins seven times over.[x] 19 I will break down your stubborn pride[y] and make the sky above you like iron and the ground beneath you like bronze.[z] 20 Your strength will be spent in vain,[a] because your soil will not yield its crops, nor will the trees of your land yield their fruit.[b]

21 " 'If you remain hostile toward me and refuse to listen to me, I will multiply your afflictions seven times over,[c] as your sins deserve. 22 I will send wild animals[d] against you, and they will rob you of your children, destroy your cattle and make you so few in number that your roads will be deserted.

23 " 'If in spite of these things you do not accept my correction[e] but continue to be hostile toward me, 24 I myself will be hostile toward you and will afflict you for your sins seven times over. 25 And I will bring the sword on you to avenge the breaking of the covenant. When you withdraw into your cities, I will send a plague[f] among you, and you will be given into enemy hands. 26 When I cut off your supply of bread,[g] ten women will be able to bake your bread in one oven, and they will dole out the bread by weight. You will eat, but you will not be satisfied.

27 " 'If in spite of this you still do not listen to me but continue to be hostile toward me, 28 then in my anger I will be hostile toward you, and I myself will punish you for your sins seven times over. 29 You will eat the flesh of your sons and the flesh of your daughters.[h] 30 I will destroy your high places,[i] cut down your incense altars[j] and pile your dead bodies[b]

[a] *11* Or *my tabernacle* [b] *30* Or *your funeral offerings*

26:4 [b] Ps 67:6
26:5 [c] Dt 11:15; Joel 2:19, 26; Am 9:13 [d] Lev 25:18
26:6 [e] Ps 29:11; 85:8; 147:14 [f] Ps 4:8 [g] Zep 3:13 [h] ver 22
26:8 [i] Dt 32:30; Jos 23:10
26:9 [j] Ge 17:6; Ne 9:23 [k] Ge 17:7
26:10 [l] Lev 25:22
26:11 [m] Ex 25:8; Ps 76:2; Eze 37:27
26:12 [n] Ge 3:8 [o] 2Co 6:16*
26:13 [p] Eze 34:27
26:14 [q] Dt 28:15-68; Mal 2:2
26:16 [r] Dt 28:22, 35 [s] 1Sa 2:33 [t] Job 31:8
26:17 [u] Lev 17:10 [v] Ps 106:41 [w] ver 36, 37; Dt 28:7, 25; Ps 53:5
26:18 [x] ver 21
26:19 [y] Isa 25:11 [z] Dt 28:23
26:20 [a] Ps 127:1; Isa 17:11 [b] Dt 11:17
26:21 [c] ver 18
26:22 [d] Dt 32:24
26:23 [e] Jer 2:30; 5:3
26:25 [f] Nu 14:12; Eze 5:17
26:26 [g] Ps 105:16; Isa 3:1; Mic 6:14
26:29 [h] Dt 28:53
26:30 [i] 2Ch 34:3; Eze 6:3 [j] Eze 6:6

26:14–39 This list of curses invokes a comprehensive catalogue of calamities. They are much more extensive than the blessings, partly because the blessings are simpler and more obvious and partly because negative motivations need to be more substantial in order to serve as an effective deterrent.

In vv. 14–17 there is fear, sickness, plunder of agricultural produce by enemies, military defeat, and subjection to enemy rulers. In vv. 18–20, introduced by another "if," the Lord threatens to multiply the punishments for their sins by seven.

26:21 The downside of covenant cause and effect is proportional to the depth or aggravation of the sin problem.

26:22 The Lord will commission beasts to thin the population of humans and domestic animals. People will be afraid to venture out.

26:24–26 If they decide not to walk with God by keeping his covenant, he will walk on a collision course with them and bring them all the miseries of military attack. They can run, but they cannot hide.

26:27–39 The dam restraining justice bursts open with a vengeance, disclosing the ultimate horrors of starvation during siege (v. 29), appalling devastation of the land (vv. 30–32), and scattering of the people into exile (vv. 33–35).

26:30 It is fitting that the presumed holiness of

on the lifeless forms of your idols,[k] and I will abhor you. 31I will turn your cities into ruins and lay waste your sanctuaries,[l] and I will take no delight in the pleasing aroma of your offerings. 32I myself will lay waste the land,[m] so that your enemies who live there will be appalled. 33I will scatter you among the nations[n] and will draw out my sword and pursue you. Your land will be laid waste, and your cities will lie in ruins. 34Then the land will enjoy its sabbath years all the time that it lies desolate and you are in the country of your enemies;[o] then the land will rest and enjoy its sabbaths. 35All the time that it lies desolate, the land will have the rest it did not have during the sabbaths you lived in it.

36" 'As for those of you who are left, I will make their hearts so fearful in the lands of their enemies that the sound of a windblown leaf will put them to flight.[p] They will run as though fleeing from the sword, and they will fall, even though no one is pursuing them. 37They will stumble over one another as though fleeing from the sword, even though no one is pursuing them. So you will not be able to stand before your enemies.[q] 38You will perish among the nations; the land of your enemies will devour you.[r] 39Those of you who are left will waste away in the lands of their enemies because of their sins; also because of their ancestors' sins they will waste away.[s]

40" 'But if they will confess their sins and the sins of their ancestors[t] — their unfaithfulness and their hostility toward me, 41which made me hostile toward them so that I sent them into the land of their enemies — then when their uncircumcised hearts[u] are humbled and they pay for their sin, 42I will remember my covenant with Jacob[v] and my covenant with Isaac[w] and my covenant with Abraham, and I will remember the land. 43For the land will be deserted by them and will enjoy its sabbaths while it lies desolate without them. They will pay for their sins because they rejected my laws and abhorred my decrees. 44Yet in spite of this, when they are in the land of their enemies, I will not reject them or abhor[x] them so as to destroy them completely,[y] breaking my covenant[z] with them. I am the LORD their God. 45But for their sake I will remember[a] the covenant with their ancestors whom I brought out of Egypt[b] in the sight of the nations to be their God. I am the LORD.' "

46These are the decrees, the laws and the regulations that the LORD established at Mount Sinai between himself and the Israelites through Moses.[c]

Redeeming What Is the LORD's

27 The LORD said to Moses, 2"Speak to the Israelites and say to them: 'If anyone makes a special vow[d] to dedicate a person to the LORD by giving the equivalent value, 3set the value of a male between the ages of twenty and sixty at

26:30 [k] Eze 6:13
26:31 [l] Ps 74:3-7
26:32 [m] Jer 9:11
26:33 [n] Dt 4:27; Eze 12:15; 20:23; Zec 7:14
26:34 [o] ver 43; 2Ch 36:21
26:36 [p] Eze 21:7
26:37 [q] Jos 7:12
26:38 [r] Dt 4:26
26:39 [s] Eze 4:17
26:40 [t] Jer 3:12-15; Lk 15:18; 1Jn 1:9
26:41 [u] Eze 44:7, 9; Ac 7:51
26:42 [v] Ge 22:15-18; 28:15 [w] Ge 26:5
26:44 [x] Ro 11:2 [y] Dt 4:31; Jer 30:11 [z] Jer 33:26
26:45 [a] Ge 17:7 [b] Ex 6:8; Lev 25:38
26:46 [c] Lev 7:38; 27:34
27:2 [d] Nu 6:2

---

these idols be defiled by corpse contamination because they are like lifeless, impure corpses anyway.

26:36–39 The survivors in exile will be a miserable lot.

26:40–45 We would expect a requirement of extreme reparation for prodigal Israel to be accepted again by the divine Father, but there are no animal sacrifices here: If the Israelites ". . . will confess their sins . . ." (v. 40) and humble themselves before the Lord—admitting they have made bad choices and putting themselves at his mercy, where they really have been all along but wouldn't admit it—then God will remember his covenant.

26:46 The expression "between himself and the Israelites" means that the legislation was placed within the framework of the covenant relationship.

✣ **26:1–46** Our pursuit of happiness will be successful only if we allow happiness to pursue us! Our approach must be indirect. As the ancient Israelites found out through long and bitter experience, directly chasing happiness will only chase it away, as if it were a wild antelope. We get happiness to pursue us by pursuing a positive relationship with God, the source of all blessings (Mt 6:33). It is a matter of priorities. If we want God first, we will have happiness, especially in the age to come (Rev 21–22).

The happiness that God gives is not exactly the same as our human definition of "happiness." It is *far better* (1Co 2:9; cf. Isa 64:4). If we are bent on finding happiness as we define it, with God left out of the picture, relegated to the sidelines or used as a mere tool, we are doomed to failure. According to the Bible, there is simply no such thing as full, genuine happiness without God and the guidance he offers.

27:1–8 The focus of this chapter on holy things links it with earlier portions of Leviticus. Verse 2 introduces the topic of promised gifts in typical case law style. Apparently, what is extraordinary about such a vow is that the gift is a human being. Verse 8 makes a concession for a poor person who wants to make such a vow but cannot afford the usual amount.

fifty shekels[a] of silver, according to the
sanctuary shekel[b];[e] 4for a female, set her
value at thirty shekels[c]; 5for a person between the ages of five and twenty, set the
value of a male at twenty shekels[d] and
of a female at ten shekels[e]; 6for a person
between one month and five years, set
the value of a male at five shekels[f][f] of silver and that of a female at three shekels[g]
of silver; 7for a person sixty years old or
more, set the value of a male at fifteen
shekels[h] and of a female at ten shekels.
8If anyone making the vow is too poor
to pay[g] the specified amount, the person being dedicated is to be presented
to the priest, who will set the value[h] according to what the one making the vow
can afford.
9"'If what they vowed is an animal that
is acceptable as an offering to the LORD,
such an animal given to the LORD becomes holy. 10They must not exchange it
or substitute a good one for a bad one, or
a bad one for a good one;[i] if they should
substitute one animal for another, both it
and the substitute become holy. 11If what
they vowed is a ceremonially unclean
animal — one that is not acceptable as an
offering to the LORD — the animal must
be presented to the priest, 12who will
judge its quality as good or bad. Whatever value the priest then sets, that is
what it will be. 13If the owner wishes to
redeem[j] the animal, a fifth must be added to its value.
14"'If anyone dedicates their house as
something holy to the LORD, the priest
will judge its quality as good or bad.
Whatever value the priest then sets, so
it will remain. 15If the one who dedicates
their house wishes to redeem it,[k] they
must add a fifth to its value, and the
house will again become theirs.
16"'If anyone dedicates to the LORD
part of their family land, its value is to
be set according to the amount of seed
required for it — fifty shekels of silver to
a homer[i] of barley seed. 17If they dedicate
a field during the Year of Jubilee, the
value that has been set remains. 18But if
they dedicate a field after the Jubilee, the
priest will determine the value according to the number of years that remain[l]
until the next Year of Jubilee, and its set
value will be reduced. 19If the one who
dedicates the field wishes to redeem it,
they must add a fifth to its value, and
the field will again become theirs. 20If,
however, they do not redeem the field,
or if they have sold it to someone else,
it can never be redeemed. 21When the
field is released in the Jubilee,[m] it will
become holy, like a field devoted to the
LORD;[n] it will become priestly property.
22"'If anyone dedicates to the LORD
a field they have bought, which is not
part of their family land, 23the priest will
determine its value up to the Year of Jubilee, and the owner must pay its value
on that day as something holy to the
LORD. 24In the Year of Jubilee the field
will revert to the person from whom it
was bought,[o] the one whose land it was.
25Every value is to be set according to
the sanctuary shekel,[p] twenty gerahs[q]
to the shekel.
26"'No one, however, may dedicate the
firstborn of an animal, since the firstborn
already belongs to the LORD;[r] whether
an ox[j] or a sheep, it is the LORD's. 27If it
is one of the unclean animals,[s] it may
be bought back at its set value, adding
a fifth of the value to it. If it is not redeemed, it is to be sold at its set value.
28"'But nothing that a person owns
and devotes[k][t] to the LORD — whether
a human being or an animal or family land — may be sold or redeemed;

27:3 [e] Ex 30:13; Nu 3:47; 18:16
27:6 [f] Nu 18:16
27:8 [g] Lev 5:11 [h] ver 12,14
27:10 [i] ver 33
27:13 [j] ver 15,19; Lev 25:25
27:15 [k] ver 13,20
27:18 [l] Lev 25:15
27:21 [m] Lev 25:10 [n] ver 28; Nu 18:14; Eze 44:29
27:24 [o] Lev 25:28
27:25 [p] Ex 30:13; Nu 18:16 [q] Nu 3:47; Eze 45:12
27:26 [r] Ex 13:2, 12
27:27 [s] ver 11
27:28 [t] Nu 18:14; Jos 6:17-19

[a] *3* That is, about 1 1/4 pounds or about 575 grams; also in verse 16 [b] *3* That is, about 2/5 ounce or about 12 grams; also in verse 25 [c] *4* That is, about 12 ounces or about 345 grams [d] *5* That is, about 8 ounces or about 230 grams [e] *5* That is, about 4 ounces or about 115 grams; also in verse 7 [f] *6* That is, about 2 ounces or about 58 grams [g] *6* That is, about 1 1/4 ounces or about 35 grams [h] *7* That is, about 6 ounces or about 175 grams [i] *16* That is, probably about 300 pounds or about 135 kilograms [j] *26* The Hebrew word can refer to either male or female. [k] *28* The Hebrew term refers to the irrevocable giving over of things or persons to the LORD.

27:9–10 If that which is vowed is a sacrificeable animal, it becomes holy so that no other animal can take its place, not even a better animal.
27:14 Unlike vows, which are conditional promises to be fulfilled in the future, such dedications go into effect immediately.
27:16–25 Either the dedicator is the original owner (vv. 16–21) or he has bought (really leased) someone else's land (vv. 22–25). Redemption by the original owner requires an extra fifth, as expected (v. 19).
27:20–21 At the next Jubilee, when the property would normally revert to the dedicator, it instead becomes the permanent property of the priesthood. It is irrevocably banished to the sphere of holiness.

everything so devoted is most holy to
the LORD.

29" 'No person devoted to destruction[a]
may be ransomed; they are to be put to
death.

30" 'A tithe[u] of everything from the
land, whether grain from the soil or fruit
from the trees, belongs to the LORD; it
is holy to the LORD. 31Whoever would
redeem any of their tithe must add a
fifth of the value to it. 32Every tithe of
the herd and flock — every tenth animal
that passes under the shepherd's rod[v] —
will be holy to the LORD. 33No one may
pick out the good from the bad or make
any substitution.[w] If anyone does make
a substitution, both the animal and its
substitute become holy and cannot be
redeemed.' "

34These are the commands the LORD
gave Moses at Mount Sinai for the Israelites.[x]

27:30 [u] Ge 28:22; 2Ch 31:6; Mal 3:8
27:32 [v] Jer 33:13; Eze 20:37
27:33 [w] ver 10
27:34 [x] Lev 26:46; Dt 4:5

Lev 27:30-33 ❖ How can we praise God with our giving, and why is it so important?

[a] 29 The Hebrew term refers to the irrevocable giving over of things or persons to the LORD, often by totally destroying them.

27:30-32 Tithes are like a firstborn animal in that they are already holy to the Lord and can be redeemed. **27:34** The book of Leviticus ends: "These are the commands the LORD gave Moses on Mount Sinai for the Israelites." This echoes the earlier conclusion in 26:46.

✜ **27:1-34** What is a person worth? A person made in the image of God (Ge 1:26; 9:6) is of inestimable value. How can anyone put a price on the image of God? Because we do not fully comprehend the Original, we cannot appraise our own worth. Life that comes from the holy Creator is sacred. Therefore, treating others as if their lives are cheap is profanity and sacrilege. God's love puts the value of every human being *way* beyond price.

Numbers

Author: Moses
Audience: God's chosen people, the Israelites
Date: Probably between 1446 and 1406 BC

Theme: God judges his rebellious people but reaffirms his intent to bring them into the promised land.

Reading Numbers

Although beginning the book of Numbers with a census and various administrative laws of the Israelites seems dull, much of this book is filled with the action-packed stories of what happened to God's people during the forty years of wandering in the wilderness.

PERSPECTIVE

It's been said that after the wedding comes the marriage. So it was with Israel and God. After the wedding at Sinai—where God proclaimed the covenant vows (Ten Commandments) with awesome splendor, Israel said, "I do," and they built a house (sanctuary) together—there was a journey through the wilderness of real life. Whatever happened, they were in it together. The vows God had given were not only for Israel to keep; they were his vows too. When he had said, "You shall have no other gods before me" (Ex 20:3)—the equivalent of "forsaking all others"—he not only forbade idol worship, but he also pledged himself to be Israel's God.

What happened after that was profoundly disturbing. While the divine Groom lavished care on his bride, bringing her breakfast in bed (manna), protecting her from danger (e.g., poisonous snakes in the Sinai peninsula), and literally hovering over her (in the *shekinah* cloud), she grumbled about the food, blamed his appointed representative (Moses) when anything went wrong, and kept saying she would rather return to the abusive home she had left (Egypt) to find a different husband. Is it any wonder that Israel's new Husband was bewildered?

As the fourth book of the Torah/Pentateuch, Numbers is like the second book (Exodus) in recounting a journey of the Israelites. Numbers picks up the travel story where Exodus leaves off, moving from the Sinai Desert to the steppes of Moab by the Jordan River at the eastern border of Canaan. Between Exodus and Numbers is Leviticus, the legislation of which continues the "wedding" begun in the latter part of Exodus. If that sounds like a long wedding, we are reminded of the fact that the Groom was a deity and the bride was a human nation.

	2200 BC	2100	2000	1900	1800	1700	1600	1500	1400
Moses' birth (c. 1526 BC)								♦	
The plagues; the Passover (c. 1446 BC)									♦
The exodus (c. 1446 BC)									♦
Desert wanderings (c. 1446–1406 BC)									▬
Exploration of Canaan (c. 1443 BC)									♦
Book of Numbers written (c. 1406 BC)									♦
Moses dies; Joshua becomes leader (c. 1406 BC)									♦
Israelites enter Canaan (c. 1406 BC)									♦

It is amazing that the omnipotent deity allows faulty people to have any choice at all. This explains why covenant "marriages" between God and human beings are so messy: He allows us to grow by making our own decisions and enjoying or suffering the consequences.

When the people of Israel make their own choices and the situation in Numbers gravitates to the drastically negative side, the book becomes downright depressing. If we step back from the story and reflect on its relationship to our own adventure, the ironic truth dawns: By showing how God not only could, but did bring his people out of desperate situations and took them to their promised home, the Bible encourages us that he can handle any crises we will ever face. So the more depressing the biblical story, the more powerful its hope for our modern story—provided we stand with Moses, Aaron, Caleb, and Joshua rather than Korah, Dathan, and Abiram.

For more perspective on this book, please see the Introduction to Leviticus.

Key Verses

"'The LORD bless you and keep you; the LORD make his face shine on you and be gracious to you; the LORD turn his face toward you and give you peace.'"

—Numbers 6:24–26

TAKING THE NEXT STEPS

The book of Numbers has two major parts. First, it is a census of the Israelites and a description of their organization around the tabernacle; included are further laws for their worship of God. Second, it is a record of the journey of God's people from Mount Sinai to the borders of Canaan, including the forty years of wandering in the wilderness after the episode of the spies. In spite of all their sins, the Israelites were still God's people; he provided food and water for them, and he protected them from their enemies. And when they did sin, Moses' intercession led to their forgiveness.

This section of God's Word contains practical insights for daily living. (1) The numerous occasions when some or all of the Israelites rebelled against the Lord, or more specifically against Moses, remind us how quickly we can allow anxiety, fear, selfishness and jealousy to take control of our lives. (2) God's anger at such sins, to the point of being ready to entirely destroy the Israelite nation, warns us how seriously God takes disobedience and our lack of trust in him. Not even Moses, when he struck the rock rather than spoke to it, escaped God's punishment. (3) But God's mercy and faithfulness to his promises is victorious over his anger and judgment. He forgives us through Jesus

Christ, who hung on the cross like the serpent in the wilderness and intercedes for us as Moses did for his people. (4) As Christians we know from experience that God provides the food for the day, the strength for the moment, the daily protection from danger. The caring God of the wilderness is the caring God of today.

WHAT TO LOOK FOR IN NUMBERS

- Israel's grumbling about manna (ch. 11)
- Miriam and Aaron's opposition to Moses (ch. 12)
- The spies and Israel's rebellion (chs. 13–14)
- The rebellion of Korah and his allies (ch. 16)
- The budding of Aaron's staff (ch. 17)
- Moses' striking the rock (ch. 20)
- The bronze serpent on a pole (ch. 21)
- Balaam's blessing rather than cursing the Israelites (chs. 22–24)

The Census

1 The LORD spoke to Moses in the tent
of meeting[a] in the Desert of Sinai[b] on
the first day of the second month[c] of the
second year after the Israelites came out
of Egypt. He said: 2"Take a census[d] of
the whole Israelite community by their
clans and families, listing every man by
name, one by one. 3You and Aaron are to
count according to their divisions all the
men in Israel who are twenty years old
or more[e] and able to serve in the army.
4One man from each tribe, each of them
the head of his family,[f] is to help you.[g]
5These are the names of the men who
are to assist you:

from Reuben,[h] Elizur son of Shedeur;
6from Simeon, Shelumiel son of Zurishaddai;
7from Judah,[i] Nahshon son of Amminadab;[j]
8from Issachar,[k] Nethanel son of Zuar;
9from Zebulun,[l] Eliab son of Helon;
10from the sons of Joseph:
from Ephraim,[m] Elishama son of Ammihud;
from Manasseh, Gamaliel son of Pedahzur;
11from Benjamin, Abidan son of Gideoni;
12from Dan,[n] Ahiezer son of Ammishaddai;
13from Asher,[o] Pagiel son of Okran;
14from Gad, Eliasaph son of Deuel;[p]
15from Naphtali,[q] Ahira son of Enan."

16These were the men appointed from
the community, the leaders[r] of their ancestral tribes. They were the heads of the
clans of Israel.[s]
17Moses and Aaron took these men
whose names had been specified, 18and
they called the whole community together on the first day of the second month.[t]
The people registered their ancestry[u] by
their clans and families, and the men
twenty years old or more were listed by

1:1 [a] Ex 40:2 [b] Ex 19:1 [c] Ex 40:17
1:2 [d] Ex 30:11-16; Nu 26:2
1:3 [e] Ex 30:14
1:4 [f] ver 16 [g] Ex 18:21; Dt 1:15
1:5 [h] Ge 29:32; Dt 33:6; Rev 7:5
1:7 [i] Ge 29:35; Ps 78:68 [j] Ru 4:20; 1Ch 2:10; Lk 3:32
1:8 [k] Ge 30:18
1:9 [l] ver 30
1:10 [m] ver 32
1:12 [n] ver 38
1:13 [o] ver 40
1:14 [p] Nu 2:14
1:15 [q] ver 42
1:16 [r] Ex 18:25 [s] ver 4; Ex 18:21; Nu 7:2
1:18 [t] ver 1 [u] Ezr 2:59; Heb 7:3

1:1–3 Just as Leviticus begins with a speech by the Lord to Moses, Numbers commences with a divine speech "in the tent of meeting" (v. 1). The Lord commands that the Israelites take a military census of men twenty years old or more who are to serve as soldiers (vv. 2–3). This is preliminary to the organization of an army that can exert maximum force to conquer Canaan.

1:3–16 As we would expect for a tribal nation, the census is structured according to hierarchical social groups determined by the patriarchal family tree (v. 2). A chieftain representing each tribe (vv. 3–16) assists Moses and Aaron, the high priest. The high priest's involvement is appropriate because the Israelites are preparing for *holy* war, which they will fight in under the Lord's direction. Also through the priest, undoubtedly by means of the Urim and Thummim in his breastplate, the army can inquire of the Lord for guidance in making military decisions (Jdg 20:27–28).

1:17–19 The fact that Moses promptly implements the census on the same day the Lord gives him the command conveys the impression that he is eager to get rolling.

name, one by one, 19as the LORD commanded Moses. And so he counted them
in the Desert of Sinai:

20 From the descendants of Reuben[v]
the firstborn son of Israel:
All the men twenty years old or
more who were able to serve in
the army were listed by name, one
by one, according to the records
of their clans and families. 21The
number from the tribe of Reuben
was 46,500.

22 From the descendants of Simeon:[w]
All the men twenty years old or
more who were able to serve in
the army were counted and listed
by name, one by one, according
to the records of their clans and
families. 23The number from the
tribe of Simeon was 59,300.

24 From the descendants of Gad:[x]
All the men twenty years old or
more who were able to serve in
the army were listed by name,
according to the records of their
clans and families. 25The number
from the tribe of Gad was 45,650.

26 From the descendants of Judah:[y]
All the men twenty years old or
more who were able to serve in
the army were listed by name,
according to the records of their
clans and families. 27The number from the tribe of Judah was
74,600.

28 From the descendants of Issachar:[z]
All the men twenty years old or
more who were able to serve in
the army were listed by name,
according to the records of their
clans and families. 29The number from the tribe of Issachar was
54,400.

30 From the descendants of Zebulun:[a]
All the men twenty years old or
more who were able to serve in
the army were listed by name,
according to the records of their
clans and families. 31The number
from the tribe of Zebulun was
57,400.

32 From the sons of Joseph:
From the descendants of Ephraim:[b]
All the men twenty years old or
more who were able to serve in
the army were listed by name,
according to the records of their
clans and families. 33The number from the tribe of Ephraim was
40,500.

34 From the descendants of Manasseh:[c]
All the men twenty years old or
more who were able to serve in
the army were listed by name,
according to the records of their
clans and families. 35The number
from the tribe of Manasseh was
32,200.

36 From the descendants of Benjamin:[d]
All the men twenty years old or
more who were able to serve in
the army were listed by name,
according to the records of their
clans and families. 37The number
from the tribe of Benjamin was
35,400.

38 From the descendants of Dan:[e]
All the men twenty years old or
more who were able to serve in
the army were listed by name,
according to the records of their
clans and families. 39The number
from the tribe of Dan was 62,700.

40 From the descendants of Asher:[f]
All the men twenty years old or
more who were able to serve in
the army were listed by name,
according to the records of their
clans and families. 41The number
from the tribe of Asher was 41,500.

42 From the descendants of Naphtali:[g]
All the men twenty years old or
more who were able to serve in
the army were listed by name,
according to the records of their
clans and families. 43The number from the tribe of Naphtali was
53,400.

1:20 [v] Nu 26:5-11; Rev 7:5
1:22 [w] Nu 26:12-14; Rev 7:7
1:24 [x] Ge 30:11; Nu 26:15-18; Rev 7:5
1:26 [y] Ge 29:35; Nu 26:19-22; Mt 1:2; Rev 7:5
1:28 [z] Nu 26:23-25; Rev 7:7
1:30 [a] Nu 26:26-27; Rev 7:8
1:32 [b] Nu 26:35-37
1:34 [c] Nu 26:28-34; Rev 7:6
1:36 [d] Nu 26:38-41; 2Ch 17:17; Rev 7:8
1:38 [e] Ge 30:6; Nu 26:42-43
1:40 [f] Nu 26:44-47; Rev 7:6
1:42 [g] Nu 26:48-50; Rev 7:6

1:20–43 These numbers list the total men from twelve tribes and range from a high of 74,600 for Judah (v. 27) to a low of 32,200 for Manasseh (v. 35). The grand total is 603,550 (v. 46). The military census does not include a thirteenth tribe—Levi—because the Levites are not to be part of the regular army. Rather, their job is to guard and take care of the tabernacle. Thus, they are counted separately later on (chs. 3–4).

44These were the men counted by
Moses and Aaron[h] and the twelve leaders of Israel, each one representing his
family. 45All the Israelites twenty years
old or more who were able to serve in
Israel's army were counted according to
their families. 46The total number was
603,550.[i]
47The ancestral tribe of the Levites,[j]
however, was not counted[k] along with
the others. 48The LORD had said to Moses: 49"You must not count the tribe of
Levi or include them in the census of
the other Israelites. 50Instead, appoint
the Levites to be in charge of the tabernacle of the covenant law[l] — over all its
furnishings and everything belonging to
it. They are to carry the tabernacle and
all its furnishings; they are to take care
of it and encamp around it. 51Whenever
the tabernacle is to move, the Levites are
to take it down, and whenever the tabernacle is to be set up, the Levites shall
do it.[m] Anyone else who approaches it
is to be put to death. 52The Israelites are
to set up their tents by divisions, each
of them in their own camp under their
standard.[n] 53The Levites, however, are to
set up their tents around the tabernacle
of the covenant law so that my wrath will
not fall[o] on the Israelite community. The
Levites are to be responsible for the care
of the tabernacle of the covenant law.[p]"
54The Israelites did all this just as the
LORD commanded Moses.

The Arrangement of the Tribal Camps

2 The LORD said to Moses and Aaron:
2"The Israelites are to camp around
the tent of meeting some distance from
it, each of them under their standard[q]
and holding the banners of their family."

1:44 [h] Nu 26:64
1:46 [i] Ex 12:37; 38:26; Nu 2:32; 26:51
1:47 [j] Nu 2:33; 26:57 [k] Nu 4:3, 49
1:50 [l] Ex 38:21; Ac 7:44
1:51 [m] Nu 3:38; 4:1-33
1:52 [n] Nu 2:2; Ps 20:5
1:53 [o] Lev 10:6; Nu 16:46; 18:5 [p] Nu 18:2-4
2:2 [q] Nu 1:52; Ps 74:4; Isa 31:9

Nu 1:53 ❖ How does the task of the Levites, camped closest around God's tabernacle, point to the work of Christ? What does this arrangement mean for our lives today?

3On the east, toward the sunrise,
the divisions of the camp of Judah
are to encamp under their standard.
The leader of the people of Judah is
Nahshon son of Amminadab.[r] 4His
division numbers 74,600.
5The tribe of Issachar will camp
next to them. The leader of the people of Issachar is Nethanel son of
Zuar.[s] 6His division numbers 54,400.
7The tribe of Zebulun will be next.
The leader of the people of Zebulun
is Eliab son of Helon.[t] 8His division
numbers 57,400.
9All the men assigned to the camp
of Judah, according to their divisions, number 186,400. They will
set out first.[u]

10On the south will be the divisions of the camp of Reuben under
their standard. The leader of the people of Reuben is Elizur son of Shedeur.[v] 11His division numbers 46,500.
12The tribe of Simeon will camp
next to them. The leader of the people of Simeon is Shelumiel son of
Zurishaddai.[w] 13His division numbers 59,300.
14The tribe of Gad will be next. The
leader of the people of Gad is Eliasaph son of Deuel.[a][x] 15His division
numbers 45,650.

2:3 [r] Nu 10:14; Ru 4:20; 1Ch 2:10
2:5 [s] Nu 1:8
2:7 [t] Nu 1:9
2:9 [u] Nu 10:14
2:10 [v] Nu 1:5
2:12 [w] Nu 1:6
2:14 [x] Nu 1:14

[a] *14* Many manuscripts of the Masoretic Text, Samaritan Pentateuch and Vulgate (see also 1:14); most manuscripts of the Masoretic Text *Reuel*

1:54 This obedience is the initial benchmark for the book of Numbers, but as the book progresses we will find that on more than one occasion the people do *everything but* what the Lord commands through Moses.

APPLICATION ✥ 1:1-54 Do Christian family members need to fight alongside one another today? In Eph 6:10-12 Paul describes a battle "against the spiritual forces of evil" in which each Christian is involved. We need each other's support as a "family" of believers (Gal 6:10; cf. 1Pe 4:17). This "family" encompasses all spiritual "brothers and sisters" (cf. Gal 3:26-29; 1Pe 3:8), including physical family members (e.g., Eph 5:21—6:4; 1Pe 3:1-7). Like the ancient Israelites, we are stronger together as bonded units than we are if we try to fight alone.

2:1-34 This chapter outlines the arrangement of tribal groups within the war camp and specifies the locations of the various tribes around the sanctuary. The twelve tribes, not including Levi, are to be divided into four groups of three tribes each. With reference to the sanctuary and Levite camp in the middle, each group of three tribes occupies a position to one of the four directions of the compass. Just as the Lord's sanctuary occupies the protected middle of the camp, which protects it in the event of an attack (cf. Ex 17:8), so it travels with the Levites in the middle of the marching column in case the Israelites are attacked in front or from behind (cf. Nu 21:1).

16All the men assigned to the camp of Reuben,[y] according to their divisions, number 151,450. They will set out second.

17Then the tent of meeting and the camp of the Levites[z] will set out in the middle of the camps. They will set out in the same order as they encamp, each in their own place under their standard.

18On the west will be the divisions of the camp of Ephraim[a] under their standard. The leader of the people of Ephraim is Elishama son of Ammihud.[b] 19His division numbers 40,500.
20The tribe of Manasseh will be next to them. The leader of the people of Manasseh is Gamaliel son of Pedahzur.[c] 21His division numbers 32,200.
22The tribe of Benjamin will be next. The leader of the people of Benjamin is Abidan son of Gideoni.[d] 23His division numbers 35,400.
24All the men assigned to the camp of Ephraim,[e] according to their divisions, number 108,100. They will set out third.[f]

25On the north will be the divisions of the camp of Dan under their standard. The leader of the people of Dan is Ahiezer son of Ammishaddai.[g] 26His division numbers 62,700.
27The tribe of Asher will camp next to them. The leader of the people of Asher is Pagiel son of Okran.[h] 28His division numbers 41,500.
29The tribe of Naphtali will be next. The leader of the people of Naphtali is Ahira son of Enan.[i] 30His division numbers 53,400.

2:16 [y] Nu 10:18
2:17 [z] Nu 1:53; 10:21
2:18 [a] Ge 48:20; Jer 31:18-20 [b] Nu 1:10
2:20 [c] Nu 1:10
2:22 [d] Nu 1:11; Ps 68:27
2:24 [e] Nu 10:22 [f] Ps 80:2
2:25 [g] Nu 1:12
2:27 [h] Nu 1:13
2:29 [i] Nu 1:15

2:31 [j] Nu 10:25
2:32 [k] Ex 38:26; Nu 1:46
2:33 [l] Nu 1:47; 26:57-62
3:1 [m] Ex 6:27
3:2 [n] Ex 6:23; Nu 26:60
3:3 [o] Ex 28:41
3:4 [p] Lev 10:2 [q] Lev 10:1 [r] 1Ch 24:1
3:6 [s] Dt 10:8; 31:9; 1Ch 15:2 [t] Nu 8:6-22; 18:1-7; 2Ch 29:11

Nu 2:34 ❖ This chapter shows the whole family of Israel being obedient to God's commands. While we know it didn't last, how can this story inspire our personal and corporate obedience to God's directives?

31All the men assigned to the camp of Dan number 157,600. They will set out last,[j] under their standards.

32These are the Israelites, counted according to their families. All the men in the camps, by their divisions, number 603,550.[k] 33The Levites, however, were not counted[l] along with the other Israelites, as the LORD commanded Moses.

34So the Israelites did everything the LORD commanded Moses; that is the way they encamped under their standards, and that is the way they set out, each of them with their clan and family.

The Levites

3 This is the account of the family of Aaron and Moses[m] at the time the LORD spoke to Moses at Mount Sinai.
2The names of the sons of Aaron were Nadab the firstborn and Abihu, Eleazar and Ithamar.[n] 3Those were the names of Aaron's sons, the anointed priests,[o] who were ordained to serve as priests.
4Nadab and Abihu, however, died before the LORD[p] when they made an offering with unauthorized fire before him in the Desert of Sinai.[q] They had no sons, so Eleazar and Ithamar served as priests during the lifetime of their father Aaron.[r]
5The LORD said to Moses, 6"Bring the tribe of Levi[s] and present them to Aaron the priest to assist him.[t] 7They are to

---

2:17 Because the order of encampment corresponds to the marching order, the Israelites can hit the road or set up camp with optimum efficiency.

✚ **2:1–34** Our modern culture revels in personal independence. Living in private dwellings, perhaps in restricted-access communities, we can live our own lives the way we want and control much of our contact with other people. Everything is designed around us for our security, convenience, and comfort. In our private cars we have wraparound sound. Commercials bombard us from all directions to reinforce what we already know: We are the center of the universe, and our desires govern it. But we cannot be the center of our own religion if we want to claim the religion of the Bible.

3:1–4 This chapter fills in details regarding the tribe of Levi, within which the family of Aaron is singled out for the priesthood. When Nadab and Abihu died, they left no sons to carry on lines of descendants. Consequently, the priesthood is limited to the two branches from Aaron's surviving sons: Eleazar and Ithamar.
3:6–9 Non-priestly Levites are to assist the priests by performing duties that serve the sanctuary

perform duties for him and for the whole community at the tent of meeting by doing the work[u] of the tabernacle. 8They are to take care of all the furnishings of the tent of meeting, fulfilling the obligations of the Israelites by doing the work of the tabernacle. 9Give the Levites to Aaron and his sons;[v] they are the Israelites who are to be given wholly to him.[a] 10Appoint Aaron and his sons to serve as priests;[w] anyone else who approaches the sanctuary is to be put to death."[x]

11The LORD also said to Moses, 12"I have taken the Levites[y] from among the Israelites in place of the first male offspring[z] of every Israelite woman. The Levites are mine,[a] 13for all the firstborn are mine.[b] When I struck down all the firstborn in Egypt, I set apart for myself every firstborn in Israel, whether human or animal. They are to be mine. I am the LORD."

14The LORD said to Moses in the Desert of Sinai, 15"Count[c] the Levites by their families and clans. Count every male a month old or more."[d] 16So Moses counted them, as he was commanded by the word of the LORD.

17These were the names of the sons of Levi:[e]
Gershon, Kohath and Merari.[f]
18These were the names of the Gershonite clans:
Libni and Shimei.[g]
19The Kohathite clans:
Amram, Izhar, Hebron and Uzziel.[h]
20The Merarite clans:[i]
Mahli and Mushi.[j]

These were the Levite clans, according to their families.

21To Gershon belonged the clans of the Libnites and Shimeites;[k] these were the Gershonite clans. 22The number of all the males a month old or more who were counted was 7,500. 23The Gershonite clans were to camp on the west, behind the tabernacle. 24The leader of the families of the Gershonites was Eliasaph son of Lael. 25At the tent of meeting the Gershonites were responsible for the care of the tabernacle[l] and tent, its coverings,[m] the curtain at the entrance[n] to the tent of meeting, 26the curtains of the courtyard[o], the curtain at the entrance to the courtyard surrounding the tabernacle and altar, and the ropes[p] — and everything related to their use.

27To Kohath belonged the clans of the Amramites, Izharites, Hebronites and Uzzielites;[q] these were the Kohathite clans. 28The number of all the males a month old or more was 8,600.[b] The Kohathites were responsible for the care of the sanctuary. 29The Kohathite clans were to camp on the south side[r] of the tabernacle. 30The leader of the families of the Kohathite clans was Elizaphan son of Uzziel. 31They were responsible for the care of the ark,[s] the table,[t] the lampstand,[u] the altars,[v] the articles of the sanctuary used in ministering, the curtain,[w] and everything related to their use.[x] 32The chief leader of the Levites was Eleazar son of Aaron, the priest. He was appointed over those who were responsible for the care of the sanctuary.

33To Merari belonged the clans of the Mahlites and the Mushites;[y] these were the Merarite clans. 34The number of all the males a month old or more who were counted was 6,200. 35The leader of the families of the Merarite clans was Zuriel

Nu 3:13 ❖ What does it mean for God to set someone apart for himself (see Ps 139:13–18)?

3:7 [u] Lev 8:35; Nu 1:50
3:9 [v] Nu 8:19; 18:6
3:10 [w] Ex 29:9 [x] Nu 1:51
3:12 [y] Mal 2:4 [z] ver 41; Nu 8:16,18 [a] Ex 13:2
3:13 [b] Ex 13:12
3:15 [c] ver 39 [d] Nu 26:62
3:17 [e] Ge 46:11 [f] Ex 6:16
3:18 [g] Ex 6:17
3:19 [h] Ex 6:18
3:20 [i] Ge 46:11 [j] Ex 6:19
3:21 [k] Ex 6:17
3:25 [l] Ex 25:9 [m] Ex 26:14 [n] Ex 26:36; Nu 4:25
3:26 [o] Ex 27:9 [p] Ex 35:18
3:27 [q] 1Ch 26:23
3:29 [r] Nu 1:53
3:31 [s] Ex 25:10-22 [t] Ex 25:23 [u] Ex 25:31 [v] Ex 27:1; 30:1 [w] Ex 26:33 [x] Nu 4:15
3:33 [y] Ex 6:19

[a] 9 Most manuscripts of the Masoretic Text; some manuscripts of the Masoretic Text, Samaritan Pentateuch and Septuagint (see also 8:16) *to me* [b] 28 Hebrew; some Septuagint manuscripts *8,300*

---

infrastructure. However, Aaron and his sons are to guard their priestly privileges.

3:14–37 Although Levites are not soldiers, it is necessary to count them and organize their workforce. Rather than counting males twenty years of age or more who can serve in the army, the register of Levites begins with one-month-old babies (v. 15) because the members of this tribe substitute for firstborn male Israelites (vv. 40–41), who are to be redeemed with five shekels when they are one month old (18:15–16).

3:21–32 Since the Kohathite clan is that of the priests, the administrative chief of all the Levites is a Kohathite: Eleazar, son of Aaron, the high priest (v. 32).

3:33–38 The Merarites are to camp on the north side of the tabernacle and take care of the entire framework of the sanctuary. The encampment of Moses and the priests is to guard the sanctuary on the east, where it is most vulnerable because that is where its entrance is located. Again the text warns that an unauthorized person who encroaches on priestly privileges is to be put to death (v. 38).

son of Abihail; they were to camp on the north side of the tabernacle.[z] 36 The Merarites were appointed[a] to take care of the frames of the tabernacle, its crossbars, posts, bases, all its equipment, and everything related to their use, 37 as well as the posts of the surrounding courtyard with their bases, tent pegs and ropes.

38 Moses and Aaron and his sons were to camp to the east[b] of the tabernacle, toward the sunrise, in front of the tent of meeting.[c] They were responsible for the care of the sanctuary[d] on behalf of the Israelites. Anyone else who approached the sanctuary was to be put to death.[e]

39 The total number of Levites counted at the LORD's command by Moses and Aaron according to their clans, including every male a month old or more, was 22,000.[f]

40 The LORD said to Moses, "Count all the firstborn Israelite males who are a month old or more[g] and make a list of their names. 41 Take the Levites for me in place of all the firstborn of the Israelites,[h] and the livestock of the Levites in place of all the firstborn of the livestock of the Israelites. I am the LORD."

42 So Moses counted all the firstborn of the Israelites, as the LORD commanded him. 43 The total number of firstborn males a month old or more, listed by name, was 22,273.[i]

44 The LORD also said to Moses, 45 "Take the Levites in place of all the firstborn of Israel, and the livestock of the Levites in place of their livestock. The Levites are to be mine. I am the LORD. 46 To redeem[j] the 273 firstborn Israelites who exceed the number of the Levites, 47 collect five shekels[a][k] for each one, according to the sanctuary shekel,[l] which weighs twenty gerahs.[m] 48 Give the money for the redemption of the additional Israelites to Aaron and his sons."

49 So Moses collected the redemption money from those who exceeded the number redeemed by the Levites. 50 From the firstborn of the Israelites he collected silver weighing 1,365 shekels,[b][n] according to the sanctuary shekel. 51 Moses gave the redemption money to Aaron and his sons, as he was commanded by the word of the LORD.

The Kohathites

4 The LORD said to Moses and Aaron: 2 "Take a census[o] of the Kohathite branch of the Levites by their clans and families. 3 Count all the men from thirty to fifty years of age[p] who come to serve in the work at the tent of meeting.

4 "This is the work of the Kohathites at the tent of meeting: the care of the most holy things.[q] 5 When the camp is to move, Aaron and his sons are to go in and take down the shielding curtain[r] and put it over the ark of the covenant law.[s] 6 Then they are to cover the curtain with a durable leather,[c] spread a cloth of solid blue over that and put the poles[t] in place.

7 "Over the table of the Presence[u] they are to spread a blue cloth and put on it the plates, dishes and bowls, and the jars for drink offerings; the bread that is continually there[v] is to remain on it. 8 They are to spread a scarlet cloth over them, cover that with the durable leather and put the poles in place.

9 "They are to take a blue cloth and cover the lampstand that is for light, together with its lamps, its wick trimmers and trays,[w] and all its jars for the olive oil used to supply it. 10 Then they are to wrap it and all its accessories in a covering of the durable leather and put it on a carrying frame.

11 "Over the gold altar[x] they are to spread a blue cloth and cover that with the durable leather and put the poles in place.

12 "They are to take all the articles used for ministering in the sanctuary, wrap them in a blue cloth, cover that with the durable leather and put them on a carrying frame.

13 "They are to remove the ashes from the bronze altar[y] and spread a purple cloth over it. 14 Then they are to place on it all the utensils used for ministering at

3:35 [z] Nu 1:53; 2:25
3:36 [a] Nu 4:32
3:38 [b] Nu 2:3 [c] Nu 1:53 [d] ver 7; Nu 18:5 [e] ver 10; Nu 1:51
3:39 [f] Nu 26:62
3:40 [g] ver 15
3:41 [h] ver 12
3:43 [i] ver 39
3:46 [j] Ex 13:13; Nu 18:15
3:47 [k] Lev 27:6 [l] Ex 30:13 [m] Lev 27:25
3:50 [n] ver 46-48

4:2 [o] Ex 30:12
4:3 [p] ver 23; Nu 8:25; 1Ch 23:3,24,27; Ezr 3:8
4:4 [q] ver 19
4:5 [r] Ex 26:31,33 [s] Ex 25:10,16
4:6 [t] Ex 25:13-15; 1Ki 8:7; 2Ch 5:8
4:7 [u] Ex 25:23, 29; Lev 24:6 [v] Ex 25:30
4:9 [w] Ex 25:31, 37,38
4:11 [x] Ex 30:1
4:13 [y] Ex 27:1-8

[a] *47* That is, about 2 ounces or about 58 grams
[b] *50* That is, about 35 pounds or about 16 kilograms
[c] *6* Possibly the hides of large aquatic mammals; also in verses 8, 10, 11, 12, 14 and 25

4:4–20 The job description of the Kohathites is by far the longest and most complicated because it involves careful coordination with the priests, who are to cover the sacred objects of furniture before the other, non-priestly Kohathites can carry them.

the altar, including the firepans, meat
forks,[z] shovels and sprinkling bowls.[a]
Over it they are to spread a covering of
the durable leather and put the poles[b]
in place.
15"After Aaron and his sons have finished covering the holy furnishings and
all the holy articles, and when the camp
is ready to move, only then are the Kohathites to come and do the carrying.[c]
But they must not touch the holy things
or they will die.[d] The Kohathites are to
carry those things that are in the tent
of meeting.
16"Eleazar[e] son of Aaron, the priest, is
to have charge of the oil for the light,[f]
the fragrant incense, the regular grain
offering[g] and the anointing oil. He is to
be in charge of the entire tabernacle and
everything in it, including its holy furnishings and articles."
17The LORD said to Moses and Aaron,
18"See that the Kohathite tribal clans are
not destroyed from among the Levites.
19So that they may live and not die when
they come near the most holy things,[h] do
this for them: Aaron and his sons are to
go into the sanctuary and assign to each
man his work and what he is to carry.
20But the Kohathites must not go in to
look[i] at the holy things, even for a moment, or they will die."

The Gershonites

21The LORD said to Moses, 22"Take a
census also of the Gershonites by their
families and clans. 23Count all the men
from thirty to fifty years of age[j] who
come to serve in the work at the tent
of meeting.
24"This is the service of the Gershonite
clans in their carrying and their other
work: 25They are to carry the curtains of
the tabernacle,[k] that is, the tent of meeting,[l] its covering[m] and its outer covering
of durable leather, the curtains for the
entrance to the tent of meeting, 26the
curtains of the courtyard surrounding
the tabernacle and altar, the curtain for
the entrance to the courtyard, the ropes
and all the equipment used in the service
of the tent. The Gershonites are to do all
that needs to be done with these things.
27All their service, whether carrying or
doing other work, is to be done under the
direction of Aaron and his sons. You shall
assign to them as their responsibility all
they are to carry. 28This is the service of
the Gershonite clans[n] at the tent of meeting. Their duties are to be under the direction of Ithamar son of Aaron, the priest.

The Merarites

29"Count the Merarites by their clans
and families.[o] 30Count all the men from
thirty to fifty years of age who come to
serve in the work at the tent of meeting.
31As part of all their service at the tent,
they are to carry the frames of the tabernacle, its crossbars, posts and bases,[p]
32as well as the posts of the surrounding
courtyard with their bases, tent pegs,
ropes, all their equipment and everything related to their use. Assign to each
man the specific things he is to carry.
33This is the service of the Merarite clans

Nu 4:25 ❖ Even carrying tabernacle curtains is a special task in God's community. What simple tasks can we do to glorify God? How can we start to engage in this way today?

4:14 [z] 2Ch 4:16 [a] Jer 52:18 [b] Ex 27:6
4:15 [c] Nu 7:9 [d] Nu 1:51; 2Sa 6:6,7
4:16 [e] Lev 10:6 [f] Ex 25:6 [g] Ex 29:41; Lev 6:14-23
4:19 [h] ver 15
4:20 [i] Ex 19:21; 1Sa 6:19
4:23 [j] ver 3; 1Ch 23:3,24,27
4:25 [k] Ex 27:10-18; Nu 3:26 [l] Nu 3:25 [m] Ex 26:14
4:28 [n] Nu 7:7
4:29 [o] Ge 46:11
4:31 [p] Nu 3:36

4:24-28 When the Kohathites have emptied the sanctuary of its furniture and utensils, the Gershonites are to pack up and carry away all the fabric and skin coverings of the sanctuary and its court, including the ropes that go with them.

4:31-33 After they have stripped the portable sanctuary down to its skeleton, the Merarites are to carry the disassembled pieces of this framework and everything pertaining to it.

✣ **3:1—4:49** At the ancient Israelite sanctuary, the Levites do what appears to be menial labor: maintenance, guarding, packing, and hauling. But all of it is honorable and vitally important because it is for the divine King. Similarly, the smallest and most insignificant task that contributes to God's work today is important: cleaning the church, changing its light bulbs, preparing food for a social event, visiting a sick person, teaching a Scriptural song to a child, encouraging a neighbor, and so on.

As in Bible times, service for God is anywhere he leads, not just at church. Some find his work in the classroom, others in the boardroom. Some help the least of Christ's brothers and sisters on the streets of San Francisco or Calcutta, others the more outwardly fortunate in posh apartments and country clubs. Everyone has a place and a role to play. For the person who seeks to do everything to God's glory (cf. 1Co 10:31), life is holy. It is as though every meal is a sacrament, every word a prayer, and every deed an act of worship.

as they work at the tent of meeting under the direction of Ithamar son of Aaron, the priest."

The Numbering of the Levite Clans

34 Moses, Aaron and the leaders of the community counted the Kohathites[q] by their clans and families. 35 All the men from thirty to fifty years of age who came to serve in the work at the tent of meeting, 36 counted by clans, were 2,750. 37 This was the total of all those in the Kohathite clans[r] who served at the tent of meeting. Moses and Aaron counted them according to the LORD's command through Moses.

38 The Gershonites[s] were counted by their clans and families. 39 All the men from thirty to fifty years of age who came to serve in the work at the tent of meeting, 40 counted by their clans and families, were 2,630. 41 This was the total of those in the Gershonite clans who served at the tent of meeting. Moses and Aaron counted them according to the LORD's command.

42 The Merarites were counted by their clans and families. 43 All the men from thirty to fifty years of age who came to serve in the work at the tent of meeting, 44 counted by their clans, were 3,200. 45 This was the total of those in the Merarite clans.[t] Moses and Aaron counted them according to the LORD's command through Moses.

46 So Moses, Aaron and the leaders of Israel counted all the Levites by their clans and families. 47 All the men from thirty to fifty years of age[u] who came to do the work of serving and carrying the tent of meeting 48 numbered 8,580.[v] 49 At the LORD's command through Moses, each was assigned his work and told what to carry.

Thus they were counted,[w] as the LORD commanded Moses.

The Purity of the Camp

5 The LORD said to Moses, 2 "Command the Israelites to send away from the camp anyone who has a defiling skin disease[a][x] or a discharge[y] of any kind, or who is ceremonially unclean[z] because of a dead body. 3 Send away male and female alike; send them outside the camp so they will not defile their camp, where I dwell among them.[a]" 4 The Israelites did so; they sent them outside the camp. They did just as the LORD had instructed Moses.

Restitution for Wrongs

5 The LORD said to Moses, 6 "Say to the Israelites: 'Any man or woman who wrongs another in any way[b] and so is unfaithful[b] to the LORD is guilty[c] 7 and must confess[d] the sin they have committed. They must make full restitution[e] for the wrong they have done, add a fifth of the value to it and give it all to the person they have wronged. 8 But if that person has no close relative to whom restitution can be made for the wrong, the restitution belongs to the LORD and must be given to the priest, along with the ram with which atonement is made for the wrongdoer.[f] 9 All the sacred contributions the Israelites bring to a priest will belong to him.[g] 10 Sacred things belong to their owners, but what they give to the priest will belong to the priest.[h]'"

The Test for an Unfaithful Wife

11 Then the LORD said to Moses, 12 "Speak to the Israelites and say to them: 'If a man's wife goes astray[i] and is unfaithful

4:34 [q] ver 2
4:37 [r] Nu 3:27
4:38 [s] Ge 46:11
4:45 [t] ver 29
4:47 [u] ver 3
4:48 [v] Nu 3:39
4:49 [w] Nu 1:47
5:2 [x] Lev 13:46 [y] Lev 15:2; Mt 9:20 [z] Lev 13:3; Nu 9:6-10
5:3 [a] Lev 26:12; Nu 35:34; 2Co 6:16
5:6 [b] Lev 6:2 [c] Lev 5:14-6:7
5:7 [d] Lev 5:5; 26:40; Jos 7:19; Lk 19:8 [e] Lev 6:5
5:8 [f] Lev 6:6, 7; 7:7
5:9 [g] Lev 6:17; 7:6-14
5:10 [h] Lev 10:13
5:12 [i] Ex 20:14

Nu 5:6 ❖ How do we respond to the fact that wronging another person is considered unfaithfulness to God? What does this show about how we treat others (see Mt 25:40)?

[a] 2 The Hebrew word for *defiling skin disease,* traditionally translated "leprosy," was used for various diseases affecting the skin. [b] 6 Or *woman who commits any wrong common to mankind*

5:1–4 The more stringent rules regarding genital discharge and corpse contamination appear to reflect an elevation in the sacral status of the Israelite war camp. The reason for sending impure persons away is not to avoid the spread of ordinary sickness but to avoid defiling the holy camp in which the Lord dwells among his people (v. 3). **5:5–10** The main innovation of the Nu 5 unit is in v. 8, which deals with the contingency that the wronged person dies and leaves no kinsman to whom reparation can be paid. The solution is that the person who committed the wrong pays the reparation to the priest, as the Lord's representative, along with the required reparation offering of a ram of "atonement" (v. 8). **5:11–31** Here a remarkable law concerning a woman

to him 13 so that another man has sexual relations with her,[j] and this is hidden from her husband and her impurity is undetected (since there is no witness against her and she has not been caught in the act), 14 and if feelings of jealousy[k] come over her husband and he suspects his wife and she is impure — or if he is jealous and suspects her even though she is not impure — 15 then he is to take his wife to the priest. He must also take an offering of a tenth of an ephah[a][l] of barley flour[m] on her behalf. He must not pour olive oil on it or put incense on it, because it is a grain offering for jealousy, a reminder-offering[n] to draw attention to wrongdoing.

16 " 'The priest shall bring her and have her stand before the LORD. 17 Then he shall take some holy water in a clay jar and put some dust from the tabernacle floor into the water. 18 After the priest has had the woman stand before the LORD, he shall loosen her hair[o] and place in her hands the reminder-offering, the grain offering for jealousy, while he himself holds the bitter water that brings a curse. 19 Then the priest shall put the woman under oath and say to her, "If no other man has had sexual relations with you and you have not gone astray[p] and become impure while married to your husband, may this bitter water that brings a curse not harm you. 20 But if you have gone astray[q] while married to your husband and you have made yourself impure by having sexual relations with a man other than your husband" — 21 here the priest is to put the woman under this curse[r] — "may the LORD cause you to become a curse[b] among your people when he makes your womb miscarry and your abdomen swell. 22 May this water[s] that brings a curse[t] enter your body so that your abdomen swells or your womb miscarries."

" 'Then the woman is to say, "Amen. So be it.[u]"

23 " 'The priest is to write these curses on a scroll[v] and then wash them off into the bitter water. 24 He shall make the woman drink the bitter water that brings a curse, and this water that brings a curse and causes bitter suffering will enter her. 25 The priest is to take from her hands the grain offering for jealousy, wave it before the LORD[w] and bring it to the altar. 26 The priest is then to take a handful of the grain offering as a memorial[c] offering and burn it on the altar; after that, he is to have the woman drink the water. 27 If she has made herself impure and been unfaithful to her husband, this will be the result: When she is made to drink the water that brings a curse and causes bitter suffering, it will enter her, her abdomen will swell and her womb will miscarry, and she will become a curse.[x] 28 If, however, the woman has not made herself impure, but is clean, she will be cleared of guilt and will be able to have children.

5:13 [j] Lev 18:20; 20:10
5:14 [k] Pr 6:34; SS 8:6
5:15 [l] Ex 16:36 [m] Lev 6:20 [n] Eze 29:16
5:18 [o] Lev 10:6; 1Co 11:6
5:19 [p] ver 12, 29
5:20 [q] ver 12
5:21 [r] Jos 6:26; 1Sa 14:24; Ne 10:29
5:22 [s] Ps 109:18 [t] ver 18 [u] Dt 27:15
5:23 [v] Jer 45:1
5:25 [w] Lev 8:27
5:27 [x] Isa 43:28; 65:15; Jer 26:6; 29:18; 42:18; 44:12, 22; Zec 8:13

[a] *15* That is, probably about 3 1/2 pounds or about 1.6 kilograms [b] *21* That is, may he cause your name to be used in cursing (see Jer. 29:22); or, may others see that you are cursed; similarly in verse 27. [c] *26* Or *representative*

---

suspected of adultery intertwines matters of impurity (vv. 13–14, 20, 27–29) and unfaithfulness to a husband (vv. 12, 27) within the social context of the Israelite community.

The case is particularly problematic because (1) it deals with suspicion rather than clear-cut guilt; (2) guilt or innocence can be impossible for a human tribunal to establish as a result of the secret nature of the offense; (3) the stakes are high—adultery is a capital offense (Lev 20:10); (4) unresolved suspicion can wreck a marriage; and (5) suspicion could be lethal to a woman, since men controlled legal matters.

5:13 The suspected-adulteress passage never uses a word that specifies adultery that is punishable by human law when the guilty parties are discovered (Lev 20:10). Only God can judge.

5:15 To request the Lord's judgment, the jealous husband must bring a grain offering without oil and incense, two elements associated with happier occasions (Lev 2:1, 15).

5:16–22 The priest takes some holy water, probably from the sacred laver/basin and adds dust from the dirt floor of the holy tabernacle (v. 17). The point is not the water's dirtiness but its holiness. He then places her under oath before the Lord (vv. 19–22).

5:21–22, 27 If a suspected adulteress is guilty, the punishment will fit the crime. The Lord will put/set her as a curse among her people by putting physical maladies in the relevant area of her body. Hebrew terminology specifies outcomes that any Israelite woman dreads: social stigma, physical suffering, and inability to bear children.

5:23–26 The priest writes the curses and then physically rubs off the words into the holy water so that it symbolically contains the curses. Next, the woman drinks the holy water that is now bitter with conditional curses. If she is guilty, the water causes the bitter suffering specified in the oath (vv. 24, 27). But if she is pure/innocent, she is vindicated and "will be able to have children" (v. 28).

29“‘This, then, is the law of jealousy
when a woman goes astray[y] and makes
herself impure while married to her
husband, 30or when feelings of jealousy
come over a man because he suspects his
wife. The priest is to have her stand before the LORD and is to apply this entire
law to her. 31The husband will be innocent of any wrongdoing, but the woman
will bear the consequences[z] of her sin.’”

The Nazirite

6 The LORD said to Moses, 2“Speak to
the Israelites and say to them: ‘If a
man or woman wants to make a special
vow[a], a vow of dedication to the LORD as a
Nazirite,[b] 3they must abstain from wine[c]
and other fermented drink and must not
drink vinegar[d] made from wine or other
fermented drink. They must not drink
grape juice or eat grapes or raisins. 4As
long as they remain under their Nazirite
vow, they must not eat anything that
comes from the grapevine, not even the
seeds or skins.

5“‘During the entire period of their
Nazirite vow, no razor[e] may be used on
their head.[f] They must be holy until the
period of their dedication to the LORD is
over; they must let their hair grow long.

6“‘Throughout the period of their dedication to the LORD, the Nazirite must not
go near a dead body.[g] 7Even if their own
father or mother or brother or sister dies,
they must not make themselves ceremonially unclean[h] on account of them,
because the symbol of their dedication
to God is on their head. 8Throughout
the period of their dedication, they are
consecrated to the LORD.

9“‘If someone dies suddenly in the
Nazirite’s presence, thus defiling the
hair that symbolizes their dedication,[i]
they must shave their head on the seventh day—the day of their cleansing.[j]
10Then on the eighth day they must
bring two doves or two young pigeons[k]
to the priest at the entrance to the tent
of meeting. 11The priest is to offer one as
a sin offering[a] and the other as a burnt
offering[l] to make atonement[m] for the
Nazirite because they sinned by being
in the presence of the dead body. That
same day they are to consecrate their
head again. 12They must rededicate
themselves to the LORD for the same
period of dedication and must bring a
year-old male lamb as a guilt offering.
The previous days do not count, because
they became defiled during their period
of dedication.

13“‘Now this is the law of the Nazirite
when the period of their dedication is

5:29 [y] ver 19
5:31 [z] Lev 5:1; 20:17
6:2 [a] Ge 28:20; Ac 21:23 [b] Jdg 13:5; 16:17; Am 2:11,12
6:3 [c] Lk 1:15 [d] Ru 2:14; Ps 69:21; Pr 10:26
6:5 [e] Ps 52:2; 57:4; 59:7; Isa 7:20; Eze 5:1 [f] 1Sa 1:11
6:6 [g] Lev 21:1-3; Nu 19:11-22
6:7 [h] Nu 9:6
6:9 [i] ver 18 [j] Lev 14:9
6:10 [k] Lev 5:7; 14:22
6:11 [l] Ge 8:20 [m] Ex 29:36

Nu 6:2–3 ❖ What is the purpose of these periods of self-denial and special devotion to God? How do we integrate such practices into our lives?

[a] *11* Or *purification offering*; also in verses 14 and 16

5:29–31 A husband’s suspicion is not an accusation for which he would be liable if she were innocent.

5:1–31 As marriage partners are to each other, God is the exclusive covenant partner of his people. Covenant intimacy demands this exclusiveness. He forbids his people to engage in idolatry or worship of other deities because he is “a jealous God” (Ex 20:5; 34:14; Dt 4:24; 5:9; 6:15).

6:1–7 There are three lifestyle restrictions that a temporary Nazirite must scrupulously observe throughout the entire period of dedication. (1) A Nazirite must remain separate from all alcoholic beverages, vinegar, and any other grape product, even if it is not fermented (vv. 3–4). (2) The Nazirite must not have his or her hair cut (v. 5). (3) The Nazirite must not go near a dead body, even that of a close relative (vv. 6–7).

6:5, 8 The Nazirite’s uncut hair is the outward symbol of separation to special holiness to the Lord. The holiness of the Nazirite is analogous in some ways to that of the high priest.

6:9–12 In addition to the usual purification for corpse contamination, the Nazirite must shave his or her head (v. 9). This removes the sign of Naziriteship. On the eighth day a sacrifice of two birds, serving as a purification offering supplemented by a burnt offering, provides compensation for the unintentional sin of breaking the vow (vv. 10–11). The same day as the purification and burnt offerings, the Israelite must begin the period of Naziriteship all over again (vv. 11–12).

6:13–21 These verses outline a ceremony for termination of a successfully completed Nazirite period, after which the Nazirite restrictions are lifted. As part of the completion ceremony, the Nazirite must shave his or her head and put the hair on the altar fire.

6:1–21 Some restrictions bring freedom. A person who abstains from alcoholic beverages (including a Nazirite) is free from fear that he or she might get into trouble as a result of being intoxicated. Faithful marriage partners spare themselves many health and emotional risks. Restrictions on leaders and their families protect them from physical or character assassination.

over.[n] They are to be brought to the entrance to the tent of meeting. 14There they are to present their offerings to the LORD: a year-old male lamb without defect for a burnt offering, a year-old ewe lamb without defect for a sin offering,[o] a ram without defect for a fellowship offering, 15together with their grain offerings and drink offerings,[p] and a basket of bread made with the finest flour and without yeast — thick loaves with olive oil mixed in, and thin loaves brushed with olive oil.[q]

16" 'The priest is to present all these before the LORD and make the sin offering and the burnt offering. 17He is to present the basket of unleavened bread and is to sacrifice the ram as a fellowship offering to the LORD, together with its grain offering and drink offering.

18" 'Then at the entrance to the tent of meeting, the Nazirite must shave off the hair that symbolizes their dedication.[r] They are to take the hair and put it in the fire that is under the sacrifice of the fellowship offering.

19" 'After the Nazirite has shaved off the hair that symbolizes their dedication, the priest is to place in their hands a boiled shoulder of the ram, and one thick loaf and one thin loaf from the basket, both made without yeast. 20The priest shall then wave these before the LORD as a wave offering; they are holy and belong to the priest, together with the breast that was waved and the thigh that was presented. After that, the Nazirite may drink wine.[s]

21" 'This is the law of the Nazirite who vows offerings to the LORD in accordance with their dedication, in addition to whatever else they can afford. They must fulfill the vows they have made, according to the law of the Nazirite.' "

6:13 [n]Ac 21:26
6:14 [o]Lev 14:10; Nu 15:27
6:15 [p]Nu 15:1-7 [q]Ex 29:2; Lev 2:4
6:18 [r]ver 9; Ac 21:24
6:20 [s]Ecc 9:7
6:23 [t]Dt 21:5; 1Ch 23:13
6:24 [u]Dt 28:3-6; Ps 28:9 [v]1Sa 2:9; Ps 17:8
6:25 [w]Job 29:24; Ps 31:16; 80:3; 119:135 [x]Ge 43:29; Ps 25:16; 86:16
6:26 [y]Ps 4:6; 44:3 [z]Ps 29:11; 37:11,37; Jn 14:27
6:27 [a]Dt 28:10; 2Sa 7:23; 2Ch 7:14; Ne 9:10; Jer 25:29
7:1 [b]Ex 40:17 [c]Ex 40:9 [d]ver 84,88; Ex 40:10
7:2 [e]Nu 1:5-16
7:7 [f]Nu 4:24-26,28

Nu 7:2-3 ❖ What material offerings or donations can we give for use in God's community?

The Priestly Blessing

22The LORD said to Moses, 23"Tell Aaron and his sons, 'This is how you are to bless[t] the Israelites. Say to them:

24" ' "The LORD bless you[u]
and keep you;[v]
25the LORD make his face shine on
you[w]
and be gracious to you;[x]
26the LORD turn his face[y] toward you
and give you peace.[z]" '

27"So they will put my name[a] on the Israelites, and I will bless them."

Offerings at the Dedication of the Tabernacle

7 When Moses finished setting up the tabernacle,[b] he anointed and consecrated it and all its furnishings.[c] He also anointed and consecrated the altar and all its utensils.[d] 2Then the leaders of Israel,[e] the heads of families who were the tribal leaders in charge of those who were counted, made offerings. 3They brought as their gifts before the LORD six covered carts and twelve oxen — an ox from each leader and a cart from every two. These they presented before the tabernacle.

4The LORD said to Moses, 5"Accept these from them, that they may be used in the work at the tent of meeting. Give them to the Levites as each man's work requires."

6So Moses took the carts and oxen and gave them to the Levites. 7He gave two carts and four oxen to the Gershonites,[f] as their work required, 8and he gave four

---

6:24–26 The blessing here is brief but poetic, with three pairs of parallels. Each pair begins with Yahweh as subject and wishes for him to have a favorable attitude: blessing, making his face shine, and lifting up his face. These ancient expressions of favor appear in other texts (Ru 2:4). The second member of each pair wishes for Yahweh to do something positive for his people: guard, be gracious, and give well-being.

✣ **6:22–27** Hebrews 4:14–16 invites Christians to ask, as they approach God's throne through their sympathetic High Priest in heaven, to receive mercy and grace in time of need. So why don't we ask more? If our prayers are real to God, are they real to us? Do we have confidence that our praises and petitions to God, feeble and unfocused as they are, have been successfully transmitted to him with the aid of his Spirit (Ro 8:26)?

7:1–9 The chieftains, representing their tribes (not including Levi), brought their gifts to the sanctuary when Moses anointed and thereby consecrated it. The chiefs gave six wagons and twelve oxen for transporting the sanctuary (vv. 3–8). The Kohathites did not need wagons because they transported the sacred furniture on their shoulders by poles (v. 9).

carts and eight oxen to the Merarites,[g] as their work required. They were all under the direction of Ithamar son of Aaron, the priest. 9But Moses did not give any to the Kohathites, because they were to carry on their shoulders[h] the holy things, for which they were responsible.

10When the altar was anointed,[i] the leaders brought their offerings for its dedication[j] and presented them before the altar. 11For the LORD had said to Moses, "Each day one leader is to bring his offering for the dedication of the altar."

12The one who brought his offering on the first day was Nahshon son of Amminadab of the tribe of Judah.

13His offering was one silver plate weighing a hundred and thirty shekels[a] and one silver sprinkling bowl weighing seventy shekels,[b] both according to the sanctuary shekel,[k] each filled with the finest flour mixed with olive oil as a grain offering;[l] 14one gold dish weighing ten shekels,[c] filled with incense;[m] 15one young bull,[n] one ram and one male lamb a year old for a burnt offering;[o] 16one male goat for a sin offering[d];[p] 17and two oxen, five rams, five male goats and five male lambs a year old to be sacrificed as a fellowship offering.[q] This was the offering of Nahshon son of Amminadab.[r]

18On the second day Nethanel son of Zuar,[s] the leader of Issachar, brought his offering.

19The offering he brought was one silver plate weighing a hundred and thirty shekels and one silver sprinkling bowl weighing seventy shekels, both according to the sanctuary shekel, each filled with the finest flour mixed with olive oil as a grain offering; 20one gold dish[t] weighing ten shekels, filled with incense; 21one young bull, one ram and one male lamb a year old for a burnt offering; 22one male goat for a sin offering; 23and two oxen, five rams, five male goats and five male lambs a year old to be sacrificed as a fellowship offering. This was the offering of Nethanel son of Zuar.

24On the third day, Eliab son of Helon,[u] the leader of the people of Zebulun, brought his offering.

25His offering was one silver plate weighing a hundred and thirty shekels and one silver sprinkling bowl weighing seventy shekels, both according to the sanctuary shekel, each filled with the finest flour mixed with olive oil as a grain offering; 26one gold dish weighing ten shekels, filled with incense; 27one young bull, one ram and one male lamb a year old for a burnt offering; 28one male goat for a sin offering; 29and two oxen, five rams, five male goats and five male lambs a year old to be sacrificed as a fellowship offering. This was the offering of Eliab son of Helon.

30On the fourth day Elizur son of Shedeur,[v] the leader of the people of Reuben, brought his offering.

31His offering was one silver plate weighing a hundred and thirty shekels and one silver sprinkling bowl weighing seventy shekels, both according to the sanctuary shekel, each filled with the finest flour mixed with olive oil as a grain offering; 32one gold dish weighing ten shekels, filled with incense; 33one young bull, one ram and one male lamb a year old for a burnt offering; 34one male goat for a sin offering; 35and two oxen, five rams, five male goats and five male lambs a year old to be sacrificed as a fellowship offering. This was the offering of Elizur son of Shedeur.

36On the fifth day Shelumiel son of Zurishaddai,[w] the leader of the people of Simeon, brought his offering.

7:8 [g] Nu 4:31-33
7:9 [h] Nu 4:15
7:10 [i] ver 1 [j] 2Ch 7:9
7:13 [k] Ex 30:13; Nu 3:47 [l] Lev 2:1
7:14 [m] Ex 30:34
7:15 [n] Ex 24:5; 29:3; Nu 28:11 [o] Lev 1:3
7:16 [p] Lev 4:3,23
7:17 [q] Lev 3:1 [r] Nu 1:7
7:18 [s] Nu 1:8
7:20 [t] ver 14
7:24 [u] Nu 1:9
7:30 [v] Nu 1:5
7:36 [w] Nu 1:6

[a] *13* That is, about 3 1/4 pounds or about 1.5 kilograms; also elsewhere in this chapter
[b] *13* That is, about 1 3/4 pounds or about 800 grams; also elsewhere in this chapter
[c] *14* That is, about 4 ounces or about 115 grams; also elsewhere in this chapter
[d] *16* Or *purification offering*; also elsewhere in this chapter

7:10–38 Having introduced the twelve tribal chieftains in ch. 7, the rest of the chapter (except for v. 89) continues with an inventory of the chieftains' other offerings, even though they brought them earlier for the service of the outer altar when it was initiated/inaugurated shortly after it was anointed (vv. 10–88; cf. v. 1).

37His offering was one silver plate
weighing a hundred and thirty
shekels and one silver sprinkling
bowl weighing seventy shekels, both
according to the sanctuary shekel,
each filled with the finest flour
mixed with olive oil as a grain offering; 38one gold dish weighing ten
shekels, filled with incense; 39one
young bull, one ram and one male
lamb a year old for a burnt offering;
40one male goat for a sin offering;
41and two oxen, five rams, five male
goats and five male lambs a year
old to be sacrificed as a fellowship
offering. This was the offering of
Shelumiel son of Zurishaddai.

42On the sixth day Eliasaph son of Deuel,[x]
the leader of the people of Gad, brought
his offering.
43His offering was one silver plate
weighing a hundred and thirty
shekels and one silver sprinkling
bowl weighing seventy shekels, both
according to the sanctuary shekel,
each filled with the finest flour
mixed with olive oil as a grain offering; 44one gold dish weighing ten
shekels, filled with incense; 45one
young bull, one ram and one male
lamb a year old for a burnt offering;
46one male goat for a sin offering;
47and two oxen, five rams, five male
goats and five male lambs a year old
to be sacrificed as a fellowship offering. This was the offering of Eliasaph
son of Deuel.

48On the seventh day Elishama son of
Ammihud,[y] the leader of the people of
Ephraim, brought his offering.
49His offering was one silver plate
weighing a hundred and thirty
shekels and one silver sprinkling
bowl weighing seventy shekels, both
according to the sanctuary shekel,
each filled with the finest flour
mixed with olive oil as a grain offering; 50one gold dish weighing ten
shekels, filled with incense; 51one
young bull, one ram and one male
lamb a year old for a burnt offering;
52one male goat for a sin offering;
53and two oxen, five rams, five male
goats and five male lambs a year
old to be sacrificed as a fellowship
offering. This was the offering of
Elishama son of Ammihud.[z]

7:42 [x] Nu 1:14
7:48 [y] Nu 1:10
7:53 [z] Nu 1:10

7:54 [a] Nu 1:10; 2:20
7:60 [b] Nu 1:11
7:66 [c] Nu 1:12; 2:25

54On the eighth day Gamaliel son of Pedahzur,[a] the leader of the people of Manasseh, brought his offering.
55His offering was one silver plate
weighing a hundred and thirty
shekels and one silver sprinkling
bowl weighing seventy shekels, both
according to the sanctuary shekel,
each filled with the finest flour
mixed with olive oil as a grain offering; 56one gold dish weighing ten
shekels, filled with incense; 57one
young bull, one ram and one male
lamb a year old for a burnt offering;
58one male goat for a sin offering;
59and two oxen, five rams, five male
goats and five male lambs a year
old to be sacrificed as a fellowship
offering. This was the offering of Gamaliel son of Pedahzur.

60On the ninth day Abidan son of Gideoni,[b] the leader of the people of Benjamin,
brought his offering.
61His offering was one silver plate
weighing a hundred and thirty
shekels and one silver sprinkling
bowl weighing seventy shekels, both
according to the sanctuary shekel,
each filled with the finest flour
mixed with olive oil as a grain offering; 62one gold dish weighing ten
shekels, filled with incense; 63one
young bull, one ram and one male
lamb a year old for a burnt offering;
64one male goat for a sin offering;
65and two oxen, five rams, five male
goats and five male lambs a year old
to be sacrificed as a fellowship offering. This was the offering of Abidan
son of Gideoni.

66On the tenth day Ahiezer son of Ammishaddai,[c] the leader of the people of
Dan, brought his offering.
67His offering was one silver plate
weighing a hundred and thirty
shekels and one silver sprinkling
bowl weighing seventy shekels, both
according to the sanctuary shekel,
each filled with the finest flour
mixed with olive oil as a grain offering; 68one gold dish weighing ten
shekels, filled with incense; 69one
young bull, one ram and one male
lamb a year old for a burnt offering;
70one male goat for a sin offering;
71and two oxen, five rams, five male
goats and five male lambs a year old

to be sacrificed as a fellowship offering. This was the offering of Ahiezer
son of Ammishaddai.

72 On the eleventh day Pagiel son of Okran,[d] the leader of the people of Asher,
brought his offering.
73 His offering was one silver plate
weighing a hundred and thirty
shekels and one silver sprinkling
bowl weighing seventy shekels, both
according to the sanctuary shekel,
each filled with the finest flour
mixed with olive oil as a grain offering; 74 one gold dish weighing ten
shekels, filled with incense; 75 one
young bull, one ram and one male
lamb a year old for a burnt offering;
76 one male goat for a sin offering;
77 and two oxen, five rams, five male
goats and five male lambs a year old
to be sacrificed as a fellowship offering. This was the offering of Pagiel
son of Okran.

78 On the twelfth day Ahira son of Enan,[e]
the leader of the people of Naphtali,
brought his offering.
79 His offering was one silver plate
weighing a hundred and thirty
shekels and one silver sprinkling
bowl weighing seventy shekels, both
according to the sanctuary shekel,
each filled with the finest flour
mixed with olive oil as a grain offering; 80 one gold dish weighing ten
shekels, filled with incense; 81 one
young bull, one ram and one male
lamb a year old for a burnt offering;
82 one male goat for a sin offering;
83 and two oxen, five rams, five male
goats and five male lambs a year old
to be sacrificed as a fellowship offering. This was the offering of Ahira
son of Enan.

84 These were the offerings of the Israelite leaders for the dedication of the
altar when it was anointed:[f] twelve silver
plates, twelve silver sprinkling bowls[g]
and twelve gold dishes.[h] 85 Each silver
plate weighed a hundred and thirty shekels, and each sprinkling bowl seventy
shekels. Altogether, the silver dishes
weighed two thousand four hundred
shekels,[a] according to the sanctuary
shekel. 86 The twelve gold dishes filled
with incense weighed ten shekels each,
according to the sanctuary shekel. Altogether, the gold dishes weighed a hundred and twenty shekels.[b] 87 The total
number of animals for the burnt offering
came to twelve young bulls, twelve rams
and twelve male lambs a year old, together with their grain offering. Twelve
male goats were used for the sin offering. 88 The total number of animals for
the sacrifice of the fellowship offering
came to twenty-four oxen, sixty rams,
sixty male goats and sixty male lambs
a year old. These were the offerings for
the dedication of the altar after it was
anointed.[i]

89 When Moses entered the tent of
meeting to speak with the LORD,[j] he
heard the voice speaking to him from
between the two cherubim above the
atonement cover[k] on the ark of the covenant law. In this way the LORD spoke
to him.

Setting Up the Lamps

8 The LORD said to Moses, 2 "Speak to
Aaron and say to him, 'When you set
up the lamps, see that all seven light up
the area in front of the lampstand.'[l] "
3 Aaron did so; he set up the lamps so
that they faced forward on the lampstand, just as the LORD commanded
Moses. 4 This is how the lampstand
was made: It was made of hammered

7:72 [d] Nu 1:13
7:78 [e] Nu 1:15; 2:29
7:84 [f] ver 1, 10 [g] Nu 4:14 [h] ver 14
7:88 [i] ver 1,10
7:89 [j] Ex 25:21, 22; 33:9,11 [k] Ps 80:1; 99:1
8:2 [l] Ex 25:37; Lev 24:2,4

[a] *85* That is, about 60 pounds or about 28 kilograms [b] *86* That is, about 3 pounds or about 1.4 kilograms

7:89 At first glance, this last verse of Nu 7 looks isolated, but it harks back to the beginning of the chapter, which refers to Moses' setting up and consecrating the sanctuary.

7:1–89 Like the Israelite chieftains who brought gifts to the Lord at the sanctuary (Nu 7) and the Magi who paid rich homage to the newborn King (Mt 2:11), we have the privilege of joyfully acknowledging God with tangible gifts as well as prayers, songs, and testimonies. When modern people initiate the use of a church and provide it with a van, kitchen utensils, and food for God's work in their community, they are following in the worthy footsteps of Nahshon, Nethanel, Eliab, and their fellow leaders.

8:1–4 Numbers 7–8 refers to initiation of all three major portions of the sanctuary: the outer altar (7:10–88), the inner sanctum (7:89), and the outer sanctum.

gold[m] — from its base to its blossoms.
The lampstand was made exactly like
the pattern[n] the LORD had shown Moses.

The Setting Apart of the Levites

5The LORD said to Moses: 6"Take the
Levites from among all the Israelites
and make them ceremonially clean.[o]
7To purify them, do this: Sprinkle the
water of cleansing[p] on them; then have
them shave their whole bodies[q] and wash
their clothes.[r] And so they will purify
themselves. 8Have them take a young
bull with its grain offering of the finest
flour mixed with olive oil;[s] then you are
to take a second young bull for a sin offering.[a] 9Bring the Levites to the front
of the tent of meeting[t] and assemble the
whole Israelite community.[u] 10You are to
bring the Levites before the LORD, and
the Israelites are to lay their hands on
them.[v] 11Aaron is to present the Levites
before the LORD as a wave offering[w] from
the Israelites, so that they may be ready
to do the work of the LORD.
12"Then the Levites are to lay their
hands on the heads of the bulls,[x] using
one for a sin offering to the LORD and
the other for a burnt offering, to make
atonement[y] for the Levites. 13Have the
Levites stand in front of Aaron and his
sons and then present them as a wave
offering to the LORD. 14In this way you
are to set the Levites apart from the other
Israelites, and the Levites will be mine.[z]
15"After you have purified the Levites
and presented them as a wave offering,[a]
they are to come to do their work at the
tent of meeting. 16They are the Israelites
who are to be given wholly to me. I have
taken them as my own in place of the
firstborn, the first male offspring[b] from
every Israelite woman. 17Every firstborn
male in Israel, whether human or animal,[c] is mine. When I struck down all
the firstborn in Egypt, I set them apart
for myself.[d] 18And I have taken the Levites in place of all the firstborn sons in
Israel.[e] 19From among all the Israelites,
I have given the Levites as gifts to Aaron
and his sons[f] to do the work at the tent
of meeting on behalf of the Israelites[g]
and to make atonement for them[h] so
that no plague will strike the Israelites
when they go near the sanctuary."
20Moses, Aaron and the whole Israelite
community did with the Levites just as
the LORD commanded Moses. 21The Levites purified themselves and washed
their clothes.[i] Then Aaron presented
them as a wave offering before the LORD
and made atonement for them to purify them.[j] 22After that, the Levites came
to do their work at the tent of meeting
under the supervision of Aaron and his
sons. They did with the Levites just as
the LORD commanded Moses.
23The LORD said to Moses, 24"This applies to the Levites: Men twenty-five
years old or more[k] shall come to take
part in the work at the tent of meeting,[l]
25but at the age of fifty, they must retire
from their regular service and work no
longer. 26They may assist their brothers
in performing their duties at the tent of
meeting, but they themselves must not
do the work. This, then, is how you are to
assign the responsibilities of the Levites."

8:4 [m] Ex 25:18, 36; 25:18 [n] Ex 25:9
8:6 [o] Lev 22:2; Isa 1:16; 52:11
8:7 [p] Nu 19:9, 17 [q] Lev 14:9; Dt 21:12 [r] Lev 14:8
8:8 [s] Lev 2:1; Nu 15:8-10
8:9 [t] Ex 40:12 [u] Lev 8:3
8:10 [v] Ac 6:6
8:11 [w] Lev 7:30
8:12 [x] Ex 29:10 [y] Ex 29:36
8:14 [z] Nu 3:12
8:15 [a] Ex 29:24
8:16 [b] Nu 3:12
8:17 [c] Ex 4:23 [d] Ex 13:2; Lk 2:23
8:18 [e] Nu 3:12
8:19 [f] Nu 3:9 [g] Nu 1:53 [h] Nu 16:46
8:21 [i] ver 7 [j] ver 12
8:24 [k] 1Ch 23:3 [l] Ex 38:21; Nu 4:3

[a] 8 Or *purification offering*; also in verse 12

Nu 8:7 ❖ Do Christians still need to purify themselves through certain actions? How does 1 John 1:7 shape our understanding of being purified for God?

8:5-19 Before the Levites can begin their sacred duties of transporting the sanctuary and its contents, they must be ritually purified and set apart from the other Israelites (v. 7).

8:9-11 Unlike the ordination of the priests, the authorization service for the Levites does not include consecration with anointing oil. Members of the Israelite community are to lay their hands on the Levites.

8:14-19 The Levites are to do the work of the sanctuary on behalf of the rest of the Israelites and are to ransom them so that no plague will strike the community.

8:23-26 The end of Nu 8 specifies the ages of men included in the Levite workforce: twenty-five to fifty. When the sanctuary later found a permanent resting place at Jerusalem and the Levites' job description changed from carrying it to less rigorous duties at the temple, David instructed that they be counted from age twenty with no upper age limit (1Ch 23:24-27).

✣ **8:1-26** Just as Levites were specially set apart to do tasks for the benefit of the priests and the Israelite community (3:6-7; 8:5-22), deacons were set apart to serve the Christian community by doing administrative tasks so that the apostles could be free for spiritual leadership (Ac 6:1-6). The dedications of Levites and deacons reinforce the concept that seemingly mundane tasks done for the Lord and his community are sacred.

The Passover

9 The LORD spoke to Moses in the Desert of Sinai in the first month[m] of the second year after they came out of Egypt.[n] He said, 2“Have the Israelites celebrate the Passover at the appointed time. 3Celebrate it at the appointed time, at twilight on the fourteenth day of this month, in accordance with all its rules and regulations.[o]”

4So Moses told the Israelites to celebrate the Passover, 5and they did so in the Desert of Sinai at twilight on the fourteenth day of the first month.[p] The Israelites did everything just as the LORD commanded Moses.

6But some of them could not celebrate the Passover on that day because they were ceremonially unclean[q] on account of a dead body. So they came to Moses and Aaron[r] that same day 7and said to Moses, “We have become unclean because of a dead body, but why should we be kept from presenting the LORD’s offering with the other Israelites at the appointed time?”

8Moses answered them, “Wait until I find out what the LORD commands concerning you.”[s]

9Then the LORD said to Moses, 10“Tell the Israelites: ‘When any of you or your descendants are unclean because of a dead body or are away on a journey, they are still to celebrate[t] the LORD’s Passover, 11but they are to do it on the fourteenth day of the second month at twilight. They are to eat the lamb, together with unleavened bread and bitter herbs.[u] 12They must not leave any of it till morning[v] or break any of its bones.[w] When they celebrate the Passover, they must follow all the regulations. 13But if anyone who is ceremonially clean and not on a journey fails to celebrate the Passover, they must be cut off from their people[x] for not presenting the LORD’s offering at the appointed time. They will bear the consequences of their sin.

14“ ‘A foreigner[y] residing among you is also to celebrate the LORD’s Passover in accordance with its rules and regulations. You must have the same regulations for both the foreigner and the native-born.’ ”

9:1 [m] Ex 40:2 [n] Nu 1:1
9:3 [o] Ex 12:2-11, 43-49; Lev 23:5-8; Dt 16:1-8
9:5 [p] Ex 12:1-13; Jos 5:10
9:6 [q] Lev 5:3 [r] Ex 18:15; Nu 27:2
9:8 [s] Ex 18:15; Nu 27:5,21; Ps 85:8
9:10 [t] 2Ch 30:2
9:11 [u] Ex 12:8
9:12 [v] Ex 12:10, 43 [w] Ex 12:46; Jn 19:36*
9:13 [x] Ge 17:14; Ex 12:15
9:14 [y] Ex 12:48, 49
9:15 [z] Ex 40:34 [a] Ex 13:21
9:17 [b] Ex 40:36-38; Nu 10:11,12; 1Co 10:1

Nu 9:17 ❖ How can we follow God’s presence today? What does this look like when we do not have a cloud or other visual symbol to follow?

The Cloud Above the Tabernacle

15On the day the tabernacle, the tent of the covenant law, was set up, the cloud[z] covered it. From evening till morning the cloud above the tabernacle looked like fire.[a] 16That is how it continued to be; the cloud covered it, and at night it looked like fire. 17Whenever the cloud lifted from above the tent, the Israelites set out; wherever the cloud settled, the Israelites encamped.[b] 18At the LORD’s command the Israelites set out, and at his command they encamped. As long as the cloud stayed over the tabernacle, they remained in camp. 19When the cloud remained over the tabernacle a long time, the Israelites obeyed the LORD’s order and did not set out. 20Sometimes the cloud was over the tabernacle only a few days; at the LORD’s command they would encamp, and then at his command they

---

9:1–5 God reminds the Israelites to celebrate Passover and makes provision for those who are ritually unclean to observe it later (vv. 9–14).
9:6–7 Some Israelites are not able to celebrate Passover at the proper time because they have become ritually impure from a corpse. Celebrating the Passover involves eating a holy sacrifice, but the Israelites are strictly forbidden to eat sacrificial food while in a state of ritual impurity (Lev 7:20–21).
9:8–12 The Lord’s solution is to establish an ongoing second date for Passover observance, a month later on the fourteenth day of the second month, for those prevented by corpse contamination from celebrating it at the normal time.
9:15–23 The desert journey resumes, guided by the divine cloud (cf. Ex 40:34–38). Its movements prompt the Israelites to either set out or to camp.

✣ **9:1–23** For the Israelites to be with God’s resident presence they must move with him. It is no use lingering to revere the spot where he has been, nor is it worthwhile trying to guess where he may go next and running ahead to get there first. The important thing is to know where his cloud is and to follow it.

God’s leadership calls for readiness to move at any time and also patience to stay put until he directs otherwise. For an individual who wants to set his or her own agenda, this arrangement can be intensely irritating and unsettling, but it is fine for someone who wants to be with God more than anything else. Such a person can feel content, like a baby carried by a parent, unworried about the specifics of the route as long as Mama or Papa is there.

would set out. 21 Sometimes the cloud stayed only from evening till morning, and when it lifted in the morning, they set out. Whether by day or by night, whenever the cloud lifted, they set out. 22 Whether the cloud stayed over the tabernacle for two days or a month or a year, the Israelites would remain in camp and not set out; but when it lifted, they would set out. 23 At the LORD's command they encamped, and at the LORD's command they set out. They obeyed the LORD's order, in accordance with his command through Moses.

The Silver Trumpets

10 The LORD said to Moses: 2 "Make two trumpets[c] of hammered silver, and use them for calling the community[d] together and for having the camps set out. 3 When both are sounded, the whole community is to assemble before you at the entrance to the tent of meeting. 4 If only one is sounded, the leaders[e] — the heads of the clans of Israel — are to assemble before you. 5 When a trumpet blast is sounded, the tribes camping on the east are to set out.[f] 6 At the sounding of a second blast, the camps on the south are to set out.[g] The blast will be the signal for setting out. 7 To gather the assembly, blow the trumpets,[h] but not with the signal for setting out.[i]

8 "The sons of Aaron, the priests, are to blow the trumpets. This is to be a lasting ordinance for you and the generations to come.[j] 9 When you go into battle in your own land against an enemy who is oppressing you,[k] sound a blast on the trumpets. Then you will be remembered[l] by the LORD your God and rescued from your enemies.[m] 10 Also at your times of rejoicing — your appointed festivals and New Moon feasts[n] — you are to sound the trumpets[o] over your burnt offerings and fellowship offerings, and they will be a memorial for you before your God. I am the LORD your God."

The Israelites Leave Sinai

11 On the twentieth day of the second month of the second year,[p] the cloud lifted[q] from above the tabernacle of the covenant law. 12 Then the Israelites set out from the Desert of Sinai and traveled from place to place until the cloud came to rest in the Desert of Paran. 13 They set out, this first time, at the LORD's command through Moses.[r]

14 The divisions of the camp of Judah went first, under their standard.[s] Nahshon son of Amminadab[t] was in command. 15 Nethanel son of Zuar was over the division of the tribe of Issachar, 16 and Eliab son of Helon was over the division of the tribe of Zebulun. 17 Then the tabernacle was taken down, and the Gershonites and Merarites, who carried it, set out.[u]

18 The divisions of the camp of Reuben went next, under their standard.[v] Elizur son of Shedeur was in command. 19 Shelumiel son of Zurishaddai was over the division of the tribe of Simeon, 20 and Eliasaph son of Deuel was over the division of the tribe of Gad. 21 Then the Kohathites set out, carrying the holy things.[w] The tabernacle was to be set up before they arrived.[x]

22 The divisions of the camp of Ephraim[y] went next, under their standard. Elishama son of Ammihud was in command. 23 Gamaliel son of Pedahzur was over the division of the tribe of Manasseh, 24 and Abidan son of Gideoni was over the division of the tribe of Benjamin.

25 Finally, as the rear guard[z] for all the units, the divisions of the camp of Dan set out under their standard. Ahiezer son of Ammishaddai was in command. 26 Pagiel son of Okran was over the division of the tribe of Asher, 27 and Ahira son of Enan was over the division of the tribe of Naphtali. 28 This was the order of march for the Israelite divisions as they set out.

Nu 10:10 ❖ What sounds are associated with rejoicing in our Christian communities and in your personal experience? How do such sounds impact our lives and worship?

10:2 [c] Ne 12:35; Ps 47:5 [d] Jer 4:5, 19; 6:1; Hos 5:8; Joel 2:1,15; Am 3:6
10:4 [e] Ex 18:21; Nu 1:16; 7:2
10:5 [f] ver 14
10:6 [g] ver 18
10:7 [h] Eze 33:3; Joel 2:1 [i] 1Co 14:8
10:8 [j] Nu 31:6
10:9 [k] Jdg 2:18; 6:9; 1Sa 10:18; Ps 106:42 [l] Ge 8:1 [m] Ps 106:4
10:10 [n] Ps 81:3 [o] Lev 23:24
10:11 [p] Ex 40:17 [q] Nu 9:17
10:13 [r] Dt 1:6
10:14 [s] Nu 2:3-9 [t] Nu 1:7
10:17 [u] Nu 4:21-32
10:18 [v] Nu 2:10-16
10:21 [w] Nu 4:20 [x] ver 17
10:22 [y] Nu 2:24
10:25 [z] Nu 2:31; Jos 6:9

10:1–8 Two signal trumpets of silver are to be blown by the priests at the sanctuary in order to assemble the people or to announce the break of camp. Different types of trumpet blasts signal a variety of activities.

10:11–12 The departure from Mount Sinai toward the Desert of Paran (v. 12) is a major transition in the Israelites' experience. The Lord has kept them at Mount Sinai long enough to make them into a functioning nation so that they can be unified

29 Now Moses said to Hobab[a] son of Reuel[b] the Midianite, Moses' father-in-law,[c] "We are setting out for the place about which the LORD said, 'I will give it to you.'[d] Come with us and we will treat you well, for the LORD has promised good things to Israel."

30 He answered, "No, I will not go;[e] I am going back to my own land and my own people."

31 But Moses said, "Please do not leave us. You know where we should camp in the wilderness, and you can be our eyes.[f] 32 If you come with us, we will share with you[g] whatever good things the LORD gives us.[h]"

33 So they set out[i] from the mountain of the LORD and traveled for three days. The ark of the covenant of the LORD[j] went before them during those three days to find them a place to rest. 34 The cloud of the LORD was over them by day when they set out from the camp.[k]

35 Whenever the ark set out, Moses said,

"Rise up, LORD!
May your enemies be scattered;[l]
may your foes flee before you.[m]"

36 Whenever it came to rest, he said,

"Return,[n] LORD,
to the countless thousands of
Israel.[o]"

Fire From the LORD

11 Now the people complained about their hardships in the hearing of the LORD, and when he heard them his anger was aroused. Then fire from the LORD burned among them[p] and consumed some of the outskirts of the camp. 2 When the people cried out to Moses, he prayed to the LORD[q] and the fire died down. 3 So that place was called Taberah,[a][r] because fire from the LORD had burned among them.

10:29 [a] Jdg 4:11 [b] Ex 2:18 [c] Ex 3:1 [d] Ge 12:7
10:30 [e] Mt 21:29
10:31 [f] Job 29:15
10:32 [g] Dt 10:18 [h] Ps 22:27-31; 67:5-7
10:33 [i] ver 12; Dt 1:33 [j] Jos 3:3
10:34 [k] Nu 9:15-23
10:35 [l] Ps 68:1 [m] Dt 7:10; 32:41; Ps 68:2; Isa 17:12-14
10:36 [n] Isa 63:17 [o] Dt 1:10
11:1 [p] Lev 10:2
11:2 [q] Nu 21:7
11:3 [r] Dt 9:22
11:4 [s] Ex 12:38 [t] Ps 78:18; 1Co 10:6
11:5 [u] Ex 16:3
11:7 [v] Ex 16:31 [w] Ge 2:12
11:9 [x] Ex 16:13

Nu 11:4-6 ❖ When have you felt ungrateful for God's provisions? What complaint did you raise, even if you didn't say it out loud?

Quail From the LORD

4 The rabble with them began to crave other food,[s] and again the Israelites started wailing[t] and said, "If only we had meat to eat! 5 We remember the fish we ate in Egypt at no cost — also the cucumbers, melons, leeks, onions and garlic.[u] 6 But now we have lost our appetite; we never see anything but this manna!"

7 The manna was like coriander seed[v] and looked like resin.[w] 8 The people went around gathering it, and then ground it in a hand mill or crushed it in a mortar. They cooked it in a pot or made it into loaves. And it tasted like something made with olive oil. 9 When the dew[x] settled on the camp at night, the manna also came down.

10 Moses heard the people of every family wailing at the entrance to their tents. The LORD became exceedingly angry, and Moses was troubled. 11 He asked the LORD, "Why have you brought this trouble on your servant? What have I done to displease you that you put the burden of

[a] 3 *Taberah* means *burning.*

---

under his benevolent rule and stay that way once they spread out in the promised land. Now they are ready to fulfill his dream and theirs!

10:29 As the Israelites are about to leave Mount Sinai, Moses urges "Hobab son of Reuel the Midianite, Moses' father-in-law," to come with them. Exodus 2:18 refers to Moses' father-in-law as Reuel, who was the "priest of Midian" (Ex 2:16), an alternative name for Jethro (Ex 3:1; 18:1).

10:35-36 Attached to the end of this chapter are two prayers that Moses pronounces: the first whenever the ark sets out, and the second whenever it comes to rest.

✣ **10:1-36** The concept that God's people benefit from cooperation with him runs through the OT. Divine-human coordination also appears in the NT. Why does the Lord have human beings do something, no matter how small, when he wants to do something amazing for them? Obviously, it is not because he cannot do those things, and far more efficiently too. Rather, it is because human activity is an expression of faith.

11:1-3 Experiencing the discomforts of travel, the people ungratefully complain. The Lord answers grumbling with destructive fire at the outskirts of the camp, reminiscent of the fire that consumed Nadab and Abihu.

11:4-15 The next episode is about the Lord's cafeteria menu, the staple of which is manna. The divine King does not take kindly to insulting rejection of the heavenly bounty that he has daily provided. Ominously, he becomes "exceedingly angry" (v. 10). Aggravating the gravity of the situation is Moses' burnout. Just as the people are sick and tired of manna, Moses is sick and tired of them!

all these people on me?[y] 12Did I conceive all these people? Did I give them birth? Why do you tell me to carry them in my arms, as a nurse carries an infant,[z] to the land you promised on oath to their ancestors?[a] 13Where can I get meat for all these people?[b] They keep wailing to me, 'Give us meat to eat!' 14I cannot carry all these people by myself; the burden is too heavy for me.[c] 15If this is how you are going to treat me, please go ahead and kill me[d] — if I have found favor in your eyes — and do not let me face my own ruin."

16The LORD said to Moses: "Bring me seventy of Israel's elders who are known to you as leaders and officials among the people. Have them come to the tent of meeting, that they may stand there with you. 17I will come down and speak with you there, and I will take some of the power of the Spirit that is on you and put it on them.[e] They will share the burden of the people with you so that you will not have to carry it alone.[f]

18"Tell the people: 'Consecrate yourselves[g] in preparation for tomorrow, when you will eat meat. The LORD heard you when you wailed,[h] "If only we had meat to eat! We were better off in Egypt!"[i] Now the LORD will give you meat, and you will eat it. 19You will not eat it for just one day, or two days, or five, ten or twenty days, 20but for a whole month — until it comes out of your nostrils and you loathe it[j] — because you have rejected the LORD,[k] who is among you, and have wailed before him, saying, "Why did we ever leave Egypt?"'"

21But Moses said, "Here I am among six hundred thousand men[l] on foot, and you say, 'I will give them meat to eat for a whole month!' 22Would they have enough if flocks and herds were slaughtered for them? Would they have enough if all the fish in the sea were caught for them?"[m]

23The LORD answered Moses, "Is the LORD's arm too short?[n] Now you will see whether or not what I say will come true for you.[o]"

24So Moses went out and told the people what the LORD had said. He brought together seventy of their elders and had them stand around the tent. 25Then the LORD came down in the cloud[p] and spoke with him,[q] and he took some of the power of the Spirit[r] that was on him and put it on the seventy elders.[s] When the Spirit rested on them, they prophesied[t] — but did not do so again.

26However, two men, whose names were Eldad and Medad, had remained in the camp. They were listed among the elders, but did not go out to the tent. Yet the Spirit also rested on them, and they prophesied in the camp. 27A young man ran and told Moses, "Eldad and Medad are prophesying in the camp."

28Joshua son of Nun, who had been Moses' aide[u] since youth, spoke up and said, "Moses, my lord, stop them!"[v]

29But Moses replied, "Are you jealous for my sake? I wish that all the LORD's people were prophets[w] and that the LORD would put his Spirit on them!" 30Then Moses and the elders of Israel returned to the camp.

31Now a wind went out from the LORD

11:11 [y] Ex 5:22
11:12 [z] Isa 40:11; 49:23 [a] Ex 13:5
11:13 [b] Jn 6:5-9
11:14 [c] Ex 18:18
11:15 [d] Ex 32:32; 1Ki 19:4; Jnh 4:3
11:17 [e] ver 25, 29; 1Sa 10:6; 2Ki 2:9,15; Joel 2:28 [f] Ex 18:18
11:18 [g] Ex 19:10 [h] Ex 16:7 [i] ver 5; Ac 7:39
11:20 [j] Ps 78:29; 106:14,15 [k] Jos 24:27; 1Sa 10:19
11:21 [l] Ex 12:37
11:22 [m] Mt 15:33
11:23 [n] Isa 50:2; 59:1 [o] Nu 23:19; Eze 12:25; 24:14
11:25 [p] Nu 12:5 [q] ver 17 [r] 1Sa 10:6 [s] Ac 2:17 [t] 1Sa 10:10
11:28 [u] Ex 33:11; Jos 1:1 [v] Mk 9:38-40
11:29 [w] 1Co 14:5

11:16–20 The Lord first addresses Moses' need, telling him to gather seventy elders (v. 16) so that they can be empowered to help him carry the burden of managing the people (v. 17). God commands that the people sanctify themselves (v. 18). Such "consecration" includes washing their clothes and abstaining from sexual relations along with bathing in preparation for a special encounter with God the next day. It sounds as though the Israelites are to enjoy sacrificial meat, but their wish-come-true will turn to punishment that fits their crime when they will have it coming out their noses (vv. 19–20).

11:24–30 When the Lord puts the Spirit on seventy elders, they temporarily prophesy. Their prophesying alarms Joshua, who is apparently concerned that leadership extending to the elders should be associated with Moses at headquarters (vv. 27–28). Rather than being jealous of the spiritual gifts granted to others, Moses rejoices and desires the best for all of God's people.

11:31–34 The biblical text says that the wind left the quail around the camp about two cubits above/on the surface of the land. This can as easily mean that the wind impels the quail to within reach of the Israelites and leaves them there just above and on the ground where they can readily be caught and slaughtered. Six hundred thousand men (v. 21) collect more than thirty-five bushels each, for a total of more than twenty-one million bushels. Even if there were only five birds per bushel (a low estimate given their relatively small size), there would be a total of more than 105 million birds.

The influx of quail in the biblical story is related to a natural phenomenon. Large numbers of quail migrate across the Sinai peninsula from Africa on their way to Europe and Asia. Since these birds have relatively heavy bodies and do not fly well, they partly depend on prevailing winds to assist their flight, and they become exhausted by long journeys. Three unusual elements signal divine

and drove quail[x] in from the sea. It scattered them up to two cubits[a] deep all around the camp, as far as a day's walk in any direction. 32 All that day and night and all the next day the people went out and gathered quail. No one gathered less than ten homers.[b] Then they spread them out all around the camp. 33 But while the meat was still between their teeth[y] and before it could be consumed, the anger of the LORD burned against the people, and he struck them with a severe plague.[z] 34 Therefore the place was named Kibroth Hattaavah,[c][a] because there they buried the people who had craved other food.

35 From Kibroth Hattaavah the people traveled to Hazeroth[b] and stayed there.

Miriam and Aaron Oppose Moses

12 Miriam and Aaron began to talk against Moses because of his Cushite wife,[c] for he had married a Cushite. 2 "Has the LORD spoken only through Moses?" they asked. "Hasn't he also spoken through us?"[d] And the LORD heard this.[e]

3 (Now Moses was a very humble man,[f] more humble than anyone else on the face of the earth.)

4 At once the LORD said to Moses, Aaron and Miriam, "Come out to the tent of meeting, all three of you." So the three of them went out. 5 Then the LORD came down in a pillar of cloud;[g] he stood at the entrance to the tent and summoned Aaron and Miriam. When the two of them stepped forward, 6 he said, "Listen to my words:

"When there is a prophet among
you,
I, the LORD, reveal myself to them
in visions,[h]
I speak to them in dreams.[i]
7 But this is not true of my servant
Moses;[j]
he is faithful in all my house.[k]
8 With him I speak face to face,
clearly and not in riddles;[l]
he sees the form of the LORD.[m]
Why then were you not afraid
to speak against my servant
Moses?"

9 The anger of the LORD burned against them, and he left them.[n]

10 When the cloud lifted from above the tent, Miriam's skin was leprous[d]—it became as white as snow.[o] Aaron turned toward her and saw that she had a defiling skin disease,[p] 11 and he said to Moses, "Please, my lord, I ask you not to hold against us the sin we have so foolishly committed.[q] 12 Do not let her be like a stillborn infant coming from its mother's womb with its flesh half eaten away."

11:31 [x] Ex 16:13; Ps 78:26-28
11:33 [y] Ps 78:30 [z] Ps 106:15
11:34 [a] Dt 9:22
11:35 [b] Nu 33:17
12:1 [c] Ex 2:21
12:2 [d] Nu 16:3 [e] Nu 11:1
12:3 [f] Mt 11:29
12:5 [g] Nu 11:25
12:6 [h] Ge 15:1; 46:2 [i] Ge 31:10; 1Ki 3:5; Heb 1:1
12:7 [j] Jos 1:1-2; Ps 105:26 [k] Heb 3:2,5
12:8 [l] Dt 34:10 [m] Ex 20:4; Ps 17:15
12:9 [n] Ge 17:22
12:10 [o] Ex 4:6; Dt 24:9 [p] 2Ki 5:1, 27
12:11 [q] 2Sa 19:19; 24:10

Nu 12:1-2 ❖ Have you ever felt envious or jealous of another person's leadership position? How did you behave?

[a] 31 That is, about 3 feet or about 90 centimeters [b] 32 That is, possibly about 1 3/4 tons or about 1.6 metric tons [c] 34 *Kibroth Hattaavah* means *graves of craving.* [d] 10 The Hebrew for *leprous* was used for various diseases affecting the skin.

intervention: The arrival of quail is timed to serve as the Lord's answer to the Israelites' demand for meat; the wind that carries the flock is from the Lord; and the number of birds is miraculous.

11:33–34 God strikes a great blow (v. 33). This may involve bacterial food poisoning that induces vomiting (possibly including out the nose). Whatever the precise nature of the plague, its acute onset is deadly, as implied by the name given to the place: Kibroth Hattaavah, meaning "the graves of craving" (v. 34).

✣ **11:1-35** Instead of simply complaining, which tends to depress ourselves and others, we can accomplish something positive if we take our complaints directly to God in prayer, believing that he will hear us. A complaint to God that is a petition of faith can end up strengthening the faith of others when the Lord answers the prayer.

12:1 Unless Moses married a second woman (for which there is no clear evidence), why would Zipporah be labeled a "Cushite" here? We don't know for sure.

12:2 Miriam and Aaron feel that Moses is unduly dominating their prophetic trio (v. 2). Why now? Moses has just appointed seventy elders to receive the prophetic gift and share responsibility with him (11:24–26), thereby moving power and influence away from Miriam and Aaron. Although the arrangement is the Lord's idea (11:16–17, 24), they can easily associate it with an earlier initiative sponsored by Jethro, Zipporah's father (Ex 18:13–26).

12:3 It can be argued that the explanation in this verse was written by an editor of the Pentateuch, not by Moses himself (cf. Ge 12:6; Dt 34).

12:4–8 While Moses does not defend himself, the Lord takes decisive action (v. 4). He does not deny the claim of Aaron and Miriam to prophetic inspiration (v. 6). But Moses has experienced more intimate access to God than any other human being (vv. 7–8) and is an active participant in dialogue with him.

12:9–12 When the divine warning is punctuated by Miriam's case of skin disease, Aaron implores Moses for forgiveness and for healing for Miriam.

JUDGMENT IN NUMBERS

REFERENCE	SIN	JUDGMENT
11:1-3	The people complain at Taberah.	Fire breaks out on the edges of the camp.
11:4-35	The people complain at Kibroth Hattaavah, seeking meat rather than manna, longing for Egypt rather than the desert.	God sends quail in great numbers along with a virulent plague.
12	Aaron and Miriam speak against Moses' leadership.	Miriam is struck with leprosy and sent outside the camp for the prescribed seven days.
14	Spies are sent to Canaan; upon returning, 10 of the 12 give an unfavorable report, discouraging the people from obeying the Lord's command to take the land.	The Lord pronounces a prolonged death sentence on the complaining generation. The 10 spies and their families are struck by plague.
16:1-40	Korah, the Levite, leads a rebellion against Moses.	The rebels and their families are swallowed by the ground.
16:41-50	The people accuse Moses and Aaron of killing Korah and those who followed him.	The Lord sends a plague; 14,700 die.
20:1-12	Moses disobeys the Lord, striking the rock rather than speaking to it.	Moses is denied entrance to the promised land.
21:4-9	The people speak against God and Moses.	The Lord sends fiery serpents.
25:1-9	Israelites join Moabites in worshiping Baal of Peor, committing sexual immorality.	Plague kills 24,000.

13So Moses cried out to the LORD,
"Please, God, heal her![r]"
14The LORD replied to Moses, "If her
father had spit in her face,[s] would she
not have been in disgrace for seven days?
Confine her outside the camp[t] for seven
days; after that she can be brought back."
15So Miriam was confined outside the
camp for seven days, and the people did
not move on till she was brought back.
16After that, the people left Hazeroth[u]
and encamped in the Desert of Paran.

Exploring Canaan

13 The LORD said to Moses, 2"Send
some men to explore[v] the land of
Canaan, which I am giving to the Israelites. From each ancestral tribe send one
of its leaders."
3So at the LORD's command Moses sent
them out from the Desert of Paran. All
of them were leaders of the Israelites.
4These are their names:

from the tribe of Reuben, Shammua son of Zakkur;
5from the tribe of Simeon, Shaphat son of Hori;
6from the tribe of Judah, Caleb son of Jephunneh;[w]
7from the tribe of Issachar, Igal son of Joseph;
8from the tribe of Ephraim, Hoshea son of Nun;
9from the tribe of Benjamin, Palti son of Raphu;
10from the tribe of Zebulun, Gaddiel son of Sodi;
11from the tribe of Manasseh (a tribe of Joseph), Gaddi son of Susi;

12:13 [r]Isa 30:26; Jer 17:14
12:14 [s]Dt 25:9; Job 17:6; 30:9-10; Isa 50:6 [t]Lev 13:46; Nu 5:2-3
12:16 [u]Nu 11:35
13:2 [v]Dt 1:22
13:6 [w]ver 30; Nu 14:6, 24; 34:19; Jdg 1:12-15

12:13-15 All Moses can do is to cry out for the Lord to heal her (v. 13). Because the Lord has disgraced Miriam, who apparently was more at fault than Aaron, it takes some time to restore her. A quick fix would trivialize the gravity of the situation. During the week of delay, all Israelites have plenty of opportunity to reflect on the deadly "disease" of rebellion against God's leadership through Moses (v. 15).

12:1-16 The fact that Moses' wife is described as "Cushite" only in the context of derogatory talk about her by Miriam and Aaron (v. 1) suggests that they look down on her for having darker skin (cf. SS 1:6). The Lord's punishment of Miriam indicates that he takes her xenophobia seriously by making her skin "as white as snow" (Nu 12:10). What is so bad about

[12]from the tribe of Dan, Ammiel son of Gemalli;
[13]from the tribe of Asher, Sethur son of Michael;
[14]from the tribe of Naphtali, Nahbi son of Vophsi;
[15]from the tribe of Gad, Geuel son of Maki.

16These are the names of the men Moses
sent to explore the land. (Moses gave
Hoshea son of Nun[x] the name Joshua.)[y]
17When Moses sent them to explore Canaan, he said, "Go up through the Negev[z]
and on into the hill country.[a] 18See what
the land is like and whether the people
who live there are strong or weak, few or
many. 19What kind of land do they live in?
Is it good or bad? What kind of towns do
they live in? Are they unwalled or fortified? 20How is the soil? Is it fertile or poor?
Are there trees in it or not? Do your best to
bring back some of the fruit of the land.[b]"
(It was the season for the first ripe grapes.)
21So they went up and explored the
land from the Desert of Zin[c] as far as
Rehob,[d] toward Lebo Hamath.[e] 22They
went up through the Negev and came
to Hebron, where Ahiman, Sheshai and
Talmai,[f] the descendants of Anak,[g] lived.
(Hebron had been built seven years
before Zoan in Egypt.)[h] 23When they
reached the Valley of Eshkol,[a] they cut
off a branch bearing a single cluster of
grapes. Two of them carried it on a pole
between them, along with some pomegranates and figs. 24That place was called
the Valley of Eshkol because of the cluster of grapes the Israelites cut off there.
25At the end of forty days they returned
from exploring the land.

13:16 [x]ver 8 [y]Dt 32:44
13:17 [z]Ge 12:9 [a]Jdg 1:9
13:20 [b]Dt 1:25
13:21 [c]Nu 20:1; 27:14; 33:36; Jos 15:1 [d]Jos 19:28 [e]Jos 13:5
13:22 [f]Jos 15:14 [g]Jos 15:13 [h]Ps 78:12, 43; Isa 19:11, 13
13:26 [i]Nu 32:8
13:27 [j]Ex 3:8 [k]Dt 1:25
13:28 [l]Dt 1:28; 9:1, 2
13:31 [m]Dt 1:28; 9:1; Jos 14:8
13:32 [n]Nu 14:36, 37 [o]Eze 36:13, 14 [p]Am 2:9
13:33 [q]Ge 6:4 [r]Dt 1:28

Nu 13:27-30 ❖ How can we have eyes of faith, like Caleb, instead of succumbing to fear like most of the spies?

Report on the Exploration

26They came back to Moses and Aaron and the whole Israelite community
at Kadesh in the Desert of Paran. There
they reported to them[i] and to the whole
assembly and showed them the fruit of
the land. 27They gave Moses this account:
"We went into the land to which you sent
us, and it does flow with milk and honey![j]
Here is its fruit.[k] 28But the people who
live there are powerful, and the cities
are fortified and very large.[l] We even saw
descendants of Anak there. 29The Amalekites live in the Negev; the Hittites,
Jebusites and Amorites live in the hill
country; and the Canaanites live near
the sea and along the Jordan."
30Then Caleb silenced the people before Moses and said, "We should go up
and take possession of the land, for we
can certainly do it."
31But the men who had gone up with
him said, "We can't attack those people; they are stronger than we are."[m]
32And they spread among the Israelites
a bad report[n] about the land they had
explored. They said, "The land we explored devours[o] those living in it. All
the people we saw there are of great
size.[p] 33We saw the Nephilim[q] there (the
descendants of Anak[r] come from the
Nephilim). We seemed like grasshoppers in our own eyes, and we looked
the same to them."

[a] 23 *Eshkol* means *cluster*; also in verse 24.

---

racism? As in the story of Miriam and Aaron, it is always about status and control, and it is always an insult to God.

13:23, 26-27 When the chieftains return to the community, they stage a much anticipated "show and tell." "Pomegranates and figs" (v. 23) confirm the land's agricultural quality, as described in the expression "flow with milk and honey" (v. 27). Most impressive is a huge "cluster" of grapes that two scouts carry between them on a pole (v. 23), the way Kohathite Levites carry sacred objects belonging to the sanctuary (4:6, 8, 11, 14; 7:9).

13:28-30 The scouts quickly move past the topic of agriculture to dwell on the human demographics of Canaan. Matching the abundant and sizeable fruits are numerous and powerful peoples with large, fortified cities (v. 28). As the people's euphoria vaporizes, there is an uproar. Observe how Caleb, the scout from Judah, needs to silence the people before telling them that they can and should go up and take the land (v. 30).

13:31-32 At this point the biased attitude of the other scouts bursts into the open as they categorically contradict Caleb and defame the land they had earlier praised, claiming that it "devours those living in it" (v. 32). The Israelites readily buy the idea that the Canaanite giants are a vastly more powerful class of human beings than they are and succumb to terror.

✣ **13:1-33** For the person of faith, obstacles are temporary because God is real. For the disbeliever, obstacles are permanent because God is not real enough. Consider this question: Is God real to me? Do I believe, act, and live as if he is alive?

PEOPLE TO KNOW // CALEB

NUMBERS 13:30: When Moses led the Israelites from Mount Sinai to the edge of the promised land, he sent twelve spies to investigate the land (Nu 13:1–3). Among those twelve spies was Caleb.

The spies stayed forty days in Canaan. Upon returning, they told the people how fruitful it was—but also despaired at its powerful inhabitants. Ten of the spies argued against entering the land for fear of the Canaanites. Joshua and Caleb, however, boldly announced that they should enter and conquer Canaan. Caleb said, "We should go up and take possession of the land, for we can certainly do it" (Nu 13:30).

Unfortunately, the Israelite people sided with the frightened ten rather than the brave two. The people grumbled that they should have never followed Moses and plotted to choose a new leader to bring them back to Egypt. Joshua and Caleb pleaded with the people to change their minds, reminding them they had God on their side, but the people threatened to stone them.

When the time came for the new generation to enter the land, Caleb was an old man in his eighties. He was, however, still vigorous and strong for battle (Jos 14:11). He received land in Canaan that was known to have mighty warriors—Anakites—but in typical Caleb fashion he simply believed, "The LORD helping me, I will drive them out" (Jos 14:12).

APPLICATION ✣ Caleb looked at the world through the eyes of faith. He did not worry about the threats that others feared; his trust was in God. God's words about Caleb were remarkable. He said Caleb had "a different spirit" and followed God wholeheartedly (Nu 14:24). What a way to be remembered! Caleb's story encourages us, too, to be people with a "different spirit"—people who demonstrate wholehearted devotion to God and see the world through not the lens of fear but rather the lens of God's all-powerful ability to see his will accomplished.

The People Rebel

14 That night all the members of the community raised their voices and wept aloud. 2All the Israelites grumbled against Moses and Aaron, and the whole assembly said to them, "If only we had died in Egypt! Or in this wilderness![s] 3Why is the LORD bringing us to this land only to let us fall by the sword? Our wives and children will be taken as plunder. Wouldn't it be better for us to go back to Egypt?" 4And they said to each other, "We should choose a leader and go back to Egypt.[t]"

5Then Moses and Aaron fell facedown[u] in front of the whole Israelite assembly gathered there. 6Joshua son of Nun and Caleb son of Jephunneh, who were among those who had explored the land, tore their clothes 7and said to the entire Israelite assembly, "The land we passed through and explored is exceedingly good.[v] 8If the LORD is pleased with us,[w] he will lead us into that land, a land flowing with milk and honey,[x] and will give it to us. 9Only do not rebel[y] against the LORD. And do not be afraid of the people of the land,[z] because we will devour them. Their protection is gone, but the LORD is with us. Do not be afraid of them."

10But the whole assembly talked about stoning[a] them. Then the glory of the LORD[b] appeared at the tent of meeting to all the Israelites. 11The LORD said to Moses, "How long will these people treat me with contempt? How long will they refuse to believe in me,[c] in spite of all the signs I have performed among them? 12I will strike them down with a plague and destroy them, but I will make you into a nation[d] greater and stronger than they."

13Moses said to the LORD, "Then the Egyptians will hear about it! By your

14:2 [s] Nu 11:1
14:4 [t] Ne 9:17
14:5 [u] Nu 16:4, 22, 45
14:7 [v] Nu 13:27; Dt 1:25
14:8 [w] Dt 10:15 [x] Nu 13:27
14:9 [y] Dt 1:26; 9:7, 23, 24 [z] Dt 1:21; 7:18; 20:1
14:10 [a] Ex 17:4 [b] Lev 9:23
14:11 [c] Ps 78:22; 106:24
14:12 [d] Ex 32:10

14:3–4 The Israelites conclude that the Lord is their enemy and their best option is to mutiny against Moses and return to Egypt.

14:5–9 With Moses and Aaron in a position of silent petition to God, Joshua and Caleb take over the defense.

14:10–12 Joshua and Caleb get nothing for their trouble except talk of stoning them, which likely threatens Moses and Aaron too (v. 10). Before this could happen, "the glory of the LORD appeared at the tent of meeting" (v. 10b). God addresses Moses to announce sentence on the rebels: death and replacement with a better nation descended from Moses (vv. 11–12).

14:13–23 Moses finds his voice to plead for the lives of those who have heaped abominable abuse on him. The Lord does indeed forgive the Israelites as Moses asks (v. 20), namely, in the sense of

power you brought these people up from among them.[e] 14And they will tell the inhabitants of this land about it. They have already heard[f] that you, LORD, are with these people and that you, LORD, have been seen face to face, that your cloud stays over them, and that you go before them in a pillar of cloud by day and a pillar of fire by night.[g] 15If you put all these people to death, leaving none alive, the nations who have heard this report about you will say, 16'The LORD was not able to bring these people into the land he promised them on oath, so he slaughtered them in the wilderness.'[h]

17"Now may the Lord's strength be displayed, just as you have declared: 18'The LORD is slow to anger, abounding in love and forgiving sin and rebellion.[i] Yet he does not leave the guilty unpunished; he punishes the children for the sin of the parents to the third and fourth generation.'[j] 19In accordance with your great love, forgive[k] the sin of these people,[l] just as you have pardoned them from the time they left Egypt until now."[m]

20The LORD replied, "I have forgiven them,[n] as you asked. 21Nevertheless, as surely as I live[o] and as surely as the glory of the LORD fills the whole earth,[p] 22not one of those who saw my glory and the signs I performed in Egypt and in the wilderness but who disobeyed me and tested me ten times[q] — 23not one of them will ever see the land I promised on oath[r] to their ancestors. No one who has treated me with contempt will ever see it.[s] 24But because my servant Caleb has a different spirit and follows me wholeheartedly,[t] I will bring him into the land he went to, and his descendants will inherit it.[u] 25Since the Amalekites and the Canaanites are living in the valleys, turn[v] back tomorrow and set out toward the desert along the route to the Red Sea.[a]"

14:13 [e] Ex 32:11-14; Ps 106:23
14:14 [f] Ex 15:14 [g] Ex 13:21
14:16 [h] Jos 7:7
14:18 [i] Ex 34:6; Ps 145:8; Jnh 4:2 [j] Ex 20:5
14:19 [k] Ex 34:9 [l] Ps 106:45 [m] Ps 78:38
14:20 [n] Ps 106:23; Mic 7:18-20
14:21 [o] Dt 32:40; Isa 49:18 [p] Ps 72:19; Isa 6:3; Hab 2:14
14:22 [q] Ex 14:11; 32:1; 1Co 10:5
14:23 [r] Nu 32:11 [s] Heb 3:18
14:24 [t] ver 6-9; Jos 14:8,14 [u] Nu 32:12
14:25 [v] Dt 1:40

Nu 14:20 ❖ How do we reconcile God's forgiveness with the severe consequences for sin? How does Christ provide hope?

26The LORD said to Moses and Aaron: 27"How long will this wicked community grumble against me? I have heard the complaints of these grumbling Israelites.[w] 28So tell them, 'As surely as I live,[x] declares the LORD, I will do to you the very thing I heard you say: 29In this wilderness your bodies will fall[y] — every one of you twenty years old or more[z] who was counted in the census and who has grumbled against me. 30Not one of you will enter the land I swore with uplifted hand to make your home, except Caleb son of Jephunneh and Joshua son of Nun. 31As for your children that you said would be taken as plunder, I will bring them in to enjoy the land you have rejected.[a] 32But as for you, your bodies will fall[b] in this wilderness. 33Your children will be shepherds here for forty years, suffering for your unfaithfulness, until the last of your bodies lies in the wilderness. 34For forty years — one year for each of the forty days you explored the land[c] — you will suffer for your sins and know what it is like to have me against you.' 35I, the LORD, have spoken, and I will surely do these things[d] to this whole wicked community, which has banded together against me. They will meet their end in this wilderness; here they will die."

36So the men Moses had sent[e] to explore the land, who returned and made the whole community grumble against him by spreading a bad report[f] about it — 37these men who were responsible

14:27 [w] Ex 16:12
14:28 [x] ver 21
14:29 [y] Nu 26:65 [z] Nu 1:45
14:31 [a] Ps 106:24
14:32 [b] 1Co 10:5
14:34 [c] Nu 13:25
14:35 [d] Nu 23:19
14:36 [e] Nu 13:4-16 [f] Nu 13:32

[a] *25 Or the Sea of Reeds*

---

preserving the corporate covenant relationship by not destroying all of them at once (v. 15). However, the Lord swears by his *life* that the people (i.e., the adult generation) who have *seen* his glory, which fills the whole earth, will *die* in the desert without *seeing* the promised land (vv. 21–23).

14:25 Accepting the Israelites' own decision to return toward Egypt, the Lord orders them back into the desert along the way leading to the Red Sea. They refuse to live in the promised land, so they will suffer by dying in the desert.

14:26–35 To make the punishment fit the crime, the Lord will bring on the Israelites the very thing they wished for when they grumbled against him. Their corpses will fall in the desert (v. 29; cf. v. 2). In this way, the Lord will accomplish his goal of purifying Israel. Ironically, the children whom the men regarded as helpless (v. 3) will be the only ones to survive (v. 31).

14:36–40 Through a divine plague, the ten spies who were the catalyst for rebellious grumbling have the distinction of being the "firstfruits" of extinction. After mourning their fate (v. 39), which kills any doubt as to the seriousness of the Lord's intentions, the Israelites arise the next morning, confess their sin, and insist they are ready to go into Canaan (v. 40).

for spreading the bad report[g] about the
land were struck down and died of a
plague[h] before the LORD. 38Of the men
who went to explore the land, only Joshua son of Nun and Caleb son of Jephunneh survived.[i]
39When Moses reported this to all the
Israelites, they mourned[j] bitterly. 40Ear-
ly the next morning they set out for the
highest point in the hill country, saying,
"Now we are ready to go up to the land the
LORD promised. Surely we have sinned![k]"
41But Moses said, "Why are you disobeying the LORD's command? This will
not succeed![l] 42Do not go up, because
the LORD is not with you. You will be defeated by your enemies,[m] 43for the Amalekites and the Canaanites will face you
there. Because you have turned away
from the LORD, he will not be with you
and you will fall by the sword."
44Nevertheless, in their presumption
they went up[n] toward the highest point
in the hill country, though neither Moses nor the ark of the LORD's covenant
moved from the camp.[o] 45Then the Amalekites and the Canaanites who lived
in that hill country came down and attacked them and beat them down all the
way to Hormah.[p]

Supplementary Offerings

15 The LORD said to Moses, 2"Speak to
the Israelites and say to them: 'After
you enter the land I am giving you[q] as a
home 3and you present to the LORD food
offerings from the herd or the flock,[r] as
an aroma pleasing to the LORD[s]—whether burnt offerings[t] or sacrifices, for special vows or freewill offerings[u] or festival offerings[v]— 4then the person who
brings an offering shall present to the
LORD a grain offering[w] of a tenth of an
ephah[a] of the finest flour mixed with a
quarter of a hin[b] of olive oil. 5With each
lamb for the burnt offering or the sacrifice, prepare a quarter of a hin of wine[x]
as a drink offering.
6" 'With a ram[y] prepare a grain offering[z] of two-tenths of an ephah[c] of the
finest flour mixed with a third of a hin[d]
of olive oil,[a] 7and a third of a hin of wine
as a drink offering. Offer it as an aroma
pleasing to the LORD.
8" 'When you prepare a young bull as
a burnt offering or sacrifice, for a special
vow or a fellowship offering[b] to the LORD,
9bring with the bull a grain offering of
three-tenths of an ephah[e][c] of the finest
flour mixed with half a hin[f] of olive oil,
10and also bring half a hin of wine as
a drink offering. This will be a food offering, an aroma pleasing to the LORD.
11Each bull or ram, each lamb or young
goat, is to be prepared in this manner.
12Do this for each one, for as many as
you prepare.
13" 'Everyone who is native-born[d] must
do these things in this way when they
present a food offering as an aroma
pleasing to the LORD. 14For the generations to come, whenever a foreigner or
anyone else living among you presents
a food offering as an aroma pleasing to
the LORD, they must do exactly as you

14:37 [g] 1Co 10:10 [h] Nu 16:49
14:38 [i] Jos 14:6
14:39 [j] Ex 33:4
14:40 [k] Dt 1:41
14:41 [l] 2Ch 24:20
14:42 [m] Dt 1:42
14:44 [n] Dt 1:43 [o] Nu 31:6
14:45 [p] Nu 21:3; Dt 1:44; Jdg 1:17
15:2 [q] Lev 23:10
15:3 [r] Lev 1:2 [s] ver 24; Ge 8:21; Ex 29:18 [t] Nu 28:19,27 [u] Lev 22:18,21; Ezr 1:4 [v] Lev 23:1-44
15:4 [w] Lev 2:1; 6:14
15:5 [x] Nu 28:7,14
15:6 [y] Lev 5:15 [z] Nu 28:12 [a] Eze 46:14
15:8 [b] Lev 1:3; 3:1
15:9 [c] Lev 14:10
15:13 [d] Lev 16:29

[a] 4 That is, probably about 3 1/2 pounds or about 1.6 kilograms [b] 4 That is, about 1 quart or about 1 liter; also in verse 5 [c] 6 That is, probably about 7 pounds or about 3.2 kilograms [d] 6 That is, about 1 1/3 quarts or about 1.3 liters; also in verse 7 [e] 9 That is, probably about 11 pounds or about 5 kilograms [f] 9 That is, about 2 quarts or about 1.9 liters; also in verse 10

14:44–45 The Israelite soldiers already doomed to die in the desert only succeed in hastening their deaths.

14:1–45 Just as modern fads sweep through society because people exert strong influence on each other, the negativity of naysaying Israelite scouts is wildly contagious to people who share a lack of adequate trust in God. How do we protect ourselves and others from negative tipping points? Here are a few tips: (1) Keep things in perspective and don't jump just because all the other lemmings do. (2) Be aware of environments that provide fertile ground for sudden change, whether for better or for worse. (3) Maintain personal anchor points of faith to hang on to when everything else seems to be shifting.

15:1–16 This passage formulates a general rule: Grain and wine offerings must accompany every sacrificial gift. The word "sacrifice" here refers not to sacrifices in general but to the class of sacrifices that includes well-being offerings, from which offerors are permitted to eat. The fact that grain and wine accompaniments are included implies that they are burned on the outer altar.

15:4–16 This section specifies in ascending order the amounts of the grain offerings and drink offerings of wine that must accompany each flock animal (sheep or goat), ram, or bull in accordance with its size/value. The same rules for sacrificial accompaniments apply to foreigners living in the land (vv. 13–16).

do. 15The community is to have the same rules for you and for the foreigner residing among you; this is a lasting ordinance for the generations to come.[e] You and the foreigner shall be the same before the LORD: 16The same laws and regulations will apply both to you and to the foreigner residing among you.[f]' "

17The LORD said to Moses, 18"Speak to the Israelites and say to them: 'When you enter the land to which I am taking you 19and you eat the food of the land,[g] present a portion as an offering to the LORD. 20Present a loaf from the first of your ground meal[h] and present it as an offering from the threshing floor.[i] 21Throughout the generations to come you are to give this offering to the LORD from the first of your ground meal.[j]

Offerings for Unintentional Sins

22" 'Now if you as a community unintentionally fail to keep any of these commands the LORD gave Moses[k] — 23any of the LORD's commands to you through him, from the day the LORD gave them and continuing through the generations to come — 24and if this is done unintentionally without the community being aware of it,[l] then the whole community is to offer a young bull for a burnt offering[m] as an aroma pleasing to the LORD, along with its prescribed grain offering and drink offering, and a male goat for a sin offering.[a][n] 25The priest is to make atonement for the whole Israelite community, and they will be forgiven,[o] for it was not intentional and they have presented to the LORD for their wrong a food offering and a sin offering. 26The whole Israelite community and the foreigners residing among them will be forgiven, because all the people were involved in the unintentional wrong.[p]

15:15 [e] ver 29; Nu 9:14
15:16 [f] Nu 9:14
15:19 [g] Jos 5:11, 12
15:20 [h] Ex 34:26; Lev 23:14; Dt 26:2, 10 [i] Lev 2:14
15:21 [j] Ro 11:16
15:22 [k] Lev 4:2
15:24 [l] Lev 5:15 [m] Lev 4:14 [n] Lev 4:3
15:25 [o] Lev 4:20; Ro 3:25; Heb 2:17
15:26 [p] ver 24
15:27 [q] Lev 4:27
15:28 [r] Lev 4:35
15:30 [s] Nu 14:40-44; Dt 1:43; 17:13; Ps 19:13 [t] ver 14
15:31 [u] 2Sa 12:9; Ps 119:126; Pr 13:13 [v] Lev 5:1; Eze 18:20
15:32 [w] Ex 31:14, 15; 35:2, 3
15:34 [x] Nu 9:8
15:35 [y] Ex 31:14, 15; Dt 21:21 [z] Lev 20:2; 24:14; Ac 7:58

Nu 15:19 ❖ What do we give back to God from the portion he has given to us?

27" 'But if just one person sins unintentionally,[q] that person must bring a year-old female goat for a sin offering. 28The priest is to make atonement before the LORD for the one who erred by sinning unintentionally, and when atonement has been made, that person will be forgiven.[r] 29One and the same law applies to everyone who sins unintentionally, whether a native-born Israelite or a foreigner residing among you.

30" 'But anyone who sins defiantly,[s] whether native-born or foreigner,[t] blasphemes the LORD and must be cut off from the people of Israel. 31Because they have despised the LORD's word and broken his commands,[u] they must surely be cut off; their guilt remains on them.[v]' "

The Sabbath-Breaker Put to Death

32While the Israelites were in the wilderness, a man was found gathering wood on the Sabbath day.[w] 33Those who found him gathering wood brought him to Moses and Aaron and the whole assembly, 34and they kept him in custody, because it was not clear what should be done to him.[x] 35Then the LORD said to Moses, "The man must die.[y] The whole assembly must stone him outside the camp.[z]" 36So the assembly took him outside the camp and stoned him to death, as the LORD commanded Moses.

Tassels on Garments

37The LORD said to Moses, 38"Speak to the Israelites and say to them: 'Throughout the generations to come you are to

[a] 24 Or *purification offering*; also in verses 25 and 27

15:17–21 When the Israelites enter the promised land, they must set aside a dedication/gift and present it to the Lord via his priest: a loaf from the first bread-making vessel(?) or dough(?) of each new harvest.

15:22–31 The text goes on to contrast forgivable inadvertent sin with defiant sin, for which there is no sacrificial remedy but only the divinely administered terminal punishment of being "cut off" (vv. 30–31).

15:32–36 Apparently to illustrate unforgivable sin, the brief narrative of a man scrounging for firewood on Sabbath is placed within the legal setting of Nu 15. This happened where the climate was warm and the people had manna to eat. It looks as though this man was going out of his way to violate the Sabbath command.

15:37–41 Numbers prescribes an ongoing strategy to jog the memory of the Israelites regarding all of the Lord's commandments—tassels on their garments to help them obey and be consecrated to the Lord rather than go wherever their hearts or eyes should lead them (v. 39).

Aside from the blue cord on the tassels in v. 38, blue cords only appear in the context of the high priest's ornate vestments, connecting the breastpiece to the ephod (Ex 28:28; 39:21) and the gold plate to the turban (Ex 28:36–37; 39:30–31).

make tassels on the corners of your garments,[a] with a blue cord on each tassel.
39You will have these tassels to look at
and so you will remember[b] all the commands of the LORD, that you may obey
them and not prostitute yourselves by
chasing after the lusts of your own hearts
and eyes. 40Then you will remember to
obey all my commands and will be consecrated to your God.[c] 41I am the LORD
your God, who brought you out of Egypt
to be your God. I am the LORD your God.'"

Korah, Dathan and Abiram

16 Korah[d] son of Izhar, the son of Kohath, the son of Levi, and certain
Reubenites — Dathan and Abiram, sons
of Eliab,[e] and On son of Peleth — became
insolent[a] 2and rose up against Moses.
With them were 250 Israelite men, well-
known community leaders who had
been appointed members of the council.[f]
3They came as a group to oppose Moses
and Aaron[g] and said to them, "You have
gone too far! The whole community is
holy,[h] every one of them, and the LORD
is with them.[i] Why then do you set yourselves above the LORD's assembly?"[j]
4When Moses heard this, he fell facedown.[k] 5Then he said to Korah and all

15:38 [a] Dt 22:12; Mt 23:5
15:39 [b] Dt 4:23; 6:12; Ps 73:27
15:40 [c] Lev 11:44; Ro 12:1; Col 1:22; 1Pe 1:15
16:1 [d] Jude 11
[e] Nu 26:8; Dt 11:6
16:2 [f] Nu 1:16; 26:9
16:3 [g] ver 7; Ps 106:16 [h] Ex 19:6 [i] Nu 14:14 [j] Nu 12:2
16:4 [k] Nu 14:5

[a] *1* Or *Peleth — took men*

15:1–41 The fact that God is incredibly merciful should bring hope to *any* sinner who desires salvation. However, it should not lead any to suppose that it is safe to presume upon his grace by believing that the gravitational pull of personal sin can be reversed at any time with a simple hop onto the "chair lift" to heaven. Going down does not make it easier to get back up. The problem is not for God to be willing to forgive but for a sinner to want to be forgiven.

16:1–3 Korah and his associates confront Moses and Aaron with fighting words. The rebels are not a disorganized mob venting riotous indignation. They are well-organized leaders who are, humanly speaking, qualified to run the nation.
16:5–7 Moses responds by challenging the rebels to burn incense in order to test their claim that their holiness is on par with that of the Aaronic priests. The test proposed by Moses is deadly dangerous, and his warning (v. 7) is no empty threat. Even though Aaron's sons Nadab and Abihu were

PEOPLE TO KNOW // KORAH

NUMBERS 16:1–50: Korah was a Levite who, along with 250 followers, rose up against Moses and Aaron (Nu 16:1–3). They accused Moses and Aaron of overextending their own authority, arguing that the whole community was holy, not just these two leaders.

Moses fell facedown when he heard this. He told Korah that the next day God would decide between the two of them who was righteous and who was wicked. Moses accused Korah and his followers of not being satisfied with their sacred task of caring for the tabernacle, a job specifically given to Korah's father's family (Nu 3:27–31). Moses accused Korah of opposing God himself.

The next day when Korah and his followers assembled, God's glory appeared, and God told Moses and Aaron to stand back while he destroyed the assembly. Moses and Aaron interceded for the people, asking God not to destroy them all for the sin of Korah.

The people moved away from Korah's group. Moses declared his own authority would be vindicated if the earth opened up and swallowed the evil men and their families, sending them alive to the realm of the dead—and that's exactly what happened (Nu 16:31–34). The fire of God then consumed Korah's 250 followers.

Tragedy continued the next day. The people blamed Moses for killing Korah and his followers, rising up once again in opposition to Moses and Aaron. In response, God unleashed a plague upon the community that killed 14,700 people before Aaron's intercession ended the devastation. Korah's rebellion was among the darkest moments the freed Israelites experienced during their years in the wilderness.

APPLICATION Jude connects Korah and his followers to certain Christians who take the grace of Christ and use it as a license for immorality (Jude 4, 11). When we feel entitled, we stray from living lives of gratitude toward God and venture into selfishness and sin. God gave Korah an honored place, caring for his tabernacle, yet Korah was unsatisfied. Unless we are careful, we can fall into the same sin. Instead of being grateful for God's grace and finding our deepest satisfaction in Christ, we can give in to our pride and envy. That road always leads to a pit of disaster.

his followers: "In the morning the LORD will show who belongs to him and who is holy,[l] and he will have that person come near him. The man he chooses[m] he will cause to come near him. 6 You, Korah, and all your followers are to do this: Take censers 7 and tomorrow put burning coals and incense in them before the LORD. The man the LORD chooses will be the one who is holy. You Levites have gone too far!"

8 Moses also said to Korah, "Now listen, you Levites! 9 Isn't it enough for you that the God of Israel has separated you from the rest of the Israelite community and brought you near himself to do the work at the LORD's tabernacle and to stand before the community and minister to them?[n] 10 He has brought you and all your fellow Levites near himself, but now you are trying to get the priesthood too.[o] 11 It is against the LORD that you and all your followers have banded together. Who is Aaron that you should grumble[p] against him?[q]"

12 Then Moses summoned Dathan and Abiram, the sons of Eliab. But they said, "We will not come! 13 Isn't it enough that you have brought us up out of a land flowing with milk and honey to kill us in the wilderness?[r] And now you also want to lord it over us![s] 14 Moreover, you haven't brought us into a land flowing with milk and honey[t] or given us an inheritance of fields and vineyards.[u] Do you want to treat these men like slaves[a]?[v] No, we will not come!"

15 Then Moses became very angry and said to the LORD, "Do not accept their offering. I have not taken so much as a donkey[w] from them, nor have I wronged any of them."

16 Moses said to Korah, "You and all your followers are to appear before the LORD tomorrow — you and they and Aaron.[x] 17 Each man is to take his censer and put incense in it — 250 censers in all — and present it before the LORD. You and Aaron are to present your censers also." 18 So each of them took his censer, put burning coals and incense in it, and stood with Moses and Aaron at the entrance to the tent of meeting. 19 When Korah had gathered all his followers in opposition to them[y] at the entrance to the tent of meeting, the glory of the LORD[z] appeared to the entire assembly. 20 The LORD said to Moses and Aaron, 21 "Separate yourselves from this assembly so I can put an end to them at once."[a]

22 But Moses and Aaron fell facedown[b] and cried out, "O God, the God who gives breath to all living things,[c] will you be angry with the entire assembly when only one man sins?"[d]

23 Then the LORD said to Moses, 24 "Say to the assembly, 'Move away from the tents of Korah, Dathan and Abiram.' "

25 Moses got up and went to Dathan and Abiram, and the elders of Israel followed him. 26 He warned the assembly, "Move back from the tents of these wicked men![e] Do not touch anything belonging to them, or you will be swept away[f] because of all their sins." 27 So they moved away from the tents of Korah, Dathan and Abiram. Dathan and Abiram had come out and were standing with their wives, children and little ones at the entrances to their tents.

28 Then Moses said, "This is how you

16:5 [l] Lev 10:3; 2Ti 2:19* [m] Nu 17:5; Ps 65:4
16:9 [n] Nu 3:6; Dt 10:8
16:10 [o] Nu 3:10; 18:7
16:11 [p] 1Co 10:10 [q] Ex 16:7
16:13 [r] Nu 14:2 [s] Ac 7:27,35
16:14 [t] Lev 20:24 [u] Ex 22:5; 23:11; Nu 20:5 [v] Jdg 16:21; 1Sa 11:2
16:15 [w] 1Sa 12:3
16:16 [x] ver 6
16:19 [y] ver 42 [z] Ex 16:7; Nu 14:10; 20:6
16:21 [a] Ex 32:10
16:22 [b] Nu 14:5 [c] Nu 27:16; Job 12:10; Heb 12:9 [d] Ge 18:23
16:26 [e] Isa 52:11 [f] Ge 19:15

Nu 16:8-11 ❖ Have you ever felt like your current calling or task isn't good enough? Why?

[a] 14 Or *to deceive these men*; Hebrew *Will you gouge out the eyes of these men*

---

authorized priests, they died for offering incense with unauthorized fire (Lev 10:1–2).

16:9–11 Moses inversely mirrors the introduction of Korah & Co.: "Is it (too) small for you . . . ?" (v. 9, alternate translation). Moses' punch line hits the proverbial nail on the head (v. 11). At issue is theocratic leadership of the community.

16:12–14 Refusing Moses' summons, Dathan and Abiram send an insulting message. As far as they are concerned, Moses is the problem blocking the way to real progress.

16:15 Moses has put up with a lot in the past, but the outrageous defamations hurled at him turn him into an anti-intercessor.

16:18–21 It is surprising that Korah & Co. show up at the court of the sanctuary the next day for an incense duel with Aaron (v. 18). Apparently ambition blinds them to the danger in which they find themselves.

16:22–27 Moses and Aaron's question of theodicy (v. 22) is reminiscent of Abraham's plea for Sodom (Ge 18:25). In response, the Lord commands Moses to save the majority of the people by isolating the rebel leaders (Nu 16:23–24). To do this, Moses goes to the Reubenite encampment of Dathan and Abiram, who have not been willing to come to him (vv. 25–27).

16:28–30 Moses proposes a test of his own divinely mandated leadership.

will know that the LORD has sent me[g]
to do all these things and that it was not
my idea: 29If these men die a natural
death and suffer the fate of all mankind,
then the LORD has not sent me.[h] 30But if
the LORD brings about something totally
new, and the earth opens its mouth and
swallows them, with everything that belongs to them, and they go down alive
into the realm of the dead,[i] then you will
know that these men have treated the
LORD with contempt."
31As soon as he finished saying all this,
the ground under them split apart[j] 32and
the earth opened its mouth and swallowed them[k] and their households, and
all those associated with Korah, together with their possessions. 33They went
down alive into the realm of the dead,
with everything they owned; the earth
closed over them, and they perished
and were gone from the community.
34At their cries, all the Israelites around
them fled, shouting, "The earth is going
to swallow us too!"
35And fire came out from the LORD[l]
and consumed[m] the 250 men who were
offering the incense.
36The LORD said to Moses, 37"Tell Eleazar son of Aaron, the priest, to remove
the censers from the charred remains
and scatter the coals some distance away,
for the censers are holy— 38the censers
of the men who sinned at the cost of their
lives.[n] Hammer the censers into sheets to
overlay the altar, for they were presented
before the LORD and have become holy.
Let them be a sign[o] to the Israelites."
39So Eleazar the priest collected the
bronze censers brought by those who had
been burned to death, and he had them
hammered out to overlay the altar, 40as
the LORD directed him through Moses.
This was to remind the Israelites that no
one except a descendant of Aaron should
come to burn incense[p] before the LORD,[q]
or he would become like Korah and his
followers.[r]
41The next day the whole Israelite
community grumbled against Moses
and Aaron. "You have killed the LORD's
people," they said.
42But when the assembly gathered
in opposition[s] to Moses and Aaron and
turned toward the tent of meeting, suddenly the cloud covered it and the glory
of the LORD appeared. 43Then Moses and
Aaron went to the front of the tent of
meeting, 44and the LORD said to Moses,
45"Get away from this assembly so I can
put an end to them at once." And they
fell facedown.
46Then Moses said to Aaron, "Take
your censer and put incense in it, along
with burning coals from the altar, and
hurry to the assembly[t] to make atonement[u] for them. Wrath has come out
from the LORD; the plague[v] has started." 47So Aaron did as Moses said, and
ran into the midst of the assembly. The
plague had already started among the
people,[w] but Aaron offered the incense
and made atonement for them. 48He
stood between the living and the dead,
and the plague stopped.[x] 49But 14,700
people died from the plague, in addition
to those who had died because of Korah.[y]
50Then Aaron returned to Moses at the
entrance to the tent of meeting, for the
plague had stopped.[a]

The Budding of Aaron's Staff

17[b] The LORD said to Moses, 2"Speak to
the Israelites and get twelve staffs
from them, one from the leader of each
of their ancestral tribes. Write the name

16:28 [g] Ex 3:12; Jn 5:36; 6:38
16:29 [h] Ecc 3:19
16:30 [i] ver 33; Ps 55:15
16:31 [j] Mic 1:3-4
16:32 [k] Nu 26:11; Dt 11:6; Ps 106:17
16:35 [l] Nu 11:1-3; 26:10 [m] Lev 10:2
16:38 [n] Pr 20:2 [o] Nu 26:10; Eze 14:8; 2Pe 2:6
16:40 [p] Ex 30:7-10; Nu 1:51 [q] 2Ch 26:18 [r] Nu 3:10
16:42 [s] ver 19; Nu 20:6
16:46 [t] Lev 10:6 [u] Nu 18:5; 25:13; Dt 9:22 [v] Nu 8:19; Ps 106:29
16:47 [w] Nu 25:6-8
16:48 [x] Nu 25:8; Ps 106:30
16:49 [y] ver 32

[a] *50* In Hebrew texts 16:36-50 is numbered 17:1-15.
[b] In Hebrew texts 17:1-13 is numbered 17:16-28.

16:31-34 Loss of any innocent family members who belong to them, such as young children, is punishment on the rebels themselves, not on the innocents.

16:1-35 It is easy to point at Korah & Co. with horror and disgust, affirming that we would never have a falling away as they did. However, the subsurface cause of their failure gives us pause because we too can neglect the private inner world where our spiritual connection to God resides. Rather than wait for that sinking feeling when we do something irreparably stupid, it is better to replenish our stores from the Source that supports the foundation of our being.

16:36-40 While the men were perishable, their censers were not. God's solution is to have Eleazar retrieve the censers and have them hammered out as a supplementary plating to overlay the outer altar, a warning against freelance priestly activities.
16:41-50 When the Israelites deliberately attribute the work of God to the powers of darkness, Aaron's mediation saves the community from extermination. The aftermath shows a high body count (v. 49).
17:1-8 To put the final nail in the coffin of opposition, the Lord sets up one final test. The extent to which the Lord abundantly emphasizes his choice is startling: Aaron's staff has also blossomed and

of each man on his staff. 3On the staff of
Levi write Aaron's name,[z] for there must
be one staff for the head of each ancestral
tribe. 4Place them in the tent of meeting
in front of the ark of the covenant law,[a]
where I meet with you.[b] 5The staff belonging to the man I choose[c] will sprout, and I
will rid myself of this constant grumbling
against you by the Israelites."
6So Moses spoke to the Israelites, and
their leaders gave him twelve staffs, one
for the leader of each of their ancestral
tribes, and Aaron's staff was among
them. 7Moses placed the staffs before
the LORD in the tent of the covenant law.[d]
8The next day Moses entered the tent
and saw that Aaron's staff, which represented the tribe of Levi, had not only
sprouted but had budded, blossomed
and produced almonds.[e] 9Then Moses
brought out all the staffs from the LORD's
presence to all the Israelites. They looked
at them, and each of the leaders took his
own staff.
10The LORD said to Moses, "Put back
Aaron's staff in front of the ark of the
covenant law, to be kept as a sign to the
rebellious.[f] This will put an end to their
grumbling against me, so that they will
not die." 11Moses did just as the LORD
commanded him.
12The Israelites said to Moses, "We will
die! We are lost, we are all lost![g] 13Anyone
who even comes near the tabernacle of
the LORD will die.[h] Are we all going to die?"

Duties of Priests and Levites

18 The LORD said to Aaron, "You,
your sons and your family are

17:3 [z] Nu 1:3
17:4 [a] ver 7 [b] Ex 25:22
17:5 [c] Nu 16:5
17:7 [d] Ex 38:21; Ac 7:44
17:8 [e] Eze 17:24; Heb 9:4
17:10 [f] Dt 9:24
17:12 [g] Isa 6:5
17:13 [h] Nu 1:51
18:1 [i] Ex 28:38
18:2 [j] Nu 3:10
18:3 [k] Nu 1:51 [l] ver 7; Nu 4:15
18:5 [m] Nu 16:46
18:6 [n] Nu 3:9
18:7 [o] Heb 9:3, 6 [p] ver 20; Ex 29:9 [q] Nu 3:10

Nu 17:6-8 ❖ How does God indicate those he has chosen for leadership among his people today?

Nu 18:7 ❖ Why is it a "gift" to serve as a priest? What does living with a priest's calling mean to believers today (see 1Pe 2:9)?

to bear the responsibility for offenses connected with the sanctuary,[i] and
you and your sons alone are to bear the
responsibility for offenses connected
with the priesthood. 2Bring your fellow
Levites from your ancestral tribe to join
you and assist you when you and your
sons minister[j] before the tent of the
covenant law. 3They are to be responsible to you and are to perform all the
duties of the tent,[k] but they must not
go near the furnishings of the sanctuary or the altar. Otherwise both they
and you will die.[l] 4They are to join you
and be responsible for the care of the
tent of meeting — all the work at the
tent — and no one else may come near
where you are.
5"You are to be responsible for the care
of the sanctuary and the altar,[m] so that
my wrath will not fall on the Israelites
again. 6I myself have selected your fellow Levites from among the Israelites
as a gift to you,[n] dedicated to the LORD
to do the work at the tent of meeting.
7But only you and your sons may serve
as priests in connection with everything
at the altar and inside the curtain.[o] I am
giving you the service of the priesthood
as a gift.[p] Anyone else who comes near
the sanctuary is to be put to death.[q]"

---

produced almonds! Why almonds? The cups of the golden lampstand in the tabernacle were "shaped like almond flowers with buds and blossoms" (Ex 25:33–34). The Hebrew word for "almond" is derived from the verb which means "watch/be awake." Watchfulness is the point of the sanctuary lamps burning all night (Ex 27:21; Lev 24:3).

✥ **16:36—17:11** The Israelites of the exodus generation had difficulty trusting authority. The Lord's example teaches us this: Love people consistently and persistently with everything you have, but if they ultimately choose to reject you, let them go because you can't force them to be grateful or to love you in return. Like Moses, Aaron, and the later Hebrew prophets, we are accountable for the quality of the service we give, not the responses we get.

17:12-13 The Israelites fear that they will die, especially if they come near the tabernacle of God's presence.
18:1-4 God calms their fears by altering the rules of engagement: The Levite tribe, including the priests, will from now on bear the liability of the sanctuary, and the priests alone will bear the liability of their priesthood (v. 1; cf. v. 23). This means that if one or more non-Levite violates the sanctity of the sanctuary, divine wrath will break out only against the Levites, in addition to the unauthorized persons themselves. If a non-priest (including a Levite) encroaches on a priestly prerogative, God will also hold the priests responsible (v. 3) because it is up to them to ensure that this does not happen. However, the Lord will no longer unleash his destruction against the whole community.
18:7 Two places of priestly service are mentioned here—outer altar and inner sanctum—but not the outer sanctum, the outermost and innermost areas of priestly service.

Offerings for Priests and Levites

8Then the LORD said to Aaron, "I myself have put you in charge of the offerings presented to me; all the holy offerings the Israelites give me I give to you and your sons as your portion, your perpetual share.[r] 9You are to have the part of the most holy offerings that is kept from the fire. From all the gifts they bring me as most holy offerings, whether grain[s] or sin[a][t] or guilt offerings,[u] that part belongs to you and your sons. 10Eat it as something most holy; every male shall eat it.[v] You must regard it as holy.

11"This also is yours: whatever is set aside from the gifts of all the wave offerings[w] of the Israelites. I give this to you and your sons and daughters as your perpetual share. Everyone in your household who is ceremonially clean[x] may eat it.

12"I give you all the finest olive oil and all the finest new wine and grain they give the LORD as the firstfruits of their harvest.[y] 13All the land's firstfruits that they bring to the LORD will be yours.[z] Everyone in your household who is ceremonially clean may eat it.

14"Everything in Israel that is devoted[b] to the LORD[a] is yours. 15The first offspring of every womb, both human and animal, that is offered to the LORD is yours.[b] But you must redeem[c] every firstborn son and every firstborn male of unclean animals.[d] 16When they are a month old, you must redeem them at the redemption price set at five shekels[c][e] of silver, according to the sanctuary shekel,[f] which weighs twenty gerahs.

17"But you must not redeem the firstborn of a cow, a sheep or a goat; they are holy.[g] Splash their blood[h] against the altar and burn their fat as a food offering, an aroma pleasing to the LORD. 18Their meat is to be yours, just as the breast of the wave offering[i] and the right thigh are yours. 19Whatever is set aside from the holy offerings the Israelites present to the LORD I give to you and your sons and daughters as your perpetual share. It is an everlasting covenant of salt[j] before the LORD for both you and your offspring."

20The LORD said to Aaron, "You will have no inheritance in their land, nor will you have any share among them;[k] I am your share and your inheritance[l] among the Israelites.

21"I give to the Levites all the tithes[m] in Israel as their inheritance[n] in return for the work they do while serving at the tent of meeting. 22From now on the Israelites must not go near the tent of meeting, or they will bear the consequences of their sin and will die.[o] 23It is the Levites who are to do the work at the tent of meeting and bear the responsibility for any offenses they commit against it. This is a lasting ordinance for the generations to come. They will receive no inheritance[p] among the Israelites. 24Instead, I give to the Levites as their inheritance the tithes that the Israelites present as an offering to the LORD. That is why I said concerning them: 'They will have no inheritance among the Israelites.'"

25The LORD said to Moses, 26"Speak to the Levites and say to them: 'When you receive from the Israelites the tithe I give you[q] as your inheritance, you must present a tenth of that tithe as the LORD's offering.[r] 27Your offering will be reckoned to you as grain from the threshing floor or juice from the winepress. 28In this way you also will present an offering to the LORD from all the tithes[s] you receive from the Israelites. From these tithes you must give the LORD's portion to Aaron the priest. 29You must present

18:8 [r] Lev 6:16; 7:6,31-34,36
18:9 [s] Lev 2:1 [t] Lev 6:25 [u] Lev 5:15; 7:7
18:10 [v] Lev 6:16
18:11 [w] Ex 29:26 [x] Lev 22:1-16
18:12 [y] Ex 23:19; Ne 10:35
18:13 [z] Ex 22:29; 23:19
18:14 [a] Lev 27:28
18:15 [b] Ex 13:2 [c] Nu 3:46 [d] Ex 13:13
18:16 [e] Lev 27:6 [f] Ex 30:13
18:17 [g] Dt 15:19 [h] Lev 3:2
18:18 [i] Lev 7:30
18:19 [j] Lev 2:13; 2Ch 13:5
18:20 [k] Dt 12:12 [l] Dt 10:9; 14:27; 18:1-2; Jos 13:33; Eze 44:28
18:21 [m] Dt 14:22; Mal 3:8 [n] Lev 27:30-33; Heb 7:5
18:22 [o] Lev 22:9; Nu 1:51
18:23 [p] ver 20
18:26 [q] ver 21 [r] Ne 10:38
18:28 [s] Mal 3:8

[a] 9 Or *purification* [b] 14 The Hebrew term refers to the irrevocable giving over of things or persons to the LORD. [c] 16 That is, about 2 ounces or about 58 grams

---

18:8-30 The remainder of Nu 18 reiterates and further details the portions of sacred gifts that belong to the priests and Levites. Placement of this legislation here accomplishes two things. (1) The Lord further affirms his choice of the Aaronic priests and the Levites who assist them. (2) The Lord rewards them for their potentially hazardous work at the sanctuary.

18:20-24 In lieu of a separate tribal territory in the promised land, the priests and other Levites will receive wages from the Lord consisting of agricultural tithes.

17:12—18:32 The NT does not specify a tithe as a means of support for the Christian ministry. However, it is easy to see how the tithe principle could be applied for maintaining a stable source of support for the Lord's work. Since most of us are not farmers, our income consists of money rather than net agricultural produce (not including seed for replanting). So, we can give a tenth of our net money income and take God up on his offer to bless us (Mal 3:10).

as the LORD's portion the best and holiest
part of everything given to you.'
30“Say to the Levites: 'When you present the best part, it will be reckoned
to you as the product of the threshing
floor or the winepress.[t] 31You and your
households may eat the rest of it anywhere, for it is your wages for your work
at the tent of meeting. 32By presenting
the best part[u] of it you will not be guilty
in this matter; then you will not defile
the holy offerings[v] of the Israelites, and
you will not die.'”

The Water of Cleansing

19 The LORD said to Moses and Aaron: 2“This is a requirement of the
law that the LORD has commanded: Tell
the Israelites to bring you a red heifer[w] without defect or blemish[x] and that
has never been under a yoke.[y] 3Give it
to Eleazar[z] the priest; it is to be taken
outside the camp[a] and slaughtered in
his presence. 4Then Eleazar the priest is
to take some of its blood on his finger
and sprinkle[b] it seven times toward the
front of the tent of meeting. 5While he
watches, the heifer is to be burned — its
hide, flesh, blood and intestines.[c] 6The
priest is to take some cedar wood, hyssop[d] and scarlet wool[e] and throw them
onto the burning heifer. 7After that, the
priest must wash his clothes and bathe
himself with water.[f] He may then come
into the camp, but he will be ceremonially unclean till evening. 8The man who
burns it must also wash his clothes and
bathe with water, and he too will be unclean till evening.

18:30 [t] ver 27
18:32 [u] Lev 22:15 [v] Lev 19:8
19:2 [w] Ge 15:9; Heb 9:13 [x] Lev 22:19-25 [y] Dt 21:3; 1Sa 6:7
19:3 [z] Nu 3:4 [a] Lev 4:12,21; Heb 13:11
19:4 [b] Lev 4:17
19:5 [c] Ex 29:14
19:6 [d] ver 18; Ps 51:7 [e] Lev 14:4
19:7 [f] Lev 11:25; 16:26,28; 22:6

Nu 19:9-10 ❖ How does the water of cleansing deepen our understanding of the work of Christ and the Spirit (see Titus 3:4-7)?

9“A man who is clean shall gather up
the ashes of the heifer[g] and put them
in a ceremonially clean place outside
the camp. They are to be kept by the Israelite community for use in the water
of cleansing;[h] it is for purification from
sin. 10The man who gathers up the ashes
of the heifer must also wash his clothes,
and he too will be unclean till evening.
This will be a lasting ordinance both for
the Israelites and for the foreigners residing among them.
11“Whoever touches a human corpse[i]
will be unclean for seven days.[j] 12They
must purify themselves with the water
on the third day and on the seventh day;[k]
then they will be clean. But if they do not
purify themselves on the third and seventh days, they will not be clean. 13If they
fail to purify themselves after touching
a human corpse,[l] they defile the LORD's
tabernacle.[m] They must be cut off from
Israel.[n] Because the water of cleansing
has not been sprinkled on them, they
are unclean;[o] their uncleanness remains
on them.
14“This is the law that applies when a
person dies in a tent: Anyone who enters
the tent and anyone who is in it will be
unclean for seven days, 15and every open
container without a lid fastened on it
will be unclean.
16“Anyone out in the open who touches

19:9 [g] Heb 9:13 [h] ver 13; Nu 8:7
19:11 [i] Lev 21:1; Nu 5:2 [j] Nu 31:19
19:12 [k] ver 19; Nu 31:19
19:13 [l] Lev 20:3 [m] Lev 15:31; 2Ch 36:14 [n] Lev 7:20; 22:3 [o] Hag 2:13

19:1-10 The victim supplied by the community is to be female, like other purification offerings for the benefit of individual commoners. It must be a cow, the largest female sacrificeable animal, so that it will supply a maximum quantity of ashes. It must be reddish to evoke the color of blood. Like other sacrificial victims, it must be unblemished. Additionally, even though the ritual is outside the camp, the cow must not have been used as a work animal.

19:3-4 The son of the high priest is to supervise the sacrificial slaughter of the cow and then “take some of its blood on his finger and sprinkle it seven times toward the front of the tent of meeting” (v. 4). Since the ritual is performed outside the sacred areas, this gesture establishes symbolic interaction with the sanctuary in order to make the procedure a sacrificial one.

19:6 Into the midst of the fire where the cow is burning, the priest must toss cedar wood, hyssop, and crimson yarn. Similarities are striking between cleansing from corpse contamination and the first-day ritual to treat a person or house for the ritual impurity of skin disease, in which hyssop, along with cedar wood and crimson yarn, was dipped into a mixture of blood and fresh water, which was then sprinkled on the person/house undergoing purification (Lev 14:4-7, 49-52). Skin disease, like corpse contamination, was closely connected with death.

19:10b-22 This section outlines the procedure and rules for applying the water and explains how this form of impurity is contracted. After the sprinkling on the seventh day, cleansing also requires laundering clothes, bathing, and waiting until evening (v. 19). Remaining in a state of impurity by neglecting the ritual will have the grave consequence of defiling the Lord's tabernacle, for which the culprit will suffer the divine penalty of being “cut off” (v. 13). The ashes are available at no charge, and the procedure is quick and easy, so there is no excuse for noncompliance.

someone who has been killed with a sword or someone who has died a natural death,[p] or anyone who touches a human bone or a grave,[q] will be unclean for seven days.

17"For the unclean person, put some ashes[r] from the burned purification offering into a jar and pour fresh water over them. 18Then a man who is ceremonially clean is to take some hyssop,[s] dip it in the water and sprinkle the tent and all the furnishings and the people who were there. He must also sprinkle anyone who has touched a human bone or a grave or anyone who has been killed or anyone who has died a natural death. 19The man who is clean is to sprinkle those who are unclean on the third and seventh days, and on the seventh day he is to purify them.[t] Those who are being cleansed must wash their clothes and bathe with water, and that evening they will be clean. 20But if those who are unclean do not purify themselves, they must be cut off from the community, because they have defiled the sanctuary of the LORD. The water of cleansing has not been sprinkled on them, and they are unclean. 21This is a lasting ordinance for them.

"The man who sprinkles the water of cleansing must also wash his clothes, and anyone who touches the water of cleansing will be unclean till evening. 22Anything that an unclean[u] person touches becomes unclean, and anyone who touches it becomes unclean till evening."

19:16 [p] Nu 31:19 [q] Mt 23:27
19:17 [r] ver 9
19:18 [s] ver 6
19:19 [t] Eze 36:25; Heb 10:22
19:22 [u] Lev 5:2; Hag 2:13,14
20:1 [v] Nu 13:21 [w] Nu 33:36 [x] Ex 15:20
20:2 [y] Ex 17:1 [z] Nu 16:19
20:3 [a] Ex 17:2 [b] Nu 14:2; 16:31-35
20:4 [c] Ex 14:11; 17:3; Nu 14:3; 16:13
20:5 [d] Nu 16:14
20:6 [e] Nu 14:5 [f] Nu 16:19
20:8 [g] Ex 4:17, 20 [h] Ex 17:6; Isa 43:20
20:9 [i] Nu 17:10

Nu 20:9-12 ❖ Has frustration with others ever affected your obedience to God? How?

Water From the Rock

20 In the first month the whole Israelite community arrived at the Desert of Zin,[v] and they stayed at Kadesh.[w] There Miriam[x] died and was buried.

2Now there was no water for the community,[y] and the people gathered in opposition[z] to Moses and Aaron. 3They quarreled[a] with Moses and said, "If only we had died when our brothers fell dead before the LORD![b] 4Why did you bring the LORD's community into this wilderness, that we and our livestock should die here?[c] 5Why did you bring us up out of Egypt to this terrible place? It has no grain or figs, grapevines or pomegranates.[d] And there is no water to drink!"

6Moses and Aaron went from the assembly to the entrance to the tent of meeting and fell facedown,[e] and the glory of the LORD[f] appeared to them. 7The LORD said to Moses, 8"Take the staff,[g] and you and your brother Aaron gather the assembly together. Speak to that rock before their eyes and it will pour out its water.[h] You will bring water out of the rock for the community so they and their livestock can drink."

9So Moses took the staff from the LORD's presence,[i] just as he commanded

---

✚ **19:1-22** Hebrews 9:13-14 speaks of another death that provides assurance. Here "the ashes" refers to application of ash water, functioning like blood, from the red cow/heifer. If this procedure could affect cleansing from ritual impurity, which was associated with mortality, how much more does the once-for-all death of the Son of God make abundant, ongoing provision for cleansing us morally, spiritually, and ultimately from mortality itself (cf. 1Co 15:51-54) by his blood?

When the Israelites sinned or encountered impurity, God gave them adequate opportunity to benefit from his remedies. In the meantime, they were covered by corporate sacrifices on their behalf, including daily burnt offerings and additional burnt and purification offerings performed on Sabbaths, new moons, and annual festivals (Nu 28-29). Having this opportunity available was no substitute for personally taking it. Similarly, Christ's sacrifice has provided the only way out of our dilemma (Ac 4:12), with daily opportunities for restoration. His sacrifice is our only assurance.

20:1 Miriam's obituary is a simple one. It appears that Miriam dies near the end of Israel's desert journey.

20:2-5 At Kadesh the Israelites dispute with Moses because there is no water. The Israelites accuse them of abusing their God-given (and therefore legal) responsibility to take care of his community (vv. 4-5).

20:7-8 The Lord instructs Moses to take the staff to a rock so that water will come out of it. At Rephidim Moses struck the rock (Ex 17:6), but this time, he and Aaron are to merely speak (plural) to the rock (Nu 20:8). This will be an even greater miracle, as there is no possibility that a physical blow will simply dislodge the natural plug to an aquifer.

20:9-10 Apparently the sight of all those recalcitrant people gathered in front of the rock is too much for Moses. Uncharacteristically "losing it," he angrily lashes out verbally and then physically, whacking the rock with his staff—not just once but twice.

him. 10He and Aaron gathered the assembly together in front of the rock
and Moses said to them, “Listen, you
rebels, must we bring you water out of
this rock?”[j] 11Then Moses raised his arm
and struck the rock twice with his staff.
Water[k] gushed out, and the community
and their livestock drank.
12But the LORD said to Moses and Aaron, “Because you did not trust in me
enough to honor me as holy[l] in the sight
of the Israelites, you will not bring this
community into the land I give them.”[m]
13These were the waters of Meribah,[a][n]
where the Israelites quarreled[o] with the
LORD and where he was proved holy
among them.

Edom Denies Israel Passage

14Moses sent messengers from Kadesh[p]
to the king of Edom,[q] saying:

“This is what your brother Israel
says: You know[r] about all the hardships that have come on us. 15Our
ancestors went down into Egypt,[s]
and we lived there many years.[t] The
Egyptians mistreated[u] us and our
ancestors, 16but when we cried out
to the LORD, he heard our cry[v] and
sent an angel[w] and brought us out
of Egypt.
“Now we are here at Kadesh, a
town on the edge of your territory. 17Please let us pass through your
country. We will not go through any
field or vineyard, or drink water
from any well. We will travel along
the King’s Highway and not turn to
the right or to the left until we have
passed through your territory.[x]”

18But Edom answered:

“You may not pass through here;
if you try, we will march out and attack you with the sword.”

19The Israelites replied:

“We will go along the main road,
and if we or our livestock[y] drink any
of your water, we will pay for it.[z] We
only want to pass through on foot—
nothing else.”

20Again they answered:

“You may not pass through.”

Then Edom came out against them
with a large and powerful army. 21Since
Edom refused to let them go through their
territory, Israel turned away from them.[a]

The Death of Aaron

22The whole Israelite community set
out from Kadesh and came to Mount
Hor.[b] 23At Mount Hor, near the border of
Edom,[c] the LORD said to Moses and Aaron, 24“Aaron will be gathered to his people.[d] He will not enter the land I give the
Israelites, because both of you rebelled
against my command[e] at the waters of
Meribah. 25Get Aaron and his son Eleazar
and take them up Mount Hor.[f] 26Remove
Aaron’s garments and put them on his

20:10 [j] Ps 106:32,33
20:11 [k] Ex 17:6; Dt 8:15; Ps 78:16; Isa 48:2; 1Co 10:4
20:12 [l] Nu 27:14 [m] ver 24; Dt 1:37; 3:27
20:13 [n] Ex 17:7 [o] Dt 33:8; Ps 95:8; 106:32
20:14 [p] Jdg 11:16-17 [q] Dt 2:4 [r] Jos 2:11; 9:9
20:15 [s] Ge 46:6 [t] Ge 15:13; Ex 12:40 [u] Ex 1:11; Dt 26:6
20:16 [v] Ex 2:23; 3:7 [w] Ex 14:19
20:17 [x] Nu 21:22
20:19 [y] Ex 12:38 [z] Dt 2:6,28
20:21 [a] Dt 2:8; Jdg 11:18
20:22 [b] Nu 33:37
20:23 [c] Nu 33:37
20:24 [d] Ge 25:8 [e] ver 10
20:25 [f] Nu 33:38

[a] 13 *Meribah* means *quarreling.*

20:12 While a lot of water gushes out for the people and their livestock, it is not the miracle God intended. Aaron did not participate in the miracle and thereby affirm his co-leadership, and Moses spoke to the people instead of the rock, which he struck. Although Moses sinned in the heat of the moment, apparently without planning to, his is a grave offense committed in full view of the community to which he is supposed to be an example. For this failure, God denies Moses and Aaron the privilege of leading the Israelites into the promised land.
20:14–21 Moses’ message to Edom in vv. 14–17 comes at the beginning of a continuous stream of events leading to the Israelite conquest. Deuteronomy 2:14 puts the encounter with Edom in relative chronological perspective. Numbers 20 skips almost everything that happens during the thirty-eight years as unworthy of mention. These are just dull decades of death in the desert.
20:22–29 Aaron’s son Eleazar accompanies Aaron and Moses up the mountain so that Moses can transfer Aaron’s high priestly garments to Eleazar. Presumably this procedure avoids corpse contamination of the sacred clothing, and Moses, not the new high priest, buries his brother. As with Miriam, Aaron also dies at the end of the desert wandering period.

20:1–29 As God’s servants our job is to do what he says and let God be God. This is easier said than done. It can be excruciating to exercise such restraint. By punishing Moses and Aaron, the Lord shows that no amount of human merit amassed through past obedience can atone for even one sin. Jesus said to his disciples, “So you also, when you have done everything you were told to do, should say, ‘We are unworthy servants; we have only done our duty’” (Lk 17:10). To be responsible for living and responding to God at a high level as an example to other people is simply one of the duties and occupational hazards of being his servant.

son Eleazar, for Aaron will be gathered
to his people;[g] he will die there."
27Moses did as the LORD commanded:
They went up Mount Hor in the sight of
the whole community. 28Moses removed
Aaron's garments and put them on his
son Eleazar.[h] And Aaron died there[i] on
top of the mountain. Then Moses and
Eleazar came down from the mountain, 29and when the whole community
learned that Aaron had died, all the Israelites mourned for him[j] thirty days.

Arad Destroyed

21 When the Canaanite king of Arad,[k]
who lived in the Negev,[l] heard that
Israel was coming along the road to Ath-
arim, he attacked the Israelites and captured some of them. 2Then Israel made
this vow to the LORD: "If you will deliver these people into our hands, we will
totally destroy[a] their cities." 3The LORD
listened to Israel's plea and gave the Canaanites over to them. They completely
destroyed them and their towns; so the
place was named Hormah.[b]

The Bronze Snake

4They traveled from Mount Hor[m] along
the route to the Red Sea,[c] to go around
Edom. But the people grew impatient
on the way;[n] 5they spoke against God[o]
and against Moses, and said, "Why have
you brought us up out of Egypt to die
in the wilderness?[p] There is no bread!
There is no water! And we detest this
miserable food!"[q]
6Then the LORD sent venomous snakes[r]
among them; they bit the people and
many Israelites died.[s] 7The people came
to Moses[t] and said, "We sinned when we
spoke against the LORD and against you.
Pray that the LORD[u] will take the snakes
away from us." So Moses prayed[v] for the
people.

20:26 [g] ver 24
20:28 [h] Ex 29:29 [i] Nu 33:38; Dt 10:6; 32:50
20:29 [j] Dt 34:8
21:1 [k] Nu 33:40; Jos 12:14 [l] Jdg 1:9,16
21:4 [m] Nu 20:22 [n] Dt 2:8; Jdg 11:18
21:5 [o] Ps 78:19 [p] Nu 14:2,3 [q] Nu 11:6
21:6 [r] Dt 8:15; Jer 8:17 [s] 1Co 10:9
21:7 [t] Ps 78:34; Hos 5:15 [u] Ex 8:8; Ac 8:24 [v] Nu 11:2

Nu 21:4-5 ❖ Can you relate to the Israelites' constant grumbling and impatience? Why? How? When? And how did God and others around you respond?

8The LORD said to Moses, "Make a
snake and put it up on a pole;[w] anyone
who is bitten can look at it and live." 9So
Moses made a bronze snake[x] and put it
up on a pole. Then when anyone was bitten by a snake and looked at the bronze
snake, they lived.[y]

The Journey to Moab

10The Israelites moved on and camped
at Oboth.[z] 11Then they set out from
Oboth and camped in Iye Abarim, in
the wilderness that faces Moab[a] toward
the sunrise. 12From there they moved
on and camped in the Zered Valley.[b]
13They set out from there and camped
alongside the Arnon[c], which is in the
wilderness extending into Amorite territory. The Arnon is the border of Moab,
between Moab and the Amorites. 14That
is why the Book of the Wars of the LORD
says:

"... Zahab[d] in Suphah and the
ravines,
the Arnon 15and[e] the slopes of the
ravines
that lead to the settlement of Ar[d]
and lie along the border of Moab."

16From there they continued on to Beer,[e]
the well where the LORD said to Moses,

21:8 [w] Jn 3:14
21:9 [x] 2Ki 18:4 [y] Jn 3:14-15
21:10 [z] Nu 33:43
21:11 [a] Nu 33:44
21:12 [b] Dt 2:13, 14
21:13 [c] Nu 22:36; Jdg 11:13,18
21:15 [d] ver 28; Dt 2:9,18
21:16 [e] Jdg 9:21

[a] 2 The Hebrew term refers to the irrevocable giving over of things or persons to the LORD, often by totally destroying them; also in verse 3. [b] 3 *Hormah* means *destruction.* [c] 4 Or *the Sea of Reeds* [d] 14 Septuagint; Hebrew *Waheb* [e] 14,15 Or *"I have been given from Suphah and the ravines / of the Arnon* 15*to*

21:1-3 Unlike the Edomites, these Canaanites are not relatives, inhabit part of the land promised to Israel, and actually attack first.
21:4-6 With all the extra travel, the Israelites become impatient (v. 4). Complaining that their appetite loathes manna, they insult God. The invasion of snakes is like the plagues on Egypt by which the Lord demonstrated his sovereignty over nature (Ex 7-10). If the Israelites prefer to live in Egypt, they will die like Egyptians.
21:8-9 God does not simply call off the serpents. Rather, he commands Moses to employ a visual antivenom, which Moses does by sculpting and displaying a snake out of bronze. The bronze snake is appointed by God, who alone is capable of healing his people. So although it is symbolic, it is not magical. To confront the serpent sculpture is to confront one's own sin and its result. It is the spiritual equivalent of looking in the mirror. That unspoken confession is all it takes to live.
21:10-15 A quotation from the "Book of the Wars of the LORD" emphasizes that the Arnon formed the border of Moab, so the Israelites are outside Moab. This lost historical source (cf. the "Book of Jashar" in Jos 10:13; 2Sa 1:18) is not mentioned anywhere else in the Bible.
21:16-18 Another potential crisis over water turns into a refreshing example of divine-human

"Gather the people together and I will
give them water."
17 Then Israel sang this song:[f]

"Spring up, O well!
Sing about it,
18 about the well that the princes dug,
that the nobles of the people
sank —
the nobles with scepters and
staffs."

Then they went from the wilderness to
Mattanah, 19 from Mattanah to Nahaliel,
from Nahaliel to Bamoth, 20 and from
Bamoth to the valley in Moab where the
top of Pisgah overlooks the wasteland.

Defeat of Sihon and Og

21 Israel sent messengers to say to Sihon[g] king of the Amorites:

22 "Let us pass through your country. We will not turn aside into any
field or vineyard, or drink water
from any well. We will travel along
the King's Highway until we have
passed through your territory.[h]"

23 But Sihon would not let Israel pass
through his territory.[i] He mustered
his entire army and marched out into
the wilderness against Israel. When he
reached Jahaz,[j] he fought with Israel.
24 Israel, however, put him to the sword[k]
and took over his land from the Arnon
to the Jabbok, but only as far as the Ammonites,[l] because their border was fortified. 25 Israel captured all the cities of
the Amorites[m] and occupied them, including Heshbon and all its surrounding
settlements. 26 Heshbon was the city of
Sihon[n] king of the Amorites, who had
fought against the former king of Moab
and had taken from him all his land as
far as the Arnon.

27 That is why the poets say:

"Come to Heshbon and let it be
rebuilt;
let Sihon's city be restored.

28 "Fire went out from Heshbon,
a blaze from the city of Sihon.[o]
It consumed Ar[p] of Moab,
the citizens of Arnon's heights.[q]
29 Woe to you, Moab![r]
You are destroyed, people of
Chemosh![s]
He has given up his sons as
fugitives[t]
and his daughters as captives[u]
to Sihon king of the Amorites.

30 "But we have overthrown them;
Heshbon's dominion has been
destroyed all the way to
Dibon.[v]
We have demolished them as far as
Nophah,
which extends to Medeba."

31 So Israel settled in the land of the
Amorites.
32 After Moses had sent spies to Jazer,[w]
the Israelites captured its surrounding
settlements and drove out the Amorites
who were there. 33 Then they turned and
went up along the road toward Bashan[x],[y]
and Og king of Bashan and his whole
army marched out to meet them in battle at Edrei.[z]
34 The LORD said to Moses, "Do not be
afraid of him, for I have delivered him
into your hands, along with his whole
army and his land. Do to him what you
did to Sihon king of the Amorites, who
reigned in Heshbon.[a]"
35 So they struck him down, together
with his sons and his whole army, leaving them no survivors. And they took
possession of his land.

21:17 [f] Ex 15:1
21:21 [g] Dt 1:4; 2:26-27; Jdg 11:19-21
21:22 [h] Nu 20:17
21:23 [i] Nu 20:21 [j] Dt 2:32; Jdg 11:20
21:24 [k] Dt 2:33; Ps 135:10-11; Am 2:9 [l] Dt 2:37
21:25 [m] Nu 13:29; Jdg 10:11; Am 2:10
21:26 [n] Dt 29:7; Ps 135:11
21:28 [o] Jer 48:45 [p] ver 15 [q] Nu 22:41; Isa 15:2
21:29 [r] Isa 25:10; Jer 48:46 [s] Jdg 11:24; 1Ki 11:7,33; 2Ki 23:13; Jer 48:7,46 [t] Isa 15:5 [u] Isa 16:2
21:30 [v] Nu 32:3; Isa 15:2; Jer 48:18,22
21:32 [w] Nu 32:1,3,35; Jer 48:32
21:33 [x] Dt 3:3 [y] Dt 3:4 [z] Dt 1:4; 3:1,10; Jos 13:12,31
21:34 [a] Dt 3:2

---

cooperation when the Israelites dig a well at the Lord's direction.

21:21–25 Not only does Sihon refuse Israel's diplomatic request with a military response as the king of Edom had; he comes out to attack Israel as the Canaanite king of Arad had. Like the Canaanites, the Amorites are not related to the Israelites, who have no qualms about crushing them and taking their land.

21:26–30 As supported by reference to some early poetry about Heshbon, Sihon's capital city, the king had earlier extended his border to the Arnon at Moab's expense.

21:33–35 Like Sihon, King Og of the fertile region of Bashan in the northern Transjordan confronts Israel with his army and suffers a similar fate.

21:1–35 When we truly sense that because Christ has already won, we who believe in him are all winners together. We too become energized, follow the game plan, and sacrifice rather than make up excuses. We too give generously, encourage rather than criticize, and assist others rather than vying with them to see who can become the greatest. Like the victorious Israelites, we can come together to a refreshing "well," a source of life that God has given to sustain us through the "desert."

Balak Summons Balaam

22 Then the Israelites traveled to the
plains of Moab and camped along
the Jordan across from Jericho.[b]
2Now Balak son of Zippor[c] saw all that
Israel had done to the Amorites, 3and
Moab was terrified because there were
so many people. Indeed, Moab was filled
with dread[d] because of the Israelites.
4The Moabites said to the elders of
Midian, "This horde is going to lick up
everything around us, as an ox licks up
the grass of the field."
So Balak son of Zippor, who was king
of Moab at that time, 5sent messengers
to summon Balaam son of Beor,[e] who
was at Pethor, near the Euphrates River,
in his native land. Balak said:

"A people has come out of Egypt;
they cover the face of the land and
have settled next to me. 6Now come
and put a curse[f] on these people,
because they are too powerful for
me. Perhaps then I will be able to
defeat them and drive them out of
the land. For I know that whoever
you bless is blessed, and whoever
you curse is cursed."

7The elders of Moab and Midian left,
taking with them the fee for divination.[g]
When they came to Balaam, they told
him what Balak had said.
8"Spend the night here," Balaam said
to them, "and I will report back to you
with the answer the LORD gives me.[h]" So
the Moabite officials stayed with him.
9God came to Balaam[i] and asked,[j]
"Who are these men with you?"
10Balaam said to God, "Balak son of
Zippor, king of Moab, sent me this message: 11'A people that has come out of
Egypt covers the face of the land. Now

22:1 [b] Nu 33:48
22:2 [c] Jdg 11:25
22:3 [d] Ex 15:15
22:5 [e] Dt 23:4; Jos 13:22; 24:9; Ne 13:2; Mic 6:5; 2Pe 2:15
22:6 [f] ver 12, 17; Nu 23:7, 11, 13
22:7 [g] Nu 23:23; 24:1
22:8 [h] ver 19
22:9 [i] Ge 20:3 [j] ver 20

22:2-3 With so many Israelites so close, King Balak and his people are seized by dread because they see what Israel has done to the Amorites, who earlier defeated Moab (21:26-30).
22:4-6 Balak comes up with a strategy to utilize a secret weapon: a curse by Balaam. Balak expects Balaam to soften up the Israelites and thereby even the odds so that his ground troops will have a fighting chance. Balaam, a diviner who originated from the northeast by the Euphrates River, has an international reputation for pronouncing effective blessings and curses.
22:8-13 This non-Israelite diviner is a kind of prophet and expects a revelation in the night. In an eighth-century BC group of inscriptions from Deir 'Alla, Jordan, Balaam son of Beor is remembered as a seer of the gods, who conveyed a disturbing message to him in an oracular vision at night.

PEOPLE TO KNOW // BALAAM

NUMBERS 22:1-34: As the Israelites passed through Moab on their journey to the promised land, the Moabites were filled with terror. Israel had just defeated the two great Amorite kings, Sihon and Og, and Moab feared they would be next. So Balak, king of Moab, hired the prophet Balaam to curse the Israelites in the hope that they could then be defeated in battle.

God told Balaam he could accompany Balak's men back to the king but warned Balaam to do only what God commanded. When Balaam saddled his donkey to travel to Balak, God's angel blocked Balaam on the road, sword in hand. What followed is one of the most bizarre stories in the Bible (Nu 22:21-41). When Balaam reached Balak, the king tried three times to make Balaam curse Israel. Instead of cursing them, Balaam blessed the Israelites. Balak became irate and told Balaam he had missed out on a generous reward by not cursing Israel. Balaam countered that he could not do anything on his own but could only obey the command of God. God's visceral and surprising reminder to Balaam to follow only what he said—delivered through the accusation of a donkey—evidently made an impression; however, it still didn't turn Balaam into a person who honored God above all.

APPLICATION ✚ The story of Balaam shows that God protects his people. When Israel's enemy tried to curse them, God turned it into a blessing. Human schemes cannot thwart God's plans.

Balaam also shows us the importance of obeying God's Word, even if others pressure us, bully us or bribe us. Balak was ready to reward Balaam richly, but Balaam had been clearly warned by God to speak only what God told him. Following God when it could mean missing out on material benefit may be difficult. Yet God's blessings for his children far outstrip the superficial rewards the world may offer.

come and put a curse on them for me.
Perhaps then I will be able to fight them
and drive them away.'"
12But God said to Balaam, "Do not go
with them. You must not put a curse on
those people, because they are blessed.[k]"
13The next morning Balaam got up and
said to Balak's officials, "Go back to your
own country, for the LORD has refused to
let me go with you."
14So the Moabite officials returned to
Balak and said, "Balaam refused to come
with us."
15Then Balak sent other officials, more
numerous and more distinguished than
the first. 16They came to Balaam and said:

"This is what Balak son of Zippor says: Do not let anything keep
you from coming to me, 17because
I will reward you handsomely[l] and
do whatever you say. Come and put
a curse[m] on these people for me."

18But Balaam answered them, "Even if
Balak gave me all the silver and gold in
his palace, I could not do anything great
or small to go beyond the command of
the LORD my God.[n] 19Now spend the night
here so that I can find out what else the
LORD will tell me.[o]"
20That night God came to Balaam[p]
and said, "Since these men have come
to summon you, go with them, but do
only what I tell you."[q]

Balaam's Donkey

21Balaam got up in the morning, saddled his donkey and went with the Moabite officials. 22But God was very angry[r]
when he went, and the angel of the LORD[s]
stood in the road to oppose him. Balaam
was riding on his donkey, and his two
servants were with him. 23When the donkey saw the angel of the LORD standing
in the road with a drawn sword[t] in his

22:12 [k] Ge 12:2; 22:17; Nu 23:20
22:17 [l] ver 37; Nu 24:11 [m] ver 6
22:18 [n] ver 38; Nu 23:12, 26; 24:13; 1Ki 22:14; 2Ch 18:13; Jer 42:4
22:19 [o] ver 8
22:20 [p] Ge 20:3 [q] ver 35, 38; Nu 23:5, 12, 16, 26; 24:13; 2Ch 18:13
22:22 [r] Ex 4:14 [s] Ge 16:7; Ex 23:20; Jdg 13:3, 6, 13
22:23 [t] Jos 5:13
[u] ver 25, 27
22:27 [v] Nu 11:1; Jas 1:19
22:28 [w] 2Pe 2:16 [x] ver 32
22:29 [y] Dt 25:4; Pr 12:10; 27:23-27; Mt 15:19
22:31 [z] Ge 21:19

Nu 22:28 ❖ What are the most surprising and unlikely means God has used to get our attention?

hand, it turned off the road into a field.
Balaam beat it[u] to get it back on the road.
24Then the angel of the LORD stood in a
narrow path through the vineyards, with
walls on both sides. 25When the donkey
saw the angel of the LORD, it pressed
close to the wall, crushing Balaam's foot
against it. So he beat the donkey again.
26Then the angel of the LORD moved
on ahead and stood in a narrow place
where there was no room to turn, either
to the right or to the left. 27When the
donkey saw the angel of the LORD, it lay
down under Balaam, and he was angry[v]
and beat it with his staff. 28Then the LORD
opened the donkey's mouth,[w] and it said
to Balaam, "What have I done to you to
make you beat me these three times?[x]"
29Balaam answered the donkey, "You
have made a fool of me! If only I had a
sword in my hand, I would kill you right
now.[y]"
30The donkey said to Balaam, "Am I
not your own donkey, which you have
always ridden, to this day? Have I been
in the habit of doing this to you?"
"No," he said.
31Then the LORD opened Balaam's
eyes,[z] and he saw the angel of the LORD
standing in the road with his sword
drawn. So he bowed low and fell facedown.
32The angel of the LORD asked him,
"Why have you beaten your donkey these
three times? I have come here to oppose
you because your path is a reckless one
before me.[a] 33The donkey saw me and
turned away from me these three times.

[a] *32* The meaning of the Hebrew for this clause is uncertain.

22:15–17 Not taking Balaam's divinely directed "no" for an answer, desperate Balak offers Balaam a tempting "blank check" to fill in any amount he wishes for his "honorarium."

22:18–19 The first part of Balaam's answer is a model of piety that would make him a biblical paradigm of loyalty to the Lord, if it were not for the rest of the story. Balaam invites the messengers to stay so that he can find out what else the Lord may have to say. Why would Balaam *hope* the Lord might change his mind? The answer to this question is rather obvious: King Balak has "upped the ante" to the point that Balaam cannot resist!

22:20–22 Surprisingly, the Lord's answer is indeed different. Balaam wastes no time lest the Lord should withdraw permission.

22:22–31 To forcefully convey divine displeasure, "the angel of the LORD" (v. 22) takes his stand in the road. Balaam is trotting into heavy opposition.

Balaam is saved by the lowly beast of burden that he mistreats for irritating him (v. 33). She is his greatest asset. When the Lord uncovers Balaam's eyes and he sees what she did, he reacts similarly (cf. v. 27) by prostrating himself before the awesome angel blocking the way with sword drawn (v. 31).

If it had not turned away, I would certainly have killed you by now,[a] but I would
have spared it."
34 Balaam said to the angel of the LORD,
"I have sinned.[b] I did not realize you were
standing in the road to oppose me. Now
if you are displeased, I will go back."
35 The angel of the LORD said to Balaam,
"Go with the men, but speak only what
I tell you." So Balaam went with Balak's
officials.
36 When Balak heard that Balaam was
coming, he went out to meet him at the
Moabite town on the Arnon[c] border, at
the edge of his territory. 37 Balak said to
Balaam, "Did I not send you an urgent
summons? Why didn't you come to me?
Am I really not able to reward you?"
38 "Well, I have come to you now," Balaam replied. "But I can't say whatever I
please. I must speak only what God puts
in my mouth."[d]
39 Then Balaam went with Balak to Kiriath Huzoth. 40 Balak sacrificed cattle and
sheep,[e] and gave some to Balaam and
the officials who were with him. 41 The
next morning Balak took Balaam up to
Bamoth Baal,[f] and from there he could
see the outskirts of the Israelite camp.[g]

Balaam's First Message

23 Balaam said, "Build me seven altars here, and prepare seven bulls
and seven rams[h] for me." 2 Balak did as
Balaam said, and the two of them offered
a bull and a ram on each altar.[i]
3 Then Balaam said to Balak, "Stay here
beside your offering while I go aside.
Perhaps the LORD will come to meet with
me.[j] Whatever he reveals to me I will tell
you." Then he went off to a barren height.
4 God met with him,[k] and Balaam said,
"I have prepared seven altars, and on
each altar I have offered a bull and a
ram."
5 The LORD put a word in Balaam's
mouth[l] and said, "Go back to Balak and
give him this word."[m]
6 So he went back to him and found
him standing beside his offering, with
all the Moabite officials.[n] 7 Then Balaam[o]
spoke his message:[p]

"Balak brought me from Aram,
the king of Moab from the eastern
mountains.
'Come,' he said, 'curse Jacob for me;
come, denounce Israel.'[q]
8 How can I curse
those whom God has not cursed?[r]
How can I denounce
those whom the LORD has not
denounced?
9 From the rocky peaks I see them,
from the heights I view them.
I see a people who live apart
and do not consider themselves
one of the nations.[s]
10 Who can count the dust of Jacob[t]
or number even a fourth of Israel?
Let me die the death of the
righteous,[u]
and may my final end be like
theirs![v]"

11 Balak said to Balaam, "What have you
done to me? I brought you to curse my

22:33 [a] ver 29
22:34 [b] Ge 39:9; Nu 14:40; 1Sa 15:24,30; 2Sa 12:13; 24:10; Job 33:27; Ps 51:4
22:36 [c] Nu 21:13
22:38 [d] Nu 23:5, 16,26
22:40 [e] Nu 23:1, 14,29; Eze 45:23
22:41 [f] Nu 21:28 [g] Nu 23:13
23:1 [h] Nu 22:40
23:2 [i] ver 14,30
23:3 [j] ver 15
23:4 [k] ver 16
23:5 [l] Dt 18:18; Jer 1:9 [m] Nu 22:20
23:6 [n] ver 17
23:7 [o] Nu 22:5 [p] ver 18; Nu 24:3,21 [q] Nu 22:6; Dt 23:4
23:8 [r] Nu 22:12
23:9 [s] Ex 33:16; Dt 32:8; 33:28
23:10 [t] Ge 13:16 [u] Ps 116:15; Isa 57:1 [v] Ps 37:37

22:34–38 Although Balaam confesses and offers to return home, as well he might, the angel tells Balaam to continue and to "speak only" what he tells him. When King Balak meets Balaam at the Moabite border, Balaam cites this condition of complete divine control as an "escape clause" in case Balak should be dissatisfied with his declarations.
22:39–40 Balak extends hospitality to Balaam by sacrificing animals and sending them to Balaam and the princes with him, apparently primarily for them to enjoy a feast. The following morning, Balak takes Balaam up to Bamoth Baal (lit., "high places of Baal"), where he can visually connect with Israel from a safe distance.

22:1–41 Balaam thought he was special because God spoke through him, but now God spoke through his donkey, to whom he considered himself so superior. Hearing God speak to us is no indication that we are unusually spiritual or mature or important. God is able to communicate with and through whomever he chooses.

23:1–5 The burnt offerings basically serve as instruments of divination to evoke communication from the deity. It appears that God meets with Balaam (vv. 4–5) *in spite of* the sacrifices.
23:7–10 Balaam is now fully aware of the identity of the people whom Balak wants him to curse: Jacob/Israel (v. 7; cf. 22:5, 11). Balaam quickly moves to the basic problem—his conflict of interest. How can he "curse . . . denounce" those whom the Lord has not cursed/denounced (23:8)?
Balaam views Israel as separate rather than just another nation, and metaphorically he refers to their innumerable multitude in terms of "dust" (v. 10). This is what God promised Abraham and Jacob that their chosen offspring would be like (Ge 13:16). Balaam wants his afterlife to be like theirs (Nu 23:10b).
23:11–12 King Balak has hired Balaam as a powerful practitioner of black magic, but he isn't even

enemies, but you have done nothing but
bless them!"[w]
[12]He answered, "Must I not speak what
the LORD puts in my mouth?"[x]

Balaam's Second Message

[13]Then Balak said to him, "Come with
me to another place where you can see
them; you will not see them all but only
the outskirts of their camp. And from
there, curse them for me." [14]So he took
him to the field of Zophim on the top
of Pisgah, and there he built seven altars and offered a bull and a ram on each
altar.[y]
[15]Balaam said to Balak, "Stay here beside your offering while I meet with him
over there."
[16]The LORD met with Balaam and put
a word in his mouth[z] and said, "Go back
to Balak and give him this word."
[17]So he went to him and found him
standing beside his offering, with the
Moabite officials. Balak asked him, "What
did the LORD say?"
[18]Then he spoke his message:

"Arise, Balak, and listen;
hear me, son of Zippor.
[19]God is not human,[a] that he should
lie,
not a human being, that he should
change his mind.[b]
Does he speak and then not act?
Does he promise and not
fulfill?
[20]I have received a command to
bless;
he has blessed,[c] and I cannot
change it.[d]

[21]"No misfortune is seen in Jacob,[e]
no misery observed[a] in Israel.[f]
The LORD their God is with them;[g]
the shout of the King[h] is among
them.
[22]God brought them out of Egypt;[i]
they have the strength of a
wild ox.[j]
[23]There is no divination against[b]
Jacob,
no evil omens[k] against[b] Israel.
It will now be said of Jacob
and of Israel, 'See what God has
done!'
[24]The people rise like a lioness;[l]
they rouse themselves like a
lion[m]
that does not rest till it devours its
prey
and drinks the blood of its
victims."

[25]Then Balak said to Balaam, "Neither
curse them at all nor bless them at all!"
[26]Balaam answered, "Did I not tell you
I must do whatever the LORD says?"

Balaam's Third Message

[27]Then Balak said to Balaam, "Come,
let me take you to another place.[n] Perhaps it will please God to let you curse
them for me from there." [28]And Balak
took Balaam to the top of Peor,[o] overlooking the wasteland.
[29]Balaam said, "Build me seven altars
here, and prepare seven bulls and sev-
en rams for me." [30]Balak did as Balaam
had said, and offered a bull and a ram
on each altar.

[a] 21 Or He has not looked on Jacob's offenses / or on the wrongs found *[b] 23 Or in*

23:11 [w]Nu 24:10; Ne 13:2
23:12 [x]Nu 22:20,38
23:14 [y]ver 2
23:16 [z]Nu 22:38
23:19 [a]Isa 55:9; Hos 11:9 [b]1Sa 15:29; Mal 3:6; Titus 1:2; Jas 1:17
23:20 [c]Ge 22:17; Nu 22:12 [d]Isa 43:13
23:21 [e]Ps 32:2,5; Ro 4:7-8 [f]Isa 40:2; Jer 50:20 [g]Ex 29:45,46; Ps 145:18 [h]Dt 33:5; Ps 89:15-18
23:22 [i]Nu 24:8 [j]Dt 33:17; Job 39:9
23:23 [k]Nu 24:1; Jos 13:22
23:24 [l]Na 2:11 [m]Ge 49:9
23:27 [n]ver 13
23:28 [o]Ps 106:28

Nu 23:26 ❖ How can we follow God's will even when pressure and potential rewards are trying to push us in another direction?

a sorcerer's apprentice. Balaam has his escape clause ready for Balak: He can only speak God's words (v. 12).
23:13–14 Not giving up, Balak hopes that moving the curser to a different location will help him delete his blessings.
23:15–25 Balaam receives his second oracle, affirming that no divination is effective against Israel. Israel is like a devouring lion (v. 24). If Balak is disappointed by Balaam's first oracle, this devastating blessing of Israel is a catastrophe. It would be better if Balaam said nothing (v. 25).
23:28 Desperate and still vainly imagining that the divine attitude can be altered by the venue, Balak relocates Balaam.
23:29–30 It is remarkable that Balaam plays along with the futile charade, directing Balak to waste fourteen more valuable animals.

23:1–30 The Lord's firm resolve to bless the children of Abraham is also for Christians who are truly God's people through faith in Christ (Gal 3:26, 29). The promise includes salvation, a future home, and adoption into a multitude of literal and spiritual descendants of Abraham—the patriarch who set the paradigm for faith (cf. Heb 11:10, 12). With the divine King in our "camp" (cf. Nu 23:21), we have ultimate "social security."

24 Now when Balaam saw that it
pleased the LORD to bless Israel,
he did not resort to divination[p] as at other times, but turned his face toward the
wilderness.[q] 2When Balaam looked out
and saw Israel encamped tribe by tribe,
the Spirit of God came on him[r] 3and he
spoke his message:

"The prophecy of Balaam son of
Beor,
the prophecy of one whose eye
sees clearly,
4the prophecy of one who hears the
words of God,[s]
who sees a vision from the
Almighty,[a][t]
who falls prostrate, and whose
eyes are opened:

5"How beautiful are your tents, Jacob,
your dwelling places, Israel!

6"Like valleys they spread out,
like gardens beside a river,
like aloes[u] planted by the LORD,
like cedars beside the waters.[v]
7Water will flow from their buckets;
their seed will have abundant
water.

"Their king will be greater than
Agag;[w]
their kingdom will be exalted.[x]

8"God brought them out of Egypt;
they have the strength of a
wild ox.
They devour hostile nations
and break their bones in pieces;[y]
with their arrows they pierce
them.[z]

24:1 [p] Nu 23:23 [q] Nu 23:28
24:2 [r] Nu 11:25, 26; 1Sa 10:10; 19:20; 2Ch 15:1
24:4 [s] Nu 22:20 [t] Ge 15:1
24:6 [u] Ps 45:8 [v] Ps 1:3; 104:16
24:7 [w] 2Sa 15:8 [x] 2Sa 5:12; 1Ch 14:2; Ps 145:11-13
24:8 [y] Ps 2:9; Jer 50:17 [z] Ps 45:5

24:9 [a] Ge 49:9; Nu 23:24 [b] Ge 12:3
24:10 [c] Eze 21:14 [d] Nu 23:11 [e] Ne 13:2
24:11 [f] Nu 22:17
24:12 [g] Nu 22:18
24:13 [h] Nu 22:18 [i] Nu 22:20
24:14 [j] Ge 49:1; Nu 31:8,16; Da 2:28; Mic 6:5

Nu 24:10 ❖ Have you ever experienced someone's becoming angry when you speak God's truth? How should you respond to that emotion?

9Like a lion they crouch and lie down,
like a lioness[a]—who dares to
rouse them?

"May those who bless you be blessed
and those who curse you be
cursed!"[b]

10Then Balak's anger burned against
Balaam. He struck his hands together[c]
and said to him, "I summoned you to
curse my enemies, but you have blessed
them[d] these three times.[e] 11Now leave at
once and go home! I said I would reward
you handsomely,[f] but the LORD has kept
you from being rewarded."
12Balaam answered Balak, "Did I not
tell the messengers you sent me,[g] 13'Even
if Balak gave me all the silver and gold in
his palace, I could not do anything of my
own accord, good or bad, to go beyond
the command of the LORD[h]—and I must
say only what the LORD says'?[i] 14Now I am
going back to my people, but come, let
me warn you of what this people will do
to your people in days to come."[j]

Balaam's Fourth Message

15Then he spoke his message:

"The prophecy of Balaam son of
Beor,
the prophecy of one whose eye
sees clearly,

[a] 4 Hebrew *Shaddai*; also in verse 16

24:1 Balaam is bent on sorcery without interference by the Source in order to satisfy Balak and claim his reward.
24:2 Since Balaam has not come to the Lord, the Lord comes to him, bypassing his human will and overpowering his ability to say anything contrary to the divine will.
24:3-9 The third oracle contains twelve parallel units. That there are twelve is appropriate because Balaam is looking at "Israel encamped tribe by tribe" (v. 2). The second member of each of the first three couplets refers to Balaam's visionary gift (vv. 3-4).

In the fourth to seventh couplets, Balaam extols Israel's war camp, of which the beauty is in tents (vv. 5-7a). The eighth couplet (v. 7b) speaks of Israel in royal terms. The tenth parallel unit (v. 8b) would be particularly disquieting to Balak because it describes Israel as devouring nations. The language is devastatingly literal, calculated to intimidate Balak into peaceful relations with Israel.

As Balaam's punch line, the twelfth and final parallel hammers home God's unequivocal "bottom line" toward Israel: "May those who bless you be blessed and those who curse you be cursed!" (v. 9b). In his first oracle, Balaam said he could not curse those whom the Lord had not cursed (23:8). Now he speaks of blessing and cursing together (cf. 22:12), adding the motivational concept that the way people treat Israel determines whether they are blessed or cursed (24:9).
24:10-14 King Balak fires Balaam and orders him to flee home without giving him any honorarium, severance package, or even a token consolation prize.
24:15-16 Before leaving, Balaam delivers unsolicited divine counsel regarding what the Israelites will do to the Moabites. Balaam describes himself as one who has access to information that is otherwise inaccessible to humans, in this case because it concerns future events.

16 the prophecy of one who hears the words of God,
who has knowledge from the Most High,
who sees a vision from the Almighty,
who falls prostrate, and whose eyes are opened:

17 "I see him, but not now;
I behold him, but not near.[k]
A star will come out of Jacob;[l]
a scepter will rise out of Israel.[m]
He will crush the foreheads of Moab,[n]
the skulls[a] of[b] all the people of Sheth.[c]
18 Edom[o] will be conquered;
Seir, his enemy, will be conquered,
but Israel will grow strong.
19 A ruler will come out of Jacob[p]
and destroy the survivors of the city."

Balaam's Fifth Message

20 Then Balaam saw Amalek[q] and spoke his message:

"Amalek was first among the nations,
but their end will be utter destruction."

Balaam's Sixth Message

21 Then he saw the Kenites[r] and spoke his message:

"Your dwelling place is secure,
your nest is set in a rock;
22 yet you Kenites will be destroyed
when Ashur[s] takes you captive."

24:17 [k] Rev 1:7 [l] Mt 2:2 [m] Ge 49:10 [n] Nu 21:29; Isa 15:1-16:14
24:18 [o] Am 9:12
24:19 [p] Ge 49:10; Mic 5:2
24:20 [q] Ex 17:14
24:21 [r] Ge 15:19
24:22 [s] Ge 10:22
24:24 [t] Ge 10:4 [u] Ge 10:21 [v] ver 20
24:25 [w] Nu 31:8
25:1 [x] Jos 2:1; Mic 6:5 [y] 1Co 10:8; Rev 2:14 [z] Nu 31:16
25:2 [a] Ex 34:15 [b] Ex 20:5; Dt 32:38; 1Co 10:20
25:3 [c] Ps 106:28; Hos 9:10
25:4 [d] Dt 4:3 [e] Dt 13:17

Nu 25:1-3 ❖ How can sexual temptation become a pathway to other forms of immorality?

Balaam's Seventh Message

23 Then he spoke his message:

"Alas! Who can live when God does this?[d]
24 Ships will come from the shores of Cyprus;[t]
they will subdue Ashur and Eber,[u]
but they too will come to ruin.[v]"

25 Then Balaam[w] got up and returned home, and Balak went his own way.

Moab Seduces Israel

25 While Israel was staying in Shittim,[x] the men began to indulge in sexual immorality[y] with Moabite women,[z] 2 who invited them to the sacrifices[a] to their gods.[b] The people ate the sacrificial meal and bowed down before these gods. 3 So Israel yoked themselves to the Baal of Peor.[c] And the LORD's anger burned against them.

4 The LORD said to Moses, "Take all the leaders of these people, kill them and expose them in broad daylight before the LORD,[d] so that the LORD's fierce anger[e] may turn away from Israel."

[a] 17 Samaritan Pentateuch (see also Jer. 48:45); the meaning of the word in the Masoretic Text is uncertain. [b] 17 Or possibly *Moab, / batter* [c] 17 Or *all the noisy boasters* [d] 23 Masoretic Text; with a different word division of the Hebrew *The people from the islands will gather from the north.*

24:17-19 Balaam sees a future ruler, whom he metaphorically depicts as a "star" or "scepter," who will originate from Israel and strike the heads of the Moabites (v. 17). This is not a conditional threat that the Moabites will be defeated if they disturb Israel (cf. vv. 8-9); rather, it is a prediction. **24:20-25** Balaam concludes his salvo with three brief discourses against other nations: (1) Amalek, (2) the Kenites, and (3) Ashur (Assyria) and Eber. Numbers 24 ends anticlimactically by simply reporting that Balaam goes home and Balak goes on his way (v. 25).

✣ **24:1-25** Today, no less than in ancient times, spokespersons for God need clear vision to see what he wants to show them, whether in his written Word, in his creation, or in providential circumstances. They need to be ready at all times to hear communication from God, even when it comes in a "gentle whisper" (cf. 1Ki 19:12), rather than drowning it out with all kinds of other "noise," including their own exuberant wordiness. They need knowledge of the Most High, including both knowledge from him and about him. They need to gain their vision from El Shaddai, be awestruck by his power and glory, fall prostrate before him in humility, and allow him to uncover their eyes to see the "angel of the LORD."

25:1-3 Camping at Shittim east of the Jordan River, the Israelites are just across from the promised land. At Shittim the Israelite men are distracted by Moabite women, who effectively use sex appeal to lure them to make sacrifices honoring Moabite gods. **25:4** To turn away divine wrath, the Lord orders Moses to take the leading culprits and expose them (i.e., their dead bodies) in full public view.

PEOPLE TO KNOW // PHINEHAS

NUMBERS 25:1–13: Phinehas was the grandson of Moses' brother Aaron. During the Israelites' wandering before they entered the promised land, they spent some time in Moab. While there, some of the men began to engage in sexual sins with Moabite women, who then led them into idolatry (Nu 25:1–2). God told Moses to put these men to death in order to turn away his anger, which had unleashed a plague in the camp.

One Israelite man brazenly took a Midianite woman into the camp and took her to his tent. Phinehas took a spear and followed them. He then stabbed the spear through both the man and woman. After this act, the plague of God's anger was stopped. God praised Phinehas for being zealous for God's honor, telling Moses that he would make a lasting covenant of peace with Phinehas (Nu 25:12).

Much later, after Israel's conquest of the promised land, Phinehas led a delegation to question the intentions of a group of Israelite soldiers, averting a civil war (Jos 22:9–12). Phinehas was a leader whose godliness and passion for God's justice echo through the ages.

APPLICATION ✥ We grieve when we see people doing things that are counter to God's commands. Around us we see evidence of sin: people who live only to satisfy their own greed, people who harm others, people who are filled with hate and cruelty. Today, in the Christian church, we are called to let God judge others, but that doesn't mean we can't act. We can pray for those lost to sin to turn to God. We can pray for and help those who are victims of sin. We can advocate for changes that bring justice and peace to our world. Phinehas was a zealous follower of God. We can also be zealous for God today.

5So Moses said to Israel's judges, "Each
of you must put to death[f] those of your
people who have yoked themselves to
the Baal of Peor."
6Then an Israelite man brought into
the camp a Midianite woman right before the eyes of Moses and the whole
assembly of Israel while they were weeping at the entrance to the tent of meeting.
7When Phinehas son of Eleazar, the
son of Aaron, the priest, saw this, he left
the assembly, took a spear in his hand
8and followed the Israelite into the tent.
He drove the spear into both of them,
right through the Israelite man and into
the woman's stomach. Then the plague
against the Israelites was stopped;[g]
9but those who died in the plague[h] numbered
24,000.[i]

10The LORD said to Moses,
11"Phinehas son of Eleazar, the son of Aaron, the
priest, has turned my anger away from
the Israelites.[j] Since he was as zealous
for my honor[k] among them as I am, I
did not put an end to them in my zeal.
12Therefore tell him I am making my
covenant of peace[l] with him.
13He and his descendants will have a covenant of a
lasting priesthood,[m] because he was zealous for the honor of his God and made
atonement[n] for the Israelites."
14The name of the Israelite who was
killed with the Midianite woman was
Zimri son of Salu, the leader of a Simeonite family.
15And the name of the Midianite woman who was put to death was
Kozbi[o] daughter of Zur, a tribal chief of
a Midianite family.[p]

25:5 [f] Ex 32:27
25:8 [g] Nu 16:46-48; Ps 106:30
25:9 [h] Nu 14:37; 1Co 10:8 [i] Nu 31:16
25:11 [j] Ps 106:30 [k] Ex 20:5; Dt 32:16,21; Ps 78:58
25:12 [l] Isa 54:10; Eze 34:25; Mal 2:4,5
25:13 [m] Ex 29:9 [n] Nu 16:46
25:15 [o] ver 18 [p] Nu 31:8; Jos 13:21

25:6–8 An Israelite man "brought . . ." (v. 6). Since this word is the usual term for bringing a sacrifice, it would be logical for the reader to expect that the Israelite devoutly sets out to make amends. Alas, his mission is not making a sacrifice but rather fornication.

Phinehas has inherited Eleazar's former position as head of the Levites, in charge of guarding the sanctuary (cf. 3:32). In the tent where the Israelite and Midianitess have gone, Phinehas summarily executes them (25:7b–8).

25:12–13 The Lord highly commends Phinehas for his decisive action and grants him a covenant of peace/well-being and of eternal priesthood (v. 13).

Who thought up the brilliant and devastatingly effective strategy of using sex and food as lethal weapons to kill Israelites? If we "connect the dots," it was Balaam who came up with a scheme and returned to counsel the Midianites and Moabites to use their women to incite Israelites to rebellion against the Lord (31:16).

25:13 Phinehas's "officiation" accomplishes a sacrifice for the Israelites in the sense of destroying offending persons to remove disruption of the covenant relationship between the Lord and his corporate people. Consequently, a plague of divine retribution against them is stopped (v. 8b).

16The LORD said to Moses, 17"Treat the
Midianites[q] as enemies and kill them.
18They treated you as enemies when they
deceived you in the Peor incident[r] involving their sister Kozbi, the daughter
of a Midianite leader, the woman who
was killed when the plague came as a
result of that incident."

The Second Census

26 After the plague the LORD said to
Moses and Eleazar son of Aaron,
the priest, 2"Take a census[s] of the whole
Israelite community by families — all
those twenty years old or more who are
able to serve in the army[t] of Israel." 3So on
the plains of Moab[u] by the Jordan across
from Jericho,[v] Moses and Eleazar the
priest spoke with them and said, 4"Take
a census of the men twenty years old or
more, as the LORD commanded Moses."

These were the Israelites who came
out of Egypt:

5The descendants of Reuben, the firstborn son of Israel, were:
through Hanok,[w] the Hanokite clan;
through Pallu,[x] the Palluite clan;
6through Hezron, the Hezronite clan;
through Karmi, the Karmite clan.
7These were the clans of Reuben; those
numbered were 43,730.
8The son of Pallu was Eliab, 9and the
sons of Eliab[y] were Nemuel, Dathan and
Abiram. The same Dathan and Abiram
were the community[z] officials who rebelled against Moses and Aaron and were
among Korah's followers when they rebelled against the LORD.[a] 10The earth
opened its mouth and swallowed them
along with Korah, whose followers died
when the fire devoured the 250 men.
And they served as a warning sign.[b] 11The
line of Korah,[c] however, did not die out.[d]

12The descendants of Simeon by their
clans were:
through Nemuel, the Nemuelite
clan;
through Jamin,[e] the Jaminite clan;
through Jakin, the Jakinite clan;
13through Zerah,[f] the Zerahite clan;
through Shaul, the Shaulite clan.
14These were the clans of Simeon; those
numbered were 22,200.[g]

15The descendants of Gad by their clans
were:
through Zephon,[h] the Zephonite
clan;
through Haggi, the Haggite clan;
through Shuni, the Shunite clan;
16through Ozni, the Oznite clan;
through Eri, the Erite clan;
17through Arodi,[a] the Arodite clan;
through Areli, the Arelite clan.
18These were the clans of Gad;[i] those
numbered were 40,500.

19Er and Onan were sons of Judah, but
they died[j] in Canaan.
20The descendants of Judah by their
clans were:
through Shelah,[k] the Shelanite clan;
through Perez, the Perezite clan;
through Zerah, the Zerahite clan.[l]
21The descendants of Perez were:
through Hezron,[m] the Hezronite
clan;
through Hamul, the Hamulite
clan.
22These were the clans of Judah;[n] those
numbered were 76,500.

23The descendants of Issachar by their
clans were:
through Tola,[o] the Tolaite clan;
through Puah, the Puite[b] clan;
24through Jashub,[p] the Jashubite clan;

25:17 [q] Nu 31:1-3
25:18 [r] Nu 31:16
26:2 [s] Ex 30:11-16; 38:25-26; Nu 1:2 [t] Nu 1:3
26:3 [u] Nu 33:48 [v] Nu 22:1
26:5 [w] Ge 46:9 [x] 1Ch 5:3
26:9 [y] Nu 16:1 [z] Nu 1:16 [a] Nu 16:2
26:10 [b] Nu 16:35, 38
26:11 [c] Ex 6:24 [d] Nu 16:33; Dt 24:16
26:12 [e] 1Ch 4:24
26:13 [f] Ge 46:10
26:14 [g] Nu 1:23
26:15 [h] Ge 46:16
26:18 [i] Nu 1:25; Jos 13:24-28
26:19 [j] Ge 38:2-10; 46:12
26:20 [k] 1Ch 2:3 [l] Jos 7:17
26:21 [m] Ru 4:19; 1Ch 2:9
26:22 [n] Nu 1:27
26:23 [o] Ge 46:13; 1Ch 7:1
26:24 [p] Ge 46:13

Nu 26:23 ❖ God apportioned the promised land based on the population size of each tribe. What did the Israelites' claims on the land mean for their history and their future?

[a] *17* Samaritan Pentateuch and Syriac (see also Gen. 46:16); Masoretic Text *Arod*
[b] *23* Samaritan Pentateuch, Septuagint, Vulgate and Syriac (see also 1 Chron. 7:1); Masoretic Text *through Puvah, the Punite*

✣ **25:1-18** When it comes to the deceptive inroads of apostasy into the church, Christians may need to face corporate conflicts head-on. Like zealous Phinehas, Christ identified with God to the extent that there was no difference between defending the honor of God and that of himself.

26:1-62 This census lists clans within each tribe that receive their names from the earliest descendants of the twelve patriarchs. Thus the chapter reads like a combination of genealogy and census. **26:9-11, 19, 33** With the genealogical component are some notices of special circumstances: the rebellion and deaths of Reubenites Dathan and Abiram along with Korah & Co.; the deaths

through Shimron, the Shimronite clan.
25 These were the clans of Issachar;[q] those numbered were 64,300.

26 The descendants of Zebulun by their clans were:
through Sered, the Seredite clan;
through Elon, the Elonite clan;
through Jahleel, the Jahleelite clan.
27 These were the clans of Zebulun;[r] those numbered were 60,500.

28 The descendants of Joseph by their clans through Manasseh and Ephraim were:

29 The descendants of Manasseh:
through Makir,[s] the Makirite clan (Makir was the father of Gilead[t]);
through Gilead, the Gileadite clan.
30 These were the descendants of Gilead:
through Iezer,[u] the Iezerite clan;
through Helek, the Helekite clan;
31 through Asriel, the Asrielite clan;
through Shechem, the Shechemite clan;
32 through Shemida, the Shemidaite clan;
through Hepher, the Hepherite clan.
33 (Zelophehad[v] son of Hepher had no sons; he had only daughters, whose names were Mahlah, Noah, Hoglah, Milkah and Tirzah.)[w]
34 These were the clans of Manasseh; those numbered were 52,700.[x]

35 These were the descendants of Ephraim by their clans:
through Shuthelah, the Shuthelahite clan;
through Beker, the Bekerite clan;
through Tahan, the Tahanite clan.
36 These were the descendants of Shuthelah:
through Eran, the Eranite clan.
37 These were the clans of Ephraim;[y] those numbered were 32,500.

These were the descendants of Joseph by their clans.

38 The descendants of Benjamin[z] by their clans were:
through Bela, the Belaite clan;
through Ashbel, the Ashbelite clan;
through Ahiram, the Ahiramite clan;
39 through Shupham,[a] the Shuphamite clan;
through Hupham, the Huphamite clan.
40 The descendants of Bela through Ard[a] and Naaman were:
through Ard,[b] the Ardite clan;
through Naaman, the Naamite clan.
41 These were the clans of Benjamin;[b] those numbered were 45,600.

42 These were the descendants of Dan by their clans:
through Shuham,[c] the Shuhamite clan.
These were the clans of Dan: 43 All of them were Shuhamite clans; and those numbered were 64,400.

44 The descendants of Asher by their clans were:
through Imnah, the Imnite clan;
through Ishvi, the Ishvite clan;
through Beriah, the Beriite clan;
45 and through the descendants of Beriah:
through Heber, the Heberite clan;
through Malkiel, the Malkielite clan.
46 (Asher had a daughter named Serah.)
47 These were the clans of Asher;[d] those numbered were 53,400.

48 The descendants of Naphtali[e] by their clans were:
through Jahzeel, the Jahzeelite clan;
through Guni, the Gunite clan;
49 through Jezer, the Jezerite clan;
through Shillem, the Shillemite clan.
50 These were the clans of Naphtali;[f] those numbered were 45,400.

51 The total number of the men of Israel was 601,730.[g]

26:25 [q] Nu 1:29
26:27 [r] Nu 1:31
26:29 [s] Jos 17:1 [t] Jdg 11:1
26:30 [u] Jos 17:2; Jdg 6:11
26:33 [v] Nu 27:1 [w] Nu 36:11
26:34 [x] Nu 1:35
26:37 [y] Nu 1:33
26:38 [z] Ge 46:21; 1Ch 7:6
26:40 [a] Ge 46:21; 1Ch 8:3
26:41 [b] Nu 1:37
26:42 [c] Ge 46:23
26:47 [d] Nu 1:41
26:48 [e] Ge 46:24; 1Ch 7:13
26:50 [f] Nu 1:43
26:51 [g] Ex 12:37; 38:26; Nu 1:46; 11:21

[a] *39* A few manuscripts of the Masoretic Text, Samaritan Pentateuch, Vulgate and Syriac (see also Septuagint); most manuscripts of the Masoretic Text *Shephupham* [b] *40* Samaritan Pentateuch and Vulgate (see also Septuagint); Masoretic Text does not have *through Ard.*

---

of Er and Onan; and the fact that Zelophehad of Manasseh has only daughters (v. 33).
26:51 Numbers adds up the total number of Israelite fighting men twenty years of age and older as 601,730. This is slightly less than the total of the first census: 603,550 (1:46). The numbers tell

52The LORD said to Moses, 53"The land
is to be allotted to them as an inheritance based on the number of names.[h]
54To a larger group give a larger inheritance, and to a smaller group a smaller
one; each is to receive its inheritance
according to the number[i] of those listed. 55Be sure that the land is distributed
by lot.[j] What each group inherits will be
according to the names for its ancestral
tribe. 56Each inheritance is to be distributed by lot among the larger and smaller
groups."

57These were the Levites[k] who were
counted by their clans:
through Gershon, the Gershonite clan;
through Kohath, the Kohathite clan;
through Merari, the Merarite clan.
58These also were Levite clans:
the Libnite clan,
the Hebronite clan,
the Mahlite clan,
the Mushite clan,
the Korahite clan.
(Kohath was the forefather of Amram;[l] 59the name of Amram's wife
was Jochebed,[m] a descendant of
Levi, who was born to the Levites[a]
in Egypt. To Amram she bore Aaron, Moses[n] and their sister Miriam.
60Aaron was the father of Nadab and
Abihu, Eleazar and Ithamar.[o] 61But
Nadab and Abihu[p] died when they
made an offering before the LORD
with unauthorized fire.)[q]

62All the male Levites a month old or
more numbered 23,000.[r] They were not
counted[s] along with the other Israelites
because they received no inheritance[t]
among them.[u]

63These are the ones counted by Moses
and Eleazar the priest when they counted
the Israelites on the plains of Moab[v] by
the Jordan across from Jericho. 64Not
one of them was among those counted[w] by Moses and Aaron the priest when
they counted the Israelites in the Desert
of Sinai. 65For the LORD had told those
Israelites they would surely die in the
wilderness,[x] and not one of them was
left except Caleb son of Jephunneh and
Joshua son of Nun.[y]

Zelophehad's Daughters

27:1–11pp // Nu 36:1–12

27 The daughters of Zelophehad[z] son
of Hepher,[a] the son of Gilead, the
son of Makir,[b] the son of Manasseh, belonged to the clans of Manasseh son of
Joseph. The names of the daughters were
Mahlah, Noah, Hoglah, Milkah and Tirzah. They came forward 2and stood before Moses, Eleazar the priest, the leaders
and the whole assembly at the entrance
to the tent of meeting and said, 3"Our father died in the wilderness.[c] He was not
among Korah's followers, who banded
together against the LORD,[d] but he died
for his own sin and left no sons.[e] 4Why
should our father's name disappear from
his clan because he had no son? Give us
property among our father's relatives."
5So Moses brought their case[f] before
the LORD,[g] 6and the LORD said to him,

[a] 59 Or *Jochebed, a daughter of Levi, who was born to Levi*

26:53 [h] Jos 11:23; 14:1; Eze 45:8
26:54 [i] Nu 33:54
26:55 [j] Nu 34:14
26:57 [k] Ge 46:11; Ex 6:16-19
26:58 [l] Ex 6:20
26:59 [m] Ex 2:1 [n] Ex 6:20
26:60 [o] Nu 3:2
26:61 [p] Lev 10:1-2 [q] Nu 3:4
26:62 [r] Nu 3:39
[s] Nu 1:47 [t] Nu 18:23 [u] Nu 2:33; Dt 10:9
26:63 [v] ver 3
26:64 [w] Nu 14:29; Dt 2:14-15; Heb 3:17
26:65 [x] Nu 14:28; 1Co 10:5 [y] Jos 14:6-10
27:1 [z] Nu 26:33 [a] Jos 17:2,3 [b] Nu 36:1
27:3 [c] Nu 26:65 [d] Nu 16:2 [e] Nu 26:33
27:5 [f] Ex 18:19 [g] Nu 9:8

---

how the various tribes fared during the decades of desert wandering. Some flourished. Others declined, most notably Simeon.

26:52-56 In addition to its military function, the second census is to determine the size of the territories that will be allotted to the tribes when they conquer the land.

26:57-62 Levites are counted separately because they do not serve in the regular army. Furthermore, they will not inherit land along with the other tribes (v. 62).

26:63-65 The second census gives the Israelites a new beginning. Except for Caleb and Joshua, the second military census includes none counted in the first census. At last, the Israelites will be permitted to enter the promised land.

✣ **26:1-65** If the strong do not cooperate with the Lord's plans, he turns to use the weak. When the Israelites lamented that any attempted invasion of Canaan would result in their children being taken captive by the enemy (14:3), God responded by saying that he would give the promised land to those same defenseless children (14:31-32). When some people do not carry out God's goals, he turns to others, and he may even wait for another generation. While the Lord inexorably moves his plans for human beings through to fulfillment, none of us is indispensable for carrying out his will.

27:1-4 Zelophehad's daughters seek to remedy inequity by asking to inherit their father's property.

27:5-7 Having no legal precedent on which to base an answer to the young women, Moses turns to the Lord, who confirms that Zelophehad's daughters are right.

7"What Zelophehad's daughters are saying is right. You must certainly give them
property as an inheritance[h] among their
father's relatives and give their father's
inheritance to them.[i]
8"Say to the Israelites, 'If a man dies
and leaves no son, give his inheritance
to his daughter. 9If he has no daughter,
give his inheritance to his brothers. 10If
he has no brothers, give his inheritance
to his father's brothers. 11If his father had
no brothers, give his inheritance to the
nearest relative in his clan, that he may
possess it. This is to have the force of
law[j] for the Israelites, as the LORD commanded Moses.'"

Joshua to Succeed Moses

12Then the LORD said to Moses, "Go up
this mountain in the Abarim Range[k] and
see the land[l] I have given the Israelites.
13After you have seen it, you too will be
gathered to your people,[m] as your brother
Aaron[n] was, 14for when the community
rebelled at the waters in the Desert of
Zin, both of you disobeyed my command
to honor me as holy[o] before their eyes."
(These were the waters of Meribah[p] Kadesh, in the Desert of Zin.)
15Moses said to the LORD, 16"May the
LORD, the God who gives breath to all
living things,[q] appoint someone over
this community 17to go out and come
in before them, one who will lead them
out and bring them in, so the LORD's
people will not be like sheep without a
shepherd."[r]
18So the LORD said to Moses, "Take
Joshua son of Nun, a man in whom is
the spirit of leadership,[a][s] and lay your
hand on him.[t] 19Have him stand before
Eleazar the priest and the entire assembly and commission him[u] in their presence.[v] 20Give him some of your authority
so the whole Israelite community will
obey him.[w] 21He is to stand before Eleazar
the priest, who will obtain decisions for
him by inquiring[x] of the Urim[y] before the
LORD. At his command he and the entire
community of the Israelites will go out,
and at his command they will come in."
22Moses did as the LORD commanded
him. He took Joshua and had him stand
before Eleazar the priest and the whole
assembly. 23Then he laid his hands on
him and commissioned him, as the LORD
instructed through Moses.

Daily Offerings

28 The LORD said to Moses, 2"Give
this command to the Israelites
and say to them: 'Make sure that you
present to me at the appointed time my
food[z] offerings, as an aroma pleasing
to me.' 3Say to them: 'This is the food
offering you are to present to the LORD:
two lambs a year old without defect, as
a regular burnt offering each day.[a] 4Of-
fer one lamb in the morning and the

27:7 [h]Job 42:15 [i]Jos 17:4
27:11 [j]Nu 35:29
27:12 [k]Nu 33:47; Jer 22:20 [l]Dt 3:23-27; 32:48-52
27:13 [m]Nu 31:2 [n]Nu 20:28
27:14 [o]Nu 20:12 [p]Ex 17:7; Dt 32:51; Ps 106:32
27:16 [q]Nu 16:22
27:17 [r]Dt 31:2; 1Ki 22:17; Eze 34:5; Zec 10:2; Mt 9:36; Mk 6:34
27:18 [s]Ge 41:38; Nu 11:25-29 [t]ver 23; Dt 34:9
27:19 [u]Dt 3:28; 31:14,23 [v]Dt 31:7
27:20 [w]Jos 1:16, 17
27:21 [x]Jos 9:14 [y]Ex 28:30
28:2 [z]Lev 3:11
28:3 [a]Ex 29:38

[a] 18 Or *the Spirit*

Nu 27:5-11 ❖ What does God's response show about his concern and care for people who are marginalized? How can we show God's love to such people today?

Nu 28:4-8 ❖ What is our daily offering or act of worship for God? How does worship of God affect our everyday lives? How can we maintain an attitude of worship every day?

27:8-11 As on other occasions, God gives Moses permanent legislation surrounding the case in question.
27:12-14 Moses will at least be permitted to see the promised land from the top of a mountain before he dies. Deuteronomy 3:27 and 34:1 identify the place as Pisgah, the same as the name of the mountain where Balaam uttered his second oracle.
27:15-21 Moses appeals to "the LORD, the God who gives breath to all living things" (v. 16), to appoint a good "shepherd" in his place. The Lord responds by identifying Joshua and instructing Moses to commission this worthy successor.
27:18-23 Transfer of power requires only a simple, straightforward but elegant ceremony in which Moses leans his hand on Joshua and then commissions him while he stands before Eleazar the high priest and the whole assembly.

✣ **27:1-23** Like sheep, people need someone they trust to lead them. Sheep need a *good* shepherd who protects his sheep with his life.

28:1-8 In the ritual calendar of Lev 23, the emphasis is on outlining overall observance of sacred times. The parallel calendar in Nu 28–29 fills in important details by providing a comprehensive inventory of public sacrifices that must be performed at the sanctuary on regular and festival occasions.
The two burnt offerings with their accompanying grain and drink offerings (28:5, 7a) constitute the daily symbolic "meals" of the Lord that are essential for maintaining his presence among the Israelites. In addition to the usual offering of wine/fermented drink at the outer altar to accompany the regular burnt offering, v. 7b prescribes a unique libation.

other at twilight, 5 together with a grain
offering of a tenth of an ephah[a] of the
finest flour mixed with a quarter of a
hin[b] of oil[b] from pressed olives. 6 This
is the regular burnt offering instituted
at Mount Sinai[c] as a pleasing aroma, a
food offering presented to the LORD. 7 The
accompanying drink offering[d] is to be a
quarter of a hin of fermented drink with
each lamb. Pour out the drink offering
to the LORD at the sanctuary.[e] 8 Offer the
second lamb at twilight, along with the
same kind of grain offering and drink
offering that you offer in the morning.
This is a food offering, an aroma pleasing
to the LORD.[f]

Sabbath Offerings

9 "'On the Sabbath[g] day, make an offering of two lambs a year old without
defect, together with its drink offering
and a grain offering of two-tenths of an
ephah[c][h] of the finest flour mixed with
olive oil. 10 This is the burnt offering for
every Sabbath, in addition to the regular
burnt offering[i] and its drink offering.

Monthly Offerings

11 "'On the first of every month,[j] present to the LORD a burnt offering of two
young bulls, one ram and seven male
lambs a year old, all without defect.[k]
12 With each bull there is to be a grain
offering[l] of three-tenths of an ephah[d][m] of
the finest flour mixed with oil; with the
ram, a grain offering of two-tenths of an
ephah of the finest flour mixed with oil;
13 and with each lamb, a grain offering[n]
of a tenth of an ephah of the finest flour
mixed with oil. This is for a burnt offering, a pleasing aroma, a food offering
presented to the LORD. 14 With each bull
there is to be a drink offering[o] of half a
hin[e] of wine; with the ram, a third of a
hin[f]; and with each lamb, a quarter of a
hin. This is the monthly burnt offering
to be made at each new moon[p] during
the year. 15 Besides the regular burnt offering[q] with its drink offering, one male
goat is to be presented to the LORD as a
sin offering.[g][r]

The Passover

28:16–25pp // Ex 12:14–20; Lev 23:4–8; Dt 16:1–8

16 "'On the fourteenth day of the first
month the LORD's Passover[s] is to be held.
17 On the fifteenth day of this month
there is to be a festival; for seven days[t]
eat bread made without yeast.[u] 18 On the
first day hold a sacred assembly and do
no regular work.[v] 19 Present to the LORD
a food offering consisting of a burnt offering of two young bulls, one ram and
seven male lambs a year old, all without
defect. 20 With each bull offer a grain offering of three-tenths of an ephah[w] of the
finest flour mixed with oil; with the ram,
two-tenths; 21 and with each of the seven
lambs, one-tenth. 22 Include one male
goat as a sin offering[x] to make atonement for you.[y] 23 Offer these in addition

28:5 [b] Lev 2:1; Nu 15:4
28:6 [c] Ex 19:3
28:7 [d] Ex 29:41 [e] Lev 3:7
28:8 [f] Lev 1:9
28:9 [g] Ex 20:10 [h] Lev 23:13
28:10 [i] ver 3
28:11 [j] Nu 10:10 [k] Lev 1:3
28:12 [l] Nu 15:6 [m] Nu 15:9
28:13 [n] Lev 6:14
28:14 [o] Nu 15:7 [p] Ezr 3:5
28:15 [q] ver 3, 24 [r] Lev 4:3
28:16 [s] Ex 12:6, 18; Lev 23:5; Dt 16:1
28:17 [t] Ex 12:19 [u] Ex 23:15; 34:18; Lev 23:6; Dt 16:3-8
28:18 [v] Ex 12:16; Lev 23:7
28:20 [w] Lev 14:10
28:22 [x] Ro 8:3 [y] Nu 15:28

[a] 5 That is, probably about 3 1/2 pounds or about 1.6 kilograms; also in verses 13, 21 and 29
[b] 5 That is, about 1 quart or about 1 liter; also in verses 7 and 14
[c] 9 That is, probably about 7 pounds or about 3.2 kilograms; also in verses 12, 20 and 28
[d] 12 That is, probably about 11 pounds or about 5 kilograms; also in verses 20 and 28
[e] 14 That is, about 2 quarts or about 1.9 liters
[f] 14 That is, about 1 1/3 quarts or about 1.3 liters
[g] 15 Or *purification offering*; also in verse 22

28:9—29:40 The calendar moves to additional sacrifices performed weekly on the Sabbath (28:9-10), monthly at new moons (28:11-15), and yearly at the annual festivals of Passover and Unleavened Bread (28:16-25), Weeks (28:26-31), Trumpets (29:1-6), the Day of Atonement (29:7-11), and Booths (29:12-38). The order is the same as in Lev 23, going from smaller to larger cycles and moving through the yearly festivals in chronological order from spring to autumn.

The number seven, which is associated with the weekly Sabbath and conveys the idea of holiness, is prominent in the Israelite system of new moons and festivals. These instances of the number seven suggest that the cyclical holy times of special worship are, in a sense, extensions of the weekly Sabbath. The large numbers of sacrifices during the Festival of Tabernacles acknowledge God's blessings at the thanksgiving season of harvest.

28:1—29:40 The earthly sanctuary and its sacrifices are gone, but there remains the need for everyone who enjoys a new covenant relationship with God to maintain it on a daily basis. We need frequent and regular reaffirmation of our connection to him.

Daily and festival sacrifices at the Israelite sanctuary, with their smoke ascending heavenward, showed that a healthy relationship with God was available to anyone, anywhere, anytime. Now our prayers ascend to where our sacrificial Lamb is depicted as if he has just been slaughtered (Rev 5:6), that is, carrying the cross event with him to continually offer its healing to all who will avail themselves of it. Those who have him have assurance of life.

to the regular morning burnt offering. 24 In this way present the food offering every day for seven days as an aroma pleasing to the LORD; it is to be offered in addition to the regular burnt offering and its drink offering. 25 On the seventh day hold a sacred assembly and do no regular work.

The Festival of Weeks

28:26–31pp // Lev 23:15–22; Dt 16:9–12

26 " 'On the day of firstfruits,[z] when you present to the LORD an offering of new grain during the Festival of Weeks,[a] hold a sacred assembly and do no regular work.[b] 27 Present a burnt offering of two young bulls, one ram and seven male lambs a year old as an aroma pleasing to the LORD. 28 With each bull there is to be a grain offering of three-tenths of an ephah of the finest flour mixed with oil; with the ram, two-tenths; 29 and with each of the seven lambs, one-tenth.[c] 30 Include one male goat to make atonement for you. 31 Offer these together with their drink offerings, in addition to the regular burnt offering[d] and its grain offering. Be sure the animals are without defect.

The Festival of Trumpets

29:1–6pp // Lev 23:23–25

29 " 'On the first day of the seventh month hold a sacred assembly and do no regular work.[e] It is a day for you to sound the trumpets. 2 As an aroma pleasing to the LORD,[f] offer a burnt offering of one young bull, one ram and seven male lambs a year old, all without defect.[g] 3 With the bull offer a grain offering of three-tenths of an ephah*[a]* of the finest flour mixed with olive oil; with the ram, two-tenths*[b]*; 4 and with each of the seven lambs, one-tenth.*[c]* 5 Include one male goat[h] as a sin offering*[d]* to make atonement for you. 6 These are in addition to the monthly[i] and daily burnt offerings[j] with their grain offerings and drink offerings as specified. They are food offerings presented to the LORD, a pleasing aroma.

The Day of Atonement

29:7–11pp // Lev 16:2–34; 23:26–32

7 " 'On the tenth day of this seventh month hold a sacred assembly. You must deny yourselves*[e]*[k] and do no work.[l] 8 Present as an aroma pleasing to the LORD a burnt offering of one young bull, one ram and seven male lambs a year old, all without defect. 9 With the bull offer a grain offering[m] of three-tenths of an ephah of the finest flour mixed with oil; with the ram, two-tenths; 10 and with each of the seven lambs, one-tenth.[n] 11 Include one male goat as a sin offering, in addition to the sin offering for atonement and the regular burnt offering[o] with its grain offering, and their drink offerings.

The Festival of Tabernacles

29:12–39pp // Lev 23:33–43; Dt 16:13–17

12 " 'On the fifteenth day of the seventh[p] month,[q] hold a sacred assembly and do no regular work. Celebrate a festival to the LORD for seven days. 13 Present as an aroma pleasing to the LORD a food offering consisting of a burnt offering of thirteen young bulls, two rams and fourteen male lambs a year old, all without defect. 14 With each of the thirteen bulls offer a grain offering[r] of three-tenths of an ephah of the finest flour mixed with oil; with each of the two rams, two-tenths; 15 and with each of the fourteen lambs, one-tenth. 16 Include one male goat as a sin offering, in addition to the regular burnt offering with its grain offering and drink offering.[s]

17 " 'On the second day[t] offer twelve young bulls, two rams and fourteen male lambs a year old, all without defect.[u] 18 With the bulls, rams and lambs, offer their grain offerings[v] and drink offerings[w] according to the number specified.[x] 19 Include one male goat as a sin offering,[y] in addition to the regular burnt offering with its grain offering, and their drink offerings.

20 " 'On the third day offer eleven bulls, two rams and fourteen male lambs a year old, all without defect.[z] 21 With the bulls, rams and lambs, offer their grain offerings and drink offerings according to the number specified.[a] 22 Include one male goat as a sin offering, in addition to the regular burnt offering with its grain offering and drink offering.

28:26 [z] Ex 34:22 [a] Ex 23:16 [b] ver 18; Dt 16:10
28:29 [c] ver 13
28:31 [d] ver 3,19
29:1 [e] Lev 23:24
29:2 [f] Nu 28:2 [g] Nu 28:3
29:5 [h] Nu 28:15
29:6 [i] Nu 28:11 [j] Nu 28:3
29:7 [k] Ac 27:9 [l] Ex 31:15; Lev 16:29; 23:26-32
29:9 [m] ver 3,18
29:10 [n] Nu 28:13
29:11 [o] Lev 16:3; Nu 28:3
29:12 [p] 1Ki 8:2 [q] Lev 23:24
29:14 [r] ver 3
29:16 [s] ver 6
29:17 [t] Lev 23:36 [u] Nu 28:3
29:18 [v] ver 9 [w] Nu 28:7 [x] Nu 15:4-12
29:19 [y] Nu 28:15
29:20 [z] ver 17
29:21 [a] ver 18

[a] *3* That is, probably about 11 pounds or about 5 kilograms; also in verses 9 and 14 *[b]* *3* That is, probably about 7 pounds or about 3.2 kilograms; also in verses 9 and 14 *[c]* *4* That is, probably about 3 1/2 pounds or about 1.6 kilograms; also in verses 10 and 15 *[d]* *5* Or *purification offering*; also elsewhere in this chapter *[e]* *7* Or *must fast*

23“ ‘On the fourth day offer ten bulls,
two rams and fourteen male lambs a
year old, all without defect. 24With the
bulls, rams and lambs, offer their grain
offerings and drink offerings according
to the number specified. 25Include one
male goat as a sin offering, in addition to
the regular burnt offering with its grain
offering and drink offering.

26“ ‘On the fifth day offer nine bulls,
two rams and fourteen male lambs a
year old, all without defect. 27With the
bulls, rams and lambs, offer their grain
offerings and drink offerings according
to the number specified. 28Include one
male goat as a sin offering, in addition to
the regular burnt offering with its grain
offering and drink offering.

29“ ‘On the sixth day offer eight bulls,
two rams and fourteen male lambs a
year old, all without defect. 30With the
bulls, rams and lambs, offer their grain
offerings and drink offerings according
to the number specified. 31Include one
male goat as a sin offering, in addition to
the regular burnt offering with its grain
offering and drink offering.

32“ ‘On the seventh day offer seven
bulls, two rams and fourteen male lambs
a year old, all without defect. 33With the
bulls, rams and lambs, offer their grain
offerings and drink offerings according
to the number specified. 34Include one
male goat as a sin offering, in addition to
the regular burnt offering with its grain
offering and drink offering.

35“ ‘On the eighth day hold a closing special assembly[b] and do no regular work.
36Present as an aroma pleasing to the
LORD[c] a food offering consisting of a burnt
offering of one bull, one ram and seven
male lambs a year old,[d] all without defect.
37With the bull, the ram and the lambs,
offer their grain offerings and drink offerings according to the number specified.
38Include one male goat as a sin offering,

29:35 [b]Lev 23:36
29:36 [c]Lev 1:9 [d]ver 2
29:39 [e]Nu 6:2 [f]Lev 23:2 [g]Lev 1:3; 1Ch 23:31; 2Ch 31:3
30:1 [h]Nu 1:4
30:2 [i]Dt 23:21-23; Jdg 11:35; Job 22:27; Ps 22:25; 50:14; 116:14; Pr 20:25; Ecc 5:4,5; Jnh 1:16
30:4 [j]ver 7
30:6 [k]Lev 5:4

Nu 29:35–39 ❖ Most Christians don’t have a culture of celebration and festivals resembling God’s instructions to the Israelites. How might Christians engage in more festivals of celebration and remembering God’s faithfulness in our families and with our Christian friends?

in addition to the regular burnt offering
with its grain offering and drink offering.

39“ ‘In addition to what you vow[e] and
your freewill offerings, offer these to the
LORD at your appointed festivals:[f] your
burnt offerings,[g] grain offerings, drink
offerings and fellowship offerings.’ ”

40Moses told the Israelites all that the
LORD commanded him.[a]

Vows

30 [b] Moses said to the heads of the
tribes of Israel:[h] “This is what the
LORD commands: 2When a man makes
a vow to the LORD or takes an oath to
obligate himself by a pledge, he must
not break his word but must do everything he said.[i]

3“When a young woman still living in
her father’s household makes a vow to
the LORD or obligates herself by a pledge
4and her father hears about her vow or
pledge but says nothing to her, then all
her vows and every pledge by which she
obligated herself will stand.[j] 5But if her
father forbids her when he hears about
it, none of her vows or the pledges by
which she obligated herself will stand;
the LORD will release her because her
father has forbidden her.

6“If she marries after she makes a vow[k]
or after her lips utter a rash promise by
which she obligates herself 7and her husband hears about it but says nothing to

[a] *40* In Hebrew texts this verse (29:40) is numbered 30:1. [b] In Hebrew texts 30:1-16 is numbered 30:2-17.

30:1–2 The main concern of Nu 30 is the tension that can arise when dependent women bind themselves by obligations to God that may conflict with the will of their fathers or husbands, to whom they are legally subordinate in ancient Israelite society (v. 16). The vows/obligations of widowed or divorced women, who are independent, are binding like those of men (v. 9).

30:3–15 Three cases are cited here, following the progression of a woman’s life from single to married status: (1) unmarried women subject to their fathers (vv. 3–5); (2) women who marry while they are under vows or pledges previously taken (vv. 6–8); (3) married women who make vows/pledges while subject to their husbands (vv. 10–15).

The Lord does not allow males to exercise their authority in an arbitrary manner. If a father or husband does not approve of the vow or pledge made by his daughter or wife, he can forbid it only when he first hears of it (vv. 5, 8, 12). If the man does not express immediate disapproval, his silence constitutes binding consent (vv. 3–4, 6–7, 10–11, 14). Therefore, if he later breaks her obligation, he will bear her accountability (v. 15).

her, then her vows or the pledges by which
she obligated herself will stand. 8But if her
husband[l] forbids her when he hears about
it, he nullifies the vow that obligates her
or the rash promise by which she obligates
herself, and the LORD will release her.
9"Any vow or obligation taken by a
widow or divorced woman will be binding on her.
10"If a woman living with her husband
makes a vow or obligates herself by a
pledge under oath 11and her husband
hears about it but says nothing to her
and does not forbid her, then all her vows
or the pledges by which she obligated
herself will stand. 12But if her husband
nullifies them when he hears about
them, then none of the vows or pledges that came from her lips will stand.[m]
Her husband has nullified them, and the
LORD will release her. 13Her husband may
confirm or nullify any vow she makes or
any sworn pledge to deny herself.[a] 14But
if her husband says nothing to her about
it from day to day, then he confirms all
her vows or the pledges binding on her.
He confirms them by saying nothing to
her when he hears about them. 15If, however, he nullifies them some time after
he hears about them, then he must bear
the consequences of her wrongdoing."
16These are the regulations the LORD
gave Moses concerning relationships between a man and his wife, and between
a father and his young daughter still living at home.

Vengeance on the Midianites

31 The LORD said to Moses, 2"Take vengeance on the Midianites[n] for the

30:8 [l] Ge 3:16
30:12 [m] Eph 5:22; Col 3:18
31:2 [n] Ge 25:2
[o] Nu 20:26; 27:13
31:3 [p] Jdg 11:36; 1Sa 24:12; 2Sa 4:8; 22:48; Ps 94:1; 149:7
31:6 [q] Nu 14:44 [r] Nu 10:9
31:7 [s] Dt 20:13; Jdg 21:11; 1Ki 11:15,16
31:8 [t] Jos 13:21 [u] Nu 25:15 [v] Jos 13:22
31:10 [w] Ge 25:16; 1Ch 6:54; Ps 69:25; Eze 25:4
31:11 [x] Dt 20:14

Nu 30:16 ❖ Do these relationships work the same way after Christ's work? Why or why not?

Nu 31:2 ❖ When is it right to take vengeance on others? Is there ever a time Christians should seek vengeance (see Ro 12:17–19)?

Israelites. After that, you will be gathered
to your people.[o]"
3So Moses said to the people, "Arm
some of your men to go to war against
the Midianites so that they may carry out
the LORD's vengeance[p] on them. 4Send
into battle a thousand men from each of
the tribes of Israel." 5So twelve thousand
men armed for battle, a thousand from
each tribe, were supplied from the clans
of Israel. 6Moses sent them into battle,
a thousand from each tribe, along with
Phinehas son of Eleazar, the priest, who
took with him articles from the sanctuary[q] and the trumpets[r] for signaling.
7They fought against Midian, as the
LORD commanded Moses, and killed every man.[s] 8Among their victims were
Evi, Rekem, Zur, Hur and Reba[t]—the
five kings of Midian.[u] They also killed
Balaam son of Beor with the sword.[v]
9The Israelites captured the Midianite
women and children and took all the
Midianite herds, flocks and goods as
plunder. 10They burned all the towns
where the Midianites had settled, as well
as all their camps.[w] 11They took all the
plunder and spoils, including the people
and animals,[x] 12and brought the captives,
spoils and plunder to Moses and Eleazar

[a] 13 Or *to fast*

30:1–16 Modern Western society is not patriarchal to the degree that men have almost exclusive control over the legal structure. Nevertheless, Nu 30 contains some important principles that transcend the differences between cultures. (1) Promises made to God are serious. (2) We should consider the effects that our vows/pledges may have on other people. (3) Family harmony within the context of a given culture should not be disturbed unless absolutely necessary. (4) By being willing to waive his own rights, the Lord teaches us that we do not always need to insist on our rights. (5) People who control other individuals should not be arbitrary or fickle. Sometimes it is necessary to annul someone's decision, but there should be a good and consistent reason for doing so.

31:1–6 One major piece of unfinished business is to fulfill the divine command issued after the Baal of Peor scandal (25:16–18). Because Midian is a tribal confederation constituting a kind of nation, corporate retributive justice requires a major military operation. This is a holy war commanded by God. Phinehas represents the Lord's presence with the troops.

31:7–12 Numbers 31 briefly describes the actual battle. Among the slain are the kings of five major subdivisions of the Midianite tribal nation. In addition, the Israelites "also killed Balaam son of Beor with the sword" (v. 8b). The unprofitable prophet must have returned from home to incite the Midianites and Moabites to deception against the Israelites at Shittim (v. 16).

31:12–16 Moses is angry with the army officers for keeping alive the Midianite women, who have been the most dangerous enemies as instruments of apostasy.

the priest and the Israelite assembly[y] at
their camp on the plains of Moab, by the
Jordan across from Jericho.
13 Moses, Eleazar the priest and all the
leaders of the community went to meet
them outside the camp. 14 Moses was angry with the officers of the army[z] — the
commanders of thousands and commanders of hundreds — who returned
from the battle.
15 "Have you allowed all the women to
live?" he asked them. 16 "They were the
ones who followed Balaam's advice[a] and
enticed the Israelites to be unfaithful to
the LORD in the Peor incident,[b] so that a
plague struck the LORD's people. 17 Now
kill all the boys. And kill every woman
who has slept with a man,[c] 18 but save
for yourselves every girl who has never
slept with a man.
19 "Anyone who has killed someone or
touched someone who was killed[d] must
stay outside the camp seven days. On the
third and seventh days you must purify
yourselves[e] and your captives. 20 Purify every garment[f] as well as everything
made of leather, goat hair or wood."
21 Then Eleazar the priest said to the
soldiers who had gone into battle, "This
is what is required by the law that the
LORD gave Moses: 22 Gold, silver, bronze,
iron,[g] tin, lead 23 and anything else that
can withstand fire must be put through
the fire,[h] and then it will be clean. But
it must also be purified with the water of cleansing.[i] And whatever cannot
withstand fire must be put through that
water. 24 On the seventh day wash your
clothes and you will be clean.[j] Then you
may come into the camp."

Dividing the Spoils

25 The LORD said to Moses, 26 "You and
Eleazar the priest and the family heads
of the community are to count all the
people[k] and animals that were captured.
27 Divide[l] the spoils equally between the
soldiers who took part in the battle and
the rest of the community. 28 From the
soldiers who fought in the battle, set
apart as tribute for the LORD[m] one out of
every five hundred, whether people, cattle, donkeys or sheep. 29 Take this tribute
from their half share and give it to Eleazar the priest as the LORD's part. 30 From
the Israelites' half, select one out of every
fifty, whether people, cattle, donkeys,
sheep or other animals. Give them to the
Levites, who are responsible for the care
of the LORD's tabernacle.[n]" 31 So Moses
and Eleazar the priest did as the LORD
commanded Moses.
32 The plunder remaining from the
spoils that the soldiers took was 675,000
sheep, 33 72,000 cattle, 34 61,000 donkeys
35 and 32,000 women who had never slept
with a man.
36 The half share of those who fought
in the battle was:

337,500 sheep, 37 of which the tribute
for the LORD[o] was 675;
38 36,000 cattle, of which the tribute
for the LORD was 72;
39 30,500 donkeys, of which the tribute
for the LORD was 61;
40 16,000 people, of whom the tribute
for the LORD was 32.

41 Moses gave the tribute to Eleazar the
priest as the LORD's part,[p] as the LORD
commanded Moses.
42 The half belonging to the Israelites, which Moses set apart from that of
the fighting men — 43 the community's
half — was 337,500 sheep, 44 36,000 cattle, 45 30,500 donkeys 46 and 16,000 people. 47 From the Israelites' half, Moses
selected one out of every fifty people and
animals, as the LORD commanded him,
and gave them to the Levites, who were
responsible for the care of the LORD's
tabernacle.
48 Then the officers who were over the
units of the army — the commanders

31:12 [y] Nu 27:2
31:14 [z] ver 48; Ex 18:21; Dt 1:15
31:16 [a] 2Pe 2:15; Rev 2:14 [b] Nu 25:1-9
31:17 [c] Dt 7:2; 20:16-18; Jdg 21:11
31:19 [d] Nu 19:16 [e] Nu 19:12
31:20 [f] Nu 19:19
31:22 [g] Jos 6:19; 22:8
31:23 [h] 1Co 3:13 [i] Nu 19:9,17
31:24 [j] Lev 11:25
31:26 [k] Nu 1:19
31:27 [l] Jos 22:8; 1Sa 30:24
31:28 [m] Nu 18:21
31:30 [n] Nu 3:7; 18:3
31:37 [o] ver 38-41
31:41 [p] Nu 5:9; 18:8

31:17–18, 35 Having attempted to destroy the Israelites, the Midianites have forfeited mercy. So, Moses orders summary execution of all captives except for 32,000 young virgin girls. These can be assimilated into the Israelite community by marrying Israelite men, who will provide them with new family identities.

31:19 All soldiers who have come in contact with corpses are required to remain outside the main encampment, where the holy sanctuary is, and to undergo ritual purification.

31:20–24 Eleazar the high priest picks up where Moses left off, conveying supplementary instructions that Moses received from the Lord (vv. 21–24). Metal objects are to be purified by fire and the "water of cleansing" (vv. 22–23a), which contains the ashes of the red cow (cf. ch. 19). Other things that cannot withstand fire are to be passed through water instead (v. 23b).

31:25–54 The rest of Nu 31 describes distribution of the spoils of war.

of thousands and commanders of hundreds — went to Moses 49and said to
him, "Your servants have counted the
soldiers under our command, and not
one is missing.[q] 50So we have brought as
an offering to the LORD the gold articles
each of us acquired — armlets, bracelets,
signet rings, earrings and necklaces — to
make atonement for ourselves[r] before
the LORD."
51Moses and Eleazar the priest accepted from them the gold — all the crafted
articles. 52All the gold from the commanders of thousands and commanders of hundreds that Moses and Eleazar
presented as a gift to the LORD weighed
16,750 shekels.[a] 53Each soldier had taken
plunder[s] for himself. 54Moses and Eleazar the priest accepted the gold from
the commanders of thousands and commanders of hundreds and brought it into
the tent of meeting as a memorial[t] for
the Israelites before the LORD.

31:49 [q] Jer 23:4
31:50 [r] Ex 30:16
31:53 [s] Dt 20:14
31:54 [t] Ex 28:12

The Transjordan Tribes

32 The Reubenites and Gadites, who
had very large herds and flocks,
saw that the lands of Jazer[u] and Gilead were suitable for livestock.[v] 2So they
came to Moses and Eleazar the priest
and to the leaders of the community,
and said, 3"Ataroth,[w] Dibon, Jazer, Nimrah,[x] Heshbon, Elealeh,[y] Sebam, Nebo
and Beon[z] — 4the land the LORD subdued[a] before the people of Israel — are
suitable for livestock,[b] and your servants
have livestock. 5If we have found favor
in your eyes," they said, "let this land be
given to your servants as our possession.
Do not make us cross the Jordan."

32:1 [u] Nu 21:32 [v] Ex 12:38
32:3 [w] ver 34 [x] ver 36 [y] ver 37; Isa 15:4; 16:9; Jer 48:34 [z] ver 38; Jos 13:17; Eze 25:9
32:4 [a] Nu 21:34 [b] Ex 12:38

Nu 32:17-18 ❖ How can we assist fellow believers in the battles they face in life? How far are we willing to go to help them?

6Moses said to the Gadites and Reubenites, "Should your fellow Israelites go to
war while you sit here? 7Why do you discourage the Israelites from crossing over
into the land the LORD has given them?[c]
8This is what your fathers did when I sent
them from Kadesh Barnea to look over
the land.[d] 9After they went up to the Valley of Eshkol[e] and viewed the land, they
discouraged the Israelites from entering
the land the LORD had given them. 10The
LORD's anger was aroused[f] that day and he
swore this oath: 11'Because they have not
followed me wholeheartedly, not one of
those who were twenty years old or more[g]
when they came up out of Egypt will see
the land I promised on oath[h] to Abraham,
Isaac and Jacob[i] — 12not one except Caleb son of Jephunneh the Kenizzite and
Joshua son of Nun, for they followed the
LORD wholeheartedly.'[j] 13The LORD's anger
burned against Israel[k] and he made them
wander in the wilderness forty years, until the whole generation of those who had
done evil in his sight was gone.[l]
14"And here you are, a brood of sinners,
standing in the place of your fathers and
making the LORD even more angry with
Israel.[m] 15If you turn away from following
him, he will again leave all this people in
the wilderness, and you will be the cause
of their destruction.[n]"

32:7 [c] Nu 13:27-14:4
32:8 [d] Nu 13:3, 26; Dt 1:19-25
32:9 [e] Nu 13:23; Dt 1:24
32:10 [f] Nu 11:1
32:11 [g] Ex 30:14 [h] Nu 14:23 [i] Nu 14:28-30
32:12 [j] Nu 14:24, 30; Dt 1:36; Ps 63:8
32:13 [k] Ex 4:14 [l] Nu 14:28-35; 26:64,65
32:14 [m] ver 10; Dt 1:34; Ps 78:59
32:15 [n] Dt 30:17-18; 2Ch 7:20

[a] *52* That is, about 420 pounds or about 190 kilograms

31:50 The army officers are grateful to God that their casualties amount to a miraculous zero. So, as a valuable offering before the Lord, they present the crafted items of gold—primarily jewelry—that they have seized (vv. 48–54).

31:54 Moses and Eleazar bring the commander's contribution into the sacred tent as a memorial/reminder for the Israelites before the Lord, testifying to the fact that their lives have been ransomed.

✚ **31:1–54** We confront the hard reality that our approach to the ethics of "holy war" genocide depends on our answer to a religious question: Which deity is true and therefore has ultimate authority over human life? Problems such as the political and ideological environment of the Middle East will never be satisfactorily and permanently solved at any conference table as long as moral attitudes and ethical judgments are founded on different religions. If we could agree that because theocracy no longer exists on Planet Earth, there is no such thing as "holy war" in the twenty-first century and therefore indiscriminate slaughter is unconscionable, inhumane, and universally condemnable, we would have a solid basis for resolution of conflict.

32:1–5 When the Reubenites and Gadites approach Moses and other leaders to request the Transjordanian territories as their possession, they cause a major misunderstanding by concluding their petition with the words: "Do not make us cross the Jordan" (v. 5).

32:6–15 Moses "hits the roof" and delivers one of the most sizzling speeches of his oratorically distinguished career. He no doubt expects the representatives of Reuben and Gad to slink away "with their tails between their legs."

16Then they came up to him and said, "We would like to build pens here for our livestock[o] and cities for our women and children. 17But we will arm ourselves for battle[a] and go ahead of the Israelites[p] until we have brought them to their place.[q] Meanwhile our women and children will live in fortified cities, for protection from the inhabitants of the land. 18We will not return to our homes until each of the Israelites has received their inheritance.[r] 19We will not receive any inheritance with them on the other side of the Jordan, because our inheritance has come to us on the east side of the Jordan."[s]

20Then Moses said to them, "If you will do this — if you will arm yourselves before the LORD for battle[t] 21and if all of you who are armed cross over the Jordan before the LORD until he has driven his enemies out before him — 22then when the land is subdued before the LORD, you may return[u] and be free from your obligation to the LORD and to Israel. And this land will be your possession before the LORD.[v]

23"But if you fail to do this, you will be sinning against the LORD; and you may be sure that your sin will find you out.[w] 24Build cities for your women and children, and pens for your flocks,[x] but do what you have promised.[y]"

25The Gadites and Reubenites said to Moses, "We your servants will do as our lord commands. 26Our children and wives, our flocks and herds will remain here in the cities of Gilead.[z] 27But your servants, every man who is armed for battle, will cross over to fight before the LORD, just as our lord says."

28Then Moses gave orders about them[a] to Eleazar the priest and Joshua son of Nun and to the family heads of the Israelite tribes. 29He said to them, "If the Gadites and Reubenites, every man armed for battle, cross over the Jordan with you before the LORD, then when the land is subdued before you, you must give them the land of Gilead as their possession. 30But if they do not cross over with you armed, they must accept their possession with you in Canaan."

31The Gadites and Reubenites answered, "Your servants will do what the LORD has said.[b] 32We will cross over before the LORD into Canaan armed, but the property we inherit will be on this side of the Jordan."

33Then Moses gave to the Gadites,[c] the Reubenites and the half-tribe of Manasseh son of Joseph the kingdom of Sihon king of the Amorites[d] and the kingdom of Og king of Bashan — the whole land with its cities and the territory around them.[e]

34The Gadites built up Dibon, Ataroth, Aroer,[f] 35Atroth Shophan, Jazer,[g] Jogbehah, 36Beth Nimrah[h] and Beth Haran as fortified cities, and built pens for their flocks. 37And the Reubenites rebuilt Heshbon, Elealeh and Kiriathaim, 38as well as Nebo[i] and Baal Meon (these names were changed) and Sibmah. They gave names to the cities they rebuilt.

39The descendants of Makir[j] son of Manasseh went to Gilead, captured it and drove out the Amorites who were there. 40So Moses gave Gilead to the Makirites,[k] the descendants of Manasseh, and they settled there. 41Jair, a descendant of Manasseh, captured their settlements and called them Havvoth Jair.[b][l] 42And Nobah captured Kenath and its surrounding settlements and called it Nobah after himself.[m]

Stages in Israel's Journey

33 Here are the stages in the journey of the Israelites when they came out of Egypt[n] by divisions under the leadership of Moses and Aaron.[o] 2At the LORD's command Moses recorded

32:16 [o] Ex 12:38; Dt 3:19
32:17 [p] Jos 4:12, 13 [q] Nu 22:4; Dt 3:20
32:18 [r] Jos 22:1-4
32:19 [s] Jos 12:1
32:20 [t] Dt 3:18
32:22 [u] Jos 22:4 [v] Dt 3:18-20
32:23 [w] Ge 4:7; 44:16; Isa 59:12
32:24 [x] ver 1, 16 [y] Nu 30:2
32:26 [z] Jos 1:14
32:28 [a] Dt 3:18-20; Jos 1:13
32:31 [b] ver 29
32:33 [c] Jos 13:24-28; 1Sa 13:7 [d] Dt 2:26 [e] Nu 21:24; Jos 12:6
32:34 [f] Dt 2:36; Jdg 11:26
32:35 [g] ver 3
32:36 [h] ver 3
32:38 [i] ver 3, Isa 15:2; Jer 48:1, 22
32:39 [j] Ge 50:23
32:40 [k] Dt 3:15; Jos 17:1
32:41 [l] Dt 3:14; Jos 13:30; Jdg 10:4; 1Ch 2:23
32:42 [m] 2Sa 18:18; Ps 49:11
33:1 [n] Mic 6:4 [o] Ps 77:20

[a] 17 Septuagint; Hebrew *will be quick to arm ourselves* [b] 41 Or *them the settlements of Jair*

32:16–19 They clarify their intentions and outline a plan for their men to not just go *with* the rest of the Israelites but to be deployed in advance of them to help them fight for their inheritance on the other side of the Jordan (vv. 16–18).

32:20–24 Moses approves, provided that they will follow through.

32:25–27 The Gadites and Reubenites reinforce their promise by repeating it, referring to their idea as their lord's (Moses') command.

32:33 The biblical text does not explain why Manasseh enters the picture at this point. Perhaps after Reuben and Gad pave the way with Moses, some Manassites decide they want to live in the Transjordan too.

33:1–3 The summary in Numbers 33 is more complete than the accounts in Exodus and earlier in Numbers, which concentrate on places where memorable events have occurred.

the stages in their journey. This is their
journey by stages:

3 The Israelites set out from Rameses on the fifteenth day of the first
month, the day after the Passover.[p]
They marched out defiantly[q] in full
view of all the Egyptians, 4 who were
burying all their firstborn, whom
the LORD had struck down among
them; for the LORD had brought
judgment on their gods.[r]
5 The Israelites left Rameses and
camped at Sukkoth.[s]
6 They left Sukkoth and camped at
Etham, on the edge of the desert.[t]
7 They left Etham, turned back to
Pi Hahiroth, to the east of Baal Zephon,[u] and camped near Migdol.[v]
8 They left Pi Hahiroth[a] and passed
through the sea[w] into the desert,
and when they had traveled for
three days in the Desert of Etham,
they camped at Marah.[x]
9 They left Marah and went to
Elim, where there were twelve
springs and seventy palm trees, and
they camped[y] there.
10 They left Elim and camped by
the Red Sea.[b]
11 They left the Red Sea and
camped in the Desert of Sin.[z]
12 They left the Desert of Sin and
camped at Dophkah.
13 They left Dophkah and camped
at Alush.
14 They left Alush and camped at
Rephidim, where there was no water
for the people to drink.
15 They left Rephidim[a] and camped
in the Desert of Sinai.[b]
16 They left the Desert of Sinai and
camped at Kibroth Hattaavah.[c]
17 They left Kibroth Hattaavah and
camped at Hazeroth.[d]
18 They left Hazeroth and camped
at Rithmah.
19 They left Rithmah and camped
at Rimmon Perez.
20 They left Rimmon Perez and
camped at Libnah.[e]
21 They left Libnah and camped
at Rissah.
22 They left Rissah and camped at
Kehelathah.
23 They left Kehelathah and
camped at Mount Shepher.
24 They left Mount Shepher and
camped at Haradah.
25 They left Haradah and camped
at Makheloth.
26 They left Makheloth and
camped at Tahath.
27 They left Tahath and camped
at Terah.
28 They left Terah and camped at
Mithkah.
29 They left Mithkah and camped
at Hashmonah.
30 They left Hashmonah and
camped at Moseroth.[f]
31 They left Moseroth and camped
at Bene Jaakan.
32 They left Bene Jaakan and
camped at Hor Haggidgad.
33 They left Hor Haggidgad and
camped at Jotbathah.[g]
34 They left Jotbathah and camped
at Abronah.
35 They left Abronah and camped
at Ezion Geber.[h]
36 They left Ezion Geber and
camped at Kadesh, in the Desert of
Zin.[i]
37 They left Kadesh and camped at
Mount Hor,[j] on the border of Edom.[k]
38 At the LORD's command Aaron the
priest went up Mount Hor, where
he died[l] on the first day of the fifth
month of the fortieth year after
the Israelites came out of Egypt.[m]
39 Aaron was a hundred and twenty-three years old when he died on
Mount Hor.
40 The Canaanite king of Arad,[n] who
lived in the Negev of Canaan, heard
that the Israelites were coming.

33:3 [p] Ex 13:4 [q] Ex 14:8
33:4 [r] Ex 12:12
33:5 [s] Ex 12:37
33:6 [t] Ex 13:20
33:7 [u] Ex 14:9 [v] Ex 14:2
33:8 [w] Ex 14:22 [x] Ex 15:23
33:9 [y] Ex 15:27
33:11 [z] Ex 16:1
33:15 [a] Ex 17:1 [b] Ex 19:1
33:16 [c] Nu 11:34
33:17 [d] Nu 11:35
33:20 [e] Jos 10:29
33:30 [f] Dt 10:6
33:33 [g] Dt 10:7
33:35 [h] Dt 2:8; 1Ki 9:26; 22:48
33:36 [i] Nu 20:1
33:37 [j] Nu 20:22 [k] Nu 20:16; 21:4
33:38 [l] Dt 10:6 [m] Nu 20:25-28
33:40 [n] Nu 21:1

[a] *8* Many manuscripts of the Masoretic Text, Samaritan Pentateuch and Vulgate; most manuscripts of the Masoretic Text *left from before Hahiroth* [b] *10* Or *the Sea of Reeds*; also in verse 11

33:3–15 These verses cover journeys from Egypt to the desert of Sinai (cf. Ex 12–19).

33:15–16 This section includes the Desert of Sinai, where the tabernacle was constructed and the laws of Leviticus were given, as just another stop along the way.

33:16–49 These verses cover the decades of travel from the Desert of Sinai to the plains of Moab by the Jordan River (cf. chs. 10–25), listing many place names that we have not encountered earlier in Numbers because no noteworthy events occurred there during the years of wandering.

41They left Mount Hor and camped
at Zalmonah.
42They left Zalmonah and camped
at Punon.
43They left Punon and camped at
Oboth.[o]
44They left Oboth and camped at
Iye Abarim, on the border of Moab.[p]
45They left Iye Abarim and
camped at Dibon Gad.
46They left Dibon Gad and camped
at Almon Diblathaim.
47They left Almon Diblathaim and
camped in the mountains of Abarim,[q] near Nebo.
48They left the mountains of Abarim and camped on the plains of
Moab by the Jordan across from Jericho.[r] 49There on the plains of Moab
they camped along the Jordan from
Beth Jeshimoth to Abel Shittim.[s]

50On the plains of Moab by the Jordan
across from Jericho the LORD said to Moses, 51"Speak to the Israelites and say to
them: 'When you cross the Jordan into
Canaan,[t] 52drive out all the inhabitants
of the land before you. Destroy all their
carved images and their cast idols, and
demolish all their high places.[u] 53Take
possession of the land and settle in it,
for I have given you the land to possess.[v]
54Distribute the land by lot, according to
your clans.[w] To a larger group give a larger inheritance, and to a smaller group a
smaller one. Whatever falls to them by
lot will be theirs. Distribute it according
to your ancestral tribes.
55" 'But if you do not drive out the inhabitants of the land, those you allow to
remain will become barbs in your eyes
and thorns[x] in your sides. They will give
you trouble in the land where you will
live. 56And then I will do to you what I
plan to do to them.' "

Boundaries of Canaan

34 The LORD said to Moses, 2"Command the Israelites and say to
them: 'When you enter Canaan, the land

33:43 [o] Nu 21:10
33:44 [p] Nu 21:11
33:47 [q] Nu 27:12
33:48 [r] Nu 22:1
33:49 [s] Nu 25:1
33:51 [t] Jos 3:17
33:52 [u] Ex 23:24; 34:13; Lev 26:1; Dt 7:2,5; 12:3; Jos 11:12; Ps 106:34-36
33:53 [v] Dt 11:31; Jos 21:43
33:54 [w] Nu 26:54
33:55 [x] Jos 23:13; Jdg 2:3; Ps 106:36
34:2 [y] Ge 17:8; Dt 1:7-8; Ps 78:54-55 [z] Eze 47:15
34:3 [a] Jos 15:1-3 [b] Ge 14:3
34:4 [c] Jos 15:3 [d] Nu 32:8
34:5 [e] Ge 15:18; Jos 15:4
34:7 [f] Eze 47:15-17
34:8 [g] Nu 13:21; Jos 13:5
34:11 [h] 2Ki 23:33; Jer 39:5 [i] Dt 3:17; Jos 11:2; 13:27
34:13 [j] Jos 14:1-5

Nu 33:55 ❖ What happens when we don't completely root out sinful behaviors from our lives? How can we drive out vices and snares completely?

Nu 34:2 ❖ What special inheritance does God give his people through Christ (see Eph 1:11-12)? What does it mean to you to have an inheritance from God?

that will be allotted to you as an inheritance[y] is to have these boundaries:[z]

3" 'Your southern side will include
some of the Desert of Zin[a] along the
border of Edom. Your southern boundary will start in the east from the southern end of the Dead Sea,[b] 4cross south
of Scorpion Pass,[c] continue on to Zin
and go south of Kadesh Barnea.[d] Then
it will go to Hazar Addar and over to Azmon, 5where it will turn, join the Wadi of
Egypt[e] and end at the Mediterranean Sea.
6" 'Your western boundary will be the
coast of the Mediterranean Sea. This will
be your boundary on the west.
7" 'For your northern boundary,[f] run
a line from the Mediterranean Sea to
Mount Hor 8and from Mount Hor to Lebo
Hamath.[g] Then the boundary will go to
Zedad, 9continue to Ziphron and end at
Hazar Enan. This will be your boundary
on the north.
10" 'For your eastern boundary, run a
line from Hazar Enan to Shepham. 11The
boundary will go down from Shepham
to Riblah[h] on the east side of Ain and
continue along the slopes east of the Sea
of Galilee.[a][i] 12Then the boundary will go
down along the Jordan and end at the
Dead Sea.
" 'This will be your land, with its
boundaries on every side.' "
13Moses commanded the Israelites:
"Assign this land by lot as an inheritance.[j]
The LORD has ordered that it be given to
the nine and a half tribes, 14because the
families of the tribe of Reuben, the tribe

[a] 11 Hebrew *Kinnereth*

33:49, 50–56 The summary of past journeys in Nu 33 returns to the present at the plains of Moab by the Jordan, where the Israelites are encamped. Here, across from Jericho, the Lord instructs them how to treat the Canaanites when they cross the Jordan: Drive them out, destroy all their objects of worship, and settle in their land, dividing it up by casting lots (vv. 50–56).

34:1–15 Numbers 34 addresses the settlement and division of the land. The boundaries of the promised land are specified as: southern (vv. 3–5), western (v. 6), northern (vv. 7–9), and eastern (vv. 10–12), aside from the Transjordanian territory of the Gadites, Reubenites, and half-tribe of Manasseh (vv. 13–15).

of Gad and the half-tribe of Manasseh
have received their inheritance.[k] 15These
two and a half tribes have received their
inheritance east of the Jordan across
from Jericho, toward the sunrise."
16The LORD said to Moses, 17"These are
the names of the men who are to assign
the land for you as an inheritance: Eleazar the priest and Joshua[l] son of Nun.
18And appoint one leader from each tribe
to help[m] assign the land. 19These are their
names:

Caleb[n] son of Jephunneh,
from the tribe of Judah;[o]
20 Shemuel son of Ammihud,
from the tribe of Simeon;[p]
21 Elidad son of Kislon,
from the tribe of Benjamin;[q]
22 Bukki son of Jogli,
the leader from the tribe of Dan;
23 Hanniel son of Ephod,
the leader from the tribe of Manasseh son of Joseph;
24 Kemuel son of Shiphtan,
the leader from the tribe of Ephraim son of Joseph;
25 Elizaphan son of Parnak,
the leader from the tribe of Zebulun;
26 Paltiel son of Azzan,
the leader from the tribe of Issachar;
27 Ahihud son of Shelomi,
the leader from the tribe of Asher;[r]
28 Pedahel son of Ammihud,
the leader from the tribe of Naphtali."

29These are the men the LORD commanded to assign the inheritance to the Israelites in the land of Canaan.

Towns for the Levites

35 On the plains of Moab by the Jordan across from Jericho, the LORD
said to Moses, 2"Command the Israelites
to give the Levites towns to live in[s] from

34:14 [k]Nu 32:33; Jos 14:3
34:17 [l]Jos 14:1
34:18 [m]Nu 1:4, 16
34:19 [n]Nu 26:65 [o]Ge 29:35; Dt 33:7
34:20 [p]Ge 49:5
34:21 [q]Ge 49:27; Ps 68:27
34:27 [r]Nu 1:40
35:2 [s]Lev 25:32-34; Jos 14:3,4
35:6 [t]Jos 20:7-9; 21:3,13
35:8 [u]Nu 26:54; 33:54; Jos 21:1-42
35:10 [v]Jos 20:2
35:11 [w]ver 22-25 [x]Ex 21:13; Dt 19:1-13

Nu 35:10-15 ❖ How can Christians practice justice for the innocent or unfairly condemned? What does the establishment of cities of refuge tell us about God's nature?

the inheritance the Israelites will possess. And give them pasturelands around
the towns. 3Then they will have towns
to live in and pasturelands for the cattle
they own and all their other animals.
4"The pasturelands around the towns
that you give the Levites will extend a
thousand cubits[a] from the town wall.
5Outside the town, measure two thousand cubits[b] on the east side, two thousand on the south side, two thousand
on the west and two thousand on the
north, with the town in the center. They
will have this area as pastureland for the
towns.

Cities of Refuge

35:6–34Ref // Dt 4:41–43; 19:1–14; Jos 20:1–9

6"Six of the towns you give the Levites will be cities of refuge, to which
a person who has killed someone may
flee.[t] In addition, give them forty-two
other towns. 7In all you must give the
Levites forty-eight towns, together with
their pasturelands. 8The towns you give
the Levites from the land the Israelites
possess are to be given in proportion to
the inheritance of each tribe: Take many
towns from a tribe that has many, but
few from one that has few."[u]
9Then the LORD said to Moses: 10"Speak
to the Israelites and say to them: 'When
you cross the Jordan into Canaan,[v] 11se-
lect some towns to be your cities of refuge, to which a person who has killed
someone[w] accidentally[x] may flee. 12They

[a] 4 That is, about 1,500 feet or about 450 meters
[b] 5 That is, about 3,000 feet or about 900 meters

34:16-29 Next, ch. 34 lists the leaders who will be responsible for dividing up the land.

✣ **32-34** If we don't feel comfortable with the strong way God and Moses ordered the Israelites to do things with an *or else* attitude, we should keep in mind that the Israelites had just come out of slavery. In many areas of life they were without the skills or motivation needed to function at a high level, so God used the "telling" approach.

35:1-8 Chapter 35 instructs the Israelite tribes to give the Levites forty-eight towns distributed throughout their territories, surrounded by pasturelands for their animals (vv. 1-8). Spreading out the Levite ministers of the Lord in this way will help to maintain the religious unity of the nation.

35:6, 9-15 Six of the Levite towns have special legal status as places of asylum/refuge to which any person who has inadvertently killed someone can flee.

CITIES OF REFUGE

The idea of providing cities of refuge (see Jos 20:1-9) for those who commit capital offenses is rooted in the tension between customary tribal law (retaliation or revenge, in which the blood relative is obligated to execute vengeance) and civil law (carried out less personally by an assembly according to a standard code of justice).

Blood feuds are usually associated with nomadic groups; legal procedures, with villages and towns. Israel, a society in the process of settling down, found it necessary to adopt an intermediate step regulating manslaughter so that an innocent person would not be killed before standing trial. Absolution was possible only by being cleared by the assembly and by the eventual death of the high priest (when there would be general amnesty).

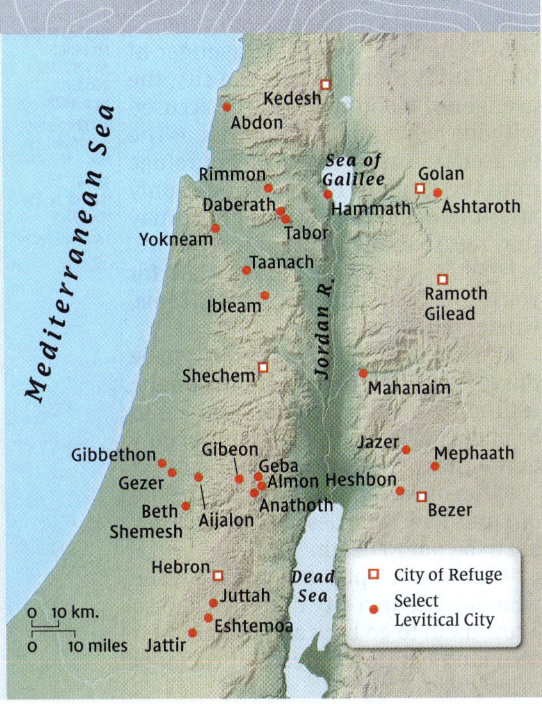

will be places of refuge from the avenger,[y] so that anyone accused of murder
may not die before they stand trial before the assembly. 13These six towns you
give will be your cities of refuge. 14Give
three on this side of the Jordan and three
in Canaan as cities of refuge. 15These six
towns will be a place of refuge for Israelites and for foreigners residing among
them, so that anyone who has killed another accidentally can flee there.
16" 'If anyone strikes someone a fatal
blow with an iron object, that person is
a murderer; the murderer is to be put to
death.[z] 17Or if anyone is holding a stone
and strikes someone a fatal blow with it,
that person is a murderer; the murderer is to be put to death. 18Or if anyone
is holding a wooden object and strikes
someone a fatal blow with it, that person
is a murderer; the murderer is to be put
to death. 19The avenger of blood shall put
the murderer to death; when the avenger
comes upon the murderer, the avenger
shall put the murderer to death.[a] 20If
anyone with malice aforethought shoves
another or throws something at them
intentionally[b] so that they die 21or if out
of enmity one person hits another with
their fist so that the other dies, that person is to be put to death; that person is a
murderer. The avenger of blood shall put
the murderer to death when they meet.
22" 'But if without enmity someone
suddenly pushes another or throws
something at them unintentionally[c] 23or,
without seeing them, drops on them a
stone heavy enough to kill them, and
they die, then since that other person
was not an enemy and no harm was intended, 24the assembly[d] must judge between the accused and the avenger of
blood according to these regulations.
25The assembly must protect the one
accused of murder from the avenger of
blood and send the accused back to the
city of refuge to which they fled. The accused must stay there until the death of
the high priest, who was anointed with
the holy oil.[e]

35:12 [y] Dt 19:6; Jos 20:3
35:16 [z] Ex 21:12; Lev 24:17
35:19 [a] ver 21
35:20 [b] Ge 4:8; Ex 21:14; Dt 19:11; 2Sa 3:27; 20:10
35:22 [c] ver 11; Ex 21:13
35:24 [d] ver 12; Jos 20:6
35:25 [e] Ex 29:7

35:16-21 Either of two criteria for what we call "first-degree murder" disqualifies a killer from asylum. **35:24-28** Once an Israelite killer runs to a town of refuge, the community will take him and judge between him and the "avenger of blood" (representing the deceased; v. 24). If the accused is acquitted, the community is to return him to the city of refuge. Only by staying there will he enjoy legal immunity to the avenger until the high priest dies, after which he is free to return home (vv. 25-28).

26" 'But if the accused ever goes outside the limits of the city of refuge to
which they fled 27and the avenger of
blood finds them outside the city, the
avenger of blood may kill the accused
without being guilty of murder. 28The
accused must stay in the city of refuge
until the death of the high priest; only
after the death of the high priest may
they return to their own property.
29" 'This is to have the force of law[f] for
you throughout the generations to come,
wherever you live.
30" 'Anyone who kills a person is to be
put to death as a murderer only on the
testimony of witnesses. But no one is to
be put to death on the testimony of only
one witness.[g]
31" 'Do not accept a ransom for the life
of a murderer, who deserves to die. They
are to be put to death.
32" 'Do not accept a ransom for anyone
who has fled to a city of refuge and so
allow them to go back and live on their
own land before the death of the high
priest.
33" 'Do not pollute the land where you
are. Bloodshed pollutes the land,[h] and
atonement cannot be made for the land
on which blood has been shed, except by
the blood of the one who shed it. 34Do not
defile the land[i] where you live and where
I dwell,[j] for I, the LORD, dwell among the
Israelites.' "

Inheritance of Zelophehad's Daughters

36:1–12pp // Nu 27:1–11

36 The family heads of the clan of
Gilead[k] son of Makir, the son of
Manasseh, who were from the clans
of the descendants of Joseph, came and
spoke before Moses and the leaders,[l] the
heads of the Israelite families. 2They
said, "When the LORD commanded my
lord to give the land as an inheritance
to the Israelites by lot, he ordered you
to give the inheritance of our brother
Zelophehad[m] to his daughters. 3Now
suppose they marry men from other Israelite tribes; then their inheritance will
be taken from our ancestral inheritance
and added to that of the tribe they marry
into. And so part of the inheritance allotted to us will be taken away. 4When the
Year of Jubilee[n] for the Israelites comes,
their inheritance will be added to that of
the tribe into which they marry, and their
property will be taken from the tribal
inheritance of our ancestors."
5Then at the LORD's command Moses
gave this order to the Israelites: "What
the tribe of the descendants of Joseph
is saying is right. 6This is what the LORD
commands for Zelophehad's daughters:
They may marry anyone they please as
long as they marry within their father's
tribal clan. 7No inheritance[o] in Israel is to
pass from one tribe to another, for every
Israelite shall keep the tribal inheritance
of their ancestors. 8Every daughter who
inherits land in any Israelite tribe must
marry someone in her father's tribal
clan,[p] so that every Israelite will possess
the inheritance of their ancestors. 9No
inheritance may pass from one tribe to

35:29 [f] Nu 27:11
35:30 [g] ver 16; Dt 17:6; 19:15; Mt 18:16; Jn 7:51; 2Co 13:1; Heb 10:28
35:33 [h] Ge 9:6; Ps 106:38; Mic 4:11
35:34 [i] Lev 18:24,25 [j] Ex 29:45
36:1 [k] Nu 26:29 [l] Nu 27:2
36:2 [m] Nu 26:33; 27:1,7
36:4 [n] Lev 25:10
36:7 [o] 1Ki 21:3
36:8 [p] 1Ch 23:22

Nu 36:3–4 ❖ Are we ever afraid of losing the good things God has given us? How can we find assurance in the face of anxiety?

35:29–34 In support of the law that a murderer must die, vv. 33–34 explain that blood(shed)/murder pollutes and defiles the land where the Lord dwells among his people. It can only be expiated/purged through the blood of the person who shed the blood.
36:1–12 This chapter consists of a postscript to 27:1–8, where the Lord allowed the daughters of Zelophehad, a Manassite descended from Gilead, to inherit his property.

✣ **35–36** It is true that Christ commanded love for enemies, forgiveness and reconciliation rather than retaliation. These principles are already in the OT. For example, Lev 19:18 says: "Do not seek revenge or bear a grudge against anyone among your people, but love your neighbor as yourself." However, a few chapters later, the same book stipulates: "Anyone who takes the life of a human being is to be put to death" (Lev 24:17). Is this a contradiction? Not if we realize that Lev 19 is addressed to individuals, but Lev 24 is for the community. God's people were not to seek revenge, but a murderer was condemned to execution by the civil community. The latter was not revenge; it was divinely mandated retributive justice.

It is important to keep in mind that although a person who justly suffers capital punishment has forfeited the present life, it is possible for him or her to enjoy the promised paradise to come. When a dying criminal on the cross next to Jesus expressed his belief and repentance, Jesus promised that the man would be with him in paradise (Lk 23:42–43).

PEOPLE TO KNOW // ZELOPHEHAD'S DAUGHTERS

NUMBERS 36:1–11: The five daughters of Zelophehad stood up for themselves and their father in a powerful way. They appealed to Moses for land, which was allotted to the men of each tribe. They explained that their father, Zelophehad of the tribe of Manasseh, had died without any sons and that his name should not for that reason disappear from his clan (Nu 27:1–7).

Moses took the daughters' case before God, and God affirmed their judgment: "What Zelophehad's daughters are saying is right" (Nu 27:7). God went on to tell Moses that when a man died with no son, his inheritance was to be given to his daughter. This may seem obvious to modern readers, but it was a new revelation to Moses—one prompted by Zelophehad's daughters.

Later some men from Manasseh pushed back against this decision. They were worried that if Zelophehad's daughters married men from another tribe, land allotted to Manasseh would be transferred to that other tribe through the women's husbands. God agreed with their concern, but God did not change his command that land should be given to the daughters. Instead, God directed that they should only marry within their father's clan in order to keep the land within their tribe (Nu 36:1–9).

When Israel entered Canaan and the land was being divided by tribe, Zelophehad's daughters reminded Joshua, Eleazar the priest and other leaders of God's promise to them through Moses (Jos 17:3–4). The promise was honored, and Zelophehad's daughters received land along with their male relatives.

APPLICATION ✣ While it is true that ancient Israel was a patriarchal culture, the story of Zelophehad's daughters shows how God affirms and honors women. Old Testament heroes like Deborah, Huldah, Esther, Ruth and Rahab give powerful witness to the fact that God calls and equips women just as he does men. This story ought to encourage us to be bold in speaking up for what is right, trusting that God is always on the side of justice and equity.

another, for each Israelite tribe is to keep
the land it inherits."
10So Zelophehad's daughters did as
the LORD commanded Moses. 11Zelophe-
had's daughters — Mahlah, Tirzah, Hoglah, Milkah and Noah[q] — married their
cousins on their father's side. 12They
married within the clans of the descendants of Manasseh son of Joseph, and
their inheritance remained in their father's tribe and clan.

13These are the commands and regulations the LORD gave through Moses[r] to
the Israelites on the plains of Moab by
the Jordan across from Jericho.[s]

36:11 [q] Nu 26:33; 27:1
36:13 [r] Lev 26:46; 27:34 [s] Nu 22:1

Deuteronomy

Author: Moses
Audience: God's chosen people, the Israelites
Date: Probably between 1446 and 1406 BC

Theme: God through Moses exhorts the new generation of Israelites to live as his obedient people in the promised land.

PERSPECTIVE

Some scholars call the book of Deuteronomy "The Gospel According to Moses." Others, instead of comparing Moses to a gospel writer, compare him to Paul, the great NT theoretician. The study notes on Deuteronomy use both these ascriptions and more to describe the incredible theological value of this OT book. Indeed, Deuteronomy is the most systematic presentation of theological truth in the entire Bible, rivaled perhaps only by Paul's letter to the Romans.

Deuteronomy? you may be wondering. *Isn't it just an OT book? How can it be "gospel" without Jesus? Doesn't it predate Jesus by at least a millennium? Isn't this kind of reliance on OT law just what Paul warns us against?*

As the writer of this commentary shows us, what Moses did was gospel. It was good news to the Israelites who heard it on the plains of Moab, and as we explore this book more deeply, it becomes gospel for us today.

First, we are surprised at who Moses is. Second, we are surprised with what Moses asks Israel to do in his speeches, not because of what he says, but because of how much sense it makes to us as non-Israelites some three-thousand-plus years after the fact.

Moses can be summed up in this statement: Moses is more of a pastor than a lawgiver. Admittedly this goes against the grain of what we think we know about him. One of our most enduring images of Moses is his Olympian moment of anger, smashing two stone tablets of law on the rocks when he saw the golden calf. At first glance this seems to be all about law. God has given the law, Moses is bringing

Reading Deuteronomy

The book of Deuteronomy takes the form of a speech of Moses (or perhaps three speeches) to the Israelites, camped east of the Jordan River and ready to enter the land of Canaan. In this long discourse, he first reviewed what had happened to them since their experience at Mount Sinai, then reminded them of the laws God had revealed to them, and concluded with a catalog of the

	2200 BC	2100	2000	1900	1800	1700	1600	1500	1400
Moses' birth (c. 1526 BC)								♦	
The plagues; the Passover (c. 1446 BC)								♦	
The exodus (c. 1446 BC)								♦	
Desert wanderings (c. 1446–1406 BC)								▬	
The Ten Commandments (c. 1445 BC)								♦	
Book of Deuteronomy written (c. 1406 BC)									♦
Moses dies; Joshua becomes leader (c. 1406 BC)									♦
Israelites enter Canaan (c. 1406 BC)									♦

the law, the children of God are breaking the law. Wasn't that really who Moses was?

But consider the occasion presented to us in Deuteronomy. The Israelites are poised to enter the promised land. It is a moment of hope. But hope, by its very nature, always has an element of uncertainty, and thus anxiety always accompanies hope. Things could go wrong. The people need the reassurance of a pastor's hand, not the discipline of an authority figure. Moses supplies that.

The second surprise is that what Moses tells the Israelites makes so much sense to us today. He tells them they need to be in a covenant relationship with God, that God wants them to be his people. Moses challenges the Israelites to respond by declaring that Yahweh alone is their God and then by doing what God asks them to do.

As you read this commentary, let the words of Deuteronomy 6:4–9 sink deeply into your heart:

> Hear, O Israel: The LORD our God, the LORD is one. Love the LORD your God with all your heart and with all your soul and with all your strength. These commandments that I give you today are to be on your hearts. Impress them on your children. Talk about them when you sit at home and when you walk along the road, when you lie down and when you get up. Tie them as symbols on your hands and bind them on your foreheads. Write them on the doorframes of your houses and on your gates.

One does not have to be an OT Israelite to fully embrace the identity that this passage describes and to live it to the full. Jesus in his teaching ministry realized the spiritual gold mine of this passage and others like it that Deuteronomy represents. In his teaching he quotes more often from Deuteronomy than from any other biblical book. And this rich resource is as available to us—perhaps even more so—as it was to Jesus.

blessings for keeping those laws and the curses for disobeying them. After Moses instructed them to keep a copy of this code in the ark, he closed with a song and with a blessing for each of the tribes. The book ends by recording Moses' death on Mount Nebo.

Key Verses

Hear, O Israel: The LORD our God, the LORD is one. Love the LORD your God with all your heart and with all your soul and with all your strength. These commandments that I give you today are to be on your hearts. Impress them on your children. Talk about them when you sit at home and when you walk along the road, when you lie down and when you get up.

—Deuteronomy 6:4–7

TAKING THE NEXT STEPS

In the book of Deuteronomy, Moses challenged the Israelites to a renewal of their covenant relationship with the Lord as they stood on the border of the land of Canaan. After all, except for Moses, Caleb and Joshua, everyone had been younger than twenty years old when the covenant was established at Mount Sinai. He reminded them that ever since the time of Abraham they had been the people of God's own choosing. God's powerful action in bringing them out of Egypt and safely through the wilderness called for a response of love for and faith in him and of loving social concern for their brothers and sisters, particularly the poor, widows, orphans and aliens.

The book outlines several important principles that are relevant to our own lives. (1) It is as easy for us to drift away from the Lord as it was for the Israelites; consequently, we too need to listen to God's Word and, like them, regularly nurture our relationship with God. (2) The command to love the Lord, given more often in this book than any other in the OT, is still valid today. (3) Just as God's special love for his people in redeeming them from Egypt and caring for them in the wilderness became the guiding principle for their treatment of others, so our redemption through Christ and his daily care in our lives is the basis of the Christian life: "As I have loved you, so you must love one another" (Jn 13:34).

WHAT TO LOOK FOR IN DEUTERONOMY

- Review of history (chs. 1–3)
- The Ten Commandments (ch. 5)
- Love and serve the Lord (chs. 6; 11)
- Never forget what God has done (ch. 8)
- True worship of the Lord (chs. 12–13)
- The care of the poor (ch. 15)
- Israel's feasts (ch. 16)
- Blessings and curses (chs. 27–30)
- The song of Moses (ch. 32)
- The blessing of Moses (ch. 33)
- The death of Moses (ch. 34)

The Command to Leave Horeb

1 These are the words Moses spoke to
all Israel in the wilderness east of the
Jordan — that is, in the Arabah — opposite Suph, between Paran and Tophel,
Laban, Hazeroth and Dizahab. 2(It takes
eleven days to go from Horeb[a] to Kadesh
Barnea[b] by the Mount Seir road.)
3In the fortieth year,[c] on the first day of
the eleventh month, Moses proclaimed[d]
to the Israelites all that the LORD had
commanded him concerning them. 4This
was after he had defeated Sihon[e] king of
the Amorites, who reigned in Heshbon,[f]
and at Edrei had defeated Og[g] king of
Bashan, who reigned in Ashtaroth.
5East of the Jordan in the territory of
Moab, Moses began to expound this law,
saying:

6The LORD our God said to us[h] at Horeb,[i] "You have stayed long enough at
this mountain. 7Break camp and advance
into the hill country of the Amorites; go

1:2 [a] Ex 3:1 [b] Nu 13:26; Dt 9:23
1:3 [c] Nu 33:38 [d] Dt 4:1-2
1:4 [e] Nu 21:21-26 [f] Nu 21:25 [g] Nu 21:33-35; Jos 13:12
1:6 [h] Nu 10:13 [i] Ex 3:1

1:1–5 The addressees are identified as "all Israel" in v. 1 and "Israelites" in v. 3. The former suggests that Moses speaks to the community of faith; the latter highlights the nation's ethnic cohesion (they are the descendants of Jacob/Israel). The syntax of v. 1b creates the impression that Moses delivered these addresses in the desert, somewhere in the Arabah.

The book opens with "These are the words Moses spoke" (v. 1). In this book Moses does not function primarily as a lawgiver but as a prophet and as the people's pastor.

APPLICATION ✣ 1:1–5 As we will see in the commentary, this book presents the gospel according to Moses. This is a gospel of divine grace lavished on undeserving human beings. Moses' vision for his own people serves as a microcosm for the divine vision of humanity as a whole. The book points the reader to the Lord God, who has redeemed his people and assigned them the mission of radiating his grace to the world.

1:6–8 Moses begins with a quotation of Yahweh's speech from thirty-eight years prior (cf. Nu 10:11–13).

to all the neighboring peoples in the Arabah, in the mountains, in the western
foothills, in the Negev[j] and along the
coast, to the land of the Canaanites and
to Lebanon,[k] as far as the great river, the
Euphrates. 8See, I have given you this
land. Go in and take possession of the
land the LORD swore[l] he would give to
your fathers — to Abraham, Isaac and
Jacob — and to their descendants after
them."

The Appointment of Leaders

9At that time I said to you, "You are too
heavy a burden for me to carry alone.[m]
10The LORD your God has increased your
numbers so that today you are as numerous[n] as the stars in the sky.[o] 11May the
LORD, the God of your ancestors, increase
you a thousand times and bless you as
he has promised![p] 12But how can I bear
your problems and your burdens and
your disputes all by myself? 13Choose
some wise, understanding and respected
men[q] from each of your tribes, and I will
set them over you."
14You answered me, "What you propose to do is good."
15So I took[r] the leading men of your
tribes, wise and respected men, and appointed them to have authority over
you — as commanders of thousands,
of hundreds, of fifties and of tens and
as tribal officials. 16And I charged your
judges at that time, "Hear the disputes
between your people and judge fairly,[s]
whether the case is between two Israelites or between an Israelite and a foreigner residing among you.[t] 17Do not
show partiality[u] in judging; hear both

1:7 [j] Jos 10:40 [k] Dt 11:24
1:8 [l] Ge 12:7; 15:18; 17:7-8; 26:4; 28:13
1:9 [m] Ex 18:18
1:10 [n] Ge 15:5 [o] Dt 10:22; 28:62
1:11 [p] Ge 22:17; Ex 32:13
1:13 [q] Ex 18:21
1:15 [r] Ex 18:25
1:16 [s] Dt 16:18; Jn 7:24 [t] Lev 24:22
1:17 [u] Lev 19:15; Dt 16:19; Pr 24:23; Jas 2:1

1:9–18 Verses 9–18 divide into three sections. (1) Moses acknowledges that the burden of the Israelites had become heavier than he could bear (v. 9). (2) Moses proposed that the people pick men from each of the tribes as leaders over them (vv. 13–15). (3) Moses reports his charge to the officials (vv. 16–18): (3a) Hear the people's disputes and judge "fairly" (v. 16b). (3b) Hear the cases of the small and the great alike (v. 17a). (3c) Judge boldly ("do not be afraid," v. 17a). (3d) Recognize their limitations (v. 17b).

✣ **1:6–18** The law was not the end goal, nor did it represent the essence of God's call. The Lord calls us that we might delight in the fulfillment of his promise and that in that fulfillment the world may see what he can do for them.

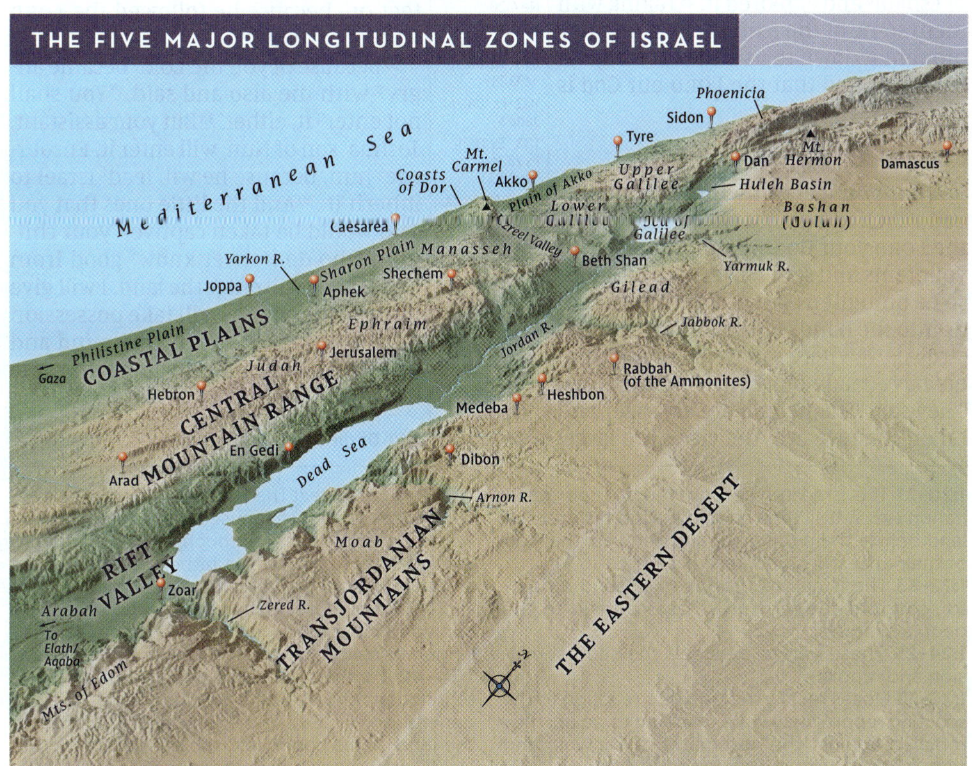

small and great alike. Do not be afraid
of anyone,[v] for judgment belongs to God.
Bring me any case too hard for you, and
I will hear it."[w] 18 And at that time I told
you everything you were to do.

Spies Sent Out

19 Then, as the LORD our God commanded us, we set out from Horeb and
went toward the hill country of the Amorites through all that vast and dreadful
wilderness[x] that you have seen, and so
we reached Kadesh Barnea.[y] 20 Then I
said to you, "You have reached the hill
country of the Amorites, which the LORD
our God is giving us. 21 See, the LORD your
God has given you the land. Go up and
take possession of it as the LORD, the God
of your ancestors, told you. Do not be
afraid;[z] do not be discouraged."

22 Then all of you came to me and said,
"Let us send men ahead to spy out the
land for us and bring back a report about
the route we are to take and the towns
we will come to."

23 The idea seemed good to me; so I
selected[a] twelve of you, one man from
each tribe. 24 They left and went up into
the hill country, and came to the Valley
of Eshkol[b] and explored it. 25 Taking with
them some of the fruit of the land, they
brought it down to us and reported,[c] "It
is a good land that the LORD our God is
giving us."

Rebellion Against the LORD

26 But you were unwilling to go up;[d]
you rebelled against the command of
the LORD your God. 27 You grumbled[e] in
your tents and said, "The LORD hates us;
so he brought us out of Egypt to deliver
us into the hands of the Amorites to destroy us. 28 Where can we go? Our brothers have made our hearts melt in fear.
They say, 'The people are stronger and
taller[f] than we are; the cities are large,

1:17 [v] 2Ch 19:6 [w] Ex 18:26
1:19 [x] Dt 8:15; Jer 2:2, 6 [y] ver 2; Nu 13:26
1:21 [z] Jos 1:6, 9, 18
1:23 [a] Nu 13:1-3
1:24 [b] Nu 13:21-25
1:25 [c] Nu 13:27
1:26 [d] Nu 14:1-4
1:27 [e] Dt 9:28; Ps 106:25
1:28 [f] Nu 13:32 [g] Nu 13:33; Dt 9:1-3
1:30 [h] Ex 14:14; Dt 3:22; Ne 4:20
1:31 [i] Dt 32:10-12; Isa 46:3-4; 63:9; Hos 11:3; Ac 13:18
1:32 [j] Ps 106:24; Jude 5
1:33 [k] Ex 13:21; Ps 78:14 [l] Nu 10:33
1:34 [m] Nu 14:23, 28-30
1:35 [n] Ps 95:11
1:36 [o] Nu 14:24; Jos 14:9
1:37 [p] Dt 3:26; 4:21 [q] Nu 20:12
1:38 [r] Nu 14:30 [s] Dt 31:7 [t] Dt 3:28
1:39 [u] Nu 14:3 [v] Isa 7:15-16
1:40 [w] Nu 14:25

Dt 1:29 ❖ How can we learn to see through eyes of faith rather than of fear?

with walls up to the sky. We even saw the
Anakites[g] there.'"

29 Then I said to you, "Do not be terrified; do not be afraid of them. 30 The
LORD your God, who is going before you,
will fight[h] for you, as he did for you in
Egypt, before your very eyes, 31 and in the
wilderness. There you saw how the LORD
your God carried[i] you, as a father carries
his son, all the way you went until you
reached this place."

32 In spite of this, you did not trust[j] in
the LORD your God, 33 who went ahead of
you on your journey, in fire by night and
in a cloud by day,[k] to search[l] out places
for you to camp and to show you the way
you should go.

34 When the LORD heard what you said,
he was angry and solemnly swore:[m] 35 "No
one from this evil generation shall see
the good land[n] I swore to give your ancestors, 36 except Caleb son of Jephunneh. He will see it, and I will give him
and his descendants the land he set his
feet on, because he followed the LORD
wholeheartedly.[o]"

37 Because of you the LORD became angry[p] with me also and said, "You shall
not enter[q] it, either. 38 But your assistant,
Joshua[r] son of Nun, will enter it. Encourage[s] him, because he will lead[t] Israel to
inherit it. 39 And the little ones that you
said would be taken captive,[u] your children who do not yet know[v] good from
bad — they will enter the land. I will give
it to them and they will take possession
of it. 40 But as for you, turn around and
set out toward the desert along the route
to the Red Sea.[a][w]"

[a] 40 Or *the Sea of Reeds*

1:20-21 The Israelites had arrived at their destination (vv. 7, 19); Yahweh had placed his grant of land before them (cf. v. 8); and Yahweh, the God of their ancestors, had kept his word.
1:22-33 The Israelites proposed to send a party to scout out the territory. Moses agreed to the people's request (v. 23).
1:24-25 These verses describe the scouts' mission and report.
1:26-33 Moses recalls the people's reaction to the scouting report. They were unwilling to go up; they rebelled against the command of Yahweh; and they muttered/grumbled in their tents.

Trying to correct the people's flawed perspective, Moses' response focused entirely on Yahweh. With a sensitive pastoral touch, Moses compared Yahweh's care to that of a father who carries his son through danger to safety. It is obvious from vv. 32-33 that Moses' exhortation had no effect. He reminded the present generation that the real challenge was neither physical nor military, but spiritual.
1:34-40 Yahweh swore he would give the land to innocent children who would replace "this evil generation" (v. 35). If the Israelites had entered the land at his command, the event recorded in Nu 20 would never have occurred.

41 Then you replied, "We have sinned
against the LORD. We will go up and fight,
as the LORD our God commanded us." So
every one of you put on his weapons,
thinking it easy to go up into the hill
country.
42 But the LORD said to me, "Tell them,
'Do not go up and fight, because I will
not be with you. You will be defeated by
your enemies.'"[x]
43 So I told you, but you would not
listen. You rebelled against the LORD's
command and in your arrogance you
marched up into the hill country. 44 The
Amorites who lived in those hills came
out against you; they chased you like a
swarm of bees[y] and beat you down from
Seir all the way to Hormah. 45 You came
back and wept before the LORD, but he
paid no attention to your weeping and
turned a deaf ear to you. 46 And so you
stayed in Kadesh[z] many days — all the
time you spent there.

Wanderings in the Wilderness

2 Then we turned back and set out toward the wilderness along the route
to the Red Sea,[a][a] as the LORD had directed
me. For a long time we made our way
around the hill country of Seir.
2 Then the LORD said to me, 3 "You have
made your way around this hill country
long enough; now turn north. 4 Give the
people these orders:[b] 'You are about to
pass through the territory of your relatives the descendants of Esau, who live
in Seir. They will be afraid of you, but be
very careful. 5 Do not provoke them to
war, for I will not give you any of their
land, not even enough to put your foot
on. I have given Esau the hill country of
Seir as his own.[c] 6 You are to pay them in
silver for the food you eat and the water
you drink.'"
7 The LORD your God has blessed you
in all the work of your hands. He has
watched[d] over your journey through this
vast wilderness. These forty years the
LORD your God has been with you, and
you have not lacked anything.
8 So we went on past our relatives the
descendants of Esau, who live in Seir.
We turned from the Arabah road, which
comes up from Elath and Ezion Geber,[e]
and traveled along the desert road of
Moab.[f]
9 Then the LORD said to me, "Do not
harass the Moabites or provoke them
to war, for I will not give you any part
of their land. I have given Ar[g] to the descendants of Lot[h] as a possession."
10 (The Emites[i] used to live there — a
people strong and numerous, and as tall
as the Anakites.[j] 11 Like the Anakites, they
too were considered Rephaites, but the
Moabites called them Emites. 12 Horites
used to live in Seir, but the descendants
of Esau drove them out. They destroyed
the Horites from before them and settled in their place, just as Israel did[k] in
the land the LORD gave them as their
possession.)
13 And the LORD said, "Now get up and
cross the Zered Valley." So we crossed
the valley.
14 Thirty-eight years passed from the
time we left Kadesh Barnea[l] until we
crossed the Zered Valley. By then, that
entire generation[m] of fighting men had
perished from the camp, as the LORD had
sworn to them.[n] 15 The LORD's hand was
against them until he had completely
eliminated[o] them from the camp.
16 Now when the last of these fighting
men among the people had died, 17 the

1:42 [x] Nu 14:41-43
1:44 [y] Ps 118:12
1:46 [z] Nu 20:1; Jdg 11:17
2:1 [a] Nu 21:4
2:4 [b] Nu 20:14-21
2:5 [c] Ge 36:8; Jos 24:4
2:7 [d] Dt 8:2-4
2:8 [e] 1Ki 9:26 [f] Jdg 11:18
2:9 [g] Nu 21:15 [h] Ge 19:36-38
2:10 [i] Ge 14:5 [j] Nu 13:22,33
2:12 [k] ver 22
2:14 [l] Nu 13:26 [m] Nu 14:29-35 [n] Dt 1:34-35
2:15 [o] Ps 106:26

Dt 2:7 ❖ When has God led you through a wilderness in life? How did you experience God's sustaining presence during that time?

[a] 1 Or *the Sea of Reeds*

1:41—2:1 The key expressions in this paragraph are "rebelled against the LORD's command" and "arrogance" (v. 43). Adding the sin of presumption to rebellion, they forgot that God is not obligated to those who do not take him seriously.

1:19—2:1 Sadly, like Israel, Christians have often proved faithless, being more impressed by the power of the enemy than the power of God.

2:2-8a In this opening episode, Moses remembers Israel's encounter with the Edomites. In vv. 2-7 he simply recalls verbatim the divinely prescribed policy for dealing with Edom.

2:8b-15 When the Israelites arrived at the edge of Moab (v. 8b), Yahweh commanded that the policy that governed their treatment of Edom was also to apply to Moab. Verses 10-12 function as a footnote, clarifying ethnographic and geographic issues raised in Moses' speech.

2:16-22 Once the last warriors of the faithless generation had died, Yahweh ordered the Israelites to move past the territory of the Ammonites. Yahweh prohibited the Israelites from harassing the Ammonites

LORD said to me, 18“Today you are to pass by the region of Moab at Ar. 19When you come to the Ammonites,[p] do not harass them or provoke them to war, for I will not give you possession of any land belonging to the Ammonites. I have given it as a possession to the descendants of Lot.[q]”

20(That too was considered a land of the Rephaites, who used to live there; but the Ammonites called them Zamzummites. 21They were a people strong and numerous, and as tall as the Anakites.[r] The LORD destroyed them from before the Ammonites, who drove them out and settled in their place. 22The LORD had done the same for the descendants of Esau, who lived in Seir,[s] when he destroyed the Horites from before them. They drove them out and have lived in their place to this day. 23And as for the Avvites[t] who lived in villages as far as Gaza, the Caphtorites[u] coming out from Caphtor[a][v] destroyed them and settled in their place.)

Defeat of Sihon King of Heshbon

24“Set out now and cross the Arnon Gorge.[w] See, I have given into your hand Sihon the Amorite, king of Heshbon, and his country. Begin to take possession of it and engage him in battle. 25This very day I will begin to put the terror[x] and fear[y] of you on all the nations under heaven. They will hear reports of you and will tremble[z] and be in anguish because of you.”

26From the Desert of Kedemoth I sent messengers to Sihon king of Heshbon offering peace and saying, 27“Let us pass through your country. We will stay on the main road; we will not turn aside to the right or to the left.[a] 28Sell us food to eat and water to drink for their price in silver. Only let us pass through on foot[b]—29as the descendants of Esau, who live in Seir, and the Moabites, who live in Ar, did for us—until we cross the Jordan into the land the LORD our God is giving us.” 30But Sihon king of Heshbon refused to let us pass through. For the LORD[c] your God had made his spirit stubborn[d] and his heart obstinate in order to give him into your hands, as he has now done.

31The LORD said to me, “See, I have begun to deliver Sihon and his country over to you. Now begin to conquer and possess his land.”[e]

32When Sihon and all his army came out to meet us in battle[f] at Jahaz, 33the LORD our God delivered him over to us and we struck him down,[g] together with his sons and his whole army. 34At that time we took all his towns and completely destroyed[b][h] them—men, women and children. We left no survivors. 35But the livestock and the plunder from the towns we had captured we carried off for ourselves. 36From Aroer[i] on the rim of the Arnon Gorge, and from the town in the gorge, even as far as Gilead, not one town was too strong for us. The LORD our God gave[j] us all of them. 37But in accordance with the command of the LORD our God,[k] you did not encroach on any of the land of the Ammonites,[l] neither the land along the course of the Jabbok[m] nor that around the towns in the hills.

Defeat of Og King of Bashan

3 Next we turned and went up along the road toward Bashan, and Og king of Bashan with his whole army marched out to meet us in battle at Edrei.[n] 2The LORD said to me, “Do not be afraid[o] of him, for I have delivered him into your hands, along with his whole army and his land. Do to him what you did to Sihon

[a] *23* That is, Crete [b] *34* The Hebrew term refers to the irrevocable giving over of things or persons to the LORD, often by totally destroying them.

2:19 [p] Ge 19:38 [q] ver 9
2:21 [r] ver 10
2:22 [s] Ge 36:8
2:23 [t] Jos 13:3 [u] Ge 10:14 [v] Am 9:7
2:24 [w] Nu 21:13-14; Jdg 11:13,18
2:25 [x] Dt 11:25 [y] Jos 2:9,11 [z] Ex 15:14-16
2:27 [a] Nu 21:21-22
2:28 [b] Nu 20:19
2:30 [c] Jos 11:20 [d] Ex 4:21; Nu 21:23; Ro 9:18
2:31 [e] Dt 1:8
2:32 [f] Nu 21:23
2:33 [g] Dt 29:7
2:34 [h] Dt 3:6; 7:2
2:36 [i] Dt 3:12; 4:48; Jos 13:9 [j] Ps 44:3
2:37 [k] ver 18-19 [l] Nu 21:24 [m] Ge 32:22; Dt 3:16
3:1 [n] Nu 21:33
3:2 [o] Nu 21:34

---

and from trying to take any of their territory, for he had given their land as their own possession.

2:23 This verse adds a puzzling reference to historical events far away. In the providence of God, the Philistines arrived in Palestine at the same time as the Israelites. Conflict was inevitable.

✣ **2:2-23** The enemies may appear numerous and strong, but the church must remember that Yahweh, the God of Israel, is mightier than all. “The one who is in you is greater than the one who is in the world” (1Jn 4:4).

2:24-37 Yahweh’s command to the Israelites consists of six imperatives (Arise! Set out! Cross! Begin! Take possession! Engage in battle! [v. 24]) and two significant promises: Yahweh had given Sihon into the Israelites’ hands, and he would cause people to tremble in fright when they heard of Israel’s triumphs.

3:1-2 Og interpreted the Israelites’ movements as a hostile military maneuver. Yahweh gave Moses a word of encouragement and a challenge (v. 2).

king of the Amorites, who reigned in Heshbon."

3So the LORD our God also gave into our hands Og king of Bashan and all his army. We struck them down, leaving no survivors.[p] 4At that time we took all his cities. There was not one of the sixty cities that we did not take from them — the whole region of Argob, Og's kingdom in Bashan.[q] 5All these cities were fortified with high walls and with gates and bars, and there were also a great many unwalled villages. 6We completely destroyed[a] them, as we had done with Sihon king of Heshbon, destroying[a r] every city — men, women and children. 7But all the livestock and the plunder from their cities we carried off for ourselves.

8So at that time we took from these two kings of the Amorites the territory east of the Jordan, from the Arnon Gorge as far as Mount Hermon. 9(Hermon is called Sirion[s] by the Sidonians; the Amorites call it Senir.)[t] 10We took all the towns on the plateau, and all Gilead, and all Bashan as far as Salekah[u] and Edrei, towns of Og's kingdom in Bashan. 11(Og king of Bashan was the last of the Rephaites.[v] His bed was decorated with iron and was more than nine cubits long and four cubits wide.[b] It is still in Rabbah[w] of the Ammonites.)

Division of the Land

12Of the land that we took over at that time, I gave the Reubenites and the Gadites the territory north of Aroer[x] by the Arnon Gorge, including half the hill country of Gilead, together with its towns. 13The rest of Gilead and also all of Bashan, the kingdom of Og, I gave to the half-tribe of Manasseh. (The whole region of Argob in Bashan used to be known as a land of the Rephaites. 14Jair,[y] a descendant of Manasseh, took the whole region of Argob as far as the border of the Geshurites and the Maakathites; it was named after him, so that to this day Bashan is called Havvoth Jair.[c]) 15And I gave Gilead to Makir.[z] 16But to the Reubenites and the Gadites I gave the territory extending from Gilead down to the Arnon Gorge (the middle of the gorge being the border) and out to the Jabbok River,[a] which is the border of the Ammonites. 17Its western border was the Jordan in the Arabah, from Kinnereth[b] to the Sea of the Arabah (that is, the Dead Sea[c]), below the slopes of Pisgah.

18I commanded you at that time: "The LORD your God has given you this land to take possession of it. But all your able-bodied men, armed for battle, must cross over ahead of the other Israelites.[d] 19However, your wives, your children and your livestock (I know you have much livestock) may stay in the towns I have given you, 20until the LORD gives rest to your fellow Israelites as he has to you, and they too have taken over the land that the LORD your God is giving them across the Jordan. After that, each of you may go back to the possession I have given you."

3:3 [p] Nu 21:35
3:4 [q] 1Ki 4:13
3:6 [r] Dt 2:24,34
3:9 [s] Dt 4:48; Ps 29:6 [t] 1Ch 5:23
3:10 [u] Jos 13:11
3:11 [v] Ge 14:5 [w] 2Sa 12:26; Jer 49:2
3:12 [x] Nu 32:32-38; Dt 2:36; Jos 13:8-13
3:14 [y] Nu 32:41; 1Ch 2:22
3:15 [z] Nu 32:39-40
3:16 [a] Nu 21:24
3:17 [b] Nu 34:11; Jos 13:27 [c] Ge 14:3; Jos 12:3
3:18 [d] Nu 32:17
3:22 [e] Dt 1:29 [f] Ex 14:14; Dt 20:4

Dt 3:21 ❖ How does recalling God's actions in the past give us strength and confidence to face the future?

Moses Forbidden to Cross the Jordan

21At that time I commanded Joshua: "You have seen with your own eyes all that the LORD your God has done to these two kings. The LORD will do the same to all the kingdoms over there where you are going. 22Do not be afraid[e] of them; the LORD your God himself will fight[f] for you."

23At that time I pleaded with the LORD:

[a] *6* The Hebrew term refers to the irrevocable giving over of things or persons to the LORD, often by totally destroying them. [b] *11* That is, about 14 feet long and 6 feet wide or about 4 meters long and 1.8 meters wide [c] *14* Or *called the settlements of Jair*

3:3–9 Moses describes the course of the battle.
3:10–11 Moses reiterates the scope of the Israelites' conquests. Moving from south to north, he lists the conquered regions.
3:12–17 Observing that the hills of Gilead and Bashan were ideal for raising livestock, the tribes of Reuben and Gad approached Moses to claim this land (Nu 32:5). Moses interpreted the request as an act of rebellion (Nu 32:14–15), but when they assured him they would cross the Jordan with the rest of the tribes and assist them in the conquest, he granted their request.
3:18–20 Having authorized the two and one-half tribes to settle east of the Jordan, Moses charged them to aid the rest of Israel in the conquest of the actual promised land (cf. Jos 1:12–15).
3:21–22 Having reminded the two and one-half tribes of their obligations to their kinsmen, Moses recalls his earlier charge to Joshua as well.
3:23–29 This prayer takes up only vv. 24 and 25,

24“Sovereign LORD, you have begun to
show to your servant your greatness[g]
and your strong hand. For what god[h] is
there in heaven or on earth who can do
the deeds and mighty works[i] you do?[j]
25Let me go over and see the good land[k]
beyond the Jordan — that fine hill country and Lebanon.”
26But because of you the LORD was angry[l] with me and would not listen to me.
“That is enough,” the LORD said. “Do not
speak to me anymore about this matter.
27Go up to the top of Pisgah and look west
and north and south and east. Look at
the land with your own eyes, since you
are not going to cross this Jordan.[m] 28But
commission[n] Joshua, and encourage and
strengthen him, for he will lead this people across[o] and will cause them to inherit
the land that you will see.” 29So we stayed
in the valley near Beth Peor.[p]

Obedience Commanded

4 Now, Israel, hear the decrees and laws I
am about to teach you. Follow them so
that you may live[q] and may go in and take
possession of the land the LORD, the God
of your ancestors, is giving you. 2Do not
add[r] to what I command you and do not
subtract from it, but keep the commands
of the LORD your God that I give you.
3You saw with your own eyes what the
LORD did at Baal Peor.[s] The LORD your
God destroyed from among you everyone who followed the Baal of Peor, 4but
all of you who held fast to the LORD your
God are still alive today.
5See, I have taught you decrees and
laws as the LORD my God commanded
me, so that you may follow them in the
land you are entering to take possession
of it. 6Observe them carefully, for this
will show your wisdom[t] and understanding to the nations, who will hear about
all these decrees and say, “Surely this
great nation is a wise and understanding
people.”[u] 7What other nation is so great[v]
as to have their gods near[w] them the way
the LORD our God is near us whenever we
pray to him? 8And what other nation is so
great as to have such righteous decrees
and laws as this body of laws I am setting
before you today?
9Only be careful,[x] and watch yourselves closely so that you do not forget
the things your eyes have seen or let
them fade from your heart as long as
you live. Teach[y] them to your children[z]
and to their children after them. 10Re-
member the day you stood before the
LORD your God at Horeb,[a] when he said
to me, “Assemble the people before me to
hear my words so that they may learn to
revere me as long as they live in the land
and may teach them to their children.”
11You came near and stood at the foot of
the mountain while it blazed with fire[b] to
the very heavens, with black clouds and
deep darkness. 12Then the LORD spoke[c]
to you out of the fire. You heard the
sound of words but saw no form; there
was only a voice. 13He declared to you his
covenant,[d] the Ten Commandments,[e]
which he commanded you to follow and
then wrote them on two stone tablets.
14And the LORD directed me at that time
to teach you the decrees and laws you are
to follow in the land that you are crossing
the Jordan to possess.

3:24 [g] Dt 11:2 [h] Ex 15:11; Ps 86:8 [i] Ps 71:16,19 [j] 2Sa 7:22
3:25 [k] Dt 4:22
3:26 [l] Dt 1:37; 31:2
3:27 [m] Nu 27:12
3:28 [n] Nu 27:18-23 [o] Dt 31:3,23
3:29 [p] Dt 4:46; 34:6
4:1 [q] Dt 5:33; 8:1; 16:20; 30:15-20; Eze 20:11; Ro 10:5
4:2 [r] Dt 12:32; Jos 1:7; Rev 22:18-19
4:3 [s] Nu 25:1-9; Ps 106:28
4:6 [t] Dt 30:19-20; Ps 19:7; Pr 1:7 [u] Job 28:28
4:7 [v] 2Sa 7:23 [w] Ps 46:1; Isa 55:6
4:9 [x] Pr 4:23 [y] Ge 18:19; Eph 6:4 [z] Ps 78:5-6
4:10 [a] Ex 19:9,16
4:11 [b] Ex 19:18; Heb 12:18-19
4:12 [c] Ex 20:22; Dt 5:4,22
4:13 [d] Dt 9:9,11 [e] Ex 24:12; 31:18; 34:28

Dt 4:9 ❖ How can we be sure to hold fast to our faith and pass it on to others, as Moses instructs?

---

but it contains several typical features of biblical prayers. Moses concludes by noting the people remained in the valley opposite Beth Peor on the plains of Moab (34:1).

4:1 In a sense, vv. 1–8 summarize the entire chapter, highlighting the importance of obedience as the proper response to Yahweh's grace expressed by the revelation of his will.

4:2-8 In this passage Moses declares that *only* that which he (on Yahweh's behalf) prescribes is normative, and by warning them not to delete anything from his word, he declares that *all* that he (on Yahweh's behalf) prescribes is normative. Obedience to the Torah is the key to life (vv. 3–4). His intent is that they might be a blessing (Ge 12:2–3) and light (Isa 42:6) to the nations.

4:1-8 A high view of God's revealed will is demonstrated in lives that conform to God's will as revealed in the Bible. The missional goal of God's people is fulfilled through the life-giving and transforming power of the divine Word.

4:9-14 Verses 9–14 involve one long sentence governed by the twofold appeal to absolute vigilance. The Israelites' greatest enemy will not be the Canaanites out there but their own minds and hearts within them.

Moses' recollections of Horeb focus on actions by the Israelites (vv. 10–11) and Yahweh (vv. 12–14). Like all covenants involving Yahweh in the OT, Yahweh defines the terms and determines the consequences for obedience or disobedience.

Idolatry Forbidden

15You saw no form[f] of any kind the day the LORD spoke to you at Horeb out of the fire. Therefore watch yourselves very carefully,[g] 16so that you do not become corrupt and make for yourselves an idol,[h] an image of any shape, whether formed like a man or a woman, 17or like any animal on earth or any bird that flies in the air, 18or like any creature that moves along the ground or any fish in the waters below. 19And when you look up to the sky and see the sun,[i] the moon and the stars — all the heavenly array[j] — do not be enticed into bowing down to them and worshiping things the LORD your God has apportioned to all the nations under heaven. 20But as for you, the LORD took you and brought you out of the iron-smelting furnace,[k] out of Egypt, to be the people of his inheritance,[l] as you now are.

21The LORD was angry with me[m] because of you, and he solemnly swore that I would not cross the Jordan and enter the good land the LORD your God is giving you as your inheritance. 22I will die in this land; I will not cross the Jordan; but you are about to cross over and take possession of that good land.[n] 23Be careful not to forget the covenant[o] of the LORD your God that he made with you; do not make for yourselves an idol[p] in the form of anything the LORD your God has forbidden. 24For the LORD your God is a consuming fire,[q] a jealous God.

25After you have had children and grandchildren and have lived in the land a long time — if you then become corrupt and make any kind of idol, doing evil[r] in the eyes of the LORD your God and arousing his anger, 26I call the heavens and the earth as witnesses against you[s] this day that you will quickly perish from the land that you are crossing the Jordan to possess. You will not live there long but will certainly be destroyed. 27The LORD will scatter[t] you among the peoples, and only a few of you will survive among the nations to which the LORD will drive you. 28There you will worship man-made gods[u] of wood and stone, which cannot see or hear or eat or smell.[v] 29But if from there you seek[w] the LORD your God, you will find him if you seek him with all your heart[x] and with all your soul.[y] 30When you are in distress and all these things have happened to you, then in later days[z] you will return to the LORD your God and obey him. 31For the LORD your God is a merciful[a] God; he will not abandon or destroy you or forget the covenant with your ancestors, which he confirmed to them by oath.

The LORD Is God

32Ask[b] now about the former days, long before your time, from the day God created human beings on the earth;[c] ask from one end of the heavens to the other.[d] Has anything so great as this ever happened, or has anything like it ever been heard of? 33Has any other people heard the voice of God[a] speaking out of fire, as you have, and lived?[e] 34Has any god ever tried to take for himself one nation out of another nation,[f] by testings, by signs[g] and wonders,[h] by war, by a mighty hand and an outstretched arm,[i] or by great and awesome deeds,[j] like all the things the LORD your God did for you in Egypt before your very eyes?

4:15 [f] Isa 40:18 [g] Jos 23:11
4:16 [h] Ex 20:4-5; 32:7; Dt 5:8; Ro 1:23
4:19 [i] Dt 17:3; Job 31:26 [j] 2Ki 17:16; 21:3; Ro 1:25
4:20 [k] 1Ki 8:51; Jer 11:4 [l] Ex 19:5; Dt 9:29
4:21 [m] Nu 20:12; Dt 1:37
4:22 [n] Dt 3:25
4:23 [o] ver 9,16 [p] Ex 20:4
4:24 [q] Ex 24:17; Dt 9:3; Heb 12:29
4:25 [r] 2Ki 17:2,17
4:26 [s] Dt 30:18-19; Isa 1:2; Mic 6:2
4:27 [t] Lev 26:33; Dt 28:36,64; Ne 1:8
4:28 [u] Dt 28:36,64; 1Sa 26:19; Jer 16:13 [v] Ps 115:4-8; 135:15-18
4:29 [w] 2Ch 15:4; Isa 55:6 [x] Jer 29:13 [y] Dt 30:1-3,10
4:30 [z] Dt 31:29; Jer 23:20; Hos 3:5
4:31 [a] 2Ch 30:9; Ne 9:31; Ps 116:5; Jnh 4:2
4:32 [b] Dt 32:7; Job 8:8 [c] Ge 1:27 [d] Mt 24:31
4:33 [e] Ex 20:22; Dt 5:24-26
4:34 [f] Ex 6:6 [g] Ex 7:3 [h] Dt 7:19; 26:8 [i] Ex 13:3 [j] Dt 34:12

[a] 33 Or *of a god*

4:15–24 Verse 20 represents the focal point of this passage, highlighting the utter treachery and perversion of idolatry. Verses 23–24 represent the climax. Moses charges his people to guard against forgetting "the covenant" (v. 23) and against manufacturing idols. He grounds this warning with, "Yahweh is Consuming Fire; he is Impassioned El" (v. 24; alternate translation). Here the fire represents not merely the presence of Yahweh but his burning fury in the face of unfaithfulness to the covenant.

4:25–31 Moses envisions Israel's descent into idolatry when they are well-established in the land. Then he lists consequences of unfaithfulness. After this coming judgment, Moses sees a change in the people's disposition. From exile, they will again seek Yahweh, and amazingly he will let himself be found by them. Israel's future is as secure as the eternal covenant and the unchangeably gracious character of God.

4:9–31 While modern Westerners tend not to create concrete objects to be worshiped, we are constantly crafting new substitutes for God. Indeed, an idol may be defined as anything (whether concrete or abstract) that rivals God—anything to which we submit and which we serve in place of God himself. When we pervert their function and treat these as ultimate things on which our well-being and destiny depend, they rival God—and that makes them an idol.

4:32–34 Moses invites his audience to engage in exhaustive historical research. Yahweh's rescue of Israel from Egypt is unparalleled.

35 You were shown these things so that
you might know that the LORD is God;
besides him there is no other.[k] 36 From
heaven he made you hear his voice[l] to
discipline you. On earth he showed you
his great fire, and you heard his words
from out of the fire. 37 Because he loved[m]
your ancestors and chose their descendants after them, he brought you out
of Egypt by his Presence and his great
strength,[n] 38 to drive out before you nations greater and stronger than you and
to bring you into their land to give it to
you for your inheritance,[o] as it is today.

39 Acknowledge and take to heart this
day that the LORD is God in heaven above
and on the earth below. There is no other.[p]
40 Keep[q] his decrees and commands, which
I am giving you today, so that it may go
well[r] with you and your children after you
and that you may live long[s] in the land
the LORD your God gives you for all time.

4:35 [k] Dt 32:39; 1Sa 2:2; Isa 45:5,18
4:36 [l] Ex 19:9,19
4:37 [m] Dt 10:15 [n] Ex 13:3, 9, 14
4:38 [o] Dt 7:1; 9:5
4:39 [p] ver 35; Jos 2:11
4:40 [q] Lev 22:31; Dt 5:33 [r] Dt 5:16 [s] Dt 6:3,18; Eph 6:2-3

Cities of Refuge

4:41–43Ref // Nu 35:6–34; Dt 19:1–14; Jos 20:1–9

41 Then Moses set aside three cities east
of the Jordan, 42 to which anyone who

4:35 Yahweh alone deserves the title God, and there is no other in his class.

4:36–38 Moses' declaration in v. 37 is revolutionary, since the notion of love is virtually absent from the vocabulary of divine-human relationships in the ancient Near East.

4:39 The people may cross the Jordan confidently, knowing that Yahweh is present with them.

4:40 Moses appeals to his people to obey the will of Yahweh for their own good and for the good of their descendants.

✣ **4:32–40** What God did for this nation of slaves sets the paradigm for what God has done for sinners, but in Christ, God's glory and grace are revealed even more dramatically.

4:41–43 By setting aside three towns of refuge east of the Jordan, Moses fulfilled part of Yahweh's instruction in Nu 35:9–34.

✣ **4:41–43** This policy illustrates the need to take into account the lives of potential secondary victims. A just society will guard against unwarranted violent responses to innocent acts.

CHARACTER OF GOD // GOD IS MERCIFUL

Deuteronomy 4:31: "For the LORD your God is a merciful God; he will not abandon or destroy you or forget the covenant with your ancestors, which he confirmed to them by oath."

There could hardly be better news than the fact that God is rich in mercy (Eph 2:4). Adam and Eve sinned, and since then, all people have been marked and marred by sin, leaving none blameless (Ps 14:3). If not for God's mercy, humanity would be left without hope.

Paul is not shy about pointing this out. He spends the opening chapters of his letter to the Romans demonstrating that each and every person has fallen into sin. In Ephesians 2:1, he tells his readers that they were dead in their trespasses and sins. No one gets a free pass; all are guilty.

But Paul doesn't leave his readers in despair; however, he begins this way in order to teach even more vividly the amazing mercy and saving love of God. God's mercy was not poured out on those who deserved it—that would be no mercy at all, merely justice. Instead, God poured out his justice on Jesus Christ at the cross so that mercy might be available to all his children.

God's mercy caused him to take those who were dead in sin and make them alive in Christ. Without ignoring justice, God made a way for sinners to come to salvation. He did this solely out of love for his creation, as John 3:16 makes clear. Of all the strong characteristics of God's nature, none is more comforting than God's mercy.

APPLICATION ✣ It is easy to get weighed down by the reality of our sins. Each one of us has done things we would rather erase from our record, and perhaps we live in shame and try to keep those items secret. The truth is that God already knows our every word, action and thought. If not for God's mercy, this would be terrifying. But mercy is a foundational part of God's nature. When we are in Christ, God sees us not according to our sins but according to Christ's righteousness. Rather than living with shame and regret, we can live with joy and freedom because in Christ we are set free and made children of God.

had killed a person could flee if they had unintentionally killed a neighbor without malice aforethought. They could flee into one of these cities and save their life. 43The cities were these: Bezer in the wilderness plateau, for the Reubenites; Ramoth in Gilead, for the Gadites; and Golan in Bashan, for the Manassites.

Introduction to the Law

44This is the law Moses set before the Israelites. 45These are the stipulations, decrees and laws Moses gave them when they came out of Egypt 46and were in the valley near Beth Peor east of the Jordan, in the land of Sihon[t] king of the Amorites, who reigned in Heshbon and was defeated by Moses and the Israelites as they came out of Egypt. 47They took possession of his land and the land of Og king of Bashan, the two Amorite kings east of the Jordan. 48This land extended from Aroer[u] on the rim of the Arnon Gorge to Mount Sirion[a][v] (that is, Hermon), 49and included all the Arabah east of the Jordan, as far as the Dead Sea,[b] below the slopes of Pisgah.

The Ten Commandments

5:6–21pp // Ex 20:1–17

5 Moses summoned all Israel and said: Hear, Israel, the decrees and laws I declare in your hearing today. Learn them and be sure to follow them. 2The LORD our God made a covenant[w] with us at Horeb. 3It was not with our ancestors[c] that the LORD made this covenant, but with us, with all of us who are alive here today.[x] 4The LORD spoke[y] to you face to face out of the fire on the mountain. 5(At that time I stood between[z] the LORD and you to declare to you the word of the LORD, because you were afraid[a] of the fire and did not go up the mountain.) And he said:

6"I am the LORD your God, who brought you out of Egypt, out of the land of slavery.

7"You shall have no other gods before[d] me.

8"You shall not make for yourself an image in the form of anything in heaven above or on the earth beneath or in the waters below. 9You shall not bow down to them or worship them; for I, the LORD your God, am a jealous God, punishing the children for the sin of the parents to the third and fourth generation of those who hate me,[b] 10but showing love to a thousand generations of those who love me and keep my commandments.[c]

11"You shall not misuse the name of the LORD your God, for the LORD will not hold anyone guiltless who misuses his name.[d]

12"Observe the Sabbath day by keeping it holy,[e] as the LORD your God has commanded you. 13Six days you shall labor and do all your work, 14but the seventh day[f] is a sabbath to the LORD your God. On it you shall not do any work, neither you, nor your son or daughter, nor your male or female servant, nor your ox, your donkey or any of your animals, nor any foreigner residing in your towns, so that your male and female servants may rest, as you do. 15Remember that you were slaves in Egypt and that the LORD your God brought

4:46 [t] Nu 21:26; Dt 3:29
4:48 [u] Dt 2:36 [v] Dt 3:9
5:2 [w] Ex 19:5
5:3 [x] Heb 8:9
5:4 [y] Dt 4:12, 33,36
5:5 [z] Gal 3:19 [a] Ex 20:18,21
5:9 [b] Ex 34:7
5:10 [c] Jer 32:18
5:11 [d] Lev 19:12; Mt 5:33-37
5:12 [e] Ex 20:8
5:14 [f] Ge 2:2; Heb 4:4

[a] 48 Syriac (see also 3:9); Hebrew *Siyon*
[b] 49 Hebrew *the Sea of the Arabah*
[c] 3 Or *not only with our parents*
[d] 7 Or *besides*

4:44–5:1a Like the introduction to the first address, the prologue to the second describes the historical context of the speech. Moses collapses the first forty years of Israel's history as a nation into one short statement.

5:1b–5 The second address divides into two parts. The first (5:1b–11:32) is sermonic; parts of the second (12:1–29:1[28:69]) are more formal, making more direct use of previously revealed prescriptions and concluding with covenant blessings and curses.

4:44–5:5 It is possible for us today to hear the voice of God and still not take it to heart. Those who abide in the vine (Jn 15:6) bear the fruit of belief and covenant commitment (love) shown in obedience to the revealed will of God. This passage declares that if we reject the revelation of God, we reject God himself.

5:7–21 This document functions as an Israelite bill of rights.

5:7–10 *Yahweh's right to exclusive allegiance.* Israel is to have no other gods.

5:11 *Yahweh's right to proper representation.* To bear the name of Yahweh means to claim him as one's owner and to accept the role of representing him.

5:12–15 *The right to humane treatment.* The weekly Sabbath was a fundamentally ethical ordinance.

PEOPLE TO KNOW // MOSES

DEUTERONOMY 5:1–5: Moses was God's chosen deliverer for the enslaved Israelites. His life divides into three forty-year periods: growing up in Egypt, living as a runaway in Midian, and leading the Israelites from Egypt to the promised land.

Moses was dramatically saved from Pharaoh's order to kill all the Hebrew baby boys (Ex 2:1–10). He was raised by Pharaoh's very own daughter. When he grew up, he saw an Egyptian beating a Hebrew slave. Thinking no one was around, Moses killed the Egyptian, but his actions were seen and word spread about what he had done. Eventually word of his actions reached Pharaoh, and Moses fled to Midian.

In Midian, Moses married Zipporah, the daughter of a Midianite priest. He lived as a shepherd until God called him to lead his people out of Egypt (Ex 3:1–10). With the help of his brother, Aaron, Moses confronted Pharaoh. God demonstrated his power in a series of plagues that led to the Egyptians wanting the Israelites to leave (Ex 7–12). The final victory over the forces of Egypt took place when Moses led the Israelites across the Red Sea on dry land. When the Egyptians pursued them, the waters closed up behind them, killing the Egyptian army (Ex 14:26–28).

Moses led the people to Sinai, where he received God's instructions for Israel. Upon arriving at the promised land, the people rejected God out of fear of the Canaanites, which led to them wandering in the wilderness for another 38 years. When Moses himself failed to follow God's clear instructions, God said that he would die before setting foot in the promised land (Nu 20:12). God brought Moses up Mount Nebo, and after Moses looked over the promised land, he died at the age of 120.

God told Moses he would raise up a prophet like him in the future, who would tell the people God's commands (Dt 18:18). This prophecy pointed to Jesus Christ, the New Moses, who interpreted and taught God's law (see Mt 5–7).

APPLICATION ✣ Moses was called to a monumental task, one he never could have done without God's power within him. Like Moses, we are called to obey God through faith in each circumstance. God will never tell us to do something that he does not intend to accomplish through us. We can follow God's will confidently, knowing that all things he calls us to are possible (Php 4:13).

you out of there with a mighty hand and an outstretched arm.[g] Therefore the LORD your God has commanded you to observe the Sabbath day.
16 "Honor your father and your mother,[h] as the LORD your God has commanded you, so that you may live long[i] and that it may go well with you in the land the LORD your God is giving you.
17 "You shall not murder.[j]
18 "You shall not commit adultery.[k]
19 "You shall not steal.
20 "You shall not give false testimony against your neighbor.
21 "You shall not covet your neighbor's wife. You shall not set your desire on your neighbor's house or land, his male or female servant, his ox or donkey, or anything that belongs to your neighbor."[l]
22 These are the commandments the LORD proclaimed in a loud voice to your

5:15 [g] Dt 4:34
5:16 [h] Ex 20:12; Lev 19:3; Dt 27:16; Eph 6:2-3*; Col 3:20 [i] Dt 4:40
5:17 [j] Mt 5:21-22*
5:18 [k] Mt 5:27-30; Lk 18:20*; Jas 2:11*
5:21 [l] Ro 7:7*; 13:9*

5:16 *Parental right to respect.* Well-being is granted by Yahweh in response to respect for one's parents.
5:17 *The right to life.* Unlike Babylonian laws, this command draws no distinctions in value of life based on status, race, or gender.
5:18 *The right to fidelity in marriage.* Adultery pollutes the land and ultimately causes it to spew out its inhabitants (Lev 18:20, 24–25).
5:19 *The right to own property.* This is a categorical prohibition of all theft.
5:20 *The right to a fair hearing.* The seriousness of false testimony is reflected by the call for the death penalty (19:15–21).
5:21a *The right to marital security.* Moses elevates the marital relationship above all other domestic relationships.
5:21b *The right to secure ownership.* These last two commands create a climate of trust and security within the community.
5:22 Moses has laid the foundations for the rest of the second address.

✣ **5:6–22** It is unrealistic to expect those who have not been redeemed to live according to the principles of the redeemed. They have

whole assembly there on the mountain
from out of the fire, the cloud and the
deep darkness; and he added nothing
more. Then he wrote them on two stone
tablets[m] and gave them to me.
23When you heard the voice out of the
darkness, while the mountain was ablaze
with fire, all the leaders of your tribes
and your elders came to me. 24And you
said, "The LORD our God has shown us
his glory and his majesty, and we have
heard his voice from the fire. Today we
have seen that a person can live even if
God speaks with them.[n] 25But now, why
should we die? This great fire will consume us, and we will die if we hear the
voice of the LORD our God any longer.[o]
26For what mortal has ever heard the
voice of the living God speaking out of
fire, as we have, and survived?[p] 27Go near
and listen to all that the LORD our God
says. Then tell us whatever the LORD our
God tells you. We will listen and obey."
28The LORD heard you when you spoke
to me, and the LORD said to me, "I have
heard what this people said to you. Everything they said was good.[q] 29Oh, that
their hearts would be inclined to fear me[r]
and keep all my commands[s] always, so
that it might go well with them and their
children forever![t]
30"Go, tell them to return to their tents.
31But you stay here[u] with me so that I
may give you all the commands, decrees
and laws you are to teach them to follow
in the land I am giving them to possess."
32So be careful to do what the LORD
your God has commanded you; do not

5:22 [m] Ex 24:12; 31:18; Dt 4:13
5:24 [n] Ex 19:19
5:25 [o] Dt 18:16
5:26 [p] Dt 4:33
5:28 [q] Dt 18:17
5:29 [r] Ps 81:8, 13 [s] Dt 11:1; Isa 48:18 [t] Dt 4:1, 40
5:31 [u] Ex 24:12
5:32 [v] Dt 17:11, 20; 28:14; Jos 1:7; 23:6; Pr 4:27
5:33 [w] Jer 7:23 [x] Dt 4:40
6:2 [y] Ex 20:20; Dt 10:12-13
6:3 [z] Dt 5:33 [a] Ex 3:8
6:4 [b] Mk 12:29*; 1Co 8:4
6:5 [c] Mt 22:37*; Mk 12:30*; Lk 10:27* [d] Dt 10:12

Dt 5:30-31 ❖ Where is God giving us opportunities to learn from him and pass on his truth to those around us?

Dt 6:4 ❖ What does loving God look like in everyday life? How can we follow this core injunction?

turn aside to the right or to the left.[v]
33Walk in obedience to all that the LORD
your God has commanded you,[w] so that
you may live and prosper and prolong
your days[x] in the land that you will possess.

Love the LORD Your God

6 These are the commands, decrees
and laws the LORD your God directed
me to teach you to observe in the land
that you are crossing the Jordan to possess, 2so that you, your children and their
children after them may fear[y] the LORD
your God as long as you live by keeping
all his decrees and commands that I give
you, and so that you may enjoy long life.
3Hear, Israel, and be careful to obey so
that it may go well with you and that you
may increase greatly[z] in a land flowing
with milk and honey,[a] just as the LORD,
the God of your ancestors, promised you.
4Hear, O Israel: The LORD our God, the
LORD is one.[a][b] 5Love[c] the LORD your God
with all your heart and with all your soul
and with all your strength.[d] 6These commandments that I give you today are to

[a] 4 Or *The LORD our God is one LORD*; or *The LORD is our God, the LORD is one*; or *The LORD is our God, the LORD alone*

---

neither the motivation nor the indwelling Spirit to empower them do so. God calls his followers to a higher standard.

5:23-27 Upon hearing the thunder of Yahweh's voice, a delegation approached Moses, requesting that Moses serve as mediator (v. 27).
5:28-31 Yahweh affirmed their response.
5:32—6:3 Moses warns the people not to get sidetracked (5:32). If they stay on course, they will reach life, well-being, and length of days. Moses' second charge (6:1-2) focuses on what Yahweh has commanded him to teach the people.

✣ **5:23—6:3** The proper disposition before the glorious and gracious God is fear, the deep sense of awe in his presence. Where there is no fear, there is no sense of obligation and no sense of gratitude that we have stood in the presence of God. Without fear, the privileged life of obedience is reduced to a burdensome duty.

6:4 By uttering the Shema, the Israelites were declaring their devotion to Yahweh. This is a cry of allegiance, an affirmation of covenant commitment.
6:5 Moses calls on the people to back up the verbal commitment expressed in v. 4 with wholehearted and full-bodied love.
6:6-9 The commitment must be a family matter (v. 7) and a public matter.

✣ **6:4-9** Moses taught his people—and he teaches us and Christians everywhere—that true spirituality arises from the heart and extends to all of life. True love for God is rooted in the heart, but it is demonstrated in life, specifically a passion to speak of one's faith in the context of the family and to declare one's allegiance publicly to the world.

be on your hearts.[e] 7Impress them on
your children. Talk about them when
you sit at home and when you walk along
the road, when you lie down and when
you get up.[f] 8Tie them as symbols on
your hands and bind them on your foreheads.[g] 9Write them on the doorframes
of your houses and on your gates.[h]
10When the LORD your God brings
you into the land he swore to your fathers, to Abraham, Isaac and Jacob, to
give you—a land with large, flourishing
cities you did not build,[i] 11houses filled
with all kinds of good things you did
not provide, wells you did not dig, and
vineyards and olive groves you did not
plant—then when you eat and are satisfied,[j] 12be careful that you do not forget
the LORD, who brought you out of Egypt,
out of the land of slavery.
13Fear the LORD[k] your God, serve him
only[l] and take your oaths in his name.
14Do not follow other gods, the gods of
the peoples around you; 15for the LORD
your God[m], who is among you, is a jealous God and his anger will burn against
you, and he will destroy you from the
face of the land. 16Do not put the LORD
your God to the test[n] as you did at Massah. 17Be sure to keep the commands of
the LORD your God and the stipulations
and decrees he has given you.[o] 18Do what
is right and good in the LORD's sight, so
that it may go well[p] with you and you
may go in and take over the good land
the LORD promised on oath to your ancestors, 19thrusting out all your enemies
before you, as the LORD said.
20In the future, when your son asks
you,[q] "What is the meaning of the stipulations, decrees and laws the LORD our
God has commanded you?" 21tell him:
"We were slaves of Pharaoh in Egypt,
but the LORD brought us out of Egypt
with a mighty hand. 22Before our eyes
the LORD sent signs and wonders—great
and terrible—on Egypt and Pharaoh and
his whole household. 23But he brought
us out from there to bring us in and give
us the land he promised on oath to our
ancestors. 24The LORD commanded us
to obey all these decrees and to fear the
LORD our God,[r] so that we might always
prosper and be kept alive, as is the case
today.[s] 25And if we are careful to obey
all this law before the LORD our God, as
he has commanded us, that will be our
righteousness.[t]"

6:6 [e] Dt 11:18
6:7 [f] Dt 4:9; 11:19; Eph 6:4
6:8 [g] Ex 13:9,16; Dt 11:18
6:9 [h] Dt 11:20
6:10 [i] Jos 24:13
6:11 [j] Dt 8:10
6:13 [k] Dt 10:20 [l] Mt 4:10*; Lk 4:8*
6:15 [m] Dt 4:24
6:16 [n] Ex 17:7; Mt 4:7*; Lk 4:12*
6:17 [o] Dt 11:22; Ps 119:4
6:18 [p] Dt 4:40
6:20 [q] Ex 13:14
6:24 [r] Dt 10:12; Jer 32:39 [s] Ps 41:2
6:25 [t] Dt 24:13; Ro 10:3,5
7:1 [u] Dt 31:3; Ac 13:19
7:2 [v] Ex 23:32 [w] Dt 13:8
7:3 [x] Ex 34:15-16; Ezr 9:2
7:4 [y] Dt 6:15

Dt 7:4 ❖ How can we stand against influences around us that might threaten to turn our hearts away from God?

Driving Out the Nations

7 When the LORD your God brings you
into the land you are entering to possess and drives out before you many
nations[u]—the Hittites, Girgashites, Amorites, Canaanites, Perizzites, Hivites
and Jebusites, seven nations larger
and stronger than you— 2and when
the LORD your God has delivered them
over to you and you have defeated them,
then you must destroy them totally.[a]
Make no treaty[v] with them, and show
them no mercy.[w] 3Do not intermarry
with them.[x] Do not give your daughters
to their sons or take their daughters for
your sons, 4for they will turn your children away from following me to serve
other gods, and the LORD's anger will
burn against you and will quickly destroy[y] you. 5This is what you are to do
to them: Break down their altars, smash
their sacred stones, cut down their

[a] 2 The Hebrew term refers to the irrevocable giving over of things or persons to the LORD, often by totally destroying them; also in verse 26.

6:10-19 Moses sets the stage for the warning in v. 12 by describing the context in which the temptation to forget Yahweh will arise (vv. 10a, 11).

6:20-25 Moses instructs his congregation on the importance of passing the faith on to succeeding generations. This short paragraph consists of a child's question (v. 20) and the adult's response (vv. 21-25).

✣ **6:10-25** Whether our buildings are sizable or small, our congregations massive or miniscule, we must make sure our commitment extends beyond glib confessions of love for God, or regurgitation of creeds, or emotionalism in worship, to the daily obedience of faith.

7:1-2a This chapter opens with a series of temporal clauses that set the stage for the presentation of the test of Israel's love for Yahweh (v. 2b). As in 6:10, the test of Israel's love for Yahweh will come when God's promises have been fulfilled.

7:2b-5 The emphatic construction rendered "you must destroy them totally" reinforces the sacred nature of the agenda. The root means "to consecrate" for divine service.

Asherah poles[a] and burn their idols in
the fire.[z] 6 For you are a people holy[a] to
the LORD your God.[b] The LORD your God
has chosen[c] you out of all the peoples
on the face of the earth to be his people,
his treasured possession.
7 The LORD did not set his affection on
you and choose you because you were
more numerous than other peoples, for
you were the fewest of all peoples.[d] 8 But
it was because the LORD loved[e] you and
kept the oath he swore[f] to your ancestors
that he brought you out with a mighty
hand and redeemed you from the land
of slavery,[g] from the power of Pharaoh
king of Egypt. 9 Know therefore that the
LORD your God is God;[h] he is the faithful
God,[i] keeping his covenant of love[j] to a
thousand generations of those who love
him and keep his commandments. 10 But

those who hate him he will repay to
their face by destruction;
he will not be slow to repay to
their face those who hate
him.

11 Therefore, take care to follow the commands, decrees and laws I give you today.
12 If you pay attention to these laws
and are careful to follow them, then the
LORD your God will keep his covenant
of love with you, as he swore to your
ancestors.[k] 13 He will love you and bless
you[l] and increase your numbers. He will
bless the fruit of your womb, the crops
of your land—your grain, new wine and
olive oil—the calves of your herds and
the lambs of your flocks in the land he
swore to your ancestors to give you.[m]
14 You will be blessed more than any other
people; none of your men or women will
be childless, nor will any of your livestock
be without young.[n] 15 The LORD will keep
you free from every disease.[o] He will not
inflict on you the horrible diseases you
knew in Egypt, but he will inflict them
on all who hate you. 16 You must destroy
all the peoples the LORD your God gives
over to you. Do not look on them with
pity[p] and do not serve their gods, for that
will be a snare[q] to you.
17 You may say to yourselves, "These
nations are stronger than we are. How
can we drive them out?[r]" 18 But do not
be afraid[s] of them; remember well what
the LORD your God did to Pharaoh and to
all Egypt.[t] 19 You saw with your own eyes
the great trials, the signs and wonders,
the mighty hand and outstretched arm,
with which the LORD your God brought
you out. The LORD your God will do the
same to all the peoples you now fear.[u]
20 Moreover, the LORD your God will send
the hornet[v] among them until even the
survivors who hide from you have perished. 21 Do not be terrified by them, for
the LORD your God, who is among you,[w]
is a great and awesome God.[x] 22 The LORD
your God will drive out those nations
before you, little by little.[y] You will not
be allowed to eliminate them all at once,
or the wild animals will multiply around
you. 23 But the LORD your God will deliver them over to you, throwing them
into great confusion until they are destroyed. 24 He will give their kings into
your hand, and you will wipe out their
names from under heaven. No one will
be able to stand up against you;[z] you will
destroy them. 25 The images of their gods
you are to burn[a] in the fire. Do not covet[b] the silver and gold on them, and do
not take it for yourselves, or you will be
ensnared[c] by it, for it is detestable[d] to
the LORD your God. 26 Do not bring a detestable thing into your house or you,

7:5 [z] Ex 23:24; Dt 12:2-3
7:6 [a] Ex 19:5-6; 1Pe 2:9 [b] Ps 50:5; Jer 2:3 [c] Dt 14:2
7:7 [d] Dt 10:22
7:8 [e] Dt 10:15 [f] Ex 32:13 [g] Ex 13:14
7:9 [h] Dt 4:35 [i] 1Co 1:9; 2Ti 2:13 [j] Ne 1:5; Da 9:4
7:12 [k] Lev 26:3-13; Dt 28:1-14; Ps 105:8-9
7:13 [l] Jn 14:21 [m] Dt 28:4
7:14 [n] Ex 23:26
7:15 [o] Ex 15:26
7:16 [p] ver 2; Ex 23:33 [q] Jdg 8:27
7:17 [r] Nu 33:53
7:18 [s] Dt 31:6 [t] Ps 105:5
7:19 [u] Dt 4:34
7:20 [v] Ex 23:28; Jos 24:12
7:21 [w] Jos 3:10 [x] Dt 10:17; Ne 9:32
7:22 [y] Ex 23:28-30
7:24 [z] Jos 23:9
7:25 [a] Ex 32:20; 1Ch 14:12 [b] Jos 7:21 [c] Jdg 8:27 [d] Dt 17:1

[a] *5* That is, wooden symbols of the goddess Asherah; here and elsewhere in Deuteronomy

---

7:6–8 Moses reflects on Israel's awesome privilege as Yahweh's covenant partner.
7:9–15 In vv. 11–12, Moses renews his charge to keep the Supreme Command (cf. 5:31; 6:1) and the blessings for those who obey.
7:16 Verse 16 is transitional, bringing the preceding conversation to a conclusion with a plea for decisive action against the Canaanites and setting the stage for v. 17.
7:17 Moses' hypothetical speaker raises a problem: the obvious numerical superiority of the nations the Israelites are about to face. Speaking for all Israel he asks, "How can I dispossess them?" (alternate translation).
7:18–26 Moses' response divides into a promise (vv. 18–24) and a warning (vv. 25–26).
7:22–24 Moses explains how God will pursue his conquest.
7:25–26 Idolatry is seductive ("a snare"), and the abomination is contagious.

7:1–26 This passage presents three keys to victory: (1) Recognize God's past grace. (2) Recognize his present power. (3) Recognize our responsibility to engage the enemy by keeping ourselves undefiled by the world.

like it, will be set apart for destruction.[e] Regard it as vile and utterly detest it, for it is set apart for destruction.

Do Not Forget the LORD

8 Be careful to follow every command I am giving you today, so that you may live[f] and increase and may enter and possess the land the LORD promised on oath to your ancestors. 2 Remember how the LORD your God led[g] you all the way in the wilderness these forty years, to humble and test you in order to know what was in your heart, whether or not you would keep his commands. 3 He humbled you, causing you to hunger and then feeding you with manna,[h] which neither you nor your ancestors had known, to teach you that man does not live on bread alone but on every word that comes from the mouth of the LORD.[i] 4 Your clothes did not wear out and your feet did not swell during these forty years.[j] 5 Know then in your heart that as a man disciplines his son, so the LORD your God disciplines you.[k]

6 Observe the commands of the LORD your God, walking in obedience to him and revering him.[l] 7 For the LORD your God is bringing you into a good land — a land with brooks, streams, and deep springs gushing out into the valleys and hills;[m] 8 a land with wheat and barley, vines and fig trees, pomegranates, olive oil and honey; 9 a land where bread will not be scarce and you will lack nothing; a land where the rocks are iron and you can dig copper out of the hills.

10 When you have eaten and are satisfied,[n] praise the LORD your God for the good land he has given you. 11 Be careful that you do not forget the LORD your God, failing to observe his commands, his laws and his decrees that I am giving you this day. 12 Otherwise, when you eat and are satisfied, when you build fine houses and settle down,[o] 13 and when your herds and flocks grow large and your silver and gold increase and all you have is multiplied, 14 then your heart will become proud and you will forget[p] the LORD your God, who brought you out of Egypt, out of the land of slavery. 15 He led you through the vast and dreadful wilderness,[q] that thirsty and waterless land, with its venomous snakes[r] and scorpions. He brought you water out of hard rock.[s] 16 He gave you manna to eat in the wilderness, something your ancestors had never known,[t] to humble and test you so that in the end it might go well with you. 17 You may say to yourself,[u] "My power and the strength of my hands have produced this wealth for me." 18 But remember the LORD your God, for it is he who gives you the ability to produce wealth,[v] and so confirms his covenant, which he swore to your ancestors, as it is today.

19 If you ever forget the LORD your God and follow other gods and worship and bow down to them, I testify against you today that you will surely be destroyed.[w] 20 Like the nations the LORD destroyed before you, so you will be destroyed for not obeying the LORD your God.

Not Because of Israel's Righteousness

9 Hear, Israel: You are now about to cross the Jordan to go in and dispossess nations greater and stronger than

7:26 [e] Lev 27:28-29
8:1 [f] Dt 4:1
8:2 [g] Am 2:10
8:3 [h] Ex 16:12, 14, 35 [i] Ex 16:2-3; Mt 4:4*; Lk 4:4*
8:4 [j] Dt 29:5; Ne 9:21
8:5 [k] 2Sa 7:14; Pr 3:11-12; Heb 12:5-11; Rev 3:19
8:6 [l] Dt 5:33
8:7 [m] Dt 11:9-12
8:10 [n] Dt 6:10-12
8:12 [o] Hos 13:6
8:14 [p] Ps 106:21
8:15 [q] Jer 2:6 [r] Nu 21:6 [s] Nu 20:11; Ps 78:15; 114:8
8:16 [t] Ex 16:15
8:17 [u] Dt 9:4, 7, 24
8:18 [v] Pr 10:22; Hos 2:8
8:19 [w] Dt 4:26; 30:18

Dt 8:3 ❖ How can we live on the words that come from the mouth of God? Why and how are God's words true nourishment?

8:1 Moses begins by reminding his audience of Yahweh's goal for Israel—life and prosperity in the land that he had sworn to give to their descendants.
8:2-5 Moses declares that Yahweh's relationship to Israel is like that of a father to a son. Yahweh's fatherly disciplinary action is always administered in love for the good of his people.
8:6-9 Moses describes the world that awaits his people beyond the Jordan.
8:10 In response to the gifts of land and food, the people were to acknowledge Yahweh.
8:11-17 Moses goes on to describe the wrong response. Instead of blessing Yahweh, the Israelites' hearts will be tempted to take credit for all their successes and to think that their wealth is the result of their own efforts.
8:18 Moses now provides the correct response.
8:19-20 If the Israelites go after other gods, they will surely perish like the nations whom Yahweh destroyed before them.

8:1-20 The first stage on the road to idolatry is ingratitude. This chapter exhibits a downward spiral, in which forgetting Yahweh (vv. 2, 11) leads to ingratitude (vv. 12-16), which leads to self-sufficiency (v. 17), which leads to idolatry (v. 19). Paul plots a similar course in Ro 1:21-23.

9:1-3 Moses promises Yahweh's fury will be turned against the enemy.

you,[x] with large cities that have walls up
to the sky.[y] 2The people are strong and
tall — Anakites! You know about them
and have heard it said: "Who can stand
up against the Anakites?"[z] 3But be assured today that the LORD your God is
the one who goes across ahead of you[a]
like a devouring fire.[b] He will destroy
them; he will subdue them before you.
And you will drive them out and annihilate them quickly,[c] as the LORD has
promised you.
4After the LORD your God has driven
them out before you, do not say to yourself,[d] "The LORD has brought me here to
take possession of this land because of
my righteousness." No, it is on account of
the wickedness of these nations[e] that the
LORD is going to drive them out before
you. 5It is not because of your righteousness or your integrity[f] that you are going
in to take possession of their land; but
on account of the wickedness of these
nations, the LORD your God will drive
them out before you, to accomplish what
he swore[g] to your fathers, to Abraham,
Isaac and Jacob. 6Understand, then, that
it is not because of your righteousness
that the LORD your God is giving you
this good land to possess, for you are a
stiff-necked people.[h]

The Golden Calf

7Remember this and never forget how
you aroused the anger of the LORD your
God in the wilderness. From the day you
left Egypt until you arrived here, you
have been rebellious against the LORD.
8At Horeb you aroused the LORD's wrath
so that he was angry enough to destroy
you.[i] 9When I went up on the mountain
to receive the tablets of stone, the tablets
of the covenant that the LORD had made
with you, I stayed on the mountain forty
days and forty nights; I ate no bread and
drank no water.[j] 10The LORD gave me two
stone tablets inscribed by the finger of
God.[k] On them were all the commandments the LORD proclaimed to you on
the mountain out of the fire, on the day
of the assembly.
11At the end of the forty days and forty
nights, the LORD gave me the two stone
tablets, the tablets of the covenant.
12Then the LORD told me, "Go down from
here at once, because your people whom
you brought out of Egypt have become
corrupt.[l] They have turned away quickly[m]
from what I commanded them and have
made an idol for themselves."
13And the LORD said to me, "I have seen
this people[n], and they are a stiff-necked
people indeed! 14Let me alone,[o] so that
I may destroy them and blot out[p] their
name from under heaven. And I will
make you into a nation stronger and
more numerous than they."
15So I turned and went down from the
mountain while it was ablaze with fire.
And the two tablets of the covenant were
in my hands.[q] 16When I looked, I saw that
you had sinned against the LORD your
God; you had made for yourselves an
idol cast in the shape of a calf.[r] You had
turned aside quickly from the way that
the LORD had commanded you. 17So I
took the two tablets and threw them out
of my hands, breaking them to pieces
before your eyes.
18Then once again I fell[s] prostrate before the LORD for forty days and forty
nights; I ate no bread and drank no water, because of all the sin you had committed, doing what was evil in the LORD's
sight and so arousing his anger. 19I feared
the anger and wrath of the LORD, for he
was angry enough with you to destroy
you.[t] But again the LORD listened to me.[u]
20And the LORD was angry enough with
Aaron to destroy him, but at that time I

Dt 9:4 ❖ Why is it tempting to think God's love for us is on account of our own righteousness? What is the true source of God's love?

9:1 [x] Dt 4:38; 11:23,31 [y] Dt 1:28
9:2 [z] Nu 13:22, 28,32-33
9:3 [a] Dt 31:3; Jos 3:11 [b] Dt 4:24; Heb 12:29 [c] Ex 23:31; Dt 7:23-24
9:4 [d] Dt 8:17 [e] Lev 18:21,24-30; Dt 18:9-14
9:5 [f] Titus 3:5 [g] Ge 12:7; 13:15; 15:7; 17:8; 26:4
9:6 [h] ver 13; Ex 32:9; Dt 31:27
9:8 [i] Ex 32:7-10; Ps 106:19
9:9 [j] Ex 24:12, 15,18; 34:28
9:10 [k] Ex 31:18; Dt 4:13
9:12 [l] Ex 32:7-8; Dt 31:29 [m] Jdg 2:17
9:13 [n] ver 6; Ex 32:9; Dt 10:16
9:14 [o] Ex 32:10 [p] Nu 14:12; Dt 29:20
9:15 [q] Ex 19:18; 32:15
9:16 [r] Ex 32:19
9:18 [s] Ex 34:28
9:19 [t] Ex 32:10-11,14 [u] Dt 10:10

9:4a Moses introduces a hypothetical speaker who imagines himself to be virtuous, but the speech indicates smug self-righteousness.
9:4b–6 The Israelites are "a stiff-necked people" (v. 6), an image of yoked oxen who often refuse to work as their master directs.
9:7–24 Moses highlights the transformation in the symbolism of Horeb from a place of grace and glory to a place of human rebellion and divine fury.
9:15–17 By smashing the tablets Moses declared the covenant null and void even before the people had a chance to see the divinely produced written documentation.
9:18–19 Moses feared that Yahweh would destroy his people. The relief is still evident thirty-eight years later, "But again the LORD listened to me" (v. 19).
9:20 Through Moses' intercession, Yahweh's threat on Aaron's life was also lifted.

prayed for Aaron too. 21 Also I took that
sinful thing of yours, the calf you had
made, and burned it in the fire. Then I
crushed it and ground it to powder as
fine as dust and threw the dust into a
stream that flowed down the mountain.[v]
22 You also made the LORD angry at
Taberah,[w] at Massah[x] and at Kibroth
Hattaavah.[y]
23 And when the LORD sent you out
from Kadesh Barnea, he said, "Go up
and take possession of the land I have
given you." But you rebelled against the
command of the LORD your God. You did
not trust[z] him or obey him. 24 You have
been rebellious against the LORD ever
since I have known you.[a]
25 I lay prostrate before the LORD those
forty days and forty nights because the
LORD had said he would destroy you.[b]
26 I prayed to the LORD and said, "Sovereign LORD, do not destroy your people,
your own inheritance that you redeemed
by your great power and brought out of
Egypt with a mighty hand.[c] 27 Remember your servants Abraham, Isaac and
Jacob. Overlook the stubbornness of this
people, their wickedness and their sin.
28 Otherwise, the country from which you
brought us will say, 'Because the LORD
was not able to take them into the land
he had promised them, and because he
hated them, he brought them out to put
them to death in the wilderness.'[d] 29 But
they are your people, your inheritance[e]
that you brought out by your great power
and your outstretched arm.[f]"

Tablets Like the First Ones

10 At that time the LORD said to me,
"Chisel out two stone tablets[g] like
the first ones and come up to me on the
mountain. Also make a wooden ark.[a] 2 I
will write on the tablets the words that
were on the first tablets, which you broke.
Then you are to put them in the ark."[h]
3 So I made the ark out of acacia wood[i]
and chiseled[j] out two stone tablets like
the first ones, and I went up on the
mountain with the two tablets in my
hands. 4 The LORD wrote on these tablets
what he had written before, the Ten Commandments he had proclaimed[k] to you
on the mountain, out of the fire, on the
day of the assembly. And the LORD gave
them to me. 5 Then I came back down the
mountain[l] and put the tablets in the ark[m]
I had made, as the LORD commanded me,
and they are there now.[n]
6 (The Israelites traveled from the wells
of Bene Jaakan to Moserah.[o] There Aaron
died and was buried, and Eleazar his son
succeeded him as priest.[p] 7 From there
they traveled to Gudgodah and on to Jotbathah, a land with streams of water.[q] 8 At
that time the LORD set apart the tribe of
Levi[r] to carry the ark of the covenant of
the LORD, to stand before the LORD to
minister[s] and to pronounce blessings[t] in
his name, as they still do today. 9 That is
why the Levites have no share or inheritance among their fellow Israelites; the
LORD is their inheritance,[u] as the LORD
your God told them.)
10 Now I had stayed on the mountain
forty days and forty nights, as I did the
first time, and the LORD listened to me
at this time also. It was not his will to
destroy you.[v] 11 "Go," the LORD said to me,
"and lead the people on their way, so that

9:21 [v] Ex 32:20
9:22 [w] Nu 11:3 [x] Ex 17:7 [y] Nu 11:34
9:23 [z] Ps 106:24
9:24 [a] ver 7; Dt 31:27
9:25 [b] ver 18
9:26 [c] Ex 32:11
9:28 [d] Ex 32:12; Nu 14:16
9:29 [e] Dt 4:20; 1Ki 8:51 [f] Dt 4:34; Ne 1:10
10:1 [g] Ex 25:10; 34:1-2
10:2 [h] Ex 25:16, 21; Dt 4:13
10:3 [i] Ex 25:5, 10; 37:1-9 [j] Ex 34:4
10:4 [k] Ex 20:1
10:5 [l] Ex 34:29 [m] Ex 40:20 [n] 1Ki 8:9
10:6 [o] Nu 33:30-31,38 [p] Nu 20:25-28
10:7 [q] Nu 33:32-34
10:8 [r] Nu 3:6 [s] Dt 18:5 [t] Dt 21:5
10:9 [u] Nu 18:20; Dt 18:1-2; Eze 44:28
10:10 [v] Ex 33:17; 34:28; Dt 9:18-19,25

[a] *1* That is, a chest

9:21 Moses concludes by describing how he disposed of the calf itself.
9:22–24 Moses summarizes in a sentence what he described in great detail in 1:26–43.

9:1–24 The call to relationship with God is never based on merit. Moses demonstrates that the Israelites had been undeserving of the mission to which God had called them. Human righteousness counts for nothing with God. Indeed, apart from God's grace we are all Canaanites.

9:25–29 Moses argues that Yahweh's own reputation was at stake. Moses concludes his prayer with a positive foundation for this appeal. Repeating his opening statements, he declares that Israel is Yahweh's people; they are his personal possession and saving them is to his advantage.

10:1–5 Moses was to cut out two tablets of stone to function like the original tablets, make an ark, and put these new tablets into it. This was not the permanent ark of the covenant.
10:6–9 Whereas the rest of the tribes of Israel would receive real estate, Yahweh promised himself as the Levites' grant.
10:10–11 *Moses' narrative epilogue*. Yahweh responded as he had done previously (cf. 9:9) and withdrew his threat to destroy his people. The reminder of his promise of land to their ancestors provides concrete proof that the covenant relationship was fully restored.

9:25—10:11 When wicked people turn from their sin in full repentance or when a righteous intercessor pleads with God on behalf of sinners, God's grace is extended to undeserving people.

they may enter and possess the land I
swore to their ancestors to give them."

Fear the LORD

12 And now, Israel, what does the LORD
your God ask of you[w] but to fear the LORD
your God, to walk in obedience to him,
to love him,[x] to serve the LORD your God
with all your heart[y] and with all your
soul, 13 and to observe the LORD's commands and decrees that I am giving you
today for your own good?
14 To the LORD your God belong the
heavens, even the highest heavens,[z]
the earth and everything in it.[a] 15 Yet the
LORD set his affection on your ancestors
and loved[b] them, and he chose you, their
descendants, above all the nations—as
it is today. 16 Circumcise[c] your hearts,
therefore, and do not be stiff-necked[d]
any longer. 17 For the LORD your God is
God of gods[e] and Lord of lords, the great
God, mighty and awesome, who shows
no partiality[f] and accepts no bribes. 18 He
defends the cause of the fatherless and
the widow,[g] and loves the foreigner residing among you, giving them food and
clothing. 19 And you are to love those who
are foreigners, for you yourselves were
foreigners in Egypt.[h] 20 Fear the LORD
your God and serve him.[i] Hold fast[j] to
him and take your oaths in his name.[k]
21 He is the one you praise;[l] he is your God,
who performed for you those great and
awesome wonders[m] you saw with your
own eyes. 22 Your ancestors who went
down into Egypt were seventy in all,[n]
and now the LORD your God has made
you as numerous as the stars in the sky.[o]

Love and Obey the LORD

11 Love[p] the LORD your God and keep his
requirements, his decrees, his laws
and his commands always.[q] 2 Remember today that your children were not
the ones who saw and experienced the
discipline of the LORD your God:[r] his majesty, his mighty hand, his outstretched
arm; 3 the signs he performed and the
things he did in the heart of Egypt, both
to Pharaoh king of Egypt and to his whole
country; 4 what he did to the Egyptian
army, to its horses and chariots, how he
overwhelmed them with the waters of
the Red Sea[a][s] as they were pursuing you,
and how the LORD brought lasting ruin
on them. 5 It was not your children who
saw what he did for you in the wilderness until you arrived at this place, 6 and
what he did[t] to Dathan and Abiram, sons
of Eliab the Reubenite, when the earth
opened its mouth right in the middle of
all Israel and swallowed them up with
their households, their tents and every
living thing that belonged to them. 7 But
it was your own eyes that saw all these
great things the LORD has done.
8 Observe therefore all the commands

10:12 [w] Mic 6:8 [x] Dt 5:33; 6:13; Mt 22:37 [y] Dt 6:5
10:14 [z] 1Ki 8:27 [a] Ex 19:5
10:15 [b] Dt 4:37
10:16 [c] Jer 4:4 [d] Dt 9:6
10:17 [e] Jos 22:22; Da 2:47 [f] Ac 10:34; Ro 2:11; Eph 6:9
10:18 [g] Ps 68:5
10:19 [h] Lev 19:34
10:20 [i] Mt 4:10 [j] Dt 11:22 [k] Ps 63:11
10:21 [l] Ex 15:2; Jer 17:14 [m] Ps 106:21-22
10:22 [n] Ge 46:26-27 [o] Ge 15:5; Dt 1:10
11:1 [p] Dt 10:12 [q] Zec 3:7
11:2 [r] Dt 5:24; 8:5
11:4 [s] Ex 14:27
11:6 [t] Nu 16:1-35

[a] 4 Or *the Sea of Reeds*

Dt 10:16 ❖ What does it mean to circumcise our hearts? Why does Moses use this vivid metaphor?

10:12a Moses begins his reflection on the practical implications of the covenant with a question.
10:12b–15 Moses' first response captures in a nutshell the message of this book, especially as it relates to the human response to divine grace. Fear is primary and love is at the core. Without these, the actions are legalistic. Without the actions, fear and love are useless and dead.
10:16–19 Moses' charge in v. 16 consists of two commands: Circumcise the foreskin of your hearts and stop stiffening your necks. Moses suggests that a circumcised heart/mind represents a disposition that is sensitive toward Yahweh and has ceased resisting his will.
10:20–22 Moses explains how Yahweh has manifested himself in Israel through "great and awesome" demonstrations of power (v. 21).
11:1 Moses reduces the divine requirement to two simple statements.

✥ **10:12—11:1** This text reminds us again that walking in the ways of the Lord and obeying his commands are the fruit he seeks as evidence of our reverent awe and covenant commitment (love) to him. Mouthing words of devotion ring hollow without the life of devotion.

11:2–7 Moses opens with a thesis statement: "Know today the lesson of Yahweh your God" (author's paraphrase). The lesson divides into two parts: Yahweh's person (v. 2b) and power (vv. 3–6). Awareness of how fearful it is to fall into the hands of the living God (Heb 10:31) should provide lasting motivation for uncompromising covenant faithfulness and a constant reminder that the benefits of covenant relationship with Yahweh should never be taken for granted (vv. 8–25).
11:8–12 Moses opens his discussion of the land with a charge to keep the Supreme Command (6:5) in all its dimensions.

I am giving you today, so that you may
have the strength to go in and take over
the land that you are crossing the Jordan to possess,[u] 9and so that you may
live long[v] in the land the LORD swore[w]
to your ancestors to give to them and
their descendants, a land flowing with
milk and honey.[x] 10The land you are entering to take over is not like the land of
Egypt, from which you have come, where
you planted your seed and irrigated it by
foot as in a vegetable garden. 11But the
land you are crossing the Jordan to take
possession of is a land of mountains and
valleys that drinks rain from heaven.[y]
12It is a land the LORD your God cares
for; the eyes[z] of the LORD your God are
continually on it from the beginning of
the year to its end.

13So if you faithfully obey[a] the commands I am giving you today — to love[b]
the LORD your God and to serve him with
all your heart and with all your soul —
14then I will send rain[c] on your land in its
season, both autumn and spring rains,[d]
so that you may gather in your grain, new
wine and olive oil. 15I will provide grass[e]
in the fields for your cattle, and you will
eat and be satisfied.[f]

16Be careful, or you will be enticed to
turn away and worship other gods and
bow down to them.[g] 17Then the LORD's
anger[h] will burn against you, and he will
shut up[i] the heavens so that it will not
rain and the ground will yield no produce, and you will soon perish[j] from
the good land the LORD is giving you.
18Fix these words of mine in your hearts
and minds; tie them as symbols on your
hands and bind them on your foreheads.[k]

11:8 [u] Jos 1:7
11:9 [v] Dt 4:40; Pr 10:27 [w] Dt 9:5 [x] Ex 3:8
11:11 [y] Dt 8:7
11:12 [z] 1Ki 9:3
11:13 [a] Dt 6:17 [b] Dt 10:12
11:14 [c] Lev 26:4; Dt 28:12 [d] Joel 2:23; Jas 5:7
11:15 [e] Ps 104:14 [f] Dt 6:11
11:16 [g] Dt 8:19; 29:18; Job 31:9, 27
11:17 [h] Dt 6:15 [i] 1Ki 8:35; 2Ch 6:26 [j] Dt 4:26
11:18 [k] Dt 6:6-8
11:19 [l] Dt 6:7 [m] Dt 4:9-10
11:20 [n] Dt 6:9
11:21 [o] Pr 3:2; 4:10 [p] Ps 72:5
11:22 [q] Dt 6:17 [r] Dt 10:20
11:23 [s] Dt 4:38; 9:1
11:24 [t] Ge 15:18; Ex 23:31; Jos 1:3; 14:9
11:25 [u] Ex 23:27; Dt 7:24
11:26 [v] Dt 30:1, 15,19
11:27 [w] Dt 28:1-14
11:28 [x] Dt 28:15

Dt 11:18 ❖ How can we tangibly keep God's Word on or near us at all times?

19Teach them to your children,[l] talking
about them when you sit at home and
when you walk along the road, when you
lie down and when you get up.[m] 20Write
them on the doorframes of your houses
and on your gates,[n] 21so that your days
and the days of your children may be
many[o] in the land the LORD swore to give
your ancestors, as many as the days that
the heavens are above the earth.[p]

22If you carefully observe[q] all these
commands I am giving you to follow —
to love the LORD your God, to walk in
obedience to him and to hold fast[r] to
him — 23then the LORD will drive out all
these nations before you, and you will
dispossess nations larger and stronger
than you.[s] 24Every place where you set
your foot will be yours:[t] Your territory
will extend from the desert to Lebanon, and from the Euphrates River to
the Mediterranean Sea. 25No one will be
able to stand against you. The LORD your
God, as he promised you, will put the
terror and fear of you on the whole land,
wherever you go.[u]

26See, I am setting before you today a
blessing and a curse[v] — 27the blessing[w]
if you obey the commands of the LORD
your God that I am giving you today;
28the curse if you disobey[x] the commands of the LORD your God and turn
from the way that I command you today
by following other gods, which you have
not known. 29When the LORD your God
has brought you into the land you are

11:13-21 The land symbolizes a choice between two ways: the way of blessing, prosperity, and life or the way of the curse, adversity, and death. The people must commit themselves wholeheartedly to the covenant. Yahweh's desire is to see their population explode as the lifespan of each generation increases on the land that he promised their ancestors.

11:22-25 Yahweh will dispossess all the Canaanite nations in advance of the Israelites (v. 23a), and Israel will "dispossess" nations stronger and mightier than they are (v. 23).

11:26-32 Moses concludes this part of the sermon with a climactic appeal for decision; he is handing the Israelites the options of "blessing" and "curse." With his call to decision, Moses challenges the new generation to respond with greater faithfulness than their parents had done. Their future in the land depends on it.

11:2-28 For those who claim to be God's people, every day is a day of decision. Our commitment to Yahweh must not only be renewed at significant junctures in our lives, but each day. The blessings associated with the covenant are not to be taken for granted or viewed as automatic rights. The covenant established by Christ involves a special relationship, which demands constant investment of energy and devotion. The options open to the Israelites—blessing and curse—are open to us, but how we experience them depends on our covenant commitment to Christ, demonstrated by active obedience.

11:29-32 Moses' attention shifts to an anticipated event on the other side of the Jordan. Having identified Mounts Gerizim and Ebal as the place

entering to possess, you are to proclaim on Mount Gerizim the blessings, and on Mount Ebal the curses.[y] 30As you know, these mountains are across the Jordan, westward, toward the setting sun, near the great trees of Moreh,[z] in the territory of those Canaanites living in the Arabah in the vicinity of Gilgal.[a] 31You are about to cross the Jordan to enter and take possession[b] of the land the LORD your God is giving you. When you have taken it over and are living there, 32be sure that you obey all the decrees and laws I am setting before you today.

The One Place of Worship

12 These are the decrees and laws you must be careful to follow in the land that the LORD, the God of your ancestors, has given you to possess—as long as you live in the land.[c] 2Destroy completely all the places on the high mountains, on the hills and under every spreading tree,[d] where the nations you are dispossessing worship their gods. 3Break down their altars, smash[e] their sacred stones and burn their Asherah poles in the fire; cut down the idols of their gods and wipe out their names from those places.

4You must not worship the LORD your God in their way. 5But you are to seek the place the LORD your God will choose from among all your tribes to put his Name there for his dwelling.[f] To that place you must go; 6there bring your burnt offerings and sacrifices, your tithes[g] and special gifts, what you have vowed to give and your freewill offerings, and the firstborn of your herds and flocks. 7There, in the presence of the LORD your God, you and your families shall eat and shall rejoice[h] in everything you have put your hand to, because the LORD your God has blessed you.

8You are not to do as we do here today, everyone doing as they see fit, 9since you have not yet reached the resting place and the inheritance the LORD your God is giving you. 10But you will cross the Jordan and settle in the land the LORD your God is giving[i] you as an inheritance, and he will give you rest from all your enemies around you so that you will live in safety. 11Then to the place the LORD your God will choose as a dwelling for his Name[j]—there you are to bring everything I command you: your burnt offerings and sacrifices, your tithes and special gifts, and all the choice possessions you have vowed to the LORD. 12And there rejoice[k] before the LORD your God—you, your sons and daughters, your male and female servants, and the Levites from your towns who have no allotment or inheritance[l] of their own. 13Be careful not to sacrifice your burnt offerings anywhere you please. 14Offer them only at the place the LORD will choose[m] in one of your tribes, and there observe everything I command you.

15Nevertheless, you may slaughter your animals in any of your towns and eat as much of the meat as you want, as if it were gazelle or deer,[n] according to the blessing the LORD your God gives you. Both the ceremonially unclean and the clean may eat it. 16But you must not eat

Dt 12:3 ❖ What can we do to root out temptation and evil from our lives?

11:29 [y] Dt 27:12-13; Jos 8:33
11:30 [z] Ge 12:6 [a] Jos 4:19
11:31 [b] Dt 9:1; Jos 1:11
12:1 [c] Dt 4:9-10; 1Ki 8:40
12:2 [d] 2Ki 16:4; 17:10
12:3 [e] Nu 33:52; Dt 7:5; Jdg 2:2
12:5 [f] ver 11,13; 2Ch 7:12,16
12:6 [g] Dt 14:22-23
12:7 [h] ver 12, 18; Lev 23:40; Dt 14:26
12:10 [i] Dt 11:31
12:11 [j] ver 5; Dt 15:20; 16:2
12:12 [k] ver 7 [l] Dt 10:9; 14:29
12:14 [m] ver 11
12:15 [n] ver 20-23; Dt 14:5; 15:22

---

for the ceremony, Moses offers a description of the location. In v. 31 Moses confidently announces the end of the journey for his people.

✣ **11:29-32** This passage reminds us that God is faithful; he always keeps his promises.

12:2-7 Moses' discourse begins with instructions on Israel's vertical relationship with Yahweh. This first version of the invitation anticipates two phases of application: purging vestiges of Canaanite idolatry (vv. 2-3) and replacing these practices with those approved by Yahweh (vv. 5-7).

12:8-12 This paragraph clarifies the key issue raised in vv. 2-7: the centralizing of national worship. Only when they have come to their "resting place" will the ideal of exclusive devotion to Yahweh be matched by exclusive worship at a central shrine (v. 9).

12:13-14 Moses concludes with a warning not to make decisions regarding worship based on personal preferences and a specific charge to offer sacrifices only at the place that Yahweh chooses.

✣ **12:1-14** Deuteronomy offers a profound theology of worship. Worship must be designed to please the object of worship, not the worshipers. Furthermore, acceptable forms and styles of worship are not determined by worshipers.

12:15-16, 20-25 Moses highlights the craving for meat (vv. 15, 20b, 21b) and responds by opening wide the door to profane consumption. This does not mean that the Israelites can treat animals callously or that this slaughter is amoral or secular.

the blood;[o] pour it out on the ground
like water.[p] 17 You must not eat in your
own towns the tithe of your grain and
new wine and olive oil, or the firstborn
of your herds and flocks, or whatever you
have vowed to give, or your freewill offerings or special gifts. 18 Instead, you are
to eat[q] them in the presence of the LORD
your God at the place the LORD your God
will choose[r] — you, your sons and daughters, your male and female servants, and
the Levites from your towns — and you
are to rejoice[s] before the LORD your God
in everything you put your hand to. 19 Be
careful not to neglect the Levites[t] as long
as you live in your land.

20 When the LORD your God has enlarged your territory[u] as he promised[v]
you, and you crave meat and say, "I
would like some meat," then you may
eat as much of it as you want. 21 If the
place where the LORD your God chooses to put his Name is too far away from
you, you may slaughter animals from the
herds and flocks the LORD has given you,
as I have commanded you, and in your
own towns you may eat as much of them
as you want. 22 Eat them as you would
gazelle or deer.[w] Both the ceremonially
unclean and the clean may eat. 23 But be
sure you do not eat the blood,[x] because
the blood is the life, and you must not
eat the life with the meat. 24 You must not
eat the blood; pour it out on the ground
like water. 25 Do not eat it, so that it may
go well[y] with you and your children after
you, because you will be doing what is
right[z] in the eyes of the LORD.

26 But take your consecrated things
and whatever you have vowed to give,[a]
and go to the place the LORD will choose.
27 Present your burnt offerings[b] on the altar of the LORD your God, both the meat
and the blood. The blood of your sacrifices must be poured beside the altar

12:16 [o] Ge 9:4; Lev 7:26; 17:10-12 [p] Dt 15:23
12:18 [q] Dt 14:23 [r] ver 5 [s] ver 7,12
12:19 [t] Dt 14:27
12:20 [u] Dt 19:8 [v] Ge 15:18; Dt 11:24
12:22 [w] ver 15
12:23 [x] ver 16; Ge 9:4; Lev 17:11,14
12:25 [y] Dt 4:40; Isa 3:10 [z] Ex 15:26; Dt 13:18; 1Ki 11:38
12:26 [a] ver 17; Nu 5:9-10
12:27 [b] Lev 1:5, 9,13
12:28 [c] ver 25; Dt 4:40
12:29 [d] Jos 23:4
12:31 [e] Dt 9:5 [f] Dt 18:10; Jer 32:35
12:32 [g] Dt 4:2; Jos 1:7; Rev 22:18-19
13:1 [h] Mt 24:24; Mk 13:22; 2Th 2:9
13:2 [i] ver 6,13
13:3 [j] Dt 8:2,16

Dt 13:3 ✧ If God knows all hearts, why would he test his people? What does the condition of our hearts reveal?

of the LORD your God, but you may eat
the meat. 28 Be careful to obey all these
regulations I am giving you, so that it
may always go well[c] with you and your
children after you, because you will be
doing what is good and right in the eyes
of the LORD your God.

29 The LORD your God will cut off[d] before you the nations you are about to
invade and dispossess. But when you
have driven them out and settled in
their land, 30 and after they have been
destroyed before you, be careful not to be
ensnared by inquiring about their gods,
saying, "How do these nations serve their
gods? We will do the same." 31 You must
not worship the LORD your God in their
way, because in worshiping their gods,
they do all kinds of detestable things the
LORD hates.[e] They even burn their sons[f]
and daughters in the fire as sacrifices
to their gods.

32 See that you do all I command you;
do not add[g] to it or take away from it.[a]

Worshiping Other Gods

13 [b] If a prophet,[h] or one who foretells
by dreams, appears among you
and announces to you a sign or wonder,
2 and if the sign or wonder spoken of
takes place, and the prophet says, "Let
us follow other gods"[i] (gods you have
not known) "and let us worship them,"
3 you must not listen to the words of that
prophet or dreamer. The LORD your God
is testing[j] you to find out whether you
love him with all your heart and with all

[a] *32* In Hebrew texts this verse (12:32) is numbered 13:1. [b] In Hebrew texts 13:1-18 is numbered 13:2-19.

12:17–19, 26–27 Animals and produce of the field that have been set apart as sacred offerings may be consumed only in the presence of Yahweh at the place he chooses. Moses specifies who may participate in these events (v. 18a) and ends with a warning not to neglect the Levite (v. 19). Verses 26–27 follow more detailed instructions on profane slaughter (vv. 20–25).

✣ **12:15–28** Even as this passage encourages us to enjoy the provision of God, it does so with a profound ethical sensitivity. The slaughter of animals could easily degenerate into a ruthless disregard for the life of the animal.

12:29–32 Moses cautions the people against fascination with the gods of the nations in Canaan.
13:1–5 False prophets represent the first potential source of spiritual sedition. The second, oneiromancy (divination through dreams), was widespread in the ancient world. Moses charges the Israelites to refuse to give prophets or dreamers who incite spiritual sedition an ear (vv. 3–4) and instructs the people on how to treat them (v. 5a).

your soul. 4It is the LORD your God you
must follow,[k] and him you must revere.
Keep his commands and obey him; serve
him and hold fast[l] to him. 5That prophet or dreamer must be put to death for
inciting rebellion against the LORD your
God, who brought you out of Egypt and
redeemed you from the land of slavery.
That prophet or dreamer tried to turn
you from the way the LORD your God
commanded you to follow. You must
purge the evil[m] from among you.
6If your very own brother, or your son
or daughter, or the wife you love, or your
closest friend secretly entices[n] you, saying, "Let us go and worship other gods"
(gods that neither you nor your ancestors
have known, 7gods of the peoples around
you, whether near or far, from one end
of the land to the other), 8do not yield[o]
to them or listen to them. Show them no
pity. Do not spare them or shield them.
9You must certainly put them to death.[p]
Your hand must be the first in putting
them to death, and then the hands of
all the people. 10Stone them to death,
because they tried to turn you away from
the LORD your God, who brought you
out of Egypt, out of the land of slavery.
11Then all Israel will hear and be afraid,[q]
and no one among you will do such an
evil thing again.
12If you hear it said about one of the
towns the LORD your God is giving you to
live in 13that troublemakers[r] have arisen
among you and have led the people of
their town astray, saying, "Let us go and
worship other gods" (gods you have not
known), 14then you must inquire, probe
and investigate it thoroughly. And if it is
true and it has been proved that this detestable thing has been done among you,
15you must certainly put to the sword
all who live in that town. You must destroy it completely,[a] both its people and
its livestock. 16You are to gather all the
plunder of the town into the middle of
the public square and completely burn
the town and all its plunder as a whole
burnt offering to the LORD your God.[s]
That town is to remain a ruin[t] forever,
never to be rebuilt, 17and none of the condemned things[a] are to be found in your
hands. Then the LORD will turn from his
fierce anger,[u] will show you mercy, and
will have compassion[v] on you. He will
increase your numbers,[w] as he promised[x]
on oath to your ancestors— 18because
you obey the LORD your God by keeping all his commands that I am giving
you today and doing what is right[y] in
his eyes.

13:4 [k] 2Ki 23:3; 2Ch 34:31 [l] Dt 10:20
13:5 [m] Dt 17:7,12; 1Co 5:13
13:6 [n] Dt 17:2-7; 29:18
13:8 [o] Pr 1:10
13:9 [p] Dt 17:5,7
13:11 [q] Dt 19:20
13:13 [r] ver 2,6; 1Jn 2:19
13:16 [s] Jos 6:24 [t] Jos 8:28; Jer 49:2
13:17 [u] Nu 25:4 [v] Dt 30:3 [w] Dt 7:13 [x] Ge 22:17; 26:4, 24; 28:14
13:18 [y] Dt 12:25, 28
14:1 [z] Lev 19:28; 21:5; Jer 16:6; 41:5; Ro 8:14; 9:8; Gal 3:26
14:2 [a] Lev 20:26 [b] Dt 7:6; 26:18-19
14:3 [c] Eze 4:14
14:4 [d] Lev 11:2-45; Ac 10:14

Dt 14:1-2 ❖ How is God calling us to visibly stand out from the world around us?

Clean and Unclean Food

14:3–20pp // Lev 11:1–23

14 You are the children[z] of the LORD
your God. Do not cut yourselves
or shave the front of your heads for the
dead, 2for you are a people holy to the
LORD your God.[a] Out of all the peoples on
the face of the earth, the LORD has chosen you to be his treasured possession.[b]
3Do not eat any detestable thing.[c]
4These are the animals you may eat:[d]
the ox, the sheep, the goat, 5the deer,
the gazelle, the roe deer, the wild goat,
the ibex, the antelope and the mountain
sheep.[b] 6You may eat any animal that has
a divided hoof and that chews the cud.
7However, of those that chew the cud or

[a] *15,17* The Hebrew term refers to the irrevocable giving over of things or persons to the LORD, often by totally destroying them. [b] *5* The precise identification of some of the birds and animals in this chapter is uncertain.

13:6–11 Moses lists five close acquaintances who might incite defection from Yahweh. To modern readers the demand to execute the conspirator in vv. 9–10a seems heartless. But allegiance to Yahweh must take precedence over family ties.

13:12–18 Because this scenario imagines rumors rather than direct contact with those who lead in the defection from Yahweh, Moses demands careful investigation (v. 14a). If the rumors prove true, Moses calls for total destruction (v. 15). The tone reflects the seriousness with which Yahweh looks on spiritual defection.

✜ **12:29—13:18** This chapter reminds Christians today that commitment to God must be rigorously pursued at the personal, family, and community level.

14:1–3 By opening this unit with "Sons you are to Yahweh your God" (v. 1; alternate translation), Moses announces that whatever follows reflects Israel's acceptance of this privileged status.

14:4–20 The meat in their diet must be like the food that God "eats" in the sacrifices offered to him. Through their dietary boundaries, the Israelites declared their unique proximity to Yahweh.

that have a divided hoof you may not
eat the camel, the rabbit or the hyrax.
Although they chew the cud, they do not
have a divided hoof; they are ceremonially unclean for you. 8The pig is also
unclean; although it has a divided hoof,
it does not chew the cud. You are not to
eat their meat or touch their carcasses.[e]
9Of all the creatures living in the water,
you may eat any that has fins and scales.
10But anything that does not have fins
and scales you may not eat; for you it
is unclean.
11You may eat any clean bird. 12But
these you may not eat: the eagle, the vulture, the black vulture, 13the red kite, the
black kite, any kind of falcon, 14any kind
of raven, 15the horned owl, the screech
owl, the gull, any kind of hawk, 16the
little owl, the great owl, the white owl,
17the desert owl, the osprey, the cormorant, 18the stork, any kind of heron, the
hoopoe and the bat.
19All flying insects are unclean to you;
do not eat them. 20But any winged creature that is clean you may eat.
21Do not eat anything you find already
dead.[f] You may give it to the foreigner
residing in any of your towns, and they
may eat it, or you may sell it to any other
foreigner. But you are a people holy to
the LORD your God.[g]
Do not cook a young goat in its mother's milk.[h]

Tithes

22Be sure to set aside a tenth[i] of all that
your fields produce each year. 23Eat the
tithe of your grain, new wine and olive oil, and the firstborn of your herds
and flocks in the presence of the LORD
your God at the place he will choose as a
dwelling for his Name,[j] so that you may
learn[k] to revere the LORD your God always. 24But if that place is too distant and
you have been blessed by the LORD your
God and cannot carry your tithe (because
the place where the LORD will choose
to put his Name is so far away), 25then
exchange your tithe for silver, and take
the silver with you and go to the place
the LORD your God will choose. 26Use the
silver to buy whatever you like: cattle,
sheep, wine or other fermented drink, or
anything you wish. Then you and your
household shall eat there in the presence
of the LORD your God and rejoice.[l] 27And
do not neglect the Levites[m] living in your
towns, for they have no allotment or inheritance of their own.[n]
28At the end of every three years, bring
all the tithes of that year's produce and
store it in your towns,[o] 29so that the Levites (who have no allotment[p] or inheritance of their own) and the foreigners,[q]
the fatherless and the widows who live
in your towns may come and eat and
be satisfied, and so that the LORD your
God may bless[r] you in all the work of
your hands.

The Year for Canceling Debts

15:1–11Ref // Lev 25:8–38

15 At the end of every seven years you
must cancel debts.[s] 2This is how it
is to be done: Every creditor shall cancel
any loan they have made to a fellow Israelite. They shall not require payment
from anyone among their own people,
because the LORD's time for canceling
debts has been proclaimed. 3You may
require payment from a foreigner,[t] but
you must cancel any debt your fellow
Israelite owes you. 4However, there need

14:8 [e] Lev 11:26-27
14:21 [f] Lev 17:15; 22:8 [g] ver 2 [h] Ex 23:19; 34:26
14:22 [i] Lev 27:30; Dt 12:6,17; Ne 10:37
14:23 [j] Dt 12:5 [k] Dt 4:10
14:26 [l] Dt 12:7-8
14:27 [m] Dt 12:19 [n] Nu 18:20
14:28 [o] Dt 26:12
14:29 [p] ver 27 [q] Dt 26:12 [r] Dt 15:10; Mal 3:10
15:1 [s] Dt 31:10
15:3 [t] Dt 23:20

14:21 The prohibition on boiling a kid in its mother's milk may allude to Canaanite fertility rites.

✣ **14:1-21** Since we no longer present these offerings to God but celebrate the sacrificial work of Jesus Christ, whenever we partake of Communion, we participate in the feast to which the Lord has graciously invited us.

14:22-26 The presentation of the tithe provided a means by which the people could participate in the kind of event that the elders of Israel experienced on Horeb (4:10; Ex 24:9-11).

14:27-29 In the third and sixth years the farmers must deposit their tithes in their towns. Here they can be stored and distributed to the Levites. Moses expands the economic safety net to include the foreigner, the fatherless, and the widow.

✣ **14:22-29** When we ask, "Do Christians need to tithe?" we have asked the wrong question. At issue is not the institution but the heart and mind of God, which should be reflected in the hearts and minds of his people. This gets us off the externals and focuses on the primary issue: soft hearts and open hands.

15:1-8 The Hebrew expression for canceling debts does not mean the cancellation of all debts. It refers to the return of all properties that a creditor is holding against loans by those indebted to him.

be no poor people among you, for in the
land the LORD your God is giving you to
possess as your inheritance, he will richly bless[u] you, 5if only you fully obey the
LORD your God and are careful to follow[v]
all these commands I am giving you today. 6For the LORD your God will bless you
as he has promised, and you will lend
to many nations but will borrow from
none. You will rule over many nations
but none will rule over you.[w]
7If anyone is poor among your fellow
Israelites in any of the towns of the land
the LORD your God is giving you, do not
be hardhearted or tightfisted[x] toward
them. 8Rather, be openhanded[y] and
freely lend them whatever they need.
9Be careful not to harbor this wicked
thought: "The seventh year, the year for
canceling debts,[z] is near," so that you
do not show ill will[a] toward the needy
among your fellow Israelites and give
them nothing. They may then appeal to
the LORD against you, and you will be
found guilty of sin.[b] 10Give generously
to them and do so without a grudging
heart;[c] then because of this the LORD
your God will bless[d] you in all your work
and in everything you put your hand
to. 11There will always be poor people
in the land. Therefore I command you
to be openhanded toward your fellow
Israelites who are poor and needy in
your land.[e]

Freeing Servants

15:12–18pp // Ex 21:2–6
15:12–18Ref // Lev 25:38–55

12If any of your people — Hebrew men
or women — sell themselves to you and
serve you six years, in the seventh year
you must let them go free.[f] 13And when
you release them, do not send them away
empty-handed. 14Supply them liberally

15:4 [u] Dt 28:8
15:5 [v] Dt 28:1
15:6 [w] Dt 28:12-13,44
15:7 [x] 1Jn 3:17
15:8 [y] Mt 5:42; Lk 6:34
15:9 [z] ver 1 [a] Mt 20:15 [b] Dt 24:15
15:10 [c] 2Co 9:5 [d] Dt 14:29; 24:19
15:11 [e] Mt 26:11; Mk 14:7; Jn 12:8
15:12 [f] Ex 21:2; Lev 25:39; Jer 34:14
15:15 [g] Dt 5:15 [h] Dt 16:12
15:19 [i] Ex 13:2
15:20 [j] Dt 12:5-7, 17,18; 14:23
15:21 [k] Lev 22:19-25
15:22 [l] Dt 12:15, 22
15:23 [m] Dt 12:16

Dt 15:4-6 ❖ How does the presence of poverty in a society serve as a barometer of its obedience to God? How can we address financial and social inequities around us?

from your flock, your threshing floor and
your winepress. Give to them as the LORD
your God has blessed you. 15Remember
that you were slaves[g] in Egypt and the
LORD your God redeemed you.[h] That is
why I give you this command today.
16But if your servant says to you, "I
do not want to leave you," because he
loves you and your family and is well off
with you, 17then take an awl and push it
through his earlobe into the door, and
he will become your servant for life. Do
the same for your female servant.
18Do not consider it a hardship to set
your servant free, because their service
to you these six years has been worth
twice as much as that of a hired hand.
And the LORD your God will bless you in
everything you do.

The Firstborn Animals

19Set apart for the LORD your God every
firstborn male[i] of your herds and flocks.
Do not put the firstborn of your cows to
work, and do not shear the firstborn of
your sheep. 20Each year you and your
family are to eat them in the presence
of the LORD your God at the place he will
choose.[j] 21If an animal has a defect, is
lame or blind, or has any serious flaw,
you must not sacrifice it to the LORD
your God.[k] 22You are to eat it in your
own towns. Both the ceremonially unclean and the clean may eat it, as if it
were gazelle or deer.[l] 23But you must not
eat the blood; pour it out on the ground
like water.[m]

15:10-11 Moses declares that Yahweh will bless the creditor "in all your work" (v. 10) and ends with another reminder that the poor will always be around.

15:12-17a Moses instructs those with means how to treat countrymen who are servants, and he contemplates the possibility of an Israelite preferring permanent servitude to economic independence.

15:1-18 God in his grace has rescued us from the bondage of sin and adopted us as his sons. We should be inspired to treat others as he has treated us.

15:19-23 The expression "each year" (v. 20) suggests the firstborn were to be presented at the central sanctuary at one of the annual festivals. Lest they become careless about their offerings, Moses reminds the Israelites that the only meat worthy of Yahweh's table is that which comes from flawless animals (v. 21).

15:19-23 This is a problem in our own day. We often view the Lord's blessing as a right rather than a privilege. But God's people cannot afford to lose sight of the grace of covenant relationship with him, confirmed in his blessing on our work and his invitation to worship in his presence.

The Passover

16:1–8pp // Ex 12:14–20; Lev 23:4–8; Nu 28:16–25

16 Observe the month of Aviv[n] and
celebrate the Passover of the LORD
your God, because in the month of Aviv
he brought you out of Egypt by night.
2Sacrifice as the Passover to the LORD
your God an animal from your flock or
herd at the place the LORD will choose
as a dwelling for his Name.[o] 3Do not eat
it with bread made with yeast, but for
seven days eat unleavened bread, the
bread of affliction,[p] because you left
Egypt in haste[q] — so that all the days of
your life you may remember the time
of your departure from Egypt.[r] 4Let no
yeast be found in your possession in all
your land for seven days. Do not let any
of the meat you sacrifice on the evening
of the first day remain until morning.[s]
5You must not sacrifice the Passover
in any town the LORD your God gives
you 6except in the place he will choose
as a dwelling for his Name. There you
must sacrifice the Passover in the evening, when the sun goes down, on the
anniversary[a][t] of your departure from
Egypt. 7Roast[u] it and eat it at the place
the LORD your God will choose. Then in
the morning return to your tents. 8For
six days eat unleavened bread and on
the seventh day hold an assembly[v] to the
LORD your God and do no work.

The Festival of Weeks

16:9–12pp // Lev 23:15–22; Nu 28:26–31

9Count off seven weeks[w] from the time
you begin to put the sickle to the standing grain.[x] 10Then celebrate the Festival of Weeks to the LORD your God by
giving a freewill offering in proportion
to the blessings the LORD your God has
given you. 11And rejoice[y] before the LORD
your God at the place he will choose as a
dwelling for his Name — you, your sons
and daughters, your male and female
servants, the Levites[z] in your towns, and
the foreigners, the fatherless and the
widows living among you. 12Remember
that you were slaves in Egypt,[a] and follow
carefully these decrees.

16:1 [n] Ex 12:2; 13:4
16:2 [o] Dt 12:5,26
16:3 [p] Ex 12:8, 39; 34:18 [q] Ex 12:11,15,19 [r] Ex 13:3,6-7
16:4 [s] Ex 12:10; 34:25
16:6 [t] Ex 12:6; Dt 12:5
16:7 [u] Ex 12:8; 2Ch 35:13
16:8 [v] Ex 12:16; 13:6; Lev 23:8
16:9 [w] Ex 34:22; Lev 23:15 [x] Ex 23:16; Nu 28:26

Dt 16:12 ❖ How do we commemorate and celebrate what God has done for us?

The Festival of Tabernacles

16:13–17pp // Lev 23:33–43; Nu 29:12–39

13Celebrate the Festival of Tabernacles
for seven days after you have gathered
the produce of your threshing floor[b] and
your winepress.[c] 14Be joyful[d] at your festival — you, your sons and daughters,
your male and female servants, and the
Levites, the foreigners, the fatherless
and the widows who live in your towns.
15For seven days celebrate the festival to
the LORD your God at the place the LORD
will choose. For the LORD your God will
bless you in all your harvest and in all
the work of your hands, and your joy[e]
will be complete.
16Three times a year all your men must
appear before the LORD your God at the
place he will choose: at the Festival of
Unleavened Bread, the Festival of Weeks
and the Festival of Tabernacles.[f] No one
should appear before the LORD empty-
handed:[g] 17Each of you must bring a gift
in proportion to the way the LORD your
God has blessed you.

16:11 [y] Dt 12:7 [z] Dt 12:12
16:12 [a] Dt 15:15
16:13 [b] Lev 23:34 [c] Ex 23:16
16:14 [d] ver 11
16:15 [e] Lev 23:39
16:16 [f] Ex 23:14, 16 [g] Ex 34:20

[a] 6 Or *down, at the time of day*

16:1 Aviv was the first month of the year, which may suggest that this celebration also functioned as a New Year festival.

16:2-7 The Passover animal is slaughtered in the evening to coincide with the timing of Israel's exodus from Egypt (v. 6). In the morning the worshipers return to the tents pitched near the sanctuary (v. 7b).

16:9 The Festivals of Unleavened Bread and Weeks respectively served as bookends of the grain harvest.

16:10-12a The Festival of Weeks is to be a joyful celebration (v. 11). By associating the festival with Egypt, Moses highlights that everything Israel has is to be received as a gift. Like his provision of salvation, Yahweh's provision of harvest calls for free and spontaneous expressions of gratitude.

16:14-15 Coming at the end of the agricultural cycle, the Festival of Booths affords the Israelites an opportunity for corporate thanksgiving in the presence of Yahweh at the place he chooses as his residence.

16:16-17 The summary statement here recalls Yahweh's words in Ex 23:14-17.

✤ 16:1-17 Even as we celebrate ecumenical festivals and commemorative festivals of our local congregations, like the ancient Israelites, we must beware of the danger of mere externalism.

Judges

18Appoint judges[h] and officials for each
of your tribes in every town the LORD
your God is giving you, and they shall
judge the people fairly. 19Do not pervert
justice[i] or show partiality.[j] Do not accept
a bribe,[k] for a bribe blinds the eyes of the
wise and twists the words of the innocent. 20Follow justice and justice alone,
so that you may live and possess the land
the LORD your God is giving you.

Worshiping Other Gods

21Do not set up any wooden Asherah
pole[l] beside the altar you build to the
LORD your God,[m] 22and do not erect a
sacred stone,[n] for these the LORD your
God hates.

17 Do not sacrifice to the LORD your
God an ox or a sheep that has any
defect[o] or flaw in it, for that would be
detestable to him.[p]

2If a man or woman living among you
in one of the towns the LORD gives you is
found doing evil in the eyes of the LORD
your God in violation of his covenant,[q]
3and contrary to my command[r] has worshiped other gods, bowing down to them
or to the sun[s] or the moon or the stars
in the sky, 4and this has been brought
to your attention, then you must investigate it thoroughly. If it is true and it has
been proved that this detestable thing
has been done in Israel,[t] 5take the man
or woman who has done this evil deed
to your city gate and stone that person
to death.[u] 6On the testimony of two or
three witnesses a person is to be put to
death, but no one is to be put to death on
the testimony of only one witness.[v] 7The
hands of the witnesses must be the first
in putting that person to death, and then
the hands of all the people. You must
purge the evil[w] from among you.

Law Courts

8If cases come before your courts
that are too difficult for you to judge—
whether bloodshed, lawsuits or assaults[x]—take them to the place the
LORD your God will choose.[y] 9Go to the
Levitical priests and to the judge who is
in office at that time. Inquire of them
and they will give you the verdict.[z]
10You must act according to the decisions they give you at the place the LORD
will choose. Be careful to do everything
they instruct you to do. 11Act according
to whatever they teach you and the decisions they give you. Do not turn aside
from what they tell you, to the right or to
the left.[a] 12Anyone who shows contempt[b]
for the judge or for the priest who stands
ministering there to the LORD your God
is to be put to death. You must purge
the evil from Israel. 13All the people will
hear and be afraid, and will not be contemptuous again.[c]

The King

14When you enter the land the LORD
your God is giving you and have taken
possession of it and settled in it, and
you say, "Let us set a king over us like
all the nations around us,"[d] 15be sure to
appoint over you a king the LORD your
God chooses. He must be from among
your fellow Israelites.[e] Do not place a
foreigner over you, one who is not an
Israelite. 16The king, moreover, must not

16:18 [h] Dt 1:16
16:19 [i] Ex 23:2, 8 [j] Lev 19:15; Dt 1:17 [k] Ecc 7:7
16:21 [l] Dt 7:5 [m] Ex 34:13; 2Ki 17:16; 21:3; 2Ch 33:3
16:22 [n] Lev 26:1
17:1 [o] Mal 1:8,13 [p] Dt 15:21
17:2 [q] Dt 13:6-11
17:3 [r] Jer 7:22-23 [s] Job 31:26
17:4 [t] Dt 13:12-14
17:5 [u] Lev 24:14
17:6 [v] Nu 35:30; Dt 19:15; Jos 7:25; Mt 18:16; Jn 8:17; 2Co 13:1; 1Ti 5:19; Heb 10:28
17:7 [w] Dt 13:5,9
17:8 [x] 2Ch 19:10 [y] Dt 12:5; Hag 2:11
17:9 [z] Dt 19:17; Eze 44:24
17:11 [a] Dt 25:1
17:12 [b] Nu 15:30
17:13 [c] Dt 13:11; 19:20
17:14 [d] Dt 11:31; 1Sa 8:5,19-20
17:15 [e] Jer 30:21

16:18-20b Moses calls on the people to imitate Yahweh in not perverting justice through partiality or bribery.

16:21—17:1 Asherah was a female goddess, the consort of El. The association of pillars with Asherim in 7:5 and 12:3 suggests this is a stone erected to symbolize Baal.

17:4b-7b Executing criminals in the gate would make a spectacle of them and demonstrate the heinousness of their "evil deed" (v. 5b).

17:8b-12b Although Moses introduces Levitical priests and a judge as final adjudicators (v. 9), his primary addressee continues to be ordinary citizens. Moses suggests that the central sanctuary will not only be a place of worship but also a court of last resort; he thus implies the role of God in the pursuit of righteousness. The priestly judge could probably use the Urim and Thummim to determine the mind of God. Refusal to listen to the priest is as reprehensible as idolatry itself and deserves the death penalty.

16:18—17:13 Righteousness is not served when those with means are able to hire the most skillful legal defense teams while people who are marginalized cannot afford representation at the same level.

17:14-20 By the act of copying the Torah, the king declared his spiritual subordination to the priests and to the Torah, the symbol of the covenant that bound Yahweh and Israel.

17:14-20 Leaders in the church *must* be walking according to the revealed will of God. In so doing, they model the link between knowing the Word and fearing and obeying the Lord.

acquire great numbers of horses for himself[f] or make the people return to Egypt[g] to get more of them,[h] for the LORD has told you, "You are not to go back that way again."[i] 17 He must not take many wives,[j] or his heart will be led astray. He must not accumulate large amounts of silver and gold.

18 When he takes the throne of his kingdom, he is to write[k] for himself on a scroll a copy of this law, taken from that of the Levitical priests. 19 It is to be with him, and he is to read it all the days of his life[l] so that he may learn to revere the LORD his God and follow carefully all the words of this law and these decrees 20 and not consider himself better than his fellow Israelites and turn from the law[m] to the right or to the left.[n] Then he and his descendants will reign a long time over his kingdom in Israel.

Offerings for Priests and Levites

18 The Levitical priests—indeed, the whole tribe of Levi—are to have no allotment or inheritance with Israel. They shall live on the food offerings presented to the LORD, for that is their inheritance.[o] 2 They shall have no inheritance among their fellow Israelites; the LORD is their inheritance, as he promised them.

3 This is the share due the priests from the people who sacrifice a bull or a sheep: the shoulder, the internal organs and the meat from the head.[p] 4 You are to give them the firstfruits of your grain, new wine and olive oil, and the first wool from the shearing of your sheep,[q] 5 for the LORD your God has chosen them[r] and their descendants out of all your tribes to stand and minister[s] in the LORD's name always.

6 If a Levite moves from one of your towns anywhere in Israel where he is living, and comes in all earnestness to the place the LORD will choose,[t] 7 he may minister in the name of the LORD his

17:16 [f] 1Ki 4:26; 10:26 [g] Isa 31:1; Hos 11:5 [h] 1Ki 10:28; Eze 17:15 [i] Ex 13:17
17:17 [j] 1Ki 11:3
17:18 [k] Dt 31:22, 24
17:19 [l] Jos 1:8
17:20 [m] 1Ki 15:5 [n] Dt 5:32
18:1 [o] Dt 10:9; 1Co 9:13
18:3 [p] Lev 7:28-34
18:4 [q] Ex 22:29; Nu 18:12
18:5 [r] Ex 28:1 [s] Dt 10:8
18:6 [t] Nu 35:2-3

18:8 [u] 2Ch 31:4; Ne 12:44, 47
18:9 [v] Dt 12:29-31
18:10 [w] Dt 12:31 [x] Lev 19:31
18:12 [y] Lev 18:24; Dt 9:4
18:15 [z] Jn 1:21; Ac 3:22*; 7:37*
18:16 [a] Ex 20:19; Dt 5:23-27

Dt 17:16–17 ❖ In what ways are these qualifications important for Christian leaders today? Where have we seen good Christian leadership practiced?

Dt 18:3–5 ❖ How can we visibly support those God has called to ordained ministry?

God like all his fellow Levites who serve there in the presence of the LORD. 8 He is to share equally in their benefits, even though he has received money from the sale of family possessions.[u]

Occult Practices

9 When you enter the land the LORD your God is giving you, do not learn to imitate[v] the detestable ways of the nations there. 10 Let no one be found among you who sacrifices their son or daughter in the fire, who practices divination[w] or sorcery, interprets omens, engages in witchcraft,[x] 11 or casts spells, or who is a medium or spiritist or who consults the dead. 12 Anyone who does these things is detestable to the LORD; because of these same detestable practices the LORD your God will drive out those nations before you.[y] 13 You must be blameless before the LORD your God.

The Prophet

14 The nations you will dispossess listen to those who practice sorcery or divination. But as for you, the LORD your God has not permitted you to do so. 15 The LORD your God will raise up for you a prophet like me from among you, from your fellow Israelites.[z] You must listen to him. 16 For this is what you asked of the LORD your God at Horeb on the day of the assembly when you said, "Let us not hear the voice of the LORD our God nor see this great fire anymore, or we will die."[a]

17 The LORD said to me: "What they

18:1–5 Yahweh offers himself as the Levitical priests' grant (v. 2b) and takes care of the Levites by means of the people's sacrifices.
18:6–8 Moses invites all Levites to participate in the prerequisites described in vv. 3–5 and designates equal prerequisites for equal service.

✚ **18:1–8** The NT teaching on the priesthood of all believers (1Pe 2:9) means that believers collectively have direct access to God and responsibility to represent him to the unbelieving world.

18:9–14 The last clause of v. 9 functions as a theme statement for vv. 9–14. Verses 10–11 provide a catalog of practices intended to manipulate spiritual forces.
18:15–20 Because Yahweh promises to provide Israel with prophets, there is no need to resort to divination, magic, and necromancy to determine his will.

say is good. 18I will raise up for them a
prophet like you from among their fellow Israelites, and I will put my words[b] in
his mouth. He will tell them everything
I command him.[c] 19I myself will call to
account[d] anyone who does not listen to
my words that the prophet speaks in my
name. 20But a prophet who presumes to
speak in my name anything I have not
commanded, or a prophet who speaks
in the name of other gods,[e] is to be put
to death."[f]

21You may say to yourselves, "How can
we know when a message has not been
spoken by the LORD?" 22If what a prophet proclaims in the name of the LORD
does not take place or come true, that is a
message the LORD has not spoken.[g] That
prophet has spoken presumptuously,[h] so
do not be alarmed.

Cities of Refuge

19:1–14Ref // Nu 35:6–34; Dt 4:41–43; Jos 20:1–9

19 When the LORD your God has destroyed the nations whose land he
is giving you, and when you have driven
them out and settled in their towns and
houses,[i] 2then set aside for yourselves
three cities in the land the LORD your
God is giving you to possess. 3Determine
the distances involved and divide into
three parts the land the LORD your God
is giving you as an inheritance, so that
a person who kills someone may flee for
refuge to one of these cities.

4This is the rule concerning anyone
who kills a person and flees there for
safety — anyone who kills a neighbor
unintentionally, without malice aforethought. 5For instance, a man may go
into the forest with his neighbor to cut
wood, and as he swings his ax to fell a
tree, the head may fly off and hit his
neighbor and kill him. That man may
flee to one of these cities and save his
life. 6Otherwise, the avenger of blood[j]
might pursue him in a rage, overtake
him if the distance is too great, and kill
him even though he is not deserving
of death, since he did it to his neighbor
without malice aforethought. 7This is
why I command you to set aside for yourselves three cities.

8If the LORD your God enlarges your
territory, as he promised on oath to your
ancestors, and gives you the whole land
he promised them, 9because you carefully follow all these laws I command you
today — to love the LORD your God and to
walk always in obedience to him[k] — then
you are to set aside three more cities.
10Do this so that innocent blood will not
be shed in your land, which the LORD
your God is giving you as your inheritance, and so that you will not be guilty
of bloodshed.[l]

11But if out of hate someone lies in
wait, assaults and kills a neighbor,[m] and
then flees to one of these cities, 12the killer shall be sent for by the town elders, be
brought back from the city, and be handed over to the avenger of blood to die.
13Show no pity.[n] You must purge from
Israel the guilt of shedding innocent
blood,[o] so that it may go well with you.

14Do not move your neighbor's boundary stone set up by your predecessors
in the inheritance you receive in the
land the LORD your God is giving you
to possess.[p]

Dt 19:11–12 ❖ Why do the motivations behind an action matter? How should we take motivations into account when we respond to wrongdoing?

18:18 [b] Isa 51:16; Jn 17:8 [c] Jn 4:25-26; 8:28; 12:49-50
18:19 [d] Ac 3:23*
18:20 [e] Jer 14:14 [f] Dt 13:1-5
18:22 [g] Jer 28:9 [h] ver 20
19:1 [i] Dt 12:29
19:6 [j] Nu 35:12
19:9 [k] Jos 20:7-8
19:10 [l] Nu 35:33; Dt 21:1-9
19:11 [m] Nu 35:16
19:13 [n] Dt 7:2 [o] 1Ki 2:31
19:14 [p] Dt 27:17; Pr 22:28; Hos 5:10

18:21–22 These verses focus on the marks of false prophecy. Moses concludes with counsel regarding the proper disposition toward prophets whose words do not come true.

✜ **18:9–22** This passage reminds readers in all ages to be vigilant in testing the validity of all who preach and teach in God's name. First John 4:1 warns Christians not to believe every spirit.

19:1–3 The Israelites were to divide the entire territory into three regions to protect those who inadvertently caused another person's death.

19:8–9 Moses calls for the addition of three more towns of refuge to serve people living beyond the narrowly defined promised land.

19:11–13 Moses reaffirms the demand in Nu 35 for discrimination between intentional murder and accidental death.

19:14 Israelite law viewed Yahweh as the true owner of the land, and the allotments to families were unchangeable.

✜ **19:1–14** Because the demand to execute the murderer is rooted in a divine charge to the ancestor of all (Noah; see Ge 9:6), this principle may not be dismissed as an Israelite civil law that is now nullified in Christ.

Witnesses

15 One witness is not enough to convict anyone accused of any crime or offense they may have committed. A matter must be established by the testimony of two or three witnesses.[q]

16 If a malicious witness[r] takes the stand to accuse someone of a crime, 17 the two people involved in the dispute must stand in the presence of the LORD before the priests and the judges[s] who are in office at the time. 18 The judges must make a thorough investigation, and if the witness proves to be a liar, giving false testimony against a fellow Israelite, 19 then do to the false witness as that witness intended to do to the other party.[t] You must purge the evil from among you. 20 The rest of the people will hear of this and be afraid,[u] and never again will such an evil thing be done among you. 21 Show no pity:[v] life for life, eye for eye, tooth for tooth, hand for hand, foot for foot.[w]

Going to War

20 When you go to war against your enemies and see horses and chariots and an army greater than yours,[x] do not be afraid[y] of them,[z] because the LORD your God, who brought you up out of Egypt, will be with you. 2 When you are about to go into battle, the priest shall come forward and address the army. 3 He shall say: "Hear, Israel: Today you are going into battle against your enemies. Do not be fainthearted[a] or afraid; do not panic or be terrified by them. 4 For the LORD your God is the one who goes with you to fight[b] for you against your enemies to give you victory."

5 The officers shall say to the army: "Has anyone built a new house and not yet begun to live in[c] it? Let him go home, or he may die in battle and someone else may begin to live in it. 6 Has anyone planted a vineyard and not begun to enjoy it? Let him go home, or he may die in battle and someone else enjoy it. 7 Has anyone become pledged to a woman and not married her? Let him go home, or he may die in battle and someone else marry her.[d]" 8 Then the officers shall add, "Is anyone afraid or fainthearted? Let him go home so that his fellow soldiers will not become disheartened too."[e] 9 When the officers have finished speaking to the army, they shall appoint commanders over it.

10 When you march up to attack a city, make its people an offer of peace.[f] 11 If they accept and open their gates, all the people in it shall be subject to forced labor[g] and shall work for you. 12 If they refuse to make peace and they engage you in battle, lay siege to that city. 13 When the LORD your God delivers it into your hand, put to the sword all the men in it.[h] 14 As for the women, the children, the livestock[i] and everything else in the city, you may take these as plunder for yourselves. And you may use the plunder the LORD your God gives you from your enemies. 15 This is how you are to treat all the cities that are at a distance from you and do not belong to the nations nearby.

16 However, in the cities of the nations the LORD your God is giving you as an inheritance, do not leave alive anything that breathes.[j] 17 Completely destroy[a] them—the Hittites, Amorites, Canaanites, Perizzites, Hivites and Jebusites—as the LORD

19:15 [q] Nu 35:30; Dt 17:6; Mt 18:16*; Jn 8:17; 2Co 13:1*; 1Ti 5:19; Heb 10:28
19:16 [r] Ex 23:1; Ps 27:12
19:17 [s] Dt 17:9
19:19 [t] Pr 19:5, 9
19:20 [u] Dt 17:13; 21:21
19:21 [v] ver 13 [w] Ex 21:24; Lev 24:20; Mt 5:38*
20:1 [x] Ps 20:7; Isa 31:1 [y] Dt 31:6, 8 [z] 2Ch 32:7-8
20:3 [a] Jos 23:10
20:4 [b] Dt 1:30; 3:22; Jos 23:10
20:5 [c] Ne 12:27
20:7 [d] Dt 24:5
20:8 [e] Jdg 7:3
20:10 [f] Lk 14:31-32
20:11 [g] 1Ki 9:21
20:13 [h] Nu 31:7
20:14 [i] Jos 8:2; 22:8
20:16 [j] Ex 23:31-33; Nu 21:2-3; Dt 7:2; Jos 11:14

[a] *17* The Hebrew term refers to the irrevocable giving over of things or persons to the LORD, often by totally destroying them.

Dt 20:4 ❖ What does victory look like in the battles we face? How do we know God is the One who gives the victory?

19:15–21 The guidelines regarding judicial proceedings flesh out the eighth commandment. The text divides into two uneven parts: (1) a call for more than one witness (v. 15) and (2) dealing with malicious witnesses (vv. 16–21).

✣ **19:15–21** We must insist that society and the courts uphold the rights of all who come before them.

20:1–4 If Yahweh defeated the Egyptians, he will overcome the Canaanites as well.

20:5–9 Verse 5 introduces officials charged with mustering the troops, keeping records, and screening recruits.

20:8–9 After those with legitimate reasons have returned home, the officials are to appoint "commanders" (v. 9) to lead the army into battle.

20:10–15 A targeted town is offered a chance to surrender. If they reject peace, then Israel may go on the offensive (v. 12).

20:16–18 Moses calls for the total destruction of Canaanite cities and their dedication to Yahweh. This policy secured their absolute transfer to the divine sphere and secured Israel's survival.

your God has commanded you. 18 Otherwise, they will teach you to follow all the detestable things they do in worshiping their gods,[k] and you will sin[l] against the LORD your God.

19 When you lay siege to a city for a long time, fighting against it to capture it, do not destroy its trees by putting an ax to them, because you can eat their fruit. Do not cut them down. Are the trees people, that you should besiege them?[a] 20 However, you may cut down trees that you know are not fruit trees and use them to build siege works until the city at war with you falls.

Atonement for an Unsolved Murder

21 If someone is found slain, lying in a field in the land the LORD your God is giving you to possess, and it is not known who the killer was, 2 your elders and judges shall go out and measure the distance from the body to the neighboring towns. 3 Then the elders of the town nearest the body shall take a heifer that has never been worked and has never worn a yoke 4 and lead it down to a valley that has not been plowed or planted and where there is a flowing stream. There in the valley they are to break the heifer's neck. 5 The Levitical priests shall step forward, for the LORD your God has chosen them to minister and to pronounce blessings[m] in the name of the LORD and to decide all cases of dispute and assault.[n] 6 Then all the elders of the town nearest the body shall wash their hands[o] over the heifer whose neck was broken in the valley, 7 and they shall declare: "Our hands did not shed this blood, nor did our eyes see it done. 8 Accept this atonement for your people Israel, whom you have redeemed, LORD, and do not hold your people guilty of the blood of an innocent person." Then the bloodshed will be atoned for,[p] 9 and you will have purged[q] from yourselves the guilt of shedding innocent blood, since you have done what is right in the eyes of the LORD.

Marrying a Captive Woman

10 When you go to war against your enemies and the LORD your God delivers them into your hands[r] and you take captives, 11 if you notice among the captives a beautiful woman and are attracted to her, you may take her as your wife. 12 Bring her into your home and have her shave her head,[s] trim her nails 13 and put aside the clothes she was wearing when captured. After she has lived in your house and mourned her father and mother for a full month,[t] then you may go to her and be her husband and she shall be your wife. 14 If you are not pleased with her, let her go wherever she wishes. You must not sell her or treat her as a slave, since you have dishonored her.[u]

The Right of the Firstborn

15 If a man has two wives, and he loves one but not the other, and both bear him sons but the firstborn is the son of the wife he does not love,[v] 16 when he wills his property to his sons, he must not give the rights of the firstborn to the son of the wife he loves in preference to his actual firstborn, the son of the wife he does not love.[w] 17 He must acknowledge the son of his unloved wife as the firstborn by giving him a double share of all he has. That son is the first sign of his father's strength.[x] The right of the firstborn belongs to him.[y]

20:18 [k] Ex 34:16; Dt 7:4; 12:30-31 [l] Ex 23:33
21:5 [m] 1Ch 23:13 [n] Dt 17:8-11
21:6 [o] Mt 27:24
21:8 [p] Nu 35:33-34
21:9 [q] Dt 19:13
21:10 [r] Jos 21:44
21:12 [s] Lev 14:9; Nu 6:9
21:13 [t] Ps 45:10
21:14 [u] Ge 34:2
21:15 [v] Ge 29:33
21:16 [w] 1Ch 26:10
21:17 [x] Ge 49:3 [y] Ge 25:31

[a] 19 Or *down to use in the siege, for the fruit trees are for the benefit of people.*

20:19–20 Since the Israelites eventually will occupy the city, it is contrary to self-interest to ruthlessly cut down the orchards around the city.

✣ **20:1–20** The church is engaged in warfare; this conflict is not against flesh and blood, but against principalities and powers arrayed against God and his church (Eph 6:12).

21:1–9 This unit shows how to resolve the spiritual crisis that an unsolved murder creates for the community. The purpose is to identify the community that should take responsibility for purging Israel of its bloodguilt. The elders represent the town and nation in the atonement ceremony. As in Moses' intercessory prayers, the elders of the town are to cast themselves and their people on the mercy of Yahweh.

✣ **21:1–9** This short unit recognizes the corporate responsibility of the entire community for the crimes of individuals. Unless the community responds to the crime, the guilt of the individual rests on the heads of all.

21:10–14 The description sounds calloused, but Moses' outlook is hinted at by the final clause (v. 14). The quarantine respects the woman's ties to her family and psychological health. He concludes with a rationale for the compassionate treatment of war brides even in divorce.

21:15–17 Moses prohibits husbands from making

A Rebellious Son

18If someone has a stubborn and rebellious son who does not obey his father
and mother[z] and will not listen to them
when they discipline him, 19his father
and mother shall take hold of him and
bring him to the elders at the gate of
his town. 20They shall say to the elders,
"This son of ours is stubborn and rebellious. He will not obey us. He is a glutton
and a drunkard." 21Then all the men of
his town are to stone him to death. You
must purge the evil[a] from among you.
All Israel will hear of it and be afraid.[b]

Various Laws

22If someone guilty of a capital offense[c] is put to death and their body is

21:18 [z] Pr 1:8; Isa 30:1; Eph 6:1-3
21:21 [a] Dt 19:19; 1Co 5:13* [b] Dt 13:11
21:22 [c] Dt 22:26; Mk 14:64; Ac 23:29

---

children pay for strained relationships between parents.

21:18–21 The description suggests the parents have done all they could to raise their son properly, but he is incorrigible.

21:22–23 How should we interpret the phrase "a curse of God"? The NIV's "[he] is under God's curse" has dominated Christian interpretation.

MAJOR SOCIAL CONCERNS IN THE COVENANT

1.	**Personhood**	Everyone's person is to be secure (Ex 20:13; Dt 5:17; Ex 21:16-21, 26-32; Lev 19:14; Dt 24:7; 27:18).
2.	**False Accusation**	Everyone is to be secure against slander and false accusation (Ex 20:16; Dt 5:20; Ex 23:1-3, 6-8; Lev 19:16; Dt 19:15-21).
3.	**Women**	No woman is to be taken advantage of within her subordinate status in society (Ex 21:7-11, 20, 26-32; 22:16-17; Nu 27:1-11; 36:1-12; Dt 21:10-14; 22:13-30; 24:1-5).
4.	**Punishment**	Punishment for wrongdoing shall not be excessive so that the culprit is dehumanized (Dt 25:1-3).
5.	**Dignity**	Every Israelite's dignity and right to be God's servant are to be honored and safeguarded (Ex 21:2, 5-6; Lev 25; Dt 15:12-18).
6.	**Inheritance**	Every Israelite's inheritance in the promised land is to be secure (Lev 25; Nu 27:5-7; 36:1-9; Dt 25:5-10).
7.	**Property**	Everyone's property is to be secure (Ex 20:15; Dt 5:19; Ex 21:33-36; 22:1-15; 23:4-5; Lev 19:35-36; Dt 22:1-4; 25:13-15).
8.	**Fruit of Labor**	All people are to receive the fruit of their labors (Lev 19:13; Dt 24:14; 25:4).
9.	**Fruit of the Ground**	Everyone is to share the fruit of the ground (Ex 23:10-11; Lev 19:9-10; 23:22; 25:3-55; Dt 14:28-29; 24:19-21).
10.	**Rest on Sabbath**	Everyone, down to the humblest servant and the resident foreigner, is to share in the weekly rest of God's Sabbath (Ex 20:8-11; Dt 5:12-15; Ex 23:12).
11.	**Marriage**	The marriage relationship is to be kept inviolate (Ex 20:14; Dt 5:18; see also Lev 18:6-23; 20:10-21; Dt 22:13-30).
12.	**Exploitation**	No one, however disabled, impoverished or powerless, is to be oppressed or exploited but is to be cared for (Ex 22:21-27; Lev 19:14, 33-34; 25:35-36; Dt 23:19; 24:6, 12-15, 17; 27:18).
13.	**Fair Trial**	Everyone is to have free access to the courts and is to be afforded a fair trial (Ex 23:6-8; Lev 19:15; Dt 1:17; 10:17-18; 16:18-20; 17:8-13; 19:15-21).
14.	**Social Order**	Every person's God-given place in the social order is to be honored (Ex 20:12; Dt 5:16; Ex 21:15, 17; 22:28; Lev 19:3, 32; 20:9; Dt 17:8-13; 21:15-21; 27:16).
15.	**Law**	No one shall be above the law, not even the king (Dt 17:18-20).
16.	**Animals**	Concern for the welfare of other creatures is to be extended to the animal world (Ex 23:5, 11; Lev 25:7; Dt 22:4, 6-7; 25:4).

exposed on a pole, 23you must not leave
the body hanging on the pole overnight.[d]
Be sure to bury it that same day, because
anyone who is hung on a pole is under
God's curse.[e] You must not desecrate[f] the
land the LORD your God is giving you as
an inheritance.

22 If you see your fellow Israelite's
ox or sheep straying, do not ignore it but be sure to take it back to its
owner.[g] 2If they do not live near you or
if you do not know who owns it, take it
home with you and keep it until they
come looking for it. Then give it back.
3Do the same if you find their donkey
or cloak or anything else they have lost.
Do not ignore it.

4If you see your fellow Israelite's donkey[h] or ox fallen on the road, do not ignore it. Help the owner get it to its feet.

5A woman must not wear men's clothing, nor a man wear women's clothing,
for the LORD your God detests anyone
who does this.

6If you come across a bird's nest beside the road, either in a tree or on the
ground, and the mother is sitting on the
young or on the eggs, do not take the
mother with the young.[i] 7You may take
the young, but be sure to let the mother
go, so that it may go well with you and
you may have a long life.[j]

8When you build a new house, make
a parapet around your roof so that you
may not bring the guilt of bloodshed on
your house if someone falls from the
roof.

9Do not plant two kinds of seed in your
vineyard;[k] if you do, not only the crops
you plant but also the fruit of the vineyard will be defiled.[a]

21:23 [d]Jos 8:29; 10:27; Jn 19:31 [e]Gal 3:13* [f]Lev 18:25; Nu 35:34
22:1 [g]Ex 23:4-5
22:4 [h]Ex 23:5
22:6 [i]Lev 22:28
22:7 [j]Dt 4:40
22:9 [k]Lev 19:19

Dt 21:23 ❖ Why is it significant that Christ died in a way that this verse describes as "under God's curse" (see also Gal 3:13)? How does this deepen our understanding of Christ's death?

Dt 22:4 ❖ What are some practical ways we can help those who find themselves in need?

10Do not plow with an ox and a donkey
yoked together.[l]

11Do not wear clothes of wool and linen
woven together.[m]

12Make tassels on the four corners of
the cloak you wear.[n]

Marriage Violations

13If a man takes a wife and, after sleeping with her[o], dislikes her 14and slanders
her and gives her a bad name, saying,
"I married this woman, but when I approached her, I did not find proof of her
virginity," 15then the young woman's father and mother shall bring to the town
elders at the gate proof that she was a
virgin. 16Her father will say to the elders,
"I gave my daughter in marriage to this
man, but he dislikes her. 17Now he has
slandered her and said, 'I did not find
your daughter to be a virgin.' But here
is the proof of my daughter's virginity."
Then her parents shall display the cloth
before the elders of the town, 18and the
elders[p] shall take the man and punish
him. 19They shall fine him a hundred
shekels[b] of silver and give them to the
young woman's father, because this man
has given an Israelite virgin a bad name.

22:10 [l]2Co 6:14
22:11 [m]Lev 19:19
22:12 [n]Nu 15:37-41; Mt 23:5
22:13 [o]Dt 24:1
22:18 [p]Ex 18:21

[a] 9 Or *be forfeited to the sanctuary* [b] 19 That is, about 2 1/2 pounds or about 1.2 kilograms

---

✣ **21:10–23** In Gal 3:13 Paul states that we all are sinners deserving the criminal's death of Dt 21:22–23. Paul also declares the glorious gospel that Christ himself became the curse that we all deserve by virtue of our sinful state.

22:1–4 The covenant love Israelites have for their neighbors extends to livestock.
22:5 To wear anything associated with the opposite gender blurs established boundaries.
22:6–8 The scope of righteous living extends to respect for the life of helpless creatures.
22:8 Without a barrier around the perimeter, people could step off the roof and fall to their deaths.
22:10 At issue is forcing a bond between clean and unclean, which happens when ox and donkey are yoked together.
22:11 These instructions draw boundaries between what is appropriate for deity (mixtures of all sorts) and mortals (no mixtures at all).
22:12 The tassels reminded the one who wore them and outsiders of Israel's special status.

✣ **22:1–12** The blurring of boundaries symbolizes chaos. The lives of the redeemed should be characterized by order and resistance to everything that causes disintegration of that order in one's life.

22:13–19 The primary issue here is the innocence of the wife.

She shall continue to be his wife; he must
not divorce her as long as he lives.
20If, however, the charge is true and no
proof of the young woman's virginity can
be found, 21she shall be brought to the
door of her father's house and there the
men of her town shall stone her to death.
She has done an outrageous thing[q] in
Israel by being promiscuous while still
in her father's house. You must purge
the evil from among you.
22If a man is found sleeping with another man's wife, both the man who slept
with her and the woman must die.[r] You
must purge the evil from Israel.
23If a man happens to meet in a town
a virgin pledged to be married and he
sleeps with her, 24you shall take both of
them to the gate of that town and stone
them to death — the young woman because she was in a town and did not
scream for help, and the man because
he violated another man's wife. You must
purge the evil from among you.[s]
25But if out in the country a man happens to meet a young woman pledged
to be married and rapes her, only the
man who has done this shall die. 26Do
nothing to the woman; she has committed no sin deserving death. This
case is like that of someone who attacks and murders a neighbor, 27for the
man found the young woman out in
the country, and though the betrothed
woman screamed, there was no one to
rescue her.
28If a man happens to meet a virgin
who is not pledged to be married and
rapes her and they are discovered,[t] 29he
shall pay her father fifty shekels[a] of silver. He must marry the young woman,
for he has violated her. He can never divorce her as long as he lives.
30A man is not to marry his father's
wife; he must not dishonor his father's
bed.[b][u]

22:21 [q] Ge 34:7; Dt 13:5; 23:17-18; Jdg 20:6; 2Sa 13:12
22:22 [r] Lev 20:10; Jn 8:5
22:24 [s] ver 21-22; 1Co 5:13*
22:28 [t] Ex 22:16

Exclusion From the Assembly

23[c] No one who has been emasculated
by crushing or cutting may enter
the assembly of the LORD.
2No one born of a forbidden marriage[d]
nor any of their descendants may enter
the assembly of the LORD, not even in
the tenth generation.
3No Ammonite or Moabite or any of
their descendants may enter the assembly of the LORD, not even in the tenth
generation.[v] 4For they did not come to
meet you with bread and water on your
way when you came out of Egypt, and
they hired Balaam[w] son of Beor from
Pethor in Aram Naharaim[e] to pronounce
a curse on you. 5However, the LORD your
God would not listen to Balaam but
turned the curse[x] into a blessing for you,
because the LORD your God loves you.
6Do not seek a treaty of friendship with
them as long as you live.[y]
7Do not despise an Edomite, for the
Edomites are related to you.[z] Do not despise an Egyptian, because you resided as
foreigners in their country.[a] 8The third
generation of children born to them may
enter the assembly of the LORD.

Uncleanness in the Camp

9When you are encamped against your
enemies, keep away from everything
impure. 10If one of your men is unclean
because of a nocturnal emission, he is
to go outside the camp and stay there.[b]
11But as evening approaches he is to wash

22:30 [u] Lev 18:8; 20:11; Dt 27:20; 1Co 5:1
23:3 [v] Ne 13:2
23:4 [w] Nu 22:5-6; 23:7; 2Pe 2:15
23:5 [x] Pr 26:2
23:6 [y] Ezr 9:12
23:7 [z] Ge 25:26; Ob 10,12 [a] Ex 22:21; 23:9; Lev 19:34; Dt 10:19
23:10 [b] Lev 15:16

[a] *29* That is, about 1 1/4 pounds or about 575 grams [b] *30* In Hebrew texts this verse (22:30) is numbered 23:1. [c] In Hebrew texts 23:1-25 is numbered 23:2-26. [d] *2* Or *one of illegitimate birth* [e] *4* That is, Northwest Mesopotamia

22:20-21 Radical surgery is required to remove those who flaunt contempt for the covenant.
22:23-27 These instructions subdivide into a primary case (vv. 23-24) and a counter case (vv. 25-27). The primary case (vv. 23-24) assumes she did not cry out, which suggests the sexual act was consensual. The counter case (vv. 25-27) highlights the role of the woman as victim.
22:28-29 The payment is considered the bride price, since she becomes his wife.

22:13-30 The narratives of the OT expose the problems with patriarchy. The solution offered by Scripture is not to replace these structures with egalitarianism but to plead for transformed leadership.

23:1-6 "Emasculated" (v. 1) seems to refer to offspring of cultic prostitutes.
23:7-8 The conciliatory tone toward Edom may reflect Yahweh's special interest in the direct descendants of Abraham.
23:9 The Israelites must guard themselves against spiritual danger.
23:10-13 The association of seminal emissions and feces suggests its impurity derives from its source inside the body.

himself, and at sunset he may return to the camp.

12 Designate a place outside the camp where you can go to relieve yourself. 13 As part of your equipment have something to dig with, and when you relieve yourself, dig a hole and cover up your excrement. 14 For the LORD your God moves[c] about in your camp to protect you and to deliver your enemies to you. Your camp must be holy,[d] so that he will not see among you anything indecent and turn away from you.

Miscellaneous Laws

15 If a slave has taken refuge with you, do not hand them over to their master.[e] 16 Let them live among you wherever they like and in whatever town they choose. Do not oppress[f] them.

17 No Israelite man[g] or woman is to become a shrine prostitute.[h] 18 You must not bring the earnings of a female prostitute or of a male prostitute[a] into the house of the LORD your God to pay any vow, because the LORD your God detests them both.

19 Do not charge a fellow Israelite interest, whether on money or food or anything else that may earn interest.[i] 20 You may charge a foreigner interest, but not a fellow Israelite, so that the LORD your God may bless[j] you in everything you put your hand to in the land you are entering to possess.

21 If you make a vow to the LORD your God, do not be slow to pay it, for the LORD your God will certainly demand it of you and you will be guilty of sin.[k] 22 But if you refrain from making a vow, you will not be guilty. 23 Whatever your lips utter you must be sure to do, because you made your vow freely to the LORD your God with your own mouth.

24 If you enter your neighbor's vineyard, you may eat all the grapes you want, but do not put any in your basket. 25 If you enter your neighbor's grainfield, you may pick kernels with your hands, but you must not put a sickle to their standing grain.[l]

24 If a man marries a woman who becomes displeasing to him[m] because he finds something indecent about her, and he writes her a certificate of divorce,[n] gives it to her and sends her from his house, 2 and if after she leaves his house she becomes the wife of another man, 3 and her second husband dislikes her and writes her a certificate of divorce, gives it to her and sends her from his house, or if he dies, 4 then her first husband, who divorced her, is not allowed to marry her again after she has been defiled. That would be detestable in the eyes of the LORD. Do not bring sin upon the land the LORD[o] your God is giving you as an inheritance.

5 If a man has recently married, he must not be sent to war or have any other duty laid on him. For one year he is to be

23:14 [c] Lev 26:12 [d] Ex 3:5
23:15 [e] 1Sa 30:15
23:16 [f] Ex 22:21
23:17 [g] Ge 19:25; 2Ki 23:7 [h] Lev 19:29; Dt 22:21
23:19 [i] Ex 22:25; Lev 25:35-37
23:20 [j] Dt 15:10; 28:12
23:21 [k] Nu 30:1-2; Ecc 5:4-5; Mt 5:33
23:25 [l] Mt 12:1; Mk 2:23; Lk 6:1
24:1 [m] Dt 22:13 [n] Mt 5:31*; 19:7-9; Mk 10:4-5
24:4 [o] Jer 3:1

[a] 18 Hebrew *of a dog*

> **Dt 23:24-25** ❖ How much generosity is it fair to expect from others? At what point might we go too far?

23:14 These clauses portray a divine commander inspecting troops.

> **23:1-14** Those who oppose covenantal standards by conduct, compromise, or indifference and opposition to the work of God are not at home in the church.

23:15-16 By calling the Israelites to provide safe haven for fugitives, Moses treats the entire land as holy ground.
23:17-18 The prostitution here reflects an imitation of foreign cults.
23:19-20 Moses makes interest-free loans a responsibility for those with means rather than a right of the poor.
23:21-23 Moses highlights three fundamental principles underlying vows. (1) Vows are optional. (2) Once made, they must be kept. (3) Yahweh holds persons accountable for their vows.
23:24-25 Moses' instructions are simultaneously realistic and responsible.

> **23:15-25** The harsh disposition toward unregistered aliens violates the spirit of Moses.

24:1a-c "Something indecent" (v. 1b) is best interpreted as some menstrual irregularity.
24:2-3 Moses imagines two developments that could complicate the woman's life.
24:4 Moses declares the original husband may not change his mind and remarry his wife.
24:5 Husbands of new brides are exempt from all communal obligations so they may devote themselves to the happiness of their wives.

> **24:1-5** The culture of divorce in the West offers Christians an opportunity to be countercultural. To the extent that we model biblical

free to stay at home and bring happiness
to the wife he has married.[p]
6 Do not take a pair of millstones — not
even the upper one — as security for a
debt, because that would be taking a person's livelihood as security.
7 If someone is caught kidnapping a
fellow Israelite and treating or selling
them as a slave, the kidnapper must die.[q]
You must purge the evil from among
you.
8 In cases of defiling skin diseases,[a] be
very careful to do exactly as the Levitical priests instruct you. You must follow
carefully what I have commanded them.[r]
9 Remember what the LORD your God did
to Miriam along the way after you came
out of Egypt.[s]
10 When you make a loan of any kind to
your neighbor, do not go into their house
to get what is offered to you as a pledge.
11 Stay outside and let the neighbor to
whom you are making the loan bring
the pledge out to you. 12 If the neighbor is
poor, do not go to sleep with their pledge
in your possession. 13 Return their cloak
by sunset[t] so that your neighbor may
sleep in it. Then they will thank you, and
it will be regarded as a righteous act in
the sight of the LORD your God.[u]
14 Do not take advantage of a hired
worker who is poor and needy, whether
that worker is a fellow Israelite or a foreigner residing in one of your towns.[v]
15 Pay them their wages each day before
sunset, because they are poor[w] and are
counting on it.[x] Otherwise they may cry
to the LORD against you, and you will be
guilty of sin.[y]
16 Parents are not to be put to death
for their children, nor children put to
death for their parents; each will die for
their own sin.[z]

24:5 [p] Dt 20:7
24:7 [q] Ex 21:16
24:8 [r] Lev 13:1-46; 14:2
24:9 [s] Nu 12:10
24:13 [t] Ex 22:26 [u] Dt 6:25; Da 4:27
24:14 [v] Lev 25:35-43; Dt 15:12-18
24:15 [w] Jer 22:13 [x] Lev 19:13 [y] Dt 15:9; Jas 5:4
24:16 [z] 2Ki 14:6; 2Ch 25:4; Jer 31:29-30; Eze 18:20

Dt 24:14-22 ❖ Who are the poor around us that we can help? How can we practice these instructions from Deuteronomy today?

17 Do not deprive the foreigner or the
fatherless of justice,[a] or take the cloak of
the widow as a pledge. 18 Remember that
you were slaves in Egypt and the LORD
your God redeemed you from there. That
is why I command you to do this.
19 When you are harvesting in your
field and you overlook a sheaf, do not
go back to get it.[b] Leave it for the foreigner, the fatherless and the widow, so
that the LORD your God may bless[c] you
in all the work of your hands. 20 When
you beat the olives from your trees, do
not go over the branches a second time.[d]
Leave what remains for the foreigner, the
fatherless and the widow. 21 When you
harvest the grapes in your vineyard, do
not go over the vines again. Leave what
remains for the foreigner, the fatherless
and the widow. 22 Remember that you
were slaves in Egypt. That is why I command you to do this.[e]
25 When people have a dispute, they
are to take it to court and the judges will decide the case,[f] acquitting the
innocent and condemning the guilty.[g] 2 If
the guilty person deserves to be beaten,[h]
the judge shall make them lie down and
have them flogged in his presence with
the number of lashes the crime deserves,
3 but the judge must not impose more
than forty lashes.[i] If the guilty party is
flogged more than that, your fellow Israelite will be degraded in your eyes.[j]

24:17 [a] Dt 1:17; 10:17-18; 16:19
24:19 [b] Lev 19:9; 23:22 [c] Pr 19:17
24:20 [d] Lev 19:10
24:22 [e] ver 18
25:1 [f] Dt 19:17 [g] Dt 1:16-17
25:2 [h] Lk 12:47-48
25:3 [i] 2Co 11:24 [j] Job 18:3

[a] 8 The Hebrew word for *defiling skin diseases,* traditionally translated "leprosy," was used for various diseases affecting the skin.

---

ideals of marriage, we declare to the world the kind of relationship people may enjoy with God through Jesus Christ.

24:6 To demand a millstone as a pledge meant depriving a household of the means for making food.
24:8-9 Moses appeals for compliance by linking the voices of Levitical priests with his own and ultimately with God's voice.
24:10-13 The illustration in vv. 10-13 gives additional instructions on how creditors may lend to the poor.
24:14-15 Moses addresses the temptation of employers to exploit their workers.
24:17-18 Moses returns to the primary issue of promoting the well-being of foreign visitors, the fatherless, and widows.
24:19-22 These instructions build on earlier legislation (Lev 19:9-10; 23:22) seeking to instill a spirit of generosity that goes far beyond the original legislation.

24:6-22 This chapter highlights the responsibility of the community to care for individuals with limited means for taking care of themselves.

25:1-3 The specific instructions on the execution of the punishment in vv. 2-3 reflect keen concern for justice for both parties.

4Do not muzzle an ox while it is treading out the grain.[k]
5If brothers are living together and
one of them dies without a son, his widow must not marry outside the family.
Her husband's brother shall take her
and marry her and fulfill the duty of a
brother-in-law to her.[l] 6The first son she
bears shall carry on the name of the dead
brother so that his name will not be blotted out from Israel.[m]
7However, if a man does not want to
marry his brother's wife, she shall go
to the elders at the town gate and say,
"My husband's brother refuses to carry
on his brother's name in Israel. He will
not fulfill the duty of a brother-in-law to
me."[n] 8Then the elders of his town shall
summon him and talk to him. If he persists in saying, "I do not want to marry
her," 9his brother's widow shall go up to
him in the presence of the elders, take
off one of his sandals,[o] spit in his face
and say, "This is what is done to the man
who will not build up his brother's family
line." 10That man's line shall be known in
Israel as The Family of the Unsandaled.
11If two men are fighting and the wife
of one of them comes to rescue her husband from his assailant, and she reaches
out and seizes him by his private parts,
12you shall cut off her hand. Show her
no pity.[p]
13Do not have two differing weights in
your bag — one heavy, one light.[q] 14Do
not have two differing measures in your
house — one large, one small. 15You must
have accurate and honest weights and
measures, so that you may live long[r] in
the land the LORD your God is giving you.
16For the LORD your God detests anyone
who does these things, anyone who deals
dishonestly.[s]
17Remember what the Amalekites[t] did
to you along the way when you came out
of Egypt. 18When you were weary and
worn out, they met you on your journey
and attacked all who were lagging behind; they had no fear of God.[u] 19When
the LORD your God gives you rest from all
the enemies around you in the land he is
giving you to possess as an inheritance,
you shall blot out the name of Amalek[v]
from under heaven. Do not forget!

25:4 [k] Pr 12:10; 1Co 9:9*; 1Ti 5:18*
25:5 [l] Mt 22:24; Mk 12:19; Lk 20:28
25:6 [m] Ge 38:9; Ru 4:5,10
25:7 [n] Ru 4:1-2, 5-6
25:9 [o] Ru 4:7-8,11
25:12 [p] Dt 19:13
25:13 [q] Lev 19:35-37; Pr 11:1; Eze 45:10; Mic 6:11
25:15 [r] Ex 20:12
25:16 [s] Pr 11:1
25:17 [t] Ex 17:8
25:18 [u] Ps 36:1; Ro 3:18
25:19 [v] 1Sa 15:2-3
26:2 [w] Ex 22:29; 23:16,19; Nu 18:13; Pr 3:9 [x] Dt 12:5

Dt 25:4 ❖ Why is God concerned with the just treatment of animals? How should Christians treat all God's living creatures?

Dt 26:2 ❖ What are the "firstfruits" that we can offer to God? How can our firstfruits be used to bless others?

Firstfruits and Tithes

26 When you have entered the land
the LORD your God is giving you
as an inheritance and have taken possession of it and settled in it, 2take some
of the firstfruits[w] of all that you produce
from the soil of the land the LORD your
God is giving you and put them in a
basket. Then go to the place the LORD
your God will choose as a dwelling for
his Name[x] 3and say to the priest in office
at the time, "I declare today to the LORD
your God that I have come to the land the
LORD swore to our ancestors to give us."
4The priest shall take the basket from
your hands and set it down in front of
the altar of the LORD your God. 5Then you
shall declare before the LORD your God:

25:5–10 A levirate marriage is a legally sanctioned union between a widow without offspring and the brother of the deceased. The brother-in-law offered her economic security and physical protection. However, the primary concern here is securing descendants for her deceased husband.
25:11–12 From the grammar and syntax of the passage as well as the severity of the punishment, her action is deliberate.
25:13–16 This text warns against having two sets of weights, the lighter one to be used when calculating payment and the heavier to calculate commodities or money one was owed.

✣ **25:1–16** Honest and fair calculation of transactions and scrupulous payment of debts should be the hallmark of those who claim to be God's people. Christians should stand out for the integrity with which they conduct their business.

25:17–19 Moses' rhetorical style cites three actions by the Amalekites against Israel that demand response.

✣ **25:17–19** Under no circumstances are these policies to be generalized into policies of genocide or justification for revenge.

26:2–3 Whereas outside Israel harvest festivals celebrated the fertility of the land, here the occasion is transformed into a commemoration of Yahweh's gift of the land itself.
26:4 The priest's actions declare that Yahweh has accepted the worshiper's devotion.
26:5–10a Many have recognized that what follows is an early creedal statement cast in celebrative prose.

BLESSINGS AND CURSES

BLESSINGS	CURSES
As Israel was faithful to their covenant calling, the Lord promised to pour out blessings.	Failure to keep covenant meant severe consequences, curses rather than blessings.
Rainfall rather than drought	Fear, disease and despair
Fruitful marriages, fields and orchards	Labor without fruit
Stored food preserved till new food could be stored; more than enough to eat	Military incursions and resultant deprivations—destroyed cities, murdered children, enslavement
Peace in the land; freedom from fear of war or wild animals	Idols destroyed and high places desecrated
Military strength and victory	Desolation
Freedom from slavery	Exile
The Lord's continued presence	Faintness of heart

"My father was a wandering Aramean,[y]
and he went down into Egypt with a few
people[z] and lived there and became a
great nation, powerful and numerous.
6But the Egyptians mistreated us and
made us suffer,[a] subjecting us to harsh
labor. 7Then we cried out to the LORD,
the God of our ancestors, and the LORD
heard our voice[b] and saw[c] our misery, toil
and oppression. 8So the LORD brought us
out of Egypt with a mighty hand and an
outstretched arm, with great terror and
with signs and wonders.[d] 9He brought
us to this place and gave us this land,
a land flowing with milk and honey;[e]
10and now I bring the firstfruits of the
soil that you, LORD, have given me." Place
the basket before the LORD your God and
bow down before him. 11Then you and
the Levites[f] and the foreigners residing
among you shall rejoice[g] in all the good
things the LORD your God has given to
you and your household.
12When you have finished setting aside
a tenth[h] of all your produce in the third
year, the year of the tithe,[i] you shall give
it to the Levite, the foreigner, the fatherless and the widow, so that they may eat
in your towns and be satisfied. 13Then say
to the LORD your God: "I have removed
from my house the sacred portion and
have given it to the Levite, the foreigner,
the fatherless and the widow, according
to all you commanded. I have not turned
aside from your commands nor have I
forgotten any of them.[j] 14I have not eaten
any of the sacred portion while I was in
mourning, nor have I removed any of it
while I was unclean,[k] nor have I offered
any of it to the dead. I have obeyed the
LORD my God; I have done everything
you commanded me. 15Look down from
heaven,[l] your holy dwelling place, and
bless your people Israel and the land you
have given us as you promised on oath to
our ancestors, a land flowing with milk
and honey."

26:5 [y]Hos 12:12 [z]Ge 43:1-2; 45:7,11; 46:27; Dt 10:22
26:6 [a]Ex 1:11,14
26:7 [b]Ex 2:23-25 [c]Ex 3:9
26:8 [d]Dt 4:34
26:9 [e]Ex 3:8
26:11 [f]Dt 12:7 [g]Dt 16:11
26:12 [h]Lev 27:30 [i]Nu 18:24; Dt 14:28-29; Heb 7:5,9
26:13 [j]Ps 119:141, 153,176
26:14 [k]Lev 7:20; Hos 9:4
26:15 [l]Isa 63:15; Zec 2:13

Follow the LORD's Commands

16The LORD your God commands you
this day to follow these decrees and laws;
carefully observe them with all your

26:10b–11 Having presented his tithe, the man is to invite his household, as well as Levites and foreigners from his town, to join him in celebrating.
26:13–15 Once a gift had been designated, its sanctity must be scrupulously guarded. The ritual concludes with a prayer (v. 15).

26:16–19 These verses summarize key theological issues of the book and provide a hinge between Moses' lengthy exposition of the specific stipulations of the covenant and his description of the consequences of the nation's response in ch. 28.

26:1–15 God's people are a thankful people. This text reminds readers of every age of the importance of specific celebrations devoted to thanksgiving.

26:16–19 Jesus reminds his disciples that his Father is glorified in this—that the disciples prove to be his disciples by bearing much fruit (Jn 15:2–5).

heart and with all your soul.[m] 17You have
declared this day that the LORD is your
God and that you will walk in obedience
to him, that you will keep his decrees,
commands and laws — that you will listen to him. 18And the LORD has declared
this day that you are his people, his treasured possession[n] as he promised, and
that you are to keep all his commands.
19He has declared that he will set you in
praise, fame and honor high above all
the nations[o] he has made and that you
will be a people holy[p] to the LORD your
God, as he promised.

The Altar on Mount Ebal

27 Moses and the elders of Israel
commanded the people: "Keep
all these commands that I give you today. 2When you have crossed the Jordan
into the land the LORD your God is giving you, set up some large stones and
coat them with plaster.[q] 3Write on them
all the words of this law when you have
crossed over to enter the land the LORD
your God is giving you, a land flowing
with milk and honey,[r] just as the LORD,
the God of your ancestors, promised you.
4And when you have crossed the Jordan,
set up these stones on Mount Ebal,[s] as I
command you today, and coat them with
plaster. 5Build there an altar[t] to the LORD
your God, an altar of stones. Do not use
any iron tool[u] on them. 6Build the altar of
the LORD your God with fieldstones and
offer burnt offerings on it to the LORD
your God. 7Sacrifice fellowship offerings
there, eating them and rejoicing in the
presence of the LORD your God. 8And you
shall write very clearly all the words of
this law on these stones you have set up."

Curses From Mount Ebal

9Then Moses and the Levitical priests
said to all Israel, "Be silent, Israel, and
listen! You have now become the people
of the LORD your God.[v] 10Obey the LORD
your God and follow his commands and
decrees that I give you today."
11On the same day Moses commanded
the people:
12When you have crossed the Jordan,
these tribes shall stand on Mount Gerizim[w] to bless the people: Simeon, Levi,
Judah, Issachar, Joseph and Benjamin.[x]
13And these tribes shall stand on Mount
Ebal to pronounce curses: Reuben, Gad,
Asher, Zebulun, Dan and Naphtali.
14The Levites shall recite to all the people of Israel in a loud voice:

15"Cursed is anyone who makes
an idol[y] — a thing detestable to the
LORD, the work of skilled hands —
and sets it up in secret."
Then all the people shall
say, "Amen!"
16"Cursed is anyone who dishonors their father or mother."[z]
Then all the people shall
say, "Amen!"
17"Cursed is anyone who moves
their neighbor's boundary stone."[a]
Then all the people shall
say, "Amen!"
18"Cursed is anyone who leads the
blind astray on the road."[b]
Then all the people shall
say, "Amen!"
19"Cursed is anyone who withholds justice from the foreigner,[c]
the fatherless or the widow."[d]
Then all the people shall
say, "Amen!"
20"Cursed is anyone who sleeps

26:16 [m] Dt 4:29
26:18 [n] Ex 6:7; 19:5; Dt 7:6; 14:2; 28:9
26:19 [o] Dt 4:7-8; 28:1,13,44 [p] Ex 19:6; Dt 7:6; 1Pe 2:9
27:2 [q] Jos 8:31
27:3 [r] Dt 26:9
27:4 [s] Dt 11:29
27:5 [t] Jos 8:31 [u] Ex 20:25
27:9 [v] Dt 26:18
27:12 [w] Dt 11:29 [x] Jos 8:35
27:15 [y] Ex 20:4; 34:17; Lev 19:4; 26:1; Dt 4:16,23; 5:8; Isa 44:9
27:16 [z] Ex 20:12; 21:17; Lev 19:3; 20:9
27:17 [a] Dt 19:14; Pr 22:28
27:18 [b] Lev 19:14
27:19 [c] Ex 22:21; Dt 24:19 [d] Dt 10:18

Dt 27:14-26 ❖ Why is it important to remember the consequences of evil? How does this benefit a person's faith?

27:2-3 Moses announces that the rituals to follow are to be performed "on the day" (alternate translation; NIV "when") the Israelites cross the Jordan into the land that Yahweh has promised them.
27:4-13 Verses 5-7 instruct the people on the rituals to be performed on Mount Ebal. Whereas the Sinai event had sealed the two-way, mutual relationship between people and deity, the third party (the land) was missing. The purpose of this ritual was to celebrate the completion of the triangle (Yahweh, Israel, the promised land). Mounts Ebal and Gerizim are present not only as witnesses to the blessings and curses, but as the repository of the Torah itself (the inscribed pillars), and the land of Canaan (now Israel) is also engaged as a vital partner in the covenantal relationship.
27:14-26 Verses 15-26 consist of twelve curses, which has led scholars to refer to this text as the "Dodecalogue" ("the twelve words").

✚ **27:1-26** These rituals signify Israel's security and hope in Yahweh. Of course, the peace they celebrate is made possible only through the work of Jesus Christ, whose sacrificial work underlies all these rituals.

with his father's wife, for he dishonors his father's bed."[e]
Then all the people shall
say, "Amen!"
21"Cursed is anyone who has sexual relations with any animal."[f]
Then all the people shall
say, "Amen!"
22"Cursed is anyone who sleeps
with his sister, the daughter of
his father or the daughter of his
mother."[g]
Then all the people shall
say, "Amen!"
23"Cursed is anyone who sleeps
with his mother-in-law."[h]
Then all the people shall
say, "Amen!"
24"Cursed is anyone who kills[i]
their neighbor secretly."
Then all the people shall
say, "Amen!"
25"Cursed is anyone who accepts
a bribe to kill an innocent person."[j]
Then all the people shall
say, "Amen!"
26"Cursed is anyone who does not
uphold the words of this law by carrying them out."[k]
Then all the people shall
say, "Amen!"

Blessings for Obedience

28 If you fully obey the LORD your
God and carefully follow all his
commands[l] I give you today, the LORD
your God will set you high above all the
nations on earth.[m] 2All these blessings
will come on you[n] and accompany you
if you obey the LORD your God:

3You will be blessed[o] in the city
and blessed in the country.[p]
4The fruit of your womb will be
blessed, and the crops of your land
and the young of your livestock —
the calves of your herds and the
lambs of your flocks.[q]
5Your basket and your kneading
trough will be blessed.

27:20 [e] Lev 18:7; Dt 22:30
27:21 [f] Lev 18:23
27:22 [g] Lev 18:9; 20:17
27:23 [h] Lev 20:14
27:24 [i] Lev 24:17; Nu 35:31
27:25 [j] Ex 23:7-8; Dt 10:17; Eze 22:12
27:26 [k] Jer 11:3; Gal 3:10*
28:1 [l] Ex 15:26; Lev 26:3; Dt 7:12-26 [m] Dt 26:19
28:2 [n] Zec 1:6
28:3 [o] Ps 128:1, 4 [p] Ge 39:5
28:4 [q] Ge 49:25; Pr 10:22

Dt 28:8 ❖ How have you experienced God's physical blessings in your life? How have you thanked God for these blessings?

6You will be blessed when you
come in and blessed when you go
out.[r]

7The LORD will grant that the enemies
who rise up against you will be defeated before you. They will come at you
from one direction but flee from you
in seven.[s]
8The LORD will send a blessing on your
barns and on everything you put your
hand to. The LORD your God will bless
you in the land he is giving you.
9The LORD will establish you as his
holy people,[t] as he promised you on
oath, if you keep the commands of the
LORD your God and walk in obedience to
him. 10Then all the peoples on earth will
see that you are called by the name[u] of
the LORD, and they will fear you. 11The
LORD will grant you abundant prosperity — in the fruit of your womb, the young
of your livestock and the crops of your
ground — in the land he swore to your
ancestors to give you.[v]
12The LORD will open the heavens, the
storehouse of his bounty, to send rain[w]
on your land in season and to bless all
the work of your hands. You will lend
to many nations but will borrow from
none.[x] 13The LORD will make you the
head, not the tail. If you pay attention
to the commands of the LORD your God
that I give you this day and carefully follow them, you will always be at the top,
never at the bottom. 14Do not turn aside
from any of the commands I give you today, to the right or to the left,[y] following
other gods and serving them.

Curses for Disobedience

15However, if you do not obey[z] the
LORD your God and do not carefully follow all his commands and decrees I am

28:6 [r] Ps 121:8
28:7 [s] Lev 26:8, 17
28:9 [t] Ex 19:6; Dt 7:6
28:10 [u] 2Ch 7:14
28:11 [v] Dt 30:9; Pr 10:22
28:12 [w] Lev 26:4 [x] Dt 15:3, 6
28:14 [y] Dt 5:32
28:15 [z] Lev 26:14

28:1-2, 15 The words for "blessings" and "curses" are concepts portrayed as animate beings that come upon their targets.
28:3-6, 16-19 While Israel's neighbors looked to fertility gods for their economic security, Israel's well-being depends on their fidelity to Yahweh.
28:7-14 Within this relationship Israel will never be able to claim credit for the blessings they enjoy, but they will be held fully liable if the blessings do not materialize. Israel was chosen to bear the name of their divine Redeemer and of the Creator of all nations (26:19). They represent humanity in microcosm, exercising authority on Yahweh's behalf and evoking the response of awe from those over whom they exercise dominion.

giving you today, all these curses will
come on you and overtake you:[a]

16You will be cursed in the city
and cursed in the country.
17Your basket and your kneading
trough will be cursed.
18The fruit of your womb will be
cursed, and the crops of your land,
and the calves of your herds and the
lambs of your flocks.
19You will be cursed when you
come in and cursed when you go
out.

20The LORD will send on you curses,[b]
confusion and rebuke[c] in everything you
put your hand to, until you are destroyed
and come to sudden ruin[d] because of the
evil you have done in forsaking him.[a]
21The LORD will plague you with diseases until he has destroyed you from the
land you are entering to possess.[e] 22The
LORD will strike you with wasting disease, with fever and inflammation, with
scorching heat and drought,[f] with blight
and mildew, which will plague you until
you perish.[g] 23The sky over your head
will be bronze, the ground beneath you
iron.[h] 24The LORD will turn the rain of
your country into dust and powder; it
will come down from the skies until you
are destroyed.
25The LORD will cause you to be defeated before your enemies. You will come at
them from one direction but flee from
them in seven,[i] and you will become a
thing of horror to all the kingdoms on
earth.[j] 26Your carcasses will be food for
all the birds and the wild animals, and
there will be no one to frighten them
away.[k] 27The LORD will afflict you with the
boils of Egypt[l] and with tumors, festering
sores and the itch, from which you cannot be cured. 28The LORD will afflict you
with madness, blindness and confusion
of mind. 29At midday you will grope[m]
about like a blind person in the dark. You
will be unsuccessful in everything you
do; day after day you will be oppressed
and robbed, with no one to rescue you.
30You will be pledged to be married to
a woman, but another will take her and
rape her.[n] You will build a house, but
you will not live in it.[o] You will plant a
vineyard, but you will not even begin to
enjoy its fruit.[p] 31Your ox will be slaughtered before your eyes, but you will eat
none of it. Your donkey will be forcibly
taken from you and will not be returned.
Your sheep will be given to your enemies,
and no one will rescue them. 32Your sons
and daughters will be given to another
nation,[q] and you will wear out your eyes
watching for them day after day, powerless to lift a hand. 33A people that you
do not know will eat what your land and
labor produce, and you will have nothing but cruel oppression all your days.[r]
34The sights you see will drive you mad.
35The LORD will afflict your knees and
legs with painful boils[s] that cannot be
cured, spreading from the soles of your
feet to the top of your head.
36The LORD will drive you and the king[t]
you set over you to a nation unknown
to you or your ancestors.[u] There you will
worship other gods, gods of wood and
stone.[v] 37You will become a thing of horror, a byword and an object of ridicule
among all the peoples where the LORD
will drive you.[w]
38You will sow much seed in the field
but you will harvest little,[x] because locusts will devour[y] it. 39You will plant
vineyards and cultivate them but you
will not drink the wine or gather the
grapes, because worms will eat them.[z]
40You will have olive trees throughout
your country but you will not use the oil,
because the olives will drop off.[a] 41You

[a] 20 Hebrew *me*

28:15 [a] Jos 23:15; Da 9:11; Mal 2:2
28:20 [b] Mal 2:2 [c] Isa 51:20; 66:15 [d] Dt 4:26
28:21 [e] Lev 26:25; Jer 24:10
28:22 [f] Lev 26:16 [g] Am 4:9
28:23 [h] Lev 26:19
28:25 [i] Isa 30:17 [j] Jer 15:4; 24:9; Eze 23:46
28:26 [k] Jer 7:33; 16:4; 34:20
28:27 [l] ver 60-61; 1Sa 5:6
28:29 [m] Job 5:14; Isa 59:10
28:30 [n] Job 31:10; Jer 8:10 [o] Am 5:11 [p] Jer 12:13
28:32 [q] ver 41
28:33 [r] Jer 5:15-17
28:35 [s] ver 27
28:36 [t] 2Ki 17:4, 6; 24:12,14; 25:7,11 [u] Jer 16:13 [v] Dt 4:28
28:37 [w] Jer 24:9
28:38 [x] Mic 6:15; Hag 1:6,9 [y] Joel 1:4
28:39 [z] Isa 5:10; 17:10-11
28:40 [a] Mic 6:15

28:20–46 Verses 20 and 45–46 frame the first volley of woes, announcing the issues involved.
28:21–26 The first alarm involves three agents of disaster: the plague (vv. 21–22a), crop failure (vv. 22b–24), and military defeat (vv. 25–26). In v. 22 Moses becomes more specific, listing seven afflictions with which Yahweh will strike his people.
28:27–34 The curses in vv. 27–29a, 34 threaten the personal health of the Israelites. Verse 28 may refer to the bewilderment that attends the kinds of disasters described in this chapter. Verse 29 illustrates how these mental disorders manifest themselves. Verse 29b announces the theme of utter futility, which is then developed by means of a series of futility curses involving grievous domestic and economic abuses.
28:35–44 Like the first alarm, this paragraph subdivides into three parts, dealing successively with illnesses (v. 35), military defeat (vv. 36–37), and famine (vv. 38–42). It ends with a warning of the internal social effects of Israel's calamities (vv. 43–44). In vv. 45–46 Moses provides a summary conclusion to the litany of disasters described in vv. 20–44.

will have sons and daughters but you will not keep them, because they will go into captivity.[b] 42Swarms of locusts will take over all your trees and the crops of your land.

43The foreigners who reside among you will rise above you higher and higher, but you will sink lower and lower.[c] 44They will lend to you, but you will not lend to them.[d] They will be the head, but you will be the tail.[e]

45All these curses will come on you. They will pursue you and overtake you until you are destroyed,[f] because you did not obey the LORD your God and observe the commands and decrees he gave you. 46They will be a sign and a wonder to you and your descendants forever.[g] 47Because you did not serve[h] the LORD your God joyfully and gladly[i] in the time of prosperity, 48therefore in hunger and thirst, in nakedness and dire poverty, you will serve the enemies the LORD sends against you. He will put an iron yoke[j] on your neck until he has destroyed you.

49The LORD will bring a nation against you from far away, from the ends of the earth,[k] like an eagle[l] swooping down, a nation whose language you will not understand, 50a fierce-looking nation without respect for the old[m] or pity for the young. 51They will devour the young of your livestock and the crops of your land until you are destroyed. They will leave you no grain, new wine or olive oil, nor any calves of your herds or lambs of your flocks until you are ruined.[n] 52They will lay siege to all the cities throughout your land until the high fortified walls in which you trust fall down. They will besiege all the cities throughout the land the LORD your God is giving you.[o]

53Because of the suffering your enemy will inflict on you during the siege, you will eat the fruit of the womb, the flesh of the sons and daughters the LORD your God has given you.[p] 54Even the most gentle and sensitive man among you will have no compassion on his own brother or the wife he loves or his surviving children, 55and he will not give to one of them any of the flesh of his children that he is eating. It will be all he has left because of the suffering your enemy will inflict on you during the siege of all your cities. 56The most gentle and sensitive[q] woman among you — so sensitive and gentle that she would not venture to touch the ground with the sole of her foot — will begrudge the husband she loves and her own son or daughter 57the afterbirth from her womb and the children she bears. For in her dire need she intends to eat them secretly because of the suffering your enemy will inflict on you during the siege of your cities.

58If you do not carefully follow all the words of this law, which are written in this book, and do not revere[r] this glorious and awesome name[s] — the LORD your God — 59the LORD will send fearful plagues on you and your descendants, harsh and prolonged disasters, and severe and lingering illnesses. 60He will bring on you all the diseases of Egypt[t] that you dreaded, and they will cling to you. 61The LORD will also bring on you every kind of sickness and disaster not recorded in this Book of the Law, until you are destroyed.[u] 62You who were as numerous as the stars in the sky[v] will be left but few in number, because you did not obey the LORD your God. 63Just as it pleased[w] the LORD to make you prosper and increase in number, so it will please[x] him to ruin and destroy you. You will be uprooted[y] from the land you are entering to possess.

64Then the LORD will scatter[z] you among all nations,[a] from one end of the earth to the other. There you will worship other gods — gods of wood and stone, which neither you nor your ancestors have known. 65Among those

28:41 [b] ver 32
28:43 [c] ver 13
28:44 [d] ver 12 [e] ver 13
28:45 [f] ver 15
28:46 [g] Isa 8:18; Eze 14:8
28:47 [h] Dt 32:15 [i] Ne 9:35
28:48 [j] Jer 28:13-14
28:49 [k] Jer 5:15; 6:22 [l] La 4:19; Hos 8:1
28:50 [m] Isa 47:6
28:51 [n] ver 33
28:52 [o] Jer 10:18; Zep 1:14-16,17
28:53 [p] Lev 26:29; 2Ki 6:28-29; Jer 19:9; La 2:20; 4:10
28:56 [q] ver 54
28:58 [r] Mal 1:14 [s] Ex 6:3
28:60 [t] ver 27
28:61 [u] Dt 4:25-26
28:62 [v] Dt 4:27; 10:22; Ne 9:23
28:63 [w] Jer 32:41 [x] Pr 1:26 [y] Jer 12:14; 45:4
28:64 [z] Lev 26:33; Dt 4:27 [a] Ne 1:8

28:47–48 Moses begins by declaring that ultimately Israel itself will be responsible for the threatened disasters (v. 47). Because the Israelites refuse to serve their benefactor, Yahweh will provide alternative masters (v. 49).
28:49–52 Moses frames this paragraph with declarations of Yahweh's involvement in Israel's demise (vv. 49, 52).
28:53–57 Borrowing images from Lev 26:27–29, this paragraph opens with a general thesis statement followed by two frightful scenes of cannibalism.
28:58–68 Moses opens this section with a reminder to his immediate audience that the horrific fate described in this chapter is inevitable if they do not live scrupulously according to "all the words of this Torah that are written in this document" (v. 58; alternate translation) and if they "do not revere this glorious and awesome name—the LORD your God" (v. 58). Moses' warning of Israel's doom concludes in v. 68 with the reversal of Israel's history—back in Egypt.

nations you will find no repose, no resting place for the sole of your foot. There the LORD will give you an anxious mind, eyes weary with longing, and a despairing heart.[b] 66You will live in constant suspense, filled with dread both night and day, never sure of your life. 67In the morning you will say, "If only it were evening!" and in the evening, "If only it were morning!" — because of the terror that will fill your hearts and the sights that your eyes will see.[c] 68The LORD will send you back in ships to Egypt on a journey I said you should never make again. There you will offer yourselves for sale to your enemies as male and female slaves, but no one will buy you.

Renewal of the Covenant

29[a] These are the terms of the covenant the LORD commanded Moses to make with the Israelites in Moab, in addition to the covenant he had made with them at Horeb.[d]

2Moses summoned all the Israelites and said to them:

Your eyes have seen all that the LORD did in Egypt to Pharaoh, to all his officials and to all his land.[e] 3With your own eyes you saw those great trials, those signs and great wonders.[f] 4But to this day the LORD has not given you a mind that understands or eyes that see or ears that hear.[g] 5Yet the LORD says, "During the forty years that I led you through the wilderness, your clothes did not wear out, nor did the sandals on your feet.[h] 6You ate no bread and drank no wine or other fermented drink. I did this so that you might know that I am the LORD your God."[i]

7When you reached this place, Sihon[j] king of Heshbon and Og king of Bashan came out to fight against us, but we defeated them.[k] 8We took their land and gave it as an inheritance to the Reubenites, the Gadites and the half-tribe of Manasseh.[l]

9Carefully follow[m] the terms of this covenant, so that you may prosper in everything you do.[n] 10All of you are standing today in the presence of the LORD your God — your leaders and chief men, your elders and officials, and all the other men of Israel, 11together with your children and your wives, and the foreigners living in your camps who chop your wood and carry your water.[o] 12You are standing here in order to enter into a covenant with the LORD your God, a covenant the LORD is making with you this day and sealing with an oath, 13to confirm you this day as his people,[p] that he may be your God[q] as he promised you and as he swore to your fathers, Abraham, Isaac and Jacob. 14I am making this covenant,[r] with its oath, not only with you 15who are standing here with us today in the presence of the LORD our God but also with those who are not here today.[s]

16You yourselves know how we lived in Egypt and how we passed through the countries on the way here. 17You saw among them their detestable images and idols of wood and stone, of silver and gold.[t] 18Make sure there is no man or woman, clan or tribe among you today whose heart turns away from the LORD our God to go and worship the gods of

28:65 [b] Lev 26:16,36
28:67 [c] ver 34; Job 7:4
29:1 [d] Dt 5:2-3
29:2 [e] Ex 19:4
29:3 [f] Dt 4:34; 7:19
29:4 [g] Isa 6:10; Ac 28:26-27; Ro 11:8*; Eph 4:18
29:5 [h] Dt 8:4
29:6 [i] Dt 8:3
29:7 [j] Dt 2:32; 3:1 [k] Nu 21:21-24,33-35
29:8 [l] Nu 32:33; Dt 3:12-13
29:9 [m] Dt 4:6; Jos 1:7 [n] 1Ki 2:3
29:11 [o] Jos 9:21,23,27
29:13 [p] Dt 28:9 [q] Ge 17:7; Ex 6:7
29:14 [r] Jer 31:31
29:15 [s] Ac 2:39
29:17 [t] Dt 28:36

[a] In Hebrew texts 29:1 is numbered 28:69, and 29:2-29 is numbered 29:1-28.

29:1 The characterization of the covenant as "that which Yahweh commanded Moses to make [lit. "cut"]" (alternate translation) highlights Moses' role as authorized interpreter. When Moses "cuts this covenant," he supervises new ceremonies whereby the new generation commits itself to the old covenant.

> ✜ **28:1—29:1** Like the Israelites of the OT, Christians may be tempted to presume upon the grace of God and take their standing with him for granted. These warnings provide an antidote to apostasy and rebellion.

29:2-9 Since most in the assembly did not witness the nation's rescue from Egypt, Moses draws them into Yahweh's actions by speaking as if they were eyewitnesses to those events. In v. 9, Moses challenges his audience to continue to prove their faith in Yahweh, keeping the words of this covenant by doing them.

29:10-13 Moses provides the longest catalog of participants in a formal religious event in the entire OT.

29:14-17 The commitments made here by Israel and Yahweh were binding for future generations. In vv. 16-17 Moses digresses with reflections on the Israelites' life in Egypt and crossing through other nations on their journey.

29:18-21 Moses warns the present and future generations that, unlike the gods of the nations, Yahweh will tolerate no rivals (v. 18). In vv. 20-21 Moses speaks of refusing forgiveness. By his idolatry and defiant response to warnings, the idolater has sealed his own fate.

those nations; make sure there is no root among you that produces such bitter poison.[u]

19 When such a person hears the words of this oath and they invoke a blessing on themselves, thinking, "I will be safe, even though I persist in going my own way," they will bring disaster on the watered land as well as the dry. 20 The LORD will never be willing to forgive them; his wrath and zeal[v] will burn[w] against them. All the curses written in this book will fall on them, and the LORD will blot[x] out their names from under heaven. 21 The LORD will single them out from all the tribes of Israel for disaster, according to all the curses of the covenant written in this Book of the Law.

22 Your children who follow you in later generations and foreigners who come from distant lands will see the calamities that have fallen on the land and the diseases with which the LORD has afflicted it.[y] 23 The whole land will be a burning waste[z] of salt[a] and sulfur — nothing planted, nothing sprouting, no vegetation growing on it. It will be like the destruction of Sodom and Gomorrah,[b] Admah and Zeboyim, which the LORD overthrew in fierce anger. 24 All the nations will ask: "Why has the LORD done this to this land?[c] Why this fierce, burning anger?"

25 And the answer will be: "It is because this people abandoned the covenant of the LORD, the God of their ancestors, the covenant he made with them when he brought them out of Egypt. 26 They went off and worshiped other gods and bowed down to them, gods they did not know, gods he had not given them. 27 Therefore the LORD's anger burned against this land, so that he brought on it all the curses written in this book.[d] 28 In furious anger and in great wrath the LORD uprooted[e] them from their land and thrust them into another land, as it is now."

29 The secret things belong to the LORD our God, but the things revealed belong to us and to our children forever, that we may follow all the words of this law.

29:18 [u] Dt 11:16; Heb 12:15
29:20 [v] Eze 23:25 [w] Ps 74:1; 79:5 [x] Ex 32:33; Dt 9:14
29:22 [y] Jer 19:8
29:23 [z] Isa 34:9 [a] Jer 17:6 [b] Ge 19:24,25; Zep 2:9
29:24 [c] 1Ki 9:8; Jer 22:8-9
29:27 [d] Da 9:11, 13,14
29:28 [e] 1Ki 14:15; 2Ch 7:20; Ps 52:5; Pr 2:22
30:1 [f] ver 15, 19; Dt 11:26 [g] Lev 26:40-45; Dt 28:64; 29:28; 1Ki 8:47
30:2 [h] Dt 4:30; Ne 1:9
30:3 [i] Ps 126:4 [j] Ps 147:2; Jer 32:37; Eze 34:13 [k] Jer 29:14
30:4 [l] Ne 1:8-9; Isa 43:6
30:5 [m] Jer 29:14
30:6 [n] Dt 10:16; Jer 32:39

Dt 29:29 ❖ What might be the "secret things" that belong to God? Why are they secret? How can we learn to be content with those things that God has chosen to reveal?

Dt 30:4 ❖ When have you felt that you are too far from God for his promises to reach you? How can this verse provide comfort in such situations?

Prosperity After Turning to the LORD

30 When all these blessings and curses[f] I have set before you come on you and you take them to heart wherever the LORD your God disperses you among the nations,[g] 2 and when you and your children return[h] to the LORD your God and obey him with all your heart and with all your soul according to everything I command you today, 3 then the LORD your God will restore your fortunes[a][i] and have compassion on you and gather[j] you again from all the nations where he scattered you.[k] 4 Even if you have been banished to the most distant land under the heavens, from there the LORD your God will gather you and bring you back.[l] 5 He will bring[m] you to the land that belonged to your ancestors, and you will take possession of it. He will make you more prosperous and numerous than your ancestors. 6 The LORD your God will circumcise your hearts and the hearts of your descendants,[n] so that you may love him with all your heart and with all your soul, and live. 7 The LORD

[a] 3 Or *will bring you back from captivity*

29:25-28 Moses does not identify the speakers behind the third speech. The speech itself divides into two virtually equal parts, the first (vv. 25-26) dealing with human causes behind Israel's fate and the second (vv. 26-27) with Yahweh's response.

✜ **29:2-28** This chapter highlights the tragic consequences of infidelity to Israel's purpose and mission. Yahweh chose Israel to be a kingdom of priests, a holy people among the nations, intervening on their behalf before him and serving as his agents of revelation and blessing.

30:1-3 When Moses' predictions have been fulfilled, Yahweh's disposition toward Israel will change; he will show compassion to them.

30:4-8 Yahweh will cause the population to exceed that of their ancestors before the exile. Moses declares that Yahweh will secure permanent and total devotion through circumcising the hearts of those whom he brings back from the exile and of their descendants. Moses' optimism presupposes a divine act of heart circumcision.

your God will put all these curses on your enemies who hate and persecute you.[o] 8You will again obey the LORD and follow all his commands I am giving you today. 9Then the LORD your God will make you most prosperous in all the work of your hands and in the fruit of your womb, the young of your livestock and the crops of your land.[p] The LORD will again delight in you and make you prosperous, just as he delighted in your ancestors, 10if you obey the LORD your God and keep his commands and decrees that are written in this Book of the Law and turn to the LORD your God with all your heart and with all your soul.[q]

The Offer of Life or Death

11Now what I am commanding you today is not too difficult for you or beyond your reach.[r] 12It is not up in heaven, so that you have to ask, "Who will ascend into heaven to get it and proclaim it to us so we may obey it?"[s] 13Nor is it beyond the sea, so that you have to ask, "Who will cross the sea to get it and proclaim it to us so we may obey it?" 14No, the word is very near you; it is in your mouth and in your heart so you may obey it.

15See, I set before you today life and prosperity, death and destruction.[t] 16For I command you today to love the LORD your God, to walk in obedience to him, and to keep his commands, decrees and laws; then you will live and increase, and the LORD your God will bless you in the land you are entering to possess.

17But if your heart turns away and you are not obedient, and if you are drawn away to bow down to other gods and worship them, 18I declare to you this day that you will certainly be destroyed.[u] You will not live long in the land you are crossing the Jordan to enter and possess.

19This day I call the heavens and the earth as witnesses against you[v] that I have set before you life and death, blessings and curses.[w] Now choose life, so that you and your children may live 20and that you may love[x] the LORD your God, listen to his voice, and hold fast to him. For the LORD is your life,[y] and he will give you many years in the land he swore to give to your fathers, Abraham, Isaac and Jacob.

Joshua to Succeed Moses

31 Then Moses went out and spoke these words to all Israel: 2"I am now a hundred and twenty years old[z] and I am no longer able to lead you.[a] The LORD has said to me, 'You shall not cross the Jordan.'[b] 3The LORD your God himself will cross[c] over ahead of you.[d] He will destroy these nations before you, and you will take possession of their land. Joshua also will cross[e] over ahead of you, as the LORD said. 4And the LORD will do to them what he did to Sihon and Og, the kings of the Amorites, whom he destroyed along with their land. 5The LORD will deliver[f] them to you, and you must do to them all that I have commanded you. 6Be strong and courageous.[g] Do not be afraid or terrified[h] because of them, for the LORD your God goes with you;[i] he will never leave you[j] nor forsake[k] you."

7Then Moses summoned Joshua and said[l] to him in the presence of all Israel, "Be strong and courageous, for you

30:7 [o] Dt 7:15
30:9 [p] Dt 28:11; Jer 31:28; 32:41
30:10 [q] Dt 4:29
30:11 [r] Isa 45:19, 23
30:12 [s] Ro 10:6*
30:15 [t] Dt 11:26
30:18 [u] Dt 8:19
30:19 [v] Dt 4:26 [w] ver 1
30:20 [x] Dt 6:5; 10:20 [y] Ps 27:1; Jn 11:25
31:2 [z] Dt 34:7 [a] Nu 27:17; 1Ki 3:7 [b] Dt 3:23, 26
31:3 [c] Nu 27:18 [d] Dt 9:3 [e] Dt 3:28
31:5 [f] Dt 7:2
31:6 [g] Jos 10:25; 1Ch 22:13 [h] Dt 7:18 [i] Dt 1:29; 20:4 [j] Jos 1:5 [k] Heb 13:5*
31:7 [l] Dt 1:38; 3:28

30:9–10 Moses closes with one more reminder that although the covenantal relationships will be restored, the Israelites must return to Yahweh with their entire being.

29:29—30:10 The work of Christ, whose mission was established before the foundation of the world (1Pe 1:18–21), provides the basis for all of God's covenants. Through Christ's work the holiness of God is satisfied and his wrath toward us is lifted and replaced with mercy.

30:11–14 Moses reiterates that the demands of covenant relationship are not unknowable, unreasonable, incomprehensible, or impossible. Verse 14 indicates the revelation is extremely near, in their mouths and in their minds/hearts.

30:15–20 Israel obeys the commands by loving Yahweh their God, by walking in his ways, and by keeping his commands. "Life" (v. 19) means the effects of sin and premature death are staved off. But it also means dwelling in the land that Yahweh had promised on oath to give to their ancestors.

30:11–20 People's standing before God and their ultimate destiny is in their own hands. Such is the gospel according to Moses, and such is the gospel according to Jesus (Mt 7:13). This is not only a warning against choosing the wrong path that leads to death and destruction but also an invitation to choose the path of life. Thanks be to God!

31:1–6 Moses announces his inability to lead the people any longer. The people will be led by Yahweh and his designated agent (v. 3a, d). Moses concludes with an impassioned appeal to his people to put full confidence in Yahweh (v. 6).

31:7–8 Moses publicly passes the mantle so that Joshua will be seen as the divinely chosen

must go with this people into the land
that the LORD swore to their ancestors
to give them, and you must divide it
among them as their inheritance. 8The
LORD himself goes before you and will be
with you;[m] he will never leave you nor
forsake you. Do not be afraid; do not be
discouraged."

Public Reading of the Law

9So Moses wrote down this law and
gave it to the Levitical priests, who carried[n] the ark of the covenant of the LORD,
and to all the elders of Israel. 10Then Moses commanded them: "At the end of every seven years, in the year for canceling
debts,[o] during the Festival of Tabernacles,[p] 11when all Israel comes to appear[q]
before the LORD your God at the place
he will choose, you shall read this law[r]
before them in their hearing. 12Assem-
ble the people — men, women and children, and the foreigners residing in your
towns — so they can listen and learn[s] to
fear the LORD your God and follow carefully all the words of this law. 13Their children,[t] who do not know this law, must
hear it and learn to fear the LORD your
God as long as you live in the land you
are crossing the Jordan to possess."

Israel's Rebellion Predicted

14The LORD said to Moses, "Now the day
of your death[u] is near. Call Joshua and
present yourselves at the tent of meeting, where I will commission him." So
Moses and Joshua came and presented
themselves at the tent of meeting.
15Then the LORD appeared at the tent
in a pillar of cloud, and the cloud stood
over the entrance to the tent.[v] 16And the
LORD said to Moses: "You are going to
rest with your ancestors, and these people will soon prostitute[w] themselves to
the foreign gods of the land they are entering. They will forsake[x] me and break
the covenant I made with them. 17And in
that day I will become angry[y] with them
and forsake[z] them; I will hide[a] my face
from them, and they will be destroyed.
Many disasters and calamities will come
on them, and in that day they will ask,
'Have not these disasters come on us because our God is not with us?'[b] 18And I
will certainly hide my face in that day
because of all their wickedness in turning to other gods.
19"Now write down this song and teach
it to the Israelites and have them sing it,
so that it may be a witness for me against
them. 20When I have brought them into
the land flowing with milk and honey,
the land I promised on oath to their ancestors,[c] and when they eat their fill and
thrive, they will turn to other gods[d] and
worship them, rejecting me and breaking
my covenant.[e] 21And when many disasters and calamities come on them,[f] this
song will testify against them, because
it will not be forgotten by their descendants. I know what they are disposed to
do,[g] even before I bring them into the
land I promised them on oath." 22So Moses wrote[h] down this song that day and
taught it to the Israelites.
23The LORD gave this command[i] to
Joshua son of Nun: "Be strong and courageous,[j] for you will bring the Israelites
into the land I promised them on oath,
and I myself will be with you."

31:8 [m] Ex 13:21; 33:14
31:9 [n] ver 25; Nu 4:15; Jos 3:3
31:10 [o] Dt 15:1 [p] Lev 23:34
31:11 [q] Dt 16:16 [r] Jos 8:34-35; 2Ki 23:2
31:12 [s] Dt 4:10
31:13 [t] Dt 11:2; Ps 78:6-7
31:14 [u] Nu 27:13; Dt 32:49-50
31:15 [v] Ex 33:9
31:16 [w] Jdg 2:12 [x] Jdg 10:6,13
31:17 [y] Jdg 2:14, 20 [z] Jdg 6:13; 2Ch 15:2 [a] Dt 32:20; Isa 1:15; 8:17 [b] Nu 14:42
31:20 [c] Dt 6:10-12 [d] Dt 32:15-17 [e] ver 16
31:21 [f] ver 17 [g] Hos 5:3
31:22 [h] ver 19
31:23 [i] ver 7 [j] Jos 1:6

Dt 31:10 ❖ What is our habit for regularly reading or hearing God's instruction? How has this pattern blessed us?

---

successor. Verse 8 offers Joshua the grounds for courage: Yahweh goes before him and guarantees his presence.

31:9–13 The narrative preamble (v. 9) highlights three specific actions by Moses in relation to the Torah. Moses wrote down this Torah. Moses hands the Torah to the Levitical priests and to all the elders of Israel. Moses charges the Levitical priests and elders to read the Torah regularly before the people.

31:14–15, 23 Yahweh appears in a pillar of cloud, which stands at the doorway of the tent. Verse 23 contains Yahweh's commissioning speech for Joshua, reassuring him that he is the divinely appointed successor.

31:16–18 Yahweh describes the Israelites' anticipated response to Moses' departure with four verbs. (1) They will "rise" (untranslated in the NIV) in rebellion against Yahweh. (2) They will "prostitute themselves" to foreign gods of the land they are entering (v. 16). (3) They will "forsake" Yahweh (v. 16). (4) They will "break the covenant" (v. 16).

The idiom "to hide the face" signifies the withdrawal of favor. The people's demise is indeed the result of divine wrath, but the ultimate cause is their abandoning of the covenant that Yahweh made with them.

31:19–21 Yahweh's primary reason for calling Moses and Joshua to the tent of meeting was to communicate a song, a sort of national anthem. The words of the song will testify to the fidelity and grace of Yahweh and the ingratitude and rebellion of his people. But the song also offers hope.

24After Moses finished writing in a
book the words of this law from beginning to end, 25he gave this command to
the Levites who carried the ark of the
covenant of the LORD: 26"Take this Book
of the Law and place it beside the ark
of the covenant of the LORD your God.
There it will remain as a witness against
you.[k] 27For I know how rebellious and
stiff-necked[l] you are. If you have been
rebellious against the LORD while I am
still alive and with you, how much more
will you rebel after I die! 28Assemble
before me all the elders of your tribes
and all your officials, so that I can speak
these words in their hearing and call the
heavens and the earth to testify against
them.[m] 29For I know that after my death
you are sure to become utterly corrupt[n]
and to turn from the way I have commanded you. In days to come, disaster[o]
will fall on you because you will do evil
in the sight of the LORD and arouse his
anger by what your hands have made."

The Song of Moses

30And Moses recited the words of this
song from beginning to end in the hearing of the whole assembly of Israel:

32 Listen, you heavens,[p] and I will
speak;
hear, you earth, the words of my
mouth.
2Let my teaching fall like rain
and my words descend like dew,[q]
like showers[r] on new grass,
like abundant rain on tender
plants.

3I will proclaim the name of the LORD.[s]
Oh, praise the greatness[t] of our
God!
4He is the Rock,[u] his works are
perfect,[v]
and all his ways are just.
A faithful God[w] who does no wrong,
upright and just is he.

5They are corrupt and not his
children;
to their shame they are a warped
and crooked generation.[x]
6Is this the way you repay[y] the LORD,
you foolish and unwise people?[z]
Is he not your Father,[a] your Creator,[a]
who made you and formed you?[b]

7Remember the days of old;
consider the generations long
past.
Ask your father and he will tell you,
your elders, and they will explain
to you.[c]
8When the Most High gave the
nations their inheritance,
when he divided all mankind,[d]
he set up boundaries for the
peoples
according to the number of the
sons of Israel.[b]
9For the LORD's portion[e] is his people,
Jacob his allotted inheritance.[f]

10In a desert[g] land he found him,
in a barren and howling waste.
He shielded him and cared for him;
he guarded him as the apple of his
eye,[h]
11like an eagle that stirs up its nest
and hovers over its young,[i]
that spreads its wings to catch them
and carries them aloft.
12The LORD alone led him;
no foreign god was with him.[j]

13He made him ride on the heights[k] of
the land

31:26 [k]ver 19
31:27 [l]Ex 32:9; Dt 9:6,24
31:28 [m]Dt 4:26; 30:19; 32:1
31:29 [n]Dt 32:5; Jdg 2:19 [o]Dt 28:15
32:1 [p]Isa 1:2
32:2 [q]Isa 55:11 [r]Ps 72:6
32:3 [s]Ex 33:19 [t]Dt 3:24
32:4 [u]ver 15,18, 30 [v]2Sa 22:31
[w]Dt 7:9
32:5 [x]Dt 31:29
32:6 [y]Ps 116:12 [z]Ps 74:2 [a]Dt 1:31; Isa 63:16 [b]ver 15
32:7 [c]Ex 13:14
32:8 [d]Ge 11:8; Ac 17:26
32:9 [e]Jer 10:16 [f]1Ki 8:51,53
32:10 [g]Jer 2:6 [h]Ps 17:8; Zec 2:8
32:11 [i]Ex 19:4
32:12 [j]ver 39
32:13 [k]Isa 58:14

[a] 6 Or *Father, who bought you* [b] 8 Masoretic Text; Dead Sea Scrolls (see also Septuagint) *sons of God*

31:24–29 Moses designates the Levites as custodians of the document. Moses' instructions concerning the song in vv. 28–29 consist of a command to the Levites to act (v. 28a), the purpose of that action (v. 28b-c), and a rationale for it (v. 29).

✣ **31:1–30** Yahweh always provides the leadership needed to fulfill his calling. The keys to the fulfillment of God's mission remain acceptance of the commission received from him and trust in his promised presence.

32:1–4 Verse 1 suggests this is a song that the world needs to hear. Verse 4 announces the theme of Israel's national anthem.

32:5–6 The first stanza indicates that corruption involves violation of the Supreme Command through idolatry. The rhetorical questions of v. 6 confirm that v. 5 has contrasted the perfections of Yahweh (v. 4) with Israel's deep-seated imperfections.

32:8–9 With elegant parallelism the elders recall the establishment of Israel's special relationship to Yahweh.

32:10–12 If the Israelites ever made it through the desert, it was entirely to Yahweh's credit (v. 12).

32:13–14 The last stanza envisions Yahweh's leading Israel through the promised land in triumphant procession.

CHARACTER OF GOD // GOD IS JUST

Deuteronomy 32:4: "He is the Rock, his works are perfect, and all his ways are just. A faithful God who does no wrong, upright and just is he."

God's justice means that he is equitable in his dealings with people. God is never petty, and he does not play favorites. Being a just judge means that all of God's judgments are right and fair.

The word *justice* is often paired with the word *righteousness*. These words communicate that God is the opposite of corrupt. All of God's ways are perfect, and his ways are just. God treats people fairly, according to what their deeds deserve.

While it is good to have a just judge—corrupt judges pervert and prevent true justice—the fact that God is perfectly just raises a serious problem for sinful humanity. If God is perfectly just and always treats sinners as they deserve, no human could ever stand before him and survive. On its own, God's justice would leave us without hope.

The good news is that while God is perfectly just, he is also full of mercy. Rather than carrying out his justice against humanity as he could have, he bore the penalty for human sin himself in Jesus Christ at the cross. Jesus Christ is God made flesh, the eternal Son of God. In his death, the justice of God meant for human sin was satisfied.

APPLICATION We are made in God's image, and therefore we should also be people of justice. We should not play favorites but rather seek to protect and promote those who suffer mistreatment. Communities that abandon justice become hostile and corrupt. God's justice also reminds us that we are sinners and, by nature, deserve God's wrath (Eph 2:3). Far from leaving us in despair, this awareness should drive us to gratitude for the costly grace of Christ.

and fed him with the fruit of the fields.
He nourished him with honey from the rock,
and with oil[l] from the flinty crag,
14 with curds and milk from herd and flock
and with fattened lambs and goats,
with choice rams of Bashan
and the finest kernels of wheat.[m]
You drank the foaming blood of the grape.[n]

15 Jeshurun[a] grew fat[o] and kicked;
filled with food, they became heavy and sleek.
They abandoned[p] the God who made them
and rejected the Rock[q] their Savior.
16 They made him jealous[r] with their foreign gods
and angered[s] him with their detestable idols.
17 They sacrificed to false gods, which are not God —
gods they had not known,[t]
gods that recently appeared,[u]
gods your ancestors did not fear.
18 You deserted the Rock, who fathered you;
you forgot[v] the God who gave you birth.

19 The LORD saw this and rejected them[w]
because he was angered by his sons and daughters.[x]
20 "I will hide my face[y] from them," he said,
"and see what their end will be;
for they are a perverse generation,[z]
children who are unfaithful.
21 They made me jealous[a] by what is no god
and angered me with their worthless idols.[b]
I will make them envious by those who are not a people;
I will make them angry by a nation that has no understanding.[c]

32:13 [l] Job 29:6
32:14 [m] Ps 81:16; 147:14 [n] Ge 49:11
32:15 [o] Dt 31:20 [p] ver 6; Isa 1:4, 28 [q] ver 4
32:16 [r] 1Co 10:22 [s] Ps 78:58
32:17 [t] Dt 28:64 [u] Jdg 5:8
32:18 [v] Isa 17:10
32:19 [w] Jer 44:21-23 [x] Ps 106:40
32:20 [y] Dt 31:17, 29 [z] ver 5
32:21 [a] 1Co 10:22 [b] 1Ki 16:13, 26 [c] Ro 10:19*

[a] 15 *Jeshurun* means *the upright one,* that is, Israel.

32:15–18 The "straight one" (alternate translation of "Jeshurun") on whom Yahweh had lavished his affection has acted perversely through devotion to other gods. In forgetting Yahweh, the Israelites have truly trampled underfoot his grace.

32:20–21 Verses 20c–21b summarize the basis for Yahweh's rejection of his people. Yahweh declares his intention in rejecting Israel.

22 For a fire will be kindled by my wrath,
one that burns down to the realm of the dead below.[d]
It will devour the earth and its harvests
and set afire the foundations of the mountains.

23 "I will heap calamities[e] on them
and spend my arrows[f] against them.
24 I will send wasting famine against them,
consuming pestilence[g] and deadly plague;[h]
I will send against them the fangs of wild beasts,[i]
the venom of vipers[j] that glide in the dust.
25 In the street the sword will make them childless;
in their homes terror will reign.[k]
The young men and young women will perish,
the infants and those with gray hair.[l]
26 I said I would scatter[m] them
and erase their name from human memory,[n]
27 but I dreaded the taunt of the enemy,
lest the adversary misunderstand
and say, 'Our hand has triumphed;
the LORD has not done all this.' "[o]

28 They are a nation without sense,
there is no discernment in them.
29 If only they were wise and would understand this[p]
and discern what their end will be!
30 How could one man chase a thousand,
or two put ten thousand to flight,[q]
unless their Rock had sold them,
unless the LORD had given them up?[r]
31 For their rock is not like our Rock,
as even our enemies concede.
32 Their vine comes from the vine of Sodom
and from the fields of Gomorrah.
Their grapes are filled with poison,
and their clusters with bitterness.
33 Their wine is the venom of serpents,
the deadly poison of cobras.[s]

34 "Have I not kept this in reserve
and sealed it in my vaults?[t]
35 It is mine to avenge; I will repay.[u]
In due time their foot will slip;[v]
their day of disaster is near
and their doom rushes upon them.[w]"

36 The LORD will vindicate his people
and relent concerning his servants[x]
when he sees their strength is gone
and no one is left, slave or free.[a]
37 He will say: "Now where are their gods,
the rock they took refuge in,[y]
38 the gods who ate the fat of their sacrifices
and drank the wine of their drink offerings?
Let them rise up to help you!
Let them give you shelter!

39 "See now that I myself am he![z]
There is no god besides me.[a]
I put to death and I bring to life,[b]
I have wounded and I will heal,[c]
and no one can deliver out of my hand.[d]
40 I lift my hand to heaven and solemnly swear:
As surely as I live forever,
41 when I sharpen my flashing sword[e]
and my hand grasps it in judgment,
I will take vengeance on my adversaries
and repay those who hate me.[f]

32:22 [d] Ps 18:7-8; Jer 15:14; La 4:11
32:23 [e] Dt 29:21 [f] Ps 7:13; Eze 5:16
32:24 [g] Dt 28:22 [h] Ps 91:6 [i] Lev 26:22 [j] Am 5:18-19
32:25 [k] Eze 7:15 [l] 2Ch 36:17; La 2:21
32:26 [m] Dt 4:27 [n] Ps 34:16
32:27 [o] Isa 10:13
32:29 [p] Dt 5:29; Ps 81:13
32:30 [q] Lev 26:8 [r] Ps 44:12
32:33 [s] Ps 58:4
32:34 [t] Jer 2:22; Hos 13:12
32:35 [u] Ro 12:19*; Heb 10:30* [v] Jer 23:12 [w] Eze 7:8-9
32:36 [x] Dt 30:1-3; Ps 135:14; Joel 2:14
32:37 [y] Jdg 10:14; Jer 2:28
32:39 [z] Isa 41:4 [a] Isa 45:5 [b] 1Sa 2:6; Ps 68:20 [c] Hos 6:1 [d] Ps 50:22
32:41 [e] Isa 34:6; 66:16; Eze 21:9-10 [f] Jer 50:29

[a] 36 Or *and they are without a ruler or leader*

32:22–25 The expression of divine fury begins cosmically (v. 22) and then zeroes in on the Israelites themselves (vv. 23–25).
32:26–35 Verse 27 explains Yahweh was troubled by the possibility that the enemies would draw false conclusions regarding their role in Israel's demise. Were the nations wise, they would get it; that is, grasp their end (cf. v. 20). With the references to Sodom and Gomorrah, Yahweh subtly hinted at the enemies' destiny (v. 29).
32:36–42 While Yahweh and Moses deem judgment to be inevitable, the second half of v. 36 sets the context of Yahweh's change in disposition. Yahweh begins by taunting the Israelites for trusting other gods. In v. 38 the mockery turns to the idols themselves. Yahweh assures Israel that he will deal with their enemies once and for all.

42 I will make my arrows drunk with
blood,[g]
while my sword devours flesh:[h]
the blood of the slain and the
captives,
the heads of the enemy leaders."
43 Rejoice,[i] you nations, with his
people,[*a,b*]
for he will avenge the blood of his
servants;[j]
he will take vengeance on his
enemies
and make atonement for his land
and people.[k]

44 Moses came with Joshua[*c*][l] son of
Nun and spoke all the words of this song
in the hearing of the people. 45 When
Moses finished reciting all these words
to all Israel, 46 he said to them, "Take
to heart all the words I have solemnly
declared to you this day,[m] so that you
may command your children to obey
carefully all the words of this law. 47 They
are not just idle words for you — they
are your life.[n] By them you will live long
in the land you are crossing the Jordan
to possess."

Moses to Die on Mount Nebo

48 On that same day the LORD told Moses, 49 "Go up into the Abarim[o] Range to
Mount Nebo in Moab, across from Jericho, and view Canaan, the land I am giving the Israelites as their own possession.
50 There on the mountain that you have
climbed you will die[p] and be gathered to
your people, just as your brother Aaron
died on Mount Hor and was gathered to
his people. 51 This is because both of you
broke faith with me in the presence of
the Israelites at the waters of Meribah
Kadesh in the Desert of Zin[q] and because
you did not uphold my holiness among
the Israelites.[r] 52 Therefore, you will see
the land only from a distance;[s] you will
not enter[t] the land I am giving to the
people of Israel."

32:42 [g] ver 23 [h] Jer 46:10,14
32:43 [i] Ro 15:10* [j] 2Ki 9:7 [k] Ps 65:3; 85:1; Rev 19:2
32:44 [l] Nu 13:8, 16
32:46 [m] Eze 40:4
32:47 [n] Dt 30:20
32:49 [o] Nu 27:12
32:50 [p] Ge 25:8
32:51 [q] Nu 20:11-13 [r] Nu 27:14
32:52 [s] Dt 34:1-3 [t] Dt 1:37
33:1 [u] Jos 14:6
33:2 [v] Ex 19:18; Ps 68:8 [w] Jdg 5:4 [x] Hab 3:3 [y] Da 7:10; Ac 7:53; Rev 5:11
33:3 [z] Hos 11:1 [a] Dt 14:2 [b] Lk 10:39
33:4 [c] Jn 1:17 [d] Ps 119:111

Dt 32:47 ❖ Do we ever treat God's instruction like "idle words"? How can we treat them like what they are: "[our] life"?

Moses Blesses the Tribes

33:1–29Ref // Ge 49:1–28

33 This is the blessing that Moses the
man of God[u] pronounced on the
Israelites before his death. 2 He said:

"The LORD came from Sinai[v]
and dawned over them from
Seir;[w]
he shone forth from Mount
Paran.[x]
He came with[*d*] myriads of holy ones[y]
from the south, from his
mountain slopes.[*e*]
3 Surely it is you who love[z] the people;
all the holy ones are in your
hand.[a]
At your feet they all bow down,[b]
and from you receive instruction,
4 the law that Moses gave us,[c]
the possession of the assembly of
Jacob.[d]
5 He was king over Jeshurun[*f*]
when the leaders of the people
assembled,
along with the tribes of Israel.

[*a*] 43 Or *Make his people rejoice, you nations* [*b*] 43 Masoretic Text; Dead Sea Scrolls (see also Septuagint) *people, / and let all the angels worship him, /* [*c*] 44 Hebrew *Hoshea,* a variant of *Joshua* [*d*] 2 Or *from* [*e*] 2 The meaning of the Hebrew for this phrase is uncertain. [*f*] 5 *Jeshurun* means *the upright one,* that is, Israel; also in verse 26.

32:43 Israel's national anthem ends on a festive note, appealing to the nations to join in the celebration of Yahweh's gracious acts on behalf of Israel.

32:44–47 Having quoted Israel's anthem, the narrator draws the reader back to the context in which the song was delivered.

32:1–47 An idol is anything that robs God of our devotion and in which we trust, anything to which we look for significance, meaning, and security. The idols of our day include money, pleasure, beauty, science, human reason, the distraction of media, and power.

32:48–52 This paragraph is cast entirely as divine speech.

32:48–52 The privilege of leadership over God's people comes with a heavy burden. From those who have been given much, much is required (Lk 12:48). Those who are called to lead must lead according to the will of the one who has called them.

33:1–5 The preamble (v. 1) reminds readers that what follows is part of Moses' preparations for his death. Moses declares publicly that although he will be departing, Israel's divine King will lead the way into the enemy territory.

6 "Let Reuben live and not die,
nor[a] his people be few."

7 And this he said about Judah:[e]

"Hear, LORD, the cry of Judah;
bring him to his people.
With his own hands he defends his cause.
Oh, be his help against his foes!"

8 About Levi he said:

"Your Thummim and Urim[f] belong
to your faithful servant.
You tested him at Massah;
you contended with him at the waters of Meribah.[g]
9 He said of his father and mother,[h]
'I have no regard for them.'
He did not recognize his brothers
or acknowledge his own children,
but he watched over your word
and guarded your covenant.[i]
10 He teaches your precepts to Jacob
and your law to Israel.[j]
He offers incense before you
and whole burnt offerings on your altar.[k]
11 Bless all his skills, LORD,
and be pleased with the work of his hands.[l]
Strike down those who rise against him,
his foes till they rise no more."

12 About Benjamin he said:

"Let the beloved of the LORD rest
secure in him,[m]
for he shields him all day long,
and the one the LORD loves rests
between his shoulders.[n]"

13 About Joseph[o] he said:

"May the LORD bless his land
with the precious dew from heaven above
and with the deep waters that lie below;[p]
14 with the best the sun brings forth
and the finest the moon can yield;

33:7 [e] Ge 49:10
33:8 [f] Ex 28:30 [g] Ex 17:7
33:9 [h] Ex 32:26-29 [i] Mal 2:5
33:10 [j] Lev 10:11; Dt 31:9-13 [k] Ps 51:19
33:11 [l] 2Sa 24:23
33:12 [m] Dt 12:10 [n] Ex 28:12
33:13 [o] Ge 49:25 [p] Ge 27:28

15 with the choicest gifts of the ancient mountains[q]
and the fruitfulness of the everlasting hills;
16 with the best gifts of the earth and its fullness
and the favor of him who dwelt in the burning bush.[r]
Let all these rest on the head of Joseph,
on the brow of the prince among[b] his brothers.
17 In majesty he is like a firstborn bull;
his horns are the horns of a wild ox.[s]
With them he will gore[t] the nations,
even those at the ends of the earth.
Such are the ten thousands of Ephraim;
such are the thousands of Manasseh."

18 About Zebulun[u] he said:

"Rejoice, Zebulun, in your going out,
and you, Issachar, in your tents.
19 They will summon peoples to the mountain[v]
and there offer the sacrifices of the righteous;[w]
they will feast on the abundance of the seas,[x]
on the treasures hidden in the sand."

20 About Gad[y] he said:

"Blessed is he who enlarges Gad's domain!
Gad lives there like a lion,
tearing at arm or head.
21 He chose the best land for himself;[z]
the leader's portion was kept for him.
When the heads of the people assembled,
he carried out the LORD's righteous will,[a]

33:15 [q] Hab 3:6
33:16 [r] Ex 3:2
33:17 [s] Nu 23:22 [t] 1Ki 22:11; Ps 44:5
33:18 [u] Ge 49:13-15
33:19 [v] Ex 15:17; Isa 2:3 [w] Ps 4:5 [x] Isa 60:5,11
33:20 [y] Ge 49:19
33:21 [z] Nu 32:1-5, 31-32 [a] Jos 4:12; 22:1-3

[a] 6 Or *but let* [b] 16 Or *of the one separated from*

33:6–7 The collection of benedictions opens unannounced with the blessing of Reuben.
33:8–11 The length of the Levites' blessing reflects Moses' relationship to this tribe (Ex 6:16–27) and their spiritual role among the people.
33:12–17 After blessing three tribes descended from Leah, the benediction turns to the tribes descended from Rachel: Benjamin and Joseph.
33:18–21 In vv. 18–25 Moses addresses the six northern tribes in five short fragments. Zebulun and Issachar are to rejoice wherever they are. The enlargement of Gad represents a fulfillment of its name, which means "good fortune."

and his judgments concerning
Israel."

22About Dan[b] he said:

"Dan is a lion's cub,
springing out of Bashan."

23About Naphtali he said:

"Naphtali is abounding with the
favor of the LORD
and is full of his blessing;
he will inherit southward to the
lake."

24About Asher[c] he said:

"Most blessed of sons is Asher;
let him be favored by his brothers,
and let him bathe his feet in oil.[d]
25The bolts of your gates will be iron
and bronze,
and your strength will equal your
days.[e]

26"There is no one like the God of
Jeshurun,[f]
who rides across the heavens to
help you[g]
and on the clouds in his majesty.
27The eternal God is your refuge,[h]
and underneath are the
everlasting arms.
He will drive out your enemies
before you,[i]
saying, 'Destroy them!'[j]
28So Israel will live in safety;[k]
Jacob will dwell[a] secure
in a land of grain and new wine,
where the heavens drop dew.[l]
29Blessed are you, Israel![m]
Who is like you,[n]
a people saved by the LORD?[o]
He is your shield and helper[p]
and your glorious sword.
Your enemies will cower before you,
and you will tread on their
heights.[q]"

33:22 [b] Ge 49:16
33:24 [c] Ge 49:21 [d] Ge 49:20; Job 29:6
33:25 [e] Dt 4:40; 32:47
33:26 [f] Ex 15:11 [g] Ps 104:3
33:27 [h] Ps 90:1 [i] Jos 24:18 [j] Dt 7:2
33:28 [k] Nu 23:9; Jer 23:6 [l] Ge 27:28
33:29 [m] Ps 144:15 [n] Ps 18:44 [o] 2Sa 7:23 [p] Ps 115:9-11 [q] Dt 32:13
34:1 [r] Dt 32:49 [s] Dt 32:52
34:2 [t] Dt 11:24
34:3 [u] Jdg 1:16; 3:13; 2Ch 28:15
34:4 [v] Ge 28:13 [w] Ge 12:7 [x] Dt 3:27
34:5 [y] Nu 12:7 [z] Dt 32:50; Jos 1:1-2
34:6 [a] Dt 3:29 [b] Jude 9
34:7 [c] Dt 31:2 [d] Ge 27:1

Dt 33:29 ❖ How is God like both a shield and a sword? How does he fight for and protect his people, and what role do we play (see Eph 6:10–17)?

The Death of Moses

34 Then Moses climbed Mount Nebo
from the plains of Moab to the top
of Pisgah, across from Jericho.[r] There
the LORD showed[s] him the whole land—
from Gilead to Dan, 2all of Naphtali, the
territory of Ephraim and Manasseh, all
the land of Judah as far as the Mediterranean Sea,[t] 3the Negev and the whole
region from the Valley of Jericho, the City
of Palms,[u] as far as Zoar. 4Then the LORD
said to him, "This is the land I promised
on oath[v] to Abraham, Isaac and Jacob
when I said, 'I will give it[w] to your descendants.' I have let you see it with your
eyes, but you will not cross[x] over into it."
5And Moses the servant of the LORD[y]
died[z] there in Moab, as the LORD had
said. 6He buried him[b] in Moab, in the
valley opposite Beth Peor,[a] but to this
day no one knows where his grave is.[b]
7Moses was a hundred and twenty years
old[c] when he died, yet his eyes were
not weak[d] nor his strength gone. 8The

[a] 28 Septuagint; Hebrew *Jacob's spring is*
[b] 6 Or *He was buried*

33:22–25 Moses' blessing of Dan is the shortest of all (v. 22). The blessing of Naphtali (v. 23) sounds like a collage of expressions that have been heard earlier and charges Naphtali to take possession of the west and the southland. In the blessing of Asher, Moses prays for both fertility and security.
33:26–29 This imagery recalls Canaanite myths of the storm god Baal, one of whose stock epithets was "rider of the clouds." The Israelites are secure because Yahweh is their defender. They are the beneficiaries of his rescue and protection.

✣ **33:1–29** As in the Lord's Prayer, issues relating to physical well-being are framed by and subordinated to the sheer privilege of calling God our Father, King, Savior, and Defender. To bear the name of Christ and to hear him address us as his beloved are reasons enough to celebrate and keep our focus on him.

34:1–6 Deuteronomy 34 recounts Moses' ascent up Mount Nebo, his observation of the land (vv. 1–4), and his death and burial (vv. 5–6). Although chapter 34 opens with a report of Moses' ascent, the bulk of the paragraph focuses on Yahweh's actions (vv. 1b, 4, 6).

The announcement of Moses' death in v. 5 is brief and to the point. But even his death confirms Yahweh's fidelity, for his death transpires "as the LORD had said." Moses was buried by Yahweh himself. Moses had reached his heavenly destination without having reached his earthly home. God had been with Moses throughout his life, and Moses was alone with God in his death.
34:7–8 As the Israelites had done for Aaron, they mourned Moses' passing for thirty days (v. 8).

Israelites grieved for Moses in the plains
of Moab thirty days, until the time of
weeping and mourning[e] was over.
9Now Joshua son of Nun was filled
with the spirit[a] of wisdom[f] because Moses had laid his hands on him.[g] So the
Israelites listened to him and did what
the LORD had commanded Moses.
10Since then, no prophet has risen in
Israel like Moses,[h] whom the LORD knew
face to face,[i] 11who did all those signs
and wonders[j] the LORD sent him to do
in Egypt — to Pharaoh and to all his officials[k] and to his whole land. 12For no
one has ever shown the mighty power
or performed the awesome deeds that
Moses did in the sight of all Israel.

34:8 [e] Ge 50:3, 10; 2Sa 11:27
34:9 [f] Ge 41:38; Isa 11:2; Da 6:3 [g] Nu 27:18, 23
34:10 [h] Dt 18:15, 18 [i] Ex 33:11; Nu 12:6, 8; Dt 5:4
34:11 [j] Dt 4:34 [k] Dt 7:19

Dt 34:9 ❖ What does it mean to be filled with the spirit of wisdom? How can we attain that spirit?

[a] 9 Or *Spirit*

34:9–12 Verse 9 shifts the attention from Moses to Joshua son of Nun, but in so doing it still honors Moses. The expression "spirit of wisdom" (v. 9) represents a special divine endowment for the fulfillment of a divinely ordained role.

✤ **34:1–12** Moses was a shepherd after the order of Christ as described in 1Pe 5:1–6 and after the order of Yahweh as celebrated in Ps 23. May the Lord raise up for his work in our day pastors in the order of Christ our Shepherd.

Author: Unknown, though certain sections may derive from Joshua himself.

Audience: God's chosen people, the Israelites

Date: Probably about 1390 BC

Theme: God enables Joshua to lead the armies of Israel to victory over the Canaanites in the promised land.

Reading Joshua

The book of Joshua divides into two sections: the first section (chs. 1–12) records the exciting stories of the conquest of Canaan; the second section (chs. 13–22) recounts the dividing up of the conquered land. The book closes with Joshua's farewell speech (ch. 23) and Israel's renewal of the covenant.

PERSPECTIVE

In the biblical book of Joshua, the author describes a time of great flux. The children of God are poised to enter the land long promised to them. Their assignment is to take the land by force. The inhabitants of the land are, according to rumor, gigantic, fierce, and ready to fight to defend their turf. Slavery in Egypt was bad. Forty years of wandering in the wilderness caused great suffering. But all-out war?

The Israelites are terrified. The promise of a new land filled with milk and honey not so long ago seemed like a dream come true. Now who can think it is possibly worth the anguish and fear that the prospects facing them will undoubtedly cause? It doesn't help that they have had a leadership change, that the man who led them for forty plus years is gone and in his place is a new, untested leader.

There were no nation-states to give Middle Eastern people of this era security. This was a tribal culture. Each tribe (extended family really) had its god. It was this family god that provided security. The god, through signs and wonders, told the people when to fight and when to flee, when to hunker down and when to move on. Security came from obeying the family god—and trusting that their family god was more powerful than their neighbor's god.

It was a world gone mad.

Two worlds, separated by up to 3,500 years and enormous social changes, faced with the same problem. Human anxiety caused by relying too much on our own technology, on our war-making ability, on false gods. Interestingly, the two worlds with the same problem have available to them the same fail-safe solution (see Jos 1:8–9).

Event	1400 BC	1300	1200	1100	1000	900	800	700	600	500	400
Israelites enter Canaan (c. 1406 BC)	♦										
Conquest of Canaan (c. 1406–1375 BC)	■										
Book of Joshua written (c. 1390 BC)	♦										
Joshua's death (c. 1390 BC)	♦										
Judges begin to rule (c. 1375 BC)	♦										
Saul named king (1050 BC)					♦						
David named king (1010 BC)					♦						
Division of the kingdom (930 BC)						♦					

The inhabitants of both the ancient and the contemporary worlds tend to make two fundamental errors that give free rein to uncontrolled angst.

The first error mistakes the source of freedom. The error is to mistakenly think that freedom comes from not having to obey anyone. *Freedom is not the absence of obedience but the result of it.* Anxiety, as we have seen, comes from the absence of obedience. True freedom comes after we choose to obey God and God's law.

The second error is to think that we are strong and courageous because we somehow find these two virtues inside ourselves. Unfortunately, we don't—they are not there. *Strength and valor come not from inside us but from God.* When God speaks to Joshua, he does not tell him to look deep inside himself and somehow release the strong and courageous being who resides there. No, God commands him to be strong and courageous. Obeying this command produces the desired emotions.

What has come in our day and age as existential angst is cured by the 3,500-year-old words recorded in the first chapter of Joshua. Read and obey.

Key Verses

"Keep this Book of the Law always on your lips; meditate on it day and night, so that you may be careful to do everything written in it. Then you will be prosperous and successful. Have I not commanded you? Be strong and courageous. Do not be afraid; do not be discouraged, for the LORD your God will be with you wherever you go."

—Joshua 1:8–9

TAKING THE NEXT STEPS

Joshua records Israel's entry into the promised land of Canaan and the victory that God gave them over the heathen nations living there. These victories, however, came only when the Israelites heard and responded to God's command to trust and obey him and to be strong and courageous in him. Once the Israelites conquered the land, Joshua and the heads of the tribes faced the challenge of dividing up Palestine and settling each tribe in a designated location. With this task completed, Joshua gathered the people together one final time at Shechem to lead them, as Moses had done in Deuteronomy, in a renewal of their covenant with the Lord.

The book contains powerful messages of encouragement to God's people today. (1) If we obey the Lord and have him on our side, we will gain the victory in our spiritual battles. God promises to be with us to strengthen us wherever we go. (2) Since victory is assured, the command to Joshua not to be afraid but to be strong and courageous is a command directed to us as well. (3) On the other hand, if we willfully disobey God's commands, do our own thing and fight in our own strength, we face insurmountable odds. (4) Every day a number of voices vie for our attention, forcing us to make difficult choices; Joshua's voice still challenges us to choose to serve the Lord in everything we do.

WHAT TO LOOK FOR IN JOSHUA

- Rahab and the spies (ch. 2)
- Crossing the Jordan River (chs. 3–4)
- The fall of Jericho (ch. 6)
- Achan and the problems at Ai (chs. 7–8)
- The battle when the sun stood still (ch. 10)
- Joshua's farewell and challenge (chs. 23–24)

Joshua Installed as Leader

1 After the death of Moses the servant
of the LORD,[a] the LORD said to Joshua[b] son of Nun, Moses' aide: 2"Moses
my servant is dead. Now then, you and
all these people, get ready to cross the
Jordan River[c] into the land I am about
to give to them — to the Israelites. 3I
will give you every place where you set
your foot,[d] as I promised Moses. 4Your
territory will extend from the desert to
Lebanon, and from the great river, the
Euphrates[e] — all the Hittite country — to
the Mediterranean Sea in the west.[f] 5No
one will be able to stand against you[g]
all the days of your life. As I was with[h]
Moses, so I will be with you; I will never
leave you nor forsake[i] you. 6Be strong
and courageous, because you will lead
these people to inherit the land I swore
to their ancestors[j] to give them.
7"Be strong and very courageous. Be
careful to obey all the law my servant
Moses gave you; do not turn from it to
the right or to the left,[k] that you may be
successful wherever you go.[l] 8Keep this
Book of the Law always on your lips; meditate on it day and night, so that you may
be careful to do everything written in it.
Then you will be prosperous and successful.[m] 9Have I not commanded you? Be
strong and courageous. Do not be afraid;[n]
do not be discouraged, for the LORD your
God will be with you wherever you go."[o]
10So Joshua ordered the officers of the
people: 11"Go through the camp and tell
the people, 'Get your provisions ready.
Three days from now you will cross the
Jordan here to go in and take possession[p]
of the land the LORD your God is giving
you for your own.'"
12But to the Reubenites, the Gadites
and the half-tribe of Manasseh,[q] Joshua
said, 13"Remember the command that

1:1 [a] Nu 12:7; Dt 34:5 [b] Ex 24:13; Dt 1:38
1:2 [c] ver 11
1:3 [d] Dt 11:24
1:4 [e] Ge 15:18 [f] Nu 34:2-12
1:5 [g] Dt 7:24 [h] Jos 3:7; 6:27 [i] Dt 31:6-8
1:6 [j] Dt 31:23
1:7 [k] Dt 5:32; 28:14 [l] Jos 11:15
1:8 [m] Dt 29:9; Ps 1:1-3
1:9 [n] Ps 27:1 [o] ver 7; Dt 31:7-8; Jer 1:8
1:11 [p] Joel 3:2
1:12 [q] Nu 32:20-22

Jos 1:6 ❖ What does it look like to be "strong and courageous" in life? Where is God calling us to be leaders or to stand up for a righteous cause?

1:1 Joshua 1 picks up where Dt 34 left off and pushes the story forward.
1:2-9 Yahweh's commissioning speech sounds like a king issuing battle plans to his field general. Joshua and Israel are to "cross the Jordan" (v. 2b). "I am about to give" stresses the land as the generous gift of Yahweh. Yahweh quotes Moses' own words in a slightly expanded form (Dt 11:24) to reiterate the promise spoken through him (Jos 1:3–4).
1:5 A divine promise reassures the new leader that no human enemy can "stand against you [Joshua]" no matter how long he lived.
1:6, 7, 9 Joshua receives Yahweh's command to "be strong and very courageous," reiterated three times.
1:7–8 Yahweh details the single provision that Joshua must observe: The success of his future endeavors hangs upon his never wavering from Moses' teachings. The key is "this Book of the Law" (v. 8) that Moses wrote shortly before his death.
1:10–11 The "officers" in v. 10 probably are civilian administrators supporting Joshua rather than military officers. They are to fan out through the camp and command the people to prepare for departure in three days.
1:12–18 Joshua deals with the tribes that settled on the east side of the Jordan—Reuben, Gad, and half of Manasseh. They have already received their inheritance from Moses. The exhortation, "Remember the command that Moses the servant of the LORD gave you" (v. 13) recalls the decrees Moses gave in Nu 32.
Joshua reiterates the two conditions that must prevail before they can go home: When Yahweh

PEOPLE TO KNOW // JOSHUA

JOSHUA 1:7–9: Joshua was the successor of Moses who led the Israelites into the promised land. The Bible introduces him as a man of war, leading Israel in battle against the Amalekites after leaving Egypt (Ex 17:8–13). He later became Moses' trusted helper and was a dedicated follower of God's plan for the Israelites. Joshua accompanied Moses partway up Mount Sinai and was not part of the sin with the golden calf (Ex 32:17).

When Moses sent twelve spies to survey the promised land, only Joshua and Caleb returned with a good report (Nu 14:6–9). The other ten spies led the people in a rebellion that resulted in Israel's wandering the wilderness for another 38 years. Only Joshua and Caleb survived from that generation.

God told Moses to give his authority to Joshua as his successor (Nu 27:18–21). In the book of Joshua, he is portrayed as a new Moses, leading the people through water on dry land as Moses did when he led the people out of Egypt. Joshua was told to take his sandals off when he encountered the commander of God's army just as Moses was told to remove his sandals when he faced God in the burning bush.

Before his death, Joshua gave a final speech just as Moses had done before he died. Joshua told the people to be faithful to God in the land. He made a covenant for the people, binding them to God's decrees. Joshua died at the age of 110.

APPLICATION ✣ God told Joshua to be strong and courageous (Jos 1:6). Like Joshua, we need to look at even the biggest challenges through the lens of God's power. Joshua and Caleb were not shaken when they saw the might of the Canaanites; they had faith in God.

God will always give us what we need to accomplish what he desires. By God's grace, we can be strong and courageous as we face each new challenge.

Moses the servant of the LORD gave you
after he said, 'The LORD your God will
give you rest[r] by giving you this land.'
14Your wives, your children and your
livestock may stay in the land that Moses gave you east of the Jordan, but all
your fighting men, ready for battle, must
cross over ahead of your fellow Israelites.
You are to help them 15until the LORD
gives them rest, as he has done for you,
and until they too have taken possession
of the land the LORD your God is giving
them. After that, you may go back and
occupy your own land, which Moses the
servant of the LORD gave you east of the
Jordan toward the sunrise."[s]

16Then they answered Joshua, "Whatever you have commanded us we will do,
and wherever you send us we will go.
17Just as we fully obeyed Moses, so we
will obey you.[t] Only may the LORD your
God be with you as he was with Moses.
18Whoever rebels against your word and
does not obey it, whatever you may command them, will be put to death. Only
be strong and courageous!"

Rahab and the Spies

2 Then Joshua son of Nun secretly
sent two spies[u] from Shittim.[v] "Go,
look over the land," he said, "especially
Jericho." So they went and entered the

1:13 [r] Dt 3:18-20
1:15 [s] Jos 22:1-4
1:17 [t] ver 5,9
2:1 [u] Jas 2:25 [v] Nu 25:1; Jos 3:1

finally has given their fellow Israelites the same "rest" they themselves have already sampled and when their west-bank kin also possess their inheritance (v. 15). All Israel will together bear its burdens, suffer its losses, pay its prices, and share in its victories.
1:16–18 The chapter concludes with the reply of the two-and-a-half tribes. A subtle argument undergirds their words: If the tribes living east of the Jordan, who have no personal interest in west-bank land, affirm what follows, how much more so will the others. The east-bank tribes promise Joshua the same obedience they gave Moses (v. 17).

APPLICATION ✣ **1:1–18** Fear lurks in the background of Jos 1. It's an emotion that all humans share. Though these words were given to God's covenant people Israel, God's people today can find relief from fears in similar ways. Joshua 1 points to four truths as the antidote to such fears: (1) our unique identity as God's people, (2) our dependence on God's word, (3) our bond of unity with other believers, and (4) God's powerful presence with us.

2:1 Despite receiving God's emphatic reassurance, Joshua opts for a cautious rather than a bold first step forward.

house of a prostitute named Rahab[w] and
stayed there.
2The king of Jericho was told, "Look,
some of the Israelites have come here
tonight to spy out the land." 3So the king
of Jericho sent this message to Rahab:
"Bring out the men who came to you
and entered your house, because they
have come to spy out the whole land."
4But the woman had taken the two
men and hidden them.[x] She said, "Yes,
the men came to me, but I did not know
where they had come from. 5At dusk,
when it was time to close the city gate,
they left. I don't know which way they
went. Go after them quickly. You may
catch up with them." 6(But she had taken
them up to the roof and hidden them under the stalks of flax[y] she had laid out on
the roof.)[z] 7So the men set out in pursuit
of the spies on the road that leads to the
fords of the Jordan, and as soon as the
pursuers had gone out, the gate was shut.
8Before the spies lay down for the
night, she went up on the roof 9and said
to them, "I know that the LORD has given
you this land and that a great fear[a] of you
has fallen on us, so that all who live in
this country are melting in fear because
of you. 10We have heard how the LORD
dried up[b] the water of the Red Sea*[a]* for
you when you came out of Egypt,[c] and
what you did to Sihon and Og,[d] the two
kings of the Amorites east of the Jordan, whom you completely destroyed.*[b]*
11When we heard of it, our hearts melted
in fear and everyone's courage failed because of you,[e] for the LORD your God is

2:1 [w] Heb 11:31
2:4 [x] 2Sa 17:19-20
2:6 [y] Jas 2:25 [z] Ex 1:17,19; 2Sa 17:19
2:9 [a] Ge 35:5; Ex 23:27; Dt 2:25
2:10 [b] Ex 14:21 [c] Nu 23:22 [d] Nu 21:21,24, 34-35
2:11 [e] Ex 15:14; Jos 5:1; 7:5; Ps 22:14; Isa 13:7

Jos 2:4-6 ❖ Is it ever okay to lie? How is Rahab a hero of faith (see Heb 11:31) and what can we learn from her part in God's plan?

God in heaven above and on the earth[f]
below.
12"Now then, please swear to me by
the LORD that you will show kindness to
my family, because I have shown kindness to you. Give me a sure sign[g] 13that
you will spare the lives of my father and
mother, my brothers and sisters, and all
who belong to them — and that you will
save us from death."
14"Our lives for your lives!" the men
assured her. "If you don't tell what we are
doing, we will treat you kindly and faithfully[h] when the LORD gives us the land."
15So she let them down by a rope
through the window,[i] for the house she
lived in was part of the city wall. 16She
said to them, "Go to the hills so the pursuers will not find you. Hide yourselves
there three days[j] until they return, and
then go on your way."[k]
17Now the men had said to her, "This
oath[l] you made us swear will not be binding on us 18unless, when we enter the
land, you have tied this scarlet cord in
the window through which you let us
down, and unless you have brought your
father and mother, your brothers and all
your family[m] into your house. 19If any

[f] Dt 4:39
2:12 [g] ver 18
2:14 [h] Jdg 1:24; Mt 5:7
2:15 [i] Ac 9:25
2:16 [j] Jas 2:25 [k] Heb 11:31
2:17 [l] Ge 24:8
2:18 [m] ver 12; Jos 6:23

[a] 10 Or *the Sea of Reeds* *[b]* 10 The Hebrew term refers to the irrevocable giving over of things or persons to the LORD, often by totally destroying them.

2:2-8 Suddenly, the mission has turned sour. But Rahab risks her life and cunningly protects her two guests. She concedes that the men "came to me" but denies knowing from where they came (v. 4). Next, Rahab lies about knowing where they are currently (v. 5). Her intervention surprisingly transforms the calamity into deliverance.

2:9-21 Rahab finally explains herself (vv. 9-11). The original language uses the perfect verb tense "has given." This tense expresses an established fact will soon become reality. The Canaanites also had warrior gods, but Rahab recognizes the superiority of Yahweh.

To conclude her explanation, Rahab returns to Yahweh, the cause of the current disarray in Canaan (v. 11b). Yahweh is not yet her God; she has not yet made him her most important—much less her only—God as an Israelite would. Rahab's words mark a step in the direction of a more complete, if not exclusive, commitment to Yahweh. More important here, and of central significance in the book, is the fact that Rahab positions herself as the spokesperson for the people of the land. They all know of Yahweh's power and intentions, yet they resist the Israelites anyway. Rahab and her family survive because of her wise choice.

2:12-13 Notice the nature of the agreement in play here. Israel is not offering the Canaanite Rahab a covenant and thereby violating its obligation to destroy Jericho. Rather, it is Rahab who affirms the sovereignty of Yahweh and accepts his purposes—a basic confession of her faith—and who, on that basis, asks Israel (and, implicitly, Yahweh) to promise to spare her life.

2:15-21 Rahab lowers the pair by a rope dropped from her window. The young spies regain the initiative and prolong the conversation rather than silently vanishing into the hills (vv. 17-20). They attach two new stipulations to the oath they have just taken. Rahab accepts the new conditions and sends them on their way (v. 21).

of them go outside your house into the
street, their blood will be on their own
heads;[n] we will not be responsible. As
for those who are in the house with you,
their blood will be on our head[o] if a hand
is laid on them. 20But if you tell what we
are doing, we will be released from the
oath you made us swear."

21"Agreed," she replied. "Let it be as
you say."

So she sent them away, and they departed. And she tied the scarlet cord in
the window.

22When they left, they went into the
hills and stayed there three days, until the pursuers had searched all along
the road and returned without finding
them. 23Then the two men started back.
They went down out of the hills, forded
the river and came to Joshua son of Nun
and told him everything that had happened to them. 24They said to Joshua,
"The LORD has surely given the whole
land into our hands;[p] all the people are
melting in fear because of us."

Crossing the Jordan

3 Early in the morning Joshua and all
the Israelites set out from Shittim[q]
and went to the Jordan, where they
camped before crossing over. 2After
three days the officers went throughout
the camp,[r] 3giving orders to the people:
"When you see the ark of the covenant[s]
of the LORD your God, and the Levitical
priests[t] carrying it, you are to move out
from your positions and follow it. 4Then
you will know which way to go, since
you have never been this way before. But
keep a distance of about two thousand
cubits[a] between you and the ark; do not
go near it."

5Joshua told the people, "Consecrate
yourselves,[u] for tomorrow the LORD will
do amazing things among you."

6Joshua said to the priests, "Take up
the ark of the covenant and pass on
ahead of the people." So they took it up
and went ahead of them.

7And the LORD said to Joshua, "Today
I will begin to exalt you[v] in the eyes of
all Israel, so they may know that I am
with you as I was with Moses.[w] 8Tell the
priests[x] who carry the ark of the covenant: 'When you reach the edge of the
Jordan's waters, go and stand in the river.'"

9Joshua said to the Israelites, "Come
here and listen to the words of the LORD
your God. 10This is how you will know
that the living God[y] is among you and
that he will certainly drive out before
you the Canaanites, Hittites, Hivites, Perizzites, Girgashites, Amorites and Jebusites.[z] 11See, the ark of the covenant of
the Lord of all the earth[a] will go into the
Jordan ahead of you. 12Now then, choose
twelve men[b] from the tribes of Israel,
one from each tribe. 13And as soon as the
priests who carry the ark of the LORD—
the Lord of all the earth[c]—set foot in the

Jos 3:6 ❖ How can we consecrate and prepare ourselves for the amazing things God has in store for us?

2:19 [n] Eze 33:4 [o] Mt 27:25
2:24 [p] ver 9; Jos 6:2
3:1 [q] Jos 2:1
3:2 [r] Jos 1:11
3:3 [s] Nu 10:33 [t] Dt 31:9
3:5 [u] Ex 19:10, 14; Lev 20:7; Jos 7:13; 1Sa 16:5; Joel 2:16
3:7 [v] Jos 4:14; 1Ch 29:25 [w] Jos 1:5
3:8 [x] ver 3
3:10 [y] Dt 5:26; 1Sa 17:26, 36; 2Ki 19:4, 16; Hos 1:10; Mt 16:16; 1Th 1:9 [z] Ex 33:2; Dt 7:1
3:11 [a] ver 13; Job 41:11; Zec 6:5
3:12 [b] Jos 4:2,4
3:13 [c] ver 11

[a] 4 That is, about 3,000 feet or about 900 meters

2:22–24 To conclude the story, the author has the spies basically borrow two of Rahab's lines (v. 24).

✜ **2:1–24** We must confess our reluctance to welcome outsiders, especially those with problematic pasts or presents. Normally, we Christians settle into comfortably snug small groups of friends who are like us. We tend to associate with people with whom we have a lot in common. Jesus models a lifestyle of hanging in with people in trouble, people in need, people on the margins: people whom others avoid. We, his followers, can do no less, but *how* can we do this? We need to overcome our natural skittishness. As Rahab welcomed the Israelite spies who were outsiders in her world, so we are to welcome outsiders into ours.

3:1–8 The morning after the spies' return, Joshua and Israel shift their camp to the Jordan (v. 1). Three days later, the officers pass through the camp to instruct Israel about the crossing (vv. 2–3). They order the people to watch for the ark with its priestly bearers and follow it (v. 3b). This comment marks the book's first mention of the ark of the covenant. Israel understood the space between the winged cherubim to be the royal throne over which Yahweh invisibly reigns. Here it symbolizes Yahweh's royal presence with Israel and his sovereign leadership over the coming invasion.

Specific instructions follow in three brief narrative snapshots (vv. 5–8). Yahweh concludes the final snapshot with a terse instruction through Joshua for the priests carrying the ark.

3:9–13 After Israel has assembled, Joshua addresses them (vv. 9–13), immediately driving home the key point: "The living God . . . among you" is, indeed, about to drive out the seven peoples inhabiting Canaan (v. 10).

Jordan, its waters flowing downstream[d] will be cut off and stand up in a heap.[e]"

[14]So when the people broke camp to cross the Jordan, the priests carrying the ark of the covenant[f] went ahead[g] of them. [15]Now the Jordan is at flood stage[h] all during harvest. Yet as soon as the priests who carried the ark reached the Jordan and their feet touched the water's edge, [16]the water from upstream stopped flowing.[i] It piled up in a heap a great distance away, at a town called Adam in the vicinity of Zarethan,[j] while the water flowing down[k] to the Sea of the Arabah[l] (that is, the Dead Sea[m]) was completely cut off. So the people crossed over opposite Jericho. [17]The priests who carried the ark of the covenant of the LORD stopped in the middle of the Jordan and stood on dry ground, while all Israel passed by until the whole nation had completed the crossing on dry ground.[n]

4 When the whole nation had finished crossing the Jordan,[o] the LORD said to Joshua, [2]"Choose twelve men[p] from among the people, one from each tribe, [3]and tell them to take up twelve stones[q] from the middle of the Jordan, from right where the priests are standing, and carry them over with you and put them down at the place where you stay tonight.[r]"

[4]So Joshua called together the twelve men he had appointed from the Israelites, one from each tribe, [5]and said to them, "Go over before the ark of the LORD your God into the middle of the Jordan. Each of you is to take up a stone on his shoulder, according to the number of the tribes of the Israelites, [6]to serve as a sign among you. In the future, when your children ask you, 'What do these stones mean?'[s] [7]tell them that the flow of the Jordan was cut off[t] before the ark of the covenant of the LORD. When it crossed the Jordan, the waters of the Jordan were cut off. These stones are to be a memorial[u] to the people of Israel forever."

[8]So the Israelites did as Joshua commanded them. They took twelve stones from the middle of the Jordan, according to the number of the tribes of the Israelites, as the LORD had told Joshua;[v] and they carried them over with them to their camp, where they put them down. [9]Joshua set up the twelve stones[w] that had been[a] in the middle of the Jordan at the spot where the priests who carried the ark of the covenant had stood. And they are there to this day.

[10]Now the priests who carried the ark remained standing in the middle of the Jordan until everything the LORD had commanded Joshua was done by the people, just as Moses had directed Joshua. The people hurried over, [11]and as soon as all of them had crossed, the ark of the LORD and the priests came to the other side while the people watched. [12]The men of Reuben, Gad and the half-tribe of Manasseh crossed over, ready for battle, in front of the Israelites,[x] as Moses had directed them. [13]About forty thousand armed for battle crossed over before the LORD to the plains of Jericho for war.

[14]That day the LORD exalted[y] Joshua in the sight of all Israel; and they stood in awe of him all the days of his life, just as they had stood in awe of Moses.

[15]Then the LORD said to Joshua, [16]"Command the priests carrying the ark of the covenant law[z] to come up out of the Jordan."

3:13 [d]ver 16 [e]Ex 15:8; Ps 78:13
3:14 [f]Ps 132:8 [g]Ac 7:44-45
3:15 [h]Jos 4:18; 1Ch 12:15
3:16 [i]Ps 66:6; 74:15 [j]1Ki 4:12; 7:46 [k]ver 13 [l]Dt 1:1 [m]Ge 14:3
3:17 [n]Ex 14:22, 29
4:1 [o]Dt 27:2
4:2 [p]Jos 3:12
4:3 [q]ver 20 [r]ver 19
4:6 [s]ver 21; Ex 12:26; 13:14
4:7 [t]Jos 3:13 [u]Ex 12:14
4:8 [v]ver 20
4:9 [w]Ge 28:18; Jos 24:26; 1Sa 7:12
4:12 [x]Nu 32:27
4:14 [y]Jos 3:7
4:16 [z]Ex 25:22

[a] 9 Or *Joshua also set up twelve stones*

3:14–17 Suddenly, the speech ends and the narrator steps forward to report that the crossing takes place exactly as expected. The trigger that ignites this event is the moment that the priests' "soles" wade into the water's edge. This event serves as a bookend to the wilderness experience parallel to the parting of the Red Sea when the Israelites left Egypt and entered the wilderness. This is also one of several indications that Joshua has inherited the mantle of Moses, and that Yahweh is indeed with him as he was with Moses (1:5).

4:1–12 The stones serve as both "sign" and "memorial" (vv. 6–7). They authenticate that the past event actually happened and remind Israel of its continuing significance for later generations. The text assumes visits to the site by future generations, probably for some ritual remembrance, if not reenactment, of the river crossing.

Parenthetically, twelve other stones unexpectedly merit mention. These are ones that Joshua himself sets up in the middle of the Jordan, right where the priests' feet stood (v. 9). With those symbolic memorials in place, the narrative resumes the main plot—the dramatic crossing.

4:13 In the OT, "forty thousand" is a round number meaning "huge army."

4:14 From this point on, Israel gives Joshua the same sincere respect given Moses during his lifetime.

4:15–24 "Waters returned" probably marks an allusion to the exodus—the return of waters over the dry path through the Red Sea. The timing of the momentous event—the tenth day of the first

CONQUEST OF CAANAN

1 ENTRY INTO CANAAN

When the Israelite tribes approached Canaan after four decades of wilderness existence, they had to overcome two Amorite kingdoms on the Medeba plateau and in Bashan (Nu 2:21-34). Under Moses' leadership, they also subdued the Midianites in order to consolidate their control over the Transjordanian region (Nu 31).

The conquest of Canaan followed a course that in retrospect appears as though it had been planned by a brilliant military strategist. Taking Jericho gave Israel control of its strategic plains, fords and roads as a base of operations. When Israel next gained control of the Bethel, Gibeon and Upper Beth Horon regions, it dominated the center of the north-south Palestinian ridge. Subsequently, Israel was able to break the power of the allied urban centers in separate campaigns south and north.

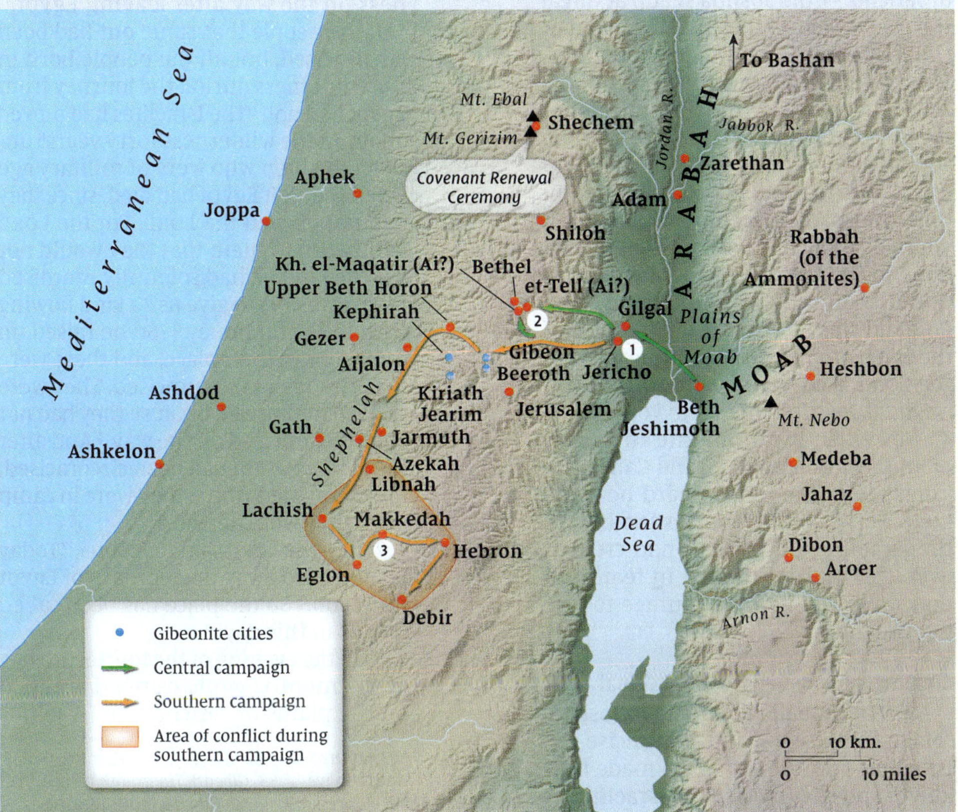

2 THE CENTRAL CAMPAIGN

The destruction of both Jericho and Ai led to a major victory against the Canaanites in the Valley of Aijalon—the battle of the long day (Jos 10:12-14)—which then allowed Joshua to proceed against the cities of the western foothills.

Archaeological evidence for the conquest is mixed, in part because the chronological problems are unsolved. On the one hand, clay tablets containing cuneiform letters to the Egyptian court have been found at Tell el-Amarna in Egypt from c. 1375 BC. These mention bands of Hapiru that threaten many of the cities of Canaan and create fear among the Canaanite inhabitants.

On the other hand, numerous towns were destroyed c. 1230 BC by unknown assailants, presumably the "Sea Peoples," but possibly including the Israelites as well. The biblical chronology based on 1Ki 6:1 seems to indicate an even earlier dating, near the end of the fifteenth century unless the numbers are symbolic.

3 THE SOUTHERN CAMPAIGN

Azekah, Libnah, Lachish, Eglon and Debir were all captured by Joshua in his campaign against the southern coalition of Canaanite cities that was led by the king of Jerusalem (Jos 10).

Several of these towns, most notably Lachish, contain destruction evidence that might possibly be correlated with the Israelite conquest, but with Jericho and Ai the historical evidence is not clear.

17 So Joshua commanded the priests, "Come up out of the Jordan."

18 And the priests came up out of the river carrying the ark of the covenant of the LORD. No sooner had they set their feet on the dry ground than the waters of the Jordan returned to their place and ran at flood stage[a] as before.

19 On the tenth day of the first month the people went up from the Jordan and camped at Gilgal[b] on the eastern border of Jericho. 20 And Joshua set up at Gilgal the twelve stones[c] they had taken out of the Jordan. 21 He said to the Israelites, "In the future when your descendants ask their parents, 'What do these stones mean?'[d] 22 tell them, 'Israel crossed the Jordan on dry ground.'[e] 23 For the LORD your God dried up the Jordan before you until you had crossed over. The LORD your God did to the Jordan what he had done to the Red Sea[*a*] when he dried it up before us until we had crossed over.[f] 24 He did this so that all the peoples of the earth might know[g] that the hand of the LORD is powerful[h] and so that you might always fear the LORD your God.[i]"

5 Now when all the Amorite kings west of the Jordan and all the Canaanite kings along the coast[j] heard how the LORD had dried up the Jordan before the Israelites until they[*b*] had crossed over, their hearts melted in fear[k] and they no longer had the courage to face the Israelites.

Circumcision and Passover at Gilgal

2 At that time the LORD said to Joshua, "Make flint knives[l] and circumcise the Israelites again." 3 So Joshua made flint knives and circumcised the Israelites at Gibeath Haaraloth.[*c*]

4:18 [a] Jos 3:15
4:19 [b] Jos 5:9
4:20 [c] ver 3,8
4:21 [d] ver 6
4:22 [e] Jos 3:17
4:23 [f] Ex 14:21
4:24 [g] 1Ki 8:42-43; 2Ki 19:19; Ps 106:8; Jer 10:7 [h] Ex 15:16; 1Ch 29:12; Ps 89:13 [i] Ex 14:31
5:1 [j] Nu 13:29 [k] Jos 2:9-11
5:2 [l] Ex 4:25

Jos 4:20-24 ❖ Joshua set up stones as a memorial of God's miraculous provision. What or who has been a "standing stone" in our lives—someone or something that reminds us of where we came from and of what God has done for us?

4 Now this is why he did so: All those who came out of Egypt—all the men of military age—died in the wilderness on the way after leaving Egypt.[m] 5 All the people that came out had been circumcised, but all the people born in the wilderness during the journey from Egypt had not. 6 The Israelites had moved about in the wilderness forty years[n] until all the men who were of military age when they left Egypt had died, since they had not obeyed the LORD. For the LORD had sworn to them that they would not see the land he had solemnly promised their ancestors to give us,[o] a land flowing with milk and honey.[p] 7 So he raised up their sons in their place, and these were the ones Joshua circumcised. They were still uncircumcised because they had not been circumcised on the way. 8 And after the whole nation had been circumcised, they remained where they were in camp until they were healed.[q]

9 Then the LORD said to Joshua, "Today I have rolled away the reproach of Egypt from you." So the place has been called Gilgal[*d*] to this day.

10 On the evening of the fourteenth day of the month,[r] while camped at Gilgal on the plains of Jericho, the Israelites

5:4 [m] Dt 2:14
5:6 [n] Dt 2:7 [o] Nu 14:23, 29-35; Dt 2:14 [p] Ex 3:8
5:8 [q] Ge 34:25
5:10 [r] Ex 12:6

[*a*] 23 Or *the Sea of Reeds* [*b*] 1 Another textual tradition *we* [*c*] 3 *Gibeath Haaraloth* means *the hill of foreskins.* [*d*] 9 *Gilgal* sounds like the Hebrew for *roll.*

month (v. 19a)—recalls dates associated with Passover, thus forging a further link between the Red Sea and Jordan crossings.

4:23 Joshua explicitly credits Yahweh with drying up the Jordan's waters and compares the act to his drying up of the Red Sea at the exodus.

5:1 With the crossing, the die is cast: Conflict with the land's inhabitants is inevitable.

✣ **3:1—5:1** We all face the problem of remembering—or, put differently, our tendency to forget—important things and events. Part of the problem is that we have so much to remember these days. The cluttered mind poses a unique danger to our lives. It makes us forget things that matter most, including our walk with Christ. Joshua erected twelve stones at Gilgal so that future Israelite generations would remember what had happened there. It would drive them back to a firm, steady, convinced, life-altering fear of God. Like Joshua, Jesus took pains to ensure that his followers remember his death. At the Last Supper, he declared, "Do this in remembrance of me" (Lk 22:19).

5:2-9 Unlike their ancestors who died in the wilderness, the generation born in the wilderness had not been circumcised. At issue is a question that echoes throughout the book: Will *this* generation obey Yahweh and keep (not lose) the land?

5:10-12 As Israel's first Passover in the new land, this celebration signals a new beginning for their

celebrated the Passover. 11The day after
the Passover, that very day, they ate some
of the produce of the land:[s] unleavened
bread and roasted grain.[t] 12The manna
stopped the day after[a] they ate this food
from the land; there was no longer any
manna for the Israelites, but that year
they ate the produce of Canaan.[u]

The Fall of Jericho

13Now when Joshua was near Jericho,
he looked up and saw a man[v] standing in
front of him with a drawn sword[w] in his
hand. Joshua went up to him and asked,
"Are you for us or for our enemies?"

14"Neither," he replied, "but as commander of the army of the LORD I have
now come." Then Joshua fell facedown[x]
to the ground in reverence, and asked
him, "What message does my Lord[b] have
for his servant?"

15The commander of the LORD's army
replied, "Take off your sandals, for the
place where you are standing is holy."[y]
And Joshua did so.

6 Now the gates of Jericho[z] were securely barred because of the Israelites. No one went out and no one
came in.

2Then the LORD said to Joshua, "See, I
have delivered[a] Jericho into your hands,
along with its king and its fighting men.
3March around the city once with all the
armed men. Do this for six days. 4Have
seven priests carry trumpets of rams'
horns in front of the ark. On the seventh
day, march around the city seven times,
with the priests blowing the trumpets.[b]
5When you hear them sound a long blast[c]
on the trumpets, have the whole army
give a loud shout;[d] then the wall of the
city will collapse and the army will go
up, everyone straight in."

6So Joshua son of Nun called the
priests and said to them, "Take up the
ark of the covenant of the LORD and
have seven priests carry trumpets in
front of it." 7And he ordered the army,
"Advance[e]! March around the city, with
an armed guard going ahead of the ark
of the LORD."

8When Joshua had spoken to the
people, the seven priests carrying the
seven trumpets before the LORD went
forward, blowing their trumpets, and
the ark of the LORD's covenant followed
them. 9The armed guard marched ahead
of the priests who blew the trumpets,
and the rear guard[f] followed the ark. All
this time the trumpets were sounding.
10But Joshua had commanded the army,
"Do not give a war cry, do not raise your
voices, do not say a word until the day I
tell you to shout. Then shout![g]" 11So he
had the ark of the LORD carried around
the city, circling it once. Then the army
returned to camp and spent the night
there.

12Joshua got up early the next morning and the priests took up the ark of
the LORD. 13The seven priests carrying the seven trumpets went forward,

5:11 [s] Nu 15:19 [t] Lev 23:14
5:12 [u] Ex 16:35
5:13 [v] Ge 18:2; 32:24 [w] Nu 22:23
5:14 [x] Ge 17:3
5:15 [y] Ex 3:5; Ac 7:33
6:1 [z] Jos 24:11
6:2 [a] Dt 7:24; Jos 2:9,24; 8:1
6:4 [b] Lev 25:9; Nu 10:8
6:5 [c] Ex 19:13
[d] ver 20; 1Sa 4:5; Ps 42:4; Isa 42:13
6:7 [e] Ex 14:15
6:9 [f] ver 13; Isa 52:12
6:10 [g] ver 20

Jos 5:13–15 ❖ What does it look like to be on God's side, rather than thinking God is on our side?

[a] 12 Or *the day* [b] 14 Or *lord*

national life. Indeed, the day after Passover the people feed themselves for the first time with food grown in their new land. Since Israel now eats off the land, their daily supply of manna stops. Ahead lies the new era of living off the land of Canaan.

5:13—6:1 The phrase "drawn sword" (v. 13) elsewhere occurs only with "the angel of the LORD" (Nu 22:23) and thus creates the expectation in readers that the "man" is in fact a divine messenger in human form. It is almost comical to watch Joshua, oblivious to the other party's true identity, commandingly confront and interrogate him.

The commander virtually quotes Yahweh's familiar orders to Moses at the burning bush (Ex 3:5). Literarily, the echoed wording links the two scenes, reconfirming Joshua as Moses' successor and—more importantly—forever marking this episode as Joshua's "burning bush experience."

6:2–25 The journeys of the ark surround Jericho in a deadly ring of Yahweh's power; the city is doomed to fall before that power. The seventh day marks the ceremony's climax.

6:6–7 Joshua issues an order to execute Yahweh's battle plan. An armed guard is to precede and follow the ark in its daily journeys around the city (vv. 7b, 9b). The front guard, rear guard, and ark together personify that Israel as a whole is engaging in Yahweh's war.

6:8–11 The combination of blowing ram's horns and dead silence may strike terror in the hearts of the Canaanites watching the scene. The human actors play important roles. But ultimately that wooden box—the symbol of Yahweh's powerful presence—commands center stage.

6:12–15 The prominence of the priests fits the chapter's pattern and presents an important theme: Israel participates ceremonially in this episode of Yahweh's war, but it is Yahweh's presence that is decisive in toppling Jericho.

Day seven begins not just "early" (v. 12) but "at

marching before the ark of the LORD and
blowing the trumpets. The armed men
went ahead of them and the rear guard
followed the ark of the LORD, while the
trumpets kept sounding. 14So on the second day they marched around the city
once and returned to the camp. They did
this for six days.

15On the seventh day, they got up at
daybreak and marched around the city
seven times in the same manner, except that on that day they circled the
city seven times.[h] 16The seventh time
around, when the priests sounded the
trumpet blast, Joshua commanded the
army, "Shout! For the LORD has given
you the city! 17The city and all that is in
it are to be devoted[a][i] to the LORD. Only
Rahab the prostitute and all who are
with her in her house shall be spared,
because she hid[j] the spies we sent. 18But
keep away from the devoted things,[k]
so that you will not bring about your
own destruction by taking any of them.
Otherwise you will make the camp of
Israel liable to destruction[l] and bring
trouble[m] on it. 19All the silver and gold
and the articles of bronze and iron[n] are
sacred to the LORD and must go into
his treasury."

20When the trumpets sounded,[o] the
army shouted, and at the sound of the
trumpet, when the men gave a loud
shout,[p] the wall collapsed; so everyone
charged straight in, and they took the
city.[q] 21They devoted the city to the LORD
and destroyed[r] with the sword every living thing in it—men and women, young
and old, cattle, sheep and donkeys.

6:15 [h] 1Ki 18:44
6:17 [i] Lev 27:28; Dt 20:17 [j] Jos 2:4
6:18 [k] Jos 7:1 [l] Jos 7:12 [m] Jos 7:25,26
6:19 [n] ver 24; Nu 31:22
6:20 [o] Jdg 6:34; Jer 4:21; Am 2:2 [p] ver 5 [q] Heb 11:30
6:21 [r] Dt 20:16

Jos 6:20 ❖ When has God shown his miraculous power and protection in your life? In the lives of other believers around you?

[a] *17* The Hebrew term refers to the irrevocable giving over of things or persons to the LORD, often by totally destroying them; also in verses 18 and 21.

daybreak," and today the whole camp ("they"), not just Joshua, rises to greet it (cf. v. 12). Today, they circle Jericho a climactic seven times as Yahweh has commanded (v. 15b; cf. v. 4).

6:16–21 Joshua commands them, "Shout!"—but then issues his final instructions concerning the city's fall, which surprisingly postpones the climactic war. The literary effect is to heighten the scene's suspense and to underscore the importance of his instructions. This marks the first mention of the important concept of "devoted things." Destruction constitutes the way Yahweh requires Israel to implement his exclusive ownership.

PEOPLE TO KNOW // RAHAB

JOSHUA 6:25: Before the Israelites entered the promised land, Joshua sent two spies to check out Jericho. The two spies came to the house of a prostitute named Rahab who lived in the city wall. Not only did Rahab protect these men from the king, she also professed a remarkable faith in God.

Rahab told the spies that stories of the Israelites' victories had reached Canaan and that the people were quaking with fear because of them. Rahab declared her conviction that their God was the God of all the earth (Jos 2:11). She then asked for mercy when the Israelites conquered Canaan, not only for herself but for her entire family. In a directive reminiscent of God's instructions during the Passover in Egypt, the spies told Rahab that if she hung a scarlet cord from her window, all who were in her house during the battle would be saved (Jos 2:17–19). In the battle, it happened as the spies promised.

Rahab had a terrible background. She was a Canaanite prostitute, yet because of her faith in God, she and her entire family were saved. Rahab is mentioned in Hebrews as a hero of faith (Heb 11:31) and is also listed in Matthew's genealogy of Jesus Christ (Mt 1:5)—one of only five women mentioned. There she is named as the mother of Boaz, who married another foreigner: Ruth.

APPLICATION ✚ God cares less about our past and our bloodline than about our faith. From the outside, everything seemed wrong with Rahab, yet she demonstrated tremendous bravery in protecting the Israelite spies. She also demonstrated tremendous faith, proclaiming the God of Israel to be Lord over all. Wherever we have come from, whatever we have done, God can use us for great things. God invites us to put our faith in him, to leave the past behind, and to join the great story of his redemption.

22Joshua said to the two men who had
spied out the land, "Go into the prostitute's house and bring her out and all
who belong to her, in accordance with
your oath to her.[s]" 23So the young men
who had done the spying went in and
brought out Rahab, her father and mother, her brothers and sisters and all who
belonged to her.[t] They brought out her
entire family and put them in a place
outside the camp of Israel.
24Then they burned the whole city
and everything in it, but they put the
silver and gold and the articles of bronze
and iron[u] into the treasury of the LORD's
house. 25But Joshua spared Rahab the
prostitute,[v] with her family and all who
belonged to her, because she hid the
men Joshua had sent as spies to Jericho[w] — and she lives among the Israelites to this day.
26At that time Joshua pronounced this
solemn oath: "Cursed before the LORD is
the one who undertakes to rebuild this
city, Jericho:

"At the cost of his firstborn son
he will lay its foundations;
at the cost of his youngest
he will set up its gates."[x]

27So the LORD was with Joshua,[y] and
his fame spread[z] throughout the land.

Achan's Sin

7 But the Israelites were unfaithful
in regard to the devoted things[a];[a]
Achan son of Karmi, the son of Zimri,[b]
the son of Zerah,[b] of the tribe of Judah,
took some of them. So the LORD's anger
burned against Israel.
2Now Joshua sent men from Jericho to
Ai, which is near Beth Aven[c] to the east
of Bethel, and told them, "Go up and spy
out the region." So the men went up and
spied out Ai.
3When they returned to Joshua, they
said, "Not all the army will have to go
up against Ai. Send two or three thousand men to take it and do not weary
the whole army, for only a few people
live there." 4So about three thousand
went up; but they were routed by the
men of Ai,[d] 5who killed about thirty-six
of them. They chased the Israelites from
the city gate as far as the stone quarries
and struck them down on the slopes. At
this the hearts of the people melted in
fear[e] and became like water.
6Then Joshua tore his clothes[f] and fell
facedown to the ground before the ark
of the LORD, remaining there till evening. The elders of Israel did the same,
and sprinkled dust[g] on their heads. 7And
Joshua said, "Alas, Sovereign LORD, why
did you ever bring this people across the
Jordan to deliver us into the hands of the
Amorites to destroy us?[h] If only we had

6:22 [s] Jos 2:14; Heb 11:31
6:23 [t] Jos 2:13
6:24 [u] ver 19
6:25 [v] Heb 11:31 [w] Jos 2:6
6:26 [x] 1Ki 16:34
6:27 [y] Ge 39:2; Jos 1:5 [z] Jos 9:1
7:1 [a] Jos 6:18 [b] Jos 22:20
7:2 [c] Jos 18:12; 1Sa 13:5; 14:23
7:4 [d] Lev 26:17; Dt 28:25
7:5 [e] Lev 26:36; Jos 2:9,11; Eze 21:7; Na 2:10
7:6 [f] Ge 37:29 [g] 1Sa 4:12; 2Sa 13:19; Ne 9:1; Job 2:12; La 2:10; Rev 18:19
7:7 [h] Ex 5:22

[a] *1* The Hebrew term refers to the irrevocable giving over of things or persons to the LORD, often by totally destroying them; also in verses 11, 12, 13 and 15. [b] *1* See Septuagint and 1 Chron. 2:6; Hebrew *Zabdi*; also in verses 17 and 18.

6:23 Rahab and her entire family are located somewhere "outside the camp of Israel," presumably to maintain its ritual cleanness.

6:26–27 Why single out Jericho for cursing? Ruined Jericho would silently warn Israel of the terrible fate awaiting those who abandon Yahweh for other gods.

Yahweh's stunning victory further enhances Joshua's public stature. It confirms convincingly that "the LORD was with Joshua" just as he promised (v. 27a). An Israelite leader can have no better reputation.

5:2—6:27 We are not at peace but at war—the Jesus War. History illustrates one important thing about the Jesus War: Jesus Christ has already won its decisive battles. To us, the tide of war often seems turned against us, but his victories have in reality decisively turned it in our favor. To paraphrase Joshua, Jesus has already "given the enemy into our hands." The cross and the resurrection mark Jesus' most decisive victory. At Calvary and the empty tomb, God through Christ decisively defeated humanity's bitterest enemies: sin and death.

7:1–14 Without preface or fanfare, the narrator describes a highly serious, treacherous breach of trust between Yahweh and Israel. As with Jericho, Joshua acts on his own, dispatching another reconnaissance team to spy out the region around Ai (v. 2). As at Jericho, the spies' report on Ai is positive (v. 3): no need to march the whole army up there.

7:5 The greatly outnumbered few kill about thirty-six Israelites, then go on the offensive, chasing the invaders from their front gate. Grave doubts suddenly plague Israel.

7:6–9 About nightfall, Joshua finally speaks, addressing God with a typical formula of deference. He then asks an accusatory question: Why did Yahweh bring "this people" across the Jordan only to hand "us" over to the Amorites for destruction? Given Joshua's ignorance of Achan's deceit, one may forgive him the frustration and indignation with which his words ring. Joshua ends his speech the way he began it—with a question to drive home what he sees as ultimately at stake here for Yahweh.

PEOPLE TO KNOW // ACHAN

JOSHUA 7:1, 19–26: The battle of Jericho was a decisive victory for Israel. God handed the city over to the Israelites in a dramatic display of power: Israel marched and shouted, and God caused Jericho's walls to crumble. Yet after this victory, one person's actions brought about a tragedy that affected the entire community. One man in the Israelite army did what Joshua had expressly forbidden. He took some of the spoils of Jericho for himself. His name was Achan (Jos 7:1).

Achan's sin was not discovered until Israel's next battle, at Ai. There Israel suffered a surprising defeat, sending the camp into a panic. Joshua tore his clothes in grief and fell in prayer before God. God then revealed to Joshua that someone in the Israelite camp had violated his command at Jericho.

The next day all the Israelites assembled before Joshua, and Achan was identified as the transgressor. Achan admitted his sin, saying that he had hidden some clothes, silver, and gold from Jericho under his tent. After Joshua verified Achan's confession, Achan paid the price for his sin—as did his entire family.

Achan provides an interesting foil to Rahab. Rahab was a Canaanite prostitute who helped the Israelites who came to Jericho to spy out the city (Jos 2:1). Though she was not of the chosen nation of Israel, her faith in God resulted in her and her entire family being saved from destruction. Achan was an Israelite and part of Israel's army, but he chose to be greedy and deceitful. History remembers his sin and his resulting punishment.

APPLICATION ✚ It is difficult to read that Achan and his whole family (and animals) were put to death for his sins of covetousness, disobedience and theft. It reminds us, however, that God's commands are not to be taken lightly. God graciously reveals his will, and we are guilty when we choose to reject it.

The theme of corporate guilt is also evident in this story. Achan's sin was a private act, but his punishment was public. Also, his one act resulted in punishment for his family, and his sin affected the entire community as they were defeated in battle at Ai. We do well to remember that even seemingly small actions can have incredibly tragic consequences.

been content to stay on the other side of
the Jordan! 8Pardon your servant, Lord.
What can I say, now that Israel has been
routed by its enemies? 9The Canaanites
and the other people of the country will
hear about this and they will surround us
and wipe out our name from the earth.[i]
What then will you do for your own great
name?"
10The LORD said to Joshua, "Stand up!
What are you doing down on your face?
11Israel has sinned; they have violated my
covenant,[j] which I commanded them to
keep. They have taken some of the devoted things; they have stolen, they have
lied,[k] they have put them with their own
possessions. 12That is why the Israelites
cannot stand against their enemies;[l] they
turn their backs and run because they
have been made liable to destruction.[m] I
will not be with you anymore unless you
destroy whatever among you is devoted
to destruction.
13"Go, consecrate the people. Tell them,
'Consecrate yourselves[n] in preparation
for tomorrow; for this is what the LORD,
the God of Israel, says: There are devoted things among you, Israel. You cannot
stand against your enemies until you
remove them.
14" 'In the morning, present yourselves
tribe by tribe. The tribe the LORD chooses[o] shall come forward clan by clan; the
clan the LORD chooses shall come forward family by family; and the family
the LORD chooses shall come forward
man by man. 15Whoever is caught with
the devoted things shall be destroyed
by fire, along with all that belongs to
him.[p] He has violated the covenant[q] of
the LORD and has done an outrageous
thing in Israel!' "[r]

7:9 [i] Ex 32:12; Dt 9:28
7:11 [j] Jos 6:17-19 [k] Ac 5:1-2
7:12 [l] Nu 14:45; Jdg 2:14 [m] Jos 6:18
7:13 [n] Jos 3:5; 6:18
7:14 [o] Pr 16:33
7:15 [p] 1Sa 14:39 [q] ver 11 [r] Ge 34:7

7:10–12 In God's eyes, Joshua's posture and procedure are totally out of line—in modern terms, he "just doesn't get it." Unless Israel does what they should have done in the first place, Yahweh refuses to be with them.

7:13–15 Yahweh spells out the conditions: Israel is to present themselves before God by tribes so that Yahweh may, step by step, sift out the mystery man's tribe, clan, and family. The penalty is severe. Singlehandedly, this one man has returned Israel to their previous state of uncleanness and has driven Yahweh from their midst.

16Early the next morning Joshua had Israel come forward by tribes, and Judah was chosen. 17The clans of Judah came forward, and the Zerahites were chosen.[s] He had the clan of the Zerahites come forward by families, and Zimri was chosen. 18Joshua had his family come forward man by man, and Achan son of Karmi, the son of Zimri, the son of Zerah, of the tribe of Judah, was chosen.

19Then Joshua said to Achan, "My son, give glory[t] to the LORD, the God of Israel, and honor him. Tell[u] me what you have done; do not hide it from me."

20Achan replied, "It is true! I have sinned against the LORD, the God of Israel. This is what I have done: 21When I saw in the plunder a beautiful robe from Babylonia,[a] two hundred shekels[b] of silver and a bar of gold weighing fifty shekels,[c] I coveted[v] them and took them. They are hidden in the ground inside my tent, with the silver underneath."

22So Joshua sent messengers, and they ran to the tent, and there it was, hidden in his tent, with the silver underneath. 23They took the things from the tent, brought them to Joshua and all the Israelites and spread them out before the LORD.

24Then Joshua, together with all Israel, took Achan son of Zerah, the silver, the robe, the gold bar, his sons and daughters, his cattle, donkeys and sheep, his tent and all that he had, to the Valley of Achor.[w] 25Joshua said, "Why have you brought this trouble[x] on us? The LORD will bring trouble on you today."

Then all Israel stoned him,[y] and after they had stoned the rest, they burned them. 26Over Achan they heaped up a large pile of rocks, which remains to this day. Then the LORD turned from his fierce anger.[z] Therefore that place has been called the Valley of Achor[d][a] ever since.

7:17 [s] Nu 26:20
7:19 [t] 1Sa 6:5; Jer 13:16; Jn 9:24* [u] 1Sa 14:43
7:21 [v] Dt 7:25; Eph 5:5; 1Ti 6:10
7:24 [w] ver 26; Jos 15:7
7:25 [x] Jos 6:18 [y] Dt 17:5
7:26 [z] Nu 25:4; Dt 13:17
[a] ver 24; Isa 65:10; Hos 2:15
8:1 [b] Dt 31:6 [c] Dt 1:21; 7:18; Jos 1:9 [d] Jos 10:7 [e] Jos 6:2
8:2 [f] ver 27; Dt 20:14
8:7 [g] Jdg 7:7; 1Sa 23:4
8:8 [h] Jdg 20:29-38 [i] ver 19

Jos 7:20-21 ❖ When has desire led us into sin? How did our actions affect others?

Ai Destroyed

8 Then the LORD said to Joshua, "Do not be afraid;[b] do not be discouraged.[c] Take the whole army[d] with you, and go up and attack Ai. For I have delivered[e] into your hands the king of Ai, his people, his city and his land. 2You shall do to Ai and its king as you did to Jericho and its king, except that you may carry off their plunder and livestock for yourselves.[f] Set an ambush behind the city."

3So Joshua and the whole army moved out to attack Ai. He chose thirty thousand of his best fighting men and sent them out at night 4with these orders: "Listen carefully. You are to set an ambush behind the city. Don't go very far from it. All of you be on the alert. 5I and all those with me will advance on the city, and when the men come out against us, as they did before, we will flee from them. 6They will pursue us until we have lured them away from the city, for they will say, 'They are running away from us as they did before.' So when we flee from them, 7you are to rise up from ambush and take the city. The LORD your God will give it into your hand.[g] 8When you have taken the city, set it on fire.[h] Do what the LORD has commanded.[i] See to it; you have my orders."

9Then Joshua sent them off, and they

[a] 21 Hebrew *Shinar* [b] 21 That is, about 5 pounds or about 2.3 kilograms [c] 21 That is, about 1 1/4 pounds or about 575 grams
[d] 26 *Achor* means *trouble.*

7:16–23 The scene is high drama, the atmosphere tense. Subdued comments probably ripple through the crowd at the shocking revelation, and a mini trial ensues. Joshua commands Achan to "give glory to the LORD . . . and . . . honor" (v. 19). The command assumes that Achan's crime somehow violates Yahweh's honor and praiseworthiness, so now Achan must offset that offense. Achan does so and provides a full accounting of his secret crime.

Joshua dispatches messengers find the stuff hidden there just as he had said (v. 22). They bring them and "spread [lit. poured] them out before the LORD" (v. 23). "Before the LORD" is appropriate in two respects: First, the goods really belong to him; second, Yahweh is the judicial authority sponsoring the trial.

7:24–26 Israel meets Yahweh's demands. They remove the "devoted things" and in so doing restore the community to its pre-Achan ritual cleanness.

8:1–2 Yahweh orders Joshua to lead "the whole army" up to attack Ai—ironically, the exact opposite advice given Joshua the last time by the returning spies (7:3). This time, Israelites may help themselves to plunder and livestock.

8:3–9 Before the elite force embarks, Joshua issues crucial orders that flesh out Yahweh's general concept into a detailed, coordinated battle plan (vv. 4–9).

went to the place of ambush[j] and lay in
wait between Bethel and Ai, to the west
of Ai — but Joshua spent that night with
the people.
10Early the next morning[k] Joshua mustered his army, and he and the leaders of
Israel[l] marched before them to Ai. 11The
entire force that was with him marched
up and approached the city and arrived
in front of it. They set up camp north of
Ai, with the valley between them and
the city. 12Joshua had taken about five
thousand men and set them in ambush
between Bethel and Ai, to the west of
the city. 13So the soldiers took up their
positions — with the main camp to the
north of the city and the ambush to the
west of it. That night Joshua went into
the valley.
14When the king of Ai saw this, he and
all the men of the city hurried out early
in the morning to meet Israel in battle at
a certain place overlooking the Arabah.[m]
But he did not know[n] that an ambush
had been set against him behind the city.
15Joshua and all Israel let themselves be
driven back[o] before them, and they fled
toward the wilderness.[p] 16All the men of
Ai were called to pursue them, and they
pursued Joshua and were lured away[q]
from the city. 17Not a man remained in
Ai or Bethel who did not go after Israel.
They left the city open and went in pursuit of Israel.
18Then the LORD said to Joshua, "Hold
out toward Ai the javelin[r] that is in your
hand,[s] for into your hand I will deliver
the city." So Joshua held out toward the
city the javelin that was in his hand.[t] 19As
soon as he did this, the men in the ambush rose quickly[u] from their position
and rushed forward. They entered the
city and captured it and quickly set it
on fire.[v]
20The men of Ai looked back and saw
the smoke of the city rising up into the
sky,[w] but they had no chance to escape
in any direction; the Israelites who had
been fleeing toward the wilderness had
turned back against their pursuers.
21For when Joshua and all Israel saw
that the ambush had taken the city and
that smoke was going up from it, they
turned around and attacked the men
of Ai. 22Those in the ambush also came
out of the city against them, so that they
were caught in the middle, with Israelites on both sides. Israel cut them down,
leaving them neither survivors nor fugitives.[x] 23But they took the king of Ai
alive[y] and brought him to Joshua.
24When Israel had finished killing all
the men of Ai in the fields and in the
wilderness where they had chased them,
and when every one of them had been
put to the sword, all the Israelites returned to Ai and killed those who were
in it. 25Twelve thousand men and wom-
en fell that day — all the people of Ai.[z]
26For Joshua did not draw back the hand
that held out his javelin until he had destroyed[a][a] all who lived in Ai.[b] 27But Israel
did carry off for themselves the livestock
and plunder of this city, as the LORD had
instructed Joshua.[c]
28So Joshua burned[d] Ai[b][e] and made it
a permanent heap of ruins,[f] a desolate
place to this day.[g] 29He impaled the body
of the king of Ai on a pole and left it there
until evening. At sunset,[h] Joshua ordered

8:9 [j] 2Ch 13:13
8:10 [k] Ge 22:3 [l] Jos 7:6
8:14 [m] Dt 1:1 [n] Jdg 20:34
8:15 [o] Jdg 20:36 [p] Jos 15:61; 16:1; 18:12
8:16 [q] Jdg 20:31
8:18 [r] Job 41:26; Ps 35:3 [s] Ex 4:2; 14:16; 17:9-12 [t] ver 26
8:19 [u] Jdg 20:33
[v] ver 8
8:20 [w] Jdg 20:40
8:22 [x] Dt 7:2; Jos 10:1
8:23 [y] 1Sa 15:8
8:25 [z] Dt 20:16-18
8:26 [a] Nu 21:2 [b] Ex 17:12
8:27 [c] ver 2
8:28 [d] Nu 31:10 [e] Jos 7:2; Jer 49:3 [f] Dt 13:16; Jos 10:1 [g] Ge 35:20
8:29 [h] Dt 21:23; Jn 19:31

[a] 26 The Hebrew term refers to the irrevocable giving over of things or persons to the LORD, often by totally destroying them. [b] *28 Ai* means *the ruin.*

8:10-13 Carefully crafted narration unfolds the dramatic scene. An opening wide shot shows Joshua mustering the army, then a close-up follows him and Israel's elders leading the troops uphill toward Ai (v. 10). The view then quickly widens to show the ascent and dramatic arrival of the entire force with Joshua at the very front of the city (v. 11). Joshua spends that night in the valley, perhaps positioning himself to lead his troops into battle (v. 13). Everyone quietly awaits the dawn.

8:14-18 Joshua and all Israel feign being routed and flee eastward down the wilderness road. Meanwhile, "lured away" from Ai (cf. v. 6) just as Joshua planned, Ai's entire military force hotly pursues them, the village's gates open and its inhabitants defenseless (v. 17). Yahweh orders Joshua to stretch out the "javelin" in his hand toward Ai because "into your hand I will deliver the city" (v. 18).

8:19-23 The visible fire and smoke confirm the successful ambush, so the fleeing Israelites turn around, springing the fatal trap (vv. 20-21). The resulting slaughter is total—there are no survivors or escapees, with one exception: The Israelites single out the king of Ai and bring him alive to Joshua, an action that signals absolute victory (v. 23).

8:24-29 Yahweh permits Israel to keep plunder and livestock from Ai. Joshua accomplishes two key things. (1) He reduces Ai to a permanent pile of burnt rubble. (2) Joshua executes the king of Ai, impaling him on a post until evening (v. 29), and then throws his corpse down at the entrance of Ai's city gate, exactly obeying Moses' instructions (Dt 21:22-23).

them to take the body from the pole and
throw it down at the entrance of the city
gate. And they raised a large pile of rocks[i]
over it, which remains to this day.

The Covenant Renewed at Mount Ebal

30Then Joshua built on Mount Ebal[j]
an altar[k] to the LORD, the God of Israel,
31as Moses the servant of the LORD had
commanded the Israelites. He built it
according to what is written in the Book
of the Law of Moses — an altar of uncut
stones, on which no iron tool[l] had been
used. On it they offered to the LORD
burnt offerings and sacrificed fellowship offerings.[m] 32There, in the presence
of the Israelites, Joshua wrote on stones
a copy of the law of Moses.[n] 33All the Israelites, with their elders, officials and
judges, were standing on both sides of
the ark of the covenant of the LORD, facing the Levitical[o] priests who carried it.
Both the foreigners living among them
and the native-born[p] were there. Half of
the people stood in front of Mount Gerizim and half of them in front of Mount
Ebal,[q] as Moses the servant of the LORD
had formerly commanded when he gave
instructions to bless the people of Israel.
34Afterward, Joshua read all the
words of the law — the blessings and
the curses — just as it is written in the
Book of the Law.[r] 35There was not a word
of all that Moses had commanded that
Joshua did not read to the whole assembly of Israel, including the women and
children, and the foreigners who lived
among them.[s]

8:29 [i] 2Sa 18:17
8:30 [j] Dt 11:29 [k] Ex 20:24
8:31 [l] Ex 20:25 [m] Dt 27:6-7
8:32 [n] Dt 27:8
8:33 [o] Dt 31:12 [p] Lev 16:29 [q] Dt 11:29; 27:11-14
8:34 [r] Dt 28:61; 31:11; Jos 1:8
8:35 [s] Ex 12:38; Dt 31:12
9:1 [t] Nu 34:6 [u] Ex 3:17; Jos 3:10
9:3 [v] ver 17; Jos 10:2; 2Sa 2:12; 2Ch 1:3; Isa 28:21

Jos 8:34-35 ❖ In what ways might we review and renew our covenant relationship with God?

The Gibeonite Deception

9 Now when all the kings west of the
Jordan heard about these things —
the kings in the hill country, in the western foothills, and along the entire coast
of the Mediterranean Sea[t] as far as Lebanon (the kings of the Hittites, Amorites,
Canaanites, Perizzites, Hivites and Jebusites)[u] — 2they came together to wage
war against Joshua and Israel.
3However, when the people of Gibeon[v] heard what Joshua had done to
Jericho and Ai, 4they resorted to a
ruse: They went as a delegation whose
donkeys were loaded[a] with worn-out
sacks and old wineskins, cracked and

[a] 4 Most Hebrew manuscripts; some Hebrew manuscripts, Vulgate and Syriac (see also Septuagint) *They prepared provisions and loaded their donkeys*

8:30-31 Joshua builds an altar, and the people immediately offer on it the "burnt offerings" and "fellowship offerings" that Moses commanded (v. 31). The wording in v. 31 echoes language in the covenant-making ceremony at Mount Sinai (Ex 24:5). Shechem also has ties to Israel's patriarchs. Both Abraham and Jacob built altars there when they, too, entered Canaan (Ge 12:7; 33:20). The altar raised by Joshua on Mount Ebal probably stakes a similar claim for the present generation.
8:32-33 The term "instruction of Moses" more likely recalls his writing of "this law" at the plains of Moab since the context has the Israelites present (Dt 31:7, 9). This ceremony serves a single purpose: to bestow on the people Yahweh's blessings.
8:34-35 Joshua reads aloud. The act is momentous—the first recorded public reading since the death of Moses. The author underscores that Joshua reads every single word (v. 35). The comment both enhances the identity of Joshua as a worthy successor to Moses and solidifies the instruction of Moses as absolutely authoritative.

✣ **7:1—8:35** What sins today might compare to Achan's? As we saw, Achan sinned by keeping to himself things that Yahweh had declared to be his own exclusive property (*herem*). The answer to our question thus lies in identifying things that God today claims to be his own. Certainly, the church and other Christians ultimately belong to only God and not to us. The church is the bride of Christ himself (Rev 19:7), a spiritual union based on Jesus' loving, sacrificial death on the cross on behalf of the church (Eph 5:25, 29). Jesus deeply cares for his bride, so it would be Achanesque to do anything to harm the church, as Achan's sin did grave harm to Israel. Therefore, the example of Achan warns against doing anything that sullies the public reputation of the church, puts a strain on its relationship with God himself, or brings disunity to the body. What applies to the church as a whole likewise applies to our treatment of fellow believers. Woe to us if we lead them astray, confuse their minds, harm their walk with Christ, or disillusion them about the gospel.

9:1-2 News of Israel's capture and the destruction of Ai (and perhaps of Jericho) galvanizes Canaan's kings into action. They recognize that the threat Israel poses is a real one.
9:3-6 Like Rahab, the Gibeonites thrust the reader eyeball-to-eyeball with real live Canaanites and their real live fears. What the Gibeonites considered "cleverness," Israel will call "treachery" here.

mended. 5 They put worn and patched sandals on their feet and wore old clothes. All the bread of their food supply was dry and moldy. 6 Then they went to Joshua in the camp at Gilgal[w] and said to him and the Israelites, "We have come from a distant country; make a treaty with us."

7 The Israelites said to the Hivites,[x] "But perhaps you live near us, so how can we make a treaty[y] with you?"

8 "We are your servants,[z]" they said to Joshua.

But Joshua asked, "Who are you and where do you come from?"

9 They answered: "Your servants have come from a very distant country[a] because of the fame of the LORD your God. For we have heard reports[b] of him: all that he did in Egypt, 10 and all that he did to the two kings of the Amorites east of the Jordan — Sihon king of Heshbon, and Og king of Bashan,[c] who reigned in Ashtaroth.[d] 11 And our elders and all those living in our country said to us, 'Take provisions for your journey; go and meet them and say to them, "We are your servants; make a treaty with us." ' 12 This bread of ours was warm when we packed it at home on the day we left to come to you. But now see how dry and moldy it is. 13 And these wineskins that we filled were new, but see how cracked they are. And our clothes and sandals are worn out by the very long journey."

14 The Israelites sampled their provisions but did not inquire[e] of the LORD. 15 Then Joshua made a treaty of peace[f] with them to let them live, and the leaders of the assembly ratified it by oath.

16 Three days after they made the treaty with the Gibeonites, the Israelites heard that they were neighbors, living near them. 17 So the Israelites set out and on the third day came to their cities: Gibeon, Kephirah, Beeroth[g] and Kiriath Jearim.[h] 18 But the Israelites did not attack them, because the leaders of the assembly had sworn an oath[i] to them by the LORD, the God of Israel.

The whole assembly grumbled[j] against the leaders, 19 but all the leaders answered, "We have given them our oath by the LORD, the God of Israel, and we cannot touch them now. 20 This is what we will do to them: We will let them live, so that God's wrath will not fall on us for breaking the oath we swore to them." 21 They continued, "Let them live,[k] but let them be woodcutters and water carriers[l] in the service of the whole assembly." So the leaders' promise to them was kept.

22 Then Joshua summoned the Gibeonites and said, "Why did you deceive us by saying, 'We live a long way[m] from you,' while actually you live near[n] us? 23 You are now under a curse:[o] You will never be released from service as woodcutters and water carriers for the house of my God."

24 They answered Joshua, "Your servants

9:6 [w] Jos 5:10
9:7 [x] ver 1; Jos 11:19 [y] Ex 23:32; Dt 7:2
9:8 [z] Dt 20:11; 2Ki 10:5
9:9 [a] Dt 20:15 [b] ver 24; Jos 2:9
9:10 [c] Nu 21:33 [d] Nu 21:24,35
9:14 [e] Nu 27:21
9:15 [f] Ex 23:32; Jos 11:19; 2Sa 21:2
9:17 [g] Jos 18:25 [h] 1Sa 7:1-2
9:18 [i] Ps 15:4 [j] Ex 15:24
9:21 [k] ver 15 [l] Dt 29:11
9:22 [m] ver 6 [n] ver 16
9:23 [o] Ge 9:25

Jos 9:26 ❖ Despite the Gibeonites' deception, Joshua honored their treaty. When have you kept a promise, even when it was difficult or inconvenient?

9:7–8 The subsequent conversation pits wary Israelites against cagey Gibeonites. Joshua presses them for details about their identity (v. 8b).

9:9–11 They emphasize the reason for their trip: The magnet of Yahweh's "fame" has drawn them to visit the Israelites. They cite reports of his victories. How could Israel ever deny a people who honor Yahweh and want peace?

9:12–16 To alleviate suspicions once and for all, the visitors point out hard evidence that verifies their "very long journey" (vv. 12–13). Some Israelite men (but not Joshua) take the bait. Their actions naively trust the matter to their human senses rather than to divine guidance. Whatever his misgivings, Joshua makes a treaty to spare the lives of these strangers, and Israel's leaders ratify it with an oath (v. 15).

9:16–18 The treaty is only three days old when Israel learns that their new "foreign" partners are in fact Gibeonites. The oath prohibits Israel from attacking their treaty partner but does not prevent the Israelite community at large from grumbling against the leaders who took it (v. 18).

9:19–21 The leaders apparently assume that Israel may not simply declare the treaty "null and void" because it was concluded under false pretenses. Again, no one consults with Yahweh, who could have either voided the treaty or voiced approval of it.

9:22–23 Joshua indicts the Gibeonites. Joshua's curse adds an important detail—the Gibeonites' woodcutting and water carrying will always serve "the house of my God" (v. 23). In assigning the Gibeonites to the sanctuary, the sacred space over which only priests preside, Joshua exercises an authority similar to that of Moses.

9:24–27 The Gibeonites defend their actions. A change to more formal literary declaration brings the scene to a close (v. 27). From distant hindsight, the narrator reiterates Joshua's twofold assignment of the Gibeonites. In a sense, this honors them: Their tasks may be lowly, but their workplace enjoys the highest rank and serves Yahweh Most High himself.

were clearly told[p] how the LORD your God had commanded his servant Moses to give you the whole land and to wipe out all its inhabitants from before you. So we feared for our lives because of you, and that is why we did this. 25We are now in your hands.[q] Do to us whatever seems good and right to you."

26So Joshua saved them from the Israelites, and they did not kill them. 27That day he made the Gibeonites woodcutters and water carriers for the assembly, to provide for the needs of the altar of the LORD at the place the LORD would choose.[r] And that is what they are to this day.

The Sun Stands Still

10 Now Adoni-Zedek king of Jerusalem[s] heard that Joshua had taken Ai[t] and totally destroyed[a][u] it, doing to Ai and its king as he had done to Jericho and its king, and that the people of Gibeon had made a treaty of peace[v] with Israel and had become their allies. 2He and his people were very much alarmed at this, because Gibeon was an important city, like one of the royal cities; it was larger than Ai, and all its men were good fighters. 3So Adoni-Zedek king of Jerusalem appealed to Hoham king of Hebron,[w] Piram king of Jarmuth, Japhia king of Lachish[x] and Debir king of Eglon. 4"Come up and help me attack Gibeon," he said, "because it has made peace[y] with Joshua and the Israelites."

5Then the five kings of the Amorites[z] — the kings of Jerusalem, Hebron, Jarmuth, Lachish and Eglon — joined forces. They moved up with all their troops and took up positions against Gibeon and attacked it.

6The Gibeonites then sent word to Joshua in the camp at Gilgal: "Do not abandon your servants. Come up to us quickly and save us! Help us, because all the Amorite kings from the hill country have joined forces against us."

7So Joshua marched up from Gilgal with his entire army,[a] including all the best fighting men. 8The LORD said to Joshua, "Do not be afraid[b] of them; I have given them into your hand. Not one of them will be able to withstand you."

9After an all-night march from Gilgal, Joshua took them by surprise. 10The LORD threw them into confusion before Israel,[c] so Joshua and the Israelites defeated them completely at Gibeon. Israel pursued them along the road going up to Beth Horon[d] and cut them down all the way to Azekah[e] and Makkedah. 11As they fled before Israel on the road down from Beth Horon to Azekah, the LORD hurled large hailstones[f] down on them, and more of them died from the hail than were killed by the swords of the Israelites.

12On the day the LORD gave the Amorites[g] over to Israel, Joshua said to the LORD in the presence of Israel:

9:24 [p] ver 9
9:25 [q] Ge 16:6
9:27 [r] Dt 12:5
10:1 [s] Jdg 1:7 [t] Jos 8:1 [u] Dt 20:16; Jos 8:22 [v] Jos 9:15
10:3 [w] Ge 13:18 [x] 2Ch 11:9; 25:27; Ne 11:30; Isa 36:2; 37:8; Jer 34:7; Mic 1:13
10:4 [y] Jos 9:15
10:5 [z] Nu 13:29
10:7 [a] Jos 8:1
10:8 [b] Dt 3:2; Jos 1:9
10:10 [c] Dt 7:23 [d] Jos 16:3,5 [e] Jos 15:35
10:11 [f] Ps 18:12; Isa 28:2,17
10:12 [g] Am 2:9

Jos 10:6–7 ❖ How can we defend the cause of the oppressed or threatened near us?

[a] *1* The Hebrew term refers to the irrevocable giving over of things or persons to the LORD, often by totally destroying them; also in verses 28, 35, 37, 39 and 40.

10:1–7 Adoni-Zedek fears a domino effect of falling cities—a seismic shift in the balance of power—that threatens his own kingdom. The five Amorite kings muster their armies at Jerusalem, proceed to Gibeon, set up camp, and lay siege to it (v. 5). In response, Joshua leads the entire army, including all its "best fighting men" (v. 7) on an all-night march to defend Israel's beleaguered ally, Gibeon.
10:8–11 As the enemy flees from Israel, Yahweh showers them with huge hailstones (v. 11). Since Israel could not have won this battle on their own, the victory ultimately belongs to Yahweh.
10:12–13 This intriguing and important text has stirred much discussion. While the cosmic scale of the text's claims is what amazes modern readers, what stuns the narrator is the earthly scene—that Joshua prays and Yahweh partners with him in fighting for Israel (v. 14). What astonishes the narrator is that God heeds a request of such cosmic magnitude.

Scholars, however, have interpreted vv. 12–13 in various ways. The traditional view, one still held by many today, assumes that the earth literally stops rotating, thereby lengthening the day to give time to attain victory. Others find that view implausible because the universe apparently shows no traces of such a cosmic event, and such a cosmic stoppage of nature seems out of keeping with God's character. Instead, they propose solutions involving natural phenomena.

An important starting point in considering this passage is to take seriously its poetic nature—that its context is phenomenological and metaphorical rather than historical or scientific. The best option is to read vv. 12–13 figuratively as a poetic depiction of the military conflict on a cosmic scale. It compares to the claim of another poem, the song of Deborah (Jdg 5:20). The poetic excerpt uses cosmic terms rhetorically to magnify the majestic power of God who won this great victory.

"Sun, stand still over Gibeon,
and you, moon, over the Valley of
Aijalon.[h]"
13 So the sun stood still,[i]
and the moon stopped,
till the nation avenged itself on[a]
its enemies,

as it is written in the Book of Jashar.[j]
The sun stopped[k] in the middle of the
sky and delayed going down about a full
day. 14 There has never been a day like
it before or since, a day when the LORD
listened to a human being. Surely the
LORD was fighting[l] for Israel!
15 Then Joshua returned with all Israel
to the camp at Gilgal.[m]

Five Amorite Kings Killed

16 Now the five kings had fled and hidden in the cave at Makkedah. 17 When
Joshua was told that the five kings had
been found hiding in the cave at Makkedah, 18 he said, "Roll large rocks up to
the mouth of the cave, and post some
men there to guard it. 19 But don't stop;
pursue your enemies! Attack them from
the rear and don't let them reach their
cities, for the LORD your God has given
them into your hand."
20 So Joshua and the Israelites defeated them completely,[n] but a few survivors
managed to reach their fortified cities.
21 The whole army then returned safely to Joshua in the camp at Makkedah,
and no one uttered a word against the
Israelites.
22 Joshua said, "Open the mouth of the
cave and bring those five kings out to
me." 23 So they brought the five kings
out of the cave — the kings of Jerusalem,
Hebron, Jarmuth, Lachish and Eglon.
24 When they had brought these kings
to Joshua, he summoned all the men of
Israel and said to the army commanders
who had come with him, "Come here
and put your feet[o] on the necks of these
kings." So they came forward and placed
their feet[p] on their necks.
25 Joshua said to them, "Do not be
afraid; do not be discouraged. Be strong
and courageous.[q] This is what the LORD
will do to all the enemies you are going
to fight." 26 Then Joshua put the kings to
death and exposed their bodies on five
poles, and they were left hanging on the
poles until evening.
27 At sunset[r] Joshua gave the order and
they took them down from the poles and
threw them into the cave where they
had been hiding. At the mouth of the
cave they placed large rocks, which are
there to this day.

Southern Cities Conquered

28 That day Joshua took Makkedah. He
put the city and its king to the sword and
totally destroyed everyone in it. He left
no survivors.[s] And he did to the king of
Makkedah as he had done to the king
of Jericho.[t]
29 Then Joshua and all Israel with him
moved on from Makkedah to Libnah and
attacked it. 30 The LORD also gave that
city and its king into Israel's hand. The
city and everyone in it Joshua put to the
sword. He left no survivors there. And
he did to its king as he had done to the
king of Jericho.
31 Then Joshua and all Israel with him
moved on from Libnah to Lachish; he
took up positions against it and attacked
it. 32 The LORD gave Lachish into Israel's
hands, and Joshua took it on the second
day. The city and everyone in it he put
to the sword, just as he had done to Libnah. 33 Meanwhile, Horam king of Gezer[u]
had come up to help Lachish, but Joshua

10:12 [h] Jdg 1:35; 12:12
10:13 [i] Hab 3:11 [j] 2Sa 1:18 [k] Isa 38:8
10:14 [l] ver 42; Ex 14:14; Dt 1:30; Ps 106:43; 136:24
10:15 [m] ver 43
10:20 [n] Dt 20:16
10:24 [o] Mal 4:3 [p] Ps 110:1
10:25 [q] Dt 31:6
10:27 [r] Dt 21:23; Jos 8:9,29
10:28 [s] Dt 20:16 [t] Jos 6:21
10:33 [u] Jos 16:3, 10; Jdg 1:29; 1Ki 9:15

[a] 13 Or *nation triumphed over*

10:15–17 The five kings hope to hide themselves out of sight until the crisis passes. However, information as to their whereabouts reaches Joshua at the Israelite camp (v. 17).

10:18–21 They roll large stones over the cave opening, making it an instant prisoner-of-war cell. This will prevent any rescue by loyal troops or an escape by the monarchs themselves (v. 18). Rather than describe the ensuing battle, the narrator skips ahead to underscore its results (v. 20-21).

10:22–27 Joshua seizes the moment for a symbolic action to benefit his troops. They can be strong and courageous because Yahweh will similarly defeat all the enemies they are now battling (v. 25b). Though it sounds inhumane to modern readers, this treatment was typical of ancient warfare.

10:28–39 Despite an astounding day of victory, other battles remain for Joshua and Israel, but to treat them the narrator adopts a style with repeated statements. The following are its core items: (1) The city's capture (vv. 28, 32, 35, 37, 39) (2) The siege and attack (vv. 29, 31, 34, 36, 38) (3) The city, everyone put to the sword (vv. 28, 30, 32, 35, 37, 39) (4) No survivors remain (vv. 28, 30, 33, 35, 37, 39) (5) The king suffers the same fate as the king of city-X (vv. 28, 30, 32, 35, 37, 39).

defeated him and his army — until no
survivors were left.
34Then Joshua and all Israel with him
moved on from Lachish to Eglon; they
took up positions against it and attacked
it. 35They captured it that same day and
put it to the sword and totally destroyed
everyone in it, just as they had done to
Lachish.
36Then Joshua and all Israel with him
went up from Eglon to Hebron[v] and attacked it. 37They took the city and put it
to the sword, together with its king, its
villages and everyone in it. They left no
survivors. Just as at Eglon, they totally
destroyed it and everyone in it.
38Then Joshua and all Israel with
him turned around and attacked Debir.[w] 39They took the city, its king and
its villages, and put them to the sword.
Everyone in it they totally destroyed.
They left no survivors. They did to Debir
and its king as they had done to Libnah
and its king and to Hebron.
40So Joshua subdued the whole region,
including the hill country, the Negev,[x]
the western foothills and the mountain
slopes,[y] together with all their kings.[z] He
left no survivors. He totally destroyed all
who breathed, just as the LORD, the God
of Israel, had commanded.[a] 41Joshua subdued them from Kadesh Barnea[b] to Gaza[c]
and from the whole region of Goshen[d] to
Gibeon. 42All these kings and their lands
Joshua conquered in one campaign, because the LORD, the God of Israel, fought[e]
for Israel.
43Then Joshua returned with all Israel
to the camp at Gilgal.[f]

Northern Kings Defeated

11 When Jabin[g] king of Hazor[h] heard
of this, he sent word to Jobab king
of Madon, to the kings of Shimron[i] and
Akshaph, 2and to the northern kings who
were in the mountains, in the Arabah[j]
south of Kinnereth,[k] in the western foothills and in Naphoth Dor[l] on the west; 3to
the Canaanites in the east and west; to the
Amorites, Hittites, Perizzites and Jebusites
in the hill country; and to the Hivites[m]
below Hermon in the region of Mizpah.[n]
4They came out with all their troops and
a large number of horses and chariots — a
huge army, as numerous as the sand on
the seashore.[o] 5All these kings joined forces[p] and made camp together at the Waters
of Merom to fight against Israel.
6The LORD said to Joshua, "Do not be
afraid of them, because by this time tomorrow I will hand[q] all of them, slain,
over to Israel. You are to hamstring[r] their
horses and burn their chariots."
7So Joshua and his whole army came
against them suddenly at the Waters
of Merom and attacked them, 8and the
LORD gave them into the hand of Israel.
They defeated them and pursued them
all the way to Greater Sidon, to Misre-
photh Maim,[s] and to the Valley of Mizpah
on the east, until no survivors were left.
9Joshua did to them as the LORD had directed: He hamstrung their horses and
burned their chariots.
10At that time Joshua turned back and
captured Hazor and put its king to the
sword. (Hazor had been the head of all
these kingdoms.) 11Everyone in it they
put to the sword. They totally destroyed[a]

10:36 [v] Jos 14:13; 15:13; Jdg 1:10
10:38 [w] Jos 15:15; Jdg 1:11
10:40 [x] Ge 12:9; Jos 12:8 [y] Dt 1:7 [z] Dt 7:24 [a] Dt 20:16-17
10:41 [b] Ge 14:7 [c] Ge 10:19 [d] Jos 11:16; 15:51
10:42 [e] ver 14
10:43 [f] ver 15; Jos 5:9
11:1 [g] Jdg 4:2, 7,23 [h] ver 10; 1Sa 12:9 [i] Jos 19:15
11:2 [j] Jos 12:3 [k] Nu 34:11 [l] Jos 17:11; Jdg 1:27; 1Ki 4:11
11:3 [m] Dt 7:1; Jdg 3:3, 5; 1Ki 9:20 [n] Ge 31:49; Jos 15:38; 18:26
11:4 [o] Jdg 7:12; 1Sa 13:5
11:5 [p] Jdg 5:19
11:6 [q] Jos 10:8 [r] 2Sa 8:4
11:8 [s] Jos 13:6

Jos 11:6 ❖ When has God sent us a message of encouragement in a time of anxiety or fear?

[a] *11* The Hebrew term refers to the irrevocable giving over of things or persons to the LORD, often by totally destroying them; also in verses 12, 20 and 21.

10:40-43 The author stakes out the boundaries of Joshua's swath of victory with the typical OT way of describing a large territory.

✜ **9:1—10:43** Joshua 9-10 in no way justifies the use of violence to achieve Christian goals. The gospel does not advance by military coercion. For Christians the war is a spiritual one. Rather than confront enemies of "flesh and blood," they face "the rulers . . . the authorities . . . the powers of this dark world and . . . the spiritual forces of evil in the heavenly realms" (Eph 6:12). Like he did with Israel, God has also dispersed his representatives—his own redeemed people—right in the middle of the world's many nations. The arrival of gospel messengers anywhere provokes modern Amorites to hostile opposition and people like the Gibeonites to peaceful inquiry.

11:1-9 In the Late Bronze Age, Hazor undoubtedly was the most influential city in all of Canaan. Its size was huge—200 acres, with an estimated population of 30,000. Joshua does precisely what Yahweh commanded (v. 9). The reader imagines a scene of fire, rising smoke, and no enemy survivors in sight.
11:10-11 Hazor finally receives its deserved reward for its previous bloodshed. Its fall destroys the last

them, not sparing anyone that breathed,[t] and he burned Hazor itself.

[12]Joshua took all these royal cities and their kings and put them to the sword. He totally destroyed them, as Moses the servant of the LORD had commanded.[u] [13]Yet Israel did not burn any of the cities built on their mounds — except Hazor, which Joshua burned. [14]The Israelites carried off for themselves all the plunder and livestock of these cities, but all the people they put to the sword until they completely destroyed them, not sparing anyone that breathed.[v] [15]As the LORD commanded his servant Moses, so Moses commanded Joshua, and Joshua did it; he left nothing undone of all that the LORD commanded Moses.[w]

[16]So Joshua took this entire land: the hill country, all the Negev, the whole region of Goshen, the western foothills,[x] the Arabah and the mountains of Israel with their foothills, [17]from Mount Halak, which rises toward Seir, to Baal Gad in the Valley of Lebanon[y] below Mount Hermon. He captured all their kings and put them to death.[z] [18]Joshua waged war against all these kings for a long time. [19]Except for the Hivites living in Gibeon,[a] not one city made a treaty of peace with the Israelites, who took them all in battle. [20]For it was the LORD himself who hardened their hearts[b] to wage war against Israel, so that he might destroy them totally, exterminating them without mercy, as the LORD had commanded Moses.[c]

[21]At that time Joshua went and destroyed the Anakites[d] from the hill country: from Hebron, Debir and Anab, from all the hill country of Judah, and from all the hill country of Israel. Joshua totally destroyed them and their towns. [22]No Anakites were left in Israelite territory; only in Gaza, Gath[e] and Ashdod[f] did any survive.

[23]So Joshua took the entire land,[g] just as the LORD had directed Moses, and he gave it as an inheritance[h] to Israel according to their tribal divisions.[i] Then the land had rest from war.[j]

11:11 [t]Dt 20:16-17
11:12 [u]Nu 33:50-52; Dt 7:2
11:14 [v]Nu 31:11-12
11:15 [w]Ex 34:11; Jos 1:7
11:16 [x]Jos 10:41
11:17 [y]Jos 12:7 [z]Dt 7:24
11:19 [a]Jos 9:3
11:20 [b]Ex 14:17; Ro 9:18 [c]Dt 7:16; Jdg 14:4
11:21 [d]Nu 13:22, 33; Dt 9:2
11:22 [e]1Sa 17:4; 1Ki 2:39; 1Ch 8:13 [f]1Sa 5:1; Isa 20:1
11:23 [g]Jos 21:43-45 [h]Dt 1:38; 12:9-10; 25:19 [i]Nu 26:53 [j]Jos 14:15
12:1 [k]Dt 3:8
12:2 [l]Dt 2:36
12:3 [m]Jos 11:2 [n]Jos 13:20
12:4 [o]Nu 21:21, 33; Dt 3:11 [p]Dt 1:4
12:5 [q]Dt 3:10 [r]1Sa 27:8 [s]Dt 3:14

List of Defeated Kings

12 These are the kings of the land whom the Israelites had defeated and whose territory they took over east of the Jordan, from the Arnon Gorge to Mount Hermon,[k] including all the eastern side of the Arabah:

[2]Sihon king of the Amorites, who reigned in Heshbon.

He ruled from Aroer on the rim of the Arnon Gorge — from the middle of the gorge — to the Jabbok River, which is the border of the Ammonites. This included half of Gilead.[l] [3]He also ruled over the eastern Arabah from the Sea of Galilee[a][m] to the Sea of the Arabah (that is, the Dead Sea), to Beth Jeshimoth,[n] and then southward below the slopes of Pisgah.

[4]And the territory of Og king of Bashan,[o] one of the last of the Rephaites, who reigned in Ashtaroth[p] and Edrei.

[5]He ruled over Mount Hermon, Salekah,[q] all of Bashan to the border of the people of Geshur[r] and Maakah,[s] and half of Gilead to the border of Sihon king of Heshbon.

[a] 3 Hebrew *Kinnereth*

---

stronghold of Canaanite rule and inaugurates the Israelite period.

11:12–15 Israel does not burn any northern cities built atop mounds except for Hazor. Presumably, this action leaves ready-made cities in Galilee in which the Israelites settle after the land distribution.

11:16–17a A survey of Canaan's major geographical regions asserts the extent of Joshua's conquests.

11:17b–20 The Canaanites could have escaped by making peace, but they refused because Yahweh steeled their resolve to attack instead. By the same token, the comment also implies that God did *not* harden the heart of the Hivites of Gibeon, leaving them free to seek peace rather than rally for war.

11:21–22 The Anakites were descendants of Anak son of Arba and, ultimately, of the fabled Nephilim (Nu 13:33). The mention of Gath is significant: It anticipates the later rise of Goliath.

11:23 The "quiet" gives Israel a chance to beat their swords into plowshares and their spears into pruning hooks (Isa 2:4). They can stop being soldiers and start being farmers, vineyard owners, and cultivators of fruit trees.

11:1–23 The encouraging words "Don't be afraid" echo across the biblical landscape. It is true that the Christian life is no lazy stroll through the park. But the reassuring "Don't be afraid" spoken by Jesus applies to fears of persecution, ostracism, and personal inadequacy. It offers us a powerful antidote to the stresses these fears inflict on us: his daily presence with us.

12:1–6 Biblical tradition remembers Sihon and Og as a "down payment" on the eventual realization of Israel's full inheritance.

6 Moses, the servant of the LORD, and
the Israelites conquered them. And Moses the servant of the LORD gave their
land to the Reubenites, the Gadites and
the half-tribe of Manasseh to be their
possession.[t]
7 Here is a list of the kings of the land
that Joshua and the Israelites conquered
on the west side of the Jordan, from Baal
Gad in the Valley of Lebanon[u] to Mount
Halak, which rises toward Seir. Joshua
gave their lands as an inheritance to the
tribes of Israel according to their tribal
divisions. 8 The lands included the hill
country, the western foothills, the Arabah, the mountain slopes, the wilderness
and the Negev.[v] These were the lands of
the Hittites, Amorites, Canaanites, Perizzites, Hivites and Jebusites. These were
the kings:

9 the king of Jericho[w] one
the king of Ai[x] (near Bethel) one
10 the king of Jerusalem[y] one
the king of Hebron one
11 the king of Jarmuth one
the king of Lachish one
12 the king of Eglon one
the king of Gezer[z] one
13 the king of Debir one
the king of Geder one
14 the king of Hormah one
the king of Arad[a] one
15 the king of Libnah one
the king of Adullam one
16 the king of Makkedah one
the king of Bethel[b] one
17 the king of Tappuah one
the king of Hepher[c] one
18 the king of Aphek[d] one
the king of Lasharon one
19 the king of Madon one
the king of Hazor one
20 the king of Shimron Meron one
the king of Akshaph[e] one
21 the king of Taanach one
the king of Megiddo one
22 the king of Kedesh[f] one
the king of Jokneam in Carmel[g] one
23 the king of Dor (in Naphoth Dor[h]) one
the king of Goyim in Gilgal one
24 the king of Tirzah one
thirty-one kings in all.[i]

12:6 [t] Nu 32:29, 33; Jos 13:8
12:7 [u] Jos 11:17
12:8 [v] Jos 11:16
12:9 [w] Jos 6:2 [x] Jos 8:29
12:10 [y] Jos 10:23
12:12 [z] Jos 10:33
12:14 [a] Nu 21:1
12:16 [b] Jos 7:2
12:17 [c] 1Ki 4:10
12:18 [d] Jos 13:4
12:20 [e] Jos 11:1
12:22 [f] Jos 19:37; 20:7; 21:32 [g] 1Sa 15:12
12:23 [h] Jos 11:2
12:24 [i] Ps 135:11; Dt 7:24
13:1 [j] Ge 24:1; Jos 14:10
13:3 [k] Jer 2:18 [l] Jdg 1:18 [m] Jdg 3:3 [n] Dt 2:23
13:4 [o] Jos 12:18; 19:30 [p] Am 2:10
13:5 [q] 1Ki 5:18; Ps 83:7; Eze 27:9 [r] Jos 12:7

Jos 12:7–24 ❖ If we were to make a list of the victories and successes God has granted us, what would be on that list?

Jos 13:1 ❖ Where is there unfinished work in our faith and discipleship?

Land Still to Be Taken

13 When Joshua had grown old,[j] the
LORD said to him, "You are now very
old, and there are still very large areas
of land to be taken over.
2 "This is the land that remains: all
the regions of the Philistines and
Geshurites, 3 from the Shihor River[k]
on the east of Egypt to the territory of
Ekron[l] on the north, all of it counted
as Canaanite though held by the five
Philistine rulers[m] in Gaza, Ashdod,
Ashkelon, Gath and Ekron; the territory of the Avvites[n] 4 on the south; all
the land of the Canaanites, from Arah
of the Sidonians as far as Aphek[o] and
the border of the Amorites;[p] 5 the area
of Byblos;[q] and all Lebanon[r] to the
east, from Baal Gad below Mount
Hermon to Lebo Hamath.

12:7–8 The report is anachronistic, affirming in advance what is to come later.
12:9–24 Except for v. 24 (one king plus the total), each line lists two kings in stereotyped form. The literary effect is to highlight their social position and the fact they are all gone. The total triumph comes from one God: Yahweh, and one united people: Israel.

✜ **12:1–24** Politicians, religious leaders, famous athletes, movie stars, rock stars, social media influencers, and founders of movements all proclaim, "Follow me!" They eagerly call for others to enthrone them as king—or, at least, as "kingpins." Given the felt need for either, many gather sizeable followings.

What rightful claim does Jesus have to being king? Why choose him over modern Canaanite ones? Jesus is a *good king*. The mind imagines him mobbed by crowds as he enters a village: Jesus mills among the locals shaking hands. Jesus loves ordinary people and loves to be with them.

Jesus is also a *king who saves*. His forgiveness unshackles the chains of sin that bind us, freeing us from our slavery to it. His grace gently lifts us up when we fall, so we can go on together with him. His soothing presence shepherds us through the dark valleys of despair through which we sometimes must pass.

13:1–7 The book's mention of unconquered areas may strike some readers as a contradiction. The comment should not surprise us, however, since the existence of areas of Canaan still awaiting

6“As for all the inhabitants of the
mountain regions from Lebanon to Mis-
rephoth Maim,[s] that is, all the Sidonians,
I myself will drive them out before the
Israelites. Be sure to allocate this land
to Israel for an inheritance, as I have instructed you,[t] 7and divide it as an inheritance[u] among the nine tribes and half
of the tribe of Manasseh.”

Division of the Land East of the Jordan

8The other half of Manasseh,[a] the Reubenites and the Gadites had received the
inheritance that Moses had given them
east of the Jordan, as he, the servant of
the LORD, had assigned[v] it to them.

9It extended from Aroer[w] on the
rim of the Arnon Gorge, and from
the town in the middle of the gorge,
and included the whole plateau[x] of
Medeba as far as Dibon,[y] 10and all
the towns of Sihon king of the Amorites, who ruled in Heshbon, out to
the border of the Ammonites.[z] 11It
also included Gilead, the territory of
the people of Geshur and Maakah,
all of Mount Hermon and all Bashan
as far as Salekah[a]— 12that is, the
whole kingdom of Og in Bashan,[b]
who had reigned in Ashtaroth[c] and
Edrei. (He was the last of the Rephaites.[d]) Moses had defeated them
and taken over their land. 13But the
Israelites did not drive out the people of Geshur[e] and Maakah,[f] so they
continue to live among the Israelites
to this day.

14But to the tribe of Levi he gave no
inheritance, since the food offerings presented to the LORD, the God of Israel, are
their inheritance, as he promised them.[g]

15This is what Moses had given to the
tribe of Reuben, according to its clans:

16The territory from Aroer[h] on the
rim of the Arnon Gorge, and from
the town in the middle of the gorge,
and the whole plateau past Medeba[i]
17to Heshbon and all its towns on the
plateau, including Dibon,[j] Bamoth
Baal, Beth Baal Meon,[k] 18Jahaz,[l] Kedemoth, Mephaath,[m] 19Kiriathaim,[n]
Sibmah, Zereth Shahar on the hill in
the valley, 20Beth Peor,[o] the slopes of
Pisgah, and Beth Jeshimoth— 21all
the towns on the plateau and the
entire realm of Sihon king of the
Amorites, who ruled at Heshbon.
Moses had defeated him and the
Midianite chiefs,[p] Evi, Rekem, Zur,
Hur and Reba[q]—princes allied with
Sihon—who lived in that country.
22In addition to those slain in battle,
the Israelites had put to the sword
Balaam son of Beor,[r] who practiced
divination. 23The boundary of the
Reubenites was the bank of the Jordan. These towns and their villages
were the inheritance of the Reubenites, according to their clans.

24This is what Moses had given to the
tribe of Gad, according to its clans:

25The territory of Jazer,[s] all the
towns of Gilead and half the Ammonite country as far as Aroer, near
Rabbah; 26and from Heshbon[t] to
Ramath Mizpah and Betonim, and
from Mahanaim to the territory of
Debir;[u] 27and in the valley, Beth Ha-
ram, Beth Nimrah, Sukkoth[v] and Zaphon with the rest of the realm of
Sihon king of Heshbon (the east side
of the Jordan, the territory up to the
end of the Sea of Galilee[b][w]). 28These
towns and their villages were the inheritance of the Gadites,[x] according
to their clans.

29This is what Moses had given to the
half-tribe of Manasseh, that is, to half the
family of the descendants of Manasseh,
according to its clans:

30The territory extending from Mahanaim[y] and including all of Bashan, the entire realm of Og king
of Bashan—all the settlements of
Jair[z] in Bashan, sixty towns, 31half
of Gilead, and Ashtaroth and Edrei
(the royal cities of Og in Bashan).
This was for the descendants of

13:6 [s] Jos 11:8 [t] Nu 33:54
13:7 [u] Jos 11:23; Ps 78:55
13:8 [v] Jos 12:6
13:9 [w] ver 16; Jdg 11:26 [x] Jer 48:8,21 [y] Nu 21:30
13:10 [z] Nu 21:24
13:11 [a] Jos 12:5
13:12 [b] Dt 3:11 [c] Jos 12:4 [d] Ge 14:5
13:13 [e] Jos 12:5 [f] Dt 3:14
13:14 [g] ver 33; Dt 18:1-2
13:16 [h] ver 9; Jos 12:2 [i] Nu 21:30
13:17 [j] Nu 32:3 [k] 1Ch 5:8
13:18 [l] Nu 21:23 [m] Jer 48:21
13:19 [n] Nu 32:37
13:20 [o] Dt 3:29
13:21 [p] Nu 25:15 [q] Nu 31:8
13:22 [r] Nu 22:5; 31:8
13:25 [s] Nu 21:32; Jos 21:39
13:26 [t] Nu 21:25; Jer 49:3 [u] Jos 10:3
13:27 [v] Ge 33:17 [w] Nu 34:11
13:28 [x] Nu 32:33
13:30 [y] Ge 32:2 [z] Nu 32:41

[a] *8* Hebrew *With it* (that is, with the other half of Manasseh) [b] *27* Hebrew *Kinnereth*

conquest is implied in the conquest narrative (chs. 6–11) and in the celebratory list of kings (ch. 12).

13:8–32 This section reviews Moses' prior land allocations east of the Jordan to two-and-a-half tribes (cf. Nu 32:33–42). Thematically, this retrospective adds details to the description in 12:1–6 and anticipates Joshua's later dismissal of the east-bank tribes to their lands (ch. 22).

Makir[a] son of Manasseh — for half
of the sons of Makir, according to
their clans.

32 This is the inheritance Moses had
given when he was in the plains of Moab
across the Jordan east of Jericho. 33 But
to the tribe of Levi, Moses had given no
inheritance; the LORD, the God of Israel, is their inheritance,[b] as he promised
them.[c]

Division of the Land West of the Jordan

14 Now these are the areas the Israelites received as an inheritance
in the land of Canaan, which Eleazar
the priest, Joshua son of Nun and the
heads of the tribal clans of Israel allotted to them.[d] 2 Their inheritances were
assigned by lot[e] to the nine and a half
tribes, as the LORD had commanded
through Moses. 3 Moses had granted the
two and a half tribes their inheritance
east of the Jordan[f] but had not granted the Levites an inheritance among
the rest,[g] 4 for Joseph's descendants
had become two tribes — Manasseh
and Ephraim.[h] The Levites received no
share of the land but only towns to live
in, with pasturelands for their flocks
and herds. 5 So the Israelites divided the
land, just as the LORD had commanded
Moses.[i]

Allotment for Caleb

6 Now the people of Judah approached
Joshua at Gilgal, and Caleb son of Jephunneh[j] the Kenizzite said to him,
"You know what the LORD said to Moses the man of God at Kadesh Barnea[k]
about you and me. 7 I was forty years old
when Moses the servant of the LORD sent
me from Kadesh Barnea to explore the

Jos 14:10-12 ❖ Caleb was one brave senior citizen! How can we imitate Caleb's strength and faith over a period of many years?

land.[l] And I brought him back a report
according to my convictions,[m] 8 but my
fellow Israelites who went up with me
made the hearts of the people melt in
fear.[n] I, however, followed the LORD my
God wholeheartedly.[o] 9 So on that day
Moses swore to me, 'The land on which
your feet have walked will be your inheritance and that of your children[p] forever,
because you have followed the LORD my
God wholeheartedly.'[a]

10 "Now then, just as the LORD promised,[q] he has kept me alive for forty-five
years since the time he said this to Moses,
while Israel moved about in the wilderness. So here I am today, eighty-five years
old! 11 I am still as strong[r] today as the day
Moses sent me out; I'm just as vigorous
to go out to battle now as I was then.
12 Now give me this hill country that the
LORD promised me that day. You yourself
heard then that the Anakites[s] were there
and their cities were large and fortified,[t]
but, the LORD helping me, I will drive
them out just as he said."

13 Then Joshua blessed[u] Caleb son of
Jephunneh and gave him Hebron[v] as his
inheritance.[w] 14 So Hebron has belonged
to Caleb son of Jephunneh the Kenizzite
ever since, because he followed the LORD,
the God of Israel, wholeheartedly. 15 (Hebron used to be called Kiriath Arba[x] after
Arba,[y] who was the greatest man among
the Anakites.)

Then the land had rest[z] from war.

13:31 [a] Ge 50:23
13:33 [b] Nu 18:20 [c] ver 14; Jos 18:7
14:1 [d] Nu 34:17-18
14:2 [e] Nu 26:55
14:3 [f] Nu 32:33 [g] Jos 13:14
14:4 [h] Ge 41:52; 48:5
14:5 [i] Nu 34:13; 35:2; Jos 21:2
14:6 [j] Nu 13:6; 14:30 [k] Nu 13:26
14:7 [l] Nu 13:17 [m] Nu 13:30; 14:6-9
14:8 [n] Nu 13:31 [o] Nu 14:24
14:9 [p] Nu 14:24; Dt 1:36
14:10 [q] Nu 14:30
14:11 [r] Dt 34:7
14:12 [s] Nu 13:33 [t] Nu 13:28
14:13 [u] Jos 22:6, 7 [v] Jos 10:36 [w] Jdg 1:20; 1Ch 6:56
14:15 [x] Ge 23:2 [y] Jos 15:13 [z] Jos 11:23

[a] 9 Deut. 1:36

13:33 For the second time the writer mentions that Moses gave no inheritance to the tribe of Levi. The rationale this time, however, is that Yahweh himself is Levi's inheritance, just as Yahweh promised them.

14:1-5 Opening and closing statements ("Now these are the areas . . .") stamp the summary as primarily retrospective—a backward look at the results of the process, not necessarily a report of how it was done. At the same time, the writer's summary report (vv. 2-5) does explain the distribution as the work of Eleazar the high priest, Joshua, and the tribal leaders. The presence of the high priest and the use of lots per Yahweh's explicit command also mark the land distribution as specifically a *sacred* act (v. 2).

14:6-15 Caleb reminds Joshua, his only ally among the spies, of "what the LORD said to Moses . . . about you and me" long ago at Kadesh Barnea (v. 6b). The promise rewards Caleb's one sterling trait: He "followed the LORD . . . God wholeheartedly," a trait the context recalls verbatim three times (vv. 8, 9, 14). In other words, what Caleb did he did wholeheartedly—obeying God's will rather than his own or that of someone else.

Caleb remarks (with apparent hyperbole) that God, as he promised, has kept him alive to age eighty-five—and just as vigorous and battle-ready as ever. The motif implicitly points the reader to the steps he followed in order to enjoy the divine blessings of long life and the retention of ancestral land.

Allotment for Judah

15:15–19pp // Jdg 1:11–15

15 The allotment for the tribe of Judah, according to its clans, extended down to the territory of Edom,[a] to
the Desert of Zin[b] in the extreme south.
2Their southern boundary started
from the bay at the southern end of
the Dead Sea, 3crossed south of Scorpion Pass,[c] continued on to Zin and
went over to the south of Kadesh
Barnea. Then it ran past Hezron up
to Addar and curved around to Kar-
ka. 4It then passed along to Azmon[d]
and joined the Wadi of Egypt,[e] ending at the Mediterranean Sea. This
is their[a] southern boundary.
5The eastern boundary[f] is the Dead
Sea as far as the mouth of the Jordan.
The northern boundary[g] started
from the bay of the sea at the mouth
of the Jordan, 6went up to Beth Hoglah[h] and continued north of Beth
Arabah to the Stone of Bohan[i] son of
Reuben. 7The boundary then went
up to Debir from the Valley of Achor[j]
and turned north to Gilgal, which
faces the Pass of Adummim south
of the gorge. It continued along
to the waters of En Shemesh and
came out at En Rogel.[k] 8Then it ran
up the Valley of Ben Hinnom along
the southern slope of the Jebusite[l]
city (that is, Jerusalem). From there
it climbed to the top of the hill west
of the Hinnom Valley at the northern end of the Valley of Rephaim.
9From the hilltop the boundary
headed toward the spring of the waters of Nephtoah,[m] came out at the
towns of Mount Ephron and went
down toward Baalah[n] (that is, Kiriath Jearim). 10Then it curved westward from Baalah to Mount Seir, ran
along the northern slope of Mount
Jearim (that is, Kesalon), continued
down to Beth Shemesh and crossed

15:1 [a] Nu 34:3 [b] Nu 33:36
15:3 [c] Nu 34:4
15:4 [d] Nu 34:5 [e] Ge 15:18
15:5 [f] Nu 34:10 [g] Jos 18:15-19
15:6 [h] Jos 18:19, 21 [i] Jos 18:17
15:7 [j] Jos 7:24 [k] 2Sa 17:17; 1Ki 1:9
15:8 [l] ver 63; Jos 18:16, 28; Jdg 1:21; 19:10
15:9 [m] Jos 18:15 [n] 1Ch 13:6
15:10 [o] Ge 38:12; Jdg 14:1
15:11 [p] Jos 19:33
15:12 [q] Nu 34:6
15:13 [r] Jos 14:13-15
15:14 [s] Nu 13:33 [t] Nu 13:22 [u] Jdg 1:10, 20
15:16 [v] Jdg 1:12
15:17 [w] Jdg 3:9, 11

Jos 15:20 ❖ What inheritance does God promise his children through Christ?

to Timnah.[o] 11It went to the northern slope of Ekron, turned toward
Shikkeron, passed along to Mount
Baalah and reached Jabneel.[p] The
boundary ended at the sea.
12The western boundary is the
coastline of the Mediterranean Sea.[q]

These are the boundaries around the
people of Judah by their clans.

13In accordance with the LORD's command to him, Joshua gave to Caleb son of
Jephunneh a portion in Judah — Kiriath
Arba, that is, Hebron. (Arba was the forefather of Anak.)[r] 14From Hebron Caleb
drove out the three Anakites[s] — Sheshai,
Ahiman and Talmai,[t] the sons of Anak.[u]
15From there he marched against the
people living in Debir (formerly called
Kiriath Sepher). 16And Caleb said, "I will
give my daughter Aksah[v] in marriage to
the man who attacks and captures Kiriath Sepher." 17Othniel[w] son of Kenaz,
Caleb's brother, took it; so Caleb gave
his daughter Aksah to him in marriage.
18One day when she came to Othniel,
she urged him[b] to ask her father for a
field. When she got off her donkey, Caleb asked her, "What can I do for you?"
19She replied, "Do me a special favor.
Since you have given me land in the Negev, give me also springs of water." So Caleb gave her the upper and lower springs.

20This is the inheritance of the tribe
of Judah, according to its clans:

21The southernmost towns of the tribe of
Judah in the Negev toward the boundary
of Edom were:

[a] 4 Septuagint; Hebrew *your* [b] 18 Hebrew and some Septuagint manuscripts; other Septuagint manuscripts (see also note at Judges 1:14) *Othniel, he urged her*

15:1–63 The larger process begins with a long report of Judah's inheritance (vv. 1–63). The boundary description (vv. 1–12) traces in considerable detail its southern (vv. 2–4), eastern (v. 5a), northern (vv. 5b–11), and western borders (v. 12).
15:13–19 Caleb returns to the stage in a brief interlude that also features his daughter Aksah. This account implies that, besides Hebron, Caleb also held territory southwest of the city in the southern hill country of Judah and the Negev.

15:20–63 The inheritance of Judah concludes with a lengthy list of Judah's towns neatly organized by four geographical regions. Many readers will find the Judah section—hands down, the largest in chs. 14–19—tediously detailed. But that is the point: Its sheer quantity underscores Judah's importance within Israel. Later history will confirm the importance of Judah's foothold in the land, for it constituted the remnant of the twelve tribes that enabled Israel to continue its mission to the world.

Kabzeel, Eder,[x] Jagur, 22Kinah, Di-
monah, Adadah, 23Kedesh, Hazor,
Ithnan, 24Ziph,[y] Telem, Bealoth,
25Hazor Hadattah, Kerioth Hezron
(that is, Hazor), 26Amam, Shema,
Moladah,[z] 27Hazar Gaddah, Hesh-
mon, Beth Pelet, 28Hazar Shual,
Beersheba,[a] Biziothiah, 29Baalah,[b]
Iyim, Ezem, 30Eltolad,[c] Kesil, Hormah, 31Ziklag,[d] Madmannah, San-
sannah, 32Lebaoth, Shilhim, Ain and
Rimmon[e] — a total of twenty-nine
towns and their villages.

33In the western foothills:
Eshtaol,[f] Zorah, Ashnah, 34Zano-
ah,[g] En Gannim, Tappuah, Enam,
35Jarmuth,[h] Adullam,[i] Sokoh, Azekah, 36Shaaraim, Adithaim and Gederah[j] (or Gederothaim)[a] — fourteen
towns and their villages.
37Zenan, Hadashah, Migdal Gad,
38Dilean, Mizpah, Joktheel,[k] 39La-
chish,[l] Bozkath,[m] Eglon, 40Kabbon,
Lahmas, Kitlish, 41Gederoth, Beth
Dagon, Naamah and Makkedah[n] —
sixteen towns and their villages.
42Libnah, Ether, Ashan,[o] 43Iphtah,
Ashnah, Nezib, 44Keilah, Akzib[p] and
Mareshah[q] — nine towns and their
villages.
45Ekron, with its surrounding
settlements and villages; 46west of
Ekron, all that were in the vicinity of Ashdod, together with their
villages; 47Ashdod,[r] its surrounding
settlements and villages; and Gaza,
its settlements and villages, as far as
the Wadi of Egypt[s] and the coastline
of the Mediterranean Sea.[t]

48In the hill country:
Shamir, Jattir,[u] Sokoh, 49Dannah,
Kiriath Sannah (that is, Debir[v]),
50Anab, Eshtemoh,[w] Anim, 51Go-
shen,[x] Holon and Giloh — eleven
towns and their villages.
52Arab, Dumah,[y] Eshan, 53Janim,
Beth Tappuah, Aphekah, 54Humtah,
Kiriath Arba (that is, Hebron) and
Zior — nine towns and their villages.
55Maon, Carmel,[z] Ziph, Juttah,
56Jezreel,[a] Jokdeam, Zanoah, 57Kain,
Gibeah[b] and Timnah — ten towns
and their villages.
58Halhul, Beth Zur,[c] Gedor, 59Maa-
rath, Beth Anoth and Eltekon — six
towns and their villages.[b]
60Kiriath Baal (that is, Kiriath Jearim[d]) and Rabbah[e] — two towns and
their villages.

61In the wilderness:
Beth Arabah, Middin, Sekakah,
62Nibshan, the City of Salt and En
Gedi[f] — six towns and their villages.
63Judah could not[g] dislodge the Jebusites[h], who were living in Jerusalem; to
this day the Jebusites live there with the
people of Judah.

Allotment for Ephraim and Manasseh

16 The allotment for Joseph began at the Jordan, east of the
springs of Jericho, and went up from
there through the desert[i] into the hill
country of Bethel. 2It went on from
Bethel (that is, Luz[j]),[c] crossed over to
the territory of the Arkites in Ataroth,
3descended westward to the territory
of the Japhletites as far as the region
of Lower Beth Horon[k] and on to Gezer,[l] ending at the Mediterranean Sea.
4So Manasseh and Ephraim, the descendants of Joseph, received their inheritance.[m]

5This was the territory of Ephraim, according to its clans:

The boundary of their inheritance went from Ataroth Addar[n] in
the east to Upper Beth Horon 6and
continued to the Mediterranean Sea.
From Mikmethath[o] on the north it
curved eastward to Taanath Shiloh,
passing by it to Janoah on the east.
7Then it went down from Janoah to
Ataroth[p] and Naarah, touched Jericho and came out at the Jordan.
8From Tappuah the border went
west to the Kanah Ravine[q] and ended at the Mediterranean Sea. This

[a] 36 Or *Gederah and Gederothaim* [b] 59 The Septuagint adds another district of eleven towns, including Tekoa and Ephrathah (Bethlehem). [c] 2 Septuagint; Hebrew *Bethel to Luz*

15:21 [x] Ge 35:21
15:24 [y] 1Sa 23:14
15:26 [z] 1Ch 4:28
15:28 [a] Ge 21:31
15:29 [b] ver 9
15:30 [c] Jos 19:4
15:31 [d] 1Sa 27:6
15:32 [e] Jdg 20:45
15:33 [f] Jdg 13:25; 16:31
15:34 [g] 1Ch 4:18; Ne 3:13
15:35 [h] Jos 10:3 [i] 1Sa 22:1
15:36 [j] 1Ch 12:4
15:38 [k] 2Ki 14:7
15:39 [l] Jos 10:3; 2Ki 14:19 [m] 2Ki 22:1
15:41 [n] Jos 10:10
15:42 [o] 1Sa 30:30
15:44 [p] Jdg 1:31 [q] Mic 1:15
15:47 [r] Jos 11:22 [s] ver 4 [t] Nu 34:6
15:48 [u] 1Sa 30:27
15:49 [v] Jos 10:3
15:50 [w] Jos 21:14
15:51 [x] Jos 10:41; 11:16
15:52 [y] Ge 25:14
15:55 [z] Jos 12:22
15:56 [a] Jos 17:16
15:57 [b] Jos 18:28; Jdg 19:12
15:58 [c] 1Ch 2:45
15:60 [d] Jos 18:14 [e] Dt 3:11
15:62 [f] 1Sa 23:29
15:63 [g] Jdg 1:21 [h] 2Sa 5:6
16:1 [i] Jos 8:15; 18:12
16:2 [j] Jos 18:13
16:3 [k] 2Ch 8:5 [l] Jos 10:33; 1Ki 9:15
16:4 [m] Jos 17:14
16:5 [n] Jos 18:13
16:6 [o] Jos 17:7
16:7 [p] 1Ch 7:28
16:8 [q] Jos 17:9

16:1—17:18 The two tribes of Joseph now receive their inheritance (16:1—17:13). The author again sounds the "did-not-destroy" theme. The Ephraimites forced the Canaanites to work for the Israelites (16:10). This seems to imply criticism of Ephraimite efforts in the matter, unless the force required to compel labor was less than that which was necessary to destroy the Canaanites.

was the inheritance of the tribe of
the Ephraimites, according to its
clans. 9It also included all the towns
and their villages that were set aside
for the Ephraimites within the inheritance of the Manassites.
10They did not dislodge the Canaanites
living in Gezer; to this day the Canaanites
live among the people of Ephraim but
are required to do forced labor.[r]
17 This was the allotment for the tribe
of Manasseh as Joseph's firstborn,[s]
that is, for Makir,[t] Manasseh's firstborn.
Makir was the ancestor of the Gileadites,
who had received Gilead and Bashan because the Makirites were great soldiers.
2So this allotment was for the rest of the
people of Manasseh — the clans of Abiezer,[u] Helek, Asriel, Shechem, Hepher
and Shemida. These are the other male
descendants of Manasseh son of Joseph
by their clans.
3Now Zelophehad son of Hepher,[v]
the son of Gilead, the son of Makir, the
son of Manasseh, had no sons but only
daughters,[w] whose names were Mahlah,
Noah, Hoglah, Milkah and Tirzah. 4They
went to Eleazar the priest, Joshua son of
Nun, and the leaders and said, "The LORD
commanded Moses to give us an inheritance among our relatives." So Joshua
gave them an inheritance along with the
brothers of their father, according to the
LORD's command.[x] 5Manasseh's share
consisted of ten tracts of land besides Gilead and Bashan east of the Jordan, 6be-
cause the daughters of the tribe of Manasseh received an inheritance among
the sons. The land of Gilead belonged to
the rest of the descendants of Manasseh.
7The territory of Manasseh extended from Asher to Mikmethath[y]
east of Shechem.[z] The boundary ran
southward from there to include the
people living at En Tappuah. 8(Manasseh had the land of Tappuah, but
Tappuah[a] itself, on the boundary of
Manasseh, belonged to the Ephraimites.) 9Then the boundary continued
south to the Kanah Ravine.[b] There
were towns belonging to Ephraim
lying among the towns of Manas-

16:10 [r] Jos 17:13; Jdg 1:28-29; 1Ki 9:16
17:1 [s] Ge 41:51 [t] Ge 50:23
17:2 [u] Nu 26:30; 1Ch 7:18
17:3 [v] Nu 27:1 [w] Nu 26:33
17:4 [x] Nu 27:5-7
17:7 [y] Jos 16:6 [z] Ge 12:6; Jos 21:21
17:8 [a] Jos 16:8
17:9 [b] Jos 16:8

Jos 16:10 ❖ What happens when we fail to completely root out sin from one area of our lives? How is this similar to the Israelites' situation with the remaining Canaanites?

Jos 17:17-18 ❖ When has Christ provided strength to do things that seemed impossible (see Php 4:13)?

seh, but the boundary of Manasseh
was the northern side of the ravine
and ended at the Mediterranean Sea.
10On the south the land belonged to
Ephraim, on the north to Manasseh.
The territory of Manasseh reached
the Mediterranean Sea and bordered
Asher on the north and Issachar[c]
on the east.
11Within Issachar and Asher, Manasseh also had Beth Shan,[d] Ibleam
and the people of Dor,[e] Endor,[f] Taanach and Megiddo,[g] together with
their surrounding settlements (the
third in the list is Naphoth[a]).
12Yet the Manassites were not able[h] to
occupy these towns, for the Canaanites
were determined to live in that region.
13However, when the Israelites grew
stronger, they subjected the Canaanites
to forced labor but did not drive them
out completely.[i]
14The people of Joseph said to Joshua,
"Why have you given us only one allotment and one portion for an inheritance?
We are a numerous people, and the LORD
has blessed us abundantly."[j]
15"If you are so numerous," Joshua answered, "and if the hill country of Ephraim is too small for you, go up into the forest and clear land for yourselves there in
the land of the Perizzites and Rephaites.[k]"
16The people of Joseph replied, "The
hill country is not enough for us, and all
the Canaanites who live in the plain have
chariots fitted with iron,[l] both those in
Beth Shan and its settlements and those
in the Valley of Jezreel."
17But Joshua said to the tribes of
Joseph — to Ephraim and Manasseh —

17:10 [c] Ge 30:18
17:11 [d] 1Sa 31:10; 1Ki 4:12; 1Ch 7:29 [e] Jos 11:2 [f] 1Sa 28:7; Ps 83:10 [g] 1Ki 9:15
17:12 [h] Jdg 1:27
17:13 [i] Jos 16:10
17:14 [j] Nu 26:28-37
17:15 [k] Ge 14:5
17:16 [l] Jdg 1:19; 4:3,13

[a] *11* That is, Naphoth Dor

17:14–18 Finally, an unexpected dialogue between the Josephites and Joshua closes both the Josephite allotment report and the larger first allotment section (vv. 14–18). The Josephites apparently have a short memory and a feeble faith. The contrast with the bold and fearless eighty-five-year-old Caleb (chs. 14–15) is stark and disappointing. Joshua's final ruling (vv. 17–18) counters both parts of the Josephite argument.

"You are numerous and very powerful.
You will have not only one allotment
18but the forested hill country as well.
Clear it, and its farthest limits will be
yours; though the Canaanites have chariots fitted with iron[m] and though they are
strong, you can drive them out."

Division of the Rest of the Land

18 The whole assembly of the Israelites gathered at Shiloh[n] and set up
the tent of meeting[o] there. The country
was brought under their control, 2but
there were still seven Israelite tribes who
had not yet received their inheritance.

3So Joshua said to the Israelites: "How
long will you wait before you begin to
take possession of the land that the LORD,
the God of your ancestors, has given you?
4Appoint three men from each tribe. I
will send them out to make a survey of
the land and to write a description of it,
according to the inheritance of each.[p]
Then they will return to me. 5You are
to divide the land into seven parts. Judah is to remain in its territory on the
south[q] and the tribes of Joseph in their
territory on the north.[r] 6After you have
written descriptions of the seven parts
of the land, bring them here to me and
I will cast lots[s] for you in the presence of
the LORD our God. 7The Levites, however,
do not get a portion among you, because
the priestly service of the LORD is their
inheritance.[t] And Gad, Reuben and the
half-tribe of Manasseh have already received their inheritance on the east side
of the Jordan. Moses the servant of the
LORD gave it to them.[u]"

8As the men started on their way to
map out the land, Joshua instructed
them, "Go and make a survey of the land
and write a description of it. Then return
to me, and I will cast lots for you here at
Shiloh[v] in the presence of the LORD." 9So
the men left and went through the land.
They wrote its description on a scroll,
town by town, in seven parts, and returned to Joshua in the camp at Shiloh.
10Joshua then cast lots[w] for them in Shiloh in the presence[x] of the LORD, and
there he distributed the land to the Israelites according to their tribal divisions.[y]

17:18 [m] ver 16
18:1 [n] Jos 19:51; 21:2; Jdg 18:31; 21:12,19; 1Sa 1:3; 4:3; Jer 7:12; 26:6 [o] Ex 27:21
18:4 [p] Mic 2:5
18:5 [q] Jos 15:1 [r] Jos 16:1-4
18:6 [s] Jos 14:2
18:7 [t] Jos 13:33 [u] Jos 13:8
18:8 [v] ver 1
18:10 [w] Nu 34:13 [x] ver 1; Jer 7:12 [y] Nu 33:54; Jos 19:51

> **Jos 18:3** ❖ When have we stalled in following God's instructions? How do we find the encouragement to move forward in such situations?

Allotment for Benjamin

11The first lot came up for the tribe of
Benjamin according to its clans. Their
allotted territory lay between the tribes
of Judah and Joseph:

12On the north side their boundary began at the Jordan, passed the
northern slope of Jericho and headed west into the hill country, coming
out at the wilderness[z] of Beth Aven.[a]
13From there it crossed to the south
slope of Luz[b] (that is, Bethel[c]) and
went down to Ataroth Addar[d] on
the hill south of Lower Beth Horon.

14From the hill facing Beth Horon[e]
on the south the boundary turned
south along the western side and
came out at Kiriath Baal (that is, Kiriath Jearim), a town of the people of
Judah. This was the western side.

15The southern side began at the
outskirts of Kiriath Jearim on the
west, and the boundary came out at
the spring of the waters of Nephtoah.[f] 16The boundary went down to
the foot of the hill facing the Valley
of Ben Hinnom, north of the Valley
of Rephaim. It continued down the
Hinnom Valley[g] along the southern
slope of the Jebusite city and so to
En Rogel.[h] 17It then curved north,
went to En Shemesh, continued
to Geliloth, which faces the Pass of
Adummim, and ran down to the
Stone of Bohan[i] son of Reuben. 18It
continued to the northern slope of
Beth Arabah[a][j] and on down into the
Arabah. 19It then went to the northern slope of Beth Hoglah and came

18:12 [z] Jos 16:1 [a] Jos 7:2
18:13 [b] Ge 28:19 [c] Jdg 1:23 [d] Jos 16:5
18:14 [e] Jos 10:10
18:15 [f] Jos 15:9
18:16 [g] Jos 15:8; 2Ki 23:10 [h] Jos 15:7
18:17 [i] Jos 15:6
18:18 [j] Jos 15:6

[a] 18 Septuagint; Hebrew *slope facing the Arabah*

18:1-10 At first hearing, Joshua's opening statement sounds like an accusation that faults the seven tribes for laziness (v. 3). In reality, his seemingly blunt statement is merely motivational rhetoric to get them moving on his plan. The plan (vv. 4–5, 8) calls for three men from each tribe to survey the land still available. Then the surveyors are to return to Joshua, who will cast lots before God and Israel to decide who gets what (vv. 6–7).

18:11—19:48 The text itself offers no explanation of the lot-casting procedure.

18:11-28 The first lot identifies Benjamin and his land. The list of Benjamite towns is the third longest after those of Judah and Levi.

out at the northern bay of the Dead
Sea,[k] at the mouth of the Jordan in
the south. This was the southern
boundary.
20The Jordan formed the boundary on the eastern side.
These were the boundaries that marked
out the inheritance of the clans of Benjamin on all sides.[l]

21The tribe of Benjamin, according to its
clans, had the following towns:
Jericho, Beth Hoglah, Emek Keziz,
22Beth Arabah, Zemaraim, Bethel,[m]
23Avvim, Parah, Ophrah, 24Kephar
Ammoni, Ophni and Geba[n] — twelve
towns and their villages.
25Gibeon,[o] Ramah,[p] Beeroth,[q]
26Mizpah,[r] Kephirah, Mozah, 27Re-
kem, Irpeel, Taralah, 28Zelah,[s] Ha-
eleph, the Jebusite city[t] (that is,
Jerusalem[u]), Gibeah[v] and Kiriath —
fourteen towns and their villages.
This was the inheritance of Benjamin
for its clans.

Allotment for Simeon

19:2–10pp // 1Ch 4:28–33

19 The second lot came out for the
tribe of Simeon according to its
clans. Their inheritance lay within the
territory of Judah.[w] 2It included:
Beersheba[x] (or Sheba),[a] Moladah,
3Hazar Shual, Balah, Ezem, 4Eltolad,
Bethul, Hormah, 5Ziklag, Beth Markaboth, Hazar Susah, 6Beth Lebaoth
and Sharuhen — thirteen towns and
their villages;
7Ain, Rimmon, Ether and
Ashan[y] — four towns and their villages — 8and all the villages around
these towns as far as Baalath Beer
(Ramah in the Negev).[z]
This was the inheritance of the tribe of
the Simeonites, according to its clans.
9The inheritance of the Simeonites was
taken from the share of Judah,[a] because
Judah's portion was more than they needed. So the Simeonites received their inheritance within the territory of Judah.[b]

18:19 [k] Ge 14:3
18:20 [l] Jos 21:4, 17; 1Sa 9:1
18:22 [m] Jos 16:1
18:24 [n] Isa 10:29
18:25 [o] Jos 9:3 [p] Jdg 4:5 [q] Jos 9:17
18:26 [r] Jos 11:3
18:28 [s] 2Sa 21:14 [t] Jos 15:8 [u] Jos 10:1 [v] Jos 15:57
19:1 [w] ver 9; Ge 49:7
19:2 [x] Ge 21:14; 1Ki 19:3
19:7 [y] Jos 15:42
19:8 [z] Jos 10:40
19:9 [a] Ge 49:7 [b] Eze 48:24
19:10 [c] Jos 21:7, 34
19:11 [d] Jos 12:22
19:13 [e] Jos 15:32
19:15 [f] Ge 35:19
19:16 [g] ver 10; Jos 21:7 [h] Eze 48:26
19:17 [i] Ge 30:18
19:18 [j] Jos 15:56 [k] 1Sa 28:4; 2Ki 4:8
19:22 [l] Jdg 4:6, 12; Ps 89:12 [m] Jos 15:10
19:23 [n] Jos 17:10 [o] Ge 49:15; Eze 48:25

Jos 19:9 ❖ How can we bless or welcome others when we have more than we need? Be specific.

Allotment for Zebulun

10The third lot came up for Zebulun[c] according to its clans:
The boundary of their inheritance
went as far as Sarid. 11Going west
it ran to Maralah, touched Dabbe-
sheth, and extended to the ravine
near Jokneam.[d] 12It turned east from
Sarid toward the sunrise to the territory of Kisloth Tabor and went on
to Daberath and up to Japhia. 13Then
it continued eastward to Gath Hepher and Eth Kazin; it came out at
Rimmon[e] and turned toward Neah.
14There the boundary went around
on the north to Hannathon and
ended at the Valley of Iphtah El.
15Included were Kattath, Nahalal,
Shimron, Idalah and Bethlehem.[f]
There were twelve towns and their
villages.
16These towns and their villages were
the inheritance of Zebulun,[g] according
to its clans.[h]

Allotment for Issachar

17The fourth lot came out for Issachar[i]
according to its clans. 18Their territory
included:
Jezreel,[j] Kesulloth, Shunem,[k]
19Hapharaim, Shion, Anaharath,
20Rabbith, Kishion, Ebez, 21Remeth,
En Gannim, En Haddah and Beth
Pazzez. 22The boundary touched
Tabor,[l] Shahazumah and Beth Shemesh,[m] and ended at the Jordan.
There were sixteen towns and their
villages.
23These towns and their villages were
the inheritance of the tribe of Issachar,[n]
according to its clans.[o]

[a] 2 Or *Beersheba, Sheba*; 1 Chron. 4:28 does not have *Sheba*.

19:1–9 The second lot identifies the inheritance of Simeon. It consists exclusively of towns within Judah's territory. The writer explains that Simeon benefited from the fact that Judah's portion exceeded Judah's needs (v. 9).

19:10–16 The third lot falls to Zebulun. Zebulun is a small tribe set snugly between Asher (west), Naphtali (north and northeast), Issachar (southeast), and West Manasseh (southwest).

19:17–23 Issachar receives its inheritance with the fall of the fourth lot. Place names and the descriptions suggest that the allotments of Zebulun, Issachar, and Napthali all meet near Mount Tabor.

DIVIDING THE LAND

Allotment for Asher

24The fifth lot came out for the tribe of
Asher[p] according to its clans. 25Their territory included:
Helkath, Hali, Beten, Akshaph,
26Allammelek, Amad and Mishal.
On the west the boundary touched
Carmel[q] and Shihor Libnath. 27It
then turned east toward Beth Dagon, touched Zebulun[r] and the Valley of Iphtah El, and went north to
Beth Emek and Neiel, passing Kabul[s]
on the left. 28It went to Abdon,[a] Rehob,[t] Hammon[u] and Kanah, as far as
Greater Sidon.[v] 29The boundary then
turned back toward Ramah[w] and
went to the fortified city of Tyre,[x]
turned toward Hosah and came out
at the Mediterranean Sea in the region of Akzib,[y] 30Ummah, Aphek
and Rehob. There were twenty-two
towns and their villages.
31These towns and their villages were
the inheritance of the tribe of Asher,[z]
according to its clans.

Allotment for Naphtali

32The sixth lot came out for Naphtali according to its clans:
33Their boundary went from He-
leph and the large tree in Zaanannim, passing Adami Nekeb and Jabneel to Lakkum and ending at the
Jordan. 34The boundary ran west
through Aznoth Tabor and came out
at Hukkok. It touched Zebulun on
the south, Asher on the west and
the Jordan[b] on the east. 35The fortified towns were Ziddim, Zer, Hammath, Rakkath, Kinnereth,[a] 36Ad-
amah, Ramah,[b] Hazor,[c] 37Kedesh,
Edrei,[d] En Hazor, 38Iron, Migdal El,
Horem, Beth Anath and Beth Shemesh. There were nineteen towns
and their villages.
39These towns and their villages were
the inheritance of the tribe of Naphtali,
according to its clans.[e]

Allotment for Dan

40The seventh lot came out for the tribe
of Dan according to its clans. 41The territory of their inheritance included:
Zorah, Eshtaol, Ir Shemesh, 42Sha-
alabbin, Aijalon,[f] Ithlah, 43Elon, Timnah,[g] Ekron, 44Eltekeh, Gibbethon,
Baalath, 45Jehud, Bene Berak, Gath
Rimmon,[h] 46Me Jarkon and Rakkon,
with the area facing Joppa.[i]
47(When the territory of the Danites
was lost to them,[j] they went up and attacked Leshem[k], took it, put it to the
sword and occupied it. They settled in
Leshem and named it Dan after their
ancestor.)[l]
48These towns and their villages were
the inheritance of the tribe of Dan,[m] according to its clans.

Allotment for Joshua

49When they had finished dividing the
land into its allotted portions, the Israelites gave Joshua son of Nun an inheritance among them, 50as the LORD had
commanded. They gave him the town he
asked for — Timnath Serah[c][n] in the hill
country of Ephraim. And he built up the
town and settled there.
51These are the territories that Eleazar the priest, Joshua son of Nun and
the heads of the tribal clans of Israel

19:24 [p] Jos 17:7
19:26 [q] Jos 12:22
19:27 [r] ver 10 [s] 1Ki 9:13
19:28 [t] Jdg 1:31 [u] 1Ch 6:76 [v] Ge 10:19; Jos 11:8
19:29 [w] Jos 18:25 [x] 2Sa 5:11; 24:7; Isa 23:1; Jer 25:22; Eze 26:2 [y] Jdg 1:31
19:31 [z] Ge 30:13; Eze 48:2
19:35 [a] Jos 11:2
19:36 [b] Jos 18:25 [c] Jos 11:1
19:37 [d] Nu 21:33
19:39 [e] Dt 33:23; Eze 48:3
19:42 [f] Jdg 1:35
19:43 [g] Ge 38:12
19:45 [h] Jos 21:24; 1Ch 6:69
19:46 [i] 2Ch 2:16; Jnh 1:3
19:47 [j] Jdg 18:1 [k] Jdg 18:7,14 [l] Jdg 18:27,29
19:48 [m] Ge 30:6
19:50 [n] Jos 24:30

[a] 28 Some Hebrew manuscripts (see also 21:30); most Hebrew manuscripts *Ebron*
[b] 34 Septuagint; Hebrew *west, and Judah, the Jordan,*
[c] 50 Also known as *Timnath Heres* (see Judges 2:9)

19:24–31 The fifth lot identifies Asher. Asher occupies a narrow swath of land east-to-west between the Mediterranean and Zebulun and south-to-north between the Kishon River and somewhere north of the Litani River.
19:32–39 The sixth lot concerns Naphtali, and again opening and closing statements (vv. 32, 39) set the section apart. The territory of Naphtali occupies the eastern part of Lower Galilee and most of Upper Galilee east of Asher and west of the Sea of Galilee and the Jordan.
19:40–48 Finally, the seventh lot falls on Dan. A parenthetical comment explains how Dan, unable to possess its allotment, militarily succeeds in settling way up north (v. 47). The comment (lit., "Dan's territory left them") seems to blame the land for getting away rather than Dan for failing. The text implies sympathy—in modern terms, "it just got away from me."
19:49–50 The allotment narrative opened with Joshua (13:1) and now fittingly returns to him (19:49). The tribes have received their allotments from Joshua, and now the collective body ("the Israelites") returns the favor, gifting him with his own inheritance.
19:51 This concluding formula looks back over the proceedings of chs. 18–19 and draws them to a close.

13:1—19:51 Joshua 13–19 begins with Yahweh's conversation with aging Joshua concerning "the land that remains" (13:2). He surveys

assigned by lot at Shiloh in the presence of the LORD at the entrance to the tent of meeting. And so they finished dividing the land.[o]

Cities of Refuge

20:1–9Ref // Nu 35:9–34; Dt 4:41–43; 19:1–14

20 Then the LORD said to Joshua: 2"Tell the Israelites to designate the cities of refuge, as I instructed you through Moses, 3so that anyone who kills a person accidentally and unintentionally[p] may flee there and find protection from the avenger of blood.[q] 4When they flee to one of these cities, they are to stand in the entrance of the city gate[r] and state their case before the elders[s] of that city. Then the elders are to admit the fugitive into their city and provide a place to live among them. 5If the avenger of blood comes in pursuit, the elders must not surrender the fugitive, because the fugitive killed their neighbor unintentionally and without malice aforethought. 6They are to stay in that city until they have stood trial before the assembly[t] and until the death of the high priest who is serving at that time. Then they may go back to their own home in the town from which they fled."

7So they set apart Kedesh[u] in Galilee in the hill country of Naphtali, Shechem[v] in the hill country of Ephraim, and Kiriath Arba (that is, Hebron[w]) in the hill country of Judah.[x] 8East of the Jordan (on the other side from Jericho) they designated Bezer[y] in the wilderness on the plateau in the tribe of Reuben, Ramoth in Gilead[z] in the tribe of Gad, and Golan in Bashan in the tribe of Manasseh. 9Any of the Israelites or any foreigner residing among them who killed someone accidentally could flee to these designated cities and not be killed by the avenger of blood prior to standing trial before the assembly.[a]

19:51 [o] Jos 14:1; 18:10; Ac 13:19
20:3 [p] Lev 4:2 [q] Nu 35:12
20:4 [r] Ru 4:1; Jer 38:7 [s] Jos 7:6
20:6 [t] Nu 35:12
20:7 [u] Jos 21:32; 1Ch 6:76 [v] Ge 12:6 [w] Jos 10:36; 21:11 [x] Lk 1:39
20:8 [y] Jos 21:36; 1Ch 6:78 [z] Jos 12:2
20:9 [a] Ex 21:13; Nu 35:15
21:1 [b] Jos 14:1
21:2 [c] Jos 18:1 [d] Nu 35:2-3
21:4 [e] ver 19
21:5 [f] ver 26
21:6 [g] Ge 30:18

Jos 20:1-6 ❖ How can Christians today provide places of sanctuary and blessing for those at risk?

Towns for the Levites

21:4–39pp // 1Ch 6:54–80

21 Now the family heads of the Levites approached Eleazar the priest, Joshua son of Nun, and the heads of the other tribal families of Israel[b] 2at Shiloh[c] in Canaan and said to them, "The LORD commanded through Moses that you give us towns to live in, with pasturelands for our livestock."[d] 3So, as the LORD had commanded, the Israelites gave the Levites the following towns and pasturelands out of their own inheritance:

4The first lot came out for the Kohathites, according to their clans. The Levites who were descendants of Aaron the priest were allotted thirteen towns from the tribes of Judah, Simeon and Benjamin.[e] 5The rest of Kohath's descendants were allotted ten towns from the clans of the tribes of Ephraim, Dan and half of Manasseh.[f]

6The descendants of Gershon were allotted thirteen towns from the clans of the tribes of Issachar,[g] Asher, Naphtali and the half-tribe of Manasseh in Bashan.

---

the terrain not yet in Israelite hands, leaving Israel to do its part and promising to drive out the Sidonians himself. An important contemporary theme emerges from this conversation: Given our human weakness, we always carry out God's tasks imperfectly, but God is strong and caring; he stands ready to aid our efforts rather than tolerate our compromise.

When we feel the weakest, that is when we are the strongest. At that moment, the powerful grace of God comes into play. The trick, of course, is to relax and let that power take over. Here is one way to surrender to God's power: Memorize Php 4:13, and when you feel yourself in need of God's power, simply say, "I can do all this through him who gives me strength." When you dread going to work: "I can do all this through him . . ." When you fail and need to repair a relationship: "I can do all this through him . . ." When you have no idea how to solve a problem, "I can do all this through him . . ." When you feel like you cannot live another day: "I can do all this through him . . ." When you repeat this assurance to yourself, you will experience the paradox of the gospel: It demonstrates its incredible power at the moment we feel at rock bottom.

20:1-9 The term "cities of refuge" links Jos 20 with the provision of Nu 35:6. The ancient custom of blood revenge—retaliation in kind against a killer by the victim's family—stands in the background of Jos 20. The provision of cities of refuge seeks to break the destructive cycle of blood revenge. But v. 3 clarifies that it only applies to accidental and unintentional killings (Nu 35:11–15).

21:1-8 Once again, a petition comes to the leaders at Shiloh. This time the petitioners ask for what Yahweh had promised them through Moses (v. 2b). Verse 8 again states that the Israelites obeyed Yahweh's command delivered by Moses.

7The descendants of Merari,[h] according to their clans, received twelve towns
from the tribes of Reuben, Gad and Zebulun.[i]
8So the Israelites allotted to the Levites these towns and their pasturelands,
as the LORD had commanded through
Moses.

9From the tribes of Judah and Simeon
they allotted the following towns by
name 10(these towns were assigned to
the descendants of Aaron who were from
the Kohathite clans of the Levites, because the first lot fell to them):
11They gave them Kiriath Arba
(that is, Hebron[j]), with its surrounding pastureland, in the hill country
of Judah. (Arba was the forefather
of Anak.) 12But the fields and villages around the city they had given
to Caleb son of Jephunneh as his
possession.
13So to the descendants of Aaron
the priest they gave Hebron (a city of
refuge for one accused of murder),
Libnah,[k] 14Jattir,[l] Eshtemoa,[m] 15Ho-
lon,[n] Debir, 16Ain, Juttah[o] and Beth
Shemesh,[p] together with their pasturelands — nine towns from these
two tribes.
17And from the tribe of Benjamin
they gave them Gibeon, Geba,[q] 18An-
athoth and Almon, together with
their pasturelands — four towns.
19The total number of towns for the
priests, the descendants of Aaron, came
to thirteen, together with their pasturelands.

20The rest of the Kohathite clans of the
Levites were allotted towns from the
tribe of Ephraim:
21In the hill country of Ephraim
they were given Shechem[r] (a city
of refuge for one accused of murder) and Gezer, 22Kibzaim and Beth
Horon,[s] together with their pasturelands — four towns.[t]
23Also from the tribe of Dan they
received Eltekeh, Gibbethon, 24Ai-
jalon and Gath Rimmon,[u] together with their pasturelands — four
towns.
25From half the tribe of Manasseh they received Taanach and Gath
Rimmon, together with their pasturelands — two towns.
26All these ten towns and their pasturelands were given to the rest of the Kohathite clans.

27The Levite clans of the Gershonites
were given:
from the half-tribe of Manasseh,
Golan in Bashan[v] (a city of refuge
for one accused of murder[w]) and Be
Eshterah, together with their pasturelands — two towns;
28from the tribe of Issachar,[x]
Kishion, Daberath, 29Jarmuth and
En Gannim, together with their pasturelands — four towns;
30from the tribe of Asher,[y]
Mishal, Abdon, 31Helkath and Rehob,
together with their pasturelands —
four towns;
32from the tribe of Naphtali,
Kedesh[z] in Galilee (a city of refuge
for one accused of murder[a]), Ham-
moth Dor and Kartan, together with
their pasturelands — three towns.
33The total number of towns of the Gershonite[b] clans came to thirteen, together
with their pasturelands.

34The Merarite clans (the rest of the Levites) were given:
from the tribe of Zebulun,[c]
Jokneam, Kartah, 35Dimnah and Nahalal, together with their pasturelands — four towns;
36from the tribe of Reuben,
Bezer,[d] Jahaz, 37Kedemoth and
Mephaath, together with their pasturelands — four towns;
38from the tribe of Gad,
Ramoth[e] in Gilead (a city of refuge

21:7 [h] Ex 6:16 [i] Jos 19:10
21:11 [j] Jos 15:13; 1Ch 6:55
21:13 [k] Jos 15:42; 1Ch 6:57
21:14 [l] Jos 15:48 [m] Jos 15:50
21:15 [n] Jos 15:51
21:16 [o] Jos 15:55 [p] Jos 15:10
21:17 [q] Jos 18:24
21:21 [r] Jos 17:7; 20:7
21:22 [s] Jos 10:10 [t] 1Sa 1:1
21:24 [u] Jos 19:45
21:27 [v] Jos 12:5 [w] Nu 35:6
21:28 [x] Ge 30:18
21:30 [y] Jos 17:7
21:32 [z] Jos 12:22 [a] Nu 35:6; Jos 20:7
21:33 [b] ver 6
21:34 [c] Jos 19:10; 1Ch 6:77
21:36 [d] Jos 20:8
21:38 [e] Dt 4:43

21:9–42 A simple, somewhat formulaic structure forms the skeleton of this long section. The underlying structure of vv. 9–42 includes the following elements: (1) Introductory formula: "to family X [they gave] . . ." (vv. 9, 11, 13, 20, 27, 34) (2) Tribal source formula: "from tribe X + town list + total number of towns" (vv. 9, 11, 13–16, 17–18, 28–29, 30–31, 32, 36–37) (3) Summary formula ("All the towns . . .") with tally (vv. 19, 26, 33, 40) (4) Grand total tally for all Levites (v. 41) (5) Conclusion (v. 42)

21:9–19 The paragraph on Aaron's descendants is the most detailed and complex one.

21:20–26 Israel gives the non-priestly Kohathites ten towns and their land belts.

21:27–33 The Gershonites also receive thirteen cities. Geographically, two of their towns lie way east of the Sea of Galilee. The rest spread north, south, and northwest of it.

21:34–40 Finally, the Merarites receive four towns from Zebulun, Reuben, and Gad (v. 39).

for one accused of murder), Mahanaim,[f] 39Heshbon and Jazer, together with their pasturelands — four
towns in all.
40The total number of towns allotted to
the Merarite clans, who were the rest of
the Levites, came to twelve.
41The towns of the Levites in the territory held by the Israelites were forty-eight in all, together with their pasturelands.[g] 42Each of these towns had
pasturelands surrounding it; this was
true for all these towns.

43So the LORD gave Israel all the land
he had sworn to give their ancestors,[h]
and they took possession[i] of it and settled there.[j] 44The LORD gave them rest[k]
on every side, just as he had sworn to
their ancestors. Not one of their enemies[l]
withstood them; the LORD gave all their
enemies[m] into their hands.[n] 45Not one of
all the LORD's good promises[o] to Israel
failed; every one was fulfilled.

Eastern Tribes Return Home

22 Then Joshua summoned the Reubenites, the Gadites and the half-
tribe of Manasseh 2and said to them,
"You have done all that Moses the servant of the LORD commanded,[p] and you
have obeyed me in everything I commanded. 3For a long time now — to this
very day — you have not deserted your
fellow Israelites but have carried out the
mission the LORD your God gave you.
4Now that the LORD your God has given
them rest as he promised, return to your
homes[q] in the land that Moses the servant of the LORD gave you on the other
side of the Jordan.[r] 5But be very careful to keep the commandment[s] and the
law that Moses the servant of the LORD
gave you: to love the LORD your God, to
walk in obedience to him, to keep his
commands,[t] to hold fast to him and to
serve him with all your heart and with
all your soul.[u]"
6Then Joshua blessed[v] them and
sent them away, and they went to their
homes. 7(To the half-tribe of Manasseh
Moses had given land in Bashan,[w] and to
the other half of the tribe Joshua gave
land on the west side[x] of the Jordan along
with their fellow Israelites.) When Joshua
sent them home, he blessed them, 8say-
ing, "Return to your homes with your
great wealth — with large herds of livestock,[y] with silver, gold, bronze and iron,
and a great quantity of clothing — and
divide[z] the plunder[a] from your enemies
with your fellow Israelites."
9So the Reubenites, the Gadites and
the half-tribe of Manasseh left the Israelites at Shiloh in Canaan to return to

21:38 [f] Ge 32:2
21:41 [g] Nu 35:7
21:43 [h] Dt 34:4 [i] Dt 11:31 [j] Dt 17:14
21:44 [k] Ex 33:14; Jos 1:13 [l] Dt 6:19 [m] Ex 23:31 [n] Dt 7:24; 21:10
21:45 [o] Jos 23:14; Ne 9:8
22:2 [p] Nu 32:25
22:4 [q] Nu 32:22; Dt 3:20 [r] Nu 32:18; Jos 1:13-15
22:5 [s] Isa 43:22 [t] Dt 5:29 [u] Dt 6:6,17
22:6 [v] Ex 39:43
22:7 [w] Nu 32:33; Jos 12:5 [x] Jos 17:2,5
22:8 [y] Dt 20:14 [z] Nu 31:27 [a] Ge 49:27; 1Sa 30:16; Isa 9:3

Jos 21:45 ❖ How has God fulfilled his "good promises" to us (see Lk 1:37)?

21:43–45 This marks one of the most important moments in the entire book, weaving together four unmistakable linguistic echoes from ch. 1 to form a thematic *inclusio* (or envelope) around chs. 1–21. (1) The writer affirms that "the LORD gave Israel all the land"; he kept his oath (v. 43a; cf. 1:6). (2) Israel "took possession of it and settled there" (v. 43b). Again, he writes retrospectively; to "take possession" was what, on Joshua's orders, the officers told the people to motivate them in their preparations for the Jordan crossing (1:11; cf. 1:15). (3) The narrator recalls another fulfilled patriarchal promise—Yahweh's gift of "rest on every side" (v. 44a). (4) The writer affirms that nothing Yahweh promised was left undone (v. 45; cf. 23:14). All credit goes to Yahweh.

✜ **20:1—21:45** The OT cities of refuge offered mercy for unfortunate Israelites. One aspect of their contemporary meaning is to challenge churches today to be "churches of refuge." What traits typify a "church of refuge"? (1) Its primary concern is with today and tomorrow, not yesterday. People sense a place where their past will never get in the way of relationships. (2) Yes, churches have rules, but refuge churches apply them only when necessary. (3) A safe church grows members who are well aware of their own faults. (4) Finally, a safe church treats people the same way God has treated them—with mercy and compassion.

22:1–6 With the fighting done and west-bank land secure, Joshua summons the east Jordanian tribes (Reuben, Gad, East Manasseh) and recalls that Moses had granted their requested inheritances east of the Jordan on one condition—that they not occupy them until they and the other tribes had together conquered the land west of the Jordan (Nu 35). Joshua affirms that they have fully met both obligations, obeying both Moses and Joshua (22:2).

Joshua makes sure the returnees remember what is ultimately most important (v. 5) and pronounces a blessing over them (v. 6).

22:9–10 The narrator invokes terminology that noticeably contrasts the east and west-bank areas. It seems to represent a west Jordanian perspective: "Shiloh in the land of Canaan" versus "the land of Gilead"; "children of Reuben, Gad, and half-Manasseh" versus "the children of Israel."

Gilead,[b] their own land, which they had
acquired in accordance with the command of the LORD through Moses.
10When they came to Geliloth near the
Jordan in the land of Canaan, the Reubenites, the Gadites and the half-tribe of
Manasseh built an imposing altar there
by the Jordan. 11And when the Israelites
heard that they had built the altar on the
border of Canaan at Geliloth near the
Jordan on the Israelite side, 12the whole
assembly of Israel gathered at Shiloh[c] to
go to war against them.
13So the Israelites sent Phinehas[d] son
of Eleazar,[e] the priest, to the land of Gilead — to Reuben, Gad and the half-tribe
of Manasseh. 14With him they sent ten
of the chief men, one from each of the
tribes of Israel, each the head of a family division among the Israelite clans.[f]
15When they went to Gilead — to Reuben, Gad and the half-tribe of Manasseh — they said to them: 16"The whole
assembly of the LORD says: 'How could
you break faith[g] with the God of Israel
like this? How could you turn away from
the LORD and build yourselves an altar
in rebellion[h] against him now? 17Was not
the sin of Peor[i] enough for us? Up to this
very day we have not cleansed ourselves
from that sin, even though a plague fell
on the community of the LORD! 18And are
you now turning away from the LORD?
"'If you rebel against the LORD today,
tomorrow he will be angry with the
whole community[j] of Israel. 19If the land
you possess is defiled, come over to the
LORD's land, where the LORD's tabernacle
stands, and share the land with us. But
do not rebel against the LORD or against
us by building an altar for yourselves,
other than the altar of the LORD our God.
20When Achan son of Zerah was unfaithful in regard to the devoted things,[a][k] did
not wrath[l] come on the whole community of Israel? He was not the only one
who died for his sin.'"[m]
21Then Reuben, Gad and the half-tribe
of Manasseh replied to the heads of the
clans of Israel: 22"The Mighty One, God,
the LORD! The Mighty One, God,[n] the
LORD![o] He knows![p] And let Israel know!
If this has been in rebellion or disobedience to the LORD, do not spare us this
day. 23If we have built our own altar to
turn away from the LORD and to offer
burnt offerings and grain offerings,[q] or
to sacrifice fellowship offerings on it,
may the LORD himself call us to account.[r]
24"No! We did it for fear that some day
your descendants might say to ours,
'What do you have to do with the LORD,
the God of Israel? 25The LORD has made
the Jordan a boundary between us and
you — you Reubenites and Gadites! You
have no share in the LORD.' So your descendants might cause ours to stop fearing the LORD.
26"That is why we said, 'Let us get
ready and build an altar — but not for
burnt offerings or sacrifices.' 27On the
contrary, it is to be a witness[s] between
us and you and the generations that

22:9 [b] Nu 32:26, 29
22:12 [c] Jos 18:1
22:13 [d] Nu 25:7 [e] Nu 3:32; Jos 24:33
22:14 [f] Nu 1:4
22:16 [g] Dt 13:14 [h] Dt 12:13-14
22:17 [i] Nu 25:1-9
22:18 [j] Lev 10:6; Nu 16:22
22:20 [k] Jos 7:1 [l] Ps 7:11 [m] Jos 7:5
22:22 [n] Dt 10:17 [o] Ps 50:1 [p] 1Ki 8:39; Job 10:7; Ps 44:21; Jer 17:10
22:23 [q] Jer 41:5 [r] Dt 12:11; 18:19; 1Sa 20:16
22:27 [s] Ge 21:30; Jos 24:27

[a] *20* The Hebrew term refers to the irrevocable giving over of things or persons to the LORD, often by totally destroying them.

22:11–14 A report (or rumor?) about an unsettling discovery conveys shocked urgency, as if the altar was scandalous and posed a serious threat to west-bank well-being. Israel meets to prepare for war against the two-and-a-half tribes. First, however, the Israelites dispatch a delegation. To put a priest in charge signals that the issue is a religious one, and this particular priest has an interesting past history (Nu 25).

22:15–20 The opening message's formula presents the speech as spoken by the community of Yahweh as a whole (v. 16). Subtly, it also implies some serious problem with the standing of the east-bank tribes in the eyes of Yahweh and Israel.

The delegation assumes that, since Yahweh has authorized only one altar—the one in Canaan (cf. v. 19)—the new altar must honor another god; it is apostasy, plain and simple. The speech moves from blunt accusation to an appeal to spare everyone terrible consequences (vv. 17–20). Peor recalls the place just east of the Jordan where Yahweh sent a terrible plague to punish Israel for worshiping an idol, the Baal of Peor, in Nu 25. The plague took 24,000 lives.

To avert this disaster, the visitors propose that the two-and-a-half tribes leave their "defiled" land east of the Jordan and settle among the other tribes in Canaan, "in the LORD's land," near the tabernacle (v. 19). They voice the west Jordanian perspective that east-bank land is not holy, as Canaan is.

22:21–29 The opening rhetorical flourish, a string of orthodox names for Israel's God, aims immediately to dispel the visitors' doubts about their religious sincerity and appropriateness (v. 22). There is, they claim, another side to this story: The altar offers tangible proof of their commitment to sacrifice only at Yahweh's west-bank sanctuary, not to fall into rebellion and apostasy.

As a final, dramatic gesture, the Transjordanians voice a negative oath: "Far be it from us" "to rebel" (v. 29) against Yahweh by sacrificing at any spot other than at the altar in front of the tabernacle.

follow, that we will worship the LORD at
his sanctuary with our burnt offerings,
sacrifices and fellowship offerings.[t] Then
in the future your descendants will not
be able to say to ours, 'You have no share
in the LORD.'
28"And we said, 'If they ever say this to
us, or to our descendants, we will answer:
Look at the replica of the LORD's altar,
which our ancestors built, not for burnt
offerings and sacrifices, but as a witness
between us and you.'
29"Far be it from us to rebel[u] against
the LORD and turn away from him today
by building an altar for burnt offerings,
grain offerings and sacrifices, other than
the altar of the LORD our God that stands
before his tabernacle.[v]"
30When Phinehas the priest and the
leaders of the community—the heads of
the clans of the Israelites—heard what
Reuben, Gad and Manasseh had to say,
they were pleased. 31And Phinehas son of
Eleazar, the priest, said to Reuben, Gad
and Manasseh, "Today we know that the
LORD is with us,[w] because you have not
been unfaithful to the LORD in this matter. Now you have rescued the Israelites
from the LORD's hand."
32Then Phinehas son of Eleazar, the
priest, and the leaders returned to Canaan from their meeting with the Reubenites and Gadites in Gilead and reported to the Israelites. 33They were glad to
hear the report and praised God.[x] And
they talked no more about going to war
against them to devastate the country
where the Reubenites and the Gadites
lived.
34And the Reubenites and the Gadites
gave the altar this name: A Witness[y] Between Us—that the LORD is God.

22:27 [t] Dt 12:6
22:29 [u] Jos 24:16 [v] Dt 12:13-14
22:31 [w] Lev 26:11-12; 2Ch 15:2
22:33 [x] 1Ch 29:20; Da 2:19; Lk 2:28

Jos 22:26-28 ❖ What are some ways Christians can commemorate and promote unity with one another today?

Joshua's Farewell to the Leaders

23 After a long time had passed and
the LORD had given Israel rest[z]
from all their enemies around them,
Joshua, by then a very old man,[a] 2sum-
moned all Israel—their elders,[b] leaders,
judges and officials[c]—and said to them:
"I am very old. 3You yourselves have seen
everything the LORD your God has done
to all these nations for your sake; it was
the LORD your God who fought for you.[d]
4Remember how I have allotted[e] as an
inheritance for your tribes all the land
of the nations that remain—the nations
I conquered—between the Jordan and
the Mediterranean Sea[f] in the west. 5The
LORD your God himself will push them
out for your sake. He will drive them out
before you, and you will take possession
of their land, as the LORD your God promised you.[g]
6"Be very strong; be careful to obey
all that is written in the Book of the Law
of Moses, without turning aside to the
right or to the left.[h] 7Do not associate
with these nations that remain among

22:34 [y] Ge 21:30
23:1 [z] Dt 12:9; Jos 21:44 [a] Jos 13:1
23:2 [b] Jos 7:6 [c] Jos 24:1
23:3 [d] Ex 14:14
23:4 [e] Jos 19:51 [f] Nu 34:6
23:5 [g] Ex 23:30; Nu 33:53
23:6 [h] Dt 5:32; Jos 1:7

22:30-31 The fact that the Transjordanians mount a defense longer than the original accusation implies that the sympathies of the biblical author lie with them. The lengthy explanation by the Transjordanians pleases the entire delegation (v. 30).
22:32-33 The centrality of Phineas the priest as hero in the narrative fully legitimates the altar. The crowd also feels a welcome sense of relief, since they immediately "praise (lit., "bless") God" and say nothing more about going to war (v. 33b).
22:34 No one tears the altar down. Instead, Reuben and Gad give it an appropriate sentence name: "A Witness Between Us—that the LORD [and absolutely no one else] is God" (v. 34). Implicit also is the unspoken tagline, "and on both sides of the river, too!"

❖ **22:1-34** The Jordan River was the symbol of theological tensions that could have divided Israel. It's possible that little Jordans, capable of eroding Christian unity, flow quietly through every congregation.

A variety of religious experiences may populate a congregation. Such differing experiences raise divisive questions about what the church should be doing. They also often cause divisions about how the church should worship: Should there be a formal, informal, or blended worship style? Rather than confront each other over every little thing, there are times simply to let things pass because we trust each other—and we trust the unseen work of the Holy Spirit. As the Transjordanians shout, "The Mighty One, God, the LORD! He knows!" (22:22).

23:1-8 Joshua summons Israel to hear his farewell address and quickly turns to remembrance (vv. 2-5), shifting the focus from himself to the audience and what "you yourselves [emphatic pronoun] have seen" (v. 3). To cling firmly to Yahweh is to embrace him so tightly—to observe such exclusive loyalty to him—as to leave not even the smallest crack for other gods between the two of you.

you; do not invoke the names of their gods or swear[i] by them. You must not serve them or bow down[j] to them. 8But you are to hold fast to the LORD[k] your God, as you have until now.

9"The LORD has driven out before you great and powerful nations;[l] to this day no one has been able to withstand you.[m]
10One of you routs a thousand,[n] because the LORD your God fights for you,[o] just as he promised. 11So be very careful to love the LORD[p] your God.

12"But if you turn away and ally yourselves with the survivors of these nations that remain among you and if you intermarry with them[q] and associate with them,[r] 13then you may be sure that the LORD your God will no longer drive out these nations before you. Instead, they will become snares[s] and traps for you, whips on your backs and thorns in your eyes,[t] until you perish from this good land, which the LORD your God has given you.

14"Now I am about to go the way of all the earth.[u] You know with all your heart and soul that not one of all the good promises the LORD your God gave you has failed. Every promise has been fulfilled; not one has failed.[v] 15But just as all the good things the LORD your God has promised you have come to you, so he will bring on you all the evil things he has threatened, until the LORD your God has destroyed you from this good land he has given you.[w] 16If you violate the covenant of the LORD your God, which he commanded you, and go and serve other gods and bow down to them, the LORD's anger will burn against you, and you will quickly perish from the good land he has given you.[x]"

23:7 [i] Ex 23:13; Ps 16:4; Jer 5:7 [j] Ex 20:5
23:8 [k] Dt 10:20
23:9 [l] Dt 11:23 [m] Dt 7:24
23:10 [n] Lev 26:8 [o] Ex 14:14; Dt 3:22
23:11 [p] Jos 22:5
23:12 [q] Dt 7:3 [r] Ex 34:16; Ps 106:34-35
23:13 [s] Ex 23:33 [t] Nu 33:55
23:14 [u] 1Ki 2:2 [v] Jos 21:45
23:15 [w] Lev 26:17; Dt 28:15
23:16 [x] Dt 4:25-26
24:1 [y] Jos 23:2
24:2 [z] Ge 11:32
24:3 [a] Ge 12:1 [b] Ge 15:5 [c] Ge 21:3
24:4 [d] Ge 25:26 [e] Dt 2:5 [f] Ge 46:5-6
24:5 [g] Ex 3:10
24:6 [h] Ex 14:9

Jos 23:8 ❖ How can we keep our devotion and obedience to God strong in the future? How can we work toward a future faithfulness through what we do today?

The Covenant Renewed at Shechem

24 Then Joshua assembled all the tribes of Israel at Shechem. He summoned the elders, leaders, judges and officials of Israel,[y] and they presented themselves before God.

2Joshua said to all the people, "This is what the LORD, the God of Israel, says: 'Long ago your ancestors, including Terah the father of Abraham and Nahor, lived beyond the Euphrates River and worshiped other gods.[z] 3But I took your father Abraham from the land beyond the Euphrates and led him throughout Canaan[a] and gave him many descendants.[b] I gave him Isaac,[c] 4and to Isaac I gave Jacob and Esau.[d] I assigned the hill country of Seir[e] to Esau, but Jacob and his family went down to Egypt.[f]

5" 'Then I sent Moses and Aaron,[g] and I afflicted the Egyptians by what I did there, and I brought you out. 6When I brought your people out of Egypt, you came to the sea, and the Egyptians pursued them with chariots and horsemen[a][h] as far as the Red Sea.[b] 7But they cried to the LORD for help, and he put

[a] 6 Or *charioteers* [b] 6 Or *the Sea of Reeds*

23:9–11 From exhortation Joshua returns again to the past deeds of Yahweh that they themselves have seen. They were so unstoppable that one solitary Israelite could rout a thousand Canaanites. For that invincibility under Yahweh to continue, Israel must "be very careful to love the LORD your God" (v. 11).

23:12–13 The long conditional warning cautions against intermarriage with the Canaanites.

23:14–16 Joshua's concluding warning dispels any illusions Israel might have about getting along with both Canaanites and Yahweh. Such attempts at accommodation are foolhardy and futile, the risks gravely serious.

✣ **23:1–16** Every Christian has his or her own story to tell of something amazing God did for them. Sometimes Jesus just lifts our spirits, gives us new insight into ourselves or others, or heals simple sicknesses. At other times his loving rebuke steers us around pitfalls, or his gentle nudge gets us past our reluctance to do the right thing. These, too, are amazing feats, albeit on a smaller scale, and rightly lead us to celebrate with gratitude and joy over what God has done.

24:1–13 Joshua launches the proceedings by addressing the assembled crowd. The address reviews Israel's ancestral history beginning with Abraham (vv. 2–4). The driving theme of the speech concerns Israel's exclusive devotion to Yahweh alone.

Israel's possession of the land is God's gift, pure and simple ("I gave you," v. 13). Yahweh generously handed over to Israel ready-made fields, vineyards, and olive groves to feed themselves, and ready-made cities in which to live. In short, the defeat of Canaan and the land gift are all Yahweh's doing. They mark the capstone of the stunning saga of salvation that he has singlehandedly orchestrated for Israel's benefit since the call of Abram.

darkness[i] between you and the Egyptians; he brought the sea over them and
covered them.[j] You saw with your own
eyes what I did to the Egyptians. Then
you lived in the wilderness for a long
time.[k]
8 " 'I brought you to the land of the
Amorites who lived east of the Jordan.
They fought against you, but I gave
them into your hands. I destroyed them
from before you, and you took possession of their land.[l] 9 When Balak son of
Zippor,[m] the king of Moab, prepared to
fight against Israel, he sent for Balaam
son of Beor to put a curse on you.[n] 10 But I
would not listen to Balaam, so he blessed
you[o] again and again, and I delivered you
out of his hand.
11 " 'Then you crossed the Jordan[p] and
came to Jericho.[q] The citizens of Jericho
fought against you, as did also the Amorites, Perizzites, Canaanites, Hittites,
Girgashites, Hivites and Jebusites, but I
gave them into your hands.[r] 12 I sent the
hornet[s] ahead of you, which drove them
out before you—also the two Amorite
kings. You did not do it with your own
sword and bow. 13 So I gave you a land
on which you did not toil and cities you
did not build; and you live in them and
eat from vineyards and olive groves that
you did not plant.'[t]
14 "Now fear the LORD and serve him
with all faithfulness.[u] Throw away the
gods[v] your ancestors worshiped beyond
the Euphrates River and in Egypt,[w] and
serve the LORD. 15 But if serving the LORD
seems undesirable to you, then choose
for yourselves this day whom you will
serve, whether the gods your ancestors
served beyond the Euphrates, or the gods
of the Amorites,[x] in whose land you are
living. But as for me and my household,
we will serve the LORD."[y]
16 Then the people answered, "Far be
it from us to forsake the LORD to serve
other gods! 17 It was the LORD our God
himself who brought us and our parents up out of Egypt, from that land of
slavery, and performed those great signs
before our eyes. He protected us on our
entire journey and among all the nations
through which we traveled. 18 And the
LORD drove out before us all the nations,
including the Amorites, who lived in the
land. We too will serve the LORD, because
he is our God."
19 Joshua said to the people, "You are
not able to serve the LORD. He is a holy
God;[z] he is a jealous God.[a] He will not
forgive your rebellion[b] and your sins. 20 If
you forsake the LORD[c] and serve foreign
gods, he will turn[d] and bring disaster on
you and make an end of you,[e] after he
has been good to you."
21 But the people said to Joshua, "No!
We will serve the LORD."
22 Then Joshua said, "You are witnesses
against yourselves that you have chosen[f]
to serve the LORD."
"Yes, we are witnesses," they replied.
23 "Now then," said Joshua, "throw
away the foreign gods[g] that are among
you and yield your hearts[h] to the LORD,
the God of Israel."
24 And the people said to Joshua, "We
will serve the LORD our God and obey
him."[i]
25 On that day Joshua made a covenant[j]
for the people, and there at Shechem he
reaffirmed for them decrees and laws.[k]
26 And Joshua recorded these things in
the Book of the Law of God.[l] Then he took
a large stone[m] and set it up there under
the oak near the holy place of the LORD.
27 "See!" he said to all the people. "This
stone will be a witness[n] against us. It has
heard all the words the LORD has said to
us. It will be a witness against you if you
are untrue to your God."
28 Then Joshua dismissed the people,
each to their own inheritance.

24:7 [i] Ex 14:20 [j] Ex 14:28 [k] Dt 1:46
24:8 [l] Nu 21:31
24:9 [m] Nu 22:2 [n] Nu 22:6
24:10 [o] Nu 23:11; Dt 23:5
24:11 [p] Jos 3:16-17 [q] Jos 6:1 [r] Ex 23:23; Dt 7:1
24:12 [s] Ex 23:28; Dt 7:20; Ps 44:3,6-7
24:13 [t] Dt 6:10-11
24:14 [u] Dt 10:12; 18:13; 1Sa 12:24; 2Co 1:12 [v] ver 23 [w] Eze 23:3
24:15 [x] Jdg 6:10; Ru 1:15 [y] Ru 1:16; 1Ki 18:21
24:19 [z] Lev 19:2; 20:26 [a] Ex 20:5 [b] Ex 23:21
24:20 [c] 1Ch 28:9, 20 [d] Ac 7:42 [e] Jos 23:15
24:22 [f] Ps 119:30,173
24:23 [g] ver 14 [h] 1Ki 8:58; Ps 119:36; 141:4
24:24 [i] Ex 19:8; 24:3,7; Dt 5:27
24:25 [j] Ex 24:8 [k] Ex 15:25
24:26 [l] Dt 31:24 [m] Ge 28:18
24:27 [n] Jos 22:27

24:14–15 A subtle, seamless shift from the divine "I" to the third person signals that Joshua speaks from here on. Israel may serve Yahweh or their ancestors' gods, but not both; polytheism is no longer an option. Joshua draws a firm line between his household and the alternatives: "We will serve the LORD." The issue is whether other Israelite households will join his or whether his alone will serve Yahweh.

24:16–24 At first glance, Joshua's reply sounds like an irritated rebuttal (v. 19). But he dispenses a strong dose of divine reality in order to dispel a dangerous delusion. The danger is that they fail to reckon fully with Yahweh's unique character compared to the gods they have known.

This leads Joshua to issue a stern conditional warning (v. 20). But Joshua's stern warning does not deter the people, who again commit themselves to serve Yahweh (cf. v. 18b). Joshua's tone now softens, and the confirmation phase of covenant-making follows (vv. 22–24).

24:25–28 The people commit to this covenant as a permanent, official, self-imposed public policy that Israel will serve Yahweh alone. (1) Joshua writes

Buried in the Promised Land

24:29–31pp // Jdg 2:6–9

29After these things, Joshua son of
Nun, the servant of the LORD, died at the
age of a hundred and ten.[o] 30And they
buried him in the land of his inheritance,
at Timnath Serah[a][p] in the hill country of
Ephraim, north of Mount Gaash.

31Israel served the LORD throughout
the lifetime of Joshua and of the elders[q]
who outlived him and who had experienced everything the LORD had done
for Israel.

32And Joseph's bones, which the Israelites had brought up from Egypt,[r] were
buried at Shechem in the tract of land[s]
that Jacob bought for a hundred pieces
of silver[b] from the sons of Hamor, the
father of Shechem. This became the inheritance of Joseph's descendants.

33And Eleazar son of Aaron[t] died and
was buried at Gibeah, which had been
allotted to his son Phinehas[u] in the hill
country of Ephraim.

24:29 [o] Jdg 2:8
24:30 [p] Jos 19:50
24:31 [q] Jdg 2:7
24:32 [r] Ge 50:25; Ex 13:19 [s] Ge 33:19; Jn 4:5; Ac 7:16
24:33 [t] Jos 22:13 [u] Ex 6:25

Jos 24:31 ❖ What is the connection between our obedience and God's action? How can we continue to obey God through seasons when we don't see his actions in our lives?

[a] *30* Also known as *Timnath Heres* (see Judges 2:9)
[b] *32* Hebrew *hundred kesitahs;* a kesitah was a unit of money of unknown weight and value.

---

down "these things" in a book of God's instruction (v. 26). (2) Joshua sets up a large stone under the oak tree at Shechem.

24:29–31 A subtle narrative touch also bestows on Joshua a telling posthumous award. His previous title had simply been "Moses' aide" (1:1), but here the writer honors him with the title "the servant of the LORD" (24:29). This is the same posthumous title awarded Moses at his death (Dt 34:5).

24:32 The box of long-carried and now-buried bones echoes the last sound of one of the book's central themes: God's fulfillment of his promise to the patriarchs.

24:33 With Eleazar's burial, a generation of Israelite leadership passes from the scene, and the momentous book of Joshua ends. The burials mark the closing bookend of the long epic from a promise received in Genesis to a promise realized in Joshua.

24:1–33 What makes something a god that is usually thought of as normal or healthy? It might be a god if we willingly yield it excessive authority to direct our lives. For example, we may follow its advice or demands without even considering whether God has anything to say about the matter. It might be a god if it in any way plays a more significant role in our lives than God does.

That was what Israel did that so seriously offended Yahweh. They trusted other gods *instead of* Yahweh; they granted those deities a large role in their lives and submitted to their authority rather than submitting to Yahweh. In short, the danger of polytheism is that we may be completely committed to the lordship of Jesus Christ yet still rely on and trust in other things with such a commitment and passion that it makes those things gods. We may worship (i.e., highly value) them, give them offerings (e.g. spend money on them), and serve them (e.g., devote time and energy). Joshua 24 calls us to renounce all other gods and to serve only Yahweh.

The three burial reports that conclude Joshua demarcate the end of one era and the dawn of another. Similarly, the resurrection of Jesus marks the crucial turning point in human history. Besides defeating death, our bitterest enemy, Jesus injects a new power—resurrection power—into our lives to strengthen us to finish the race.

Judges

Author: Unknown, though certain sections may derive from the prophet Samuel

Audience: God's chosen people, the Israelites

Date: Probably about 1000 BC

Theme: Through leaders known as "judges," God again and again delivers the Israelites, who are in danger of losing the promised land through their unfaithfulness.

PERSPECTIVE

We may wonder if the name of this book points toward judgment of some kind; with today's strong reaction against judging or being judged on any level, such an idea might seem out of place in today's world. But "judging" in the ancient world meant something quite different from what it does now—not someone who decides cases in a court of law but someone who helped deliver people from enemies and encouraged them to stay on the morally straight and narrow path. To put it another way, a biblical judge was a leader who helped save people from external and internal enemies.

That said, is there anything in the biblical understanding of "judges" that can help us cope with the modern-day discomfort of being judged?

Absolutely! The core issue in Judges is not whether or not judging is done but rather with whom is God's representative doing the judging—in other words, who is the authority behind the judge? Then as today, leaders were flawed men and women who delivered people only because they were doing the work of the true Judge. One understands the book of Judges only when the focus is put on the necessity of doing the work assigned by God rather than on the "heroes" of the story.

The most important issue is for us to recognize today is that judgment gets done by God no matter what. God's people must figure out how that judgment, those teachings and assignments from God based on the Scriptures, is best communicated to the church and to the whole world. As we think about our original definition above, we can begin to understand that it is more productive to focus less on

Reading Judges

Most of the book of Judges contains familiar stories of God's deliverance through such leaders as Ehud, Deborah, Gideon, Jephthah and Samson. The later chapters of the book, however (chs. 17–21), describe how the Israelites' sin increased as everyone did whatever they wanted and ignored God's law.

	1400 BC	1300	1200	1100	1000	900	800	700	600	500	400
Israelites enter Canaan (c. 1406 BC)											
Deborah's rule (c. 1209–1169 BC)											
Gideon's rule (c. 1162–1122 BC)											
Samuel's birth (c. 1105 BC)											
Jephthah's rule (c. 1078–1072 BC)											
Samson's rule (c. 1075–1055 BC)											
Book of Judges written (c. 1000 BC)											
Division of the kingdom (930 BC)											

Key Verse

When they cried out to the LORD, he raised up for them a deliverer.

—Judges 3:9

individuals and more on the community of believers as the models of what God's standards for us are.

Perhaps the model here for us is not one of the judges but Ruth. Why is it that when the great leaders of the biblical texts are listed, Ruth is rarely on the list? Not that she is ignored. Almost anyone who reads the story of Ruth notices an extraordinary person. But "leader" is not the label we usually affix to her name. We more often see Ruth as a model of a good citizen, ready to help any and all so that the "family" remains strong, faithful, effective.

Perhaps this is where the functions of protecting the community from external enemies and keeping us all aware of the righteousness demanded by God should lie today. Failure of relatively unknown individuals to do so typically does not have the disastrous consequences as the fall of a well-known leader. Despite human frailty, however, God's judgment—rather, God's righteousness—will reign as his flawed creation moves toward reconciliation.

TAKING THE NEXT STEPS

The book of Judges describes the life of the Israelites in Canaan after the death of Joshua and before the Lord had given them kings. Because of their sin against the Lord in failing to destroy all their enemies and in serving the heathen gods of the Canaanites, the Lord allowed their enemies to gain power over them and to destroy their land. When they poured out their hurt to the Lord, the Lord was faithful to his promises, and, in his grace, he sent them judges to deliver them and rule over them. Each time a judge died, however, the people once again regressed to the worship of idols. This cycle characterizes much of the book of Judges.

This book directs our attention to some basic truths about us and about God. (1) The tendency to turn our backs on the Lord and choose gods of our own making is as much a danger for us as it was for the Israelites. In so doing, we only make more problems for ourselves. (2) We cannot expect the Lord to bless us if we reject him and his will. (3) God is faithful to his promises; regardless of how badly we may have messed up our lives, he will forgive us whenever we sincerely confess our sin and set our lives in the direction of living for him. (4) When God gives us his grace and strength, nothing stands in the way of victory. The more we depend on him, the stronger we become.

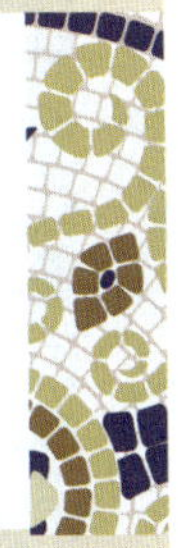

WHAT TO LOOK FOR IN JUDGES

- The story of left-handed Ehud (ch. 3)
- The story of Deborah (chs. 4–5)
- The story of Gideon (chs. 6–8)
- The story of Jephthah (chs. 10–12)
- The story of Samson (chs. 13–16)

Israel Fights the Remaining Canaanites

1:11–15pp // Jos 15:15–19

1 After the death[a] of Joshua, the Israelites asked the LORD, "Who of us is to go up first[b] to fight against the Canaanites?[c]"

2 The LORD answered, "Judah[d] shall go up; I have given the land into their hands.[e]"

3 The men of Judah then said to the Simeonites their fellow Israelites, "Come up with us into the territory allotted to us, to fight against the Canaanites. We in turn will go with you into yours." So the Simeonites[f] went with them.

4 When Judah attacked, the LORD gave the Canaanites and Perizzites[g] into their hands, and they struck down ten thousand men at Bezek.[h] 5 It was there that they found Adoni-Bezek and fought against him, putting to rout the Canaanites and Perizzites. 6 Adoni-Bezek fled, but they chased him and caught him, and cut off his thumbs and big toes.

7 Then Adoni-Bezek said, "Seventy kings with their thumbs and big toes cut off have picked up scraps under my table. Now God has paid me back[i] for what I did to them." They brought him to Jerusalem, and he died there.

8 The men of Judah attacked Jerusalem[j] also and took it. They put the city to the sword and set it on fire.

9 After that, Judah went down to fight against the Canaanites living in the hill country,[k] the Negev[l] and the western foothills. 10 They advanced against the Canaanites living in Hebron[m] (formerly called Kiriath Arba[n]) and defeated Sheshai, Ahiman and Talmai.[o] 11 From there they advanced against the people living in Debir[p] (formerly called Kiriath Sepher).

12 And Caleb said, "I will give my daughter Aksah in marriage to the man who attacks and captures Kiriath Sepher." 13 Othniel son of Kenaz, Caleb's younger brother, took it; so Caleb gave his daughter Aksah to him in marriage.

14 One day when she came to Othniel, she urged him[a] to ask her father for a field. When she got off her donkey, Caleb asked her, "What can I do for you?"

15 She replied, "Do me a special favor. Since you have given me land in the Negev, give me also springs of water." So Caleb gave her the upper and lower springs.

16 The descendants of Moses' father-in-law,[q] the Kenite,[r] went up from the City of Palms[b][s] with the people of Judah to live among the inhabitants of the Desert of Judah in the Negev near Arad.[t]

17 Then the men of Judah went with the Simeonites[u] their fellow Israelites and attacked the Canaanites living in

1:1 [a] Jos 24:29 [b] Nu 27:21 [c] ver 27; Jdg 3:1-6
1:2 [d] Ge 49:8 [e] ver 4; Jdg 3:28
1:3 [f] ver 17
1:4 [g] Ge 13:7; Jos 3:10 [h] 1Sa 11:8
1:7 [i] Lev 24:19
1:8 [j] ver 21; Jos 15:63
1:9 [k] Nu 13:17 [l] Nu 21:1
1:10 [m] Ge 13:18 [n] Ge 35:27 [o] Jos 15:14
1:11 [p] Jos 15:15
1:16 [q] Nu 10:29 [r] Ge 15:19; Jdg 4:11 [s] Dt 34:3; Jdg 3:13 [t] Nu 21:1
1:17 [u] ver 3

> **Jdg 1:4** ❖ How has God given us victories over difficult situations in our lives?

[a] 14 Hebrew; Septuagint and Vulgate *Othniel, he urged her* [b] 16 That is, Jericho

1:1–2a The phrase "the Israelites asked the LORD" (v. 1) expresses the idea of obtaining a declaration of the divine will. The question they want the answer to is, Which tribe will be the first to fight against the Canaanites?

1:2b–21 God intended that each tribe trust him in the process of conquering its allotment. Thus, by making a treaty, the two tribes undercut this process. Even so, the Judahites and Simeonites will see general success in their campaigns since they are willing to go up and fight the Canaanites.

1:8–11 The Judahites have great success.

1:12–15 The story demonstrates that the claim of the descendants of Othniel and Aksah to this land is based on a legal gift by the original recipient of the territory. Aksah's request is not short-term; rather, it is generational in its impact.

1:17 It is ironic that the Simeonites, a numerically insignificant tribe, are the only tribe in the story of the occupation of the land who obey Yahweh and "totally" destroy the city. Yet they will not be mentioned in the book of Judges again.

JUDGES OF ISRAEL
SHAMGAR ?
Hazor (Jabin)
Mediterranean Sea
ELON
Sea of Galilee
Mt. Carmel
Kishon R.
Jezreel Valley
Kedesh (of Naphtali) (Barak)
JAIR
Havvoth Jair
Mt. Tabor
GIDEON
Hill of Moreh
Megiddo
En Harod
Kamon
Ophrah
Taanach
Jabesh Gilead
Abel Meholah
TOLA
Jordan R.
JEPHTHAH
Shamir
Zaphon
ABDON
Mt. Ebal
Penuel/Peniel
Shechem
Pirathon
Sukkoth
Jabbok R.
Mt. Gerizim
AMMONITES
Mizpah
Shiloh
DEBORAH
Gilead
Bethel
EHUD
Mizpah
Gilgal
Rabbah (of the Ammonites)
Ramah
Sorek Valley
Timnah
Jericho (City of Palms)
Eshtaol
Gibeah
Zorah
Jerusalem
IBZAN
SAMSON
Bethlehem
Ashkelon
Tableland of Moab (Mishor)
PHILISTINES
SHAMGAR ?
Gaza
Hebron
Dead Sea
OTHNIEL
Debir
Arnon R.
Beersheba
0 10 km.
0 10 miles
MAJOR JUDGE
MINOR JUDGE

HEROES OF THE FAITH

NAME	EVENTS	YEARS OF REST	PASSAGES
Othniel	Raised up to lead Israel against Cushan-Rishathaim, king of Mesopotamia, after eight years of forced service	40	3:7-11
Ehud	Assassinates Eglon, king of Moab, and leads Israel in battle against Moab	80	3:12-30
Shamgar	Defeats six hundred Philistines	–	3:31
Deborah	Prophetess and judge called to encourage Barak, commander of Israel, and to help lead Israel in victory over King Jabin of Canaan and his commander Sisera	40	4-5
Gideon	Leads three hundred Israelites in battle against the combined might of the Midianites, Amalekites and "other eastern peoples," defeating them; falls into idolatry late in life	40	6-8
Tola	Leads Israel after Abimelek's bloody coup	23	10:1-2
Jephthah	Though of questionable birth, leads his people against the Ammonites; sacrifices only daughter because of rash vow	6	11:1—12:7
Samson	Fights the Philistines; snared by his sinful relationship with Delilah; redeemed in the end, defeating three thousand Philistines	20	13-16

Zephath, and they totally destroyed[a] the
city. Therefore it was called Hormah.[b][v]
18 Judah also took[c] Gaza,[w] Ashkelon and
Ekron — each city with its territory.
19 The LORD was with[x] the men of Judah. They took possession of the hill
country, but they were unable to drive
the people from the plains, because they
had chariots fitted with iron.[y] 20 As Moses had promised, Hebron[z] was given to
Caleb, who drove from it the three sons
of Anak.[a] 21 The Benjamites, however, did
not drive out[b] the Jebusites, who were
living in Jerusalem;[c] to this day the Jebusites live there with the Benjamites.
22 Now the tribes of Joseph attacked
Bethel, and the LORD was with them.
23 When they sent men to spy out Bethel (formerly called Luz),[d] 24 the spies saw
a man coming out of the city and they
said to him, "Show us how to get into the
city and we will see that you are treated
well."[e] 25 So he showed them, and they
put the city to the sword but spared[f] the
man and his whole family. 26 He then
went to the land of the Hittites, where
he built a city and called it Luz, which is
its name to this day.
27 But Manasseh did not drive out the
people of Beth Shan or Taanach or Dor or
Ibleam[g] or Megiddo and their surrounding settlements, for the Canaanites[h] were
determined to live in that land. 28 When
Israel became strong, they pressed the
Canaanites into forced labor but never
drove them out completely. 29 Nor did
Ephraim drive out the Canaanites living

1:17 [v] Nu 21:3
1:18 [w] Jos 11:22
1:19 [x] ver 2 [y] Jos 17:16
1:20 [z] Jos 14:9; 15:13-14 [a] ver 10; Jos 14:13
1:21 [b] Jos 15:63 [c] ver 8
1:23 [d] Ge 28:19
1:24 [e] Jos 2:12, 14
1:25 [f] Jos 6:25
1:27 [g] Jos 17:11 [h] ver 1

[a] 17 The Hebrew term refers to the irrevocable giving over of things or persons to the LORD, often by totally destroying them. [b] 17 *Hormah* means *destruction*. [c] 18 Hebrew; Septuagint *Judah did not take*

1:19–21 The Benjamite failure in v. 21 contrasts starkly with the general success of the Judahites. **1:22–36** The process of subjugation is observable in a four-stage decline in Israelite spirituality. (1) The general success of Judah is recounted through a number of very short stories. The Judahites, having enlisted the Simeonites as their allies, are able to "drive out" the Canaanites everywhere except in the plain. No Canaanites "live among" the Judahites (vv. 1–20). (2) Benjamin, Manasseh, Ephraim, and Zebulun do "not drive out" the Canaanites, and the Canaanites "live among" them, though some Canaanites are forced laborers (vv. 21–30; cf. Jos 16:10; 18:11–28). (3) Asher and Naphtali do "not drive out" the Canaanites, the inhabitants of the land, but instead these tribes "live among" the Canaanites. A few Canaanites become forced laborers (vv. 31–33). (4) There is no statement about "driving out" or "living among." Instead, the Amorites oppress or confine the tribe of Dan, not allowing them into the plain (v. 34). This utter failure of the Danites anticipates their move in ch. 18. Translated "oppressing" in Ex 3:9, where the Egyptians "oppress" the Israelites, it anticipates 2:18; 4:3; 6:9; 10:12.

in Gezer,[i] but the Canaanites continued
to live there among them.[j] 30Neither did
Zebulun drive out the Canaanites living
in Kitron or Nahalol, so these Canaanites
lived among them, but Zebulun did subject them to forced labor. 31Nor did Asher
drive out those living in Akko or Sidon
or Ahlab or Akzib[k] or Helbah or Aphek
or Rehob. 32The Asherites lived among
the Canaanite inhabitants of the land
because they did not drive them out.
33Neither did Naphtali drive out those
living in Beth Shemesh or Beth Anath[l];
but the Naphtalites too lived among the
Canaanite inhabitants of the land, and
those living in Beth Shemesh and Beth
Anath became forced laborers for them.
34The Amorites[m] confined the Danites
to the hill country, not allowing them
to come down into the plain. 35And the
Amorites were determined also to hold
out in Mount Heres, Aijalon[n] and Shaalbim, but when the power of the tribes of
Joseph increased, they too were pressed
into forced labor. 36The boundary of the
Amorites was from Scorpion Pass[o] to Sela
and beyond.

The Angel of the LORD at Bokim

2 The angel of the LORD[p] went up from
Gilgal to Bokim[q] and said, "I brought
you up out of Egypt[r] and led you into the
land I swore to give to your ancestors.[s]
I said, 'I will never break my covenant
with you,[t] 2and you shall not make a covenant with the people of this land,[u] but
you shall break down their altars.[v]' Yet
you have disobeyed me. Why have you
done this? 3And I have also said, 'I will
not drive them out before you;[w] they will
become traps[x] for you, and their gods will
become snares[y] to you.' "

1:29 [i] 1Ki 9:16 [j] Jos 16:10
1:31 [k] Jdg 10:6
1:33 [l] Jos 19:38
1:34 [m] Ex 3:17
1:35 [n] Jos 19:42
1:36 [o] Jos 15:3
2:1 [p] Jdg 6:11 [q] ver 5 [r] Ex 20:2 [s] Ge 17:8 [t] Lev 26:42-44; Dt 7:9
2:2 [u] Ex 23:32; 34:12; Dt 7:2 [v] Ex 34:13
2:3 [w] Jos 23:13 [x] Nu 33:55 [y] Dt 7:16; Jdg 3:6; Ps 106:36
2:9 [z] Jos 19:50
2:10 [a] Ex 5:2; 1Sa 2:12; 1Ch 28:9; Gal 4:8
2:11 [b] Jdg 3:12; 4:1; 6:1; 10:6 [c] Jdg 3:7; 8:33
2:12 [d] Ps 106:36 [e] Dt 31:16; Jdg 10:6
2:13 [f] Jdg 10:6
2:14 [g] Dt 31:17

> **Jdg 2:10** ❖ What causes children to walk away from the faith of their parents? How can faith be effectively passed on to the next generation?

4When the angel of the LORD had spoken these things to all the Israelites, the
people wept aloud, 5and they called that
place Bokim.[a] There they offered sacrifices to the LORD.

Disobedience and Defeat

2:6–9pp // Jos 24:29–31

6After Joshua had dismissed the Israelites, they went to take possession of the
land, each to their own inheritance. 7The
people served the LORD throughout the
lifetime of Joshua and of the elders who
outlived him and who had seen all the
great things the LORD had done for Israel.
8Joshua son of Nun, the servant of the
LORD, died at the age of a hundred and
ten. 9And they buried him in the land
of his inheritance, at Timnath Heres[b][z]
in the hill country of Ephraim, north of
Mount Gaash.
10After that whole generation had been
gathered to their ancestors, another generation grew up who knew neither the
LORD nor what he had done for Israel.[a]
11Then the Israelites did evil in the eyes
of the LORD[b] and served the Baals.[c] 12They
forsook the LORD, the God of their ancestors, who had brought them out of
Egypt. They followed and worshiped various gods[d] of the peoples around them.[e]
They aroused the LORD's anger 13because
they forsook him and served Baal and
the Ashtoreths.[f] 14In his anger[g] against

[a] 5 *Bokim* means *weepers*. [b] 9 Also known as *Timnath Serah* (see Joshua 19:50 and 24:30)

2:1–5 The process of occupation would have been completed in due course if the Israelites had fulfilled their obligations to Yahweh, but now their disobedience has put the completion of the conquest in jeopardy (v. 3).

> **APPLICATION** ✣ **1:1—2:5** Like ancient Israel, Christians also are in covenant relationship with God, albeit through a better covenant. Nevertheless, the stipulations of that covenant—the law of love, as Paul describes it—require obedience (Ro 13:8–10; see also Jas 1:25). While the warfare in which Christians are engaged is not physical but spiritual, the necessity of walking by faith in loyalty to Christ's covenant is the only hope of victory.

2:6–11 In vv. 6–10 there is a specific contrast between two different generations: the faithfulness of Joshua's day and the unfaithfulness of the subsequent generation. The description of this second generation is stark (v. 10); the result is anticipated (v. 11). This was an active choice on their part, as Jos 24 reinforces.
2:11–13 The initial statement that "the Israelites did evil in the eyes of the LORD" will be the opening declaration for every major judge story in the book (v. 11). The idea of "going" or "walking after other gods" clearly contrasts with the biblical idea of walking with the Lord. And the idea of worshiping these other gods is a blatant violation of Ex 20:5, "You shall not bow down to them."
2:14–15 In this second part, Yahweh's anger at the Israelites results in the oppressions that he brings

Israel the LORD gave them into the hands[h] of raiders who plundered them. He sold them[i] into the hands of their enemies all around, whom they were no longer able to resist.[j] 15 Whenever Israel went out to fight, the hand of the LORD was against them to defeat them, just as he had sworn to them. They were in great distress.

16 Then the LORD raised up judges,[a][k] who saved[l] them out of the hands of these raiders. 17 Yet they would not listen to their judges but prostituted[m] themselves to other gods and worshiped them. They quickly turned from the ways of their ancestors, who had been obedient to the LORD's commands.[n] 18 Whenever the LORD raised up a judge for them, he was with the judge and saved them out of the hands of their enemies as long as the judge lived; for the LORD relented[o] because of their groaning[p] under those who oppressed and afflicted them. 19 But when the judge died, the people returned to ways even more corrupt[q] than those of their ancestors, following other gods and serving and worshiping them.[r] They refused to give up their evil practices and stubborn ways.

20 Therefore the LORD was very angry[s] with Israel and said, "Because this nation has violated the covenant I ordained for their ancestors and has not listened to me, 21 I will no longer drive out[t] before them any of the nations Joshua left when he died. 22 I will use them to test[u] Israel and see whether they will keep the way of the LORD and walk in it as their ancestors did." 23 The LORD had allowed those nations to remain; he did not drive them out at once by giving them into the hands of Joshua.

2:14 [h] Ps 106:41 [i] Dt 32:30; Jdg 3:8 [j] Dt 28:25
2:16 [k] Ac 13:20 [l] Ps 106:43
2:17 [m] Ex 34:15 [n] ver 7
2:18 [o] Dt 32:36; Jos 1:5 [p] Ps 106:44
2:19 [q] Jdg 3:12 [r] Jdg 4:1; 8:33
2:20 [s] ver 14; Jos 23:16
2:21 [t] Jos 23:13
2:22 [u] Dt 8:2,16; Jdg 3:1,14

3 These are the nations the LORD left to test[v] all those Israelites who had not experienced any of the wars in Canaan 2 (he did this only to teach warfare to the descendants of the Israelites who had not had previous battle experience): 3 the five[w] rulers of the Philistines, all the Canaanites, the Sidonians, and the Hivites living in the Lebanon mountains from Mount Baal Hermon to Lebo Hamath. 4 They were left to test[x] the Israelites to see whether they would obey the LORD's commands, which he had given their ancestors through Moses.

5 The Israelites lived[y] among the Canaanites, Hittites, Amorites, Perizzites, Hivites and Jebusites. 6 They took their daughters in marriage and gave their own daughters to their sons, and served their gods.[z]

Othniel

7 The Israelites did evil in the eyes of the LORD; they forgot the LORD[a] their God and served the Baals and the Asherahs.[b] 8 The anger of the LORD burned against Israel so that he sold[c] them into the hands of Cushan-Rishathaim king of Aram Naharaim,[b] to whom the Israelites were subject for eight years. 9 But when they cried out[d] to the LORD, he raised up for them a deliverer, Othniel[e] son of Kenaz, Caleb's younger brother, who saved them. 10 The Spirit of the LORD came on

3:1 [v] Jdg 2:21-22
3:3 [w] Jos 13:3
3:4 [x] Dt 8:2; Jdg 2:22
3:5 [y] Ps 106:35
3:6 [z] Ex 34:16; Dt 7:3-4
3:7 [a] Dt 4:9 [b] Ex 34:13; Jdg 2:11,13
3:8 [c] Jdg 2:14
3:9 [d] ver 15; Jdg 6:6,7; 10:10; Ps 106:44 [e] Jdg 1:13

[a] 16 Or *leaders*; similarly in verses 17-19
[b] 8 That is, Northwest Mesopotamia

---

on them as punishment. Because the Israelites did "evil," Yahweh ensured that when they went out to battle, the outcome was a calamitous disaster.

2:16–19 The text clearly implies that each successive generation experiences a greater degeneration into sin and corruption than did the previous one (v. 19). Thus, the picture is not just cyclical but downward. Israel is spiraling down into a spiritual abyss.

2:20—3:4 Yahweh's punishment is a fulfillment and expansion of his promise in 2:3.

3:5–6 This passage stresses three things: (1) The Israelites "lived among" the peoples of the land (v. 5); (2) they intermarried with the peoples there; and (3) they "served" their gods (v. 6).

2:6—3:6 The myth of secularism is that there are no idols because there is no God. But if idolatry is worshiping the creation, or some part of it, instead of the Creator (cf. Ro 1:18–23), then the process of sacralization (the process by which created things become central to life, invoking religious-like awe and submission) provides numerous examples of idolatry in modern contexts.

One example of sacralization is the relentless pursuit of money and material possessions. This is the idol Matthew talks about in his Gospel (Mt 6:24); following this idol leads to sins such as greed and covetousness. Underlying this idol is the fundamental belief that the essence of life is material well-being.

3:7–8 Yahweh subjects those who have served foreign Baals and Asherim to serve a foreign king for eight years.

3:9 This is not a penitential plea, as though the Israelites have repented. Rather, it is simply an anguished cry of pain. Yahweh intervenes on the basis of his compassion, not the people's repentance.

3:10 Cushan-Rishathaim means "dark, doubly wicked" and is clearly a derogatory term.

him,[f] so that he became Israel's judge[a] and went to war. The LORD gave Cushan-Rishathaim king of Aram into the hands of Othniel, who overpowered him. 11So the land had peace for forty years, until Othniel son of Kenaz died.

Ehud

12Again the Israelites did evil in the eyes of the LORD,[g] and because they did this evil the LORD gave Eglon king of Moab[h] power over Israel. 13Getting the Ammonites and Amalekites to join him, Eglon came and attacked Israel, and they took possession of the City of Palms.[b][i] 14The Israelites were subject to Eglon king of Moab for eighteen years.

15Again the Israelites cried out to the LORD, and he gave them a deliverer[j]—Ehud, a left-handed man, the son of Gera the Benjamite. The Israelites sent him with tribute to Eglon king of Moab. 16Now Ehud had made a double-edged sword about a cubit[c] long, which he strapped to his right thigh under his clothing. 17He presented the tribute to Eglon king of Moab, who was a very fat man.[k] 18After Ehud had presented the tribute, he sent on their way those who had carried it. 19But on reaching the stone images near Gilgal he himself went back to Eglon and said, "Your Majesty, I have a secret message for you."

The king said to his attendants, "Leave us!" And they all left.

20Ehud then approached him while he was sitting alone in the upper room of his palace[d] and said, "I have a message from God for you." As the king rose from his seat, 21Ehud reached with his

3:10 [f] Nu 11:25, 29; 24:2; Jdg 6:34; 11:29; 13:25; 14:6,19; 1Sa 11:6
3:12 [g] Jdg 2:11, 14 [h] 1Sa 12:9
3:13 [i] Jdg 1:16
3:15 [j] ver 9; Ps 78:34; 107:13
3:17 [k] ver 12

[a] *10* Or *leader* [b] *13* That is, Jericho [c] *16* That is, about 18 inches or about 45 centimeters
[d] *20* The meaning of the Hebrew for this word is uncertain; also in verse 24.

3:7–11 In an age when many choose a different path, not uncommonly bringing on themselves oppression that is the result of sin, it is wonderful to see a model like Othniel who simply walks in step with God and overcomes evil. The simplicity and faithfulness of Othniel stands in radical contrast to the complexity and self-gratification of Samson, the final judge of the book of Judges.

3:12–15a Only here does the writer say that Yahweh actively "gave . . . power" (v. 12) to or strengthened/empowered the oppressor against Israel. Yahweh raises up Ehud. This left-handed savior is ironically a Benjamite (meaning "son of the right hand"). The palace guards, assuming he is right-handed, would not have checked for a left-handed weapon-carrier.

3:15b–18 Ehud's improvisation is undoubtedly a foreshadowing of other improvised weapons in Judges: Shamgar's oxgoad (v. 31), Jael's tent peg (4:21–22), Gideon's jars and torches (7:20), the woman's millstone (9:53), and Samson's donkey jawbone (15:15).

3:19–26a The execution of the plot is heightened by satire and irony. The satire centers mainly on Eglon's famed obesity. While his size symbolizes his greed, it also hints at his vulnerability. Ehud's words, like his double-edged dagger, have a double meaning: The "secret message" from God is a dagger (v. 19).

PEOPLE TO KNOW // EHUD

JUDGES 3:12–26: Ehud was a judge from the tribe of Benjamin (Jdg 3:15) who happened to be left-handed. This itself is somewhat ironic since the name Benjamin can be translated "son of my right hand." But Ehud's left-handedness was more than a joke. It was a critical factor in allowing him to carry out God's plan.

Ehud's story began when Israel was oppressed by the Moabites. The king of Moab, Eglon, was an especially corpulent man who harassed Israel for eighteen years. When Israel cried out to God in distress, God called Ehud to deliver them (Jdg 3:15). Ehud was able to conceal a dagger where Eglon's guards did not expect and assassinate the wicked king.

Ehud went on to lead Israel to victory over Moab, and the land enjoyed peace for eighty years.

APPLICATION Sometimes we think that our different qualities are liabilities. Ehud's story shows that a trait as simple as being left-handed can be used by God for great purposes. Like Ehud, we should trust God to lead us into the tasks he has set before us. The thing that makes us different might be just the quality in us that God intends to use to further his purposes in the world.

left hand, drew the sword from his right thigh and plunged it into the king's belly. 22Even the handle sank in after the blade, and his bowels discharged. Ehud did not pull the sword out, and the fat closed in over it. 23Then Ehud went out to the porch[a]; he shut the doors of the upper room behind him and locked them.

24After he had gone, the servants came and found the doors of the upper room locked. They said, "He must be relieving himself[l] in the inner room of the palace." 25They waited to the point of embarrassment,[m] but when he did not open the doors of the room, they took a key and unlocked them. There they saw their lord fallen to the floor, dead.

26While they waited, Ehud got away. He passed by the stone images and escaped to Seirah. 27When he arrived there, he blew a trumpet[n] in the hill country of Ephraim, and the Israelites went down with him from the hills, with him leading them.

28"Follow me," he ordered, "for the LORD has given Moab, your enemy, into your hands.[o]" So they followed him down and took possession of the fords of the Jordan[p] that led to Moab; they allowed no one to cross over. 29At that time they struck down about ten thousand Moabites, all vigorous and strong; not one escaped. 30That day Moab was made subject to Israel, and the land had peace[q] for eighty years.

3:24 [l]1Sa 24:3
3:25 [m]2Ki 2:17; 8:11
3:27 [n]Jdg 6:34; 1Sa 13:3
3:28 [o]Jdg 7:9, 15 [p]Jos 2:7; Jdg 7:24; 12:5
3:30 [q]ver 11

3:31 [r]Jdg 5:6 [s]Jos 23:10
4:1 [t]Jdg 2:19
4:2 [u]Jos 11:1 [v]ver 13,16; 1Sa 12:9; Ps 83:9
4:3 [w]Jdg 1:19 [x]Ps 106:42
4:5 [y]Ge 35:8
4:6 [z]Heb 11:32

> **Jdg 3:21** ❖ Ehud's left-handedness was a trait God used. What special characteristics has God given you that he can use for his purposes?

Shamgar

31After Ehud came Shamgar son of Anath,[r] who struck down six hundred[s] Philistines with an oxgoad. He too saved Israel.

Deborah

4 Again the Israelites did evil[t] in the eyes of the LORD, now that Ehud was dead. 2So the LORD sold them into the hands of Jabin king of Canaan, who reigned in Hazor.[u] Sisera,[v] the commander of his army, was based in Harosheth Haggoyim. 3Because he had nine hundred chariots fitted with iron[w] and had cruelly oppressed[x] the Israelites for twenty years, they cried to the LORD for help.

4Now Deborah, a prophet, the wife of Lappidoth, was leading[b] Israel at that time. 5She held court under the Palm of Deborah between Ramah and Bethel[y] in the hill country of Ephraim, and the Israelites went up to her to have their disputes decided. 6She sent for Barak son of Abinoam[z] from Kedesh in Naphtali and said to him, "The LORD, the God of Israel, commands you: 'Go, take with

[a] *23* The meaning of the Hebrew for this word is uncertain. [b] *4* Traditionally *judging*

The actual description of the killing (i.e., sacrifice) is given in grotesque detail. The term translated "fat" is the sacrificial term used for the entrails. The scatological satire continues with the comic scene of vv. 24–25, in which Eglon's servants belatedly discover their master's corpse.

3:26b–29 The Moabite despot has already been given into the hand of Ehud and is dead. For Ehud, the entire process has been a matter of trust in Yahweh and assurance of Yahweh's deliverance.

> ✣ **3:12–30** How are we to wage spiritual warfare against those who abuse, exploit, and persecute the church? While the warfare in which Christians are engaged is spiritual, not physical, the necessity of walking by faith in loyalty to Christ's covenant is the only hope of victory. We are certainly not to fashion our own daggers as Ehud did but rather to engage the world with a better weapon already supplied—the sword of the Spirit, the Word of God.

3:31 Again, the enemy is not only defeated but made to look utterly ridiculous, as the reader's attention is drawn to the improvised weapon.

> ✣ **3:31** See the comments at the end of the last three minor judges (12:8–15).

4:1–24 "Jabin king of Canaan" only plays a role in the story's prologue and epilogue, but immediately the prologue introduces Jabin's commander, Sisera, who will be the up-front antagonist in the story.

4:4 Deborah (meaning "honeybee"), a prophetess, is leading/judging Israel. As a prophetess, Deborah stands in a long tradition, starting with Miriam (Ex 15:20) and continuing throughout the OT.

4:6–7 Barak (meaning "lightning") is introduced. Clearly Deborah is the one who is taking the initiative, not Barak. Deborah is used as a foil to promote Barak's negative characterization. The first rhetorical question (v. 6) literally reads: "Has not Yahweh, the God of Israel, commanded, Go?" Thus, this is not her opinion about his calling and how things ought to work out but the sure word of Yahweh.

you ten thousand men of Naphtali and Zebulun and lead them up to Mount Tabor. 7 I will lead Sisera, the commander of Jabin's army, with his chariots and his troops to the Kishon River[a] and give him into your hands.'"

8 Barak said to her, "If you go with me, I will go; but if you don't go with me, I won't go."

9 "Certainly I will go with you," said Deborah. "But because of the course you are taking, the honor will not be yours, for the LORD will deliver Sisera into the hands of a woman." So Deborah went with Barak to Kedesh.[b] 10 There Barak summoned[c] Zebulun and Naphtali, and ten thousand men went up under his command. Deborah also went up with him.

11 Now Heber the Kenite had left the other Kenites,[d] the descendants of Hobab,[e] Moses' brother-in-law,[a] and pitched his tent by the great tree in Zaanannim[f] near Kedesh.

12 When they told Sisera that Barak son of Abinoam had gone up to Mount Tabor, 13 Sisera summoned from Harosheth Haggoyim to the Kishon River all his men and his nine hundred chariots fitted with iron.[g]

14 Then Deborah said to Barak, "Go! This is the day the LORD has given Sisera into your hands. Has not the LORD gone ahead[h] of you?" So Barak went down Mount Tabor, with ten thousand men following him. 15 At Barak's advance, the LORD routed[i] Sisera and all his chariots and army by the sword, and Sisera got down from his chariot and fled on foot.

16 Barak pursued the chariots and army as far as Harosheth Haggoyim, and all Sisera's troops fell by the sword; not a man was left.[j] 17 Sisera, meanwhile, fled on foot to the tent of Jael, the wife of Heber the Kenite, because there was an alliance between Jabin king of Hazor and the family of Heber the Kenite.

Jdg 4:14 ❖ What comfort can we take in knowing God goes ahead of us into every battle and trial we face?

18 Jael went out to meet Sisera and said to him, "Come, my lord, come right in. Don't be afraid." So he entered her tent, and she covered him with a blanket.

19 "I'm thirsty," he said. "Please give me some water." She opened a skin of milk,[k] gave him a drink, and covered him up.

20 "Stand in the doorway of the tent," he told her. "If someone comes by and asks you, 'Is anyone in there?' say 'No.'"

21 But Jael, Heber's wife, picked up a tent peg and a hammer and went quietly to him while he lay fast asleep, exhausted. She drove the peg through his temple into the ground, and he died.[l]

22 Just then Barak came by in pursuit of Sisera, and Jael went out to meet him. "Come," she said, "I will show you the man you're looking for." So he went in with her, and there lay Sisera with the tent peg through his temple—dead.

23 On that day God subdued[m] Jabin king of Canaan before the Israelites. 24 And the hand of the Israelites pressed harder and harder against Jabin king of Canaan until they destroyed him.

The Song of Deborah

5 On that day Deborah and Barak son of Abinoam sang this song:[n]

2 "When the princes in Israel take the lead,
when the people willingly offer[o] themselves—
praise the LORD![p]

4:7 [a] Ps 83:9
4:9 [b] ver 21; Jdg 2:14
4:10 [c] ver 14; Jdg 5:15,18
4:11 [d] Jdg 1:16 [e] Nu 10:29 [f] Jos 19:33
4:13 [g] ver 3
4:14 [h] Dt 9:3; 2Sa 5:24; Ps 68:7
4:15 [i] Jos 10:10; Ps 83:9-10
4:16 [j] Ps 83:9
4:19 [k] Jdg 5:25
4:21 [l] Jdg 5:26
4:23 [m] Ne 9:24; Ps 18:47
5:1 [n] Ex 15:1
5:2 [o] 2Ch 17:16; Ps 110:3 [p] ver 9

[a] 11 Or *father-in-law*

4:9 Deborah issues another prophecy. The reader has only one woman to suspect as the possible fulfillment—Deborah. But the ironic twist is just over the horizon.
4:14 Deborah's question underscores the certainty of the victory and highlights Barak's reluctance.
4:15 The Hebrew literally states: "Yahweh threw Sisera . . . into a panic . . ."
4:18–19 Jael is a non-Israelite, specifically a Kenite. Her words (v. 18) and her hospitality disarm the Canaanite warlord. Jael demonstrates ancient Near Eastern hospitality in giving him milk and covering him up.
4:21 To the attentive reader, the similarities between Jael's murder of Sisera and Ehud's assassination of Eglon are transparent (3:21–22). The result is to ironically picture Barak playing a role similar to that of Eglon's attendants. Without his general Sisera, Jabin is no threat and is quickly subdued.
5:1–31 After the prose setting of the song (v. 1), an initial call to praise contains a report of Israel's need (vv. 2–8). It opens with a summons to praise Yahweh (v. 2). The act continues with a call especially addressed to royalty—that is, to kings and rulers (v. 3)—to pay attention. Yahweh's epiphany is described in terms of storms and earthquakes.

PEOPLE TO KNOW // DEBORAH

JUDGES 5:1-31: Deborah served as a prophet and judge after Ehud. When an enemy commander named Sisera oppressed Israel, the people cried out to God in distress. God used Deborah's leadership to defeat Israel's enemies.

To oppose the threat of Sisera and his Canaanite forces, Deborah sent Barak to lead an army into war, promising that God would deliver Sisera into Barak's hands (Jdg 4:7). But Barak was afraid. He told Deborah he would only go if she went with him. Deborah told him she would go but that because of his hesitation, the honor of victory would not be his. God would deliver Sisera into the hands of a woman, a prediction that shortly came to pass (Jdg 4:17-22).

APPLICATION ✚ Deborah was the only female judge, and she was also a prophet. God used her as a mighty leader for the people. Her bravery and trust in God outshined that of her army commander, Barak. Deborah reminds us that our strength and security do not depend on external factors. Instead, true strength and security come from trusting in God alone and following his ways, regardless of what battles we may face.

3 "Hear this, you kings! Listen, you
rulers!
I, even I, will sing to[a] the LORD;
I will praise the LORD, the God of
Israel, in song.[q]

4 "When you, LORD, went out from
Seir,[r]
when you marched from the land
of Edom,
the earth shook, the heavens
poured,
the clouds poured down water.[s]
5 The mountains quaked[t] before the
LORD, the One of Sinai,
before the LORD, the God of Israel.

6 "In the days of Shamgar son of
Anath,[u]
in the days of Jael,[v] the highways[w]
were abandoned;
travelers took to winding paths.
7 Villagers in Israel would not fight;
they held back until I, Deborah,
arose,
until I arose, a mother in Israel.
8 God chose new leaders[x]
when war came to the city gates,
but not a shield or spear was seen
among forty thousand in Israel.
9 My heart is with Israel's princes,
with the willing volunteers[y]
among the people.
Praise the LORD!

10 "You who ride on white donkeys,[z]
sitting on your saddle blankets,
and you who walk along the road,
consider 11 the voice of the singers[b] at
the watering places.
They recite the victories[a] of the
LORD,
the victories of his villagers in
Israel.

"Then the people of the LORD
went down to the city gates.[b]
12 'Wake up,[c] wake up, Deborah!
Wake up, wake up, break out in
song!
Arise, Barak!
Take captive your captives,[d] son of
Abinoam.'

13 "The remnant of the nobles came
down;
the people of the LORD came down
to me against the mighty.
14 Some came from Ephraim, whose
roots were in Amalek;[e]

5:3 [q] Ps 27:6
5:4 [r] Dt 33:2 [s] Ps 68:8
5:5 [t] Ex 19:18; Ps 68:8; 97:5; Isa 64:3
5:6 [u] Jdg 3:31 [v] Jdg 4:17 [w] Isa 33:8
5:8 [x] Dt 32:17
5:9 [y] ver 2
5:10 [z] Jdg 10:4; 12:14
5:11 [a] 1Sa 12:7; Mic 6:5 [b] ver 8
5:12 [c] Ps 57:8 [d] Ps 68:18; Eph 4:8
5:14 [e] Jdg 3:13

[a] 3 Or *of* [b] 11 The meaning of the Hebrew for this word is uncertain.

5:7 The phrase "mother in Israel" is a significant metaphor. In the context of the song, there is obviously the later contrast with the mother of Sisera (v. 28).

There are two causes for the praise and response of the people (v. 11 and vv. 12-13). (1) The voices of the singers at the watering places relating Yahweh's victories and those of his warriors stimulate a response. (2) The leadership of Deborah and then Barak is highlighted.

5:11 In the ancient Near East, victory songs usually extol the might and power of the king in his victory over his enemies. Only a victory song for "the people of the LORD" would choose to extol the inferiority of its own army in the face of oppression to praise the people's king, Yahweh.

5:14-18 The third and central act of the song is a recognition and assessment of the tribes who participated and those who did not (vv. 14-18). The

Benjamin was with the people
who followed you.
From Makir captains came down,
from Zebulun those who bear a
commander's[a] staff.
15 The princes of Issachar were with
Deborah;[f]
yes, Issachar was with Barak,
sent under his command into the
valley.
In the districts of Reuben
there was much searching of heart.
16 Why did you stay among the sheep
pens[b]
to hear the whistling for the
flocks?[g]
In the districts of Reuben
there was much searching of
heart.
17 Gilead stayed beyond the Jordan.
And Dan, why did he linger by the
ships?
Asher remained on the coast[h]
and stayed in his coves.
18 The people of Zebulun risked their
very lives;
so did Naphtali on the terraced
fields.[i]

19 "Kings came[j], they fought,
the kings of Canaan fought.
At Taanach, by the waters of
Megiddo,[k]
they took no plunder of silver.[l]
20 From the heavens[m] the stars fought,
from their courses they fought
against Sisera.
21 The river Kishon[n] swept them away,
the age-old river, the river Kishon.
March on, my soul; be strong!
22 Then thundered the horses'
hooves —
galloping, galloping go his mighty
steeds.
23 'Curse Meroz,' said the angel of the
LORD.
'Curse its people bitterly,
because they did not come to help
the LORD,
to help the LORD against the
mighty.'

24 "Most blessed of women be Jael,[o]
the wife of Heber the Kenite,
most blessed of tent-dwelling
women.
25 He asked for water, and she gave him
milk;[p]
in a bowl fit for nobles she
brought him curdled milk.
26 Her hand reached for the tent peg,
her right hand for the workman's
hammer.
She struck Sisera, she crushed his
head,
she shattered and pierced his
temple.[q]
27 At her feet he sank,
he fell; there he lay.
At her feet he sank, he fell;
where he sank, there he fell —
dead.

28 "Through the window peered Sisera's
mother;
behind the lattice she cried out,[r]
'Why is his chariot so long in coming?
Why is the clatter of his chariots
delayed?'
29 The wisest of her ladies answer her;
indeed, she keeps saying to
herself,
30 'Are they not finding and dividing
the spoils:[s]
a woman or two for each man,
colorful garments as plunder for
Sisera,
colorful garments embroidered,
highly embroidered garments for
my neck —
all this as plunder?'

5:15 [f] Jdg 4:10
5:16 [g] Nu 32:1
5:17 [h] Jos 19:29
5:18 [i] Jdg 4:6,10
5:19 [j] Jos 11:5; Jdg 4:13 [k] Jdg 1:27 [l] ver 30
5:20 [m] Jos 10:11
5:21 [n] Jdg 4:7
5:24 [o] Jdg 4:17
5:25 [p] Jdg 4:19
5:26 [q] Jdg 4:21
5:28 [r] Pr 7:6
5:30 [s] Ex 15:9; 1Sa 30:24

[a] *14* The meaning of the Hebrew for this word is uncertain. [b] *16* Or *the campfires*; or *the saddlebags*

Israelites display a serious deficiency of political and military unity.

5:20–21 The poetry paints a magnificent portrait of divine intervention. It is interesting that not one line of the poem shows the Israelites directly involved in the work of warfare. The poet seems to purposely choose not to give such a description to allow all the honor to go to Yahweh.

5:23 From the placement of the curse it is possible to interpret the failure of Meroz as one of denying immediate aid to the pursuing Israelite warriors rather than as a failure to enlist troops at the beginning of the campaign.

5:24–30 The fifth and final act is a double portrait of Jael's deed and Sisera's mother, which leads to the climactic conclusion of this song. Jael risked everything to aid God's people. By contrast, the Israelite tribes and city of Meroz, who could be expected to participate and render aid, did not.

The picture shifts to Sisera's mother anxiously awaiting the return of her son. The lady and her attendants fantasize about a huge amount of

31 “So may all your enemies perish,
LORD!
But may all who love you be like
the sun[t]
when it rises in its strength.”

Then the land had peace[u] forty years.

Gideon

6 The Israelites did evil in the eyes of
the LORD,[v] and for seven years he
gave them into the hands of the Midianites.[w] 2 Because the power of Midian was
so oppressive,[x] the Israelites prepared
shelters for themselves in mountain
clefts, caves and strongholds.[y] 3 Whenever the Israelites planted their crops,
the Midianites, Amalekites[z] and other
eastern peoples invaded the country.
4 They camped on the land and ruined
the crops[a] all the way to Gaza and did
not spare a living thing for Israel, neither
sheep nor cattle nor donkeys. 5 They came
up with their livestock and their tents
like swarms of locusts.[b] It was impossible to count them or their camels;[c] they
invaded the land to ravage it. 6 Midian
so impoverished the Israelites that they
cried out[d] to the LORD for help.
7 When the Israelites cried out to the
LORD because of Midian, 8 he sent them
a prophet, who said, “This is what the
LORD, the God of Israel, says: I brought
you up out of Egypt,[e] out of the land of
slavery. 9 I rescued you from the hand of
the Egyptians. And I delivered you from
the hand of all your oppressors; I drove
them out before you and gave you their
land.[f] 10 I said to you, ‘I am the LORD your
God; do not worship[g] the gods of the Amorites,[h] in whose land you live.’ But you
have not listened to me.”
11 The angel of the LORD[i] came and sat
down under the oak in Ophrah that belonged to Joash the Abiezrite,[j] where his
son Gideon[k] was threshing wheat in a
winepress to keep it from the Midianites.
12 When the angel of the LORD appeared
to Gideon, he said, “The LORD is with
you,[l] mighty warrior.”
13 “Pardon me, my lord,” Gideon replied, “but if the LORD is with us, why
has all this happened to us? Where are
all his wonders that our ancestors told[m]
us about when they said, ‘Did not the
LORD bring us up out of Egypt?’ But now
the LORD has abandoned[n] us and given
us into the hand of Midian.”
14 The LORD turned to him and said,
“Go in the strength you have[o] and save
Israel out of Midian’s hand. Am I not
sending you?”
15 “Pardon me, my lord,” Gideon replied,

5:31 [t] 2Sa 23:4; Ps 19:4; 89:36 [u] Jdg 3:11
6:1 [v] Jdg 2:11 [w] Nu 25:15-18; 31:1-3
6:2 [x] 1Sa 13:6; Isa 8:21 [y] Heb 11:38
6:3 [z] Jdg 3:13
6:4 [a] Lev 26:16; Dt 28:30,51
6:5 [b] Jdg 7:12 [c] Jdg 8:10
6:6 [d] Jdg 3:9
6:8 [e] Jdg 2:1
6:9 [f] Ps 44:2
6:10 [g] 2Ki 17:35 [h] Jer 10:2
6:11 [i] Ge 16:7 [j] Jos 17:2 [k] Heb 11:32
6:12 [l] Jos 1:5; Jdg 13:3; Lk 1:11, 28
6:13 [m] Ps 44:1 [n] 2Ch 15:2
6:14 [o] Heb 11:34

Jdg 5:31 ❖ How does the song of Deborah and Barak depict the fates of those who hate God and those who love God? Have we seen such fates befall people?

Jdg 6:15-16 ❖ When we feel too small or insignificant to be used by God, what encouragement does God give us in our doubts?

---

plunder (ironically including women) as the cause for his delay; they never (openly) suspect the possibility of his death.

5:31 The climactic conclusion is a double prayer for God to bring such a judgment to pass on all who defy him and for God to bring blessing on those who love him.

4:1–5:31 Both the narrative and the song celebrate the saving work of Yahweh. The double accounting in prose and poetry stresses God’s sovereignty over human events. This passage encourages us to perceive God’s sovereignty over history and our own lives. Whether it is in his discipline, in his compassionate deliverance, in his financial provision, or in his leading and guiding decisions, God is sovereign over all of life, and he is at work bringing his plan to fruition.

6:1 The opening component stands in stark contrast to the praise of Yahweh that has just been sung in the previous chapter.

6:2-3 The Israelites revert to living in caves. By contrast, the nomadic Midianites come and take over the land.

6:8 The prophet is formally indicting the Israelites for a breach of the covenant.

6:1-10 We turn to God in a moment of need, even when we have not been walking in his ways. Yet we expect God to answer our prayers because we are in need. Over and over the Bible addresses this issue of manipulation in prayer (e.g., Jas 4:1-6). Being in relationship with the living God is never a mechanical process.

6:11-12 Gideon is the only judge in the book of Judges who is called by God personally through a theophany. There is great irony in the angel’s statement, as Gideon is hiding from the Midianites, threshing wheat in a winepress.

6:13-16 In the dialogue with the angel of the Lord, Gideon will mount a three-point opposition, which, in each case, anticipates later plot complications. (1) His response to the angel of the Lord’s initial

PEOPLE TO KNOW // GIDEON

JUDGES 6:17–24: When God called Gideon, he looked nothing like a military champion. He was threshing wheat in the worst possible place, down in a winepress, because he was terrified of the Midianites. Even after God's call, Gideon proceeded timidly. He tore down his father's idols but did so under cover of darkness out of fear of his neighbors (Jdg 6:27). Before facing the Midianites, Gideon twice tested God with his fleece instead of immediately obeying, yet again showing his cowardly character (Jdg 6:36–40).

God used Gideon to deliver Israel from the Midianites in dramatic fashion. With only three hundred soldiers, armed only with trumpets, clay pots and torches, the Israelites took their enemies by surprise. In a panic, their enemies attacked one another.

After Gideon's victory, some wanted to make Gideon king. He refused, but then led the people into idol worship in a moment reminiscent of the golden calf story at Sinai. Gideon had many wives and concubines who bore him seventy sons. His son Abimelek went on to become a murderous leader who declared himself king. Gideon himself named Abimelek—a small detail that shows Gideon's pride and moral decline—Abimelek means "my father is king."

APPLICATION Gideon's story is both an encouragement and a caution. Gideon shows that God can choose unlikely candidates to do great things. God's power was greater than Gideon's weakness, and when he trusted God, God used him powerfully.

Gideon also shows the seductive nature of positions of power. After his military victory, Gideon became prideful and sinful. When God uses us, we should never think God's work is actually our own greatness. We need to remain humble and grateful, no matter what God does through us.

"but how can I save Israel? My clan is the
weakest in Manasseh, and I am the least
in my family.[p]"
16The LORD answered, "I will be with
you[q], and you will strike down all the
Midianites, leaving none alive."
17Gideon replied, "If now I have found
favor in your eyes, give me a sign[r] that
it is really you talking to me. 18Please do
not go away until I come back and bring
my offering and set it before you."
And the LORD said, "I will wait until
you return."
19Gideon went inside, prepared a
young goat, and from an ephah[a] of flour
he made bread without yeast. Putting the
meat in a basket and its broth in a pot,
he brought them out and offered them
to him under the oak.[s]
20The angel of God said to him, "Take
the meat and the unleavened bread,
place them on this rock,[t] and pour out
the broth." And Gideon did so. 21Then the
angel of the LORD touched the meat and
the unleavened bread[u] with the tip of
the staff that was in his hand. Fire flared
from the rock, consuming the meat and
the bread. And the angel of the LORD
disappeared. 22When Gideon realized[v]
that it was the angel of the LORD, he exclaimed, "Alas, Sovereign LORD! I have
seen the angel of the LORD face to face!"[w]
23But the LORD said to him, "Peace! Do
not be afraid.[x] You are not going to die."
24So Gideon built an altar to the LORD
there and called[y] it The LORD Is Peace.
To this day it stands in Ophrah[z] of the
Abiezrites.
25That same night the LORD said to

6:15 [p] Ex 3:11; 1Sa 9:21
6:16 [q] Ex 3:12; Jos 1:5
6:17 [r] ver 36-37; Ge 24:14; Isa 38:7-8
6:19 [s] Ge 18:7-8
6:20 [t] Jdg 13:19
6:21 [u] Lev 9:24
6:22 [v] Jdg 13:16, 21 [w] Ge 32:30; Ex 33:20; Jdg 13:22
6:23 [x] Da 10:19
6:24 [y] Ge 22:14 [z] Jdg 8:32

[a] *19* That is, probably about 36 pounds or about 16 kilograms

call is a dull, cynical question and diatribe about God's treatment of the nation (v. 13). He displays a detached disregard for Yahweh's primary concern about Israel's covenantal disloyalty (anticipating vv. 25–32; 8:24–27). (2) Although Yahweh encourages Gideon, Gideon's objection in 6:15 is an attempt to evade personal responsibility for the conquest because of his clan's small size (anticipating 7:2–8). (3) After Yahweh's assurance (6:16), Gideon's request for a sign in v. 17 demonstrates his need for tangible manifestations of the divine (anticipating vv. 36–37, 39; 7:10–15; and especially 8:24–27).

6:17 Gideon begins his requests for signs. Gideon's offering is not in accordance with any Levitical sacrifice. Nevertheless, the Lord accepts the sacrifices. God's actions are not just concerned with Gideon but are centered on delivering Israel.

6:25 God's command to Gideon contains two demands. By commanding Gideon to destroy the pagan altar and rebuild a proper altar to Yahweh

him, "Take the second bull from your
father's herd, the one seven years old.[a]
Tear down your father's altar to Baal and
cut down the Asherah pole[b][a] beside it.
26 Then build a proper kind of[c] altar to the
LORD your God on the top of this height.
Using the wood of the Asherah pole that
you cut down, offer the second[d] bull as
a burnt offering."
27 So Gideon took ten of his servants
and did as the LORD told him. But because he was afraid of his family and the
townspeople, he did it at night rather
than in the daytime.
28 In the morning when the people of
the town got up, there was Baal's altar,[b]
demolished, with the Asherah pole beside it cut down and the second bull sacrificed on the newly built altar!
29 They asked each other, "Who did
this?"
When they carefully investigated, they
were told, "Gideon son of Joash did it."
30 The people of the town demanded of
Joash, "Bring out your son. He must die,
because he has broken down Baal's altar
and cut down the Asherah pole beside it."
31 But Joash replied to the hostile crowd
around him, "Are you going to plead Baal's cause? Are you trying to save him?
Whoever fights for him shall be put to
death by morning! If Baal really is a god,
he can defend himself when someone
breaks down his altar." 32 So because Gideon broke down Baal's altar, they gave him
the name Jerub-Baal[e][c] that day, saying,
"Let Baal contend with him."
33 Now all the Midianites, Amalekites
and other eastern peoples[d] joined forces
and crossed over the Jordan and camped
in the Valley of Jezreel.[e] 34 Then the Spirit of the LORD came on[f] Gideon, and he
blew a trumpet,[g] summoning the Abiezrites to follow him. 35 He sent messengers
throughout Manasseh, calling them to
arms, and also into Asher, Zebulun and
Naphtali,[h] so that they too went up to
meet them.
36 Gideon said to God, "If you will save[i]
Israel by my hand as you have promised— 37 look, I will place a wool fleece
on the threshing floor.[j] If there is dew
only on the fleece and all the ground is
dry, then I will know[k] that you will save
Israel by my hand, as you said." 38 And
that is what happened. Gideon rose early

6:25 [a] Ex 34:13; Dt 7:5
6:28 [b] 1Ki 16:32
6:32 [c] Jdg 7:1; 8:29,35; 1Sa 12:11
6:33 [d] ver 3 [e] Jos 17:16
6:34 [f] Jdg 3:10; 1Ch 12:18; 2Ch 24:20 [g] Jdg 3:27
6:35 [h] Jdg 4:6
6:36 [i] ver 14
6:37 [j] Ex 4:3-7 [k] Ge 24:14

[a] 25 Or *Take a full-grown, mature bull from your father's herd* [b] 25 That is, a wooden symbol of the goddess Asherah; also in verses 26, 28 and 30 [c] 26 Or *build with layers of stone an* [d] 26 Or *full-grown*; also in verse 28 [e] 32 *Jerub-Baal* probably means *let Baal contend.*

---

on this pagan site, Yahweh seems to be ordering him to reclaim this apostate shrine's location.

6:26–30 Gideon carries out Yahweh's orders under the cover of night. The utter outrage and hostility of the town reflects the true spiritual condition of the nation: The Israelites are so disloyal to God's covenant that they are willing to kill a fellow Israelite for the cause of Baal.

6:31–32 Joash's decision is a ploy to save face, and to save Gideon at the same time, by referring the case to higher authority (v. 31). The townspeople back down, and Gideon receives a new name: Jerub-Baal (v. 32, meaning "Let/May Baal contend/indict").

6:11–32 On the divine level, this section of the Gideon/Abimelek cycle emphasizes the grace of Yahweh. God's compassion for his people, with all of their grave transgressions and weaknesses, provides once again the impetus to deliver Israel. Moreover, God surprises us by remaining faithful in the midst of persistent cynicism and doubt.

On the human level, the story of Gideon's call serves as a notable illustration of the dangers of not remembering God's mighty acts. The end result can be cynicism and an inability to perceive God at work. It can lead to an ignorance and misunderstanding of God's Word and questioning as to why things happen in the world.

6:33–35 Like the Moabites (and their allies) in 3:13 and the massively armed Canaanites in 4:13, this horde presents an almost insurmountable challenge to the underequipped and overmatched Israelites.

6:34–40 While the phrase "the Spirit of the LORD came on Gideon" (v. 34) sounds spiritually positive, the Spirit's work reflects God's sovereign will to set things in motion for the deliverance he has planned; it has nothing to do with Gideon's condition of faith or spirituality. Gideon's almost immediate "fleecing" of God speaks to his unbelief, his lack of spirituality: Gideon is trying to manipulate God.

This fleecing process is nothing short of a pagan test of the Deity. Apparently being clothed with the Spirit is not sufficient. Gideon needs tangible signs obtained through divinatory processes to believe God. Just as Yahweh uses the fleece requests with their pagan overtones to encourage Gideon to deliver Israel, he will also use two Midianites—one relating his dream, the other interpreting it (also with pagan overtones)—to encourage and motivate Gideon to action. What great lengths God is going to in order to save Israel from the hand of Midian! In short, God performs the signs with the fleece because he intends to save Israel; he will not let Gideon's unbelief derail his plan.

the next day; he squeezed the fleece and
wrung out the dew — a bowlful of water.
39 Then Gideon said to God, "Do not be
angry with me. Let me make just one
more request.[l] Allow me one more test
with the fleece, but this time make the
fleece dry and let the ground be covered
with dew." 40 That night God did so. Only
the fleece was dry; all the ground was
covered with dew.

Gideon Defeats the Midianites

7 Early in the morning, Jerub-Baal[m]
(that is, Gideon) and all his men
camped at the spring of Harod. The camp
of Midian was north of them in the valley
near the hill of Moreh.[n] 2 The LORD said to
Gideon, "You have too many men. I cannot deliver Midian into their hands, or
Israel would boast against me, 'My own
strength[o] has saved me.' 3 Now announce
to the army, 'Anyone who trembles with
fear may turn back and leave Mount Gilead.[p]'" So twenty-two thousand men left,
while ten thousand remained.
4 But the LORD said to Gideon, "There
are still too many[q] men. Take them down
to the water, and I will thin them out for
you there. If I say, 'This one shall go with
you,' he shall go; but if I say, 'This one
shall not go with you,' he shall not go."
5 So Gideon took the men down to the
water. There the LORD told him, "Separate those who lap the water with their
tongues as a dog laps from those who
kneel down to drink." 6 Three hundred of
them drank from cupped hands, lapping
like dogs. All the rest got down on their
knees to drink.
7 The LORD said to Gideon, "With the

6:39 [l] Ge 18:32
7:1 [m] Jdg 6:32 [n] Ge 12:6
7:2 [o] Dt 8:17; 2Co 4:7
7:3 [p] Dt 20:8
7:4 [q] 1Sa 14:6

7:7 [r] 1Sa 14:6
7:9 [s] Jos 2:24; 10:8; 11:6
7:12 [t] Jdg 8:10 [u] Jdg 6:5 [v] Jer 49:29 [w] Jos 11:4

Jdg 7:7 ❖ Where have we seen God do incredible things with seemingly meager resources?

three hundred men that lapped I will
save you and give the Midianites into
your hands. Let all the others go home."[r]
8 So Gideon sent the rest of the Israelites
home but kept the three hundred, who
took over the provisions and trumpets
of the others.
Now the camp of Midian lay below him
in the valley. 9 During that night the LORD
said to Gideon, "Get up, go down against
the camp, because I am going to give it
into your hands.[s] 10 If you are afraid to
attack, go down to the camp with your
servant Purah 11 and listen to what they
are saying. Afterward, you will be encouraged to attack the camp." So he and
Purah his servant went down to the outposts of the camp. 12 The Midianites, the
Amalekites[t] and all the other eastern
peoples had settled in the valley, thick as
locusts.[u] Their camels[v] could no more be
counted than the sand on the seashore.[w]
13 Gideon arrived just as a man was telling a friend his dream. "I had a dream,"
he was saying. "A round loaf of barley
bread came tumbling into the Midianite
camp. It struck the tent with such force
that the tent overturned and collapsed."
14 His friend responded, "This can be
nothing other than the sword of Gideon
son of Joash, the Israelite. God has given
the Midianites and the whole camp into
his hands."
15 When Gideon heard the dream and
its interpretation, he bowed down and

7:1–8 The two central episodes deal with the issue of fear. The double reduction of Gideon's fighting force begins with the removal of all the fearful Israelites. The result is a twenty-two-thousand-man reduction. Then God directs Gideon to go down to the water for the further reduction of his remaining ten-thousand-man force (vv. 4–8).

It seems best to understand the reduction process as based on purely arbitrary criteria. Along with this drastic reduction in his forces comes a further word of reassurance (v. 7). The reason for the reductions is stated explicitly in v. 2.

7:9–11 God has clearly devised his own sign for Gideon. Gideon hears the exact same words that Yahweh had already spoken to him (v. 14; cf. 6:16, 36). The irony is rich: Hearing the promise directly from Yahweh did not convince Gideon; however, hearing it from the lips of a Midianite soldier does convince him.

7:15–18 The dream has its intended effect on Gideon: He worships God (v. 15). Gideon now gathers his small band of men with the confidence that Yahweh will truly give them the victory. At this moment, he believes God and worships God as the result of this final sign. After this, Judges does not show Gideon worshiping God again.

✣ **6:33–7:18** It is impossible to engender faith without the Word of God. General revelation demonstrates that there is a God (Ro 1:18–23), but only the Word of God reveals his attributes, his character, and his person. It is difficult, if not impossible, to have faith in someone that you don't know or barely know. It is extremely hard to trust someone that you misunderstand or are misinformed about. Gideon's ignorance about the Word of God was a strong factor in his inability to trust Yahweh, for he had

worshiped.[x] He returned to the camp of Israel and called out, "Get up! The LORD has given the Midianite camp into your hands." 16Dividing the three hundred men[y] into three companies,[z] he placed trumpets and empty jars in the hands of all of them, with torches inside.

17"Watch me," he told them. "Follow my lead. When I get to the edge of the camp, do exactly as I do. 18When I and all who are with me blow our trumpets,[a] then from all around the camp blow yours and shout, 'For the LORD and for Gideon.'"

19Gideon and the hundred men with him reached the edge of the camp at the beginning of the middle watch, just after they had changed the guard. They blew their trumpets and broke the jars that were in their hands. 20The three companies blew the trumpets and smashed the jars. Grasping the torches in their left hands and holding in their right hands the trumpets they were to blow, they shouted, "A sword[b] for the LORD and for Gideon!" 21While each man held his position around the camp, all the Midianites ran, crying out as they fled.[c]

22When the three hundred trumpets sounded,[d] the LORD caused the men throughout the camp to turn on each other[e] with their swords. The army fled to Beth Shittah toward Zererah as far as the border of Abel Meholah[f] near Tabbath. 23Israelites from Naphtali, Asher and all Manasseh were called out,[g] and they pursued the Midianites. 24Gideon sent messengers throughout the hill country of Ephraim, saying, "Come down against the Midianites and seize the waters of the Jordan[h] ahead of them as far as Beth Barah."

So all the men of Ephraim were called out and they seized the waters of the Jordan as far as Beth Barah. 25They also captured two of the Midianite leaders, Oreb and Zeeb[i]. They killed Oreb at the rock of Oreb,[j] and Zeeb at the winepress of Zeeb. They pursued the Midianites and brought the heads of Oreb and Zeeb to Gideon, who was by the Jordan.[k]

7:15 [x] 1Sa 15:31
7:16 [y] Ge 14:15 [z] 2Sa 18:2
7:18 [a] Jdg 3:27
7:20 [b] ver 14
7:21 [c] 2Ki 7:7
7:22 [d] Jos 6:20 [e] 1Sa 14:20; 2Ch 20:23 [f] 1Ki 4:12; 19:16
7:23 [g] Jdg 6:35
7:24 [h] Jdg 3:28
7:25 [i] Jdg 8:3; Ps 83:11 [j] Isa 10:26 [k] Jdg 8:4
8:1 [l] Jdg 12:1 [m] 2Sa 19:41
8:3 [n] Jdg 7:25; Pr 15:1
8:4 [o] Jdg 7:25
8:5 [p] Ge 33:17 [q] Ps 83:11
8:6 [r] 1Sa 25:11 [s] ver 15
8:7 [t] Jdg 7:15
8:8 [u] Ge 32:30; 1Ki 12:25

Zebah and Zalmunna

8 Now the Ephraimites asked Gideon, "Why have you treated us like this? Why didn't you call us when you went to fight Midian?"[l] And they challenged him vigorously.[m]

2But he answered them, "What have I accomplished compared to you? Aren't the gleanings of Ephraim's grapes better than the full grape harvest of Abiezer? 3God gave Oreb and Zeeb,[n] the Midianite leaders, into your hands. What was I able to do compared to you?" At this, their resentment against him subsided.

4Gideon and his three hundred men, exhausted yet keeping up the pursuit, came to the Jordan[o] and crossed it. 5He said to the men of Sukkoth,[p] "Give my troops some bread; they are worn out, and I am still pursuing Zebah and Zalmunna,[q] the kings of Midian."

6But the officials of Sukkoth said, "Do you already have the hands of Zebah and Zalmunna in your possession? Why should we give bread[r] to your troops?"[s]

7Then Gideon replied, "Just for that, when the LORD has given Zebah and Zalmunna[t] into my hand, I will tear your flesh with desert thorns and briers."

8From there he went up to Peniel[a][u] and made the same request of them, but they answered as the men of Sukkoth had. 9So he said to the men of Peniel,

[a] 8 Hebrew *Penuel,* a variant of *Peniel;* also in verses 9 and 17

misconceptions about Yahweh and misunderstood the very nature and character of God. If we do not implant the Word of God in our lives (Ro 10:17), we will manifest the same unbelief—even stubbornness to believe—that Gideon did.

7:19—8:3 Gideon and his men reach the Midianite camp at just the right time: the changing of the guard. Once again the narrator shows that Yahweh's sovereign hand is at work in the victory.

The pursuit of the defeated Midianites is narrated in two stages. In the initial stage (7:22b–23), the troops from Naphtali, Asher, and all Manasseh are called out to pursue the Midianites along a route described in 7:22b. In the second stage (7:24–25), Gideon calls out the troops of Ephraim.

8:4–21 If the narrative ended with v. 3, Gideon would be considered one of the heroic judges of ancient Israel, notwithstanding his problem with fear and lack of faith. However, the narration continues, and the portrayal of Gideon becomes more and more bleak.

8:5 There are no indications of Yahweh's involvement in this second battle. Yahweh's silence and noninvolvement in this second battle and subsequent events foreshadow the Jephthah narrative, in which Yahweh's silence and noninvolvement are paramount.

"When I return in triumph, I will tear
down this tower."[v]
10 Now Zebah and Zalmunna were
in Karkor with a force of about fifteen
thousand men, all that were left of the
armies of the eastern peoples; a hundred
and twenty thousand swordsmen had
fallen.[w] 11 Gideon went up by the route
of the nomads east of Nobah[x] and Jogbehah[y] and attacked the unsuspecting
army. 12 Zebah and Zalmunna, the two
kings of Midian, fled, but he pursued
them and captured them, routing their
entire army.
13 Gideon son of Joash then returned
from the battle by the Pass of Heres.
14 He caught a young man of Sukkoth
and questioned him, and the young
man wrote down for him the names of
the seventy-seven officials of Sukkoth,
the elders of the town. 15 Then Gideon
came and said to the men of Sukkoth,
"Here are Zebah and Zalmunna, about
whom you taunted me by saying, 'Do
you already have the hands of Zebah
and Zalmunna in your possession? Why
should we give bread to your exhausted men?[z]'" 16 He took the elders of the
town and taught the men of Sukkoth a
lesson[a] by punishing them with desert
thorns and briers. 17 He also pulled down
the tower of Peniel and killed the men
of the town.[b]
18 Then he asked Zebah and Zalmunna, "What kind of men did you kill at
Tabor?[c]"
"Men like you," they answered, "each
one with the bearing of a prince."
19 Gideon replied, "Those were my
brothers, the sons of my own mother.
As surely as the LORD lives, if you had
spared their lives, I would not kill you."
20 Turning to Jether, his oldest son, he
said, "Kill them!" But Jether did not draw
his sword, because he was only a boy and
was afraid.
21 Zebah and Zalmunna said, "Come,
do it yourself. 'As is the man, so is his
strength.'" So Gideon stepped forward
and killed them, and took the ornaments[d] off their camels' necks.

Gideon's Ephod

22 The Israelites said to Gideon, "Rule
over us — you, your son and your grandson — because you have saved us from
the hand of Midian."
23 But Gideon told them, "I will not rule
over you, nor will my son rule over you.
The LORD will rule[e] over you." 24 And he
said, "I do have one request, that each of
you give me an earring from your share
of the plunder." (It was the custom of
the Ishmaelites[f] to wear gold earrings.)
25 They answered, "We'll be glad to give
them." So they spread out a garment,
and each of them threw a ring from his
plunder onto it. 26 The weight of the gold
rings he asked for came to seventeen
hundred shekels,[a] not counting the ornaments, the pendants and the purple
garments worn by the kings of Midian
or the chains that were on their camels'
necks. 27 Gideon made the gold into an

8:9 [v] ver 17
8:10 [w] Jdg 6:5; 7:12; Isa 9:4
8:11 [x] Nu 32:42 [y] Nu 32:35
8:15 [z] ver 6
8:16 [a] ver 7
8:17 [b] ver 9
8:18 [c] Jos 19:22; Jdg 4:6
8:21 [d] ver 26; Ps 83:11
8:23 [e] Ex 16:8; 1Sa 8:7; 10:19; 12:12
8:24 [f] Ge 25:13

[a] *26* That is, about 43 pounds or about 20 kilograms

8:18–19 Gideon's motive in pursuing the two Midianite kings is revealed: revenge.

✣ 7:19—8:21 We can be thankful that we have the example of Gideon's obedience and victory over the Midianites. The story of God working by calling Gideon is an encouragement to Christians: God can use us, imperfect as we are, to accomplish beneficial results for the kingdom of Christ. Positive examples of faith can enhance the application of faith in our lives. Marvelous is the victory when it is solely of God. Gideon and his puny three hundred were not the reason for the victory in this battle; rather, they were simply used by God to achieve his victory. When we trust God and see his great victory, so often in spite of us, we need to give him the glory.

8:22–23 The Israelites make three errors in their proposition. (1) Gideon cannot be king over them since Yahweh is already supposed to be king over them. (2) Yahweh is the one who has saved Israel, not Gideon. Yet Gideon does not correct their mistake. (3) According to the Israelites' logic, the one who has saved them should be their king. The text shows that the Israelites do exactly the opposite of what their own thesis requires, for their deliverer has been Yahweh.

8:24–27 Gideon's creation of an ephod from the Midianite (Ishmaelite) golden earrings hearkens back to Aaron's casting the golden calf from the Egyptians' golden earrings (Ex 32:1–8). It is possible that Gideon had divinatory intentions when he made the ephod. He wanted to create a way to understand the will of God.

8:27 Gideon creates his own idol and clothes it with pagan materials. If Yahweh's altar effectively replaced Baal's altar at Ophrah, then Gideon's cult image, the ephod, effectively replaces the Asherah cult image.

At the beginning of the Gideon story, Ophrah

ephod,[g] which he placed in Ophrah, his
town. All Israel prostituted themselves
by worshiping it there, and it became a
snare[h] to Gideon and his family.

Gideon's Death

28 Thus Midian was subdued before the
Israelites and did not raise its head again.
During Gideon's lifetime, the land had
peace[i] forty years.
29 Jerub-Baal[j] son of Joash went back
home to live. 30 He had seventy sons[k] of
his own, for he had many wives. 31 His
concubine, who lived in Shechem, also
bore him a son, whom he named Abimelek.[l] 32 Gideon son of Joash died at a good
old age[m] and was buried in the tomb of
his father Joash in Ophrah of the Abiezrites.
33 No sooner had Gideon died than the
Israelites again prostituted themselves
to the Baals.[n] They set up Baal-Berith[o] as
their god[p] 34 and did not remember[q] the
LORD their God, who had rescued them
from the hands of all their enemies on
every side. 35 They also failed to show any
loyalty to the family of Jerub-Baal (that
is, Gideon) in spite of all the good things
he had done for them.[r]

Abimelek

9 Abimelek[s] son of Jerub-Baal went to
his mother's brothers in Shechem
and said to them and to all his mother's
clan, 2 "Ask all the citizens of Shechem,
'Which is better for you: to have all seventy of Jerub-Baal's sons rule over you,
or just one man?' Remember, I am your
flesh and blood.[t]"
3 When the brothers repeated all this
to the citizens of Shechem, they were inclined to follow Abimelek, for they said,
"He is related to us." 4 They gave him seventy shekels[a] of silver from the temple
of Baal-Berith,[u] and Abimelek used it to
hire reckless scoundrels,[v] who became
his followers. 5 He went to his father's
home in Ophrah and on one stone murdered his seventy brothers,[w] the sons of
Jerub-Baal. But Jotham, the youngest
son of Jerub-Baal, escaped by hiding.[x]
6 Then all the citizens of Shechem and
Beth Millo gathered beside the great
tree at the pillar in Shechem to crown
Abimelek king.
7 When Jotham was told about this, he
climbed up on the top of Mount Gerizim[y]
and shouted to them, "Listen to me, citizens of Shechem, so that God may listen
to you. 8 One day the trees went out to
anoint a king for themselves. They said
to the olive tree, 'Be our king.'
9 "But the olive tree answered, 'Should
I give up my oil, by which both gods and
humans are honored, to hold sway over
the trees?'
10 "Next, the trees said to the fig tree,
'Come and be our king.'

8:27 [g] Jdg 17:5; 18:14 [h] Dt 7:16; Ps 106:39
8:28 [i] Jdg 5:31
8:29 [j] Jdg 7:1
8:30 [k] Jdg 9:2, 5,18,24
8:31 [l] Jdg 9:1
8:32 [m] Ge 25:8
8:33 [n] Jdg 2:11, 13,19 [o] Jdg 9:4 [p] Jdg 9:27,46
8:34 [q] Jdg 3:7; Dt 4:9; Ps 78:11, 42
8:35 [r] Jdg 9:16
9:1 [s] Jdg 8:31
9:2 [t] Ge 29:14; Jdg 8:30
9:4 [u] Jdg 8:33 [v] Jdg 11:3; 2Ch 13:7
9:5 [w] ver 2, Jdg 8:30 [x] 2Ki 11:2
9:7 [y] Dt 11:29; 27:12; Jn 4:20

[a] 4 That is, about 1 3/4 pounds or about 800 grams

Jdg 8:27 ❖ What sometimes causes God's children to fall into sin even after God's merciful acts on their behalf?

Jdg 9:5-6 ❖ How can a thirst for power lead a person to do awful things? Where have we witnessed this?

---

is the hub of a clan cult, a family affair. At the end, it is a center for national religious prostitution (under Gideon's oversight). Thus, things have come full circle.

8:28–32 The introduction of the ephod worship above and the epilogue set the stage for the sequel that follows.

❖ **8:22–32** When God works through us, whether in a formal or informal ministry situation, we must give him the honor and glory. The deep-rooted pride of achievement can blur our vision as to how we got to where we are. God has gifted men and women, and therefore God ultimately gets the credit for whatever they accomplish. The athlete, the intellectual, the businessperson, the preacher—all owe their achievements and accomplishments to God's gifts and plan.

8:33–35 The Israelites set Baal-Berith (or, "lord or master of the covenant," v. 33) as their god (even though Yahweh is the Lord of the covenant).

9:1–24 Abimelek is not happy with his position as an outsider, and he is dominated by a ruthless craving to change his marginal existence.

9:2–6 Abimelek murders his (paternal) brothers on a single stone (ironically a single stone will kill Abimelek, v. 53). With seemingly all opposition removed, Abimelek is made king in Shechem.

9:7–15 Jotham, the lone survivor of the Ophrah massacre, appears to confront the men of Shechem with the evil they have done. He adapts a four-part fable to his purpose. The fable is relatively straightforward. Jotham's implication is this: Since the trees (i.e., the citizens/lords of Shechem) have absurdly tried to make the thornbush (i.e., Abimelek) their king, then perhaps fire will come out of the thornbush and consume the trees and forest.

11“But the fig tree replied, ‘Should I
give up my fruit, so good and sweet, to
hold sway over the trees?’
12“Then the trees said to the vine,
‘Come and be our king.’
13“But the vine answered, ‘Should I
give up my wine,[z] which cheers both
gods and humans, to hold sway over
the trees?’
14“Finally all the trees said to the
thornbush, ‘Come and be our king.’
15“The thornbush said to the trees, ‘If
you really want to anoint me king over
you, come and take refuge in my shade;[a]
but if not, then let fire come out[b] of the
thornbush and consume the cedars of
Lebanon!’[c]
16“Have you acted honorably and in
good faith by making Abimelek king?
Have you been fair to Jerub-Baal and
his family? Have you treated him as he
deserves? 17Remember that my father
fought for you and risked his life to rescue you from the hand of Midian. 18But
today you have revolted against my father’s family. You have murdered his seventy sons[d] on a single stone and have
made Abimelek, the son of his female
slave, king over the citizens of Shechem
because he is related to you. 19So have
you acted honorably and in good faith
toward Jerub-Baal and his family today?
If you have, may Abimelek be your joy,
and may you be his, too! 20But if you have
not, let fire come out[e] from Abimelek
and consume you, the citizens of Shechem and Beth Millo, and let fire come
out from you, the citizens of Shechem
and Beth Millo, and consume Abimelek!”
21Then Jotham fled, escaping to Beer,
and he lived there because he was afraid
of his brother Abimelek.

9:13 [z] Ecc 2:3
9:15 [a] Isa 30:2 [b] ver 20 [c] Isa 2:13
9:18 [d] ver 5-6; Jdg 8:30
9:20 [e] ver 15
9:23 [f] 1Sa 16:14, 23; 18:10; 1Ki 22:22; Isa 19:14; 33:1
9:24 [g] Nu 35:33; 1Ki 2:32 [h] ver 56-57 [i] Dt 27:25
9:27 [j] Am 9:13 [k] Jdg 8:33
9:28 [l] 1Sa 25:10; 1Ki 12:16 [m] Ge 34:2,6
9:29 [n] 2Sa 15:4
9:32 [o] Jos 8:2

22After Abimelek had governed Israel
three years, 23God stirred up animosity[f]
between Abimelek and the citizens of
Shechem so that they acted treacherously against Abimelek. 24God did this
in order that the crime against Jerub-
Baal’s seventy sons, the shedding[g] of
their blood, might be avenged[h] on their
brother Abimelek and on the citizens
of Shechem, who had helped him[i] murder his brothers. 25In opposition to him
these citizens of Shechem set men on
the hilltops to ambush and rob everyone
who passed by, and this was reported to
Abimelek.
26Now Gaal son of Ebed moved with
his clan into Shechem, and its citizens
put their confidence in him. 27After they
had gone out into the fields and gathered the grapes and trodden[j] them, they
held a festival in the temple of their god.[k]
While they were eating and drinking,
they cursed Abimelek. 28Then Gaal son
of Ebed said, “Who[l] is Abimelek, and why
should we Shechemites be subject to
him? Isn’t he Jerub-Baal’s son, and isn’t
Zebul his deputy? Serve the family of
Hamor,[m] Shechem’s father! Why should
we serve Abimelek? 29If only this people
were under my command![n] Then I would
get rid of him. I would say to Abimelek,
‘Call out your whole army!’ ”[a]
30When Zebul the governor of the city
heard what Gaal son of Ebed said, he was
very angry. 31Under cover he sent messengers to Abimelek, saying, “Gaal son of
Ebed and his clan have come to Shechem
and are stirring up the city against you.
32Now then, during the night you and
your men should come and lie in wait[o]

[a] 29 Septuagint; Hebrew *him.” Then he said to Abimelek, “Call out your whole army!”*

9:16–20 The curse is conditional (though rhetorical). The conditional clause contains two possible situations that the NIV translates as three questions: (1) “Have you acted honorably and in good faith by making Abimelek king?” (2) “Have you been fair to Jerub-Baal and his family?” (3) “Have you treated him as he deserves?” (v. 16). The implied answer is that the Shechemites have not acted in a blameless and honest manner; they have not acted with integrity.
9:18–20 Jotham reminds them that Gideon took great personal risk, yet the citizens/lords of Shechem “have revolted” (v. 18) against Gideon’s family, murdering his sons and installing Abimelek, an illegitimate son (hence a “thorn”), to the throne. Verse 19 resumes the question or condition and concludes with a sarcastic statement. Verse 20, however, gives the second situation and the real, intended curse. Because the crime has already been committed and the outcomes are irrevocable, the curse is really a pronouncement of sure judgment.
9:22–24 The time period is by far the shortest of any oppression or judgeship in the book. God does not put up with Abimelek and the Shechemites for very long. It is important to recognize that it is God who begins the process of avenging the wrongs done by both Abimelek and the Shechemites.
9:25–57 The entrance of the character Gaal is deliberately patterned after that of Abimelek. Gaal (like Abimelek earlier) uses rhetorical questions to heighten his popularity and undermine that of the current government.

in the fields. 33In the morning at sunrise, advance against the city. When Gaal and his men come out against you, seize the opportunity to attack them.[p]"

34So Abimelek and all his troops set out by night and took up concealed positions near Shechem in four companies. 35Now Gaal son of Ebed had gone out and was standing at the entrance of the city gate just as Abimelek and his troops came out from their hiding place.[q]

36When Gaal saw them, he said to Zebul, "Look, people are coming down from the tops of the mountains!"

Zebul replied, "You mistake the shadows of the mountains for men."

37But Gaal spoke up again: "Look, people are coming down from the central hill,[a] and a company is coming from the direction of the diviners' tree."

38Then Zebul said to him, "Where is your big talk now, you who said, 'Who is Abimelek that we should be subject to him?' Aren't these the men you ridiculed?[r] Go out and fight them!"

39So Gaal led out[b] the citizens of Shechem and fought Abimelek. 40Abimelek chased him all the way to the entrance of the gate, and many were killed as they fled. 41Then Abimelek stayed in Arumah, and Zebul drove Gaal and his clan out of Shechem.

42The next day the people of Shechem went out to the fields, and this was reported to Abimelek. 43So he took his men, divided them into three companies[s] and set an ambush in the fields. When he saw the people coming out of the city, he rose to attack them. 44Abimelek and the companies with him rushed forward to a position at the entrance of the city gate. Then two companies attacked those in the fields and struck them down. 45All that day Abimelek pressed his attack against the city until he had captured it and killed its people. Then he destroyed the city[t] and scattered salt[u] over it.

46On hearing this, the citizens in the tower of Shechem went into the stronghold of the temple[v] of El-Berith. 47When Abimelek heard that they had assembled there, 48he and all his men went up Mount Zalmon.[w] He took an ax and cut off some branches, which he lifted to his shoulders. He ordered the men with him, "Quick! Do what you have seen me do!" 49So all the men cut branches and followed Abimelek. They piled them against the stronghold and set it on fire with the people still inside. So all the people in the tower of Shechem, about a thousand men and women, also died.

50Next Abimelek went to Thebez[x] and besieged it and captured it. 51Inside the city, however, was a strong tower, to which all the men and women — all the people

9:33 [p] 1Sa 10:7
9:35 [q] Ps 32:7; Jer 49:10
9:38 [r] ver 28-29
9:43 [s] Jdg 7:16
9:45 [t] ver 20; 2Ki 3:25 [u] Dt 29:23
9:46 [v] Jdg 8:33
9:48 [w] Ps 68:14
9:50 [x] 2Sa 11:21

[a] 37 The Hebrew for this phrase means *the navel of the earth.* [b] 39 Or *Gaal went out in the sight of*

9:34–41 Abimelek deploys his troops to ambush the city (v. 34). Abimelek's ambush succeeds, and Abimelek slays many while chasing Gaal to the entrance of Shechem (vv. 39–40). Abimelek stays in Arumah while Zebul expels Gaal and his brothers from Shechem (v. 41). At this, one might expect the conflict to be resolved. But Abimelek is the son of Jerub-Baal, and his personal revenge is only now beginning.

9:42–45 The use of the term "people" (v. 42) indicates that this group includes women. The helpless victims are slaughtered in the fields, putting up whatever feeble resistance that they can. The scattering of salt over the ground of the city is an attempt to condemn it to perpetual barrenness and desolation. Just as Abimelek has made Jerub-Baal's family barren, so now he makes Shechem barren.

9:46–49 All of the people—men and women, one thousand in number—die in the conflagration (v. 49b). Once again, one might now expect the conflict between Abimelek and Shechem to be resolved, but his campaign for personal revenge is still far from over.

9:50–55 Based on the repetition of the previous reprisals, the reader's expectations are set for another of Abimelek's massacres. However, unexpectedly the narrative introduces "a woman" who drops an upper millstone on Abimelek's head and cracks his skull (v. 53). The upper millstone, usually made of basalt, though sometimes sandstone, was the smaller upper stone of a hand mill that was worked against a larger stone to grind grain. For most women, grinding grain was a daily domestic task. It was humiliating for a man to do such work. Therefore, it was also humiliating to be struck by such a stone hurled by a woman. As in the case of Jael in 4:21, this woman takes what is normally a domestic, everyday object and turns it into weapon.

God has repaid the evil committed by Abimelek and the evil committed by the men of Shechem. The curse of Jotham, son of Jerub-Baal, comes on them. In this way Yahweh works vindication and justice.

The primary theme of the Abimelek account is the notion of revenge: getting even (when in the human context) or retribution (when in the divine context). The pattern of divine retribution in the cycles section so far has been one of sin / punishment / compassion / deliverance. In the Abimelek narrative, however, the pattern appears to be sin / exact retribution.

of the city—had fled. They had locked
themselves in and climbed up on the
tower roof. 52Abimelek went to the tower and attacked it. But as he approached
the entrance to the tower to set it on fire,
53a woman dropped an upper millstone
on his head and cracked his skull.[y]
54Hurriedly he called to his armor-
bearer, "Draw your sword and kill me,[z] so
that they can't say, 'A woman killed him.'"
So his servant ran him through, and he
died. 55When the Israelites saw that
Abimelek was dead, they went home.
56Thus God repaid the wickedness that
Abimelek had done to his father by murdering his seventy brothers. 57God also
made the people of Shechem pay for all
their wickedness.[a] The curse of Jotham
son of Jerub-Baal came on them.

Tola

10 After the time of Abimelek, a man
of Issachar[b] named Tola son of
Puah,[c] the son of Dodo, rose to save[d] Israel. He lived in Shamir, in the hill country
of Ephraim. 2He led[a] Israel twenty-three
years; then he died, and was buried in
Shamir.

Jair

3He was followed by Jair of Gilead, who
led Israel twenty-two years. 4He had thirty sons, who rode thirty donkeys. They
controlled thirty towns in Gilead, which
to this day are called Havvoth Jair.[b][e]
5When Jair died, he was buried in Kamon.

Jephthah

6Again the Israelites did evil in the
eyes of the LORD.[f] They served the Baals
and the Ashtoreths,[g] and the gods of
Aram, the gods of Sidon, the gods of
Moab, the gods of the Ammonites and the
gods of the Philistines.[h] And because the
Israelites forsook the LORD[i] and no longer served him, 7he became angry[j] with
them. He sold them[k] into the hands of
the Philistines and the Ammonites, 8who
that year shattered and crushed them.
For eighteen years they oppressed all the
Israelites on the east side of the Jordan
in Gilead, the land of the Amorites. 9The
Ammonites also crossed the Jordan to
fight against Judah, Benjamin and Ephraim; Israel was in great distress. 10Then
the Israelites cried out to the LORD, "We
have sinned against you, forsaking our
God and serving the Baals."[l]
11The LORD replied, "When the Egyptians,[m] the Amorites, the Ammonites,[n]
the Philistines,[o] 12the Sidonians, the Amalekites and the Maonites[c] oppressed
you[p] and you cried to me for help, did
I not save you from their hands? 13But
you have forsaken me and served other
gods, so I will no longer save you. 14Go
and cry out to the gods you have chosen. Let them save you when you are in
trouble![q]"
15But the Israelites said to the LORD,
"We have sinned. Do with us whatever

9:53 [y] 2Sa 11:21
9:54 [z] 1Sa 31:4; 2Sa 1:9
9:57 [a] ver 20
10:1 [b] Ge 30:18 [c] Ge 46:13 [d] Jdg 2:16; 6:14
10:4 [e] Nu 32:41
10:6 [f] Jdg 2:11 [g] Jdg 2:13 [h] Jdg 2:12 [i] Dt 32:15
10:7 [j] Dt 31:17 [k] Dt 32:30; Jdg 2:14; 1Sa 12:9
10:10 [l] 1Sa 12:10
10:11 [m] Ex 14:30 [n] Nu 21:21; Jdg 3:13 [o] Jdg 3:31
10:12 [p] Ps 106:42
10:14 [q] Dt 32:37

[a] 2 Traditionally *judged;* also in verse 3 [b] 4 Or *called the settlements of Jair* [c] 12 Hebrew; some Septuagint manuscripts *Midianites*

Jdg 10:15–16 ❖ What does it feel like to acknowledge sin openly before God? How has he shown us his mercy when we have confessed our sin (see Ps 32:5)?

8:33—9:57 This text certainly underscores the results of sin. Our sins cannot be measured in a lifetime; they have an impact on the next generation and beyond. Whether it is our families, our communities, or our nation, the impact of personal sin will be felt. The harvest of the seeds of sin may not necessarily come in our generation, but it will come in innumerable ones beyond us.

10:1–2 Tola's genealogical connection is given back to a third generation. Often in the OT, such a genealogical statement is evidence of high social standing.

10:3–5 In order to have thirty sons, one has to have a harem. Following as it does so soon after the Gideon/Abimelek cycle, the issue of kingship seems to be clearly in view.

10:1–5 See the comments at the end of the last three minor judges (12:8–15).

10:6–16 By identifying seven sets of deities, the text is meant to be symbolic, conveying that the Israelites went completely after other deities. Israel's confession seems on the surface to reflect a genuine repentance, but their hearts are not really devoted to God for any reason except for convenience.

10:6–16 Believers are entirely capable of going through the motions, of offering God insincere and superficial repentance. They can perform the right rituals, play their parts, and certainly put on a convincing performance, at least as far as other human beings are concerned. But the Lord sees through the charade; he knows our hearts. He will not be manipulated.

you think best,[r] but please rescue us now." 16Then they got rid of the foreign gods among them and served the LORD.[s] And he could bear Israel's misery[t] no longer.[u]

17When the Ammonites were called to arms and camped in Gilead, the Israelites assembled and camped at Mizpah.[v] 18The leaders of the people of Gilead said to each other, "Whoever will take the lead in attacking the Ammonites will be head[w] over all who live in Gilead."

11 Jephthah[x] the Gileadite was a mighty warrior.[y] His father was Gilead; his mother was a prostitute. 2Gilead's wife also bore him sons, and when they were grown up, they drove Jephthah away. "You are not going to get any inheritance in our family," they said, "because you are the son of another woman." 3So Jephthah fled from his brothers and settled in the land of Tob,[z] where a gang of scoundrels[a] gathered around him and followed him.

4Some time later, when the Ammonites[b] were fighting against Israel, 5the elders of Gilead went to get Jephthah from the land of Tob. 6"Come," they said, "be our commander, so we can fight the Ammonites."

7Jephthah said to them, "Didn't you hate me and drive me from my father's house?[c] Why do you come to me now, when you're in trouble?"

8The elders of Gilead said to him, "Nevertheless, we are turning to you now; come with us to fight the Ammonites, and you will be head[d] over all of us who live in Gilead."

9Jephthah answered, "Suppose you take me back to fight the Ammonites and the LORD gives them to me — will I really be your head?"

10The elders of Gilead replied, "The LORD is our witness;[e] we will certainly do as you say." 11So Jephthah went with the elders of Gilead, and the people made him head and commander over them. And he repeated all his words before the LORD in Mizpah.[f]

12Then Jephthah sent messengers to the Ammonite king with the question: "What do you have against me that you have attacked my country?"

13The king of the Ammonites answered Jephthah's messengers, "When Israel came up out of Egypt, they took away my land from the Arnon to the Jabbok,[g] all the way to the Jordan. Now give it back peaceably."

14Jephthah sent back messengers to the Ammonite king, 15saying:

> "This is what Jephthah says: Israel did not take the land of Moab[h] or the land of the Ammonites.[i] 16But when they came up out of Egypt, Israel went through the wilderness to the Red Sea[a][j] and on to Kadesh.[k] 17Then

10:15 [r] 1Sa 3:18; 2Sa 15:26
10:16 [s] Jos 24:23; Jer 18:8 [t] Isa 63:9 [u] Dt 32:36; Ps 106:44-45
10:17 [v] Ge 31:49; Jdg 11:29
10:18 [w] Jdg 11:8,9
11:1 [x] Heb 11:32 [y] Jdg 6:12
11:3 [z] 2Sa 10:6,8 [a] Jdg 9:4
11:4 [b] Jdg 10:9
11:7 [c] Ge 26:27
11:8 [d] Jdg 10:18
11:10 [e] Ge 31:50; Jer 42:5
11:11 [f] Jos 11:3; Jdg 10:17; 20:1; 1Sa 10:17
11:13 [g] Ge 32:22; Nu 21:24
11:15 [h] Dt 2:9 [i] Dt 2:19
11:16 [j] Nu 14:25; Dt 1:40 [k] Nu 20:1

[a] 16 Or *the Sea of Reeds*

10:17–18 The leaders of Gilead do not depend on the Lord to raise up a deliverer. Instead, they choose their own. Presumably this is why it is not said of Jephthah that Yahweh raises him up to deliver Israel.

11:1–3 The first thing emphasized in the narrative introduction is that "Jephthah . . . was a mighty warrior" (v. 1; cf. Gideon in 6:12). But the second part of the verse adds a problem: His father was a man named Gilead, but his mother was a prostitute. His brothers went to court to sue on the grounds that Jephthah's adoption was not valid, and the elders ruled in favor of the brothers and legally disinherited Jephthah. Verse 3 explains how Jephthah became known as a mighty warrior.

11:4–6 The elders' initial offer of 10:18 was that "whoever" saved them would become their tribal chief. But they make the lesser offer of "commander" (11:6). It may be because Jephthah had been disinherited.

11:7 Jephthah rejects the elders. After Jephthah's objection, they raise the offer back to its initial level. Their haggling shows how unprincipled these opportunists are.

11:9 The elders without hesitation reverse their earlier decision and disinherit Jephthah's brothers in order to get their man. Their ritual ceremony uses the Lord's name, but the Lord is absent from the process of raising up Jephthah. Just using the divine name does not mean that God is in it.

> ✣ **10:17—11:11** What is especially disturbing in this passage is that the opportunists are the political and spiritual leaders of Israel. Could such raw opportunists be found in the church today? It is a chilling thought, but the better part of wisdom recognizes that such situations can and do exist.

11:12–13 The Ammonite king's response is hardly satisfying. In the lengthy speech that follows, Jephthah communicates using a common ancient Near Eastern form known as the royal covenant/treaty disputation.

11:15–24 Jephthah starts the speech with an assertion. Israel cannot give back to Ammon that which was never Ammon's. Not only does Jephthah's rehearsal of the area's history function to undercut the Ammonite claim, it also functions as a mocking warning to the Ammonite monarch.

Israel sent messengers[l] to the king
of Edom, saying, 'Give us permission
to go through your country,'[m] but
the king of Edom would not listen.
They sent also to the king of Moab,
and he refused.[n] So Israel stayed at
Kadesh.
18"Next they traveled through
the wilderness, skirted the lands
of Edom[o] and Moab, passed along
the eastern side[p] of the country of
Moab, and camped on the other side
of the Arnon.[q] They did not enter
the territory of Moab, for the Arnon
was its border.
19"Then Israel sent messengers
to Sihon king of the Amorites, who
ruled in Heshbon, and said to him,
'Let us pass through your country to
our own place.'[r] 20Sihon, however,
did not trust Israel[a] to pass through
his territory. He mustered all his
troops and encamped at Jahaz and
fought with Israel.[s]
21"Then the LORD, the God of Israel, gave Sihon and his whole army
into Israel's hands, and they defeated them. Israel took over all the land
of the Amorites who lived in that
country, 22capturing all of it from
the Arnon to the Jabbok and from
the desert to the Jordan.[t]
23"Now since the LORD, the God of
Israel, has driven the Amorites out

11:17 [l] Nu 20:14 [m] Nu 20:18,21 [n] Jos 24:9
11:18 [o] Nu 21:4 [p] Dt 2:8 [q] Nu 21:13
11:19 [r] Nu 21:21-22; Dt 2:26-27
11:20 [s] Nu 21:23; Dt 2:32
11:22 [t] Dt 2:36
11:24 [u] Nu 21:29; Jos 3:10; 1Ki 11:7
11:25 [v] Nu 22:2 [w] Jos 24:9
11:26 [x] Nu 21:25
11:27 [y] Ge 18:25 [z] Ge 16:5; 31:53; 1Sa 24:12,15
11:29 [a] Nu 11:25; Jdg 3:10; 6:34; 14:6,19; 15:14; 1Sa 11:6; 16:13; Isa 11:2

Jdg 11:30-31 ❖ Have we ever tried to make a selfish and foolish bargain with God? What happened?

before his people Israel, what right
have you to take it over? 24Will you
not take what your god Chemosh[u]
gives you? Likewise, whatever the
LORD our God has given us, we will
possess. 25Are you any better than
Balak son of Zippor,[v] king of Moab?
Did he ever quarrel with Israel or
fight with them?[w] 26For three hundred years Israel occupied[x] Heshbon, Aroer, the surrounding settlements and all the towns along
the Arnon. Why didn't you retake
them during that time? 27I have not
wronged you, but you are doing me
wrong by waging war against me.
Let the LORD, the Judge,[y] decide[z] the
dispute this day between the Israelites and the Ammonites."
28The king of Ammon, however, paid
no attention to the message Jephthah
sent him.
29Then the Spirit[a] of the LORD
came on Jephthah. He crossed Gilead
and Manasseh, passed through Mizpah of Gilead, and from there he advanced against the Ammonites. 30And

[a] *20* Or *however, would not make an agreement for Israel*

11:23 Jephthah uses what appears to be a logical argument—an argument commonly asserted in the ancient Near East: A people must accept the will of its god. For all his apparent piety, Jephthah localizes Yahweh as though he is just like Chemosh, Milcom, Baal, or any other false god.
11:25-26 The essence of the argument is this: Since no Ammonite king (or Moabite, either, for that matter) has ever attempted to claim the land area in dispute for over three hundred years, nobody in his right mind would claim it now. Thus, the claim is rejected.
11:27 Jephthah's conclusion is found here. Jephthah mocks the Ammonite king for considering war with the Israelites, since war with them is war with Yahweh. Jephthah voices a recognition that the victory belongs to Yahweh (vv. 21, 27). But like his negotiations with the elders, this is only a tacit recognition, for Jephthah is a pragmatic Yahwist.

✣ **11:12-28** Theological ignorance and error lead to devastating results. In addition, we live in a world that has, over the course of a century, continually depreciated the worth of theological matters.

Having a knowledge of the Bible is not considered important today. In our drive for the advantages and distractions afforded by technology, knowing God's Word is seen as having little or no value. Knowing the Bible "does not put bread on the table," so the argument goes. And yet Christians know that nothing could ever be more valuable than a working knowledge of God's written revelation to his people.

11:29 As pointed out in the discussion of Gideon (6:34-35), this does not presuppose any particular level of spirituality on the part of the recipient.
11:29-32 The irony is stark. Jephthah delivers the Israelites from the Ammonites, who along with their neighbors sacrifice their children to their gods; then he sacrifices his daughter to Yahweh, who does not accept human sacrifice.

It may seem odd to Western readers to anticipate that sheep or cattle might come out of one's house. But the typical four-room house of this period contained a room that housed animals.

The focus is on the daughter's innocence and Jephthah's ignorance: God did provide for the monetary redemption of vows made without fully

PEOPLE TO KNOW // JEPHTHAH

JUDGES 11:29–40: Jephthah was a judge from Gilead, on the east side of the Jordan River. His mother was a prostitute, so the other sons of his father drove him away (Jdg 11:1–2). Jephthah struck off on his own and surrounded himself with a gang of thugs.

When the Ammonites oppressed Israel, the elders of Gilead begged Jephthah for help, promising to make him their leader if he defeated their enemies. Jephthah tried to reason with the Ammonite king, but his message was rejected. Then, filled with the Spirit of God, he advanced against his enemies. However, he made a foolish vow to God. He promised that if God gave him victory, he would sacrifice as a burnt offering the first thing that came out of his house when he came home (Jdg 11:31).

God gave Jephthah a decisive victory over the Ammonites, but when he returned home the first thing out of his house was his beloved daughter, his only child. She came dancing and celebrating, but Jephthah was anguished. He told his daughter about his vow to God, and she accepted that he must keep it.

The book of Judges describes the failure of the Israelites to fully commit to God as they settled the promised land. Jephthah's story illustrates that even the chosen judges of Israel were becoming more and more corrupt and disobedient. Jephthah's sin in sacrificing his daughter and violence toward the Ephraimites show that the people of Israel were continuing to reap the consequences of their failure to follow God.

APPLICATION Jephthah demonstrates a lack of understanding God. With his foolish vow, he tried to manipulate God in order to secure victory. Sometimes it can be tempting to try bargaining with God to get what we want, but it does not work. God cannot be manipulated, and any attempts to do so will end in failure and tragedy. The heartbreaking reality is that God would have used Jephthah to deliver his people without Jephthah taking the fateful vow. Jephthah's daughter was a victim of Jephthah's tragic lack of trust in the Lord.

Jephthah made a vow[b] to the LORD: "If
you give the Ammonites into my hands,
31whatever comes out of the door of
my house to meet me when I return
in triumph from the Ammonites will
be the LORD's, and I will sacrifice it as
a burnt offering."
32Then Jephthah went over to fight
the Ammonites, and the LORD gave them
into his hands. 33He devastated twenty
towns from Aroer to the vicinity of Minnith,[c] as far as Abel Keramim. Thus Israel
subdued Ammon.
34When Jephthah returned to his
home in Mizpah, who should come out
to meet him but his daughter, dancing
to the sound of timbrels![d] She was an
only child. Except for her he had neither
son nor daughter. 35When he saw her, he
tore his clothes and cried, "Oh no, my
daughter! You have brought me down
and I am devastated. I have made a vow
to the LORD that I cannot break.[e]"
36"My father," she replied, "you have
given your word to the LORD. Do to me
just as you promised,[f] now that the LORD
has avenged you of your enemies,[g] the
Ammonites. 37But grant me this one request," she said. "Give me two months to
roam the hills and weep with my friends,
because I will never marry."
38"You may go," he said. And he let her
go for two months. She and her friends
went into the hills and wept because
she would never marry. 39After the two
months, she returned to her father, and
he did to her as he had vowed. And she
was a virgin.
From this comes the Israelite tradition
40that each year the young women of Israel go out for four days to commemorate
the daughter of Jephthah the Gileadite.

11:30 [b] Ge 28:20
11:33 [c] Eze 27:17
11:34 [d] Ex 15:20; Jer 31:4
11:35 [e] Nu 30:2; Ecc 5:2,4,5
11:36 [f] Lk 1:38 [g] 2Sa 18:19

considering their ramifications (Lev 27:1–8). Tragically, had he known about this, Jephthah could have redeemed his daughter.

11:29–40 The tragedy of this passage is repeated again and again in our modern society. Jephthah was an illegitimate son, born of a prostitute, and rejected. He became a man who was hurt, angry, ambition-driven, and abusive to his daughter. He blamed his daughter for the disaster that he would inflict on her and made himself the victim. In many ways this nameless daughter represents all the courageous daughters of abusive fathers.

Jephthah and Ephraim

12 The Ephraimite forces were called
out, and they crossed over to Zaphon. They said to Jephthah, "Why did
you go to fight the Ammonites without calling us to go with you?[h] We're
going to burn down your house over
your head."
2Jephthah answered, "I and my people
were engaged in a great struggle with the
Ammonites, and although I called, you
didn't save me out of their hands. 3When
I saw that you wouldn't help, I took my
life in my hands[i] and crossed over to
fight the Ammonites, and the LORD gave
me the victory over them. Now why have
you come up today to fight me?"
4Jephthah then called together the
men of Gilead and fought against Ephraim. The Gileadites struck them down because the Ephraimites had said, "You
Gileadites are renegades from Ephraim
and Manasseh." 5The Gileadites captured
the fords of the Jordan[j] leading to Ephraim, and whenever a survivor of Ephraim said, "Let me cross over," the men of
Gilead asked him, "Are you an Ephraimite?" If he replied, "No," 6they said,
"All right, say 'Shibboleth.'" If he said,
"Sibboleth," because he could not pronounce the word correctly, they seized
him and killed him at the fords of the
Jordan. Forty-two thousand Ephraimites
were killed at that time.
7Jephthah led[a] Israel six years. Then
Jephthah the Gileadite died and was buried in a town in Gilead.

12:1 [h] Jdg 8:1
12:3 [i] 1Sa 19:5; 28:21; Job 13:14
12:5 [j] Jos 22:11; Jdg 3:28

> **Jdg 12:5-6** ❖ Where have we seen division and conflict between God's people? How might this have been avoided?
>
> **Jdg 13:1** ❖ How can we tell when bad circumstances are the result of sin?

Ibzan, Elon and Abdon

8After him, Ibzan of Bethlehem led
Israel. 9He had thirty sons and thirty
daughters. He gave his daughters away
in marriage to those outside his clan, and
for his sons he brought in thirty young
women as wives from outside his clan.
Ibzan led Israel seven years. 10Then Ibzan died and was buried in Bethlehem.
11After him, Elon the Zebulunite led
Israel ten years. 12Then Elon died and was
buried in Aijalon in the land of Zebulun.
13After him, Abdon son of Hillel, from
Pirathon, led Israel. 14He had forty sons
and thirty grandsons,[k] who rode on seventy donkeys.[l] He led Israel eight years.
15Then Abdon son of Hillel died and was
buried at Pirathon in Ephraim, in the hill
country of the Amalekites.[m]

The Birth of Samson

13 Again the Israelites did evil in the
eyes of the LORD, so the LORD delivered them into the hands of the Philistines[n] for forty years.
2A certain man of Zorah,[o] named
Manoah, from the clan of the Danites,

12:14 [k] Jdg 10:4 [l] Jdg 5:10
12:15 [m] Jdg 5:14
13:1 [n] Jdg 2:11; 1Sa 12:9
13:2 [o] Jos 15:33; 19:41

[a] 7 Traditionally *judged*; also in verses 8-14

12:1 The Ephraimite accusation and threat come from the ancient Near Eastern context of the covenant disputation.
12:2-3 Without waiting for a response to his rhetorical question at the end of v. 3, Jephthah calls out the Gileadites and fights against the Ephraimites.
12:4-7 This is an intertribal feud that God has hardly sanctioned. This episode is a foretaste of the intertribal war that erupts in chs. 19–21.

> ✤ **12:1-7** Contentious people produce contention. Jealousy, envy, and every sort of evil (Jas 3:14-18) can consume God's people. So it is with the petty, unimportant, and unnecessary fights that consume many a church: The emotional and physical damage can be astronomical. There is a need for humility and repentance.

12:8-10 From Gideon on, judgeship is always on the verge of turning into kingship, with sons succeeding fathers to office.
12:11-12 Nothing is really reported about Elon the Zebulunite except the length of his judgeship and the place of his burial.
12:13-15 Oddly, Abdon has fewer grandsons than sons. In light of the covenantal blessings and cursings (namely, Dt 28:4, 18), this could potentially be a subtle allusion to Abdon's unfaithfulness.

> ✤ **12:8-15** The minor judges give evidence (like their major judge counterparts) of a spiritual and moral degeneration. Such a negative characterization serves as a warning to us today: Starting well means nothing unless we commit to finishing well and then faithfully follow through.

13:1-2 The length of the oppression is forty years, double the next longest oppression. This may speak to its severity. Instead of the usual "and the Israelites cried out to the LORD," there is only silence. Considering Israel's stubborn rebellion at this time, it is remarkable that Yahweh will intervene through a miraculous birth reminiscent of the one he gave to Abraham and Sarah. This demonstrates the tremendous, long-suffering grace of God.

had a wife who was childless, unable to
give birth. 3The angel of the LORD[p] appeared to her[q] and said, "You are barren
and childless, but you are going to become pregnant and give birth to a son.[r]
4Now see to it that you drink no wine
or other fermented drink and that you
do not eat anything unclean.[s] 5You will
become pregnant and have a son whose
head is never to be touched by a razor[t]
because the boy is to be a Nazirite,[u] dedicated to God from the womb. He will
take the lead[v] in delivering Israel from
the hands of the Philistines."
6Then the woman went to her husband and told him, "A man of God[w] came
to me. He looked like an angel of God,[x]
very awesome. I didn't ask him where
he came from, and he didn't tell me
his name. 7But he said to me, 'You will
become pregnant and have a son. Now
then, drink no wine or other fermented drink and do not eat anything unclean, because the boy will be a Nazirite
of God from the womb until the day of
his death.'"
8Then Manoah prayed to the LORD:
"Pardon your servant, Lord. I beg you to
let the man of God you sent to us come
again to teach us how to bring up the
boy who is to be born."
9God heard Manoah, and the angel of
God came again to the woman while she
was out in the field; but her husband
Manoah was not with her. 10The woman
hurried to tell her husband, "He's here!
The man who appeared to me the other day!"
11Manoah got up and followed his wife.
When he came to the man, he said, "Are
you the man who talked to my wife?"
"I am," he said.
12So Manoah asked him, "When your
words are fulfilled, what is to be the rule
that governs the boy's life and work?"
13The angel of the LORD answered,
"Your wife must do all that I have told
her. 14She must not eat anything that
comes from the grapevine, nor drink any
wine or other fermented drink[y] nor eat
anything unclean.[z] She must do everything I have commanded her."
15Manoah said to the angel of the LORD,
"We would like you to stay until we prepare a young goat[a] for you."
16The angel of the LORD replied, "Even
though you detain me, I will not eat any
of your food. But if you prepare a burnt
offering,[b] offer it to the LORD." (Manoah
did not realize that it was the angel of
the LORD.)
17Then Manoah inquired of the angel of the LORD, "What is your name,[c]
so that we may honor you when your
word comes true?"
18He replied, "Why do you ask my
name?[d] It is beyond understanding.[a]"
19Then Manoah took a young goat, together with the grain offering, and sacrificed it on a rock[e] to the LORD. And
the LORD did an amazing thing while
Manoah and his wife watched: 20As the
flame[f] blazed up from the altar toward
heaven, the angel of the LORD ascended
in the flame. Seeing this, Manoah and his
wife fell with their faces to the ground.[g]
21When the angel of the LORD did not
show himself again to Manoah and his
wife, Manoah realized[h] that it was the
angel of the LORD.
22"We are doomed[i] to die!" he said to
his wife. "We have seen[j] God!"
23But his wife answered, "If the LORD
had meant to kill us, he would not have
accepted a burnt offering and grain offering from our hands, nor shown us all
these things or now told us this."[k]
24The woman gave birth to a boy and

13:3 [p] ver 6,8; Jdg 6:12 [q] ver 10 [r] Lk 1:13
13:4 [s] ver 14; Nu 6:2-4; Lk 1:15
13:5 [t] Nu 6:5; 1Sa 1:11 [u] Nu 6:2, 13 [v] 1Sa 7:13
13:6 [w] ver 8; 1Sa 2:27; 9:6 [x] ver 17-18; Mt 28:3
13:14 [y] Nu 6:4 [z] ver 4
13:15 [a] ver 3; Jdg 6:19
13:16 [b] Jdg 6:20
13:17 [c] Ge 32:29
13:18 [d] Isa 9:6
13:19 [e] Jdg 6:20
13:20 [f] Lev 9:24 [g] 1Ch 21:16; Eze 1:28; Mt 17:6
13:21 [h] ver 16; Jdg 6:22
13:22 [i] Dt 5:26 [j] Ge 32:30; Jdg 6:22
13:23 [k] Ps 25:14

[a] 18 Or *is wonderful*

13:3–7 The first prediction is fulfilled in v. 24. The second prediction is fulfilled progressively over chs. 14–16: Samson only begins the process of deliverance; he will not accomplish it.

The Nazirite vow included three basic prohibitions: (1) to refrain from consuming intoxicating drink (Nu 6:1–4); (2) to refrain from cutting one's hair for the duration of the vow (Nu 6:5); and (3) to avoid coming into contact with a dead body (Nu 6:6–12).

13:8–23 Manoah is unwilling to trust his wife's testimony, and, as a result, he unnecessarily delays the fulfillment of God's plan. No additional revelation concerning Samson is communicated through the angel's second visit. In the end, it only reveals Manoah's unwillingness to believe what was announced in the angel's first visit to his wife.

13:16 Apparently, Manoah's intention is to detain and obligate his divine visitor through feeding, a concept well-attested in ancient Near Eastern religions, where feeding a deity or his envoy provided the basis for the petitioner's expectation of divine action on his behalf.

13:17 In the ancient Near Eastern context, people believed that knowing the name of a heavenly being provided power over that being.

13:24–25 Ironically, it is his mother who gives the baby the name Samson (v. 24a), which is also the

named him Samson.[l] He grew[m] and the
LORD blessed him,[n] 25and the Spirit of
the LORD began to stir[o] him while he
was in Mahaneh Dan,[p] between Zorah
and Eshtaol.

Samson's Marriage

14 Samson went down to Timnah[q]
and saw there a young Philistine
woman. 2When he returned, he said to
his father and mother, "I have seen a
Philistine woman in Timnah; now get
her for me as my wife."[r]
3His father and mother replied, "Isn't
there an acceptable woman among your
relatives or among all our people?[s] Must
you go to the uncircumcised[t] Philistines
to get a wife?[u]"
But Samson said to his father, "Get her
for me. She's the right one for me." 4(His
parents did not know that this was from
the LORD, who was seeking an occasion to
confront the Philistines;[v] for at that time
they were ruling over Israel.)[w]
5Samson went down to Timnah together with his father and mother. As
they approached the vineyards of Timnah, suddenly a young lion came roaring toward him. 6The Spirit of the LORD
came powerfully upon him[x] so that he
tore the lion apart with his bare hands
as he might have torn a young goat. But
he told neither his father nor his mother
what he had done. 7Then he went down
and talked with the woman, and he liked
her.
8Some time later, when he went back
to marry her, he turned aside to look
at the lion's carcass, and in it he saw a
swarm of bees and some honey. 9He
scooped out the honey with his hands
and ate as he went along. When he re-
joined his parents, he gave them some,
and they too ate it. But he did not tell
them that he had taken the honey from
the lion's carcass.
10Now his father went down to see the
woman. And there Samson held a feast,
as was customary for young men. 11When
the people saw him, they chose thirty
men to be his companions.
12"Let me tell you a riddle,[y]" Samson
said to them. "If you can give me the
answer within the seven days of the
feast,[z] I will give you thirty linen garments and thirty sets of clothes.[a] 13If you
can't tell me the answer, you must give
me thirty linen garments and thirty sets
of clothes."
"Tell us your riddle," they said. "Let's
hear it."
14He replied,

"Out of the eater, something to eat;
out of the strong, something
sweet."

For three days they could not give the
answer.

13:24 [l] Heb 11:32 [m] 1Sa 3:19 [n] Lk 1:80
13:25 [o] Jdg 3:10 [p] Jdg 18:12
14:1 [q] Ge 38:12
14:2 [r] Ge 21:21; 34:4
14:3 [s] Ge 24:4 [t] Dt 7:3 [u] Ex 34:16
14:4 [v] Jos 11:20 [w] Jdg 13:1
14:6 [x] Jdg 3:10; 13:25
14:12 [y] 1Ki 10:1; Eze 17:2 [z] Ge 29:27 [a] Ge 45:22; 2Ki 5:5

---

name of the Canaanite sun-god (as well as in other Semitic languages). This is hardly a name that would be expected after such a double theophany of Yahweh to his mother. Even so, by God's grace, the boy grows up, and Yahweh blesses him.

> **13:1–25** This passage calls us to an attitude check. Have we grown apathetic in our Christianity? Are we sensitive to God's calling in our lives? Has compromise with the world caused us to be unresponsive to God's Word, to his standards of morality, to his promises and expectations for our lives? Have we become dull, not being able to discern his voice? Do we demand personal verification, unwilling to trust his self-revelation in his Word? Are we moving forward by faith, or demanding that we will only move forward by sight?

14:1–20 The text's emphasis on "seeing" stresses that Samson is a man dominated by his senses, not logic. These carnal appetites overwhelm his perception of important matters—things that any thinking man would understand. Moreover, Samson's demand to his parents reveals a total disregard for authority in his life, whether parental or divine.
14:4 The parenthetical statement of this verse suggests that Samson's sinful actions are turned by Yahweh to accomplish his will.
14:5–7 Samson's parents capitulate and go down to Timnah with Samson to arrange the marriage. Samson easily tears a lion in two. While this is a truly marvelous feat, Samson deliberately withholds any mention of this incident to his parents. Why?

Samson has, in dealing with the lion, produced a corpse. According to the Nazirite vow, after touching a corpse one had to go immediately to the tabernacle and undergo a lengthy restoration ritual, but Samson refuses to do so. This indicates that God and his law are not important to Samson, only what is right in his own eyes.
14:8–9 Some time later Samson returns to marry the Timnite. Samson should have left the honey in the corpse alone (Lev 11:24–40, esp. 27); as a Nazirite, even more so. Not only does he not care about his own ritually unclean status, but he cares little for that of others, including his parents, who are now ritually unclean because of his action. The only thing that matters to Samson is the satisfaction of his own appetites and cravings.
14:11–18 Ironically, Samson, who refused to tell his own mother and father about the lion, gives in to his bride's hounding on the final day.

15 On the fourth[a] day, they said to Samson's wife, "Coax[b] your husband into
explaining the riddle for us, or we will
burn you and your father's household
to death.[c] Did you invite us here to steal
our property?"
16 Then Samson's wife threw herself on
him, sobbing, "You hate me! You don't
really love me.[d] You've given my people a riddle, but you haven't told me the
answer."
"I haven't even explained it to my
father or mother," he replied, "so why
should I explain it to you?" 17 She cried
the whole seven days[e] of the feast. So on
the seventh day he finally told her, because she continued to press him. She in
turn explained the riddle to her people.
18 Before sunset on the seventh day the
men of the town said to him,

"What is sweeter than honey?
  What is stronger than a lion?"[f]

Samson said to them,

"If you had not plowed with my
    heifer,
  you would not have solved my
    riddle."

19 Then the Spirit of the LORD came
powerfully upon him.[g] He went down
to Ashkelon, struck down thirty of their
men, stripped them of everything and
gave their clothes to those who had explained the riddle. Burning with anger,[h]
he returned to his father's home. 20 And
Samson's wife was given to one of his
companions[i] who had attended him at
the feast.

Samson's Vengeance on the Philistines

15 Later on, at the time of wheat harvest, Samson took a young goat[j]
and went to visit his wife. He said, "I'm
going to my wife's room." But her father
would not let him go in.

2 "I was so sure you hated her," he said,
"that I gave her to your companion.[k] Isn't
her younger sister more attractive? Take
her instead."
3 Samson said to them, "This time I
have a right to get even with the Philistines; I will really harm them." 4 So he
went out and caught three hundred foxes
and tied them tail to tail in pairs. He then
fastened a torch to every pair of tails,
5 lit the torches and let the foxes loose
in the standing grain of the Philistines.
He burned up the shocks and standing
grain, together with the vineyards and
olive groves.
6 When the Philistines asked, "Who did
this?" they were told, "Samson, the Timnite's son-in-law, because his wife was
given to his companion."
So the Philistines went up and burned
her and her father to death.[l] 7 Samson
said to them, "Since you've acted like
this, I swear that I won't stop until I get
my revenge on you." 8 He attacked them
viciously and slaughtered many of them.
Then he went down and stayed in a cave
in the rock of Etam.
9 The Philistines went up and camped
in Judah, spreading out near Lehi.[m] 10 The
people of Judah asked, "Why have you
come to fight us?"
"We have come to take Samson prisoner," they answered, "to do to him as
he did to us."

14:15 [b] Jdg 16:5; Ecc 7:26 [c] Jdg 15:6
14:16 [d] Jdg 16:15
14:17 [e] Est 1:5
14:18 [f] ver 14
14:19 [g] Nu 11:25; Jdg 3:10; 6:34; 11:29; 13:25; 15:14; 1Sa 11:6; 16:13; 1Ki 18:46; 2Ch 24:20; Isa 11:2 [h] 1Sa 11:6
14:20 [i] Jdg 15:2, 6; Jn 3:29
15:1 [j] Ge 38:17
15:2 [k] Jdg 14:20
15:6 [l] Jdg 14:15
15:9 [m] ver 14, 17,19

[a] *15* Some Septuagint manuscripts and Syriac; Hebrew *seventh*

Jdg 14:19 ❖ God used Samson despite his character flaws. What does this show us about God? How does this encourage us?

Jdg 15:3 ❖ Is it ever right to take justice into our own hands (see Ro 12:19)? How can we tell if we are acting according to God's will?

14:19–20 Samson's unbridled anger sets the stage for his bride being given to another. His father-in-law sees an opportunity to marry his daughter to one of his own people—no doubt a better social move on his part.

15:1–20 Samson's father-in-law proposes a new arrangement: that Samson take his younger daughter, who is more attractive than her older sister (v. 2). Samson takes revenge. While truly an amazing feat, it is motivated purely by Samson's desire for retaliation.

The Philistines, having determined Samson's guilt, burn his wife and father-in-law. So the conflict escalates even more (v. 7). While revenge was a common motivation for action in the ancient Near East, Yahweh had declared that vengeance belongs to him (Dt 32:35).

15:10–11 The series of dialogues between the Judahites and Philistines and between the Judahites and Samson is revealing. All three parties are concerned about what is being or has been done to them. For the Philistines, Judahites, and Samson, the only thing that matters is reprisal and counter reprisal.

11Then three thousand men from Judah went down to the cave in the rock of Etam and said to Samson, "Don't you realize that the Philistines are rulers over us?[n] What have you done to us?"

He answered, "I merely did to them what they did to me."

12They said to him, "We've come to tie you up and hand you over to the Philistines."

Samson said, "Swear to me that you won't kill me yourselves."

13"Agreed," they answered. "We will only tie you up and hand you over to them. We will not kill you." So they bound him with two new ropes and led him up from the rock. 14As he approached Lehi, the Philistines came toward him shouting. The Spirit of the LORD came powerfully upon him.[o] The ropes on his arms became like charred flax, and the bindings dropped from his hands. 15Finding a fresh jawbone of a donkey, he grabbed it and struck down a thousand men.[p]

16Then Samson said,

"With a donkey's jawbone
  I have made donkeys of them.[a]
With a donkey's jawbone
  I have killed a thousand men."

17When he finished speaking, he threw away the jawbone; and the place was called Ramath Lehi.[b]

18Because he was very thirsty, he cried out to the LORD,[q] "You have given your servant this great victory. Must I now die of thirst and fall into the hands of the uncircumcised?" 19Then God opened up the hollow place in Lehi, and water came out of it. When Samson drank, his strength returned and he revived.[r] So the spring was called En Hakkore,[c] and it is still there in Lehi.

20Samson led[d] Israel for twenty years[s] in the days of the Philistines.

Samson and Delilah

16 One day Samson went to Gaza, where he saw a prostitute. He went in to spend the night with her. 2The people of Gaza were told, "Samson is here!" So they surrounded the place and lay in wait for him all night at the city gate.[t] They made no move during the night, saying, "At dawn we'll kill him."

3But Samson lay there only until the middle of the night. Then he got up and took hold of the doors of the city gate, together with the two posts, and tore them loose, bar and all. He lifted them to his shoulders and carried them to the top of the hill that faces Hebron.[u]

4Some time later, he fell in love[v] with a woman in the Valley of Sorek whose name was Delilah. 5The rulers of the

15:11 [n] Jdg 13:1; 14:4; Ps 106:40-42
15:14 [o] Jdg 3:10; 14:19; 1Sa 11:6
15:15 [p] Lev 26:8; Jos 23:10; Jdg 3:31
15:18 [q] Jdg 16:28
15:19 [r] Ge 45:27; Isa 40:29
15:20 [s] Jdg 13:1; 16:31; Heb 11:32
16:2 [t] 1Sa 23:26; Ps 118:10-12; Ac 9:24
16:3 [u] Jos 10:36
16:4 [v] Ge 24:67

[a] 16 Or *made a heap or two*; the Hebrew for *donkey* sounds like the Hebrew for *heap*.
[b] 17 *Ramath Lehi* means *jawbone hill*.
[c] 19 *En Hakkore* means *caller's spring*.
[d] 20 Traditionally *judged*

15:15–20 Practically speaking, Samson uses what is available, but it is ritually unclean. So, in picking up this item, he again shows his disregard for his Nazirite vow.

The epilogue to this climactic slaughter of the Philistines shows Samson's first recorded prayer (v. 18). But it is immediately plain that this is only due to his exhaustion from the massacre: It is a desperation of thirst. From the tone of Samson's prayer, it seems clear that this is little more than a demand for water (cf. Israel's demands in the wilderness).

✣ **14:1—15:20** This passage is a warning to us concerning what characteristics we should not want in our lives. In Samson, Israel has a judge who determines what is right and wrong purely based on his senses. Today we are encouraged to live life in this way. We are persuaded by commercials that if we like something, we need to go for it. Ads are directed to our senses—appearance is everything. If you don't have the right stuff, you're nothing. Sex is used to sell everything from cars to ice cream. Samson lived in a fashion that our culture would endorse—at least in his willingness to gratify every inclination of his heart (see Ge 6:5).

16:1–22 Samson's going to a prostitute once again indicates of his lack of regard for God's law.

16:2–3 His insolent act endangers him. City gates were not light objects. The distance between Gaza and Hebron is about 40 miles (64.4 km) and involves an ascent of more than 2,000 feet. But Samson only acts to save himself. He has not delivered one Israelite from the hands of their oppressors, the Philistines.

16:4–5 Once again, through his sensual weakness Samson supplies the Philistines with the opportunity to try to overcome him. Significantly, Delilah is the only woman in the Samson cycle whose name is supplied. By only supplying Delilah's name and using it seven times, the narrator singles her out as the most threatening of the four women in the story.

16:5 The "rulers" (lit., "tyrants") of the Philistines each offer her 1,100 shekels of silver, giving her a total of 5,500 shekels (an absurdly fantastic amount of money for this time period). This demonstrates how much they want Samson out of the way.

Philistines[w] went to her and said, "See if you can lure[x] him into showing you the secret of his great strength and how we can overpower him so we may tie him up and subdue him. Each one of us will give you eleven hundred shekels[a] of silver."[y]

6 So Delilah said to Samson, "Tell me the secret of your great strength and how you can be tied up and subdued."

7 Samson answered her, "If anyone ties me with seven fresh bowstrings that have not been dried, I'll become as weak as any other man."

8 Then the rulers of the Philistines brought her seven fresh bowstrings that had not been dried, and she tied him with them. 9 With men hidden in the room,[z] she called to him, "Samson, the Philistines are upon you!" But he snapped the bowstrings as easily as a piece of string snaps when it comes close to a flame. So the secret of his strength was not discovered.

10 Then Delilah said to Samson, "You have made a fool of me;[a] you lied to me. Come now, tell me how you can be tied."

11 He said, "If anyone ties me securely with new ropes[b] that have never been used, I'll become as weak as any other man."

12 So Delilah took new ropes and tied him with them. Then, with men hidden in the room, she called to him, "Samson, the Philistines are upon you!" But he snapped the ropes off his arms as if they were threads.

13 Delilah then said to Samson, "All this time you have been making a fool of me and lying to me. Tell me how you can be tied."

He replied, "If you weave the seven braids of my head into the fabric on the loom and tighten it with the pin, I'll become as weak as any other man." So while he was sleeping, Delilah took the seven braids of his head, wove them into the fabric 14 and[b] tightened it with the pin.

Again she called to him, "Samson, the Philistines are upon you!"[c] He awoke from his sleep and pulled up the pin and the loom, with the fabric.

15 Then she said to him, "How can you say, 'I love you,'[d] when you won't confide in me? This is the third time[e] you have made a fool of me and haven't told me the secret of your great strength."[f] 16 With such nagging she prodded him day after day until he was sick to death of it.

17 So he told her everything.[g] "No razor has ever been used on my head," he said, "because I have been a Nazirite[h] dedicated to God from my mother's womb. If my head were shaved, my strength would leave me, and I would become as weak as any other man."

18 When Delilah saw that he had told her everything, she sent word to the rulers of the Philistines[i], "Come back once more; he has told me everything." So the rulers of the Philistines returned with the silver in their hands. 19 After putting him to sleep on her lap, she called for someone to shave off the seven braids of his hair, and so began to subdue him.[c] And his strength left him.[j]

20 Then she called, "Samson, the Philistines are upon you!"

He awoke from his sleep and thought, "I'll go out as before and shake myself free." But he did not know that the LORD had left him.[k]

21 Then the Philistines[l] seized him, gouged out his eyes[m] and took him down to Gaza. Binding him with bronze shackles, they set him to grinding grain[n] in the

16:5 [w] Jos 13:3 [x] Ex 10:7; Jdg 14:15 [y] ver 18
16:9 [z] ver 12
16:10 [a] ver 13
16:11 [b] Jdg 15:13
16:14 [c] ver 9,20
16:15 [d] Jdg 14:16 [e] Nu 24:10 [f] ver 5
16:17 [g] Mic 7:5 [h] Nu 6:2,5; Jdg 13:5
16:18 [i] Jos 13:3; 1Sa 5:8
16:19 [j] Pr 7:26-27
16:20 [k] Nu 14:42; Jos 7:12; 1Sa 16:14; 18:12; 28:15
16:21 [l] Jer 47:1 [m] Nu 16:14 [n] Job 31:10; Isa 47:2

[a] 5 That is, about 28 pounds or about 13 kilograms [b] 13,14 Some Septuagint manuscripts; Hebrew *replied, "I can if you weave the seven braids of my head into the fabric on the loom."* 14 *So she* [c] 19 Hebrew; some Septuagint manuscripts *and he began to weaken*

16:13 Delilah unleashes a verbal attack on Samson to subdue him and receive her payment. In her third attempt, Delilah repeats the same line as the second. Samson's answer is perilously near the truth since it concerns his hair. This may indicate that his will is breaking.

16:15–17 In her final attempt, Delilah crowns her attack: "How can you say, 'I love you,' when you won't confide in me?" (v. 15). Sadly, Samson's confession demonstrates that he has known all along that he is a Nazirite. This is a powerful comment on all of Samson's previous acts in which he has demonstrated total disregard for his Nazirite status. Instead of the judge overthrowing the oppressor (e.g., Ehud vs. Eglon), the judge is undone by the oppressors' hired gun.

16:20–22 This is perhaps one of the most tragic passages in the OT. The Spirit of Yahweh is no longer empowering Samson. Grinding grain was considered a slave or female occupation, and so the Philistines greatly humble their nemesis with their actions. From their perspective there is ironic justice in Samson's grinding the grain, since he earlier burned up their grain.

prison. 22But the hair on his head began
to grow again after it had been shaved.

The Death of Samson

23Now the rulers of the Philistines
assembled to offer a great sacrifice to
Dagon[o] their god and to celebrate, saying, "Our god has delivered Samson, our
enemy, into our hands."
24When the people saw him, they
praised their god,[p] saying,

"Our god has delivered our enemy
into our hands,[q]
the one who laid waste our land
and multiplied our slain."

25While they were in high spirits,[r] they
shouted, "Bring out Samson to entertain us." So they called Samson out of
the prison, and he performed for them.
When they stood him among the pillars, 26Samson said to the servant who
held his hand, "Put me where I can feel
the pillars that support the temple, so
that I may lean against them." 27Now
the temple was crowded with men and
women; all the rulers of the Philistines
were there, and on the roof[s] were about
three thousand men and women watching Samson perform. 28Then Samson
prayed to the LORD,[t] "Sovereign LORD,

16:23 [o] 1Sa 5:2; 1Ch 10:10
16:24 [p] Da 5:4 [q] 1Sa 31:9; 1Ch 10:9
16:25 [r] Jdg 9:27; Ru 3:7; Est 1:10
16:27 [s] Dt 22:8; Jos 2:8
16:28 [t] Jdg 15:18

Jdg 16:28 ❖ How have we seen God help his children even after their own moral failure?

16:23–31 Dagon is the Hebrew word form of the important Upper Mesopotamian and West Semitic deity Dagan, an important grain deity. In this connection, Samson's burning of the grain stocks is seen to be more serious. Likewise, in their excitement over the capture of Samson, it is understandable why the Philistines in their victory give the credit to Dagon.

To complete the humiliation, the Philistines bring Samson out of prison to the temple to perform. The temple is fully crowded with men and women, with some three thousand on the roof. In this context, Samson utters his second prayer to Yahweh.
16:28 The first line of this prayer raises expectations that perhaps finally Samson is genuinely turning to

PEOPLE TO KNOW // SAMSON

JUDGES 16:23–31: Ecclesiastes 1:8 says, "The eye never has enough of seeing." How true that was for Samson! Samson had a roving eye—he was never satisfied. Yet God was able to use this man, who was driven by his appetites, to deliver his people.

Samson did not live a righteous life. He had a weakness for Philistine women and had a problem controlling his anger. Still, when God's Spirit filled Samson, no one on earth could match his strength. He killed a lion with his bare hands and killed a thousand Philistines armed with only a donkey's jawbone (Jdg 15:15).

Samson's most fateful encounter was with Delilah. She was a Philistine woman living in the Valley of Sorek. The location itself sets off warning alarms. "Sorek" refers to grapevines. As a Nazirite, Samson was not allowed to drink wine or eat anything from a grapevine, so he should have stayed away from a place known for its vineyards. Delilah, at the urging of Philistine leaders, coaxed the secret of Samson's strength from him. Of course, once Delilah knew his secret, she was able to cut his hair while he was sleeping. When he awoke, the Philistines overpowered him, gouged out his eyes, and chained him to a millstone to grind grain in prison. Samson, whose name can mean "little light," had lost his light.

God was not finished with Samson, however. One day the Philistines gathered for a celebration at the temple of Dagon. They brought Samson out to mock him. Samson prayed to God for one last moment of strength, and he toppled the central temple pillars. The building crumbled, killing three thousand people, including Samson himself. The last word in the story sums up this wayward man's violent life: "Thus he killed many more when he died than while he lived" (Jdg 16:30).

APPLICATION ✚ Samson was blessed by God with strength, but he failed to use his gifts wisely. Instead of letting God guide him in his actions, he acted impulsively and without any self-control. He gave in to anger, lust and self-gratification.

Today, with internet access at our fingertips and a culture of moral relativism, Christians need to cultivate a lifestyle that shows the fruit of the Spirit: self-control, goodness and faithfulness. When we let the Spirit guide our actions, we can resist temptations and demonstrate a righteous lifestyle.

remember me. Please, God, strengthen
me just once more, and let me with one
blow get revenge[u] on the Philistines for
my two eyes." 29 Then Samson reached toward the two central pillars on which the
temple stood. Bracing himself against
them, his right hand on the one and his
left hand on the other, 30 Samson said,
"Let me die with the Philistines!" Then
he pushed with all his might, and down
came the temple on the rulers and all the
people in it. Thus he killed many more
when he died than while he lived.
31 Then his brothers and his father's
whole family went down to get him.
They brought him back and buried him
between Zorah and Eshtaol in the tomb
of Manoah[v] his father. He had led[a w] Israel
twenty years.[x]

Micah's Idols

17 Now a man named Micah[y] from the
hill country of Ephraim 2 said to his
mother, "The eleven hundred shekels[b]
of silver that were taken from you and
about which I heard you utter a curse — I
have that silver with me; I took it."
Then his mother said, "The LORD bless
you,[z] my son!"
3 When he returned the eleven hundred
shekels of silver to his mother, she said,
"I solemnly consecrate my silver to the
LORD for my son to make an image overlaid with silver.[a] I will give it back to you."
4 So after he returned the silver to his
mother, she took two hundred shekels[c]
of silver and gave them to a silversmith,
who used them to make the idol.[b] And
it was put in Micah's house.
5 Now this man Micah had a shrine,[c]
and he made an ephod[d] and some household gods[e] and installed[f] one of his sons
as his priest.[g] 6 In those days Israel had
no king;[h] everyone did as they saw fit.[i]
7 A young Levite from Bethlehem in
Judah,[j] who had been living within the
clan of Judah, 8 left that town in search of
some other place to stay. On his way[d] he
came to Micah's house in the hill country
of Ephraim.
9 Micah asked him, "Where are you
from?"
"I'm a Levite from Bethlehem in Judah," he said, "and I'm looking for a place
to stay."

16:28 [u] Jer 15:15
16:31 [v] Jdg 13:2 [w] Ru 1:1; 1Sa 4:18 [x] Jdg 15:20
17:1 [y] Jdg 18:2, 13
17:2 [z] Ru 2:20; 1Sa 15:13; 2Sa 2:5
17:3 [a] Ex 20:4, 23; 34:17; Lev 19:4
17:4 [b] Ex 32:4; Isa 17:8
17:5 [c] Isa 44:13; Eze 8:10 [d] Jdg 8:27 [e] Ge 31:19; Jdg 18:14 [f] Nu 16:10 [g] Ex 29:9; Jdg 18:24
17:6 [h] Jdg 18:1; 19:1; 21:25 [i] Dt 12:8
17:7 [j] Jdg 19:1; Ru 1:1-2; Mic 5:2; Mt 2:1

> **Jdg 17:10-13** ❖ Where have we seen people try to "buy" God's favor for selfish reasons?

[a] *31* Traditionally *judged* [b] *2* That is, about 28 pounds or about 13 kilograms [c] *4* That is, about 5 pounds or about 2.3 kilograms [d] *8* Or *To carry on his profession*

Yahweh in humility and proper faith. But this is truly an egocentric prayer. Samson is not concerned about Yahweh's reputation, only his personal revenge on the Philistines for gouging out his eyes.

16:30 It is perhaps ironic that unwittingly Samson keeps the law about tearing down cultic installations (Dt 12:2–3) when Yahweh empowers him to destroy the temple of Dagon. Samson serves as a microcosm of Israel for its respective failures to fulfill their obligations to Yahweh.

> ✣ **16:1-31** Samson's spiritual apathy is truly stupefying. Spiritual apathy concerning one's calling can lead to open rebellion, as Samson's union with the prostitute of Gaza illustrates. Throughout the Samson cycle, self-interest serves as the motivation—not only for his exploits but also for Delilah, the one who brings him down. When self-interest serves as the motivational factor in one's life, eventual devastation will come—in some cases not surprisingly from another person whose motivation is also driven by self-interest.

17:1-6 The Israelites are now capable of manufacturing their own idols. The name Micah means "Who is like Yahweh?" This is ironic since Yahweh is so absent from this story.

17:2 This sum (1,100 shekels of silver) is precisely the amount Delilah took from each of the five Philistine rulers (16:5). What seems to underlie Micah's mother's curse and blessing is the ancient Near Eastern concept of magic.

17:3 Micah's mother solemnly consecrates the silver to Yahweh in order for her son to make an idolatrous object (or objects).

17:4-6 The mother contributes the silver for the production of the "idol" (v. 4), emphasizing the fabricated aspect of the image. Micah contributes the material for the production of the ephod. Micah places all the religious paraphernalia in his own house, where he makes a shrine and installs one of his sons as the shrine's priest.

Ironically, while thinking that they are doing right, both Micah and his mother perform actions contrary to Yahweh's requirements as prescribed in Dt 12. The story ends with the first occurrence of the refrain, "In those days Israel had no king; everyone did as they saw fit" (v. 6).

17:7-13 Bethlehem is not a Levitical town in Judah. Thus, this Levite should not have been living in Bethlehem in Judah. In light of the offer that Micah makes to him in v. 10, it is clear that the Levite is motivated primarily by material concerns. Having a genuine Levite as his priest gives Micah's shrine an air of legitimacy and prestige. But here Micah demonstrates an ignorance of the law in its most basic teachings.

10 Then Micah said to him, "Live with me and be my father and priest,[k] and I'll give you ten shekels[a] of silver a year, your clothes and your food." 11 So the Levite agreed to live with him, and the young man became like one of his sons to him. 12 Then Micah installed[l] the Levite, and the young man became his priest and lived in his house. 13 And Micah said, "Now I know that the LORD will be good to me, since this Levite has become my priest."

The Danites Settle in Laish

18 In those days Israel had no king.[m] And in those days the tribe of the Danites was seeking a place of their own where they might settle, because they had not yet come into an inheritance among the tribes of Israel.[n] 2 So the Danites[o] sent five of their leading men from Zorah and Eshtaol to spy out the land and explore it. These men represented all the Danites. They told them, "Go, explore the land."[p]

So they entered the hill country of Ephraim and came to the house of Micah,[q] where they spent the night. 3 When they were near Micah's house, they recognized the voice of the young Levite; so they turned in there and asked him, "Who brought you here? What are you doing in this place? Why are you here?"

4 He told them what Micah had done for him, and said, "He has hired me and I am his priest.[r]"

5 Then they said to him, "Please inquire of God[s] to learn whether our journey will be successful."

6 The priest answered them, "Go in peace[t]. Your journey has the LORD's approval."

7 So the five men left and came to Laish,[u] where they saw that the people were living in safety, like the Sidonians, at peace and secure. And since their land lacked nothing, they were prosperous.[b] Also, they lived a long way from the Sidonians[v] and had no relationship with anyone else.[c]

8 When they returned to Zorah and Eshtaol, their fellow Danites asked them, "How did you find things?"

9 They answered, "Come on, let's attack them! We have seen the land, and it is very good. Aren't you going to do something? Don't hesitate to go there and take it over.[w] 10 When you get there, you will find an unsuspecting people and a spacious land that God has put into your hands, a land that lacks nothing[x] whatever.[y]"

11 Then six hundred men[z] of the Danites,[a] armed for battle, set out from Zorah and Eshtaol. 12 On their way they set up camp near Kiriath Jearim in Judah. This is why the place west of Kiriath Jearim is called Mahaneh Dan[d][b] to this day. 13 From there they went on to the hill country of Ephraim and came to Micah's house.

14 Then the five men who had spied out the land of Laish said to their fellow Danites, "Do you know that one of these houses has an ephod, some household gods and an image overlaid with silver?[c] Now you know what to do." 15 So they turned in there and went to the house of the young Levite at Micah's place and greeted him. 16 The six hundred Danites,[d] armed for battle, stood at the entrance of the gate. 17 The five men who had spied out the land went inside and took the idol, the ephod and the household gods[e] while the priest and the six hundred armed men stood at the entrance of the gate.

18 When the five men went into Micah's house and took[f] the idol, the ephod and the household gods, the priest said to them, "What are you doing?"

19 They answered him, "Be quiet![g] Don't

17:10 [k] Jdg 18:19
17:12 [l] Nu 16:10
18:1 [m] Jdg 17:6; 19:1 [n] Jos 19:47
18:2 [o] Jdg 13:25 [p] Jos 2:1 [q] Jdg 17:1
18:4 [r] Jdg 17:12
18:5 [s] 1Ki 22:5
18:6 [t] 1Ki 22:6
18:7 [u] Jos 19:47 [v] ver 28
18:9 [w] Nu 13:30; 1Ki 22:3
18:10 [x] ver 7, 27; Dt 8:9 [y] 1Ch 4:40
18:11 [z] ver 16, 17 [a] Jdg 13:2
18:12 [b] Jdg 13:25
18:14 [c] Ge 31:19; Jdg 17:5
18:16 [d] ver 11
18:17 [e] Ge 31:19; Mic 5:13
18:18 [f] Isa 46:2; Jer 43:11; Hos 10:5
18:19 [g] Job 21:5; 29:9; 40:4; Mic 7:16

[a] *10* That is, about 4 ounces or about 115 grams
[b] *7* The meaning of the Hebrew for this clause is uncertain.
[c] *7* Hebrew; some Septuagint manuscripts *with the Arameans*
[d] *12* *Mahaneh Dan* means *Dan's camp.*

18:1–31 Just as the wayward Levite sought a place to settle, so now the text describes a wayward tribe seeking a place to settle. They recognize "the voice" (v. 3) of the young Levite. The word "voice" probably refers to the Levite's accent. Consequently, they bombard the Levite with questions.

18:4–6 The answer does not disturb the Danites in the least. Instead, they ask him to pray to God for an answer. Notice that they use the term "God," not Yahweh. Ironically, the Levite, who has barely found his own way, now confidently and authoritatively pronounces Yahweh's approval of theirs.

18:7–10 Without proper defenses or effective alliances, Laish was easy prey. The spies return to Zorah and Eshtaol (v. 8) and give their report, which stresses the prosperity of the land and the vulnerability of its inhabitants (vv. 9–10). The writer portrays the Danites and their spies as eager perpetrators of injustice.

18:18–20 Arriving at Micah's house, the five scouts

say a word. Come with us, and be our father and priest.[h] Isn't it better that you
serve a tribe and clan in Israel as priest
rather than just one man's household?"
20The priest was very pleased. He took
the ephod, the household gods and the
idol and went along with the people.
21Putting their little children, their livestock and their possessions in front of
them, they turned away and left.

22When they had gone some distance
from Micah's house, the men who lived
near Micah were called together and
overtook the Danites. 23As they shouted
after them, the Danites turned and said
to Micah, "What's the matter with you
that you called out your men to fight?"

24He replied, "You took the gods I
made, and my priest, and went away.
What else do I have? How can you ask,
'What's the matter with you?' "

25The Danites answered, "Don't argue with us, or some of the men may
get angry and attack you, and you and
your family will lose your lives." 26So the
Danites went their way, and Micah, seeing that they were too strong for him,[i]
turned around and went back home.

27Then they took what Micah had
made, and his priest, and went on to Laish, against a people at peace and secure.[j]
They attacked them with the sword and
burned down their city.[k] 28There was no
one to rescue them because they lived
a long way from Sidon[l] and had no relationship with anyone else. The city was
in a valley near Beth Rehob.[m]

18:19 [h] Jdg 17:10
18:26 [i] Ps 18:17; 35:10
18:27 [j] ver 7, 10 [k] Ge 49:17; Jos 19:47
18:28 [l] ver 7 [m] Nu 13:21; 2Sa 10:6
18:29 [n] Ge 14:14 [o] Jos 19:47; 1Ki 15:20
18:30 [p] Ex 2:22; Jdg 17:3,5
18:31 [q] Jdg 19:18 [r] Jos 18:1; Jer 7:14
19:1 [s] Jdg 18:1 [t] Ru 1:1

Jdg 18:19-20 ❖ When have we seen people use their religious status for personal gain? Has that ever been true of us?

The Danites rebuilt the city and settled there. 29They named it Dan[n] after
their ancestor Dan, who was born to Israel — though the city used to be called
Laish.[o] 30There the Danites set up for
themselves the idol, and Jonathan son
of Gershom,[p] the son of Moses,[a] and his
sons were priests for the tribe of Dan until the time of the captivity of the land.
31They continued to use the idol Micah
had made, all the time the house of God[q]
was in Shiloh.[r]

A Levite and His Concubine

19 In those days Israel had no king.
Now a Levite who lived in a remote
area in the hill country of Ephraim[s] took
a concubine from Bethlehem in Judah.[t]
2But she was unfaithful to him. She left
him and went back to her parents' home
in Bethlehem, Judah. After she had been
there four months, 3her husband went
to her to persuade her to return. He had
with him his servant and two donkeys.
She took him into her parents' home,
and when her father saw him, he gladly
welcomed him. 4His father-in-law, the

[a] *30* Many Hebrew manuscripts, some Septuagint manuscripts and Vulgate; many other Hebrew manuscripts and some other Septuagint manuscripts *Manasseh*

inform their tribesmen that the house contains a shrine with all the trappings. The Levite priest questions them, but they make him an offer (v. 19). They appeal to his vanity and materialism, and they gain his commitment.

18:22-24 Ironically, Micah is concerned about the loss of gods who could not even protect themselves or their maker. Micah, who at the beginning of the story was portrayed as a thief, is now himself the victim of theft.

18:25-28 Micah departs without his gods, and the Danites continue on their quest. In the same ruthless manner that they had stolen from Micah, the Danites exterminate the helpless inhabitants of Laish.

18:30 The Levite's Yahwistic name, Jonathan (meaning "Yahweh has given"), and his genealogical connections to Moses heighten the irony of the entire story.

18:31 It is interesting that Jdg 17-18 conclude with a reference to the legitimate "house of God" at Shiloh. This is a clear condemnation of Micah's illegitimate shrine and the cult objects he made.

✣ **17:1—18:31** When God's word is unknown or ignored, the results are human-manufactured, culturally conditioned innovations. Self-consumed individuals (and a group) dominate this passage, which is itself at its very root immersed in the misconception that humans can manipulate deity (i.e., idolatry). The participants in both parts of the story here appear quite ridiculous in all their efforts and activities. Don't they realize what they are doing?

19:1-2 By focusing on Levites in the concluding episodes, the narrator communicates the extent of Israel's moral decline. A concubine was a second-class wife—a woman who performed marriage duties without the same legal rights as a full wife. The young woman initiates a separation and goes straight for her father's house in Bethlehem.

19:3-8 The Levite speaks kindly to her. This may suggest that she has not left without some provocation on his part (his later callousness toward her seems to be a strong indication of this). The

woman's father, prevailed on him to stay;
so he remained with him three days, eating and drinking,[u] and sleeping there.
5On the fourth day they got up early
and he prepared to leave, but the woman's father said to his son-in-law, "Refresh yourself[v] with something to eat;
then you can go." 6So the two of them
sat down to eat and drink together. Afterward the woman's father said, "Please
stay tonight and enjoy yourself.[w]" 7And
when the man got up to go, his father-
in-law persuaded him, so he stayed there
that night. 8On the morning of the fifth
day, when he rose to go, the woman's
father said, "Refresh yourself. Wait till
afternoon!" So the two of them ate together.
9Then when the man, with his concubine and his servant, got up to leave, his
father-in-law, the woman's father, said,
"Now look, it's almost evening. Spend
the night here; the day is nearly over.
Stay and enjoy yourself. Early tomorrow morning you can get up and be on
your way home." 10But, unwilling to stay
another night, the man left and went toward Jebus[x] (that is, Jerusalem), with his
two saddled donkeys and his concubine.
11When they were near Jebus and the
day was almost gone, the servant said to
his master, "Come, let's stop at this city
of the Jebusites[y] and spend the night."
12His master replied, "No. We won't
go into any city whose people are not
Israelites. We will go on to Gibeah." 13He
added, "Come, let's try to reach Gibeah or Ramah[z] and spend the night in
one of those places." 14So they went on,
and the sun set as they neared Gibeah
in Benjamin.[a] 15There they stopped to
spend the night. They went and sat in
the city square,[b] but no one took them
in for the night.

19:4 [u] Ex 32:6
19:5 [v] ver 8; Ge 18:5
19:6 [w] ver 9, 22; Jdg 16:25
19:10 [x] Ge 10:16; Jos 15:8; 1Ch 11:4-5
19:11 [y] Jos 3:10
19:13 [z] Jos 18:25
19:14 [a] 1Sa 10:26; Isa 10:29
19:15 [b] Ge 19:2
19:16 [c] Ps 104:23 [d] ver 1
19:17 [e] Ge 29:4
19:18 [f] Jdg 18:31
19:19 [g] Ge 24:25 [h] Ge 14:18
19:21 [i] Ge 24:32-33; Lk 7:44
19:22 [j] Jdg 16:25 [k] Dt 13:13 [l] Ge 19:4-5; Jdg 20:5; Ro 1:26-27
19:23 [m] Ge 19:6 [n] Ge 34:7; Lev 19:29; Dt 22:21; Jdg 20:6; 2Sa 13:12; Ro 1:27
19:24 [o] Ge 19:8; Dt 21:14

16That evening[c] an old man from the
hill country of Ephraim,[d] who was living
in Gibeah (the inhabitants of the place
were Benjamites), came in from his work
in the fields. 17When he looked and saw
the traveler in the city square, the old
man asked, "Where are you going? Where
did you come from?"[e]
18He answered, "We are on our way
from Bethlehem in Judah to a remote
area in the hill country of Ephraim where
I live. I have been to Bethlehem in Judah
and now I am going to the house of the
LORD.[a][f] No one has taken me in for the
night. 19We have both straw and fodder[g]
for our donkeys and bread and wine[h]
for ourselves your servants — me, the
woman and the young man with us. We
don't need anything."
20"You are welcome at my house," the
old man said. "Let me supply whatever
you need. Only don't spend the night
in the square." 21So he took him into his
house and fed his donkeys. After they
had washed their feet, they had something to eat and drink.[i]
22While they were enjoying themselves,[j] some of the wicked men[k] of the
city surrounded the house. Pounding on
the door, they shouted to the old man
who owned the house, "Bring out the
man who came to your house so we can
have sex with him.[l]"
23The owner of the house went outside[m] and said to them, "No, my friends,
don't be so vile. Since this man is my
guest, don't do this outrageous thing.[n]
24Look, here is my virgin daughter,[o] and
his concubine. I will bring them out to
you now, and you can use them and do to
them whatever you wish. But as for this
man, don't do such an outrageous thing."

[a] *18* Hebrew, Vulgate, Syriac and Targum; Septuagint *going home*

---

father-in-law's hospitality borders on the excessive: Six times he offers hospitality, persuading the Levite to spend five days with him.

19:12–15 Ironically, by seeking to avoid the potential inhospitality of a foreign city, the Levite and his party suffer that very fate, or even worse, in Gibeah, an Israelite city. The people of Gibeah abuse (in general) the Levite and his party passively (by refusing basic hospitality) before the rapists actively abuse the concubine (vv. 15, 22).

19:16–20 Finally, an old man from Ephraim, a temporary resident in Gibeah and not a Benjamite, comes by and questions the party. The old man welcomes them to spend the night at his house, "only don't spend the night in the square" (v. 20). The latter clause is reminiscent of the story of Lot in Sodom in Ge 19:1–11.

19:23–25 The old man, who appears initially to be the model host, ends up being the one who comes up with the idea of throwing the concubine (and his own virgin daughter) to the horde at the door. The man condemns the horde for thinking of doing this outrageous act upon the Levite and yet, ironically, ends up doing a foolish thing in making such an offer. Amazingly, there is no protest from the Levite. When they refuse to listen to the old man, it is the Levite who seizes his concubine and hands her over to the horde.

25But the men would not listen to him.
So the man took his concubine and sent
her outside to them, and they raped her
and abused her[p] throughout the night,
and at dawn they let her go. 26At daybreak the woman went back to the house
where her master was staying, fell down
at the door and lay there until daylight.
27When her master got up in the morning and opened the door of the house
and stepped out to continue on his way,
there lay his concubine, fallen in the
doorway of the house, with her hands
on the threshold. 28He said to her, "Get
up; let's go." But there was no answer.
Then the man put her on his donkey and
set out for home.
29When he reached home, he took a
knife[q] and cut up his concubine, limb
by limb, into twelve parts and sent them
into all the areas of Israel.[r] 30Everyone
who saw it was saying to one another,
"Such a thing has never been seen or
done, not since the day the Israelites
came up out of Egypt.[s] Just imagine!
We must do something! So speak up![t]"

The Israelites Punish the Benjamites

20 Then all Israel[u] from Dan to Beersheba[v] and from the land of Gilead came together as one[w] and assembled[x]
before the LORD in Mizpah. 2The leaders
of all the people of the tribes of Israel
took their places in the assembly of God's
people, four hundred thousand men[y]
armed with swords. 3(The Benjamites
heard that the Israelites had gone up to
Mizpah.) Then the Israelites said, "Tell us
how this awful thing happened."
4So the Levite, the husband of the
murdered woman, said, "I and my concubine came to Gibeah[z] in Benjamin to
spend the night.[a] 5During the night the
men of Gibeah came after me and surrounded the house, intending to kill me.[b]
They raped my concubine, and she died.[c]
6I took my concubine, cut her into pieces
and sent one piece to each region of Israel's inheritance,[d] because they committed this lewd and outrageous act[e] in Israel. 7Now, all you Israelites, speak up and
tell me what you have decided to do.[f]"
8All the men rose up together as one,
saying, "None of us will go home. No, not
one of us will return to his house. 9But
now this is what we'll do to Gibeah: We'll
go up against it in the order decided by
casting lots.[g] 10We'll take ten men out
of every hundred from all the tribes of
Israel, and a hundred from a thousand,

19:25 [p] 1Sa 31:4
19:29 [q] Ge 22:6 [r] Jdg 20:6; 1Sa 11:7
19:30 [s] Hos 9:9 [t] Jdg 20:7; Pr 13:10
20:1 [u] Jdg 21:5 [v] 1Sa 3:20; 2Sa 3:10; 1Ki 4:25 [w] 1Sa 11:7 [x] 1Sa 7:5
20:2 [y] Jdg 8:10
20:4 [z] Jos 15:57 [a] Jdg 19:15
20:5 [b] Jdg 19:22 [c] Jdg 19:25-26
20:6 [d] Jdg 19:29 [e] Jos 7:15; Jdg 19:23
20:7 [f] Jdg 19:30
20:9 [g] Lev 16:8

Jdg 19:30 ❖ What might cause God's own people to fall into complete moral corruption?

19:27–28 If the people of Gibeah were callous to the sons of Belial, then this Levite shows a deeper level of callousness, because this is a woman with whom he is in relationship. The Levite commands her with almost unbelievable callousness to "get up" (v. 28) because he is ready to go.

19:29–30 What are the real motives of this nameless Levite? The act of dismemberment is a graphic means of calling everyone to arms. It is highly ironic that the one who issues such a call for justice is himself so selfishly insensitive and self-involved regarding the crime itself.

19:1–30 There are many victims like the concubine in our world today. They are the hapless, ill-fated casualties of a world that either ignores God or outright rejects him. These victims most often are what our society, in one way or another, deems the "less important" people: women, children, and disadvantaged or marginalized people who have no power to defend themselves. These people deserve our compassion and pursuit of justice on their behalf. They also desperately need to hear about Jesus Christ's love.

20:1–17 The reader knows the Levite's dismemberment of the concubine is nothing but an expression of the self-centered callousness he displayed toward her at Gibeah; however, those who have received the ghastly pieces interpret it as a zealous act of covenant faithfulness and a call to religious war.

20:4–7 Here the Levite bears false witness. The general storyline is correct, but his testimony conceals his own involvement in the incident at Gibeah. In the previous account, the wicked men demanded that the old man bring the Levite out so that they could have sex with him (19:22). The Levite now testifies: "Me they intended to kill" (20:5; alternate translation).

20:8–11 Without any additional testimony (contrary to Dt 19:15), the tribal assembly condemns the crime against the Levite's concubine and takes steps to punish the guilty. It seems that the procedure for condemning Gibeah derives from a law recorded in Dt 13:12–18. While the law there specifically applies to idolatry, the abomination committed by the wicked men of Gibeah may have been understood as contrary to proper covenantal behavior.

Unfortunately, the Israelites do not follow the stipulations of this law when they implement it. The leadership of the assembly does not "inquire, probe and investigate it thoroughly" (Dt 13:14a). They simply accept the Levite's version of what has happened.

and a thousand from ten thousand, to
get provisions for the army. Then, when
the army arrives at Gibeah[a] in Benjamin,
it can give them what they deserve for
this outrageous act done in Israel." 11So
all the Israelites got together and united
as one against the city.[h]
12The tribes of Israel sent messengers
throughout the tribe of Benjamin, saying, "What about this awful crime that
was committed among you? 13Now turn
those wicked men[i] of Gibeah over to us
so that we may put them to death and
purge the evil from Israel.[j]"
But the Benjamites would not listen to
their fellow Israelites. 14From their towns
they came together at Gibeah to fight
against the Israelites. 15At once the Benjamites mobilized twenty-six thousand
swordsmen from their towns, in addition
to seven hundred able young men from
those living in Gibeah. 16Among all these
soldiers there were seven hundred select
troops who were left-handed,[k] each of
whom could sling a stone at a hair and
not miss.
17Israel, apart from Benjamin, mustered four hundred thousand swordsmen, all of them fit for battle.
18The Israelites went up to Bethel[b]
and inquired of God.[l] They said, "Who
of us is to go up first to fight[m] against
the Benjamites?"
The LORD replied, "Judah shall go first."
19The next morning the Israelites
got up and pitched camp near Gibeah.
20The Israelites went out to fight the
Benjamites and took up battle positions
against them at Gibeah. 21The Benjamites came out of Gibeah and cut down
twenty-two thousand Israelites[n] on the
battlefield that day. 22But the Israelites
encouraged one another and again took
up their positions where they had stationed themselves the first day. 23The
Israelites went up and wept before the
LORD until evening,[o] and they inquired
of the LORD. They said, "Shall we go up
again to fight[p] against the Benjamites,
our fellow Israelites?"
The LORD answered, "Go up against
them."
24Then the Israelites drew near to Benjamin the second day. 25This time, when
the Benjamites came out from Gibeah
to oppose them, they cut down another
eighteen thousand Israelites,[q] all of them
armed with swords.
26Then all the Israelites, the whole
army, went up to Bethel, and there they
sat weeping before the LORD.[r] They fasted that day until evening and presented
burnt offerings and fellowship offerings
to the LORD.[s] 27And the Israelites inquired of the LORD. (In those days the ark
of the covenant of God[t] was there, 28with
Phinehas son of Eleazar,[u] the son of Aaron, ministering before it.)[v] They asked,
"Shall we go up again to fight against the
Benjamites, our fellow Israelites, or not?"
The LORD responded, "Go, for tomorrow I will give them into your hands.[w]"
29Then Israel set an ambush[x] around
Gibeah. 30They went up against the Benjamites on the third day and took up positions against Gibeah as they had done
before. 31The Benjamites came out to
meet them and were drawn away[y] from
the city. They began to inflict casualties on the Israelites as before, so that
about thirty men fell in the open field
and on the roads — the one leading to
Bethel and the other to Gibeah. 32While

Jdg 20:26–28 ❖ Why is it important to practice lament and have a contrite heart before God?

20:11 [h] ver 1
20:13 [i] Dt 13:13; Jdg 19:22 [j] Dt 17:12
20:16 [k] Jdg 3:15; 1Ch 12:2
20:18 [l] ver 26-27; Nu 27:21 [m] ver 23,28
20:21 [n] ver 25
20:23 [o] Jos 7:6 [p] ver 18
20:25 [q] ver 21
20:26 [r] ver 23 [s] Jdg 21:4
20:27 [t] Jos 18:1
20:28 [u] Jos 24:33 [v] Dt 18:5 [w] Jdg 7:9
20:29 [x] Jos 8:2,4
20:31 [y] Jos 8:16

[a] *10* One Hebrew manuscript; most Hebrew manuscripts *Geba,* a variant of *Gibeah* [b] *18* Or *to the house of God*; also in verse 26

20:18–48 The Israelites' first inquiry is, "Who of us is to go up first to fight against the Benjamites?" (v. 18a). Yahweh's response is that Judah is to go first, but there is no promise of victory (v. 18b). Though the Israelites attack Gibeah en masse, they are severely defeated (vv. 19–21).
20:22–25 The Israelites once again attack en masse, and once again they are defeated severely by the Benjamites, though not quite as badly (vv. 24–25).
20:26–28 Before the second battle, the Israelites wept before Yahweh; now before they ask of God again, they weep, fast, and offer sacrifices (v. 26). Then the Israelites set an ambush and destroy all the towns, including the animals.

✠ **20:1–48** It is not uncommon today that the religious charlatan, the spiritual quack (like the Levite in this narrative), gets the biggest response from gullible Christians who do not inquire about the real credentials of the impostor. Yet the truly biblical preacher may find the assembly to which he speaks emotionally moved, but with no real resolve to follow God's directives.

the Benjamites were saying, "We are
defeating them as before,"[z] the Israelites were saying, "Let's retreat and draw
them away from the city to the roads."
33All the men of Israel moved from
their places and took up positions at
Baal Tamar, and the Israelite ambush
charged out of its place[a] on the west[a] of
Gibeah.[b] 34Then ten thousand of Israel's
able young men made a frontal attack
on Gibeah. The fighting was so heavy
that the Benjamites did not realize[b] how
near disaster was.[c] 35The LORD defeated
Benjamin[d] before Israel, and on that day
the Israelites struck down 25,100 Benjamites, all armed with swords. 36Then the
Benjamites saw that they were beaten.
Now the men of Israel had given way[e]
before Benjamin, because they relied on
the ambush they had set near Gibeah.
37Those who had been in ambush made a
sudden dash into Gibeah, spread out and
put the whole city to the sword.[f] 38The
Israelites had arranged with the ambush
that they should send up a great cloud
of smoke[g] from the city, 39and then the
Israelites would counterattack.
The Benjamites had begun to inflict
casualties on the Israelites (about thirty),
and they said, "We are defeating them
as in the first battle."[h] 40But when the
column of smoke began to rise from the
city, the Benjamites turned and saw the
whole city going up in smoke.[i] 41Then
the Israelites counterattacked, and the
Benjamites were terrified, because they
realized that disaster had come on them.
42So they fled before the Israelites in the
direction of the wilderness, but they
could not escape the battle. And the Israelites who came out of the towns cut
them down there. 43They surrounded
the Benjamites, chased them and easily[c]
overran them in the vicinity of Gibeah
on the east. 44Eighteen thousand Benjamites fell, all of them valiant fighters.[j]
45As they turned and fled toward the
wilderness to the rock of Rimmon,[k] the
Israelites cut down five thousand men
along the roads. They kept pressing after the Benjamites as far as Gidom and
struck down two thousand more.
46On that day twenty-five thousand
Benjamite swordsmen fell, all of them
valiant fighters. 47But six hundred of
them turned and fled into the wilderness to the rock of Rimmon, where they
stayed four months. 48The men of Israel
went back to Benjamin and put all the
towns to the sword, including the animals and everything else they found.
All the towns they came across they set
on fire.[l]

Wives for the Benjamites

21 The men of Israel had taken an
oath[m] at Mizpah:[n] "Not one of us
will give[o] his daughter in marriage to a
Benjamite."
2The people went to Bethel,[d] where
they sat before God until evening, raising their voices and weeping bitterly.
3"LORD, God of Israel," they cried, "why
has this happened to Israel? Why should
one tribe be missing from Israel today?"
4Early the next day the people built an
altar and presented burnt offerings and
fellowship offerings.[p]
5Then the Israelites asked, "Who from
all the tribes of Israel[q] has failed to assemble before the LORD?" For they had
taken a solemn oath that anyone who
failed to assemble before the LORD at
Mizpah was to be put to death.
6Now the Israelites grieved for the
tribe of Benjamin, their fellow Israelites. "Today one tribe is cut off from Israel," they said. 7"How can we provide
wives for those who are left, since we
have taken an oath[r] by the LORD not
to give them any of our daughters in

20:32 [z] ver 39
20:33 [a] Jos 8:19
20:34 [b] Jos 8:14 [c] Isa 47:11
20:35 [d] 1Sa 9:21
20:36 [e] Jos 8:15
20:37 [f] Jos 8:19
20:38 [g] Jos 8:20
20:39 [h] ver 32
20:40 [i] Jos 8:20
20:44 [j] Ps 76:5
20:45 [k] Jos 15:32; Jdg 21:13
20:48 [l] Jdg 21:23
21:1 [m] Jos 9:18 [n] Jdg 20:1 [o] ver 7,18
21:4 [p] Jdg 20:26; 2Sa 24:25
21:5 [q] Jdg 5:23; 20:1
21:7 [r] ver 1

[a] *33* Some Septuagint manuscripts and Vulgate; the meaning of the Hebrew for this word is uncertain. [b] *33* Hebrew *Geba,* a variant of *Gibeah* [c] *43* The meaning of the Hebrew for this word is uncertain. [d] *2* Or *to the house of God*

21:1–5 The Israelites have sworn two oaths at Mizpah before the battles, and these create dilemmas. The first, given in parenthetical flashback in v. 1, is that the Israelites had promised not to give their daughters in marriage to the Benjamites. The excessive slaughter of the Benjamites and the danger of tribal extinction expose the rashness of that oath.

The people assemble at Bethel, raising their voices and weeping bitterly, but Yahweh does not answer. Early the next day the Israelites resume the inquiry by building an altar and presenting burnt offerings and fellowship offerings (v. 4).

21:6–14 Verses 6–7 record the emotional dilemma created by the Israelites' first oath. Ironically, they discover that Jabesh Gilead did not send any contingent to the war. So the second oath sworn at Mizpah (v. 5) is now conveniently implemented. Just as the Danites had attacked the unsuspecting town of Laish (18:27–28), so the Israelites attack the unsuspecting town of Jabesh Gilead.

marriage?" 8Then they asked, "Which one of the tribes of Israel failed to assemble before the LORD at Mizpah?" They discovered that no one from Jabesh Gilead[s] had come to the camp for the assembly. 9For when they counted the people, they found that none of the people of Jabesh Gilead were there.

10So the assembly sent twelve thousand fighting men with instructions to go to Jabesh Gilead and put to the sword those living there, including the women and children. 11"This is what you are to do," they said. "Kill every male and every woman who is not a virgin.[t]" 12They found among the people living in Jabesh Gilead four hundred young women who had never slept with a man, and they took them to the camp at Shiloh[u] in Canaan.

13Then the whole assembly sent an offer of peace[v] to the Benjamites at the rock of Rimmon.[w] 14So the Benjamites returned at that time and were given the women of Jabesh Gilead who had been spared. But there were not enough for all of them.

15The people grieved for Benjamin,[x] because the LORD had made a gap in the tribes of Israel. 16And the elders of the assembly said, "With the women of Benjamin destroyed, how shall we provide wives for the men who are left? 17The Benjamite survivors must have heirs," they said, "so that a tribe of Israel will not be wiped out. 18We can't give them our daughters as wives, since we Israelites have taken this oath: 'Cursed be anyone who gives[y] a wife to a Benjamite.' 19But look, there is the annual festival of the LORD in Shiloh,[z] which lies north of Bethel, east of the road that goes from Bethel to Shechem, and south of Lebonah."

20So they instructed the Benjamites, saying, "Go and hide in the vineyards 21and watch. When the young women of Shiloh come out to join in the dancing,[a] rush from the vineyards and each of you seize one of them to be your wife. Then return to the land of Benjamin. 22When their fathers or brothers complain to us, we will say to them, 'Do us the favor of helping them, because we did not get wives for them during the war. You will not be guilty of breaking your oath because you did not give[b] your daughters to them.' "

23So that is what the Benjamites did. While the young women were dancing, each man caught one and carried her off to be his wife. Then they returned to their inheritance and rebuilt the towns and settled in them.[c]

24At that time the Israelites left that place and went home to their tribes and clans, each to his own inheritance.

25In those days Israel had no king; everyone did as they saw fit.[d]

21:8 [s] 1Sa 11:1; 31:11
21:11 [t] Nu 31:17-18
21:12 [u] Jos 18:1
21:13 [v] Dt 20:10 [w] Jdg 20:47
21:15 [x] ver 6
21:18 [y] ver 1
21:19 [z] Jos 18:1; Jdg 18:31; 1Sa 1:3
21:21 [a] Ex 15:20; Jdg 11:34
21:22 [b] ver 1,18
21:23 [c] Jdg 20:48
21:25 [d] Dt 12:8; Jdg 17:6; 18:1; 19:1

Jdg 21:25 ❖ What happens when people do as they see fit and act as though they are in charge of their own lives? How do we see this happening in the world today?

21:13–14 The operation yields only four hundred young women, so they are two hundred short of the required total. This shortfall will lead the Israelites to their final solution.

21:15–25 The only other time that the elders of the entire nation of Israel are mentioned in this book is 2:7. In contrast, the elders in 21:15–25 are the ones who devise a shameful plan to supply the Benjamites with the women needed to make up the shortage from Jabesh Gilead. In so doing, the elders devise a plan that is nothing short of another mass rape.

21:19–20 The annual festival may have been a local one, or in light of the reference to vineyards (v. 20), it may refer to the Festival of Tabernacles.

21:22–23 With the Benjamites "seizing" wives, the fathers are not technically "giving" them to the Benjamites. The Benjamites return and rebuild their cities (v. 23). In the end, what has been accomplished? Not only has justice not been served, but many injustices have happened in the feeble attempt to implement justice for the original atrocity.

21:25 The book ends with the powerful refrain, "In those days Israel had no king; every man did what was right in his own eyes" (alternate translation). Sadly, the accuracy of the second line of the refrain is forcefully demonstrated in this final story.

✜ **21:1–25** Whenever religious reasons are used to justify actions, there is room for a closer look. If in the process God's moral laws are broken, the actions are invariably wrong. We should be careful never to use one law or oath to circumvent another, for destruction and tragedy will surely follow.

When God's kingship is unacknowledged—when his law is ignored, when the morality that he advocates is circumvented—incredible, appalling disasters are the outcome. When rash oaths in his name are used to manipulate and abuse people, when leaders use the ends to justify the means, when God does not exist in the lives of his people, the consequences are outrageously appalling.

Ruth

Author: Unknown

Audience: God's chosen people, the Israelites

Date: Ruth lived during the time of the judges; the book was written sometime after David became king in about 1010 BC

Theme: God uses the faithfulness of Ruth and Boaz to fill Naomi's emptiness by sustaining her life and providing an heir.

PERSPECTIVE

The book of Ruth contains a wonderful love story, which, while set in the period of the judges, contrasts greatly with the general chaos and disobedience of that period. In a refreshing way the book provides an antithesis to the incessantly negative message about the conditions in Israel during that time by underscoring God's tremendous blessing in the midst of great familial distress.

Ruth's is a story of great personal devotion and of God's quiet care for the disenfranchised and disadvantaged through the bonds of family. In it we see God's plan to establish the foundations of the lineage of Jesus.

For additional perspective on Ruth's story, turn to the Introduction to Judges.

Reading Ruth

The book of Ruth should be read at one time, for these four brief chapters constitute a single story. Since this story happened during the time of the judges, you may wish to review the Introduction to the book of Judges.

TAKING THE NEXT STEPS

Through this brief story, centering on one particular family and occurring at the time of the judges (see 1:1), the Israelites discovered that the Lord was not only their personal God but the universal God, the God for all nations. Ruth, a Moabitess, was taken into the tribe of Judah, and through a series of events guided by God's providence, she became an ancestor of the great King David.

In reading the story, we become convinced of several things. (1) Since sin was rampant during the time of the judges, we are reminded that

Event	Date
Israelites enter Canaan (c. 1406 BC)	1400 BC
Judges begin to rule (c. 1375 BC)	
Deborah's rule (c. 1209-1169 BC)	
Samuel's birth (c. 1105 BC)	
Samson's rule (c. 1075-1055 BC)	
David named king (c. 1010 BC)	
Book of Ruth written (c. 1000 BC)	
Division of the kingdom (930 BC)	

Timeline scale: 1400 BC, 1300, 1200, 1100, 1000, 900, 800, 700, 600, 500, 400

even in the worst of times, God is still at work. (2) God loves every one of us, regardless of our racial or national background; all those who commit themselves to the Lord Jesus Christ he accepts as his children. (3) God places a high priority on the family and wants us to do everything we can to preserve it for his sake. (4) In guarding the sanctity of our families, we are not alone, for God cares for us and he will have his way in our lives.

Key Verse

Ruth replied, "Don't urge me to leave you or to turn back from you. Where you go I will go, and where you stay I will stay. Your people will be my people and your God my God."

—Ruth 1:16

WHAT TO LOOK FOR IN RUTH

- Ruth decides to join the tribe of Judah (ch. 1)
- Boaz is kind to Ruth (ch. 2)
- Ruth courageously reaches out to Boaz, who responds generously (ch. 3)
- Boaz and Ruth marry and have a child, Obed (ch. 4)

Naomi Loses Her Husband and Sons

1 In the days when the judges ruled,[a][a] there was a famine in the land.[b] So a man from Bethlehem in Judah, together with his wife and two sons, went to live for a while in the country of Moab.[c] 2The man's name was Elimelek, his wife's name was Naomi, and the names of his two sons were Mahlon and Kilion. They were Ephrathites from Bethlehem,[d] Judah. And they went to Moab and lived there.

3Now Elimelek, Naomi's husband, died, and she was left with her two sons. 4They married Moabite women, one named Orpah and the other Ruth.[e] After they had lived there about ten years, 5both Mahlon and Kilion also died, and Naomi was left without her two sons and her husband.

Naomi and Ruth Return to Bethlehem

6When Naomi heard in Moab that the LORD had come to the aid of his people[f] by providing food[g] for them, she and her daughters-in-law prepared to return home from there. 7With her two

1:1 [a]Jdg 2:16-18 [b]Ge 12:10; Ps 105:16 [c]Jdg 3:30
1:2 [d]Ge 35:19
1:4 [e]Mt 1:5
1:6 [f]Ex 4:31; Jer 29:10; Zep 2:7 [g]Ps 132:15; Mt 6:11

[a] 1 Traditionally *judged*

1:1–2 The story is set in the period of the judges (v. 1a). To its original hearers, such an allusion must have conjured up visions of the moral depravity that prevailed in that time. Ironically, the man comes from Bethlehem, which means "house of bread," but there is no bread/food in that city.
1:3–5 Naomi is left battered by the relentless onslaught of one tragic event after another.
1:6 This is the first time Yahweh is mentioned in the story, and it is in the context of his compassionate provision for his people. As Yahweh has provided food for his people, will he yet provide fertility to Ruth and an offspring for Naomi?
1:7–13 Naomi's urging must have been with some mixed feelings. To urge Orpah and Ruth to return to Moab necessitates that she will travel home completely alone. Naomi pronounces a blessing on the women, making it abundantly clear that, at least in her understanding, she is the target of God's overwhelming power and wrath.

daughters-in-law she left the place where
she had been living and set out on the
road that would take them back to the
land of Judah.
8Then Naomi said to her two daughters-in-law, "Go back, each of you, to your
mother's home. May the LORD show you
kindness,[h] as you have shown kindness
to your dead husbands[i] and to me. 9May
the LORD grant that each of you will find
rest[j] in the home of another husband."
Then she kissed them goodbye and
they wept aloud 10and said to her, "We
will go back with you to your people."
11But Naomi said, "Return home, my
daughters. Why would you come with
me? Am I going to have any more sons,
who could become your husbands?[k] 12Re-
turn home, my daughters; I am too old to
have another husband. Even if I thought
there was still hope for me—even if I
had a husband tonight and then gave
birth to sons— 13would you wait until
they grew up? Would you remain unmarried for them? No, my daughters. It is
more bitter for me than for you, because
the LORD's hand has turned against me![l]"
14At this they wept aloud again. Then
Orpah kissed her mother-in-law[m] goodbye, but Ruth clung to her.[n]
15"Look," said Naomi, "your sister-in-
law is going back to her people and her
gods.[o] Go back with her."
16But Ruth replied, "Don't urge me
to leave you[p] or to turn back from you.
Where you go I will go, and where you

1:8 [h] Ru 2:20; 2Ti 1:16 [i] ver 5
1:9 [j] Ru 3:1
1:11 [k] Ge 38:11; Dt 25:5
1:13 [l] Jdg 2:15; Job 4:5; 19:21; Ps 32:4
1:14 [m] Ru 2:11 [n] Pr 17:17; 18:24
1:15 [o] Jos 24:14; Jdg 11:24
1:16 [p] 2Ki 2:2

1:14–19a Orpah kisses Naomi goodbye, but Ruth swears her commitment to Naomi in the name of Israel's God, thus acknowledging him as her God. The essence of the oath is that only death will separate Ruth from Naomi.

PEOPLE TO KNOW // RUTH

RUTH 1:16–18: Deuteronomy 23:3 directed that no Moabite can enter the assembly of God's people, even in the tenth generation. How surprising, then, to read the story of Ruth here in the OT.

Ruth married an Israelite named Mahlon whose family had moved to Moab to escape a severe famine. In time, Mahlon, his father, and his brother died, leaving his mother Naomi alone with her two Moabite daughters-in-law. When Naomi learned the famine in Bethlehem had passed, she decided to return home. She asked her daughters-in-law to stay in Moab. Ruth refused, pledging full devotion to Naomi and to Naomi's God (Ru 1:16–17).

In Bethlehem, Ruth bravely volunteered to glean in the fields at harvest time to find food for herself and Naomi. In the fields, she caught the eye of Boaz, the field owner. Boaz turned out to be a relative of Naomi's deceased husband, and he praised Ruth for her loyalty to Naomi. He promised Ruth protection in his fields and provided generously for her and Naomi.

Ruth showed her loyalty once again when she followed Naomi's instructions to approach Boaz at the threshing floor at night to propose marriage to him. As a Moabite, this was a risky action. But Boaz responded graciously, promising to do whatever he could to provide for Ruth and Naomi. In the end, Ruth and Boaz married, and she soon had a son they named Obed—the grandfather of King David.

Matthew lists Ruth in the genealogy of Jesus, one of only five women he includes (Mt 1:5). Not only was Ruth the great-grandmother of David; she is in the lineage of the King of kings!

APPLICATION ✤ Boaz calls Ruth "a woman of noble character" (Ru 3:11). Ruth first demonstrated her nobility through her deep loyalty to Naomi. She worked to provide for Naomi, even though she herself was a vulnerable foreigner from the despised land of Moab.

Sometimes when we feel uncomfortable or out of place, we may try to hide or withdraw from contact with others. We think we can't make a difference in the world because we're not in a position of power or one of the "elite." But Ruth shows that all our actions—being loyal to a friend, helping someone less fortunate, being faithful to a promise—all these things become our witness and show our character to others. We don't have to wait until we fit in or become influential. We can serve God's purposes in whatever situation God places us.

stay I will stay. Your people will be my
people and your God my God.[q] 17Where
you die I will die, and there I will be buried. May the LORD deal with me, be it ever
so severely,[r] if even death separates you
and me." 18When Naomi realized that
Ruth was determined to go with her, she
stopped urging her.[s]

19So the two women went on until
they came to Bethlehem. When they
arrived in Bethlehem, the whole town
was stirred[t] because of them, and the
women exclaimed, "Can this be Naomi?"

20"Don't call me Naomi,[a]" she told
them. "Call me Mara,[b] because the Almighty[c][u] has made my life very bitter.[v]
21I went away full, but the LORD has
brought me back empty.[w] Why call me
Naomi? The LORD has afflicted[d] me;
the Almighty has brought misfortune
upon me."

22So Naomi returned from Moab accompanied by Ruth the Moabite, her
daughter-in-law, arriving in Bethlehem
as the barley harvest[x] was beginning.[y]

Ruth Meets Boaz in the Grain Field

2 Now Naomi had a relative[z] on her
husband's side, a man of standing
from the clan of Elimelek,[a] whose name
was Boaz.[b]

2And Ruth the Moabite said to Naomi,
"Let me go to the fields and pick up the
leftover grain[c] behind anyone in whose
eyes I find favor."

Naomi said to her, "Go ahead, my
daughter." 3So she went out, entered a
field and began to glean behind the harvesters. As it turned out, she was working
in a field belonging to Boaz, who was
from the clan of Elimelek.

4Just then Boaz arrived from Bethlehem and greeted the harvesters, "The
LORD be with you![d]"

"The LORD bless you![e]" they answered.

5Boaz asked the overseer of his harvesters, "Who does that young woman
belong to?"

6The overseer replied, "She is the Moabite[f] who came back from Moab with
Naomi. 7She said, 'Please let me glean
and gather among the sheaves behind
the harvesters.' She came into the field
and has remained here from morning
till now, except for a short rest in the
shelter."

8So Boaz said to Ruth, "My daughter,
listen to me. Don't go and glean in another field and don't go away from here.
Stay here with the women who work for
me. 9Watch the field where the men are

1:16 [q] Ru 2:11,12
1:17 [r] 1Sa 3:17; 25:22; 2Sa 19:13; 2Ki 6:31
1:18 [s] Ac 21:14
1:19 [t] Mt 21:10
1:20 [u] Ex 6:3 [v] ver 13; Job 6:4
1:21 [w] Job 1:21
1:22 [x] Ex 9:31; Ru 2:23 [y] 2Sa 21:9
2:1 [z] Ru 3:2,12 [a] Ru 1:2 [b] Ru 4:21
2:2 [c] ver 7; Lev 19:9; 23:22; Dt 24:19
2:4 [d] Jdg 6:12; Lk 1:28; 2Th 3:16 [e] Ps 129:7-8
2:6 [f] Ru 1:22

Ru 1:16–17 ❖ How can we show Ruth-like loyalty and love to those who are in need?

Ru 2:3 ❖ How does God work through seemingly random coincidences? Where have we witnessed God's hand in the mundane?

[a] 20 *Naomi* means *pleasant.* [b] 20 *Mara* means *bitter.* [c] 20 Hebrew *Shaddai*; also in verse 21
[d] 21 Or *has testified against*

1:19b–22 Naomi has returned home empty, unfulfilled, and bitter. In a subtle touch of the narrator, Naomi utters her complaint as though Ruth, whose words of loving commitment still ring in the readers' ears, has never pronounced these words at all. Yahweh has indeed not brought Naomi back empty.

APPLICATION ✚ 1:1–22 What the world attributes to large impersonal forces of nature and chance, the Scriptures attribute to the sovereignty of God. This is a fundamental teaching of the Bible, and the book of Ruth stresses that teaching throughout its chapters. How we respond to the circumstances that God may bring into our lives often determines further outcomes.

2:1–3 Verse 1 serves as a parenthetical digression in which one of the major characters is introduced. This relative is described as "a man of standing" from the family/clan of Elimelek (v. 1b).

The storyteller adds an important clause: "As it turned out, she was working in a field belonging to Boaz . . ." (v. 3). God, who is constantly working behind the scenes, is pictured as directing and controlling this situation through his gracious providence.

2:4–5 The initial greetings between Boaz and his workers in v. 4 builds suspense by focusing on Boaz, a man whose first words are a blessing on his workers in the name of Yahweh. Such a greeting speaks to his character and foreshadows his generosity.

Boaz immediately questions his overseer about the identity of the unknown young woman gleaning in his field by asking about her origins (v. 5). The overseer insinuates that she is gathering too much grain.

2:6–9 Boaz addresses Ruth, not the overseer. In a series of six short statements with a final seventh conditional statement, Boaz outlines a graciously generous program for Ruth in his field despite the fact that she is a Moabite woman. In his seven statements Boaz is granting her more than the ordinary rights of gleaning. Boaz's provision in Ruth's situation is extraordinary.

harvesting, and follow along after the
women. I have told the men not to lay
a hand on you. And whenever you are
thirsty, go and get a drink from the water
jars the men have filled."
10 At this, she bowed down with her
face to the ground.[g] She asked him, "Why
have I found such favor in your eyes that
you notice me[h] — a foreigner?[i]"
11 Boaz replied, "I've been told all
about what you have done for your
mother-in-law[j] since the death of your
husband — how you left your father and
mother and your homeland and came
to live with a people you did not know
before.[k] 12 May the LORD repay you for
what you have done. May you be richly
rewarded by the LORD,[l] the God of Israel,
under whose wings[m] you have come to
take refuge.[n]"
13 "May I continue to find favor in your
eyes, my lord," she said. "You have put
me at ease by speaking kindly to your
servant — though I do not have the
standing of one of your servants."
14 At mealtime Boaz said to her, "Come
over here. Have some bread and dip it in
the wine vinegar."
When she sat down with the harvesters, he offered her some roasted grain.
She ate all she wanted and had some left
over.[o] 15 As she got up to glean, Boaz gave
orders to his men, "Let her gather among
the sheaves and don't reprimand her.
16 Even pull out some stalks for her from
the bundles and leave them for her to
pick up, and don't rebuke her."
17 So Ruth gleaned in the field until
evening. Then she threshed the barley
she had gathered, and it amounted to
about an ephah.[a] 18 She carried it back
to town, and her mother-in-law saw
how much she had gathered. Ruth also
brought out and gave her what she had
left over[p] after she had eaten enough.
19 Her mother-in-law asked her, "Where
did you glean today? Where did you
work? Blessed be the man who took
notice of you![q]"
Then Ruth told her mother-in-law
about the one at whose place she had
been working. "The name of the man
I worked with today is Boaz," she said.
20 "The LORD bless him!" Naomi said to
her daughter-in-law. "He has not stopped
showing his kindness[r] to the living and
the dead." She added, "That man is our
close relative; he is one of our guardian-
redeemers.[b][s]"
21 Then Ruth the Moabite said, "He
even said to me, 'Stay with my workers until they finish harvesting all my
grain.'"
22 Naomi said to Ruth her daughter-in-law, "It will be good for you, my

2:10 [g] 1Sa 25:23 [h] Ps 41:1 [i] Dt 15:3
2:11 [j] Ru 1:14 [k] Ru 1:16-17
2:12 [l] 1Sa 24:19 [m] Ps 17:8; 36:7; 57:1; 61:4; 63:7; 91:4 [n] Ru 1:16
2:14 [o] ver 18
2:18 [p] ver 14
2:19 [q] ver 10; Ps 41:1
2:20 [r] Ru 3:10; 2Sa 2:5; Pr 17:17 [s] Ru 3:9,12; 4:1,14

[a] *17* That is, probably about 30 pounds or about 13 kilograms [b] *20* The Hebrew word for *guardian-redeemer* is a legal term for one who has the obligation to redeem a relative in serious difficulty (see Lev. 25:25-55).

2:10 Overwhelmed by Boaz's unexpected protection and generosity, Ruth falls to the ground. This gesture consists of dropping to the knees and touching the forehead to the ground. She is completely surprised. Boaz's action is once again evidence of God's providence.
2:11-12 Boaz's reply is permeated with praise and admiration. He affirms what Ruth has solemnly vowed to Naomi. Boaz then wishes that Yahweh will "repay" Ruth for her actions and prays that she may "be richly rewarded by the LORD" (v. 12).
2:13 Ruth expresses her gratitude, referring to herself here as "servant," although she does not really even have this status. The term is an expression of Ruth's humility.
2:14-16 Boaz welcomes her to the intimacy of the noon meal, invites her to eat, and bestows so much roasted grain on her that she eats all she wants and still has some left over.
2:17b-19 Ruth has threshed roughly enough for the two women to eat for a little more than a week. The large quantity and leftovers from the noon meal clearly lead into Naomi's surprised reaction and excited questions in v. 19a. It is clear from Naomi's two questions that she is not concerned about finding out a particular geographic location where Ruth has gleaned but is concerned about who the owner of the field is.
2:20-21 Naomi pronounces a blessing on Boaz. Naomi also now adds some crucial information: Naomi's revelation of Boaz's relationship to them is important to the plot because it creates anticipation of events to come.
2:22-23 The end of this passage stresses that Ruth is still living with her mother-in-law, which is significant to the plot of the story. Ruth has gleaned for both the barley and wheat harvests in the fields of Boaz, but there has been no development in their relationship. What looked like a clear potential solution to their widowed situation seems to have died out.

2:1-23 It is certainly the case that Boaz and Ruth represent ideal models of extraordinary character. It is not in some religious setting that Ruth or Boaz manifest graciousness and loving-kindness toward each other. Rather, it is in the daily workplace, the place where too often such consideration is lacking. Such manifestations of this kind of love are the result of commitment to the Lord, and both Ruth and Boaz exhibit these qualities to those around them. Certainly,

ISRAEL AND MOAB

Born of the incestuous relationship between Lot and his daughter, Moab represented a constant threat to the Israelites. In every way, they embodied the dangers and temptations God wanted Israel to eschew. And yet, it was a Moabite named Ruth who would stand in direct relation to Jesus. This chart examines the biblical history of Israel and Moab.

STORIES OF CONFLICT	STORIES OF COMPROMISE	WORDS OF CONDEMNATION
Throughout the OT, Israel and Moab were in constant military conflict.	Though Israel was called to be holy and set apart, we find them constantly compromising this call in favor of other gods, including those of Moab.	God spoke through his prophets not only to Israel, but also to nations around them. Moab was addressed many times in prophetic literature.
Numbers 22–24 As the Israelites approach the promised land, the Moabites enlist Balaam to curse God's people. Ironically, each attempt to curse results instead in blessing. (Cf. Jos 24:9–10; Mic 6:5.)	***Genesis 19:37*** Moab is born through the incestuous relations of Lot and his daughter.	***Deuteronomy 23:3*** The Lord forbids any Moabite to enter the assembly of the LORD.
Judges 3 God delivers Israel from Moabite oppression through Ehud's daring assassination of Moab's king.	***Numbers 25*** Just as God delivers Israel from Balaam's cursing, Israel turns to sexual immorality with the Moabites, resulting in spiritual adultery—idolatry.	***Psalm 60:8*** "Moab is my washbasin" (cf. Ps 108:9).
1 Samuel 14:47 Saul assumes the kingship and fights against Israel's enemies, including Moab.	***Judges 10*** Again, Israel runs after Moab's gods.	***Isaiah 11:14; 15; 16:2; 25:10*** The prophet Isaiah condemns Moab.
2 Samuel 8:2 King David defeats the Moabites, killing two-thirds of their fighting force and forcing the rest into servitude (cf. 1Ch 18:2).	***1 Kings 11*** King Solomon, called to lead Israel in worship of the true God, instead builds altars to Chemosh, Moab's chief deity. As was so often the case, he was led astray through his marriage to a Moabite (cf. 2Ki 23).	***Jeremiah 9:26; 25:21; 27:3; 48*** "'Whoever flees from the terror will fall into a pit, whoever climbs out of the pit will be caught in a snare; for I will bring on Moab the year of her punishment,' declares the LORD."
2 Kings 3 The Moabites rebel against Israel; the divided kingdom is united momentarily and empowered to defeat Moab through the prophetic encouragement of Elisha.	***Nehemiah 13:23*** Nehemiah discovers the post-exilic community has defiled itself by intermarrying with the Moabites.	***Ezekiel 25:11*** "I will inflict punishment on Moab. Then they will know that I am the LORD."
2 Kings 13:20 Israel and Moab were regularly in conflict (cf. 2Ki 24:2).		***Amos 2:2*** "I will send fire on Moab . . . Moab will go down in great tumult."
2 Chronicles 20 God miraculously delivers Jehoshaphat from the Moabite coalition through songs of praise; not a sword was needed.		***Zephaniah 2:8–9*** "I have heard the insults of Moab . . . who insulted my people . . . Therefore, as surely as I live . . . Moab will become like Sodom."

daughter, to go with the women who work for him, because in someone else's field you might be harmed."

23So Ruth stayed close to the women of Boaz to glean until the barley and wheat harvests[t] were finished. And she lived with her mother-in-law.

Ruth and Boaz at the Threshing Floor

3 One day Ruth's mother-in-law Naomi said to her, "My daughter, I must find a home[a][u] for you, where you will be well provided for. 2Now Boaz, with whose women you have worked, is a relative[v] of ours. Tonight he will be winnowing barley on the threshing floor. 3Wash, put on perfume,[w] and get dressed in your best clothes. Then go down to the threshing floor, but don't let him know you are there until he has finished eating and drinking. 4When he lies down, note the place where he is lying. Then go and uncover his feet and lie down. He will tell you what to do."

5"I will do whatever you say,"[x] Ruth answered. 6So she went down to the threshing floor and did everything her mother-in-law told her to do.

7When Boaz had finished eating and drinking and was in good spirits,[y] he went over to lie down at the far end of the grain pile. Ruth approached quietly, uncovered his feet and lay down. 8In the middle of the night something startled the man; he turned—and there was a woman lying at his feet!

9"Who are you?" he asked.

"I am your servant Ruth," she said. "Spread the corner of your garment[z] over me, since you are a guardian-redeemer[b][a] of our family."

2:23 [t]Dt 16:9
3:1 [u]Ru 1:9
3:2 [v]Dt 25:5-10; Ru 2:1
3:3 [w]2Sa 14:2
3:5 [x]Eph 6:1; Col 3:20
3:7 [y]Jdg 19:6, 9, 22; 2Sa 13:28; 1Ki 21:7; Est 1:10
3:9 [z]Eze 16:8 [a]ver 12; Ru 2:20
3:11 [b]Pr 12:4; 31:10
3:12 [c]ver 9 [d]Ru 4:1
3:13 [e]Dt 25:5; Ru 4:5; Mt 22:24 [f]Jdg 8:19; Jer 4:2
3:14 [g]Ro 14:16; 2Co 8:21

Ru 3:11 ❖ How can we live in such a way that all who know us see us as people of noble character?

10"The LORD bless you, my daughter," he replied. "This kindness is greater than that which you showed earlier: You have not run after the younger men, whether rich or poor. 11And now, my daughter, don't be afraid. I will do for you all you ask. All the people of my town know that you are a woman of noble character.[b] 12Although it is true that I am a guardian-redeemer of our family,[c] there is another who is more closely related than[d] I. 13Stay here for the night, and in the morning if he wants to do his duty as your guardian-redeemer,[e] good; let him redeem you. But if he is not willing, as surely as the LORD lives[f] I will do it. Lie here until morning."

14So she lay at his feet until morning, but got up before anyone could be recognized; and he said, "No one must know that a woman came to the threshing floor."[g]

15He also said, "Bring me the shawl you are wearing and hold it out." When she did so, he poured into it six measures of barley and placed the bundle on her. Then he[c] went back to town.

16When Ruth came to her mother-in-

[a] *1* Hebrew *find rest* (see 1:9) [b] *9* The Hebrew word for *guardian-redeemer* is a legal term for one who has the obligation to redeem a relative in serious difficulty (see Lev. 25:25-55); also in verses 12 and 13. [c] *15* Most Hebrew manuscripts; many Hebrew manuscripts, Vulgate and Syriac *she*

---

the writer intends that his readers (both ancient and modern) look to these two individuals as models to follow for living a moral life.

3:1-5 This change in Ruth's appearance, with its symbolic meaning, will indicate to Boaz both her availability and the seriousness of her intentions. It should be remembered that things could go wrong with this plan. Yet Ruth demonstrates her radical commitment to and trust in Naomi's wisdom.
3:6-8 Verse 7 shows Boaz in good spirits. Thus, he will be receptive to the request communicated by Ruth's symbolic actions. Ruth approaches, uncovers his feet, and lies down. The narrator has built the suspense to a peak.
3:9 The utter surprise of Boaz is captured in the narration. Ruth's words are carefully chosen, suggesting a female petitioner's weakness and need for help or protection when presenting a request before a more powerful male.

Next, Ruth invokes Boaz to "spread the corner of your garment over me." The choice of the term can be construed as a general plea for protection. The term may also refer to the symbolic investment connected with marriage. Boaz takes it to be an invitation to marriage.

There is no doubt that this scene on the threshing floor is sexually provocative. But the narrator constantly and consistently depicts both Ruth and Boaz as individuals of unmatched character. The narrator uses the sexual connotations of the scene to convey the sexual and emotional tension felt by the characters.
3:10-14 Boaz's first words are a blessing. He goes on to assure Ruth of his good intentions toward her. Boaz acknowledges his responsibility, but he also recognizes the hierarchy within the clan structure.
3:15 It is clear the generous gift of grain is meant as a symbol of his commitment to the relationship.

law, Naomi asked, "How did it go, my
daughter?"
Then she told her everything Boaz
had done for her 17and added, "He gave
me these six measures of barley, saying, 'Don't go back to your mother-in-law
empty-handed.'"
18Then Naomi said, "Wait, my daughter, until you find out what happens. For
the man will not rest until the matter is
settled today."[h]

Boaz Marries Ruth

4 Meanwhile Boaz went up to the town
gate and sat down there just as the
guardian-redeemer[a] he had mentioned[i]
came along. Boaz said, "Come over here,
my friend, and sit down." So he went over
and sat down.
2Boaz took ten of the elders[j] of the
town and said, "Sit here," and they did
so. 3Then he said to the guardian-redeemer, "Naomi, who has come back
from Moab, is selling the piece of land
that belonged to our relative Elimelek.
4I thought I should bring the matter to

3:18 [h] Ps 37:3-5
4:1 [i] Ru 3:12
4:2 [j] 1Ki 21:8; Pr 31:23

[a] 1 The Hebrew word for *guardian-redeemer* is a legal term for one who has the obligation to redeem a relative in serious difficulty (see Lev. 25:25-55); also in verses 3, 6, 8 and 14.

3:16–18 This dialogue between Ruth and Naomi comprises the last words that either of them utter in the story. Poised on the threshold of fulfillment, they both step aside, with Boaz taking center stage. His action will now dominate the story's resolution.

✤ **3:1–18** Ruth and Boaz demonstrate their pure motives in this chapter, which speaks to the very essence of integrity. As Christians, ultimately we are called to serve the Lord and therefore ought to speak and act out of pure motives that will bring honor and glory to his name. Honesty with God and honesty with ourselves as we reflect on what we are doing and why we are doing it goes a long way in helping us to evaluate our motives and, by extension, to act with integrity toward others.

4:1–2 Boaz, true to his words, "went up to the town gate and sat down there just as the guardian-redeemer he had mentioned came along" (v. 1). This is not simply a coincidence but the hidden hand of Yahweh at work.

4:3–4 Having assembled the elders, Boaz confronts the unnamed "guardian-redeemer." It is clear that the text refers to a transaction in which only the right of use of the land is being transferred for a stipulated value. Boaz appeals to the nearer redeemer to buy back the rights from the unnamed third party.

In contrast to Boaz, the guardian-redeemer has done nothing. In all probability, he knows about the field of Elimelek. Since there is no descendant of Elimelek, the field will, at a certain point, merge into his possession. Whatever price he pays for

PEOPLE TO KNOW // BOAZ

RUTH 4:1–12: Boaz was a man from Bethlehem who showed kindness to Ruth and Naomi. Though Ruth was a Moabite, word had reached Boaz of how faithful Ruth had been to her mother-in-law, Naomi. Boaz was related to Noami through her deceased husband, Elimelek.

Ruth risked her safety by venturing into fields to glean behind harvesters in order to bring some food home to Naomi. Providentially, she ended up in Boaz's field. When Boaz learned who she was, he showed her kindness (Ru 2:15–18). He told Ruth not to gather in any other field, where she might be harmed.

When Ruth told Naomi she had been in the field of Boaz, Naomi revealed that Boaz was one of their guardian-redeemers (Ru 2:20). Ruth continued to gather in Boaz's field through the barley and wheat harvests. Then Naomi told Ruth to do something bold: sneak onto the threshing floor at night and ask Boaz to marry her. Ruth bravely obeyed, and Boaz was moved by Ruth's further act of loyalty to Naomi. He praised her noble character, which he said was known to all in the town (Ru 3:10–11). After clearing the arrangement with another potential guardian-redeemer who was a closer relative of Naomi's late husband, Boaz took Ruth as his wife. They had a son named Obed, the grandfather of King David.

APPLICATION ✤ Despite the Israelites' dislike for Moabites and Moses' instructions prohibiting them from God's assembly (Dt 23:3), Boaz chose the Moabite Ruth as his wife. The OT demonstrates God's concern for people who are marginalized, especially foreigners, orphans and widows (Dt 10:18–19). Like Boaz, our hearts should be drawn to those in need, and our actions should exemplify the love of God to others. The ministry of justice and mercy is central to our obedience to God.

your attention and suggest that you buy
it in the presence of these seated here
and in the presence of the elders of my
people. If you will redeem it, do so. But
if you[a] will not, tell me, so I will know.
For no one has the right to do it except
you,[k] and I am next in line."
"I will redeem it," he said.
5Then Boaz said, "On the day you buy
the land from Naomi, you also acquire
Ruth the Moabite, the[b] dead man's widow, in order to maintain the name of the
dead with his property."[l]
6At this, the guardian-redeemer said,
"Then I cannot redeem[m] it because I
might endanger my own estate. You redeem it yourself. I cannot do it."
7(Now in earlier times in Israel, for
the redemption and transfer of property to become final, one party took off
his sandal and gave it to the other. This
was the method of legalizing transactions in Israel.)[n]
8So the guardian-redeemer said to
Boaz, "Buy it yourself." And he removed
his sandal.
9Then Boaz announced to the elders
and all the people, "Today you are witnesses that I have bought from Naomi
all the property of Elimelek, Kilion and
Mahlon. 10I have also acquired Ruth the
Moabite, Mahlon's widow, as my wife, in
order to maintain the name of the dead
with his property, so that his name will
not disappear from among his family
or from his hometown.[o] Today you are
witnesses!"
11Then the elders and all the people
at the gate said, "We are witnesses.[p]
May the LORD make the woman who is
coming into your home like Rachel and
Leah,[q] who together built up the family
of Israel. May you have standing in Ephrathah[r] and be famous in Bethlehem.
12Through the offspring the LORD gives
you by this young woman, may your
family be like that of Perez,[s] whom Tamar bore to Judah."

4:4 [k] Lev 25:25; Jer 32:7-8
4:5 [l] Ge 38:8; Dt 25:5-6; Ru 3:13; Mt 22:24
4:6 [m] Lev 25:25; Ru 3:13
4:7 [n] Dt 25:7-9
4:10 [o] Dt 25:6
4:11 [p] Dt 25:9 [q] Ps 127:3; 128:3 [r] Ge 35:16
4:12 [s] ver 18; Ge 38:29
4:13 [t] Ge 29:31; 33:5; Ru 3:11
4:14 [u] Lk 1:58
4:15 [v] Ru 1:16-17; 2:11-12; 1Sa 1:8
4:17 [w] ver 22; 1Sa 16:1,18; 1Ch 2:12,13
4:18 [x] Mt 1:3-6

Ru 4:9-10 ❖ Where are there opportunities for us to show the kind of selfless care and mercy for others that Boaz showed?

Naomi Gains a Son

13So Boaz took Ruth and she became
his wife. When he made love to her, the
LORD enabled her to conceive,[t] and she
gave birth to a son. 14The women[u] said to
Naomi: "Praise be to the LORD, who this
day has not left you without a guardian-redeemer. May he become famous
throughout Israel! 15He will renew your
life and sustain you in your old age. For
your daughter-in-law, who loves you and
who is better to you than seven sons,[v]
has given him birth."
16Then Naomi took the child in her
arms and cared for him. 17The women
living there said, "Naomi has a son!" And
they named him Obed. He was the father
of Jesse,[w] the father of David.

The Genealogy of David

4:18–22pp // 1Ch 2:5–15; Mt 1:3–6; Lk 3:31–33

18This, then, is the family line of Perez[x]:

[a] 4 Many Hebrew manuscripts, Septuagint, Vulgate and Syriac; most Hebrew manuscripts *he*
[b] 5 Vulgate and Syriac; Hebrew (see also Septuagint) *Naomi and from Ruth the Moabite, you acquire the*

---

the redemption will be offset by the annual crop yields. With such self-interest in mind, the nearer redeemer quickly consents to redeem the field.

4:5–8 Boaz now drives home the second responsibility: "On the day you buy the land from Naomi, you also acquire Ruth the Moabite, the dead man's widow, in order to maintain the name of the dead with his property" (v. 5).

Confronted with this reality, the nearer redeemer is not up to fulfilling his social and moral responsibilities. Nonverbal action closes the scene. The nearer redeemer removes his sandal and hands it to Boaz as a symbolic act declaring his abdication of his own right of redemption.

4:9–10 Through solemn and emphatic declaration, Boaz reinforces the issue of restoration of the clan—the memory of the deceased may not perish.

4:11–12 The elders and all those at the gate declare their witness of the legal proceedings. They then pronounce a threefold blessing on Boaz.

4:13–16 Naomi's resolution to the death and emptiness that have afflicted her is truly resolved in these few verses. She who was left alone without her two sons now takes the boy, holds him, and becomes the one who cares for him (v. 16).

4:17 Finally, a surprise identification is given. The child is "the father of Jesse, the father of David." It is at this point that the reader can perceive how precarious the situation was: Without Ruth, the line of Elimelek would have been extinguished, as would the line of Boaz, and hence there would have been no David. This is God at work.

4:18–22 Far from being peripheral to the main narrative sequence of the Bible, the book of Ruth

Perez was the father of Hezron,
19 Hezron the father of Ram,
Ram the father of Amminadab,[y]
20 Amminadab the father of Nahshon,
Nahshon the father of Salmon,[a]
21 Salmon the father of Boaz,[z]
Boaz the father of Obed,
22 Obed the father of Jesse,
and Jesse the father of David.

4:19 [y] Ex 6:23
4:21 [z] Ru 2:1

[a] *20* A few Hebrew manuscripts, some Septuagint manuscripts and Vulgate (see also verse 21 and Septuagint of 1 Chron. 2:11); most Hebrew manuscripts *Salma*

---

dramatizes its principal theme: the continuity of the people Israel in the land that God had given them. Moreover, in Yahweh's providence, the love of Boaz, Ruth, and Naomi lays the foundation for a salvation that extends to the ends of a lost world.

4:1–22 Christians can learn much from Boaz. Because we live in a world that demands to get its own way and is often more than willing to bypass or short-circuit any ethical issue that stands in the way, the church finds itself infected with this way of living. Clear scriptural directives for reconciliation are ignored in order to achieve one's goals. Unsupported testimony (i.e., gossip) filters its way throughout congregations to gain its intended aims. The very idea of showing love does not cross the minds of many church attendees, who are more interested in having their needs met.

The story of Naomi, Ruth, and Boaz models a pervasive integrity and trust in the Lord that we in the church can and should follow today.

Author: Unknown

Audience: God's chosen people, the Israelites

Date: Sometime after Israel was divided into the northern and southern kingdoms in about 930 BC

Theme: God exalts the weak and humbles the proud, as evidenced by accounts of Hannah, Samuel and King Saul.

PERSPECTIVE

If playwright Arthur Miller was correct in defining a great play as one in which you discover facets of your own character, then the two books of Samuel can be read as great plays. From Hannah's reaction to her infertility in 1 Samuel to David's desperate act of worship to stop the plague in 2 Samuel 24, these two books seem like nonstop character studies.

If you like to read biographies, the two Samuels are for you. If you are in need of a surefire series to teach, the life of King David will keep people coming, as the application of biblical truth to everyday living is immediate and direct. God speaks through these pages.

Why do we hear God's voice so clearly through the lives of Hannah, Samuel, Eli and his sons, Saul, David, and David's family? What is it about the stories of these people that make us think we have met them? How do they remind us of people we know in everyday life?

Samuel was a priest; David was a king. They lived three thousand years ago under circumstances so foreign to our way of life; we can hardly imagine it. But the reason we find the applications so immediate has deep theological roots. No matter what role we play, what deeds we do, or what culture gives form to our humanity, we are all created in God's image. We all have the same Father. We are made the same way. If you dig deep enough, underneath every role, deed, and culture you find a person made to seek God. It is the deepest, most basic urge we have. That is why we can read biographies of kings and arch criminals and see ourselves in them.

Reading 1 Samuel

First Samuel narrates two main stories that intersect with each other: the story of Samuel and the story of Israel's first king, Saul. It contains many well-known Bible stories.

	1400 BC	1300	1200	1100	1000	900	800	700	600	500	400
Israelites enter Canaan (c. 1406 BC)											
Judges begin to rule (c. 1375 BC)											
Saul named king (1050 BC)											
David kills Goliath (c. 1025 BC)											
Saul dies; David named king (1010 BC)											
Solomon's reign (970–930 BC)											
Division of the kingdom (930 BC)											
Book of 1 Samuel written (c. 925 BC)											

Key Verse

Samuel took the horn of oil and anointed [David] in the presence of his brothers, and from that day on the Spirit of the LORD came powerfully upon David.

—1 Samuel 16:13

There is a second reason why we find these applications so immediate. It is because we are all sinners saved by grace. We recognize not only our parentage; we recognize our common condition. When the prophet Nathan accuses David of murder and adultery in 2 Samuel 12, he points a long, bony finger at David and says, "You are the man," and all of us flinch. We have not all committed adultery, yet in the deepest recesses of our hearts we all have sins we are desperately trying to hide.

Similarly, when David sings his beautiful song of praise to God in 2 Samuel 22, thanking his Creator for delivering him from all his enemies, both external and internal, we immediately feel the warmth surrounding our hearts. We remember all the times in our lives when God's grace was sufficient to overcome the worst we could manage.

The books of Samuel remind us of the importance of similarity. We are so different from Samuel and David. But the same God made us, the same God saved us, and the same God keeps us safe. We call to that God who is worthy of praise, and we are saved from our enemies.

TAKING THE NEXT STEPS

The book of I Samuel tells how kingship came to the nation of Israel during the time of Samuel, the last judge. In Israel's wars with the Philistines, and in the conflicts between Saul and David, it is shown that success comes with God's help—never by human ingenuity. At the same time, the importance of obedience is stressed—that God helps those who obey his commands but withdraws from those who disobey.

Several principles of practical guidance for our lives stand out in this book. (1) God never abandons his people; even when the situation deteriorates, as it did during the time of Eli and his sons, God brings hope, just as he did through the birth of Samuel. (2) God cannot be forced or manipulated into serving our wants, but he will help those who depend on him and seek to do his will. (3) Even our religious worship of God is without value if we do not accompany it with obedience. (4) Outward appearance means nothing to God; what he wants is a heart dedicated to his service. (5) Those who let jealousy control their lives hurt themselves more than they hurt their fellow human beings.

WHAT TO LOOK FOR IN 1 SAMUEL

- Hannah's prayer and the birth of Samuel (ch. 1)
- God's call of young Samuel (ch. 3)
- The Philistines' capture and return of the ark (chs. 4–6)
- The Israelites' request for a king (ch. 8)
- Saul, Israel's first king (chs. 9–11)
- Samuel's rebuke of Saul for his disobedience (chs. 13; 15)
- David's anointing as king (ch. 16)
- David and Goliath (ch. 17)
- Jealous Saul's attempt to kill David (chs. 19; 23–24; 26)
- David's friendship with Jonathan (ch. 20)

The Birth of Samuel

1 There was a certain man from Ramathaim, a Zuphite[a] from the hill
country[a] of Ephraim, whose name was
Elkanah[b] son of Jeroham, the son of Elihu, the son of Tohu, the son of Zuph, an
Ephraimite. 2He had two wives;[c] one was
called Hannah and the other Peninnah.
Peninnah had children, but Hannah had
none.
3Year after year[d] this man went up
from his town to worship[e] and sacrifice
to the LORD Almighty at Shiloh,[f] where
Hophni and Phinehas, the two sons of
Eli, were priests of the LORD. 4Whenever
the day came for Elkanah to sacrifice,[g] he
would give portions of the meat to his
wife Peninnah and to all her sons and
daughters. 5But to Hannah he gave a double portion because he loved her, and the
LORD had closed her womb.[h] 6Because
the LORD had closed Hannah's womb,
her rival kept provoking her in order to
irritate her.[i] 7This went on year after year.
Whenever Hannah went up to the house
of the LORD, her rival provoked her till
she wept and would not eat. 8Her husband Elkanah would say to her, "Hannah,
why are you weeping? Why don't you eat?
Why are you downhearted? Don't I mean
more to you than ten sons?[j]"
9Once when they had finished eating
and drinking in Shiloh, Hannah stood up.
Now Eli the priest was sitting on his chair
by the doorpost of the LORD's house.[k] 10In
her deep anguish[l] Hannah prayed to the
LORD, weeping bitterly. 11And she made
a vow, saying, "LORD Almighty, if you
will only look on your servant's misery
and remember[m] me, and not forget your
servant but give her a son, then I will
give him to the LORD for all the days of
his life, and no razor[n] will ever be used
on his head."
12As she kept on praying to the LORD,

1Sa 1:10 ❖ When have you come to God in prayer in deep anguish? What was the outcome?

1:1 [a] Jos 17:17-18 [b] 1Ch 6:27,34
1:2 [c] Dt 21:15-17; Lk 2:36
1:3 [d] ver 21; Ex 23:14; 34:23; Lk 2:41 [e] Dt 12:5-7 [f] Jos 18:1
1:4 [g] Dt 12:17-18
1:5 [h] Ge 16:1; 30:2
1:6 [i] Job 24:21
1:8 [j] Ru 4:15
1:9 [k] 1Sa 3:3
1:10 [l] Job 7:11
1:11 [m] Ge 8:1; 28:20; 29:32 [n] Nu 6:1-21; Jdg 13:5

[a] *1* See Septuagint and 1 Chron. 6:26-27,33-35; or *from Ramathaim Zuphim.*

1:1-28 This opening paragraph contains several features that illustrate the righteousness of Samuel's parents. Elkanah is depicted as an upstanding Israelite who cares deeply for his family and carefully attends to his religious commitments. The Law of Moses mandated regular trips to the tabernacle to worship (Dt 16:16), and Elkanah is a faithful Israelite, concerned to fulfill his vows to Yahweh.
1:4 Elkanah carefully and generously distributes meat to his family, likely a common practice during the festivals in which certain sacrifices were offered.
1:5-8 Elkanah loves Hannah deeply, despite her unenviable position as a barren wife. Hannah's intense pain is aggravated by the insufferable cruelty inflicted on her by her counterpart, Peninnah.
1:9-10 While at the Lord's temple for the festival at Shiloh, Hannah weeps and prays earnestly, making a vow to Yahweh (v. 11), which implies the so-called Nazirite vow. The term "Nazirite" is defined in Nu 6, explaining that a man or woman can make a special vow of separation to Yahweh. After the period of separation is over, there's a ritual for terminating the vow (Nu 6). Hannah is offering her unborn child as a permanent Nazirite, whose life will be wholly and exclusively God's.
1:11-18 The encounter between Eli and Hannah contains an ironic twist. The spiritual leader of the nation is unable to discern the spiritual significance of this woman's struggle. In the end, he recognizes in her the faith he was supposed to represent (v. 17).

Eli observed her mouth. 13Hannah was
praying in her heart, and her lips were
moving but her voice was not heard. Eli
thought she was drunk 14and said to her,
"How long are you going to stay drunk?
Put away your wine."
15"Not so, my lord," Hannah replied,
"I am a woman who is deeply troubled.
I have not been drinking wine or beer;
I was pouring[o] out my soul to the LORD.
16Do not take your servant for a wicked
woman; I have been praying here out of
my great anguish and grief."
17Eli answered, "Go in peace,[p] and may
the God of Israel grant you what you have
asked of him.[q]"
18She said, "May your servant find favor in your eyes.[r]" Then she went her way
and ate something, and her face was no
longer downcast.[s]
19Early the next morning they arose
and worshiped before the LORD and then
went back to their home at Ramah. Elkanah made love to his wife Hannah, and
the LORD remembered[t] her. 20So in the
course of time Hannah became pregnant
and gave birth to a son. She named[u] him
Samuel,[a] saying, "Because I asked the
LORD for him."

Hannah Dedicates Samuel

21When her husband Elkanah went up
with all his family to offer the annual[v]
sacrifice to the LORD and to fulfill his
vow,[w] 22Hannah did not go. She said to
her husband, "After the boy is weaned,
I will take him and present[x] him before
the LORD, and he will live there always."[b]

1:15 [o] Ps 42:4; 62:8; La 2:19
1:17 [p] Jdg 18:6; 1Sa 25:35; 2Ki 5:19; Mk 5:34 [q] Ps 20:3-5
1:18 [r] Ru 2:13 [s] Ecc 9:7; Ro 15:13
1:19 [t] Ge 4:1; 30:22
1:20 [u] Ge 41:51-52; Ex 2:10,22; Mt 1:21
1:21 [v] ver 3 [w] Dt 12:11
1:22 [x] ver 11,28; Lk 2:22
1:23 [y] ver 17; Nu 30:7
1:24 [z] Nu 15:8-10; Dt 12:5; Jos 18:1
1:27 [a] ver 11-13; Ps 66:19-20
1:28 [b] ver 11,22; Ge 24:26,52
2:1 [c] Lk 1:46-55 [d] Ps 9:14; 13:5 [e] Ps 89:17,24; 92:10; Isa 12:2-3

23"Do what seems best to you," her
husband Elkanah told her. "Stay here
until you have weaned him; only may
the LORD make good[y] his[c] word." So the
woman stayed at home and nursed her
son until she had weaned him.
24After he was weaned, she took the
boy with her, young as he was, along
with a three-year-old bull,[d][z] an ephah[e]
of flour and a skin of wine, and brought
him to the house of the LORD at Shiloh.
25When the bull had been sacrificed,
they brought the boy to Eli, 26and she
said to him, "Pardon me, my lord. As
surely as you live, I am the woman who
stood here beside you praying to the
LORD. 27I prayed[a] for this child, and the
LORD has granted me what I asked of
him. 28So now I give him to the LORD.
For his whole life[b] he will be given over
to the LORD." And he worshiped the LORD
there.

Hannah's Prayer

2 Then Hannah prayed and said:[c]

"My heart rejoices[d] in the LORD;
in the LORD my horn[f][e] is lifted
high.

[a] 20 *Samuel* sounds like the Hebrew for *heard by God.* [b] 22 Masoretic Text; Dead Sea Scrolls *always. I have dedicated him as a Nazirite—all the days of his life."* [c] 23 Masoretic Text; Dead Sea Scrolls, Septuagint and Syriac *your* [d] 24 Dead Sea Scrolls, Septuagint and Syriac; Masoretic Text *with three bulls* [e] 24 That is, probably about 36 pounds or about 16 kilograms [f] 1 *Horn* here symbolizes strength; also in verse 10.

1:19–20 These verses reveal a quick answer to Hannah's prayer. Birth narratives play an important role in biblical literature. Clearly the birth of Samuel into such circumstances marked for the narrator the dawning of a new day in Israel. Hannah's naming of Samuel emphasizes her confidence in God's faithfulness to answer prayer.

1:21–24 Hannah decides not to accompany Elkanah and the rest of the family during the annual festival. But when the boy is old enough to live in Shiloh permanently (two or three years old), Hannah feels able to fulfill her vow. She takes him to Shiloh and worships Yahweh in gratitude for his gracious gift.

1:25–28 In language that illustrates how appropriate her response is, Hannah dedicates Samuel to Yahweh for all his life. Having come to God with nothing, she now returns to Shiloh to give back that which means everything.

APPLICATION ✣ 1:1–28 When a nation is in such despair, the only hope is the actions of righteous individuals, both in national leadership and in the common citizenry. First Samuel 1 announces both. Samuel is the coming new leadership, and he is given to the nation through a righteous family.

God desires to use godly leaders to reform nations. Through her suffering and trials, God used Hannah to initiate spiritual rebirth in Israel. Like Elizabeth and Mary after her, God honored Hannah with miraculous conception to show his mercy and grace and to continue his salvation story. But without a host of other nameless Israelites, who also prayed and lived their lives in quiet devotion, such reform would not have been possible.

2:1–11 This little poem plays an important structuring role in 1–2 Samuel generally. It corresponds in a kind of point-counterpoint fashion with two poems near the conclusion of the two-volume book (2Sa 22:1–51; 23:1–7). Hannah begins 1–2 Samuel

PEOPLE TO KNOW // HANNAH

1 SAMUEL 2:1–11: Hannah lived at the end of the period of the judges before Israel had a king. Her husband, Elkanah, had another wife named Peninnah, who was able to have children, but Hannah had none. This was a source of deep pain for Hannah, worsened by the fact that Peninnah harassed her for being barren. Elkanah, however, loved Hannah deeply.

At God's sanctuary in Shiloh, Hannah prayed fervently for a child. After mistaking her distress for intoxication and hearing Hannah's troubled explanation, the priest Eli blessed her, saying, "May the God of Israel grant you what you have asked of him" (1Sa 1:17).

Soon Hannah became pregnant and gave birth to her son, whom she named Samuel. When the child was weaned, she brought him to the tabernacle at Shiloh where he was raised by Eli. Each year Hannah visited Samuel and brought him a new robe she had made for him (1Sa 2:19).

Hannah's beautiful prayer in 1 Samuel 2:1–10 praises God for lifting up the lowly and bringing down the proud. It proclaims God's sovereignty over all human affairs. Readers have long recognized parallels between Hannah's prayer and Mary's song in Luke 1:46–55.

APPLICATION ✤ Hannah's story illustrates the divine truth that God raises the humble and humbles the proud. Hannah's grateful, humble and generous spirit is shown in the fact that she gave her precious son into the Lord's service. Hannah kept her promise to God and showed her gratitude for his blessings.

A common theme in the Bible is abundance out of barrenness. Women who were unable to have children ended up being the mothers of some of the most important characters in the Bible: Isaac, Jacob, Joseph and Benjamin, Samson, Samuel and John the Baptist. God repeatedly brings life where there is no life. Hannah's story can inspire us to praise for the new life God has provided to us in his Son, Jesus Christ.

My mouth boasts over my enemies,
for I delight in your deliverance.

2 "There is no one holy[f] like the LORD;
there is no one besides you;
there is no Rock[g] like our God.

3 "Do not keep talking so proudly
or let your mouth speak such
arrogance,[h]
for the LORD is a God who knows,
and by him deeds[i] are weighed.[j]

4 "The bows of the warriors are
broken,[k]
but those who stumbled are
armed with strength.
5 Those who were full hire themselves
out for food,
but those who were hungry are
hungry no more.
She who was barren[l] has borne
seven children,
but she who has had many sons
pines away.

6 "The LORD brings death and makes
alive;[m]
he brings down to the grave and
raises up.[n]
7 The LORD sends poverty and
wealth;[o]
he humbles and he exalts.[p]
8 He raises[q] the poor from the
dust
and lifts the needy from the
ash heap;
he seats them with princes
and has them inherit a throne of
honor.[r]

2:2 [f] Ex 15:11; Lev 19:2 [g] Dt 32:30-31; 2Sa 22:2,32
2:3 [h] Pr 8:13 [i] 1Sa 16:7; 1Ki 8:39 [j] Pr 16:2; 24:11-12
2:4 [k] Ps 37:15
2:5 [l] Ps 113:9; Jer 15:9
2:6 [m] Dt 32:39 [n] Isa 26:19
2:7 [o] Dt 8:18 [p] Job 5:11; Ps 75:7
2:8 [q] Ps 113:7-8 [r] Job 36:7

1Sa 2:8 ✤ Where have we seen God raise up the humble and humble the proud?

---

by celebrating what Yahweh has done and will do while David concludes the book by celebrating Yahweh's faithfulness.

Hannah's prayer spans the height and depth of Israelite theology and relates it to her circumstances. Her joy and triumph are firmly rooted in the singular holiness of Yahweh. Only he represents pure power and moral character. Her confidence flows from this certainty, and she bursts forth in a stream of truths that result from it.

The concluding phrases of Hannah's song emphasize the Lord's anointed as especially chosen by God and empowered for the task of leading Israel. This description of Yahweh's anointed becomes a template for the stories that follow.

"For the foundations[s] of the earth
are the LORD's;
on them he has set the world.
9 He will guard the feet[t] of his faithful
servants,
but the wicked will be silenced in
the place of darkness.[u]

"It is not by strength[v] that one
prevails;
10 those who oppose the LORD will be
broken.[w]
The Most High will thunder[x] from
heaven;
the LORD will judge[y] the ends of
the earth.

"He will give strength[z] to his king
and exalt the horn[a] of his
anointed."

11 Then Elkanah went home to Ramah,
but the boy ministered[b] before the LORD
under Eli the priest.

Eli's Wicked Sons

12 Eli's sons were scoundrels; they had
no regard[c] for the LORD. 13 Now it was
the practice of the priests that, whenever any of the people offered a sacrifice, the priest's servant would come
with a three-pronged fork in his hand
while the meat[d] was being boiled 14 and
would plunge the fork into the pan or
kettle or caldron or pot. Whatever the
fork brought up the priest would take
for himself. This is how they treated all
the Israelites who came to Shiloh. 15 But
even before the fat was burned, the
priest's servant would come and say to
the person who was sacrificing, "Give the
priest some meat to roast; he won't accept boiled meat from you, but only raw."
16 If the person said to him, "Let the fat
be burned first, and then take whatever
you want," the servant would answer,
"No, hand it over now; if you don't, I'll
take it by force."
17 This sin of the young men was very
great in the LORD's sight, for they[a] were
treating the LORD's offering with contempt.[e]
18 But Samuel was ministering[f] before
the LORD — a boy wearing a linen ephod.[g]
19 Each year his mother made him a little
robe and took it to him when she went
up with her husband to offer the annual[h]
sacrifice. 20 Eli would bless Elkanah and
his wife, saying, "May the LORD give you
children by this woman to take the place
of the one she prayed[i] for and gave to[b]
the LORD." Then they would go home.
21 And the LORD was gracious to Hannah;[j]
she gave birth to three sons and two
daughters. Meanwhile, the boy Samuel
grew[k] up in the presence of the LORD.
22 Now Eli, who was very old, heard
about everything his sons were doing
to all Israel and how they slept with the
women[l] who served at the entrance to
the tent of meeting. 23 So he said to them,
"Why do you do such things? I hear from
all the people about these wicked deeds
of yours. 24 No, my sons; the report I hear
spreading among the LORD's people is not
good. 25 If one person sins against another,
God[c] may mediate for the offender; but if
anyone sins against the LORD, who will[m]
intercede[n] for them?" His sons, however,
did not listen to their father's rebuke, for
it was the LORD's will to put them to death.
26 And the boy Samuel continued to
grow[o] in stature and in favor with the
LORD and with people.

Prophecy Against the House of Eli

27 Now a man of God[p] came to Eli and
said to him, "This is what the LORD says:

2:8 [s]Job 38:4
2:9 [t]Ps 91:12 [u]Mt 8:12 [v]Ps 33:16-17
2:10 [w]Ps 2:9 [x]Ps 18:13 [y]Ps 96:13 [z]Ps 21:1 [a]Ps 89:24
2:11 [b]ver 18; 1Sa 3:1
2:12 [c]Jer 2:8; 9:6
2:13 [d]Lev 7:29-34
2:17 [e]Mal 2:7-9
2:18 [f]ver 11; 1Sa 3:1 [g]ver 28
2:19 [h]1Sa 1:3
2:20 [i]1Sa 1:11, 27-28; Lk 2:34
2:21 [j]Ge 21:1 [k]ver 26; Jdg 13:24; 1Sa 3:19; Lk 2:40
2:22 [l]Ex 38:8
2:25 [m]Nu 15:30; Jos 11:20 [n]Dt 1:17; 1Sa 3:14; Heb 10:26
2:26 [o]ver 21; Lk 2:52
2:27 [p]Ex 4:14-16; 1Ki 13:1

[a] *17* Dead Sea Scrolls and Septuagint; Masoretic Text *people* [b] *20* Dead Sea Scrolls; Masoretic Text *and asked from* [c] *25* Or *the judges*

2:12–17 The designation "scoundrels" ("sons of Belial") in these opening chapters of 1 Samuel refers to people who had a lack of regard for the proper worship of Yahweh. It is ironic that Eli earlier mistakenly assumed Hannah was a "wicked woman" (1:16; "daughter of Belial"). The specific nature of the sins of Hophni and Phinehas has to do with their rights as priests. The narrator summarizes their great sin as "treating the LORD's offering with contempt" (2:17).

2:18–21 The linen ephod was a garment worn by priests, and Samuel's "little robe" (v. 19) supplied by his mother each year may have been an outer cloak worn over the ephod.

2:22–26 Eli is either unwilling or unable to control his wayward sons, who reject his rebuke. Samuel, by contrast, continues to mature physically as well as spiritually.

2:27–36 The specifics of God's judgment against Eli are both corporate and personal. The entire house of Eli will suffer the consequences of the present wickedness. Every one of its members will die early, making Eli the last old man in his priestly line (v. 22). But the immediate and personal application for Eli relates to his sons, Hophni and Phinehas (vv. 34–36): They will both die on the same day. Yahweh will raise up in their place a

'Did I not clearly reveal myself to your
ancestor's family when they were in
Egypt under Pharaoh? 28I chose[q] your
ancestor out of all the tribes of Israel
to be my priest, to go up to my altar, to
burn incense, and to wear an ephod[r] in
my presence. I also gave your ancestor's
family all the food offerings presented
by the Israelites. 29Why do you[a] scorn my
sacrifice and offering[s] that I prescribed
for my dwelling?[t] Why do you honor
your sons more than me by fattening
yourselves on the choice parts of every
offering made by my people Israel?'

30"Therefore the LORD, the God of Israel, declares: 'I promised that members of
your family would minister before me forever.[u]' But now the LORD declares: 'Far be it
from me! Those who honor me I will hon-
or,[v] but those who despise[w] me will be disdained. 31The time is coming when I will
cut short your strength and the strength
of your priestly house, so that no one in it
will reach old age,[x] 32and you will see distress in my dwelling. Although good will
be done to Israel, no one in your family
line will ever reach old age.[y] 33Every one
of you that I do not cut off from serving at
my altar I will spare only to destroy your
sight and sap your strength, and all your
descendants will die in the prime of life.

34" 'And what happens to your two
sons, Hophni and Phinehas, will be a sign
to you — they will both die[z] on the same
day.[a] 35I will raise up for myself a faithful
priest,[b] who will do according to what is
in my heart and mind. I will firmly establish his priestly house, and they will
minister before my anointed[c] one always. 36Then everyone left in your family
line will come and bow down before him
for a piece of silver and a loaf of bread
and plead, "Appoint me to some priestly
office so I can have food to eat.[d]" ' "

2:28 [q] Ex 28:1 [r] Lev 8:7-8
2:29 [s] ver 12-17 [t] Dt 12:5; Mt 10:37
2:30 [u] Ex 29:9 [v] Ps 50:23; 91:15 [w] Mal 2:9
2:31 [x] 1Sa 4:11-18; 22:16-20
2:32 [y] 1Ki 2:26-27; Zec 8:4
2:34 [z] 1Sa 4:11 [a] 1Ki 13:3
2:35 [b] 1Sa 12:3; 1Ki 2:35 [c] 1Sa 16:13; 2Sa 7:11, 27; 1Ki 11:38
2:36 [d] 1Ki 2:27

The LORD Calls Samuel

3 The boy Samuel ministered[e] before
the LORD under Eli. In those days the
word of the LORD was rare;[f] there were
not many visions.[g]

2One night Eli, whose eyes[h] were becoming so weak that he could barely see,
was lying down in his usual place. 3The
lamp[i] of God had not yet gone out, and
Samuel was lying down in the house
of the LORD, where the ark of God was.
4Then the LORD called Samuel.

Samuel answered, "Here I am.[j]" 5And
he ran to Eli and said, "Here I am; you
called me."

But Eli said, "I did not call; go back
and lie down." So he went and lay down.

6Again the LORD called, "Samuel!" And
Samuel got up and went to Eli and said,
"Here I am; you called me."

"My son," Eli said, "I did not call; go
back and lie down."

7Now Samuel did not yet know the
LORD: The word of the LORD had not yet
been revealed[k] to him.

8A third time the LORD called, "Samuel!" And Samuel got up and went to
Eli and said, "Here I am; you called me."

Then Eli realized that the LORD was
calling the boy. 9So Eli told Samuel, "Go
and lie down, and if he calls you, say,
'Speak, LORD, for your servant is listening.' " So Samuel went and lay down in
his place.

10The LORD came and stood there,
calling as at the other times, "Samuel!
Samuel!"

Then Samuel said, "Speak, for your
servant is listening."

11And the LORD said to Samuel: "See, I
am about to do something in Israel that
will make the ears of everyone who hears

3:1 [e] 1Sa 2:11 [f] Ps 74:9 [g] Am 8:11
3:2 [h] 1Sa 4:15
3:3 [i] Lev 24:1-4
3:4 [j] Isa 6:8
3:7 [k] Ac 19:12

[a] *29* The Hebrew is plural.

---

faithful priest (v. 35). The fulfillment of this prophecy comes in stages.

> **2:1-36** The contrast between Samuel and Eli's sons in this chapter is a lesson for all religious professionals, as well as for individuals deeply involved in the life of their local congregation. It reminds us all that proximity to God's work is no substitute for submission to the commands and the grace of God.

3:1 Our author has a special appreciation for the importance of living under the authority of Yahweh's word. Without such direction, the nation (or any individual) will wander aimlessly and eventually fall into self-destructive behavior.

3:2-10 Samuel's recurring self-announcement ("Here I am; you called me") is the expression of those who volunteer themselves for service. It is especially significant when someone hears and obeys the divine call (Ge 22:1, 11; Ex 3:4; Isa 6:8).

After calling Samuel three times, Yahweh now "came and stood there" (1Sa 3:10). Apparently, Samuel is now receiving not only a word but also a vision, which is significant because we have been told that both word and vision were rare in those days (v. 1).

3:11-14 The call of Samuel thus far has been an idyllic, childlike exchange. But when Yahweh reveals the message to Samuel, it is anything but idyllic or

about it tingle.[l] 12At that time I will carry out against Eli everything[m] I spoke against his family — from beginning to end. 13For I told him that I would judge his family forever because of the sin he knew about; his sons blasphemed God,[a] and he failed to restrain[n] them. 14Therefore I swore to the house of Eli, 'The guilt of Eli's house will never be atoned[o] for by sacrifice or offering.' "

15Samuel lay down until morning and then opened the doors of the house of the LORD. He was afraid to tell Eli the vision, 16but Eli called him and said, "Samuel, my son."

Samuel answered, "Here I am."

17"What was it he said to you?" Eli asked. "Do not hide it from me. May God deal with you, be it ever so severely,[p] if you hide from me anything he told you." 18So Samuel told him everything, hiding nothing from him. Then Eli said, "He is the LORD; let him do what is good in his eyes."[q]

19The LORD was with[r] Samuel as he grew[s] up, and he let none[t] of Samuel's words fall to the ground. 20And all Israel from Dan to Beersheba[u] recognized that Samuel was attested as a prophet of the LORD. 21The LORD continued to appear at Shiloh, and there he revealed[v] himself to Samuel through his word.

4 And Samuel's word came to all Israel.

The Philistines Capture the Ark

Now the Israelites went out to fight against the Philistines. The Israelites camped at Ebenezer,[w] and the Philistines at Aphek.[x] 2The Philistines deployed their forces to meet Israel, and as the battle spread, Israel was defeated by the Philistines, who killed about four thousand of them on the battlefield. 3When the soldiers returned to camp, the elders of Israel asked, "Why[y] did the LORD bring defeat on us today before the Philistines? Let us bring the ark[z] of the LORD's covenant from Shiloh, so that he may go with us and save us from the hand of our enemies."

4So the people sent men to Shiloh, and they brought back the ark of the covenant of the LORD Almighty, who is enthroned between the cherubim.[a] And Eli's two sons, Hophni and Phinehas, were there with the ark of the covenant of God.

5When the ark of the LORD's covenant came into the camp, all Israel raised such a great shout[b] that the ground shook. 6Hearing the uproar, the Philistines asked, "What's all this shouting in the Hebrew camp?"

When they learned that the ark of the LORD had come into the camp, 7the Philistines were afraid.[c] "A god has[b] come

3:11 [l]2Ki 21:12; Jer 19:3
3:12 [m]1Sa 2:27-36
3:13 [n]1Sa 2:12, 17, 22, 29-31
3:14 [o]Lev 15:30-31; 1Sa 2:25; Isa 22:14
3:17 [p]Ru 1:17; 2Sa 3:35
3:18 [q]Job 2:10; Isa 39:8
3:19 [r]Ge 21:22; 39:2 [s]1Sa 2:21 [t]1Sa 9:6
3:20 [u]Jdg 20:1
3:21 [v]ver 10
4:1 [w]1Sa 7:12 [x]Jos 12:18; 1Sa 29:1
4:3 [y]Jos 7:7 [z]Nu 10:35; Jos 6:7
4:4 [a]Ex 25:22; 2Sa 6:2
4:5 [b]Jos 6:5, 10
4:7 [c]Ex 15:14

1Sa 3:13 ❖ When is it right to intervene when family members are acting sinfully? How should we address their sin?

1Sa 4:4 ❖ How do people try to use God as a "good luck charm" or to curry special favor? How does it turn out?

[a] *13* An ancient Hebrew scribal tradition (see also Septuagint); Masoretic Text *sons made themselves contemptible* [b] *7* Or *"Gods have* (see Septuagint)

childlike. Yahweh informs Samuel that he is about to fulfill his word regarding the end of Eli's priesthood (2:27–36). There is no turning back now (3:14).

3:15-18 Samuel tells Eli the dreadful message, to which Eli responds with gloomy resignation. Surely he understands that the sovereign Yahweh is free to punish sin and is just in doing so.

3:19-21 The emphasis of these verses is the validity of Samuel's prophetic ministry.

✣ **3:1—4:1a** In God's appearance to Samuel, his word functions both to inform and to invite. God's word in the Bible refers to things around us, but it also relates to us directly. He speaks both to *inform* us and to *form* us, both for *information* and for *formation*. The word that God addresses to contemporary believers is both an instrument of government, whereby he informs us how we ought to live, and also a means of fellowship, whereby he invites us into personal relationship with him.

4:1-4 The question asked by the elders of Israel in v. 3 about this defeat reflects the Israelite concept of the sovereignty of Yahweh. They assume that Yahweh has brought this defeat on them; in a sense, they are right. The sins of Eli and his sons Hophni and Phinehas have national and military consequences.

The subtle reference in v. 4b reminds the reader that along with the ark come the wicked sons of Eli. As long as this situation persists, Yahweh will not bless Israel's wars, and the ark will not serve a military role.

4:5-9 Ironically, while the Philistines recognize that Israel's God is more powerful than anything they have ever experienced (v. 7), Israel has become negligent in its worship of this miracle-working God.

into the camp," they said. "Oh no! Nothing like this has happened before. 8We're
doomed! Who will deliver us from the
hand of these mighty gods? They are the
gods who struck the Egyptians with all
kinds of plagues in the wilderness. 9Be
strong, Philistines! Be men, or you will
be subject to the Hebrews, as they[d] have
been to you. Be men, and fight!"
10So the Philistines fought, and the Israelites were defeated[e] and every man fled
to his tent. The slaughter was very great;
Israel lost thirty thousand foot soldiers.
11The ark of God was captured, and Eli's
two sons, Hophni and Phinehas, died.[f]

Death of Eli

12That same day a Benjamite ran from
the battle line and went to Shiloh with
his clothes torn and dust[g] on his head.
13When he arrived, there was Eli[h] sitting on his chair by the side of the road,
watching, because his heart feared for
the ark of God. When the man entered
the town and told what had happened,
the whole town sent up a cry.
14Eli heard the outcry and asked,
"What is the meaning of this uproar?"
The man hurried over to Eli, 15who was
ninety-eight years old and whose eyes[i]
had failed so that he could not see. 16He
told Eli, "I have just come from the battle
line; I fled from it this very day."
Eli asked, "What happened, my son?"
17The man who brought the news replied, "Israel fled before the Philistines,
and the army has suffered heavy losses.
Also your two sons, Hophni and Phinehas, are dead, and the ark of God has
been captured."

4:9 [d] Jdg 13:1; 1Co 16:13
4:10 [e] ver 2; Dt 28:25; 2Sa 18:17; 2Ki 14:12
4:11 [f] 1Sa 2:34; Ps 78:61,64
4:12 [g] Jos 7:6; 2Sa 1:2; 15:32; Ne 9:1; Job 2:12
4:13 [h] ver 18; 1Sa 1:9
4:15 [i] 1Sa 3:2

4:10–11 The loss described here may well be a metaphorical statement for an excessively large number of military casualties. Regardless, the losses of vv. 1–11 are due to a theological crisis in Israelite society that goes far beyond a failed military strategy. The culmination of Samuel's prophecy in ch. 3 and its acceptance by Eli, along with vv. 12–22, remove all doubt: Israel lost this war with the Philistines because of the wickedness of Eli and his sons.

✜ **4:1b–11** Living for Jesus does not mean we are always right or that we will always "win." Sometimes we will need correction and the discipline provided by others. Unlike the Israelites in this passage, we must never assume that God owes us something or that we can control the outcome of personal conflict by appealing to our relationship with God. After all, our life with God centers around God's grace and depends not one bit on our own merit.

4:12–18 The messenger's pitiable report contains four parts that build in climactic fashion (v. 17). We are not told of Eli's reaction to the first three pieces of news. But at the mention of the ark's capture, he falls and dies. The narrator intends us to understand that Eli is practically unaffected by the news of his sons' deaths, supposing that he has given up on them as hopeless.

PEOPLE TO KNOW // ELI

1 SAMUEL 4:12–18: Eli was a priest of God at Shiloh. Though being a priest meant he was a spiritual leader, his story is ultimately one of failure.

Eli's sons, Hophni and Phinehas, were wicked. They greedily took food for themselves from sacrifices offered to God, especially desiring the fat, which was supposed to be God's portion (Lev 3:16). In God's eyes, their actions were blasphemous (1Sa 3:13).

God told young Samuel, who was growing up under Eli's care, that Eli's house would come to destruction. Hophni and Phinehas were doing wrong, but Eli was guilty of not restraining his sons from their evil. God punished the two sons; they were killed in a battle against the Philistines, having taken the ark to the battlefield in a vain attempt to use it as a good luck charm.

When word reached Eli of his sons' deaths and the capture of the ark, Eli fell backward off his chair, broke his neck, and died, "for he was an old man, and he was heavy" (1Sa 4:18). With this last comment, the Bible hints that the sins of Eli's sons, which included gluttony, were passed on to them by Eli.

APPLICATION ✜ Sadly, corrupt religious leaders are not only a thing of the past. Still today there are all too many examples of church leaders who engage in greed, sexual sins and other offenses. Eli's story reminds us that these sins are detestable to God, and God will hold such leaders accountable for their offenses. God demands righteousness and purity, and God holds spiritual leaders to the highest standards.

18 When he mentioned the ark of God, Eli fell backward off his chair by the side of the gate. His neck was broken and he died, for he was an old man, and he was heavy. He had led[a][j] Israel forty years.

19 His daughter-in-law, the wife of Phinehas, was pregnant and near the time of delivery. When she heard the news that the ark of God had been captured and that her father-in-law and her husband were dead, she went into labor and gave birth, but was overcome by her labor pains. 20 As she was dying, the women attending her said, "Don't despair; you have given birth to a son." But she did not respond or pay any attention.

21 She named the boy Ichabod,[b][k] saying, "The Glory[l] has departed from Israel" — because of the capture of the ark of God and the deaths of her father-in-law and her husband. 22 She said, "The Glory has departed from Israel, for the ark of God has been captured."

The Ark in Ashdod and Ekron

5 After the Philistines had captured the ark of God, they took it from Ebenezer[m] to Ashdod.[n] 2 Then they carried the ark into Dagon's temple and set it beside Dagon.[o] 3 When the people of Ashdod rose early the next day, there was Dagon, fallen[p] on his face on the ground before the ark of the LORD! They took Dagon and put him back in his place. 4 But the following morning when they rose, there was Dagon, fallen on his face on the ground before the ark of the LORD! His head and hands had been broken[q] off and were lying on the threshold; only his body remained. 5 That is why to this day neither the priests of Dagon nor any others who enter Dagon's temple at Ashdod step on the threshold.[r]

6 The LORD's hand[s] was heavy on the people of Ashdod and its vicinity; he brought devastation[t] on them and afflicted them with tumors.[c][u] 7 When the people of Ashdod saw what was happening, they said, "The ark of the god of Israel must not stay here with us, because his hand is heavy on us and on Dagon our god." 8 So they called together all the rulers of the Philistines and asked them, "What shall we do with the ark of the god of Israel?"

They answered, "Have the ark of the god of Israel moved to Gath.[v]" So they moved the ark of the God of Israel.

9 But after they had moved it, the LORD's hand was against that city, throwing it into a great panic.[w] He afflicted the people of the city, both young and old, with an outbreak of tumors.[d] 10 So they sent the ark of God to Ekron.

As the ark of God was entering Ekron, the people of Ekron cried out, "They

4:18 [j] ver 13
4:21 [k] Ge 35:18 [l] Ps 26:8; Jer 2:11
5:1 [m] 1Sa 4:1; 7:12 [n] Jos 13:3
5:2 [o] Jdg 16:23
5:3 [p] Isa 19:1; 46:7
5:4 [q] Eze 6:6; Mic 1:7
5:5 [r] Zep 1:9
5:6 [s] ver 7; Ex 9:3; Ps 32:4; Ac 13:11 [t] ver 11; Ps 78:66 [u] Dt 28:27; 1Sa 6:5
5:8 [v] ver 11
5:9 [w] ver 6, 11; Dt 2:15; 1Sa 7:13; Ps 78:66

1Sa 5:11 ❖ Why is God's presence such a fearful thing for those who don't follow him?

[a] 18 Traditionally *judged* [b] 21 *Ichabod* means *no glory.* [c] 6 Hebrew; Septuagint and Vulgate *tumors. And rats appeared in their land, and there was death and destruction throughout the city* [d] 9 Or *with tumors in the groin* (see Septuagint)

4:19–22 The narrator patterns the story of the birth and naming of Ichabod after the birth of Benjamin to Rachel (Ge 35:16–19). But in this case, the wife of Phinehas seems to draw no comfort from the fact that she is delivering a son (1Sa 4:20). The name "Ichabod" presumably means "no glory." Another possibility is that the name means "Where is the glory?" The focusing restatement of this situation in v. 22 removes all doubt about the source of this mother's distress as she passes.

✣ **4:12–22** The deaths of Eli and his sons had been announced by the anonymous "man of God" and by the young Samuel; this chapter describes the nation's defeat at the hands of the Philistines and the death of Eli and his sons. The point of this prophecy-fulfillment pattern is that these events are divinely driven, that God's word through his prophets is true, and that God's will is being accomplished in and through these events. Prophetic history marches with certainty from word to fulfillment. God's word is to be trusted and his prophets believed.

5:1–5 On the first morning after placing the ark next to Dagon, the Philistines find Dagon in a position of subservience and worship, prostrate before Yahweh's ark (v. 3). On the following morning, Dagon has lost his head and hands (v. 4): a sign of military defeat. The superstitious custom of jumping over the threshold of a sacred place was known in ancient Israel, even practiced by idolatrous priests in Jerusalem (Zep 1:4, 9).

5:6–12 In the Philistine mind, there is no doubt that the plague of tumors is due to the hand of Yahweh. The Philistines have now learned the hard lesson that the Israelites themselves learned in ch. 4: No one can manipulate or control Yahweh in any way, let alone by simply obtaining possession of the ark of the covenant. Both the Israelites and the Philistines have grossly underestimated God's power and holiness.

have brought the ark of the god of Israel around to us to kill us and our people."
11So they called together all the rulers[x] of
the Philistines and said, "Send the ark of
the god of Israel away; let it go back to
its own place, or it[a] will kill us and our
people." For death had filled the city with
panic; God's hand was very heavy on it.
12Those who did not die were afflicted
with tumors, and the outcry of the city
went up to heaven.

The Ark Returned to Israel

6 When the ark of the LORD had
been in Philistine territory sev-
en months, 2the Philistines called for
the priests and the diviners[y] and said,
"What shall we do with the ark of the
LORD? Tell us how we should send it
back to its place."
3They answered, "If you return the ark
of the god of Israel, do not send it back
to him without a gift;[z] by all means send
a guilt offering[a] to him. Then you will be
healed, and you will know why his hand[b]
has not been lifted from you."
4The Philistines asked, "What guilt offering should we send to him?"
They replied, "Five gold tumors and
five gold rats, according to the number[c] of the Philistine rulers, because the
same plague has struck both you and
your rulers. 5Make models of the tumors[d] and of the rats that are destroying
the country, and give glory[e] to Israel's
god. Perhaps he will lift his hand from
you and your gods and your land. 6Why
do you harden[f] your hearts as the Egyptians and Pharaoh did? When Israel's god
dealt harshly with them, did they[g] not
send the Israelites out so they could go
on their way?
7"Now then, get a new cart[h] ready, with
two cows that have calved and have never
been yoked.[i] Hitch the cows to the cart,
but take their calves away and pen them
up. 8Take the ark of the LORD and put it on
the cart, and in a chest beside it put the
gold objects you are sending back to him
as a guilt offering. Send it on its way, 9but
keep watching it. If it goes up to its own
territory, toward Beth Shemesh,[j] then the
LORD has brought this great disaster on
us. But if it does not, then we will know
that it was not his hand that struck us but
that it happened to us by chance."
10So they did this. They took two such
cows and hitched them to the cart and
penned up their calves. 11They placed the
ark of the LORD on the cart and along
with it the chest containing the gold rats
and the models of the tumors. 12Then the
cows went straight up toward Beth Shemesh, keeping on the road and lowing all
the way; they did not turn to the right or
to the left. The rulers of the Philistines
followed them as far as the border of
Beth Shemesh.
13Now the people of Beth Shemesh
were harvesting their wheat in the valley, and when they looked up and saw the
ark, they rejoiced at the sight. 14The cart
came to the field of Joshua of Beth Shemesh, and there it stopped beside a large
rock. The people chopped up the wood
of the cart and sacrificed the cows as a
burnt offering[k] to the LORD. 15The Levites[l]
took down the ark of the LORD, together

5:11 [x]ver 6, 8-9
6:2 [y]Ge 41:8; Ex 7:11; Isa 2:6
6:3 [z]Ex 23:15; Dt 16:16 [a]Lev 5:15 [b]ver 9
6:4 [c]ver 17-18; Jos 13:3; Jdg 3:3
6:5 [d]1Sa 5:6-11 [e]Jos 7:19; Isa 42:12; Jn 9:24; Rev 14:7
6:6 [f]Ex 7:13; 8:15; 9:34; 14:17 [g]Ex 12:31, 33
6:7 [h]2Sa 6:3 [i]Nu 19:2
6:9 [j]ver 3; Jos 15:10; 21:16
6:14 [k]2Sa 24:22; 1Ki 19:21
6:15 [l]Jos 3:3

[a] *11* Or *he*

6:1-6 The terrified Philistines decide they have seen enough; it is time to return the ark to Israel. In a fascinating turn of events, the Philistine priests and diviners are now urging their people to give glory and honor to Yahweh, the God of Israel.
6:7-12 The proof that Yahweh was the genuine source of the Philistines' afflictions comes in the nature of the ark's return to Israel. The cows act against nature (walking away from their new calves) and under divine compulsion (without turning to the right or to the left), taking the cart straight to Beth Shemesh.
6:13—7:1 The driving question of the citizens of Beth Shemesh is: who should house the ark now that they have lost Shiloh and now that Eli's family is dead. The people of Kiriath Jearim accept the task, consecrating Eleazar, the son of Abinadab, to "guard" (lit., "keep"; 7:1) the ark. These events form the inspiration for the psalmist's meditations in Ps 78:60-62, 65-69.

5:1—7:1 At the very time when many people are seeking God in illegitimate ways, God seems evermore distant. Deism still clings, for God seems for many to be as far away as ever. But Christians know that God, the transcendent Creator of the universe, is also immanently involved in the world.

In this text God crashed into the Philistine world to teach them that their various ways of explaining and understanding divine presence are all wrong. The message of this text is greatly needed in today's world. It illustrates that the Philistine worldview—which is so similar in many ways to today's postmodern New Age perspective—is inadequate. God is not susceptible to the forces of magic or idolatry. He cannot be manipulated or pressed into service whenever we feel threatened or at risk.

with the chest containing the gold objects, and placed them on the large rock.
On that day the people of Beth Shemesh
offered burnt offerings and made sacrifices to the LORD. 16 The five rulers of the
Philistines saw all this and then returned
that same day to Ekron.
17 These are the gold tumors the Philistines sent as a guilt offering to the
LORD — one each[m] for Ashdod, Gaza,
Ashkelon, Gath and Ekron. 18 And the
number of the gold rats was according
to the number of Philistine towns belonging to the five rulers — the fortified
towns with their country villages. The
large rock on which the Levites set the
ark of the LORD is a witness to this day
in the field of Joshua of Beth Shemesh.
19 But God struck down[n] some of the
inhabitants of Beth Shemesh, putting
seventy[a] of them to death because they
looked[o] into the ark of the LORD. The
people mourned because of the heavy
blow the LORD had dealt them. 20 And
the people of Beth Shemesh asked, "Who
can stand[p] in the presence of the LORD,
this holy[q] God? To whom will the ark go
up from here?"
21 Then they sent messengers to the
people of Kiriath Jearim,[r] saying, "The
Philistines have returned the ark of the
LORD. Come down and take it up to your
7 town." 1 So the men of Kiriath Jearim
came and took up the ark of the LORD.
They brought it to Abinadab's[s] house
on the hill and consecrated Eleazar his
son to guard the ark of the LORD. 2 The
ark remained at Kiriath Jearim a long
time — twenty years in all.

6:17 [m] ver 4
6:19 [n] 2Sa 6:7 [o] Ex 19:21; Nu 4:5,15,20
6:20 [p] 2Sa 6:9; Mal 3:2; Rev 6:17 [q] Lev 11:45
6:21 [r] Jos 9:17; 15:9,60; 1Ch 13:5-6
7:1 [s] 2Sa 6:3

1Sa 6:19–20 ❖ Does God show favoritism to his own people? Why or why not?

1Sa 7:4 ❖ What is God calling us to "put away" to serve him only?

Samuel Subdues the Philistines at Mizpah

Then all the people of Israel turned
back to the LORD. 3 So Samuel said to all
the Israelites, "If you are returning[t] to
the LORD with all your hearts, then rid[u]
yourselves of the foreign gods and the
Ashtoreths[v] and commit[w] yourselves to
the LORD and serve him only,[x] and he
will deliver you out of the hand of the
Philistines." 4 So the Israelites put away
their Baals and Ashtoreths, and served
the LORD only.
5 Then Samuel said, "Assemble all Israel at Mizpah,[y] and I will intercede with
the LORD for you." 6 When they had assembled at Mizpah, they drew water and
poured[z] it out before the LORD. On that
day they fasted and there they confessed,
"We have sinned against the LORD." Now
Samuel was serving as leader[b][a] of Israel
at Mizpah.
7 When the Philistines heard that Israel
had assembled at Mizpah, the rulers of the

7:3 [t] Dt 30:10; Isa 55:7; Hos 6:1 [u] Ge 35:2; Jos 24:14 [v] Jdg 2:12-13; 1Sa 31:10 [w] Joel 2:12 [x] Dt 6:13; Mt 4:10; Lk 4:8
7:5 [y] Jdg 20:1
7:6 [z] Ps 62:8; La 2:19 [a] Jdg 10:10; Ne 9:1; Ps 106:6

[a] *19* A few Hebrew manuscripts; most Hebrew manuscripts and Septuagint *50,070*
[b] *6* Traditionally *judge*; also in verse 15

The God of Israel is in fact immanent and in control; he is victorious over all the forces of our world, just as he was victorious over the Philistine god Dagon.

7:2 Israel has been plagued with sin and failure, but through it all, God graciously continues to find a way to draw Israel closer to himself. Whereas their mourning in 6:19 was the result of the tragedy at Beth Shemesh, their remorse in this verse is accompanied by seeking after Yahweh.

7:3 To "return" to the Lord implies acknowledging, confessing, and forsaking sinful behavior, making it possible to be reinstated in a right relationship with him. The combination of "returning" with "all your hearts" refers to the seat of one's intellectual commitments rather than singularly to human emotions.

7:4 The paragraph ends with a terse but encouraging statement. Samuel's preaching is effective, and the Israelites are now prepared to be led into their future.

✣ **7:2–4** This passage teaches there is a natural connection between committing ourselves to the Lord exclusively and ridding ourselves of foreign gods, whatever they may be in our contemporary context. For today's believers, any object of our affection may potentially become a "foreign god," interfering with our relationship with God. Whenever and wherever this happens, the message of the prophet needs to be heard again.

7:5–6 Israel's confession in v. 6 makes a significant contribution to the overall message of 1–2 Samuel "We have sinned against the LORD." The historian responsible for the books of Samuel seems especially interested in defining and illustrating the nature of genuine confession and repentance.

7:7–11 In 1Sa 4 the Israelites lost to the Philistines because they attempted to manipulate God by bringing the ark of the covenant into the battle. They had no leadership to warn them against such action, and the military defeat was at the same

Philistines came up to attack them. When
the Israelites heard of it, they were afraid[b]
because of the Philistines. 8They said to
Samuel, "Do not stop crying[c] out to the
LORD our God for us, that he may rescue us
from the hand of the Philistines." 9Then
Samuel[d] took a suckling lamb and sacrificed it as a whole burnt offering to the
LORD. He cried out to the LORD on Israel's
behalf, and the LORD answered him.[e]
10While Samuel was sacrificing the
burnt offering, the Philistines drew near
to engage Israel in battle. But that day
the LORD thundered[f] with loud thunder
against the Philistines and threw them
into such a panic[g] that they were routed
before the Israelites. 11The men of Israel
rushed out of Mizpah and pursued the
Philistines, slaughtering them along the
way to a point below Beth Kar.
12Then Samuel took a stone[h] and set it
up between Mizpah and Shen. He named
it Ebenezer,[a] saying, "Thus far the LORD
has helped us."
13So the Philistines were subdued[i] and
they stopped invading Israel's territory.
Throughout Samuel's lifetime, the hand
of the LORD was against the Philistines.
14The towns from Ekron to Gath that the
Philistines had captured from Israel were
restored to Israel, and Israel delivered
the neighboring territory from the hands
of the Philistines. And there was peace
between Israel and the Amorites.
15Samuel[j] continued as Israel's leader
all the days of his life. 16From year to
year he went on a circuit from Bethel
to Gilgal to Mizpah, judging Israel in all
those places. 17But he always went back to
Ramah,[k] where his home was, and there
he also held court for Israel. And he built
an altar[l] there to the LORD.

7:7 [b] 1Sa 17:11
7:8 [c] 1Sa 12:19, 23; Isa 37:4; Jer 15:1
7:9 [d] Ps 99:6 [e] Jer 15:1
7:10 [f] 1Sa 2:10; 2Sa 22:14-15 [g] Jos 10:10
7:12 [h] Ge 35:14; Jos 4:9
7:13 [i] Jdg 13:1,5; 1Sa 13:5
7:15 [j] ver 6; 1Sa 12:11
7:17 [k] 1Sa 1:19; 8:4 [l] Jdg 21:4
8:1 [m] Dt 16:18-19
8:2 [n] Ge 22:19; 1Ki 19:3; Am 5:4-5
8:3 [o] Ex 23:8; Dt 16:19; Ps 15:5
8:4 [p] 1Sa 7:17
8:5 [q] Dt 17:14-20
8:6 [r] 1Sa 15:11

1Sa 8:3 ❖ How can parents pass on their Christian faith and practice to their children? Is it the parents' fault when their children fail?

Israel Asks for a King

8 When Samuel grew old, he appointed[m] his sons as Israel's leaders.[b] 2The
name of his firstborn was Joel and the
name of his second was Abijah, and they
served at Beersheba.[n] 3But his sons did
not follow his ways. They turned aside
after dishonest gain and accepted bribes[o]
and perverted justice.
4So all the elders of Israel gathered
together and came to Samuel at Ramah.[p]
5They said to him, "You are old, and your
sons do not follow your ways; now appoint a king[q] to lead[c] us, such as all the
other nations have."
6But when they said, "Give us a king
to lead us," this displeased[r] Samuel; so
he prayed to the LORD. 7And the LORD
told him: "Listen to all that the people
are saying to you; it is not you they have

[a] 12 *Ebenezer* means *stone of help.*
[b] 1 Traditionally *judges*
[c] 5 Traditionally *judge*; also in verses 6 and 20

time a spiritual failure. Now, the people implore Samuel to continue interceding on their behalf (7:8). Nothing has really changed—and yet everything has changed.

7:12–14 This stone monument is more than a reminder for future generations that Yahweh helped in this battle against the Philistines. It also serves the present generation by acknowledging that this victory is not a result of their own strength or brilliant military strategy. Yahweh had spoken with a loud thunder (v. 10), and this stone acknowledges his help.

7:15–17 The spectacular victory over the Philistines and the concluding reference to "peace" in v. 14 draw deliberate comparisons between Samuel and the charismatic leaders in the book of Judges. But Samuel's jurisdiction is broader than that of previous judges, and he represents the transition from Israel as a tribal confederation under the temporary leadership of various judges to a centralized, king-ruled government.

✜ **7:5–17** As important and meaningful as modern national monuments are, the "Ebenezer" (meaning "stone of help"; v. 12) stood in Samuel's day as a reminder of what *God* had done for the nation of Israel. God had been faithful to his word; God had *acted* on their behalf. Our modern nations could use such a monument. How do we remember God's mighty acts in our own life, family, and church?

8:1–6 The Israelites are justified in planning for the future, but requesting a "king to lead" (v. 6) is tantamount to a rejection of Samuel's godly judgeship and ministry of prophecy. The statement "such as all the other nations have" (v. 5) reveals the people are grasping for something they fail to understand and will lose the very things they hope to ensure by having a king.

8:7–9 This speech of Yahweh uses characteristic vocabulary to illustrate that the people's request is tantamount to other episodes of rebellion from Israel's history: "forsaking me and serving other gods" (v. 8). He is painfully aware that even given the warnings against kingship, Israel will not relent.

rejected, but they have rejected me as
their king.[s] 8 As they have done from the
day I brought them up out of Egypt until
this day, forsaking me and serving other
gods, so they are doing to you. 9 Now listen to them; but warn them solemnly and
let them know[t] what the king who will
reign over them will claim as his rights."
10 Samuel told all the words of the LORD
to the people who were asking him for
a king. 11 He said, "This is what the king
who will reign over you will claim as his
rights: He will take[u] your sons and make
them serve with his chariots and horses,
and they will run in front of his chariots.[v]
12 Some he will assign to be commanders[w] of thousands and commanders of
fifties, and others to plow his ground and
reap his harvest, and still others to make
weapons of war and equipment for his
chariots. 13 He will take your daughters to
be perfumers and cooks and bakers. 14 He
will take the best of your[x] fields and vineyards[y] and olive groves and give them to
his attendants. 15 He will take a tenth of
your grain and of your vintage and give
it to his officials and attendants. 16 Your
male and female servants and the best
of your cattle[a] and donkeys he will take
for his own use. 17 He will take a tenth of
your flocks, and you yourselves will become his slaves. 18 When that day comes,
you will cry out for relief from the king
you have chosen, but the LORD will not
answer[z] you in that day."
19 But the people refused[a] to listen to
Samuel. "No!" they said. "We want a king
over us. 20 Then we will be like all the other nations,[b] with a king to lead us and to
go out before us and fight our battles."
21 When Samuel heard all that the people said, he repeated[c] it before the LORD.

8:7 [s] Ex 16:8; 1Sa 10:19
8:9 [t] ver 11-18; 1Sa 10:25
8:11 [u] 1Sa 10:25; 14:52 [v] Dt 17:16; 2Sa 15:1
8:12 [w] 1Sa 22:7
8:14 [x] Eze 46:18 [y] 1Ki 21:7,15
8:18 [z] Pr 1:28; Isa 1:15; Mic 3:4
8:19 [a] Isa 66:4; Jer 44:16
8:20 [b] ver 5
8:21 [c] Jdg 11:11
8:22 [d] ver 7
9:1 [e] 1Sa 14:51; 1Ch 8:33; 9:39
9:2 [f] 1Sa 10:24 [g] 1Sa 10:23
9:4 [h] Jos 24:33 [i] 2Ki 4:42
9:5 [j] 1Sa 1:1 [k] 1Sa 10:2
9:6 [l] Dt 33:1; 1Ki 13:1 [m] 1Sa 3:19

1Sa 9:6 ❖ When have you sought the advice of a devout follower of God?

22 The LORD answered, "Listen[d] to them
and give them a king."
Then Samuel said to the Israelites,
"Everyone go back to your own town."

Samuel Anoints Saul

9 There was a Benjamite, a man of
standing, whose name was Kish[e] son
of Abiel, the son of Zeror, the son of Be-
korath, the son of Aphiah of Benjamin.
2 Kish had a son named Saul, as handsome a young man as could be found[f]
anywhere in Israel, and he was a head
taller[g] than anyone else.
3 Now the donkeys belonging to Saul's
father Kish were lost, and Kish said to his
son Saul, "Take one of the servants with
you and go and look for the donkeys."
4 So he passed through the hill[h] country
of Ephraim and through the area around
Shalisha,[i] but they did not find them.
They went on into the district of Sha-
alim, but the donkeys were not there.
Then he passed through the territory of
Benjamin, but they did not find them.
5 When they reached the district of
Zuph,[j] Saul said to the servant who was
with him, "Come, let's go back, or my
father will stop thinking about the donkeys and start worrying[k] about us."
6 But the servant replied, "Look, in this
town there is a man of God;[l] he is highly respected, and everything[m] he says
comes true. Let's go there now. Perhaps
he will tell us what way to take."
7 Saul said to his servant, "If we go,
what can we give the man? The food in

[a] *16* Septuagint; Hebrew *young men*

8:10–18 The portrait of kingship that Samuel paints appears to be an authentic description of the Canaanite political structure as it existed prior to and during the time of Samuel. He warns the people that having a king like "all the other nations" (v. 5) will lead ultimately to enslavement.

8:19–22 Israel's desire to be "like all the other nations" is repeated (vv. 5, 20). To this is added, "with a king to lead us and to go out before us and fight our battles" (v. 20). The lust for territorial security is stated in general terms here. Apparently, the people of Israel do not remember how their genuine repentance brought them a glorious victory over the Philistines (ch. 7).

✥ **8:1–22** All too often, Christians become more like Israel than we care to admit, forsaking the security of the lordship of God and grasping after a compromised authority to become something we were never meant to be. In our clearest and most honest moments, we all too often seek security by conforming to the spirit of the times rather than serving in the world as God's counterculture, as we were created to do. Like Israel, we tend to forfeit the lordship of God in order to become "like all the other nations" (v. 20). And we pay the price.

9:1–15 Saul is an impressive young man. His father's lengthy genealogy implies the family has great wealth. Saul himself strikes an imposing figure, literally standing out in the crowd (v. 2; 10:23–24).

PEOPLE TO KNOW // SAUL

1 SAMUEL 9:1–27: Saul's story began hopeful but quickly became a long series of failures. When Israel asked for a king, Samuel anointed Saul, who initially seemed promising. God changed Saul's heart and sent his Spirit powerfully upon him (1Sa 10:9–10).

But Saul never lived up to his potential. He failed to wait for Samuel to offer a sacrifice to God, instead offering the sacrifice himself. When Samuel arrived, he told Saul that because of this sin Saul's kingdom would not endure (1Sa 13:14). Saul also failed to completely destroy the Amalekites as God had ordered, causing Samuel to tell him again that God would rip the kingdom away from him. Though Saul was the tallest man in Israel, and only he and his son had decent weaponry (1Sa 13:22), Saul failed to fight Goliath, allowing the Philistine to taunt him and his troops. When David stepped up and confronted Goliath and thus became more popular than Saul, Saul obsessively tried to kill David, God's next anointed king.

In his later days, Saul consulted a medium to summon Samuel's spirit after Samuel's death. Samuel told Saul that he and his sons would join the realm of the dead the next day (1Sa 28:19). The following day, Saul and three of his sons died on the battlefield (1Sa 31:6).

APPLICATION ✤ Saul's life is a warning against pride, disobedience and envy. Saul failed to follow God's clear commands, to his own detriment. His pride and his envy toward David drove him to persistent evil. When we disobey God's instructions, we abandon the guardrails of God's merciful design. Rejecting God yields hazardous consequences. Saul's story is a warning to all who read it to stay humble and obedient to the Lord.

our sacks is gone. We have no gift[n] to take
to the man of God. What do we have?"
8 The servant answered him again.
"Look," he said, "I have a quarter of a
shekel[a] of silver. I will give it to the man
of God so that he will tell us what way to
take." 9 (Formerly in Israel, if someone
went to inquire of God, they would say,
"Come, let us go to the seer," because
the prophet of today used to be called
a seer.)[o]
10 "Good," Saul said to his servant.
"Come, let's go." So they set out for the
town where the man of God was.
11 As they were going up the hill to the
town, they met some young women coming out to draw[p] water, and they asked
them, "Is the seer here?"
12 "He is," they answered. "He's ahead
of you. Hurry now; he has just come to
our town today, for the people have a
sacrifice[q] at the high place.[r] 13 As soon
as you enter the town, you will find him
before he goes up to the high place to eat.
The people will not begin eating until he
comes, because he must bless the sacrifice; afterward, those who are invited
will eat. Go up now; you should find him
about this time."
14 They went up to the town, and as
they were entering it, there was Samuel,
coming toward them on his way up to
the high place.
15 Now the day before Saul came,
the LORD had revealed this to Samuel:
16 "About this time tomorrow I will send
you a man from the land of Benjamin.
Anoint[s] him ruler over my people Israel; he will deliver[t] them from the hand
of the Philistines. I have looked on my
people, for their cry has reached me."
17 When Samuel caught sight of Saul,
the LORD said to him, "This[u] is the man
I spoke to you about; he will govern my
people."
18 Saul approached Samuel in the gateway and asked, "Would you please tell
me where the seer's house is?"
19 "I am the seer," Samuel replied. "Go
up ahead of me to the high place, for
today you are to eat with me, and in the
morning I will send you on your way and

9:7 [n] 1Ki 14:3; 2Ki 5:5,15; 8:8
9:9 [o] 2Sa 24:11; 2Ki 17:13; 1Ch 9:22; 26:28; 29:29; Isa 30:10; Am 7:12
9:11 [p] Ge 24:11, 13
9:12 [q] Nu 28:11-15; 1Sa 7:17 [r] Ge 31:54; 1Sa 10:5; 1Ki 3:2
9:16 [s] 1Sa 10:1 [t] Ex 3:7-9
9:17 [u] 1Sa 16:12

[a] *8* That is, about 1/10 ounce or about 3 grams

9:15–16 Yahweh has prepared Samuel to anoint Saul as "ruler" ("prince," "leader") over the nation of Israel. This term is used in Samuel and Kings for the one officially chosen and appointed by Yahweh to rule over his people Israel.

9:17 Saul and Samuel meet for the first time. Saul is to be a ruler-deliverer who operates under the direct authority of Yahweh and his prophet.

9:18–25 Samuel includes his guests in a banquet that evening at the high place outside the town.

will tell you all that is in your heart. 20 As for the donkeys[v] you lost three days ago, do not worry about them; they have been found. And to whom is all the desire[w] of Israel turned, if not to you and your whole family line?"

21 Saul answered, "But am I not a Benjamite, from the smallest tribe[x] of Israel, and is not my clan the least of all the clans of the tribe of Benjamin?[y] Why do you say such a thing to me?"

22 Then Samuel brought Saul and his servant into the hall and seated them at the head of those who were invited—about thirty in number. 23 Samuel said to the cook, "Bring the piece of meat I gave you, the one I told you to lay aside."

24 So the cook took up the thigh[z] with what was on it and set it in front of Saul. Samuel said, "Here is what has been kept for you. Eat, because it was set aside for you for this occasion from the time I said, 'I have invited guests.'" And Saul dined with Samuel that day.

25 After they came down from the high place to the town, Samuel talked with Saul on the roof[a] of his house. 26 They rose about daybreak, and Samuel called to Saul on the roof, "Get ready, and I will send you on your way." When Saul got ready, he and Samuel went outside together. 27 As they were going down to the edge of the town, Samuel said to Saul, "Tell the servant to go on ahead of us"—and the servant did so—"but you stay here for a while, so that I may give you a message from God."

10 Then Samuel took a flask[b] of olive oil and poured it on Saul's head and kissed him, saying, "Has not the LORD anointed[c] you ruler over his inheritance?[a][d] 2 When you leave me today, you will meet two men near Rachel's tomb,[e] at Zelzah on the border of Benjamin. They will say to you, 'The donkeys[f] you set out to look for have been found. And now your father has stopped thinking about them and is worried[g] about you. He is asking, "What shall I do about my son?"'

3 "Then you will go on from there until you reach the great tree of Tabor. Three men going up to worship God at Bethel[h] will meet you there. One will be carrying three young goats, another three loaves of bread, and another a skin of wine. 4 They will greet you and offer you two loaves of bread, which you will accept from them.

5 "After that you will go to Gibeah of God, where there is a Philistine outpost.[i] As you approach the town, you will meet a procession of prophets coming down from the high place[j] with lyres, timbrels, pipes and harps[k] being played before them, and they will be prophesying.[l] 6 The Spirit[m] of the LORD will come powerfully upon you, and you will prophesy with them; and you will be changed into a different person. 7 Once these signs are fulfilled, do whatever[n] your hand finds to do, for God is with[o] you.

8 "Go down ahead of me to Gilgal.[p] I will surely come down to you to sacrifice burnt offerings and fellowship offerings, but you must wait seven days until I come to you and tell you what you are to do."

Saul Made King

9 As Saul turned to leave Samuel, God changed[q] Saul's heart, and all these signs were fulfilled that day. 10 When he and his servant arrived at Gibeah, a procession

9:20 [v] ver 3 [w] 1Sa 8:5; 12:13
9:21 [x] 1Sa 15:17 [y] Jdg 20:35,46
9:24 [z] Lev 7:32-34; Nu 18:18
9:25 [a] Dt 22:8; Ac 10:9
10:1 [b] 1Sa 16:13; 2Ki 9:1,3,6 [c] Ps 2:12 [d] Dt 32:9; Ps 78:62,71
10:2 [e] Ge 35:20 [f] 1Sa 9:4
[g] 1Sa 9:5
10:3 [h] Ge 28:22; 35:7-8
10:5 [i] 1Sa 13:3 [j] 1Sa 9:12 [k] 2Ki 3:15 [l] 1Sa 19:20; 1Co 14:1
10:6 [m] ver 10; Nu 11:25; 1Sa 19:23-24
10:7 [n] Ecc 9:10 [o] Jos 1:5; Jdg 6:12; Heb 13:5
10:8 [p] 1Sa 11:14-15
10:9 [q] ver 6

1Sa 10:9 ❖ How can we tell if God has changed our hearts? How will it affect us?

[a] 1 Hebrew; Septuagint and Vulgate *over his people Israel? You will reign over the LORD's people and save them from the power of their enemies round about. And this will be a sign to you that the LORD has anointed you ruler over his inheritance:*

Saul becomes the center of attention, being given a place of honor and a specially designated portion of food.

9:26–10:1 In the morning, Samuel prepares Saul to receive a private word from God by asking that he send his servant on ahead of them (9:27). Once alone, Samuel anoints Saul. The use of oil is a symbol of the spirit of Yahweh in several OT passages and represents the empowerment of Yahweh.

10:2–8 Samuel concludes his description of three signs of confirmation with a command for Saul to wait for seven days at Gilgal to receive further instructions. At that time, Samuel will sacrifice burnt offerings and fellowship offerings (v. 8).

10:9–16 The question "Is Saul also among the prophets?" (v. 11) serves as a rhetorical question expecting a negative answer. In this light, the question affirms Saul's new spiritual gifts, not because he belongs naturally to the band of prophets but because he is the legitimate new ruler of Israel. It affirms his anointing by Samuel, and he accepts his new role.

of prophets met him; the Spirit of God
came powerfully upon him, and he
joined in their prophesying.[r] 11When all
those who had formerly known him saw
him prophesying with the prophets, they
asked each other, "What is this[s] that has
happened to the son of Kish? Is Saul also
among the prophets?"[t]
12A man who lived there answered,
"And who is their father?" So it became
a saying: "Is Saul also among the prophets?" 13After Saul stopped prophesying,
he went to the high place.
14Now Saul's uncle[u] asked him and his
servant, "Where have you been?"
"Looking for the donkeys," he said.
"But when we saw they were not to be
found, we went to Samuel."
15Saul's uncle said, "Tell me what Samuel said to you."
16Saul replied, "He assured us that the
donkeys[v] had been found." But he did
not tell his uncle what Samuel had said
about the kingship.
17Samuel summoned the people of Israel to the LORD at Mizpah[w] 18and said to
them, "This is what the LORD, the God
of Israel, says: 'I brought Israel up out
of Egypt, and I delivered you from the
power of Egypt and all the kingdoms
that oppressed[x] you.' 19But you have now
rejected your God, who saves you out of
all your disasters and calamities. And you
have said, 'No, appoint a king[y] over us.'
So now present[z] yourselves before the
LORD by your tribes and clans."
20When Samuel had all Israel come
forward by tribes, the tribe of Benjamin
was taken by lot. 21Then he brought forward the tribe of Benjamin, clan by clan,
and Matri's clan was taken. Finally Saul
son of Kish was taken. But when they
looked for him, he was not to be found.

10:10 [r]ver 5-6; 1Sa 19:20
10:11 [s]Mt 13:54; Jn 7:15 [t]1Sa 19:24
10:14 [u]1Sa 14:50
10:16 [v]1Sa 9:20
10:17 [w]Jdg 20:1; 1Sa 7:5
10:18 [x]Jdg 6:8-9
10:19 [y]1Sa 8:5-7; 12:12 [z]Jos 7:14; 24:1
10:22 [a]1Sa 23:2, 4,9-11
10:23 [b]1Sa 9:2
10:24 [c]Dt 17:15; 2Sa 21:6 [d]1Ki 1:25,34,39
10:25 [e]Dt 17:14-20; 1Sa 8:11-18
10:26 [f]1Sa 11:4
10:27 [g]Dt 13:13 [h]1Ki 10:25; 2Ch 17:5
11:1 [i]1Sa 12:12 [j]Jdg 21:8 [k]1Ki 20:34; Eze 17:13
11:2 [l]Nu 16:14 [m]1Sa 17:26

22So they inquired[a] further of the LORD,
"Has the man come here yet?"
And the LORD said, "Yes, he has hidden
himself among the supplies."
23They ran and brought him out, and
as he stood among the people he was
a head taller[b] than any of the others.
24Samuel said to all the people, "Do you
see the man the LORD has chosen?[c] There
is no one like him among all the people."
Then the people shouted, "Long live[d]
the king!"
25Samuel explained to the people the
rights and duties[e] of kingship. He wrote
them down on a scroll and deposited it
before the LORD. Then Samuel dismissed
the people to go to their own homes.
26Saul also went to his home in Gibeah,[f] accompanied by valiant men whose
hearts God had touched. 27But some
scoundrels[g] said, "How can this fellow
save us?" They despised him and brought
him no gifts.[h] But Saul kept silent.

Saul Rescues the City of Jabesh

11 Nahash[a][i] the Ammonite went up and
besieged Jabesh Gilead.[j] And all the
men of Jabesh said to him, "Make a treaty[k] with us, and we will be subject to you."
2But Nahash the Ammonite replied,
"I will make a treaty with you only on
the condition that I gouge[l] out the right
eye of every one of you and so bring disgrace[m] on all Israel."

[a] 1 Masoretic Text; Dead Sea Scrolls *gifts. Now Nahash king of the Ammonites oppressed the Gadites and Reubenites severely. He gouged out all their right eyes and struck terror and dread in Israel. Not a man remained among the Israelites beyond the Jordan whose right eye was not gouged out by Nahash king of the Ammonites, except that seven thousand men fled from the Ammonites and entered Jabesh Gilead. About a month later,* [1]*Nahash*

10:17-27 Samuel calls another national convocation at Mizpah, the site of Israel's humble repentance and victory (7:5-17). Interestingly, the prophetic speech pattern used here is one well known throughout the OT for announcing judgment. In fact, the selection of Saul is inserted at the very point where we would expect an announcement of judgment. This being the case, Yahweh's act of providing a king for Israel is itself an act of divine wrath (see Hos 13:11).

When Saul is selected by a process of elimination, he is nowhere to be found. Because this king-designate has been prophetically anointed, has received three signs confirming his divine appointment (1Sa 10:1-7), and has been empowered by the spirit of God, this hesitancy to take up the task reflects badly on Saul.

Once located, Saul is presented to the people, who enthusiastically approve.

9:1—10:27 An awareness that God is at work in the world today should make believers more sensitive to his unexpected and unseen influence in our everyday lives. God does not miraculously send us a prophetic word every day or meet us in a burning bush (Ex 3). Nevertheless, we should learn to be faithful while attending to the routine, the ordinary, and the familiar. For in these, God often leads and directs his people.

3The elders of Jabesh said to him, "Give
us seven days so we can send messengers throughout Israel; if no one comes
to rescue us, we will surrender to you."
4When the messengers came to Gibeah[n] of Saul and reported these terms to
the people, they all wept[o] aloud. 5Just
then Saul was returning from the fields,
behind his oxen, and he asked, "What
is wrong with everyone? Why are they
weeping?" Then they repeated to him
what the men of Jabesh had said.
6When Saul heard their words, the
Spirit[p] of God came powerfully upon
him, and he burned with anger. 7He
took a pair of oxen, cut them into pieces, and sent the pieces by messengers
throughout Israel,[q] proclaiming, "This is
what will be done to the oxen of anyone[r]
who does not follow Saul and Samuel."
Then the terror of the LORD fell on the
people, and they came out together as
one. 8When Saul mustered[s] them at Bezek,[t] the men of Israel numbered three
hundred thousand and those of Judah
thirty thousand.
9They told the messengers who had
come, "Say to the men of Jabesh Gilead,
'By the time the sun is hot tomorrow,
you will be rescued.'" When the messengers went and reported this to the men
of Jabesh, they were elated. 10They said
to the Ammonites, "Tomorrow we will
surrender[u] to you, and you can do to us
whatever you like."

11:4 [n]1Sa 10:5, 26; 15:34 [o]Jdg 2:4; 1Sa 30:4
11:6 [p]Jdg 3:10; 6:34; 13:25; 14:6; 1Sa 10:10; 16:13
11:7 [q]Jdg 19:29 [r]Jdg 21:5
11:8 [s]Jdg 20:2 [t]Jdg 1:4
11:10 [u]ver 3

1Sa 11:6 ❖ How can we tell whether we are burning with the righteous anger of God or our own human and sinful anger?

11The next day Saul separated his men
into three divisions;[v] during the last
watch of the night they broke into the
camp of the Ammonites and slaughtered
them until the heat of the day. Those who
survived were scattered, so that no two
of them were left together.

Saul Confirmed as King

12The people then said to Samuel,
"Who[w] was it that asked, 'Shall Saul reign
over us?' Turn these men over to us so
that we may put them to death."
13But Saul said, "No one will be put to
death today,[x] for this day the LORD has
rescued[y] Israel."
14Then Samuel said to the people,
"Come, let us go to Gilgal[z] and there renew the kingship.[a]" 15So all the people
went to Gilgal[b] and made Saul king in
the presence of the LORD. There they
sacrificed fellowship offerings before
the LORD, and Saul and all the Israelites
held a great celebration.

Samuel's Farewell Speech

12 Samuel said to all Israel, "I have
listened[c] to everything you said to
me and have set a king[d] over you. 2Now

11:11 [v]Jdg 7:16
11:12 [w]1Sa 10:27; Lk 19:27
11:13 [x]2Sa 19:22 [y]Ex 14:13; 1Sa 19:5
11:14 [z]1Sa 10:8 [a]1Sa 10:25
11:15 [b]1Sa 10:8, 17
12:1 [c]1Sa 8:7 [d]1Sa 10:24; 11:15

11:1–3 During the judges period, the Ammonites had threatened Israelite territory more than once (3:13; 10:6–9; 11:4). The question that plagues the minds of the elders of Jabesh Gilead is whether there is anyone to rescue them. Thus, the text establishes the suspense: Will Israel's new king be up to the task, or will he fail to deliver, as the troublemakers of 10:27 suspect?

11:4–5 This passage is especially reminiscent of Jdg 19–21.

11:6–8 As in the previous passage, the "Spirit of God" comes on Saul to empower him (v. 6). The text uses nearly identical phraseology as in Judges. The Spirit fills the judge with divine indignation and empowers him for military service. The earlier Spirit-empowerment of Saul was temporary, but this one is apparently more permanent, continuing until Samuel anoints David as Saul's replacement.

11:9–11 The victory over the Ammonites functions as Saul's first test and prepares him and the nation for his final coronation at Gilgal.

11:12–15 This short passage illustrates the role of the king as the anointed one whom Yahweh has publicly confirmed. He is the only one who has the ability to forgive crimes and abolish the demands of divine justice—similar to the OT's prophetic descriptions of the long-awaited Messiah.

11:1–15 It is not always easy to know whether we are definitely moved by God's spirit or by our natural instincts. It is easy to be confused about what we are supposed to do and when we are supposed to do it. In this text, we are presented with an OT example of a chosen servant of God, prepared in many ways to fulfill God's mission for his life and also open and responsive to God's prodding, direction, and timing. We can learn much from such examples.

12:1–5 It is time for Samuel to clear the air. Under his tenure, things were fair and equitable. The claim that Samuel has not *taken* anything unlawfully or unjustly relates this speech with the one in 8:11–18. There Samuel detailed "the way of the king," who would "take" everything they hold dear, including their freedom. In Samuel's reference to the Lord's "anointed" (12:5), he stresses the role of the new king to uphold Yahweh's rule among his people. Now the burden rests on Saul.

PEOPLE TO KNOW // SAMUEL

1 SAMUEL 12:1–5: Samuel was the miracle son of Hannah, who had been barren and prayed to God for a son (1Sa 1:20). Samuel was a literal answer to prayer. Hannah had told God she would give this child to him once he was old enough to serve, so Samuel grew up in the temple under the care of Eli the priest. God called to Samuel one night in the temple to announce his judgment upon Eli's family for their wickedness (1Sa 3:11–18).

When he grew up, Samuel became a prophetic leader in Israel. However, his sons were evil and not fit to lead after him, so the people asked Samuel for a king (1Sa 8:1–5). Samuel warned them against this decision, but the people insisted. God instructed Samuel to give the people a king, and Samuel anointed Saul (1Sa 10:1). After Saul failed to follow God's directives, God sent Samuel to anoint David. Samuel was first impressed by the look of David's older brother Eliab, but God told Samuel that while people look only at the outside, God looks at the heart (1Sa 16:7). David was the youngest of his brothers and relegated to the lowly task of shepherding, yet he was the one God had Samuel anoint as king.

After Samuel's death, King Saul summoned Samuel's spirit through a medium at Endor. Saul asked Samuel for help since God had refused to answer the king. Samuel, however, replied that the very next day Saul and his sons would join him in the realm of the dead (1Sa 28:19). The next day, Saul and three of his sons died on the battlefield (1Sa 31:6).

APPLICATION It is hard to speak bold messages of truth or judgment to those in power, but that's exactly what Samuel had to do, both with Eli and Saul. Samuel reminds us not to fear human authorities, but to fear only God. God will honor his faithful servants. Even when it is difficult, we must be messengers of God's truth.

you have a king as your leader.[e] As for
me, I am old and gray, and my sons are
here with you. I have been your leader
from my youth until this day. 3Here I
stand. Testify against me in the presence
of the LORD and his anointed.[f] Whose ox
have I taken? Whose donkey[g] have I tak-
en? Whom have I cheated? Whom have
I oppressed? From whose hand have I
accepted a bribe[h] to make me shut my
eyes? If I have done[i] any of these things,
I will make it right."
4"You have not cheated or oppressed
us," they replied. "You have not taken
anything from anyone's hand."
5Samuel said to them, "The LORD is
witness against you, and also his anointed is witness this day, that you have not
found anything[j] in my hand.[k]"
"He is witness," they said.
6Then Samuel said to the people, "It
is the LORD who appointed Moses and
Aaron and brought[l] your ancestors up
out of Egypt. 7Now then, stand here, because I am going to confront[m] you with
evidence before the LORD as to all the
righteous acts performed by the LORD
for you and your ancestors.
8"After Jacob entered Egypt, they
cried[n] to the LORD for help, and the LORD
sent[o] Moses and Aaron, who brought
your ancestors out of Egypt and settled
them in this place.
9"But they forgot[p] the LORD their
God; so he sold them into the hand of
Sisera,[q] the commander of the army of
Hazor, and into the hands of the Philistines[r] and the king of Moab,[s] who fought
against them. 10They cried out to the
LORD and said, 'We have sinned; we have
forsaken[t] the LORD and served the Baals
and the Ashtoreths.[u] But now deliver
us from the hands of our enemies, and
we will serve you.' 11Then the LORD sent

12:2 [e]1Sa 8:5
12:3 [f]1Sa 10:1; 24:6; 2Sa 1:14 [g]Nu 16:15 [h]Dt 16:19 [i]Ac 20:33
12:5 [j]Ac 23:9; 24:20 [k]Ex 22:4
12:6 [l]Ex 6:26; Mic 6:4
12:7 [m]Isa 1:18; Mic 6:1-5
12:8 [n]Ex 2:23 [o]Ex 3:10; 4:16
12:9 [p]Jdg 3:7 [q]Jdg 4:2 [r]Jdg 10:7; 13:1 [s]Jdg 3:12
12:10 [t]Jdg 10:10,15 [u]Jdg 2:13

12:6–15 The expression "present yourselves" in vv. 7, 16 mark these units as distinct (NIV "stand here" and "stand still"). Both usages prepare the audience to consider the mighty deeds of Yahweh. Samuel emphasizes in particular the judges period in order to show that regardless of how far short their ancestors fell, Yahweh never abandoned them. The cycle of sin, oppression, repentance, and judge-provided deliverance was oft repeated and had, in fact, preserved the nation. Now this current generation of Israelites has grown dissatisfied with the theocratic system, just as their ancestors had grown tired of the manna in the desert.

So, Samuel drives home their choice. He forces them to face the reality of a human king as opposed to the divinely provided judge-deliverers. Verse 13

Jerub-Baal,[a][v] Barak,[b][w] Jephthah[x] and Samuel,[c] and he delivered you from the hands of your enemies all around you, so that you lived in safety.

12"But when you saw that Nahash[y] king[z] of the Ammonites was moving against you, you said to me, 'No, we want a king to rule[a] over us'—even though the LORD your God was your king. 13Now here is the king[b] you have chosen, the one you asked[c] for; see, the LORD has set a king over you. 14If you fear[d] the LORD and serve and obey him and do not rebel against his commands, and if both you and the king who reigns over you follow the LORD your God—good! 15But if you do not obey the LORD, and if you rebel against[e] his commands, his hand will be against you, as it was against your ancestors.

16"Now then, stand still and see[f] this great thing the LORD is about to do before your eyes! 17Is it not wheat harvest[g] now? I will call[h] on the LORD to send thunder and rain.[i] And you will realize what an evil[j] thing you did in the eyes of the LORD when you asked for a king."

18Then Samuel called on the LORD, and that same day the LORD sent thunder and rain. So all the people stood in awe[k] of the LORD and of Samuel.

19The people all said to Samuel, "Pray[l] to the LORD your God for your servants so that we will not die, for we have added to all our other sins the evil of asking for a king."

20"Do not be afraid," Samuel replied. "You have done all this evil; yet do not turn away from the LORD, but serve the LORD with all your heart. 21Do not turn away after useless[m] idols.[n] They can do you no good, nor can they rescue you, because they are useless. 22For the sake[o] of his great name[p] the LORD will not reject[q] his people, because the LORD was pleased to make[r] you his own. 23As for me, far be it from me that I should sin against the LORD by failing to pray[s] for you. And I will teach[t] you the way that is good and right. 24But be sure to fear[u] the LORD and serve him faithfully with all your heart; consider[v] what great[w] things he has done for you. 25Yet if you persist[x] in doing evil, both you and your king will perish."[y]

12:11 [v]Jdg 6:14, 32 [w]Jdg 4:6 [x]Jdg 11:1
12:12 [y]1Sa 11:1 [z]1Sa 8:5 [a]Jdg 8:23; 1Sa 8:6,19
12:13 [b]1Sa 8:5; Hos 13:11 [c]1Sa 10:24
12:14 [d]Jos 24:14
12:15 [e]ver 9; Jos 24:20; Isa 1:20
12:16 [f]Ex 14:13
12:17 [g]1Sa 7:9-10 [h]Jas 5:18 [i]Pr 26:1 [j]1Sa 8:6-7
12:18 [k]Ex 14:31
12:19 [l]ver 23; Ex 9:28; Jas 5:18; 1Jn 5:16
12:21 [m]Isa 41:24, 29; Jer 16:19; Hab 2:18 [n]Dt 11:16
12:22 [o]Ps 106:8 [p]Jos 7:9 [q]1Ki 6:13 [r]Dt 7:7; 1Pe 2:9
12:23 [s]Ro 1:9-10; Col 1:9; 2Ti 1:3 [t]1Ki 8:36; Ps 34:11; Pr 4:11
12:24 [u]Ecc 12:13 [v]Isa 5:12 [w]Dt 10:21
12:25 [x]1Sa 31:1-5 [y]Jos 24:20
13:2 [z]1Sa 10:26

1Sa 12:23 ❖ Who is God calling us to pray for? How can we help teach them "the way that is good and right"?

Samuel Rebukes Saul

13 Saul was thirty[d] years old when he became king, and he reigned over Israel forty-[e] two years.

2Saul chose three thousand men from Israel; two thousand were with him at Mikmash and in the hill country of Bethel, and a thousand were with Jonathan at Gibeah[z] in Benjamin. The rest of the men he sent back to their homes.

[a] *11* Also called *Gideon* [b] *11* Some Septuagint manuscripts and Syriac; Hebrew *Bedan* [c] *11* Hebrew; some Septuagint manuscripts and Syriac *Samson* [d] *1* A few late manuscripts of the Septuagint; Hebrew does not have *thirty.* [e] *1* Probable reading of the original Hebrew text (see Acts 13:21); Masoretic Text does not have *forty-.*

is the hinge or central theme of the chapter. To prove that this is no omnipotent monarchy, Samuel outlines the conditions for its success (vv. 14–15).

12:16–25 For the sake of future generations, it is critically important for the Israelites to properly define and understand the role of the new king. But just as important is the role of prophets in the new government. Israel may have a new king and a new political structure, but they must never neglect the word of the servants of Yahweh, the prophets.

Samuel's words and the miraculous storm drive the people to repentance and to a plea for Samuel to intercede on their behalf (v. 19). Samuel reiterates that they have acted wickedly, but they are not without hope. If they remain true to Yahweh, avoiding all idolatry, he will not reject them. Despite the new political system, Yahweh still wants an intimate relationship with Israel, but only under the old-covenant terms.

Having duly charged the people to remain faithful, the rest of Samuel's answer addresses his own responsibilities (vv. 23–25): Samuel's new role arises from his prophetic relationship with Yahweh.

12:1–25 God was constantly giving Israel second chances. At some point, one would wonder if God's grace might give out: When does one exhaust the mercy of God and begin to worry that God might withhold his forgiveness?

Samuel's speech tells us that God's grace to forgive takes shape first of all as grace to convict and uncover the hidden sinfulness of the human heart. Most Christians today stress only forgiveness as the ministry of God's grace. But here the hard words of the prophet, bringing awareness that one is in need of forgiveness, are also a gift of God's grace.

13:1–4 Jonathan appears for the first time with little fanfare. He is not identified specifically as Saul's son until v. 16. His skirmish with a Philistine outpost escalates into the full-fledged war that

3Jonathan attacked the Philistine outpost[a] at Geba, and the Philistines heard
about it. Then Saul had the trumpet
blown throughout the land and said,
"Let the Hebrews hear!" 4So all Israel
heard the news: "Saul has attacked the
Philistine outpost, and now Israel has
become obnoxious[b] to the Philistines."
And the people were summoned to join
Saul at Gilgal.

5The Philistines assembled to fight Israel, with three thousand[a] chariots, six
thousand charioteers, and soldiers as
numerous as the sand[c] on the seashore.
They went up and camped at Mikmash,
east of Beth Aven. 6When the Israelites
saw that their situation was critical and
that their army was hard pressed, they
hid in caves and thickets, among the
rocks, and in pits and cisterns.[d] 7Some
Hebrews even crossed the Jordan to the
land of Gad[e] and Gilead.

Saul remained at Gilgal, and all the
troops with him were quaking with fear.
8He waited seven[f] days, the time set by
Samuel; but Samuel did not come to Gilgal, and Saul's men began to scatter. 9So
he said, "Bring me the burnt offering
and the fellowship offerings." And Saul
offered[g] up the burnt offering. 10Just as
he finished making the offering, Samuel[h]
arrived, and Saul went out to greet him.

11"What have you done?" asked Samuel.

Saul replied, "When I saw that the men
were scattering, and that you did not
come at the set time, and that the Philistines were assembling at Mikmash,[i] 12I
thought, 'Now the Philistines will come
down against me at Gilgal, and I have
not sought the LORD's favor.[j]' So I felt
compelled to offer the burnt offering."

13:3 [a] 1Sa 10:5
13:4 [b] Ge 34:30
13:5 [c] Jos 11:4
13:6 [d] Jdg 6:2
13:7 [e] Nu 32:33
13:8 [f] 1Sa 10:8
13:9 [g] 2Sa 24:25; 1Ki 3:4
13:10 [h] 1Sa 15:13
13:11 [i] ver 2,5, 16,23
13:12 [j] Jer 26:19
13:13 [k] 2Ch 16:9 [l] 1Sa 15:23,24
13:14 [m] 1Sa 15:28 [n] Ac 7:46; 13:22 [o] 2Sa 6:21
13:15 [p] 1Sa 14:2
13:17 [q] 1Sa 14:15 [r] Jos 18:23
13:18 [s] Jos 18:13-14 [t] Ne 11:34
13:19 [u] 2Ki 24:14; Jer 24:1

1Sa 13:11-12 ❖ When has fear or impatience led us to make a bad choice?

13"You have done a foolish thing,[k]"
Samuel said. "You have not kept[l] the
command the LORD your God gave you;
if you had, he would have established
your kingdom over Israel for all time.
14But now your kingdom[m] will not endure; the LORD has sought out a man
after his own heart[n] and appointed[o] him
ruler of his people, because you have not
kept the LORD's command."

15Then Samuel left Gilgal[b] and went up
to Gibeah[p] in Benjamin, and Saul counted the men who were with him. They
numbered about six hundred.

Israel Without Weapons

16Saul and his son Jonathan and the
men with them were staying in Gibeah[c] in Benjamin, while the Philistines
camped at Mikmash. 17Raiding[q] parties
went out from the Philistine camp in
three detachments. One turned toward
Ophrah[r] in the vicinity of Shual, 18an-
other toward Beth Horon,[s] and the third
toward the borderland overlooking the
Valley of Zeboyim[t] facing the wilderness.

19Not a blacksmith[u] could be found
in the whole land of Israel, because the
Philistines had said, "Otherwise the Hebrews will make swords or spears!" 20So
all Israel went down to the Philistines to
have their plow points, mattocks, axes

[a] 5 Some Septuagint manuscripts and Syriac; Hebrew *thirty thousand* [b] 15 Hebrew; Septuagint *Gilgal and went his way; the rest of the people went after Saul to meet the army, and they went out of Gilgal* [c] 16 Two Hebrew manuscripts; most Hebrew manuscripts *Geba*, a variant of *Gibeah*

---

everyone is expecting and for which Saul has been anointed king.

13:5–7 When the Philistines muster what seems like insurmountable odds, many of Saul's troops begin to scatter.

15:8–15 Saul has been directed by Samuel to wait seven days, after which the prophet will arrive, offer the appropriate sacrifices, and commission Saul and the troops to enter the battle. Standing beside every Israelite king was to be a prophet speaking God's word for the situation.

Saul's offense is not the mere fact that he offers a sacrifice but that he disobeys God's word through the prophet Samuel. No sooner has Saul finished than Samuel appears to announce that Saul has lost the opportunity to establish an eternal dynasty. He himself will keep the throne, but it will not pass to his descendants and endure forever, as eventually will be promised to David. Instead, Yahweh will give the kingdom to "a man after his own heart" (v. 14).

13:16–22 The Philistines hold decisive military superiority over the Israelites during this period. They substantially outnumber the troops of Saul and Jonathan, and by controlling a monopoly in metallurgical technology and technicians, the Philistines are able to limit Israel's arsenal. The result is that on the day of battle, only Saul and Jonathan among the Israelites are armed (v. 22). Presumably the Philistines know how inadequately Israel is prepared for war. It seems clear: Saul and his forces are in danger of annihilation.

and sickles[a] sharpened. 21The price was two-thirds of a shekel[b] for sharpening plow points and mattocks, and a third of a shekel[c] for sharpening forks and axes and for repointing goads.

22So on the day of the battle not a soldier with Saul and Jonathan[v] had a sword or spear[w] in his hand; only Saul and his son Jonathan had them.

Jonathan Attacks the Philistines

23Now a detachment of Philistines had gone out to the pass[x] at Mikmash.

14 1One day Jonathan son of Saul said to his young armor-bearer, "Come, let's go over to the Philistine outpost on the other side." But he did not tell his father.

2Saul was staying on the outskirts of Gibeah[y] under a pomegranate tree in Migron.[z] With him were about six hundred men, 3among whom was Ahijah, who was wearing an ephod. He was a son of Ichabod's[a] brother Ahitub[b] son of Phinehas, the son of Eli,[c] the LORD's priest in Shiloh. No one was aware that Jonathan had left.

4On each side of the pass[d] that Jonathan intended to cross to reach the Philistine outpost was a cliff; one was called Bozez and the other Seneh. 5One cliff stood to the north toward Mikmash, the other to the south toward Geba.

6Jonathan said to his young armor-bearer, "Come, let's go over to the outpost of those uncircumcised[e] men. Perhaps the LORD will act in our behalf. Nothing[f] can hinder the LORD from saving, whether by many[g] or by few.[h]"

7"Do all that you have in mind," his armor-bearer said. "Go ahead; I am with you heart and soul."

8Jonathan said, "Come on, then; we will cross over toward them and let them see us. 9If they say to us, 'Wait there until we come to you,' we will stay where we are and not go up to them. 10But if they say, 'Come up to us,' we will climb up, because that will be our sign[i] that the LORD has given them into our hands."

11So both of them showed themselves to the Philistine outpost. "Look!" said the Philistines. "The Hebrews are crawling out of the holes they were hiding[j] in." 12The men of the outpost shouted to Jonathan and his armor-bearer, "Come up to us and we'll teach you a lesson.[k]"

So Jonathan said to his armor-bearer, "Climb up after me; the LORD has given them into the hand[l] of Israel."

13Jonathan climbed up, using his hands and feet, with his armor-bearer right behind him. The Philistines fell before Jonathan, and his armor-bearer followed and killed behind him. 14In that first attack Jonathan and his armor-bearer killed some twenty men in an area of about half an acre.

Israel Routs the Philistines

15Then panic[m] struck the whole army — those in the camp and field, and those in the outposts and raiding[n] parties — and the ground shook. It was a panic sent by God.[d]

13:22 [v] 1Ch 9:39 [w] Jdg 5:8
13:23 [x] 1Sa 14:4
14:2 [y] 1Sa 13:15 [z] Isa 10:28
14:3 [a] 1Sa 4:21 [b] 1Sa 22:11,20 [c] 1Sa 2:28
14:4 [d] 1Sa 13:23
14:6 [e] 1Sa 17:26, 36; Jer 9:26 [f] Heb 11:34 [g] Jdg 7:4 [h] 1Sa 17:46-47
14:10 [i] Ge 24:14; Jdg 6:36-37
14:11 [j] 1Sa 13:6
14:12 [k] 1Sa 17:43-44 [l] 2Sa 5:24
14:15 [m] Ge 35:5; 2Ki 7:5-7 [n] 1Sa 13:17

[a] *20* Septuagint; Hebrew *plow points* [b] *21* That is, about 1/4 ounce or about 8 grams [c] *21* That is, about 1/8 ounce or about 4 grams [d] *15* Or *a terrible panic*

13:1-22 Consider the features of Saul's actions that contribute to the anatomy of sin: (1) Saul allows the circumstances of his current crisis to overtake him. (2) Saul commits himself to partial obedience. (3) When Samuel confronts Saul with this infraction, he fails to accept responsibility.

In taking this action and explaining himself to Samuel, Saul continues the kind of self-justification we have come to expect (and use ourselves) since the Garden of Eden.

13:23—14:6 The unit opens with the account of Jonathan's daring raid on the Philistine detachment at Mikmash. Jonathan is unimpressed by the enemy's greater numbers and undeterred in his belief that Yahweh will deliver Israel from this dreaded enemy. His words to the armor-bearer reveal his character and commitment.

14:3 While Jonathan and his armor-bearer are on their secret mission, Saul is in Gibeah administering his kingdom. The passing reference to Ahijah in this verse is important for our reading of this unit. What is remarkable here is Ahijah's carefully phrased genealogy. The narrator has detoured from direct descent in the line of Aaron to highlight an uncle, Ichabod, thus recalling the checkered history of Eli, Phinehas, and Hophni. The reference in this verse to the rejected priestly house stresses the rejection of Saul's royal house. Moreover, it reveals something of the inner life of Saul, who has apparently lost the prophet Samuel as his spiritual advisor.

14:7-14 The Lord honors Jonathan's brave leadership. By implication the paragraph is showing what kind of king Jonathan would have been as his father's successor. But alas, the text has already informed us that Jonathan will not be king because of Saul's unfaithfulness (13:13-14).

14:15-19 This paragraph continues the contrast between Saul and Jonathan by illustrating how

16Saul's lookouts[o] at Gibeah in Benjamin saw the army melting away in all
directions. 17Then Saul said to the men
who were with him, "Muster the forces
and see who has left us." When they did,
it was Jonathan and his armor-bearer
who were not there.
18Saul said to Ahijah, "Bring[p] the ark
of God." (At that time it was with the Israelites.)[a] 19While Saul was talking to the
priest, the tumult in the Philistine camp
increased more and more. So Saul said
to the priest,[q] "Withdraw your hand."
20Then Saul and all his men assembled
and went to the battle. They found the
Philistines in total confusion, striking[r]
each other with their swords. 21Those
Hebrews who had previously been with
the Philistines and had gone up with
them to their camp went[s] over to the
Israelites who were with Saul and Jonathan. 22When all the Israelites who had
hidden[t] in the hill country of Ephraim
heard that the Philistines were on the
run, they joined the battle in hot pursuit. 23So on that day the LORD saved[u]
Israel, and the battle moved on beyond
Beth Aven.[v]

Jonathan Eats Honey

24Now the Israelites were in distress
that day, because Saul had bound the
people under an oath,[w] saying, "Cursed
be anyone who eats food before evening
comes, before I have avenged myself on
my enemies!" So none of the troops tasted food.
25The entire army entered the woods,
and there was honey on the ground.
26When they went into the woods, they
saw the honey oozing out; yet no one
put his hand to his mouth, because they
feared the oath. 27But Jonathan had not
heard that his father had bound the people with the oath, so he reached out the
end of the staff that was in his hand
and dipped it into the honeycomb.[x] He
raised his hand to his mouth, and his
eyes brightened.[b] 28Then one of the soldiers told him, "Your father bound the
army under a strict oath, saying, 'Cursed
be anyone who eats food today!' That is
why the men are faint."
29Jonathan said, "My father has made
trouble[y] for the country. See how my eyes
brightened when I tasted a little of this
honey. 30How much better it would have
been if the men had eaten today some
of the plunder they took from their enemies. Would not the slaughter of the
Philistines have been even greater?"
31That day, after the Israelites had
struck down the Philistines from Mikmash to Aijalon,[z] they were exhausted.
32They pounced on the plunder[a] and,
taking sheep, cattle and calves, they
butchered them on the ground and ate
them, together with the blood.[b] 33Then
someone said to Saul, "Look, the men
are sinning against the LORD by eating
meat that has blood in it."
"You have broken faith," he said. "Roll
a large stone over here at once." 34Then
he said, "Go out among the men and tell
them, 'Each of you bring me your cattle
and sheep, and slaughter them here and
eat them. Do not sin against the LORD by
eating meat with blood still in it.' "
So everyone brought his ox that night
and slaughtered it there. 35Then Saul

14:16 [o] 2Sa 18:24
14:18 [p] 1Sa 30:7
14:19 [q] Nu 27:21
14:20 [r] Jdg 7:22; 2Ch 20:23
14:21 [s] 1Sa 29:4
14:22 [t] 1Sa 13:6
14:23 [u] Ex 14:30; Ps 44:6-7 [v] 1Sa 13:5
14:24 [w] Jos 6:26
14:27 [x] ver 43; 1Sa 30:12
14:29 [y] Jos 7:25; 1Ki 18:18
14:31 [z] Jos 10:12
14:32 [a] 1Sa 15:19 [b] Ge 9:4; Lev 3:17; 7:26; 17:10-14; 19:26; Dt 12:16, 23-24

[a] *18* Hebrew; Septuagint *"Bring the ephod." (At that time he wore the ephod before the Israelites.)*
[b] *27* Or *his strength was renewed;* similarly in verse 29

Jonathan is a leader who takes action, while Saul simply responds. When Saul sees what is happening, he calls for Ahijah to bring the ark, apparently planning to ask Yahweh whether he should join the battle with the Philistines or not.

14:20–23 Inexplicably, Saul suddenly stops the inquiry and rushes to the battlefield. Such sudden reversals expose Saul's uncertainty and remind the reader of his previous failure to wait for Samuel's arrival to offer a sacrifice. The battle appears to have been nearly won before Saul even arrives on the scene (v. 20).

14:24–26 Saul's impetuous, even careless, decree disallowing his troops to eat food during the day of battle may have been motivated by a desire to create a "holy war" setting, which is reasonable in this context. But however commendable his reasons for such a ban, the result is that his troops are famished and exhausted.

14:27–30 This passage's unusual events illustrate again the contrast between Jonathan and Saul. Jonathan, unaware of his father's foolish ban, does not hesitate to refresh himself with honey. His "brightened" condition (vv. 27, 29) proves that he has better understood God's will for the troops than his father. He quickly condemns Saul's ban and accuses him of making trouble for Israel (v. 29).

14:31–37 Later when Saul seeks divine guidance concerning a surprise night attack, there is no response from Yahweh. This divine silence is tantamount to divine displeasure, and Saul begins an investigation to find the guilty party who violated the order. When Jonathan proves to be the guilty party, Saul is faced with revolt in his own army.

built an altar[c] to the LORD; it was the
first time he had done this.
36 Saul said, "Let us go down and pursue the Philistines by night and plunder
them till dawn, and let us not leave one
of them alive."
"Do whatever seems best to you," they
replied.
But the priest said, "Let us inquire of
God here."
37 So Saul asked God, "Shall I go down
and pursue the Philistines? Will you give
them into Israel's hand?" But God did not
answer[d] him that day.
38 Saul therefore said, "Come here, all
you who are leaders of the army, and let
us find out what sin has been committed[e] today. 39 As surely as the LORD who
rescues Israel lives,[f] even if the guilt lies
with my son Jonathan, he must die." But
not one of them said a word.
40 Saul then said to all the Israelites,
"You stand over there; I and Jonathan
my son will stand over here."
"Do what seems best to you," they replied.
41 Then Saul prayed to the LORD, the
God of Israel, "Why have you not answered your servant today? If the fault
is in me or my son Jonathan, respond
with Urim, but if the men of Israel are at
fault,[a] respond with Thummim." Jonathan and Saul were taken by lot, and the
men were cleared. 42 Saul said, "Cast the
lot between me and Jonathan my son."
And Jonathan was taken.
43 Then Saul said to Jonathan, "Tell me
what you have done."[g]
So Jonathan told him, "I tasted a little
honey[h] with the end of my staff. And
now I must die!"
44 Saul said, "May God deal with me,
be it ever so severely,[i] if you do not die,
Jonathan.[j]"

14:35 [c] 1Sa 7:17
14:37 [d] 1Sa 10:22; 28:6,15
14:38 [e] Jos 7:11; 1Sa 10:19
14:39 [f] 2Sa 12:5
14:43 [g] Jos 7:19 [h] ver 27
14:44 [i] Ru 1:17 [j] ver 39
14:45 [k] 1Ki 1:52; Lk 21:18; Ac 27:34 [l] 2Sa 14:11
14:47 [m] 1Sa 11:1-13 [n] ver 52; 2Sa 10:6
14:48 [o] 1Sa 15:2,7
14:49 [p] 1Sa 31:2; 1Ch 8:33 [q] 1Sa 18:17-20
14:51 [r] 1Sa 9:1

1Sa 14:45 ❖ How can we find the courage to speak up for what is right, even when it opposes those with great power?

45 But the men said to Saul, "Should
Jonathan die — he who has brought
about this great deliverance in Israel?
Never! As surely as the LORD lives, not a
hair[k] of his head will fall to the ground,
for he did this today with God's help." So
the men rescued[l] Jonathan, and he was
not put to death.
46 Then Saul stopped pursuing the
Philistines, and they withdrew to their
own land.
47 After Saul had assumed rule over
Israel, he fought against their enemies
on every side: Moab, the Ammonites,[m]
Edom, the kings[b] of Zobah,[n] and the
Philistines. Wherever he turned, he
inflicted punishment on them.[c] 48 He
fought valiantly and defeated the Amalekites,[o] delivering Israel from the
hands of those who had plundered
them.

Saul's Family

49 Saul's sons were Jonathan, Ishvi
and Malki-Shua.[p] The name of his older daughter was Merab, and that of the
younger was Michal.[q] 50 His wife's name
was Ahinoam daughter of Ahimaaz. The
name of the commander of Saul's army
was Abner son of Ner, and Ner was Saul's
uncle. 51 Saul's father Kish[r] and Abner's
father Ner were sons of Abiel.
52 All the days of Saul there was bitter
war with the Philistines, and whenever

[a] 41 Septuagint; Hebrew does not have *"Why . . . at fault.* [b] 47 Masoretic Text; Dead Sea Scrolls and Septuagint *king* [c] 47 Hebrew; Septuagint *he was victorious*

14:38–46 Saul has gradually alienated himself first from Samuel, then from his army with the foolish ban against eating, and now finally from his own son (v. 39). The result is a lost opportunity. The day that began with prospects of a final and decisive victory over the Philistines ends in a draw (v. 46).

14:47–52 These brief notices about Saul's reign are typical of the OT royal summaries; for example, for David and for other kings in the books of 1–2 Kings. It has been suggested that Saul's summary is more notable for what it does *not* say than for what it does say. Unlike David's summary, for example, there is no mention of Yahweh. Especially important is the concluding verse (v. 52). The Philistine threat was Saul's reason for serving Israel as king (9:16). But the final subjugation of Philistia would have to await a greater king.

13:23—14:52 Christians are not supposed to navigate their own course. We must recognize that we are incapable of finding within our own beings the measure by which we must rule our lives. Just as Saul needed Samuel to direct and guide him, so we need God to shine his light on our paths (Ps 119:105). As Saul was condemned once he turned from Samuel to find guidance in other sources, so modern believers must be warned against neglecting or abandoning God as the source of truth and light.

Saul saw a mighty or brave man, he took[s]
him into his service.

The LORD Rejects Saul as King

15 Samuel said to Saul, "I am the one
the LORD sent to anoint[t] you king
over his people Israel; so listen now to
the message from the LORD. 2This is what
the LORD Almighty says: 'I will punish
the Amalekites[u] for what they did to
Israel when they waylaid them as they
came up from Egypt. 3Now go, attack
the Amalekites and totally[v] destroy[a] all
that belongs to them. Do not spare them;
put to death men and women, children
and infants, cattle and sheep, camels and
donkeys.' "

4So Saul summoned the men and
mustered them at Telaim — two hundred thousand foot soldiers and ten
thousand from Judah. 5Saul went to
the city of Amalek and set an ambush
in the ravine. 6Then he said to the Kenites,[w] "Go away, leave the Amalekites
so that I do not destroy you along with
them; for you showed kindness to all
the Israelites when they came up out of
Egypt." So the Kenites moved away from
the Amalekites.

7Then Saul attacked the Amalekites[x] all
the way from Havilah to Shur,[y] near the
eastern border of Egypt. 8He took Agag
king of the Amalekites alive,[z] and all
his people he totally destroyed with the
sword. 9But Saul and the army spared[a]
Agag and the best of the sheep and cattle,
the fat calves[b] and lambs — everything
that was good. These they were unwilling
to destroy completely, but everything
that was despised and weak they totally
destroyed.

10Then the word of the LORD came to
Samuel: 11"I regret[b] that I have made Saul
king, because he has turned[c] away from
me and has not carried out my instructions."[d] Samuel was angry,[e] and he cried
out to the LORD all that night.

12Early in the morning Samuel got up
and went to meet Saul, but he was told,
"Saul has gone to Carmel.[f] There he has
set up a monument in his own honor and
has turned and gone on down to Gilgal."

13When Samuel reached him, Saul said,
"The LORD bless you! I have carried out
the LORD's instructions."

14But Samuel said, "What then is this
bleating of sheep in my ears? What is this
lowing of cattle that I hear?"

15Saul answered, "The soldiers brought
them from the Amalekites; they spared
the best of the sheep and cattle to sacrifice to the LORD your God, but we totally
destroyed the rest."

16"Enough!" Samuel said to Saul. "Let
me tell you what the LORD said to me
last night."

"Tell me," Saul replied.

17Samuel said, "Although you were
once small[g] in your own eyes, did you
not become the head of the tribes of Israel? The LORD anointed you king over
Israel. 18And he sent you on a mission,
saying, 'Go and completely destroy those

14:52 [s]1Sa 8:11
15:1 [t]1Sa 9:16
15:2 [u]Ex 17:8-14; Nu 24:20; Dt 25:17-19
15:3 [v]Nu 24:20; Dt 20:16-18; Jos 6:17; 1Sa 22:19
15:6 [w]Ex 18:10, 19; Nu 10:29-32; 24:22; Jdg 1:16; 4:1
15:7 [x]1Sa 14:48 [y]Ge 16:7; 25:17-18; Ex 15:22
15:8 [z]1Sa 30:1
15:9 [a]ver 3,15
15:11 [b]Ge 6:6; 2Sa 24:16 [c]Jos 22:16 [d]1Sa 13:13; 1Ki 9:6-7 [e]ver 35
15:12 [f]Jos 15:55
15:17 [g]1Sa 9:21

[a] 3 The Hebrew term refers to the irrevocable giving over of things or persons to the LORD, often by totally destroying them; also in verses 8, 9, 15, 18, 20 and 21. [b] 9 Or *the grown bulls*; the meaning of the Hebrew for this phrase is uncertain.

15:1–2 The Amalekites were the first people to oppose the Israelites after the exodus (Ex 17:8–16). Because of their cowardly tactics on an unsuspecting nation, Yahweh promised to extract vengeance against them in some future day when Israel was established in the promised land (Ex 17:8–16; cf. Dt 25:17–19).

Samuel returns to announce that now is the time to accomplish Yahweh's vengeance against Amalek (1Sa 15:2–3), and Saul is the king to do this. Yahweh still has an important mission for Saul, even though his destiny is uncertain.

15:3–9 Samuel's instructions for warfare are clear (v. 3). The description given is familiar to us as what has become known as "holy war," though this terminology is not used in the OT itself. In such wars, Yahweh himself initiates the conflict and ensures its success.

The term "totally destroy" occurs eight times in this chapter and is an important concept in understanding why Saul is rejected. The word denotes a special act of consecration to God. This passage ends on a note that indicates Saul and his army are *selectively* obedient to Yahweh's instructions.

15:10–13 Yahweh informs Samuel that he regrets making Saul king (v. 11). This precipitates an encounter between Samuel and Saul, in which Saul fails to take responsibility for his actions.

15:14–19 Samuel's blunt questions shatter the delusional world in which Saul is living (v. 14). Saul has rationalized his sparing of Agag and the best of the cattle; in Saul's mind, this is only a temporary postponement in fulfilling Yahweh's command. But Samuel's booming "What then is this bleating of sheep?" (v. 14) breaks into Saul's world and reveals his deception for what it truly is—a selfish rejection of God's message. Samuel reminds the king that it is Yahweh's command that made him king and that it is also Yahweh's command that he has now rejected (vv. 17–19).

wicked people, the Amalekites; wage war
against them until you have wiped them
out.' 19Why did you not obey the LORD?
Why did you pounce on the plunder[h] and
do evil in the eyes of the LORD?"
20"But I did obey[i] the LORD," Saul said.
"I went on the mission the LORD assigned
me. I completely destroyed the Amalekites and brought back Agag their king.
21The soldiers took sheep and cattle from
the plunder, the best of what was devoted to God, in order to sacrifice them to
the LORD your God at Gilgal."
22But Samuel replied:

"Does the LORD delight in burnt
offerings and sacrifices
as much as in obeying the LORD?
To obey is better than sacrifice,[j]
and to heed is better than the fat
of rams.
23For rebellion is like the sin of
divination,[k]
and arrogance like the evil of
idolatry.
Because you have rejected[l] the word
of the LORD,
he has rejected you as king."

24Then Saul said to Samuel, "I have
sinned.[m] I violated the LORD's command
and your instructions. I was afraid[n] of the
men and so I gave in to them. 25Now I beg
you, forgive[o] my sin and come back with
me, so that I may worship the LORD."

15:19 [h] 1Sa 14:32
15:20 [i] ver 13
15:22 [j] Ps 40:6-8; 51:16; Isa 1:11-15; Jer 7:22; Hos 6:6; Mic 6:6-8; Mt 12:7; Mk 12:33; Heb 10:6-9
15:23 [k] Dt 18:10 [l] 1Sa 13:13
15:24 [m] 2Sa 12:13 [n] Pr 29:25; Isa 51:12-13
15:25 [o] Ex 10:17
15:26 [p] 1Sa 13:14
15:27 [q] 1Ki 11:11, 31
15:28 [r] 1Sa 28:17; 1Ki 11:31
15:29 [s] 1Ch 29:11; Titus 1:2 [t] Nu 23:19; Eze 24:14
15:30 [u] Isa 29:13; Jn 5:44; 12:43

1Sa 15:29 ❖ How do we find comfort in knowing that God does not change his mind the way people so often do?

26But Samuel said to him, "I will not
go back with you. You have rejected[p] the
word of the LORD, and the LORD has rejected you as king over Israel!"
27As Samuel turned to leave, Saul
caught hold of the hem of his robe, and
it tore.[q] 28Samuel said to him, "The LORD
has torn[r] the kingdom of Israel from you
today and has given it to one of your
neighbors — to one better than you.
29He who is the Glory of Israel does not
lie[s] or change[t] his mind; for he is not a
human being, that he should change
his mind."
30Saul replied, "I have sinned. But
please honor[u] me before the elders of
my people and before Israel; come back
with me, so that I may worship the LORD
your God." 31So Samuel went back with
Saul, and Saul worshiped the LORD.
32Then Samuel said, "Bring me Agag
king of the Amalekites."
Agag came to him in chains.[a] And he
thought, "Surely the bitterness of death
is past."
33But Samuel said,

[a] *32* The meaning of the Hebrew for this phrase is uncertain.

15:20–21 The series of statements made by the king in his defense before Samuel reveals a pitiable soul who is sorry only that he has been caught. His instincts are to defend himself against his accuser.

Once deflection of blame fails, Saul's second strategy is argumentation. In his own defense, he redefines Yahweh's command. In one breath, Saul argues that he did in fact execute the terms of holy war (i.e., complete annihilation of the enemy) *and* he brought back Agag the king. But this is a self-condemning contradiction. In the face of exposed disobedience, many have attempted to redefine what it actually means to obey.

15:22–23 Samuel's response is unequivocal. Yahweh desires obedience over everything else. Even sacrifice is unacceptable if it becomes only a ruse for real submission to God's will. Samuel announces the judgment of Yahweh, which is strictly commensurate with the nature of Saul's sin (v. 23). Now Saul has lost not only his dynasty (as in ch. 13) but also his right to serve as king.

15:24–25 After hearing the irrefutable statement of rejection, Saul changes his strategy again and for the first time we hear something like a confession; it turns out to be self-serving. Technically, Saul uses the right words, but these are followed by many more words revealing the obligatory nature of that confession; it is contrived and motivated by Saul's self-interest.

15:26–29 After Saul's disingenuous confession, and Samuel responds by reaffirming that Yahweh has rejected Saul as king.

15:30–31 The repetition of Saul's confession (vv. 24–25, 30) is common in OT narrative as a technique for emphasis. Saul's second confession serves a climactic role near the end of a unit and reveals the spirit of Saul's ploy. He has replaced "forgive my sin" with "honor me before the elders" (cf. vv. 25, 30). Saul seems more concerned with his people than with Samuel's God.

15:32–35 In the closing scene of this chapter, Samuel executes the Amalekite king. The job unfinished by the king is now left for the prophet himself, who gave the original order (see v. 3). The public execution of Agag is itself an implicit rebuke of Saul, who allowed him to live in the first place.

After this, Samuel mourns for Saul, and Yahweh is grieved that he made Saul king. Everyone seems full of sorrow and regret—except Saul. Implicit in the text is that while others are sorrowful, Saul is unrepentant, showing no true remorse.

"As your sword has made women
childless,
so will your mother be childless
among women."[v]

And Samuel put Agag to death before
the LORD at Gilgal.
34Then Samuel left for Ramah,[w] but
Saul went up to his home in Gibeah[x] of
Saul. 35Until the day Samuel[y] died, he did
not go to see Saul again, though Samuel mourned[z] for him. And the LORD
regretted that he had made Saul king
over Israel.

15:33 [v] Ge 9:6; Jdg 1:7
15:34 [w] 1Sa 7:17 [x] 1Sa 11:4
15:35 [y] 1Sa 19:24 [z] 1Sa 16:1

Samuel Anoints David

16 The LORD said to Samuel, "How
long will you mourn[a] for Saul, since
I have rejected[b] him as king over Israel?
Fill your horn with oil[c] and be on your
way; I am sending you to Jesse[d] of Bethlehem. I have chosen[e] one of his sons to
be king."

16:1 [a] 1Sa 15:35 [b] 1Sa 15:23 [c] 2Ki 9:1 [d] Ru 4:17; 1Sa 9:16 [e] Ps 78:70; Ac 13:22

15:1-35 It is possible simply to go through the motions while neglecting the internal realities of our tortured souls. Samuel reminds us with his word to Saul that obedience is better than sacrifice. If we miss the reality of internal worship and confession, no amount of attention to externals, such as church attendance or involvement in Christian causes, will atone for disobeying God's Word.

16:1 Yahweh commands his prophet to move forward regardless of his sense of personal loss. Jesse is the grandson of Ruth and Boaz (Ru 4:17-22) and comes from the tribe of Judah (Ru 4:12). From this time forward, the name of Jesse, the city of Bethlehem, and the tribe of Judah will always be linked to Israel's Messiah.

The last phrase of 1Sa 16:1 contains a subtle but powerful statement about David. A perhaps more descriptive translation of the sentence is: "I have provided *for myself* a king from among his sons" (alternate translation). This suggests a contrast with the circumstances surrounding Saul's selection, when Yahweh made a concession for the sake of the people (8:22).

PEOPLE TO KNOW // DAVID

1 SAMUEL 16:1-13: When the prophet Samuel confronted King Saul for failing to keep God's commands, Samuel told Saul God had chosen another to be king, a man after God's own heart (1Sa 13:13-14). That man was David.

David was the youngest of seven brothers, tasked with watching his father's sheep. Yet God was not looking for a king who was in a powerful position or looked good on the outside (like Saul); he wanted someone with a righteous heart.

David became a well-known and popular figure in the kingdom after defeating the giant Goliath (1Sa 17:48-51). This made Saul envious, and he tried to kill David. But when David had a chance to kill Saul, he spared Saul's life, declaring he would not touch the Lord's anointed (1Sa 24:5-7; 26:11).

After Saul's death, David became king; he made Jerusalem his royal city and brought the ark of God there. God promised that David's dynasty would be established forever (2Sa 7:5-16).

Perhaps David's greatest recorded failure came when he took Bathsheba, a married woman, for his own sexual gratification and then ordered the death of her husband to hide his sin (2Sa 11). After this, David's reign was marred by chaos. He allowed one of his sons to rape his daughter Tamar without any consequence. Another son and the brother of Tamar, Absalom, rebelled and tried to take the throne. Another son, Adonijah tried to make himself king instead of David's son Solomon. And when David was near death, his final instructions to Solomon included a mandate to carry out a series of revenge killings (1Ki 2:5-9).

Despite David's failures, his legacy is one of faithfulness to God and repentance when he failed (see Ps 51 and David's many other psalms). His name became synonymous with God's everlasting promise to Israel—a promise that pointed to David's descendant, Jesus Christ.

APPLICATION David did not lead a perfect life, but his story is a rich demonstration of God's faithfulness. God called David from humble beginnings to do great things. When David failed, God punished him; when David repented, God forgave him. The power of David's story is not in his military exploits or kingly successes. It is in God's everlasting love and promise to his people. David's life points us to Jesus Christ, the true and perfect King who reigns forever.

2 But Samuel said, "How can I go? If
Saul hears about it, he will kill me."
The LORD said, "Take a heifer with you
and say, 'I have come to sacrifice to the
LORD.' 3 Invite Jesse to the sacrifice, and
I will show[f] you what to do. You are to
anoint[g] for me the one I indicate."
4 Samuel did what the LORD said. When
he arrived at Bethlehem,[h] the elders of
the town trembled when they met him.
They asked, "Do you come in peace?[i]"
5 Samuel replied, "Yes, in peace; I have
come to sacrifice to the LORD. Consecrate[j]
yourselves and come to the sacrifice with
me." Then he consecrated Jesse and his
sons and invited them to the sacrifice.
6 When they arrived, Samuel saw Eliab[k]
and thought, "Surely the LORD's anointed
stands here before the LORD."
7 But the LORD said to Samuel, "Do not
consider his appearance or his height, for
I have rejected him. The LORD does not
look at the things people look at. People
look at the outward appearance,[l] but the
LORD looks at the heart."[m]
8 Then Jesse called Abinadab[n] and had
him pass in front of Samuel. But Samuel
said, "The LORD has not chosen this one
either." 9 Jesse then had Shammah pass
by, but Samuel said, "Nor has the LORD
chosen this one." 10 Jesse had seven of
his sons pass before Samuel, but Samuel
said to him, "The LORD has not chosen
these." 11 So he asked Jesse, "Are these all[o]
the sons you have?"
"There is still the youngest," Jesse answered. "He is tending the sheep."
Samuel said, "Send for him; we will
not sit down until he arrives."
12 So he[p] sent for him and had him
brought in. He was glowing with health
and had a fine appearance and handsome[q] features.
Then the LORD said, "Rise and anoint
him; this is the one."
13 So Samuel took the horn of oil and
anointed him in the presence of his
brothers, and from that day on the Spirit
of the LORD[r] came powerfully upon David.[s] Samuel then went to Ramah.

16:3 [f] Ex 4:15 [g] Dt 17:15; 1Sa 9:16
16:4 [h] Ge 48:7; Lk 2:4 [i] 1Ki 2:13; 2Ki 9:17
16:5 [j] Ex 19:10, 22
16:6 [k] 1Sa 17:13
16:7 [l] Ps 147:10 [m] 1Ki 8:39; 1Ch 28:9; Isa 55:8
16:8 [n] 1Sa 17:13
16:11 [o] 1Sa 17:12
16:12 [p] 1Sa 9:17 [q] Ge 39:6; 1Sa 17:42
16:13 [r] Nu 27:18; Jdg 11:29 [s] 1Sa 10:1, 6, 9-10; 11:6
16:14 [t] Jdg 16:20 [u] Jdg 9:23; 1Sa 18:10

1Sa 16:7 ❖ How can we see people the way God sees them rather than looking "at the things people look at"?

David in Saul's Service

14 Now the Spirit of the LORD had departed[t] from Saul, and an evil[a] spirit[u]
from the LORD tormented him.
15 Saul's attendants said to him, "See, an
evil spirit from God is tormenting you.

[a] 14 Or *and a harmful*; similarly in verses 15, 16 and 23

16:2-3 Samuel is evidently aware of Saul's hostile intent toward him because he fears for his life, should it become known that he has anointed David. But Yahweh assures Samuel that he will make known to the prophet what he should do.
16:4-5 Samuel consecrates Jesse and his sons and invites them (and presumably the elders of Bethlehem) to the sacrifice.
16:6-7 People and God do not perceive reality in the same way. In order to anoint the correct son of Jesse, Samuel will have to overcome his human reliance on his own ability to see.
16:8-10 The other sons of Jesse parade before the great prophet, but none is the "chosen" one.
16:11-13 The youngest son of Jesse is apparently so unlikely a candidate it hardly seems necessary to summon him from his work "tending the sheep" (v. 11). Once he is summoned, however, Yahweh quickly confirms his choice (v. 12). Samuel immediately obeys and anoints David in this private setting.

As in the case of Saul, anointing for kingship is accompanied by the arrival of the spirit of Yahweh, empowering the king-designate for service.

✤ **16:1-13** This text is especially concerned with the kind of person God seeks. When we consider the qualities of the people around us, we are inevitably influenced by what we see with our eyes. But God also uses the uneducated, the poor, the disenfranchised to work in powerful ways for his kingdom. The fact is that we simply cannot see the human heart the way God does; thus, we may often be surprised by what God sees in others.

16:14 Just as the arrival of the spirit of Yahweh marked David as someone destined and supremely fitted to *become* king of Israel (v. 13), so the departure of the Spirit from Saul marks him as destined not to *remain* king.

The spirit of Yahweh comes to impart strength and power for service, while the evil spirit *from* Yahweh torments. The ruinous spirit comes from Yahweh because of Saul's persistent and unrepentant stance, and it is the source of his problems, plaguing him throughout the rest of the narrative.
16:15-18 Saul's attendants believe music is the answer to Saul's tortured condition. They offer to find an appropriate harpist to smooth the ailing Saul whenever his fits occur. David has now become well known, at least to this unnamed attendant, who uses several important descriptors for David. The most ironic and telling, however, is the last: "The LORD is with him" (v. 18). Here the contrast is established between Saul and David.

16 Let our lord command his servants here
to search for someone who can play the
lyre.[v] He will play when the evil spirit
from God comes on you, and you will
feel better."
17 So Saul said to his attendants, "Find
someone who plays well and bring him
to me."
18 One of the servants answered, "I
have seen a son of Jesse of Bethlehem
who knows how to play the lyre. He is a
brave man and a warrior. He speaks well
and is a fine-looking man. And the LORD
is with[w] him."
19 Then Saul sent messengers to Jesse and said, "Send me your son David,
who is with the sheep." 20 So Jesse took
a donkey loaded with bread,[x] a skin of
wine and a young goat and sent them
with his son David to Saul.
21 David came to Saul and entered his
service.[y] Saul liked him very much, and
David became one of his armor-bearers.
22 Then Saul sent word to Jesse, saying,
"Allow David to remain in my service,
for I am pleased with him."
23 Whenever the spirit from God came
on Saul, David would take up his lyre
and play. Then relief would come to Saul;
he would feel better, and the evil spirit[z]
would leave him.

David and Goliath

17 Now the Philistines gathered their
forces for war and assembled[a] at
Sokoh in Judah. They pitched camp at
Ephes Dammim, between Sokoh[b] and
Azekah. 2 Saul and the Israelites assembled and camped in the Valley of Elah[c]
and drew up their battle line to meet the
Philistines. 3 The Philistines occupied one
hill and the Israelites another, with the
valley between them.
4 A champion named Goliath,[d] who was
from Gath, came out of the Philistine
camp. His height was six cubits and a
span.[a] 5 He had a bronze helmet on his
head and wore a coat of scale armor of
bronze weighing five thousand shekels[b];
6 on his legs he wore bronze greaves, and
a bronze javelin[e] was slung on his back.
7 His spear shaft was like a weaver's rod,[f]
and its iron point weighed six hundred
shekels.[c] His shield bearer[g] went ahead
of him.
8 Goliath stood and shouted to the
ranks of Israel, "Why do you come out
and line up for battle? Am I not a Philistine, and are you not the servants of
Saul? Choose[h] a man and have him come
down to me. 9 If he is able to fight and
kill me, we will become your subjects;
but if I overcome him and kill him, you
will become our subjects and serve us."
10 Then the Philistine said, "This day I
defy[i] the armies of Israel! Give me a man

16:16 [v] ver 23; 1Sa 18:10; 19:9; 2Ki 3:15
16:18 [w] 1Sa 3:19; 17:32-37
16:20 [x] 1Sa 10:27; Pr 18:16
16:21 [y] Ge 41:46; Pr 22:29
16:23 [z] ver 14-16
17:1 [a] 1Sa 13:5
[b] Jos 15:35; 2Ch 28:18
17:2 [c] 1Sa 21:9
17:4 [d] Jos 11:21-22; 2Sa 21:19
17:6 [e] ver 45
17:7 [f] 2Sa 21:19 [g] ver 41
17:8 [h] 1Sa 8:17
17:10 [i] ver 26, 45; 2Sa 21:21

[a] 4 That is, about 9 feet 9 inches or about 3 meters [b] 5 That is, about 125 pounds or about 58 kilograms [c] 7 That is, about 15 pounds or about 6.9 kilograms

---

16:19–23 This short passage introduces three themes that will recur in chs. 17–31: Saul is in decline, David prospers because "the LORD is with him" (v. 18), and Saul is deeply attached to David.

> ✣ **16:14–23** As Christians, we are committed to the *idea* that God is at work in our lives, but we are not often *consciously aware* of the specifics of his involvement. Little does David realize that God will use his musical talents to have David gain access to the court, furthering Samuel's action in anointing him with oil.
>
> All this will happen sooner rather than later in David's life, but he has to walk through these circumstances somewhat in the dark. David is left simply to do his best without having the big picture. So it often is with modern believers.

17:1–3 The battleground between Sokoh and Azekah places this event in the western foothills of Judah. The Valley of Elah (Valley of the Terebinth) separates the opposing armies, presumably with the Philistine troops on the southern slopes of the valley and the Israelite forces on the northern slopes.

17:4–11 Peculiar to this Israelite-Philistine battle is the appearance of a single infantryman who challenges Israel to match him in representative combat. Single combat as a substitute for full-fledged battle between opposing armies was possible in the ancient world as a means of settling disputes without extensive bloodshed. However, representative individual combat seldom succeeded as a means of limiting warfare. As in our text, the warring parties often continued with the battle after the contest was over (vv. 52–54).

Goliath is not designated a "giant"; rather, he is portrayed as an exceedingly tall warrior whose very height strikes terror in the hearts of his potential foes. The NIV's note "9 feet 9 inches" tall (v. 4) represents the Hebrew text.

The description of Goliath's impressive stature reminds the reader of another impressive leader (10:23). In other words, Saul is the best match for Goliath. Indeed, there is an implicit condemnation of Saul in Goliath's description, since King Saul would be expected not only to motivate his troops but to lead them into battle against the Philistines. But on hearing Goliath's words, "Saul and all the Israelites" are paralyzed with fear (17:11).

and let us fight each other." 11On hearing the Philistine's words, Saul and all the Israelites were dismayed and terrified.

12Now David was the son of an Ephrathite named Jesse,[j] who was from Bethlehem[k] in Judah. Jesse had eight[l] sons, and in Saul's time he was very old. 13Jesse's three oldest sons had followed Saul to the war: The firstborn was Eliab;[m] the second, Abinadab; and the third, Shammah.[n] 14David was the youngest. The three oldest followed Saul, 15but David went back and forth from Saul to tend his father's sheep[o] at Bethlehem.

16For forty days the Philistine came forward every morning and evening and took his stand.

17Now Jesse said to his son David, "Take this ephah[*a*] of roasted grain[p] and these ten loaves of bread for your brothers and hurry to their camp. 18Take along these ten cheeses to the commander of their unit. See how your brothers[q] are and bring back some assurance[*b*] from them. 19They are with Saul and all the men of Israel in the Valley of Elah, fighting against the Philistines."

20Early in the morning David left the flock in the care of a shepherd, loaded up and set out, as Jesse had directed. He reached the camp as the army was going out to its battle positions, shouting the war cry. 21Israel and the Philistines were drawing up their lines facing each other. 22David left his things with the keeper of supplies, ran to the battle lines and asked his brothers how they were. 23As he was talking with them, Goliath, the Philistine champion from Gath, stepped out from his lines and shouted his usual[r] defiance, and David heard it. 24Whenever the Israelites saw the man, they all fled from him in great fear.

25Now the Israelites had been saying, "Do you see how this man keeps coming out? He comes out to defy Israel. The king will give great wealth to the man who kills him. He will also give him his daughter[s] in marriage and will exempt his family from taxes in Israel."

26David asked the men standing near him, "What will be done for the man who kills this Philistine and removes this disgrace[t] from Israel? Who is this uncircumcised[u] Philistine that he should defy[v] the armies of the living[w] God?"

27They repeated to him what they had been saying and told him, "This is what will be done for the man who kills him."

28When Eliab, David's oldest brother, heard him speaking with the men, he burned with anger[x] at him and asked, "Why have you come down here? And with whom did you leave those few sheep in the wilderness? I know how conceited you are and how wicked your heart is; you came down only to watch the battle."

29"Now what have I done?" said David. "Can't I even speak?" 30He then turned away to someone else and brought up the same matter, and the men answered him as before. 31What David said was overheard and reported to Saul, and Saul sent for him.

32David said to Saul, "Let no one lose heart[y] on account of this Philistine; your servant will go and fight him."

33Saul replied,[z] "You are not able to go out against this Philistine and fight him;

17:12 [j] Ru 4:17; 1Ch 2:13-15 [k] Ge 35:19 [l] 1Sa 16:11
17:13 [m] 1Sa 16:6 [n] 1Sa 16:9
17:15 [o] 1Sa 16:19
17:17 [p] 1Sa 25:18
17:18 [q] Ge 37:14
17:23 [r] ver 8-10
17:25 [s] Jos 15:16; 1Sa 18:17
17:26 [t] 1Sa 11:2 [u] 1Sa 14:6 [v] ver 10 [w] Dt 5:26
17:28 [x] Ge 37:4, 8, 11; Pr 18:19; Mt 10:36
17:32 [y] Dt 20:3; 1Sa 16:18
17:33 [z] Nu 13:31

[*a*] *17* That is, probably about 36 pounds or about 16 kilograms [*b*] *18* Or *some token*; or *some pledge of spoils*

17:12-16 Goliath is enormous, protected by impressive armor, armed with potent weapons, and accompanied by his own shield bearer for added protection. He must have looked overpowering, even invincible. By contrast, David can hardly look more vulnerable and insignificant.

The text further characterizes David by contrasting him with everyone else in the story. His oldest brothers are in Saul's military, stationed at the camp of the Israelites. Goliath is in the habit of taking his defiant stand morning and evening for 40 days. The descriptions of Goliath and David in vv. 4–16 subtly differentiate the powerful and defiant enemies of God in the world from the unassuming innocence of God's faithful shepherd boy from Bethlehem.

17:17-25 David has been given the menial task of carrying provisions to the commander of his brothers' unit when he personally witnesses Goliath's defiant challenge.

17:26-28 The central question of the passage is David's in v. 26. The Israelite troops see a terrifying and seemingly invincible warrior who brings reproach on all Israel. But David sees only an uncircumcised Philistine who worships dead idols yet has the audacity to reproach the armies of the living God. Thus, the soldiers' words of resignation are contrasted with David's words of indignation. David has learned to see things others cannot see.

17:29-31 David has matured enough to speak for himself, and he ignores his brother's disapproval.

17:31-33 David's conversations with the troops contain an implicit offer to fight Goliath. Saul is at least willing to entertain the possibility. But when

you are only a young man, and he has
been a warrior from his youth."
34 But David said to Saul, "Your servant has been keeping his father's sheep.
When a lion[a] or a bear came and carried
off a sheep from the flock, 35 I went after
it, struck it and rescued the sheep from
its mouth. When it turned on me, I seized
it by its hair, struck it and killed it. 36 Your
servant has killed both the lion and the
bear; this uncircumcised Philistine will
be like one of them, because he has defied the armies of the living God. 37 The
LORD who rescued[b] me from the paw of
the lion[c] and the paw of the bear will rescue me from the hand of this Philistine."
Saul said to David, "Go, and the LORD
be with[d] you."
38 Then Saul dressed David in his own
tunic. He put a coat of armor on him and
a bronze helmet on his head. 39 David
fastened on his sword over the tunic and
tried walking around, because he was
not used to them.
"I cannot go in these," he said to Saul,
"because I am not used to them." So he
took them off. 40 Then he took his staff
in his hand, chose five smooth stones
from the stream, put them in the pouch
of his shepherd's bag and, with his sling
in his hand, approached the Philistine.
41 Meanwhile, the Philistine, with his
shield bearer in front of him, kept coming closer to David. 42 He looked David
over and saw that he was little more than
a boy, glowing with health and handsome,[e] and he despised[f] him. 43 He said
to David, "Am I a dog,[g] that you come
at me with sticks?" And the Philistine
cursed David by his gods. 44 "Come here,"
he said, "and I'll give your flesh to the
birds and the wild animals![h]"
45 David said to the Philistine, "You
come against me with sword and spear
and javelin, but I come against you in
the name[i] of the LORD Almighty, the God
of the armies of Israel, whom you have
defied.[j] 46 This day the LORD will deliver
you into my hands, and I'll strike you
down and cut off your head. This very
day I will give the carcasses[k] of the Philistine army to the birds and the wild
animals, and the whole world[l] will know
that there is a God in Israel.[m] 47 All those
gathered here will know that it is not by
sword[n] or spear that the LORD saves;[o] for
the battle[p] is the LORD's, and he will give
all of you into our hands."
48 As the Philistine moved closer to attack him, David ran quickly toward the
battle line to meet him. 49 Reaching into
his bag and taking out a stone, he slung it
and struck the Philistine on the forehead.
The stone sank into his forehead, and he
fell facedown on the ground.
50 So David triumphed over the Philistine with a sling[q] and a stone; without
a sword in his hand he struck down the
Philistine and killed him.
51 David ran and stood over him. He
took hold of the Philistine's sword and
drew it from the sheath. After he killed
him, he cut[r] off his head with the sword.[s]

17:34 [a] Jer 49:19; Am 3:12
17:37 [b] 2Co 1:10 [c] 2Ti 4:17 [d] 1Sa 20:13; 1Ch 22:11,16
17:42 [e] 1Sa 16:12 [f] Ps 123:3-4; Pr 16:18
17:43 [g] 1Sa 24:14; 2Sa 3:8; 9:8; 2Ki 8:13
17:44 [h] 1Ki 20:10-11
17:45 [i] 2Sa 22:33, 35; 2Ch 32:8; Ps 124:8; Heb 11:32-34 [j] ver 10
17:46 [k] Dt 28:26 [l] Jos 4:24; 1Ki 8:43; Isa 52:10 [m] 1Ki 18:36; 2Ki 19:19; Isa 37:20
17:47 [n] Hos 1:7; Zec 4:6 [o] 1Sa 14:6; 2Ch 14:11 [p] 2Ch 20:15; Ps 44:6-7
17:50 [q] 2Sa 23:21
17:51 [r] Heb 11:34 [s] 1Sa 21:9

1Sa 17:45–47 ❖ How can we demonstrate David's confidence and faith in the battles and challenges we face?

---

they meet and David volunteers to fight Goliath, Saul cannot accept the idea that this inexperienced youth could successfully combat Goliath.

17:34–37 David's explanation of how he might be able to prevail against the Philistine also reveals his profound faith in Yahweh. Since the Hebrew word translated "paw" in v. 37 is the same for "hand," David is relating the hand/power of the Philistine with that of the lion or bear. In young David's mind, all the enemies of God are reduced to the same level; they are nothing but dumb beasts. David has moved from reciting his own bravery and skill (vv. 34–36) to acknowledging that Yahweh is the source of deliverance (v. 37).

17:38–39 It is possible that Saul's offer for David to use his royal armor is a calculated effort to bind the two together in a way that will make it possible for Saul to take credit for David's victory, should he actually succeed in defeating the Philistine champion. In any event, Saul appears all too willing to loan his fighting gear to someone else, since he is not prepared to use it himself, especially against Goliath.

17:40–47 The text portrays David as fearless in the face of this enormous warrior, and he shakes off Goliath's threats. In a beautiful speech that dramatizes the conflict between Israel and the enemy nations around them, David emphasizes that Goliath is trusting in his own superior military resources. In contrast, David repeats his theme by promising that everyone present, both Israelite and Philistine, will learn that the battle already belongs to the Lord (v. 47). The narrator later returns to this theme to stress its centrality (v. 50).

17:48–51 No doubt this young shepherd boy is unlike any other warrior Goliath has ever seen. But superior strength and military resources are useless against the representative of Yahweh. The contest is over before it begins: David kills Goliath with one of his choice stones. Since he does the job without a sword in his hand, Yahweh has been true to David's word: He saved "not by sword or spear" (v. 47).

When the Philistines saw that their hero was dead, they turned and ran.
52Then the men of Israel and Judah surged forward with a shout and pursued the Philistines to the entrance of Gath[a] and to the gates of Ekron.[t] Their dead were strewn along the Shaaraim[u] road to Gath and Ekron.
53When the Israelites returned from chasing the Philistines, they plundered their camp.
54David took the Philistine's head and brought it to Jerusalem; he put the Philistine's weapons in his own tent.
55As Saul watched David[v] going out to meet the Philistine, he said to Abner, commander of the army, "Abner, whose son is that young man?"

Abner replied, "As surely as you live, Your Majesty, I don't know."
56The king said, "Find out whose son this young man is."
57As soon as David returned from killing the Philistine, Abner took him and brought him before Saul, with David still holding the Philistine's head.
58"Whose son are you, young man?" Saul asked him.

David said, "I am the son of your servant Jesse[w] of Bethlehem."

Saul's Growing Fear of David

18 After David had finished talking with Saul, Jonathan became one in spirit with David, and he loved[x] him as himself.[y]
2From that day Saul kept David with him and did not let him return home to his family.
3And Jonathan made a covenant[z] with David because he loved him as himself.
4Jonathan took off the robe[a] he was wearing and gave it to David, along with his tunic, and even his sword, his bow and his belt.
5Whatever mission Saul sent him on, David was so successful that Saul gave him a high rank in the army. This pleased all the troops, and Saul's officers as well.
6When the men were returning home after David had killed the Philistine, the women came out from all the towns of Israel to meet King Saul with singing and dancing,[b] with joyful songs and with

17:52 [t] Jos 15:11 [u] Jos 15:36
17:55 [v] 1Sa 16:21
17:58 [w] ver 12
18:1 [x] 2Sa 1:26 [y] Ge 44:30
18:3 [z] 1Sa 20:8, 16, 17, 42
18:4 [a] Ge 41:42
18:6 [b] Ex 15:20

[a] 52 Some Septuagint manuscripts; Hebrew *of a valley*

17:52-54 The location of the account is a deliberate narrative technique in the book's structure. After Saul's anointing, the narrator recorded the new king's military victory over the Ammonites (10:1-2; 11:1-11). So here the text moves from David's anointing to this victory over Goliath and the Philistine nation generally (16:13 and ch. 17). It seems important to illustrate in each case that Yahweh's chosen is qualified to lead Israel victoriously into battle.

17:55-58 Some have speculated that Saul's unstable mental condition has resulted in a loss of memory (see 16:14), or perhaps Saul wants to know more about David's parentage because he had promised to give his daughter in marriage to the one who killed Goliath (17:25).

> ✣ **17:1-58** Christians should not be surprised when they encounter opposition to what God has called them to do. The Bible teaches in a variety of ways that there will often be challenges to God's sovereign rule in the world. Church history presents many examples of Christians who failed to interact to change hostile surrounding cultures. For example, the majority of the Christian community in Germany failed to reject radical nationalism and to oppose vigorously the growth of Nazism in the early twentieth century. The church essentially failed to function as a transforming element of the culture. The way in which today's Christians in North America respond to the growing reality of anti-Christian sentiment and practice may pose an upsetting parallel.

18:1-4 The specific Hebrew verb for "love" used here has important political overtones (v. 1). So, for example, Saul loved David in 16:21, and Hiram king of Tyre loved David in 1Ki 5:1. Indeed, the relationship between David and Jonathan is a classic example of a covenant between individuals, and the language used to characterize that relationship is typical of ancient kinship and mutual kinship obligation. The political overtones of Jonathan's love for David are marked by their "covenant" (1Sa 18:3) and by Jonathan's extravagant gifts (v. 4).

It is also possible that the specific idiom for "became one in spirit" (v. 1) has a similar kind of double meaning, inferring again the political nature of their relationship. David and Jonathan's immediate bonding and personal friendship apparently lead the crown prince to renounce his throne, and the gifts of v. 4 are symbolic of his commitment to defer to David's right to be king.

18:5-9 This section emphasizes Saul's anger and jealousy of David. The author carefully sets up a screen around David's intimate responses to other characters and to events as they unfold by withholding from the reader David's thoughts or feelings. We learn what kind of person he is by his speeches, by his impressive military exploits, and by what other characters feel about him. But the narrator never makes statements about *David's* feelings or reveals his inner thoughts.

By contrast, the narrator exposes in this chapter the feelings and emotions of everyone around David. This technique focuses our attention squarely on David as the central figure, as everyone around him seems likewise focused.

timbrels[c] and lyres. 7As they danced, they
sang:[d]

> "Saul has slain his thousands,
> and David his tens[e] of thousands."

8Saul was very angry; this refrain displeased him greatly. "They have credited David with tens of thousands," he
thought, "but me with only thousands.
What more can he get but the kingdom?[f]" 9And from that time on Saul kept
a close eye on David.
10The next day an evil[a] spirit[g] from
God came forcefully on Saul. He was
prophesying in his house, while David
was playing the lyre, as he usually[h] did.
Saul had a spear in his hand 11and he
hurled it, saying to himself,[i] "I'll pin David to the wall." But David eluded[j] him
twice.
12Saul was afraid[k] of David, because the
LORD[l] was with[m] David but had departed
from Saul. 13So he sent David away from
him and gave him command over a thousand men, and David led[n] the troops in
their campaigns.[o] 14In everything he did
he had great success,[p] because the LORD
was with[q] him. 15When Saul saw how
successful he was, he was afraid of him.
16But all Israel and Judah loved David,
because he led them in their campaigns.[r]
17Saul said to David, "Here is my older
daughter[s] Merab. I will give her to you
in marriage; only serve me bravely and
fight the battles[t] of the LORD." For Saul
said to himself,[u] "I will not raise a hand
against him. Let the Philistines do that!"
18But David said to Saul, "Who am
I,[v] and what is my family or my clan in
Israel, that I should become the king's
son-in-law?[w]" 19So[b] when the time came
for Merab,[x] Saul's daughter, to be given
to David, she was given in marriage to
Adriel of Meholah.[y]
20Now Saul's daughter Michal[z] was in
love with David, and when they told Saul
about it, he was pleased. 21"I will give her
to him," he thought, "so that she may
be a snare[a] to him and so that the hand
of the Philistines may be against him."
So Saul said to David, "Now you have a
second opportunity to become my son-
in-law."
22Then Saul ordered his attendants:
"Speak to David privately and say, 'Look,
the king likes you, and his attendants all
love you; now become his son-in-law.' "
23They repeated these words to David.
But David said, "Do you think it is a small
matter to become the king's son-in-law?
I'm only a poor man and little known."
24When Saul's servants told him what
David had said, 25Saul replied, "Say to

1Sa 18:8 ❖ Envy is a deadly sin. How can God's children avoid falling into it?

18:6 [c]Jdg 11:34; Ps 68:25
18:7 [d]Ex 15:21 [e]1Sa 21:11; 29:5
18:8 [f]1Sa 15:8
18:10 [g]1Sa 16:14 [h]1Sa 19:7
18:11 [i]1Sa 20:7, 33 [j]1Sa 19:10
18:12 [k]ver 15, 29 [l]1Sa 16:13 [m]1Sa 28:15
18:13 [n]ver 16; Nu 27:17 [o]2Sa 5:2
18:14 [p]Ge 39:3 [q]Ge 39:2, 23; Jos 6:27; 1Sa 16:18
18:16 [r]ver 5
18:17 [s]1Sa 17:25 [t]Nu 21:14; 1Sa 25:28 [u]ver 25
18:18 [v]1Sa 9:21; 2Sa 7:18 [w]ver 23
18:19 [x]2Sa 21:8 [y]Jdg 7:22
18:20 [z]ver 28
18:21 [a]ver 17, 26

[a] *10* Or *a harmful* [b] *19* Or *However,*

18:10–16 Saul obviously is experiencing deep psychological problems. This chapter contains the first of several references to his fits of jealousy over David's popularity, and Saul is afraid. But as often in biblical narrative, the historian is more interested in the theological causes than historical details.

The theme of the paragraph is repeated twice: Yahweh is with David, and Saul is afraid of David (vv. 12, 14–15; cf. vv. 28–29). These statements form the theological centerpiece of the chapter and give the narrator's underlying foundations for what is happening historically in the family of Saul and in Saul himself. The text is also clear about the causal connection between Saul's fear and David's successes. Yahweh is with David to make successful everything he attempts, and therefore Saul is afraid (vv. 12, 14–15). The irony that plays out in the subsequent narrative is that David will not himself raise a hand against Saul, who is still Yahweh's anointed.

18:17–19 The rest of the chapter relates Saul's attempts to rid himself of David. First, he offers in marriage his oldest daughter to David, which is the expected reward for the warrior who defeated Goliath. Saul's motive is revealed in v. 17, but Saul changes his mind and gives Merab to another man.

18:20–30 When Saul learns of Michal's love for David, he sees it as another opportunity to ensnare the young rival (v. 21). Saul is "pleased" (v. 20) because he sees Michal's love for David as another opportunity to entrap David, but David is "pleased" (v. 26) because he sees it as an opportunity to become the king's son-in-law. This ironic twist illustrates the nature of Saul's relationship with David.

✚ **18:1–30** Even when an enemy of God, motivated by anger, jealousy, or hatred, attempts to intervene forcibly against the progress of what God is accomplishing, that very intervention itself can be used by God to further his purposes. Christians are called to refuse retaliation and to live in such a way as not only to *overcome* but to *transform* their oppressors. Though Saul had set his course and would not allow himself to be deterred, David was faithful to what God placed before him, and God was "with" David (v. 12). As Christians, we must bear testimony to God's grace in our lives in good times and in bad, and we must remember that a loving response to opposition can transform our enemies and transform ourselves as well.

David, 'The king wants no other price[b]
for the bride than a hundred Philistine
foreskins, to take revenge on his enemies.'" Saul's plan[c] was to have David fall
by the hands of the Philistines.
26When the attendants told David
these things, he was pleased to become
the king's son-in-law. So before the allotted time elapsed, 27David took his men
with him and went out and killed two
hundred Philistines and brought back
their foreskins. They counted out the full
number to the king so that David might
become the king's son-in-law. Then Saul
gave him his daughter Michal[d] in marriage.
28When Saul realized that the LORD
was with David and that his daughter
Michal loved David, 29Saul became still
more afraid of him, and he remained his
enemy the rest of his days.
30The Philistine commanders continued to go out to battle, and as often as
they did, David met with more success[e]
than the rest of Saul's officers, and his
name became well known.

Saul Tries to Kill David

19 Saul told his son Jonathan[f] and all
the attendants to kill[g] David. But
Jonathan had taken a great liking to David 2and warned him, "My father Saul is
looking for a chance to kill you. Be on
your guard tomorrow morning; go into
hiding and stay there. 3I will go out and
stand with my father in the field where
you are. I'll speak[h] to him about you and
will tell you what I find out."
4Jonathan spoke[i] well of David to Saul
his father and said to him, "Let not the
king do wrong[j] to his servant David; he
has not wronged you, and what he has
done has benefited you greatly. 5He took
his life in his hands when he killed the
Philistine. The LORD won a great victory[k]
for all Israel, and you saw it and were
glad. Why then would you do wrong to
an innocent[l] man like David by killing
him for no reason?"
6Saul listened to Jonathan and took
this oath: "As surely as the LORD lives,
David will not be put to death."
7So Jonathan called David and told
him the whole conversation. He brought
him to Saul, and David was with Saul as
before.[m]
8Once more war broke out, and David
went out and fought the Philistines. He
struck them with such force that they
fled before him.
9But an evil[a] spirit[n] from the LORD
came on Saul as he was sitting in his
house with his spear in his hand. While
David was playing the lyre, 10Saul tried to
pin him to the wall with his spear, but David eluded[o] him as Saul drove the spear
into the wall. That night David made
good his escape.
11Saul sent men to David's house to
watch[p] it and to kill him in the morning.
But Michal, David's wife, warned him,
"If you don't run for your life tonight,
tomorrow you'll be killed." 12So Michal
let David down through a window,[q] and
he fled and escaped. 13Then Michal took
an idol and laid it on the bed, covering it
with a garment and putting some goats'
hair at the head.
14When Saul sent the men to capture
David, Michal said,[r] "He is ill."
15Then Saul sent the men back to see
David and told them, "Bring him up to

[a] 9 Or *But a harmful*

18:25 [b] Ge 34:12; Ex 22:17; 1Sa 14:24 [c] ver 17
18:27 [d] ver 13; 2Sa 3:14
18:30 [e] ver 5; 2Sa 11:1
19:1 [f] 1Sa 18:1 [g] 1Sa 18:9
19:3 [h] 1Sa 20:12
19:4 [i] 1Sa 20:32; Pr 31:8, 9; Jer 18:20 [j] Ge 42:22; Pr 17:13
19:5 [k] 1Sa 11:13; 17:49-50; 1Ch 11:14 [l] Dt 19:10-13; 1Sa 20:32; Mt 27:4
19:7 [m] 1Sa 16:21; 18:2, 13
19:9 [n] 1Sa 16:14; 18:10-11
19:10 [o] 1Sa 18:11
19:11 [p] Ps 59 Title
19:12 [q] Jos 2:15; Ac 9:25
19:14 [r] Jos 2:4

1Sa 19:4-6 ❖ Where can we be a bold voice for people who are innocent and oppressed?

19:1-7 The opening verse of the text states that Saul now resolves to draw others into his conspiracy against David. Because of his friendship and commitment to David, Jonathan arranges to serve as an intermediary to accomplish a reconciliation with his father. Jonathan's logic and eloquence win the day, and his father and friend are reconciled. But the peaceable relations are short-lived.

19:8-10 More military glory for David results again in more problems with Saul. As before, his victories ignite jealousy in Saul, which leads to yet another attempt on David's life.

19:11-17 Michal's ruse shows just how morbid and insane Saul's preoccupation with David is. The precise nature of the "idol" (vv. 12, 16) she places in the bed is much disputed.

The ruse works, giving David time to escape. But when Saul realizes what Michal has done, he becomes angry with her. In order to calm the unpredictable Saul, she deceives him, now for a second time. Michal appears to have no hesitation about the deceptions, and the narrator relates the events in an apparently approving tone.

19:1-17 Saul was obsessed with killing David; therefore Jonathan and Michal were justified in their actions. We should be careful here

me in his bed so that I may kill him."
16But when the men entered, there was
the idol in the bed, and at the head was
some goats' hair.
17Saul said to Michal, "Why did you
deceive me like this and send my enemy
away so that he escaped?"
Michal told him, "He said to me, 'Let
me get away. Why should I kill you?' "
18When David had fled and made his
escape, he went to Samuel at Ramah[s]
and told him all that Saul had done to
him. Then he and Samuel went to Naioth and stayed there. 19Word came to
Saul: "David is in Naioth at Ramah"; 20so
he sent men to capture him. But when
they saw a group of prophets[t] prophesying, with Samuel standing there as their
leader, the Spirit of God came on[u] Saul's
men, and they also prophesied.[v] 21Saul
was told about it, and he sent more men,
and they prophesied too. Saul sent men

19:18 [s]1Sa 7:17
19:20 [t]ver 11, 14; Jn 7:32, 45 [u]Nu 11:25 [v]1Sa 10:5; Joel 2:28

---

and not assume that in our own situations it would be appropriate to mislead or deceive another person.

19:18–21 David returns to Samuel, who is evidently active as the leader of a band of prophets at Ramah. The irony of David's presence in Ramah with Samuel should not escape us. Though the text of ch. 10 does not say so explicitly, it appears that this is also where Saul first received the promise of the Spirit of God and where his heart was transformed (10:6, 9). Now, however, the tide has turned.

Samuel takes David to "Naioth at Ramah" (19:18–19). The Hebrew word translated "Naioth" is probably a reference to camps: remote country dwelling places that could become the residences of shepherds and could be associated with the dwelling place of God. When Saul's espionage sources tell him where David is, he sends three detachments to these camps at Ramah to capture David. But in all three instances, his envoys become enamored with the feverish worship, and they also prophesy in the Spirit of God and are distracted from their task.

LOCATIONS OF EVENTS IN DAVID'S LIFE

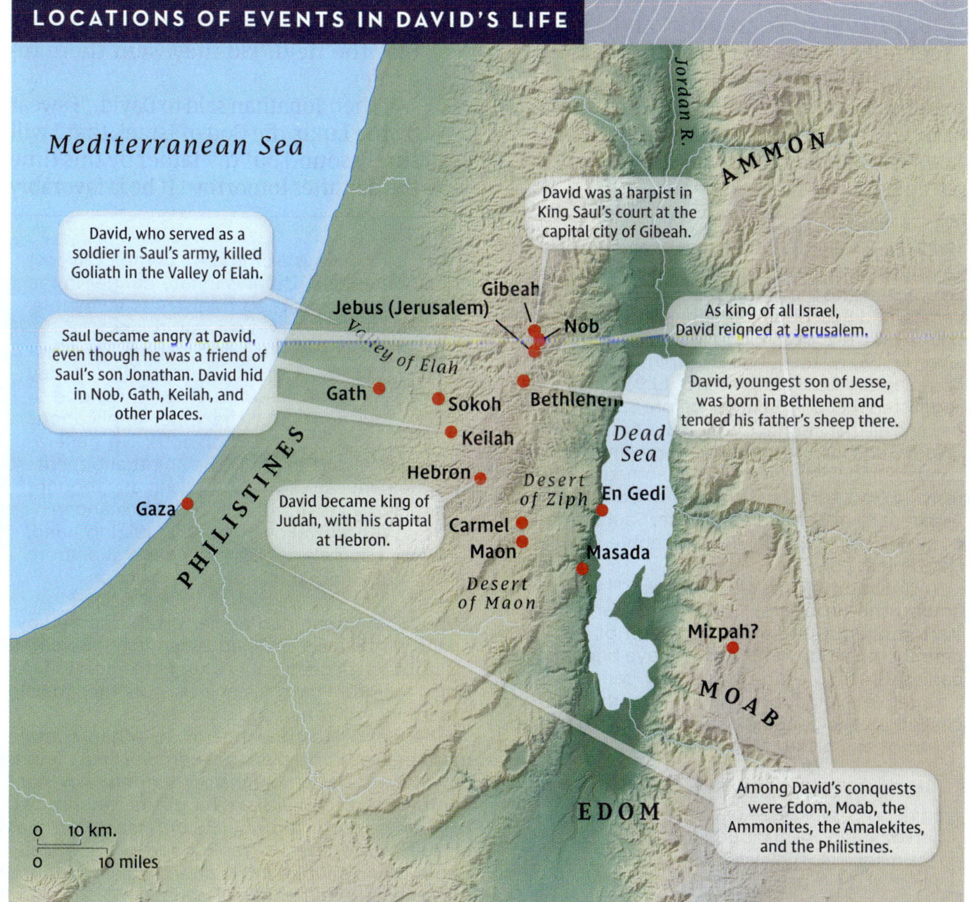

a third time, and they also prophesied.
22Finally, he himself left for Ramah and
went to the great cistern at Seku. And he
asked, "Where are Samuel and David?"
"Over in Naioth at Ramah," they said.
23So Saul went to Naioth at Ramah.
But the Spirit of God came even on him,
and he walked along prophesying[w] until he came to Naioth. 24He stripped[x] off
his garments, and he too prophesied in
Samuel's presence. He lay naked all that
day and all that night. This is why people
say, "Is Saul also among the prophets?"[y]

David and Jonathan

20 Then David fled from Naioth at
Ramah and went to Jonathan and
asked, "What have I done? What is my
crime? How have I wronged[z] your father,
that he is trying to kill me?"
2"Never!" Jonathan replied. "You are
not going to die! Look, my father doesn't
do anything, great or small, without letting me know. Why would he hide this
from me? It isn't so!"
3But David took an oath[a] and said,
"Your father knows very well that I have
found favor in your eyes, and he has said
to himself, 'Jonathan must not know this
or he will be grieved.' Yet as surely as the
LORD lives and as you live, there is only
a step between me and death."
4Jonathan said to David, "Whatever
you want me to do, I'll do for you."
5So David said, "Look, tomorrow is the
New Moon feast,[b] and I am supposed to
dine with the king; but let me go and
hide[c] in the field until the evening of
the day after tomorrow. 6If your father
misses me at all, tell him, 'David earnestly asked my permission to hurry to
Bethlehem,[d] his hometown, because an
annual[e] sacrifice is being made there for
his whole clan.' 7If he says, 'Very well,'
then your servant is safe. But if he loses
his temper,[f] you can be sure that he is
determined to harm me. 8As for you,
show kindness to your servant, for you
have brought him into a covenant[g] with
you before the LORD. If I am guilty, then
kill[h] me yourself! Why hand me over to
your father?"
9"Never!" Jonathan said. "If I had the
least inkling that my father was determined to harm you, wouldn't I tell you?"
10David asked, "Who will tell me if your
father answers you harshly?"
11"Come," Jonathan said, "let's go out
into the field." So they went there together.
12Then Jonathan said to David, "I swear
by the LORD, the God of Israel, that I will
surely sound out my father by this time
the day after tomorrow! If he is favorably

19:23 [w]1Sa 10:13
19:24 [x]2Sa 6:20; Isa 20:2; Mic 1:8 [y]1Sa 10:11
20:1 [z]1Sa 24:9
20:3 [a]Dt 6:13
20:5 [b]Nu 10:10; 28:11 [c]1Sa 19:2
20:6 [d]1Sa 17:58 [e]Dt 12:5
20:7 [f]1Sa 25:17
20:8 [g]1Sa 18:3; 23:18 [h]2Sa 14:32

19:22–24 Finally, out of frustration and desperation Saul goes himself to the camps at Ramah. But before he even reaches the group, the "Spirit of God" (v. 23) comes, and Saul begins prophesying as the others before him. It is possible to interpret this "Spirit of God" (v. 23) as the same evil spirit *from* God that had plagued Saul (16:14; 18:10; 19:9). Others have suggested that only Saul lies before Samuel "all that day and all that night" (19:24) in this ecstatic state of external unconsciousness. In this reading, the text is condemning Saul irrevocably as someone who has resisted God's grace and opposed God's purposes with regard to David. In any case, Saul's prophetic ecstasy before Samuel lasts an entire day, giving David plenty of time to escape.

A question closes the chapter: "Is Saul also among the prophets?" (v. 24). Its earlier use in 10:11 implied a positive evaluation of Saul. But here the question, which must have been used in earliest times to characterize Saul, can only imply a negative evaluation. The irony of the question challenges the genuine nature of Saul's prophetic behavior and also his legitimacy as king of Israel.

19:18–24 The presence of God's empowering Spirit is no *guarantee* of future blessing. Gifted persons and inspired leaders often begin to feel invincible. The evangelical church has seen some of its most visible leaders fail in sin in very public ways; some have completely lost their ministries. There is innate danger in the heresy that Spirit-led ministry is invincible, irrespective of continued faithfulness.

This, of course, has implications for all of us as individuals since we cannot live today on the spiritual blessings of our childhood or early adulthood. But the wider implications for the church are also obvious: No generation can afford to enjoy the spiritual benefits of their ancestors without giving any thought to their own responsibility in service and ministry. Without following God's guiding hand, the church is always only one generation from complete ineffectiveness or extinction.

20:1–23 Jonathan had earlier established a covenant with David and had essentially abdicated his right to succeed Saul as king of Israel (18:1–4). David therefore feels he can trust Jonathan to help determine what he should do next.

The elaborate speeches of Jonathan contain more than a simple plan to determine Saul's intentions toward David. Jonathan confirms his covenant commitment to David and his desire that his own children be protected when David in fact becomes king. He also speaks frankly and prophetically about David's future international rule, which is a new theme in the books of Samuel.

disposed toward you, will I not send you word and let you know? 13But if my father intends to harm you, may the LORD deal with Jonathan, be it ever so severely,[i] if I do not let you know and send you away in peace. May the LORD be with[j] you as he has been with my father. 14But show me unfailing kindness like the LORD's kindness as long as I live, so that I may not be killed, 15and do not ever cut off your kindness from my family[k] — not even when the LORD has cut off every one of David's enemies from the face of the earth."

16So Jonathan made a covenant[l] with the house of David, saying, "May the LORD call David's enemies to account." 17And Jonathan had David reaffirm his oath[m] out of love for him, because he loved him as he loved himself.

18Then Jonathan said to David, "Tomorrow is the New Moon feast. You will be missed, because your seat will be empty.[n] 19The day after tomorrow, toward evening, go to the place where you hid[o] when this trouble began, and wait by the stone Ezel. 20I will shoot three arrows to the side of it, as though I were shooting at a target. 21Then I will send a boy and say, 'Go, find the arrows.' If I say to him, 'Look, the arrows are on this side of you; bring them here,' then come, because, as surely as the LORD lives, you are safe; there is no danger. 22But if I say to the boy, 'Look, the arrows are beyond[p] you,' then you must go, because the LORD has sent you away. 23And about the matter you and I discussed — remember, the LORD is witness[q] between you and me forever."

24So David hid in the field, and when the New Moon feast came, the king sat down to eat. 25He sat in his customary place by the wall, opposite Jonathan,[a] and Abner sat next to Saul, but David's place was empty.[r] 26Saul said nothing that day, for he thought, "Something must have happened to David to make him ceremonially unclean — surely he is unclean.[s]" 27But the next day, the second day of the month, David's place was empty again. Then Saul said to his son Jonathan, "Why hasn't the son of Jesse come to the meal, either yesterday or today?"

28Jonathan answered, "David earnestly asked me for permission[t] to go to Bethlehem. 29He said, 'Let me go, because our family is observing a sacrifice in the town and my brother has ordered me to be there. If I have found favor in your eyes, let me get away to see my brothers.' That is why he has not come to the king's table."

30Saul's anger flared up at Jonathan and he said to him, "You son of a perverse and rebellious woman! Don't I know that you have sided with the son of Jesse to your own shame and to the shame of the mother who bore you? 31As long as the son of Jesse lives on this earth, neither you nor your kingdom will be established. Now send someone to bring him to me, for he must die!"

32"Why[u] should he be put to death? What[v] has he done?" Jonathan asked his father. 33But Saul hurled his spear at him to kill him. Then Jonathan knew that his father intended[w] to kill David.

34Jonathan got up from the table in fierce anger; on that second day of the feast he did not eat, because he was grieved at his father's shameful treatment of David.

35In the morning Jonathan went out to

20:13 [i] Ru 1:17; 1Sa 3:17 [j] Jos 1:5; 1Sa 17:37; 18:12; 1Ch 22:11,16
20:15 [k] 2Sa 9:7
20:16 [l] 1Sa 25:22
20:17 [m] 1Sa 18:3
20:18 [n] ver 5,25
20:19 [o] 1Sa 19:2
20:22 [p] ver 37
20:23 [q] ver 14-15; Ge 31:50
20:25 [r] ver 18
20:26 [s] Lev 7:20-21; 15:5; 1Sa 16:5
20:28 [t] ver 6
20:32 [u] 1Sa 19:4; Mt 27:23 [v] Ge 31:36; Lk 23:22
20:33 [w] ver 7; 1Sa 18:11,17

[a] *25* Septuagint; Hebrew *wall. Jonathan arose*

20:24–29 At first glance, David's absence at Saul's table seems like no more than a simple gaffe in social etiquette. But Saul may have assumed that David's absence betrayed his own royal aspirations.
20:30–34 After hearing the full explanation for David's absence (vv. 28–29), Saul erupts into a full-fledged tirade in which he insults Jonathan personally. Saul's shocking outburst reveals a new element in his obsession with David and helps explain why Jonathan and David finally realize they must abandon all hopes of reconciliation with Saul. In v. 31, Saul's suspicion of David becomes a conviction that David's rapid rise not only threatens Saul personally but also Jonathan and the hopes of Saul's family dynasty in Israel.

When Jonathan tries yet again to defend David's motives, Saul reaches for his spear to kill even Jonathan! Now Jonathan is sure of Saul's resolve to kill his friend. Jonathan must remain with Saul; David cannot.
20:35–42 Jonathan meets his friend at the predetermined location and communicates the bad news by the agreed-upon ruse. After the youngster is sent away, the two bid farewell in an emotional scene. Characterized as it is by physical signs of respect, mutual devotion, and sorrow (bowing, embracing, and weeping), this text powerfully illustrates the depth and profound nature of the relationship between Jonathan and David. In this tearful goodbye, it is Jonathan who recognizes their only recourse:

the field for his meeting with David. He
had a small boy with him, 36and he said to
the boy, "Run and find the arrows I shoot."
As the boy ran, he shot an arrow beyond
him. 37When the boy came to the place
where Jonathan's arrow had fallen, Jonathan called out after him, "Isn't the arrow
beyond[x] you?" 38Then he shouted, "Hurry!
Go quickly! Don't stop!" The boy picked
up the arrow and returned to his master.
39(The boy knew nothing about all this;
only Jonathan and David knew.) 40Then
Jonathan gave his weapons to the boy
and said, "Go, carry them back to town."

20:37 [x] ver 22

20:42 [y] ver 22; 1Sa 1:17 [z] 2Sa 1:26; Pr 18:24

1Sa 20:42 ❖ How does Jonathan model what it means to be a godly and loyal friend even through difficult circumstances?

41After the boy had gone, David got
up from the south side of the stone and
bowed down before Jonathan three
times, with his face to the ground.
Then they kissed each other and wept
together — but David wept the most.
42Jonathan said to David, "Go in peace,[y]
for we have sworn friendship[z] with each

"Go in peace" (v. 42). This he follows with one last reminder that their oath of loyalty is witnessed by Yahweh himself, which Jonathan hopes will assure peaceable relations between his descendants and David's. This text, of course, creates a tension throughout the rest of 1 and 2 Samuel, resolved finally in David's relationship with Jonathan's son, Mephibosheth (2Sa 9; 21:1–14). After this scene, David and Jonathan will only see each other on one other occasion (1Sa 23:16–18).

✜ **20:1–42** The message of faithfulness in relationships speaks as powerfully today as it did in the biblical context. Especially compelling is the *permanency* of the commitment between David and Jonathan, which grew out of their covenant relationship rooted in love (v. 17). The relevance of this discussion on faithfulness for contemporary culture in North America should be readily apparent and applicable on several levels. Our society today longs for models of such permanency or lasting commitment in relationships.

Generally, Christians today bemoan what is happening in our culture: children are abandoned by parents, traditional marriages crumble, friendships end over petty squabbles, and business relationships are broken and dishonorable. Thus, the Bible opens up a whole different perspective into the potential of human relationships. Against much of modern popular culture, this text teaches that it is possible for humans to build relationships that are durable and part of God's plan for the future.

PEOPLE TO KNOW // JONATHAN

1 SAMUEL 20:41: Jonathan was the son of King Saul. As such, he dealt with the frustration and danger of having a reckless father. On one occasion, Saul made a foolish order that none of his soldiers could eat before his battle was won (1Sa 14:24). Jonathan did not hear the order, and he ate some honey. Saul ordered Jonathan to be killed for this. Fortunately, Saul's soldiers intervened.

Jonathan became best friends with David, which caused more conflict with his father because of Saul's jealousy of David. Saul tried to get Jonathan to help kill David, who had become popular with the people. Jonathan, however, protected David (1Sa 19:1–6). Jonathan even made a covenant to protect the future king. Saul was so livid at Jonathan's loyalty to David that he tried to kill Jonathan again.

Later, when Saul was in constant pursuit of David, Jonathan risked a visit to his friend and helped David find strength in God (1Sa 23:17). He affirmed God's plan for David, declaring that David would one day be king over Israel.

Sadly, Jonathan died on the battlefield in a fight with the Philistines. When word reached David, he lamented the death of his beloved friend (2Sa 1:19–27).

Jonathan was caught in a difficult place, between loyalty to his father and loyalty to his friend. He bravely stood up for David, and he faced Saul's wrath because of it. He knew, however, that God was with David and that David would become Israel's next king.

APPLICATION ✜ Those who find themselves caught between their families and God's will can relate to Jonathan. It is difficult to disappoint, and perhaps even anger, our families when we choose to follow God's ways. Nevertheless, God's call on our lives is more important than earthly relationships. It's important to honor and respect our families, but our ultimate allegiance belongs to God alone.

other in the name of the LORD, saying,
'The LORD is witness between you and
me, and between your descendants and
my descendants forever.'" Then David
left, and Jonathan went back to the town.[a]

David at Nob

21[b] David went to Nob,[a] to Ahimelek
the priest. Ahimelek trembled[b]
when he met him, and asked, "Why are
you alone? Why is no one with you?"
2David answered Ahimelek the priest,
"The king sent me on a mission and said
to me, 'No one is to know anything about
the mission I am sending you on.' As for
my men, I have told them to meet me at
a certain place. 3Now then, what do you
have on hand? Give me five loaves of
bread, or whatever you can find."
4But the priest answered David, "I
don't have any ordinary bread[c] on hand;
however, there is some consecrated[d]
bread here — provided the men have
kept[e] themselves from women."
5David replied, "Indeed women have
been kept from us, as usual whenever[c] I
set out. The men's bodies are holy[f] even
on missions that are not holy. How much
more so today!" 6So the priest gave him
the consecrated bread,[g] since there was
no bread there except the bread of the
Presence that had been removed from
before the LORD and replaced by hot
bread on the day it was taken away.
7Now one of Saul's servants was there
that day, detained before the LORD; he
was Doeg[h] the Edomite,[i] Saul's chief
shepherd.
8David asked Ahimelek, "Don't you
have a spear or a sword here? I haven't
brought my sword or any other weapon,
because the king's mission was urgent."
9The priest replied, "The sword[j] of Goliath the Philistine, whom you killed in
the Valley of Elah,[k] is here; it is wrapped
in a cloth behind the ephod. If you want
it, take it; there is no sword here but that
one."
David said, "There is none like it; give
it to me."

David at Gath

10That day David fled from Saul and
went[l] to Achish king of Gath. 11But the
servants of Achish said to him, "Isn't this

21:1 [a] 1Sa 14:3; 22:9,19; Ne 11:32; Isa 10:32 [b] 1Sa 16:4
21:4 [c] Lev 24:8-9 [d] Ex 25:30; Mt 12:4 [e] Ex 19:15
21:5 [f] 1Th 4:4
21:6 [g] Lev 24:8-9; Mt 12:3-4; Mk 2:25-28; Lk 6:1-5
21:7 [h] 1Sa 22:9, 22 [i] 1Sa 14:47; Ps 52 Title
21:9 [j] 1Sa 17:51 [k] 1Sa 17:2
21:10 [l] 1Sa 27:2

a 42 In Hebrew texts this sentence (20:42b) is numbered 21:1. *b* In Hebrew texts 21:1-15 is numbered 21:2-16. *c* 5 Or *from us in the past few days since*

1Sa 21:6 ❖ When might it be okay to break the letter of the law for a greater purpose (see Mk 2:23–28)?

21:1-9 One can learn a lot about a person by seeing where they turn in times of trouble. When David first found it necessary to run from Saul, he went to Samuel at Ramah. Now officially on the run, David goes to Ahimelek, the priest at Nob, where he receives "the bread of the Presence" (v. 6) of Yahweh and the sword of Goliath, which is unique in its ability to prompt images of strength and victory in Yahweh's cause.

Earlier David received the aid of the old prophet Samuel; now he gets the assistance of a priest of Yahweh in the old traditions of the tabernacle at Shiloh. The reminder of the military victories of his youth in the name of Yahweh are referred to twice here in vv. 9, 11; in his greatest hour of need, David is reminded that Yahweh has been his help in time of trouble.

21:10-15 Having benefited all he could and not

David, the king of the land? Isn't he the
one they sing about in their dances:

"'Saul has slain his thousands,
and David his tens of
thousands'?"[m]

12 David took these words to heart and
was very much afraid of Achish king of
Gath. 13 So he pretended to be insane[n] in
their presence; and while he was in their
hands he acted like a madman, making
marks on the doors of the gate and letting saliva run down his beard.
14 Achish said to his servants, "Look at
the man! He is insane! Why bring him to
me? 15 Am I so short of madmen that you
have to bring this fellow here to carry on
like this in front of me? Must this man
come into my house?"

David at Adullam and Mizpah

22 David left Gath and escaped to
the cave[o] of Adullam. When his
brothers and his father's household
heard about it, they went down to him
there. 2 All those who were in distress
or in debt or discontented gathered[p]
around him, and he became their commander. About four hundred men were
with him.
3 From there David went to Mizpah
in Moab and said to the king of Moab,
"Would you let my father and mother
come and stay with you until I learn
what God will do for me?" 4 So he left
them with the king of Moab, and they
stayed with him as long as David was in
the stronghold.
5 But the prophet Gad[q] said to David,
"Do not stay in the stronghold. Go into
the land of Judah." So David left and
went to the forest of Hereth.

Saul Kills the Priests of Nob

6 Now Saul heard that David and his
men had been discovered. And Saul was
seated,[r] spear in hand, under the tamarisk[s] tree on the hill at Gibeah, with all
his officials standing at his side. 7 He said
to them, "Listen, men of Benjamin! Will
the son of Jesse give all of you fields and
vineyards? Will he make all of you commanders[t] of thousands and commanders
of hundreds? 8 Is that why you have all
conspired against me? No one tells me
when my son makes a covenant[u] with the
son of Jesse. None of you is concerned[v]
about me or tells me that my son has
incited my servant to lie in wait for me,
as he does today."
9 But Doeg[w] the Edomite, who was
standing with Saul's officials, said, "I saw
the son of Jesse come to Ahimelek son
of Ahitub at Nob.[x] 10 Ahimelek inquired[y]
of the LORD for him; he also gave him
provisions[z] and the sword of Goliath the
Philistine."
11 Then the king sent for the priest
Ahimelek son of Ahitub and all the men
of his family, who were the priests at Nob,
and they all came to the king. 12 Saul said,
"Listen now, son of Ahitub."
"Yes, my lord," he answered.
13 Saul said to him, "Why have you conspired[a] against me, you and the son of
Jesse, giving him bread and a sword and
inquiring of God for him, so that he has
rebelled against me and lies in wait for
me, as he does today?"
14 Ahimelek answered the king, "Who[b]
of all your servants is as loyal as David,
the king's son-in-law, captain of your
bodyguard and highly respected in your
household? 15 Was that day the first time
I inquired of God for him? Of course not!

21:11 [m] 1Sa 18:7; 29:5; Ps 56 Title
21:13 [n] Ps 34 Title
22:1 [o] 2Sa 23:13; Ps 57 Title; 142 Title
22:2 [p] 1Sa 23:13; 25:13; 2Sa 15:20
22:5 [q] 2Sa 24:11; 1Ch 21:9; 29:29; 2Ch 29:25
22:6 [r] Jdg 4:5 [s] Ge 21:33
22:7 [t] 1Sa 8:14
22:8 [u] 1Sa 18:3; 20:16 [v] 1Sa 23:21
22:9 [w] 1Sa 21:7; Ps 52 Title [x] 1Sa 21:1
22:10 [y] Nu 27:21; 1Sa 10:22 [z] 1Sa 21:6
22:13 [a] ver 8
22:14 [b] 1Sa 19:4

wishing to further endanger the gracious priests at Nob, David needs to continue to distance himself from Saul. Interestingly, the servants of Achish identify David as "king of the land" (v. 11), which probably means they think of him as a local chieftain or ruler. At any rate, they must not have realized his real status as a refugee on the run from Saul.

22:1–5 Being driven off by the Philistines, David now withdraws to Adullam, where he is met by family members and four hundred malcontents, who join forces with him in a loosely organized army. It is from this motley band of men that David begins to form a fiercely loyal inner circle of followers, which is to become a personal army. This group will grow into at least six hundred and become an important factor in the rest of his rule over Israel.

22:6–8 As the scene opens, Saul is surrounded with all the trappings of power: He is seated on a hill in the royal city, spear in hand, with powerful officials all around (v. 6). Yet the point of the narrative is that he is in fact powerless to do anything about David, no matter how outrageous and abhorrent his attempts.

22:9–19 Doeg, being an Edomite and having no compulsion about sparing David or the priests at Nob, sees this as an opportunity to turn his good fortune into political advantage. He informs Saul about Ahimelek's aid for David (Doeg was introduced in passing in 21:7), and Saul promptly condemns the priests to death, despite Ahimelek's denial of participation in a conspiracy. When the Israelite officials uniformly refuse to carry out Saul's death sentence, Doeg is conscripted to perform the ghastly service for Saul.

Let not the king accuse your servant or
any of his father's family, for your servant knows nothing at all about this
whole affair."
16But the king said, "You will surely die, Ahimelek, you and your whole
family."
17Then the king ordered the guards
at his side: "Turn and kill the priests of
the LORD, because they too have sided
with David. They knew he was fleeing,
yet they did not tell me."
But the king's officials were unwilling[c] to raise a hand to strike the priests
of the LORD.
18The king then ordered Doeg, "You
turn and strike down the priests." So
Doeg the Edomite turned and struck
them down. That day he killed eighty-five
men who wore the linen ephod.[d] 19He
also put to the sword[e] Nob, the town of
the priests, with its men and women,
its children and infants, and its cattle,
donkeys and sheep.
20But one son of Ahimelek son of Ahitub, named Abiathar,[f] escaped and fled
to join David.[g] 21He told David that Saul
had killed the priests of the LORD. 22Then
David said to Abiathar, "That day, when
Doeg[h] the Edomite was there, I knew he
would be sure to tell Saul. I am responsible for the death of your whole family.
23Stay with me; don't be afraid. The man
who wants to kill you[i] is trying to kill me
too. You will be safe with me."

22:17 [c] Ex 1:17
22:18 [d] 1Sa 2:18, 31
22:19 [e] 1Sa 15:3
22:20 [f] 1Sa 23:6, 9; 30:7; 1Ki 2:22, 26, 27 [g] 1Sa 2:32
22:22 [h] 1Sa 21:7
22:23 [i] 1Ki 2:26

1Sa 22:18 ❖ What can cause people to lose their moral compass and commit senseless acts of violence or evil?

David Saves Keilah

23 When David was told, "Look, the
Philistines are fighting against
Keilah[j] and are looting the threshing
floors," 2he inquired[k] of the LORD, saying,
"Shall I go and attack these Philistines?"
The LORD answered him, "Go, attack
the Philistines and save Keilah."
3But David's men said to him, "Here
in Judah we are afraid. How much more,
then, if we go to Keilah against the Philistine forces!"
4Once again David inquired of the
LORD, and the LORD answered him, "Go
down to Keilah, for I am going to give
the Philistines into your hand.[l]" 5So David and his men went to Keilah, fought
the Philistines and carried off their livestock. He inflicted heavy losses on the
Philistines and saved the people of Keilah. 6(Now Abiathar[m] son of Ahimelek
had brought the ephod down with him
when he fled to David at Keilah.)

Saul Pursues David

7Saul was told that David had gone to
Keilah, and he said, "God has delivered
him into my hands, for David has imprisoned himself by entering a town with
gates and bars." 8And Saul called up all

23:1 [j] Jos 15:44
23:2 [k] ver 4, 12; 1Sa 30:8; 2Sa 5:19, 23
23:4 [l] Jos 8:7; Jdg 7:7
23:6 [m] 1Sa 22:20

22:20–21 Only one member of the priestly family escapes: Abiathar. When he runs to David with the news, David takes full responsibility for the terrible consequences of his relationship with Ahimelek. However, the reader knows that which David can only suspect: The real causes for the disaster are Saul's irrational pursuit of David and the treachery of Doeg the Edomite.

22:22–23 David begs Abiathar to remain with him where he will be safe so that David becomes the protector of the last surviving priest. As a result, king-elect and priest-elect join forces as fellow fugitives, and they forge a relationship that will last throughout David's reign.

✣ 21:1—22:23 The overarching theme of the text is that God's word is certain and true. Certainly, our world needs to hear precisely this message. The emerging generation rejects the idea that truth is absolute and purely rational. In the face of such shifting sands it is still necessary to communicate this simple truth of the gospel: God will be faithful to his Word. This message comes as comfort to the believer and cause for alarm for the unbeliever.

23:1–6 The reference to Abiathar and the priestly ephod ties these events together with the previous episode and presumably means David's inquiries are answered by means of the sacred lots: the Urim and Thummim stored in the ephod. The specifics of how these worked is not clear, but they served as a form of divinely sanctioned lot-casting, which may have functioned something like our "heads or tails."

This important feature of David's relationship with God is central in the contrast between Saul and David. Yahweh has long since stopped answering Saul's inquiries, presumably because Saul has made up his mind before asking. By contrast, Ahimelek earlier inquired of Yahweh on David's behalf, which may be when David learned the value of such inquiries.

23:7–14 Saul should have rejoiced in the deliverance of Keilah from the Philistines. But his only thoughts are of how much easier it will now be to trap David. David is still painfully aware of his role in the tragic deaths of the citizens of Nob, and he fears the same will happen now at Keilah, as his prayer reveals (v. 10). It is a shocking fact that Saul is mustering his troops to capture *David*

his forces for battle, to go down to Keilah
to besiege David and his men.
9When David learned that Saul was
plotting against him, he said to Abiathar[n]
the priest, "Bring the ephod." 10David
said, "LORD, God of Israel, your servant
has heard definitely that Saul plans to
come to Keilah and destroy the town on
account of me. 11Will the citizens of Keilah surrender me to him? Will Saul come
down, as your servant has heard? LORD,
God of Israel, tell your servant."
And the LORD said, "He will."
12Again David asked, "Will the citizens
of Keilah surrender[o] me and my men
to Saul?"
And the LORD said, "They will."
13So David and his men,[p] about six
hundred in number, left Keilah and kept
moving from place to place. When Saul
was told that David had escaped from
Keilah, he did not go there.
14David stayed in the wilderness
strongholds and in the hills of the Desert of Ziph.[q] Day after day Saul searched[r]
for him, but God did not[s] give David into
his hands.
15While David was at Horesh in the Desert of Ziph, he learned that[a] Saul had
come out to take his life. 16And Saul's
son Jonathan went to David at Horesh
and helped him find strength[t] in God.
17"Don't be afraid," he said. "My father
Saul will not lay a hand on you. You will
be king[u] over Israel, and I will be second
to you. Even my father Saul knows this."
18The two of them made a covenant[v]
before the LORD. Then Jonathan went
home, but David remained at Horesh.
19The Ziphites[w] went up to Saul at
Gibeah and said, "Is not David hiding
among us[x] in the strongholds at Horesh,
on the hill of Hakilah,[y] south of Jeshimon? 20Now, Your Majesty, come down
whenever it pleases you to do so, and we
will be responsible for giving[z] him into
your hands."
21Saul replied, "The LORD bless you for
your concern[a] for me. 22Go and get more
information. Find out where David usually goes and who has seen him there.
They tell me he is very crafty. 23Find out
about all the hiding places he uses and
come back to me with definite information. Then I will go with you; if he is in

23:9 [n] ver 6; 1Sa 22:20; 30:7
23:12 [o] ver 20
23:13 [p] 1Sa 22:2; 25:13
23:14 [q] Jos 15:24, 55 [r] Ps 54:3-4 [s] Ps 32:7
23:16 [t] 1Sa 30:6
23:17 [u] 1Sa 20:31; 24:20
23:18 [v] 1Sa 18:3; 20:16,42; 2Sa 9:1; 21:7
23:19 [w] 1Sa 26:1 [x] Ps 54 Title [y] 1Sa 26:3
23:20 [z] ver 12
23:21 [a] 1Sa 22:8

1Sa 23:16 ❖ How can we help a friend in distress find strength in God?

[a] 15 Or *he was afraid because*

---

rather than to take advantage of the victory to pursue the Philistines further.

The citizens of Keilah would be anxious to avoid the same fate as Nob, regardless of how grateful they may be to David. They would be compelled to surrender David to Saul. In order to avoid more innocent bloodshed, David and his men escape into the Desert of Ziph.

As Saul's hostility against David intensifies, the narrator informs us that "God did not give David into his hands" (v. 14). This reminder keeps before us the question of royal authority in Israel. Yahweh, the true king of Israel, is in charge, and ultimately his plan will be accomplished.

23:15-18 As in other texts where Jonathan and David appear together, the crown prince acknowledges the future greatness of David, though v. 17 is the most explicit statement of all. David is encouraged no doubt by their long-standing friendship but perhaps more by Jonathan's certainty and optimism about the future.

23:19-29 The same Yahweh who delivered the Philistines into David's hands now protects David from the hand of Saul. The irony here is again the role of the Philistines. Just as Saul is closing in on David and feels he has him trapped at long last, word comes of another Philistine raid, forcing Saul to abandon his pursuit of David. The hand of Yahweh is clearly behind these events, since he is free to use any means necessary to protect David—even the perennial threat of the Philistines.

Saul has long since stopped seeking messages from Yahweh, depending instead on his own political and strategic decision-making abilities. In his desperate obsession with killing David, he is completely dependent on his own wisdom and whatever intelligence he can gather from informants. All of this transpires while the king should have been concerned instead about the Philistines.

By contrast, David is himself inflicting losses on the Philistines and doing so with the help of Abiathar; on two occasions David consults the priestly ephod for guidance. Consulting Yahweh becomes David's standard practice throughout much of his reign. By contrast, Saul has executed the priests who could have helped him, and he seems incapable of hearing God's word.

✣ **23:1-29** What are the primary methods by which God communicates today? Without denying a role for modern prophets or the *possibility* of audible voices or some other dramatic means of communication, we must begin by stating that God's *primary* means of communication today is through Scripture. Our identity as Christians means we are a people of the Book—more specifically, 66 books divided into the OT and NT. In seeking the guidance of God, we should never separate the work of the Holy Spirit from the role of Scripture (Eph 6:17).

the area, I will track him down among
all the clans of Judah."
24So they set out and went to Ziph
ahead of Saul. Now David and his men
were in the Desert of Maon,[b] in the Arabah south of Jeshimon. 25Saul and his
men began the search, and when David
was told about it, he went down to the
rock and stayed in the Desert of Maon.
When Saul heard this, he went into the
Desert of Maon in pursuit of David.
26Saul[c] was going along one side of
the mountain, and David and his men
were on the other side, hurrying to get
away from Saul. As Saul and his forces
were closing in on David and his men
to capture them, 27a messenger came to
Saul, saying, "Come quickly! The Philistines are raiding the land." 28Then Saul
broke off his pursuit of David and went to
meet the Philistines. That is why they call
this place Sela Hammahlekoth.[a] 29And
David went up from there and lived in
the strongholds of En Gedi.[b][d]

David Spares Saul's Life

24 [c] After Saul returned from pursuing the Philistines, he was told,
"David is in the Desert of En Gedi.[e]" 2So
Saul took three thousand able young
men from all Israel and set out to look[f]
for David and his men near the Crags of
the Wild Goats.
3He came to the sheep pens along the
way; a cave[g] was there, and Saul went in
to relieve[h] himself. David and his men
were far back in the cave. 4The men said,
"This is the day the LORD spoke[i] of when
he said[d] to you, 'I will give your enemy
into your hands for you to deal with as
you wish.'"[j] Then David crept up unnoticed and cut off a corner of Saul's robe.
5Afterward, David was conscience-
stricken[k] for having cut off a corner of
his robe. 6He said to his men, "The LORD
forbid that I should do such a thing to
my master, the LORD's anointed,[l] or lay
my hand on him; for he is the anointed
of the LORD." 7With these words David
sharply rebuked his men and did not
allow them to attack Saul. And Saul left
the cave and went his way.
8Then David went out of the cave and
called out to Saul, "My lord the king!"
When Saul looked behind him, David
bowed down and prostrated himself with
his face to the ground.[m] 9He said to Saul,
"Why do you listen when men say, 'David is bent on harming you'? 10This day
you have seen with your own eyes how
the LORD delivered you into my hands
in the cave. Some urged me to kill you,
but I spared you; I said, 'I will not lay
my hand on my lord, because he is the
LORD's anointed.' 11See, my father, look
at this piece of your robe in my hand! I
cut off the corner of your robe but did
not kill you. See that there is nothing
in my hand to indicate that I am guilty[n]
of wrongdoing or rebellion. I have not
wronged you, but you are hunting[o] me
down to take my life. 12May the LORD

23:24 [b] Jos 15:55; 1Sa 25:2
23:26 [c] Ps 17:9
23:29 [d] 2Ch 20:2
24:1 [e] 1Sa 23:28-29
24:2 [f] 1Sa 26:2
24:3 [g] Ps 57 Title; 142 Title [h] Jdg 3:24
24:4 [i] 1Sa 25:28-30 [j] 1Sa 23:17; 26:8
24:5 [k] 2Sa 24:10
24:6 [l] 1Sa 26:11
24:8 [m] 1Sa 25:23-24
24:11 [n] Ps 7:3 [o] 1Sa 23:14, 23; 26:20

[a] 28 *Sela Hammahlekoth* means *rock of parting.*
[b] 29 In Hebrew texts this verse (23:29) is numbered 24:1.
[c] In Hebrew texts 24:1-22 is numbered 24:2-23.
[d] 4 Or *"Today the LORD is saying*

24:1-7 Saul's desperate state of mind is illustrated by his willingness to deploy significant military resources to pursue David, even while the Philistine threat still looms in the shadows. The assumption on the part of David's men that Yahweh has miraculously provided this opportunity to kill Saul is only natural; God has delivered Saul into David's "hands" (v. 4).

24:4-5 David's cutting a corner of Saul's robe is probably more than a means of proving his good will toward Saul. It seems likely here that this action has enormous symbolic significance, indicating perhaps not only that Saul's hold on the kingdom is over but that David's has now begun. So, David takes a portion of Saul's garment rather than his life.

24:6-7 As we have seen in 1 Samuel, Yahweh's anointed is endowed with Yahweh's Spirit, and the idea of striking such a one is repulsive to David. Even in the case of Saul, from whom the spirit of Yahweh has departed, David's act symbolizing the transfer of power is in a sense lifting the hand against Yahweh's anointed.

24:8-22 David's eloquent speech in vv. 9-15 is juxtaposed with Saul's choked cry in vv. 16-21. Saul's speech culminates in an admission that David is in the right and will in fact be king. Nothing validates David's reign more than a confession on the lips of Saul himself that David is the legitimate anointed one (v. 20).

After acknowledging that David is in the right, Saul makes a profound confession (v. 20). Here there is no recrimination, as we have come to expect from Saul (cf. 15:10-31). He seems genuinely to understand that he will be placed aside in favor of David.

Most of Saul's sons are eventually killed by the Philistines (31:2) and the Gibeonites (2Sa 21:1-14). The historians responsible for the books of Samuel want the reader to understand that David does keep his promises to Jonathan and Saul. Unlike most ancient monarchs, David shows a God-pleasing, compassionate attitude toward his enemies; in this sense, he is truly a man after God's own heart.

judge[p] between you and me. And may
the LORD avenge[q] the wrongs you have
done to me, but my hand will not touch
you. 13As the old saying goes, 'From evildoers come evil deeds,'[r] so my hand will
not touch you.
14"Against whom has the king of Israel come out? Who are you pursuing?
A dead dog?[s] A flea?[t] 15May the LORD be
our judge[u] and decide between us. May
he consider my cause and uphold[v] it;
may he vindicate[w] me by delivering[x] me
from your hand."
16When David finished saying this,
Saul asked, "Is that your voice,[y] David
my son?" And he wept aloud. 17"You are
more righteous than I,"[z] he said. "You
have treated me well,[a] but I have treated you badly. 18You have just now told
me about the good you did to me; the
LORD delivered[b] me into your hands,
but you did not kill me. 19When a man
finds his enemy, does he let him get away
unharmed? May the LORD reward you
well for the way you treated me today.
20I know that you will surely be king[c]
and that the kingdom[d] of Israel will be
established in your hands. 21Now swear[e]
to me by the LORD that you will not kill
off my descendants or wipe out my name
from my father's family.[f]"
22So David gave his oath to Saul. Then
Saul returned home, but David and his
men went up to the stronghold.[g]

David, Nabal and Abigail

25 Now Samuel died,[h] and all Israel assembled and mourned[i] for
him; and they buried him at his home
in Ramah.[j] Then David moved down into
the Desert of Paran.[a]

1Sa 24:17 ❖ What experience has caused you to face and acknowledge your own sin and failure?

2A certain man in Maon,[k] who had
property there at Carmel, was very
wealthy. He had a thousand goats and
three thousand sheep, which he was
shearing in Carmel. 3His name was Nabal and his wife's name was Abigail.[l] She
was an intelligent and beautiful woman,
but her husband was surly and mean in
his dealings—he was a Calebite.[m]
4While David was in the wilderness, he
heard that Nabal was shearing sheep. 5So
he sent ten young men and said to them,
"Go up to Nabal at Carmel and greet him
in my name. 6Say to him: 'Long life to
you! Good health[n] to you and your household! And good health to all that is yours![o]
7" 'Now I hear that it is sheep-shearing
time. When your shepherds were with
us, we did not mistreat[p] them, and the
whole time they were at Carmel nothing
of theirs was missing. 8Ask your own
servants and they will tell you. Therefore
be favorable toward my men, since we
come at a festive time. Please give your
servants and your son David whatever[q]
you can find for them.' "
9When David's men arrived, they gave
Nabal this message in David's name.
Then they waited.
10Nabal answered David's servants,
"Who[r] is this David? Who is this son
of Jesse? Many servants are breaking
away from their masters these days.

24:12 [p] Ge 16:5; 31:53; Job 5:8 [q] Jdg 11:27; 1Sa 26:10
24:13 [r] Mt 7:20
24:14 [s] 1Sa 17:43; 2Sa 9:8 [t] 1Sa 26:20
24:15 [u] ver 12 [v] Ps 35:1, 23; Mic 7:9 [w] Ps 43:1 [x] Ps 119:134, 154
24:16 [y] 1Sa 26:17
24:17 [z] Ge 38:26; 1Sa 26:21 [a] Mt 5:44
24:18 [b] 1Sa 26:23
24:20 [c] 1Sa 23:17 [d] 1Sa 13:14
24:21 [e] Ge 21:23; 2Sa 21:1-9 [f] 1Sa 20:14-15
24:22 [g] 1Sa 23:29
25:1 [h] 1Sa 28:3 [i] Nu 20:29; Dt 34:8 [j] Ge 21:21; 2Ch 33:20
25:2 [k] Jos 15:55; 1Sa 23:24
25:3 [l] Pr 31:10 [m] Jos 15:13
25:6 [n] Ps 122:7; Lk 10:5 [o] 1Ch 12:18
25:7 [p] ver 15
25:8 [q] Ne 8:10
25:10 [r] Jdg 9:28

[a] *1* Hebrew and some Septuagint manuscripts; other Septuagint manuscripts *Maon*

✜ **24:1–22** The text's message of reverence and trust speaks volumes. David in this text exemplified a radical reverence for God that controlled his thoughts and actions. He refused to succumb to a bloody resolution to his problems, even while his trusted allies around him assured him it was "God's will" that he kill Saul. This is vital reverence resulting in obedience, even when it is unclear which action is the obedient action to take.

25:1 It is not insignificant that the reference to Samuel's death follows immediately on the heels of Saul's confession in 24:20–21, which was a public announcement accepting Samuel's judgment on him. Saul has now come to see the truth of what Samuel predicted concerning him and his reign, though he is seeing it too late (chs. 13–15).

25:2–13 Here we encounter for the first time Nabal, who is wealthy and boorish. His name in Hebrew means "foolish," which becomes an ironic part of the narrative (v. 25). However, as rude and unsavory as Nabal is, his wife Abigail is "intelligent and beautiful" (v. 3). Her name means "my father is joy(ous)," and her beauty is more than skin deep.

David's delegation asks Nabal for no more than payment for protection they have voluntarily rendered earlier. Indeed, ancient Near Eastern customs of hospitality and OT laws suggest that Nabal, who is more than able to provide such modest provisions, is under obligation to aid David.

Nabal's response brings a swift reaction. David's command "Strap on your sword" (v. 13) leaves no doubt about his intentions. Here David acts impetuously and violently, which does not bode well for his future as ruler over Israel.

11 Why should I take my bread[s] and water, and the meat I have slaughtered for
my shearers, and give it to men coming
from who knows where?"
12 David's men turned around and went
back. When they arrived, they reported every word. 13 David said to his men,
"Each of you strap on your sword!" So
they did, and David strapped his on as
well. About four hundred men went[t] up
with David, while two hundred stayed
with the supplies.[u]
14 One of the servants told Abigail, Nabal's wife, "David sent messengers from
the wilderness to give our master his
greetings,[v] but he hurled insults at them.
15 Yet these men were very good to us.
They did not mistreat[w] us, and the whole
time we were out in the fields near them
nothing was missing.[x] 16 Night and day
they were a wall[y] around us the whole
time we were herding our sheep near
them. 17 Now think it over and see what
you can do, because disaster is hanging
over our master and his whole household. He is such a wicked[z] man that no
one can talk to him."

25:11 [s]Jdg 8:6
25:13 [t]1Sa 23:13 [u]1Sa 30:24
25:14 [v]1Sa 13:10
25:15 [w]ver 7 [x]ver 21
25:16 [y]Ex 14:22; Job 1:10
25:17 [z]1Sa 20:7
25:18 [a]1Ch 12:40 [b]2Sa 16:1
25:19 [c]Ge 32:20
25:21 [d]Ps 109:5
25:22 [e]1Sa 3:17; 20:13 [f]1Ki 14:10; 21:21; 2Ki 9:8
25:23 [g]1Sa 20:41

18 Abigail acted quickly. She took two
hundred loaves of bread, two skins of
wine, five dressed sheep, five seahs[a] of
roasted grain, a hundred cakes of raisins[a]
and two hundred cakes of pressed figs,
and loaded them on donkeys.[b] 19 Then
she told her servants, "Go on ahead;[c] I'll
follow you." But she did not tell her husband Nabal.
20 As she came riding her donkey into
a mountain ravine, there were David
and his men descending toward her, and
she met them. 21 David had just said, "It's
been useless — all my watching over this
fellow's property in the wilderness so
that nothing of his was missing. He has
paid[d] me back evil for good. 22 May God
deal with David,[b] be it ever so severely,[e]
if by morning I leave alive one male[f] of
all who belong to him!"
23 When Abigail saw David, she quickly
got off her donkey and bowed down before David with her face to the ground.[g]
24 She fell at his feet and said: "Pardon

[a] *18* That is, probably about 60 pounds or about 27 kilograms [b] *22* Some Septuagint manuscripts; Hebrew *with David's enemies*

25:14–23 Nabal's servants feel it useless to try to reason with him directly. Instead, one of them goes immediately to his remarkable wife, Abigail. She recognizes the seriousness of the situation at once and takes decisive action. Just as she and David approach each other, David is considering the vengeful action he is about to take (vv. 21–22). His intentions are clear, and his mind is set.

25:24–31 Abigail's speech shows remarkable wisdom and skill. She softens David's rage with her

PEOPLE TO KNOW // ABIGAIL

1 SAMUEL 25:14–40: The Bible calls Abigail "an intelligent and beautiful woman" (1Sa 25:3). Her first husband, Nabal, on the other hand, is described as surly and mean.

Abigail and Nabal encountered David when he was on the run from King Saul. David sent his men to request some much-needed assistance from Nabal. David reminded Nabal that his men had been helpful to Nabal in the past. Nabal, however, disrespectfully rejected David's request for help.

When word reached Abigail of what Nabal had done, she demonstrated her true character. She prepared a feast and sent it to David and his men. She also bowed down before David, admitting that her husband was living up to his name, which means "fool." Abigail spoke more than she knew when she declared that God would make David's family into a lasting dynasty (1Sa 25:28). David responded by praising God for sending Abigail to him, averting the bloody vengeance he had intended to carry out against Nabal.

Abigail boldly corrected Nabal's wrongdoing by standing strong against it, generously providing food for David's men and apologizing on behalf of her husband. David, duly impressed by this strong and wise woman, asked her to be his wife.

APPLICATION It's not easy to stand up for what is right, especially when it means going against family or friends. Abigail offers an example of doing the right thing even when it is hard. While we ought to be supportive of our family members, when they do what is wrong, we need the strength and courage, like Abigail, to follow God's way instead of theirs.

your servant, my lord, and let me speak
to you; hear what your servant has to
say. 25Please pay no attention, my lord,
to that wicked man Nabal. He is just like
his name—his name means Fool,[h] and
folly goes with him. And as for me, your
servant, I did not see the men my lord
sent. 26And now, my lord, as surely as
the LORD your God lives and as you live,
since the LORD has kept you from bloodshed[i] and from avenging[j] yourself with
your own hands, may your enemies and
all who are intent on harming my lord
be like Nabal.[k] 27And let this gift,[l] which
your servant has brought to my lord, be
given to the men who follow you.

28"Please forgive[m] your servant's presumption. The LORD your God will certainly make a lasting[n] dynasty for my
lord, because you fight the LORD's battles,[o] and no wrongdoing[p] will be found
in you as long as you live. 29Even though
someone is pursuing you to take your
life, the life of my lord will be bound
securely in the bundle of the living by
the LORD your God, but the lives of your
enemies he will hurl[q] away as from the
pocket of a sling. 30When the LORD has
fulfilled for my lord every good thing
he promised concerning him and has
appointed him ruler[r] over Israel, 31my
lord will not have on his conscience the
staggering burden of needless bloodshed
or of having avenged himself. And when
the LORD your God has brought my lord
success, remember[s] your servant."

32David said to Abigail, "Praise[t] be

25:25 [h] Pr 14:16
25:26 [i] ver 33 [j] Heb 10:30 [k] 2Sa 18:32
25:27 [l] Ge 33:11; 1Sa 30:26
25:28 [m] ver 24 [n] 2Sa 7:11, 26 [o] 1Sa 18:17 [p] 1Sa 24:11
25:29 [q] Jer 10:18
25:30 [r] 1Sa 13:14
25:31 [s] Ge 40:14
25:32 [t] Ge 24:27; Ex 18:10; Lk 1:68
25:33 [u] ver 26
25:35 [v] Ge 19:21; 1Sa 20:42; 2Ki 5:19
25:36 [w] 2Sa 13:23 [x] Pr 20:1; Isa 5:11, 22; Hos 4:11 [y] ver 19
25:38 [z] 1Sa 26:10; 2Sa 6:7

1Sa 25:32–34 ❖ Why are vengeance and punishment best left to God rather than taken into our own hands?

to the LORD, the God of Israel, who has
sent you today to meet me. 33May you
be blessed for your good judgment and
for keeping me from bloodshed[u] this day
and from avenging myself with my own
hands. 34Otherwise, as surely as the LORD,
the God of Israel, lives, who has kept me
from harming you, if you had not come
quickly to meet me, not one male belonging to Nabal would have been left
alive by daybreak."

35Then David accepted from her hand
what she had brought him and said, "Go
home in peace. I have heard your words
and granted[v] your request."

36When Abigail went to Nabal, he was
in the house holding a banquet like that
of a king. He was in high[w] spirits and very
drunk.[x] So she told[y] him nothing at all
until daybreak. 37Then in the morning,
when Nabal was sober, his wife told him
all these things, and his heart failed him
and he became like a stone. 38About ten
days later, the LORD struck[z] Nabal and
he died.

39When David heard that Nabal was
dead, he said, "Praise be to the LORD, who
has upheld my cause against Nabal for
treating me with contempt. He has kept
his servant from doing wrong and has
brought Nabal's wrongdoing down on
his own head."

"present" in v. 27 and addresses him as a superior (v. 24).

25:32–35 Abigail has made it nearly impossible for David to exact his revenge on this beautiful and gifted woman, who so humbly and persuasively intervenes on behalf of her master's servants and herself. More importantly, she has reminded David of who he is. David recognizes that Abigail has saved him from wrongdoing and that Yahweh himself is at work in these events to prevent the guilt of bloodshed.

25:36–44 Not only does Nabal's death suddenly confirm David's actions, but it makes the way clear for this remarkable woman, Abigail, to become David's wife. Her wisdom and strong character make her a suitable partner for David, and she is in many respects his equal.

The political significance of his marriage should not be missed. David's exile from Saul's court means he has lost his power base in Gibeah, where he was hailed as a military hero. His marriages to Abigail and Ahinoam give him ties to the Hebron and Jezreel areas, perhaps giving him a new power base among the inhabitants of Judah. David's compliance and teachability are turned to good use in the movement toward a new kingdom; once again the Lord hammers out his will on the anvil of human circumstances.

✤ **25:1–44** The issues we have discussed in this previous section have to do with discipleship. The nature of Christian discipleship involves "learning," since a disciple is, after all, a "learner" and the rabbi is a "teacher." This text serves as a reminder that disciples must be teachable; they receive the word of God and must act on it, adjusting their lives accordingly. David learns that patience and personal restraint are a better, God-pleasing way of acting as king. All of us are on a journey to somewhere; all of us are in the process of becoming someone. Christian discipleship adopts a certain understanding of the nature of growth in grace. So, a new believer, immature in faith at first, should grow naturally into a mature believer.

Then David sent word to Abigail, asking her to become his wife. 40 His servants went to Carmel and said to Abigail,
"David has sent us to you to take you to
become his wife."
41 She bowed down with her face to the
ground and said, "I am your servant and
am ready to serve you and wash the feet
of my lord's servants." 42 Abigail[a] quickly
got on a donkey and, attended by her
five female servants, went with David's
messengers and became his wife. 43 David
had also married Ahinoam[b] of Jezreel,
and they both were his wives.[c] 44 But Saul
had given his daughter Michal, David's
wife, to Paltiel[a][d] son of Laish, who was
from Gallim.[e]

David Again Spares Saul's Life

26 The Ziphites[f] went to Saul at Gibeah and said, "Is not David hid-
ing[g] on the hill of Hakilah, which faces
Jeshimon?"
2 So Saul went down to the Desert of
Ziph, with his three thousand select Israelite troops, to search[h] there for David.
3 Saul made his camp beside the road on
the hill of Hakilah facing Jeshimon, but
David stayed in the wilderness. When he
saw that Saul had followed him there, 4 he
sent out scouts and learned that Saul had
definitely arrived.
5 Then David set out and went to the
place where Saul had camped. He saw
where Saul and Abner[i] son of Ner, the
commander of the army, had lain down.
Saul was lying inside the camp, with the
army encamped around him.
6 David then asked Ahimelek the Hittite and Abishai son of Zeruiah,[j] Joab's
brother, "Who will go down into the
camp with me to Saul?"
"I'll go with you," said Abishai.

25:42 [a] Ge 24:61-67
25:43 [b] Jos 15:56 [c] 1Sa 27:3; 30:5
25:44 [d] 2Sa 3:15 [e] Isa 10:30
26:1 [f] 1Sa 23:19 [g] Ps 54 Title
26:2 [h] 1Sa 13:2; 24:2
26:5 [i] 1Sa 14:50; 17:55
26:6 [j] Jdg 7:10-11; 1Ch 2:16
26:9 [k] 2Sa 1:14 [l] 1Sa 24:5
26:10 [m] 1Sa 25:38; Ro 12:19 [n] Ge 47:29; Dt 31:14; Ps 37:13 [o] 1Sa 31:6; 2Sa 1:1
26:12 [p] Ge 2:21; 15:12

1Sa 26:10 ❖ How can we be like David in leaving the important matters in God's hands, even when it looks like we have the opportunity to take matters into our own?

7 So David and Abishai went to the
army by night, and there was Saul, lying asleep inside the camp with his spear
stuck in the ground near his head. Abner
and the soldiers were lying around him.
8 Abishai said to David, "Today God has
delivered your enemy into your hands.
Now let me pin him to the ground with
one thrust of the spear; I won't strike
him twice."
9 But David said to Abishai, "Don't destroy him! Who can lay a hand on the
LORD's anointed[k] and be guiltless?[l] 10 As
surely as the LORD lives," he said, "the
LORD himself will strike[m] him, or his time[n]
will come and he will die,[o] or he will go
into battle and perish. 11 But the LORD forbid that I should lay a hand on the LORD's
anointed. Now get the spear and water
jug that are near his head, and let's go."
12 So David took the spear and water
jug near Saul's head, and they left. No
one saw or knew about it, nor did anyone wake up. They were all sleeping,
because the LORD had put them into a
deep sleep.[p]
13 Then David crossed over to the other
side and stood on top of the hill some
distance away; there was a wide space
between them. 14 He called out to the
army and to Abner son of Ner, "Aren't
you going to answer me, Abner?"
Abner replied, "Who are you who calls
to the king?"
15 David said, "You're a man, aren't you?

[a] 44 Hebrew *Palti,* a variant of *Paltiel*

26:1–12 The Ziphites were Saul's informants once before concerning David's location. They were apparently spying out David's movements throughout their areas of southern Judah in order to gain the favor of King Saul.

When David learns that Saul has camped in a vulnerable location, he daringly enters the camp with Abishai. Saul was once before supernaturally hindered from finding David, when the Spirit of God prevented him from apprehending David (19:23–24). Now Saul and his entire regiment are unaware of David's presence because of God-induced sleep. In both episodes, the text emphasizes Yahweh's personal and active involvement in David's rise to power.

When Abishai wants to take advantage of Saul's vulnerability, David's reaction is similar to his own in the cave of En Gedi. There is significance in David's ideas for the variety of ways in which Saul might meet his end (26:10). The idea that Saul might die in battle anticipates ch. 31. But David has also learned his lesson from the Nabal episode (ch. 25), that the Lord might directly strike his adversary with untimely death.

26:13–25 Having escaped with Saul's spear and water jug, David now confronts Saul with the irrationality and injustice of his pursuit. In the ensuing dialogue, David pleads his innocence and pleads with the king to consider how irrational is his obsession with capturing David. David again implies that the king's reckless pursuit is useless because he, David, is harmless (v. 20; cf. 24:14).

26:15–21 Saul admits his guilt and makes more

PEOPLE TO KNOW // ABISHAI

1 SAMUEL 26:8–11: Abishai was one of King David's army commanders and also David's nephew. He entered the story when David was on the run from King Saul. Saul set up camp with his three thousand men, and David asked who would join him in sneaking into Saul's camp—a very dangerous mission. Abishai bravely volunteered: "I'll go with you" (1Sa 26:6).

Though Abishai was brave, he also had a vengeful streak. When he and David were in Saul's camp, Abishai asked David's permission to kill Saul in his sleep. David, however, knew this was not the right thing to do. Though Saul had become wicked, he was still the Lord's anointed.

Later, as David fled Jerusalem during Absalom's rebellion, a member of Saul's family named Shimei taunted and cursed David. Again, Abishai asked for permission to kill the king's enemy. Yet again, David wisely denied Abishai's request. (Curiously, as David prepared to pass the kingship on to his son, Solomon, one of his instructions to Solomon was to ensure Shimei indeed was killed for cursing him [1Ki 2:8–9].)

Abishai demonstrated his loyalty and bravery over the course of David's life. He was always willing to fight for David, as he showed when David sent him out to defeat the rebel Sheba (2Sa 20). Abishai also courageously saved David's life from the mighty Ishbi-Benob, a Philistine champion who intended to kill the king.

APPLICATION True loyalty is hard to come by. Abishai shows what a long life of faithfulness and loyalty looks like. However, his life is also a cautionary tale of the temptation and danger of vengeance. The Bible says God will take vengeance on those who deserve it (Dt 32:43); it is not our job to mete out divine punishment.

And who is like you in Israel? Why didn't
you guard your lord the king? Someone came to destroy your lord the king.
16What you have done is not good. As
surely as the LORD lives, you and your
men must die, because you did not guard
your master, the LORD's anointed. Look
around you. Where are the king's spear
and water jug that were near his head?"
17Saul recognized David's voice and
said, "Is that your voice,[q] David my son?"
David replied, "Yes it is, my lord the
king." 18And he added, "Why is my
lord pursuing his servant? What have I
done, and what wrong[r] am I guilty of?
19Now let my lord the king listen to his
servant's words. If the LORD has incited you against me, then may he accept
an offering.[s] If, however, people have
done it, may they be cursed before the
LORD! They have driven me today from
my share in the LORD's inheritance[t] and
have said, 'Go, serve other gods.' 20Now
do not let my blood fall to the ground
far from the presence of the LORD. The
king of Israel has come out to look for a
flea[u] — as one hunts a partridge in the
mountains."
21Then Saul said, "I have sinned.[v] Come
back, David my son. Because you considered my life precious[w] today, I will not try
to harm you again. Surely I have acted
like a fool and have been terribly wrong."
22"Here is the king's spear," David answered. "Let one of your young men
come over and get it. 23The LORD rewards[x]

26:17 [q] 1Sa 24:16
26:18 [r] 1Sa 24:9, 11-14
26:19 [s] 2Sa 16:11 [t] 2Sa 14:16
26:20 [u] 1Sa 24:14
26:21 [v] Ex 9:27; 1Sa 15:24 [w] 1Sa 24:17
26:23 [x] Ps 62:12

concessions than he has before (v. 21). David merely returns Saul's spear and expresses his faith that God will honor his actions and deliver him from trouble (v. 24). David concludes it is safer to rely on Yahweh for protection, even in exile in the desert, than to trust Saul and his unpredictable temperament.

26:22–25 Saul's parting words, "You will do great things and surely triumph" (v. 25), are more prophetic than Saul could have known and certainly more than he intends. This is to be the last meeting between the two anointed ones. David "went on his way" (v. 25) with the blessing and protection of Yahweh. Saul "returned home," a king in name only (v. 25).

26:1–25 David is convinced of God's guidance, even if he does not have immediate confirmation. This is also a natural part of Christian discipleship. As we grow and mature in our faith, we also become more confident about God's guidance, and we spend less time seeking constantly for evidence of his moving.

Unfortunately, in our modern context, the opposite development is taking place. As Christians become more comfortable in the conviction that God is at work in the details of life, the world around us has made less and less room for God. The premise that God exists

everyone for their righteousness[y] and faithfulness. The LORD delivered you into my hands today, but I would not lay a hand on the LORD's anointed. 24As surely as I valued your life today, so may the LORD value my life and deliver[z] me from all trouble."

25Then Saul said to David, "May you be blessed, David my son; you will do great things and surely triumph."

So David went on his way, and Saul returned home.

David Among the Philistines

27 But David thought to himself, "One of these days I will be destroyed by the hand of Saul. The best thing I can do is to escape to the land of the Philistines. Then Saul will give up searching for me anywhere in Israel, and I will slip out of his hand."

2So David and the six hundred men[a] with him left and went[b] over to Achish[c] son of Maok king of Gath. 3David and his men settled in Gath with Achish. Each man had his family with him, and David had his two wives:[d] Ahinoam of Jezreel and Abigail of Carmel, the widow of Nabal. 4When Saul was told that David had fled to Gath, he no longer searched for him.

5Then David said to Achish, "If I have found favor in your eyes, let a place be assigned to me in one of the country towns, that I may live there. Why should your servant live in the royal city with you?"

6So on that day Achish gave him Ziklag,[e] and it has belonged to the kings of Judah ever since. 7David lived[f] in Philistine territory a year and four months.

8Now David and his men went up and raided the Geshurites,[g] the Girzites and the Amalekites.[h] (From ancient times these peoples had lived in the land extending to Shur[i] and Egypt.) 9Whenever David attacked an area, he did not leave a man or woman alive,[j] but took sheep and cattle, donkeys and camels, and clothes. Then he returned to Achish.

10When Achish asked, "Where did you go raiding today?" David would say, "Against the Negev of Judah" or "Against the Negev of Jerahmeel[k]" or "Against the Negev of the Kenites.[l]" 11He did not leave a man or woman alive to be brought to Gath, for he thought, "They might inform on us and say, 'This is what David did.'" And such was his practice as long as he lived in Philistine territory. 12Achish trusted David and said to himself, "He has become so obnoxious to his people, the Israelites, that he will be my servant for life."

26:23 [y]Ps 7:8; 18:20,24
26:24 [z]Ps 54:7
27:2 [a]1Sa 25:13 [b]1Sa 21:10 [c]1Ki 2:39
27:3 [d]1Sa 25:43; 30:3
27:6 [e]Jos 15:31; 19:5; Ne 11:28
27:7 [f]1Sa 29:3
27:8 [g]Jos 13:2, 13 [h]Ex 17:8; 1Sa 15:7-8 [i]Ex 15:22
27:9 [j]1Sa 15:3
27:10 [k]1Sa 30:29; 1Ch 2:9,25 [l]Jdg 1:16

1Sa 27:1 ❖ Where can we go for safety when we feel threatened (see Ps 46:1)? How does God show his love in these moments?

---

and that he defines human moral responsibilities has been an underlying principle of Western civilization. But in the last few decades, Western cultures have been experimenting with the prospects of defining our responsibilities without the benefit of God. Modern humankind has learned to live without God.

27:1–7 This is David's most desperate hour. He realizes his only lasting means of escaping Saul's evil intentions is to go into exile in Philistia (v. 1). He is being driven from Yahweh's presence and forced to live where the inhabitants serve pagan gods. As David once fled from Gibeah and the royal court (19:18–24), now he is forced to flee from the desert recesses of southern Judah.

We have encountered Achish before (21:10–15). His city, Gath, is one of the five principal cities of the Philistines, governed in a so-called pentapolis. It is not to David's advantage to settle actually *in* the city of Gath. As we will learn, David must operate somewhat independently of Achish's close observation, and Ziklag appears to be ideal for David's purposes. In 27:6 the narrator gives a hint at the success with which David occupies Ziklag.

27:8–12 David's custom during the 16 months he lives in Philistia (v. 7) is to conduct raids against Judah's desert neighbors. While living in Philistia on the run from King Saul, he has actually become a defender of Judahite causes. At the same time, he is also able to endear himself to the Philistine king, leading him to think David is fighting Philistia's enemies. David has it both ways: the inhabitants of Judah and the Philistine king love him.

The Philistine ruler naively believes David has burned his bridges, irreparably alienating himself from his own people. He accepts David's word and assumes the citizens of Israel must hate David so much by now that he will have no choice but to remain loyal to his new Philistine colleague (v. 12).

✣ **27:1–12** David takes decisive action that will affect the role he will play in God's plans for the future. He bases his decisions on the logical and rational circumstances around him and appears to have simply trusted God to guide the process. Because we often lust for the tangible and the safety of the discernible, this type of trust is usually difficult for us.

28 In those days the Philistines gathered[m] their forces to fight against
Israel. Achish said to David, "You must
understand that you and your men will
accompany me in the army."
2 David said, "Then you will see for
yourself what your servant can do."
Achish replied, "Very well, I will make
you my bodyguard for life."

Saul and the Medium at Endor

3 Now Samuel was dead,[n] and all Israel
had mourned for him and buried him
in his own town of Ramah.[o] Saul had
expelled the mediums and spiritists[p]
from the land.
4 The Philistines assembled and came
and set up camp at Shunem,[q] while Saul
gathered all Israel and set up camp at Gilboa.[r] 5 When Saul saw the Philistine army,
he was afraid; terror filled his heart. 6 He
inquired[s] of the LORD, but the LORD did
not answer him by dreams[t] or Urim[u] or
prophets. 7 Saul then said to his attendants, "Find me a woman who is a medium,[v] so I may go and inquire of her."
"There is one in Endor,[w]" they said.
8 So Saul disguised[x] himself, putting
on other clothes, and at night he and
two men went to the woman. "Consult[y]
a spirit for me," he said, "and bring up
for me the one I name."
9 But the woman said to him, "Surely
you know what Saul has done. He has cut
off[z] the mediums and spiritists from the
land. Why have you set a trap for my life
to bring about my death?"
10 Saul swore to her by the LORD, "As
surely as the LORD lives, you will not be
punished for this."
11 Then the woman asked, "Whom shall
I bring up for you?"
"Bring up Samuel," he said.
12 When the woman saw Samuel, she
cried out at the top of her voice and said
to Saul, "Why have you deceived me?
You are Saul!"
13 The king said to her, "Don't be afraid.
What do you see?"
The woman said, "I see a ghostly figure[a] coming up out of the earth."
14 "What does he look like?" he asked.
"An old man wearing a robe[a] is coming
up," she said.
Then Saul knew it was Samuel, and
he bowed down and prostrated himself
with his face to the ground.
15 Samuel said to Saul, "Why have you
disturbed me by bringing me up?"
"I am in great distress," Saul said. "The

28:1 [m] 1Sa 29:1
28:3 [n] 1Sa 25:1 [o] 1Sa 7:17 [p] Ex 22:18; Lev 19:31; 20:27; Dt 18:10-11; 1Sa 15:23
28:4 [q] Jos 19:18; 2Ki 4:8 [r] 1Sa 31:1,3
28:6 [s] 1Sa 14:37; 1Ch 10:13-14; Pr 1:28 [t] Nu 12:6 [u] Ex 28:30; Nu 27:21
28:7 [v] Ac 16:16 [w] Jos 17:11
28:8 [x] 2Ch 18:29; 35:22 [y] Dt 18:10-11; 1Ch 10:13; Isa 8:19
28:9 [z] ver 3
28:14 [a] 1Sa 15:27; 24:8

1Sa 28:6 ❖ Can we sin to the point that God stops listening to us (see Heb 13:5)? Why or why not?

[a] *13* Or *see spirits*; or *see gods*

28:1–2 David is now in an impossible situation. Achish joins his fellow Philistine commanders in mustering their forces against Israel's heartland, and it is time for David to "fish or cut bait." David's response seems carefully crafted to be noncommittal, though it satisfies Achish.

28:3–6 The narrator anticipates the medium's initial objections (v. 9). Even Saul himself, at some point earlier in his reign—perhaps under the direction of Samuel—had forbidden the use of mediums (v. 3). But as we will soon see, driving this specific sin from Saul's land did not drive the roots of that sin from his heart.

The narrator prepares us further for what follows by exposing Saul's inner life. The statement that he "inquired of the LORD" (v. 6) is significant in light of this phrase's other occurrences in 1 Samuel. For Saul, it is too late. Yahweh has long since stopped answering Saul; as king, he is more inclined to make up his mind before asking. When his "foxhole" prayer brings no satisfaction, he becomes desperate to discern the plan of God. His next action represents the lowest point of his troubled reign as king over Israel.

28:7–14 Against the wishes of the prophets and the religious leaders in ancient Israel, some Israelites apparently persisted in the Canaanite custom of necromancy and other death rituals. Saul's visit at night may have been a simple military necessity. But nighttime may also have been the approved time for such séances, the darkness of night being the appropriate time to communicate with those who live in darkness. The idea that Saul needs the medium to "bring up" (v. 8) someone reflects the concept of Sheol as a place for the dead beneath the earth's surface, to which people descend at death.

28:9–11 Ironically, the medium is hesitant. But once Saul guarantees her safety, the medium is ready to hear the name of the departed individual whom Saul wishes to contact. Now we learn for the first time that it is Samuel.

28:12–14 At his appearance, the woman shrieks and immediately recognizes her client (v. 12). At this point in the narrative, we are left with unanswered questions. Why precisely should the woman be shocked at the apparition if she were accustomed to such séances? Does Samuel's appearance differ significantly from other specters? Why does she suddenly discern Saul's identity?

Without becoming sidetracked with questions that are finally unanswerable, we can state that the essentials are clear. Samuel appears to Saul one last time and communicates with him through this medium (v. 14).

28:15–25 Given an audience with his former mentor,

Philistines are fighting against me, and God has departed[b] from me. He no longer answers me, either by prophets or by dreams. So I have called on you to tell me what to do."

16Samuel said, "Why do you consult me, now that the LORD has departed from you and become your enemy? 17The LORD has done what he predicted through me. The LORD has torn[c] the kingdom out of your hands and given it to one of your neighbors — to David. 18Because you did not obey[d] the LORD or carry out his fierce wrath[e] against the Amalekites, the LORD has done this to you today. 19The LORD will deliver both Israel and you into the hands of the Philistines, and tomorrow you and your sons[f] will be with me. The LORD will also give the army of Israel into the hands of the Philistines."

20Immediately Saul fell full length on the ground, filled with fear because of Samuel's words. His strength was gone, for he had eaten nothing all that day and all that night.

21When the woman came to Saul and saw that he was greatly shaken, she said, "Look, your servant has obeyed you. I took my life[g] in my hands and did what you told me to do. 22Now please listen to your servant and let me give you some food so you may eat and have the strength to go on your way."

23He refused[h] and said, "I will not eat."

But his men joined the woman in urging him, and he listened to them. He got up from the ground and sat on the couch.

24The woman had a fattened calf at the house, which she butchered at once. She took some flour, kneaded it and baked bread without yeast. 25Then she set it before Saul and his men, and they ate. That same night they got up and left.

28:15 [b] ver 6; 1Sa 18:12
28:17 [c] 1Sa 15:28
28:18 [d] 1Sa 15:20 [e] 1Ki 20:42
28:19 [f] 1Sa 31:2
28:21 [g] Jdg 12:3; 1Sa 19:5; Job 13:14
28:23 [h] 2Ki 5:13

Achish Sends David Back to Ziklag

29 The Philistines gathered[i] all their forces at Aphek,[j] and Israel camped by the spring in Jezreel.[k] 2As the Philistine rulers marched with their units of hundreds and thousands, David and his men were marching at the rear[l] with Achish. 3The commanders of the Philistines asked, "What about these Hebrews?"

Achish replied, "Is this not David, who was an officer of Saul king of Israel? He has already been with me for over a year,[m] and from the day he left Saul until now, I have found no fault in him."

4But the Philistine commanders were angry with Achish and said, "Send[n] the man back, that he may return to the place you assigned him. He must not go with us into battle, or he will turn[o] against us during the fighting. How better could he regain his master's favor than by taking the heads of our own men? 5Isn't this the David they sang about in their dances:

"'Saul has slain his thousands,
and David his tens of
thousands'?"[p]

6So Achish called David and said to him, "As surely as the LORD lives, you have been reliable, and I would be pleased to have you serve with me in the army. From the day[q] you came to me until today, I have found no fault in you, but the rulers[r] don't approve of you. 7Now turn back and go in peace; do nothing to displease the Philistine rulers."

8"But what have I done?" asked David. "What have you found against your

29:1 [i] 1Sa 28:1 [j] Jos 12:18; 1Sa 4:1 [k] 2Ki 9:30
29:2 [l] 1Sa 28:2
29:3 [m] 1Sa 27:7; Da 6:5
29:4 [n] 1Ch 12:19 [o] 1Sa 14:21
29:5 [p] 1Sa 18:7; 21:11
29:6 [q] 1Sa 27:8-12 [r] ver 3

Saul summarizes his situation succinctly and factually (v. 15). The message of the deceased Samuel is the same as the living Samuel: He simply reiterates the divine judgment against the king announced when he was alive. Though there is no advice concerning the Philistines, there is this: "Tomorrow you and your sons will be with me" (v. 19). The time of Saul's judgment has arrived. The theme of Yahweh's rejection of the first anointed one, Saul, peaks in v. 20.

28:1-25 It would be simplistic for us to limit the application of this text to blatant heretical practices such as pursuing occult practices. Rather, we should also consider how easy it is to use good things in a "magical" way in an attempt to manipulate God. Some believers come to expect good things from God—and maybe even believe that God *owes* them something—because they (we!) have fulfilled certain obligations. One's relationship with God can be quickly reduced to a sort of quid pro quo in which all we have to do is keep our end of the bargain, and God will be forced to keep his. Such is never the case.

29:1-11 The generals are aware of the danger of mixed loyalties during the strain of combat, and they apparently have experience with Hebrew soldiers who have easily switched from one army to another. They insist that Achish send David away. **29:8** David's questions feign shock and disappointment. Achish would naturally assume that he himself is the king David refers to, but the reader must assume, in light of the context, that David is loyal only to Saul and the Israelite troops. For

servant from the day I came to you until now? Why can't I go and fight against
the enemies of my lord the king?"
9Achish answered, "I know that you
have been as pleasing in my eyes as an
angel[s] of God; nevertheless, the Philistine commanders[t] have said, 'He must
not go up with us into battle.' 10Now
get up early, along with your master's
servants who have come with you, and
leave[u] in the morning as soon as it is
light."
11So David and his men got up early
in the morning to go back to the land of
the Philistines, and the Philistines went
up to Jezreel.

David Destroys the Amalekites

30 David and his men reached Ziklag[v]
on the third day. Now the Amalekites[w] had raided the Negev and Ziklag.
They had attacked Ziklag and burned it,
2and had taken captive the women and
everyone else in it, both young and old.
They killed none of them, but carried
them off as they went on their way.
3When David and his men reached
Ziklag, they found it destroyed by fire
and their wives and sons and daughters
taken captive. 4So David and his men
wept aloud until they had no strength
left to weep. 5David's two wives[x] had
been captured — Ahinoam of Jezreel and Abigail, the widow of Nabal of
Carmel. 6David was greatly distressed
because the men were talking of stoning[y] him; each one was bitter in spirit
because of his sons and daughters. But
David found strength[z] in the LORD his
God.
7Then David said to Abiathar[a] the
priest, the son of Ahimelek, "Bring me
the ephod.[b]" Abiathar brought it to him,
8and David inquired[c] of the LORD, "Shall
I pursue this raiding party? Will I overtake them?"
"Pursue them," he answered. "You will
certainly overtake them and succeed[d] in
the rescue."
9David and the six hundred men[e] with
him came to the Besor Valley, where
some stayed behind. 10Two hundred of
them were too exhausted[f] to cross the
valley, but David and the other four hundred continued the pursuit.
11They found an Egyptian in a field

29:9 [s]2Sa 14:17, 20; 19:27 [t]ver 4
29:10 [u]1Ch 12:19
30:1 [v]1Sa 29:4, 11 [w]1Sa 15:7; 27:8
30:5 [x]1Sa 25:43; 2Sa 2:2
30:6 [y]Ex 17:4; Jn 8:59 [z]Ps 27:14; 56:3-4,11; Ro 4:20
30:7 [a]1Sa 22:20 [b]1Sa 23:9
30:8 [c]1Sa 23:2 [d]ver 18
30:9 [e]1Sa 27:2
30:10 [f]ver 9,21

1Sa 29:9 ❖ What does it take to live in a way that even our enemies praise our character (see 1Pe 2:12)?

1Sa 30:6 ❖ How can we find strength in God when those around us mistreat us?

David, the real "enemies" *are* the Philistines, and "my lord the king" must refer to Saul. This question implies that if David were forced to join the battle, he would indeed turn on the Philistines.

29:9–10 The irony of Achish's speech is impressive. David's worst-case scenario has developed, and he appears to have no means of avoiding the battle. Ironically Achish now praises David's character and reluctantly *prohibits* him from staying. Achish thinks he is disappointing David by driving him away. The manner in which David is released from this trap leaves us breathless.

30:1–6 The importance of David and his rule over Israel is demonstrated in this fact: David is the instrument of Yahweh's vengeance against Amalek. The Amalekites have plundered David's adopted city, taking alive all the women and children of his men—including David's own two wives, Ahinoam and Abigail. As if this were not enough, David's own men for the first time question his leadership (v. 6). Their bitterness over losing their families is so severe that they now talk of stoning David.

This brings us to another crisis in David's life, narrated in such a way as to heighten the contrast between him and Saul. Like Saul in ch. 28, David is now surrounded with trouble. Saul was pressed all around by the Philistines with little hope of victory, while David is surrounded by his own grieving men and likewise appears to have no hope of retrieving their families. These stories show both men at their lowest ebb.

In Saul's greatest moment of crisis, he had tried to inquire of Yahweh but found that the Lord had abandoned him (28:6). The contrast between Saul and David becomes most apparent in the closing phrase of this passage: "But David found strength in the LORD his God" (30:6). Even though God graciously makes faith possible, it is up to us to respond to his grace. Here David musters up his strength in his greatest moment of crisis.

30:7–10 David calls for Abiathar to bring the priestly ephod containing the Urim and Thummim, the divinely sanctioned and approved means of seeking divine guidance. The particular terminology used in vv. 7–8 refers to the practice of "inquiring" (lit., "asking") of Yahweh—that is, seeking his will in specific situations. David's rise to kingship is characterized by the importance he attached to seeking guidance from God.

30:11–25 The victory over the Amalekite marauders is narrated in such a way as to highlight an important feature of David's character: He identifies with people and understands their needs. First Samuel 30 highlights two such episodes: (1) David is generous and gracious in his treatment of an Egyptian who had been an Amalekite slave (vv. 11–15). (2) David decides to include in receiving plunder those too exhausted to make the journey to the Amalekite

and brought him to David. They gave
him water to drink and food to eat—
12part of a cake of pressed figs and two
cakes of raisins. He ate and was revived,[g] for he had not eaten any food
or drunk any water for three days and
three nights.
13David asked him, "Who do you belong to? Where do you come from?"
He said, "I am an Egyptian, the slave
of an Amalekite. My master abandoned
me when I became ill three days ago.
14We raided the Negev of the Kerethites,[h]
some territory belonging to Judah and
the Negev of Caleb.[i] And we burned[j]
Ziklag."
15David asked him, "Can you lead me
down to this raiding party?"
He answered, "Swear to me before God
that you will not kill me or hand me over
to my master, and I will take you down
to them."
16He led David down, and there they
were, scattered over the countryside,
eating, drinking and reveling[k] because
of the great amount of plunder[l] they
had taken from the land of the Philistines and from Judah. 17David fought[m]
them from dusk until the evening of the
next day, and none of them got away,
except four hundred young men who
rode off on camels and fled.[n] 18David
recovered[o] everything the Amalekites
had taken, including his two wives.
19Nothing was missing: young or old,
boy or girl, plunder or anything else
they had taken. David brought everything back. 20He took all the flocks and
herds, and his men drove them ahead
of the other livestock, saying, "This is
David's plunder."
21Then David came to the two hundred
men who had been too exhausted[p] to
follow him and who were left behind at
the Besor Valley. They came out to meet
David and the men with him. As David
and his men approached, he asked them
how they were. 22But all the evil men and
troublemakers among David's followers
said, "Because they did not go out with
us, we will not share with them the plunder we recovered. However, each man
may take his wife and children and go."
23David replied, "No, my brothers, you
must not do that with what the LORD has
given us. He has protected us and delivered into our hands the raiding party
that came against us. 24Who will listen
to what you say? The share of the man
who stayed with the supplies is to be the
same as that of him who went down to
the battle. All will share alike.[q]" 25David
made this a statute and ordinance for
Israel from that day to this.
26When David reached Ziklag, he sent
some of the plunder to the elders of Judah, who were his friends, saying, "Here
is a gift for you from the plunder of the
LORD's enemies."
27David sent it to those who were in
Bethel,[r] Ramoth[s] Negev and Jattir;[t] 28to
those in Aroer,[u] Siphmoth, Eshtemoa[v]
29and Rakal; to those in the towns of the
Jerahmeelites[w] and the Kenites;[x] 30to
those in Hormah,[y] Bor Ashan,[z] Athak
31and Hebron;[a] and to those in all the
other places where he and his men had
roamed.

30:12 [g] Jdg 15:19
30:14 [h] 2Sa 8:18; 1Ki 1:38, 44; Eze 25:16; Zep 2:5 [i] ver 16; Jos 14:13; 15:13 [j] ver 1
30:16 [k] Lk 12:19 [l] ver 14
30:17 [m] 1Sa 11:11 [n] 1Sa 15:3
30:18 [o] Ge 14:16
30:21 [p] ver 10
30:24 [q] Nu 31:27; Jos 22:8
30:27 [r] Jos 7:2 [s] Jos 19:8 [t] Jos 15:48
30:28 [u] Jos 13:16 [v] Jos 15:50
30:29 [w] 1Sa 27:10 [x] Jdg 1:16; 1Sa 15:6
30:30 [y] Nu 14:45; Jdg 1:17 [z] Jos 15:42
30:31 [a] Jos 14:13; 2Sa 2:1, 4

---

encampment and who stayed with the supplies. Here David establishes the principle of equality that lasts throughout his reign (v. 24).

Through David's faith in Yahweh and his resolve to avenge his losses and those of his men, God turns an impossible and hopeless situation into a great victory. While Saul is preparing for his final battle, which is doomed to failure, David is leading his meager forces in victory against one of Israel's greatest enemies. Saul has proven himself ill-equipped and inadequate for leading God's people; David seems perfectly suited for the task.

30:26-31 With this victory, David now takes the daring step of sharing the spoils with his "friends" in Judah (v. 26). By giving them portions of "the plunder of the LORD's enemies" (v. 26), David continues to endear himself to the citizens of Judah, whom he will soon rule as king. Presumably many of these "friends" are the same who will shortly anoint him king "over the tribe of Judah" at Hebron (2Sa 2:4).

29:1—30:31 Where do we turn for help in our time of need? As modern believers, we seek God through the portals of his written Word. Being convinced by the truth in his Word, we must seek to act boldly on it, with confidence and hope.

By the living of our everyday lives, we establish patterns of seeking advice and help, either from Endor (ch. 28) or from Abiathar (ch. 29)—that is, finding answers either apart from God or directly from the God of heaven and earth, who has revealed his truth in Scripture. These are really the only two options. If we choose the first, in time we will become like Saul, incapable of making right decisions; if we decide to continually pursue God's will, we will become like David, who makes right decisions almost instinctively.

Saul Takes His Life

31:1–13pp // 2Sa 1:4–12; 1Ch 10:1–12

31 Now the Philistines fought against
Israel; the Israelites fled before
them, and many fell dead on Mount
Gilboa.[b] 2The Philistines were in hot
pursuit of Saul and his sons, and they
killed his sons Jonathan, Abinadab
and Malki-Shua. 3The fighting grew
fierce around Saul, and when the archers overtook him, they wounded[c]
him critically.

4Saul said to his armor-bearer, "Draw
your sword and run me through,[d] or
these uncircumcised[e] fellows will come
and run me through and abuse me."

But his armor-bearer was terrified and
would not do it; so Saul took his own
sword and fell on it. 5When the armor-
bearer saw that Saul was dead, he too
fell on his sword and died with him. 6So
Saul and his three sons and his armor-
bearer and all his men died together that
same day.

7When the Israelites along the valley
and those across the Jordan saw that the
Israelite army had fled and that Saul and
his sons had died, they abandoned their
towns and fled. And the Philistines came
and occupied them.

8The next day, when the Philistines
came to strip the dead, they found Saul
and his three sons fallen on Mount Gilboa.
9They cut off his head and stripped off his
armor, and they sent messengers throughout the land of the Philistines to proclaim
the news[f] in the temple of their idols and
among their people.[g] 10They put his armor
in the temple of the Ashtoreths[h] and fastened his body to the wall of Beth Shan.[i]

11When the people of Jabesh Gilead[j]
heard what the Philistines had done to
Saul, 12all their valiant men marched
through the night to Beth Shan. They
took down the bodies of Saul and his
sons from the wall of Beth Shan and went
to Jabesh, where they burned[k] them.
13Then they took their bones[l] and buried
them under a tamarisk[m] tree at Jabesh,
and they fasted[n] seven days.[o]

31:1 [b] 1Sa 28:4; 1Ch 10:1-12
31:3 [c] 2Sa 1:6
31:4 [d] Jdg 9:54; 2Sa 1:6,10 [e] 1Sa 14:6
31:9 [f] 2Sa 1:20 [g] Jdg 16:24
31:10 [h] Jdg 2:12-13; 1Sa 7:3 [i] Jos 17:11; 2Sa 21:12
31:11 [j] 1Sa 11:1
31:12 [k] 2Sa 2:4-7; 2Ch 16:14; Am 6:10
31:13 [l] 2Sa 21:12-14 [m] 1Sa 22:6 [n] 2Sa 1:12 [o] Ge 50:10

1Sa 31:2 ❖ When have we seen one person's sin have devastating effects on their family? How does this amplify the importance of practicing righteousness?

31:1–6 The description of Saul's death brings the contrast between David and Saul to a climax. Chapter 30 has just related David's great success against the Amalekites; he rescued Ziklag and saved the lives of everyone associated with him. By contrast, Saul and everyone associated with him die in this losing battle with the Philistines. Saul had been commissioned as king specifically to provide victory against the Philistines (9:16), which makes his death at their hands especially ironic.

31:7–10 The result of the debacle at Mount Gilboa is devastating for Israel. The subsequent evacuation of the towns in the area leaves the Philistine military in control of Israelite territory. Saul's armor is placed in "the temple of the Ashtoreths" (v. 10), which may refer to the goddess Astarte, worshiped principally at Sidon, but is more likely a derogatory reference to the unnamed principal goddess of Beth Shan.

Saul's worst fears of bodily desecration at the hands of the Philistines become a reality. Moreover, his defeat and death become occasions for celebrations in the temples of foreign idol gods, implying the victory of those gods over Yahweh in the minds of the Philistines. The national tragedy, painful though it is, serves merely as the backdrop for Saul's failure to vigorously defend and honor the name of Yahweh.

31:11–13 Even in this dreary moment, the anointed of Yahweh cannot be left in such degrading circumstances. The residents of Jabesh Gilead never forgot how Saul rescued them from the Ammonites (ch. 11). Now they will repay his kindness with their loyalty.

Their actions pay homage to the king of Israel as the anointed one of Yahweh. Their kindness in return for Saul's kindness provides the king some dignity in his otherwise shameful death.

✜ **31:1–13** Death is not the end of our story. Contemporary believers should read 1Sa 31 in a way that leads to hope for the future. Just as ancient Israelite readers would have read this text in anticipation of the coronation of David and the rule of the ideal anointed one, so we know there is more to the story. The coming of David's greater Son has given us reason to hope that a new day will dawn in which death will no more claim its wretched price (1Co 15:54–57).

2 Samuel

Author: Unknown

Audience: God's chosen people, the Israelites

Date: Sometime after Israel was divided into the northern and southern kingdoms in about 930 BC

Theme: God exalts the weak and humbles the proud, as evidenced by accounts of events during the reign of King David.

PERSPECTIVE

While 1 Samuel details the transition from theocracy to monarchy, 2 Samuel narrates its growth. Second Samuel 1–20 describes the consolidation of the monarchy under David, while chs. 21–24 function as an epilogue to the books generally.

See also the Introduction to 1 Samuel for more perspective on this book.

TAKING THE NEXT STEPS

The book of 2 Samuel records how David ruled the kingdom that God had chosen him to lead. God established an everlasting covenant with David, making that kingship secure for him and for his descendants. One of his first acts as king was to conquer the city of Jerusalem and to make it the capital city; this city remained important throughout the rest of Bible times. The most important theme running through the book, however, is that only by obedience to God could David expect success in battle and in his personal life.

Throughout this book God tells us how to live as his children. (1) We may lay out ambitious goals for our lives, such as David's plan to build a temple, but God may have other plans in store for us. (2) If we want the Lord to bless us, we must be obedient to his will; otherwise, disaster will follow. Sin has its consequences. (3) As the David and Bathsheba story indicates, we so often spin a tangled web when we try to cover

Reading 2 Samuel

In the first half of this book, David consolidated his power until he finally becomes king over all the twelve tribes. With the Lord on his side, he was successful, both in battle and as the leader of Israel. The second half of the book, however, recounts the personal and family difficulties that plague David after his act of adultery with Bathsheba and his murder of her husband.

Event	1400 BC	1300	1200	1100	1000	900	800	700	600	500	400
Israelites enter Canaan (c. 1406 BC)											
Judges begin to rule (c. 1375 BC)											
Saul's reign (1050–1010 BC)											
David's reign (1010–970 BC)											
Division of the kingdom (930 BC)											
Book of 2 Samuel written (c. 925 BC)											
Exile of Israel (722 BC)											
Fall of Jerusalem (586 BC)											

Key Verses

"How great you are, Sovereign LORD! There is no one like you, and there is no God but you, as we have heard with our own ears. . . . You have established your people Israel as your very own forever, and you, LORD, have become their God."

—2 Samuel 7:22, 24

up our sins. If we confess our sins, however, God will always forgive, though the results from those sins may still be very painful.

WHAT TO LOOK FOR IN 2 SAMUEL

- David becomes king of all Israel (chs. 2–5)
- The ark brought to Jerusalem (ch. 6)
- God's covenant with David (ch. 7)
- The David and Bathsheba episode (chs. 11–12)
- David's difficulties with his son Amnon (ch. 13)
- David's difficulties with his son Absalom (chs. 14–18)
- David's pride in counting his mighty men (ch. 24)

David Hears of Saul's Death

1:4–12pp // 1Sa 31:1–13; 1Ch 10:1–12

1 After the death[a] of Saul, David returned from striking down[b] the Amalekites and stayed in Ziklag two days. 2On
the third day a man[c] arrived from Saul's
camp with his clothes torn and dust on
his head.[d] When he came to David, he fell
to the ground to pay him honor.
3"Where have you come from?" David
asked him.
He answered, "I have escaped from
the Israelite camp."
4"What happened?" David asked.
"Tell me."
"The men fled from the battle," he replied. "Many of them fell and died. And
Saul and his son Jonathan are dead."
5Then David said to the young man
who brought him the report, "How do
you know that Saul and his son Jonathan are dead?"
6"I happened to be on Mount Gilboa,[e]" the young man said, "and there
was Saul, leaning on his spear, with the
chariots and their drivers in hot pursuit.

1:1 [a] 1Sa 31:6 [b] 1Sa 30:17
1:2 [c] 2Sa 4:10 [d] 1Sa 4:12
1:6 [e] 1Sa 28:4; 31:2-4

1:1–10 The reference to David's recent military campaign against and defeat of the Amalekites not only places this text in historical perspective but prepares us for the irony of what follows (v. 1). David's return and the conclusion of the battle on Mount Gilboa happen at roughly the same time.

The messenger is not identified as an Amalekite until his speech to David (v. 8). This messenger is not likely to arouse sympathy among those who have just rescued their families from the Amalekites.

How the royal insignia of crown and armlet come to be in David's possession is an important issue to clarify (v. 10). Perhaps many in Israel suspect David has in fact killed Saul and Jonathan. By explaining the timeline, the narrator has made it clear that David is probably just returning from the Amalekite campaign while the debacle at Mount

7When he turned around and saw me,
he called out to me, and I said, 'What
can I do?'
8"He asked me, 'Who are you?'
"'An Amalekite,[f]' I answered.
9"Then he said to me, 'Stand here
by me and kill me! I'm in the throes of
death, but I'm still alive.'
10"So I stood beside him and killed
him, because I knew that after he had
fallen he could not survive. And I took
the crown[g] that was on his head and the
band on his arm and have brought them
here to my lord."
11Then David and all the men with him
took hold of their clothes and tore[h] them.
12They mourned and wept and fasted till
evening for Saul and his son Jonathan,
and for the army of the LORD and for the
nation of Israel, because they had fallen
by the sword.
13David said to the young man who
brought him the report, "Where are you
from?"
"I am the son of a foreigner, an Amalekite,[i]" he answered.
14David asked him, "Why weren't you
afraid to lift your hand to destroy the
LORD's anointed?[j]"
15Then David called one of his men and
said, "Go, strike him down!"[k] So he struck
him down, and he died.[l] 16For David had
said to him, "Your blood be on your own
head.[m] Your own mouth testified against
you when you said, 'I killed the LORD's
anointed.'"

David's Lament for Saul and Jonathan

17David took up this lament[n] concerning Saul and his son Jonathan, 18and he
ordered that the people of Judah be
taught this lament of the bow (it is written in the Book of Jashar):[o]

1:8 [f] 1Sa 15:2; 30:13,17
1:10 [g] Jdg 9:54; 2Ki 11:12
1:11 [h] Ge 37:29; 2Sa 3:31; 13:31
1:13 [i] ver 8
1:14 [j] 1Sa 24:6; 26:9
1:15 [k] 2Sa 4:12 [l] 2Sa 4:10
1:16 [m] Lev 20:9; 2Sa 3:28-29; 1Ki 2:32; Mt 27:24-25; Ac 18:6
1:17 [n] 2Ch 35:25
1:18 [o] Jos 10:13; 1Sa 31:3

1:19 [p] ver 27
1:20 [q] Mic 1:10 [r] 1Sa 31:8 [s] Ex 15:20; 1Sa 18:6
1:21 [t] ver 6; 1Sa 31:1 [u] Eze 31:15 [v] Isa 21:5
1:22 [w] Isa 34:3, 7 [x] Dt 32:42; 1Sa 18:4
1:23 [y] Dt 28:49; Jer 4:13 [z] Jdg 14:18

2Sa 1:17–18 ❖ What is the role of lament in your faith life? How have you practiced lament in the past?

19"A gazelle[a] lies slain on your heights,
Israel.
How the mighty have fallen![p]

20"Tell it not in Gath,[q]
proclaim it not in the streets of
Ashkelon,
lest the daughters of the Philistines[r]
be glad,
lest the daughters of the
uncircumcised rejoice.[s]

21"Mountains of Gilboa,[t]
may you have neither dew nor
rain,
may no showers fall on your
terraced fields.[b][u]
For there the shield of the mighty
was despised,
the shield of Saul—no longer
rubbed with oil.[v]

22"From the blood[w] of the slain,
from the flesh of the mighty,
the bow[x] of Jonathan did not turn
back,
the sword of Saul did not return
unsatisfied.
23Saul and Jonathan—
in life they were loved and
admired,
and in death they were not
parted.
They were swifter than eagles,[y]
they were stronger than lions.[z]

24"Daughters of Israel,
weep for Saul,

[a] 19 *Gazelle* here symbolizes a human dignitary.
[b] 21 Or / *nor fields that yield grain for offerings*

Gilboa is taking place. He simply could not have killed Saul and Jonathan because he could not have been in two places at once. More importantly, David's loyalties have always been with Yahweh's anointed one and his son Jonathan.

1:11–16 Some may have expected David and his men to rejoice at the death of Saul. But David demonstrates that he has the highest reverence for the Israelite king, the anointed one of Yahweh.

1:17–27 In one of the most emotional and moving scenes of the Bible, David's genuine pain comes through with singular clarity. The theme of the dirge is clear from the phrase repeated three times (vv. 19, 25, 27). This simple phrase (only three words in Hebrew) powerfully captures the depth of David's emotions and serves as a literary marker for the structure of the poem.

APPLICATION ✚ 1:1–27 Power itself is not inherently evil, but the way people use it often is. The Bible has much to teach us on this point. At this transitional chapter in the books of Samuel, it is appropriate to consider Saul's abuse of power as narrated in 1 Samuel; this chapter serves to demonstrate the results. Conversely, David has served in 1 Samuel as an example of the right use of power, and he will continue to serve this way in the next few chapters. Unfortunately, however, David will not be so exemplary throughout all of this book.

who clothed you in scarlet and
finery,
who adorned your garments with
ornaments of gold.

25 "How the mighty have fallen in
battle!
Jonathan lies slain on your
heights.
26 I grieve for you, Jonathan my
brother;[a]
you were very dear to me.
Your love for me was wonderful,[b]
more wonderful than that of
women.

27 "How the mighty have fallen!
The weapons of war have
perished!"[c]

David Anointed King Over Judah

2 In the course of time, David inquired[d]
of the LORD. "Shall I go up to one of
the towns of Judah?" he asked.
The LORD said, "Go up."
David asked, "Where shall I go?"
"To Hebron,"[e] the LORD answered.
2 So David went up there with his two
wives,[f] Ahinoam of Jezreel and Abigail,[g]
the widow of Nabal of Carmel. 3 David
also took the men who were with him,[h]
each with his family, and they settled in
Hebron and its towns. 4 Then the men of
Judah came to Hebron,[i] and there they

1:26 [a] 1Sa 20:42 [b] 1Sa 18:1
1:27 [c] ver 19, 25; 1Sa 2:4
2:1 [d] 1Sa 23:2, 11-12 [e] Ge 13:18; 1Sa 30:31
2:2 [f] 1Sa 25:43; 30:5 [g] 1Sa 25:42
2:3 [h] 1Sa 27:2; 30:9
2:4 [i] 1Sa 30:31 [j] 1Sa 2:35; 2Sa 5:3-5 [k] 1Sa 31:11-13
2:5 [l] 1Sa 23:21
2:6 [m] Ex 34:6; 1Ti 1:16
2:8 [n] 1Sa 14:50 [o] Ge 32:2
2:9 [p] Nu 32:26 [q] Jdg 1:32 [r] 1Ch 12:29

2Sa 2:1 ❖ How can we remember to ask for God's wisdom before making important decisions?

anointed[j] David king over the tribe of
Judah.
When David was told that it was the
men from Jabesh Gilead[k] who had buried
Saul, 5 he sent messengers to them to say
to them, "The LORD bless[l] you for showing this kindness to Saul your master by
burying him. 6 May the LORD now show
you kindness and faithfulness,[m] and I
too will show you the same favor because
you have done this. 7 Now then, be strong
and brave, for Saul your master is dead,
and the people of Judah have anointed
me king over them."

War Between the Houses of David and Saul

3:2–5pp // 1Ch 3:1–4

8 Meanwhile, Abner[n] son of Ner, the
commander of Saul's army, had taken
Ish-Bosheth son of Saul and brought
him over to Mahanaim.[o] 9 He made him
king over Gilead,[p] Ashuri[q] and Jezreel,
and also over Ephraim, Benjamin and
all Israel.[r]
10 Ish-Bosheth son of Saul was forty
years old when he became king over Israel, and he reigned two years. The tribe

2:1–4a Now is the time for David to move into action and claim the promises of God. But how will David know when to take action? The expression "David inquired of the LORD" (v. 1) tells it all. His dependence on Yahweh for guidance characterizes David and is partly what the text refers to when it describes him as the ideal king of Israel.

With God's guidance revealed clearly through the Urim and Thummim, surrounded by his retinue of family and personal troops, David is finally ready to be anointed king by the inhabitants of Judah. Prophetic anointing indicates divine approval; here, however, anointing is by the people, which represents the public acceptance of David as king.

2:4b–7 The loyalty of the people of Jabesh Gilead is a significant confirmation of David's right to rule the whole of Israel rather than Judah only.

Presumably the rise of the Philistines and Saul's death will once again threaten Jabesh Gilead; David encourages them to strengthen themselves for the future and decide to transform their loyalty to Saul into loyalty for David (v. 7).

✚ **2:1–7** Perhaps you have heard it said, or have said yourself: "If only I could have the same kind of experience with God as Moses (or David, or any biblical saint), then surely I would be as faithful as they were." In reality, we have the advantage over these biblical saints because of where we stand in relation to God's redemptive acts in history and because we have in our possession the entire Bible. We read these stories with the perspective that they are the foundations that underpin the story of Jesus' work on our behalf.

2:8–11 Events in the north quickly move against David. For the first time, our historian tells us of "Ish-Bosheth son of Saul" (v. 8), who is backed by Abner, Saul's rugged military leader. All hopes for a lasting dynasty for Saul rested with him. Abner and Ish-Bosheth make a bold play when they assert their control over "all Israel" (v. 9). Unfortunately for these conspirators, the house of Judah follows David (v. 10).

The specific wording of this paragraph underscores the contrast between David and Ish-Bosheth. Unlike David's rise to power, there is no mention here of divine direction or approval, nor is there mention of public anointing or popular support. Ish-Bosheth is part of a political power move. By contrast, David rises to power through sensitivity to Yahweh's guidance and timing. David's is no power play; rather, his is a "faith play."

of Judah, however, remained loyal to
David. 11 The length of time David was
king in Hebron over Judah was seven
years and six months.[s]
12 Abner son of Ner, together with the
men of Ish-Bosheth son of Saul, left Mahanaim and went to Gibeon.[t] 13 Joab[u] son
of Zeruiah and David's men went out
and met them at the pool of Gibeon. One
group sat down on one side of the pool
and one group on the other side.
14 Then Abner said to Joab, "Let's have
some of the young men get up and fight
hand to hand in front of us."
"All right, let them do it," Joab said.
15 So they stood up and were counted off — twelve men for Benjamin and
Ish-Bosheth son of Saul, and twelve for
David. 16 Then each man grabbed his opponent by the head and thrust his dagger
into his opponent's side, and they fell
down together. So that place in Gibeon
was called Helkath Hazzurim.[a]
17 The battle that day was very fierce,
and Abner and the Israelites were defeated[v] by David's men.
18 The three sons of Zeruiah[w] were
there: Joab,[x] Abishai[y] and Asahel.[z] Now
Asahel was as fleet-footed as a wild gazelle.[a] 19 He chased Abner, turning neither
to the right nor to the left as he pursued
him. 20 Abner looked behind him and
asked, "Is that you, Asahel?"
"It is," he answered.
21 Then Abner said to him, "Turn aside
to the right or to the left; take on one
of the young men and strip him of his
weapons." But Asahel would not stop
chasing him.
22 Again Abner warned Asahel, "Stop
chasing me! Why should I strike you
down? How could I look your brother
Joab in the face?"[b]
23 But Asahel refused to give up the
pursuit; so Abner thrust the butt of his
spear into Asahel's stomach,[c] and the
spear came out through his back. He fell
there and died on the spot. And every
man stopped when he came to the place
where Asahel had fallen and died.[d]
24 But Joab and Abishai pursued Abner,
and as the sun was setting, they came to

2:11 [s] 2Sa 5:5
2:12 [t] Jos 18:25
2:13 [u] 2Sa 8:16; 1Ch 2:16; 11:6
2:17 [v] 2Sa 3:1
2:18 [w] 2Sa 3:39
[x] 2Sa 3:30
[y] 1Sa 26:6
[z] 1Ch 2:16
[a] 1Ch 12:8
2:22 [b] 2Sa 3:27
2:23 [c] 2Sa 3:27; 4:6 [d] 2Sa 20:12

[a] 16 *Helkath Hazzurim* means *field of daggers* or *field of hostilities.*

2:12–32 The account of the civil war between the house of David in the south and the house of Ish-Bosheth in the north is held together literarily by the march of the generals with their armies from their respective capitals to Gibeon (vv. 12–13) and by their return after the conflict (vv. 29–32).

Joab's presence at Gibeon in Benjamin, the home tribe of Saul, may indicate Joab's army had made successful advances north into Ish-Bosheth's territory. The episode between Abner and Joab's brother Asahel serves two purposes in the narrative (vv. 18–28). First, in the immediate context it explains how the death of Asahel sickens both sides (v. 23); they lose the heart and will for warfare and declare a truce (v. 28). Second, this episode explains why hostility between Joab and Abner continues.

PEOPLE TO KNOW // ASAHEL

2 SAMUEL 2:18–23: Asahel was a nephew of king David and a brother of Joab and Abishai. The Bible describes Asahel as being a particularly good runner, "as fleet-footed as a wild gazelle" (2Sa 2:18). Asahel fought for David when Abner made King Saul's son Ish-Bosheth a rival king.

At the battle of Gibeon, Asahel pursued Abner relentlessly. Abner tried to convince Asahel to give up the chase and turn off to the right or left, but Asahel pressed on. Abner warned Asahel that if he did not give up the chase, Abner would strike him down. Finally, Abner thrust the butt of his spear into Asahel's stomach, and the spear shaft impaled him. Joab and Abishai later avenged their brother by killing Abner, against King David's wishes (2Sa 3:30).

Though Asahel died before David became the sole king of Israel, Asahel is counted among David's mighty warriors. In fact, in the list of David's Thirty great warriors (2Sa 23:24; 1Ch 11:26), Asahel is listed first.

APPLICATION Asahel gave his all for King David. He did not back down from danger or give in when his enemy told him to abandon the chase. Though tragically cut short, Asahel's story is a witness to the power of commitment and bravery. When we commit our full selves to the task God has before us and don't give up, our efforts can become a lasting legacy.

the hill of Ammah, near Giah on the way
to the wasteland of Gibeon. 25 Then the
men of Benjamin rallied behind Abner.
They formed themselves into a group
and took their stand on top of a hill.
26 Abner called out to Joab, "Must the
sword devour[e] forever? Don't you realize that this will end in bitterness? How
long before you order your men to stop
pursuing their fellow Israelites?"
27 Joab answered, "As surely as God
lives, if you had not spoken, the men
would have continued pursuing them
until morning."
28 So Joab[f] blew the trumpet,[g] and all
the troops came to a halt; they no longer pursued Israel, nor did they fight
anymore.
29 All that night Abner and his men
marched through the Arabah. They
crossed the Jordan, continued through the
morning hours[a] and came to Mahanaim.[h]
30 Then Joab stopped pursuing Abner
and assembled the whole army. Besides
Asahel, nineteen of David's men were
found missing. 31 But David's men had
killed three hundred and sixty Benjamites who were with Abner. 32 They took
Asahel and buried him in his father's
tomb[i] at Bethlehem. Then Joab and his
men marched all night and arrived at
Hebron by daybreak.

3 The war between the house of Saul
and the house of David lasted a long
time.[j] David grew stronger and stronger,[k]
while the house of Saul grew weaker and
weaker.[l]

2 Sons were born to David in Hebron:
His firstborn was Amnon the son
of Ahinoam[m] of Jezreel;
3 his second, Kileab the son of Abigail[n] the widow of Nabal of Carmel;
the third, Absalom[o] the son of Maakah daughter of Talmai king of
Geshur;[p]
4 the fourth, Adonijah[q] the son of
Haggith;
the fifth, Shephatiah the son of
Abital;
5 and the sixth, Ithream the son of
David's wife Eglah.
These were born to David in Hebron.

Abner Goes Over to David

6 During the war between the house of
Saul and the house of David, Abner had
been strengthening his own position in
the house of Saul. 7 Now Saul had had
a concubine[r] named Rizpah[s] daughter
of Aiah. And Ish-Bosheth said to Abner,
"Why did you sleep with my father's concubine?"
8 Abner was very angry because of what
Ish-Bosheth said. So he answered, "Am I
a dog's head[t] — on Judah's side? This very
day I am loyal to the house of your father Saul and to his family and friends.
I haven't handed you over to David. Yet
now you accuse me of an offense involving this woman! 9 May God deal with Abner, be it ever so severely, if I do not do
for David what the LORD promised[u] him
on oath 10 and transfer the kingdom from
the house of Saul and establish David's
throne over Israel and Judah from Dan to
Beersheba."[v] 11 Ish-Bosheth did not dare
to say another word to Abner, because
he was afraid of him.
12 Then Abner sent messengers on his
behalf to say to David, "Whose land is it?
Make an agreement with me, and I will
help you bring all Israel over to you."
13 "Good," said David. "I will make an
agreement with you. But I demand one
thing of you: Do not come into my presence unless you bring Michal daughter of
Saul when you come to see me."[w] 14 Then
David sent messengers to Ish-Bosheth
son of Saul, demanding, "Give me my
wife Michal,[x] whom I betrothed to myself for the price of a hundred Philistine
foreskins."

[a] 29 See Septuagint; the meaning of the Hebrew for this phrase is uncertain.

2:26 [e] Dt 32:42; Jer 46:10,14
2:28 [f] 2Sa 18:16 [g] Jdg 3:27
2:29 [h] ver 8
2:32 [i] Ge 49:29
3:1 [j] 1Ki 14:30 [k] 2Sa 5:10 [l] 2Sa 2:17
3:2 [m] 1Sa 25:43; 1Ch 3:1-3
3:3 [n] 1Sa 25:42 [o] 2Sa 13:1,28 [p] 1Sa 27:8; 2Sa 13:37; 14:32; 15:8
3:4 [q] 1Ki 1:5,11
3:7 [r] 2Sa 16:21-22 [s] 2Sa 21:8-11
3:8 [t] 1Sa 24:14; 2Sa 9:8; 16:9
3:9 [u] 1Sa 15:28; 1Ki 19:2
3:10 [v] Jdg 20:1; 1Sa 3:20
3:13 [w] Ge 43:5; 1Sa 18:20
3:14 [x] 1Sa 18:27

3:1–5 Rather than recount further gruesome details of the civil war, the text merely states that it goes on "a long time" (v. 1). The inclusion of a list of David's sons seems curious here. Most likely this list of David's sons born while he rules from Hebron is intended to intensify the contrast between David's growing strength and Ish-Bosheth's waning influence.
3:6–20 Abner, the general of Ish-Bosheth's army, has grown in political influence and strength in the house of Saul (v. 6). Ish-Bosheth suspects Abner will use his strength to take the throne of the northern kingdom; Abner is insulted by Ish-Bosheth's accusation against him (v. 8) and expresses twice his decision to do for David what Yahweh has promised to do—that is, to transfer the house of Saul into David's hands (vv. 9, 18). Abner does not offer ulterior motives. He appears to be doing the best he can in a nearly impossible situation.

PEOPLE TO KNOW // ABNER

2 SAMUEL 3:6–21: Abner was a cousin of King Saul and the commander of Saul's army. When David killed Goliath, Saul asked Abner who David was. Abner replied that he did not know, but he sought out David in the camp and then presented David, who still had Goliath's head in his hands, to Saul (1Sa 17:55–58).

Abner was close to Saul throughout Saul's reign. He ate at the king's table and aided Saul in his attempts to kill David. After Saul's death, Abner initially maintained his loyalty to Saul's family. He opposed David as king, anointing one of Saul's sons, Ish-Bosheth, as the new king in Saul's place.

When King Ish-Bosheth accused Abner of sleeping with Saul's concubine, Rizpah, the accusation angered Abner enough to switch his loyalty to David, a critical step in uniting Israel under David's throne. David received Abner's service with gratitude.

APPLICATION ✣ Abner was a man of loyalty. He stood by Saul's side throughout Saul's reign and then continued to show loyalty to Saul's son as the next king. Yet when Saul's son accused Abner of wrongdoing, Abner came to recognize that David was God's chosen king over Israel. It is not easy to change one's perspective or allegiance, and sometimes God uses circumstances to help us repent and turn to follow his way. Abner's final act of pledging loyalty to David helped unify Israel. His life shows the importance of allowing God to change our minds and seeking God's plans rather than stubbornly clinging to our own goals.

15So Ish-Bosheth gave orders and had
her taken away from her husband[y] Paltiel[z] son of Laish. 16Her husband, however, went with her, weeping behind
her all the way to Bahurim.[a] Then Abner said to him, "Go back home!" So he
went back.
17Abner conferred with the elders[b]
of Israel and said, "For some time you
have wanted to make David your king.
18Now do it! For the LORD promised David, 'By my servant David I will rescue
my people Israel from the hand of the
Philistines[c] and from the hand of all their
enemies.[d]'"
19Abner also spoke to the Benjamites
in person. Then he went to Hebron to
tell David everything that Israel and the
whole tribe of Benjamin[e] wanted to do.
20When Abner, who had twenty men
with him, came to David at Hebron, David prepared a feast for him and his men.
21Then Abner said to David, "Let me go
at once and assemble all Israel for my
lord the king, so that they may make a
covenant[f] with you, and that you may
rule over all that your heart desires."[g]
So David sent Abner away, and he went
in peace.

3:15 [y] Dt 24:1-4 [z] 1Sa 25:44
3:16 [a] 2Sa 16:5; 19:16
3:17 [b] Jdg 11:11
3:18 [c] 1Sa 9:16 [d] 1Sa 15:28; 2Sa 8:6
3:19 [e] 1Sa 10:20-21; 1Ch 12:2, 16,29
3:21 [f] ver 10,12 [g] 1Ki 11:37
3:27 [h] 2Sa 2:8

2Sa 3:27 ❖ How can God's children resist the urge to take revenge after they have been badly wronged?

Joab Murders Abner

22Just then David's men and Joab returned from a raid and brought with
them a great deal of plunder. But Abner was no longer with David in Hebron,
because David had sent him away, and
he had gone in peace. 23When Joab and
all the soldiers with him arrived, he was
told that Abner son of Ner had come to
the king and that the king had sent him
away and that he had gone in peace.
24So Joab went to the king and said,
"What have you done? Look, Abner came
to you. Why did you let him go? Now he
is gone! 25You know Abner son of Ner; he
came to deceive you and observe your
movements and find out everything you
are doing."
26Joab then left David and sent messengers after Abner, and they brought
him back from the cistern at Sirah. But
David did not know it. 27Now when Abner[h] returned to Hebron, Joab took him
aside into an inner chamber, as if to speak

3:21–39 In narrating Joab's murder of Abner, the narrator goes to great lengths to emphasize David's innocence. David sent him away "in peace" (three times in vv. 21–23). When Joab summons Abner with the clearly premeditated intent to kill him, we are told explicitly, "David did not know it" (v. 26). Finally, David personally leads the throng at the funeral for Abner (vv. 31–35). All the people of Israel accept David's innocence and are greatly pleased by everything he has done (vv. 36–37).

with him privately. And there, to avenge the blood of his brother Asahel, Joab stabbed him in the stomach, and he died.[i]

28Later, when David heard about this, he said, "I and my kingdom are forever innocent[j] before the LORD concerning the blood of Abner son of Ner. 29May his blood[k] fall on the head of Joab and on his whole family![l] May Joab's family never be without someone who has a running sore[m] or leprosy[a] or who leans on a crutch or who falls by the sword or who lacks food."

30(Joab and his brother Abishai murdered Abner because he had killed their brother Asahel in the battle at Gibeon.)

31Then David said to Joab and all the people with him, "Tear your clothes and put on sackcloth[n] and walk in mourning[o] in front of Abner." King David himself walked behind the bier. 32They buried Abner in Hebron, and the king wept[p] aloud at Abner's tomb. All the people wept also.

33The king sang this lament[q] for Abner:

"Should Abner have died as the
lawless die?
34 Your hands were not bound,
your feet were not fettered.
You fell as one falls before the
wicked."

And all the people wept over him again.

35Then they all came and urged David to eat something while it was still day; but David took an oath, saying, "May God deal with me, be it ever so severely,[r] if I taste bread[s] or anything else before the sun sets!"

36All the people took note and were pleased; indeed, everything the king did pleased them. 37So on that day all the people there and all Israel knew that the king had no part[t] in the murder of Abner son of Ner.

38Then the king said to his men, "Do you not realize that a commander and a great man has fallen[u] in Israel this day? 39And today, though I am the anointed king, I am weak, and these sons of Zeruiah[v] are too strong for me.[w] May the LORD repay[x] the evildoer according to his evil deeds!"

Ish-Bosheth Murdered

4 When Ish-Bosheth son of Saul heard that Abner[y] had died in Hebron, he lost courage, and all Israel became alarmed. 2Now Saul's son had two men who were leaders of raiding bands. One was named Baanah and the other Rekab; they were sons of Rimmon the Beerothite from the tribe of Benjamin — Beeroth[z] is considered part of Benjamin, 3because the people of Beeroth fled to Gittaim[a] and have resided there as foreigners to this day.

4(Jonathan[b] son of Saul had a son who was lame in both feet. He was five years old when the news[c] about Saul and Jonathan came from Jezreel. His nurse picked him up and fled, but as she hurried to leave, he fell and became disabled.[d] His name was Mephibosheth.)[e]

5Now Rekab and Baanah, the sons of Rimmon the Beerothite, set out for the house of Ish-Bosheth,[f] and they arrived there in the heat of the day while he was taking his noonday rest. 6They went into the inner part of the house as if to get some wheat, and they stabbed[g] him in the stomach. Then Rekab and his brother Baanah slipped away.

7They had gone into the house while he was lying on the bed in his bedroom. After they stabbed and killed him, they cut off his head. Taking it with them,

3:27 [i] 2Sa 2:22; 20:9-10; 1Ki 2:5
3:28 [j] ver 37; Dt 21:9
3:29 [k] Lev 20:9 [l] 1Ki 2:31-33 [m] Lev 15:2
3:31 [n] 2Sa 1:2, 11; Ps 30:11; Isa 20:2 [o] Ge 37:34
3:32 [p] Nu 14:1; Pr 24:17
3:33 [q] 2Sa 1:17
3:35 [r] Ru 1:17; 1Sa 3:17 [s] 1Sa 31:13; 2Sa 1:12; 12:17; Jer 16:7
3:37 [t] ver 28
3:38 [u] 2Sa 1:19
3:39 [v] 2Sa 2:18 [w] 2Sa 19:5-7 [x] 1Ki 2:5-6, 33-34; Ps 41:10; 101:8
4:1 [y] 2Sa 3:27; Ezr 4:4
4:2 [z] Jos 9:17; 18:25
4:3 [a] Ne 11:33
4:4 [b] 1Sa 18:1 [c] 1Sa 31:1-4 [d] Lev 21:18 [e] 2Sa 9:3, 6; 1Ch 8:34; 9:40
4:5 [f] 2Sa 2:8
4:6 [g] 2Sa 2:23

[a] 29 The Hebrew for *leprosy* was used for various diseases affecting the skin.

4:1–12 As in the narration of Abner's death, the biblical historian is concerned to document David's innocence. David's quote reminds us there is a right way and a wrong way to become king, and the cruel murder of "an innocent man" is not the right way (vv. 9–11).

The mention of disabled Mephibosheth (v. 4) reminds us that David's coming rule over all Israel has a corresponding truth: Saul's descendants will *not* rule Israel.

2:8—4:12 David is celebrated in these texts as the ideal king who willingly submits to God's timing and direction and consistently renounces the way of power politics and force. Jesus fulfills all that was right about David. Like David, he could have chosen the wrong way to accomplish his divine mission. In fact, Satan even tempted him with that (Mt 4:1-11). But Jesus is the ideal king of Israel because he became king in the right way, through submission to his divine vocation as the son of David and through patient waiting and service.

they traveled all night by way of the Arabah. 8 They brought the head of Ish-Bosheth to David at Hebron and said to the king, "Here is the head of Ish-Bosheth son of Saul,[h] your enemy, who tried to kill you. This day the LORD has avenged my lord the king against Saul and his offspring."

9 David answered Rekab and his brother Baanah, the sons of Rimmon the Beerothite, "As surely as the LORD lives, who has delivered[i] me out of every trouble, 10 when someone told me, 'Saul is dead,' and thought he was bringing good news, I seized him and put him to death in Ziklag.[j] That was the reward I gave him for his news! 11 How much more — when wicked men have killed an innocent man in his own house and on his own bed — should I not now demand his blood[k] from your hand and rid the earth of you!"

12 So David gave an order to his men, and they killed them.[l] They cut off their hands and feet and hung the bodies by the pool in Hebron. But they took the head of Ish-Bosheth and buried it in Abner's tomb at Hebron.

David Becomes King Over Israel

5:1–3pp // 1Ch 11:1–3

5 All the tribes of Israel[m] came to David at Hebron and said, "We are your own flesh and blood.[n] 2 In the past, while Saul was king over us, you were the one who led Israel on their military campaigns.[o] And the LORD said to you, 'You will shepherd[p] my people Israel, and you will become their ruler.[q]' "

3 When all the elders of Israel had come to King David at Hebron, the king made a covenant[r] with them at Hebron before the LORD, and they anointed[s] David king over Israel.

4 David was thirty years old[t] when he became king, and he reigned[u] forty[v] years. 5 In Hebron he reigned over Judah seven years and six months,[w] and in Jerusalem he reigned over all Israel and Judah thirty-three years.

4:8 [h] 1Sa 24:4; 25:29
4:9 [i] Ge 48:16; 1Ki 1:29
4:10 [j] 2Sa 1:2-16
4:11 [k] Ge 9:5; Ps 9:12
4:12 [l] 2Sa 1:15
5:1 [m] 2Sa 19:43 [n] 1Ch 11:1
5:2 [o] 1Sa 18:5, 13,16 [p] 1Sa 16:1; 2Sa 7:7 [q] 1Sa 25:30
5:3 [r] 2Sa 3:21 [s] 2Sa 2:4
5:4 [t] Lk 3:23 [u] 1Ki 2:11; 1Ch 3:4 [v] 1Ch 26:31; 29:27
5:5 [w] 2Sa 2:11; 1Ch 3:4
5:6 [x] Jdg 1:8 [y] Jos 15:8
5:7 [z] 2Sa 6:12, 16; 1Ki 2:10
5:9 [a] ver 7; 1Ki 9:15,24
5:10 [b] 2Sa 3:1
5:11 [c] 1Ki 5:1,18; 1Ch 14:1

2Sa 4:8 ❖ Where have we seen people do evil things in an attempt to win the favor of powerful people?

2Sa 5:6 ❖ Why does pride so often come before a fall (see Pr 16:18)? How can we avoid becoming prideful?

David Conquers Jerusalem

5:6–10pp // 1Ch 11:4–9
5:11–16pp // 1Ch 3:5–9; 14:1–7

6 The king and his men marched to Jerusalem[x] to attack the Jebusites,[y] who lived there. The Jebusites said to David, "You will not get in here; even the blind and the lame can ward you off." They thought, "David cannot get in here." 7 Nevertheless, David captured the fortress of Zion — which is the City of David.[z]

8 On that day David had said, "Anyone who conquers the Jebusites will have to use the water shaft to reach those 'lame and blind' who are David's enemies.[a]" That is why they say, "The 'blind and lame' will not enter the palace."

9 David then took up residence in the fortress and called it the City of David. He built up the area around it, from the terraces[b][a] inward. 10 And he became more and more powerful,[b] because the LORD God Almighty was with him.

11 Now Hiram[c] king of Tyre sent envoys to David, along with cedar logs and carpenters and stonemasons, and they built a palace for David. 12 Then David knew that the LORD had established him as king over Israel and had exalted his

[a] 8 Or *are hated by David* [b] 9 Or *the Millo*

5:1–5 The importance of this part in our story is highlighted by the presence of "all the tribes of Israel" with David at Hebron (v. 1). Also here are the "elders of Israel," who deal directly with "King David," a term that takes on new meaning from this point forward (v. 3). The elders assert something equally significant: "We are your own flesh and blood" (v. 1). This is a high-water mark to which the narrative has been building since 1Sa 16. David now reigns as king over all Israel.

5:6–10 Without doubt, Jerusalem is the most important city of the Bible; it is mentioned over 800 times. The name "Zion" occurs over 150 times in the OT and refers originally to the southeastern hill of the city, which is equated in this passage with the "City of David" (v. 7). Zion comes to be used as a synonym of Jerusalem and takes on enormous theological significance in Psalms, Isaiah, and elsewhere.

5:11–12 The events narrated in this section are not given in chronological sequence. The biblical historian has collected events topically in this unit to produce the full impact of David under the blessing of Yahweh (v. 10). These historical developments serve to confirm in the reader's mind that God has blessed David and established his kingdom (v. 12).

kingdom for the sake of his people Israel.

13After he left Hebron, David took more concubines and wives[d] in Jerusalem, and more sons and daughters were born to him. 14These are the names of the children born to him there:[e] Shammua, Shobab, Nathan, Solomon, 15Ibhar, Elishua, Nepheg, Japhia, 16Elishama, Eliada and Eliphelet.

David Defeats the Philistines

5:17–25pp // 1Ch 14:8–17

17When the Philistines heard that David had been anointed king over Israel, they went up in full force to search for him, but David heard about it and went down to the stronghold.[f] 18Now the Philistines had come and spread out in the Valley of Rephaim;[g] 19so David inquired[h] of the LORD, "Shall I go and attack the Philistines? Will you deliver them into my hands?"

The LORD answered him, "Go, for I will surely deliver the Philistines into your hands."

20So David went to Baal Perazim, and there he defeated them. He said, "As waters break out, the LORD has broken out against my enemies before me." So that place was called Baal Perazim.[a][i] 21The Philistines abandoned their idols there, and David and his men carried them off.[j]

22Once more the Philistines came up and spread out in the Valley of Rephaim; 23so David inquired of the LORD, and he answered, "Do not go straight up, but circle around behind them and attack them in front of the poplar trees. 24As soon as you hear the sound[k] of marching in the tops of the poplar trees, move quickly, because that will mean the LORD has gone out in front[l] of you to strike the Philistine army." 25So David did as the LORD commanded him, and he struck down the Philistines all the way from Gibeon[b][m] to Gezer.[n]

The Ark Brought to Jerusalem

6:1–11pp // 1Ch 13:1–14
6:12–19pp // 1Ch 15:25—16:3

6 David again brought together all the able young men of Israel — thirty thousand. 2He and all his men went to Baalah[c][o] in Judah to bring up from there the ark[p] of God, which is called by the Name,[d][q] the name of the LORD Almighty, who is enthroned[r] between the cherubim[s] on the ark. 3They set the ark of God on a new cart[t] and brought it from the house of Abinadab, which was on the hill. Uzzah and Ahio, sons of Abinadab, were guiding the new cart 4with the ark of God on it,[e] and Ahio was walking in front of it. 5David and all Israel were celebrating with all their might before the LORD, with castanets,[f] harps, lyres, timbrels, sistrums and cymbals.[u]

5:13 [d] Dt 17:17; 1Ch 3:9
5:14 [e] 1Ch 3:5
5:17 [f] 2Sa 23:14; 1Ch 11:16
5:18 [g] Jos 15:8; 17:15; 18:16
5:19 [h] 1Sa 23:2; 2Sa 2:1
5:20 [i] Isa 28:21
5:21 [j] Dt 7:5; 1Ch 14:12; Isa 46:2
5:24 [k] 2Ki 7:6 [l] Jdg 4:14
5:25 [m] Isa 28:21 [n] 1Ch 14:16
6:2 [o] Jos 15:9 [p] 1Sa 4:4; 7:1 [q] Lev 24:16; Isa 63:14 [r] Ps 99:1 [s] Ex 25:22; 1Ch 13:5-6
6:3 [t] Nu 7:4-9; 1Sa 6:7
6:5 [u] 1Sa 18:6-7; Ezr 3:10; Ps 150:5

[a] *20* *Baal Perazim* means *the lord who breaks out.*
[b] *25* Septuagint (see also 1 Chron. 14:16); Hebrew *Geba*
[c] *2* That is, Kiriath Jearim (see 1 Chron. 13:6)
[d] *2* Hebrew; Septuagint and Vulgate do not have *the Name.*
[e] *3,4* Dead Sea Scrolls and some Septuagint manuscripts; Masoretic Text *cart 4and they brought it with the ark of God from the house of Abinadab, which was on the hill*
[f] *5* Masoretic Text; Dead Sea Scrolls and Septuagint (see also 1 Chron. 13:8) *songs*

5:13–16 There may be hints of future trouble here: The new king has taken more wives and concubines in direct violation of the royal law of Dt 17:17.

5:17–25 The Philistines attack Judah's heartland in an apparent attempt to drive a wedge between David's two constituencies and prevent the unification of Israel under David's rule. As we have seen throughout this unit, the events are reported thematically, not in chronological sequence.

It is difficult to overstress the joy and celebration in the narrator's voice in reporting these Israelite triumphs over the Philistines. The significance of these victories is highlighted by subtle references in the text. (1) The idea that the Philistines abandon their idols is a powerful image (v. 21). David's glorious victory is a reversal of the account in 1Sa 4:1–11. (2) Yahweh's "going" in front of Israel's army (v. 25) is reminiscent of ancient theophanic poetry in which Yahweh and his celestial armies come to help in holy war. (3) The repeated information that "David inquired of the LORD" is a familiar theme (vv. 19, 23). Now that David is king, he defeats the hated foe of God. But he continues to take steps that are directed and guided by Yahweh's loving response. Here again, David becomes the portrait of the ideal king of Israel.

6:1–5 This chapter's location is significant in light of the immediately preceding paragraphs. The new political role for Jerusalem is now supplemented by a new religious significance. The entrance of the ark of the covenant into the city is the culmination of a long and painful journey since the fall of Shiloh (1Sa 4:12–22). Thus, the chapter's location builds on the political and military accomplishments of David in 2Sa 5:6–25 by narrating an event of substantial religious significance.

While the theological importance of this move of the ark to Jerusalem seems central, it clearly has political significance as well. David is most likely attempting to transfer the former authority and power of Shiloh, now sadly lost for decades, to the newly designated capital city.

6 When they came to the threshing floor of Nakon, Uzzah reached out and took hold of[v] the ark of God, because the oxen stumbled. 7 The LORD's anger burned against Uzzah because of his irreverent act;[w] therefore God struck him down,[x] and he died there beside the ark of God.

8 Then David was angry because the LORD's wrath[y] had broken out against Uzzah, and to this day that place is called Perez Uzzah.[a][z]

9 David was afraid of the LORD that day and said, "How[a] can the ark of the LORD ever come to me?" 10 He was not willing to take the ark of the LORD to be with him in the City of David. Instead, he took it to the house of Obed-Edom[b] the Gittite. 11 The ark of the LORD remained in the house of Obed-Edom the Gittite for three months, and the LORD blessed him and his entire household.[c]

12 Now King David[d] was told, "The LORD has blessed the household of Obed-Edom and everything he has, because of the ark of God." So David went to bring up the ark of God from the house of Obed-Edom to the City of David with rejoicing. 13 When those who were carrying the ark of the LORD had taken six steps, he sacrificed[e] a bull and a fattened calf. 14 Wearing a linen ephod,[f] David was dancing[g] before the LORD with all his might, 15 while he and all Israel were bringing up the ark of the LORD with shouts and the sound of trumpets.[h]

16 As the ark of the LORD was entering the City of David,[i] Michal daughter of Saul watched from a window. And when she saw King David leaping and dancing before the LORD, she despised him in her heart.

17 They brought the ark of the LORD and set it in its place inside the tent that David had pitched for it,[j] and David sacrificed burnt offerings[k] and fellowship offerings before the LORD. 18 After he had finished sacrificing[l] the burnt offerings and fellowship offerings, he blessed the people in the name of the LORD Almighty. 19 Then he gave a loaf of bread, a cake of dates and a cake of raisins[m] to each person in the whole crowd of Israelites, both men and women.[n] And all the people went to their homes.

20 When David returned home to bless his household, Michal daughter of Saul came out to meet him and said, "How the king of Israel has distinguished himself today, going around half-naked[o] in full view of the slave girls of his servants as any vulgar fellow would!"

21 David said to Michal, "It was before the LORD, who chose me rather than your father or anyone from his house when he appointed[p] me ruler over the LORD's people Israel—I will celebrate before the LORD. 22 I will become even more undignified than this, and I will be humiliated in my own eyes. But by these slave girls you spoke of, I will be held in honor."

23 And Michal daughter of Saul had no children to the day of her death.

6:6 [v] Nu 4:15, 19-20; 1Ch 13:9
6:7 [w] 1Ch 15:13-15 [x] Ex 19:22; 1Sa 6:19
6:8 [y] Ps 7:11 [z] Ge 38:29
6:9 [a] Ps 119:120
6:10 [b] 1Ch 13:13; 26:4-5
6:11 [c] Ge 30:27; 39:5
6:12 [d] 1Ki 8:1; 1Ch 15:25
6:13 [e] 1Ki 8:5, 62
6:14 [f] Ex 19:6; 1Sa 2:18 [g] Ex 15:20
6:15 [h] Ps 47:5; 98:6
6:16 [i] 2Sa 5:7
6:17 [j] 1Ch 15:1; 2Ch 1:4 [k] Lev 1:1-17; 1Ki 8:62-64
6:18 [l] 1Ki 8:22
6:19 [m] Hos 3:1 [n] Ne 8:10
6:20 [o] ver 14, 16
6:21 [p] 1Sa 13:14; 15:28

2Sa 6:13 ❖ What are ways we can reverently and joyfully celebrate God?

[a] 8 *Perez Uzzah* means *outbreak against Uzzah.*

6:6–11 The process of bringing the ark into the city is disastrous. In a way that seems especially foreign to present-day readers, the unfortunate Uzzah illustrates the holiness of God present in the ark. The Israelites have not taken his power and holiness seriously enough, and now David is left with the question in v. 9. The text implies that the ark (and hence God's presence) can and will come into David's life, but God's power and holiness come with it.

6:12–23 Note that Michal is identified in her first appearance in this unit as the "daughter of Saul" (v. 16) rather than the "wife of David." In her objections and demeanor, she manifests her father's disposition rather than her husband's. Whatever the details of Michal's objections may have been, she functions in this text as a remnant of her father's family line. The closing phrase of the chapter implies that childlessness is her punishment. Saul, Jonathan, and Ish-Bosheth are dead; Mephibosheth is disabled; Michal is barren.

5:1—6:23 The Christian reader recognizes at once that David's accomplishments are nothing less than laying the foundation for the Lord's Zion, the city of all future salvation. By affirming Christian faith and becoming a member of the community, a person today joins in the journey to Zion.

Having the rest of the story gives today's Christian readers an appreciation for David's anointing and his building of Jerusalem. We know where these events will ultimately lead. With Christ before us as the son of David and his eternal city as our destination, we march onward in faith. These two—king and city—symbolize our "hope of glory" in that we expect to participate in King Jesus' resurrection glory, a hope kept alive in us by his presence within (Col 1:27).

God's Promise to David

7:1–17pp // 1Ch 17:1–15

7 After the king was settled in his palace[q] and the LORD had given him rest
from all his enemies around him, 2he
said to Nathan the prophet, "Here I am,
living in a house[r] of cedar, while the ark
of God remains in a tent."[s]
3Nathan replied to the king, "Whatever
you have in mind, go ahead and do it, for
the LORD is with you."
4But that night the word of the LORD
came to Nathan, saying:

5"Go and tell my servant David,
'This is what the LORD says: Are
you[t] the one to build me a house
to dwell in?[u] 6I have not dwelt in a
house from the day I brought the
Israelites up out of Egypt to this day.
I have been moving from place to
place with a tent[v] as my dwelling.[w]
7Wherever I have moved with all the
Israelites,[x] did I ever say to any of
their rulers whom I commanded to
shepherd[y] my people Israel, "Why
have you not built me a house of
cedar?[z]"'
8"Now then, tell my servant David, 'This is what the LORD Almighty
says: I took you from the pasture,
from tending the flock,[a] and appointed you ruler[b] over my people Israel.[c] 9I have been with you
wherever you have gone,[d] and I
have cut off all your enemies from
before you.[e] Now I will make your
name great, like the names of the
greatest men on earth. 10And I will
provide a place for my people Israel
and will plant[f] them so that they can
have a home of their own and no
longer be disturbed. Wicked[g] people
will not oppress them anymore,[h] as

7:1 [q]1Ch 17:1
7:2 [r]2Sa 5:11 [s]Ex 26:1; Ac 7:45-46
7:5 [t]1Ki 8:19; 1Ch 22:8 [u]1Ki 5:3-5
7:6 [v]Ex 40:18, 34 [w]1Ki 8:16
7:7 [x]Dt 23:14 [y]2Sa 5:2 [z]Lev 26:11-12
7:8 [a]1Sa 16:11 [b]2Sa 6:21 [c]Ps 78:70-72; 2Co 6:18*
7:9 [d]2Sa 5:10 [e]Ps 18:37-42
7:10 [f]Ex 15:17; Isa 5:1-7 [g]Ps 89:22-23 [h]Isa 60:18

7:1–3 With the reference to David's "palace" in v. 1, the narrator introduces a theme word for the chapter—"house"—which occurs fifteen times. It will recur several times in the next few verses, all referring to a physical structure—either a royal palace (as here in v. 1) or a temple.

7:4–5 During the night, Yahweh reverses the plan. Will David refuse to hear the divine message as Saul did, or will he submit to Yahweh's will? This chapter, more than any other, answers these questions irrevocably: David is not like Saul. He is as much an ideal ruler of God's people as Saul was an inadequate one.

7:6–7 Yahweh's objection to David's plan has historical reasons. Temples were for deities who were tied down. Israel's God cannot be manipulated or contained in a temple, a point made carefully when the temple *was* eventually built (see 1Ki 8:27).

7:8–11a Yahweh's alternate plan (vv. 8–17) emphasizes the special relationship Yahweh has with David (vv. 5, 8). David is the legitimate anointed one who suitably rules God's people because he is the Immanuel figure; God is with him. Through David, Yahweh will provide security for all Israel and will "give [them] rest" (v. 11) from their enemies.

PEOPLE TO KNOW // NATHAN

2 SAMUEL 7:4–17: Nathan was a prophet during the reign of King David. When David wanted to build a temple to God, Nathan delivered God's message to David that he was not the one who would build the temple. He also told David of God's promise to make David's line into an everlasting dynasty (2Sa 7:4–16).

When David sinned by committing adultery with Bathsheba and having her husband, Uriah, killed, God sent Nathan to confront David. Nathan told a clever parable to reveal to David his guilt (2Sa 12:1–14). Nathan told David that his and Bathsheba's son would die as a result of David's sin, and it happened as Nathan said.

Later, when David was an old man, his son Adonijah tried to make himself king instead of Solomon; Nathan advocated for Solomon's cause. He sent Bathsheba to David to remind David of his word that Solomon would be the next king. David affirmed his wish to have Solomon reign as king after him, and Nathan and Zadok anointed Solomon king over Israel (1Ki 1:45).

APPLICATION ✚ Being prophet to a king would not be easy. Telling the rich and powerful what they may not want to hear carries obvious occupational hazards. Nathan's life shows, however, that obedience to God is always better than bending to human pressure. Nathan boldly confronted David about his sin. He listened to God and spoke with conviction. His actions are an example for all God's children. When God calls us to speak, then we must speak.

they did at the beginning [11]and have
done ever since the time I appointed leaders[a][i] over my people Israel. I
will also give you rest from all your
enemies.[j]
"'The LORD declares to you that
the LORD himself will establish[k] a
house[l] for you: [12]When your days
are over and you rest[m] with your ancestors, I will raise up your offspring
to succeed you, your own flesh and
blood,[n] and I will establish his kingdom. [13]He is the one who will build
a house for my Name,[o] and I will
establish the throne of his kingdom
forever.[p] [14]I will be his father, and
he will be my son.[q] When he does
wrong, I will punish him with a rod[r]
wielded by men, with floggings inflicted by human hands. [15]But my
love will never be taken away from
him, as I took it away from Saul,[s]
whom I removed from before you.
[16]Your house and your kingdom will
endure forever before me[b]; your
throne[t] will be established forever.[u]'"

[17]Nathan reported to David all the
words of this entire revelation.

David's Prayer

7:18–29pp // 1Ch 17:16–27

[18]Then King David went in and sat before the LORD, and he said:

"Who am I,[v] Sovereign LORD, and
what is my family, that you have
brought me this far? [19]And as if
this were not enough in your sight,
Sovereign LORD, you have also spoken about the future of the house
of your servant—and this decree,[w]
Sovereign LORD, is for a mere human![c]
[20]"What more can David say to
you? For you know[x] your servant,[y]
Sovereign LORD. [21]For the sake of
your word and according to your
will, you have done this great thing
and made it known to your servant.
[22]"How great[z] you are,[a] Sovereign
LORD! There is no one like you, and
there is no God[b] but you, as we have
heard with our own ears.[c] [23]And who
is like your people Israel[d]—the one
nation on earth that God went out to
redeem as a people for himself, and
to make a name for himself, and to
perform great and awesome wonders[e] by driving out nations and
their gods from before your people,
whom you redeemed[f] from Egypt?[d]
[24]You have established your people
Israel as your very own[g] forever, and
you, LORD, have become their God.[h]
[25]"And now, LORD God, keep forever the promise you have made
concerning your servant and his

7:11 [i]Jdg 2:16; 1Sa 12:9-11 [j]ver 1 [k]1Sa 25:28 [l]ver 27
7:12 [m]1Ki 2:1 [n]Ps 132:11-12
7:13 [o]1Ki 5:5; 8:19,29 [p]Isa 9:7
7:14 [q]Ps 89:26; Heb 1:5* [r]Ps 89:30-33
7:15 [s]1Sa 15:23, 28
7:16 [t]Ps 89:36-37 [u]ver 13
7:18 [v]Ex 3:11; 1Sa 18:18
7:19 [w]Isa 55:8-9
7:20 [x]Jn 21:17 [y]1Sa 16:7
7:22 [z]Ps 48:1; 86:10; Jer 10:6 [a]Dt 3:24 [b]Ex 15:11 [c]Ex 10:2; Ps 44:1
7:23 [d]Dt 4:32-38 [e]Dt 10:21 [f]Dt 9:26; 15:15
7:24 [g]Dt 26:18 [h]Ex 6:6-7; Ps 48:14

2Sa 7:18–29 ❖ What things should we praise God for in view of all he has done for us? What petitions should we make to God for the days ahead?

[a] *11* Traditionally *judges* [b] *16* Some Hebrew manuscripts and Septuagint; most Hebrew manuscripts *you* [c] *19* Or *for the human race* [d] *23* See Septuagint and 1 Chron. 17:21; Hebrew *wonders for your land and before your people, whom you redeemed from Egypt, from the nations and their gods.*

7:11b–17 Next, Yahweh details his plan more specifically for David. Rather than David's building a "house" for Yahweh, God declares he instead will build a "house" for David (v. 11b). David will be succeeded by a son, thus establishing the first royal dynasty in Israel. That son will build the temple (v. 13). Saul's family line will not last; David's will last forever (v. 16).

7:18–21 Perhaps here more than anywhere else we see the contrast between David and Saul. Put simply, David acquiesces to "the word of the LORD" (v. 4). Yahweh will make David's house stand forever, and David is greatly humbled by the promise. David's opening question is also reminiscent of Saul's (1Sa 9:21). But the similarity ends there.

7:22–24 David is driven from humility to adoration of God's greatness. Israel has become Yahweh's people, and he is her God (v. 24), which is covenant language again linking this promise to David with God's mighty acts of the past.

7:25–29 As elsewhere in the OT, Israel's prayers, when at their best, call on God to be fully God in their lives and base the request on God's own reputation and character (v. 26).

✥ **7:1–29** David's prayer is a model of yielding to God while at the same time boldly asking that God truly be God, faithfully keeping his promises. Likewise, present-day believers must take advantage of every opportunity to receive the grace of God: church attendance, Bible study, prayer, involvement in missions and outreach, commitment to serve the poor, and so on. Just as David lived close to the established means of God's grace, so must today's believers learn to explore the different ways in which God calls us to action.

house. Do as you promised, 26so
that your name will be great forever. Then people will say, 'The LORD
Almighty is God over Israel!' And the
house of your servant David will be
established in your sight.

27"LORD Almighty, God of Israel,
you have revealed this to your servant, saying, 'I will build a house
for you.' So your servant has found
courage to pray this prayer to you.
28Sovereign LORD, you are God! Your
covenant is trustworthy,[i] and you
have promised these good things
to your servant. 29Now be pleased
to bless the house of your servant,
that it may continue forever in your
sight; for you, Sovereign LORD, have
spoken, and with your blessing[j] the
house of your servant will be blessed
forever."

David's Victories

8:1–14pp // 1Ch 18:1–13

8 In the course of time, David defeated
the Philistines and subdued them,
and he took Metheg Ammah from the
control of the Philistines.

2David also defeated the Moabites.[k] He
made them lie down on the ground and
measured them off with a length of cord.
Every two lengths of them were put to
death, and the third length was allowed
to live. So the Moabites became subject
to David and brought him tribute.

3Moreover, David defeated Hadadezer[l] son of Rehob, king of Zobah,[m] when
he went to restore his monument at[a]
the Euphrates River. 4David captured a
thousand of his chariots, seven thousand
charioteers[b] and twenty thousand foot
soldiers. He hamstrung[n] all but a hundred of the chariot horses.

5When the Arameans of Damascus[o]
came to help Hadadezer king of Zobah,
David struck down twenty-two thousand
of them. 6He put garrisons in the Aramean kingdom of Damascus, and the
Arameans became subject to him and
brought tribute. The LORD gave David
victory wherever he went.[p]

7David took the gold shields[q] that belonged to the officers of Hadadezer and
brought them to Jerusalem. 8From Tebah[c] and Berothai,[r] towns that belonged
to Hadadezer, King David took a great
quantity of bronze.

9When Tou[d] king of Hamath[s] heard
that David had defeated the entire army
of Hadadezer, 10he sent his son Joram[e]
to King David to greet him and congratulate him on his victory in battle over
Hadadezer, who had been at war with
Tou. Joram brought with him articles of
silver, of gold and of bronze.

11King David dedicated[t] these articles
to the LORD, as he had done with the
silver and gold from all the nations he
had subdued: 12Edom[f] and Moab,[u] the
Ammonites[v] and the Philistines,[w] and
Amalek.[x] He also dedicated the plunder taken from Hadadezer son of Rehob,
king of Zobah.

13And David became famous[y] after he
returned from striking down eighteen
thousand Edomites[g] in the Valley of Salt.[z]

14He put garrisons throughout Edom,
and all the Edomites[a] became subject
to David.[b] The LORD gave David victory
wherever he went.[c]

2Sa 8:14 ❖ What kind of victories has God given us? How do we know certain successes are from God (see Jas 1:17)?

7:28 [i] Ex 34:6; Jn 17:17
7:29 [j] Nu 6:23-27
8:2 [k] Ge 19:37; Nu 24:17
8:3 [l] 2Sa 10:16, 19 [m] 1Sa 14:47
8:4 [n] Jos 11:9
8:5 [o] 1Ki 11:24
8:6 [p] ver 14; 2Sa 3:18; 7:9
8:7 [q] 1Ki 10:16
8:8 [r] Eze 47:16
8:9 [s] 1Ki 8:65; 2Ch 8:4
8:11 [t] 1Ki 7:51; 1Ch 26:26
8:12 [u] ver 2 [v] 2Sa 10:14 [w] 2Sa 5:25 [x] 1Sa 27:8
8:13 [y] 2Sa 7:9 [z] 2Ki 14:7; 1Ch 18:12
8:14 [a] Nu 24:17-18 [b] Ge 27:29, 37-40 [c] ver 6

[a] 3 Or *his control along* [b] 4 Septuagint (see also Dead Sea Scrolls and 1 Chron. 18:4); Masoretic Text *captured seventeen hundred of his charioteers* [c] 8 See some Septuagint manuscripts (see also 1 Chron. 18:8); Hebrew *Betah.* [d] 9 Hebrew *Toi,* a variant of *Tou;* also in verse 10 [e] 10 A variant of *Hadoram* [f] 12 Some Hebrew manuscripts, Septuagint and Syriac (see also 1 Chron. 18:11); most Hebrew manuscripts *Aram* [g] 13 A few Hebrew manuscripts, Septuagint and Syriac (see also 1 Chron. 18:12); most Hebrew manuscripts *Aram* (that is, Arameans)

8:1–6 Shortly after his coronation, David drove the Philistines from Judah's heartland and confined them to the coastal plains (5:17-25). The victory mentioned here probably indicates that he reclaims disputed territory and almost completely defeats them (8:1). The rest of the paragraph lists David's victories over enemies in the Transjordan (Moab) and the north (the Arameans of Zobah and Damascus).

8:7–14 David consistently "dedicated" (v. 11) the captured articles to Yahweh. Once again we learn more about Israel's king in contrast to Saul. When God blesses, King David gives thanks and obeys.

David has reached a point where he can turn his attention to Israel's long-term foes to the east and south (Edom, Moab, and Ammon).

David's Officials

8:15–18pp // 1Ch 18:14–17

15David reigned over all Israel, doing what was just and right for all his people. 16Joab[d] son of Zeruiah was over the army; Jehoshaphat[e] son of Ahilud was recorder; 17Zadok[f] son of Ahitub and Ahimelek son of Abiathar were priests; Seraiah was secretary;[g] 18Benaiah[h] son of Jehoiada was over the Kerethites[i] and Pelethites; and David's sons were priests.[a]

David and Mephibosheth

9 David asked, "Is there anyone still left of the house of Saul to whom I can show kindness for Jonathan's sake?"[j]

2Now there was a servant of Saul's household named Ziba.[k] They summoned him to appear before David, and the king said to him, "Are you Ziba?"

"At your service," he replied.

3The king asked, "Is there no one still alive from the house of Saul to whom I can show God's kindness?"

Ziba answered the king, "There is still a son of Jonathan;[l] he is lame[m] in both feet."

4"Where is he?" the king asked.

Ziba answered, "He is at the house of Makir[n] son of Ammiel in Lo Debar."

5So King David had him brought from Lo Debar, from the house of Makir son of Ammiel.

8:16 [d] 2Sa 19:13; 1Ch 11:6 [e] 2Sa 20:24; 1Ki 4:3
8:17 [f] 2Sa 15:24, 29; 1Ch 16:39; 24:3 [g] 1Ki 4:3; 2Ki 12:10
8:18 [h] 2Sa 20:23; 1Ki 1:8, 38; 1Ch 18:17 [i] 1Sa 30:14
9:1 [j] 1Sa 20:14-17, 42
9:2 [k] 2Sa 16:1-4; 19:17, 26, 29
9:3 [l] 1Sa 20:14 [m] 2Sa 4:4
9:4 [n] 2Sa 17:27-29
9:6 [o] 2Sa 16:4; 19:24-30
9:7 [p] ver 1, 3; 2Sa 12:8; 19:28; 1Ki 2:7; 2Ki 25:29
9:8 [q] 2Sa 16:9
9:10 [r] ver 7, 11, 13; 2Sa 19:28

2Sa 9:1 ❖ How does David model the words of Christ? What are ways we can "love [our] enemies" (Mt 5:44)?

6When Mephibosheth son of Jonathan, the son of Saul, came to David, he bowed down to pay him honor.[o]

David said, "Mephibosheth!"

"At your service," he replied.

7"Don't be afraid," David said to him, "for I will surely show you kindness for the sake of your father Jonathan. I will restore to you all the land that belonged to your grandfather Saul, and you will always eat at my table.[p]"

8Mephibosheth bowed down and said, "What is your servant, that you should notice a dead dog[q] like me?"

9Then the king summoned Ziba, Saul's steward, and said to him, "I have given your master's grandson everything that belonged to Saul and his family. 10You and your sons and your servants are to farm the land for him and bring in the crops, so that your master's grandson[r] may be provided for. And Mephibosheth, grandson of your master, will always eat at my table." (Now Ziba had fifteen sons and twenty servants.)

11Then Ziba said to the king, "Your servant will do whatever my lord the

[a] *18* Or *were chief officials* (see Septuagint and Targum; see also 1 Chron. 18:17)

8:15–18 With this list of royal officials, we discover that the previous social stratification based on kinship has given way to a structure based more on skill and ability. So, in this list of royal officers, a series of functional roles has replaced the elders of Israel and Judah as the power structure.

David is Yahweh's chosen anointed one who rules as Yahweh himself wants his people to be governed. David becomes the example for all future kings—the standard by which they will be judged. But as we will see in the rest of this book, this is not the whole story.

✣ **8:1–18** This chapter illustrates that God is faithful to his word and strengthens his servants for the task to which he has called them. So, what can it mean for today's believers to have victory wherever we go? It means that God has already won the victory and has promised to strengthen us for the tasks we are called to perform in the church and in the world. As David defeated Israel's enemies, so today's believers can expect to accomplish successfully our God-given and God-ordained tasks, with the help of his Holy Spirit. God is still at work fulfilling his Word through his people.

9:1–5 The military summary provided in ch. 8 fulfills the words of Jonathan in 1Sa 20:15. So now is the time for David to keep the covenant he and Jonathan established. David's motives are singularly focused on Jonathan; his reasons for showing kindness now are simply "for Jonathan's sake" (2Sa 9:1, 7).

9:6–13 Regardless of what Mephibosheth may have hoped, it can hardly be good news for him to be summoned to the royal palace. David brings him from obscurity in Lo Debar and identifies him as the son of Jonathan and grandson of Saul (v. 6). In the central and pivotal section of our text (v. 7), David begins by alleviating his visitor's fears. The king will not only permit Mephibosheth to live, but he will show kindness to him for Jonathan's sake.

That kindness takes the form of two blessings. First, David will give him the property of Saul's estate, instantly making Mephibosheth a wealthy man. Next, David grants the privilege that was lost to Mephibosheth when Saul and Jonathan were killed; that is, the right to eat at the king's table.

king commands his servant to do." So
Mephibosheth ate at David's[a] table like
one of the king's sons.[s]
12Mephibosheth had a young son
named Mika, and all the members of
Ziba's household were servants of Mephibosheth.[t] 13And Mephibosheth lived
in Jerusalem, because he always ate at
the king's table; he was lame in both feet.

David Defeats the Ammonites

10:1–19pp // 1Ch 19:1–19

10 In the course of time, the king of
the Ammonites died, and his son
Hanun succeeded him as king. 2David
thought, "I will show kindness to Hanun
son of Nahash,[u] just as his father showed
kindness to me." So David sent a delegation to express his sympathy to Hanun
concerning his father.
When David's men came to the land
of the Ammonites, 3the Ammonite commanders said to Hanun their lord, "Do
you think David is honoring your father
by sending envoys to you to express
sympathy? Hasn't David sent them to
you only to explore the city and spy
it out and overthrow it?" 4So Hanun
seized David's envoys, shaved off half
of each man's beard,[v] cut off their garments at the buttocks,[w] and sent them
away.
5When David was told about this, he
sent messengers to meet the men, for
they were greatly humiliated. The king
said, "Stay at Jericho till your beards have
grown, and then come back."

9:11 [s]Job 36:7; Ps 113:8
9:12 [t]1Ch 8:34
10:2 [u]1Sa 11:1
10:4 [v]Lev 19:27; Isa 15:2; Jer 48:37 [w]Isa 20:4
10:6 [x]Ge 34:30 [y]2Sa 8:5 [z]Jdg 18:28 [a]Dt 3:14
10:12 [b]Dt 31:6; 1Co 16:13; Eph 6:10 [c]Jdg 10:15; 1Sa 3:18; Ne 4:14

2Sa 10:1–5 ❖ How do we respond when acts of kindness or mercy are rejected or perceived the wrong way?

6When the Ammonites realized that
they had become obnoxious[x] to David,
they hired twenty thousand Aramean[y]
foot soldiers from Beth Rehob[z] and Zobah, as well as the king of Maakah[a] with a
thousand men, and also twelve thousand
men from Tob.
7On hearing this, David sent Joab out
with the entire army of fighting men.
8The Ammonites came out and drew up
in battle formation at the entrance of
their city gate, while the Arameans of
Zobah and Rehob and the men of Tob
and Maakah were by themselves in the
open country.
9Joab saw that there were battle lines
in front of him and behind him; so he
selected some of the best troops in Israel
and deployed them against the Arameans. 10He put the rest of the men under
the command of Abishai his brother and
deployed them against the Ammonites. 11Joab said, "If the Arameans are
too strong for me, then you are to come
to my rescue; but if the Ammonites are
too strong for you, then I will come to
rescue you. 12Be strong,[b] and let us fight
bravely for our people and the cities of
our God. The LORD will do what is good
in his sight."[c]

[a] *11* Septuagint; Hebrew *my*

9:1–13 We may be tempted to show kindness and to keep our covenant commitments only when it is convenient to do so or when it shows particular promise of return. In the workplace, in schools, even in the church, we tend to keep our promises to those who will repay us in some way. In this text, David serves as an example because he keeps covenant and shows mercy to someone who cannot benefit him. David uses power *in this passage* in a way that is consistent with his calling as shepherd of God's flock. As such, he also anticipates his greater Son, who will use his power only for the advancement of his Father's kingdom. Unfortunately, David will not always represent such an example of the use of power, as later chapters reveal.

10:1–5 Nahash, the Ammonite king who has died here (v. 1) and an old adversary of Saul (1Sa 11), was likely David's ally during the difficult days of Saul's reign.

Details on why the shaved beard and cut garments represented the ultimate insult are not entirely clear (v. 4). The beard was apparently the pride and joy of an Israelite male, which was cut only for periods of mourning or as an act of humiliation. Since garments in the biblical world often reflected status, power, or identity, the added insult of cutting their garments at their hips exposes David's men to further humiliation.

David's decisive victory over the Arameans brings the power motif into focus and characterizes him as the legitimate king of Israel (vv. 15–19), who has God-given power and authority. David does indeed have royal power, and as we will see, this motif returns in frightening ways in chs. 11 and 12.

10:6–8 The first battle described here takes place near the city of Rabbah, which was the royal citadel of the Ammonites (12:26).

10:9–12 Once the Arameans arrive in the Transjordan, they successfully outmaneuver Joab so that he is forced to fight on two separate fronts. The short-tempered general is seldom a model of virtue, but here Joab's quote (v. 12) illustrates the healthy balance between effort and faith.

13 Then Joab and the troops with him
advanced to fight the Arameans, and
they fled before him. 14 When the Ammonites realized that the Arameans were
fleeing, they fled before Abishai and
went inside the city. So Joab returned
from fighting the Ammonites and came
to Jerusalem.
15 After the Arameans saw that they had
been routed by Israel, they regrouped.
16 Hadadezer had Arameans brought from
beyond the Euphrates River; they went
to Helam, with Shobak the commander
of Hadadezer's army leading them.
17 When David was told of this, he
gathered all Israel, crossed the Jordan and went to Helam. The Arameans
formed their battle lines to meet David
and fought against him. 18 But they fled
before Israel, and David killed seven
hundred of their charioteers and forty
thousand of their foot soldiers.[a] He also
struck down Shobak the commander of
their army, and he died there. 19 When all
the kings who were vassals of Hadadezer
saw that they had been routed by Israel,
they made peace with the Israelites and
became subject[d] to them.
So the Arameans[e] were afraid to help
the Ammonites anymore.

David and Bathsheba

11 In the spring,[f] at the time when
kings go off to war, David sent Joab[g]
out with the king's men and the whole
Israelite army.[h] They destroyed the Ammonites and besieged Rabbah.[i] But David
remained in Jerusalem.
2 One evening David got up from his
bed and walked around on the roof[j] of
the palace. From the roof he saw[k] a woman bathing. The woman was very beautiful, 3 and David sent someone to find out
about her. The man said, "She is Bathsheba,[l] the daughter of Eliam[m] and the
wife of Uriah[n] the Hittite." 4 Then David
sent messengers to get her.[o] She came
to him, and he slept[p] with her. (Now she
was purifying herself from her monthly uncleanness.)[q] Then she went back
home. 5 The woman conceived and sent
word to David, saying, "I am pregnant."
6 So David sent this word to Joab: "Send
me Uriah[r] the Hittite." And Joab sent him

10:19 [d] 2Sa 8:6
[e] 1Ki 11:25; 2Ki 5:1
11:1 [f] 1Ki 20:22, 26 [g] 2Sa 2:18 [h] 1Ch 20:1 [i] 2Sa 12:26-28
11:2 [j] Dt 22:8; Jos 2:8 [k] Mt 5:28
11:3 [l] 1Ch 3:5 [m] 2Sa 23:34 [n] 2Sa 23:39
11:4 [o] Lev 20:10; Ps 51 Title; Jas 1:14-15 [p] Dt 22:22 [q] Lev 15:25-30; 18:19
11:6 [r] 1Ch 11:41

[a] *18* Some Septuagint manuscripts (see also 1 Chron. 19:18); Hebrew *horsemen*

10:13–14 To the disappointment of the Ammonites, their Aramean allies flee before Joab. The Israelite victory is probably tempered by losses so that Joab is unable to continue his siege on the city itself and has no alternative but to return to Jerusalem (v. 14).

10:15–19 The next battle is between Israel and the Arameans themselves and will determine the fate of all of Syria-Palestine. David leads the troops himself this time in what becomes a decisive victory. With the Aramean allies effectively neutralized, all that remains for David to control the Transjordan area is to conquer Ammon itself (12:26–31).

11:1 The text is concerned with showing that David's adultery with Bathsheba occurs approximately one year after the Ammonite-Aramean wars began. In a striking irony, David is described as performing his rightful role as king of Israel; that is, he is defending the nation. The irony, of course, is that David stays home and rather than defend his subjects, he abuses them (i.e., Bathsheba and her family). By placing in the foreground the picture of Israel's adversary kings marching off to war, the narrator has put the spotlight on David sitting at home.

11:2 The narrator emphasizes Bathsheba's beauty and immediately alerts the reader that danger lurks around the corner.

11:3–5 The narration is further characterized by three occurrences of a theme word, ("sent") (vv. 3, 4, 5). David *sends* someone to find out more about Bathsheba. David then *sends* again, this time with the intention of fetching Bathsheba to the palace. The specific verbs used in v. 4 to describe David's actions are painfully clear: He sends, he takes her, and he lies with her. Mercifully brief, the verse coldly recounts David's crime.

The little phrase near the end of v. 4 sounds an ominous note. The point of the clause is that Bathsheba is cleansing herself ritually because of menstruation. Such a detail clarifies a few further facts about the episode. (1) She is not currently pregnant prior to intercourse with David. (2) Intercourse with David takes place precisely at the most opportune time for conception. (3) Since Uriah is off in the battlefield, he cannot possibly be the father.

11:5 David is not the only character who "sends" in this episode, for Bathsheba *sends* a succinct message that changes everything. David exercised power in ch. 10 and thus far in ch. 11 by "sending." But when Bathsheba "sends," David must deal with a different kind of power. The power of wronged Bathsheba, the power of David's own sin—these are powers that David will now attempt to answer with more "sending" (v. 6). But ultimately, Yahweh will "send," and David will relent (12:1).

11:6 The second episode of ch. 11 narrates David's first attempts to cover up the unfortunate consequences of his episode with Bathsheba. Our unit's theme word ("sent") occurs three times in this verse. In order to cover his guilt, David tries deception and deceit. He has faith in his plan, and he believes his royal power is sufficient for the task. So, as elsewhere, David *sends* in order to control and dominate, and also this time to conceal.

PEOPLE TO KNOW // BATHSHEBA

2 SAMUEL 11:1–27: Bathsheba, the wife of one of King David's soldiers, is known for her relationship with David. Scripture tells us that when David saw Bathsheba bathing, he desired her, sent for her and slept with her. Shortly after, Bathsheba sent word to David that she was pregnant. In a desperate attempt to hide his flagrant sin, David had Bathsheba's husband, Uriah, brought home from battle, hoping that Uriah would sleep with Bathsheba so that the baby would be assumed to be his. When this ploy failed, David commanded his army officer Joab to ensure Uriah's death on the battlefield.

Bathsheba mourned for her slain husband, but soon David summoned her to his palace and married her. She had a son, but the child died as judgment for David's sin, adding to Bathsheba's grief. Bathsheba and David had a second son together, Solomon, who became king after David.

When David was near death, another son named Adonijah tried to claim the throne for himself. At Nathan's bidding, Bathsheba bravely approached David to advocate for Solomon as the next king (1Ki 1:28–31). David honored Bathsheba's request and ensured that Solomon took the throne before David himself died.

In the NT, Bathsheba is one of only five women mentioned in Matthew's genealogy of Jesus (Mt 1:6). She is forever honored in the list of Jesus' ancestors.

APPLICATION It's difficult to know how to read Bathsheba's story since she is not given a voice in the text. Based on Nathan's rebuke of David (2Sa 12), Nathan considered Bathsheba innocent of wrongdoing when King David sent for her and slept with her. We also read of Bathsheba's grief in losing a husband and son.

Yet while Bathsheba suffered tragic events, she used the opportunities given to her and found a way forward. She raised a son who loved God and asked God for wisdom to be a good king. She advocated for her son and refused to let circumstances dictate the end of her story.

to David. 7When Uriah came to him, David asked him how Joab was, how the
soldiers were and how the war was going. 8Then David said to Uriah, "Go down
to your house and wash your feet."[s] So
Uriah left the palace, and a gift from the
king was sent after him. 9But Uriah slept
at the entrance to the palace with all his
master's servants and did not go down
to his house.
10David was told, "Uriah did not go
home." So he asked Uriah, "Haven't you
just come from a military campaign?
Why didn't you go home?"
11Uriah said to David, "The ark[t] and Israel and Judah are staying in tents,[a] and
my commander Joab and my lord's men
are camped in the open country. How
could I go to my house to eat and drink
and make love to my wife? As surely as
you live, I will not do such a thing!"
12Then David said to him, "Stay here
one more day, and tomorrow I will send
you back." So Uriah remained in Jerusalem that day and the next. 13At David's
invitation, he ate and drank with him,
and David made him drunk. But in the
evening Uriah went out to sleep on his
mat among his master's servants; he did
not go home.
14In the morning David wrote a letter[u]
to Joab and sent it with Uriah. 15In it he
wrote, "Put Uriah out in front where the

11:8 [s] Ge 18:4; 43:24; Lk 7:44
11:11 [t] 2Sa 7:2
11:14 [u] 1Ki 21:8

[a] 11 *Or staying at Sukkoth*

11:7 When Uriah arrives in Jerusalem, David's hypocritical questions are likely intended to give Uriah the impression that David has summoned him from the battlefield to get an accurate military report.
11:8–13 David's pathetic attempts to manipulate and control Uriah bring the king's hypocrisy to the foreground. Obviously, David wants Uriah to spend a night at home with his wife, creating the possibility later that Uriah is the father of Bathsheba's child. David has grossly underestimated Uriah's character. The great irony of our text is that this convert of foreign ancestry is more righteous than the Israelite king. King David, the anointed one of Yahweh, has abused his God-given power and attempts to manipulate a faithful and righteous servant in a desperate scam to save himself.
11:14–25 The third episode is the shocking account of murder. David is not finished *sending* yet. His next step is to write Uriah's own death warrant and "send" it to Joab by Uriah's own hand (v. 14). His powerful royal prerogative has been turned to evil purposes; his attempts to save himself jeopardize his army's actions against Rabbah and trivialize the deaths of Israelite soldiers that he himself

fighting is fiercest. Then withdraw from
him so he will be struck down[v] and die.[w]"
16So while Joab had the city under
siege, he put Uriah at a place where he
knew the strongest defenders were.
17When the men of the city came out and
fought against Joab, some of the men in
David's army fell; moreover, Uriah the
Hittite died.
18Joab sent David a full account of the
battle. 19He instructed the messenger:
"When you have finished giving the
king this account of the battle, 20the
king's anger may flare up, and he may
ask you, 'Why did you get so close to the
city to fight? Didn't you know they would
shoot arrows from the wall? 21Who killed
Abimelek[x] son of Jerub-Besheth[a]? Didn't
a woman drop an upper millstone on him
from the wall,[y] so that he died in Thebez?
Why did you get so close to the wall?' If he
asks you this, then say to him, 'Moreover,
your servant Uriah the Hittite is dead.'"
22The messenger set out, and when he
arrived he told David everything Joab
had sent him to say. 23The messenger
said to David, "The men overpowered us
and came out against us in the open, but
we drove them back to the entrance of
the city gate. 24Then the archers shot arrows at your servants from the wall, and
some of the king's men died. Moreover,
your servant Uriah the Hittite is dead."
25David told the messenger, "Say this
to Joab: 'Don't let this upset you; the
sword devours one as well as another.
Press the attack against the city and destroy it.' Say this to encourage Joab."
26When Uriah's wife heard that her
husband was dead, she mourned for him.
27After the time of mourning was over,
David had her brought to his house, and
she became his wife and bore him a son.
But the thing David had done displeased[z]
the LORD.

11:15 [v] 2Sa 12:9 [w] 2Sa 12:12
11:21 [x] Jdg 8:31 [y] Jdg 9:50-54
11:27 [z] 2Sa 12:9; Ps 51:4-5

12:1 [a] 2Sa 7:2; 1Ki 20:35-41 [b] Ps 51 Title [c] 2Sa 14:4
12:5 [d] 1Ki 20:40
12:6 [e] Ex 22:1; Lk 19:8
12:7 [f] 1Sa 16:13 [g] 1Ki 20:42
12:8 [h] 2Sa 9:7
12:9 [i] Nu 15:31; 1Sa 15:19 [j] 2Sa 11:15

2Sa 11:17 ❖ David's sin spiraled from negligence, to lust and adultery, to deceit and murder. How can we keep sin from spiraling out of control? Why does one sin often lead to more?

Nathan Rebukes David

11:1; 12:29–31pp // 1Ch 20:1–3

12 The LORD sent Nathan[a] to David.[b]
When he came to him,[c] he said,
"There were two men in a certain town,
one rich and the other poor. 2The rich
man had a very large number of sheep
and cattle, 3but the poor man had nothing except one little ewe lamb he had
bought. He raised it, and it grew up with
him and his children. It shared his food,
drank from his cup and even slept in his
arms. It was like a daughter to him.
4"Now a traveler came to the rich man,
but the rich man refrained from taking
one of his own sheep or cattle to prepare
a meal for the traveler who had come to
him. Instead, he took the ewe lamb that
belonged to the poor man and prepared
it for the one who had come to him."
5David[d] burned with anger against
the man and said to Nathan, "As surely
as the LORD lives, the man who did this
must die! 6He must pay for that lamb
four times over,[e] because he did such a
thing and had no pity."
7Then Nathan said to David, "You are
the man! This is what the LORD, the God
of Israel, says: 'I anointed[f] you[g] king over
Israel, and I delivered you from the hand
of Saul. 8I gave your master's house to
you,[h] and your master's wives into your
arms. I gave you all Israel and Judah.
And if all this had been too little, I would
have given you even more. 9Why did you
despise[i] the word of the LORD by doing
what is evil in his eyes? You struck down[j]

[a] *21* Also known as *Jerub-Baal* (that is, Gideon)

has caused. His flippant response to the news of Uriah's death (v. 25) is a shocking illustration of how far David has gone.

11:26–27 The fourth part of our chapter is the (apparent) conclusion of the story (vv. 26–27): David takes Bathsheba as his wife, and she bears him a son. David "sent and brought her" (alternate translation, v. 27; NIV "had her brought") to the royal palace. This is the last time in our text David is the subject of *sending*. From now on, God or Joab will do the *sending* (12:1, 25, 27). From David's perspective, that is the end of the matter. However, in God's eyes this is only the beginning of the struggle.

12:1–6 The best way to expose David's hypocrisy is to have him condemn himself. Nathan's parable arouses David's indignation, and he quickly condemns himself by condemning the rich man.

12:7–10 David has announced his official royal judgment on any man who would behave in such a way. Nathan comes immediately to the point of his parable (v. 7): "You are the man!" David's sin is that he has "despise[d] the word of the LORD" by committing evil in God's sight (cf. 1Sa 15:23, 26). As David chose the way of violence to cover his sin, so the sword will never depart from his royal dynasty. God's punishment matches the crime.

Uriah the Hittite with the sword and took
his wife to be your own. You killed him
with the sword of the Ammonites. 10Now,
therefore, the sword[k] will never depart
from your house, because you despised
me and took the wife of Uriah the Hittite
to be your own.'
11"This is what the LORD says: 'Out of
your own household I am going to bring
calamity on you.[l] Before your very eyes
I will take your wives and give them to
one who is close to you, and he will sleep
with your wives in broad daylight. 12You
did it in secret,[m] but I will do this thing in
broad daylight[n] before all Israel.' "
13Then David said to Nathan, "I have
sinned[o] against the LORD."
Nathan replied, "The LORD has taken
away[p] your sin.[q] You are not going to
die.[r] 14But because by doing this you have
shown utter contempt for[a] the LORD,[s] the
son born to you will die."
15After Nathan had gone home, the
LORD struck[t] the child that Uriah's wife
had borne to David, and he became ill.
16David pleaded with God for the child.
He fasted and spent the nights lying[u]
in sackcloth[b] on the ground. 17The elders of his household stood beside him
to get him up from the ground, but he
refused, and he would not eat any food
with them.[v]
18On the seventh day the child died.
David's attendants were afraid to tell
him that the child was dead, for they
thought, "While the child was still living,
he wouldn't listen to us when we spoke to
him. How can we now tell him the child is
dead? He may do something desperate."

12:10 [k]2Sa 13:28; 18:14-15; 1Ki 2:25
12:11 [l]Dt 28:30; 2Sa 16:21-22
12:12 [m]2Sa 11:4-15 [n]2Sa 16:22
12:13 [o]Ge 13:13; Nu 22:34; 1Sa 15:24; 2Sa 24:10 [p]Ps 32:1-5; 51:1,9; 103:12; Zec 3:4,9 [q]Pr 28:13; Mic 7:18-19 [r]Lev 20:10; 24:17
12:14 [s]Isa 52:5; Ro 2:24
12:15 [t]1Sa 25:38
12:16 [u]2Sa 13:31; Ps 5:7
12:17 [v]2Sa 3:35
12:20 [w]Mt 6:17 [x]Job 1:20
12:21 [y]Jdg 20:26
12:22 [z]Jnh 3:9 [a]Isa 38:1-5
12:23 [b]Ge 37:35 [c]1Sa 31:13; 2Sa 13:39; Job 7:10; 10:21
12:24 [d]1Ki 1:11 [e]1Ki 1:10; 1Ch 22:9; 28:5; Mt 1:6
12:25 [f]Ne 13:26

2Sa 12:13 ❖ When have we been painfully confronted with our own sin?

19David noticed that his attendants
were whispering among themselves, and
he realized the child was dead. "Is the
child dead?" he asked.
"Yes," they replied, "he is dead."
20Then David got up from the ground.
After he had washed,[w] put on lotions and
changed his clothes,[x] he went into the
house of the LORD and worshiped. Then
he went to his own house, and at his request they served him food, and he ate.
21His attendants asked him, "Why are
you acting this way? While the child was
alive, you fasted and wept,[y] but now that
the child is dead, you get up and eat!"
22He answered, "While the child was
still alive, I fasted and wept. I thought,
'Who knows?[z] The LORD may be gracious
to me and let the child live.'[a] 23But now
that he is dead, why should I go on fasting? Can I bring him back again? I will go
to him,[b] but he will not return to me."[c]
24Then David comforted his wife Bathsheba,[d] and he went to her and made
love to her. She gave birth to a son, and
they named him Solomon.[e] The LORD
loved him; 25and because the LORD loved
him, he sent word through Nathan the
prophet to name him Jedidiah.[c][f]
26Meanwhile Joab fought against

[a] *14* An ancient Hebrew scribal tradition; Masoretic Text *for the enemies of* [b] *16* Dead Sea Scrolls and Septuagint; Masoretic Text does not have *in sackcloth.* [c] *25* *Jedidiah* means *loved by the LORD.*

12:11–12 Calamity will arise against David from within his own household.

12:13 Here we learn David's real character. Certainly, he is remembered for the heinous sins of ch. 11. But his response to the prophetic word in this verse is why David became known as Israel's ideal king. David's words are full of genuine remorse and sorrow. True repentance (v. 13a) is met instantly with genuine forgiveness (v. 13b). God is merciful.

12:14–23 At the same time as v. 13 illustrates God's merciful forgiveness, v. 14 illustrates the consequences of sin, even though forgiven by God. The aftermath of sin remains; the child will die. Sin that has been forgiven and forgotten by God may still leave human scars.

The episode of the child's death and David's reversal of conventional mourning customs leaves many interpreters perplexed (vv. 15–23). The normal period of mourning lasted seven days, and the child died on the seventh day (v. 18). Since David assumed an attitude of mourning while he prayed for the sick boy, he had already fulfilled the customary period of mourning, and there was no need to continue his futile prayers for the boy's life (vv. 21–23). There may be nothing more intended here than indicating the depth of David's passion and hope in God.

12:24–25 The birth of another son between David and Bathsheba holds great symbolic significance. Bathsheba is called David's "wife" rather than the "wife of Uriah the Hittite" (cf. 11:3; 12:10). More importantly, Yahweh loves the new son; he bears two names, Solomon and Jedidiah. Though other children are born to this union, he will have special significance in fulfilling the covenant promises of 2Sa 7.

12:26–31 This paragraph is a historical flashback used as a literary frame. It serves together with 10:1—11:1 to create a literary envelope for the whole.

Joab and the army (formerly including Uriah the Hittite) capture Rabbah's water supply, and it will

Rabbah[g] of the Ammonites and captured the royal citadel. 27 Joab then sent
messengers to David, saying, "I have
fought against Rabbah and taken its water supply. 28 Now muster the rest of the
troops and besiege the city and capture
it. Otherwise I will take the city, and it
will be named after me."
29 So David mustered the entire army
and went to Rabbah, and attacked and
captured it. 30 David took the crown[h] from
their king's[a] head, and it was placed on
his own head. It weighed a talent[b] of
gold, and it was set with precious stones.
David took a great quantity of plunder
from the city 31 and brought out the people who were there, consigning them
to labor with saws and with iron picks
and axes, and he made them work at
brickmaking.[c] David did this to all the
Ammonite[i] towns. Then he and his entire
army returned to Jerusalem.

Amnon and Tamar

13 In the course of time, Amnon[j] son of
David fell in love with Tamar,[k] the
beautiful sister of Absalom[l] son of David.
2 Amnon became so obsessed with his
sister Tamar that he made himself ill. She
was a virgin, and it seemed impossible
for him to do anything to her.
3 Now Amnon had an adviser named
Jonadab son of Shimeah,[m] David's brother. Jonadab was a very shrewd man. 4 He
asked Amnon, "Why do you, the king's
son, look so haggard morning after
morning? Won't you tell me?"
Amnon said to him, "I'm in love with
Tamar, my brother Absalom's sister."
5 "Go to bed and pretend to be ill," Jonadab said. "When your father comes to see
you, say to him, 'I would like my sister
Tamar to come and give me something
to eat. Let her prepare the food in my
sight so I may watch her and then eat it
from her hand.'"
6 So Amnon lay down and pretended
to be ill. When the king came to see him,
Amnon said to him, "I would like my
sister Tamar to come and make some
special bread in my sight, so I may eat
from her hand."
7 David sent word to Tamar at the palace: "Go to the house of your brother Amnon and prepare some food for him." 8 So
Tamar went to the house of her brother
Amnon, who was lying down. She took
some dough, kneaded it, made the bread
in his sight and baked it. 9 Then she took
the pan and served him the bread, but
he refused to eat.
"Send everyone out of here,"[n] Amnon
said. So everyone left him. 10 Then Amnon said to Tamar, "Bring the food here
into my bedroom so I may eat from your
hand." And Tamar took the bread she had

12:26 [g] Dt 3:11; 1Ch 20:1-3
12:30 [h] 1Ch 20:2; Est 8:15; Ps 21:3; 132:18
12:31 [i] 1Sa 14:47
13:1 [j] 2Sa 3:2 [k] 2Sa 14:27; 1Ch 3:9 [l] 2Sa 3:3
13:3 [m] 1Sa 16:9
13:9 [n] Ge 45:1

[a] *30* Or *from Milkom's* (that is, Molek's)
[b] *30* That is, about 75 pounds or about 34 kilograms
[c] *31* The meaning of the Hebrew for this clause is uncertain.

only be a matter of time before the city falls into Israelite hands. In the last occurrence of our passage's theme word, Joab uses his power to "send" (12:27) a message to David. Just as the war was precipitated by the sending of messengers (10:2, 4), so now it is concluded.

✣ **10:1–12:31** American culture has believed the lie that our highest human fulfillment is partially achievable through self-indulgent, unrestrained erotic expression rather than through faithful, enduring, monogamous love. It's a lie that's as old as human civilization itself, and this text reveals the ancient lie for what it is. David surrenders impulsively to his most basic instincts, which lead him down a path that grows darker with each step. Rather than reaching his highest level of personal fulfillment, David discovers the darkness of his own soul. It is a hopeless cycle that ends only and always in chaos, pain, regret, and death (Pr 7:21–23, 27).

13:1-2 The narrator lifts Absalom into the foreground and makes us aware that this is not simply a story about Amnon and Tamar; rather, this account participates in the larger narrative of Absalom. Since ch. 14 ends with the word "Absalom," these two chapters begin and end with Absalom. Amnon's crude but honest explanation for his lovesickness (13:2) shows that his "love" for Tamar is not love in any meaningful sense but only lust.

13:3-5 The previous two verses presented Amnon's problem: He cannot have the woman he desires. Here we meet his solution: the nefarious advice of a cousin. Now we get a picture of the strife permeating David's extended family.

13:6-14 The Hebrew of this text uses a wide array of literary devices to emphasize the irony and injustice of the shameful act. Tamar's impressive speech desperately raises numerous objections and shows her to be a woman of integrity. Her prohibition, "Don't force me!" uses a specific verb decrying the act for what it would be: rape. His proposal is a "wicked thing" and will only make a fool of him. This narrator is fond of thematic analogies between episodes. Amnon's actions are subtly drawn together with David's in a cause-and-effect relationship: David's sin has come to rest now in his immediate family.

prepared and brought it to her brother
Amnon in his bedroom. 11But when she
took it to him to eat, he grabbed[o] her and
said, "Come to bed with me, my sister."[p]
12"No, my brother!" she said to him.
"Don't force me! Such a thing should not
be done in Israel![q] Don't do this wicked
thing.[r] 13What about me?[s] Where could I
get rid of my disgrace? And what about
you? You would be like one of the wicked
fools in Israel. Please speak to the king;
he will not keep me from being married
to you." 14But he refused to listen to her,
and since he was stronger than she, he
raped her.[t]
15Then Amnon hated her with intense
hatred. In fact, he hated her more than
he had loved her. Amnon said to her, "Get
up and get out!"
16"No!" she said to him. "Sending me
away would be a greater wrong than
what you have already done to me."
But he refused to listen to her. 17He
called his personal servant and said, "Get
this woman out of my sight and bolt the
door after her." 18So his servant put her
out and bolted the door after her. She was
wearing an ornate[a] robe,[u] for this was the
kind of garment the virgin daughters
of the king wore. 19Tamar put ashes[v] on
her head and tore the ornate robe she
was wearing. She put her hands on her
head and went away, weeping aloud as
she went.
20Her brother Absalom said to her,
"Has that Amnon, your brother, been

13:11 [o] Ge 39:12 [p] Ge 38:16
13:12 [q] Lev 20:17; Jdg 20:6 [r] Ge 34:7; Jdg 19:23
13:13 [s] Ge 20:12; Lev 18:9; Dt 22:21,23-24
13:14 [t] Ge 34:2; Dt 22:25; Eze 22:11
13:18 [u] Ge 37:23; Jdg 5:30
13:19 [v] Jos 7:6; 1Sa 4:12; 2Sa 1:2; Est 4:1; Da 9:3
13:21 [w] Ge 34:7
13:22 [x] Ge 31:24 [y] Lev 19:17-18; 1Jn 2:9-11
13:23 [z] 1Sa 25:7

2Sa 13:20 ❖ Despite his character flaws that became obvious later, Absalom showed kindness to Tamar in this moment. How can we show kindness and mercy to those who are bereaved and desolate?

with you? Be quiet for now, my sister;
he is your brother. Don't take this thing
to heart." And Tamar lived in her brother Absalom's house, a desolate woman.
21When King David heard all this, he
was furious.[w] 22And Absalom never said
a word to Amnon, either good or bad;[x] he
hated[y] Amnon because he had disgraced
his sister Tamar.

Absalom Kills Amnon

23Two years later, when Absalom's
sheepshearers[z] were at Baal Hazor near
the border of Ephraim, he invited all the
king's sons to come there. 24Absalom
went to the king and said, "Your servant
has had shearers come. Will the king and
his attendants please join me?"
25"No, my son," the king replied. "All
of us should not go; we would only be a
burden to you." Although Absalom urged
him, he still refused to go but gave him
his blessing.
26Then Absalom said, "If not, please
let my brother Amnon come with us."
The king asked him, "Why should he

[a] *18* The meaning of the Hebrew for this word is uncertain; also in verse 19.

13:15–17 After the act is complete, Amnon in his hatred wants to drive Tamar away (v. 15). But Israelite law (and presumably earlier Hebrew mores) required that a man who had sexual intercourse with a virgin must marry her. Tamar objects that "sending" her away now will be worse than Amnon's first offense (v. 16)—a reference to the OT provision for divorcing a wife (Dt 24:1). Amnon and Tamar are not married, of course, but Tamar's use of the technical term for divorce is a plea, a reminder that two wrongs do not make a right.
13:18–19 The mention of Tamar's "ornate robe" is interesting because this is the only other example of the expression used to describe Joseph's famous coat (Ge 37:3). Tamar's robe signifies her status as an unmarried princess. Once she tears it, the robe symbolizes the ruin of her life.
13:20–22 Verse 21 states that when David learns what has happened, he is furious. The abrupt ending of the verse is an indictment of his inactivity. It seems likely that David's consciousness of his own guilt paralyzes him. How can he chastise Amnon in light of his own sin? Here he appears the overindulgent father who becomes a passive, silent sufferer throughout the rest of the extended narrative (i.e., through ch. 20). Absalom refuses to speak to Amnon, but he treasures the hatred in his heart (v. 22). The narrative that began with love (vv. 1–2) now ends with hatred (vv. 21–22). At its center stands the act of violence that has turned love into hatred (vv. 14–15).
13:23–36 Absalom's two-year wait, during which he likely nurtures his hatred and plots his revenge, comes to fruition in the murder of Amnon. Though rape is roundly condemned in the OT, the punishment was not murder, and Absalom's actions are totally unjustified. Not unlike David's murder of Uriah, Absalom's execution of Amnon involves cold-blooded intrigue and secrecy.

The expression "all the king's sons" (vv. 23, 29, 30, 33; without "all" in vv. 35, 36) is probably a technical term designating those sons of David besides the crown prince, who is himself in line to inherit the throne. Amnon is the crown prince and the object of Absalom's plot, while the other princes are only a decoy (v. 27). The question of succession to David's kingdom is a theme just below the surface of this text. Amnon's murder serves both to avenge his shameful rape of Tamar and to clear the way for Absalom to claim the royal throne.

go with you?" 27But Absalom urged him,
so he sent with him Amnon and the rest
of the king's sons.
28Absalom[a] ordered his men, "Listen!
When Amnon is in high[b] spirits from
drinking wine and I say to you, 'Strike
Amnon down,' then kill him. Don't be
afraid. Haven't I given you this order?
Be strong and brave.[c]" 29So Absalom's
men did to Amnon what Absalom had
ordered. Then all the king's sons got up,
mounted their mules and fled.
30While they were on their way, the
report came to David: "Absalom has
struck down all the king's sons; not one
of them is left." 31The king stood up, tore[d]
his clothes and lay down on the ground;
and all his attendants stood by with their
clothes torn.
32But Jonadab son of Shimeah, David's
brother, said, "My lord should not think
that they killed all the princes; only Amnon is dead. This has been Absalom's
express intention ever since the day Amnon raped his sister Tamar. 33My lord the
king should not be concerned about the
report that all the king's sons are dead.
Only Amnon is dead."
34Meanwhile, Absalom had fled.
Now the man standing watch looked
up and saw many people on the road
west of him, coming down the side of
the hill. The watchman went and told
the king, "I see men in the direction of
Horonaim, on the side of the hill."[a]
35Jonadab said to the king, "See, the
king's sons have come; it has happened
just as your servant said."
36As he finished speaking, the king's
sons came in, wailing loudly. The king,
too, and all his attendants wept very bitterly.
37Absalom fled and went to Talmai[e]
son of Ammihud, the king of Geshur.
But King David mourned many days for
his son.
38After Absalom fled and went to Geshur, he stayed there three years. 39And
King David longed to go to Absalom,[f]
for he was consoled[g] concerning Amnon's death.

Absalom Returns to Jerusalem

14 Joab[h] son of Zeruiah knew that
the king's heart longed for Absalom. 2So Joab sent someone to Tekoa[i]
and had a wise woman[j] brought from
there. He said to her, "Pretend you are
in mourning. Dress in mourning clothes,
and don't use any cosmetic lotions.[k] Act
like a woman who has spent many days
grieving for the dead. 3Then go to the
king and speak these words to him." And
Joab[l] put the words in her mouth.
4When the woman from Tekoa went[b]
to the king, she fell with her face to the
ground to pay him honor, and she said,
"Help me, Your Majesty!"
5The king asked her, "What is troubling you?"
She said, "I am a widow; my husband is
dead. 6I your servant had two sons. They
got into a fight with each other in the
field, and no one was there to separate
them. One struck the other and killed
him. 7Now the whole clan has risen up
against your servant; they say, 'Hand over
the one who struck his brother down, so
that we may put him to death[m] for the
life of his brother whom he killed; then
we will get rid of the heir[n] as well.' They
would put out the only burning coal I
have left,[o] leaving my husband neither
name nor descendant on the face of the
earth."
8The king said to the woman, "Go
home,[p] and I will issue an order in your
behalf."

13:28 [a]2Sa 3:3 [b]Jdg 19:6, 9, 22; Ru 3:7; 1Sa 25:36 [c]2Sa 12:10
13:31 [d]Nu 14:6; 2Sa 1:11; 12:16
13:37 [e]ver 34; 2Sa 3:3; 14:23, 32
13:39 [f]2Sa 14:13 [g]2Sa 12:19-23
14:1 [h]2Sa 2:18
14:2 [i]2Ch 11:6; Ne 3:5; Jer 6:1; Am 1:1 [j]2Sa 20:16 [k]Ru 3:3; 2Sa 12:20; Isa 1:6
14:3 [l]ver 19
14:7 [m]Nu 35:19 [n]Mt 21:38 [o]Dt 19:10-13
14:8 [p]1Sa 25:35

[a] 34 Septuagint; Hebrew does not have this sentence. [b] 4 Many Hebrew manuscripts, Septuagint, Vulgate and Syriac; most Hebrew manuscripts *spoke*

13:37–39 The narrator gives a brief report of the ensuing three years. Absalom is forced into exile in Geshur. David is incapable of administering justice in his own family, and Absalom is unable to return home. Later David is able to deal with the loss of Amnon and is ready for reconciliation with Absalom.

14:1–20 Being fully aware of David's desire (v. 1), Joab makes arrangements to persuade David that it is acceptable to bring Absalom home. To do so, Joab is in need of a gifted and eloquent actress in order to persuade David to take action. In Tekoa, he finds a remarkable woman noted for her articulate, persuasive speech. Joab supplies the words, the woman the speaking and acting skills.

As supreme judge of the nation, David must have felt an obligation to avenge Amnon's death as required by law. Keeping Absalom safely tucked away in Geshur saved David from any unpleasantness and made it possible for him to avoid taking action. But once he declares that the woman's son will be spared, it suddenly becomes admissible to consider an exception in the case of Absalom.

9But the woman from Tekoa said to
him, "Let my lord the king pardon[q] me
and my family,[r] and let the king and his
throne be without guilt.[s]"
10The king replied, "If anyone says
anything to you, bring them to me, and
they will not bother you again."
11She said, "Then let the king invoke
the LORD his God to prevent the avenger[t]
of blood from adding to the destruction,
so that my son will not be destroyed."
"As surely as the LORD lives," he said,
"not one hair[u] of your son's head will fall
to the ground.[v]"
12Then the woman said, "Let your servant speak a word to my lord the king."
"Speak," he replied.
13The woman said, "Why then have
you devised a thing like this against
the people of God? When the king says
this, does he not convict himself,[w] for
the king has not brought back his banished son?[x] 14Like water[y] spilled on the
ground, which cannot be recovered, so
we must die.[z] But that is not what God
desires; rather, he devises ways so that a
banished person[a] does not remain banished from him.
15"And now I have come to say this to
my lord the king because the people have
made me afraid. Your servant thought,
'I will speak to the king; perhaps he will
grant his servant's request. 16Perhaps
the king will agree to deliver his servant
from the hand of the man who is trying
to cut off both me and my son from God's
inheritance.'[b]
17"And now your servant says, 'May
the word of my lord the king secure
my inheritance, for my lord the king
is like an angel[c] of God in discerning[d]
good and evil. May the LORD your God
be with you.' "
18Then the king said to the woman,
"Don't keep from me the answer to what
I am going to ask you."
"Let my lord the king speak," the woman said.
19The king asked, "Isn't the hand of
Joab[e] with you in all this?"
The woman answered, "As surely as
you live, my lord the king, no one can
turn to the right or to the left from anything my lord the king says. Yes, it was
your servant Joab who instructed me to
do this and who put all these words into
the mouth of your servant. 20Your servant Joab did this to change the present
situation. My lord has wisdom[f] like that
of an angel of God — he knows everything that happens in the land.[g]"
21The king said to Joab, "Very well, I
will do it. Go, bring back the young man
Absalom."
22Joab fell with his face to the ground
to pay him honor, and he blessed the
king.[h] Joab said, "Today your servant
knows that he has found favor in your
eyes, my lord the king, because the king
has granted his servant's request."
23Then Joab went to Geshur and
brought Absalom back to Jerusalem.
24But the king said, "He must go to his
own house; he must not see my face." So
Absalom went to his own house and did
not see the face of the king.
25In all Israel there was not a man so
highly praised for his handsome appearance as Absalom. From the top of his
head to the sole of his foot there was

14:9 [q] 1Sa 25:24 [r] Mt 27:25 [s] 1Sa 25:28; 1Ki 2:33
14:11 [t] Nu 35:12, 21 [u] Mt 10:30 [v] 1Sa 14:45
14:13 [w] 2Sa 12:7; 1Ki 20:40 [x] 2Sa 13:38-39
14:14 [y] Job 14:11; Ps 58:7; Isa 19:5 [z] Job 10:8; 17:13; 30:23; Ps 22:15; Heb 9:27 [a] Nu 35:15, 25-28; Job 34:15
14:16 [b] Ex 34:9; 1Sa 26:19
14:17 [c] ver 20; 1Sa 29:9; 2Sa 19:27 [d] 1Ki 3:9; Da 2:21
14:19 [e] ver 3
14:20 [f] 1Ki 3:12, 28; Isa 28:6 [g] ver 17; 2Sa 18:13; 19:27
14:22 [h] Ge 47:7

14:21–33 The rest of this chapter characterizes Absalom further and prepares us as readers for the tragic events to follow. Absalom's impressive appearance is prelude to his claim to be king. Just as Saul's height and David's manly appearance served them well, so Absalom's striking good looks will serve him well. The physical characteristic of full, thick hair is an important detail that the narrator hopes we will remember (see 18:9). His manipulative and violent treatment of Joab further warns us of an ambitious side to Absalom that does not bode well for the future.

13:1—14:33 The vicious cycle of apparently unending hatred and violence is characteristic of human nature. Our world is filled with examples, each with its own lengthy string of unforgiving acts of violence. From news reports of domestic disputes that turn startlingly violent to the devastating actions and images of international war, we see the darkness of the human heart nearly everywhere we look. The sad fact is that each of us repeats the failures of Adam and Eve in the primeval garden, eating the fruit of the tree of the knowledge of good and evil to learn for ourselves. Thus, each of us contributes to the communal hatred that plagues humankind and constantly threatens to erupt at any moment in self-destructive violence. This is the additional lesson of the story of David's family: All hate-driven violence inflicts as much harm on the avenger as the victim. Amnon and Absalom both come to a violent death, which contributes to our fuller understanding of the nature of sin.

no blemish in him. 26Whenever he cut
the hair of his head[i] — he used to cut his
hair once a year because it became too
heavy for him — he would weigh it, and
its weight was two hundred shekels[a] by
the royal standard.
27Three sons[j] and a daughter were
born to Absalom. His daughter's name
was Tamar,[k] and she became a beautiful
woman.
28Absalom lived two years in Jerusalem without seeing the king's face.
29Then Absalom sent for Joab in order
to send him to the king, but Joab refused
to come to him. So he sent a second time,
but he refused to come. 30Then he said
to his servants, "Look, Joab's field is next
to mine, and he has barley[l] there. Go and
set it on fire." So Absalom's servants set
the field on fire.
31Then Joab did go to Absalom's house,
and he said to him, "Why have your servants set my field on fire?[m]"
32Absalom said to Joab, "Look, I sent
word to you and said, 'Come here so I
can send you to the king to ask, "Why
have I come from Geshur?[n] It would be
better for me if I were still there!"' Now
then, I want to see the king's face, and
if I am guilty of anything, let him put
me to death."[o]
33So Joab went to the king and told
him this. Then the king summoned Absalom, and he came in and bowed down
with his face to the ground before the
king. And the king kissed[p] Absalom.

Absalom's Conspiracy

15 In the course of time,[q] Absalom
provided himself with a chariot[r]
and horses and with fifty men to run
ahead of him. 2He would get up early and
stand by the side of the road leading to
the city gate.[s] Whenever anyone came
with a complaint to be placed before the
king for a decision, Absalom would call
out to him, "What town are you from?"
He would answer, "Your servant is from
one of the tribes of Israel." 3Then Absalom would say to him, "Look, your
claims are valid and proper, but there
is no representative of the king to hear
you."[t] 4And Absalom would add, "If only
I were appointed judge in the land![u] Then
everyone who has a complaint or case
could come to me and I would see that
they receive justice."
5Also, whenever anyone approached
him to bow down before him, Absalom
would reach out his hand, take hold of
him and kiss him. 6Absalom behaved
in this way toward all the Israelites who
came to the king asking for justice, and so
he stole the hearts[v] of the people of Israel.
7At the end of four[b] years, Absalom
said to the king, "Let me go to Hebron
and fulfill a vow I made to the LORD.
8While your servant was living at Geshur[w] in Aram, I made this vow:[x] 'If the
LORD takes me back to Jerusalem, I will
worship the LORD in Hebron.[c]'"
9The king said to him, "Go in peace."
So he went to Hebron.
10Then Absalom sent secret messengers throughout the tribes of Israel to
say, "As soon as you hear the sound of
the trumpets,[y] then say, 'Absalom is king

14:26 [i] 2Sa 18:9; Eze 44:20
14:27 [j] 2Sa 18:18 [k] 2Sa 13:1
14:30 [l] Ex 9:31
14:31 [m] Jdg 15:5
14:32 [n] 2Sa 3:3 [o] 1Sa 20:8
14:33 [p] Ge 33:4; Lk 15:20
15:1 [q] 2Sa 12:11 [r] 1Sa 8:11; 1Ki 1:5
15:2 [s] Ge 23:10; 2Sa 19:8
15:3 [t] Pr 12:2
15:4 [u] Jdg 9:29
15:6 [v] Ro 16:18
15:8 [w] 2Sa 3:3; 13:37-38 [x] Ge 28:20
15:10 [y] 1Ki 1:34, 39; 2Ki 9:13

2Sa 14:33 ❖ When have you experienced reconciliation in a difficult family relationship?

2Sa 15:6 ❖ What happens when we value the praise of people over obedience to God?

[a] *26* That is, about 5 pounds or about 2.3 kilograms [b] *7* Some Septuagint manuscripts, Syriac and Josephus; Hebrew *forty* [c] *8* Some Septuagint manuscripts; Hebrew does not have *in Hebron.*

15:1-12 The theme of this passage is the summarizing statement that Absalom "stole the hearts" of the Israelites (v. 6). The "heart" in OT Hebrew is often the seat of one's intellect as well as one's emotions. This paragraph, then, demonstrates how Absalom strategized in his efforts to deceive and distort what mattered to the people in the attempt to overthrow David.

After four years of building his base, Absalom is now ready to instigate open rebellion against his father (v. 7). He appears as patient and calculated in rebellion as he was in revenge. His request to go to Hebron to fulfill a vow to the Lord sounds suspiciously like his earlier request to allow Amnon his brother to join his sheepshearers at Baal Hazor (13:23-27).

The narrator is clear that the 200 men accompanying Absalom are duped into being present; they do not know about "the matter" (15:11). Once there, they will automatically be associated with the rebellion, and any attempts to walk away from it will be nearly impossible. Ahithophel, a key figure in the story, is introduced into the narrative here for the first time (v. 12). He is a powerful ally because his counsel is valued so highly by both Absalom and David (16:23).

PEOPLE TO KNOW // ABSALOM

2 SAMUEL 15:1–12: Absalom was one of King David's sons. He is introduced as the brother of Tamar, who is described as a beautiful daughter of the king. Amnon, another of David's sons, raped his half sister Tamar, and Absalom had Amnon killed in response to his crime. Absalom then fled from Jerusalem and lived in Geshur for three years (2Sa 13).

After some time, David longed to be reconciled to his son, and Absalom returned to Jerusalem. But Absalom used his good looks and charm to win over the people's love. The Bible describes Absalom's physical beauty and long flowing hair (2Sa 14:25–26). Absalom promoted himself among the people and sowed discontent toward his father David. Once Absalom saw he had won the hearts of the people, he staged a military rebellion in Hebron and announced himself king.

Absalom's support was strong enough that David was forced to flee Jerusalem. Absalom took over the city, even going so far as to have sex with David's concubines on the palace roof. This fulfilled the prophet Nathan's words to David after David's sin with Bathsheba (2Sa 12:11).

Although David was in exile, he had allies in Absalom's court. He was aware when Absalom set out to engage him in battle. Yet David's love for his son was such that he asked his men to spare Absalom's life in the fight. During the conflict Absalom's mule ran under a tree, causing Absalom's abundant hair to become tangled in the branches. Absalom hung helpless while David's commander Joab killed him.

David mourned for his son Absalom, but Joab rebuked David for showing such lack of gratitude toward the men who risked their lives for him. David then returned to Jerusalem as Israel's king once again.

APPLICATION ✚ It seems that David's children paid the price for his lack of good parenting. Amnon, Tamar and Absalom all suffered because David didn't discipline and guide them as he should have. However, even in the face of poor parenting, people are responsible for their actions. Absalom was spoiled and vain. Yet he could have chosen to work on his areas of weakness instead of indulging in actions that he knew were wrong. He chose to use his good looks and charm to betray his own father and usurp Israel's throne. In the end, he found out—as have so many others throughout history—that treachery carries a heavy cost.

in Hebron.'" 11Two hundred men from
Jerusalem had accompanied Absalom.
They had been invited as guests and
went quite innocently, knowing nothing
about the matter. 12While Absalom was
offering sacrifices, he also sent for Ahithophel[z] the Gilonite, David's counselor,[a]
to come from Giloh,[b] his hometown. And
so the conspiracy gained strength, and
Absalom's following kept on increasing.[c]

David Flees

13A messenger came and told David,
"The hearts of the people of Israel are
with Absalom."
14Then David said to all his officials
who were with him in Jerusalem, "Come!
We must flee,[d] or none of us will escape
from Absalom.[e] We must leave immediately, or he will move quickly to overtake
us and bring ruin on us and put the city
to the sword."
15The king's officials answered him,
"Your servants are ready to do whatever
our lord the king chooses."
16The king set out, with his entire
household following him; but he left ten
concubines[f] to take care of the palace.
17So the king set out, with all the people
following him, and they halted at the
edge of the city. 18All his men marched
past him, along with all the Kerethites[g]
and Pelethites; and all the six hundred
Gittites who had accompanied him from
Gath marched before the king.
19The king said to Ittai[h] the Gittite,

15:12 [z] ver 31, 34; 2Sa 16:15, 23; 1Ch 27:33 [a] Job 19:14; Ps 41:9; 55:13; Jer 9:4 [b] Jos 15:51 [c] Ps 3:1
15:14 [d] 2Sa 12:11; 1Ki 2:26; Ps 3 Title; 132:1
[e] 2Sa 19:9
15:16 [f] 2Sa 16:21-22; 20:3
15:18 [g] 1Sa 30:14; 2Sa 8:18; 20:7, 23; 1Ki 1:38, 44; 1Ch 18:17
15:19 [h] 2Sa 18:2

15:13–23 David wisely discerns that he will need time to organize his forces and prepare for a defense against Absalom (v. 14). Though fleeing for his life, David's popularity among the country citizens is apparent by the loud weeping that's heard as he and his entire entourage cross the valley.

The text emphasizes especially the foreign troops who have remained loyal to David over the years. The phrase "Kerethites and Pelethites" points to a royal bodyguard David assembled while living in exile at Ziklag (v. 18). These experienced troops were attached directly to the king and were loyal only to him.

“Why should you come along with us?
Go back and stay with King Absalom.
You are a foreigner,[i] an exile from your
homeland. 20You came only yesterday.
And today shall I make you wander[j]
about with us, when I do not know where
I am going? Go back, and take your people with you. May the LORD show you
kindness and faithfulness.”[a][k]
21But Ittai replied to the king, “As surely as the LORD lives, and as my lord the
king lives, wherever my lord the king
may be, whether it means life or death,
there will your servant be.”[l]
22David said to Ittai, “Go ahead, march
on.” So Ittai the Gittite marched on with
all his men and the families that were
with him.
23The whole countryside wept aloud as
all the people passed by. The king also
crossed the Kidron Valley,[m] and all the
people moved on toward the wilderness.
24Zadok[n] was there, too, and all the Levites who were with him were carrying
the ark[o] of the covenant of God. They
set down the ark of God, and Abiathar[p]
offered sacrifices until all the people had
finished leaving the city.
25Then the king said to Zadok, “Take
the ark of God back into the city. If I find
favor in the LORD’s eyes, he will bring me
back and let me see it and his dwelling
place[q] again. 26But if he says, ‘I am not
pleased with you,’ then I am ready; let
him do to me whatever seems good to
him.[r]”
27The king also said to Zadok the
priest, “Do you understand?[s] Go back
to the city with my blessing. Take your
son Ahimaaz with you, and also Abiathar’s son Jonathan.[t] You and Abiathar
return with your two sons. 28I will wait
at the fords[u] in the wilderness until word
comes from you to inform me.” 29So Zadok and Abiathar took the ark of God
back to Jerusalem and stayed there.
30But David continued up the Mount
of Olives, weeping[v] as he went; his head[w]
was covered and he was barefoot. All the
people with him covered their heads too
and were weeping as they went up. 31Now
David had been told, “Ahithophel[x] is
among the conspirators with Absalom.”
So David prayed, “LORD, turn Ahithophel’s counsel into foolishness.”
32When David arrived at the summit,
where people used to worship God, Hushai the Arkite[y] was there to meet him,
his robe torn and dust[z] on his head.
33David said to him, “If you go with me,
you will be a burden[a] to me. 34But if you
return to the city and say to Absalom,
‘Your Majesty, I will be your servant; I
was your father’s servant in the past, but
now I will be your servant,’[b] then you
can help me by frustrating Ahithophel’s
advice. 35Won’t the priests Zadok and
Abiathar be there with you? Tell them
anything you hear in the king’s palace.[c]
36Their two sons, Ahimaaz son of Zadok
and Jonathan[d] son of Abiathar, are there
with them. Send them to me with anything you hear.”
37So Hushai,[e] David’s confidant, arrived

15:19 [i] Ge 31:15
15:20 [j] 1Sa 23:13 [k] 2Sa 2:6
15:21 [l] Ru 1:16-17; Pr 17:17
15:23 [m] 2Ch 29:16
15:24 [n] 2Sa 8:17 [o] Nu 4:15 [p] 1Sa 22:20
15:25 [q] Ex 15:13; Ps 43:3; Jer 25:30
15:26 [r] 1Sa 3:18; 2Sa 22:20; 1Ki 10:9
15:27 [s] 1Sa 9:9 [t] 2Sa 17:17
15:28 [u] 2Sa 17:16
15:30 [v] 2Sa 19:4; Ps 126:6 [w] Est 6:12; Isa 20:2-4
15:31 [x] ver 12; 2Sa 16:23; 17:14,23
15:32 [y] Jos 16:2 [z] 2Sa 1:2
15:33 [a] 2Sa 19:35
15:34 [b] 2Sa 16:19
15:35 [c] 2Sa 17:15-16
15:36 [d] ver 27; 2Sa 17:17
15:37 [e] 2Sa 16:16-17; 1Ch 27:33

[a] 20 Septuagint; Hebrew *May kindness and faithfulness be with you*

15:24–30 The next portion of the narrative continues David’s flight from the city. Now begins the series of so-called meeting scenes. David first encounters Zadok the priest, then Hushai, Ziba, and Shimei. The action is delayed while important speeches carry forward the relevant ideas in this unit.

These scenes portray David’s reactions under fire. David calmly works through his grief with resolve and wisdom, always with a righteous respect for Yahweh’s will. He is a man of great faith but also of great planning and strategy. He is being humbled by the course of political events, but he need not be naïve.

15:25–26 David’s resignation is not simple fatalism. Rather, he seems to acknowledge the events as the just punishment for his sins, and he submits to the will of God, whatever the outcome. At this sad moment in his life, David is not the least bit grasping or manipulative. He appears utterly submissive to Yahweh’s will.

15:27–30 David’s decision to send the ark of the covenant back into Jerusalem illustrates that he has learned to see beyond personal ambition and accomplishment. He would rather be right in his relationship with Yahweh than be the winner of this conflict. He refuses to turn possession of the ark to political advantage, but he humbly trusts God to do what is best in his life.

15:31 As if David needs more bad news, he learns that his trusted counselor, Ahithophel, is among the conspirators. But again, we see a combination of faith and strategy in David’s prayer that Yahweh will turn Ahithophel’s counsel—otherwise always dependable—into foolishness.

15:32–37 David’s arrangement with Hushai the Arkite has him returning to Jerusalem prepared to serve as a double agent. He will offer his services to Absalom, but his mission will be to counter the advice of Ahithophel. David also informs Hushai of the ring of priestly spies prepared to carry the information to the king in the desert (vv. 27–28). The suspense and intrigue begin to build.

at Jerusalem as Absalom[f] was entering the city.

David and Ziba

16 When David had gone a short distance beyond the summit, there was Ziba,[g] the steward of Mephibosheth, waiting to meet him. He had a string of donkeys saddled and loaded with two hundred loaves of bread, a hundred cakes of raisins, a hundred cakes of figs and a skin of wine.[h]

2The king asked Ziba, "Why have you brought these?"

Ziba answered, "The donkeys are for the king's household to ride on, the bread and fruit are for the men to eat, and the wine is to refresh[i] those who become exhausted in the wilderness."

3The king then asked, "Where is your master's grandson?"[j]

Ziba said to him, "He is staying in Jerusalem, because he thinks, 'Today the Israelites will restore to me my grandfather's kingdom.'"

4Then the king said to Ziba, "All that belonged to Mephibosheth is now yours."

"I humbly bow," Ziba said. "May I find favor in your eyes, my lord the king."

Shimei Curses David

5As King David approached Bahurim,[k] a man from the same clan as Saul's family came out from there. His name was Shimei[l] son of Gera, and he cursed[m] as he came out. 6He pelted David and all the king's officials with stones, though all the troops and the special guard were on David's right and left. 7As he cursed, Shimei said, "Get out, get out, you murderer, you scoundrel! 8The LORD has repaid you for all the blood you shed in the household of Saul, in whose place you have reigned.[n] The LORD has given the kingdom into the hands of your son Absalom. You have come to ruin because you are a murderer!"

9Then Abishai[o] son of Zeruiah said to the king, "Why should this dead dog curse my lord the king? Let me go over and cut off his head."[p]

10But the king said, "What does this have to do with you, you sons of Zeruiah?[q] If he is cursing because the LORD said to him, 'Curse David,' who can ask, 'Why do you do this?'"[r]

11David then said to Abishai and all his officials, "My son,[s] my own flesh and blood, is trying to kill me. How much more, then, this Benjamite! Leave him alone; let him curse, for the LORD has told him to.[t] 12It may be that the LORD will look upon my misery[u] and restore to me his covenant blessing[v] instead of his curse today.[w]"

13So David and his men continued along the road while Shimei was going along the hillside opposite him, cursing as he went and throwing stones at him and showering him with dirt. 14The king and all the people with him arrived at their destination exhausted.[x] And there he refreshed himself.

The Advice of Ahithophel and Hushai

15Meanwhile, Absalom[y] and all the men of Israel came to Jerusalem, and Ahithophel[z] was with him. 16Then Hushai[a] the

> **2Sa 16:16** ❖ When might it be okay to lie or deceive for a good cause? Are there times when deceit is the best course of action?

15:37 [f] 2Sa 16:15
16:1 [g] 2Sa 9:1-13 [h] 1Sa 25:18
16:2 [i] 2Sa 17:27-29
16:3 [j] 2Sa 9:9-10; 19:26-27
16:5 [k] 2Sa 3:16 [l] 2Sa 19:16-23; 1Ki 2:8-9,36,44 [m] Ex 22:28
16:8 [n] 2Sa 21:9
16:9 [o] 2Sa 9:8 [p] Ex 22:28; Lk 9:54
16:10 [q] 2Sa 19:22 [r] Ro 9:20
16:11 [s] 2Sa 12:11 [t] Ge 45:5
16:12 [u] Ps 4:1; 25:18 [v] Dt 23:5; Ro 8:28 [w] Ps 109:28
16:14 [x] 2Sa 17:2
16:15 [y] 2Sa 15:37 [z] 2Sa 15:12
16:16 [a] 2Sa 15:37

16:1–4 Just beyond the summit of the Mount of Olives, David meets Ziba. The picture of a representative of Saul's house meeting and supporting David at this moment is somehow ironic. David is, after all, running from his own son, just as he once ran from Saul. This image contributes to the theme of loyalty in this extended narrative. Who is loyal to whom?

16:5–14 As the king and his entourage pass his town, Shimei, in an act also related to the house of Saul, takes the opportunity to pour down on them insults, dirt, and stones. It seems likely that Shimei is expressing the resentment of others who felt David's rise to power was illegitimate and not condoned by Yahweh.

David reacts humbly and indicates that now is not the time for further violence, especially against the family of Saul, the former anointed of Yahweh. David wants to be submissive to the Lord's will in every respect. Perhaps this curse is itself from God (vv. 10–11). Even these many years after Saul's death and in such extreme circumstances in which his own son and close advisers have proven disloyal, David by contrast remains loyal to Saul, the anointed of the Lord, and to Yahweh's will, whatever his own fate.

16:15–16 The opening paragraph reminds us of the narrative's central theme—that is, loyalty. Upon learning that his trusted counselor failed to remain loyal, David prayed that the Lord would turn Ahithophel's counsel into foolishness, and he sent Hushai to make it possible (15:31–37). Now the question becomes: Will Hushai be loyal, or will he too join the conspiracy?

Arkite, David's confidant, went to Absalom and said to him, "Long live the king!
Long live the king!"
17 Absalom said to Hushai, "So this is
the love you show your friend? If he's
your friend, why didn't you go with
him?"[b]
18 Hushai said to Absalom, "No, the one
chosen by the LORD, by these people, and
by all the men of Israel — his I will be,
and I will remain with him. 19 Furthermore, whom should I serve? Should I
not serve the son? Just as I served your
father, so I will serve you."[c]
20 Absalom said to Ahithophel, "Give us
your advice. What should we do?"
21 Ahithophel answered, "Sleep with
your father's concubines whom he left to
take care of the palace. Then all Israel will
hear that you have made yourself obnoxious to your father, and the hands of everyone with you will be more resolute."
22 So they pitched a tent for Absalom on
the roof, and he slept with his father's
concubines in the sight of all Israel.[d]
23 Now in those days the advice[e] Ahithophel gave was like that of one who inquires of God. That was how both David[f]
and Absalom regarded all of Ahithophel's
advice.

17 Ahithophel said to Absalom, "I
would[a] choose twelve thousand
men and set out tonight in pursuit of
David. 2 I would attack him while he is
weary and weak.[g] I would strike him with
terror, and then all the people with him
will flee. I would strike down only the
king[h] 3 and bring all the people back to
you. The death of the man you seek will
mean the return of all; all the people will
be unharmed." 4 This plan seemed good
to Absalom and to all the elders of Israel.
5 But Absalom said, "Summon also Hushai[i] the Arkite, so we can hear what he
has to say as well." 6 When Hushai came
to him, Absalom said, "Ahithophel has
given this advice. Should we do what he
says? If not, give us your opinion."
7 Hushai replied to Absalom, "The advice Ahithophel has given is not good
this time. 8 You know your father and his
men; they are fighters, and as fierce as
a wild bear robbed of her cubs.[j] Besides,
your father is an experienced fighter;[k] he
will not spend the night with the troops.
9 Even now, he is hidden in a cave or some
other place.[l] If he should attack your
troops first,[b] whoever hears about it will
say, 'There has been a slaughter among
the troops who follow Absalom.' 10 Then
even the bravest soldier, whose heart is
like the heart of a lion,[m] will melt[n] with
fear, for all Israel knows that your father
is a fighter and that those with him are
brave.[o]
11 "So I advise you: Let all Israel, from
Dan to Beersheba[p] — as numerous as the
sand[q] on the seashore — be gathered to
you, with you yourself leading them
into battle. 12 Then we will attack him

16:17 [b] 2Sa 19:25
16:19 [c] 2Sa 15:34
16:22 [d] 2Sa 12:11-12; 15:16
16:23 [e] 2Sa 17:14,23 [f] 2Sa 15:12
17:2 [g] 2Sa 16:14
[h] 1Ki 22:31; Zec 13:7
17:5 [i] 2Sa 15:32
17:8 [j] Hos 13:8 [k] 1Sa 16:18
17:9 [l] Jer 41:9
17:10 [m] 1Ch 12:8 [n] Jos 2:9, 11; Eze 21:15 [o] 2Sa 23:8; 1Ch 11:11
17:11 [p] Jdg 20:1 [q] Ge 12:2; 22:17; Jos 11:4

[a] 1 Or *Let me* [b] 9 Or *When some of the men fall at the first attack*

When Hushai meets Absalom, he repeats the standard loyalty oath (16:16): "Long live the king!" In this context, the expression raises further the question: Does Hushai intend to support Absalom or David? By pledging loyalty to "the king," does he mean the young usurper king or the banished King David?

16:17–19 Absalom may have become suspicious, so he pushes Hushai further about his loyalty to David (v. 17). Absalom's question puts Hushai in a tight spot. His response is the picture of diplomacy, and it admirably convinces Absalom that Hushai is wise and can be trusted (vv. 18–19).

16:20–23 Hushai's task is a difficult one. Ahithophel's counsel is nearly always right, as though God himself has spoken from Mount Sinai (v. 23). His first piece of advice is rather strange: Absalom should appear publicly sleeping with David's royal harem (v. 21). Sexual relations with a king's wife or concubine was equivalent to claiming that king's throne. Absalom quickly obeys Ahithophel's advice, which is also the fulfillment of Nathan's pronouncement to David in 12:11–12. This act must have given the impression to the inhabitants of Jerusalem that the insurrection was in fact successful, and Absalom is king (16:22). It also constitutes a definite and irreversible break between Absalom and David. Here we see again that David continues to reap what he has sown.

17:1–14 The conflict between Ahithophel's counsel (16:20—17:4) and Hushai's (17:5–14) is carefully explained to increase the tension in this story. Ahithophel advocates striking while David's position is weakened, while Hushai argues that only a carefully planned and well-staffed attack will be successful against so experienced an opponent as David. Hushai's speech is once again impressive, and Absalom and all the men of Israel are persuaded. Ahithophel's advice is disregarded (v. 14a).

However, lest we place too much credit on Hushai's rhetorical abilities, the narrator intrudes with a rare, explicitly stated theological assessment (v. 14b). This pronouncement is the turning point—the moment at which the reader learns how the story will end. God has acted, and we have only to follow the course of events as Absalom's otherwise successful rebellion comes to ruin and David is restored to the throne.

wherever he may be found, and we will
fall on him as dew settles on the ground.
Neither he nor any of his men will be left
alive. 13If he withdraws into a city, then
all Israel will bring ropes to that city, and
we will drag it down to the valley[r] until
not so much as a pebble is left."
14Absalom and all the men of Israel
said, "The advice[s] of Hushai the Arkite
is better than that of Ahithophel."[t] For
the LORD had determined to frustrate[u]
the good advice of Ahithophel in order
to bring disaster[v] on Absalom.[w]
15Hushai told Zadok and Abiathar, the
priests, "Ahithophel has advised Absalom
and the elders of Israel to do such and
such, but I have advised them to do so
and so. 16Now send a message at once
and tell David, 'Do not spend the night
at the fords in the wilderness;[x] cross over
without fail, or the king and all the people with him will be swallowed up.[y]' "
17Jonathan[z] and Ahimaaz were staying
at En Rogel.[a] A female servant was to go
and inform them, and they were to go
and tell King David, for they could not
risk being seen entering the city. 18But
a young man saw them and told Absalom. So the two of them left at once and
went to the house of a man in Bahurim.[b]
He had a well in his courtyard, and they
climbed down into it. 19His wife took a
covering and spread it out over the opening of the well and scattered grain over
it. No one knew anything about it.[c]
20When Absalom's men came to the
woman[d] at the house, they asked, "Where
are Ahimaaz and Jonathan?"
The woman answered them, "They
crossed over the brook."[a] The men
searched but found no one, so they returned to Jerusalem.
21After they had gone, the two climbed
out of the well and went to inform King
David. They said to him, "Set out and
cross the river at once; Ahithophel has

17:13 [r] Mic 1:6
17:14 [s] 2Sa 16:23 [t] 2Sa 15:12 [u] 2Sa 15:34; Ne 4:15 [v] Ps 9:16 [w] 2Ch 10:8
17:16 [x] 2Sa 15:28 [y] 2Sa 15:35
17:17 [z] 2Sa 15:27, 36 [a] Jos 15:7; 18:16
17:18 [b] 2Sa 3:16; 16:5
17:19 [c] Jos 2:6
17:20 [d] Ex 1:19; Jos 2:3-5; 1Sa 19:12-17
17:23 [e] 2Sa 15:12; 16:23 [f] 2Ki 20:1; Mt 27:5
17:24 [g] Ge 32:2; 2Sa 2:8
17:25 [h] 2Sa 19:13; 20:4,9-12; 1Ki 2:5,32; 1Ch 12:18 [i] 1Ch 2:13-17
17:27 [j] 1Sa 11:1 [k] Dt 3:11; 2Sa 10:1-2; 12:26,29 [l] 2Sa 9:4 [m] 2Sa 19:31-39; 1Ki 2:7 [n] 2Sa 19:31; Ezr 2:61
17:29 [o] 1Ch 12:40 [p] 2Sa 16:2; Ro 12:13

2Sa 17:27–29 ❖ How can we help meet the material needs of those around us?

advised such and such against you." 22So
David and all the people with him set out
and crossed the Jordan. By daybreak, no
one was left who had not crossed the
Jordan.
23When Ahithophel saw that his advice[e] had not been followed, he saddled
his donkey and set out for his house in
his hometown. He put his house in order[f]
and then hanged himself. So he died and
was buried in his father's tomb.

Absalom's Death

24David went to Mahanaim,[g] and Absalom crossed the Jordan with all the
men of Israel. 25Absalom had appointed
Amasa[h] over the army in place of Joab.
Amasa was the son of Jether,[b][i] an Ishmaelite[c] who had married Abigail,[d] the
daughter of Nahash and sister of Zeruiah
the mother of Joab. 26The Israelites and
Absalom camped in the land of Gilead.
27When David came to Mahanaim, Sho-
bi son of Nahash[j] from Rabbah[k] of the
Ammonites, and Makir[l] son of Ammiel
from Lo Debar, and Barzillai[m] the Gileadite[n] from Rogelim 28brought bedding
and bowls and articles of pottery. They
also brought wheat and barley, flour and
roasted grain, beans and lentils,[e] 29honey
and curds, sheep, and cheese from cows'
milk for David and his people to eat.[o]
For they said, "The people have become
exhausted and hungry and thirsty in the
wilderness.[p]"

[a] 20 Or *"They passed by the sheep pen toward the water."* [b] 25 Hebrew *Ithra,* a variant of *Jether* [c] 25 Some Septuagint manuscripts (see also 1 Chron. 2:17); Hebrew and other Septuagint manuscripts *Israelite* [d] 25 Hebrew *Abigal,* a variant of *Abigail* [e] 28 Most Septuagint manuscripts and Syriac; Hebrew *lentils, and roasted grain*

17:15–22 This passage shows David's espionage ring in action. The sons of Zadok and Abiathar are well positioned to take reports of Ahithophel's advice to David (see 15:27–29, 35–36). The two younger priests narrowly escape capture, and they successfully reach David with the vital information. David and everyone with him cross the river and head to Mahanaim in order to prepare for the coming battle (17:22).

17:23 The brief note on Ahithophel's disgraceful death is surprising. We can only assume this seasoned politician realizes his cause is irreversibly lost once Absalom rejects his advice. David's prayer has been answered (15:31).

17:24–29 Absalom and "all the men of Israel" enter the Transjordan and set up camp in Gilead. Interestingly, Mahanaim was the center of Ish-Bosheth's power (2:8–9), and the northern Transjordan area was important for Saul's reign. The irony of David escaping from Absalom and finding shelter here is heightened when he is met by friendly local authorities who support him and his troops with much-needed provisions.

18 David mustered the men who were with him and appointed over them commanders of thousands and commanders of hundreds. 2 David sent out his troops,[q] a third under the command of Joab, a third under Joab's brother Abishai[r] son of Zeruiah, and a third under Ittai[s] the Gittite. The king told the troops, "I myself will surely march out with you."

3 But the men said, "You must not go out; if we are forced to flee, they won't care about us. Even if half of us die, they won't care; but you are worth ten[t] thousand of us.[a] It would be better now for you to give us support from the city."[u]

4 The king answered, "I will do whatever seems best to you."

So the king stood beside the gate while all his men marched out in units of hundreds and of thousands. 5 The king commanded Joab, Abishai and Ittai, "Be gentle with the young man Absalom for my sake." And all the troops heard the king giving orders concerning Absalom to each of the commanders.

6 David's army marched out of the city to fight Israel, and the battle took place in the forest[v] of Ephraim. 7 There Israel's troops were routed by David's men, and the casualties that day were great — twenty thousand men. 8 The battle spread out over the whole countryside, and the forest swallowed up more men that day than the sword.

9 Now Absalom happened to meet David's men. He was riding his mule, and as the mule went under the thick branches of a large oak, Absalom's hair[w] got caught in the tree. He was left hanging in midair, while the mule he was riding kept on going.

10 When one of the men saw what had happened, he told Joab, "I just saw Absalom hanging in an oak tree."

11 Joab said to the man who had told him this, "What! You saw him? Why didn't you strike[x] him to the ground right there? Then I would have had to give you ten shekels[b] of silver and a warrior's belt.[y]"

12 But the man replied, "Even if a thousand shekels[c] were weighed out into my hands, I would not lay a hand on the king's son. In our hearing the king commanded you and Abishai and Ittai, 'Protect the young man Absalom for my sake.[d]' 13 And if I had put my life in jeopardy[e] — and nothing is hidden from the king[z] — you would have kept your distance from me."

14 Joab[a] said, "I'm not going to wait like this for you." So he took three javelins in his hand and plunged them into Absalom's heart while Absalom was still alive in the oak tree. 15 And ten of Joab's armor-bearers surrounded Absalom, struck him and killed him.[b]

16 Then Joab[c] sounded the trumpet, and the troops stopped pursuing Israel, for Joab halted them. 17 They took

18:2 [q] Jdg 7:16; 1Sa 11:11 [r] 1Sa 26:6 [s] 2Sa 15:19
18:3 [t] 1Sa 18:7 [u] 2Sa 21:17
18:6 [v] Jos 17:18
18:9 [w] 2Sa 14:26
18:11 [x] 2Sa 3:39 [y] 1Sa 18:4
18:13 [z] 2Sa 14:19-20
18:14 [a] 2Sa 2:18; 14:30
18:15 [b] 2Sa 12:10
18:16 [c] 2Sa 2:28; 20:22

2Sa 18:14 ❖ How did Absalom's death affect the life of David? How has the treachery and fall of a close friend or family member affected your life?

[a] 3 Two Hebrew manuscripts, some Septuagint manuscripts and Vulgate; most Hebrew manuscripts *care; for now there are ten thousand like us* [b] 11 That is, about 4 ounces or about 115 grams [c] 12 That is, about 25 pounds or about 12 kilograms [d] 12 A few Hebrew manuscripts, Septuagint, Vulgate and Syriac; most Hebrew manuscripts may be translated *Absalom, whoever you may be.* [e] 13 Or *Otherwise, if I had acted treacherously toward him*

18:1–5 Apparently Hushai's delay tactics have given David enough time to reach the safety of Mahanaim. He originally planned to join the troops in the field but is deterred by their pleas that he will be worth more in the city than in the field of battle (v. 3).

18:6–8 The account of the actual battle is brief. The rebellion has a superior force, and it appears to command an impressive advantage. The significance of the "forest of Ephraim," however, is clear: It is difficult terrain for fighting and gives the advantage to David's men (v. 8).

18:9 The historian tells us that Absalom's hair is caught in a tree and the mule rides on, leaving him dangling. The symbolism of Absalom's predicament is clear: As Absalom has lost his mule from under him, so he has also lost his royal seat. There may be further symbolism intended in Absalom's suspension "between heaven and earth" (another possible translation of NIV "in midair"). His rebellion has left him without the ground beneath his feet, unable to fulfill his life as prince or king and incapable of serving in the kingdom of God.

18:10–20 David's prebattle instructions are preoccupied with Absalom's safekeeping (v. 5). Once Absalom is captured, one of Joab's men reminds him of David's concerns (v. 12).

When Joab sends a Cushite to David with the news of Absalom's death, one recalls the story of the Amalekite who reported Saul's death (1:1–16). Joab takes no chances here. This will not be good news for David, and he refuses to send Ahimaaz son of Zadok (18:19–20).

PEOPLE TO KNOW // JOAB

2 SAMUEL 18:14–15: Joab was King David's army commander and nephew. Joab and his brothers were all warriors and demonstrated their valor and military strength in battle. Because Joab was David's army commander, he was with David at many of the significant events of David's reign. When David committed adultery with Bathsheba and she became pregnant, David sent Joab instructions to ensure Uriah's death on the battlefield (2Sa 11:14–15). When David's son Absalom killed his brother Amnon, Absalom fled to Geshur. Knowing David longed to see Absalom again, Joab orchestrated their reunion (2Sa 14:1–23). Shortly thereafter, Absalom rebelled and announced himself king. Joab led David's men against Absalom's forces, killing Absalom in battle. David mourned for his son, but Joab rebuked the king for not showing gratitude to his soldiers, who had risked their lives for him.

When David was old and nearing death, his son Adonijah tried to make himself king instead of Solomon. Joab chose to support Adonijah as king (1Ki 1:7). For this act, David instructed Solomon to ensure Joab's death. In the hope of saving his own life, Joab ran into God's tabernacle, but Solomon told his officer Benaiah to strike him down and kill him where he stood (1Ki 2:34).

APPLICATION ✣ Joab was a man of war and viewed the world through the lens of warfare, vengeance and power. Against David's wishes, he killed Abner (2Sa 3:27), Absalom (2Sa 18:14–15) and Amasa (2Sa 20:9–10). Joab also supported Adonijah as king instead of Solomon—an allegiance that led to his death.

Joab's life shows the old truth that those who live by the sword often die by it (see Mt 26:52). While Joab did much to help David, he failed to recognize God's anointed power on David's dynasty, which was passed through Solomon. Godly leadership does not win through violence and earthly power; it brings transformation through righteousness and justice.

Absalom, threw him into a big pit in the
forest and piled up[d] a large heap of rocks[e]
over him. Meanwhile, all the Israelites
fled to their homes.
18During his lifetime Absalom had tak-
en a pillar and erected it in the King's
Valley[f] as a monument[g] to himself, for
he thought, "I have no son[h] to carry on
the memory of my name." He named
the pillar after himself, and it is called
Absalom's Monument to this day.

David Mourns

19Now Ahimaaz[i] son of Zadok said,
"Let me run and take the news to the
king that the LORD has vindicated him
by delivering him from the hand of his
enemies.[j]"
20"You are not the one to take the news
today," Joab told him. "You may take the
news another time, but you must not do
so today, because the king's son is dead."
21Then Joab said to a Cushite, "Go, tell
the king what you have seen." The Cushite bowed down before Joab and ran off.
22Ahimaaz son of Zadok again said to
Joab, "Come what may, please let me run
behind the Cushite."
But Joab replied, "My son, why do you
want to go? You don't have any news that
will bring you a reward."
23He said, "Come what may, I want to
run."
So Joab said, "Run!" Then Ahimaaz
ran by way of the plain[a] and outran the
Cushite.
24While David was sitting between the
inner and outer gates, the watchman[k]
went up to the roof of the gateway by

18:17 [d] Jos 7:26 [e] Jos 8:29
18:18 [f] Ge 14:17 [g] Ge 50:5; Nu 32:42; 1Sa 15:12 [h] 2Sa 14:27
18:19 [i] 2Sa 15:36 [j] ver 31; Jdg 11:36
18:24 [k] 1Sa 14:16; 2Sa 19:8; 2Ki 9:17; Jer 51:12

[a] 23 That is, the plain of the Jordan

18:19—19:4 The account of the two messengers running to David slowly builds suspense as we are forced to wait for David's reactions (18:19—19:7). Ahimaaz appears to have been genuinely ignorant about the specifics of Absalom's death (18:29). When he is forced to "stand aside" (18:30) and wait for the Cushite to deliver the vital piece of missing information, we as readers are also left waiting for the moment when David learns of Absalom's death. David's powerful sense of loss (18:33) towers over the landscape of this narrative, turning the army's spectacular military achievement into defeat (19:2). His anguished "my son" is repeated five times in 18:33 (and another three times in 19:4) and reflects David's inconsolable attempt to comprehend the loss.

the wall. As he looked out, he saw a man
running alone. 25The watchman called
out to the king and reported it.
The king said, "If he is alone, he must
have good news." And the runner came
closer and closer.
26Then the watchman saw another
runner, and he called down to the gatekeeper, "Look, another man running
alone!"
The king said, "He must be bringing
good news,[l] too."
27The watchman said, "It seems to me
that the first one runs like[m] Ahimaaz
son of Zadok."
"He's a good man," the king said. "He
comes with good news."
28Then Ahimaaz called out to the king,
"All is well!" He bowed down before the
king with his face to the ground and said,
"Praise be to the LORD your God! He has
delivered up those who lifted their hands
against my lord the king."
29The king asked, "Is the young man
Absalom safe?"
Ahimaaz answered, "I saw great confusion just as Joab was about to send the
king's servant and me, your servant, but
I don't know what it was."
30The king said, "Stand aside and wait
here." So he stepped aside and stood
there.
31Then the Cushite arrived and said,
"My lord the king, hear the good news!
The LORD has vindicated you today by
delivering you from the hand of all who
rose up against you."
32The king asked the Cushite, "Is the
young man Absalom safe?"
The Cushite replied, "May the enemies
of my lord the king and all who rise up
to harm you be like that young man."[n]
33The king was shaken. He went up to
the room over the gateway and wept. As
he went, he said: "O my son Absalom!
My son, my son Absalom! If only I had
died[o] instead of you — O Absalom, my
son, my son!"[a][p]

19[b] Joab was told, "The king is weeping and mourning for Absalom."
2And for the whole army the victory that
day was turned into mourning, because
on that day the troops heard it said, "The
king is grieving for his son." 3The men
stole into the city that day as men steal
in who are ashamed when they flee from
battle. 4The king covered his face and
cried aloud, "O my son Absalom! O Absalom, my son, my son!"
5Then Joab went into the house to the
king and said, "Today you have humiliated all your men, who have just saved
your life and the lives of your sons and
daughters and the lives of your wives and
concubines. 6You love those who hate
you and hate those who love you. You
have made it clear today that the commanders and their men mean nothing
to you. I see that you would be pleased
if Absalom were alive today and all of us
were dead. 7Now go out and encourage
your men. I swear by the LORD that if
you don't go out, not a man will be left
with you by nightfall. This will be worse
for you than all the calamities that have
come on you from your youth till now."[q]
8So the king got up and took his seat
in the gateway. When the men were told,
"The king is sitting in the gateway,[r]" they
all came before him.
Meanwhile, the Israelites had fled to
their homes.

David Returns to Jerusalem

9Throughout the tribes of Israel, all the
people were arguing among themselves,
saying, "The king delivered us from the
hand of our enemies; he is the one who
rescued us from the hand of the Philistines.[s] But now he has fled the country
to escape from Absalom;[t] 10and Absalom,
whom we anointed to rule over us, has
died in battle. So why do you say nothing
about bringing the king back?"
11King David sent this message to

18:26 [l] 1Ki 1:42; Isa 52:7; 61:1
18:27 [m] 2Ki 9:20
18:32 [n] Jdg 5:31; 1Sa 25:26
18:33 [o] Ex 32:32 [p] Ge 43:14; 2Sa 19:4; Ro 9:3
19:7 [q] Pr 14:28
19:8 [r] 2Sa 15:2
19:9 [s] 2Sa 8:1-14 [t] 2Sa 15:14

2Sa 19:7-8 ❖ When does leadership responsibility eclipse personal concerns? How can leaders lead well in the face of difficulty?

[a] *33* In Hebrew texts this verse (18:33) is numbered 19:1. [b] In Hebrew texts 19:1-43 is numbered 19:2-44.

19:5–7 Life must go on, even if David cannot bear to imagine it without Absalom. Joab takes the role of the realist, who convinces David to continue with life without trying to talk him out of his grief.
19:8b–10 Now that Absalom is dead, the pro-David voices among the northern tribes argue that they should move quickly to bring David back into power in Jerusalem (vv. 9–10).
19:11–15 Judah is apparently slower to act, and David realizes he can never rule effectively in Jerusalem

Zadok[u] and Abiathar, the priests: "Ask
the elders of Judah, 'Why should you
be the last to bring the king back to his
palace, since what is being said throughout Israel has reached the king at his
quarters? 12You are my relatives, my own
flesh and blood. So why should you be
the last to bring back the king?' 13And
say to Amasa,[v] 'Are you not my own flesh
and blood?[w] May God deal with me, be
it ever so severely,[x] if you are not the
commander of my army for life in place
of Joab.[y]' "

14He won over the hearts of the men of
Judah so that they were all of one mind.
They sent word to the king, "Return, you
and all your men." 15Then the king returned and went as far as the Jordan.

Now the men of Judah had come to
Gilgal[z] to go out and meet the king and
bring him across the Jordan. 16Shimei[a]
son of Gera, the Benjamite from Bahurim, hurried down with the men of Judah to meet King David. 17With him were
a thousand Benjamites, along with Ziba,[b]
the steward of Saul's household,[c] and his
fifteen sons and twenty servants. They
rushed to the Jordan, where the king
was. 18They crossed at the ford to take the
king's household over and to do whatever he wished.

When Shimei son of Gera crossed the
Jordan, he fell prostrate before the king
19and said to him, "May my lord not hold
me guilty. Do not remember how your
servant did wrong on the day my lord the
king left Jerusalem.[d] May the king put
it out of his mind. 20For I your servant
know that I have sinned, but today I have
come here as the first from the tribes
of Joseph to come down and meet my
lord the king."

21Then Abishai[e] son of Zeruiah said,
"Shouldn't Shimei be put to death for
this? He cursed[f] the LORD's anointed."[g]

22David replied, "What does this have
to do with you, you sons of Zeruiah?[h]
What right do you have to interfere?
Should anyone be put to death in Israel today?[i] Don't I know that today I am
king over Israel?" 23So the king said to
Shimei, "You shall not die." And the king
promised him on oath.[j]

24Mephibosheth,[k] Saul's grandson, also
went down to meet the king. He had not
taken care of his feet or trimmed his
mustache or washed his clothes from
the day the king left until the day he
returned safely. 25When he came from
Jerusalem to meet the king, the king
asked him, "Why didn't you go with me,[l]
Mephibosheth?"

26He said, "My lord the king, since I
your servant am lame,[m] I said, 'I will
have my donkey saddled and will ride
on it, so I can go with the king.' But Ziba[n]
my servant betrayed me. 27And he has
slandered your servant to my lord the
king. My lord the king is like an angel[o]
of God; so do whatever you wish. 28All
my grandfather's descendants deserved
nothing but death[p] from my lord the
king, but you gave your servant a place
among those who eat at your table.[q] So
what right do I have to make any more
appeals to the king?"

29The king said to him, "Why say
more? I order you and Ziba to divide
the land."

30Mephibosheth said to the king, "Let
him take everything, now that my lord
the king has returned home safely."

31Barzillai[r] the Gileadite also came
down from Rogelim to cross the Jordan
with the king and to send him on his way
from there. 32Now Barzillai was very old,
eighty years of age. He had provided for
the king during his stay in Mahanaim,
for he was a very wealthy[s] man. 33The
king said to Barzillai, "Cross over with

19:11 [u] 2Sa 15:24
19:13 [v] 2Sa 17:25 [w] Ge 29:14 [x] Ru 1:17; 1Ki 19:2; 8:16 [y] 2Sa 2:13
19:15 [z] Jos 5:9; 1Sa 11:15
19:16 [a] 2Sa 16:5-13; 1Ki 2:8
19:17 [b] 2Sa 9:2; 16:1-2 [c] Ge 43:16
19:19 [d] 1Sa 22:15; 2Sa 16:6-8
19:21 [e] 1Sa 26:6 [f] Ex 22:28 [g] 1Sa 12:3; 26:9; 2Sa 16:7-8
19:22 [h] 2Sa 2:18; 16:10 [i] 1Sa 11:13
19:23 [j] 1Ki 2:8, 42
19:24 [k] 2Sa 4:4; 9:6-10
19:25 [l] 2Sa 16:17
19:26 [m] Lev 21:18 [n] 2Sa 9:2
19:27 [o] 1Sa 29:9; 2Sa 14:17,20
19:28 [p] 2Sa 16:8; 21:6-9 [q] 2Sa 9:7, 13
19:31 [r] 2Sa 17:27-29; 1Ki 2:7
19:32 [s] 1Sa 25:2; 2Sa 17:27

---

without Judah's support. He sends messengers to the "elders of Judah," stressing his kinship with them and offering to make Amasa the general of the Israelite army. All Judah acts to bring David back across the Jordan River. They meet him at Gilgal to escort him back into the city.

19:16–23 Shimei is of course anxious to make amends. David's generosity is a picture of a true anointed one who is confident enough of his reign to forgive a man like Shimei.

19:24–30 David meets Mephibosheth, who argues passionately for his innocence against the slander of Ziba. This is a case of conflicting testimonies, and David sees immediately that he will not quickly be able to sort it all out. David's compromise leaves Mephibosheth with something and still rewards Ziba for his support during the crisis.

19:31–39 Barzillai had been part of the delegation from the Transjordan that supported David during the crisis. David always appears ready to reward loyalty, and he wants to reward the powerful Barzillai. But Barzillai is beyond caring for palace attractions (v. 35) and prefers instead to live out the rest of his life at home. In his place he offers Kimham, assumed by most interpreters to be one of his younger sons.

me and stay with me in Jerusalem, and
I will provide for you."
34But Barzillai answered the king,
"How many more years will I live, that I
should go up to Jerusalem with the king?
35I am now eighty[t] years old. Can I tell
the difference between what is enjoyable
and what is not? Can your servant taste
what he eats and drinks? Can I still hear
the voices of male and female singers?[u]
Why should your servant be an added[v]
burden to my lord the king? 36Your servant will cross over the Jordan with the
king for a short distance, but why should
the king reward me in this way? 37Let
your servant return, that I may die in
my own town near the tomb of my father[w] and mother. But here is your servant Kimham.[x] Let him cross over with
my lord the king. Do for him whatever
you wish."
38The king said, "Kimham shall cross
over with me, and I will do for him whatever you wish. And anything you desire
from me I will do for you."
39So all the people crossed the Jordan,
and then the king crossed over. The king
kissed Barzillai and bid him farewell,[y]
and Barzillai returned to his home.
40When the king crossed over to Gilgal,
Kimham crossed with him. All the troops
of Judah and half the troops of Israel had
taken the king over.
41Soon all the men of Israel were coming to the king and saying to him, "Why
did our brothers, the men of Judah, steal
the king away and bring him and his
household across the Jordan, together
with all his men?"[z]
42All the men of Judah answered the
men of Israel, "We did this because the
king is closely related to us. Why are you
angry about it? Have we eaten any of the
king's provisions? Have we taken anything for ourselves?"
43Then the men of Israel[a] answered
the men of Judah, "We have ten shares
in the king; so we have a greater claim on
David than you have. Why then do you
treat us with contempt? Weren't we the
first to speak of bringing back our king?"
But the men of Judah pressed their
claims even more forcefully than the
men of Israel.

Sheba Rebels Against David

20 Now a troublemaker named
Sheba son of Bikri, a Benjamite,
happened to be there. He sounded the
trumpet and shouted,

"We have no share[b] in David,[c]
  no part in Jesse's son![d]
Every man to his tent, Israel!"

2So all the men of Israel deserted David to follow Sheba son of Bikri. But the
men of Judah stayed by their king all
the way from the Jordan to Jerusalem.
3When David returned to his palace in
Jerusalem, he took the ten concubines[e]
he had left to take care of the palace and
put them in a house under guard. He
provided for them but had no sexual
relations with them. They were kept in
confinement till the day of their death,
living as widows.
4Then the king said to Amasa,[f] "Summon the men of Judah to come to me
within three days, and be here yourself."
5But when Amasa went to summon Judah, he took longer than the time the
king had set for him.
6David said to Abishai,[g] "Now Sheba
son of Bikri will do us more harm than

19:35 [t] Ps 90:10 [u] 2Ch 35:25; Ezr 2:65; Ecc 2:8; 12:1; Isa 5:11-12 [v] 2Sa 15:33
19:37 [w] Ge 49:29; 1Ki 2:7 [x] ver 40; Jer 41:17
19:39 [y] Ge 31:55; 47:7
19:41 [z] Jdg 8:1; 12:1
19:43 [a] 2Sa 5:1
20:1 [b] Ge 31:14 [c] Ge 29:14; 1Ki 12:16 [d] 1Sa 22:7-8; 2Ch 10:16
20:3 [e] 2Sa 15:16; 16:21-22
20:4 [f] 2Sa 17:25; 19:13
20:6 [g] 2Sa 21:17

19:40–43 Unfortunately, the end of Absalom's conspiracy is not the end of David's difficulties (as Nathan predicted, 12:10). The final paragraph of this unit illustrates the divide between Judah and the northern tribes (vv. 40–43). Even during David's exemplary reign the union threatens to dissolve into intertribal conflict at the slightest provocation. This hostility sets the stage for the open conflict described in the next chapter.

20:1–3 The description of Sheba as "a troublemaker" (v. 1) is the OT way of describing someone who is a worthless scoundrel. His cry of revolution in v. 1 is similar to that of secessionists after Solomon's death (1Ki 12:16) and may be a conventional rallying cry for traditionalists in the north. The phrase "all the men of Israel" (2Sa 20:2) indicates the geography of the secessionists, not the number of people involved in the rebellion.

20:4–10 When David returned to the throne after Absalom's conspiracy, he promised to replace Joab with Amasa as the commander of the army (19:13). Since Amasa himself commanded Absalom's army during the revolt, this is a certain compromise meant to appease those who objected to Joab's leadership (17:25). However, in Amasa's first assignment as the commander of the army for David, he fails (20:5).

Absalom's rebellion posed a threat to the king; Sheba's revolt threatens the kingdom itself. David can ill afford to delay in responding to the threat, and perhaps he is having doubts about Amasa's loyalty. His solution is to send out his best soldiers as an advance party under the leadership of Joab's brother, Abishai.

Absalom did. Take your master's men
and pursue him, or he will find fortified
cities and escape from us."[a] 7So Joab's
men and the Kerethites[h] and Pelethites
and all the mighty warriors went out
under the command of Abishai. They
marched out from Jerusalem to pursue
Sheba son of Bikri.
8While they were at the great rock
in Gibeon,[i] Amasa came to meet them.
Joab[j] was wearing his military tunic, and
strapped over it at his waist was a belt
with a dagger in its sheath. As he stepped
forward, it dropped out of its sheath.
9Joab said to Amasa, "How are you, my
brother?" Then Joab took Amasa by the
beard with his right hand to kiss him.
10Amasa was not on his guard against
the dagger[k] in Joab's[l] hand, and Joab
plunged it into his belly, and his intestines spilled out on the ground. Without
being stabbed again, Amasa died. Then
Joab and his brother Abishai pursued
Sheba son of Bikri.
11One of Joab's men stood beside Amasa and said, "Whoever favors Joab,
and whoever is for David, let him follow Joab!" 12Amasa lay wallowing in his
blood in the middle of the road, and the
man saw that all the troops came to a
halt[m] there. When he realized that everyone who came up to Amasa stopped, he
dragged him from the road into a field
and threw a garment over him. 13After
Amasa had been removed from the road,
everyone went on with Joab to pursue
Sheba son of Bikri.
14Sheba passed through all the tribes of
Israel to Abel Beth Maakah and through
the entire region of the Bikrites,[b][n] who
gathered together and followed him.
15All the troops with Joab came and besieged Sheba in Abel Beth Maakah.[o] They
built a siege ramp[p] up to the city, and it
stood against the outer fortifications.
While they were battering the wall to
bring it down, 16a wise woman[q] called

20:7 [h] 1Sa 30:14; 2Sa 8:18; 15:18; 1Ki 1:38
20:8 [i] Jos 9:3 [j] 2Sa 2:18
20:10 [k] Jdg 3:21; 2Sa 2:23; 3:27 [l] 1Ki 2:5
20:12 [m] 2Sa 2:23
20:14 [n] Nu 21:16
20:15 [o] 1Ki 15:20; 2Ki 15:29 [p] 2Ki 19:32; Isa 37:33; Jer 6:6; 32:24
20:16 [q] 2Sa 14:2

2Sa 20:9-10 ❖ What causes someone to be as vengeful as Joab? How can we learn to walk in a more Christlike way?

from the city, "Listen! Listen! Tell Joab
to come here so I can speak to him." 17He
went toward her, and she asked, "Are
you Joab?"
"I am," he answered.
She said, "Listen to what your servant
has to say."
"I'm listening," he said.
18She continued, "Long ago they used
to say, 'Get your answer at Abel,' and that
settled it. 19We are the peaceful[r] and
faithful in Israel. You are trying to destroy a city that is a mother in Israel. Why
do you want to swallow up the LORD's
inheritance?"[s]
20"Far be it from me!" Joab replied,
"Far be it from me to swallow up or
destroy! 21That is not the case. A man
named Sheba son of Bikri, from the hill
country of Ephraim, has lifted up his
hand against the king, against David.
Hand over this one man, and I'll withdraw from the city."
The woman said to Joab, "His head[t]
will be thrown to you from the wall."
22Then the woman went to all the people with her wise advice,[u] and they cut off
the head of Sheba son of Bikri and threw
it to Joab. So he sounded the trumpet,
and his men dispersed from the city, each
returning to his home. And Joab went
back to the king in Jerusalem.

David's Officials

23Joab[v] was over Israel's entire army;
Benaiah son of Jehoiada was over the Kerethites and Pelethites; 24Adoniram[c][w] was
in charge of forced labor; Jehoshaphat[x]

20:19 [r] Dt 2:26 [s] 1Sa 26:19; 2Sa 21:3
20:21 [t] 2Sa 4:8
20:22 [u] Ecc 9:13
20:23 [v] 2Sa 2:28; 8:16-18; 24:2
20:24 [w] 1Ki 4:6; 5:14; 12:18; 2Ch 10:18 [x] 2Sa 8:16; 1Ki 4:3

[a] 6 Or *and do us serious injury* [b] 14 See Septuagint and Vulgate; Hebrew *Berites.* [c] 24 Some Septuagint manuscripts (see also 1 Kings 4:6 and 5:14); Hebrew *Adoram*

20:11–13 When Amasa greets Joab as an ally, Joab strikes him down in a single blow. As Amasa draws his last breath, no one cares beyond removing him as a mere inconvenience from the path so the troops can get on with their business.
20:14–22 As it turns out, Sheba's revolt is not serious. Joab is able to easily corner this rebel. But ironically, in the midst of all this military power and strategy, it is a "wise woman" (v. 16) who intervenes and delivers the town from destruction. Her persuasive use of words and skillful rhetoric save the town and the kingdom.
20:23–26 The literary unit beginning in ch. 15 is now concluded with a little paragraph corresponding to a similar list at 8:15–18. These were probably lists of officials from, respectively, early and late in David's reign. They serve literarily to conclude extended narratives in 2 Samuel and to summarize the organization of David's government. Thus, the entire narrative in chs. 9–20 finds conclusion

son of Ahilud was recorder; 25Sheva was secretary; Zadok[y] and Abiathar were priests; 26and Ira the Jairite[a] was David's priest.

20:25 [y] 1Sa 2:35; 2Sa 8:17
21:1 [z] Ge 12:10; Dt 32:24
[a] Ex 32:11

The Gibeonites Avenged

21 During the reign of David, there was a famine[z] for three successive years; so David sought[a] the face of the LORD. The LORD said, "It is on account of Saul and his blood-stained house; it is because he put the Gibeonites to death."

21:2 [b] Jos 9:15
21:3 [c] 1Sa 26:19; 2Sa 20:19

2The king summoned the Gibeonites[b] and spoke to them. (Now the Gibeonites were not a part of Israel but were survivors of the Amorites; the Israelites had sworn to spare them, but Saul in his zeal for Israel and Judah had tried to annihilate them.) 3David asked the Gibeonites, "What shall I do for you? How shall I make atonement so that you will bless the LORD's inheritance?"[c]

[a] *26* Hebrew; some Septuagint manuscripts and Syriac (see also 23:38) *Ithrite*

---

in these words, which signal the end of the action of Absalom's rebellion and Sheba's revolt. Things are getting back to normal in Jerusalem.

Ironically, Joab is back in power (20:23). David attempted to replace him, but Joab is not a man easily persuaded to give up power. The lessons of the wise woman of Abel seem to have been lost on Joab.

15:1—20:26 Rebellion can often look like vocation. In other words, we easily justify our rebellion because it appears to be a way to accomplish something we are genuinely called to accomplish. Taking Absalom as our departure point, it is clear that he, as crown prince, had at his disposal large amounts of legitimate power. He could probably assume that he would one day become David's successor and rule all Israel. Over time, he began to believe he had no reason to wait for David's (and God's) timing. As David sent and took Bathsheba simply because he *could*, so Absalom took the kingdom because he believed it was eventually to be his anyway, and *he had the ability* to take it. It was one way of fulfilling his calling.

This is often the nature of temptation. In fact, temptations are hard to recognize because they regularly offer us ways to take control and use our own (God-given) power to falsely realize a true vocation. The abuse of God-given power to accomplish a God-given mission is a great temptation for believers today. Absalom serves precisely in this way as a warning for all of us who fail to resist this temptation.

21:1-9 After three years of famine, David fervently prays to discover the cause of the plague. The Lord reveals to David that the famine is the result of Saul's treason against the Gibeonites. The text

PEOPLE TO KNOW // RIZPAH

2 SAMUEL 21:1-14: Rizpah is a tragic character. She was a concubine of King Saul. After Saul's death, Saul's son Ish-Bosheth accused his general Abner of sleeping with Rizpah (2Sa 3:7). To sleep with the wife or a concubine of a king signaled laying a claim to the throne. (Notice how Solomon responded when his brother Adonijah asked for David's servant Abishag in marriage [1Ki 2:22].)

Abner was incensed by Ish-Bosheth's accusation, but he did not directly deny the charge. Rizpah may indeed have been a victim of Abner's conspiracy.

Rizpah reappears in 2Sa 21:1-14. God told David that a famine in Israel was due to Saul's violence against the Gibeonites, which violated the treaty Joshua had made with them (Jos 9). In order to placate the Gibeonites, David handed over seven of Saul's grandsons to be killed. Two of the seven were sons of Rizpah.

The bodies of Saul's grandsons were left exposed on a hill. Rizpah sat on sackcloth and stayed with the bodies. Day and night she guarded them from birds and wild animals. When word reached David of Rizpah's vigil, David finally gathered and buried the bones of Saul's slain grandsons, along with bones of Saul and Jonathan. When David did this, "God answered prayer in behalf of the land" (2Sa 21:14). The rains returned.

APPLICATION Rizpah was a silent but powerful witness. She was caught in the crossfire of political machinations beyond her control. The two stories the Bible recounts about her are tragic. Yet through her grieving and her commitment to the dignity of her slain sons, she had a powerful impact.

Sometimes we are beaten down by life. We are often victims of tragedies we neither choose nor control. Even so, God can use our quiet witness and commitment to accomplish good in the world.

4The Gibeonites answered him, "We
have no right to demand silver or gold
from Saul or his family, nor do we have
the right to put anyone in Israel to
death."[d]
"What do you want me to do for you?"
David asked.
5They answered the king, "As for the
man who destroyed us and plotted
against us so that we have been decimated and have no place anywhere in
Israel, 6let seven of his male descendants
be given to us to be killed and their bodies exposed[e] before the LORD at Gibeah
of Saul — the LORD's chosen[f] one."
So the king said, "I will give them to
you."
7The king spared Mephibosheth[g] son
of Jonathan, the son of Saul, because of
the oath[h] before the LORD between David and Jonathan son of Saul. 8But the
king took Armoni and Mephibosheth,
the two sons of Aiah's daughter Rizpah,[i]
whom she had borne to Saul, together
with the five sons of Saul's daughter Merab,[a] whom she had borne to Adriel son
of Barzillai the Meholathite.[j] 9He handed
them over to the Gibeonites, who killed
them and exposed their bodies on a hill
before the LORD. All seven of them fell
together; they were put to death[k] during
the first days of the harvest, just as the
barley harvest was beginning.[l]
10Rizpah daughter of Aiah took sackcloth and spread it out for herself on a
rock. From the beginning of the harvest till the rain poured down from the
heavens on the bodies, she did not let
the birds touch them by day or the wild
animals by night.[m] 11When David was
told what Aiah's daughter Rizpah, Saul's
concubine, had done, 12he went and took
the bones of Saul[n] and his son Jonathan
from the citizens of Jabesh Gilead. (They
had stolen their bodies from the public
square at Beth Shan,[o] where the Philistines had hung[p] them after they struck
Saul down on Gilboa.) 13David brought
the bones of Saul and his son Jonathan
from there, and the bones of those who
had been killed and exposed were gathered up.
14They buried the bones of Saul and
his son Jonathan in the tomb of Saul's
father Kish, at Zela[q] in Benjamin, and did
everything the king commanded. After
that,[r] God answered prayer[s] in behalf
of the land.

21:4 [d]Nu 35:33-34
21:6 [e]Nu 25:4 [f]1Sa 10:24
21:7 [g]2Sa 4:4 [h]1Sa 18:3; 20:8, 15; 2Sa 9:7
21:8 [i]2Sa 3:7 [j]1Sa 18:19
21:9 [k]2Sa 16:8 [l]Ru 1:22
21:10 [m]ver 8; Dt 21:23; 1Sa 17:44
21:12 [n]1Sa 31:11-13 [o]Jos 17:11 [p]1Sa 31:10
21:14 [q]Jos 18:28 [r]Jos 7:26 [s]2Sa 24:25
21:15 [t]2Sa 5:25
21:17 [u]2Sa 20:6

2Sa 21:14 ❖ What is the appropriate way to honor the deceased? Do you think God cares about this? Why or why not?

Wars Against the Philistines

21:15–22pp // 1Ch 20:4–8

15Once again there was a battle between the Philistines[t] and Israel. David went down with his men to fight
against the Philistines, and he became
exhausted. 16And Ishbi-Benob, one
of the descendants of Rapha, whose
bronze spearhead weighed three hundred shekels[b] and who was armed with
a new sword, said he would kill David.
17But Abishai[u] son of Zeruiah came to
David's rescue; he struck the Philistine

[a] *8* Two Hebrew manuscripts, some Septuagint manuscripts and Syriac (see also 1 Samuel 18:19); most Hebrew and Septuagint manuscripts *Michal*
[b] *16* That is, about 7 1/2 pounds or about 3.5 kilograms

---

recalls Jos 9:3–27 in which the Gibeonites, non-Israelite residents of cities north of Jerusalem, tricked Joshua into a peace treaty.

21:10-13 Rizpah loses two sons in the carnage (v. 8). David does what Rizpah cannot do: He gives the fallen from the house of Saul a proper burial in their own family tomb. All these many years later, and near the conclusion of 1–2 Samuel, the house of Saul is finally laid to rest.

21:14 Apparently, David's actions meet the needs of justice and honor, and God answers prayer "in behalf of the land." Israel is delivered from the famine. The portrait of Israel's king solidifies the ideal anointed king for Israel's future: David's repentant leadership provides a context in which Yahweh can answer prayer.

21:15-22 These four episodes presumably occur at various times in David's early wars with the Philistines and are held together literarily by two common threads (summarized in the concluding v. 22).

The descendants of Rapha are a frightening lot. They were probably a distinct group of the Rephaim in the OT and may have been the Transjordanian equivalent of the Anakites west of the Jordan. In light of references to the weight and size of their spears (vv. 16, 19), we can probably assume they are giants like Goliath in 1Sa 17, making this a list of David's "giant-killers." The unnamed "huge man" with six digits on each hand and foot (2Sa 21:20) is especially compelling. More importantly, this list illustrates that giants in the Bible generally portray a negative image, usually representing pagans who deserve God's displeasure and are worthy of his wrath. When the large man taunts Israel, David's nephew Jonathan justifiably cuts him down (v. 21).

down and killed him. Then David's men
swore to him, saying, "Never again will
you go out with us to battle, so that
the lamp[v] of Israel will not be extinguished.[w]"
18In the course of time, there was another battle with the Philistines, at Gob.
At that time Sibbekai[x] the Hushathite
killed Saph, one of the descendants of
Rapha.
19In another battle with the Philistines
at Gob, Elhanan son of Jair[a] the Bethle-
hemite killed the brother of[b] Goliath the
Gittite, who had a spear with a shaft like
a weaver's rod.[y]
20In still another battle, which took
place at Gath, there was a huge man with
six fingers on each hand and six toes on
each foot — twenty-four in all. He also
was descended from Rapha. 21When he
taunted Israel, Jonathan son of Shimeah,[z] David's brother, killed him.
22These four were descendants of Rapha in Gath, and they fell at the hands
of David and his men.

21:17 [v]1Ki 11:36 [w]2Sa 18:3
21:18 [x]1Ch 11:29; 20:4; 27:11
21:19 [y]1Sa 17:7
21:21 [z]1Sa 16:9
22:1 [a]Ex 15:1; Jdg 5:1; Ps 18:2-50
22:2 [b]Dt 32:4; Ps 71:3 [c]Ps 31:3; 91:2 [d]Ps 144:2
22:3 [e]Dt 32:37; Jer 16:19 [f]Ge 15:1 [g]Lk 1:69

David's Song of Praise

22:1–51pp // Ps 18:1–50

22 David sang[a] to the LORD the words
of this song when the LORD delivered him from the hand of all his enemies and from the hand of Saul. 2He said:

"The LORD is my rock,[b] my fortress[c]
and my deliverer;[d]
3 my God is my rock, in whom I take
refuge,[e]
my shield[c][f] and the horn[d][g] of my
salvation.

2Sa 22:2-3 ❖ How is a rock an appropriate metaphor for God? What does it teach about God's nature and provision?

He is my stronghold,[h] my refuge and
my savior —
from violent people you save me.

4"I called to the LORD, who is worthy[i]
of praise,
and have been saved from my
enemies.
5The waves[j] of death swirled
about me;
the torrents of destruction
overwhelmed me.
6The cords of the grave[k] coiled
around me;
the snares of death
confronted me.

7"In my distress[l] I called[m] to the LORD;
I called out to my God.
From his temple he heard my voice;
my cry came to his ears.
8The earth[n] trembled and quaked,[o]
the foundations[p] of the heavens[e]
shook;
they trembled because he was
angry.
9Smoke rose from his nostrils;
consuming fire[q] came from his
mouth,

[h]Ps 9:9
22:4 [i]Ps 48:1; 96:4
22:5 [j]Ps 69:14-15; 93:4; Jnh 2:3
22:6 [k]Ps 116:3
22:7 [l]Ps 120:1 [m]Ps 34:6,15; 116:4
22:8 [n]Jdg 5:4; Ps 97:4 [o]Ps 77:18 [p]Job 26:11
22:9 [q]Ps 97:3; Heb 12:29

[a] 19 See 1 Chron. 20:5; Hebrew *Jaare-Oregim.* [b] 19 See 1 Chron. 20:5; Hebrew does not have *the brother of.* [c] 3 *Or sovereign* [d] 3 *Horn* here symbolizes strength. [e] 8 Hebrew; Vulgate and Syriac (see also Psalm 18:7) *mountains*

22:1-4 The poems at the beginning and end of the books of Samuel serve an important function as literary frames for the whole (Hannah's prayer in 1Sa 2:1-11 and David's psalm and last words in 2Sa 22:1—23:7). The poetic frame articulates more directly and explicitly the books' core theological statements. Fittingly, then, in these concluding sections of 1-2 Samuel, the historian has included this praise song, which should be taken as a theological commentary on the entire history of David.

This particular psalm (repeated in Ps 18) is of a type most often called a "song of thanksgiving," though it is also a "royal psalm." At the heart of thanksgiving psalms is typically a story of deliverance or salvation, which may be summarized succinctly at the beginning, as it is in the introduction to our psalm (2Sa 22:4).

22:5-7 As is typical for Hebrew thanksgiving psalms, the general statement of deliverance in v. 4 is expanded significantly in this passage. David defines his situation as that of certain and imminent death (note the theme "death," "destruction," and "grave/Sheol," vv. 5-6). This is followed again by the assertion that he called out to God in the midst of his distress, and God heard his earnest and righteous prayer.

22:8-20 Yahweh (here described in terms of a theophany) delivers the king in his time of trouble and equips him for warfare. The primary image associated with Yahweh throughout the theophany is that of the Divine Warrior. He comes as the warrior storm god, shaking the earth, breathing smoke and spewing consuming fire (vv. 8-9). His thunderous arrival is meant to strike terror in the hearts of his enemies, a terror justified because of the arrows and bolts of lightning he uses against them (vv. 13-15).

The conclusion of the spectacular theophany is that Yahweh has brought David out "into a spacious place" (v. 20). He has reached into David's tight spot and has set him down safely in the open.

burning coals blazed out of it.
10 He parted the heavens and came down;
dark clouds[r] were under his feet.
11 He mounted the cherubim and flew;
he soared[a] on the wings of the wind.[s]
12 He made darkness his canopy around him—
the dark[b] rain clouds of the sky.
13 Out of the brightness of his presence
bolts of lightning[t] blazed forth.
14 The LORD thundered[u] from heaven;
the voice of the Most High resounded.
15 He shot his arrows[v] and scattered the enemy,
with great bolts of lightning he routed them.
16 The valleys of the sea were exposed
and the foundations of the earth laid bare
at the rebuke[w] of the LORD,
at the blast of breath from his nostrils.

17 "He reached down from on high[x] and took hold of me;
he drew[y] me out of deep waters.
18 He rescued me from my powerful enemy,
from my foes, who were too strong for me.
19 They confronted me in the day of my disaster,
but the LORD was my support.[z]
20 He brought me out into a spacious[a] place;
he rescued[b] me because he delighted[c] in me.[d]

21 "The LORD has dealt with me according to my righteousness;[e]
according to the cleanness of my hands[f] he has rewarded me.
22 For I have kept[g] the ways of the LORD;
I am not guilty of turning from my God.
23 All his laws are before me;[h]
I have not turned[i] away from his decrees.
24 I have been blameless[j] before him
and have kept myself from sin.
25 The LORD has rewarded me according to my righteousness,[k]
according to my cleanness[c] in his sight.

26 "To the faithful you show yourself faithful,
to the blameless you show yourself blameless,
27 to the pure[l] you show yourself pure,
but to the devious you show yourself shrewd.[m]
28 You save the humble,[n]
but your eyes are on the haughty to bring them low.[o]
29 You, LORD, are my lamp;[p]
the LORD turns my darkness into light.
30 With your help I can advance against a troop[d];
with my God I can scale a wall.

31 "As for God, his way is perfect:[q]
The LORD's word is flawless;[r]
he shields all who take refuge in him.
32 For who is God besides the LORD?
And who is the Rock[s] except our God?

22:10 [r] 1Ki 8:12; Na 1:3
22:11 [s] Ps 104:3
22:13 [t] ver 9
22:14 [u] 1Sa 2:10
22:15 [v] Dt 32:23
22:16 [w] Na 1:4
22:17 [x] Ps 144:7 [y] Ex 2:10
22:19 [z] Ps 23:4
22:20 [a] Ps 31:8 [b] Ps 118:5 [c] Ps 22:8 [d] 2Sa 15:26
22:21 [e] 1Sa 26:23 [f] Ps 24:4
22:22 [g] Ge 18:19; Ps 128:1; Pr 8:32
22:23 [h] Dt 6:4-9; Ps 119:30-32 [i] Ps 119:102
22:24 [j] Ge 6:9; Eph 1:4
22:25 [k] ver 21
22:27 [l] Mt 5:8 [m] Lev 26:23-24
22:28 [n] Ex 3:8; Ps 72:12-13 [o] Isa 2:12,17; 5:15
22:29 [p] Ps 27:1
22:31 [q] Dt 32:4; Mt 5:48 [r] Ps 12:6; 119:140; Pr 30:5-6
22:32 [s] 1Sa 2:2

[a] *11* Many Hebrew manuscripts (see also Psalm 18:10); most Hebrew manuscripts *appeared* [b] *12* Septuagint (see also Psalm 18:11); Hebrew *massed* [c] *25* Hebrew; Septuagint and Vulgate (see also Psalm 18:24) *to the cleanness of my hands* [d] *30* Or *can run through a barricade*

22:21–30 David's hymn of praise now takes a turn that seems unusual for modern readers. In the next section, the king maintains his innocence and righteousness and asserts that Yahweh was only being faithful in saving David. Yahweh has dealt with David in wonderful ways in accordance with the king's righteousness and clean hands (v. 21). In general, David claims to have maintained his relationship with God by keeping the law and spurning evil (vv. 22–25).

David is not claiming here to have never sinned, a claim that can hardly be read seriously based on what we learned about David in ch. 11. Rather, he is taking the standard OT view that deliverance is also vindication of one's relationship with God.

22:31–37 The next section of the poem celebrates David's military victories, all of which have been won in the strength of Yahweh. David extols the incomparability of Yahweh in the form of two rhetorical questions (v. 32) that call for an emphatic negative answer ("No one!"), and they contain an implicit belief in God as the one God. It is Yahweh who made David swift in flight (which he often needed against Saul) and strong in battle (vv. 33–35).

33 It is God who arms me with
strength[a]
and keeps my way secure.
34 He makes my feet like the feet of a
deer;[t]
he causes me to stand on the
heights.[u]
35 He trains my hands[v] for battle;
my arms can bend a bow of
bronze.
36 You make your saving help my
shield;[w]
your help has made[b] me great.
37 You provide a broad path[x] for my
feet,
so that my ankles do not give way.

38 "I pursued my enemies and crushed
them;
I did not turn back till they were
destroyed.
39 I crushed[y] them completely, and
they could not rise;
they fell beneath my feet.
40 You armed me with strength for
battle;
you humbled my adversaries
before me.[z]
41 You made my enemies turn their
backs[a] in flight,
and I destroyed my foes.
42 They cried for help,[b] but there was
no one to save them —[c]
to the LORD, but he did not
answer.
43 I beat them as fine as the dust of the
earth;
I pounded and trampled[d] them
like mud[e] in the streets.

44 "You have delivered[f] me from the
attacks of the peoples;
you have preserved[g] me as the
head of nations.
People[h] I did not know now
serve me,
45 foreigners cower[i] before me;
as soon as they hear of me, they
obey me.
46 They all lose heart;
they come trembling[c][j] from their
strongholds.

47 "The LORD lives! Praise be to my
Rock!
Exalted be my God, the Rock, my
Savior![k]
48 He is the God who avenges me,[l]
who puts the nations under me,
49 who sets me free from my
enemies.[m]
You exalted me above my foes;
from a violent man you
rescued me.
50 Therefore I will praise you, LORD,
among the nations;
I will sing the praises of your
name.[n]

51 "He gives his king great victories;[o]
he shows unfailing kindness to his
anointed,[p]
to David[q] and his descendants
forever."[r]

David's Last Words

23 These are the last words of David:

"The inspired utterance of David son
of Jesse,
the utterance of the man exalted[s]
by the Most High,

22:34 [t] Hab 3:19 [u] Dt 32:13
22:35 [v] Ps 144:1
22:36 [w] Eph 6:16
22:37 [x] Pr 4:11
22:39 [y] Mal 4:3
22:40 [z] Ps 44:5
22:41 [a] Ex 23:27
22:42 [b] Isa 1:15 [c] Ps 50:22
22:43 [d] Mic 7:10 [e] Isa 10:6; Mic 7:10
22:44 [f] 2Sa 3:1 [g] Dt 28:13
[h] 2Sa 8:1-14; Isa 55:3-5
22:45 [i] Ps 66:3; 81:15
22:46 [j] Mic 7:17
22:47 [k] Ps 89:26
22:48 [l] Ps 94:1; 144:2; 1Sa 25:39
22:49 [m] Ps 140:1,4
22:50 [n] Ro 15:9*
22:51 [o] Ps 144:9-10 [p] Ps 89:20 [q] 2Sa 7:13 [r] Ps 89:24,29
23:1 [s] 2Sa 7:8-9; Ps 78:70-71; 89:27

[a] *33* Dead Sea Scrolls, some Septuagint manuscripts, Vulgate and Syriac (see also Psalm 18:32); Masoretic Text *who is my strong refuge*
[b] *36* Dead Sea Scrolls; Masoretic Text *shield; / you stoop down to make*
[c] *46* Some Septuagint manuscripts and Vulgate (see also Psalm 18:45); Masoretic Text *they arm themselves*

22:38–46 David lists his great military victories in which he has subdued all his enemies. As a hymn of praise, the poem offers these victories as evidence of God's strength and power, not of David's own military might. It celebrates the king as a great warrior—but only because it knows that Yahweh, not David, is the One who wins the battles.
22:47–51 At the close of the hymn, the psalmist bursts forth in praise. In this closing stanza, we encounter again themes used elsewhere in the psalm: God as rock and salvation and victory over enemies.

There is, however, something new here. For the first time in the poem, the term "anointed" (v. 51) is used specifically to refer to David. This is yet another way in which our psalm is similar to Hannah's prayer, because it likewise concludes with a reference to the anointed one of God (1Sa 2:10). But the way in which blessing and favor are specifically tied to David in 2Sa 22:51 is noteworthy.

As we near the conclusion of this book in which we learned about the Lord's promise of an eternal dynasty for David (ch. 7), the final phrase of the poem becomes even more significant, especially for Christian readers. This king whom God has blessed with such favor is no singular individual but David *and* his offspring forever (v. 51b), which refers then to the royal family of David and ultimately to Christ (Mt 1:6–16).
23:1–7 In the thanksgiving psalm of the previous

the man anointed[t] by the God of Jacob,
the hero of Israel's songs:

2 "The Spirit[u] of the LORD spoke through me;
his word was on my tongue.
3 The God of Israel spoke,
the Rock[v] of Israel said to me:
'When one rules over people in righteousness,[w]
when he rules in the fear of God,[x]
4 he is like the light of morning at sunrise[y]
on a cloudless morning,
like the brightness after rain
that brings grass from the earth.'

5 "If my house were not right with God,
surely he would not have made with me an everlasting covenant,[z]
arranged and secured in every part;
surely he would not bring to fruition my salvation
and grant me my every desire.
6 But evil men are all to be cast aside like thorns,[a]
which are not gathered with the hand.
7 Whoever touches thorns
uses a tool of iron or the shaft of a spear;
they are burned up where they lie."

23:1 [t] 1Sa 16:12-13; Ps 89:20
23:2 [u] Mt 22:43; 2Pe 1:21
23:3 [v] Dt 32:4; 2Sa 22:2, 32 [w] Ps 72:2 [x] 2Ch 19:7, 9; Isa 11:1-5
23:4 [y] Jdg 5:31; Ps 89:36
23:5 [z] Ps 89:29; Isa 55:3
23:6 [a] Mt 13:40-41

David's Mighty Warriors

23:8–39pp // 1Ch 11:10–41

8 These are the names of David's
mighty warriors:
Josheb-Basshebeth,[a] a Tahkemonite,[b]
was chief of the Three; he raised his spear
against eight hundred men, whom he
killed[c] in one encounter.
9 Next to him was Eleazar son of Dodai[b]
the Ahohite.[c] As one of the three mighty
warriors, he was with David when they
taunted the Philistines gathered at Pas
Dammim[d] for battle. Then the Israelites
retreated, 10 but Eleazar stood his ground
and struck down the Philistines till his
hand grew tired and froze to the sword.
The LORD brought about a great victory
that day. The troops returned to Eleazar,
but only to strip the dead.
11 Next to him was Shammah son of

23:9 [b] 1Ch 27:4 [c] 1Ch 8:4

[a] 8 Hebrew; some Septuagint manuscripts suggest *Ish-Bosheth*, that is, *Esh-Baal* (see also 1 Chron. 11:11 *Jashobeam*). [b] 8 Probably a variant of *Hakmonite* (see 1 Chron. 11:11) [c] 8 Some Septuagint manuscripts (see also 1 Chron. 11:11); Hebrew and other Septuagint manuscripts *Three; it was Adino the Eznite who killed eight hundred men* [d] 9 See 1 Chron. 11:13; Hebrew *gathered there.*

---

section, David has looked back at the mercy and faithfulness of Yahweh during his life and reign. Here in his last words, he looks forward, trusting in the promises he has received from God. David extols the benefits and virtues of a righteous kingship. His must be just such a kingship because God has made "an everlasting covenant" with him (v. 5).

The designation of David as "the man anointed" (v. 1), or "Messiah," links this poem with the preceding one because of its use of the same term in its concluding verse (22:51). Together they form a poetic core at the center of the passage's structure.

23:2-7 The prophet-like speech of David commends the beautiful benefits of righteous rulership for all who are so ruled. But David then turns to an even more meaningful concept. His own kingship is regarded by Yahweh as acceptable because his dynasty has been granted an "everlasting covenant" (v. 5). This is a technical term in the OT that has semantic parallels in the ancient Near East related to legal contracts with no anticipated ending point; that is, they exist in perpetuity. The expression is used in the OT for all of the covenants (Noahic, Abrahamic, Mosaic, and Davidic). Thus, David's kingship is both a blessing for all humankind and an enduring promise more specifically to Israel. Such concepts became foundational for Israel's messianic hopes, pointing toward just the king that Israel longs for.

More specifically, the three poetic sections that provide literary shape for 1–2 Samuel also give theological shape to the books' portrayal of David (1Sa 2:1-10; 2Sa 22:1-51; 23:1-7). In fact, the messianic themes of the narratives are clarified, perhaps even intensified, by the poetic frame. Thus, Hannah's prayer, David's thanksgiving psalm, and his last words bring into sharp focus the most important themes in the narratives, especially those with messianic implications.

23:8-12 We come now to a military honor roll, which matches the list at 21:15-22 and like it may have come from an official military archive. In succinct fashion, this passage lists the heroes who supported David along with a few of their more spectacular exploits. From a human perspective, these are the valiant and loyal soldiers who made David's kingdom possible, and our historian honors them enthusiastically with this Soldiers' Hall of Fame. After relating two of their amazing feats, the text adds "the LORD brought about a great victory" (23:10, 12): Even when celebrating the decorated war heroes, one must remember the source of their strength.

Agee the Hararite. When the Philistines
banded together at a place where there
was a field full of lentils, Israel's troops
fled from them. 12But Shammah took
his stand in the middle of the field. He
defended it and struck the Philistines
down, and the LORD brought about a
great victory.

13During harvest time, three of the
thirty chief warriors came down to David at the cave of Adullam,[d] while a
band of Philistines was encamped in
the Valley of Rephaim.[e] 14At that time
David was in the stronghold,[f] and the
Philistine garrison was at Bethlehem.[g]
15David longed for water and said, "Oh,
that someone would get me a drink of
water from the well near the gate of
Bethlehem!" 16So the three mighty warriors broke through the Philistine lines,
drew water from the well near the gate
of Bethlehem and carried it back to David. But he refused to drink it; instead,
he poured[h] it out before the LORD. 17"Far
be it from me, LORD, to do this!" he said.
"Is it not the blood[i] of men who went at
the risk of their lives?" And David would
not drink it.

Such were the exploits of the three
mighty warriors.

18Abishai[j] the brother of Joab son of
Zeruiah was chief of the Three.[a] He raised
his spear against three hundred men,
whom he killed, and so he became as
famous as the Three. 19Was he not held
in greater honor than the Three? He became their commander, even though he
was not included among them.

20Benaiah[k] son of Jehoiada, a valiant
fighter from Kabzeel,[l] performed great
exploits. He struck down Moab's two
mightiest warriors. He also went down
into a pit on a snowy day and killed a
lion. 21And he struck down a huge Egyptian. Although the Egyptian had a spear
in his hand, Benaiah went against him
with a club. He snatched the spear from
the Egyptian's hand and killed him with
his own spear. 22Such were the exploits
of Benaiah son of Jehoiada; he too was
as famous as the three mighty warriors.
23He was held in greater honor than any
of the Thirty, but he was not included
among the Three. And David put him in
charge of his bodyguard.

24Among the Thirty were:
Asahel[m] the brother of Joab,
Elhanan son of Dodo from Bethlehem,
25Shammah the Harodite,[n]
Elika the Harodite,
26Helez[o] the Paltite,
Ira son of Ikkesh from Tekoa,
27Abiezer from Anathoth,[p]
Sibbekai[b] the Hushathite,
28Zalmon the Ahohite,
Maharai[q] the Netophathite,[r]
29Heled[c] son of Baanah the Netophathite,
Ithai son of Ribai from Gibeah[s] in
Benjamin,
30Benaiah the Pirathonite,[t]
Hiddai[d] from the ravines of Gaash,[u]
31Abi-Albon the Arbathite,
Azmaveth the Barhumite,[v]
32Eliahba the Shaalbonite,
the sons of Jashen,

23:13 [d]1Sa 22:1 [e]2Sa 5:18
23:14 [f]1Sa 22:4-5 [g]Ru 1:19
23:16 [h]Ge 35:14
23:17 [i]Lev 17:10-12
23:18 [j]2Sa 10:10,14; 1Ch 11:20
23:20 [k]2Sa 8:18; 20:23 [l]Jos 15:21
23:24 [m]2Sa 2:18
23:25 [n]Jdg 7:1; 1Ch 11:27
23:26 [o]1Ch 27:10
23:27 [p]Jos 21:18
23:28 [q]1Ch 27:13 [r]2Ki 25:23; Ne 7:26
23:29 [s]Jos 15:57
23:30 [t]Jdg 12:13 [u]Jos 24:30
23:31 [v]2Sa 3:16

[a] *18* Most Hebrew manuscripts (see also 1 Chron. 11:20); two Hebrew manuscripts and Syriac *Thirty*
[b] *27* Some Septuagint manuscripts (see also 21:18; 1 Chron. 11:29); Hebrew *Mebunnai*
[c] *29* Some Hebrew manuscripts and Vulgate (see also 1 Chron. 11:30); most Hebrew manuscripts *Heleb*
[d] *30* Hebrew; some Septuagint manuscripts (see also 1 Chron. 11:32) *Hurai*

23:13–17 The water retrieved by the three unnamed soldiers illustrates not only their love and loyalty to David but his own devout instincts, which, of course, made his men love him all the more. After his men risked their lives to bring him the water he longed for to satisfy his nostalgia, his reaction may seem ungrateful to modern readers. But the particular verb for "poured it out" (v. 16) refers to the pouring out of libations, and when poured out "before the LORD," this is terminology specifically reminiscent of offerings to Yahweh as an act of devotion. David honors his men even more by offering the water to Yahweh as a sacrifice.

23:18–23 The "Three" and the "Thirty" referred to in this text were presumably ranks of honor whose precise relationship to the other larger groups is unclear. Their members changed over time as some died and others were replaced, so at the time of this list there were actually 37 in the "Thirty" (v. 39). These two groups were special corps of David's elite troops.

23:24–38 The names of the soldiers appear to have no particular order in this list. Surprisingly Joab is not mentioned, though his armor-bearer is powerful enough to make the list (v. 37). Perhaps Joab is so powerful it is not necessary to include him. His influence and power stand at the top of this list, just as his presence is felt throughout the narratives related to David.

Jonathan [33]son of[a] Shammah the
Hararite,
Ahiam son of Sharar[b] the Hararite,
[34]Eliphelet son of Ahasbai the Maakathite,
Eliam[w] son of Ahithophel[x] the Gilonite,
[35]Hezro the Carmelite,[y]
Paarai the Arbite,
[36]Igal son of Nathan from Zobah,[z]
the son of Hagri,[c]
[37]Zelek the Ammonite,
Naharai the Beerothite, the armor-
bearer of Joab son of Zeruiah,
[38]Ira the Ithrite,[a]
Gareb the Ithrite
[39]and Uriah[b] the Hittite.
There were thirty-seven in all.

David Enrolls the Fighting Men

24:1–17pp // 1Ch 21:1–17

24 Again[c] the anger of the LORD
burned against Israel, and he incited David against them, saying, "Go
and take a census of[d] Israel and Judah."
[2]So the king said to Joab[e] and the army
commanders[d] with him, "Go throughout
the tribes of Israel from Dan to Beersheba[f] and enroll the fighting men, so that I
may know how many there are."
[3]But Joab replied to the king, "May
the LORD your God multiply the troops a
hundred times over,[g] and may the eyes of
my lord the king see it. But why does my
lord the king want to do such a thing?"
[4]The king's word, however, overruled
Joab and the army commanders; so they
left the presence of the king to enroll the
fighting men of Israel.

23:34 [w]2Sa 11:3 [x]2Sa 15:12
23:35 [y]Jos 12:22
23:36 [z]1Sa 14:47
23:38 [a]2Sa 20:26; 1Ch 2:53
23:39 [b]2Sa 11:3
24:1 [c]Jos 9:15 [d]1Ch 27:23
24:2 [e]2Sa 20:23 [f]Jdg 20:1; 2Sa 3:10
24:3 [g]Dt 1:11
24:5 [h]Dt 2:36; Jos 13:9 [i]Nu 21:32
24:6 [j]Ge 10:19; Jos 19:28; Jdg 1:31
24:7 [k]Jos 19:29 [l]Ge 21:22-33 [m]Dt 1:7; Jos 11:3
24:9 [n]Nu 1:44-46; 1Ch 21:5
24:10 [o]1Sa 24:5 [p]2Sa 12:13 [q]Nu 12:11; 1Sa 13:13
24:11 [r]1Sa 22:5 [s]1Sa 9:9; 1Ch 29:29

2Sa 23:39 ❖ Bathsheba's husband, Uriah, was one of David's best soldiers. What is a godly response when a person is betrayed?

[5]After crossing the Jordan, they
camped near Aroer,[h] south of the town
in the gorge, and then went through Gad
and on to Jazer.[i] [6]They went to Gilead
and the region of Tahtim Hodshi, and on
to Dan Jaan and around toward Sidon.[j]
[7]Then they went toward the fortress of
Tyre[k] and all the towns of the Hivites
and Canaanites. Finally, they went on
to Beersheba[l] in the Negev[m] of Judah.
[8]After they had gone through the entire land, they came back to Jerusalem at
the end of nine months and twenty days.
[9]Joab reported the number of the
fighting men to the king: In Israel there
were eight hundred thousand able-bodied men who could handle a sword, and
in Judah five hundred thousand.[n]
[10]David was conscience-stricken[o] after
he had counted the fighting men, and he
said to the LORD, "I have sinned[p] greatly
in what I have done. Now, LORD, I beg
you, take away the guilt of your servant.
I have done a very foolish thing.[q]"
[11]Before David got up the next morning, the word of the LORD had come to
Gad[r] the prophet, David's seer:[s] [12]"Go and

[a] 33 Some Septuagint manuscripts (see also 1 Chron. 11:34); Hebrew does not have *son of.* [b] 33 Hebrew; some Septuagint manuscripts (see also 1 Chron. 11:35) *Sakar* [c] 36 Some Septuagint manuscripts (see also 1 Chron. 11:38); Hebrew *Haggadi* [d] 2 Septuagint (see also verse 4 and 1 Chron. 21:2); Hebrew *Joab the army commander*

23:39 If so much subtlety is involved in the list, then certainly the last item is intended to convey irony: "and Uriah the Hittite" (v. 39). As impressive as these war heroes were, here is a stinging reminder that even David, the greatest warrior of them all, was flawed.

24:1–2 At first glance, our historian appears to have chosen a peculiar way to conclude 1–2 Samuel. Upon further reflection, this narrative plays a role in the overall contribution of chs. 21–24 generally to the message of 1–2 Samuel. Chapter 24 returns to one of the central characterizing features of David as the ideal king of Israel. In short, this narrative reinforces the ideal portrait of David as someone willing to place aside his royal power in deference to Yahweh's will and authority.

The opening verse of this text presents modern readers with a number of perplexing questions. Why is the Lord angry? Here we are simply not told why Yahweh is angry with David, and to read emotions or motivations into the text is to be guilty of "psychologizing" the character of God.

24:2–7 The text assumes through the words of Joab that the census reflects a shift in David's object of faith—a shift from reliance on Yahweh to win battles to a reliance on access to military might (v. 3). It is sinful because David is acting like a typical ancient Near Eastern king instead of an Israelite king.

24:8–9 After nearly ten months of arduous work, Joab is able to give David a report of the census.

24:10 David has a change of heart. Interestingly, this verse gives no hint of prophetic intervention. The real point of the narrative seems to be David's important words, "I have sinned" (v. 17). The confession is strategically placed to remind us of another time David used almost the identical words to admit his guilt before Nathan and Yahweh (12:13), only this time there is no prophetic "You are the man" (12:7) to expose David's hypocrisy and call for repentance.

24:11–12 Gad the prophet comes to David the

tell David, 'This is what the LORD says:
I am giving you three options. Choose
one of them for me to carry out against
you.' "
13So Gad went to David and said to him,
"Shall there come on you three[a] years of
famine[t] in your land? Or three months
of fleeing from your enemies while they
pursue you? Or three days of plague[u] in
your land? Now then, think it over and
decide how I should answer the one who
sent me."
14David said to Gad, "I am in deep distress. Let us fall into the hands of the
LORD, for his mercy[v] is great; but do not
let me fall into human hands."
15So the LORD sent a plague on Israel
from that morning until the end of the
time designated, and seventy thousand
of the people from Dan to Beersheba
died.[w] 16When the angel stretched out
his hand to destroy Jerusalem, the LORD
relented[x] concerning the disaster and
said to the angel who was afflicting the
people, "Enough! Withdraw your hand."
The angel of the LORD[y] was then at the
threshing floor of Araunah the Jebusite.
17When David saw the angel who was
striking down the people, he said to the
LORD, "I have sinned; I, the shepherd,[b]
have done wrong. These are but sheep.[z]
What have they done? Let your hand fall
on me and my family."[a]

24:13 [t] Dt 28:38-42,48; Eze 14:21 [u] Lev 26:25
24:14 [v] Ne 9:28; Ps 51:1; 103:8,13; 130:4
24:15 [w] 1Ch 27:24
24:16 [x] Ge 6:6; 1Sa 15:11 [y] Ex 12:23; Ac 12:23
24:17 [z] Ps 74:1 [a] Jnh 1:12
24:21 [b] Nu 16:44-50
24:22 [c] 1Sa 6:14; 1Ki 19:21
24:23 [d] Eze 20:40-41

2Sa 24:17 ❖ How can we repent of our failure if we fail in a leadership role?

David Builds an Altar

24:18–25pp // 1Ch 21:18–26

18On that day Gad went to David and
said to him, "Go up and build an altar to
the LORD on the threshing floor of Araunah the Jebusite." 19So David went up,
as the LORD had commanded through
Gad. 20When Araunah looked and saw
the king and his officials coming toward
him, he went out and bowed down before the king with his face to the ground.
21Araunah said, "Why has my lord the
king come to his servant?"
"To buy your threshing floor," David
answered, "so I can build an altar to the
LORD, that the plague on the people may
be stopped."[b]
22Araunah said to David, "Let my lord
the king take whatever he wishes and
offer it up. Here are oxen[c] for the burnt
offering, and here are threshing sledges
and ox yokes for the wood. 23Your Majesty, Araunah[c] gives[d] all this to the king."

[a] *13* Septuagint (see also 1 Chron. 21:12); Hebrew *seven* [b] *17* Dead Sea Scrolls and Septuagint; Masoretic Text does not have *the shepherd.*
[c] *23* Some Hebrew manuscripts and Septuagint; most Hebrew manuscripts *King Araunah*

---

next day, *after* David has confessed and pleaded for forgiveness. This final narrative of 1–2 Samuel portrays David as a king who has learned how to confess and seek forgiveness and restoration. This time he does not need a prophetic intermediary to threaten him or to persuade him of his guilt. David sees his own guilt, and he quickly and genuinely repents and seeks to reverse what he has done.

24:13–14 Yahweh makes David "pick his poison." Required to choose between famine, military defeat, or plague (v. 13), David surprises us again. He concludes that the judgment of humans is unpredictable, and God's judgment is consistently tempered by his mercy (v. 14). He trusts God enough to fling himself on God's mercy rather than calculate the costs of suffering at the hands of mortals. In this, again David has become this narrative's portrait of the ideal king of Israel.

24:15–17 In the closing paragraphs of this book, we encounter another rather bizarre episode. The tender-hearted King David is tortured by the realization that his people (v. 17) suffer because of his actions. He intervenes on their behalf, pleading that the Lord lay his vengeful wrath on him and his own family rather than on the people of Jerusalem, which the angel of death is about to strike with the plague (v. 16).

24:18–24 At Gad's instruction, David acquires "the threshing floor of Araunah the Jebusite" (v. 18), builds an altar to Yahweh on it, and offers burnt offerings and fellowship offerings. The Lord responds, and the plague ends. At the end of the day, it is David's relationship with Yahweh that saves Jerusalem. All is well.

Threshing floors were normally on a hill where the grain was collected for threshing and winnowing. They were also traditional sites for theophanies and receiving divine messages. The context of this final paragraph implies that the threshing floor in question is north of David's city. The Chronicler provides the missing detail that, in fact, this threshing floor becomes the site chosen for Solomon's temple, having been duly purchased with David's money and made sacred by his offerings (1Ch 22:1; 2Ch 3:1). The final paragraph, therefore, establishes the sanctity of the future site of the temple.

Moreover, the cost of Araunah's threshing floor is significant. David insists on paying a fair price, and his assertion about the nature of sacrifice in 2Sa 24:24 has profound significance. David understands the need to sacrifice a portion of his personal wealth to honor Yahweh. Otherwise, his worship will be cheap and his service meaningless.

Araunah also said to him, "May the LORD your God accept you."

[24]But the king replied to Araunah, "No, I insist on paying you for it. I will not sacrifice to the LORD my God burnt offerings that cost me nothing."[e]

So David bought the threshing floor and the oxen and paid fifty shekels[a] of silver for them. [25]David built an altar[f] to the LORD there and sacrificed burnt offerings and fellowship offerings. Then the LORD answered his prayer[g] in behalf of the land, and the plague on Israel was stopped.

24:24 [e] Mal 1:13-14

24:25 [f] 1Sa 7:17 [g] 2Sa 21:14

[a] 24 That is, about 1 1/4 pounds or about 575 grams

24:25 The final verse of the books of Samuel therefore produces an interesting reminder: "David built an *altar* to the LORD there" instead of "David built the *temple* of the LORD there." David is the ideal anointed one because he is repentant and forgiven by Yahweh, the true King of Israel. He is ideal because he trusts in the mercy of God rather than the fickle judgment of mortals (v. 14) and because he pays the cost of true worship (v. 24). David is someone well suited for kingship in Israel.

All others in Israel's future will be measured by David as the standard of Israelite kingship. But few will measure up. Each royal failure only serves to drive the hope, the longing, for an ideal son of David further into the future. So, Jesus becomes the fulfillment of this longing for another David. Jesus fulfills David's promise in an unexpected way and in a way no one else could (Mt 4:17).

21:1—24:25 The NT found this portrait of the ideal king of Israel useful for its Christological affirmations. In the first Gospel, the prophecy-fulfillment motif leans heavily on the Davidic ancestry of the Messiah. This is especially apparent in Matthew's carefully constructed genealogy of Jesus, where Abraham and David are benchmarks (Mt 1:1, 17). The title "Son of David" is commonly heard from those who need help from Jesus (Mt 9:27; 15:22; 20:30; see also 12:23; 21:9, 15). This title in Matthew is equivalent to "Messiah" and provides an explicit link to the Davidic roots of Israel's messianic expectation.

In Luke-Acts, the promise-fulfillment pattern gives way to an emphasis on the flow of salvation history, which continues to give a central role to the messianic foreshadowing of David's rule. In a critical text for Luke's Gospel, several features of Nathan's prophecy appear together (Lk 1:32–33): Jesus will be made great, he will be considered the Son of God, he will inherit the throne of his ancestor David, and he will rule over God's people forever. Jesus is the Lord's Anointed One, born in Bethlehem of David (Lk 1:27; 2:4, 11, 26). Jesus' resurrection is the fulfillment of the Davidic promise in Ps 16 (Ac 2:24–32), and Jesus' ascension into heaven is the fulfillment of the Davidic promise in Ps 110 (Ac 2:33–36). Paul's use of the expression "descendant of David" (lit., "seed of David") appears to be a proof of Jesus' Messiahship based on the Davidic covenant (Ro 1:3–5; 2Ti 2:8; cf. 2Sa 7:12, 14).

Jesus comes to establish the kingdom of God, as David established and built the kingdom of God in old Israel. Like David, Jesus is upheld by God's power and is victorious over God's enemies. Jesus is God's Anointed One, the Messiah, who rules his people in justice and truth.

As the One sent from God, Jesus prods us, as he did his first disciples, with the questions "But what about you? . . . Who do you say I am?" With Peter and Christians everywhere, we assert, "You are the Messiah" (Mk 8:29). At least a portion of what we mean in our confession of Jesus as the Christ affirms the messianic expectations of 1–2 Samuel, their interpretation in Israel's Scriptures, and the Christological development of these expectations in the pages of the NT.

1 Kings

Author: Unknown

Audience: God's chosen people, the Israelites

Date: Probably about 550 BC, during the Babylonian exile

Theme: God judges and eventually expels Israel and Judah from his presence in the promised land when their kings turn away from his covenant law.

PERSPECTIVE

The separation of church and state, a cornerstone of modern, religiously plural democracies, leaves unclear the relationship between prophet and king. The two books of Kings are crystal clear on the issue—the prophet has authority over the king.

To be sure, some present-day commentators are sure that modern Western democracies are clear on the relationship between prophet and king. The king (or president or prime minister or whatever the political ruler is called) rules. No ambiguity there, they say. Others hesitate to answer.

Some of the confusion has to do with what is understood by the three terms in the phrase, "the prophet has authority over the king." What is a prophet? What is a king? What is authority? Some of the confusion can be traced to the different ways the biblical writer of 1 and 2 Kings understood these three terms and the way those of us in modern democratic pluralisms understand them.

The writer of Kings thought of a "prophet" as a charismatic person given a special message from God to present to a backsliding king of Israel. He considered a "king" a person anointed by God to politically rule over Israel. "Authority" was a kind of moral commitment and example on the part of either the prophet or king. The prophet, for example, demonstrated his "authority" by delivering his unpopular message from God to the king regardless of the danger or personal cost. The king, by contrast, demonstrated his authority by personal model—the people's character was represented by the

Reading 1 Kings

The book of 1 Kings has three main sections: the kingdom of Solomon, the split of the kingdom at the beginning of Rehoboam's reign, and the subsequent reign and interaction of the kings of Israel and Judah.

	1400 BC	1300	1200	1100	1000	900	800	700	600	500	400
David's reign (1010–970 BC)											
Solomon's reign (970–930 BC)											
Building of the temple (966–959 BC)											
Division of the kingdom (930 BC)											
Elijah's ministry in Israel (c. 875–848 BC)											
Ahab's reign (874–853 BC)											
Elisha's ministry in Israel (c. 848–797 BC)											
Book of 1 Kings written (c. 560–550 BC)											

Key Verses

Solomon . . . said . . . "Now LORD, the God of Israel, keep for your servant David my father the promises you made to him when you said, 'You shall never fail to have a successor to sit before me on the throne of Israel, if only your descendants are careful in all they do to walk before me faithfully as you have done.'"

—1 Kings 8:22–23, 25

king's character. When the king sinned, the people sinned; when the king was faithful and just, the people were considered faithful and just.

Part of the challenge facing readers today is that none of these three terms is understood this way in modern (particularly Western), religiously plural democracies. Who is a "prophet" today? Whereas biblical prophets were specially called individuals, the prophetic function today rests largely with the voice of the church. While some might identify prominent Christian leaders of the past and present as having a prophetic voice, most will point toward the prophetic role of the entire church rather than special individuals.

Who is a "king" today? Whereas biblical kings ruled by law and God's anointing, political leaders in representative governments "rule" not by God's anointing but by making decisions based largely on the majority will of the people who elected them. What is "authority" today? The authority of political leaders does not rest in their personal faithfulness in living a sanctified Christian life. Yet we would be naïve to claim that the personal life and commitment of elected leaders has no "authority" in our lives. And what of the authority of prophets? Of the rare individuals on whom we confer the title, too often they find themselves having to seek political power to change things, becoming politicians themselves in the process. More pertinent is the question of what is the authority of the church, today's prophetic voice. People believe in and desire this unofficial relationship between church and state much more than they do the official separation laws. Perhaps this implicit double standard is the way forward to make sure that the prophet always has a say in the work of the king. The message of 1–2 Kings is that no matter how we do it, the "prophet" must have a voice. God rules and we must tell the world of that fact.

TAKING THE NEXT STEPS

The author of the book of 1 Kings continues the account of the kings of God's people by telling the stories of the succession of King Solomon to the throne, the division of the united kingdom into the northern kingdom of Israel and the southern kingdom of Judah, and the various kings up to the time of Ahab and Jehoshaphat. The kingdom was at the pinnacle of glory during the time of Solomon. He began his reign by building the temple of the Lord God in Jerusalem. What lay behind his success was his obedience to the Lord, but his disobedience later in life spelled disaster. As the kings began less and less to exercise spiritual leadership for God's people, God began to speak through the prophets, who frequently confronted kings with the will of God.

As with the other historical books of the OT, we can find important guidelines here as to how God relates to us. (1) As long as we believe in the Lord and obey his will, we will experience his presence in our lives. (2) The most important quality we need in our lives is spiritual wisdom, something that comes only as a gift from the Lord. (3) When those whom God has appointed to lead his people fail to do so, God raises up other servants (such as the prophets) to bring forth his word. (4) The five prayers of Elijah (see also Jas 5:17–18) present a powerful pattern for our prayer life and remind us of God's faithfulness to his promises.

WHAT TO LOOK FOR IN 1 KINGS

- Solomon becomes king (chs. 1–2)
- Solomon asks for wisdom (ch. 3)
- The building of the temple (chs. 5–6)
- The dedication of the temple (ch. 8)
- Solomon's downfall through mixed marriages (ch. 11)
- The division of the kingdom after Solomon (ch. 12)
- The story of the prophet Elijah (chs. 17–19; 21)

Adonijah Sets Himself Up as King

1 When King David was very old, he
could not keep warm even when they
put covers over him. 2So his attendants
said to him, "Let us look for a young virgin to serve the king and take care of
him. She can lie beside him so that our
lord the king may keep warm."
3Then they searched throughout Israel
for a beautiful young woman and found
Abishag, a Shunammite,[a] and brought
her to the king. 4The woman was very
beautiful; she took care of the king and
waited on him, but the king had no sexual relations with her.
5Now Adonijah,[b] whose mother was
Haggith, put himself forward and said,
"I will be king." So he got chariots[c] and
horses[a] ready, with fifty men to run
ahead of him. 6(His father had never rebuked[d] him by asking, "Why do you behave as you do?" He was also very handsome and was born next after Absalom.)
7Adonijah conferred with Joab[e] son of
Zeruiah and with Abiathar[f] the priest,
and they gave him their support. 8But
Zadok[g] the priest, Benaiah[h] son of Jehoiada, Nathan[i] the prophet, Shimei[j] and
Rei and David's special guard[k] did not
join Adonijah.

1:3 [a] Jos 19:18
1:5 [b] 2Sa 3:4
[c] 2Sa 15:1
1:6 [d] 2Sa 3:3-4
1:7 [e] 1Ki 2:22, 28; 1Ch 11:6 [f] 1Sa 22:20; 2Sa 20:25
1:8 [g] 2Sa 20:25 [h] 2Sa 8:18 [i] 2Sa 12:1 [j] 1Ki 4:18 [k] 2Sa 23:8

[a] 5 Or *charioteers*

1:1–4 The inability of David to function as king creates a crisis in the young kingdom. His powerlessness to stay warm is a sign of impending death. David's protectors attempt to assist him by seeking out a beautiful young woman to provide him with personal care. None of this would be unusual in a society that expected kings to have a large harem. The narrative provides no indication that Abishag is sought for the purpose of restoring virility.

1:5–10 The attempted coup by Adonijah and the counter coup of Solomon are the outcome of moral compromises of David's reign. Adonijah is David's fourth and apparently the oldest surviving son (2Sa 3:4). Absalom killed Amnon, David's oldest son, because he raped Absalom's sister Tamar (2Sa 13:28–29). Absalom himself, the third oldest son, died in his revolt against David (2Sa 18:14–15).

Adonijah is aggressive in seizing the throne (vv. 5, 7, 9). He employs a personal chariot force and guard of honor to give him the status of king and to prepare for his coup. Joab, the powerful military leader of David's army, joins in the revolt, along with Abiathar, a leading priest.

Joab is a relative of David and the ruthless leader of David's army (2Sa 3:27; 18:15). With Joab at the head of the conspirators, Adonijah has access to the entire army, a far greater force than the palace guard of Benaiah. Abiathar the priest has served David from the beginning of his struggles. Adonijah calls together the royal family and all the men of Judah, his own clansmen, who under Joab constitute the striking force of the national army.

Adonijah underestimated the resistance of those loyal to Solomon, and he overestimated the power of his forces to overcome them (v. 12).

9Adonijah then sacrificed sheep, cattle and fattened calves at the Stone of
Zoheleth near En Rogel.[l] He invited all
his brothers, the king's sons, and all the
royal officials of Judah, 10but he did not
invite Nathan the prophet or Benaiah
or the special guard or his brother Solomon.[m]
11Then Nathan asked Bathsheba,[n] Solomon's mother, "Have you not heard that
Adonijah,[o] the son of Haggith, has become king, and our lord David knows
nothing about it? 12Now then, let me advise[p] you how you can save your own life
and the life of your son Solomon. 13Go in
to King David and say to him, 'My lord
the king, did you not swear[q] to me your
servant: "Surely Solomon your son shall
be king after me, and he will sit on my
throne"? Why then has Adonijah become
king?' 14While you are still there talking
to the king, I will come in and add my
word to what you have said."
15So Bathsheba went to see the aged
king in his room, where Abishag[r] the
Shunammite was attending him. 16Bath-
sheba bowed down, prostrating herself
before the king.
"What is it you want?" the king asked.
17She said to him, "My lord, you yourself swore[s] to me your servant by the
LORD your God: 'Solomon your son shall
be king after me, and he will sit on my
throne.' 18But now Adonijah has become
king, and you, my lord the king, do not
know about it. 19He has sacrificed[t] great
numbers of cattle, fattened calves, and
sheep, and has invited all the king's sons,
Abiathar the priest and Joab the commander of the army, but he has not invited Solomon your servant. 20My lord the
king, the eyes of all Israel are on you, to
learn from you who will sit on the throne
of my lord the king after him. 21Other-
wise, as soon as my lord the king is laid
to rest[u] with his ancestors, I and my son
Solomon will be treated as criminals."
22While she was still speaking with the
king, Nathan the prophet arrived. 23And
the king was told, "Nathan the prophet
is here." So he went before the king and
bowed with his face to the ground.
24Nathan said, "Have you, my lord
the king, declared that Adonijah shall
be king after you, and that he will sit on
your throne? 25Today he has gone down
and sacrificed great numbers of cattle,
fattened calves, and sheep. He has invited all the king's sons, the commanders of
the army and Abiathar the priest. Right
now they are eating and drinking with
him and saying, 'Long live King Adonijah!' 26But me your servant, and Zadok
the priest, and Benaiah son of Jehoiada,
and your servant Solomon he did not
invite.[v] 27Is this something my lord the
king has done without letting his servants know who should sit on the throne
of my lord the king after him?"

David Makes Solomon King

1:28–53pp // 1Ch 29:21–25

28Then King David said, "Call in Bathsheba." So she came into the king's presence and stood before him.
29The king then took an oath: "As surely as the LORD lives, who has delivered
me out of every trouble,[w] 30I will surely
carry out this very day what I swore[x] to
you by the LORD, the God of Israel: Solomon your son shall be king after me, and
he will sit on my throne in my place."
31Then Bathsheba bowed down with
her face to the ground, prostrating herself before the king, and said, "May my
lord King David live forever!"

1:9 [l] 2Sa 17:17
1:10 [m] 2Sa 12:24
1:11 [n] 2Sa 12:24 [o] 2Sa 3:4
1:12 [p] Pr 15:22
1:13 [q] ver 30; 1Ch 22:9-13
1:15 [r] ver 1
1:17 [s] ver 13,30
1:19 [t] ver 9
1:21 [u] Dt 31:16; 1Ki 2:10
1:26 [v] ver 8,10
1:29 [w] 2Sa 4:9
1:30 [x] ver 13,17

1:11-14 Adonijah believes he is entitled to be heir and attempts to take over the throne; David is either negligent in the matter of not fulfilling his earlier oath to Bathsheba (vv. 13, 17, 30), or he secretly sympathizes with the ambitions of Adonijah.

Nathan the prophet intervenes. David has not been in control of his own household (v. 6), a pattern seen during his reign.

Nathan emerged after David took office in Jerusalem (2Sa 7:2). He was always associated with the king and had sufficient influence that he could confront and correct the king, as in the Bathsheba episode (2Sa 12:1–15).

1:15-27 Nathan the prophet has previously served as the conscience to the king. Knowing the oath of succession, Nathan is committed to ensuring the promise is fulfilled. This time Nathan brings his rebuke through the influence of Bathsheba. The prophet arrives as a messenger to report to David that the investiture of Adonijah is in progress. As on previous occasions, Nathan directly addresses the failure of the king without rousing the king's anger.

1:28-37 When confronted with his failures, David accepts responsibility for his wrong. He assures Nathan and Bathsheba that he will keep the vow made earlier (vv. 29–30). He commands prophet, priest, and general (Nathan, Zadok, and Benaiah) to commence the coronation of Solomon immediately. Solomon sits on David's private mule, dramatic and visual evidence that royal authority has been turned over to the rightful heir.

CHRONOLOGY OF FOREIGN KINGS

THIS IS A CHRONOLOGY OF SELECTED FOREIGN KINGS MENTIONED IN THIS STUDY BIBLE.

ARAM	Ben-Hadad I	c. 895-860*
	Ben-Hadad II (Hadadezer)	c. 860-843
	Hazael	c. 843-796
	Ben-Hadad III	c. 796-770
	Rezin	740s-732
ASSYRIA	Tiglath-Pileser III	745-727
	Shalmaneser V	727-722
	Sargon II	721-705
	Sennacherib	705-681
	Esarhaddon	681-669
	Ashurbanipal	669-627
BABYLONIA	Marduk-Baladan II	722-710,703
	Nebuchadnezzar II	605-562
	Amel-Marduk	562-560
	Nabonidus	556-539
	Belshazzar (Coregency with Nabonidus)	553(?)-539
EGYPT	Ahmose I	1550-1525**
	Thutmose II	1491-1479
	Thutmose III	1479-1425
	Tutankhamun	1333-1323
	Seti I	1289-1278
	Rameses II	1279-1212
	Merneptah	1212-1202
	Siamun	978-959
	Psusennes II	959-945
	Shishak I	945-924
	Osorkon I	924-889
	Shabako	716-702
	Shebitku	701-690
	Tirhakah	690-664
	Psammetichus I	664-610
	Necho II	610-595
	Psammetichus II	595-589
	Hophra	589-570
	Amasis	570-526
PERSIA	Cyrus the Great	559-530
	Cambyses II	530-522
	Darius I the Great	522-486
	Xerxes (Ahasuerus)	486-465
	Artaxerxes I	465-424
	Darius II	423-404

*All dates are BC and are those of the kings' reigns.
**The earlier Egyptian dates assigned here are less certain than the later ones; there were also a few coregencies.

32King David said, "Call in Zadok the
priest, Nathan the prophet and Benaiah
son of Jehoiada." When they came before the king, 33he said to them: "Take
your lord's servants with you and have
Solomon my son mount my own mule[y]
and take him down to Gihon.[z] 34There
have Zadok the priest and Nathan the
prophet anoint[a] him king over Israel.
Blow the trumpet[b] and shout, 'Long live
King Solomon!' 35Then you are to go up
with him, and he is to come and sit on my
throne and reign in my place. I have appointed him ruler over Israel and Judah."
36Benaiah son of Jehoiada answered
the king, "Amen! May the LORD, the God
of my lord the king, so declare it. 37As the
LORD was with my lord the king, so may
he be with[c] Solomon to make his throne
even greater[d] than the throne of my lord
King David!"
38So Zadok[e] the priest, Nathan the
prophet, Benaiah son of Jehoiada, the
Kerethites[f] and the Pelethites went down
and had Solomon mount King David's
mule, and they escorted him to Gihon.[g]
39Zadok the priest took the horn of oil[h]
from the sacred tent and anointed Solomon. Then they sounded the trumpet
and all the people shouted,[i] "Long live
King Solomon!" 40And all the people
went up after him, playing pipes and rejoicing greatly, so that the ground shook
with the sound.
41Adonijah and all the guests who were
with him heard it as they were finishing
their feast. On hearing the sound of the
trumpet, Joab asked, "What's the meaning of all the noise in the city?"
42Even as he was speaking, Jonathan[j]
son of Abiathar the priest arrived. Adonijah said, "Come in. A worthy man like
you must be bringing good news."[k]
43"Not at all!" Jonathan answered. "Our
lord King David has made Solomon king.
44The king has sent with him Zadok the
priest, Nathan the prophet, Benaiah
son of Jehoiada, the Kerethites and the
Pelethites, and they have put him on
the king's mule, 45and Zadok the priest
and Nathan the prophet have anointed him king at Gihon. From there they
have gone up cheering, and the city resounds[l] with it. That's the noise you hear.
46Moreover, Solomon has taken his seat
on the royal throne. 47Also, the royal officials have come to congratulate our lord
King David, saying, 'May your God make
Solomon's name more famous than yours
and his throne greater[m] than yours!' And
the king bowed in worship on his bed
48and said, 'Praise be to the LORD, the
God of Israel, who has allowed my eyes
to see a successor[n] on my throne today.'"
49At this, all Adonijah's guests rose in
alarm and dispersed. 50But Adonijah, in
fear of Solomon, went and took hold of
the horns[o] of the altar. 51Then Solomon
was told, "Adonijah is afraid of King Solomon and is clinging to the horns of the
altar. He says, 'Let King Solomon swear to
me today that he will not put his servant
to death with the sword.'"
52Solomon replied, "If he shows himself to be worthy, not a hair[p] of his head
will fall to the ground; but if evil is found
in him, he will die." 53Then King Solomon
sent men, and they brought him down
from the altar. And Adonijah came and
bowed down to King Solomon, and Solomon said, "Go to your home."

1Ki 1:52 ❖ Should showing mercy to others be conditional? Why or why not?

1:33 [y] 2Sa 20:6-7 [z] 2Ch 32:30; 33:14
1:34 [a] 1Sa 10:1; 16:3,12; 1Ki 19:16; 2Ki 9:3, 13 [b] ver 25; 2Sa 5:3; 15:10
1:37 [c] Jos 1:5, 17; 1Sa 20:13 [d] ver 47
1:38 [e] ver 8 [f] 2Sa 8:18 [g] ver 33
1:39 [h] Ex 30:23-32; Ps 89:20 [i] ver 34; 1Sa 10:24
1:42 [j] 2Sa 15:27, 36 [k] 2Sa 18:26
1:45 [l] ver 40
1:47 [m] ver 37; Ge 47:31
1:48 [n] 2Sa 7:12; 1Ki 3:6
1:50 [o] 1Ki 2:28
1:52 [p] 1Sa 14:45; 2Sa 14:11
2:1 [q] Ge 47:29; Dt 31:14

David's Charge to Solomon

2:10–12pp // 1Ch 29:26–28

2 When the time drew near for David
to die,[q] he gave a charge to Solomon
his son.

1:38-40 Zadok the priest anoints Solomon as king with the authority of Nathan the prophet. The trumpet blast announces the installation of the new king. With this, prophet, priest, and general set out with the royal guard. A joyful procession follows, marking this a most significant occasion.
1:41-48 The tumult of the coronation attracts the attention of Adonijah's allies just down the valley. Jonathan, the son of Abiathar the priest and a man of status, is apparently present at the proceedings of Solomon's anointing and reports everything that has transpired. The last word, spoken by David himself, is a thanksgiving prayer that the dynasty will continue (v. 48).
1:49-53 The allies of Adonijah quickly disperse, unwilling to challenge the will of David and the forces who are with Solomon. Adonijah himself seeks refuge in the sanctuary; the sanctuary protects the innocent, but it is of no help to the guilty. Adonijah seems to think he is able to bargain for mercy. Solomon grants him security on the condition that he conduct himself with loyalty and honor.
2:1-6 The previous episode of Solomon gaining the throne is continued by describing the role

2“I am about to go the way of all the
earth,”[r] he said. “So be strong,[s] act like a
man, 3and observe[t] what the LORD your
God requires: Walk in obedience to him,
and keep his decrees and commands,
his laws and regulations, as written in
the Law of Moses. Do this so that you
may prosper[u] in all you do and wherever you go 4and that the LORD may keep
his promise[v] to me: ‘If your descendants
watch how they live, and if they walk
faithfully[w] before me with all their heart
and soul, you will never fail to have a
successor on the throne of Israel.’
5“Now you yourself know what Joab[x]
son of Zeruiah did to me—what he did
to the two commanders of Israel's armies, Abner[y] son of Ner and Amasa[z]
son of Jether. He killed them, shedding
their blood in peacetime as if in battle,
and with that blood he stained the belt
around his waist and the sandals on his
feet. 6Deal with him according to your
wisdom,[a] but do not let his gray head
go down to the grave in peace.
7“But show kindness to the sons of Barzillai[b] of Gilead and let them be among
those who eat at your table.[c] They stood
by me when I fled from your brother
Absalom.
8“And remember, you have with you
Shimei[d] son of Gera, the Benjamite from
Bahurim, who called down bitter curses on me the day I went to Mahanaim.
When he came down to meet me at the
Jordan, I swore[e] to him by the LORD: ‘I

2:2 [r]Jos 23:14 [s]Dt 31:7,23; Jos 1:6
2:3 [t]Dt 17:14-20; Jos 1:7 [u]1Ch 22:13
2:4 [v]2Sa 7:13,25; 1Ki 8:25 [w]2Ki 20:3; Ps 132:12
2:5 [x]2Sa 2:18; 18:5,12,14 [y]2Sa 3:27 [z]2Sa 20:10
2:6 [a]ver 9
2:7 [b]2Sa 17:27; 19:31-39 [c]2Sa 9:7
2:8 [d]2Sa 16:5-13 [e]2Sa 19:18-23
2:9 [f]ver 6
2:10 [g]Ac 2:29; 13:36 [h]2Sa 5:7
2:11 [i]2Sa 5:4,5
2:12 [j]1Ch 29:23 [k]2Ch 1:1
2:13 [l]1Sa 16:4

1Ki 2:2-4 ❖ What advice can we give at the end of our lives to our children or to a younger friend? What would we say about God and about how to live?

will not put you to death by the sword.’
9But now, do not consider him innocent.
You are a man of wisdom;[f] you will know
what to do to him. Bring his gray head
down to the grave in blood.”
10Then David rested with his ancestors
and was buried[g] in the City of David.[h]
11He had reigned[i] forty years over Israel—seven years in Hebron and thirty-
three in Jerusalem. 12So Solomon sat on
the throne[j] of his father David, and his
rule was firmly established.[k]

Solomon's Throne Established

13Now Adonijah, the son of Haggith,
went to Bathsheba, Solomon's mother.
Bathsheba asked him, “Do you come
peacefully?”[l]
He answered, “Yes, peacefully.” 14Then
he added, “I have something to say to
you.”
“You may say it,” she replied.
15“As you know,” he said, “the kingdom was mine. All Israel looked to me as
their king. But things changed, and the
kingdom has gone to my brother; for it
has come to him from the LORD. 16Now
I have one request to make of you. Do
not refuse me.”
“You may make it,” she said.

David had in securing the throne in the midst of various rivalries that carried over from his time.

2:2–4 The charge of David to Solomon is typical Deuteronomistic theology; it expresses the ideology of the kingdom. The fundamental obligation of the king is to carefully observe the divine mandate (2:3a), which is “written in the Law of Moses”—that is, Deuteronomy. Faithfulness to the covenant is the single discriminating factor in determining whether kings are good or bad. These final words of David are the fundamental first words for every succeeding king.

2:5–6 As is the case in any transition of power, some matters need immediate attention to prevent the kind of conflict experienced with Adonijah. David's instructions to Solomon in this passage wrap up David's unfinished business.

2:7 David owes a favor to Barzillai, a Gileadite of Rogelim, who brought food and supplies to him and his followers at Mahanaim during Absalom's rebellion (2Sa 17:27–29). David insists that the sons be rewarded for this deed of loyalty.

2:8–9 David was never able to overcome the hostility between Benjamin and Judah. The rift of north and south was evident during the rebellion of Absalom when Shimei, a Benjamite relative of Saul, publicly cursed David and accused him of bloodguilt in succeeding the house of Saul (2Sa 16:5–13). When the rebellion was put down, Shimei petitioned David for his life, and David granted him leniency (2Sa 19:16–23). Solomon cannot now allow such resistance to go unchecked, and David instructs him to find occasion to deal with it.

2:10–11 David dies and is buried in the city of David, the walled fortress of the Jebusites that was first conquered by David and his personal striking force (2Sa 5:6–9). Though Peter makes reference to the tomb of David as known in his time (Ac 2:29), it is no longer possible to authenticate the place. The summary of David's reign recaps several key events in the life of David.

2:12–17 The selection of Solomon to be king does not settle the question of succession. Adonijah uses the influence of Bathsheba to rally support for his right to rule as the older brother. Adonijah's request to be given Abishag as his wife becomes the occasion for Solomon to rid himself of the adversary he has reluctantly spared (cf. 1:52).

17So he continued, "Please ask King Solomon — he will not refuse you — to give me Abishag[m] the Shunammite as my wife."

18"Very well," Bathsheba replied, "I will speak to the king for you."

19When Bathsheba went to King Solomon to speak to him for Adonijah, the king stood up to meet her, bowed down to her and sat down on his throne. He had a throne brought for the king's mother,[n] and she sat down at his right hand.[o]

20"I have one small request to make of you," she said. "Do not refuse me."

The king replied, "Make it, my mother; I will not refuse you."

21So she said, "Let Abishag[p] the Shunammite be given in marriage to your brother Adonijah."

22King Solomon answered his mother, "Why do you request Abishag[q] the Shunammite for Adonijah? You might as well request the kingdom for him — after all, he is my older brother[r] — yes, for him and for Abiathar the priest and Joab son of Zeruiah!"

23Then King Solomon swore by the LORD: "May God deal with me, be it ever so severely,[s] if Adonijah does not pay with his life for this request! 24And now, as surely as the LORD lives — he who has established me securely on the throne of my father David and has founded a dynasty for me as he promised[t] — Adonijah shall be put to death today!" 25So King Solomon gave orders to Benaiah[u] son of Jehoiada, and he struck down Adonijah and he died.

26To Abiathar[v] the priest the king said, "Go back to your fields in Anathoth.[w] You deserve to die, but I will not put you to death now, because you carried the ark[x] of the Sovereign LORD before my father David and shared all my father's hardships."[y] 27So Solomon removed Abiathar from the priesthood of the LORD, fulfilling[z] the word the LORD had spoken at Shiloh about the house of Eli.

28When the news reached Joab, who had conspired with Adonijah though not with Absalom, he fled to the tent of the LORD and took hold of the horns[a] of the altar. 29King Solomon was told that Joab had fled to the tent of the LORD and was beside the altar. Then Solomon ordered Benaiah[b] son of Jehoiada, "Go, strike him down!"

30So Benaiah entered the tent of the LORD and said to Joab, "The king says, 'Come out![c]'"

But he answered, "No, I will die here."

Benaiah reported to the king, "This is how Joab answered me."

31Then the king commanded Benaiah, "Do as he says. Strike him down and bury him, and so clear me and my whole family of the guilt of the innocent blood[d] that Joab shed. 32The LORD will repay[e] him for the blood he shed,[f] because without my father David knowing it he attacked two men and killed them with the sword. Both of them — Abner son of Ner, commander of Israel's army, and Amasa[g] son of Jether, commander of Judah's army — were better[h] men and more upright than he. 33May the guilt of their blood rest on the head of Joab and his descendants forever. But on David and his descendants, his house and his throne, may there be the LORD's peace forever."

34So Benaiah son of Jehoiada went up and struck down Joab and killed him, and he was buried at his home out in the country. 35The king put Benaiah[i] son of Jehoiada over the army in Joab's position and replaced Abiathar with Zadok[j] the priest.

36Then the king sent for Shimei[k] and said to him, "Build yourself a house in Jerusalem and live there, but do not go anywhere else. 37The day you leave and

2:17 [m] 1Ki 1:3
2:19 [n] 1Ki 15:13 [o] Ps 45:9
2:21 [p] 1Ki 1:3
2:22 [q] 2Sa 12:8; 1Ki 1:3 [r] 1Ch 3:2
2:23 [s] Ru 1:17
2:24 [t] 2Sa 7:11; 1Ch 22:10
2:25 [u] 2Sa 8:18
2:26 [v] 1Sa 22:20 [w] Jos 21:18 [x] 2Sa 15:24 [y] 1Sa 23:6
2:27 [z] 1Sa 2:27-36
2:28 [a] 1Ki 1:7,50
2:29 [b] ver 25
2:30 [c] Ex 21:14
2:31 [d] Nu 35:33; Dt 19:13; 21:8-9
2:32 [e] Jdg 9:57; Ps 7:16 [f] Jdg 9:24 [g] 2Sa 3:27; 20:10 [h] 2Ch 21:13
2:35 [i] 1Ki 4:4 [j] ver 27; 1Ch 29:22
2:36 [k] ver 8; 2Sa 16:5

2:18-25 The role of Bathsheba in the proceedings is somewhat perplexing. Bathsheba is well aware of Solomon's claim to the throne because of the promise to David (2:24), so it is possible that in delivering the request she knows Solomon will respond by using this as a way to eliminate his rival.

2:26-27 Solomon bans Abiathar to Anathoth, where he can no longer function as a priest; according to the judgment of Deuteronomistic theology, this is a consequence of the sins of the house of Eli in Shiloh (1Sa 3:12-14). The genealogy from Eli to Ahimelech, priest of Nob, Abiathar's father, is never given explicitly (1Ki 22:20), but there may have been independent tradition to confirm it.

2:28-35 The banishment of Abiathar signals to Joab that his time is up. He may have hoped that Solomon would not resort to execution, at least not in the temple, but Solomon's resolve is undeterred.

2:36-38 Solomon gives amnesty to Shimei but at a considerable cost: He is confined to Jerusalem, which prevents him from again rallying support against the Davidic dynasty in the Benjamite country-

cross the Kidron Valley,[l] you can be sure
you will die; your blood will be on your
own head."[m]
38 Shimei answered the king, "What
you say is good. Your servant will do as
my lord the king has said." And Shimei
stayed in Jerusalem for a long time.
39 But three years later, two of Shimei's
slaves ran off to Achish[n] son of Maakah,
king of Gath, and Shimei was told, "Your
slaves are in Gath." 40 At this, he saddled his donkey and went to Achish at
Gath in search of his slaves. So Shimei
went away and brought the slaves back
from Gath.
41 When Solomon was told that Shimei
had gone from Jerusalem to Gath and
had returned, 42 the king summoned
Shimei and said to him, "Did I not make
you swear by the LORD and warn you,
'On the day you leave to go anywhere
else, you can be sure you will die'? At
that time you said to me, 'What you say
is good. I will obey.' 43 Why then did you
not keep your oath to the LORD and obey
the command I gave you?"
44 The king also said to Shimei, "You
know in your heart all the wrong[o] you
did to my father David. Now the LORD
will repay you for your wrongdoing.
45 But King Solomon will be blessed, and
David's throne will remain secure[p] before
the LORD forever."
46 Then the king gave the order to Benaiah son of Jehoiada, and he went out
and struck Shimei down and he died.
The kingdom was now established[q] in
Solomon's hands.

Solomon Asks for Wisdom

3:4–15pp // 2Ch 1:2–13

3 Solomon made an alliance with Pharaoh king of Egypt and married[r] his
daughter.[s] He brought her to the City
of David[t] until he finished building his
palace[u] and the temple of the LORD, and
the wall around Jerusalem. 2 The people, however, were still sacrificing at the
high places,[v] because a temple had not
yet been built for the Name of the LORD.
3 Solomon showed his love[w] for the LORD
by walking according to the instructions[x]
given him by his father David, except
that he offered sacrifices and burned incense on the high places.
4 The king went to Gibeon[y] to offer
sacrifices, for that was the most important high place, and Solomon offered a

2:37 [l] 2Sa 15:23 [m] Lev 20:9; Jos 2:19; 2Sa 1:16
2:39 [n] 1Sa 27:2
2:44 [o] 1Sa 25:39; 2Sa 16:5-13; Eze 17:19
2:45 [p] 2Sa 7:13; Pr 25:5
2:46 [q] ver 12; 2Ch 1:1
3:1 [r] 1Ki 7:8 [s] 1Ki 9:24 [t] 2Sa 5:7 [u] 1Ki 7:1; 9:15,19
3:2 [v] Lev 17:3-5; Dt 12:2,4-5; 1Ki 22:43
3:3 [w] Dt 6:5; Ps 31:23; 1Co 8:3 [x] 1Ki 2:3; 9:4; 11:4,6,38
3:4 [y] 1Ch 16:39

---

side. Shimei goes south and west to Gath, perhaps taking literally the prohibition of not crossing the Kidron, in the hope that this will not violate his oath. He returns with his servants before Solomon finds out about his departure, but this does not spare him. Solomon executes the oath according to its intent, if not the exact letter of the law.

APPLICATION ✣ 1:1—2:46 The enthusiastic statements about the celebration of Solomon's rule leave no doubt about the conviction narrator (1:47–48). For the sake of the kingdom of God, it is important that the throne be made secure under Solomon's dominion, and to that end it is necessary that all opposition to his rule be stopped. How do we discern God's will in the methods of Solomon? Do the ends justify the means? The contemporary Christian faces a similar cynicism when attempting to discern God's will in current events.

There is no flattering portrayal of a champion in this narrative; the deeds of each individual are frankly described, even though this may diminish the reader's estimation of all of the characters. The narrator holds God in highest esteem; God alone is allowed to be the hero in an otherwise sordid tale. Understanding the dynamic between human will and action and divine purpose becomes particularly difficult in dealing with the depraved behavior of human conflict.

In a democratic society, Christians are asked to be a part of the process by which leaders come into power. Admittedly the procedures are often not fair and equitable, and inevitably the leaders are flawed. Nevertheless, these procedures are regarded as a means ordained by God to accomplish his purpose in the world in which his people live. As with Solomon, God carries out his purposes through imperfect people using imperfect methods of achieving their goals.

3:1–3 The introductory note about Solomon's marriage to the daughter of Pharaoh is significant in relation to Solomon's worship at Gibeon and the building of the temple. Solomon has become allied to Pharaoh, likely in connection with Egyptian campaigns into Philistine country (9:16). The mention of Pharaoh's daughter calls attention to Solomon's prominent international position early in his reign.

3:4 Solomon's choice to worship outside of Jerusalem is normal before the completion of the temple (v. 2), but the choice of Gibeon is politically advantageous. Gibeonite territory was one of the first areas to become a part of Saul's kingdom, and a new king would need to renew the connection with the Gibeonites to become recognized as their ruler. Gibeon is also home to the largest high place in the country, a prominent location for Yahweh worship before the temple in Jerusalem is established.

thousand burnt offerings on that altar.
5At Gibeon the LORD appeared[z] to Solomon during the night in a dream,[a] and
God said, "Ask for whatever you want me
to give you."
6Solomon answered, "You have shown
great kindness to your servant, my father David, because he was faithful[b] to
you and righteous and upright in heart.
You have continued this great kindness
to him and have given him a son[c] to sit
on his throne this very day.
7"Now, LORD my God, you have made
your servant king in place of my father
David. But I am only a little child[d] and
do not know how to carry out my duties.
8Your servant is here among the people
you have chosen,[e] a great people, too
numerous to count or number.[f] 9So give
your servant a discerning[g] heart to govern your people and to distinguish[h] between right and wrong. For who is able[i]
to govern this great people of yours?"
10The Lord was pleased that Solomon
had asked for this. 11So God said to him,
"Since you have asked[j] for this and not
for long life or wealth for yourself, nor
have asked for the death of your enemies but for discernment in administering justice, 12I will do what you have
asked.[k] I will give you a wise[l] and discerning heart, so that there will never
have been anyone like you, nor will there
ever be. 13Moreover, I will give you what
you have not[m] asked for—both wealth
and honor[n]—so that in your lifetime

3:5 [z] 1Ki 9:2 [a] Nu 12:6; Mt 1:20
3:6 [b] 1Ki 2:4; 9:4 [c] 1Ki 1:48
3:7 [d] Nu 27:17; 1Ch 29:1
3:8 [e] Dt 7:6 [f] Ge 15:5
3:9 [g] 2Sa 14:17; Jas 1:5 [h] Pr 2:3-9; Heb 5:14 [i] Ps 72:1-2
3:11 [j] Jas 4:3
3:12 [k] 1Jn 5:14-15 [l] 1Ki 4:29,30, 31; 5:12; 10:23; Ecc 1:16
3:13 [m] Mt 6:33; Eph 3:20 [n] 1Ki 4:21-24; Pr 3:1-2,16

1Ki 3:5 ❖ If God made you this offer, what would you want to ask for? Why?

3:5–8 Solomon is seeking guidance and blessing from Yahweh. When Yahweh appears in the dream, Solomon makes his request in terms of the covenant relationship established with David his father (v. 6). "Great kindness" is an expression of covenant loyalty, describing integrity in a relationship.

3:9–15 As king, Solomon has the well-being of the people at heart; his request is to be able to rule with justice, having a discerning mind (v. 9). As a king whose first concern is the welfare of the people, Solomon is also granted that which he does not request: wealth, honor, and a long life.

PEOPLE TO KNOW // SOLOMON

1 KINGS 3:9–10: Solomon was Israel's wealthiest and wisest king. He reigned during a time of peace and prosperity. He accomplished lavish building projects, most notably the ornate and stunning temple of God. When the temple was inaugurated, God's presence occupied it in the form of a thick cloud (1Ki 8:10).

God showed favor to Solomon from a young age, appearing to him in a dream and offering him anything he asked for. God was pleased when Solomon asked for wisdom (1Ki 3:9–10). Solomon's wisdom became legendary, and people came from far and wide to hear his decrees.

Solomon slipped away from righteousness, however. By the end of his reign, he looked like the opposite of what Moses said a king of Israel should be (Dt 17:16–17). Solomon's heart was led astray by his many wives and concubines, and he allowed the worship of other gods. He subjected the people to harsh forced labor to accomplish his building projects, as Pharaoh had done to the Israelites in Egypt. Solomon had storage cities built simply to accommodate his many horses and chariots. The house he built for himself was bigger than the house he built for God.

God raised up adversaries against Solomon because of his sin—most notably Jeroboam, who went on to take most of the kingdom away from Solomon's heir, Rehoboam (1Ki 11:26). While the kingdom did not crumble during Solomon's reign, his sin set a course of events in motion that had devastating effects.

APPLICATION ✣ Solomon was blessed by God, but he did not keep his eyes and heart fixed on God. Wealth, envy, lust and power can lead even the wisest heart astray. Jesus warned against the deceitfulness of riches (Mk 4:19), and Solomon's life is a testimony to that truth.

Wealth and power are not evil, but the pursuit of wealth and power can distract us from following God's plans. When we set our hearts on wanting more and more, we will end up turning away from God. Solomon should have abided by the wisdom of one of his own proverbs: "Better a little with the fear of the LORD than great wealth with turmoil" (Pr 15:16).

you will have no equal[o] among kings.
14And if you walk[p] in obedience to me
and keep my decrees and commands as
David your father did, I will give you a
long life."[q] 15Then Solomon awoke[r] — and
he realized it had been a dream.
He returned to Jerusalem, stood before the ark of the Lord's covenant and
sacrificed burnt offerings[s] and fellowship
offerings.[t] Then he gave a feast[u] for all
his court.

A Wise Ruling

16Now two prostitutes came to the king
and stood before him. 17One of them said,
"Pardon me, my lord. This woman and I
live in the same house, and I had a baby
while she was there with me. 18The third
day after my child was born, this woman
also had a baby. We were alone; there was
no one in the house but the two of us.
19"During the night this woman's
son died because she lay on him. 20So
she got up in the middle of the night
and took my son from my side while I
your servant was asleep. She put him
by her breast and put her dead son by
my breast. 21The next morning, I got
up to nurse my son — and he was dead!
But when I looked at him closely in the
morning light, I saw that it wasn't the
son I had borne."
22The other woman said, "No! The living one is my son; the dead one is yours."
But the first one insisted, "No! The
dead one is yours; the living one is
mine." And so they argued before the
king.

TRADE ROUTES IN ISRAEL

3:13 [o] 1Ki 10:23
3:14 [p] ver 6; Pr 3:1-2,16 [q] Ps 61:6; 91:16
3:15 [r] Ge 41:7 [s] 1Ki 8:65 [t] Mk 6:21 [u] Est 1:3,9; Da 5:1
3:26 [v] Ge 43:30; Isa 49:15; Jer 31:20; Hos 11:8

23The king said, "This one says, 'My
son is alive and your son is dead,' while
that one says, 'No! Your son is dead and
mine is alive.'"
24Then the king said, "Bring me a
sword." So they brought a sword for the
king. 25He then gave an order: "Cut the
living child in two and give half to one
and half to the other."
26The woman whose son was alive was
deeply moved[v] out of love for her son
and said to the king, "Please, my lord,
give her the living baby! Don't kill him!"
But the other said, "Neither I nor you
shall have him. Cut him in two!"
27Then the king gave his ruling: "Give
the living baby to the first woman. Do
not kill him; she is his mother."
28When all Israel heard the verdict the
king had given, they held the king in

3:16–23 The exceptional wisdom granted to Solomon is next demonstrated in a difficult judicial case. It is his responsibility to render a decision when there are no independent witnesses and where there is a great deal of bitterness between the two parties involved. Ancient prostitutes were generally slaves, often daughters who had been sold by their own parents. Or they were poor women who had never had an opportunity to marry or who had lost their husbands and were not supported by their own families. Note how Solomon has time for the most vulnerable of his subjects, not only in terms of their poverty but also in terms of their vices.

3:24–26 The judgment of Solomon shows both mercy and justice. Solomon's judgment does not deal with the circumstances of the death of the child or with the various accusations being made. His concern is with the bonding relationship of a mother and her child, which he presumes to be present by virtue of the fact that the case has come before him.

3:27 Once Solomon knows the identity of the true mother, he does not engage in further punishments. Justice is best served when tempered with mercy; the life of a child is preserved and the bond of motherhood restored, and there is renewed opportunity to make the best of a bad situation.

3:28 The judgment of the new king causes the people to be filled with awe: People recognize that Solomon has received a divine gift that is at work in enabling him to resolve an otherwise impossible case.

3:1–28 Under the new covenant no single government represents the kingdom of God, but government makes it possible for the kingdom to advance. This is true even when a government is hostile and restricts or persecutes expressions of faith in Christ. Consider that the apostle Paul was able to spread the gospel across Asia Minor and as far as Rome because of the security and order provided by *Pax Romana*. Prayer for government is

awe, because they saw that he had wisdom[w] from God to administer justice.

Solomon's Officials and Governors

4 So King Solomon ruled over all Israel. 2And these were his chief officials:

Azariah[x] son of Zadok — the priest;
3Elihoreph and Ahijah, sons of Shisha — secretaries;
Jehoshaphat[y] son of Ahilud — recorder;
4Benaiah[z] son of Jehoiada — commander in chief;
Zadok[a] and Abiathar — priests;
5Azariah son of Nathan — in charge of the district governors;
Zabud son of Nathan — a priest and adviser to the king;
6Ahishar — palace administrator;
Adoniram son of Abda — in charge of forced labor.

7Solomon had twelve district governors over all Israel, who supplied provisions for the king and the royal household. Each one had to provide supplies for one month in the year. 8These are their names:

Ben-Hur — in the hill country[b] of Ephraim;
9Ben-Deker — in Makaz, Shaalbim,[c] Beth Shemesh[d] and Elon Bethhanan;
10Ben-Hesed — in Arubboth (Sokoh[e] and all the land of Hepher[f] were his);
11Ben-Abinadab — in Naphoth Dor[g] (he was married to Taphath daughter of Solomon);
12Baana son of Ahilud — in Taanach and Megiddo, and in all of Beth Shan[h] next to Zarethan[i] below Jezreel, from Beth Shan to Abel Meholah[j] across to Jokmeam;[k]
13Ben-Geber — in Ramoth Gilead (the settlements of Jair[l] son of Manasseh in Gilead were his, as well as the region of Argob in Bashan and its sixty large walled cities[m] with bronze gate bars);
14Ahinadab son of Iddo — in Mahanaim;[n]
15Ahimaaz[o] — in Naphtali (he had married Basemath daughter of Solomon);
16Baana son of Hushai[p] — in Asher and in Aloth;
17Jehoshaphat son of Paruah — in Issachar;
18Shimei[q] son of Ela — in Benjamin;
19Geber son of Uri — in Gilead (the country of Sihon king of the Amorites and the country of Og[r] king of Bashan). He was the only governor over the district.

Solomon's Daily Provisions

20The people of Judah and Israel were
as numerous as the sand[s] on the seashore; they ate, they drank and they
were happy. 21And Solomon ruled[t] over all the kingdoms from the Euphrates River[u] to the land of the Philistines, as far as the border of Egypt.[v] These countries brought tribute[w] and were Solomon's subjects all his life.
22Solomon's daily provisions were thirty cors[a] of the finest flour and sixty cors[b] of meal,
23ten head of stall-fed cattle, twenty of pasture-fed cattle and a hundred sheep and goats, as well as deer,

[a] 22 That is, probably about 5 1/2 tons or about 5 metric tons [b] 22 That is, probably about 11 tons or about 10 metric tons

3:28 [w] ver 9, 11-12; Col 2:3
4:2 [x] 1Ch 6:10
4:3 [y] 2Sa 8:16
4:4 [z] 1Ki 2:35 [a] 1Ki 2:27
4:8 [b] Jos 24:33
4:9 [c] Jdg 1:35 [d] Jos 21:16
4:10 [e] Jos 15:35 [f] Jos 12:17
4:11 [g] Jos 11:2
4:12 [h] Jos 17:11; Jdg 5:19 [i] Jos 3:16 [j] 1Ki 19:16 [k] 1Ch 6:68
4:13 [l] Nu 32:41 [m] Dt 3:4
4:14 [n] Jos 13:26
4:15 [o] 2Sa 15:27
4:16 [p] 2Sa 15:32
4:18 [q] 1Ki 1:8
4:19 [r] Dt 3:8-10
4:20 [s] Ge 22:17; 32:12; 1Ki 3:8
4:21 [t] 2Ch 9:26; Ps 72:11 [u] Jos 1:4; Ps 72:8 [v] Ge 15:18 [w] Ps 68:29

important not only to provide for good order but because it is God's will that all should be saved and come to knowledge of the truth (1Ti 2:3–4).

4:1-6 The roster of chief officials mentions eight distinct offices as compared with five in 2Sa 8:16–18 and six in 2Sa 20:23–25. The list has been transmitted with variations, the result of historical and textual developments.
4:7-20 The districts of Solomon's administration are defined according to tribal territory and groups of cities. This is the only administrative document pertaining to the official organization of the kingdom. The administrative list in Kings has been incorporated into the narrative to show how the practical wisdom of Solomon brings satisfaction to his citizens (v. 20).
4:21 The extent of Solomon's kingdom and the prosperity of the people are fulfillments of the covenant with Abraham (Ge 15:18). Solomon reigns from the Euphrates River to the border of Egypt (v. 21); the record of kings bringing tribute to Solomon comprises a territory more vast than the land God had promised Abraham.
4:22-28 The list of provisions for a single day are for the entire palatial establishment, including servants and guests. A comparison of the texts for Solomon's stalls suggests that 4,000 is the original number. The records indicate that Solomon has 12,000 horses in 4,000 stalls and probably about 3,000 chariots, a formidable force comparable to others of the time.

gazelles, roebucks and choice fowl. 24For
he ruled over all the kingdoms west of
the Euphrates River, from Tiphsah[x] to
Gaza, and had peace[y] on all sides. 25Dur-
ing Solomon's lifetime Judah and Israel,
from Dan to Beersheba,[z] lived in safety,[a]
everyone under their own vine and under their own fig tree.[b]
26Solomon had four[a] thousand stalls
for chariot horses,[c] and twelve thousand
horses.[b]
27The district governors,[d] each in his
month, supplied provisions for King
Solomon and all who came to the king's
table. They saw to it that nothing was
lacking. 28They also brought to the
proper place their quotas of barley and
straw for the chariot horses and the other horses.

Solomon's Wisdom

29God gave Solomon wisdom[e] and
very great insight, and a breadth of understanding as measureless as the sand
on the seashore. 30Solomon's wisdom
was greater than the wisdom of all the
people of the East,[f] and greater than all
the wisdom of Egypt.[g] 31He was wiser[h]
than anyone else, including Ethan the
Ezrahite—wiser than Heman, Kalkol
and Darda, the sons of Mahol. And his
fame spread to all the surrounding nations. 32He spoke three thousand proverbs[i] and his songs[j] numbered a thousand and five. 33He spoke about plant
life, from the cedar of Lebanon to the
hyssop that grows out of walls. He also
spoke about animals and birds, reptiles
and fish. 34From all nations people came
to listen to Solomon's wisdom, sent by all
the kings[k] of the world, who had heard
of his wisdom.[c]

4:24 [x] Ps 72:11 [y] 1Ch 22:9
4:25 [z] Jdg 20:1 [a] Jer 23:6 [b] Mic 4:4; Zec 3:10
4:26 [c] 1Ki 10:26; 2Ch 1:14
4:27 [d] ver 7
4:29 [e] 1Ki 3:12
4:30 [f] Ge 25:6 [g] Ac 7:22
4:31 [h] 1Ki 3:12; 1Ch 2:6; 6:33; 15:19; Ps 89 Title
4:32 [i] Pr 1:1; Ecc 12:9 [j] SS 1:1
4:34 [k] 1Ki 10:1; 2Ch 9:23
5:1 [l] ver 10, 18; 2Sa 5:11; 1Ch 14:1

1Ki 4:34 ❖ Why is wisdom among the most important traits for a leader? How do we acquire godly wisdom?

Preparations for Building the Temple

5:1–16pp // 2Ch 2:1–18

5[d] When Hiram[l] king of Tyre heard
that Solomon had been anointed
king to succeed his father David, he sent
his envoys to Solomon, because he had
always been on friendly terms with David. 2Solomon sent back this message
to Hiram:

[a] *26* Some Septuagint manuscripts (see also 2 Chron. 9:25); Hebrew *forty* [b] *26* Or *charioteers* [c] *34* In Hebrew texts 4:21-34 is numbered 5:1-14. [d] In Hebrew texts 5:1-18 is numbered 5:15-32.

4:29–31 In addition to the wisdom required to govern a vast kingdom, Solomon has a breadth of knowledge that rivals that of all ancient peoples. Mesopotamia and Egypt were famous for wisdom, some aspects of which are preserved to the present time. Ethan and Heman are noted in their contribution to the Psalter (Ps 88–89). "Sons of Mahol" (v. 31) does not refer to physical ancestry but to their skill as musicians or dancers. Wisdom, poetry, and music are closely connected. "Ezrahite" (v. 31) means native and may indicate that this knowledge of musical instruments and poetry goes back to the pre-Israelite occupants of Canaan. Wisdom is expressed with skill and impact by means of poetry and song.

4:32–34 Solomon is not only known for his songs (v. 32) but also for his proverbs. There are collections of Solomon's proverbs, as indicated by the divisions in Proverbs. The "proverbs of Solomon" (Pr 10:1—22:16) contain 475 proverbs, the numerical value of the name Solomon. The proverbs of Solomon inspire other collections of proverbs (e.g., Pr 25:1; 30; 31:1-9) long after Solomon's death.

Ancient wisdom encompassed not only music and poetry along with proverbial sayings for prudent conduct, but also much of what is now called science. The reference to Solomon's wisdom concerning nature (v. 33) is not just that nature served as a basis for proverbial sayings. Solomon's classification of creatures into beasts, birds, reptiles, and fish may have been another aspect of his comprehensive knowledge.

✣ **4:1–34** Wisdom is knowledge of how to live with other people and how to live in harmony with the world of nature. These two kinds of knowledge are the basis of getting on well in this world. Living in harmony with the world of nature is a continuing challenge as environmental issues emerge and persist. Wisdom of how to live with people can be an even greater challenge. Conflict and violence are part of social relations from the smallest units of society to the largest: homes, communities, nations, and between nations. The ideals of Solomon's wisdom and administration are rightly remembered as the goal toward which every society must strive.

5:1–6 Hiram's alliance with David and Solomon serves as the grounds for Solomon to make his appeal for building materials. Solomon first explains the delay in building the temple: David has been involved in warfare to gain control over his empire. Chronicles develops the theological reason why David could not build the temple (1Ch 22:7–8; 28:2–3); Solomon gives a historical reason: David was too occupied by warfare, and the peace of God's kingdom is inconsistent with a person constantly involved in warfare.

3“You know that because of the
wars[m] waged against my father David
from all sides, he could not build a
temple for the Name of the LORD his
God until the LORD put his enemies
under his feet. 4But now the LORD
my God has given me rest[n] on every
side, and there is no adversary or disaster. 5I intend, therefore, to build
a temple[o] for the Name of the LORD
my God, as the LORD told my father
David, when he said, ‘Your son whom
I will put on the throne in your place
will build the temple for my Name.’[p]
6“So give orders that cedars of
Lebanon be cut for me. My men will
work with yours, and I will pay you
for your men whatever wages you
set. You know that we have no one
so skilled in felling timber as the
Sidonians.”

7When Hiram heard Solomon’s message, he was greatly pleased and said,
“Praise be to the LORD today, for he has
given David a wise son to rule over this
great nation.”
8So Hiram sent word to Solomon:

“I have received the message you
sent me and will do all you want in
providing the cedar and juniper
logs. 9My men will haul them down
from Lebanon to the Mediterranean
Sea[q], and I will float them as rafts by
sea to the place you specify. There I
will separate them and you can take
them away. And you are to grant my
wish by providing food[r] for my royal
household.”

10In this way Hiram kept Solomon
supplied with all the cedar and juniper
logs he wanted, 11and Solomon gave Hiram twenty thousand cors[a] of wheat as

1Ki 5:13–18 ❖ Was Solomon’s labor force appropriate? When does ambition become greed?

food for his household, in addition to
twenty thousand baths[b,c] of pressed olive oil. Solomon continued to do this for
Hiram year after year. 12The LORD gave
Solomon wisdom,[s] just as he had promised him. There were peaceful relations
between Hiram and Solomon, and the
two of them made a treaty.[t]
13King Solomon conscripted laborers[u]
from all Israel—thirty thousand men.
14He sent them off to Lebanon in shifts of
ten thousand a month, so that they spent
one month in Lebanon and two months
at home. Adoniram[v] was in charge of the
forced labor. 15Solomon had seventy thousand carriers and eighty thousand stonecutters in the hills, 16as well as thirty-three
hundred[d] foremen[w] who supervised the
project and directed the workers. 17At the
king’s command they removed from the
quarry[x] large blocks of high-grade stone[y]
to provide a foundation of dressed stone
for the temple. 18The craftsmen of Solomon and Hiram and workers from Byblos[z]
cut and prepared the timber and stone for
the building of the temple.

Solomon Builds the Temple

6:1–29pp // 2Ch 3:1–14

6 In the four hundred and eightieth[e]
year after the Israelites came out of
Egypt, in the fourth year of Solomon’s

[a] *11* That is, probably about 3,600 tons or about 3,250 metric tons [b] *11* Septuagint (see also 2 Chron. 2:10); Hebrew *twenty cors* [c] *11* That is, about 120,000 gallons or about 440,000 liters
[d] *16* Hebrew; some Septuagint manuscripts (see also 2 Chron. 2:2,18) *thirty-six hundred*
[e] *1* Hebrew; Septuagint *four hundred and fortieth*

5:3 [m] 1Ch 22:8; 28:3
5:4 [n] 1Ki 4:24; 1Ch 22:9
5:5 [o] 1Ch 17:12 [p] 2Sa 7:13; 1Ch 22:10
5:9 [q] Ezr 3:7 [r] Eze 27:17; Ac 12:20
5:12 [s] 1Ki 3:12 [t] Am 1:9
5:13 [u] 1Ki 9:15
5:14 [v] 1Ki 4:6; 2Ch 10:18
5:16 [w] 1Ki 9:23
5:17 [x] 1Ki 6:7 [y] 1Ch 22:2
5:18 [z] Jos 13:5

5:7-10 Hiram’s response is to praise Solomon’s God for the succession of a wise king like Solomon (v. 7). Hiram’s reply is constructed around his obligation and Solomon’s obligation: Hiram will give Solomon trees, and Solomon will give Hiram food (vv. 8–9).

The cedar tree (vv. 8, 10) is renowned for its beauty and impressive height, reaching as high as 30 meters (nearly 100 feet). The kings of Egypt, Mesopotamia, Phoenicia, Assyria, Babylon, Persia, and Greece all used cedar timber for building temples and palaces. Cedar wood was also desired for its fragrance. The trees were bound together in rafts so they could be driven by water as far as Joppa, where they could be disassembled and taken overland to Jerusalem.

5:11-12 Solomon provides Hiram annually with over fifty thousand bushels of grain and over one hundred thousand gallons of the finest oil. The oil was of exceptional quality for the lamps in the tabernacle (Ex 27:20) and the preparation of flour offerings (Ex 29:40). The treaty is of mutual benefit, since the cliffs of Tyre are not conducive to producing food and Solomon requires the skills and materials of the Phoenicians.

5:13–18 The second section of building preparations gives some detail of the work of Adoniram (cf. 4:6), the chief officer in charge of the conscripted labor force. Hiram’s workers will bring the cedars down from Lebanon (5:9) assisted by Solomon’s workforce. The amount of labor required to quarry and shape the stones to lay the foundation of the temple made them costly (v. 17).

6:1 The description of the temple construction

reign over Israel, in the month of Ziv, the second month, he began to build the temple of the LORD.[a]

2The temple[b] that King Solomon built for the LORD was sixty cubits long, twenty wide and thirty high.[a] 3The portico at the front of the main hall of the temple extended the width of the temple, that is twenty cubits,[b] and projected ten cubits[c] from the front of the temple. 4He made narrow windows[c] high up in the temple walls. 5Against the walls of the main hall and inner sanctuary he built a structure around the building, in which there were side rooms.[d] 6The lowest floor was five cubits[d] wide, the middle floor six cubits[e] and the third floor seven.[f] He made offset ledges around the outside of the temple so that nothing would be inserted into the temple walls.

7In building the temple, only blocks dressed[e] at the quarry were used, and no hammer, chisel or any other iron tool[f] was heard at the temple site while it was being built.

8The entrance to the lowest[g] floor was on the south side of the temple; a stairway led up to the middle level and from there to the third. 9So he built the temple and completed it, roofing it with beams and cedar[g] planks. 10And he built the side rooms all along the temple. The height of each was five cubits, and they were attached to the temple by beams of cedar.

11The word of the LORD came to Solomon: 12"As for this temple you are building, if you follow my decrees, observe my laws and keep all my commands and obey them, I will fulfill through you the promise[h] I gave to David your father. 13And I will live among the Israelites and will not abandon[i] my people Israel."

14So Solomon built the temple and completed[j] it. 15He lined its interior walls with cedar boards, paneling them from the floor of the temple to the ceiling,[k] and covered the floor of the temple with planks of juniper. 16He partitioned off twenty cubits at the rear of the temple with cedar boards from floor to ceiling to form within the temple an inner sanctuary, the Most Holy Place.[l] 17The main hall in front of this room was forty cubits[h] long. 18The inside of the temple

1Ki 6:11-13 ❖ How does Solomon's temple foreshadow life with the Spirit for God's followers today (see 2Pe 2:5)?

6:1 [a] Ac 7:47
6:2 [b] Eze 41:1
6:4 [c] Eze 40:16; 41:16
6:5 [d] ver 16, 19-21; Eze 41:5-6
6:7 [e] Ex 20:25 [f] Dt 27:5
6:9 [g] ver 14, 38
6:12 [h] 2Sa 7:12-16; 1Ki 2:4; 9:5
6:13 [i] Ex 25:8; Lev 26:11; Dt 31:6; Heb 13:5
6:14 [j] ver 9, 38
6:15 [k] 1Ki 7:7
6:16 [l] Ex 26:33; Lev 16:2; 1Ki 8:6

[a] 2 That is, about 90 feet long, 30 feet wide and 45 feet high or about 27 meters long, 9 meters wide and 14 meters high [b] 3 That is, about 30 feet or about 9 meters; also in verses 16 and 20 [c] 3 That is, about 15 feet or about 4.5 meters; also in verses 23-26 [d] 6 That is, about 7 1/2 feet or about 2.3 meters; also in verses 10 and 24 [e] 6 That is, about 9 feet or about 2.7 meters [f] 6 That is, about 11 feet or about 3.2 meters [g] 8 Septuagint; Hebrew *middle* [h] 17 That is, about 60 feet or about 18 meters

begins and ends with a chronological notice (vv. 1, 37–38). The introduction sets the month in which the foundation is laid in reference to the exodus. This is significant for two reasons. First, the temple represents the worldview of the Israelites that Yahweh rules in all the earth, so they calculate their chronology from the founding of the temple. Second, the exodus is the redemptive event through which the Israelites experience the rule of God in the world (Ex 15:13, 18).

The account of the temple construction consists of three sections. The first describes the exterior of the temple (vv. 2–14), the second its interior (vv. 15–28), and the third particular features of the furnishings of the temple and court (vv. 29–36).

6:2–6 The description of the exterior concludes with a statement that the building has been completed (v. 9a); this is followed by a parenthetical note on the construction of the roof, the room extensions around the sides of the building, and the exterior paneling (vv. 9b–10). This section ends with an exhortation to obey the covenant (vv. 11–13); the covenant, not the temple, is the means to divine presence. The building account resumes with a repetition of the statement that Solomon built and completed the temple (v. 14; cf. v. 9); this repetition marks the transition to the second section.

6:7–14 The use of undressed stones taken directly from the quarry conforms to the requirement that no iron tools were to be used on stones for altars used in worship (v. 7; Ex 20:25; Dt 27:5–6). The prohibition against dressed stones is another way of distinguishing an Israelite place of worship from the Canaanite shrines. Israelite altars are to be unadorned, made of earth or rough stones and without steps (Ex 20:24–26). The temple symbolizes the divine rule but in no sense the actual image of a king, not even in the construction of the building itself.

6:15–18 The temple's interior is finished with costly materials: cedar for the wall panels and juniper for the floor panels (vv. 15–16). The interior walls of the temple have carvings of gourds and open flowers, cherubs and palmettes (vv. 18, 29). At the extreme interior of the hall a special area is constructed as the Most Holy Place (v. 16b). It is constructed with equal lengths in all directions, extending 20 cubits into the hall and 20 cubits toward the ceiling (cf. 2Ch 3:8).

SOLOMON'S TEMPLE

The temple of Solomon, located near the king's palace, functioned as God's royal palace and Israel's national center of worship. The Lord said to Solomon, "I have consecrated this temple . . . by putting my Name there forever. My eyes and my heart will always be there" (1Ki 9:3). By its cosmological and royal symbolism, the sanctuary taught the absolute sovereignty of the Lord over the whole creation and his special headship over Israel.

The floor plan is a type that has a long history in Semitic religion, particularly among the West Semites. An early example of the tripartite division into portico, main hall and inner sanctuary has been found at Syrian Ebla (c. 2300 BC) and, much later but more contemporaneous with Solomon, at 'Ain Dara in north Syria (tenth century BC) and at Tell Tayinat in southeast Turkey (eighth century BC). Like Solomon's, the temples at 'Ain Dara and at Tell Tayinat had three divisions, had two columns supporting the entrance, and were located adjacent to the royal palace.

Many archaeological parallels can be drawn to the methods of construction used in the temple, e.g., the "dressed stone and ... cedar beams" technique described in 1Ki 6:36. Interestingly, evidence for the largest bronze-casting industry ever found in the Holy Land comes from the same locale and period as that indicated in Scripture: Zarethan in the Jordan valley c. 1000 BC.

960-586 BC

Historical accounts of temple architecture are imprecise and subject to academic interpretation; subsequently, artistic representations vary.

This model (p. 525) recognizes influence from the wilderness tabernacle, accepts general Near Eastern cultural diffusion, and rejects overt pagan Canaanite symbols. It uses known archaeological parallels to supplement the text and assumes interior dimensions from 1Ki 6:17-20.

was cedar,[m] carved with gourds and open
flowers. Everything was cedar; no stone
was to be seen.
19He prepared the inner sanctuary[n]
within the temple to set the ark of the
covenant[o] of the LORD there. 20The inner
sanctuary[p] was twenty cubits long, twenty wide and twenty high. He overlaid
the inside with pure gold, and he also
overlaid the altar of cedar. 21Solomon
covered the inside of the temple with
pure gold, and he extended gold chains
across the front of the inner sanctuary,
which was overlaid with gold. 22So he
overlaid the whole interior with gold.
He also overlaid with gold the altar that
belonged to the inner sanctuary.
23For the inner sanctuary he made
a pair of cherubim[q] out of olive wood,
each ten cubits high. 24One wing of the
first cherub was five cubits long, and
the other wing five cubits—ten cubits
from wing tip to wing tip. 25The second
cherub also measured ten cubits, for the
two cherubim were identical in size and
shape. 26The height of each cherub was
ten cubits. 27He placed the cherubim[r] inside the innermost room of the temple,
with their wings spread out. The wing
of one cherub touched one wall, while
the wing of the other touched the other
wall, and their wings touched each other
in the middle of the room. 28He overlaid
the cherubim with gold.
29On the walls all around the temple,
in both the inner and outer rooms, he
carved cherubim,[s] palm trees and open
flowers. 30He also covered the floors of

6:18 [m] 1Ki 7:24; Ps 74:6
6:19 [n] 1Ki 8:6 [o] 1Sa 3:3
6:20 [p] Eze 41:3-4
6:23 [q] Ex 37:1-9
6:27 [r] Ex 25:20; 37:9; 1Ki 8:7; 2Ch 5:8
6:29 [s] ver 32,35

6:19-22 The Most Holy Place is prepared as a repository for the ark, which contains the terms of the Mosaic covenant. The interior of the Most Holy Place is covered with pure gold (v. 20). Nothing is said about the veil in front of the Most Holy Place (cf. 2Ch 3:14), but reference is made to gold chains pulled across its front (v. 21). Perhaps the curtain was pulled with these chains.

An altar built of cedar stands in front of the Most Holy Place. Though not stated, the altar inside the temple is for offering incense, as in the tabernacle (Ex 30:1-10; 1Ch 28:18).

6:23-28 Cherubim were a distinguishing feature of thrones in ancient Mesopotamia, Syria, and Canaan. They were composite creatures, signifying union of the highest powers of strength, speed, and wisdom. The cherubim of Solomon's temple are distinct because they are not designed to serve as a human throne. They are attached to the ark, which serves as a footstool to God's throne (cf. 1Ch 28:2).

6:29-33 The third section of the temple description notes particular features about the larger temple complex. Cherubim, palm trees, and open flowers are engraved on all the walls, inside and outside. Special attention is given to the wood doors leading to the Most Holy Place.

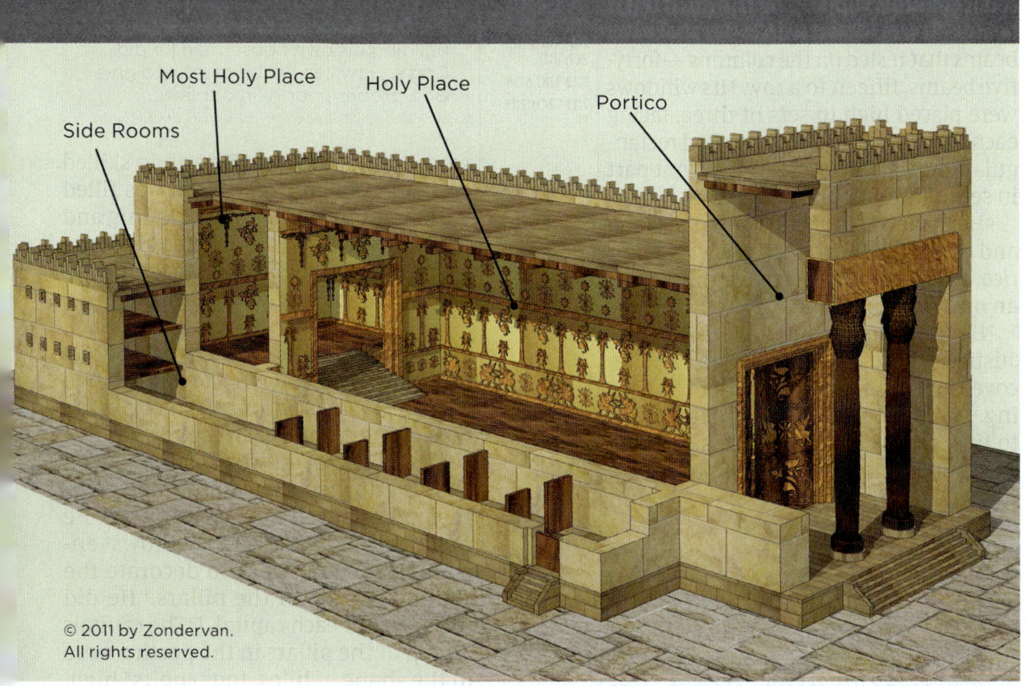

both the inner and outer rooms of the
temple with gold.
31For the entrance to the inner sanctuary he made doors out of olive wood that
were one fifth of the width of the sanctuary. 32And on the two olive-wood doors
he carved cherubim, palm trees and open
flowers, and overlaid the cherubim and
palm trees with hammered gold. 33In the
same way, for the entrance to the main
hall he made doorframes out of olive
wood that were one fourth of the width
of the hall. 34He also made two doors
out of juniper wood, each having two
leaves that turned in sockets. 35He carved
cherubim, palm trees and open flowers
on them and overlaid them with gold
hammered evenly over the carvings.
36And he built the inner courtyard of
three courses[t] of dressed stone and one
course of trimmed cedar beams.
37The foundation of the temple of the
LORD was laid in the fourth year, in the
month of Ziv. 38In the eleventh year in
the month of Bul, the eighth month, the
temple was finished in all its details according to its specifications.[u] He had
spent seven years building it.

Solomon Builds His Palace

7 It took Solomon thirteen years, however, to complete the construction of his
palace.[v] 2He built the Palace[w] of the Forest
of Lebanon[x] a hundred cubits long, fifty
wide and thirty high,[a] with four rows of

6:36 [t] 1Ki 7:12; Ezr 6:4
6:38 [u] Heb 8:5
7:1 [v] 1Ki 9:10; 2Ch 8:1
7:2 [w] 2Sa 7:2 [x] 1Ki 10:17; 2Ch 9:16

[a] 2 That is, about 150 feet long, 75 feet wide and 45 feet high or about 45 meters long, 23 meters wide and 14 meters high

6:34–35 The design of the doors is unclear. The two doors of juniper wood providing entrance into the main hall each have two panels. For the first time it is explained that the gold is inlaid over the engraved figures.

6:36—7:1 A wall consisting of three layers of shaped stones with an ornate cedar beam on the top encloses the temple in an inner court. The temple is a separate section within the great court, which includes the temple and the entire palace compound. The concluding chronological reference to the seven years of temple building includes notice of the thirteen years it took to build the palace.

7:2–5 The first building described is the great assembly hall, which also serves as an armory. It is known as the "Palace of the Forest of Lebanon" because its many pillars give it the appearance of a great forest. The structure of the building, however, is not clear; salient features are given to indicate its grandeur.

The three sets of doorways serve as entrances to the great halls and are perhaps placed at the ends, opposite each other. The doorways and doorposts are square. Whatever the arrangement of the rooms, doors, and windows, the "Forest of Lebanon" is a hall fit for a great assembly with plenty of room for an armory.

cedar columns supporting trimmed cedar
beams. 3It was roofed with cedar above the
beams that rested on the columns—forty-
five beams, fifteen to a row. 4Its windows
were placed high in sets of three, facing
each other. 5All the doorways had rectangular frames; they were in the front part
in sets of three, facing each other.[a]
6He made a colonnade fifty cubits long
and thirty wide.[b] In front of it was a portico, and in front of that were pillars and
an overhanging roof.
7He built the throne hall, the Hall of
Justice, where he was to judge,[y] and he
covered it with cedar from floor to ceiling.[cz] 8And the palace in which he was
to live, set farther back, was similar in
design. Solomon also made a palace like
this hall for Pharaoh's daughter, whom
he had married.[a]
9All these structures, from the outside
to the great courtyard and from foundation to eaves, were made of blocks
of high-grade stone cut to size and
smoothed on their inner and outer faces. 10The foundations were laid with large
stones of good quality, some measuring
ten cubits[d] and some eight.[e] 11Above were
high-grade stones, cut to size, and cedar
beams. 12The great courtyard was surrounded by a wall of three courses[b] of
dressed stone and one course of trimmed
cedar beams, as was the inner courtyard
of the temple of the LORD with its portico.

The Temple's Furnishings

7:23–26pp // 2Ch 4:2–5
7:38–51pp // 2Ch 4:6,10—5:1

13King Solomon sent to Tyre and
brought Huram,[fc] 14whose mother was
a widow from the tribe of Naphtali and
whose father was from Tyre and a skilled
craftsman in bronze. Huram was filled
with wisdom,[d] with understanding and
with knowledge to do all kinds of bronze
work. He came to King Solomon and did
all[e] the work assigned to him.
15He cast two bronze pillars,[f] each
eighteen cubits high and twelve cubits
in circumference.[g] 16He also made two
capitals[g] of cast bronze to set on the
tops of the pillars; each capital was five
cubits[h] high. 17A network of interwoven
chains adorned the capitals on top of
the pillars, seven for each capital. 18He
made pomegranates in two rows[i] encircling each network to decorate the
capitals on top of the pillars.[j] He did
the same for each capital. 19The capitals
on top of the pillars in the portico were
in the shape of lilies, four cubits[k] high.

7:7 [y] Ps 122:5; Pr 20:8 [z] 1Ki 6:15
7:8 [a] 1Ki 3:1; 2Ch 8:11
7:12 [b] 1Ki 6:36
7:13 [c] 2Ch 2:13
7:14 [d] Ex 31:2-5; 35:31; 36:1; 2Ch 2:14 [e] 2Ch 4:11,16
7:15 [f] 2Ki 25:17; 2Ch 3:15; 4:12; Jer 52:17,21
7:16 [g] 2Ki 25:17

> **1Ki 7:1** ❖ Solomon spent more time building his own house than he did God's. How can we be careful to give God proper priority in our lives?

[a] *5* The meaning of the Hebrew for this verse is uncertain. [b] *6* That is, about 75 feet long and 45 feet wide or about 23 meters long and 14 meters wide [c] *7* Vulgate and Syriac; Hebrew *floor* [d] *10* That is, about 15 feet or about 4.5 meters; also in verse 23 [e] *10* That is, about 12 feet or about 3.6 meters [f] *13* Hebrew *Hiram,* a variant of *Huram;* also in verses 40 and 45 [g] *15* That is, about 27 feet high and 18 feet in circumference or about 8.1 meters high and 5.4 meters in circumference [h] *16* That is, about 7 1/2 feet or about 2.3 meters; also in verse 23 [i] *18* Two Hebrew manuscripts and Septuagint; most Hebrew manuscripts *made the pillars, and there were two rows* [j] *18* Many Hebrew manuscripts and Syriac; most Hebrew manuscripts *pomegranates* [k] *19* That is, about 6 feet or about 1.8 meters; also in verse 38

7:6–8 The hall of pillars does not seem to be an independent building but a colonnade that serves as an entrance to the great assembly hall. A hall along the front of the porch has a protective barrier guarding the entrance into the building. It is likely that this porch is built to serve as the judgment hall.

The palace of Solomon and the quarters for all his servants are set in another court back (west) of the hall. The public buildings are situated in a separate court; the palace is not accessible to the public but has an entrance to the public court as well as to the inner court of the temple. The palace of Solomon and that of Pharaoh's daughter are similar in construction to the other buildings, since all of them are royal structures.

7:9–12 Special notice is made of the costly stonework that is part of the buildings and the courts. Dressed stone is used from the foundation to the framework—or to the roof overhang, if stonework is mixed with the woodwork, as is often done. This seems to have been the case in the royal buildings, as the stonework and woodwork are made to measure on the upper levels (v. 11). The stonework extends as far as the large public court. The foundation stones are large (3.5 to 4.5 meters; 11.5 to 14.6 feet) but not excessive by building standards. The larger outer court is built with three levels of stone and a row of cedar timbers (v. 12), like the inner temple court (cf. 6:36).

7:15–16 The first of the artifacts described are the two pillars set in the porch of the temple. They are made of bronze and are 8 meters (about 27 feet) in height. Their circumference is over 5 meters (17.5 feet), making them almost 2 meters (6 feet) in diameter.

7:17–22 The height of each pillar is extended by a

TEMPLE FURNISHINGS

Glimpses of the rich ornamentation of Solomon's temple can be gained through recent discoveries that illumine the text of 1Ki 6–7.

1 ARK OF THE COVENANT
Cherubim with wings flanking a royal throne are attested in Egyptian, Israelite and Phoenician art (e.g., at Megiddo).

2 MOVABLE BRONZE BASIN
An extremely close parallel to the wheeled portable basins used in the courtyard of the temple has come from archaeological excavations on Cyprus. This representation combines elements from the biblical text with the archaeological evidence.

3 INCENSE ALTAR
A stone incense altar having four horns on the corners was found at Megiddo. It provides a clear idea of the shape of the gold incense altar in the temple.

4 TABLE FOR THE BREAD OF THE PRESENCE
The table for the bread of the Presence was made of gold.

5 LAMPSTAND
Ten lampstands were in the temple, five on each side of the sanctuary (1Ki 7:49), to which were added ten tables (2Ch 4:8). Ritual sevenfold lamps have been found at several places in Israel, including Hazor and Dothan. The stand itself is modeled on bronze ones from the excavations at Megiddo.

20On the capitals of both pillars, above
the bowl-shaped part next to the network, were the two hundred pomegranates[h] in rows all around. 21He erected
the pillars at the portico of the temple.
The pillar to the south he named Jakin[a]
and the one to the north Boaz.[b i] 22The
capitals on top were in the shape of lilies. And so the work on the pillars was
completed.
23He made the Sea[j] of cast metal, circular in shape, measuring ten cubits
from rim to rim and five cubits high. It
took a line of thirty cubits[c] to measure
around it. 24Below the rim, gourds encircled it — ten to a cubit. The gourds
were cast in two rows in one piece with
the Sea.
25The Sea stood on twelve bulls,[k] three
facing north, three facing west, three facing south and three facing east. The Sea
rested on top of them, and their hindquarters were toward the center. 26It was
a handbreadth[d] in thickness, and its rim
was like the rim of a cup, like a lily blossom. It held two thousand baths.[e]

7:20 [h] 2Ch 3:16; 4:13; Jer 52:23
7:21 [i] 1Ki 6:3; 2Ch 3:17
7:23 [j] 2Ki 25:13; 1Ch 18:8; Jer 52:17
7:25 [k] 2Ch 4:4-5; Jer 52:20

[a] 21 *Jakin* probably means *he establishes.*
[b] 21 *Boaz* probably means *in him is strength.*
[c] 23 That is, about 45 feet or about 14 meters
[d] 26 That is, about 3 inches or about 7.5 centimeters
[e] 26 That is, about 12,000 gallons or about 44,000 liters; the Septuagint does not have this sentence.

---

bronze capital at the top, just over 2 meters (7 feet) in height (v. 16). These are ornately decorated. The pillar to the south is named Jakin and the pillar to the north Boaz; the significance of the names can only be guessed: Jakin ("he establishes") may refer to the promise of the kingdom, and Boaz ("in him is strength") may have been a prayer for the king. The pillars perhaps have a structural as well as symbolic function.

7:23–26 The second item described is a giant water container, over 4 meters (15 feet) in diameter and over 2 meters (7.5 feet) in height, cast with two

27He also made ten movable stands[l] of
bronze; each was four cubits long, four
wide and three high.[a] 28This is how the
stands were made: They had side panels
attached to uprights. 29On the panels
between the uprights were lions, bulls
and cherubim — and on the uprights
as well. Above and below the lions and
bulls were wreaths of hammered work.
30Each stand[m] had four bronze wheels
with bronze axles, and each had a basin resting on four supports, cast with
wreaths on each side. 31On the inside
of the stand there was an opening that
had a circular frame one cubit[b] deep.
This opening was round, and with its
basework it measured a cubit and a half.[c]
Around its opening there was engraving.
The panels of the stands were square, not
round. 32The four wheels were under the
panels, and the axles of the wheels were
attached to the stand. The diameter of
each wheel was a cubit and a half. 33The
wheels were made like chariot wheels;
the axles, rims, spokes and hubs were
all of cast metal.

34Each stand had four handles, one on
each corner, projecting from the stand.
35At the top of the stand there was a circular band half a cubit[d] deep. The supports and panels were attached to the top
of the stand. 36He engraved cherubim,
lions and palm trees on the surfaces of
the supports and on the panels, in every
available space, with wreaths all around.
37This is the way he made the ten stands.
They were all cast in the same molds and
were identical in size and shape.

38He then made ten bronze basins,[n]
each holding forty baths[e] and measuring four cubits across, one basin to go on
each of the ten stands. 39He placed five of
the stands on the south side of the temple and five on the north. He placed the
Sea on the south side, at the southeast
corner of the temple. 40He also made the
pots[f] and shovels and sprinkling bowls.

So Huram finished all the work he
had undertaken for King Solomon in
the temple of the LORD:

41 the two pillars;
the two bowl-shaped capitals on top of the pillars;
the two sets of network decorating the two bowl-shaped capitals on top of the pillars;
42 the four hundred pomegranates for the two sets of network (two rows of pomegranates for each network decorating the bowl-shaped capitals[o] on top of the pillars);
43 the ten stands with their ten basins;
44 the Sea and the twelve bulls under it;
45 the pots, shovels and sprinkling bowls.[p]

All these objects that Huram made
for King Solomon for the temple of the
LORD were of burnished bronze. 46The
king had them cast in clay molds in the

7:27 [l] ver 38; 2Ch 4:14
7:30 [m] 2Ki 16:17
7:38 [n] Ex 30:18; 2Ch 4:6
7:42 [o] ver 20
7:45 [p] Ex 27:3

[a] *27* That is, about 6 feet long and wide and about 4 1/2 feet high or about 1.8 meters long and wide and 1.4 meters high [b] *31* That is, about 18 inches or about 45 centimeters [c] *31* That is, about 2 1/4 feet or about 68 centimeters; also in verse 32 [d] *35* That is, about 9 inches or about 23 centimeters [e] *38* That is, about 240 gallons or about 880 liters [f] *40* Many Hebrew manuscripts, Septuagint, Syriac and Vulgate (see also verse 45 and 2 Chron. 4:11); many other Hebrew manuscripts *basins*

---

rows of gourds beneath its rim, which have the shape of a lily. It holds about 11,000 gallons of water. Its significance is to be found in the name "Sea." Water has a practical use in ritual cleansings in Solomon's temple (2Ch 4:6), but the size of the great water basin is not practical for that purpose. Its primary purpose in the temple court is to represent the rule of God over the cosmos.
7:27–35 In addition to the great Sea, the temple has ten water tanks in the shape of a bowl to distribute water for cleansing purposes. Each of these tanks is 6 feet in diameter and holds about 220 gallons of water (v. 38). It is estimated that the weight of each stand with its water reservoir full would be 3.5 tons. They are equipped with wheels, but they are not readily mobile.

The bases for these tanks are elaborately decorated with cherub figures and borders, above and below, with delicately worked spiral designs (v. 29). The opening of the box-shaped frame has within it a circular rim to support the laver (v. 31), with engravings on the square frame that hold the laver support. The wheels are over 2 feet in diameter (v. 32), similar to a chariot wheel with rims, spokes, and a hub cast together (v. 33) and attached to the legs with axles in sockets.
7:36–39 All the space on the panels, frames, and handles is appropriately decorated with cherubim and palm trees (v. 36). All ten lavers are identical (v. 37), disposed in two groups at the south and north corners of the temple (v. 39), with the great Sea being further to the east on the south side.
7:40–47 Huram is responsible for a variety of artifacts used for the altars, including ash containers and shovels and containers for sprinkling (cf. Ex 27:3). The bowl shape of the capitals has not been mentioned previously. The items are made with polished bronze and smelted in earthen molds in the Jordan Valley north of Jerusalem, just north of the Jabbok River east of the Jordan.

plain[q] of the Jordan between Sukkoth[r]
and Zarethan.[s] 47Solomon left all these
things unweighed,[t] because there were
so many; the weight of the bronze was
not determined.

48Solomon also made all the furnishings that were in the LORD's temple:

the golden altar;
the golden table[u] on which was the
bread of the Presence;[v]
49the lampstands[w] of pure gold (five
on the right and five on the left,
in front of the inner sanctuary);
the gold floral work and lamps and
tongs;
50the pure gold basins, wick trimmers,
sprinkling bowls, dishes and censers;[x]
and the gold sockets for the doors
of the innermost room, the Most
Holy Place, and also for the doors
of the main hall of the temple.

51When all the work King Solomon
had done for the temple of the LORD was
finished, he brought in the things his
father David had dedicated[y] — the silver and gold and the furnishings — and
he placed them in the treasuries of the
LORD's temple.

7:46 [q]2Ch 4:17 [r]Ge 33:17; Jos 13:27 [s]Jos 3:16
7:47 [t]1Ch 22:3
7:48 [u]Ex 37:10 [v]Ex 25:30
7:49 [w]Ex 25:31-38
7:50 [x]2Ki 25:13
7:51 [y]2Sa 8:11
8:1 [z]Nu 7:2 [a]2Sa 6:17 [b]2Sa 5:7
8:2 [c]2Ch 7:8 [d]Lev 23:34
8:3 [e]Nu 7:9; Jos 3:3
8:4 [f]1Ki 3:4; 2Ch 1:3
8:5 [g]2Sa 6:13
8:6 [h]2Sa 6:17

The Ark Brought to the Temple

8:1–21pp // 2Ch 5:2—6:11

8 Then King Solomon summoned into
his presence at Jerusalem the elders
of Israel, all the heads of the tribes and
the chiefs[z] of the Israelite families, to
bring up the ark[a] of the LORD's covenant
from Zion, the City of David.[b] 2All the Israelites came together to King Solomon
at the time of the festival[c] in the month
of Ethanim, the seventh month.[d]
3When all the elders of Israel had arrived, the priests[e] took up the ark, 4and
they brought up the ark of the LORD and
the tent of meeting[f] and all the sacred
furnishings in it. The priests and Levites
carried them up, 5and King Solomon and
the entire assembly of Israel that had
gathered about him were before the ark,
sacrificing[g] so many sheep and cattle that
they could not be recorded or counted.
6The priests then brought the ark
of the LORD's covenant[h] to its place in
the inner sanctuary of the temple, the
Most Holy Place, and put it beneath the

7:48-51 The gold items are located inside the building next to the specially constructed throne room at the back. The incense altar (cf. 6:20, 22), the table with bread, and the ten lampstands (each with seven arms) are elements in the temple to represent access to the presence of the divine. Other floral decorations are part of the lampstands and lamps, which provide decoration and light. The highest quality of metal distinguishes the sacredness of the area.

5:1–7:51a The detail and precision described in these chapters point to Solomon's desire for excellence in building the temple as a way to honor a perfect and holy God. Artists, composers, sculptors, and the builders of massive cathedrals and churches throughout history have had no less desire for excellence than Solomon did as they have built edifices and created music and artwork to honor God.

However, later in Israelite history the leaders of Judah reduced the temple to a place of ritual; their sacrifices, festivals, and even their prayers in the temple were an abomination to God (Isa 1:11-15). Though they had intense dedication to the temple, their city and land were equivalent to Sodom and Gomorrah (Isa 1:10). The grandeur that Solomon carefully built into the temple was not sufficient to assure that God would be honored in the land of Israel.

One of the most decisive influences in the lives of the faithful is their understanding of God. A subtle deception for Christians is the assumption that belief in the Bible will lead to a true understanding of the God of the Bible. Though mortals can never understand God fully, it is possible and necessary to seek to understand God rightly. It is also possible to come to a seriously distorted understanding of God through improper, however sincere, reading of the Scriptures. Misunderstanding God may be no less disastrous for a church than it was for those who celebrated the construction of Solomon's temple.

7:51b After the building is completed, its function as a temple must be established. The articles dedicated to God by a vow are brought to its treasuries, and the ark is placed in the Most Holy Place.

8:1-3 Solomon assembles the elders of Israel, the heads of the tribes, and the ancestral chieftains to bring the ark up to the temple. Several groups of people are distinguished: The ordinary people are brought together with their leaders, while the priests actually carry the ark (vv. 2-3).

8:4-7 The ark processional takes place in the seventh month. Since the temple was completed in the eighth month (6:38), the inauguration of the temple seems to be almost a year later. The ark and the "tent of meeting" are brought up to the temple—the former to be put in the sacred throne room, the latter to be stored with the other sacred items. With the building of the temple the tabernacle has no further function but is kept as a sacred treasure.

wings of the cherubim.[i] 7The cherubim
spread their wings over the place of the
ark and overshadowed the ark and its
carrying poles. 8These poles were so long
that their ends could be seen from the
Holy Place in front of the inner sanctuary, but not from outside the Holy Place;
and they are still there today.[j] 9There
was nothing in the ark except the two
stone tablets[k] that Moses had placed in
it at Horeb, where the LORD made a covenant with the Israelites after they came
out of Egypt.
10When the priests withdrew from the
Holy Place, the cloud[l] filled the temple
of the LORD. 11And the priests could not
perform their service because of the
cloud, for the glory of the LORD filled
his temple.
12Then Solomon said, "The LORD has
said that he would dwell in a dark cloud;[m]
13I have indeed built a magnificent temple for you, a place for you to dwell[n] forever."
14While the whole assembly of Israel was standing there, the king turned
around and blessed[o] them. 15Then he
said:

> "Praise be to the LORD,[p] the God of
> Israel, who with his own hand has
> fulfilled what he promised with his
> own mouth to my father David. For
> he said, 16'Since the day I brought
> my people Israel out of Egypt, I have
> not chosen a city in any tribe of Isra-
> el to have a temple built so that my
> Name[q] might be there, but I have
> chosen[r] David[s] to rule my people
> Israel.'
> 17"My father David had it in his
> heart to build a temple[t] for the
> Name of the LORD, the God of Isra-
> el. 18But the LORD said to my father
> David, 'You did well to have it in
> your heart to build a temple for my
> Name. 19Nevertheless, you[u] are not
> the one to build the temple, but your
> son, your own flesh and blood — he
> is the one who will build the temple
> for my Name.'[v]
> 20"The LORD has kept the promise
> he made: I have succeeded David my
> father and now I sit on the throne
> of Israel, just as the LORD promised,
> and I have built[w] the temple for the
> Name of the LORD, the God of Israel.
> 21I have provided a place there for
> the ark, in which is the covenant
> of the LORD that he made with our
> ancestors when he brought them
> out of Egypt."

Solomon's Prayer of Dedication
8:22–53pp // 2Ch 6:12–40

22Then Solomon stood before the altar of the LORD in front of the whole assembly of Israel, spread out his hands[x]
toward heaven 23and said:

8:6 [i] 1Ki 6:19,27
8:8 [j] Ex 25:13-15
8:9 [k] Ex 24:7-8; 25:21; 40:20; Dt 10:2-5; Heb 9:4
8:10 [l] Ex 40:34-35; 2Ch 7:1-2
8:12 [m] Ps 18:11; 97:2
8:13 [n] Ex 15:17; 2Sa 7:13; Ps 132:13
8:14 [o] 2Sa 6:18
8:15 [p] 2Sa 7:12-13; 1Ch 29:10, 20; Ne 9:5; Lk 1:68
8:16 [q] Dt 12:5 [r] 1Sa 16:1 [s] 2Sa 7:4-6,8
8:17 [t] 2Sa 7:2; 1Ch 17:1
8:19 [u] 2Sa 7:5 [v] 2Sa 7:13; 1Ki 5:3,5
8:20 [w] 1Ch 28:6
8:22 [x] Ex 9:29; Ezr 9:5

8:8–9 When the ark is placed beneath the cherubs, the poles are still visible. The poles, as a permanent fixture, indicate the presence of the ark. The ark contains only the tablets of the covenant (cf. Ex 25:21; Dt 10:5). The pot of manna (Ex 16:33) and the staff of Aaron that budded (Nu 17:10) are also sacred objects associated with the temple or Holy Place but are never said to be actually inside the ark in the OT.
8:10–11 When the priests bring the ark into Solomon's sanctuary, the glory of the divine presence takes possession of it, just as the same glory accompanied it in the desert.
8:12–13 The ark is set in the Most Holy Place in thick darkness. A poem recited by Solomon celebrates the significance of this "magnificent temple." God's temple is the heavens (vv. 39, 43, 49), but the Most Holy Place with the ark and the cherubs now represents his heavenly temple.
8:14–16 The blessing of the assembly begins with a declaration of the blessedness of God (vv. 14–15). Blessedness is a description of God, an acknowledgment that he is the source and dispenser of blessing. The blessedness of God is his fulfillment of the promise that the son of David was destined to build a temple as a focus for Israel's prayers and worship.
8:17–21 Solomon's words express the importance of the temple in the history of the nation and the role it will have in future relationships between God and his people. The presence of the temple assures the people that God has secured a royal dynasty for his people (cf. 2Sa 7:12–17). The temple is the place where the ark of God's covenant finds its rest (8:21). The ark represents the special legal bond uniting God and Israel. The presence of the ark of the covenant makes the temple the focal point for prayer, no matter where the prayer is uttered.
8:22–26 Solomon takes a position at the altar in front of all the people and begins his prayer of dedication. Standing with one's hands spread toward heaven is a customary posture of prayer, though Solomon is later said to have been kneeling (v. 54). Standing before a seated deity signifies an attitude of readiness for service; kneeling or sitting depicts humility in the presence of the deity.
Solomon's prayer emphasizes the loyal faithfulness of God in his covenant with those who are faithful; "covenant of love" (v. 23) is a paraphrase for loyalty. Divine loyalty is evident in the promise to David already fulfilled; Solomon's prayer is that the divine promise might now be fulfilled in the continuity of David's descendants on the

"LORD, the God of Israel, there is no God like[y] you in heaven above or on earth below—you who keep your covenant of love[z] with your servants who continue wholeheartedly in your way. 24You have kept your promise to your servant David my father; with your mouth you have promised and with your hand you have fulfilled it—as it is today.

25"Now LORD, the God of Israel, keep for your servant David my father the promises[a] you made to him when you said, 'You shall never fail to have a successor to sit before me on the throne of Israel, if only your descendants are careful in all they do to walk before me faithfully as you have done.' 26And now, God of Israel, let your word that you promised[b] your servant David my father come true.

27"But will God really dwell[c] on earth? The heavens, even the highest heaven, cannot contain[d] you. How much less this temple I have built! 28Yet give attention to your servant's prayer and his plea for mercy, LORD my God. Hear the cry and the prayer that your servant is praying in your presence this day. 29May your eyes be open[e] toward[f] this temple night and day, this place of which you said, 'My Name[g] shall be there,' so that you will hear the prayer your servant prays toward this place. 30Hear the supplication of your servant and of your people Israel when they pray toward this place. Hear from heaven, your dwelling place, and when you hear, forgive.[h]

31"When anyone wrongs their neighbor and is required to take an oath and they come and swear the oath[i] before your altar in this temple, 32then hear from heaven and act. Judge between your servants, condemning the guilty by bringing down on their heads what they have done, and vindicating the innocent by treating them in accordance with their innocence.[j]

33"When your people Israel have been defeated[k] by an enemy because they have sinned[l] against you, and when they turn back to you and give praise to your name, praying and making supplication to you in this temple, 34then hear from heaven and forgive the sin of your people Israel and bring them back to the land you gave to their ancestors.

35"When the heavens are shut up and there is no rain[m] because your people have sinned against you, and when they pray toward this place and give praise to your name and turn from their sin because you have afflicted them, 36then hear from heaven and forgive the sin of your servants, your people Israel. Teach[n] them the right way[o] to live, and send rain on the land you gave your people for an inheritance.

37"When famine[p] or plague comes to the land, or blight[q] or mildew, locusts or grasshoppers, or when an enemy besieges them in any of their cities, whatever disaster or disease may come, 38and when a prayer or plea is made by anyone among your people Israel—being aware of the afflictions of their own hearts, and spreading out their hands toward this temple— 39then hear from heaven, your dwelling place. Forgive and act; deal with everyone according to all they do, since you know[r] their hearts (for you alone know

8:23 [y] 1Sa 2:2; 2Sa 7:22 [z] Dt 7:9,12; Ne 1:5; 9:32; Da 9:4
8:25 [a] 1Ki 2:4
8:26 [b] 2Sa 7:25
8:27 [c] Ac 7:48 [d] 2Ch 2:6; Ps 139:7-16; Isa 66:1; Jer 23:24
8:29 [e] 2Ch 7:15; Ne 1:6 [f] Da 6:10 [g] Dt 12:11
8:30 [h] Ps 85:2
8:31 [i] Ex 22:11
8:32 [j] Dt 25:1
8:33 [k] Lev 26:17; Dt 28:25 [l] Lev 26:39
8:35 [m] Lev 26:19; Dt 28:24
8:36 [n] 1Sa 12:23; Ps 25:4; 94:12 [o] Ps 5:8; 27:11; Jer 6:16
8:37 [p] Lev 26:26 [q] Dt 28:22
8:39 [r] 1Sa 16:7; 1Ch 28:9; Ps 11:4; Jer 17:10; Jn 2:24; Ac 1:24

throne. The covenant blessing is conditional on the faithfulness of the covenant partners (v. 46). Solomon pleads for the people to receive divine mercy when they pray (v. 30).

8:27–30 The presence of God is not limited to the temple, since even the heavens cannot contain the Creator (v. 27); this is the place God has chosen for his "Name" (v. 29). Solomon prays that "the eyes" of the LORD will always be open to the place where petitions are made (vv. 29, 52).

8:31–32 In the prayer, seven petitions are intended to be representative of any future situation that the people of the covenant might encounter. Solomon's first request is that justice might function as it should in the determination of guilt and innocence.

8:33–40 The petitions of Solomon make specific reference to the curses of Deuteronomy. One of the curses of covenant disobedience is that Israel will be struck by her enemies (v. 33). There may also come a time when no rain falls, when the sky turns to bronze and the earth to iron (vv. 35–36). Enemies will attack their fortified cities (v. 37). War and illness are both matters of individual as well as national concern (v. 38). God is the one who knows the inner attitude (v. 39) and who can forgive the truly penitent.

every human heart), 40 so that they
will fear[s] you all the time they live
in the land you gave our ancestors.
41 "As for the foreigner who does
not belong to your people Israel but
has come from a distant land because of your name — 42 for they will
hear of your great name and your
mighty hand[t] and your outstretched
arm — when they come and pray
toward this temple, 43 then hear
from heaven, your dwelling place.
Do whatever the foreigner asks of
you, so that all the peoples of the
earth may know[u] your name and
fear[v] you, as do your own people Israel, and may know that this house
I have built bears your Name.
44 "When your people go to war
against their enemies, wherever you
send them, and when they pray to
the LORD toward the city you have
chosen and the temple I have built
for your Name, 45 then hear from
heaven their prayer and their plea,
and uphold their cause.
46 "When they sin against you —
for there is no one who does not
sin[w] — and you become angry with
them and give them over to their
enemies, who take them captive[x]
to their own lands, far away or
near; 47 and if they have a change
of heart in the land where they are
held captive, and repent and plead[y]
with you in the land of their captors and say, 'We have sinned, we
have done wrong, we have acted
wickedly';[z] 48 and if they turn back
to you with all their heart[a] and soul
in the land of their enemies who
took them captive, and pray[b] to you
toward the land you gave their ancestors, toward the city you have
chosen and the temple[c] I have built
for your Name; 49 then from heav-
en, your dwelling place, hear their
prayer and their plea, and uphold
their cause. 50 And forgive your people, who have sinned against you;
forgive all the offenses they have
committed against you, and cause
their captors to show them mercy;[d]
51 for they are your people and your
inheritance,[e] whom you brought out
of Egypt, out of that iron-smelting
furnace.[f]
52 "May your eyes be open to your
servant's plea and to the plea of your
people Israel, and may you listen to
them whenever they cry out to you.
53 For you singled them out from all
the nations of the world to be your
own inheritance,[g] just as you declared through your servant Moses
when you, Sovereign LORD, brought
our ancestors out of Egypt."

54 When Solomon had finished all these
prayers and supplications to the LORD, he
rose from before the altar of the LORD,

1Ki 8:41-43 ❖ Solomon prays for those who do not know God. How might we pray for those who do not yet have a relationship with the Lord?

8:40 [s] Ps 130:4
8:42 [t] Dt 3:24
8:43 [u] 1Sa 17:46; 2Ki 19:19 [v] Ps 102:15
8:46 [w] Pr 20:9; Ecc 7:20; Ro 3:9; 1Jn 1:8-10 [x] Lev 26:33-39; Dt 28:64
8:47 [y] Lev 26:40; Ne 1:6 [z] Ps 106:6; Da 9:5
8:48 [a] Dt 4:29; Jer 29:12-14 [b] Da 6:10 [c] Jnh 2:4
8:50 [d] 2Ch 30:9; Ps 106:46
8:51 [e] Dt 4:20; 9:29; Ne 1:10 [f] Jer 11:4
8:53 [g] Ex 19:5; Dt 9:26-29

8:41-43 There will be those from other nations who voluntarily join the society of the covenant (see Dt 4:6-8). Solomon's prayer is that they, in the same way as other Israelites, might find mercy before God.

8:44-45 Solomon's petition returns to the themes of war and exile (vv. 46-53). In war the people experience God's judgment. Solomon prays that God may "uphold their cause" (v. 45). This is an appropriate request that God act on their behalf to give them justice; however, it may be impossible for God to defend his people in war because of their covenant violation.

8:46-51 Exile is the consequence of a ruptured relationship with God. Captors may take them into an enemy land (v. 46), but if they turn in their minds and make confession to God (vv. 47-48), God may hear and forgive (vv. 49-50). Defeat by enemies is evidence of sin and failure (v. 46); the only recourse in captivity is to turn back to God in repentance, remembering his covenant and his promise. God redeemed his people and made them his special possession at Mount Sinai (8:53; cf. Ex 19:5-6). Solomon's prayer is that God's work may be completed.

8:52-53 The prophetic concerns of a total exile are evident in the final two petitions of this prayer. There were many exiles in the history of Israel, but complete destruction of Jerusalem and its temple will be the greatest challenge to faith. The mention of land, city, and temple suggests total destruction, not a partial exile (v. 48). The promise of the exodus (v. 53) has to be reaffirmed. The petitions (vv. 45, 50) and the covenant promise (vv. 51-53) are particularly important in a time when the temple might no longer be present. Even then, prayer could be directed to God in heaven, who would hear and forgive.

8:54-61 Following the long dedicatory prayer, Solomon stands to bless the people by giving praise to God for fulfilling his word. The prayer switches to the first person with two concluding petitions. Solomon asks for justice as each day requires, so that all nations may know the truth

where he had been kneeling with his hands spread out toward heaven. 55He stood and blessed[h] the whole assembly of Israel in a loud voice, saying:

56"Praise be to the LORD, who has given rest[i] to his people Israel just as he promised. Not one word has failed of all the good promises[j] he gave through his servant Moses. 57May the LORD our God be with us as he was with our ancestors; may he never leave us nor forsake[k] us. 58May he turn our hearts[l] to him, to walk in obedience to him and keep the commands, decrees and laws he gave our ancestors. 59And may these words of mine, which I have prayed before the LORD, be near to the LORD our God day and night, that he may uphold the cause of his servant and the cause of his people Israel according to each day's need, 60so that all the peoples[m] of the earth may know that the LORD is God and that there is no other.[n] 61And may your hearts be fully committed[o] to the LORD our God, to live by his decrees and obey his commands, as at this time."

The Dedication of the Temple

8:62–66pp // 2Ch 7:1–10

62Then the king and all Israel with him offered sacrifices before the LORD. 63Solomon offered a sacrifice of fellowship offerings to the LORD: twenty-two thousand cattle and a hundred and twenty thousand sheep and goats. So the king and all the Israelites dedicated the temple of the LORD.

64On that same day the king consecrated the middle part of the courtyard in front of the temple of the LORD, and there he offered burnt offerings, grain offerings and the fat of the fellowship offerings, because the bronze altar[p] that stood before the LORD was too small to hold the burnt offerings, the grain offerings and the fat of the fellowship offerings.

65So Solomon observed the festival[q] at that time, and all Israel with him—a vast assembly, people from Lebo Hamath[r] to the Wadi of Egypt.[s] They celebrated it before the LORD our God for seven days and seven days more, fourteen days in all. 66On the following day he sent the people away. They blessed the king and then went home, joyful and glad in heart for all the good things the LORD had done for his servant David and his people Israel.

The LORD Appears to Solomon

9:1–9pp // 2Ch 7:11–22

9 When Solomon had finished[t] building the temple of the LORD and the royal palace, and had achieved all he had desired to do, 2the LORD appeared[u] to him a second time, as he had appeared to him at Gibeon. 3The LORD said to him:

"I have heard[v] the prayer and plea you have made before me; I have consecrated this temple, which you have built, by putting my Name there forever. My eyes[w] and my heart will always be there.

4"As for you, if you walk before me faithfully with integrity of heart[x] and uprightness, as David[y] your father did, and do all I command and observe my decrees and laws, 5I will establish[z] your royal throne over Israel forever, as I promised David your father when I said, 'You shall never fail[a] to have a successor on the throne of Israel.'

6"But if you[a] or your descendants

8:55 [h] ver 14; 2Sa 6:18
8:56 [i] Dt 12:10 [j] Jos 21:45; 23:15
8:57 [k] Dt 31:6; Jos 1:5; Heb 13:5
8:58 [l] Ps 119:36
8:60 [m] Jos 4:24; 1Sa 17:46 [n] Dt 4:35; 1Ki 18:39; Jer 10:10-12
8:61 [o] 1Ki 11:4; 15:3,14; 2Ki 20:3
8:64 [p] 2Ch 4:1
8:65 [q] ver 2; Lev 23:34 [r] Nu 34:8; Jos 13:5; Jdg 3:3; 2Ki 14:25 [s] Ge 15:18
9:1 [t] 1Ki 7:1; 2Ch 8:6
9:2 [u] 1Ki 3:5
9:3 [v] 2Ki 20:5; Ps 10:17 [w] Dt 11:12; 1Ki 8:29
9:4 [x] Ge 17:1 [y] 1Ki 15:5
9:5 [z] 1Ch 22:10 [a] 2Sa 7:15; 1Ki 2:4

[a] 6 The Hebrew is plural.

---

declared at Mount Sinai: There is but one Lord (v. 60; cf. Dt 4:35, 39). Solomon in turn petitions for undivided loyalty from the people. Ironically, the requests of this prayer fail to be realized in Solomon's lifetime (11:4).

8:62–66 The closing summary of the temple dedication at the Festival of Tabernacles brings the account back to the events of the introduction (cf. vv. 1–2). Further details are added: The sacrifices previously described as being without number (v. 5) are here described in terms of number of oxen and sheep (v. 63). Communal peace offerings introduce the sacrifices and appear to be the central aspect of the dedication. The main function of these offerings is to provide food for the table; these sacrifices are for joyous occasions of celebration. The quantity of these offerings is so great that the great bronze altar does not have sufficient capacity (v. 64). The entire court was consecrated for the occasion.

9:1–9 God appears to Solomon to warn him about the consequences of covenant failure. The promise of an eternal house of David is always contingent on the absolute faithfulness of the Davidic kings (vv. 6–7). This is not to dismiss the possibility of grace and forgiveness; the problem is to expect grace while unrepentant. No beautiful building or eloquent prayer can serve as a substitute for

turn away[b] from me and do not observe the commands and decrees I
have given you[a] and go off to serve
other gods and worship them, 7then
I will cut off Israel from the land[c] I
have given them and will reject this
temple I have consecrated for my
Name.[d] Israel will then become a
byword[e] and an object of ridicule[f]
among all peoples. 8This temple
will become a heap of rubble. All[b]
who pass by will be appalled and
will scoff and say, 'Why has the LORD
done such a thing to this land and
to this temple?'[g] 9People will answer, 'Because they have forsaken
the LORD their God, who brought
their ancestors out of Egypt, and
have embraced other gods, worshiping and serving them — that is why
the LORD brought all this disaster
on them.' "

Solomon's Other Activities

9:10–28pp // 2Ch 8:1–18

10At the end of twenty years, during
which Solomon built these two buildings — the temple of the LORD and the
royal palace — 11King Solomon gave
twenty towns in Galilee to Hiram king
of Tyre, because Hiram had supplied him
with all the cedar and juniper and gold[h]
he wanted. 12But when Hiram went from
Tyre to see the towns that Solomon had
given him, he was not pleased with them.
13"What kind of towns are these you have
given me, my brother?" he asked. And he
called them the Land of Kabul,[c i] a name
they have to this day. 14Now Hiram had
sent to the king 120 talents[d] of gold.

9:6 [b] 2Sa 7:14
9:7 [c] 2Ki 17:23; 25:21 [d] Jer 7:14 [e] Ps 44:14 [f] Dt 28:37
9:8 [g] Dt 29:24; Jer 22:8-9
9:11 [h] 2Ch 8:2
9:13 [i] Jos 19:27

> **1Ki 9:6-8** ❖ Why does God issue stern warnings to his people? How can such warnings build a person's faith?

15Here is the account of the forced labor King Solomon conscripted[j] to build
the LORD's temple, his own palace, the
terraces,[e k] the wall of Jerusalem, and
Hazor,[l] Megiddo and Gezer.[m] 16(Pharaoh
king of Egypt had attacked and captured
Gezer. He had set it on fire. He killed its
Canaanite inhabitants and then gave it as
a wedding gift to his daughter, Solomon's
wife. 17And Solomon rebuilt Gezer.) He
built up Lower Beth Horon,[n] 18Baalath,[o]
and Tadmor[f] in the desert, within his
land, 19as well as all his store cities[p] and
the towns for his chariots[q] and for his
horses[g] — whatever he desired to build
in Jerusalem, in Lebanon and throughout all the territory he ruled.
20There were still people left from the
Amorites, Hittites, Perizzites, Hivites and
Jebusites (these peoples were not Israelites). 21Solomon conscripted the descendants[r] of all these peoples remaining in
the land — whom the Israelites could not
exterminate[h s] — to serve as slave labor,[t]
as it is to this day. 22But Solomon did not

9:15 [j] Jos 16:10; 1Ki 5:13 [k] ver 24; 2Sa 5:9 [l] Jos 19:36 [m] Jos 17:11
9:17 [n] Jos 16:3; 2Ch 8:5
9:18 [o] Jos 19:44
9:19 [p] ver 1 [q] 1Ki 4:26
9:21 [r] Ge 9:25-26 [s] Jos 15:63; 17:12; Jdg 1:21, 27,29 [t] Ezr 2:55, 58

[a] 6 The Hebrew is plural. [b] 8 See some Septuagint manuscripts, Old Latin, Syriac, Arabic and Targum; Hebrew *And though this temple is now imposing, all* [c] 13 *Kabul* sounds like the Hebrew for *good-for-nothing.* [d] 14 That is, about 4 1/2 tons or about 4 metric tons [e] 15 Or *the Millo*; also in verse 24 [f] 18 The Hebrew may also be read *Tamar.* [g] 19 Or *charioteers* [h] 21 The Hebrew term refers to the irrevocable giving over of things or persons to the LORD, often by totally destroying them.

---

obedience (v. 8). The demand for obedience not only pertains to the king but also pertains to the entire people (vv. 6–9).

> **7:51b—9:9** Solomon's mission in building the temple was to memorialize and perpetuate the great works of Yahweh, the kingdom anticipated in the promise to David. The calling of the Christian church is to show the purpose of God for creation as it is accomplished in his world. Belonging to the church demands that Christians learn to live in harmony and unity with each other (Eph 4:1-3). Fundamentally, living as a Christian requires a new way of thinking (Eph 4:17-24). Outside of Christ, human values are governed by self-interest and the deceit of greed. Christ bridges all divisions among his people: All races and classes are brought into harmony, as they are transformed in the knowledge of their joint identity and purpose in reflecting God's image (Col 3:10-11).

9:10-14 It is not clear why Solomon gives territory to Hiram, but Hiram apparently thinks twenty settlements in northern Galilee are not nearly enough compensation for the amount of gold given. At minimum Hiram has given Solomon several tons of gold.
9:15-19 The account of conscripted labor enumerates the various projects that form a part of Solomon's building activities. Six cities are named as part of the fortifications; these form a line of defense from north to south. Excavations at cities like Lachish have revealed large buildings with long, narrow rooms that served for storage.
9:20-22 The conscripted labor that Solomon uses to maintain his building projects consists of native

make slaves[u] of any of the Israelites; they were his fighting men, his government officials, his officers, his captains, and the commanders of his chariots and charioteers. 23They were also the chief officials[v] in charge of Solomon's projects — 550 officials supervising those who did the work.

24After Pharaoh's daughter[w] had come up from the City of David to the palace Solomon had built for her, he constructed the terraces.[x]

25Three[y] times a year Solomon sacrificed burnt offerings and fellowship offerings on the altar he had built for the LORD, burning incense before the LORD along with them, and so fulfilled the temple obligations.

26King Solomon also built ships[z] at Ezion Geber,[a] which is near Elath in Edom, on the shore of the Red Sea.[a] 27And Hiram sent his men — sailors[b] who knew the sea — to serve in the fleet with Solomon's men. 28They sailed to Ophir[c] and brought back 420 talents[b] of gold, which they delivered to King Solomon.

The Queen of Sheba Visits Solomon

10:1–13pp // 2Ch 9:1–12

10 When the queen of Sheba[d] heard about the fame of Solomon and his relationship to the LORD, she came to test Solomon with hard questions.[e] 2Arriving at Jerusalem with a very great caravan — with camels carrying spices, large quantities of gold, and precious stones — she came to Solomon and talked with him about all that she had on her mind. 3Solomon answered all her questions; nothing was too hard for the king to explain to her. 4When the queen of Sheba saw all the wisdom of Solomon and the palace he had built, 5the food on his table,[f] the seating of his officials, the attending servants in their robes, his cupbearers, and the burnt offerings he made at[c] the temple of the LORD, she was overwhelmed.

6She said to the king, "The report I heard in my own country about your achievements and your wisdom is true. 7But I did not believe these things until I came and saw with my own eyes. Indeed, not even half was told me; in wisdom and wealth[g] you have far exceeded the report I heard. 8How happy your people must be! How happy your officials, who continually stand before you and hear[h] your wisdom! 9Praise[i] be to the LORD your God, who has delighted in you and placed you on the throne of Israel. Because of the LORD's eternal love for Israel, he has made you king to maintain justice[j] and righteousness."

10And she gave the king 120 talents[d] of gold,[k] large quantities of spices, and precious stones. Never again were so many spices brought in as those the queen of Sheba gave to King Solomon.

11(Hiram's ships brought gold from Ophir;[l] and from there they brought great cargoes of almugwood[e] and precious stones. 12The king used the almugwood to make supports[f] for the temple of the LORD and for the royal palace, and to make harps and lyres for the musicians. So much almugwood has never been imported or seen since that day.)

> **1Ki 10:9** ❖ How can we demonstrate a faith that makes other people praise God?

9:22 [u] Lev 25:39
9:23 [v] 1Ki 5:16
9:24 [w] 1Ki 3:1; 7:8 [x] 2Sa 5:9; 1Ki 11:27; 2Ch 32:5
9:25 [y] Ex 23:14; 2Ch 8:12-13,16
9:26 [z] 1Ki 22:48 [a] Nu 33:35; Dt 2:8
9:27 [b] 1Ki 10:11; Eze 27:8
9:28 [c] 1Ch 29:4
10:1 [d] Ge 10:7, 28; Mt 12:42; Lk 11:31 [e] Jdg 14:12
10:5 [f] 1Ch 26:16
10:7 [g] 1Ch 29:25
10:8 [h] Pr 8:34
10:9 [i] 1Ki 5:7 [j] 2Sa 8:15; Ps 33:5; 72:2
10:10 [k] ver 2
10:11 [l] Ge 10:29; 1Ki 9:27-28

[a] 26 Or *the Sea of Reeds* [b] 28 That is, about 16 tons or about 14 metric tons [c] 5 Or *the ascent by which he went up to* [d] 10 That is, about 4 1/2 tons or about 4 metric tons [e] 11 Probably a variant of *algumwood*; also in verse 12 [f] 12 The meaning of the Hebrew for this word is uncertain.

Canaanite peoples who lived as subordinates after the conquest; these are different from the temporary conscriptions that Solomon established to construct the buildings (5:13).

9:23–25 The offerings Solomon makes are not to suggest he is acting as a priest but rather to show he makes provision for daily and yearly rituals of the temple (v. 25b).

9:26–28 In addition to internal administration of his kingdom, Solomon has extensive involvement in foreign affairs. These include trade with distant lands, which he carries out in cooperation with Hiram (see 10:22). The shipbuilders of Tyre had access to many types of wood and imported materials for sails and ornamentation.

10:1–5 The account of the queen of Sheba further illustrates the fame, wisdom, and wealth of Solomon. This queen controlled an enormous amount of wealth, as indicated in the size of the caravan that attended her (v. 2). His answers to her questions and his accomplishments are enough to take away her breath (v. 5).

10:6–15 Solomon's wealth is indicated by the enormous gifts the queen needs to give in order to be significant (v. 10); the gold alone is equivalent to what Solomon has received from Hiram (cf. 9:14). Wealth is stressed as much as wisdom in the queen's visit.

13 King Solomon gave the queen of Sheba all she desired and asked for, besides what he had given her out of his royal bounty. Then she left and returned with her retinue to her own country.

Solomon's Splendor

10:14–29pp // 2Ch 1:14–17; 9:13–28

14 The weight of the gold[m] that Solomon received yearly was 666 talents,[a] 15 not including the revenues from merchants and traders and from all the Arabian kings and the governors of the territories.

16 King Solomon made two hundred large shields[n] of hammered gold; six hundred shekels[b] of gold went into each shield. 17 He also made three hundred small shields of hammered gold, with three minas[c] of gold in each shield. The king put them in the Palace of the Forest of Lebanon.[o]

18 Then the king made a great throne covered with ivory and overlaid with fine gold. 19 The throne had six steps, and its back had a rounded top. On both sides of the seat were armrests, with a lion standing beside each of them. 20 Twelve lions stood on the six steps, one at either end of each step. Nothing like it had ever been made for any other kingdom. 21 All King Solomon's goblets were gold, and all the household articles in the Palace of the Forest of Lebanon were pure gold. Nothing was made of silver, because silver was considered of little value in Solomon's days. 22 The king had a fleet of trading ships[d][p] at sea along with the ships of Hiram. Once every three years it returned, carrying gold, silver and ivory, and apes and baboons.

23 King Solomon was greater in riches[q] and wisdom[r] than all the other kings of the earth. 24 The whole world sought audience with Solomon to hear the wisdom[s] God had put in his heart. 25 Year after year, everyone who came brought a gift — articles of silver and gold, robes, weapons and spices, and horses and mules.

26 Solomon accumulated chariots and horses;[t] he had fourteen hundred chari-

10:14 [m] 1Ki 9:28
10:16 [n] 1Ki 14:26-28
10:17 [o] 1Ki 7:2
10:22 [p] 1Ki 9:26
10:23 [q] 1Ki 3:13 [r] 1Ki 4:30
10:24 [s] 1Ki 3:9, 12, 28
10:26 [t] Dt 17:16; 1Ki 4:26; 9:19; 2Ch 1:14; 9:25

[a] 14 That is, about 25 tons or about 23 metric tons
[b] 16 That is, about 15 pounds or about 6.9 kilograms; also in verse 29
[c] 17 That is, about 3 3/4 pounds or about 1.7 kilograms; or perhaps reference is to double minas, that is, about 7 1/2 pounds or about 3.5 kilograms.
[d] 22 Hebrew *of ships of Tarshish*

10:16–17 Large shields were body length, possibly three sided; small shields were a light protection worn on the arm. The weight of gold in each small shield is just over 3.5 pounds, just under 2 kilos. The weight measure of the large shields is likely four times that of the small shields. Guards display the shields as the king goes up to the temple (cf. 14:27–28).

10:18–25 The throne of Solomon was a work of grandeur. The throne had ivory inlays and was covered with gold. The rest of the passage describes other aspects of Solomon's fantastic accumulation of wealth.

10:26–29 Solomon's vast wealth provides for a strong military and security as well as spectacular luxury in the capital city. The amounts of horses, chariots, and military cities mentioned summarizes information given earlier (4:26; 9:19). Solomon's merchants buy horses and chariots and trade them along the way with the Hittite and Aramean kings (10:29). Egypt may have been a recipient in the trade of horses and chariots; Solomon may have controlled trade between Egypt and Syria.

9:10—10:29 Wealth is never an individual matter; no one can achieve wealth in isolation from a community or a broad work environment, and people with wealth should always honor God as the giver. We must live our Christian lives with these principles in mind. The use of money is fundamental to living out our Christian values. The story of Solomon has important lessons on God's view of wealth, its significance, and its use.

God granted wealth to Israel in the same way as he provided manna in the desert. The Israelites were to remember that they were unable to become independently wealthy. Theologically, resources are a gift from God; sociologically, they are received as a community and are a product of the collective work of individuals.

Christians need to think carefully about their view of the world in relation to wealth. They need to remember that resources are limited for particular people in particular places. Not everyone is able to generate a living, let alone wealth, through relentless hard work. Those in the kingdom of God must look beyond their own interests both in how they acquire wealth and in how they share it with those who do not have the same opportunities.

Solomon is an important example to all Christians who have considerable material well-being in comparison to other people of the world. We must honor God with the riches he has given us through the collective support of a whole economic system. We are privileged to have the blessing; our challenge is to use this blessing to bring about peace and good—the kind of kingdom that encompassed Solomon's vision (Ps 72).

ots and twelve thousand horses,[a] which
he kept in the chariot cities and also with
him in Jerusalem. 27 The king made silver
as common[u] in Jerusalem as stones, and
cedar as plentiful as sycamore-fig trees
in the foothills. 28 Solomon's horses were
imported from Egypt and from Kue[b] —
the royal merchants purchased them
from Kue at the current price. 29 They
imported a chariot from Egypt for six
hundred shekels of silver, and a horse for
a hundred and fifty.[c] They also exported
them to all the kings of the Hittites[v] and
of the Arameans.

Solomon's Wives

11 King Solomon, however, loved many
foreign women[w] besides Pharaoh's
daughter — Moabites, Ammonites,
Edomites, Sidonians and Hittites. 2 They
were from nations about which the LORD
had told the Israelites, "You must not intermarry[x] with them, because they will
surely turn your hearts after their gods."
Nevertheless, Solomon held fast to them
in love. 3 He had seven hundred wives of
royal birth and three hundred concubines, and his wives led him astray. 4 As
Solomon grew old, his wives turned his
heart after other gods, and his heart was
not fully devoted[y] to the LORD his God, as
the heart of David his father had been.
5 He followed Ashtoreth[z] the goddess of
the Sidonians, and Molek[a] the detestable
god of the Ammonites. 6 So Solomon did
evil in the eyes of the LORD; he did not
follow the LORD completely, as David his
father had done.
7 On a hill east[b] of Jerusalem, Solomon
built a high place for Chemosh[c] the detestable god of Moab, and for Molek[d] the
detestable god of the Ammonites. 8 He
did the same for all his foreign wives,
who burned incense and offered sacrifices to their gods.
9 The LORD became angry with Solomon because his heart had turned away
from the LORD, the God of Israel, who had
appeared[e] to him twice. 10 Although he
had forbidden Solomon to follow other
gods,[f] Solomon did not keep the LORD's
command.[g] 11 So the LORD said to Solomon, "Since this is your attitude and
you have not kept my covenant and my
decrees, which I commanded you, I will
most certainly tear[h] the kingdom away
from you and give it to one of your subordinates. 12 Nevertheless, for the sake of
David your father, I will not do it during
your lifetime. I will tear it out of the hand
of your son. 13 Yet I will not tear the whole
kingdom from him, but will give him one
tribe[i] for the sake[j] of David my servant
and for the sake of Jerusalem, which I
have chosen."[k]

Solomon's Adversaries

14 Then the LORD raised up against Solomon an adversary, Hadad the Edomite,
from the royal line of Edom. 15 Earlier

1Ki 11:9–11 ❖ What can cause even the greatest leaders to fall from virtue to evil? How does Solomon's life provide a cautionary example of what to avoid?

10:27 [u] Dt 17:17
10:29 [v] 2Ki 7:6-7
11:1 [w] Dt 17:17; Ne 13:26
11:2 [x] Ex 34:16; Dt 7:3-4
11:4 [y] 1Ki 8:61; 9:4
11:5 [z] ver 33; Jdg 2:13; 2Ki 23:13 [a] ver 7
11:7 [b] 2Ki 23:13 [c] Nu 21:29; Jdg 11:24 [d] Lev 20:2-5; Ac 7:43
11:9 [e] ver 2-3; 1Ki 3:5; 9:2
11:10 [f] 1Ki 9:6 [g] 1Ki 6:12
11:11 [h] ver 31; 1Ki 12:15-16; 2Ki 17:21
11:13 [i] 1Ki 12:20 [j] 2Sa 7:15 [k] Dt 12:11

[a] 26 Or *charioteers* [b] 28 Probably *Cilicia*
[c] 29 That is, about 3 3/4 pounds or about 1.7 kilograms

11:1–4 Solomon attaches himself to foreign women, accommodating their practices. Though he builds altars for them in the presence of the temple (vv. 7–8), it doesn't say that he actually worships with these women. The covenant contained specific warnings about intermarriage with the nations (Dt 7:1–5); this review of Solomon's reign focuses specifically on that failure.

The wives are all princesses, women of high political rank (1Ki 11:3). Though these relationships may have begun as a matter of political expediency, the end result is the catastrophe Deuteronomy warned would happen.

11:5–10 "Ashtoreth" is a form of the name of the Canaanite goddess Ashtart. She was the Canaanite goddess of war and sexuality. Molek (also called Milcom), a name that meant "kingship," is the national god of the Ammonites (v. 7). This god is associated with child sacrifice (Jer 32:35).

11:11–13 The indictment on Solomon is given as a word from Yahweh without specifically revealing the manner in which that word is delivered (vv. 11–13). Judgment against Solomon is mitigated by the promise to David (vv. 12–13).

11:14–22 God assigned Solomon's enemies as human political opponents to punish Solomon (vv. 14, 23, 25). In later Hebrew this word for "adversary" meant "prosecutor," in some instances a member of God's court (Job 1:9; 2:2; Zec 3:1–2); eventually the term became a name to describe the devil.

Two kings named Hadad are known from the genealogies of Edom (Ge 36:31–39). David conquered Edom as one of the expansions of his empire (2Sa 8:13–14).

Nothing is said of the fate of Hadad, but when David and Joab die, Hadad renounces the security and luxury of Egypt and enters into some type of guerilla warfare against Solomon (11:25).

THE DIVIDED KINGDOMS OF ISRAEL AND JUDAH
Sidon
PHOENICIA
Damascus
ARAM DAMASCUS
Tyre
Dan
Mediterranean Sea
Hazor
GESHUR
Akko
Geshur
Sea of Galilee
Karnaim
Ashtaroth
Dor
Shunem
Megiddo
Jezreel
Taanach
Beth Shan
Ramoth Gilead
Rehob
ISRAEL
Samaria
Tirzah
Shechem
Penuel/Peniel
Joppa
Aphek
Jordan R.
Rabbah (of the Ammonites)
Bethel
Gibbethon
Gezer
Gibeon
AMMON
Ekron
Ashdod
Jerusalem
Ashkelon
Gath
JUDAH
Gaza
Lachish
Hebron
Dead Sea
Dibon
Sharuhen
PHILISTIA
Arnon R.
Raphia
Arad
MOAB
Beersheba
Zered R.
Tamar
Sela
Fortresses in Negev
Bozrah
Kadesh Barnea
EDOM
0 20 km.
0 20 miles
Kingdom of Israel
Kingdom of Judah
Jeroboam's worship centers

when David was fighting with Edom,
Joab the commander of the army, who
had gone up to bury the dead, had struck
down all the men in Edom.[l] 16Joab and
all the Israelites stayed there for six
months, until they had destroyed all
the men in Edom. 17But Hadad, still only
a boy, fled to Egypt with some Edomite officials who had served his father.
18They set out from Midian and went to
Paran.[m] Then taking people from Paran
with them, they went to Egypt, to Pharaoh king of Egypt, who gave Hadad a
house and land and provided him with
food.
19Pharaoh was so pleased with Hadad
that he gave him a sister of his own wife,
Queen Tahpenes, in marriage. 20The sister of Tahpenes bore him a son named
Genubath, whom Tahpenes brought up
in the royal palace. There Genubath lived
with Pharaoh's own children.
21While he was in Egypt, Hadad heard
that David rested with his ancestors and
that Joab the commander of the army
was also dead. Then Hadad said to Pharaoh, "Let me go, that I may return to my
own country."
22"What have you lacked here that you
want to go back to your own country?"
Pharaoh asked.
"Nothing," Hadad replied, "but do let
me go!"
23And God raised up against Solomon
another adversary,[n] Rezon son of Eliada,
who had fled from his master, Hadadezer[o] king of Zobah. 24When David destroyed Zobah's army, Rezon gathered
a band of men around him and became
their leader; they went to Damascus,[p]
where they settled and took control.
25Rezon was Israel's adversary as long
as Solomon lived, adding to the trouble caused by Hadad. So Rezon ruled in
Aram[q] and was hostile toward Israel.

11:15 [l] Dt 20:13; 2Sa 8:14; 1Ch 18:12
11:18 [m] Nu 10:12
11:23 [n] ver 14 [o] 2Sa 8:3
11:24 [p] 2Sa 8:5; 10:8,18
11:25 [q] 2Sa 10:19

Jeroboam Rebels Against Solomon

26Also, Jeroboam son of Nebat rebelled[r] against the king. He was one of
Solomon's officials, an Ephraimite from
Zeredah, and his mother was a widow
named Zeruah.
27Here is the account of how he rebelled against the king: Solomon had
built the terraces[a][s] and had filled in the
gap in the wall of the city of David his
father. 28Now Jeroboam was a man of
standing,[t] and when Solomon saw how
well[u] the young man did his work, he put
him in charge of the whole labor force
of the tribes of Joseph.
29About that time Jeroboam was going
out of Jerusalem, and Ahijah[v] the prophet of Shiloh met him on the way, wearing
a new cloak. The two of them were alone
out in the country, 30and Ahijah took
hold of the new cloak he was wearing and
tore[w] it into twelve pieces. 31Then he said
to Jeroboam, "Take ten pieces for yourself, for this is what the LORD, the God of
Israel, says: 'See, I am going to tear[x] the
kingdom out of Solomon's hand and give
you ten tribes. 32But for the sake of my
servant David and the city of Jerusalem,
which I have chosen out of all the tribes
of Israel, he will have one tribe. 33I will
do this because they have[b] forsaken me
and worshiped[y] Ashtoreth the goddess
of the Sidonians, Chemosh the god of
the Moabites, and Molek the god of the
Ammonites, and have not walked in obedience to me, nor done what is right in
my eyes, nor kept my decrees[z] and laws
as David, Solomon's father, did.
34" 'But I will not take the whole kingdom out of Solomon's hand; I have made
him ruler all the days of his life for the
sake of David my servant, whom I chose
and who obeyed my commands and

11:26 [r] 2Sa 20:21; 1Ki 12:2; 2Ch 13:6
11:27 [s] 1Ki 9:24
11:28 [t] Ru 2:1 [u] Pr 22:29
11:29 [v] 1Ki 12:15; 14:2; 2Ch 9:29
11:30 [w] 1Sa 15:27
11:31 [x] ver 11
11:33 [y] ver 5-7 [z] 1Ki 3:3

[a] 27 Or *the Millo* [b] 33 Hebrew; Septuagint, Vulgate and Syriac *because he has*

11:23–25 David's defeat of Hadadezer king of Zobah is described in some detail (2Sa 8:3–8). Rezon, a rebel against Hadadezer, organized a guerilla movement and eventually gained control of Damascus. He founded a dynasty that became the kingdom of Aram-Damascus, the most powerful Syrian state in the days following Solomon. As an independent power he resisted Solomon during the whole time of his rule.
11:26–28 Jeroboam, Solomon's servant, becomes his successor (vv. 11, 27–28).
11:29 Jeroboam flees to Egypt and seeks refuge there until Solomon dies (v. 40). Where the prophet meets Jeroboam is not specified, but it is not a coincidental encounter.
11:30–33 Prophets often communicate in dramatic fashion (e.g., Isa 20:1–6). The action of Ahijah is particularly dramatic as he tears up Jeroboam's new garment. The fact that it is a new garment is stressed twice, making it a fit item for the prophetic sign.
11:34–37 Jeroboam's insurrection against Solomon gains him nothing more than exile in Egypt (v. 40). God will grant Jeroboam his desire to rule (v. 37), but it will not happen because of his own initiative. Ahijah's words amplify the judgment given earlier in the narrative: it comes as the result of Solomon

decrees. 35I will take the kingdom from
his son's hands and give you ten tribes.
36I will give one tribe[a] to his son so that
David my servant may always have a
lamp[b] before me in Jerusalem, the city
where I chose to put my Name. 37How-
ever, as for you, I will take you, and you
will rule over all that your heart desires;[c]
you will be king over Israel. 38If you do
whatever I command you and walk in
obedience to me and do what is right
in my eyes by obeying my decrees[d] and
commands, as David my servant did, I
will be with you. I will build you a dynasty[e] as enduring as the one I built for
David and will give Israel to you. 39I will
humble David's descendants because of
this, but not forever.'"

40Solomon tried to kill Jeroboam, but
Jeroboam fled to Egypt, to Shishak[f] the
king, and stayed there until Solomon's
death.

Solomon's Death

11:41–43pp // 2Ch 9:29–31

41As for the other events of Solomon's
reign — all he did and the wisdom he
displayed — are they not written in the
book of the annals of Solomon? 42Solo-
mon reigned in Jerusalem over all Israel
forty years. 43Then he rested with his
ancestors and was buried in the city of
David his father. And Rehoboam[g] his son
succeeded him as king.

11:36 [a] ver 13; 1Ki 12:17 [b] 1Ki 15:4; 2Ki 8:19
11:37 [c] 2Sa 3:21
11:38 [d] Dt 17:19 [e] Jos 1:5; 2Sa 7:11, 27
11:40 [f] 2Ch 12:2
11:43 [g] 1Ki 14:21; Mt 1:7

12:2 [h] 1Ki 11:40
12:4 [i] 1Sa 8:11-18; 1Ki 4:20-28
12:6 [j] 1Ki 4:2
12:7 [k] Pr 15:1

1Ki 12:7-11 ❖ To whom do we go for wise advice? How can we tell when advice we receive is good?

Israel Rebels Against Rehoboam

12:1–24pp // 2Ch 10:1—11:4

12 Rehoboam went to Shechem, for
all Israel had gone there to make
him king. 2When Jeroboam son of Nebat
heard this (he was still in Egypt, where
he had fled[h] from King Solomon), he returned from[a] Egypt. 3So they sent for Jeroboam, and he and the whole assembly
of Israel went to Rehoboam and said to
him: 4"Your father put a heavy yoke[i] on
us, but now lighten the harsh labor and
the heavy yoke he put on us, and we will
serve you."

5Rehoboam answered, "Go away for
three days and then come back to me."
So the people went away.

6Then King Rehoboam consulted the
elders[j] who had served his father Solomon during his lifetime. "How would
you advise me to answer these people?"
he asked.

7They replied, "If today you will be a
servant to these people and serve them
and give them a favorable answer,[k] they
will always be your servants."

8But Rehoboam rejected the advice
the elders gave him and consulted the

[a] 2 Or *he remained in*

---

promoting worship of foreign gods (v. 33). A son of Solomon will continue to rule one tribe to preserve the line of David (v. 36); this acknowledges the political reality that territorially the tribes of Benjamin and Simeon are absorbed, and Judah exists as a single territory.

11:38–40 Ahijah declares Jeroboam to be a true successor of David; the promise of dynasty applies to Jeroboam as it had to David. This discourse sounds similar to Nathan's prophecy to the king, legitimizing the northern kingdom (2Sa 7:9a, 16a). Unlike David, to whom the kingdom is promised in perpetuity, Jeroboam's promise is contingent on his total obedience. The house of David will be humbled, but a ruler will remain in Jerusalem for the sake of the covenant God made with David (v. 34).

When Solomon becomes aware of Jeroboam's plot, Jeroboam finds refuge in the court of Shishak, the first king of the Twenty-Second Dynasty in Egypt (c. 945–924 BC). Shishak's treatment of Jeroboam indicates a change in Egyptian policy toward Solomon.

✣ **11:1–43** The lessons of Solomon taught in the narrative of Kings are sobering: A great and wise king may at the same time be a foolish and weak king. This is the irony of Solomon's life: Wisdom has the power to produce wealth, but the seductive power of wealth can erode the wisdom of following God. The narrative of Kings calls everyone to be a person greater than Solomon. While no one may compare to Solomon in his glory, wealth or wisdom, everyone needs the wisdom of faithfulness to God.

The persistent lesson of Solomon for those who live under a new covenant is the importance of faithfulness. Success at any one point in the life of an individual—spiritually, materially, or both—is no assurance of continued loyalty to God; in fact, the opposite may be more the case. This message is skillfully related in the story of Solomon's reign.

12:1–7 Dynastic succession did not have an established procedure in the early days of the kingdom. Solomon had to overcome the forces of Adonijah in succeeding David to the throne. In the same way, Rehoboam, son of Solomon, has to travel to Shechem to develop a consensus on his claim to the throne.

12:8–14 The elders of Israel were an influential

young men who had grown up with him and were serving him. 9He asked them, "What is your advice? How should we answer these people who say to me, 'Lighten the yoke your father put on us'?"

10The young men who had grown up with him replied, "These people have said to you, 'Your father put a heavy yoke on us, but make our yoke lighter.' Now tell them, 'My little finger is thicker than my father's waist. 11My father laid on you a heavy yoke; I will make it even heavier. My father scourged you with whips; I will scourge you with scorpions.'"

12Three days later Jeroboam and all the people returned to Rehoboam, as the king had said, "Come back to me in three days." 13The king answered the people harshly. Rejecting the advice given him by the elders, 14he followed the advice of the young men and said, "My father made your yoke heavy; I will make it even heavier. My father scourged[l] you with whips; I will scourge you with scorpions." 15So the king did not listen to the people, for this turn of events was from the LORD,[m] to fulfill the word the LORD had spoken to Jeroboam son of Nebat through Ahijah[n] the Shilonite.

16When all Israel saw that the king refused to listen to them, they answered the king:

> "What share do we have in David,
> what part in Jesse's son?
> To your tents, Israel![o]
> Look after your own house,
> David!"

So the Israelites went home. 17But as for the Israelites who were living in the towns of Judah,[p] Rehoboam still ruled over them.

18King Rehoboam sent out Adoniram,[a][q] who was in charge of forced labor, but all Israel stoned him to death. King Rehoboam, however, managed to get into his chariot and escape to Jerusalem. 19So Israel has been in rebellion against the house of David[r] to this day.

20When all the Israelites heard that Jeroboam had returned, they sent and called him to the assembly and made him king over all Israel. Only the tribe of Judah remained loyal to the house of David.[s]

21When Rehoboam arrived in Jerusalem, he mustered all Judah and the tribe of Benjamin—a hundred and eighty thousand able young men—to go to war[t] against Israel and to regain the kingdom for Rehoboam son of Solomon.

22But this word of God came to Shemaiah[u] the man of God: 23"Say to Rehoboam son of Solomon king of Judah, to all Judah and Benjamin, and to the rest of the people, 24'This is what the LORD says: Do not go up to fight against your brothers, the Israelites. Go home, every one of you, for this is my doing.'" So they obeyed the word of the LORD and went home again, as the LORD had ordered.

Golden Calves at Bethel and Dan

25Then Jeroboam fortified Shechem[v] in the hill country of Ephraim and lived there. From there he went out and built up Peniel.[b][w]

12:14 [l] Ex 1:14; 5:5-9,16-18 12:15 [m] ver 24; Dt 2:30; Jdg 14:4; 2Ch 22:7; 25:20 [n] 1Ki 11:29 12:16 [o] 2Sa 20:1 12:17 [p] 1Ki 11:13, 36 12:18 [q] 2Sa 20:24; 1Ki 4:6; 5:14 12:19 [r] 2Ki 17:21 12:20 [s] 1Ki 11:13, 32 12:21 [t] 2Ch 11:1 12:22 [u] 2Ch 12:5-7 12:25 [v] Jdg 9:45 [w] Jdg 8:8,17

[a] *18* Some Septuagint manuscripts and Syriac (see also 4:6 and 5:14); Hebrew *Adoram*
[b] *25* Hebrew *Penuel,* a variant of *Peniel*

---

force in critical decisions (2Sa 17:4, 15; 19:11). The "young men" are described as those who have grown up with Rehoboam. Since Rehoboam is forty-one years old when he becomes king (14:21), it seems that the reference to "young men" does not necessarily imply youth. Rather, they belong to another generation and have different values from the more experienced elders. As might be expected, the opinions of the two groups of advisors are diametrically opposed.

Though Rehoboam makes a foolish political choice, he is not influenced by politics alone. The values of the covenant have already been lost by Solomon. It's apparent that Rehoboam has no inner desire to follow Yahweh or the way of the covenant. He makes choices according to his own values, a practice he has learned through his father.

12:15–20 Rehoboam proceeds to follow the path of political coercion and sends Adoniram to deal with the unrest, but the people are in no mood to listen to these harsh new policies. They kill Adoniram, and Rehoboam flees to Jerusalem.

The death of Solomon and the revolt of the northern tribes provides the occasion for Jeroboam to return from his exile in Egypt and assume leadership over the new political entity of Israel (v. 20). It seems that Jeroboam is not summoned to the assembly until after the murder of Adoniram, when it becomes known he has returned from Egypt.

12:21–24 Rehoboam has not lost all capacity to respect the prophetic word. As he prepares a considerable army to enforce his will over the rebellious tribes, a godly man named Shemaiah reminds him that the tribes' rejection of his rule is evidence of a divine judgment against Rehoboam himself. Rehoboam respects this judgment sufficiently to refrain from further political conflict and self-destruction.

12:25–31 Jeroboam creates a distinct kingdom in the north by initiating various changes. He fortifies

26 Jeroboam thought to himself, "The
kingdom will now likely revert to the
house of David. 27 If these people go up to
offer sacrifices at the temple of the LORD
in Jerusalem,[x] they will again give their
allegiance to their lord, Rehoboam king
of Judah. They will kill me and return to
King Rehoboam."
28 After seeking advice, the king made
two golden calves.[y] He said to the people, "It is too much for you to go up to
Jerusalem. Here are your gods, Israel,
who brought you up out of Egypt."[z] 29 One
he set up in Bethel,[a] and the other in
Dan.[b] 30 And this thing became a sin;[c]
the people came to worship the one at
Bethel and went as far as Dan to worship
the other.[a]
31 Jeroboam built shrines[d] on high
places and appointed priests[e] from all
sorts of people, even though they were
not Levites. 32 He instituted a festival on
the fifteenth day of the eighth[f] month,
like the festival held in Judah, and offered sacrifices on the altar. This he did
in Bethel, sacrificing to the calves he had
made. And at Bethel he also installed
priests at the high places he had made.
33 On the fifteenth day of the eighth
month, a month of his own choosing,
he offered sacrifices on the altar he had
built at Bethel.[g] So he instituted the festival for the Israelites and went up to the
altar to make offerings.

The Man of God From Judah

13 By the word of the LORD a man of
God[h] came from Judah to Bethel,[i]
as Jeroboam was standing by the altar

12:27 [x] Dt 12:5-6
12:28 [y] Ex 32:4; 2Ki 10:29; 17:16 [z] Ex 32:8
12:29 [a] Ge 28:19 [b] Jdg 18:27-31
12:30 [c] 1Ki 13:34; 2Ki 17:21
12:31 [d] 1Ki 13:32 [e] Nu 3:10; 1Ki 13:33; 2Ki 17:32; 2Ch 11:14-15; 13:9
12:32 [f] Lev 23:33-34; Nu 29:12
12:33 [g] Nu 15:39; 1Ki 13:1; Am 7:13
13:1 [h] 2Ki 23:17 [i] 1Ki 12:32-33

[a] *30* Probable reading of the original Hebrew text; Masoretic Text *people went to the one as far as Dan*

Shechem to make it a royal residence, then establishes places of worship in Bethel and Dan so the people will not go to Jerusalem for the pilgrimage festivals. To do this, he makes the Canaanite calf the symbol of divine presence and providence.

Archaeological evidence indicates that in the days of Jeroboam the sanctuary at Dan extended over a relatively large area. This area, with its various structures, storerooms, and open spaces paved with stone, may be the various "shrines on high places" (v. 31).

12:32-33 Jeroboam alters the priesthood; he establishes the eighth month as the time of the great fall pilgrimage. The ordination of non-Levitical priests may have been part of the policy to split the kingdoms of David and Jeroboam. Levitical priests would naturally have had a loyalty to the temple as well as to David, and most may have been unwilling to serve at a separate shrine. Jeroboam's ascent to the altar on the first day of the festival is the initiation of the high place he has built.

13:1-10 A man of God from Judah calls Jeroboam to

PEOPLE TO KNOW // JEROBOAM

1 KINGS 12:25-33: Jeroboam was an official of King Solomon who oversaw the labor forces of Ephraim and Manasseh (1Ki 11:28). One day the prophet Ahijah met Jeroboam in the country. Ahijah tore his new cloak into twelve pieces and told Jeroboam to take ten, announcing that God was ripping the kingdom away from Solomon for his sin and would give ten tribes to Jeroboam as king (1Ki 11:29-31). Ahijah promised that if Jeroboam honored God, God would make his family into a dynasty like David's.

Solomon tried to kill Jeroboam, who fled to Egypt until Solomon's death (1Ki 11:40). When Solomon's son Rehoboam became king, Israel turned from Rehoboam and made Jeroboam king; only Judah and Benjamin remained under Rehoboam. Ahijah's word proved true: Jeroboam reigned over the ten northern tribes.

Unfortunately, Jeroboam was a terrible king. Afraid his kingdom would reunite with Judah if the people continued to worship God in Jerusalem, Jeroboam set up golden calves for his people to worship at the northern and southern ends of his kingdom (1Ki 12:26-30). He abandoned God's ways and led his people into sin. The prophet Ahijah pronounced God's judgment against Jeroboam, declaring that God would raise up another king who would cut off Jeroboam's family in Israel (1Ki 14:14).

APPLICATION Jeroboam's story is sad. He had leadership skills and qualities that led to him rising to a high position in Solomon's court. God chose him to be king over the northern tribes. Yet when he became king, he immediately turned to evil. His life is an important reminder that giftedness alone does not lead to success. We need to humble ourselves before God and use our gifts for his glory. If we use our gifts for our own glory instead of for God's purposes, we will fail like Jeroboam.

to make an offering. 2By the word of the
LORD he cried out against the altar: "Altar, altar! This is what the LORD says: 'A
son named Josiah[j] will be born to the
house of David. On you he will sacrifice
the priests of the high places who make
offerings here, and human bones will
be burned on you.'" 3That same day the
man of God gave a sign:[k] "This is the sign
the LORD has declared: The altar will be
split apart and the ashes on it will be
poured out."
4When King Jeroboam heard what the
man of God cried out against the altar at
Bethel, he stretched out his hand from
the altar and said, "Seize him!" But the
hand he stretched out toward the man
shriveled up, so that he could not pull
it back. 5Also, the altar was split apart
and its ashes poured out according to
the sign given by the man of God by the
word of the LORD.
6Then the king said to the man of God,
"Intercede[l] with the LORD your God and
pray for me that my hand may be restored." So the man of God interceded
with the LORD, and the king's hand was
restored and became as it was before.
7The king said to the man of God,
"Come home with me for a meal, and I
will give you a gift."[m]
8But the man of God answered the
king, "Even if you were to give me half
your possessions,[n] I would not go with
you, nor would I eat bread[o] or drink
water here. 9For I was commanded by
the word of the LORD: 'You must not eat
bread or drink water or return by the way
you came.'" 10So he took another road
and did not return by the way he had
come to Bethel.
11Now there was a certain old prophet living in Bethel, whose sons came
and told him all that the man of God
had done there that day. They also told
their father what he had said to the king.

13:2 [j] 2Ki 23:15-16,20
13:3 [k] Jdg 6:17; Isa 7:14; Jn 2:11; 1Co 1:22
13:6 [l] Ex 8:8; 9:28; 10:17; Lk 6:27-28; Ac 8:24; Jas 5:16
13:7 [m] 1Sa 9:7; 2Ki 5:15
13:8 [n] Nu 22:18; 24:13 [o] ver 16
13:16 [p] ver 8
13:18 [q] Dt 13:3
13:21 [r] ver 26

1Ki 13:18 ❖ How can we tell when someone is a false prophet, speaking things about God that are not true (see Mt 7:15–20)?

12Their father asked them, "Which way
did he go?" And his sons showed him
which road the man of God from Judah had taken. 13So he said to his sons,
"Saddle the donkey for me." And when
they had saddled the donkey for him, he
mounted it 14and rode after the man of
God. He found him sitting under an oak
tree and asked, "Are you the man of God
who came from Judah?"
"I am," he replied.
15So the prophet said to him, "Come
home with me and eat."
16The man of God said, "I cannot turn
back and go with you, nor can I eat
bread[p] or drink water with you in this
place. 17I have been told by the word of
the LORD: 'You must not eat bread or
drink water there or return by the way
you came.'"
18The old prophet answered, "I too am
a prophet, as you are. And an angel said
to me by the word of the LORD: 'Bring
him back with you to your house so that
he may eat bread and drink water.'" (But
he was lying[q] to him.) 19So the man of
God returned with him and ate and
drank in his house.
20While they were sitting at the table, the word of the LORD came to the
old prophet who had brought him back.
21He cried out to the man of God who had
come from Judah, "This is what the LORD
says: 'You have defied[r] the word of the
LORD and have not kept the command
the LORD your God gave you. 22You came
back and ate bread and drank water in
the place where he told you not to eat or
drink. Therefore your body will not be
buried in the tomb of your ancestors.'"

---

account for his worship at Bethel. Three times we are told the man of God from Judah is not to eat bread, drink water, or return by the way he came. The first occurs in his encounter with Jeroboam. In return for healing, the king offers the man of God hospitality, possibly as a sign of solidarity and affirmation of his new position. The prophet refuses, citing God's command.

13:11–17 When the old prophet from Bethel invites the man from Judah to return for food and drink, the latter repeats God's command (vv. 16–17).

13:18–22 The prophet from Bethel lies; believing the lie does not excuse the man from Judah, who has demonstrated with a sign that he knows the word of Yahweh (v. 5). The word of judgment that comes to the prophet from Bethel repeats God's prohibition of eating and drinking (v. 22). The disobedience of the prophet from Judah and the successive judgment becomes a demonstration of the judgment that rests on the house of Jeroboam for disobeying God's commands to be faithful. The donkey stands helplessly beside the man's body, just as Jeroboam stood beside the shattered altar. In subtle terms, this scene shows Jeroboam to be a dumb animal.

23When the man of God had finished
eating and drinking, the prophet who
had brought him back saddled his donkey for him. 24As he went on his way, a
lion[s] met him on the road and killed him,
and his body was left lying on the road,
with both the donkey and the lion standing beside it. 25Some people who passed
by saw the body lying there, with the lion
standing beside the body, and they went
and reported it in the city where the old
prophet lived.
26When the prophet who had brought
him back from his journey heard of it,
he said, "It is the man of God who defied
the word of the LORD. The LORD has given
him over to the lion, which has mauled
him and killed him, as the word of the
LORD had warned him."
27The prophet said to his sons, "Saddle the donkey for me," and they did so.
28Then he went out and found the body
lying on the road, with the donkey and
the lion standing beside it. The lion had
neither eaten the body nor mauled the
donkey. 29So the prophet picked up the
body of the man of God, laid it on the
donkey, and brought it back to his own
city to mourn for him and bury him.
30Then he laid the body in his own tomb,
and they mourned over him and said,
"Alas, my brother!"[t]
31After burying him, he said to his sons,
"When I die, bury me in the grave where
the man of God is buried; lay my bones[u]
beside his bones. 32For the message he
declared by the word of the LORD against
the altar in Bethel and against all the
shrines on the high places[v] in the towns
of Samaria[w] will certainly come true."[x]
33Even after this, Jeroboam did not
change his evil ways, but once more appointed priests for the high places from
all sorts[y] of people. Anyone who wanted
to become a priest he consecrated for the
high places. 34This was the sin[z] of the
house of Jeroboam that led to its downfall and to its destruction[a] from the face
of the earth.

13:24 [s]1Ki 20:36
13:30 [t]Jer 22:18
13:31 [u]2Ki 23:18
13:32 [v]ver 2; Lev 26:30 [w]1Ki 16:24,28 [x]2Ki 23:16
13:33 [y]1Ki 12:31; 2Ch 11:15; 13:9
13:34 [z]1Ki 12:30 [a]1Ki 14:10
14:2 [b]1Sa 28:8; 2Sa 14:2; 1Ki 11:29
14:3 [c]1Sa 9:7
14:7 [d]2Sa 12:7-8; 1Ki 16:2
14:8 [e]1Ki 11:31, 33,38 [f]1Ki 15:5

Ahijah's Prophecy Against Jeroboam

14 At that time Abijah son of Jeroboam became ill, 2and Jeroboam
said to his wife, "Go, disguise yourself,
so you won't be recognized as the wife of
Jeroboam. Then go to Shiloh. Ahijah[b] the
prophet is there — the one who told me
I would be king over this people. 3Take
ten loaves of bread[c] with you, some cakes
and a jar of honey, and go to him. He will
tell you what will happen to the boy." 4So
Jeroboam's wife did what he said and
went to Ahijah's house in Shiloh.
Now Ahijah could not see; his sight
was gone because of his age. 5But the
LORD had told Ahijah, "Jeroboam's wife
is coming to ask you about her son, for
he is ill, and you are to give her such and
such an answer. When she arrives, she
will pretend to be someone else."
6So when Ahijah heard the sound of
her footsteps at the door, he said, "Come
in, wife of Jeroboam. Why this pretense?
I have been sent to you with bad news.
7Go, tell Jeroboam that this is what the
LORD, the God of Israel, says: 'I raised you
up from among the people and appointed you ruler[d] over my people Israel. 8I
tore[e] the kingdom away from the house
of David and gave it to you, but you have
not been like my servant David, who kept
my commands and followed me with all
his heart, doing only what was right[f] in
my eyes. 9You have done more evil than

13:23–32 In the final scene the prophet from Bethel retrieves the body from the presence of the lion, which has not molested the body or mauled the donkey (vv. 25b–32). That the lion refrained from eating serves to emphasize retrospectively the sin of the man of God, who ate prohibited food.
13:33–34 The warning at the altar does nothing to change Jeroboam's ways: He proceeds to ordain priests to serve at the high places. This sin of Jeroboam leads to the dissolution of the nation and its ultimate destruction.
14:1–8 Judgment against the house of Jeroboam begins with the illness and death of his son Abijah. The name of his son meant "my father is Yah(weh)," suggesting a pretentious claim on the part of the king. Desperate for help, Jeroboam seeks the help of the prophet Ahijah, who brought him the original message of his appointment as king. The king sends his wife to Shiloh in Ephraim in the hopes of receiving a more favorable response. The physical sight of Ahijah has failed, but he has inspired vision—one that enables him not only to identify his visitor but also to declare the harsh message he has for her.
14:9–11 The condemnation of Jeroboam is in terms of his call (vv. 7–11; cf. 11:33–35). Jeroboam has received the kingdom at the expense of the Davidic dynasty because Solomon failed to be loyal to God. That Jeroboam is "more evil than all who lived before [him]" (v. 9) is stereotyped language found repeatedly in Kings; David was not evil (v. 8), but Jeroboam has committed the same sins as Solomon and leaders before David. Like Solomon, Jeroboam will come under judgment.

all who lived before you. You have made
for yourself other gods, idols[g] made of
metal; you have aroused my anger and
turned your back on me.[h]
10 "'Because of this, I am going to bring
disaster on the house of Jeroboam. I will
cut off from Jeroboam every last male in
Israel — slave or free.[a][i] I will burn up the
house of Jeroboam as one burns dung,
until it is all gone.[j] 11 Dogs[k] will eat those
belonging to Jeroboam who die in the
city, and the birds will feed on those who
die in the country. The LORD has spoken!'
12 "As for you, go back home. When you
set foot in your city, the boy will die. 13 All
Israel will mourn for him and bury him.
He is the only one belonging to Jeroboam who will be buried, because he is the
only one in the house of Jeroboam in
whom the LORD, the God of Israel, has
found anything good.[l]
14 "The LORD will raise up for himself
a king over Israel who will cut off the
family of Jeroboam. Even now this is beginning to happen.[b] 15 And the LORD will
strike Israel, so that it will be like a reed
swaying in the water. He will uproot[m]
Israel from this good land that he gave
to their ancestors and scatter them beyond the Euphrates River, because they
aroused[n] the LORD's anger by making
Asherah[o] poles.[c] 16 And he will give Israel up because of the sins[p] Jeroboam
has committed and has caused Israel to
commit."
17 Then Jeroboam's wife got up and
left and went to Tirzah.[q] As soon as she
stepped over the threshold of the house,
the boy died. 18 They buried him, and all
Israel mourned for him, as the LORD had
said through his servant the prophet Ahijah.
19 The other events of Jeroboam's reign,
his wars and how he ruled, are written
in the book of the annals of the kings of
Israel. 20 He reigned for twenty-two years
and then rested with his ancestors. And
Nadab his son succeeded him as king.

Rehoboam King of Judah

14:21,25–31pp // 2Ch 12:9–16

21 Rehoboam son of Solomon was king
in Judah. He was forty-one years old
when he became king, and he reigned
seventeen years in Jerusalem, the city
the LORD had chosen out of all the tribes
of Israel in which to put his Name. His
mother's name was Naamah; she was an
Ammonite.[r]
22 Judah[s] did evil in the eyes of the
LORD. By the sins they committed they
stirred up his jealous anger[t] more than
those who were before them had done.
23 They also set up for themselves high
places, sacred stones[u] and Asherah
poles on every high hill and under every spreading tree.[v] 24 There were even
male shrine prostitutes[w] in the land;
the people engaged in all the detestable
practices of the nations the LORD had
driven out before the Israelites.
25 In the fifth year of King Rehoboam,
Shishak king of Egypt attacked[x] Jerusalem. 26 He carried off the treasures of the

14:9 [g] Ex 34:17; 1Ki 12:28; 2Ch 11:15 [h] Ne 9:26; Ps 50:17; Eze 23:35
14:10 [i] Dt 32:36; 1Ki 21:21; 2Ki 9:8-9; 14:26 [j] 1Ki 15:29
14:11 [k] 1Ki 16:4; 21:24
14:13 [l] 2Ch 12:12; 19:3
14:15 [m] Dt 29:28; 2Ki 15:29; 17:6; Ps 52:5 [n] Jos 23:15-16 [o] Ex 34:13; Dt 12:3
14:16 [p] 1Ki 12:30; 13:34; 15:30, 34; 16:2
14:17 [q] ver 12; 1Ki 15:33; 16:6-9
14:21 [r] ver 31; 1Ki 11:1; 2Ch 12:13
14:22 [s] 2Ch 12:1 [t] Dt 32:21; Ps 78:58; 1Co 10:22
14:23 [u] Dt 16:22; 2Ki 17:9-10; Eze 16:24-25 [v] Dt 12:2; Isa 57:5
14:24 [w] Dt 23:17; 1Ki 15:12; 2Ki 23:7
14:25 [x] 1Ki 11:40; 2Ch 12:2

[a] *10* Or *Israel — every ruler or leader* [b] *14* The meaning of the Hebrew for this sentence is uncertain. [c] *15* That is, wooden symbols of the goddess Asherah; here and elsewhere in 1 Kings

---

His whole royal house will die without receiving a proper burial (vv. 10–11).

14:12–16 The judgment against Jeroboam begins the moment his wife enters the city. Yahweh will raise up another king in place of the descendants of Jeroboam, but ultimately the whole nation will go into exile beyond the Euphrates because of his sins. The metaphor of a reed shaken in the water may refer to the many dynastic changes that will shortly take place or to the uncertainty that comes with the instability of leadership. The Asherah poles, which are so offensive to Yahweh, are associated with the worship of Baal, representing the goddess of fertility.

14:19–20 The concluding notice of the reign of Jeroboam makes special note of his great feats in warfare and rule. Information from the royal annals of the kings must have been incorporated into the sources the prophetic authors used to compile their history. Reference to these records becomes a fixed and formalized framework for the reign of each king.

14:21–24 This passage introduces Rehoboam at the death of Solomon; he reigns from 930–913 BC. Most notable about Rehoboam is the way he leads Judah in the sins of Canaanite worship, no less than what Jeroboam does in the north. Worst of all are the "shrine prostitutes" (v. 24). Sexual relations were part of sacrificial rites as a means of achieving fertility and prosperity (Hos 4:14). Cult practices and prostitution were explicitly forbidden by the covenant (Dt 23:18).

14:25–31 One of the main events of the reign of Rehoboam is the invasion of Shishak of Egypt. Of greatest significance is the cost of the campaign to the wealth and splendor that Solomon accumulated. The temple and palace are stripped; mere bronze shields replace the gold ones Solomon made. The ceremonial marches to the temple lose much of their former splendor.

temple[y] of the LORD and the treasures of the royal palace. He took everything, including all the gold shields[z] Solomon had made. 27 So King Rehoboam made bronze shields to replace them and assigned these to the commanders of the guard on duty at the entrance to the royal palace. 28 Whenever the king went to the LORD's temple, the guards bore the shields, and afterward they returned them to the guardroom.

29 As for the other events of Rehoboam's reign, and all he did, are they not written in the book of the annals of the kings of Judah? 30 There was continual warfare[a] between Rehoboam and Jeroboam. 31 And Rehoboam rested with his ancestors and was buried with them in the City of David. His mother's name was Naamah; she was an Ammonite.[b] And Abijah[a] his son succeeded him as king.

Abijah King of Judah

15:1–2,6–8pp // 2Ch 13:1–2,22—14:1

15 In the eighteenth year of the reign of Jeroboam son of Nebat, Abijah[b] became king of Judah, 2 and he reigned in Jerusalem three years. His mother's name was Maakah[c] daughter of Abishalom.[c]

3 He committed all the sins his father had done before him; his heart was not fully devoted[d] to the LORD his God, as the heart of David his forefather had been. 4 Nevertheless, for David's sake the LORD his God gave him a lamp[e] in Jerusalem by raising up a son to succeed him and by making Jerusalem strong. 5 For David had done what was right in the eyes of the LORD and had not failed to keep[f] any of the LORD's commands all the days of his life—except in the case of Uriah[g] the Hittite.

6 There was war[h] between Abijah[d] and Jeroboam throughout Abijah's lifetime. 7 As for the other events of Abijah's reign, and all he did, are they not written in the book of the annals of the kings of Judah? There was war between Abijah and Jeroboam. 8 And Abijah rested with his ancestors and was buried in the City of David. And Asa his son succeeded him as king.

Asa King of Judah

15:9–22pp // 2Ch 14:2–3; 15:16—16:6
15:23–24pp // 2Ch 16:11—17:1

9 In the twentieth year of Jeroboam king of Israel, Asa became king of Judah, 10 and he reigned in Jerusalem forty-one

14:26 [y] 1Ki 15:15, 18 [z] 1Ki 10:17
14:30 [a] 1Ki 12:21; 15:6
14:31 [b] ver 21; 2Ch 12:16
15:2 [c] 2Ch 11:20; 13:2
15:3 [d] 1Ki 11:4; Ps 119:80
15:4 [e] 2Sa 21:17; 1Ki 11:36; 2Ch 21:7
15:5 [f] 1Ki 9:4; 14:8 [g] 2Sa 11:2-27; 12:9
15:6 [h] 1Ki 14:30

1Ki 14:30 ❖ Why do God's people sometimes fight with each other? How might they find peace with one another through Christ?

1Ki 15:3 ❖ Where have we seen generational sins passed down through a family? How can such a cycle of sin be broken?

[a] *31* Some Hebrew manuscripts and Septuagint (see also 2 Chron. 12:16); most Hebrew manuscripts *Abijam* [b] *1* Some Hebrew manuscripts and Septuagint (see also 2 Chron. 12:16); most Hebrew manuscripts *Abijam*; also in verses 7 and 8 [c] *2* A variant of *Absalom*; also in verse 10 [d] *6* Some Hebrew manuscripts and Syriac *Abijam* (that is, Abijah); most Hebrew manuscripts *Rehoboam*

12:1—14:31 Jesus, in his high priestly prayer for his disciples, did not ask that God take them out of the world, but that God would keep them from the evil one; they were not of this world, just as Jesus himself was not of this world (Jn 17:15-16). Christians have struggled with this concept and debated it in many ways. Christians understand that they live by the values and conduct of the kingdom of God, but it is not easy to know how these are to be exercised in particular circumstances. To some extent believers must conform to the culture around them as part of the world they live in, but in certain ways their lives need to display a different value system.

As in the days of Jeroboam and Rehoboam, there exists an expression of faith that has compromised biblical life and values so much that it is indistinguishable from the surrounding culture. Jesus did not ask that his followers be taken from the world, but that they would be sanctified in the truth of God's Word and sent into the world (Jn 17:17-18). Purity from this world must begin with clear Christian thinking. Failure to clearly distinguish Christian faith from postmodern relativism will lead Christians to conform too much to the ways of the world (see Ro 12:2).

15:1-2 Abijah (Abijam in Hebrew) succeeds Rehoboam. His mother Maakah may have been a foreigner, possibly of Aramean descent, which may account for her idolatry (15:13).
15:3-8 Kings condemns Abijah; he follows in the idolatry of Rehoboam. Abijah continues his father's policy of war with Israel (vv. 6-7), but the text doesn't acknowledge any divine blessing on his reign.
15:9-13 The forty-one years of Asa are from 910-869 BC. He takes initiative against the male and

years. His grandmother's name was Maakah[i] daughter of Abishalom.
11Asa did what was right in the eyes of
the LORD, as his father David had done.
12He expelled the male shrine prostitutes[j] from the land and got rid of all
the idols his ancestors had made. 13He
even deposed his grandmother Maakah
from her position as queen mother, because she had made a repulsive image
for the worship of Asherah. Asa cut it
down[k] and burned it in the Kidron Valley.
14Although he did not remove the high
places, Asa's heart was fully committed[l]
to the LORD all his life. 15He brought into
the temple of the LORD the silver and
gold and the articles that he and his father had dedicated.[m]
16There was war[n] between Asa and
Baasha king of Israel throughout their
reigns. 17Baasha king of Israel went up
against Judah and fortified Ramah[o] to
prevent anyone from leaving or entering
the territory of Asa king of Judah.
18Asa then took all the silver and gold
that was left in the treasuries of the
LORD's temple[p] and of his own palace.
He entrusted it to his officials and sent[q]
them to Ben-Hadad[r] son of Tabrimmon,
the son of Hezion, the king of Aram, who
was ruling in Damascus. 19"Let there be
a treaty between me and you," he said,
"as there was between my father and
your father. See, I am sending you a gift
of silver and gold. Now break your treaty with Baasha king of Israel so he will
withdraw from me."
20Ben-Hadad agreed with King Asa
and sent the commanders of his forces against the towns of Israel. He conquered[s] Ijon, Dan, Abel Beth Maakah and
all Kinnereth in addition to Naphtali.
21When Baasha heard this, he stopped
building Ramah and withdrew to Tirzah.
22Then King Asa issued an order to all
Judah — no one was exempt — and they
carried away from Ramah the stones and
timber Baasha had been using there.
With them King Asa built up Geba[t] in
Benjamin, and also Mizpah.
23As for all the other events of Asa's
reign, all his achievements, all he did and
the cities he built, are they not written
in the book of the annals of the kings
of Judah? In his old age, however, his
feet became diseased. 24Then Asa rested
with his ancestors and was buried with
them in the city of his father David. And
Jehoshaphat[u] his son succeeded him as
king.

Nadab King of Israel

25Nadab son of Jeroboam became king
of Israel in the second year of Asa king
of Judah, and he reigned over Israel two
years. 26He did evil in the eyes of the
LORD, following the ways of his father[v]
and committing the same sin his father
had caused Israel to commit.
27Baasha son of Ahijah from the tribe
of Issachar plotted against him, and he
struck him down[w] at Gibbethon,[x] a Philistine town, while Nadab and all Israel
were besieging it. 28Baasha killed Nadab
in the third year of Asa king of Judah and
succeeded him as king.
29As soon as he began to reign, he
killed Jeroboam's whole family.[y] He
did not leave Jeroboam anyone that
breathed, but destroyed them all, according to the word of the LORD given
through his servant Ahijah the Shilonite.

15:10 [i] ver 2
15:12 [j] 1Ki 14:24; 22:46
15:13 [k] Ex 32:20
15:14 [l] ver 3; 1Ki 8:61; 22:43
15:15 [m] 1Ki 7:51
15:16 [n] ver 32
15:17 [o] Jos 18:25; 1Ki 12:27
15:18 [p] ver 15; 1Ki 14:26 [q] 2Ki 12:18 [r] 1Ki 11:23-24
15:20 [s] Jdg 18:29; 2Sa 20:14; 2Ki 15:29
15:22 [t] Jos 18:24; 21:17
15:24 [u] Mt 1:8
15:26 [v] 1Ki 12:30; 14:16
15:27 [w] 1Ki 14:14 [x] Jos 19:44; 21:23
15:29 [y] 1Ki 14:10, 14

---

female cult prostitutes serving at the country shrines and removes Maakah as the leading lady. Official functions of the office of queen mother in Israelite monarchy are nowhere more specific than in 15:13.

15:14–15 Though Asa is unable to remove the shrines, he is committed to the restoration of the temple treasuries. He is able to restore some of the artifacts of the temple through plunder from his enemies, which he and his father dedicate for temple use.

15:16–19 The war with Baasha brings the Arameans into conflict with Israel. Asa takes whatever treasures Shishak has left behind and whatever he has managed to restore and sends them as a bribe to the Aramean king Ben-Hadad to attack Baasha. The mention of Asa's father may indicate that Abijah has already made an agreement with Ben-Hadad (v. 19).

15:19–20 Ben-Hadad is more than willing to accept money from both Baasha and Asa in their war against each other. The Aramean breaks his treaty and attacks northern Israel, capturing all the land of Naphtali. The northern attack forces Baasha to abandon his southern fortification.

15:21–24 After the withdrawal of Baasha, Asa conscripts workers to use the materials at Ramah to rebuild Geba and Mizpah along with other cities in Judah. His death from disease was regarded as evidence of divine disfavor.

15:25–32 The only son of Jeroboam to succeed him is Nadab (909–908 BC). Baasha not only assassinates Nadab but also carries out a blood purge against the entire royal lineage of Jeroboam, fulfilling the judgment that Ahijah the prophet proclaimed against him.

30 This happened because of the sins[z]
Jeroboam had committed and had
caused Israel to commit, and because
he aroused the anger of the LORD, the
God of Israel.
31 As for the other events of Nadab's
reign, and all he did, are they not written
in the book of the annals of the kings
of Israel? 32 There was war[a] between Asa
and Baasha king of Israel throughout
their reigns.

Baasha King of Israel

33 In the third year of Asa king of Judah, Baasha son of Ahijah became king
of all Israel in Tirzah, and he reigned
twenty-four years. 34 He did evil[b] in the
eyes of the LORD, following the ways of
Jeroboam and committing the same sin
Jeroboam had caused Israel to commit.
16 Then the word of the LORD came
to Jehu[c] son of Hanani[d] concerning Baasha: 2 "I lifted you up from the
dust[e] and appointed you ruler[f] over my
people Israel, but you followed the ways
of Jeroboam and caused[g] my people
Israel to sin and to arouse my anger by
their sins. 3 So I am about to wipe out
Baasha and his house,[h] and I will make
your house like that of Jeroboam son
of Nebat. 4 Dogs[i] will eat those belonging to Baasha who die in the city, and
birds will feed on those who die in the
country."
5 As for the other events of Baasha's
reign, what he did and his achievements,
are they not written in the book of the
annals[j] of the kings of Israel? 6 Baasha
rested with his ancestors and was buried
in Tirzah.[k] And Elah his son succeeded
him as king.
7 Moreover, the word of the LORD came[l]
through the prophet Jehu[m] son of Hanani to Baasha and his house, because
of all the evil he had done in the eyes
of the LORD, arousing his anger by the
things he did, becoming like the house
of Jeroboam — and also because he destroyed it.

Elah King of Israel

8 In the twenty-sixth year of Asa king
of Judah, Elah son of Baasha became
king of Israel, and he reigned in Tirzah
two years.
9 Zimri, one of his officials, who had
command of half his chariots, plotted
against him. Elah was in Tirzah at the
time, getting drunk[n] in the home of
Arza, the palace administrator[o] at Tirzah. 10 Zimri came in, struck him down
and killed him in the twenty-seventh
year of Asa king of Judah. Then he succeeded him as king.
11 As soon as he began to reign and was
seated on the throne, he killed off Baasha's whole family.[p] He did not spare a
single male, whether relative or friend.
12 So Zimri destroyed the whole family of
Baasha, in accordance with the word of
the LORD spoken against Baasha through
the prophet Jehu — 13 because of all the
sins Baasha and his son Elah had committed and had caused Israel to commit,
so that they aroused the anger of the
LORD, the God of Israel, by their worthless idols.[q]
14 As for the other events of Elah's
reign, and all he did, are they not written in the book of the annals of the kings
of Israel?

Zimri King of Israel

15 In the twenty-seventh year of Asa
king of Judah, Zimri reigned in Tirzah
seven days. The army was encamped near
Gibbethon,[r] a Philistine town. 16 When the
Israelites in the camp heard that Zimri
had plotted against the king and murdered him, they proclaimed Omri, the
commander of the army, king over Israel
that very day there in the camp. 17 Then
Omri and all the Israelites with him withdrew from Gibbethon and laid siege to
Tirzah. 18 When Zimri saw that the city was
taken, he went into the citadel of the royal
palace and set the palace on fire around
him. So he died, 19 because of the sins he
had committed, doing evil in the eyes

15:30 [z] 1Ki 14:9, 16
15:32 [a] ver 16
15:34 [b] ver 26; 1Ki 12:28-29; 13:33; 14:16
16:1 [c] ver 7; 2Ch 19:2; 20:34 [d] 2Ch 16:7
16:2 [e] 1Sa 2:8 [f] 1Ki 14:7-9 [g] 1Ki 15:34
16:3 [h] ver 11; 1Ki 14:10; 15:29; 21:22
16:4 [i] 1Ki 14:11
16:5 [j] 1Ki 14:19; 15:31
16:6 [k] 1Ki 14:17; 15:33
16:7 [l] 1Ki 15:27, 29 [m] ver 1
16:9 [n] 2Ki 9:30-33 [o] 1Ki 18:3
16:11 [p] ver 3
16:13 [q] Dt 32:21; 1Sa 12:21; Isa 41:29
16:15 [r] Jos 19:44; 1Ki 15:27

15:33–34 Baasha's guilt lies in following the sins of Jeroboam; Jehu son of Hanani delivers the sentence.
16:1–4 The speech against Baasha is given in similar rhetoric to that found in the judgment against Jeroboam. Baasha is appointed as a leader over Israel but causes Israel to sin and offends Yahweh (v. 2, cf. 14:9; v. 3, cf. 14:10; v. 4, cf. 14:11).
16:5–7 The summary of Baasha's reign includes the activity of Jehu the prophet, which makes explicit the parallel to Jeroboam.
16:8–14 The house of Baasha ends with the type of violence Baasha inflicted on the house of Jeroboam. The judgment announced by the prophet Jehu is fulfilled, just as that announced by Abijah against Jeroboam (vv. 12–13; cf. 15:29–30).
16:15–20 Zimri is included as one of the kings of Israel even though his reign only lasts seven days.

of the LORD and following the ways of
Jeroboam and committing the same sin
Jeroboam had caused Israel to commit.
20 As for the other events of Zimri's
reign, and the rebellion he carried out,
are they not written in the book of the
annals of the kings of Israel?

Omri King of Israel

21 Then the people of Israel were split
into two factions; half supported Tibni
son of Ginath for king, and the other half
supported Omri. 22 But Omri's followers proved stronger than those of Tibni
son of Ginath. So Tibni died and Omri
became king.
23 In the thirty-first year of Asa king of
Judah, Omri became king of Israel, and
he reigned twelve years, six of them in
Tirzah.[s] 24 He bought the hill of Samaria
from Shemer for two talents[a] of silver
and built a city on the hill, calling it Samaria,[t] after Shemer, the name of the
former owner of the hill.
25 But Omri did evil[u] in the eyes of the
LORD and sinned more than all those before him. 26 He followed completely the
ways of Jeroboam son of Nebat, committing the same sin Jeroboam had caused[v]
Israel to commit, so that they aroused
the anger of the LORD, the God of Israel,
by their worthless idols.[w]
27 As for the other events of Omri's
reign, what he did and the things he
achieved, are they not written in the
book of the annals of the kings of Israel?

16:23 [s] 1Ki 15:21
16:24 [t] 1Ki 13:32; Jn 4:4
16:25 [u] Dt 4:25; Mic 6:16
16:26 [v] ver 19 [w] Dt 32:21
16:30 [x] ver 25; 1Ki 14:9
16:31 [y] Dt 7:3; 1Ki 11:2 [z] Jdg 18:7; 2Ki 9:34 [a] 2Ki 10:18; 17:16
16:32 [b] 2Ki 10:21, 27; 11:18
16:33 [c] 2Ki 13:6 [d] ver 29, 30; 1Ki 14:9; 21:25
16:34 [e] Jos 6:26

1Ki 16:21-22 ❖ What does society look like when "might makes right"? How would Jesus teach a better way (see Mt 5:38-42)?

28 Omri rested with his ancestors and was
buried in Samaria. And Ahab his son succeeded him as king.

Ahab Becomes King of Israel

29 In the thirty-eighth year of Asa king
of Judah, Ahab son of Omri became king
of Israel, and he reigned in Samaria over
Israel twenty-two years. 30 Ahab son of
Omri did more[x] evil in the eyes of the
LORD than any of those before him. 31 He
not only considered it trivial to commit
the sins of Jeroboam son of Nebat, but
he also married[y] Jezebel daughter[z] of
Ethbaal king of the Sidonians, and began to serve Baal[a] and worship him. 32 He
set up an altar for Baal in the temple[b] of
Baal that he built in Samaria. 33 Ahab also
made an Asherah pole[c] and did more[d] to
arouse the anger of the LORD, the God
of Israel, than did all the kings of Israel
before him.
34 In Ahab's time, Hiel of Bethel rebuilt
Jericho. He laid its foundations at the cost
of his firstborn son Abiram, and he set up
its gates at the cost of his youngest son
Segub, in accordance with the word of
the LORD spoken by Joshua son of Nun.[e]

[a] *24* That is, about 150 pounds or about 68 kilograms

16:21-28 The twelve-year reign of Omri is shared with Tibni for the first five years (885–874 BC). Tibni the son of Ginath makes a bid for the throne (v. 21), so the country is divided for a period of about four years (cf. vv. 21–22). Omri receives the briefest attention; his great deeds are mentioned in a general summarizing fashion (v. 27). The one achievement mentioned is the establishment of a new state capital, Samaria (v. 24).
16:29–33 The twenty-two-year reign of Ahab (874–853 BC) ends with the battle at Qarqar. The summary of his reign occurs several chapters later (22:39–40) since his story is intertwined with the Elijah accounts. Ahab extends the idolatry of Israel; he builds a temple for Baal in Samaria and promotes the cult of Asherah. His infamous marriage to Jezebel, daughter of the Sidonian king (v. 31), facilitates the state promotion of the Baal cult.
16:34 Rebuilding Jericho, one of many cities Ahab restores, brings about the curse of Joshua.

✣ **15:1—16:34** Most of the Christian past involves conflict, as with the history of Israel and Judah. This conflict goes back to the earliest times of the NT itself. The apostle Paul encounters intense conflict with the church at Corinth and avoids a further personal confrontation by writing a painful letter (2Co 1:23—2:4). Others took satisfaction in the suffering and imprisonment of the apostle Paul and preached Christ with the goal of adding difficulty to his life in prison (Php 1:15–18).

As Christians look back on their past it is important to have a clear perspective on the way in which the church struggles and fails in dealing with the forces of each age. Then it becomes more feasible to respect considerable differences within the Christian faith. Above all, it is important to see how God continues to be at work accomplishing his purposes—sometimes through the deeds of wicked individuals who seek only to promote their own interests and sometimes through individuals willing to sacrifice their lives in doing the will of God on earth.

PEOPLE TO KNOW // AHAB

1 KINGS 16:29–34: Ahab was among the most wicked kings of the northern kingdom of Israel, doing more evil in God's eyes than all the kings before him (1Ki 16:30).

Chief among Ahab's misdeeds was his marriage to the wicked Jezebel, who led him and his kingdom deep into idolatry. Ahab filled his royal court with false prophets and built places of worship to false gods.

Ahab's sin led to a prolonged famine in Israel. Instead of realizing it was his own fault, Ahab blamed the national crisis on Elijah, God's prophet. After three years of famine, Elijah challenged Ahab's prophets to the famous showdown on Mount Carmel (1Ki 18:16–46). God answered with fire from the sky, and the people killed Baal's prophets. In spite of the failures of the priests of Baal, Ahab maintained his contempt for God's prophets.

Ahab showed further wickedness when he had Naboth killed simply because he wanted Naboth's vineyard. For this sin, Elijah declared Ahab would die a violent death and have his blood licked up by dogs (1Ki 21:19). Later, during an intense battle, an arrow was shot at random in the heat of fighting and struck Ahab. He was wounded and watched the battle from his chariot while he bled and then died. When the chariot was washed, his blood was licked up by dogs as God had foretold (1Ki 22:38).

APPLICATION Ahab chose evil over good. He married into a wicked family and followed in the ways of his evil ancestors. His story reminds us of the importance of surrounding ourselves with the right kind of influences and of letting God work in our lives to break negative family patterns and generational sins. Though Ahab did display one instance of humble repentance that pleased God (1Ki 21:25–29), his legacy is ultimately one of failure. His life shows how destruction and chaos result from rejecting God and chasing after sin and idols.

Elijah Announces a Great Drought

17 Now Elijah[f] the Tishbite, from Tish-
be[a] in Gilead,[g] said to Ahab, "As the
LORD, the God of Israel, lives, whom I
serve, there will be neither dew nor rain[h]
in the next few years except at my word."

Elijah Fed by Ravens

2 Then the word of the LORD came to
Elijah: 3 "Leave here, turn eastward and
hide in the Kerith Ravine, east of the
Jordan. 4 You will drink from the brook,
and I have directed the ravens[i] to supply
you with food there."

5 So he did what the LORD had told
him. He went to the Kerith Ravine, east
of the Jordan, and stayed there. 6 The
ravens brought him bread and meat in
the morning[j] and bread and meat in the
evening, and he drank from the brook.

Elijah and the Widow at Zarephath

7 Some time later the brook dried up
because there had been no rain in the
land. 8 Then the word of the LORD came
to him: 9 "Go at once to Zarephath[k] in the
region of Sidon and stay there. I have directed a widow[l] there to supply you with
food." 10 So he went to Zarephath. When
he came to the town gate, a widow was
there gathering sticks. He called to her
and asked, "Would you bring me a little
water in a jar so I may have a drink?"[m]
11 As she was going to get it, he called,
"And bring me, please, a piece of bread."

12 "As surely as the LORD your God
lives," she replied, "I don't have any
bread — only a handful of flour in a jar
and a little olive oil[n] in a jug. I am gath-

17:1 [f] Mal 4:5; Jas 5:17 [g] Jdg 12:4 [h] Dt 10:8; 1Ki 18:1; 2Ki 3:14; Lk 4:25
17:4 [i] Ge 8:7
17:6 [j] Ex 16:8
17:9 [k] Ob 20 [l] Lk 4:26
17:10 [m] Ge 24:17; Jn 4:7
17:12 [n] ver 1; 2Ki 4:2

[a] 1 Or *Tishbite, of the settlers*

17:1 The threat of drought by the oath of Yahweh is a direct challenge to the powers of Baal. Baal was the rider of the clouds—the god of rain and fertility, and therefore of riches. The protagonist and antagonist in the present story are Yahweh and Baal, represented by Elijah and Ahab, respectively.

17:2–6 Immediately after delivering the message, presumably in Samaria, Elijah is directed to go outside Ahab's territory. Elijah needs sustenance and protection, and provision for Elijah becomes even more dramatic after the brook dries up.

17:7–11 Not only is Baal incapable of overcoming the drought, but Yahweh's provision for the faithful prophet takes place right in the heart of Baal territory.

17:12–16 The widow to whom God directs Elijah is herself preparing to die with her son because the drought has exhausted their entire food supply. Despite her dire situation, the woman answers the prophet's request in the name of the God of Elijah. The woman trusts the God of the prophet and does as he instructs. Her faith is rewarded,

ering a few sticks to take home and make
a meal for myself and my son, that we
may eat it — and die."
13Elijah said to her, "Don't be afraid. Go
home and do as you have said. But first
make a small loaf of bread for me from
what you have and bring it to me, and
then make something for yourself and
your son. 14For this is what the LORD, the
God of Israel, says: 'The jar of flour will
not be used up and the jug of oil will not
run dry until the day the LORD sends rain
on the land.'"
15She went away and did as Elijah had
told her. So there was food every day for
Elijah and for the woman and her family. 16For the jar of flour was not used
up and the jug of oil did not run dry, in
keeping with the word of the LORD spoken by Elijah.
17Some time later the son of the woman who owned the house became ill.
He grew worse and worse, and finally
stopped breathing. 18She said to Elijah,
"What do you have against me, man of
God? Did you come to remind me of my
sin[o] and kill my son?"
19"Give me your son," Elijah replied. He
took him from her arms, carried him to
the upper room where he was staying,
and laid him on his bed. 20Then he cried
out to the LORD, "LORD my God, have you
brought tragedy even on this widow I
am staying with, by causing her son to
die?" 21Then he stretched[p] himself out
on the boy three times and cried out to
the LORD, "LORD my God, let this boy's
life return to him!"
22The LORD heard Elijah's cry, and the
boy's life returned to him, and he lived.
23Elijah picked up the child and carried
him down from the room into the house.
He gave him to his mother and said,
"Look, your son is alive!"

17:18 [o] 2Ki 3:13; Lk 5:8
17:21 [p] 2Ki 4:34; Ac 20:10
17:24 [q] Jn 3:2; 16:30 [r] Ps 119:43; Jn 17:17
18:1 [s] 1Ki 17:1; Lk 4:25; Jas 5:17 [t] Dt 28:12
18:3 [u] 1Ki 16:9 [v] Ne 7:2
18:4 [w] 2Ki 9:7 [x] ver 13; Isa 16:3
18:7 [y] 2Ki 1:8
18:10 [z] 1Ki 17:3

1Ki 17:14–16 ❖ How can we experience God's sustaining power during the dry seasons in life?

24Then the woman said to Elijah, "Now
I know[q] that you are a man of God and
that the word of the LORD from your
mouth is the truth."[r]

Elijah and Obadiah

18 After a long time, in the third[s] year,
the word of the LORD came to Elijah: "Go and present yourself to Ahab,
and I will send rain[t] on the land." 2So
Elijah went to present himself to Ahab.
Now the famine was severe in Samaria,
3and Ahab had summoned Obadiah, his
palace administrator.[u] (Obadiah was a
devout believer[v] in the LORD. 4While Jezebel[w] was killing off the LORD's prophets,
Obadiah had taken a hundred prophets
and hidden[x] them in two caves, fifty in
each, and had supplied them with food
and water.) 5Ahab had said to Obadiah,
"Go through the land to all the springs
and valleys. Maybe we can find some
grass to keep the horses and mules alive
so we will not have to kill any of our animals." 6So they divided the land they
were to cover, Ahab going in one direction and Obadiah in another.
7As Obadiah was walking along, Elijah met him. Obadiah recognized[y] him,
bowed down to the ground, and said, "Is
it really you, my lord Elijah?"
8"Yes," he replied. "Go tell your master,
'Elijah is here.'"
9"What have I done wrong," asked Obadiah, "that you are handing your servant over to Ahab to be put to death? 10As
surely as the LORD your God lives, there
is not a nation or kingdom where my
master has not sent someone to look[z] for

---

the prophetic word is confirmed, and the God of Israel is shown to be the giver of life.

17:17–21 The illness and death of the woman's son is taken as evidence that Elijah is not a benevolent prophet to a foreign woman; instead, she is being punished for her sins. Elijah's action to revive the boy may be an acted-out prayer typical of the prophets, but it could also be a self-sacrificial intercession in which he takes the role of the sacrificial victim, identifying himself with the ultimate uncleanness of death.

17:22–24 God restores life to the child, demonstrating that God, not Baal, is the giver of life.

18:1–6 In the face of this extended drought, Ahab has completely misplaced priorities. He is busy trying to preserve the animals but apparently has no concern for the prophets whom Jezebel has cut off. There are two droughts in the land; while hunger from drought is severe, hunger for the prophets is caused by the wiles of a wicked woman. Ahab and Obadiah are not only going in different directions geographically in their search for water, they are in pursuit of opposing values.

18:7–15 While the pagan widow immediately complied with a demanding request (17:13–15), the man who fears Yahweh responds with fear. As the widow makes Elijah responsible for the death of her son by bringing her sin to light (17:18), so Obadiah feels that Elijah will be the cause of his death if he should report to Ahab (18:9, 12, 14).

you. And whenever a nation or kingdom
claimed you were not there, he made
them swear they could not find you.
11But now you tell me to go to my master and say, 'Elijah is here.' 12I don't know
where the Spirit[a] of the LORD may carry you when I leave you. If I go and tell
Ahab and he doesn't find you, he will kill
me. Yet I your servant have worshiped
the LORD since my youth. 13Haven't you
heard, my lord, what I did while Jezebel
was killing the prophets of the LORD? I
hid a hundred of the LORD's prophets
in two caves, fifty in each, and supplied
them with food and water. 14And now
you tell me to go to my master and say,
'Elijah is here.' He will kill me!"
15Elijah said, "As the LORD Almighty
lives, whom I serve, I will surely present[b]
myself to Ahab today."

Elijah on Mount Carmel

16So Obadiah went to meet Ahab and
told him, and Ahab went to meet Elijah.
17When he saw Elijah, he said to him, "Is
that you, you troubler[c] of Israel?"
18"I have not made trouble for Israel," Elijah replied. "But you[d] and your
father's family have. You have abandoned[e] the LORD's commands and have
followed the Baals. 19Now summon the
people from all over Israel to meet me
on Mount Carmel.[f] And bring the four
hundred and fifty prophets of Baal and
the four hundred prophets of Asherah,
who eat at Jezebel's table."
20So Ahab sent word throughout all
Israel and assembled the prophets on
Mount Carmel. 21Elijah went before the
people and said, "How long will you waver[g] between two opinions? If the LORD

18:12 [a] 2Ki 2:16; Eze 3:14; Ac 8:39
18:15 [b] 1Ki 17:1
18:17 [c] Jos 7:25; 1Ki 21:20; Ac 16:20
18:18 [d] 1Ki 16:31, 33; 21:25 [e] 2Ch 15:2
18:19 [f] Jos 19:26
18:21 [g] Jos 24:15; 2Ki 17:41; Mt 6:24
18:22 [h] 1Ki 19:10 [i] ver 19
18:24 [j] ver 38; 1Ch 21:26
18:26 [k] Ps 115:4-5; Jer 10:5; 1Co 8:4; 12:2
18:27 [l] Hab 2:19
18:28 [m] Lev 19:28; Dt 14:1

1Ki 18:21 ❖ Where do we see people wavering between commitments rather than devoting themselves fully to God? Where might we see this wavering in our own hearts?

is God, follow him; but if Baal is God,
follow him."
But the people said nothing.
22Then Elijah said to them, "I am the
only one of the LORD's prophets left,[h]
but Baal has four hundred and fifty
prophets.[i] 23Get two bulls for us. Let Baal's prophets choose one for themselves,
and let them cut it into pieces and put it
on the wood but not set fire to it. I will
prepare the other bull and put it on the
wood but not set fire to it. 24Then you call
on the name of your god, and I will call
on the name of the LORD. The god who
answers by fire[j] — he is God."
Then all the people said, "What you
say is good."
25Elijah said to the prophets of Baal,
"Choose one of the bulls and prepare it
first, since there are so many of you. Call
on the name of your god, but do not light
the fire." 26So they took the bull given
them and prepared it.
Then they called on the name of Baal
from morning till noon. "Baal, answer
us!" they shouted. But there was no response;[k] no one answered. And they
danced around the altar they had made.
27At noon Elijah began to taunt them.
"Shout louder!" he said. "Surely he is a
god! Perhaps he is deep in thought, or
busy, or traveling. Maybe he is sleeping and must be awakened."[l] 28So they
shouted louder and slashed[m] themselves
with swords and spears, as was their cus-

18:16–18 The meeting between Elijah and Ahab contrasts Ahab's apostasy with the faithfulness of Obadiah (vv. 16–20). While the latter has respectfully greeted Elijah by falling to the ground (v. 7), Ahab accuses Elijah of being the one who had put a hex on Israel (v. 17). This accusation is itself a contradiction: If Baal is truly a god, Elijah could have no power over Israel at all. If Elijah does have power to bring drought, then Baal is not really a god.

18:19–20 The choice of Mount Carmel is significant as the center for the worship of a local deity that functioned as Canaanite Baal. Its proximity to the Phoenician border places the challenge to Jezebel right at her doorstep. Carmel is also the natural place to worship the storm god who can calm the winter gales and turn the storms into rain.

18:21–25 The contest at Mount Carmel shows that the Lord of Israel will tolerate no compromise; the contest Elijah proposes shows the folly of attempting to serve two masters (vv. 22–24).

18:26–28 The prophets' ritual dance, which may have included music and song, is meant to attract the attention of their god. Baal rituals seem to be alluded to in Elijah's taunting questions. In the assumption that Baal rituals follow a seasonal pattern, the death of Baal alluded to in the prophet's mention of sleep would signify the hot dry period of summer. The customary gashing with knives and blades may be part of a blood ritual seeking the first rainfall. Bloodletting was a rite of imitative magic to prompt a release of vital rain. These rituals would take place at a fall festival for the Baal cult in anticipation of the early rains.

tom, until their blood flowed. 29 Midday
passed, and they continued their frantic prophesying until the time for the
evening sacrifice.[n] But there was no response, no one answered, no one paid
attention.[o]
30 Then Elijah said to all the people,
"Come here to me." They came to him,
and he repaired the altar[p] of the LORD,
which had been torn down. 31 Elijah
took twelve stones, one for each of the
tribes descended from Jacob, to whom
the word of the LORD had come, saying,
"Your name shall be Israel."[q] 32 With the
stones he built an altar in the name[r] of the
LORD, and he dug a trench around it large
enough to hold two seahs[a] of seed. 33 He
arranged[s] the wood, cut the bull into pieces and laid it on the wood. Then he said to
them, "Fill four large jars with water and
pour it on the offering and on the wood."
34 "Do it again," he said, and they did
it again.
"Do it a third time," he ordered, and
they did it the third time. 35 The water ran
down around the altar and even filled
the trench.
36 At the time of sacrifice, the prophet Elijah stepped forward and prayed:
"LORD, the God of Abraham,[t] Isaac and
Israel, let it be known[u] today that you are
God in Israel and that I am your servant
and have done all these things at your
command.[v] 37 Answer me, LORD, answer
me, so these people will know that you,
LORD, are God, and that you are turning
their hearts back again."
38 Then the fire[w] of the LORD fell and
burned up the sacrifice, the wood, the
stones and the soil, and also licked up
the water in the trench.

18:29 [n] Ex 29:41 [o] ver 26
18:30 [p] 1Ki 19:10
18:31 [q] Ge 32:28; 35:10; 2Ki 17:34
18:32 [r] Col 3:17
18:33 [s] Ge 22:9; Lev 1:6-8
18:36 [t] Ex 3:6; Mt 22:32 [u] 1Ki 8:43; 2Ki 19:19 [v] Nu 16:28
18:38 [w] Lev 9:24; Jdg 6:21; 1Ch 21:26; 2Ch 7:1; Job 1:16
18:39 [x] ver 24
18:40 [y] Jdg 4:7 [z] Dt 13:5; 18:20; 2Ki 10:24-25
18:42 [a] ver 19-20; Jas 5:18
18:44 [b] Lk 12:54
18:46 [c] 2Ki 3:15 [d] 2Ki 4:29; 9:1
19:1 [e] 1Ki 18:40

39 When all the people saw this, they
fell prostrate and cried, "The LORD—he
is God! The LORD—he is God!"[x]
40 Then Elijah commanded them,
"Seize the prophets of Baal. Don't let
anyone get away!" They seized them,
and Elijah had them brought down to the
Kishon Valley[y] and slaughtered[z] there.
41 And Elijah said to Ahab, "Go, eat and
drink, for there is the sound of a heavy
rain." 42 So Ahab went off to eat and drink,
but Elijah climbed to the top of Carmel,
bent down to the ground and put his
face between his knees.[a]
43 "Go and look toward the sea," he told
his servant. And he went up and looked.
"There is nothing there," he said.
Seven times Elijah said, "Go back."
44 The seventh time the servant reported, "A cloud[b] as small as a man's hand is
rising from the sea."
So Elijah said, "Go and tell Ahab, 'Hitch
up your chariot and go down before the
rain stops you.'"
45 Meanwhile, the sky grew black with
clouds, the wind rose, a heavy rain
started falling and Ahab rode off to Jezreel. 46 The power[c] of the LORD came on
Elijah and, tucking his cloak into his
belt,[d] he ran ahead of Ahab all the way
to Jezreel.

Elijah Flees to Horeb

19 Now Ahab told Jezebel everything
Elijah had done and how he had
killed[e] all the prophets with the sword.
2 So Jezebel sent a messenger to Elijah
to say, "May the gods deal with me,

[a] *32* That is, probably about 24 pounds or about 11 kilograms

---

18:29–37 Elijah's offering takes place on an altar restored for the purpose (18:30); disrepair of the altar is presumably a result of the oppression Jezebel has inflicted on the prophets. The animal is prepared on the wood, and everything is soaked with water three times. Elijah's prayer that the hearts of the people will be turned back to Yahweh brings fire to consume the offering.

The actions of Elijah signal the restoration of Israel. An altar of twelve stones and twelve dousings with water (four jars emptied three times) both recall the twelve tribes and the crossing of the Jordan. Building an altar, forsaking false gods, and restoring the name Israel (vv. 30–31) follow the pattern of Jacob when he built the altar at Bethel.

18:38 The "fire of the LORD" indicates the divine presence. Fire may indicate both the divine presence and approval of the sacrifice, as with Gideon and Moses.

18:39–40 The Carmel event is no less significant than the exodus; the renewal of Israel does not allow for the continuance of Baalism.

18:41–46 With Israel reborn, Elijah turns his attention to Ahab, who must prepare for a feast to celebrate the coming of rain. As Ahab rides furiously toward Jezreel, Elijah runs on ahead. Running before the king indicates service to that king, now with the intent that the king will fulfill his proper mission in service to God.

19:1–2 After the slaughter of the prophets of Baal, Jezebel asserts her authority as the patron of the Baal cult. Jezebel (meaning "Where is the prince [Baal]?") is pitted against Elijah (meaning "Yah[weh] is my God").

Jezebel sends her messenger with a verbal threat.

be it ever so severely,[f] if by this time
tomorrow I do not make your life like
that of one of them."
3Elijah was afraid[a] and ran[g] for his life.
When he came to Beersheba in Judah, he
left his servant there, 4while he himself
went a day's journey into the wilderness.
He came to a broom bush, sat down under it and prayed that he might die. "I
have had enough, LORD," he said. "Take
my life;[h] I am no better than my ancestors." 5Then he lay down under the bush
and fell asleep.[i]
All at once an angel touched him
and said, "Get up and eat." 6He looked
around, and there by his head was some
bread baked over hot coals, and a jar of
water. He ate and drank and then lay
down again.
7The angel of the LORD came back a
second time and touched him and said,
"Get up and eat, for the journey is too
much for you." 8So he got up and ate
and drank. Strengthened by that food,
he traveled forty[j] days and forty nights
until he reached Horeb,[k] the mountain
of God. 9There he went into a cave[l] and
spent the night.

The LORD Appears to Elijah

And the word of the LORD came to him:
"What are you doing here, Elijah?"
10He replied, "I have been very zealous[m] for the LORD God Almighty. The Israelites have rejected your covenant, torn
down your altars, and put your prophets
to death with the sword. I am the only
one left,[n] and now they are trying to kill
me too."
11The LORD said, "Go out and stand on
the mountain[o] in the presence of the
LORD, for the LORD is about to pass by."
Then a great and powerful wind[p] tore
the mountains apart and shattered the
rocks before the LORD, but the LORD was
not in the wind. After the wind there was
an earthquake, but the LORD was not in
the earthquake. 12After the earthquake
came a fire, but the LORD was not in
the fire. And after the fire came a gentle whisper.[q] 13When Elijah heard it, he
pulled his cloak over his face[r] and went
out and stood at the mouth of the cave.
Then a voice said to him, "What are
you doing here, Elijah?"
14He replied, "I have been very zealous
for the LORD God Almighty. The Israelites have rejected your covenant, torn
down your altars, and put your prophets
to death with the sword. I am the only
one left,[s] and now they are trying to kill
me too."
15The LORD said to him, "Go back the
way you came, and go to the Desert of

1Ki 19:12-13 ❖ How have we experienced the gentle whisper of God during a difficult season? What messages of assurance has God given us in such times?

19:2 [f] 1Ki 20:10; 2Ki 6:31; Ru 1:17
19:3 [g] Ge 31:21
19:4 [h] Nu 11:15; Jer 20:18; Jnh 4:8
19:5 [i] Ge 28:11
19:8 [j] Ex 24:18; 34:28; Dt 9:9-11, 18; Mt 4:2 [k] Ex 3:1
19:9 [l] Ex 33:22
19:10 [m] Nu 25:13 [n] 1Ki 18:4, 22; Ro 11:3*
19:11 [o] Ex 24:12 [p] Eze 1:4; 37:7
19:12 [q] Job 4:16; Zec 4:6
19:13 [r] ver 9; Ex 3:6
19:14 [s] ver 10

[a] 3 Or *Elijah saw*

If she can persuade Elijah to leave the country, she can pursue her goals without interference from the prophet and without risking violent conflict, as Elijah has gained a following with the people.

19:3–5a The prophet Elijah appears to be a contradiction of himself in his fearful withdrawal from Jezebel and his accusations against the faithlessness of the people (v. 10). He seems to have felt confident in confronting Ahab, but he is not prepared to face the real advocate of the Baal cult in spite of the dramatic victory that has just taken place on the mountain. He ignores the dramatic conversion of the people (18:39), forgets the courageous faithfulness of the prophet Obadiah (18:3–4), blames the people for the vengeful attack of Jezebel (19:10, 14), and regards himself as utterly isolated in his struggle against the Baal cult.

Alone in the desert, Elijah desires nothing other than death. "No better than my ancestors" (v. 4) may recall Moses, who asks for death when the people grumble about their conditions in the desert (Nu 11:15).

19:5b–9a Elijah is twice strengthened by divine provision of food and refreshed by sleep before he continues his journey toward Horeb for forty days and forty nights.

19:9b–14 Elijah's answer to Yahweh's question shows that he is a prophet worthy of encountering Yahweh at his mountain (v. 11a); his function as a prophet is restored. The narrative intentionally makes Elijah a prophet like Moses. Storm, earthquake, and fire recall the original appearance of God to the people at Mount Sinai. Elijah wraps his face in his garment, the equivalent of Moses being protected by the rock as the glory of Yahweh passed by (v. 13; cf. Ex 33:21–22).

Elijah has restored the people to a relationship with God after failure. Like Moses, Elijah has brought God's word to the people (cf. Dt 18:16–18); he occupies a position above that of the other prophets. Elijah experiences the divine presence: After the storm, earthquake, and fire, God speaks in the silence. The divine word comes to Elijah, renewing his commission to judge Israel's compromise of the covenant and bringing about a spiritual renewal.

19:15–18 The commission of Elijah is the pledge that conflict with Baal will end in victory over the house of Ahab: Anointing the kings of Aram and

Damascus. When you get there, anoint
Hazael[t] king over Aram. 16 Also, anoint[u]
Jehu son of Nimshi king over Israel,
and anoint Elisha[v] son of Shaphat from
Abel Meholah to succeed you as prophet.
17 Jehu will put to death any who escape
the sword of Hazael,[w] and Elisha will put
to death any who escape the sword of
Jehu. 18 Yet I reserve[x] seven thousand in
Israel — all whose knees have not bowed
down to Baal and whose mouths have
not kissed[y] him."

The Call of Elisha

19 So Elijah went from there and found
Elisha son of Shaphat. He was plowing
with twelve yoke of oxen, and he himself
was driving the twelfth pair. Elijah went
up to him and threw his cloak[z] around
him. 20 Elisha then left his oxen and ran
after Elijah. "Let me kiss my father and
mother goodbye,"[a] he said, "and then I
will come with you."

"Go back," Elijah replied. "What have
I done to you?"

21 So Elisha left him and went back. He
took his yoke of oxen[b] and slaughtered
them. He burned the plowing equipment
to cook the meat and gave it to the people, and they ate. Then he set out to follow Elijah and became his servant.[c]

Ben-Hadad Attacks Samaria

20 Now Ben-Hadad[d] king of Aram
mustered his entire army. Accompanied by thirty-two kings with their
horses and chariots, he went up and besieged Samaria and attacked it. 2 He sent
messengers into the city to Ahab king of
Israel, saying, "This is what Ben-Hadad
says: 3 'Your silver and gold are mine, and
the best of your wives and children are
mine.' "

4 The king of Israel answered, "Just as
you say, my lord the king. I and all I have
are yours."

5 The messengers came again and said,
"This is what Ben-Hadad says: 'I sent to
demand your silver and gold, your wives
and your children. 6 But about this time
tomorrow I am going to send my officials
to search your palace and the houses of
your officials. They will seize everything
you value and carry it away.' "

19:15 [t] 2Ki 8:7-15
19:16 [u] 2Ki 9:1-3, 6 [v] ver 21; 2Ki 2:9,15
19:17 [w] 2Ki 8:12, 29; 9:14; 13:3, 7,22
19:18 [x] Ro 11:4* [y] Hos 13:2
19:19 [z] 2Ki 2:8, 14
19:20 [a] Mt 8:21-22; Lk 9:61
19:21 [b] 2Sa 24:22 [c] ver 16
20:1 [d] 1Ki 15:18; 22:31; 2Ki 6:24

Israel is the harbinger of judgment on the nation for its political compromise and of a purge of the Baal cult within Israel.

19:19 The anointing of Elisha assures Elijah that the prophetic challenge will not end with him. Transfer of the garment signifies a transmission of the mission and the ability to accomplish it.

19:20-21 Elisha recognizes God's call and prepares to separate from his family. There is no indication that Elijah's question to Elisha is a rebuke; it may indicate that the calling of Elisha does not need to sever natural family affection.

Elisha's sacrifice is a thank offering for his call, in which neighbors are naturally invited to join. The burning of the yoke of the oxen signifies a complete break with the past. From that time on Elisha becomes the protégé of Elijah.

17:1—19:21 In ancient times, material well-being required that the gods be satisfied in order for them to bestow their bounty. In part, religion served materialist desires; in modern times, materialism has itself become a religion.

Modern society continues to operate largely on the materialistic premises of such thinkers as Charles Darwin, Karl Marx, and Sigmund Freud. Convinced that the only reality is material, true explanations become reductive. Thought is treated as the irrational product of environment or brain chemistry. Reductionism permeates society—from politics and social sciences to literature and the performing arts.

One of the legacies of materialism is the belief that the perfect society may be engineered through social science and planning. In the name of humanity, social scientists claim the right to remake society without having to obtain its consent. They believe in their own power to bring about complete material well-being and implicitly believe that this is the highest good, since it is the basis of fulfilling all other desires.

Such objectives, even if achievable, cannot bring about the promise of some sort of heaven on earth. Materialist doctrines of moral relativism and denial of personal responsibility undermine the ideal society of materialist dreams. Materialist religion is as deceptive, destructive, and pervasive as Baalism in Ahab's Israel.

20:1-4 The battle for Samaria results when negotiations break down between the Aramean king and his Israelite vassal. Aram is an ethnic rather than a geographic term, and the thirty-two "kings" were not heads of state but tribal chieftains who roamed with semi-independence in the area of Damascus. The title "king of Aram" (v. 1) refers to the control Ben-Hadad has in mustering these chieftains against Ahab.

20:5-11 Ben-Hadad demands that his officers conduct the taxation as they see fit, including possession of members of the royal family, leaving Ahab to rule as a vassal. Ahab follows the advice of his elders in resisting this demand. Ben-Hadad responds to this with an oath that he will turn Samaria into dust scooped up by his soldiers, but Ahab replies with a proverb of his own (v. 11): Boasting only comes after the battle.

7The king of Israel summoned all
the elders of the land and said to them,
"See how this man is looking for trouble![e] When he sent for my wives and my
children, my silver and my gold, I did
not refuse him."
8The elders and the people all answered, "Don't listen to him or agree to
his demands."
9So he replied to Ben-Hadad's messengers, "Tell my lord the king, 'Your servant will do all you demanded the first
time, but this demand I cannot meet.'"
They left and took the answer back to
Ben-Hadad.
10Then Ben-Hadad sent another message to Ahab: "May the gods deal with
me, be it ever so severely, if enough dust[f]
remains in Samaria to give each of my
men a handful."
11The king of Israel answered, "Tell
him: 'One who puts on his armor should
not boast[g] like one who takes it off.'"
12Ben-Hadad heard this message while
he and the kings were drinking[h] in their
tents,[a] and he ordered his men: "Prepare
to attack." So they prepared to attack the
city.

Ahab Defeats Ben-Hadad

13Meanwhile a prophet came to Ahab
king of Israel and announced, "This is
what the LORD says: 'Do you see this vast
army? I will give it into your hand today, and then you will know[i] that I am
the LORD.'"
14"But who will do this?" asked Ahab.
The prophet replied, "This is what the
LORD says: 'The junior officers under the
provincial commanders will do it.'"
"And who will start[j] the battle?" he
asked.
The prophet answered, "You will."
15So Ahab summoned the 232 junior officers under the provincial commanders.
Then he assembled the rest of the Israelites, 7,000 in all. 16They set out at noon
while Ben-Hadad and the 32 kings allied with him were in their tents getting
drunk.[k] 17The junior officers under the
provincial commanders went out first.
Now Ben-Hadad had dispatched
scouts, who reported, "Men are advancing from Samaria."
18He said, "If they have come out for
peace, take them alive; if they have come
out for war, take them alive."
19The junior officers under the provincial commanders marched out of the city
with the army behind them 20and each
one struck down his opponent. At that,
the Arameans fled, with the Israelites
in pursuit. But Ben-Hadad king of Aram
escaped on horseback with some of his
horsemen. 21The king of Israel advanced
and overpowered the horses and chariots and inflicted heavy losses on the
Arameans.
22Afterward, the prophet[l] came to the
king of Israel and said, "Strengthen your
position and see what must be done, because next spring[m] the king of Aram will
attack you again."
23Meanwhile, the officials of the king
of Aram advised him, "Their gods are
gods[n] of the hills. That is why they were
too strong for us. But if we fight them
on the plains, surely we will be stronger
than they. 24Do this: Remove all the kings
from their commands and replace them
with other officers. 25You must also raise
an army like the one you lost — horse
for horse and chariot for chariot — so
we can fight Israel on the plains. Then
surely we will be stronger than they." He
agreed with them and acted accordingly.
26The next spring[o] Ben-Hadad mustered the Arameans and went up to
Aphek[p] to fight against Israel. 27When
the Israelites were also mustered and

20:7 [e] 2Ki 5:7
20:10 [f] 2Sa 22:43; 1Ki 19:2
20:11 [g] Pr 27:1; Jer 9:23
20:12 [h] ver 16; 1Ki 16:9
20:13 [i] ver 28; Ex 6:7
20:14 [j] Jdg 1:1
20:16 [k] ver 12; 1Ki 16:9
20:22 [l] ver 13 [m] ver 26; 2Sa 11:1
20:23 [n] 1Ki 14:23; Ro 1:21-23
20:26 [o] ver 22 [p] 2Ki 13:17

[a] *12* Or *in Sukkoth*; also in verse 16

20:12–15 Ahab is given assurance by an unnamed prophet that God will win the battle as in the time of the exodus, so the Israelites may know the meaning of the name Yahweh (v. 13). The word of proof offered by the prophet is that Ahab will appoint 232 elite troops engaged in the protection of the provinces, who will be joined by seven thousand of the regular troops marshaled for the occasion.
20:16–21 The Israelites meet the Aramean army man for man, pursue them, and inflict heavy casualties. Ben-Hadad manages to escape with his horsemen, but the Israelites decimate their cavalry as well.
20:22–26 The Aramean king is advised to abandon the ineffective alliances with area chieftains and bring his military forces directly under his control, with officials he appoints himself. He further needs to tally a force equal to the troops and cavalry that desert him.
20:27–28 When the entire Israelite army is mustered, it looks small and weak in comparison to the vast opposition (v. 27). The prophet responds with a message identical to the one given before the first battle (v. 28), with the same assurance the God of the exodus will be with them in defeat of his enemies.

given provisions, they marched out to
meet them. The Israelites camped opposite them like two small flocks of goats,
while the Arameans covered the countryside.[q]
28The man of God came up and told
the king of Israel, "This is what the LORD
says: 'Because the Arameans think the
LORD is a god of the hills and not a god[r]
of the valleys, I will deliver this vast army
into your hands, and you will know[s] that
I am the LORD.'"
29For seven days they camped opposite each other, and on the seventh day
the battle was joined. The Israelites inflicted a hundred thousand casualties
on the Aramean foot soldiers in one day.
30The rest of them escaped to the city
of Aphek,[t] where the wall collapsed on
twenty-seven thousand of them. And
Ben-Hadad fled to the city and hid[u] in
an inner room.
31His officials said to him, "Look, we
have heard that the kings of Israel are
merciful. Let us go to the king of Israel
with sackcloth[v] around our waists and
ropes around our heads. Perhaps he will
spare your life."
32Wearing sackcloth around their
waists and ropes around their heads,
they went to the king of Israel and said,
"Your servant Ben-Hadad says: 'Please
let me live.'"
The king answered, "Is he still alive?
He is my brother."
33The men took this as a good sign and
were quick to pick up his word. "Yes, your
brother Ben-Hadad!" they said.
"Go and get him," the king said. When
Ben-Hadad came out, Ahab had him
come up into his chariot.
34"I will return the cities[w] my father
took from your father," Ben-Hadad offered. "You may set up your own market

20:27 [q] Jdg 6:6; 1Sa 13:6
20:28 [r] ver 23 [s] ver 13
20:30 [t] ver 26 [u] 1Ki 22:25; 2Ch 18:24
20:31 [v] Ge 37:34
20:34 [w] 1Ki 15:20
[x] Jer 49:23-27
[y] Ex 23:32
20:35 [z] 1Ki 13:21; 2Ki 2:3-7
20:36 [a] 1Ki 13:24
20:39 [b] 2Ki 10:24

1Ki 20:28 ❖ Have we ever tried to keep God in one corner of life, forgetting that he is Lord over all? How is God's omnipresence a blessing and a comfort?

areas in Damascus,[x] as my father did in
Samaria."
Ahab said, "On the basis of a treaty[y]
I will set you free." So he made a treaty
with him, and let him go.

A Prophet Condemns Ahab

35By the word of the LORD one of the
company of the prophets said to his companion, "Strike me with your weapon,"
but he refused.[z]
36So the prophet said, "Because you
have not obeyed the LORD, as soon as
you leave me a lion[a] will kill you." And
after the man went away, a lion found
him and killed him.
37The prophet found another man and
said, "Strike me, please." So the man
struck him and wounded him. 38Then
the prophet went and stood by the road
waiting for the king. He disguised himself with his headband down over his
eyes. 39As the king passed by, the prophet
called out to him, "Your servant went
into the thick of the battle, and someone came to me with a captive and said,
'Guard this man. If he is missing, it will
be your life for his life,[b] or you must pay
a talent[a] of silver.' 40While your servant
was busy here and there, the man disappeared."
"That is your sentence," the king of
Israel said. "You have pronounced it
yourself."
41Then the prophet quickly removed

[a] 39 That is, about 75 pounds or about 34 kilograms

20:29–30 The battle at Aphek is described briefly, depicting the victory in terms of holy war: The armies face each other seven days and the walls of Aphek fall (see Jos 6:1–20). With God's help, the Israelites shatter the Arameans.
20:31 Ben-Hadad is left with no alternative but to appeal to treaty loyalty, which he expects from Ahab (20:31). "Merciful" is a covenant term denoting loyalty to a relationship. Coarse black cloth attached to the waist is a sign of penitence. A rope on the head indicates servitude.
20:32–34 Ahab responds to this with a willingness to continue a treaty relationship. The envoys test Ahab by suggesting a renewed loyalty. The deal Ahab strikes with Ben-Hadad sends the enemy king away with his life.
20:35–37 A message for Ahab comes from one of the "company of the prophets," a group associated with Elisha, mentioned only here in connection with Elijah.
20:38–40 Ahab fails to realize that "your life for his life" is a verdict he is bringing on himself and his people.
20:41–43 The doctrine of holy war requires that the spoils belong entirely to God (cf. Jos 6:18). A prisoner in such a case cannot be treated as common property; anything so devoted cannot be sold or redeemed by substituting something

the headband from his eyes, and the king
of Israel recognized him as one of the
prophets. 42He said to the king, "This is
what the LORD says: 'You have set free
a man I had determined should die.[a][c]
Therefore it is your life for his life,[d] your
people for his people.'" 43Sullen and angry,[e] the king of Israel went to his palace
in Samaria.

Naboth's Vineyard

21 Some time later there was an incident involving a vineyard belonging to Naboth[f] the Jezreelite. The vineyard was in Jezreel,[g] close to the palace
of Ahab king of Samaria. 2Ahab said to
Naboth, "Let me have your vineyard to
use for a vegetable garden, since it is
close to my palace. In exchange I will
give you a better vineyard or, if you prefer, I will pay you whatever it is worth."
3But Naboth replied, "The LORD forbid
that I should give you the inheritance[h]
of my ancestors."
4So Ahab went home, sullen and angry[i]
because Naboth the Jezreelite had said,
"I will not give you the inheritance of
my ancestors." He lay on his bed sulking
and refused to eat.
5His wife Jezebel came in and asked
him, "Why are you so sullen? Why won't
you eat?"
6He answered her, "Because I said to
Naboth the Jezreelite, 'Sell me your vineyard; or if you prefer, I will give you another vineyard in its place.' But he said,
'I will not give you my vineyard.'"
7Jezebel his wife said, "Is this how you
act as king over Israel? Get up and eat!
Cheer up. I'll get you the vineyard[j] of
Naboth the Jezreelite."
8So she wrote letters in Ahab's name,
placed his seal[k] on them, and sent them
to the elders and nobles who lived in
Naboth's city with him. 9In those letters
she wrote:

> "Proclaim a day of fasting and seat
> Naboth in a prominent place among
> the people. 10But seat two scoun-
> drels[l] opposite him and have them
> bring charges that he has cursed[m]
> both God and the king. Then take
> him out and stone him to death."

11So the elders and nobles who lived
in Naboth's city did as Jezebel directed
in the letters she had written to them.
12They proclaimed a fast[n] and seated Naboth in a prominent place among the
people. 13Then two scoundrels came and
sat opposite him and brought charges
against Naboth before the people, saying,
"Naboth has cursed both God and the
king." So they took him outside the city
and stoned him to death.[o] 14Then they

20:42 [c] Jer 48:10 [d] ver 39; Jos 2:14; 1Ki 22:31-37
20:43 [e] 1Ki 21:4
21:1 [f] 2Ki 9:21 [g] 1Ki 18:45-46
21:3 [h] Lev 25:23; Nu 36:7; Eze 46:18
21:4 [i] 1Ki 20:43
21:7 [j] 1Sa 8:14
21:8 [k] Ge 38:18; Est 3:12; 8:8,10
21:10 [l] Ac 6:11 [m] Ex 22:28; Lev 24:15-16
21:12 [n] Isa 58:4
21:13 [o] 2Ki 9:26

[a] *42* The Hebrew term refers to the irrevocable giving over of things or persons to the LORD, often by totally destroying them.

---

else; therefore it is not Ahab's prerogative to make a treaty with him. The king, learning of the judgment pronounced on him and his country, returns to his capital resentful and angry.

> ✣ **20:1-43** Judgment is conspicuously absent in contemporary concepts of God. The church may shoulder its share of blame for this perception; divine punishment has often been attached to rules that have little to do with morality or to requirements of faith that have little to do with biblical theology. It may also be the consequence of a permissive culture in pursuit of personal freedom without responsibility for the consequences of such choices. A therapeutic culture has replaced judgment with validation of feelings. But sin is still sin, and still requires that the believer repent and ask for forgiveness.

21:1-2 The royal center at Jezreel was built concurrently with Samaria; the planners and architects of both sites followed the same architectural layout. The various buildings included a central building that served as a royal residence. The size and imposing nature of the fortifications express the need to show the strength and position of the royal dynasty. These grandiose public works are a means of social control over the local population. This function of Jezreel in the royal priorities clarifies Ahab's desire to enhance his presence by taking possession of Naboth's vineyard.

21:3 Naboth appropriately refuses Ahab's offer of purchase from the viewpoint of ancestral inheritance: All the land belongs to God; the Israelites are sojourners. It is not their right to sell land and so alienate it from the family.

21:4-8 Jezebel perceives Ahab's response as weakness, and moves to write letters and sign them in the name of the king: If Ahab won't act within the power of his office, Jezebel will resort to treachery.

21:9-14 Naboth himself appears to have been the head of an influential local family, as he is given a place of honor at the sacred occasion. However, refusing to cooperate with the royal request makes him a rival to the supporters of the king. It is an offense to curse a ruler of the people (Ex 22:28), so it is simple for unscrupulous witnesses to bring a sentence of death against Naboth. The ease with which such a plot is accomplished demonstrates the pervasive corruption of Ahab's reign.

sent word to Jezebel: "Naboth has been
stoned to death."
15 As soon as Jezebel heard that Naboth
had been stoned to death, she said to
Ahab, "Get up and take possession of the
vineyard[p] of Naboth the Jezreelite that he
refused to sell you. He is no longer alive,
but dead." 16 When Ahab heard that Naboth was dead, he got up and went down
to take possession of Naboth's vineyard.
17 Then the word of the LORD came to
Elijah the Tishbite: 18 "Go down to meet
Ahab king of Israel, who rules in Samaria. He is now in Naboth's vineyard, where
he has gone to take possession of it. 19 Say
to him, 'This is what the LORD says: Have
you not murdered a man and seized his
property?' Then say to him, 'This is what
the LORD says: In the place where dogs
licked up Naboth's blood,[q] dogs[r] will lick
up your blood — yes, yours!' "
20 Ahab said to Elijah, "So you have
found me, my enemy!"[s]
"I have found you," he answered, "because you have sold[t] yourself to do evil
in the eyes of the LORD. 21 He says, 'I am
going to bring disaster on you. I will wipe
out your descendants and cut off from
Ahab every last male[u] in Israel — slave or
free.[a] 22 I will make your house[v] like that
of Jeroboam son of Nebat and that of
Baasha son of Ahijah, because you have
aroused my anger and have caused Israel to sin.'[w]
23 "And also concerning Jezebel the
LORD says: 'Dogs[x] will devour Jezebel
by the wall of[b] Jezreel.'
24 "Dogs[y] will eat those belonging to
Ahab who die in the city, and the birds
will feed on those who die in the country."
25 (There was never[z] anyone like Ahab,
who sold himself to do evil in the eyes of
the LORD, urged on by Jezebel his wife.
26 He behaved in the vilest manner by
going after idols, like the Amorites[a] the
LORD drove out before Israel.)
27 When Ahab heard these words, he
tore his clothes, put on sackcloth[b] and

21:15 [p] 1Sa 8:14
21:19 [q] 2Ki 9:26; Ps 9:12; Isa 14:20 [r] 1Ki 22:38
21:20 [s] 1Ki 18:17 [t] ver 25; 2Ki 17:17; Ro 7:14
21:21 [u] 1Ki 14:10; 2Ki 9:8
21:22 [v] 1Ki 15:29; 16:3 [w] 1Ki 12:30
21:23 [x] 2Ki 9:10, 34-36
21:24 [y] 1Ki 14:11; 16:4
21:25 [z] ver 20; 1Ki 16:33
21:26 [a] Ge 15:16; Lev 18:25-30; 2Ki 21:11
21:27 [b] Ge 37:34; 2Sa 3:31; 2Ki 6:30

1Ki 21:27-29 ❖ God listens to prayers of repentance made in true humility, even when they come from someone as evil as Ahab. What does true repentance before God look like?

[a] *21* Or *Israel — every ruler or leader* [b] *23* Most Hebrew manuscripts; a few Hebrew manuscripts, Vulgate and Syriac (see also 2 Kings 9:26) *the plot of ground at*

21:15-16 Jezebel informs her husband that the vineyard is now his for the taking. This criminal act has been achieved with full judicial authority.
21:17-18 Ahab has gone from Samaria to Jezreel to inspect his property (vv. 16, 18b); Ahab "who rules in Samaria" (v. 18) is a reference to his royal residence rather than his personal presence in Samaria. Yahweh instructs Elijah to confront Ahab at the scene of the crime.
21:19 The judgment against Ahab matches the fate of Naboth. The dogs do literally lick up the blood of Ahab in Samaria when the chariot in which he dies is washed (22:38), but they also lick up his blood in the vineyard of Naboth when the body of his son Joram is thrown there (2Ki 9:25-26). Human injustice is answered by divine judgment in a double sense: Ahab will die in battle, and his dynasty will end with the death of his son. The deaths of Ahab and Jezebel are described in the terms of Jeroboam and Baasha (21:23-24; cf. 14:10-11; 16:4).
21:20-25 Ahab's response to Elijah betrays knowledge of his own guilt: Elijah is Ahab's enemy because the latter has violated his responsibility as a king under the covenant. Elijah describes Ahab's guilt for what it is (v. 20). Greed has led Ahab into the sin of murder and theft, so there is none who can be compared to him.
21:26 Though Jezebel is an accomplice in his crime, Ahab is still at fault as the instigator of her actions. Murder and theft are the results of desecrating the covenant, a manifestation of Ahab's disrespect for God and for the relationships that are divinely ordained.
21:27-29 The ending of the narrative offers a surprising turn: Ahab shows his repentance by wearing sackcloth, fasting, and conducting his affairs with gentleness. God responds to that humbling. Though Ahab does die violently in battle, he is buried in the royal tomb (22:39-40) and his dynasty continues for another fourteen years under the rule of his sons.

✜ **21:1-29** The story of Naboth is a biblical model for injustice, as it demonstrates how the powerful take advantage of the weak to add to their wealth. It has all the features that are typical of such instances: The actions are done "legally" because they are in the power of the state; they are justified by the people in power, so the victims may not even be able to make a case for the injustice of their case. As a society becomes corrupt because of oppressive leaders, there is increased opportunity for such individuals to ply their trade.

Christians who see such injustice also know how God feels when the powerful oppress their weaker counterparts (see Ps 9:9). As we strive to reflect God's purposes in our own lives, we can also strive to create a more just society: first by not perpetrating injustice in our own actions and attitudes, and second by vigorously defending the rights of the downtrodden.

fasted. He lay in sackcloth and went around meekly.

28Then the word of the LORD came to Elijah the Tishbite: 29"Have you noticed how Ahab has humbled himself before me? Because he has humbled himself, I will not bring this disaster in his day, but I will bring it on his house in the days of his son."[c]

Micaiah Prophesies Against Ahab

22:1–28pp // 2Ch 18:1–27

22 For three years there was no war between Aram and Israel. 2But in the third year Jehoshaphat king of Judah went down to see the king of Israel. 3The king of Israel had said to his officials, "Don't you know that Ramoth Gilead[d] belongs to us and yet we are doing nothing to retake it from the king of Aram?"

4So he asked Jehoshaphat, "Will you go with me to fight[e] against Ramoth Gilead?"

Jehoshaphat replied to the king of Israel, "I am as you are, my people as your people, my horses as your horses." 5But Jehoshaphat also said to the king of Israel, "First seek the counsel[f] of the LORD."

6So the king of Israel brought together the prophets—about four hundred men—and asked them, "Shall I go to war against Ramoth Gilead, or shall I refrain?"

"Go,"[g] they answered, "for the Lord will give it into the king's hand."

7But Jehoshaphat asked, "Is there no longer a prophet[h] of the LORD here whom we can inquire of?"

8The king of Israel answered Jehoshaphat, "There is still one prophet through whom we can inquire of the LORD, but I hate[i] him because he never prophesies anything good[j] about me, but always bad. He is Micaiah son of Imlah."

21:29 [c] 2Ki 9:26
22:3 [d] Dt 4:43; Jos 21:38
22:4 [e] 2Ki 3:7
22:5 [f] Ex 33:7; 2Ki 3:11
22:6 [g] 1Ki 18:19
22:7 [h] 2Ki 3:11
22:8 [i] Am 5:10 [j] Isa 5:20
22:10 [k] ver 6
22:11 [l] Dt 33:17; Zec 1:18-21
22:14 [m] Nu 22:18; 24:13; 1Ki 18:10, 15

1Ki 22:8 ❖ Why do some resist hearing the true words of God? Where have we seen people resist God's messengers?

"The king should not say such a thing," Jehoshaphat replied.

9So the king of Israel called one of his officials and said, "Bring Micaiah son of Imlah at once."

10Dressed in their royal robes, the king of Israel and Jehoshaphat king of Judah were sitting on their thrones at the threshing floor[k] by the entrance of the gate of Samaria, with all the prophets prophesying before them. 11Now Zedekiah son of Kenaanah had made iron horns[l] and he declared, "This is what the LORD says: 'With these you will gore the Arameans until they are destroyed.'"

12All the other prophets were prophesying the same thing. "Attack Ramoth Gilead and be victorious," they said, "for the LORD will give it into the king's hand."

13The messenger who had gone to summon Micaiah said to him, "Look, the other prophets without exception are predicting success for the king. Let your word agree with theirs, and speak favorably."

14But Micaiah said, "As surely as the LORD lives, I can tell him only what the LORD tells me."[m]

15When he arrived, the king asked him, "Micaiah, shall we go to war against Ramoth Gilead, or not?"

"Attack and be victorious," he answered, "for the LORD will give it into the king's hand."

16The king said to him, "How many times must I make you swear to tell me nothing but the truth in the name of the LORD?"

22:1-3 Three years is a typological number rather than an exact chronological statement. Plans for the attack are laid during a state visit by Jehoshaphat. Ahab's question concerning Ramoth Gilead is intended to arouse shame and resentment (v. 3), since the Arameans are violating the agreement made earlier at Aphek.

22:4 Ahab does not have sufficient resources to attack the Arameans on his own, so he solicits help from his ally in enforcing the treaty. Jehoshaphat affirms his support, but he wisely refuses to proceed unless there is divine confirmation that this action is within God's will.

22:5-12 The inquiry unfolds in two scenes in which the prophets affirm Ahab's goals (vv. 5–6, 10–12). Their leader Zedekiah reaffirms their opinion by acting out the message of how the Arameans will be utterly defeated. The agreement of the prophets is emphatic (v. 12).

22:13-18 The prophet Micaiah is asked and answers, but the king knows Micaiah is only giving him the answer that will confirm the loyalty of his prophets rather than the divine word. So Micaiah elaborates that the armies of Israel will be scattered like sheep without a shepherd and will return home without a leader (v. 17). In other words, Ahab will die.

17Then Micaiah answered, "I saw all
Israel scattered on the hills like sheep
without a shepherd,[n] and the LORD said,
'These people have no master. Let each
one go home in peace.'"
18The king of Israel said to Jehoshaphat, "Didn't I tell you that he never
prophesies anything good about me, but
only bad?"
19Micaiah continued, "Therefore hear
the word of the LORD: I saw the LORD
sitting on his throne[o] with all the multitudes[p] of heaven standing around him
on his right and on his left. 20And the
LORD said, 'Who will entice Ahab into
attacking Ramoth Gilead and going to
his death there?'
"One suggested this, and another that.
21Finally, a spirit came forward, stood before the LORD and said, 'I will entice him.'
22" 'By what means?' the LORD asked.
" 'I will go out and be a deceiving[q] spirit in the mouths of all his prophets,' he
said.
" 'You will succeed in enticing him,'
said the LORD. 'Go and do it.'
23"So now the LORD has put a deceiving
spirit in the mouths of all these prophets[r]
of yours. The LORD has decreed disaster
for you."
24Then Zedekiah[s] son of Kenaanah
went up and slapped[t] Micaiah in the
face. "Which way did the spirit from[a]
the LORD go when he went from me to
speak to you?" he asked.
25Micaiah replied, "You will find out
on the day you go to hide[u] in an inner
room."
26The king of Israel then ordered,
"Take Micaiah and send him back to
Amon the ruler of the city and to Joash
the king's son 27and say, 'This is what the
king says: Put this fellow in prison[v] and
give him nothing but bread and water
until I return safely.'"
28Micaiah declared, "If you ever return
safely, the LORD has not spoken[w] through
me." Then he added, "Mark my words,
all you people!"

Ahab Killed at Ramoth Gilead

22:29–36pp // 2Ch 18:28–34

29So the king of Israel and Jehoshaphat king of Judah went up to Ramoth
Gilead. 30The king of Israel said to Jehoshaphat, "I will enter the battle in disguise,[x] but you wear your royal robes."
So the king of Israel disguised himself
and went into battle.
31Now the king of Aram had ordered
his thirty-two chariot commanders, "Do
not fight with anyone, small or great,
except the king[y] of Israel." 32When the
chariot commanders saw Jehoshaphat,
they thought, "Surely this is the king of
Israel." So they turned to attack him, but
when Jehoshaphat cried out, 33the chariot commanders saw that he was not the
king of Israel and stopped pursuing him.
34But someone drew his bow[z] at

22:17 [n]ver 34-36; Nu 27:17; Mt 9:36
22:19 [o]Isa 6:1; Eze 1:26; Da 7:9 [p]Job 1:6; 2:1; Ps 103:20-21; Mt 18:10; Heb 1:7,14
22:22 [q]Jdg 9:23; 1Sa 16:14; 18:10; 19:9; Eze 14:9; 2Th 2:11
22:23 [r]Eze 14:9
22:24 [s]ver 11 [t]Ac 23:2
22:25 [u]1Ki 20:30
22:27 [v]2Ch 16:10
22:28 [w]Dt 18:22
22:30 [x]2Ch 35:32
22:31 [y]2Sa 17:2
22:34 [z]2Ch 35:23

[a] 24 Or *Spirit of*

22:19–23 The contradiction with Micaiah's first response is clarified with a vision which explains the behavior of Ahab's prophets and how it is possible for the initial words of Micaiah to conform to them.

A crux in this passage is the intent of the enticement as a "deceiving spirit" (v. 23). The question as to how the spirit will try to persuade Ahab suggests that the message is not a deception on the part of the messenger but a description of the effect his message will have on the king. Ahab is deluded; this delusion begins when he adopts the message of his own prophets and is confirmed when he recognizes that Micaiah speaks the truth, contrary to the other prophets.

22:24–28 Micaiah does not claim, as charged by Zedekiah, that the spirit of Yahweh has left Zedekiah and gone over to him. Micaiah can only speak the truth he has seen in the vision (v. 14). The punishment on Ahab and his prophets is determined by their own hardness of heart, just as Pharaoh hardened his heart and then came under divine judgment of an unchanging will that led to his destruction (Ex 9:12, 34; 10:1, 20).

The confrontation with Micaiah reaches its climax when Zedekiah assaults him and the king confines him until the truth of his words can be verified. Imprisonment will keep Micaiah from dissenting from the other prophets in front of the people. Micaiah, for his part, simply responds according to the prophetic test of truth as found in Dt 18:21–22. If Zedekiah and Ahab are vindicated, death is his well-deserved fate.

22:29–30 With the consultation at an impasse, the scene moves to the battlefront. The king's disguise is his response to the prophecy that the army will return without its king (v. 17). Though Ahab has chosen to disregard the prophecy, he is not able to ignore it.

22:31–33 The Aramean chariot commanders plan to single out the king of Israel, and Ahab's ruse works, but only for a moment: Jehoshaphat's outcry informs them he is not the king of Israel.

22:34–36 That Ahab is shot is not an accident; rather, it confirms the judgment that Micaiah pronounced.

The wounded king demands to be taken from the troops; this is the first step in separating his

RULERS OF THE DIVIDED KINGDOM OF ISRAEL AND JUDAH

DATA AND DATES IN ORDER OF SEQUENCE

	SCRIPTURE	KINGS	SYNCHRONISM OR CORRELATION	LENGTH OF REIGN	HISTORICAL DATA	DATES
1.	*1Ki 12:1–24* *1Ki 14:21–31*	***Rehoboam*** *(Judah)*		*17 years*		*930-913*
2.	1Ki 12:25—14:20	**Jeroboam I** (Israel)		22 years		930-909
3.	*1Ki 15:1–8*	***Abijah*** *(Judah)*	*18th of Jeroboam*	*3 years*		*913-910*
4.	*1Ki 15:9–24*	***Asa*** *(Judah)*	*20th of Jeroboam*	*41 years*		*910-869*
5.	1Ki 15:25–31	**Nadab** (Israel)	2nd of Asa	2 years		909-908
6.	1Ki 15:32—16:7	**Baasha** (Israel)	3rd of Asa	24 years		908-886
7.	1Ki 16:8–14	**Elah** (Israel)	26th of Asa	2 years		886-885
8.	1Ki 16:15–20	**Zimri** (Israel)	27th of Asa	7 days		885
9.	1Ki 16:21–22	**Tibni** (Israel)			Overlap with Omri	885-880
10.	1Ki 16:23–28	**Omri** (Israel)	27th of Asa 31st of Asa	12 years	Made king by the people Overlap with Tibni Official reign = 11 actual years Sole reign	885 885-880 885-874 880-874
11.	1Ki 16:29—22:40	**Ahab** (Israel)	38th of Asa	22 years	Official reign = 21 actual years	874-853
12.	*1Ki 22:41–50*	***Jehoshaphat*** *(Judah)*	*4th of Ahab*	*25 years*	*Coregency with Asa* *Official reign* *Sole reign* *Has Jehoram as regent*	*872-869* *872-848* *869-853* *853-848*
13.	1Ki 22:51— 2Ki 1:18	**Ahaziah** (Israel)	17th of Jehoshaphat	2 years	Official reign = 1 year actual reign	853-852
14.	2Ki 1:17 2Ki 3:1—8:15	**Joram** (Israel)	2nd of Jehoram 18th of Jehoshaphat	12 years	Official reign = 11 actual years	852 852-841
15.	*2Ki 8:16–24*	***Jehoram*** *(Judah)*	*5th of Joram*	*8 years*	*Coregency with Jehoshaphat* *Sole reign* *Official reign = 7 actual years*	*853-848* *848-841* *848-841*
16.	*2Ki 8:25–29* *2Ki 9:29*	***Ahaziah*** *(Judah)*	*12th of Joram* *11th of Joram*	*1 year*	*Nonaccession-year reckoning* *Accession-year reckoning*	*841* *841*
17.	2Ki 9:30—10:36	**Jehu** (Israel)		28 years		841-814
18.	*2Ki 11*	***Athaliah*** *(Judah)*		*7 years*		*841-835*
19.	*2Ki 12*	***Joash*** *(Judah)*	*7th of Jehu*	*40 years*		*835-796*
20.	2Ki 13:1–9	**Jehoahaz** (Israel)	23rd of Joash	17 years		814-798
21.	2Ki 13:10–25	**Jehoash** (Israel)	37th of Joash	16 years		798-782

Italics denote rulers of ***Judah***. Non-italic type denotes rulers of **Israel**. All dates are BC.

	SCRIPTURE	KINGS	SYNCHRONISM OR CORRELATION	LENGTH OF REIGN	HISTORICAL DATA	DATES
22.	*2Ki 14:1-22*	***Amaziah*** *(Judah)*	*2nd of Jehoash*	*29 years*		*796-767*
					Overlap with Azariah	*792-767*
23.	2Ki 14:23-29	**Jeroboam II** (Israel)		41 years	Coregency with Jehoash	793-782
					Total reign	793-753
			15th of Amaziah		Sole reign	782-753
24.	2Ki 15:1-7	***Azariah*** *(Judah) (=* ***Uzziah****)*	27th of Jeroboam		Overlap with Amaziah	792-767
				52 years	Total reign	792-740
					Sole reign	767-750
25.	2Ki 15:8-12	**Zechariah** (Israel)	38th of Azariah	6 months		753
26.	2Ki 15:13-15	**Shallum** (Israel)	39th of Azariah	1 month		752
27.	2Ki 15:16-22	**Menahem** (Israel)	39th of Azariah	10 years	Ruled in Samaria	752-742
28.	2Ki 15:23-26	**Pekahiah** (Israel)	50th of Azariah	2 years		742-740
29.	2Ki 15:27-31	**Pekah** (Israel)			In Gilead; overlapping years	752-740
				20 years	Total reign	752-732
			52nd of Azariah		Sole reign	740-732
30.	*2Ki 15:32-38*	***Jotham*** *(Judah)*	*2nd of Pekah*		*Coregency with Azariah*	*750-740*
	2Ki 15:30			*16 years*	*Official reign*	*750-735*
					Reign to his 20th year	*750-732*
31.	*2Ki 16*	***Ahaz*** *(Judah)*			*Total reign*	*735-715*
			17th of Pekah			*735*
				16 years	*From 20th of Jotham*	*732-715*
32.	2Ki 15:30	**Hoshea** (Israel)			20th of Jotham	732
	2Ki 17		12th of Ahaz	9 years		732-722
33.	*2Ki 18:1—20:21*	***Hezekiah*** *(Judah)*	*3rd of Hoshea*	*29 years*		*715-686*
					Coregency with Ahaz	*729-715*
34.	*2Ki 21:1-18*	***Manasseh*** *(Judah)*			*Coregency with Hezekiah*	*697-686*
				55 years	*Total reign*	*697-642*
35.	*2Ki 21:19-26*	***Amon*** *(Judah)*		*2 years*		*642-640*
36.	*2Ki 22:1—23:30*	***Josiah*** *(Judah)*		*31 years*		*640-609*
37.	*2Ki 23:31-33*	***Jehoahaz*** *(Judah)*		*3 months*		*609*
38.	*2Ki 23:34—24:7*	***Jehoiakim*** *(Judah)*		*11 years*		*609-598*
39.	*2Ki 24:8-17*	***Jehoiachin*** *(Judah)*		*3 months*		*598-597*
40.	*2Ki 24:18—25:26*	***Zedekiah*** *(Judah)*		*11 years*		*597-586*

random and hit the king of Israel between the sections of his armor. The king told his chariot driver, "Wheel around and get me out of the fighting. I've been wounded." 35 All day long the battle raged, and the king was propped up in his chariot facing the Arameans. The blood from his wound ran onto the floor of the chariot, and that evening he died. 36 As the sun was setting, a cry spread through the army: "Every man to his town. Every man to his land!"[a]

37 So the king died and was brought to Samaria, and they buried him there. 38 They washed the chariot at a pool in Samaria (where the prostitutes bathed),[a] and the dogs[b] licked up his blood, as the word of the LORD had declared.

39 As for the other events of Ahab's reign, including all he did, the palace he built and adorned with ivory,[c] and the cities he fortified, are they not written in the book of the annals of the kings of Israel? 40 Ahab rested with his ancestors. And Ahaziah his son succeeded him as king.

22:36 [a] 2Ki 14:12
22:38 [b] 1Ki 21:19
22:39 [c] 2Ch 9:17; Am 3:15

Jehoshaphat King of Judah

22:41–50pp // 2Ch 20:31—21:1

41 Jehoshaphat son of Asa became king of Judah in the fourth year of Ahab king of Israel. 42 Jehoshaphat was thirty-five years old when he became king, and he reigned in Jerusalem twenty-five years. His mother's name was Azubah daughter of Shilhi. 43 In everything he followed the ways of his father Asa[d] and did not stray from them; he did what was right in the eyes of the LORD. The high places,[e] however, were not removed, and the people continued to offer sacrifices and burn incense there.[b] 44 Jehoshaphat was also at peace with the king of Israel.

45 As for the other events of Jehoshaphat's reign, the things he achieved and his military exploits, are they not written in the book of the annals of the kings of Judah? 46 He rid the land of the rest of the male shrine prostitutes[f] who remained there even after the reign of his father Asa. 47 There was then no king[g] in Edom; a provincial governor ruled.

48 Now Jehoshaphat built a fleet of trading ships[c][h] to go to Ophir for gold, but they never set sail — they were wrecked at Ezion Geber. 49 At that time Ahaziah son of Ahab said to Jehoshaphat, "Let my men sail with yours," but Jehoshaphat refused.

50 Then Jehoshaphat rested with his ancestors and was buried with them in the city of David his father. And Jehoram his son succeeded him as king.

Ahaziah King of Israel

51 Ahaziah son of Ahab became king of Israel in Samaria in the seventeenth

22:43 [d] 2Ch 17:3 [e] 1Ki 3:2; 15:14; 2Ki 12:3
22:46 [f] Dt 23:17; 1Ki 14:24; 15:12
22:47 [g] 2Sa 8:14; 2Ki 3:9; 8:20
22:48 [h] 1Ki 9:26; 10:22

[a] 38 Or *Samaria and cleaned the weapons*
[b] 43 In Hebrew texts this sentence (22:43b) is numbered 22:44, and 22:44-53 is numbered 22:45-54.
[c] 48 Hebrew *of ships of Tarshish*

---

fate from that of the army, and the end of the day seals the separate destinies of king and army. At evening the king dies, the blood from his mortal wound draining and collecting at the bottom of the chariot. At sunset the army disperses; each of the soldiers returns to his own place of residence. By the end of the day the king's effort to subvert the word of doom spoken against him fails.

22:37–38 The death of the king is the first prophecy to receive fulfillment on that fateful day. The body of the king is returned to Samaria, where the chariot is washed. Dogs lick up the blood of the slain king, fulfilling the word pronounced by Elijah (cf. 21:19). The defiance of Ahab in his death stands as a stark contrast to his earlier humility when Elijah denounced him for the murder of Naboth (21:27–29).

22:39–40 The epilogue on Ahab's reign notes his significant achievements and his royal burial as a great king. The reign of Ahab is among the most influential and, by temporal standards, an almost incomparable success.

22:41–50 In Kings, Jehoshaphat is given credit for purging the "male shrine prostitutes" (v. 46) allowed by his father. He also apparently attempted to renovate the ships used by Solomon, but they proved to be unseaworthy and never left port. Jehoshaphat also refuses the assistance of Ahaziah, whose alliance with Phoenician shipbuilding expertise may have been of great assistance (v. 49).

The two kingdoms ally themselves against the Arameans, but Jehoshaphat determines to maintain his economic and territorial independence. His control of Edom supports Israel because it cuts off Aramean access to the Red Sea. For this reason, Israel, Judah, and Edom unite to resist Moabite attempts for independence (2Ki 3:4–27).

22:51–53 The introductory summary of Ahaziah's reign provides us with the length of his reign. The last year of the reign of Ahab was the battle of Qarqar in 853 BC, a firm date in ancient Syrian chronology.

22:1–50 Though the secular role of the state is necessary, it is absurd to think that faith is a purely private matter. If religion has no role

year of Jehoshaphat king of Judah, and
he reigned over Israel two years. 52He
did evil[i] in the eyes of the LORD, because
he followed the ways of his father and
mother and of Jeroboam son of Nebat,
who caused Israel to sin. 53He served and
worshiped Baal[j] and aroused the anger
of the LORD, the God of Israel, just as his
father[k] had done.

22:52 [i] 1Ki 15:26; 21:25
22:53 [j] Jdg 2:11 [k] 1Ki 16:30-32

---

in public society, then secularism becomes a state religion of its own, imposing its own values on people of all faiths and religions. This is really no different from Ahab choosing his own prophets to agree with him.

Values for ethics and law cannot be established apart from convictions that have a personal faith base, and in that sense are always religious. Freedom of religion in the secular state must not only allow for the public expression of various faiths; it must also allow for rational expression of faith convictions. To the extent that a state fails to do this, it will fall victim to its own vices, just like Ahab and the state of Israel did in listening only to their own prophets.

Christians often find themselves in the unhappy position of Jehoshaphat. Having a desire to seek an independent course of action, they are pressured in various ways to conform, even at risk to their own well-being. While they seek to do what is right, the "high places" remain and compromise the way of life they value most.

2 Kings

Author: Unknown

Audience: God's chosen people, the Israelites

Date: Probably about 550 BC, during the Babylonian exile

Theme: God judges and eventually expels Israel and Judah from his presence in the promised land when their kings turn away from his covenant law.

Reading 2 Kings

Second Kings begins with the transfer of Elijah's power to Elisha, and then recounts numerous episodes in Elisha's life, including several miracles. The rest of the book is an account of the acts of various kings of Israel and Judah, culminating in two major events: the destruction of Samaria and the destruction of Jerusalem.

PERSPECTIVE

Second Kings continues the narrative of 1 Kings. Its separation into two books is otherwise artificial. The book records the ups and downs of the divided kingdom and concludes with the fall of both. The story continues to describe the prophetic ministries of Elijah and Elisha and introduces the ministry of the prophet Isaiah during the Assyrian crisis. See also the Introduction to 1 Kings for more perspective on the books of 1–2 Kings.

TAKING THE NEXT STEPS

In the book of 2 Kings, the author describes the end of both the northern kingdom of Israel and the southern kingdom of Judah. The principle of obedience reached its final end: Because the kings and the people persistently refused to obey him, God—faithful to his word—judged Samaria by allowing Assyria to destroy it and deport its people, and judged Jerusalem by allowing Babylon to destroy it and carry its people into exile. They had refused to heed the frequent warnings of the prophets.

God has important messages for us in this book. (1) God calls us to listen to the word of the Lord as revealed through the prophets and to respond in humble obedience. (2) God shows amazing patience with us in our sinfulness, but his longsuffering love has limits. And once his threatened judgment begins, he will bring it to swift completion. (3) At the same time, God will remain faithful to his promise never to

1400 BC 1300 1200 1100 1000 900 800 700 600 500 400

Division of the kingdom (930 BC)
Elijah's ministry in Israel (c. 875–848 BC)
Elisha's ministry in Israel (c. 848–797 BC)
Exile of Israel (722 BC)
Hezekiah's reign (715–686 BC)
Fall of Jerusalem (586 BC)
King Jehoiachin released from prison (c. 561 BC)
Book of 2 Kings written (c. 560–550 BC)

wipe out his people completely; he will preserve a faithful remnant until the return of the Lord Jesus Christ, who now makes salvation available to all nations.

Key Verse

Nevertheless, for the sake of his servant David, the LORD was not willing to destroy Judah. He had promised to maintain a lamp for David and his descendants forever.

—2 Kings 8:19

WHAT TO LOOK FOR IN 2 KINGS

- Elijah's fiery ascent into heaven (ch. 2)
- Miracles of Elisha (chs. 4–6)
- The destruction of Ahab's family (chs. 9–10)
- King Joash and the repair of the temple (chs. 11–12)
- The destruction of Samaria and end of the northern kingdom (ch. 17)
- The reign of Hezekiah and his victory over Sennacherib (chs. 18–20)
- King Josiah and the finding of the Law (chs. 22–23)
- The fall of Jerusalem and the exile (ch. 25)

The LORD's Judgment on Ahaziah

1 After Ahab's death, Moab[a] rebelled
against Israel. 2Now Ahaziah had fallen
through the lattice of his upper room in
Samaria and injured himself. So he sent
messengers,[b] saying to them, "Go and
consult Baal-Zebub,[c] the god of Ekron,[d]
to see if I will recover[e] from this injury."
3But the angel[f] of the LORD said to Elijah[g] the Tishbite, "Go up and meet the
messengers of the king of Samaria and
ask them, 'Is it because there is no God in
Israel[h] that you are going off to consult
Baal-Zebub, the god of Ekron?' 4There-
fore this is what the LORD says: 'You will
not leave[i] the bed you are lying on. You
will certainly die!' " So Elijah went.
5When the messengers returned to
the king, he asked them, "Why have you
come back?"

1:1 [a] Ge 19:37; 2Sa 8:2; 2Ki 3:5
1:2 [b] ver 16 [c] Mk 3:22 [d] 1Sa 6:2; Isa 2:6; 14:29; Mt 10:25 [e] Jdg 18:5; 2Ki 8:7-10
1:3 [f] ver 15; Ge 16:7 [g] 1Ki 17:1 [h] 1Sa 28:8
1:4 [i] ver 6,16; Ps 41:8

1:1 The death of Ahab brings about a new era: Moab rebels almost immediately, with both Edom and Libnah gaining independence during the reign of Joram. The days of the Israelite kingdom are over and this spells the end of a period of international influence for Israel.

1:2 Ahaziah is an apostate like his parents, but his particular sin is the act of seeking a prophetic message from Baal-Zebub, a god of the Philistines. Baal-Zebub (meaning "lord of the flies") may have been a god to control disease. It is likely that the name was originally Baal-Zebul ("lord of a lofty or exalted place"), a description used for Baal in Ugaritic literature.

1:3–4 The king's desire to receive an answer from Baal-Zebub, as if there were no God in Israel (v. 3), becomes the occasion for Elijah to confront once again the apostate king. The impact of the struggle in the narrative is achieved through the double meaning of the word "messenger." This Hebrew word refers to both the "angel [of the LORD]" and to the "messengers [of the king]." God exercises his authority through the first messenger, while King Ahaziah can do nothing more than extend his power through military messengers.

1:5–6 The king's messengers in effect return with a prophetic message from Yahweh rather than from Baal-Zebub.

6“A man came to meet us,” they replied. “And he said to us, ‘Go back to the
king who sent you and tell him, “This is
what the LORD says: Is it because there
is no God in Israel that you are sending
messengers to consult Baal-Zebub, the
god of Ekron? Therefore you will not
leave the bed you are lying on. You will
certainly die!” ’ ”
7The king asked them, “What kind of
man was it who came to meet you and
told you this?”
8They replied, “He had a garment of
hair[a][j] and had a leather belt around his
waist.”
The king said, “That was Elijah the
Tishbite.”
9Then he sent[k] to Elijah a captain[l] with
his company of fifty men. The captain
went up to Elijah, who was sitting on
the top of a hill, and said to him, “Man of
God, the king says, ‘Come down!’ ”
10Elijah answered the captain, “If I am
a man of God, may fire come down from
heaven and consume you and your fifty
men!” Then fire[m] fell from heaven and
consumed the captain and his men.
11At this the king sent to Elijah another captain with his fifty men. The
captain said to him, “Man of God, this
is what the king says, ‘Come down at
once!’ ”
12“If I am a man of God,” Elijah replied,
“may fire come down from heaven and
consume you and your fifty men!” Then
the fire of God fell from heaven and consumed him and his fifty men.

1:8 [j] 1Ki 18:7; Zec 13:4; Mt 3:4; Mk 1:6
1:9 [k] 2Ki 6:14 [l] Ex 18:25; Isa 3:3
1:10 [m] 1Ki 18:38; Lk 9:54; Rev 11:5; 13:13

2Ki 1:16 ❖ Why might desperation send people running for help to other gods? Where do people today run for help rather than turning to God?

13So the king sent a third captain with
his fifty men. This third captain went up
and fell on his knees before Elijah. “Man
of God,” he begged, “please have respect
for my life[n] and the lives of these fifty
men, your servants! 14See, fire has fallen
from heaven and consumed the first two
captains and all their men. But now have
respect for my life!”
15The angel[o] of the LORD said to Elijah,
“Go down with him; do not be afraid[p] of
him.” So Elijah got up and went down
with him to the king.
16He told the king, “This is what the
LORD says: Is it because there is no God
in Israel for you to consult that you have
sent messengers[q] to consult Baal-Zebub,
the god of Ekron? Because you have done
this, you will never leave[r] the bed you are
lying on. You will certainly die!” 17So he
died,[s] according to the word of the LORD
that Elijah had spoken.
Because Ahaziah had no son, Joram[b][t]
succeeded him as king in the second year
of Jehoram son of Jehoshaphat king of
Judah. 18As for all the other events of
Ahaziah’s reign, and what he did, are
they not written in the book of the annals of the kings of Israel?

1:13 [n] 1Sa 26:21; Ps 72:14
1:15 [o] ver 3 [p] Isa 51:12; 57:11; Jer 1:17; Eze 2:6
1:16 [q] ver 2 [r] ver 4
1:17 [s] 2Ki 8:15; Jer 20:6; 28:17 [t] 2Ki 3:1; 8:16

[a] 8 Or *He was a hairy man* [b] 17 Hebrew *Jehoram*, a variant of *Joram*

1:7–12 The king recognizes Elijah by his description and takes up the challenge by immediately sending a military unit to arrest him. The military officers are no match for the power of Yahweh through Elijah.

1:15 In the end the king’s messengers finally get their way, but it has nothing to do with their power.

1:16–17a When the king gets his request to meet his nemesis Elijah face to face, the prophet repeats the inevitable message of doom. Each of Ahaziah’s actions moves him inevitably toward the judgment reserved for him because he has rejected the God of the covenant.

1:17b–18 With Elijah’s appearance before the king, Ahaziah’s death is simply reported. The narrative concludes with the summary of his reign and the introduction of the next king.

APPLICATION ✚ 1:1–18 Elijah’s authority was grounded in his uncompromising allegiance to God in the teaching of the covenant. Jesus’ authority was established with the people through his use of the Scriptures. He promised that this power would be with his followers always, even to the end of the world (Mt 28:20).

This Spirit-enabled power continues to be the authority of the church. The church has often claimed and used temporal powers, but while temporal power does not always help the church to accomplish its mission, neither can temporal power prevent the growth of the church.

It is vital that Christian leaders always adhere to the genuine source of their authority, which is found in being faithful to the revelation of God for his world. Their power lies in teaching the people this truth, which believers are also responsible to follow. When Christians and their institutions are faithful to God’s revelation, the governmental powers of this world cannot control this kingdom-building power.

Elijah Taken Up to Heaven

2 When the LORD was about to take[u]
Elijah up to heaven in a whirlwind,[v]
Elijah and Elisha[w] were on their way from
Gilgal.[x] 2Elijah said to Elisha, "Stay here;[y]
the LORD has sent me to Bethel."
But Elisha said, "As surely as the LORD
lives and as you live, I will not leave
you."[z] So they went down to Bethel.
3The company[a] of the prophets at
Bethel came out to Elisha and asked, "Do
you know that the LORD is going to take
your master from you today?"
"Yes, I know," Elisha replied, "so be
quiet."
4Then Elijah said to him, "Stay here,
Elisha; the LORD has sent me to Jericho.[b]"
And he replied, "As surely as the LORD
lives and as you live, I will not leave you."
So they went to Jericho.
5The company[c] of the prophets at Jericho went up to Elisha and asked him, "Do
you know that the LORD is going to take
your master from you today?"
"Yes, I know," he replied, "so be quiet."
6Then Elijah said to him, "Stay here;[d]
the LORD has sent me to the Jordan."[e]
And he replied, "As surely as the LORD
lives and as you live, I will not leave
you."[f] So the two of them walked on.
7Fifty men from the company of the
prophets went and stood at a distance,
facing the place where Elijah and Elisha
had stopped at the Jordan. 8Elijah took
his cloak,[g] rolled it up and struck[h] the
water with it. The water divided[i] to the

2:1 [u] Ge 5:24; Heb 11:5 [v] ver 11; 1Ki 19:11; Isa 5:28; 66:15; Jer 4:13; Na 1:3 [w] 1Ki 19:16, 21 [x] Dt 11:30; 2Ki 4:38
2:2 [y] ver 6 [z] Ru 1:16; 1Sa 1:26; 2Ki 4:30
2:3 [a] 1Sa 10:5; 2Ki 4:1,38
2:4 [b] Jos 3:16; 6:26
2:5 [c] ver 3
2:6 [d] ver 2 [e] Jos 3:15 [f] Ru 1:16
2:8 [g] 1Ki 19:19 [h] ver 14 [i] Ex 14:21

2:1 The force and power of the wind that will take Elijah up to heaven are symbolic of the majestic and holy presence of the divine. During the time of Samuel, Gilgal became an important religious center and may have been the site of an ancient temple.

2:2–8 The whole narrative is designed to build suspense. Arriving at Bethel, Elijah and Elisha hear a prophetic revelation that is later repeated. Mixed emotions of impatience, sorrow, and anger may be intended in the words, "I know. Be quiet!" (vv. 3, 5; alternate translation). But Elisha is determined to follow his master, refusing to compromise his vow though repeatedly challenged.

PEOPLE TO KNOW // ELIJAH

2 KINGS 2:1–11: Elijah was a prophet of God in Israel during the reign of the wicked King Ahab and Queen Jezebel. Elijah was an intense and emotional messenger for God.

Elijah told Ahab that God was bringing a drought on Israel, which did not put Elijah in the king's good graces (1Ki 17:1). After three years, Elijah challenged Ahab's false prophets to a showdown on Mount Carmel. In a dramatic display of power, God sent fire down from heaven to burn Elijah's sacrifice and altar (1Ki 18:38). The prophets of Baal were humiliated, and the people put them to the sword.

Queen Jezebel intended to kill Elijah for this. In desperation, he fled south. Dejected, lonely and depressed, Elijah prayed for God to end his life. Instead, God led Elijah to Mount Horeb and showed Elijah his presence in a way reminiscent of God's appearing to Moses (1Ki 19:11–12; see Ex 33:22). God gently told Elijah he was not alone; there were seven thousand others in Israel who were faithful to God.

Elijah became a mentor to a younger prophet, Elisha. The day God was going to take Elijah to heaven, Elisha refused to leave him. Together, the older and younger prophets experienced miracles: crossing the Jordan River on dry ground and seeing up close a chariot of fire from heaven. God took Elijah home to heaven in the chariot, and this miracle was witnessed by Elisha and other prophets.

Centuries later, the prophet Malachi envisioned Elijah's return before the day of the Lord (Mal 4:5). Jesus said this prophecy was fulfilled through John the Baptist (Mt 11:14).

APPLICATION ✣ Elijah knew what it was like to be exhausted, depressed and lonely. He had served and obediently worked for the Lord in the face of opposition and danger. After facing threats to his life from the most powerful people in the land, he did not want to go on. God dealt gently with Elijah in his time of darkness, caring for his physical needs (1Ki 19:5–8) and speaking encouragement to him in a gentle whisper (1Ki 19:12). Elijah's story reminds us that many of us struggle with challenges to our physical and mental health. When we are in a place of despair, God will lavish his love on us. And when we know of those who struggle, we can learn from God's tender actions toward Elijah and treat others with gentleness and care.

right and to the left, and the two of them
crossed over on dry[j] ground.
9When they had crossed, Elijah said
to Elisha, "Tell me, what can I do for you
before I am taken from you?"
"Let me inherit a double[k] portion of
your spirit,"[l] Elisha replied.
10"You have asked a difficult thing,"
Elijah said, "yet if you see me when I am
taken from you, it will be yours — otherwise, it will not."
11As they were walking along and talking together, suddenly a chariot of fire[m]
and horses of fire appeared and separated the two of them, and Elijah went
up to heaven[n] in a whirlwind.[o] 12Elisha
saw this and cried out, "My father! My
father! The chariots[p] and horsemen of
Israel!" And Elisha saw him no more.
Then he took hold of his garment and
tore[q] it in two.
13Elisha then picked up Elijah's cloak
that had fallen from him and went back
and stood on the bank of the Jordan. 14He
took the cloak[r] that had fallen from Elijah and struck[s] the water with it. "Where
now is the LORD, the God of Elijah?" he
asked. When he struck the water, it divided to the right and to the left, and he
crossed over.
15The company[t] of the prophets from
Jericho, who were watching, said, "The
spirit[u] of Elijah is resting on Elisha." And
they went to meet him and bowed to
the ground before him. 16"Look," they
said, "we your servants have fifty able
men. Let them go and look for your master. Perhaps the Spirit[v] of the LORD has
picked him up[w] and set him down on
some mountain or in some valley."

2:8 [j] Ex 14:22,29
2:9 [k] Dt 21:17 [l] Nu 11:17
2:11 [m] 2Ki 6:17; Ps 68:17; 104:3, 4; Isa 66:15; Hab 3:8; Zec 6:1 [n] Ge 5:24 [o] ver 1
2:12 [p] 2Ki 6:17; 13:14 [q] Ge 37:29
2:14 [r] 1Ki 19:19 [s] ver 8
2:15 [t] ver 7; 1Sa 10:5 [u] Nu 11:17
2:16 [v] 1Ki 18:12 [w] Ac 8:39

2Ki 2:9-10 ❖ What do we most want to learn from our spiritual mentors or guides? Why?

"No," Elisha replied, "do not send
them."
17But they persisted until he was too
embarrassed[x] to refuse. So he said, "Send
them." And they sent fifty men, who
searched for three days but did not find
him. 18When they returned to Elisha, who
was staying in Jericho, he said to them,
"Didn't I tell you not to go?"

Healing of the Water

19The people of the city said to Elisha,
"Look, our lord, this town is well situated,
as you can see, but the water is bad and
the land is unproductive."
20"Bring me a new bowl," he said, "and
put salt in it." So they brought it to him.
21Then he went out to the spring and
threw[y] the salt into it, saying, "This is
what the LORD says: 'I have healed this
water. Never again will it cause death or
make the land unproductive.'" 22And the
water has remained pure[z] to this day, according to the word Elisha had spoken.

Elisha Is Jeered

23From there Elisha went up to Bethel.
As he was walking along the road, some
boys came out of the town and jeered[a] at
him. "Get out of here, baldy!" they said.
"Get out of here, baldy!" 24He turned
around, looked at them and called down
a curse[b] on them in the name[c] of the
LORD. Then two bears came out of the
woods and mauled forty-two of the boys.

2:17 [x] 2Ki 8:11
2:21 [y] Ex 15:25; 2Ki 4:41; 6:6
2:22 [z] Ex 15:25
2:23 [a] Ex 22:28; 2Ch 36:16; Job 19:18; Ps 31:18
2:24 [b] Ge 4:11; Ne 13:25-27 [c] Dt 18:19

2:9-11 Elisha asks for a double portion of Elijah's spirit, an expression used elsewhere to refer to the right of inheritance of the firstborn as double that of the others (Dt 21:17). Elisha is not requesting twice the prophetic spirit of Elijah, but rather the right to the office of Elijah.

2:12-14 "My father" is repeated, an expression of the honor attributed to the leader. "The chariots and horseman of Israel" likely refers to the vision of Elijah departing into glory. Elijah introduced the cloak as a symbol of succession when he first anointed Elisha as his successor (1Ki 19:19). The same miraculous crossing assures Elisha that he is indeed the true successor to Elijah.

2:15-18 The prophetic band in Jericho confirms that Elisha will continue the work of Elijah.

2:19-22 This first event confirms that Elisha has succeeded Elijah as a prophet like Moses (see Ex 15:22-26). The effect of the sterility caused by the water is not clear; it could be that it caused the land to be unproductive, or that it caused the people to be childless.

The salt in the new bowl distinguishes this prophetic action from all other common techniques that might be used in "healing" the water; it remains pure until the time the accounts of Elisha are recorded (v. 22).

2:23-24 The taunting from the young men should not be viewed as immature juvenile activity. If a prophet were known because he was a hairy man (see 1:8), taunting Elisha as a bald man is to deny that he is a prophet, or at least to deny that he is a prophet like Elijah. The mauling of the youthful mob is not vindictive anger on behalf of Elisha but divine judgment for denial of the divine purpose. The bears are no less divinely appointed than the fish that swallowed Jonah.

25And he went on to Mount Carmel[d] and from there returned to Samaria.

Moab Revolts

3 Joram[a][e] son of Ahab became king of Israel in Samaria in the eighteenth year of Jehoshaphat king of Judah, and he reigned twelve years. 2He did evil[f] in the eyes of the LORD, but not as his father[g] and mother had done. He got rid of the sacred stone[h] of Baal that his father had made. 3Nevertheless he clung to the sins[i] of Jeroboam son of Nebat, which he had caused Israel to commit; he did not turn away from them.

4Now Mesha king of Moab[j] raised sheep, and he had to pay the king of Israel a tribute of a hundred thousand lambs[k] and the wool of a hundred thousand rams. 5But after Ahab died, the king of Moab rebelled[l] against the king of Israel. 6So at that time King Joram set out from Samaria and mobilized all Israel. 7He also sent this message to Jehoshaphat king of Judah: "The king of Moab has rebelled against me. Will you go with me to fight[m] against Moab?"

"I will go with you," he replied. "I am as you are, my people as your people, my horses as your horses."

8"By what route shall we attack?" he asked.

"Through the Desert of Edom," he answered.

9So the king of Israel set out with the king of Judah and the king of Edom.[n] After a roundabout march of seven days, the army had no more water for themselves or for the animals with them.

10"What!" exclaimed the king of Israel. "Has the LORD called us three kings together only to deliver us into the hands of Moab?"

11But Jehoshaphat asked, "Is there no prophet of the LORD here, through whom we may inquire[o] of the LORD?"

An officer of the king of Israel answered, "Elisha[p] son of Shaphat is here. He used to pour water on the hands of Elijah.[b][q]"

12Jehoshaphat said, "The word[r] of the LORD is with him." So the king of Israel and Jehoshaphat and the king of Edom went down to him.

13Elisha said to the king of Israel, "Why do you want to involve me? Go to the prophets of your father and the prophets of your mother."

"No," the king of Israel answered, "because it was the LORD who called us three kings together to deliver us into the hands of Moab."

14Elisha said, "As surely as the LORD Almighty lives, whom I serve, if I did not have respect for the presence of Jehoshaphat king of Judah, I would not

2:25 [d] 1Ki 18:20; 2Ki 4:25
3:1 [e] 2Ki 1:17
3:2 [f] 1Ki 15:26 [g] 1Ki 16:30-32 [h] Ex 23:24; 2Ki 10:18, 26-28
3:3 [i] 1Ki 12:28-32; 14:9,16
3:4 [j] Ge 19:37; 2Ki 1:1 [k] Ezr 7:17; Isa 16:1
3:5 [l] 2Ki 1:1
3:7 [m] 1Ki 22:4
3:9 [n] 1Ki 22:47
3:11 [o] Ge 25:22; 1Ki 22:7 [p] Ge 20:7 [q] 1Ki 19:16
3:12 [r] Nu 11:17

[a] *1* Hebrew *Jehoram,* a variant of *Joram;* also in verse 6 [b] *11* That is, he was Elijah's personal servant.

2:25 With the return to Mount Carmel, Elisha completes the transition to being successor to Elijah.

> **2:1–25** God has always chosen and empowered his leaders for times of political threat against his people. Jesus gave his followers the same assurance that the kingdom of God would prevail. The "keys of the kingdom" were entrusted to Peter (Mt 16:19) with the assurance that no earthly power would ever be able to stop the will of God on earth.
>
> Though Jesus directed his words specifically at Peter (Mt 16:17), it must be remembered that the blessing belonged to all the disciples (cf. Mt 13:16–17; 18:18). The heavenly Father had revealed his Son to his disciples (Mt 11:25–30). The church was built on the foundation of the apostles and prophets (Eph 2:20) as a sacred temple to the Lord. Christians who make up the church today are still an integral part of that legacy.

3:1–2 Joram is credited with removing the memorial pillar that Ahab had set up in honor of Baal. Standing stones were objects of veneration and worship, as they were not symbols of a transcendent deity but evoked an actual presence.

3:3–8 After David defeated the Moabites (2Sa 8:2), they were required to pay Israel tribute. Mesha's refusal to pay that tribute is the result of the weakening military control of Israel. Joram musters his forces with reinforcements from Judah and Edom.

3:9 Traveling the route of attack around the Dead Sea would have taken considerable time. In typical prophetic style it is described as "a march of seven days," the emphasis being on the time-consuming effort of a difficult journey rather than a precise calculation of time.

3:10–12 Joram realizes that the imminent failure of his armies is a sign of divine judgment on him. Jehoshaphat comes to the rescue in a nonmilitary fashion by proposing they seek direction from Elisha, whom he recognizes as a true prophet.

3:13–14 Joram has been alienated from Elisha and could not have sought his assistance without the mediation of Jehoshaphat. Joram knows that only the God of Elisha can be of assistance. Elisha grants Joram a concession; though he regards Joram, the leader of the group, with disdain, Jehoshaphat is worthy of receiving a word from Yahweh.

pay any attention to you. 15But now bring
me a harpist."[s]
While the harpist was playing, the
hand[t] of the LORD came on Elisha 16and
he said, "This is what the LORD says: I
will fill this valley with pools of water.
17For this is what the LORD says: You will
see neither wind nor rain, yet this valley
will be filled with water,[u] and you, your
cattle and your other animals will drink.
18This is an easy[v] thing in the eyes of
the LORD; he will also deliver Moab into
your hands. 19You will overthrow every
fortified city and every major town. You
will cut down every good tree, stop up
all the springs, and ruin every good field
with stones."
20The next morning, about the time[w]
for offering the sacrifice, there it was—
water flowing from the direction of
Edom! And the land was filled with water.[x]
21Now all the Moabites had heard that
the kings had come to fight against
them; so every man, young and old,
who could bear arms was called up and
stationed on the border. 22When they
got up early in the morning, the sun
was shining on the water. To the Moabites across the way, the water looked
red—like blood. 23"That's blood!" they
said. "Those kings must have fought and
slaughtered each other. Now to the plunder, Moab!"
24But when the Moabites came to the
camp of Israel, the Israelites rose up and
fought them until they fled. And the Israelites invaded the land and slaughtered the Moabites. 25They destroyed
the towns, and each man threw a stone
on every good field until it was covered.
They stopped up all the springs and cut
down every good tree. Only Kir Hareseth[y] was left with its stones in place,
but men armed with slings surrounded
it and attacked it.
26When the king of Moab saw that the
battle had gone against him, he took
with him seven hundred swordsmen
to break through to the king of Edom,
but they failed. 27Then he took his firstborn[z] son, who was to succeed him as
king, and offered him as a sacrifice on
the city wall. The fury against Israel was
great; they withdrew and returned to
their own land.

3:15 [s] 1Sa 16:23 [t] Jer 15:17; Eze 1:3
3:17 [u] Ps 107:35; Isa 32:2; 35:6; 41:18
3:18 [v] Ge 18:14; 2Ki 20:10; Isa 49:6; Jer 32:17, 27; Mk 10:27
3:20 [w] Ex 29:39-40 [x] Ex 17:6
3:25 [y] ver 19; Isa 15:1; 16:7; Jer 48:31, 36
3:27 [z] Dt 12:31; 2Ki 16:3; 21:6; 2Ch 28:3; Ps 106:38; Jer 19:4-5; Am 2:1; Mic 6:7

2Ki 3:16-20 ❖ When has God given us living water to sustain us in what looked like a hopeless situation (see Isa 58:11)?

3:15 The procedures for entering the mystic state of prophecy are veiled in tantalizing incidental comments. Elisha calls for music in order that he might experience the power of the Lord. The use of music is only one means of entering the mystical experience.
3:16-18 Elisha declares that the valley itself will become a pool. Though such occurrences were not infrequent, there is nothing natural about the deliverance experienced by the three parched armies. The water comes from God according to the word of the prophet.
3:19-20 Through experiencing this miracle, Joram and his allies trust that they will be successful in the upcoming battle. The ruin described in the victory over Moab is a contradiction to the rules for war provided in the covenant (Dt 20:19). Elisha does not order the destruction of trees and farmland but describes the totality of the ruin that will come to Moab in the conflict.
3:21-23 The soldiers who muster at the border to meet the coalition are described as bearing weapons, meaning they are lightly armed soldiers who carry swords. There is a notable wordplay here; while waiting in the red sandstone ground of Edom (meaning "red"), the Moabites mistake water that appears bloodred for actual blood.
3:24-25 The Moabites' mistake is a fatal error. The resulting destruction is exactly as the prophet predicted.
3:26-27 The final outcome of the Israelites' campaign fails to regain control over the territory and restore the tribute of Moab. Neither the presence of Jehoshaphat nor the word of Elisha can turn the tide of judgment against Israel. In spite of the rout of the Moabites through divine intervention, Joram cannot achieve his goal; he is forced to retreat.

3:1-27 Christians must reconcile the doctrine of the Divine Warrior with the particular historical wars that are a part of the present order. Just as God was active in human affairs in times past, exercising his rule among human kingdoms and giving them to whomever he willed (Da 5:21), so God continues to be at work in human affairs.

A particularly difficult question for the faithful is how to relate to the government in its legitimate role of controlling violence and exercising judgment. Though this is a God-ordained function, it is scarcely possible to point to a government at any time that consistently carried out this function as a legitimate representative of divine authority. War is a matter of fallible human governments making judgments in matters of life and death. At their best they have their share of evil, and at their worst they are the greatest enemy to their own people.

PEOPLE TO KNOW // **ELISHA**

2 KINGS 4:1-37: Elisha was a disciple of the prophet Elijah. When Elijah found him, Elisha was plowing in a field. After being called, Elisha slaughtered his oxen, gave the meat to his community and followed Elijah (1Ki 19:19-21).

When Elijah was taken up to heaven, he made Elisha his successor by giving him a "double portion" of his prophetic spirit (2Ki 2:9-10). After Elijah was taken to heaven in a fiery chariot, Elisha picked up his master's cloak, struck the Jordan River with it, and crossed on dry ground as Elijah had done earlier.

Elisha's flurry of miracles certainly sets him apart from most other OT prophets. Elisha's ministry as a miracle worker points to Jesus, who also fed multitudes (2Ki 4:42-44; Mt 14:13-21), raised the dead (2Ki 4:32-35; Mk 5:21-43) and cured leprosy (2Ki 5; Mk 1:40-45). Elisha's best-known miracles demonstrate God's kindness and compassion toward those in need.

APPLICATION Elisha's name means "God saves." Jesus' name means the same thing. Elisha revealed God's salvation in his own time; he saw God at work when others could not (e.g., 2Ki 6:15-17). His ministry of miracles and compassion also points to God's salvation through Jesus Christ. While we do not have the same ministry as Elisha, our task is the same: to serve God and to point others to God's salvation.

The Widow's Olive Oil

4 The wife of a man from the company[a]
of the prophets cried out to Elisha,
"Your servant my husband is dead, and
you know that he revered the LORD. But
now his creditor[b] is coming to take my
two boys as his slaves."
2Elisha replied to her, "How can I help
you? Tell me, what do you have in your
house?"
"Your servant has nothing there at all,"
she said, "except a small jar of olive oil."[c]
3Elisha said, "Go around and ask all
your neighbors for empty jars. Don't ask
for just a few. 4Then go inside and shut
the door behind you and your sons. Pour
oil into all the jars, and as each is filled,
put it to one side."
5She left him and shut the door behind
her and her sons. They brought the jars
to her and she kept pouring. 6When all
the jars were full, she said to her son,
"Bring me another one."
But he replied, "There is not a jar left."
Then the oil stopped flowing.
7She went and told the man of God,[d]
and he said, "Go, sell the oil and pay your
debts. You and your sons can live on what
is left."

The Shunammite's Son Restored to Life

8One day Elisha went to Shunem.[e]
And a well-to-do woman was there, who
urged him to stay for a meal. So whenever he came by, he stopped there to eat.
9She said to her husband, "I know that
this man who often comes our way is a
holy man of God. 10Let's make a small
room on the roof and put in it a bed and a
table, a chair and a lamp for him. Then he
can stay[f] there whenever he comes to us."
11One day when Elisha came, he went
up to his room and lay down there. 12He
said to his servant Gehazi, "Call the Shunammite."[g] So he called her, and she
stood before him. 13Elisha said to him,

4:1 [a] 1Sa 10:5; 2Ki 2:3 [b] Ex 22:26; Lev 25:39-43; Ne 5:3-5; Job 22:6; 24:9 4:2 [c] 1Ki 17:12 4:7 [d] 1Ki 12:22 4:8 [e] Jos 19:18 4:10 [f] Mt 10:41; Ro 12:13 4:12 [g] 2Ki 8:1

4:1-7 The oil is a divine gift that is not dependent on the presence of the man of God and cannot be viewed as some kind of trick. No details are given following Elisha's final instruction (v. 7), but it may be assumed that the woman obeys without question. Her debts are paid, and her family remains together.
4:8-10 Like Samuel (1Sa 7:15-17), Elisha probably follows a circuit in the administration of his duties. Regarded as a holy man, Elisha is distinguished from the other prophets who continue to have regular vocations. The room is furnished simply but adequately for a regular guest.
4:11-13 The second part of the story introduces Gehazi, the assistant to Elisha, as intermediary between Elisha and the woman. The scene depicts a deference and appropriate protocol between Elisha and his patron. Elisha poses the same question to his benefactor as he did to the widow who came to plead her case (cf. v. 2). His suggestions of intervening with the king or military commander show that Elisha has come into a position of political influence. As wealthy people, the woman and her husband carry a heavy liability for maintaining the state and its military. The woman declines political intervention; she has no need of social or material assistance, unlike the first woman who is about to lose her sons.

"Tell her, 'You have gone to all this trouble for us. Now what can be done for you?
Can we speak on your behalf to the king
or the commander of the army?'"
She replied, "I have a home among
my own people."
14"What can be done for her?" Elisha
asked.
Gehazi said, "She has no son, and her
husband is old."
15Then Elisha said, "Call her." So he
called her, and she stood in the doorway. 16"About this time[h] next year," Elisha
said, "you will hold a son in your arms."
"No, my lord!" she objected. "Please,
man of God, don't mislead your servant!"
17But the woman became pregnant,
and the next year about that same time
she gave birth to a son, just as Elisha had
told her.
18The child grew, and one day he went
out to his father, who was with the reapers.[i] 19He said to his father, "My head!
My head!"
His father told a servant, "Carry him to
his mother." 20After the servant had lifted him up and carried him to his mother,
the boy sat on her lap until noon, and
then he died. 21She went up and laid him
on the bed[j] of the man of God, then shut
the door and went out.
22She called her husband and said,
"Please send me one of the servants and
a donkey so I can go to the man of God
quickly and return."
23"Why go to him today?" he asked.
"It's not the New Moon[k] or the Sabbath."
"That's all right," she said.
24She saddled the donkey and said to
her servant, "Lead on; don't slow down
for me unless I tell you." 25So she set out
and came to the man of God at Mount
Carmel.[l]
When he saw her in the distance, the
man of God said to his servant Gehazi,
"Look! There's the Shunammite! 26Run to
meet her and ask her, 'Are you all right?
Is your husband all right? Is your child
all right?'"
"Everything is all right," she said.
27When she reached the man of God at
the mountain, she took hold of his feet.
Gehazi came over to push her away, but
the man of God said, "Leave her alone!
She is in bitter distress,[m] but the LORD
has hidden it from me and has not told
me why."
28"Did I ask you for a son, my lord?"
she said. "Didn't I tell you, 'Don't raise
my hopes'?"
29Elisha said to Gehazi, "Tuck your cloak
into your belt,[n] take my staff[o] in your
hand and run. Don't greet anyone you
meet, and if anyone greets you, do not
answer. Lay my staff on the boy's face."
30But the child's mother said, "As
surely as the LORD lives and as you live,
I will not leave you." So he got up and
followed her.
31Gehazi went on ahead and laid the
staff on the boy's face, but there was no
sound or response. So Gehazi went back
to meet Elisha and told him, "The boy
has not awakened."
32When Elisha reached the house,
there was the boy lying dead on his
couch.[p] 33He went in, shut the door on
the two of them and prayed[q] to the LORD.
34Then he got on the bed and lay on the
boy, mouth to mouth, eyes to eyes, hands
to hands. As he stretched[r] himself out on
him, the boy's body grew warm. 35Elisha

4:16 [h] Ge 18:10
4:18 [i] Ru 2:3
4:21 [j] ver 32
4:23 [k] Nu 10:10; 1Ch 23:31; Ps 81:3
4:25 [l] 1Ki 18:20; 2Ki 2:25
4:27 [m] 1Sa 1:15
4:29 [n] 1Ki 18:46; 2Ki 2:8,14; 9:1 [o] Ex 4:2; 7:19; 14:16
4:32 [p] ver 21
4:33 [q] 1Ki 17:20; Mt 6:6
4:34 [r] 1Ki 17:21; Ac 20:10

4:14–17 Unlike the widow, she cannot lose her children because she has none. Elisha asks her to be present in person for his announcement that in a year she will embrace a son. Like Sarah at the announcement of Isaac (Ge 18:12), the woman finds the promise incredible; in spite of her doubts, her desire for a child is fulfilled.

4:18–21 The narrative immediately advances to another day, some years later, when the child has grown. Now this woman is distraught, as was the widow: Despite the miraculous birth, she does not now have a son. When the child dies in her arms, she immediately lays the body on the bed of the man of God and prepares to confront him.

4:22–23 The husband is presented as uncompassionate and skeptical. The woman silences her husband with a single word for well-being; an amorphous term, it can be interpreted as a dismissal or a confidence.

4:24–28 The woman is resolute: She will express her distress to the man of God himself. Like the woman at Zarephath (1Ki 17:18), the woman from Shunem feels that Elisha has deceived her. Surprisingly, Elisha confesses to being mystified by this turn of events.

4:29–32 The final division of the story shows that the woman has not lost her faith in God or his servant. Despite her hurt, confusion, and anxiety, she refuses to go back to her son with Gehazi; her vow to stay with Elisha is identical to that of Elisha in his refusal to leave Elijah (cf. 2:2, 4, 6).

4:33–37 This miracle is private, as was the multiplication of the oil (vv. 4–5). Here Elisha's actions are described in detail, as opposed to an earlier miracle (1Ki 17:17–23).

turned away and walked back and forth
in the room and then got on the bed and
stretched out on him once more. The
boy sneezed seven times[s] and opened
his eyes.[t]
36 Elisha summoned Gehazi and said,
"Call the Shunammite." And he did.
When she came, he said, "Take your
son."[u] 37 She came in, fell at his feet and
bowed to the ground. Then she took her
son and went out.

Death in the Pot

38 Elisha returned to Gilgal[v] and there
was a famine[w] in that region. While the
company of the prophets was meeting
with him, he said to his servant, "Put
on the large pot and cook some stew for
these prophets."
39 One of them went out into the fields
to gather herbs and found a wild vine
and picked as many of its gourds as his
garment could hold. When he returned,
he cut them up into the pot of stew,
though no one knew what they were.
40 The stew was poured out for the men,
but as they began to eat it, they cried out,
"Man of God, there is death in the pot!"
And they could not eat it.
41 Elisha said, "Get some flour." He put
it into the pot and said, "Serve it to the
people to eat." And there was nothing
harmful in the pot.[x]

Feeding of a Hundred

42 A man came from Baal Shalishah,[y]
bringing the man of God twenty loaves[z]

4:35 [s] Jos 6:15 [t] 2Ki 8:5
4:36 [u] Heb 11:35
4:38 [v] 2Ki 2:1 [w] Lev 26:26; 2Ki 8:1
4:41 [x] Ex 15:25; 2Ki 2:21
4:42 [y] 1Sa 9:4 [z] Mt 14:17; 15:36

[a] 1Sa 9:7
4:43 [b] Lk 9:13 [c] Mt 14:20; Jn 6:12
5:1 [d] Ge 10:22; 2Sa 10:19 [e] Ex 4:6; Nu 12:10; Lk 4:27
5:2 [f] 2Ki 6:23; 13:20; 24:2
5:3 [g] Ge 20:7

2Ki 4:43–44 ❖ How does Elisha's ministry foreshadow Christ? What can we offer God from our lives that he can multiply and use for great purposes?

of barley bread[a] baked from the first
ripe grain, along with some heads of
new grain. "Give it to the people to eat,"
Elisha said.
43 "How can I set this before a hundred
men?" his servant asked.
But Elisha answered, "Give it to the
people to eat.[b] For this is what the LORD
says: 'They will eat and have some left
over.[c]'" 44 Then he set it before them, and
they ate and had some left over, according to the word of the LORD.

Naaman Healed of Leprosy

5 Now Naaman was commander of the
army of the king of Aram.[d] He was
a great man in the sight of his master
and highly regarded, because through
him the LORD had given victory to
Aram. He was a valiant soldier, but he
had leprosy.[a][e]
2 Now bands of raiders[f] from Aram had
gone out and had taken captive a young
girl from Israel, and she served Naaman's
wife. 3 She said to her mistress, "If only
my master would see the prophet[g] who
is in Samaria! He would cure him of his
leprosy."

[a] 1 The Hebrew for *leprosy* was used for various diseases affecting the skin; also in verses 3, 6, 7, 11 and 27.

4:38–41 Two stories involve the prophetic groups that support Elisha in his efforts to teach the ways of the covenant in a state devoted to the Baal cult. In this first story, a famine leaves the group foraging for what they can find, with near-disastrous results. Elisha responds immediately to the crisis with the authority that is his alone as the man of God.

4:42–44 In the second story, food is multiplied as it will be later with Jesus' miracles (Mt 14:13–21; 15:29–39). Through Elisha, God provides for these prophets just as he had for the widow.

✤ **4:1–44** Life in this world is characterized by need and struggle as typified in these stories about Elisha. The pain of various situations and individuals is not really comparable; who is to say that losing a child to a creditor is more painful than never having had a child at all (4:1, 14), or that the pain of food deprivation is more difficult than the loss of children (vv. 38, 43)?

Empathy is a somewhat risky business, since one can never know the feelings or pain of another. Perhaps this unknown is part of the divine mystery of grace. God sovereignly dispenses his mercy to particular situations in his care for all his children. Mercy by its very nature is not justice, so people are not able to demand whatever they consider to be their right, nor can they expect that their experience with God will be like that of someone else. Every age has a need for a mission like that of Elisha: to care for the needy, intervene for justice, and provide for the well-being of the marginalized.

5:1 Naaman's fame and valor are expanded three times to emphasize his distinction (v. 1). He also has one other distinction: He is a leper. This single word at the end of a string of accolades compromises all the others.

5:2–3 This slave girl's remark begins a series of transmissions that travel like lightning.

PEOPLE TO KNOW // NAAMAN

2 KINGS 5:1–19: Naaman was the commander of the Aramean army, highly regarded by his king because of his military victories. He had a problem, however. Naaman had leprosy (2Ki 5:1).

Within Naaman's house, his wife had a young Israelite slave serving her. The girl was moved with compassion for Naaman's illness and told her mistress that there was a prophet in Israel who could cure Naaman. With the king of Aram's blessing, Naaman set off for Israel, freighted with generous gifts for the man who he hoped could cure him.

The prophet Elisha did not even step out of his house to greet Naaman when he arrived; he simply sent out his servant telling Naaman to wash in the Jordan River seven times (2Ki 5:10). Naaman was incensed and resolved to leave, but his men reasoned with him to try this simple thing. Naaman conceded and dipped himself in the Jordan seven times, and his skin became as clear as that of a young child.

Overcome with gratitude, Naaman returned to Elisha and praised the God of Israel. He urged Elisha to take his generous gifts, but Elisha refused. Naaman then asked for permission to take some earth from Israel with him back to Aram so that he could worship God on Israel's soil back home. Then he asked forgiveness for the fact that he would need to help the frail king of Aram bow down to his false god, Rimmon. Elisha simply replied, "Go in peace" (2Ki 5:19).

APPLICATION Naaman's story shows a surprising reversal. The enemy of Israel becomes a devoted worshiper of God. We cannot predict whose hearts will be open to God's transforming power, and sometimes it is the people we least expect. God's love and his will are amazing and surprising. Naaman also models the gratitude and generosity of spirit that should accompany repentance and true faith. Rather than being selfish with our praise and gifts to God, we must be selfless.

4Naaman went to his master and told
him what the girl from Israel had said.
5"By all means, go," the king of Aram
replied. "I will send a letter to the king
of Israel." So Naaman left, taking with
him ten talents[a] of silver, six thousand
shekels[b] of gold and ten sets of clothing.[h]
6The letter that he took to the king of Israel read: "With this letter I am sending
my servant Naaman to you so that you
may cure him of his leprosy."
7As soon as the king of Israel read the
letter,[i] he tore his robes and said, "Am I
God?[j] Can I kill and bring back to life?[k]
Why does this fellow send someone to
me to be cured of his leprosy? See how
he is trying to pick a quarrel[l] with me!"
8When Elisha the man of God heard
that the king of Israel had torn his robes,
he sent him this message: "Why have you
torn your robes? Have the man come
to me and he will know that there is a
prophet[m] in Israel." 9So Naaman went
with his horses and chariots and stopped
at the door of Elisha's house. 10Elisha sent
a messenger to say to him, "Go, wash[n]
yourself seven times[o] in the Jordan, and
your flesh will be restored and you will
be cleansed."
11But Naaman went away angry and
said, "I thought that he would surely
come out to me and stand and call on
the name of the LORD his God, wave his
hand[p] over the spot and cure me of my
leprosy. 12Are not Abana and Pharpar,
the rivers of Damascus, better than all
the waters[q] of Israel? Couldn't I wash in
them and be cleansed?" So he turned
and went off in a rage.[r]
13Naaman's servants went to him
and said, "My father,[s] if the prophet

5:5 [h] ver 22; Ge 24:53; Jdg 14:12; 1Sa 9:7
5:7 [i] 2Ki 19:14 [j] Ge 30:2 [k] Dt 32:39; 1Sa 2:6 [l] 1Ki 20:7
5:8 [m] 1Ki 22:7
5:10 [n] Jn 9:7 [o] Ge 33:3; Lev 14:7
5:11 [p] Ex 7:19
5:12 [q] Isa 8:6 [r] Pr 14:17,29; 19:11; 29:11
5:13 [s] 2Ki 6:21; 13:14

[a] *5* That is, about 750 pounds or about 340 kilograms [b] *5* That is, about 150 pounds or about 69 kilograms

5:4 Naaman's disease has caused whiteness (v. 27), perhaps something like vitiligo in which pigment is lost from areas of the skin. Naaman continued to have access to the court of the king of Aram in Damascus, indicating that he is likely not contagious.
5:5–6 The content of the letter sent by Naaman's king shifts the focus to the dramatic response of the Israelite king. The story mocks the impotence of kings and royal protocol, especially when the God of the covenant is being actively rejected.
5:7–12 Naaman's pride shows up; he interprets the prophet's indifference to royal protocol as an affront to his own status. The prophet's instructions only make the situation worse.
5:13–14 Reason convinces this conqueror to humble himself and take action.

had told you to do some great thing,
would you not have done it? How much
more, then, when he tells you, 'Wash
and be cleansed'!" 14So he went down
and dipped himself in the Jordan seven
times,[t] as the man of God had told him,
and his flesh was restored[u] and became
clean like that of a young boy.[v]
15Then Naaman and all his attendants
went back to the man of God[w]. He stood
before him and said, "Now I know[x] that
there is no God in all the world except
in Israel. So please accept a gift[y] from
your servant."
16The prophet answered, "As surely as
the LORD lives, whom I serve, I will not
accept a thing." And even though Naaman urged him, he refused.[z]
17"If you will not," said Naaman,
"please let me, your servant, be given
as much earth[a] as a pair of mules can
carry, for your servant will never again
make burnt offerings and sacrifices to
any other god but the LORD. 18But may
the LORD forgive your servant for this
one thing: When my master enters the
temple of Rimmon to bow down and
he is leaning[b] on my arm and I have to
bow there also — when I bow down in
the temple of Rimmon, may the LORD
forgive your servant for this."
19"Go in peace,"[c] Elisha said.
After Naaman had traveled some distance, 20Gehazi, the servant of Elisha
the man of God, said to himself, "My
master was too easy on Naaman, this
Aramean, by not accepting from him
what he brought. As surely as the LORD[d]
lives, I will run after him and get something from him."
21So Gehazi hurried after Naaman.
When Naaman saw him running toward
him, he got down from the chariot to
meet him. "Is everything all right?" he
asked.
22"Everything is all right," Gehazi answered. "My master sent me to say, 'Two
young men from the company of the
prophets have just come to me from
the hill country of Ephraim. Please give
them a talent[a] of silver and two sets of
clothing.'"[e]
23"By all means, take two talents,"
said Naaman. He urged Gehazi to accept
them, and then tied up the two talents
of silver in two bags, with two sets of
clothing. He gave them to two of his servants, and they carried them ahead of
Gehazi. 24When Gehazi came to the hill,
he took the things from the servants and
put them away in the house. He sent the
men away and they left.
25When he went in and stood before
his master, Elisha asked him, "Where
have you been, Gehazi?"

2Ki 5:13–14 ❖ Who has encouraged you to stick with your faith when it seemed foolish? What blessings followed?

5:14 [t] Ge 33:3; Lev 14:7; Jos 6:15 [u] Ex 4:7 [v] Job 33:25; Lk 4:27
5:15 [w] Jos 2:11 [x] Jos 4:24; 1Sa 17:46; Da 2:47 [y] 1Sa 9:7; 25:27
5:16 [z] ver 20, 26; Ge 14:23; Da 5:17
5:17 [a] Ex 20:24
5:18 [b] 2Ki 7:2
5:19 [c] 1Sa 1:17; Ac 15:33
5:20 [d] Ex 20:7
5:22 [e] ver 5; Ge 45:22

[a] *22* That is, about 75 pounds or about 34 kilograms

5:15 Naaman's arrogance has become humility; he now qualifies to have a direct audience with the prophet. He makes his confession to the God of Israel, proving the earlier words of Elisha to be true (v. 8). The master of the servant girl now becomes the servant of the Israelite prophet.
5:16 Grace granted by God cannot be rewarded with material benefits.
5:17–19 Naaman acknowledges no God in all the earth except the God of Israel. When the healed general details what he will have to do as the king's right-hand man, Elisha dismisses him with a simple blessing: "Go in peace." Elisha does not question Naaman's loyalty. His humble petition serves as its own affirmation of his genuine faith.
5:20–22 Naaman shows the true character of faith while Gehazi, the servant of the prophet, betrays his master and his trust in God. Though Gehazi professes that all is at peace, he is in the very process of violating that peace. He not only prepares to lie but puts the lie in the mouth of his master.
5:23–24 While Naaman's reputation precedes him (v. 1), the servants precede Gehazi with the plunder of his treachery.
5:25–27 The closing episode shows Elisha to be a true prophet who is fully aware of the implications of what has transpired. Strangely, Elisha goes on to name items Gehazi has not actually taken: fields of olives and vineyards, sheep, cattle, and servants. His question to Gehazi indicates that this servant's sin is not merely greed and theft: His envy is immoral, as is his indifference to the Naaman's profound conversion and trust in the God of Israel.

✜ **5:1–27** Naaman's dramatic conversion stands in sharp contrast to Gehazi's callous indifference to Elisha's specifically stated wishes. In one instance, the proud warrior humbles himself to bathe in a dirty river. Due to his humble obedience, he experiences healing. In the next, a supposedly humble servant selfishly defies Elisha and then expects to experience no consequences. His expectation is sorely misplaced.

How often do we as Christians today not see the hypocrisy of our statements and actions, even in the face of others' true repentance? How often do we disobey God's stated instructions

"Your servant didn't go anywhere,"
Gehazi answered.
26 But Elisha said to him, "Was not
my spirit with you when the man got
down from his chariot to meet you? Is
this the time[f] to take money or to accept
clothes — or olive groves and vineyards,
or flocks and herds, or male and female
slaves?[g] 27 Naaman's leprosy[h] will cling
to you and to your descendants forever."
Then Gehazi[i] went from Elisha's presence
and his skin was leprous — it had become
as white as snow.[j]

An Axhead Floats

6 The company[k] of the prophets said
to Elisha, "Look, the place where we
meet with you is too small for us. 2 Let us
go to the Jordan, where each of us can
get a pole; and let us build a place there
for us to meet."
And he said, "Go."
3 Then one of them said, "Won't you
please come with your servants?"
"I will," Elisha replied. 4 And he went
with them.
They went to the Jordan and began
to cut down trees. 5 As one of them was
cutting down a tree, the iron axhead fell
into the water. "Oh no, my lord!" he cried
out. "It was borrowed!"
6 The man of God asked, "Where did
it fall?" When he showed him the place,
Elisha cut a stick and threw[l] it there, and
made the iron float. 7 "Lift it out," he said.
Then the man reached out his hand and
took it.

Elisha Traps Blinded Arameans

8 Now the king of Aram was at war with
Israel. After conferring with his officers,
he said, "I will set up my camp in such
and such a place."

5:26 [f] ver 16 [g] Jer 45:5
5:27 [h] Nu 12:10; 2Ki 15:5 [i] Col 3:5 [j] Ex 4:6
6:1 [k] 1Sa 10:5; 2Ki 4:38
6:6 [l] Ex 15:25; 2Ki 2:21
6:9 [m] ver 12
6:10 [n] Jer 11:18
6:12 [o] ver 9
6:13 [p] Ge 37:17
6:14 [q] 2Ki 1:9
6:16 [r] Ge 15:1 [s] 2Ch 32:7; Ps 55:18; Ro 8:31; 1Jn 4:4
6:17 [t] 2Ki 2:11, 12; Ps 68:17; Zec 6:1-7

2Ki 6:16-18 ❖ Have your eyes ever been opened to the larger reality of what God is doing around you? What did you perceive in that situation?

9 The man of God sent word to the
king[m] of Israel: "Beware of passing
that place, because the Arameans are
going down there." 10 So the king of Israel checked on the place indicated by
the man of God. Time and again Elisha
warned[n] the king, so that he was on his
guard in such places.
11 This enraged the king of Aram. He
summoned his officers and demanded
of them, "Tell me! Which of us is on the
side of the king of Israel?"
12 "None of us, my lord the king[o],"
said one of his officers, "but Elisha, the
prophet who is in Israel, tells the king of
Israel the very words you speak in your
bedroom."
13 "Go, find out where he is," the king
ordered, "so I can send men and capture him." The report came back: "He is
in Dothan."[p] 14 Then he sent[q] horses and
chariots and a strong force there. They
went by night and surrounded the city.
15 When the servant of the man of
God got up and went out early the next
morning, an army with horses and chariots had surrounded the city. "Oh no,
my lord! What shall we do?" the servant
asked.
16 "Don't be afraid,"[r] the prophet answered. "Those who are with us are
more[s] than those who are with them."
17 And Elisha prayed, "Open his eyes,
LORD, so that he may see." Then the LORD
opened the servant's eyes, and he looked
and saw the hills full of horses and chariots[t] of fire all around Elisha.

---

and blithely believe that God will look the other way? Surely Jesus' parable of the speck and the plank (Mt 7:1-5) applies just as urgently to us today as it did to Jesus' original hearers. At the end of this story, whatever speck may have remained in Naaman's life pales in comparison to the plank in Gehazi's. Thankfully, true repentance offers a way for both to be reconciled to God (1Jn 1:9).

6:1-7 The "iron axhead" was undoubtedly a valuable instrument and was "borrowed" (literally "begged or prayed for"), making the loss so much more distressing. The connection for its being placed here in the Elisha accounts is that it relates another miracle of Elisha at the Jordan (cf. the Naaman story in ch. 5).

6:8-10 The first episode of this story presents Elisha as a God-equipped spy in the Aramean camp. This prophet knows exactly how to warn the king of Israel.

6:11-14 The king of Aram is determined to capture Elisha, either to avenge the sabotage of his army or to enlist him as an intelligence informant in his own forces. To ensure the success of his efforts, he dispatches a heavy force deep into the Israelite territory.

6:15-17 This passage contrasts the Aramean army with the army of God. The Arameans are no match for one man of God surrounded by the chariots of Yahweh's army.

ELISHA
Mediterranean Sea
PHOENICIA
SYRIA
Elisha predicted that the wicked Hazael would succeed Ben-Hadad as King of Syria
Sidon
Zarephath
Mt. Hermon
Damascus
Tyre
Dan
Pharpar R.
GALILEE
ARAM
Sea of Galilee
Mt. Carmel
Kishon R.
Yarmuk R.
Elisha restores Shunammite's son to life
Shunem
Jezreel
Jordan R.
Ramoth Gilead
Elisha born
Dothan
Elisha protected the cities of Dothan and Samaria through chariots of fire and by bringing blindness upon the Syrian army
SAMARIA
Abel Meholah?
Samaria
Kerith Ravine
Jabbok R.
GILEAD
Joppa
Shiloh
Bethel
The prophet Elisha continued Elijah's work in the northern kingdom of Israel, from Syria in the north to Edom in the south.
Gilgal
Ramah
Jericho
Jerusalem
AMMON
Moresheth Gath
Tekoa
JUDAH
Besor Valley
Dead Sea
Arnon R.
PHILISTIA
Beersheba
Arad
MOAB
Kir Hareseth
Desert of Beersheba
Zered R.
EDOM
10,000 ft 3050 m
5000 ft 1525 m
2000 ft 610 m
1000 ft 305 m
0 (sea level) 0 (sea level)
-1640 ft -500 m
0 40 km.
0 40 miles

18 As the enemy came down toward
him, Elisha prayed to the LORD, "Strike
this army with blindness."[u] So he struck
them with blindness, as Elisha had
asked.
19 Elisha told them, "This is not the
road and this is not the city. Follow me,
and I will lead you to the man you are
looking for." And he led them to Samaria.
20 After they entered the city, Elisha
said, "LORD, open the eyes of these men
so they can see." Then the LORD opened
their eyes and they looked, and there
they were, inside Samaria.
21 When the king of Israel saw them,
he asked Elisha, "Shall I kill them, my
father?[v] Shall I kill them?"
22 "Do not kill them," he answered.
"Would you kill those you have captured[w]
with your own sword or bow? Set food
and water before them so that they may
eat and drink and then go back to their
master." 23 So he prepared a great feast
for them, and after they had finished
eating and drinking, he sent them away,
and they returned to their master. So
the bands[x] from Aram stopped raiding
Israel's territory.

Famine in Besieged Samaria

24 Some time later, Ben-Hadad[y] king
of Aram mobilized his entire army and
marched up and laid siege[z] to Samaria.
25 There was a great famine[a] in the city;
the siege lasted so long that a donkey's
head sold for eighty shekels[*a*] of silver,
and a quarter of a cab[*b*] of seed pods[*c*][b]
for five shekels.[*d*]
26 As the king of Israel was passing by
on the wall, a woman cried to him, "Help
me, my lord the king!"
27 The king replied, "If the LORD does
not help you, where can I get help for
you? From the threshing floor? From
the winepress?" 28 Then he asked her,
"What's the matter?"
She answered, "This woman said to
me, 'Give up your son so we may eat him
today, and tomorrow we'll eat my son.'
29 So we cooked my son and ate[c] him.
The next day I said to her, 'Give up your
son so we may eat him,' but she had hidden him."
30 When the king heard the woman's
words, he tore[d] his robes. As he went
along the wall, the people looked, and
they saw that, under his robes, he had
sackcloth[e] on his body. 31 He said, "May
God deal with me, be it ever so severely,
if the head of Elisha son of Shaphat remains on his shoulders today!"
32 Now Elisha was sitting in his house,
and the elders[f] were sitting with him.
The king sent a messenger ahead, but
before he arrived, Elisha said to the elders, "Don't you see how this murderer[g]
is sending someone to cut off my head?[h]
Look, when the messenger comes, shut
the door and hold it shut against him.
Is not the sound of his master's footsteps behind him?" 33 While he was still
talking to them, the messenger came
down to him.
The king said, "This disaster is from
the LORD. Why should I wait[i] for the LORD
any longer?"
7 Elisha replied, "Hear the word of the
LORD. This is what the LORD says:
About this time tomorrow, a seah[*e*] of

6:18 [u] Ge 19:11; Ac 13:11
6:21 [v] 2Ki 5:13
6:22 [w] Dt 20:11; 2Ch 28:8-15; Ro 12:20
6:23 [x] 2Ki 5:2
6:24 [y] 1Ki 15:18; 20:1; 2Ki 8:7 [z] Dt 28:52
6:25 [a] Lev 26:26; Ru 1:1 [b] Isa 36:12
6:29 [c] Lev 26:29; Dt 28:53-55
6:30 [d] 2Ki 18:37; Isa 22:15 [e] Ge 37:34; 1Ki 21:27
6:32 [f] Eze 8:1; 14:1; 20:1 [g] 1Ki 18:4 [h] ver 31
6:33 [i] Lev 24:11; Job 2:9; 14:14; Isa 40:31

[*a*] *25* That is, about 2 pounds or about 920 grams
[*b*] *25* That is, probably about 1/4 pound or about 100 grams
[*c*] *25* Or *of doves' dung*
[*d*] *25* That is, about 2 ounces or about 58 grams
[*e*] *1* That is, probably about 12 pounds or about 5.5 kilograms of flour; also in verses 16 and 18

6:18–20 The Aramean army is not struck down by the swords of soldiers but by a blinding light. Elisha takes the Aramean army captive to the capital where he prays a prayer virtually identical to the one that enabled his servant to see the heavenly armies (cf. v. 17).
6:21–23 The king of Israel has not been responsible for taking the soldiers captive and requires permission from the prophet, respectfully and unusually addressed as "father." Elisha's gracious instructions result in a halt of the border wars.
6:24–25 Ben-Hadad was probably a dynastic name for Aramean kings. The usual assumption of historians is that the Ben-Hadad in this Elisha story is Ben-Hadad son of Hazael (cf. 13:3).
6:26–29 The heart-rending atrocity of this story is the woman's apparent lack of feeling for the death of her own child and that of her neighbor; the normal compassion of motherhood is subordinated to the desperation to survive.
6:30–31 When the king learns of the real concern of the woman, he can only tear his clothes in grief. The rip reveals his own despair, as it exposes the coarse cloth of lament he is wearing underneath his regular tunic. Elisha is a logical target for the frustrations of an impotent king.
6:32–33 The threat the king makes against Elisha is irrational, but it is not idle. Elisha is fully aware of the king's intentions; he knows the king is right behind the messenger and that he has relented from his rash order.
7:1–2 The narrative moves quickly, showing the

the finest flour will sell for a shekel[a] and
two seahs[b] of barley for a shekel[j] at the
gate of Samaria."
2The officer on whose arm the king
was leaning[k] said to the man of God,
"Look, even if the LORD should open the
floodgates[l] of the heavens, could this
happen?"
"You will see it with your own eyes,"
answered Elisha, "but you will not eat[m]
any of it!"

The Siege Lifted

3Now there were four men with leprosy[c][n] at the entrance of the city gate.
They said to each other, "Why stay here
until we die? 4If we say, 'We'll go into the
city'—the famine is there, and we will
die. And if we stay here, we will die. So
let's go over to the camp of the Arameans
and surrender. If they spare us, we live;
if they kill us, then we die."
5At dusk they got up and went to
the camp of the Arameans. When they
reached the edge of the camp, no one
was there, 6for the Lord had caused the
Arameans to hear the sound[o] of chariots
and horses and a great army, so that they
said to one another, "Look, the king of
Israel has hired[p] the Hittite[q] and Egyptian kings to attack us!" 7So they got up
and fled[r] in the dusk and abandoned
their tents and their horses and donkeys. They left the camp as it was and
ran for their lives.
8The men who had leprosy[s] reached
the edge of the camp, entered one of the
tents and ate and drank. Then they took
silver, gold and clothes, and went off and
hid them. They returned and entered
another tent and took some things from
it and hid them also.
9Then they said to each other, "What
we're doing is not right. This is a day of
good news and we are keeping it to ourselves. If we wait until daylight, punishment will overtake us. Let's go at once
and report this to the royal palace."
10So they went and called out to the
city gatekeepers and told them, "We
went into the Aramean camp and no one
was there—not a sound of anyone—
only tethered horses and donkeys, and
the tents left just as they were." 11The
gatekeepers shouted the news, and it
was reported within the palace.
12The king got up in the night and said
to his officers, "I will tell you what the Arameans have done to us. They know we
are starving; so they have left the camp to
hide[t] in the countryside, thinking, 'They
will surely come out, and then we will
take them alive and get into the city.'"
13One of his officers answered, "Have
some men take five of the horses that are
left in the city. Their plight will be like
that of all the Israelites left here—yes,
they will only be like all these Israelites
who are doomed. So let us send them to
find out what happened."
14So they selected two chariots with
their horses, and the king sent them after the Aramean army. He commanded
the drivers, "Go and find out what has
happened." 15They followed them as far
as the Jordan, and they found the whole
road strewn with the clothing and equipment the Arameans had thrown away
in their headlong flight. So the messengers returned and reported to the king.
16Then the people went out and plundered[u] the camp of the Arameans. So a
seah of the finest flour sold for a shekel,
and two seahs of barley sold for a shekel,[v]
as the LORD had said.

7:1 [j] ver 16
7:2 [k] 2Ki 5:18 [l] ver 19; Ge 7:11; Ps 78:23; Mal 3:10 [m] ver 17
7:3 [n] Lev 13:45-46; Nu 5:1-4
7:6 [o] Ex 14:24; 2Sa 5:24; Eze 1:24 [p] 2Sa 10:6; Jer 46:21 [q] Nu 13:29
7:7 [r] Jdg 7:21; Ps 48:4-6; Pr 28:1; Isa 30:17
7:8 [s] Isa 33:23; 35:6
7:12 [t] Jos 8:4; 2Ki 6:25-29
7:16 [u] Isa 33:4, 23 [v] ver 1

2Ki 7:8-9 ❖ God can choose unlikely people to deliver lifesaving news. Which unlikely messengers has God used in our lives to point to his grace and mercy, and how did their message impact us?

[a] *1* That is, about 2/5 ounce or about 12 grams; also in verses 16 and 18 [b] *1* That is, probably about 20 pounds or about 9 kilograms of barley; also in verses 16 and 18 [c] *3* The Hebrew for *leprosy* was used for various diseases affecting the skin; also in verse 8.

---

control of the prophet and the despair of the king. Elisha's bold prediction shocks the officer who hears it.

7:3–5 Caught in a death trap, four lepers decide to desert to the enemy camp. When they arrive, they find the enemy has fled in terror.

7:6–7 The narrator gives us a glimpse of God's mighty act in terrifying this enormous army.

7:8–15 The king, acting with prudent skepticism, suspects an enemy ploy to dupe his soldiers, draw them out of the city, capture them alive, and take the city. Subordinates point out that the Aramean army has been defeated (v. 15).

7:16–17 Food prices become exactly as the prophet earlier announced, and Elisha's statement to the officer (v. 2) also comes to pass.

17 Now the king had put the officer on
whose arm he leaned in charge of the
gate, and the people trampled him in
the gateway, and he died,[w] just as the
man of God had foretold when the king
came down to his house. 18 It happened
as the man of God had said to the king:
"About this time tomorrow, a seah of the
finest flour will sell for a shekel and two
seahs of barley for a shekel at the gate
of Samaria."
19 The officer had said to the man of God,
"Look, even if the LORD should open the
floodgates[x] of the heavens, could this happen?" The man of God had replied, "You
will see it with your own eyes, but you will
not eat any of it!" 20 And that is exactly
what happened to him, for the people
trampled him in the gateway, and he died.

The Shunammite's Land Restored

8 Now Elisha had said to the woman[y]
whose son he had restored to life,
"Go away with your family and stay for
a while wherever you can, because the
LORD has decreed a famine[z] in the land
that will last seven years."[a] 2 The woman
proceeded to do as the man of God said.
She and her family went away and stayed
in the land of the Philistines seven years.
3 At the end of the seven years she
came back from the land of the Philistines and went to appeal to the king for
her house and land. 4 The king was talking to Gehazi, the servant of the man of
God, and had said, "Tell me about all the
great things Elisha has done." 5 Just as
Gehazi was telling the king how Elisha
had restored[b] the dead to life, the woman whose son Elisha had brought back
to life came to appeal to the king for her
house and land.
Gehazi said, "This is the woman, my
lord the king, and this is her son whom
Elisha restored to life." 6 The king asked
the woman about it, and she told him.

7:17 [w] ver 2; 2Ki 6:32
7:19 [x] ver 2
8:1 [y] 2Ki 4:8-37 [z] Lev 26:26; Dt 28:22; Ru 1:1 [a] Ge 12:10; Ps 105:16; Hag 1:11
8:5 [b] 2Ki 4:35
8:7 [c] 2Sa 8:5; 1Ki 11:24 [d] 2Ki 6:24
8:8 [e] 1Ki 19:15 [f] Ge 32:20; 1Sa 9:7; 2Ki 1:2 [g] Jdg 18:5
8:10 [h] Isa 38:1
8:11 [i] Jdg 3:25 [j] Lk 19:41
8:12 [k] 1Ki 19:17; 2Ki 10:32; 12:17; 13:3,7 [l] Ps 137:9; Isa 13:16; Hos 13:16; Na 3:10; Lk 19:44 [m] Ge 34:29 [n] 2Ki 15:16; Am 1:13
8:13 [o] 1Sa 17:43; 2Sa 3:8 [p] 1Ki 19:15

Then he assigned an official to her case
and said to him, "Give back everything
that belonged to her, including all the
income from her land from the day she
left the country until now."

Hazael Murders Ben-Hadad

7 Elisha went to Damascus,[c] and Ben-
Hadad[d] king of Aram was ill. When the
king was told, "The man of God has come
all the way up here," 8 he said to Hazael,[e]
"Take a gift[f] with you and go to meet the
man of God. Consult[g] the LORD through
him; ask him, 'Will I recover from this
illness?' "
9 Hazael went to meet Elisha, taking
with him as a gift forty camel-loads of
all the finest wares of Damascus. He went
in and stood before him, and said, "Your
son Ben-Hadad king of Aram has sent me
to ask, 'Will I recover from this illness?' "
10 Elisha answered, "Go and say to him,
'You will certainly recover.'[h] Nevertheless,[a] the LORD has revealed to me that
he will in fact die." 11 He stared at him
with a fixed gaze until Hazael was embarrassed.[i] Then the man of God began
to weep.[j]
12 "Why is my lord weeping?" asked
Hazael.
"Because I know the harm[k] you will
do to the Israelites," he answered. "You
will set fire to their fortified places, kill
their young men with the sword, dash[l]
their little children[m] to the ground, and
rip open[n] their pregnant women."
13 Hazael said, "How could your servant,
a mere dog,[o] accomplish such a feat?"
"The LORD has shown me that you will
become king[p] of Aram," answered Elisha.
14 Then Hazael left Elisha and returned
to his master. When Ben-Hadad asked,
"What did Elisha say to you?" Hazael

[a] *10* The Hebrew may also be read *Go and say, 'You will certainly not recover,' for.*

7:18–20 The final verses bring closure to the story by repeating the prophetic word, which determines the course of events.

8:1–6 The arrival of the Shunammite woman to lodge her complaint, accompanied by her son, provides an immediate opportunity to verify the event of his being raised back to life. The king is moved by her story and acts much more nobly than his predecessor Ahab, who had no hesitation in confiscating the property owned by Naboth.

8:7–13 Elisha is in Damascus on the occasion of King Ben-Hadad's illness. The king sends Hazael, one of his trusted deputies, with an enormous gift to receive a word from the prophet, though "forty camel-loads" should be read as hyperbole (v. 9).

God has already declared that Hazael will be the instrument of punishment to Israel (1Ki 19:15–17); here stands the man who will crush innocent citizens of Israel.

8:14–15 Events transpire as the prophet says; Hazael is well known in history as the usurper who took over the Aramean throne in Damascus. The "feat" that Hazael will accomplish (8:13) is described from an Aramean point of view.

PEOPLE TO KNOW // GEHAZI

2 KINGS 8:4–5: Gehazi was a faithful servant of Elisha. He witnessed, and even participated in, many of the miracles that Elisha performed during his amazing ministry. Most memorable was when Elisha sent him to bring his staff and lay it on the Shunammite woman's son who had passed away. Gehazi witnessed the young man restored to life (2Ki 4:22–37). Later in 2 Kings we read that after Elisha instructed Naaman as to how to be cleansed of his leprosy, Naaman offered to give Elisha gifts of silver and clothing as a way of thanking the prophet. Elisha refused the gifts, but Gehazi had other ideas (2Ki 5:20). He hurried to catch up with Naaman, then lied to this foreign army commander and told him that Elisha had decided to take his offer of silver and clothing after all. Gehazi's greed got the best of him.

Elisha, of course, knew that this was happening, so when he confronted Gehazi and received more lies in return, Elisha cursed his servant with Naaman's leprosy: Gehazi's skin turned white as snow, and Elisha said to him, "Naaman's leprosy will cling to you and to your descendants forever" (2Ki 5:27).

APPLICATION ✣ Our human nature is sometimes stupendously fickle. In the book of Genesis, God said to Cain, "If you do not do what is right, sin is crouching at your door; it desires to have you, but you must rule over it" (Ge 4:7). Gehazi, as with many other characters in the Bible, failed to rule over his baser instincts. He lied to Elisha and paid a shocking price.

Greed is a corrupting impulse; it's a thief that will steal our contentment. Acting on our greed may not give us a disease, but it will undermine our relationships and corrode our souls.

replied, "He told me that you would
certainly recover." 15But the next day
he took a thick cloth, soaked it in water and spread it over the king's face, so
that he died.[q] Then Hazael succeeded
him as king.

Jehoram King of Judah

8:16–24pp // 2Ch 21:5–10,20

16In the fifth year of Joram[r] son of
Ahab king of Israel, when Jehoshaphat
was king of Judah, Jehoram[s] son of Jehoshaphat began his reign as king of
Judah. 17He was thirty-two years old
when he became king, and he reigned
in Jerusalem eight years. 18He followed
the ways of the kings of Israel, as the
house of Ahab had done, for he married
a daughter[t] of Ahab. He did evil in the
eyes of the LORD. 19Nevertheless, for the
sake of his servant David, the LORD was
not willing to destroy[u] Judah. He had

8:15 [q] 2Ki 1:17
8:16 [r] 2Ki 1:17; 3:1 [s] 2Ch 21:1-4
8:18 [t] ver 26; 2Ki 11:1
8:19 [u] Ge 6:13

✣ **6:1—8:15** The Israelites experience the activity of the Divine Warrior in many different ways depending on their situation, but the presence and activity of God is at work through his prophets. The rule of God is demonstrated through Elisha the man of God rather than the king. Protecting the poor, bringing life and justice, leading armies, and acting as a covenant champion are all part of the ideal royal profile.

The apostle Paul reminds the Ephesians that the situation is no different for them (Eph 6:10-13). They need to be strong in the Lord and in the power of his might; they must put on the whole armor of God so that they can take their stand against the tricks of the devil. Equipped with the spiritual armor of God, it is possible for Christians in this world to stand against such forces. This spiritual armor is nothing other than faith in the truth of the gospel (Eph 6:14-17); above all it is prayer to the Divine Warrior (Eph 6:18) and steadfast prayer at all times for all the saints.

In the essentials of spiritual warfare, the present world is no different from the tortured topsy-turvy world of Elisha. Christians in many different places are ravaged by the turbulence of war, just as the faithful were in the days of Elisha. Where actual physical warfare is not present, Christians struggle against ideologies and social forces designed to undermine the rule of God in this world, the way of life God has ordained through his Word for those created to represent him as his image.

Everywhere the faithful are called to be like Elisha and his followers; they must resist evil and show mercy as they are able. As with Elisha, their weapon is prayer, and their assurance is that the Divine Warrior will act on their behalf even as he did in the distressing days of Israelite apostasy.

8:16–24 The promise to David is a light that continues to shine (vv. 18–19). Though the dynasty

promised to maintain a lamp[v] for David
and his descendants forever.
20 In the time of Jehoram, Edom rebelled against Judah and set up its own
king.[w] 21 So Jehoram[a] went to Zair with all
his chariots. The Edomites surrounded
him and his chariot commanders, but
he rose up and broke through by night;
his army, however, fled back home. 22 To
this day Edom has been in rebellion[x]
against Judah. Libnah[y] revolted at the
same time.
23 As for the other events of Jehoram's
reign, and all he did, are they not written
in the book of the annals of the kings of
Judah? 24 Jehoram rested with his ancestors and was buried with them in the City
of David. And Ahaziah his son succeeded
him as king.

Ahaziah King of Judah

8:25–29pp // 2Ch 22:1–6

25 In the twelfth[z] year of Joram son of
Ahab king of Israel, Ahaziah son of Jehoram king of Judah began to reign. 26 Ahaziah was twenty-two years old when he
became king, and he reigned in Jerusalem one year. His mother's name was
Athaliah,[a] a granddaughter of Omri[b] king
of Israel. 27 He followed the ways of the
house of Ahab[c] and did evil[d] in the eyes
of the LORD, as the house of Ahab had
done, for he was related by marriage to
Ahab's family.
28 Ahaziah went with Joram son of
Ahab to war against Hazael king of
Aram at Ramoth Gilead.[e] The Arameans wounded Joram; 29 so King Joram
returned to Jezreel[f] to recover from the
wounds the Arameans had inflicted on
him at Ramoth[b] in his battle with Hazael[g]
king of Aram.
Then Ahaziah son of Jehoram king of
Judah went down to Jezreel to see Joram son of Ahab, because he had been
wounded.

8:19 [v] 2Sa 21:17; 7:13; 1Ki 11:36; Rev 21:23
8:20 [w] 1Ki 22:47
8:22 [x] Ge 27:40 [y] Nu 33:20; Jos 21:13; 2Ki 19:8
8:25 [z] 2Ki 9:29
8:26 [a] ver 18 [b] 1Ki 16:23
8:27 [c] 1Ki 16:30 [d] 1Ki 15:26
8:28 [e] Dt 4:43; 1Ki 22:3,29
8:29 [f] 2Ki 9:15 [g] 1Ki 19:15,17

9:1 [h] 1Sa 10:5 [i] 2Ki 4:29 [j] 1Sa 10:1 [k] 2Ki 8:28
9:3 [l] 1Ki 19:16
9:6 [m] 1Ki 19:16; 2Ch 22:7
9:7 [n] Ge 4:24; Rev 6:10 [o] Dt 32:43 [p] 1Ki 18:4; 21:15
9:8 [q] 2Ki 10:17 [r] Dt 32:36; 1Sa 25:22; 1Ki 21:21; 2Ki 14:26

2Ki 8:19 ❖ How have we seen God's faithfulness to his promises displayed even in the face of great sin?

2Ki 9:6–7 ❖ Why does God exact judgment upon sin? How should the reality of God's justice shape a person's behavior?

Jehu Anointed King of Israel

9 The prophet Elisha summoned a man
from the company[h] of the prophets
and said to him, "Tuck your cloak into
your belt,[i] take this flask of olive oil[j] with
you and go to Ramoth Gilead.[k] 2 When
you get there, look for Jehu son of Jehoshaphat, the son of Nimshi. Go to him,
get him away from his companions and
take him into an inner room. 3 Then take
the flask and pour the oil[l] on his head
and declare, 'This is what the LORD says:
I anoint you king over Israel.' Then open
the door and run; don't delay!"
4 So the young prophet went to Ramoth
Gilead. 5 When he arrived, he found the
army officers sitting together. "I have a
message for you, commander," he said.
"For which of us?" asked Jehu.
"For you, commander," he replied.
6 Jehu got up and went into the house.
Then the prophet poured the oil[m] on Jehu's head and declared, "This is what the
LORD, the God of Israel, says: 'I anoint
you king over the LORD's people Israel.
7 You are to destroy the house of Ahab
your master, and I will avenge[n] the blood
of my servants[o] the prophets and the
blood of all the LORD's servants shed
by Jezebel.[p] 8 The whole house[q] of Ahab
will perish. I will cut off from Ahab every last male[r] in Israel—slave or free.[c]
9 I will make the house of Ahab like the

[a] 21 Hebrew *Joram,* a variant of *Jehoram;* also in verses 23 and 24 [b] 29 Hebrew *Ramah,* a variant of *Ramoth* [c] 8 Or *Israel—every ruler or leader*

is preserved, Judah suffers the loss of territory and influence.

The note that the revolt of Edom continues "until this day" (v. 22) shows a special interest in territorial claims when Judah regains its military strength.

8:25–29 Ahaziah's mother is Athaliah, here said to be a "granddaughter [descendant] of Omri" (v. 26). The queen mother could exercise considerable influence in affairs of the court, as we saw in the case of Maakah (cf. 1Ki 15:13). Jezebel's influence in fostering foreign cults in Jerusalem continues through her daughter Athaliah. These individuals are best described in terms of "the house of Ahab" (v. 27), who was renowned for his support of the prophets of Baal against Elijah.

9:1–10 Jehu's anointing takes place hastily and in secret, as is necessary if the revolt is to take place with the army leaders while they are on active duty. The prophetic prediction (vv. 7–10) against the house of Ahab is certainly exploited by Jehu and his party.

The prediction has two standard elements: immediate judgment followed by a stereotyped curse. The message against Jezebel is specifically

house of Jeroboam[s] son of Nebat and
like the house of Baasha[t] son of Ahijah.
10 As for Jezebel, dogs[u] will devour her
on the plot of ground at Jezreel, and no
one will bury her.' " Then he opened the
door and ran.
11 When Jehu went out to his fellow
officers, one of them asked him, "Is everything all right? Why did this maniac[v]
come to you?"
"You know the man and the sort of
things he says," Jehu replied.
12 "That's not true!" they said. "Tell us."
Jehu said, "Here is what he told me:
'This is what the LORD says: I anoint you
king over Israel.' "
13 They quickly took their cloaks and
spread[w] them under him on the bare
steps. Then they blew the trumpet[x] and
shouted, "Jehu is king!"

Jehu Kills Joram and Ahaziah

9:21–29pp // 2Ch 22:7–9

14 So Jehu son of Jehoshaphat, the son
of Nimshi, conspired against Joram.
(Now Joram and all Israel had been defending Ramoth Gilead[y] against Hazael king of Aram, 15 but King Joram[a] had
returned to Jezreel to recover[z] from the
wounds the Arameans had inflicted on
him in the battle with Hazael king of
Aram.) Jehu said, "If you desire to make
me king, don't let anyone slip out of the
city to go and tell the news in Jezreel."
16 Then he got into his chariot and rode
to Jezreel, because Joram was resting
there and Ahaziah[a] king of Judah had
gone down to see him.
17 When the lookout[b] standing on the
tower in Jezreel saw Jehu's troops approaching, he called out, "I see some
troops coming."
"Get a horseman," Joram ordered.
"Send him to meet them and ask, 'Do
you come in peace?[c]' "
18 The horseman rode off to meet Jehu
and said, "This is what the king says: 'Do
you come in peace?' "
"What do you have to do with peace?"
Jehu replied. "Fall in behind me."
The lookout reported, "The messenger
has reached them, but he isn't coming
back."
19 So the king sent out a second horseman. When he came to them he said,
"This is what the king says: 'Do you come
in peace?' "
Jehu replied, "What do you have to do
with peace? Fall in behind me."
20 The lookout reported, "He has
reached them, but he isn't coming back
either. The driving is like[d] that of Jehu
son of Nimshi—he drives like a maniac."
21 "Hitch up my chariot," Joram ordered. And when it was hitched up, Joram king of Israel and Ahaziah king of
Judah rode out, each in his own chariot,
to meet Jehu. They met him at the plot
of ground that had belonged to Naboth[e]
the Jezreelite. 22 When Joram saw Jehu he
asked, "Have you come in peace, Jehu?"
"How can there be peace," Jehu replied,
"as long as all the idolatry and witchcraft
of your mother Jezebel[f] abound?"
23 Joram turned about and fled, calling
out to Ahaziah, "Treachery,[g] Ahaziah!"
24 Then Jehu drew his bow[h] and shot
Joram between the shoulders. The arrow
pierced his heart and he slumped down
in his chariot. 25 Jehu said to Bidkar, his
chariot officer, "Pick him up and throw
him on the field that belonged to Naboth
the Jezreelite. Remember how you and I

a 15 Hebrew *Jehoram*, a variant of *Joram*; also in verses 17 and 21-24

9:9 [s] 1Ki 14:10; 15:29; 16:3,11 [t] 1Ki 16:3
9:10 [u] ver 35-36; 1Ki 21:23
9:11 [v] Jer 29:26; Jn 10:20; Ac 26:24
9:13 [w] Mt 21:8; Lk 19:36 [x] 2Sa 15:10; 1Ki 1:34,39
9:14 [y] Dt 4:43; 2Ki 8:28
9:15 [z] 2Ki 8:29
9:16 [a] 2Ch 22:7
9:17 [b] Isa 21:6 [c] 1Sa 16:4
9:20 [d] 2Sa 18:27
9:21 [e] ver 26; 1Ki 21:1-7,15-19
9:22 [f] 1Ki 16:30-33; 18:19; 2Ch 21:13; Rev 2:20
9:23 [g] 2Ki 11:14
9:24 [h] 1Ki 22:34

---

a fulfillment of the prophetic word (1Ki 21:23). The judgment speech summarizes the accumulated sins of Israel from Jeroboam to Joram.

9:11–13 Calling the prophet a "maniac" is a derogatory reference to the eccentric nature of prophets. But prophets did have influence, and even though the prophet is spoken of disparagingly, his word is effective. Following the accession ceremony, a proclamation to announce the anointed as king was normal procedure.

9:14–16 The narrative moves to the scene at Jezreel where the coup actually takes place. Joram will naturally expect that his chief officer is bringing him news from the battlefront when the watchmen see him approach.

9:17–18 Jehu's response to the king's question brings his mission into focus. The rider is in the service of a king who represents the crime of Ahab against Naboth in spilling innocent blood; he has nothing whatever to do with peace. Jehu is bringing revolution to Jezreel.

9:19–23 Joram acts in naivety, denial, or desperation; the narrative is ambiguous regarding his state of mind. Perhaps he thinks his presence can change the course of Jehu's action. But Jehu has come unannounced, with a formidable force, and has not allowed the messengers to return. There can be no peace for Joram. The reign of Ahab was characterized by lies and deceit. His dynasty ends by means of the same treachery that characterized it.

9:24–26 The callous violence of Jehu is carried out in the sense of fulfilling divine judgment.

were riding together in chariots behind
Ahab his father when the LORD spoke
this prophecy[i] against him: 26'Yesterday I saw the blood of Naboth[j] and the
blood of his sons, declares the LORD, and
I will surely make you pay for it on this
plot of ground, declares the LORD.'[a] Now
then, pick him up and throw him on that
plot, in accordance with the word of the
LORD."[k]
27When Ahaziah king of Judah saw
what had happened, he fled up the
road to Beth Haggan.[b] Jehu chased him,
shouting, "Kill him too!" They wounded
him in his chariot on the way up to Gur
near Ibleam,[l] but he escaped to Megiddo[m] and died there. 28His servants took
him by chariot[n] to Jerusalem and buried
him with his ancestors in his tomb in the
City of David. 29(In the eleventh[o] year of
Joram son of Ahab, Ahaziah had become
king of Judah.)

9:25 [i] 1Ki 21:19-22,24-29
9:26 [j] 1Ki 21:19 [k] 1Ki 21:29
9:27 [l] Jdg 1:27 [m] 2Ki 23:29
9:28 [n] 2Ki 14:20; 23:30
9:29 [o] 2Ki 8:25
9:30 [p] Jer 4:30; Eze 23:40
9:31 [q] 1Ki 16:9-10
9:33 [r] Ps 7:5
9:34 [s] 1Ki 16:31; 21:25

Jezebel Killed

30Then Jehu went to Jezreel. When Jezebel heard about it, she put on eye makeup,[p] arranged her hair and looked out of
a window. 31As Jehu entered the gate,
she asked, "Have you come in peace, you
Zimri,[q] you murderer of your master?"[c]
32He looked up at the window and
called out, "Who is on my side? Who?"
Two or three eunuchs looked down at
him. 33"Throw her down!" Jehu said. So
they threw her down, and some of her
blood spattered the wall and the horses
as they trampled her underfoot.[r]
34Jehu went in and ate and drank.
"Take care of that cursed woman," he
said, "and bury her, for she was a king's
daughter."[s] 35But when they went out
to bury her, they found nothing except

[a] *26* See 1 Kings 21:19. [b] *27* Or *fled by way of the garden house* [c] *31* Or *"Was there peace for Zimri, who murdered his master?"*

9:27–29 Jehu is determined to remove not only the ruling descendant of Ahab but also members of the royal family. The summary of the reign of Ahaziah is inserted as the conclusion to his burial.
9:30–33 Jehu then returns to Jezreel to deal with Jezebel.
9:34–37 The abandonment of the body of Jezebel to the scavenger animals is a particularly disparaging insult against the woman who was queen; it emphasizes the fulfillment of the prophetic word (cf. 1Ki 21:23). The proverb about her body being as dung is possibly a further insult to her name, calling attention to a second meaning for *zebel* as "manure."

PEOPLE TO KNOW // JEZEBEL

2 KINGS 9:30–37: Jezebel was the daughter of the king of Sidon. She married King Ahab of Israel, and together, she and her husband led the nation into all kinds of evil (1Ki 16:30–33). She turned the people's hearts to idolatry and sought to kill all the prophets of God. After Elijah's victory over the prophets of Baal on Mount Carmel, which led to those prophets being put to death, Jezebel became intent on killing Elijah (1Ki 19:2). Elijah fled to Mount Horeb, where God gave him encouragement.

When Ahab became envious of Naboth's vineyard, Jezebel had an easy solution: Kill Naboth and take his land. Ahab did so. For this and her other sins, Jezebel was judged by God. Elijah prophesied that she would be devoured by dogs (1Ki 21:23).

Later, Elijah's successor, Elisha, sent one of the prophets to anoint Jehu king over Israel and instruct him to destroy Ahab's household (2Ki 9:6–10). Jehu went to Jezreel, and Jezebel spoke to him to him through a window. Jehu called for the eunuchs near her to throw her out the window, which they did, killing her. Jehu entered the palace and ate, and then told his men to take care of Jezebel's body. When they went outside, they found that she had been eaten by dogs. All that remained was her skull, hands and feet.

APPLICATION Jezebel is an example of passion and commitment for the wrong things. She was intent on bringing others to the worship of false gods. In her zeal, she rejected the true God and led others away from him. She used her power for evil instead of for good. She let nothing stand in the way of her goals, even to the point of violence and murder. Even when God demonstrated his miraculous power at Carmel, Jezebel was not moved. Having devotion and dedication are good things, but we need to be sure that our passions are for the right things; we must choose our goals with wisdom and prayer. And then, we should go about those goals with passion and commitment.

her skull, her feet and her hands. 36They went back and told Jehu, who said, "This is the word of the LORD that he spoke through his servant Elijah the Tishbite: On the plot of ground at Jezreel dogs[t] will devour Jezebel's flesh.[a][u] 37Jezebel's body will be like dung[v] on the ground in the plot at Jezreel, so that no one will be able to say, 'This is Jezebel.'"

Ahab's Family Killed

10 Now there were in Samaria[w] seventy sons[x] of the house of Ahab. So Jehu wrote letters and sent them to Samaria: to the officials of Jezreel,[b][y] to the elders and to the guardians[z] of Ahab's children. He said, 2"You have your master's sons with you and you have chariots and horses, a fortified city and weapons. Now as soon as this letter reaches you, 3choose the best and most worthy of your master's sons and set him on his father's throne. Then fight for your master's house."

4But they were terrified and said, "If two kings could not resist him, how can we?"

5So the palace administrator, the city governor, the elders and the guardians sent this message to Jehu: "We are your servants[a] and we will do anything you say. We will not appoint anyone as king; you do whatever you think best."

6Then Jehu wrote them a second letter, saying, "If you are on my side and will obey me, take the heads of your master's sons and come to me in Jezreel by this time tomorrow."

Now the royal princes, seventy of them, were with the leading men of the city, who were rearing them. 7When the letter arrived, these men took the princes and slaughtered all seventy[b] of them. They put their heads[c] in baskets and sent them to Jehu in Jezreel. 8When the messenger arrived, he told Jehu, "They have brought the heads of the princes."

Then Jehu ordered, "Put them in two piles at the entrance of the city gate until morning."

9The next morning Jehu went out. He stood before all the people and said, "You are innocent. It was I who conspired against my master and killed him, but who killed all these? 10Know, then, that not a word the LORD has spoken against the house of Ahab will fail. The LORD has done what he announced[d] through his servant Elijah."[e] 11So Jehu[f] killed everyone in Jezreel who remained of the house of Ahab, as well as all his chief men, his close friends and his priests, leaving him no survivor.[g]

12Jehu then set out and went toward Samaria. At Beth Eked of the Shepherds, 13he met some relatives of Ahaziah king of Judah and asked, "Who are you?"

They said, "We are relatives of Ahaziah,[h] and we have come down to greet the families of the king and of the queen mother.[i]"

14"Take them alive!" he ordered. So they took them alive and slaughtered them by the well of Beth Eked—forty-two of them. He left no survivor.

15After he left there, he came upon Jehonadab[j] son of Rekab,[k] who was on his way to meet him. Jehu greeted him and said, "Are you in accord with me, as I am with you?"

"I am," Jehonadab answered.

"If so," said Jehu, "give me your hand."[l] So he did, and Jehu helped him up into the chariot. 16Jehu said, "Come with me and see my zeal[m] for the LORD." Then he had him ride along in his chariot.

9:36 [t] Ps 68:23; Jer 15:3 [u] 1Ki 21:23
9:37 [v] Ps 83:10; Isa 5:25; Jer 8:2; 9:22; 16:4; 25:33; Zep 1:17
10:1 [w] 1Ki 13:32 [x] Jdg 8:30 [y] 1Ki 21:1 [z] ver 5
10:5 [a] Jos 9:8; 1Ki 20:4,32
10:7 [b] 1Ki 21:21 [c] 2Sa 4:8
10:10 [d] 2Ki 9:7-10 [e] 1Ki 21:29
10:11 [f] Hos 1:4 [g] ver 14; Job 18:19
10:13 [h] 2Ki 8:24, 29; 2Ch 22:8 [i] 1Ki 2:19
10:15 [j] Jer 35:6, 14-19 [k] 1Ch 2:55; Jer 35:2 [l] Ezr 10:19; Eze 17:18
10:16 [m] Nu 25:13; 1Ki 19:10

[a] *36* See 1 Kings 21:23. [b] *1* Hebrew; some Septuagint manuscripts and Vulgate *of the city*

10:1–8 Jehu's objective is to eliminate all claimants to the throne, described as seventy sons of Ahab. The letters he sends challenge the members of the former regime to contest the rule of Jehu if they are so inclined. After the guardians of the royal heads refuse to install a rival king, Jehu's response appears deliberately ambiguous: "heads" as in a generic term for people, or actual heads? This may be the ruse Jehu uses to claim innocence in the whole affair and imply the massacre is the result of a popular rebellion against Joram. The bloody spectacle at the city gate is an effective tactic of intimidation.

10:9–14 Once Jehu has the situation in Jezreel fully in his control, he proceeds to the capital, Samaria. The narrative does not explain the circumstances of this encounter with the brothers of Ahaziah, but the text may be read to say their intent is to avenge the deaths of the family members of Joram and Jezebel. The massacre indicates Jehu's need to control resistance movements in Judah, as there are undoubtedly loyalties to the house of Ahab there as well.

10:15–17 Jeremiah describes the Rekabites (Jer 35:5–11) as examples of fidelity to their word, in contrast to Judah. Jehonadab joins Jehu in his chariot to Samaria, where Jehu immediately eliminates all the remnants of the house of Ahab.

17 When Jehu came to Samaria, he
killed all who were left there of Ahab's
family;[n] he destroyed them, according
to the word of the LORD spoken to Elijah.

Servants of Baal Killed

18 Then Jehu brought all the people together and said to them, "Ahab
served[o] Baal a little; Jehu will serve him
much. 19 Now summon[p] all the prophets of Baal, all his servants and all his
priests. See that no one is missing, because I am going to hold a great sacrifice for Baal. Anyone who fails to come
will no longer live." But Jehu was acting
deceptively in order to destroy the servants of Baal.
20 Jehu said, "Call an assembly[q] in hon-
or of Baal." So they proclaimed it. 21 Then
he sent word throughout Israel, and all
the servants of Baal came; not one stayed
away. They crowded into the temple of
Baal until it was full from one end to
the other. 22 And Jehu said to the keeper of the wardrobe, "Bring robes for all
the servants of Baal." So he brought out
robes for them.
23 Then Jehu and Jehonadab son of Rekab went into the temple of Baal. Jehu
said to the servants of Baal, "Look around
and see that no one who serves the LORD
is here with you—only servants of Baal."
24 So they went in to make sacrifices and
burnt offerings. Now Jehu had posted
eighty men outside with this warning:
"If one of you lets any of the men I am
placing in your hands escape, it will be
your life for his life."[r]
25 As soon as Jehu had finished making
the burnt offering, he ordered the guards
and officers: "Go in and kill[s] them; let
no one escape."[t] So they cut them down
with the sword. The guards and officers
threw the bodies out and then entered
the inner shrine of the temple of Baal.
26 They brought the sacred stone[u] out of
the temple of Baal and burned it. 27 They
demolished the sacred stone of Baal and
tore down the temple[v] of Baal, and people have used it for a latrine to this day.
28 So Jehu[w] destroyed Baal worship in
Israel. 29 However, he did not turn away
from the sins[x] of Jeroboam son of Nebat, which he had caused Israel to commit—the worship of the golden calves[y]
at Bethel[z] and Dan.
30 The LORD said to Jehu, "Because you
have done well in accomplishing what is
right in my eyes and have done to the
house of Ahab all I had in mind to do,
your descendants will sit on the throne
of Israel to the fourth generation."[a] 31 Yet
Jehu was not careful[b] to keep the law of
the LORD, the God of Israel, with all his
heart. He did not turn away from the
sins[c] of Jeroboam, which he had caused
Israel to commit.

10:17 [n] 2Ki 9:8
10:18 [o] Jdg 2:11; 1Ki 16:31-32
10:19 [p] 1Ki 18:19; 22:6
10:20 [q] Ex 32:5; Joel 1:14
10:24 [r] 1Ki 20:39
10:25 [s] Ex 22:20; 2Ki 11:18 [t] 1Ki 18:40
10:26 [u] 1Ki 14:23
10:27 [v] 1Ki 16:32
10:28 [w] 1Ki 19:17
10:29 [x] 1Ki 12:30 [y] 1Ki 12:28-29 [z] 1Ki 12:32
10:30 [a] ver 35; 2Ki 15:12
10:31 [b] Pr 4:23 [c] 1Ki 12:30

2Ki 10:31 ❖ God wants full-heart commitment. How can we ensure our devotion to God is not half-hearted?

10:18–28 The second objective of Jehu in Samaria is to purge the ministers of the Baal cult and destroy its temple. The whole temple complex is torn to the ground; it is unlikely the whole complex is a "latrine" (v. 27) but is more likely a permanent public dump.

10:29–36 The summary of Jehu's reign gives Jehu credit for the change of religion he has brought about in Samaria. The dynasty of Jehu endures for almost a hundred years—by far the longest in Israel. This achievement is not without compromise or cost. It is twice noted that Jehu fails to rectify the fundamental problem of cultic worship at Dan and Bethel (vv. 29, 31).

✣ **8:16—10:36** Injustice must be addressed, but not in a manner that creates an equal evil in turn. This is what we see in the actions of Jehu as king.

As Aquinas observed, the passion most immediately associated with injustice is anger. Anger is often justified, inspired by love and respect for those persons whose rights are perceived as being violated. Anger recoils at injustice; it strikes out at what is wrong. It strains to change unjust structures that deprive the vulnerable of political, social, economic, or personal rights that human dignity demands. A good dose of anger can be helpful; anger is creative energy that can be used for positive action. It is like a fire; in a controlled environment, it is a powerful force for good, but out of control it can do irreparable damage. Anger can lash out in harsh words, biting insults, violence, riots, and even war.

Jehu's brutal actions are designed to achieve his personal ambitions as a military leader under the guise of terminating the injustices of the previous regime. Though he was anointed by God's prophet and acted on God's behalf, the prophet Hosea condemns Jehu's methods as bringing inevitable judgment (Hos 1:4). It's a poignant reminder that as we work for good and justice in our modern world, we must be careful to understand all the repercussions of our actions.

[32]In those days the LORD began to reduce[d] the size of Israel. Hazael[e] overpowered the Israelites throughout their territory [33]east of the Jordan in all the land of Gilead (the region of Gad, Reuben and Manasseh), from Aroer[f] by the Arnon Gorge through Gilead to Bashan. [34]As for the other events of Jehu's reign, all he did, and all his achievements, are they not written in the book of the annals[g] of the kings of Israel?

[35]Jehu rested with his ancestors and was buried in Samaria. And Jehoahaz his son succeeded him as king. [36]The time that Jehu reigned over Israel in Samaria was twenty-eight years.

Athaliah and Joash

11:1–21pp // 2Ch 22:10—23:21

11 When Athaliah[h] the mother of Ahaziah saw that her son was dead, she proceeded to destroy the whole royal family. [2]But Jehosheba, the daughter of King Jehoram[a] and sister of Ahaziah, took Joash[i] son of Ahaziah and stole him away from among the royal princes, who were about to be murdered. She put him and his nurse in a bedroom to hide him from Athaliah; so he was not killed.[j] [3]He remained hidden with his nurse at the temple of the LORD for six years while Athaliah ruled the land.

[4]In the seventh year Jehoiada sent for the commanders of units of a hundred, the Carites[k] and the guards and had them brought to him at the temple of the LORD. He made a covenant with them and put them under oath at the temple of the LORD. Then he showed them the king's son. [5]He commanded them, saying, "This is what you are to do: You who are in the three companies that are going on duty on the Sabbath[l] — a third of you guarding the royal palace,[m] [6]a third at the Sur Gate, and a third at the gate

10:32 [d]2Ki 13:25 [e]1Ki 19:17; 2Ki 8:12
10:33 [f]Nu 32:34; Dt 2:36; Jdg 11:26; Isa 17:2
10:34 [g]1Ki 15:31
11:1 [h]2Ki 8:18
11:2 [i]ver 21; 2Ki 12:1 [j]Jdg 9:5
11:4 [k]ver 19
11:5 [l]1Ch 9:25 [m]1Ki 14:27

2Ki 11:2 ❖ Where have we seen God's dramatic protection of his children? What does this tell us about God's care?

[a] 2 Hebrew *Joram,* a variant of *Jehoram*

11:1-3 Athaliah's conduct is consistent with that of Jehoram, who killed all the other sons of Jehoshaphat when he came to the throne (2Ch 21:4). Athaliah may have prevented Jehu from entering Judah to reunite Judah and Israel. She is able to retain control of the army and retain the independence of Judah for six years. However, one young man escapes Athaliah's notice.

11:4-11 Jehoiada summons all the temple guards, who take their stations with their weapons as instructed. The focus of activity shifts to anointing the young king at the temple on this extraordinary Sabbath day.

PEOPLE TO KNOW // ATHALIAH

2 KINGS 11:1-20: Athaliah was the only queen to reign in Judah on David's throne. She was the daughter of King Ahab and Queen Jezebel of Israel—her parents were known for their wickedness. Athaliah became part of the kingdom of Judah when she married King Jehoram (2Ki 8:18). After Jehoram's death, Athaliah's son Ahaziah became king. He reigned for only one year, however, before his death at the hands of Jehu, king of Israel.

Following the death of her son, Athaliah took the throne of Judah herself and ruled as monarch. She tried to kill off the whole royal family of David in order to eliminate any challengers to the throne. Yet Joash, son of Ahaziah, was saved by Jehosheba, one of the deceased king's sisters. Joash was raised in secret at the temple for six years while Athaliah ruled Judah (2Ki 11:1-3).

After those six years, the priest Jehoiada led Judah's army commanders to stage a rebellion. They surrounded the young Joash with military protection, placed the crown on his head, and proclaimed him king. When Athaliah heard the noise and saw the young king, she cried out, "Treason! Treason!" (2Ki 11:14). Jehoiada ordered the army commanders to kill her. The people rejoiced when the wicked queen was killed, and Joash became Judah's youngest king at the age of seven.

APPLICATION ✣ Athaliah came from a wicked family, and she carried on their wicked ways. Instead of following God's commands and making new and better choices, she sought power and dominion of the nation. The people of Judah suffered during her reign. We don't know why God allows evil people to ascend to positions of power. Yet we can find comfort in the fact that God will ultimately bring them to justice.

behind the guard, who take turns guarding the temple— 7and you who are in
the other two companies that normally
go off Sabbath duty are all to guard the
temple for the king. 8Station yourselves
around the king, each of you with weapon in hand. Anyone who approaches your
ranks[a] is to be put to death. Stay close to
the king wherever he goes."
9The commanders of units of a hundred did just as Jehoiada the priest ordered. Each one took his men—those
who were going on duty on the Sabbath
and those who were going off duty—and
came to Jehoiada the priest. 10Then he
gave the commanders the spears and
shields[n] that had belonged to King David and that were in the temple of the
LORD. 11The guards, each with weapon in
hand, stationed themselves around the
king—near the altar and the temple,
from the south side to the north side of
the temple.
12Jehoiada brought out the king's son
and put the crown on him; he presented
him with a copy of the covenant[o] and
proclaimed him king. They anointed[p]
him, and the people clapped their hands[q]
and shouted, "Long live the king!"[r]
13When Athaliah heard the noise made
by the guards and the people, she went
to the people at the temple of the LORD.
14She looked and there was the king,
standing by the pillar,[s] as the custom
was. The officers and the trumpeters
were beside the king, and all the people
of the land were rejoicing and blowing
trumpets.[t] Then Athaliah tore[u] her robes
and called out, "Treason! Treason!"[v]
15Jehoiada the priest ordered the commanders of units of a hundred, who were
in charge of the troops: "Bring her out
between the ranks[b] and put to the sword
anyone who follows her." For the priest
had said, "She must not be put to death
in the temple[w] of the LORD." 16So they
seized her as she reached the place where
the horses enter[x] the palace grounds, and
there she was put to death.[y]
17Jehoiada then made a covenant[z] between the LORD and the king and people
that they would be the LORD's people.
He also made a covenant between the
king and the people.[a] 18All the people of
the land went to the temple[b] of Baal and
tore it down. They smashed[c] the altars
and idols to pieces and killed Mattan the
priest[d] of Baal in front of the altars.
Then Jehoiada the priest posted
guards at the temple of the LORD. 19He
took with him the commanders of hundreds, the Carites,[e] the guards and all the
people of the land, and together they
brought the king down from the temple of the LORD and went into the palace, entering by way of the gate of the
guards. The king then took his place on
the royal throne. 20All the people of the

11:10 [n] 2Sa 8:7; 1Ch 18:7
11:12 [o] Ex 25:16; 2Ki 23:3 [p] 1Sa 9:16; 1Ki 1:39 [q] Ps 47:1; 98:8; Isa 55:12 [r] 1Sa 10:24
11:14 [s] 1Ki 7:15; 2Ki 23:3; 2Ch 34:31 [t] 1Ki 1:39 [u] Ge 37:29 [v] 2Ki 9:23
11:15 [w] 1Ki 2:30
11:16 [x] Ne 3:28; Jer 31:40 [y] Ge 4:14
11:17 [z] Ex 24:8; 2Sa 5:3; 2Ch 15:12; 23:3; 29:10; 34:31; Ezr 10:3 [a] 2Ki 23:3; Jer 34:8
11:18 [b] 1Ki 16:32 [c] Dt 12:3 [d] 1Ki 18:40; 2Ki 10:25; 23:20
11:19 [e] ver 4

[a] 8 *Or approaches the precincts* [b] 15 *Or out from the precincts*

11:12 Once the officers and guards are stationed, the king is brought out for the ceremony. The anointing with oil, the blowing of the horns, and the shouts of the people are reminiscent of the coronation of Solomon (1Ki 1:39–40) or Jehu (2Ki 9:13). The king was required to keep with him a testimony of the covenant as a constant reminder that he must rule according to divine order (Dt 17:18–19).

11:13–21 When Athaliah sees the king, she recognizes immediately that her time as queen is over; she is seized by force and taken to the entrance of the Horse Gate where she is summarily executed, allowing no time for her supporters to raise resistance to the new king.

11:17–18 The anointing of a new king requires renewal of the covenant. This is the first occasion that the making of a covenant is mentioned during the time of the monarchy.

Both the Chronicler (2Ch 23:16, 18) and Josephus emphasize the restoration of the Davidic line. This is critical, since the "lamp" of David's legacy has come to near extinction. The renewal of the Davidic dynasty includes the commitment of the king to lead the people according to the Book of the Covenant.

The leaders then follow the pattern of Jehu in the north by purging the land of Baal influence. This is not the end of Baal cult in Jerusalem, however; Hezekiah again removes altars and shrines of Canaanite religion (18:4), as does Josiah following the days of Manasseh (23:4). But a new beginning is established with Joash.

11:19–20 The restoration of a true Davidic king and the death of Athaliah bring an end to the domination of the Baal cult in Judah.

11:1–20 The church in this world may feel threatened, even as the temple seemed to be threatened in the time of Athaliah. At the confession at Caesarea Philippi, Jesus assures Peter that he is the rock on which the church will be built, and the "gates of Hades" will not prevail against it (Mt 16:13–18). The light of the church is as secure as the lamp of David (v. 19); indeed, it is a lamp shining in its own right. Matthew's Gospel is the account of Jesus Christ, Son of David, Son of Abraham (Mt 1:1). Both the blessing of Abraham and the promise to David find their fulfillment in the person of Christ.

land rejoiced,[f] and the city was calm, because Athaliah had been slain with the
sword at the palace.
21 Joash[a] was seven years old when he
began to reign.[b]

Joash Repairs the Temple

12:1–21pp // 2Ch 24:1–14; 24:23–27

12 [c] In the seventh year of Jehu, Joash[dg] became king, and he reigned
in Jerusalem forty years. His mother's
name was Zibiah; she was from Beersheba. 2 Joash did what was right in the eyes
of the LORD all the years Jehoiada the
priest instructed him. 3 The high places,[h]
however, were not removed; the people
continued to offer sacrifices and burn
incense there.
4 Joash said to the priests, "Collect[i] all
the money that is brought as sacred offerings[j] to the temple of the LORD — the
money collected in the census,[k] the money received from personal vows and the
money brought voluntarily[l] to the temple. 5 Let every priest receive the money
from one of the treasurers, then use it
to repair whatever damage is found in
the temple."
6 But by the twenty-third year of King
Joash the priests still had not repaired
the temple. 7 Therefore King Joash summoned Jehoiada the priest and the other priests and asked them, "Why aren't
you repairing the damage done to the
temple? Take no more money from your
treasurers, but hand it over for repairing the temple." 8 The priests agreed that
they would not collect any more money
from the people and that they would not
repair the temple themselves.
9 Jehoiada the priest took a chest and
bored a hole in its lid. He placed it beside
the altar, on the right side as one enters
the temple of the LORD. The priests who
guarded the entrance[m] put into the chest
all the money[n] that was brought to the
temple of the LORD. 10 Whenever they saw
that there was a large amount of money
in the chest, the royal secretary[o] and the
high priest came, counted the money
that had been brought into the temple
of the LORD and put it into bags. 11 When
the amount had been determined, they
gave the money to the men appointed to
supervise the work on the temple. With
it they paid those who worked on the
temple of the LORD — the carpenters and
builders, 12 the masons and stonecutters.[p]
They purchased timber and blocks of
dressed stone for the repair of the temple of the LORD, and met all the other
expenses of restoring the temple.
13 The money brought into the temple was not spent for making silver basins, wick trimmers, sprinkling bowls,
trumpets or any other articles of gold[q]
or silver for the temple of the LORD; 14 it
was paid to the workers, who used it to
repair the temple. 15 They did not require
an accounting from those to whom they
gave the money to pay the workers, because they acted with complete honesty.[r]
16 The money from the guilt offerings[s]
and sin offerings[et] was not brought into
the temple of the LORD; it belonged[u] to
the priests.
17 About this time Hazael[v] king of
Aram went up and attacked Gath and
captured it. Then he turned to attack

11:20 [f] Pr 11:10; 28:12; 29:2
12:1 [g] 2Ki 11:2
12:3 [h] 1Ki 3:3; 2Ki 14:4; 15:35; 18:4
12:4 [i] 2Ki 22:4 [j] Ex 35:5 [k] Ex 30:12 [l] Ex 35:29; 1Ch 29:3-9
12:9 [m] Jer 35:4 [n] 2Ch 24:8; Mk 12:41; Lk 21:1
12:10 [o] 2Sa 8:17
12:12 [p] 2Ki 22:5-6
12:13 [q] 1Ki 7:48-51; 2Ch 24:14
12:15 [r] 2Ki 22:7; 1Co 4:2
12:16 [s] Lev 5:14-19; Nu 18:9 [t] Lev 4:1-35 [u] Lev 7:7
12:17 [v] 2Ki 8:12

2Ki 12:5 ❖ What repair work might need to happen in our own faith (see 1Pe 2:5)?

[a] *21* Hebrew *Jehoash*, a variant of *Joash* [b] *21* In Hebrew texts this verse (11:21) is numbered 12:1. [c] In Hebrew texts 12:1-21 is numbered 12:2-22. [d] *1* Hebrew *Jehoash*, a variant of *Joash*; also in verses 2, 4, 6, 7 and 18 [e] *16* Or *purification offerings*

The threat of another Athaliah determined to eliminate the worship of God will continue to arise in different places and at different times. The church must not fear—not even at the prospect of great suffering, as has happened so frequently. The "lamp" of David, embodied in the church that Jesus himself established, will not be snuffed out.

11:21—12:21 Jehoiada has taught the king well and apparently has considerable influence early in his reign, even choosing his wives (2 Chr 24:3). The priestly training of Joash influences him to take the initiative in temple restoration, with Jehoiada playing a minor role.

12:4–12 The temple restoration under Joash refers to two sources of income for repair: the funds brought to the temple and the money in the possession of the priests (v. 5), which never comes to the temple (v. 16).

12:13–16 The refurbishing of the temple artifacts used in worship is temporarily suspended to concentrate on the building itself.

12:17–21 Joash successfully buys off Hazael with the sacred vessels and temple treasures. Hazael does not seriously consider a conquest of Judah;

Jerusalem. 18But Joash king of Judah took all the sacred objects dedicated by his predecessors — Jehoshaphat, Jehoram and Ahaziah, the kings of Judah — and the gifts he himself had dedicated and all the gold found in the treasuries of the temple of the LORD and of the royal palace, and he sent[w] them to Hazael king of Aram, who then withdrew[x] from Jerusalem.

19As for the other events of the reign of Joash, and all he did, are they not written in the book of the annals of the kings of Judah? 20His officials[y] conspired against him and assassinated[z] him at Beth Millo,[a] on the road down to Silla. 21The officials who murdered him were Jozabad son of Shimeath and Jehozabad son of Shomer. He died and was buried with his ancestors in the City of David. And Amaziah his son succeeded him as king.

Jehoahaz King of Israel

13 In the twenty-third year of Joash son of Ahaziah king of Judah, Jehoahaz son of Jehu became king of Israel in Samaria, and he reigned seventeen years. 2He did evil[b] in the eyes of the LORD by following the sins of Jeroboam son of Nebat, which he had caused Israel to commit, and he did not turn away from them. 3So the LORD's anger[c] burned against Israel, and for a long time he kept them under the power[d] of Hazael king of Aram and Ben-Hadad[e] his son.

12:18 [w]1Ki 15:18; 2Ch 21:16-17 [x]1Ki 15:21
12:20 [y]2Ki 14:5 [z]2Ch 24:25 [a]Jdg 9:6
13:2 [b]1Ki 12:26-33
13:3 [c]Dt 31:17; Jdg 2:14 [d]1Ki 8:12; 12:17; 19:17 [e]ver 24
13:4 [f]Dt 4:29; Ps 78:34 [g]Ex 3:7; Dt 26:7 [h]2Ki 14:26
13:5 [i]ver 25; 2Ki 14:25,27
13:6 [j]1Ki 12:30 [k]1Ki 16:33
13:7 [l]2Ki 10:32-33 [m]2Sa 22:43

2Ki 13:4-5 ❖ How can we better share and demonstrate God's heart for people who are oppressed? Who are those around us that we can bless?

4Then Jehoahaz sought[f] the LORD's favor, and the LORD listened to him, for he saw[g] how severely the king of Aram was oppressing[h] Israel. 5The LORD provided a deliverer[i] for Israel, and they escaped from the power of Aram. So the Israelites lived in their own homes as they had before. 6But they did not turn away from the sins[j] of the house of Jeroboam, which he had caused Israel to commit; they continued in them. Also, the Asherah pole[a][k] remained standing in Samaria.

7Nothing had been left[l] of the army of Jehoahaz except fifty horsemen, ten chariots and ten thousand foot soldiers, for the king of Aram had destroyed the rest and made them like the dust[m] at threshing time.

8As for the other events of the reign of Jehoahaz, all he did and his achievements, are they not written in the book of the annals of the kings of Israel? 9Jehoahaz rested with his ancestors and was buried in Samaria. And Jehoash[b] his son succeeded him as king.

[a] 6 That is, a wooden symbol of the goddess Asherah; here and elsewhere in 2 Kings
[b] 9 Hebrew *Joash*, a variant of *Jehoash*; also in verses 12-14 and 25

---

his goal is to control Joash, providing himself taxation revenues in the process. His main goal is to control trade routes along the coast as he had in the Transjordan.

Chronicles adds to the story of Joash's reign by describing dissension within the priesthood that results in Joash's killing Zechariah, son of Jehoiada (2Ch 24:20–21). No explanation is given for the assassination of Joash, but his capitulation to Hazael and stripping the temple likely bring about political discontent.

✣ **11:21—12:21** The church is best served when it is not supported by the state beyond the right to be protected by the state. Often the church today faces the hostility of the state; this should not be surprising. The state represents the world, the powers of this age. Jesus warns his followers to expect the hostility of the world (Jn 15:18–20). The church cannot expect understanding from the world; it can only hope for tolerance and equal treatment with all other groups in society.

The tension between the secular and the sacred today remains as difficult as the cooperation of royalty and priesthood under the covenant in OT. The story of Joash is a warning of the dangers that can lead to self-destructive conflict. Avenues of compromise will be found on many issues if the church is to live in harmony with the state and if Christians are to participate in secular power with ethical integrity. And yet believers must do so to influence our society for Christ.

13:1–3 The purge executed by Jehu decimated the power of Israel; that allowed for Aramean expansion in the Transjordan (10:32–33).

13:4–6 Hazael and his successor Ben-Hadad III are able to oppress Jehoahaz king of Israel during most of his seventeen-year reign. Even so, a prophetic word declares that Yahweh will send deliverance to Israel, which enables the dynasty to survive.

13:7–9 The ten thousand foot soldiers of Jehoahaz (v. 7) are a marked contrast to the ten chariots left to his forces; a large number of infantry does not provide resistance to the speed of chariots. Aram crushes Israel's military.

Jehoash King of Israel

10 In the thirty-seventh year of Joash
king of Judah, Jehoash son of Jehoahaz
became king of Israel in Samaria, and he
reigned sixteen years. 11 He did evil in the
eyes of the LORD and did not turn away
from any of the sins of Jeroboam son
of Nebat, which he had caused Israel to
commit; he continued in them.

12 As for the other events of the reign
of Jehoash, all he did and his achievements, including his war against Amaziah[n] king of Judah, are they not written
in the book of the annals[o] of the kings
of Israel? 13 Jehoash rested with his ancestors, and Jeroboam[p] succeeded him
on the throne. Jehoash was buried in
Samaria with the kings of Israel.

14 Now Elisha had been suffering from
the illness from which he died. Jehoash
king of Israel went down to see him and
wept over him. "My father! My father!"
he cried. "The chariots[q] and horsemen
of Israel!"

15 Elisha said, "Get a bow and some arrows,"[r] and he did so. 16 "Take the bow
in your hands," he said to the king of
Israel. When he had taken it, Elisha put
his hands on the king's hands.

17 "Open the east window," he said, and
he opened it. "Shoot!"[s] Elisha said, and
he shot. "The LORD's arrow of victory,
the arrow of victory over Aram!" Elisha
declared. "You will completely destroy
the Arameans at Aphek."[t]

18 Then he said, "Take the arrows," and
the king took them. Elisha told him,
"Strike the ground." He struck it three
times and stopped. 19 The man of God was
angry with him and said, "You should
have struck the ground five or six times;
then you would have defeated Aram and
completely destroyed it. But now you will
defeat it only three times."[u]

20 Elisha died and was buried.

Now Moabite raiders[v] used to enter the
country every spring. 21 Once while some
Israelites were burying a man, suddenly
they saw a band of raiders; so they threw
the man's body into Elisha's tomb. When
the body touched Elisha's bones, the man
came to life[w] and stood up on his feet.

22 Hazael king of Aram oppressed[x] Israel throughout the reign of Jehoahaz.
23 But the LORD was gracious to them and
had compassion and showed concern
for them because of his covenant[y] with
Abraham, Isaac and Jacob. To this day he
has been unwilling to destroy[z] them or
banish them from his presence.[a]

24 Hazael king of Aram died, and Ben-
Hadad[b] his son succeeded him as king.
25 Then Jehoash son of Jehoahaz recap-
tured from Ben-Hadad son of Hazael the
towns he had taken in battle from his
father Jehoahaz. Three times[c] Jehoash
defeated him, and so he recovered[d] the
Israelite towns.

Amaziah King of Judah

14:1–7pp // 2Ch 25:1–4,11–12
14:8–22pp // 2Ch 25:17—26:2

14 In the second year of Jehoash[a] son
of Jehoahaz king of Israel, Amaziah son of Joash king of Judah began
to reign. 2 He was twenty-five years old

[a] *1* Hebrew *Joash,* a variant of *Jehoash;* also in verses 13, 23 and 27

13:12 [n] 2Ki 14:15 [o] 1Ki 15:31
13:13 [p] 2Ki 14:23; Hos 1:1
13:14 [q] 2Ki 2:12
13:15 [r] 1Sa 20:20
13:17 [s] Jos 8:18 [t] 1Ki 20:26
13:19 [u] ver 25
13:20 [v] 2Ki 3:7; 24:2
13:21 [w] Mt 27:52
13:22 [x] 1Ki 19:17; 2Ki 8:12
13:23 [y] Ge 13:16-17; Ex 2:24 [z] Dt 29:20 [a] Ex 33:15; 2Ki 14:27; 17:18; 24:3,20
13:24 [b] ver 3
13:25 [c] ver 18,19 [d] 2Ki 10:32

13:10–13 The significant events of the reign of Jehoash are only mentioned within the summary of his reign (see also vv. 22–25 and 14:8–14). The fortunes of Israel begin to rise significantly during the reign of Jehoash until it becomes a formidable and wealthy country under his son, Jeroboam II.
13:14 Jehoash visits Elisha to pay his respects, approaching him in the same way Elisha did his master, Elijah (cf. 2:12). Elisha, unlike Elijah, has had active military leadership in the conflicts of Israel against the Arameans (cf. 3:11–19; 6:13–17); the words of Jehoash acknowledge that role and place Elisha on a prophetic par with Elijah.
13:15–19 Elisha's last action is to give a message of promise to the dynasty of Jehu, not unlike the final blessing of other leaders. The significance of Elisha's instruction is like that of the prophet Ahijah in the call of Jeroboam (1Ki 11:29–32). They are communicative and interactive, and the message that accompanies it is impacted by the action itself.
13:20–21 The legacy of Elisha is last of all remembered in a story about his burial. His prophetic anointing is reiterated after his death, as contact with his bones leads to life-giving power; this signifies the life-giving power of the prophet for the nation as he declared the divine will.
13:22–25 The aggression of Hazael impacted the greater part of the reign of Jehoahaz, whose seventeen-year rule extended into the eighth century BC. Again the covenant with the patriarchs is mentioned in this context (cf. Dt 6:10–12).
14:1–4 Amaziah's succession to the throne is not without conflict. His father Joash was assassinated in a political plot (12:21); Amaziah does not deal with the assassins until he has secured his place on the throne (14:5). Though Amaziah is said to do what is right, the ominous note of his rule is sounded in the observation that his reign is not like that of David but rather like that of his father Joash (vv. 3–4). Amaziah's unsuccessful war against Jehoash demonstrates the dominance of Israel (vv. 8–12).

when he became king, and he reigned in Jerusalem twenty-nine years. His mother's name was Jehoaddan; she was from Jerusalem. 3He did what was right in the eyes of the LORD, but not as his father David had done. In everything he followed the example of his father Joash. 4The high places,[e] however, were not removed; the people continued to offer sacrifices and burn incense there.

5After the kingdom was firmly in his grasp, he executed[f] the officials[g] who had murdered his father the king. 6Yet he did not put the children of the assassins to death, in accordance with what is written in the Book of the Law[h] of Moses where the LORD commanded: "Parents are not to be put to death for their children, nor children put to death for their parents; each will die for their own sin."[a][i]

7He was the one who defeated ten thousand Edomites in the Valley of Salt[j] and captured Sela[k] in battle, calling it Joktheel, the name it has to this day.

8Then Amaziah sent messengers to Jehoash son of Jehoahaz, the son of Jehu, king of Israel, with the challenge: "Come, let us face each other in battle."

9But Jehoash king of Israel replied to Amaziah king of Judah: "A thistle[l] in Lebanon sent a message to a cedar in Lebanon, 'Give your daughter to my son in marriage.' Then a wild beast in Lebanon came along and trampled the thistle underfoot. 10You have indeed defeated Edom and now you are arrogant.[m] Glory in your victory, but stay at home! Why ask for trouble and cause your own downfall and that of Judah also?"

11Amaziah, however, would not listen, so Jehoash king of Israel attacked. He and Amaziah king of Judah faced each other at Beth Shemesh[n] in Judah. 12Judah was routed by Israel, and every man fled to his home.[o] 13Jehoash king of Israel captured Amaziah king of Judah, the son of Joash, the son of Ahaziah, at Beth Shemesh. Then Jehoash went to Jerusalem and broke down the wall[p] of Jerusalem from the Ephraim Gate[q] to the Corner Gate[r]—a section about four hundred cubits long.[b] 14He took all the gold and silver and all the articles found in the temple of the LORD and in the treasuries of the royal palace. He also took hostages and returned to Samaria.

15As for the other events of the reign of Jehoash, what he did and his achievements, including his war[s] against Amaziah king of Judah, are they not written in the book of the annals of the kings of Israel? 16Jehoash rested with his ancestors and was buried in Samaria with the kings of Israel. And Jeroboam his son succeeded him as king.

17Amaziah son of Joash king of Judah lived for fifteen years after the death of Jehoash son of Jehoahaz king of Israel. 18As for the other events of Amaziah's reign, are they not written in the book of the annals of the kings of Judah?

19They conspired[t] against him in Jerusalem, and he fled to Lachish,[u] but they sent men after him to Lachish and

14:4 [e] 2Ki 12:3; 16:4
14:5 [f] 2Ki 21:24 [g] 2Ki 12:20
14:6 [h] Dt 28:61 [i] Nu 26:11; Job 21:20; Jer 31:30; 44:3; Eze 18:4,20
14:7 [j] 2Sa 8:13; 2Ch 25:11 [k] Jdg 1:36
14:9 [l] Jdg 9:8-15
14:10 [m] Dt 8:14; 2Ch 26:16; 32:25
14:11 [n] Jos 15:10
14:12 [o] 2Sa 18:17
14:13 [p] 1Ki 3:1; 2Ch 33:14; 36:19; Jer 39:2 [q] Ne 8:16; 12:39 [r] 2Ch 25:23; Jer 31:38; Zec 14:10
14:15 [s] 2Ki 13:12
14:19 [t] 2Ki 12:20 [u] Jos 10:3; 2Ki 18:14,17

2Ki 14:3 ❖ How has our faith been shaped by our parents? In what ways did they give us a positive or negative model of faith?

[a] 6 Deut. 24:16 [b] 13 That is, about 600 feet or about 180 meters

14:5–6 Special care is taken to point out that Amaziah follows the covenant regulation in carrying out the executions of those who had killed his father (Dt 24:16).

14:7 The circumstances of the battle with Edom are not specified, though Chronicles indicates that Amaziah initiates the attack (2Ch 25:11).

14:8–11 If Amaziah has allied with Jehoash of Israel in his efforts to gain control of lucrative trade routes, the cooperation ends in sharp disagreement. Amaziah seriously overestimates his military capability after his defeat of Edom. Jehoash is not intimidated; his reply is laced with scorn.

14:12–14 In a decisive victory, Jehoash takes Amaziah prisoner, then marches unhindered to Jerusalem, breaks down part of its wall, and plunders it. The plundering of the temple is reminiscent of the attack of Hazael against Joash (12:17–18); the hostages are likely nobility or members of the royal family, kept under guard or held for ransom.

14:15–22 Amaziah's death and the succession of Azariah are unexpected after the closing notice of his reign (v. 18). The narrative sequence may be explained by the unusual circumstances of his succession. After Amaziah's death and burial Judah installs Azariah as king in his place (v. 21). A crown prince normally succeeds at the death of his father, but the statement indicates that Azariah begins to rule while his father is still alive and Amaziah continues to be king, though only in a purely formal sense. The instability of his position is indicated by the measures Amaziah takes to secure his rule (v. 5) and by the fact that he is driven into exile and executed (v. 19).

killed him there. 20He was brought back
by horse[v] and was buried in Jerusalem
with his ancestors, in the City of David.
21Then all the people of Judah took
Azariah,[aw] who was sixteen years old,
and made him king in place of his father
Amaziah. 22He was the one who rebuilt
Elath[x] and restored it to Judah after Amaziah rested with his ancestors.

Jeroboam II King of Israel

23In the fifteenth year of Amaziah son
of Joash king of Judah, Jeroboam[y] son
of Jehoash king of Israel became king in
Samaria, and he reigned forty-one years.
24He did evil in the eyes of the LORD and
did not turn away from any of the sins
of Jeroboam son of Nebat, which he had
caused Israel to commit.[z] 25He was the
one who restored the boundaries of Israel from Lebo Hamath[a] to the Dead Sea,[bb]
in accordance with the word of the LORD,
the God of Israel, spoken through his servant Jonah[c] son of Amittai, the prophet
from Gath Hepher.
26The LORD had seen how bitterly everyone in Israel, whether slave or free,[d]
was suffering;[ce] there was no one to help
them.[f] 27And since the LORD had not said
he would blot out[g] the name of Israel
from under heaven, he saved[h] them by
the hand of Jeroboam son of Jehoash.
28As for the other events of Jeroboam's reign, all he did, and his military
achievements, including how he recovered for Israel both Damascus[i] and Hamath,[j] which had belonged to Judah, are
they not written in the book of the annals[k] of the kings of Israel? 29Jeroboam
rested with his ancestors, the kings of
Israel. And Zechariah his son succeeded
him as king.

Azariah King of Judah

15:1–7pp // 2Ch 26:3–4,21–23

15 In the twenty-seventh year of Jeroboam king of Israel, Azariah[dl] son
of Amaziah king of Judah began to reign.
2He was sixteen years old when he became king, and he reigned in Jerusalem
fifty-two years. His mother's name was
Jekoliah; she was from Jerusalem. 3He
did what was right in the eyes of the
LORD, just as his father Amaziah had
done. 4The high places, however, were
not removed; the people continued to
offer sacrifices and burn incense there.
5The LORD afflicted[m] the king with leprosy[e] until the day he died, and he lived
in a separate house.[fn] Jotham[o] the king's
son had charge of the palace[p] and governed the people of the land.

[a] *21* Also called *Uzziah* [b] *25* Hebrew *the Sea of the Arabah* [c] *26* Or *Israel was suffering. They were without a ruler or leader, and* [d] *1* Also called *Uzziah*; also in verses 6, 7, 8, 17, 23 and 27 [e] *5* The Hebrew for *leprosy* was used for various diseases affecting the skin. [f] *5* Or *in a house where he was relieved of responsibilities*

14:20 [v] 2Ki 9:28
14:21 [w] 2Ki 15:1; 2Ch 26:23
14:22 [x] 1Ki 9:26; 2Ki 16:6
14:23 [y] 2Ki 13:13
14:24 [z] 1Ki 15:30
14:25 [a] Nu 13:21; 1Ki 8:65 [b] Dt 3:17 [c] Jnh 1:1; Mt 12:39
14:26 [d] Dt 32:36 [e] 2Ki 13:4 [f] Ps 18:41; 22:11; 72:12; 107:12; Isa 63:5; La 1:7
14:27 [g] 2Ki 13:23 [h] Jdg 6:14
14:28 [i] 2Sa 8:5; 1Ki 11:24 [j] 2Ch 8:3 [k] 1Ki 15:31
15:1 [l] ver 32; 2Ki 14:21
15:5 [m] Ge 12:17 [n] Lev 13:46 [o] 2Ch 27:1 [p] Ge 41:40

14:23–29 Judah's political power is eclipsed by Israel under the reign of Jeroboam, the successor to Jehoash. The fortunes of the Jehu dynasty rise to impressive heights during the forty-one-year reign of Jeroboam. His victories reestablish the territorial limits of the reign of Solomon (v. 25; cf. 1Ki 5:1; 8:65).

With the death of Jehoash and the rule of Azariah in Judah, it seems the royal houses of Samaria and Israel come to a new level of cooperation. Vast areas of productive agricultural land, from the prairies of Bashan (Am 4:1) to the plantations of Carmel, produce abundant harvests of grain, wine, and oil (Hos 7:14). The Transjordan caravan routes, as well as the Jezreel Valley and the Sharon Plain, are under Israelite control.

13:1–14:29 The religious leaders of Israel prioritize immediate and lavish material gains; these are achieved with disregard to the injury done to the powerless and will bring death to the nation in just one generation.

The prophetic warnings of judgment against the oppressive rich continue for the modern church. The safety of the church depends on her having no association with this Babylon, the great representative of wealth and oppression in the world, and its sins (Rev 18:2–3, 4–8). Individual Christians and congregations are by necessity a part of this admonition. They must be vigilant in using wealth to seek first the kingdom of God. This is the only way to dissociate from Babylon, to avoid participating in her sins (Rev 18:4). Seeking first God's kingdom in the wealth of this world is a daily discipline, a continuous and conscious choice to use money and resources to further the values of the kingdom of God and to bring others into that kingdom. The choices are not easy; however, we must always seek to use our influence to bring justice and Good News to the weak and the needy.

15:1–7 Outside of Kings, Azariah is known by the name Uzziah (2Ch 26–27; Isa 1:1; 6:1). Though Azariah has a long and prosperous reign, his achievements are left unrecorded in the OT. The single detail of his life for which he is remembered is that he has leprosy (15:5) and is unable to perform his administrative and official duties. Jotham is appointed to carry out the responsibilities of the king in place of his father.

6 As for the other events of Azariah's reign, and all he did, are they not written in the book of the annals of the kings of Judah? 7 Azariah rested[q] with his ancestors and was buried near them in the City of David. And Jotham[r] his son succeeded him as king.

Zechariah King of Israel

8 In the thirty-eighth year of Azariah king of Judah, Zechariah son of Jeroboam became king of Israel in Samaria, and he reigned six months. 9 He did evil[s] in the eyes of the LORD, as his predecessors had done. He did not turn away from the sins of Jeroboam son of Nebat, which he had caused Israel to commit.

10 Shallum son of Jabesh conspired against Zechariah. He attacked him in front of the people,[a] assassinated[t] him and succeeded him as king. 11 The other events of Zechariah's reign are written in the book of the annals[u] of the kings of Israel. 12 So the word of the LORD spoken to Jehu was fulfilled:[v] "Your descendants will sit on the throne of Israel to the fourth generation."[b]

Shallum King of Israel

13 Shallum son of Jabesh became king in the thirty-ninth year of Uzziah king of Judah, and he reigned in Samaria[w] one month. 14 Then Menahem son of Gadi went from Tirzah[x] up to Samaria. He attacked Shallum son of Jabesh in Samaria, assassinated[y] him and succeeded him as king.

15 The other events of Shallum's reign, and the conspiracy he led, are written in the book of the annals[z] of the kings of Israel.

16 At that time Menahem, starting out from Tirzah, attacked Tiphsah[a] and everyone in the city and its vicinity, because they refused to open[b] their gates. He sacked Tiphsah and ripped open all the pregnant women.

15:7 [q] Isa 6:1; 14:28 [r] ver 5
15:9 [s] 1Ki 15:26
15:10 [t] 2Ki 12:20
15:11 [u] 1Ki 15:31
15:12 [v] 2Ki 10:30
15:13 [w] ver 1, 8
15:14 [x] 1Ki 14:17 [y] 2Ki 12:20
15:15 [z] 1Ki 15:31
15:16 [a] 1Ki 4:24 [b] 2Ki 8:12; Hos 13:16

2Ki 15:18–20 ❖ Sin always makes us pay a price. How have we experienced this in our life and seen it in the lives of those around us?

Menahem King of Israel

17 In the thirty-ninth year of Azariah king of Judah, Menahem son of Gadi became king of Israel, and he reigned in Samaria ten years. 18 He did evil in the eyes of the LORD. During his entire reign he did not turn away from the sins of Jeroboam son of Nebat, which he had caused Israel to commit.

19 Then Pul[c][c] king of Assyria invaded the land, and Menahem gave him a thousand talents[d] of silver to gain his support and strengthen his own hold on the kingdom. 20 Menahem exacted this money from Israel. Every wealthy person had to contribute fifty shekels[e] of silver to be given to the king of Assyria. So the king of Assyria withdrew[d] and stayed in the land no longer.

21 As for the other events of Menahem's reign, and all he did, are they not written in the book of the annals of the kings of Israel? 22 Menahem rested with his ancestors. And Pekahiah his son succeeded him as king.

Pekahiah King of Israel

23 In the fiftieth year of Azariah king of Judah, Pekahiah son of Menahem became king of Israel in Samaria, and he reigned two years. 24 Pekahiah did evil in the eyes of the LORD. He did not turn away from the sins of Jeroboam son of Nebat, which he had caused Israel to commit. 25 One of his chief officers, Pekah[e] son of Remaliah, conspired against him. Taking fifty men of Gilead

15:19 [c] 1Ch 5:6, 26
15:20 [d] 2Ki 12:18
15:25 [e] 2Ch 28:6; Isa 7:1

[a] *10* Hebrew; some Septuagint manuscripts *in Ibleam* [b] *12* 2 Kings 10:30 [c] *19* Also called *Tiglath-Pileser* [d] *19* That is, about 38 tons or about 34 metric tons [e] *20* That is, about 1 1/4 pounds or about 575 grams

---

15:8–12 The death of Jeroboam brings an end to the dynasty of Jehu, which was prophesied to continue for four generations (10:30). Social and moral decay, vividly chronicled in Amos, has its effect in the territorial and political upheavals that come with the death of Jeroboam (15:8, 13).
15:13–16 Shallum's reign is described primarily in terms of his defeat by Menahem.
15:17–20 Menahem can only achieve and maintain his power through alliance with the king of Assyria. Pul is also known as Tiglath-Pileser III (cf. v. 29). Menahem submits to the Assyrians in payment of tribute and in return gains their support so he can secure his kingdom.
15:23–26 The ten-year reign of Menahem is followed by a two-year reign of his son Pekahiah (742–740 BC). He is assassinated by Pekah, his chief officer, who is assisted by a military unit from Gilead.

with him, he assassinated[f] Pekahiah,
along with Argob and Arieh, in the citadel of the royal palace at Samaria. So
Pekah killed Pekahiah and succeeded
him as king.
26 The other events of Pekahiah's reign,
and all he did, are written in the book of
the annals of the kings of Israel.

Pekah King of Israel

27 In the fifty-second year of Azariah
king of Judah, Pekah[g] son of Remaliah[h]
became king of Israel in Samaria, and
he reigned twenty years. 28 He did evil
in the eyes of the LORD. He did not turn
away from the sins of Jeroboam son of
Nebat, which he had caused Israel to
commit.
29 In the time of Pekah king of Israel,
Tiglath-Pileser[i] king of Assyria came and
took Ijon,[j] Abel Beth Maakah, Janoah,
Kedesh and Hazor. He took Gilead and
Galilee, including all the land of Naphtali,[k] and deported[l] the people to Assyria.
30 Then Hoshea[m] son of Elah conspired
against Pekah son of Remaliah. He attacked and assassinated[n] him, and then
succeeded him as king in the twentieth
year of Jotham son of Uzziah.
31 As for the other events of Pekah's
reign, and all he did, are they not written
in the book of the annals of the kings
of Israel?

Jotham King of Judah

15:33–38pp // 2Ch 27:1–4,7–9

32 In the second year of Pekah son of
Remaliah king of Israel, Jotham[o] son of
Uzziah king of Judah began to reign. 33 He
was twenty-five years old when he became king, and he reigned in Jerusalem
sixteen years. His mother's name was
Jerusha daughter of Zadok. 34 He did what
was right[p] in the eyes of the LORD, just as
his father Uzziah had done. 35 The high
places,[q] however, were not removed; the
people continued to offer sacrifices and
burn incense there. Jotham rebuilt the
Upper Gate[r] of the temple of the LORD.
36 As for the other events of Jotham's
reign, and what he did, are they not
written in the book of the annals of the
kings of Judah? 37 (In those days the LORD
began to send Rezin[s] king of Aram and
Pekah son of Remaliah against Judah.)
38 Jotham rested with his ancestors and
was buried with them in the City of David, the city of his father. And Ahaz his
son succeeded him as king.

Ahaz King of Judah

16:1–20pp // 2Ch 28:1–27

16 In the seventeenth year of Pekah son of Remaliah, Ahaz[t] son of
Jotham king of Judah began to reign.
2 Ahaz was twenty years old when he became king, and he reigned in Jerusalem

15:25 [f] 2Ki 12:20
15:27 [g] 2Ch 28:6; Isa 7:1 [h] Isa 7:4
15:29 [i] 2Ki 16:7; 17:6; 1Ch 5:26; 2Ch 28:20; Jer 50:17 [j] 1Ki 15:20 [k] 2Ki 16:9; 17:24; 2Ch 16:4; Isa 9:1 [l] 2Ki 24:14-16; 1Ch 5:22; Isa 14:6,17; 36:17; 45:13
15:30 [m] 2Ki 17:1 [n] 2Ki 12:20
15:32 [o] 1Ch 5:17
15:34 [p] ver 3; 1Ki 14:8; 2Ch 26:4-5
15:35 [q] 2Ki 12:3 [r] 2Ch 23:20
15:37 [s] 2Ki 16:5; Isa 7:1
16:1 [t] Isa 1:1; 14:28

15:27–31 The year of Pekah's ascension to the throne in Samaria is the same year that King Azariah (Uzziah) dies (cf. Isa 6:1). From that point on, the politics of both Damascus and Samaria are dominated entirely by the activities of Tiglath-Pileser III (v. 29).

15:32–38 The reigns of Azariah and Jotham overlap with those of the last kings of Israel; the fate of Judah is determined by Israel's change in circumstances. The complexity of the stories of overlapping reigns points to the political turbulence of this period; political struggles lead to various alliances vying for power.

Jotham begins to reign in 750 BC, ten years before the death of Azariah. Rezin of Aramea and Pekah of Israel attempt to coerce Jotham into an alliance against Assyria (v. 37), but Ahaz attempts to gain independence from them through the assistance of the Assyrians (16:5–9). The pro-Assyrian policy effectively ends the reign of Jotham, but it does not deliver Judah; within a generation the armies of Assyria surround Jerusalem, and citizens from Judah are exiled as well.

Aside from the notation that Jotham exercises royal authority in the place of his father (v. 5), the only achievement of his reign given in Kings is that he renovates one of the gateways of the temple (v. 35), which is of special interest to the worship concerns of the historian.

✣ **15:1–38** From a political perspective, the kingdoms of Jeroboam and Uzziah can be regarded as a remarkable success. From the perspective of observing the values of God's kingdom, they are failures, parts of a dark period that comes under divine judgment.

Though human kingdoms fail, God's kingdom does not fail. It finds fulfillment in the proclamation of the Savior who came as the child promised by Isaiah in those dark days. The kingdom of God continues to find expression within the great kingdoms of this world. These kingdoms will crumble, just as surely as all the others before them, but Christ "will build [his] church, and the gates of Hades will not overcome it" (Mt 16:18).

16:1–9 Ahaz becomes king twelve years before Hoshea begins to reign (17:1). The historian portrays Ahaz as idolatrous and wicked, and as voluntarily submitting to the Assyrian yoke—a grievous misdeed in addition to his promoting idolatry in the high places.

ASSYRIAN CAMPAIGNS AGAINST ISRAEL AND JUDAH

The Assyrian invasions of the eighth century BC were the most traumatic political events in the entire history of Israel.

The brutal Assyrian style of warfare relied on massive armies, superbly equipped with the world's first great siege machines manipulated by an efficient corps of engineers.

Psychological terror, however, was Assyria's most effective weapon. It was ruthlessly applied, with corpses impaled on stakes, severed heads stacked in heaps, and captives skinned alive.

The shock of bloody military sieges on both Israel and Judah was profound. The prophets did not fail to speak out against their horror, while at the same time pleading with the people to see God's hand in history, to recognize spiritual causes in the present punishment.

1. CAMPAIGNS OF TIGLATH-PILESER III (738–732 BC)

King Tiglath-Pileser of Assyria (745–727 BC) proved to be a vigorous campaigner, first exacting tribute from Menahem and then annexing Hamath, Philistia, Galilee, Gilead and Damascus (738–732 BC) during the reign of Pekah.

The ferocious onslaught against the northern tribes left only central Israel and the capital city of Samaria intact.

By this time Israel was a tiny nation racked by pro- and anti-Assyrian factions, multiple assassinations, hypocrisy, arrogance and fear.

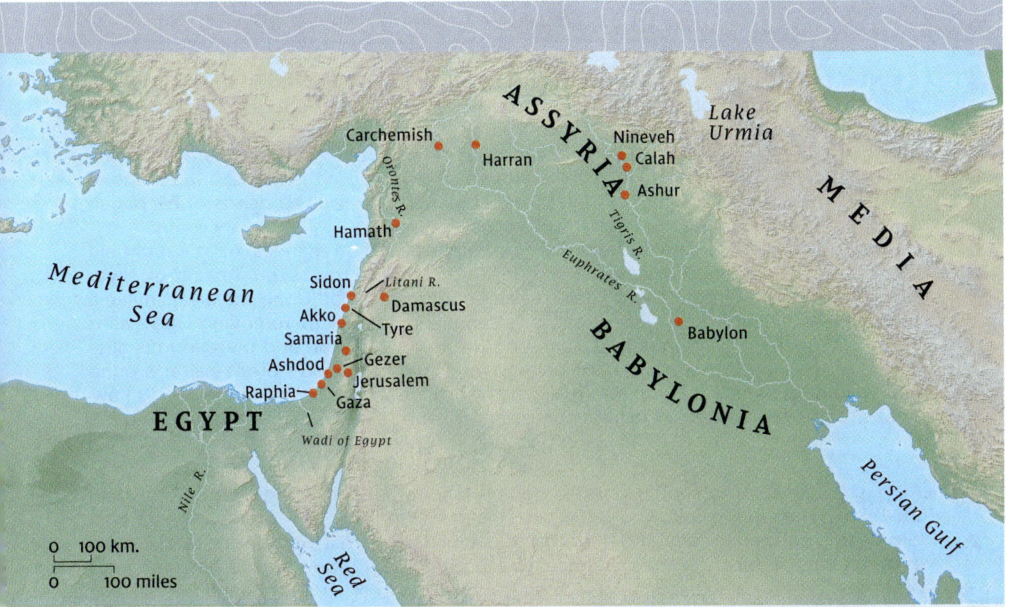

2. CAMPAIGN OF SHALMANESER V (725–722 BC)

The last king of Israel, Hoshea, conspired with Egypt and withheld the annual tribute to the Assyrians.

A protracted three-year siege conducted by Shalmaneser and concluded by Sargon II saw the end of the Israelite kingdom in 722–721 BC.

At that time, according to Assyrian annals, "I [Sargon] besieged and conquered Samaria, led away as plunder 27,290 inhabitants . . . I installed over [those remaining] an officer of mine and imposed upon them the tribute of the former king."

3. SENNACHERIB'S CAMPAIGN AGAINST JUDAH (701 BC)

In the 14th year of Hezekiah, the Assyrians finally attacked Judah. The Prism of Sennacherib calls Hezekiah "overbearing and proud," indicating that he was part of Philistia's and Egypt's effort to rebel against Assyria.

A battle in the plain of Eltekeh was won by Assyria; the Egyptian and Cushite charioteers fled. Lachish was besieged and taken. Sennacherib's annals note: "As for Hezekiah the Jew, he did not submit to my yoke. I laid siege to 46 of his strong cities, walled forts and the countless small villages in their vicinity, and conquered them by means of well-tamped earth ramps and battering-rams brought near to the walls combined with the attack by foot-soldiers, using mines, breaches and sapper work. I drove out 200,150 people, young and old, male and female, horses, mules, donkeys, camels, large and small cattle beyond counting, and considered them plunder. Himself I made a prisoner in Jerusalem, his royal residence, like a bird in a cage."

Nowhere, however, does the boastful Assyrian king record the disaster mentioned in 2Ki 19:35-36; 2Ch 32:21; Isa 37:36-37.

PEOPLE TO KNOW // AHAZ

2 KINGS 16:1–20: Ahaz was a descendant of David and a king of the southern kingdom of Judah. His father Jotham and his grandfather Uzziah were both good kings. Ahaz's son Hezekiah was one of Judah's greatest kings.

Unfortunately, righteousness skipped a generation with Ahaz. He was among the most wicked kings of Judah. He even sacrificed his own son in the fire (2Ki 16:3), one of the most detestable acts in God's eyes. Ahaz practiced the wicked deeds of his pagan neighbors rather than dedicating himself to God's ways.

Instead of turning to God for help when he was attacked by enemies, Ahaz sought aid from Tiglath-Pileser, king of Assyria. In order to pay tribute to Assyria, Ahaz took silver and gold from the temple and palace treasuries. Ahaz also had Uriah the priest make a copy of a pagan altar and place it at God's temple in Jerusalem, removing God's altar from its prominent place. While desecrating the temple of God and pledging his allegiance to the king of Assyria, Ahaz declared he would keep God's bronze altar around for "seeking guidance" (2Ki 16:15). This type of divination was forbidden by God's Law. Ahaz's reign was marked by failure, persistent evil and religious corruption.

APPLICATION ✜ Ahaz should have learned from his father and grandfather to obey and trust God. Instead, he followed his wicked heart. His reliance on foreign powers cost him dearly, both financially and morally. Ahaz didn't fully trust God but instead looked everywhere else for help and guidance: to other people, to idols and to false religious practices. When we abandon God to seek guidance from other people and human wisdom, only failure and misery will follow.

sixteen years. Unlike David his father, he
did not do what was right[u] in the eyes
of the LORD his God. 3He followed the
ways of the kings of Israel and even sacrificed his son[v] in the fire, engaging in
the detestable[w] practices of the nations
the LORD had driven out before the Israelites. 4He offered sacrifices and burned
incense at the high places, on the hilltops
and under every spreading tree.[x]
5Then Rezin[y] king of Aram and Pekah
son of Remaliah king of Israel marched
up to fight against Jerusalem and besieged Ahaz, but they could not overpower him. 6At that time, Rezin[z] king of
Aram recovered Elath[a] for Aram by driving out the people of Judah. Edomites
then moved into Elath and have lived
there to this day.
7Ahaz sent messengers to say to Tiglath-Pileser[b] king of Assyria, "I am your
servant and vassal. Come up and save[c]
me out of the hand of the king of Aram
and of the king of Israel, who are attacking me." 8And Ahaz took the silver and
gold found in the temple of the LORD
and in the treasuries of the royal palace and sent it as a gift[d] to the king of

16:2 [u] 1Ki 14:8
16:3 [v] Lev 18:21; 2Ki 21:6 [w] Lev 18:3; Dt 9:4; 12:31
16:4 [x] Dt 12:2; Eze 6:13
16:5 [y] 2Ki 15:37; Isa 7:1,4
16:6 [z] Isa 9:12 [a] 2Ki 14:22; 2Ch 26:2
16:7 [b] 2Ki 15:29 [c] Isa 2:6; Jer 2:18; Eze 16:28; Hos 10:6
16:8 [d] 2Ki 12:18
16:9 [e] 2Ki 15:29 [f] Isa 22:6; Am 1:5; 9:7
16:10 [g] Isa 8:2
16:12 [h] 2Ch 26:16
16:13 [i] Lev 6:8-13 [j] Lev 7:11-21
16:14 [k] 2Ch 4:1

2Ki 16:10 ❖ How might worldly influences affect true worship of God? How can believers resist such influences?

Assyria. 9The king of Assyria complied
by attacking Damascus[e] and capturing it.
He deported its inhabitants to Kir[f] and
put Rezin to death.
10Then King Ahaz went to Damascus
to meet Tiglath-Pileser king of Assyria.
He saw an altar in Damascus and sent
to Uriah[g] the priest a sketch of the altar, with detailed plans for its construction. 11So Uriah the priest built an altar
in accordance with all the plans that
King Ahaz had sent from Damascus and
finished it before King Ahaz returned.
12When the king came back from Damascus and saw the altar, he approached it
and presented offerings[ah] on it. 13He offered up his burnt offering[i] and grain
offering, poured out his drink offering,
and splashed the blood of his fellowship offerings[j] against the altar. 14As for
the bronze altar[k] that stood before the

[a] 12 Or *and went up*

16:10–14 The political compliance to Tiglath-Pileser III requires Ahaz to meet him in Damascus to bring tribute. While there, he sees an altar, a blueprint of which he sends to Uriah the faithful high priest (Isa 8:2), who builds it according to Ahaz's model. When Ahaz returns from Damascus he conducts the inaugural sacrificial ceremony, just as Solomon did at the dedication of the temple.

LORD, he brought it from the front of the temple — from between the new altar and the temple of the LORD — and put it on the north side of the new altar.

15 King Ahaz then gave these orders to Uriah the priest: "On the large new altar, offer the morning[l] burnt offering and the evening grain offering, the king's burnt offering and his grain offering, and the burnt offering of all the people of the land, and their grain offering and their drink offering. Splash against this altar the blood of all the burnt offerings and sacrifices. But I will use the bronze altar for seeking guidance."[m] 16 And Uriah the priest did just as King Ahaz had ordered.

17 King Ahaz cut off the side panels and removed the basins from the movable stands. He removed the Sea from the bronze bulls that supported it and set it on a stone base.[n] 18 He took away the Sabbath canopy[a] that had been built at the temple and removed the royal entryway outside the temple of the LORD, in deference to the king of Assyria.[o]

19 As for the other events of the reign of Ahaz, and what he did, are they not written in the book of the annals of the kings of Judah? 20 Ahaz rested with his ancestors and was buried with them in the City of David. And Hezekiah his son succeeded him as king.

16:15 [l] Ex 29:38-41 [m] 1Sa 9:9
16:17 [n] 1Ki 7:27
16:18 [o] Eze 16:28

Hoshea Last King of Israel

17:3–7pp // 2Ki 18:9–12

17 In the twelfth year of Ahaz king of Judah, Hoshea[p] son of Elah became king of Israel in Samaria, and he reigned nine years. 2 He did evil in the eyes of the LORD, but not like the kings of Israel who preceded him.

3 Shalmaneser[q] king of Assyria came up to attack Hoshea, who had been Shalmaneser's vassal and had paid him tribute. 4 But the king of Assyria discovered that Hoshea was a traitor, for he had sent envoys to So[b] king of Egypt, and he no longer paid tribute to the king of Assyria, as he had done year by year. Therefore Shalmaneser seized him and put him in prison. 5 The king of Assyria invaded the entire land, marched against Samaria and laid siege[r] to it for three years. 6 In the ninth year of Hoshea, the king of Assyria captured Samaria[s] and deported[t] the Israelites to Assyria. He settled them in Halah, in Gozan[u] on the Habor River and in the towns of the Medes.

Israel Exiled Because of Sin

7 All this took place because the Israelites had sinned[v] against the LORD their

17:1 [p] 2Ki 15:30
17:3 [q] 2Ki 18:9-12; Hos 10:14
17:5 [r] Hos 13:16
17:6 [s] Hos 13:16 [t] Dt 28:36, 64; 2Ki 18:10-11 [u] 1Ch 5:26
17:7 [v] Jos 23:16; Jdg 6:10

[a] 18 Or *the dais of his throne* (see Septuagint)
[b] 4 *So* is probably an abbreviation for *Osorkon.*

16:15–20 Ahaz directs that all the regular offerings for the king and his officials are to be brought to the new altar. The old altar is for the exclusive use of the king, where he will worship and pray. The sense of how Ahaz will seek Yahweh is not specified. All the other changes Ahaz makes are regarded negatively as an accommodation to Assyrian influence.

✤ **16:1–20** In seeking to protect his earthly inheritance, Ahaz loses it all. Had he been willing to trust God with his kingdom, he and his people could have been secure.

Jesus promises his followers that all the needs of this earthly life will be provided to those who make the kingdom of God their concern (Mt 6:25–33). By contrast, those who seek treasure on this earth will find it will rust and decay (Mt 6:19–21). Either that or it will be taken away, in the same way Tiglath-Pileser III strips the treasures of the temple.

The choices of Ahaz are typical of the values of the wealthy seeking security for their possessions: He chooses to trust political and economic forces rather than God. In so doing he is willing to desecrate the temple by robbing it of its valuable metals and setting up foreign altars in its precincts.

In all of this, God is still with Ahaz. During his reign the kingdom of Israel (the nation he so fears) disappears entirely, and his own people come under the domination of the Assyrians.

Wealth is important to life in this world but not as an end in itself. Wealth used in dependence on God and in furthering the kingdom of God enables his presence and blessing. But Ahaz chooses to make his wealth his god, and in so doing he loses the blessing of the sign of Immanuel. Christians who have experienced the blessing of the fulfillment of Immanuel must beware of falling into the same pattern.

17:1–6 The end of Hoshea's reign is described in two-verse pairs (vv. 3–4 and 5–6), each of which notes an invasion by Shalmaneser V. The report begins with an emphatic irony: Hoshea, who did not sin as did the kings of Israel before him, is the king whom Shalmaneser V attacks. The author recalls the vivid memory of the attack that ended the nation of Israel and the reason for it. The author then describes the effect of the invasion for the city of Samaria and the population of the country.
17:7–23 A prophetic sermon details the sins that are responsible for the fall of Israel (and Judah; cf. v. 19). The only mention of Israel's kings here is in the general introduction of the sins of Israel

EXILE OF THE NORTHERN KINGDOM

The mass deportation policy of the Assyrians was a companion piece to the brutal and calculated terror initiated by Ashurnasirpal and followed by all his successors. It was intended to forestall revolts but, like all draconian measures, it merely spread misery and engendered hatred. In the end, it hastened the disintegration of the Assyrian Empire.

There is some evidence that Israel experienced its first deportations under Tiglath-Pileser III (745–727 BC), a cruelty repeated by Sargon II (721–705) at the time of the fall of Samaria. The latter king's inscriptions boast of carrying away 27,290 inhabitants of the city "as plunder." According to 2Ki 17:6, they were sent to Assyria, to Halah, to Gozan on the Habor River, and apparently to the eastern frontiers of the empire (to the towns of the Medes, most probably somewhere in the vicinity of Ecbatana, the modern Hamadan).

The sequel is provided by the inscriptions of Sargon: "The Arabs who live far away in the desert, who know neither overseers nor officials, and who had not yet brought their tribute to any king, I deported ... and settled them in Samaria."

Much mythology has developed around the theme of the so-called ten "lost" tribes of Israel. A close examination of Assyrian records reveals that the deportations approximated only a limited percentage of the population, usually consisting of noble families. Agricultural workers, no doubt the majority, were deliberately left to care for the crops (cf. the Babylonian practice, 2Ki 24:14; 25:12).

God, who had brought them up out of Egypt[w] from under the power of Pharaoh king of Egypt. They worshiped other gods 8and followed the practices of the nations[x] the LORD had driven out before them, as well as the practices that the kings of Israel had introduced. 9The Israelites secretly did things against the LORD their God that were not right. From watchtower to fortified city[y] they built themselves high places in all their towns. 10They set up sacred stones and Asherah poles[z] on every high hill and under every spreading tree.[a] 11At every high place they burned incense, as the nations whom the LORD had driven out before them had done. They did wicked things that aroused the LORD's anger. 12They worshiped idols,[b] though the LORD had said, "You shall not do this."[a] 13The LORD warned Israel and Judah through all his prophets and seers:[c] "Turn from your evil ways.[d] Observe my commands and decrees, in accordance with the entire Law that I commanded your ancestors to obey and that I delivered to you through my servants the prophets."

14But they would not listen and were as stiff-necked[e] as their ancestors, who did not trust in the LORD their God. 15They rejected his decrees and the covenant[f] he had made with their ancestors and the statutes he had warned them to keep. They followed worthless idols[g] and themselves became worthless. They imitated the nations[h] around them although the LORD had ordered them, "Do not do as they do."

16They forsook all the commands of the LORD their God and made for themselves two idols cast in the shape of calves,[i] and an Asherah[j] pole. They bowed down to all the starry hosts,[k] and they worshiped Baal.[l] 17They sacrificed[m] their sons and daughters in the fire. They practiced divination and sought omens[n] and sold[o] themselves to do evil in the eyes of the LORD, arousing his anger.

18So the LORD was very angry with Israel and removed them from his presence. Only the tribe of Judah was left, 19and even Judah did not keep the commands of the LORD their God. They followed the practices Israel had introduced.[p] 20Therefore the LORD rejected all the people of Israel; he afflicted them and gave them into the hands of plunderers,[q] until he thrust them from his presence.

21When he tore[r] Israel away from the house of David, they made Jeroboam son of Nebat their king.[s] Jeroboam enticed Israel away from following the LORD and caused them to commit a great sin. 22The Israelites persisted in all the sins of Jeroboam and did not turn away from them 23until the LORD removed them from his presence, as he had warned through all his servants the prophets. So the people of Israel were taken from their homeland into exile in Assyria, and they are still there.

Samaria Resettled

24The king of Assyria[t] brought people from Babylon, Kuthah, Avva, Hamath and Sepharvaim[u] and settled them in the towns of Samaria to replace the Israelites. They took over Samaria and lived in its towns. 25When they first lived there, they did not worship the LORD; so he sent lions[v] among them and they killed some of the people. 26It was reported to the king of Assyria: "The people you deported and resettled in the towns of Samaria do not know what the god of that country requires. He has sent lions among them, which are killing them off, because the people do not know what he requires."

27Then the king of Assyria gave this order: "Have one of the priests you took captive from Samaria go back to live there and teach the people what the god of the land requires." 28So one of the priests who had been exiled from Samaria came to live in Bethel and taught them how to worship the LORD.

29Nevertheless, each national group

17:7 [w] Ex 14:15-31
17:8 [x] Lev 18:3; Dt 18:9; 2Ki 16:3
17:9 [y] 2Ki 18:8
17:10 [z] Ex 34:13; Mic 5:14 [a] 1Ki 14:23
17:12 [b] Ex 20:4
17:13 [c] 1Sa 9:9 [d] Jer 18:11; 25:5; 35:15
17:14 [e] Ex 32:9; Dt 31:27; Ac 7:51
17:15 [f] Dt 29:25 [g] Dt 32:21; Ro 1:21-23 [h] Dt 12:30-31
17:16 [i] 1Ki 12:28 [j] 1Ki 14:15, 23 [k] 2Ki 21:3 [l] 1Ki 16:31
17:17 [m] Dt 18:10-12; 2Ki 16:3 [n] Lev 19:26 [o] 1Ki 21:20
17:19 [p] 1Ki 14:22-23; 2Ki 16:3
17:20 [q] 2Ki 15:29
17:21 [r] 1Ki 11:11 [s] 1Ki 12:20
17:24 [t] Ezr 4:2, 10 [u] 2Ki 18:34
17:25 [v] Ge 37:20

[a] *12* Exodus 20:4,5

(v. 8b). Their apostasy involved the adoption of foreign practices introduced into the worship of Yahweh, such as the erection of stone pillars and Asherah poles. This litany of sins against God's expressed commands continued until God finally had enough (v. 23).

17:24–33 The exiled Israelites are replaced with people from other lands. The five nationalities noted in v. 24 correspond with Mesopotamian locations conquered by Sargon II in the latter part of the eighth century BC. The repatriation of a priest to Bethel to teach the newcomers how to fear Yahweh (vv. 27–28) also fits well with known Sargonic policy. The peoples brought to repopulate Israel add Yahweh to the gods from their homelands as another god to worship (v. 33).

made its own gods in the several towns[w]
where they settled, and set them up in
the shrines[x] the people of Samaria had
made at the high places.[y] 30The people
from Babylon made Sukkoth Benoth,
those from Kuthah made Nergal, and
those from Hamath made Ashima; 31the
Avvites made Nibhaz and Tartak, and
the Sepharvites burned their children
in the fire as sacrifices to Adrammelek[z]
and Anammelek, the gods of Sepharvaim.[a] 32They worshiped the LORD, but they
also appointed all sorts[b] of their own
people to officiate for them as priests
in the shrines at the high places. 33They
worshiped the LORD, but they also served
their own gods in accordance with the
customs of the nations from which they
had been brought.

34To this day they persist in their former practices. They neither worship the
LORD nor adhere to the decrees and regulations, the laws and commands that
the LORD gave the descendants of Jacob,
whom he named Israel.[c] 35When the LORD
made a covenant with the Israelites, he
commanded them: "Do not worship[d] any
other gods or bow down to them, serve
them or sacrifice to them. 36But the LORD,
who brought you up out of Egypt with
mighty power and outstretched arm,[e] is
the one you must worship. To him you
shall bow down and to him offer sacrifices. 37You must always be careful[f] to keep
the decrees and regulations, the laws and
commands he wrote for you. Do not worship other gods. 38Do not forget[g] the covenant I have made with you, and do not
worship other gods. 39Rather, worship the
LORD your God; it is he who will deliver
you from the hand of all your enemies."

40They would not listen, however,
but persisted in their former practices.
41Even while these people were worshiping the LORD,[h] they were serving their
idols. To this day their children and
grandchildren continue to do as their
ancestors did.

2Ki 17:41 ❖ Divided hearts lead people to serve the Lord while still following practices he prohibits. How can God's children avoid this sin (see Mt 5:8)?

Hezekiah King of Judah

18:2–4pp // 2Ch 29:1–2; 31:1
18:5–7pp // 2Ch 31:20–21
18:9–12pp // 2Ki 17:3–7

18 In the third year of Hoshea son of
Elah king of Israel, Hezekiah[i] son
of Ahaz king of Judah began to reign.
2He was twenty-five years old when he

17:29 [w] Jer 2:28 [x] 1Ki 12:31 [y] Mic 4:5
17:31 [z] 2Ki 19:37 [a] ver 24
17:32 [b] 1Ki 12:31
17:34 [c] Ge 32:28; 35:10; 1Ki 18:31
17:35 [d] Ex 20:5; Jdg 6:10
17:36 [e] Ex 3:20; 6:6; Ps 136:12
17:37 [f] Dt 5:32
17:38 [g] Dt 4:23; 6:12
17:41 [h] ver 32-33; 1Ki 18:21; Mt 6:24
18:1 [i] Isa 1:1; 2Ch 28:27

17:34–41 In the worship fostered at Bethel and the other high places before the deportation, the people did not fear the Lord; they included unacceptable elements of other religions and, of course, did not accept or use the temple at Jerusalem.

The end of Israel becomes the occasion for a concluding observation on Israel's failure to observe and obey the covenant from the time of the exodus "to this day," which is repeated twice (vv. 34, 40–41). Repetitive phrases are typical in Hebrew narrative to mark the beginning and end of a distinct literary unit within a larger composition.

✣ **17:1–41** The people failed to honor God with their worship, leading to a fundamental misunderstanding of the covenant relationship that continued to distort a true understanding of a genuine relationship with God. Merely observing rituals misses the point of pursuing true relationship with God. God created Israel to be his bride, his "treasured possession" (Dt 7:6); he voluntarily entered into an oath with them. The fundamental requirement of that relationship is stated in the primary confession of the covenant book: "Love the LORD your God with all your heart and with all your soul and with all your strength" (Dt 6:5). God never demands perfection in keeping the pledge; his love is perfect and abundant to pardon. Our God is one who will always forgive our sins and heal our diseases (Ps 103:3). God requires a loyalty to that promise; as with the oath of marriage, the covenant partners must always promise and pursue uncompromised faithfulness.

The failure of the covenant relationship that resulted in the exile did not bring an end to the promise of God or his love for his people. The church continues the work of God for which the prophets longed. In this new covenant there is forgiveness of sins; we who believe can encourage each other in our walk with the Lord as we wait for the day when everyone will know the Lord as Jeremiah promised (Jer 31:34).

Jesus turns the Passover into a confession of this new covenant. The wine is his blood of the covenant, shed for many for the forgiveness of sins (Mt 26:28). Paul declares the cup of the Passover is the new covenant in the blood of Christ; eating the bread and drinking the wine must be done in remembrance of Christ until he comes (1Co 11:25–26).

The Lord's Supper is the representation of the new redemption that follows the failures of the old covenant. When believers participate in this sacrament, they recognize and participate in the redemption that God had planned before the beginning of the world.

PEOPLE TO KNOW // HEZEKIAH

2 KINGS 18:1–8: Hezekiah's father was King Ahaz, one of Judah's worst kings. Hezekiah, however, did what was right in God's eyes by rooting out idol worship. He trusted in God, and God was with him (2Ki 18:3–8).

One day King Sennacherib of Assyria sent Hezekiah a threatening message that Jerusalem would be destroyed just like all of Assyria's other victims. Rather than panic, Hezekiah went to God's temple and prayed (2Ki 19:14–19). God miraculously delivered Jerusalem from Sennacherib's army, sending the angel of death upon the Assyrians at night. Sennacherib's own account of his victories, which archaeologists have discovered, confirms that Sennacherib could not destroy Jerusalem.

Later when Hezekiah became sick, God sent Isaiah to tell him he would die of his illness (Isa 38:1). Hezekiah prayed fervently, and God sent Isaiah back to tell Hezekiah God would add fifteen years to his life (Isa 38:5). God caused a shadow to go backwards as a sign that his promise to extend Hezekiah's life was certain (Isa 38:8).

APPLICATION ✣ Hezekiah was considered a righteous king, yet his father and son, Ahaz and Manasseh, were considered two of Judah's most wicked kings. If we come from families that do not honor God, it can be difficult to break free of sinful patterns. Hezekiah shows that choosing our own path is possible. No matter our background, we can break wicked cycles and follow the Lord. When we do that, we should pray that God will help us pass on a godly legacy to those who follow.

became king, and he reigned in Jerusalem twenty-nine years.[j] His mother's
name was Abijah[a] daughter of Zechariah.
3He did what was right in the eyes of the
LORD, just as his father David[k] had done.
4He removed[l] the high places, smashed
the sacred stones[m] and cut down the
Asherah poles. He broke into pieces the
bronze snake[n] Moses had made, for up to
that time the Israelites had been burning
incense to it. (It was called Nehushtan.[b])
5Hezekiah trusted[o] in the LORD, the
God of Israel. There was no one like him
among all the kings of Judah, either before him or after him. 6He held fast[p] to
the LORD and did not stop following him;
he kept the commands the LORD had giv-
en Moses. 7And the LORD was with him;
he was successful[q] in whatever he undertook. He rebelled[r] against the king
of Assyria and did not serve him. 8From
watchtower to fortified city,[s] he defeated the Philistines, as far as Gaza and its
territory.
9In King Hezekiah's fourth year,[t] which
was the seventh year of Hoshea son of
Elah king of Israel, Shalmaneser king of
Assyria marched against Samaria and
laid siege to it. 10At the end of three
years the Assyrians took it. So Samaria
was captured in Hezekiah's sixth year,
which was the ninth year of Hoshea king
of Israel. 11The king[u] of Assyria deported
Israel to Assyria and settled them in Halah, in Gozan on the Habor River and in
towns of the Medes. 12This happened because they had not obeyed the LORD their
God, but had violated his covenant[v] — all
that Moses the servant of the LORD commanded.[w] They neither listened to the
commands[x] nor carried them out.

18:2 [j] Isa 38:5
18:3 [k] Isa 38:5
18:4 [l] 2Ch 31:1 [m] Ex 23:24 [n] Nu 21:9
18:5 [o] 2Ki 19:10; 23:25
18:6 [p] Dt 10:20; Jos 23:8
18:7 [q] Ge 39:3; 1Sa 18:14 [r] 2Ki 16:7
18:8 [s] 2Ki 17:9; Isa 14:29
18:9 [t] Isa 1:1
18:11 [u] Isa 37:12
18:12 [v] 2Ki 17:15 [w] Da 9:6,10 [x] 1Ki 9:6

2Ki 18:1–4 ❖ Hezekiah's father, Ahaz, was wicked. How can we resist evil family influences while striving to be righteous followers of God?

[a] 2 Hebrew *Abi*, a variant of *Abijah*
[b] 4 *Nehushtan* sounds like the Hebrew for both *bronze* and *snake*.

18:1–3 In contrast to all the previous kings of Israel and Judah, Hezekiah is introduced as a faithful king, one who reformed Judean worship and moved Judah toward the ideal of the covenant.
18:4–6 Hezekiah is the very model of the Davidic ideal. His faithfulness results in the preservation of Jerusalem, a stark contrast to the captivity of Israel.
18:7–12 Hezekiah's independent rule begins in 715 BC, fourteen years before the siege against Jerusalem. He is rewarded for his faithfulness, not only in successfully resisting the Assyrian advances but also in securing his boundaries toward the Philistine territories. Hezekiah's trust is particularly evident when he refuses to yield to the Assyrians, even when the fortified cities of Judah are destroyed and the Assyrian armies have encircled Jerusalem.

13In the fourteenth year of King Hezekiah's reign, Sennacherib king of Assyria attacked all the fortified cities of Judah[y] and captured them. 14So Hezekiah king of Judah sent this message to the king of Assyria at Lachish: "I have done wrong.[z] Withdraw from me, and I will pay whatever you demand of me." The king of Assyria exacted from Hezekiah king of Judah three hundred talents[a] of silver and thirty talents[b] of gold. 15So Hezekiah gave[a] him all the silver that was found in the temple of the LORD and in the treasuries of the royal palace.

16At this time Hezekiah king of Judah stripped off the gold with which he had covered the doors and doorposts of the temple of the LORD, and gave it to the king of Assyria.

Sennacherib Threatens Jerusalem

18:13,17–37pp // Isa 36:1–22
18:17–35pp // 2Ch 32:9–19

17The king of Assyria sent his supreme commander,[b] his chief officer and his field commander with a large army, from Lachish to King Hezekiah at Jerusalem. They came up to Jerusalem and stopped at the aqueduct of the Upper Pool,[c] on the road to the Washerman's Field. 18They called for the king; and Eliakim[d] son of Hilkiah the palace administrator, Shebna[e] the secretary, and Joah son of Asaph the recorder went out to them.

19The field commander said to them, "Tell Hezekiah:

"'This is what the great king, the king of Assyria, says: On what are you basing this confidence of yours? 20You say you have the counsel and the might for war—but you speak only empty words. On whom are you depending, that you rebel against me? 21Look, I know you are depending on Egypt,[f] that splintered reed of a staff,[g] which pierces the hand of anyone who leans on it! Such is Pharaoh king of Egypt to all who depend on him. 22But if you say to me, "We are depending on the LORD our God"—isn't he the one whose high places and altars Hezekiah removed, saying to Judah and Jerusalem, "You must worship before this altar in Jerusalem"?

23"'Come now, make a bargain with my master, the king of Assyria: I will give you two thousand horses—if you can put riders on them! 24How can you repulse one officer[h] of the least of my master's officials, even though you are depending on Egypt for chariots and horsemen[c]? 25Furthermore, have I come to attack and destroy this place without word from the LORD?[i] The LORD himself told me to march against this country and destroy it.'"

26Then Eliakim son of Hilkiah, and Shebna and Joah said to the field commander, "Please speak to your servants in Aramaic,[j] since we understand it. Don't speak to us in Hebrew in the hearing of the people on the wall."

27But the commander replied, "Was it only to your master and you that my master sent me to say these things, and not to the people sitting on the wall—who, like you, will have to eat their own excrement and drink their own urine?"

28Then the commander stood and called out in Hebrew, "Hear the word of the great king, the king of Assyria! 29This is what the king says: Do not let Hezekiah deceive[k] you. He cannot deliver you from

18:13 [y] 2Ch 32:1; Isa 1:7; Mic 1:9
18:14 [z] Isa 24:5
18:15 [a] 1Ki 15:18; 2Ki 16:8
18:17 [b] Isa 20:1 [c] 2Ki 20:20; 2Ch 32:4,30; Isa 7:3
18:18 [d] 2Ki 19:2; Isa 22:20 [e] Isa 22:15
18:21 [f] Isa 20:5; Eze 29:6 [g] Isa 30:5,7
18:24 [h] Isa 10:8
18:25 [i] 2Ki 19:6, 22
18:26 [j] Ezr 4:7
18:29 [k] 2Ki 19:10

[a] *14* That is, about 11 tons or about 10 metric tons
[b] *14* That is, about 1 ton or about 1 metric ton
[c] *24* Or *charioteers*

18:13–16 The success and prosperity of Hezekiah come to an abrupt end with Assyria's invasion of Judah. A monumental wall relief from the palace of Sennacherib in Nineveh commemorates the battle over Lachish and the deportation of its inhabitants, demonstrating its strategic importance in Assyria's military advance.

18:17–18 The biblical events are part of a larger Assyrian campaign into Philistia and Judah. In the ensuing speech, Hezekiah is always referred to by his personal name, while the Assyrian king is designated "the great king."

18:19–25 The field commander is the spokesman for the Assyrians, quite possibly because of his fluency in languages (vv. 26–27). His attack centers on the question of trust (vv. 21–25). Trust in God is undermined because presumably Hezekiah has insulted Yahweh by removing the high places; thus, the only reasonable alternative is to enter an agreement with the Assyrians.

18:26–30 The shouting to the people on the wall is designed to intimidate. Though the envoys of Sennacherib and the Jerusalem delegates know Aramaic well, as it was the international language of the day, the field commander insists on speaking the Hebrew dialect of the south. He threatens the people with the dire consequences of starvation, which is the typical result of siege warfare (cf. 6:24–31).

my hand. 30Do not let Hezekiah persuade
you to trust in the LORD when he says,
'The LORD will surely deliver us; this city
will not be given into the hand of the
king of Assyria.'
31"Do not listen to Hezekiah. This is
what the king of Assyria says: Make
peace with me and come out to me. Then
each of you will eat fruit from your own
vine and fig tree[l] and drink water from
your own cistern,[m] 32until I come and
take you to a land like your own—a land
of grain and new wine, a land of bread
and vineyards, a land of olive trees and
honey. Choose life[n] and not death!
"Do not listen to Hezekiah, for he is
misleading you when he says, 'The LORD
will deliver us.' 33Has the god[o] of any
nation ever delivered his land from the
hand of the king of Assyria? 34Where are
the gods of Hamath[p] and Arpad?[q] Where
are the gods of Sepharvaim, Hena and
Ivvah? Have they rescued Samaria from
my hand? 35Who of all the gods of these
countries has been able to save his land
from me? How then can the LORD deliver
Jerusalem from my hand?"[r]
36But the people remained silent and
said nothing in reply, because the king
had commanded, "Do not answer him."
37Then Eliakim son of Hilkiah the palace administrator, Shebna the secretary,
and Joah son of Asaph the recorder went
to Hezekiah, with their clothes torn,[s] and
told him what the field commander had
said.

Jerusalem's Deliverance Foretold

19:1–13pp // Isa 37:1–13

19 When King Hezekiah heard this, he
tore[t] his clothes and put on sackcloth and went into the temple of the
LORD. 2He sent Eliakim the palace administrator, Shebna the secretary and
the leading priests, all wearing sackcloth, to the prophet Isaiah[u] son of Amoz.
3They told him, "This is what Hezekiah
says: This day is a day of distress and
rebuke and disgrace, as when children
come to the moment of birth and there
is no strength to deliver them. 4It may
be that the LORD your God will hear all
the words of the field commander, whom
his master, the king of Assyria, has sent
to ridicule[v] the living God, and that he
will rebuke[w] him for the words the LORD
your God has heard. Therefore pray for
the remnant that still survives."
5When King Hezekiah's officials came
to Isaiah, 6Isaiah said to them, "Tell your
master, 'This is what the LORD says: Do
not be afraid of what you have heard—
those words with which the underlings
of the king of Assyria have blasphemed[x]
me. 7Listen! When he hears a certain report, I will make him want to return to
his own country, and there I will have
him cut down with the sword.[y]'"
8When the field commander heard
that the king of Assyria had left Lachish,[z]
he withdrew and found the king fighting
against Libnah.
9Now Sennacherib received a report
that Tirhakah, the king of Cush,[a] was
marching out to fight against him. So
he again sent messengers to Hezekiah
with this word: 10"Say to Hezekiah king
of Judah: Do not let the god you depend[a]
on deceive[b] you when he says, 'Jerusalem will not be given into the hands of
the king of Assyria.' 11Surely you have
heard what the kings of Assyria have
done to all the countries, destroying
them completely. And will you be delivered? 12Did the gods of the nations
that were destroyed by my predecessors
deliver[c] them—the gods of Gozan,[d] Harran,[e] Rezeph and the people of Eden who
were in Tel Assar? 13Where is the king
of Hamath or the king of Arpad? Where
are the kings of Lair, Sepharvaim, Hena
and Ivvah?"[f]

Hezekiah's Prayer

19:14–19pp // Isa 37:14–20

14Hezekiah received the letter from the
messengers and read it. Then he went

18:31 [l]Nu 13:23; 1Ki 4:25 [m]Jer 14:3; La 4:4
18:32 [n]Dt 8:7-9; 30:19
18:33 [o]2Ki 19:12; Isa 10:10-11
18:34 [p]2Ki 17:24; 19:13 [q]Isa 10:9
18:35 [r]Ps 2:1-2
18:37 [s]2Ki 6:30
19:1 [t]Ge 37:34; 1Ki 21:27; 2Ch 32:20-22
19:2 [u]Isa 1:1
19:4 [v]2Ki 18:35 [w]2Sa 16:12
19:6 [x]2Ki 18:25
19:7 [y]ver 37
19:8 [z]2Ki 18:14
19:10 [a]2Ki 18:5 [b]2Ki 18:29
19:12 [c]2Ki 18:33 [d]2Ki 17:6 [e]Ge 11:31
19:13 [f]2Ki 18:34

[a] 9 That is, the upper Nile region

18:31-32 As is typical of brutal conquerors, his promise is one of prosperity and independence.
18:33—19:4 When Sennacherib boasts about previous conquests, Hezekiah is duly humbled by this intimidation (19:3); it is a day of distress, rebuke, and contempt.
19:5-7 In spite of all of Sennacherib's threats through his commander, the prophet Isaiah assures Hezekiah that Sennacherib will soon hear news that will drive him back to his own land.
19:8-13 The message of Isaiah leads to a transition in the narrative. When the Egyptians approach, the Assyrians temporarily withdraw.
19:14-19 The repeated boasts of Assyrian conquests are impressive (v. 12). In response to such taunts, Hezekiah prays; he is granted access to

up to the temple of the LORD and spread
it out before the LORD. 15 And Hezekiah
prayed to the LORD: "LORD, the God of Israel, enthroned between the cherubim,[g]
you alone are God over all the kingdoms
of the earth. You have made heaven and
earth. 16 Give ear,[h] LORD, and hear;[i] open
your eyes,[j] LORD, and see; listen to the
words Sennacherib has sent to ridicule
the living God.

17 "It is true, LORD, that the Assyrian
kings have laid waste these nations and
their lands. 18 They have thrown their
gods into the fire and destroyed them,
for they were not gods[k] but only wood
and stone, fashioned by human hands.[l]
19 Now, LORD our God, deliver us from his
hand, so that all the kingdoms[m] of the
earth may know[n] that you alone, LORD,
are God."

Isaiah Prophesies Sennacherib's Fall

19:20–37pp // Isa 37:21–38
19:35–37pp // 2Ch 32:20–21

20 Then Isaiah son of Amoz sent a message to Hezekiah: "This is what the LORD,
the God of Israel, says: I have heard[o] your
prayer concerning Sennacherib king of
Assyria. 21 This is the word that the LORD
has spoken against him:

"'Virgin Daughter[p] Zion
despises you and mocks[q] you.
Daughter Jerusalem
tosses her head[r] as you flee.
22 Who is it you have ridiculed and
blasphemed?
Against whom have you raised
your voice
and lifted your eyes in pride?
Against the Holy One[s] of Israel!
23 By your messengers
you have ridiculed the Lord.
And you have said,[t]
"With my many chariots[u]
I have ascended the heights of the
mountains,
the utmost heights of Lebanon.
I have cut down its tallest cedars,
the choicest of its junipers.
I have reached its remotest parts,
the finest of its forests.
24 I have dug wells in foreign lands
and drunk the water there.
With the soles of my feet
I have dried up all the streams of
Egypt."

25 "'Have you not heard?[v]
Long ago I ordained it.
In days of old I planned[w] it;
now I have brought it to pass,
that you have turned fortified
cities
into piles of stone.[x]
26 Their people, drained of power,
are dismayed[y] and put to
shame.
They are like plants in the field,
like tender green shoots,[z]
like grass sprouting on the roof,
scorched[a] before it grows up.

27 "'But I know[b] where you are
and when you come and go
and how you rage against me.
28 Because you rage against me
and because your insolence has
reached my ears,
I will put my hook[c] in your nose
and my bit[d] in your mouth,
and I will make you return[e]
by the way you came.'

29 "This will be the sign[f] for you, Hezekiah:

19:15 [g] Ex 25:22
19:16 [h] Ps 31:2 [i] 1Ki 8:29 [j] ver 4; 2Ch 6:40
19:18 [k] Isa 44:9-11; Jer 10:3-10 [l] Ps 115:4; Ac 17:29
19:19 [m] 1Ki 8:43 [n] Ps 83:18
19:20 [o] 2Ki 20:5
19:21 [p] Jer 14:17; La 2:13 [q] Ps 22:7-8 [r] Job 16:4; Ps 109:25
19:22 [s] Ps 71:22; Isa 5:24
19:23 [t] Isa 10:18 [u] Ps 20:7
19:25 [v] Isa 40:21,28 [w] Isa 10:5; 45:7 [x] Mic 1:6
19:26 [y] Ps 6:10 [z] Isa 4:2 [a] Ps 129:6
19:27 [b] Ps 139:1-4
19:28 [c] Eze 19:9; 29:4 [d] Isa 30:28 [e] ver 33
19:29 [f] 2Ki 20:8-9; Lk 2:12

2Ki 19:14–15 ❖ When have you gone to God in prayer after receiving bad news? How did God answer that prayer?

the temple where he prays before the cherubim (v. 15), who represent the throne of the Creator of the universe.

19:20–28 Isaiah delivers an answer to Hezekiah's prayer as a mocking song. The sentiment of the song is typical of Isaiah; the divine plan has been determined from the beginning of the world (v. 25; Isa 40:21; 46:10). The Assyrians will not escape the destruction of war, which they have executed as part of God's judgment (cf. Isa 10:5–7). God knows their every action, their every pursuit (19:27). The Assyrians will be led away as prisoners in the same manner as they have led away their war prisoners.

19:29–34 Isaiah twice assures Hezekiah that Sennacherib will be turned back to the way he came (vv. 28c, 33–34). Judah will feel the effects of the foreign presence; it will be two years before a normal agricultural cycle of sowing and harvest can resume (vv. 29–30). Though many will be deported, those who survive will take root as a healthy plant, once again making the country prosperous. There was no actual siege against Jerusalem as at Lachish and the other fortified cities of Judah (vv. 32–34). God protects Jerusalem for the sake of his own name and because of his promise to David.

"This year you will eat what grows
by itself,[g]
and the second year what springs
from that.
But in the third year sow and reap,
plant vineyards[h] and eat their fruit.
30 Once more a remnant of the
kingdom of Judah
will take root[i] below and bear fruit
above.
31 For out of Jerusalem will come a
remnant,
and out of Mount Zion a band of
survivors.

"The zeal[j] of the LORD Almighty will accomplish this.

32 "Therefore this is what the LORD says
concerning the king of Assyria:

" 'He will not enter this city
or shoot an arrow here.
He will not come before it with
shield
or build a siege ramp against it.
33 By the way that he came he will
return;[k]
he will not enter this city,
declares the LORD.
34 I will defend[l] this city and save it,
for my sake and for the sake of
David[m] my servant.' "

35 That night the angel of the LORD[n]
went out and put to death a hundred
and eighty-five thousand in the Assyrian camp. When the people got up the
next morning—there were all the dead
bodies![o] 36 So Sennacherib king of Assyria
broke camp and withdrew. He returned
to Nineveh[p] and stayed there.
37 One day, while he was worshiping in
the temple of his god Nisrok, his sons
Adrammelek and Sharezer killed him
with the sword,[q] and they escaped to the
land of Ararat.[r] And Esarhaddon[s] his son
succeeded him as king.

Hezekiah's Illness

20:1–11pp // 2Ch 32:24–26; Isa 38:1–8

20 In those days Hezekiah became ill
and was at the point of death. The
prophet Isaiah son of Amoz went to him

19:29 [g] Lev 25:5 [h] Ps 107:37
19:30 [i] 2Ch 32:22-23
19:31 [j] Isa 9:7
19:33 [k] ver 28
19:34 [l] 2Ki 20:6 [m] 1Ki 11:12-13
19:35 [n] Ex 12:23 [o] Job 24:24
19:36 [p] Ge 10:11; Jnh 1:2
19:37 [q] ver 7 [r] Ge 8:4 [s] Ezr 4:2

20:3 [t] Ne 13:22 [u] 2Ki 18:3-6
20:5 [v] 1Sa 9:16; 1Ki 9:3; 2Ki 19:20 [w] Ps 39:12; 56:8
20:6 [x] 2Ki 19:34
20:7 [y] Isa 38:21
20:9 [z] Dt 13:2; Jer 44:29
20:11 [a] Jos 10:13

2Ki 20:5 ❖ How does it comfort us to know that God hears our prayers and sees our sorrows?

and said, "This is what the LORD says:
Put your house in order, because you
are going to die; you will not recover."
2 Hezekiah turned his face to the wall
and prayed to the LORD, 3 "Remember,[t]
LORD, how I have walked before you
faithfully[u] and with wholehearted devotion and have done what is good in
your eyes." And Hezekiah wept bitterly.
4 Before Isaiah had left the middle
court, the word of the LORD came to him:
5 "Go back and tell Hezekiah, the ruler of
my people, 'This is what the LORD, the
God of your father David, says: I have
heard[v] your prayer and seen your tears;[w]
I will heal you. On the third day from
now you will go up to the temple of the
LORD. 6 I will add fifteen years to your
life. And I will deliver you and this city
from the hand of the king of Assyria. I
will defend[x] this city for my sake and for
the sake of my servant David.' "
7 Then Isaiah said, "Prepare a poultice
of figs." They did so and applied it to the
boil,[y] and he recovered.
8 Hezekiah had asked Isaiah, "What
will be the sign that the LORD will heal
me and that I will go up to the temple
of the LORD on the third day from now?"
9 Isaiah answered, "This is the LORD's
sign[z] to you that the LORD will do what
he has promised: Shall the shadow go
forward ten steps, or shall it go back ten
steps?"
10 "It is a simple matter for the shadow
to go forward ten steps," said Hezekiah.
"Rather, have it go back ten steps."
11 Then the prophet Isaiah called on the
LORD, and the LORD made the shadow go
back[a] the ten steps it had gone down on
the stairway of Ahaz.

Envoys From Babylon

20:12–19pp // Isa 39:1–8
20:20–21pp // 2Ch 32:32–33

12 At that time Marduk-Baladan son of
Baladan king of Babylon sent Hezekiah

19:35–37 The Bible ignores the twenty years that elapse before the assassination of Sennacherib. The point is that divine judgment is meted out on the cruel Assyrian invader.
20:1–3 Isaiah's message for Jerusalem is positive, but initially not so for its king. On receiving the news of his impending death, King Hezekiah turns to God.
20:4–11 Isaiah returns with the message that Hezekiah will be delivered, as will Jerusalem, because of God's reputation and the promise made to David.
20:12–15 The visit of the Babylonian envoys has

letters and a gift, because he had heard
of Hezekiah's illness. 13Hezekiah received
the envoys and showed them all that was
in his storehouses — the silver, the gold,
the spices and the fine olive oil — his
armory and everything found among
his treasures. There was nothing in his
palace or in all his kingdom that Hezekiah did not show them.
14Then Isaiah the prophet went to
King Hezekiah and asked, "What did
those men say, and where did they come
from?"
"From a distant land," Hezekiah replied. "They came from Babylon."
15The prophet asked, "What did they
see in your palace?"
"They saw everything in my palace,"
Hezekiah said. "There is nothing among
my treasures that I did not show them."
16Then Isaiah said to Hezekiah, "Hear
the word of the LORD: 17The time will
surely come when everything in your
palace, and all that your predecessors
have stored up until this day, will be
carried off to Babylon.[b] Nothing will be
left, says the LORD. 18And some of your
descendants,[c] your own flesh and blood
who will be born to you, will be taken
away, and they will become eunuchs in
the palace of the king of Babylon."
19"The word of the LORD you have spoken is good," Hezekiah replied. For he
thought, "Will there not be peace and
security in my lifetime?"
20As for the other events of Hezekiah's
reign, all his achievements and how he
made the pool[d] and the tunnel by which
he brought water into the city, are they
not written in the book of the annals of
the kings of Judah? 21Hezekiah rested
with his ancestors. And Manasseh his
son succeeded him as king.

20:17 [b]2Ki 24:13; 25:13; 2Ch 36:10; Jer 27:22; 52:17-23
20:18 [c]2Ki 24:15; 2Ch 33:11; Da 1:3
20:20 [d]Ne 3:16

Manasseh King of Judah

21:1–10pp // 2Ch 33:1–10
21:17–18pp // 2Ch 33:18–20

21 Manasseh was twelve years old
when he became king, and he
reigned in Jerusalem fifty-five years. His

---

the same general chronological link to the time of the Assyrian siege. The sequence is arranged to show the threat to Jerusalem and the Davidic dynasty. No purpose for the visit is stated; it is probably an effort to maintain goodwill between common enemies of the Assyrians.

20:16-19 For this activity with the Babylonians, Hezekiah receives the ultimate judgment; his dynasty will end with his descendants going into exile.

20:20-21 Hezekiah resigns himself to the judgment he will receive; the word of Yahweh is appropriate. The statement of self-interest, that there will be peace during his days, is drawn into Kings from Isaiah's account. The failure of peace is a motif in Isaiah (Isa 48:22; 57:21). Hezekiah does not fall into the category of the wicked, but his faithlessness in this matter is one more example of why Judah goes into exile.

18:1—20:21 Faithfulness is a primary requirement in any healthy relationship and is the most fundamental requirement in a relationship with God. A covenant is the highest commitment of faithfulness; for Hezekiah, the covenant is both collective and personal: He represents the people who have entered into a divine covenant and leads them to faithfully observe it.

In the same way, Christians are called to faithfulness—both collectively and individually. Paul writes that as stewards responsible for the work of the kingdom in this world, faithfulness is the one fundamental requirement (1Co 4:2). Such stewardship is much more than just giving money or being prudent with material possessions. Being effective stewards means that we use every moment of time as a gift from God in a way that honors God. Hezekiah is a model of the exhortation the apostle Paul leaves Christians. The motives of Hezekiah can be questioned in the way he dealt with the Assyrians, in his prayer during the time of his illness, and particularly in exposing his wealth and military capabilities to the Babylonian emissaries. In all of these matters, Hezekiah is simply presented as a king in pursuit of faithfulness, doing the best he can within his own circumstances.

21:1-6 The dates of Manasseh's reign must be calculated from the time of the captivity. The reign of Manasseh likely began in 696 BC, giving him a ten-year coregency with Hezekiah. Manasseh reigned the longest of all the Judean kings.

Manasseh must have had the support of the leaders of Judah in his practice of foreign worship. Assyria has not yet met the disaster declared by Isaiah (Isa 10:12-19), and Manasseh reverses the policies of his father, both in the practice of faith and in the submission to Assyria.

Manasseh's act of passing the sons through the fire is named along with sorcery and his consulting mediums. These and other practices are specific violations of the covenant (Dt 18:10-11). Passing one's sons through the fire probably concerns funeral rites, as may be suggested by its pairing with consulting ghosts and spirits of the dead. Rituals that involved children do not necessarily indicate that the children were slaughtered for these rites (cf. Jer 7:32; 19:5; 32:35). Incineration of bodies took place at a dedicated location called a *tophet* by archaeologists (based on the Hebrew references). Such a place had a low enclosure wall and was used for generations. Those buried were primarily premature, stillborn, and young infants who didn't survive, buried with a special ceremony.

PEOPLE TO KNOW // MANASSEH

2 KINGS 21:1–18: Manasseh became king of Judah after his father, Hezekiah. Hezekiah was one of the best kings Judah ever had. Manasseh was arguably its worst.

Manasseh rebuilt the pagan worship centers his father had destroyed. He erected an Asherah pole and altars to Baal. He worshiped the "starry host" (2Ki 21:3). He placed altars to other deities in God's temple. He consulted mediums and spiritists. He even sacrificed his own son in flames. He also "shed so much innocent blood that he filled Jerusalem from end to end" (2Ki 21:16).

The book of 2 Kings tells us that Manasseh was more wicked than the nations God had driven out when he brought them into the promised land and credits Manasseh's sins for the eventual destruction of Jerusalem at the hands of Babylon.

Chronicles, written later than Kings, adds a fascinating epilogue to Manasseh's story. According to the writer of Chronicles, Manasseh was dragged to Babylon by his Assyrian enemies. From Babylon, Manasseh humbled himself and prayed to God. God was moved by his prayers and restored him to his throne in Jerusalem, where Manasseh enacted civic and religious reforms that honored God (2Ch 33:12–16).

APPLICATION ✣ Manasseh failed to learn how to love God from his father, Hezekiah. Though the Bible does not tell us what kind of father Hezekiah was, we know he was a righteous man. Those who have parents who honor God should gratefully carry on the faith passed onto them. Those who do not can look to the example of Manasseh's grandson, Josiah. Despite Josiah's evil father, Amon, and his evil grandfather, Manasseh, Josiah broke the cycle of evil and became one of Judah's most righteous kings. We can also take an important lesson from the Chronicles account of Manasseh's life: Even the worst sins can be forgiven when we come humbly to God and ask for forgiveness (1Jn 1:9). This promise is sealed for us by the grace of Jesus Christ.

mother's name was Hephzibah.[e] 2He did
evil[f] in the eyes of the LORD, following
the detestable practices[g] of the nations
the LORD had driven out before the Israelites. 3He rebuilt the high places[h] his
father Hezekiah had destroyed; he also
erected altars to Baal[i] and made an Asherah pole, as Ahab king of Israel had done.
He bowed down to all the starry hosts[j]
and worshiped them. 4He built altars[k]
in the temple of the LORD, of which the
LORD had said, "In Jerusalem I will put
my Name."[l] 5In the two courts[m] of the
temple of the LORD, he built altars to all
the starry hosts. 6He sacrificed his own
son[n] in the fire, practiced divination,
sought omens, and consulted mediums
and spiritists.[o] He did much evil in the
eyes of the LORD, arousing his anger.

7He took the carved Asherah pole[p] he
had made and put it in the temple, of
which the LORD had said to David and to
his son Solomon, "In this temple and in
Jerusalem, which I have chosen out of all
the tribes of Israel, I will put my Name[q]
forever. 8I will not again[r] make the feet
of the Israelites wander from the land I
gave their ancestors, if only they will be
careful to do everything I commanded
them and will keep the whole Law that
my servant Moses[s] gave them." 9But the
people did not listen. Manasseh led them
astray, so that they did more evil[t] than
the nations[u] the LORD had destroyed before the Israelites.

10The LORD said through his servants
the prophets: 11"Manasseh king of Judah
has committed these detestable sins. He
has done more evil[v] than the Amorites[w]

21:1 [e] Isa 62:4
21:2 [f] Jer 15:4 [g] 2Ki 16:3
21:3 [h] 2Ki 18:4 [i] Jdg 6:28; 1Ki 16:32 [j] Dt 17:3; 2Ki 17:16
21:4 [k] Jer 32:34 [l] 2Sa 7:13; 1Ki 8:29
21:5 [m] 1Ki 7:12; 2Ki 23:12
21:6 [n] Lev 18:21; Dt 18:10; 2Ki 16:3; 17:17 [o] Lev 19:31
21:7 [p] Dt 16:21; 2Ki 23:4 [q] 2Sa 7:13; 1Ki 8:29; 9:3; 2Ki 23:27; Jer 32:34
21:8 [r] 2Sa 7:10 [s] 2Ki 18:12
21:9 [t] Pr 29:12 [u] Dt 9:4
21:11 [v] 2Ki 24:3-4 [w] Ge 15:16; 1Ki 21:26

2Ki 21:10–15 ❖ When does God's patience for sin run out? How does this show the need for the grace of Christ?

21:7–13 The carved image of the Asherah implies something even worse than the standard Asherah pole. Setting the image in the temple is a desecration of the one place that represented divine ownership and fulfillment of the promise to David.

The "plumb line" of Samaria (v. 13) is a graphic image used by the earlier prophets (cf. Am 7:7–8). Ordinary tools of construction become God's standard of destruction. Jerusalem's being wiped clean as a washed pan turned upside down is an equally graphic proverb. God has had his fill of Judah's sinning; the city will be emptied out, its social order turned completely upside down.

who preceded him and has led Judah
into sin with his idols. 12 Therefore this
is what the LORD, the God of Israel, says:
I am going to bring such disaster[x] on
Jerusalem and Judah that the ears of
everyone who hears of it will tingle.[y] 13 I
will stretch out over Jerusalem the measuring line used against Samaria and the
plumb line[z] used against the house of
Ahab. I will wipe[a] out Jerusalem as one
wipes a dish, wiping it and turning it
upside down. 14 I will forsake[b] the remnant[c] of my inheritance and give them
into the hands of enemies. They will be
looted and plundered by all their enemies; 15 they have done evil[d] in my eyes
and have aroused[e] my anger from the
day their ancestors came out of Egypt
until this day."

16 Moreover, Manasseh also shed so
much innocent blood[f] that he filled Jerusalem from end to end — besides the sin
that he had caused Judah to commit, so
that they did evil in the eyes of the LORD.

17 As for the other events of Manasseh's
reign, and all he did, including the sin
he committed, are they not written in
the book of the annals of the kings of
Judah? 18 Manasseh rested with his ancestors and was buried in his palace garden,[g]
the garden of Uzza. And Amon his son
succeeded him as king.

Amon King of Judah

21:19–24pp // 2Ch 33:21–25

19 Amon was twenty-two years old
when he became king, and he reigned
in Jerusalem two years. His mother's
name was Meshullemeth daughter of
Haruz; she was from Jotbah. 20 He did
evil[h] in the eyes of the LORD, as his father
Manasseh had done. 21 He followed completely the ways of his father, worshiping
the idols his father had worshiped, and
bowing down to them. 22 He forsook the
LORD, the God of his ancestors, and did
not walk[i] in obedience to him.

23 Amon's officials conspired against
him and assassinated[j] the king in his palace. 24 Then the people of the land killed[k]
all who had plotted against King Amon,
and they made Josiah his son king in
his place.

25 As for the other events of Amon's
reign, and what he did, are they not written in the book of the annals of the kings
of Judah? 26 He was buried in his tomb in
the garden[l] of Uzza. And Josiah his son
succeeded him as king.

The Book of the Law Found

22:1–20pp // 2Ch 34:1–2,8–28

22 Josiah was eight years old when
he became king, and he reigned in
Jerusalem thirty-one years. His mother's
name was Jedidah daughter of Adaiah;
she was from Bozkath.[m] 2 He did what was
right[n] in the eyes of the LORD and followed completely the ways of his father
David, not turning aside to the right[o] or
to the left.

3 In the eighteenth year of his reign,
King Josiah sent the secretary, Shaphan[p]
son of Azaliah, the son of Meshullam,

21:12 [x] 2Ki 23:26; 24:3; Jer 15:4 [y] 1Sa 3:11; Jer 19:3
21:13 [z] Isa 34:11; La 2:8; Am 7:7-9 [a] 2Ki 23:27
21:14 [b] Ps 78:58-60 [c] 2Ki 19:4; Mic 2:12
21:15 [d] Ex 32:22 [e] Jer 25:7
21:16 [f] 2Ki 24:4
21:18 [g] ver 26
21:20 [h] ver 2-6
21:22 [i] 1Ki 11:33
21:23 [j] 2Ki 12:20; 2Ch 33:24-25
21:24 [k] 2Ki 14:5
21:26 [l] ver 18
22:1 [m] Jos 15:39
22:2 [n] Dt 17:19 [o] Dt 5:32
22:3 [p] 2Ch 34:20; Jer 39:14

21:14–18 The good remnant found in the reforms of Hezekiah will be uprooted and cast out. The nation is no longer God's inheritance, unique among the other nations. The shedding of innocent blood is also a metaphor for injustice against the poor, one of the greatest offenses committed by those who had themselves once been slaves (Isa 1:15–17). Manasseh is the only king to have his misdeeds noted in the concluding formula (21:17).

21:19–26 Amon is born when his father is forty-five, making it unlikely that he is the oldest son. The reign of Amon is brought to an abrupt end by conspirators from his own court. Perhaps this is an anti-Assyrian uprising, possibly in connection with disturbances during the reign of Ashurbanipal (640 BC). Whatever the case, the plot fails. Representative civic leaders dispatch the conspirators and make Amon's son Josiah king.

21:1–26 The effects of the sins of one person can extend to many others. Other individuals are drawn into errant ways, and many victims suffer the results of evil. This is particularly true when transgressions are committed by persons in political power. Most often oppressive actions are exercised as necessary for peace and liberty. Commonly, the results are irreversible for generations and many pay a terrible price, as is the case with Manasseh. Misguided religion and racially motivated violence have often been a part of the evil exercised against others throughout history. Our calling as believers is to prayerfully recognize and reverse that history in the name of our loving Savior.

22:1–2 Josiah's reign begins in 640 BC, and he rules during the declining years of the Assyrian Empire. The reign of Josiah takes place during massive transitions of power in international affairs. The account of Josiah's reign is introduced (v. 2) and concluded (23:25) with the standard formulas for keeping the covenant: He does not turn to the right or to the left (Dt 5:32; 17:20) but loves God with all his heart, soul, and strength (Dt 6:5).

22:3–7 The disastrous state of the temple must have taken place during the apostate reign of

to the temple of the LORD. He said: 4"Go
up to Hilkiah the high priest and have
him get ready the money that has been
brought into the temple of the LORD,
which the doorkeepers have collected[q]
from the people. 5Have them entrust it to
the men appointed to supervise the work
on the temple. And have these men pay
the workers who repair[r] the temple of the
LORD— 6the carpenters, the builders and
the masons. Also have them purchase
timber and dressed stone to repair the
temple.[s] 7But they need not account for
the money entrusted to them, because
they are honest in their dealings."[t]
8Hilkiah the high priest said to Shaphan the secretary, "I have found the
Book of the Law[u] in the temple of the
LORD." He gave it to Shaphan, who read it.
9Then Shaphan the secretary went to the
king and reported to him: "Your officials
have paid out the money that was in the
temple of the LORD and have entrusted
it to the workers and supervisors at the
temple." 10Then Shaphan the secretary
informed the king, "Hilkiah the priest
has given me a book." And Shaphan read
from it in the presence of the king.[v]
11When the king heard the words of
the Book of the Law, he tore his robes.
12He gave these orders to Hilkiah the
priest, Ahikam[w] son of Shaphan, Akbor
son of Micaiah, Shaphan the secretary
and Asaiah the king's attendant: 13"Go
and inquire of the LORD for me and
for the people and for all Judah about
what is written in this book that has
been found. Great is the LORD's anger[x]
that burns against us because those who
have gone before us have not obeyed the
words of this book; they have not acted in accordance with all that is written
there concerning us."
14Hilkiah the priest, Ahikam, Akbor,

22:4 [q] 2Ki 12:4-5
22:5 [r] 2Ki 12:5, 11-14
22:6 [s] 2Ki 12:11-12
22:7 [t] 2Ki 12:15
22:8 [u] Dt 31:24
22:10 [v] Jer 36:21
22:12 [w] 2Ki 25:22; Jer 26:24
22:13 [x] Dt 29:24-28; 31:17
22:16 [y] Dt 31:29; Jos 23:15 [z] Dt 29:27; Da 9:11
22:17 [a] Dt 29:25-27
22:18 [b] 2Ch 34:26; Jer 21:2
22:19 [c] Ex 10:3; 1Ki 21:29; Ps 51:17; Isa 57:15; Mic 6:8 [d] Jer 26:6 [e] Lev 26:31
22:20 [f] Isa 57:1

2Ki 22:8–13 ❖ What happens to communities when God's Word is lost and forgotten? What happens to our faith when we neglect reading God's Word?

Shaphan and Asaiah went to speak to
the prophet Huldah, who was the wife of
Shallum son of Tikvah, the son of Harhas, keeper of the wardrobe. She lived in
Jerusalem, in the New Quarter.
15She said to them, "This is what the
LORD, the God of Israel, says: Tell the
man who sent you to me, 16'This is what
the LORD says: I am going to bring disaster[y] on this place and its people, according to everything written in the book[z]
the king of Judah has read. 17Because
they have forsaken[a] me and burned
incense to other gods and aroused my
anger by all the idols their hands have
made,[a] my anger will burn against
this place and will not be quenched.'
18Tell the king of Judah, who sent you
to inquire[b] of the LORD, 'This is what
the LORD, the God of Israel, says concerning the words you heard: 19Because
your heart was responsive and you humbled[c] yourself before the LORD when you
heard what I have spoken against this
place and its people — that they would
become a curse[b][d] and be laid waste[e] —
and because you tore your robes and
wept in my presence, I also have heard
you, declares the LORD. 20Therefore I
will gather you to your ancestors, and
you will be buried in peace.[f] Your eyes
will not see all the disaster I am going
to bring on this place.'"
So they took her answer back to the
king.

[a] 17 *Or by everything they have done* [b] 19 That is, their names would be used in cursing (see Jer. 29:22); or, others would see that they are cursed.

Manasseh. In that time the Book of the Covenant seems to have been entirely forgotten. Josiah begins to seek the God of David in the eighth year of his reign and to remove the idolatrous high places from Judah and Jerusalem in the twelfth (2Ch 34:3). The temple purification begins in his eighteenth year, at which time the Book of the Covenant is discovered (2Ch 34:8, 14). So reforms begin before the discovery of that book.

It is not difficult to understand why the Book of the Covenant may have been moved from its proper place beside the ark of the covenant (Dt 31:26); Manasseh would not have wanted it there, nor would the priests have wanted to provoke him by leaving it there.

22:8–17 The book found in the temple is readily identified as "the Law." Josiah becomes profoundly repentant and takes immediate action when he learns about the neglect of the covenant. He dispatches a delegation to Huldah, the court prophetess. Her message is an unequivocal application of the book's message to the inhabitants of Judah and Jerusalem. The curse of the covenant rests on them (e.g., Dt 28:58–68).

22:18–20 Huldah only mitigates this curse by telling the king that his penitence will prevent the disaster of the exile from taking place during his lifetime. The "curse" on the inhabitants of the kingdom cannot be averted, but Josiah will die in peace. In all other circumstances this would signify a natural

Josiah Renews the Covenant

23:1–3pp // 2Ch 34:29–32
23:4–20Ref // 2Ch 34:3–7,33
23:21–23pp // 2Ch 35:1,18–19
23:28–30pp // 2Ch 35:20—36:1

23 Then the king called together all
the elders of Judah and Jerusalem. 2He went up to the temple of the
LORD with the people of Judah, the inhabitants of Jerusalem, the priests and
the prophets — all the people from the
least to the greatest. He read[g] in their
hearing all the words of the Book of the
Covenant, which had been found in the
temple of the LORD. 3The king stood by
the pillar and renewed the covenant[h] in
the presence of the LORD — to follow[i] the
LORD and keep his commands, statutes
and decrees with all his heart and all his
soul, thus confirming the words of the
covenant written in this book. Then all
the people pledged themselves to the
covenant.
4The king ordered Hilkiah the high
priest, the priests next in rank and the
doorkeepers[j] to remove[k] from the temple of the LORD all the articles made for
Baal and Asherah and all the starry hosts.
He burned them outside Jerusalem in
the fields of the Kidron Valley and took
the ashes to Bethel. 5He did away with
the idolatrous priests appointed by the
kings of Judah to burn incense on the
high places of the towns of Judah and
on those around Jerusalem — those who
burned incense to Baal, to the sun and
moon, to the constellations and to all
the starry hosts.[l] 6He took the Asherah
pole from the temple of the LORD to the
Kidron Valley outside Jerusalem and
burned it there. He ground it to powder
and scattered the dust over the graves
of the common people.[m] 7He also tore
down the quarters of the male shrine

23:2 [g] Dt 31:11; 2Ki 22:8
23:3 [h] 2Ki 11:14, 17 [i] Dt 13:4
23:4 [j] 2Ki 25:18 [k] 2Ki 21:7
23:5 [l] 2Ki 21:3; Jer 8:2
23:6 [m] Jer 26:23

> **2Ki 23:1–3** ❖ Where have we witnessed the transforming power of the Bible?

prostitutes[n] that were in the temple of
the LORD, the quarters where women did
weaving for Asherah.
8Josiah brought all the priests from
the towns of Judah and desecrated the
high places, from Geba[o] to Beersheba,
where the priests had burned incense. He
broke down the gateway at the entrance
of the Gate of Joshua, the city governor,
which was on the left of the city gate.
9Although the priests of the high places
did not serve[p] at the altar of the LORD in
Jerusalem, they ate unleavened bread
with their fellow priests.
10He desecrated Topheth,[q] which was
in the Valley of Ben Hinnom,[r] so no one
could use it to sacrifice their son[s] or
daughter in the fire to Molek. 11He removed from the entrance to the temple
of the LORD the horses that the kings of
Judah had dedicated to the sun. They
were in the court[a] near the room of an
official named Nathan-Melek. Josiah
then burned the chariots dedicated to
the sun.[t]
12He pulled down the altars the kings
of Judah had erected on the roof[u] near
the upper room of Ahaz, and the altars
Manasseh had built in the two courts[v]
of the temple of the LORD. He removed
them from there, smashed them to pieces and threw the rubble into the Kidron
Valley. 13The king also desecrated the
high places that were east of Jerusalem
on the south of the Hill of Corruption —
the ones Solomon[w] king of Israel had

23:7 [n] 1Ki 14:24; 15:12; Eze 16:16
23:8 [o] 1Ki 15:22
23:9 [p] Eze 44:10-14
23:10 [q] Isa 30:33; Jer 7:31,32; 19:6 [r] Jos 15:8 [s] Lev 18:21; Dt 18:10
23:11 [t] Dt 4:19
23:12 [u] Jer 19:13; Zep 1:5 [v] 2Ki 21:5
23:13 [w] 1Ki 11:7

[a] *11* The meaning of the Hebrew for this word is uncertain.

---

death, not a death in war as Josiah experiences (23:29–30). Peace for Josiah means he will be buried in his own grave with other distinguished kings of Judah.

23:1–3 The inclusion of both civil and religious leaders as representatives makes the covenant effective in both civil and religious jurisdictions. This is a high point in the history of the nation; the people not only enter into a covenant with God, but the covenant becomes the legal foundation of the political order. Josiah enacts this renewal of the covenant by calling for the purification of worship.

23:4–7 Purification begins in Jerusalem; it focuses on the temple and extends to destroying idolatrous objects and those who led in such practices.

23:8–11 Nothing is known of cultic installations at the city gates, nor is a Joshua Gate known in Jerusalem. The rural priests who come into Jerusalem do not have the same status in Jerusalem, but they do have food provided to them. Their restrictions are similar to physically blemished priests (Lev 21:22–23); their limited rank is likely dictated by the nature of the reform in the allocation of priests.

23:12–14 Josiah's purifications involve the removal of shrines that go back to the time of Solomon (1Ki 11:5–7). The "Hill of Corruption" is a wordplay on the Mount of Olives; instead of the "Mount of Anointing" it is the "Mount of Destruction." Filling the idolatrous places with human bones renders them untouchable (cf. Nu 19:16).

built for Ashtoreth the vile goddess of
the Sidonians, for Chemosh the vile god
of Moab, and for Molek the detestable
god of the people of Ammon. 14Josiah
smashed[x] the sacred stones and cut down
the Asherah poles and covered the sites
with human bones.
15Even the altar[y] at Bethel, the high
place made by Jeroboam[z] son of Nebat,
who had caused Israel to sin — even that
altar and high place he demolished. He
burned the high place and ground it to
powder, and burned the Asherah pole
also. 16Then Josiah[a] looked around, and
when he saw the tombs that were there
on the hillside, he had the bones removed from them and burned on the
altar to defile it, in accordance with the
word of the LORD proclaimed by the man
of God who foretold these things.
17The king asked, "What is that tomb-
stone I see?"
The people of the city said, "It marks
the tomb of the man of God who came
from Judah and pronounced against the
altar of Bethel the very things you have
done to it."
18"Leave it alone," he said. "Don't let
anyone disturb his bones[b]." So they
spared his bones and those of the prophet who had come from Samaria.
19Just as he had done at Bethel, Josiah
removed all the shrines at the high places that the kings of Israel had built in the
towns of Samaria and that had aroused
the LORD's anger. 20Josiah slaughtered[c]
all the priests of those high places on
the altars and burned human bones[d] on
them. Then he went back to Jerusalem.

21The king gave this order to all the
people: "Celebrate the Passover[e] to the
LORD your God, as it is written in this
Book of the Covenant." 22Neither in the
days of the judges who led Israel nor in
the days of the kings of Israel and the
kings of Judah had any such Passover
been observed. 23But in the eighteenth
year of King Josiah, this Passover was
celebrated to the LORD in Jerusalem.
24Furthermore, Josiah got rid of the
mediums and spiritists,[f] the household
gods,[g] the idols and all the other detestable things seen in Judah and Jerusalem.
This he did to fulfill the requirements of
the law written in the book that Hilkiah
the priest had discovered in the temple
of the LORD. 25Neither before nor after
Josiah was there a king like him who
turned[h] to the LORD as he did — with all
his heart and with all his soul and with
all his strength, in accordance with all
the Law of Moses.
26Nevertheless, the LORD did not turn
away from the heat of his fierce anger,
which burned against Judah because of
all that Manasseh[i] had done to arouse his
anger. 27So the LORD said, "I will remove[j]
Judah also from my presence[k] as I removed Israel, and I will reject Jerusalem,
the city I chose, and this temple, about
which I said, 'My Name shall be there.'[a]"
28As for the other events of Josiah's
reign, and all he did, are they not written
in the book of the annals of the kings
of Judah?
29While Josiah was king, Pharaoh
Necho[l] king of Egypt went up to the

23:14 [x] Ex 23:24; Dt 7:5, 25
23:15 [y] 1Ki 13:1-3 [z] 1Ki 12:33
23:16 [a] 1Ki 13:2
23:18 [b] 1Ki 13:31
23:20 [c] Ex 22:20; 2Ki 10:25; 11:18 [d] 1Ki 13:2
23:21 [e] Ex 12:11; Nu 9:2; Dt 16:1-8
23:24 [f] Lev 19:31; Dt 18:11; 2Ki 21:6 [g] Ge 31:19
23:25 [h] 2Ki 18:5
23:26 [i] 2Ki 21:12; Jer 15:4
23:27 [j] 2Ki 21:13 [k] 2Ki 18:11
23:29 [l] Jer 46:2

[a] 27 1 Kings 8:29

23:15-16 Josiah has a special interest in Bethel as a territory that once belonged to Judah. Jeroboam set up a border shrine there in establishing his kingdom. Josiah's desecration of the altar by burning the bones of the graves on it fulfills the words of the prophet from Judah in the time of Jeroboam (1Ki 13:1-2).

23:17-20 The purging of the shrines in the cities of Samaria also fulfills prophecy (1Ki 13:32). Josiah shows no tolerance for the priests of those high places but punishes them according to the instructions found for the treatment of idolatrous cities (Dt 13:13-18).

23:21-23 Celebrating the Passover is an essential aspect of covenant renewal. Its introduction resumes the account of the renewal ceremony (vv. 1-3), which is interrupted by the lengthy description of Josiah's reforms. Prior to this, the last reported covenant renewal was in the days of Joshua (Jos 8:30-35); this covenant renewal marks the first occasion since Joshua's time when the Passover was celebrated as a national festival with government officials involved.

23:24-25 The renewal also involves purging all false prophecy in Israel. Consultation with the dead was a usual method for attempting to receive a divine message. "Mediums and spiritists" refers to some type of necromancy—or attempting to communicate with the dead. The use of "household gods" also goes back to ancient practice (Ge 31:19). These images were of various sizes and were always associated with trying to communicate with a deity.

23:26-30 Josiah's encounter with the Egyptians at Megiddo meets with disaster. His tragic death is a calamity. According to the Chronicler, Jeremiah composed a long lament song for his funeral, which remains to his time (2Ch 35:25). As at other times, certain civic officials assume leadership and appoint one of Josiah's younger sons to the throne.

Euphrates River to help the king of Assyria. King Josiah marched out to meet
him in battle, but Necho faced him and
killed him at Megiddo.[m] 30Josiah's servants brought his body in a chariot[n] from
Megiddo to Jerusalem and buried him
in his own tomb. And the people of the
land took Jehoahaz son of Josiah and
anointed him and made him king in
place of his father.

Jehoahaz King of Judah

23:31–34pp // 2Ch 36:2–4

31Jehoahaz[o] was twenty-three years old
when he became king, and he reigned in
Jerusalem three months. His mother's
name was Hamutal[p] daughter of Jeremiah; she was from Libnah. 32He did evil in
the eyes of the LORD, just as his predecessors had done. 33Pharaoh Necho put
him in chains at Riblah[q] in the land of
Hamath[r] so that he might not reign in
Jerusalem, and he imposed on Judah a
levy of a hundred talents[a] of silver and
a talent[b] of gold. 34Pharaoh Necho made
Eliakim[s] son of Josiah king in place of
his father Josiah and changed Eliakim's
name to Jehoiakim. But he took Jehoahaz and carried him off to Egypt, and
there he died.[t] 35Jehoiakim paid Pharaoh
Necho the silver and gold he demanded. In order to do so, he taxed the land
and exacted the silver and gold from the
people of the land according to their as-
sessments.[u]

23:29 [m] Zec 12:11
23:30 [n] 2Ki 9:28
23:31 [o] 1Ch 3:15; Jer 22:11 [p] 2Ki 24:18
23:33 [q] 2Ki 25:6 [r] 1Ki 8:65
23:34 [s] 1Ch 3:15; 2Ch 36:5-8 [t] Jer 22:12; Eze 19:3-4
23:35 [u] ver 33

23:36 [v] Jer 26:1
24:1 [w] Jer 25:1, 9; Da 1:1
24:2 [x] Jer 35:11 [y] Jer 25:9
24:3 [z] 2Ki 18:25 [a] 2Ki 21:12; 23:26
24:4 [b] 2Ki 21:16
24:6 [c] Jer 22:19

Jehoiakim King of Judah

23:36—24:6pp // 2Ch 36:5–8

36Jehoiakim[v] was twenty-five years old
when he became king, and he reigned
in Jerusalem eleven years. His mother's
name was Zebidah daughter of Pedaiah;
she was from Rumah. 37And he did evil
in the eyes of the LORD, just as his predecessors had done.

24 During Jehoiakim's reign, Nebuchadnezzar[w] king of Babylon invaded the land, and Jehoiakim became
his vassal for three years. But then he
turned against Nebuchadnezzar and rebelled. 2The LORD sent Babylonian,[c] Aramean,[x] Moabite and Ammonite raiders
against him to destroy[y] Judah, in accordance with the word of the LORD proclaimed by his servants the prophets.
3Surely these things happened to Judah
according to the LORD's command,[z] in
order to remove them from his presence
because of the sins of Manasseh[a] and all
he had done, 4including the shedding of
innocent blood.[b] For he had filled Jerusalem with innocent blood, and the LORD
was not willing to forgive.

5As for the other events of Jehoiakim's
reign, and all he did, are they not written
in the book of the annals of the kings
of Judah? 6Jehoiakim rested[c] with his

[a] 33 That is, about 3 3/4 tons or about 3.4 metric tons [b] 33 That is, about 75 pounds or about 34 kilograms [c] 2 Or *Chaldean*

22:1–23:30 Josiah reads like a story of too little, too late, but this would likely not have been his own assessment of his life's work. The Book of the Law instructs him as to his course of action. His reforms are right, irrespective of the eventual outcome for Judah. His action is to the glory of God—which is always the ultimate goal and a goal that is achievable. But if Josiah had as his only goal the preservation of Judah, it is indeed too little, too late.

Success in leadership must be measured by the impact it has on people. Within his time, Josiah is an immensely successful reformer—more so than any other king who preceded him. He leads the nation in an unprecedented revival, going back to times before the monarchy even began (v. 22).

Though the fate of the nation is sealed, Josiah is instrumental in preserving the covenant. This is especially evident in the life of Jeremiah, who carries a message of judgment to the people who defy that covenant.

23:31–35 The civic leaders of Israel appoint Shallum to succeed Josiah (v. 30). Shallum is the fourth son of Josiah according to the genealogy in 1Chr 3:15; he receives the throne name Jehoahaz when he is anointed king. Jehoahaz is appointed by the same leaders who made Josiah king (2Ki 21:24) in the hopes that he will continue the policies of his father. There is no concluding summary of the reign of Jehoahaz, since he dies in Egypt; the place of his tomb is not known. Necho makes Eliakim the king of Judah on his successful return from Haran.
23:36–37 Political forces change during Jehoiakim's reign. Pharoah Necho fails to restrict the power of the Babylonians at Haran. Egypt controls the Levant for about four years, until the Babylonians conquer Carchemish in 605 BC. Jehoiakim, enthroned by the Egyptians, soon comes under the domination of the Babylonians, the successors of the Neo-Assyrian Empire.
24:1–7 Nebuchadnezzar marches to Egypt in his fourth year but fails to gain a victory. Necho follows up his victory by invading the southern coast and taking Gaza (cf. Jer 47:1). This is the time of Jehoiakim's rebellion against Babylon. Jehoiakim is caught in the power struggle.

ancestors. And Jehoiachin his son succeeded him as king.
7The king of Egypt[d] did not march out
from his own country again, because the
king of Babylon[e] had taken all his territory, from the Wadi of Egypt to the Euphrates River.

Jehoiachin King of Judah

24:8–17pp // 2Ch 36:9–10

8Jehoiachin[f] was eighteen years old
when he became king, and he reigned
in Jerusalem three months. His mother's
name was Nehushta daughter of Elnathan; she was from Jerusalem. 9He did
evil in the eyes of the LORD, just as his
father had done.
10At that time the officers of Nebuchadnezzar[g] king of Babylon advanced
on Jerusalem and laid siege to it, 11and
Nebuchadnezzar himself came up to the
city while his officers were besieging it.
12Jehoiachin king of Judah, his mother,
his attendants, his nobles and his officials all surrendered[h] to him.
In the eighth year of the reign of the
king of Babylon, he took Jehoiachin
prisoner. 13As the LORD had declared,[i]
Nebuchadnezzar removed the treasures[j]
from the temple of the LORD and from
the royal palace, and cut up the gold articles[k] that Solomon[l] king of Israel had
made for the temple of the LORD. 14He
carried all Jerusalem into exile:[m] all the
officers and fighting men, and all the
skilled workers and artisans — a total of
ten thousand. Only the poorest[n] people
of the land were left.
15Nebuchadnezzar took Jehoiachin
captive to Babylon. He also took from
Jerusalem to Babylon the king's mother,[o]

24:7 [d]Ge 15:18 [e]Jer 37:5-7; 46:2
24:8 [f]1Ch 3:16
24:10 [g]Da 1:1
24:12 [h]2Ki 25:27; Jer 22:24-30; 24:1; 25:1; 29:2; 52:28
24:13 [i]2Ki 20:17 [j]2Ki 25:15; Isa 39:6 [k]2Ki 25:14; Jer 20:5 [l]1Ki 7:51
24:14 [m]Jer 24:1; 52:28 [n]2Ki 25:12; Jer 40:7; 52:16
24:15 [o]Jer 22:24-28 [p]Est 2:6; Eze 17:12-14
24:16 [q]Jer 52:28
24:17 [r]1Ch 3:15; 2Ch 36:11; Jer 37:1
24:18 [s]Jer 52:1 [t]2Ki 23:31
24:20 [u]Dt 4:26; 29:27
25:1 [v]Jer 34:1-7 [w]Eze 24:2

2Ki 24:14 ❖ In the OT, rebellion leads to exile. How does Judah's fate point us to Jesus Christ (see Jn 14:6)?

his wives, his officials and the prominent
people[p] of the land. 16The king of Babylon also deported to Babylon the entire
force of seven thousand fighting men,
strong and fit for war, and a thousand
skilled workers and artisans.[q] 17He made
Mattaniah, Jehoiachin's uncle, king in his
place and changed his name to Zedekiah.[r]

Zedekiah King of Judah

24:18–20pp // 2Ch 36:11–16; Jer 52:1–3

18Zedekiah[s] was twenty-one years old
when he became king, and he reigned
in Jerusalem eleven years. His mother's
name was Hamutal[t] daughter of Jeremiah; she was from Libnah. 19He did evil in
the eyes of the LORD, just as Jehoiakim
had done. 20It was because of the LORD's
anger that all this happened to Jerusalem and Judah, and in the end he thrust[u]
them from his presence.

The Fall of Jerusalem

25:1–12pp // Jer 39:1–10
25:1–21pp // 2Ch 36:17–20; Jer 52:4–27
25:22–26pp // Jer 40:7–9; 41:1–3,16–18

Now Zedekiah rebelled against the
king of Babylon.
25 So in the ninth year of Zedekiah's
reign, on the tenth day of the tenth
month, Nebuchadnezzar[v] king of Babylon marched against Jerusalem with his
whole army. He encamped outside the
city and built siege works[w] all around it.
2The city was kept under siege until the
eleventh year of King Zedekiah.

24:8-9 Jehoiakim dies before Jerusalem surrenders and is succeeded by his eighteen-year-old son, Jehoiachin, who reigns only three months (v. 8).
24:10-12 Nebuchadnezzar himself arrives to join the army besieging Jerusalem, and Jehoiachin surrenders, which spares the city from destruction. Jehoiachin pays for the policy of his father with exile.
24:13-16 It was common practice for conquering armies to plunder temple and palace treasures.
24:17-18 Before leaving Jerusalem, Nebuchadnezzar installs Mattaniah, the youngest son of Josiah, as his vassal king. His throne name is Zedekiah; he rules until the fate of the kingdom of Judah is sealed.

23:31—24:17 It is said that God is all you need, but you do not know that until God is all you have. That was certainly true for the Israelites in exile, who suffered alienation and humiliation. The story preserved in Kings is testimony to the strength and resolution of their faith.

24:18-19 Zedekiah takes the throne as a sworn vassal of Nebuchadnezzar. The Babylonians expect little resistance from Judah; the deportation of military personnel and high officials requires that a new administration must be structured. Zedekiah has a difficult time maneuvering among the various factions.
25:1-3 It is not clear what inspires Zedekiah's rebellion, but he breaks his treaty with Babylon by sending messengers to Egypt to ask for horses and troops (Eze 17:15). In response, Nebuchadnezzar marches through Palestine and chooses to attack Jerusalem first, besieging it in 588 BC.

NEBUCHADNEZZAR'S CAMPAIGNS AGAINST JUDAH

605–586 BC

Events in Judah moved swiftly following the death of Josiah. Pharaoh Necho pressed his advantage by deporting Jehoahaz, the new ruler, and appointing a second son of Josiah, Jehoiakim, as king.

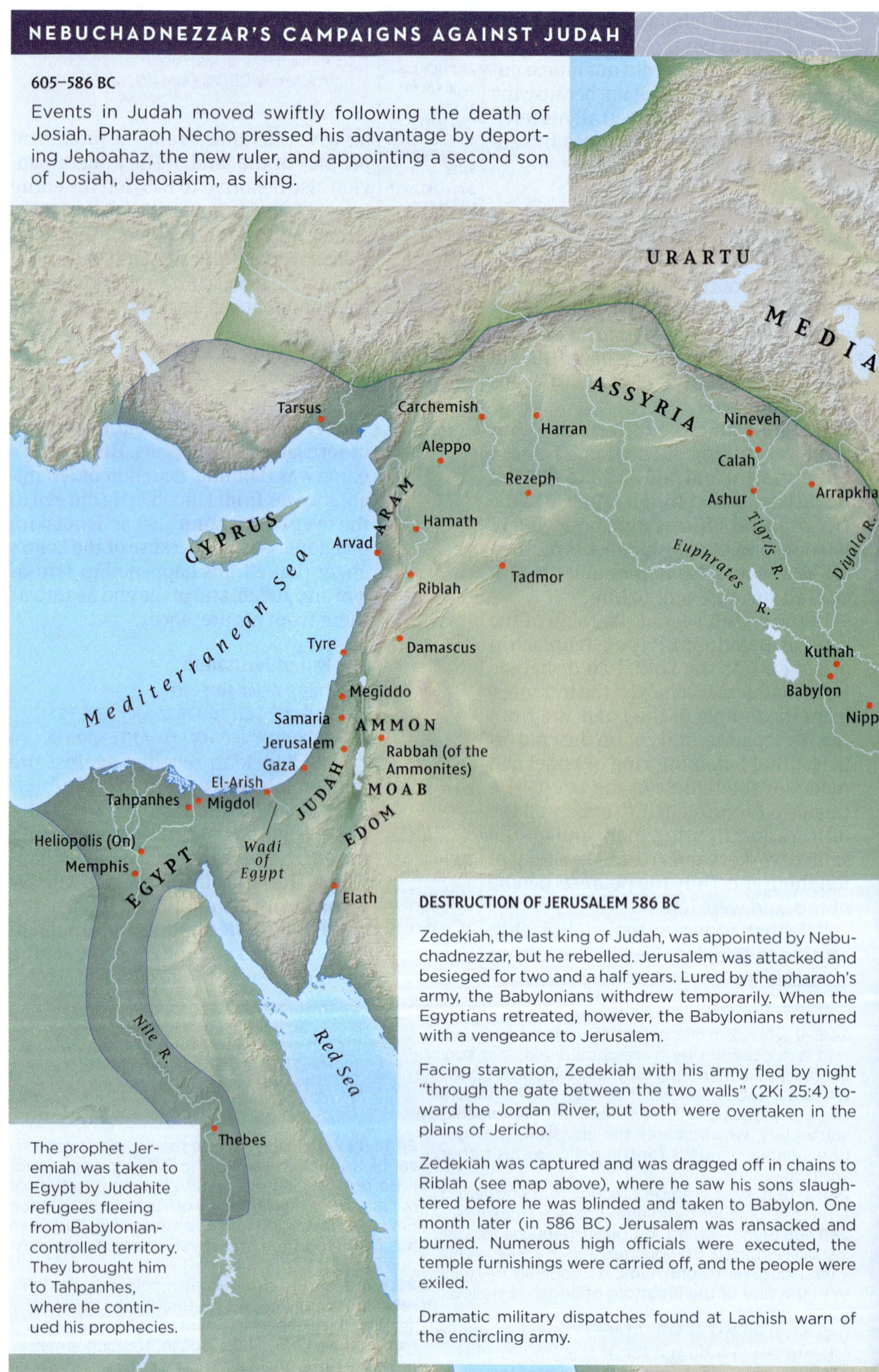

The prophet Jeremiah was taken to Egypt by Judahite refugees fleeing from Babylonian-controlled territory. They brought him to Tahpanhes, where he continued his prophecies.

DESTRUCTION OF JERUSALEM 586 BC

Zedekiah, the last king of Judah, was appointed by Nebuchadnezzar, but he rebelled. Jerusalem was attacked and besieged for two and a half years. Lured by the pharaoh's army, the Babylonians withdrew temporarily. When the Egyptians retreated, however, the Babylonians returned with a vengeance to Jerusalem.

Facing starvation, Zedekiah with his army fled by night "through the gate between the two walls" (2Ki 25:4) toward the Jordan River, but both were overtaken in the plains of Jericho.

Zedekiah was captured and was dragged off in chains to Riblah (see map above), where he saw his sons slaughtered before he was blinded and taken to Babylon. One month later (in 586 BC) Jerusalem was ransacked and burned. Numerous high officials were executed, the temple furnishings were carried off, and the people were exiled.

Dramatic military dispatches found at Lachish warn of the encircling army.

The Chaldeans (Kaldu), as the Neo-Babylonians were called, had important connections at Ur and Harran, centers of worship of the moon-god Sin. They also developed the trade routes across North Arabia, where Tema was particularly important, becoming the residence of Nabonidus during the last days of the kingdom.

CONQUEST OF JERUSALEM C. 597 BC

Soon a stronger power appeared in the north in the person of Nebuchadnezzar, king of the Chaldeans (Neo-Babylonians), who determined to follow the fierce policies of his Assyrian predecessors.

The tribute of Jehoiakim was paid at a distance when he heard of Nebuchadnezzar's approach. After three years as a Babylonian vassal, he rebelled, bringing a rapid response in the form of small-scale raids from Babylonians, Arameans, Moabites and Ammonites (c. 602 BC). Finally, Nebuchadnezzar's forces controlled all of the coastal territory north of the Wadi of Egypt (see previous page).

When 18-year-old Jehoiachin had ruled just three months (597 BC), the main Babylonian army struck, capturing Jerusalem and exiling the king as a captive in Babylon. Ten thousand persons were deported.

PEOPLE TO KNOW // ZEDEKIAH

2 KINGS 24:18–20: Zedekiah was the final king of Judah, installed into this position by King Nebuchadnezzar of Babylon. Zedekiah was the son of the great king Josiah. Two of his brothers and his nephew were kings before him. Unlike his father, however, Zedekiah did evil in God's eyes (2Ki 24:19).

Zedekiah refused to heed the warnings of the prophet Jeremiah, who urged Zedekiah to serve the king of Babylon (Jer 27:12). Zedekiah imprisoned Jeremiah for prophesying bad news for Jerusalem (Jer 32:3). Jeremiah prophesied that though Jerusalem would be destroyed, and Zedekiah would be taken captive to Babylon, the king would not die by the sword but would die peacefully (Jer 34:4–5).

When Zedekiah's officials wanted to kill Jeremiah for prophesying against Judah, Zedekiah allowed them to do what they wanted with the prophet. They threw Jeremiah into a cistern to die, but Ebed-Melek, with Zedekiah's permission, saved Jeremiah from death. Zedekiah secretly spoke with Jeremiah and expressed his own fear, but he ordered Jeremiah not to speak of their conversation (Jer 38:19–26).

For the last two years of Zedekiah's reign, Jerusalem was under siege by Babylon. When battle broke out, Zedekiah was captured and taken before Nebuchadnezzar. The Babylonians killed Zedekiah's sons in front of him and then gouged out his eyes. He was put in shackles and taken to Babylon, where he died in prison (2Ki 25:6–7; Jer 52:11).

APPLICATION ✣ Zedekiah refused to heed the word of God's messenger. Sometimes when God's Word is difficult to follow or inconveniences us in our pursuit of what we want or think is best, we tune it out and keep living our own way. Perhaps we have fallen into a lifestyle pattern that we know is out of sync with God's will, and we plug our ears to God's warnings. Zedekiah's story shows that we cannot ignore God and get away with it forever. The Good News is that, when we do fail, God provides us a way to be reconciled to himself through Jesus Christ.

3By the ninth day of the fourth[a] month
the famine[x] in the city had become so
severe that there was no food for the people to eat. 4Then the city wall was broken
through,[y] and the whole army fled at
night through the gate between the two
walls near the king's garden, though the
Babylonians[b] were surrounding[z] the city.
They fled toward the Arabah,[c] 5but the
Babylonian[d] army pursued the king and
overtook him in the plains of Jericho. All
his soldiers were separated from him
and scattered,[a] 6and he was captured.[b]

He was taken to the king of Babylon at
Riblah,[c] where sentence was pronounced
on him. 7They killed the sons of Zedekiah before his eyes. Then they put out his
eyes, bound him with bronze shackles
and took him to Babylon.[d]

8On the seventh day of the fifth
month, in the nineteenth year of Nebuchadnezzar king of Babylon, Nebuzaradan commander of the imperial guard,
an official of the king of Babylon, came
to Jerusalem. 9He set fire[e] to the temple
of the LORD, the royal palace and all the
houses of Jerusalem. Every important
building he burned down.[f] 10The whole
Babylonian army under the commander
of the imperial guard broke down the
walls[g] around Jerusalem. 11Nebuzaradan
the commander of the guard carried into

25:3 [x]Jer 14:18; La 4:9
25:4 [y]Eze 33:21 [z]Jer 4:17
25:5 [a]Eze 12:14
25:6 [b]Jer 34:21-22 [c]2Ki 23:33
25:7 [d]Jer 21:7; 32:4-5; Eze 12:11
25:9 [e]Isa 60:7 [f]Ps 74:3-8; Jer 2:15; Am 2:5; Mic 3:12
25:10 [g]Ne 1:3

2Ki 25:8–17 ✣ Where can we go for comfort and strength when everything we know and love falls apart (see Ps 91:1–2)?

[a] *3* Probable reading of the original Hebrew text (see Jer. 52:6); Masoretic Text does not have *fourth.* [b] *4* Or *Chaldeans;* also in verses 13, 25 and 26 [c] *4* Or *the Jordan Valley* [d] *5* Or *Chaldean;* also in verses 10 and 24

25:4–7 The royal party is captured in the level area at Jericho. The group is taken to the military headquarters in Riblah, where the king witnesses the death of his sons before being cruelly blinded and led to Babylon.
25:8–21 The destruction of Jerusalem is thorough. Temple, palaces, and houses are burned, the temple vessels—including the enormous bronze Sea, the wheeled bronze stands—all those items described in the account of Solomon's construction of the temple—are broken and taken as plunder. With the capture and destruction of Jerusalem, the kingdom of Judah ceases to exist.

exile[h] the people who remained in the
city, along with the rest of the populace
and those who had deserted to the king
of Babylon.[i] 12But the commander left
behind some of the poorest people[j] of
the land to work the vineyards and fields.
13The Babylonians broke up the bronze
pillars, the movable stands and the
bronze Sea that were at the temple of
the LORD and they carried the bronze to
Babylon. 14They also took away the pots,
shovels, wick trimmers, dishes and all
the bronze articles[k] used in the temple
service. 15The commander of the imperial guard took away the censers and
sprinkling bowls — all that were made
of pure gold or silver.
16The bronze from the two pillars, the
Sea and the movable stands, which Solomon had made for the temple of the
LORD, was more than could be weighed.
17Each pillar[l] was eighteen cubits[a] high.
The bronze capital on top of one pillar
was three cubits[b] high and was decorated with a network and pomegranates of
bronze all around. The other pillar, with
its network, was similar.
18The commander of the guard took
as prisoners Seraiah[m] the chief priest,
Zephaniah[n] the priest next in rank and
the three doorkeepers. 19Of those still in
the city, he took the officer in charge of
the fighting men, and five royal advisers.
He also took the secretary who was chief
officer in charge of conscripting the people of the land and sixty of the conscripts
who were found in the city. 20Nebuzara-
dan the commander took them all and
brought them to the king of Babylon at
Riblah. 21There at Riblah, in the land of
Hamath, the king had them executed.
So Judah went into captivity, away
from her land.[o]
22Nebuchadnezzar king of Babylon appointed Gedaliah[p] son of Ahikam, the
son of Shaphan, to be over the people he
had left behind in Judah. 23When all the
army officers and their men heard that
the king of Babylon had appointed Gedaliah as governor, they came to Gedaliah
at Mizpah — Ishmael son of Nethaniah,
Johanan son of Kareah, Seraiah son of
Tanhumeth the Netophathite, Jaazaniah the son of the Maakathite, and their
men. 24Gedaliah took an oath to reassure
them and their men. "Do not be afraid of
the Babylonian officials," he said. "Settle
down in the land and serve the king of
Babylon, and it will go well with you."
25In the seventh month, however, Ishmael son of Nethaniah, the son of Elishama, who was of royal blood, came with
ten men and assassinated Gedaliah and
also the men of Judah and the Babylonians who were with him at Mizpah. 26At
this, all the people from the least to the
greatest, together with the army officers,
fled to Egypt[q] for fear of the Babylonians.

Jehoiachin Released

25:27–30pp // Jer 52:31–34

27In the thirty-seventh year of the exile
of Jehoiachin king of Judah, in the year

25:11 [h] 2Ki 24:14 [i] 2Ki 24:1
25:12 [j] 2Ki 24:14
25:14 [k] Ex 27:3; 1Ki 7:47-50
25:17 [l] 1Ki 7:15-22
25:18 [m] 1Ch 6:14; Ezr 7:1; Ne 11:11 [n] Jer 21:1; 29:25
25:21 [o] Ge 12:7; Dt 28:64; Jos 23:13; 2Ki 23:27
25:22 [p] Jer 39:14; 40:5,7
25:26 [q] Isa 30:2; Jer 43:7

[a] 17 That is, about 27 feet or about 8.1 meters
[b] 17 That is, about 4 1/2 feet or about 1.4 meters

25:22–24 Gedaliah belongs to a prominent noble family; his grandfather was a scribe during the days of Josiah (22:3); his father was a member of the mission sent to Huldah (22:12), and he also intervened to save Jeremiah from the mob (Jer 26:24). Jeremiah supports Gedaliah, who is appointed by the Babylonians as governor at Mizpah (Jer 39:14). The army officers enter into an oath with Gedaliah; they need assurance there will be no reprisals for their having fought against the Babylonians. They are granted amnesty to now serve the Babylonians.
25:25–26 After a short time, Gedaliah and the Babylonians at Mizpah are murdered by a band led by Ishmael son of Nethaniah, a member of the royal family. It is not certain if Ishmael is contesting Gedaliah's position as a leader of Judah. The murder is a vendetta against those who are viewed as collaborating with the Babylonians.

The people of Judah, fearful of Babylonian revenge, flee to Egypt, forcing Jeremiah and Baruch to go with them (Jer 43:4–7). The report of their flight indicates that the judgment of exile is carried out in totality. Gedaliah's death marks the extinction of all national existence.
25:27–30 Awel-Marduk, son and successor of Nebuchadnezzar, reigns for two years (561–560 BC). His accession year becomes the occasion to grant amnesty to prisoners. Jehoiachin is then granted a favored status in relation to other captive kings; it is not specified what these privileges actually mean. He is confined to the court of the Babylonian king, with his family. Seven sons are born to him in exile (1Ch 3:17–18).

24:1–25:30 Death is a process. The process itself can be long and agonizing, or it can be swift and unexpected, whether it be the death of an individual, a marriage, or any other relationship. Depending on the process and the circumstances, the pain is experienced in different ways and at different levels.

In many respects, the death of a marriage in divorce or the death of a community is more

EXILE OF THE SOUTHERN KINGDOM

Knowledge about the destiny of the captives from Israel and Judah is sparse in the period following the capture of Samaria and the later destruction of Jerusalem.

Assyrians and Babylonians treated their subject peoples essentially the same: overwhelming military force used in a manner inspiring psychological terror, along with mass deportations and heavy tribute.

Three deportations are mentioned in Jer 52:28-30, the largest one consisting of 10,000 Jews (2Ki 24:14) who were taken to Babylon along with King Jehoiachin in 597 BC.

After the destruction of Jerusalem by Nebuzaradan, the commander of the Babylonian army, hundreds of exiles were taken to Riblah in the land of Hamath, where, in addition to Zedekiah's sons, at least 61 were executed.

Clay tablets from the fifth century BC called the Murashu archives have been found at Nippur. They document the commercial transactions with Jewish families who remained in Mesopotamia following Ezra's return to Jerusalem.

Eze 1:1-3 and 3:15 indicate that other captives were placed at Tel Aviv and at the Kebar River, both probably in the locale of Nippur, as were other villages mentioned in Ezr 2:59; 8:15,17; Ne 7:61.

Jehoiachin and his family were kept in Babylon, where clay ration receipts bearing his name and the names of his sons have been found.

Awel-Marduk became king of Babylon,
he released Jehoiachin[r] king of Judah
from prison. He did this on the twenty-
seventh day of the twelfth month. 28He
spoke kindly to him and gave him a seat
of honor[s] higher than those of the other
kings who were with him in Babylon.
29So Jehoiachin put aside his prison
clothes and for the rest of his life ate
regularly at the king's table.[t] 30Day by
day the king gave Jehoiachin a regular
allowance as long as he lived.[u]

25:27 [r]2Ki 24:12; Jer 52:31-34
25:28 [s]Ezr 5:5; Ne 2:1; Da 2:48
25:29 [t]2Sa 9:7
25:30 [u]Est 2:9; Jer 28:4

---

painful than physical death. In physical death there is an absolute termination; the death of a marriage or community is like a death that does not die. If children are involved in the death of a marriage, some continuity with the former relationship is unavoidable. In the death of a community, like that of Judah, there is much continuity with the past but also much alienation in which highly valued relationships and customs end.

It is said that those who lose all their possessions lose a lot, those who lose their friends lose a lot more, and those who lose hope have lost everything. The exiles have lost their possessions and are separated from many of their friends, but they never lose hope. Their memory of the exile is one expression of the faithfulness of God—and implicitly therefore of hope in the faithfulness of God for the future. When we experience loss, the same God promises to be with us in our troubles (2Co 1:3–7).

Author: Unknown, possibly Ezra

Audience: The people of Judah who had returned from exile in Babylon

Date: Between 450 and 400 BC

Theme: Chronicles encourages postexilic Israel with an account focused on God's promises to faithful Davidic kings (especially David and Solomon), ensuring Israel's future.

Reading 1 Chronicles

The first part of this book reads like a family tree; beginning with Adam, it is a list of all those who formed links in the chain of the covenant. Then, after a brief chapter on the reign of King Saul, the rest of the book is a record of what David did as king of all Israel and ends with an account of David's death.

PERSPECTIVE

Why should we have hope that the future will bring good? The world is at war. Environmental resources are disappearing at an alarming rate. Signs of cultural decline—crime rates, increasing fragmentation of society, immorality—are increasing. Individual well-being plummets as depression and suicide rates rise. Where is the hope in all that?

Chronicles explains why we should have hope. Hope, Chronicles tells us, rests not in world peace or in environmental restoration or in cultural rejuvenation, although all of those things are welcome. Chronicles tells us hope rests in the Lord.

But how can we communicate that hope to hopeless generations? The destructive character of hopelessness is that it closes us off to even the most legitimate messengers of hope. We hear but do not understand; we read but do not comprehend. Feeling becomes disconnected from the facts. How, then, does the Chronicler do it?

First, he does it by retelling in some detail the story of God's chosen people up to this point. The Chronicler begins with Adam and traces the line of descent through the twelve tribes and the conquest of Canaan. By his selection of certain incidents and his omission of others, it is obvious that the author wants this story to come across well. The characters are true heroes; the events are inspiring acts of God. King David's strengths are stressed while his failures are forgotten. God's acts of judgment are redemptive, not punitive.

By the way the story is told, it becomes obvious that the hearers are meant to focus on the big picture—the community of people who have gone before, not on themselves. So the lesson is that hopelessness feeds

	1400 BC	1300	1200	1100	1000	900	800	700	600	500	400
Saul's reign (1050–1010 BC)											
David's reign (1010–970 BC)											
Solomon's reign (970–930 BC)											
Building of the temple (966–959 BC)											
Division of the kingdom (930 BC)											
Exile of Israel (722 BC)											
Fall of Jerusalem (586 BC)											
Book of 1 Chronicles written (c. 450–400 BC)											

on self-absorption. Hope, by contrast, feeds on other-absorption—to some extent the human community, but especially on God.

The second technique the Chronicler uses is to imply that readers have a commitment to act, but nowhere does the Chronicler explicitly call for action. Why does he do that?

A story well told transports us from our outsider status to full involvement. We become a part of the story by reading about it and becoming inspired by it. In 1 Chronicles 12:17, men from the tribe of Benjamin come to join David's army. David expects them to not just fight as soldiers but to join the story: "If you have come to me in peace, to help me, I am ready for you to join me."

They were not expected to just join in the story; they were expected to join for the specific reason of making the story line better for future generations. It is clear that David himself did what he did so that his son, heir, and successor, Solomon, would have an even greater kingdom to rule over (1Ch 28–29). Clearly, the Chronicler's theory is that hope comes from pointing away from the self—toward God, toward others, and toward the future.

One final strategy: The Chronicler sets the venue for discovering and recapturing hope. The venue is not the home or the marketplace; it is neither the nation nor the world. All of these venues are susceptible to the dangers of self-absorption.

No, the Chronicler's venue is worship, liturgical and otherwise. Worship is the antithesis of self-absorption. Worship is God-absorption. It defeats hopelessness. It makes us hope.

Key Verse

Then you will have success if you are careful to observe the decrees and laws that the LORD gave Moses for Israel. Be strong and courageous. Do not be afraid or discouraged.

—1 Chronicles 22:13

TAKING THE NEXT STEPS

The author of the books of 1 and 2 Chronicles (possibly Ezra, compare 2Ch 36:22–23 with Ezr 1:1–4), writing after the exile in Babylon, reworked the material in 1 Samuel through 2 Kings into a second account of the history of God's people, omitting most of the history of the northern kingdom of Israel and adding significant details to the history of the southern kingdom. His goal was to inspire the small band of Jews who returned from Babylon to rebuild Jerusalem. In the face of smashed villages, hostile neighbors and a pile of rubble that once was the holy city with its temple, such encouragement was desperately needed. The author therefore emphasized through genealogies that these returned exiles were part of a long history of God's people, and drew special attention to those elements of the life of the people that still existed—namely, the line of David, organized worship of the Lord God, and adherence to God's law.

These themes in the book of 1 Chronicles have several important implications for our lives. (1) No matter how difficult and depressing our circumstances in life, recalling and reviewing God's care in the past will renew our faith and inspire us to continue to work for him. (2) God is not pleased with shoddy and apathetic worship of the Lord; he wants it to be organized in an orderly and disciplined fashion. (3) As long as our lives are centered around God and his will, we can expect God to bless us, even though we may experience disappointments in fulfilling our own goals and dreams. (4) To be able to give for the temple of the Lord (which today corresponds to the church; see 1Co 3:16–17) ought to thrill our hearts.

WHAT TO LOOK FOR IN 1 CHRONICLES

- Death of Saul (ch. 10)
- The ark brought to Jerusalem (chs. 13; 15–16)
- God's covenant with David (ch. 17)
- David's pride in counting his mighty men (ch. 21)
- David's extensive plans for the temple (chs. 22; 28–29)

Historical Records From Adam to Abraham

To Noah's Sons

1 Adam,[a] Seth, Enosh, 2Kenan,[b] Mahalalel,[c] Jared,[d] 3Enoch,[e] Methuselah,[f]
Lamech,[g] Noah.[h]

4The sons of Noah:[a][i]
Shem, Ham and Japheth.[j]

The Japhethites

1:5–7pp // Ge 10:2–5

5The sons[b] of Japheth:
Gomer, Magog, Madai, Javan, Tubal, Meshek and Tiras.

6The sons of Gomer:
Ashkenaz, Riphath[c] and Togarmah.

7The sons of Javan:
Elishah, Tarshish, the Kittites and the Rodanites.

1:1 [a] Ge 5:1-32; Lk 3:36-38
1:2 [b] Ge 5:9 [c] Ge 5:12 [d] Ge 5:15
1:3 [e] Ge 5:18; Jude 14 [f] Ge 5:21 [g] Ge 5:25 [h] Ge 5:29
1:4 [i] Ge 6:10; 10:1 [j] Ge 5:32

1Ch 1:1 ❖ Why is it important to remember those who have gone before us? What legacy have our fore-bearers left behind?

The Hamites

1:8–16pp // Ge 10:6–20

8The sons of Ham:
Cush, Egypt, Put and Canaan.

9The sons of Cush:
Seba, Havilah, Sabta, Raamah and Sabteka.
The sons of Raamah:
Sheba and Dedan.

[a] 4 Septuagint; Hebrew does not have this line. [b] 5 *Sons* may mean *descendants* or *successors* or *nations*; also in verses 6-9, 17 and 23. [c] 6 Many Hebrew manuscripts and Vulgate (see also Septuagint and Gen. 10:3); most Hebrew manuscripts *Diphath*

1:1 The genealogical prologue found in chs. 1–9 contains the most extensive and complex genealogies of the entire Bible. The basic purpose of the genealogy is to identify kinship relationships among individuals, families, and people groups. It is evident the genealogies of chs. 1–9 serve multiple purposes, especially in (1) legitimizing the authority of the Levitical priesthood as the rightful successors to the royal authority of Davidic kingship and (2) asserting the continuity of the Hebrew people through the national distress of the Babylonian exile. There is even a sense in which the juxtaposition of certain genealogies (e.g., that of Esau and Israel or Saul and David) works to express movement in history according to God's redemptive plan.

APPLICATION ✣ **1:1—2:2** For the Chronicler, the theological center of Scripture's "big picture" storyline is the God of Israel. The Chronicler's theology of hope is credible for the Jewish community because the God of Israel has proven faithful to his word across the generations from Adam to all those listed in his genealogy—the prominent and the obscure.

By appealing to those books and records

[10]Cush was the father[a] of
Nimrod, who became a mighty warrior on earth.
[11]Egypt was the father of
the Ludites, Anamites, Lehabites, Naphtuhites, [12]Pathrusites,
Kasluhites (from whom the Philistines came) and Caphtorites.
[13]Canaan was the father of
Sidon his firstborn,[b] and of the Hittites, [14]Jebusites, Amorites,
Girgashites, [15]Hivites, Arkites, Sinites, [16]Arvadites, Zemarites and
Hamathites.

The Semites
1:17–23pp // Ge 10:21–31; 11:10–27

[17]The sons of Shem:
Elam, Ashur, Arphaxad, Lud and Aram.
The sons of Aram:[c]
Uz, Hul, Gether and Meshek.
[18]Arphaxad was the father of Shelah, and Shelah the father of Eber.
[19]Two sons were born to Eber:
One was named Peleg,[d] because in his time the earth was divided; his brother was named Joktan.
[20]Joktan was the father of
Almodad, Sheleph, Hazarmaveth,
Jerah, [21]Hadoram, Uzal, Diklah,
[22]Obal,[e] Abimael, Sheba, [23]Ophir,
Havilah and Jobab. All these were sons of Joktan.

[24]Shem,[k] Arphaxad,[f] Shelah,
[25]Eber, Peleg, Reu,
[26]Serug, Nahor, Terah
[27]and Abram (that is, Abraham).

The Family of Abraham

[28]The sons of Abraham:
Isaac and Ishmael.

Descendants of Hagar
1:29–31pp // Ge 25:12–16

[29]These were their descendants:
Nebaioth the firstborn of Ishmael,
Kedar, Adbeel, Mibsam, [30]Mishma, Dumah, Massa, Hadad, Tema,
[31]Jetur, Naphish and Kedemah.
These were the sons of Ishmael.

Descendants of Keturah
1:32–33pp // Ge 25:1–4

[32]The sons born to Keturah, Abraham's concubine:[l]
Zimran, Jokshan, Medan, Midian, Ishbak and Shuah.
The sons of Jokshan:
Sheba and Dedan.[m]
[33]The sons of Midian:
Ephah, Epher, Hanok, Abida and Eldaah.
All these were descendants of Keturah.

Descendants of Sarah
1:35–37pp // Ge 36:10–14

[34]Abraham[n] was the father of Isaac.[o]
The sons of Isaac:
Esau and Israel.[p]

Esau's Sons

[35]The sons of Esau:[q]
Eliphaz, Reuel,[r] Jeush, Jalam and Korah.
[36]The sons of Eliphaz:
Teman, Omar, Zepho,[g] Gatam and Kenaz;
by Timna: Amalek.[h][s]
[37]The sons of Reuel:[t]
Nahath, Zerah, Shammah and Mizzah.

The People of Seir in Edom
1:38–42pp // Ge 36:20–28

[38]The sons of Seir:
Lotan, Shobal, Zibeon, Anah, Dishon, Ezer and Dishan.
[39]The sons of Lotan:

1:24 [k] Ge 10:21-25; Lk 3:34-36
1:32 [l] Ge 22:24 [m] Ge 10:7
1:34 [n] Lk 3:34 [o] Ge 21:2-3; Mt 1:2; Ac 7:8 [p] Ge 17:5; 25:25-26
1:35 [q] Ge 36:19 [r] Ge 36:4
1:36 [s] Ex 17:14
1:37 [t] Ge 36:17

[a] 10 *Father* may mean *ancestor* or *predecessor* or *founder*; also in verses 11, 13, 18 and 20. [b] 13 Or *of the Sidonians, the foremost* [c] 17 One Hebrew manuscript and some Septuagint manuscripts (see also Gen. 10:23); most Hebrew manuscripts do not have this line. [d] 19 *Peleg* means *division.* [e] 22 Some Hebrew manuscripts and Syriac (see also Gen. 10:28); most Hebrew manuscripts *Ebal* [f] 24 Hebrew; some Septuagint manuscripts *Arphaxad, Cainan* (see also note at Gen. 11:10) [g] 36 Many Hebrew manuscripts, some Septuagint manuscripts and Syriac (see also Gen. 36:11); most Hebrew manuscripts *Zephi* [h] 36 Some Septuagint manuscripts (see also Gen. 36:12); Hebrew *Gatam, Kenaz, Timna and Amalek*

already a part of the Hebrew Bible as resources for his preaching and teaching, the Chronicler offers his audience the flawless, true, and eternal word of God himself. Such is the pattern for apostolic preaching in the NT, and so it remains for preaching, teaching, and discipleship in the church today. The unfolding drama of God's redemption of humanity as recorded in Scripture continues to provide the "big picture" storyline for the Christian faith.

Hori and Homam. Timna was Lotan's sister.
40 The sons of Shobal:
Alvan,[a] Manahath, Ebal, Shepho and Onam.
The sons of Zibeon:
Aiah and Anah.[u]
41 The son of Anah:
Dishon.
The sons of Dishon:
Hemdan,[b] Eshban, Ithran and Keran.
42 The sons of Ezer:
Bilhan, Zaavan and Akan.[c]
The sons of Dishan[d]:
Uz and Aran.

The Rulers of Edom

1:43–54pp // Ge 36:31–43

43 These were the kings who reigned in Edom before any Israelite king reigned:
Bela son of Beor, whose city was named Dinhabah.
44 When Bela died, Jobab son of Zerah from Bozrah succeeded him as king.
45 When Jobab died, Husham from the land of the Temanites[v] succeeded him as king.
46 When Husham died, Hadad son of Bedad, who defeated Midian in the country of Moab, succeeded him as king. His city was named Avith.
47 When Hadad died, Samlah from Masrekah succeeded him as king.
48 When Samlah died, Shaul from Rehoboth on the river[e] succeeded him as king.
49 When Shaul died, Baal-Hanan son of Akbor succeeded him as king.
50 When Baal-Hanan died, Hadad succeeded him as king. His city was named Pau,[f] and his wife's name was Mehetabel daughter of Matred, the daughter of Me-Zahab.
51 Hadad also died.

The chiefs of Edom were:
Timna, Alvah, Jetheth, 52 Oholibamah, Elah, Pinon, 53 Kenaz, Teman,
Mibzar, 54 Magdiel and Iram. These were the chiefs of Edom.

1:40 [u] Ge 36:2
1:45 [v] Ge 36:11

1Ch 2:7 ❖ Achar (Achan in the book of Joshua) is remembered for his sin. Consider how Jesus' work and our confession removes our sin (see 1Jn 1:9). How do we want to be remembered?

Israel's Sons

2:1–2pp // Ge 35:23–26

2 These were the sons of Israel:
Reuben, Simeon, Levi, Judah, Issachar, Zebulun, 2 Dan, Joseph, Benjamin, Naphtali, Gad and Asher.

Judah

2:5–15pp // Ru 4:18–22; Mt 1:3–6

To Hezron's Sons

3 The sons of Judah:[w]
Er, Onan and Shelah.[x] These three were born to him by a Canaanite woman, the daughter of Shua.[y] Er, Judah's firstborn, was wicked in the LORD's sight; so the LORD put him to death.[z] 4 Judah's daughter-in-law[a] Tamar[b] bore Perez[c] and Zerah to Judah. He had five sons in all.

5 The sons of Perez:[d]
Hezron[e] and Hamul.
6 The sons of Zerah:
Zimri, Ethan, Heman, Kalkol and Darda[g] — five in all.
7 The son of Karmi:

2:3 [w] Ge 29:35; 38:2-10 [x] Ge 38:5 [y] Ge 38:2 [z] Nu 26:19
2:4 [a] Ge 11:31 [b] Ge 38:11-30 [c] Ge 38:29
2:5 [d] Ge 46:12 [e] Nu 26:21

[a] *40* Many Hebrew manuscripts and some Septuagint manuscripts (see also Gen. 36:23); most Hebrew manuscripts *Alian* [b] *41* Many Hebrew manuscripts and some Septuagint manuscripts (see also Gen. 36:26); most Hebrew manuscripts *Hamran* [c] *42* Many Hebrew and Septuagint manuscripts (see also Gen. 36:27); most Hebrew manuscripts *Zaavan, Jaakan* [d] *42* See Gen. 36:28; Hebrew *Dishon,* a variant of *Dishan* [e] *48* Possibly the Euphrates [f] *50* Many Hebrew manuscripts, some Septuagint manuscripts, Vulgate and Syriac (see also Gen. 36:39); most Hebrew manuscripts *Pai* [g] *6* Many Hebrew manuscripts, some Septuagint manuscripts and Syriac (see also 1 Kings 4:31); most Hebrew manuscripts *Dara*

2:3–8 The Chronicler promotes inclusivism, highlighting non-Hebrew women. Other theological themes include the demotion of the firstborn son (v. 3; cf. 5:1), God's justice in his punishment of wickedness (v. 3; cf. 5:26), and God's faithfulness in sustaining the line of Judah (v. 4; cf. 4:10).

2:9–17 The Chronicler showcases Ram because his interest in Judah centers on the family of David through Ram (vv. 13–17; see also Ru 4:19).

Achar,[a][f] who brought trouble on
Israel by violating the ban on taking devoted things.[b][g]
8 The son of Ethan:
Azariah.
9 The sons born to Hezron[h] were:
Jerahmeel, Ram and Caleb.[c]

From Ram Son of Hezron

10 Ram[i] was the father of
Amminadab[j], and Amminadab
the father of Nahshon,[k] the leader
of the people of Judah. 11 Nahshon
was the father of Salmon,[d] Salmon the father of Boaz, 12 Boaz[l]
the father of Obed and Obed the
father of Jesse.[m]
13 Jesse[n] was the father of
Eliab[o] his firstborn; the second
son was Abinadab, the third Shimea, 14 the fourth Nethanel, the fifth
Raddai, 15 the sixth Ozem and the
seventh David. 16 Their sisters
were Zeruiah[p] and Abigail. Zeruiah's[q] three sons were Abishai,
Joab[r] and Asahel. 17 Abigail was the
mother of Amasa,[s] whose father
was Jether the Ishmaelite.

Caleb Son of Hezron

18 Caleb son of Hezron had children by
his wife Azubah (and by Jerioth).
These were her sons: Jesher, Shobab and Ardon. 19 When Azubah
died, Caleb[t] married Ephrath, who
bore him Hur. 20 Hur was the father of Uri, and Uri the father of
Bezalel.[u]
21 Later, Hezron, when he was sixty
years old, married the daughter
of Makir the father of Gilead.[v] He
made love to her, and she bore him
Segub. 22 Segub was the father of
Jair, who controlled twenty-three
towns in Gilead. 23 (But Geshur and
Aram captured Havvoth Jair,[e][w] as
well as Kenath[x] with its surrounding settlements — sixty towns.) All
these were descendants of Makir
the father of Gilead.

24 After Hezron died in Caleb Ephrathah, Abijah the wife of Hezron
bore him Ashhur[y] the father[f] of
Tekoa.

Jerahmeel Son of Hezron

25 The sons of Jerahmeel the firstborn
of Hezron:
Ram his firstborn, Bunah, Oren,
Ozem and[g] Ahijah. 26 Jerahmeel
had another wife, whose name
was Atarah; she was the mother
of Onam.
27 The sons of Ram the firstborn of Jerahmeel:
Maaz, Jamin and Eker.
28 The sons of Onam:
Shammai and Jada.
The sons of Shammai:
Nadab and Abishur.
29 Abishur's wife was named Abihail,
who bore him Ahban and Molid.
30 The sons of Nadab:
Seled and Appaim. Seled died
without children.
31 The son of Appaim:
Ishi, who was the father of Sheshan.
Sheshan was the father of Ahlai.
32 The sons of Jada, Shammai's brother:
Jether and Jonathan. Jether died
without children.
33 The sons of Jonathan:
Peleth and Zaza.
These were the descendants of Jerahmeel.
34 Sheshan had no sons — only daughters.
He had an Egyptian servant
named Jarha. 35 Sheshan gave his
daughter in marriage to his servant Jarha, and she bore him Attai.
36 Attai was the father of Nathan,
Nathan the father of Zabad,[z]
37 Zabad the father of Ephlal,
Ephlal the father of Obed,
38 Obed the father of Jehu,
Jehu the father of Azariah,

2:7 [f] Jos 7:1 [g] Jos 6:18
2:9 [h] Nu 26:21
2:10 [i] Lk 3:32-33 [j] Ex 6:23 [k] Nu 1:7
2:12 [l] Ru 2:1 [m] Ru 4:17
2:13 [n] Ru 4:17 [o] 1Sa 16:6
2:16 [p] 1Sa 26:6 [q] 2Sa 2:18 [r] 2Sa 2:13
2:17 [s] 2Sa 17:25
2:19 [t] ver 42,50
2:20 [u] Ex 31:2
2:21 [v] Nu 27:1
2:23 [w] Nu 32:41; Dt 3:14; Jos 13:30 [x] Nu 32:42
2:24 [y] 1Ch 4:5
2:36 [z] 1Ch 11:41

[a] 7 *Achar* means *trouble*; *Achar* is called *Achan* in Joshua. [b] 7 The Hebrew term refers to the irrevocable giving over of things or persons to the LORD, often by totally destroying them.
[c] 9 Hebrew *Kelubai*, a variant of *Caleb*
[d] 11 Septuagint (see also Ruth 4:21); Hebrew *Salma* [e] 23 Or *captured the settlements of Jair*
[f] 24 *Father* may mean *civic leader* or *military leader*; also in verses 42, 45, 49-52 and possibly elsewhere. [g] 25 Or *Oren and Ozem, by*

2:25–41 The Chronicler's interest in the role of non-Hebrews surfaces in the reference to the Egyptian named Jarha (v. 34).

39 Azariah the father of Helez,
Helez the father of Eleasah,
40 Eleasah the father of Sismai,
Sismai the father of Shallum,
41 Shallum the father of Jekamiah,
and Jekamiah the father of Elishama.

The Clans of Caleb

42 The sons of Caleb[a] the brother of Jerahmeel:
Mesha his firstborn, who was the father of Ziph, and his son Mareshah,[a] who was the father of Hebron.
43 The sons of Hebron:
Korah, Tappuah, Rekem and Shema.
44 Shema was the father of Raham, and Raham the father of Jorkeam. Rekem was the father of Shammai.
45 The son of Shammai was Maon[b], and Maon was the father of Beth Zur.[c]
46 Caleb's concubine Ephah was the mother of Haran, Moza and Gazez. Haran was the father of Gazez.
47 The sons of Jahdai:
Regem, Jotham, Geshan, Pelet, Ephah and Shaaph.
48 Caleb's concubine Maakah was the mother of Sheber and Tirhanah.
49 She also gave birth to Shaaph the father of Madmannah[d] and to Sheva the father of Makbenah and Gibea. Caleb's daughter was Aksah.[e]
50 These were the descendants of Caleb.

The sons of Hur[f] the firstborn of Ephrathah:
Shobal the father of Kiriath Jearim,[g]
51 Salma the father of Bethlehem, and Hareph the father of Beth Gader.
52 The descendants of Shobal the father of Kiriath Jearim were:
Haroeh, half the Manahathites,
53 and the clans of Kiriath Jearim: the Ithrites,[h] Puthites, Shumathites and Mishraites. From these descended the Zorathites and Eshtaolites.
54 The descendants of Salma:
Bethlehem, the Netophathites,[i] Atroth Beth Joab, half the Manahathites, the Zorites,
55 and the clans of scribes[b] who lived at Jabez: the Tirathites, Shimeathites and Sucathites. These are the Kenites[j] who came from Hammath,[k] the father of the Rekabites.[c][l]

2:42 [a] ver 19
2:45 [b] Jos 15:55 [c] Jos 15:58
2:49 [d] Jos 15:31 [e] Jos 15:16
2:50 [f] 1Ch 4:4 [g] ver 19
2:53 [h] 2Sa 23:38
2:54 [i] Ezr 2:22; Ne 7:26; 12:28
2:55 [j] Ge 15:19; Jdg 1:16; Jdg 4:11 [k] Jos 19:35 [l] 2Ki 10:15,23; Jer 35:2-19
3:1 [m] 1Ch 14:3; 28:5 [n] Jos 15:56 [o] 1Sa 25:42
3:2 [p] 1Ki 2:22
3:4 [q] 2Sa 5:4; 1Ch 29:27 [r] 2Sa 2:11; 5:5
3:5 [s] 2Sa 11:3; 12:24

The Sons of David

3:1–4pp // 2Sa 3:2–5
3:5–8pp // 2Sa 5:14–16; 1Ch 14:4–7

3 These were the sons of David[m] born to him in Hebron:
The firstborn was Amnon the son of Ahinoam of Jezreel;[n]
the second, Daniel the son of Abigail[o] of Carmel;
2 the third, Absalom the son of Maakah daughter of Talmai king of Geshur;
the fourth, Adonijah[p] the son of Haggith;
3 the fifth, Shephatiah the son of Abital;
and the sixth, Ithream, by his wife Eglah.
4 These six were born to David in Hebron,[q] where he reigned seven years and six months.[r]
David reigned in Jerusalem thirty-three years,
5 and these were the children born to him there:
Shammua,[d] Shobab, Nathan and Solomon. These four were by Bathsheba[e][s] daughter of Ammiel.

[a] *42* The meaning of the Hebrew for this phrase is uncertain. [b] *55* Or *of the Sopherites* [c] *55* Or *father of Beth Rekab* [d] *5* Hebrew *Shimea*, a variant of *Shammua* [e] *5* One Hebrew manuscript and Vulgate (see also Septuagint and 2 Samuel 11:3); most Hebrew manuscripts *Bathshua*

2:42–55 Caleb's descendants are ordered according to their different mothers, including an unnamed wife (vv. 42–45), a concubine named Ephah (vv. 46–47), and a concubine named Maacah (vv. 48–50a). The reference to Bethlehem is a natural prelude to the family tree of David.

3:1–24 The family of David is the featured attraction of Judah's genealogy. The Chronicler's emphasis stems from prophetic statements about God's unbreakable covenant with David and the re-establishment of Davidic kingship (cf. Jer 33:19–22).

3:1–5 David's sons are registered in two lists according to the capital city in which they were born: Hebron or Jerusalem. The birth reports citing the name of the individual mothers of David's sons recall the annals of the kings of Judah (e.g., 1Ki 15:2). Theologically, the practice reflects the association of the "offspring of the woman" promise (Ge 3:15) with the line of David (cf. 2Sa 7:16).

6 There were also Ibhar, Elishua,[a] Eliphelet, 7 Nogah, Nepheg, Japhia, 8 Elishama, Eliada and Eliphelet — nine in all. 9 All these were the sons of David, besides his sons by his concubines. And Tamar[t] was their sister.[u]

The Kings of Judah

10 Solomon's son was Rehoboam,[v]
Abijah his son,
Asa his son,
Jehoshaphat[w] his son,
11 Jehoram[b][x] his son,
Ahaziah[y] his son,
Joash[z] his son,
12 Amaziah[a] his son,
Azariah his son,
Jotham[b] his son,
13 Ahaz[c] his son,
Hezekiah[d] his son,
Manasseh[e] his son,
14 Amon[f] his son,
Josiah[g] his son.
15 The sons of Josiah:
Johanan the firstborn,
Jehoiakim[h] the second son,
Zedekiah[i] the third,
Shallum[j] the fourth.
16 The successors of Jehoiakim:
Jehoiachin[c][k] his son,
and Zedekiah.[l]

The Royal Line After the Exile

17 The descendants of Jehoiachin the captive:
Shealtiel[m] his son, 18 Malkiram,
Pedaiah, Shenazzar,[n] Jekamiah,
Hoshama and Nedabiah.[o]
19 The sons of Pedaiah:
Zerubbabel[p] and Shimei.
The sons of Zerubbabel:
Meshullam and Hananiah.
Shelomith was their sister.
20 There were also five others:
Hashubah, Ohel, Berekiah, Hasadiah and Jushab-Hesed.
21 The descendants of Hananiah:
Pelatiah and Jeshaiah, and the sons of Rephaiah, of Arnan, of Obadiah and of Shekaniah.
22 The descendants of Shekaniah:
Shemaiah and his sons:
Hattush,[q] Igal, Bariah, Neariah and Shaphat — six in all.
23 The sons of Neariah:
Elioenai, Hizkiah and Azrikam — three in all.
24 The sons of Elioenai:
Hodaviah, Eliashib, Pelaiah, Akkub, Johanan, Delaiah and Anani — seven in all.

Other Clans of Judah

4 The descendants of Judah:[r]
Perez, Hezron,[s] Karmi, Hur and Shobal.

3:9 [t] 2Sa 13:1 [u] 1Ch 14:4
3:10 [v] 1Ki 11:43; 14:21-31; 2Ch 12:16 [w] 2Ch 17:1-21:3
3:11 [x] 2Ki 8:16-24; 2Ch 21:1 [y] 2Ch 22:1-10 [z] 2Ki 11:1-12:21
3:12 [a] 2Ki 14:1-22; 2Ch 25:1-28 [b] Isa 1:1; Hos 1:1; Mic 1:1
3:13 [c] 2Ki 16:1-20; 2Ch 28:1; Isa 7:1 [d] 2Ki 18:1-20:21; 2Ch 29:1; Jer 26:19 [e] 2Ch 33:1
3:14 [f] 2Ki 21:19-26; 2Ch 33:21; Zep 1:1 [g] 2Ch 34:1; Jer 1:2; 3:6; 25:3
3:15 [h] 2Ki 23:34 [i] Jer 37:1 [j] 2Ki 23:31
3:16 [k] 2Ki 24:6, 8; Mt 1:11 [l] 2Ki 24:18
3:17 [m] Ezr 3:2
3:18 [n] Ezr 1:8; 5:14 [o] Jer 22:30
3:19 [p] Ezr 2:2; 3:2; 5:2; Ne 7:7; 12:1; Hag 1:1; 2:2; Zec 4:6
3:22 [q] Ezr 8:2-3
4:1 [r] Ge 29:35; 46:12; 1Ch 2:3 [s] Nu 26:21

1Ch 3:9 ❖ In the line of David's sons, one daughter is mentioned: Tamar (see 2Sa 13:1-22). How might we remember and honor those whose stories are particularly painful?

[a] 6 Two Hebrew manuscripts (see also 2 Samuel 5:15 and 1 Chron. 14:5); most Hebrew manuscripts *Elishama* [b] 11 Hebrew *Joram,* a variant of *Jehoram* [c] 16 Hebrew *Jeconiah,* a variant of *Jehoiachin;* also in verse 17

3:10–16 The Chronicler reports the complete list of Davidic kings reigning in the southern kingdom of Judah during the period of the divided Hebrew monarchies. Jehoiachin's (v. 16) release from prison serves as the postscript for the book of Jeremiah (Jer 52:31–34) and rekindled hope for the restoration of the Davidic monarchy after the Babylonian exile. This is why the Chronicler introduces the last section of the Davidic genealogy with King Jehoiachin "the captive" (3:17).

3:17–24 The final section of the royal genealogy contains the register of the postexilic descendants of David. The key figures include Shenazzar (v. 18), who led the initial wave of Jewish immigrants back to Jerusalem with the help of King Cyrus of Persia (cf. Ezr 1:8–11), and Zerubbabel, who headed up a second Hebrew migration from Persia sometime later (Ezr 2:2).

✣ **2:3—3:24** The Chronicler's genealogical prologue works for his audience because they have been initiated into the shared secret of the community of faith—a covenant relationship with Yahweh, the covenant maker. They have also experienced the disruption of the Babylonian exile as threatened by the prophets. For these reasons, they are in a position to embrace the wisdom of the Chronicler's theology of hope, which is rooted in God's faithfulness over the course of their history as illustrated in the genealogical record.

Appropriately, the Chronicler calls his contemporaries to respond to his historical sermon with praise and worship of the God of their Hebrew ancestors. As believers, we are called to similar worship as we wonder in gratitude for God's faithfulness to his people over the centuries.

4:1–8 The initial portion of the genealogical appendix to the tribe of Judah emphasizes how the restoration community continues past Israelite history.

[2]Reaiah son of Shobal was the father of Jahath, and Jahath the father of Ahumai and Lahad. These were the clans of the Zorathites.
[3]These were the sons[a] of Etam:
Jezreel, Ishma and Idbash. Their sister was named Hazzelelponi.
[4]Penuel was the father of Gedor, and Ezer the father of Hushah.
These were the descendants of Hur,[t] the firstborn of Ephrathah and father[b] of Bethlehem.[u]
[5]Ashhur[v] the father of Tekoa had two wives, Helah and Naarah.
[6]Naarah bore him Ahuzzam, Hepher, Temeni and Haahashtari. These were the descendants of Naarah.
[7]The sons of Helah:
Zereth, Zohar, Ethnan, [8]and Koz, who was the father of Anub and Hazzobebah and of the clans of Aharhel son of Harum.

[9]Jabez was more honorable than his
brothers. His mother had named him

4:4 [t]1Ch 2:50 [u]Ru 1:19
4:5 [v]1Ch 2:24

1Ch 4:9-10 ❖ How might we put the prayer of Jabez into our own words to express our longings to God?

Jabez,[c] saying, "I gave birth to him in pain."
[10]Jabez cried out to the God of Israel, "Oh, that you would bless me and enlarge my territory! Let your hand be with me, and keep me from harm so that I will be free from pain." And God granted his request.

[11]Kelub, Shuhah's brother, was the father of Mehir, who was the father of Eshton. [12]Eshton was the father of Beth Rapha, Paseah and Tehinnah the father of Ir Nahash.[d] These were the men of Rekah.

[a] 3 Some Septuagint manuscripts (see also Vulgate); Hebrew *father* [b] 4 *Father* may mean *civic leader* or *military leader*; also in verses 12, 14, 17, 18 and possibly elsewhere. [c] 9 *Jabez* sounds like the Hebrew for *pain.* [d] 12 Or *of the city of Nahash*

4:3-8 The name Hazzelelponi (v. 3) is a curiosity but should be retained as original to the text. Women (wives as well as sisters) are featured in the Chronicler's genealogies. The expression "father of" common to the genealogies in this section may be understood in the sense of "ancestor" and/or as "settler" or even "founding father" of a town or village.

4:9-10 The effectiveness of prayer to the God of Israel is an important theme in Chronicles. God's responsiveness to prayer in the past is an invitation to offer prayers addressing present needs and concerns.

4:11-12 None of the persons included in this section of the genealogy are mentioned elsewhere in the OT.

PEOPLE TO KNOW // JABEZ

1 CHRONICLES 4:9-10: Genealogies are often considered boring—who wants to read a long list of ancient names? Often, however, genealogies have fascinating details embedded within them. Such is the case with the mention of Jabez.

Jabez appears in only one place in the Bible, in the middle of a genealogy (1Ch 4:9-10). The writer pauses on Jabez's name to give some details. Jabez was "more righteous" than his brothers. His mother gave him his name because she gave birth to him in pain. And Jabez lifted a prayerful cry to God, asking for blessing, territory, God's presence to be with him, and freedom from pain. All of these petitions are relatable even to people reading this passage today. The Bible then says, with intriguing brevity and no further explanation, "And God granted his request" (1Ch 4:9).

Questions about this little passage abound, but anything more that could be said about Jabez, his situation, and his prayer is mere speculation. He remains a mysterious figure tucked into a genealogy—a man known for being righteous and for having his prayer answered by God.

APPLICATION ✚ Today many people preach a kind of "prosperity gospel": *ask God for wealth and happiness, and you're sure to get it.* Such teaching often makes God out to be a mere instrument for fulfilling our selfish desires rather than the Lord of the universe. Jabez reminds us that we need to bring our prayers to God in righteousness, not in selfishness. It is not wrong to bring prayers for prosperity before God, but those prayers need to come from a God-honoring heart. God is not our heavenly credit card. He is our holy King.

[13]The sons of Kenaz:
Othniel[w] and Seraiah.
The sons of Othniel:
Hathath and Meonothai.[a] [14]Meon-
othai was the father of Ophrah.
Seraiah was the father of Joab,
the father of Ge Harashim.[b] It was called this because its people were skilled workers.
[15]The sons of Caleb son of Jephunneh:
Iru, Elah and Naam.
The son of Elah:
Kenaz.
[16]The sons of Jehallelel:
Ziph, Ziphah, Tiria and Asarel.
[17]The sons of Ezrah:
Jether, Mered, Epher and Jalon.
One of Mered's wives gave birth to Miriam,[x] Shammai and Ishbah the father of Eshtemoa.
[18](His wife from the tribe of Judah gave birth to Jered the father of Gedor, Heber the father of Soko, and Jekuthiel the father of Zanoah.[y]) These were the children of Pharaoh's daughter Bithiah, whom Mered had married.
[19]The sons of Hodiah's wife, the sister of Naham:
the father of Keilah[z] the Garmite, and Eshtemoa the Maakathite.[a]
[20]The sons of Shimon:
Amnon, Rinnah, Ben-Hanan and Tilon.
The descendants of Ishi:
Zoheth and Ben-Zoheth.
[21]The sons of Shelah[b] son of Judah:
Er the father of Lekah, Laadah the father of Mareshah and the clans of the linen workers at Beth Ashbea,
[22]Jokim, the men of Kozeba, and Joash and Saraph, who ruled in Moab and Jashubi Lehem. (These records are from ancient times.)
[23]They were the potters who lived at Netaim and Gederah; they stayed there and worked for the king.

Simeon

4:28–33pp // Jos 19:2–10

[24]The descendants of Simeon:[c]
Nemuel, Jamin, Jarib,[d] Zerah and Shaul;
[25]Shallum was Shaul's son, Mibsam his son and Mishma his son.
[26]The descendants of Mishma:
Hammuel his son, Zakkur his son and Shimei his son.

4:13 [w] Jos 15:17
4:17 [x] Ex 15:20
4:18 [y] Jos 15:34
4:19 [z] Jos 15:44 [a] Dt 3:14
4:21 [b] Ge 38:5
4:24 [c] Ge 29:33 [d] Nu 26:12

[a] *13* Some Septuagint manuscripts and Vulgate; Hebrew does not have *and Meonothai.*
[b] *14* *Ge Harashim* means *valley of skilled workers.*

4:13–16 The Chronicler includes the genealogies of Othniel and Caleb because both were responsible for expanding the boundaries of Israel during the days of the judges. Their example was meant to remind the people that God was still capable of enlarging the borders of diminished Judah through the efforts of faithful individuals.

4:17–20 This section of the extended Judahite genealogy is interesting because of the prominent place it gives to women, especially Miriam (a Calebite relative of Ezrah, v. 17) and Bithiah (daughter of Pharaoh, v. 18).

4:21–23 The reference to Shelah, the oldest surviving son of Judah, echoes 2:3 and forms an *inclusio* (or envelope) construction marking 2:3—4:23 as a larger literary unit.

4:1–23 The Chronicler's subtle call to his postexilic audience for an "evangelistic openness" to relationships with non-Jews calls to mind the parable Jesus told about the good Samaritan (Lk 10:25–37). The story is well-known and often told. The question raised in applying the parable today still challenges the Christian and the Christian church: "Who is my neighbor?"

4:24–43 Theologically, the focus of this genealogy is faithfulness—the faithfulness of God's word concerning the destiny of Simeon (Ge 49:5–7), the faithfulness of the Simeonites in possessing the land that Joshua allotted to them, the faithfulness of God in helping the Simeonites overcome their enemies (cf. Dt 1:30; 3:22), and the faithfulness of Shimei's family in trusting God to expand Simeonite tribal holdings (1Ch 4:38–43).

4:24–43 The Chronicler seeks to reconcile the disparity between the Davidic ideal—the way things should optimally be for the people of God—and the reality of the Persians occupying Judah. He writes to a discouraged audience in postexilic Jerusalem.

The NT mentions other kinds of tensions between the biblical ideal and actual human experience that have the potential to produce similar feelings of anxiety and despair in individual believers and in the Christian community at large. For example, witness the amount of time Paul, called to be a great evangelist, spent locked up in prison. The greater the disconnection between the ideal and the actual, the more room for seeds of doubt to germinate, undermining one's hope in God and robbing one of the joy of the Lord.

And yet throughout history God has proven that he is unchanging and faithful in his promises to his people. Using our earlier NT example, Paul's time in prison allowed him to write the Spirit-inspired letters to the early NT churches that still instruct and inspire us today. No matter the situation, God remains actively in control and is moving his purposes forward.

27 Shimei had sixteen sons and six
daughters, but his brothers did not have
many children; so their entire clan did
not become as numerous as the people
of Judah. 28 They lived in Beersheba,[e]
Moladah,[f] Hazar Shual, 29 Bilhah, Ezem,[g]
Tolad, 30 Bethuel, Hormah,[h] Ziklag, 31 Beth
Markaboth, Hazar Susim, Beth Biri and
Shaaraim.[i] These were their towns until
the reign of David. 32 Their surrounding
villages were Etam, Ain,[j] Rimmon, Token
and Ashan[k] — five towns — 33 and all the
villages around these towns as far as Baalath.[a] These were their settlements. And
they kept a genealogical record.

34 Meshobab, Jamlech, Joshah son of
Amaziah, 35 Joel, Jehu son of Josh-
ibiah, the son of Seraiah, the son
of Asiel, 36 also Elioenai, Jaakobah,
Jeshohaiah, Asaiah, Adiel, Jesimiel,
Benaiah, 37 and Ziza son of Shiphi,
the son of Allon, the son of Jedaiah, the son of Shimri, the son of
Shemaiah.

38 The men listed above by name were
leaders of their clans. Their families increased greatly, 39 and they went to the
outskirts of Gedor[l] to the east of the valley in search of pasture for their flocks.
40 They found rich, good pasture, and the
land was spacious, peaceful and quiet.[m]
Some Hamites had lived there formerly.
41 The men whose names were listed
came in the days of Hezekiah king of Judah. They attacked the Hamites in their
dwellings and also the Meunites[n] who
were there and completely destroyed[b]
them, as is evident to this day. Then they
settled in their place, because there was
pasture for their flocks. 42 And five hundred of these Simeonites, led by Pelatiah,
Neariah, Rephaiah and Uzziel, the sons
of Ishi, invaded the hill country of Seir.[o]
43 They killed the remaining Amalekites[p]
who had escaped, and they have lived
there to this day.

Reuben

5 The sons of Reuben[q] the firstborn of
Israel (he was the firstborn, but when
he defiled his father's marriage bed,[r] his
rights as firstborn were given to the sons
of Joseph[s] son of Israel;[t] so he could not be
listed in the genealogical record in accordance with his birthright,[u] 2 and though
Judah[v] was the strongest of his brothers
and a ruler[w] came from him, the rights of
the firstborn[x] belonged to Joseph) — 3 the
sons of Reuben[y] the firstborn of Israel:
Hanok, Pallu,[z] Hezron and Karmi.
4 The descendants of Joel:
Shemaiah his son, Gog his son,
Shimei his son, 5 Micah his son,
Reaiah his son, Baal his son,
6 and Beerah his son, whom Tiglath-
Pileser[c][a] king of Assyria took into
exile. Beerah was a leader of the
Reubenites.
7 Their relatives by clans,[b] listed according to their genealogical records:
Jeiel the chief, Zechariah, 8 and
Bela son of Azaz, the son of Shema, the son of Joel. They settled
in the area from Aroer[c] to Nebo
and Baal Meon. 9 To the east they
occupied the land up to the edge
of the desert that extends to the
Euphrates River, because their
livestock had increased in Gilead.[d]
10 During Saul's reign they waged
war against the Hagrites[e], who were
defeated at their hands; they occupied the dwellings of the Hagrites
throughout the entire region east
of Gilead.

Gad

11 The Gadites[f] lived next to them in
Bashan, as far as Salekah:[g]
12 Joel was the chief, Shapham the
second, then Janai and Shaphat,
in Bashan.

1Ch 5:1 ❖ How has God given the rights of the firstborn to his children through Christ (see Ro 8:17)?

4:28 [e] Ge 21:14 [f] Jos 15:26
4:29 [g] Jos 15:29
4:30 [h] Nu 14:45
4:31 [i] Jos 15:36
4:32 [j] Nu 34:11 [k] Jos 15:42
4:39 [l] Jos 15:58
4:40 [m] Jdg 18:7-10
4:41 [n] 2Ch 20:1; 26:7
4:42 [o] Ge 14:6
4:43 [p] 1Sa 15:8; 30:17; 2Sa 8:12; Est 3:1; 9:16
5:1 [q] Ge 29:32 [r] Ge 35:22; 49:4 [s] Ge 48:16, 22; 49:26 [t] Ge 48:5 [u] 1Ch 26:10
5:2 [v] Ge 49:10, 12 [w] 1Sa 9:16; 12:12; 2Sa 6:21; 1Ch 11:2; 2Ch 7:18; Ps 60:7; Mic 5:2; Mt 2:6 [x] Ge 25:31
5:3 [y] Ge 29:32; 46:9; Ex 6:14; Nu 26:5-11 [z] Nu 26:5
5:6 [a] ver 26; 2Ki 15:19; 16:10; 2Ch 28:20
5:7 [b] ver 17
5:8 [c] Nu 32:34
5:9 [d] Nu 32:26; Jos 22:9
5:10 [e] ver 18-21
5:11 [f] Jos 13:24-28 [g] Dt 3:10; Jos 13:11

[a] *33* Some Septuagint manuscripts (see also Joshua 19:8); Hebrew *Baal* [b] *41* The Hebrew term refers to the irrevocable giving over of things or persons to the LORD, often by totally destroying them. [c] *6* Hebrew *Tilgath-Pilneser,* a variant of *Tiglath-Pileser;* also in verse 26

5:1–10 The Chronicler recounts Reuben's crime of engaging in sexual intercourse with his father's concubine (Bilhah) to explain why the tribes of Judah and Joseph were so prominent in later Israelite history. From Judah came the "ruler" (v. 2), a reference to King David. And the firstborn rights of Reuben were transferred to Joseph's sons Ephraim and Manasseh (Ge 48:5–20).
5:11–22 The genealogy of Gad is unusual in that it begins with a geographical note (v. 11) and omits

13Their relatives, by families, were:
Michael, Meshullam, Sheba, Jorai,
Jakan, Zia and Eber — seven in all.
14These were the sons of Abihail son
of Huri, the son of Jaroah, the son
of Gilead, the son of Michael, the
son of Jeshishai, the son of Jahdo,
the son of Buz.
15Ahi son of Abdiel, the son of Guni,
was head of their family.
16The Gadites lived in Gilead, in Bashan and its outlying villages, and
on all the pasturelands of Sharon
as far as they extended.
17All these were entered in the genealogical records during the reigns of
Jotham[h] king of Judah and Jeroboam[i]
king of Israel.

18The Reubenites, the Gadites and the
half-tribe of Manasseh had 44,760 men
ready for military service[j] — able-bodied men who could handle shield and
sword, who could use a bow, and who
were trained for battle. 19They waged war
against the Hagrites, Jetur,[k] Naphish and
Nodab. 20They were helped[l] in fighting
them, and God delivered the Hagrites
and all their allies into their hands, because they cried[m] out to him during the
battle. He answered their prayers, because they trusted[n] in him. 21They seized
the livestock of the Hagrites — fifty thousand camels, two hundred fifty thousand
sheep and two thousand donkeys. They
also took one hundred thousand people captive, 22and many others fell slain,
because the battle[o] was God's. And they
occupied the land until the exile.[p]

The Half-Tribe of Manasseh

23The people of the half-tribe of Manasseh were numerous; they settled in
the land from Bashan to Baal Hermon,
that is, to Senir (Mount Hermon).[q]
24These were the heads of their families: Epher, Ishi, Eliel, Azriel, Jeremiah,
Hodaviah and Jahdiel. They were brave
warriors, famous men, and heads of
their families. 25But they were unfaithful[r] to the God of their ancestors and
prostituted[s] themselves to the gods of
the peoples of the land, whom God had
destroyed before them. 26So the God of
Israel stirred up the spirit of Pul[t] king of
Assyria (that is, Tiglath-Pileser[u] king of
Assyria), who took the Reubenites, the
Gadites and the half-tribe of Manasseh
into exile. He took them to Halah,[v] Habor, Hara and the river of Gozan, where
they are to this day.

Levi

6 [a] The sons of Levi:[w]
Gershon, Kohath and Merari.
2The sons of Kohath:
Amram, Izhar, Hebron and Uzziel.

[a] In Hebrew texts 6:1-15 is numbered 5:27-41, and 6:16-81 is numbered 6:1-66.

5:17 [h] 2Ki 15:32 [i] 2Ki 14:16,28
5:18 [j] Nu 1:3
5:19 [k] ver 10; Ge 25:15; 1Ch 1:31
5:20 [l] Ps 37:40 [m] 1Ki 8:44; 2Ch 13:14; 14:11; Ps 20:7-9; 22:5 [n] Ps 26:1; Da 6:23
5:22 [o] 2Ch 32:8 [p] 2Ki 15:29; 17:6
5:23 [q] Dt 3:8,9; SS 4:8
5:25 [r] Dt 32:15-18; 2Ki 17:7; 1Ch 9:1; 2Ch 26:16 [s] Ex 34:15
5:26 [t] 2Ki 15:19 [u] 2Ki 15:29 [v] 2Ki 17:6; 18:11
6:1 [w] Ge 46:11; Ex 6:16; Nu 26:57; 1Ch 23:6

materials from the other Gadite genealogies (e.g., Ge 46:16; Nu 26:15–18; 1Ch 12:9–13). This emphasis on the territorial holdings of Gad forms an envelope for the genealogical record.

5:17 There is some question concerning the reference to "Jotham king of Judah" in the chronological footnote since the Transjordan tribes were part of the northern kingdom. It seems likely that events in Israel were synchronized by reference to whomever occupied the throne in Judah.

5:18–22 The Chronicler's focus is on the theology of warfare. The war with the Hagrites and their allies was God's battle (v. 22). The people trusted in God and he answered their prayers (vv. 20–21).

5:23–26 Once the Israelites became guilty of the sins for which God punished the Canaanites, the covenant promise was in jeopardy. The Chronicler's consistent understanding of God's sovereignty is worth noting: It is God who stirred the spirit of the king of Assyria to judge the sin of Israel (v. 26).

✣ **5:1–26** One way in which the NT enhances the message of Chronicles is that of example through character study. For instance, we have the account of the life of the apostle Paul, introduced to us as the "worst of sinners" (cf. 1Ti 1:16) but transformed into the apostle to the Gentiles (Ac 9:15). The name Demas is associated with the more tragic story of one who apparently started well (cf. Col 4:14) but who quit the race and deserted Paul because "he loved this world" (2Ti 4:10).

Indeed, the reality of life in a world filled with distraction and misplaced priorities still plagues believers today. But sincerely focusing on the words and priorities of God (Mt 6:33) leads to a life well lived in service to God regardless of the surrounding circumstances or culture.

6:1–15 The focus of the initial genealogy of Levi is Kohath (v. 2) since he was the ancestor of the Aaronite high priests (v. 3). The listing of the Aaronite high priests preserves twenty-one generations from Eleazar to Jozadak, but it is not a complete genealogical record.

Azariah served as priest in Solomon's temple (v. 10), and Jozadak was deported to Babylonia at the time of Jerusalem's exile (v. 15). Both events were watershed moments in Israelite history.

[3]The children of Amram:
Aaron, Moses and Miriam.
The sons of Aaron:
Nadab, Abihu,[x] Eleazar and Ithamar.
[4]Eleazar was the father of Phinehas,
Phinehas the father of Abishua,
[5]Abishua the father of Bukki,
Bukki the father of Uzzi,
[6]Uzzi the father of Zerahiah,
Zerahiah the father of Meraioth,
[7]Meraioth the father of Amariah,
Amariah the father of Ahitub,
[8]Ahitub the father of Zadok,[y]
Zadok the father of Ahimaaz,
[9]Ahimaaz the father of Azariah,
Azariah the father of Johanan,
[10]Johanan the father of Azariah[z] (it was he who served as priest in the temple Solomon built in Jerusalem),
[11]Azariah the father of Amariah,
Amariah the father of Ahitub,
[12]Ahitub the father of Zadok,
Zadok the father of Shallum,
[13]Shallum the father of Hilkiah,[a]
Hilkiah the father of Azariah,
[14]Azariah the father of Seraiah,[b]
and Seraiah the father of Jozadak.[a]
[15]Jozadak[c] was deported when the LORD sent Judah and Jerusalem into exile by the hand of Nebuchadnezzar.

[16]The sons of Levi:[d]
Gershon,[b] Kohath and Merari.[e]
[17]These are the names of the sons of Gershon:
Libni and Shimei.
[18]The sons of Kohath:
Amram, Izhar, Hebron and Uzziel.
[19]The sons of Merari:[f]
Mahli and Mushi.
These are the clans of the Levites listed according to their fathers:

6:3 [x]Lev 10:1
6:8 [y]2Sa 8:17; 15:27; Ezr 7:2
6:10 [z]1Ki 4:2; 6:1; 2Ch 3:1; 26:17-18
6:13 [a]2Ki 22:1-20; 2Ch 34:9; 35:8
6:14 [b]2Ki 25:18; Ezr 2:2; Ne 11:11
6:15 [c]2Ki 25:18; Ne 12:1; Hag 1:1, 14; 2:2,4; Zec 6:11
6:16 [d]Ge 29:34; Ex 6:16; Nu 3:17-20 [e]Nu 26:57
6:19 [f]Ge 46:11; 1Ch 23:21; 24:26
6:22 [g]Ex 6:24
6:24 [h]1Ch 15:5
6:27 [i]1Sa 1:1 [j]1Sa 1:20
6:28 [k]ver 33; 1Sa 8:2
6:31 [l]1Ch 25:1; 2Ch 29:25-26; Ne 12:45 [m]1Ch 9:33; 15:19; Ezr 3:10; Ps 68:25

1Ch 6:31 ❖ Why is music is an important part of following God?

[20]Of Gershon:
Libni his son, Jahath his son,
Zimmah his son, [21]Joah his son,
Iddo his son, Zerah his son
and Jeatherai his son.
[22]The descendants of Kohath:
Amminadab his son, Korah[g] his son,
Assir his son, [23]Elkanah his son,
Ebiasaph his son, Assir his son,
[24]Tahath his son, Uriel[h] his son,
Uzziah his son and Shaul his son.
[25]The descendants of Elkanah:
Amasai, Ahimoth,
[26]Elkanah his son,[c] Zophai his son,
Nahath his son, [27]Eliab his son,
Jeroham his son, Elkanah[i] his son
and Samuel[j] his son.[d]
[28]The sons of Samuel:
Joel[e][k] the firstborn
and Abijah the second son.
[29]The descendants of Merari:
Mahli, Libni his son,
Shimei his son, Uzzah his son,
[30]Shimea his son, Haggiah his son
and Asaiah his son.

The Temple Musicians
6:54–80pp // Jos 21:4–39

[31]These are the men[l] David put in charge of the music[m] in the house of the

[a] *14* Hebrew *Jehozadak,* a variant of *Jozadak;* also in verse 15 [b] *16* Hebrew *Gershom,* a variant of *Gershon;* also in verses 17, 20, 43, 62 and 71 [c] *26* Some Hebrew manuscripts, Septuagint and Syriac; most Hebrew manuscripts *Ahimoth* [26]*and Elkanah. The sons of Elkanah:* [d] *27* Some Septuagint manuscripts (see also 1 Samuel 1:19,20 and 1 Chron. 6:33,34); Hebrew does not have *and Samuel his son.* [e] *28* Some Septuagint manuscripts and Syriac (see also 1 Samuel 8:2 and 1 Chron. 6:33); Hebrew does not have *Joel.*

6:16–30 This section of the genealogy introduces the three sons of Levi, each one as a founding ancestor of a major division of the Levitical corps: Gershon, Kohath, and Merari. The clan genealogies appear to descend (i.e., arranged from father to son) to the time of Saul and David (given the reference to Samuel's sons in v. 28 [cf. 1Sa 8:2–3] and the reference to Asaiah in v. 30 [cf. 15:6]).

The tragic record of Samuel's sons is found in 1Sa 8:2–3. As a result of their corrupt leadership, the Israelites requested a king to rule the tribes (1Sa 8:4–5).

6:31–47 King David's preparations for building the temple in which to worship Yahweh necessitated a reorganization of the nonpriestly Levites, whose services were no longer required as porters, assemblers, and custodians of the portable tabernacle. The Chronicler summarizes the reassignment of Levitical duties under the dual headings of music for the house of God (vv. 31–32) and duties related to the tabernacle (v. 48).

Heman (v. 33) oversaw the ministry of music in the house of the Lord (v. 31; cf. 15:16–17). Asaph was appointed the first associate of Heman ("served at his right hand," v. 39). Ethan headed a third musical guild as a result of the reorganization of the Levites by King David (vv. 44–47; cf. 15:16–17).

LORD after the ark came to rest there.
32They ministered with music before the
tabernacle, the tent of meeting, until
Solomon built the temple of the LORD in
Jerusalem. They performed their duties
according to the regulations laid down
for them.

33Here are the men who served, together with their sons:

From the Kohathites:

Heman,[n] the musician,
the son of Joel,[o] the son of Samuel,
34the son of Elkanah,[p] the son of Jeroham,
the son of Eliel, the son of Toah,
35the son of Zuph, the son of Elkanah,
the son of Mahath, the son of Amasai,
36the son of Elkanah, the son of Joel,
the son of Azariah, the son of Zephaniah,
37the son of Tahath, the son of Assir,
the son of Ebiasaph, the son of Korah,[q]
38the son of Izhar,[r] the son of Kohath,
the son of Levi, the son of Israel;

39and Heman's associate Asaph,[s] who served at his right hand:

Asaph son of Berekiah, the son of Shimea,[t]
40the son of Michael, the son of Baaseiah,[a]
the son of Malkijah, 41the son of Ethni,
the son of Zerah, the son of Adaiah,
42the son of Ethan, the son of Zimmah,
the son of Shimei, 43the son of Jahath,
the son of Gershon, the son of Levi;

44and from their associates, the Merarites, at his left hand:

Ethan son of Kishi, the son of Abdi,
the son of Malluk, 45the son of Hashabiah,
the son of Amaziah, the son of Hilkiah,
46the son of Amzi, the son of Bani,
the son of Shemer, 47the son of Mahli,
the son of Mushi, the son of Merari,
the son of Levi.

48Their fellow Levites[u] were assigned
to all the other duties of the tabernacle,
the house of God. 49But Aaron and his descendants were the ones who presented
offerings on the altar[v] of burnt offering
and on the altar of incense[w] in connection with all that was done in the Most
Holy Place, making atonement for Israel,
in accordance with all that Moses the
servant of God had commanded.

50These were the descendants of Aaron:

Eleazar his son, Phinehas his son,
Abishua his son, 51Bukki his son,
Uzzi his son, Zerahiah his son,
52Meraioth his son, Amariah his son,
Ahitub his son, 53Zadok[x] his son
and Ahimaaz his son.

54These were the locations of their
settlements[y] allotted as their territory
(they were assigned to the descendants
of Aaron who were from the Kohathite
clan, because the first lot was for them):
55They were given Hebron
in Judah with its surrounding

6:33 [n]1Ki 4:31; 1Ch 15:17; 25:1 [o]ver 28
6:34 [p]1Sa 1:1
6:37 [q]Ex 6:24
6:38 [r]Ex 6:21
6:39 [s]1Ch 25:1, 9; 2Ch 29:13; Ne 11:17 [t]1Ch 15:17
6:48 [u]1Ch 23:32
6:49 [v]Ex 27:1-8 [w]Ex 30:1-7,10; 2Ch 26:18
6:53 [x]2Sa 8:17
6:54 [y]Nu 31:10

[a] *40* Most Hebrew manuscripts; some Hebrew manuscripts, one Septuagint manuscript and Syriac *Maaseiah*

6:48–49 Here the Chronicler distinguishes between the "fellow Levites" (v. 48) and the priesthood descended from Aaron (v. 49) with respect to liturgical duties. The context indicates that the Chronicler differentiates between the Levitical musicians (vv. 31–47) and the priests assigned to perform the sacrificial liturgy of the sanctuary (vv. 48–49). The priests were responsible for the altar of burnt offering, the altar of incense, and the work of the Most Holy Place in general (v. 49; cf. Nu 18:5).

6:50–53 Zadok was a contemporary of David (2Sa 15:27; 19:11), while Ahimaaz was the high priest during a portion of Solomon's reign (6:8–9). David reorganized the priesthood (vv. 31–32) and Solomon built the temple where divinely ordained priestly tasks were performed (v. 49).

6:54–81 The Chronicler's list of Levitical cities is parallel to Joshua's allotment of towns to the Levites (Jos 21:5–39). The Chronicler also reorders the Levitical settlement list from Joshua, placing the allotment of towns for the descendants of Aaron first (vv. 54–60; cf. Jos 21:9–19), calling attention to the centrality of the priestly line in postexilic Judah.

6:1–81 Israel's right relationship with God was to be accomplished primarily through the teaching ministry of the Levitical corps (Dt 33:10). The curriculum for this educational initiative in "spiritual literacy" is the law of God.

pasturelands. 56But the fields and
villages around the city were given
to Caleb son of Jephunneh.[z]
57So the descendants of Aaron
were given Hebron (a city of refuge), and Libnah,[aa] Jattir,[b] Eshtemoa,
58Hilen, Debir,[c] 59Ashan,[d] Juttah[b] and
Beth Shemesh, together with their
pasturelands. 60And from the tribe
of Benjamin they were given Gibeon,[c] Geba, Alemeth and Anathoth,[e]
together with their pasturelands.
The total number of towns distributed among the Kohathite clans
came to thirteen.
61The rest of Kohath's descendants
were allotted ten towns from the clans
of half the tribe of Manasseh.
62The descendants of Gershon, clan
by clan, were allotted thirteen towns
from the tribes of Issachar, Asher and
Naphtali, and from the part of the tribe
of Manasseh that is in Bashan.
63The descendants of Merari, clan by
clan, were allotted twelve towns from
the tribes of Reuben, Gad and Zebulun.
64So the Israelites gave the Levites
these towns[f] and their pasturelands.
65From the tribes of Judah, Simeon and
Benjamin they allotted the previously
named towns.
66Some of the Kohathite clans were
given as their territory towns from the
tribe of Ephraim.
67In the hill country of Ephraim
they were given Shechem (a city of
refuge), and Gezer,[dg] 68Jokmeam,[h]
Beth Horon,[i] 69Aijalon[j] and Gath
Rimmon,[k] together with their pasturelands.
70And from half the tribe of Manasseh the Israelites gave Aner and
Bileam, together with their pasturelands, to the rest of the Kohathite
clans.

71The Gershonites[l] received the following:
From the clan of the half-tribe of
Manasseh
they received Golan in Bashan[m]
and also Ashtaroth, together with
their pasturelands;
72from the tribe of Issachar
they received Kedesh, Daberath,[n]
73Ramoth and Anem, together
with their pasturelands;
74from the tribe of Asher
they received Mashal, Abdon,[o]
75Hukok[p] and Rehob,[q] together
with their pasturelands;
76and from the tribe of Naphtali
they received Kedesh in Galilee,
Hammon[r] and Kiriathaim,[s] together with their pasturelands.

77The Merarites (the rest of the Levites) received the following:
From the tribe of Zebulun
they received Jokneam, Kartah,[e]
Rimmono and Tabor, together
with their pasturelands;
78from the tribe of Reuben across the
Jordan east of Jericho
they received Bezer[t] in the wilderness, Jahzah, 79Kedemoth[u] and
Mephaath, together with their
pasturelands;
80and from the tribe of Gad
they received Ramoth in Gilead,[v]
Mahanaim,[w] 81Heshbon and Jazer,[x] together with their pasturelands.[y]

Issachar

7 The sons of Issachar:[z]
Tola, Puah,[a] Jashub and Shimron — four in all.
2The sons of Tola:
Uzzi, Rephaiah, Jeriel, Jahmai,
Ibsam and Samuel — heads of
their families. During the reign
of David, the descendants of Tola

6:56 [z] Jos 14:13; 15:13
6:57 [a] Nu 33:20 [b] Jos 15:48
6:58 [c] Jos 10:3
6:59 [d] Jos 15:42
6:60 [e] Jer 1:1
6:64 [f] Nu 35:1-8; Jos 21:3, 41-42
6:67 [g] Jos 10:33
6:68 [h] 1Ki 4:12 [i] Jos 10:10
6:69 [j] Jos 10:12 [k] Jos 19:45
6:71 [l] 1Ch 23:7
[m] Jos 20:8
6:72 [n] Jos 19:12
6:74 [o] Jos 19:28
6:75 [p] Jos 19:34 [q] Nu 13:21
6:76 [r] Jos 19:28 [s] Nu 32:37
6:78 [t] Jos 20:8
6:79 [u] Dt 2:26
6:80 [v] Jos 20:8 [w] Ge 32:2
6:81 [x] Nu 21:32 [y] 2Ch 11:14
7:1 [z] Ge 30:18; Nu 26:23 [a] Ge 46:13

[a] 57 See Joshua 21:13; Hebrew *given the cities of refuge: Hebron, Libnah.* [b] 59 Syriac (see also Septuagint and Joshua 21:16); Hebrew does not have *Juttah.* [c] 60 See Joshua 21:17; Hebrew does not have *Gibeon.* [d] 67 See Joshua 21:21; Hebrew *given the cities of refuge: Shechem, Gezer.* [e] 77 See Septuagint and Joshua 21:34; Hebrew does not have *Jokneam, Kartah.*

Historically, the church of Jesus Christ has spread his gospel in a similar manner—by clergy invested with the office gift of pastor-teacher and by laypeople endowed with the spiritual gift of teaching. The goal of this instruction is consistent with that of the priestly ministry: freeing people from bondage to sin through a knowledge of God's truth about the human condition and his redemptive plan to remedy our plight (cf. Jn 8:32; 2Ti 3:14–16).

7:1-5 Issachar means "hired workman," and Jacob's deathbed blessing of Issachar plays on that mean-

listed as fighting men in their genealogy numbered 22,600.
3 The son of Uzzi:
Izrahiah.
The sons of Izrahiah:
Michael, Obadiah, Joel and Ishiah. All five of them were chiefs. 4 According to their family genealogy, they had 36,000 men ready for battle, for they had many wives and children.
5 The relatives who were fighting men belonging to all the clans of Issachar, as listed in their genealogy, were 87,000 in all.

Benjamin

6 Three sons of Benjamin:[b]
Bela, Beker and Jediael.
7 The sons of Bela:
Ezbon, Uzzi, Uzziel, Jerimoth and Iri, heads of families — five in all. Their genealogical record listed 22,034 fighting men.
8 The sons of Beker:
Zemirah, Joash, Eliezer, Elioenai, Omri, Jeremoth, Abijah, Anathoth and Alemeth. All these were the sons of Beker. 9 Their genealogical record listed the heads of families and 20,200 fighting men.
10 The son of Jediael:
Bilhan.
The sons of Bilhan:
Jeush, Benjamin, Ehud, Kenaanah, Zethan, Tarshish and Ahishahar. 11 All these sons of Jediael were heads of families. There were 17,200 fighting men ready to go out to war.
12 The Shuppites and Huppites were the descendants of Ir, and the Hushites[a] the descendants of Aher.

7:6 [b] Ge 46:21; Nu 26:38; 1Ch 8:1-40
7:13 [c] Ge 30:8; 46:24
7:14 [d] Ge 41:51; Jos 17:1; 1Ch 5:23 [e] Nu 26:30
7:15 [f] Nu 26:33; 36:1-12
7:17 [g] Nu 26:30; 1Sa 12:11
7:18 [h] Jos 17:2
7:20 [i] Ge 41:52; Nu 1:33; 26:35

Naphtali

13 The sons of Naphtali:[c]
Jahziel, Guni, Jezer and Shillem[b] — the descendants of Bilhah.

Manasseh

14 The descendants of Manasseh:[d]
Asriel was his descendant through his Aramean concubine. She gave birth to Makir the father of Gilead.[e] 15 Makir took a wife from among the Huppites and Shuppites. His sister's name was Maakah.
Another descendant was named Zelophehad,[f] who had only daughters.
16 Makir's wife Maakah gave birth to a son and named him Peresh. His brother was named Sheresh, and his sons were Ulam and Rakem.
17 The son of Ulam:
Bedan.
These were the sons of Gilead[g] son of Makir, the son of Manasseh. 18 His sister Hammoleketh gave birth to Ishhod, Abiezer[h] and Mahlah.
19 The sons of Shemida were:
Ahian, Shechem, Likhi and Aniam.

Ephraim

20 The descendants of Ephraim:[i]
Shuthelah, Bered his son,
Tahath his son, Eleadah his son,
Tahath his son, 21 Zabad his son
and Shuthelah his son.
Ezer and Elead were killed by the native-born men of Gath, when they went down to seize their livestock.

[a] *12* Or *Ir. The sons of Dan: Hushim,* (see Gen. 46:23); Hebrew does not have *The sons of Dan.*
[b] *13* Some Hebrew and Septuagint manuscripts (see also Gen. 46:24 and Num. 26:49); most Hebrew manuscripts *Shallum*

---

ing in predicting that Issachar's descendants will toil in forced labor gangs (Ge 49:15).

7:6–12 The name Benjamin was given by his father and means literally "son of the right hand." The insertion of the Benjamite genealogy at this juncture serves to introduce the more extensive family tree of Benjamin that follows in ch. 8.

7:13 Bilhah was one of Jacob's concubines and the mother of Naphtali (Ge 46:24–25).

7:14–29 Manasseh and Ephraim were the sons of Joseph by his Egyptian wife Asenath (Ge 41:50–51). Manasseh and Ephraim are the so-called "half-tribes" or "Joseph tribes" of Israel. It is helpful to remember that the Chronicler has selected and arranged genealogical materials from a number of ancient sources for theological purposes related to the postexilic restoration of Judah. The Chronicler has included genealogical records of the Joseph tribes primarily to round out the ideal number of the twelve tribes.

7:20–29 Often Ephraim is placed first when paired with Manasseh because of Jacob's blessing of Ephraim prior to Manasseh (Ge 48:20). The reference to Joshua (1Ch 7:27) is in keeping with the Chronicler's emphasis on the Israelite conquest and occupation of the land that God had promised to Israel.

The story of Ezer and Elead is unique to Chronicles. The Chronicler inserts the account as an example of temporary loss and setback overcome providentially by human initiative.

[22]Their father Ephraim mourned
for them many days, and his relatives came to comfort him. [23]Then
he made love to his wife again, and
she became pregnant and gave birth
to a son. He named him Beriah,[a] because there had been misfortune in
his family. [24]His daughter was Sheerah, who built Lower and Upper Beth
Horon[j] as well as Uzzen Sheerah.
[25]Rephah was his son, Resheph his
son,[b]
Telah his son, Tahan his son,
[26]Ladan his son, Ammihud his son,
Elishama his son, [27]Nun his son
and Joshua his son.
[28]Their lands and settlements included
Bethel and its surrounding villages, Naa-
ran to the east, Gezer[k] and its villages to
the west, and Shechem and its villages all
the way to Ayyah and its villages. [29]Along
the borders of Manasseh were Beth Shan,[l]
Taanach, Megiddo and Dor,[m] together
with their villages. The descendants of
Joseph son of Israel lived in these towns.

Asher

[30]The sons of Asher:[n]
Imnah, Ishvah, Ishvi and Beriah.
Their sister was Serah.
[31]The sons of Beriah:
Heber and Malkiel, who was the
father of Birzaith.
[32]Heber was the father of Japhlet, Shomer and Hotham and of their sister Shua.
[33]The sons of Japhlet:
Pasak, Bimhal and Ashvath.
These were Japhlet's sons.
[34]The sons of Shomer:
Ahi, Rohgah,[c] Hubbah and Aram.
[35]The sons of his brother Helem:
Zophah, Imna, Shelesh and Amal.
[36]The sons of Zophah:
Suah, Harnepher, Shual, Beri,
Imrah, [37]Bezer, Hod, Shamma,
Shilshah, Ithran[d] and Beera.
[38]The sons of Jether:
Jephunneh, Pispah and Ara.
[39]The sons of Ulla:
Arah, Hanniel and Rizia.
[40]All these were descendants of Asher—heads of families, choice men, brave
warriors and outstanding leaders. The
number of men ready for battle, as listed
in their genealogy, was 26,000.

7:24 [j]Jos 10:10; 16:3,5
7:28 [k]Jos 10:33; 16:7
7:29 [l]Jos 17:11 [m]Jos 11:2
7:30 [n]Ge 46:17; Nu 1:40; 26:44

1Ch 7:22-23 ❖ How do we commemorate past misfortunes? How might misfortunes bring us closer to God?

The Genealogy of Saul the Benjamite

8:28–38pp // 1Ch 9:34–44

8 Benjamin[o] was the father of Bela his
firstborn,
Ashbel the second son, Aharah
the third,
[2]Nohah the fourth and Rapha the
fifth.
[3]The sons of Bela were:
Addar,[p] Gera, Abihud,[e] [4]Abishua,
Naaman, Ahoah,[q] [5]Gera, Shephu-
phan and Huram.
[6]These were the descendants of
Ehud,[r] who were heads of families of those living in Geba and
were deported to Manahath:
[7]Naaman, Ahijah, and Gera, who
deported them and who was the
father of Uzza and Ahihud.
[8]Sons were born to Shaharaim in
Moab after he had divorced his
wives Hushim and Baara. [9]By his

8:1 [o]Ge 46:21; 1Ch 7:6
8:3 [p]Ge 46:21
8:4 [q]2Sa 23:9
8:6 [r]Jdg 3:12-30; 1Ch 2:52

[a] 23 *Beriah* sounds like the Hebrew for *misfortune.* [b] 25 Some Septuagint manuscripts; Hebrew does not have *his son.* [c] 34 Or *of his brother Shomer: Rohgah* [d] 37 Possibly a variant of *Jether* [e] 3 Or *Gera the father of Ehud*

7:30-40 Asher was the son of Zilpah, the handmaid of Leah (Ge 46:18). Asher concludes the tribal list. The attrition in the number of soldiers to 26,000 (7:40) from 41,500 (Nu 1:40-41) testifies to the misfortunes experienced by this tribe.

✣ **7:1-40** The theme of including the Gentiles in the covenant promises to Israel encases the message of the entire Bible, much like an envelope or even bookends. The opening chapters of Genesis introduce the table of nations (Ge 10) and God's promise to bless all nations (Ge 12:1-3), and the concluding book of the Bible depicts the nations surrounding the throne of God in worship (Rev 5:9-10; 7:9-10). Jesus' call to "go and make disciples of all nations" (Mt 28:19) challenges all believers who read his words to act on their part in fulfilling that mission.

8:1-7 The focal point of the genealogy is the clan of Ehud more than the family tree of the tribal patriarch Benjamin.

8:8-13 Moab was a satellite state under Israelite control during the reigns of David and Solomon (cf. 2Sa 8:2). The curious report of sons born to

wife Hodesh he had Jobab, Zibia, Mesha, Malkam, 10 Jeuz, Sakia
and Mirmah. These were his sons,
heads of families. 11 By Hushim he
had Abitub and Elpaal.
12 The sons of Elpaal:
Eber, Misham, Shemed (who built Ono[s] and Lod with its surrounding villages), 13 and Beriah and
Shema, who were heads of families of those living in Aijalon[t] and who drove out the inhabitants of Gath.[u]
14 Ahio, Shashak, Jeremoth, 15 Zebadiah, Arad, Eder, 16 Michael, Ishpah
and Joha were the sons of Beriah.
17 Zebadiah, Meshullam, Hizki, Heber,
18 Ishmerai, Izliah and Jobab were the sons of Elpaal.
19 Jakim, Zikri, Zabdi, 20 Elienai, Zillethai, Eliel, 21 Adaiah, Beraiah
and Shimrath were the sons of Shimei.
22 Ishpan, Eber, Eliel, 23 Abdon, Zikri,
Hanan, 24 Hananiah, Elam, Anthothijah, 25 Iphdeiah and Penuel
were the sons of Shashak.
26 Shamsherai, Shehariah, Athaliah,
27 Jaareshiah, Elijah and Zikri were
the sons of Jeroham.
28 All these were heads of families, chiefs as listed in their genealogy, and they lived in Jerusalem.

29 Jeiel[a] the father[b] of Gibeon lived in Gibeon.[v]
His wife's name was Maakah,
30 and his firstborn son was Abdon, followed by Zur, Kish, Baal,
Ner,[c] Nadab, 31 Gedor, Ahio, Zeker
32 and Mikloth, who was the father
of Shimeah. They too lived near their relatives in Jerusalem.

8:12 [s] Ezr 2:33; Ne 6:2; 7:37; 11:35
8:13 [t] Jos 10:12 [u] Jos 11:22
8:29 [v] Jos 9:3
8:33 [w] 1Sa 28:19 [x] 1Sa 9:1 [y] 1Sa 14:49 [z] 2Sa 2:8
8:34 [a] 2Sa 9:12 [b] 2Sa 4:4
8:40 [c] Nu 26:38

1Ch 8:8 ❖ Family dysfunction leaves lasting wounds. How can we heal scars from our family's past?

33 Ner[w] was the father of Kish,[x] Kish
the father of Saul[y], and Saul the father of Jonathan, Malki-Shua, Abinadab and Esh-Baal.[dz]
34 The son of Jonathan:[a]
Merib-Baal,[eb] who was the father of Micah.
35 The sons of Micah:
Pithon, Melek, Tarea and Ahaz.
36 Ahaz was the father of Jehoaddah, Jehoaddah was the father of Alemeth, Azmaveth and Zimri, and Zimri was the father of Moza.
37 Moza was the father of Binea;
Raphah was his son, Eleasah his son and Azel his son.
38 Azel had six sons, and these were their names:
Azrikam, Bokeru, Ishmael, Sheariah, Obadiah and Hanan. All these were the sons of Azel.
39 The sons of his brother Eshek:
Ulam his firstborn, Jeush the second son and Eliphelet the third.
40 The sons of Ulam were brave
warriors who could handle the bow. They had many sons and grandsons — 150 in all.
All these were the descendants of Benjamin.[c]

[a] *29* Some Septuagint manuscripts (see also 9:35); Hebrew does not have *Jeiel.* [b] *29 Father* may mean *civic leader* or *military leader.* [c] *30* Some Septuagint manuscripts (see also 9:36); Hebrew does not have *Ner.* [d] *33* Also known as *Ish-Bosheth* [e] *34* Also known as *Mephibosheth*

Shaharaim (8:8) is in keeping with the Chronicler's style of personalizing the genealogies with sidebars that highlight unusual events or that call attention to marginalized people (like women and non-Hebrews).

8:14–28 Perhaps geography is an organizing principle in the gathering of the Benjamite history since there is a general movement from the outskirts of the territory of Benjamin to the city of Jerusalem. This illustrates that the city of Jerusalem belongs to all Israel as it records citizens from several tribes resettling there after the exile (9:3).

8:29–40 The list is the most extensive record of Saul's family in the Bible and is repeated (with minor variations) in 9:35–44 as an introduction to the death of King Saul (ch. 10).

✜ **8:1—9:1a** Part of the story of the Bible is the conflict between faith in God (and the truth he has disclosed through general and special revelation) and false gods and false teaching espoused by humanistic philosophies and superstitious religions. In recent decades the church has had to combat an equally insidious false teaching that promotes health, wealth, and happiness. Such teaching makes the Christian life more a quest for personal success than a call to suffer for the cause of Christ (see Mt 10:22; 24:9). This gospel of "gain with no pain" ignores biblical stories that feature the adversity and suffering of God's people.

9 All Israel was listed in the genealogies recorded in the book of the kings
of Israel and Judah. They were taken
captive to Babylon because of their unfaithfulness.[d]

The People in Jerusalem

9:1–17pp // Ne 11:3–19

2 Now the first to resettle on their own
property in their own towns[e] were some
Israelites, priests, Levites and temple
servants.[f]
3 Those from Judah, from Benjamin,
and from Ephraim and Manasseh who
lived in Jerusalem were:
4 Uthai son of Ammihud, the son of
Omri, the son of Imri, the son of
Bani, a descendant of Perez son
of Judah.[g]
5 Of the Shelanites[a]:
Asaiah the firstborn and his sons.
6 Of the Zerahites:
Jeuel.
The people from Judah numbered
690.
7 Of the Benjamites:
Sallu son of Meshullam, the son of
Hodaviah, the son of Hassenuah;
8 Ibneiah son of Jeroham; Elah son
of Uzzi, the son of Mikri; and Meshullam son of Shephatiah, the
son of Reuel, the son of Ibnijah.
9 The people from Benjamin, as listed in their genealogy, numbered
956. All these men were heads of
their families.
10 Of the priests:
Jedaiah; Jehoiarib; Jakin;
11 Azariah son of Hilkiah, the son
of Meshullam, the son of Zadok,
the son of Meraioth, the son of
Ahitub, the official in charge of
the house of God;
12 Adaiah son of Jeroham, the son
of Pashhur,[h] the son of Malkijah;
and Maasai son of Adiel, the son of
Jahzerah, the son of Meshullam,
the son of Meshillemith, the son
of Immer.
13 The priests, who were heads of
families, numbered 1,760. They
were able men, responsible for
ministering in the house of God.
14 Of the Levites:
Shemaiah son of Hasshub, the son
of Azrikam, the son of Hashabiah,
a Merarite; 15 Bakbakkar, Heresh,
Galal and Mattaniah[i] son of Mika,
the son of Zikri, the son of Asaph;
16 Obadiah son of Shemaiah, the
son of Galal, the son of Jeduthun;
and Berekiah son of Asa, the son
of Elkanah, who lived in the villages of the Netophathites.[j]
17 The gatekeepers:[k]
Shallum, Akkub, Talmon, Ahiman
and their fellow Levites, Shallum
their chief 18 being stationed at the
King's Gate[l] on the east, up to the
present time. These were the gatekeepers belonging to the camp
of the Levites. 19 Shallum[m] son of
Kore, the son of Ebiasaph, the son
of Korah, and his fellow gatekeepers from his family (the Korahites)
were responsible for guarding the
thresholds of the tent just as their
ancestors had been responsible
for guarding the entrance to the
dwelling of the LORD. 20 In earlier
times Phinehas[n] son of Eleazar was
the official in charge of the gatekeepers, and the LORD was with
him. 21 Zechariah[o] son of Meshelemiah was the gatekeeper at the
entrance to the tent of meeting.
22 Altogether, those chosen to be gatekeepers[p] at the thresholds numbered
212. They were registered by genealogy
in their villages. The gatekeepers had
been assigned to their positions of trust
by David and Samuel the seer.[q] 23 They

9:1 [d] 1Ch 5:25
9:2 [e] Jos 9:27; Ezr 2:70 [f] Ezr 2:43,58; 8:20; Ne 7:60
9:4 [g] Ge 38:29; 46:12
9:12 [h] Ezr 2:38; 10:22; Ne 10:3; Jer 21:1; 38:1
9:15 [i] 2Ch 20:14; Ne 11:22
9:16 [j] Ne 12:28
9:17 [k] ver 22; 1Ch 26:1; 2Ch 8:14; 31:14; Ezr 2:42; Ne 7:45
9:18 [l] 1Ch 26:14; Eze 43:1; 46:1
9:19 [m] Jer 35:4
9:20 [n] Nu 25:7-13
9:21 [o] 1Ch 26:2, 14
9:22 [p] ver 17; 1Ch 26:1-2; 2Ch 31:15,18 [q] 1Sa 9:9

[a] 5 See Num. 26:20; Hebrew *Shilonites.*

9:1b–34 The repetition of "Israel" in 2:1 and 9:1a suggests an envelope construction encasing the genealogies of 2:1—9:1a as a complete literary unit. The genealogy as a whole calls attention to the priests, Levites, and temple personnel resettling Jerusalem.

9:2–3 The introduction to the list of people resettling Judah after the Babylonian exile subtly confirms the link between the postexilic Jewish community and the earlier nation of Israel.

9:4–6 The Chronicler abbreviates the list of descendants of Judah found in the parallel of Ne 11:4–6.

9:7–9 The Chronicler's list contains variations from the parallel account in Ne 11:7–9. Each writer makes selective use of a common and more complete genealogical record.

9:17 Four chief gatekeepers are identified, as there were four entrances to the temple precincts. A gate was located on each of the cardinal compass points, with the east gate being the most important. The gatekeepers worked their shifts in pairs for seven-day periods (v. 25), and in all they manned twenty-two stations around the clock (26:17–18).

and their descendants were in charge
of guarding the gates of the house of
the LORD — the house called the tent of
meeting. 24The gatekeepers were on the
four sides: east, west, north and south.
25Their fellow Levites in their villages
had to come from time to time and share
their duties for seven-day[r] periods. 26But
the four principal gatekeepers, who were
Levites, were entrusted with the responsibility for the rooms and treasuries[s] in
the house of God. 27They would spend
the night stationed around the house of
God,[t] because they had to guard it; and
they had charge of the key[u] for opening
it each morning.
28Some of them were in charge of the
articles used in the temple service; they
counted them when they were brought
in and when they were taken out. 29Oth-
ers were assigned to take care of the furnishings and all the other articles of the
sanctuary,[v] as well as the special flour
and wine, and the olive oil, incense and
spices. 30But some[w] of the priests took
care of mixing the spices. 31A Levite
named Mattithiah, the firstborn son of
Shallum the Korahite, was entrusted
with the responsibility for baking the
offering bread. 32Some of the Kohathites,
their fellow Levites, were in charge of
preparing for every Sabbath the bread
set out on the table.[x]
33Those who were musicians,[y] heads of
Levite families, stayed in the rooms of
the temple and were exempt from other
duties because they were responsible for
the work day and night.[z]
34All these were heads of Levite families, chiefs as listed in their genealogy,
and they lived in Jerusalem.

The Genealogy of Saul

9:34–44pp // 1Ch 8:28–38

35 Jeiel[a] the father[a] of Gibeon lived in
Gibeon.

9:25 [r]2Ki 11:5; 2Ch 23:8
9:26 [s]1Ch 26:22
9:27 [t]Nu 3:38; 1Ch 23:30-32 [u]Isa 22:22
9:29 [v]Nu 3:28; 1Ch 23:29
9:30 [w]Ex 30:23-25
9:32 [x]Lev 24:5-8; 1Ch 23:29; 2Ch 13:11
9:33 [y]1Ch 6:31; 25:1-31 [z]Ps 134:1
9:35 [a]1Ch 8:29

> **1Ch 9:22** ❖ Should God's assembly have "gatekeepers" today? Why or why not?

His wife's name was Maakah,
36and his firstborn son was Abdon, followed by Zur, Kish, Baal,
Ner, Nadab, 37Gedor, Ahio, Zechariah and Mikloth. 38Mikloth was the
father of Shimeam. They too lived
near their relatives in Jerusalem.
39 Ner[b] was the father of Kish,[c] Kish
the father of Saul, and Saul the
father of Jonathan,[d] Malki-Shua,
Abinadab and Esh-Baal.[b][e]
40 The son of Jonathan:
Merib-Baal,[c][f] who was the father
of Micah.
41 The sons of Micah:
Pithon, Melek, Tahrea and Ahaz.[d]
42 Ahaz was the father of Jadah, Jadah[e] was the father of Alemeth,
Azmaveth and Zimri, and Zimri
was the father of Moza. 43Moza
was the father of Binea; Rephaiah
was his son, Eleasah his son and
Azel his son.
44 Azel had six sons, and these were
their names:
Azrikam, Bokeru, Ishmael, Sheariah, Obadiah and Hanan. These
were the sons of Azel.

9:39 [b]1Ch 8:33 [c]1Sa 9:1 [d]1Sa 13:22 [e]2Sa 2:8
9:40 [f]2Sa 4:4

Saul Takes His Life

10:1–12pp // 1Sa 31:1–13; 2Sa 1:4–12

10 Now the Philistines fought against
Israel; the Israelites fled before
them, and many fell dead on Mount Gilboa. 2The Philistines were in hot pursuit

[a] 35 *Father* may mean *civic leader* or *military leader.* [b] 39 Also known as *Ish-Bosheth* [c] 40 Also known as *Mephibosheth* [d] 41 Vulgate and Syriac (see also Septuagint and 8:35); Hebrew does not have *and Ahaz.* [e] 42 Some Hebrew manuscripts and Septuagint (see also 8:36); most Hebrew manuscripts *Jarah, Jarah*

9:27–29 The gatekeepers provided leadership in the day-to-day operations of the temple by continually guarding the premises and its contents and opening the gates for temple services every morning. **9:33** The word translated "musicians" can also signify "singers." It is unclear if the singers are the Levites mentioned in vv. 14–16 or gatekeepers (vv. 17–32) who double as temple musicians. **9:35–44** This genealogy repeats the register of Saul's family tree (with minor variations) found in 8:29–38 as one segment of the genealogy of Benjamin. These minor differences may be explained as either textual variation or an ongoing process of transformation of names because of language changes over time.

> ✜ **9:1b–44** The story of Israel is a story of fresh starts by God's grace. In fact, the story of the Bible is the story of God making and remaking, doing "new things" (Isa 43:19; cf. Jer 31:22; Rev 21:5). These new beginnings, flashing like meteor showers across the timeline of church history, testify to the faithfulness of God through the ages.

of Saul and his sons, and they killed his sons Jonathan, Abinadab and Malki-Shua. 3 The fighting grew fierce around Saul, and when the archers overtook him, they wounded him.

4 Saul said to his armor-bearer, "Draw your sword and run me through, or these uncircumcised fellows will come and abuse me."

But his armor-bearer was terrified and would not do it; so Saul took his own sword and fell on it. 5 When the armor-bearer saw that Saul was dead, he too fell on his sword and died. 6 So Saul and his three sons died, and all his house died together.

7 When all the Israelites in the valley saw that the army had fled and that Saul and his sons had died, they abandoned their towns and fled. And the Philistines came and occupied them.

8 The next day, when the Philistines came to strip the dead, they found Saul and his sons fallen on Mount Gilboa. 9 They stripped him and took his head and his armor, and sent messengers throughout the land of the Philistines to proclaim the news among their idols and their people. 10 They put his armor in the temple of their gods and hung up his head in the temple of Dagon.[g]

11 When all the inhabitants of Jabesh Gilead[h] heard what the Philistines had done to Saul, 12 all their valiant men went and took the bodies of Saul and his sons and brought them to Jabesh. Then they buried their bones under the great tree in Jabesh, and they fasted seven days.

13 Saul died[i] because he was unfaithful[j] to the LORD; he did not keep[k] the word of the LORD and even consulted a medium[l] for guidance, 14 and did not inquire of the LORD. So the LORD put him to death and turned[m] the kingdom[n] over to David son of Jesse.

David Becomes King Over Israel

11:1–3pp // 2Sa 5:1–3

11 All Israel[o] came together to David at Hebron[p] and said, "We are your own flesh and blood. 2 In the past, even while Saul was king, you were the one who led Israel on their military campaigns.[q] And the LORD your God said to you, 'You will shepherd[r] my people Israel, and you will become their ruler.[s]'"

3 When all the elders of Israel had come to King David at Hebron, he made a covenant with them at Hebron before the LORD, and they anointed[t] David king over Israel, as the LORD had promised through Samuel.

David Conquers Jerusalem

11:4–9pp // 2Sa 5:6–10

4 David and all the Israelites marched to Jerusalem (that is, Jebus). The Jebusites[u] who lived there 5 said to David, "You will not get in here." Nevertheless, David captured the fortress of Zion — which is the City of David.

6 David had said, "Whoever leads the attack on the Jebusites will become commander in chief." Joab[v] son of Zeruiah

1Ch 10:13–14 ❖ Where do we go for guidance? How can we be sure the influences in our lives are godly?

1Ch 11:2 ❖ Why should godly leaders be like shepherds to their people? What are the positive qualities of shepherds that good leaders should demonstrate?

10:10 [g] Jdg 16:23
10:11 [h] Jdg 21:8
10:13 [i] 2Sa 1:1 [j] 1Sa 15:23; 1Ch 5:25 [k] 1Sa 13:13 [l] Lev 19:31; 20:6; Dt 18:9-14; 1Sa 28:7
10:14 [m] 1Ch 12:23 [n] 1Sa 13:14; 15:28
11:1 [o] 1Ch 9:1 [p] Ge 13:18; 23:19
11:2 [q] 1Sa 18:5, 16 [r] Ps 78:71; Mt 2:6 [s] 1Ch 5:2
11:3 [t] 1Sa 16:1-13
11:4 [u] Ge 10:16; 15:18-21; Jos 3:10; 15:8; Jdg 1:21; 19:10
11:6 [v] 2Sa 2:13; 8:16

10:1–7 Saul was anointed king to deliver God's people "from the hand of the Philistines" (1Sa 9:16). Ironically, Saul and his sons were killed by these very same Philistines. The national hopes that fueled the fervent clamor for a king were dashed. The Chronicler offers no theological commentary on the morality of Saul's suicide, which is a rare occurrence in the Bible.

10:8–12 The rescue of the exposed corpses of Saul and his sons by the valiant men of Jabesh Gilead may have been prompted by King Saul's deliverance of Jabesh Gilead from the aggression of Nahash the Ammonite (1Sa 11:1–11).

10:13–14 Saul failed miserably on three crucial counts: he was unfaithful, he did not keep the word of the Lord, and he neglected to seek guidance from the Lord. Unfaithfulness and failure to seek the Lord are prominent themes in Chronicles; these actions inevitably result in divine judgment.

11:1–3 The passage references several key concepts connected with kingship after the Davidic ideal: the pastoral image of king as shepherd of the people, the "king" as "ruler" (the term has military connotations and calls to mind the language of the Davidic covenant, 2Sa 7:7–8), and the act of anointing (cf. 1Sa 16:3, 12).

11:4–9 According to the Chronicler, the conquest of Jerusalem is the first major act of David's kingship. In contrast to Saul's unfaithfulness (10:13), David expands his base of power in Israel "because the LORD Almighty was with him" (11:9). David's faithfulness to God and his obedience to God's law is the standard by which his successors will be measured.

went up first, and so he received the
command.
7David then took up residence in the
fortress, and so it was called the City of
David. 8He built up the city around it,
from the terraces[a][w] to the surrounding
wall, while Joab restored the rest of the
city. 9And David became more and more
powerful,[x] because the LORD Almighty
was with him.

David's Mighty Warriors

11:10–41pp // 2Sa 23:8–39

10These were the chiefs of David's
mighty warriors — they, together with
all Israel,[y] gave his kingship strong support to extend it over the whole land, as
the LORD had promised[z] — 11this is the
list of David's mighty warriors:[a]
Jashobeam,[b] a Hakmonite, was chief of
the officers[c]; he raised his spear against
three hundred men, whom he killed in
one encounter.
12Next to him was Eleazar son of Dodai the Ahohite, one of the three mighty
warriors. 13He was with David at Pas
Dammim when the Philistines gathered
there for battle. At a place where there
was a field full of barley, the troops fled
from the Philistines. 14But they took their
stand in the middle of the field. They
defended it and struck the Philistines
down, and the LORD brought about a
great victory.[b]
15Three of the thirty chiefs came down
to David to the rock at the cave of Adullam, while a band of Philistines was encamped in the Valley[c] of Rephaim. 16At
that time David was in the stronghold,[d]
and the Philistine garrison was at Bethlehem. 17David longed for water and
said, "Oh, that someone would get me
a drink of water from the well near the
gate of Bethlehem!" 18So the Three broke
through the Philistine lines, drew water
from the well near the gate of Bethlehem and carried it back to David. But he
refused to drink it; instead, he poured[e]
it out to the LORD. 19"God forbid that I
should do this!" he said. "Should I drink
the blood of these men who went at the
risk of their lives?" Because they risked
their lives to bring it back, David would
not drink it.
Such were the exploits of the three
mighty warriors.
20Abishai[f] the brother of Joab was
chief of the Three. He raised his spear
against three hundred men, whom he
killed, and so he became as famous as the
Three. 21He was doubly honored above
the Three and became their commander,
even though he was not included among
them.
22Benaiah son of Jehoiada, a valiant
fighter from Kabzeel,[g] performed great
exploits. He struck down Moab's two
mightiest warriors. He also went down
into a pit on a snowy day and killed a
lion.[h] 23And he struck down an Egyptian
who was five cubits[d] tall. Although the
Egyptian had a spear like a weaver's rod[i]
in his hand, Benaiah went against him
with a club. He snatched the spear from
the Egyptian's hand and killed him with
his own spear. 24Such were the exploits
of Benaiah son of Jehoiada; he too was
as famous as the three mighty warriors.
25He was held in greater honor than any
of the Thirty, but he was not included
among the Three. And David put him in
charge of his bodyguard.

26The mighty warriors were:
Asahel[j] the brother of Joab,
Elhanan son of Dodo from Bethlehem,
27Shammoth[k] the Harorite,

11:8 [w] 2Sa 5:9; 2Ch 32:5
11:9 [x] 2Sa 3:1; Est 9:4
11:10 [y] ver 1 [z] ver 3; 1Ch 12:23
11:11 [a] 2Sa 17:10
11:14 [b] Ex 14:30; 1Sa 11:13
11:15 [c] 1Ch 14:9; Isa 17:5
11:16 [d] 2Sa 5:17
11:18 [e] Dt 12:16
11:20 [f] 1Sa 26:6
11:22 [g] Jos 15:21 [h] 1Sa 17:36
11:23 [i] 1Sa 17:7
11:26 [j] 2Sa 2:18
11:27 [k] 1Ch 27:8

[a] 8 Or *the Millo* [b] 11 Possibly a variant of *Jashob-Baal* [c] 11 Or *Thirty*; some Septuagint manuscripts *Three* (see also 2 Samuel 23:8) [d] 23 That is, about 7 feet 6 inches or about 2.3 meters

---

11:10–47 The lists of soldiers in both 2 Samuel and the Chronicles makes reference to the "Three" and the "Thirty" (vv. 15, 20, 25; 2Sa 23:8, 13, 17, 23). These elite troops are the ancient equivalent of both the modern-day special forces military units and a secret service charged with the protection of the highest elected officials.

The roster of David's mighty men begins with the names and exploits of those known as "the Three": Jashobeam, Eleazar, and Shammah (vv. 11–14). Perhaps the most striking feature of this passage is the theological assessment of the heroism of the Three, that "the LORD brought about a great victory" (v. 14). The Chronicler emphasizes David's ability to inspire remarkable bravery and unshakable loyalty among his followers.

11:25 Benaiah is accorded special honor because of his role as the chief of King David's bodyguards.

11:26–47 The list of David's "mighty men" is longer than the parallel found in 2Sa 23:24–39. The differences in the two lists of David's mighty men suggests not only the Chronicler's access to additional historical sources but also the natural fluidity present in a group of military heroes during David's long reign.

Helez the Pelonite,
28 Ira son of Ikkesh from Tekoa,
Abiezer[l] from Anathoth,
29 Sibbekai[m] the Hushathite,
Ilai the Ahohite,
30 Maharai the Netophathite,
Heled son of Baanah the Netophathite,
31 Ithai son of Ribai from Gibeah in Benjamin,
Benaiah[n] the Pirathonite,[o]
32 Hurai from the ravines of Gaash,
Abiel the Arbathite,
33 Azmaveth the Baharumite,
Eliahba the Shaalbonite,
34 the sons of Hashem the Gizonite,
Jonathan son of Shagee the Hararite,
35 Ahiam son of Sakar the Hararite,
Eliphal son of Ur,
36 Hepher the Mekerathite,
Ahijah the Pelonite,
37 Hezro the Carmelite,
Naarai son of Ezbai,
38 Joel the brother of Nathan,
Mibhar son of Hagri,
39 Zelek the Ammonite,
Naharai the Berothite, the armor-bearer of Joab son of Zeruiah,
40 Ira the Ithrite,
Gareb the Ithrite,
41 Uriah[p] the Hittite,
Zabad[q] son of Ahlai,
42 Adina son of Shiza the Reubenite, who was chief of the Reubenites, and the thirty with him,
43 Hanan son of Maakah,
Joshaphat the Mithnite,
44 Uzzia the Ashterathite,[r]
Shama and Jeiel the sons of Hotham the Aroerite,
45 Jediael son of Shimri,
his brother Joha the Tizite,
46 Eliel the Mahavite,
Jeribai and Joshaviah the sons of Elnaam,
Ithmah the Moabite,
47 Eliel, Obed and Jaasiel the Mezobaite.

Warriors Join David

12 These were the men who came to
David at Ziklag,[s] while he was banished from the presence of Saul son of
Kish (they were among the warriors who
helped him in battle; 2 they were armed
with bows and were able to shoot arrows or to sling stones right-handed or
left-handed;[t] they were relatives of Saul[u]
from the tribe of Benjamin):

3 Ahiezer their chief and Joash the
sons of Shemaah the Gibeathite;
Jeziel and Pelet the sons of Azmaveth; Berakah, Jehu the Anathothite, 4 and Ishmaiah the Gibeonite, a
mighty warrior among the Thirty,
who was a leader of the Thirty; Jeremiah, Jahaziel, Johanan, Jozabad
the Gederathite,[a][v] 5 Eluzai, Jerimoth,
Bealiah, Shemariah and Shephati-
ah the Haruphite; 6 Elkanah, Ishiah,
Azarel, Joezer and Jashobeam the
Korahites; 7 and Joelah and Zebadiah
the sons of Jeroham from Gedor.[w]

8 Some Gadites[x] defected to David at his
stronghold in the wilderness. They were
brave warriors, ready for battle and able
to handle the shield and spear. Their faces were the faces of lions,[y] and they were
as swift as gazelles[z] in the mountains.
9 Ezer was the chief,
Obadiah the second in command,
Eliab the third,
10 Mishmannah the fourth, Jeremiah the fifth,
11 Attai the sixth, Eliel the seventh,
12 Johanan the eighth, Elzabad the ninth,
13 Jeremiah the tenth and Makbannai the eleventh.
14 These Gadites were army command-
ers; the least was a match for a hundred,[a]
and the greatest for a thousand.[b] 15 It was
they who crossed the Jordan in the first
month when it was overflowing all its

[a] 4 In Hebrew texts the second half of this verse (*Jeremiah . . . Gederathite*) is numbered 12:5, and 12:5-40 is numbered 12:6-41.

11:28 [l] 1Ch 27:12
11:29 [m] 2Sa 21:18
11:31 [n] 1Ch 27:14 [o] Jdg 12:13
11:41 [p] 2Sa 11:6 [q] 1Ch 2:36
11:44 [r] Dt 1:4
12:1 [s] Jos 15:31; 1Sa 27:2-6
12:2 [t] Jdg 3:15; 20:16 [u] 2Sa 3:19
12:4 [v] Jos 15:36
12:7 [w] Jos 15:58
12:8 [x] Ge 30:11 [y] 2Sa 17:10 [z] 2Sa 2:18
12:14 [a] Lev 26:8 [b] Dt 32:30

12:1–7 This section of the larger literary unit (chs. 10–12) furthers the Chronicler's theme of the wide support King David enjoys from all Israel. The purpose of ch. 12 seems to be that of telling the story of the building of David's "great army" (v. 22).

The ambidextrous skill of these Benjamite warriors as both slingers and bowmen is noteworthy. We learn from ancient correspondence that a small group of experienced archers could turn the tide of a battle.

12:8–15 Unlike the archers and slingers from the tribe of Benjamin, the Gadite soldiers excel in hand-to-hand combat because of their speed and strength.

banks,[c] and they put to flight everyone
living in the valleys, to the east and to
the west.
16 Other Benjamites[d] and some men
from Judah also came to David in his
stronghold. 17 David went out to meet
them and said to them, "If you have come
to me in peace to help me, I am ready for
you to join me. But if you have come to
betray me to my enemies when my hands
are free from violence, may the God of
our ancestors see it and judge you."
18 Then the Spirit[e] came on Amasai,[f]
chief of the Thirty, and he said:

"We are yours, David!
  We are with you, son of Jesse!
Success,[g] success to you,
  and success to those who help you,
    for your God will help you."

So David received them and made
them leaders of his raiding bands.
19 Some of the tribe of Manasseh defected to David when he went with the
Philistines to fight against Saul. (He and
his men did not help the Philistines because, after consultation, their rulers
sent him away. They said, "It will cost
us our heads if he deserts to his master
Saul.")[h] 20 When David went to Ziklag,[i]
these were the men of Manasseh who
defected to him: Adnah, Jozabad, Jediael, Michael, Jozabad, Elihu and Zillethai, leaders of units of a thousand in
Manasseh. 21 They helped David against
raiding bands, for all of them were brave
warriors, and they were commanders in
his army. 22 Day after day men came to
help David, until he had a great army,
like the army of God.[a]

Others Join David at Hebron

23 These are the numbers of the men
armed for battle who came to David at
Hebron[j] to turn[k] Saul's kingdom over to
him, as the LORD had said:[l]

24 from Judah, carrying shield and spear — 6,800 armed for battle;

25 from Simeon, warriors ready for battle — 7,100;

26 from Levi — 4,600, 27 including Jehoiada, leader of the family of Aaron, with 3,700 men, 28 and Zadok,[m] a brave young warrior, with 22 officers from his family;

29 from Benjamin,[n] Saul's tribe — 3,000, most[o] of whom had remained loyal to Saul's house until then;

30 from Ephraim, brave warriors, famous in their own clans — 20,800;

31 from half the tribe of Manasseh, designated by name to come and make David king — 18,000;

32 from Issachar, men who understood the times and knew what Israel should do[p] — 200 chiefs, with all their relatives under their command;

33 from Zebulun, experienced soldiers prepared for battle with every type of weapon, to help David with undivided loyalty — 50,000;

34 from Naphtali — 1,000 officers, together with 37,000 men carrying shields and spears;

35 from Dan, ready for battle — 28,600;

36 from Asher, experienced soldiers prepared for battle — 40,000;

37 and from east of the Jordan, from Reuben, Gad and the half-tribe of Manasseh, armed with every type of weapon — 120,000.

38 All these were fighting men who
volunteered to serve in the ranks. They
came to Hebron fully determined to
make David king over all Israel.[q] All the
rest of the Israelites were also of one

1Ch 12:38 ❖ What qualities attract people to a godly leader? What characteristics might we look for in a leader for our faith community or church?

12:15 [c] Jos 3:15
12:16 [d] 2Sa 3:19
12:18 [e] Jdg 3:10; 6:34; 1Ch 28:12; 2Ch 15:1; 20:14; 24:20 [f] 2Sa 17:25 [g] 1Sa 25:5-6
12:19 [h] 1Sa 29:2-11
12:20 [i] 1Sa 27:6
12:23 [j] 2Sa 2:3-4 [k] 1Ch 10:14 [l] 1Sa 16:1; 1Ch 11:10
12:28 [m] 2Sa 8:17; 1Ch 6:8; 15:11; 16:39; 27:17
12:29 [n] 2Sa 3:19 [o] 2Sa 2:8-9
12:32 [p] Est 1:13
12:38 [q] 2Sa 5:1-3; 1Ch 9:1

[a] *22* *Or a great and mighty army*

12:16–18 The reference to the "Spirit" coming on Amasai signifies the anointing of God's Spirit and marks his speech as a type of prophetic utterance. The Chronicler essentially tells his audience that "God helps those who help David and his descendants." **12:19–22** Amasai's generalized prophecy of God's "help" in bringing about success for David's kingship (v. 18) is fulfilled through the loyal "help" of others against the Amalekite bandits.

12:23–40 The purpose of this report of the tribal gathering at Hebron is the transfer of Saul's kingdom to David (v. 23). The Chronicler also notes that all this is done according to the word of the Lord. The section concludes with representatives from the Hebrew tribes gathered at Hebron for the crowning of David as king over all Israel (vv. 38–40). David's coronation sets the stage for the rest of the Chronicler's history.

mind to make David king. 39 The men spent three days there with David, eating and drinking,[r] for their families had supplied provisions for them. 40 Also, their neighbors from as far away as Issachar, Zebulun and Naphtali came bringing food on donkeys, camels, mules and oxen. There were plentiful supplies[s] of flour, fig cakes, raisin[t] cakes, wine, olive oil, cattle and sheep, for there was joy[u] in Israel.

Bringing Back the Ark

13:1–14pp // 2Sa 6:1–11

13 David conferred with each of his officers, the commanders of thousands and commanders of hundreds. 2 He then said to the whole assembly of Israel, "If it seems good to you and if it is the will of the LORD our God, let us send word far and wide to the rest of our people throughout the territories of Israel, and also to the priests and Levites who are with them in their towns and pasturelands, to come and join us. 3 Let us bring the ark of our God back to us,[v] for we did not inquire[w] of[a] it[b] during the reign of Saul." 4 The whole assembly agreed to do this, because it seemed right to all the people.

5 So David assembled all Israel,[x] from the Shihor River[y] in Egypt to Lebo Hamath,[z] to bring the ark of God from Kiriath Jearim.[a] 6 David and all Israel went to Baalah[b] of Judah (Kiriath Jearim) to bring up from there the ark of God the LORD, who is enthroned between the cherubim[c] — the ark that is called by the Name.

7 They moved the ark of God from Abinadab's[d] house on a new cart, with Uzzah and Ahio guiding it. 8 David and all the Israelites were celebrating with all their might before God, with songs and with harps, lyres, timbrels, cymbals and trumpets.[e]

9 When they came to the threshing floor of Kidon, Uzzah reached out his hand to steady the ark, because the oxen stumbled. 10 The LORD's anger[f] burned against Uzzah, and he struck him down[g] because he had put his hand on the ark. So he died there before God.

11 Then David was angry because the LORD's wrath had broken out against Uzzah, and to this day that place is called Perez Uzzah.[c][h]

12 David was afraid of God that day and asked, "How can I ever bring the ark of God to me?" 13 He did not take the ark to be with him in the City of David. Instead, he took it to the house of Obed-Edom[i] the Gittite. 14 The ark of God remained with the family of Obed-Edom in his house for three months, and the LORD blessed his household[j] and everything he had.

1Ch 13:12 ❖ How does Jesus solve the problem of sinful humans coming in contact with a holy God (see Ro 5:1–2)?

12:39 [r] 2Sa 3:20; Isa 25:6-8
12:40 [s] 2Sa 16:1; 17:29 [t] 1Sa 25:18 [u] 1Ch 29:22
13:3 [v] 1Sa 7:1-2 [w] 2Ch 1:5
13:5 [x] 1Ch 11:1; 15:3 [y] Jos 13:3 [z] Nu 13:21 [a] 1Sa 6:21; 7:2
13:6 [b] Jos 15:9; 2Sa 6:2 [c] Ex 25:22; 2Ki 19:15
13:7 [d] Nu 4:15; 1Sa 7:1
13:8 [e] 2Sa 6:5; 1Ch 15:16,19, 24; 2Ch 5:12; Ps 92:3
13:10 [f] 1Ch 15:13, 15 [g] Lev 10:2
13:11 [h] 1Ch 15:13; Ps 7:11
13:13 [i] 1Ch 15:18, 24; 16:38; 26:4-5,15
13:14 [j] 2Sa 6:11; 1Ch 26:4-5

[a] *3* Or *we neglected* [b] *3* Or *him* [c] *11* Perez Uzzah means *outbreak against Uzzah.*

✣ **10:1—12:40** The crisis of loyalty addressed by the Chronicler is not as far removed from the Christian church as we might think. The contemporary social doctrine of "political correctness" permeates popular culture. To be politically correct means that language and practices that might offend another sociopolitical or religious group are to be eliminated. Therefore the Christian church is now embroiled in an internal controversy involving the exclusive claims of the gospel of Jesus Christ and its implications for the doctrine of salvation in an age of religious pluralism.

13:1–14 David consults with not only his military leaders but also the religious leadership of Israel (priests and Levites) and the general populace (v. 2). Implicit in David's summons to restore the ark to its proper place is the cause-and-effect link between Saul's defeat by the Philistines and the neglect of the ark of God (v. 3).

13:5, 6, 8 Affirming the prominent theme of Israelite unity under King David, the Chronicler indicates in threefold repetition that "all" the Israelites participate in the processional to return the ark of God.

13:6 The mysterious and majestic presence of God enthroned between the cherubim of the ark of the covenant is based on the understanding that this is where God meets his people (Ex 25:22).

13:9–11 The death of Uzzah from steadying the ark of the covenant is one of two failures of King David reported by the Chronicler (the other is the census-taking, ch. 21). God is a consuming fire, and he will show himself holy before all people. The Chronicler's repetition of the word "break out" in this section of the narrative seems to draw attention to this terrifying dimension of God's character (cf. v. 11; 14:11; 15:13).

13:13–14 David's disposition to deposit the ark at the nearest convenient location indicates his submission to God's will. Whether out of abject fear or outright reverence, David refuses to manipulate God for personal advantage through control of the sacred symbol of divine presence.

David's House and Family

14:1–7pp // 2Sa 5:11–16; 1Ch 3:5–8

14 Now Hiram king of Tyre sent messengers to David, along with cedar
logs,[k] stonemasons and carpenters to
build a palace for him. 2And David knew
that the LORD had established him as
king over Israel and that his kingdom
had been highly exalted[l] for the sake of
his people Israel.

3In Jerusalem David took more wives
and became the father of more sons[m]
and daughters. 4These are the names of
the children born to him there:[n] Shammua, Shobab, Nathan, Solomon, 5Ibhar,
Elishua, Elpelet, 6Nogah, Nepheg, Japhia,
7Elishama, Beeliada[a] and Eliphelet.

David Defeats the Philistines

14:8–17pp // 2Sa 5:17–25

8When the Philistines heard that David
had been anointed king over all Israel,[o]
they went up in full force to search for
him, but David heard about it and went
out to meet them. 9Now the Philistines
had come and raided the Valley[p] of Rephaim; 10so David inquired of God: "Shall
I go and attack the Philistines? Will you
deliver them into my hands?"

The LORD answered him, "Go, I will
deliver them into your hands."

11So David and his men went up to Baal
Perazim,[q] and there he defeated them.
He said, "As waters break out, God has
broken out against my enemies by my
hand." So that place was called Baal Perazim.[b] 12The Philistines had abandoned
their gods there, and David gave orders
to burn[r] them in the fire.[s]

13Once more the Philistines raided the
valley;[t] 14so David inquired of God again,
and God answered him, "Do not go directly after them, but circle around them
and attack them in front of the poplar
trees. 15As soon as you hear the sound
of marching in the tops of the poplar
trees, move out to battle, because that
will mean God has gone out in front of
you to strike the Philistine army." 16So
David did as God commanded him, and
they struck down the Philistine army, all
the way from Gibeon[u] to Gezer.[v]

17So David's fame[w] spread throughout
every land, and the LORD made all the
nations fear[x] him.

1Ch 14:2 ❖ Why is it important to remember that God is the One who gives us our role or position? What happens when we forget this?

The Ark Brought to Jerusalem

15:25—16:3pp // 2Sa 6:12–19

15 After David had constructed buildings for himself in the City of David,
he prepared[y] a place for the ark of God
and pitched[z] a tent for it. 2Then David
said, "No one but the Levites[a] may carry[b]
the ark of God, because the LORD chose
them to carry the ark of the LORD and to
minister[c] before him forever."

3David assembled all Israel[d] in Jerusalem to bring up the ark of the LORD
to the place he had prepared for it. 4He
called together the descendants of Aaron
and the Levites:

5From the descendants of Kohath,
Uriel the leader and 120 relatives;
6from the descendants of Merari,
Asaiah the leader and 220 relatives;
7from the descendants of Gershon,[c]
Joel the leader and 130 relatives;
8from the descendants of Elizaphan,[e]
Shemaiah the leader and 200 relatives;

14:1 [k]2Ch 2:3; Ezr 3:7
14:2 [l]Nu 24:7; Dt 26:19
14:3 [m]1Ch 3:1
14:4 [n]1Ch 3:9
14:8 [o]1Ch 11:1
14:9 [p]ver 13; Jos 15:8; 1Ch 11:15
14:11 [q]Isa 28:21
14:12 [r]Ex 32:20 [s]Jos 7:15
14:13 [t]ver 9
14:16 [u]Jos 9:3 [v]Jos 10:33
14:17 [w]Jos 6:27; 2Ch 26:8 [x]Ex 15:14-16; Dt 2:25
15:1 [y]Ps 132:1-18 [z]1Ch 16:1; 17:1
15:2 [a]Nu 4:15; Dt 10:8; 2Ch 5:5 [b]Dt 31:9 [c]1Ch 23:13
15:3 [d]1Ki 8:1; 1Ch 13:5
15:8 [e]Ex 6:22

[a] 7 A variant of *Eliada* [b] 11 *Baal Perazim* means *the lord who breaks out.* [c] 7 Hebrew *Gershom,* a variant of *Gershon*

14:1-2 King Hiram of Tyre was an ally of both David and Solomon. Most likely Hiram ruled from about 980–950 BC, but scholarly estimates vary widely.
14:3 Unlike King Saul's dynasty, which died out (10:6), David's house is a "fruitful vine" (cf. Ps 128:3).
14:8-12 Unlike King Saul, who "inquired" of the medium of Endor (1Sa 28:7), David "inquired" of the Lord and was assured victory (14:10). The Philistines abandon their gods on the battlefield (v. 12), symbolic of their impotence before Yahweh, the true God.
14:13-17 Once again, David is assured of God's help in battle, but this time the tactics are changed. The rustling of the leaves in the trees is most likely the Spirit of God, since David is told God will go before him in battle. As God blesses David's faithfulness, so David's success brings glory and honor to God.
15:1-24 This time the ark is to be carried by the Levites, not driven on a cart. God himself may have revealed this to David through the king's study of the Mosaic law (Dt 10:8; 18:5). In his appointment of the proper Levitical clan to transport the ark, King David again demonstrates his faithfulness to God's commands. This time David and the religious leaders of Israel follow the prescriptions of the Mosaic code.

9 from the descendants of Hebron,[f]
Eliel the leader and 80 relatives;
10 from the descendants of Uzziel,
Amminadab the leader and 112
relatives.

11 Then David summoned Zadok[g] and Abiathar[h] the priests, and Uriel, Asaiah, Joel, Shemaiah, Eliel and Amminadab the Levites. 12 He said to them, "You are the heads of the Levitical families; you and your fellow Levites are to consecrate[i] yourselves and bring up the ark of the LORD, the God of Israel, to the place I have prepared for it. 13 It was because you, the Levites,[j] did not bring it up the first time that the LORD our God broke out in anger against us.[k] We did not inquire of him about how to do it in the prescribed way." 14 So the priests and Levites consecrated themselves in order to bring up the ark of the LORD, the God of Israel. 15 And the Levites carried the ark of God with the poles on their shoulders, as Moses had commanded[l] in accordance with the word of the LORD.

16 David told the leaders of the Levites to appoint their fellow Levites as musicians[m] to make a joyful sound with musical instruments: lyres, harps and cymbals.[n]

17 So the Levites appointed Heman[o] son of Joel; from his relatives, Asaph[p] son of Berekiah; and from their relatives the Merarites,[q] Ethan son of Kushaiah; 18 and with them their relatives next in rank: Zechariah,[a] Jaaziel, Shemiramoth, Jehiel, Unni, Eliab, Benaiah, Maaseiah, Mattithiah, Eliphelehu, Mikneiah, Obed-Edom[r] and Jeiel,[b] the gatekeepers.

19 The musicians Heman,[s] Asaph and Ethan were to sound the bronze cymbals; 20 Zechariah, Jaaziel,[c] Shemiramoth, Jehiel, Unni, Eliab, Maaseiah and Benaiah were to play the lyres according to *alamoth*,[d] 21 and Mattithiah, Eliphelehu, Mikneiah, Obed-Edom, Jeiel and Azaziah were to play the harps, directing according to *sheminith*.[d] 22 Kenaniah the head Levite was in charge of the singing; that was his responsibility because he was skillful at it.

23 Berekiah and Elkanah were to be doorkeepers for the ark. 24 Shebaniah, Joshaphat, Nethanel, Amasai, Zechariah, Benaiah and Eliezer the priests were to

15:9 [f] Ex 6:18
15:11 [g] 1Ch 12:28 [h] 1Sa 22:20
15:12 [i] Ex 19:14-15; Lev 11:44; 2Ch 35:6
15:13 [j] 1Ki 8:4 [k] 2Sa 6:3; 1Ch 13:7-10
15:15 [l] Ex 25:14; Nu 4:5,15
15:16 [m] Ps 68:25 [n] 1Ch 13:8; 25:1; Ne 12:27,36
15:17 [o] 1Ch 6:33 [p] 1Ch 6:39 [q] 1Ch 6:44
15:18 [r] 1Ch 26:4-5
15:19 [s] 1Ch 25:6

[a] *18* Three Hebrew manuscripts and most Septuagint manuscripts (see also verse 20 and 16:5); most Hebrew manuscripts *Zechariah son and* or *Zechariah, Ben and* [b] *18* Hebrew; Septuagint (see also verse 21) *Jeiel and Azaziah* [c] *20* See verse 18; Hebrew *Aziel*, a variant of *Jaaziel*. [d] *20,21* Probably a musical term

15:16–24 The concluding section showcases the priests and Levites as musicians, another theme in Chronicles.

PEOPLE TO KNOW // ABIATHAR

1 CHRONICLES 15:11: Abiathar's story begins sadly. King Saul conscripted Doeg the Edomite to kill God's priests, and Abiathar alone survived from his family (1Sa 22:2–23). Abiathar escaped and joined David, who later made Abiathar high priest along with Zadok. As high priest, one of Abiathar's important tasks was to bring offerings before God.

Abiathar proved himself useful to King David when David's son, Absalom, rebelled against the king. Forced to flee Jerusalem, David sent Abiathar back to the city with the ark of the covenant. Abiathar was among a small group of subjects loyal to David who were able to warn the king of Absalom's schemes.

Abiathar's story ends in disappointment. When King David was old and near death, his chosen heir for the throne was Solomon. Abiathar, however, supported Adonijah, another of David's sons, as the next king of Israel. This act of rebellion resulted in Abiathar being stripped of the role of high priest. The Bible states that this fulfilled God's word of judgment to remove the family of Eli from priestly service (1Ki 2:27).

APPLICATION Priests in Israel were consecrated for the Lord's service. Abiathar filled this role faithfully during the time of David, even after his own family tragedy. Abiathar shows us the importance of serving God with commitment.

But Abiathar's life also serves as a warning. When Abiathar supported Adonijah as the next king of Israel instead of Solomon, Abiathar chose a strong-looking human leader rather than God's anointed. Still today we may get caught up in supporting human leaders who are engaging or charismatic instead of putting our full trust in the Lord and looking to follow his servants.

PEOPLE TO KNOW // MICHAL

1 CHRONICLES 15:29: Michal was a daughter of King Saul. After David began to serve Saul in the palace, Michal met and fell in love with him, and David must have felt something for her because he wanted to marry her. Saul tried to use their relationship to plot David's death, telling David all he was required to pay as a bride price to marry Michal was one hundred Philistine foreskins (1Sa 18:25). Saul's hope was that David would be killed in acquiring these, but David instead went above and beyond and gave Saul two hundred Philistine foreskins in exchange for Michal's hand in marriage.

Michal then saved David from another of Saul's schemes to kill him. When Saul sent men to their home, Michal helped David escape through the window. She took an idol and laid it in his bed, putting some goat hair around its head, and told the men David was ill. Saul demanded they get David anyway, but they discovered that David had escaped with Michal's help (1Sa 19:11–17).

With David on the run, Saul gave Michal in marriage to another man. When David became king of Judah, however, he took Michal back (2Sa 3:13–16), destroying the new life she had made in spite of the political maneuverings of her father. Michal's anger and contempt toward David are well known. After David became king and established Jerusalem as his capital, he brought the ark of God into the city with much fanfare and celebration. Michal criticized his celebration of worship and dancing. David told her that his shameless display was for God alone. The last word about Michal is that she had no children to the day of her death (2Sa 6:16–23).

APPLICATION ✣ Michal's story is a complicated one, since we have little information about her motives or faith. She bravely protected David from her own father, showing admirable courage. She was forced to marry someone else after David fled from her father. She may have found happiness in her second marriage, but after David became king and compelled her to return to him, we see that anger and bitterness consumed her. When we are put into difficult situations through no fault of our own, it's easy to become bitter. Sometimes we are so grieved and frustrated that we lash out in anger. Instead of acting out in anger, we can let God work to heal our hearts. It's not a sin to be angry or to give voice to our feelings, but we need to be careful that in our anger, we do not sin by our actions (Eph 4:26).

blow trumpets[t] before the ark of God.
Obed-Edom and Jehiah were also to be
doorkeepers for the ark.
25So David and the elders of Israel and
the commanders of units of a thousand
went to bring up the ark[u] of the covenant of the LORD from the house of
Obed-Edom, with rejoicing. 26Because
God had helped the Levites who were
carrying the ark of the covenant of the
LORD, seven bulls and seven rams[v] were
sacrificed. 27Now David was clothed in a
robe of fine linen, as were all the Levites
who were carrying the ark, and as were
the musicians, and Kenaniah, who was in
charge of the singing of the choirs. David
also wore a linen ephod. 28So all Israel
brought up the ark of the covenant of the
LORD with shouts, with the sounding of
rams' horns[w] and trumpets, and of cymbals, and the playing of lyres and harps.
29As the ark of the covenant of the
LORD was entering the City of David,
Michal daughter of Saul watched from
a window. And when she saw King David
dancing and celebrating, she despised
him in her heart.

15:24 [t] ver 28; 1Ch 16:6; 2Ch 7:6
15:25 [u] 1Ch 13:13; 2Ch 1:4
15:26 [v] Nu 23:1-4,29
15:28 [w] 1Ch 13:8

1Ch 15:22 ✣ What skills can we offer to God in worship?

Ministering Before the Ark

16:8–22pp // Ps 105:1–15
16:23–33pp // Ps 96:1–13
16:34–36pp // Ps 106:1,47–48

16 They brought the ark of God and
set it inside the tent that David had

15:25—16:3 David's priestly role in the processional is tacitly approved by the detailed reference to the king's garb: a linen robe and linen ephod like that of the Levites (15:27; cf. Ex 39:27–29). By contrast, David earns the disapproval of his wife Michal (15:29), Saul's daughter. In one sense she represents the last vestige of King Saul's unfaithfulness, and her story provides further justification for God's rejection of Saul's dynasty.
16:1-3 The "burnt offerings" are sacrifices for sin

pitched[x] for it, and they presented burnt
offerings and fellowship offerings before
God. 2After David had finished sacrificing the burnt offerings and fellowship
offerings, he blessed[y] the people in the
name of the LORD. 3Then he gave a loaf
of bread, a cake of dates and a cake of
raisins to each Israelite man and woman.
4He appointed some of the Levites to
minister[z] before the ark of the LORD, to
extol,[a] thank, and praise the LORD, the
God of Israel: 5Asaph was the chief, and
next to him in rank were Zechariah, then
Jaaziel,[b] Shemiramoth, Jehiel, Mattithiah, Eliab, Benaiah, Obed-Edom and Jeiel.
They were to play the lyres and harps,
Asaph was to sound the cymbals, 6and
Benaiah and Jahaziel the priests were to
blow the trumpets regularly before the
ark of the covenant of God.

7That day David first appointed Asaph
and his associates to give praise[a] to the
LORD in this manner:

8 Give praise[b] to the LORD, proclaim his name;
make known among the nations[c] what he has done.
9 Sing to him, sing praise[d] to him;
tell of all his wonderful acts.
10 Glory in his holy name;
let the hearts of those who seek the LORD rejoice.
11 Look to the LORD and his strength;
seek[e] his face always.

12 Remember[f] the wonders he has done,
his miracles,[g] and the judgments he pronounced,
13 you his servants, the descendants of Israel,
his chosen ones, the children of Jacob.
14 He is the LORD our God;
his judgments[h] are in all the earth.

15 He remembers[c] his covenant forever,
the promise he made, for a thousand generations,
16 the covenant[i] he made with Abraham,
the oath he swore to Isaac.
17 He confirmed it to Jacob[j] as a decree,
to Israel as an everlasting covenant:
18 "To you I will give the land of Canaan[k]
as the portion you will inherit."

19 When they were but few in number,[l]
few indeed, and strangers in it,
20 they[d] wandered from nation to nation,
from one kingdom to another.
21 He allowed no one to oppress them;
for their sake he rebuked kings:[m]
22 "Do not touch my anointed ones;
do my prophets[n] no harm."

23 Sing to the LORD, all the earth;
proclaim his salvation day after day.
24 Declare his glory among the nations,
his marvelous deeds among all peoples.

25 For great is the LORD and most worthy of praise;[o]
he is to be feared[p] above all gods.[q]
26 For all the gods of the nations are idols,
but the LORD made the heavens.[r]
27 Splendor and majesty are before him;
strength and joy are in his dwelling place.

16:1 [x] 1Ch 15:1 16:2 [y] Ex 39:43 16:4 [z] 1Ch 15:2 16:7 [a] 2Sa 23:1 16:8 [b] ver 34; Ps 136:1 [c] 2Ki 19:19 16:9 [d] Ex 15:1 16:11 [e] 1Ch 28:9; 2Ch 7:14; Ps 24:6; 119:2, 58 16:12 [f] Ps 77:11 [g] Ps 78:43 16:14 [h] Isa 26:9 16:16 [i] Ge 12:7; 15:18; 17:2; 22:16-18; 26:3; 28:13; 35:11 16:17 [j] Ge 35:9-12 16:18 [k] Ge 13:14-17 16:19 [l] Ge 34:30; Dt 7:7 16:21 [m] Ge 12:17; 20:3; Ex 7:15-18 16:22 [n] Ge 20:7 16:25 [o] Ps 48:1 [p] Ps 76:7; 89:7 [q] Dt 32:39 16:26 [r] Lev 19:4; Ps 102:25

[a] *4* Or *petition;* or *invoke* [b] *5* See 15:18,20; Hebrew *Jeiel,* possibly another name for *Jaaziel.* [c] *15* Some Septuagint manuscripts (see also Psalm 105:8); Hebrew *Remember* [d] *18-20* One Hebrew manuscript, Septuagint and Vulgate (see also Psalm 105:12); most Hebrew manuscripts *inherit, / 19though you are but few in number, / few indeed, and strangers in it." / 20They*

and demonstrate dedication to God. The "fellowship offerings" signify the completion of a vow (13:3) and thankfulness on the part of all Israel for the blessings of God in sustaining the nation and establishing David as king. The communal blessing and ritual meal are part of a covenant renewal ceremony (cf. Ex 24:11).

16:4–43 The psalm of thanksgiving is the theological center of the Chronicler's retelling of Israel's history. The Chronicler's song celebrates God as both covenant maker and covenant keeper, the linchpin in his theology of hope for postexilic Judah.

16:8–36 The psalm of thanksgiving is a composite of selections from three psalms (Ps 105:1–15; 96:1–13; 106:1, 47–48). The Chronicler has been influenced in his selection of poems from the Psalter by the vocabulary found in the immediate context of the narrative. The theological themes of the three divisions of the composite psalm rehearse the key emphases of 1–2Ch as a "biography" of God.

16:7–22 The first unit from Ps 105 highlights God as a covenant maker and keeper and Israel's unique place among the nations as his elect (vv. 15–17).

16:23–33 The second unit from Ps 96 extols God as creator and sovereign over all the nations and over all their gods.

28 Ascribe to the LORD, all you families of nations,
ascribe to the LORD glory and strength.[s]
29 Ascribe to the LORD the glory due his name;
bring an offering and come before him.
Worship the LORD in the splendor of his[a] holiness.[t]
30 Tremble[u] before him, all the earth!
The world is firmly established; it cannot be moved.

31 Let the heavens rejoice, let the earth be glad;[v]
let them say among the nations, "The LORD reigns![w]"
32 Let the sea resound, and all that is in it;[x]
let the fields be jubilant, and everything in them!
33 Let the trees[y] of the forest sing,
let them sing for joy before the LORD,
for he comes to judge[z] the earth.

34 Give thanks[a] to the LORD, for he is good;[b]
his love endures forever.[c]
35 Cry out, "Save us, God our Savior;[d]
gather us and deliver us from the nations,
that we may give thanks to your holy name,
and glory in your praise."
36 Praise be to the LORD, the God of Israel,[e]
from everlasting to everlasting.

Then all the people said "Amen" and "Praise the LORD."

37 David left Asaph and his associates
before the ark of the covenant of the
LORD to minister there regularly, according to each day's requirements.[f] 38 He also
left Obed-Edom[g] and his sixty-eight associates to minister with them. Obed-Edom
son of Jeduthun, and also Hosah,[h] were
gatekeepers.

39 David left Zadok[i] the priest and his
fellow priests before the tabernacle of
the LORD at the high place in Gibeon[j]
40 to present burnt offerings to the LORD
on the altar of burnt offering regularly, morning and evening, in accordance
with everything written in the Law[k] of
the LORD, which he had given Israel.
41 With them were Heman[l] and Jeduthun and the rest of those chosen and
designated by name to give thanks to
the LORD, "for his love endures forever."
42 Heman and Jeduthun were responsible
for the sounding of the trumpets and
cymbals and for the playing of the other
instruments for sacred song.[m] The sons
of Jeduthun were stationed at the gate.

43 Then all the people left, each for their
own home, and David returned home to
bless his family.

God's Promise to David

17:1–15pp // 2Sa 7:1–17

17 After David was settled in his palace, he said to Nathan the prophet,
"Here I am, living in a house of cedar,
while the ark of the covenant of the LORD
is under a tent.[n]"

2 Nathan replied to David, "Whatever you have in mind,[o] do it, for God is
with you."

3 But that night the word of God came
to Nathan, saying:

1Ch 16:34 ❖ What are we giving thanks to God for right now? How has he showed his love to us?

16:28 [s] Ps 29:1-2 16:29 [t] Ps 29:1-2 16:30 [u] Ps 114:7 16:31 [v] Isa 44:23; 49:13 [w] Ps 93:1 16:32 [x] Ps 98:7 16:33 [y] Isa 55:12 [z] Ps 96:10; 98:9 16:34 [a] ver 8 [b] Na 1:7 [c] 2Ch 5:13; 7:3; Ezr 3:11; Ps 136:1-26; Jer 33:11 16:35 [d] Mic 7:7 16:36 [e] Dt 27:15; 1Ki 8:15; Ps 72:18-19 16:37 [f] 2Ch 8:14 16:38 [g] 1Ch 13:13 [h] 1Ch 26:10 16:39 [i] 2Sa 8:17; 1Ch 15:11 [j] 1Ki 3:4; 2Ch 1:3 16:40 [k] Ex 29:38; Nu 28:1-8 16:41 [l] 1Ch 6:33; 25:1-6; 2Ch 5:13 16:42 [m] 2Ch 7:6 17:1 [n] 1Ch 15:1 17:2 [o] 2Ch 6:7

[a] 29 Or LORD *with the splendor of*

16:34–36 The third unit from Ps 106 praises the goodness and mercy of the God of salvation. Last, and not to be overlooked, the entire composite psalm repeats the covenant name Yahweh some sixteen times.

16:39 The reference to the Gibeon sanctuary is important because it demonstrates that King David has not neglected the Mosaic tabernacle. Likewise, the continuation of the morning and evening sacrifices commanded by the Torah is further evidence of David's faithfulness to the Law of Moses.

16:41–42 Both Heman and Jeduthun are known elsewhere as directors of Levitical musical guilds (cf. 25:1, 6).

17:1-27 David's desire to build a temple for Yahweh is typical of royal behavior in the biblical world.

17:1-3 The idea behind the word "prophet" in the OT world is that of a servant who stands in the council of the gods and then reports exactly what he hears as a divine messenger or herald. Nathan is a strategic religious-political adviser in the early Hebrew monarchy as evidenced by his role in securing Solomon's succession to David's throne (cf. 1Ki 1). Elsewhere we learn that Nathan the prophet is also a court historian since the Chronicler references his "records" (cf. 29:29; 2 Chr 9:29). However, in this case God rebuffs the combined good intentions of King David and the blessing of the prophet Nathan.

4“Go and tell my servant David,
‘This is what the LORD says: You[p] are
not the one to build me a house to
dwell in. 5I have not dwelt in a house
from the day I brought Israel up out
of Egypt to this day. I have moved
from one tent site to another, from
one dwelling place to another.
6Wherever I have moved with all
the Israelites, did I ever say to any of
their leaders[a] whom I commanded
to shepherd my people, “Why have
you not built me a house of cedar?”’
7“Now then, tell my servant David, ‘This is what the LORD Almighty
says: I took you from the pasture,
from tending the flock, and appointed you ruler[q] over my people Israel.
8I have been with you wherever you
have gone, and I have cut off all your
enemies from before you. Now I will
make your name like the names of
the greatest men on earth. 9And I
will provide a place for my people Israel and will plant them so that they
can have a home of their own and no
longer be disturbed. Wicked people
will not oppress them anymore, as
they did at the beginning 10and have
done ever since the time I appointed
leaders[r] over my people Israel. I will
also subdue all your enemies.
“‘I declare to you that the LORD
will build a house for you: 11When
your days are over and you go to
be with your ancestors, I will raise
up your offspring to succeed you,
one of your own sons, and I will
establish his kingdom. 12He is the

1Ch 17:9 ❖ How has God shown us his protection? Where has he given us a place of belonging and security?

one who will build[s] a house for me,
and I will establish his throne forever.[t] 13I will be his father,[u] and he
will be my son.[v] I will never take
my love away from him, as I took
it away from your predecessor. 14I
will set him over my house and my
kingdom forever; his throne[w] will
be established forever.[x]’”
15Nathan reported to David all the
words of this entire revelation.

David's Prayer

17:16–27pp // 2Sa 7:18–29

16Then King David went in and sat before the LORD, and he said:

“Who am I, LORD God, and what
is my family, that you have brought
me this far? 17And as if this were not
enough in your sight, my God, you
have spoken about the future of the
house of your servant. You, LORD
God, have looked on me as though I
were the most exalted of men.
18“What more can David say to
you for honoring your servant? For
you know your servant, 19LORD. For
the sake[y] of your servant and according to your will, you have done this
great thing and made known all
these great promises.[z]

17:4 [p] 1Ch 28:3
17:7 [q] 2Sa 6:21
17:10 [r] Jdg 2:16
17:12 [s] 1Ki 5:5 [t] 2Ch 7:18
17:13 [u] 2Co 6:18 [v] Lk 1:32; Heb 1:5*
17:14 [w] 1Ki 2:12; 1Ch 28:5 [x] Ps 132:11; Jer 33:17
17:19 [y] 2Sa 7:16-17; 2Ki 20:6; Isa 9:7; 37:35; 55:3 [z] 2Sa 7:25

[a] 6 Traditionally *judges*; also in verse 10

17:4–15 The problem is not building a temple for Yahweh, but David's legacy as a warrior means he will serve only as Solomon's contractor for the temple (cf. 22:8; 28:3). The temple as “God's house” can have significance for God's people only after God has built “David's house.”

17:16–27 Biblical commentators have noted a high degree of connection between David's prayer here and its precursor in 2Sa 7:18–29. This is the first of several prayers offered to God by Israelite kings inserted in the Chronicler's retelling of Israelite history. In fact, this is a subtle agenda item of the Chronicler—to draw the people of postexilic Judah back into conversation with God through prayer. The emphasis on prayer fits naturally into his concern for worship renewal because prayer ultimately ushers in the glory of God (v. 24).

✜ **13:1—17:27** The community of faith in ancient Israel and the early Christian church used signs in much the same way. A sign conveys information that leads to personal action. For example, the sign of Christian baptism points to the theological idea of the “virtual” death, burial, and resurrection of the believer in Jesus Christ (cf. Ro 6:3–4).

The religious symbol points to a spiritual reality outside of itself, participates in its power, and clarifies its meaning. So the dove is a symbol of the reality of the empowering Holy Spirit (Mt 3:16), and the sacrificial lamb is a symbol of the reality of the redemptive nature of Jesus Christ's life and ministry (Jn 1:29; Rev 5:6). For the sake of continuing to teach the legacy of Christian worship, instruction, and evangelism to the generations now being raised in this age of technology and visual media culture, the church must rediscover the value of these historically important religious symbols and the deep truths they communicate.

20"There is no one like you, LORD,
and there is no God but you,[a] as
we have heard with our own ears.
21And who is like your people Israel — the one nation on earth whose
God went out to redeem[b] a people
for himself, and to make a name for
yourself, and to perform great and
awesome wonders by driving out
nations from before your people,
whom you redeemed from Egypt?
22You made your people Israel your
very own forever,[c] and you, LORD,
have become their God.
23"And now, LORD, let the promise[d] you have made concerning your
servant and his house be established
forever. Do as you promised, 24so
that it will be established and that
your name will be great forever.
Then people will say, 'The LORD Almighty, the God over Israel, is Israel's
God!' And the house of your servant
David will be established before you.
25"You, my God, have revealed to
your servant that you will build a
house for him. So your servant has
found courage to pray to you. 26You,
LORD, are God! You have promised
these good things to your servant.
27Now you have been pleased to
bless the house of your servant,
that it may continue forever in your
sight;[e] for you, LORD, have blessed it,
and it will be blessed forever."

David's Victories

18:1–13pp // 2Sa 8:1–14

18 In the course of time, David defeated the Philistines and subdued
them, and he took Gath and its surrounding villages from the control of the Philistines.
2David also defeated the Moabites,[f]
and they became subject to him and
brought him tribute.
3Moreover, David defeated Hadadezer
king of Zobah,[g] in the vicinity of Hamath,
when he went to set up his monument
at[a] the Euphrates River.[h] 4David captured
a thousand of his chariots, seven thousand charioteers and twenty thousand
foot soldiers. He hamstrung[i] all but a
hundred of the chariot horses.
5When the Arameans of Damascus[j]
came to help Hadadezer king of Zobah,
David struck down twenty-two thousand
of them. 6He put garrisons in the Aramean kingdom of Damascus, and the
Arameans became subject to him and
brought him tribute. The LORD gave David victory wherever he went.
7David took the gold shields carried by
the officers of Hadadezer and brought
them to Jerusalem. 8From Tebah[b] and
Kun, towns that belonged to Hadadezer,
David took a great quantity of bronze,
which Solomon used to make the bronze
Sea,[k] the pillars and various bronze articles.
9When Tou king of Hamath heard that
David had defeated the entire army of
Hadadezer king of Zobah, 10he sent his
son Hadoram to King David to greet him
and congratulate him on his victory in
battle over Hadadezer, who had been
at war with Tou. Hadoram brought all
kinds of articles of gold, of silver and
of bronze.
11King David dedicated these articles to
the LORD, as he had done with the silver
and gold he had taken from all these nations: Edom[l] and Moab, the Ammonites
and the Philistines, and Amalek.[m]
12Abishai son of Zeruiah struck down
eighteen thousand Edomites[n] in the Valley of Salt. 13He put garrisons in Edom,
and all the Edomites became subject
to David. The LORD gave David victory
wherever he went.

1Ch 18:11 ❖ All victories come from God. How can we dedicate or offer back to God some of what he has given us?

17:20 [a] Ex 8:10; 9:14; 15:11; Isa 44:6; 46:9
17:21 [b] Ex 6:6
17:22 [c] Ex 19:5-6
17:23 [d] 1Ki 8:25
17:27 [e] Ps 16:11; 21:6
18:2 [f] Nu 21:29
18:3 [g] 1Ch 19:6
[h] Ge 2:14
18:4 [i] Ge 49:6
18:5 [j] 2Ki 16:9; 1Ch 19:6
18:8 [k] 1Ki 7:23; 2Ch 4:12,15-16
18:11 [l] Nu 24:18 [m] Nu 24:20
18:12 [n] 1Ki 11:15

[a] 3 Or *to restore his control over*
[b] 8 Hebrew *Tibhath*, a variant of *Tebah*

18:1–13 Subduing the Philistines secures the western flank of David's empire. Among the spoils David takes are large quantities of bronze, later used by Solomon in casting the bronze vessels for the temple (vv. 7–8). This is another way in which the Chronicler connects David to the building of Yahweh's temple.
18:9–10 The news of Israel's success against the kingdom of Zobah and the Arameans of Damascus prompts Tou, king of Hamath, to forge a political alliance.
18:12–13 Edom is among the nations paying tribute to Israel during the reign of Solomon (cf. 1Ki 4:21). The God who "gave David victory" is the God of the postexilic Judah. That same blessing of divine approval awaits those who dedicate themselves in expectant faith to the spiritual and physical restoration of Jerusalem.

David's Officials

18:14–17pp // 2Sa 8:15–18

[14]David reigned[o] over all Israel,[p] doing
what was just and right for all his people.
[15]Joab[q] son of Zeruiah was over the army;
Jehoshaphat son of Ahilud was recorder;
[16]Zadok[r] son of Ahitub and Ahimelek[a][s]
son of Abiathar were priests; Shavsha
was secretary; [17]Benaiah son of Jehoiada
was over the Kerethites and Pelethites;[t]
and David's sons were chief officials at
the king's side.

David Defeats the Ammonites

19:1–19pp // 2Sa 10:1–19

19 In the course of time, Nahash
king of the Ammonites[u] died, and
his son succeeded him as king. [2]David
thought, "I will show kindness to Hanun son of Nahash, because his father
showed kindness to me." So David sent
a delegation to express his sympathy to
Hanun concerning his father.

When David's envoys came to Hanun
in the land of the Ammonites to express
sympathy to him, [3]the Ammonite commanders said to Hanun, "Do you think David is honoring your father by sending envoys to you to express sympathy? Haven't
his envoys come to you only to explore
and spy out[v] the country and overthrow
it?" [4]So Hanun seized David's envoys,
shaved them, cut off their garments at
the buttocks, and sent them away.

[5]When someone came and told David
about the men, he sent messengers to
meet them, for they were greatly humiliated. The king said, "Stay at Jericho
till your beards have grown, and then
come back."

[6]When the Ammonites realized that
they had become obnoxious[w] to David,
Hanun and the Ammonites sent a thousand talents[b] of silver to hire chariots
and charioteers from Aram Naharaim,[c]
Aram Maakah and Zobah.[x] [7]They hired
thirty-two thousand chariots and charioteers, as well as the king of Maakah with
his troops, who came and camped near
Medeba,[y] while the Ammonites were
mustered from their towns and moved
out for battle.

[8]On hearing this, David sent Joab out
with the entire army of fighting men.
[9]The Ammonites came out and drew up
in battle formation at the entrance to
their city, while the kings who had come
were by themselves in the open country.

[10]Joab saw that there were battle lines
in front of him and behind him; so he
selected some of the best troops in Israel
and deployed them against the Arameans. [11]He put the rest of the men under
the command of Abishai[z] his brother,
and they were deployed against the Ammonites. [12]Joab said, "If the Arameans
are too strong for me, then you are to
rescue me; but if the Ammonites are too
strong for you, then I will rescue you.
[13]Be strong, and let us fight bravely for
our people and the cities of our God. The
LORD will do what is good in his sight."

[14]Then Joab and the troops with him
advanced to fight the Arameans, and
they fled before him. [15]When the Ammonites realized that the Arameans were
fleeing, they too fled before his brother
Abishai and went inside the city. So Joab
went back to Jerusalem.

[16]After the Arameans saw that they
had been routed by Israel, they sent
messengers and had Arameans brought
from beyond the Euphrates River, with
Shophak the commander of Hadadezer's
army leading them.

1Ch 19:2 ❖ What are ways we can show kindness to those who have been good to us? How do such acts honor God?

18:14 [o]1Ch 29:26 [p]1Ch 11:1
18:15 [q]2Sa 5:6-8; 1Ch 11:6
18:16 [r]2Sa 8:17; 1Ch 6:8 [s]1Ch 24:6
18:17 [t]1Sa 30:14; 2Sa 8:18; 15:18
19:1 [u]Ge 19:38; Jdg 10:17-11:33; 2Ch 20:1-2; Zep 2:8-11
19:3 [v]Nu 21:32
19:6 [w]Ge 34:30 [x]1Ch 18:3, 5, 9
19:7 [y]Nu 21:30; Jos 13:9, 16
19:11 [z]1Sa 26:6

[a] *16* Some Hebrew manuscripts, Vulgate and Syriac (see also 2 Samuel 8:17); most Hebrew manuscripts *Abimelek* [b] *6* That is, about 38 tons or about 34 metric tons [c] *6* That is, Northwest Mesopotamia

18:14–17 Three distinct departments comprise David's royal cabinet: a war office, a priestly office, and an administrative office.
19:1—20:3 The beard was the symbol of manhood in the ancient world, so to shave off half a man's beard was both an insult to the Israelite emissaries and an affront to the virility of King David (19:4–5).
19:6–7 The thousand talents of silver translates into more than 37 tons of the precious metal.
19:13 Finally, Joab encourages his troops by alluding to Yahweh's covenant with Israel and to the conquest of Canaan by Joshua. Joab prayerfully commits the outcome of the battle to the sovereignty and goodness of God.
19:15 It may have already been late in the year, and the winter rains would prevent any prolonged siege of the city. Joab's defeat of the coalition of Ammonite and Aramean armies is not decisive.

17When David was told of this, he gathered all Israel[a] and crossed the Jordan; he
advanced against them and formed his
battle lines opposite them. David formed
his lines to meet the Arameans in battle, and they fought against him. 18But
they fled before Israel, and David killed
seven thousand of their charioteers and
forty thousand of their foot soldiers. He
also killed Shophak the commander of
their army.
19When the vassals of Hadadezer saw
that they had been routed by Israel, they
made peace with David and became subject to him.
So the Arameans were not willing to
help the Ammonites anymore.

The Capture of Rabbah

20:1–3pp // 2Sa 11:1; 12:29–31

20 In the spring, at the time when
kings go off to war, Joab led out
the armed forces. He laid waste the land
of the Ammonites and went to Rabbah[b]
and besieged it, but David remained in
Jerusalem. Joab attacked Rabbah and left
it in ruins.[c] 2David took the crown from
the head of their king[a]—its weight was
found to be a talent[b] of gold, and it was set
with precious stones—and it was placed
on David's head. He took a great quantity
of plunder from the city 3and brought out
the people who were there, consigning
them to labor with saws and with iron
picks and axes.[d] David did this to all the
Ammonite towns. Then David and his
entire army returned to Jerusalem.

19:17 [a]1Ch 9:1
20:1 [b]Dt 3:11; 2Sa 12:26 [c]Am 1:13-15
20:3 [d]Dt 29:11

1Ch 20:7 ❖ What does true valor look like for followers of God today?

War With the Philistines

20:4–8pp // 2Sa 21:15–22

4In the course of time, war broke out
with the Philistines, at Gezer.[e] At that
time Sibbekai the Hushathite killed Sip-
pai, one of the descendants of the Rephaites,[f] and the Philistines were subjugated.
5In another battle with the Philistines,
Elhanan son of Jair killed Lahmi the
brother of Goliath the Gittite, who had
a spear with a shaft like a weaver's rod.[g]
6In still another battle, which took
place at Gath, there was a huge man with
six fingers on each hand and six toes on
each foot—twenty-four in all. He also
was descended from Rapha. 7When he
taunted Israel, Jonathan son of Shimea,
David's brother, killed him.
8These were descendants of Rapha in
Gath, and they fell at the hands of David
and his men.

David Counts the Fighting Men

21:1–26pp // 2Sa 24:1–25

21 Satan[h] rose up against Israel and
incited David to take a census[i] of Israel. 2So David said to Joab and the commanders of the troops, "Go and count[j]
the Israelites from Beersheba to Dan.
Then report back to me so that I may
know how many there are."

20:4 [e]Jos 10:33 [f]Ge 14:5
20:5 [g]1Sa 17:7
21:1 [h]2Ch 18:21; Ps 109:6 [i]2Ch 14:8; 25:5
21:2 [j]1Ch 27:23-24

[a] 2 Or *of Milkom*, that is, Molek [b] 2 That is, about 75 pounds or about 34 kilograms

20:1 The Chronicler omits the story of David's episode with Bathsheba (2Sa 11:2—12:25), although a hint is retained in the cryptic reference to the king's decision to remain behind.
20:2 A talent of gold would weigh more than 75 pounds. The piece in question is probably an ornamental crown symbolizing Ammonite kingship and may have been displayed at certain royal occasions.
20:4-8 The passage consists of three battle reports, each of which records a contest between an Israelite warrior and a Philistine warrior descended from the Rephaites. The relationship of the Philistine Rephaites to the giants of the Transjordan, also called "Rephaim" or "Anakim," is unclear (cf. Dt 2:10-11).

✚ **18:1—20:8** The warfare motif is not restricted to the OT. The church at Ephesus learned about spiritual warfare—an ongoing cosmic battle between God and the unseen powers of evil—from the apostle Paul (Eph 6:11-12; cf. 2Co 10:3-4). The kingdom of God ushered in at the second coming of Jesus Christ will result in a new heaven and earth and will rid evil from God's creation once and for all. In fact, according to Paul, Jesus Christ will yield his kingdom to the Father only after he has defeated all dominions and powers, subdued all his enemies, and destroyed the last enemy: death (1Co 15:21-26).
As was the case in the OT with David's wars, so too the battle belongs to God in the NT era. King David sang with joyful confidence that "with God we will gain the victory" (Ps 60:12). In like manner, the apostle Paul rejoiced with the Corinthian church that God "gives us the victory" over sin and death "through our Lord Jesus Christ" (1Co 15:57).

21:1—22:1 The Chronicler's primary concern is the relationship of the census-taking story to the Jerusalem temple. In the Chronicler's opinion, what better place for God's permanent sanctuary than the site identified as the prime location for repentant prayer and divine absolution?
21:1-7 It is God's prerogative to use Satan as his

3 But Joab replied, "May the LORD multiply his troops a hundred times over.[k]
My lord the king, are they not all my
lord's subjects? Why does my lord want
to do this? Why should he bring guilt
on Israel?"
4 The king's word, however, overruled
Joab; so Joab left and went throughout
Israel and then came back to Jerusalem. 5 Joab reported the number of the
fighting men to David: In all Israel[l] there
were one million one hundred thousand
men who could handle a sword, including four hundred and seventy thousand
in Judah.
6 But Joab did not include Levi and
Benjamin in the numbering, because
the king's command was repulsive to
him. 7 This command was also evil in the
sight of God; so he punished Israel.
8 Then David said to God, "I have
sinned greatly by doing this. Now, I beg
you, take away the guilt of your servant.
I have done a very foolish thing."
9 The LORD said to Gad,[m] David's seer,[n]
10 "Go and tell David, 'This is what the
LORD says: I am giving you three options.
Choose one of them for me to carry out
against you.'"
11 So Gad went to David and said to him,
"This is what the LORD says: 'Take your
choice: 12 three years of famine,[o] three
months of being swept away[a] before
your enemies, with their swords over-
taking you, or three days of the sword[p]
of the LORD[q]—days of plague in the land,
with the angel of the LORD ravaging every part of Israel.' Now then, decide how
I should answer the one who sent me."
13 David said to Gad, "I am in deep distress. Let me fall into the hands of the
LORD, for his mercy[r] is very great; but
do not let me fall into human hands."
14 So the LORD sent a plague on Israel,
and seventy thousand men of Israel fell
dead.[s] 15 And God sent an angel[t] to destroy Jerusalem.[u] But as the angel was
doing so, the LORD saw it and relented[v]

21:3 [k] Dt 1:11
21:5 [l] 1Ch 9:1
21:9 [m] 1Sa 22:5 [n] 1Sa 9:9
21:12 [o] Dt 32:24 [p] Eze 30:25 [q] Ge 19:13
21:13 [r] Ps 6:4; 86:15; 130:4,7
21:14 [s] 1Ch 27:24
21:15 [t] Ge 32:1 [u] Ps 125:2 [v] Ge 6:6; Ex 32:14

1Ch 21:8 ❖ How can we show true sorrow and repentance to God when God reveals sin in our lives? How do we find hope when we come humbly before God in repentance (see 1Jn 1:9)?

concerning the disaster and said to the
angel who was destroying[w] the people,
"Enough! Withdraw your hand." The angel of the LORD was then standing at the
threshing floor of Araunah[b] the Jebusite.
16 David looked up and saw the angel of
the LORD standing between heaven and
earth, with a drawn sword in his hand
extended over Jerusalem. Then David
and the elders, clothed in sackcloth, fell
facedown.[x]
17 David said to God, "Was it not I who
ordered the fighting men to be counted?
I, the shepherd,[c] have sinned and done
wrong. These are but sheep.[y] What have
they done? LORD my God, let your hand
fall on me and my family,[z] but do not
let this plague remain on your people."

David Builds an Altar

18 Then the angel of the LORD ordered
Gad to tell David to go up and build an
altar to the LORD on the threshing floor[a]
of Araunah the Jebusite. 19 So David went
up in obedience to the word that Gad had
spoken in the name of the LORD.
20 While Araunah was threshing
wheat,[b] he turned and saw the angel;
his four sons who were with him hid
themselves. 21 Then David approached,
and when Araunah looked and saw him,
he left the threshing floor and bowed
down before David with his face to the
ground.
22 David said to him, "Let me have the

[w] Ge 19:13
21:16 [x] Nu 14:5; Jos 7:6
21:17 [y] 2Sa 7:8; Ps 74:1 [z] Jnh 1:12
21:18 [a] 2Ch 3:1
21:20 [b] Jdg 6:11

[a] *12* Hebrew; Septuagint and Vulgate (see also 2 Samuel 24:13) *of fleeing* [b] *15* Hebrew *Ornan,* a variant of *Araunah;* also in verses 18-28
[c] *17* Probable reading of the original Hebrew text (see 2 Samuel 24:17 and note); Masoretic Text does not have *the shepherd.*

---

agent of testing and/or judgment to accomplish his redemptive purposes in the created order. This fact, however, does not absolve David of his personal guilt in the matter.

21:8–17 It seems the offense is not so much a breach of ritual protocol as it is David's motive. David orders the census as a tribute to his own strength and power rather than as a testimony to God (v. 3).

21:16–17 The reaction of David and the elders of Israel to the sight of the destroying angel suggests they expected greater leniency in submitting to three days of the sword of Yahweh.

21:18–27 God commands David, through Gad, to build an altar at the site of Araunah's threshing floor. The Chronicler interprets this command as legitimizing a new altar for the sacrificial worship of the central shrine (cf. vv. 28–29).

site of your threshing floor so I can build
an altar to the LORD, that the plague on
the people may be stopped. Sell it to me
at the full price."
23 Araunah said to David, "Take it! Let
my lord the king do whatever pleases
him. Look, I will give the oxen for the
burnt offerings, the threshing sledges
for the wood, and the wheat for the grain
offering. I will give all this."
24 But King David replied to Araunah,
"No, I insist on paying the full price. I
will not take for the LORD what is yours,
or sacrifice a burnt offering that costs
me nothing."
25 So David paid Araunah six hundred
shekels[a] of gold for the site. 26 David built
an altar to the LORD there and sacrificed
burnt offerings and fellowship offerings.
He called on the LORD, and the LORD answered him with fire[c] from heaven on
the altar of burnt offering.
27 Then the LORD spoke to the angel,
and he put his sword back into its sheath.
28 At that time, when David saw that the
LORD had answered him on the threshing floor of Araunah the Jebusite, he offered sacrifices there. 29 The tabernacle
of the LORD, which Moses had made in
the wilderness, and the altar of burnt
offering were at that time on the high
place at Gibeon.[d] 30 But David could not
go before it to inquire of God, because
he was afraid of the sword of the angel
of the LORD.

22 Then David said, "The house of
the LORD God[e] is to be here, and
also the altar of burnt offering for Israel."

Preparations for the Temple

2 So David gave orders to assemble the
foreigners[f] residing in Israel, and from
among them he appointed stonecutters[g]
to prepare dressed stone for building
the house of God. 3 He provided a large
amount of iron to make nails for the
doors of the gateways and for the fit-
tings, and more bronze than could be
weighed.[h] 4 He also provided more cedar
logs[i] than could be counted, for the Sidonians and Tyrians had brought large
numbers of them to David.
5 David said, "My son Solomon is young[j]
and inexperienced, and the house to be
built for the LORD should be of great magnificence and fame and splendor in the
sight of all the nations. Therefore I will
make preparations for it." So David made
extensive preparations before his death.
6 Then he called for his son Solomon
and charged him to build[k] a house for
the LORD, the God of Israel. 7 David said
to Solomon: "My son, I had it in my heart[l]
to build[m] a house for the Name[n] of the
LORD my God. 8 But this word of the LORD
came to me: 'You have shed much blood
and have fought many wars.[o] You are not
to build a house for my Name,[p] because
you have shed much blood on the earth
in my sight. 9 But you will have a son who
will be a man of peace[q] and rest, and I
will give him rest from all his enemies on
every side. His name will be Solomon,[b][r]
and I will grant Israel peace and quiet[s]
during his reign. 10 He is the one who will
build a house for my Name.[t] He will be
my son,[u] and I will be his father. And I
will establish the throne of his kingdom
over Israel forever.'[v]
11 "Now, my son, the LORD be with[w] you,
and may you have success and build the
house of the LORD your God, as he said
you would. 12 May the LORD give you
discretion and understanding[x] when
he puts you in command over Israel, so
that you may keep the law of the LORD
your God. 13 Then you will have success
if you are careful to observe the decrees
and laws[y] that the LORD gave Moses for

21:26 [c] Lev 9:24; Jdg 6:21
21:29 [d] 1Ki 3:4; 1Ch 16:39
22:1 [e] Ge 28:17; 1Ch 21:18-29; 2Ch 3:1
22:2 [f] 1Ki 9:21; Isa 56:6 [g] 1Ki 5:17-18
22:3 [h] ver 14; 1Ki 7:47; 1Ch 29:2-5
22:4 [i] 1Ki 5:6
22:5 [j] 1Ki 3:7; 1Ch 29:1
22:6 [k] Ac 7:47
22:7 [l] 1Ch 17:2 [m] 2Sa 7:2; 1Ki 8:17 [n] Dt 12:5,11
22:8 [o] 1Ki 5:3 [p] 1Ch 28:3
22:9 [q] 1Ki 5:4 [r] 2Sa 12:24 [s] 1Ki 4:20
22:10 [t] 1Ch 17:12 [u] 2Sa 7:13 [v] 2Sa 7:14; 2Ch 6:15
22:11 [w] ver 16
22:12 [x] 1Ki 3:9-12; 2Ch 1:10
22:13 [y] 1Ch 28:7

[a] *25* That is, about 15 pounds or about 6.9 kilograms [b] *9* *Solomon* sounds like and may be derived from the Hebrew for *peace.*

1Ch 22:9 ❖ How has God granted us peace and rest?

21:26 David's prayer for God's mercy is answered by the sign of fire sent from heaven. This is seen as divine confirmation of this shift in the location for Israel's worship center.
22:2–5 The temple is a theological statement to the nations that God is faithful to his covenant with David and that his kingdom is embodied in the Israelite monarchy.
22:6–16 David's counsel recorded here is a private charge to his son Solomon to build Yahweh's temple. It anticipates the later public commissioning of the crown prince (cf. 28:9–10).
22:11–13 The transfer of royal authority from David to Solomon reflects the account of Joshua being commissioned by Moses as his successor (cf. Dt 31; Jos 1). For example, because of their life choices, both Moses and David are disqualified from achieving their ultimate goals, while both Joshua and Solomon lead God's people into an era of "rest" and "blessing."

Israel. Be strong and courageous.[z] Do not
be afraid or discouraged.
14"I have taken great pains to provide
for the temple of the LORD a hundred
thousand talents[a] of gold, a million talents[b] of silver, quantities of bronze and
iron too great to be weighed, and wood
and stone. And you may add to them.[a]
15You have many workers: stonecutters,
masons and carpenters, as well as those
skilled in every kind of work 16in gold
and silver, bronze and iron — craftsmen[b]
beyond number. Now begin the work,
and the LORD be with you."
17Then David ordered[c] all the leaders
of Israel to help his son Solomon. 18He
said to them, "Is not the LORD your God
with you? And has he not granted you
rest[d] on every side?[e] For he has given the
inhabitants of the land into my hands,
and the land is subject to the LORD and to
his people. 19Now devote your heart and
soul to seeking the LORD your God.[f] Begin
to build the sanctuary of the LORD God,
so that you may bring the ark of the covenant of the LORD and the sacred articles
belonging to God into the temple that
will be built for the Name of the LORD."

The Levites

23 When David was old and full of
years, he made his son Solomon[g]
king over Israel.[h]
2He also gathered together all the leaders of Israel, as well as the priests and Levites. 3The Levites thirty years old or more[i]
were counted, and the total number of
men was thirty-eight thousand.[j] 4David
said, "Of these, twenty-four thousand are
to be in charge[k] of the work of the temple
of the LORD and six thousand are to be officials and judges.[l] 5Four thousand are to
be gatekeepers and four thousand are to
praise the LORD with the musical instruments[m] I have provided for that purpose."[n]
6David separated[o] the Levites into
divisions corresponding to the sons of
Levi: Gershon, Kohath and Merari.

Gershonites

7Belonging to the Gershonites:
Ladan and Shimei.
8The sons of Ladan:
Jehiel the first, Zetham and Joel —
three in all.
9The sons of Shimei:
Shelomoth, Haziel and Haran —
three in all.
These were the heads of the families of Ladan.
10And the sons of Shimei:
Jahath, Ziza,[c] Jeush and Beriah.
These were the sons of Shimei —
four in all.
11Jahath was the first and Ziza the
second, but Jeush and Beriah did
not have many sons; so they were
counted as one family with one
assignment.

Kohathites

12The sons of Kohath:[p]
Amram, Izhar, Hebron and
Uzziel — four in all.
13The sons of Amram:[q]
Aaron and Moses.
Aaron was set apart,[r] he and his
descendants forever, to consecrate the most holy things, to offer sacrifices before the LORD, to
minister before him and to pronounce blessings[s] in his name
forever. 14The sons of Moses the
man[t] of God were counted as part
of the tribe of Levi.

22:13 [z] Dt 31:6; Jos 1:6-9; 1Ch 28:20
22:14 [a] ver 3; 1Ch 29:2-5,19
22:16 [b] ver 11; 2Ch 2:7
22:17 [c] 1Ch 28:1-6
22:18 [d] ver 9; 1Ch 23:25 [e] 2Sa 7:1
22:19 [f] ver 7; 1Ki 8:6; 1Ch 28:9; 2Ch 5:7; 7:14
23:1 [g] 1Ki 1:33-39; 1Ch 28:5 [h] 1Ki 1:30; 1Ch 29:28
23:3 [i] ver 24; Nu 8:24 [j] Nu 4:3-49
23:4 [k] Ezr 3:8 [l] 1Ch 26:29; 2Ch 19:8
23:5 [m] 1Ch 15:16 [n] Ne 12:45
23:6 [o] 2Ch 8:14; 29:25
23:12 [p] Ex 6:18
23:13 [q] Ex 6:20; 28:1 [r] Ex 30:7-10; Dt 21:5 [s] Nu 6:23
23:14 [t] Dt 33:1

[a] *14* That is, about 3,750 tons or about 3,400 metric tons [b] *14* That is, about 37,500 tons or about 34,000 metric tons [c] *10* One Hebrew manuscript, Septuagint and Vulgate (see also verse 11); most Hebrew manuscripts *Zina*

22:14 The main focus is not on the opulence of the temple but on David's understanding of the inestimable worth of God.

22:17–19 This building project demands the full support of the nation. David envisions two distinct purposes for the temple: (1) housing the sacred vessels and furniture essential to Israel's worship and (2) exalting the name of the Lord before his people and the nations.

23:1 The expression "old and full of years" indicates great honor (e.g., Abraham, Ge 25:8; Isaac, 35:29; Moses, Dt 34:7; Job, Job 42:17).

23:2–6a This census should not be seen as a contradiction to the ill-advised military census (ch. 21). The purpose of this census is to establish a rotation of Levitical service for temple worship.

23:6b–24 The genealogical table of Levi highlights his three sons in keeping with the order found elsewhere: Gershon, Kohath, and Merari. Apart from Moses (vv. 15–17), each family in the register is represented by three generations of descendants. The expression "heads of families" (v. 24) in Chronicles denotes clan leaders or family elders (cf. 27:1).

23:13 Both the priests and the Levites are called "to minister" before the Lord and "pronounce blessings" in his name (cf. Dt 10:8). The distinctive service of the priests consists of consecrating holy things and of offering sacrifices.

15 The sons of Moses:
Gershom and Eliezer.[u]
16 The descendants of Gershom:[v]
Shubael was the first.
17 The descendants of Eliezer:
Rehabiah was the first.
Eliezer had no other sons, but the
sons of Rehabiah were very numerous.
18 The sons of Izhar:
Shelomith was the first.
19 The sons of Hebron:[w]
Jeriah the first, Amariah the second, Jahaziel the third and Jekameam the fourth.
20 The sons of Uzziel:
Micah the first and Ishiah the
second.

Merarites

21 The sons of Merari:[x]
Mahli and Mushi.
The sons of Mahli:
Eleazar and Kish.
22 Eleazar died without having sons:
he had only daughters. Their
cousins, the sons of Kish, married them.
23 The sons of Mushi:
Mahli, Eder and Jerimoth — three
in all.

24 These were the descendants of Levi by
their families — the heads of families as
they were registered under their names
and counted individually, that is, the
workers twenty years old or more[y] who
served in the temple of the LORD. 25 For David had said, "Since the LORD, the God of
Israel, has granted rest[z] to his people and
has come to dwell in Jerusalem forever,
26 the Levites no longer need to carry the
tabernacle or any of the articles used in its
service."[a] 27 According to the last instructions of David, the Levites were counted
from those twenty years old or more.
28 The duty of the Levites was to help
Aaron's descendants in the service of the
temple of the LORD: to be in charge of
the courtyards, the side rooms, the purification[b] of all sacred things and the
performance of other duties at the house
of God. 29 They were in charge of the bread
set out on the table,[c] the special flour for
the grain offerings,[d] the thin loaves made
without yeast, the baking and the mixing, and all measurements of quantity
and size.[e] 30 They were also to stand every
morning to thank and praise the LORD.
They were to do the same in the evening[f]
31 and whenever burnt offerings were presented to the LORD on the Sabbaths, at the
New Moon[g] feasts and at the appointed
festivals.[h] They were to serve before the
LORD regularly in the proper number and
in the way prescribed for them.
32 And so the Levites[i] carried out their
responsibilities for the tent of meeting,[j]
for the Holy Place and, under their relatives the descendants of Aaron, for the
service of the temple of the LORD.[k]

1Ch 23:28-31 ❖ How can we contribute to corporate worship in our setting? What tasks can we help with in church or in our worshiping communities?

1Ch 24:5 ❖ Where do we see favoritism or status separating ministry workers today? How do we think God views this?

The Divisions of Priests

24 These were the divisions[l] of the
descendants of Aaron:[m]
The sons of Aaron were Nadab, Abihu, Eleazar and Ithamar.[n] 2 But Nadab
and Abihu died before their father did,[o]
and they had no sons; so Eleazar and
Ithamar served as the priests. 3 With the
help of Zadok[p] a descendant of Eleazar
and Ahimelek a descendant of Ithamar,
David separated them into divisions
for their appointed order of ministering. 4 A larger number of leaders were
found among Eleazar's descendants
than among Ithamar's, and they were
divided accordingly: sixteen heads of
families from Eleazar's descendants and
eight heads of families from Ithamar's
descendants. 5 They divided them impartially by casting lots,[q] for there were

23:15 [u] Ex 18:4
23:16 [v] 1Ch 26:24-28
23:19 [w] 1Ch 24:23
23:21 [x] 1Ch 24:26
23:24 [y] Nu 4:3; 10:17,21
23:25 [z] 1Ch 22:9
23:26 [a] Nu 4:5, 15; 7:9; Dt 10:8
23:28 [b] 2Ch 29:15; Ne 13:9; Mal 3:3
23:29 [c] Ex 25:30 [d] Lev 2:4-7; 6:20-23 [e] Lev 19:35-36; 1Ch 9:29,32
23:30 [f] 1Ch 9:33; Ps 134:1
23:31 [g] 2Ki 4:23 [h] Lev 23:4; Nu 28:9-29:39; Isa 1:13-14; Col 2:16
23:32 [i] Nu 1:53; 1Ch 6:48 [j] Nu 3:6-8,38 [k] 2Ch 23:18; 31:2; Eze 44:14
24:1 [l] 1Ch 23:6; 28:13; 2Ch 5:11; 8:14; 23:8; 31:2; 35:4,5; Ezr 6:18 [m] Nu 3:2-4 [n] Ex 6:23
24:2 [o] Lev 10:1-2; Nu 3:4
24:3 [p] 2Sa 8:17
24:5 [q] ver 31; 1Ch 25:8

23:25-32 The shift from a portable to a permanent sanctuary for Israel's worship of Yahweh means that the duties for the Levites must be reassigned. **23:30-31** In addition to their role as a supporting cast to the priesthood, the Levites are also in charge of the music that accompanies the rituals of temple worship.

24:1-19 The emphasis here is not one of liturgical function but rather one of organization for service (vv. 1-5). The writer's concern is twofold: the formal sanctioning of the duty roster by King David (v. 3) and the propriety of carefully ordering priestly service by means of lot-casting (v. 5).

officials of the sanctuary and officials
of God among the descendants of both
Eleazar and Ithamar.
6The scribe Shemaiah son of Nethanel, a Levite, recorded their names in the
presence of the king and of the officials:
Zadok the priest, Ahimelek[r] son of Abiathar and the heads of families of the
priests and of the Levites — one family
being taken from Eleazar and then one
from Ithamar.

7The first lot fell to Jehoiarib,
the second to Jedaiah,[s]
8the third to Harim,[t]
the fourth to Seorim,
9the fifth to Malkijah,
the sixth to Mijamin,
10the seventh to Hakkoz,
the eighth to Abijah,[u]
11the ninth to Jeshua,
the tenth to Shekaniah,
12the eleventh to Eliashib,
the twelfth to Jakim,
13the thirteenth to Huppah,
the fourteenth to Jeshebeab,
14the fifteenth to Bilgah,
the sixteenth to Immer,[v]
15the seventeenth to Hezir,[w]
the eighteenth to Happizzez,
16the nineteenth to Pethahiah,
the twentieth to Jehezkel,
17the twenty-first to Jakin,
the twenty-second to Gamul,
18the twenty-third to Delaiah
and the twenty-fourth to Maaziah.

19This was their appointed order of
ministering when they entered the temple of the LORD, according to the regulations prescribed for them by their
ancestor Aaron, as the LORD, the God of
Israel, had commanded him.

The Rest of the Levites

20As for the rest of the descendants of
Levi:[x]
from the sons of Amram: Shubael;
from the sons of Shubael: Jehdeiah.

24:6 [r]1Ch 18:16
24:7 [s]Ezr 2:36; Ne 12:6
24:8 [t]Ezr 2:39; Ne 10:5
24:10 [u]Ne 12:4, 17; Lk 1:5
24:14 [v]Jer 20:1
24:15 [w]Ne 10:20
24:20 [x]1Ch 23:6
24:21 [y]1Ch 23:17
24:23 [z]1Ch 23:19
24:26 [a]1Ch 6:19; 23:21
24:31 [b]ver 5
25:1 [c]1Ch 6:39 [d]1Ch 6:33 [e]1Ch 16:41, 42; Ne 11:17 [f]1Sa 10:5; 2Ki 3:15 [g]1Ch 15:16 [h]1Ch 6:31 [i]2Ch 5:12; 8:14; 34:12; 35:15; Ezr 3:10

21As for Rehabiah,[y] from his sons:
Ishiah was the first.
22From the Izharites: Shelomoth;
from the sons of Shelomoth: Jahath.
23The sons of Hebron:[z] Jeriah the
first,[a] Amariah the second, Jahaziel the third and Jekameam the
fourth.
24The son of Uzziel: Micah;
from the sons of Micah: Shamir.
25The brother of Micah: Ishiah;
from the sons of Ishiah: Zechariah.
26The sons of Merari:[a] Mahli and Mushi.
The son of Jaaziah: Beno.
27The sons of Merari:
from Jaaziah: Beno, Shoham, Zakkur and Ibri.
28From Mahli: Eleazar, who had no
sons.
29From Kish: the son of Kish:
Jerahmeel.
30And the sons of Mushi: Mahli, Eder
and Jerimoth.

These were the Levites, according to
their families. 31They also cast lots,[b] just
as their relatives the descendants of Aaron did, in the presence of King David
and of Zadok, Ahimelek, and the heads
of families of the priests and of the Levites. The families of the oldest brother
were treated the same as those of the
youngest.

The Musicians

25 David, together with the commanders of the army, set apart
some of the sons of Asaph,[c] Heman[d] and
Jeduthun[e] for the ministry of prophesying,[f] accompanied by harps, lyres and
cymbals.[g] Here is the list of the men[h]
who performed this service:[i]

[a] 23 Two Hebrew manuscripts and some Septuagint manuscripts (see also 23:19); most Hebrew manuscripts *The sons of Jeriah:*

24:20–31 This section reporting the divisions of the priests supplements the report of David's reorganization of the Levites (ch. 23).
25:1–7 The Chronicler traces the origin of the temple music ministry in three Levitical families: Asaph, Heman, and Jeduthun. There is a sense in which these families represent musical guilds, as witnessed in their contribution to the Psalms (cf. Ps 73–89). David's organization of a corps of Levitical temple musicians is important to the legitimacy of music in worship as temple liturgy developed.
25:1a Although strong associations between musicians and the military are known in the ancient world, it is unclear whether these consultants are military personnel or Levitical officers since the meaning of the word "army" is flexible. It is not surprising that David organizes the Levitical musical guilds responsible for the music of the temple liturgy since he himself accounts for nearly half of the songs in the Psalter.

2 From the sons of Asaph:
Zakkur, Joseph, Nethaniah and Asarelah. The sons of Asaph were under the supervision of Asaph, who
prophesied under the king's supervision.
3 As for Jeduthun, from his sons:[j]
Gedaliah, Zeri, Jeshaiah, Shimei,[a]
Hashabiah and Mattithiah, six in all,
under the supervision of their father
Jeduthun, who prophesied, using
the harp[k] in thanking and praising
the LORD.
4 As for Heman, from his sons:
Bukkiah, Mattaniah, Uzziel, Shubael
and Jerimoth; Hananiah, Hanani,
Eliathah, Giddalti and Romamti-
Ezer; Joshbekashah, Mallothi, Hothir and Mahazioth.
5 (All these were
sons of Heman the king's seer. They
were given him through the promises of God to exalt him. God gave
Heman fourteen sons and three
daughters.)

6 All these men were under the supervision of their father[l] for the music of
the temple of the LORD, with cymbals,
lyres and harps, for the ministry at the
house of God.
Asaph, Jeduthun and Heman[m] were
under the supervision of the king.[n]
7 Along with their relatives — all of
them trained and skilled in music for
the LORD — they numbered 288.
8 Young
and old alike, teacher as well as student,
cast lots[o] for their duties.

9 The first lot, which was for Asaph,[p] fell to Joseph,
his sons and relatives[b] 12[c]
the second to Gedaliah,
him and his relatives and sons 12
10 the third to Zakkur,
his sons and relatives 12
11 the fourth to Izri,[d]
his sons and relatives 12
12 the fifth to Nethaniah,
his sons and relatives 12
13 the sixth to Bukkiah,
his sons and relatives 12
14 the seventh to Jesarelah,[e]
his sons and relatives 12
15 the eighth to Jeshaiah,
his sons and relatives 12
16 the ninth to Mattaniah,
his sons and relatives 12
17 the tenth to Shimei,
his sons and relatives 12
18 the eleventh to Azarel,[f]
his sons and relatives 12
19 the twelfth to Hashabiah,
his sons and relatives 12
20 the thirteenth to Shubael,
his sons and relatives 12
21 the fourteenth to Mattithiah,
his sons and relatives 12
22 the fifteenth to Jerimoth,
his sons and relatives 12
23 the sixteenth to Hananiah,
his sons and relatives 12
24 the seventeenth to Joshbekashah,
his sons and relatives 12
25 the eighteenth to Hanani,
his sons and relatives 12
26 the nineteenth to Mallothi,
his sons and relatives 12
27 the twentieth to Eliathah,
his sons and relatives 12
28 the twenty-first to Hothir,
his sons and relatives 12
29 the twenty-second to Giddalti,
his sons and relatives 12
30 the twenty-third to Mahazioth,
his sons and relatives 12
31 the twenty-fourth to Romamti-Ezer,
his sons and relatives 12.[q]

25:3 [j] 1Ch 16:41-42 [k] Ge 4:21; Ps 33:2
25:6 [l] 1Ch 15:16 [m] 1Ch 15:19 [n] 2Ch 23:18; 29:25
25:8 [o] 1Ch 26:13
25:9 [p] 1Ch 6:39
25:31 [q] 1Ch 9:33

1Ch 25:6 ❖ What role does music play in our faith and worship? How does music honor God?

[a] *3* One Hebrew manuscript and some Septuagint manuscripts (see also verse 17); most Hebrew manuscripts do not have *Shimei.*
[b] *9* See Septuagint; Hebrew does not have *his sons and relatives.* [c] *9* See the total in verse 7; Hebrew does not have *twelve.* [d] *11* A variant of *Zeri* [e] *14* A variant of *Asarelah* [f] *18* A variant of *Uzziel*

25:6-7 The three families of musicians trace their lineage to Levi. The four sons of Asaph, the six sons of Jeduthun, and the fourteen sons of Heman account for the twenty-four divisions of temple musicians.
25:8-31 The reference to "young and old alike, teacher as well as student" (v. 8) suggests a conservatory-like environment with emphasis on becoming proficient in technique and skill level through training and rehearsal in addition to scheduled appearances for music ministry in the temple liturgy.

The Gatekeepers

26 The divisions of the gatekeepers:[r]

From the Korahites: Meshelemiah son of Kore, one of the sons of Asaph.
2 Meshelemiah had sons:
Zechariah[s] the firstborn,
Jediael the second,
Zebadiah the third,
Jathniel the fourth,
3 Elam the fifth,
Jehohanan the sixth
and Eliehoenai the seventh.
4 Obed-Edom also had sons:
Shemaiah the firstborn,
Jehozabad the second,
Joah the third,
Sakar the fourth,
Nethanel the fifth,
5 Ammiel the sixth,
Issachar the seventh
and Peullethai the eighth.
(For God had blessed Obed-Edom.[t])

6 Obed-Edom's son Shemaiah also had sons, who were leaders in their father's family because they were very capable men.
7 The sons of Shemaiah: Othni, Rephael, Obed and Elzabad; his relatives Elihu and Semakiah were also able men.
8 All these were descendants of Obed-Edom; they and their sons and their relatives were capable men with the strength to do the work — descendants of Obed-Edom, 62 in all.
9 Meshelemiah had sons and relatives, who were able men — 18 in all.

10 Hosah the Merarite had sons: Shimri the first (although he was not the firstborn, his father had appointed him the first),[u]
11 Hilkiah the second, Tabaliah the third and Zechariah the fourth. The sons and relatives of Hosah were 13 in all.

12 These divisions of the gatekeepers, through their leaders, had duties for ministering[v] in the temple of the LORD, just as their relatives had.
13 Lots[w] were cast for each gate, according to their families, young and old alike.
14 The lot for the East Gate[x] fell to Shelemiah.[a] Then lots were cast for his son Zechariah,[y] a wise counselor, and the lot for the North Gate fell to him.
15 The lot for the South Gate fell to Obed-Edom,[z] and the lot for the storehouse fell to his sons.
16 The lots for the West Gate and the Shalleketh Gate on the upper road fell to Shuppim and Hosah.
Guard was alongside of guard:
17 There were six Levites a day on the east, four a day on the north, four a day on the south and two at a time at the storehouse.
18 As for the court[b] to the west, there were four at the road and two at the court[b] itself.
19 These were the divisions of the gatekeepers who were descendants of Korah and Merari.[a]

The Treasurers and Other Officials

20 Their fellow Levites[b] were[c] in charge of the treasuries of the house of God and the treasuries for the dedicated things.[c]
21 The descendants of Ladan, who were Gershonites through Ladan and who were heads of families belonging to Ladan the Gershonite,[d] were Jehieli,
22 the sons of Jehieli, Zetham and his brother

26:1 [r] 1Ch 9:17
26:2 [s] 1Ch 9:21
26:5 [t] 2Sa 6:10; 1Ch 13:13; 16:38
26:10 [u] Dt 21:16; 1Ch 5:1
26:12 [v] 1Ch 9:22
26:13 [w] 1Ch 24:5, 31; 25:8
26:14 [x] 1Ch 9:18 [y] 1Ch 9:21
26:15 [z] 1Ch 13:13; 2Ch 25:24
26:19 [a] 2Ch 35:15; Ne 7:1; Eze 44:11
26:20 [b] 2Ch 24:5 [c] 1Ch 28:12
26:21 [d] 1Ch 23:7; 29:8

[a] 14 A variant of *Meshelemiah* [b] 18 The meaning of the Hebrew for this word is uncertain. [c] 20 Septuagint; Hebrew *As for the Levites, Ahijah was*

26:1–19 The first section of this chapter identifies two families of Levitical gatekeepers: Meshelemiah (vv. 1-3, 9) and Hosah (vv. 10-11). The family of Meshelemiah traces its heritage to the line of Korah through the family of Izhar and ultimately Kohath, one of the three sons of Levi (6:1-2, 22; 26:1). The family of Hosah are descendants of Merari, another son of Levi (cf. Ex 6:16-19).
26:12–18 The next unit is a table of organization outlining the service assignments of the temple gatekeepers. The essential purpose of expanding this record of temple gatekeepers is to recount the ceremony for the specific gatekeeper assignments.
26:16–18 The final unit of this section recounts a duty roster of sorts, indicating the number of Levites stationed at the various posts during the daily watches. The temple gatekeepers serve two by two, and there are apparently twenty-four daily assignments.
26:20–32 The second section of this chapter may be divided into two distinct units: the list of Levites who serve as treasurers (vv. 20-28) and those who hold administrative posts outside the temple precinct of Jerusalem (vv. 29-32). The two rosters complete the catalog of the various registers of Levites and their assigned duties (chs. 23-26). The two paragraphs are unified by the genealogical framework of the four Kohathite families mentioned by the Chronicler or his source (26:23).

Joel. They were in charge of the treasuries[e] of the temple of the LORD.
23From the Amramites, the Izharites, the Hebronites and the Uzzielites:[f]

24Shubael,[g] a descendant of Gershom son of Moses, was the official in charge of the treasuries. 25His relatives through Eliezer: Rehabiah his son, Jeshaiah his son, Joram his son, Zikri his son and Shelomith[h] his son. 26Shelomith and his relatives were in charge of all the treasuries for the things dedicated[i] by King David, by the heads of families who were the commanders of thousands and commanders of hundreds, and by the other army commanders. 27Some of the plunder taken in battle they dedicated for the repair of the temple of the LORD. 28And everything dedicated by Samuel the seer[j] and by Saul son of Kish, Abner son of Ner and Joab son of Zeruiah, and all the other dedicated things were in the care of Shelomith and his relatives.
29From the Izharites: Kenaniah and his sons were assigned duties away from the temple, as officials and judges[k] over Israel.
30From the Hebronites: Hashabiah[l] and his relatives — seventeen hundred able men — were responsible in Israel west of the Jordan for all the work of the LORD and for the king's service. 31As for the Hebronites,[m] Jeriah was their chief according to the genealogical records of their families. In the fortieth[n] year of David's reign a search was made in the records, and capable men among the Hebronites were found at Jazer in Gilead. 32Jeriah had twenty-seven hundred relatives, who were able men and heads of families, and King David put them in charge of the Reubenites, the Gadites and the half-tribe of Manasseh for every matter pertaining to God and for the affairs of the king.

26:22 [e] 1Ch 9:26
26:23 [f] Nu 3:27
26:24 [g] 1Ch 23:16
26:25 [h] 1Ch 23:18
26:26 [i] 2Sa 8:11
26:28 [j] 1Sa 9:9
26:29 [k] Dt 17:8-13; 1Ch 23:4; Ne 11:16
26:30 [l] 1Ch 27:17
26:31 [m] 1Ch 23:19 [n] 2Sa 5:4

1Ch 26:32 ❖ Jeriah's descendants were known for their wisdom in political and religious matters. Are we similarly trustworthy with "every matter pertaining to God and for the affairs of the king?"

Army Divisions

27 This is the list of the Israelites — heads of families, commanders of thousands and commanders of hundreds, and their officers, who served the king in all that concerned the army divisions that were on duty month by month throughout the year. Each division consisted of 24,000 men.

2In charge of the first division, for the first month, was Jashobeam[o] son of Zabdiel. There were 24,000 men in his division. 3He was a descendant of Perez and chief of all the army officers for the first month.
4In charge of the division for the second month was Dodai[p] the Ahohite; Mikloth was the leader of his division. There were 24,000 men in his division.
5The third army commander, for the third month, was Benaiah[q] son of Jehoiada the priest. He was chief and there were 24,000 men in his division. 6This was the Benaiah who was a mighty warrior among the Thirty and was over the Thirty. His son Ammizabad was in charge of his division.
7The fourth, for the fourth month, was Asahel[r] the brother of Joab; his son Zebadiah was his successor. There were 24,000 men in his division.
8The fifth, for the fifth month, was the commander Shamhuth[s] the Izrahite. There were 24,000 men in his division.

27:2 [o] 2Sa 23:8; 1Ch 11:11
27:4 [p] 2Sa 23:9
27:5 [q] 2Sa 23:20
27:7 [r] 2Sa 2:18; 1Ch 11:26
27:8 [s] 1Ch 11:27

26:29–32 Two special groups of Levites are placed in charge of public administration in regions west of the Jordan River. The date formula (v. 31) suggests these Levitical assignments are made in the last year of David's reign. The Chronicler's purpose in reporting that the Levites had a presence in the public administration of the united monarchy is unclear. He may be either (1) attempting to legitimize the role of the Levites in offices of civil service at his own time or (2) calling for their involvement in that role based on the earlier precedent.
27:1–15 The military divisions described here represent a militia or citizen army, perhaps similar to the National Guard in the US. David carefully organizes his army into twelve divisions.

9 The sixth, for the sixth month, was Ira[t] the son of Ikkesh the Tekoite. There were 24,000 men in his division.

10 The seventh, for the seventh month, was Helez[u] the Pelonite, an Ephraimite. There were 24,000 men in his division.

11 The eighth, for the eighth month, was Sibbekai[v] the Hushathite, a Zerahite. There were 24,000 men in his division.

12 The ninth, for the ninth month, was Abiezer[w] the Anathothite, a Benjamite. There were 24,000 men in his division.

13 The tenth, for the tenth month, was Maharai[x] the Netophathite, a Zerahite. There were 24,000 men in his division.

14 The eleventh, for the eleventh month, was Benaiah[y] the Pirathonite, an Ephraimite. There were 24,000 men in his division.

15 The twelfth, for the twelfth month, was Heldai[z] the Netophathite, from the family of Othniel.[a] There were 24,000 men in his division.

Leaders of the Tribes

16 The leaders of the tribes of Israel:

over the Reubenites: Eliezer son of Zikri;
over the Simeonites: Shephatiah son of Maakah;
17 over Levi: Hashabiah[b] son of Kemuel;
over Aaron: Zadok;[c]
18 over Judah: Elihu, a brother of David;
over Issachar: Omri son of Michael;
19 over Zebulun: Ishmaiah son of Obadiah;
over Naphtali: Jerimoth son of Azriel;
20 over the Ephraimites: Hoshea son of Azaziah;
over half the tribe of Manasseh: Joel son of Pedaiah;
21 over the half-tribe of Manasseh in Gilead: Iddo son of Zechariah;

27:9 [t] 2Sa 23:26; 1Ch 11:28
27:10 [u] 2Sa 23:26; 1Ch 11:27
27:11 [v] 2Sa 21:18
27:12 [w] 2Sa 23:27; 1Ch 11:28
27:13 [x] 2Sa 23:28; 1Ch 11:30
27:14 [y] 1Ch 11:31
27:15 [z] 2Sa 23:29 [a] Jos 15:17
27:17 [b] 1Ch 26:30 [c] 2Sa 8:17; 1Ch 12:28

1Ch 27:23–24 ❖ What did David's census reveal about where he placed his trust? In what do we place our trust today?

over Benjamin: Jaasiel son of Abner;
22 over Dan: Azarel son of Jeroham.
These were the leaders of the tribes of Israel.

23 David did not take the number of
the men twenty years old or less,[d] because the LORD had promised to make
Israel as numerous as the stars[e] in the
sky. 24 Joab son of Zeruiah began to
count the men but did not finish. God's
wrath came on Israel on account of this
numbering,[f] and the number was not
entered in the book[a] of the annals of
King David.

The King's Overseers

25 Azmaveth son of Adiel was in charge of the royal storehouses.

Jonathan son of Uzziah was in charge of the storehouses in the outlying districts, in the towns, the villages and the watchtowers.

26 Ezri son of Kelub was in charge of the workers who farmed the land.

27 Shimei the Ramathite was in charge of the vineyards.

Zabdi the Shiphmite was in charge of the produce of the vineyards for the wine vats.

28 Baal-Hanan the Gederite was in charge of the olive and sycamore-fig[g] trees in the western foothills.

Joash was in charge of the supplies of olive oil.

29 Shitrai the Sharonite was in charge of the herds grazing in Sharon.

Shaphat son of Adlai was in charge of the herds in the valleys.

30 Obil the Ishmaelite was in charge of the camels.

Jehdeiah the Meronothite was in charge of the donkeys.

27:23 [d] 1Ch 21:2-5 [e] Ge 15:5
27:24 [f] 2Sa 24:15; 1Ch 21:7
27:28 [g] 1Ki 10:27; 2Ch 1:15

[a] *24* Septuagint; Hebrew *number*

27:16–24 The record notes Joab's aversion to the task of this census; it also reiterates God's judgment against David and Israel for the king's sin of equating political strength with the size of his military forces (2Sa 24:3, 10; cf. 1Ch 21:3, 7–8). Implicit in the reference to the Abrahamic covenant (27:23) is the sovereignty of God in "growing" Israel as a nation (cf. Ge 12:2). David has compromised his commitment to acknowledge God's rule over Israel.

27:25–31 Material wealth is not only necessary to offset expenditures of the centralized government, but it also enhances the king's prestige. Generally, the OT sees such wealth as a sign of God's blessing on the king's reign, although Moses' instruction was that the king not amass large treasuries (Dt 17:17).

31 Jaziz the Hagrite[h] was in charge of
the flocks.
All these were the officials in charge
of King David's property.

32 Jonathan, David's uncle, was a counselor, a man of insight and a scribe. Jehiel
son of Hakmoni took care of the king's
sons.
33 Ahithophel[i] was the king's counselor.
Hushai[j] the Arkite was the king's confidant. 34 Ahithophel was succeeded by Jehoiada son of Benaiah and by Abiathar.[k]
Joab[l] was the commander of the royal army.

David's Plans for the Temple

28 David summoned all the officials[m]
of Israel to assemble at Jerusa-
lem: the officers over the tribes, the commanders of the divisions in the service of
the king, the commanders of thousands
and commanders of hundreds, and the
officials in charge of all the property and
livestock belonging to the king and his
sons, together with the palace officials,
the warriors and all the brave fighting
men.
2 King David rose to his feet and said:
"Listen to me, my fellow Israelites, my
people. I had it in my heart[n] to build a
house as a place of rest for the ark of the
covenant of the LORD, for the footstool[o]
of our God, and I made plans to build
it. 3 But God said to me,[p] 'You are not to
build a house for my Name,[q] because
you are a warrior and have shed blood.'[r]
4 "Yet the LORD, the God of Israel, chose
me[s] from my whole family[t] to be king
over Israel forever. He chose Judah[u] as
leader, and from the tribe of Judah he
chose my family, and from my father's
sons he was pleased to make me king
over all Israel. 5 Of all my sons — and
the LORD has given me many[v] — he has
chosen my son Solomon[w] to sit on the
throne of the kingdom of the LORD over
Israel. 6 He said to me: 'Solomon your
son is the one who will build my house
and my courts, for I have chosen him
to be my son,[x] and I will be his father.
7 I will establish his kingdom forever if
he is unswerving in carrying out my
commands and laws,[y] as is being done
at this time.'
8 "So now I charge you in the sight of all
Israel and of the assembly of the LORD,
and in the hearing of our God: Be careful
to follow all the commands[z] of the LORD
your God, that you may possess this good
land and pass it on as an inheritance to
your descendants forever.[a]
9 "And you, my son Solomon, acknowledge the God of your father, and serve
him with wholehearted devotion[b] and
with a willing mind, for the LORD searches every heart[c] and understands every
desire and every thought. If you seek
him,[d] he will be found by you; but if you
forsake[e] him, he will reject[f] you forever.
10 Consider now, for the LORD has chosen
you to build a house as the sanctuary. Be
strong and do the work."

27:31 [h] 1Ch 5:10
27:33 [i] 2Sa 15:12 [j] 2Sa 15:37
27:34 [k] 1Ki 1:7 [l] 1Ch 11:6
28:1 [m] 1Ch 11:10; 27:1-31
28:2 [n] 1Ch 17:2 [o] Ps 99:5; 132:7
28:3 [p] 2Sa 7:5 [q] 1Ch 22:8 [r] 1Ki 5:3; 1Ch 17:4
28:4 [s] 1Ch 17:23, 27; 2Ch 6:6 [t] 1Sa 16:1-13 [u] Ge 49:10; 1Ch 5:2
28:5 [v] 1Ch 3:1 [w] 1Ch 22:9; 23:1
28:6 [x] 2Sa 7:13; 1Ch 22:9-10
28:7 [y] 1Ch 22:13
28:8 [z] Dt 6:1 [a] Dt 4:1
28:9 [b] 1Ch 29:19 [c] 1Sa 16:7; Ps 7:9 [d] Ps 40:16; Jer 29:13 [e] Jos 24:20; 2Ch 15:2 [f] Ps 44:23

1Ch 28:9 ❖ What does wholehearted devotion to God look like? How can we continue to seek God, as David encouraged Solomon to do?

27:32–34 It seems clear that the contents of the roster span the long reign of King David. Beyond recounting David's governmental organization, the real purpose of chs. 23–27 for the Chronicler is the important message that "all Israel" is behind the king in his plans to build the temple.
28:1–8 This group of leaders is probably distinct from the "whole assembly" in 29:1 since the "people" were a part of that larger gathering (see 29:9).
28:2–3 The expressions "house . . . of rest" for the temple and "footstool" for the ark of the covenant are found only in Ps 132 and Chronicles. Clearly, Ps 132 is important to the Chronicler because it contains reflections about David's restless ambition to build a sanctuary for God.
28:4–8 It is widely agreed that the next segment of David's speech to the officials of Israel serves to legitimize his dynasty. David traces his lineage to the tribe of Judah, the tribe given the "scepter" in Jacob's blessing of his sons (cf. Ge 49:8–12). The emphasis on Solomon as the "chosen . . . son" (v. 6) among David's children leads naturally to the understanding that God's kingdom and David's kingdom are inseparably linked. Perhaps most important as David passes the baton to his son Solomon, he exhorts Israel to look to God for their hope and help—not to himself or even to his dynasty (v. 8).
28:9–10 The public transfer of power accomplished "in the sight of all Israel" (v. 8) completes the succession ritual begun with David's private charge to his son (22:11–13).
28:10 The Chronicler's understanding of Solomon's divine election to the throne of his father is unusual in that he is the only OT writer to apply the word "chosen" to Solomon. Solomon's accession is also out of the ordinary in that he is not David's oldest living son and is therefore not the logical heir to the throne.

11 Then David gave his son Solomon
the plans[g] for the portico of the temple,
its buildings, its storerooms, its upper
parts, its inner rooms and the place of
atonement. 12 He gave him the plans of
all that the Spirit[h] had put in his mind
for the courts of the temple of the LORD
and all the surrounding rooms, for the
treasuries of the temple of God and for
the treasuries for the dedicated things.[i]
13 He gave him instructions for the divisions[j] of the priests and Levites, and for
all the work of serving in the temple of
the LORD, as well as for all the articles to
be used in its service. 14 He designated the
weight of gold for all the gold articles
to be used in various kinds of service,
and the weight of silver for all the silver
articles to be used in various kinds of
service: 15 the weight of gold for the gold
lampstands[k] and their lamps, with the
weight for each lampstand and its lamps;
and the weight of silver for each silver
lampstand and its lamps, according to
the use of each lampstand; 16 the weight
of gold for each table[l] for consecrated
bread; the weight of silver for the silver
tables; 17 the weight of pure gold for the
forks, sprinkling bowls[m] and pitchers;
the weight of gold for each gold dish;
the weight of silver for each silver dish;
18 and the weight of the refined gold for
the altar of incense.[n] He also gave him
the plan for the chariot,[o] that is, the cherubim of gold that spread their wings and
overshadow[p] the ark of the covenant of
the LORD.

28:11 [g] Ex 25:9
28:12 [h] 1Ch 12:18 [i] 1Ch 26:20
28:13 [j] 1Ch 24:1
28:15 [k] Ex 25:31
28:16 [l] Ex 25:23
28:17 [m] Ex 27:3
28:18 [n] Ex 30:1-10 [o] Ex 25:18-22 [p] Ex 25:20
28:19 [q] 1Ki 6:38 [r] Ex 25:9
28:20 [s] Dt 31:6; 1Ch 22:13; 2Ch 19:11; Hag 2:4 [t] Dt 4:31; Jos 24:20 [u] 1Ki 6:14; 2Ch 7:11
28:21 [v] Ex 35:25-36:5
29:1 [w] 1Ki 3:7; 1Ch 22:5; 2Ch 13:7
29:2 [x] ver 7, 14, 16; Ezr 1:4; 6:5; Hag 2:8 [y] Isa 54:11 [z] 1Ch 22:2-5

19 "All this," David said, "I have in writing as a result of the LORD's hand on me,
and he enabled me to understand all the
details[q] of the plan.[r]"
20 David also said to Solomon his son,
"Be strong and courageous,[s] and do the
work. Do not be afraid or discouraged,
for the LORD God, my God, is with you.
He will not fail you or forsake[t] you until
all the work for the service of the temple
of the LORD is finished.[u] 21 The divisions
of the priests and Levites are ready for
all the work on the temple of God, and
every willing person skilled[v] in any craft
will help you in all the work. The officials
and all the people will obey your every
command."

Gifts for Building the Temple

29 Then King David said to the whole
assembly: "My son Solomon, the
one whom God has chosen, is young and
inexperienced.[w] The task is great, because this palatial structure is not for
man but for the LORD God. 2 With all
my resources I have provided for the
temple of my God—gold[x] for the gold
work, silver for the silver, bronze for the
bronze, iron for the iron and wood for the
wood, as well as onyx for the settings,
turquoise,[a][y] stones of various colors, and
all kinds of fine stone and marble—all
of these in large quantities.[z] 3 Besides, in
my devotion to the temple of my God I

[a] *2* The meaning of the Hebrew for this word is uncertain.

28:11–21 The detailed instructions handed over to Solomon deal with temple architecture (vv. 11–12), temple personnel (v. 13), temple furnishings (vv. 14–19), and the final commissioning of Solomon as the crown prince (vv. 20–21). The influence of the tabernacle narrative is clearly evident in the vocabulary and theology of the passage. For the Chronicler, the temple is the continuation of all that the tabernacle represented in Israelite religion, and David plays a role similar to that of Moses as God's agent in establishing the institution.
28:11–19 The exact nature of the plans and instructions David gives to Solomon for the execution of the temple building project is unknown. It seems clear they are written plans, probably sketches or blueprints of sorts containing specific directions. The portico, the anterooms, and the courts are new elements in the construction plans, and they receive primary attention (v. 11). The two treasuries are prominently featured in the plans (v. 12), most likely because they were cited previously in connection with the duties of the Levites (26:22–28).
28:14–17 The gold and silver vessels are especially important to the Chronicler because they are among the goods the Persians returned to the Jews when they came back to Jerusalem after the Babylonian exile (cf. Ezr 1:7–11). Thus they connect temple worship from before and after the exile, but more importantly, they are tokens of God's faithfulness in preserving and restoring his covenant people.
28:20–21 It is significant that the third and final charge to Solomon as he is inducted into office mentions a supporting cast that includes the religious leaders, the various guilds of craftsmen, the political leaders, and all the people. The temple is to be a national response to the God of Israel by his covenant people—not a monument to King David.
29:1–5 This third speech to the people provides a way that the gathered listeners can demonstrate their devotion to God and their support for the crown prince Solomon—by sacrificially giving of their material resources to the temple building fund.
29:3 The phrase "personal treasures" is typically

now give my personal treasures of gold
and silver for the temple of my God, over
and above everything I have provided[a]
for this holy temple: 4three thousand talents[a] of gold (gold of Ophir)[b] and seven
thousand talents[b] of refined silver,[c] for
the overlaying of the walls of the buildings, 5for the gold work and the silver
work, and for all the work to be done
by the craftsmen. Now, who is willing
to consecrate themselves to the LORD
today?"
6Then the leaders of families, the officers of the tribes of Israel, the commanders of thousands and commanders of hundreds, and the officials[d] in
charge of the king's work gave willingly.[e] 7They[f] gave toward the work on the
temple of God five thousand talents[c]
and ten thousand darics[d] of gold, ten
thousand talents[e] of silver, eighteen
thousand talents[f] of bronze and a hundred thousand talents[g] of iron. 8Anyone
who had precious stones[g] gave them to
the treasury of the temple of the LORD
in the custody of Jehiel the Gershonite.[h] 9The people rejoiced at the willing response of their leaders, for they
had given freely and wholeheartedly[i] to

29:3 [a]2Ch 24:10; 31:3; 35:8 29:4 [b]Ge 10:29 [c]1Ch 22:14 29:6 [d]1Ch 27:1; 28:1 [e]ver 9; Ex 25:1-8; 35:20-29; 36:2; 2Ch 24:10; Ezr 7:15 29:7 [f]Ex 25:2; Ne 7:70-71 29:8 [g]Ex 35:27 [h]1Ch 26:21 29:9 [i]1Ki 8:61; 2Co 9:7 29:11 [j]Ps 24:8; 59:17; 62:11 [k]Ps 89:11

1Ch 29:10 ❖ How can we encourage and lead others to worship God?

the LORD. David the king also rejoiced
greatly.

David's Prayer

10David praised the LORD in the presence of the whole assembly, saying,

"Praise be to you, LORD,
the God of our father Israel,
from everlasting to everlasting.
11Yours, LORD, is the greatness and the
power[j]
and the glory and the majesty and
the splendor,
for everything in heaven and
earth is yours.[k]
Yours, LORD, is the kingdom;

[a] 4 That is, about 110 tons or about 100 metric tons [b] 4 That is, about 260 tons or about 235 metric tons [c] 7 That is, about 190 tons or about 170 metric tons [d] 7 That is, about 185 pounds or about 84 kilograms [e] 7 That is, about 380 tons or about 340 metric tons [f] 7 That is, about 675 tons or about 610 metric tons [g] 7 That is, about 3,800 tons or about 3,400 metric tons

---

used to describe Israel as God's "special possession." David's example of selflessly giving the wealth stored for his own personal security becomes the catalyst for others to generously give gifts.

29:4 The identification of the gold given by David as "gold of Ophir" probably refers as much to the quality of the gold as to its source of origin. As was true with the tabernacle, only the best of natural and human resources is to be given for the construction of Yahweh's earthly sanctuary.

29:5 "Gave willingly" introduces a key theme in the entire chapter (cf. vv. 5, 6, 9, 14, 17). The word often denotes freewill gifts and offerings—giving that is not required but is prompted by a willing heart or spirit.

29:6–9 The open-handed giving of Israelite leaders serves to inspire the people to give in a similar way.

✜ **21:1—29:9** Leadership is a matter of universal importance, and effective supervision is essential to the survival of any social group, political organization, or religious institution. No biblical character is more prominent as an example of leadership than King David, and a review of his intentional actions as leader can inspire us still today: (1) David had charisma. More important than his abilities, however, was the empowerment of the Holy Spirit in his life (1Sa 16:13). (2) David well understood the importance of vision, as demonstrated in his conquest of Jerusalem (2Sa 5:6-10). That victory legitimized King David and propelled Israel into nationhood. It also became the impetus for David's lifelong quest to build a sanctuary for Yahweh in the very city that God helped him capture (cf. 1Ch 22:1). (3) This section of 1Ch (21:1—29:9) offers an excellent illustration of David's ability to define the vision (i.e., build a house for Yahweh), structure the plan to accomplish the vision, and motivate others to implement and fulfill the vision. (4) David clearly understood the benefits of delegating authority to others as evidenced by his roster of cabinet appointees. (5) David shows us that a servant-leader can survive a grave mistake, an error of judgment, or a near fatal flaw because of God's mercy. (6) David's final acts of kingship included naming his successor and providing that individual with all the resources needed to carry on David's vision for Israel (cf. 21:1—29:9). Through his instructions to Solomon, David built a bridge to the future for all Israel to follow for several centuries beyond his own death.

29:10–12 David "blesses" God as an act of homage or reverence because God is the source of all blessing. David acknowledges that earthly human kingdoms can only thrive as they concede that all power, strength, honor, and wealth belong to God alone.

you are exalted as head over all.[l]
12 Wealth and honor[m] come from you;
you are the ruler[n] of all things.
In your hands are strength and
power
to exalt and give strength to all.
13 Now, our God, we give you thanks,
and praise your glorious name.

14 "But who am I, and who are my people, that we should be able to give as
generously as this? Everything comes
from you, and we have given you only
what comes from your hand. 15 We are
foreigners and strangers[o] in your sight,
as were all our ancestors. Our days on
earth are like a shadow,[p] without hope.
16 LORD our God, all this abundance that
we have provided for building you a
temple for your Holy Name comes from
your hand, and all of it belongs to you.
17 I know, my God, that you test the heart[q]
and are pleased with integrity. All these
things I have given willingly and with
honest intent. And now I have seen with
joy how willingly your people who are
here have given to you.[r] 18 LORD, the God
of our fathers Abraham, Isaac and Israel,
keep these desires and thoughts in the
hearts of your people forever, and keep
their hearts loyal to you. 19 And give my
son Solomon the wholehearted devotion[s] to keep your commands, statutes
and decrees[t] and to do everything to
build the palatial structure for which I
have provided."[u]

20 Then David said to the whole assembly, "Praise the LORD your God." So
they all praised the LORD, the God of
their fathers; they bowed down, prostrating themselves before the LORD and
the king.

Solomon Acknowledged as King

29:21–25pp // 1Ki 1:28–53

21 The next day they made sacrifices to the LORD and presented burnt
offerings to him:[v] a thousand bulls, a
thousand rams and a thousand male
lambs, together with their drink offerings, and other sacrifices in abundance
for all Israel. 22 They ate and drank with
great joy[w] in the presence of the LORD
that day.

Then they acknowledged Solomon son
of David as king a second time, anointing him before the LORD to be ruler and
Zadok[x] to be priest. 23 So Solomon sat on
the throne[y] of the LORD as king in place
of his father David. He prospered and all
Israel obeyed him. 24 All the officers and
warriors, as well as all of King David's
sons, pledged their submission to King
Solomon.

25 The LORD highly exalted Solomon
in the sight of all Israel and bestowed
on him royal splendor[z] such as no king
over Israel ever had before.[a]

The Death of David

29:26–28pp // 1Ki 2:10–12

26 David son of Jesse was king[b] over
all Israel. 27 He ruled over Israel forty
years — seven in Hebron and thirty-three
in Jerusalem.[c] 28 He died[d] at a good old
age, having enjoyed long life, wealth and
honor. His son Solomon succeeded him
as king.[e]
29 As for the events of King David's

29:11 [l] Rev 5:12-13
29:12 [m] 2Ch 1:12 [n] 2Ch 20:6; Ro 11:36
29:15 [o] Ps 39:12; Heb 11:13 [p] Job 14:2
29:17 [q] Ps 139:23; Pr 15:11; 17:3; Jer 11:20; 17:10 [r] 1Ch 28:9; Ps 15:1-5
29:19 [s] 1Ch 28:9 [t] Ps 72:1 [u] 1Ch 22:14
29:21 [v] 1Ki 8:62
29:22 [w] 1Ch 23:1 [x] 1Ki 1:33-39
29:23 [y] 1Ki 2:12
29:25 [z] 2Ch 1:1, 12 [a] 1Ki 3:13; Ecc 2:9
29:26 [b] 1Ch 18:14
29:27 [c] 2Sa 5:4-5; 1Ki 2:11; 1Ch 3:4
29:28 [d] Ge 15:15; Ac 13:36 [e] 1Ch 23:1

29:14–16 David appeals to the imagery of the resident alien to remind his audience that they are utterly dependent on God for their security and physical well-being.

29:17–19 The heart is crucial to physical and spiritual life. David petitions for his son Solomon, that he might exhibit "wholehearted devotion" (v. 19) by obeying the law of God.

29:20 The throne of Israel belongs to Yahweh, and to bow to the king is ultimately to bow to God, who has installed the king as his agent of justice and righteousness.

29:21–25 It seems likely this installation ceremony for King Solomon is the formal and public sequel to the earlier hurried and private appointment of Solomon as David's successor.

29:24–25 The stability of the Davidic throne was twice challenged by rivals within the royal family (2Sa 15–18; 1Ki 1). Solomon knows that such an oath of allegiance is crucial to the smooth transfer of power in the aftermath of Adonijah's attempted coup. The summary statement calls attention to the place of "all Israel" in this new regime, a key theme in Chronicles. It expresses both the totality of God's rule and the unity of the Israelites as God's people.

29:26–30 The Chronicler uses the phrase "son of Jesse" to remind his audience of the selection process by which David came to the throne of Israel (cf. 1Sa 16).

29:29 This chapter's recounting of Solomon as David's successor is a subtle reminder that, in Solomon, God has fulfilled his promise to the house of David through Nathan the prophet. The citation to the records of the prophets Samuel, Nathan, and Gad probably refers to the books of Samuel and Kings and perhaps an additional source available to the Chronicler. The record of David's reign is based reliably on the authoritative word of God's prophets.

reign, from beginning to end, they are
written in the records of Samuel the seer,[f]
the records of Nathan[g] the prophet and
the records of Gad[h] the seer, 30together
with the details of his reign and power,
and the circumstances that surrounded
him and Israel and the kingdoms of all
the other lands.

29:29 [f] 1Sa 9:9 [g] 2Sa 7:2 [h] 1Sa 22:5

29:10–30 Social critics have observed that the American right to pursue happiness in the form of instant emotional "fixes" has created a society addicted to fun but lacking joy. The Chronicler's report that the people of Israel "ate and drank with great joy in the presence of the LORD" at the coronation of King Solomon (29:22) interestingly reflects the thematic structure of the psalm of lament. These psalms typically conclude with a "vow of praise" that testifies that God is sovereign in human circumstance (i.e., Yahweh has the ability to change the situation if he wills to intervene) and points to the goodness of God's character (i.e., recognizing that God is good whether or not he chooses to intervene and remedy a situation). In reflecting these truths, the Chronicler affirms the theological truth that joy is connected to the person and presence of God (cf. 16:27).

2 Chronicles

Author: Unknown

Audience: The people of Judah who had returned from exile in Babylon

Date: Between 450 and 400 BC

Theme: Chronicles encourages postexilic Israel with an account focused on God's promises to faithful Davidic kings (especially David and Solomon) ensuring Israel's future.

Reading 2 Chronicles

Flowing as a chronological record of the kings of Judah from Solomon on, the unique feature of this book is its full description of the reigns of those kings who did right in the eyes of the Lord; those who did evil receive relatively little comment.

PERSPECTIVE

Second Chronicles begins with Solomon's reign of the united kingdom. His rule includes the construction and dedication of the temple (chs. 2–7). Upon Solomon's death (ch. 9), the narrative turns to describe the long history of the divided kingdom and the eventual demise of both kingdoms. The last chapter in the book details the fall of Jerusalem (36:15–21).

See also the Introduction to 1 Chronicles for more perspective on the books of 1–2 Chronicles.

TAKING THE NEXT STEPS

The author of the book of 2 Chronicles (probably Ezra; see Introduction to 1 Chronicles) continues his history of the nation of Judah from the reign of King Solomon to the exile into Babylon and the return to Canaan. Again, his goal was to inspire the small band of discouraged Jews who had returned to the promised land. He assured them that from God's standpoint, they were the true Israel of God. He stressed for them the continuity of the stories of their lives in the present with the stories of God's people in the past, particularly in the three most important elements of Israelite worship: temple, music, and law. Finally, he reminded them of one of the most important principles that God operates on: If they truly depended on the Lord, he would intervene in even the most hopeless of circumstances and rescue them from the dangers that confronted them.

	1400 BC	1300	1200	1100	1000	900	800	700	600	500	400
Solomon's reign (970–930 BC)											
Building of the temple (966–959 BC)											
Division of the kingdom (930 BC)											
Exile of Israel (722 BC)											
Fall of Jerusalem (586 BC)											
First return of exiles to Jerusalem (538 BC)											
Completion of temple (516 BC)											
Book of 2 Chronicles written (c. 450–400 BC)											

In addition to the practical applications noted for the book of 1 Chronicles, we can see several others. (1) When we note how often reforms were necessary because of idolatry in the nation of Judah, we realize how easy it is to depart from the Lord. In fact, if we are not growing in our faith, we are probably sliding backward. (2) True success in life ought never to be defined in terms of how many goods we have accumulated, but by our commitment to and relationship with the Lord. (3) One of the most important qualities that God looks for in us is humility.

Key Verse

If my people, who are called by my name, will humble themselves and pray and seek my face and turn from their wicked ways, then I will hear from heaven, and I will forgive their sin and will heal their land.

—2 Chronicles 7:14

WHAT TO LOOK FOR IN 2 CHRONICLES

- Solomon builds the temple (chs. 1–9)
- Rehoboam and the dividing of the kingdom (chs. 10–12)
- Abijah and his victory over Jeroboam (ch. 13)
- Asa and his reforms (chs. 14–16)
- Jehoshaphat and his miraculous victory over Moab (chs. 17; 19–20)
- Joash and his repair of the temple (chs. 23–24)
- Uzziah and Judah in its glory (ch. 26)
- Hezekiah and the destruction of Sennacherib (chs. 29–32)
- Josiah and the rediscovery of the law (chs. 34–35)

Solomon Asks for Wisdom

1:2–13pp // 1Ki 3:4–15
1:14–17pp // 1Ki 10:26–29; 2Ch 9:25–28

1 Solomon son of David established[a]
himself firmly over his kingdom, for
the LORD his God was with[b] him and
made him exceedingly great.[c]
2Then Solomon spoke to all Israel[d]—
to the commanders of thousands and
commanders of hundreds, to the judges
and to all the leaders in Israel, the heads
of families— 3and Solomon and the
whole assembly went to the high place
at Gibeon, for God's tent of meeting[e] was
there, which Moses[f] the LORD's servant
had made in the wilderness. 4Now David had brought up the ark[g] of God from
Kiriath Jearim to the place he had prepared for it, because he had pitched a
tent[h] for it in Jerusalem. 5But the bronze
altar[i] that Bezalel[j] son of Uri, the son of
Hur, had made was in Gibeon in front of
the tabernacle of the LORD; so Solomon
and the assembly inquired[k] of him there.
6Solomon went up to the bronze altar before the LORD in the tent of meeting and
offered a thousand burnt offerings on it.
7That night God appeared[l] to Solomon
and said to him, "Ask for whatever you
want me to give you."
8Solomon answered God, "You have
shown great kindness to David my father
and have made me[m] king in his place.
9Now, LORD God, let your promise[n] to
my father David be confirmed, for you
have made me king over a people who
are as numerous as the dust of the earth.[o]
10Give me wisdom and knowledge, that
I may lead[p] this people, for who is able
to govern this great people of yours?"
11God said to Solomon, "Since this is
your heart's desire and you have not
asked for wealth,[q] possessions or honor,
nor for the death of your enemies, and
since you have not asked for a long life
but for wisdom and knowledge to govern
my people over whom I have made you
king, 12therefore wisdom and knowledge
will be given you. And I will also give you
wealth, possessions and honor,[r] such as
no king who was before you ever had
and none after you will have.[s]"
13Then Solomon went to Jerusalem
from the high place at Gibeon, from before the tent of meeting. And he reigned
over Israel.
14Solomon accumulated chariots[t] and
horses; he had fourteen hundred chariots and twelve thousand horses,[a] which
he kept in the chariot cities and also with
him in Jerusalem. 15The king made silver and gold[u] as common in Jerusalem
as stones, and cedar as plentiful as sycamore-fig trees in the foothills. 16Solo-
mon's horses were imported from Egypt
and from Kue[b]—the royal merchants
purchased them from Kue at the current
price. 17They imported a chariot[v] from
Egypt for six hundred shekels[c] of silver,
and a horse for a hundred and fifty.[d] They
also exported them to all the kings of the
Hittites and of the Arameans.

1:1 [a] 1Ki 2:12, 26; 2Ch 12:1 [b] Ge 21:22; 39:2; Nu 14:43 [c] 1Ch 29:25
1:2 [d] 1Ch 9:1; 28:1
1:3 [e] Ex 36:8 [f] Ex 40:18
1:4 [g] 2Sa 6:2; 1Ch 15:25 [h] 2Sa 6:17; 1Ch 15:1
1:5 [i] Ex 38:2 [j] Ex 31:2 [k] 1Ch 13:3
1:7 [l] 2Ch 7:12
1:8 [m] 1Ch 23:1; 28:5
1:9 [n] 2Sa 7:25; 1Ki 8:25 [o] Ge 12:2
1:10 [p] Nu 27:17; 2Sa 5:2; Pr 8:15-16
1:11 [q] Dt 17:17
1:12 [r] 1Ch 29:12 [s] 1Ch 29:25; 2Ch 9:22; Ne 13:26
1:14 [t] 1Sa 8:11; 1Ki 4:26; 9:19
1:15 [u] 1Ki 9:28; Isa 60:5
1:17 [v] SS 1:9

2Ch 1:12 ❖ When we ask for the right things, God often gives more than we ask for (see Mt 6:33). How have you experienced God's generous heart?

[a] 14 Or *charioteers* [b] 16 Probably Cilicia
[c] 17 That is, about 15 pounds or about 6.9 kilograms [d] 17 That is, about 3 3/4 pounds or about 1.7 kilograms

1:1–6 Solomon begins his rule over Israel with an act of public worship. In terms of biblical chronology, Solomon's accession to David's throne occurs around 970 BC. Solomon's petition for wisdom and knowledge (v. 10) is rooted in his worship experience before Bezalel's altar (cf. Ex 38:1–2). It is clear that in identifying Solomon as a "second Bezalel," the Chronicler understands that the greatest demonstration of Solomon's wisdom is building the temple itself.

1:7–13 Here Solomon is a model of how the righteous should pray because he first inquires of or seeks God. He then couches his prayer in the history of God's "great kindness" to David (v. 8), acknowledging that the Lord has indeed proven himself as a good God. Next, Solomon voices his humility and dependence on God in his rhetorical question, "Who is able to govern this great people of yours?" (v. 10). Beyond this, Solomon seeks spiritual blessing over material blessing when he asks God for wisdom and knowledge to rule instead of personal wealth and riches (vv. 10–11).

1:13 The summary statement "and he reigned over Israel" reconnects the Gibeon experience with Solomon's efforts to establish himself as king in Israel. The Chronicler wants his audience to understand a cause-and-effect relationship between Solomon's worship of God and his firm rule of Israel.

1:14–17 The Chronicler's rationale for framing the story of Solomon with the description of the staggering wealth possessed by the king is to demonstrate God's faithfulness in fulfilling his promise cited in v. 12. Implicit in the reference to the size of Solomon's vast wealth is the idea of God's favor resting on a faithful king.

Preparations for Building the Temple

2:1–18pp // 1Ki 5:1–16

2[a] Solomon gave orders to build a temple[w] for the Name of the LORD and a
royal palace for himself.[x] 2 He conscripted 70,000 men as carriers and 80,000
as stonecutters in the hills and 3,600 as
foremen over them.[y]

3 Solomon sent this message to Hiram[bz] king of Tyre:

"Send me cedar logs[a] as you did
for my father David when you sent
him cedar to build a palace to live in.
4 Now I am about to build a temple[b]
for the Name of the LORD my God
and to dedicate it to him for burning fragrant incense[c] before him, for
setting out the consecrated bread[d]
regularly, and for making burnt offerings[e] every morning and evening
and on the Sabbaths,[f] at the New
Moons and at the appointed festivals of the LORD our God. This is a
lasting ordinance for Israel.

5 "The temple I am going to build
will be great,[g] because our God is
greater than all other gods.[h] 6 But
who is able to build a temple for
him, since the heavens, even the
highest heavens, cannot contain
him?[i] Who then am I[j] to build a temple for him, except as a place to burn
sacrifices before him?

7 "Send me, therefore, a man skilled
to work in gold and silver, bronze and
iron, and in purple, crimson and blue
yarn, and experienced in the art of
engraving, to work in Judah and Jerusalem with my skilled workers,[k]
whom my father David provided.

8 "Send me also cedar, juniper and
algum[c] logs from Lebanon, for I know
that your servants are skilled in cutting timber there. My servants will
work with yours 9 to provide me with
plenty of lumber, because the temple
I build must be large and magnificent. 10 I will give your servants, the
woodsmen who cut the timber, twenty thousand cors[d] of ground wheat,
twenty thousand cors[e] of barley,
twenty thousand baths[f] of wine and
twenty thousand baths of olive oil.[l]"

11 Hiram king of Tyre replied by letter
to Solomon:

"Because the LORD loves[m] his people, he has made you their king."

12 And Hiram added:

"Praise be to the LORD, the God
of Israel, who made heaven and
earth![n] He has given King David a
wise son, endowed with intelligence
and discernment, who will build a
temple for the LORD and a palace
for himself.

13 "I am sending you Huram-Abi,[o]
a man of great skill, 14 whose mother
was from Dan[p] and whose father was
from Tyre. He is trained[q] to work
in gold and silver, bronze and iron,
stone and wood, and with purple
and blue[r] and crimson yarn and fine
linen. He is experienced in all kinds
of engraving and can execute any
design given to him. He will work
with your skilled workers and with
those of my lord, David your father.

15 "Now let my lord send his servants the wheat and barley and the
olive oil[s] and wine he promised,
16 and we will cut all the logs from
Lebanon that you need and will float
them as rafts by sea down to Joppa.[t] You can then take them up to
Jerusalem."

2:1 [w] Dt 12:5 [x] Ecc 2:4
2:2 [y] ver 18; 2Ch 10:4
2:3 [z] 2Sa 5:11 [a] 1Ch 14:1
2:4 [b] ver 1; Dt 12:5 [c] Ex 30:7 [d] Ex 25:30 [e] Ex 29:42; 2Ch 13:11 [f] Nu 28:9-10
2:5 [g] 1Ch 22:5; Ps 135:5 [h] 1Ch 16:25
2:6 [i] 1Ki 8:27; 2Ch 6:18; Jer 23:24 [j] Ex 3:11
2:7 [k] ver 13-14; Ex 35:31; 1Ch 22:16
2:10 [l] Ezr 3:7
2:11 [m] 1Ki 10:9; 2Ch 9:8
2:12 [n] Ne 9:6; Ps 8:3; 33:6; 102:25
2:13 [o] 1Ki 7:13
2:14 [p] Ex 31:6 [q] Ex 35:31 [r] Ex 35:35
2:15 [s] ver 10; Ezr 3:7
2:16 [t] Jos 19:46; Jnh 1:3

2Ch 2:6 ❖ How does Solomon's statement result in awe of the fact that God chooses to dwell within his people by his Spirit (see 1Co 6:19)?

[a] In Hebrew texts 2:1 is numbered 1:18, and 2:2-18 is numbered 2:1-17. [b] *3* Hebrew *Huram,* a variant of *Hiram;* also in verses 11 and 12 [c] *8* Probably a variant of *almug* [d] *10* That is, probably about 3,600 tons or about 3,200 metric tons of wheat [e] *10* That is, probably about 3,000 tons or about 2,700 metric tons of barley [f] *10* That is, about 120,000 gallons or about 440,000 liters

2:1–18 The Chronicler understands Solomon's building campaign as a two-phased undertaking—the "temple for the Name of the LORD" (v. 1) and his own royal palace. The actual construction of the temple begins in the fourth year of Solomon's reign (c. 966 BC; cf. 1Ki 6:1) and is completed six years later (960 BC).

2:3–9 In return for raw building materials, Solomon will provide Hiram with supplies of wheat, barley, honey, and olive oil (v. 10). The more interesting features of the correspondence are the synopsis of temple worship (v. 4) and theological treatise (vv. 5–6) Solomon offers the Phoenician king.

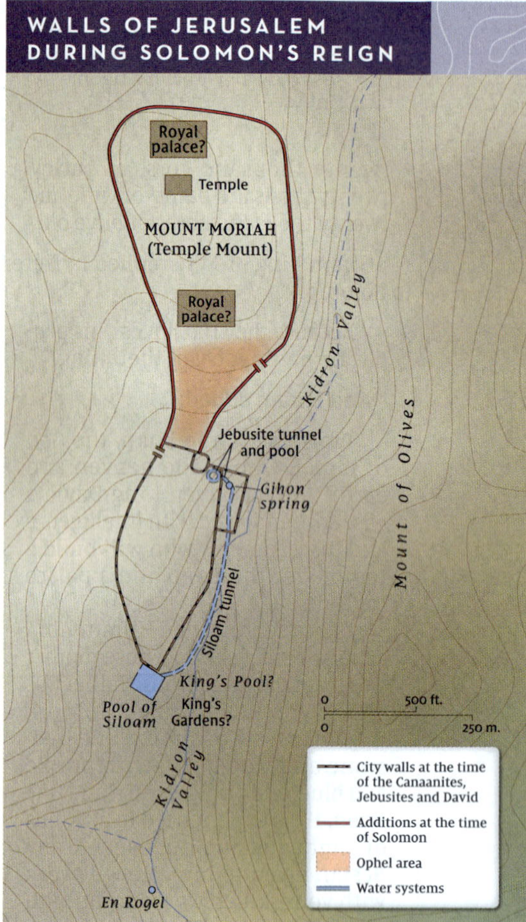

[17]Solomon took a census of all the foreigners[u] residing in Israel, after the census[v] his father David had taken; and they
were found to be 153,600. [18]He assigned[w]
70,000 of them to be carriers and 80,000
to be stonecutters in the hills, with 3,600
foremen over them to keep the people
working.

2:17 [u]1Ch 22:2 [v]2Sa 24:2
2:18 [w]ver 2; 1Ch 22:2; 2Ch 8:8
3:1 [x]Ac 7:47 [y]Ge 28:17 [z]2Sa 24:18; 1Ch 21:18
3:2 [a]Ezr 5:11

2Ch 3:1 ❖ Mount Moriah was the location Abraham went to sacrifice Isaac before God stopped him and provided a substitute for the sacrifice (see Ge 22). Why might it be significant that Solomon built God's temple at this location?

Solomon Builds the Temple

3:1–14pp // 1Ki 6:1–29

3 Then Solomon began to build[x] the
temple of the LORD[y] in Jerusalem on
Mount Moriah, where the LORD had appeared to his father David. It was on the
threshing floor of Araunah[a][z] the Jebusite,
the place provided by David. [2]He began
building on the second day of the second
month in the fourth year of his reign.[a]
[3]The foundation Solomon laid for
building the temple of God was sixty
cubits long and twenty cubits wide[b][b] (using the cubit of the old standard). [4]The
portico at the front of the temple was
twenty cubits[c] long across the width of
the building and twenty[d] cubits high.
He overlaid the inside with pure gold.
[5]He paneled the main hall with juniper and covered it with fine gold and
decorated it with palm tree[c] and chain
designs. [6]He adorned the temple with
precious stones. And the gold he used
was gold of Parvaim. [7]He overlaid the
ceiling beams, doorframes, walls and
doors of the temple with gold, and he
carved cherubim[d] on the walls.

[a] *1* Hebrew *Ornan,* a variant of *Araunah*
[b] *3* That is, about 90 feet long and 30 feet wide or about 27 meters long and 9 meters wide
[c] *4* That is, about 30 feet or about 9 meters; also in verses 8, 11 and 13
[d] *4* Some Septuagint and Syriac manuscripts; Hebrew *and a hundred and twenty*

3:3 [b]Eze 41:2 3:5 [c]Eze 40:16 3:7 [d]Ge 3:24; 1Ki 6:29-35; Eze 41:18

2:17–18 The census of Solomon's labor force clarifies the earlier report of the numbers of workers conscripted for the temple and palace building projects (v. 2). This census clearly followed the ill-fated numbering of Israel by David (v. 17b).

3:1–17 The building of Yahweh's temple at Mount Moriah fulfills the plans made by David for the structure in the purchase of Araunah's threshing floor (v. 1; cf. 1Ch 21:25–26). The reference to Mount Moriah awakens memories of the Lord's appearance to Abraham at the near sacrifice of his son Isaac (cf. Ge 22).

3:3 The dimensions of Solomon's temple rendered in contemporary measurements are as follows: The sanctuary proper is 90 feet long, 30 feet wide, and 45 feet high (with the Holy Place measuring 60′ × 30′ by 45′ and the Most Holy Place measuring 30′ × 30′ × 45′); the porch or portico extends the temple by another 15 feet in length (i.e., 30′ wide × 30′ high). The walls of the portico are overlaid with gold (3:4b), not only enhancing the beauty of the entrance but having the practical effect of reflecting light into the building.

3:5–7 The combination of extensive gold overlay and the presence of the cherubim represent the beauty and majesty of a royal throne room, a fitting dwelling place for the Lord. The repeated artistic motifs of the palm tree and the chain design may represent the ideas of life and eternality—the domains of God as creator.

3:8–14 Like the cherubim that guarded the entrance to the garden after the fall (Ge 3:24), these crea-

8 He built the Most Holy Place,[e] its length corresponding to the width of the temple — twenty cubits long and twenty cubits wide. He overlaid the inside with six hundred talents[a] of fine gold. 9 The gold nails[f] weighed fifty shekels.[b] He also overlaid the upper parts with gold.

10 For the Most Holy Place he made a pair[g] of sculptured cherubim and overlaid them with gold. 11 The total wingspan of the cherubim was twenty cubits. One wing of the first cherub was five cubits[c] long and touched the temple wall, while its other wing, also five cubits long, touched the wing of the other cherub. 12 Similarly one wing of the second cherub was five cubits long and touched the other temple wall, and its other wing, also five cubits long, touched the wing of the first cherub. 13 The wings of these cherubim[h] extended twenty cubits. They stood on their feet, facing the main hall.[d]

14 He made the curtain[i] of blue, purple and crimson yarn and fine linen, with cherubim[j] worked into it.

15 For the front of the temple he made two pillars,[k] which together were thirty-five cubits[e] long, each with a capital[l] five cubits high. 16 He made interwoven chains[f][m] and put them on top of the pillars. He also made a hundred pomegranates[n] and attached them to the chains. 17 He erected the pillars in the front of the temple, one to the south and one to the north. The one to the south he named Jakin[g] and the one to the north Boaz.[h]

The Temple's Furnishings

4:2–6,10—5:1pp // 1Ki 7:23–26,38–51

4 He made a bronze altar[o] twenty cubits long, twenty cubits wide and ten cubits high.[i] 2 He made the Sea[p] of cast metal, circular in shape, measuring ten cubits from rim to rim and five cubits[j] high. It took a line of thirty cubits[k] to measure around it. 3 Below the rim, figures of bulls encircled it — ten to a cubit.[l] The bulls were cast in two rows in one piece with the Sea.

> **2Ch 4:11** ❖ How can we use our skills to serve God in our faith community?

4 The Sea stood on twelve bulls, three facing north, three facing west, three facing south and three facing east.[q] The Sea rested on top of them, and their hindquarters were toward the center. 5 It was a handbreadth[m] in thickness, and its rim was like the rim of a cup, like a lily blossom. It held three thousand baths.[n]

6 He then made ten basins[r] for washing and placed five on the south side and five on the north. In them the things to be used for the burnt offerings[s] were rinsed, but the Sea was to be used by the priests for washing.

7 He made ten gold lampstands[t] according to the specifications[u] for them and placed them in the temple, five on the south side and five on the north.

8 He made ten tables[v] and placed them in the temple, five on the south side and five on the north. He also made a hundred gold sprinkling bowls.[w]

9 He made the courtyard[x] of the priests, and the large court and the doors for the court, and overlaid the doors with bronze. 10 He placed the Sea on the south side, at the southeast corner.

11 And Huram also made the pots and shovels and sprinkling bowls.

So Huram finished[y] the work he had

3:8 [e] Ex 26:33
3:9 [f] Ex 26:32
3:10 [g] Ex 25:18
3:13 [h] Ex 25:18
3:14 [i] Ex 26:31, 33; Heb 9:3 [j] Ge 3:24
3:15 [k] 1Ki 7:15; Rev 3:12 [l] 1Ki 7:22
3:16 [m] 1Ki 7:17 [n] 1Ki 7:20
4:1 [o] Ex 20:24; 27:1-2; 40:6; 1Ki 8:64; 2Ki 16:14
4:2 [p] Rev 4:6; 15:2
4:4 [q] Nu 2:3-25; Eze 48:30-34; Rev 21:13
4:6 [r] Ex 30:18 [s] Ne 13:5,9; Eze 40:38
4:7 [t] Ex 25:31 [u] Ex 25:40
4:8 [v] Ex 25:23 [w] Nu 4:14
4:9 [x] 1Ki 6:36; 2Ki 21:5; 2Ch 33:5
4:11 [y] 1Ki 7:14

[a] *8* That is, about 23 tons or about 21 metric tons
[b] *9* That is, about 1 1/4 pounds or about 575 grams
[c] *11* That is, about 7 1/2 feet or about 2.3 meters; also in verse 15
[d] *13* Or *facing inward*
[e] *15* That is, about 53 feet or about 16 meters
[f] *16* Or possibly *made chains in the inner sanctuary*; the meaning of the Hebrew for this phrase is uncertain.
[g] *17* *Jakin* probably means *he establishes.*
[h] *17* *Boaz* probably means *in him is strength.*
[i] *1* That is, about 30 feet long and wide and 15 feet high or about 9 meters long and wide and 4.5 meters high
[j] *2* That is, about 7 1/2 feet or about 2.3 meters
[k] *2* That is, about 45 feet or about 14 meters
[l] *3* That is, about 18 inches or about 45 centimeters
[m] *5* That is, about 3 inches or about 7.5 centimeters
[n] *5* That is, about 18,000 gallons or about 66,000 liters

---

tures guard the ark of the covenant eventually installed in the Most Holy Place (2Ch 5:7–8). A veil woven of blue, purple, and scarlet yarn separated the Holy Place from the Most Holy Place in the Mosaic tabernacle (Ex 26:31–36).

3:15–17 As with the veil, the bronze pillars in the front of the temple are given separate attention. Jakin means "it is firm" or "he establishes," and Boaz may mean "in strength."

4:1—5:1 The Sea of cast metal (4:2–5) replaces the laver of the Mosaic tabernacle (cf. Ex 30:17–21). It holds about 11,000 gallons. The ten golden lampstands replace the one lampstand featured in the Mosaic tabernacle (4:7; cf. Ex 25:31–36). The Chronicler seems to assume that the ten lampstands rest on ten tables. The summary of Huram-Abi's achievements (4:11–16) completes the record of the skilled smiths sent by King Hiram of Tyre (2:13–14).

undertaken for King Solomon in the
temple of God:

[12]the two pillars;
the two bowl-shaped capitals on top of the pillars;
the two sets of network decorating the two bowl-shaped capitals on top of the pillars;
[13]the four hundred pomegranates for the two sets of network (two rows of pomegranates for each network, decorating the bowl-shaped capitals on top of the pillars);
[14]the stands[z] with their basins;
[15]the Sea and the twelve bulls under it;
[16]the pots, shovels, meat forks and all related articles.

All the objects that Huram-Abi[a] made
for King Solomon for the temple of the
LORD were of polished bronze. [17]The
king had them cast in clay molds in the
plain of the Jordan between Sukkoth[b]
and Zarethan.[a] [18]All these things that
Solomon made amounted to so much
that the weight of the bronze[c] could not
be calculated.

[19]Solomon also made all the furnishings that were in God's temple:

the golden altar;
the tables[d] on which was the bread of the Presence;
[20]the lampstands[e] of pure gold with their lamps, to burn in front of the inner sanctuary as prescribed;
[21]the gold floral work and lamps and tongs (they were solid gold);
[22]the pure gold wick trimmers, sprinkling bowls, dishes[f] and censers;[g] and the gold doors of the temple: the inner doors to the Most Holy Place and the doors of the main hall.

5 When all the work Solomon had done
for the temple of the LORD was finished,[h] he brought in the things his father David had dedicated[i] — the silver
and gold and all the furnishings — and
he placed them in the treasuries of God's
temple.

The Ark Brought to the Temple

5:2—6:11pp // 1Ki 8:1–21

[2]Then Solomon summoned to Jerusalem the elders of Israel, all the heads
of the tribes and the chiefs of the Israelite families, to bring up the ark[j] of the
LORD's covenant from Zion, the City of
David. [3]And all the Israelites[k] came together to the king at the time of the festival in the seventh month.

[4]When all the elders of Israel had arrived, the Levites took up the ark, [5]and
they brought up the ark and the tent of
meeting and all the sacred furnishings
in it. The Levitical priests[l] carried them
up; [6]and King Solomon and the entire assembly of Israel that had gathered about
him were before the ark, sacrificing so
many sheep and cattle that they could
not be recorded or counted.

[7]The priests then brought the ark[m] of
the LORD's covenant to its place in the
inner sanctuary of the temple, the Most
Holy Place, and put it beneath the wings
of the cherubim. [8]The cherubim[n] spread
their wings over the place of the ark and
covered the ark and its carrying poles.
[9]These poles were so long that their ends,
extending from the ark, could be seen
from in front of the inner sanctuary, but
not from outside the Holy Place; and they
are still there today. [10]There was nothing
in the ark except[o] the two tablets[p] that
Moses had placed in it at Horeb, where
the LORD made a covenant with the Israelites after they came out of Egypt.

[11]The priests then withdrew from the
Holy Place. All the priests who were there
had consecrated themselves, regardless
of their divisions.[q] [12]All the Levites who
were musicians[r] — Asaph, Heman, Jeduthun and their sons and relatives — stood
on the east side of the altar, dressed in

4:14 [z]1Ki 7:27-30
4:16 [a]1Ki 7:13
4:17 [b]Ge 33:17
4:18 [c]1Ki 7:23
4:19 [d]Ex 25:23, 30
4:20 [e]Ex 25:31
4:22 [f]Nu 7:14 [g]Lev 10:1
5:1 [h]1Ki 6:14 [i]2Sa 8:11
5:2 [j]Nu 3:31; 2Sa 6:12; 1Ch 15:25
5:3 [k]1Ch 9:1; 2Ch 7:8-10
5:5 [l]Nu 3:31; 1Ch 15:2
5:7 [m]Rev 11:19
5:8 [n]Ge 3:24
5:10 [o]Heb 9:4 [p]Ex 16:34; Dt 10:2
5:11 [q]1Ch 24:1
5:12 [r]1Ki 10:12; 1Ch 25:1; Ps 68:25

a 17 Hebrew *Zeredatha,* a variant of *Zarethan*

5:1 The reference to the deposit of David's war plunder in the temple treasuries serves as a transition to the account of the installation of the ark of the covenant.
5:2—6:2 The transfer of the ark of the covenant comes almost verbatim from 1Ki 8:1-13. The installation of the ark and the dedication of the temple are held in conjunction with the Festival of Tabernacles (v. 3). The rest of the sacred furniture from the tent of meeting, as well as the tent itself, is also transported to the temple precinct (vv. 4-5).
5:6-10 The reference to the tablets of Moses as the only contents of the ark of the covenant indicates that the Chronicler is familiar with the tradition that the ark held additional contents at one time.
5:11-13 The reference to the Levitical musicians reflects the Chronicler's special interest in the musical tradition of the temple.

fine linen and playing cymbals, harps
and lyres. They were accompanied by
120 priests sounding trumpets.[s] 13The
trumpeters and musicians joined in
unison to give praise and thanks to the
LORD. Accompanied by trumpets, cymbals and other instruments, the singers
raised their voices in praise to the LORD
and sang:

"He is good;
his love endures forever."[t]

Then the temple of the LORD was filled
with the cloud, 14and the priests could
not perform[u] their service because of the
cloud,[v] for the glory[w] of the LORD filled
the temple of God.

6 Then Solomon said, "The LORD has
said that he would dwell in a dark
cloud;[x] 2I have built a magnificent temple for you, a place for you to dwell forever.[y]"

3While the whole assembly of Israel was standing there, the king turned
around and blessed them. 4Then he said:

"Praise be to the LORD, the God
of Israel, who with his hands has
fulfilled what he promised with his
mouth to my father David. For he
said, 5'Since the day I brought my
people out of Egypt, I have not chosen a city in any tribe of Israel to
have a temple built so that my Name
might be there, nor have I chosen
anyone to be ruler over my people
Israel. 6But now I have chosen Jerusalem[z] for my Name[a] to be there,
and I have chosen David[b] to rule my
people Israel.'

7"My father David had it in his
heart[c] to build a temple for the

5:12 [s]1Ch 13:8; 15:24
5:13 [t]1Ch 16:34, 41; 2Ch 7:3; 20:21; Ezr 3:11; Ps 100:5; 136:1; Jer 33:11
5:14 [u]Ex 40:35; Rev 15:8 [v]Ex 19:16 [w]Ex 29:43; 2Ch 7:2
6:1 [x]Ex 19:9; 1Ki 8:12-50
6:2 [y]Ezr 6:12; 7:15; Ps 135:21
6:6 [z]Dt 12:5; Isa 14:1 [a]Ex 20:24; 2Ch 12:13 [b]1Ch 28:4
6:7 [c]1Sa 10:7; 1Ch 17:2; 28:2; Ac 7:46
6:11 [d]Dt 10:2; 2Ch 5:10; Ps 25:10; 50:5
6:13 [e]Ne 8:4 [f]Ps 95:6

2Ch 5:13-14 ❖ When have we felt the powerful presence of God during worship?

Name of the LORD, the God of Israel. 8But the LORD said to my father
David, 'You did well to have it in
your heart to build a temple for my
Name. 9Nevertheless, you are not
the one to build the temple, but your
son, your own flesh and blood — he
is the one who will build the temple
for my Name.'

10"The LORD has kept the promise
he made. I have succeeded David my
father and now I sit on the throne
of Israel, just as the LORD promised,
and I have built the temple for the
Name of the LORD, the God of Israel. 11There I have placed the ark, in
which is the covenant[d] of the LORD
that he made with the people of Israel."

Solomon's Prayer of Dedication

6:12–40pp // 1Ki 8:22–53
6:41–42pp // Ps 132:8–10

12Then Solomon stood before the altar
of the LORD in front of the whole assembly of Israel and spread out his hands.
13Now he had made a bronze platform,[e]
five cubits long, five cubits wide and
three cubits high,[a] and had placed it in
the center of the outer court. He stood
on the platform and then knelt down[f]
before the whole assembly of Israel and
spread out his hands toward heaven. 14He
said:

[a] 13 That is, about 7 1/2 feet long and wide and 4 1/2 feet high or about 2.3 meters long and wide and 1.4 meters high

---

5:14 This account of the event is told from a priestly perspective in terms of their service rendered in the temple. Later the event is retold from the perspective of Solomon and the assembly of Israel (7:1–2).
6:3–11 Like his father David, Solomon assumes a priestly or pastoral role when addressing the nation of Israel (cf. 1Ch 16:43).
6:4–6 The reference to the "God of Israel" and the repetition of the word "chosen" allude to the Abrahamic covenant (Ge 12:1–3). The allusion to the exodus reveals that Solomon understands the continuity between the Mosaic covenant and the Davidic covenant. Finally, the acknowledgment that Jerusalem is now the place identified with God's "Name" (v. 6) demonstrates Solomon's awareness of the teaching of Deuteronomy concerning an eventual permanent worship site in Israel (cf. Dt 12:11, 21).
6:7–11 The second half of Solomon's address to the people of Israel is basically a prayer of thanksgiving, acknowledging God as a promise keeper.
6:12–42 The fact that Solomon's prayer occupies more text than the account of the actual construction of the temple further substantiates the argument that the Chronicler is making a theological statement to his own audience: Prayer is central in the life of the postexilic community.
6:12–13 The opening paragraph lists the preparations undertaken by Solomon for his dedicatory prayer for the Jerusalem temple. The backdrop of the bronze altar of burnt offering for the prayer of dedication points to the idea that prayer is also a form of sacrifice.
6:14–17 The threefold repetition of God's covenant name, "LORD, the God of Israel" (vv. 14, 16, 17),

"LORD, the God of Israel, there is
no God like you[g] in heaven or on
earth—you who keep your covenant of love[h] with your servants
who continue wholeheartedly in
your way. 15You have kept your
promise to your servant David my
father; with your mouth you have
promised[i] and with your hand you
have fulfilled it—as it is today.
16"Now, LORD, the God of Israel,
keep for your servant David my father the promises you made to him
when you said, 'You shall never fail[j]
to have a successor to sit before me
on the throne of Israel, if only your
descendants are careful in all they
do to walk before me according to
my law,[k] as you have done.' 17And
now, LORD, the God of Israel, let your
word that you promised your servant David come true.
18"But will God really dwell[l] on
earth with humans? The heavens,[m]
even the highest heavens, cannot
contain you. How much less this
temple I have built! 19Yet, LORD my
God, give attention to your servant's
prayer and his plea for mercy. Hear
the cry and the prayer that your servant is praying in your presence.
20May your eyes[n] be open toward
this temple day and night, this place
of which you said you would put
your Name[o] there. May you hear[p]
the prayer your servant prays toward this place. 21Hear the supplications of your servant and of your
people Israel when they pray toward
this place. Hear from heaven, your
dwelling place; and when you hear,
forgive.[q]
22"When anyone wrongs their
neighbor and is required to take an
oath[r] and they come and swear the
oath before your altar in this temple,
23then hear from heaven and act.
Judge between your servants, condemning[s] the guilty and bringing
down on their heads what they have
done, and vindicating the innocent
by treating them in accordance with
their innocence.
24"When your people Israel have
been defeated[t] by an enemy because
they have sinned against you and
when they turn back and give praise
to your name, praying and making
supplication before you in this temple, 25then hear from heaven and
forgive the sin of your people Israel
and bring them back to the land you
gave to them and their ancestors.
26"When the heavens are shut up
and there is no rain[u] because your
people have sinned against you, and
when they pray toward this place
and give praise to your name and
turn from their sin because you have
afflicted them, 27then hear from
heaven and forgive[v] the sin of your
servants, your people Israel. Teach
them the right way to live, and send
rain on the land you gave your people for an inheritance.
28"When famine[w] or plague comes
to the land, or blight or mildew, locusts or grasshoppers, or when enemies besiege them in any of their
cities, whatever disaster or disease
may come, 29and when a prayer or
plea is made by anyone among your
people Israel—being aware of their
afflictions and pains, and spreading
out their hands toward this temple— 30then hear from heaven,
your dwelling place. Forgive,[x] and
deal with everyone according to all
they do, since you know their hearts
(for you alone know the human

6:14 [g] Ex 8:10; 15:11 [h] Dt 7:9
6:15 [i] 1Ch 22:10
6:16 [j] 2Sa 7:13, 15; 1Ki 2:4; 2Ch 7:18; 23:3 [k] Ps 132:12
6:18 [l] Rev 21:3 [m] 2Ch 2:6; Ps 11:4; Isa 40:22; 66:1; Ac 7:49
6:20 [n] Ex 3:16; Ps 34:15 [o] Dt 12:11 [p] 2Ch 7:14; 30:20
6:21 [q] Ps 51:1; Isa 33:24; 40:2; 43:25; 44:22; 55:7; Mic 7:18
6:22 [r] Ex 22:11
6:23 [s] Isa 3:11; 65:6; Mt 16:27
6:24 [t] Lev 26:17
6:26 [u] Lev 26:19; Dt 11:17; 28:24; 2Sa 1:21; 1Ki 17:1
6:27 [v] ver 30, 39; 2Ch 7:14
6:28 [w] 2Ch 20:9
6:30 [x] ver 27

---

addresses his majesty as Lord of creation, while the emphasis on his covenant love speaks to his uniqueness and incomparability as the one true God (v. 14). Solomon's prayer for the continuation of the Davidic dynasty is ultimately the Chronicler's prayer as well.

6:18–39 This section of Solomon's prayer includes two distinct segments: the fundamental theological principles of intercessory prayer and the circumstances prompting intercession (vv. 22–39). (1) To understand prayer is to acknowledge the paradoxical truth of God's nature—so vast and expansive, yet so close at the same time. If the heavens cannot contain the Creator, how much less can a building like the temple (v. 18). Yet somehow the temple becomes the symbolic focal point of God's interest in and care for humanity, for it is here that his eyes and ears are continually open to the prayers of both Israelite and foreigner alike (v. 21; cf. vv. 32–33). (2) The list of circumstances prompting intercessory prayer should be regarded as representative and not comprehensive (vv. 22–39). The examples of personal injustices, warfare, and natural calamities are universal experiences in the agricultural society of biblical times.

heart),[y] 31 so that they will fear you[z] and walk in obedience to you all the time they live in the land you gave our ancestors.

32 "As for the foreigner who does not belong to your people Israel but has come[a] from a distant land because of your great name and your mighty hand[b] and your outstretched arm—when they come and pray toward this temple, 33 then hear from heaven, your dwelling place. Do whatever the foreigner[c] asks of you, so that all the peoples of the earth may know your name and fear you, as do your own people Israel, and may know that this house I have built bears your Name.

34 "When your people go to war against their enemies,[d] wherever you send them, and when they pray[e] to you toward this city you have chosen and the temple I have built for your Name, 35 then hear from heaven their prayer and their plea, and uphold their cause.

36 "When they sin against you—for there is no one who does not sin[f]—and you become angry with them and give them over to the enemy, who takes them captive[g] to a land far away or near; 37 and if they have a change of heart[h] in the land where they are held captive, and repent and plead with you in the land of their captivity and say, 'We have sinned, we have done wrong and acted wickedly'; 38 and if they turn back to you with all their heart and soul in the land of their captivity where they were taken, and pray toward the land you gave their ancestors, toward the city you have chosen and toward the temple I have built for your Name; 39 then from heaven, your dwelling place, hear their prayer and their pleas, and uphold their cause. And forgive your people, who have sinned against you.

40 "Now, my God, may your eyes be open and your ears attentive[i] to the prayers offered in this place.

41 "Now arise,[j] LORD God, and come
to your resting place,[k]
you and the ark of your
might.
May your priests,[l] LORD God, be
clothed with salvation,
may your faithful people
rejoice in your
goodness.[m]
42 LORD God, do not reject your
anointed one.
Remember the great love[n]
promised to David your
servant."

The Dedication of the Temple

7:1–10pp // 1Ki 8:62–66

7 When Solomon finished praying, fire[o] came down from heaven and consumed the burnt offering and the sacrifices, and the glory of the LORD filled[p] the temple.[q] 2 The priests could not enter[r] the temple of the LORD because the glory[s] of the LORD filled it. 3 When all the Israelites saw the fire coming down and the glory of the LORD above the temple, they knelt on the pavement with their faces to the ground, and they worshiped and gave thanks to the LORD, saying,

"He is good;
his love endures forever."[t]

4 Then the king and all the people offered sacrifices before the LORD. 5 And King Solomon offered a sacrifice of twenty-two

6:30 [y] 1Sa 16:7; 1Ch 28:9; Ps 7:9; 44:21; Pr 16:2; 17:3
6:31 [z] Ps 103:11, 13; Pr 8:13
6:32 [a] 2Ch 9:6; Jn 12:20; Ac 8:27 [b] Ex 3:19, 20
6:33 [c] 2Ch 7:14
6:34 [d] Dt 28:7 [e] 1Ch 5:20
6:36 [f] Job 15:14; Ps 143:2; Ecc 7:20; Jer 17:9; Jas 3:1; 1Jn 1:8-10 [g] Lev 26:44
6:37 [h] 2Ch 7:14; 33:12, 19, 23; Jer 29:13
6:40 [i] 2Ch 7:15; Ne 1:6, 11; Ps 17:1, 6
6:41 [j] Isa 33:10 [k] 1Ch 28:2 [l] Ps 132:16 [m] Ps 116:12
6:42 [n] Ps 89:24, 28; Isa 55:3
7:1 [o] Lev 9:24; 1Ki 18:38 [p] Ex 16:10 [q] Ps 26:8
7:2 [r] 1Ki 8:11 [s] Ex 29:43; 40:35; 2Ch 5:14
7:3 [t] 1Ch 16:34; 2Ch 5:13; 20:21

2Ch 6:30–31 ❖ Solomon prayed for the future forgiveness of the Israelites for sins not yet committed. What does this show about the human heart?

6:40–42 The parallel in 1Ki 8:50b–53 shows us that Solomon expects a favorable response to the prayer from God by virtue of the special relationship between Yahweh and Israel established by the Mosaic covenant. By contrast, the Chronicler omits the reference to Moses and the exodus and grounds this expectation in God's promises to David.

7:1–10 God's action in issuing fire from heaven on an altar is a familiar motif in the OT. In a similar manner, each aspect of God's divine response to the temple dedication ceremonies, all of which have been organized and orchestrated by Solomon, is crucial to the establishment of the new sanctuary as the central Israelite worship center.

7:4–6 The number of animals sacrificed can be understood as either literal or symbolic; however, the point is to observe the magnitude of this worship response to God. Solomon's new bronze altar is, in fact, inadequate for the task (cf. v. 7).

thousand head of cattle and a hundred
and twenty thousand sheep and goats. So
the king and all the people dedicated the
temple of God. 6 The priests took their positions, as did the Levites[u] with the LORD's
musical instruments,[v] which King David
had made for praising the LORD and which
were used when he gave thanks, saying,
"His love endures forever." Opposite the
Levites, the priests blew their trumpets,
and all the Israelites were standing.
7 Solomon consecrated the middle part
of the courtyard in front of the temple
of the LORD, and there he offered burnt
offerings and the fat of the fellowship offerings, because the bronze altar he had
made could not hold the burnt offerings,
the grain offerings and the fat portions.
8 So Solomon observed the festival[w] at
that time for seven days, and all Israel
with him — a vast assembly, people from
Lebo Hamath to the Wadi of Egypt.[x] 9 On
the eighth day they held an assembly, for
they had celebrated the dedication of the
altar for seven days and the festival[y] for
seven days more. 10 On the twenty-third
day of the seventh month he sent the
people to their homes, joyful and glad
in heart for the good things the LORD
had done for David and Solomon and
for his people Israel.

The LORD Appears to Solomon

7:11–22pp // 1Ki 9:1–9

11 When Solomon had finished the temple of the LORD and the royal palace, and
had succeeded in carrying out all he had
in mind to do in the temple of the LORD
and in his own palace, 12 the LORD appeared to him at night and said:

"I have heard your prayer and
have chosen this place for myself[z]
as a temple for sacrifices.
13 "When I shut up the heavens so

2Ch 7:14 ❖ What might it look like for us to humble ourselves and seek God's face? What areas of our lives can we more fully dedicate to this task?

that there is no rain,[a] or command
locusts to devour the land or send
a plague among my people, 14 if my
people, who are called by my name,
will humble[b] themselves and pray
and seek my face[c] and turn[d] from
their wicked ways, then I will hear
from heaven, and I will forgive[e]
their sin and will heal[f] their land.
15 Now my eyes will be open and my
ears attentive to the prayers offered
in this place.[g] 16 I have chosen[h] and
consecrated this temple so that my
Name may be there forever. My eyes
and my heart will always be there.
17 "As for you, if you walk before
me faithfully[i] as David your father
did, and do all I command, and observe my decrees and laws, 18 I will
establish your royal throne, as I
covenanted with David your father
when I said, 'You shall never fail to
have a successor[j] to rule over Israel.'[k]
19 "But if you[a] turn away[l] and forsake[m] the decrees and commands I
have given you[a] and go off to serve
other gods and worship them,
20 then I will uproot[n] Israel from my
land,[o] which I have given them, and
will reject this temple I have consecrated for my Name. I will make it
a byword and an object of ridicule[p]
among all peoples. 21 This temple
will become a heap of rubble. All[b]

7:6 [u] 1Ch 15:16 [v] 2Ch 5:12
7:8 [w] 2Ch 30:26 [x] Ge 15:18
7:9 [y] Lev 23:36
7:12 [z] Dt 12:5
7:13 [a] 2Ch 6:26-28; Am 4:7
7:14 [b] Lev 26:41; 2Ch 6:37; Jas 4:10 [c] 1Ch 16:11 [d] Isa 55:7; Zec 1:4 [e] 2Ch 6:27 [f] 2Ch 30:20; Isa 30:26; 57:18
7:15 [g] 2Ch 6:40
7:16 [h] ver 12; 2Ch 6:6
7:17 [i] 1Ki 9:4
7:18 [j] 2Ch 6:16 [k] 2Sa 7:13; 2Ch 13:5
7:19 [l] Dt 28:15 [m] Lev 26:14,33
7:20 [n] Dt 29:28 [o] 1Ki 14:15 [p] Dt 28:37

[a] *19* The Hebrew is plural. [b] *21* See some Septuagint manuscripts, Old Latin, Syriac, Arabic and Targum; Hebrew *And though this temple is now so imposing, all*

7:8 The reference to "Lebo Hamath to the Wadi of Egypt" constitutes the ideal boundaries of ancient Israel, the possession promised to the patriarchs (cf. Ge 15:18; Nu 34:5, 8).

7:9 The weeklong dedication of the temple precedes the weeklong Festival of Tabernacles celebration. Solomon holds a sacred assembly on the eighth day.

7:11–22 The dream report may be divided into two uneven segments: an introduction (vv. 11–12a) and the divine address (vv. 12b–22).

7:13–18 The promise will be fulfilled under two separate but related conditions. The first is that the people must obey the laws of God (vv. 13–16); the second is that the king must also obey those same divine decrees and laws (vv. 17–18).

7:13–16 The word "humble" means to subdue one's pride and submit in self-denying loyalty to God and his will. "Pray" is a shameless acknowledgment of personal sin and a plea for God's mercy. "Seek" is often used in desperate situations in which God is the only possible hope for deliverance. "Turn" signifies a complete change of direction away from sin and toward God.

7:19–22 Although the Lord's threat is addressed to Solomon and the people of Israel, the Chronicler clearly understands that the threat of divine punishment is still in force for his own audience.

who pass by will be appalled and
say,[q] 'Why has the LORD done such
a thing to this land and to this temple?' 22People will answer, 'Because
they have forsaken the LORD, the
God of their ancestors, who brought
them out of Egypt, and have embraced other gods, worshiping
and serving them — that is why he
brought all this disaster on them.'"

7:21 [q] Dt 29:24
8:5 [r] 1Ch 7:24; 2Ch 14:7
8:7 [s] Ge 10:16
8:8 [t] 1Ki 4:6; 9:21

Solomon's Other Activities

8:1–18pp // 1Ki 9:10–28

8 At the end of twenty years, during
which Solomon built the temple of
the LORD and his own palace, 2Solomon
rebuilt the villages that Hiram[a] had giv-
en him, and settled Israelites in them.
3Solomon then went to Hamath Zobah
and captured it. 4He also built up Tadmor in the desert and all the store cities
he had built in Hamath. 5He rebuilt Upper Beth Horon[r] and Lower Beth Horon
as fortified cities, with walls and with
gates and bars, 6as well as Baalath and
all his store cities, and all the cities for
his chariots and for his horses[b] — whatever he desired to build in Jerusalem, in
Lebanon and throughout all the territory
he ruled.
7There were still people left from the
Hittites, Amorites, Perizzites, Hivites
and Jebusites[s] (these people were not
Israelites). 8Solomon conscripted[t] the
descendants of all these people remaining in the land — whom the Israelites
had not destroyed — to serve as slave
labor, as it is to this day. 9But Solomon
did not make slaves of the Israelites for
his work; they were his fighting men,
commanders of his captains, and commanders of his chariots and charioteers.
10They were also King Solomon's chief

8:11 [u] 1Ki 3:1; 7:8
8:12 [v] 1Ki 8:64; 2Ch 4:1; 15:8
8:13 [w] Ex 29:38; Nu 28:3 [x] Nu 28:9 [y] Ex 23:14; Dt 16:16 [z] Ex 23:16
8:14 [a] 1Ch 24:1 [b] 1Ch 25:1 [c] 1Ch 9:17; 26:1 [d] Ne 12:24, 36 [e] 1Ch 23:6; Ne 12:45

2Ch 8:8 ❖ How could Israel, a nation freed from slavery in Egypt, make their neighbors slaves? Was Solomon right to do this? Why or why not? Do we ever find ourselves in the position of being an oppressor? How?

officials — two hundred and fifty officials
supervising the men.
11Solomon brought Pharaoh's daughter[u] up from the City of David to the palace he had built for her, for he said, "My
wife must not live in the palace of David
king of Israel, because the places the ark
of the LORD has entered are holy."
12On the altar[v] of the LORD that he had
built in front of the portico, Solomon
sacrificed burnt offerings to the LORD,
13according to the daily requirement[w] for
offerings commanded by Moses for the
Sabbaths,[x] the New Moons and the three[y]
annual festivals — the Festival of Unleavened Bread, the Festival of Weeks[z] and
the Festival of Tabernacles. 14In keeping
with the ordinance of his father David, he
appointed the divisions[a] of the priests for
their duties, and the Levites[b] to lead the
praise and to assist the priests according to
each day's requirement. He also appointed
the gatekeepers[c] by divisions for the various gates, because this was what David
the man of God[d] had ordered.[e] 15They did
not deviate from the king's commands to
the priests or to the Levites in any matter,
including that of the treasuries.
16All Solomon's work was carried out,
from the day the foundation of the temple of the LORD was laid until its completion. So the temple of the LORD was
finished.

[a] 2 Hebrew *Huram,* a variant of *Hiram;* also in verse 18 [b] 6 Or *charioteers*

8:1-6 The report of the cities given by Hiram of Tyre to Solomon seems to reverse the report found in the parallel in the book of Kings (1Ki 9:10-14). It may be possible to harmonize the reports in one of two ways. (1) Perhaps Kings and Chronicles refer to two different occasions or communications between Hiram and Solomon. (2) Chronicles may be the sequel to the account in Kings that Hiram held the twenty cities temporarily as collateral for the timber supplied to Solomon until such time as a cash payment (of gold) could be made.
8:3 The capture of Hamath is the only reference to a military campaign by King Solomon in all of Chronicles.
8:6 The emphasis on store cites and chariot cities highlights the priority Solomon gives to the related activities of trade and military defense.
8:7-10 The writer emphasizes how Solomon puts fellow countrymen in positions of leadership.
8:11 Only Chronicles records the rationale for the displacement of Solomon's Egyptian wife, ostensibly because of issues of ritual purity.
8:12-15 Not only does King Solomon obey the Law of Moses, but he is also careful to implement his father's instructions concerning the reorganization of the priests and Levites (cf. 1Ch 23–26).
8:16-18 This summary statement conveys the idea that Solomon cuts no corners and spares no expense in getting the job done. For the Chronicler, Solomon's role as king is summed up in his work of completing the temple.

17Then Solomon went to Ezion Geber
and Elath on the coast of Edom. 18And
Hiram sent him ships commanded by
his own men, sailors who knew the sea.
These, with Solomon's men, sailed to
Ophir and brought back four hundred
and fifty talents[a] of gold,[f] which they
delivered to King Solomon.

The Queen of Sheba Visits Solomon

9:1–12pp // 1Ki 10:1–13

9 When the queen of Sheba[g] heard of
Solomon's fame, she came to Jerusalem to test him with hard questions. Arriving with a very great caravan — with
camels carrying spices, large quantities
of gold, and precious stones — she came
to Solomon and talked with him about
all she had on her mind. 2Solomon answered all her questions; nothing was
too hard for him to explain to her. 3When
the queen of Sheba saw the wisdom of
Solomon,[h] as well as the palace he had
built, 4the food on his table, the seating
of his officials, the attending servants
in their robes, the cupbearers in their
robes and the burnt offerings he made
at[b] the temple of the LORD, she was overwhelmed.
5She said to the king, "The report I
heard in my own country about your
achievements and your wisdom is true.
6But I did not believe what they said until I came[i] and saw with my own eyes.
Indeed, not even half the greatness of
your wisdom was told me; you have far
exceeded the report I heard. 7How happy
your people must be! How happy your
officials, who continually stand before
you and hear your wisdom! 8Praise be to
the LORD your God, who has delighted in
you and placed you on his throne[j] as king
to rule for the LORD your God. Because
of the love of your God for Israel and his
desire to uphold them forever, he has
made you king[k] over them, to maintain
justice and righteousness."
9Then she gave the king 120 talents[c]
of gold,[l] large quantities of spices, and
precious stones. There had never been
such spices as those the queen of Sheba
gave to King Solomon.

8:18 [f] 2Ch 9:9
9:1 [g] Ge 10:7; Eze 23:42; Mt 12:42; Lk 11:31
9:3 [h] 1Ki 5:12
9:6 [i] 2Ch 6:32
9:8 [j] 1Ki 2:12; 1Ch 17:14; 28:5; 29:23; 2Ch 13:8 [k] 2Ch 2:11
9:9 [l] 2Ch 8:18
9:10 [m] 2Ch 8:18
9:14 [n] 2Ch 17:11; Isa 21:13; Jer 25:24; Eze 27:21; 30:5
9:16 [o] 2Ch 12:9 [p] 1Ki 7:2
9:17 [q] 1Ki 22:39

2Ch 9:8 ❖ How can we live in such a way that those around us praise God (see Mt 5:16)?

10(The servants of Hiram and the servants of Solomon brought gold from
Ophir;[m] they also brought algumwood[d]
and precious stones. 11The king used the
algumwood to make steps for the temple
of the LORD and for the royal palace, and
to make harps and lyres for the musicians. Nothing like them had ever been
seen in Judah.)
12King Solomon gave the queen of Sheba all she desired and asked for; he gave
her more than she had brought to him.
Then she left and returned with her retinue to her own country.

Solomon's Splendor

9:13–28pp // 1Ki 10:14–29; 2Ch 1:14–17

13The weight of the gold that Solomon received yearly was 666 talents,[e]
14not including the revenues brought
in by merchants and traders. Also all the
kings of Arabia[n] and the governors of
the territories brought gold and silver
to Solomon.
15King Solomon made two hundred
large shields of hammered gold; six hundred shekels[f] of hammered gold went
into each shield. 16He also made three
hundred small shields[o] of hammered
gold, with three hundred shekels[g] of gold
in each shield. The king put them in the
Palace of the Forest of Lebanon.[p]
17Then the king made a great throne
covered with ivory[q] and overlaid with
pure gold. 18The throne had six steps,
and a footstool of gold was attached to it.
On both sides of the seat were armrests,
with a lion standing beside each of them.
19Twelve lions stood on the six steps,
one at either end of each step. Nothing

[a] 18 That is, about 17 tons or about 15 metric tons
[b] 4 Or *and the ascent by which he went up to*
[c] 9 That is, about 4 1/2 tons or about 4 metric tons
[d] 10 Probably a variant of *almugwood*
[e] 13 That is, about 25 tons or about 23 metric tons
[f] 15 That is, about 15 pounds or about 6.9 kilograms
[g] 16 That is, about 7 1/2 pounds or about 3.5 kilograms

9:1–12 The story of the queen of Sheba's visit illustrates the key theme of the larger literary unit (chs. 1–9); namely, that Solomon's wisdom, wealth, and fame are all gifts from God.

9:13–21 The review of the opulence of Solomon's kingdom further enhanced the king's (and Israel's) reputation among all the other kingdoms (v. 19). The account stands as a testimony to God's faithfulness in keeping his promise to give Solomon unsurpassed wealth and honor (cf. 1:11–12).

like it had ever been made for any other
kingdom. 20All King Solomon's goblets
were gold, and all the household articles
in the Palace of the Forest of Lebanon
were pure gold. Nothing was made of
silver, because silver was considered of
little value in Solomon's day. 21The king
had a fleet of trading ships[a] manned by
Hiram's[b] servants. Once every three years
it returned, carrying gold, silver and ivory, and apes and baboons.
22King Solomon was greater in riches
and wisdom than all the other kings of
the earth.[r] 23All the kings[s] of the earth
sought audience with Solomon to hear
the wisdom God had put in his heart.
24Year after year, everyone who came
brought a gift[t]—articles of silver and
gold, and robes, weapons and spices, and
horses and mules.
25Solomon had four thousand stalls for
horses and chariots,[u] and twelve thousand horses,[c] which he kept in the chariot cities and also with him in Jerusalem.
26He ruled[v] over all the kings from the
Euphrates River[w] to the land of the Philistines, as far as the border of Egypt.[x]
27The king made silver as common in
Jerusalem as stones, and cedar as plentiful as sycamore-fig trees in the foothills.
28Solomon's horses were imported from
Egypt and from all other countries.

Solomon's Death

9:29–31pp // 1Ki 11:41–43

29As for the other events of Solomon's
reign, from beginning to end, are they
not written in the records of Nathan[y] the
prophet, in the prophecy of Ahijah[z] the
Shilonite and in the visions of Iddo the
seer concerning Jeroboam[a] son of Nebat?
30Solomon reigned in Jerusalem over all
Israel forty years. 31Then he rested with
his ancestors and was buried in the city
of David[b] his father. And Rehoboam his
son succeeded him as king.

Israel Rebels Against Rehoboam

10:1—11:4pp // 1Ki 12:1–24

10 Rehoboam went to Shechem, for
all Israel had gone there to make
him king. 2When Jeroboam[c] son of Nebat
heard this (he was in Egypt, where he had
fled[d] from King Solomon), he returned
from Egypt. 3So they sent for Jeroboam,
and he and all Israel[e] went to Rehoboam and said to him: 4"Your father put a
heavy yoke on us,[f] but now lighten the
harsh labor and the heavy yoke he put
on us, and we will serve you."
5Rehoboam answered, "Come back to
me in three days." So the people went
away.
6Then King Rehoboam consulted the
elders[g] who had served his father Solomon during his lifetime. "How would
you advise me to answer these people?"
he asked.
7They replied, "If you will be kind to
these people and please them and give

9:22 [r] 1Ki 3:13; 2Ch 1:12
9:23 [s] 1Ki 4:34
9:24 [t] 2Ch 32:23; Ps 45:12; 68:29; 72:10; Isa 18:7
9:25 [u] 1Sa 8:11; 1Ki 4:26
9:26 [v] 1Ki 4:21 [w] Ps 72:8-9 [x] Ge 15:18-21
9:29 [y] 2Sa 7:2; 1Ch 29:29 [z] 1Ki 11:29 [a] 2Ch 10:2
9:31 [b] 1Ki 2:10
10:2 [c] 2Ch 9:29 [d] 1Ki 11:40
10:3 [e] 1Ch 9:1
10:4 [f] 2Ch 2:2
10:6 [g] Job 8:8-9; 12:12; 15:10; 32:7

[a] 21 Hebrew *of ships that could go to Tarshish*
[b] 21 Hebrew *Huram,* a variant of *Hiram*
[c] 25 Or *charioteers*

9:22–28 By way of literary structure, this passage completes the envelope construction introduced in 1:14–17. The two texts recite the symbols of Solomon's great wealth and in so doing frame the entire literary unit (chs. 1–9).

9:29–31 The phrase "rested with his ancestors" (v. 31) signifies both a peaceful death and a long and prosperous life. The Chronicler omits altogether the unfavorable theological review of Solomon's idolatry-tainted reign found in 1Ki 11:1–13 as well as the opposition recorded in 1Ki 11:14–40.

APPLICATION ✣ 1:1—9:31 The establishment of Solomon's temple in Jerusalem brings a renewed emphasis on prayer to Israelite religious thought and life. Christian prayer is first and foremost a matter of heart and attitude, not vain repetition.

Participation in the daily cycle of prayer hearkens back to the temple as the house of prayer and the idea that prayer was, for the Israelites, one means for recovering order out of chaos. It can mean the same for believers today as individuals surrender their lives to God's will and seek him first when confronting daily questions, reasons for praise, and needs: "Pray in the Spirit on all occasions with all kinds of prayers and requests. With this in mind, be alert and always keep on praying for all the Lord's people" (Eph 6:18).

10:1–4 Rehoboam may be hoping the long Israelite tradition associated with this site will contribute to easing political tensions. Jeroboam makes his way to Shechem during the interim period between the national mourning over Solomon's death and the installation of the new king.

Two issues of primary concern must be settled in order for the northern tribes to guarantee loyalty to the new king: easing the "harsh labor" (e.g., forced labor gangs) and "heavy yoke" (e.g., taxation, v. 4) that they experienced under Solomon.

10:5–11 The advice of Solomon's elders is conciliatory (v. 7) to the people's request. The advice of Rehoboam's cronies (vv. 8–9), by contrast, threatens

acted wisely, dispersing some of his sons
throughout the districts of Judah and
Benjamin, and to all the fortified cities.
He gave them abundant provisions and
took many wives for them.

Shishak Attacks Jerusalem

12:9–16pp // 1Ki 14:21,25–31

12 After Rehoboam's position as king
was established[e] and he had become strong,[f] he and all Israel[a] with him
abandoned the law of the LORD. 2Because
they had been unfaithful[g] to the LORD,
Shishak[h] king of Egypt attacked Jerusalem in the fifth year of King Rehoboam.
3With twelve hundred chariots and sixty
thousand horsemen and the innumerable troops of Libyans, Sukkites and Cushites[b][i] that came with him from Egypt, 4he
captured the fortified cities[j] of Judah and
came as far as Jerusalem.

5Then the prophet Shemaiah[k] came to
Rehoboam and to the leaders of Judah
who had assembled in Jerusalem for fear
of Shishak, and he said to them, "This
is what the LORD says, 'You have abandoned me; therefore, I now abandon[l]
you to Shishak.' "

6The leaders of Israel and the king
humbled themselves and said, "The
LORD is just."[m]

7When the LORD saw that they humbled themselves, this word of the LORD
came to Shemaiah: "Since they have
humbled themselves, I will not destroy
them but will soon give them deliverance.[n] My wrath will not be poured out
on Jerusalem through Shishak. 8They
will, however, become subject[o] to him,
so that they may learn the difference between serving me and serving the kings
of other lands."

9When Shishak king of Egypt attacked
Jerusalem, he carried off the treasures
of the temple of the LORD and the treasures of the royal palace. He took everything, including the gold shields[p] Sol-

12:1 [e] ver 13 [f] 2Ch 11:17
12:2 [g] 1Ki 14:22-24 [h] 1Ki 11:40
12:3 [i] 2Ch 16:8; Na 3:9
12:4 [j] 2Ch 11:10
12:5 [k] 2Ch 11:2 [l] Dt 28:15; 2Ch 15:2
12:6 [m] Ex 9:27; Da 9:14
12:7 [n] 1Ki 21:29; Ps 78:38
12:8 [o] Dt 28:48
12:9 [p] 2Ch 9:16
12:12 [q] 1Ki 14:13; 2Ch 19:3
12:13 [r] Dt 12:5; 2Ch 6:6
12:15 [s] 2Ch 9:29; 11:2
12:16 [t] 2Ch 11:20

2Ch 12:7 ❖ How does God's forgiving nature comfort us? How can we live a life of thanksgiving for God's merciful grace?

omon had made. 10So King Rehoboam
made bronze shields to replace them
and assigned these to the commanders
of the guard on duty at the entrance to
the royal palace. 11Whenever the king
went to the LORD's temple, the guards
went with him, bearing the shields, and
afterward they returned them to the
guardroom.

12Because Rehoboam humbled himself, the LORD's anger turned from him,
and he was not totally destroyed. Indeed,
there was some good[q] in Judah.

13King Rehoboam established himself
firmly in Jerusalem and continued as
king. He was forty-one years old when he
became king, and he reigned seventeen
years in Jerusalem, the city the LORD
had chosen out of all the tribes of Israel
in which to put his Name.[r] His mother's
name was Naamah; she was an Ammonite. 14He did evil because he had not set
his heart on seeking the LORD.

15As for the events of Rehoboam's
reign, from beginning to end, are they
not written in the records of Shemaiah[s]
the prophet and of Iddo the seer that
deal with genealogies? There was continual warfare between Rehoboam and
Jeroboam. 16Rehoboam rested with his
ancestors and was buried in the City of
David. And Abijah[t] his son succeeded
him as king.

Abijah King of Judah

13:1–2,22—14:1pp // 1Ki 15:1–2,6–8

13 In the eighteenth year of the reign
of Jeroboam, Abijah became king
of Judah, 2and he reigned in Jerusalem

[a] *1* That is, Judah, as frequently in 2 Chronicles
[b] *3* That is, people from the upper Nile region

12:1–12 The Chronicler understands Shishak's invasion of Judah as punishment for sin. The phrase "he had become strong" (v. 1) suggests that pride and self-reliance have replaced Rehoboam's dependence on God.

12:5–8 Shemaiah the prophet brings a message of both judgment and mercy to Rehoboam and the leaders of Judah. The response by Rehoboam and the leaders of Judah is essentially a confession of sin. God mercifully decrees that Judah will experience a qualified deliverance from Shishak, but the people will not escape the consequences of their disobedience.

12:12 The phrase "humbled himself" means to forsake one's pride and yield in self-denying loyalty to God.

12:13–16 The Chronicler places blame for idolatry directly on Rehoboam.

13:1–2a Jeroboam ruled as king of Israel for twenty-two years (930–909 BC). Abijah's three-year reign over Judah is thus fixed from 913–910 BC.

three years. His mother's name was Maakah,[a] a daughter[b] of Uriel of Gibeah.
There was war between Abijah[u] and
Jeroboam.[v] 3Abijah went into battle with
an army of four hundred thousand able
fighting men, and Jeroboam drew up a
battle line against him with eight hundred thousand able troops.
4Abijah stood on Mount Zemaraim,[w]
in the hill country of Ephraim, and said,
"Jeroboam and all Israel,[x] listen to me!
5Don't you know that the LORD, the God
of Israel, has given the kingship of Israel
to David and his descendants forever[y] by
a covenant of salt?[z] 6Yet Jeroboam son of
Nebat, an official of Solomon son of David, rebelled[a] against his master. 7Some
worthless scoundrels[b] gathered around
him and opposed Rehoboam son of Solomon when he was young and indecisive
and not strong enough to resist them.
8"And now you plan to resist the kingdom of the LORD, which is in the hands
of David's descendants. You are indeed
a vast army and have with you the gold-
en calves[c] that Jeroboam made to be
your gods. 9But didn't you drive out the
priests of the LORD,[d] the sons of Aaron,
and the Levites, and make priests of your
own as the peoples of other lands do?
Whoever comes to consecrate himself
with a young bull[e] and seven rams may
become a priest of what are not gods.[f]
10"As for us, the LORD is our God, and
we have not forsaken him. The priests
who serve the LORD are sons of Aaron,
and the Levites assist them. 11Every
morning and evening[g] they present
burnt offerings and fragrant incense
to the LORD. They set out the bread on
the ceremonially clean table[h] and light
the lamps on the gold lampstand every
evening. We are observing the requirements of the LORD our God. But you have

13:2 [u] 2Ch 11:20 [v] 1Ki 15:6
13:4 [w] Jos 18:22 [x] 1Ch 11:1
13:5 [y] 2Sa 7:13 [z] Lev 2:13; Nu 18:19
13:6 [a] 1Ki 11:26
13:7 [b] Jdg 9:4
13:8 [c] 1Ki 12:28; 2Ch 11:15
13:9 [d] 2Ch 11:14-15 [e] Ex 29:35-36 [f] Jer 2:11
13:11 [g] Ex 29:39; 2Ch 2:4 [h] Lev 24:5-9
13:12 [i] Nu 10:8-9 [j] Ac 5:39
13:13 [k] Jos 8:9
13:14 [l] 2Ch 14:11
13:15 [m] 2Ch 14:12
13:16 [n] 2Ch 16:8
13:18 [o] 1Ch 5:20; 2Ch 14:11; Ps 22:5

2Ch 13:15 ❖ God won the battle for Judah. What victories has God given us?

forsaken him. 12God is with us; he is our
leader. His priests with their trumpets
will sound the battle cry against you.[i]
People of Israel, do not fight against the
LORD,[j] the God of your ancestors, for you
will not succeed."
13Now Jeroboam had sent troops
around to the rear, so that while he was
in front of Judah the ambush[k] was behind them. 14Judah turned and saw that
they were being attacked at both front
and rear. Then they cried out[l] to the
LORD. The priests blew their trumpets
15and the men of Judah raised the battle
cry. At the sound of their battle cry, God
routed Jeroboam and all Israel[m] before
Abijah and Judah. 16The Israelites fled
before Judah, and God delivered[n] them
into their hands. 17Abijah and his troops
inflicted heavy losses on them, so that
there were five hundred thousand casualties among Israel's able men. 18The
Israelites were subdued on that occasion,
and the people of Judah were victorious
because they relied[o] on the LORD, the God
of their ancestors.
19Abijah pursued Jeroboam and took
from him the towns of Bethel, Jeshanah
and Ephron, with their surrounding villages. 20Jeroboam did not regain power
during the time of Abijah. And the LORD
struck him down and he died.
21But Abijah grew in strength. He married fourteen wives and had twenty-two
sons and sixteen daughters.
22The other events of Abijah's reign,

[a] 2 Most Septuagint manuscripts and Syriac (see also 11:20 and 1 Kings 15:2); Hebrew *Micaiah*
[b] 2 Or *granddaughter*

13:2b–3 The story begins with a blunt announcement that civil war has erupted between Israel (led by Jeroboam) and Judah (led by Abijah). The troops of Israel outnumber the troops of Judah two to one.

13:4–12 Abijah's speech is propagandistic, contrasting the faithfulness and loyalty of Abijah with the rebellion and disloyalty of Jeroboam in two issues: the Davidic covenant (vv. 4-8a) and God's temple in Jerusalem (vv. 8b–12). Implicitly, Jeroboam has rebelled against God since God has given the kingdom to David and his descendants (v. 5).

The most damning indictment against the northern tribes are "the golden calves that Jeroboam made to be your gods" (v. 8b). The punch line of Abijah's speech is eminently theological and decidedly practical: "God is with us" (v. 12a). What kind of folly is it to "fight against the LORD" (v. 12b)?

13:13–19 The entire battle report turns on a key verb—the men of Judah are victorious "because they *relied on* the LORD" (v. 18, emphasis added). The significance of the phrase "God of their ancestors" in the same verse should not be missed—God has done this kind of thing before.

13:20–21 The verb "strike down" (v. 20) often denotes a divine plague or blow executed by God as the divine Warrior who brings judgment on rebellious and sinful people.

what he did and what he said, are written in the annotations of the prophet Iddo.

14 [a] And Abijah rested with his ancestors and was buried in the City of David. Asa his son succeeded him as king, and in his days the country was at peace for ten years.

Asa King of Judah

14:2–3pp // 1Ki 15:11–12

2Asa did what was good and right in the eyes of the LORD his God. 3He removed the foreign altars and the high places, smashed the sacred stones and cut down the Asherah poles.[b][p] 4He commanded Judah to seek the LORD, the God of their ancestors, and to obey his laws and commands. 5He removed the high places and incense altars[q] in every town in Judah, and the kingdom was at peace under him. 6He built up the fortified cities of Judah, since the land was at peace. No one was at war with him during those years, for the LORD gave him rest.[r]

7"Let us build up these towns," he said to Judah, "and put walls around them, with towers, gates and bars. The land is still ours, because we have sought the LORD our God; we sought him and he has given us rest on every side." So they built and prospered.

8Asa had an army of three hundred thousand men from Judah, equipped with large shields and with spears, and two hundred and eighty thousand from Benjamin, armed with small shields and with bows. All these were brave fighting men.

9Zerah the Cushite[s] marched out against them with an army of thousands upon thousands and three hundred chariots, and came as far as Mareshah.[t] 10Asa went out to meet him, and they took up battle positions in the Valley of Zephathah near Mareshah.

11Then Asa called[u] to the LORD his God and said, "LORD, there is no one like you to help the powerless against the mighty. Help us, LORD our God, for we rely[v] on you, and in your name[w] we have come against this vast army. LORD, you are our God; do not let mere mortals prevail[x] against you."

12The LORD struck down[y] the Cushites before Asa and Judah. The Cushites fled, 13and Asa and his army pursued them as far as Gerar.[z] Such a great number of Cushites fell that they could not recover; they were crushed before the LORD and his forces. The men of Judah carried off a large amount of plunder. 14They destroyed all the villages around Gerar, for the terror[a] of the LORD had fallen on them. They looted all these villages, since there was much plunder there. 15They also attacked the camps of the herders and carried off droves of sheep and goats and camels. Then they returned to Jerusalem.

> **2Ch 14:3** ❖ How can we root out of our lives the things that distract us or lead us away from God? Be specific.

Asa's Reform

15:16–19pp // 1Ki 15:13–16

15 The Spirit of God came on[b] Azariah son of Oded. 2He went out to meet Asa and said to him, "Listen to me, Asa and all Judah and Benjamin. The LORD is with you[c] when you are with him.[d] If you seek[e] him, he will be found by you, but if you forsake him, he will forsake you.[f] 3For a long time Israel was without the true God, without a priest to teach[g] and without the law.[h] 4But in their distress they turned to the LORD, the God of Israel, and sought him,[i] and he was found by them. 5In those days it was not safe to travel about,[j] for all the inhabitants of the lands were in great turmoil. 6One nation was being crushed by another and one city by another,[k] because God

14:3 [p] Ex 34:13; Dt 7:5; 1Ki 15:12-14
14:5 [q] 2Ch 34:4,7
14:6 [r] 1Ch 22:9; 2Ch 15:15
14:9 [s] 2Ch 12:3; 16:8 [t] 2Ch 11:8
14:11 [u] 2Ch 13:14 [v] 2Ch 13:18
[w] 1Sa 17:45 [x] 1Sa 14:6; Ps 9:19
14:12 [y] 2Ch 13:15
14:13 [z] Ge 10:19
14:14 [a] Ge 35:5; 2Ch 17:10
15:1 [b] Nu 11:25, 26; 24:2; 2Ch 20:14; 24:20
15:2 [c] ver 4, 15; 2Ch 20:17 [d] Jas 4:8 [e] Jer 29:13 [f] 1Ch 28:9; 2Ch 24:20
15:3 [g] Lev 10:11 [h] 2Ch 17:9; La 2:9
15:4 [i] Dt 4:29
15:5 [j] Jdg 5:6
15:6 [k] Mt 24:7

[a] In Hebrew texts 14:1 is numbered 13:23, and 14:2-15 is numbered 14:1-14. [b] 3 That is, wooden symbols of the goddess Asherah; here and elsewhere in 2 Chronicles

14:2-15 King Asa was a religious reformer (14:3-5) and built fortifications for the defense of Judah's perimeter (v. 7). The repetition of the idea of seeking the Lord in vv. 4 and 7 sets the theme for the entire section.

14:8-15 The story turns on Asa's prayer for "help" from the Lord (v. 11). His prayer seems to be modeled on Solomon's exhortation that the Israelites pray toward the temple; then God will hear from heaven and "uphold their cause" (6:34-35).

15:1-19 These are the themes highlighted in the prophet's message: God is with those who side with him, and he rewards obedience (vv. 2, 7); and God will be found by those who seek him but forsakes those who abandon him (v. 2). In good homiletical style, the sermon ends with an exhortation to continue the good work already begun because God will honor it (v. 7).

was troubling them with every kind of
distress. 7But as for you, be strong[l] and
do not give up, for your work will be rewarded."[m]
8When Asa heard these words and the
prophecy of Azariah son of[a] Oded the
prophet, he took courage. He removed
the detestable idols from the whole land
of Judah and Benjamin and from the
towns he had captured[n] in the hills of
Ephraim. He repaired the altar[o] of the
LORD that was in front of the portico of
the LORD's temple.
9Then he assembled all Judah and
Benjamin and the people from Ephraim,
Manasseh and Simeon who had settled
among them, for large numbers[p] had
come over to him from Israel when they
saw that the LORD his God was with him.
10They assembled at Jerusalem in the
third month of the fifteenth year of Asa's
reign. 11At that time they sacrificed to the
LORD seven hundred head of cattle and
seven thousand sheep and goats from
the plunder[q] they had brought back.
12They entered into a covenant[r] to seek
the LORD,[s] the God of their ancestors,
with all their heart and soul. 13All who
would not seek the LORD, the God of Israel, were to be put to death,[t] whether
small or great, man or woman. 14They
took an oath to the LORD with loud
acclamation, with shouting and with
trumpets and horns. 15All Judah rejoiced
about the oath because they had sworn
it wholeheartedly. They sought God[u] eagerly, and he was found by them. So the
LORD gave them rest[v] on every side.
16King Asa also deposed his grandmother Maakah from her position as
queen mother, because she had made a
repulsive image for the worship of Asherah.[w] Asa cut it down, broke it up and
burned it in the Kidron Valley. 17Although
he did not remove the high places from
Israel, Asa's heart was fully committed
to the LORD all his life. 18He brought into
the temple of God the silver and gold
and the articles that he and his father
had dedicated.
19There was no more war until the thir-
ty-fifth year of Asa's reign.

15:7 [l]Jos 1:7,9 [m]Ps 58:11
15:8 [n]2Ch 13:19 [o]2Ch 8:12
15:9 [p]2Ch 11:16-17
15:11 [q]2Ch 14:13
15:12 [r]2Ki 11:17; 2Ch 23:16; 34:31 [s]1Ch 16:11
15:13 [t]Ex 22:20; Dt 13:9-16
15:15 [u]Dt 4:29 [v]1Ch 22:9; 2Ch 14:7
15:16 [w]Ex 34:13; 2Ch 14:2-5

2Ch 15:16 ❖ Confronting a family member about a moral or spiritual issue can be difficult. How can we find courage to do this when necessary?

Asa's Last Years

16:1–6pp // 1Ki 15:17–22
16:11—17:1pp // 1Ki 15:23–24

16 In the thirty-sixth year of Asa's
reign Baasha[x] king of Israel went
up against Judah and fortified Ramah to
prevent anyone from leaving or entering
the territory of Asa king of Judah.
2Asa then took the silver and gold out
of the treasuries of the LORD's temple
and of his own palace and sent it to Ben-
Hadad king of Aram, who was ruling in
Damascus. 3"Let there be a treaty[y] between me and you," he said, "as there
was between my father and your father.
See, I am sending you silver and gold.
Now break your treaty with Baasha king
of Israel so he will withdraw from me."
4Ben-Hadad agreed with King Asa
and sent the commanders of his forces
against the towns of Israel. They conquered Ijon, Dan, Abel Maim[b] and all the
store cities of Naphtali. 5When Baasha
heard this, he stopped building Ramah
and abandoned his work. 6Then King Asa
brought all the men of Judah, and they
carried away from Ramah the stones
and timber Baasha had been using. With
them he built up Geba and Mizpah.
7At that time Hanani[z] the seer came to

16:1 [x]Jer 41:9
16:3 [y]2Ch 20:35
16:7 [z]1Ki 16:1

[a] 8 Vulgate and Syriac (see also Septuagint and verse 1); Hebrew does not have *Azariah son of.*
[b] 4 Also known as *Abel Beth Maakah*

15:8–15 The king's obedience to God's word through the prophet Azariah launches sweeping religious reforms in Judah. The covenant ceremony may have been associated with the Festival of Weeks or Pentecost. The word "rest" occurs three times in the review of Asa's reign (14:6, 7; 15:15) and signifies the blessing of God for a peaceful and prosperous life as a reward for covenant obedience.
15:16 The Asherah pole was a cultic symbol of the Canaanite fertility goddess Asherah in the form of a tree or tree trunk. The pole represented the tree of life in Canaanite religion.
15:17 Rather than see this as a contradiction to the record of the king's reforms (cf. 14:2), it is probably better to assume that the writer distinguishes between the high places of Judah and Israel.
16:1–10 King Baasha of Israel is the aggressor in that the defensive measures he takes to fortify Ramah also threaten the territory of Judah economically and militarily. Asa resorts to paying tribute to a third party for the purpose of engaging Baasha's army on a second front, thereby splitting his focus and strength.
16:7–9 The key word in the prophet's speech is

Asa king of Judah and said to him: "Because you relied on the king of Aram and
not on the LORD your God, the army of
the king of Aram has escaped from your
hand. 8Were not the Cushites[a][a] and Libyans a mighty army with great numbers
of chariots and horsemen[b]? Yet when
you relied on the LORD, he delivered[b]
them into your hand. 9For the eyes[c] of
the LORD range throughout the earth
to strengthen those whose hearts are
fully committed to him. You have done
a foolish[d] thing, and from now on you
will be at war."

10Asa was angry with the seer because
of this; he was so enraged that he put
him in prison. At the same time Asa brutally oppressed some of the people.

11The events of Asa's reign, from beginning to end, are written in the book
of the kings of Judah and Israel. 12In
the thirty-ninth year of his reign Asa
was afflicted with a disease in his feet.
Though his disease was severe, even
in his illness he did not seek help from
the LORD,[e] but only from the physicians.
13Then in the forty-first year of his reign
Asa died and rested with his ancestors.
14They buried him in the tomb that he
had cut out for himself in the City of
David. They laid him on a bier covered
with spices and various blended perfumes,[f] and they made a huge fire[g] in
his honor.

Jehoshaphat King of Judah

17 Jehoshaphat his son succeeded him
as king and strengthened himself
against Israel. 2He stationed troops in all
the fortified cities of Judah and put garrisons in Judah and in the towns of Ephraim that his father Asa had captured.[h]
3The LORD was with Jehoshaphat because he followed the ways of his father
David[i] before him. He did not consult the
Baals 4but sought[j] the God of his father
and followed his commands rather than
the practices of Israel. 5The LORD established the kingdom under his control;
and all Judah brought gifts[k] to Jehoshaphat, so that he had great wealth and
honor.[l] 6His heart was devoted[m] to the
ways of the LORD; furthermore, he removed the high places[n] and the Asherah
poles[o] from Judah.[p]

7In the third year of his reign he sent
his officials Ben-Hail, Obadiah, Zechariah, Nethanel and Micaiah to teach[q] in the
towns of Judah. 8With them were certain
Levites[r] — Shemaiah, Nethaniah, Zebadiah, Asahel, Shemiramoth, Jehonathan,
Adonijah, Tobijah and Tob-Adonijah —
and the priests Elishama and Jehoram.
9They taught throughout Judah, taking
with them the Book of the Law[s] of the
LORD; they went around to all the towns
of Judah and taught the people.

10The fear[t] of the LORD fell on all the
kingdoms of the lands surrounding
Judah, so that they did not go to war
against Jehoshaphat. 11Some Philistines
brought Jehoshaphat gifts and silver as
tribute, and the Arabs[u] brought him

2Ch 16:10 ❖ What causes people to become angry with God's messengers? Where do we see this today?

2Ch 17:3-6 ❖ This passage talks about faithfulness leading to God's blessings. How can we integrate this principle into our own lives and remove the idols that can distract us from God's mission?

16:8 [a]2Ch 12:3; 14:9 [b]2Ch 13:16
16:9 [c]Pr 15:3; Jer 16:17; Zec 4:10 [d]1Sa 13:13
16:12 [e]Jer 17:5-6
16:14 [f]Ge 50:2; Jn 19:39-40 [g]2Ch 21:19; Jer 34:5
17:2 [h]2Ch 15:8
17:3 [i]1Ki 22:43
17:4 [j]1Ki 12:28; 2Ch 22:9
17:5 [k]1Sa 10:27 [l]2Ch 18:1
17:6 [m]1Ki 8:61; 2Ch 15:17 [n]1Ki 15:14; 2Ch 19:3; 20:33 [o]Ex 34:13 [p]2Ch 21:12
17:7 [q]Lev 10:11; Dt 6:4-9; 2Ch 15:3; 35:3
17:8 [r]2Ch 19:8; Ne 8:7-8
17:9 [s]Dt 6:4-9; 28:61
17:10 [t]Ge 35:5; Dt 2:25; 2Ch 14:14
17:11 [u]2Ch 9:14; 26:8

[a] 8 That is, people from the upper Nile region
[b] 8 Or *charioteers*

"rely" (v. 7). History should have been Asa's teacher (v. 8). Here in this crisis, Asa shuns divine aid and trusts in his political savvy and human instincts to deliver Judah. Asa's response to Hanani constitutes the first record of a prophet of God being persecuted by a king in the OT (v. 10).

16:11–14 The statement that Asa seeks human help in the form of physicians rather than divine help for healing (v. 12b) impugns his faith in God, not in ancient medical practitioners.

17:1–5 Jehoshaphat is compared favorably to David because he is single-minded in his obedience to God (v. 3). God demonstrates his faithfulness to his word by continuing the Davidic dynasty through Jehoshaphat (v. 1). God cut off the enemies of Judah (v. 2).

17:6 Jehoshaphat demonstrated wholehearted devotion to God by removing the symbols and practices of false worship. God blessed Jehoshaphat's leadership as he has shepherded the people into the way of God through religious reforms.

17:7–9 This "theological faculty" engages in "distance learning" of sorts, in that they launch an itinerant teaching ministry throughout the towns of Judah.

17:10–19 God's blessing rests on Jehoshaphat's reign; as a result, "the fear of the LORD" falls on Judah's neighbors. Respect for Judah's political clout results in people to the west and south paying tribute.

The flow of wealth into Judah permits the building of fortifications and store cities (vv. 12–13). Jehoshaphat's army totals 1,160,000 soldiers.

flocks:[v] seven thousand seven hundred
rams and seven thousand seven hundred goats.
12 Jehoshaphat became more and more
powerful; he built forts and store cities
in Judah 13 and had large supplies in the
towns of Judah. He also kept experienced
fighting men in Jerusalem. 14 Their en-
rollment[w] by families was as follows:

From Judah, commanders of units of 1,000:
Adnah the commander, with 300,000 fighting men;
15 next, Jehohanan the commander, with 280,000;
16 next, Amasiah son of Zikri, who volunteered[x] himself for the service of the LORD, with 200,000.
17 From Benjamin:[y]
Eliada, a valiant soldier, with 200,000 men armed with bows and shields;
18 next, Jehozabad, with 180,000 men armed for battle.

19 These were the men who served the
king, besides those he stationed in the
fortified cities[z] throughout Judah.[a]

Micaiah Prophesies Against Ahab

18:1–27pp // 1Ki 22:1–28

18 Now Jehoshaphat had great wealth
and honor,[b] and he allied[c] himself
with Ahab[d] by marriage. 2 Some years
later he went down to see Ahab in Samaria. Ahab slaughtered many sheep
and cattle for him and the people with
him and urged him to attack Ramoth
Gilead. 3 Ahab king of Israel asked Jehoshaphat king of Judah, "Will you go
with me against Ramoth Gilead?"
Jehoshaphat replied, "I am as you are,
and my people as your people; we will
join you in the war." 4 But Jehoshaphat
also said to the king of Israel, "First seek
the counsel of the LORD."
5 So the king of Israel brought together
the prophets—four hundred men—and
asked them, "Shall we go to war against
Ramoth Gilead, or shall I not?"

17:11 [v] 2Ch 21:16
17:14 [w] 2Sa 24:2
17:16 [x] Jdg 5:9; 1Ch 29:9
17:17 [y] Nu 1:36
17:19 [z] 2Ch 11:10 [a] 2Ch 25:5
18:1 [b] 2Ch 17:5 [c] 2Ch 19:1-3; 22:3 [d] 2Ch 21:6
18:11 [e] 2Ch 22:5
18:13 [f] Nu 22:18, 20,35

2Ch 18:12–13 ❖ When someone pressures us to change what we say about God or the Bible, how can we stand firm in the truth?

"Go," they answered, "for God will give
it into the king's hand."
6 But Jehoshaphat asked, "Is there no
longer a prophet of the LORD here whom
we can inquire of?"
7 The king of Israel answered Jehoshaphat, "There is still one prophet through
whom we can inquire of the LORD, but
I hate him because he never prophesies
anything good about me, but always bad.
He is Micaiah son of Imlah."
"The king should not say such a thing,"
Jehoshaphat replied.
8 So the king of Israel called one of his
officials and said, "Bring Micaiah son of
Imlah at once."
9 Dressed in their royal robes, the king
of Israel and Jehoshaphat king of Judah were sitting on their thrones at the
threshing floor by the entrance of the
gate of Samaria, with all the prophets
prophesying before them. 10 Now Zedekiah son of Kenaanah had made iron
horns, and he declared, "This is what
the LORD says: 'With these you will gore
the Arameans until they are destroyed.'"
11 All the other prophets were prophesying the same thing. "Attack Ramoth
Gilead[e] and be victorious," they said,
"for the LORD will give it into the king's
hand."
12 The messenger who had gone to
summon Micaiah said to him, "Look,
the other prophets without exception
are predicting success for the king. Let
your word agree with theirs, and speak
favorably."
13 But Micaiah said, "As surely as the
LORD lives, I can tell him only what my
God says."[f]
14 When he arrived, the king asked him,
"Micaiah, shall we go to war against Ramoth Gilead, or shall I not?"
"Attack and be victorious," he answered,
"for they will be given into your hand."

18:1–4 The gist of the opening report is King Jehoshaphat's consent to partner with King Ahab in a war against Ramoth Gilead. Jehoshaphat wisely requests that Ahab "seek the counsel of the LORD" (v. 4) before they move ahead.

18:5–27 Jehoshaphat knows that the true prophets are often dissenters in the face of popular opinion, and he requests yet another prophetic judgment (v. 6).

The king's envoy attempts to coach Micaiah as he enters the situation (v. 12). But Micaiah staunchly refuses to compromise any message from the Lord

15The king said to him, "How many
times must I make you swear to tell me
nothing but the truth in the name of
the LORD?"
16Then Micaiah answered, "I saw all
Israel[g] scattered on the hills like sheep
without a shepherd,[h] and the LORD said,
'These people have no master. Let each
one go home in peace.' "
17The king of Israel said to Jehoshaphat, "Didn't I tell you that he never
prophesies anything good about me, but
only bad?"
18Micaiah continued, "Therefore hear
the word of the LORD: I saw the LORD
sitting on his throne[i] with all the multitudes of heaven standing on his right
and on his left. 19And the LORD said, 'Who
will entice Ahab king of Israel into attacking Ramoth Gilead and going to his
death there?'
"One suggested this, and another that.
20Finally, a spirit came forward, stood before the LORD and said, 'I will entice him.'
" 'By what means?' the LORD asked.
21" 'I will go and be a deceiving spirit[j] in
the mouths of all his prophets,' he said.
" 'You will succeed in enticing him,'
said the LORD. 'Go and do it.'
22"So now the LORD has put a deceiving
spirit in the mouths of these prophets
of yours.[k] The LORD has decreed disaster for you."
23Then Zedekiah son of Kenaanah
went up and slapped[l] Micaiah in the
face. "Which way did the spirit from[a]
the LORD go when he went from me to
speak to you?" he asked.
24Micaiah replied, "You will find out on
the day you go to hide in an inner room."
25The king of Israel then ordered,
"Take Micaiah and send him back to
Amon the ruler of the city and to Joash
the king's son, 26and say, 'This is what the

18:16 [g] 1Ch 9:1 [h] Nu 27:17; Eze 34:5-8
18:18 [i] Da 7:9
18:21 [j] 1Ch 21:1; Job 1:6; Zec 3:1; Jn 8:44
18:22 [k] Job 12:16; Isa 19:14; Eze 14:9
18:23 [l] Jer 20:2; Mk 14:65; Ac 23:2
18:26 [m] 2Ch 16:10; Heb 11:36
18:29 [n] 1Sa 28:8
18:31 [o] 2Ch 13:14
18:34 [p] 2Ch 22:5
19:2 [q] 1Ki 16:1

king says: Put this fellow in prison[m] and
give him nothing but bread and water
until I return safely.' "
27Micaiah declared, "If you ever return
safely, the LORD has not spoken through
me." Then he added, "Mark my words,
all you people!"

Ahab Killed at Ramoth Gilead

18:28–34pp // 1Ki 22:29–36

28So the king of Israel and Jehoshaphat king of Judah went up to Ramoth
Gilead. 29The king of Israel said to Jehoshaphat, "I will enter the battle in disguise, but you wear your royal robes." So
the king of Israel disguised[n] himself and
went into battle.
30Now the king of Aram had ordered
his chariot commanders, "Do not fight
with anyone, small or great, except
the king of Israel." 31When the chariot
commanders saw Jehoshaphat, they
thought, "This is the king of Israel." So
they turned to attack him, but Jehoshaphat cried out,[o] and the LORD helped
him. God drew them away from him,
32for when the chariot commanders saw
that he was not the king of Israel, they
stopped pursuing him.
33But someone drew his bow at random and hit the king of Israel between
the breastplate and the scale armor.
The king told the chariot driver, "Wheel
around and get me out of the fighting.
I've been wounded." 34All day long the
battle raged, and the king of Israel
propped himself up in his chariot facing the Arameans until evening. Then
at sunset he died.[p]
19 When Jehoshaphat king of Judah
returned safely to his palace in
Jerusalem, 2Jehu[q] the seer, the son of
Hanani, went out to meet him and said

[a] 23 Or *Spirit of*

(v. 13). His response to Ahab's initial inquiry must have been sarcastic, a parody of the king's four hundred "yes men" (v. 14).

18:16–17 Ahab presumes the prophet predicts his death in battle, which he does. But Micaiah's message has a double meaning, in that the people of Israel currently "have no master" (18:16b). Ahab's corrupt rule has led the people far from God—how scathing is the statement that the sheep will have "peace" (18:16c) when the shepherd is gone.

18:18–22 Micaiah's second vision offers a window into the throne room of God, where the divine council discusses the battle of Ramoth Gilead and the fate of King Ahab. Micaiah's message about the "deceiving spirit" (v. 22) sent from God unmasks the fraudulent prophets of Ahab.

18:27 The king's death in battle will vindicate Micaiah and verify the truth of his message.

18:28–34 Ahab fulfills Micaiah's prophecy about the king being lured to his own destruction. Ahab's ploy to disguise himself is perhaps an attempt to thwart the word of the prophet that the king fears may be true. The Chronicler interprets Jehoshaphat's cry as a prayer and adds the clause "and the LORD helped him" (v. 31).

19:1–3 Jehu the seer is the son of Hanani the seer, who rebuked King Asa of Judah for entering into a foreign alliance with Ben-Hadad of Aram (16:1–9).

to the king, "Should you help the wicked[r] and love[a] those who hate the LORD?[s]
Because of this, the wrath[t] of the LORD is
on you. 3There is, however, some good[u]
in you, for you have rid the land of the
Asherah poles[v] and have set your heart
on seeking God.[w]"

Jehoshaphat Appoints Judges

4Jehoshaphat lived in Jerusalem, and
he went out again among the people
from Beersheba to the hill country of
Ephraim and turned them back to the
LORD, the God of their ancestors. 5He
appointed judges[x] in the land, in each
of the fortified cities of Judah. 6He told
them, "Consider carefully what you do,[y]
because you are not judging for mere
mortals[z] but for the LORD, who is with
you whenever you give a verdict. 7Now
let the fear of the LORD be on you. Judge
carefully, for with the LORD our God there
is no injustice[a] or partiality[b] or bribery."
8In Jerusalem also, Jehoshaphat appointed some of the Levites, priests and
heads of Israelite families to administer[c] the law of the LORD and to settle disputes. And they lived in Jerusalem. 9He
gave them these orders: "You must serve
faithfully and wholeheartedly in the fear
of the LORD. 10In every case that comes
before you from your people who live in
the cities — whether bloodshed or other
concerns of the law, commands, decrees
or regulations — you are to warn them
not to sin against the LORD;[d] otherwise
his wrath will come on you and your people. Do this, and you will not sin.
11"Amariah the chief priest will be over
you in any matter concerning the LORD,
and Zebadiah son of Ishmael, the leader
of the tribe of Judah, will be over you in
any matter concerning the king, and the
Levites will serve as officials before you.
Act with courage,[e] and may the LORD be
with those who do well."

19:2 [r]2Ch 16:2-9 [s]Ps 139:21-22 [t]2Ch 24:18; 32:25; Ps 7:11
19:3 [u]1Ki 14:13; 2Ch 12:12 [v]2Ch 17:6 [w]2Ch 18:1; 20:35; 25:7; Ezr 7:10
19:5 [x]Ge 47:6; Ex 18:26
19:6 [y]Lev 19:15 [z]Dt 1:17; 16:18-20; 17:8-13
19:7 [a]Ge 18:25; Dt 32:4 [b]Dt 10:17; Job 34:19; Ro 2:11; Col 3:25
19:8 [c]2Ch 17:8-9
19:10 [d]Dt 17:8-13
19:11 [e]1Ch 28:20
20:1 [f]1Ch 4:41
20:2 [g]Ge 14:7
20:3 [h]1Sa 7:6; 2Ch 19:3; Ezr 8:21; Jer 36:9; Jnh 3:5,7

2Ch 19:4 ❖ Jehoshaphat went beyond the borders of his kingdom trying to restore worship of God in Israel. Where might God be calling us to go beyond our comfort zone for the gospel?

2Ch 20:2-4 ❖ Under threat, Jehoshaphat went straight to God and led his people to God. How can we follow Jehoshaphat's example in challenging times?

Jehoshaphat Defeats Moab and Ammon

20 After this, the Moabites and Ammonites with some of the Meunites[b][f] came to wage war against Jehoshaphat.
2Some people came and told Jehoshaphat, "A vast army is coming against
you from Edom,[c] from the other side
of the Dead Sea. It is already in Hazezon Tamar[g]" (that is, En Gedi). 3Alarmed,
Jehoshaphat resolved to inquire of the
LORD, and he proclaimed a fast[h] for all Judah. 4The people of Judah came together to seek help from the LORD; indeed,
they came from every town in Judah to
seek him.
5Then Jehoshaphat stood up in the
assembly of Judah and Jerusalem at
the temple of the LORD in the front of
the new courtyard 6and said:

[a] *2 Or and make alliances with* [b] *1* Some Septuagint manuscripts; Hebrew *Ammonites* [c] *2* One Hebrew manuscript; most Hebrew manuscripts, Septuagint and Vulgate *Aram*

The evil of *alliances* with foreign nations in lieu of *reliance* on God is a repeated theme in Chronicles.
19:4 The section opens with a brief account of Jehoshaphat's activity as an evangelist throughout Judah after the debacle at Ramoth Gilead.
19:5–11 The strategic location of these fortified cities makes them accessible for the general population. In addition to hearing cases and rendering fair verdicts, the judge must also warn (or instruct) the citizenry who come before the bench not to commit further sin against the Lord, lest the "wrath" of God come against them and their families (vv. 9–10). To ensure separation of power and introduce a checks-and-balances mechanism into the judicial organization, the king gives the chief priest Amariah jurisdiction over religious matters (v. 11a). He grants jurisdiction in civil matters to Zebadiah (v. 11b). The Levites serve as "officials" and assist the courts as clerks and bailiffs (v. 11c). The king exhorts them to "act with courage" and invokes the Lord's presence with them as they discharge their duties (v. 11d).
20:1–4 The expression "vast army" is the Chronicler's way of describing the overwhelming numerical superiority of the invaders. The fact that people from "every town" in Judah rally together to seek the Lord indicates the lasting spiritual impact Jehoshaphat's revival has upon the nation.
20:5–12 Jehoshaphat's prayer-speech appeals widely to other OT texts. For example, his address to God, "LORD, the God of our ancestors" (v. 6) echoes David's prayer before the assembly of Israel after the gifts for the temple were collected (1Ch 29:10–13). Jehoshaphat's prayer makes allusions to three important OT covenants: the Abrahamic covenant, the Mosaic covenant, and the Davidic covenant.

"LORD, the God of our ancestors,[i]
are you not the God who is in heav-
en?[j] You rule over all the kingdoms[k]
of the nations. Power and might are
in your hand, and no one can withstand you. 7Our God, did you not
drive out the inhabitants of this land
before your people Israel and give it
forever to the descendants of Abraham your friend?[l] 8They have lived
in it and have built in it a sanctuary[m]
for your Name, saying, 9'If calamity
comes upon us, whether the sword
of judgment, or plague or famine,[n]
we will stand in your presence before
this temple that bears your Name
and will cry out to you in our distress,
and you will hear us and save us.'

10"But now here are men from
Ammon, Moab and Mount Seir,
whose territory you would not allow Israel to invade when they came
from Egypt;[o] so they turned away
from them and did not destroy
them. 11See how they are repaying
us by coming to drive us out of the
possession[p] you gave us as an inheritance. 12Our God, will you not judge
them?[q] For we have no power to face
this vast army that is attacking us.
We do not know what to do, but our
eyes are on you.[r]"

13All the men of Judah, with their
wives and children and little ones, stood
there before the LORD.

14Then the Spirit[s] of the LORD came
on Jahaziel son of Zechariah, the son of
Benaiah, the son of Jeiel, the son of Mattaniah, a Levite and descendant of Asaph,
as he stood in the assembly.

15He said: "Listen, King Jehoshaphat
and all who live in Judah and Jerusalem!
This is what the LORD says to you: 'Do not
be afraid or discouraged[t] because of this
vast army. For the battle[u] is not yours, but
God's. 16Tomorrow march down against
them. They will be climbing up by the
Pass of Ziz, and you will find them at the
end of the gorge in the Desert of Jeruel.
17You will not have to fight this battle.
Take up your positions; stand firm and
see[v] the deliverance the LORD will give
you, Judah and Jerusalem. Do not be
afraid; do not be discouraged. Go out to
face them tomorrow, and the LORD will
be with you.'"

18Jehoshaphat bowed down[w] with his
face to the ground, and all the people of
Judah and Jerusalem fell down in worship before the LORD. 19Then some Levites from the Kohathites and Korahites
stood up and praised the LORD, the God
of Israel, with a very loud voice.

20Early in the morning they left for the
Desert of Tekoa. As they set out, Jehoshaphat stood and said, "Listen to me, Judah
and people of Jerusalem! Have faith[x] in
the LORD your God and you will be upheld; have faith in his prophets and you
will be successful.[y]" 21After consulting
the people, Jehoshaphat appointed men
to sing to the LORD and to praise him for
the splendor of his[a] holiness[z] as they
went out at the head of the army, saying:

"Give thanks to the LORD,
for his love endures forever."[a]

22As they began to sing and praise, the
LORD set ambushes[b] against the men of
Ammon and Moab and Mount Seir who
were invading Judah, and they were defeated. 23The Ammonites[c] and Moabites
rose up against the men from Mount
Seir[d] to destroy and annihilate them.
After they finished slaughtering the men
from Seir, they helped to destroy one
another.[e]

20:6 [i]Mt 6:9 [j]Dt 4:39 [k]1Ch 29:11-12
20:7 [l]Isa 41:8; Jas 2:23
20:8 [m]2Ch 6:20
20:9 [n]2Ch 6:28
20:10 [o]Nu 20:14-21; Dt 2:4-6, 9, 18-19
20:11 [p]Ps 83:1-12
20:12 [q]Jdg 11:27 [r]Ps 25:15; 121:1-2
20:14 [s]2Ch 15:1
20:15 [t]2Ch 32:7 [u]Ex 14:13-14; 1Sa 17:47
20:17 [v]Ex 14:13; 2Ch 15:2
20:18 [w]Ex 4:31
20:20 [x]Isa 7:9 [y]Ge 39:3; Pr 16:3
20:21 [z]1Ch 16:29; Ps 29:2 [a]2Ch 5:13; Ps 136:1
20:22 [b]Jdg 7:22; 2Ch 13:13
20:23 [c]Ge 19:38 [d]2Ch 21:8 [e]Jdg 7:22; 1Sa 14:20; Eze 38:21

[a] 21 Or *him with the splendor of*

20:13–17 A number of the Yahweh-war motifs are continued in the prophetic speech of Jahaziel: the exhortation to take courage and stand firm (vv. 15, 17); the numerical superiority of the enemy armies ("vast army," v. 15); the Israelites not having to fight because Yahweh will wage war for them (vv. 15, 17); and the promise of certain victory because God will sustain his people with his presence (vv. 16–17). The prediction that the people of Judah will see God's victory "tomorrow" (v. 17) is a reminder of the urgency of the situation.

20:18–19 The response has affinities to both covenant-renewal liturgy and temple liturgy in OT corporate worship: worship proper (demonstrated by lying prostrate before God) followed by enthusiastic praise (cf. Neh 9–10; Ps 95).

20:20–26 Jehoshaphat paraphrases the priestly exhortation and adds "have faith in his prophets and you will be successful" (v. 20). This statement affirms the effectiveness of the prophetic word prompted by the Spirit of God and may even signify canonical prophetic literature by this time.

Interestingly, the Levitical chorus initiates God's battle strategy against the enemy coalition. God stirs the Transjordan armies into a spirit of frenzied self-destruction (vv. 22–23). The name given to the valley where the Lord upheld his people is the Valley of Berakah, meaning "praise" (v. 26; cf. v. 20).

24When the men of Judah came to
the place that overlooks the desert and
looked toward the vast army, they saw
only dead bodies lying on the ground;
no one had escaped. 25So Jehoshaphat
and his men went to carry off their
plunder, and they found among them a
great amount of equipment and clothing[a] and also articles of value — more
than they could take away. There was
so much plunder that it took three days
to collect it. 26On the fourth day they assembled in the Valley of Berakah, where
they praised the LORD. This is why it is
called the Valley of Berakah[b] to this day.
27Then, led by Jehoshaphat, all the
men of Judah and Jerusalem returned
joyfully to Jerusalem, for the LORD had
given them cause to rejoice over their
enemies. 28They entered Jerusalem and
went to the temple of the LORD with
harps and lyres and trumpets.
29The fear[f] of God came on all the surrounding kingdoms when they heard
how the LORD had fought[g] against the
enemies of Israel. 30And the kingdom
of Jehoshaphat was at peace, for his God
had given him rest[h] on every side.

The End of Jehoshaphat's Reign

20:31—21:1pp // 1Ki 22:41–50

31So Jehoshaphat reigned over Judah.
He was thirty-five years old when he became king of Judah, and he reigned in
Jerusalem twenty-five years. His mother's name was Azubah daughter of Shilhi. 32He followed the ways of his father
Asa and did not stray from them; he did
what was right in the eyes of the LORD.
33The high places,[i] however, were not
removed, and the people still had not
set their hearts on the God of their ancestors.
34The other events of Jehoshaphat's
reign, from beginning to end, are written in the annals of Jehu[j] son of Hanani,
which are recorded in the book of the
kings of Israel.
35Later, Jehoshaphat king of Judah
made an alliance[k] with Ahaziah king of
Israel, whose ways were wicked.[l] 36He
agreed with him to construct a fleet of
trading ships.[c] After these were built at
Ezion Geber, 37Eliezer son of Dodavahu
of Mareshah prophesied against Jehoshaphat, saying, "Because you have made
an alliance with Ahaziah, the LORD will
destroy what you have made." The ships[m]
were wrecked and were not able to set
sail to trade.[d]

21 Then Jehoshaphat rested with his
ancestors and was buried with
them in the City of David. And Jehoram[n] his son succeeded him as king.
2Jehoram's brothers, the sons of Jehoshaphat, were Azariah, Jehiel, Zechariah,
Azariahu, Michael and Shephatiah. All
these were sons of Jehoshaphat king of
Israel.[e] 3Their father had given them
many gifts[o] of silver and gold and articles of value, as well as fortified cities[p]
in Judah, but he had given the kingdom
to Jehoram because he was his firstborn
son.

20:29 [f] Ge 35:5; Dt 2:25; 2Ch 14:14; 17:10 [g] Ex 14:14
20:30 [h] 1Ch 22:9; 2Ch 14:6-7; 15:15
20:33 [i] 2Ch 17:6; 19:3
20:34 [j] 1Ki 16:1
20:35 [k] 2Ch 16:3 [l] 2Ch 19:1-3
20:37 [m] 1Ki 9:26; 2Ch 9:21
21:1 [n] 1Ch 3:11
21:3 [o] 2Ch 11:23 [p] 2Ch 11:10

[a] 25 Some Hebrew manuscripts and Vulgate; most Hebrew manuscripts *corpses*
[b] 26 *Berakah* means *praise.*
[c] 36 Hebrew *of ships that could go to Tarshish*
[d] 37 Hebrew *sail for Tarshish*
[e] 2 That is, Judah, as frequently in 2 Chronicles

20:27–28 The musical instruments that accompanied the singing of the Levites in battle (v. 21) are now employed in the joyful celebration.
20:31—21:3 King Jehoshaphat's twenty-five-year reign may be dated between 872 and 848 BC (v. 31). Much like his father, Jehoshaphat was rebuked by God's prophet for entering into foreign political alliances (19:1-3; cf. 16:7-9), and he failed to remove completely the high places (20:33; cf. 15:17). Although Jehoshaphat "followed the ways of his father Asa" (v. 32), neither Asa nor Jehoshaphat is given the epitaph of Hezekiah and Josiah (29:2; 34:2).
20:34 The "annals of Jehu" are part of larger historical materials documenting the Israelite monarchies.
20:37 The prophecy from Eliezer predicting catastrophe for Jehoshaphat's fleet fits a pattern of prophetic rebuke and divine judgment of the king of Judah for entering into political and commercial alliances with the northern kingdom of Israel or other foreign nations.

10:1—21:3 King Jehoshaphat's charge to "have faith in his prophets" (20:20) is still our directive in the sense that we too accept the OT prophets as Yahweh's divinely commissioned messengers. The Chronicler would call us to "have faith" in these prophets to the point where we indeed believe that they spoke the very words of God.

There are practical benefits of exploring how the messages of the OT prophets speak to the Christian church today. We live in a similar time and cultural context: one that celebrates religious pluralism, which is what the OT prophets vehemently spoke against (e.g., Eze 33:10-11).

Jehoram King of Judah

21:5–10,20pp // 2Ki 8:16–24

4When Jehoram established[q] himself
firmly over his father's kingdom, he put
all his brothers[r] to the sword along with
some of the officials of Israel. 5Jehoram
was thirty-two years old when he became
king, and he reigned in Jerusalem eight
years. 6He followed the ways of the kings
of Israel,[s] as the house of Ahab had done,
for he married a daughter of Ahab.[t] He
did evil in the eyes of the LORD. 7Nev-
ertheless, because of the covenant the
LORD had made with David,[u] the LORD
was not willing to destroy the house of
David.[v] He had promised to maintain
a lamp[w] for him and his descendants
forever.

8In the time of Jehoram, Edom[x] rebelled against Judah and set up its own
king. 9So Jehoram went there with his
officers and all his chariots. The Edomites surrounded him and his chariot
commanders, but he rose up and broke
through by night. 10To this day Edom has
been in rebellion against Judah.

Libnah[y] revolted at the same time, because Jehoram had forsaken the LORD,
the God of his ancestors. 11He had also
built high places on the hills of Judah
and had caused the people of Jerusalem to prostitute themselves and had
led Judah astray.

12Jehoram received a letter from Elijah[z] the prophet, which said:

> "This is what the LORD, the God of
> your father[a] David, says: 'You have
> not followed the ways of your fa-
> ther Jehoshaphat or of Asa[b] king
> of Judah. 13But you have followed
> the ways of the kings of Israel, and
> you have led Judah and the people
> of Jerusalem to prostitute them-
> selves, just as the house of Ahab
> did.[c] You have also murdered your
> own brothers, members of your
> own family, men who were bet-
> ter[d] than you. 14So now the LORD is
> about to strike your people, your
> sons, your wives and everything
> that is yours, with a heavy blow.
> 15You yourself will be very ill with
> a lingering disease[e] of the bowels,
> until the disease causes your bowels
> to come out.'"

16The LORD aroused against Jehoram
the hostility of the Philistines and of
the Arabs[f] who lived near the Cushites.
17They attacked Judah, invaded it and
carried off all the goods found in the
king's palace, together with his sons and
wives. Not a son was left to him except
Ahaziah,[a] the youngest.[g]

18After all this, the LORD afflicted Jehoram with an incurable disease of the
bowels. 19In the course of time, at the
end of the second year, his bowels came
out because of the disease, and he died
in great pain. His people made no funeral fire in his honor,[h] as they had for his
predecessors.

20Jehoram was thirty-two years old
when he became king, and he reigned in
Jerusalem eight years. He passed away,
to no one's regret, and was buried[i] in
the City of David, but not in the tombs
of the kings.

[a] 17 Hebrew *Jehoahaz,* a variant of *Ahaziah*

21:4 [q] 1Ki 2:12 [r] Jdg 9:5
21:6 [s] 1Ki 12:28-30 [t] 2Ch 18:1; 22:3
21:7 [u] 2Sa 7:13 [v] 2Sa 7:15; 2Ch 23:3 [w] 2Sa 21:17; 1Ki 11:36
21:8 [x] 2Ch 20:22-23
21:10 [y] Nu 33:20
21:12 [z] 2Ki 1:16-17 [a] 2Ch 17:3-6 [b] 2Ch 14:2
21:13 [c] ver 6, 11; 1Ki 16:29-33 [d] ver 4; 1Ki 2:32
21:15 [e] ver 18-19; Nu 12:10
21:16 [f] 2Ch 17:10-11; 22:1; 26:7
21:17 [g] 2Ki 12:18; 2Ch 22:1; 25:23; Joel 3:5
21:19 [h] 2Ch 16:14
21:20 [i] 2Ch 24:25; 28:27; 33:20; Jer 22:18, 28

2Ch 21:4 ❖ Lust for power causes people to do awful things. Where have we seen power misused? How can we use power for godly purposes?

21:4–20 The affiliation of the house of Judah with the house of Ahab through the marriage of Jehoram and Athaliah (v. 6; 22:1–2) is a recipe for self-destruction.

21:8–11 There is a direct correlation between a king's increasing political power and his faithfulness to the covenant. The author's theological commentary on the two revolts against Jehoram places blame directly on the king's sin of idolatry (vv. 10b–11).

21:12–15 Elijah was alive during part of Jehoram's reign since Jehoram was apparently a coregent with Jehoshaphat as early as 853 BC. The body of Elijah's letter is characteristic of OT prophetic speech. The pattern of presenting an indictment followed by pronouncing judgment is typical of the structure of preexilic prophetic messages. The phrase "the ways of the kings of Israel" refers to Jeroboam's sin of idolatry, perpetuated by all his successors in Israel (1Ki 14:9; cf. 15:34).

21:15 The king's punishment exposes his mortality and mocks his dignity as royalty.

21:16–17 The report of the revolt on the part of the Philistines and Arabs validates the prophecy of Elijah and underscores the theme of immediate divine retribution in Chronicles.

21:18–19 Tragically, this descendant of David dies dishonorably, and even his own people refuse to honor him in death (cf. 16:14).

Ahaziah King of Judah

22:1–6pp // 2Ki 8:25–29
22:7–9pp // 2Ki 9:21–29

22 The people[j] of Jerusalem[k] made Ahaziah, Jehoram's youngest son, king in his place, since the raiders,[l] who came with the Arabs into the camp, had killed all the older sons. So Ahaziah son of Jehoram king of Judah began to reign.

2 Ahaziah was twenty-two[a] years old when he became king, and he reigned in Jerusalem one year. His mother's name was Athaliah, a granddaughter of Omri.

3 He too followed[m] the ways of the house of Ahab,[n] for his mother encouraged him to act wickedly. 4 He did evil in the eyes of the LORD, as the house of Ahab had done, for after his father's death they became his advisers, to his undoing. 5 He also followed their counsel when he went with Joram[b] son of Ahab king of Israel to wage war against Hazael king of Aram at Ramoth Gilead.[o] The Arameans wounded Joram; 6 so he returned to Jezreel to recover from the wounds they had inflicted on him at Ramoth[c] in his battle with Hazael[p] king of Aram.

Then Ahaziah[d] son of Jehoram king of Judah went down to Jezreel to see Joram son of Ahab because he had been wounded.

7 Through Ahaziah's[q] visit to Joram, God brought about Ahaziah's downfall. When Ahaziah arrived, he went out with Joram to meet Jehu son of Nimshi, whom the LORD had anointed to destroy the house of Ahab. 8 While Jehu was executing judgment on the house of Ahab,[r] he found the officials of Judah and the sons of Ahaziah's relatives, who had been attending Ahaziah, and he killed them. 9 He then went in search of Ahaziah, and his men captured him while he was hiding[s] in Samaria. He was brought to Jehu and put to death. They buried him, for they said, "He was a son of Jehoshaphat, who sought[t] the LORD with all his heart." So there was no one in the house of Ahaziah powerful enough to retain the kingdom.

22:1 [j] 2Ch 33:25; 36:1 [k] 2Ch 23:20-21; 26:1 [l] 2Ch 21:16-17
22:3 [m] 2Ch 18:1 [n] 2Ch 21:6
22:5 [o] 2Ch 18:11, 34
22:6 [p] 1Ki 19:15; 2Ki 8:13-15; 9:15
22:7 [q] 2Ki 9:16; 2Ch 10:15
22:8 [r] 2Ki 10:13
22:9 [s] Jdg 9:5 [t] 2Ch 17:4

2Ch 22:3 ❖ What can we do to withstand wicked influences around us, perhaps even from people very close to us?

Athaliah and Joash

22:10—23:21pp // 2Ki 11:1–21

10 When Athaliah the mother of Ahaziah saw that her son was dead, she proceeded to destroy the whole royal family of the house of Judah. 11 But Jehosheba,[e] the daughter of King Jehoram, took Joash son of Ahaziah and stole him away from among the royal princes who were about to be murdered and put him and his nurse in a bedroom. Because Jehosheba,[e] the daughter of King Jehoram and wife of the priest Jehoiada, was Ahaziah's sister, she hid the child from Athaliah so she could not kill him. 12 He remained hidden with them at the temple of God for six years while Athaliah ruled the land.

23 In the seventh year Jehoiada showed his strength. He made a covenant with the commanders of units of a hundred: Azariah son of Jeroham,

[a] *2* Some Septuagint manuscripts and Syriac (see also 2 Kings 8:26); Hebrew *forty-two*
[b] *5* Hebrew *Jehoram,* a variant of *Joram;* also in verses 6 and 7
[c] *6* Hebrew *Ramah,* a variant of *Ramoth*
[d] *6* Some Hebrew manuscripts, Septuagint, Vulgate and Syriac (see also 2 Kings 8:29); most Hebrew manuscripts *Azariah*
[e] *11* Hebrew *Jehoshabeath,* a variant of *Jehosheba*

22:1–6 The account of King Ahaziah's reign consists of three brief reports: the résumé and theological review (vv. 1–4), the alliance with Joram of Israel (vv. 5–6a), and the death report (vv. 6b–9). The one-year reign of Ahaziah is dated anywhere from 845–841 BC, depending on the source. His brief tenure in the royal office is best placed in 842 or 841 BC.
22:7–9 The Chronicler's theological commentary bluntly states that God "brought about Ahaziah's downfall" (v. 7). The message of the passage is alarmingly clear: God repays evil for evil almost immediately on those who fail to emulate David's example of righteous rule. Although the sins of the house of Ahab perpetuated by King Ahaziah are unnamed in Chronicles, it seems they include idolatry, witchcraft, and a failure to trust in God as the sovereign of Judah—evidenced by "unholy" political alliances.
22:10–12 It seems likely that Athaliah is the daughter of the Phoenician princess Jezebel and King Ahab of Israel. Like her mother, she worships the Canaanite fertility god Baal and imposes Baal worship on the people of the kingdom by manipulating the king. She attempts to completely destroy the house of David and rules the land for six years.

The name Jehosheba means "Yahweh vows." Fittingly, God uses this faithful woman to keep his oath to maintain the family dynasty of David (cf. 21:7).
23:1–11 The coup led by Jehoiada the priest occurs during the seventh year of Athaliah's rule (or about

Ishmael son of Jehohanan, Azariah son of Obed, Maaseiah son of Adaiah, and Elishaphat son of Zikri. 2They went throughout Judah and gathered the Levites[u] and the heads of Israelite families from all the towns. When they came to Jerusalem, 3the whole assembly made a covenant[v] with the king at the temple of God.

Jehoiada said to them, "The king's son shall reign, as the LORD promised concerning the descendants of David.[w] 4Now this is what you are to do: A third of you priests and Levites who are going on duty on the Sabbath are to keep watch at the doors, 5a third of you at the royal palace and a third at the Foundation Gate, and all the others are to be in the courtyards of the temple of the LORD. 6No one is to enter the temple of the LORD except the priests and Levites on duty; they may enter because they are consecrated, but all the others are to observe[x] the LORD's command not to enter.[a] 7The Levites are to station themselves around the king, each with weapon in hand. Anyone who enters the temple is to be put to death. Stay close to the king wherever he goes."

8The Levites and all the men of Judah did just as Jehoiada the priest ordered.[y] Each one took his men — those who were going on duty on the Sabbath and those who were going off duty — for Jehoiada the priest had not released any of the divisions.[z] 9Then he gave the commanders of units of a hundred the spears and the large and small shields that had belonged to King David and that were in the temple of God. 10He stationed all the men, each with his weapon in his hand, around the king — near the altar and the temple, from the south side to the north side of the temple.

11Jehoiada and his sons brought out the king's son and put the crown on him; they presented him with a copy[a] of the covenant and proclaimed him king. They anointed him and shouted, "Long live the king!"

12When Athaliah heard the noise of the people running and cheering the king, she went to them at the temple of the LORD. 13She looked, and there was the king,[b] standing by his pillar[c] at the entrance. The officers and the trumpeters were beside the king, and all the people of the land were rejoicing and blowing trumpets, and musicians with their instruments were leading the praises. Then Athaliah tore her robes and shouted, "Treason! Treason!"

14Jehoiada the priest sent out the commanders of units of a hundred, who were in charge of the troops, and said to them: "Bring her out between the ranks[b] and put to the sword anyone who follows her." For the priest had said, "Do not put her to death at the temple of the LORD." 15So they seized her as she reached the entrance of the Horse Gate[d] on the palace grounds, and there they put her to death.

16Jehoiada then made a covenant[e] that he, the people and the king[c] would be the LORD's people. 17All the people went to the temple of Baal and tore it down. They smashed the altars and idols and killed[f] Mattan the priest of Baal in front of the altars.

18Then Jehoiada placed the oversight of the temple of the LORD in the hands of

23:2 [u] Nu 35:2-5
23:3 [v] 2Ki 11:17 [w] 2Sa 7:12; 1Ki 2:4; 2Ch 6:16; 7:18; 21:7
23:6 [x] 1Ch 23:28-29; Zec 3:7
23:8 [y] 2Ki 11:9 [z] 1Ch 24:1
23:11 [a] Ex 25:16; Dt 17:18; 1Sa 10:24
23:13 [b] 1Ki 1:41 [c] 1Ki 7:15
23:15 [d] Ne 3:28; Jer 31:40
23:16 [e] 2Ch 29:10; 34:31; Ne 9:38
23:17 [f] Dt 13:6-9

2Ch 23:16–19 ❖ Do we need to renew our covenant with God? How might God be calling us to deeper worship and devotion?

[a] 6 Or *are to stand guard where the LORD has assigned them* [b] 14 Or *out from the precincts* [c] 16 Or *covenant between the LORD and the people and the king that they* (see 2 Kings 11:17)

---

837 BC). Jehoiada is not driven by selfish motives; rather, he appeals to the promise of God anchored in the Davidic covenant (v. 3b).

Jehoiada plans his coup in three stages: first assembling a coalition of conspirators, then strategically deploying armed guards to ensure the safety of the king, and finally presenting Joash for public installation as king of Judah. The installation of a king includes a coronation, anointing with oil, and the presentation of a "copy of the covenant" (v. 11).

23:12–15 The cooperation of the priests with army commanders suggests that this coalition is responsible for the coup that elevates Joash to the throne. Jehoiada the priest also decrees that Athaliah be executed outside temple precincts to avoid defiling the sacred site.

23:16–19 The coronation of Joash climaxes with a covenant-renewal ceremony led by Jehoiada the priest. Two distinct but related covenants are enacted in the aftermath of the coup against Athaliah: The first covenant is ratified by the king and the people of Jerusalem, reestablishing the authority of Davidic kingship in Judah; the second pact is a covenant-renewal ceremony binding king and people in obedience to the Law of Moses.

the Levitical priests,[g] to whom David had
made assignments in the temple,[h] to present the burnt offerings of the LORD as
written in the Law of Moses, with rejoicing and singing, as David had ordered.
19 He also stationed gatekeepers[i] at the
gates of the LORD's temple so that no one
who was in any way unclean might enter.
20 He took with him the commanders
of hundreds, the nobles, the rulers of the
people and all the people of the land and
brought the king down from the temple
of the LORD. They went into the palace
through the Upper Gate[j] and seated the
king on the royal throne. 21 All the people of the land rejoiced, and the city was
calm, because Athaliah had been slain
with the sword.[k]

Joash Repairs the Temple

24:1–14pp // 2Ki 12:1–16
24:23–27pp // 2Ki 12:17–21

24 Joash was seven years old when
he became king, and he reigned
in Jerusalem forty years. His mother's
name was Zibiah; she was from Beersheba. 2 Joash did what was right in the
eyes of the LORD[l] all the years of Jehoiada
the priest. 3 Jehoiada chose two wives for
him, and he had sons and daughters.
4 Some time later Joash decided to restore the temple of the LORD. 5 He called
together the priests and Levites and said
to them, "Go to the towns of Judah and
collect the money[m] due annually from
all Israel,[n] to repair the temple of your
God. Do it now." But the Levites[o] did not
act at once.
6 Therefore the king summoned Jehoiada the chief priest and said to him,
"Why haven't you required the Levites to
bring in from Judah and Jerusalem the
tax imposed by Moses the servant of the
LORD and by the assembly of Israel for
the tent of the covenant law?"[p]
7 Now the sons of that wicked woman
Athaliah had broken into the temple of
God and had used even its sacred objects
for the Baals.
8 At the king's command, a chest was
made and placed outside, at the gate of
the temple of the LORD. 9 A proclamation was then issued in Judah and Jerusalem that they should bring to the
LORD the tax that Moses the servant of
God had required of Israel in the wilderness. 10 All the officials and all the people brought their contributions gladly,[q]
dropping them into the chest until it was
full. 11 Whenever the chest was brought in
by the Levites to the king's officials and
they saw that there was a large amount
of money, the royal secretary and the
officer of the chief priest would come
and empty the chest and carry it back
to its place. They did this regularly and
collected a great amount of money. 12 The
king and Jehoiada gave it to those who
carried out the work required for the
temple of the LORD. They hired[r] masons
and carpenters to restore the LORD's temple, and also workers in iron and bronze
to repair the temple.
13 The men in charge of the work were
diligent, and the repairs progressed under them. They rebuilt the temple of God

23:18 [g] 1Ch 23:28-32; 2Ch 5:5 [h] 1Ch 23:6; 25:6
23:19 [i] 1Ch 9:22
23:20 [j] 2Ki 15:35
23:21 [k] 2Ch 22:1
24:2 [l] 2Ch 25:2; 26:5
24:5 [m] Ex 30:16; Ne 10:32-33; Mt 17:24 [n] 1Ch 11:1 [o] 1Ch 26:20
24:6 [p] Ex 30:12-16; Nu 1:50
24:10 [q] Ex 25:2; 1Ch 29:3,6,9
24:12 [r] 2Ch 34:11

2Ch 24:2 ❖ Jehoiada the priest had a profoundly positive influence on Joash. How have we been mentored and guided by God's servants?

23:20–21 The installation of Joash on the royal throne marks the end of Athaliah. Thanks to Jehosheba and Jehoiada, there has been, in one sense, no interruption of Davidic kingship in Judah—Joash has been there all along, although in hiding.

✣ 21:4—23:21 The Chronicler's emphasis on named individuals in the history of the Israelite monarchies reminds each of us of our uniqueness and importance. In the stories of a man like Jehoiada and a woman like Jehosheba, the Chronicler reminds us that each person of faith in the God of the Bible becomes an integral player on the stage of redemptive history as he or she steps out and "shows strength" (23:1) with the help of the Holy Spirit.

24:1–3 The forty-year reign of Joash is dated variously between 840 and 796 BC. The Chronicler divides the reign of Joash into two distinct and contrasting periods: the good years of his early rule under the instruction of Jehoiada and the later years of apostasy.

24:4–16 The favorable report concerning Joash's reign centers on two themes: the renovation of Yahweh's temple and the figure of Jehoiada as the ideal high priest. Jehoiada is the model high priest for the Chronicler because of his role as royal guardian and adviser.

The expression "old and full of years" (v. 15) is an idiom signifying honor and respect, and Jehoiada's longevity is a sign of divine favor. Jehoiada is remembered especially for two things: leading Judah in covenant faithfulness and leading in the initiative to refurbish the temple.

18 But Jehoash king of Israel replied to Amaziah king of Judah: "A thistle[x] in Lebanon sent a message to a cedar in Lebanon, 'Give your daughter to my son in marriage.' Then a wild beast in Lebanon came along and trampled the thistle underfoot. 19 You say to yourself that you have defeated Edom, and now you are arrogant and proud. But stay at home! Why ask for trouble and cause your own downfall and that of Judah also?"

20 Amaziah, however, would not listen, for God so worked that he might deliver them into the hands of Jehoash, because they sought the gods of Edom.[y] 21 So Jehoash king of Israel attacked. He and Amaziah king of Judah faced each other at Beth Shemesh in Judah. 22 Judah was routed by Israel, and every man fled to his home. 23 Jehoash king of Israel captured Amaziah king of Judah, the son of Joash, the son of Ahaziah,[a] at Beth Shemesh. Then Jehoash brought him to Jerusalem and broke down the wall of Jerusalem from the Ephraim Gate[z] to the Corner Gate[a]—a section about four hundred cubits[b] long. 24 He took all the gold and silver and all the articles found in the temple of God that had been in the care of Obed-Edom,[b] together with the palace treasures and the hostages, and returned to Samaria.

25 Amaziah son of Joash king of Judah lived for fifteen years after the death of Jehoash son of Jehoahaz king of Israel. 26 As for the other events of Amaziah's reign, from beginning to end, are they not written in the book of the kings of Judah and Israel? 27 From the time that Amaziah turned away from following the LORD, they conspired against him in Jerusalem and he fled to Lachish[c], but they sent men after him to Lachish and killed him there. 28 He was brought back by horse and was buried with his ancestors in the City of Judah.[c]

25:18 [x] Jdg 9:8-15
25:20 [y] 1Ki 12:15; 2Ch 10:15; 22:7
25:23 [z] 2Ki 14:13; Ne 8:16; 12:39 [a] 2Ch 26:9; Jer 31:38
25:24 [b] 1Ch 26:15
25:27 [c] Jos 10:3

Uzziah King of Judah

26:1–4pp // 2Ki 14:21–22; 15:1–3
26:21–23pp // 2Ki 15:5–7

26 Then all the people of Judah[d] took Uzziah,[d] who was sixteen years old, and made him king in place of his father Amaziah. 2 He was the one who rebuilt Elath and restored it to Judah after Amaziah rested with his ancestors.

3 Uzziah was sixteen years old when he became king, and he reigned in Jerusalem fifty-two years. His mother's name was Jekoliah; she was from Jerusalem. 4 He did what was right in the eyes of the LORD, just as his father Amaziah had done. 5 He sought God during the days of Zechariah, who instructed him in the fear[e] of God.[e] As long as he sought the LORD, God gave him success.[f]

6 He went to war against the Philistines[g] and broke down the walls of Gath, Jabneh and Ashdod.[h] He then rebuilt towns near Ashdod and elsewhere among the Philistines. 7 God helped him against the Philistines and against the Arabs[i] who lived in Gur Baal and against the Meunites.[j] 8 The Ammonites[k] brought tribute to Uzziah, and his fame spread as far as the border of Egypt, because he had become very powerful.

9 Uzziah built towers in Jerusalem at the Corner Gate,[l] at the Valley Gate[m] and at the angle of the wall, and he fortified them. 10 He also built towers in the wilderness and dug many cisterns, because he had much livestock in the foothills and in the plain. He had people working his fields and vineyards in the hills and in the fertile lands, for he loved the soil.

26:1 [d] 2Ch 22:1
26:5 [e] 2Ch 15:2; 24:2; Da 1:17 [f] 2Ch 27:6
26:6 [g] Isa 2:6; 11:14; 14:29; Jer 25:20 [h] Am 1:8; 3:9
26:7 [i] 2Ch 21:16 [j] 2Ch 20:1
26:8 [k] Ge 19:38; 2Ch 17:11
26:9 [l] 2Ki 14:13; 2Ch 25:23 [m] Ne 2:13; 3:13

[a] 23 Hebrew *Jehoahaz*, a variant of *Ahaziah*
[b] 23 That is, about 600 feet or about 180 meters
[c] 28 Most Hebrew manuscripts; some Hebrew manuscripts, Septuagint, Vulgate and Syriac (see also 2 Kings 14:20) *David*
[d] 1 Also called *Azariah*
[e] 5 Many Hebrew manuscripts, Septuagint and Syriac; other Hebrew manuscripts *vision*

25:25–28 The report of Amaziah's assassination includes his flight to Lachish. Assassins from Jerusalem hunt him down there, execute him, and bring his body back to Jerusalem for burial in the royal tomb complex.

26:1–5 The Chronicler's assessment of Uzziah as one who does "right . . . just as his father Amaziah had done" (v. 4) is hardly a ringing endorsement, since in the end Amaziah was an apostate king (25:27). Uzziah rules the kingdom of Judah for fifty-five years, from approximately 792 to 740 BC.

26:6–15 The litany of achievements indicating God's favor include military victory over Judah's archenemies (vv. 6–8), extensive building activity and agricultural bounty (vv. 9–10), and the marshalling of a large, well-trained, well-equipped army (vv. 11–15).

A considerable amount of archaeological data supports the biblical account of Uzziah's building activity, especially the reference to towers and cisterns (v. 10). Not since Solomon has there been a king with such agrarian interests (cf. 1Ki 4:33).

[11]Uzziah had a well-trained army, ready
to go out by divisions according to their
numbers as mustered by Jeiel the secretary and Maaseiah the officer under the
direction of Hananiah, one of the royal
officials. [12]The total number of family
leaders over the fighting men was 2,600.
[13]Under their command was an army of
307,500 men trained for war, a powerful
force to support the king against his enemies. [14]Uzziah provided shields, spears,
helmets, coats of armor, bows and slingstones for the entire army.[n] [15]In Jerusalem he made devices invented for use on
the towers and on the corner defenses so
that soldiers could shoot arrows and hurl
large stones from the walls. His fame
spread far and wide, for he was greatly
helped until he became powerful.

[16]But after Uzziah became powerful,
his pride[o] led to his downfall.[p] He was
unfaithful[q] to the LORD his God, and entered the temple of the LORD to burn
incense[r] on the altar of incense. [17]Azari-
ah[s] the priest with eighty other courageous priests of the LORD followed him
in. [18]They confronted King Uzziah and
said, "It is not right for you, Uzziah, to
burn incense to the LORD. That is for the
priests,[t] the descendants[u] of Aaron,[v] who
have been consecrated to burn incense.[w]
Leave the sanctuary, for you have been
unfaithful; and you will not be honored
by the LORD God."

26:14 [n]Jer 46:4
26:16 [o]2Ki 14:10 [p]Dt 32:15; 2Ch 25:19 [q]1Ch 5:25 [r]2Ki 16:12
26:17 [s]1Ki 4:2; 1Ch 6:10
26:18 [t]Nu 16:39 [u]Nu 18:1-7 [v]Ex 30:7 [w]1Ch 6:49
26:19 [x]Nu 12:10; 2Ki 5:25-27
26:21 [y]Ex 4:6; Lev 13:46; 14:8; Nu 5:2; 19:12
26:22 [z]2Ki 15:1; Isa 1:1; 6:1
26:23 [a]Isa 1:1; 6:1 [b]2Ki 14:21; 15:7; Am 1:1

2Ch 26:16 ❖ How does pride damage faith? What are a few ways we can deal with pride in our lives?

[19]Uzziah, who had a censer in his hand
ready to burn incense, became angry.
While he was raging at the priests in their
presence before the incense altar in the
LORD's temple, leprosy[a][x] broke out on
his forehead. [20]When Azariah the chief
priest and all the other priests looked
at him, they saw that he had leprosy on
his forehead, so they hurried him out.
Indeed, he himself was eager to leave,
because the LORD had afflicted him.

[21]King Uzziah had leprosy until the day
he died. He lived in a separate house[b][y]—
leprous, and banned from the temple
of the LORD. Jotham his son had charge
of the palace and governed the people
of the land.

[22]The other events of Uzziah's reign,
from beginning to end, are recorded by
the prophet Isaiah[z] son of Amoz. [23]Uz-
ziah[a] rested with his ancestors and was
buried near them in a cemetery that
belonged to the kings, for people said,
"He had leprosy." And Jotham his son
succeeded him as king.[b]

[a] *19* The Hebrew for *leprosy* was used for various diseases affecting the skin; also in verses 20, 21 and 23. [b] *21* Or *in a house where he was relieved of responsibilities*

26:16–21 The report of Uzziah's pride is the focal point of the Chronicler's review of his reign. The ominous words "after Uzziah became powerful" (v. 16a) link the commentary on the two phases of Uzziah's rule: the early years of God's blessing (vv. 5–15) and the later years of divine judgment (vv. 16–21). The expression "was unfaithful" (v. 16) becomes a regular theme in the Chronicler's retelling of the history of Davidic kingship (cf. 28:19, 22; 29:6, 19; 30:7; 33:19).

26:17–18 Only members of the Aaronic priesthood were allowed to attend to the altar and burn incense there. The priest's challenge to royal authority is done at great risk, given the recent horror of Joash's murder of the priest Zechariah (cf. 24:22). Azariah's threat to Uzziah is generally cast as God choosing to no longer honor this unfaithful king.

26:19–21 It is important to notice that God's anger breaks out against Uzziah only after the king has vented his anger against the priests. Uzziah's disregard for the Lord's priests and for the Lord's sanctuary implicitly signals a disregard for God himself. Uzziah thus joins the list of other notorious kings immediately afflicted by God because of their unfaithfulness. More significant is the dishonor of being excluded from worship in the temple of the Lord.

26:22–23 The record of Isaiah son of Amoz is one of several prophetic resources in the Chronicler's bibliography.

✜ **24:1–26:23** We have already learned from the lives of kings Joash, Amaziah, and Uzziah that receiving instruction and accepting counsel demand listening skills and that such skills are directly related to "the fear of the LORD." It is the biblical notion of the fear of the Lord that fosters reliance on God and receptivity to divine wisdom, in contrast to self-reliance and dependence on one's own understanding.

The writer of Proverbs reinforces God's attitudes toward those who renounce their devotion to him in favor of self-reliance: "I hate pride and arrogance, evil behavior and perverse speech" (Pr 8:13); "When pride comes, then comes disgrace, but with humility comes wisdom" (Pr 11:2); "The LORD detests all the proud of heart. Be sure of this: They will not go unpunished" (Pr 16:5).

Jotham King of Judah

27:1–4,7–9pp // 2Ki 15:33–38

27 Jotham[c] was twenty-five years
old when he became king, and he
reigned in Jerusalem sixteen years. His
mother's name was Jerusha daughter
of Zadok. 2He did what was right in the
eyes of the LORD, just as his father Uzziah had done, but unlike him he did not
enter the temple of the LORD. The people,
however, continued their corrupt practices. 3Jotham rebuilt the Upper Gate of
the temple of the LORD and did extensive
work on the wall at the hill of Ophel.[d] 4He
built towns in the hill country of Judah
and forts and towers in the wooded areas.
5Jotham waged war against the king
of the Ammonites[e] and conquered them.
That year the Ammonites paid him a hundred talents[a] of silver, ten thousand cors[b]
of wheat and ten thousand cors[c] of barley.
The Ammonites brought him the same
amount also in the second and third years.
6Jotham grew powerful[f] because he
walked steadfastly before the LORD his
God.
7The other events in Jotham's reign,
including all his wars and the other
things he did, are written in the book of
the kings of Israel and Judah. 8He was
twenty-five years old when he became
king, and he reigned in Jerusalem sixteen
years. 9Jotham rested with his ancestors
and was buried in the City of David. And
Ahaz his son succeeded him as king.

Ahaz King of Judah

28:1–27pp // 2Ki 16:1–20

28 Ahaz[g] was twenty years old when
he became king, and he reigned
in Jerusalem sixteen years. Unlike David
his father, he did not do what was right
in the eyes of the LORD. 2He followed
the ways of the kings of Israel and also
made idols[h] for worshiping the Baals.
3He burned sacrifices in the Valley of Ben
Hinnom[i] and sacrificed his children[j] in
the fire, engaging in the detestable[k] practices of the nations the LORD had driven
out before the Israelites. 4He offered sacrifices and burned incense at the high
places, on the hilltops and under every
spreading tree.
5Therefore the LORD his God delivered him into the hands of the king of
Aram.[l] The Arameans defeated him and
took many of his people as prisoners and
brought them to Damascus.
He was also given into the hands of the
king of Israel, who inflicted heavy casualties on him. 6In one day Pekah[m] son of
Remaliah killed a hundred and twenty
thousand soldiers in Judah[n] — because
Judah had forsaken the LORD, the God
of their ancestors. 7Zikri, an Ephraimite warrior, killed Maaseiah the king's
son, Azrikam the officer in charge of the
palace, and Elkanah, second to the king.
8The men of Israel took captive from
their fellow Israelites who were from Judah[o] two hundred thousand wives, sons
and daughters. They also took a great

2Ch 27:6 ❖ What does this statement about Jotham tell us about the blessings of walking steadfastly with God? In what ways can we implement this practice in our lives today?

27:1 [c] 2Ki 15:5, 32; 1Ch 3:12
27:3 [d] 2Ch 33:14; Ne 3:26
27:5 [e] Ge 19:38
27:6 [f] 2Ch 26:5
28:1 [g] 1Ch 3:13; Isa 1:1
28:2 [h] Ex 34:17; 2Ch 22:3
28:3 [i] Jos 15:8; 2Ki 23:10 [j] Lev 18:21; 2Ki 3:27; 2Ch 33:6; Eze 20:26 [k] Dt 18:9; 2Ch 33:2
28:5 [l] Isa 7:1
28:6 [m] 2Ki 15:25, 27 [n] ver 8; Isa 9:21; 11:13
28:8 [o] Dt 28:25-41; 2Ch 11:4

[a] *5* That is, about 3 3/4 tons or about 3.4 metric tons [b] *5* That is, probably about 1,800 tons or about 1,600 metric tons of wheat [c] *5* That is, probably about 1,500 tons or about 1,350 metric tons of barley

27:1-9 The brief report of King Jotham's reign is little more than a postscript to King Uzziah's tenure on the throne of Judah. Typically, his sixteen-year rule is dated from 750–735 BC. It appears that Jotham served as a coregent with his father Uzziah for the first ten years of his kingship (750–740 BC). The reference to the twentieth year of King Jotham (2Ki 15:30) is usually understood to mean that Jotham's reign also overlapped with that of his son Ahaz. If so, then Ahaz is coregent and junior partner with his father Jotham commencing in 735 BC. Jotham probably dies in 732 BC.

The Chronicler's review of Jotham's reign applauds achievements on three fronts: his building program, his military success, and his consolidation of political power (vv. 3–6). Jotham's war with the Ammonites (v. 5) is not mentioned elsewhere in the OT, but the campaign extends his father's military expansion from areas southwest of Judah to the east. But unlike his father, Jotham does not fall prey to the temptation of pride and turn away from God. His success is attributed directly to the fact that he "walked steadfastly before the LORD" (v. 6).

28:1-4 The Chronicler's negative theological review of Ahaz is supported by a shocking list of covenant violations, such as idolatry, child sacrifice, and participation in the false worship associated with the Canaanite high places.

28:5-15 Beyond the sheer totals, the devastating losses to Judah are compounded by the deaths of key officials (v. 7). The deaths of three members of Ahaz's "cabinet" would have had a crippling effect in the administration of political and military affairs in Judah.

deal of plunder, which they carried back
to Samaria.[p]
9 But a prophet of the LORD named
Oded was there, and he went out to meet
the army when it returned to Samaria.
He said to them, "Because the LORD, the
God of your ancestors, was angry[q] with
Judah, he gave them into your hand. But
you have slaughtered them in a rage that
reaches to heaven.[r] 10 And now you intend to make the men and women of
Judah and Jerusalem your slaves.[s] But
aren't you also guilty of sins against the
LORD your God? 11 Now listen to me! Send
back your fellow Israelites you have tak-
en as prisoners, for the LORD's fierce anger rests on you.[t]"
12 Then some of the leaders in Ephraim — Azariah son of Jehohanan, Berekiah son of Meshillemoth, Jehizkiah
son of Shallum, and Amasa son of Had-
lai — confronted those who were arriving from the war. 13 "You must not bring
those prisoners here," they said, "or we
will be guilty before the LORD. Do you
intend to add to our sin and guilt? For
our guilt is already great, and his fierce
anger rests on Israel."
14 So the soldiers gave up the prisoners
and plunder in the presence of the officials and all the assembly. 15 The men designated by name took the prisoners, and
from the plunder they clothed all who
were naked. They provided them with
clothes and sandals, food and drink,[u]
and healing balm. All those who were
weak they put on donkeys. So they took
them back to their fellow Israelites at
Jericho, the City of Palms,[v] and returned
to Samaria.
16 At that time King Ahaz sent to the
kings[a] of Assyria[w] for help. 17 The Edomites[x] had again come and attacked Judah
and carried away prisoners,[y] 18 while the
Philistines[z] had raided towns in the foothills and in the Negev of Judah. They
captured and occupied Beth Shemesh,
Aijalon[a] and Gederoth, as well as Soko,
Timnah and Gimzo, with their surrounding villages. 19 The LORD had humbled
Judah because of Ahaz king of Israel,[b] for
he had promoted wickedness in Judah
and had been most unfaithful[b] to the
LORD. 20 Tiglath-Pileser[c][c] king of Assyria
came to him, but he gave him trouble
instead of help.[d] 21 Ahaz took some of
the things from the temple of the LORD
and from the royal palace and from the
officials and presented them to the king
of Assyria, but that did not help him.
22 In his time of trouble King Ahaz became even more unfaithful[e] to the LORD.
23 He offered sacrifices to the gods[f] of Damascus, who had defeated him; for he
thought, "Since the gods of the kings of
Aram have helped them, I will sacrifice
to them so they will help me."[g] But they
were his downfall and the downfall of
all Israel.
24 Ahaz gathered together the furnishings from the temple of God[h] and cut
them in pieces. He shut the doors[i] of the
LORD's temple and set up altars[j] at every
street corner in Jerusalem. 25 In every
town in Judah he built high places to

2Ch 28:23 ❖ When we see people around us idolizing things or worshiping God in ways that are not right, how can we avoid falling into these practices?

28:8 [p] 2Ch 29:9
28:9 [q] 2Ch 25:15; Isa 10:6; 47:6; Zec 1:15 [r] Ezr 9:6; Rev 18:5
28:10 [s] Lev 25:39-46
28:11 [t] 2Ch 11:4; Jas 2:13
28:15 [u] 2Ki 6:22; Pr 25:21-22 [v] Dt 34:3; Jdg 1:16
28:16 [w] 2Ki 16:7
28:17 [x] Ps 137:7; Isa 34:5 [y] 2Ch 29:9
28:18 [z] Eze 16:27,57 [a] Jos 10:12
28:19 [b] 2Ch 21:2
28:20 [c] 2Ki 15:29; 1Ch 5:6 [d] 2Ki 16:7
28:22 [e] Jer 5:3
28:23 [f] 2Ch 25:14 [g] Jer 44:17-18
28:24 [h] 2Ki 16:18 [i] 2Ch 29:7 [j] 2Ch 30:14

[a] *16* Most Hebrew manuscripts; one Hebrew manuscript, Septuagint and Vulgate (see also 2 Kings 16:7) *king* [b] *19* That is, Judah, as frequently in 2 Chronicles [c] *20* Hebrew *Tilgath-Pilneser,* a variant of *Tiglath-Pileser*

28:9–14 Oded is a prophet of Yahweh from Israel whose ministry is centered in Samaria; clearly God still has a voice in the northern kingdom. Unlike King Ahaz and their Judean counterparts, the leadership of Israel responds to the word of God through the prophet Oded and repent of their actions.

28:16–21 The heavy losses suffered at the hands of the invading Israelites and Arameans (vv. 5–15) force Ahaz to seek the "help" (v. 16) of Tiglath-Pileser III, king of Assyria (745–727 BC). This dangerous diplomacy of playing one ancient superpower (i.e., Assyria) against another (i.e., Egypt) as an ally in petty border wars was a tactic soundly condemned by Hosea the prophet (Hos 7:11). However, it was a ploy of the northern kingdom of Israel during the reign of Jeroboam II.

According to the Chronicler, all this comes about to "humble Judah" (v. 19) because of the wickedness of Ahaz. Rather than "help," Ahaz receives "trouble" from the Assyrians (v. 20). Judah also loses its political autonomy as Judah, Ammon, Moab, Ashkelon, Edom, and Gaza are all subordinated to Assyria as vassal states.

28:22–25 Ahaz's "time of trouble" (v. 22) affords the king the opportunity to seek the Lord in penitent prayer. But instead of turning to God, he strays even further by worshiping the gods of the victorious Syrians or Arameans (v. 23). Like King Ahab of Israel, Ahaz institutionalizes the worship of false gods as the state religion.

burn sacrifices to other gods and aroused
the anger of the LORD, the God of his ancestors.
26The other events of his reign and
all his ways, from beginning to end, are
written in the book of the kings of Judah and Israel. 27Ahaz rested[k] with his
ancestors and was buried[l] in the city of
Jerusalem, but he was not placed in the
tombs of the kings of Israel. And Hezekiah his son succeeded him as king.

Hezekiah Purifies the Temple

29:1–2pp // 2Ki 18:2–3

29 Hezekiah[m] was twenty-five years
old when he became king, and he
reigned in Jerusalem twenty-nine years.
His mother's name was Abijah daughter
of Zechariah. 2He did what was right in
the eyes of the LORD, just as his father
David[n] had done.
3In the first month of the first year
of his reign, he opened the doors of the
temple of the LORD and repaired[o] them.
4He brought in the priests and the Levites, assembled them in the square on
the east side 5and said: "Listen to me,
Levites! Consecrate[p] yourselves now and
consecrate the temple of the LORD, the
God of your ancestors. Remove all defilement from the sanctuary. 6Our parents[q]
were unfaithful;[r] they did evil in the eyes
of the LORD our God and forsook him.
They turned their faces away from the
LORD's dwelling place and turned their
backs on him. 7They also shut the doors
of the portico and put out the lamps.
They did not burn incense or present
any burnt offerings at the sanctuary to
the God of Israel. 8Therefore, the anger
of the LORD has fallen on Judah and Jerusalem; he has made them an object of
dread and horror[s] and scorn,[t] as you can
see with your own eyes. 9This is why our
fathers have fallen by the sword and why
our sons and daughters and our wives
are in captivity.[u] 10Now I intend to make
a covenant[v] with the LORD, the God of
Israel, so that his fierce anger will turn
away from us. 11My sons, do not be negligent now, for the LORD has chosen you to
stand before him and serve him,[w] to minister[x] before him and to burn incense."
12Then these Levites[y] set to work:

from the Kohathites,
Mahath son of Amasai and Joel son of Azariah;
from the Merarites,
Kish son of Abdi and Azariah son of Jehallelel;
from the Gershonites,
Joah son of Zimmah and Eden[z] son of Joah;
13from the descendants of Elizaphan,
Shimri and Jeiel;
from the descendants of Asaph,[a]
Zechariah and Mattaniah;
14from the descendants of Heman,
Jehiel and Shimei;
from the descendants of Jeduthun,
Shemaiah and Uzziel.

15When they had assembled their fellow Levites and consecrated themselves,
they went in to purify[b] the temple of the
LORD, as the king had ordered, following the word of the LORD. 16The priests
went into the sanctuary of the LORD to
purify it. They brought out to the courtyard of the LORD's temple everything
unclean that they found in the temple
of the LORD. The Levites took it and carried it out to the Kidron Valley.[c] 17They
began the consecration on the first day
of the first month, and by the eighth day

2Ch 29:6 ❖ Are there sins or behaviors in our family line for which we need to repent? How can we repent of family sins?

28:27 [k] Isa 14:28-32 [l] 2Ch 21:20; 24:25
29:1 [m] 1Ch 3:13
29:2 [n] 2Ch 28:1; 34:2
29:3 [o] 2Ch 28:24
29:5 [p] 2Ch 35:6
29:6 [q] Ps 106:6-47; Jer 2:27 [r] 1Ch 5:25; Eze 8:16
29:8 [s] Dt 28:25; 2Ch 24:18 [t] Jer 18:16; 19:8; 25:9,18
29:9 [u] 2Ch 28:5-8,17
29:10 [v] 2Ch 15:12; 23:16
29:11 [w] Nu 3:6; 8:6,14 [x] 1Ch 15:2
29:12 [y] Nu 3:17-20 [z] 2Ch 31:15
29:13 [a] 1Ch 6:39
29:15 [b] ver 5; 1Ch 23:28; 2Ch 30:12
29:16 [c] 2Sa 15:23

28:26–27 Like King Uzziah before him (26:23), Ahaz is denied the honor of proper burial "in the tombs of the kings of Israel"—the ultimate negative theological review by the Chronicler.
29:1–2 King Hezekiah is compared to David (v. 2). In fact, the reference to David foreshadows several direct analogies between that ideal king and Hezekiah later in the narrative.
29:3–11 The king's speech to the priests and Levites contains two injunctions: a call to the religious leadership to "consecrate" themselves and an instruction to them to "remove all defilement from the sanctuary" (v. 5). The rest of the royal address rehearses the neglect of the temple by Hezekiah's predecessors. Hezekiah is almost a Moses-type figure, acting as intercessor for the nation (v. 10). Hezekiah encourages the priests and Levites to reject apathy and to perform their duty (v. 11).
29:12–19 The Chronicler records the names of fourteen individuals who serve as the leaders of the purification ritual of the temple. The actual cleansing of the temple takes two weeks: one week for the outer courts and another week to purge the sanctuary itself (vv. 15–17). The Chronicler is careful to indicate the work is done in accordance with the "the word of the LORD" (v. 15).

of the month they reached the portico
of the LORD. For eight more days they
consecrated the temple of the LORD itself, finishing on the sixteenth day of
the first month.
18 Then they went in to King Hezekiah and reported: "We have purified the
entire temple of the LORD, the altar of
burnt offering with all its utensils, and
the table for setting out the consecrated bread, with all its articles. 19 We have
prepared and consecrated all the articles[d]
that King Ahaz removed in his unfaithfulness while he was king. They are now
in front of the LORD's altar."
20 Early the next morning King Hezekiah gathered the city officials together
and went up to the temple of the LORD.
21 They brought seven bulls, seven rams,
seven male lambs and seven male goats
as a sin offering[a][e] for the kingdom, for
the sanctuary and for Judah. The king
commanded the priests, the descendants of Aaron, to offer these on the altar of the LORD. 22 So they slaughtered
the bulls, and the priests took the blood
and splashed it against the altar; next
they slaughtered the rams and splashed
their blood against the altar; then they
slaughtered the lambs and splashed their
blood[f] against the altar. 23 The goats for
the sin offering were brought before
the king and the assembly, and they
laid their hands[g] on them. 24 The priests
then slaughtered the goats and presented their blood on the altar for a sin offering to atone[h] for all Israel, because the
king had ordered the burnt offering and
the sin offering for all Israel.
25 He stationed the Levites in the temple of the LORD with cymbals, harps and
lyres in the way prescribed by David[i]
and Gad[j] the king's seer and Nathan
the prophet; this was commanded by
the LORD through his prophets. 26 So
the Levites stood ready with David's instruments,[k] and the priests with their
trumpets.[l]
27 Hezekiah gave the order to sacrifice the burnt offering on the altar. As
the offering began, singing to the LORD
began also, accompanied by trumpets
and the instruments[m] of David king of
Israel. 28 The whole assembly bowed in
worship, while the musicians played and
the trumpets sounded. All this continued
until the sacrifice of the burnt offering
was completed.
29 When the offerings were finished,
the king and everyone present with him
knelt down and worshiped.[n] 30 King Hezekiah and his officials ordered the Levites to praise the LORD with the words
of David and of Asaph the seer. So they
sang praises with gladness and bowed
down and worshiped.
31 Then Hezekiah said, "You have now
dedicated yourselves to the LORD. Come
and bring sacrifices[o] and thank offerings to the temple of the LORD." So the
assembly brought sacrifices and thank
offerings, and all whose hearts were willing[p] brought burnt offerings.
32 The number of burnt offerings the
assembly brought was seventy bulls, a
hundred rams and two hundred male
lambs — all of them for burnt offerings
to the LORD. 33 The animals consecrated
as sacrifices amounted to six hundred
bulls and three thousand sheep and
goats. 34 The priests, however, were too
few to skin all the burnt offerings;[q] so
their relatives the Levites helped them
until the task was finished and until other priests had been consecrated,[r] for the
Levites had been more conscientious in
consecrating themselves than the priests

[a] 21 Or *purification offering*; also in verses 23 and 24

29:19 [d] 2Ch 28:24
29:21 [e] Lev 4:13-14
29:22 [f] Lev 4:18
29:23 [g] Lev 4:15
29:24 [h] Ex 29:36; Lev 4:26
29:25 [i] 1Ch 25:6; 2Ch 8:14 [j] 1Sa 22:5; 2Sa 24:11
29:26 [k] 1Ch 15:16 [l] 1Ch 15:24; 23:5; 2Ch 5:12
29:27 [m] 2Ch 23:18
29:29 [n] 2Ch 20:18
29:31 [o] Heb 13:15-16 [p] Ex 25:2; 35:22
29:34 [q] 2Ch 35:11 [r] 2Ch 30:3,15

29:20–36 The ceremony for the consecration of the temple is a multifaceted event. (1) The initial phase addresses the issues of sin and purification in the community (vv. 20–24). (2) The next phase features burnt offerings signifying the dedication of the religious and civic leaders and the sanctuary to the service of God (vv. 25–30). (3) The final stage includes participation by the assembly of people from Jerusalem and Judah (vv. 31–36).

The Chronicler takes great pains to demonstrate direct connections to earlier traditions originating with David and sanctioned by God's word through the prophets (vv. 25–26).

29:29–30 It is clear to all that Yahweh is King in Israel, not Hezekiah, for the king also bows before the Lord with the assembly. The reference to Asaph the seer recalls the commissioning of certain members of the Levitical musical guilds for the ministry of prophesying.

29:31–36 During the final phase of the consecration ceremony, the rites of purification and dedication are extended to the "assembly" (v. 31) and "all the people" of Judah (v. 36). The Chronicler commends the spirit of the Levites who assisted the priests in preparing the animals for sacrifice (v. 34a). That the restoration of temple worship is truly an act of God is seen in the fact that it is accomplished so quickly (v. 36).

had been. 35 There were burnt offerings in abundance, together with the fat[s] of the fellowship offerings[t] and the drink offerings[u] that accompanied the burnt offerings.

So the service of the temple of the LORD was reestablished. 36 Hezekiah and all the people rejoiced at what God had brought about for his people, because it was done so quickly.

Hezekiah Celebrates the Passover

30 Hezekiah sent word to all Israel and Judah and also wrote letters to Ephraim and Manasseh,[v] inviting them to come to the temple of the LORD in Jerusalem and celebrate the Passover[w] to the LORD, the God of Israel. 2 The king and his officials and the whole assembly in Jerusalem decided to celebrate[x] the Passover in the second month. 3 They had not been able to celebrate it at the regular time because not enough priests had consecrated[y] themselves and the people had not assembled in Jerusalem. 4 The plan seemed right both to the king and to the whole assembly. 5 They decided to send a proclamation throughout Israel, from Beersheba to Dan,[z] calling the people to come to Jerusalem and celebrate the Passover to the LORD, the God of Israel. It had not been celebrated in large numbers according to what was written.

6 At the king's command, couriers went throughout Israel and Judah with letters from the king and from his officials, which read:

"People of Israel, return to the LORD, the God of Abraham, Isaac and Israel, that he may return to you who are left, who have escaped from the hand of the kings of Assyria. 7 Do not be like your parents[a] and your fellow Israelites, who were unfaithful to the LORD, the God of their ancestors, so that he made them an object of horror,[b] as you see. 8 Do not be stiff-necked,[c] as your ancestors were; submit to the LORD. Come to his sanctuary, which he has consecrated forever. Serve the LORD your God, so that his fierce anger[d] will turn away from you. 9 If you return[e] to the LORD, then your fellow Israelites and your children will be shown compassion[f] by their captors and will return to this land, for the LORD your God is gracious and compassionate.[g] He will not turn his face from you if you return to him."

10 The couriers went from town to town in Ephraim and Manasseh, as far as Zebulun, but people scorned and ridiculed[h] them. 11 Nevertheless, some from Asher, Manasseh and Zebulun humbled themselves and went to Jerusalem.[i] 12 Also in Judah the hand of God was on the people to give them unity[j] of mind to carry out what the king and his officials had ordered, following the word of the LORD.

13 A very large crowd of people assembled in Jerusalem to celebrate the Festival of Unleavened Bread[k] in the second month. 14 They removed the altars[l] in Jerusalem and cleared away the incense altars and threw them into the Kidron Valley.[m]

15 They slaughtered the Passover lamb on the fourteenth day of the second month. The priests and the Levites were ashamed and consecrated[n] themselves and brought burnt offerings to the

29:35 [s] Ex 29:13; Lev 3:16 [t] Lev 7:11-21 [u] Nu 15:5-10
30:1 [v] Ge 41:52 [w] Ex 12:11; Nu 28:16
30:2 [x] Nu 9:10
30:3 [y] 2Ch 29:34
30:5 [z] Jdg 20:1
30:7 [a] Ps 78:8, 57; 106:6; Eze 20:18 [b] 2Ch 29:8
30:8 [c] Ex 32:9 [d] Nu 25:4; 2Ch 29:10
30:9 [e] Dt 30:2-5; Isa 1:16; 55:7 [f] 1Ki 8:50; Ps 106:46 [g] Ex 34:6-7; Dt 4:31; Mic 7:18
30:10 [h] 2Ch 36:16
30:11 [i] ver 25
30:12 [j] Jer 32:39; Eze 11:19; Php 2:13
30:13 [k] Nu 28:16
30:14 [l] 2Ch 28:24 [m] 2Sa 15:23
30:15 [n] 2Ch 29:34

2Ch 30:1 ❖ Hezekiah invited those outside of the kingdom of Judah to celebrate Passover at God's temple. How can we invite outsiders into our faith?

30:1–5 The introductory section of the chapter recounts the decision to celebrate the Passover in Jerusalem at the reopened temple.

30:6–9 The actual text of Hezekiah's letter is summarized in the second section of the unit. Curiously, the letter itself does not mention the Passover celebration—although this is the theme of the entire passage. Israelites who live anywhere in the land are invited to the Passover celebration.

30:6–12 In addition to calling the people to repentance, Hezekiah's letter admonishes the Israelites to cease being "unfaithful" (v. 7) and "stiff-necked" (v. 8) like their ancestors. Hezekiah's letter holds out hope to those who have escaped the wrath of God meted out through Assyrian kings. The appeal to the Lord, who "is gracious and compassionate" (v. 9), seems to allude once again to Solomon's dedicatory prayer (cf. 1Ki 8:50).

30:13—31:1 The Chronicler's report alternates between the description of the Festival of Unleavened Bread (vv. 13–14, 21–27) and the Passover (vv. 15–20). Hezekiah's festival may be outlined in three broad movements: the assembling of large numbers of Israelites making the pilgrimage to Jerusalem (vv. 13, 17–18), the cleansing and consecration rituals (vv. 14–16, 19), and the "sacrifice" of joyful praise extended over a two-week period (vv. 21–27).

temple of the LORD. 16 Then they took up their regular positions[o] as prescribed in the Law of Moses the man of God. The priests splashed against the altar the blood handed to them by the Levites. 17 Since many in the crowd had not consecrated themselves, the Levites had to kill[p] the Passover lambs for all those who were not ceremonially clean and could not consecrate their lambs[a] to the LORD. 18 Although most of the many people who came from Ephraim, Manasseh, Issachar and Zebulun had not purified themselves,[q] yet they ate the Passover, contrary to what was written. But Hezekiah prayed for them, saying, "May the LORD, who is good, pardon everyone 19 who sets their heart on seeking God — the LORD, the God of their ancestors — even if they are not clean according to the rules of the sanctuary." 20 And the LORD heard[r] Hezekiah and healed[s] the people.[t]

21 The Israelites who were present in Jerusalem celebrated the Festival of Unleavened Bread[u] for seven days with great rejoicing, while the Levites and priests praised the LORD every day with resounding instruments dedicated to the LORD.[b]

22 Hezekiah spoke encouragingly to all the Levites, who showed good understanding of the service of the LORD. For the seven days they ate their assigned portion and offered fellowship offerings and praised[c] the LORD, the God of their ancestors.

23 The whole assembly then agreed to celebrate[v] the festival seven more days; so for another seven days they celebrated joyfully. 24 Hezekiah king of Judah provided[w] a thousand bulls and seven thousand sheep and goats for the assembly, and the officials provided them with a thousand bulls and ten thousand sheep and goats. A great number of priests consecrated themselves. 25 The entire assembly of Judah rejoiced, along with the priests and Levites and all who had assembled from Israel[x], including the foreigners who had come from Israel and also those who resided in Judah. 26 There was great joy in Jerusalem, for since the days of Solomon[y] son of David king of Israel there had been nothing like this in Jerusalem. 27 The priests and the Levites stood to bless[z] the people, and God heard them, for their prayer reached heaven, his holy dwelling place.

30:16 [o]2Ch 35:10
30:17 [p]2Ch 29:34
30:18 [q]Ex 12:43-49; Nu 9:6-10
30:20 [r]2Ch 6:20 [s]2Ch 7:14; Mal 4:2 [t]Jas 5:16
30:21 [u]Ex 12:15, 17; 13:6
30:23 [v]1Ki 8:65; 2Ch 7:9
30:24 [w]1Ki 8:5; 2Ch 29:34; 35:7; Ezr 6:17; 8:35
30:25 [x]ver 11
30:26 [y]2Ch 7:8
30:27 [z]Ex 39:43; Nu 6:23; Dt 26:15; 2Ch 23:18; Ps 68:5
31:1 [a]2Ki 18:4; 2Ch 32:12; Isa 36:7
31:2 [b]2Ch 29:9 [c]1Ch 24:1 [d]1Ch 15:2 [e]Ps 7:17; 9:2; 47:6; 71:22 [f]1Ch 23:28-32
31:3 [g]1Ch 29:3; 2Ch 35:7; Eze 45:17 [h]Nu 28:1-29:40
31:4 [i]Nu 18:8; Dt 18:8; Ne 13:10; Mal 2:7
31:5 [j]Nu 18:12, 24; Ne 13:12; Eze 44:30

2Ch 31:4-5 ❖ How might God be stirring our hearts to generously support gospel ministries? Where can we contribute to help spread God's kingdom?

31 When all this had ended, the Israelites who were there went out to the towns of Judah, smashed the sacred stones and cut down[a] the Asherah poles. They destroyed the high places and the altars throughout Judah and Benjamin and in Ephraim and Manasseh. After they had destroyed all of them, the Israelites returned to their own towns and to their own property.

Contributions for Worship

31:20–21pp // 2Ki 18:5–7

2 Hezekiah[b] assigned the priests and Levites to divisions[c] — each of them according to their duties as priests or Levites — to offer burnt offerings and fellowship offerings, to minister,[d] to give thanks and to sing praises[e] at the gates of the LORD's dwelling.[f] 3 The king contributed[g] from his own possessions for the morning and evening burnt offerings and for the burnt offerings on the Sabbaths, at the New Moons and at the appointed festivals as written in the Law of the LORD.[h] 4 He ordered the people living in Jerusalem to give the portion[i] due the priests and Levites so they could devote themselves to the Law of the LORD. 5 As soon as the order went out, the Israelites generously gave the firstfruits[j]

[a] 17 Or *consecrate themselves* [b] 21 Or *priests sang to the LORD every day, accompanied by the LORD's instruments of praise* [c] 22 Or *and confessed their sins to*

30:18–19 The Chronicler makes an important theological observation that intent of heart and acts of repentance, when combined with intercessory prayer, override the letter of the law when it comes to the worship of God.
31:2–21 Hezekiah reinstates the system of tithes and offerings designed both to show worship to God and to financially underwrite the ministry of the priests and Levites (30:2–3). This enables the temple personnel to devote themselves to the study and teaching of "the Law of the LORD" (v. 4).
31:5–8 The Chronicler notes the overwhelming response to the king's command to bring the firstfruits of the produce of the field and a tithe of the herds and flocks.

of their grain, new wine,[k] olive oil and
honey and all that the fields produced.
They brought a great amount, a tithe of
everything. 6The people of Israel and
Judah who lived in the towns of Judah
also brought a tithe[l] of their herds and
flocks and a tithe of the holy things dedicated to the LORD their God, and they
piled them in heaps.[m] 7They began doing
this in the third month and finished in
the seventh month.[n] 8When Hezekiah
and his officials came and saw the heaps,
they praised the LORD and blessed[o] his
people Israel.

9Hezekiah asked the priests and Levites about the heaps; 10and Azariah the
chief priest, from the family of Zadok,[p]
answered, "Since the people began to
bring their contributions to the temple
of the LORD, we have had enough to eat
and plenty to spare, because the LORD
has blessed his people, and this great
amount is left over."[q]

11Hezekiah gave orders to prepare
storerooms in the temple of the LORD,
and this was done. 12Then they faithfully
brought in the contributions, tithes and
dedicated gifts. Konaniah,[r] a Levite, was
the overseer in charge of these things,
and his brother Shimei was next in rank.
13Jehiel, Azaziah, Nahath, Asahel, Jerimoth, Jozabad,[s] Eliel, Ismakiah, Mahath
and Benaiah were assistants of Konaniah
and Shimei his brother. All these served
by appointment of King Hezekiah and
Azariah the official in charge of the temple of God.

14Kore son of Imnah the Levite, keeper of the East Gate, was in charge of the
freewill offerings given to God, distributing the contributions made to the LORD
and also the consecrated gifts. 15Eden,[t]
Miniamin, Jeshua, Shemaiah, Amariah
and Shekaniah assisted him faithfully
in the towns[u] of the priests, distributing
to their fellow priests according to their
divisions, old and young alike.

16In addition, they distributed to the
males three years old or more whose
names were in the genealogical records[v] — all who would enter the temple
of the LORD to perform the daily duties
of their various tasks, according to their
responsibilities and their divisions. 17And
they distributed to the priests enrolled
by their families in the genealogical records and likewise to the Levites twenty
years old or more, according to their responsibilities and their divisions. 18They
included all the little ones, the wives,
and the sons and daughters of the whole
community listed in these genealogical
records. For they were faithful in consecrating themselves.

19As for the priests, the descendants
of Aaron, who lived on the farmlands
around their towns or in any other
towns,[w] men were designated by name to
distribute portions to every male among
them and to all who were recorded in the
genealogies of the Levites.

20This is what Hezekiah did throughout Judah, doing what was good and
right and faithful[x] before the LORD his
God. 21In everything that he undertook
in the service of God's temple and in obedience to the law and the commands, he
sought his God and worked wholeheartedly. And so he prospered.[y]

Sennacherib Threatens Jerusalem

32:9–19pp // 2Ki 18:17–35; Isa 36:2–20
32:20–21pp // 2Ki 19:35–37; Isa 37:36–38

32 After all that Hezekiah had so
faithfully done, Sennacherib[z] king
of Assyria came and invaded Judah. He
laid siege to the fortified cities, thinking
to conquer them for himself. 2When Hezekiah saw that Sennacherib had come
and that he intended to wage war against
Jerusalem,[a] 3he consulted with his officials and military staff about blocking
off the water from the springs outside
the city, and they helped him. 4They

31:5 [k] Dt 12:17
31:6 [l] Lev 27:30; Ne 13:10-12 [m] Dt 14:28; Ru 3:7
31:7 [n] Ex 23:16
31:8 [o] Ps 144:13-15
31:10 [p] 2Sa 8:17 [q] Ex 36:5; Eze 44:30; Mal 3:10-12
31:12 [r] 2Ch 35:9
31:13 [s] 2Ch 35:9
31:15 [t] 2Ch 29:12 [u] Jos 21:9-19
31:16 [v] 1Ch 23:3; Ezr 3:4
31:19 [w] ver 12-15; Lev 25:34; Nu 35:2-5
31:20 [x] 2Ki 20:3; 22:2
31:21 [y] Dt 29:9
32:1 [z] 2Ki 18:13-19; Isa 36:1; 37:9,17,37
32:2 [a] Isa 22:7; Jer 1:15

31:11–19 The Chronicler reports that the bounty of goods received is carefully inventoried, properly stored and maintained, and distributed with equity among the families of the priests and Levites.
31:20–21 The concluding theological review of Hezekiah is an extension of the favorable assessment found in the opening (29:1–2). The review also links Hezekiah with David in his wholehearted devotion to God and with Solomon in his concern for the Lord's temple, ranking him among the great kings of Israel (cf. 7:11).
32:1–23 Sennacherib's invasion of Judah is one of the most important events in the history of the southern kingdom. The Assyrian campaign is dated to 701 BC, during the fourteenth year of Hezekiah.
32:1–8 Hezekiah's defensive precautions should not be interpreted as a lack of faith in God but rather as an example of prudence on the part of a wise king. As commander-in-chief he encourages the people with a motivational speech (vv. 6–8a). The king's appeal to the people is a theological treatise, not a nationalistic or patriotic rallying cry.

gathered a large group of people who
blocked all the springs[b] and the stream
that flowed through the land. "Why
should the kings[a] of Assyria come and
find plenty of water?" they said. 5Then
he worked hard repairing all the broken
sections of the wall[c] and building towers
on it. He built another wall outside that
one and reinforced the terraces[bd] of the
City of David. He also made large numbers of weapons[e] and shields.

6He appointed military officers over
the people and assembled them before
him in the square at the city gate and
encouraged them with these words: 7"Be
strong and courageous.[f] Do not be afraid
or discouraged[g] because of the king of
Assyria and the vast army with him, for
there is a greater power with us than
with him.[h] 8With him is only the arm of
flesh,[i] but with us[j] is the LORD our God
to help us and to fight our battles."[k] And
the people gained confidence from what
Hezekiah the king of Judah said.

9Later, when Sennacherib king of Assyria and all his forces were laying siege
to Lachish,[l] he sent his officers to Jerusalem with this message for Hezekiah
king of Judah and for all the people of
Judah who were there:

10"This is what Sennacherib king
of Assyria says: On what are you
basing your confidence,[m] that you
remain in Jerusalem under siege?
11When Hezekiah says, 'The LORD
our God will save us from the hand
of the king of Assyria,' he is misleading[n] you, to let you die of hunger
and thirst. 12Did not Hezekiah himself remove this god's high places
and altars, saying to Judah and Jerusalem, 'You must worship before
one altar[o] and burn sacrifices on it'?

13"Do you not know what I and
my predecessors have done to all
the peoples of the other lands?
Were the gods of those nations
ever able to deliver their land from
my hand?[p] 14Who of all the gods of
these nations that my predecessors
destroyed has been able to save his
people from me? How then can your
god deliver you from my hand?
15Now do not let Hezekiah deceive[q]
you and mislead you like this. Do
not believe him, for no god of any
nation or kingdom has been able to
deliver[r] his people from my hand or
the hand of my predecessors.[s] How
much less will your god deliver you
from my hand!"

16Sennacherib's officers spoke further
against the LORD God and against his
servant Hezekiah. 17The king also wrote
letters[t] ridiculing[u] the LORD, the God of
Israel, and saying this against him: "Just
as the gods[v] of the peoples of the other
lands did not rescue their people from
my hand, so the god of Hezekiah will not
rescue his people from my hand." 18Then
they called out in Hebrew to the people
of Jerusalem who were on the wall, to
terrify them and make them afraid in
order to capture the city. 19They spoke
about the God of Jerusalem as they did
about the gods of the other peoples of
the world — the work of human hands.[w]

20King Hezekiah and the prophet
Isaiah son of Amoz cried out in prayer
to heaven about this. 21And the LORD
sent an angel,[x] who annihilated all the
fighting men and the commanders and

32:4 [b] 2Ki 18:17; 20:20; Isa 22:9, 11; Na 3:14
32:5 [c] 2Ch 25:23; Isa 22:10 [d] 1Ki 9:24; 1Ch 11:8 [e] Isa 22:8
32:7 [f] Dt 31:6; 1Ch 22:13 [g] 2Ch 20:15 [h] Nu 14:9; 2Ki 6:16
32:8 [i] Job 40:9; Isa 52:10; Jer 17:5; 32:21 [j] Dt 3:22; 1Sa 17:45; 2Ch 13:12 [k] 1Ch 5:22; 2Ch 20:17; Ps 20:7; Isa 28:6
32:9 [l] Jos 10:3, 31
32:10 [m] Eze 29:16
32:11 [n] Isa 37:10
32:12 [o] 2Ch 31:1
32:13 [p] ver 15
32:15 [q] Isa 37:10 [r] Da 3:15 [s] Ex 5:2
32:17 [t] Isa 37:14 [u] Ps 74:22; Isa 37:4, 17 [v] 2Ki 19:12
32:19 [w] 2Ki 19:18; Ps 115:4-8; Isa 2:8; 17:8
32:21 [x] Ge 19:13

2Ch 32:7 ❖ How can we gain eyes to see that there is a greater power at work within us than all that looks threatening in the world (see 1Jn 4:4)?

[a] 4 Hebrew; Septuagint and Syriac *king* [b] 5 Or *the Millo*

32:9–19 The reason for Sennacherib's failure to withdraw from Judah after receiving Hezekiah's tribute is unclear, although the Assyrian king is no doubt motivated by greed to possess all the wealth of the Jerusalem temple—not just a portion of it.
32:10–15 The message delivered to King Hezekiah by the officers of Sennacherib is a call to surrender the city of Jerusalem or die in the siege.
32:16–19 The final section of the Assyrian message is a taunt against the God of Israel, mocking his impotence in the current crisis.
32:20–23 God's deliverance of Hezekiah and the people of Judah is achieved through prayer. After God's decisive action against the Assyrian army and its leaders, Sennacherib withdraws from Jerusalem in disgrace and returns to Assyria with the remnants of his decimated army. This account compresses time in such a way to suggest that Sennacherib is assassinated immediately upon his return to Nineveh, perhaps to accent the retribution principle for his audience. In actuality, Sennacherib is murdered by his son Adrammelech while worshiping in the temple of Nisroch some twenty years later (c. 681 BC).

officers in the camp of the Assyrian king.
So he withdrew to his own land in disgrace. And when he went into the temple of his god, some of his sons, his own
flesh and blood, cut him down with the
sword.[y]
22 So the LORD saved Hezekiah and the
people of Jerusalem from the hand of
Sennacherib king of Assyria and from
the hand of all others. He took care of
them[a] on every side. 23 Many brought
offerings to Jerusalem for the LORD and
valuable gifts[z] for Hezekiah king of Judah. From then on he was highly regarded by all the nations.

Hezekiah's Pride, Success and Death

32:24–33pp // 2Ki 20:1–21; Isa 37:21–38; 38:1–8

24 In those days Hezekiah became ill
and was at the point of death. He prayed
to the LORD, who answered him and gave
him a miraculous sign. 25 But Hezekiah's
heart was proud[a] and he did not respond
to the kindness shown him; therefore
the LORD's wrath[b] was on him and on
Judah and Jerusalem. 26 Then Hezekiah
repented[c] of the pride of his heart, as
did the people of Jerusalem; therefore
the LORD's wrath did not come on them
during the days of Hezekiah.[d]
27 Hezekiah had very great wealth
and honor,[e] and he made treasuries for
his silver and gold and for his precious
stones, spices, shields and all kinds of
valuables. 28 He also made buildings to
store the harvest of grain, new wine and
olive oil; and he made stalls for various
kinds of cattle, and pens for the flocks.
29 He built villages and acquired great
numbers of flocks and herds, for God
had given him very great riches.[f]
30 It was Hezekiah who blocked[g] the
upper outlet of the Gihon[h] spring and
channeled the water down to the west
side of the City of David. He succeeded
in everything he undertook. 31 But when
envoys were sent by the rulers of Babylon[i] to ask him about the miraculous
sign[j] that had occurred in the land, God
left him to test[k] him and to know everything that was in his heart.
32 The other events of Hezekiah's reign
and his acts of devotion are written in
the vision of the prophet Isaiah son of
Amoz in the book of the kings of Judah
and Israel. 33 Hezekiah rested with his ancestors and was buried on the hill where
the tombs of David's descendants are. All
Judah and the people of Jerusalem honored him when he died. And Manasseh
his son succeeded him as king.

Manasseh King of Judah

33:1–10pp // 2Ki 21:1–10
33:18–20pp // 2Ki 21:17–18

33 Manasseh[l] was twelve years old
when he became king, and he
reigned in Jerusalem fifty-five years.
2 He did evil in the eyes of the LORD,[m]
following the detestable[n] practices of the
nations the LORD had driven out before

32:21 [y] 2Ki 19:7
32:23 [z] 2Ch 9:24; 17:5; Isa 45:14; Zec 14:16-17
32:25 [a] 2Ki 14:10; 2Ch 26:16 [b] 2Ch 19:2; 24:18
32:26 [c] Jer 26:18-19 [d] 2Ch 34:27,28; Isa 39:8
32:27 [e] 1Ch 29:12
32:29 [f] 1Ch 29:12
32:30 [g] 2Ki 18:17 [h] 1Ki 1:33
32:31 [i] Isa 39:1 [j] ver 24; Isa 38:7 [k] Ge 22:1; Dt 8:16
33:1 [l] 1Ch 3:13
33:2 [m] Jer 15:4 [n] Dt 18:9; 2Ch 28:3

[a] 22 Hebrew; Septuagint and Vulgate *He gave them rest*

32:22 Far more important to the Chronicler is God's deliverance of Hezekiah and Judah from the superior forces of the Assyrians.

32:24–33 The expression "in those days" (v. 24) is intended to closely link Hezekiah's illness with the Assyrian invasion in a chronological sense. The direct relationship between divine blessing and God's forgiveness recorded in vv. 27–31 repeats a motif associated with righteous kings (e.g., David, Solomon, Jehoshaphat, Uzziah). The reference to Hezekiah's "great wealth and honor" (v. 27) is another parallel the Chronicler draws between this king and Solomon (cf. 1:12; 9:22).

27:1—32:33 Hezekiah's ability to encourage others is indeed a commendable trait—and one certainly worth emulating. To encourage is to embolden another to overcome a paralyzing fear or deep-seated reluctance. To encourage is to inspire, to boost, and to offer hope to another through word or deed.

The NT values encouragement as a Christian virtue because it serves to embolden the timid in the service of Christ (1Th 5:14). The apostle Paul directs believers who have the gift of encouragement to use it whenever the opportunity presents itself (Ro 12:6–8). Those who encourage others and reflect the grace and truth of Jesus in doing so help to build God's kingdom on earth (see Mt 13:31–32).

33:1–10 Manasseh's fifty-five-year reign probably includes a coregency of several years with his father, Hezekiah. The dates of his reign extend from about 696 to 642 BC. Manasseh was probably born into the royal family during the fifteen-year extension of Hezekiah's life (cf. 2Ki 20:1–6).

The specific catalog of abominations promoted by Manasseh as "alternative religion" invites comparison with the Mosaic prohibitions against false worship. Among the abominations borrowed wholesale from Canaanite culture are idolatry associated with the fertility cult deities Asherah and Baal, astral worship, infanticide, and the occult (vv. 3–6).

the Israelites. 3He rebuilt the high places his father Hezekiah had demolished; he also erected altars to the Baals and made Asherah poles.[o] He bowed down[p] to all the starry hosts and worshiped them. 4He built altars in the temple of the LORD, of which the LORD had said, "My Name[q] will remain in Jerusalem forever." 5In both courts of the temple of the LORD,[r] he built altars to all the starry hosts. 6He sacrificed his children[s] in the fire in the Valley of Ben Hinnom, practiced divination and witchcraft, sought omens, and consulted mediums[t] and spiritists.[u] He did much evil in the eyes of the LORD, arousing his anger.

7He took the image he had made and put it in God's temple,[v] of which God had said to David and to his son Solomon, "In this temple and in Jerusalem, which I have chosen out of all the tribes of Israel, I will put my Name forever. 8I will not again make the feet of the Israelites leave the land[w] I assigned to your ancestors, if only they will be careful to do everything I commanded them concerning all the laws, decrees and regulations given through Moses." 9But Manasseh led Judah and the people of Jerusalem astray, so that they did more evil than the nations the LORD had destroyed before the Israelites.[x]

10The LORD spoke to Manasseh and his people, but they paid no attention. 11So the LORD brought against them the army commanders of the king of Assyria, who took Manasseh prisoner,[y] put a hook in his nose, bound him with bronze shackles[z] and took him to Babylon. 12In his distress he sought the favor of the LORD his God and humbled[a] himself greatly before the God of his ancestors. 13And when he prayed to him, the LORD was moved by his entreaty and listened to his plea; so he brought him back to Jerusalem and to his kingdom. Then Manasseh knew that the LORD is God.

14Afterward he rebuilt the outer wall of the City of David, west of the Gihon[b] spring in the valley, as far as the entrance of the Fish Gate[c] and encircling the hill of Ophel;[d] he also made it much higher. He stationed military commanders in all the fortified cities in Judah.

15He got rid of the foreign gods and removed[e] the image from the temple of the LORD, as well as all the altars he had built on the temple hill and in Jerusalem; and he threw them out of the city. 16Then he restored the altar of the LORD and sacrificed fellowship offerings and thank offerings[f] on it, and told Judah to serve the LORD, the God of Israel. 17The people, however, continued to sacrifice at the high places, but only to the LORD their God.

18The other events of Manasseh's reign, including his prayer to his God and the words the seers spoke to him in the name of the LORD, the God of Israel, are written in the annals of the kings of Israel.[a] 19His prayer and how God was moved by his entreaty, as well as all his sins and unfaithfulness, and the sites where he built high places and set up Asherah poles and idols before he humbled[g] himself—all these are written in the records of the seers.[b][h] 20Manasseh rested with his ancestors and was buried[i] in his palace. And Amon his son succeeded him as king.

2Ch 33:12–13 ❖ Even someone as wicked as Manasseh is able to repent and find forgiveness in God. What might God be calling us to repent of to draw us closer to him?

Amon King of Judah

33:21–25pp // 2Ki 21:19–24

21Amon[j] was twenty-two years old when he became king, and he reigned in Jerusalem two years. 22He did evil in the

33:3 [o] Dt 16:21-22 [p] Dt 17:3; 2Ch 31:1
33:4 [q] 2Ch 7:16
33:5 [r] 2Ch 4:9
33:6 [s] Lev 18:21; Dt 18:10; 2Ch 28:3 [t] Lev 19:31 [u] 1Sa 28:13
33:7 [v] 2Ch 7:16
33:8 [w] 2Sa 7:10
33:9 [x] Jer 15:4
33:11 [y] Dt 28:36 [z] Ps 149:8
33:12 [a] 2Ch 6:37; 32:26; 1Pe 5:6
33:14 [b] 1Ki 1:33 [c] Ne 3:3; 12:39; Zep 1:10 [d] 2Ch 27:3; Ne 3:26
33:15 [e] ver 3-7; 2Ki 23:12
33:16 [f] Lev 7:11-18
33:19 [g] 2Ch 6:37 [h] 2Ki 21:17
33:20 [i] 2Ki 21:18; 2Ch 21:20
33:21 [j] 1Ch 3:14

[a] *18* That is, Judah, as frequently in 2 Chronicles
[b] *19* One Hebrew manuscript and Septuagint; most Hebrew manuscripts *of Hozai*

33:11–13 The nose "hook" and "bronze shackles" are typical of the humiliation inflicted on captives in the biblical world. Unlike King Ahaz, Manasseh turns to God in his distress and finds favor with the Almighty. The expression "the LORD was moved" (v. 13) is unusual and marks a theological distinctive of the God of the Bible.

33:14–17 Manasseh's reforms are both political and religious in nature. The depth, extent, and duration of Manasseh's religious reforms remain an open question. The impact of Manasseh's religious reforms seems restricted to Jerusalem and its immediate surroundings, given the Chronicler's reference to ongoing worship in the high places (v. 17).

33:18–20 Manasseh's concluding résumé is significant theologically because of the emphasis on the king's prayer of entreaty and God's response to his repentance.

33:21–25 Amon's rule lasts only two years (642–640 BC). He is judged an evil king because he perpetuates the false worship established in Judah by his father.

eyes of the LORD, as his father Manasseh had done. Amon worshiped and offered sacrifices to all the idols Manasseh had made. 23But unlike his father Manasseh, he did not humble[k] himself before the LORD; Amon increased his guilt.

24Amon's officials conspired against him and assassinated him in his palace. 25Then the people[l] of the land killed all who had plotted against King Amon, and they made Josiah his son king in his place.

Josiah's Reforms

34:1–2pp // 2Ki 22:1–2
34:3–7Ref // 2Ki 23:4–20
34:8–13pp // 2Ki 22:3–7

34 Josiah[m] was eight years old when he became king,[n] and he reigned in Jerusalem thirty-one years. 2He did what was right in the eyes of the LORD and followed the ways of his father David,[o] not turning aside to the right or to the left.

3In the eighth year of his reign, while he was still young, he began to seek the God[p] of his father David. In his twelfth year he began to purge Judah and Jerusalem of high places, Asherah poles and idols. 4Under his direction the altars of the Baals were torn down; he cut to pieces the incense altars that were above them, and smashed the Asherah poles[q] and the idols. These he broke to pieces and scattered over the graves of those who had sacrificed to them.[r] 5He burned[s] the bones of the priests on their altars, and so he purged Judah and Jerusalem. 6In the towns of Manasseh, Ephraim and Simeon, as far as Naphtali, and in the ruins around them, 7he tore down the altars and the Asherah poles and crushed the idols to powder[t] and cut to pieces all the incense altars throughout Israel. Then he went back to Jerusalem.

8In the eighteenth year of Josiah's reign, to purify the land and the temple, he sent Shaphan son of Azaliah and Maaseiah the ruler of the city, with Joah son of Joahaz, the recorder, to repair the temple of the LORD his God.

9They went to Hilkiah[u] the high priest and gave him the money that had been brought into the temple of God, which the Levites who were the gatekeepers had collected from the people of Manasseh, Ephraim and the entire remnant of Israel and from all the people of Judah and Benjamin and the inhabitants of Jerusalem. 10Then they entrusted it to the men appointed to supervise the work on the LORD's temple. These men paid the workers who repaired and restored the temple. 11They also gave money[v] to the carpenters and builders to purchase dressed stone, and timber for joists and beams for the buildings that the kings of Judah had allowed to fall into ruin.[w]

12The workers labored faithfully.[x] Over them to direct them were Jahath and Obadiah, Levites descended from Merari, and Zechariah and Meshullam, descended from Kohath. The Levites—all who were skilled in playing musical instruments—[y] 13had charge of the laborers[z] and supervised all the workers from job to job. Some of the Levites were secretaries, scribes and gatekeepers.

The Book of the Law Found

34:14–28pp // 2Ki 22:8–20
34:29–32pp // 2Ki 23:1–3

14While they were bringing out the money that had been taken into the temple of the LORD, Hilkiah the priest found the Book of the Law of the LORD that had been given through Moses. 15Hilkiah said to Shaphan the secretary, "I have found the Book of the Law[a] in the temple of the LORD." He gave it to Shaphan.

16Then Shaphan took the book to the king and reported to him: "Your officials are doing everything that has been

33:23 [k] ver 12; Ex 10:3; 2Ch 7:14; Ps 18:27; 147:6; Pr 3:34
33:25 [l] 2Ch 22:1
34:1 [m] 1Ch 3:14 [n] Zep 1:1
34:2 [o] 2Ch 29:2
34:3 [p] 1Ki 13:2; 1Ch 16:11; 2Ch 15:2; 33:17,22
34:4 [q] Ex 34:13 [r] Ex 32:20; Lev 26:30; 2Ki 23:11; Mic 1:5
34:5 [s] 1Ki 13:2
34:7 [t] Ex 32:20; 2Ch 31:1
34:9 [u] 1Ch 6:13; 2Ch 35:8
34:11 [v] 2Ch 24:12 [w] 2Ch 33:4-7
34:12 [x] 2Ki 12:15 [y] 1Ch 25:1
34:13 [z] 1Ch 23:4
34:15 [a] 2Ki 22:8; Ezr 7:6; Ne 8:1

34:1–7 Josiah's reign can be dated with confidence to 640–609 BC. The age of twenty was the age of majority in Hebrew culture and, more than coincidentally for the Chronicler, the age when the Levites began their service to Yahweh (cf. Nu 1:3; 1Ch 23:24).
34:8–13 The need for skilled craftsmen such as carpenters and masons indicates the temple is in a serious state of disrepair (vv. 10–11). Chronicles places blame for the ruin of the temple on the kings of Judah. The Chronicler connects the success of the temple repairs to the faithfulness of the workers and effective supervision by the Levites (vv. 12–13).
34:14–18 The puzzling question for biblical scholars has been the identity of the book mentioned in v. 14. The general consensus favors the book of Deuteronomy or an earlier version of it. Presumably the scroll fell out of circulation because of the need to hide it at the threat of military invasion, or else it was censored by rulers and/or concealed by the priests during one of the eras when Israel lapsed into religious apostasy.

committed to them. 17They have paid
out the money that was in the temple of
the LORD and have entrusted it to the supervisors and workers." 18Then Shaphan
the secretary informed the king, "Hilkiah the priest has given me a book." And
Shaphan read from it in the presence
of the king.

19When the king heard the words of
the Law,[b] he tore[c] his robes. 20He gave
these orders to Hilkiah, Ahikam son of
Shaphan[d], Abdon son of Micah,[a] Shaphan
the secretary and Asaiah the king's attendant: 21"Go and inquire of the LORD
for me and for the remnant in Israel and
Judah about what is written in this book
that has been found. Great is the LORD's
anger that is poured out[e] on us because
those who have gone before us have not
kept the word of the LORD; they have
not acted in accordance with all that is
written in this book."

22Hilkiah and those the king had sent
with him[b] went to speak to the prophet[f]
Huldah, who was the wife of Shallum son
of Tokhath,[c] the son of Hasrah,[d] keeper
of the wardrobe. She lived in Jerusalem,
in the New Quarter.

23She said to them, "This is what the
LORD, the God of Israel, says: Tell the
man who sent you to me, 24'This is what
the LORD says: I am going to bring disaster[g] on this place and its people[h] — all
the curses[i] written in the book that has
been read in the presence of the king
of Judah. 25Because they have forsaken
me[j] and burned incense to other gods
and aroused my anger by all that their
hands have made,[e] my anger will be
poured out on this place and will not
be quenched.' 26Tell the king of Judah,
who sent you to inquire of the LORD,
'This is what the LORD, the God of Israel,

34:19 [b] Dt 28:3-68 [c] Jos 7:6; Isa 36:22; 37:1
34:20 [d] 2Ki 22:3
34:21 [e] 2Ch 29:8; La 2:4; 4:11; Eze 36:18
34:22 [f] Ex 15:20; Ne 6:14
34:24 [g] Pr 16:4; Isa 3:9; Jer 40:2; 42:10; 44:2,11 [h] 2Ch 36:14-20 [i] Dt 28:15-68
34:25 [j] 2Ch 33:3-6; Jer 22:9

[a] *20* Also called *Akbor son of Micaiah*
[b] *22* One Hebrew manuscript, Vulgate and Syriac; most Hebrew manuscripts do not have *had sent with him.* [c] *22* Also called *Tikvah* [d] *22* Also called *Harhas* [e] *25* Or *by everything they have done*

34:19–28 Recognizing the message of the scroll as the very word of God, Josiah tears his clothes—a tangible expression of grief in response to personal or national crises.

34:22–28 Huldah is not mentioned elsewhere in the OT. She is respected as a servant of Yahweh, and her interpretation of the law scroll is received as a word from God.

That interpretation is delivered in a two-part message. (1) A message of punishment (vv. 24–25) assumes the curses of Dt 28. (2) A message of salvation (vv. 26–28a) is prompted by Josiah's repentance.

PEOPLE TO KNOW // **HULDAH**

2 CHRONICLES 34:22–28: Huldah was a prophet in Jerusalem during the time of King Josiah and one of only three female prophets mentioned in the OT (with Miriam and Deborah).

In the eighteenth year of Josiah's reign, Hilkiah the priest found a copy of the Book of the Law of God in the temple (2Ki 22:8). Josiah's secretary, Shaphan, brought the book to the king and read to him from it.

Upon hearing the words of God's instruction, Josiah tore his robes (2Ki 22:11). He knew that the kingdom of Judah had strayed from God's commands revealed in his Law. Josiah told Hilkiah, Shaphan and other officials to go inquire of the Lord about the words in the book. To learn God's will, they went to the prophet Huldah.

All the Bible tells us about Huldah is that she was a prophet, the wife of Shallum, and she lived in the New Quarter of Jerusalem (2Ki 22:14). Huldah explained God's words to Josiah's officials and also gave them a prophetic message. She told them that God would bring disaster upon Judah for its sins. God also told her to tell the king's officials that because Josiah had humbled himself, he himself would not see the disaster God would bring upon Jerusalem. The officials relayed Huldah's message back to Josiah.

After this, Josiah instituted sweeping religious reforms in Judah. He rid the kingdom of idolatry and led the people back to proper worship of God.

APPLICATION ✜ Spiritual revival often begins with a faithful few. Huldah was a prophet of God when Judah had fallen deep into idol worship. Huldah's story reminds us to stay faithful even when society around us moves away from God. When the time for revival comes, God will speak through his faithful people, helping them deliver his word of truth to the world.

says concerning the words you heard:
27Because your heart was responsive[k]
and you humbled[l] yourself before God
when you heard what he spoke against
this place and its people, and because
you humbled yourself before me and
tore your robes and wept in my presence, I have heard you, declares the
LORD. 28Now I will gather you to your
ancestors,[m] and you will be buried in
peace. Your eyes will not see all the disaster I am going to bring on this place
and on those who live here.' "[n]

So they took her answer back to the
king.

29Then the king called together all
the elders of Judah and Jerusalem. 30He
went up to the temple of the LORD[o] with
the people of Judah, the inhabitants of
Jerusalem, the priests and the Levites —
all the people from the least to the greatest. He read in their hearing all the words
of the Book of the Covenant, which had
been found in the temple of the LORD.
31The king stood by his pillar[p] and renewed the covenant[q] in the presence
of the LORD — to follow[r] the LORD and
keep his commands, statutes and decrees
with all his heart and all his soul, and to
obey the words of the covenant written
in this book.

32Then he had everyone in Jerusalem
and Benjamin pledge themselves to it;
the people of Jerusalem did this in accordance with the covenant of God, the
God of their ancestors.

33Josiah removed all the detestable[s]
idols from all the territory belonging to
the Israelites, and he had all who were
present in Israel serve the LORD their
God. As long as he lived, they did not
fail to follow the LORD, the God of their
ancestors.

34:27 [k] 2Ch 12:7; 32:26 [l] Ex 10:3; 2Ch 6:37
34:28 [m] 2Ch 35:20-25 [n] 2Ch 32:26
34:30 [o] 2Ki 23:2; Ne 8:1-3
34:31 [p] 1Ki 7:15; 2Ki 11:14 [q] 2Ki 11:17; 2Ch 23:16; 29:10 [r] Dt 13:4
34:33 [s] ver 3-7; Dt 18:9
35:1 [t] Ex 12:1-30; Nu 9:3; 28:16
35:3 [u] Dt 33:10; 1Ch 23:26; 2Ch 5:7; 17:7
35:4 [v] ver 10; 1Ch 9:10-13; 24:1; 2Ch 8:14; Ezr 6:18
35:6 [w] Lev 11:44; 2Ch 29:5,15
35:7 [x] 2Ch 30:24 [y] 2Ch 31:3
35:8 [z] 1Ch 29:3; 2Ch 29:31-36 [a] 1Ch 6:13

2Ch 34:27 ❖ How can we foster a more responsive heart before God?

Josiah Celebrates the Passover

35:1,18–19pp // 2Ki 23:21–23

35 Josiah celebrated the Passover[t]
to the LORD in Jerusalem, and the
Passover lamb was slaughtered on the
fourteenth day of the first month. 2He
appointed the priests to their duties and
encouraged them in the service of the
LORD's temple. 3He said to the Levites,
who instructed[u] all Israel and who had
been consecrated to the LORD: "Put the
sacred ark in the temple that Solomon
son of David king of Israel built. It is not
to be carried about on your shoulders.
Now serve the LORD your God and his
people Israel. 4Prepare yourselves by
families in your divisions,[v] according
to the instructions written by David king
of Israel and by his son Solomon.

5"Stand in the holy place with a group
of Levites for each subdivision of the
families of your fellow Israelites, the lay
people. 6Slaughter the Passover lambs,
consecrate yourselves[w] and prepare the
lambs for your fellow Israelites, doing
what the LORD commanded through
Moses."

7Josiah provided for all the lay people
who were there a total of thirty thousand
lambs and goats for the Passover offerings,[x] and also three thousand cattle —
all from the king's own possessions.[y]

8His officials also contributed[z] voluntarily to the people and the priests and
Levites. Hilkiah,[a] Zechariah and Jehiel,
the officials in charge of God's temple,
gave the priests twenty-six hundred
Passover offerings and three hundred

34:29-33 Covenant renewal for ancient Israel was repairing or restoring a relationship with God that had been broken by their willful violation of the conditions regulating the relationship. Repentance or humbling oneself is the first step in renewing a covenant relationship with God. Josiah's covenant-renewal ceremony combines elements of the Mosaic covenant and of the Davidic covenant. In keeping with the prescription of the Mosaic law, all the people gather for the reading of the law scroll and the covenant-ratification ceremony.

35:1-19 The Passover, more than any other Hebrew religious festival, drew the nation of Israel back to its roots since it was at Mount Sinai that the former Hebrew slaves were constituted as the people of God.

35:1-6 The Chronicler specifies the precise date for the observance of the Passover to demonstrate that Josiah is in compliance with Mosaic law.

Quite apart from the technicalities of sacrificial worship, we cannot overlook the essential calling of the Levitical priesthood as mediators (vv. 3, 5-6). The Levitical priests are to mediate the holy presence of God in Israel by making atonement first for their own sins and then for the sins of the people (Lev 9:7).

35:7-10 The Chronicler notes that the civil and religious leaders of Judah are not only generous but also willing (v. 8). No doubt the Chronicler seeks to impress the importance of the virtue of generosity on his audience as well.

PEOPLE TO KNOW // **JOSIAH**

2 CHRONICLES 34–35: Long before Josiah was born, a prophet foretold that he would be a king who would root out idolatry (1Ki 13:2). Josiah was one of the last kings of Judah, but also one of the best. His father and grandfather were exceedingly wicked kings, but Josiah honored God.

Josiah was only eight years old when he took the throne in Jerusalem. In the eighteenth year of his reign, a copy of God's Law was found in the temple. When it was read to Josiah, he tore his robes in lament for the ways Judah had failed to keep God's commands (2Ki 22:11). Josiah then led the people in sweeping religious reforms, renewing their covenant with God and vowing to keep God's decrees. He removed idol worship from the land, destroying the places where it was practiced. He led the nation in a Passover celebration like they had never had before. The Bible says there was no king before or after Josiah who turned to the Lord as he did (2Ki 23:25).

Despite Josiah's righteousness, God did not turn from his judgment against Judah that had been prophesied during the reign of wicked King Manasseh (2Ki 23:26). The nation's future had been set, but God did not carry out the final judgement on Judah during Josiah's lifetime. He was spared that horror. However, he did die on the battlefield, trying to stop the Egyptian army from coming to the aid of Assyria when Assyria was being pummeled by Babylon.

APPLICATION Josiah's life shows the transformative power of God's Word. When we read the Bible, it should radically reform our lives and lead us to obedience and love for God. Just as Josiah had to "clean house" in the kingdom to get it on track with God, taking God's Word seriously will require us to perform a makeover of our lives. Thankfully, God grants us his Holy Spirit to lead us in this work of sanctification.

cattle. 9Also Konaniah[b] along with Shemaiah and Nethanel, his brothers, and Hashabiah, Jeiel and Jozabad,[c] the leaders of the Levites, provided five thousand Passover offerings and five hundred head of cattle for the Levites.

10The service was arranged and the priests stood in their places with the Levites in their divisions[d] as the king had ordered.[e] 11The Passover lambs were slaughtered,[f] and the priests splashed against the altar the blood handed to them, while the Levites skinned the animals. 12They set aside the burnt offerings to give them to the subdivisions of the families of the people to offer to the LORD, as it is written in the Book of Moses. They did the same with the cattle. 13They roasted the Passover animals over the fire as prescribed,[g] and boiled the holy offerings in pots, caldrons and pans and served them quickly to all the people. 14After this, they made preparations for themselves and for the priests, because the priests, the descendants of Aaron, were sacrificing the burnt offerings and the fat portions[h] until nightfall. So the Levites made preparations for themselves and for the Aaronic priests.

15The musicians,[i] the descendants of Asaph, were in the places prescribed by David, Asaph, Heman and Jeduthun the king's seer. The gatekeepers at each gate did not need to leave their posts, because their fellow Levites made the preparations for them.

16So at that time the entire service of the LORD was carried out for the celebration of the Passover and the offering of burnt offerings on the altar of the LORD, as King Josiah had ordered. 17The Israelites who were present celebrated the Passover at that time and observed the Festival of Unleavened Bread for seven

35:9 [b] 2Ch 31:12 [c] 2Ch 31:13
35:10 [d] ver 4; Ezr 6:18 [e] 2Ch 30:16
35:11 [f] 2Ch 29:22,34; 30:17
35:13 [g] Ex 12:2-11; Lev 6:25; 1Sa 2:13-15
35:14 [h] Ex 29:13
35:15 [i] 1Ch 25:1; 26:12-19; 2Ch 29:30; Ne 12:46; Ps 68:25

35:11–15 The Passover ceremony consists of two segments: offering the animal sacrifices and eating the Passover meal. The shift in the locus of the Passover from the home to the temple as the central shrine radically alters the ritual character of the Passover. The priests and attending Levites supervise the roasting of the sacrificial animals and serve the Passover meal to the assembly. The Chronicler emphasizes how the priests and Levites fulfill all the requirements of the ceremony demanded by the king and the Law of Moses (vv. 10, 16).

35:16–19 The declaration that Josiah's Passover is unrivaled as a religious festival in Israel anticipates a comparison with Hezekiah's Passover celebration (cf. 30:26). The Chronicler is probably referring to the centralized celebration of the Passover linked to the Jerusalem temple.

KINGS AND PROPHETS

KINGS AND PROPHETS OF THE SOUTHERN KINGDOM		KINGS AND PROPHETS OF THE NORTHERN KINGDOM	
			Amos 760
Jotham 759-744			Hosea 760-730
		Menahem 746-737	
Ahaz 743-728	Isaiah 740-700	Pekahiah 736-735	
		Pekah 734-731	
Hezekiah 727-699	Micah 737-690	Hoshea 730-722	
Manasseh 698-644			
Amon 643-642			
Josiah 641-610	Habakkuk 630		
Jehoahaz 3 months	Zephaniah 627		
Jehoiakim 608-598	Jeremiah 627-580	EXILE	
Jehoiachin 3 months	Daniel 605-530		
Zedekiah 596-586	Ezekiel 593-570		

All dates are approximate. Information derived from Tom Watson, *Chronological and Background Charts of the Old Testament*, rev. and exp. ed. (Grand Rapids: Zondervan, 1994), 30, 52.

days. 18The Passover had not been observed like this in Israel since the days
of the prophet Samuel; and none of the
kings of Israel had ever celebrated such
a Passover as did Josiah, with the priests,
the Levites and all Judah and Israel who
were there with the people of Jerusalem. 19This Passover was celebrated in
the eighteenth year of Josiah's reign.

The Death of Josiah

35:20—36:1pp // 2Ki 23:28–30

20After all this, when Josiah had set
the temple in order, Necho king of Egypt
went up to fight at Carchemish[j] on the
Euphrates,[k] and Josiah marched out to
meet him in battle. 21But Necho sent
messengers to him, saying, "What quarrel is there, king of Judah, between you
and me? It is not you I am attacking at
this time, but the house with which I am
at war. God has told[l] me to hurry; so stop
opposing God, who is with me, or he will
destroy you."
22Josiah, however, would not turn

35:20 [j] Isa 10:9; Jer 46:2 [k] Ge 2:14
35:21 [l] 1Ki 13:18; 2Ki 18:25

2Ch 35:18 ❖ What are a few ways we can extravagantly celebrate God's goodness and our redemption?

35:20–25 The expression "after all this" (v. 20) cues the reader that some time has elapsed since Josiah's celebration of the Passover. Specifically, the narrative leaps chronologically from the Passover festival in Jerusalem in 622 BC to Josiah's death in battle at Megiddo in 609 BC.

The Megiddo pass lies on the international coastal highway, an ancient trade route connect-

away from him, but disguised[m] himself
to engage him in battle. He would not
listen to what Necho had said at God's
command but went to fight him on the
plain of Megiddo.
23 Archers[n] shot King Josiah, and he
told his officers, "Take me away; I am
badly wounded." 24 So they took him out
of his chariot, put him in his other chariot and brought him to Jerusalem, where
he died. He was buried in the tombs of
his ancestors, and all Judah and Jerusalem mourned for him.
25 Jeremiah composed laments for Josiah, and to this day all the male and
female singers commemorate Josiah in
the laments.[o] These became a tradition
in Israel and are written in the Laments.
26 The other events of Josiah's reign
and his acts of devotion in accordance
with what is written in the Law of the
LORD— 27 all the events, from beginning
to end, are written in the book of the
36 kings of Israel and Judah. 1 And the
people of the land took Jehoahaz
son of Josiah and made him king in Jerusalem in place of his father.

Jehoahaz King of Judah

36:2–4pp // 2Ki 23:31–34

2 Jehoahaz[a] was twenty-three years old
when he became king, and he reigned
in Jerusalem three months. 3 The king
of Egypt dethroned him in Jerusalem
and imposed on Judah a levy of a hundred talents[b] of silver and a talent[c] of
gold. 4 The king of Egypt made Eliakim,
a brother of Jehoahaz, king over Judah
and Jerusalem and changed Eliakim's
name to Jehoiakim. But Necho[p] took
Eliakim's brother Jehoahaz and carried
him off to Egypt.

Jehoiakim King of Judah

36:5–8pp // 2Ki 23:36—24:6

5 Jehoiakim[q] was twenty-five years old
when he became king, and he reigned in
Jerusalem eleven years. He did evil in the
eyes of the LORD his God. 6 Nebuchadnezzar[r] king of Babylon attacked him
and bound him with bronze shackles to
take him to Babylon.[s] 7 Nebuchadnezzar
also took to Babylon articles from the
temple of the LORD and put them in his
temple[d] there.[t]
8 The other events of Jehoiakim's reign,
the detestable things he did and all that
was found against him, are written in
the book of the kings of Israel and Judah. And Jehoiachin his son succeeded
him as king.

Jehoiachin King of Judah

36:9–10pp // 2Ki 24:8–17

9 Jehoiachin[u] was eighteen[e] years old
when he became king, and he reigned in

35:22 [m] Jdg 5:19; 1Sa 28:8; 2Ch 18:29
35:23 [n] 1Ki 22:34
35:25 [o] Jer 22:10,15-16
36:4 [p] Jer 22:10-12
36:5 [q] Jer 22:18; 26:1; 35:1
36:6 [r] Jer 25:9; 27:6; Eze 29:18 [s] 2Ch 33:11; Eze 19:9; Da 1:1
36:7 [t] 2Ki 24:13; Ezr 1:7; Da 1:2
36:9 [u] Jer 22:24-28; 52:31

[a] 2 Hebrew *Joahaz*, a variant of *Jehoahaz*; also in verse 4 [b] 3 That is, about 3 3/4 tons or about 3.4 metric tons [c] 3 That is, about 75 pounds or about 34 kilograms [d] 7 Or *palace*
[e] 9 One Hebrew manuscript, some Septuagint manuscripts and Syriac (see also 2 Kings 24:8); most Hebrew manuscripts *eight*

---

ing Egypt with Syria, northern Mesopotamia, and Anatolia. It is at this strategic location that Josiah (foolishly) chooses to intercept Pharaoh Necho and the Egyptian army. Previously, Josiah was commended for his responsiveness to God (34:27). Now he actually stands in opposition to God's word spoken through Pharaoh Necho—to his own destruction (v. 21b).

The Chronicler is careful to note that Josiah receives a proper burial in the "tombs of his ancestors" (35:24). The shock wave of Josiah's death sends tremors through Judah from which the nation never recovers.

35:26—36:1 The expression "acts of devotion" (v. 26) can also be rendered "covenant loyalty," commemorating the covenant-renewal ceremony convened by Josiah and ratified by all Judah (34:29–31).

33:1—36:1 The preacher both comforts and disturbs the audience through proclaiming the word of God. The messenger must deliver the message of the One who sends the servant—not an invented message (cf. Am 3:8; 2Pe 1:21).

The preacher grounds the word in the world by communicating God's truth with relevance and pertinence to our ever-changing society. The "preaching" of Chronicles informs contemporary preaching at two levels. (1) In terms of content, the disturbing message of preaching is the call to repentance. (2) In terms of style, the narrative approach permits the preacher to locate the disturbing message in a larger story that also includes the message of comfort.

36:2–14 The four brief accounts of the reigns of Jehoahaz, Jehoiakim, Jehoiachin, and Zedekiah summarize the deadly game of "musical thrones" that sees the end of the kingdom of Judah. This final section of the Chronicler's history is driven by both a documentary impulse (i.e., telling *what* happened) and the literary impulse (i.e., telling *how* it happened). The repetition of the twin themes of the exile of the last Judahite kings and the repeated plundering of the Lord's temple explains *what* happens to the kingdom of Judah (vv. 4, 6–7, 10, 18, 20).

Jerusalem three months and ten days.
He did evil in the eyes of the LORD. 10In
the spring, King Nebuchadnezzar sent
for him and brought him to Babylon,[v]
together with articles of value from the
temple of the LORD, and he made Jehoiachin's uncle,[a] Zedekiah, king over Judah
and Jerusalem.

Zedekiah King of Judah

36:11–16pp // 2Ki 24:18–20; Jer 52:1–3

11Zedekiah[w] was twenty-one years old
when he became king, and he reigned
in Jerusalem eleven years. 12He did evil
in the eyes of the LORD[x] his God and did
not humble[y] himself before Jeremiah
the prophet, who spoke the word of the
LORD. 13He also rebelled against King
Nebuchadnezzar, who had made him
take an oath[z] in God's name. He became
stiff-necked[a] and hardened his heart and
would not turn to the LORD, the God of
Israel. 14Furthermore, all the leaders of
the priests and the people became more
and more unfaithful,[b] following all the
detestable practices of the nations and
defiling the temple of the LORD, which
he had consecrated in Jerusalem.

The Fall of Jerusalem

36:17–20pp // 2Ki 25:1–21; Jer 52:4–27
36:22–23pp // Ezr 1:1–3

15The LORD, the God of their ancestors,
sent word to them through his messengers[c] again and again,[d] because he had
pity on his people and on his dwelling

36:10 [v] ver 18; 2Ki 20:17; Ezr 1:7; Jer 22:25; 24:1; 29:1; 37:1; Eze 17:12
36:11 [w] 2Ki 24:17; Jer 27:1; 28:1
36:12 [x] Jer 37:1-39:18 [y] Dt 8:3; 2Ch 7:14; 33:23; Jer 21:3-7
36:13 [z] Eze 17:13 [a] 2Ki 17:14; 2Ch 30:8
36:14 [b] 1Ch 5:25
36:15 [c] Isa 5:4; 44:26; Jer 7:25; Hag 1:13; Zec 1:4; Mal 2:7; 3:1 [d] Jer 7:13, 25; 25:3-4; 35:14, 15; 44:4-6

[a] *10* Hebrew *brother,* that is, relative (see 2 Kings 24:17)

36:14 The corporate interpretation of the exile is a key component in the "all Israel" theology of the Chronicler.

36:15–21 The Chronicler offers his generation a twofold rationale for Judah's expulsion from the land of promise. (1) Both king and people have rejected God's word spoken by his prophetic messengers (v. 16). (2) The people of Judah have failed to keep the covenant stipulation of giving the land "its sabbath rests" (v. 21).

The Lord handed his people over to Nebuchadnezzar in fulfillment of the words of Jeremiah the prophet (vv. 17, 21; cf. Jer 25:8–11; 29:10). The postexilic generation needs assurance that God keeps his word, whether it be a word of blessing or of judgment (Ps 33:4–5).

✣ **36:2–21** The righteous should not necessarily expect to escape the problem of evil in this fallen world. Instead, they are assured God will uphold them in their suffering by the help of his Holy Spirit (Ro 8:9–11; 1Co 10:13). Only a sovereign God of infinite power and eternal goodness is able to use human suffering to cultivate godly virtues in the righteous that lead to the crown of life (Ro 5:3–4; Jas 1:12).

PEOPLE TO KNOW // CYRUS

2 CHRONICLES 36:22–23: In 586 BC King Nebuchadnezzar of Babylon devastated Judah, destroyed Jerusalem and dragged the people into exile (2Ki 25). Soon, however, the power of Babylon fell to the power of Persia, and in 539 BC Cyrus of Persia decreed that the exiles could return home and rebuild their city and their lives (2Ch 36:22–23).

Remarkably, Isaiah the prophet mentioned Cyrus by name, even calling the Persian king God's "shepherd" and "anointed" one (Isa 44:28—45:1). God told Isaiah that Cyrus would "rebuild my city and set my exiles free" (Isa 45:13). The book of Ezra shows Cyrus doing just that.

Cyrus sent the exiles back with articles that had been taken from God's temple in Nebuchadnezzar's attack (Ezr 1:7–11). He authorized building materials for building a new temple (Ezr 3:7). Cyrus's decrees were recorded in the royal annals of Persia. When the Jews faced opposition in their rebuilding efforts, they appealed to Cyrus's decisions on their behalf in order to gain protection and authority from later kings of Persia. Cyrus's decisions and actions on behalf of the Jews continued to benefit them even after his death.

APPLICATION ✣ God said of Cyrus, "He is my shepherd and will accomplish all that I please" (Isa 44:28). Sometimes God's choice of servants is surprising, even shocking. Cyrus was the most powerful man in his time and place. He had no personal connection to the Jews, and yet God inclined his heart to be merciful to them. While we don't know what Cyrus's relationship with God was like, his story shows us that God can use anyone—even the most unlikely people—to accomplish his will.

place. [16]But they mocked God's messengers, despised his words and scoffed[e] at
his prophets until the wrath[f] of the LORD
was aroused against his people and there
was no remedy.[g] [17]He brought up against
them the king of the Babylonians,[a] who
killed their young men with the sword in
the sanctuary, and did not spare young
men[h] or young women, the elderly or the
infirm. God gave them all into the hands
of Nebuchadnezzar.[i] [18]He carried to Babylon all the articles[j] from the temple of
God, both large and small, and the treasures of the LORD's temple and the treasures of the king and his officials. [19]They
set fire[k] to God's temple[l] and broke down
the wall[m] of Jerusalem; they burned all
the palaces and destroyed[n] everything
of value there.[o]

[20]He carried into exile[p] to Babylon the
remnant, who escaped from the sword,
and they became servants[q] to him and
his successors until the kingdom of Persia came to power. [21]The land enjoyed its
sabbath rests;[r] all the time of its desolation it rested,[s] until the seventy years[t]
were completed in fulfillment of the
word of the LORD spoken by Jeremiah.

[22]In the first year of Cyrus[u] king of
Persia, in order to fulfill the word of
the LORD spoken by Jeremiah, the LORD
moved the heart of Cyrus king of Persia
to make a proclamation throughout his
realm and also to put it in writing:

[23]"This is what Cyrus king of Persia
says:

> " 'The LORD, the God of heaven, has given me all the kingdoms of the earth and he has appointed[v] me to build a temple for him at Jerusalem in Judah. Any of his people among you may go up, and may the LORD their God be with them.' "

36:16 [e] 2Ki 2:23; Pr 1:25; Jer 5:13 [f] Ezr 5:12; Pr 1:30-31 [g] 2Ch 30:10; Pr 29:1; Zec 1:2
36:17 [h] Jer 6:11 [i] Ezr 5:12; Jer 32:28
36:18 [j] ver 7,10
36:19 [k] Jer 11:16; 17:27; 21:10, 14; 22:7; 32:29; 39:8; La 4:11; Eze 20:47; Am 2:5; Zec 11:1 [l] 1Ki 9:8-9 [m] 2Ki 14:13 [n] La 2:6 [o] Ps 79:1-3
36:20 [p] Lev 26:44; 2Ki 24:14; Ezr 2:1; Ne 7:6 [q] Jer 27:7
36:21 [r] Lev 25:4; 26:34 [s] 1Ch 22:9 [t] Jer 1:1; 25:11; 27:22; 29:10; 40:1; Da 9:2; Zec 1:12; 7:5
36:22 [u] Isa 44:28; 45:1, 13; Jer 25:12; 29:10; Da 1:21; 6:28; 10:1
36:23 [v] Jdg 4:10

[a] 17 Or *Chaldeans*

2Ch 36:22–23 ❖ God can move even in the heart of an enemy king to accomplish his good purposes. What does this show us about God and how the world really works?

36:22–23 The quotation of Cyrus's decree offers a hopeful summary statement to the Chronicler's history and directs the audience to the continuation of the story found in the books of Ezra–Nehemiah.

The epilogue includes a date formula, "the first year of Cyrus king of Persia" (v. 22; the year is 538 BC). The famous clay barrel (or inscribed cylinder) of Cyrus records his conquest of Babylon. Although the Hebrews are not specifically mentioned in the text of the Cyrus Cylinder, the decree includes those Israelites previously exiled by the Assyrians and Babylonians.

In one sense, not only is King Cyrus Yahweh's "shepherd," but he is also Yahweh's "prophet" in that his proclamation permits Jerusalem to be restored and the temple to be rebuilt. The aftermath of Cyrus's decree is recorded in the books of Ezra–Nehemiah.

✣ **36:22–23** On the one hand, the Bible declares with certainty that God is the sovereign Lord of the nations. Yet on the other hand, the "Assyrias," "Babylonias" and "Persias" of contemporary history still rage against God and persecute the church of Jesus Christ.

This side of the second coming of Jesus, we still need to consider the truths behind the Chronicler's concern for the doctrine of God's sovereignty. After all, we still live with the political reality of the nations roaring like the waves of the sea as they churn up the mud and mire of wickedness and rebellion against God (cf. Isa 17:12–13; 57:20–21).

There is something significant in the incomplete citation of Ezr 1:3 in the Chronicler's epilogue. The expression "may go up" (36:23) is both an invitation and a directive to worship. The Chronicler's call for postexilic Judah to "go up" to the temple and worship makes the apostle Peter's words all the more penetrating when he says:

"But you are a chosen people, a royal priesthood, a holy nation, God's special possession, that you may declare the praises of him who called you out of darkness into his wonderful light" (1Pe 2:9).

Ezra

Author: Probably Ezra

Audience: The people of Judah who had returned from exile in Babylonia

Date: Sometime after 440 BC

Theme: God directs a remnant of the Israelites, who had been exiled to Babylonia, to return to Jerusalem to rebuild the temple.

Reading Ezra

Ezra divides into two parts, each telling the story of a homecoming. The first one, led by Zerubbabel and Joshua took place in the first year of Cyrus, king of Persia. Ezra led a second group back to the promised land about sixty years after the first group.

PERSPECTIVE

The books of Ezra and Nehemiah (originally one book) tell the story of Israel's return to Zion during a hundred-year period from 539 BC to 433 BC. The return was led first by a scribe and priest, Ezra, who brought a group of Babylonian exiles back to Jerusalem, and later by a governor appointed by the Persian ruler Artaxerxes, an Israelite politician named Nehemiah. In keeping with their complementary roles as religious and political leaders, Ezra emphasized the need to reestablish the Law of Moses, while Nehemiah advocated and oversaw the rebuilding of the gates and walls of the city.

Both Ezra and Nehemiah were responding to a 559 BC proclamation by Cyrus the Great, king of Persia. Cyrus, whose heart was moved by the Lord (Ezr 1:1), announced that the God of heaven had appointed him to build a temple in Jerusalem—not only build it but raise the funds to pay for it. Ezra and Nehemiah ended up being Cyrus's representatives in fulfilling this divine command.

Yet there was an even bigger motivation at work here. For both Ezra and Nehemiah, law-keeping and wall-building were manifestations of a larger purpose—a purpose larger even than Cyrus's proclamation. Both Ezra and Nehemiah believed that a successful return from Babylon to Jerusalem was based on a theological task: renewing the returned exiles' worship of Yahweh.

Before jumping to any conclusions about how this story might have meaning for those of us who live in the twenty-first-century West, we should note some pretty dramatic cultural differences between our day and the Middle East in the sixth century BC.

1400 BC 1300 1200 1100 1000 900 800 700 600 500 400

Fall of Jerusalem (586 BC)
Persia's conquest of Babylon (539 BC)
First return of exiles to Jerusalem (538 BC)
Ministries of Haggai and Zechariah (c. 520–480 BC)
Completion of temple (516 BC)
Second return to Jerusalem under Ezra (458 BC)
Third return to Jerusalem under Nehemiah (444 BC)
Book of Ezra written (c. 440 BC)

For starters, we are not physically exiled, looking for a way to get back to our promised land. God's people had been militarily conquered and physically removed from their land and lived in exile in Babylon. Our predicament today as religious people is that we are being culturally exiled even as we continue to live on the same streets that once showcased our churches and provided places for our food pantries, soup kitchens, and shelters for people experiencing stormy times.

And we are not looking for a return to some sort of religiously homogeneous culture. We are not looking for endorsement of our particular religious views. We can, however, resonate with a few of the tasks taken on by these returned exiles: Cyrus's declaration that the temple be reconstructed, Ezra's reestablishment of the law, Nehemiah's rebuilding of the walls. That is, we can easily identify a current need for church revitalization that can learn from Cyrus's burden. We need a strong church in the face of record numbers of Americans turning away from the Christian church. Behind each of these resonances lies a deeper vacuum, a loss of a sense of human beings as worshiping beings. What is missing from public discourse and private convictions alike is a constant awareness that we are created beings, creatures of a Creator who is beyond time and space, all-powerful and totally good. This awareness of God can only be nurtured by congregations in worshiping churches, law-making that looks far beyond immediate political advantage to laws that encourage true justice and compassion, and the contextual safety of a country that sees its citizens' devotion to transcendent religion as a strength rather than a weakness. Ezra and Nehemiah demanded that this be the foundation of the re-civilization of the promised land; we need to learn this critical lesson once again.

Key Verses

Praise be to the LORD, the God of our ancestors, who has put it into the king's heart to bring honor to the house of the LORD in Jerusalem in this way and who has extended his good favor to me before the king and his advisers and all the king's powerful officials. Because the hand of the LORD my God was on me, I took courage and gathered leaders from Israel to go up with me.

—Ezra 7:27–28

TAKING THE NEXT STEPS

Ezra records the story of God's people coming home from the captivity in Babylon to the promised land in order to rebuild the temple of God and reestablish their homes. They were certain they were not on their own, for God was guiding them by his providence. And even though the Jews no longer had their own king, God still provided them with powerful leaders such as Zerubbabel and Ezra, who showed them by word and deed what true service to God involved.

This short book reminds us of several characteristics of God that are important in our daily lives. (1) God is a forgiving God, who does not stay angry forever; even if we sin against him grievously, he gives us new opportunities to serve him. (2) God is a caring God, who will accomplish his will in spite of opposition, and whose protection in our daily lives is all that we really need to make it through each day. (3) God is the one and only God, and he expects us to worship him and him alone, and not cooperate with those who oppose his will.

WHAT TO LOOK FOR IN EZRA

- The return to Canaan ordered by Cyrus (ch. 1)
- Rebuilding the temple (chs. 3–6)
- The return to Canaan led by Ezra (chs. 7–8)
- The problem of mixed marriages (chs. 9–10)

Cyrus Helps the Exiles to Return

1:1–3pp // 2Ch 36:22–23

1 In the first year of Cyrus king of Persia,
in order to fulfill the word of the LORD
spoken by Jeremiah,[a] the LORD moved
the heart[b] of Cyrus king of Persia to make
a proclamation throughout his realm
and also to put it in writing:

2"This is what Cyrus king of Persia
says:
"'The LORD, the God of heaven,
has given me all the kingdoms of
the earth and he has appointed[c] me
to build[d] a temple for him at Jerusalem in Judah. 3Any of his people
among you may go up to Jerusalem
in Judah and build the temple of the
LORD, the God of Israel, the God who
is in Jerusalem, and may their God
be with them. 4And in any locality
where survivors[e] may now be living, the people are to provide them
with silver and gold, with goods and
livestock, and with freewill offerings[f] for the temple of God in Jerusalem.'"[g]

5Then the family heads of Judah and
Benjamin,[h] and the priests and Levites—
everyone whose heart God had moved[i]—
prepared to go up and build the house[j] of
the LORD in Jerusalem. 6All their neighbors assisted them with articles of silver
and gold, with goods and livestock, and
with valuable gifts, in addition to all the
freewill offerings.
7Moreover, King Cyrus brought out the

1:1 [a]Jer 25:11-12; 29:10-14 [b]2Ch 36:22,23
1:2 [c]Isa 44:28; 45:13 [d]Ezr 5:13
1:4 [e]Isa 10:20-22 [f]Nu 15:3; Ps 50:14; 54:6; 116:17 [g]Ezr 4:3; 5:13; 6:3,14
1:5 [h]Ezr 4:1; Ne 11:4 [i]ver 1; Ex 35:20-22; 2Ch 36:22; Hag 1:14; Php 2:13 [j]Ps 127:1

Ezr 1:5 ❖ What is God moving our hearts to do for him?

1:1 In 539 BC the Persians together with the Medes diverted the waters of the Euphrates and marched into well-fortified Babylon (Da 5). The author of Ezra wants the reader to see that Cyrus's first year as king was not to be interpreted merely from the vantage of international politics. It was much more. Through Cyrus, God takes action and intervenes to end the captivity of his people.
1:2a Cyrus acknowledges his successful military acquisition derives from "the LORD."
1:2b–3 Cyrus acknowledges the scope of the task of [re]building Yahweh's earthly dwelling in Jerusalem (v. 2b) and his support for it. This would include providing financial backing and any other resources needed to make it happen.

Cyrus's surprising use of the covenantal name Yahweh (NIV "LORD") is not an acknowledgment that Cyrus had experienced Yahweh in the same way as an Israelite. Rather, it is an acknowledgment that Yahweh is Israel's God who resides in Jerusalem. Embedded in the edict are two important factors for the successful execution of the project. On the one hand it depends upon the willingness of some people to leave Babylon. On the other hand, it depends entirely on divine presence/favor, as Cyrus states, "May their God be with them" (v. 3).
1:4a The king enables those who wish to go up by rallying support, first from those Jews who wish to stay but also from the non-Judean community.
1:4b The building project required not only willing souls but also money and materials.
1:5 As the numbers in ch. 2 make clear, not many Israelites chose to return. The author deliberately mentions that priests and Levites were among a second group who also responded. Without these spiritual leaders, the renewal process would not have been possible.
1:6 The Hebrew can also be rendered, "they strengthened their hands." The way the neighbors supported those returning to Jerusalem was through giving.
1:7–8 Roughly two hundred years earlier, Isaiah prophesied that God's people would return to

articles belonging to the temple of the LORD, which Nebuchadnezzar had carried away from Jerusalem and had placed in the temple of his god.[a][k] 8Cyrus king of Persia had them brought by Mithredath the treasurer, who counted them out to Sheshbazzar[l] the prince of Judah.
9This was the inventory:

gold dishes	30
silver dishes	1,000
silver pans[b]	29
10gold bowls	30
matching silver bowls	410
other articles	1,000

11In all, there were 5,400 articles of gold and of silver. Sheshbazzar brought all these along with the exiles when they came up from Babylon to Jerusalem.

The List of the Exiles Who Returned

2:1–70pp // Ne 7:6–73

2 Now these are the people of the province who came up from the captivity of the exiles,[m] whom Nebuchadnezzar king of Babylon[n] had taken captive to Babylon (they returned to Jerusalem and Judah, each to their own town,[o] 2in company with Zerubbabel,[p] Joshua,[q] Nehemiah, Seraiah,[r] Reelaiah, Mordecai, Bilshan, Mispar, Bigvai, Rehum and Baanah):

The list of the men of the people of Israel:

3the descendants of Parosh[s]	2,172
4of Shephatiah	372
5of Arah	775
6of Pahath-Moab (through the line of Jeshua and Joab)	2,812
7of Elam	1,254
8of Zattu	945
9of Zakkai	760
10of Bani	642
11of Bebai	623
12of Azgad	1,222
13of Adonikam[t]	666
14of Bigvai	2,056
15of Adin	454
16of Ater (through Hezekiah)	98
17of Bezai	323
18of Jorah	112
19of Hashum	223
20of Gibbar	95

21the men of Bethlehem[u]	123
22of Netophah	56
23of Anathoth	128
24of Azmaveth	42
25of Kiriath Jearim,[c] Kephirah and Beeroth	743
26of Ramah[v] and Geba	621
27of Mikmash	122
28of Bethel and Ai[w]	223
29of Nebo	52
30of Magbish	156
31of the other Elam	1,254
32of Harim	320
33of Lod, Hadid and Ono	725
34of Jericho[x]	345
35of Senaah	3,630

36The priests:

the descendants of Jedaiah[y] (through the family of Jeshua)	973

1:7 [k] 2Ki 24:13; 2Ch 36:7,10; Ezr 5:14; 6:5
1:8 [l] Ezr 5:14
2:1 [m] 2Ch 36:20; Ne 7:6 [n] 2Ki 24:16; 25:12 [o] Ne 7:73
2:2 [p] 1Ch 3:19 [q] Ezr 3:2 [r] Ne 10:2
2:3 [s] Ezr 8:3
2:13 [t] Ezr 8:13
2:21 [u] Mic 5:2
2:26 [v] Jos 18:25
2:28 [w] Ge 12:8
2:34 [x] 1Ki 16:34; 2Ch 28:15
2:36 [y] 1Ch 24:7

[a] 7 Or *gods* [b] 9 The meaning of the Hebrew for this word is uncertain. [c] 25 See Septuagint (see also Neh. 7:29); Hebrew *Kiriath Arim.*

Jerusalem and that "the articles of the LORD's house" would be involved (Isa 52:11–12).

1:9–11 All of this empirical evidence affirms Cyrus's best wishes (v. 3). It is the author's implicit way of showing that the Lord is with his people, thus practically fulfilling his word spoken by Jeremiah (Jer 30:3).

APPLICATION ✣ 1:1–11 God is going to keep his word no matter what obstacles are stacked against the plan he enacts. It's critical that we realize how significant it is that God keeps his word to restore all things to himself, especially in times of separation from him due to sin's consequences. Without such a worldview, we lose our view and perspective on life. And with it, our hope (see Jos 1:9; Ro 15:13).

2:1–2 The captive people return to their homeland. Another exodus is taking place, one promised by Isaiah (Isa 48:20–22).

Zerubbabel and Joshua, the first two names on the list, emerge as key players in the restoration and rebuilding process. Zerubbabel has a position in the Davidic line—a hope of reestablishing kingship. Joshua, as Judah's high priest, gives solid spiritual leadership and is associated with rebuilding the altar (3:2).

2:2b–20 The use of the phrase "the people of Israel" (v. 2) is a reminder of the ties and connections these people have to a past that defined them. Using the ancestral name rather than the current family head is the author's implicit way of stating that these people have a legal connection to the land.

2:21–35 Twenty-one geographical names emerge on the list. The list associates the people who are going up to Jerusalem and Judah with towns in the region, not with an ancestor.

2:36–58 After naming returning laypeople (vv. 3–35), the author lists five distinct categories of ministers who return (priests, Levites, musicians,

[37]of Immer[z] 1,052
[38]of Pashhur[a] 1,247
[39]of Harim[b] 1,017

[40]The Levites:[c]

the descendants of Jeshua[d]
and Kadmiel (of the line
of Hodaviah) 74

[41]The musicians:[e]

the descendants of Asaph 128

[42]The gatekeepers[f] of the temple:

the descendants of
Shallum, Ater, Talmon,
Akkub, Hatita and Shobai 139

[43]The temple servants:[g]

the descendants of
Ziha, Hasupha, Tabbaoth,
[44]Keros, Siaha, Padon,
[45]Lebanah, Hagabah, Akkub,
[46]Hagab, Shalmai, Hanan,
[47]Giddel, Gahar, Reaiah,
[48]Rezin, Nekoda, Gazzam,
[49]Uzza, Paseah, Besai,
[50]Asnah, Meunim, Nephusim,
[51]Bakbuk, Hakupha, Harhur,

2:37 [z]1Ch 24:14
2:38 [a]1Ch 9:12
2:39 [b]1Ch 24:8
2:40 [c]Ge 29:34; Nu 3:9; Dt 18:6-7; 1Ch 16:4; Ezr 7:7; 8:15; Ne 12:24 [d]Ezr 3:9
2:41 [e]1Ch 15:16
2:42 [f]1Sa 3:15; 1Ch 9:17
2:43 [g]1Ch 9:2; Ne 11:21

gatekeepers, and temple servants). Four families of priests are noted first (vv. 36–39). Along with the priests, two families of Levites are named (v. 40).

The list also includes musicians associated with the "descendants of Asaph" (v. 41). There is mention also of six families of gatekeepers (v. 42). As with the musicians, David organized the gatekeepers. The list concludes with thirty-five families of temple servants and an additional ten families associated with the servants of Solomon (vv. 43–58).

RETURN FROM EXILE

Restoration of the Jewish exiles began under Cyrus (559–530 BC), who allowed them to return to Judah with the captured temple treasures. The temple was consecrated in 516 BC by official permission of Darius I (522–486 BC).

Ezra won the approval of Artaxerxes I (465–424 BC) to return with additional exiles and to promote obedience to the law; Nehemiah, to rebuild the walls of Jerusalem.

Babylon and its vicinity long retained a large and prosperous Jewish community, as clay tablets from the Murashu archives at Nippur testify.

[52]Bazluth, Mehida, Harsha,
[53]Barkos, Sisera, Temah,
[54]Neziah and Hatipha

[55]The descendants of the servants of Solomon:

the descendants of
Sotai, Hassophereth, Peruda,
[56]Jaala, Darkon, Giddel,
[57]Shephatiah, Hattil,
Pokereth-Hazzebaim and Ami

[58]The temple servants[h] and the descendants of the servants of Solomon 392

[59]The following came up from
the towns of Tel Melah, Tel Harsha,
Kerub, Addon and Immer, but they
could not show that their families
were descended[i] from Israel:

[60]The descendants of
Delaiah, Tobiah and
Nekoda 652

[61]And from among the priests:

The descendants of
Hobaiah, Hakkoz and Barzillai
(a man who had married
a daughter of Barzillai the
Gileadite[j] and was called by
that name).

[62]These searched for their family records, but they could not find
them and so were excluded from
the priesthood[k] as unclean. [63]The
governor ordered them not to eat
any of the most sacred food[l] until
there was a priest ministering with
the Urim and Thummim.[m]

[64]The whole company numbered
42,360, [65]besides their 7,337 male and
female slaves; and they also had 200
male and female singers.[n] [66]They
had 736 horses,[o] 245 mules, [67]435
camels and 6,720 donkeys.

[68]When they arrived at the house of
the LORD in Jerusalem, some of the heads
of the families[p] gave freewill offerings
toward the rebuilding of the house of
God on its site. [69]According to their ability they gave to the treasury for this work
61,000 darics[a] of gold, 5,000 minas[b] of
silver and 100 priestly garments.

[70]The priests, the Levites, the musicians, the gatekeepers and the temple
servants settled in their own towns,
along with some of the other people,
and the rest of the Israelites settled in
their towns.[q]

2:58 [h] 1Ki 9:21; 1Ch 9:2
2:59 [i] Nu 1:18
2:61 [j] 2Sa 17:27
2:62 [k] Nu 3:10; 16:39-40
2:63 [l] Lev 2:3, 10 [m] Ex 28:30; Nu 27:21
2:65 [n] 2Sa 19:35
2:66 [o] Isa 66:20
2:68 [p] Ex 25:2
2:70 [q] ver 1; 1Ch 9:2; Ne 11:3-4
3:1 [r] Ne 7:73; 8:1 [s] Lev 23:24

Ezr 2:68 ❖ What are we able to offer for the building or rebuilding of worshiping communities?

Rebuilding the Altar

3 When the seventh month came and
the Israelites had settled in their
towns,[r] the people assembled[s] together

[a] 69 That is, about 1,100 pounds or about 500 kilograms [b] 69 That is, about 3 tons or about 2.8 metric tons

2:59–70 Although family records were apparently lost for both laypeople and priests (vv. 59, 62), the wording of the latter verse draws attention to the specific search pertaining to the priests since exclusion from the priesthood is mentioned as a result of the unsuccessful search. The Urim and Thummim would ultimately determine God's intentions for them once a priest was again officiating with these sacred instruments. The larger point of the account here is that it remains unclear whether the priests under scrutiny could be consecrated for the Lord's work. Reestablishing true worship in Israel cannot effectively be done if laypeople and ministers of the Lord have a questionable identity as the people of God.

2:64–70 Verse 64 functions as a numerical summary. The chapter concludes with what appears to be a total head count of people and their possessions, including servants and animals, that set out and eventually settled in Jerusalem. The total of the "whole company" listed in 2:64 does not mathematically equate when adding the numbers together, but that is not surprising as often such lists are not intended to be exhaustive and are therefore incomplete.

2:1–70 As we journey in becoming the people of God, we need to be reassured that when we lose our spiritual markers of identity because of our own wrongdoing or life's circumstances, we are still God's possession.

The fact of the matter is this: We make our own markers of identity as a result of trying to figure out who we are. The problem with the markers of identity that we establish is that they do not stand the test of time because they are of human origin. We need, therefore, to have a purpose that is not grounded in ourselves. It might be summed up this way: We don't know *who* we are until we know *whose* we are.

3:1–2 The "seventh month" (v. 1) signals movement forward from both a practical point of view (to rebuild the temple) and a theological perspective (to rebuild worship).

as one in Jerusalem. 2Then Joshua[t] son
of Jozadak[u] and his fellow priests and
Zerubbabel son of Shealtiel[v] and his associates began to build the altar of the God
of Israel to sacrifice burnt offerings on it,
in accordance with what is written in the
Law of Moses[w] the man of God. 3Despite
their fear[x] of the peoples around them,
they built the altar on its foundation
and sacrificed burnt offerings on it to
the LORD, both the morning and evening
sacrifices.[y] 4Then in accordance with what
is written, they celebrated the Festival of
Tabernacles[z] with the required number of
burnt offerings prescribed for each day.
5After that, they presented the regular
burnt offerings, the New Moon[a] sacrifices
and the sacrifices for all the appointed
sacred festivals of the LORD,[b] as well as
those brought as freewill offerings to the
LORD. 6On the first day of the seventh
month they began to offer burnt offerings
to the LORD, though the foundation of
the LORD's temple had not yet been laid.

Rebuilding the Temple

7Then they gave money to the masons
and carpenters, and gave food and drink
and olive oil to the people of Sidon and
Tyre, so that they would bring cedar logs[c]
by sea from Lebanon[d] to Joppa, as authorized by Cyrus[e] king of Persia.
8In the second month of the second
year after their arrival at the house of God
in Jerusalem, Zerubbabel[f] son of Shealtiel,
Joshua son of Jozadak and the rest of the
people (the priests and the Levites and
all who had returned from the captivity
to Jerusalem) began the work. They appointed Levites twenty[g] years old and older to supervise the building of the house
of the LORD. 9Joshua[h] and his sons and
brothers and Kadmiel and his sons (descendants of Hodaviah[a]) and the sons of
Henadad and their sons and brothers—all
Levites—joined together in supervising
those working on the house of God.
10When the builders laid[i] the foundation of the temple of the LORD, the
priests in their vestments and with trumpets,[j] and the Levites (the sons of Asaph)
with cymbals, took their places to praise[k]
the LORD, as prescribed by David[l] king of
Israel.[m] 11With praise and thanksgiving
they sang to the LORD:

"He is good;
his love toward Israel endures
forever."[n]

And all the people gave a great shout[o] of
praise to the LORD, because the foundation of the house of the LORD was laid.
12But many of the older priests and

3:2 [t] Ezr 2:2; Ne 12:1, 8; Hag 2:2 [u] Hag 1:1; Zec 6:11 [v] 1Ch 3:17 [w] Ex 20:24; Dt 12:5-6
3:3 [x] Ezr 4:4; Da 9:25 [y] Ex 29:39; Nu 28:1-8
3:4 [z] Ex 23:16; Nu 29:12-38; Ne 8:14-18; Zec 14:16-19
3:5 [a] Nu 28:3, 11,14; Col 2:16 [b] Lev 23:1-44; Nu 29:39
3:7 [c] 1Ch 14:1 [d] Isa 35:2 [e] Ezr 1:2-4; 6:3
3:8 [f] Zec 4:9 [g] 1Ch 23:24
3:9 [h] Ezr 2:40
3:10 [i] Ezr 5:16 [j] Nu 10:2; 1Ch 16:6 [k] 1Ch 25:1 [l] 1Ch 6:31 [m] Zec 6:12
3:11 [n] 1Ch 16:34, 41; 2Ch 7:3; Ps 107:1; 118:1 [o] Ne 12:24

Ezr 3:3 ❖ Have we ever been afraid to worship God because of those around us? How can we overcome these fears?

[a] 9 Hebrew *Yehudah,* a variant of *Hodaviah*

3:2 As Joshua and Zerubbabel provide spiritual and administrative leadership, this verse orients the reader to the specific goals of the covenantal community. It announces the stated project, "to build the altar of the God of Israel," but the verse also reflects the stated purpose for building the altar, "to sacrifice burnt offerings on it." Furthermore, Joshua and company have the stated authority backing their efforts, "in accordance with what is written in the Law of Moses the man of God." Their worship is rooted and grounded in the Word of God.

3:3 With the altar rebuilt according to Mosaic specifications, the people were ready to reengage in worshiping Yahweh on a daily basis. Although the returnees labored under adverse conditions, they were not paralyzed by fear; they continued the work on the altar.

3:4–5 The Festival of Tabernacles was a celebration deriving from the fact that God graciously protected and provided for Israel's ancestors when they lived in tents during their forty-year desert discipline. The people who had returned to Jerusalem were ready to engage the Lord with all the required sacrifices built into their calendar year.

3:6 In the seventh month the altar was rebuilt; most of Israel's sacrificial system was in place, and all this happened prior to the building of the temple. This indicates that true worship was possible even without the temple.

3:7–9 After completing the altar, the returnees immediately turn their attention to preparations for rebuilding the temple, starting with the foundation. The administrative and spiritual leaders (Zerubbabel and Joshua, respectively), as well as the priests, Levites, and "all who had returned" (v. 8), worked. The Levites who were age twenty and older were appointed to supervise all the work. This appointment parallels that of King David to some degree (1Ch 23:4–32). Here it seems evident that the author intentionally attempts to make connections with the past.

3:10–11 The praise of the returnees was rooted in a keen awareness of Yahweh's strong and unshakable character, without which the return from exile and the completion of the temple foundation would not have been possible.

3:12 Although the environment was joyful, people who had seen Solomon's temple firsthand were underwhelmed at what they saw and wept loudly.

Levites and family heads, who had seen the former temple,[p] wept aloud when they saw the foundation of this temple being laid, while many others shouted for joy. 13No one could distinguish the sound of the shouts of joy[q] from the sound of weeping, because the people made so much noise. And the sound was heard far away.

Opposition to the Rebuilding

4 When the enemies of Judah and Benjamin heard that the exiles were building a temple for the LORD, the God of Israel, 2they came to Zerubbabel and to the heads of the families and said, "Let us help you build because, like you, we seek your God and have been sacrificing to him since the time of Esarhaddon[r] king of Assyria, who brought us here."[s]

3But Zerubbabel, Joshua and the rest of the heads of the families of Israel answered, "You have no part with us in building a temple to our God. We alone will build it for the LORD, the God of Israel, as King Cyrus, the king of Persia, commanded us."[t]

4Then the peoples around them set out to discourage the people of Judah and make them afraid to go on building.[a][u] 5They bribed officials to work against them and frustrate their plans during the entire reign of Cyrus king of Persia and down to the reign of Darius king of Persia.

Later Opposition Under Xerxes and Artaxerxes

6At the beginning of the reign of Xerxes,[b][v] they lodged an accusation against the people of Judah and Jerusalem.[w]

7And in the days of Artaxerxes[x] king of Persia, Bishlam, Mithredath, Tabeel and the rest of his associates wrote a letter to Artaxerxes. The letter was written in Aramaic script and in the Aramaic[y] language.[c,d]

8Rehum the commanding officer and Shimshai the secretary wrote a letter against Jerusalem to Artaxerxes the king as follows:

9Rehum the commanding officer and Shimshai the secretary, together

3:12 [p] Hag 2:3,9
3:13 [q] Job 8:21; Ps 27:6; Isa 16:9
4:2 [r] 2Ki 17:24; 19:37 [s] 2Ki 17:41
4:3 [t] Ezr 1:1-4; Ne 2:20
4:4 [u] Ezr 3:3
4:6 [v] Est 1:1; Da 9:1 [w] Est 3:13; 9:5
4:7 [x] Ezr 7:1; Ne 2:1 [y] 2Ki 18:26; Isa 36:11; Da 2:4

[a] 4 Or *and troubled them as they built*
[b] 6 Hebrew *Ahasuerus*
[c] 7 Or *written in Aramaic and translated*
[d] 7 The text of 4:8 – 6:18 is in Aramaic.

3:13 The author wants the reader to know that not only was the sound of Israel's praises to the Lord loud (indicative of a renewed heart), but also the sound reverberated outside the community. In fact, their renewed witness in the land sets the stage for the trouble described in the chapter that follows.

3:1-13 God's character enables us to look at life's difficulties (self-imposed or otherwise) and see God presently as good. But it also enables us to look forward with great assurance when we will face more of life's difficulties (self-imposed or otherwise) and see that God will still be good.

4:1-5, 24 The biblical writer intentionally gives a lot of literary space to the topic of opposition and only ten verses to narrate the completion and celebration of the rebuilt temple (6:13-22). One must understand the completed task in light of its opposition.

4:1-2 The narrator identifies "the enemies of Judah and Benjamin" (v. 1). But in the recorded speech, they self-identify as exiles. The boast "like you, we seek your God" becomes their rationale for offering assistance (v. 2). Perhaps they were prompted by a sense of entitlement based on their long residence in the land.

4:3 Israel's leaders respond with discernment and uncompromising theological conviction. A lack of purity could not be tolerated given their sordid past, especially in light of this second chance.

4:4-5 The wise decision to exclude these folks because of legal and theological convictions was not without a cost for the reestablished community. Those excluded most likely felt angry and rejected, which led to retaliation. The goal of their tactic was to "discourage," which can also be rendered, "weakening the hands of," the people of Judah (v. 4). When this phrase appears elsewhere in the Bible, it describes a crippling effect caused by deep despair and dismay. Indeed, the enemies' tactic, whatever it was, produced fruit. Eventually the Jews, worn out by the opposition, voluntarily stopped their work on the house of God for sixteen years (v. 24).

4:1-5 This short narrative invites the reader, but especially a leader, to lead with conviction and to count the cost of conviction. It shows that such a thing exists as a theology of saying no. There is a time for religious intolerance when the purity of a task or an idea is at stake. During such times, believers must be discerning and prayerful in their decisions (see Php 1:9-11), relying on the Holy Spirit's direction.

4:6 The first of the two instances of opposition concern an accusation leveled at the people early in the reign of Xerxes. The author offers no information about the nature of this complaint but merely lists it first.

4:7-13 The second instance of opposition concerns a piece of correspondence. The recipient is King Artaxerxes of Persia. The complaint has the backing of people of rank and carries some weight.

with the rest of their associates[z]—
the judges, officials and administrators over the people from Persia,
Uruk and Babylon, the Elamites of
Susa, 10 and the other people whom
the great and honorable Ashurbanipal deported and settled in the
city of Samaria and elsewhere in
Trans-Euphrates.[a]

11 (This is a copy of the letter they sent
him.)

To King Artaxerxes,

From your servants in Trans-Euphrates:

12 The king should know that the
people who came up to us from you
have gone to Jerusalem and are rebuilding that rebellious and wicked
city. They are restoring the walls and
repairing the foundations.[b]
13 Furthermore, the king should
know that if this city is built and its
walls are restored, no more taxes,
tribute or duty[c] will be paid, and
eventually the royal revenues will
suffer.[a] 14 Now since we are under
obligation to the palace and it is
not proper for us to see the king
dishonored, we are sending this
message to inform the king, 15 so
that a search may be made in the
archives[d] of your predecessors. In
these records you will find that this
city is a rebellious city, troublesome
to kings and provinces, a place with
a long history of sedition. That is
why this city was destroyed.[e] 16 We
inform the king that if this city is
built and its walls are restored, you
will be left with nothing in Trans-
Euphrates.

17 The king sent this reply:

To Rehum the commanding officer,
Shimshai the secretary and the rest
of their associates living in Samaria
and elsewhere in Trans-Euphrates:[f]

Greetings.

18 The letter you sent us has been
read and translated in my presence.
19 I issued an order and a search was
made, and it was found that this city
has a long history of revolt[g] against
kings and has been a place of rebellion and sedition. 20 Jerusalem
has had powerful kings ruling over
the whole of Trans-Euphrates,[h] and
taxes, tribute and duty were paid
to them. 21 Now issue an order to
these men to stop work, so that
this city will not be rebuilt until I
so order. 22 Be careful not to neglect
this matter. Why let this threat grow,
to the detriment of the royal interests?[i]

4:9 [z] Ezr 5:6; 6:6,13
4:10 [a] ver 17; Ne 4:2
4:12 [b] Ezr 5:3,9
4:13 [c] Ezr 7:24; Ne 5:4
4:15 [d] Ezr 5:17; 6:1
[e] Est 3:8
4:17 [f] ver 10
4:19 [g] 2Ki 18:7
4:20 [h] Ge 15:18-21; Ex 23:31; Jos 1:4; 1Ki 4:21; 1Ch 18:3; Ps 72:8-11
4:22 [i] Da 6:2

[a] *13* The meaning of the Aramaic for this clause is uncertain.

4:14–16 The heart of this complaint pertains to loyalty. Those crafting the letter prop themselves up and appear to have a staunch loyalty to the distant king. Since rebuilding a city wall is akin to gaining strength and independence, this construction project was viewed as a compromise of loyalties, posing a serious threat to the empire.

The informants describe Jerusalem's interactions with past political administrations as rebellious. According to the king's informants, the city was destroyed on account of such rebellion (v. 15), and they are justified in their complaint. Their human perspective, however, contrasts with the divine perspective about the city's fall (2Ch 36:15–19).

4:17–23 The section closes with a record of the king's response and action to the supposed threat. It speaks of three orders: one to look into the matter, another to stop the work, and a hypothetical order that might grant rebuilding at a future time. This literary interlude (vv. 6–23) fills out the bigger picture of opposition that the Jews faced.

4:6–24 The staunch opposition and nasty accusations lodged against the Jews in their effort to rebuild reflect what we know, this side of the cross, to be spiritual warfare. What looks like a fight against flesh and blood is really a fight against the principalities and powers in the heavenly places (Eph 6:10–12).

We often forget, and perhaps even deny, that theologically speaking we are in a time of war, not peace. With Jesus's resurrection, the age to come has broken into this present age. But the present age is not benign. It is the present evil age (Eph 6:12). This is why some receive salvation and others do not. This is why we see some healings, but not all the time. This is why we ultimately experience opposition—both individually and corporately as the church. This is the reason why the nations are not yet reached for the gospel. This is why some nations remain closed to Christianity. This is why evil prevails. This is why the church looks defeated, thwarted, and even stopped. We are living in the age of tension between what is now and what we long for in the future (see Rev 21:4).

Ezr 4:23 ❖ How do conflicts and rivalries hinder the work of believers today?

Ezr 5:5 ❖ How can we remain resilient in our faith against obstacles and opposition?

23 As soon as the copy of the letter of King Artaxerxes was read to Rehum and Shimshai the secretary and their associates,[j] they went immediately to the Jews in Jerusalem and compelled them by force to stop.

24 Thus the work on the house of God in Jerusalem came to a standstill until the second year of the reign of Darius[k] king of Persia.

Tattenai's Letter to Darius

5 Now Haggai[l] the prophet and Zechariah[m] the prophet, a descendant of Iddo, prophesied[n] to the Jews in Judah and Jerusalem in the name of the God of Israel, who was over them. 2 Then Zerubbabel[o] son of Shealtiel and Joshua[p] son of Jozadak set to work[q] to rebuild the house of God in Jerusalem. And the prophets of God were with them, supporting them.

3 At that time Tattenai,[r] governor of Trans-Euphrates, and Shethar-Bozenai[s] and their associates went to them and asked, "Who authorized you to rebuild this temple and to finish it?"[t] 4 They[a] also asked, "What are the names of those who are constructing this building?" 5 But the eye of their God[u] was watching over the elders of the Jews, and they were not stopped until a report could go to Darius and his written reply be received.

6 This is a copy of the letter that Tattenai, governor of Trans-Euphrates, and Shethar-Bozenai and their associates, the officials of Trans-Euphrates, sent to King Darius. 7 The report they sent him read as follows:

To King Darius:

Cordial greetings.

8 The king should know that we went to the district of Judah, to the temple of the great God. The people are building it with large stones and placing the timbers in the walls. The work[v] is being carried on with diligence and is making rapid progress under their direction.

9 We questioned the elders and asked them, "Who authorized you to rebuild this temple and to finish it?"[w] 10 We also asked them their names, so that we could write down the names of their leaders for your information.

11 This is the answer they gave us:

"We are the servants of the God of heaven and earth, and we are rebuilding the temple[x] that was built many years ago, one that a great king of Israel built and finished. 12 But because our ancestors angered[y] the God of heaven, he gave them into the hands of Nebuchadnezzar the Chaldean, king of Babylon, who destroyed this temple and deported the people to Babylon.[z]

13 "However, in the first year of Cyrus king of Babylon, King Cyrus issued a decree[a] to rebuild this house of God. 14 He even removed from the temple[b] of Babylon the

4:23 [j] ver 9
4:24 [k] Ne 2:1-8; Da 9:25; Hag 1:1,15; Zec 1:1
5:1 [l] Ezr 6:14; Hag 1:1,3,12; 2:1,10,20 [m] Zec 1:1; 7:1 [n] Hag 1:14-2:9; Zec 4:9-10; 8:9
5:2 [o] 1Ch 3:19; Hag 1:14; 2:21; Zec 4:6-10 [p] Ezr 2:2; 3:2 [q] ver 8; Hag 2:2-5
5:3 [r] Ezr 6:6 [s] Ezr 6:6 [t] ver 9; Ezr 1:3; 4:12
5:5 [u] 2Ki 25:28; Ezr 7:6,9,28; 8:18,22,31; Ne 2:8,18; Ps 33:18; Isa 66:14
5:8 [v] ver 2
5:9 [w] Ezr 4:12
5:11 [x] 1Ki 6:1; 2Ch 3:1-2
5:12 [y] 2Ch 36:16 [z] Dt 21:10; 28:36; 2Ki 24:1; 25:8,9,11; Jer 1:3
5:13 [a] Ezr 1:1

[a] 4 See Septuagint; Aramaic *We*. [b] 14 Or *palace*

5:1 God intervenes after the long sixteen-year hiatus to fulfill the intended goal of rebuilding the temple (1:1–11).

5:2 This verse demonstrates how true prophecy was meant to motivate, bring change, and work in the lives of God's covenantal people.

5:3–5 Once again Persian officials challenge the Jews about the rebuilding process but with an entirely different spirit. Their challenge is not necessarily to deter but to do things according to government regulations. Verse 5 reveals the heart of the matter—God's seeing eye leads to protection from harm.

5:6–10 The officials are loyal informants of the king but of a different type from those mentioned in 4:12–16. They simply wish to obtain government clearance on the building project.

The Persians do not acknowledge Israel's God as the only God, but as one among many (see 1:1–3). He was, however, the only God for the Israelites. No malice seems intended in the investigation. In fact, the Persian officials affirmed both the workers and the work (v. 8). These officials also wanted to know names of those from the Jewish community; the more information, the better in bringing the matter to a conclusion.

5:11–17 The Jews confidently provide Darius with a historical sketch about the temple. Notice that Solomon's name is omitted above in reference to the first temple (v. 12). The Jews may have put forward only the names of those who could be traced in the official documents. The focus in ch. 3 pertains to the building, but here in ch. 5 the focus is on the evidence allowing the Jews to build.

gold and silver articles of the house of God, which Nebuchadnezzar had taken from the temple in Jerusalem and brought to the temple[a] in Babylon.[b] Then King Cyrus gave them to a man named Sheshbazzar,[c] whom he had appointed governor, 15and he told him, 'Take these articles and go and deposit them in the temple in Jerusalem. And rebuild the house of God on its site.'

16"So this Sheshbazzar came and laid the foundations of the house of God[d] in Jerusalem. From that day to the present it has been under construction but is not yet finished."

17Now if it pleases the king, let a search be made in the royal archives[e] of Babylon to see if King Cyrus did in fact issue a decree to rebuild this house of God in Jerusalem. Then let the king send us his decision in this matter.

The Decree of Darius

6 King Darius then issued an order, and they searched in the archives[f] stored in the treasury at Babylon. 2A scroll was found in the citadel of Ecbatana in the province of Media, and this was written on it:

Memorandum:

3In the first year of King Cyrus, the king issued a decree concerning the temple of God in Jerusalem:

Let the temple be rebuilt as a place to present sacrifices, and let its foundations be laid.[g] It is to be sixty cubits[b] high and sixty cubits wide, 4with three courses[h] of large stones and one of timbers. The costs are to be paid by the royal treasury.[i] 5Also, the gold[j] and silver articles of the house of God, which Nebuchadnezzar took from the temple in Jerusalem and brought to Babylon, are to be returned to their places in the temple in Jerusalem; they are to be deposited in the house of God.[k]

6Now then, Tattenai,[l] governor of Trans-Euphrates, and Shethar-Bozenai[m] and you other officials of that province, stay away from there. 7Do not interfere with the work on this temple of God. Let the governor of the Jews and the Jewish elders rebuild this house of God on its site.

8Moreover, I hereby decree what you are to do for these elders of the Jews in the construction of this house of God:

Their expenses are to be fully paid out of the royal treasury,[n] from the revenues[o] of Trans-Euphrates, so that the work will not stop. 9Whatever is needed — young bulls, rams, male lambs for burnt offerings[p] to the God of heaven, and wheat, salt, wine and olive oil, as requested by the priests in Jerusalem — must be given them daily without fail, 10so that they may offer sacrifices pleasing to the God of heaven and pray for the well-being of the king and his sons.[q]

5:14 [b] Ezr 1:7; 6:5; Da 5:2 [c] 1Ch 3:18
5:16 [d] Ezr 3:10; 6:15
5:17 [e] Ezr 4:15; 6:1,2
6:1 [f] Ezr 4:15; 5:17
6:3 [g] Ezr 3:10; Hag 2:3
6:4 [h] 1Ki 6:36 [i] ver 8; Ezr 7:20
6:5 [j] 1Ch 29:2 [k] Ezr 1:7; 5:14
6:6 [l] Ezr 5:3 [m] Ezr 5:3
6:8 [n] ver 4 [o] 1Sa 9:20
6:9 [p] Lev 1:3,10
6:10 [q] Ezr 7:23; 1Ti 2:1-2

[a] 14 Or *palace* [b] 3 That is, about 90 feet or about 27 meters

Ezr 6:6-12 ❖ When has God given you special protection and support in a task he called you to accomplish?

5:1-17 Not unlike the Israelites under Persian rule, US residents have legal recourse to protect their First Amendment rights (freedom of speech). Free debate is encouraged, and there is an ability to seek help and reform through democratic means.

Historically and legally, freedom of religion allows one to defend the Christian worldview. On this basis, it would appear that a Christian in the US (and other parts of the Western world) may be able to stand somewhat secure in their rights and freedom to worship (unlike the suffering and persecuted underground church elsewhere in the world). Nevertheless, this sense of security is false in many aspects since our confidence and freedom must stem from something more certain than political constitutional rights.

6:1-5 The needed documentary evidence was found in Ecbatana, the summer residence of Persian kings.

6:6-10 This passage contains Darius's letter of response to Tattenai. He prohibits physical interference (v. 6b). In addition, v. 8 suggests that the king prohibited any financial interference. It was not uncommon for Persian kings to look after the religious interests of their subjects, attempting to secure both public and divine favor from the gods their subjects served.

11 Furthermore, I decree that if anyone defies this edict, a beam is to be pulled from their house and they are to be impaled[r] on it. And for this crime their house is to be made a pile of rubble.[s] 12 May God, who has caused his Name to dwell there,[t] overthrow any king or people who lifts a hand to change this decree or to destroy this temple in Jerusalem.

I Darius[u] have decreed it. Let it be carried out with diligence.

Completion and Dedication of the Temple

13 Then, because of the decree King Darius had sent, Tattenai, governor of Trans-Euphrates, and Shethar-Bozenai and their associates[v] carried it out with diligence. 14 So the elders of the Jews continued to build and prosper under the preaching[w] of Haggai the prophet and Zechariah, a descendant of Iddo. They finished building the temple according to the command of the God of Israel and the decrees of Cyrus,[x] Darius[y] and Artaxerxes,[z] kings of Persia. 15 The temple was completed on the third day of the month Adar, in the sixth year of the reign of King Darius.[a]

16 Then the people of Israel — the priests, the Levites and the rest of the exiles — celebrated the dedication[b] of the house of God with joy. 17 For the dedication of this house of God they offered[c] a hundred bulls, two hundred rams, four hundred male lambs and, as a sin offering[a] for all Israel, twelve male goats, one for each of the tribes of Israel. 18 And they installed the priests in their divisions[d] and the Levites in their groups[e] for the service of God at Jerusalem, according to what is written in the Book of Moses.[f]

The Passover

19 On the fourteenth day of the first month, the exiles celebrated the Passover.[g] 20 The priests and Levites had

6:11 [r] Dt 21:22-23; Est 2:23; 5:14; 9:14 [s] Ezr 7:26; Da 2:5; 3:29
6:12 [t] Ex 20:24; Dt 12:5; 1Ki 9:3; 2Ch 6:2 [u] ver 14
6:13 [v] Ezr 4:9
6:14 [w] Ezr 5:1 [x] Ezr 1:1-4 [y] ver 12 [z] Ezr 7:1; Ne 2:1
6:15 [a] Zec 1:1; 4:9
6:16 [b] 1Ki 8:63; 2Ch 7:5
6:17 [c] 2Sa 6:13; 2Ch 29:21; 30:24; Ezr 8:35
6:18 [d] 1Ch 23:6; 2Ch 35:4; Lk 1:5 [e] 1Ch 24:1 [f] Nu 3:6-9; 8:9-11; 18:1-32
6:19 [g] Ex 12:11; Nu 28:16

[a] 17 Or *purification offering*

6:11–12 Finally, Darius closes his response with the enforcement of a penalty to those who would disobey the decree. Such threats of punishment and curses for disobedient subjects were typical parts of covenantal agreements in the ancient Near East.

Darius not only sanctioned that the work continued, but he also guaranteed the protection of God's people in the process of its completion. Opposition does not last forever because God eventually (on his timetable) intervenes in governments of the world. But divine intervention here is twofold. Not only does God intervene by raising up the prophets Haggai and Zechariah from within the covenantal community (5:1–5), but God also intervenes by raising up individuals, outside the covenantal community and from the government, to support and encourage his people and to achieve his broader purposes. It is fitting, therefore, that 6:1–12 concludes the narrator's discussion on temple-building opposition with such a definitive statement.

✣ **6:1–12** If the restoration of Zion is nonnegotiable because it is tied to the very promises of God that "whoever curses you I will curse" (Ge 12:3), then God's people can have a staunch assurance that opposition toward all of God's kingdom work will end. While it can be difficult to wait for God's wheels of justice to grind, we can be assured that in the end, God will do something radical to oppose those who are opposed to him. "Many are the plans in a person's heart, but it is the LORD's purpose that prevails" (Pr 19:21).

6:13–15 Ezra shows in a succinct summary statement how, why, and when the rebuilding was completed, as well as the results. First, from a practical point of view, the lack of governmental interference enabled the Jews to continue to build. Second, from a spiritual point of view, the "preaching" of the prophets motivated the Jews, enabling them "to build and prosper" (v. 14).

Verses 13–14 communicate how and why the temple ultimately was rebuilt. The human side of the equation (work decreed by Persian kings) operated in tandem with the divine side (work commanded by God). The "command of the God of Israel" (v. 14) likely refers to the prophetic words of Haggai and Zechariah that enabled the finished project.

Verse 15 also gives the answer to the "when" question. The date corresponds to March 12, 515 BC, some years after Haggai and Zechariah started preaching in August to December of 520 BC (Hag 1:1; Zec 1:1, second year of Darius).

6:16–18 As was done in earlier building phases, the returnees celebrated and worshiped. The previous celebrations, however, were a mixed bag (3:3, 12–13). Joy alone characterizes this present celebration (6:16, 22).

This moment recalls, too, the dedication of Solomon's temple when the king, along with all Israel, offered sacrifices before the Lord (1Ki 8:62–63). This building dedication, installation, and celebration was just as valid as previous building dedications.

6:19–22 With all the religious installations in place (including a new temple and the presence of qualified personnel to lead worship), the community resumes and conducts worship in the traditional way with the celebration of Passover. The day of Passover was followed by the weeklong Festival of Unleavened Bread. These combined festivals were intended to bring the worshiper back to God, to

purified themselves and were all ceremonially clean. The Levites slaughtered[h]
the Passover lamb for all the exiles, for
their relatives the priests and for themselves. 21So the Israelites who had returned from the exile ate it, together
with all who had separated themselves[i]
from the unclean practices[j] of their Gentile neighbors in order to seek the LORD,[k]
the God of Israel. 22For seven days they
celebrated with joy the Festival of Unleavened Bread,[l] because the LORD had
filled them with joy by changing the attitude[m] of the king of Assyria so that he
assisted them in the work on the house
of God, the God of Israel.

Ezra Comes to Jerusalem

7 After these things, during the reign
of Artaxerxes[n] king of Persia, Ezra
son of Seraiah, the son of Azariah, the
son of Hilkiah,[o] 2the son of Shallum,
the son of Zadok,[p] the son of Ahitub,[q]
3the son of Amariah, the son of Azariah,
the son of Meraioth, 4the son of Zerahiah, the son of Uzzi, the son of Bukki,
5the son of Abishua, the son of Phinehas,
the son of Eleazar, the son of Aaron the
chief priest— 6this Ezra[r] came up from
Babylon. He was a teacher well versed in
the Law of Moses, which the LORD, the God
of Israel, had given. The king had granted
him everything he asked, for the hand of
the LORD his God was on him.[s] 7Some of
the Israelites, including priests, Levites,
musicians, gatekeepers and temple servants, also came up to Jerusalem in the
seventh year of King Artaxerxes.[t]
8Ezra arrived in Jerusalem in the fifth
month of the seventh year of the king.
9He had begun his journey from Babylon on the first day of the first month,
and he arrived in Jerusalem on the first
day of the fifth month, for the gracious
hand of his God was on him.[u] 10For Ezra
had devoted himself to the study and

6:20 [h]2Ch 30:15,17; 35:11
6:21 [i]Ezr 9:1; Ne 9:2 [j]Dt 18:9; Ezr 9:11; Eze 36:25 [k]1Ch 22:19; Ps 14:2
6:22 [l]Ex 12:17 [m]Ezr 1:1
7:1 [n]Ezr 4:7; 6:14; Ne 2:1 [o]2Ki 22:4
7:2 [p]1Ki 1:8; 1Ch 6:8 [q]Ne 11:11
7:6 [r]Ne 12:36 [s]Ezr 5:5; Isa 41:20
7:7 [t]Ezr 8:1
7:9 [u]ver 6

Ezr 7:10 ❖ What role does the Bible play in our lives? How might we dedicate ourselves to study and teaching, like Ezra?

---

remind the worshiper who was responsible for the joyous occasion. This celebration of Passover in Ezra not only connects the worshipers with their past, but it celebrates another rescue mission—Israel's deliverance from exile—and the motif of the second exodus resurfaces.

Measures are taken to ensure a proper celebration. The Levites slaughter the Passover lamb (v. 20). Likewise, those partaking in the meal have to demonstrate purity. The exclusive rather than inclusive nature of those participating in worship is important because the identity and purity of God's people is at stake.

Thus in vv. 13–22 the narrator summarizes how, why, and when the second temple was completed but zooms in on the ultimate result—the worship of Yahweh and the people's reestablished relationship with their God, who is mighty to protect and save. The real victor over all obstacles and opposition is not Cyrus, not Darius, but Yahweh.

6:13–22 As temples of the living God, our lives should be marked by full service and dedication to God. Celebration leading to worship should naturally flow from our lives/temples as a result of what God has done; it should be our goal to "keep the Festival" as Paul exhorts (1Co 5:8). Peter asserts that the OT Passover lamb, although a reality for the Israelites, merely foreshadowed the ultimate and final Passover Lamb, Jesus. Through his perfect life and sacrificial death, Jesus rescues us from condemnation and raises us from death to life (1Pe 1:19–21).

7:1–6 Ezra's lineage ties him to a great lineup of staunchly loyal and prestigious priests who served in powerful regimes.

Next, the author reveals Ezra's social and religious standing within the priesthood (v. 6b). The designations show that Ezra fulfilled an important role in the postexile phase: a role further unpacked by the statement in v. 10.

7:10 Ezra had a strong resolve. An alternate reading would be "he made firm his heart" or "had set his heart" to a task. The Hebrew verbal form used indicates an internally causative action.

Ezra's entire life was oriented toward the word of God. The fruit of his study was personal piety and application of the truths of God's law. Thus this verse highlights Ezra's critical role and his depth of character. The divine favor Ezra experienced was because of one main reason: "The hand of the LORD his God was on him" (v. 6). Here the author shows how and why Ezra ended up in Jerusalem—God moved him to act for the divine purpose of reviving the law in the covenantal community after years of neglect.

7:1–10 Placing a premium on studying and applying God's Word has the power to bring revival to individuals and churches. Church history testifies to this fact.

What place does the Word hold in our churches and lives? While it is true that not everyone is called to be a scribe of the caliber of Ezra or a reformer of the caliber of Luther, the former's specialized role does reveal the continued need to have experts in the church to help restore God's people.

Institutions like Bible colleges and seminaries have a critical role to play as a result. In this regard professors with a heart for the Word, teaching at a seminary, are critical to the church's mission.

observance of the Law of the LORD, and
to teaching[v] its decrees and laws in Israel.

King Artaxerxes' Letter to Ezra

11 This is a copy of the letter King Artaxerxes had given to Ezra the priest,
a teacher of the Law, a man learned in
matters concerning the commands and
decrees of the LORD for Israel:

12 Artaxerxes, king of kings,[w]

To Ezra the priest, teacher of the Law
of the God of heaven:

Greetings.

13 Now I decree that any of the Israelites in my kingdom, including
priests and Levites, who volunteer
to go to Jerusalem with you, may
go. 14 You are sent by the king and
his seven advisers[x] to inquire about
Judah and Jerusalem with regard to
the Law of your God, which is in your
hand. 15 Moreover, you are to take
with you the silver and gold that
the king and his advisers have freely
given[y] to the God of Israel, whose
dwelling[z] is in Jerusalem, 16 together with all the silver and gold[a] you
may obtain from the province of
Babylon, as well as the freewill offerings of the people and priests for
the temple of their God in Jerusalem.[b] 17 With this money be sure to
buy bulls, rams and male lambs,[c]
together with their grain offerings
and drink offerings,[d] and sacrifice[e]
them on the altar of the temple of
your God in Jerusalem.
18 You and your fellow Israelites
may then do whatever seems best
with the rest of the silver and gold,
in accordance with the will of your
God. 19 Deliver[f] to the God of Jerusalem all the articles entrusted to you
for worship in the temple of your
God. 20 And anything else needed
for the temple of your God that you
are responsible to supply, you may
provide from the royal treasury.[g]
21 Now I, King Artaxerxes, decree
that all the treasurers of Trans-Euphrates are to provide with diligence
whatever Ezra the priest, the teacher of the Law of the God of heaven,
may ask of you — 22 up to a hundred
talents[a] of silver, a hundred cors[b] of
wheat, a hundred baths[c] of wine,
a hundred baths[c] of olive oil, and
salt without limit. 23 Whatever the
God of heaven has prescribed, let
it be done with diligence for the
temple of the God of heaven. Why
should his wrath fall on the realm
of the king and of his sons?[h] 24 You
are also to know that you have no
authority to impose taxes, tribute or
duty[i] on any of the priests, Levites,
musicians, gatekeepers, temple servants or other workers at this house
of God.[j]
25 And you, Ezra, in accordance
with the wisdom of your God, which
you possess, appoint[k] magistrates
and judges to administer justice to
all the people of Trans-Euphrates —
all who know the laws of your God.
And you are to teach[l] any who do
not know them. 26 Whoever does not
obey the law of your God and the law

7:10 [v] ver 25; Dt 33:10; Ne 8:1-8
7:12 [w] Eze 26:7; Da 2:37
7:14 [x] Est 1:14
7:15 [y] 1Ch 29:6 [z] 1Ch 29:6,9; 2Ch 6:2
7:16 [a] Ezr 8:25 [b] Zec 6:10
7:17 [c] 2Ki 3:4 [d] Nu 15:5-12 [e] Dt 12:5-11
7:19 [f] Ezr 5:14; Jer 27:22
7:20 [g] Ezr 6:4
7:23 [h] Ezr 6:10
7:24 [i] Ezr 4:13 [j] Ezr 8:36
7:25 [k] Ex 18:21, 26; Dt 16:18 [l] ver 10; Lev 10:11

[a] *22* That is, about 3 3/4 tons or about 3.4 metric tons [b] *22* That is, probably about 18 tons or about 16 metric tons [c] *22* That is, about 600 gallons or about 2,200 liters

---

7:12–20 In the first set of orders Artaxerxes entrusts Ezra with two main things: amassing a volunteer team of people (vv. 13–14) and the acquisition of financial aid (vv. 15–20).
7:12–14 The statement here is revealing. Artaxerxes, without knowing it, portrays Ezra as a lawgiver and keeper akin to Moses (Ex 31:18) or one of the nation's great kings, such as Josiah (2Ki 22:1—23:32) or Hezekiah (2Ch 31:21). Ezra, like Moses, was a lawgiver, another important tie to preexilic Israel.
7:15–20 The second item the king entrusts Ezra with concerns money. Artaxerxes entrusts Ezra with a large amount of financial support to aid sacrifices for temple worship. In this context Artaxerxes also trusts that any financial surplus not used for temple services would be used by Ezra "in accordance with the will of your God" (v. 18). The will of God is knowable because Ezra possesses God's will in his hand (v. 14). The law of God and God's will are one and the same.
7:21–24 The king requires that government workers in his territories abroad, relative to matters of worship, trust Ezra upon his arrival. Likewise, the treasurers may not collect any revenues (taxes) from the temple clergy (v. 24).
7:25–26 The last part of the letter is orders directed toward Ezra: "And you, Ezra" (v. 25). Artaxerxes thereby entrusts Ezra with governmental affairs, asking him to dispense justice in the land by delegating people like himself to the task, people "who know the laws of your God" (v. 25a). Finally, this section closes with a strong word reminding Ezra of the consequences for those who break either God's or the king's laws. Disobedience to

of the king must surely be punished by death, banishment, confiscation of property, or imprisonment.[a][m]

27Praise be to the LORD, the God of our ancestors, who has put it into the king's heart[n] to bring honor[o] to the house of the LORD in Jerusalem in this way 28and who has extended his good favor[p] to me before the king and his advisers and all the king's powerful officials. Because the hand of the LORD my God was on me,[q] I took courage and gathered leaders from Israel to go up with me.

List of the Family Heads Returning With Ezra

8 These are the family heads and those registered with them who came up with me from Babylon during the reign of King Artaxerxes:[r]

2of the descendants of Phinehas, Gershom;
of the descendants of Ithamar, Daniel;
of the descendants of David, Hattush
3of the descendants of Shekaniah;[s]

of the descendants of Parosh,[t] Zechariah, and with him were registered 150 men;
4of the descendants of Pahath-Moab,[u] Eliehoenai son of Zerahiah, and with him 200 men;
5of the descendants of Zattu,[b]

7:26 [m]Ezr 6:11 7:27 [n]Ezr 1:1; 6:22 [o]1Ch 29:12 7:28 [p]2Ki 25:28 [q]Ezr 5:5; 9:9 8:1 [r]Ezr 7:7 8:3 [s]1Ch 3:22 [t]Ezr 2:3 8:4 [u]Ezr 2:6

[a] *26* The text of 7:12-26 is in Aramaic. [b] *5* Some Septuagint manuscripts (also 1 Esdras 8:32); Hebrew does not have *Zattu.*

the law would not be tolerated, and Ezra, along with those appointed by Ezra, were to hold lawbreakers accountable.

7:27-28 The final section of this chapter brings Ezra's personal point of view back to the reader. It is Ezra's first-person interpretation of how and why he ended up taking the trek to Jerusalem and a preface to the list of people who volunteered to follow him in this new exodus.

7:11-28 Ezra and the Persian king hoped that the nation would be transformed by applying the truths and principles of God's Word. Still today the Bible is a critical source of wisdom, not just at the personal level but in the public sphere as well.

The presence or absence of godly principles directly affects the well-being of a nation. To remain Christian and have an influence means we need to retain the Bible. America and other Western nations threaten to spiral into decline by turning away from the Bible.

A nation that has the Word or is attempting to apply its principles (however those principles have come to that nation such as a pagan king, a missionary, a pastor/teacher) will discover the real benefits of following God's directives: "The LORD reigns forever; he has established his throne for judgment. He rules the world in righteousness and judges the peoples with equity. The LORD is a refuge for the oppressed, a stronghold in times of trouble. Those who know your name trust in you, for you, LORD, have never forsaken those who seek you" (Ps 9:7-10).

8:1-14 This list commences with the needed workers for temple services in Jerusalem: family heads

PEOPLE TO KNOW // EZRA

EZRA 7:27-28: Ezra was a priest during the Babylonian exile. He began his life in Babylon but was allowed to travel to Jerusalem by permission of King Artaxerxes of Persia (Ezr 7:1-6), along with others who were returning to their ancestral land. Artaxerxes showed favor to Ezra, giving him everything he asked for and sending him well-supplied with money and food.

While Zerubbabel and Nehemiah focused on physical rebuilding efforts in Jerusalem, Ezra's rebuilding project was spiritual in nature. He sought to bring the Jews back into conformity to the Law of Moses (Ezr 7:10). He led a group of priests on this mission.

Later, Ezra read the Law of Moses for all the people (Ne 8:1). As he read, some Levites helped interpret the meaning of the words. The people celebrated the fact that they could hear God's Word read and explained to them. Learning God's directions for the Festival of Tabernacles, they celebrated the festival together. The public reading of the Law also led the people to confess their sins and the sins of their ancestors.

APPLICATION Ezra was zealous to share God's Word. One of the many lessons of his life is that we can emulate Ezra's passion for obeying God and living holy lives according to God's Word. Like the Jews in Ezra's day, we too stray from God's ways and need to be called back, by God's grace, to live godly lives.

Shekaniah son of Jahaziel, and
with him 300 men;
6 of the descendants of Adin,[v] Ebed son
of Jonathan, and with him 50 men;
7 of the descendants of Elam, Jeshaiah
son of Athaliah, and with him 70
men;
8 of the descendants of Shephatiah,
Zebadiah son of Michael, and with
him 80 men;
9 of the descendants of Joab, Obadiah
son of Jehiel, and with him 218
men;
10 of the descendants of Bani,[a] Shelomith son of Josiphiah, and with
him 160 men;
11 of the descendants of Bebai, Zechariah son of Bebai, and with him
28 men;
12 of the descendants of Azgad, Johanan son of Hakkatan, and with
him 110 men;
13 of the descendants of Adonikam,[w]
the last ones, whose names were
Eliphelet, Jeuel and Shemaiah,
and with them 60 men;
14 of the descendants of Bigvai, Uthai
and Zakkur, and with them 70
men.

The Return to Jerusalem

15 I assembled them at the canal that
flows toward Ahava,[x] and we camped
there three days. When I checked among
the people and the priests, I found no
Levites[y] there. 16 So I summoned Eliezer,
Ariel, Shemaiah, Elnathan, Jarib, Elnathan, Nathan, Zechariah and Meshullam,
who were leaders, and Joiarib and Elnathan, who were men of learning, 17 and
I ordered them to go to Iddo, the leader
in Kasiphia. I told them what to say to
Iddo and his fellow Levites, the temple
servants[z] in Kasiphia, so that they might
bring attendants to us for the house of
our God. 18 Because the gracious hand
of our God was on us,[a] they brought us
Sherebiah, a capable man, from the descendants of Mahli son of Levi, the son
of Israel, and Sherebiah's sons and brothers, 18 in all; 19 and Hashabiah, together
with Jeshaiah from the descendants of
Merari, and his brothers and nephews,
20 in all. 20 They also brought 220 of the
temple servants[b] — a body that David
and the officials had established to assist
the Levites. All were registered by name.
21 There, by the Ahava Canal,[c] I proclaimed a fast, so that we might humble
ourselves before our God and ask him for
a safe journey[d] for us and our children,
with all our possessions. 22 I was ashamed
to ask the king for soldiers[e] and horsemen to protect us from enemies on the
road, because we had told the king, "The
gracious hand of our God is on everyone[f]
who looks to him, but his great anger is
against all who forsake him.[g]" 23 So we
fasted[h] and petitioned our God about
this, and he answered our prayer.
24 Then I set apart twelve of the leading
priests, namely, Sherebiah,[i] Hashabiah

Ezr 8:21 ❖ What important moments, events, or decisions have led us to come before God asking for a special measure of help and protection? How do we approach God at such times?

8:6 [v] Ezr 2:15; Ne 7:20; 10:16
8:13 [w] Ezr 2:13
8:15 [x] ver 21, 31 [y] Ezr 2:40; 7:7
8:17 [z] Ezr 2:43
8:18 [a] Ezr 5:5
8:20 [b] 1Ch 9:2; Ezr 2:43
8:21 [c] ver 15; 2Ch 20:3 [d] Ps 5:8; 107:7
8:22 [e] Ne 2:9; Ezr 7:6, 9, 28 [f] Ezr 5:5 [g] Dt 31:17; 2Ch 15:2
8:23 [h] 2Ch 20:3; 33:13
8:24 [i] ver 18

[a] *10* Some Septuagint manuscripts (also 1 Esdras 8:36); Hebrew does not have *Bani.*

---

associated with the priestly lines of Phinehas and Ithamar and descendants of David (vv. 2–3).

8:15–20 Ezra chooses to send "leaders" and "men of learning" who "go to Iddo, the leader in Kasiphia" to recruit attendants for the house of God (vv. 16–17). Among the recruits were also 220 temple servants to aid the Levites (v. 20). The mention of David here recalls 3:10. Once again, the author wishes to reestablish that the nation must follow the directives for worship observed by the people of Israel before the exile.

Ezra attributes the success in recruiting Levites to God's good hand on them (8:18). Ezra understood that the practical things that fall into place, such as safety in travel and recruiting the right Levites to do the work, all stem from God's provision.

8:21–36 Before the journey could begin, Ezra put into place two more preparatory elements. The first concerned a fast for their physical safety; the second was a delegation of the finances for safekeeping to the priests and Levites (vv. 28–29).

The outcome of fasting and praying was not just a request for a safe journey to Jerusalem but a testimony of God's character to the king. Accordingly, in Ezra's mind there was more on the line than just a safe journey physically to Jerusalem. Yahweh was clearly different from the gods of the Persian pantheon.

8:24–30 Ezra's concern is for the safekeeping of the finances that poured in from donors back in Babylon. These donations were to be handled by twelve priests. Both the donations and those bearing them were deemed "consecrated to the Lord" (v. 28). All of this (the holiness and purpose of finances) was an indirect charge to be faithful to the task. It reflects the importance Ezra placed on godly stewardship leading to worship of Yahweh.

and ten of their brothers, 25and I weighed
out[j] to them the offering of silver and
gold and the articles that the king, his
advisers, his officials and all Israel present there had donated for the house of
our God. 26I weighed out to them 650
talents[a] of silver, silver articles weighing
100 talents,[b] 100 talents[b] of gold, 2720
bowls of gold valued at 1,000 darics,[c] and
two fine articles of polished bronze, as
precious as gold.

28I said to them, "You as well as these
articles are consecrated to the LORD.[k] The
silver and gold are a freewill offering
to the LORD, the God of your ancestors.
29Guard them carefully until you weigh
them out in the chambers of the house of
the LORD in Jerusalem before the leading
priests and the Levites and the family
heads of Israel." 30Then the priests and
Levites received the silver and gold and
sacred articles that had been weighed
out to be taken to the house of our God
in Jerusalem.

31On the twelfth day of the first month
we set out from the Ahava Canal[l] to go
to Jerusalem. The hand of our God was
on us, and he protected us from enemies and bandits along the way. 32So we
arrived in Jerusalem, where we rested
three days.[m]

33On the fourth day, in the house of our
God, we weighed out the silver and gold
and the sacred articles into the hands
of Meremoth[n] son of Uriah, the priest.
Eleazar son of Phinehas was with him,
and so were the Levites Jozabad son of
Jeshua and Noadiah son of Binnui.[o] 34Ev-
erything was accounted for by number
and weight, and the entire weight was
recorded at that time.

35Then the exiles who had returned
from captivity sacrificed burnt offerings
to the God of Israel: twelve bulls for all
Israel, ninety-six rams, seventy-seven
male lambs and, as a sin offering,[d] twelve
male goats.[p] All this was a burnt offering
to the LORD. 36They also delivered the
king's orders[q] to the royal satraps and to
the governors of Trans-Euphrates, who
then gave assistance to the people and
to the house of God.[r]

8:25 [j] ver 33; Ezr 7:15,16
8:28 [k] Lev 21:6; 22:2-3
8:31 [l] ver 15
8:32 [m] Ge 40:13; Ne 2:11
8:33 [n] Ne 3:4,21 [o] Ne 3:24
8:35 [p] 2Ch 29:21; Ezr 6:17
8:36 [q] Ezr 7:21-24 [r] Est 9:3
9:1 [s] Ezr 6:21; Ne 9:2 [t] Ge 19:38 [u] Ex 13:5
9:2 [v] Ex 34:16 [w] Ex 22:31 [x] Ezr 10:2

Ezr 9:3-4 ❖ When have we come before God in sorrow and repentance?

Ezra's Prayer About Intermarriage

9 After these things had been done, the
leaders came to me and said, "The
people of Israel, including the priests and
the Levites, have not kept themselves
separate[s] from the neighboring peoples
with their detestable practices, like those
of the Canaanites, Hittites, Perizzites, Jebusites, Ammonites,[t] Moabites, Egyptians
and Amorites.[u] 2They have taken some of
their daughters[v] as wives for themselves
and their sons, and have mingled the
holy race[w] with the peoples around them.
And the leaders and officials have led the
way in this unfaithfulness."[x]

3When I heard this, I tore my tunic

[a] *26* That is, about 24 tons or about 22 metric tons [b] *26* That is, about 3 3/4 tons or about 3.4 metric tons [c] *27* That is, about 19 pounds or about 8.4 kilograms [d] *35* Or *purification offering*

8:31-32 These verses show how God answered the people's pleas for help through fasting and praying. On the journey, the returnees were indeed "rescued" (alternate translation) from opposition.

8:33-34 Likewise, all was carried out as planned with the finances.

8:35-36 These verses mark a return to third-person narrative, and the chapter closes with a note of celebration. Now with the lawgiver and his entourage back in Jerusalem, yet another celebration ensues, and Ezra has made it abundantly clear that divine assistance was given to the people of God every step of the way.

✤ 8:1-36 This Ezra passage invites us to contemplate our own perspectives about the journey we are on in life. Navigation in this world to do kingdom work is not easy or without hassle, but God has graciously given us a system to navigate it with success. The text invites us to recall that we are on a journey with a clear destination—to arrive home safely at the house of our God, to be in relationship with him. It also reminds us that the journey is not hassle free. Needed help may not necessarily be available, and at times it may be unsafe. Moreover, the journey requires a God-dependent mindset: That is, we must be aware and assured of divine assistance when problems arise.

9:1-2 The leaders, priests, and Levites have defiled themselves as did the people of Israel of old. The mission to restore the sanctity of Zion faces an existential threat.

9:3-5 In this entire act of mourning, subduing his bodily desires and dying to self, Ezra revealed a visceral reaction to sin. All he had to fall back on was his deep awareness of God's merciful and gracious character.

and cloak, pulled hair from my head and
beard and sat down appalled. 4Then everyone who trembled[y] at the words of
the God of Israel gathered around me
because of this unfaithfulness of the exiles. And I sat there appalled until the
evening sacrifice.

5Then, at the evening sacrifice,[z] I rose
from my self-abasement, with my tunic
and cloak torn, and fell on my knees with
my hands spread out to the LORD my God
6and prayed:

"I am too ashamed and disgraced,
my God, to lift up my face to you,
because our sins are higher than our
heads and our guilt has reached to
the heavens.[a] 7From the days of our
ancestors[b] until now, our guilt has
been great. Because of our sins, we
and our kings and our priests have
been subjected to the sword[c] and
captivity,[d] to pillage and humiliation[e] at the hand of foreign kings,
as it is today.

8"But now, for a brief moment,
the LORD our God has been gracious[f]
in leaving us a remnant[g] and giving
us a firm place[a][h] in his sanctuary,
and so our God gives light to our
eyes[i] and a little relief in our bondage. 9Though we are slaves,[j] our God
has not forsaken us in our bondage.
He has shown us kindness[k] in the
sight of the kings of Persia: He has
granted us new life to rebuild the
house of our God and repair its ruins,[l] and he has given us a wall of
protection in Judah and Jerusalem.

10"But now, our God, what can we
say after this? For we have forsaken
the commands[m] 11you gave through
your servants the prophets when
you said: 'The land you are entering to possess is a land polluted[n]
by the corruption of its peoples. By
their detestable practices[o] they have
filled it with their impurity from
one end to the other. 12Therefore, do
not give your daughters in marriage
to their sons or take their daughters
for your sons. Do not seek a treaty of
friendship with them[p] at any time,
that you may be strong and eat the
good things of the land and leave it
to your children as an everlasting
inheritance.'

13"What has happened to us is
a result of our evil deeds and our
great guilt, and yet, our God, you

9:4 [y] Ezr 10:3
9:5 [z] Ex 29:41
9:6 [a] 2Ch 28:9; Job 42:6; Ps 38:4; Rev 18:5
9:7 [b] 2Ch 29:6 [c] Eze 21:1-32 [d] Dt 28:64 [e] Dt 28:37
9:8 [f] Ps 25:16; Isa 33:2 [g] Ge 45:7 [h] Ecc 12:11; Isa 22:23 [i] Ps 13:3
9:9 [j] Ex 1:14; Ne 9:36 [k] Ezr 7:28 [l] Ps 69:35; Isa 43:1; Jer 32:44
9:10 [m] Dt 11:8; Isa 1:19-20
9:11 [n] Lev 18:25-28 [o] Dt 9:4
9:12 [p] Ex 34:15; Dt 7:3; 23:6

[a] 8 *Or a foothold*

9:6–7 The grief and guilt associated with lifestyle choices not aligned with God's Word weighed Ezra down physically and spiritually. Just as the Israelites before the exile were guilty, so is postexilic Israel. Even after suffering the exile, God's people were still prone to wander away from God's law.

9:8–9 As Ezra's prayer continues, the awareness of God's grace takes center stage. The Hebrew of v. 8 says that the two purposes of God's grace manifested itself in "leaving an escaped remnant" and "giving us a peg" (alternate translation). The term for "peg" is rendered as "secure hold" or "firm place" in English translations. It is a term associated with the instrument that holds up the tabernacle (Ex 27:19; 35:18). The metaphor affirms that God has given them something firm in the renewed sanctuary: a secure place where, indeed, one can tangibly see a manifestation of God's grace. Ezra's interpretive lens for dealing with sin is God's relentless, gracious, and merciful character.

9:10–12 The rhetorical question in v. 10 captures the intensity of the moment. The answer, of course, is "nothing." Their neglectful behavior relative to the application of God's Word is yet another connection to preexilic Israel. Their character flaw is great (lack of loyalty in the relationship), and they deserve his wrath, not his mercy.

9:13–15 As Ezra's prayer draws to a close, he asks in v. 14, "Would you not be angry enough with us to destroy us?" He concedes that the people's ongoing guilt deserves God's full wrath, particularly in light of his grace. The existence of God's people hangs in the balance, not unlike the threat that existed with the golden calf prior to Moses' intercession (Ex 32–34).

The theology that surfaces from this part of Ezra's prayer reveals how the sin-guilt cycle prevalent with God's people exposes a bigger problem: Guilty people cannot legally stand before a holy God. Ezra knows that the future existence of the exiles is based solely on the fact that God is and always will be the God of Israel.

✣ **9:1–15** God's people defy him by engaging in a particular unfaithfulness resulting in sin's consequences (the equivalent of the exile). Because of God's merciful restoration (the equivalent of the return from exile), they experience his grace and joy. For a time, and out of deep, genuine gratitude, they do everything according to the Word of God as it relates to regulating their worship of him (chs. 1–6). With the passing of time, gratitude for his mercy and favor fade, and people can easily slip back into their old patterns of unfaithfulness. When it comes to the attention of our spiritual leaders that we have fallen back, the hope is that they are grieved and cry out to God on our behalf, revealing our own need for repentance and restoration.

have punished us less than our
sins deserved[q] and have given us
a remnant like this. 14Shall we then
break your commands again and
intermarry[r] with the peoples who
commit such detestable practices?
Would you not be angry enough
with us to destroy us,[s] leaving us no
remnant[t] or survivor? 15LORD, the
God of Israel, you are righteous![u]
We are left this day as a remnant.
Here we are before you in our guilt,
though because of it not one of us
can stand[v] in your presence.[w]"

The People's Confession of Sin

10 While Ezra was praying and confessing,[x] weeping and throwing
himself down before the house of God, a
large crowd of Israelites — men, women
and children — gathered around him.
They too wept bitterly. 2Then Shekaniah
son of Jehiel, one of the descendants of
Elam, said to Ezra, "We have been unfaithful[y] to our God by marrying foreign
women from the peoples around us. But
in spite of this, there is still hope for Israel.[z] 3Now let us make a covenant[a] before
our God to send away[b] all these women
and their children, in accordance with
the counsel of my lord and of those who
fear the commands of our God. Let it be
done according to the Law. 4Rise up; this
matter is in your hands. We will support
you, so take courage and do it."
5So Ezra rose up and put the leading
priests and Levites and all Israel under
oath[c] to do what had been suggested.
And they took the oath. 6Then Ezra withdrew from before the house of God and
went to the room of Jehohanan son of
Eliashib. While he was there, he ate no
food and drank no water,[d] because he
continued to mourn over the unfaithfulness of the exiles.
7A proclamation was then issued
throughout Judah and Jerusalem for
all the exiles to assemble in Jerusalem.
8Anyone who failed to appear within
three days would forfeit all his property, in accordance with the decision of the
officials and elders, and would himself be
expelled from the assembly of the exiles.

9Within the three days, all the men
of Judah and Benjamin[e] had gathered
in Jerusalem. And on the twentieth day
of the ninth month, all the people were
sitting in the square before the house of
God, greatly distressed by the occasion
and because of the rain. 10Then Ezra the
priest stood up and said to them, "You
have been unfaithful; you have married
foreign women, adding to Israel's guilt.
11Now honor[a] the LORD, the God of your

[a] 11 Or *Now make confession to*

9:13 [q] Job 11:6; Ps 103:10
9:14 [r] Ne 13:27 [s] Dt 9:8 [t] Dt 9:14
9:15 [u] Ge 18:25; Ps 51:4; Jer 12:1; Da 9:7 [v] Ne 9:33; Ps 130:3; Mal 3:2 [w] 1Ki 8:47
10:1 [x] 2Ch 20:9; Da 9:20
10:2 [y] Ezr 9:2; Ne 13:27 [z] Dt 30:8-10
10:3 [a] 2Ch 34:31 [b] Ex 34:16; Dt 7:2-3; Ezr 9:4
10:5 [c] Ne 5:12; 13:25
10:6 [d] Ex 34:28; Dt 9:18
10:9 [e] Ezr 1:5

Ezr 10:11 ❖ Did God support this instruction from the Jewish leaders? Why or why not? How does 1Co 7:12–14 apply to this situation?

10:1 The shift to third-person narrative gives attention to those in the community and their critical viewpoint on the event. Now we learn that the emotional effects of sin in the camp were not confined just to Ezra.

10:2–4 Shekaniah confesses two things: their unfaithfulness and yet their hope, two seemingly contradictory points. Hope is obviously needed because the threat of destruction or another exile looms large yet again (9:14–15).

The "covenant" in 10:3 was to be agreed upon by Ezra and other leaders. How could sending away the women and children be done according to the law? In the statement, "Let it be done according to the Law" (v. 4), the "it" refers to the terms of the covenant and the legal requirement of the oath associated with covenant-making.

10:5–6 Ezra acts in two specific ways. First, he secures the group's consensus by calling for an oath or pledge of allegiance to be acted upon. Second, Ezra returns praying and fasting in hopes to avert God's wrath. Accordingly, he continues to mourn. Likewise, the assembled group recognizes the urgent need to avert God's fierce anger.

10:7–8 A communication was then put out for "all the exiles" (v. 7). The stern nature of the communication was expressed by two parts: First, if they fail to appear they will forfeit property; second, they would become exiles among the exiles. In other words, they would become like the ones they had married: non-Yahwist foreigners.

10:9–10 Ezra cuts to the chase and does what a faithful priest in the covenant community ought to have done. As their spiritual leader he holds them accountable for their actions and calls them to reform their ways. An alternate translation of v. 10 points to the emphasis of the original. The Hebrew reads, "You, you have been unfaithful" or "You yourselves have been unfaithful." This statement by Ezra reinforces the accountability of God's people for their actions expressed in Shekaniah's confession (v. 2). Not only was preexilic Israel guilty, but now postexilic Israel is guilty.

10:11 Ezra commands them accordingly to "honor the LORD, the God of your ancestors, and do his will" (v. 11a, b). Doing God's will entails both praise and reform. This leads to the third command, "separate yourselves" (v. 11c). He reminds them of the

ancestors, and do his will. Separate yourselves from the peoples around you and
from your foreign wives."[f]
12 The whole assembly responded with
a loud voice:[g] "You are right! We must do
as you say. 13 But there are many people
here and it is the rainy season; so we cannot stand outside. Besides, this matter
cannot be taken care of in a day or two,
because we have sinned greatly in this
thing. 14 Let our officials act for the whole
assembly. Then let everyone in our towns
who has married a foreign woman come
at a set time, along with the elders and
judges[h] of each town, until the fierce anger[i] of our God in this matter is turned
away from us." 15 Only Jonathan son of
Asahel and Jahzeiah son of Tikvah, supported by Meshullam and Shabbethai[j]
the Levite, opposed this.
16 So the exiles did as was proposed.
Ezra the priest selected men who were
family heads, one from each family
division, and all of them designated
by name. On the first day of the tenth
month they sat down to investigate the
cases, 17 and by the first day of the first
month they finished dealing with all the
men who had married foreign women.

Those Guilty of Intermarriage

18 Among the descendants of the
priests, the following had married foreign women:[k]

From the descendants of Joshua[l]
son of Jozadak, and his brothers:
Maaseiah, Eliezer, Jarib and Gedaliah. 19 (They all gave their hands[m]
in pledge to put away their wives,
and for their guilt they each presented a ram from the flock as a
guilt offering.)[n]
20 From the descendants of Immer:[o]
Hanani and Zebadiah.
21 From the descendants of Harim:[p]
Maaseiah, Elijah, Shemaiah, Jehiel
and Uzziah.
22 From the descendants of Pashhur:[q]
Elioenai, Maaseiah, Ishmael, Nethanel, Jozabad and Elasah.

23 Among the Levites:[r]

Jozabad, Shimei, Kelaiah (that is,
Kelita), Pethahiah, Judah and Eli-
ezer.
24 From the musicians:
Eliashib.[s]
From the gatekeepers:
Shallum, Telem and Uri.

25 And among the other Israelites:

From the descendants of Parosh:[t]
Ramiah, Izziah, Malkijah, Mijamin, Eleazar, Malkijah and Benaiah.
26 From the descendants of Elam:[u]
Mattaniah, Zechariah, Jehiel, Abdi,
Jeremoth and Elijah.
27 From the descendants of Zattu:
Elioenai, Eliashib, Mattaniah, Jeremoth, Zabad and Aziza.
28 From the descendants of Bebai:
Jehohanan, Hananiah, Zabbai and
Athlai.

10:11 [f] ver 3; Dt 24:1; Ne 9:2; Mal 2:10-16
10:12 [g] Jos 6:5
10:14 [h] Dt 16:18 [i] Nu 25:4; 2Ch 29:10; 30:8
10:15 [j] Ne 11:16
10:18 [k] Jdg 3:6 [l] Ezr 2:2
10:19 [m] 2Ki 10:15 [n] Lev 5:15; 6:6
10:20 [o] 1Ch 24:14
10:21 [p] 1Ch 24:8
10:22 [q] 1Ch 9:12
10:23 [r] Ne 8:7; 9:4
10:24 [s] Ne 3:1; 12:10; 13:7,28
10:25 [t] Ezr 2:3
10:26 [u] ver 2

---

previously agreed-upon action of sending away what appears to be the defilement in the land: their foreign wives and children (v. 3).

Ironically, the returnees are re-defiling the land by affiliating with women who worship other gods, a defilement that God warned about previously (9:11–12; cf. Dt 13). Thus, the forced departure is not unlike the forced removal that God imposed on the inhabitants of Canaan through Joshua's conquests. The expulsion of the women and children represents a reconquering of the promised land. It is a cleansing of the land that would enable the returned exiles to remain in the land and for the promises of God to be furthered in the life of the community.

10:12–17 The people's swift response shows awareness, not denial, of their transgression and guilt, and a healthy fear of God's just anger with respect to it (vv. 13–14). They actually believe their reforms will avert God's wrath and more consequences for sin, which is not an unhealthy motivation for change. With the exception of four people who stood against the idea for unknown reasons (v. 15), Ezra gets the surprising but hoped-for cooperation evidenced in the unified and loud voice of the assembly (v. 12). This loud, unified voice should not be glossed over. Rarely does one see such quick admission of wrongdoing in the biblical text. The people of God admit and confess to their guilt, then promise to reform.

10:18–22 The offending priests are noted. At the top of the list is Joshua, the son of Jozadak, the high priest at the time. Those following Joshua in the priestly lineup derive from the family of the high priest. Their poor example is now made right. Thus, the offending priests confess their own sins, and, by offering a guilt offering, they are ministering as appropriate in the community for unfaithfulness (Lev 5:14–19).

10:25–43 The list of offending laypeople comes next. From the general population of Israelites, noteworthy is the mention of the descendants of Elam, who include Mattaniah, Zechariah, Jehiel, Abdi, Jeremoth, and Elijah (v. 26).

29 From the descendants of Bani:
Meshullam, Malluk, Adaiah, Jashub, Sheal and Jeremoth.
30 From the descendants of Pahath-Moab:
Adna, Kelal, Benaiah, Maaseiah, Mattaniah, Bezalel, Binnui and Manasseh.
31 From the descendants of Harim:
Eliezer, Ishijah, Malkijah, Shemaiah, Shimeon,
32 Benjamin, Malluk and Shemariah.
33 From the descendants of Hashum:
Mattenai, Mattattah, Zabad, Eliphelet, Jeremai, Manasseh and Shimei.
34 From the descendants of Bani:
Maadai, Amram, Uel,
35 Benaiah, Bedeiah, Keluhi,
36 Vaniah, Meremoth, Eliashib,
37 Mattaniah, Mattenai and Jaasu.
38 From the descendants of Binnui:[a]
Shimei,
39 Shelemiah, Nathan, Adaiah,
40 Maknadebai, Shashai, Sharai,
41 Azarel, Shelemiah, Shemariah,
42 Shallum, Amariah and Joseph.
43 From the descendants of Nebo:
Jeiel, Mattithiah, Zabad, Zebina, Jaddai, Joel and Benaiah.

44 All these had married foreign women, and some of them had children by these wives.[b]

[a] *37,38* See Septuagint (also 1 Esdras 9:34); Hebrew *Jaasu* [38]*and Bani and Binnui,* [b] *44* Or *and they sent them away with their children*

10:44 This verse represents a final summary statement by the author with respect to the events that unfolded beginning in ch. 9.

10:1–44 There is still hope for God's guilty people. The wrongdoing in our lives clearly makes us guilty, but how do we handle both the ongoing wrong and the feelings of deep guilt associated with it? Perhaps we handle it by harsh judgment and condemnation of ourselves and of others. Some of us prefer our own rigid works of righteousness that we feel will appease our guilty consciences. If you find yourself working to make things right after confession and repentance, it might suggest a turn toward self-reliance and away from God-reliance. Ultimately, we must look to the cross where our true hope for forgiveness and reform is found.

Nehemiah

Author: Probably Ezra, appropriating Nehemiah's memoirs

Audience: The people of Judah who had returned from exile in Babylonia

Date: Sometime after 430 BC

Theme: God uses Nehemiah to lead his people to rebuild the walls of Jerusalem and to rebuild their distinctive identity as God's people.

PERSPECTIVE

The book of Nehemiah details the third return (continued from the book of Ezra) under the leadership of the governor Nehemiah. Chapters 1–13 narrate the restoration of the walls and sanctity of Zion. The book concludes in 13:4–31 with an epilogue, noting Nehemiah's final attempts at reform.

See the Introduction to Ezra for more perspective on the books of Ezra and Nehemiah.

TAKING THE NEXT STEPS

In this book Nehemiah personally narrated how he administered the affairs of the Jews in the promised land during the time that Ezra was there. He began by expressing his intense concern for their plight, especially in that the walls of Jerusalem had not been rebuilt. He realized this was a matter of prayer, but to Nehemiah, prayer must always be accompanied with work. Consequently, he asked King Artaxerxes to allow him to give leadership to the Jews, not only in rebuilding Jerusalem but also in serving as their governor for two terms.

From the example of Nehemiah, we can learn much about how God wants us to conduct our lives. (1) His deep concern and passion for what God's people were going through and his intense desire to help them is a model for all of us to follow. (2) Nehemiah's style of active leadership was as proper as Ezra's more passive style. God uses a

Reading Nehemiah

The first twelve chapters of Nehemiah describe in great detail what this leader of the Jews did during his first term as governor of the Jews: rebuilding the walls of Jerusalem, dealing with social and economic problems, and assisting Ezra in the reestablishment of the worship of the true God. The last chapter summarizes various episodes of his second term as governor.

1400 BC 1300 1200 1100 1000 900 800 700 600 500 400

- Fall of Jerusalem (586 BC)
- Persia's conquest of Babylon (539 BC)
- First return of exiles to Jerusalem (538 BC)
- Ministries of Haggai and Zechariah (c. 520–480 BC)
- Temple restoration completed (516 BC)
- Second return to Jerusalem under Ezra (458 BC)
- Third return to Jerusalem under Nehemiah (444 BC)
- Jerusalem's wall rebuilt (444 BC)
- Book of Nehemiah written (c. 430 BC)

variety of personalities to lead the church today, and no one method is necessarily better than any other. The Bible says the key issue is servant leadership motivated out of love for the Lord and love for one another. (3) It is never enough simply to pray to God: We must accompany our prayers by putting forth every effort to do what God wants us to do. (4) The elements of worship evident in chs. 8 and 9, namely, listening to the Word of God, praising him, confessing our sins and renewing our relationship with the Lord, are important elements of Christian worship today.

Key Verses

Ezra the priest brought the Law before the assembly, which was made up of men and women and all who were able to understand. He read it aloud from daybreak till noon ... in the presence of the men, women and others who could understand. And all the people listened attentively to the Book of the Law.

—Nehemiah 8:2-3

WHAT TO LOOK FOR IN NEHEMIAH

- Nehemiah's concern for the Jews' situation (chs. 1-2)
- Rebuilding the walls of Jerusalem (chs. 3-4; 6)
- Handling the exploitation of the poor (ch. 5)
- Organizing the true worship of the Lord (ch. 9)
- Episodes of Nehemiah's dynamic style of leadership (ch. 13)

Nehemiah's Prayer

1 The words of Nehemiah son of Hakaliah:

In the month of Kislev[a] in the twentieth year, while I was in the citadel of
Susa, 2 Hanani,[b] one of my brothers, came
from Judah with some other men, and I
questioned them about the Jewish remnant[c] that had survived the exile, and
also about Jerusalem.
3 They said to me, "Those who survived
the exile and are back in the province are
in great trouble and disgrace. The wall of
Jerusalem is broken down, and its gates
have been burned with fire.[d]"
4 When I heard these things, I sat down
and wept.[e] For some days I mourned
and fasted[f] and prayed before the God
of heaven. 5 Then I said:

"LORD, the God of heaven, the
great and awesome God,[g] who
keeps his covenant of love[h] with
those who love him and keep his
commandments, 6 let your ear be attentive and your eyes open to hear[i]
the prayer[j] your servant is praying
before you day and night for your
servants, the people of Israel. I confess the sins we Israelites, including
myself and my father's family, have
committed against you. 7 We have
acted very wickedly[k] toward you.
We have not obeyed the commands,
decrees and laws you gave your servant Moses.
8 "Remember[l] the instruction you
gave your servant Moses, saying, 'If
you are unfaithful, I will scatter[m]
you among the nations, 9 but if you
return to me and obey my commands, then even if your exiled people are at the farthest horizon, I will
gather[n] them from there and bring
them to the place I have chosen as
a dwelling for my Name.'[o]
10 "They are your servants and
your people, whom you redeemed
by your great strength and your
mighty hand.[p] 11 Lord, let your ear
be attentive[q] to the prayer of this
your servant and to the prayer of
your servants who delight in revering your name. Give your servant
success today by granting him favor
in the presence of this man."

I was cupbearer[r] to the king.

Artaxerxes Sends Nehemiah to Jerusalem

2 In the month of Nisan in the twentieth year of King Artaxerxes,[s] when

1:1 [a] Ne 10:1; Zec 7:1
1:2 [b] Ne 7:2 [c] Jer 52:28
1:3 [d] 2Ki 25:10; Ne 2:3,13,17
1:4 [e] Ps 137:1 [f] Ezr 9:4
1:5 [g] Dt 7:21; Ne 4:14 [h] Ex 20:6; Da 9:4
1:6 [i] 1Ki 8:29 [j] Da 9:17
1:7 [k] Dt 28:14-15; Ps 106:6
1:8 [l] 2Ki 20:3 [m] Lev 26:33
1:9 [n] Dt 30:4 [o] 1Ki 8:48; Jer 29:14
1:10 [p] Ex 32:11; Dt 9:29
1:11 [q] ver 6 [r] Ge 40:1
2:1 [s] Ezr 7:1

Ne 1:4 ❖ When have we lamented over a situation involving other believers? What prayers can we offer to God in such situations?

1:1-4 The plot of the book is wrapped in the report provided by Hanani. The devastating news of Jerusalem's condition fits squarely within the Sinaitic covenant equation of judgment-destruction (Dt 28:52). Verse 4 breaks down Nehemiah's reaction to the report. The context suggests the idea of many days passing, since the next chronological marker is found in 2:1: "in the month of Nisan," some four months later.
1:5-6 By attaching the familiar "God of heaven" to Yahweh (NIV "LORD"; v. 5), Nehemiah's invocation anchors the prayer to the revelation of God to Moses at Sinai (Ex 6:2-3) and thereby sets the theological context for the rest of the prayer. The "covenant of love" (Ne 1:5) gives Nehemiah the boldness to petition Yahweh. Nehemiah's prayer reflects a conviction that without a confession of sin, no promises of God can be fulfilled for the exiles.
1:7 This verse continues the confession of sin: "We have not obeyed the commands, decrees and laws," which is the typical three-part designation for Deuteronomic law (Dt 4:44-45). Here Nehemiah appeals to truths that Yahweh originated and gave to his servant Moses.
1:8-10 This passage marks the shift in the prayer from confession to petition by appealing directly to the Deuteronomic promise of return from exile after the people repent (Dt 30:1-5) to "the place the LORD your God will choose from among all your tribes to put his Name there for his dwelling" (Dt 12:5). This rich and textured theological phrase emphasizes the significance of Jerusalem in the Deuteronomic theology of the divine presence.

APPLICATION ✣ **1:1-11** Nehemiah's opening prayer underscores the idea that confession of sin is significant in our own lives, in those of our family, and in the lives of others. We as Christians have a responsibility in our own particular cultural contexts to identify and weep over the consequences that come in the aftermath of the sins of our ancestors. A posture of humility will prevent us, in turn, from smugness, arrogance, and defensiveness when confronted with our own sinful past.

2:1-2 As a result of a brief exchange, Nehemiah will pack up his bags and find himself in Yehud (the Neo-Babylonian name for the province in which Jerusalem was located), placed in charge of the restoration of Zion. As soon as the king notices Nehemiah's incongruous mood, Nehemiah

wine was brought for him, I took the
wine and gave it to the king. I had not
been sad in his presence before, 2so the
king asked me, "Why does your face look
so sad when you are not ill? This can be
nothing but sadness of heart."
I was very much afraid, 3but I said to
the king, "May the king live forever![t]
Why should my face not look sad when
the city[u] where my ancestors are buried
lies in ruins, and its gates have been destroyed by fire?[v]"
4The king said to me, "What is it you
want?"

Then I prayed to the God of heaven,
5and I answered the king, "If it pleases
the king and if your servant has found
favor in his sight, let him send me to the
city in Judah where my ancestors are
buried so that I can rebuild it."
6Then the king[w], with the queen sitting beside him, asked me, "How long
will your journey take, and when will
you get back?" It pleased the king to send
me; so I set a time.
7I also said to him, "If it pleases the
king, may I have letters to the governors of Trans-Euphrates,[x] so that they

2:3 [t]1Ki 1:31; Da 2:4; 5:10; 6:6,21 [u]Ps 137:6 [v]Ne 1:3
2:6 [w]Ne 5:14; 13:6
2:7 [x]Ezr 8:36

---

becomes convinced he has reached the point of no return. Will he find favor with the king as he has been praying for several weeks now?

2:3 Nehemiah's rhetorical response, "Why should my face not look sad," deftly omits the political designation of the "city" as Jerusalem and places the emphasis on Nehemiah's ancestral roots.

2:4–5 Nehemiah himself might have been taken aback at how effective his own planning panned out since the text interjects a new line in the narrative sequence. We expect the framing formula of "and I answered the king" (v. 5), but instead we hear that Nehemiah prayed (v. 4). In this heightened tension, he draws closer to the God of heaven.

In presenting his formal request for a commission, Nehemiah's goal is plainly stated: "so that I can rebuild it" (v. 5). Nehemiah enters the arena and hopes to become the lead character in this process of rebuilding Zion.

2:7–8 The next and final section of the formal exchange at the court represents a unit that we might call the "let's put this in writing part." This action reveals just how well-prepared Nehemiah was for the meeting, as there is no indicator that the events described at the court happened over an extended period of time.

✜ **2:1–8** There are numerous examples in church history of when the people of God prayed to

PEOPLE TO KNOW // ARTAXERXES

NEHEMIAH 2:1–9: After Cyrus of Persia allowed the Jewish exiles to return home from Babylon in 539 BC, the people began rebuilding Jerusalem and its temple. The returnees faced opposition from some of their neighbors in these rebuilding efforts, however. Some of their opponents sent a letter to Artaxerxes, the new king of Persia, urging him to order the Jews to stop rebuilding on the grounds that they would stop paying taxes if Jerusalem were rebuilt (Ezr 4:11–16).

In response to this letter, Artaxerxes ordered work in Jerusalem to cease. The rebuilding was later resumed by decree of King Darius (Ezr 6:3–12).

Artaxerxes's influence on the returned exiled community was not all bad. He granted the priest Ezra everything he asked, allowing Ezra and many with him to return to Jerusalem. Artaxerxes even sent gold and silver along with Ezra as an offering to the priests and temple in Jerusalem. He provided generously for Ezra, not only with silver and gold but also with food (Ezr 7:21–22).

Artaxerxes was also responsible for sending Nehemiah, his royal cupbearer, to Jerusalem (Ne 2:1–8). He sent Nehemiah with a letter, allowing him to carry out his rebuilding efforts and sent army officers and cavalry with him. Nehemiah went on to lead the rebuilding of the wall in Jerusalem and was appointed governor of Judah by Artaxerxes. Later, Artaxerxes welcomed Nehemiah back in Persia and subsequently allowed him to return to Jerusalem a second time (Ne 13:6–7).

APPLICATION ✜ Like Cyrus, Artaxerxes shows the amazing way God can use unexpected people to accomplish his will. Artaxerxes was the king of the superpower Persia, and yet God inclined his heart to the cause of some exiles struggling to rebuild Jerusalem.

God has long been in the habit of making surprising choices. We cannot predict whom God will use to accomplish his plans. This is a reminder of God's sovereignty: God is not only Lord of his followers—he is Lord over all the peoples, all the earth and all the universe.

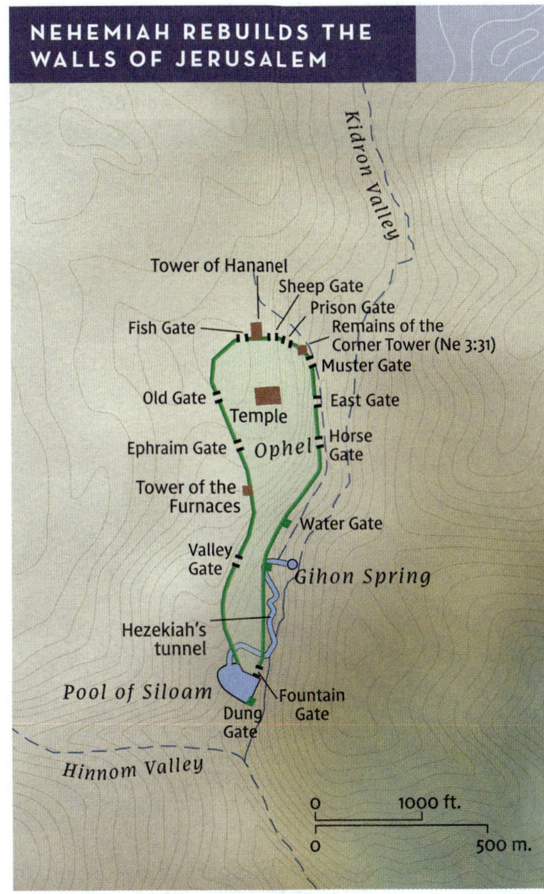

will provide me safe-conduct until I arrive in Judah? 8And may I have a letter to
Asaph, keeper of the royal park, so he will
give me timber to make beams for the
gates of the citadel[y] by the temple and
for the city wall and for the residence I
will occupy?" And because the gracious
hand of my God was on me,[z] the king
granted my requests. 9So I went to the

2:8 [y] Ne 7:2 [z] ver 18; Ezr 5:5; 7:6
2:9 [a] Ezr 8:22
2:10 [b] ver 19; Ne 4:1,7 [c] Ne 4:3; 13:4-7 [d] Est 10:3
2:11 [e] Ge 40:13
2:13 [f] 2Ch 26:9 [g] Ne 3:13 [h] Ne 1:3

governors of Trans-Euphrates and gave
them the king's letters. The king had also
sent army officers and cavalry[a] with me.
10When Sanballat[b] the Horonite and
Tobiah[c] the Ammonite official heard
about this, they were very much disturbed that someone had come to promote the welfare of the Israelites.[d]

Nehemiah Inspects Jerusalem's Walls

11I went to Jerusalem, and after staying
there three days[e] 12I set out during the
night with a few others. I had not told anyone what my God had put in my heart to
do for Jerusalem. There were no mounts
with me except the one I was riding on.
13By night I went out through the Valley Gate[f] toward the Jackal[a] Well and
the Dung Gate,[g] examining the walls[h]
of Jerusalem, which had been broken
down, and its gates, which had been destroyed by fire. 14Then I moved on toward the Fountain Gate[i] and the King's
Pool,[j] but there was not enough room
for my mount to get through; 15so I went
up the valley by night, examining the
wall. Finally, I turned back and reentered
through the Valley Gate. 16The officials
did not know where I had gone or what
I was doing, because as yet I had said
nothing to the Jews or the priests or nobles or officials or any others who would
be doing the work.
17Then I said to them, "You see the
trouble we are in: Jerusalem lies in ruins, and its gates have been burned with
fire.[k] Come, let us rebuild the wall[l] of
Jerusalem, and we will no longer be in
disgrace.[m]" 18I also told them about the

[a] 13 Or *Serpent* or *Fig*

2:14 [i] Ne 3:15 [j] 2Ki 18:17 2:17 [k] Ne 1:3 [l] Ps 102:16; Isa 30:13; 58:12 [m] Eze 5:14

---

see the will of the Lord accomplished. The work of God in building the spiritual building of the church continues to this day. This is the ministry to which believers have been called as intercessors. We should not think that this kind of direct answer to prayer is restricted to the covenant people in the history of redemption. As God's people, we too are writing the history of redemption with the people the Lord has placed on our path; and we too are called to see the rebuilding of the church take place—both on a local and on a global scale.

2:9–10 The mention of an imperial escort stresses Nehemiah's role as a new political force to be reckoned with in the eyes of the regional establishment. Verse 10 launches a major theme of Nehemiah's memoirs: opposition.

2:11–15 Literarily, the description of the night survey introduces us to the actual building project described in both chs. 3 and 4 of Nehemiah.

2:16–18 The "officials" (mentioned twice in v. 16) refer to the local Jewish officials that would answer to Nehemiah as the newly positioned governor of Yehud. Nehemiah's succinct address intentionally repeats the familiar vocabulary of both ch. 1 and his address to the king in ch. 2. The removal of "disgrace" (v. 17) recalls the cause-and-effect relationship between the restoration of Zion and the absence of disgrace. Verse 18 describes another foundational theme in this book: answered prayer.

DECREES AND ACCOMPLISHMENTS

	538 BC	458 BC	444 BC
Reference	Ezra 1-6	Ezra 7-10	Nehemiah 1-13
Persian King	Cyrus	Artaxerxes	Artaxerxes
Jewish Leaders	Sheshbazzar Zerubbabel Joshua	Ezra	Nehemiah
Decree	As many as wished could return. Temple could be rebuilt, partially financed by royal treasury. Vessels returned.	As many as wished could return. Finances provided by royal treasury. Allowed to have own civil magistrates.	Allowed to rebuild the wall.
Accomplishments	Temple begun; sacrifices made and Feast of Tabernacles celebrated. Samaritans made trouble, and work ceased until 520. Temple completed in 516.	Problems with intermarriage.	Wall rebuilt in 52 days, despite opposition from Sanballat, Tobiah, and Geshem. Walls dedicated and Law read.

Information from John Walton, *Chronological and Background Charts of the Old Testament*, rev. and exp. ed. (Grand Rapids: Zondervan, 1994), 35.

gracious hand of my God on me[n] and
what the king had said to me.
They replied, "Let us start rebuilding."
So they began this good work.
19 But when Sanballat the Horonite, Tobiah the Ammonite official and Geshem[o]
the Arab heard about it, they mocked
and ridiculed us.[p] "What is this you are
doing?" they asked. "Are you rebelling
against the king?"
20 I answered them by saying, "The God
of heaven will give us success. We his
servants will start rebuilding, but as for
you, you have no share[q] in Jerusalem or
any claim or historic right to it."

2:18 [n] 2Sa 2:7
2:19 [o] Ne 6:1, 2, 6 [p] Ps 44:13-16
2:20 [q] Ezr 4:3
3:1 [r] Ezr 10:24 [s] Isa 58:12 [t] ver 32; Ne 12:39

Ne 2:19 ❖ How should we respond when we are mocked for living out our faith, both in big and small ways?

Builders of the Wall

3 Eliashib[r] the high priest and his fellow priests went to work and rebuilt[s]
the Sheep Gate.[t] They dedicated it and
set its doors in place, building as far as

2:19–20 His counterparts' strong reaction in v. 10 is developed in vv. 19–20 and underscores the epic political struggle Nehemiah faces with the local governors of the Trans-Euphrates. However, Nehemiah is equally forceful in his reply. These three antagonists have no claim to Zion in the past, present, or future.

✜ **2:9–20** Just as the early church faced the reality of opposition, we will face opposition in the building of Zion, the people of God in the new covenant. Nehemiah's approach may sound intolerant in an age of pluralism, tolerance, and inclusivity. However, in the eyes of the majority church elsewhere in the world, especially in areas facing persecutions, this no-compromise approach makes sense since it is a matter of the physical survival of the community of believers.

3:1–32 Chapter 3 builds on the string of Nehemiah's successes following his extended time of prayer and mourning: both the king and the people wholeheartedly embrace Nehemiah's project of restoration, and now the diverse community of Yehud gets involved.

Formulaic emphasis. Nehemiah skillfully structures his name list with formulaic language. Beyond identifying the participants, the chapter recounts the restoration of the enclosure wall with a particular emphasis on rebuilding and restoring some gates in the first half of the account (vv. 1–15), and the wall in relationship to individuals' houses and other landmarks in the second half (vv. 16–32).

Building and repairing. When Nehemiah writes about gates being rebuilt, we should probably understand this to mean new doors were installed. This new construction would provide an explanation as to why the high priest felt the need to dedicate the Sheep Gate (in the sense of making it holy, v. 1).

For building activities pertaining to walls, the

the Tower of the Hundred, which they
dedicated, and as far as the Tower of Hananel.[u] 2The men of Jericho[v] built the adjoining section, and Zakkur son of Imri
built next to them.

3The Fish Gate[w] was rebuilt by the sons
of Hassenaah. They laid its beams and
put its doors and bolts and bars in place.
4Meremoth son of Uriah, the son of Hakkoz, repaired the next section. Next to
him Meshullam son of Berekiah, the son
of Meshezabel, made repairs, and next
to him Zadok son of Baana also made
repairs. 5The next section was repaired
by the men of Tekoa,[x] but their nobles
would not put their shoulders to the
work under their supervisors.[a]

6The Jeshanah[b] Gate[y] was repaired by
Joiada son of Paseah and Meshullam son
of Besodeiah. They laid its beams and
put its doors with their bolts and bars
in place. 7Next to them, repairs were
made by men from Gibeon[z] and Mizpah — Melatiah of Gibeon and Jadon of
Meronoth — places under the authority
of the governor of Trans-Euphrates. 8Uz-
ziel son of Harhaiah, one of the goldsmiths, repaired the next section; and
Hananiah, one of the perfume-makers,
made repairs next to that. They restored
Jerusalem as far as the Broad Wall.[a] 9Re-
phaiah son of Hur, ruler of a half-district
of Jerusalem, repaired the next section.

3:1 [u] Ne 12:39; Jer 31:38; Zec 14:10
3:2 [v] Ne 7:36
3:3 [w] 2Ch 33:14; Ne 12:39
3:5 [x] 2Sa 14:2
3:6 [y] Ne 12:39
3:7 [z] Jos 9:3; Ne 2:7
3:8 [a] Ne 12:38
3:11 [b] Ne 12:38
3:13 [c] 2Ch 26:9 [d] Jos 15:34 [e] Ne 2:13
3:14 [f] Jer 6:1
3:15 [g] Isa 8:6; Jn 9:7

10Adjoining this, Jedaiah son of Haru-
maph made repairs opposite his house,
and Hattush son of Hashabneiah made
repairs next to him. 11Malkijah son of
Harim and Hasshub son of Pahath-Moab
repaired another section and the Tower
of the Ovens.[b] 12Shallum son of Hallo-
hesh, ruler of a half-district of Jerusalem,
repaired the next section with the help
of his daughters.

13The Valley Gate[c] was repaired by
Hanun and the residents of Zanoah.[d]
They rebuilt it and put its doors with
their bolts and bars in place. They also
repaired a thousand cubits[c] of the wall
as far as the Dung Gate.[e]

14The Dung Gate was repaired by Malkijah son of Rekab, ruler of the district of
Beth Hakkerem.[f] He rebuilt it and put its
doors with their bolts and bars in place.

15The Fountain Gate was repaired by
Shallun son of Kol-Hozeh, ruler of the
district of Mizpah. He rebuilt it, roofing it over and putting its doors and
bolts and bars in place. He also repaired
the wall of the Pool of Siloam,[d][g] by the
King's Garden, as far as the steps going
down from the City of David. 16Beyond
him, Nehemiah son of Azbuk, ruler of a

[a] 5 Or *their Lord* or *the governor* [b] 6 Or *Old*
[c] 13 That is, about 1,500 feet or about 450 meters
[d] 15 Hebrew *Shelah*, a variant of *Shiloah*, that is, Siloam

---

verb "to repair" dominates the account. The needed stonework would be recycled from the existing building materials found in the debris caused by the damage of the destruction of the walls in 586 BC.

Identification and individuals. Next to the actual parts of the walls that were affected, the identification of individuals dominates the chapter, and significant elements for interpretation are embedded into the names, occupations, and tasks.

"Priests" (vv. 1, 22) feature prominently at the beginning of the list and also toward the end. Other members of the religious class include "Levites" (v. 17) and "temple servants" (v. 26). These three groups play a central role later in the account (see chs. 8–12).

Specialized craftsmen, "goldsmiths" (vv. 8, 31; or "refiners"), perfumers (v. 8) and "merchants" (v. 32), are involved as well. Further pointing to socio-organizational diversity, the daughters of Shallum, "ruler of a half-district of Jerusalem" (v. 12) also participated in repairing a section of the wall.

Gates and walls. Details on the gates' construction (vv. 1–15) are covered by the recurring phrase "[they] put its doors with their bolts and bars in place." The phrase emphasizes that the sanctity of the site has been restored and also confirms the gates as the focal point of the Babylonian and subsequent destructions (e.g., 1:3).

Supplementary details occur for every gate except for the Sheep Gate and the Dung Gate. These details offer us a window into the extent of the damage and where most of the work needed to take place. We may assume other gates mentioned in the second part of the report required no work (e.g., the "Water Gate," 3:26; see also 8:1) since they are not mentioned as repair projects.

✣ **3:1–32** What is clearly intentional in this account is an emphasis on the remarkable socioeconomic diversity represented in the building project. People of all walks of life participated. The qualification for taking part does not relate to one's particular skill set but is based on the desire to rebuild Zion, which for us today means the edification and sanctification of the body of Christ. This image painted by Ne 3 prepares us for the unity of the body of Christ reflected in the list of Ro 12:1–8; this list allows a diversity of role and functions so that the whole body/temple (1Co 3:16; Eph 2:22) is built together.

half-district of Beth Zur,[h] made repairs
up to a point opposite the tombs[a][i] of David, as far as the artificial pool and the
House of the Heroes.
17Next to him, the repairs were made
by the Levites under Rehum son of Bani.
Beside him, Hashabiah, ruler of half the
district of Keilah,[j] carried out repairs for
his district. 18Next to him, the repairs
were made by their fellow Levites under
Binnui[b] son of Henadad, ruler of the other half-district of Keilah. 19Next to him,
Ezer son of Jeshua, ruler of Mizpah, repaired another section, from a point facing the ascent to the armory as far as the
angle of the wall. 20Next to him, Baruch
son of Zabbai zealously repaired another
section, from the angle to the entrance
of the house of Eliashib the high priest.
21Next to him, Meremoth[k] son of Uriah, the son of Hakkoz, repaired another
section, from the entrance of Eliashib's
house to the end of it.
22The repairs next to him were made
by the priests from the surrounding
region. 23Beyond them, Benjamin and
Hasshub made repairs in front of their
house; and next to them, Azariah son
of Maaseiah, the son of Ananiah, made
repairs beside his house. 24Next to him,
Binnui[l] son of Henadad repaired another section, from Azariah's house to the
angle and the corner, 25and Palal son of
Uzai worked opposite the angle and the
tower projecting from the upper palace
near the court of the guard.[m] Next to
him, Pedaiah son of Parosh[n] 26and the
temple servants[o] living on the hill of
Ophel[p] made repairs up to a point opposite the Water Gate[q] toward the east
and the projecting tower. 27Next to them,
the men of Tekoa[r] repaired another section, from the great projecting tower[s] to
the wall of Ophel.

28Above the Horse Gate,[t] the priests
made repairs, each in front of his own
house. 29Next to them, Zadok son of Immer made repairs opposite his house.
Next to him, Shemaiah son of Shekaniah, the guard at the East Gate, made
repairs. 30Next to him, Hananiah son of
Shelemiah, and Hanun, the sixth son of
Zalaph, repaired another section. Next
to them, Meshullam son of Berekiah
made repairs opposite his living quarters. 31Next to him, Malkijah, one of the
goldsmiths, made repairs as far as the
house of the temple servants and the
merchants, opposite the Inspection Gate,
and as far as the room above the corner;
32and between the room above the corner and the Sheep Gate[u] the goldsmiths
and merchants made repairs.

3:16 [h] Jos 15:58 [i] Ac 2:29
3:17 [j] Jos 15:44
3:21 [k] Ezr 8:33
3:24 [l] Ezr 8:33
3:25 [m] Jer 32:2; 37:21; 39:14 [n] Ezr 2:3
3:26 [o] Ne 7:46; 11:21 [p] 2Ch 33:14 [q] Ne 8:1,3,16; 12:37
3:27 [r] ver 5 [s] Ps 48:12
3:28 [t] 2Ki 11:16; 2Ch 23:15; Jer 31:40

Ne 3:28 ❖ What does this verse tell us about doing the work of God in our own communities and neighborhoods?

Opposition to the Rebuilding

4 [c] When Sanballat[v] heard that we were
rebuilding the wall, he became angry and was greatly incensed. He ridiculed the Jews, 2and in the presence of
his associates[w] and the army of Samaria,
he said, "What are those feeble Jews doing? Will they restore their wall? Will they
offer sacrifices? Will they finish in a day?
Can they bring the stones back to life
from those heaps of rubble[x]—burned
as they are?"
3Tobiah[y] the Ammonite, who was at
his side, said, "What they are building—
even a fox climbing up on it would break
down their wall of stones!"[z]

4Hear us, our God, for we are despised.[a]
Turn their insults back on their own
heads. Give them over as plunder in a
land of captivity. 5Do not cover up their
guilt[b] or blot out their sins from your
sight,[c] for they have thrown insults in
the face of[d] the builders.

6So we rebuilt the wall till all of it
reached half its height, for the people
worked with all their heart.

3:32 [u] ver 1; Jn 5:2
4:1 [v] Ne 2:10
4:2 [w] Ezr 4:9-10 [x] Ps 79:1; Jer 26:18
4:3 [y] Ne 2:10 [z] Job 13:12; 15:3
4:4 [a] Ps 44:13; 79:12; 123:3-4; Jer 33:24
4:5 [b] Isa 2:9; La 1:22 [c] 2Ki 14:27; Ps 51:1; 69:27-28; 109:14; Jer 18:23

[a] *16* Hebrew; Septuagint, some Vulgate manuscripts and Syriac *tomb*
[b] *18* Two Hebrew manuscripts and Syriac (see also Septuagint and verse 24); most Hebrew manuscripts *Bavvai*
[c] In Hebrew texts 4:1-6 is numbered 3:33-38, and 4:7-23 is numbered 4:1-17.
[d] *5* Or *have aroused your anger before*

4:1-3 Sanballat gives a counterpart speech to motivate his troops as Nehemiah did to the leaders of Yehud in 2:17–18, with equal success. "Tobiah the Ammonite" (v. 3) is reintroduced without his title of "servant," but the echo-chamber effect of his rhetorical question supports the idea of his role as Sanballat's junior partner.

4:4-6 Nehemiah himself led this prayer, rather than the religious authorities. The prayer fits the genre of imprecation, common in the psalms, where the

7But when Sanballat, Tobiah,[d] the
Arabs, the Ammonites and the people
of Ashdod heard that the repairs to Jerusalem's walls had gone ahead and that
the gaps were being closed, they were
very angry. 8They all plotted together[e]
to come and fight against Jerusalem and
stir up trouble against it. 9But we prayed
to our God and posted a guard day and
night to meet this threat.
10Meanwhile, the people in Judah said,
"The strength of the laborers[f] is giving
out, and there is so much rubble that we
cannot rebuild the wall."
11Also our enemies said, "Before they
know it or see us, we will be right there
among them and will kill them and put
an end to the work."
12Then the Jews who lived near them
came and told us ten times over, "Wherever you turn, they will attack us."
13Therefore I stationed some of the
people behind the lowest points of the
wall at the exposed places, posting them
by families, with their swords, spears
and bows. 14After I looked things over, I
stood up and said to the nobles, the officials and the rest of the people, "Don't
be afraid[g] of them. Remember[h] the Lord,
who is great and awesome,[i] and fight[j] for
your families, your sons and your daughters, your wives and your homes."
15When our enemies heard that we
were aware of their plot and that God
had frustrated it,[k] we all returned to the
wall, each to our own work.
16From that day on, half of my men
did the work, while the other half were
equipped with spears, shields, bows and
armor. The officers posted themselves
behind all the people of Judah 17who
were building the wall. Those who carried materials did their work with one
hand and held a weapon[l] in the other, 18and each of the builders wore his
sword at his side as he worked. But the
man who sounded the trumpet[m] stayed
with me.
19Then I said to the nobles, the officials
and the rest of the people, "The work is
extensive and spread out, and we are
widely separated from each other along
the wall. 20Wherever you hear the sound
of the trumpet,[n] join us there. Our God
will fight[o] for us!"
21So we continued the work with half
the men holding spears, from the first
light of dawn till the stars came out. 22At
that time I also said to the people, "Have
every man and his helper stay inside Jerusalem at night, so they can serve us
as guards by night and as workers by

4:7 [d] Ne 2:10
4:8 [e] Ps 2:2; 83:1-18
4:10 [f] 1Ch 23:4
4:14 [g] Ge 28:15; Nu 14:9; Dt 1:29 [h] Ne 1:8 [i] Ne 1:5 [j] 2Sa 10:12
4:15 [k] 2Sa 17:14; Job 5:12
4:17 [l] Ps 149:6
4:18 [m] Nu 10:2
4:20 [n] Eze 33:3 [o] Ex 14:14; Dt 1:30; 20:4; Jos 10:14

Ne 4:13 ❖ How can we defend ourselves against threats to our faith?

---

individual prays down curses upon his enemies' heads. Verse 6 prepares us for the impending struggle of the rest of the chapter.

4:7–9 As in vv. 4–5, the escalating threat is met by the prayers of the community, which points to the determination of the community to face the threat with keen spiritual awareness as well as personal preparedness. The people know that countering the physical threat will require spiritual means.

4:10–15 Three reported speeches expose the depth of the threat at the halfway mark and set the stage for the events narrated in the rest of the chapter.

4:10 The first speech reflects the sentiment of the community at large: the extent of the devastation seriously hampers the debris-clearing process.

4:11 The second speech shifts the focus to an impending threat from the "enemies."

4:12 The third speech continues the movement toward an escalation of the conflict, now outside the bounds of Jerusalem proper. Jews in outlying communities are feeling the imposition from Sanballat's tribal alliance. This in turn places intense pressure on Nehemiah at the outset of his governorship to provide protection for the Jewish communities living outside Jerusalem.

4:13–14 The rest of the section chronicles the success of Nehemiah's approach and speaks to his deftness as a motivator in the community. By calling the workers to remember and fight, Nehemiah accomplished the dual purpose of not only averting a serious physical threat to the work but also motivating the community to return to their work in spite of the logistical difficulties.

4:15 This verse represents a significant marker in Nehemiah's narrative and provides the theological summary of why the community went from a high state of military readiness to the resumption of the work. To the end of the chapter, and in the rest of the account, the community will not face a similar sense of physical danger.

4:16–23 The builders have regained the initiative. Preparedness, solidarity, and unity of purpose dominate the account. Nehemiah makes a significant shift to the strategy of rebuilding.

4:19–20 Verse 19 introduces us to Nehemiah's next major speech in his memoirs. Nehemiah again looks beyond the adverse circumstances, as he did during his time of prayer and fasting, and looks up to "our God" who "will fight for us" (v. 20), but not without addressing the question of preparedness in the case of an attack.

4:21–22 These verses provide another summary of the situation.

8I sent him this reply: "Nothing like what you are saying is happening; you are just making it up out of your head."

9They were all trying to frighten us, thinking, "Their hands will get too weak for the work, and it will not be completed."

But I prayed, "Now strengthen my hands."

10One day I went to the house of Shemaiah son of Delaiah, the son of Mehetabel, who was shut in at his home. He said, "Let us meet in the house of God, inside the temple[p], and let us close the temple doors, because men are coming to kill you—by night they are coming to kill you."

11But I said, "Should a man like me run away? Or should someone like me go into the temple to save his life? I will not go!" 12I realized that God had not sent him, but that he had prophesied against me[q] because Tobiah and Sanballat[r] had hired him. 13He had been hired to intimidate me so that I would commit a sin by doing this, and then they would give me a bad name to discredit me.[s]

14Remember[t] Tobiah and Sanballat,[u] my God, because of what they have done; remember also the prophet[v] Noadiah and how she and the rest of the prophets[w] have been trying to intimidate me. 15So the wall was completed on the twenty-fifth of Elul, in fifty-two days.

Opposition to the Completed Wall

16When all our enemies heard about this, all the surrounding nations were afraid and lost their self-confidence, because they realized that this work had been done with the help of our God.

17Also, in those days the nobles of Judah were sending many letters to Tobiah, and replies from Tobiah kept coming to them. 18For many in Judah were under oath to him, since he was son-in-law to Shekaniah son of Arah, and his son Jehohanan had married the daughter of Meshullam son of Berekiah. 19Moreover, they kept reporting to me his good deeds and then telling him what I said. And Tobiah sent letters to intimidate me.

7 After the wall had been rebuilt and I had set the doors in place, the gatekeepers,[x] the musicians[y] and the Levites[z] were appointed. 2I put in charge of Jerusalem my brother Hanani,[a] along with Hananiah[b] the commander of the citadel,[c] because he was a man of integrity and feared[d] God more than most people

6:10 [p] Nu 18:7
6:12 [q] Eze 13:22-23 [r] Ne 2:10
6:13 [s] Jer 20:10
6:14 [t] Ne 1:8 [u] Ne 2:10 [v] Ex 15:20; Eze 13:17-23; Ac 21:9; Rev 2:20 [w] Ne 13:29; Jer 23:9-40; Zec 13:2-3
7:1 [x] 1Ch 9:27; 26:12-19; Ne 6:1, 15 [y] Ps 68:25 [z] Ne 8:9
7:2 [a] Ne 1:2 [b] Ne 10:23 [c] Ne 2:8 [d] 1Ki 18:3

6:10–15 The identity of Shemaiah remains a mystery beyond this incident. From the context of v. 12 ("he had prophesied"), we can safely assume he belonged to the guild of prophets, along with a female prophet named Noadiah.

The specificity of the designation "temple" and the call to "close the temple doors" (v. 10) raises red flags in Nehemiah's mind. Nehemiah would know that no one is allowed in this sacred space, let alone to be confined inside the temple with its doors closed. His greatest concern is not his own personal safety but the sanctity of Yahweh's sacred space. By entering the temple's sacred space, Nehemiah would have been discredited in the eyes of the faithful community of believers. This would have seriously compromised his larger plan to restore the sanctity of Zion.

6:17–18 The text does not elaborate on the content of the letters; unlike the correspondence between Sanballat and Nehemiah, their mail remains unopened to us. However, v. 18 explicitly states why open channels of communication existed between Tobiah and the nobles: "Many in Judah were under oath to him" because of marriage alliances that spanned two generations (v. 18). This list of family names speaks to the extent of the alliance and circles back to the reasons why Ezra and Nehemiah both speak so strongly against intermarriage within the context of the sanctity of Zion.

6:19 This verse adds an additional layer of correspondence. Clearly these nobles were not on the side of Zion. Tobiah in turn tried also to "intimidate" (see v. 14) Nehemiah in his work. This verse therefore holds interpretive significance for the whole of Nehemiah's opposition and qualifies the sense of unity that existed at the outset of his mission in chs. 1–3. His situation remained precarious throughout since some remained very much in the camp of the local authorities.

6:1–19 Dealing with bullies: Nehemiah's experience of betrayal by those he thought he could trust is not an unfamiliar one in ministry. It would be naïve to think that everyone has our best interests at heart as we focus on the building up and edification of God's people in our respective callings. We should not be surprised how entangled the ministry of the gospel can be with folks with ulterior motives such as greed and power. Opposition to the building up of Zion comes in all sorts of ways, and Nehemiah offers some solid advice on how to conduct ourselves, especially among those friends-turned-foes, whether through bullying, intimidation, or the uncovering of hidden ungodly alliances.

7:1–3 Nehemiah will only entrust the guarding of the "citadel" to his own trusted blood brother. Hananiah's credentials are then listed. Nehemiah knows to focus first on the character of a person in relationship to God. Verse 3 details three specific instructions given to both Hanani and Hananiah ("I said to them").

do. [3]I said to them, "The gates of Jerusalem are not to be opened until the sun
is hot. While the gatekeepers are still on
duty, have them shut the doors and bar
them. Also appoint residents of Jerusalem as guards, some at their posts and
some near their own houses."

The List of the Exiles Who Returned

7:6–73pp // Ezr 2:1–70

[4]Now the city was large and spacious,
but there were few people in it,[e] and the
houses had not yet been rebuilt. [5]So my
God put it into my heart to assemble
the nobles, the officials and the common people for registration by families.
I found the genealogical record of those
who had been the first to return. This is
what I found written there:

[6]These are the people of the province who came up from the captivity of the exiles[f] whom Nebuchadnezzar king of Babylon had taken
captive (they returned to Jerusalem
and Judah, each to his own town, [7]in
company with Zerubbabel,[g] Joshua,
Nehemiah, Azariah, Raamiah, Naha-
mani, Mordecai, Bilshan, Mispereth,
Bigvai, Nehum and Baanah):

The list of the men of Israel:

[8]the descendants of Parosh 2,172
[9]of Shephatiah 372
[10]of Arah 652
[11]of Pahath-Moab (through the line of Jeshua and Joab) 2,818
[12]of Elam 1,254
[13]of Zattu 845
[14]of Zakkai 760
[15]of Binnui 648
[16]of Bebai 628
[17]of Azgad 2,322
[18]of Adonikam 667
[19]of Bigvai 2,067
[20]of Adin[h] 655
[21]of Ater (through Hezekiah) 98
[22]of Hashum 328
[23]of Bezai 324
[24]of Hariph 112
[25]of Gibeon 95

[26]the men of Bethlehem and Netophah[i] 188
[27]of Anathoth[j] 128
[28]of Beth Azmaveth 42
[29]of Kiriath Jearim, Kephirah[k] and Beeroth[l] 743
[30]of Ramah and Geba 621
[31]of Mikmash 122
[32]of Bethel and Ai[m] 123
[33]of the other Nebo 52
[34]of the other Elam 1,254
[35]of Harim 320
[36]of Jericho[n] 345
[37]of Lod, Hadid and Ono[o] 721
[38]of Senaah 3,930

[39]The priests:

the descendants of Jedaiah (through the family of Jeshua) 973
[40]of Immer 1,052
[41]of Pashhur 1,247
[42]of Harim 1,017

[43]The Levites:

the descendants of Jeshua (through Kadmiel through the line of Hodaviah) 74

7:4 [e]Ne 11:1
7:6 [f]2Ch 36:20; Ezr 2:1-70; Ne 1:2
7:7 [g]1Ch 3:19; Ezr 2:2
7:20 [h]Ezr 8:6
7:26 [i]2Sa 23:28; 1Ch 2:54
7:27 [j]Jos 21:18
7:29 [k]Jos 18:26 [l]Jos 18:25
7:32 [m]Ge 12:8
7:36 [n]Ne 3:2
7:37 [o]1Ch 8:12

Ne 7:2 ❖ Hananiah is described as a person of integrity who "feared God more than most people do." Who do we know who most closely fits this description? How might we imitate Hananiah?

7:4–5 Nehemiah is now setting his sights on the next task: rebuilding the city itself and setting up a relocation program so that people of the province of Yehud actually move back permanently. Nehemiah plainly and clearly explains why he is summoning the people: He needs legal evidence that the people he is gathering actually belong to Israel, a noted designation that symbolizes the beginning of the restoration promised by the prophets.

7:6–73a Nehemiah lists the returnees who will repopulate Zion after the wall and gates are rebuilt.

✣ **7:1–73a** Nehemiah's divine prompting to find lists of names is equal to the divine promptings others receive to go preach the gospel to a particular land/place/city/people. Divine guidance is not only for tasks pertaining to spiritual activities alone. In the comprehensive call to restore the sanctity of Zion and to prepare the city of God for the return of the King, we should take seriously the so-called menial tasks of data entry, compiling directories, or coordinating schedules. Legitimate membership in the community of faith is especially important since we too face strong opponents in the proclamation of the gospel. We need to know who is who—or perhaps, who is whose.

44 The musicians:[p]

the descendants of Asaph 148

45 The gatekeepers:[q]

the descendants of
Shallum, Ater, Talmon,
Akkub, Hatita and Shobai 138

46 The temple servants:[r]

the descendants of
Ziha, Hasupha, Tabbaoth,
47 Keros, Sia, Padon,
48 Lebana, Hagaba, Shalmai,
49 Hanan, Giddel, Gahar,
50 Reaiah, Rezin, Nekoda,
51 Gazzam, Uzza, Paseah,
52 Besai, Meunim, Nephusim,
53 Bakbuk, Hakupha, Harhur,
54 Bazluth, Mehida, Harsha,
55 Barkos, Sisera, Temah,
56 Neziah and Hatipha

57 The descendants of the servants of Solomon:

the descendants of
Sotai, Sophereth, Perida,
58 Jaala, Darkon, Giddel,
59 Shephatiah, Hattil,
Pokereth-Hazzebaim and
Amon

60 The temple servants and the descendants of the servants of Solomon[s] 392

61 The following came up from the towns of Tel Melah, Tel Harsha, Kerub, Addon and Immer, but they could not show that their families were descended from Israel:

62 the descendants of
Delaiah, Tobiah and
Nekoda 642

63 And from among the priests:

the descendants of
Hobaiah, Hakkoz and Barzillai
(a man who had married
a daughter of Barzillai the
Gileadite and was called by
that name).

7:44 [p] Ne 11:23
7:45 [q] 1Ch 9:17
7:46 [r] Ne 3:26
7:60 [s] 1Ch 9:2
7:65 [t] Ex 28:30; Ne 8:9
7:71 [u] 1Ch 29:7
7:72 [v] Ex 25:2
7:73 [w] Ne 1:10; Ps 34:22; 103:21; 113:1; 135:1 [x] Ezr 3:1; Ne 11:1 [y] Ezr 3:1
8:1 [z] Ne 3:26 [a] Dt 28:61; 2Ch 34:15; Ezr 7:6
8:2 [b] Lev 23:23-25; Nu 29:1-6 [c] Dt 31:11

64 These searched for their family records, but they could not find
them and so were excluded from the
priesthood as unclean. 65 The governor, therefore, ordered them not to
eat any of the most sacred food until
there should be a priest ministering
with the Urim and Thummim.[t]

66 The whole company numbered
42,360, 67 besides their 7,337 male and
female slaves; and they also had 245
male and female singers. 68 There
were 736 horses, 245 mules,[a] 69 435
camels and 6,720 donkeys.

70 Some of the heads of the families contributed to the work. The
governor gave to the treasury 1,000
darics[b] of gold, 50 bowls and 530
garments for priests. 71 Some of the
heads of the families[u] gave to the
treasury for the work 20,000 darics[c]
of gold and 2,200 minas[d] of silver.
72 The total given by the rest of the
people was 20,000 darics of gold,
2,000 minas[e] of silver and 67 garments for priests.[v]
73 The priests, the Levites, the
gatekeepers, the musicians and the
temple servants,[w] along with certain
of the people and the rest of the Israelites, settled in their own towns.[x]

Ezra Reads the Law

When the seventh month came and
the Israelites had settled in their towns,[y]
8 1 all the people came together as one
in the square before the Water Gate.[z]
They told Ezra the teacher of the Law to
bring out the Book of the Law of Moses,[a] which the LORD had commanded
for Israel.
2 So on the first day of the seventh
month[b] Ezra the priest brought the Law[c]

[a] *68* Some Hebrew manuscripts (see also Ezra 2:66); most Hebrew manuscripts do not have this verse. [b] *70* That is, about 19 pounds or about 8.4 kilograms [c] *71* That is, about 375 pounds or about 170 kilograms; also in verse 72 [d] *71* That is, about 1 1/3 tons or about 1.2 metric tons [e] *72* That is, about 1 1/4 tons or about 1.1 metric tons

7:73b—8:8 Along with the first month and the Passover in the spring (Lev 23:6), the seventh month represents the high point in the Jewish calendar year (Lev 23:23, 26, 33) with the Festival of Trumpets (today's Rosh Hashanah) on the first day, the Day of Atonement (today's Yom Kippur) on the tenth, and the Festival of Tabernacles on the fifteenth. As the narrative unfolds, however, it is the third festival that receives special attention. **8:1–2** Ezra is curator of the Law when asked to bring out the Book of the Law, but as he is about to read from it, he is designated "priest," as he "brought the Law before the assembly."

before the assembly, which was made up
of men and women and all who were able
to understand. 3He read it aloud from
daybreak till noon as he faced the square
before the Water Gate[d] in the presence of
the men, women and others who could
understand. And all the people listened
attentively to the Book of the Law.
4Ezra the teacher of the Law stood on a
high wooden platform[e] built for the occasion. Beside him on his right stood Mattithiah, Shema, Anaiah, Uriah, Hilkiah and
Maaseiah; and on his left were Pedaiah,
Mishael, Malkijah, Hashum, Hashbadda-
nah, Zechariah and Meshullam.
5Ezra opened the book. All the people
could see him because he was standing[f]
above them; and as he opened it, the
people all stood up. 6Ezra praised the
LORD, the great God; and all the people lifted their hands[g] and responded,
"Amen! Amen!" Then they bowed down
and worshiped the LORD with their faces
to the ground.
7The Levites[h] — Jeshua, Bani, Sherebiah, Jamin, Akkub, Shabbethai, Hodiah,
Maaseiah, Kelita, Azariah, Jozabad, Hanan and Pelaiah — instructed[i] the people
in the Law while the people were standing there. 8They read from the Book of
the Law of God, making it clear[a] and
giving the meaning so that the people
understood what was being read.
9Then Nehemiah the governor, Ezra
the priest and teacher of the Law, and the
Levites[j] who were instructing the people
said to them all, "This day is holy to the
LORD your God. Do not mourn or weep."[k]
For all the people had been weeping as
they listened to the words of the Law.

8:3 [d] Ne 3:26
8:4 [e] 2Ch 6:13
8:5 [f] Jdg 3:20
8:6 [g] Ex 4:31; Ezr 9:5; 1Ti 2:8
8:7 [h] Ezr 10:23 [i] Lev 10:11; 2Ch 17:7
8:9 [j] Ne 7:1, 65, 70 [k] Dt 12:7, 12; 16:14-15
8:10 [l] 1Sa 25:8; Lk 14:12-14 [m] Lev 23:40; Dt 12:18; 16:11, 14-15
8:12 [n] Est 9:22

Ne 8:1-8 ❖ How might we share God's Word and its truth with more people?

10Nehemiah said, "Go and enjoy choice
food and sweet drinks, and send some to
those who have nothing[l] prepared. This
day is holy to our Lord. Do not grieve, for
the joy[m] of the LORD is your strength."
11The Levites calmed all the people,
saying, "Be still, for this is a holy day.
Do not grieve."
12Then all the people went away to eat
and drink, to send portions of food and
to celebrate with great joy,[n] because they
now understood the words that had been
made known to them.
13On the second day of the month, the
heads of all the families, along with the
priests and the Levites, gathered around
Ezra the teacher to give attention to the
words of the Law. 14They found written in
the Law, which the LORD had commanded through Moses, that the Israelites
were to live in temporary shelters during
the festival of the seventh month 15and
that they should proclaim this word and
spread it throughout their towns and in
Jerusalem: "Go out into the hill country
and bring back branches from olive and
wild olive trees, and from myrtles, palms
and shade trees, to make temporary shelters" — as it is written.[b]
16So the people went out and brought
back branches and built themselves temporary shelters on their own roofs, in
their courtyards, in the courts of the
house of God and in the square by the

[a] 8 Or *God, translating it* [b] 15 See Lev. 23:37-40.

8:3 Ezra read aloud to a captive audience from dawn to noon, which at this time of year represents about six hours. The imagery is that everyone was leaning forward to pay attention. Their ears are opened, and they have become active listeners.
8:4–5 These verses provide further background to the morning scene of Ezra reading the Law described in vv. 2–3. The overall picture is similar to Israel's great addresses in the past (Dt 29; Jos 8:30–35) and the covenant renewals during the late Judean period.
8:6 That "all the people" lifted their hands was a clear sign of worship, adoration, and honor to God. We will never know what specific words Ezra used to bless the Lord, but we do know what all the people said in response: "Amen! Amen!" which is connected to the meaning "believe, trust."
8:7–8 Thirteen Levites functioned as simultaneous interpreters, probably providing quick words of clarification, all without disrupting the actual reading of the Law by Ezra.
8:9–12 The statement to the assembly "do not mourn or weep" (v. 9) goes at the heart of the mood of the day. There will be time for repentance and confession (see ch. 9)—but not today. In v. 10 Nehemiah commissions a celebration banquet.
8:13–14 Under Ezra's leadership, the tribal leaders reconvened by themselves the following day. They "found written in the Law" (v. 14) that the whole assembly should immediately regather to Jerusalem and celebrate the Festival of Tabernacles, which required that people build and live in temporary shelters.
8:15–17 As on the first day, the people respond right away and return and build temporary shelters within the city of Jerusalem at specific locations. The exceptional nature of this particular addition cannot be overstated, since now Zion stands again as a protected sacred site. Indeed, "their joy was very great" (v. 17), which is in response to Nehemiah's instruction for the people to rejoice.

Water Gate and the one by the Gate of Ephraim.[o] 17The whole company that had returned from exile built temporary shelters and lived in them. From the days of Joshua son of Nun until that day, the Israelites had not celebrated[p] it like this. And their joy was very great.

18Day after day, from the first day to the last, Ezra read[q] from the Book of the Law of God. They celebrated the festival for seven days, and on the eighth day, in accordance with the regulation,[r] there was an assembly.

The Israelites Confess Their Sins

9 On the twenty-fourth day of the same month, the Israelites gathered together, fasting and wearing sackcloth and putting dust on their heads.[s] 2Those of Israelite descent had separated themselves from all foreigners.[t] They stood in their places and confessed their sins and the sins of their ancestors.[u] 3They stood where they were and read from the Book of the Law of the LORD their God for a quarter of the day, and spent another quarter in confession and in worshiping the LORD their God. 4Standing on the stairs of the Levites[v] were Jeshua, Bani, Kadmiel, Shebaniah, Bunni, Sherebiah, Bani and Kenani. They cried out with loud voices to the LORD their God. 5And the Levites — Jeshua, Kadmiel, Bani, Hashabneiah, Sherebiah, Hodiah, Shebaniah and Pethahiah — said: "Stand up and praise the LORD your God,[w] who is from everlasting to everlasting.[*a*]"

"Blessed be your glorious name, and may it be exalted above all blessing and praise. 6You alone are the LORD.[x] You made the heavens,[y] even the highest heavens, and all their starry host, the earth[z] and all that is on it, the seas[a] and all that is in them.[b] You give life to everything, and the multitudes of heaven worship you.

7"You are the LORD God, who chose Abram and brought him out of Ur of the Chaldeans[c] and named him Abraham.[d] 8You found his heart faithful to you, and you made a covenant with him to give to his descendants the land of the Canaanites, Hittites, Amorites, Perizzites, Jebusites and Girgashites.[e] You have kept your promise[f] because you are righteous.[g]

9"You saw the suffering of our ancestors in Egypt;[h] you heard their cry at the Red Sea.[*b*][i] 10You sent signs[j] and wonders against Pharaoh, against all his officials and all the people of his land, for you knew how arrogantly the Egyptians treated them. You made a name[k] for yourself, which remains to this day. 11You divided the sea before them,[l] so that they passed through it on dry ground, but you hurled their pursuers into the depths, like a stone into mighty waters.[m] 12By day you led[n] them with a pillar of cloud,[o] and

8:16 [o] 2Ki 14:13; Ne 12:39
8:17 [p] 2Ch 7:8; 8:13; 30:21
8:18 [q] Dt 31:11 [r] Lev 23:36, 40; Nu 29:35
9:1 [s] Jos 7:6; 1Sa 4:12
9:2 [t] Ne 13:3, 30 [u] Ezr 10:11; Ps 106:6
9:4 [v] Ezr 10:23
9:5 [w] Ps 78:4
9:6 [x] Dt 6:4 [y] 2Ki 19:15 [z] Ge 1:1; Isa 37:16 [a] Ps 95:5 [b] Dt 10:14
9:7 [c] Ge 11:31 [d] Ge 17:5
9:8 [e] Ge 15:18-21 [f] Jos 21:45 [g] Ge 15:6; Ezr 9:15
9:9 [h] Ex 3:7 [i] Ex 14:10-30
9:10 [j] Ex 10:1 [k] Jer 32:20; Da 9:15
9:11 [l] Ex 14:21; Ps 78:13 [m] Ex 15:4-5, 10; Heb 11:29
9:12 [n] Ex 15:13 [o] Ex 13:21

Ne 9:2–3 ❖ What sins of our ancestors might we need to confess before God? Why should people confess the sins of those who have gone before?

a 5 Or *God for ever and ever* *b* 9 Or *the Sea of Reeds*

8:18 In conclusion, the account fittingly summarizes the role of Ezra, who daily read the "Book of the Law of God." It also summarizes the atmosphere of celebration that lasted the duration of the feast.

✤ 7:73b—8:18 The obvious application of this text across cultural and ethnic fault lines centers on the centrality of God's Word in Christian ministry, regardless of our diversity. The history of Christian mission attests to the amazing adaptability of the Word of God to different cultures. The common denominator underlying global ministry will be a high view of Scripture and its authority to inform and direct our life and practice.

9:1–5 The time of confession is set in the broader context of a public reading of the "Book of the Law of the LORD their God" (v. 3) that alternated between times of confession and repentance and the reading of the Word.

9:6 "You alone are the LORD" captures only a fraction of the emphatic nature in the original: "You are he Yahweh, you alone, you, you made the heavens . . . [and] the earth" (alternate translation).

9:7–8 His faithfulness to the promise to Abraham reveals that Yahweh is righteous.

9:9–11 The exodus event was the crowning moment of Yahweh's revelation as the uncontested, one God over all the gods of Egypt (Ex 15:11): "You made a name for yourself" (Ne 9:10).

9:12–15 The Sinai account circles back to the wilderness journey by highlighting God's provision for his wandering people.

by night with a pillar of fire to give
them light on the way they were
to take.
13"You came down on Mount Si-
nai;[p] you spoke[q] to them from heav-
en. You gave them regulations and
laws that are just[r] and right, and decrees and commands that are good.[s]
14You made known to them your
holy Sabbath[t] and gave them commands, decrees and laws through
your servant Moses. 15In their hunger you gave them bread from heav-
en[u] and in their thirst you brought
them water from the rock;[v] you told
them to go in and take possession
of the land you had sworn with uplifted hand to give them.[w]
16"But they, our ancestors, became arrogant and stiff-necked,
and they did not obey your commands.[x] 17They refused to listen and
failed to remember[y] the miracles
you performed among them. They
became stiff-necked and in their rebellion appointed a leader in order
to return to their slavery.[z] But you
are a forgiving God, gracious and
compassionate, slow to anger[a] and
abounding in love.[b] Therefore you
did not desert them,[c] 18even when
they cast for themselves an image
of a calf[d] and said, 'This is your god,
who brought you up out of Egypt,'
or when they committed awful blasphemies.
19"Because of your great compassion you did not abandon them in
the wilderness. By day the pillar of
cloud did not fail to guide them
on their path, nor the pillar of fire
by night to shine on the way they
were to take. 20You gave your good
Spirit[e] to instruct them. You did not
withhold your manna[f] from their
mouths, and you gave them water[g]

9:13 [p] Ex 19:11 [q] Ex 19:19 [r] Ps 119:137 [s] Ex 20:1
9:14 [t] Ge 2:3; Ex 20:8-11
9:15 [u] Ex 16:4; Jn 6:31 [v] Ex 17:6; Nu 20:7-13 [w] Dt 1:8, 21
9:16 [x] Dt 1:26-33; 31:29
9:17 [y] Ps 78:42 [z] Nu 14:1-4 [a] Ex 34:6 [b] Nu 14:17-19 [c] Ps 78:11
9:18 [d] Ex 32:4
9:20 [e] Nu 11:17; Isa 63:11, 14 [f] Ex 16:15 [g] Ex 17:6

9:16–18 In response to this perfect record of faithfulness, "they, our ancestors became arrogant" (v. 16). In response to this paradigm of inflexibility and rebellion, the prayer pivots to Yahweh's revelation of his character, which serves as a point-by-point response to the Israelites' rebellion (v. 17b).

9:19–21 The recalling of Israel's wilderness years (see Dt 8:1–4) concludes the whole first part of the history of Israel. The appeal is to the character of Yahweh as revealed in the declaration of the divine name at Sinai.

CHARACTER OF GOD // GOD IS PATIENT

Nehemiah 9:17: They refused to listen and failed to remember the miracles you performed among them. They became stiff-necked and in their rebellion appointed a leader in order to return to their slavery. But you are a forgiving God, gracious and compassionate, slow to anger and abounding in love.

God described his nature to Moses as being "slow to anger" (Ex 34:6). To some readers, this might seem strange. After all, God had just carried out his judgment upon the Israelite camp for their sin with the golden calf. However, throughout the Bible this aspect of God's character is repeated and affirmed: God is indeed patient and slow to anger.

When the Jewish exiles returned from captivity in Babylon and began rebuilding their homes, Nehemiah served as governor of Judah. Leading the people in spiritual renewal, he stood before the community and offered a prayer, proclaiming again that God was "slow to anger" (Ne 9:17). This was a remarkable thing to pray in a context when God's punishment for Judah's sin was still fresh in their minds.

It is good news that God is slow to anger. If God were reactive and volatile, we would have no hope. Instead, God is patient with human failure. While God does punish sin, there are plenty of cases in the Bible where God shows remarkable restraint (Ps 103:10–12). God's patience allows for repentance and renewal. Rather than striking them down, God gives his children time to repent and return to him (2Pe 3:9).

APPLICATION ✣ There are few things worse than someone who is quick to anger. We tread lightly around them, always walking on eggshells, afraid they might explode at any moment. We never feel safe around such people. The good news is that God is nothing like that. God is not a vengeful tyrant ready to lash out in anger at any moment. God's justice is measured by God's patience. Despite human sin, God is slow to anger, desiring instead that his children come to him in repentance and faith.

for their thirst. 21 For forty years you
sustained them in the wilderness;
they lacked nothing,[h] their clothes
did not wear out nor did their feet
become swollen.[i]
22 "You gave them kingdoms and
nations, allotting to them even the
remotest frontiers. They took over
the country of Sihon[a][j] king of Heshbon and the country of Og king of
Bashan.[k] 23 You made their children
as numerous as the stars in the sky,
and you brought them into the land
that you told their parents to enter
and possess. 24 Their children went
in and took possession of the land.[l]
You subdued before them the Canaanites, who lived in the land;
you gave the Canaanites into their
hands, along with their kings and
the peoples of the land, to deal with
them as they pleased. 25 They captured fortified cities and fertile land;
they took possession of houses filled
with all kinds of good things, wells
already dug, vineyards, olive groves
and fruit trees in abundance. They
ate to the full and were well-nour-
ished;[m] they reveled in your great
goodness.[n]
26 "But they were disobedient and
rebelled against you; they turned
their backs on your law.[o] They killed
your prophets,[p] who had warned
them in order to turn them back to
you; they committed awful blasphemies.[q] 27 So you delivered them into
the hands of their enemies,[r] who
oppressed them. But when they
were oppressed they cried out to
you. From heaven you heard them,
and in your great compassion[s] you
gave them deliverers, who rescued
them from the hand of their enemies.
28 "But as soon as they were at
rest, they again did what was evil
in your sight. Then you abandoned
them to the hand of their enemies
so that they ruled over them. And
when they cried out to you again,
you heard from heaven, and in your
compassion you delivered them[t]
time after time.
29 "You warned them in order to
turn them back to your law, but they
became arrogant[u] and disobeyed
your commands. They sinned
against your ordinances, of which
you said, 'The person who obeys
them will live by them.'[v] Stubbornly they turned their backs on you,
became stiff-necked and refused to
listen.[w] 30 For many years you were
patient with them. By your Spirit
you warned them through your
prophets.[x] Yet they paid no attention, so you gave them into the
hands of the neighboring peoples.
31 But in your great mercy you did
not put an end[y] to them or abandon them, for you are a gracious
and merciful God.
32 "Now therefore, our God, the
great God, mighty[z] and awesome,
who keeps his covenant of love,[a] do
not let all this hardship seem trifling
in your eyes — the hardship that has
come on us, on our kings and leaders, on our priests and prophets, on
our ancestors and all your people,
from the days of the kings of Assyria until today. 33 In all that has
happened to us, you have remained
righteous;[b] you have acted faithfully, while we acted wickedly.[c] 34 Our
kings,[d] our leaders, our priests and
our ancestors[e] did not follow your
law; they did not pay attention to

9:21 [h] Dt 2:7 [i] Dt 8:4
9:22 [j] Nu 21:21 [k] Nu 21:33
9:24 [l] Jos 11:23
9:25 [m] Dt 6:10-12 [n] Nu 13:27; Dt 32:12-15
9:26 [o] 1Ki 14:9 [p] Mt 21:35-36 [q] Jdg 2:12-13
9:27 [r] Jdg 2:14 [s] Ps 106:45
9:28 [t] Ps 106:43
9:29 [u] Ps 5:5; Isa 2:11; Jer 43:2 [v] Dt 30:16 [w] Zec 7:11-12
9:30 [x] 2Ki 17:13-18; 2Ch 36:16
9:31 [y] Isa 48:9; Jer 4:27
9:32 [z] Ps 24:8 [a] Dt 7:9
9:33 [b] Ge 18:25 [c] Jer 44:3; Da 9:7-8,14
9:34 [d] 2Ki 23:11 [e] Jer 44:17

[a] *22* One Hebrew manuscript and Septuagint; most Hebrew manuscripts *Sihon, that is, the country of the*

9:22–25 Verse 22 returns to a well-rehearsed dimension to the conquest of Canaan in Israelite lore (Nu 21:23–35; Dt 2:24–27; 3:1–11). The prayer pointedly recalls that the promise of land to occupy is not complete without the presence of "children as numerous as the stars in the sky" (Ne 9:23) along with the accompanying defeat of the Canaanites and numerous material blessings as fruit of conquest.

9:26–31 The people's response to Yahweh at the time of the exodus (v. 17a) is matched at the time of the settlement in Canaan and throughout the time of the monarchy. But there were many times (NIV "time after time") that Yahweh continued to display his "compassion" (v. 28) by delivering them. In spite of the catastrophic failures on the part of Israel, Yahweh's "great mercy" (v. 31) prevails in the end.

9:32–35 Yahweh has been fully justified in his actions to judge Israel and the verdict is in: Yahweh is righteous, while the people "acted wickedly" (v. 33). The returned community recognizes the universal and pervasive guilt shared by every sphere of society. Yahweh's character of faithful-

your commands or the statutes you
warned them to keep. 35Even while
they were in their kingdom, enjoying your great goodness[f] to them
in the spacious and fertile land you
gave them, they did not serve you[g]
or turn from their evil ways.
36"But see, we are slaves[h] today,
slaves in the land you gave our ancestors so they could eat its fruit and
the other good things it produces.
37Because of our sins, its abundant
harvest goes to the kings you have
placed over us. They rule over our
bodies and our cattle as they please.
We are in great distress.[i]

9:35 [f] Isa 63:7 [g] Dt 28:45-48
9:36 [h] Dt 28:48; Ezr 9:9
9:37 [i] Dt 28:33; La 5:5

ness is not only the centerpiece of their appeal—it is the only one.

9:36–37 If there is a formal petition, it is intentionally oblique ("we are slaves today," v. 36) and remains permeated with a deep sense of the fact that their fate is fully deserved ("because of our sins," v. 37) and of the undeserved favor of God toward them (the squandered gift of the land). We are essentially taken back to square one in this sweeping overview of the history of Israel, which parallels Ezra's own prayer in Ezr 9:9.

9:1–37 The biblical narrative is our narrative. It is our story.

One of the great themes of the story of God's people is that once they lost the narrative of Scripture, they lost the narrative of their lives. Without spending time in the Scripture, we are flying blind and remain woefully unaware of our sinful condition. The Scripture provides a type of diagnostic spiritual health report of where we stand and what adjustments we need to make to stay close to God. Without these regular checkups, we do not know how healthy or unhealthy we are. Just as with our own physical health, avoiding doctor checkups and regular diagnostics (what to eat or not eat, etc.) is akin to flying blind. We do not have a sense of what is ahead on the journey.

We should not wait until we crash and burn spiritually to get our lives with God back on track. The Scripture is our guide. Nehemiah 9 is a bitter recounting of a hard lesson learned: that without God's Word, the Israelites grew cold and stiff-necked toward him, both in Egypt and in their more recent history.

We need to heed the wise words of the psalmist: "I have hidden your word in my heart that I might not sin against you" (Ps 119:11). By embracing the narrative of Scripture and the big picture of the cycles of creation-sin-judgment-deliverance-redemption in our lives, we grow in our dependence upon God's compassion as revealed in the person of Jesus Christ. Despite our repeated journeys through this cycle, believers are still rooted in him, the One who has fulfilled all righteousness.

CHARACTER OF GOD // GOD IS MERCIFUL

Nehemiah 9:31: "But in your great mercy you did not put an end to them or abandon them, for you are a gracious and merciful God."

God described himself as merciful to Moses (Ex 34:6). Before the Israelites entered the promised land, Moses reminded them that God is merciful and would not abandon or forget them (Dt 4:31).

God's mercy means that his children do not receive the punishment for sin they deserve. Each person has sinned and strayed from God's will, yet God chooses to show mercy. By sheer grace, God made sinners alive in Christ even when they were dead in sin (Eph 2:4–5). He gives them his Spirit to lead them into living righteous lives. Furthermore, when they do sin, God shows his patience and mercy by allowing his children to repent and to be restored to him (1Jn 2:1).

At first, God's mercy might seem to be in conflict with God's justice. If justice demands punishment for sin, how can God instead show mercy? God reconciles his justice and mercy at the cross of Jesus Christ. Far from abandoning justice, the punishment for sin was poured out on Jesus Christ instead of on God's people. Since God's justice was satisfied at the cross, God's mercy is not a denial of his justice. Instead, it is a stunning display of his grace and love.

APPLICATION God could have carried out the full weight of his justice upon each one of us, as he did with the world during the flood, saving only Noah and his family (Heb 11:7). Instead, God acts mercifully toward us, and the cross of Christ shows us the measure of God's mercy. God does not treat us as our sins deserve, but instead extends to us the priceless gift of eternal life. This is not because of anything we have done or could do; it is only because God is rich in mercy (Eph 2:4).

The Agreement of the People

38"In view of all this, we are making a
binding agreement,[j] putting it in writing,[k] and our leaders, our Levites and
our priests are affixing their seals to it."[a]

10

[b] Those who sealed it were:

Nehemiah the governor, the son of Hakaliah.

Zedekiah, 2Seraiah,[l] Azariah, Jeremiah,
3Pashhur,[m] Amariah, Malkijah,
4Hattush, Shebaniah, Malluk,
5Harim,[n] Meremoth, Obadiah,
6Daniel, Ginnethon, Baruch,
7Meshullam, Abijah, Mijamin,
8Maaziah, Bilgai and Shemaiah.
These were the priests.

9The Levites:[o]

Jeshua son of Azaniah, Binnui of the sons of Henadad, Kadmiel,
10and their associates: Shebaniah, Hodiah, Kelita, Pelaiah, Hanan,
11Mika, Rehob, Hashabiah,
12Zakkur, Sherebiah, Shebaniah,
13Hodiah, Bani and Beninu.

14The leaders of the people:

Parosh, Pahath-Moab, Elam, Zattu, Bani,
15Bunni, Azgad, Bebai,
16Adonijah, Bigvai, Adin,[p]
17Ater, Hezekiah, Azzur,
18Hodiah, Hashum, Bezai,
19Hariph, Anathoth, Nebai,
20Magpiash, Meshullam, Hezir,[q]
21Meshezabel, Zadok, Jaddua,
22Pelatiah, Hanan, Anaiah,
23Hoshea, Hananiah,[r] Hasshub,
24Hallohesh, Pilha, Shobek,

9:38 [j] 2Ch 23:16 [k] Isa 44:5
10:2 [l] Ezr 2:2
10:3 [m] 1Ch 9:12
10:5 [n] 1Ch 24:8
10:9 [o] Ne 12:1
10:16 [p] Ezr 8:6
10:20 [q] 1Ch 24:15
10:23 [r] Ne 7:2

Ne 10:32-39 ❖ What responsibility do Christians have to support and maintain their church? How can we contribute to this mission?

25Rehum, Hashabnah, Maaseiah,
26Ahiah, Hanan, Anan,
27Malluk, Harim and Baanah.

28"The rest of the people—
priests, Levites, gatekeepers, musicians, temple servants[s] and all
who separated themselves from the
neighboring peoples[t] for the sake
of the Law of God, together with
their wives and all their sons and
daughters who are able to understand— 29all these now join their
fellow Israelites the nobles, and
bind themselves with a curse and
an oath[u] to follow the Law of God
given through Moses the servant
of God and to obey carefully all the
commands, regulations and decrees
of the LORD our Lord.
30"We promise not to give our
daughters in marriage to the peoples around us or take their daughters for our sons.[v]
31"When the neighboring peoples
bring merchandise or grain to sell
on the Sabbath,[w] we will not buy
from them on the Sabbath or on
any holy day. Every seventh year we
will forgo working the land[x] and will
cancel all debts.[y]
32"We assume the responsibility
for carrying out the commands to

10:28 [s] Ps 135:1 [t] 2Ch 6:26; Ne 9:2
10:29 [u] Nu 5:21; Ps 119:106
10:30 [v] Ex 34:16; Dt 7:3; Ne 13:23
10:31 [w] Ne 13:16, 18; Jer 17:27; Eze 23:38; Am 8:5 [x] Ex 23:11; Lev 25:1-7 [y] Dt 15:1

[a] *38* In Hebrew texts this verse (9:38) is numbered 10:1. [b] In Hebrew texts 10:1-39 is numbered 10:2-40.

9:38 While the word "covenant" is not actually present in this verse, the verb used ("we are making") is the idiomatic "cutting," which is always used in the context of covenant-making (Ge 15:18). Thus it indicates, "we are cutting a binding agreement" (alternate translation).
10:1–27 Weaving in names that hark back to the past along with names from the present reflects the tribal characteristics of belonging in a past, present, and future sense.
10:28–29 Verse 28 adds "the rest of the people" to the list of those who are also committing themselves to what now unmistakably references Sinaitic covenantal terms: They are entering into a "curse and an oath" (v. 29) in a ceremony strongly reminiscent of the one in the plains of Moab (Dt 30:11–19) and at Mount Ebal (Jos 8:30–35; cf. Dt 27).
10:30–31 The first set of three promises is strongly reminiscent of a form found in OT laws such as the Ten Commandments (e.g., "you shall not . . ." Dt 5:8).
The first relates to the practice of intermarriage (cf. Ne 10:28). In effect, the people are making a promise not to repeat the mistakes of the past. The second keeps the focus on the peoples of the land but now extends to economic partnerships (v. 31a). The third directly connects to the commitment not to repeat the problems of injustice described in ch. 5.
10:32–34 The rest of the promises are specifically tied to the worship of Yahweh and "the service of the house of our God" (v. 32). Heading off the list of promises is the collection of a temple tax for maintenance: "offerings," including "grain," "burnt," and "sin offerings to make atonement for

give a third of a shekel[a] each year for
the service of the house of our God:
33 for the bread set out on the table;[z]
for the regular grain offerings and
burnt offerings; for the offerings
on the Sabbaths, at the New Moon[a]
feasts and at the appointed festivals; for the holy offerings; for sin
offerings[b] to make atonement for
Israel; and for all the duties of the
house of our God.[b]
34 "We — the priests, the Levites
and the people — have cast lots[c] to
determine when each of our families is to bring to the house of our
God at set times each year a contribution of wood[d] to burn on the altar
of the LORD our God, as it is written
in the Law.
35 "We also assume responsibility for bringing to the house of the
LORD each year the firstfruits[e] of our
crops and of every fruit tree.[f]
36 "As it is also written in the Law,
we will bring the firstborn[g] of our
sons and of our cattle, of our herds
and of our flocks to the house of
our God, to the priests ministering
there.[h]
37 "Moreover, we will bring to the
storerooms of the house of our God,
to the priests, the first of our ground
meal, of our grain offerings, of the
fruit of all our trees and of our new
wine and olive oil.[i] And we will bring
a tithe[j] of our crops to the Levites,[k]
for it is the Levites who collect the
tithes in all the towns where we

10:33 [z] Lev 24:6 [a] Nu 10:10; Ps 81:3; Isa 1:14 [b] 2Ch 24:5
10:34 [c] Lev 16:8 [d] Ne 13:31
10:35 [e] Ex 22:29; 23:19; Nu 18:12 [f] Dt 26:1-11
10:36 [g] Ex 13:2; Nu 18:14-16 [h] Ne 13:31
10:37 [i] Lev 23:17; Nu 18:12 [j] Lev 27:30; Nu 18:21 [k] Dt 14:22-29
[l] Eze 44:30
10:38 [m] Nu 18:26
10:39 [n] Dt 12:6; Ne 13:11,12
11:1 [o] Ne 7:4 [p] ver 18; Isa 48:2; 52:1; 64:10; Zec 14:20-21 [q] Ne 7:73

Ne 11:1-3 ❖ Why is it important that the leaders of God's people come together rather than remaining "lone wolves"?

work.[l] 38 A priest descended from
Aaron is to accompany the Levites
when they receive the tithes, and
the Levites are to bring a tenth of
the tithes[m] up to the house of our
God, to the storerooms of the treasury. 39 The people of Israel, including the Levites, are to bring their
contributions of grain, new wine
and olive oil to the storerooms,
where the articles for the sanctuary and for the ministering priests,
the gatekeepers and the musicians
are also kept.
"We will not neglect the house of
our God."[n]

The New Residents of Jerusalem

11:3–19pp // 1Ch 9:1–17

11 Now the leaders of the people settled
in Jerusalem. The rest of the people
cast lots to bring one out of every ten
of them to live in Jerusalem,[o] the holy
city,[p] while the remaining nine were to
stay in their own towns.[q] 2 The people
commended all who volunteered to live
in Jerusalem.
3 These are the provincial leaders who
settled in Jerusalem (now some Israelites, priests, Levites, temple servants and

[a] *32* That is, about 1/8 ounce or about 4 grams
[b] *33* Or *purification offerings*

Israel" (v. 33). Following the temple tax, the text is almost disarming in its practicality: Without wood supplies, there can be no sacrifice.

10:35–38 Another essential dimension to worship was the bringing of "firstfruits" (v. 35) to Yahweh and the "storerooms" (v. 37) of the temple. The "tithes" (v. 37), another well-known revenue stream in the law, must be collected through the Levites. In turn, from this tithe a tenth must go to the "house of our God" to be stored in the "storerooms of the treasury" (v. 38).

10:39 As a final note, all "the people of Israel" are responsible to bring in "contributions of grain, new wine and olive oil" to the storerooms "for the ministering priests, the gatekeepers and the musicians." Without the people's active involvement in supplying provisions to the temple personnel, worship will not be sustainable.

✣ **9:38–10:39** Making a commitment to support the work and worship of God is not optional if we desire to participate in continuous worship among God's people. It is hard to imagine proper worship without sacrifices and consistent contributions to the house of the Lord and the work of God. In other words, supporting the material needs of worship on a permanent basis is an essential part of worship. It is not enough to build programs, read the Bible, and confess sins; worship always involves giving of one's time, finances, and personal efforts. The imagery of supplying firewood evokes the mundane and unappealing. However, appeals for these supplies in a modern context are equally important (building maintenance and payroll come to mind).

11:1–3 In this introductory and formal record of who repopulated the "holy city" (v. 1), the theme of contribution to the work of the house of the Lord continues from the preceding chapter.

descendants of Solomon's servants lived in the towns of Judah, each on their own property in the various towns,[r] 4while other people from both Judah and Benjamin[s] lived in Jerusalem):[t]

From the descendants of Judah:

Athaiah son of Uzziah, the son of Zechariah, the son of Amariah, the son of Shephatiah, the son of Mahalalel, a descendant of Perez; 5and Maaseiah son of Baruch, the son of Kol-Hozeh, the son of Hazaiah, the son of Adaiah, the son of Joiarib, the son of Zechariah, a descendant of Shelah. 6The descendants of Perez who lived in Jerusalem totaled 468 men of standing.

7From the descendants of Benjamin:

Sallu son of Meshullam, the son of Joed, the son of Pedaiah, the son of Kolaiah, the son of Maaseiah, the son of Ithiel, the son of Jeshaiah, 8and his followers, Gabbai and Sallai—928 men. 9Joel son of Zikri was their chief officer, and Judah son of Hassenuah was over the New Quarter of the city.

10From the priests:

Jedaiah; the son of Joiarib; Jakin; 11Seraiah[u] son of Hilkiah, the son of Meshullam, the son of Zadok, the son of Meraioth, the son of Ahitub,[v] the official in charge of the house of God, 12and their associates, who carried on work for the temple—822 men; Adaiah son of Jeroham, the son of Pelaliah, the son of Amzi, the son of Zechariah, the son of Pashhur, the son of Malkijah, 13and his associates, who were heads of families—242 men; Amashsai son of Azarel, the son of Ahzai, the son of Meshillemoth, the son of Immer, 14and his[a] associates, who were men of standing—128. Their chief officer was Zabdiel son of Haggedolim.

15From the Levites:

Shemaiah son of Hasshub, the son of Azrikam, the son of Hashabiah, the son of Bunni; 16Shabbethai[w] and Jozabad,[x] two of the heads of the Levites, who had charge of the outside work of the house of God; 17Mattaniah[y] son of Mika, the son of Zabdi, the son of Asaph,[z] the director who led in thanksgiving and prayer; Bakbukiah, second among his associates; and Abda son of Shammua, the son of Galal, the son of Jeduthun.[a] 18The Levites in the holy city[b] totaled 284.

19The gatekeepers:

Akkub, Talmon and their associates, who kept watch at the gates—172 men.

20The rest of the Israelites, with the priests and Levites, were in all the towns of Judah, each on their ancestral property.

21The temple servants[c] lived on the hill of Ophel, and Ziha and Gishpa were in charge of them.

22The chief officer of the Levites in Jerusalem was Uzzi son of Bani, the son of Hashabiah, the son of Mattaniah,[d] the son of Mika. Uzzi was one of Asaph's descendants, who were the musicians responsible for the service of the house of God. 23The musicians[e] were under the king's orders, which regulated their daily activity.

24Pethahiah son of Meshezabel, one of the descendants of Zerah[f] son of Judah, was the king's agent in all affairs relating to the people.

25As for the villages with their fields,

11:3 [r] 1Ch 9:2-3; Ezr 2:1
11:4 [s] Ezr 1:5 [t] Ezr 2:70
11:11 [u] 2Ki 25:18; Ezr 2:2 [v] Ezr 7:2
11:16 [w] Ezr 10:15 [x] Ezr 8:33
11:17 [y] 1Ch 9:15; Ne 12:8 [z] 2Ch 5:12 [a] 1Ch 25:1
11:18 [b] Rev 21:2
11:21 [c] Ezr 2:43; Ne 3:26
11:22 [d] 1Ch 9:15
11:23 [e] Ne 7:44
11:24 [f] Ge 38:30

[a] *14* Most Septuagint manuscripts; Hebrew *their*

11:4–9 The list begins appropriately with the one surviving eponymous tribe, Judah, with a list of "men of standing" (v. 6) that further underscores the courage and the honor given to them for living in Jerusalem. Of note, the list of "descendants of Benjamin" outnumbers the list of Judah (v. 7).
11:10–14 The term "Haggedolim" (v. 14) probably was a term meaning "the great one" rather than a proper name per se, and reflects the warriors of ages past in Israel.
11:15–19 The mixing of religious duties and protective duties continues with the list of Levites.
11:20–24 The musicians come under Persian supervisory rule (v. 23). The crown will allow the worship of Yahweh to proceed but not entirely without supervision.
11:25–36 The settlement patterns in fifth-century BC Yehud strongly suggest that designations such as "Judah" and "Benjamin" should not be taken at face value or in a literal territorial sense. In other words, "X marks the spot" only indicates that Israelite presence was in a particular settlement, which may or may not have overlapped sites historically connected to named territories before

some of the people of Judah lived in Kiriath Arba[g] and its surrounding settlements, in Dibon[h] and its settlements, in
Jekabzeel and its villages, 26in Jeshua, in
Moladah, in Beth Pelet,[i] 27in Hazar Shual,
in Beersheba[j] and its settlements, 28in
Ziklag,[k] in Mekonah and its settlements,
29in En Rimmon, in Zorah,[l] in Jarmuth,[m]
30Zanoah, Adullam[n] and their villages, in
Lachish[o] and its fields, and in Azekah[p]
and its settlements. So they were living
all the way from Beersheba[q] to the Valley
of Hinnom.

31The descendants of the Benjamites
from Geba[r] lived in Mikmash,[s] Aija, Bethel and its settlements, 32in Anathoth,[t]
Nob[u] and Ananiah, 33in Hazor,[v] Ramah
and Gittaim,[w] 34in Hadid, Zeboim[x] and
Neballat, 35in Lod and Ono,[y] and in Ge
Harashim.

36Some of the divisions of the Levites
of Judah settled in Benjamin.

Priests and Levites

12 These were the priests[z] and Levites
who returned with Zerubbabel[a] son
of Shealtiel and with Joshua:[b]

Seraiah,[c] Jeremiah, Ezra,
2Amariah, Malluk, Hattush,
3Shekaniah, Rehum, Meremoth,
4Iddo,[d] Ginnethon,[a] Abijah,[e]
5Mijamin,[b] Moadiah, Bilgah,
6Shemaiah, Joiarib, Jedaiah,[f]
7Sallu, Amok, Hilkiah and Jedaiah.

These were the leaders of the priests and
their associates in the days of Joshua.

8The Levites were Jeshua, Binnui, Kadmiel, Sherebiah, Judah, and also Mattaniah,[g] who, together with his associates,
was in charge of the songs of thanksgiving. 9Bakbukiah and Unni, their associates, stood opposite them in the services.

10Joshua was the father of Joiakim,
Joiakim the father of Eliashib,[h] Eliashib
the father of Joiada, 11Joiada the father
of Jonathan, and Jonathan the father
of Jaddua.

12In the days of Joiakim, these were
the heads of the priestly families:

of Seraiah's family, Meraiah;
of Jeremiah's, Hananiah;
13of Ezra's, Meshullam;
of Amariah's, Jehohanan;
14of Malluk's, Jonathan;
of Shekaniah's,[c] Joseph;
15of Harim's, Adna;
of Meremoth's,[d] Helkai;
16of Iddo's,[i] Zechariah;
of Ginnethon's, Meshullam;
17of Abijah's, Zikri;
of Miniamin's and of Moadiah's,
Piltai;
18of Bilgah's, Shammua;
of Shemaiah's, Jehonathan;

11:25 g Ge 35:27; Jos 14:15 h Nu 21:30
11:26 i Jos 15:27
11:27 j Ge 21:14
11:28 k 1Sa 27:6
11:29 l Jos 15:33 m Jos 10:3
11:30 n Jos 15:35 o Jos 10:3 p Jos 10:10 q Jos 15:28
11:31 r Jos 21:17; Isa 10:29 s 1Sa 13:2
11:32 t Jos 21:18; Isa 10:30 u 1Sa 21:1
11:33 v Jos 11:1 w 2Sa 4:3
11:34 x 1Sa 13:18
11:35 y 1Ch 8:12
12:1 z Ne 10:1-8 a 1Ch 3:19 b Ezr 2:2 c Ezr 2:2
12:4 d Zec 1:1 e Lk 1:5
12:6 f 1Ch 24:7
12:8 g Ne 11:17
12:10 h Ezr 10:24
12:16 i ver 4

[a] *4* Many Hebrew manuscripts and Vulgate (see also verse 16); most Hebrew manuscripts *Ginnethoi* [b] *5* A variant of *Miniamin* [c] *14* Very many Hebrew manuscripts, some Septuagint manuscripts and Syriac (see also verse 3); most Hebrew manuscripts *Shebaniah's* [d] *15* Some Septuagint manuscripts (see also verse 3); Hebrew *Meraioth's*

the exile. The protection of Yahweh's sacred space continues to take precedence over the reality that the people of Yahweh continue to be very much a minority in the land.

11:1–36 Through the ages of Christian history, believers have not always applied the principles outlined above. Material desires, career aspirations and ambitions for territorial expansion have to give way to the focal point of maintaining the sanctity of Zion, which now is defined as the people of God.

Paul compares the church to a "foundation of the truth" in 1Ti 3:15, and thus Scripture continues to challenge us by giving us marching orders away from unhealthy attachments to earthly categories (buildings, rituals, and career aspirations) and toward spiritual ones.

Like the remnant who returned to the region around Jerusalem, we need to realize we will never be a majority voice in the "present evil age," from which Jesus came to save us (Gal 1:3–5). Even in the age of megachurches in the West and parts of Asia and Africa, from a standpoint of demographics, what is, for example, a 20,000-member church in a city of 5 million people? The Christian patterns of settlement in the present evil age will never be swayed in our favor. This radical redistribution will only occur in the new heaven and new earth when Christ establishes his kingdom on earth (Isa 65:17; 66:22; 2Pe 3:13; Rev 21).

Our global map will always resemble the postexilic patterns of settlement in Yehud rather than the settlement patterns of the time of Joshua and Judges. Thus, our task remains the same as those of the temple attendants in Yehud. We, as Levites ("a royal priesthood," 1Pe 2:9), are called to populate the holy city with God's people from the Jerusalem "above" (Gal 4:26), making sure that we remain holy as he is holy (1Pe 1:16).

12:1–26 This genealogy targets the priests and Levites in a more comprehensive way than the list of Ne 7, along with a practical rationale—the resumption of worship can begin in earnest since everything and everyone is in place.

19 of Joiarib's, Mattenai;
of Jedaiah's, Uzzi;
20 of Sallu's, Kallai;
of Amok's, Eber;
21 of Hilkiah's, Hashabiah;
of Jedaiah's, Nethanel.

22 The family heads of the Levites in the days of Eliashib, Joiada, Johanan and Jaddua, as well as those of the priests, were recorded in the reign of Darius the Persian. 23 The family heads among the descendants of Levi up to the time of Johanan son of Eliashib were recorded in the book of the annals. 24 And the leaders of the Levites[j] were Hashabiah, Sherebiah, Jeshua son of Kadmiel, and their associates, who stood opposite them to give praise and thanksgiving, one section responding to the other, as prescribed by David the man of God.

25 Mattaniah, Bakbukiah, Obadiah, Meshullam, Talmon and Akkub were gatekeepers who guarded the storerooms at the gates. 26 They served in the days of Joiakim son of Joshua, the son of Jozadak, and in the days of Nehemiah the governor and of Ezra the priest, the teacher of the Law.

Dedication of the Wall of Jerusalem

27 At the dedication[k] of the wall of Jerusalem, the Levites were sought out from where they lived and were brought to Jerusalem to celebrate joyfully the dedication with songs of thanksgiving and with the music of cymbals,[l] harps and lyres.[m] 28 The musicians also were brought together from the region around Jerusalem — from the villages of the Netophathites,[n] 29 from Beth Gilgal, and from the area of Geba and Azmaveth, for the musicians had built villages for themselves around Jerusalem. 30 When the priests and Levites had purified themselves ceremonially, they purified the people,[o] the gates and the wall.

Ne 12:27 ❖ What occasions in church merit such celebration? How can we joyfully celebrate these moments with fellow children of God?

31 I had the leaders of Judah go up on top of[a] the wall. I also assigned two large choirs to give thanks. One was to proceed on top of[b] the wall to the right, toward the Dung Gate.[p] 32 Hoshaiah and half the leaders of Judah followed them, 33 along with Azariah, Ezra, Meshullam, 34 Judah, Benjamin,[q] Shemaiah, Jeremiah, 35 as well as some priests with trumpets,[r] and also Zechariah son of Jonathan, the son of Shemaiah, the son of Mattaniah, the son of Micaiah, the son of Zakkur, the son of Asaph, 36 and his associates — Shemaiah, Azarel, Milalai, Gilalai, Maai, Nethanel, Judah and Hanani — with musical instruments[s] prescribed by David the man of God.[t] Ezra[u] the teacher of the Law led the procession. 37 At the Fountain Gate[v] they continued directly up the steps of the City of David on the ascent to the wall and passed above the site of David's palace to the Water Gate[w] on the east.

38 The second choir proceeded in the opposite direction. I followed them on top of[c] the wall, together with half the people — past the Tower of the Ovens[x] to the Broad Wall,[y] 39 over the Gate of Ephraim,[z] the Jeshanah[d] Gate,[a] the Fish Gate,[b] the Tower of Hananel[c] and the Tower of the Hundred,[d] as far as the Sheep Gate.[e] At the Gate of the Guard they stopped.

40 The two choirs that gave thanks then took their places in the house of God; so did I, together with half the officials, 41 as well as the priests — Eliakim, Maaseiah, Miniamin, Micaiah, Elioenai, Zechariah and Hananiah with their trumpets —

[a] 31 Or *go alongside* [b] 31 Or *proceed alongside*
[c] 38 Or *them alongside* [d] 39 Or *Old*

12:24 [j] Ezr 2:40
12:27 [k] Dt 20:5 [l] 2Sa 6:5 [m] 1Ch 15:16, 28; 25:6; Ps 92:3
12:28 [n] 1Ch 2:54; 9:16
12:30 [o] Ex 19:10; Job 1:5
12:31 [p] Ne 2:13
12:34 [q] Ezr 1:5
12:35 [r] Ezr 3:10
12:36 [s] 1Ch 15:16 [t] 2Ch 8:14 [u] Ezr 7:6
12:37 [v] Ne 2:14; 3:15 [w] Ne 3:26
12:38 [x] Ne 3:11 [y] Ne 3:8
12:39 [z] 2Ki 14:13; Ne 8:16 [a] Ne 3:6 [b] 2Ch 33:14; Ne 3:3 [c] Ne 3:1 [d] Ne 3:1 [e] Ne 3:1

12:27–43 Before the celebration can begin, the priests and Levites "purified themselves" and "purified the people, the gates and the wall" (v. 30). The restoration project thus has come full circle from its beginning in ch. 3.

The second action verb after "took their places" in v. 40 is the first of several verbs that creates a dynamic picture ("on that day," v. 43) and serves as the fitting and dramatic conclusion to an extraordinary past few months for Nehemiah and the rest of the people: (1) The "choirs sang" (v. 42; "caused to hear," alternate translation) (2) "under the direction of Jezrahiah" (v. 42). (3) They offered "great sacrifices" (v. 43, which then explains why so many of them are mentioned by name). (4) They rejoiced (v. 43).

As in a crescendo, the atmosphere of rejoicing receives one last main verb describing a mood of extraordinary joy: "Rejoicing in Jerusalem could be heard far away" (v. 43). The projected and public nature of the joy serves as a fitting conclusion that the enemies of Zion could not prevail and take away the joy of a community who put their faith in Yahweh.

[42]and also Maaseiah, Shemaiah, Eleazar, Uzzi, Jehohanan, Malkijah, Elam and Ezer. The choirs sang under the direction of Jezrahiah. [43]And on that day they offered great sacrifices, rejoicing because God had given them great joy. The women and children also rejoiced. The sound of rejoicing in Jerusalem could be heard far away.

[44]At that time men were appointed to be in charge of the storerooms[f] for the contributions, firstfruits and tithes.[g] From the fields around the towns they were to bring into the storerooms the portions required by the Law for the priests and the Levites, for Judah was pleased with the ministering priests and Levites.[h] [45]They performed the service of their God and the service of purification, as did also the musicians and gatekeepers, according to the commands of David[i] and his son Solomon.[j] [46]For long ago, in the days of David and Asaph,[k] there had been directors for the musicians and for the songs of praise[l] and thanksgiving to God. [47]So in the days of Zerubbabel and of Nehemiah, all Israel contributed the daily portions for the musicians and the gatekeepers. They also set aside the portion for the other Levites, and the Levites set aside the portion for the descendants of Aaron.[m]

12:44 [f]Ne 13:4, 13 [g]Lev 27:30 [h]Dt 18:8
12:45 [i]1Ch 25:1; 2Ch 8:14 [j]1Ch 6:31; 23:5
12:46 [k]2Ch 35:15 [l]2Ch 29:27; Ps 137:4
12:47 [m]Nu 18:21; Dt 18:8
13:1 [n]ver 23; Dt 23:3
13:2 [o]Nu 22:3-11 [p]Nu 23:7; Dt 23:3 [q]Nu 23:11; Dt 23:4-5
13:3 [r]ver 23; Ne 9:2
13:4 [s]Ne 12:44 [t]Ne 2:10
13:5 [u]Lev 27:30; Nu 18:21

Ne 13 ❖ Is Nehemiah being self-righteous in his final moments? Why or why not? How should Christians respond to his exclusionist practices (see Gal 3:28)?

Nehemiah's Final Reforms

13 On that day the Book of Moses was read aloud in the hearing of the people and there it was found written that no Ammonite or Moabite should ever be admitted into the assembly of God,[n] [2]because they had not met the Israelites with food and water but had hired Balaam[o] to call a curse down on them.[p] (Our God, however, turned the curse into a blessing.)[q] [3]When the people heard this law, they excluded from Israel all who were of foreign descent.[r]

[4]Before this, Eliashib the priest had been put in charge of the storerooms[s] of the house of our God. He was closely associated with Tobiah,[t] [5]and he had provided him with a large room formerly used to store the grain offerings and incense and temple articles, and also the tithes[u] of grain, new wine and olive oil prescribed for the Levites, musicians and gatekeepers, as well as the contributions for the priests.

[6]But while all this was going on, I was

12:44–47 Nehemiah knows that unless people willingly contribute to the service of the house of the Lord, as promised in ch. 10, his efforts and success in restoring Zion could be reversed, especially since Jerusalem remains surrounded by hostile neighbors. As the current governor of Judah and successor of Zerubbabel, he is also accountable to the crown to make sure that the groups involved in the service of the temple are supported to fulfill their respective duties, including temple security and the protection of the sanctity of the site.

As a concluding thought, "all Israel" (v. 47) was true to the promise to provide for the affairs of the temple attendants (musicians, gatekeepers, Levites, and descendants of Aaron). The obvious parallel between the "days of Zerubbabel" in the first return and those "of Nehemiah" strongly hints at the success of Nehemiah's mission (v. 47).

13:1–3 The final act of "that day" is the public reading of "the Book of Moses," which underscores its newly gained importance (v. 1). The community has gathered around the hearing of the law one more time. On this occasion, however, the reading appears brief and targeted to what is essentially a direct quotation from Dt 23:3–5. The added interpretation "Our God, however, turned the curse into a blessing" (v. 2) recalls the work of the Levites among the people in ch. 8 to clarify the law. Upon hearing this injunction, "they excluded from Israel all who were of foreign descent" (v. 3), which is a further connection with Israel's distant past.

✚ **12:1—13:3** In the West, Christian short-term outreach teams routinely do prayer walks, as do church staff members in their neighborhoods. What is the significance of all these processions? The proclamation of God's faithfulness in a very public way is an act of worship to him. Those who take these walks are declaring to the world around them that God is at work and that he is faithful to carry out his purposes.

It took courage for the fledgling minority in Yehud to have such a public display on the walls of the city, but they (men, women, and children) did it with their whole heart—so much so that their joy was heard from afar (12:43).

13:4–9 At the heart of what Eliashib had done was an illicit partnership with Tobiah (e.g., Lev 21:1). Tobiah needs no introduction in his twin role as joint-chief protagonist and double agent by marriage alliance (6:18), and this enemy of Israel, unbelievably, had an office in the temple itself. The word "catastrophe" does not even begin to describe what is going on, and it thrusts us back to the dark ages of the systemic neglect of the worship in Judah before the exile.

PEOPLE TO KNOW // NEHEMIAH

NEHEMIAH 13:1-31: Nehemiah was the cupbearer of King Artaxerxes of Persia. When word reached Nehemiah that the wall of Jerusalem was in disrepair, Nehemiah wept for his land and his people. Artaxerxes noticed Nehemiah's sadness, and when Nehemiah told him the reason, the king sent Nehemiah to Jerusalem with supplies and support (Ne 2:1-9).

When Nehemiah reached Jerusalem, he assessed the situation. He then led the Jews to start rebuilding the wall and repairing its gates. The workers soon faced opposition from neighboring peoples, however (Ne 4:1-3). Furthermore, the strength of the workers began to give out. Nehemiah divided the people up, half working while the other half stood guard, and the work continued.

Appointed governor by Artaxerxes, Nehemiah also worked to rectify injustice in Jerusalem. The poor were being charged interest by the rich and even being forced into slavery (Ne 5:7-8). Nehemiah made the leaders take an oath to change their ways and protect the needs of the poor.

Despite continued outside opposition, the wall was completed. The people dedicated the wall with great rejoicing (Ne 12:27). Some time later when Nehemiah made another visit to Jerusalem from Persia, he was distraught to see the positive religious reforms that had taken effect in the city abandoned. Nehemiah's last words are a sad prayer asking God to remember to his credit the good things he tried to do (Ne 13:31).

APPLICATION ✥ It is important to protect and promote the integrity of God's community. Nehemiah saw that things were not the way they should have been within the city of Jerusalem, and he worked tirelessly to make changes. Our own faith sometimes needs some rebuilding, and though certain people—or old habits—will oppose the rebuilding efforts, we need to continue to work toward becoming God's living stones, built into his spiritual house (1Pe 2:5). And every time we look to team up with others to strengthen our efforts to build into God's kingdom on earth, we imitate the tireless work and passion of Nehemiah.

not in Jerusalem, for in the thirty-sec-
ond year of Artaxerxes[v] king of Babylon
I had returned to the king. Some time
later I asked his permission 7and came
back to Jerusalem. Here I learned about
the evil thing Eliashib[w] had done in providing Tobiah a room in the courts of the
house of God. 8I was greatly displeased
and threw all Tobiah's household goods
out of the room.[x] 9I gave orders to purify the rooms,[y] and then I put back into
them the equipment of the house of
God, with the grain offerings and the
incense.

10I also learned that the portions assigned to the Levites had not been given
to them,[z] and that all the Levites and
musicians responsible for the service had
gone back to their own fields. 11So I rebuked the officials and asked them, "Why
is the house of God neglected?"[a] Then I
called them together and stationed them
at their posts.

12All Judah brought the tithes[b] of
grain, new wine and olive oil into the
storerooms.[c] 13I put Shelemiah the priest,
Zadok the scribe, and a Levite named
Pedaiah in charge of the storerooms and
made Hanan son of Zakkur, the son of
Mattaniah, their assistant, because they
were considered trustworthy. They were
made responsible for distributing the
supplies to their fellow Levites.[d]

14Remember[e] me for this, my God, and
do not blot out what I have so faithfully
done for the house of my God and its
services.

15In those days I saw people in Judah
treading winepresses on the Sabbath

13:6 [v] Ne 2:6; 5:14
13:7 [w] Ezr 10:24
13:8 [x] Mt 21:12-13; Jn 2:13-16
13:9 [y] 1Ch 23:28; 2Ch 29:5
13:10 [z] Dt 12:19
13:11 [a] Ne 10:37-39; Hag 1:1-9
13:12 [b] 2Ch 31:6 [c] 1Ki 7:51; Ne 10:37-39; Mal 3:10
13:13 [d] Ne 12:44; Ac 6:1-5
13:14 [e] Ge 8:1

13:10-14 Nehemiah's response mirrors his decisiveness in dealing with Tobiah. Nehemiah promptly transitions Eliashib out of his position and replaces him with three individuals all mentioned by name. In this intercessory prayer, Nehemiah realizes all too well that the work accomplished to restore Zion could quickly be wiped out as a result of Eliashib's grievous failure. The uncompromising standards of holiness in the worship of Yahweh continue to loom large in this narrative.

13:15-16 The reforms continue at a rapid pace, organized by three pointed addresses. Nehemiah "warned" (v. 15) those who were violating the Sabbath. The people had stopped caring for the

and bringing in grain and loading it on
donkeys, together with wine, grapes, figs
and all other kinds of loads. And they
were bringing all this into Jerusalem on
the Sabbath.[f] Therefore I warned them
against selling food on that day. 16People
from Tyre who lived in Jerusalem were
bringing in fish and all kinds of merchandise and selling them in Jerusalem
on the Sabbath[g] to the people of Judah.
17I rebuked the nobles of Judah and said
to them, "What is this wicked thing you
are doing — desecrating the Sabbath
day? 18Didn't your ancestors do the same
things, so that our God brought all this
calamity on us and on this city? Now you
are stirring up more wrath against Israel
by desecrating the Sabbath."[h]
19When evening shadows fell on the
gates of Jerusalem before the Sabbath,[i]
I ordered the doors to be shut and not
opened until the Sabbath was over. I
stationed some of my own men at the
gates so that no load could be brought
in on the Sabbath day. 20Once or twice
the merchants and sellers of all kinds of
goods spent the night outside Jerusalem.
21But I warned them and said, "Why do
you spend the night by the wall? If you
do this again, I will arrest you." From that
time on they no longer came on the Sabbath. 22Then I commanded the Levites
to purify themselves and go and guard
the gates in order to keep the Sabbath
day holy.

Remember[j] me for this also, my God,
and show mercy to me according to your
great love.

23Moreover, in those days I saw men
of Judah who had married[k] women from
Ashdod, Ammon and Moab.[l] 24Half of
their children spoke the language of
Ashdod or the language of one of the
other peoples, and did not know how to
speak the language of Judah. 25I rebuked
them and called curses down on them.
I beat some of the men and pulled out
their hair. I made them take an oath[m] in
God's name and said: "You are not to give
your daughters in marriage to their sons,
nor are you to take their daughters in
marriage for your sons or for yourselves.
26Was it not because of marriages like
these that Solomon king of Israel sinned?
Among the many nations there was no
king like him.[n] He was loved by his God,[o]
and God made him king over all Israel,
but even he was led into sin by foreign
women.[p] 27Must we hear now that you
too are doing all this terrible wickedness
and are being unfaithful to our God by
marrying[q] foreign women?"
28One of the sons of Joiada son of

13:15 [f] Ex 20:8-11; 34:21; Dt 5:12-15; Ne 10:31
13:16 [g] Ne 10:31
13:18 [h] Ne 10:31; Jer 17:21-23
13:19 [i] Lev 23:32
13:22 [j] Ge 8:1; Ne 12:30
13:23 [k] Ezr 9:1-2; Mal 2:11 [l] ver 1; Ne 10:30
13:25 [m] Ezr 10:5
13:26 [n] 1Ki 3:13; 2Ch 1:12 [o] 2Sa 12:25 [p] 1Ki 11:3
13:27 [q] Ezr 9:14; 10:2

---

house of Yahweh and conducted business as if the worship of Yahweh was unimportant.

13:17–22 The second address elicits a second question: "What is this wicked thing you are doing?" (v. 17). The focus of Nehemiah's anger, the fish trade from Tyre on the Sabbath (v. 16), combines the violation of the Sabbath law along with trading with the non-Israelite peoples of the land. In conclusion, the purpose of the Sabbath reform is made explicitly clear: "in order to keep the Sabbath day holy" (v. 22).

13:23–27 The tempo continues unabated and returns to a well-worn theme. The oath focuses on the exchange of "daughters" and "sons" (v. 25) and essentially repeats the oath that had already been taken in 10:30. Nehemiah's final question to them underscores their "terrible wickedness" and their unfaithfulness "to our God by marrying foreign women" (v. 27).

13:28–31 The final round of reform focuses on priestly leadership, starting at the highest level. Nehemiah holds both the high priest and the culprit in equal contempt of God's law. The reference to the "covenant of the priesthood" (v. 29) is unique but may very well deal with the covenantal obligations pertaining to them within the broader covenant of Sinai.

Nehemiah concludes his account with the focus on what ultimately mattered most to him: the preservation of the sanctity of Zion, including its leadership. All these tasks were, of course, supposed to be overseen by the priests and Levites themselves. However, in light of the catastrophic failure witnessed upon his return, he, as a governor and non-Levite, took it upon himself to carry out the maintenance of the worship in Jerusalem, the holy city.

In the context of this tremendous (and lonely) responsibility comes the final "remember" prayer (v. 31). Nehemiah thus ends his account on a wonderfully hopeful note. Nehemiah's prayer has been answered in ways far greater than he could have ever imagined.

13:4–31 The call to remember the zeal of Nehemiah is also our call. We want to be remembered for what we have accomplished for the Lord. We, too, uphold the sanctity of Zion as the will of God for our lives (see 1Th 4:3). Now, however, Christ is the one who makes us holy by faith in him (Ac 26:18).

The human zeal of Nehemiah ultimately falls short, as did that of Saul of Tarsus (Gal 1:14) and everyone else who thinks building the kingdom of God is accomplished through our own willpower, aptitudes, or an unhealthy focus on

Eliashib[r] the high priest was son-in-law to Sanballat[s] the Horonite. And I drove him away from me.

29Remember[t] them, my God, because they defiled the priestly office and the covenant of the priesthood and of the Levites.

30So I purified the priests and the Levites of everything foreign,[u] and assigned them duties, each to his own task. 31I also made provision for contributions of wood[v] at designated times, and for the firstfruits.

Remember[w] me with favor, my God.

13:28 [r] Ezr 10:24 [s] Ne 2:10
13:29 [t] Ne 6:14
13:30 [u] Ne 10:30
13:31 [v] Ne 10:34 [w] ver 14,22; Ge 8:1

ritual (see Mt 23). The sanctifying process of Zion finds its fulfillment, as our zeal for God's people and the establishment of his kingdom, in Christ alone. He alone is our sanctification (1Co 1:30), and he is the one at work in us to do and move according to his good and perfect will. We offer ourselves as "living sacrifice[s]," which is our "true and proper worship" (Ro 12:1-2). At the cross, Jesus reveals for us the weightier matters of the law: displaying self-sacrifice, love of enemies, and self-emptying (Php 2), rather than the pursuit of ambition to prop up our own pride.

Christ's work on the cross was not a senseless act of violence; rather, it was a self-sacrifice by God the Son who chose to offer himself up as an atoning sacrifice for the despondent people of all time—Zion in Yehud, in our days, and in the future—until he returns to establish his kingdom. Thus, apart from Christ's work on the cross, we will not understand the ruthlessness of God's holiness and his complete intolerance for the existence of sin in his presence (including Ezra's actions to break up marriages and Nehemiah's advocacy to separate).

However complex these ethical questions get, we do know that at the cross, Jesus Christ, as a perfect man and an innocent individual, experienced the injustice of a violent death. Christ tasted injustice; therefore we put our trust in him and in his vindication against all injustice.

Jesus' resurrection is the beginning of the restoration of justice that will be fulfilled when he returns. He will judge everyone according to what he or she has done (Ro 14:10). Those who have placed their faith in him will be found justified (whose justified state will be justified by their just actions) and those who continued to reject his gracious offer of salvation will find themselves permanently outside the gates of the holy city (Rev 22:15).

Thus, as we, too, are the guardians of Zion, we continue to open the gates of the city at daytime, as it were, so that whosoever believes in him "shall not perish but have eternal life" (Jn 3:16).

Esther

Author: Unknown

Audience: The Jewish people

Date: Sometime after 460 BC

Theme: God providentially positions Esther and Mordecai to bring the Jews of Persia deliverance from their enemies.

PERSPECTIVE

Esther was a powerful woman, and her story is without a doubt both an inspiration and one of the great teaching resources of the church. What is the key to unlocking the great lessons of this book? It is this: Read correctly, the lead character of the book of Esther is not even Esther, but God. Esther should definitely get an Oscar® nomination as best supporting actress, but the conclusions one draws from the book don't work unless God plays the lead.

To be sure, this reading is a bit difficult to advocate since God is not mentioned anywhere in the book. Martin Luther, in fact, challenged the book's proper place in the canon because of this fact. But God is the lead character, no doubt. The great lesson of Esther is that it is the story of God's keeping promises in spite of the political configuration of the world. It is not an end-justifies-the-means argument. It is not a model of how a powerful woman should work her way up the corporate ladder. It is not a handbook on Christian leadership.

The story of Esther is perfect guidance for us when we find ourselves in a situation where right and wrong are not clearly defined. It is perfect inspiration for us when we find ourselves in situations we never sought, never planned for, and don't think we have the gifts to succeed at. It tells us what to do: Trust these situations to the Lord and move on.

There are no books, secular or biblical, that give us step-by-step procedures for what to do in tough situations. But all sixty-six books of the Bible rest their cases on the fact that God is the lead character of the universe, and that our initial response to that and to all the situations confronting us is prayerful acknowledgment that God rules.

Reading Esther

The use of poetic license in biblical narrative to interpret the significance of the events told does not compromise the integrity of Scripture. Some of the questions scholars have and "problems" they perceive with the book of Esther arise because we value historical accuracy and precision where the author valued poetic license for the purpose of interpretation. Those of us who rightly insist on the historical veracity of

	1400 BC	1300	1200	1100	1000	900	800	700	600	500	400
Fall of Jerusalem (586 BC)									♦		
Persia's conquest of Babylon (539 BC)										♦	
First return of exiles to Jerusalem (538 BC)										♦	
Xerxes' reign in Persia (486–465 BC)										■	
Esther becomes queen of Persia (479 BC)										♦	
Second return to Jerusalem under Ezra (458 BC)										♦	
Third return to Jerusalem under Nehemiah (444 BC)										♦	
Jerusalem's wall rebuilt (444 BC)										♦	
Book of Esther written (c. 460–350 BC)										▬	▬

biblical events must also fully appreciate the literary genre and the author's use of poetic license, and not press the story historically where the author did not intend his readers to do so. One ought to read the book of Esther as a short story from history; it can be read in about half an hour.

Key Verses

"If you remain silent at this time, relief and deliverance for the Jews will arise from another place, but you and your father's family will perish. And who knows but that you have come to your royal position for such a time as this?" . . . "When this is done, I will go to the king, even though it is against the law. And if I perish, I perish."

—Esther 4:14, 16

TAKING THE NEXT STEPS

The book of Esther contains a remarkable story of God's deliverance of his people from a severe crisis that threatened to destroy them completely. Even though the word "God" or "Lord" does not appear in this book, God is very much behind the scenes, guiding the affairs in Susa by his providence. The means God used to accomplish this were rather unusual: He took two people (Mordecai and Esther) at a very low point in their spiritual lives, and through spiritual growth, enabled them to function as saviors of his people.

This story in the Bible sheds light on some of the basic principles on which God operates in our lives. (1) God is always behind the scenes in our lives, controlling the things that happen. (2) Coincidences in our lives are not accidents but are God's way of demonstrating to us that he is present and that he is having his way in our lives. (3) God can take even our sins and mistakes and use them in his service. (4) God is faithful to his promises; even though there is no reference to this in Esther, it is obvious that God's promise throughout the OT to bring a Savior into the world stands behind his decision to save the Jews from annihilation.

WHAT TO LOOK FOR IN ESTHER

- Vashti's removal as queen (ch. 1)
- Esther chosen as the new queen (ch. 2)
- Haman's plot to destroy the Jews (ch. 3)
- Esther's decision to plead before the king (chs. 4–5; 7)
- Jewish victory and the feast of Purim (chs. 8–9)

Queen Vashti Deposed

1 This is what happened during the time
of Xerxes,[a][a] the Xerxes who ruled over
127 provinces[b] stretching from India to
Cush[b]:[c] 2 At that time King Xerxes reigned
from his royal throne in the citadel of
Susa,[d] 3 and in the third year of his reign
he gave a banquet[e] for all his nobles and
officials. The military leaders of Persia
and Media, the princes, and the nobles
of the provinces were present.
4 For a full 180 days he displayed the
vast wealth of his kingdom and the
splendor and glory of his majesty. 5 When
these days were over, the king gave a
banquet, lasting seven days,[f] in the enclosed garden[g] of the king's palace, for all
the people from the least to the greatest
who were in the citadel of Susa. 6 The
garden had hangings of white and blue
linen, fastened with cords of white linen
and purple material to silver rings on
marble pillars. There were couches[h] of
gold and silver on a mosaic pavement of
porphyry, marble, mother-of-pearl and
other costly stones. 7 Wine was served in
goblets of gold, each one different from
the other, and the royal wine was abundant, in keeping with the king's liberality.[i] 8 By the king's command each guest
was allowed to drink with no restrictions,
for the king instructed all the wine stewards to serve each man what he wished.
9 Queen Vashti also gave a banquet[j] for
the women in the royal palace of King
Xerxes.
10 On the seventh day, when King Xerxes was in high spirits[k] from wine,[l] he
commanded the seven eunuchs who
served him — Mehuman, Biztha, Harbona,[m] Bigtha, Abagtha, Zethar and
Karkas — 11 to bring[n] before him Queen
Vashti, wearing her royal crown, in order to display her beauty[o] to the people
and nobles, for she was lovely to look at.
12 But when the attendants delivered the
king's command, Queen Vashti refused
to come. Then the king became furious
and burned with anger.[p]
13 Since it was customary for the king
to consult experts in matters of law and
justice, he spoke with the wise men who
understood the times[q] 14 and were closest
to the king — Karshena, Shethar, Adma-
tha, Tarshish, Meres, Marsena and Memukan, the seven nobles[r] of Persia and
Media who had special access to the king
and were highest in the kingdom.
15 "According to law, what must be done
to Queen Vashti?" he asked. "She has not
obeyed the command of King Xerxes that
the eunuchs have taken to her."
16 Then Memukan replied in the presence of the king and the nobles, "Queen
Vashti has done wrong, not only against
the king but also against all the nobles

1:1 [a] Ezr 4:6; Da 9:1 [b] Est 9:30; Da 3:2; 6:1 [c] Est 8:9
1:2 [d] Ezr 4:9; Ne 1:1; Est 2:8
1:3 [e] 1Ki 3:15; Est 2:18
1:5 [f] Jdg 14:17 [g] 2Ki 21:18; Est 7:7-8
1:6 [h] Est 7:8; Eze 23:41; Am 3:12; 6:4
1:7 [i] Est 2:18; Da 5:2
1:9 [j] 1Ki 3:15
1:10 [k] Jdg 16:25; Ru 3:7 [l] Ge 14:18; Est 3:15; 5:6; 7:2; Pr 31:4-7; Da 5:1-4 [m] Est 7:9
1:11 [n] SS 2:4 [o] Ps 45:11; Eze 16:14
1:12 [p] Ge 39:19; Est 2:21; 7:7; Pr 19:12
1:13 [q] 1Ch 12:32; Jer 10:7; Da 2:12
1:14 [r] 2Ki 25:19; Ezr 7:14

Est 1:11 ❖ Where do we see objectification of women continue in today's society? How might Christians stand against this?

[a] *1* Hebrew *Ahasuerus*; here and throughout Esther [b] *1* That is, the upper Nile region

1:1-3 Xerxes, the Persian king who reigned from 486 to 465 BC, was known for his consolidation of the Persian Empire.

1:4-8 The might and glory of the Persian Empire were at Xerxes' disposal in order to reward those who would remain loyal to his cause and obedient to his command.

APPLICATION ✜ **1:1-8** Through the centuries and around the world, political and military might have been glorified as the epitome of a nation's strength. America and other Western powers must take heed that, though perhaps founded for Christian liberty, their might and power are nonetheless worldly might and power, subject to the continuing grace and favor of God.

1:9-12 Because Xerxes was displaying his power and might in order to solidify the loyalty of his nobles as he went to war against Greece, the refusal of his own queen to obey his command must have been extremely embarrassing. He needed his men to obey his commands, but in his own palace he could not even get his own wife to obey.

✜ **1:9-12** Like Vashti, people today unwittingly make decisions that have long-reaching consequences. These events may be completely secular and perhaps made by people who give Christ no thought. Nonetheless, through them God is moving all of history forward to accomplish all that must happen before the return of his Son, Jesus Christ, the true King of kings.

1:13-15 What began as an issue between two people suddenly is escalated into a crisis of empire-wide proportions.

1:16-20 Vashti is assumed to have such influence on the women of the empire that when they hear of her disobedience, they will similarly respond to their husbands. Therefore, the king must make sure that these women also hear that Vashti has been deposed as a result of her insolence.

PEOPLE TO KNOW // XERXES

ESTHER 1:1–22: Xerxes was the king of Persia during the time of Esther. While he was king of a mighty empire, Xerxes seemed incapable of making any decision on his own.

Xerxes banished his wife, Vashti, after she refused to be paraded in front of a group of his guests at a banquet (of course, the sentence of banishment was not Xerxes' own idea). His advisers then told him to make a search for a new queen, which led him to crown Esther, a Jewish woman who had kept her nationality a secret (Est 2:17).

Esther's cousin, Mordecai, learned that Xerxes' top official, Haman, planned to have all the Jews killed. Haman told Xerxes to enact this decree, and of course Xerxes blindly followed Haman's advice. Mordecai asked Esther to speak to Xerxes on behalf of the Jews. Esther knew, however, that anyone who approached the king uninvited could be sentenced to death if the king did not welcome them. Summoning her courage, Esther went before Xerxes, who was pleased to see her.

Esther revealed to Xerxes that she was Jewish and that Haman had decreed that all her people be killed. Incensed, Xerxes had Haman killed and gave Mordecai his position.

APPLICATION Xerxes provides a negative example of someone easily manipulated. Xerxes did not seem to be able to make a decision on his own, likely because he didn't know what he believed to be right and wrong.

When we know what we believe and act consistently within those beliefs, we can stand firm against the lies of the enemy. By immersing ourselves in the Word of God and listening to the Holy Spirit in our hearts, we can cultivate a firm foundation of faith in Christ, an understanding of the will of God, and we can then live a life of conviction based on that foundation.

and the peoples of all the provinces of
King Xerxes. 17For the queen's conduct
will become known to all the women,
and so they will despise their husbands
and say, 'King Xerxes commanded Queen
Vashti to be brought before him, but she
would not come.' 18This very day the Persian and Median women of the nobility
who have heard about the queen's conduct will respond to all the king's nobles
in the same way. There will be no end of
disrespect and discord.[s]
19"Therefore, if it pleases the king,[t]
let him issue a royal decree and let it be
written in the laws of Persia and Media,
which cannot be repealed,[u] that Vashti is
never again to enter the presence of King
Xerxes. Also let the king give her royal
position to someone else who is better
than she. 20Then when the king's edict
is proclaimed throughout all his vast
realm, all the women will respect their
husbands, from the least to the greatest."
21The king and his nobles were pleased
with this advice, so the king did as Memukan proposed. 22He sent dispatches
to all parts of the kingdom, to each province in its own script and to each people
in their own language,[v] proclaiming that
every man should be ruler over his own
household, using his native tongue.

Esther Made Queen

2 Later when King Xerxes' fury had
subsided,[w] he remembered Vashti
and what she had done and what he had
decreed about her. 2Then the king's personal attendants proposed, "Let a search
be made for beautiful young virgins for
the king. 3Let the king appoint commissioners in every province of his realm to
bring all these beautiful young women

1:18 [s] Pr 19:13; 27:15
1:19 [t] Ecc 8:4 [u] Est 8:8; Da 6:8,12
1:22 [v] Ne 13:24; Est 8:9; Eph 5:22-24; 1Ti 2:12
2:1 [w] Est 1:19-20; 7:10

1:20–22 Xerxes and the seven nobles find this reasoning to be sound, and so the king issues a decree to this effect.

1:13–22 The scene in vv. 13–22 is an inside look at just what makes the world go 'round. Law and justice may be the public ideal of every great government, but people in power, compelled by their own fears and anxieties, all too often abuse the power with which they have been entrusted. Absolute power held by flawed leaders is a terrifying scenario.

2:1–11 Vashti refused to come to King Xerxes in the third year of his reign, 483 BC. Esther was made queen in the seventh year of his reign, 479 BC (vv. 16–17). During the intervening years Xerxes was off fighting a disastrous war with Greece. Shortly after his return from Greece, Esther was chosen as his new consort.

into the harem at the citadel of Susa. Let
them be placed under the care of Hegai,
the king's eunuch, who is in charge of
the women; and let beauty treatments
be given to them. 4Then let the young
woman who pleases the king be queen
instead of Vashti." This advice appealed
to the king, and he followed it.
5Now there was in the citadel of Susa
a Jew of the tribe of Benjamin, named
Mordecai son of Jair, the son of Shimei,
the son of Kish,[x] 6who had been carried
into exile from Jerusalem by Nebuchadnezzar king of Babylon, among those
taken captive with Jehoiachin[a][y] king of
Judah.[z] 7Mordecai had a cousin named
Hadassah, whom he had brought up because she had neither father nor mother.
This young woman, who was also known
as Esther,[a] had a lovely figure[b] and was
beautiful. Mordecai had taken her as
his own daughter when her father and
mother died.

2:5 [x] 1Sa 9:1; Est 3:2
2:6 [y] 2Ki 24:6, 15; 2Ch 36:10, 20 [z] Da 1:1-5; 5:13
2:7 [a] Ge 41:45 [b] Ge 39:6
2:8 [c] ver 3,15; Ne 1:1; Est 1:2; Da 8:2
2:9 [d] Ge 39:21 [e] ver 3,12; Ge 37:3; 1Sa 9:22-24; 2Ki 25:30; Eze 16:9-13; Da 1:5
2:10 [f] ver 20

Est 2:7 ❖ How might we, like Mordecai, care for those who have been beaten down by tragic life circumstances?

8When the king's order and edict had
been proclaimed, many young wom-
en were brought to the citadel of Susa[c]
and put under the care of Hegai. Esther
also was taken to the king's palace and
entrusted to Hegai, who had charge of
the harem. 9She pleased him and won
his favor.[d] Immediately he provided her
with her beauty treatments and special
food.[e] He assigned to her seven female
attendants selected from the king's palace and moved her and her attendants
into the best place in the harem.
10Esther had not revealed her nationality and family background, because
Mordecai had forbidden her to do so.[f]

[a] 6 Hebrew *Jeconiah,* a variant of *Jehoiachin*

2:5–6 The author's point in mentioning the exile of the king of Judah is to associate Mordecai with the exile of the Israelites from the promised land, providing a historical context within which to understand the events that are about to transpire.
2:7 The name Esther may be the Persian word for "star," or it may be a Hebrew transliteration of Ishtar, the name of the Babylonian goddess of love and war.
2:8 Esther "was taken" into the harem, regardless of how she felt about it. The use of the passive voice is appropriate in this story, for it expresses life from the perspective of being caught up in and swept along by circumstances beyond one's control.
2:10 Mordecai commands Esther to conceal her "nationality and family background," even though

THE ANCIENT PERSIAN EMPIRE

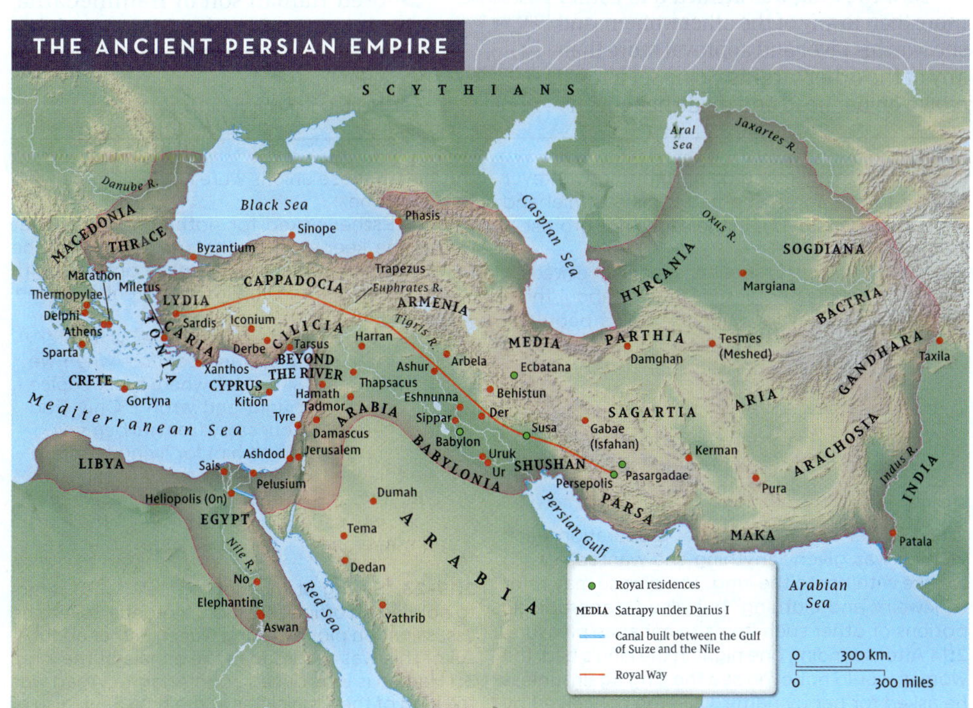

11Every day he walked back and forth
near the courtyard of the harem to find
out how Esther was and what was happening to her.
12Before a young woman's turn came
to go in to King Xerxes, she had to complete twelve months of beauty treatments prescribed for the women, six
months with oil of myrrh and six with
perfumes[g] and cosmetics. 13And this is
how she would go to the king: Anything
she wanted was given her to take with
her from the harem to the king's palace.
14In the evening she would go there and
in the morning return to another part of
the harem to the care of Shaashgaz, the
king's eunuch who was in charge of the
concubines.[h] She would not return to the
king unless he was pleased with her and
summoned her by name.[i]
15When the turn came for Esther (the
young woman Mordecai had adopted,
the daughter of his uncle Abihail[j]) to go
to the king,[k] she asked for nothing other
than what Hegai, the king's eunuch who
was in charge of the harem, suggested.
And Esther won the favor[l] of everyone
who saw her. 16She was taken to King
Xerxes in the royal residence in the tenth
month, the month of Tebeth, in the seventh year of his reign.
17Now the king was attracted to Esther
more than to any of the other women, and
she won his favor and approval more than
any of the other virgins. So he set a royal
crown on her head and made her queen[m]
instead of Vashti. 18And the king gave a
great banquet,[n] Esther's banquet, for all
his nobles and officials.[o] He proclaimed
a holiday throughout the provinces and
distributed gifts with royal liberality.[p]

2:12 [g] Pr 27:9; SS 1:3; Isa 3:24
2:14 [h] 1Ki 11:3; SS 6:8; Da 5:2 [i] Est 4:11
2:15 [j] Est 9:29 [k] Ps 45:14 [l] Ge 18:3; 30:27; Est 5:8
2:17 [m] Est 1:11; Eze 16:9-13
2:18 [n] 1Ki 3:15; Est 1:3 [o] Ge 40:20 [p] Est 1:7
2:19 [q] ver 21; Est 3:2; 4:2; 5:13
2:20 [r] ver 10
2:21 [s] Ge 40:2; Est 6:2 [t] Est 1:12; 3:5; 5:9; 7:7
2:23 [u] Ge 40:19; Ps 7:14-16; Pr 26:27 [v] Est 6:1; 10:2
3:1 [w] ver 10; Ex 17:8-16; Nu 24:7; Dt 25:17-19; 1Sa 14:48; Est 5:11

Mordecai Uncovers a Conspiracy

19When the virgins were assembled a
second time, Mordecai was sitting at the
king's gate.[q] 20But Esther had kept secret
her family background and nationality
just as Mordecai had told her to do, for
she continued to follow Mordecai's instructions as she had done when he was
bringing her up.[r]
21During the time Mordecai was sitting
at the king's gate, Bigthana[a] and Teresh,
two of the king's officers[s] who guarded
the doorway, became angry[t] and conspired to assassinate King Xerxes. 22But
Mordecai found out about the plot and
told Queen Esther, who in turn reported
it to the king, giving credit to Mordecai.
23And when the report was investigated
and found to be true, the two officials
were impaled[u] on poles. All this was recorded in the book of the annals[v] in the
presence of the king.

Haman's Plot to Destroy the Jews

3 After these events, King Xerxes honored Haman son of Hammedatha,
the Agagite,[w] elevating him and giving
him a seat of honor higher than that of

[a] *21* Hebrew *Bigthan,* a variant of *Bigthana*

---

it would certainly mean compromising whatever fidelity to the Torah she had. Unlike Daniel and his friends (Da 1:8–17), Esther does not protest.

2:1-11 The story is not about conflict between any two hostile peoples; rather, it is about the hostility of the world against God's people. Against all odds, in some inscrutable and mysterious way, the events of human history work to fulfill the promises of the covenant the Lord made with his people at Sinai. While God may be good to all his creatures in general, he is in a special relationship of protection and preservation with his covenant people.

2:12-13 After twelve months of preparation, each woman was given "anything she wanted" (v. 13) to take with her to the king. The phrase may refer to jewelry and clothing, but also to aphrodisiac potions or other such items to enhance pleasure.
2:14 After spending one night in the king's bed, the woman would not even see the king again, unless he asked for her by name. Children conceived by the king in these unions were not legitimate heirs to the throne.
2:15-18 Esther asked for nothing except what Hegai, the keeper of the harem, suggested she take with her. Esther's deference contrasts with Vashti's defiance and implies a different outcome.

2:12-18 This episode from Esther's life offers great encouragement and comfort when we find ourselves in situations where every choice is an odd mix of right and wrong. Only God knows the end of our story from its beginning. We are responsible to him for living faithfully in obedience to his word in every situation as we best know how. Esther's story shows that we can entrust our circumstances to the Lord and move on.

2:19-23 "Sitting at the king's gate" (v. 19) refers to holding an official position. Mordecai foiled the assassination plot by telling Queen Esther about it. All of this was recorded in the annals of the king.
3:1 Haman is introduced as an Agagite. Agag was the king of the Amalekites at the time Saul (also of

PEOPLE TO KNOW // **ESTHER**

ESTHER 4:12–16: Esther was a Jewish woman living in Persia. She was raised by her cousin, Mordecai (Est 2:7). They were from the tribe of Benjamin.

When King Xerxes conducted a search for a new queen after banishing Queen Vashti, beautiful Esther was taken into the king's palace. At Mordecai's bidding, she did not reveal that she was a Jew. Of all the women brought to him, Xerxes favored Esther and made her queen of Persia.

One of Xerxes' officials, Haman, hated Mordecai, and this hatred extended to all Jews. Haman's anger led him to convince Xerxes to decree that all Jews were to be killed (Est 3:6). Xerxes, of course, did not know his own queen was Jewish.

Mordecai persuaded Esther to intercede with the king on behalf of her people—a scary task, as anyone who approached the king uninvited could be sentenced to death. Mordecai told Esther that perhaps the reason she had become queen was "for such a time as this" (Est 4:14).

After a series of events, Esther revealed her Jewish identity and told Xerxes how Haman had plotted the destruction of her people. Incensed, Xerxes had Haman executed. Furthermore, at Esther's bidding, he issued a new decree that the Jews could defend themselves on what would have been the day of their destruction (Est 8:11).

APPLICATION God delivered the Jews through the bravery and obedience of Esther. This young woman found herself in a position of power and influence. She could have chosen to spend the rest of her life living at ease in the palace. But she risked everything to stand up for the cause of justice, and her actions helped to save an entire group of people.

We need to obey God even when it is risky. Esther's bravery was rewarded. But as the martyrs of the church prove, not every brave person will have a story of freedom and success. But the actions and choices we make do influence the world. We need to choose wisely.

I and my attendants will fast as you do. When this is done, I will go to the king, even though it is against the law. And if I perish, I perish."[h]

17So Mordecai went away and carried out all of Esther's instructions.

Esther's Request to the King

5 On the third day Esther put on her royal robes[i] and stood in the inner court of the palace, in front of the king's[j] hall. The king was sitting on his royal throne in the hall, facing the entrance.
2When he saw Queen Esther standing in the court, he was pleased with her and held out to her the gold scepter that was in his hand. So Esther approached and touched the tip of the scepter.[k]

3Then the king asked, "What is it, Queen Esther? What is your request? Even up to half the kingdom,[l] it will be given you."

4"If it pleases the king," replied Esther, "let the king, together with Haman, come today to a banquet I have prepared for him."

5"Bring Haman at once," the king said, "so that we may do what Esther asks."

So the king and Haman went to the banquet Esther had prepared. 6As they were drinking wine,[m] the king again asked Esther, "Now what is your petition?

4:16 [h] Ge 43:14
5:1 [i] Est 4:16; Eze 16:13 [j] Est 6:4; Pr 21:1
5:2 [k] Est 4:11; 8:4; Pr 21:1
5:3 [l] Est 7:2; Da 5:16; Mk 6:23
5:6 [m] Est 1:10

continuous sequence of defining moments throughout life as we daily face decisions that demand we choose either to identify ourselves with Christ, by obedience to his Word, or to live as pagans in that moment.

5:1 Esther does not just try to make herself beautiful for her uninvited audience with the king; she appears before him in her "royal robes." At the same time as she decides to identify with her people, she also claims her authority and power as the Queen of Persia.

5:2–3 For the first time in the story, Esther is directly addressed as "Queen Esther." The king was disposed to be generous in meeting her request.

5:4–7 Esther now has Xerxes and Haman, the two most powerful men in the Persian Empire, responding to her initiative. While the king is drinking wine, he again asks Esther why she appeared uninvited in her royal robes in the throne room. Using a delay tactic, Esther again asks only that Haman and the king come to a second banquet on the next day. The suspense is heightened—not only for the king but also for the reader.

It will be given you. And what is your
request? Even up to half the kingdom,[n]
it will be granted."[o]
7Esther replied, "My petition and my
request is this: 8If the king regards me
with favor[p] and if it pleases the king to
grant my petition and fulfill my request,
let the king and Haman come tomorrow
to the banquet[q] I will prepare for them.
Then I will answer the king's question."

Haman's Rage Against Mordecai

9Haman went out that day happy and
in high spirits. But when he saw Mordecai at the king's gate and observed that
he neither rose nor showed fear in his
presence, he was filled with rage[r] against
Mordecai.[s] 10Nevertheless, Haman restrained himself and went home.
Calling together his friends and Zeresh,[t] his wife, 11Haman boasted[u] to them
about his vast wealth, his many sons,[v]
and all the ways the king had honored
him and how he had elevated him above
the other nobles and officials. 12"And
that's not all," Haman added. "I'm the
only person[w] Queen Esther invited to
accompany the king to the banquet she
gave. And she has invited me along with
the king tomorrow. 13But all this gives
me no satisfaction as long as I see that
Jew Mordecai sitting at the king's gate.[x]"
14His wife Zeresh and all his friends
said to him, "Have a pole set up, reaching
to a height of fifty cubits,[a][y] and ask the
king in the morning to have Mordecai
impaled[z] on it. Then go with the king
to the banquet and enjoy yourself." This
suggestion delighted Haman, and he had
the pole set up.

5:6 [n] Mk 6:23 [o] Est 7:2; 9:12
5:8 [p] Est 2:15; 7:3; 8:5 [q] 1Ki 3:15; Est 6:14
5:9 [r] Est 2:21; Pr 14:17 [s] Est 3:3,5
5:10 [t] Est 6:13
5:11 [u] Pr 13:16 [v] Est 9:7-10,13
5:12 [w] Job 22:29; Pr 16:18; 29:23
5:13 [x] Est 2:19
5:14 [y] Est 7:9 [z] Ezr 6:11; Est 6:4
6:1 [a] Da 2:1; 6:18 [b] Est 2:23; 10:2
6:3 [c] Ecc 9:13-16
6:8 [d] Ge 41:42; Isa 52:1

Est 5:9–13 ❖ Why is boasting such an easy sin to fall into? What does God think of those who boast in their own efforts (see Jas 4:16)?

Est 6:6–13 ❖ Where have we seen God humble the proud and raise the humble (see 1Sa 2:7–8)? How can we foster a spirit of true humility?

Mordecai Honored

6 That night the king could not sleep;[a]
so he ordered the book of the chronicles,[b] the record of his reign, to be brought
in and read to him. 2It was found recorded
there that Mordecai had exposed Bigthana and Teresh, two of the king's officers
who guarded the doorway, who had conspired to assassinate King Xerxes.
3"What honor and recognition has Mordecai received for this?" the king asked.
"Nothing has been done for him,"[c] his
attendants answered.
4The king said, "Who is in the court?"
Now Haman had just entered the outer
court of the palace to speak to the king
about impaling Mordecai on the pole he
had set up for him.
5His attendants answered, "Haman is
standing in the court."
"Bring him in," the king ordered.
6When Haman entered, the king asked
him, "What should be done for the man
the king delights to honor?"
Now Haman thought to himself, "Who
is there that the king would rather hon-
or than me?" 7So he answered the king,
"For the man the king delights to honor,
8have them bring a royal robe[d] the king

[a] *14* That is, about 75 feet or about 23 meters

5:9–14 When Mordecai again refuses to bow, Haman plots his revenge against Mordecai himself by building a gallows of extraordinary size—75 feet high—on which to display Mordecai's lifeless body. He does this not realizing that its size is the measure of his own pride.

5:1–14 We have the benefit of knowing the end of the story and how Esther's decision led her to power and fame. But at the time Esther made that decision, she did not know how her story would end.

Like Esther, we too need a transformation of our character so that we may no longer live as pagans. Without this transformation of character by the Holy Spirit, none of us can attain the full potential of our humanity. Without the work of God's Spirit, we cannot be the persons God created us to be, nor can we attain fully to the purpose of our lives as agents of God's redemptive work in history.

6:1–3 While Haman plots Mordecai's outrageous death, the king plans to honor Mordecai's faithful service. "The book of the chronicles" (v. 1) was the official record of the Persian kings. From this official transcript the king would draw up a list of those who were to be rewarded for faithful service to the throne.

6:4–7 Haman's intention is foiled at the moment he is to tell the king about his plan for Mordecai's death. He is stopped short by the king's question, and we watch as his pride swells in this moment. But his expectation of honor will soon be radically reversed.

6:7–9 Haman's request was intended both to honor

PEOPLE TO KNOW // MORDECAI

ESTHER 6:1–13: Mordecai was Esther's cousin who raised her after her parents died (Est 2:7). When Esther was taken to the palace and selected as the new queen of Persia, Mordecai cautioned her not to reveal her Jewish nationality (Est 2:20).

The story of Esther portrays Mordecai as upright and loyal to Esther and the king. However, he refused to honor Xerxes' chief official, Haman, by bowing down to him. Haman was so furious that he convinced Xerxes to decree that all Jews should be put to death.

Mordecai pleaded with Esther to go before Xerxes on behalf of her people, telling her that perhaps she had become queen "for such a time as this" (Est 4:14). Esther bravely approached the king and invited him to a banquet with Haman. Haman left the banquet in high spirits, until he saw Mordecai and remembered his hatred. Haman set up a pole to impale Mordecai on, intending to ask the king's permission to kill Mordecai the next morning.

When Esther revealed to Xerxes that the people Haman planned to kill were her own, Xerxes sentenced Haman to be impaled on the very gallows Haman had set up for Mordecai. Mordecai was then raised to Haman's position in the kingdom, where he acted quickly to preserve his people.

APPLICATION ✣ Mordecai showed compassion and bravery. He raised his cousin as his own child and cared for her. He aided her in her position of power, offering advice and guidance. God calls all his children to care for those in need (Mt 25:35–40). Further, like Mordecai, God calls believers to stand up to injustice and to give voice to the cause of people who are oppressed. Honoring God includes defending the powerless and the marginalized.

has worn and a horse[e] the king has ridden, one with a royal crest placed on its
head. 9Then let the robe and horse be
entrusted to one of the king's most noble
princes. Let them robe the man the king
delights to honor, and lead him on the
horse through the city streets, proclaiming before him, 'This is what is done for
the man the king delights to honor![f]' "
10"Go at once," the king commanded Haman. "Get the robe and the horse
and do just as you have suggested for
Mordecai the Jew, who sits at the king's
gate. Do not neglect anything you have
recommended."
11So Haman got[g] the robe and the
horse. He robed Mordecai, and led him
on horseback through the city streets,
proclaiming before him, "This is what
is done for the man the king delights
to honor!"
12Afterward Mordecai returned to the
king's gate. But Haman rushed home,
with his head covered[h] in grief, 13and
told Zeresh[i] his wife and all his friends
everything that had happened to him.
His advisers and his wife Zeresh said to
him, "Since Mordecai, before whom your
downfall[j] has started, is of Jewish origin,
you cannot stand against him — you will
surely come to ruin!" 14While they were
still talking with him, the king's eunuchs
arrived and hurried Haman away to the
banquet[k] Esther had prepared.

6:8 [e] 1Ki 1:33
6:9 [f] Ge 41:43
6:11 [g] Ge 41:42
6:12 [h] 2Sa 15:30; Jer 14:3,4; Mic 3:7
6:13 [i] Est 5:10 [j] Ps 57:6; Pr 26:27; 28:18
6:14 [k] 1Ki 3:15; Est 5:8

the king and to reinforce Haman's relationship with him. For Haman no other honor was left to him but to partake of the king's own power, prestige, and stature. To have such an intimate gesture bestowed instead on Mordecai, the Jew, is a crushing humiliation. With this account, the full extent of Haman's tragic miscalculation begins to emerge.

✣ **6:1–14** The author of Esther implies a consistency in God's rule of human history that is based on his word, not on circumstances. Regardless of how circumstances appear, God is ruling history according to the ancient covenant he made with Israel at Sinai (Ex 19). God's promise to Israel made at the beginning of their nation still stood.

God was not capricious like the false gods of the pagans. He was not locked in some struggle with other supposed deities that gave him control only on certain days or in certain situations.

What a great God we serve! Our God is so great, so powerful, that he can work without miracles through the ordinary events of billions of human lives through millennia of time to accomplish his eternal purposes and ancient promises. He can, and he does, and he will.

Haman Impaled

7 So the king and Haman went to Queen Esther's banquet,[l] 2and as they were drinking wine[m] on the second day, the king again asked, "Queen Esther, what is your petition? It will be given you. What is your request? Even up to half the kingdom,[n] it will be granted.[o]"

3Then Queen Esther answered, "If I have found favor[p] with you, Your Majesty, and if it pleases you, grant me my life — this is my petition. And spare my people — this is my request. 4For I and my people have been sold to be destroyed, killed and annihilated.[q] If we had merely been sold as male and female slaves, I would have kept quiet, because no such distress would justify disturbing the king.[a]"

5King Xerxes asked Queen Esther, "Who is he? Where is he — the man who has dared to do such a thing?"

6Esther said, "An adversary and enemy! This vile Haman!"

Then Haman was terrified before the king and queen. 7The king got up in a rage,[r] left his wine and went out into the palace garden.[s] But Haman, realizing that the king had already decided his fate,[t] stayed behind to beg Queen Esther for his life.

8Just as the king returned from the palace garden to the banquet hall, Haman was falling on the couch[u] where Esther was reclining.[v]

The king exclaimed, "Will he even molest the queen while she is with me in the house?"[w]

As soon as the word left the king's mouth, they covered Haman's face.[x] 9Then Harbona,[y] one of the eunuchs attending the king, said, "A pole reaching to a height of fifty cubits[b][z] stands by Haman's house. He had it set up for Mordecai, who spoke up to help the king."

The king said, "Impale him on it!"[a] 10So they impaled Haman[b] on the pole[c] he had set up for Mordecai.[d] Then the king's fury subsided.[e]

7:1 [l] Ge 40:20-22; Mt 22:1-14
7:2 [m] Est 1:10 [n] Est 5:3 [o] Est 9:12
7:3 [p] Est 2:15
7:4 [q] Est 3:9
7:7 [r] Ge 34:7; Est 1:12; Pr 19:12; 20:1-2 [s] 2Ki 21:18 [t] Est 6:13
7:8 [u] Est 1:6 [v] Ge 39:14 [w] Ge 34:7 [x] Est 6:12
7:9 [y] Est 1:10 [z] Est 5:14 [a] Ps 7:14-16; 9:16; Pr 11:5-6; 26:27; Mt 7:2
7:10 [b] Pr 10:28 [c] Est 9:25 [d] Da 6:24 [e] Est 2:1
8:1 [f] Est 2:7; 7:6; Pr 22:22-23
8:2 [g] Ge 41:42; Est 3:10 [h] Pr 13:22; Da 2:48
8:4 [i] Est 4:11; 5:2

Est 7:3 ❖ Are there people for whom we can speak up whose lives and safety are threatened? How might we advocate for people who are oppressed or voiceless?

Est 8:5 ❖ Which laws and policies do we believe Christians should advocate to restrict evil? Why?

The King's Edict in Behalf of the Jews

8 That same day King Xerxes gave Queen Esther the estate of Haman,[f] the enemy of the Jews. And Mordecai came into the presence of the king, for Esther had told how he was related to her. 2The king took off his signet ring,[g] which he had reclaimed from Haman, and presented it to Mordecai. And Esther appointed him over Haman's estate.[h]

3Esther again pleaded with the king, falling at his feet and weeping. She begged him to put an end to the evil plan of Haman the Agagite, which he had devised against the Jews. 4Then the king extended the gold scepter[i] to Esther and she arose and stood before him.

5"If it pleases the king," she said, "and if he regards me with favor and thinks it

[a] 4 Or *quiet, but the compensation our adversary offers cannot be compared with the loss the king would suffer* [b] 9 That is, about 75 feet or about 23 meters

7:1–2 Xerxes asks Queen Esther for the third time to reveal her request and again assures her of his positive and generous response.
7:3–5 Esther quotes the exact words of Haman's edict (cf. 3:13), but by using the passive voice, she delays mentioning Haman's name or the fact that it was the king himself who sold the Jewish people into this predicament. Xerxes' indignation and anger erupt with the demand that she tell him, "Who is he? Where is he—the man . . . ?" (v. 5).
7:6–7 Haman's only chance of survival lies in the hands of Esther. Harem protocol dictated that no one but the king could be left alone with a woman of the harem. That Haman should actually fall on the couch where Esther is reclining is unthinkable.
7:8–10 Haman's dangerous pride and vicious plans are rewarded in kind (see Mt 26:52).

✜ **7:1–10** Human evil, wherever it occurs and for whatever motivation, always sets itself against God, because God is the definition of goodness and righteousness. Divine justice inevitably and inextricably means the destruction of evil. In order to deliver the Jewish people from annihilation as God promised in his covenant with them, God necessarily had to destroy the evil that threatened their existence. In this case that evil came in the person of Haman. Mercy on Haman would have been inconsistent with God's covenant.

8:1–2 In a great reversal Mordecai is vested with all the power and authority previously wielded by Haman (cf. 3:10).
8:3–6 The decree of death for the Jews that Haman

the right thing to do, and if he is pleased
with me, let an order be written overrul-
ing the dispatches that Haman son of
Hammedatha, the Agagite, devised and
wrote to destroy the Jews in all the king's
provinces. 6 For how can I bear to see disaster fall on my people? How can I bear
to see the destruction of my family?"[j]
7 King Xerxes replied to Queen Esther
and to Mordecai the Jew, "Because Haman attacked the Jews, I have given his
estate to Esther, and they have impaled
him on the pole he set up. 8 Now write
another decree[k] in the king's name in
behalf of the Jews as seems best to you,
and seal it with the king's signet ring[l] —
for no document written in the king's
name and sealed with his ring can be
revoked."[m]
9 At once the royal secretaries were
summoned — on the twenty-third day
of the third month, the month of Sivan.
They wrote out all Mordecai's orders to
the Jews, and to the satraps, governors
and nobles of the 127 provinces stretching from India to Cush.[a][n] These orders
were written in the script of each province and the language of each people and
also to the Jews in their own script and
language.[o] 10 Mordecai wrote in the name
of King Xerxes, sealed the dispatches
with the king's signet ring, and sent
them by mounted couriers, who rode
fast horses especially bred for the king.
11 The king's edict granted the Jews
in every city the right to assemble and
protect themselves; to destroy, kill and
annihilate the armed men of any nationality or province who might attack them
and their women and children,[b] and to
plunder[p] the property of their enemies.
12 The day appointed for the Jews to do
this in all the provinces of King Xerxes
was the thirteenth day of the twelfth
month, the month of Adar.[q] 13 A copy of
the text of the edict was to be issued as
law in every province and made known
to the people of every nationality so that
the Jews would be ready on that day[r] to
avenge themselves on their enemies.
14 The couriers, riding the royal horses, went out, spurred on by the king's
command, and the edict was issued in
the citadel of Susa.

The Triumph of the Jews

15 When Mordecai[s] left the king's presence, he was wearing royal garments of
blue and white, a large crown of gold
and a purple robe of fine linen.[t] And the
city of Susa held a joyous celebration.[u]
16 For the Jews it was a time of happiness
and joy,[v] gladness and honor.[w] 17 In every
province and in every city to which the
edict of the king came, there was joy[x]
and gladness among the Jews, with feasting and celebrating. And many people of
other nationalities became Jews because
fear[y] of the Jews had seized them.[z]

9 On the thirteenth day of the twelfth
month, the month of Adar,[a] the edict
commanded by the king was to be carried
out. On this day the enemies of the Jews

8:6 [j] Est 7:4; 9:1
8:8 [k] Est 3:12-14 [l] Ge 41:42 [m] Est 1:19; Da 6:15
8:9 [n] Est 1:1 [o] Est 1:22
8:11 [p] Est 9:10, 15,16
8:12 [q] Est 3:13; 9:1
8:13 [r] Est 3:14
8:15 [s] Est 9:4 [t] Ge 41:42 [u] Est 3:15
8:16 [v] Ps 97:10-12 [w] Ps 112:4
8:17 [x] Est 9:19, 27; Ps 35:27; Pr 11:10 [y] Ex 15:14,16; Dt 11:25 [z] Est 9:3
9:1 [a] Est 8:12

[a] 9 That is, the upper Nile region [b] 11 Or *province, together with their women and children, who might attack them;*

---

proposed and the king signed is irrevocable. The only solution to their dilemma is to write another decree to counteract the first with equal force.

8:9–10 Mordecai's message is that the Jews may take whatever measures are necessary to defend themselves. He seals the edict with the king's signet ring—the same one also used by Haman to seal the decree of death.

8:17 Some have argued that the Persians recognized the improbable series of events as the hand of God and thus responded in true, heartfelt conversion to the God of the Jews.

✣ **8:1–17** From the beginning of time God's war has been against sin and evil. It is easy to think wrongly of sin and evil as being abstractions apart from people. We seem to want God to destroy sin and evil but leave people alone. However, sin and evil do not exist apart from beings who sin and beings who do evil, whether angelic or human.

Because we are all sinners and evildoers, we all have God's irrevocable decree of death against us. God could have justly destroyed the earth and everyone on it, for none of us is good by God's high standards. Instead, he chose to issue a counter-decree to redeem a people out of sin and evil and into righteousness, removing them from the realm of his destruction to the realm of deliverance. The gift of the sacrifice and resurrection of his Son Jesus guarantees that deliverance to all who place their trust in him for their salvation (Ro 10:9–10).

9:1–10 In the armed conflict on Adar 13, 75,000 died throughout the empire. The author is careful to say three times that the Jews "did not lay their hands on the plunder" (vv. 10, 15, 16) even though Mordecai's decree allowed it. The Jews understood the implementation of Mordecai's decree as governed by the ancient command of holy war against the Amalekites (1Sa 15:3).

had hoped to overpower them, but now
the tables were turned and the Jews got
the upper hand[b] over those who hated
them.[c] 2The Jews assembled in their cities[d] in all the provinces of King Xerxes to
attack those determined to destroy them.
No one could stand against them,[e] because the people of all the other nationalities were afraid of them. 3And all the
nobles of the provinces, the satraps, the
governors and the king's administrators
helped the Jews,[f] because fear of Mordecai had seized them. 4Mordecai was
prominent[g] in the palace; his reputation
spread throughout the provinces, and
he became more and more powerful.[h]
5The Jews struck down all their enemies with the sword, killing and destroying them,[i] and they did what they
pleased to those who hated them. 6In
the citadel of Susa, the Jews killed and
destroyed five hundred men. 7They also
killed Parshandatha, Dalphon, Aspatha,
8Poratha, Adalia, Aridatha, 9Parmash-
ta, Arisai, Aridai and Vaizatha, 10the ten
sons[j] of Haman son of Hammedatha, the
enemy of the Jews. But they did not lay
their hands on the plunder.[k]
11The number of those killed in the
citadel of Susa was reported to the king
that same day. 12The king said to Queen
Esther, "The Jews have killed and destroyed five hundred men and the ten
sons of Haman in the citadel of Susa.
What have they done in the rest of the
king's provinces? Now what is your petition? It will be given you. What is your
request? It will also be granted."[l]
13"If it pleases the king," Esther answered, "give the Jews in Susa permission to carry out this day's edict tomorrow also, and let Haman's ten sons[m] be
impaled[n] on poles."
14So the king commanded that this be
done. An edict was issued in Susa, and
they impaled[o] the ten sons of Haman.
15The Jews in Susa came together on the
fourteenth day of the month of Adar, and
they put to death in Susa three hundred
men, but they did not lay their hands on
the plunder.[p]
16Meanwhile, the remainder of the
Jews who were in the king's provinces
also assembled to protect themselves
and get relief[q] from their enemies.[r] They
killed seventy-five thousand of them[s]
but did not lay their hands on the plunder. 17This happened on the thirteenth
day of the month of Adar, and on the
fourteenth they rested and made it a
day of feasting[t] and joy.
18The Jews in Susa, however, had assembled on the thirteenth and fourteenth, and then on the fifteenth they
rested and made it a day of feasting and
joy.
19That is why rural Jews — those living
in villages — observe the fourteenth of
the month of Adar[u] as a day of joy and
feasting, a day for giving presents to each
other.[v]

Purim Established

20Mordecai recorded these events, and
he sent letters to all the Jews throughout the provinces of King Xerxes, near
and far, 21to have them celebrate annually the fourteenth and fifteenth days of
the month of Adar 22as the time when
the Jews got relief[w] from their enemies,
and as the month when their sorrow was
turned into joy and their mourning into
a day of celebration.[x] He wrote them to
observe the days as days of feasting and
joy and giving presents of food[y] to one
another and gifts to the poor.
23So the Jews agreed to continue the
celebration they had begun, doing what

9:1 [b] Jer 29:4-7 [c] Est 3:12-14; Pr 22:22-23
9:2 [d] ver 15-18 [e] Est 8:11,17; Ps 71:13,24
9:3 [f] Ezr 8:36
9:4 [g] Ex 11:3 [h] 2Sa 3:1; 1Ch 11:9
9:5 [i] Ezr 4:6
9:10 [j] Est 5:11 [k] Ge 14:23; 1Sa 14:32; Est 3:13; 8:11
9:12 [l] Est 5:6; 7:2
9:13 [m] Est 5:11 [n] Dt 21:22-23
9:14 [o] Ezr 6:11
9:15 [p] Ge 14:23; Est 8:11
9:16 [q] Est 4:14 [r] Dt 25:19 [s] 1Ch 4:43
9:17 [t] 1Ki 3:15
9:19 [u] Est 3:7 [v] ver 22; Dt 16:11,14; Ne 8:10, 12; Est 2:9; Rev 11:10
9:22 [w] Est 4:14 [x] Ne 8:12; Ps 30:11-12 [y] 2Ki 25:30

9:13 Though perhaps barbaric by modern standards, this also was a custom in ancient warfare. Esther's reasons for the second day of killing in Susa may have been legitimate, even though they are unknown to us and were also possibly unknown to the author. Haman was, after all, second only to the king, and he likely had many in Susa who were loyal to him and his decree.

✣ **9:1–19** The Bible assures us that the full expanse of human history, including the days in which we now live, is encompassed by God's redemptive plan. Even those whose sinful pride, like Haman's, pit them against God and the gospel are in the final analysis players in the universal plan of redemption. One would hope that before their end they will turn to Christ and be counted among the people whom God has called out from both the Jews and Gentiles to be saved from his destruction of evil. For all who have come to trust in Christ alone for salvation have been saved from God's wrath, whether they be Jew or Gentile.

9:20–22 It is fitting that the fulfillment of God's promise to the Jews in Persia should also be written down and commemorated.
9:23–28 The authority on which Purim is based is

Mordecai had written to them. 24For Haman son of Hammedatha, the Agagite,[z]
the enemy of all the Jews, had plotted
against the Jews to destroy them and
had cast the *pur*[a] (that is, the lot[b]) for
their ruin and destruction. 25But when
the plot came to the king's attention,[a]
he issued written orders that the evil
scheme Haman had devised against the
Jews should come back onto his own
head,[c] and that he and his sons should
be impaled[d] on poles.[e] 26(Therefore these
days were called Purim, from the word
pur.[f]) Because of everything written in
this letter and because of what they had
seen and what had happened to them,
27the Jews took it on themselves to establish the custom that they and their
descendants and all who join them
should without fail observe these two
days every year, in the way prescribed
and at the time appointed. 28These days
should be remembered and observed in
every generation by every family, and
in every province and in every city. And
these days of Purim should never fail to
be celebrated by the Jews — nor should
the memory of these days die out among
their descendants.

29So Queen Esther, daughter of Abihail,[g]
along with Mordecai the Jew, wrote with
full authority to confirm this second letter
concerning Purim. 30And Mordecai sent
letters to all the Jews in the 127 provinces[h]
of Xerxes' kingdom — words of goodwill
and assurance — 31to establish these days
of Purim at their designated times, as
Mordecai the Jew and Queen Esther had
decreed for them, and as they had established for themselves and their descendants in regard to their times of fasting[i]
and lamentation.[j] 32Esther's decree confirmed these regulations about Purim,
and it was written down in the records.

The Greatness of Mordecai

10 King Xerxes imposed tribute
throughout the empire, to its distant shores.[k] 2And all his acts of power
and might, together with a full account
of the greatness of Mordecai,[l] whom
the king had promoted,[m] are they not
written in the book of the annals[n] of the
kings of Media and Persia? 3Mordecai the
Jew was second[o] in rank[p] to King Xerxes,[q] preeminent among the Jews, and
held in high esteem by his many fellow
Jews, because he worked for the good of
his people and spoke up for the welfare
of all the Jews.[r]

9:24 [z] Ex 17:8-16 [a] Est 3:7 [b] Lev 16:8
9:25 [c] Ps 7:16 [d] Dt 21:22-23 [e] Est 7:10
9:26 [f] ver 20; Est 3:7
9:29 [g] Est 2:15
9:30 [h] Est 1:1
9:31 [i] Est 4:16 [j] Est 4:1-3
10:1 [k] Ps 72:10; 97:1; Isa 24:15
10:2 [l] Est 8:15; 9:4 [m] Ge 41:44 [n] Est 2:23
10:3 [o] Da 5:7 [p] Ge 41:43 [q] Ge 41:40 [r] Ne 2:10; Jer 29:4-7; Da 6:3

[a] 25 Or *when Esther came before the king*

Est 9:23-28 ❖ How do we celebrate the redemption God has accomplished for us? How do we share this celebration with fellow believers?

Est 10:1-3 ❖ Mordecai is portrayed as a faithful servant throughout the book of Esther. How can we emulate Mordecai's faithfulness as we go out into the secular world?

---

unlike that of the feasts commanded by Moses in the Pentateuch. The celebration of Purim is therefore different from the festivals prescribed by the Torah. Rather than being imposed on the people from above as God's commandment, Purim began as the spontaneous response of God's people to his omnipotent faithfulness to the promises of the covenant.

✣ 9:20-28 The book of Esther is part of the spiritual heritage of Christians given to us by Jesus Christ. Its significance has been transformed by his resurrection. The deliverance of the Jews in Persia foreshadows the redemption of those from all nations who enter into God's covenant through Jesus the Messiah. Christ reveals a new destiny: a destiny beyond death in eternal life.

9:29-31 At the beginning of her story, Esther is referred to as "the young woman Mordecai had adopted, the daughter of his uncle Abihail" (2:15). At the end of her story her Jewish identity and Persian position are integrated in the reference to her as "Queen Esther, daughter of Abihail" (9:29).

10:1-3 When Haman had worn Xerxes' signet ring, he was effectively the king over the enemies of the Jews. Now Mordecai wears that same ring and is effectively king over the Jews.

✣ 9:29—10:3 Both Esther and Mordecai were used by God in this work to accomplish his purposes and save the Jewish people from destruction. Although God's name is not mentioned in this book, we see in the timing of these events, and their ultimate conclusion, that God was working behind the scenes to orchestrate the elimination of evil and protect his chosen people.

The celebration of Purim is a foreshadowing of the day when God's plan for the renewal of creation is complete and the treachery and threat of evil is no more. On that day, believers will celebrate God's wondrous work in restoring the beauty and perfection of his creation once again (Isa 11:6; Rev 21:1-4).

Author: Unknown

Audience: God's people

Date: Unknown, though Job himself probably lived during the patriarchal period

Theme: God is active in realms beyond human understanding, even in the midst of great suffering.

Reading Job

The book of Job begins and ends with a narrative section on what happened to Job, and it includes conversations between God and Satan about Job. Most of the book, however, is a series of speeches of Job and four of his friends, attempting to come to grips with Job's suffering. If we wish to discover God's message for us in this book, we must be careful with these conversations, for much of what is said

PERSPECTIVE

There is good reason why Christian theologians consider theodicy—the defense of God's goodness in the face of the reality of evil and suffering in the world—the unsolvable theological issue. The reason is this: It is unsolvable. Yet this does not stop generation after generation of theological scholars from trying to solve it. And the biblical text they most often reference in this task is the book of Job.

To ask why God blesses, or doesn't bless, the righteous, or why God punishes, or doesn't punish, the wicked is to ask the wrong question when trying to understand this classic work. God's justice is ultimately unfathomable to us. God is just—we know that by faith—but we can't know *how* God is just. Thus, the book of Job does not answer that question; rather, it answers another question. Our task in reading Job is to read it as the answer to an unspoken question and then from the answer infer the correct question.

We have all gained some comfort in knowing that others, like us, all experience undeserved suffering. Once we get the core question right, all of the other wisdom we have learned about Job remains just as meaningful to us, but with a slightly different twist and a more satisfying context—the context set by the right question.

Unlike many books of the Bible, we don't know the author of Job or its date of composition. We do not really know whether it is based on historical events (and a historical person named Job) or whether it is a purely literary construction. This book cannot be fully understood without relating it to real life—not just the legendary Job, but our own experience or the experience of someone we

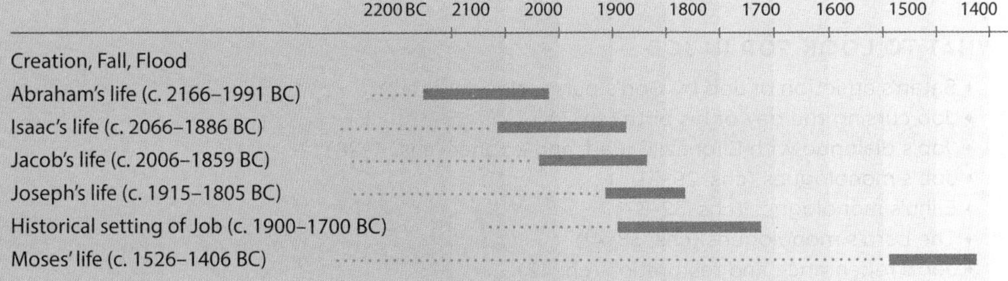

know, here in the 21st century. Suffering is not, in the end, a philosophical, or even a theological problem, but a human problem. We all suffer; some more than others, but the quantity really doesn't matter. What matters is what suffering teaches us about God. Job's response to God's answer to his questioning in this book (42:1-6) is perhaps the most instructive response ever uttered to the problem of suffering in the world.

does not reflect God's own perspective as seen elsewhere in the Bible. This book fits in the literary genre of wisdom literature, not historical narrative. Therefore, we must not take all the accounts in this book, such as the exchanges between God and Satan in the first part of the book, as literal fact; rather, we must examine each element in the book in relationship to the whole book and to the whole Bible.

TAKING THE NEXT STEPS

Most Bible students think that Job lived about the time of Abraham, though the story was probably put down into writing much later. In this book the writer struggles with the problem of human suffering and pain: Why do bad things happen to people who live good lives? The basic answer is the freedom of God: God knows what he is doing, and he is free to act as he sees fit. We cannot prove this by what we see happening around us, but we accept it through faith. Furthermore, by means of the story of Job, God assures us that he deals with us not according to the demands of his justice but according to his grace—grace that we experience through a mediator between us and God.

For anyone who is experiencing pain in his or her life, the book of Job is invaluable, for we learn several important lessons. (1) Pain and suffering are common to all people: good and bad, rich and poor; no categories of people are exempt. (2) Devout children of God can feel such intense pain that they will say things they would not otherwise say. (3) Whenever we suffer, we must realize that there may be spiritual realities (such as the conversation between God and Satan) beyond our awareness. But God is under no obligation to reveal these other facts to us. (4) Whenever we experience affliction, we must never forget that Satan is under the control of God; he is not free to do as he pleases. (5) God remains true to the principle that the righteous are rewarded and evil people punished, even though this may not become apparent until the end of time.

Key Verses

I know that my redeemer lives, and that in the end he will stand on the earth. And after my skin has been destroyed, yet in my flesh I will see God; I myself will see him with my own eyes—I, and not another.

—Job 19:25-27

WHAT TO LOOK FOR IN JOB

- Satan's affliction of Job by God's permission (chs. 1–2)
- Job cursing the day of his birth (ch. 3)
- Job's dialogue with Eliphaz, Bildad, and Zophar (chs. 4–28)
- Job's monologues (chs. 29–31)
- Elihu's monologues (chs. 32–37)
- The Lord's monologues (chs. 38–41)
- Job's repentance and restoration (ch. 42)

Prologue

1 In the land of Uz[a] there lived a man
whose name was Job.[b] This man was
blameless[c] and upright; he feared God[d]
and shunned evil. 2He had seven sons
and three daughters,[e] 3and he owned
seven thousand sheep, three thousand
camels, five hundred yoke of oxen and
five hundred donkeys, and had a large
number of servants. He was the greatest
man[f] among all the people of the East.
4His sons used to hold feasts in their
homes on their birthdays, and they
would invite their three sisters to eat
and drink with them. 5When a period
of feasting had run its course, Job would
make arrangements for them to be purified. Early in the morning he would
sacrifice a burnt offering[g] for each of
them, thinking, "Perhaps my children
have sinned[h] and cursed God[i] in their
hearts." This was Job's regular custom.
6One day the angels*a*[j] came to present
themselves before the LORD, and Satan*b*
also came with them.[k] 7The LORD said to
Satan, "Where have you come from?"
Satan answered the LORD, "From
roaming throughout the earth, going
back and forth on it."[l]
8Then the LORD said to Satan, "Have
you considered my servant Job?[m] There
is no one on earth like him; he is blameless and upright, a man who fears God
and shuns evil."[n]
9"Does Job fear God for nothing?"[o] Satan replied. 10"Have you not put a hedge
around him and his household and everything he has?[p] You have blessed the
work of his hands, so that his flocks and
herds are spread throughout the land.[q]
11But now stretch out your hand and
strike everything he has,[r] and he will
surely curse you to your face."[s]

1:1 [a] Jer 25:20 [b] Eze 14:14,20; Jas 5:11 [c] Ge 6:9; 17:1 [d] Ge 22:12; Ex 18:21
1:2 [e] Job 42:13
1:3 [f] Job 29:25
1:5 [g] Ge 8:20; Job 42:8 [h] Job 8:4 [i] 1Ki 21:10,13
1:6 [j] Job 38:7 [k] Job 2:1
1:7 [l] 1Pe 5:8
1:8 [m] Jos 1:7; Job 42:7-8 [n] ver 1
1:9 [o] 1Ti 6:5
1:10 [p] Ps 34:7 [q] ver 3; Job 29:6; 31:25; Ps 128:1-2
1:11 [r] Job 19:21 [s] Job 2:5

Job 1:9-12 ❖ Do we follow and respect God only because he has blessed us? Or do we not follow him because he hasn't? What motivates our relationship with the Lord?

a 6 Hebrew *the sons of God* *b* 6 Hebrew *satan* means *adversary.*

1:1 The terms "blameless" and "upright" in v. 1 do not describe people who live lives of sinless perfection; rather, they describe those who have found favor in the eyes of God and other people. Job is also described as one who "feared God." In a non-Israelite context, fearing God could refer to being ritually or ethically conscientious. In sum, Job is a model of devotion and integrity.
1:2-3 Job's prosperity is described in terms of his family and his possessions. Job is portrayed as the ultimate example of a person who is beyond reproach and who has achieved success by the highest standards.
1:4-5 Why does Job imagine his family might curse God at their feasts? If Job is engaged in an appeasement mentality, he wants to reap benefits from a god that he is serving. The stage is set for the challenger to raise the issue of Job's motives and God's policies.
1:6-12 In ancient Near Eastern polytheistic cultures, the divine council was populated by the chief gods. In OT monotheism this concept is revised. These angels, as administrative functionaries, possess no independent divine authority, but they do have delegated roles in administrating Yahweh's authority.
1:6 The Hebrew word transliterated as the proper name "Satan" refers to one who challenges. We are not in a position to claim that the challenger in Job should be identified with Satan as we know him in the NT.
1:7-12 The challenger is questioning the validity of a moral order in which the righteous unfailingly prosper, or what we can call the "retribution principle." He raises the point that Job's motives are open to question: Is he truly righteous or just acting in ways that will benefit him and his family?
The challenger's claim stems not from some identified flaw in Job but from his experience with

12The LORD said to Satan, "Very well, then, everything he has is in your power, but on the man himself do not lay a finger."

Then Satan went out from the presence of the LORD.

13One day when Job's sons and daughters were feasting and drinking wine at the oldest brother's house, 14a messenger came to Job and said, "The oxen were plowing and the donkeys were grazing nearby, 15and the Sabeans[t] attacked and made off with them. They put the servants to the sword, and I am the only one who has escaped to tell you!"

16While he was still speaking, another messenger came and said, "The fire of God fell from the heavens[u] and burned up the sheep and the servants,[v] and I am the only one who has escaped to tell you!"

17While he was still speaking, another messenger came and said, "The Chaldeans[w] formed three raiding parties and swept down on your camels and made off with them. They put the servants to the sword, and I am the only one who has escaped to tell you!"

18While he was still speaking, yet another messenger came and said, "Your sons and daughters were feasting and drinking wine at the oldest brother's house, 19when suddenly a mighty wind[x] swept in from the desert and struck the four corners of the house. It collapsed on them and they are dead, and I am the only one who has escaped to tell you!"

20At this, Job got up and tore his robe[y] and shaved his head. Then he fell to the ground in worship[z] 21and said:

"Naked I came from my mother's
womb,
and naked I will depart.[a][a]
The LORD gave and the LORD has
taken away;[b]
may the name of the LORD be
praised."[c]

22In all this, Job did not sin by charging God with wrongdoing.[d]

2 On another day the angels[b] came to present themselves before the LORD, and Satan also came with them[e] to present himself before him. 2And the LORD said to Satan, "Where have you come from?"

Satan answered the LORD, "From roaming throughout the earth, going back and forth on it."

3Then the LORD said to Satan, "Have you considered my servant Job? There is no one on earth like him; he is blameless and upright, a man who fears God and shuns evil.[f] And he still maintains his integrity,[g] though you incited me against him to ruin him without any reason."[h]

4"Skin for skin!" Satan replied. "A man will give all he has for his own life. 5But now stretch out your hand and strike his flesh and bones,[i] and he will surely curse you to your face."[j]

6The LORD said to Satan, "Very well, then, he is in your hands; but you must spare his life."[k]

7So Satan went out from the presence of the LORD and afflicted Job with painful sores from the soles of his feet to

1:15 [t] Ge 10:7; Job 6:19
1:16 [u] Ge 19:24 [v] Lev 10:2; Nu 11:1-3
1:17 [w] Ge 11:28, 31
1:19 [x] Jer 4:11; 13:24
1:20 [y] Ge 37:29 [z] 1Pe 5:6
1:21 [a] Ecc 5:15; 1Ti 6:7 [b] 1Sa 2:7 [c] Job 2:10; Eph 5:20; 1Th 5:18
1:22 [d] Job 2:10
2:1 [e] Job 1:6
2:3 [f] Job 1:1, 8 [g] Job 27:6 [h] Job 9:17
2:5 [i] Job 19:20 [j] Job 1:11
2:6 [k] Job 1:12

[a] 21 Or *will return there* [b] 1 Hebrew *the sons of God*

---

human nature. The challenger's assertion is that God's policy is misguided and ill-advised.

1:13–19 An Israelite audience would readily recognize all the disasters because they are among those presented in the covenant curses for disobedience (Dt 28:31-35). This recognition would remind them of the principles of retribution theology—here on the communal level.

1:20–22 Job's initial response to this utterly devastating news reflects the normal customs of mourning. Job acknowledges by his prostration that God has performed a remarkable act, and Job accepts it as such; he abases himself in response to the great power that God has demonstrated. The challenger said Job would "curse" God to his face (v. 11), but Job does not attribute wrongdoing to God, nor is he calling God to accountability. This is not Job's final posture, but his reflection at this stage; we will later see that Job does call God to account.

APPLICATION ✣ 1:1–22 We should not conclude that the text is providing us with a biblically authorized response to suffering in the character of Job; we must maintain the distinction between description and prescription. Undoubtedly God was pleased with Job's response, but a variety of other responses may have been just as acceptable. This part of the book is not designed to detail "the" right response to suffering.

2:1–6 Yahweh is accountable and responsible despite the role that the challenger plays. Job's righteousness continues to be confirmed from all sources. If the retribution principle represents justice, it must be carried out in proportion: The punishment must suit the crime. In Job's case, no such proportionality can be sustained.

2:7–10 The first round of trials brought mental

the crown of his head.[l] 8Then Job took a
piece of broken pottery and scraped himself with it as he sat among the ashes.[m]
9His wife said to him, "Are you still
maintaining your integrity? Curse God
and die!"
10He replied, "You are talking like a
foolish[a] woman. Shall we accept good
from God, and not trouble?"[n]
In all this, Job did not sin in what he
said.[o]

11When Job's three friends, Eliphaz
the Temanite,[p] Bildad the Shuhite[q] and
Zophar the Naamathite, heard about all
the troubles that had come upon him,
they set out from their homes and met
together by agreement to go and sympathize with him and comfort him.[r]
12When they saw him from a distance,
they could hardly recognize him; they
began to weep aloud, and they tore their
robes and sprinkled dust on their heads.[s]
13Then they sat on the ground with him
for seven days and seven nights.[t] No one
said a word to him, because they saw how
great his suffering was.

Job Speaks

3 After this, Job opened his mouth and
cursed the day of his birth. 2He said:

3"May the day of my birth perish,
and the night that said, 'A boy is conceived!'[u]
4That day—may it turn to darkness;
may God above not care about it;
may no light shine on it.
5May gloom and utter darkness[v]
claim it once more;

2:7 [l] Dt 28:35; Job 7:5
2:8 [m] Job 42:6; Jer 6:26; Eze 27:30; Mt 11:21
2:10 [n] Job 1:21 [o] Job 1:22; Ps 39:1; Jas 1:12; 5:11
2:11 [p] Ge 36:11; Jer 49:7 [q] Ge 25:2 [r] Job 42:11; Ro 12:15
2:12 [s] Jos 7:6; Ne 9:1; La 2:10; Eze 27:30
2:13 [t] Ge 50:10; Eze 3:15
3:3 [u] Job 10:18-19; Jer 20:14-18
3:5 [v] Job 10:21, 22; Ps 23:4; Jer 2:6; 13:16
3:6 [w] Job 23:17
3:8 [x] Job 41:1, 8, 10, 25
3:9 [y] Job 41:18
3:11 [z] Job 10:18
3:12 [a] Ge 30:3; Isa 66:12

Job 2:9 ❖ How can we stand firm in our faith when those closest to us are pressuring us to do otherwise?

Job 3:11–19 ❖ What causes a person to despair of life itself? How can we help such people or find hope and comfort in the midst of such times?

may a cloud settle over it;
may blackness overwhelm it.
6That night—may thick darkness[w]
seize it;
may it not be included among the
days of the year
nor be entered in any of the
months.
7May that night be barren;
may no shout of joy be heard in it.
8May those who curse days[b] curse
that day,
those who are ready to rouse
Leviathan.[x]
9May its morning stars become dark;
may it wait for daylight in vain
and not see the first rays of
dawn,[y]
10for it did not shut the doors of the
womb on me
to hide trouble from my eyes.

11"Why did I not perish at birth,
and die as I came from the
womb?[z]
12Why were there knees to receive me[a]
and breasts that I might be
nursed?

[a] *10* The Hebrew word rendered *foolish* denotes moral deficiency. [b] *8* Or *curse the sea*

---

anguish associated with loss. The second brings physical problems associated with pain. Job accepts God's right to do both, and he refuses to curse God, despite the advice of Job's wife, who has encouraged her husband to capitulate to his tragic fate by cursing God (v. 9) and accept the inevitable punishment of death. Contrary to cursing God to his face, Job has not sinned with his lips.

2:11–13 Eliphaz, Bildad, and Zophar now enter the picture with a specific purpose: to commiserate or sympathize with Job and to offer condolences in an attempt to alleviate his grief.

✣ **2:1–13** Job assumed that his suffering came from the hand of God. God did indeed play an active role, but we must remember that the book is not trying to give us a model for how God is regularly involved in what people suffer.

What vocabulary should we use to describe God's involvement? Consider that one of the major lessons of the book of Job is that no such language suffices. Whenever we choose a verb to communicate God's relationship to suffering, we are proposing what can only be a simplistic understanding of what God does. In the scenario laid out in Job, the individual happened to be right—his circumstances were from the hand of God. But it would be reductionistic and inaccurate for us to characterize all suffering as coming directly from the hand of God.

3:1–7 In this chapter, we find the only curse Job utters, focused on the day of his birth rather than on God.

3:8–10 Who are "those who curse days" (v. 8)? In ancient Near Eastern literature, demons were considered responsible for disruption of order.

3:11–19 Job depicts the netherworld as a place of comfort, rest, ease, and tranquility. In modern-day terms, a parallel might be someone who was starving looking forward to prison, where they could at least get three meals a day.

[13]For now I would be lying down[b] in
peace;
I would be asleep and at rest[c]
[14]with kings and rulers of the earth,[d]
who built for themselves places
now lying in ruins,[e]
[15]with princes[f] who had gold,
who filled their houses with
silver.[g]
[16]Or why was I not hidden away in the
ground like a stillborn child,[h]
like an infant who never saw the
light of day?
[17]There the wicked cease from
turmoil,
and there the weary are at rest.[i]
[18]Captives also enjoy their ease;
they no longer hear the slave
driver's shout.[j]
[19]The small and the great are there,
and the slaves are freed from their
owners.

[20]"Why is light given to those in
misery,
and life to the bitter of soul,[k]
[21]to those who long for death that
does not come,[l]
who search for it more than for
hidden treasure,[m]
[22]who are filled with gladness
and rejoice when they reach the
grave?
[23]Why is life given to a man
whose way is hidden,
whom God has hedged in?[n]
[24]For sighing has become my daily
food;[o]
my groans pour out like water.[p]
[25]What I feared has come upon me;
what I dreaded[q] has happened
to me.

3:13 [b]Job 17:13 [c]Job 7:8-10, 21; 10:22; 14:10-12; 19:27; 21:13, 23
3:14 [d]Job 12:17 [e]Job 15:28
3:15 [f]Job 12:21 [g]Job 27:17
3:16 [h]Ps 58:8; Ecc 6:3
3:17 [i]Job 17:16
3:18 [j]Job 39:7
3:20 [k]1Sa 1:10; Jer 20:18; Eze 27:30-31
3:21 [l]Rev 9:6 [m]Pr 2:4
3:23 [n]Job 19:6, 8, 12; Ps 88:8; La 3:7
3:24 [o]Job 6:7; 33:20 [p]Ps 42:3, 4
3:25 [q]Job 30:15
3:26 [r]Job 7:4, 14
4:2 [s]Job 32:20
4:3 [t]Isa 35:3; Heb 12:12
4:4 [u]Isa 35:3; Heb 12:12
4:5 [v]Job 19:21 [w]Job 6:14
4:6 [x]Pr 3:26 [y]Job 1:1
4:7 [z]Job 36:7 [a]Job 8:20; Ps 37:25
4:8 [b]Job 15:35 [c]Pr 22:8; Hos 10:13; Gal 6:7-8
4:9 [d]Job 15:30; Isa 30:33; 2Th 2:8

Job 4:7 ❖ Eliphaz blames Job's sin for his suffering. How should we instead reach out to someone in the depths of sorrow and pain?

[26]I have no peace, no quietness;
I have no rest,[r] but only turmoil."

Eliphaz

4 Then Eliphaz the Temanite replied:

[2]"If someone ventures a word with
you, will you be impatient?
But who can keep from
speaking?[s]
[3]Think how you have instructed
many,
how you have strengthened feeble
hands.[t]
[4]Your words have supported those
who stumbled;
you have strengthened faltering
knees.[u]
[5]But now trouble comes to you, and
you are discouraged;
it strikes[v] you, and you are
dismayed.[w]
[6]Should not your piety be your
confidence[x]
and your blameless[y] ways your
hope?

[7]"Consider now: Who, being innocent,
has ever perished?[z]
Where were the upright ever
destroyed?[a]
[8]As I have observed, those who plow
evil[b]
and those who sow trouble
reap it.[c]
[9]At the breath of God[d] they perish;

3:20–26 Job's fears have been realized (v. 25), though he can imagine no actions of his that could have been the cause of his circumstances. Job's words do not demonstrate the reasons for his foreboding apprehension, and so the book remains ambiguous concerning Job's motives (and now his fears). We are left wondering, what truly drives Job's virtuous life?

✚ **3:1–26** God can take actions that we perceive as negative, but which are ultimately for our good—that is, disciplinary actions that are not necessarily punitive. In Hos 2:6 God describes building a hedge around Israel to prevent the nation from finding their way. The hedge is intended to drive them back to their Lord, to prevent them from wandering. It manifests itself not in misfortunes but in lack of success in worldly endeavors. When we experience these, we should reconsider our motives and make it our goal to pursue greater dependence on God.

4:1–11 Eliphaz's first exhortation for Job occurs in the problematic verse 6. Given Eliphaz's observations in vv. 7–11, he seems to be accusing Job of denial in v. 6. In this interpretation, an alternate translation might be something more like, "Is not your [self-proclaimed] piety the basis for this irrational confidence? Is your only hope really in the [presumed] blamelessness of your ways?" In Eliphaz's view, the incontestable retribution principle (vv. 7–11) reveals Job as deluded by his own self-professed righteousness and exposes his hope as vain.

at the blast of his anger they are no more.[e]
10 The lions may roar and growl,
yet the teeth of the great lions are broken.[f]
11 The lion perishes for lack of prey,[g]
and the cubs of the lioness are scattered.

12 "A word was secretly brought to me,
my ears caught a whisper[h] of it.[i]
13 Amid disquieting dreams in the night,
when deep sleep falls on people,[j]
14 fear and trembling seized me
and made all my bones shake.[k]
15 A spirit glided past my face,
and the hair on my body stood on end.
16 It stopped,
but I could not tell what it was.
A form stood before my eyes,
and I heard a hushed voice:
17 'Can a mortal be more righteous than God?[l]
Can even a strong man be more pure than his Maker?[m]
18 If God places no trust in his servants,
if he charges his angels with error,[n]
19 how much more those who live in houses of clay,[o]
whose foundations[p] are in the dust,[q]
who are crushed more readily than a moth!
20 Between dawn and dusk they are broken to pieces;
unnoticed, they perish forever.[r]
21 Are not the cords of their tent pulled up,[s]
so that they die without wisdom?'[t]

5 "Call if you will, but who will answer you?
To which of the holy ones[u] will you turn?
2 Resentment kills a fool,
and envy slays the simple.[v]
3 I myself have seen a fool taking root,[w]

4:9 [e] Job 40:13
4:10 [f] Job 5:15; Ps 58:6
4:11 [g] Job 27:14; Ps 34:10
4:12 [h] Job 26:14 [i] Job 33:14
4:13 [j] Job 33:15
4:14 [k] Jer 23:9; Hab 3:16
4:17 [l] Job 9:2 [m] Job 35:10
4:18 [n] Job 15:15
4:19 [o] Job 10:9 [p] Job 22:16 [q] Ge 2:7
4:20 [r] Job 14:2, 20; 20:7; Ps 90:5-6
4:21 [s] Job 8:22 [t] Job 18:21; 36:12
5:1 [u] Job 15:15
5:2 [v] Pr 12:16
5:3 [w] Ps 37:35; Jer 12:2
[x] Job 24:18
5:4 [y] Job 4:11 [z] Am 5:12
5:5 [a] Job 18:8-10
5:7 [b] Job 14:1
5:8 [c] Ps 35:23; 50:15
5:9 [d] Job 42:3; Ps 40:5
5:10 [e] Job 36:28
5:11 [f] Ps 113:7-8
5:12 [g] Ne 4:15; Ps 33:10
5:13 [h] 1Co 3:19*
5:14 [i] Job 12:25 [j] Dt 28:29
5:15 [k] Ps 35:10 [l] Job 4:10

Job 5:7 ❖ How do we know when the hardships we face are God's way of correcting us? How can we tell when they are something else?

but suddenly his house was cursed.[x]
4 His children are far from safety,[y]
crushed in court[z] without a defender.
5 The hungry consume his harvest,[a]
taking it even from among thorns,
and the thirsty pant after his wealth.
6 For hardship does not spring from the soil,
nor does trouble sprout from the ground.
7 Yet man is born to trouble[b]
as surely as sparks fly upward.

8 "But if I were you, I would appeal to God;
I would lay my cause before him.[c]
9 He performs wonders that cannot be fathomed,[d]
miracles that cannot be counted.
10 He provides rain for the earth;
he sends water on the countryside.[e]
11 The lowly he sets on high,[f]
and those who mourn are lifted to safety.
12 He thwarts the plans[g] of the crafty,
so that their hands achieve no success.
13 He catches the wise in their craftiness,[h]
and the schemes of the wily are swept away.
14 Darkness[i] comes upon them in the daytime;
at noon they grope as in the night.[j]
15 He saves the needy[k] from the sword in their mouth;
he saves them from the clutches of the powerful.[l]

4:12–21 Eliphaz's main point reflects ancient Near Eastern beliefs—namely, that the gods have far more regulations than humans know or recognize; there are so many ways one might offend the gods in one's ritual performance, one can never claim not to deserve what the deity has sent. In that case, Job's confidence would truly be irrational.

5:1–7 Eliphaz speaks of "the holy ones" (v. 1), members of the divine council (i.e., the "sons of God"). Eliphaz is more correct than he knows. Eliphaz, however, implies that summoning one of the council would be fruitless (vv. 6–7).

5:8–16 Instead, Eliphaz counsels Job to appeal directly to God and then explains why by reciting many of God's attributes.

[16]So the poor have hope,
and injustice shuts its mouth.[m]

[17]"Blessed is the one whom God
corrects;[n]
so do not despise the discipline[o] of
the Almighty.[a][p]
[18]For he wounds, but he also binds
up;[q]
he injures, but his hands also heal.[r]
[19]From six calamities he will rescue
you;
in seven no harm will touch you.[s]
[20]In famine[t] he will deliver you from
death,
and in battle from the stroke of
the sword.[u]
[21]You will be protected from the lash
of the tongue,[v]
and need not fear[w] when
destruction comes.
[22]You will laugh at destruction and
famine,
and need not fear the wild
animals.[x]
[23]For you will have a covenant with the
stones[y] of the field,
and the wild animals will be at
peace with you.[z]
[24]You will know that your tent is
secure;
you will take stock of your
property and find nothing
missing.[a]
[25]You will know that your children
will be many,[b]
and your descendants like the
grass of the earth.[c]
[26]You will come to the grave in full
vigor,[d]
like sheaves gathered in season.

[27]"We have examined this, and it is
true.
So hear it and apply it to yourself."

Job

6 Then Job replied:

[2]"If only my anguish could be
weighed
and all my misery be placed on
the scales![e]
[3]It would surely outweigh the sand[f] of
the seas —
no wonder my words have been
impetuous.[g]
[4]The arrows[h] of the Almighty are in
me,[i]
my spirit drinks[j] in their poison;
God's terrors[k] are marshaled
against me.[l]
[5]Does a wild donkey bray when it has
grass,
or an ox bellow when it has
fodder?
[6]Is tasteless food eaten without
salt,
or is there flavor in the sap of the
mallow[b]?
[7]I refuse to touch it;
such food makes me ill.[m]

[8]"Oh, that I might have my request,
that God would grant what I hope
for,[n]
[9]that God would be willing to
crush me,
to let loose his hand and cut off
my life![o]
[10]Then I would still have this
consolation —
my joy in unrelenting pain —
that I had not denied the words[p]
of the Holy One.[q]

[11]"What strength do I have, that I
should still hope?
What prospects, that I should be
patient?[r]
[12]Do I have the strength of stone?
Is my flesh bronze?
[13]Do I have any power to help myself,[s]
now that success has been driven
from me?

[14]"Anyone who withholds kindness
from a friend
forsakes the fear of the Almighty.

5:16 [m]Ps 107:42
5:17 [n]Jas 1:12 [o]Ps 94:12; Pr 3:11 [p]Heb 12:5-11
5:18 [q]Isa 30:26 [r]1Sa 2:6
5:19 [s]Ps 34:19; 91:10
5:20 [t]Ps 33:19 [u]Ps 144:10
5:21 [v]Ps 31:20 [w]Ps 91:5
5:22 [x]Ps 91:13; Eze 34:25
5:23 [y]Ps 91:12 [z]Isa 11:6-9
5:24 [a]Job 8:6
5:25 [b]Ps 112:2 [c]Ps 72:16; Isa 44:3-4
5:26 [d]Ge 15:15
6:2 [e]Job 31:6
6:3 [f]Pr 27:3 [g]Job 23:2
6:4 [h]Ps 38:2 [i]Job 16:12, 13 [j]Job 21:20 [k]Job 30:15 [l]Ps 88:15-18
6:7 [m]Job 3:24
6:8 [n]Job 14:13
6:9 [o]Nu 11:15; 1Ki 19:4
6:10 [p]Job 22:22; 23:12 [q]Lev 19:2; Isa 57:15
6:11 [r]Job 21:4
6:13 [s]Job 26:2

[a] 17 Hebrew *Shaddai*; here and throughout Job
[b] 6 The meaning of the Hebrew for this phrase is uncertain.

5:17 Eliphaz points out that Job should look at his situation as the disciplinary correction of God.
5:18–27 Job can now have confidence that God, because of who he is, will respond to Job's repentance and bring restoration. The rest of Eliphaz's speech anticipates this restoration.
6:1–10 Job is prepared to face the facts and wishes for death. He finds consolation only in his refusal to accept a sugar-coated view of reality (v. 10).
6:14–30 Job launches into his first verbal assault on his friends. He challenges them to reveal his specific offense (v. 24) because his integrity is at stake (v. 29).

15 But my brothers are as
undependable as intermittent
streams,[t]
as the streams that overflow
16 when darkened by thawing ice
and swollen with melting snow,
17 but that stop flowing in the dry
season,
and in the heat[u] vanish from their
channels.
18 Caravans turn aside from their
routes;
they go off into the wasteland and
perish.
19 The caravans of Tema[v] look for
water,
the traveling merchants of Sheba
look in hope.
20 They are distressed, because they
had been confident;
they arrive there, only to be
disappointed.[w]
21 Now you too have proved to be of no
help;
you see something dreadful and
are afraid.[x]
22 Have I ever said, 'Give something on
my behalf,
pay a ransom for me from your
wealth,
23 deliver me from the hand of the
enemy,
rescue me from the clutches of the
ruthless'?

24 "Teach me, and I will be quiet;[y]
show me where I have been
wrong.
25 How painful are honest words![z]
But what do your arguments
prove?
26 Do you mean to correct what I say,
and treat my desperate words as
wind?[a]
27 You would even cast lots[b] for the
fatherless
and barter away your friend.

28 "But now be so kind as to look
at me.
Would I lie to your face?[c]
29 Relent, do not be unjust;
reconsider, for my integrity is at
stake.[a][d]

6:15 [t] Ps 38:11; Jer 15:18
6:17 [u] Job 24:19
6:19 [v] Ge 25:15; Isa 21:14
6:20 [w] Jer 14:3
6:21 [x] Ps 38:11
6:24 [y] Ps 39:1
6:25 [z] Ecc 12:11
6:26 [a] Job 8:2; 15:3
6:27 [b] Joel 3:3; Na 3:10; 2Pe 2:3
6:28 [c] Job 27:4; 33:1,3; 36:3,4
6:29 [d] Job 23:7, 10; 34:5,36; 42:6
6:30 [e] Job 27:4 [f] Job 12:11
7:1 [g] Job 14:14; Isa 40:2 [h] Job 5:7 [i] Job 14:6
7:2 [j] Lev 19:13
7:3 [k] Job 16:7; Ps 6:6
7:4 [l] Dt 28:67
7:5 [m] Job 17:14; Isa 14:11
7:6 [n] Job 9:25 [o] Job 13:15; 17:11,15
7:7 [p] Ps 78:39; Jas 4:14 [q] Job 9:25
7:8 [r] Job 20:7, 9,21
7:9 [s] Job 11:8 [t] 2Sa 12:23; Job 30:15
7:10 [u] Job 27:21, 23 [v] Job 8:18
7:11 [w] Ps 40:9

Job 6:15–17 ❖ How does God sustain us when those around us are undependable?

Job 7:11 ❖ When is it an appropriate time to voice our anguish and misery? When is it better to remain quiet?

30 Is there any wickedness on my lips?[e]
Can my mouth not discern[f]
malice?

7 "Do not mortals have hard service[g]
on earth?[h]
Are not their days like those of
hired laborers?[i]
2 Like a slave longing for the evening
shadows,
or a hired laborer waiting to be
paid,[j]
3 so I have been allotted months of
futility,
and nights of misery have been
assigned to me.[k]
4 When I lie down I think, 'How long
before I get up?'[l]
The night drags on, and I toss and
turn until dawn.
5 My body is clothed with worms[m] and
scabs,
my skin is broken and festering.

6 "My days are swifter than a weaver's
shuttle,[n]
and they come to an end without
hope.[o]
7 Remember, O God, that my life is but
a breath;[p]
my eyes will never see happiness
again.[q]
8 The eye that now sees me will see
me no longer;
you will look for me, but I will be
no more.[r]
9 As a cloud vanishes and is gone,
so one who goes down to the
grave[s] does not return.[t]
10 He will never come to his house
again;
his place[u] will know him no more.[v]

11 "Therefore I will not keep silent;[w]

[a] 29 Or *my righteousness still stands*

7:7–21 After rehearsing his troubles in vv. 1–6, Job here primarily accuses God of being overattentive and unrealistic in his expectations. Job claims that, unlike the chaos creatures (v. 12), he is no threat to order and therefore doesn't warrant God's constant attention. Job conveys the terrifying prospect of God's singling out a single person on whom to focus his wrath.

I will speak out in the anguish of
my spirit,
I will complain in the bitterness of
my soul.[x]
12 Am I the sea, or the monster of the
deep,[y]
that you put me under guard?
13 When I think my bed will
comfort me
and my couch will ease my
complaint,[z]
14 even then you frighten me with
dreams
and terrify[a] me with visions,
15 so that I prefer strangling and
death,[b]
rather than this body of mine.
16 I despise my life;[c] I would not live
forever.
Let me alone; my days have no
meaning.

17 "What is mankind that you make so
much of them,
that you give them so much
attention,[d]
18 that you examine them every
morning
and test them every moment?[e]
19 Will you never look away from me,
or let me alone even for an
instant?[f]
20 If I have sinned, what have I done to
you,[g]
you who see everything we do?
Why have you made me your
target?[h]
Have I become a burden to you?[a]
21 Why do you not pardon my offenses
and forgive my sins?[i]
For I will soon lie down in the dust;[j]
you will search for me, but I will
be no more."

Bildad

8 Then Bildad the Shuhite replied:

2 "How long will you say such things?
Your words are a blustering wind.[k]
3 Does God pervert justice?[l]
Does the Almighty pervert what is
right?[m]
4 When your children sinned against
him,
he gave them over to the penalty
of their sin.[n]
5 But if you will seek God earnestly
and plead[o] with the Almighty,
6 if you are pure and upright,
even now he will rouse himself on
your behalf[p]
and restore you to your
prosperous state.[q]
7 Your beginnings will seem humble,
so prosperous[r] will your future be.

8 "Ask the former generation[s]
and find out what their ancestors
learned,
9 for we were born only yesterday and
know nothing,[t]
and our days on earth are but a
shadow.[u]
10 Will they not instruct you and tell
you?
Will they not bring forth words
from their understanding?
11 Can papyrus grow tall where there is
no marsh?
Can reeds thrive without water?
12 While still growing and uncut,
they wither more quickly than
grass.[v]
13 Such is the destiny of all who forget
God;[w]
so perishes the hope of the
godless.[x]
14 What they trust in is fragile[b];
what they rely on is a spider's web.[y]

Job 8:5–7 ❖ Bildad has decent theology but poor sensitivity. How can we be appropriately sensitive to those who are hurting around us?

7:11 [x] 1Sa 1:10
7:12 [y] Eze 32:2-3
7:13 [z] Job 9:27
7:14 [a] Job 9:34
7:15 [b] 1Ki 19:4
7:16 [c] Job 9:21; 10:1
7:17 [d] Ps 8:4; 144:3; Heb 2:6
7:18 [e] Job 14:3
7:19 [f] Job 9:18
7:20 [g] Job 35:6 [h] Job 16:12
7:21 [i] Job 10:14 [j] Job 10:9; Ps 104:29
8:2 [k] Job 6:26
8:3 [l] Dt 32:4; 2Ch 19:7; Ro 3:5 [m] Ge 18:25
8:4 [n] Job 1:19
8:5 [o] Job 11:13
8:6 [p] Ps 7:6 [q] Job 5:24
8:7 [r] Job 42:12
8:8 [s] Dt 4:32; 32:7; Job 15:18
8:9 [t] Ge 47:9 [u] 1Ch 29:15; Job 7:6
8:12 [v] Ps 129:6; Jer 17:6
8:13 [w] Ps 9:17 [x] Job 11:20; 13:16; 15:34; Pr 10:28
8:14 [y] Isa 59:5

[a] *20* A few manuscripts of the Masoretic Text, an ancient Hebrew scribal tradition and Septuagint; most manuscripts of the Masoretic Text *I have become a burden to myself.* [b] *14* The meaning of the Hebrew for this word is uncertain.

8:1–4 Bildad launches into a speech filled with rhetorical questions designed to affirm that God upholds justice. In these statements he denies that God would "pervert" justice and righteousness (v. 3). Job has not charged God with perverting justice (yet), but in Bildad's view of the world, that would be the only logical conclusion if Job can sustain his claim of innocence.

8:5–22 Bildad is simply patronizing Job (v. 6), but he also has his own implied accusations as he unwraps the implications of the retribution principle: "Surely God does not reject one who is blameless or strengthen the hands of evildoers" (v. 20). These convictions lead him to characterize Job implicitly as "godless" (v. 13) and one who forgets God.

15 They lean on the web,[z] but it gives
way;
they cling to it, but it does not
hold.[a]
16 They are like a well-watered plant in
the sunshine,
spreading its shoots[b] over the
garden;[c]
17 it entwines its roots around a pile of
rocks
and looks for a place among the
stones.
18 But when it is torn from its spot,
that place disowns it and says, 'I
never saw you.'[d]
19 Surely its life withers[e] away,
and[a] from the soil other plants
grow.[f]

20 "Surely God does not reject one who
is blameless[g]
or strengthen the hands of
evildoers.[h]
21 He will yet fill your mouth with
laughter[i]
and your lips with shouts of joy.[j]
22 Your enemies will be clothed in
shame,[k]
and the tents of the wicked will be
no more."[l]

Job

9 Then Job replied:

2 "Indeed, I know that this is true.
But how can mere mortals prove
their innocence before God?[m]
3 Though they wished to dispute with
him,
they could not answer him one
time out of a thousand.[n]
4 His wisdom[o] is profound, his power
is vast.[p]
Who has resisted him and come
out unscathed?[q]
5 He moves mountains without their
knowing it
and overturns them in his anger.[r]

8:15 [z] Job 27:18 [a] Ps 49:11
8:16 [b] Ps 80:11 [c] Ps 37:35; Jer 11:16
8:18 [d] Job 7:8; Ps 37:36
8:19 [e] Job 20:5 [f] Ecc 1:4
8:20 [g] Job 1:1 [h] Job 21:30
8:21 [i] Job 5:22 [j] Ps 126:2; 132:16
8:22 [k] Ps 35:26; 109:29; 132:18 [l] Job 18:6,14,21
9:2 [m] Job 4:17; Ps 143:2; Ro 3:20
9:3 [n] Job 10:2; 40:2
9:4 [o] Job 11:6 [p] Job 36:5 [q] 2Ch 13:12
9:5 [r] Mic 1:4
9:6 [s] Isa 2:21; Hag 2:6; Heb 12:26 [t] Job 26:11
9:7 [u] Isa 13:10; Eze 32:8
9:8 [v] Ge 1:6; Ps 104:2-3 [w] Job 38:16; Ps 77:19
9:9 [x] Ge 1:16; Job 38:31; Am 5:8
9:10 [y] Ps 71:15 [z] Job 5:9
9:11 [a] Job 23:8-9; 35:14
9:12 [b] Job 11:10 [c] Isa 45:9; Ro 9:20
9:13 [d] Job 26:12; Ps 89:10; Isa 30:7; 51:9
9:15 [e] Job 10:15 [f] Job 8:5
9:17 [g] Job 16:12 [h] Job 30:22 [i] Job 16:14 [j] Job 2:3

Job 9:16 ❖ Do we ever feel like God doesn't want to give us a hearing? Why?

6 He shakes the earth[s] from its place
and makes its pillars tremble.[t]
7 He speaks to the sun and it does not
shine;
he seals off the light of the stars.[u]
8 He alone stretches out the heavens[v]
and treads on the waves of the
sea.[w]
9 He is the Maker of the Bear[b] and
Orion,
the Pleiades and the constellations
of the south.[x]
10 He performs wonders[y] that cannot
be fathomed,
miracles that cannot be counted.[z]
11 When he passes me, I cannot see
him;
when he goes by, I cannot perceive
him.[a]
12 If he snatches away, who can stop
him?[b]
Who can say to him, 'What are you
doing?'[c]
13 God does not restrain his anger;
even the cohorts of Rahab[d]
cowered at his feet.

14 "How then can I dispute with him?
How can I find words to argue
with him?
15 Though I were innocent, I could not
answer him;[e]
I could only plead[f] with my Judge
for mercy.
16 Even if I summoned him and he
responded,
I do not believe he would give me
a hearing.
17 He would crush me[g] with a storm[h]
and multiply[i] my wounds for no
reason.[j]

[a] 19 Or *Surely all the joy it has / is that* [b] 9 Or *of Leo*

9:1–13 Job's hymn (vv. 4–13) explains why Job trembles at the thought of opposing God in court.
9:5–9 Verse 5 could also be translated "God traverses the mountains." This would parallel his treading on the seas in v. 8. The first clause of v. 6 contains terminology commonly used for earthquakes. The earthquake continues the theme of punishment against those who resist.
9:7 The punishment theme moves heavenward. Sealing the stars would refer to shutting them out so they could not enter the paths to shine in the heavens.
9:9–12 Constellations often are the subject of omens (for good or ill) in Akkadian literature. God uses all of the cosmos against those who would oppose him.
9:13 In the Babylonian creation epic, *Enuma Elish*, Tiamat, the chaos creature associated with the sea, rebels against the gods with the aid of her consorts. The section that this verse closes shows God handily defeating even the most fearsome chaos creatures.

18 He would not let me catch my breath
but would overwhelm me with misery.[k]
19 If it is a matter of strength, he is mighty!
And if it is a matter of justice, who can challenge him[a]?
20 Even if I were innocent, my mouth would condemn me;
if I were blameless, it would pronounce me guilty.

21 "Although I am blameless,[l]
I have no concern for myself;
I despise my own life.[m]
22 It is all the same; that is why I say,
'He destroys both the blameless and the wicked.'[n]
23 When a scourge[o] brings sudden death,
he mocks the despair of the innocent.[p]
24 When a land falls into the hands of the wicked,[q]
he blindfolds its judges.[r]
If it is not he, then who is it?

25 "My days are swifter than a runner;[s]
they fly away without a glimpse of joy.
26 They skim past like boats of papyrus,[t]
like eagles swooping down on their prey.[u]
27 If I say, 'I will forget my complaint,[v]
I will change my expression, and smile,'
28 I still dread[w] all my sufferings,
for I know you will not hold me innocent.[x]
29 Since I am already found guilty,
why should I struggle in vain?[y]
30 Even if I washed myself with soap
and my hands[z] with cleansing powder,[a]
31 you would plunge me into a slime pit
so that even my clothes would detest me.

9:18 [k] Job 7:19; 27:2
9:21 [l] Job 1:1 [m] Job 7:16
9:22 [n] Job 10:8; Ecc 9:2, 3; Eze 21:3
9:23 [o] Heb 11:36 [p] Job 24:1, 12
9:24 [q] Job 10:3; 16:11 [r] Job 12:6
9:25 [s] Job 7:6
9:26 [t] Isa 18:2 [u] Hab 1:8
9:27 [v] Job 7:11
9:28 [w] Job 3:25; Ps 119:120 [x] Job 7:21
9:29 [y] Ps 37:33
9:30 [z] Job 31:7 [a] Jer 2:22
9:32 [b] Ro 9:20 [c] Ps 143:2; Ecc 6:10
9:33 [d] 1Sa 2:25
9:34 [e] Job 13:21; Ps 39:10
9:35 [f] Job 13:21
10:1 [g] 1Ki 19:4 [h] Job 7:11
10:2 [i] Job 9:29
10:3 [j] Job 9:22 [k] Job 14:15; Ps 138:8; Isa 64:8 [l] Job 21:16; 22:18
10:4 [m] 1Sa 16:7
10:5 [n] Ps 90:2, 4; 2Pe 3:8
10:6 [o] Job 14:16
10:8 [p] Ps 119:73

Job 9:33-35 ❖ How does Jesus Christ solve these longings?

32 "He is not a mere mortal like me that I might answer him,[b]
that we might confront each other in court.[c]
33 If only there were someone to mediate between us,[d]
someone to bring us together,
34 someone to remove God's rod from me,[e]
so that his terror would frighten me no more.
35 Then I would speak up without fear of him,
but as it now stands with me, I cannot.[f]

10 "I loathe my very life;[g]
therefore I will give free rein to my complaint
and speak out in the bitterness of my soul.[h]
2 I say to God: Do not declare me guilty,
but tell me what charges[i] you have against me.
3 Does it please you to oppress me,[j]
to spurn the work of your hands,[k]
while you smile on the plans of the wicked?[l]
4 Do you have eyes of flesh?
Do you see as a mortal sees?[m]
5 Are your days like those of a mortal
or your years like those of a strong man,[n]
6 that you must search out my faults
and probe after my sin[o] —
7 though you know that I am not guilty
and that no one can rescue me from your hand?

8 "Your hands shaped[p] me and made me.

[a] 19 See Septuagint; Hebrew *me*.

9:21–22 Job's rhetoric escalates as he throws caution to the wind and makes his boldest statement yet: "He [God] destroys both the blameless and the wicked" (v. 22).
9:29–33 Though Job identifies God as the source of destruction for all, he still believes there is a justice system at work. Job has not claimed there is no justice, only that God is the sole target of his complaint. Job requests a courtroom scenario in which an arbitrator will serve on his behalf (v. 33) so he can state his case (v. 35).
10:3 Job continues to think the world ought to operate according to the retribution principle. Job questions God's omniscience as part of his defense.
10:8–12 The biblical and ancient Near Eastern accounts demonstrate the view that it was not just the first human who was made of dust/clay. Every human is molded by deity and returns to dust.

Will you now turn and
destroy me?
9 Remember that you molded me like
clay.[q]
Will you now turn me to dust
again?[r]
10 Did you not pour me out like milk
and curdle me like cheese,
11 clothe me with skin and flesh
and knit me together[s] with bones
and sinews?
12 You gave me life[t] and showed me
kindness,
and in your providence watched
over my spirit.

13 "But this is what you concealed in
your heart,
and I know that this was in your
mind:[u]
14 If I sinned, you would be
watching me
and would not let my offense go
unpunished.[v]
15 If I am guilty — woe to me![w]
Even if I am innocent, I cannot lift
my head,[x]
for I am full of shame
and drowned in[a] my affliction.
16 If I hold my head high, you stalk me
like a lion[y]
and again display your awesome
power against me.[z]
17 You bring new witnesses against
me[a]
and increase your anger toward
me;[b]
your forces come against me wave
upon wave.

18 "Why then did you bring me out of
the womb?[c]
I wish I had died before any eye
saw me.
19 If only I had never come into being,
or had been carried straight from
the womb to the grave!
20 Are not my few days[d] almost over?[e]
Turn away from me[f] so I can have
a moment's joy
21 before I go to the place of no return,[g]
to the land of gloom and utter
darkness,[h]
22 to the land of deepest night,
of utter darkness and disorder,
where even the light is like
darkness."

10:9 [q] Isa 64:8 [r] Ge 2:7
10:11 [s] Ps 139:13, 15
10:12 [t] Job 33:4
10:13 [u] Job 23:13
10:14 [v] Job 7:21
10:15 [w] Job 9:13; Isa 3:11 [x] Job 9:15
10:16 [y] Isa 38:13; La 3:10 [z] Job 5:9
10:17 [a] Job 16:8 [b] Ru 1:21
10:18 [c] Job 3:11
10:20 [d] Job 14:1 [e] Job 7:19 [f] Job 7:16
10:21 [g] 2Sa 12:23; Job 3:13; 16:22 [h] Ps 23:4; 88:12
11:2 [i] Job 8:2
11:3 [j] Job 17:2; 21:3
11:4 [k] Job 6:10 [l] Job 10:7
11:6 [m] Job 9:4 [n] Ezr 9:13; Job 15:5
11:7 [o] Ecc 3:11; Ro 11:33
11:8 [p] Job 22:12

Job 10:16–17 ❖ Is Job's characterization of God going after him in a negative way appropriate? Why or why not?

Zophar

11 Then Zophar the Naamathite replied:

2 "Are all these words to go
unanswered?[i]
Is this talker to be vindicated?
3 Will your idle talk reduce others to
silence?
Will no one rebuke you when you
mock?[j]
4 You say to God, 'My beliefs are
flawless[k]
and I am pure[l] in your sight.'
5 Oh, how I wish that God would
speak,
that he would open his lips
against you
6 and disclose to you the secrets of
wisdom,[m]
for true wisdom has two sides.
Know this: God has even forgotten
some of your sin.[n]

7 "Can you fathom[o] the mysteries of
God?
Can you probe the limits of the
Almighty?
8 They are higher than the heavens[p]
above — what can you do?
They are deeper than the depths
below — what can you know?
9 Their measure is longer than the
earth
and wider than the sea.

[a] *15* Or *and aware of*

10:13 Job stunningly claims to know the mind of God. This brash and arrogant declaration shows once again Job's deficient view of God.
10:18–22 Job finishes his speech of despair (over getting a fair trial) by wishing again for death, a reprise of his lament in ch. 3.
11:1–20 Zophar characterizes Job's stance about his innocence as a foolish charade. As he wishes for God to address this subject, Zophar observes that "true wisdom has two sides" (v. 6), perhaps implying that Job is not perceiving the other side.
11:7–12 Zophar thinks that Job takes too much on himself in supposing that he can match God in court. In one sense this anticipates part of what God will say when he appears in ch. 38. This illustrates that the words of Job's friends are not utter foolishness.

CHARACTER OF GOD // GOD IS OMNISCIENT

Job 11:7–9: Can you fathom the mysteries of God? Can you probe the limits of the Almighty? They are higher than the heavens above—what can you do? They are deeper than the depths below—what can you know? Their measure is longer than the earth and wider than the sea.

God's omniscience refers to his all-knowing nature. There is no corner of reality that God does not know fully. This includes not only human actions, but even our thoughts. The same God who created everything knows that creation completely.

Job 11:7–9 praises this quality in God, proclaiming that his understanding and limits are beyond measure. It might be disturbing to some to realize that God knows all our inner thoughts and desires, but it is important to remember this in the context of God's love. God is not looking for reasons to accuse or condemn. He fully understands human weakness (Ps 103:14). This, too, is due to his omniscience.

God's omniscience extends not only to every place in creation, including our hearts and minds; his omniscience also extends into all times. God knows the end from the beginning. He knows what tomorrow will bring. The world is not governed by chance. God knows the plans he has for the future, and he is all-powerful: His plans for the future are certain to occur.

APPLICATION ✣ Understanding God's omniscience can lead us to be more open in prayer and confession (see Job's reaction in Job 42:1–3), which will in turn deepen our communion with God. Furthermore, God's omniscience can fill us with hope for the future. After all, God already knows the future completely. If we stand with God, nothing to come can ultimately stand against us.

10 "If he comes along and confines you
in prison
and convenes a court, who can
oppose him?[q]
11 Surely he recognizes deceivers;
and when he sees evil, does he not
take note?[r]
12 But the witless can no more become
wise
than a wild donkey's colt can be
born human.[a]

13 "Yet if you devote your heart[s] to him
and stretch out your hands to
him,[t]
14 if you put away the sin that is in your
hand
and allow no evil[u] to dwell in your
tent,[v]
15 then, free of fault, you will lift up
your face;[w]
you will stand firm and without
fear.
16 You will surely forget your trouble,[x]
recalling it only as waters gone by.[y]
17 Life will be brighter than noonday,[z]
and darkness will become like
morning.

11:10 [q]Job 9:12; Rev 3:7
11:11 [r]Job 34:21-25; Ps 10:14
11:13 [s]1Sa 7:3; Ps 78:8 [t]Ps 88:9
11:14 [u]Ps 101:4 [v]Job 22:23
11:15 [w]Job 22:26; 1Jn 3:21
11:16 [x]Isa 65:16 [y]Job 22:11
11:17 [z]Job 22:28; Ps 37:6; Isa 58:8,10

Job 11:11 ❖ Why should we be careful not to blame those in difficult circumstances for what they are going through? What other explanations might there be for misfortune in a person's life?

18 You will be secure, because there is
hope;
you will look about you and take
your rest[a] in safety.[b]
19 You will lie down, with no one to
make you afraid,[c]
and many will court your favor.[d]
20 But the eyes of the wicked will fail,[e]
and escape will elude them;[f]
their hope will become a dying
gasp."[g]

Job

12 Then Job replied:

2 "Doubtless you are the only people
who matter,
and wisdom will die with you![h]

11:18 [a]Ps 3:5 [b]Lev 26:6; Pr 3:24
11:19 [c]Lev 26:6 [d]Isa 45:14
11:20 [e]Dt 28:65; Job 17:5 [f]Job 27:22; 34:22 [g]Job 8:13
12:2 [h]Job 17:10

[a] 12 Or *wild donkey can be born tame*

11:13–20 Zophar lays out his recommended course of action. He assumes that Job has sinned and brought this punishment down on himself (vv. 15–20)—a flawed conclusion. The goal he holds out for Job is that his prosperity will be restored.
12:1–6 Job asserts that God should be concerned

[3] But I have a mind as well as you;
I am not inferior to you.
Who does not know all these things?[i]

[4] "I have become a laughingstock[j] to my friends,
though I called on God and he answered[k] —
a mere laughingstock, though righteous and blameless![l]
[5] Those who are at ease have contempt for misfortune
as the fate of those whose feet are slipping.
[6] The tents of marauders are undisturbed,[m]
and those who provoke God are secure[n] —
those God has in his hand.[a]

[7] "But ask the animals, and they will teach you,
or the birds in the sky, and they will tell you;
[8] or speak to the earth, and it will teach you,
or let the fish in the sea inform you.
[9] Which of all these does not know
that the hand of the LORD has done this?[o]
[10] In his hand is the life of every creature
and the breath of all mankind.[p]
[11] Does not the ear test words
as the tongue tastes food?[q]
[12] Is not wisdom found among the aged?[r]
Does not long life bring understanding?[s]

[13] "To God belong wisdom[t] and power;[u]
counsel and understanding are his.[v]
[14] What he tears down[w] cannot be rebuilt;[x]
those he imprisons cannot be released.
[15] If he holds back the waters,[y] there is drought;[z]
if he lets them loose, they devastate the land.[a]

12:3 [i] Job 13:2
12:4 [j] Job 21:3 [k] Ps 91:15 [l] Job 6:29
12:6 [m] Job 22:18 [n] Job 9:24; 21:9
12:9 [o] Isa 41:20
12:10 [p] Job 27:3; 33:4; Ac 17:28
12:11 [q] Job 34:3
12:12 [r] Job 15:10 [s] Job 32:7,9
12:13 [t] Job 11:6 [u] Job 9:4 [v] Job 32:8; 38:36
12:14 [w] Job 19:10 [x] Job 37:7; Isa 25:2
12:15 [y] 1Ki 8:35 [z] 1Ki 17:1 [a] Ge 7:11

Job 12:13 ❖ How can we proclaim God's wisdom and power even in the most painful moments? Why is this an important exercise?

[16] To him belong strength and insight;
both deceived and deceiver are his.[b]
[17] He leads rulers away stripped[c]
and makes fools of judges.[d]
[18] He takes off the shackles[e] put on by kings
and ties a loincloth[b] around their waist.
[19] He leads priests away stripped
and overthrows officials long established.[f]
[20] He silences the lips of trusted advisers
and takes away the discernment of elders.[g]
[21] He pours contempt on nobles
and disarms the mighty.
[22] He reveals the deep things of darkness[h]
and brings utter darkness[i] into the light.[j]
[23] He makes nations great, and destroys them;[k]
he enlarges nations,[l] and disperses them.
[24] He deprives the leaders of the earth of their reason;
he makes them wander in a trackless waste.[m]
[25] They grope in darkness with no light;[n]
he makes them stagger like drunkards.[o]

13 "My eyes have seen all this,
my ears have heard and understood it.
[2] What you know, I also know;
I am not inferior to you.[p]
[3] But I desire to speak to the Almighty
and to argue my case with God.[q]
[4] You, however, smear me with lies;[r]
you are worthless physicians, all of you!

12:16 [b] Job 13:7,9
12:17 [c] Job 19:9 [d] Job 3:14
12:18 [e] Ps 116:16
12:19 [f] Job 24:12, 22; 34:20, 28; 35:9
12:20 [g] Job 32:9
12:22 [h] 1Co 4:5 [i] Job 3:5 [j] Da 2:22
12:23 [k] Jer 25:9 [l] Ps 107:38; Isa 9:3; 26:15
12:24 [m] Ps 107:40
12:25 [n] Job 5:14 [o] Ps 107:27; Isa 24:20
13:2 [p] Job 12:3
13:3 [q] Job 23:3-4
13:4 [r] Ps 119:69; Jer 23:32

[a] 6 Or *those whose god is in their own hand*
[b] 18 Or *shackles of kings / and ties a belt*

---

about those who are wicked and hold them in contempt (vv. 5–6). This observation rests on the premise that justice should be proportional and relative.

12:10–25 This section, which is laid out like a hymn, expresses God's authority to revoke the power of corrupt or repressive leaders.

13:4–8 Job turns his attention back to his desired

[5]If only you would be altogether
silent!
For you, that would be wisdom.[s]
[6]Hear now my argument;
listen to the pleas of my lips.
[7]Will you speak wickedly on God's
behalf?
Will you speak deceitfully for
him?[t]
[8]Will you show him partiality?[u]
Will you argue the case for God?
[9]Would it turn out well if he
examined you?
Could you deceive him as you
might deceive a mortal?[v]
[10]He would surely call you to account
if you secretly showed partiality.
[11]Would not his splendor[w] terrify you?
Would not the dread of him fall on
you?
[12]Your maxims are proverbs of ashes;
your defenses are defenses of clay.

[13]"Keep silent and let me speak;
then let come to me what may.
[14]Why do I put myself in jeopardy
and take my life in my hands?
[15]Though he slay me, yet will I hope[x]
in him;[y]
I will surely[a] defend my ways to
his face.[z]
[16]Indeed, this will turn out for my
deliverance,[a]
for no godless person would dare
come before him!
[17]Listen carefully to what I say;[b]
let my words ring in your ears.
[18]Now that I have prepared my case,[c]
I know I will be vindicated.
[19]Can anyone bring charges against
me?[d]
If so, I will be silent and die.[e]

[20]"Only grant me these two things,
God,
and then I will not hide from you:
[21]Withdraw your hand[f] far from me,
and stop frightening me with your
terrors.

13:5 [s]Pr 17:28
13:7 [t]Job 36:4
13:8 [u]Lev 19:15
13:9 [v]Job 12:16; Gal 6:7
13:11 [w]Job 31:23
13:15 [x]Job 7:6 [y]Ps 23:4; Pr 14:32 [z]Job 27:5
13:16 [a]Isa 12:1
13:17 [b]Job 21:2
13:18 [c]Job 23:4
13:19 [d]Job 40:4; Isa 50:8 [e]Job 10:8
13:21 [f]Ps 39:10
13:22 [g]Job 14:15 [h]Job 9:16
13:23 [i]1Sa 26:18
13:24 [j]Dt 32:20; Ps 13:1; Isa 8:17 [k]Job 19:11; La 2:5
13:25 [l]Lev 26:36 [m]Job 21:18; Isa 42:3
13:26 [n]Ps 25:7
13:27 [o]Job 33:11
13:28 [p]Isa 50:9; Jas 5:2
14:1 [q]Job 5:7; Ecc 2:23
14:2 [r]Jas 1:10 [s]Ps 90:5-6 [t]Job 8:9
14:3 [u]Ps 8:4; 144:3 [v]Ps 143:2

Job 13:4–5 ❖ Job sternly corrected those who tried to adjust his own understanding of God and justice. When is it appropriate to boldly correct the understanding of those around us?

Job 14:1–2 ❖ How does the fleeting nature of life impact how carefully we consider how we live each day?

[22]Then summon me and I will
answer,[g]
or let me speak, and you reply to
me.[h]
[23]How many wrongs and sins have I
committed?[i]
Show me my offense and my sin.
[24]Why do you hide your face[j]
and consider me your enemy?[k]
[25]Will you torment a windblown leaf?[l]
Will you chase after dry chaff?[m]
[26]For you write down bitter things
against me
and make me reap the sins of my
youth.[n]
[27]You fasten my feet in shackles;[o]
you keep close watch on all my
paths
by putting marks on the soles of
my feet.

[28]"So man wastes away like something
rotten,
like a garment eaten by moths.[p]

14 "Mortals, born of woman,
are of few days and full of
trouble.[q]
[2]They spring up like flowers[r] and
wither away;[s]
like fleeting shadows,[t] they do not
endure.
[3]Do you fix your eye on them?[u]
Will you bring them[b] before you
for judgment?[v]

[a] 15 Or *He will surely slay me; I have no hope — / yet I will* [b] 3 Septuagint, Vulgate and Syriac; Hebrew *me*

---

court case, beginning with a rebuke to the friends (v. 4). He accuses them of speaking "wickedly on God's behalf" (v. 7). The friends presume to represent God's testimony about Job and his supposed sin.
13:15 Unfortunately, the most familiar and popular sections in Job are often among the most difficult. The Hebrew verb here could describe "hoping" or "waiting." It could also be translated, "Even though he may slay me, I will not wait [in silence]"—that is, Job will continue to press for the court appearance for which he's been asking.
13:28—14:13 After concluding his plea for a legitimate hearing, Job shifts to a discussion of human mortality and frailty. Like nearly everyone in the ancient world, Job believes that life continues after death, but such a belief offers little hope if life in the netherworld is dreary and filled with drudgery. Job wishes he could take refuge in the grave and then be brought back to life (14:13), but he realizes that such an option does not exist.

4 Who can bring what is pure[w] from
the impure?[x]
No one![y]
5 A person's days are determined;
you have decreed the number of
his months[z]
and have set limits he cannot
exceed.
6 So look away from him and let him
alone,[a]
till he has put in his time like a
hired laborer.[b]

7 "At least there is hope for a tree:
If it is cut down, it will sprout
again,
and its new shoots will not fail.
8 Its roots may grow old in the ground
and its stump die in the soil,
9 yet at the scent of water it will bud
and put forth shoots like a plant.
10 But a man dies and is laid low;
he breathes his last and is no
more.[c]
11 As the water of a lake dries up
or a riverbed becomes parched
and dry,[d]
12 so he lies down and does not rise;
till the heavens are no more,[e]
people will not awake
or be roused from their sleep.[f]

13 "If only you would hide me in the
grave
and conceal me till your anger has
passed![g]
If only you would set me a time
and then remember me!
14 If someone dies, will they live
again?
All the days of my hard service
I will wait for my renewal[a] to
come.
15 You will call and I will answer you;[h]
you will long for the creature your
hands have made.
16 Surely then you will count my steps[i]
but not keep track of my sin.[j]
17 My offenses will be sealed up in a
bag;[k]
you will cover over my sin.[l]

18 "But as a mountain erodes and
crumbles
and as a rock is moved from its
place,
19 as water wears away stones
and torrents wash away the soil,
so you destroy a person's hope.[m]
20 You overpower them once for all,
and they are gone;
you change their countenance and
send them away.
21 If their children are honored, they
do not know it;
if their offspring are brought low,
they do not see it.[n]
22 They feel but the pain of their own
bodies
and mourn only for themselves."

Eliphaz

15 Then Eliphaz the Temanite replied:

2 "Would a wise person answer with
empty notions
or fill their belly with the hot east
wind?[o]
3 Would they argue with useless words,
with speeches that have no value?

14:4 [w] Ps 51:10 [x] Eph 2:1-3 [y] Jn 3:6; Ro 5:12
14:5 [z] Job 21:21
14:6 [a] Job 7:19 [b] Job 7:1, 2; Ps 39:13
14:10 [c] Job 13:19
14:11 [d] Isa 19:5
14:12 [e] Rev 20:11; 21:1 [f] Ac 3:21
14:13 [g] Isa 26:20
14:15 [h] Job 13:22
14:16 [i] Ps 139:1-3; Pr 5:21; Jer 32:19 [j] Job 10:6
14:17 [k] Dt 32:34 [l] Hos 13:12
14:19 [m] Job 7:6
14:21 [n] Ecc 9:5; Isa 63:16
15:2 [o] Job 6:26

[a] 14 Or *release*

14:14 Job is hoping that his turn will come.
14:15–17 Job's objective is restored relationship, not restored benefits. This continues to be the most important aspect of Job's posture.

4:1—14:22 We must ask whether our faith can be sustained when our desires are not granted; when healing does not come; when broken homes are not restored; when the goals we pursue remain beyond our reach.

As Christians we must first conclude that being motivated by righteousness and faith rather than by benefits should be our goal. Some people never get there: They only think of Christianity as a benefits system, and if there is nothing in it for them, they lose all motivation. Yet Christ has told us that the cost of discipleship is high. In following Jesus we lose our lives; we don't gain or enrich them (Mt 16:25).

Once this course is set, we must determine that righteous behavior earns us nothing and that even if it gains us nothing, God is worthy of our devotion. He is a righteous God and has created us with the capacity to imitate him. It is in the imitation of him that we find relationship with him—our highest joy.

Our faith and its accompanying righteousness ought not to be self-serving. Righteousness should have its desired end in relationship with God, not in gaining reward from God. This is the teaching of the book of Job, and it is a lesson we still desperately need to learn.

15:1–4 Eliphaz makes six accusations in three parallel pairs (vv. 4–6), but he first says that Job's words have nullified his claims to piety and undermined his claim against the deity (v. 4).

4 But you even undermine piety
and hinder devotion to God.
5 Your sin prompts your mouth;
you adopt the tongue of the crafty.[p]
6 Your own mouth condemns you, not mine;
your own lips testify against you.[q]

7 "Are you the first man ever born?[r]
Were you brought forth before the hills?[s]
8 Do you listen in on God's council?[t]
Do you have a monopoly on wisdom?
9 What do you know that we do not know?
What insights do you have that we do not have?[u]
10 The gray-haired and the aged[v] are on our side,
men even older than your father.
11 Are God's consolations[w] not enough for you,
words[x] spoken gently to you?[y]
12 Why has your heart[z] carried you away,
and why do your eyes flash,
13 so that you vent your rage against God
and pour out such words from your mouth?

14 "What are mortals, that they could be pure,
or those born of woman,[a] that they could be righteous?[b]
15 If God places no trust in his holy ones,
if even the heavens are not pure in his eyes,[c]
16 how much less mortals, who are vile and corrupt,[d]
who drink up evil like water![e]

17 "Listen to me and I will explain to you;
let me tell you what I have seen,

15:5 [p] Job 5:13
15:6 [q] Lk 19:22
15:7 [r] Job 38:21 [s] Ps 90:2; Pr 8:25
15:8 [t] Ro 11:34; 1Co 2:11
15:9 [u] Job 13:2
15:10 [v] Job 32:6-7
15:11 [w] 2Co 1:3-4 [x] Zec 1:13 [y] Job 36:16
15:12 [z] Job 11:13
15:14 [a] Job 14:4; 25:4 [b] Pr 20:9; Ecc 7:20
15:15 [c] Job 4:18; 25:5
15:16 [d] Ps 14:1 [e] Job 34:7; Pr 19:28
15:18 [f] Job 8:8
15:20 [g] Job 24:1; 27:13-23
15:21 [h] Job 18:11; 20:25 [i] Job 27:20; 1Th 5:3
15:22 [j] Job 19:29; 27:14
15:23 [k] Ps 59:15; 109:10 [l] Job 18:12
15:25 [m] Job 36:9
15:27 [n] Ps 17:10
15:28 [o] Isa 5:9 [p] Job 3:14
15:29 [q] Job 27:16-17
15:30 [r] Job 5:14 [s] Job 22:20

Job 15:10 ❖ Are older believers always wiser? Why or why not (see 1Ti 4:2)?

18 what the wise have declared,
hiding nothing received from their ancestors[f]
19 (to whom alone the land was given
when no foreigners moved among them):
20 All his days the wicked man suffers torment,
the ruthless man through all the years stored up for him.[g]
21 Terrifying sounds fill his ears;[h]
when all seems well, marauders attack him.[i]
22 He despairs of escaping the realm of darkness;
he is marked for the sword.[j]
23 He wanders about[k] for food like a vulture;
he knows the day of darkness is at hand.[l]
24 Distress and anguish fill him with terror;
troubles overwhelm him, like a king poised to attack,
25 because he shakes his fist at God
and vaunts himself against the Almighty,[m]
26 defiantly charging against him
with a thick, strong shield.

27 "Though his face is covered with fat
and his waist bulges with flesh,[n]
28 he will inhabit ruined towns
and houses where no one lives,[o]
houses crumbling to rubble.[p]
29 He will no longer be rich and his wealth will not endure,[q]
nor will his possessions spread over the land.
30 He will not escape the darkness;[r]
a flame[s] will wither his shoots,

15:5 The second pair of accusations concerns Job's motives and methods. Eliphaz is suggesting that Job has rationalized his sins, so much so that he is not aware of them. Eliphaz is accusing Job of what we today call "spin."
15:6 In the third parallel set Eliphaz expresses his assessment of Job's current position—Job stands condemned by his own words. Eliphaz then attacks what he assesses is Job's arrogance.
15:11 Eliphaz may here refer to the revelation that he disclosed in 4:12–21. This speech would have been considered a consoling word because it suggests that Job is not alone—all humanity shares his deficiency of righteousness (4:17).
15:14–15 As in 4:18, Eliphaz follows his initial statement with an assertion concerning God's lack of trust in his holy ones. Eliphaz is suggesting that even those things that seem to be unblemished from our perspective are not so to God.
15:17–35 This speech primarily focuses on the destiny of the wicked. In v. 25, Eliphaz unequivocally places Job in the category of the wicked.

and the breath of God's mouth[t]
will carry him away.
31 Let him not deceive himself by
trusting what is worthless,[u]
for he will get nothing in return.
32 Before his time[v] he will wither,[w]
and his branches will not flourish.[x]
33 He will be like a vine stripped of its
unripe grapes,[y]
like an olive tree shedding its
blossoms.
34 For the company of the godless will
be barren,
and fire will consume the tents of
those who love bribes.[z]
35 They conceive trouble and give birth
to evil;[a]
their womb fashions deceit."

Job

16 Then Job replied:

2 "I have heard many things like
these;
you are miserable comforters, all
of you![b]
3 Will your long-winded speeches
never end?
What ails you that you keep on
arguing?[c]
4 I also could speak like you,
if you were in my place;
I could make fine speeches against
you
and shake my head[d] at you.
5 But my mouth would encourage you;
comfort from my lips would bring
you relief.

6 "Yet if I speak, my pain is not
relieved;
and if I refrain, it does not go
away.
7 Surely, God, you have worn me out;[e]
you have devastated my entire
household.
8 You have shriveled me up — and it
has become a witness;
my gauntness[f] rises up and
testifies against me.[g]
9 God assails me and tears[h] me in his
anger

15:30 [t] Job 4:9
15:31 [u] Isa 59:4
15:32 [v] Ecc 7:17 [w] Job 22:16; Ps 55:23 [x] Job 18:16
15:33 [y] Hab 3:17
15:34 [z] Job 8:22
15:35 [a] Ps 7:14; Isa 59:4; Hos 10:13
16:2 [b] Job 13:4
16:3 [c] Job 6:26
16:4 [d] Ps 22:7; 109:25; La 2:15; Zep 2:15; Mt 27:39
16:7 [e] Job 7:3
16:8 [f] Job 19:20 [g] Job 10:17
16:9 [h] Hos 6:1 [i] Ps 35:16; La 2:16; Ac 7:54 [j] Job 13:24
16:10 [k] Ps 22:13 [l] Isa 50:6; La 3:30; Mic 5:1; Ac 23:2 [m] Ps 35:15
16:11 [n] Job 1:15, 17
16:12 [o] Job 9:17 [p] La 3:12
16:13 [q] Job 20:24
16:14 [r] Job 9:17 [s] Joel 2:7
16:15 [t] Ge 37:34
16:17 [u] Isa 59:6; Jnh 3:8
16:18 [v] Isa 26:21 [w] Ps 66:18-19
16:19 [x] Ge 31:50; Ro 1:9; 1Th 2:5
16:20 [y] La 2:19
16:21 [z] Ps 9:4
16:22 [a] Ecc 12:5
17:1 [b] Ps 88:3-4

Job 16:2-5 ❖ How can we be the kind of comforters Job describes? To whom in our lives can we bring this comfort?

and gnashes his teeth at me;[i]
my opponent fastens on me his
piercing eyes.[j]
10 People open their mouths[k] to jeer
at me;
they strike my cheek[l] in scorn
and unite together against me.[m]
11 God has turned me over to the
ungodly
and thrown me into the clutches
of the wicked.[n]
12 All was well with me, but he
shattered me;
he seized me by the neck and
crushed me.[o]
He has made me his target;[p]
13 his archers surround me.
Without pity, he pierces[q] my kidneys
and spills my gall on the ground.
14 Again and again[r] he bursts upon me;
he rushes at me like a warrior.[s]

15 "I have sewed sackcloth[t] over my skin
and buried my brow in the dust.
16 My face is red with weeping,
dark shadows ring my eyes;
17 yet my hands have been free of
violence[u]
and my prayer is pure.

18 "Earth, do not cover my blood;[v]
may my cry never be laid to rest![w]
19 Even now my witness[x] is in heaven;
my advocate is on high.
20 My intercessor is my friend[a]
as my eyes pour out[y] tears to God;
21 on behalf of a man he pleads[z] with
God
as one pleads for a friend.

22 "Only a few years will pass
before I take the path of no
return.[a]

17 1 My spirit is broken,
my days are cut short,
the grave awaits me.[b]

[a] 20 Or *My friends treat me with scorn*

16:1-17 Job continues to delineate new charges against God. Though he voices accusations in vv. 11-14, his main charge is summarized in v. 9.
16:18-21 If we combine information from the context of Job, the OT, and documents from the ancient Near East, we can infer that Job hopes for a member of the divine council to call God to account on his behalf.
17:1-16 Job returns to the topic of death. He sees no vindication after the grave; death offers no

[2]Surely mockers[c] surround me;
my eyes must dwell on their hostility.

[3]"Give me, O God, the pledge you demand.[d]
Who else will put up security[e] for me?[f]
[4]You have closed their minds to understanding;
therefore you will not let them triumph.
[5]If anyone denounces their friends for reward,
the eyes of their children will fail.[g]

[6]"God has made me a byword[h] to everyone,
a man in whose face people spit.
[7]My eyes have grown dim with grief;[i]
my whole frame is but a shadow.
[8]The upright are appalled at this;
the innocent are aroused[j] against the ungodly.
[9]Nevertheless, the righteous[k] will hold to their ways,
and those with clean hands[l] will grow stronger.

[10]"But come on, all of you, try again!
I will not find a wise man among you.[m]
[11]My days have passed, my plans are shattered.
Yet the desires of my heart[n]
[12]turn night into day;
in the face of the darkness light is near.
[13]If the only home I hope for is the grave,[o]
if I spread out my bed in the realm of darkness,
[14]if I say to corruption,[p] 'You are my father,'
and to the worm,[q] 'My mother' or 'My sister,'
[15]where then is my hope —[r]
who can see any hope for me?
[16]Will it go down to the gates of death?[s]
Will we descend together into the dust?"

17:2 [c]1Sa 1:6-7
17:3 [d]Ps 119:122 [e]Pr 6:1 [f]Isa 38:14
17:5 [g]Job 11:20
17:6 [h]Job 30:9
17:7 [i]Job 16:8
17:8 [j]Job 22:19
17:9 [k]Pr 4:18 [l]Job 22:30
17:10 [m]Job 12:2
17:11 [n]Job 7:6
17:13 [o]Job 3:13
17:14 [p]Job 13:28; 30:28,30; Ps 16:10 [q]Job 21:26
17:15 [r]Job 7:6
17:16 [s]Job 3:17-19; Jnh 2:6

Job 17:15-16 ❖ How does the death and resurrection of Christ bring the kind of hope Job longs for, even in the face of death (see 1Co 15:54-58)?

Job 18:5-21 ❖ What causes people like Bildad to be so sure in their condemnation of others? How can we avoid this same kind of judgmentalism?

Bildad

18 Then Bildad the Shuhite replied:

[2]"When will you end these speeches?
Be sensible, and then we can talk.
[3]Why are we regarded as cattle
and considered stupid in your sight?[t]
[4]You who tear yourself[u] to pieces in your anger,
is the earth to be abandoned for your sake?
Or must the rocks be moved from their place?

[5]"The lamp of a wicked man is snuffed out;[v]
the flame of his fire stops burning.
[6]The light in his tent becomes dark;
the lamp beside him goes out.
[7]The vigor of his step is weakened;[w]
his own schemes[x] throw him down.[y]
[8]His feet thrust him into a net;[z]
he wanders into its mesh.
[9]A trap seizes him by the heel;
a snare holds him fast.
[10]A noose is hidden for him on the ground;
a trap lies in his path.
[11]Terrors startle him on every side[a]
and dog[b] his every step.
[12]Calamity is hungry[c] for him;
disaster is ready for him when he falls.
[13]It eats away parts of his skin;
death's firstborn devours his limbs.[d]
[14]He is torn from the security of his tent[e]
and marched off to the king of terrors.

18:3 [t]Ps 73:22
18:4 [u]Job 13:14
18:5 [v]Job 21:17; Pr 13:9; 20:20; 24:20
18:7 [w]Pr 4:12 [x]Job 5:13 [y]Job 15:6
18:8 [z]Job 22:10; Ps 9:15; 35:7
18:11 [a]Job 15:21; Jer 6:25; 20:3 [b]Job 20:8
18:12 [c]Isa 8:21
18:13 [d]Zec 14:12
18:14 [e]Job 8:22

relief (vv. 1, 13). In vv. 15–16 he again makes clear that he has no hope in the afterlife. Chapter 17 also affirms Job's view of righteousness: Truly righteous people are concerned about their integrity, not the rewards they receive.

18:1–21 Bildad, the traditionalist in the group, reasserts traditional wisdom concerning the plight of the wicked. It is one thing to say that the wicked will suffer, but it is quite another to conclude that anyone who is suffering must be wicked; this, however, is the inference that the friends are drawing.

18:13 The description speaks not of a slowly

15 Fire resides[a] in his tent;
burning sulfur[f] is scattered over his dwelling.
16 His roots dry up below[g]
and his branches wither above.[h]
17 The memory of him perishes from the earth;
he has no name in the land.[i]
18 He is driven from light into the realm of darkness[j]
and is banished from the world.
19 He has no offspring[k] or descendants[l] among his people,
no survivor where once he lived.[m]
20 People of the west are appalled at his fate;[n]
those of the east are seized with horror.
21 Surely such is the dwelling[o] of an evil man;
such is the place of one who does not know God."[p]

Job

19

Then Job replied:

2 "How long will you torment me
and crush me with words?
3 Ten times now you have reproached me;
shamelessly you attack me.
4 If it is true that I have gone astray,
my error[q] remains my concern alone.
5 If indeed you would exalt yourselves above me[r]
and use my humiliation against me,
6 then know that God has wronged me[s]
and drawn his net[t] around me.

7 "Though I cry, 'Violence!' I get no response;[u]
though I call for help, there is no justice.[v]
8 He has blocked my way so I cannot pass;[w]
he has shrouded my paths in darkness.[x]
9 He has stripped[y] me of my honor
and removed the crown from my head.[z]
10 He tears me down[a] on every side till I am gone;
he uproots my hope[b] like a tree.[c]
11 His anger[d] burns against me;
he counts me among his enemies.[e]
12 His troops advance in force;[f]
they build a siege ramp[g] against me
and encamp around my tent.

13 "He has alienated my family[h] from me;
my acquaintances are completely estranged from me.[i]
14 My relatives have gone away;
my closest friends have forgotten me.
15 My guests and my female servants count me a foreigner;
they look on me as on a stranger.
16 I summon my servant, but he does not answer,
though I beg him with my own mouth.
17 My breath is offensive to my wife;
I am loathsome to my own family.
18 Even the little boys[j] scorn me;
when I appear, they ridicule me.
19 All my intimate friends[k] detest me;[l]
those I love have turned against me.
20 I am nothing but skin and bones;[m]
I have escaped only by the skin of my teeth.[b]

21 "Have pity on me, my friends, have pity,
for the hand of God has struck me.
22 Why do you pursue[n] me as God does?
Will you never get enough of my flesh?[o]

23 "Oh, that my words were recorded,
that they were written on a scroll,[p]

18:15 [f] Ps 11:6
18:16 [g] Isa 5:24; Hos 9:1-16; Am 2:9 [h] Job 15:30; Mal 4:1
18:17 [i] Ps 34:16; Pr 2:22; 10:7
18:18 [j] Job 5:14
18:19 [k] Jer 22:30 [l] Isa 14:22 [m] Job 27:14-15
18:20 [n] Ps 37:13; Jer 50:27,31
18:21 [o] Job 21:28 [p] Jer 9:3; 1Th 4:5
19:4 [q] Job 6:24
19:5 [r] Ps 35:26; 38:16; 55:12
19:6 [s] Job 27:2 [t] Job 18:8
19:7 [u] Job 30:20 [v] Job 9:24; Hab 1:2-4
19:8 [w] Job 3:23; La 3:7 [x] Job 30:26
19:9 [y] Job 12:17 [z] Ps 89:39,44; La 5:16
19:10 [a] Job 12:14 [b] Job 7:6 [c] Job 24:20
19:11 [d] Job 16:9 [e] Job 13:24
19:12 [f] Job 16:13 [g] Job 30:12
19:13 [h] Ps 69:8 [i] Job 16:7; Ps 88:8
19:18 [j] 2Ki 2:23
19:19 [k] Ps 55:12-13 [l] Ps 38:11
19:20 [m] Job 33:21; Ps 102:5
19:22 [n] Job 13:25; 16:11 [o] Ps 69:26
19:23 [p] Isa 30:8

[a] 15 Or *Nothing he had remains* [b] 20 Or *only by my gums*

progressing disease but of the total destruction of the body in the grave.
18:21 Bildad describes the plight of the wicked using several statements that coincide with Job's experiences. In this verse he concludes that such things happen to those who do not know God. This is a devastating judgment.
19:1–29 Job's sense of abandonment leads him to reiterate that his friends have deserted him and God has wronged him (v. 6). This begins a series of accusations specifying how God has brought disaster. Job, however, still refuses to admit that this treatment might be God's response to his behavior.
19:23–24 Because Job does not expect to be

[24]that they were inscribed with an iron
tool on[a] lead,
or engraved in rock forever!
[25]I know that my redeemer[b][q] lives,[r]
and that in the end he will stand
on the earth.[c]
[26]And after my skin has been
destroyed,
yet[d] in[e] my flesh I will see God;[s]
[27]I myself will see him
with my own eyes—I, and not
another.
How my heart yearns[t] within me!

[28]"If you say, 'How we will hound him,
since the root of the trouble lies in
him,[f]'
[29]you should fear the sword yourselves;
for wrath will bring punishment
by the sword,[u]
and then you will know that there
is judgment.[g]"[v]

Zophar

20

Then Zophar the Naamathite replied:

[2]"My troubled thoughts prompt me to
answer
because I am greatly disturbed.
[3]I hear a rebuke[w] that dishonors me,
and my understanding inspires
me to reply.

[4]"Surely you know how it has been
from of old,
ever since mankind[h] was placed
on the earth,
[5]that the mirth of the wicked is brief,
the joy of the godless lasts but a
moment.[x]
[6]Though the pride of the godless
person reaches to the
heavens
and his head touches the clouds,[y]
[7]he will perish forever,[z] like his own
dung;
those who have seen him will say,
'Where is he?'[a]
[8]Like a dream[b] he flies away,[c] no more
to be found,
banished[d] like a vision of the
night.[e]
[9]The eye that saw him will not see
him again;
his place will look on him no more.[f]
[10]His children[g] must make amends to
the poor;
his own hands must give back his
wealth.[h]
[11]The youthful vigor[i] that fills his
bones
will lie with him in the dust.[j]

[12]"Though evil is sweet in his mouth
and he hides it under his tongue,
[13]though he cannot bear to let it go
and lets it linger in his mouth,[k]
[14]yet his food will turn sour in his
stomach;
it will become the venom of
serpents within him.
[15]He will spit out the riches he
swallowed;
God will make his stomach vomit
them up.

19:25 [q] Ps 78:35; Pr 23:11; Isa 43:14; Jer 50:34 [r] Job 16:19
19:26 [s] Ps 17:15; Mt 5:8; 1Co 13:12; 1Jn 3:2
19:27 [t] Ps 73:26
19:29 [u] Job 15:22 [v] Job 22:4; Ps 1:5; 9:7
20:3 [w] Job 19:3
20:5 [x] Job 8:12; Ps 37:35-36; 73:19
20:6 [y] Isa 14:13-14; Ob 3-4
20:7 [z] Job 4:20 [a] Job 7:10; 8:18
20:8 [b] Ps 73:20 [c] Job 27:21-23 [d] Job 18:18 [e] Ps 90:5
20:9 [f] Job 7:8
20:10 [g] Job 5:4 [h] Job 27:16-17
20:11 [i] Job 13:26 [j] Job 21:26
20:13 [k] Nu 11:18-20

Job 19:25 ❖ How does hope in a Redeemer carry us through the worst of life's sufferings (see Ro 8:38-39)?

Job 20:2-3 ❖ How does Zophar embody Paul's statement that "knowledge puffs up while love builds up" (1Co 8:1)? What might a more loving response to people who are hurting look like?

[a] *24* Or *and* [b] *25* Or *vindicator* [c] *25* Or *on my grave* [d] *26* Or *And after I awake, / though this body has been destroyed, / then* [e] *26* Or *destroyed, / apart from* [f] *28* Many Hebrew manuscripts, Septuagint and Vulgate; most Hebrew manuscripts *me* [g] *29* Or *sword, / that you may come to know the Almighty* [h] *4* Or *Adam*

around much longer to present his case personally, he wishes for a permanent record of his sufferings and claims for posterity.

19:25 A "redeemer" is also one who enters a legal situation on behalf of another. Their job is to recover losses and to salvage the dignity of one who has suffered loss. Job expects his "redeemer" to arrive and testify on his behalf.

19:27 Job's statement further substantiates the idea that Job will enjoy restored favor with God in his own flesh. Job hopes that God will no longer treat him as a stranger; he hopes that if he is no longer an outsider, Job will be welcomed back into fellowship with God.

20:1-29 Zophar grounds his argument in God's actions against the wicked: He takes away their riches (v. 15), rains down blows on them (v. 23), and carries away all that they have (vv. 28-29). The reader knows that even though Job has experienced these things, they do not result from the wrath of God, as Zophar suggests (v. 28). Zophar indirectly accuses Job of pride (v. 6) and of concealing evil (v. 12). As always, the friends observe Job's circumstances but draw illegitimate conclusions about God's motives and Job's conduct.

16 He will suck the poison[l] of serpents;
the fangs of an adder will kill
him.[m]
17 He will not enjoy the streams,
the rivers flowing with honey[n]
and cream.[o]
18 What he toiled for he must give back
uneaten;
he will not enjoy the profit from
his trading.
19 For he has oppressed the poor and
left them destitute;[p]
he has seized houses he did not
build.

20 "Surely he will have no respite from
his craving;[q]
he cannot save himself by his
treasure.
21 Nothing is left for him to devour;
his prosperity will not endure.[r]
22 In the midst of his plenty, distress
will overtake him;
the full force of misery will come
upon him.
23 When he has filled his belly,
God will vent his burning anger
against him
and rain down his blows on him.[s]
24 Though he flees[t] from an iron
weapon,
a bronze-tipped arrow pierces
him.
25 He pulls it out of his back,
the gleaming point out of his
liver.
Terrors[u] will come over him;[v]
26 total darkness[w] lies in wait for his
treasures.
A fire unfanned will consume him[x]
and devour what is left in his tent.
27 The heavens will expose his guilt;
the earth will rise up against him.[y]
28 A flood will carry off his house,[z]
rushing waters[a] on the day of
God's wrath.[a]
29 Such is the fate God allots the
wicked,
the heritage appointed for them
by God."[b]

Job

21

Then Job replied:

2 "Listen carefully to my words;
let this be the consolation you
give me.
3 Bear with me while I speak,

20:16 [l] Dt 32:32 [m] Dt 32:24
20:17 [n] Dt 32:13 [o] Job 29:6
20:19 [p] Job 24:4,14; 35:9
20:20 [q] Ecc 5:12-14
20:21 [r] Job 15:29
20:23 [s] Ps 78:30-31
20:24 [t] Isa 24:18; Am 5:19
20:25 [u] Job 18:11 [v] Job 16:13
20:26 [w] Job 18:18 [x] Ps 21:9
20:27 [y] Dt 31:28
20:28 [z] Dt 28:31 [a] Job 21:17, 20,30
20:29 [b] Job 27:13

21:3 [c] Job 16:10
21:4 [d] Job 6:11
21:5 [e] Jdg 18:19; Job 29:9; 40:4
21:7 [f] Job 12:6; Ps 73:3; Jer 12:1; Hab 1:13
21:8 [g] Ps 17:14
21:9 [h] Ps 73:5
21:10 [i] Ex 23:26
21:12 [j] Ps 81:2
21:13 [k] Job 36:11
21:14 [l] Job 22:17 [m] Pr 1:29
21:15 [n] Ex 5:2; Job 34:9; Mal 3:14
21:17 [o] Job 18:5

Job 21:7-21 ❖ How would we answer Job's anguished question about why the wicked often prosper? Why does God often allow the wicked to live long, comfortable lives?

and after I have spoken, mock
on.[c]

4 "Is my complaint directed to a
human being?
Why should I not be impatient?[d]
5 Look at me and be appalled;
clap your hand over your mouth.[e]
6 When I think about this, I am
terrified;
trembling seizes my body.
7 Why do the wicked live on,
growing old and increasing in
power?[f]
8 They see their children established
around them,
their offspring before their eyes.[g]
9 Their homes are safe and free from
fear;[h]
the rod of God is not on them.
10 Their bulls never fail to breed;
their cows calve and do not
miscarry.[i]
11 They send forth their children as a
flock;
their little ones dance about.
12 They sing to the music of timbrel
and lyre;
they make merry to the sound of
the pipe.[j]
13 They spend their years in prosperity[k]
and go down to the grave in
peace.[b]
14 Yet they say to God, 'Leave us alone![l]
We have no desire to know your
ways.[m]
15 Who is the Almighty, that we should
serve him?
What would we gain by praying to
him?'[n]
16 But their prosperity is not in their
own hands,
so I stand aloof from the plans of
the wicked.

17 "Yet how often is the lamp of the
wicked snuffed out?[o]
How often does calamity come
upon them,
the fate God allots in his anger?

[a] 28 Or *The possessions in his house will be carried off, / washed away* [b] 13 Or *in an instant*

18 How often are they like straw before the wind,
like chaff[p] swept away by a gale?
19 It is said, 'God stores up the punishment of the wicked for their children.'[q]
Let him repay the wicked, so that they themselves will experience it!
20 Let their own eyes see their destruction;
let them drink[r] the cup of the wrath of the Almighty.[s]
21 For what do they care about the families they leave behind
when their allotted months[t] come to an end?

22 "Can anyone teach knowledge to God,[u]
since he judges even the highest?[v]
23 One person dies in full vigor,
completely secure and at ease,
24 well nourished in body,[a]
bones rich with marrow.[w]
25 Another dies in bitterness of soul,
never having enjoyed anything good.
26 Side by side they lie in the dust,
and worms cover them both.[x]

27 "I know full well what you are thinking,
the schemes by which you would wrong me.
28 You say, 'Where now is the house of the great,[y]
the tents where the wicked lived?'[z]
29 Have you never questioned those who travel?
Have you paid no regard to their accounts —
30 that the wicked are spared from the day of calamity,[a]
that they are delivered from[b] the day of wrath?[b]
31 Who denounces their conduct to their face?
Who repays them for what they have done?
32 They are carried to the grave,
and watch is kept over their tombs.
33 The soil in the valley is sweet to them;[c]
everyone follows after them,
and a countless throng goes[c] before them.[d]

34 "So how can you console me[e] with your nonsense?
Nothing is left of your answers but falsehood!"

21:18 [p] Job 13:25; Ps 1:4
21:19 [q] Ex 20:5; Jer 31:29; Eze 18:2
21:20 [r] Ps 75:8; Isa 51:17 [s] Jer 25:15; Rev 14:10
21:21 [t] Job 14:5
21:22 [u] Job 35:11; 36:22; Isa 40:13-14; Ro 11:34 [v] Ps 82:1
21:24 [w] Pr 3:8
21:26 [x] Job 24:20; Ecc 9:2-3; Isa 14:11
21:28 [y] Job 1:3; 12:21; 31:37 [z] Job 8:22
21:30 [a] Pr 16:4 [b] Job 20:22, 28; 2Pe 2:9
21:33 [c] Job 3:22; 17:16; 24:24 [d] Job 3:19
21:34 [e] Job 16:2

[a] *24* The meaning of the Hebrew for this word is uncertain. [b] *30* Or *wicked are reserved for the day of calamity, / that they are brought forth to* [c] *33* Or *them, / as a countless throng went*

21:1-34 In response to the three speeches about the plight and destiny of the wicked, Job offers his own observations about the wicked. These are diametrically opposed to the neat and tidy perspective of the friends. Job confronts them with evidence that contradicts the traditions they have been spouting—the wicked, in fact, often do prosper (vv. 7-33). This is information that the friends all know but prefer to ignore. Job is preparing his case that the system is broken, for whether people have a secure and prosperous life or a miserable life of destitution, they all die (v. 26). This sentiment picks up a theme well-known from Ecclesiastes.

15:1—21:34 The force of the argument in this second series of dialogues concerns the suffering of the wicked. Job's friends insist that the wicked do suffer, and Job's concluding speech questions whether human experience affirms such consistency. What should we think about this, and how does it factor into our own worldview?

Certainly, both OT and NT encourage us to think that God delights in good behavior and that he will judge the wicked. We reap what we sow (Gal 6:7), yet our own experiences and observations lead us to share in Job's skepticism. Perhaps we should adopt a modified view of the retribution principle, understood in proverbial and theological terms. In other words, the retribution principle is useful to describe God's nature, and it therefore helps us to identify general trends in human experience, but it offers no guarantees and cannot be applied consistently or universally in this fallen world.

This interpretation suggests several important conclusions: (1) We cannot draw conclusions about people's behavior from their circumstances. (2) We should not expect wicked people to get their just punishment in this life. (3) We should never rejoice in the misfortune of an enemy, though we may take consolation that justice is sometimes served in this world.

On the last point we must distinguish between judicial actions and personal circumstances. In the former case, justice is vindicated when a corrupt politician is caught, indicted, tried, and punished for his or her crimes. Without indulging vindictive feelings, we can rejoice that justice was served and that the system worked. However, we should not respond gleefully when someone we consider

Eliphaz

22 Then Eliphaz the Temanite replied:

2 "Can a man be of benefit to God?[f]
Can even a wise person benefit him?
3 What pleasure would it give the Almighty if you were righteous?
What would he gain if your ways were blameless?

4 "Is it for your piety that he rebukes you
and brings charges against you?[g]
5 Is not your wickedness great?
Are not your sins[h] endless?
6 You demanded security[i] from your relatives for no reason;
you stripped people of their clothing, leaving them naked.
7 You gave no water to the weary
and you withheld food from the hungry,[j]
8 though you were a powerful man, owning land—
an honored man,[k] living on it.
9 And you sent widows away empty-handed[l]
and broke the strength of the fatherless.
10 That is why snares are all around you,
why sudden peril terrifies you,
11 why it is so dark[m] you cannot see,
and why a flood of water covers you.[n]

12 "Is not God in the heights of heaven?[o]
And see how lofty are the highest stars!
13 Yet you say, 'What does God know?[p]
Does he judge through such darkness?[q]
14 Thick clouds[r] veil him, so he does not see us
as he goes about in the vaulted heavens.'
15 Will you keep to the old path
that the wicked have trod?
16 They were carried off before their time,[s]
their foundations washed away by a flood.[t]
17 They said to God, 'Leave us alone!
What can the Almighty do to us?'[u]
18 Yet it was he who filled their houses with good things,[v]
so I stand aloof from the plans of the wicked.[w]
19 The righteous see their ruin and rejoice;[x]
the innocent mock[y] them, saying,
20 'Surely our foes are destroyed,
and fire[z] devours their wealth.'

21 "Submit to God and be at peace with him;
in this way prosperity will come to you.[a]
22 Accept instruction from his mouth
and lay up his words in your heart.
23 If you return[b] to the Almighty, you will be restored:[c]
If you remove wickedness far from your tent[d]
24 and assign your nuggets to the dust,

22:2 [f] Lk 17:10
22:4 [g] Job 14:3; 19:29; Ps 143:2
22:5 [h] Job 11:6; 15:5
22:6 [i] Ex 22:26; Dt 24:6,17; Eze 18:12,16
22:7 [j] Job 31:17, 21,31
22:8 [k] Isa 3:3; 9:15
22:9 [l] Job 24:3, 21
22:11 [m] Job 5:14 [n] Ps 69:1-2; 124:4-5; La 3:54
22:12 [o] Job 11:8
22:13 [p] Ps 10:11; Isa 29:15 [q] Eze 8:12
22:14 [r] Job 26:9
22:16 [s] Job 15:32 [t] Job 14:19; Mt 7:26-27
22:17 [u] Job 21:15
22:18 [v] Job 12:6 [w] Job 21:16
22:19 [x] Ps 58:10; 107:42 [y] Ps 52:6
22:20 [z] Job 15:30
22:21 [a] Ps 34:8-10
22:23 [b] Job 8:5; Isa 31:6; Zec 1:3 [c] Isa 19:22; Ac 20:32 [d] Job 11:14

Job 22:5 ❖ Why do self-righteous people sometimes lash out in anger? How can we control this impulse in our own lives?

---

an enemy or a wicked person suffers personal tragedies (i.e., they lose a loved one or contract a serious disease). We should rather defer to Christ's exhortation that we love even our enemies (Mt 5:43–48) and realize that we cannot legitimately assess their circumstances, whether good or bad, as God's judgment of wickedness.

22:1-30 Eliphaz's opening line sets the tone for the remainder of his speech as he targets the issue that Job has been holding as his defense. In vv. 2–3 Eliphaz is in effect saying, "A mediator will do you no good; your proposed lawsuit would have no chance of success."
22:6-9 Here we find the friends' only attempt to accuse Job of specific sins, alleging injustice toward three vulnerable classes: the debtor (v. 6), the hungry/thirsty (vv. 7–8), and the widow/orphan (v. 9).
22:15–18 Eliphaz is urging Job not to think that he can follow the path of the wicked that Job has just described. His comments in vv. 17–18 contain the same wording that Job attributes to the wicked in 21:14–16.
22:21–22 Eliphaz advises Job to reengage with God and stop arguing.
22:23–27 Concluding his final speech, Eliphaz emphasizes restored favor with God (vv. 25–27) but with the twist that renewed favor will put Job in a position to influence God. This alludes to a subtle temptation for Job to pursue benefits rather than seek righteousness for righteousness' sake.

your gold of Ophir to the rocks in
the ravines,[e]
25 then the Almighty will be your gold,
the choicest silver for you.[f]
26 Surely then you will find delight in
the Almighty[g]
and will lift up your face to God.
27 You will pray to him,[h] and he will
hear you,
and you will fulfill your vows.
28 What you decide on will be done,
and light will shine on your ways.
29 When people are brought low and
you say, 'Lift them up!'
then he will save the downcast.[i]
30 He will deliver even one who is not
innocent,
who will be delivered through the
cleanness of your hands."[j]

Job

23

Then Job replied:

2 "Even today my complaint[k] is bitter;[l]
his hand[a] is heavy in spite of[b] my
groaning.
3 If only I knew where to find him;
if only I could go to his dwelling!
4 I would state my case[m] before him
and fill my mouth with
arguments.
5 I would find out what he would
answer me,
and consider what he would say
to me.
6 Would he vigorously oppose me?[n]
No, he would not press charges
against me.
7 There the upright can establish their
innocence before him,[o]
and there I would be delivered
forever from my judge.
8 "But if I go to the east, he is not
there;
if I go to the west, I do not find
him.
9 When he is at work in the north, I do
not see him;
when he turns to the south, I
catch no glimpse of him.[p]
10 But he knows the way that I take;
when he has tested me,[q] I will
come forth as gold.[r]
11 My feet have closely followed his
steps;[s]
I have kept to his way without
turning aside.[t]
12 I have not departed from the
commands of his lips;[u]
I have treasured the words of his
mouth more than my daily
bread.[v]

13 "But he stands alone, and who can
oppose him?
He does whatever he pleases.[w]
14 He carries out his decree against me,
and many such plans he still has
in store.[x]
15 That is why I am terrified before
him;
when I think of all this, I fear
him.
16 God has made my heart faint;[y]
the Almighty[z] has terrified me.
17 Yet I am not silenced by the
darkness,[a]
by the thick darkness that covers
my face.

24

"Why does the Almighty not set
times for judgment?[b]
Why must those who know him
look in vain for such days?[c]
2 There are those who move boundary
stones;[d]
they pasture flocks they have
stolen.
3 They drive away the orphan's
donkey

Job 23:8-12 ❖ Even when we are faithfully following his ways, we can at times feel that God is distant from us. When that happens, how can we find hope and assurance (see Mt 28:20)?

Job 24:1-12 ❖ How do we reconcile all the pain in the world with God's loving hand? Why do some people seem to be given more than their share of sorrows and suffering?

22:24 [e] Job 31:25
22:25 [f] Isa 33:6
22:26 [g] Job 27:10; Isa 58:14
22:27 [h] Job 33:26; 34:28; Isa 58:9
22:29 [i] Mt 23:12; 1Pe 5:5
22:30 [j] Job 42:7-8
23:2 [k] Job 7:11 [l] Job 6:3
23:4 [m] Job 13:18
23:6 [n] Job 9:4
23:7 [o] Job 13:3
23:9 [p] Job 9:11
23:10 [q] Ps 66:10; 139:1-3 [r] 1Pe 1:7
23:11 [s] Ps 17:5 [t] Ps 44:18
23:12 [u] Job 6:10 [v] Jn 4:32,34
23:13 [w] Ps 115:3
23:14 [x] 1Th 3:3
23:16 [y] Dt 20:3; Ps 22:14; Jer 51:46 [z] Job 27:2
23:17 [a] Job 19:8
24:1 [b] Jer 46:10 [c] Ac 1:7
24:2 [d] Dt 19:14; 27:17; Pr 23:10

[a] 2 Septuagint and Syriac; Hebrew / *the hand on me* [b] 2 Or *heavy on me in*

22:30 Perhaps Eliphaz is suggesting that when Job is restored, he could help people who are suffering the same things he has endured.
23:1—24:25 In ch. 23 Job ponders his status before God. He is torn between optimistic confidence (vv. 6b–7, 10) and frustrated attempts at justification (vv. 8–9). He is filled with continuing plans for his legal defense (vv. 4–5) and affirmations of his righteousness (vv. 11–12). Both his suffering (v. 2) and his terror of God (vv. 13–17) remain.

and take the widow's ox in pledge.[e]
4 They thrust the needy from the path
and force all the poor[f] of the land
into hiding.[g]
5 Like wild donkeys in the desert,
the poor go about their labor[h] of
foraging food;
the wasteland provides food for
their children.
6 They gather fodder in the fields
and glean in the vineyards of the
wicked.
7 Lacking clothes, they spend the
night naked;
they have nothing to cover
themselves in the cold.[i]
8 They are drenched by mountain rains
and hug[j] the rocks for lack of
shelter.
9 The fatherless[k] child is snatched
from the breast;
the infant of the poor is seized for
a debt.
10 Lacking clothes, they go about
naked;
they carry the sheaves, but still go
hungry.
11 They crush olives among the
terraces[a];
they tread the winepresses, yet
suffer thirst.
12 The groans of the dying rise from
the city,
and the souls of the wounded cry
out for help.[l]
But God charges no one with
wrongdoing.[m]

13 "There are those who rebel against
the light,[n]
who do not know its ways
or stay in its paths.[o]
14 When daylight is gone, the murderer
rises up,
kills the poor and needy,
and in the night steals forth like a
thief.[p]
15 The eye of the adulterer watches for
dusk;[q]
he thinks, 'No eye will see me,'[r]
and he keeps his face concealed.
16 In the dark, thieves break into
houses,[s]
but by day they shut themselves in;
they want nothing to do with the
light.[t]
17 For all of them, midnight is their
morning;
they make friends with the terrors
of darkness.

18 "Yet they are foam[u] on the surface of
the water;[v]
their portion of the land is cursed,
so that no one goes to the
vineyards.
19 As heat and drought snatch away the
melted snow,[w]
so the grave[x] snatches away those
who have sinned.
20 The womb forgets them,
the worm feasts on them;
the wicked are no longer
remembered[y]
but are broken like a tree.[z]
21 They prey on the barren and
childless woman,
and to the widow they show no
kindness.[a]
22 But God drags away the mighty by
his power;
though they become established,
they have no assurance of life.[b]
23 He may let them rest in a feeling of
security,[c]
but his eyes are on their ways.[d]
24 For a little while they are exalted,
and then they are gone;[e]
they are brought low and gathered
up like all others;
they are cut off like heads of
grain.[f]

25 "If this is not so, who can prove me
false
and reduce my words to
nothing?"[g]

Bildad

25 Then Bildad the Shuhite replied:

2 "Dominion and awe belong to God;[h]
he establishes order in the heights
of heaven.

[a] 11 The meaning of the Hebrew for this word is uncertain.

24:3 [e] Dt 24:6, 10,12,17; Job 22:6
24:4 [f] Job 29:12; 30:25; Ps 41:1 [g] Pr 28:28
24:5 [h] Ps 104:23
24:7 [i] Ex 22:27; Job 22:6
24:8 [j] La 4:5
24:9 [k] Dt 24:17
24:12 [l] Eze 26:15 [m] Job 9:23
24:13 [n] Jn 3:19-20 [o] Isa 5:20
24:14 [p] Ps 10:9
24:15 [q] Pr 7:8-9 [r] Ps 10:11
24:16 [s] Ex 22:2; Mt 6:19 [t] Jn 3:20
24:18 [u] Job 9:26 [v] Job 22:16
24:19 [w] Job 6:17 [x] Job 21:13
24:20 [y] Job 18:17; Pr 10:7 [z] Ps 31:12; Da 4:14
24:21 [a] Job 22:9
24:22 [b] Dt 28:66
24:23 [c] Job 12:6 [d] Job 11:11
24:24 [e] Job 14:21; Ps 37:10 [f] Isa 17:5
24:25 [g] Job 6:28; 27:4
25:2 [h] Job 9:4; Rev 1:6

24:12–17 Job turns his attention to the injustice in the world. He wonders why God does not respond. Job here complains, "God charges no one with wrongdoing" (v. 12).

24:22–23 In this analysis, Job observes that wickedness offers no advantage. The wicked fall prey to their own schemes and to their own mortality.

25:1–6 Bildad's last speech is only six verses long.

[3]Can his forces be numbered?
On whom does his light not rise?[i]
[4]How then can a mortal be righteous before God?
How can one born of woman be pure?[j]
[5]If even the moon[k] is not bright
and the stars are not pure in his eyes,[l]
[6]how much less a mortal, who is but a maggot —
a human being,[m] who is only a worm!"[n]

Job

26 Then Job replied:

[2]"How you have helped the powerless![o]
How you have saved the arm that is feeble![p]
[3]What advice you have offered to one without wisdom!
And what great insight you have displayed!
[4]Who has helped you utter these words?
And whose spirit spoke from your mouth?

[5]"The dead are in deep anguish,[q]
those beneath the waters and all that live in them.
[6]The realm of the dead[r] is naked before God;
Destruction[a] lies uncovered.[s]
[7]He spreads out the northern skies[t]
over empty space;
he suspends the earth over nothing.
[8]He wraps up the waters[u] in his clouds,[v]
yet the clouds do not burst under their weight.
[9]He covers the face of the full moon,
spreading his clouds[w] over it.
[10]He marks out the horizon on the face of the waters[x]
for a boundary between light and darkness.[y]
[11]The pillars of the heavens quake,
aghast at his rebuke.
[12]By his power he churned up the sea;[z]
by his wisdom[a] he cut Rahab to pieces.
[13]By his breath the skies became fair;
his hand pierced the gliding serpent.[b]
[14]And these are but the outer fringe of his works;
how faint the whisper we hear of him!
Who then can understand the thunder of his power?"[c]

Job's Final Word to His Friends

27 And Job continued his discourse:[d]

[2]"As surely as God lives, who has denied me justice,[e]
the Almighty, who has made my life bitter,[f]

25:3 [i] Jas 1:17
25:4 [j] Job 4:17; 14:4
25:5 [k] Job 31:26 [l] Job 15:15
25:6 [m] Job 7:17 [n] Ps 22:6
26:2 [o] Job 6:12 [p] Ps 71:9
26:5 [q] Ps 88:10
26:6 [r] Ps 139:8 [s] Job 41:11; Pr 15:11; Heb 4:13
26:7 [t] Job 9:8
26:8 [u] Pr 30:4 [v] Job 37:11
26:9 [w] Job 22:14; Ps 97:2
26:10 [x] Pr 8:27, 29 [y] Job 38:8-11
26:12 [z] Ex 14:21; Isa 51:15; Jer 31:35 [a] Job 12:13
26:13 [b] Isa 27:1
26:14 [c] Job 36:29
27:1 [d] Job 29:1
27:2 [e] Job 34:5 [f] Job 9:18

Job 25:6 ❖ Do you agree with Bildad's description of humans? Why or why not?

Job 26:12-14 ❖ Should God's power frighten humans? Why or why not?

Job 27:2-4 ❖ How can we keep our words righteous even when our life situations are bitter? Why is this often difficult?

[a] 6 Hebrew *Abaddon*

His entrenched traditionalism has reduced him to platitudes and repetition of previous points.

26:1—27:23 The Akkadian myth "The Descent of Ishtar to the Underworld" recounts Ishtar's passage through the seven gates of the netherworld. It is intriguing to see similar themes in both Job and the "The Descent," but the contexts are very different.

26:5-8 In the ancient view, people saw the earth/netherworld as suspended on the functionless cosmic waters below, parallel to the heaven and stretched out over the upper cosmic waters. The imagery of cloud-enveloped waters in v. 8 likewise fits the ideas that were widely held in the ancient world.

26:11 More ancient imagery: Just as the earth is supported by pillars, so too are the heavens. The pillars may refer to mountains since some mountains were believed to intersect the sky and perhaps hold it up.

26:12-13 The churning of the sea has been generally considered an element of the typical mythical scene in which the restless cosmic ocean disturbs the creatures (monsters, beasts) that represent chaos and disorder. The cosmic creature Rahab is roused when the sea is agitated.

27:1-6 Job gives a final response to his friends. The oath formula shows that Job is delivering an ultimatum to his friends—further debate will be useless.

27:2 Job describes what God has done to him: "denied me justice" and "made my life bitter." These two statements summarize Job's flawed view of God. The flaw is not in the blunt facts (Job's suffering at God's hand) but in what he implies about God's character as he reiterates those facts.

[3]as long as I have life within me,
the breath of God[g] in my nostrils,
[4]my lips will not say anything wicked,
and my tongue will not utter lies.[h]
[5]I will never admit you are in the right;
till I die, I will not deny my integrity.[i]
[6]I will maintain my innocence and never let go of it;
my conscience will not reproach me as long as I live.[j]

[7]"May my enemy be like the wicked,
my adversary like the unjust!
[8]For what hope have the godless[k]
when they are cut off,
when God takes away their life?[l]
[9]Does God listen to their cry
when distress comes upon them?[m]
[10]Will they find delight in the Almighty?[n]
Will they call on God at all times?

[11]"I will teach you about the power of God;
the ways of the Almighty I will not conceal.
[12]You have all seen this yourselves.
Why then this meaningless talk?
[13]"Here is the fate God allots to the wicked,
the heritage a ruthless man receives from the Almighty:[o]
[14]However many his children, their fate is the sword;[p]
his offspring will never have enough to eat.[q]
[15]The plague will bury those who survive him,
and their widows will not weep for them.[r]
[16]Though he heaps up silver like dust
and clothes like piles of clay,[s]
[17]what he lays up the righteous will wear,[t]
and the innocent will divide his silver.
[18]The house he builds is like a moth's cocoon,[u]
like a hut[v] made by a watchman.
[19]He lies down wealthy, but will do so no more;[w]
when he opens his eyes, all is gone.
[20]Terrors overtake him like a flood;[x]
a tempest snatches him away in the night.[y]
[21]The east wind carries him off, and he is gone;
it sweeps him out of his place.[z]
[22]It hurls itself against him without mercy[a]
as he flees headlong from its power.[b]
[23]It claps its hands in derision
and hisses him out of his place."[c]

27:3 [g] Job 32:8; 33:4
27:4 [h] Job 6:28
27:5 [i] Job 2:9; 13:15
27:6 [j] Job 2:3
27:8 [k] Job 8:13 [l] Job 11:20; Lk 12:20
27:9 [m] Job 35:12; Pr 1:28; Isa 1:15; Jer 14:12; Mic 3:4
27:10 [n] Job 22:26
27:13 [o] Job 15:20; 20:29
27:14 [p] Dt 28:41; Job 15:22; Hos 9:13 [q] Job 20:10
27:15 [r] Ps 78:64
27:16 [s] Zec 9:3
27:17 [t] Pr 28:8; Ecc 2:26
27:18 [u] Job 8:14 [v] Isa 1:8
27:19 [w] Job 7:8
27:20 [x] Job 15:21 [y] Job 20:8
27:21 [z] Job 7:10; 21:18
27:22 [a] Jer 13:14; Eze 5:11; 24:14 [b] Job 11:20
27:23 [c] Job 18:18

Interlude: Where Wisdom Is Found

28 There is a mine for silver
and a place where gold is refined.

27:4-6 Job nonetheless expresses his lifelong commitment to doing what is right.
27:7-10 Job begins by cursing his enemies. His three "advisers" have opposed and condemned him. Just as they have implicitly condemned him, he now does the same to them.
27:11-12 Job initially asked for his friends' instruction (6:24). Now Job turns the tables, assessing their instruction as nothing but "meaningless talk" (27:12).
27:13-23 Job now returns to a discussion of God's interaction with the wicked. Job specifically mentions God's retributive action (though God is only named in v. 13).

22:1—27:23 Humans (especially Americans) tend to be motivated by self-interest: "What is in it for me?" we ask. We have not only adopted our own self-fulfillment and happiness as a goal, but nearly consider it a right. Not only has happiness become our ambition, it has often become a spiritual expectation. Often in the process we expect much of God and little of ourselves.

If the book of Job promotes righteousness for its own sake as a moral principle, we should explore what this value looks like: What does it look like for our faith to get beyond our self-interest? Taking the lead from the book of Job, we would have to conclude that such a faith would not abandon belief even if life gets difficult. But it is important that we also consider the proper motives for our behavior and our choices. How should we discern what God expects of us and what we should expect of ourselves? How should we live if we want to pursue a faith not based on our own self-interest?

Ideally we should aspire to holiness, not because of benefits we can gain as a result but because God is God, and our righteous behavior is one of the ways we honor him. Regardless of whether we experience any advantages in life because of these decisions, we choose this path because of who God is.

28:1-11 Mining was an important industry in the ancient world. As the passage outlines, mining

[2]Iron is taken from the earth,
and copper is smelted from ore.[d]
[3]Mortals put an end to the darkness;[e]
they search out the farthest recesses
for ore in the blackest darkness.
[4]Far from human dwellings they cut a shaft,
in places untouched by human feet;
far from other people they dangle and sway.
[5]The earth, from which food comes,[f]
is transformed below as by fire;
[6]lapis lazuli comes from its rocks,
and its dust contains nuggets of gold.
[7]No bird of prey knows that hidden path,
no falcon's eye has seen it.
[8]Proud beasts do not set foot on it,
and no lion prowls there.
[9]People assault the flinty rock with their hands
and lay bare the roots of the mountains.
[10]They tunnel through the rock;
their eyes see all its treasures.
[11]They search[a] the sources of the rivers
and bring hidden things to light.

[12]But where can wisdom be found?[g]
Where does understanding dwell?
[13]No mortal comprehends its worth;[h]
it cannot be found in the land of the living.
[14]The deep says, "It is not in me";
the sea says, "It is not with me."
[15]It cannot be bought with the finest gold,
nor can its price be weighed out in silver.[i]
[16]It cannot be bought with the gold of Ophir,
with precious onyx or lapis lazuli.
[17]Neither gold nor crystal can compare with it,
nor can it be had for jewels of gold.[j]
[18]Coral and jasper are not worthy of mention;
the price of wisdom is beyond rubies.[k]
[19]The topaz of Cush cannot compare with it;
it cannot be bought with pure gold.[l]

[20]Where then does wisdom come from?
Where does understanding dwell?[m]
[21]It is hidden from the eyes of every living thing,
concealed even from the birds in the sky.
[22]Destruction[b][n] and Death say,
"Only a rumor of it has reached our ears."
[23]God understands the way to it
and he alone knows where it dwells,[o]
[24]for he views the ends of the earth[p]
and sees everything under the heavens.[q]
[25]When he established the force of the wind
and measured out the waters,[r]
[26]when he made a decree for the rain
and a path for the thunderstorm,[s]
[27]then he looked at wisdom and appraised it;
he confirmed it and tested it.

28:2 [d]Dt 8:9
28:3 [e]Ecc 1:13
28:5 [f]Ps 104:14
28:12 [g]Ecc 7:24
28:13 [h]Pr 3:15; Mt 13:44-46
28:15 [i]Pr 3:13-14; 8:10-11; 16:16
28:17 [j]Pr 16:16
28:18 [k]Pr 3:15
28:19 [l]Pr 8:19
28:20 [m]ver 23, 28
28:22 [n]Job 26:6
28:23 [o]Pr 8:22-31
28:24 [p]Ps 33:13-14 [q]Pr 15:3
28:25 [r]Job 12:15; Ps 135:7
28:26 [s]Job 37:3, 8, 11; 38:25, 27

Job 28:20-28 ❖ True wisdom is hard to find. How can we lay hold of it (see 1Co 1:24)?

[a] *11* Septuagint, Aquila and Vulgate; Hebrew *They dam up* [b] *22* Hebrew *Abaddon*

requires delving deep into dark places and produces stunning products from what looks common (dust, rock). These aspects will be applied to the search for wisdom.

28:12–19 One can search for precious metals. It is possible to explore and discover the sources of rivers. In contrast, wisdom is inaccessible and invaluable.

28:20-28 The previous passage (vv. 12–19) declares that wisdom cannot be "found." This passage suggests that wisdom comes from God. The first concerns a *search* which is ultimately unsuccessful; the second concerns a *source*. Since wisdom is hidden from every living thing, Destruction and Death are consulted (v. 22). They confess that wisdom is not to be found in their realm either. In other words, Sheol offers no heightened levels of awareness.

28:23–27 The poem begins moving to its conclusion with the first reference to God, who then becomes the subject of the remainder of the sentences. Previously the path to wisdom and its place of dwelling were unknown; now the poem affirms that God knows both path and place. God's relationship to wisdom is elaborated in this passage.

28 And he said to the human race,
"The fear of the Lord — that is wisdom,
and to shun evil is understanding."[t]

Job's Final Defense

29 Job continued his discourse:[u]

2 "How I long for the months gone by,
for the days when God watched over me,[v]
3 when his lamp shone on my head
and by his light I walked through darkness![w]
4 Oh, for the days when I was in my prime,
when God's intimate friendship blessed my house,[x]
5 when the Almighty was still with me
and my children were around me,
6 when my path was drenched with cream[y]
and the rock[z] poured out for me streams of olive oil.[a]

7 "When I went to the gate[b] of the city
and took my seat in the public square,
8 the young men saw me and stepped aside
and the old men rose to their feet;
9 the chief men refrained from speaking
and covered their mouths with their hands;[c]
10 the voices of the nobles were hushed,
and their tongues stuck to the roof of their mouths.[d]
11 Whoever heard me spoke well of me,
and those who saw me commended me,

28:28 [t] Dt 4:6; Ps 111:10; Pr 1:7; 9:10
29:1 [u] Job 13:12; 27:1
29:2 [v] Jer 31:28
29:3 [w] Job 11:17
29:4 [x] Ps 25:14; Pr 3:32
29:6 [y] Job 20:17 [z] Ps 81:16 [a] Dt 32:13
29:7 [b] Job 31:21
29:9 [c] Job 21:5
29:10 [d] Ps 137:6
29:12 [e] Job 24:4 [f] Job 31:17, 21 [g] Ps 72:12; Pr 21:13
29:13 [h] Job 31:20 [i] Job 22:9
29:14 [j] Job 27:6; Ps 132:9; Isa 59:17; 61:10; Eph 6:14
29:15 [k] Nu 10:31
29:16 [l] Job 24:4; Pr 29:7
29:17 [m] Ps 3:7
29:18 [n] Ps 30:6
29:19 [o] Job 18:16; Jer 17:8
29:20 [p] Ps 18:34 [q] Ge 49:24
29:22 [r] Dt 32:2

Job 29:4-6 ❖ Is it good for us to look back with longing at more vibrant times in our faith? How can we move closer to God when our faith doesn't feel as active?

12 because I rescued the poor[e] who cried for help,
and the fatherless[f] who had none to assist them.[g]
13 The one who was dying blessed me;[h]
I made the widow's[i] heart sing.
14 I put on righteousness[j] as my clothing;
justice was my robe and my turban.
15 I was eyes[k] to the blind
and feet to the lame.
16 I was a father to the needy;[l]
I took up the case of the stranger.
17 I broke the fangs of the wicked
and snatched the victims from their teeth.[m]

18 "I thought, 'I will die in my own house,
my days as numerous as the grains of sand.[n]
19 My roots will reach to the water,[o]
and the dew will lie all night on my branches.
20 My glory will not fade;
the bow[p] will be ever new in my hand.'[q]

21 "People listened to me expectantly,
waiting in silence for my counsel.
22 After I had spoken, they spoke no more;
my words fell gently on their ears.[r]
23 They waited for me as for showers
and drank in my words as the spring rain.

28:28 Fear of the Lord is expressed in righteous behavior. Fear of the Lord does not appease a needy god so that he will leave us alone; rather, fear of the Lord pursues true, ethical righteousness.

✚ **28:1-28** We express our fear of the Lord when we trust him with our circumstances—as uncomfortable or confusing as they may be. We trust him enough to accept that there need not be an explanation. We trust that his just nature is unassailable even though there is no identifiable justice in the circumstances in which we find ourselves. We trust that he has set up the system in the very best (wisest) way possible even when we are suffering the consequences of a system broken by the fall. We trust his love for us, and we trust that even in our difficulties he can show his love and strengthen us through our persistent trials.

29:1-25 Job never suggests he has earned God's blessing in his life. The reference to God's "intimate friendship" in v. 4 is of particular interest.
29:7-10, 21-23 Job describes the universal respect he once received from leaders and the general populace. Job's best qualities may have contributed to the respect he enjoyed; ultimately, however, his success and prosperity were the primary factors behind his social position. When he lost his prosperity, he lost respect from those around him.

24 When I smiled at them, they scarcely
believed it;
the light of my face was precious
to them.[a]
25 I chose the way for them and sat as
their chief;
I dwelt as a king[s] among his
troops;
I was like one who comforts
mourners.[t]

30 "But now they mock me,[u]
men younger than I,
whose fathers I would have
disdained
to put with my sheep dogs.
2 Of what use was the strength of their
hands to me,
since their vigor had gone from
them?
3 Haggard from want and hunger,
they roamed[b] the parched land
in desolate wastelands at night.
4 In the brush they gathered salt
herbs,
and their food[c] was the root of the
broom bush.
5 They were banished from human
society,
shouted at as if they were thieves.
6 They were forced to live in the dry
stream beds,
among the rocks and in holes in
the ground.
7 They brayed among the bushes
and huddled in the undergrowth.
8 A base and nameless brood,
they were driven out of the land.

9 "And now those young men mock
me[v] in song;[w]
I have become a byword[x] among
them.
10 They detest me and keep their
distance;
they do not hesitate to spit in my
face.[y]
11 Now that God has unstrung my bow
and afflicted me,[z]
they throw off restraint[a] in my
presence.

29:25 [s] Job 1:3; 31:37 [t] Job 4:4
30:1 [u] Job 12:4
30:9 [v] Ps 69:11 [w] Job 12:4; La 3:14, 63 [x] Job 17:6
30:10 [y] Nu 12:14; Dt 25:9; Isa 50:6; Mt 26:67
30:11 [z] Ru 1:21 [a] Ps 32:9
30:12 [b] Ps 140:4-5 [c] Job 19:12
30:13 [d] Isa 3:12
30:15 [e] Job 31:23; Ps 55:4-5 [f] Job 3:25; Hos 13:3
30:16 [g] Job 3:24; Ps 22:14; 42:4
30:19 [h] Ps 69:2, 14
30:20 [i] Job 19:7
30:21 [j] Job 19:6, 22 [k] Job 16:9,14 [l] Job 10:3
30:22 [m] Job 27:21 [n] Job 9:17
30:23 [o] Job 9:22; 10:8

Job 30:20 ❖ Where can we find comfort when God seems far off and silent (see Mt 27:46)?

12 On my right the tribe[d] attacks;
they lay snares for my feet,[b]
they build their siege ramps
against me.[c]
13 They break up my road;[d]
they succeed in destroying me.
'No one can help him,' they say.
14 They advance as through a gaping
breach;
amid the ruins they come
rolling in.
15 Terrors overwhelm me;[e]
my dignity is driven away as by
the wind,
my safety vanishes like a cloud.[f]

16 "And now my life ebbs away;[g]
days of suffering grip me.
17 Night pierces my bones;
my gnawing pains never rest.
18 In his great power God becomes like
clothing to me[e];
he binds me like the neck of my
garment.
19 He throws me into the mud,[h]
and I am reduced to dust and
ashes.

20 "I cry out to you, God, but you do not
answer;[i]
I stand up, but you merely look
at me.
21 You turn on me ruthlessly;[j]
with the might of your hand[k] you
attack me.[l]
22 You snatch me up and drive me
before the wind;[m]
you toss me about in the
storm.[n]
23 I know you will bring me down to
death,[o]

[a] *24* The meaning of the Hebrew for this clause is uncertain. [b] *3* Or *gnawed* [c] *4* Or *fuel*
[d] *12* The meaning of the Hebrew for this word is uncertain. [e] *18* Hebrew; Septuagint *power he grasps my clothing*

29:25 These phrases suggest unquestioned loyalty from his followers and portray Job as a compassionate leader, not an oppressive tyrant ruling over unwilling subjects.
30:1–31 It would be bad enough to be passively neglected by upstanding citizens, but it is far worse to be subject to abuse by the dregs of society.
30:15 The word "terrors" was used in 18:14 when Bildad spoke of a "king of terrors" in a string of personifications. If Terrors is indeed a personal entity, "Night" in 30:17 may also be a personification parallel to Terrors.
30:20–23 Job has returned his attention to God. God has joined Terrors and Night in behaving toward Job as a chaos creature, as an author of disorder and death.

to the place appointed for all the
living.[p]

24 "Surely no one lays a hand on a
broken man
when he cries for help in his
distress.[q]

25 Have I not wept for those in trouble?
Has not my soul grieved for the
poor?[r]

26 Yet when I hoped for good, evil
came;
when I looked for light, then came
darkness.[s]

27 The churning inside me never
stops;[t]
days of suffering confront me.

28 I go about blackened,[u] but not by the
sun;
I stand up in the assembly and cry
for help.[v]

29 I have become a brother of jackals,[w]
a companion of owls.[x]

30 My skin grows black and peels;[y]
my body burns with fever.[z]

31 My lyre is tuned to mourning,[a]
and my pipe to the sound of
wailing.

31 "I made a covenant with my eyes
not to look lustfully at a young
woman.[b]

2 For what is our lot from God above,
our heritage from the Almighty
on high?[c]

3 Is it not ruin[d] for the wicked,
disaster for those who do wrong?[e]

4 Does he not see my ways[f]
and count my every step?[g]

5 "If I have walked with falsehood
or my foot has hurried after
deceit[h] —

6 let God weigh me in honest scales[i]
and he will know that I am
blameless —

7 if my steps have turned from the
path,[j]
if my heart has been led by my
eyes,
or if my hands[k] have been defiled,

8 then may others eat what I have
sown,[l]
and may my crops be uprooted.[m]

9 "If my heart has been enticed[n] by a
woman,
or if I have lurked at my
neighbor's door,

10 then may my wife grind another
man's grain,
and may other men sleep with
her.[o]

11 For that would have been wicked,
a sin to be judged.[p]

12 It is a fire[q] that burns to
Destruction[a];[r]
it would have uprooted my
harvest.[s]

13 "If I have denied justice to any of my
servants,
whether male or female,
when they had a grievance against
me,[t]

14 what will I do when God
confronts me?
What will I answer when called to
account?

15 Did not he who made me in the
womb make them?

[a] 12 Hebrew *Abaddon*

30:23 [p] Job 3:19
30:24 [q] Job 19:7
30:25 [r] Job 24:4; Ps 35:13-14; Ro 12:15
30:26 [s] Job 3:25-26; 19:8; Jer 8:15
30:27 [t] La 2:11
30:28 [u] Ps 38:6; 42:9; 43:2 [v] Job 19:7
30:29 [w] Ps 44:19 [x] Ps 102:6; Mic 1:8
30:30 [y] La 4:8 [z] Ps 102:3
30:31 [a] Isa 24:8
31:1 [b] Mt 5:28
31:2 [c] Job 20:29
31:3 [d] Job 21:30 [e] Job 34:22
31:4 [f] 2Ch 16:9 [g] Pr 5:21
31:5 [h] Mic 2:11
31:6 [i] Job 6:2; 27:5-6
31:7 [j] Job 23:11 [k] Job 9:30
31:8 [l] Lev 26:16; Job 20:18 [m] Mic 6:15
31:9 [n] Job 24:15
31:10 [o] Dt 28:30; Jer 8:10
31:11 [p] Ge 38:24; Lev 20:10; Dt 22:22-24
31:12 [q] Job 15:30 [r] Job 26:6 [s] Job 20:28
31:13 [t] Dt 24:14-15

Job 31:1 ❖ Our eyes can lead us into all kinds of sin. How can we, like Job, make a covenant with our eyes to not fall into these sins?

30:27–31 God has allowed disaster in Job's life and refuses to respond to Job's pleas. As a result, Job himself has become an outcast (v. 29). He is now the mourner (v. 31) with no one to comfort him.
31:1–40 A large harem was an indicator of power and status in the ancient world. Job shuns the idea of amassing multiple wives and concubines, and he characterizes this decision as a "covenant" (v. 1) he made with his eyes in order to underscore the point that he is not even remotely "on the prowl." Job avoids the obsessive pursuit of prestige that might trip up other people in his position.
31:2–4 Job is committed to the retribution principle, asserting that the wicked will suffer. Verse 4 affirms that God scrutinizes Job's actions; therefore if God does not act against Job, Job may claim vindication.
31:9–12 The image of Job's wife "grind[ing] another man's grain" (v. 10) is a sexual euphemism: She will process what another man produces (i.e., children). The wisdom saying that closes the section (v. 12) bears resemblance to Song of Songs: "Love is as strong as death, its jealousy unyielding as the grave. It burns like a blazing fire, like a mighty flame" (SS 8:6). Passion cannot easily be extinguished and, as the text indicates, will burn "to Destruction" (Job 31:12).
31:13–23 The person who does justice shows compassion and performs acts of charity. Job took every available opportunity to enact compassion and justice, as anyone who is able should, and therefore he considered himself above reproach.

Did not the same one form us
both within our mothers?[u]

16 "If I have denied the desires of the
poor[v]
or let the eyes of the widow[w] grow
weary,
17 if I have kept my bread to myself,
not sharing it with the
fatherless[x] —
18 but from my youth I reared them as
a father would,
and from my birth I guided the
widow —
19 if I have seen anyone perishing for
lack of clothing,[y]
or the needy[z] without garments,
20 and their hearts did not bless me
for warming them with the fleece
from my sheep,
21 if I have raised my hand against the
fatherless,[a]
knowing that I had influence in
court,
22 then let my arm fall from the
shoulder,
let it be broken off at the joint.[b]
23 For I dreaded destruction from God,
and for fear of his splendor[c] I
could not do such things.

24 "If I have put my trust in gold[d]
or said to pure gold, 'You are my
security,'[e]
25 if I have rejoiced over my great
wealth,[f]
the fortune my hands had gained,
26 if I have regarded the sun[g] in its
radiance
or the moon moving in splendor,
27 so that my heart was secretly enticed
and my hand offered them a kiss
of homage,
28 then these also would be sins to be
judged,[h]
for I would have been unfaithful
to God on high.

29 "If I have rejoiced at my enemy's
misfortune[i]
or gloated over the trouble that
came to him[j] —
30 I have not allowed my mouth to sin
by invoking a curse against their
life —
31 if those of my household have never
said,
'Who has not been filled with Job's
meat?'[k] —
32 but no stranger had to spend the
night in the street,
for my door was always open to
the traveler[l] —
33 if I have concealed[m] my sin as people
do,[a]
by hiding[n] my guilt in my heart
34 because I so feared the crowd[o]
and so dreaded the contempt of
the clans
that I kept silent and would not go
outside —
35 ("Oh, that I had someone to hear
me![p]
I sign now my defense — let the
Almighty answer me;

31:15 [u] Job 10:3
31:16 [v] Job 5:16; 20:19 [w] Job 22:9
31:17 [x] Job 22:7; 29:12
31:19 [y] Job 22:6 [z] Job 24:4
31:21 [a] Job 22:9
31:22 [b] Job 38:15
31:23 [c] Job 13:11
31:24 [d] Job 22:25 [e] Mt 6:24; Mk 10:24
31:25 [f] Ps 62:10
31:26 [g] Eze 8:16
31:28 [h] Dt 17:2-7
31:29 [i] Ob 12 [j] Pr 17:5; 24:17-18
31:31 [k] Job 22:7
31:32 [l] Ge 19:2-3; Ro 12:13
31:33 [m] Pr 28:13 [n] Ge 3:8
31:34 [o] Ex 23:2
31:35 [p] Job 19:7; 30:28

[a] 33 *Or as Adam did*

31:24–28 Job raises two possible sources of trust and security: the first is material wealth; the second is the gods, particularly the astral deities (sun and moon). Job reminds God that he is obliged to act if Job has committed any of these errors. The word rendered "unfaithful" often suggests disowning (v. 28). Job identifies such behavior as sufficiently serious to require retribution from God.
31:29–32, 38–40 The overarching theme of these verses may be termed "grace to outsiders"—those who are not members in good standing in the community.
31:33–37 Job adds his signature to his oath. He has not hidden his offense. Job calls on El Shaddai (NIV "the Almighty") to answer him. Job's imagery in v. 36 suggests that he will publicize any claims against him. He is eager for the opportunity to respond to formal legal charges.

Job's final formal speech thus concludes on one of the book's high points. He has adamantly denied any wrongdoing and has taken a decisive (and risky) step to try to force a response from God. If God remains silent, Job, though undoubtedly still dissatisfied, could at least theoretically claim vindication (i.e., God did not strike him dead for a false oath) in order to make way for his return to society and to restore his status in the community. Such an accomplishment would enable Job to restore his sense of coherence and order—he could make sense of his life once again in the midst of his disastrous situation.

29:1—31:40 What theological price are we willing to pay in order to achieve order and logic in our lives? Do we prioritize our rationality above God's reputation? Do we give more concern to our reputation than God's reputation? If we truly believe what we say we believe about the Bible—that it is God's revelation of his character—then that biblical revelation takes precedence over our feeble attempts to discern what feels like order in our world. It also supersedes any defense we may wish to raise around our reputation.

let my accuser[q] put his indictment in writing.
36 Surely I would wear it on my shoulder,
I would put it on like a crown.
37 I would give him an account of my every step;
I would present it to him as to a ruler.[r]) —

38 "if my land cries out against me[s]
and all its furrows are wet with tears,
39 if I have devoured its yield without payment[t]
or broken the spirit of its tenants,[u]
40 then let briers[v] come up instead of wheat
and stinkweed instead of barley."

The words of Job are ended.

Elihu

32 So these three men stopped answering Job, because he was righteous in his own eyes.[w] 2 But Elihu son
of Barakel the Buzite,[x] of the family of
Ram, became very angry with Job for
justifying himself rather than God.[y] 3 He
was also angry with the three friends,
because they had found no way to refute Job, and yet had condemned him.[a]
4 Now Elihu had waited before speaking
to Job because they were older than he.
5 But when he saw that the three men
had nothing more to say, his anger was
aroused.
6 So Elihu son of Barakel the Buzite
said:

"I am young in years,
and you are old;[z]
that is why I was fearful,
not daring to tell you what I know.
7 I thought, 'Age should speak;
advanced years should teach wisdom.'
8 But it is the spirit[b] in a person,
the breath of the Almighty,[a] that gives them understanding.[b]
9 It is not only the old[c] who are wise,[c]
not only the aged who understand what is right.

10 "Therefore I say: Listen to me;
I too will tell you what I know.
11 I waited while you spoke,
I listened to your reasoning;
while you were searching for words,
12 I gave you my full attention.
But not one of you has proved Job wrong;
none of you has answered his arguments.
13 Do not say, 'We have found wisdom;[d]
let God, not a man, refute him.'
14 But Job has not marshaled his words against me,
and I will not answer him with your arguments.

15 "They are dismayed and have no more to say;
words have failed them.
16 Must I wait, now that they are silent,
now that they stand there with no reply?
17 I too will have my say;
I too will tell what I know.
18 For I am full of words,

Job 32:6–9 ❖ Why do people sometimes think too highly of their knowledge? What kind of wisdom can age bring (see Jn 8:7–9)?

31:35 q Job 27:7; 35:14
31:37 r Job 1:3; 29:25
31:38 s Ge 4:10
31:39 t 1Ki 21:19 u Lev 19:13; Jas 5:4
31:40 v Ge 3:18
32:1 w Job 10:7; 33:9
32:2 x Ge 22:21 y Job 27:5; 30:21
32:6 z Job 15:10
32:8 a Job 27:3; 33:4 b Pr 2:6
32:9 c 1Co 1:26
32:13 d Jer 9:23

[a] 3 Masoretic Text; an ancient Hebrew scribal tradition *Job, and so had condemned God* [b] 8 Or *Spirit*; also in verse 18 [c] 9 Or *many*; or *great*

32:1–5 Buz was a brother of Uz in Ge 22:20–21. Thus, Elihu is related to the Israelites as part of the international family of Abram. Job's friends represented the common logic of the ancient Near East. Elihu represents a more theologically sophisticated opinion that might have predominated among the Israelites. Those Israelites would likely find Elihu's thinking more persuasive.

Elihu is seen as a raging, angry young man who is enraged because Job regards his own righteousness more highly than God's. Elihu directs his anger against the incompetence of the friends on two counts: (1) They have condemned Job without having found fault. (2) They have run out of arguments without having succeeded.

32:6–22 In v. 8 Elihu asserts, "But it is the spirit in a person, the breath of the Almighty, that gives them understanding." This spirit within a person (not the Holy Spirit) compels Elihu in v. 18; he is energized and impatient to speak and be heard.
32:12–14 Elihu reiterates the failure of the friends and differentiates himself from them.
32:15–22 Elihu's description of himself resembles Jeremiah's description of how he is compelled to deliver his prophetic message. We should not, however, conclude that Elihu is claiming a prophetic office or role. When Job's friends began their speeches, they acknowledged the wisdom and righteousness of Job. Elihu jumps directly to confrontation.

and the spirit within me
compels me;
19 inside I am like bottled-up wine,
like new wineskins ready to burst.
20 I must speak and find relief;
I must open my lips and reply.
21 I will show no partiality,[e]
nor will I flatter anyone;
22 for if I were skilled in flattery,
my Maker would soon take me
away.

33 "But now, Job, listen to my
words;
pay attention to everything I say.[f]
2 I am about to open my mouth;
my words are on the tip of my
tongue.
3 My words come from an upright
heart;
my lips sincerely speak what I
know.[g]
4 The Spirit of God has made me;[h]
the breath of the Almighty[i] gives
me life.
5 Answer me[j] then, if you can;
stand up[k] and argue your case
before me.
6 I am the same as you in God's sight;
I too am a piece of clay.[l]
7 No fear of me should alarm you,
nor should my hand be heavy on
you.[m]

8 "But you have said in my hearing —
I heard the very words —
9 'I am pure,[n] I have done no wrong;[o]
I am clean and free from sin.
10 Yet God has found fault with me;
he considers me his enemy.[p]
11 He fastens my feet in shackles;[q]
he keeps close watch on all my
paths.'[r]

12 "But I tell you, in this you are not
right,
for God is greater than any
mortal.[s]
13 Why do you complain to him[t]

32:21 [e] Lev 19:15; Job 13:10; Mt 22:16
33:1 [f] Job 13:6
33:3 [g] Job 6:28; 27:4; 36:4
33:4 [h] Ge 2:7; Job 10:3 [i] Job 27:3
33:5 [j] ver 32 [k] Job 13:18
33:6 [l] Job 4:19
33:7 [m] Job 9:34; 13:21; 2Co 2:4
33:9 [n] Job 10:7 [o] Job 13:23; 16:17
33:10 [p] Job 13:24
33:11 [q] Job 13:27 [r] Job 14:16
33:12 [s] Ecc 7:20
33:13 [t] Job 40:2; Isa 45:9

Job 33:19-30 ❖ When has God "chastened" us through a period of pain (v. 19)? Does Elihu have a point here?

that he responds to no one's
words[a]?
14 For God does speak[u] — now one way,
now another —
though no one perceives it.
15 In a dream,[v] in a vision of the
night,
when deep sleep falls on people
as they slumber in their beds,
16 he may speak[w] in their ears
and terrify them with warnings,
17 to turn them from wrongdoing
and keep them from pride,
18 to preserve them from the pit,[x]
their lives from perishing by the
sword.[b][y]

19 "Or someone may be chastened on a
bed of pain
with constant distress in their
bones,[z]
20 so that their body finds food[a]
repulsive
and their soul loathes the choicest
meal.[b]
21 Their flesh wastes away to nothing,
and their bones, once hidden, now
stick out.[c]
22 They draw near to the pit,
and their life to the messengers of
death.[c][d]
23 Yet if there is an angel at their side,
a messenger, one out of a
thousand,
sent to tell them how to be
upright,[e]
24 and he is gracious to that person and
says to God,
'Spare them from going down to
the pit;[f]

33:14 [u] Ps 62:11
33:15 [v] Job 4:13
33:16 [w] Job 36:10,15
33:18 [x] ver 22, 24,28,30 [y] Job 15:22
33:19 [z] Job 30:17
33:20 [a] Ps 107:18 [b] Job 3:24; 6:6
33:21 [c] Job 16:8; 19:20
33:22 [d] Ps 88:3
33:23 [e] Mic 6:8
33:24 [f] Isa 38:17

[a] 13 Or *that he does not answer for any of his actions* [b] 18 Or *from crossing the river* [c] 22 Or *to the place of the dead*

33:1-33 The statement that the Spirit "has made me" is parallel to the statement that God's breath "gives me life" (v. 4). God "made" Elihu by giving him life and wisdom.

33:8-12 Elihu warns Job that no one can "out-God" God (v. 12). This theological commitment is Elihu's strength, and it is what makes his position more acceptable than Job's.

33:15-18 Elihu contends that God has not been silent; rather, Job has not been listening on the right frequency. He identifies several communication strategies as having corrective intentions (vv. 15-16). In other words, Elihu considers these communications to be instructive and constructive rather than punitive.

33:23-28 Is the messenger (NIV "angel," v. 23) an angelic mediator or a human one? Elihu may view himself as the messenger/mediator who is going to interpret Job's situation and advise him. Elihu is serving as a mediator to bring the two sides to a mutual understanding.

I have found a ransom for them —
25 let their flesh be renewed like a child's;
let them be restored as in the days of their youth'[g] —
26 then that person can pray to God and find favor with him,[h]
they will see God's face and shout for joy;[i]
he will restore them to full well-being.[j]
27 And they will go to others and say,
'I have sinned,[k] I have perverted what is right,[l]
but I did not get what I deserved.[m]
28 God has delivered me from going down to the pit,
and I shall live to enjoy the light of life.'[n]

29 "God does all these things to a person[o] —
twice, even three times —
30 to turn them back from the pit,
that the light of life[p] may shine on them.

31 "Pay attention, Job, and listen to me;
be silent, and I will speak.
32 If you have anything to say, answer me;
speak up, for I want to vindicate you.
33 But if not, then listen to me;
be silent, and I will teach you wisdom.[q]"

34

Then Elihu said:

2 "Hear my words, you wise men;
listen to me, you men of learning.
3 For the ear tests words
as the tongue tastes food.[r]
4 Let us discern for ourselves what is right;
let us learn together what is good.[s]

5 "Job says, 'I am innocent,[t]
but God denies me justice.[u]
6 Although I am right,
I am considered a liar;
although I am guiltless,
his arrow inflicts an incurable wound.'[v]
7 Is there anyone like Job,
who drinks scorn like water?[w]
8 He keeps company with evildoers;
he associates with the wicked.[x]
9 For he says, 'There is no profit
in trying to please God.'[y]

10 "So listen to me, you men of understanding.
Far be it from God to do evil,[z]
from the Almighty to do wrong.[a]
11 He repays everyone for what they have done;[b]
he brings on them what their conduct deserves.[c]
12 It is unthinkable that God would do wrong,
that the Almighty would pervert justice.[d]
13 Who appointed him over the earth?
Who put him in charge of the whole world?[e]
14 If it were his intention
and he withdrew his spirit[a] and breath,[f]
15 all humanity would perish together
and mankind would return to the dust.[g]

16 "If you have understanding, hear this;
listen to what I say.
17 Can someone who hates justice govern?[h]

Job 34:11 ❖ What can we make of the statement that God repays everyone for what they have done and treats them as they deserve (see Ps 103:10)?

33:25 [g] 2Ki 5:14
33:26 [h] Job 34:28 [i] Job 22:26 [j] Ps 50:15; 51:12
33:27 [k] 2Sa 12:13 [l] Lk 15:21 [m] Ro 6:21
33:28 [n] Job 22:28
33:29 [o] 1Co 12:6; Eph 1:11; Php 2:13
33:30 [p] Ps 56:13
33:33 [q] Ps 34:11
34:3 [r] Job 12:11
34:4 [s] 1Th 5:21
34:5 [t] Job 33:9 [u] Job 27:2
34:6 [v] Job 6:4
34:7 [w] Job 15:16
34:8 [x] Job 22:15; Ps 50:18
34:9 [y] Job 21:15; 35:3
34:10 [z] Ge 18:25 [a] Dt 32:4; Job 8:3; Ro 9:14
34:11 [b] Ps 62:12; Mt 16:27; Ro 2:6; 2Co 5:10 [c] Jer 32:19; Eze 33:20
34:12 [d] Job 8:3
34:13 [e] Job 38:4,6
34:14 [f] Ps 104:29
34:15 [g] Ge 3:19; Job 9:22
34:17 [h] 2Sa 23:3-4

[a] 14 Or *Spirit*

34:1-37 In vv. 7-9, Job is being accused of engaging in mockery of God and of aligning himself philosophically with evildoers by default when he sets himself against God. In this deduction, Elihu is wrong.

Elihu assumes that if Job finds no benefit in loyalty to God, he plans to join the wicked. Though Job *is* guilty of self-righteousness and disparaging God's justice (as Elihu contends), he is *not* guilty of following God only for the blessings. In this misrepresentation of Job, Elihu does not misrepresent God as the friends do; he is wrong in his inference about Job's motivation.

34:10-20 Elihu's insistence that God would not pervert justice (v. 10) echoes the words of Bildad (8:3).

34:13-15 Elihu continues to speak eloquently about the loftiness of God. He affirms that God is not dependent on anyone or anything. Conversely, human beings are absolutely and totally reliant on God's provision for their very existence. Consequently, we do not surpass God in his attributes, including that of his justice.

Will you condemn the just and
mighty One?[i]
18 Is he not the One who says to kings,
'You are worthless,'
and to nobles, 'You are wicked,'[j]
19 who shows no partiality[k] to princes
and does not favor the rich over
the poor,[l]
for they are all the work of his
hands?[m]
20 They die in an instant, in the middle
of the night;[n]
the people are shaken and they
pass away;
the mighty are removed without
human hand.[o]

21 "His eyes are on the ways of mortals;
he sees their every step.[p]
22 There is no deep shadow,[q] no utter
darkness,[r]
where evildoers can hide.
23 God has no need to examine people
further,
that they should come before him
for judgment.[s]
24 Without inquiry he shatters the
mighty[t]
and sets up others in their place.[u]
25 Because he takes note of their deeds,
he overthrows them in the night
and they are crushed.
26 He punishes them for their
wickedness
where everyone can see them,
27 because they turned from following
him[v]
and had no regard for any of his
ways.[w]
28 They caused the cry of the poor to
come before him,
so that he heard the cry of the
needy.[x]
29 But if he remains silent, who can
condemn him?
If he hides his face, who can see
him?
Yet he is over individual and nation
alike,
30 to keep the godless from ruling,
from laying snares for the people.[y]

31 "Suppose someone says to God,
'I am guilty but will offend no
more.
32 Teach me what I cannot see;[z]
if I have done wrong, I will not do
so again.'[a]
33 Should God then reward you on your
terms,
when you refuse to repent?[b]
You must decide, not I;
so tell me what you know.

34 "Men of understanding declare,
wise men who hear me say to me,
35 'Job speaks without knowledge;[c]
his words lack insight.'
36 Oh, that Job might be tested to the
utmost
for answering like a wicked
man![d]
37 To his sin he adds rebellion;
scornfully he claps his hands[e]
among us
and multiplies his words against
God."[f]

35 Then Elihu said:

2 "Do you think this is just?
You say, 'I am in the right, not
God.'
3 Yet you ask him, 'What profit is it
to me,[a]

34:17 [i] Job 40:8
34:18 [j] Ex 22:28
34:19 [k] Dt 10:17; Ac 10:34 [l] Lev 19:15 [m] Job 10:3
34:20 [n] Ex 12:29 [o] Job 12:19
34:21 [p] Job 31:4; Pr 15:3
34:22 [q] Am 9:2-3 [r] Ps 139:12
34:23 [s] Job 11:11
34:24 [t] Job 12:19 [u] Da 2:21
34:27 [v] Ps 28:5; Isa 5:12 [w] 1Sa 15:11
34:28 [x] Ex 22:23; Job 35:9; Jas 5:4
34:30 [y] Pr 29:2-12
34:32 [z] Job 35:11; Ps 25:4 [a] Job 33:27
34:33 [b] Job 41:11
34:35 [c] Job 35:16; 38:2
34:36 [d] Job 22:15
34:37 [e] Job 27:23 [f] Job 23:2

[a] 3 Or *you*

34:17b–20 No one has suggested that God hates justice, but Job has wondered whether God carries it out consistently. Elihu's case is weakened by hyperbole. Yet as he returns to expressing the attributes of God, his affirmations are legitimate. The question that Elihu fails to consider is whether God has options. Job has drawn false inferences about the execution of the retribution principle. Elihu is drawing other inferences (based on his reinterpretation of the retribution principle). Both comprehend God's attributes, but each is wrong (in different ways) about what we can understand of God's actions.
34:21–30 God has access to every place and all pieces of evidence as he considers the actions of humanity. In vv. 29–30 Elihu wonders, What if God remains silent? Then he asserts that God has a right to such silence. Job is presumptuous to criticize God on this count.
34:31–33 Having offered a defense of God's apparent indifference, Elihu now proposes a hypothetical course of action. As Job has refused to repent, Elihu makes his case as he asks Job what he expects God to do (v. 33). Elihu implies that he has expressed Job's expectations and insinuates that Job's request is ungodly.
34:36–37 Elihu's assessment is that Job wants God to "reward" him on Job's terms. This summarizes what he perceives to be Job's offense. That offense is not something that occurred prior to Job's downfall, but it has become evident in his response to his downfall.
35:1–16 Elihu accuses Job of expecting to benefit from his righteous behavior (v. 3). That may

37 "At this my heart pounds
and leaps from its place.
2 Listen! Listen to the roar of his voice,
to the rumbling that comes from his mouth.[j]
3 He unleashes his lightning beneath the whole heaven
and sends it to the ends of the earth.
4 After that comes the sound of his roar;
he thunders with his majestic voice.
When his voice resounds,
he holds nothing back.
5 God's voice thunders in marvelous ways;
he does great things beyond our understanding.[k]
6 He says to the snow,[l] 'Fall on the earth,'
and to the rain shower, 'Be a mighty downpour.'[m]
7 So that everyone he has made may know his work,
he stops all people from their labor.[a][n]
8 The animals take cover;
they remain in their dens.[o]
9 The tempest comes out from its chamber,
the cold from the driving winds.
10 The breath of God produces ice,
and the broad waters become frozen.[p]
11 He loads the clouds with moisture;
he scatters his lightning through them.[q]
12 At his direction they swirl around
over the face of the whole earth
to do whatever he commands them.[r]
13 He brings the clouds to punish people,[s]
or to water his earth and show his love.[t]

14 "Listen to this, Job;
stop and consider God's wonders.
15 Do you know how God controls the clouds
and makes his lightning flash?
16 Do you know how the clouds hang poised,
those wonders of him who has perfect knowledge?[u]
17 You who swelter in your clothes
when the land lies hushed under the south wind,
18 can you join him in spreading out the skies,[v]
hard as a mirror of cast bronze?

19 "Tell us what we should say to him;
we cannot draw up our case because of our darkness.
20 Should he be told that I want to speak?
Would anyone ask to be swallowed up?
21 Now no one can look at the sun,
bright as it is in the skies
after the wind has swept them clean.

37:2 [j] Ps 29:3-9
37:5 [k] Job 5:9
37:6 [l] Job 38:22 [m] Job 36:27
37:7 [n] Job 12:14
37:8 [o] Job 38:40; Ps 104:22
37:10 [p] Job 38:29-30; Ps 147:17
37:11 [q] Job 36:27,29
37:12 [r] Ps 148:8
37:13 [s] 1Sa 12:17 [t] Ex 9:18; 1Ki 18:45; Job 38:27
37:16 [u] Job 36:4
37:18 [v] Job 9:8; Ps 104:2; Isa 44:24

[a] 7 Or *work, / he fills all people with fear by his power*

Job 37:14 ❖ How does considering God's wonders reorient us in confusing or difficult times?

37:6–13 God's justice is the focus of Elihu's discussion. Elihu illustrates the way this unfathomable instrument of judgment works. Through this activity God punishes or shows his favor—weather is an instrument of his justice (v. 13).
37:14–24 Elihu poses rhetorical questions to prompt Job's recognition of God's great works in nature (vv. 15–16). This foreshadows God's approach in the next chapter. Elihu's description of God's majesty (v. 22) anticipates Yahweh's entrance a few verses later. Elihu mistakenly asserts that God is beyond human reach. He is right that God is exalted in power (v. 23).

✣ **32:1—37:24** Elihu's opinion was that when anyone thinks of God as paying close attention to the details of our lives and micromanaging our circumstances, we are giving ourselves too much importance and trivializing God's role in the cosmos. Yet what is the alternative? Do we believe that God is not really involved in the details and is only engaged in the larger issues?
Here lies mystery. While we can err on the deism extreme (asserting that God is distant and disinterested in life on earth) or on the micromanagement extreme, we can also err by thinking we can sort it all out and figure out how God works or does not work. The error of "God too small" is committed when we misrepresent at one extreme or the other, but it is also committed when we think we can fully describe the nature of his involvement. To believe that his work could so easily be defined is to reduce him to something manageable. We must be content with mystery.

22 Out of the north he comes in golden
splendor;
God comes in awesome majesty.
23 The Almighty is beyond our reach
and exalted in power;[w]
in his justice[x] and great
righteousness, he does not
oppress.[y]
24 Therefore, people revere him,[z]
for does he not have regard for all
the wise[a] in heart?[a]"

The LORD Speaks

38 Then the LORD spoke to Job out
of the storm.[b] He said:

2 "Who is this that obscures my plans
with words without knowledge?[c]
3 Brace yourself like a man;
I will question you,
and you shall answer me.[d]

4 "Where were you when I laid the
earth's foundation?[e]
Tell me, if you understand.
5 Who marked off its dimensions?[f]
Surely you know!

37:23 [w] Job 9:4; 36:4; 1Ti 6:16 [x] Job 8:3 [y] Isa 63:9; Eze 18:23,32
37:24 [z] Mt 10:28 [a] Mt 11:25
38:1 [b] Job 40:6
38:2 [c] Job 35:16; 42:3; 1Ti 1:7
38:3 [d] Job 40:7
38:4 [e] Ps 104:5; Pr 8:29
38:5 [f] Pr 8:29; Isa 40:12

Job 38:1-41 ❖ How did God's flood of questions make Job feel? What feelings do these questions evoke about our position in regard to God and his power in creation?

[a] 24 Or *for he does not have regard for any who think they are wise.*

38:1-3 Throughout the dialogues and discourses of the book, the deity has most often been identified as El Shaddai ("Almighty") or Elohim ("God"). The use of Yahweh in the prologue (chs. 1-2) and now in the divine speeches is significant: Yahweh comes in the storm; the storm sets the tone for the speeches. The storm does not simply convey his power; it conveys his wrath.

This chapter contrasts with Yahweh's open admiration of Job expressed in the prologue. The contrast is not contradictory; it asserts that although Job's conduct is above reproach, his understanding is flawed. Yahweh is about to offer a corrective.

38:4-38 In these verses Yahweh expresses his control, which comprises his power and wisdom. Throughout the Bible God communicates to his people on the basis of their understanding when it comes to scientific matters. He pushes them beyond their cultural understandings in theological matters.

CHARACTER OF GOD // GOD IS WISE

Job 38:1-4: "Who is this that obscures my plans with words without knowledge? Brace yourself like a man; I will question you, and you shall answer me. Where were you when I laid the earth's foundation? Tell me, if you understand."

Isaiah says that God's thoughts are not like human thoughts: "As the heavens are higher than the earth, so are my ways higher than your ways and my thoughts than your thoughts" (Isa 55:9). In Romans 11:33, Paul describes God's wisdom as unsearchable and beyond human ability to trace out.

Job experienced the wisdom of God in a tangible way. Job had been afflicted by tragic events. His friends told him that there must be some wickedness in his life—some unconfessed sin—that accounted for his misfortune. Job, however, maintained his innocence and demanded his day in court with God, where God would explain to Job exactly what was going on. God came to Job, but he did not give Job the explanation he wanted. Instead, God took Job on a tour of the mysteries of creation (Job 38–41). He asked Job if he could understand where light comes from, what was at the bottom of the sea, if he had seen where rain and snow are made, or if he could harness the stars. He asked if Job had the power to send lightning or teach birds the wisdom they need to live in the wild. In the end, God did not give Job an explanation of his suffering, but Job received a profound awareness of the unsearchable wisdom of God. He replied to God that in God's creation are "things too wonderful for me to know" (Job 42:3).

APPLICATION ❖ No one knows a house better than the builder, and no one knows the universe better than the Creator. From microscopic particles to the laws of physics to the farthest stars and galaxies, God knows it all because he made it all. God also understands our minds and our hearts. Our thoughts are not hidden from him (Ps 139:2). While we can never understand the mind of God, in his mercy he has revealed himself to us in his Word and in his world. The Bible tells us all we need to know and serve God. It does not scratch the depths of God's wisdom, but it reveals God's heart.

Who stretched a measuring line
across it?
6 On what were its footings set,
or who laid its cornerstone[g] —
7 while the morning stars sang
together
and all the angels[a] shouted for
joy?

8 "Who shut up the sea behind doors[h]
when it burst forth from the
womb,[i]
9 when I made the clouds its garment
and wrapped it in thick darkness,
10 when I fixed limits for it[j]
and set its doors and bars in
place,[k]
11 when I said, 'This far you may come
and no farther;
here is where your proud waves
halt'?[l]

12 "Have you ever given orders to the
morning,
or shown the dawn its place,
13 that it might take the earth by the
edges
and shake the wicked[m] out of it?
14 The earth takes shape like clay
under a seal;
its features stand out like those of
a garment.
15 The wicked are denied their light,[n]
and their upraised arm is broken.[o]

16 "Have you journeyed to the springs
of the sea
or walked in the recesses of the
deep?[p]
17 Have the gates of death[q] been shown
to you?
Have you seen the gates of the
deepest darkness?
18 Have you comprehended the vast
expanses of the earth?[r]
Tell me, if you know all this.

19 "What is the way to the abode of
light?
And where does darkness reside?

38:6 [g] Job 26:7
38:8 [h] Jer 5:22 [i] Ge 1:9-10
38:10 [j] Ps 33:7; 104:9 [k] Job 26:10
38:11 [l] Ps 89:9
38:13 [m] Ps 104:35
38:15 [n] Job 18:5 [o] Ps 10:15
38:16 [p] Ps 77:19
38:17 [q] Ps 9:13
38:18 [r] Job 28:24
38:20 [s] Job 26:10
38:21 [t] Job 15:7
38:22 [u] Job 37:6
38:23 [v] Isa 30:30; Eze 13:11 [w] Ex 9:18; Jos 10:11; Rev 16:21
38:25 [x] Job 28:26
38:26 [y] Job 36:27
38:27 [z] Ps 104:14; 107:35
38:28 [a] Ps 147:8; Jer 14:22
38:29 [b] Ps 147:16-17
38:30 [c] Job 37:10
38:31 [d] Job 9:9; Am 5:8
38:33 [e] Ps 148:6; Jer 31:36

20 Can you take them to their places?
Do you know the paths[s] to their
dwellings?
21 Surely you know, for you were
already born![t]
You have lived so many years!

22 "Have you entered the storehouses
of the snow[u]
or seen the storehouses of the
hail,
23 which I reserve for times of trouble,[v]
for days of war and battle?[w]
24 What is the way to the place where
the lightning is dispersed,
or the place where the east winds
are scattered over the earth?
25 Who cuts a channel for the torrents
of rain,
and a path for the thunderstorm,[x]
26 to water[y] a land where no one lives,
an uninhabited desert,
27 to satisfy a desolate wasteland
and make it sprout with grass?[z]
28 Does the rain have a father?[a]
Who fathers the drops of dew?
29 From whose womb comes the ice?
Who gives birth to the frost from
the heavens[b]
30 when the waters become hard as
stone,
when the surface of the deep is
frozen?[c]

31 "Can you bind the chains[b] of the
Pleiades?
Can you loosen Orion's belt?[d]
32 Can you bring forth the
constellations in their
seasons[c]
or lead out the Bear[d] with its
cubs?
33 Do you know the laws[e] of the
heavens?
Can you set up God's[e] dominion
over the earth?

[a] *7* Hebrew *the sons of God* [b] *31* Septuagint; Hebrew *beauty* [c] *32* Or *the morning star in its season* [d] *32* Or *out Leo* [e] *33* Or *their*

38:7 This is one of the few references in the OT to the "sons of God" (see NIV footnote; NIV "angels"). The association between the members of the divine council and the stars also occurs in ancient Near Eastern literature. The difference is that in Israelite theology, the divine council is not composed of gods with whom Yahweh shares divine authority.

38:25–27 Throughout the book, Job has assumed the retribution principle, which has led him to believe that the world operates according to justice. This logic is flawed. One cannot assume that because God is just, the world necessarily operates in a just way. Yahweh makes this point when he notes that rain falls in places where no one lives. If justice reigned in the cosmos, rain would target the deserving. Though God controls nature, he doesn't micromanage the system with justice in mind for each moment's activity. Job's reliance on the retribution principle crumbles under scrutiny.

34 "Can you raise your voice to the
clouds
and cover yourself with a flood of
water?[f]
35 Do you send the lightning bolts on
their way?[g]
Do they report to you, 'Here we
are'?
36 Who gives the ibis wisdom[a][h]
or gives the rooster
understanding?[b][i]
37 Who has the wisdom to count the
clouds?
Who can tip over the water jars of
the heavens
38 when the dust becomes hard
and the clods of earth stick
together?

39 "Do you hunt the prey for the lioness
and satisfy the hunger of the lions[j]
40 when they crouch in their dens[k]
or lie in wait in a thicket?
41 Who provides food for the raven[l]
when its young cry out to God
and wander about for lack of
food?[m]

39 "Do you know when the
mountain goats[n] give birth?
Do you watch when the doe bears
her fawn?
2 Do you count the months till they
bear?
Do you know the time they give
birth?
3 They crouch down and bring forth
their young;
their labor pains are ended.
4 Their young thrive and grow strong
in the wilds;
they leave and do not return.

5 "Who let the wild donkey[o] go free?
Who untied its ropes?
6 I gave it the wasteland[p] as its home,
the salt flats as its habitat.[q]
7 It laughs at the commotion in the
town;
it does not hear a driver's shout.[r]
8 It ranges the hills for its pasture
and searches for any green thing.

9 "Will the wild ox[s] consent to serve
you?
Will it stay by your manger at
night?
10 Can you hold it to the furrow with a
harness?
Will it till the valleys behind you?
11 Will you rely on it for its great
strength?
Will you leave your heavy work
to it?
12 Can you trust it to haul in your grain
and bring it to your threshing
floor?

13 "The wings of the ostrich flap
joyfully,
though they cannot compare
with the wings and feathers of the
stork.
14 She lays her eggs on the ground
and lets them warm in the sand,
15 unmindful that a foot may crush
them,
that some wild animal may
trample them.
16 She treats her young harshly,[t] as if
they were not hers;
she cares not that her labor was in
vain,
17 for God did not endow her with
wisdom
or give her a share of good sense.[u]
18 Yet when she spreads her feathers to
run,
she laughs at horse and rider.

19 "Do you give the horse its strength

38:34 [f] Job 22:11; 36:27-28
38:35 [g] Job 36:32; 37:3
38:36 [h] Job 9:4 [i] Job 32:8; Ps 51:6; Ecc 2:26
38:39 [j] Ps 104:21
38:40 [k] Job 37:8
38:41 [l] Lk 12:24 [m] Ps 147:9; Mt 6:26
39:1 [n] Dt 14:5
39:5 [o] Job 6:5; 11:12; 24:5
39:6 [p] Job 24:5; Ps 107:34; Jer 2:24 [q] Hos 8:9
39:7 [r] Job 3:18
39:9 [s] Nu 23:22; Dt 33:17
39:16 [t] La 4:3
39:17 [u] Job 35:11

[a] *36* That is, wisdom about the flooding of the Nile
[b] *36* That is, understanding of when to crow; the meaning of the Hebrew for this verse is uncertain.

Job 39:1-30 ❖ Why is it important to remember that God is active and powerful in areas beyond our own lives and understanding? Do we ever try to reduce God's work to our own concerns? How can we foster a larger perspective?

38:39—39:30 Academics in the ancient world commonly made lists of plants, animals, stars, and many other things. Such lists were a type of wisdom, so it is no surprise to find a list such as this in a biblical wisdom book.
39:13-18 Some have objected that Yahweh's description does not accurately portray ostrich behavior, but it should be noted that the comments in the text deal with perception. Yahweh is adopting the perspective common to humans at the time rather than making universally verifiable statements about the nature of ostriches or of any other creature described in chs. 38–39.

or clothe its neck with a flowing
mane?
20 Do you make it leap like a locust,[v]
striking terror with its proud
snorting?[w]
21 It paws fiercely, rejoicing in its
strength,
and charges into the fray.[x]
22 It laughs at fear, afraid of nothing;
it does not shy away from the
sword.
23 The quiver rattles against its side,
along with the flashing spear and
lance.
24 In frenzied excitement it eats up the
ground;
it cannot stand still when the
trumpet sounds.[y]
25 At the blast of the trumpet[z] it snorts,
'Aha!'
It catches the scent of battle from
afar,
the shout of commanders and the
battle cry.[a]

26 "Does the hawk take flight by your
wisdom
and spread its wings toward the
south?
27 Does the eagle soar at your
command
and build its nest on high?[b]
28 It dwells on a cliff and stays there at
night;
a rocky crag is its stronghold.
29 From there it looks for food;[c]
its eyes detect it from afar.
30 Its young ones feast on blood,
and where the slain are, there
it is."[d]

40 The LORD said to Job:[e]
2 "Will the one who contends with the
Almighty correct him?
Let him who accuses God answer
him!"

3 Then Job answered the LORD:

4 "I am unworthy[f] — how can I reply to
you?
I put my hand over my mouth.[g]
5 I spoke once, but I have no
answer[h] —
twice, but I will say no more."[i]

6 Then the LORD spoke to Job out of
the storm:[j]

7 "Brace yourself like a man;
I will question you,
and you shall answer me.[k]

8 "Would you discredit my justice?[l]
Would you condemn me to justify
yourself?
9 Do you have an arm like God's,[m]
and can your voice thunder like
his?[n]
10 Then adorn yourself with glory and
splendor,
and clothe yourself in honor and
majesty.[o]
11 Unleash the fury of your wrath,[p]
look at all who are proud and
bring them low,[q]
12 look at all who are proud and
humble them,[r]
crush[s] the wicked where they
stand.
13 Bury them all in the dust together;
shroud their faces in the grave.
14 Then I myself will admit to you
that your own right hand can save
you.[t]

15 "Look at Behemoth,
which I made along with you

Job 40:4-5 ❖ When is it best to fall silent before God? Why?

39:20 [v] Joel 2:4-5 [w] Jer 8:16
39:21 [x] Jer 8:6
39:24 [y] Jer 4:5, 19; Eze 7:14; Am 3:6
39:25 [z] Jos 6:5 [a] Am 1:14; 2:2
39:27 [b] Jer 49:16; Ob 4
39:29 [c] Job 9:26
39:30 [d] Mt 24:28; Lk 17:37
40:1 [e] Job 10:2; 13:3; 23:4; 31:35; 33:13
40:4 [f] Job 42:6 [g] Job 29:9
40:5 [h] Job 9:3 [i] Job 9:15
40:6 [j] Job 38:1
40:7 [k] Job 38:3; 42:4
40:8 [l] Job 27:2; Ro 3:3
40:9 [m] 2Ch 32:8 [n] Job 37:5; Ps 29:3-4
40:10 [o] Ps 93:1; 104:1
40:11 [p] Isa 42:25; Na 1:6 [q] Isa 2:11, 12,17; Da 4:37
40:12 [r] 1Sa 2:7 [s] Isa 13:11; 63:2-3,6
40:14 [t] Ps 20:6; 60:5; 108:6

40:1-14 In vv. 1-2 Yahweh demands an answer from Job. Job's reply (vv. 4-5) is appropriately one of submission and humility, but he stops short of recanting.
40:7-8 As in 38:3, Yahweh challenges Job to prepare to answer as one who has wisdom. Job is identified as one who has discredited Yahweh's justice. Yahweh is taking Job to task for not valuing God's justice more than his own righteousness.
Yahweh offers a challenge: Let Job take up control of the cosmos using the retribution principle that he has adopted and imposed on Yahweh. If Job were "God for a day," could he execute the retribution principle consistently in bringing justice?
If Job could exercise divine power and prove his view of justice, his righteousness would be vindicated. He must demonstrate that the system he envisions (and to which he wants God held accountable) can actually work. Only in such a system would suffering be taken as evidence of unrighteousness.
40:15—41:34 Job is compared to Behemoth (40:15). Job, like Behemoth, is the first of God's works (cf. 15:7) and withstands all turbulence. God brings his sword against Job (40:19), and by a snare he

and which feeds on grass like
an ox.
16 What strength it has in its loins,
what power in the muscles of its
belly!
17 Its tail sways like a cedar;
the sinews of its thighs are
close-knit.
18 Its bones are tubes of bronze,
its limbs like rods of iron.
19 It ranks first among the works of
God,[u]
yet its Maker can approach it with
his sword.
20 The hills bring it their produce,[v]
and all the wild animals play[w]
nearby.
21 Under the lotus plants it lies,
hidden among the reeds in the
marsh.
22 The lotuses conceal it in their
shadow;
the poplars by the stream[x]
surround it.
23 A raging river does not alarm it;
it is secure, though the Jordan
should surge against its
mouth.
24 Can anyone capture it by the eyes,
or trap it and pierce its nose?[y]

41 [a] "Can you pull in Leviathan[z] with
a fishhook
or tie down its tongue with a
rope?
2 Can you put a cord through its nose
or pierce its jaw with a hook?[a]
3 Will it keep begging you for mercy?
Will it speak to you with gentle
words?

40:19 [u] Job 41:33
40:20 [v] Ps 104:14 [w] Ps 104:26
40:22 [x] Isa 44:4
40:24 [y] Job 41:2,7,26
41:1 [z] Job 3:8; Ps 104:26; Isa 27:1
41:2 [a] Isa 37:29

Job 41:1–11 ❖ Why is it important to remember the limits of our own strength and righteousness before God?

[a] In Hebrew texts 41:1-8 is numbered 40:25-32, and 41:9-34 is numbered 41:1-26.

---

penetrates Job's anger (40:24). Yahweh does not speak of Job doing anything *to* Behemoth. Like Leviathan (41:1–3, 10–11, 34), Yahweh won't beg for mercy; you can't put him on a leash, subdue him, or rouse him. These all discuss what *Job* can't do to Leviathan. Job must also learn he cannot do them to Yahweh.

Yahweh's message seems to be: "Job, be strong and content like Behemoth, and don't think that you can domesticate or subdue me any more than you can Leviathan." Job needs to have more respect for Yahweh. The point is not that God can subdue Leviathan and therefore he can subdue Job—that was never in question. Rather, the passage indicates that since Job cannot bring Leviathan to heel, he cannot expect to domesticate Yahweh.

38:1—41:34 The book of Job is not intended to bring comfort to the suffering, but to bring understanding that might prevent us from simply blaming God for it. The alternative is to trust in the wisdom of God, and thereby the book gives us a focus for our faith.

Too often we focus our faith on believing that God will heal, relieve our suffering, or protect us from pain. Sometimes our faith lies in the belief that God will somehow come to us and give us explanations for why things have happened. At other times we place our faith in our ability to force our experiences into a coherent, meaningful narrative. All these approaches are unrealistic. Our faith should be directed toward embracing an all-wise God and asking him for help to live well before him regardless of our plight in this world that continues to display both order and disorder.

We should recognize, then, that the book of Job does not seek to explain God to us—such an endeavor would be impossible, as the book demonstrates. The book instead exposes our false and misguided ideas about God, the world, and suffering. It does not replace the rejected concepts with a comprehensive list of particulars but simply gives direction for thinking. If we can avoid the standard list of misperceptions and begin moving in the right direction, the book will have achieved its purpose.

That does not mean that there are never reasons for suffering that might need to be recognized. Sometimes we suffer the consequences of bad choices, and we need to acknowledge those and make changes. Overall, however, we are not encouraged to immerse ourselves in anguish over what may have caused our suffering. We definitely should not assume that if we are suffering, we must have done something to deserve it. People are often prone to respond to suffering with the question, "Why me?" But consider that it is when we have *not* suffered or when we are unexpectedly granted *relief* from suffering that we should pose the puzzled question, "Why me?"

If we shouldn't expect explanations or relief, what should we expect? We should expect that God is able to sustain us through suffering and even strengthen us through it. We please and honor God by trusting him in faith. We find purpose in suffering if we allow it to draw us closer to him in dependence instead of driving us further from him (though this should not be confused with ultimate cause or treated as a reason for our suffering). We serve and honor God by being people of faith and helping others who might also be suffering to find the same solutions.

4 Will it make an agreement with you
for you to take it as your slave for life?[b]
5 Can you make a pet of it like a bird
or put it on a leash for the young women in your house?
6 Will traders barter for it?
Will they divide it up among the merchants?
7 Can you fill its hide with harpoons
or its head with fishing spears?
8 If you lay a hand on it,
you will remember the struggle
and never do it again!
9 Any hope of subduing it is false;
the mere sight of it is overpowering.
10 No one is fierce enough to rouse it.[c]
Who then is able to stand against me?[d]
11 Who has a claim against me that I must pay?[e]
Everything under heaven belongs to me.[f]

12 "I will not fail to speak of Leviathan's limbs,
its strength and its graceful form.
13 Who can strip off its outer coat?
Who can penetrate its double coat of armor*[a]*?
14 Who dares open the doors of its mouth,
ringed about with fearsome teeth?
15 Its back has*[b]* rows of shields
tightly sealed together;
16 each is so close to the next
that no air can pass between.
17 They are joined fast to one another;
they cling together and cannot be parted.
18 Its snorting throws out flashes of light;
its eyes are like the rays of dawn.[g]
19 Flames stream from its mouth;
sparks of fire shoot out.
20 Smoke pours from its nostrils
as from a boiling pot over burning reeds.
21 Its breath[h] sets coals ablaze,
and flames dart from its mouth.[i]
22 Strength resides in its neck;
dismay goes before it.
23 The folds of its flesh are tightly joined;
they are firm and immovable.
24 Its chest is hard as rock,
hard as a lower millstone.
25 When it rises up, the mighty are terrified;
they retreat before its thrashing.
26 The sword that reaches it has no effect,
nor does the spear or the dart or the javelin.
27 Iron it treats like straw
and bronze like rotten wood.
28 Arrows do not make it flee;
slingstones are like chaff to it.
29 A club seems to it but a piece of straw;
it laughs at the rattling of the lance.
30 Its undersides are jagged potsherds,
leaving a trail in the mud like a threshing sledge.[j]
31 It makes the depths churn like a boiling caldron
and stirs up the sea like a pot of ointment.
32 It leaves a glistening wake behind it;
one would think the deep had white hair.
33 Nothing on earth is its equal[k] —
a creature without fear.
34 It looks down on all that are haughty;
it is king over all that are proud.[l]"

Job

42

Then Job replied to the LORD:

2 "I know that you can do all things;[m]
no purpose of yours can be thwarted.[n]
3 You asked, 'Who is this that obscures my plans without knowledge?'[o]
Surely I spoke of things I did not understand,
things too wonderful for me to know.[p]

4 "You said, 'Listen now, and I will speak;
I will question you,
and you shall answer me.'[q]
5 My ears had heard of you[r]
but now my eyes have seen you.[s]

41:4 [b] Ex 21:6
41:10 [c] Job 3:8 [d] Jer 50:44
41:11 [e] Ro 11:35 [f] Ex 19:5; Dt 10:14; Ps 24:1; 50:12; 1Co 10:26
41:18 [g] Job 3:9
41:21 [h] Isa 40:7 [i] Ps 18:8
41:30 [j] Isa 41:15
41:33 [k] Job 40:19
41:34 [l] Job 28:8
42:2 [m] Ge 18:14; Mt 19:26 [n] 2Ch 20:6
42:3 [o] Job 38:2 [p] Ps 40:5; 131:1; 139:6
42:4 [q] Job 38:3; 40:7
42:5 [r] Job 26:14; Ro 10:17 [s] Jdg 13:22; Isa 6:5; Eph 1:17-18

[a] *13* Septuagint; Hebrew *double bridle* [b] *15* Or *Its pride is its*

42:1-6 Job concedes that he spoke of things "too wonderful for me to know" (v. 3).

42:5-6 Job distinguishes between secondhand experience ("my ears had heard") and firsthand

PEOPLE TO KNOW // JOB

JOB 42:1–6: Job was a righteous man, but he experienced many tragedies in his life. In a mysterious glimpse into God's throne room, Job 1 depicts Satan challenging God to a test, with Job as their subject. Satan presumes Job is only good because he is blessed; God contends Job will remain good even if his blessings are taken (Job 1:6–12).

Satan brings disaster upon Job's life. His children die, his servants die, his livestock die. When Job remained righteous through all of this, Satan struck Job's body with excruciating sores (Job 2:7–8). Job's own wife told him to curse God for all that had happened to him, but Job refused (Job 2:9–10).

Job was then visited by friends who had a lot of theological knowledge but no pastoral sensitivity. They each told Job that there must have been something he did—some sin he had committed—to bring about these misfortunes. In spite of his friends' lengthy discussions, Job would not be swayed; he continued to claim that he was innocent of wrong. He demanded his day in court with God (Job 31:5–8).

God spoke to Job and gave him a tour of the marvels of creation. God revealed his own wisdom and power, and Job was faced with the reality of how little he himself truly understood about the universe and the power and wisdom of God. He acknowledged he was only one small part of God's creation and repented of challenging God. God then restored Job's fortunes, giving him twice as much as he had before (Job 42:10).

APPLICATION ✥ Job shows us that blessings and hardships cannot easily be correlated with righteousness and wickedness. It is true that good actions often lead to good results and wicked actions usually yield bad results (see the book of Proverbs). However, it is also true that sometimes the righteous suffer and the wicked prosper. Job's story is an example for us: Whatever our circumstances, God's plans are bigger than we can comprehend. God is God, and we are not. We can also take comfort in the fact that, even after all his suffering, Job found God to be good.

6 Therefore I despise myself[t]
and repent in dust and ashes."[u]

Epilogue

7 After the LORD had said these things
to Job, he said to Eliphaz the Temanite, "I
am angry with you and your two friends,[v]
because you have not spoken the truth
about me, as my servant Job has. 8 So
now take seven bulls and seven rams[w]
and go to my servant Job and sacrifice
a burnt offering[x] for yourselves. My servant
Job will pray for you, and I will accept
his prayer[y] and not deal with you
according to your folly.[z] You have not
spoken the truth about me, as my servant
Job has." 9 So Eliphaz the Temanite,
Bildad the Shuhite and Zophar the Naamathite
did what the LORD told them;
and the LORD accepted Job's prayer.
10 After Job had prayed for his friends,
the LORD restored his fortunes[a] and gave
him twice as much as he had before.[b]
11 All his brothers and sisters and everyone
who had known him before[c] came

42:6 [t] Job 40:4 [u] Ezr 9:6
42:7 [v] Job 32:3
42:8 [w] Nu 23:1, 29 [x] Job 1:5 [y] Ge 20:17; Jas 5:15-16; 1Jn 5:16 [z] Job 22:30
42:10 [a] Dt 30:3; Ps 14:7 [b] Job 1:3; Ps 85:1-3; 126:5-6
42:11 [c] Job 19:13

Job 42:7 ✥ How can we be careful not to fall into the same mistake as Job's friends when we speak about God? What can we learn from this story about how God dealt with both Job and his friends?

---

experience ("now my eyes have seen," v. 5). Considering this experience, he repents (v. 6). "Repent" means to reconsider something or to put something out of mind—to forget all about it. He has thereby announced the end to his mourning as he has accepted his reality.
42:7–17 The epilogue involves two parts: the reprimand and reconciliation of Job's friends (vv. 7–9) and the restoration of Job's prosperity (vv. 10–16).
42:7–8 Job did speak what is right (or valid) in certain ways, even though in other ways he misspoke. Although Job spoke more truly than his friends, God does not exonerate his behavior as a whole. God threatens that Job's friends are vulnerable to loss and misery, contrary to their confidence in the retribution principle.
42:10–17 Job offers a prayer for his friends as in ch. 1, where Job offered sacrifices for his children. When Job acted as priest for his children, his behavior revealed flaws in his theology. This exposed him to questions regarding his motivations, which led to his suffering. When Job acts as an intercessor for his friends, he trusts in God's compassion. He is not suspicious of God's character. As a result, this behavior leads to Job's restoration (v. 10).

and ate with him in his house. They comforted and consoled him over all the trouble the LORD had brought on him, and each one gave him a piece of silver[a] and a gold ring.

12The LORD blessed the latter part of
Job's life more than the former part. He had fourteen thousand sheep, six thousand camels, a thousand yoke of oxen and a thousand donkeys.
13And he also had seven sons and three daughters.
14The first daughter he named Jemimah, the second Keziah and the third Keren-Happuch.
15Nowhere in all the land were there found women as beautiful as Job's daughters, and their father granted them an inheritance along with their brothers.

16After this, Job lived a hundred and forty years; he saw his children and their children to the fourth generation.
17And so Job died, an old man and full of years.[d]

42:17 [d] Ge 15:15; 25:8

[a] *11* Hebrew *him a kesitah;* a kesitah was a unit of money of unknown weight and value.

42:1-17 God desires that we learn perseverance and wisdom and that we mature, and suffering is part of the disorder in the world that we learn from: God can bring good from it. Disorder has remained part of the cosmos as part of God's plan. But instead of responding to this disorder righteously, we have responded to this disorder with sin, which sometimes results in suffering. We should not rejoice over our sin and over the chaos and suffering that ensue as a result. Positive results can follow sin when we recognize it, suffer the consequences, repent, and thereby grow strong against it. But that does not make sin God's will.

God can teach us lessons through our suffering, but we should not think of it as his will to do so. Likewise, we should not think in terms of "blaming the world." We must resist finding a focus for blame, for that is not the point.

God's plan for history and the cosmos entails a gradual process of expanding order. While that process remains incomplete, we cope with the disorder that remains. God could have chosen to act differently, but it is not our role to second-guess God or to suggest better options, as the book of Job has taught us. We cannot reduce God's policies to a simple formula that fits our limited understanding.

Authors: David, Asaph, the Sons of Korah, Solomon, Heman, Ethan, Moses and unknown authors

Audience: God's people

Date: Between the time of Moses (probably about 1440 BC) and the time following the Babylonian exile (after 538 BC)

Theme: God the Great King inspires the psalmists' words of lament and praise that are appropriate responses to God.

PERSPECTIVE

It may be that the book of Psalms is the most complete revelation in all of Christendom. Properly read, the 150 psalms touch every aspect of what it means to be fully human, created in the image of God. The Psalter tells the story of God's working in the world and with humanity. Yet the psalms tell the story using one of our primary means of artistic expression: song. And, yes, there is a moral to each of the 150 mini-stories in David, Solomon, and others' compositions; sometimes more than one. When you put the wisdom, art, and ethics of the psalms together it feels like one can almost reach out and touch God as our head, heart, and hands fade away in a wave of blissful relationship.

The book of Psalms is complete in another way. It is both revelation—God's words to us—and meditation—our words to God. There is a reason why the psalms are read every day in liturgies around the world. They are like public prayer conversations with God set to music. They can be read privately or corporately but never without a two-way engagement with the Author of our being.

When the psalms were written, their function was their use in worship as either praise or lament or thanksgiving. The wholeness and simplicity of that function in OT times has been shattered and dispersed today. We talk about the psalms' usefulness—what is of advantage to us. And we talk about the psychological, the sociological, and the philosophical functions of the psalms. They are worth much to each of us as individuals and as communities, as they spread across the disciplines of life. Yet there must be more to them than that.

Reading Psalms

In reading the psalms, we must remember that we are reading poetry. Hebrew poetry is quite different from the poetry that most of us are familiar with; its key features are a love of structure (sometimes as simple as the use of the Hebrew alphabet in Ps 119, sometimes highly complex) and the use of parallelism (such as two parts of a verse saying

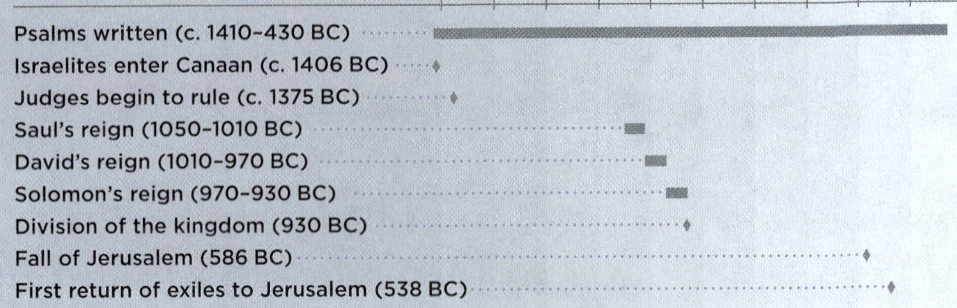

essentially the same thing). The Psalter is arranged into five books, though there is no general theme to each book. Probably there were smaller collections of psalms preceding the one collection of 150 we have today.

Key Verses

Blessed is the one who does not walk in step with the wicked or stand in the way that sinners take or sit in the company of mockers, but whose delight is in the law of the LORD, and who meditates on his law day and night. That person is like a tree planted by streams of water, which yields its fruit in season and whose leaf does not wither—whatever they do prospers.

—Psalm 1:1–3

In the midst of this discussion of the psalms' utility, something has been lost, something we might call "the wholeness of the worship of God." And this is precisely what the Psalter can restore to us. When we read the psalms, God's promises come alive. When we sing the psalms, our hearts are filled with joy. God speaks through the psalms to our everyday burdens and cares. All of this is enhanced by learning more about the text we have before us. We read, then, the study notes to this book with one eye on learning all we can but with our other eye on being embraced by the wholeness of God's amazing love.

TAKING THE NEXT STEPS

The book of Psalms is the prayer book of the Bible. The psalmists find occasion to pray in every imaginable situation and express the whole breadth of human emotions in their prayers. These prayers include praise, thanksgiving, acknowledgements of faith and trust in God, confession of sin, and even complaints against God concerning the way that they are being treated. The psalmists address these psalms to God—God not as an abstract being but as One who is at the center of their everyday lives.

The believer today will find in this book a pattern for prayer life. (1) There is not a human feeling that we have, negative or positive, that cannot be brought before God in prayer. We can praise God with exhilarating songs, and we can complain to him in our deepest despair. (2) God wants us to meditate on him and on his Word as our only source of faith, hope, and love. (3) God wants us to reach out to him for protection in our day-to-day lives, considering him alone as our help and our strength. (4) God wants us to recall regularly his care for his people, both in past history and in our own personal lives. Such remembering cannot help but make us rejoice in him.

WHAT TO LOOK FOR IN PSALMS

- Psalms of trust in God (11; 16; 23; 27; 46; 91; 121; 125; 131)
- Psalms of praise to God (33; 66; 95–101; 103; 111; 113; 117; 145–150)
- Psalms telling stories of history (18; 78; 81; 105–107; 135; 136)
- Psalms of thanksgiving (30; 32; 34; 75; 100; 116; 118; 138)
- Psalms by or for the king (2; 18; 20; 21; 45; 72; 101; 110; 144)
- Psalms of nature (8; 19; 104; 148)
- Psalms of meditation (1; 19; 36; 37; 49; 73; 112; 127; 128; 133)
- Psalms of confession of sin (6; 32; 38; 51; 130; 143)
- Psalms of individual complaint (3–7; 9–11; 13–14; 22; 25–28; 41–43; 52–57; 71; 77; 86; 88–89; 120; 141–142)
- Psalms of community complaint (12; 44; 60; 74; 80; 83; 85; 90; 94; 123; 126; 129)
- Psalms against one's enemies (35; 55; 58–59; 69–70; 79; 109; 137; 140)

BOOK I

Psalms 1 – 41

Psalm 1

1 Blessed is the one
who does not walk[a] in step with
the wicked
or stand in the way that sinners
take
or sit[b] in the company of mockers,
2 but whose delight[c] is in the law of
the LORD,[d]
and who meditates[e] on his law day
and night.
3 That person is like a tree[f] planted by
streams of water,[g]
which yields its fruit[h] in season
and whose leaf does not wither —
whatever they do prospers.[i]

4 Not so the wicked!
They are like chaff[j]
that the wind blows away.

1:1 [a] Pr 4:14 [b] Ps 26:4; Jer 15:17
1:2 [c] Ps 119:16, 35 [d] Ps 119:1 [e] Jos 1:8
1:3 [f] Ps 128:3 [g] Jer 17:8 [h] Eze 47:12 [i] Ge 39:3
1:4 [j] Job 21:18; Isa 17:13

Ps 1:1-3 ❖ Why is a tree planted by streams of water an apt image for a righteous person? How can we be like such a tree?

5 Therefore the wicked will not stand[k]
in the judgment,[l]
nor sinners in the assembly of the
righteous.

6 For the LORD watches over[m] the way
of the righteous,
but the way of the wicked leads to
destruction.[n]

Psalm 2

1 Why do the nations conspire[a]
and the peoples plot[o] in vain?
2 The kings[p] of the earth rise up
and the rulers band together
against the LORD and against his
anointed,[q] saying,

1:5 [k] Ps 5:5 [l] Ps 9:7-8,16
1:6 [m] Ps 37:18; 2Ti 2:19 [n] Ps 9:6
2:1 [o] Ps 21:11
2:2 [p] Ps 48:4 [q] Ps 74:18, 23; Jn 1:41; Ac 4:25-26*

[a] 1 Hebrew; Septuagint *rage*

1:1-2 The lifestyle described in v. 1 is one to be avoided, not emulated. Most likely Torah ("law," v. 2) here implies the traditional commandments of God in *the* Torah as well as the life-giving guidance God gives elsewhere in Scripture. Psalm 1 stresses careful, diligent attention to Scripture in seeking God's guidance for life.
1:3 The image of the tree is known from the similar passage in Jer 17:7-8.
1:4-6 The reader is presented with a choice: the way of righteousness that God oversees or the way of wickedness that will ultimately perish.

APPLICATION ✚ **1:1-6** When we meditate on and memorize the Psalms, we are planting our roots deeply into the life-giving water of God's Word. This is the same "living water" that Jesus offers to the Samaritan woman at the well (Jn 4).

2:1-3 The opening section of Ps 2 describes an international conspiracy against the authority of Yahweh and his "anointed" representative (v. 2c).

THE PSALMS

CATEGORY	DEFINING FEATURES	BOOK 1	BOOKS 2 AND 3	BOOKS 4 AND 5
Lament Psalms	Corporately or individually call upon God in a time of crisis—stating the dilemma, trusting him to deliver and promising to praise	3; 4; 5; 6; 7; 10; 12; 13; 16; 17; 22:1-21; 25; 26; 27:7-14; 28; 35; 38; 39; 40:11-17; 41	42; 43; 44; 51; 54; 55; 56; 57; 58; 60; 61; 63; 64; 69; 70; 71; 74; 77; 79; 80; 82; 83; 85; 86; 88; 89:38-51	90; 94; 102:1-11; 108; 109; 120; 129; 130; 137; 139; 140; 141; 142; 143; 144:3-15
Songs of Praise	Individually give thanks for God's action to save or corporately praise him for his greatness exhibited in creation and history	8; 9; 11; 18; 22:22-31; 27:1-6; 29; 30; 31; 32; 33; 34; 40:1-10	46; 47; 48; 63; 65; 66; 67; 68; 75; 76; 81; 84; 89:1-18	92; 93; 95; 96; 97; 98; 99; 100; 101; 103; 104; 105; 106:1-5; 107; 111; 112; 113; 116; 117; 118; 124; 134; 135; 136; 138; 144:1-4; 145; 146; 147; 148; 149; 150
Royal Psalms	Celebrate the Davidic King's special relationship to God or reveal the King's speech	2; 18; 20; 21	45; 72; 89	101; 110; 144
Wisdom Psalms	Resemble Wisdom Literature in language and tone	1; 14; 15; 19; 23; 24; 31; 36; 37	49; 52; 53; 59; 62; 73; 78; 82	119; 127; 128; 132

For extensive classification, see Tom Watson, *Chronological and Background Charts of the Old Testament*, rev. and exp. ed. (Grand Rapids: Zondervan, 1994), 48-50.

3 "Let us break their chains
and throw off their shackles."[r]

4 The One enthroned in heaven
laughs;[s]
the Lord scoffs at them.
5 He rebukes them in his anger
and terrifies them in his wrath,[t]
saying,
6 "I have installed my king
on Zion, my holy mountain."

7 I will proclaim the LORD's decree:

He said to me, "You are my son;
today I have become your
father.[u]
8 Ask me,
and I will make the nations your
inheritance,
the ends of the earth[v] your
possession.
9 You will break them with a rod of
iron[a];[w]
you will dash them to pieces[x] like
pottery.[y]"

2:3 [r] Jer 5:5
2:4 [s] Ps 37:13; 59:8; Pr 1:26
2:5 [t] Ps 21:9; 78:49-50
2:7 [u] Ac 13:33*; Heb 1:5*
2:8 [v] Ps 22:27
2:9 [w] Rev 12:5 [x] Ps 89:23 [y] Rev 2:27*

Ps 2:1-6 ❖ What does this passage tell us about rebellious leaders in our world? What about the rebellion in our own hearts?

[a] 9 Or *will rule them with an iron scepter* (see Septuagint and Syriac)

2:4-6 Yahweh sees these human beings, knows their plots, and is unconcerned. Divine laughter turns to "anger" and scoffing to "rebuke" (v. 5) as Yahweh himself pronounces judgment on the assembled conspirators.

2:7-9 The king takes center stage to testify in his own voice to the authorizing covenant established between Yahweh and the king. The background of this relationship is clearly the Davidic covenant described in 2Sa 7:4-16. The nations are to become the king's "inheritance" (Ps 2:8).

2:10-12 The narrator returns in the final section of the psalm to issue a stern warning to the rebellious kings.

2:1-12 Whenever we buy into the world's way of placing self before all else, we become "the nations," negating the work of Christ to bring us into the family of God and hampering our witness to the world.

10 Therefore, you kings, be wise;
be warned, you rulers of the earth.
11 Serve the LORD with fear
and celebrate his rule[z] with trembling.[a]
12 Kiss his son,[b] or he will be angry
and your way will lead to your destruction,
for his wrath[c] can flare up in a moment.
Blessed are all who take refuge[d] in him.

Psalm 3[a]

A psalm of David. When he fled from his son Absalom.[e]

1 LORD, how many are my foes!
How many rise up against me!
2 Many are saying of me,
"God will not deliver him."[f][b]

3 But you, LORD, are a shield[g] around me,
my glory, the One who lifts my head high.[h]
4 I call out to the LORD,
and he answers me from his holy mountain.[i]

5 I lie down and sleep;[j]
I wake again, because the LORD sustains me.
6 I will not fear[k] though tens of thousands
assail me on every side.

7 Arise,[l] LORD!
Deliver me,[m] my God!
Strike[n] all my enemies on the jaw;
break the teeth[o] of the wicked.

8 From the LORD comes deliverance.[p]
May your blessing be on your people.

2:11 [z] Heb 12:28 [a] Ps 119:119-120
2:12 [b] Jn 5:23 [c] Rev 6:16 [d] Ps 34:8; Ro 9:33
3:Title [e] 2Sa 15:14
3:2 [f] Ps 71:11
3:3 [g] Ge 15:1; Ps 28:7 [h] Ps 27:6
3:4 [i] Ps 2:6
3:5 [j] Lev 26:6; Pr 3:24
3:6 [k] Ps 27:3
3:7 [l] Ps 7:6 [m] Ps 6:4 [n] Job 16:10 [o] Ps 58:6
3:8 [p] Isa 43:3,11

Ps 3:3-6 ❖ How can we find comfort in these verses and apply these teachings to the struggles we face every day?

Ps 4:2 ❖ What delusions and false gods do we see people chasing after today? What are ways we might point people to the true God?

Psalm 4[c]

For the director of music. With stringed instruments. A psalm of David.

1 Answer me when I call to you,
my righteous God.
Give me relief from my distress;
have mercy[q] on me and hear my prayer.[r]

2 How long will you people turn my glory into shame?
How long will you love delusions
and seek false gods[d]?[e][s]
3 Know that the LORD has set apart his faithful servant[t] for himself;
the LORD hears[u] when I call to him.

4 Tremble and[f] do not sin;[v]
when you are on your beds,[w]
search your hearts and be silent.
5 Offer the sacrifices of the righteous
and trust in the LORD.[x]

6 Many, LORD, are asking, "Who will bring us prosperity?"
Let the light of your face shine on us.[y]

4:1 [q] Ps 25:16 [r] Ps 17:6
4:2 [s] Ps 31:6
4:3 [t] Ps 31:23 [u] Ps 6:8
4:4 [v] Eph 4:26* [w] Ps 77:6
4:5 [x] Dt 33:19; Ps 37:3
4:6 [y] Nu 6:25

[a] In Hebrew texts 3:1-8 is numbered 3:2-9.
[b] 2 The Hebrew has *Selah* (a word of uncertain meaning) here and at the end of verses 4 and 8.
[c] In Hebrew texts 4:1-8 is numbered 4:2-9.
[d] 2 Or *seek lies* [e] 2 The Hebrew has *Selah* (a word of uncertain meaning) here and at the end of verse 4. [f] 4 Or *In your anger* (see Septuagint)

3:1-2 One can almost sense the panic as the psalmist sees only the multitude of enemies about to overwhelm him.
3:3-4 The psalmist responds with a cry of his own directed to God. The cry of confidence has the appearance of hindsight gained after the fact of actual deliverance.
3:5-8 The final segment of the psalm projects an almost eerie sense of confidence and security. Yahweh is the unshakable source of human dignity and honor.

✣ **3:1-8** Sometimes when we are under attack, we can begin to question our own worth to others, to ourselves, even to God. At moments like these we need to tap into the vision that proceeds from God and gives us hope.

4:1-2 The opening section of Ps 4 is divided into a plea directed to Yahweh (v. 1) and a rebuke directed to the psalmist's own people (v. 2).
4:3-5 Having condemned the opponents for worshiping false gods, the psalmist now advises them to offer right sacrifices.
4:6-8 The "who" (v. 6) of this sentence clearly refers to the multiple gods and goddesses of the pagan pantheon. In contrast, the psalmist trusts in the steadfast love of Yahweh—a love that never ceases.

[7]Fill my heart[z] with joy[a]
when their grain and new wine
abound.

[8]In peace I will lie down and sleep,[b]
for you alone, LORD,
make me dwell in safety.[c]

Psalm 5[a]

For the director of music. For pipes. A psalm of David.

[1]Listen to my words, LORD,
consider my lament.
[2]Hear my cry for help,[d]
my King and my God,[e]
for to you I pray.

[3]In the morning,[f] LORD, you hear my
voice;
in the morning I lay my requests
before you
and wait expectantly.
[4]For you are not a God who is pleased
with wickedness;
with you, evil people[g] are not
welcome.
[5]The arrogant[h] cannot stand[i]
in your presence.
You hate[j] all who do wrong;
[6]you destroy those who tell lies.[k]
The bloodthirsty and deceitful
you, LORD, detest.
[7]But I, by your great love,
can come into your house;
in reverence I bow down[l]
toward your holy temple.

[8]Lead me, LORD, in your
righteousness[m]
because of my enemies —
make your way straight[n] before me.
[9]Not a word from their mouth can be
trusted;
their heart is filled with malice.
Their throat is an open grave;[o]
with their tongues they tell lies.[p]
[10]Declare them guilty, O God!
Let their intrigues be their
downfall.
Banish them for their many sins,[q]
for they have rebelled[r] against
you.
[11]But let all who take refuge in you be
glad;
let them ever sing for joy.[s]
Spread your protection over
them,
that those who love your name[t]
may rejoice in you.[u]

[12]Surely, LORD, you bless the
righteous;
you surround them[v] with your
favor as with a shield.

Psalm 6[b]

For the director of music. With stringed instruments. According to sheminith.[c] A psalm of David.

[1]LORD, do not rebuke me in your
anger[w]
or discipline me in your wrath.
[2]Have mercy on me, LORD, for I am
faint;
heal me,[x] LORD, for my bones are
in agony.[y]

4:7 [z]Ac 14:17 [a]Isa 9:3
4:8 [b]Ps 3:5 [c]Lev 25:18
5:2 [d]Ps 3:4 [e]Ps 84:3
5:3 [f]Ps 88:13
5:4 [g]Ps 11:5; 92:15
5:5 [h]Ps 73:3 [i]Ps 1:5 [j]Ps 11:5
5:6 [k]Ps 55:23; Rev 21:8
5:7 [l]Ps 138:2
5:8 [m]Ps 31:1 [n]Ps 27:11
5:9 [o]Lk 11:44 [p]Ro 3:13*
5:10 [q]Ps 9:16 [r]Ps 107:11
5:11 [s]Ps 2:12 [t]Ps 69:36 [u]Isa 65:13
5:12 [v]Ps 32:7
6:1 [w]Ps 38:1
6:2 [x]Hos 6:1 [y]Ps 22:14; 31:10

Ps 5:11–12 ❖ When has God's protection over us been like a shield?

Ps 6:2–3 ❖ Have we offered laments like this before to God? How have we felt God's presence during those periods?

[a] In Hebrew texts 5:1-12 is numbered 5:2-13. [b] In Hebrew texts 6:1-10 is numbered 6:2-11. [c] Title: Probably a musical term

4:1–8 This psalm is a call to practicing the presence of God.

5:1–3 The psalmist's speech is a loud "cry for help" (v. 2) rather than any other form of quiet meditation or reflection.
5:4–6 The psalmist finds the grounds of confidence to approach Yahweh in the very character of God himself.
5:7–8 Yahweh's holiness is incompatible with evil; it is also characterized by relentless goodness. From the beginning, God's only intent was and still is to bless his creation. Relentless goodness is the flip side of incompatibility with evil.
5:11–12 Trust is more than a temporary desire for protection or security. It signals a willingness to commit one's whole destiny to God.

5:1–12 Those who take refuge in God find hope in his holiness. Why? Because he is incompatible with evil and because he is relentlessly good.

6:1–5 The first subsection pleads that Yahweh will not prove himself right at the psalmist's expense. The second subsection changes to pleas for divine action. The third subsection describes a change of action or direction. If Yahweh continues to "forget" the faithful in this life, there will be no one left above ground to praise him.

3 My soul is in deep anguish.[z]
How long,[a] LORD, how long?

4 Turn, LORD, and deliver me;
save me because of your unfailing love.[b]
5 Among the dead no one proclaims your name.
Who praises you from the grave?[c]

6 I am worn out[d] from my groaning.

All night long I flood my bed with weeping
and drench my couch with tears.[e]
7 My eyes grow weak[f] with sorrow;
they fail because of all my foes.

8 Away from me,[g] all you who do evil,[h]
for the LORD has heard my weeping.
9 The LORD has heard my cry for mercy;[i]
the LORD accepts my prayer.
10 All my enemies will be overwhelmed with shame and anguish;
they will turn back and suddenly be put to shame.[j]

Psalm 7[a]

A shiggaion[b] of David, which he sang to the LORD concerning Cush, a Benjamite.

1 LORD my God, I take refuge in you;
save and deliver me from all who pursue me,[k]
2 or they will tear me apart like a lion[l]
and rip me to pieces with no one to rescue[m] me.

3 LORD my God, if I have done this
and there is guilt on my hands[n] —
4 if I have repaid my ally with evil
or without cause have robbed my foe —
5 then let my enemy pursue and overtake me;
let him trample my life to the ground
and make me sleep in the dust.[c]

6 Arise,[o] LORD, in your anger;
rise up against the rage of my enemies.[p]
Awake,[q] my God; decree justice.
7 Let the assembled peoples gather around you,
while you sit enthroned over them on high.
8 Let the LORD judge the peoples.
Vindicate me, LORD, according to my righteousness,[r]
according to my integrity, O Most High.
9 Bring to an end the violence of the wicked
and make the righteous secure —[s]
you, the righteous God[t]
who probes minds and hearts.[u]

10 My shield[d] is God Most High,
who saves the upright in heart.[v]
11 God is a righteous judge,[w]
a God who displays his wrath every day.
12 If he does not relent,
he[e] will sharpen his sword;[x]
he will bend and string his bow.
13 He has prepared his deadly weapons;
he makes ready his flaming arrows.

14 Whoever is pregnant with evil
conceives trouble and gives birth[y] to disillusionment.

6:3 [z] Jn 12:27 [a] Ps 90:13
6:4 [b] Ps 17:13
6:5 [c] Ps 30:9; 88:10-12; Ecc 9:10; Isa 38:18
6:6 [d] Ps 69:3 [e] Ps 42:3
6:7 [f] Ps 31:9
6:8 [g] Ps 119:115 [h] Mt 7:23; Lk 13:27
6:9 [i] Ps 116:1
6:10 [j] Ps 71:24; 73:19
7:1 [k] Ps 31:15
7:2 [l] Isa 38:13 [m] Ps 50:22
7:3 [n] 1Sa 24:11; Isa 59:3
7:6 [o] Ps 94:2 [p] Ps 138:7 [q] Ps 44:23
7:8 [r] Ps 18:20; 96:13
7:9 [s] Ps 37:23 [t] Jer 11:20 [u] 1Ch 28:9; Ps 26:2; Rev 2:23
7:10 [v] Ps 125:4
7:11 [w] Ps 50:6
7:12 [x] Dt 32:41
7:14 [y] Job 15:35; Isa 59:4; Jas 1:15

[a] In Hebrew texts 7:1-17 is numbered 7:2-18.
[b] Title: Probably a literary or musical term
[c] 5 The Hebrew has *Selah* (a word of uncertain meaning) here.
[d] 10 Or *sovereign*
[e] 12 Or *If anyone does not repent, / God*

6:6–7 The extended suffering prompted by Yahweh's inaction has reduced the psalmist to weeping and anguish.
6:8–10 Yahweh will deliver the psalmist, and the opponents will receive a public punishment.

6:1–10 Experiences of personal pain are evidence that we live in a disordered world. In many ways, it is a world that defies the good intentions of the Creator.

7:1–2 The psalmist is in trouble. He takes refuge in Yahweh.
7:3–5 The passage is divided into an "if" section describing possible wrongs of which the psalmist claims innocence and a "then" section where consequences of proven guilt are laid out.
7:6–9 Having established innocence, the psalmist turns to Yahweh as the righteous judge. He calls on Yahweh to arise in righteous indignation and to assume his seat as judge.
7:10–13 God judges righteously and metes out that judgment's consequences. Yahweh now responds as a "shield" and defender for those proven to be righteous. He also prepares to dispense judgment on the wicked.
7:14–16 The psalmist moves on to describe the fate of the wicked themselves. Heaping up words

15 Whoever digs a hole and scoops it out
falls into the pit they have made.[z]
16 The trouble they cause recoils on
them;
their violence comes down on
their own heads.

17 I will give thanks to the LORD
because of his righteousness;[a]
I will sing the praises[b] of the name
of the LORD Most High.

Psalm 8[a]

For the director of music. According to gittith.[b] *A psalm of David.*

1 LORD, our Lord,
how majestic is your name in all
the earth!

You have set your glory
in the heavens.[c]
2 Through the praise of children and
infants
you have established a
stronghold[d] against your
enemies,
to silence the foe[e] and the avenger.
3 When I consider your heavens,[f]
the work of your fingers,
the moon and the stars,[g]
which you have set in place,
4 what is mankind that you are
mindful of them,
human beings that you care for
them?[c][h]

5 You have made them[d] a little lower
than the angels[e]
and crowned them[d] with glory
and honor.[i]

7:15 [z] Job 4:8
7:17 [a] Ps 71:15-16 [b] Ps 9:2
8:1 [c] Ps 57:5; 113:4; 148:13
8:2 [d] Mt 21:16* [e] Ps 44:16; 1Co 1:27
8:3 [f] Ps 89:11 [g] Ps 136:9
8:4 [h] Job 7:17; Ps 144:3; Heb 2:6
8:5 [i] Ps 21:5; 103:4
8:6 [j] Ge 1:28 [k] 1Co 15:25, 27*; Eph 1:22; Heb 2:6-8*
8:9 [l] ver 1
9:1 [m] Ps 86:12 [n] Ps 26:7

Ps 7:15 ❖ When have we seen God give wicked people what they deserve? How did they fall into the pit they had dug?

Ps 8:6 ❖ What area of ruling has God tasked us with in creation? How can we rule in that area for God's glory?

6 You made them rulers[j] over the
works of your hands;
you put everything under their[f]
feet:[k]
7 all flocks and herds,
and the animals of the wild,
8 the birds in the sky,
and the fish in the sea,
all that swim the paths of the seas.

9 LORD, our Lord,
how majestic is your name in all
the earth![l]

Psalm 9[g,h]

For the director of music. To the tune of "The Death of the Son." A psalm of David.

1 I will give thanks to you, LORD, with
all my heart;[m]
I will tell of all your wonderful
deeds.[n]

[a] In Hebrew texts 8:1-9 is numbered 8:2-10. [b] Title: Probably a musical term [c] 4 Or *what is a human being that you are mindful of him, / a son of man that you care for him?* [d] 5 Or *him* [e] 5 Or *than God* [f] 6 Or *made him ruler . . . ; / . . . his* [g] Psalms 9 and 10 may originally have been a single acrostic poem in which alternating lines began with the successive letters of the Hebrew alphabet. In the Septuagint they constitute one psalm. [h] In Hebrew texts 9:1-20 is numbered 9:2-21.

---

relating to conception and birth, the psalmist scorns the one who is "pregnant with evil" (v. 14) and trouble. The enemy ultimately falls into the pit prepared for the psalmist.

7:17 Yahweh is to be praised because he is a righteous judge who can be trusted to uphold the righteous and punish the wicked.

✚ **7:1-17** How comforting it is to think of God as our refuge. Yet often, precisely when we need that refuge most, we feel unable or unworthy to enter in. As a result, we do not take the steps to healing and wholeness that God provides.

8:1a Earth and heaven mark the two extremes of God's creation and declare Yahweh's majestic name.

8:1b-2 Toddlers and nursing children are particularly dependent on others. The psalmist creates a contrast with the presumed power of those who oppose God and his faithful ones.

8:3-4 The psalmist begins with Yahweh's creative power and then reflects on the significance of earthbound humans.

8:5-8 Humans, who can seem so powerless and small in the scheme of things, are invested with stupendous worth and responsibility by the creator.

8:9 Praise began by affirming the magnificence of the Creator. It ends in awe that God has elevated humanity to unimaginable heights.

✚ **8:1-9** This psalm opens a new window on who we really are. Although we see ourselves as weak and insignificant, God sees us as only a little lower than the angels themselves.

9:1—10:18 Psalms 9 and 10 were originally read together as a single composition.

9:1-3 The psalmist is still suffering yet begins with an expression of confident thanksgiving.

[2]I will be glad and rejoice[o] in you;
I will sing the praises of your name,[p] O Most High.

[3]My enemies turn back;
they stumble and perish before you.
[4]For you have upheld my right and my cause,[q]
sitting enthroned as the righteous judge.[r]
[5]You have rebuked the nations and destroyed the wicked;
you have blotted out their name[s] for ever and ever.
[6]Endless ruin has overtaken my enemies,
you have uprooted their cities;
even the memory of them[t] has perished.

[7]The LORD reigns forever;
he has established his throne[u] for judgment.
[8]He rules the world in righteousness[v]
and judges the peoples with equity.
[9]The LORD is a refuge for the oppressed,
a stronghold in times of trouble.[w]
[10]Those who know your name[x] trust in you,
for you, LORD, have never forsaken[y] those who seek you.

[11]Sing the praises of the LORD, enthroned in Zion;[z]
proclaim among the nations[a] what he has done.[b]
[12]For he who avenges blood[c] remembers;
he does not ignore the cries of the afflicted.

[13]LORD, see how my enemies[d] persecute me!
Have mercy and lift me up from the gates of death,
[14]that I may declare your praises[e]
in the gates of Daughter Zion,
and there rejoice in your salvation.[f]

[15]The nations have fallen into the pit they have dug;[g]
their feet are caught in the net they have hidden.[h]
[16]The LORD is known by his acts of justice;
the wicked are ensnared by the work of their hands.[a]
[17]The wicked go down to the realm of the dead,[i]
all the nations that forget God.[j]
[18]But God will never forget the needy;
the hope[k] of the afflicted[l] will never perish.

[19]Arise, LORD, do not let mortals triumph;
let the nations be judged in your presence.
[20]Strike them with terror, LORD;
let the nations know they are only mortal.[m]

Psalm 10[b]

[1]Why, LORD, do you stand far off?[n]
Why do you hide yourself[o] in times of trouble?

[2]In his arrogance the wicked man hunts down the weak,
who are caught in the schemes he devises.
[3]He boasts[p] about the cravings of his heart;

9:2 [o]Ps 5:11 [p]Ps 92:1; 83:18
9:4 [q]Ps 140:12 [r]1Pe 2:23
9:5 [s]Pr 10:7
9:6 [t]Ps 34:16
9:7 [u]Ps 89:14
9:8 [v]Ps 96:13
9:9 [w]Ps 32:7
9:10 [x]Ps 91:14 [y]Ps 37:28
9:11 [z]Ps 76:2 [a]Ps 107:22 [b]Ps 105:1
9:12 [c]Ge 9:5
9:13 [d]Ps 38:19
9:14 [e]Ps 106:2 [f]Ps 13:5; 51:12
9:15 [g]Ps 7:15-16 [h]Ps 35:8; 57:6
9:17 [i]Ps 49:14 [j]Job 8:13; Ps 50:22
9:18 [k]Ps 71:5; Pr 23:18 [l]Ps 12:5
9:20 [m]Ps 62:9; Isa 31:3
10:1 [n]Ps 22:1,11 [o]Ps 13:1
10:3 [p]Ps 94:4

Ps 9:1 ❖ Whom can we tell of God's wonderful deeds? What deeds can we proclaim to them?

[a] *16* The Hebrew has *Higgaion* and *Selah* (words of uncertain meaning) here; *Selah* occurs also at the end of verse 20. [b] Psalms 9 and 10 may originally have been a single acrostic poem in which alternating lines began with the successive letters of the Hebrew alphabet. In the Septuagint they constitute one psalm.

9:4–8 The dominant emphasis in these verses is on Yahweh's character as a "righteous judge" (v. 4). In a series of parallel phrases, the psalmist describes the divine judgment on the opposing nations.
9:9–14 The same Hebrew word appears behind the NIV translation for both "refuge" and "stronghold" in v. 9. This word describes a high, rocky spot that is inaccessible and thus provides protection from enemies.
9:15–20 Psalm 9 concludes by describing the just punishment of the wicked. Once again, the interplay in these verses between the "nations" and the "wicked" allows flexibility in understanding the enemy as the wicked individuals opposing the psalmist or as the evil nations oppressing Israel.
10:1–11 Psalm 10 opens with agonized questions directed to God. The questions and the attendant sense of abandonment set the stage for the scathing description of the arrogant wicked that dominates vv. 2–11.

he blesses the greedy and reviles
the LORD.
4 In his pride the wicked man does not
seek him;
in all his thoughts there is no
room for God.[q]
5 His ways are always prosperous;
your laws are rejected by[a] him;
he sneers at all his enemies.
6 He says to himself, "Nothing will
ever shake me."
He swears, "No one will ever do
me harm."[r]

7 His mouth is full[s] of lies and threats;[t]
trouble and evil are under his
tongue.[u]
8 He lies in wait near the villages;
from ambush he murders the
innocent.[v]
His eyes watch in secret for his
victims;
9 like a lion in cover he lies in wait.
He lies in wait to catch the helpless;[w]
he catches the helpless and drags
them off in his net.
10 His victims are crushed, they
collapse;
they fall under his strength.
11 He says to himself, "God will never
notice;[x]
he covers his face and never sees."

12 Arise, LORD! Lift up your hand,[y]
O God.
Do not forget the helpless.[z]
13 Why does the wicked man revile
God?
Why does he say to himself,
"He won't call me to account"?
14 But you, God, see the trouble[a] of the
afflicted;

10:4 [q] Ps 14:1; 36:1
10:6 [r] Rev 18:7
10:7 [s] Ro 3:14* [t] Ps 73:8 [u] Ps 140:3
10:8 [v] Ps 94:6
10:9 [w] Ps 17:12; 59:3; 140:5
10:11 [x] Job 22:13
10:12 [y] Ps 17:7; Mic 5:9 [z] Ps 9:12
10:14 [a] Ps 22:11

Ps 10:12–15 ❖ What do we see in the world around us that makes us cry out for God's justice?

you consider their grief and take it
in hand.
The victims commit themselves to
you;[b]
you are the helper[c] of the
fatherless.
15 Break the arm of the wicked man;[d]
call the evildoer to account for his
wickedness
that would not otherwise be
found out.

16 The LORD is King for ever and ever;[e]
the nations[f] will perish from his
land.
17 You, LORD, hear the desire of the
afflicted;[g]
you encourage them, and you
listen to their cry,
18 defending the fatherless[h] and the
oppressed,[i]
so that mere earthly mortals
will never again strike terror.

Psalm 11

For the director of music. Of David.

1 In the LORD I take refuge.[j]
How then can you say to me:
"Flee like a bird to your mountain.
2 For look, the wicked bend their
bows;
they set their arrows[k] against the
strings

[b] Ps 37:5 [c] Ps 68:5
10:15 [d] Ps 37:17
10:16 [e] Ps 29:10 [f] Dt 8:20
10:17 [g] 1Ch 29:18; Ps 34:15
10:18 [h] Ps 82:3 [i] Ps 9:9
11:1 [j] Ps 56:11
11:2 [k] Ps 7:13

[a] 5 See Septuagint; Hebrew / *they are haughty, and your laws are far from*

10:12–15 The psalmist suggests that God's absence or delay has allowed opportunity for the wicked to work. Now he follows his critique with a call for divine action. He questions the assumption of God's ignorance or unconcern (vv. 12–13).
10:16–18 The combined psalm concludes by acknowledging Yahweh as the eternal King, Protector of the afflicted and Defender of "the fatherless and the oppressed" (v. 18). Since Yahweh is the eternal righteous King, he will take the side of the weak.

✣ **9:1—10:18** The arrogant pride that marks the wicked in Ps 10 in particular (vv. 2–11) has none of the sense of wonder and awe that marks the psalmist's encounter with the Creator in Ps 8. Set immediately following the wondrous pronouncements of Ps 8, the wicked person's prideful dismissal of God is stated in its most shocking and extreme fashion. The result is a rebuke of the faithless for their ignorance and pride, but it is also a warning for the faithful: They should not allow the seeming absence of God (10:1) to erode their confidence in his active concern and presence.

11:1 The psalm draws a contrast between the fear generated by those who advise others to flee and the confidence of the psalmist, who takes refuge in Yahweh.
11:2–3 "Upright" (v. 2b) can be applied to unwavering, smooth roads or unwavering, direct persons. These people may be attacked by the wicked, but they will be justified by Yahweh.

to shoot from the shadows
at the upright in heart.[l]
3 When the foundations[m] are being destroyed,
what can the righteous do?"

4 The LORD is in his holy temple;[n]
the LORD is on his heavenly throne.[o]
He observes everyone on earth;[p]
his eyes examine[q] them.
5 The LORD examines the righteous,[r]
but the wicked, those who love violence,
he hates with a passion.[s]
6 On the wicked he will rain
fiery coals and burning sulfur;[t]
a scorching wind[u] will be their lot.

7 For the LORD is righteous,[v]
he loves justice;[w]
the upright will see his face.[x]

11:2 [l] Ps 64:3-4
11:3 [m] Ps 82:5
11:4 [n] Ps 18:6 [o] Ps 103:19 [p] Ps 33:13 [q] Ps 34:15-16
11:5 [r] Ge 22:1; Jas 1:12 [s] Ps 5:5
11:6 [t] Eze 38:22 [u] Jer 4:11-12
11:7 [v] Ps 7:9,11; 45:7 [w] Ps 33:5 [x] Ps 17:15

12:1 [y] Isa 57:1
12:2 [z] Ps 10:7; 41:6; 55:21; Ro 16:18

Ps 11:4–5, 7 ❖ From what we know about God in our own lives, how is his rule and reign made manifest?

Ps 12:1–2 ❖ How can society reform to become more righteous? What can God's servants do to help this happen?

Psalm 12[a]

For the director of music. According to sheminith.[b] *A psalm of David.*

1 Help, LORD, for no one is faithful anymore;[y]
those who are loyal have vanished from the human race.
2 Everyone lies to their neighbor;
they flatter with their lips
but harbor deception in their hearts.[z]

[a] In Hebrew texts 12:1-8 is numbered 12:2-9.
[b] Title: Probably a musical term

11:4–6 Yahweh is in control. From his vantage point in the heavens he can examine the chaotic human events on the earth and render righteous judgments.
11:7 This psalm affirms Yahweh's righteousness and love of justice. These twin attributes provide the basis of the psalmist's confident hope.

✚ **11:1–7** According to this psalm, in foundation-shaking circumstances we have two basic choices: Either we can flee to the hills, which may provide a refuge that is temporary at best, or we can take refuge in God.

12:1–2 The psalmist drives home the complaint in the language of hyperbole. This heightens the sense of oppression and leaves God little choice but to act.

CHARACTER OF GOD // GOD IS RIGHTEOUS

Psalm 11:7: For the LORD is righteous, he loves justice; the upright will see his face.

Righteousness and justice are closely linked. In fact, they often appear together in the Bible (Am 5:24). In human terms, justice usually refers to our relationships with one another and righteousness refers to our relationship with God. When the psalmist asks, "Who may stand in [God's] holy place?" the answer is "The one who has clean hands and a pure heart" (Ps 24:4). "Clean hands" refers to justice; a "pure heart" refers to righteousness.

God's righteousness, of course, is of a different kind than ours. God's *righteousness* refers to his absolute moral perfection. God cannot—never has and never will—sin (1Jn 3:5). Righteousness is like a perfectly straight line. In this analogy God is neither bent nor crooked; he is completely consistent, completely upright, completely moral.

Cultures around the Israelites, such as the Babylonians and later the Greeks, believed in a pantheon of gods. These gods were given to all sorts of vices and deceits. They would lie, fight and behave promiscuously. The Bible never describes God in such ways. God never behaves in a way that is evil; he cannot even be tempted to do so (Jas 1:13).

APPLICATION ✚ Despite God's complete lack of any sin, Paul writes in 2Co 5:21 that Christ himself became sin for us so that we might become the righteousness of God. This means that if we are in Christ and have accepted his salvation, God the Father looks on us not on the basis of our failings but on the basis of his righteousness. Because of this, we can stand before God without fault and without blemish (Jude 24). Paul looks forward with hope to meeting his "righteous Judge," confident that God will bestow on all his children a "crown of righteousness" (2Ti 4:8).

[3]May the LORD silence all flattering
lips
and every boastful tongue —[a]
[4]those who say,
"By our tongues we will prevail;
our own lips will defend us — who
is lord over us?"

[5]"Because the poor are plundered and
the needy groan,
I will now arise," says the LORD.
"I will protect them[b] from those
who malign them."
[6]And the words of the LORD are
flawless,[c]
like silver purified in a crucible,
like gold[a] refined seven times.

[7]You, LORD, will keep the needy safe
and will protect us forever from
the wicked,[d]
[8]who freely strut[e] about
when what is vile is honored by
the human race.

Psalm 13[b]

For the director of music.
A psalm of David.

[1]How long, LORD? Will you forget me
forever?
How long will you hide your face[f]
from me?
[2]How long must I wrestle with my
thoughts[g]
and day after day have sorrow in
my heart?
How long will my enemy triumph
over me?[h]

[3]Look on me and answer,[i] LORD my
God.
Give light to my eyes,[j] or I will
sleep in death,[k]
[4]and my enemy will say, "I have
overcome him,[l]"
and my foes will rejoice when I
fall.

[5]But I trust in your unfailing love;[m]
my heart rejoices in your
salvation.[n]
[6]I will sing[o] the LORD's praise,
for he has been good to me.

Psalm 14

14:1–7pp // Ps 53:1–6

For the director of music. Of David.

[1]The fool[c] says in his heart,
"There is no God."[p]
They are corrupt, their deeds are vile;
there is no one who does good.

12:3 [a]Da 7:8; Rev 13:5
12:5 [b]Ps 10:18; 34:6
12:6 [c]2Sa 22:31; Ps 18:30; Pr 30:5
12:7 [d]Ps 37:28
12:8 [e]Ps 55:10-11
13:1 [f]Job 13:24; Ps 44:24
13:2 [g]Ps 42:4 [h]Ps 42:9
13:3 [i]Ps 5:1 [j]Ezr 9:8 [k]Jer 51:39
13:4 [l]Ps 25:2
13:5 [m]Ps 52:8 [n]Ps 9:14
13:6 [o]Ps 116:7
14:1 [p]Ps 10:4

Ps 13:6 ❖ How can a prayer that starts so dark end on such a note of praise? When has God met you in your darkness?

Ps 14:1-7 ❖ What aspects of the description of the "fool" in this psalm can we chase out of our own lives today?

[a] *6* Probable reading of the original Hebrew text; Masoretic Text *earth* [b] In Hebrew texts 13:1-6 is numbered 13:2-6. [c] *1* The Hebrew words rendered *fool* in Psalms denote one who is morally deficient.

12:3-4 The self-absorption of the wicked is reflected in their own arrogant words.
12:5 Yahweh takes seriously his kingly role as protector of the defenseless.
12:6-7 Using the analogy of purifying precious metal, the psalmist describes the "words of the LORD" (v. 6).
12:8 The wicked still "strut about" unhindered, but the faithful see that Yahweh is the God of the pure, effective Word. He takes the side of the needy when others malign them.

✚ **12:1-8** Most people could provide a long list of ways that words are used deceptively. It is usually easier to point to others in this regard; however, we also need to look at the ways we use words with those with whom we interact. Are we honoring God with our words, or are we using them as a form of self-protection? Are we building up or breaking down our relationships with others?

13:1-2 This questioning is a response to the experience of the hiddenness of God. Such questions reveal a faith seeking to understand amid painful experiences.
13:3-4 The psalmist can only anticipate rapid decline, defeat, and death without the hoped-for divine intervention.
13:5-6 This psalm concludes with confidence based on understanding God's character and the psalmist's previous experience of Yahweh's goodness.

✚ **13:1-6** Many today struggle with feelings of unworthiness, believing them to be the result of some wrong within themselves. Such inner turmoil often grows out of self-condemnation and can lead to anger, paralysis, and despair. Verses 5 and 6 provide a much-needed response to this kind of thinking.

14:1-3 The foolish wicked are led astray by assuming their power has no limits. Folly is not simply

[2]The LORD looks down from heaven[q]
on all mankind
to see if there are any who
understand,[r]
any who seek God.
[3]All have turned away, all have
become corrupt;[s]
there is no one who does good,[t]
not even one.[u]

[4]Do all these evildoers know
nothing?[v]

They devour my people[w] as though
eating bread;
they never call on the LORD.[x]
[5]But there they are, overwhelmed
with dread,
for God is present in the company
of the righteous.
[6]You evildoers frustrate the plans of
the poor,
but the LORD is their refuge.[y]

[7]Oh, that salvation for Israel would
come out of Zion!
When the LORD restores[z] his
people,
let Jacob rejoice and Israel be glad!

Psalm 15

A psalm of David.

[1]LORD, who may dwell in your sacred
tent?[a]
Who may live on your holy
mountain?[b]

[2]The one whose walk is blameless,
who does what is righteous,
who speaks the truth[c] from their
heart;
[3]whose tongue utters no slander,[d]
who does no wrong to a neighbor,
and casts no slur on others;
[4]who despises a vile person
but honors[e] those who fear the
LORD;
who keeps an oath[f] even when it
hurts,
and does not change their mind;
[5]who lends money to the poor
without interest;[g]
who does not accept a bribe[h]
against the innocent.

Whoever does these things
will never be shaken.[i]

Psalm 16

A miktam[a] of David.

[1]Keep me safe,[j] my God,
for in you I take refuge.[k]

[2]I say to the LORD, "You are my Lord;
apart from you I have no good
thing."[l]
[3]I say of the holy people who are in
the land,[m]
"They are the noble ones in whom
is all my delight."

[a] Title: Probably a literary or musical term

14:2 [q] Ps 33:13 [r] Ps 92:6
14:3 [s] Ps 58:3 [t] Ps 143:2 [u] Ro 3:10-12*
14:4 [v] Ps 82:5 [w] Ps 27:2 [x] Ps 79:6; Isa 64:7
14:6 [y] Ps 9:9; 40:17
14:7 [z] Ps 53:6
15:1 [a] Ps 27:5-6 [b] Ps 24:3-5
15:2 [c] Ps 24:4; Zec 8:3,16; Eph 4:25
15:3 [d] Ex 23:1
15:4 [e] Ac 28:10 [f] Jdg 11:35
15:5 [g] Ex 22:25 [h] Ex 23:8; Dt 16:19 [i] 2Pe 1:10
16:1 [j] Ps 17:8 [k] Ps 7:1
16:2 [l] Ps 73:25
16:3 [m] Ps 101:6

Ps 15:2-5 ❖ No one can live up to this standard. Where, then, do we turn for hope (see 2Co 5:21)?

Ps 16:2 ❖ How is this amazing statement true of believers today? How can we cultivate a sense of thankfulness to God every day?

---

uninformed stupidity but a moral decision to do evil. These verses repeat at 53:1-3.

14:4-6 The foolish wicked are identified as "evildoers" (v. 4). The question the psalmist asks in this same verse provides us with all the perspective we need.

14:7 The psalm concludes with the experience of the exiled community expressing the desire for restoration.

14:1-7 What immediately comes to your mind as you read vv. 1-6? When we hurry to identify ourselves with the righteous poor, we often fail to acknowledge the many ways our abundant lifestyle is founded on the exploitation of the majority world who have so little.

15:2-5b The psalmist supplies 11 answers to the foundational questions of v. 1. These answers offer a response to the central concern of the psalm: What style of living prepares one for living in the presence of Yahweh?

15:5c Whoever lives in the manner described need never fear being "shaken." This verb describes the insecurity experienced when one's feet are on rough, untrustworthy ground.

15:1-5 The one who lives a life of trust, discipline, and transparency is ready to meet God.

16:1 This is a plea for continued protection.

16:2 Competing translations of v. 2 concern who is speaking in v. 2a, either the psalmist or another person. The choice depends on the understanding of who the "holy people" and "noble ones" are in v. 3.

16:3-4 The NIV takes v. 3a to mean "holy people" and connects the verse with vv. 1–2. Other

4 Those who run after other gods[n] will
suffer[o] more and more.
I will not pour out libations of
blood to such gods
or take up their names[p] on my
lips.

5 LORD, you alone are my portion[q] and
my cup;[r]
you make my lot secure.
6 The boundary lines have fallen for
me in pleasant places;
surely I have a delightful
inheritance.[s]
7 I will praise the LORD, who counsels
me;[t]
even at night[u] my heart
instructs me.
8 I keep my eyes always on the LORD.
With him at my right hand,[v] I will
not be shaken.

9 Therefore my heart is glad[w] and my
tongue rejoices;
my body also will rest secure,[x]
10 because you will not abandon me to
the realm of the dead,
nor will you let your faithful[a] one
see decay.[y]
11 You make known to me the path of
life;[z]
you will fill me with joy in your
presence,[a]
with eternal pleasures[b] at your
right hand.

Psalm 17

A prayer of David.

1 Hear me, LORD, my plea is just;
listen to my cry.[c]
Hear my prayer —
it does not rise from deceitful
lips.[d]
2 Let my vindication come from you;
may your eyes see what is right.

3 Though you probe my heart,
though you examine me at night
and test me,[e]
you will find that I have planned no
evil;[f]
my mouth has not transgressed.[g]
4 Though people tried to bribe me,
I have kept myself from the ways
of the violent
through what your lips have
commanded.
5 My steps have held to your paths;[h]
my feet have not stumbled.[i]

6 I call on you, my God, for you will
answer me;[j]
turn your ear to me[k] and hear my
prayer.[l]
7 Show me the wonders of your great
love,[m]
you who save by your right hand[n]
those who take refuge in you from
their foes.
8 Keep me as the apple of your eye;[o]
hide me in the shadow of your
wings
9 from the wicked who are out to
destroy me,
from my mortal enemies who
surround me.[p]

10 They close up their callous hearts,[q]
and their mouths speak with
arrogance.[r]

16:4 [n] Ps 106:37-38 [o] Ps 32:10 [p] Ex 23:13
16:5 [q] Ps 73:26 [r] Ps 23:5
16:6 [s] Ps 78:55; Jer 3:19
16:7 [t] Ps 73:24 [u] Ps 77:6
16:8 [v] Ps 73:23
16:9 [w] Ps 4:7; 30:11 [x] Ps 4:8
16:10 [y] Ac 13:35*
16:11 [z] Mt 7:14 [a] Ac 2:25-28* [b] Ps 36:7-8
17:1 [c] Ps 61:1 [d] Isa 29:13
17:3 [e] Ps 26:2; 66:10 [f] Job 23:10; Jer 50:20 [g] Ps 39:1
17:5 [h] Ps 44:18; 119:133 [i] Ps 18:36
17:6 [j] Ps 86:7 [k] Ps 116:2 [l] Ps 88:2
17:7 [m] Ps 31:21 [n] Ps 20:6
17:8 [o] Dt 32:10
17:9 [p] Ps 31:20; 109:3
17:10 [q] Ps 73:7 [r] 1Sa 2:3

[a] 10 Or *holy*

---

commentators draw on evidence that the Hebrew word refers to Canaanite deities, linking v. 3 with the negative comments in v. 4. In this case, the "noble ones" (v. 3) represent those who practice false allegiance to pagan gods.

16:5-8 The pleasant circumstances that surround the psalmist are the result of the blessing of Yahweh.

16:9-11 The reasons for the psalmist's feeling of security fall into three categories: (1) deliverance from death (v. 10); (2) continued guidance (v. 11a); and (3) the gift of divine presence (v. 11b-c).

16:1-11 Where do we find security? Concern for security against robbery is epidemic in a society obsessed with possessions. Concern for building a nest egg that will assure our comfort in our old age bolsters that same obsession. Even at the most unstable moments, Yahweh is *still* our "portion and . . . cup" (v. 5). When we trust in God's provision, we have the right perspective on our possessions because we know where our security lies (see Mt 6:19-21).

17:1-5 From the beginning, Ps 17 is couched in the voice of the innocent sufferer. Yahweh is called to "hear" and "listen" (v. 1) since the psalmist's declaration is without deceit.

The psalmist invites divine scrutiny and examination, confident there is no fault to be uncovered. The final statement of v. 5 may function either as evidence of loyalty to Yahweh's teaching or as an acknowledgment of divine guidance.

17:6-12 The pupil of the eye (v. 8) is to be carefully guarded from injury. The "shadow of [God's] wings" in the same verse refers to small birds under the wings of their hovering parent. Surrounding enemies are like hungry lions moving in for the kill.

11 They have tracked me down, they
now surround me,[s]
with eyes alert, to throw me to the
ground.
12 They are like a lion[t] hungry for prey,
like a fierce lion crouching in
cover.

13 Rise up, LORD, confront them, bring
them down;[u]
with your sword rescue me from
the wicked.
14 By your hand save me from such
people, LORD,
from those of this world[v] whose
reward is in this life.
May what you have stored up for the
wicked fill their bellies;
may their children gorge
themselves on it,
and may there be leftovers[w] for
their little ones.

15 As for me, I will be vindicated and
will see your face;
when I awake, I will be satisfied
with seeing your likeness.[x]

Psalm 18[a]

18:Title—50pp // 2Sa 22:1–51

For the director of music. Of David the servant of the LORD. He sang to the LORD the words of this song when the LORD delivered him from the hand of all his enemies and from the hand of Saul. He said:

1 I love you, LORD, my strength.

2 The LORD is my rock,[y] my fortress
and my deliverer;
my God is my rock, in whom I take
refuge,
my shield[b][z] and the horn[c] of my
salvation,[a] my stronghold.

17:11 [s] Ps 37:14; 88:17
17:12 [t] Ps 7:2; 10:9
17:13 [u] Ps 7:12; 22:20; 73:18
17:14 [v] Lk 16:8 [w] Ps 73:3-7
17:15 [x] Nu 12:8; Ps 4:6-7; 16:11; 1Jn 3:2
18:2 [y] Ps 19:14 [z] Ps 59:11 [a] Ps 75:10

18:3 [b] Ps 48:1
18:4 [c] Ps 116:3 [d] Ps 124:4
18:5 [e] Ps 116:3
18:6 [f] Ps 34:15
18:7 [g] Jdg 5:4 [h] Ps 68:7-8
18:8 [i] Ps 50:3
18:9 [j] Ps 144:5
18:10 [k] Ps 80:1 [l] Ps 104:3
18:11 [m] Dt 4:11; Ps 97:2

Ps 17:15 ❖ How has God vindicated you in the trials you have faced that have been caused by other people?

3 I called to the LORD, who is worthy of
praise,[b]
and I have been saved from my
enemies.
4 The cords of death[c] entangled me;
the torrents[d] of destruction
overwhelmed me.
5 The cords of the grave coiled
around me;
the snares of death[e]
confronted me.

6 In my distress I called to the LORD;
I cried to my God for help.
From his temple he heard my voice;[f]
my cry came before him, into his
ears.
7 The earth trembled and quaked,[g]
and the foundations of the
mountains shook;
they trembled because he was
angry.[h]
8 Smoke rose from his nostrils;
consuming fire[i] came from his
mouth,
burning coals blazed out of it.
9 He parted the heavens and came
down;[j]
dark clouds were under his feet.
10 He mounted the cherubim[k] and
flew;
he soared on the wings of the
wind.[l]
11 He made darkness his covering,[m] his
canopy around him—
the dark rain clouds of the sky.

[a] In Hebrew texts 18:1-50 is numbered 18:2-51.
[b] 2 Or *sovereign* [c] 2 *Horn* here symbolizes strength.

17:13–15 Yahweh stands to render judgment and enforce it. The psalmist recognizes only the righteous can stand in Yahweh's presence and hope to "be satisfied with seeing" (v. 15) the likeness of God.

17:1–15 The "face of the Lord" has fearsome potential for judgment (1Pe 3:12). By contrast, the faithful "will *see his face*" (Rev 22:3–4, emphasis added). In other words, the NT preserves the same tension as the OT between the wicked, who experience the face of God as judgment, and the faithful, who discover God's face shining on them with blessing and satisfaction.

18:1–3 The psalmist begins with a first-person address of his love to Yahweh (v. 1). He then heaps up titles of Yahweh that call forth his praise. These titles respond to Yahweh as a source of refuge, protection, and deliverance.
18:4–5 The attack experienced by the psalmist is life-threatening. Life is going under and only Yahweh can save.
18:6 When the psalmist calls, Yahweh hears and responds.
18:7–15 The awesome power and majesty of the divine glory entering the human world is not business as usual. The created world cannot contain the Creator, and its usual laws and order are stretched to the breaking point by this divine intrusion.

12 Out of the brightness of his
presence[n] clouds advanced,
with hailstones and bolts of
lightning.[o]
13 The LORD thundered[p] from heaven;
the voice of the Most High
resounded.[a]
14 He shot his arrows and scattered the
enemy,
with great bolts of lightning he
routed them.[q]
15 The valleys of the sea were exposed
and the foundations of the earth
laid bare
at your rebuke,[r] LORD,
at the blast of breath from your
nostrils.

16 He reached down from on high and
took hold of me;
he drew me out of deep waters.[s]
17 He rescued me from my powerful
enemy,
from my foes, who were too
strong for me.[t]
18 They confronted me in the day of
my disaster,
but the LORD was my support.[u]
19 He brought me out into a spacious
place;[v]
he rescued me because he
delighted in me.[w]

20 The LORD has dealt with
me according to my
righteousness;
according to the cleanness of my
hands[x] he has rewarded me.
21 For I have kept the ways of the
LORD;[y]
I am not guilty of turning[z] from
my God.
22 All his laws are before me;[a]
I have not turned away from his
decrees.
23 I have been blameless before him

18:12 [n] Ps 104:2 [o] Ps 97:3
18:13 [p] Ps 29:3; 104:7
18:14 [q] Ps 144:6
18:15 [r] Ps 76:6; 106:9
18:16 [s] Ps 144:7
18:17 [t] Ps 35:10
18:18 [u] Ps 59:16
18:19 [v] Ps 31:8 [w] Ps 118:5
18:20 [x] Ps 24:4
18:21 [y] 2Ch 34:33 [z] Ps 119:102
18:22 [a] Ps 119:30

Ps 18:24 ❖ Does God reward us for our own righteousness? Why or why not (see 1Pe 2:24)?

and have kept myself from sin.
24 The LORD has rewarded
me according to my
righteousness,[b]
according to the cleanness of my
hands in his sight.

25 To the faithful[c] you show yourself
faithful,
to the blameless you show
yourself blameless,
26 to the pure you show yourself pure,
but to the devious you show
yourself shrewd.[d]
27 You save the humble
but bring low those whose eyes
are haughty.[e]
28 You, LORD, keep my lamp burning;
my God turns my darkness into
light.[f]
29 With your help[g] I can advance
against a troop[b];
with my God I can scale a wall.

30 As for God, his way is perfect:[h]
The LORD's word is flawless;[i]
he shields all who take refuge[j] in
him.
31 For who is God besides the LORD?[k]
And who is the Rock[l] except our
God?
32 It is God who arms me with
strength[m]
and keeps my way secure.
33 He makes my feet like the feet of a
deer;[n]

18:24 [b] 1Sa 26:23
18:25 [c] 1Ki 8:32; Ps 62:12; Mt 5:7
18:26 [d] Pr 3:34
18:27 [e] Pr 6:17
18:28 [f] Job 18:6; 29:3
18:29 [g] Heb 11:34
18:30 [h] Dt 32:4; Rev 15:3 [i] Ps 12:6 [j] Ps 17:7
18:31 [k] Dt 32:39; 86:8; Isa 45:5, 6,14,18,21 [l] Dt 32:31; 1Sa 2:2
18:32 [m] Isa 45:5
18:33 [n] Hab 3:19

[a] *13* Some Hebrew manuscripts and Septuagint (see also 2 Samuel 22:14); most Hebrew manuscripts *resounded, / amid hailstones and bolts of lightning* [b] *29* Or *can run through a barricade*

18:16–19 The final segment of the narrative shifts the focus from the power of Yahweh to the psalmist's personal experience of deliverance. This connection is made by viewing the distress as being overwhelmed by "deep waters," from which Yahweh extracts the psalmist (v. 16). Divine aid is the consequence of God's divine "delight" (v. 19) in the psalmist.

18:20–29 The first subsection is clearly marked off by almost identical verses at beginning and end (vv. 20, 24). The psalmist is asserting that divine deliverance is a consequence of personal righteousness, loyalty, and cleanness of hands.

The second subsection (vv. 25–26) encourages the faithful to adopt a fruitful relation to Yahweh.

The third subsection (vv. 27–29) moves from the general acknowledgment of the previous section that Yahweh is the hope of the faithful (vv. 25–26) to the personal recognition that Yahweh is the psalmist's source of strength.

18:30–31 The faithful experience peace and confidence when they trust in the "perfect" (v. 30) way of Yahweh. Yahweh can be trusted to do what he says, to act according to his promises and commitments.

18:32–34 Along with giving strength, Yahweh also provides sure footing in the conflicts of life (vv. 32b–33).

he causes me to stand on the
heights.[o]
34 He trains my hands for battle;[p]
my arms can bend a bow of
bronze.
35 You make your saving help my
shield,
and your right hand sustains[q] me;
your help has made me great.
36 You provide a broad path for my
feet,
so that my ankles do not give way.

37 I pursued my enemies[r] and overtook
them;
I did not turn back till they were
destroyed.
38 I crushed them so that they could
not rise;[s]
they fell beneath my feet.[t]
39 You armed me with strength for
battle;
you humbled my adversaries
before me.
40 You made my enemies turn their
backs[u] in flight,
and I destroyed[v] my foes.
41 They cried for help, but there was no
one to save them[w]—
to the LORD, but he did not
answer.[x]
42 I beat them as fine as windblown
dust;
I trampled them[a] like mud in the
streets.
43 You have delivered me from the
attacks of the people;
you have made me the head of
nations.[y]
People I did not know[z] now
serve me,
44 foreigners[a] cower before me;
as soon as they hear of me, they
obey me.
45 They all lose heart;
they come trembling from their
strongholds.[b]

46 The LORD lives! Praise be to my
Rock!
Exalted be God my Savior![c]
47 He is the God who avenges me,
who subdues nations[d] under me,
48 who saves[e] me from my enemies.
You exalted me above my foes;
from a violent man you
rescued me.
49 Therefore I will praise you, LORD,
among the nations;
I will sing[f] the praises of your
name.[g]

50 He gives his king great victories;
he shows unfailing love to his
anointed,
to David[h] and to his descendants
forever.[i]

Psalm 19[b]

For the director of music.
A psalm of David.

1 The heavens[j] declare[k] the glory of
God;
the skies proclaim the work of his
hands.
2 Day after day they pour forth speech;
night after night they reveal
knowledge.[l]

18:33 [o] Dt 32:13 18:34 [p] Ps 144:1 18:35 [q] Ps 119:116 18:37 [r] Ps 37:20; 44:5 18:38 [s] Ps 36:12 [t] Ps 47:3 18:40 [u] Ps 21:12 [v] Ps 94:23 18:41 [w] Ps 50:22 [x] Job 27:9; Pr 1:28 18:43 [y] 2Sa 8:1-14 [z] Isa 52:15; 55:5
18:44 [a] Ps 66:3 18:45 [b] Mic 7:17 18:46 [c] Ps 51:14 18:47 [d] Ps 47:3 18:48 [e] Ps 59:1 18:49 [f] Ps 108:1 [g] Ro 15:9* 18:50 [h] Ps 144:10 [i] Ps 89:4 19:1 [j] Isa 40:22 [k] Ps 50:6; Ro 1:19 19:2 [l] Ps 74:16

[a] 42 Many Hebrew manuscripts, Septuagint, Syriac and Targum (see also 2 Samuel 22:43); Masoretic Text *I poured them out* [b] In Hebrew texts 19:1-14 is numbered 19:2-15.

18:35–45 In a series of "you" statements the psalmist describes Yahweh's saving and equipping acts (cf. vv. 35–36, 39–40, 43). Then in each case he moves to describe a personal experience of the consequences of this divine empowerment (vv. 37–38, 41–42, 44–45).

18:46–50 The psalm concludes with a song of praise to Yahweh for deliverance and victory. Yahweh is the "Rock" (v. 46), linking back to the opening lines of the psalm (v. 2) as well as to the opening of the previous section (v. 31), and bringing this important theme of the psalm to an appropriate end.

The psalmist's promise to "sing the praises" to the name of Yahweh among the nations (v. 49) clearly took on heightened significance for the exilic community, who were "scattered . . . among the nations" (cf. 44:11).

18:1–50 Many of us today have real difficulty imagining the presence of God in earthshaking and awe-inspiring terms. In many contemporary congregations, God through Jesus has become a familiar friend rather than a holy God. While it is important to understand that God is our helper and friend, perhaps something essential is lost when we *never* experience the shock of God's holy presence. We need to experience God as both holy God and loyal friend if we are to keep our faith in the right perspective.

19:1–4b Inanimate creation is given voice as the heavens and skies "declare," "proclaim," and "pour forth speech" (vv. 1–2) in praise of the Creator. This is a continual outcry of nature—from the past until now and into the future.

3 They have no speech, they use no
words;
no sound is heard from them.
4 Yet their voice[a] goes out into all the
earth,
their words to the ends of the
world.[m]
In the heavens God has pitched a
tent[n] for the sun.
5 It is like a bridegroom coming out of
his chamber,
like a champion rejoicing to run
his course.
6 It rises at one end of the heavens
and makes its circuit to the other;[o]
nothing is deprived of its warmth.

7 The law of the LORD is perfect,
refreshing the soul.[p]
The statutes of the LORD are
trustworthy,[q]
making wise the simple.[r]
8 The precepts of the LORD are right,[s]
giving joy to the heart.
The commands of the LORD are
radiant,
giving light to the eyes.
9 The fear of the LORD is pure,
enduring forever.
The decrees of the LORD are firm,
and all of them are righteous.[t]

10 They are more precious than gold,[u]
than much pure gold;
they are sweeter than honey,
than honey from the honeycomb.
11 By them your servant is warned;
in keeping them there is great
reward.
12 But who can discern their own errors?
Forgive my hidden faults.[v]
13 Keep your servant also from willful
sins;
may they not rule over me.
Then I will be blameless,
innocent of great transgression.

19:4 [m] Ro 10:18* [n] Ps 104:2
19:6 [o] Ps 113:3; Ecc 1:5
19:7 [p] Ps 23:3 [q] Ps 93:5; 111:7 [r] Ps 119:98-100
19:8 [s] Ps 12:6; 119:128
19:9 [t] Ps 119:138, 142
19:10 [u] Pr 8:10
19:12 [v] Ps 51:2; 90:8; 139:6
19:14 [w] Ps 104:34 [x] Ps 18:2 [y] Isa 47:4
20:1 [z] Ps 46:7,11 [a] Ps 91:14
20:2 [b] Ps 3:4
20:3 [c] Ac 10:4 [d] Ps 51:19
20:4 [e] Ps 21:2; 145:16,19
20:5 [f] Ps 9:14; 60:4 [g] 1Sa 1:17
20:6 [h] Ps 28:8; 41:11; Isa 58:9

Ps 19:6 ❖ How do we see God's glory and work displayed in creation? What part of creation makes us marvel the most in the Creator?

Ps 20:4 ❖ What is the true "desire of your heart"? How well does it reflect God's will?

14 May these words of my mouth and
this meditation of my heart
be pleasing[w] in your sight,
LORD, my Rock[x] and my
Redeemer.[y]

Psalm 20[b]

For the director of music.
A psalm of David.

1 May the LORD answer you when you
are in distress;
may the name of the God of Jacob[z]
protect you.[a]
2 May he send you help from the
sanctuary[b]
and grant you support from Zion.
3 May he remember[c] all your sacrifices
and accept your burnt offerings.[c][d]
4 May he give you the desire of your
heart[e]
and make all your plans succeed.
5 May we shout for joy over your
victory
and lift up our banners[f] in the
name of our God.

May the LORD grant all your
requests.[g]

6 Now this I know:
The LORD gives victory to his
anointed.[h]

[a] 4 Septuagint, Jerome and Syriac; Hebrew *measuring line* [b] In Hebrew texts 20:1-9 is numbered 20:2-10. [c] 3 The Hebrew has *Selah* (a word of uncertain meaning) here.

19:4c–6 The description of the sun moves from the more general "works" of God—heavens, firmament—to a specific example of those works.
19:7–11 The divine scrutiny illustrated by the constant arcing of the sun overhead implies the need for a guide to how humans can satisfy God's will. The psalm moves to consider how the Torah (the Law) fulfills that role (v. 11), revealing Yahweh's will.
19:12–14 The psalmist has wondered at the revelation of God declared through nature and rejoiced in the guidance offered through God's Torah. He turns to the appropriate human response. The final statement models the kind of submission to the will of God that the rest of the psalm describes.

19:1–14 Humans are not left alone and forlorn with no purpose or meaning in life. God's Word is a delight because through it we discover who God is and how to assume our place within his creation.

20:1–5 The first section of the poem contains a string of eight linked pairs. They ask for divine hearing and protection (v. 1), divine help and support from the temple (v. 2), God's favorable response to the king's offerings and sacrifices (v. 3), and successful fulfillment of the king's military plans (v. 4).
20:6 The identity of the speaker is not clear from

He answers him from his heavenly sanctuary
with the victorious power of his right hand.
7 Some trust in chariots and some in horses,[i]
but we trust in the name of the LORD our God.[j]
8 They are brought to their knees and fall,
but we rise up[k] and stand firm.[l]
9 LORD, give victory to the king!
Answer us[m] when we call!

Psalm 21[a]

For the director of music. A psalm of David.

1 The king rejoices in your strength, LORD.
How great is his joy in the victories you give![n]

2 You have granted him his heart's desire[o]
and have not withheld the request of his lips.[b]
3 You came to greet him with rich blessings
and placed a crown of pure gold[p] on his head.
4 He asked you for life, and you gave it to him—
length of days, for ever and ever.[q]
5 Through the victories[r] you gave, his glory is great;
you have bestowed on him splendor and majesty.
6 Surely you have granted him unending blessings
and made him glad with the joy[s] of your presence.[t]
7 For the king trusts in the LORD;
through the unfailing love of the Most High
he will not be shaken.

8 Your hand will lay hold[u] on all your enemies;
your right hand will seize your foes.
9 When you appear for battle,
you will burn them up as in a blazing furnace.
The LORD will swallow them up in his wrath,
and his fire will consume them.[v]
10 You will destroy their descendants from the earth,
their posterity from mankind.[w]
11 Though they plot evil[x] against you
and devise wicked schemes,[y] they cannot succeed.
12 You will make them turn their backs[z]
when you aim at them with drawn bow.

13 Be exalted in your strength, LORD;
we will sing and praise your might.

Ps 21:7 ❖ What does this verse say to believers today?

20:7 [i] Ps 33:17; Isa 31:1 [j] 2Ch 32:8
20:8 [k] Mic 7:8 [l] Ps 37:23
20:9 [m] Ps 3:7; 17:6
21:1 [n] Ps 59:16-17
21:2 [o] Ps 37:4
21:3 [p] 2Sa 12:30
21:4 [q] Ps 61:5-6; 91:16; 133:3
21:5 [r] Ps 18:50
21:6 [s] Ps 43:4 [t] 1Ch 17:27
21:8 [u] Isa 10:10
21:9 [v] Ps 50:3; La 2:2; Mal 4:1
21:10 [w] Dt 28:18; Ps 37:28
21:11 [x] Ps 2:1 [y] Ps 10:2
21:12 [z] Ps 7:12-13; 18:40

[a] In Hebrew texts 21:1-13 is numbered 21:2-14.
[b] 2 The Hebrew has *Selah* (a word of uncertain meaning) here.

the context. He may be one of the Levites serving in the temple, speaking prophetically to assure the king and people.
20:7–8 By trusting in "chariots" and "horses" (v. 7a) the misguided opponents are doomed to fall. In contrast, those who trust in Yahweh "rise up and stand firm" (v. 8b).
20:9 The psalm concludes with a final plea connecting the intercessory and personal prayers of the assembly.

✣ **20:1–9** We are called to trust in the God who has delivered us; he has called us into a relationship of commitment and trust that can and should inform and guide every day of our earthly lives.

21:1 Psalm 21 begins with the king's rejoicing in the strength of Yahweh, which provides the king with victories.
21:2–6 The king is a model of integrity; what he desires in his heart, he requests with his lips. Yahweh's response to the king's integrity pours out in blessing.
21:7 In this central verse, the king responds to the description of divine blessing and presence with a confession of trust in Yahweh.
21:8–12 The presence of God is a two-edged sword. For the faithful who trust in him, God brings blessing and salvation. For the rebellious, God's coming means judgment. In this passage the psalmist describes the hoped-for consequences of Yahweh's "appearing" (v. 9) on his enemies.
21:13 The final call is for Yahweh to be "exalted" because of his many acts of strength.

✣ **21:1–13** We want to be in control of our lives, and we want to take credit for the victories we achieve. Yet we are too often forced to admit just how little control we really have. Do we understand our victories—however great or small—as God's acting on our behalf and bringing deliverance and success?

Psalm 22[a]

For the director of music. To the tune of "The Doe of the Morning." A psalm of David.

1 My God, my God, why have you
forsaken me?[a]
Why are you so far[b] from
saving me,
so far from my cries of anguish?
2 My God, I cry out by day, but you do
not answer,
by night,[c] but I find no rest.[b]

3 Yet you are enthroned as the Holy
One;[d]
you are the one Israel praises.[ce]
4 In you our ancestors put their trust;
they trusted and you delivered
them.
5 To you they cried out and were saved;
in you they trusted and were not
put to shame.[f]

6 But I am a worm[g] and not a man,
scorned by everyone,[h] despised[i] by
the people.
7 All who see me mock me;
they hurl insults,[j] shaking their
heads.[k]
8 "He trusts in the LORD," they say,
"let the LORD rescue him.[l]
Let him deliver him,
since he delights[m] in him."

9 Yet you brought me out of the
womb;[n]
you made me trust in you, even at
my mother's breast.
10 From birth[o] I was cast on you;
from my mother's womb you have
been my God.

11 Do not be far from me,
for trouble is near
and there is no one to help.[p]

12 Many bulls[q] surround me;
strong bulls of Bashan[r]
encircle me.

22:1 [a] Mt 27:46*; Mk 15:34* [b] Ps 10:1
22:2 [c] Ps 42:3
22:3 [d] Ps 99:9 [e] Dt 10:21
22:5 [f] Isa 49:23
22:6 [g] Job 25:6; Isa 41:14 [h] Ps 31:11 [i] Isa 49:7; 53:3
22:7 [j] Mt 27:39, 44 [k] Mk 15:29
22:8 [l] Ps 91:14 [m] Mt 27:43
22:9 [n] Ps 71:6
22:10 [o] Isa 46:3
22:11 [p] Ps 72:12
22:12 [q] Ps 68:30 [r] Dt 32:14
22:13 [s] Ps 17:12 [t] Ps 35:21
22:14 [u] Ps 31:10 [v] Job 30:16; Da 5:6
22:15 [w] Ps 38:10; Jn 19:28 [x] Ps 104:29
22:16 [y] Ps 59:6 [z] Isa 53:5; Zec 12:10; Jn 19:34
22:17 [a] Lk 23:35 [b] Lk 23:27
22:18 [c] Mt 27:35*; Lk 23:34; Jn 19:24*
22:19 [d] Ps 70:5
22:20 [e] Ps 35:17

Ps 22:1–2 ❖ When have we felt forsaken by God? How does Christ help us in moments like these (see Mt 27:46)?

13 Roaring lions[s] that tear their prey
open their mouths wide[t]
against me.
14 I am poured out like water,
and all my bones are out of joint.[u]
My heart has turned to wax;
it has melted[v] within me.
15 My mouth[d] is dried up like a
potsherd,
and my tongue sticks to the roof
of my mouth;[w]
you lay me in the dust[x] of death.

16 Dogs[y] surround me,
a pack of villains encircles me;
they pierce[ez] my hands and my
feet.
17 All my bones are on display;
people stare[a] and gloat over me.[b]
18 They divide my clothes among them
and cast lots[c] for my garment.

19 But you, LORD, do not be far from me.
You are my strength; come
quickly[d] to help me.
20 Deliver me from the sword,
my precious life[e] from the power
of the dogs.
21 Rescue me from the mouth of the
lions;
save me from the horns of the
wild oxen.

22 I will declare your name to my
people;

[a] In Hebrew texts 22:1-31 is numbered 22:2-32.
[b] 2 Or *night, and am not silent* [c] 3 Or *Yet you are holy, / enthroned on the praises of Israel*
[d] 15 Probable reading of the original Hebrew text; Masoretic Text *strength* [e] 16 Dead Sea Scrolls and some manuscripts of the Masoretic Text, Septuagint and Syriac; most manuscripts of the Masoretic Text *me, / like a lion*

22:1 The opening words of this psalm have become so familiar to us from Jesus' use of them from the cross that it is difficult for us to separate them from that much later context. If we read these words *only* as words about Jesus, we ignore the original and continuing word of God to *us*.

22:2–11 The first major section of the psalm emphasizes the theme of abandonment through two sets of contrasts. The first contrast focuses on God's *silence* (vv. 2–5) while the second is concerned with God's *failure to act* (vv. 6–11).

22:12–21 Fierce attack reduces the psalmist to fear and weakness. His strength departs like water "poured out" (v. 14a) on the ground. His body feels out of control ("all my bones are out of joint," v. 14b). Similarly, the psalmist's "heart" (or courage, v. 14c-d) melts away like wax. He feels weakened by fear (v. 15a) and his mouth is bone-dry (v. 15b) as he fears the approach of death (v. 15c).

22:22–25 The first subsection of this final stanza begins with a vow to declare Yahweh's name in worship. The phrases "in the assembly" (v. 22b)

in the assembly I will praise you.[f]
23 You who fear the LORD, praise him![g]
All you descendants of Jacob,
honor him!
Revere him,[h] all you descendants
of Israel!
24 For he has not despised or scorned
the suffering of the afflicted one;
he has not hidden his face[i] from him
but has listened to his cry for
help.[j]

25 From you comes the theme of my
praise in the great assembly;[k]
before those who fear you[a] I will
fulfill my vows.[l]
26 The poor will eat[m] and be satisfied;
those who seek the LORD will
praise him —[n]
may your hearts live forever!

27 All the ends of the earth[o]
will remember and turn to the
LORD,
and all the families of the nations
will bow down before him,[p]
28 for dominion belongs to the LORD[q]
and he rules over the nations.

29 All the rich[r] of the earth will feast
and worship;
all who go down to the dust[s] will
kneel before him —
those who cannot keep
themselves alive.
30 Posterity[t] will serve him;
future generations will be told
about the Lord.
31 They will proclaim his
righteousness,
declaring to a people yet unborn:[u]
He has done it!

22:22 [f]Heb 2:12*
22:23 [g]Ps 86:12; 135:19 [h]Ps 33:8
22:24 [i]Ps 69:17 [j]Heb 5:7
22:25 [k]Ps 35:18 [l]Ecc 5:4
22:26 [m]Ps 107:9 [n]Ps 40:16
22:27 [o]Ps 2:8 [p]Ps 86:9
22:28 [q]Ps 47:7-8
22:29 [r]Ps 45:12 [s]Isa 26:19
22:30 [t]Ps 102:28
22:31 [u]Ps 78:6
23:1 [v]Isa 40:11; Jn 10:11; 1Pe 2:25 [w]Php 4:19
23:2 [x]Eze 34:14; Rev 7:17
23:3 [y]Ps 19:7 [z]Ps 5:8; 85:13
23:4 [a]Job 10:21-22 [b]Ps 3:6; 27:1 [c]Isa 43:2
23:5 [d]Ps 92:10 [e]Ps 16:5

Ps 23:4 ❖ How have we felt God's comfort and guidance through every journey of life?

Psalm 23

A psalm of David.

1 The LORD is my shepherd,[v] I lack
nothing.[w]
2 He makes me lie down in green
pastures,
he leads me beside quiet waters,[x]
3 he refreshes my soul.[y]
He guides me along the right paths[z]
for his name's sake.
4 Even though I walk
through the darkest valley,[b][a]
I will fear no evil,[b]
for you are with me;[c]
your rod and your staff,
they comfort me.

5 You prepare a table before me
in the presence of my enemies.
You anoint my head with oil;[d]
my cup[e] overflows.
6 Surely your goodness and love will
follow me
all the days of my life,

[a] 25 Hebrew *him* [b] 4 Or *the valley of the shadow of death*

---

and "in the great assembly" (v. 25a) indicate he speaks of temple worship.

22:26–31 The concluding praise section of the psalm describes the global effects of Yahweh's righteous rule. The psalmist envisions a future in which the current state of affairs will be reversed and the true purposes of Yahweh will be realized. God will come near, and humanity will acknowledge his lordship and bow before him.

✣ **22:1–31** The faith modeled by Jesus on the cross was no fair-weather religion that trusted in God only when the going was good. In that situation, Jesus experienced the worst the world had to offer. When it was darkest, as life was slipping away, he was able to proclaim with a final certainty: "It is finished" (Jn 19:30). Having won his way through to the end, Jesus surrendered his spirit into the hand of God the Father (Lk 23:46). Psalm 22, with its hopeful vision of a future creation restored to its original purposes, encourages us to do the same.

23:1 David speaks of Yahweh as "*my* shepherd" (emphasis added), acknowledging Yahweh is indeed the power behind the throne of David.

23:2–3 The shepherd "makes" his sheep rest when he determines it's needed. He also "leads" his sheep forward into pleasant places full of all the necessities of life.

23:4 From a life of abundant care and ready resources, the psalmist moves to a description of a fearful threat.

23:5 To sit at Yahweh's table is to enjoy fellowship and communion with him. To do so "in the presence of my enemies" is to have one's special relationship to God declared publicly in a context of divine blessing and security.

23:6 To "dwell" with God is a potent image of eternal security and ongoing relationship.

✣ **23:1–6** Being in Christ does not mean that the troubles of this world are simply removed from us. Sometimes illness, injury, disappointment and the cares of this life necessitate a

CHARACTER OF GOD // GOD IS A SHEPHERD

Psalm 23:1: The LORD is my shepherd, I lack nothing.

When Ps 23:1 says, "The LORD is my shepherd," David is putting himself in the place of sheep. David uses an image from his own experience. Before becoming the great king of Israel, he was a shepherd who cared for his father's flocks (1Sa 16:11).

David understood what shepherds do. They protect their flocks from predators (1Sa 17:34–35). Shepherds lead their flocks to pastures and water. And when a sheep goes missing, the shepherd goes out and finds it (Mt 18:12).

All these are things David relates to God. As Shepherd, God leads his children. God also protects his children; as David says, "You prepare a table before me in the presence of my enemies" (Ps 23:5). David knew what it was like to watch his flocks eat while predators lurked in nearby mountain crags. David also knew that God's presence and mercy would follow him wherever he might wander: "Surely your goodness and love will follow me all the days of my life" (Ps 23:6).

God as a Shepherd was a perfect analogy. Jesus Christ used the same image. Jesus said, "I am the good shepherd. The good shepherd lays down his life for the sheep" (Jn 10:11). With this metaphor, Jesus showed the depth of his love for his followers.

APPLICATION Knowing that we have a heavenly Shepherd reminds us that we are not traveling through life alone. We have a guide who will lead us on the paths of righteousness. He will ensure our needs are met. He will protect us from threats, both small and great. He will even pursue us when we wander. Most important of all, we have a Shepherd who was willing to lay down his life so that we might have salvation.

and I will dwell in the house of the LORD
forever.

Psalm 24

Of David. A psalm.

1 The earth is the LORD's,[f] and everything in it,
the world, and all who live in it;[g]
2 for he founded it on the seas
and established it on the waters.

3 Who may ascend the mountain[h] of the LORD?
Who may stand in his holy place?[i]
4 The one who has clean hands[j] and a pure heart,[k]
who does not trust in an idol
or swear by a false god.[a]
5 They will receive blessing from the LORD
and vindication from God their Savior.
6 Such is the generation of those who seek him,
who seek your face,[l] God of Jacob.[b,c]

24:1 [f] Ex 9:29; Job 41:11; Ps 89:11 [g] 1Co 10:26* 24:3 [h] Ps 2:6 [i] Ps 15:1; 65:4 24:4 [j] Job 17:9 [k] Mt 5:8 24:6 [l] Ps 27:8

Ps 24:1–4 What does the psalmist's call for "clean hands and a pure heart" mean for believers today?

[a] 4 Or *swear falsely* [b] 6 Two Hebrew manuscripts and Syriac (see also Septuagint); most Hebrew manuscripts *face, Jacob* [c] 6 The Hebrew has *Selah* (a word of uncertain meaning) here and at the end of verse 10.

need to rest, and God "makes" us lie down for a time. However, the green pastures in which we lie are still his. We walk through dark valleys, but God is always with us. We sometimes stand "in the presence of [our] enemies" (v. 5); even there, God provides.

The images of God's loving care and concern in this psalm have reassured believers throughout history of God's great love and personal care for them. Whatever our struggle, we need to constantly and gratefully assess the ways God is setting a table for *us* in the presence of our enemies: whether those be human enemies or negative circumstances.

24:1–2 Because he created it, the earth belongs to Yahweh. In certain passages "earth" and "world" emphasize the stable character of the cosmos Yahweh creates and sustains (1Sa 2:8; 1Ch 16:30). In other contexts, the emphasis is on Yahweh's authority as Creator (Ps 33:8–9; 89:11).

24:3–6 The psalm turns its gaze on the creature who would enter God's presence. The psalm's liturgical nature becomes clearer in a series of questions and answers. A throng of pilgrim

[7]Lift up your heads, you gates;[m]
be lifted up, you ancient doors,
that the King of glory[n] may
come in.
[8]Who is this King of glory?
The LORD strong and mighty,
the LORD mighty in battle.[o]
[9]Lift up your heads, you gates;
lift them up, you ancient doors,
that the King of glory may
come in.
[10]Who is he, this King of glory?
The LORD Almighty—
he is the King of glory.

Psalm 25[a]

Of David.

[1]In you, LORD my God,
I put my trust.[p]

[2]I trust in you;[q]
do not let me be put to shame,
nor let my enemies triumph
over me.
[3]No one who hopes in you
will ever be put to shame,[r]
but shame will come on those
who are treacherous without
cause.

[4]Show me your ways, LORD,
teach me your paths.[s]
[5]Guide me in your truth and
teach me,
for you are God my Savior,
and my hope is in you all day long.
[6]Remember, LORD, your great mercy
and love,[t]
for they are from of old.
[7]Do not remember the sins of my
youth[u]
and my rebellious ways;
according to your love[v]
remember me,
for you, LORD, are good.

[8]Good and upright[w] is the LORD;
therefore he instructs[x] sinners in
his ways.
[9]He guides[y] the humble in what is
right
and teaches them[z] his way.
[10]All the ways of the LORD are loving
and faithful[a]
toward those who keep the
demands of his covenant.[b]
[11]For the sake of your name,[c] LORD,
forgive my iniquity, though it is
great.

[12]Who, then, are those who fear the
LORD?
He will instruct them in the ways[d]
they should choose.[b]
[13]They will spend their days in
prosperity,[e]
and their descendants will inherit
the land.[f]
[14]The LORD confides[g] in those who
fear him;
he makes his covenant known[h] to
them.
[15]My eyes are ever on the LORD,[i]
for only he will release my feet
from the snare.

[16]Turn to me[j] and be gracious to me,
for I am lonely and afflicted.

24:7 [m] Isa 26:2 [n] Ps 97:6; 1Co 2:8
24:8 [o] Ps 76:3-6
25:1 [p] Ps 86:4
25:2 [q] Ps 41:11
25:3 [r] Isa 49:23
25:4 [s] Ex 33:13
25:6 [t] Ps 103:17; Isa 63:7,15
25:7 [u] Job 13:26; Jer 3:25 [v] Ps 51:1
25:8 [w] Ps 92:15 [x] Ps 32:8
25:9 [y] Ps 23:3 [z] Ps 27:11
25:10 [a] Ps 40:11 [b] Ps 103:18
25:11 [c] Ps 31:3; 79:9
25:12 [d] Ps 37:23
25:13 [e] Pr 19:23 [f] Ps 37:11
25:14 [g] Pr 3:32 [h] Jn 7:17
25:15 [i] Ps 141:8
25:16 [j] Ps 69:16

Ps 25:11 ❖ Why is God's loving forgiveness not only for our benefit but also for the sake of his name?

[a] This psalm is an acrostic poem, the verses of which begin with the successive letters of the Hebrew alphabet. [b] *12* Or *ways he chooses*

---

worshipers approaches the Temple Mount in Jerusalem.

24:7–10 The gathered pilgrim worshipers anticipate the arrival of Yahweh himself. The temple can never fully contain the glory that is Yahweh; rather, it serves only as the meeting place of God and humans.

24:1–10 When we realize that our life is in God's hands, we are emboldened to make decisions that are based on the well-being of the whole earth—all of God's kingdom—not just things that impact our own personal benefit or concern.

25:1–3 The psalm begins with a confident declaration of trust in Yahweh, followed immediately by a plea that the speaker not be "put to shame" (v. 2) or defeated by the enemy. Because Yahweh will never allow those who trust in him to be put to shame, the psalmist is free to claim personal application of that truth.

25:8–10 The content shifts to descriptive praise of Yahweh for his enduring love and faithfulness (v. 10a). This section responds point for point to the pleas in vv. 4–7.

25:12–15 These verses describe the blessings that accrue to those who "fear the LORD" (vv. 12a, 14a). The section moves in two directions: It admonishes the larger community to adopt the stance of fearing Yahweh, and it provides a foundation for the psalmist's confidence of deliverance (cf. v. 15a).

25:16–21 The final section of the psalm directly addresses the asked-for actions of Yahweh. A new

17 Relieve the troubles of my heart
and free me from my anguish.[k]
18 Look on my affliction and my distress[l]
and take away all my sins.
19 See how numerous are my enemies[m]
and how fiercely they hate me!

20 Guard my life[n] and rescue me;
do not let me be put to shame,
for I take refuge in you.
21 May integrity[o] and uprightness protect me,
because my hope, LORD,[a] is in you.

22 Deliver Israel,[p] O God,
from all their troubles!

Psalm 26

Of David.

1 Vindicate me, LORD,
for I have led a blameless life;[q]
I have trusted[r] in the LORD
and have not faltered.[s]
2 Test me,[t] LORD, and try me,
examine my heart and my mind;[u]
3 for I have always been mindful of your unfailing love
and have lived[v] in reliance on your faithfulness.

4 I do not sit[w] with the deceitful,
nor do I associate with hypocrites.
5 I abhor[x] the assembly of evildoers
and refuse to sit with the wicked.
6 I wash my hands in innocence,[y]
and go about your altar, LORD,
7 proclaiming aloud your praise
and telling of all your wonderful deeds.[z]

25:17 [k]Ps 107:6
25:18 [l]2Sa 16:12
25:19 [m]Ps 3:1
25:20 [n]Ps 86:2
25:21 [o]Ps 41:12
25:22 [p]Ps 130:8
26:1 [q]Ps 7:8; Pr 20:7 [r]Ps 28:7 [s]2Ki 20:3; Heb 10:23
26:2 [t]Ps 17:3 [u]Ps 7:9
26:3 [v]2Ki 20:3
26:4 [w]Ps 1:1
26:5 [x]Ps 31:6; 139:21
26:6 [y]Ps 73:13
26:7 [z]Ps 9:1

Ps 26:4-6 ❖ How do we keep ourselves upright despite the evil that goes on around us?

8 LORD, I love[a] the house where you live,
the place where your glory dwells.
9 Do not take away my soul along with sinners,
my life with those who are bloodthirsty,[b]
10 in whose hands are wicked schemes,
whose right hands are full of bribes.[c]
11 I lead a blameless life;
deliver me[d] and be merciful to me.

12 My feet stand on level ground;[e]
in the great congregation[f] I will praise the LORD.

Psalm 27

Of David.

1 The LORD is my light[g] and my salvation[h] —
whom shall I fear?
The LORD is the stronghold of my life —
of whom shall I be afraid?[i]

2 When the wicked advance against me
to devour[b] me,
it is my enemies and my foes
who will stumble and fall.[j]

26:8 [a]Ps 27:4
26:9 [b]Ps 28:3
26:10 [c]1Sa 8:3
26:11 [d]Ps 69:18
26:12 [e]Ps 27:11; 40:2 [f]Ps 22:22
27:1 [g]Isa 60:19 [h]Ex 15:2 [i]Ps 118:6
27:2 [j]Ps 9:3; 14:4

[a] 21 Septuagint; Hebrew does not have *LORD*.
[b] 2 Or *slander*

---

string of seven imperative verb forms signal the psalmist's final plea for deliverance.
25:22 This final verse identifies the pleas of the individual psalmist with the redemption of Israel "from all their troubles."

✚ **25:1-22** The message of both OT and NT is clear: Those who enter the eternal kingdom of God's grace are those who acknowledge their sin and trust in the gracious mercy of God while surrendering self-reliance and pride.

26:1 The invitation to judge prepares the way for the following verbs of examination and scrutiny in v. 2.
26:2-7 The repeated synonyms for "testing" drive home the psalmist's willing submission to God's examination. By offering these parts of life to God's scrutiny the psalmist is demonstrating complete openness.
26:8-11 The psalmist is filled by a sense of love for the temple as the place where God and humans come together.
26:12 The psalm ends with a statement of the psalmist's firm conviction that God will act in his behalf. All fear of slipping is gone. As a result, the psalmist's praise of Yahweh wells forth in the "great congregation."

✚ **26:1-12** As Ro 5:1-5 makes abundantly clear, Jesus' righteousness and his saving work on our behalf give us confidence to stand in the presence of a holy God without fear and to anticipate with great joy "the hope of the glory of God" (Ro 5:2).

27:1-3 Yahweh is the light that vanquishes the "darkest valley" (23:4). That light marks out the "right paths" (cf. 23:3). Yahweh is also the life-saving stronghold that delivers the psalmist. Because of that guidance and protection, he is unafraid

[3]Though an army besiege me,
my heart will not fear;[k]
though war break out against me,
even then I will be confident.[l]

[4]One thing[m] I ask from the LORD,
this only do I seek:
that I may dwell in the house of the LORD
all the days of my life,[n]
to gaze on the beauty of the LORD
and to seek him in his temple.
[5]For in the day of trouble
he will keep me safe in his dwelling;
he will hide me[o] in the shelter of his sacred tent
and set me high upon a rock.[p]

[6]Then my head will be exalted[q]
above the enemies who surround me;
at his sacred tent I will sacrifice[r] with shouts of joy;
I will sing and make music to the LORD.

[7]Hear my voice when I call, LORD;
be merciful to me and answer me.[s]
[8]My heart says of you, "Seek his face!"
Your face, LORD, I will seek.
[9]Do not hide your face[t] from me,
do not turn your servant away in anger;
you have been my helper.
Do not reject me or forsake me,
God my Savior.
[10]Though my father and mother forsake me,
the LORD will receive me.

27:3 [k]Ps 3:6 [l]Job 4:6
27:4 [m]Ps 90:17 [n]Ps 23:6; 26:8
27:5 [o]Ps 17:8; 31:20 [p]Ps 40:2
27:6 [q]Ps 3:3 [r]Ps 107:22
27:7 [s]Ps 13:3
27:9 [t]Ps 69:17
27:11 [u]Ps 5:8; 25:4; 86:11
27:12 [v]Mt 26:60; Ac 9:1
27:13 [w]Ps 31:19 [x]Jer 11:19; Eze 26:20
27:14 [y]Ps 40:1
28:1 [z]Ps 83:1 [a]Ps 88:4
28:2 [b]Ps 138:2; 140:6 [c]Ps 5:7

Ps 27:4 ❖ If you could ask "one thing" from the Lord, what would it be? Why?

Ps 28:1-2, 6-7 ❖ How can these verses help us as believers today as we face our own trials?

[11]Teach me your way, LORD;
lead me in a straight path[u]
because of my oppressors.
[12]Do not turn me over to the desire of my foes,
for false witnesses[v] rise up against me,
spouting malicious accusations.

[13]I remain confident of this:
I will see the goodness of the LORD[w]
in the land of the living.[x]
[14]Wait[y] for the LORD;
be strong and take heart
and wait for the LORD.

Psalm 28

Of David.

[1]To you, LORD, I call;
you are my Rock,
do not turn a deaf ear to me.
For if you remain silent,[z]
I will be like those who go down to the pit.[a]
[2]Hear my cry for mercy[b]
as I call to you for help,
as I lift up my hands
toward your Most Holy Place.[c]
[3]Do not drag me away with the wicked,
with those who do evil,

(27:1b, d). The protective presence and care of Yahweh encourages the psalmist in the face of enemy attack (vv. 2–3).
27:4–6 There is a protective benefit to the nearness of God. Freed from fear of the enemy by the presence of Yahweh, the psalmist is free to sing praises and to offer sacrifices of thanksgiving to God.
27:7–12 This cry underscores the reality of the poet's suffering in spite of a strong confidence in Yahweh's saving nature. The rest of the plea is divided into a desire for divine presence in the face of God's seeming absence (vv. 8–10), a desire for divine instruction in the right way (v. 11), and a desire for divine vindication in the face of "false witnesses" (v. 12).
27:13–14 The psalmist returns to the confident stance of vv. 1–3. The two verbs "be strong" and "take heart" are the same used in Joshua to encourage the Israelites as they cross the Jordan River.

✜ **27:1–14** Where or to whom do you go when life seems too much to handle? Perhaps to your spouse or a close friend, a trusted pastor, your parents or other family? For the psalmist, God is the stronghold of his life—the secure place when all else fails.

28:1–2 The psalmist asks Yahweh not to "turn a deaf ear" (v. 1b) to his cries. If God does "remain silent," the psalmist will "be like" those who descend to death in Sheol (v. 1c). He pleads with Yahweh as "my Rock" (v. 1a). God is the psalmist's secure high place.
28:3–5 The wicked use a facade of cordiality to mask malice. God expects a person's attitudes,

who speak cordially with their neighbors
but harbor malice in their hearts.[d]
4 Repay them for their deeds
and for their evil work;
repay them for what their hands have done[e]
and bring back on them what they deserve.[f]

5 Because they have no regard for the deeds of the LORD
and what his hands have done,[g]
he will tear them down
and never build them up again.

6 Praise be to the LORD,
for he has heard my cry for mercy.
7 The LORD is my strength[h] and my shield;
my heart trusts[i] in him, and he helps me.
My heart leaps for joy,
and with my song I praise him.[j]

8 The LORD is the strength of his people,
a fortress of salvation for his anointed one.[k]
9 Save your people and bless your inheritance;[l]
be their shepherd[m] and carry them[n] forever.

Psalm 29

A psalm of David.

1 Ascribe to the LORD,[o] you heavenly beings,
ascribe to the LORD glory[p] and strength.

Ps 29:2 ❖ How can we ascribe to God "the glory due his name"? What does this mean?

2 Ascribe to the LORD the glory due his name;
worship the LORD in the splendor of his[a] holiness.[q]

3 The voice[r] of the LORD is over the waters;
the God of glory thunders,[s]
the LORD thunders over the mighty waters.
4 The voice of the LORD is powerful;[t]
the voice of the LORD is majestic.
5 The voice of the LORD breaks the cedars;
the LORD breaks in pieces the cedars of Lebanon.[u]
6 He makes Lebanon leap[v] like a calf,
Sirion[b][w] like a young wild ox.
7 The voice of the LORD strikes
with flashes of lightning.
8 The voice of the LORD shakes the desert;
the LORD shakes the Desert of Kadesh.[x]
9 The voice of the LORD twists the oaks[c]
and strips the forests bare.
And in his temple all cry, "Glory!"[y]

10 The LORD sits enthroned over the flood;[z]

[a] 2 Or *LORD with the splendor of* [b] 6 That is, Mount Hermon [c] 9 Or *LORD makes the deer give birth*

28:3 [d] Ps 12:2; Ps 26:9; Jer 9:8
28:4 [e] 2Ti 4:14; Rev 22:12 [f] Rev 18:6
28:5 [g] Isa 5:12
28:7 [h] Ps 18:1 [i] Ps 13:5 [j] Ps 40:3; 69:30
28:8 [k] Ps 20:6
28:9 [l] Dt 9:29; Ezr 1:4 [m] Isa 40:11 [n] Dt 1:31; 32:11
29:1 [o] 1Ch 16:28 [p] Ps 96:7-9
29:2 [q] 2Ch 20:21
29:3 [r] Job 37:5 [s] Ps 18:13
29:4 [t] Ps 68:33
29:5 [u] Jdg 9:15
29:6 [v] Ps 114:4 [w] Dt 3:9
29:8 [x] Nu 13:26
29:9 [y] Ps 26:8
29:10 [z] Ge 6:17

---

desires, and commitment to be consistent with their outwardly observable actions.

28:6-7 The psalmist's certainty is expressed in words that almost parallel the plea itself in v. 2. Because of this assurance he praises Yahweh (vv. 6–7).

28:8-9 The individual image of Yahweh as the psalmist's "strength" and "shield" (v. 7) has been expanded to include the whole community in v. 8.

✤ **28:1-9** God's purpose in calling his church out of the world is not to escape. He has called us out to experience a new wholeness and to experience the world's brokenness for what it really is—a direct contradiction of God's intention for humanity and his whole creation. Living as we do in the midst of that brokenness every day, we can become less sensitive to the ways in which some of our cultural realities offend the righteousness of the holy God (see Ro 12:1-2).

29:1-2 The Hebrew word for the term "heavenly beings" in v. 1 is the plural of the common ancient Near Eastern word for "god." Its purpose is to enhance the majesty of Yahweh at the expense of foreign deities, bowing down in worship of his holiness.

29:3-9 The phrase "the voice of the LORD" appears eight times in this passage. The descriptive phrases picture a massive storm originating over the Mediterranean Sea (v. 3), moving ashore at the heavily forested Lebanon range to the far north of Israel (vv. 5–6), and then heading across the Desert of Kadesh (v. 8). The pinnacle and climax of the theophany comes at the height of the storm's power, as all those gathered in the temple worship Yahweh.

29:10-11 The ark of the covenant served as the place where God sat enthroned between the wings of the cherubim as Israel's king.

CHARACTER OF GOD // GOD IS GLORIOUS

Psalm 29:1-2: Ascribe to the LORD, you heavenly beings, ascribe to the LORD glory and strength. Ascribe to the LORD the glory due his name; worship the LORD in the splendor of his holiness.

Glory seems like an abstract concept to many. How is glory different from beauty or splendor? The Hebrew word for *glory* (*kavod*) gives the idea of heaviness or weight. God's presence was so intense and powerful that it was perceived as being heavy or weighty. When we think of God's glory, it's helpful to also remember his power, might and greatness.

When the Israelites completed the tabernacle in the wilderness, the cloud of God's glorious presence filled it in such a way that Moses could not enter it (Ex 40:35). God's glory filled it, and that glory was too heavy for anyone to walk into. When Solomon completed the Lord's temple, the same thing occurred: The priests could not enter because of the intense glory of God's holy presence (1Ki 8:11).

Isaiah the prophet experienced the glory of the Lord in the temple (Isa 6). Through a dramatic vision, Isaiah saw God on his throne, surrounded by angels announcing God's holiness. Isaiah was overwhelmed by God's presence and immediately felt the depth of his own sin. The angels announced that the whole earth is filled with God's glory.

In the NT, we encounter a different picture of God's glory. John 1:14 says that in Jesus Christ, the Word made flesh, we see the glory of God. Christ came as a human baby, taking on the nature of a servant who laid down his life for sinners (Php 2:7-8). However, when Christ returns, he will come with greater power and glory than the world has ever seen. He will sit on his throne as the righteous Lord over all (Mt 25:31).

APPLICATION ✤ Psalm 29:1-2 invites believers to ascribe glory to God. Certainly, God is already full of glory and does not need anything from us. Yet the Bible wants us to recognize and proclaim God's glory. This is not because God is vain but because when we praise God, we are reminded of who we are and who God is. Ascribing glory to God orients us toward worshiping the One who made us, the One who loves us and the One who saves us.

the LORD is enthroned as King
forever.[a]
11 The LORD gives strength to his
people;[b]
the LORD blesses his people with
peace.[c]

Psalm 30[a]

A psalm. A song. For the dedication of the temple.[b] Of David.

1 I will exalt you, LORD,
for you lifted me out of the
depths
and did not let my enemies gloat
over me.[d]
2 LORD my God, I called to you for
help,[e]
and you healed me.[f]
3 You, LORD, brought me up from the
realm of the dead;
you spared me from going down
to the pit.[g]
4 Sing the praises of the LORD, you his
faithful people;[h]
praise his holy name.[i]
5 For his anger[j] lasts only a moment,
but his favor lasts a lifetime;
weeping may stay for the night,
but rejoicing comes in the
morning.[k]

29:10 [a] Ps 10:16
29:11 [b] Ps 28:8 [c] Ps 37:11
30:1 [d] Ps 25:2; 28:9
30:2 [e] Ps 88:13 [f] Ps 6:2
30:3 [g] Ps 28:1; 86:13
30:4 [h] Ps 149:1 [i] Ps 97:12
30:5 [j] Ps 103:9 [k] 2Co 4:17

Ps 30:1 ✤ What "depths" has God lifted you out of? How have you offered your thanksgiving to him?

[a] In Hebrew texts 30:1-12 is numbered 30:2-13.
[b] Title: Or *palace*

✤ **29:1-11** How long has it been since you were overwhelmed in this way by a sense of God's powerful presence? The next time you experience an awe-inspiring weather event, think about this psalm.

30:1-3 The psalmist's suffering may have been occasioned by a desperate illness. The psalmist appears almost to have been plucked out of the line of those waiting to enter Sheol.
30:4-5 The psalmist calls on the listening/reading "faithful people" (v. 4) to join in the praise of Yahweh.

6 When I felt secure, I said,
"I will never be shaken."
7 LORD, when you favored me,
you made my royal mountain[a]
stand firm;
but when you hid your face,[l]
I was dismayed.

8 To you, LORD, I called;
to the Lord I cried for mercy:
9 "What is gained if I am silenced,
if I go down to the pit?
Will the dust praise you?
Will it proclaim your
faithfulness?[m]
10 Hear, LORD, and be merciful to me;
LORD, be my help."

11 You turned my wailing into dancing;
you removed my sackcloth and
clothed me with joy,[n]
12 that my heart may sing your praises
and not be silent.
LORD my God, I will praise[o] you
forever.[p]

Psalm 31[b]

31:1–4pp // Ps 71:1–3

For the director of music.
A psalm of David.

1 In you, LORD, I have taken refuge;
let me never be put to shame;
deliver me in your righteousness.
2 Turn your ear to me,
come quickly to my rescue;
be my rock of refuge,[q]
a strong fortress to save me.
3 Since you are my rock and my
fortress,[r]
for the sake of your name[s] lead
and guide me.
4 Keep me free from the trap that is
set for me,
for you are my refuge.[t]
5 Into your hands I commit my spirit;[u]
deliver me, LORD, my faithful God.

6 I hate those who cling to worthless
idols;
as for me, I trust in the LORD.[v]
7 I will be glad and rejoice in your
love,
for you saw my affliction[w]
and knew the anguish[x] of my soul.
8 You have not given me into the
hands[y] of the enemy
but have set my feet in a spacious
place.

9 Be merciful to me, LORD, for I am in
distress;
my eyes grow weak with sorrow,[z]
my soul and body with grief.
10 My life is consumed by anguish
and my years by groaning;[a]
my strength fails because of my
affliction,[c]
and my bones grow weak.[b]
11 Because of all my enemies,
I am the utter contempt of my
neighbors[c]
and an object of dread to my closest
friends—
those who see me on the street
flee from me.
12 I am forgotten as though I were
dead;[d]
I have become like broken pottery.

30:7 [l] Dt 31:17; Ps 104:29
30:9 [m] Ps 6:5
30:11 [n] Ps 4:7; Jer 31:4,13
30:12 [o] Ps 16:9 [p] Ps 44:8
31:2 [q] Ps 18:2
31:3 [r] Ps 18:2 [s] Ps 23:3
31:4 [t] Ps 25:15
31:5 [u] Lk 23:46; Ac 7:59
31:6 [v] Jnh 2:8
31:7 [w] Ps 90:14 [x] Ps 10:14; Jn 10:27
31:8 [y] Dt 32:30
31:9 [z] Ps 6:7
31:10 [a] Ps 13:2 [b] Ps 38:3; 39:11
31:11 [c] Job 19:13; Ps 38:11; 64:8; Isa 53:4
31:12 [d] Ps 88:4

[a] 7 That is, Mount Zion [b] In Hebrew texts 31:1-24 is numbered 31:2-25. [c] 10 Or *guilt*

30:6–7 In the rest of the psalm, the psalmist gives an account of the changing mental and emotional processes that accompanied his downfall and deliverance. The psalmist begins with an almost naive sense of safety and security (v. 6). The tension between real and false security is played out in v. 7.
30:8–10 The rhetorical questions at the end of v. 9—each assuming the answer "No!"—realize that the only "profit" that humans represent to God lies in their praise and acknowledgment of his faithfulness.
30:11–12 Psalm 30 concludes with the psalmist's joyful memory of deliverance realized. His rites of mourning have become instead a dance.

✣ **30:1–12** When we acknowledge that without God life is formless and void, when we acknowledge that he alone has the power to save, then regardless of its circumstances, life with God at the center can be marked with enduring contentment.

31:1–4 The related terms pile up in these verses ("refuge" in vv. 1, 2, 4; "rock" and "fortress" in vv. 2, 3), emphasizing the theme of reliance and trust that underlies the whole psalm.
31:5 To commit one's "spirit" to God is not simply to trust for physical deliverance but also to surrender everything into God's care. The psalmist's act of commitment reflects complete surrender of control and submission to God's will.
31:6–8 The phrase "worthless idols" (v. 6) refers pointedly to the emptiness of idols on which the wicked rely. The remaining verses celebrate the psalmist's assurance of Yahweh's love and deliverance.
31:9–13 The psalmist's plea introduces an extended narrative of suffering that serves as the motivation for divine deliverance. The disgraceful public

[13]For I hear many whispering,
"Terror on every side!"[e]
They conspire against me
and plot to take my life.[f]

[14]But I trust[g] in you, LORD;
I say, "You are my God."
[15]My times[h] are in your hands;
deliver me from the hands of my enemies,
from those who pursue me.
[16]Let your face shine[i] on your servant;
save me in your unfailing love.
[17]Let me not be put to shame,[j] LORD,
for I have cried out to you;
but let the wicked be put to shame
and be silent[k] in the realm of the dead.
[18]Let their lying lips[l] be silenced,
for with pride and contempt
they speak arrogantly[m] against the righteous.

[19]How abundant are the good things[n]
that you have stored up for those who fear you,
that you bestow in the sight of all,[o]
on those who take refuge in you.
[20]In the shelter of your presence you hide[p] them
from all human intrigues;[q]
you keep them safe in your dwelling
from accusing tongues.

[21]Praise be to the LORD,
for he showed me the wonders of his love[r]
when I was in a city under siege.[s]
[22]In my alarm[t] I said,
"I am cut off from your sight!"
Yet you heard my cry[u] for mercy
when I called to you for help.

31:13 [e]Jer 20:3, 10; La 2:22 [f]Mt 27:1
31:14 [g]Ps 140:6
31:15 [h]Job 24:1; Ps 143:9
31:16 [i]Nu 6:25; Ps 4:6
31:17 [j]Ps 25:2-3 [k]Ps 115:17
31:18 [l]Ps 120:2 [m]Ps 94:4
31:19 [n]Ro 11:22 [o]Isa 64:4
31:20 [p]Ps 27:5 [q]Job 5:21
31:21 [r]Ps 17:7 [s]1Sa 23:7
31:22 [t]Ps 116:11 [u]La 3:54
31:23 [v]Ps 34:9 [w]Ps 145:20 [x]Ps 94:2
31:24 [y]Ps 27:14
32:1 [z]Ps 85:2
32:2 [a]Ro 4:7-8*; 2Co 5:19 [b]Jn 1:47
32:3 [c]Ps 31:10
32:4 [d]Job 33:7

Ps 31:20 ❖ How has God's presence sheltered us from threats or conflicts around us?

Ps 32:5 ❖ Why is open confession of sin so important? When have we experienced the blessings that follow honest confession before God?

[23]Love the LORD, all his faithful people![v]
The LORD preserves those who are true to him,[w]
but the proud he pays back[x] in full.
[24]Be strong and take heart,[y]
all you who hope in the LORD.

Psalm 32

Of David. A maskil.[a]

[1]Blessed is the one
whose transgressions are forgiven,
whose sins are covered.[z]
[2]Blessed is the one
whose sin the LORD does not count against them[a]
and in whose spirit is no deceit.[b]

[3]When I kept silent,
my bones wasted away[c]
through my groaning all day long.
[4]For day and night
your hand was heavy[d] on me;
my strength was sapped
as in the heat of summer.[b]

[5]Then I acknowledged my sin to you
and did not cover up my iniquity.

[a] Title: Probably a literary or musical term
[b] 4 The Hebrew has *Selah* (a word of uncertain meaning) here and at the end of verses 5 and 7.

shame the psalmist experiences is falsely induced: The psalmist feels terrified, under attack, and threatened.

31:14–18 It is as if the psalmist says: "Contrary to what one might expect under the circumstances, I do not despair, *but I* surrender in trust to the hand of God" (vv. 14–15). Yahweh is the only source of hope. This is a call to be perceptive observers of life and sensitive to the character and purpose of God, and to respond appropriately.

31:19–20 His experiences are seen not as isolated personal events but as part of the tapestry of dealing between God and his people. As God has stored up goodness for those who fear him, so goodness is in store for the suffering psalmist.

31:21–24 The focus returns to his more specific context. The object is to give testimony to this larger group from his own experience.

✣ **31:1–24** If our context should change—a job lost, a spouse divorced or passed away, a moral failure tarnishing a reputation—then our value and identity feels tarnished as well. In what appear to be hopeless circumstances, God arrives to provide refuge and hope.

32:1–2 The psalm begins with a twofold repetition of "blessed"—the same word that begins the whole Psalter (1:1). Forgiveness comes to the one who confesses sin completely and openly without deceit or reservation.

32:3–5 In Ps 32, the psalmist's sin has led to illness. The destructive effects of repressed and unexpressed emotions and anxieties can be powerfully experienced in physical pain and psychological disintegration.

I said, "I will confess[e]
my transgressions[f] to the LORD."
And you forgave
the guilt of my sin.[g]

6 Therefore let all the faithful pray to
you
while you may be found;[h]
surely the rising of the mighty
waters
will not reach them.[i]
7 You are my hiding place;
you will protect me from trouble[j]
and surround me with songs of
deliverance.[k]

8 I will instruct[l] you and teach you in
the way you should go;
I will counsel you with my loving
eye on[m] you.
9 Do not be like the horse or the mule,
which have no understanding
but must be controlled by bit and
bridle[n]
or they will not come to you.
10 Many are the woes of the wicked,[o]
but the LORD's unfailing love
surrounds the one who trusts[p] in
him.

11 Rejoice in the LORD[q] and be glad, you
righteous;
sing, all you who are upright in
heart!

Psalm 33

1 Sing joyfully to the LORD, you
righteous;
it is fitting[r] for the upright[s] to
praise him.
2 Praise the LORD with the harp;
make music to him on the
ten-stringed lyre.[t]
3 Sing to him a new song;[u]
play skillfully, and shout for joy.

4 For the word of the LORD is right[v]
and true;
he is faithful in all he does.
5 The LORD loves righteousness and
justice;[w]
the earth is full of his unfailing
love.[x]

6 By the word[y] of the LORD the
heavens were made,
their starry host by the breath of
his mouth.
7 He gathers the waters of the sea into
jars[a];
he puts the deep into storehouses.
8 Let all the earth fear the LORD;
let all the people of the world
revere him.[z]
9 For he spoke, and it came to be;
he commanded,[a] and it stood
firm.

10 The LORD foils the plans of the
nations;[b]
he thwarts the purposes of the
peoples.
11 But the plans of the LORD stand firm
forever,
the purposes[c] of his heart through
all generations.

12 Blessed is the nation whose God is
the LORD,[d]
the people he chose[e] for his
inheritance.
13 From heaven the LORD looks down
and sees all mankind;[f]
14 from his dwelling place[g] he watches
all who live on earth —

32:5 [e] Pr 28:13 [f] Ps 103:12 [g] Lev 26:40
32:6 [h] Ps 69:13; Isa 55:6 [i] Isa 43:2
32:7 [j] Ps 9:9 [k] Ex 15:1
32:8 [l] Ps 25:8 [m] Ps 33:18
32:9 [n] Pr 26:3
32:10 [o] Ro 2:9 [p] Pr 16:20
32:11 [q] Ps 64:10
33:1 [r] Ps 147:1 [s] Ps 32:11
33:2 [t] Ps 92:3
33:3 [u] Ps 96:1
33:4 [v] Ps 19:8
33:5 [w] Ps 11:7 [x] Ps 119:64
33:6 [y] Heb 11:3
33:8 [z] Ps 67:7; 96:9
33:9 [a] Ge 1:3; Ps 148:5
33:10 [b] Isa 8:10
33:11 [c] Job 23:13
33:12 [d] Ps 144:15 [e] Ex 19:5; Dt 7:6
33:13 [f] Job 28:24; Ps 11:4
33:14 [g] 1Ki 8:39

[a] 7 Or *sea as into a heap*

32:6–7 The exhortation in these two verses is styled as a direct address to God. The purpose is to encourage humans to hold on to the hope of divine grace offered in response to honest confession.
32:8–10 The readers are warned not to resist the divine will and face "many . . . woes" (v. 10a). By contrast, those wise ones who trust in Yahweh find themselves surrounded by his "unfailing love" (v. 10b).

✣ **32:1–11** Our failure to live up to the "should haves" and "ought tos" of our lives causes many of us to hide our failings. But freedom is found in having a community of faith willing to hear your wrongs as fellow sinners rather than as perfectionistic judges.

33:1–3 A "new song" (v. 3) is a logical response to a "new act" of deliverance. For such new joy, the old expressions of joy will simply not do.
33:4–11 Motivation to praise falls into three categories: the right and faithful *character* of God (vv. 4–5), the powerful and creative *word* of God (vv. 6–9), and the enduring and unshakable *purpose* of God (vv. 10–11).
33:12 Israel's plans and purposes are subjected to the same sovereign will of Yahweh as the rest of the nations. Israel is "blessed" (v. 12a) above all other nations because it has become God's "inheritance" (v. 12b).
33:13–19 The remainder of the section balances the preceding section: Divine scrutiny holds humans to the standard of Yahweh's righteousness (vv. 13–15); human power is doomed to failure compared to

[15]he who forms[h] the hearts of all,
who considers everything they do.[i]

[16]No king is saved by the size of his army;[j]
no warrior escapes by his great strength.
[17]A horse[k] is a vain hope for deliverance;
despite all its great strength it cannot save.
[18]But the eyes[l] of the LORD are on those who fear him,
on those whose hope is in his unfailing love,[m]
[19]to deliver them from death
and keep them alive in famine.[n]

[20]We wait[o] in hope for the LORD;
he is our help and our shield.
[21]In him our hearts rejoice,[p]
for we trust in his holy name.
[22]May your unfailing love be with us, LORD,
even as we put our hope in you.

Psalm 34[a,b]

Of David. When he pretended to be insane before Abimelek, who drove him away, and he left.

[1]I will extol the LORD at all times;[q]
his praise will always be on my lips.
[2]I will glory[r] in the LORD;
let the afflicted hear and rejoice.[s]
[3]Glorify the LORD with me;
let us exalt[t] his name together.

[4]I sought the LORD,[u] and he answered me;
he delivered me from all my fears.
[5]Those who look to him are radiant;[v]
their faces are never covered with shame.[w]
[6]This poor man called, and the LORD heard him;
he saved him out of all his troubles.
[7]The angel of the LORD[x] encamps around those who fear him,
and he delivers them.

[8]Taste and see that the LORD is good;[y]
blessed is the one who takes refuge[z] in him.
[9]Fear the LORD, you his holy people,
for those who fear him lack nothing.[a]
[10]The lions may grow weak and hungry,
but those who seek the LORD lack no good thing.[b]
[11]Come, my children, listen to me;
I will teach you[c] the fear of the LORD.
[12]Whoever of you loves life[d]
and desires to see many good days,
[13]keep your tongue from evil
and your lips from telling lies.[e]
[14]Turn from evil and do good;[f]
seek peace[g] and pursue it.

33:15 [h] Job 10:8 [i] Jer 32:19
33:16 [j] Ps 44:6
33:17 [k] Ps 20:7; Pr 21:31
33:18 [l] Job 36:7; Ps 34:15 [m] Ps 147:11
33:19 [n] Job 5:20
33:20 [o] Ps 130:6
33:21 [p] Zec 10:7; Jn 16:22
34:1 [q] Ps 71:6; Eph 5:20
34:2 [r] Jer 9:24; 1Co 1:31 [s] Ps 119:74
34:3 [t] Lk 1:46
34:4 [u] Mt 7:7
34:5 [v] Ps 36:9 [w] Ps 25:3
34:7 [x] 2Ki 6:17; Da 6:22
34:8 [y] 1Pe 2:3 [z] Ps 2:12
34:9 [a] Ps 23:1
34:10 [b] Ps 84:11
34:11 [c] Ps 32:8
34:12 [d] 1Pe 3:10
34:13 [e] 1Pe 2:22
34:14 [f] Ps 37:27 [g] Heb 12:14

[a] This psalm is an acrostic poem, the verses of which begin with the successive letters of the Hebrew alphabet. [b] In Hebrew texts 34:1-22 is numbered 34:2-23.

Ps 33:16–17 ❖ Where do we see people placing hope in politicians or armies? How can we resist placing our hope in such things?

Ps 34:2 ❖ What fears has God delivered us from? How has he answered us when we sought his face?

Yahweh's (vv. 16–17); and Yahweh's purpose for the faithful is deliverance (vv. 18–19).

33:20–22 The speakers trust Yahweh because his covering is like a shield protecting a soldier in hand-to-hand combat.

✣ **33:1–22** Psalm 33 celebrates the enduring quality of God's creation. But it is not the enduring creation—as lasting and stable as it appears to be—that fills the psalmist with trust. It is, instead, the Creator God himself who inspires hope and confidence.

34:1–3 Psalm 34 begins with an invocation to praise Yahweh, in which the psalmist first proclaims his personal pledge (vv. 1–2) and then invites the listener/reader to join with him.

34:4–7 The psalmist here presents a personal testimony of deliverance by Yahweh, interwoven with encouragement to others to entrust themselves to his care.

34:8–9 Verse 8 is an exhortation to discover the goodness that Yahweh represents and to "take refuge in him." Those who "fear the LORD" (v. 9) receive what they need from him.

34:11–20 The psalmist describes the nature of this most important relationship (vv. 11–14). The next two verses contrast Yahweh's response to the righteous and those "who do evil" (v. 16). Verses 17–20 are intended to be an encouragement that Yahweh hears and acts on behalf of the righteous.

CHARACTER OF GOD // GOD IS GOOD

Psalm 34:8: Taste and see that the LORD is good; blessed is the one who takes refuge in him.

It may sound like an understatement to say that God is good. After all, "good" is a rather small and mundane word. Saying something is good does not evoke a sense of divine grandeur. A simple meal might be called "good."

The Hebrew word for *good (tov)*, however, is wonderfully wide. When God spoke creation into being and ordered it to work as it should, he called it "good" (Ge 1:4). The word *tov* appears seven times in Ge 1, showing the complete goodness of God's creation. At the end of six days of creation, God saw that all he had made was "very good" (Ge 1:31).

Describing the majesty and wonder of creation as "good" helps us understand the scope and weight of this small word. To say God is good is not mundane. God's goodness speaks to the way he relates to his creation and creatures. The fact that God is good fills us with hope that he is strong and faithful. As Ps 34:8 says, God's goodness means we can take refuge in him.

APPLICATION ✣ There is so much brokenness and hurt in the world. What could be better news than that the God over all, who holds the future in his hands, is good? God will not give his creation up to mere chance. Just as he is good, his plans are good. The universe is not run by an impersonal force; it is held in the loving hands of a God who is sovereign and good.

15 The eyes of the LORD[h] are on the
righteous,[i]
and his ears are attentive to their
cry;
16 but the face of the LORD is against[j]
those who do evil,[k]
to blot out their name[l] from the
earth.

17 The righteous cry out, and the LORD
hears[m] them;
he delivers them from all their
troubles.
18 The LORD is close[n] to the
brokenhearted[o]
and saves those who are crushed
in spirit.

19 The righteous person may have
many troubles,[p]
but the LORD delivers him from
them all;[q]
20 he protects all his bones,
not one of them will be
broken.[r]

21 Evil will slay the wicked;[s]
the foes of the righteous will be
condemned.
22 The LORD will rescue[t] his servants;
no one who takes refuge in him
will be condemned.

34:15 [h] Ps 33:18 [i] Job 36:7
34:16 [j] Lev 17:10; Jer 44:11 [k] 1Pe 3:10-12* [l] Pr 10:7
34:17 [m] Ps 145:19
34:18 [n] Ps 145:18 [o] Isa 57:15
34:19 [p] ver 17 [q] ver 4,6; Pr 24:16
34:20 [r] Jn 19:36*
34:21 [s] Ps 94:23
34:22 [t] 1Ki 1:29; Ps 71:23
35:1 [u] Ps 43:1
35:2 [v] Ps 62:2

Ps 35:1-3 ❖ How can we let God fight our battles for us? Why is this difficult to do at times?

Psalm 35

Of David.

1 Contend, LORD, with those who
contend with me;
fight[u] against those who fight
against me.
2 Take up shield and armor;
arise[v] and come to my aid.
3 Brandish spear and javelin[a]
against those who pursue me.

[a] 3 Or *and block the way*

34:21-22 Evil acts lead to divine condemnation. By contrast, those who "take refuge in" Yahweh need not fear condemnation.

✣ **34:1-22** We too often identify divine blessing with "getting the goods" in one way or another. The trouble is that we may come to associate divine blessing *exclusively* with such external evidence. The people of Jesus' day struggled with this sort of thinking (Jn 9:1-12).

35:1-3 Yahweh should "contend" with those who "contend" and should "fight" with those who "fight" (v. 1). The remainder of the introductory plea describes Yahweh's action in more militaristic terms.

Say to me,
"I am your salvation."

4 May those who seek my life
be disgraced[w] and put to shame;
may those who plot my ruin
be turned back in dismay.
5 May they be like chaff[x] before the wind,
with the angel of the LORD driving them away;
6 may their path be dark and slippery,
with the angel of the LORD pursuing them.

7 Since they hid their net for me without cause
and without cause dug a pit for me,
8 may ruin overtake them by surprise —[y]
may the net they hid entangle them,
may they fall into the pit,[z] to their ruin.
9 Then my soul will rejoice[a] in the LORD
and delight in his salvation.[b]
10 My whole being will exclaim,
"Who is like you,[c] LORD?
You rescue the poor from those too strong[d] for them,
the poor and needy[e] from those who rob them."

11 Ruthless witnesses[f] come forward;
they question me on things I know nothing about.
12 They repay me evil for good[g]
and leave me like one bereaved.
13 Yet when they were ill, I put on sackcloth
and humbled myself with fasting.[h]
When my prayers returned to me unanswered,
14 I went about mourning
as though for my friend or brother.
I bowed my head in grief
as though weeping for my mother.
15 But when I stumbled, they gathered in glee;
assailants gathered against me
without my knowledge.
They slandered[i] me without ceasing.
16 Like the ungodly they maliciously mocked;[a]
they gnashed their teeth[j] at me.

17 How long,[k] Lord, will you look on?
Rescue me from their ravages,
my precious life[l] from these lions.
18 I will give you thanks in the great assembly;[m]
among the throngs I will praise you.[n]
19 Do not let those gloat over me
who are my enemies without cause;
do not let those who hate me
without reason[o]
maliciously wink the eye.[p]
20 They do not speak peaceably,
but devise false accusations
against those who live quietly in the land.
21 They sneer[q] at me and say, "Aha! Aha![r]
With our own eyes we have seen it."

22 LORD, you have seen[s] this; do not be silent.
Do not be far[t] from me, Lord.

35:4 [w] Ps 70:2
35:5 [x] Job 21:18; Ps 1:4; Isa 29:5
35:8 [y] 1Th 5:3 [z] Ps 9:15
35:9 [a] Lk 1:47 [b] Isa 61:10
35:10 [c] Ex 15:11 [d] Ps 18:17 [e] Ps 37:14
35:11 [f] Ps 27:12
35:12 [g] Jn 10:32
35:13 [h] Job 30:25; Ps 69:10
35:15 [i] Job 30:1,8
35:16 [j] Job 16:9; La 2:16
35:17 [k] Hab 1:13 [l] Ps 22:20
35:18 [m] Ps 22:25 [n] Ps 22:22
35:19 [o] Ps 38:19; 69:4; Jn 15:25* [p] Ps 13:4; Pr 6:13
35:21 [q] Ps 22:13 [r] Ps 40:15
35:22 [s] Ex 3:7 [t] Ps 10:1; 28:1

[a] 16 Septuagint; Hebrew may mean *Like an ungodly circle of mockers,*

35:4–6 The psalmist turns to a plea for retribution. Like chaff blown by the wind, they will be driven away.
35:7–8 The punishment received is equivalent to the offense committed. Those who hid a net will be entangled. Those who dug a pit will fall into it instead.
35:9–10 The various verbs used to express the psalmist's testimony of rejoicing and delight emphasize a visible and audible expression of joy in a public setting. That testimony is encapsulated in the exclamation preserved in v. 10—a rhetorical question with only a single obvious answer: "No one!"
35:11–16 The psalmist is opposed by "ruthless witnesses" (v. 11). What is depicted is damaging false testimony in a case involving the death penalty. To return evil for good is one of the greatest insults imaginable and a rejection of one's authority.
35:17–18 The psalmist questions "how long" (v. 17) God can view the enemies' attacks and sit still without acting?
35:19–27 The psalmist begs for deliverance (vv. 19–21), vindication (vv. 22–25), and retribution (vv. 26–27) directed toward those who rejoice (vv. 19, 24, 26) over the psalmist's distress. Once again, he characterizes these attacks as baseless (v. 19; cf. v. 7). The psalmist's enemies are hostile and present false testimony, claiming to be eyewitnesses (vv. 20–21).

The caustic exclamation "Aha! Aha!" (v. 21) is a public form of "finger pointing" that intends to cause public shame and disgrace.

23 Awake,[u] and rise to my defense!
Contend for me, my God and Lord.
24 Vindicate me in your righteousness, LORD my God;
do not let them gloat over me.
25 Do not let them think, "Aha, just what we wanted!"
or say, "We have swallowed him up."[v]

26 May all who gloat over my distress
be put to shame[w] and confusion;
may all who exalt themselves over me[x]
be clothed with shame and disgrace.
27 May those who delight in my vindication[y]
shout for joy[z] and gladness;
may they always say, "The LORD be exalted,
who delights[a] in the well-being of his servant."

28 My tongue will proclaim your righteousness,[b]
your praises all day long.

Psalm 36[a]

For the director of music. Of David the servant of the LORD.

1 I have a message from God in my heart
concerning the sinfulness of the wicked:[b]
There is no fear of God
before their eyes.[c]

2 In their own eyes they flatter themselves
too much to detect or hate their sin.
3 The words of their mouths[d] are wicked and deceitful;
they fail to act wisely[e] or do good.[f]
4 Even on their beds they plot evil;[g]
they commit themselves to a sinful course[h]
and do not reject what is wrong.[i]

5 Your love, LORD, reaches to the heavens,
your faithfulness to the skies.
6 Your righteousness is like the highest mountains,
your justice like the great deep.[j]
You, LORD, preserve both people and animals.
7 How priceless is your unfailing love, O God!
People take refuge in the shadow of your wings.[k]
8 They feast on the abundance of your house;[l]
you give them drink from your river[m] of delights.
9 For with you is the fountain of life;[n]
in your light[o] we see light.

10 Continue your love to those who know you,
your righteousness to the upright in heart.
11 May the foot of the proud not come against me,
nor the hand of the wicked drive me away.

Ps 36:2 ❖ Why do those who flatter themselves fail to detect their own sin? How can we protect ourselves against such pride?

35:23 [u] Ps 44:23
35:25 [v] La 2:16
35:26 [w] Ps 40:14; 109:29 [x] Ps 38:16
35:27 [y] Ps 9:4 [z] Ps 32:11 [a] Ps 40:16; 147:11
35:28 [b] Ps 51:14
36:1 [c] Ro 3:18*
36:3 [d] Ps 10:7 [e] Ps 94:8 [f] Jer 4:22
36:4 [g] Pr 4:16; Mic 2:1 [h] Isa 65:2 [i] Ps 52:3; Ro 12:9
36:6 [j] Job 11:8; Ps 77:19; Ro 11:33
36:7 [k] Ru 2:12; Ps 17:8
36:8 [l] Ps 65:4 [m] Job 20:17; Rev 22:1
36:9 [n] Jer 2:13 [o] 1Pe 2:9

[a] In Hebrew texts 36:1-12 is numbered 36:2-13.
[b] 1 Or *A message from God: The transgression of the wicked / resides in their hearts.*

35:28 The psalm concludes with the hopeful psalmist promising to testify regarding Yahweh's righteousness that has vindicated him against the false witnesses.

❖ **35:1–28** The psalm cautions us to be clear about our motives when we seek public vindication for ourselves and even wish for the downfall of our detractors. God is not on call to exact vengeance for us. There is innocent suffering that needs to be confronted and judged, but the psalmist reminds us that what is finally at stake is not *our* reputation or even our well-being but *God's* glory and righteousness.

36:1–4 Psalm 36 provides an "insight" into the fate of the arrogant who exhibit no "fear of God" (v. 1) and yet often seem to prosper.
36:5–9 The psalmist praises Yahweh's love that fills the whole of creation—reaching from heaven to earth, from the mighty mountains to the great deep. Not only does Yahweh's love provide abundant pleasures, but it also offers access to the "river of delights" (v. 8) and the "fountain of life" (v. 9).
36:10–11 In calling for divine action, the writer is

12 See how the evildoers lie fallen —
thrown down, not able to rise![p]

Psalm 37[a]

Of David.

1 Do not fret because of those who are evil
or be envious[q] of those who do wrong;[r]
2 for like the grass they will soon wither,
like green plants they will soon die away.[s]

3 Trust in the LORD and do good;
dwell in the land[t] and enjoy safe pasture.[u]
4 Take delight[v] in the LORD,
and he will give you the desires of your heart.

5 Commit your way to the LORD;
trust in him[w] and he will do this:
6 He will make your righteous reward[x]
shine like the dawn,[y]
your vindication like the noonday sun.

7 Be still[z] before the LORD
and wait patiently[a] for him;
do not fret when people succeed in their ways,
when they carry out their wicked schemes.

8 Refrain from anger[b] and turn from wrath;
do not fret — it leads only to evil.
9 For those who are evil will be destroyed,
but those who hope in the LORD
will inherit the land.[c]

10 A little while, and the wicked will be no more;[d]
though you look for them, they will not be found.

36:12 [p] Ps 140:10
37:1 [q] Pr 23:17-18 [r] Ps 73:3
37:2 [s] Ps 90:6
37:3 [t] Dt 30:20 [u] Isa 40:11; Jn 10:9
37:4 [v] Isa 58:14
37:5 [w] Ps 4:5; Ps 55:22; Pr 16:3; 1Pe 5:7
37:6 [x] Mic 7:9 [y] Job 11:17
37:7 [z] Ps 62:5; La 3:26 [a] Ps 40:1
37:8 [b] Eph 4:31; Col 3:8
37:9 [c] Isa 57:13; 60:21
37:10 [d] Job 7:10; 24:24

Ps 37:1-4 ❖ Are we ever envious of those who do wrong? How does this psalm reorient our understanding?

11 But the meek will inherit the land[e]
and enjoy peace and prosperity.

12 The wicked plot against the righteous
and gnash their teeth[f] at them;
13 but the Lord laughs at the wicked,
for he knows their day is coming.[g]

14 The wicked draw the sword
and bend the bow[h]
to bring down the poor and needy,[i]
to slay those whose ways are upright.
15 But their swords will pierce their own hearts,[j]
and their bows will be broken.

16 Better the little that the righteous have
than the wealth[k] of many wicked;
17 for the power of the wicked will be broken,[l]
but the LORD upholds the righteous.

18 The blameless spend their days
under the LORD's care,[m]
and their inheritance will endure forever.
19 In times of disaster they will not wither;
in days of famine they will enjoy plenty.

20 But the wicked will perish:
Though the LORD's enemies are
like the flowers of the field,
they will be consumed, they will
go up in smoke.[n]

37:11 [e] Mt 5:5
37:12 [f] Ps 35:16
37:13 [g] 1Sa 26:10; Ps 2:4
37:14 [h] Ps 11:2 [i] Ps 35:10
37:15 [j] Ps 9:16
37:16 [k] Pr 15:16
37:17 [l] Job 38:15; Ps 10:15
37:18 [m] Ps 1:6
37:20 [n] Ps 102:3

[a] This psalm is an acrostic poem, the stanzas of which begin with the successive letters of the Hebrew alphabet.

---

expressing his personal desire and aligning that personal desire with the will and purpose of Yahweh.
36:12 In the eye of the psalmist, God has implanted a vision of the fall of the wicked that exposes their apparent present dominance and power for what it truly is.

✤ **36:1-12** The poet finds the strength to live today, not in some hoped-for future but in the ongoing provision of God for the faithful; his unfailing love provides refuge as well as the abundant delights of God's house.

37:1-11 Verses 1–2 admonish the reader/listener not to be concerned because of the apparent success and invulnerability of the wicked. Their ultimate destiny is defeat and destruction.
37:10-11 The unit concludes with the basis of a positive response to the psalmist's demands. The evil have only "a little while" before they are "no more," but the "meek" who "hope in the LORD" (v. 9) will "inherit the land."
37:12-22 Four illustrations of the futility of wicked attempts at self-power (vv. 12–13, 14–15, 20, 21–22) bracket a call to righteousness (vv. 16–19). The

21 The wicked borrow and do not repay,
but the righteous give generously;[o]
22 those the LORD blesses will inherit the land,
but those he curses[p] will be destroyed.

23 The LORD makes firm the steps[q]
of the one who delights[r] in him;
24 though he may stumble, he will not fall,[s]
for the LORD upholds[t] him with his hand.

25 I was young and now I am old,
yet I have never seen the righteous forsaken[u]
or their children begging bread.
26 They are always generous and lend freely;
their children will be a blessing.[a][v]

27 Turn from evil and do good;[w]
then you will dwell in the land forever.
28 For the LORD loves the just
and will not forsake his faithful ones.

Wrongdoers will be completely destroyed[b];
the offspring of the wicked will perish.[x]
29 The righteous will inherit the land[y]
and dwell in it forever.

30 The mouths of the righteous utter wisdom,
and their tongues speak what is just.
31 The law of their God is in their hearts;[z]
their feet do not slip.[a]

32 The wicked lie in wait[b] for the righteous,
intent on putting them to death;
33 but the LORD will not leave them in the power of the wicked
or let them be condemned when brought to trial.[c]

34 Hope in the LORD[d]
and keep his way.
He will exalt you to inherit the land;
when the wicked are destroyed, you will see[e] it.

35 I have seen a wicked and ruthless man
flourishing[f] like a luxuriant native tree,
36 but he soon passed away and was no more;
though I looked for him, he could not be found.[g]

37 Consider the blameless, observe the upright;
a future awaits those who seek peace.[c][h]
38 But all sinners will be destroyed;
there will be no future[d] for the wicked.[i]

39 The salvation[j] of the righteous comes from the LORD;
he is their stronghold in time of trouble.[k]
40 The LORD helps[l] them and delivers[m] them;

37:21 [o] Ps 112:5
37:22 [p] Job 5:3; Pr 3:33
37:23 [q] 1Sa 2:9 [r] Ps 147:11
37:24 [s] Pr 24:16 [t] Ps 145:14; 147:6
37:25 [u] Heb 13:5
37:26 [v] Ps 147:13
37:27 [w] Ps 34:14
37:28 [x] Ps 21:10; Isa 14:20
37:29 [y] ver 9; Pr 2:21
37:31 [z] Dt 6:6; Ps 40:8; Isa 51:7 [a] ver 23
37:32 [b] Ps 10:8
37:33 [c] Ps 109:31; 2Pe 2:9
37:34 [d] Ps 27:14 [e] Ps 52:6
37:35 [f] Job 5:3
37:36 [g] Job 20:5
37:37 [h] Isa 57:1-2
37:38 [i] Ps 1:4
37:39 [j] Ps 3:8 [k] Ps 9:9
37:40 [l] 1Ch 5:20 [m] Isa 31:5

[a] 26 Or *freely; / the names of their children will be used in blessings* (see Gen. 48:20); or *freely; / others will see that their children are blessed* [b] 28 See Septuagint; Hebrew *They will be protected forever* [c] 37 Or *upright; / those who seek peace will have posterity* [d] 38 Or *posterity*

---

purpose is to contrast the secure future of the righteous with the certain disappearance of the wicked.

37:23–29 The psalm now moves from describing the fate of the wicked to considering the blessings of the faithful. Yahweh's protective care makes the path of the righteous sure and firm and offers help should the righteous stumble (vv. 23–24). The wicked are "completely destroyed," and the righteous will "inherit the land" (vv. 28–29).

37:30–34 An extended wisdom saying about the present reality of the righteous (vv. 30–31) is followed by a contrasting picture of the devious plots of the wicked (vv. 32–33). The psalmist exhorts the faithful to wait patiently for Yahweh while keeping "his way" (v. 34). Yahweh will act.

37:35–36 Just as the righteous and wicked occupy conflicting positions in the present, so the future holds much the same in store. The wicked that seemed rooted like a flourishing tree will suddenly, unexpectedly, disappear.

37:37–38 If the reader/listener will but "consider the blameless" and "observe the upright," they will reach the same conclusion.

37:39–40 Once again, the theme of Yahweh as refuge and "stronghold" of the righteous takes the stage. Because the body of the psalm is preoccupied with the eventual demise of the wicked, the conclusion offers a hopeful way forward.

37:1–40 The realization of this darkness without and within can tempt us to view God

he delivers them from the wicked
and saves them,
because they take refuge in him.

Psalm 38[a]

A psalm of David. A petition.

1 LORD, do not rebuke me in your
anger
or discipline me in your wrath.[n]
2 Your arrows[o] have pierced me,
and your hand has come down
on me.
3 Because of your wrath there is no
health in my body;
there is no soundness in my
bones[p] because of my sin.
4 My guilt has overwhelmed me
like a burden too heavy to bear.[q]

5 My wounds fester and are
loathsome
because of my sinful folly.[r]
6 I am bowed down and brought very
low;
all day long I go about
mourning.[s]
7 My back is filled with searing pain;[t]
there is no health in my body.
8 I am feeble and utterly crushed;
I groan[u] in anguish of heart.

9 All my longings lie open before you,
Lord;
my sighing[v] is not hidden from
you.
10 My heart pounds, my strength
fails[w] me,
even the light has gone from my
eyes.[x]

38:1 [n] Ps 6:1
38:2 [o] Job 6:4; Ps 32:4
38:3 [p] Ps 6:2; Isa 1:6
38:4 [q] Ezr 9:6
38:5 [r] Ps 69:5
38:6 [s] Job 30:28; Ps 35:14; 42:9
38:7 [t] Ps 102:3
38:8 [u] Ps 22:1
38:9 [v] Job 3:24; Ps 6:6; 10:17
38:10 [w] Ps 31:10 [x] Ps 6:7

Ps 38:5–8 ❖ Have you ever felt physically ill due to your sin? How do you find relief in God?

11 My friends and companions avoid
me because of my wounds;[y]
my neighbors stay far away.
12 Those who want to kill me set their
traps,[z]
those who would harm me talk of
my ruin;[a]
all day long they scheme and lie.[b]

13 I am like the deaf, who cannot hear,
like the mute, who cannot speak;
14 I have become like one who does not
hear,
whose mouth can offer no reply.
15 LORD, I wait[c] for you;
you will answer,[d] Lord my God.
16 For I said, "Do not let them gloat[e]
or exalt themselves over me when
my feet slip."[f]

17 For I am about to fall,
and my pain is ever with me.
18 I confess my iniquity;[g]
I am troubled by my sin.
19 Many have become my enemies[h]
without cause[b];
those who hate me without
reason[i] are numerous.
20 Those who repay my good with evil[j]
lodge accusations against me,
though I seek only to do what is
good.

38:11 [y] Ps 31:11
38:12 [z] Ps 140:5 [a] Ps 35:4; 54:3 [b] Ps 35:20
38:15 [c] Ps 39:7 [d] Ps 17:6
38:16 [e] Ps 35:26 [f] Ps 13:4
38:18 [g] Ps 32:5
38:19 [h] Ps 18:17 [i] Ps 35:19
38:20 [j] Ps 35:12; 1Jn 3:12

[a] In Hebrew texts 38:1-22 is numbered 38:2-23.
[b] *19* One Dead Sea Scrolls manuscript; Masoretic Text *my vigorous enemies*

---

as the "big fix," which can take us out of our suffering and pain. When we set aside this unrealistic view of being in relationship with God, we can, little by little, begin to experience the presence of God *within* the distorted world in which we live when God chooses not to change our circumstances.

38:1–4 The psalmist experiences physical suffering as the rebuke of Yahweh for personal sin. He does not deny the assumed accusation but freely admits his guilt (vv. 3–4).

From the psalmist's view Yahweh is acting out of "anger" and "wrath" (vv. 1, 3)—regular terms used to describe the experience of God's displeasure with human sin. However, the harshness of God's anger/wrath is mitigated as the psalmist understands it as a part of divine instruction.

The consequences of the disease are all-consuming (v. 3), presenting as inner as well as outer physical pain and deterioration. Add to this the psychological torment of "guilt" (v. 4), and the psalmist's absorption by disease is complete.
38:5–9 The afflicted psalmist's diseased body exhibits sores that emit a foul odor. The psalmist experiences searing back pain. He acknowledges the suffering results from personal sin and "folly" (v. 5), responding with mourning and repentance. The psalmist feels "feeble and utterly crushed" (vv. 8–9), responding with groans and sighs.
38:11–12 Former friends distance themselves. Opponents consider the sickness an opportunity to exploit.
38:13–20 The psalmist waits for Yahweh. The author feels at a crisis point and is wracked with pain. This sense of vulnerability and lack of control leads him at last to the full confession of sin and an expression of remorse (v. 18).

[21]LORD, do not forsake me;
do not be far[k] from me, my God.
[22]Come quickly to help me,[l]
my Lord and my Savior.[m]

Psalm 39[a]

For the director of music. For Jeduthun. A psalm of David.

[1]I said, "I will watch my ways[n]
and keep my tongue from sin;[o]
I will put a muzzle on my mouth
while in the presence of the wicked."
[2]So I remained utterly silent,[p]
not even saying anything good.
But my anguish increased;
[3] my heart grew hot within me.
While I meditated, the fire burned;
then I spoke with my tongue:

[4]"Show me, LORD, my life's end
and the number of my days;[q]
let me know how fleeting my life is.[r]
[5]You have made my days[s] a mere handbreadth;
the span of my years is as nothing before you.
Everyone is but a breath,[t]
even those who seem secure.[b]

[6]"Surely everyone goes around like a mere phantom;[u]
in vain they rush about,[v] heaping up wealth
without knowing whose it will finally be.[w]

Ps 39:4-5 ❖ Why is remembering the short number of days of this life a good discipline for growing in righteousness?

[7]"But now, Lord, what do I look for?
My hope is in you.[x]
[8]Save me[y] from all my transgressions;[z]
do not make me the scorn of fools.
[9]I was silent; I would not open my mouth,[a]
for you are the one who has done this.
[10]Remove your scourge from me;
I am overcome by the blow of your hand.[b]
[11]When you rebuke[c] and discipline anyone for their sin,
you consume their wealth like a moth[d] —
surely everyone is but a breath.

[12]"Hear my prayer, LORD,
listen to my cry for help;
do not be deaf to my weeping.
I dwell with you as a foreigner,[e]
a stranger,[f] as all my ancestors were.
[13]Look away from me, that I may enjoy life again
before I depart and am no more."[g]

38:21 [k]Ps 35:22
38:22 [l]Ps 40:13 [m]Ps 27:1
39:1 [n]1Ki 2:4 [o]Job 2:10; Jas 3:2
39:2 [p]Ps 38:13
39:4 [q]Ps 90:12 [r]Ps 103:14
39:5 [s]Ps 89:45 [t]Ps 62:9
39:6 [u]1Pe 1:24 [v]Ps 127:2 [w]Lk 12:20
39:7 [x]Ps 38:15
39:8 [y]Ps 51:9 [z]Ps 44:13
39:9 [a]Job 2:10
39:10 [b]Job 9:34; Ps 32:4
39:11 [c]2Pe 2:16 [d]Job 13:28
39:12 [e]1Pe 2:11 [f]Heb 11:13
39:13 [g]Job 10:21; 14:10

[a] In Hebrew texts 39:1-13 is numbered 39:2-14.
[b] 5 The Hebrew has *Selah* (a word of uncertain meaning) here and at the end of verse 11.

38:21–22 Nearing the end of personal resources and hope, he recognizes that Yahweh is synonymous with salvation.

✣ **38:1–22** Often Christian leaders enmeshed in moral failures feel unable to confess their sin or to seek help, pursuing radical means of covering their sin rather than confession. This psalm helps us to see that acknowledging sin is the only way out of this trap of fear and destruction.

39:1–3 It is difficult to know what words might be considered "sin" (v. 1). The key may be v. 2, where the psalmist says that silence only increased his anguish. In this event the speech he "muzzles" would be a bitter complaint against the "wicked" (v. 1). The struggle is between verbally assaulting the wicked or speaking something "good" (v. 2). The inner turmoil ultimately forces him to break his self-imposed silence with the "good" word.
39:4–6 Rather than complaining, the psalmist offers a meditation on human frailty. The psalmist wishes to know the "end" of his life and the "number" of his days (v. 4) to gain an appropriate appreciation for the fragile nature of human existence.
39:7–11 The psalmist finds hope for deliverance in Yahweh. Deliverance comes through confession of sin; the psalmist acknowledges that the suffering endured is from God and is intended as "rebuke and discipline" (v. 11).
39:12–13 The psalmist concludes with a final plea to Yahweh for deliverance. Unless Yahweh relents and ends the punishment, he has no hope but to depart and be no more.

✣ **39:1–13** Meditative silence can allow us time to reflect on the real reasons behind our anger and pain. It's good to reflect on these root causes before our lashing out jeopardizes relationships by distorting and confusing the real issues involved.

Psalm 40[a]

40:13–17pp // Ps 70:1–5

For the director of music. Of David. A psalm.

1 I waited patiently[h] for the LORD;
he turned to me and heard my cry.[i]
2 He lifted me out of the slimy pit,
out of the mud and mire;[j]
he set my feet on a rock[k]
and gave me a firm place to stand.
3 He put a new song[l] in my mouth,
a hymn of praise to our God.
Many will see and fear the LORD
and put their trust in him.

4 Blessed is the one[m]
who trusts in the LORD,[n]
who does not look to the proud,
to those who turn aside to false gods.[b]
5 Many, LORD my God,
are the wonders[o] you have done,
the things you planned for us.
None can compare[p] with you;
were I to speak and tell of your deeds,
they would be too many to declare.

6 Sacrifice and offering you did not desire —[q]
but my ears you have opened[c] —
burnt offerings[r] and sin offerings[d] you did not require.
7 Then I said, "Here I am, I have come —
it is written about me in the scroll.[e]
8 I desire to do your will,[s] my God;
your law is within my heart."[t]

9 I proclaim your saving acts in the great assembly;[u]
I do not seal my lips, LORD,
as you know.[v]
10 I do not hide your righteousness in my heart;
I speak of your faithfulness[w] and your saving help.
I do not conceal your love and your faithfulness
from the great assembly.[x]

11 Do not withhold your mercy from me, LORD;
may your love[y] and faithfulness[z] always protect me.
12 For troubles[a] without number surround me;
my sins have overtaken me, and I cannot see.[b]
They are more than the hairs of my head,[c]
and my heart fails[d] within me.
13 Be pleased to save me, LORD;

40:1 [h] Ps 27:14 [i] Ps 34:15 **40:2** [j] Ps 69:14 [k] Ps 27:5 **40:3** [l] Ps 33:3 **40:4** [m] Ps 34:8 [n] Ps 84:12 **40:5** [o] Ps 136:4 [p] Ps 139:18; Isa 55:8 **40:6** [q] 1Sa 15:22; Am 5:22 [r] Isa 1:11 **40:8** [s] Jn 4:34 [t] Ps 37:31 **40:9** [u] Ps 22:25 [v] Jos 22:22; Ps 119:13 **40:10** [w] Ps 89:1 [x] Ac 20:20 **40:11** [y] Pr 20:28 [z] Ps 43:3 **40:12** [a] Ps 116:3 [b] Ps 38:4 [c] Ps 69:4 [d] Ps 73:26

[a] In Hebrew texts 40:1-17 is numbered 40:2-18. [b] 4 Or *to lies* [c] 6 Hebrew; some Septuagint manuscripts *but a body you have prepared for me* [d] 6 Or *purification offerings* [e] 7 Or *come / with the scroll written for me*

Ps 40:9–10 ❖ Where do we have the opportunity to boldly proclaim God's saving acts and righteousness? Why should God's children do this?

40:1–4 The purpose of the "new song" (v. 3) is testimony. It will draw others to "fear" Yahweh. In our passage, the positive content of fearing Yahweh is put forward as "trust" in him (v. 3) and is clarified further by the blessing in v. 4.

40:5–10 In this new section the psalmist testifies to the "wonders" Yahweh has done (vv. 5–6) and declares personal loyalty to him (vv. 7–10). Verses 6–8 may refer only to the specific experience of the psalmist. In this case the psalmist is testifying that rather than demanding gifts and sacrifices as payment for the psalmist's sin, what Yahweh really wanted was the "opened" (v. 6) ears of the psalmist and a heart willing to allow the Torah ("law," v. 8) to guide it.

40:11–12 After establishing a foundation of personal faithfulness, the psalmist appeals to Yahweh for mercy. Isolated and desperate, the psalmist is on the brink of losing all hope ("my heart fails," v. 12).

40:13–17 Verses 13–17 bring Ps 40 to a conclusion in an unexpected fashion. The earlier part of the psalm was directed to the psalmist's testimony to the faithfulness of God and desire for deliverance. These final verses, which essentially repeat the entirety of Ps 70, focus on the psalmist's enemies. The one link with the earlier portion of Ps 40 is the continuing theme of trusting Yahweh.

40:1–17 Our communities of worship and faith must take care that the important role of confession as a means of proclaiming God's righteousness, truth, and salvation does not become the exclusive domain of twelve-step programs and other psychological support groups, as effective as those may be. Confession always has been and always will be a critical part of communal worship in the church.

come quickly, LORD, to
help me.[e]

14 May all who want to take my life
be put to shame and confusion;
may all who desire my ruin[f]
be turned back in disgrace.
15 May those who say to me, "Aha!
Aha!"
be appalled at their own
shame.
16 But may all who seek you
rejoice and be glad in you;
may those who long for your saving
help always say,
"The LORD is great!"[g]

17 But as for me, I am poor and
needy;
may the Lord think of me.
You are my help and my deliverer;
you are my God, do not delay.[h]

Psalm 41[a]

For the director of music.
A psalm of David.

1 Blessed are those who have regard
for the weak;[i]
the LORD delivers them in times of
trouble.
2 The LORD protects and preserves
them —
they are counted among the
blessed in the land —[j]
he does not give them over to the
desire of their foes.[k]
3 The LORD sustains them on their
sickbed
and restores them from their bed
of illness.

4 I said, "Have mercy[l] on me, LORD;
heal me, for I have sinned[m]
against you."
5 My enemies say of me in malice,

40:13 [e] Ps 70:1
40:14 [f] Ps 35:4
40:16 [g] Ps 35:27
40:17 [h] Ps 70:5
41:1 [i] Ps 82:3-4; Pr 14:21
41:2 [j] Ps 37:22 [k] Ps 27:12
41:4 [l] Ps 6:2 [m] Ps 51:4

Ps 41:9 ❖ How does God sustain us when we have been betrayed by someone close to us?

"When will he die and his name
perish?[n]"
6 When one of them comes to
see me,
he speaks falsely,[o] while his heart
gathers slander;[p]
then he goes out and spreads it
around.

7 All my enemies whisper together[q]
against me;
they imagine the worst for me,
saying,
8 "A vile disease has afflicted him;
he will never get up from the
place where he lies."
9 Even my close friend,[r]
someone I trusted,
one who shared my bread,
has turned[b] against me.[s]

10 But may you have mercy on me,
LORD;
raise me up,[t] that I may repay
them.
11 I know that you are pleased
with me,[u]
for my enemy does not triumph
over me.[v]
12 Because of my integrity you
uphold me[w]
and set me in your presence
forever.[x]

13 Praise be to the LORD, the God of
Israel,[y]
from everlasting to everlasting.
Amen and Amen.[z]

41:5 [n] Ps 38:12
41:6 [o] Ps 12:2 [p] Pr 26:24
41:7 [q] Ps 56:5; 71:10-11
41:9 [r] 2Sa 15:12; Ps 55:12 [s] Job 19:19; Ps 55:20; Mt 26:23; Jn 13:18*
41:10 [t] Ps 3:3
41:11 [u] Ps 147:11 [v] Ps 25:2
41:12 [w] Ps 37:17 [x] Job 36:7
41:13 [y] Ps 72:18 [z] Ps 89:52; 106:48

[a] In Hebrew texts 41:1-13 is numbered 41:2-14.
[b] 9 Hebrew *has lifted up his heel*

41:1-3 Those who know how to care appropriately for the weak can anticipate appropriate treatment from Yahweh when weakness overtakes them.
41:4-9 Two stanzas of three verses each expound the malice of the psalmist's enemies (vv. 5-6) and friends (v. 9), who speak false cheer to the patient, spread groundless rumors, and plot together to take advantage of the situation. The section is introduced by the psalmist's confession of sin and a plea to Yahweh for mercy.
41:10-12 The psalmist's hope is not only for forgiveness and restored health but also for justice.
41:13 Verse 13 presents the first of four similar doxologies. These mark the conclusion of the first four books of the Psalter. This verse marks the end of the first Davidic collection of psalms (Ps 3-41).

✣ **41:1-13** Psalm 41 offers insight into the kind of integrity that leads to being upheld by God. This kind of integrity is a consistent way of acting that has its beginning and end in God. There may be individual stumbles along the way, but the person of integrity is the one whose eyes remain firmly fixed on the goal.

BOOK II

Psalms 42–72

Psalm 42[a,b]

For the director of music. A maskil[c] of the Sons of Korah.

1 As the deer pants for streams of
water,
so my soul pants[a] for you, my
God.
2 My soul thirsts[b] for God, for the
living God.[c]
When can I go[d] and meet with
God?
3 My tears[e] have been my food
day and night,
while people say to me all day long,
"Where is your God?"[f]
4 These things I remember
as I pour out my soul:
how I used to go to the house of
God[g]
under the protection of the
Mighty One[d]
with shouts of joy and praise[h]
among the festive throng.

5 Why, my soul, are you downcast?[i]
Why so disturbed within me?
Put your hope in God,[j]
for I will yet praise him,
my Savior[k] and my God.

6 My soul is downcast within me;
therefore I will remember you
from the land of the Jordan,
the heights of Hermon—from
Mount Mizar.
7 Deep calls to deep
in the roar of your waterfalls;
all your waves and breakers
have swept over me.[l]

42:1 [a] Ps 119:131
42:2 [b] Ps 63:1 [c] Jer 10:10 [d] Ps 43:4
42:3 [e] Ps 80:5 [f] Ps 79:10
42:4 [g] Isa 30:29 [h] Ps 100:4
42:5 [i] Ps 38:6; 77:3 [j] La 3:24 [k] Ps 44:3
42:7 [l] Ps 88:7; Jnh 2:3
42:8 [m] Ps 57:3 [n] Job 35:10 [o] Ps 63:6; 149:5
42:9 [p] Ps 38:6
42:11 [q] Ps 43:5
43:1 [r] 1Sa 24:15; Ps 26:1; 35:1 [s] Ps 5:6
43:2 [t] Ps 44:9 [u] Ps 42:9

Ps 42:11 ❖ How can we find hope in God when our souls are downcast?

Ps 43:1 ❖ What prayers of intercession can we raise to God when our nation is unfaithful?

8 By day the LORD directs his
love,[m]
at night[n] his song[o] is with me—
a prayer to the God of my life.

9 I say to God my Rock,
"Why have you forgotten me?
Why must I go about mourning,[p]
oppressed by the enemy?"
10 My bones suffer mortal agony
as my foes taunt me,
saying to me all day long,
"Where is your God?"

11 Why, my soul, are you downcast?
Why so disturbed within me?
Put your hope in God,
for I will yet praise him,
my Savior and my God.[q]

Psalm 43[a]

1 Vindicate me, my God,
and plead my cause[r]
against an unfaithful nation.
Rescue me from those who are
deceitful and wicked.[s]
2 You are God my stronghold.
Why have you rejected[t] me?
Why must I go about mourning,
oppressed by the enemy?[u]

[a] In many Hebrew manuscripts Psalms 42 and 43 constitute one psalm. [b] In Hebrew texts 42:1-11 is numbered 42:2-12. [c] Title: Probably a literary or musical term [d] 4 See Septuagint and Syriac; the meaning of the Hebrew for this line is uncertain.

42:1-5 Psalms 42 and 43 should be read as a unified composition. Few images in the Psalter exceed the beauty of the opening lines of Ps 42. The emphasis is the pleasure of being in God's presence which the psalmist misses and longs to restore.
42:6-11 The psalmist acknowledges his "soul is downcast" (v. 6a). Immediately, he enters a new terrain of hope (v. 6b). He now remembers the living God, the source of life and hope. God is the "Rock" (v. 9) who provides firm footing and protection.
43:1-5 The first two pleas express the desire that the psalmist's hope and faith in God will be rewarded and publicly acknowledged. The poet pictures himself enthusiastically praising God to the tune of the harp.

42:1—43:5 The psalmist suggests another way to remember God's faithfulness: discover opportunities to worship God with others. Even if we feel distant or abandoned, the communal celebration will have the effect of renewing our certainty and hope. One of the roles of the worshiping congregation is to worship when others cannot, to celebrate the resurrection of Christ when others are mourning the death of a loved one or struggling with their own sin. The congregation is to declare the wonderful works of God even when other individuals can no longer see him or sense his presence, thereby encouraging the one experiencing difficulty.

3 Send me your light[v] and your
faithful care,
let them lead me;
let them bring me to your holy
mountain,[w]
to the place where you dwell.[x]
4 Then I will go to the altar[y] of God,
to God, my joy and my delight.
I will praise you with the lyre,[z]
O God, my God.

5 Why, my soul, are you downcast?
Why so disturbed within me?
Put your hope in God,
for I will yet praise him,
my Savior and my God.[a]

Psalm 44[a]

For the director of music. Of the Sons of Korah. A maskil.[b]

1 We have heard it with our ears, O God;
our ancestors have told us[b]
what you did in their days,
in days long ago.
2 With your hand you drove out[c] the
nations
and planted[d] our ancestors;
you crushed the peoples
and made our ancestors flourish.[e]
3 It was not by their sword[f] that they
won the land,
nor did their arm bring them
victory;
it was your right hand, your arm,[g]
and the light of your face, for you
loved[h] them.

4 You are my King[i] and my God,
who decrees[c] victories for Jacob.
5 Through you we push back our
enemies;
through your name we trample[j]
our foes.
6 I put no trust in my bow,[k]
my sword does not bring me
victory;
7 but you give us victory[l] over our
enemies,
you put our adversaries to
shame.[m]
8 In God we make our boast[n] all day
long,
and we will praise your name
forever.[d][o]

9 But now you have rejected[p] and
humbled us;
you no longer go out with our
armies.[q]
10 You made us retreat[r] before the
enemy,
and our adversaries have
plundered us.
11 You gave us up to be devoured like
sheep[s]
and have scattered us among the
nations.[t]
12 You sold your people for a pittance,[u]
gaining nothing from their sale.

13 You have made us a reproach to our
neighbors,[v]
the scorn[w] and derision of those
around us.
14 You have made us a byword among
the nations;
the peoples shake their heads[x]
at us.
15 I live in disgrace all day long,
and my face is covered with
shame
16 at the taunts of those who reproach
and revile[y] me,
because of the enemy, who is bent
on revenge.

17 All this came upon us,
though we had not forgotten[z] you;

43:3 [v] Ps 36:9 [w] Ps 42:4 [x] Ps 84:1
43:4 [y] Ps 26:6 [z] Ps 33:2
43:5 [a] Ps 42:6
44:1 [b] Ex 12:26; Ps 78:3
44:2 [c] Ps 78:55 [d] Ex 15:17 [e] Ps 80:9
44:3 [f] Dt 8:17; Jos 24:12 [g] Ps 77:15 [h] Dt 4:37; 7:7-8
44:4 [i] Ps 74:12
44:5 [j] Ps 108:13
44:6 [k] Ps 33:16
44:7 [l] Ps 136:24 [m] Ps 53:5
44:8 [n] Ps 34:2 [o] Ps 30:12
44:9 [p] Ps 74:1 [q] Ps 60:1,10
44:10 [r] Lev 26:17; Jos 7:8; Ps 89:41
44:11 [s] Ro 8:36 [t] Dt 4:27; 28:64; Ps 106:27
44:12 [u] Isa 52:3; Jer 15:13
44:13 [v] Ps 79:4; 80:6 [w] Dt 28:37
44:14 [x] Ps 109:25; Jer 24:9
44:16 [y] Ps 74:10
44:17 [z] Ps 78:7, 57; Da 9:13

[a] In Hebrew texts 44:1-26 is numbered 44:2-27.
[b] Title: Probably a literary or musical term
[c] 4 Septuagint, Aquila and Syriac; Hebrew *King, O God; / command*
[d] 8 The Hebrew has *Selah* (a word of uncertain meaning) here.

44:1–3 The psalmist describes how the history of God's activity with the ancestors of the faith provides the foundation of confidence to present believers.

44:4–8 Faced with suffering, the people *remember* past evidence of Yahweh's good intent and powerful action. The single voice may well be the king; he acknowledges that human rulers must submit to God's ultimate sovereignty. The singular voice reappears again and again in what follows (cf. vv. 6, 15–16), leading the people to recognize their dependence on the gracious mercy of God.

44:9–16 Israel's experience did not live up to their expectations. Victory eluded them, and the reality of defeat took its place. The description suggests severe destruction, societal dislocation, and even deportation (v. 11). The psalm would have resonated with the Diaspora community—ethnic Jews scattered throughout the nations.

The emphatic litany of "You" in vv. 9–14 is directed to God. The embarrassing words of shame and disgrace pile up like a monument of stones intended to mark the scene of some infamous event.

44:17–22 The new departure in this segment is

we had not been false to your
covenant.
18 Our hearts had not turned[a] back;
our feet had not strayed from your
path.
19 But you crushed[b] us and made us a
haunt for jackals;
you covered us over with deep
darkness.[c]

20 If we had forgotten[d] the name of our
God
or spread out our hands to a
foreign god,[e]
21 would not God have discovered it,
since he knows the secrets of the
heart?[f]
22 Yet for your sake we face death all
day long;
we are considered as sheep to be
slaughtered.[g]

23 Awake,[h] Lord! Why do you sleep?[i]
Rouse yourself! Do not reject us
forever.[j]
24 Why do you hide your face[k]
and forget our misery and
oppression?[l]

25 We are brought down to the dust;[m]
our bodies cling to the ground.
26 Rise up[n] and help us;
rescue[o] us because of your
unfailing love.

Psalm 45[a]

For the director of music. To the tune of "Lilies." Of the Sons of Korah. A maskil.[b] A wedding song.

1 My heart is stirred by a noble
theme
as I recite my verses for the king;
my tongue is the pen of a skillful
writer.

44:18 [a] Job 23:11
44:19 [b] Ps 51:8 [c] Job 3:5
44:20 [d] Ps 78:11 [e] Dt 6:14; Ps 81:9
44:21 [f] Ps 139:1-2; Jer 17:10
44:22 [g] Isa 53:7; Ro 8:36*
44:23 [h] Ps 7:6 [i] Ps 78:65 [j] Ps 77:7
44:24 [k] Job 13:24 [l] Ps 42:9
44:25 [m] Ps 119:25
44:26 [n] Ps 35:2 [o] Ps 25:22
45:2 [p] Lk 4:22
45:3 [q] Heb 4:12; Rev 1:16 [r] Isa 9:6
45:4 [s] Rev 6:2
45:6 [t] Ps 93:2; 98:9
45:7 [u] Ps 33:5 [v] Isa 61:1 [w] Ps 21:6; Heb 1:8-9*
45:8 [x] SS 1:3

Ps 44:23–24 ❖ Why does it sometimes feel as though God is distant or sleeping? How can we find hope in such times (see 121:3–4)?

2 You are the most excellent of men
and your lips have been anointed
with grace,[p]
since God has blessed you forever.

3 Gird your sword[q] on your side, you
mighty one;[r]
clothe yourself with splendor and
majesty.
4 In your majesty ride forth
victoriously[s]
in the cause of truth, humility and
justice;
let your right hand achieve
awesome deeds.
5 Let your sharp arrows pierce the
hearts of the king's enemies;
let the nations fall beneath your
feet.
6 Your throne, O God,[c] will last for ever
and ever;[t]
a scepter of justice will be the
scepter of your kingdom.
7 You love righteousness[u] and hate
wickedness;
therefore God, your God, has set
you above your companions
by anointing[v] you with the oil of
joy.[w]
8 All your robes are fragrant[x] with
myrrh and aloes and cassia;
from palaces adorned with ivory
the music of the strings makes
you glad.

[a] In Hebrew texts 45:1-17 is numbered 45:2-18.
[b] Title: Probably a literary or musical term
[c] 6 Here the king is addressed as God's representative.

---

not that Israel suffers defeat and exile. It is not even that the exile is attributed to God. Where Ps 44 departs is in the community's earnest assertion that they are innocent of any guilt that might justify exile.
44:23–26 With typical language intended to rouse the hearer to action, the beleaguered community makes its desire for deliverance known.

✣ **44:1–26** The community's protest is no claim of complete sinlessness but a claim to have fulfilled their essential obligations to the covenant. Most of us would have to admit that accepting the sacrificial death of Christ as Savior has not yet perfectly removed all our tendencies toward selfishness, anger, lust, greed, and other more subtle forms of sin. Our moments of weakness and failure, while serious in their own right and in need of repentance and confession, do not drive an irreparable wedge between us and God.

45:1 Perhaps the king is the poet's patron who has commissioned this poem for his wedding day.
45:2–9 The psalmist praises the king and encourages him to exercise his power in the service of "truth, humility and justice" (v. 4). The anticipated result of this display of kingly power is the defeat of his enemies and the establishment of an eternal kingdom of justice and peace.

9 Daughters of kings[y] are among your honored women;
at your right hand[z] is the royal bride in gold of Ophir.

10 Listen, daughter, and pay careful attention:
Forget your people[a] and your father's house.
11 Let the king be enthralled by your beauty;
honor[b] him, for he is your lord.[c]
12 The city of Tyre will come with a gift,[a][d]
people of wealth will seek your favor.
13 All glorious[e] is the princess within her chamber;
her gown is interwoven with gold.
14 In embroidered garments she is led to the king;[f]
her virgin companions follow her—
those brought to be with her.
15 Led in with joy and gladness,
they enter the palace of the king.

16 Your sons will take the place of your fathers;
you will make them princes throughout the land.

17 I will perpetuate your memory through all generations;[g]
therefore the nations will praise you[h] for ever and ever.

Psalm 46[b]

For the director of music. Of the Sons of Korah. According to alamoth.[c] *A song.*

1 God is our refuge[i] and strength,
an ever-present[j] help in trouble.
2 Therefore we will not fear,[k] though the earth give way[l]
and the mountains fall[m] into the heart of the sea,
3 though its waters roar[n] and foam
and the mountains quake with their surging.[d]

4 There is a river whose streams make glad the city of God,[o]
the holy place where the Most High dwells.
5 God is within her,[p] she will not fall;
God will help[q] her at break of day.
6 Nations[r] are in uproar, kingdoms[s] fall;
he lifts his voice, the earth melts.[t]

7 The LORD Almighty is with us;[u]
the God of Jacob is our fortress.[v]

8 Come and see what the LORD has done,[w]
the desolations[x] he has brought on the earth.
9 He makes wars[y] cease
to the ends of the earth.
He breaks the bow[z] and shatters the spear;

45:9 [y] SS 6:8 [z] 1Ki 2:19 45:10 [a] Dt 21:13 45:11 [b] Ps 95:6 [c] Isa 54:5 45:12 [d] Ps 22:29; Isa 49:23 45:13 [e] Isa 61:10 45:14 [f] SS 1:4 45:17 [g] Mal 1:11 [h] Ps 138:4 46:1 [i] Ps 9:9; 14:6 [j] Dt 4:7 46:2 [k] Ps 23:4 [l] Ps 82:5 [m] Ps 18:7 46:3 [n] Ps 93:3 46:4 [o] Ps 48:1, 8; Isa 60:14 46:5 [p] Isa 12:6; Eze 43:7 [q] Ps 37:40 46:6 [r] Ps 2:1 [s] Ps 68:32 [t] Mic 1:4 46:7 [u] 2Ch 13:12 [v] Ps 9:9 46:8 [w] Ps 66:5 [x] Isa 61:4 46:9 [y] Isa 2:4 [z] Ps 76:3

[a] 12 Or *A Tyrian robe is among the gifts* [b] In Hebrew texts 46:1-11 is numbered 46:2-12. [c] Title: Probably a musical term [d] 3 The Hebrew has *Selah* (a word of uncertain meaning) here and at the end of verses 7 and 11.

Ps 45:17 ❖ What opportunities do we have to share God's mighty acts with the next generation?

Ps 46:9-10 ❖ How can we find space in the busyness of life to "be still" (v. 10) and meditate on God's power and presence?

45:10-15 The bride is depicted as a "daughter" (v. 10) who forsakes her people to become the king's wife. The king craves the bride's "beauty" (v. 11a), while the bride is counseled to "honor" the king because he is her "lord" (v. 11b). This rather one-sided relationship is consistent with what is known of the ancient Near East during this period.
45:16-17 Besides the possibility of political alliance, the marriage represents the potential for dynastic succession through sons. This description assumes a long line of royal family that preceded the present king.

✣ **45:1-17** The ambiguous statement in v. 6, "Your throne, O God, will last for ever and ever," seems to equate the bridegroom king with God himself. This ambiguous statement allows the possibility that the king, who appears here to be called "God," is in fact being understood as the Messiah who will usher in God's kingdom. If so, then the marriage ceremony may well already be understood as between Messiah and the people of God, as in the later understanding of this psalm.

46:1-3 The radical confidence of the psalmist is exhibited in an ability to stand without fear in the face of what constitutes a threat of massive natural upheaval (cf. Ge 6–9).
46:4-7 Rather than destruction, this river offers rejoicing. Unlike the mountains in v. 2, the city of God "will not fall" (v. 5).
46:8-11 The invitation to "come and see what the LORD has done" (v. 8) introduces a series of parallel

he burns the shields[a] with fire.[a]
10 He says, "Be still, and know that I am
God;[b]
I will be exalted[c] among the
nations,
I will be exalted in the earth."
11 The LORD Almighty is with us;
the God of Jacob is our fortress.

Psalm 47[b]

For the director of music. Of the Sons of Korah. A psalm.

1 Clap your hands,[d] all you nations;
shout to God with cries of joy.[e]

2 For the LORD Most High is awesome,[f]
the great King[g] over all the earth.
3 He subdued[h] nations under us,
peoples under our feet.
4 He chose our inheritance[i] for us,
the pride of Jacob, whom he loved.[c]

5 God has ascended amid shouts of joy,
the LORD amid the sounding of
trumpets.[j]
6 Sing praises[k] to God, sing praises;
sing praises to our King, sing
praises.
7 For God is the King of all the earth;[l]
sing to him a psalm[m] of praise.

8 God reigns[n] over the nations;
God is seated on his holy throne.
9 The nobles of the nations assemble
as the people of the God of
Abraham,
for the kings[d] of the earth belong to
God;[o]
he is greatly exalted.[p]

46:9 [a] Eze 39:9
46:10 [b] Ps 100:3 [c] Isa 2:11
47:1 [d] Ps 98:8; Isa 55:12 [e] Ps 106:47
47:2 [f] Dt 7:21 [g] Mal 1:14
47:3 [h] Ps 18:39, 47
47:4 [i] 1Pe 1:4
47:5 [j] Ps 68:33; 98:6
47:6 [k] Ps 68:4; 89:18
47:7 [l] Zec 14:9 [m] Col 3:16
47:8 [n] 1Ch 16:31
47:9 [o] Ps 72:11; 89:18 [p] Ps 97:9

Ps 47:5–7 ❖ In what ways can we as believers today integrate this kind of praise into our daily lives?

Psalm 48[e]

A song. A psalm of the Sons of Korah.

1 Great is the LORD,[q] and most worthy
of praise,
in the city of our God,[r] his holy
mountain.[s]

2 Beautiful[t] in its loftiness,
the joy of the whole earth,
like the heights of Zaphon[f] is Mount
Zion,
the city of the Great King.[u]
3 God is in her citadels;
he has shown himself to be her
fortress.[v]

4 When the kings joined forces,
when they advanced together,[w]
5 they saw her and were astounded;
they fled in terror.[x]
6 Trembling seized them there,
pain like that of a woman in
labor.
7 You destroyed them like ships of
Tarshish
shattered by an east wind.[y]

8 As we have heard,
so we have seen

48:1 [q] Ps 96:4 [r] Ps 46:4 [s] Isa 2:2-3; Mic 4:1; Zec 8:3
48:2 [t] Ps 50:2; La 2:15 [u] Mt 5:35
48:3 [v] Ps 46:7
48:4 [w] 2Sa 10:1-19
48:5 [x] Ex 15:16
48:7 [y] Jer 18:17; Eze 27:26

[a] 9 Or *chariots* [b] In Hebrew texts 47:1-9 is numbered 47:2-10. [c] 4 The Hebrew has *Selah* (a word of uncertain meaning) here. [d] 9 Or *shields* [e] In Hebrew texts 48:1-14 is numbered 48:2-15. [f] 2 *Zaphon* was the most sacred mountain of the Canaanites.

---

lines describing militant actions. These works of God are warnings to those who want to rule the earth with military might.

46:1–11 When we participate in war, justified as it may be, we are not participating in what God intended for his creation; rather, we're involved in something that grew out of human sin and disobedience. We are not even participating in something that will last—wars will eventually cease to the ends of the earth—and we thank God for that.

47:1–4 The Hebrew expression translated "clap the hands . . . of joy" (v. 1) may mean "strike hands" as confirmation of a bargain or contract. The "nations" (v. 1) are being called to come to an agreement regarding their relationship to Yahweh, God of Israel.
47:5–9 The second stanza focuses on Yahweh's kingship. This is reiterated three times (vv. 6b, 7a, 8a) and mentions his enthronement as well (v. 8b). The kings of the earth in their submission to Yahweh have become his possession (v. 9), and there are no longer any who compete with the divine authority of Yahweh as King.

47:1–9 God's purposes move unhindered to their completion despite the chaotic brokenness of our world. God subdues the nations and provides Israel with their true inheritance.

48:1–3 The psalm begins typically for a song in praise of Yahweh, focusing on the city/mountain where Yahweh makes himself present.
48:4–7 The opposing kings join forces for a combined attack (v. 4) reminiscent of 2:2. The response of the enemy to what they see is described in a series of verbs and expressions indicating astonishment and terror. The result is destruction.
48:8 The enemy hosts look on Mount Zion, tremble,

in the city of the LORD Almighty,
in the city of our God:
God makes her secure
forever.[a][z]

9 Within your temple, O God,
we meditate on your unfailing
love.[a]
10 Like your name,[b] O God,
your praise reaches to the ends of
the earth;[c]
your right hand is filled with
righteousness.
11 Mount Zion rejoices,
the villages of Judah are glad
because of your judgments.[d]

12 Walk about Zion, go around her,
count her towers,
13 consider well her ramparts,
view her citadels,[e]
that you may tell of them
to the next generation.[f]

14 For this God is our God for ever and
ever;
he will be our guide[g] even to the
end.

Psalm 49[b]

For the director of music. Of the Sons of Korah. A psalm.

1 Hear this, all you peoples;[h]
listen, all who live in this
world,[i]
2 both low and high,
rich and poor alike:
3 My mouth will speak words of
wisdom;[j]
the meditation of my heart will
give you understanding.[k]
4 I will turn my ear to a proverb;[l]
with the harp I will expound my
riddle:[m]

5 Why should I fear[n] when evil days
come,
when wicked deceivers surround
me —
6 those who trust in their wealth[o]
and boast of their great riches?
7 No one can redeem the life of
another
or give to God a ransom for
them —
8 the ransom for a life is costly,
no payment is ever enough — [p]
9 so that they should live on[q]
forever
and not see decay.
10 For all can see that the wise die,[r]
that the foolish and the senseless
also perish,
leaving their wealth to others.[s]
11 Their tombs will remain their
houses[c] forever,
their dwellings for endless
generations,
though they had[d] named[t] lands
after themselves.

12 People, despite their wealth, do not
endure;

48:8 [z] Ps 87:5
48:9 [a] Ps 26:3
48:10 [b] Dt 28:58; Jos 7:9 [c] Isa 41:10
48:11 [d] Ps 97:8
48:13 [e] ver 3; Ps 122:7 [f] Ps 78:6
48:14 [g] Ps 23:4
49:1 [h] Ps 78:1 [i] Ps 33:8
49:3 [j] Ps 37:30 [k] Ps 119:130
49:4 [l] Ps 78:2 [m] Nu 12:8
49:5 [n] Ps 23:4
49:6 [o] Job 31:24
49:8 [p] Mt 16:26
49:9 [q] Ps 22:29; 89:48
49:10 [r] Ecc 2:16 [s] Ecc 2:18,21
49:11 [t] Ge 4:17; Dt 3:14

Ps 48:9 ❖ Do you spend time meditating on God's love? What does God's love mean to us as believers (see 1Jn 4:10)?

[a] 8 The Hebrew has *Selah* (a word of uncertain meaning) here. [b] In Hebrew texts 49:1-20 is numbered 49:2-21. [c] *11* Septuagint and Syriac; Hebrew *In their thoughts their houses will remain* [d] *11* Or *generations, / for they have*

---

and flee to their destruction (vv. 5–7). By contrast, the psalmist and his readers look at the "city of our God" (v. 8) and find enduring security.
48:9–11 The emphasis here is on the temple as God's home—where he is present among his people as King. Because of Yahweh's righteous judgments, Israel rejoices.
48:12–14 The psalm concludes with a mental tour of the defensive structures of Zion. Yahweh is the eternal God who protects and guides his people like a shepherd.

✣ **48:1–14** No matter how impressive our battle works, they are an empty hope to defend us unless God is there.

49:1–4 The psalmist begins with a pluralized form of the classic opening to the Shema—Israel's call to faith—"Hear!" Those called to hear are also described as those "who live in this world" (v. 1b). The emphasis is on those who live in this transitory age. Since the heart is the seat of moral reasoning and decision-making, such "heart talk" represents the deep outflow of the speaker's moral character.
49:5–12 The prosperity of the wicked does not undermine the psalmist's confidence in God's good intent for the righteous. He acknowledges the reality of "evil days" (v. 5a) and "wicked deceivers" (v. 5b) who use wealth to oppress the poor.
49:11 The naming of lands after oneself was a choice normally reserved for conquering kings. Here the rich practice the naming of lands in a vain attempt to ensure some immortality for themselves.

they are like the beasts that
perish.
[13]This is the fate of those who trust in
themselves,[u]
and of their followers, who
approve their sayings.[a]
[14]They are like sheep and are destined
to die;[v]
death will be their shepherd
(but the upright will prevail[w] over
them in the morning).
Their forms will decay in the grave,
far from their princely mansions.
[15]But God will redeem me from the
realm of the dead;[x]
he will surely take me to himself.[y]
[16]Do not be overawed when others
grow rich,
when the splendor of their houses
increases;
[17]for they will take nothing with them
when they die,
their splendor will not descend
with them.[z]
[18]Though while they live they count
themselves blessed — [a]
and people praise you when you
prosper —
[19]they will join those who have gone
before them,[b]
who will never again see the light[c]
of life.
[20]People who have wealth but lack
understanding
are like the beasts that perish.[d]

Psalm 50

A psalm of Asaph.

[1]The Mighty One, God, the LORD,[e]
speaks and summons the earth
from the rising of the sun to
where it sets.[f]
[2]From Zion, perfect in beauty,[g]
God shines forth.[h]
[3]Our God comes[i]
and will not be silent;
a fire devours before him,[j]
and around him a tempest rages.
[4]He summons the heavens above,
and the earth,[k] that he may judge
his people:
[5]"Gather to me this consecrated
people,[l]
who made a covenant[m] with me
by sacrifice."
[6]And the heavens proclaim[n] his
righteousness,
for he is a God of justice.[b,c,o]
[7]"Listen, my people, and I will speak;
I will testify[p] against you, Israel:
I am God, your God.[q]
[8]I bring no charges against you
concerning your sacrifices
or concerning your burnt
offerings,[r] which are ever
before me.
[9]I have no need of a bull[s] from your
stall
or of goats from your pens,
[10]for every animal of the forest is mine,
and the cattle on a thousand hills.[t]

Ps 49:13 ❖ How does God give us hope beyond death? How does this hope shape the way we live?

49:13 [u] Lk 12:20 **49:14** [v] Job 24:19; Ps 9:17 [w] Da 7:18; Mal 4:3; 1Co 6:2; Rev 2:26 **49:15** [x] Ps 56:13; Hos 13:14 [y] Ps 73:24 **49:17** [z] Ps 17:14; 1Ti 6:7 **49:18** [a] Dt 29:19; Lk 12:19 **49:19** [b] Ge 15:15 [c] Job 33:30 **49:20** [d] Ecc 3:19 **50:1** [e] Jos 22:22 [f] Ps 113:3 **50:2** [g] Ps 48:2 [h] Dt 33:2; Ps 80:1 **50:3** [i] Ps 96:13 [j] Ps 97:3; Da 7:10 **50:4** [k] Dt 4:26; Isa 1:2 **50:5** [l] Ps 30:4 [m] Ex 24:7 **50:6** [n] Ps 89:5 [o] Ps 75:7 **50:7** [p] Ps 81:8 [q] Ex 20:2 **50:8** [r] Ps 40:6; Hos 6:6 **50:9** [s] Ps 69:31 **50:10** [t] Ps 104:24

[a] *13* The Hebrew has *Selah* (a word of uncertain meaning) here and at the end of verse 15.
[b] *6* With a different word division of the Hebrew; Masoretic Text *for God himself is judge*
[c] *6* The Hebrew has *Selah* (a word of uncertain meaning) here.

49:13–20 The attitude of self-reliance that refuses to acknowledge dependence on Yahweh alone is the real issue. Accepting one's absolute dependence on Yahweh's undeserved mercy is at the core of fearing the Lord. Such fear is not terror; rather, it is submission of one's whole being to Yahweh's control. This is what the arrogant rich lack.

✚ **49:1–20** Those who trust in themselves and their own wealth or power are doomed to the decay of death. However, those who trust in God will find their significance there.

50:1–6 God subpoenas both witnesses ("heavens" and "earth") and defendants ("this consecrated people," v. 5) to gather for the hearing of the case.
50:7–13 The first accusation is a parody of the Shema (Dt 6:4). By bringing together both Shema and the giving of the Law, the psalmist emphasizes the core of the covenant tradition as allegiance to Yahweh alone and obedience to his covenant demands.

The intersection of faithfulness to the covenant and sacrifice is at issue in the remainder of the psalm. God does not rebuke Israel for failing to sacrifice (Ps 50:8). Israel's *understanding* of sacrifice appears to be defective.

In this first section, the problem seems to be that those who sacrifice believe their sacrifices are *essential* to God—that in some sense their sacrifices meet a need that God has. Some in Israel must have agreed with the general Mesopotamian view that sacrifice met the needs of deities and offered an opportunity for humans to manipulate them.

[11]I know every bird in the mountains,
and the insects in the fields are mine.
[12]If I were hungry I would not tell you,
for the world[u] is mine, and all that is in it.
[13]Do I eat the flesh of bulls
or drink the blood of goats?

[14]"Sacrifice thank offerings[v] to God,
fulfill your vows[w] to the Most High,
[15]and call[x] on me in the day of trouble;
I will deliver you, and you will honor[y] me."

[16]But to the wicked person, God says:

"What right have you to recite my laws
or take my covenant on your lips?[z]
[17]You hate my instruction
and cast my words behind[a] you.
[18]When you see a thief, you join[b] with him;
you throw in your lot with adulterers.
[19]You use your mouth for evil
and harness your tongue to deceit.[c]
[20]You sit and testify against your brother[d]
and slander your own mother's son.
[21]When you did these things and I kept silent,[e]
you thought I was exactly[a] like you.
But I now arraign you
and set my accusations[f] before you.

[22]"Consider this, you who forget God,[g]
or I will tear you to pieces, with no one to rescue you:[h]
[23]Those who sacrifice thank offerings honor me,
and to the blameless[b] I will show my salvation.[i]"

50:12 [u]Ex 19:5
50:14 [v]Heb 13:15 [w]Dt 23:21
50:15 [x]Ps 81:7 [y]Ps 22:23
50:16 [z]Isa 29:13
50:17 [a]Ne 9:26; Ro 2:21-22
50:18 [b]Ro 1:32; 1Ti 5:22
50:19 [c]Ps 10:7; 52:2
50:20 [d]Mt 10:21
50:21 [e]Ecc 8:11; Isa 42:14 [f]Ps 90:8
50:22 [g]Job 8:13; Ps 9:17 [h]Ps 7:2
50:23 [i]Ps 91:16
51:1 [j]Ac 3:19 [k]Isa 43:25; Col 2:14
51:2 [l]1Jn 1:9 [m]Heb 9:14
51:3 [n]Isa 59:12
51:4 [o]Ge 20:6; Lk 15:21 [p]Ro 3:4*
51:5 [q]Job 14:4
51:6 [r]Pr 2:6 [s]Ps 15:2

Ps 50:9–10 ❖ God does not need our material offerings. Instead, what does God deeply desire from his children?

Psalm 51[c]

For the director of music. A psalm of David. When the prophet Nathan came to him after David had committed adultery with Bathsheba.

[1]Have mercy on me, O God,
according to your unfailing love;
according to your great compassion
blot out[j] my transgressions.[k]
[2]Wash away[l] all my iniquity
and cleanse[m] me from my sin.

[3]For I know my transgressions,
and my sin is always before me.[n]
[4]Against you, you only, have I sinned
and done what is evil in your sight;[o]
so you are right in your verdict
and justified when you judge.[p]
[5]Surely I was sinful[q] at birth,
sinful from the time my mother conceived me.
[6]Yet you desired faithfulness even in the womb;
you taught me wisdom[r] in that secret place.[s]

[a] 21 *Or thought the 'I AM' was* [b] 23 Probable reading of the original Hebrew text; the meaning of the Masoretic Text for this phrase is uncertain. [c] In Hebrew texts 51:1-19 is numbered 51:3-21.

50:14–15 The section concludes with an exhortation to right sacrifice.
50:16–23 Israel lacks the inner commitment to Yahweh that would give their ritual sacrifice meaning (v. 17). The psalm offers six examples of covenant-breaking wickedness, presented in synonymous pairs. In a general sense, the psalmist envisions failure to maintain relationships of honesty and respect.

✣ **50:1–23** True worship requires the fear of Yahweh, acknowledgment of sin, and repentance. True worship involves seeing the hurts of the world. It means acting on what we see. When we do, our praise will have meaning beyond our own well-being and will sound with new sweetness in God's ears.

51:1–2 The psalmist appeals to the "unfailing love" (v. 1) of God as the basis of hope for forgiveness. Although the psalmist has failed by sinning, Yahweh does not fail; he continues in his commitment to sinful humans who acknowledge their sin and rely on God's merciful forgiveness and love. The psalmist's confession is far-reaching and complete.
51:3–6 That the sin is against Yahweh "only" (v. 4) may seem to belittle the offense against Bathsheba, Uriah, or society as a whole. But the intent is to acknowledge that violations of the covenant are offenses against God. The psalmist concedes that his sin proceeds from a longstanding sinful nature. In his expressions of self-awareness, the psalmist exhibits the kind of transparency God desires (v. 6).

[7]Cleanse me with hyssop,[t] and I will
be clean;
wash me, and I will be whiter than
snow.[u]
[8]Let me hear joy and gladness;[v]
let the bones you have crushed
rejoice.
[9]Hide your face from my sins[w]
and blot out all my iniquity.

[10]Create in me a pure heart,[x] O God,
and renew a steadfast spirit
within me.[y]
[11]Do not cast me from your presence
or take your Holy Spirit[z] from me.
[12]Restore to me the joy of your
salvation[a]
and grant me a willing spirit, to
sustain me.

[13]Then I will teach transgressors your
ways,[b]
so that sinners will turn back to
you.[c]
[14]Deliver me from the guilt of
bloodshed,[d] O God,
you who are God my Savior,[e]
and my tongue will sing of your
righteousness.[f]
[15]Open my lips, Lord,[g]
and my mouth will declare your
praise.
[16]You do not delight in sacrifice,[h] or I
would bring it;
you do not take pleasure in burnt
offerings.
[17]My sacrifice, O God, is[a] a broken spirit;
a broken and contrite heart[i]
you, God, will not despise.

[18]May it please you to prosper Zion,[j]
to build up the walls of Jerusalem.
[19]Then you will delight in the
sacrifices of the righteous,[k]
in burnt offerings[l] offered whole;
then bulls[m] will be offered on your
altar.

51:7 [t]Lev 14:4; Heb 9:19 [u]Isa 1:18
51:8 [v]Isa 35:10
51:9 [w]Jer 16:17
51:10 [x]Ps 78:37; Ac 15:9 [y]Eze 18:31
51:11 [z]Eph 4:30
51:12 [a]Ps 13:5
51:13 [b]Ac 9:21-22 [c]Ps 22:27
51:14 [d]2Sa 12:9 [e]Ps 25:5 [f]Ps 35:28
51:15 [g]Ps 9:14
51:16 [h]1Sa 15:22; Ps 40:6
51:17 [i]Ps 34:18
51:18 [j]Ps 102:16; Isa 51:3
51:19 [k]Ps 4:5
[l]Ps 66:13 [m]Ps 66:15
52:Title [n]1Sa 22:9
52:1 [o]Ps 94:4
52:2 [p]Ps 50:19 [q]Ps 57:4
52:3 [r]Jer 9:5
52:4 [s]Ps 120:2,3
52:5 [t]Isa 22:19 [u]Pr 2:22 [v]Ps 27:13
52:6 [w]Job 22:19; Ps 37:34; 40:3

Ps 51:7-12 ❖ What sins do we need to confess to God? How can we be truly cleansed of our sin and guilt (see 1Jn 1:7)?

Psalm 52[b]

For the director of music. A maskil[c] *of David. When Doeg the Edomite*[n] *had gone to Saul and told him: "David has gone to the house of Ahimelek."*

[1]Why do you boast of evil, you
mighty hero?
Why do you boast[o] all day long,
you who are a disgrace in the eyes
of God?
[2]You who practice deceit,[p]
your tongue plots destruction;
it is like a sharpened razor.[q]
[3]You love evil rather than good,
falsehood[r] rather than speaking
the truth.[d]
[4]You love every harmful word,
you deceitful tongue![s]

[5]Surely God will bring you down to
everlasting ruin:
He will snatch you up and pluck[t]
you from your tent;
he will uproot[u] you from the land
of the living.[v]
[6]The righteous will see and fear;
they will laugh[w] at you, saying,

[a] *17* Or *The sacrifices of God are* [b] In Hebrew texts 52:1-9 is numbered 52:3-11. [c] Title: Probably a literary or musical term [d] *3* The Hebrew has *Selah* (a word of uncertain meaning) here and at the end of verse 5.

51:7–9 The psalmist pleads with Yahweh in v. 9 to "hide [his] face"—not from the psalmist but from his *sins*. Such an act implies that God chooses not to take one's failings into account.
51:10–12 In these verses, the psalmist emphasizes the need for a transformed inner attitude.
51:13–17 The psalmist's acts of praise and contrition provide an example for other sinners (v. 13). Deliverance leads to public praise (vv. 14–15).
51:18–19 The concern expressed for the rebuilding of Jerusalem adapts this individual plea for deliverance to the circumstances of the Jewish community in exile.

✜ **51:1–19** Admitting sin and working on it is painful, and no one likes to face pain. But David's story and his response to being called to account (2Sa 11) provides believers with a model for repentance. David's emotional response to his sin in this psalm is worthy of close study.

52:1–5 The tongue of the wicked almost takes on a life of its own as it plots out its destructive course. The psalmist puts its deceptive power to lie and mislead in the foreground. The result of the enemy's arrogant falsehood and deceit is judgment (v. 5).
52:6–7 The fall of the wicked provides an object lesson for the righteous. Behind the laughter (v. 6) stands a clear admonition not to follow this path to destruction.

7 "Here now is the man
who did not make God his
stronghold
but trusted in his great wealth[x]
and grew strong by destroying
others!"

8 But I am like an olive tree[y]
flourishing in the house of God;
I trust[z] in God's unfailing love
for ever and ever.
9 For what you have done I will always
praise you[a]
in the presence of your faithful
people.
And I will hope in your name,
for your name is good.[b]

Psalm 53[a]

53:1–6pp // Ps 14:1–7

For the director of music. According to mahalath.[b] *A* maskil[c] *of David.*

1 The fool[c] says in his heart,
"There is no God."[d]
They are corrupt, and their ways are
vile;
there is no one who does good.

2 God looks down from heaven[e]
on all mankind
to see if there are any who
understand,
any who seek God.[f]
3 Everyone has turned away, all have
become corrupt;
there is no one who does good,
not even one.[g]

4 Do all these evildoers know nothing?

They devour my people as though
eating bread;
they never call on God.

52:7 [x] Ps 49:6
52:8 [y] Jer 11:16 [z] Ps 13:5
52:9 [a] Ps 30:12 [b] Ps 54:6
53:1 [c] Ps 14:1-7; Ro 3:10 [d] Ps 10:4
53:2 [e] Ps 33:13 [f] 2Ch 15:2
53:3 [g] Ro 3:10-12*
53:5 [h] Lev 26:17 [i] Eze 6:5
54:1 [j] Ps 20:1 [k] 2Ch 20:6
54:2 [l] Ps 5:1; 55:1
54:3 [m] Ps 86:14 [n] Ps 40:14 [o] Ps 36:1

Ps 52:7 ❖ Where do we see people trusting in their wealth rather than God? What becomes of such people in the end?

Ps 53:1 ❖ Why is it foolish to say there is no God? To what kind of life will such a belief lead?

5 But there they are, overwhelmed
with dread,
where there was nothing to
dread.[h]
God scattered the bones[i] of those
who attacked you;
you put them to shame, for God
despised them.

6 Oh, that salvation for Israel would
come out of Zion!
When God restores his people,
let Jacob rejoice and Israel be
glad!

Psalm 54[d]

For the director of music. With stringed instruments. A maskil[c] *of David. When the Ziphites had gone to Saul and said, "Is not David hiding among us?"*

1 Save me, O God, by your name;[j]
vindicate me by your might.[k]
2 Hear my prayer, O God;[l]
listen to the words of my mouth.

3 Arrogant foes are attacking me;[m]
ruthless people are trying to kill
me[n] —
people without regard for God.[e][o]

[a] In Hebrew texts 53:1-6 is numbered 53:2-7.
[b] Title: Probably a musical term [c] Title: Probably a literary or musical term [d] In Hebrew texts 54:1-7 is numbered 54:3-9. [e] 3 The Hebrew has *Selah* (a word of uncertain meaning) here.

52:8–9 Unlike the wicked (v. 5), the psalmist will be like a tree planted deep. Yahweh's continued presence is linked to the psalmist's trust in God's "unfailing love" (v. 8).

52:1–9 Believers need not experience the rooting out reserved for the wicked. When we trust in God rather than in ourselves for deliverance and security, we look for God's salvation and direction in every circumstance.

53:1–3 See the commentary on 14:1–3 for discussion on these verses.
53:4–5 Having described the corruption of human beings (v. 2) in terms that seem absolute, the wicked are condemned for treating the poor as consumable objects. God's power is unleashed in judgment on the wicked.
53:6 The psalm concludes with an expression of the people's hope for restoration.

53:1–6 The corruption of human beings finds its way into all kinds of societal evils. Treating oppressed people as consumable objects is nothing new, and it continues today in many forms. Believers do well to check their actions and activities for any signs of this in their own lives, and to defend those whom they see suffering such oppression.

54:1–2 Along with deliverance, the psalmist also desires vindication (v. 1b).
54:3 The attackers are described with a Hebrew term that normally refers to a non-Israelite. Per-

[4]Surely God is my help;[p]
the Lord is the one who sustains me.[q]
[5]Let evil recoil[r] on those who slander me;
in your faithfulness[s] destroy them.
[6]I will sacrifice a freewill offering[t] to you;
I will praise your name, LORD, for it is good.[u]
[7]You have delivered me[v] from all my troubles,
and my eyes have looked in triumph on my foes.[w]

Psalm 55[a]

For the director of music. With stringed instruments. A maskil[b] *of David.*

[1]Listen to my prayer, O God,
do not ignore my plea;[x]
[2] hear me and answer me.[y]
My thoughts trouble me and I am distraught[z]
[3] because of what my enemy is saying,
because of the threats of the wicked;
for they bring down suffering on me[a]
and assail me in their anger.[b]

[4]My heart is in anguish within me;
the terrors[c] of death have fallen on me.
[5]Fear and trembling[d] have beset me;
horror has overwhelmed me.
[6]I said, "Oh, that I had the wings of a dove!
I would fly away and be at rest.

54:4 [p]Ps 118:7 [q]Ps 41:12
54:5 [r]Ps 94:23 [s]Ps 89:49; 143:12
54:6 [t]Ps 50:14 [u]Ps 52:9
54:7 [v]Ps 34:6 [w]Ps 59:10
55:1 [x]Ps 27:9; 61:1
55:2 [y]Ps 66:19 [z]Ps 77:3; Isa 38:14
55:3 [a]2Sa 16:6-8; Ps 17:9 [b]Ps 71:11
55:4 [c]Ps 116:3
55:5 [d]Job 21:6; Ps 119:120

Ps 54:1 ❖ From what are we praying for God to save us? What spiritual or physical threats might we need to lift to him in prayer?

[7]I would flee far away
and stay in the desert;[c]
[8]I would hurry to my place of shelter,
far from the tempest and storm.[e]"

[9]Lord, confuse the wicked, confound their words,
for I see violence and strife[f] in the city.
[10]Day and night they prowl about on its walls;
malice and abuse are within it.
[11]Destructive forces[g] are at work in the city;
threats and lies[h] never leave its streets.

[12]If an enemy were insulting me,
I could endure it;
if a foe were rising against me,
I could hide.
[13]But it is you, a man like myself,
my companion, my close friend,[i]
[14]with whom I once enjoyed sweet fellowship
at the house of God,[j]
as we walked about
among the worshipers.

[15]Let death take my enemies by surprise;[k]
let them go down alive to the realm of the dead,[l]

55:8 [e]Isa 4:6
55:9 [f]Jer 6:7
55:11 [g]Ps 5:9 [h]Ps 10:7
55:13 [i]2Sa 15:12; Ps 41:9
55:14 [j]Ps 42:4
55:15 [k]Ps 64:7 [l]Nu 16:30,33

[a] In Hebrew texts 55:1-23 is numbered 55:2-24.
[b] Title: Probably a literary or musical term
[c] 7 The Hebrew has *Selah* (a word of uncertain meaning) here and in the middle of verse 19.

haps the intent is to emphasize just how far they are from true covenant relationship.
54:4 The central message of the psalm is confidence in God.
54:5 The psalmist asks God to render justice.
54:6–7 As in many laments, this psalm concludes with a vow to offer sacrifice and praise.

54:1–7 When we keep our eyes on God and allow him to help us, we can know fulfillment even when our most intimate human connections fail to provide that for us.

55:1–2a The speaker of vv. 1–2 pleads with God to "answer."
55:2b–5 The psalmist's circumstance is dominated by mental and emotional turmoil. The enemy's angry attack is described with a Hebrew term normally rendered "bear a grudge against" or "harbor animosity toward."
55:6–8 The psalmist wishes only to flee. Wild "doves" (v. 6) often nested in remote and inaccessible cliffs. The poet is tempted not to wait for divine deliverance but to exercise *self*-deliverance by fleeing to a "place of shelter" (v. 8).
55:9–11 The enemy's hostile speech inspires the psalmist's appeal to God to "confuse" (or split, v. 9) the enemy's tongue. The psalmist may be drawing on the tower of Babel narrative to speak a word of divine condemnation to the current culture (Ge 11).
55:12–14 The attacker is a "close" confidant (v. 13). The location of the "sweet fellowship" (v. 14) is the temple, so the two have been spiritually connected and compatible. This last comment heightens the tragic betrayal.
55:15 Tricked by death, they should be brought

for evil finds lodging among
them.

16 As for me, I call to God,
and the LORD saves me.
17 Evening,[m] morning[n] and noon
I cry out in distress,
and he hears my voice.
18 He rescues me unharmed
from the battle waged against me,
even though many oppose me.
19 God, who is enthroned from of old,[o]
who does not change —
he will hear[p] them and humble
them,
because they have no fear of God.

20 My companion attacks his friends;[q]
he violates his covenant.[r]
21 His talk is smooth as butter,
yet war is in his heart;
his words are more soothing than
oil,[s]
yet they are drawn swords.[t]

22 Cast your cares on the LORD
and he will sustain you;[u]
he will never let
the righteous be shaken.[v]
23 But you, God, will bring down the
wicked
into the pit[w] of decay;
the bloodthirsty and deceitful[x]
will not live out half their days.[y]

But as for me, I trust in you.[z]

Psalm 56[a]

For the director of music. To the tune of "A Dove on Distant Oaks." Of David. A miktam.[b] *When the Philistines had seized him in Gath.*

1 Be merciful to me, my God,
for my enemies are in hot
pursuit;[a]
all day long they press their
attack.
2 My adversaries pursue me all day
long;[b]
in their pride many are
attacking me.[c]

3 When I am afraid,[d] I put my trust in
you.
4 In God, whose word I praise —
in God I trust and am not afraid.
What can mere mortals do
to me?[e]

5 All day long they twist my words;[f]
all their schemes are for my ruin.
6 They conspire,[g] they lurk,
they watch my steps,
hoping to take my life.[h]
7 Because of their wickedness do not[c]
let them escape;
in your anger, God, bring the
nations down.[i]

8 Record my misery;
list my tears on your scroll[d] —
are they not in your record?[j]
9 Then my enemies will turn back[k]
when I call for help.[l]
By this I will know that God is for
me.[m]

55:17 [m] Ps 141:2; Ac 3:1 [n] Ps 5:3
55:19 [o] Dt 33:27 [p] Ps 78:59
55:20 [q] Ps 7:4 [r] Ps 89:34
55:21 [s] Pr 5:3 [t] Ps 28:3; 57:4; 59:7
55:22 [u] Ps 37:5; Mt 6:25-34; 1Pe 5:7 [v] Ps 37:24
55:23 [w] Ps 73:18 [x] Ps 5:6 [y] Job 15:32; Pr 10:27 [z] Ps 25:2
56:1 [a] Ps 57:1-3
56:2 [b] Ps 57:3 [c] Ps 35:1
56:3 [d] Ps 55:4-5
56:4 [e] Ps 118:6; Heb 13:6
56:5 [f] Ps 41:7
56:6 [g] Ps 59:3 [h] Ps 71:10
56:7 [i] Ps 36:12; 55:23
56:8 [j] Mal 3:16
56:9 [k] Ps 9:3 [l] Ps 102:2 [m] Ro 8:31

Ps 55:17 ❖ How can hard times actually make our prayer lives better? When have you experienced this firsthand?

Ps 56:3-4 ❖ How can we put our trust in God even when we feel afraid (see 1Jn 4:18)?

[a] In Hebrew texts 56:1-13 is numbered 56:2-14.
[b] Title: Probably a literary or musical term
[c] 7 Probable reading of the original Hebrew text; Masoretic Text does not have *do not.*
[d] 8 Or *misery; / put my tears in your wineskin*

down to Sheol (NIV "realm of the dead") while still alive—abrupt and unexpected.
55:16-19 The psalmist's confidence is founded on Yahweh, the King (v. 19).
55:20-21 The enemy's words appear "more soothing than oil" used to anoint and soften. In reality, their intent is to cut and maim like "drawn swords" (v. 21).
55:22-23 The psalmist calls others to trust God by casting their cares on him, confident of the coming judgment on the wicked.

❖ **55:1-23** Just to be associated with certain words is destructive, especially if the words are untrue. Our words can affect the way someone is viewed by others and even undermine the way one feels about oneself. As always, believers need to be careful to consider the impact of their words (Jas 3:7-8).

56:1-4 The enemy is depicted as being like a hound in full pursuit. The attack is continual, but the psalmist relies on God's protection.
56:5-11 The wicked "twist [his] words" (v. 5), plot harm, and wait for the opportunity to snuff out his life. The psalmist appeals to God for compensation. But he makes an unexpected turn by requesting that God bring down "the nations" (v. 7), a reference to the ethnic and tribal communities that make up the world population. This broadened

[10] In God, whose word I praise,
in the LORD, whose word I praise—
[11] in God I trust and am not afraid.
What can man do to me?

[12] I am under vows[n] to you, my God;
I will present my thank offerings to you.
[13] For you have delivered me from death[o]
and my feet from stumbling,
that I may walk before God
in the light of life.[p]

Psalm 57[a]

57:7–11pp // Ps 108:1–5

For the director of music. To the tune of "Do Not Destroy." Of David. A miktam.[b] *When he had fled from Saul into the cave.*

[1] Have mercy on me, my God, have mercy on me,
for in you I take refuge.[q]
I will take refuge in the shadow of your wings[r]
until the disaster has passed.[s]

[2] I cry out to God Most High,
to God, who vindicates me.[t]
[3] He sends from heaven and saves me,[u]
rebuking those who hotly pursue me—[c][v]
God sends forth his love and his faithfulness.[w]

[4] I am in the midst of lions;[x]
I am forced to dwell among ravenous beasts—
men whose teeth are spears and arrows,
whose tongues are sharp swords.[y]

[5] Be exalted, O God, above the heavens;
let your glory be over all the earth.[z]

[6] They spread a net for my feet—
I was bowed down[a] in distress.
They dug a pit[b] in my path—
but they have fallen into it themselves.[c]

[7] My heart, O God, is steadfast,
my heart is steadfast;[d]
I will sing and make music.
[8] Awake, my soul!
Awake, harp and lyre![e]
I will awaken the dawn.

[9] I will praise you, Lord, among the nations;
I will sing of you among the peoples.
[10] For great is your love, reaching to the heavens;
your faithfulness reaches to the skies.[f]

[11] Be exalted, O God, above the heavens;
let your glory be over all the earth.[g]

56:12 [n] Ps 50:14
56:13 [o] Ps 116:8 [p] Job 33:30
57:1 [q] Ps 2:12 [r] Ps 17:8 [s] Isa 26:20
57:2 [t] Ps 138:8
57:3 [u] Ps 18:9, 16 [v] Ps 56:1 [w] Ps 40:11
57:4 [x] Ps 35:17 [y] Ps 55:21; Pr 30:14
57:5 [z] Ps 108:5
57:6 [a] Ps 145:14 [b] Ps 35:7 [c] Ps 7:15; Pr 28:10
57:7 [d] Ps 108:1
57:8 [e] Ps 16:9; 30:12; 150:3
57:10 [f] Ps 36:5; 103:11
57:11 [g] ver 5

Ps 57:4 ❖ What dangers lurking around us remind us of our need for God and his protection?

[a] In Hebrew texts 57:1-11 is numbered 57:2-12.
[b] Title: Probably a literary or musical term
[c] *3* The Hebrew has *Selah* (a word of uncertain meaning) here and at the end of verse 6.

reference probably reflects the viewpoint of the Jewish population that was exiled from Israel and scattered around the nations.

The psalmist wants God to record his lament. The psalmist seems to imply that if God remembers the plea, he will act (vv. 8–9).

56:12–13 Fulfillment of a vow normally took place in the context of public worship.

✣ **56:1–13** God's Word is a source of confidence to those who are beset by enemies. Only God sees the true state of our affairs. Only he is able to judge human righteousness and failure.

57:1–5 The psalmist's desire to seek refuge is based on an understanding of God that inspires confidence. "God sends forth his love and his faithfulness" (v. 3) and rules over everything.

57:6–8 The evil acts of the opponents return on them (v. 6c-d). The placement of the refrain (v. 5) in the middle of the discussion of the enemy attack demonstrates what the psalmist hopes to experience in reality: God's protective presence amid trouble.

57:9–11 As did Ps 56, this psalm shifts somewhat to include a more international perspective. This may represent an adaptation of this psalm from being individually focused to being community focused and speaking to the circumstances of the Jews after the exile.

✣ **57:1–11** Yahweh is *above* the heavens, outside what he made. Yet God's glory can fill creation. This God can be known, loves, and can be loved in return.

Psalm 58[a]

For the director of music. To the tune of "Do Not Destroy." Of David. A miktam.[b]

1 Do you rulers indeed speak justly?[h]
Do you judge people with equity?
2 No, in your heart you devise injustice,
and your hands mete out violence on the earth.[i]

3 Even from birth the wicked go astray;
from the womb they are wayward, spreading lies.
4 Their venom is like the venom of a snake,[j]
like that of a cobra that has stopped its ears,
5 that will not heed the tune of the charmer,
however skillful the enchanter may be.

6 Break the teeth in their mouths, O God;[k]
LORD, tear out the fangs of those lions![l]
7 Let them vanish like water that flows away;[m]
when they draw the bow, let their arrows fall short.[n]
8 May they be like a slug that melts away as it moves along,
like a stillborn child[o] that never sees the sun.

9 Before your pots can feel the heat of the thorns[p] —
whether they be green or dry —
the wicked will be swept away.[c][q]
10 The righteous will be glad when they are avenged,[r]
when they dip their feet in the blood of the wicked.[s]
11 Then people will say,
"Surely the righteous still are rewarded;
surely there is a God who judges the earth."[t]

58:1 [h] Ps 82:2
58:2 [i] Ps 94:20; Mal 3:15
58:4 [j] Ps 140:3; Ecc 10:11
58:6 [k] Ps 3:7 [l] Job 4:10
58:7 [m] Jos 7:5; Ps 112:10 [n] Ps 64:3
58:8 [o] Job 3:16
58:9 [p] Ps 118:12 [q] Pr 10:25
58:10 [r] Ps 64:10; 91:8 [s] Ps 68:23
58:11 [t] Ps 9:8; 18:20
59:1 [u] Ps 143:9
59:2 [v] Ps 139:19
59:3 [w] Ps 56:6
59:4 [x] Ps 35:19, 23

Ps 58:1-2 ❖ Where do you see wicked leadership? What kind of leaders does God call for? How can believers emulate those qualities?

Psalm 59[d]

For the director of music. To the tune of "Do Not Destroy." Of David. A miktam.[b] *When Saul had sent men to watch David's house in order to kill him.*

1 Deliver me from my enemies, O God;[u]
be my fortress against those who are attacking me.
2 Deliver me from evildoers
and save me from those who are after my blood.[v]

3 See how they lie in wait for me!
Fierce men conspire[w] against me
for no offense or sin of mine, LORD.
4 I have done no wrong, yet they are ready to attack me.[x]
Arise to help me; look on my plight!
5 You, LORD God Almighty,
you who are the God of Israel,

[a] In Hebrew texts 58:1-11 is numbered 58:2-12. [b] Title: Probably a literary or musical term [c] 9 The meaning of the Hebrew for this verse is uncertain. [d] In Hebrew texts 59:1-17 is numbered 59:2-18.

58:1-5 Corrupt judges are likened to cobras: so intent on evil that they are immune to persuasion, wanting only to lash out and harm.
58:6-8 The psalmist calls on God to render corrupt judges impotent and toothless. The psalmist wishes that the wicked had never been born, that their wickedness (cf. v. 3) had never even begun.
58:9-11 Bathing one's feet in the blood of the enemy is a traditional ancient Near Eastern way of expressing the enemy's utter defeat as the victorious soldier walks through the aftermath of a vicious battle. Vindication comes when the righteous are publicly "rewarded" (v. 11) by God.

✚ **58:1-11** Believers long for the restoration of creation, when evil will be destroyed and harmony reigns at last between individuals, people groups, humans and animals, and all of us with the physical world itself (Rev 21:1-5).

59:1-2 The psalmist pleads for deliverance and protection from enemies.
59:3-9 The enemy lies in wait/ambushes and attacks (cf. 56:6) the psalmist without cause. The enemy is characterized as a pack of dogs looking for vulnerable prey. The enemy's verbal attacks are likened to vicious thrusts with a sword (59:7b).

Like the watchman of a besieged city straining to see the expected arrival of the reinforcements, the psalmist watches for the appearance of "my God on whom I can rely" (v. 10a).

rouse yourself to punish all the nations;
show no mercy to wicked traitors.[a][y]

6 They return at evening,
snarling like dogs,[z]
and prowl about the city.
7 See what they spew from their mouths—
the words from their lips are sharp as swords,[a]
and they think, "Who can hear us?"[b]
8 But you laugh at them, LORD;[c]
you scoff at all those nations.[d]

9 You are my strength, I watch for you;
you, God, are my fortress,[e]
10 my God on whom I can rely.

God will go before me
and will let me gloat over those who slander me.
11 But do not kill them, Lord our shield,[b][f]
or my people will forget.[g]
In your might uproot them
and bring them down.[h]
12 For the sins of their mouths,[i]
for the words of their lips,[j]
let them be caught in their pride.[k]
For the curses and lies they utter,
13 consume them in your wrath,
consume them till they are no more.[l]
Then it will be known to the ends of the earth
that God rules over Jacob.[m]

14 They return at evening,
snarling like dogs,
and prowl about the city.
15 They wander about for food[n]
and howl if not satisfied.
16 But I will sing of your strength,[o]
in the morning[p] I will sing of your love;[q]
for you are my fortress,
my refuge in times of trouble.[r]

17 You are my strength, I sing praise to you;
you, God, are my fortress,
my God on whom I can rely.

59:5 [y] Jer 18:23
59:6 [z] ver 14
59:7 [a] Ps 57:4 [b] Ps 10:11
59:8 [c] Ps 37:13; Pr 1:26 [d] Ps 2:4
59:9 [e] Ps 9:9; 62:2
59:11 [f] Ps 84:9 [g] Dt 4:9 [h] Ps 106:27
59:12 [i] Ps 10:7 [j] Pr 12:13 [k] Zep 3:11
59:13 [l] Ps 104:35 [m] Ps 83:18
59:15 [n] Job 15:23
59:16 [o] Ps 21:13 [p] Ps 88:13 [q] Ps 101:1
[r] Ps 46:1

Ps 59:16 ❖ How can praising God with songs bolster our strength? What are your favorite hymns or worship songs?

Psalm 60[c]

60:5–12pp // Ps 108:6–13

For the director of music. To the tune of "The Lily of the Covenant." A miktam[d] of David. For teaching. When he fought Aram Naharaim[e] and Aram Zobah,[f] and when Joab returned and struck down twelve thousand Edomites in the Valley of Salt.

1 You have rejected us,[s] God, and burst upon us;
you have been angry[t]—now restore us![u]
2 You have shaken the land[v] and torn it open;
mend its fractures,[w] for it is quaking.
3 You have shown your people desperate times;[x]
you have given us wine that makes us stagger.[y]
4 But for those who fear you, you have raised a banner
to be unfurled against the bow.[g]

60:1 [s] 2Sa 5:20; Ps 44:9 [t] Ps 79:5 [u] Ps 80:3
60:2 [v] Ps 18:7 [w] 2Ch 7:14
60:3 [x] Ps 71:20 [y] Isa 51:17; Jer 25:16

[a] 5 The Hebrew has *Selah* (a word of uncertain meaning) here and at the end of verse 13. [b] 11 Or *sovereign* [c] In Hebrew texts 60:1-12 is numbered 60:3-14. [d] Title: Probably a literary or musical term [e] Title: That is, Arameans of Northwest Mesopotamia [f] Title: That is, Arameans of central Syria [g] 4 The Hebrew has *Selah* (a word of uncertain meaning) here.

59:10–17 The psalmist desires public vindication and the enemy's destruction. This object lesson has two purposes: (1) to punish the enemy for their arrogant slander (v. 12); (2) to make it clear that God rules Israel (v. 13). In v. 9, the psalmist watched for God's deliverance. Here God's "strength" (v. 16) has already become a cause for praise.

59:1–17 God is sovereign and all-powerful; he is loving as well. Without the last, God would be a powerful deity, but we would not likely *trust* him. Without God's love, we could recognize God's power over life and death and over all aspects of our world, but we might have a difficult time trusting it. Thankfully, as believers we don't have to live our lives outside of God's love (1Jn 4:8).

60:1–4 This psalm laments a particularly significant defeat that is interpreted as divine judgment on Israel. The "banner" (v. 4) is a type of flag used in battle to offer a rallying point.

[5]Save us and help us with your right
hand,[z]
that those you love[a] may be
delivered.
[6]God has spoken from his sanctuary:
"In triumph I will parcel out
Shechem[b]
and measure off the Valley of
Sukkoth.
[7]Gilead[c] is mine, and Manasseh is
mine;
Ephraim is my helmet,
Judah[d] is my scepter.[e]
[8]Moab is my washbasin,
on Edom I toss my sandal;
over Philistia I shout in
triumph.[f]"

[9]Who will bring me to the fortified
city?
Who will lead me to Edom?
[10]Is it not you, God, you who have now
rejected us
and no longer go out with our
armies?[g]
[11]Give us aid against the enemy,
for human help is worthless.[h]
[12]With God we will gain the victory,
and he will trample down our
enemies.[i]

Psalm 61[a]

For the director of music. With stringed instruments. Of David.

[1]Hear my cry, O God;[j]
listen to my prayer.[k]

[2]From the ends of the earth I call to
you,
I call as my heart grows faint;[l]
lead me to the rock[m] that is higher
than I.

60:5 [z] Ps 17:7; 108:6 [a] Ps 127:2
60:6 [b] Ge 12:6
60:7 [c] Jos 13:31 [d] Dt 33:17 [e] Ge 49:10
60:8 [f] 2Sa 8:1
60:10 [g] Jos 7:12; Ps 44:9; 108:11
60:11 [h] Ps 146:3
60:12 [i] Nu 24:18; Ps 44:5
61:1 [j] Ps 64:1 [k] Ps 86:6
61:2 [l] Ps 77:3 [m] Ps 18:2

61:3 [n] Ps 62:7 [o] Pr 18:10
61:4 [p] Ps 23:6 [q] Ps 91:4
61:5 [r] Ps 56:12 [s] Ps 86:11
61:6 [t] Ps 21:4
61:7 [u] Ps 41:12 [v] Ps 40:11
61:8 [w] Ps 65:1; 71:22
62:1 [x] Ps 33:20

Ps 60:7 ❖ Gilead was across the Jordan River from most of Israel. As God's people, we can experience seasons when we feel like we live beyond the boundaries of his love and care, or outside of the care of his people. How can we find reassurance that God loves all of those who will turn to him, no matter the circumstances?

Ps 61:4 ❖ How does this verse parallel Jesus' teaching about the vine and the branches in Jn 15?

[3]For you have been my refuge,[n]
a strong tower against the foe.[o]

[4]I long to dwell[p] in your tent forever
and take refuge in the shelter of
your wings.[b][q]
[5]For you, God, have heard my vows;[r]
you have given me the heritage of
those who fear your name.[s]

[6]Increase the days of the king's life,
his years for many generations.[t]
[7]May he be enthroned in God's
presence forever;[u]
appoint your love and faithfulness
to protect him.[v]

[8]Then I will ever sing in praise of
your name[w]
and fulfill my vows day after day.

Psalm 62[c]

For the director of music. For Jeduthun. A psalm of David.

[1]Truly my soul finds rest[x] in God;
my salvation comes from him.

[a] In Hebrew texts 61:1-8 is numbered 61:2-9.
[b] 4 The Hebrew has *Selah* (a word of uncertain meaning) here.
[c] In Hebrew texts 62:1-12 is numbered 62:2-13.

60:5-8 This section begins with a renewed plea for deliverance and continues with a word from God himself.
60:9-12 The psalmist calls on God directly to aid his people against their enemies and acknowledges that human power is ultimately of no avail. The confident assurance of v. 12 must be read as a hopeful profession of faith, standing as it does in such close proximity with the preceding pictures of divine abandonment and human powerlessness.

✣ **60:1-12** Our failures do not mean that God has failed. Destruction, no matter how desperate, can be mended (v. 2). God offers deliverance from sin to those who repent and trust in him for salvation.

61:1-5 One can almost see the psalmist frantically reaching upward along the rock and seeking the outstretched hand of God to pull him to safety. The psalmist's vow to praise God's name in the face of such threatening isolation is a measure of his faith.
61:6-7 In an unexpected shift, the psalmist moves from an individual plea for protection to a prayer for long life and enduring reign for the king.
61:8 The psalm ends with a promise to praise God's name daily as a fulfillment of the vow mentioned earlier in v. 5.

✣ **61:1-8** The psalmist cries despite his weak heart (v. 2) because God has been a refuge and a strong tower against the foe in the past.

62:1-6 The assault by the wicked is described in two central verses (vv. 3-4) bracketed by trust in

[2]Truly he is my rock[y] and my
salvation;
he is my fortress, I will never be
shaken.

[3]How long will you assault me?
Would all of you throw me down —
this leaning wall,[z] this tottering
fence?
[4]Surely they intend to topple me
from my lofty place;
they take delight in lies.
With their mouths they bless,
but in their hearts they curse.[a][a]

[5]Yes, my soul, find rest in God;
my hope comes from him.
[6]Truly he is my rock and my
salvation;
he is my fortress, I will not be
shaken.
[7]My salvation and my honor depend
on God[b];
he is my mighty rock, my refuge.[b]
[8]Trust in him at all times, you people;
pour out your hearts to him,[c]
for God is our refuge.

[9]Surely the lowborn are but a breath,[d]
the highborn are but a lie.
If weighed on a balance,[e] they are
nothing;
together they are only a breath.
[10]Do not trust in extortion
or put vain hope in stolen goods;[f]
though your riches increase,
do not set your heart on them.[g]

[11]One thing God has spoken,
two things I have heard:
"Power belongs to you, God,
[12] and with you, Lord, is unfailing
love";
and, "You reward everyone
according to what they have
done."[h]

62:2 [y]Ps 89:26
62:3 [z]Isa 30:13
62:4 [a]Ps 28:3
62:7 [b]Ps 46:1; 85:9; Jer 3:23
62:8 [c]1Sa 1:15; Ps 42:4; La 2:19
62:9 [d]Ps 39:5,11 [e]Isa 40:15
62:10 [f]Isa 61:8 [g]Job 31:25; 1Ti 6:6-10
62:12 [h]Job 34:11; Mt 16:27

Ps 62:10 ❖ How can we keep from setting our hearts on riches or possessions (see Mt 6:19–21)?

Ps 63:1 ❖ When has your life felt like a parched land with no water? How did you rely on God through those times?

Psalm 63[c]

A psalm of David. When he was in the Desert of Judah.

[1]You, God, are my God,
earnestly I seek you;
I thirst for you,[i]
my whole being longs for you,
in a dry and parched land
where there is no water.
[2]I have seen you in the sanctuary[j]
and beheld your power and your
glory.
[3]Because your love is better than life,[k]
my lips will glorify you.
[4]I will praise you as long as I live,[l]
and in your name I will lift up my
hands.[m]
[5]I will be fully satisfied as with the
richest of foods;[n]
with singing lips my mouth will
praise you.

[6]On my bed I remember you;
I think of you through the watches
of the night.[o]
[7]Because you are my help,[p]
I sing in the shadow of your
wings.
[8]I cling to you;
your right hand upholds me.[q]

63:1 [i]Ps 42:2; 84:2
63:2 [j]Ps 27:4
63:3 [k]Ps 69:16
63:4 [l]Ps 104:33 [m]Ps 28:2
63:5 [n]Ps 36:8
63:6 [o]Ps 42:8
63:7 [p]Ps 27:9
63:8 [q]Ps 18:35

[a] 4 The Hebrew has *Selah* (a word of uncertain meaning) here and at the end of verse 8. [b] 7 Or */ God Most High is my salvation and my honor* [c] In Hebrew texts 63:1-11 is numbered 63:2-12.

God as "my rock," "my salvation," and "my fortress" (vv. 1–2, 5–6). The effect is to surround the attacking enemy with the power of God.
62:7–8 These central verses provide the transition from the more individual reflections to community-oriented themes in the last verses.
62:9–12 These sayings are similar in structure, content, and vocabulary with comparable sayings from Wisdom Literature. God can be trusted.

✥ **62:1–12** With eyes on the storm, there seems no hope to overcome it. With eyes turned toward self, there is no personal power equal to the task. Only when one can focus on God alone does the power of the storm recede in response to his command: "Quiet! Be still!" (Mk 4:39).

63:1 The psalmist begins with imagery of a parched traveler searching for life as if looking for water. God is just such a rare and life-giving commodity. The verb "seek" has the edge of an "earnest, intent, focused" search.
63:2–8 The psalmist's vision is of God "in the sanctuary" (v. 2), reminiscent of Isaiah's vision (Isa 6:1–9). The remainder of this section of the psalm follows this division as the psalmist first praises God for his power and then commits faithfully to cling to God's sustaining love.

[9]Those who want to kill me will be
destroyed;[r]
they will go down to the depths of
the earth.[s]
[10]They will be given over to the sword
and become food for jackals.

[11]But the king will rejoice in God;
all who swear by God will glory in
him,[t]
while the mouths of liars will be
silenced.

Psalm 64[a]

For the director of music.
A psalm of David.

[1]Hear me, my God, as I voice my
complaint;[u]
protect my life from the threat of
the enemy.[v]

[2]Hide me from the conspiracy of the
wicked,[w]
from the plots of evildoers.
[3]They sharpen their tongues like
swords
and aim cruel words like deadly
arrows.[x]
[4]They shoot from ambush at the
innocent;[y]
they shoot suddenly, without
fear.[z]

[5]They encourage each other in evil
plans,
they talk about hiding their
snares;
they say, "Who will see it[b]?"[a]
[6]They plot injustice and say,
"We have devised a perfect plan!"
Surely the human mind and heart
are cunning.

[7]But God will shoot them with his
arrows;

63:9 [r]Ps 40:14 [s]Ps 55:15
63:11 [t]Dt 6:13; Ps 21:1; Isa 45:23
64:1 [u]Ps 55:2 [v]Ps 140:1
64:2 [w]Ps 56:6; 59:2
64:3 [x]Ps 58:7
64:4 [y]Ps 11:2 [z]Ps 55:19
64:5 [a]Ps 10:11
64:8 [b]Ps 9:3; Pr 18:7 [c]Ps 22:7
64:9 [d]Jer 51:10
64:10 [e]Ps 25:20 [f]Ps 32:11
65:1 [g]Ps 116:18
65:2 [h]Isa 66:23
65:3 [i]Ps 38:4 [j]Heb 9:14
65:4 [k]Ps 4:3; 33:12

Ps 64:1-10 ❖ How does David's confidence in God's salvation reassure us in the face of the everyday trials we encounter?

Ps 65:2 ❖ When have you experienced God's power to answer prayers?

they will suddenly be struck
down.
[8]He will turn their own tongues
against them[b]
and bring them to ruin;
all who see them will shake their
heads[c] in scorn.
[9]All people will fear;
they will proclaim the works of
God
and ponder what he has done.[d]

[10]The righteous will rejoice in the
LORD
and take refuge in him;[e]
all the upright in heart will glory
in him![f]

Psalm 65[c]

For the director of music.
A psalm of David. A song.

[1]Praise awaits[d] you, our God, in
Zion;
to you our vows will be fulfilled.[g]
[2]You who answer prayer,
to you all people will come.[h]
[3]When we were overwhelmed by
sins,[i]
you forgave[e] our transgressions.[j]
[4]Blessed are those you choose[k]

[a] In Hebrew texts 64:1-10 is numbered 64:2-11. [b] 5 Or *us* [c] In Hebrew texts 65:1-13 is numbered 65:2-14. [d] 1 Or *befits*; the meaning of the Hebrew for this word is uncertain. [e] 3 Or *made atonement for*

63:9-11 The lives of the enemies are "given over to the sword" (v. 10), and their bodies lie unburied and exposed.

✣ **63:1-11** The teaching of both the OT and NT agrees that knowing God and his love is more satisfying than life itself.

64:1-2 The problem is a terrifying and life-threatening attack by the psalmist's enemies.
64:3-6 The deadly words of the enemies cut and pierce. The utter arrogance of the wicked is displayed in their sense of impunity. The section concludes with the ironic comment of the narrator. One can almost see the psalmist's head shaking with ironic confusion over the enemy's misguided conclusion.
64:7-8 Far from carrying out their plot in secret, they will be exposed to public ridicule as "all who see them" unite in shaking "their heads in scorn" (v. 8).
64:9-10 The righteous need have no fear of such attackers but should take refuge in Yahweh, assured of his protective care.

✣ **64:1-10** Hope for justice has a double edge. We sinners should have no complaint when we receive from God the justice we have wished on others because of our own sin.

65:1-4 Distress is the result of sin and praise is a response to God's forgiveness (v. 3).

and bring near to live in your courts!
We are filled with the good things of your house,[l]
of your holy temple.

5 You answer us with awesome and righteous deeds,
God our Savior,[m]
the hope of all the ends of the earth
and of the farthest seas,[n]
6 who formed the mountains by your power,
having armed yourself with strength,[o]
7 who stilled the roaring of the seas,[p]
the roaring of their waves,
and the turmoil of the nations.[q]
8 The whole earth is filled with awe at your wonders;
where morning dawns, where evening fades,
you call forth songs of joy.

9 You care for the land and water it;[r]
you enrich it abundantly.
The streams of God are filled with water
to provide the people with grain,[s]
for so you have ordained it.[a]
10 You drench its furrows and level its ridges;
you soften it with showers and bless its crops.
11 You crown the year with your bounty,
and your carts overflow with abundance.
12 The grasslands of the wilderness overflow;[t]
the hills are clothed with gladness.
13 The meadows are covered with flocks[u]
and the valleys are mantled with grain;[v]
they shout for joy and sing.[w]

65:4 [l] Ps 36:8
65:5 [m] Ps 85:4 [n] Ps 107:23
65:6 [o] Ps 93:1
65:7 [p] Mt 8:26 [q] Isa 17:12-13
65:9 [r] Ps 68:9-10 [s] Ps 46:4; 104:14
65:12 [t] Job 28:26
65:13 [u] Ps 144:13 [v] Ps 72:16 [w] Ps 98:8; Isa 55:12

Ps 66:5-6 ❖ Why is it important to remember and proclaim God's mighty deeds?

Psalm 66

For the director of music. A song. A psalm.

1 Shout for joy to God, all the earth![x]
2 Sing the glory of his name;[y]
make his praise glorious.
3 Say to God, "How awesome are your deeds![z]
So great is your power
that your enemies cringe[a] before you.
4 All the earth bows down[b] to you;
they sing praise[c] to you,
they sing the praises of your name."[b]

5 Come and see what God has done,
his awesome deeds[d] for mankind!
6 He turned the sea into dry land,[e]
they passed through the waters on foot—
come, let us rejoice in him.
7 He rules forever[f] by his power,
his eyes watch[g] the nations—
let not the rebellious[h] rise up against him.

8 Praise[i] our God, all peoples,
let the sound of his praise be heard;
9 he has preserved our lives
and kept our feet from slipping.[j]
10 For you, God, tested us;
you refined us like silver.[k]
11 You brought us into prison
and laid burdens[l] on our backs.
12 You let people ride over our heads;[m]
we went through fire and water,

66:1 [x] Ps 100:1
66:2 [y] Ps 79:9
66:3 [z] Ps 65:5 [a] Ps 18:44
66:4 [b] Ps 22:27 [c] Ps 67:3
66:5 [d] Ps 106:22
66:6 [e] Ex 14:22
66:7 [f] Ps 145:13 [g] Ps 11:4 [h] Ps 140:8
66:8 [i] Ps 98:4
66:9 [j] Ps 121:3
66:10 [k] Ps 17:3; Isa 48:10; Zec 13:9; 1Pe 1:6-7
66:11 [l] La 1:13
66:12 [m] Isa 51:23

[a] 9 Or *for that is how you prepare the land*
[b] 4 The Hebrew has *Selah* (a word of uncertain meaning) here and at the end of verses 7 and 15.

65:5-8 God forgives sin and provides stability. God hears the sinner's prayer and responds "with awesome and righteous deeds" (v. 5). God provided boundaries to the chaotic waters at creation and will similarly provide limits to the power of the nations and the "turmoil" (v. 7) that results from their striving. All are amazed by God's wondrous and righteous power (cf. vv. 5, 8) and are inspired to shouts of joy.
65:9-13 God so loves the land that he pours out his blessing on it. All this excess is attributed to the care and power of God (v. 8). As a result, the land throws a party (v. 13).

✣ **65:1-13** God's redemption is *inclusive* and not *exclusive*. God wants peoples near and far to fear his wondrous works—not by standing on the outside and looking in longingly but by standing shoulder to shoulder and joining in the chorus of praise with other believers.

66:1-15 The first subdivision (vv. 1-4) opens with a call to the universal praise of God by "all the earth" (v. 1). The second subsection (vv. 5-7) describes the works of God. The third subsection (vv. 8-12) begins, as did the first, with a universal call to

but you brought us to a place of
abundance.[n]
13 I will come to your temple with
burnt offerings
and fulfill my vows[o] to you—
14 vows my lips promised and my
mouth spoke
when I was in trouble.
15 I will sacrifice fat animals to you
and an offering of rams;
I will offer bulls and goats.[p]

16 Come and hear,[q] all you who fear
God;
let me tell[r] you what he has done
for me.
17 I cried out to him with my mouth;
his praise was on my tongue.
18 If I had cherished sin in my heart,
the Lord would not have listened;[s]
19 but God has surely listened
and has heard[t] my prayer.
20 Praise be to God,
who has not rejected[u] my prayer
or withheld his love from me!

Psalm 67[a]

For the director of music. With stringed instruments. A psalm. A song.

1 May God be gracious to us and
bless us
and make his face shine on us—[b][v]
2 so that your ways may be known on
earth,
your salvation[w] among all
nations.[x]

66:12 [n] Isa 43:2
66:13 [o] Ecc 5:4
66:15 [p] Nu 6:14; Ps 51:19
66:16 [q] Ps 34:11 [r] Ps 71:15,24
66:18 [s] Job 36:21; Isa 1:15; Jas 4:3
66:19 [t] Ps 116:1-2
66:20 [u] Ps 22:24; 68:35
67:1 [v] Nu 6:24-26; Ps 4:6
67:2 [w] Isa 52:10 [x] Titus 2:11
67:4 [y] Ps 96:10-13
67:6 [z] Lev 26:4; Ps 85:12; Eze 34:27
67:7 [a] Ps 33:8
68:1 [b] Nu 10:35; Isa 33:3
68:2 [c] Hos 13:3 [d] Isa 9:18; Mic 1:4

Ps 67:6 ❖ What blessings have you received from God in the past year? How have you praised him for these gifts?

3 May the peoples praise you, God;
may all the peoples praise you.
4 May the nations be glad and sing for
joy,
for you rule the peoples with
equity[y]
and guide the nations of the earth.
5 May the peoples praise you, God;
may all the peoples praise you.

6 The land yields its harvest;[z]
God, our God, blesses us.
7 May God bless us still,
so that all the ends of the earth
will fear him.[a]

Psalm 68[c]

For the director of music. Of David. A psalm. A song.

1 May God arise, may his enemies be
scattered;
may his foes flee[b] before him.
2 May you blow them away like
smoke—[c]
as wax melts[d] before the fire,
may the wicked perish before
God.

[a] In Hebrew texts 67:1-7 is numbered 67:2-8.
[b] *1* The Hebrew has *Selah* (a word of uncertain meaning) here and at the end of verse 4.
[c] In Hebrew texts 68:1-35 is numbered 68:2-36.

---

praise God. What follows constitutes Israel's personal testimony before the nations.

66:16–20 The final section of the psalm begins again with an invitation to a larger community of participants—presumably those gathered to worship in the temple. Psalm 66 becomes the testimony of Israel among the nations that God is in decisive control over the world (vv. 2–7) and delivers those who adopt the proper attitude of repentance for their sin (vv. 17–20). The goal of this testimony is to call "all the earth" (v. 1) and the "peoples" (v. 8) to experience the blessing and to join in the praise of God.

✜ **66:1–20** We sometimes think that God's power can only be displayed when we live charmed, painless lives of abundant goodness. Such a perspective inhibits us from talking honestly and openly about the failures, struggles, hurts, and attacks that characterize our lives. But it is in our weakness that the power of God is made known (2Co 12:10).

67:1–3 Verses 1–3 describe the salvation of God as extending to other nations who learn to "fear him" (v. 7).

67:4–5 Verses 4–5 continue the note of universal thanksgiving.

67:6–7 The final verse reintroduces the theme that stitches together Ps 56–68. The growing theme has reached its climax, and all is ready for the celebration to begin.

✜ **67:1–7** God has promised to guide us himself, to go before us and to make his way known. Our attention to the details of God's rule among us will sharpen our vision along with our faith to follow him.

68:1–3 The psalmist uses the imagery of vanishing smoke and melting wax to describe the utter defeat of God's enemies. While the wicked will perish when God comes, the righteous have nothing to fear.

[3]But may the righteous be glad
and rejoice[e] before God;
may they be happy and joyful.

[4]Sing to God, sing in praise of his
name,[f]
extol him who rides on the
clouds[a][g];
rejoice before him — his name is
the LORD.[h]
[5]A father to the fatherless,[i] a defender
of widows,[j]
is God in his holy dwelling.[k]
[6]God sets the lonely in families,[b][l]
he leads out the prisoners[m] with
singing;
but the rebellious live in a
sun-scorched land.[n]

[7]When you, God, went out[o] before
your people,
when you marched through the
wilderness,[c]
[8]the earth shook, the heavens poured
down rain,[p]
before God, the One of Sinai,[q]
before God, the God of Israel.
[9]You gave abundant showers,[r] O God;
you refreshed your weary
inheritance.
[10]Your people settled in it,
and from your bounty, God, you
provided[s] for the poor.

[11]The Lord announces the word,
and the women who proclaim it
are a mighty throng:
[12]"Kings and armies flee[t] in haste;
the women at home divide the
plunder.
[13]Even while you sleep among the
sheep pens,[d][u]
the wings of my dove are sheathed
with silver,
its feathers with shining gold."
[14]When the Almighty[e] scattered[v] the
kings in the land,
it was like snow fallen on Mount
Zalmon.

[15]Mount Bashan, majestic mountain,
Mount Bashan, rugged mountain,
[16]why gaze in envy, you rugged
mountain,
at the mountain where God
chooses[w] to reign,
where the LORD himself will dwell
forever?
[17]The chariots of God are tens of
thousands
and thousands of thousands;[x]
the Lord has come from Sinai into
his sanctuary.[f]
[18]When you ascended on high,
you took many captives;[y]
you received gifts from people,[z]
even from[g] the rebellious —
that you,[h] LORD God, might dwell
there.

[19]Praise be to the Lord, to God our
Savior,[a]
who daily bears our burdens.[b]

Ps 68:5-6 ❖ How can we better share and demonstrate God's heart for people who are poor or oppressed?

68:3 [e]Ps 32:11
68:4 [f]Ps 66:2 [g]Dt 33:26 [h]Ex 6:3; Ps 83:18
68:5 [i]Ps 10:14 [j]Dt 10:18 [k]Dt 26:15
68:6 [l]Ps 113:9 [m]Ac 12:6 [n]Ps 107:34
68:7 [o]Ex 13:21; Jdg 4:14
68:8 [p]Jdg 5:4 [q]Ex 19:16,18
68:9 [r]Dt 11:11
68:10 [s]Ps 74:19
68:12 [t]Jos 10:16
68:13 [u]Ge 49:14
68:14 [v]Jos 10:10
68:16 [w]Dt 12:5
68:17 [x]Dt 33:2; Da 7:10
68:18 [y]Jdg 5:12 [z]Eph 4:8*
68:19 [a]Ps 65:5 [b]Ps 55:22

[a] 4 Or *name, / prepare the way for him who rides through the deserts* [b] 6 Or *the desolate in a homeland* [c] 7 The Hebrew has *Selah* (a word of uncertain meaning) here and at the end of verses 19 and 32. [d] 13 Or *the campfires*; or *the saddlebags* [e] 14 Hebrew *Shaddai* [f] 17 Probable reading of the original Hebrew text; Masoretic Text *Lord is among them at Sinai in holiness* [g] 18 Or *gifts for people, / even* [h] 18 Or *they*

68:4–6 The coming of God is an occasion for great joy, and the gathered worshipers are called to join in singing his praise. God appears in association with the power of the storm (cf. vv. 33–34) and is proclaimed the one "who rides on the clouds" (v. 4)—a description also known to be applied to the Canaanite deity Baal.
68:7–10 In contrast to the "rebellious" (v. 6), the faithful experience Yahweh as refreshing showers. In an allusion to the exodus and conquest of Canaan, God goes before his people "through the wilderness" (v. 7). This allusion is heightened in the following verses by the phrases "God, the One of Sinai" (v. 8), "inheritance" (v. 9), and "settled in it" (v. 10).
68:11–14 When Yahweh arrives, "kings and armies flee" (v. 12) and are scattered like snow on the mountaintops (v. 14). Just the prospect of God's coming is enough to send the mighty kings of the earth into a panic.
68:15–16 The craggy mountains of Bashan gaze down with envy on Zion because it is the place "where God chooses to reign" (v. 16).
68:17–18 The victory procession of a returning king was common in the ancient Near East. Captives were paraded as a visible representation of the king's far-flung conquests. Even the "rebellious" (v. 18) will hurry with gifts.
68:19–27 God's presence in his sanctuary is a source of hope for his people. The conquered come from Bashan. The "sea" mentioned (v. 22) is the Mediterranean, which borders Israel on the west. The psalmist mixes the image of the victorious king entering his capital city with the procession of celebrants to the Jerusalem temple.

20 Our God is a God who saves;
from the Sovereign LORD comes escape from death.[c]
21 Surely God will crush the heads[d] of his enemies,
the hairy crowns of those who go on in their sins.
22 The Lord says, "I will bring them from Bashan;
I will bring them from the depths of the sea,[e]
23 that your feet may wade in the blood of your foes,[f]
while the tongues of your dogs[g] have their share."

24 Your procession, God, has come into view,
the procession of my God and King into the sanctuary.[h]
25 In front are the singers, after them the musicians;
with them are the young women playing the timbrels.[i]
26 Praise God in the great congregation;
praise the LORD in the assembly of Israel.[j]
27 There is the little tribe[k] of Benjamin, leading them,
there the great throng of Judah's princes,
and there the princes of Zebulun and of Naphtali.

28 Summon your power, God[a];
show us your strength, our God, as you have done before.
29 Because of your temple at Jerusalem
kings will bring you gifts.[l]
30 Rebuke the beast among the reeds,
the herd of bulls[m] among the calves of the nations.
Humbled, may the beast bring bars of silver.
Scatter the nations[n] who delight in war.

68:20 [c] Ps 56:13
68:21 [d] Ps 110:5; Hab 3:13
68:22 [e] Nu 21:33
68:23 [f] Ps 58:10 [g] 1Ki 21:19
68:24 [h] Ps 63:2
68:25 [i] Jdg 11:34; 1Ch 13:8
68:26 [j] Ps 26:12; Isa 48:1
68:27 [k] 1Sa 9:21
68:29 [l] Ps 72:10
68:30 [m] Ps 22:12 [n] Ps 89:10
68:31 [o] Isa 19:19; 45:14
68:33 [p] Ps 18:10 [q] Ps 29:4
68:34 [r] Ps 29:1
68:35 [s] Ps 29:11 [t] Ps 66:20
69:1 [u] Jnh 2:5
69:2 [v] Ps 40:2
69:3 [w] Ps 6:6 [x] Ps 119:82; Isa 38:14
69:4 [y] Jn 15:25* [z] Ps 35:19; 38:19

31 Envoys will come from Egypt;[o]
Cush[b] will submit herself to God.

32 Sing to God, you kingdoms of the earth,
sing praise to the Lord,
33 to him who rides[p] across the highest heavens, the ancient heavens,
who thunders with mighty voice.[q]
34 Proclaim the power[r] of God,
whose majesty is over Israel,
whose power is in the heavens.
35 You, God, are awesome in your sanctuary;
the God of Israel gives power and strength to his people.[s]

Praise be to God![t]

Psalm 69[c]

For the director of music. To the tune of "Lilies." Of David.

1 Save me, O God,
for the waters have come up to my neck.[u]
2 I sink in the miry depths,[v]
where there is no foothold.
I have come into the deep waters;
the floods engulf me.
3 I am worn out calling for help;[w]
my throat is parched.
My eyes fail,[x]
looking for my God.
4 Those who hate me without reason[y]
outnumber the hairs of my head;
many are my enemies without cause,[z]
those who seek to destroy me.
I am forced to restore
what I did not steal.

[a] *28* Many Hebrew manuscripts, Septuagint and Syriac; most Hebrew manuscripts *Your God has summoned power for you* [b] *31* That is, the upper Nile region [c] In Hebrew texts 69:1-36 is numbered 69:2-37.

68:28–31 Because of his "power" and "strength" (v. 28), the nations hurry to bring Yahweh gifts and tribute, acknowledging their allegiance to him (vv. 29–30).

68:32–35 Having seen his glory, rebellious nations praise God, who is King both in the heavens and on the earth (v. 34). Yahweh's power is manifest in his temple, and his presence in Israel imparts "power and strength to his people" (v. 35).

68:1–35 To experience God in this way is to experience him with one's guard let down and the boundaries removed. It is to know the terrible, awesome, fearsome, threatening being of the One who created us and yet is now unleashed among us to challenge our sinful nature. The image of sinful nations bringing tribute is an appropriate depiction of the individual sinner's response to a holy God.

69:1–4 The psalmist chooses the desperate struggle of a shipwreck survivor to symbolize his own struggle. The real threat is not the pounding waves of the sea but the pounding attack of enemies who seek to destroy.

5 You, God, know my folly;[a]
my guilt is not hidden from you.[b]

6 Lord, the LORD Almighty,
may those who hope in you
not be disgraced because of me;
God of Israel,
may those who seek you
not be put to shame because
of me.
7 For I endure scorn for your sake,[c]
and shame covers my face.[d]
8 I am a foreigner to my own family,
a stranger to my own mother's
children;[e]
9 for zeal for your house consumes
me,[f]
and the insults of those who insult
you fall on me.[g]
10 When I weep and fast,[h]
I must endure scorn;
11 when I put on sackcloth,[i]
people make sport of me.
12 Those who sit at the gate mock me,
and I am the song of the
drunkards.[j]

13 But I pray to you, LORD,
in the time of your favor;[k]
in your great love,[l] O God,
answer me with your sure
salvation.
14 Rescue me from the mire,
do not let me sink;
deliver me from those who hate me,
from the deep waters.[m]
15 Do not let the floodwaters[n]
engulf me
or the depths swallow me up[o]
or the pit close its mouth over me.

16 Answer me, LORD, out of the
goodness of your love;[p]
in your great mercy turn to me.
17 Do not hide your face[q] from your
servant;
answer me quickly, for I am in
trouble.[r]
18 Come near and rescue me;
deliver[s] me because of my foes.

19 You know how I am scorned,[t]
disgraced and shamed;
all my enemies are before you.
20 Scorn has broken my heart
and has left me helpless;
I looked for sympathy, but there was
none,
for comforters,[u] but I found none.[v]
21 They put gall in my food
and gave me vinegar for my
thirst.[w]

22 May the table set before them
become a snare;
may it become retribution and[a] a
trap.
23 May their eyes be darkened so they
cannot see,
and their backs be bent forever.[x]
24 Pour out your wrath[y] on them;
let your fierce anger overtake
them.
25 May their place be deserted;[z]
let there be no one to dwell in
their tents.[a]
26 For they persecute those you wound
and talk about the pain of those
you hurt.[b]
27 Charge them with crime upon
crime;[c]
do not let them share in your
salvation.[d]
28 May they be blotted out of the book
of life[e]

[a] 22 Or *snare / and their fellowship become*

69:5 [a] Ps 38:5 [b] Ps 44:21
69:7 [c] Jer 15:15 [d] Ps 44:15
69:8 [e] Ps 31:11; Isa 53:3
69:9 [f] Jn 2:17* [g] Ps 89:50-51; Ro 15:3*
69:10 [h] Ps 35:13
69:11 [i] Ps 35:13
69:12 [j] Job 30:9
69:13 [k] Isa 49:8; 2Co 6:2 [l] Ps 51:1
69:14 [m] ver 2; Ps 144:7
69:15 [n] Ps 124:4-5 [o] Nu 16:33
69:16 [p] Ps 63:3
69:17 [q] Ps 27:9 [r] Ps 66:14
69:18 [s] Ps 49:15
69:19 [t] Ps 22:6
69:20 [u] Job 16:2 [v] Isa 63:5
69:21 [w] Mt 27:34; Mk 15:23; Jn 19:28-30
69:23 [x] Isa 6:9-10; Ro 11:9-10*
69:24 [y] Ps 79:6
69:25 [z] Mt 23:38 [a] Ac 1:20*
69:26 [b] Isa 53:4; Zec 1:15
69:27 [c] Ne 4:5 [d] Ps 109:14; Isa 26:10
69:28 [e] Ex 32:32-33; Lk 10:20; Php 4:3

Ps 69:9 ❖ How can we show our zeal for God's house, sharing Christ's passion for the Father's honor (see Jn 2:17)?

69:5–12 Whatever the nature of the guilt the psalmist admits to God in v. 5, the scorn he experiences results from his "zeal" for God's house (v. 9).
69:10–12 The public response to the psalmist's fervent and visible grief is ridicule and mocking.
69:13–18 The psalmist's desperation is highlighted by the repeated appearance of the call "answer me" in vv. 13, 16, 17. God's "great love" (v. 13; cf. v. 16) and "mercy" (v. 16) serve as the grounds for his plea. For God to "hide [his] face" (v. 17) from his covenant people was considered a sign of divine rejection and punishment for sin.
69:19–21 This sadistic toying with the one suffering is used in the NT to describe the suffering of Christ on the cross.
69:22–24 The "snare" and "trap" (v. 22) are frequently used metaphorically for sudden entrapment of humans by their own deeds. These honest expressions of anger are placed within the context of anticipated *divine* retribution (v. 24). The blindness, constant burdens, decimation of descendants, and striking of the enemy's name from the "book of life" (v. 28) are God's actions against those who injure people under his protection.
69:26–27 In calling for divine action against the

and not be listed with the
righteous.[f]

29 But as for me, afflicted and in pain —
may your salvation, God, protect
me.[g]

30 I will praise God's name in song[h]
and glorify him[i] with
thanksgiving.
31 This will please the LORD more than
an ox,
more than a bull with its horns
and hooves.[j]
32 The poor will see and be glad[k] —
you who seek God, may your
hearts live![l]
33 The LORD hears the needy[m]
and does not despise his captive
people.

34 Let heaven and earth praise him,
the seas and all that move in
them,[n]
35 for God will save Zion[o]
and rebuild the cities of Judah.[p]
Then people will settle there and
possess it;
36 the children of his servants will
inherit it,
and those who love his name will
dwell there.[q]

Psalm 70[a]

70:1–5pp // Ps 40:13–17

For the director of music.
Of David. A petition.

1 Hasten, O God, to save me;
come quickly, LORD, to help me.[r]

2 May those who want to take my life[s]
be put to shame and confusion;
may all who desire my ruin
be turned back in disgrace.[t]
3 May those who say to me, "Aha!
Aha!"
turn back because of their shame.
4 But may all who seek you
rejoice and be glad in you;
may those who long for your saving
help always say,
"The LORD is great!"

5 But as for me, I am poor and needy;[u]
come quickly to me,[v] O God.
You are my help and my deliverer;
LORD, do not delay.

Psalm 71

71:1–3pp // Ps 31:1–4

1 In you, LORD, I have taken refuge;
let me never be put to shame.[w]
2 In your righteousness, rescue me
and deliver me;
turn your ear[x] to me and save me.
3 Be my rock of refuge,
to which I can always go;
give the command to save me,
for you are my rock and my
fortress.[y]
4 Deliver me, my God, from the hand
of the wicked,[z]
from the grasp of those who are
evil and cruel.

5 For you have been my hope,
Sovereign LORD,
my confidence[a] since my youth.

Ps 70:1 ❖ What situations in life send you crying out for God's saving help?

69:28 [f] Eze 13:9
69:29 [g] Ps 59:1; 70:5
69:30 [h] Ps 28:7 [i] Ps 34:3
69:31 [j] Ps 50:9-13
69:32 [k] Ps 34:2 [l] Ps 22:26
69:33 [m] Ps 12:5; 68:6
69:34 [n] Ps 96:11; 148:1; Isa 44:23; 49:13; 55:12
69:35 [o] Ob 17 [p] Ps 51:18; Isa 44:26
69:36 [q] Ps 37:29; 102:28
70:1 [r] Ps 40:13
70:2 [s] Ps 35:4 [t] Ps 35:26
70:5 [u] Ps 40:17 [v] Ps 141:1
71:1 [w] Ps 25:2-3; 31:1
71:2 [x] Ps 17:6
71:3 [y] Ps 18:2; 31:2-3; 44:4
71:4 [z] Ps 140:4
71:5 [a] Job 4:6; Jer 17:7

[a] In Hebrew texts 70:1-5 is numbered 70:2-6.

---

enemy, the psalmist acknowledges that God is already in the process of disciplining him as well.
69:29 The psalmist concludes this section with a plea for God's salvation and protection.
69:30-33 Here a shift occurs. This change of mood comes with a vow to "praise God's name in song" (v. 30).
69:34-36 In the final segment of the psalm, the psalmist calls "heaven and earth," the "seas," and their inhabitants (v. 34) to join in the praise of God. The shift begun at the end of v. 33 continues as he envisions God's salvation of Zion and the reconstruction and repopulation of the devastated cities of Judah.

✣ **69:1-36** What identifies salt, Jesus says, is *invisible* to the eye (Mk 9:50). But just put a bit on the tip of your tongue and you will know: It *tastes* like salt. Similarly, if we are connected to God through his Son, that relationship will work itself out in visible ways; we will be obviously and distinctively different from those who have not entered God's kingdom.

70:1-5 Psalm 70 serves to introduce the more extensive plea of Ps 71.
71:1-4 The opening section of Ps 71 introduces the new theme of "refuge" that dominates vv. 1-8. The theme of shame and disgrace reappears as well. The refuge God provides is always available to those in need (v. 3).
71:5-9 For the first time it becomes clear that the psalmist is speaking from the experience and vulnerability of old age. He realizes that dependence

6 From birth[b] I have relied on you;
you brought me forth from my mother's womb.[c]
I will ever praise[d] you.
7 I have become a sign[e] to many;
you are my strong refuge.[f]
8 My mouth[g] is filled with your praise,
declaring your splendor[h] all day long.

9 Do not cast[i] me away when I am old;[j]
do not forsake me when my strength is gone.
10 For my enemies speak against me;
those who wait to kill[k] me conspire[l] together.
11 They say, "God has forsaken him;
pursue him and seize him,
for no one will rescue[m] him."
12 Do not be far[n] from me, my God;
come quickly, God, to help[o] me.
13 May my accusers perish in shame;
may those who want to harm me
be covered with scorn and disgrace.[p]

14 As for me, I will always have hope;[q]
I will praise you more and more.

15 My mouth will tell[r] of your righteous deeds,
of your saving acts all day long —
though I know not how to relate them all.
16 I will come and proclaim your mighty acts,[s] Sovereign LORD;
I will proclaim your righteous deeds, yours alone.

71:6 [b] Ps 22:10 [c] Ps 22:9; Isa 46:3 [d] Ps 9:1; 34:1; 52:9; 119:164; 145:2
71:7 [e] Isa 8:18; 1Co 4:9 [f] 2Sa 22:3; Ps 61:3
71:8 [g] Ps 51:15; 63:5 [h] Ps 35:28; 96:6; 104:1
71:9 [i] Ps 51:11 [j] ver 18; Ps 92:14; Isa 46:4
71:10 [k] Ps 10:8; 59:3; Pr 1:18 [l] Ps 31:13; 56:6; Mt 12:14
71:11 [m] Ps 7:2
71:12 [n] Ps 35:22; 38:21 [o] Ps 38:22; 70:1
71:13 [p] ver 24
71:14 [q] Ps 130:7
71:15 [r] Ps 35:28; 40:5
71:16 [s] Ps 106:2
71:17 [t] Dt 4:5 [u] Ps 26:7
71:18 [v] ver 9 [w] Ps 22:30, 31; 78:4
71:19 [x] Ps 36:5; 57:10 [y] Ps 126:2; Lk 1:49 [z] Ps 35:10
71:20 [a] Ps 60:3 [b] Hos 6:2
71:21 [c] Ps 18:35 [d] Ps 23:4; 86:17; Isa 12:1; 49:13
71:22 [e] Ps 33:2 [f] Ps 92:3; 144:9 [g] 2Ki 19:22
71:23 [h] Ps 103:4
71:24 [i] Ps 35:28 [j] ver 13

Ps 71:5–18 ❖ How does God work in believers' lives to establish our faith in him?

17 Since my youth, God, you have taught[t] me,
and to this day I declare your marvelous deeds.[u]
18 Even when I am old and gray,[v]
do not forsake me, my God,
till I declare your power to the next generation,
your mighty acts to all who are to come.[w]

19 Your righteousness, God, reaches to the heavens,[x]
you who have done great things.[y]
Who is like you, God?[z]
20 Though you have made me see troubles,[a]
many and bitter,
you will restore[b] my life again;
from the depths of the earth
you will again bring me up.
21 You will increase my honor[c]
and comfort[d] me once more.

22 I will praise you with the harp[e]
for your faithfulness, my God;
I will sing praise to you with the lyre,[f]
Holy One of Israel.[g]
23 My lips will shout for joy
when I sing praise to you —
I whom you have delivered.[h]
24 My tongue will tell of your righteous acts
all day long,[i]
for those who wanted to harm me[j]
have been put to shame and confusion.

---

on Yahweh predates even birth, to the time when he was being formed in his mother's womb.
71:10–13 The opponents are pictured watching closely for an opportunity to attack. The psalmist turns desperately to God for immediate deliverance and desires shame and disgrace to pour out on his enemies.
71:14–24 Two elements dominate this expression of praise and confidence: the righteousness of Yahweh and his saving acts. The former is mentioned three times (vv. 15, 16, 19) while the latter appears four times (vv. 15, 16, 17, 19).
71:19 "Who is like you, God?" This expression of God's incomparability is on the one hand the pinnacle of the psalmist's praise of Yahweh, while on the other hand it provides the foundation for his confidence expressed in vv. 20–21.
71:20–23 "From the depths of the earth" in v. 20 might suggest resurrection from the grave, but it probably indicates the psalmist's confidence of being delivered from a life-threatening circumstance.
71:24 Verse 24 returns to the concerns expressed at the beginning of chs. 70–71. There the psalmist called on Yahweh for speedy deliverance (70:2–4). In 71:24 he concludes with the answering assurance.

✣ **70:1—71:24** While aging is becoming an increasing concern of modern society, our concern should be to enhance the spiritual, emotional, and physical health and satisfaction among the aging population rather than to simply and vainly strive to delay or eliminate the effects of aging.

Psalm 72

Of Solomon.

1 Endow the king with your justice, O God,
the royal son with your righteousness.
2 May he judge your people in righteousness,[k]
your afflicted ones with justice.

3 May the mountains bring prosperity to the people,
the hills the fruit of righteousness.
4 May he defend the afflicted among the people
and save the children of the needy;[l]
may he crush the oppressor.
5 May he endure[a] as long as the sun,
as long as the moon, through all generations.
6 May he be like rain[m] falling on a mown field,
like showers watering the earth.
7 In his days may the righteous flourish[n]
and prosperity abound till the moon is no more.

8 May he rule from sea to sea
and from the River[b][o] to the ends of the earth.[p]
9 May the desert tribes bow before him
and his enemies lick the dust.
10 May the kings of Tarshish and of distant shores
bring tribute to him.
May the kings of Sheba[q] and Seba
present him gifts.[r]
11 May all kings bow down to him
and all nations serve him.

72:2 [k] Isa 9:7; 11:4-5; 32:1
72:4 [l] Isa 11:4
72:6 [m] Dt 32:2; Hos 6:3
72:7 [n] Ps 92:12; Isa 2:4
72:8 [o] Ex 23:31 [p] Zec 9:10
72:10 [q] Ge 10:7 [r] 2Ch 9:24

Ps 72:8-11 ❖ How do we see God's kingdom spreading in every corner of the globe? How can we support this mission?

12 For he will deliver the needy who cry out,
the afflicted who have no one to help.
13 He will take pity on the weak and the needy
and save the needy from death.
14 He will rescue[s] them from oppression and violence,
for precious[t] is their blood in his sight.

15 Long may he live!
May gold from Sheba[u] be given him.
May people ever pray for him
and bless him all day long.
16 May grain abound throughout the land;
on the tops of the hills may it sway.
May the crops flourish like Lebanon[v]
and thrive[c] like the grass of the field.
17 May his name endure forever;[w]
may it continue as long as the sun.[x]

Then all nations will be blessed through him,[d]
and they will call him blessed.[y]

18 Praise be to the LORD God, the God of Israel,[z]
who alone does marvelous deeds.[a]

72:14 [s] Ps 69:18 [t] 1Sa 26:21; Ps 116:15
72:15 [u] Isa 60:6
72:16 [v] Ps 104:16
72:17 [w] Ex 3:15 [x] Ps 89:36 [y] Ge 12:3; Lk 1:48
72:18 [z] 1Ch 29:10; Ps 41:13; 106:48 [a] Job 5:9

[a] *5* Septuagint; Hebrew *You will be feared* [b] *8* That is, the Euphrates [c] *16* Probable reading of the original Hebrew text; Masoretic Text *Lebanon, / from the city* [d] *17* Or *will use his name in blessings* (see Gen. 48:20)

72:1 The psalm opens with a direct appeal for God to empower "the king" with the necessary resources for just and righteous rule.
72:2–4 God is the source of right rule. Monarchs empowered by him will rule so that the defenseless are protected, the oppressor crushed.
72:5–7 The "sun" and "moon" (v. 5), established by God at creation, serve as symbols of longevity and endurance. Because the monarch pours righteous judgment on the land, the "righteous" will "flourish" (v. 7).
72:8–11 The king is envisioned as establishing the intended creation order—God's kingdom—throughout the whole earth. Ultimately "all kings . . . and all nations" (v. 11) will submit to his authority. The language expresses the hopes of the exilic community for a future "son of David"—the Messiah—who will usher in the kingdom of God.
72:12–14 The king has the task of defending those who are unable to defend themselves in society.
72:15–17 Such a king will be loved by his people, who will pray daily for his well-being and bless him. In a subtle interweaving of the covenantal promises to David and Abraham, the nations are said to "be blessed through him" at the same time they "call him blessed" (v. 17).
72:18–19 This sentiment is another one particularly well suited to bring to a close the developing theme of the preceding group of Ps 56–72.

19 Praise be to his glorious name
forever;
may the whole earth be filled with
his glory.[b]
Amen and Amen.[c]

20 This concludes the prayers of David
son of Jesse.

BOOK III

Psalms 73 – 89

Psalm 73

A psalm of Asaph.

1 Surely God is good to Israel,
to those who are pure in heart.[d]

2 But as for me, my feet had almost
slipped;
I had nearly lost my foothold.
3 For I envied[e] the arrogant
when I saw the prosperity of the
wicked.[f]

4 They have no struggles;
their bodies are healthy and
strong.[a]
5 They are free[g] from common human
burdens;
they are not plagued by human
ills.
6 Therefore pride is their necklace;[h]
they clothe themselves with
violence.[i]
7 From their callous hearts[j] comes
iniquity[b];
their evil imaginations have no
limits.
8 They scoff, and speak with malice;
with arrogance[k] they threaten
oppression.
9 Their mouths lay claim to heaven,
and their tongues take possession
of the earth.
10 Therefore their people turn to them
and drink up waters in
abundance.[c]
11 They say, "How would God know?
Does the Most High know
anything?"

12 This is what the wicked are like —
always free of care, they go on
amassing wealth.[l]

13 Surely in vain[m] I have kept my heart
pure
and have washed my hands in
innocence.[n]
14 All day long I have been afflicted,
and every morning brings new
punishments.

15 If I had spoken out like that,
I would have betrayed your
children.
16 When I tried to understand[o] all this,
it troubled me deeply
17 till I entered the sanctuary[p] of God;
then I understood their final
destiny.[q]

18 Surely you place them on slippery
ground;[r]
you cast them down to ruin.

72:19 [b] Nu 14:21; Ne 9:5 [c] Ps 41:13
73:1 [d] Mt 5:8
73:3 [e] Ps 37:1; Pr 23:17 [f] Job 21:7; Jer 12:1
73:5 [g] Job 21:9
73:6 [h] Ge 41:42 [i] Ps 109:18
73:7 [j] Ps 17:10
73:8 [k] Ps 17:10; Jude 16
73:12 [l] Ps 49:6
73:13 [m] Job 21:15; 34:9 [n] Ps 26:6
73:16 [o] Ecc 8:17
73:17 [p] Ps 77:13 [q] Ps 37:38
73:18 [r] Ps 35:6

Ps 73:1–17 ❖ Have you ever envied carefree people who give no thought to God yet are wealthy and healthy? How can entering God's sanctuary clear our vision?

[a] *4* With a different word division of the Hebrew; Masoretic Text *struggles at their death; / their bodies are healthy* [b] *7* Syriac (see also Septuagint); Hebrew *Their eyes bulge with fat* [c] *10* The meaning of the Hebrew for this verse is uncertain.

72:20 The term for "prayers" most commonly reflects petition or entreaty on behalf of the sufferer.

72:1–20 Psalm 72 calls us to pray not only for the well-being of our leaders but also for their wisdom to see that all justice is ultimately God's justice. Righteousness is not measured by what works but by the character of God. He empowers leaders and will ultimately set all things right (v. 8).

73:1 Asaph reminds the reader that "surely God is good," and in v. 28 he states that "it is good to be near God."
73:2–14 Why do the wicked prosper when God's people seem to struggle so much? Asaph *believes* that God is good, but he *knows* that he is suffering (vv. 13–14). Herein lies the crisis of faith and experience: Asaph believes one thing, but his experience tells another.
73:15–17 This passage marks a turning point in the psalm, pivoting from lament to praise and declaration of faith. Clearly, it is in meeting with God in his sanctuary that Asaph's internal torment finds release. The psalmist came to see things from God's perspective (vv. 21–22).
73:18–28 It was ignorance of God's mystery and his inability to bring to mind the fact that God is simply bigger than our human understanding that led to Asaph's overemphasis on temporal as

19 How suddenly[s] are they destroyed,
completely swept away by terrors!
20 They are like a dream[t] when one
awakes;[u]
when you arise, Lord,
you will despise them as fantasies.

21 When my heart was grieved
and my spirit embittered,
22 I was senseless[v] and ignorant;
I was a brute beast[w] before you.

23 Yet I am always with you;
you hold me by my right hand.
24 You guide[x] me with your counsel,[y]
and afterward you will take me
into glory.
25 Whom have I in heaven but you?
And earth has nothing I desire
besides you.[z]
26 My flesh and my heart[a] may fail,[b]
but God is the strength of my
heart
and my portion forever.

27 Those who are far from you will
perish;[c]
you destroy all who are unfaithful
to you.
28 But as for me, it is good to be near
God.[d]
I have made the Sovereign LORD
my refuge;
I will tell of all your deeds.[e]

Psalm 74

A maskil[a] of Asaph.

1 O God, why have you rejected us
forever?[f]
Why does your anger smolder
against the sheep of your
pasture?[g]
2 Remember the nation you
purchased[h] long ago,[i]
the people of your inheritance,
whom you redeemed[j]—
Mount Zion, where you dwelt.[k]
3 Turn your steps toward these
everlasting ruins,
all this destruction the enemy has
brought on the sanctuary.

4 Your foes roared[l] in the place where
you met with us;
they set up their standards[m] as
signs.
5 They behaved like men wielding
axes
to cut through a thicket of trees.[n]
6 They smashed all the carved[o]
paneling
with their axes and hatchets.
7 They burned your sanctuary to the
ground;
they defiled the dwelling place of
your Name.
8 They said in their hearts, "We will
crush[p] them completely!"
They burned every place where
God was worshiped in the
land.

9 We are given no signs from God;
no prophets[q] are left,
and none of us knows how long
this will be.
10 How long will the enemy mock you,
God?
Will the foe revile[r] your name
forever?
11 Why do you hold back your hand,
your right hand?[s]

73:19 [s] Isa 47:11
73:20 [t] Job 20:8 [u] Ps 78:65
73:22 [v] Ps 49:10; 92:6 [w] Ecc 3:18
73:24 [x] Ps 48:14 [y] Ps 32:8
73:25 [z] Php 3:8
73:26 [a] Ps 84:2 [b] Ps 40:12
73:27 [c] Ps 119:155
73:28 [d] Heb 10:22; Jas 4:8 [e] Ps 40:5
74:1 [f] Dt 29:20; Ps 44:23 [g] Ps 79:13; 95:7; 100:3
74:2 [h] Ex 15:16 [i] Dt 32:7 [j] Ex 15:13 [k] Ps 68:16
74:4 [l] La 2:7 [m] Nu 2:2
74:5 [n] Jer 46:22
74:6 [o] 1Ki 6:18
74:8 [p] Ps 83:4
74:9 [q] 1Sa 3:1
74:10 [r] Ps 44:16
74:11 [s] La 2:3

[a] Title: Probably a literary or musical term

Ps 74:1 ❖ Why do those who are in Christ not need to fear God's rejection (see Ro 8:1)?

opposed to eternal reality (vv. 21–22). Meeting with God awakens the poet to a profound awareness of the immense gift of divine presence. Asaph realizes he is truly rich (vv. 25–27).

73:27–28 God's justice will not be denied. Sometimes it is realized by the way he intervenes into current events of humankind, but we are certain it will become clear at the final judgment.

73:1–28 The sovereign God sees our hearts and knows our moods and precisely how we see things. If we are disappointed or angry with God he is fully aware of that fact, and there is no point in offering a politely dishonest prayer.

74:1–3 As is so often the way in the Psalms, despair leads to prayer. The irony of this passage is that the *enemies* of Judah have become the *instruments* of Yahweh.

74:4–9 The psalmist points to the great offense perpetrated by Judah's enemies in their assault on the temple. The lack of "signs" (v. 9) may refer to the silence of God in response to the fall of Jerusalem. What is more, there are no prophets, and the people do not know how long this state of affairs will continue.

74:10–11 Knowing that Yahweh is capable of acting makes his inactivity all the more inexplicable from the psalmist's perspective.

Take it from the folds of your
garment and destroy them!

12 But God is my King[t] from long
ago;
he brings salvation on the
earth.

13 It was you who split open the sea[u] by
your power;
you broke the heads of the
monster[v] in the waters.

14 It was you who crushed the heads of
Leviathan
and gave it as food to the
creatures of the desert.

15 It was you who opened up springs[w]
and streams;
you dried up[x] the ever-flowing
rivers.

16 The day is yours, and yours also the
night;
you established the sun and
moon.[y]

17 It was you who set all the
boundaries[z] of the earth;
you made both summer and
winter.[a]

18 Remember how the enemy has
mocked you, LORD,
how foolish people[b] have reviled
your name.

19 Do not hand over the life of your
dove to wild beasts;
do not forget the lives of your
afflicted[c] people forever.

20 Have regard for your covenant,[d]
because haunts of violence fill the
dark places of the land.

21 Do not let the oppressed[e] retreat in
disgrace;
may the poor and needy[f] praise
your name.

22 Rise up, O God, and defend your
cause;
remember how fools[g] mock you
all day long.

23 Do not ignore the clamor of your
adversaries,[h]
the uproar of your enemies, which
rises continually.

74:12 [t] Ps 44:4
74:13 [u] Ex 14:21 [v] Isa 51:9; Eze 29:3
74:15 [w] Ex 17:6; Nu 20:11 [x] Jos 2:10; 3:13
74:16 [y] Ge 1:16; Ps 136:7-9
74:17 [z] Dt 32:8; Ac 17:26 [a] Ge 8:22
74:18 [b] Dt 32:6; Ps 39:8
74:19 [c] Ps 9:18
74:20 [d] Ge 17:7; Ps 106:45
74:21 [e] Ps 103:6 [f] Ps 35:10
74:22 [g] Ps 53:1
74:23 [h] Ps 65:7

Psalm 75[a]

For the director of music. To the tune of "Do Not Destroy." A psalm of Asaph. A song.

1 We praise you, God,
we praise you, for your Name is
near;[i]
people tell of your wonderful
deeds.[j]

2 You say, "I choose the appointed
time;
it is I who judge with equity.

3 When the earth and all its people
quake,[k]
it is I who hold its pillars[l] firm.[b]

4 To the arrogant I say, 'Boast no
more,'
and to the wicked, 'Do not lift up
your horns.[c][m]

5 Do not lift your horns against
heaven;
do not speak so defiantly.' "

6 No one from the east or the west
or from the desert can exalt
themselves.

7 It is God who judges:[n]
He brings one down, he exalts
another.[o]

75:1 [i] Ps 145:18 [j] Ps 44:1; 71:16
75:3 [k] Isa 24:19 [l] 1Sa 2:8
75:4 [m] Zec 1:21
75:7 [n] Ps 50:6 [o] 1Sa 2:7; Ps 147:6; Da 2:21

[a] In Hebrew texts 75:1-10 is numbered 75:2-11.
[b] 3 The Hebrew has *Selah* (a word of uncertain meaning) here.
[c] 4 *Horns* here symbolize strength; also in verses 5 and 10.

74:12–21 The psalmist speaks of Yahweh's intrinsic character (v. 12), which cannot change even if the community's present circumstances are difficult to understand. The graphic presentation of Yahweh in vv. 13–16 is designed to illustrate his power over chaos.
74:18–23 The psalmist asks Yahweh to remember Judah's enemies mocking his name, to remember his covenant, and not to forget his afflicted people forever. The command to "rise up" (v. 22) is directed toward Yahweh as Judge. The loss of the temple was a challenge to the very nature of Yahweh.

74:1–23 It may be hard for us to discern just how God's hand is at work in the (often traumatic) events of our own experience. Challenging as it may be, we should practice such discernment. We should ask God to reveal to us how and where he is at work in our own situations and also ask what role he would have us play to move his purposes forward.

75:1 It is poignant that the psalmist celebrates the nearness of God's "Name" following a lament over the loss of the temple.
75:2–5 Not only will God judge, but God holds the earth and keeps it secure—he will deal with the arrogant and the mocker.
75:6–8 In these verses the psalmist himself portrays God first as the exalting and humbling God and then as Judge.

[8]In the hand of the LORD is a cup
full of foaming wine mixed[p] with
spices;
he pours it out, and all the wicked of
the earth
drink it down to its very dregs.[q]

[9]As for me, I will declare[r] this
forever;
I will sing praise to the God of
Jacob,
[10]who says, "I will cut off the horns of
all the wicked,
but the horns of the righteous will
be lifted up."[s]

Psalm 76[a]

For the director of music. With stringed instruments. A psalm of Asaph. A song.

[1]God is renowned in Judah;
in Israel his name is great.
[2]His tent is in Salem,[t]
his dwelling place in Zion.
[3]There he broke the flashing arrows,
the shields and the swords, the
weapons of war.[b][u]

[4]You are radiant with light,
more majestic than mountains
rich with game.
[5]The valiant lie plundered,
they sleep their last sleep;[v]
not one of the warriors
can lift his hands.
[6]At your rebuke, God of Jacob,
both horse and chariot[w] lie still.

[7]It is you alone who are to be feared.[x]
Who can stand[y] before you when
you are angry?[z]
[8]From heaven you pronounced
judgment,
and the land feared[a] and was
quiet—
[9]when you, God, rose up to judge,[b]
to save all the afflicted of the
land.
[10]Surely your wrath against mankind
brings you praise,[c]
and the survivors of your wrath
are restrained.[c]

[11]Make vows to the LORD your God and
fulfill them;[d]
let all the neighboring lands
bring gifts[e] to the One to be
feared.
[12]He breaks the spirit of rulers;
he is feared by the kings of the
earth.

Psalm 77[d]

For the director of music. For Jeduthun. Of Asaph. A psalm.

[1]I cried out to God[f] for help;
I cried out to God to hear me.
[2]When I was in distress,[g] I sought the
Lord;

75:8 [p] Pr 23:30 [q] Job 21:20; Jer 25:15
75:9 [r] Ps 40:10
75:10 [s] Ps 89:17; 92:10; 148:14
76:2 [t] Ge 14:18
76:3 [u] Ps 46:9
76:5 [v] Ps 13:3
76:6 [w] Ex 15:1
76:7 [x] 1Ch 16:25 [y] Ezr 9:15; Rev 6:17 [z] Ps 2:5; Na 1:6
76:8 [a] 1Ch 16:30; 2Ch 20:29-30
76:9 [b] Ps 9:8
76:10 [c] Ex 9:16; Ro 9:17
76:11 [d] Ps 50:14; Ecc 5:4-5 [e] 2Ch 32:23; Ps 68:29
77:1 [f] Ps 3:4
77:2 [g] Ps 50:15; Isa 26:9,16

Ps 75:8 ❖ God's cup of judgment was taken up by Christ on behalf of God's children (see Lk 22:42). How does this knowledge bring us comfort and assurance?

Ps 76:11 ❖ What vows have you made to God? How can you fulfill them?

[a] In Hebrew texts 76:1-12 is numbered 76:2-13.
[b] 3 The Hebrew has *Selah* (a word of uncertain meaning) here and at the end of verse 9.
[c] 10 Or *Surely the wrath of mankind brings you praise, / and with the remainder of wrath you arm yourself*
[d] In Hebrew texts 77:1-20 is numbered 77:2-21.

75:9-10 The psalm closes with a double declaration. The first statement is the psalmist's determination to declare God's authority and "sing praise to the God of Jacob" (v. 9). The final declaration of judgment is another divine message.

75:1-10 Often the way we see our reality is very different from God's perspective. God intends to bless us for our *eternal good,* though not necessarily for our *present ease.*

76:1-3 God is not distant. God still dwells in Zion. Israel's God ends their wars.
76:4-6 The imagery in this passage speaks of God's great and unquestionable majesty. The God who ends wars leaves rebellious armies devastated and powerless.

76:7-10 The idea of a sovereign's being "feared" (v. 7) in the ancient world was used in much the same way as we would use the word *awed.*
76:11-12 The aim of God's justice is always to bring peace and restore righteousness. God saves his people by ending rebellion and transforming the rebels. This final stanza sets out to answer the question of how we respond to such a God.

76:1-12 Jesus made a public spectacle of all the powers of evil that would keep us from coming to God—he triumphed over them by the cross.

77:1-2 The psalmist is relating an account of a protracted time when he grappled with God in prayer.

at night I stretched out untiring
hands,[h]
and I would not be comforted.[i]
3 I remembered you, God, and I
groaned;
I meditated, and my spirit grew
faint.[a][j]
4 You kept my eyes from closing;
I was too troubled to speak.
5 I thought about the former days,[k]
the years of long ago;
6 I remembered my songs in the
night.
My heart meditated and my spirit
asked:

7 "Will the Lord reject forever?
Will he never show his favor[l]
again?
8 Has his unfailing love vanished
forever?
Has his promise[m] failed for all
time?
9 Has God forgotten to be merciful?[n]
Has he in anger withheld his
compassion?[o]"

10 Then I thought, "To this I will
appeal:
the years when the Most High
stretched out his right hand.[p]
11 I will remember the deeds of the
LORD;
yes, I will remember your
miracles[q] of long ago.
12 I will consider all your works
and meditate on all your mighty
deeds."

13 Your ways, God, are holy.
What god is as great as our God?[r]
14 You are the God who performs
miracles;
you display your power among the
peoples.

77:2 [h] Job 11:13 [i] Ge 37:35
77:3 [j] Ps 143:4
77:5 [k] Dt 32:7; Ps 44:1; 143:5; Isa 51:9
77:7 [l] Ps 85:1
77:8 [m] 2Pe 3:9
77:9 [n] Ps 25:6; 40:11; 51:1 [o] Isa 49:15
77:10 [p] Ps 31:22
77:11 [q] Ps 143:5
77:13 [r] Ex 15:11; Ps 71:19; 86:8

Ps 77:10 ❖ How can remembering God's mighty acts of the past anchor us through current trials? What circumstances are you experiencing that may spur you to recall God's faithfulness?

15 With your mighty arm you
redeemed your people,[s]
the descendants of Jacob and
Joseph.

16 The waters[t] saw you, God,
the waters saw you and
writhed;[u]
the very depths were convulsed.
17 The clouds poured down water,[v]
the heavens resounded with
thunder;
your arrows flashed back and
forth.
18 Your thunder was heard in the
whirlwind,
your lightning lit up the world;
the earth trembled and quaked.[w]
19 Your path led through the sea,[x]
your way through the mighty
waters,
though your footprints were not
seen.

20 You led your people[y] like a flock[z]
by the hand of Moses and Aaron.

Psalm 78

A maskil[b] of Asaph.

1 My people, hear my teaching;[a]
listen to the words of my mouth.
2 I will open my mouth with a
parable;[b]

77:15 [s] Ex 6:6; Dt 9:29
77:16 [t] Ex 14:21, 28; Hab 3:8 [u] Ps 114:4; Hab 3:10
77:17 [v] Jdg 5:4
77:18 [w] Jdg 5:4
77:19 [x] Hab 3:15
77:20 [y] Ex 13:21 [z] Ps 78:52; Isa 63:11
78:1 [a] Isa 51:4; 55:3
78:2 [b] Ps 49:4; Mt 13:35*

[a] 3 The Hebrew has *Selah* (a word of uncertain meaning) here and at the end of verses 9 and 15.
[b] Title: Probably a literary or musical term

77:3–6 The poet's memory of past grace made his present suffering even more difficult to bear. It is possible that the songs which the speaker remembered in the night were songs of praise to Yahweh.
77:7–9 This self-interrogation reminds the speaker of what he knows about his God. This reminder brings remarkable transformation.
77:10–15 Verse 10 serves as the pivot around which this poem revolves. Equally, the verses that follow speak of the poet's remembrance of the saving works of Yahweh in the past and his goodness toward his own people. Israel's God has not changed.
77:16–20 The poet commemorates the parting of the Red Sea (Ex 14). Clouds, thunder, lightning, and the quaking of the earth typically mark the physical manifestation of God on earth in the OT.
77:20 The image of God as Shepherd in the ancient Near East speaks of both divine kingship and of divine care. Just as the flock is obliged to follow the shepherd, so also the shepherd is expected to look after the sheep.

✜ **77:1–20** Our spirituality must be marked by remembrance of the past as much as it is marked by vision for the future. God has been, is, and always will be faithful to his promises.

78:1–8 Verses 1–2 present the reader with a context for understanding what is to follow.

I will utter hidden things, things
from of old —
3 things we have heard and known,
things our ancestors have told us.[c]
4 We will not hide them from their
descendants;[d]
we will tell the next generation
the praiseworthy deeds[e] of the
LORD,
his power, and the wonders he has
done.
5 He decreed statutes[f] for Jacob[g]
and established the law in Israel,
which he commanded our ancestors
to teach their children,
6 so the next generation would know
them,
even the children yet to be born,[h]
and they in turn would tell their
children.
7 Then they would put their trust in
God
and would not forget[i] his deeds
but would keep his commands.[j]
8 They would not be like their
ancestors[k] —
a stubborn[l] and rebellious[m]
generation,
whose hearts were not loyal to God,
whose spirits were not faithful to
him.

9 The men of Ephraim, though armed
with bows,[n]
turned back on the day of battle;[o]
10 they did not keep God's covenant[p]
and refused to live by his law.
11 They forgot what he had done,[q]
the wonders he had shown them.
12 He did miracles[r] in the sight of their
ancestors
in the land of Egypt,[s] in the region
of Zoan.[t]
13 He divided the sea[u] and led them
through;
he made the water stand up like a
wall.[v]
14 He guided them with the cloud by
day
and with light from the fire all
night.[w]
15 He split the rocks[x] in the wilderness
and gave them water as abundant
as the seas;
16 he brought streams out of a rocky
crag
and made water flow down like
rivers.

17 But they continued to sin[y] against
him,
rebelling in the wilderness against
the Most High.
18 They willfully put God to the test[z]
by demanding the food they
craved.[a]
19 They spoke against God;[b]
they said, "Can God really
spread a table in the wilderness?
20 True, he struck the rock,
and water gushed out,[c]
streams flowed abundantly,
but can he also give us bread?
Can he supply meat[d] for his
people?"
21 When the LORD heard them, he was
furious;
his fire broke out[e] against Jacob,
and his wrath rose against Israel,
22 for they did not believe in God
or trust[f] in his deliverance.
23 Yet he gave a command to the skies
above
and opened the doors of the
heavens;[g]
24 he rained down manna[h] for the
people to eat,
he gave them the grain of heaven.
25 Human beings ate the bread of
angels;

78:3 [c] Ps 44:1
78:4 [d] Dt 11:19 [e] Ps 26:7; 71:17
78:5 [f] Ps 19:7; 81:5 [g] Ps 147:19
78:6 [h] Ps 22:31; 102:18
78:7 [i] Dt 6:12 [j] Dt 5:29
78:8 [k] 2Ch 30:7 [l] Ex 32:9 [m] ver 37; Isa 30:9
78:9 [n] ver 57; 1Ch 12:2 [o] Jdg 20:39
78:10 [p] 2Ki 17:15
78:11 [q] Ps 106:13
78:12 [r] Ps 106:22 [s] Ex 7-12 [t] Nu 13:22
78:13 [u] Ex 14:21; Ps 136:13
[v] Ex 15:8
78:14 [w] Ex 13:21; Ps 105:39
78:15 [x] Nu 20:11; 1Co 10:4
78:17 [y] Dt 9:22; Isa 63:10; Heb 3:16
78:18 [z] 1Co 10:9 [a] Ex 16:2; Nu 11:4
78:19 [b] Nu 21:5
78:20 [c] Nu 20:11 [d] Nu 11:18
78:21 [e] Nu 11:1
78:22 [f] Dt 1:32; Heb 3:19
78:23 [g] Ge 7:11; Mal 3:10
78:24 [h] Ex 16:4; Jn 6:31*

The psalmist continues his instructional theme by discussing the transmission of teaching from one generation to the next. Each generation learns to have the commandments of the Lord on their hearts. They bear the obligation to teach these commandments to the succeeding generation. As well as cultivating trust and obedience, the education is so that those who follow will avoid the failings of their predecessors.

78:9–16 The poet describes Ephraim's downfall as having a threefold cause: failure to keep God's covenant, refusal to walk in the ways of God's law, and forgetfulness regarding God's miraculous works in the past (vv. 12–16).

78:17–31 The Israelites constantly tested Yahweh, and by doing so they cast doubt on both *his love* for them (Ex 14:11) and, as in this case, *his ability* to help them (Ps 78:19–20). The harm of forgetfulness is illustrated by God's response in vv. 21–22.

Despite the rebellion of the people, Yahweh continued to prove his character and competence by providing the very things they had so skeptically demanded (vv. 23–29). The provision is gracious and generous, and is not a tacit acceptance of the people's rebellious behavior and distrust (vv. 17–21). Verses 30–31 make it quite clear that Israel's God is not to be toyed with.

he sent them all the food they
could eat.
26 He let loose the east wind[i] from the
heavens
and by his power made the south
wind blow.
27 He rained meat down on them like
dust,
birds like sand on the seashore.
28 He made them come down inside
their camp,
all around their tents.
29 They ate till they were gorged —[j]
he had given them what they
craved.
30 But before they turned from what
they craved,
even while the food was still in
their mouths,[k]
31 God's anger rose against them;
he put to death the sturdiest[l]
among them,
cutting down the young men of
Israel.

32 In spite of all this, they kept on
sinning;
in spite of his wonders,[m] they did
not believe.[n]
33 So he ended their days in futility[o]
and their years in terror.
34 Whenever God slew them, they
would seek[p] him;
they eagerly turned to him
again.
35 They remembered that God was
their Rock,[q]
that God Most High was their
Redeemer.[r]
36 But then they would flatter him with
their mouths,[s]
lying to him with their tongues;
37 their hearts were not loyal[t] to him,
they were not faithful to his
covenant.
38 Yet he was merciful;[u]
he forgave[v] their iniquities[w]
and did not destroy them.

78:26 [i] Nu 11:31
78:29 [j] Nu 11:20
78:30 [k] Nu 11:33
78:31 [l] Isa 10:16
78:32 [m] ver 11 [n] ver 22
78:33 [o] Nu 14:29,35
78:34 [p] Hos 5:15
78:35 [q] Dt 32:4 [r] Dt 9:26
78:36 [s] Eze 33:31
78:37 [t] ver 8; Ac 8:21
78:38 [u] Ex 34:6 [v] Isa 48:10 [w] Nu 14:18,20
78:39 [x] Ge 6:3; Ps 103:14 [y] Job 7:7; Jas 4:14
78:40 [z] Heb 3:16 [a] Ps 95:8; 106:14 [b] Eph 4:30
78:41 [c] Nu 14:22 [d] 2Ki 19:22; Ps 89:18
78:44 [e] Ex 7:20-21; Ps 105:29
78:45 [f] Ex 8:24; Ps 105:31 [g] Ex 8:2,6
78:46 [h] Ex 10:13
78:47 [i] Ex 9:23; Ps 105:32
78:48 [j] Ex 9:25
78:49 [k] Ex 15:7

Ps 78:40–43 ❖ When have we been forgetful of what God has done for us? How can we foster a continual posture of gratitude?

Time after time he restrained his
anger
and did not stir up his full wrath.
39 He remembered that they were but
flesh,[x]
a passing breeze[y] that does not
return.

40 How often they rebelled[z] against him
in the wilderness[a]
and grieved him[b] in the wasteland!
41 Again and again they put God to the
test;[c]
they vexed the Holy One of Israel.[d]
42 They did not remember his power —
the day he redeemed them from
the oppressor,
43 the day he displayed his signs in
Egypt,
his wonders in the region of Zoan.
44 He turned their river into blood;[e]
they could not drink from their
streams.
45 He sent swarms of flies[f] that
devoured them,
and frogs[g] that devastated them.
46 He gave their crops to the
grasshopper,
their produce to the locust.[h]
47 He destroyed their vines with hail[i]
and their sycamore-figs with sleet.
48 He gave over their cattle to the hail,
their livestock[j] to bolts of
lightning.
49 He unleashed against them his hot
anger,[k]
his wrath, indignation and
hostility —
a band of destroying angels.
50 He prepared a path for his anger;
he did not spare them from death
but gave them over to the plague.

78:32–33 Despite divine judgment, this generation *continued* to rebel. The irony is that this generation is freed from slavery.

78:34–35 These verses present a picture similar to the cycle of sin, crying out, and God's help recorded in the book of Judges.

78:36–39 God's rebuke would bring a "repentance" that was far from genuine. The people would, in a sense, say the right things and, in a sense, do the right things, but their words and deeds were only superficial and did not reflect a true change of heart. Remarkably, Yahweh's character remains unchanged despite his people's failings.

78:40–55 Time and again, this newborn nation rebelled against their Redeemer. They forgot God's miraculous power and his shepherding care (vv. 52–55). God's manifest power should have made Israel fearful of forgetting; his loving care should have inspired an affection that kept Israel from forgetting.

51 He struck down all the firstborn of Egypt,[l]
the firstfruits of manhood in the tents of Ham.[m]
52 But he brought his people out like a flock;[n]
he led them like sheep through the wilderness.
53 He guided them safely, so they were unafraid;
but the sea engulfed[o] their enemies.[p]
54 And so he brought them to the border of his holy land,
to the hill country his right hand[q] had taken.
55 He drove out nations[r] before them
and allotted their lands to them as an inheritance;[s]
he settled the tribes of Israel in their homes.

56 But they put God to the test
and rebelled against the Most High;
they did not keep his statutes.
57 Like their ancestors[t] they were disloyal and faithless,
as unreliable as a faulty bow.[u]
58 They angered him[v] with their high places;[w]
they aroused his jealousy with their idols.[x]
59 When God heard them, he was furious;
he rejected Israel[y] completely.
60 He abandoned the tabernacle of Shiloh,[z]
the tent he had set up among humans.

78:51 [l] Ex 12:29; Ps 135:8 [m] Ps 105:23; 106:22
78:52 [n] Ps 77:20
78:53 [o] Ex 14:28 [p] Ps 106:10
78:54 [q] Ex 15:17; Ps 44:3
78:55 [r] Ps 44:2 [s] Jos 13:7
78:57 [t] Eze 20:27 [u] Hos 7:16
78:58 [v] Jdg 2:12 [w] Lev 26:30 [x] Ex 20:4; Dt 32:21
78:59 [y] Dt 32:19
78:60 [z] Jos 18:1

78:61 [a] Ps 132:8 [b] 1Sa 4:17
78:63 [c] Nu 11:1 [d] Jer 7:34; 16:9
78:64 [e] 1Sa 4:17; 22:18
78:65 [f] Ps 44:23
78:66 [g] 1Sa 5:6
78:68 [h] Ps 87:2
78:70 [i] 1Sa 16:1
78:71 [j] 2Sa 5:2; Ps 28:9
78:72 [k] 1Ki 9:4

61 He sent the ark of his might[a] into captivity,[b]
his splendor into the hands of the enemy.
62 He gave his people over to the sword;
he was furious with his inheritance.
63 Fire consumed[c] their young men,
and their young women had no wedding songs;[d]
64 their priests were put to the sword,[e]
and their widows could not weep.

65 Then the Lord awoke as from sleep,[f]
as a warrior wakes from the stupor of wine.
66 He beat back his enemies;
he put them to everlasting shame.[g]
67 Then he rejected the tents of Joseph,
he did not choose the tribe of Ephraim;
68 but he chose the tribe of Judah,
Mount Zion,[h] which he loved.
69 He built his sanctuary like the heights,
like the earth that he established forever.
70 He chose David[i] his servant
and took him from the sheep pens;
71 from tending the sheep he brought him
to be the shepherd[j] of his people Jacob,
of Israel his inheritance.
72 And David shepherded them with integrity of heart;[k]
with skillful hands he led them.

78:56–64 The people repeated the mistakes of their ancestors in *testing* God and *rebelling* against him (v. 56, as is made explicit in v. 57). The people in the land resorted to idolatry. Verses 59–64 highlight Israel's unfaithfulness by recounting the severity of Yahweh's response to it. When God heard their prayers to lifeless statues—with the ironic implication that *Yahweh alone* hears these prayers—he became very angry. The consequences of Israel's idolatry were stark (vv. 61–64).

78:65–72 Once Yahweh's attention is refocused on Israel's plight, the people witness again the raw power of the warrior God who freed his people from Egypt with a mighty hand (vv. 42–51). The remarkable surprise of these verses is compounded by the very fact that no reason is given for the sudden change of heart.

This lengthy psalm ends with the poignant image of David as the shepherd-king. He is chosen by God, and the pastoral imagery of caring for sheep is transposed to caring for God's people on a national scale. We see here the author's hope in a coming king from the line of David who would truly represent the best of everything the historical David offered.

78:1–72 Christians living in the twenty-first century should not be too quick to shake our heads at the fickleness of the exodus generation. We often fall prey to exactly the same tendencies. It is easy to look at the licentiousness and permissiveness of the world in which we live and to say, "It's too hard to be a Christian! Why should I deny myself? I want to go back to the life I had before!" But the benefits of following Jesus far outweigh the so-called losses of not indulging ourselves and trying to make our own way in the world (Jn 14:6).

Psalm 79

A psalm of Asaph.

1 O God, the nations have invaded
your inheritance;[l]
they have defiled your holy
temple,
they have reduced Jerusalem to
rubble.[m]
2 They have left the dead bodies of
your servants
as food for the birds of the sky,
the flesh of your own people for
the animals of the wild.[n]
3 They have poured out blood like
water
all around Jerusalem,
and there is no one to bury the
dead.[o]
4 We are objects of contempt to our
neighbors,
of scorn and derision to those
around us.[p]

5 How long,[q] LORD? Will you be angry[r]
forever?
How long will your jealousy burn
like fire?[s]
6 Pour out your wrath[t] on the nations
that do not acknowledge[u] you,
on the kingdoms
that do not call on your name;[v]
7 for they have devoured Jacob
and devastated his homeland.

8 Do not hold against us the sins of
past generations;[w]
may your mercy come quickly to
meet us,
for we are in desperate need.[x]
9 Help us,[y] God our Savior,
for the glory of your name;
deliver us and forgive our sins
for your name's sake.[z]
10 Why should the nations say,
"Where is their God?"[a]

Before our eyes, make known
among the nations
that you avenge[b] the outpoured
blood of your servants.
11 May the groans of the prisoners
come before you;
with your strong arm preserve
those condemned to die.
12 Pay back into the laps[c] of our
neighbors seven times[d]
the contempt they have hurled at
you, Lord.
13 Then we your people, the sheep of
your pasture,[e]
will praise you forever;[f]
from generation to generation
we will proclaim your praise.

79:1 [l] Ps 74:2 [m] 2Ki 25:9
79:2 [n] Dt 28:26; Jer 7:33
79:3 [o] Jer 16:4
79:4 [p] Ps 44:13; 80:6
79:5 [q] Ps 74:10 [r] Ps 74:1; 85:5 [s] Dt 29:20; Ps 89:46; Zep 3:8
79:6 [t] Ps 69:24; Rev 16:1 [u] Jer 10:25; 2Th 1:8 [v] Ps 14:4
79:8 [w] Isa 64:9 [x] Ps 116:6; 142:6
79:9 [y] 2Ch 14:11 [z] Ps 25:11; 31:3; Jer 14:7
79:10 [a] Ps 42:10 [b] Ps 94:1
79:12 [c] Isa 65:6; Jer 32:18 [d] Ge 4:15
79:13 [e] Ps 74:1; 95:7 [f] Ps 44:8
80:1 [g] Ps 77:20 [h] Ex 25:22
80:2 [i] Nu 2:18-24 [j] Ps 35:23

Ps 79:5-7 ❖ What events in the world around us make us cry out for God to enact his justice?

Psalm 80[a]

For the director of music. To the tune of "The Lilies of the Covenant." Of Asaph. A psalm.

1 Hear us, Shepherd of Israel,
you who lead Joseph like a flock.[g]
You who sit enthroned between the
cherubim,[h]
shine forth 2 before Ephraim,
Benjamin and Manasseh.[i]
Awaken[j] your might;
come and save us.

[a] In Hebrew texts 80:1-19 is numbered 80:2-20.

79:1-4 Moses' prayer in Deuteronomy that Yahweh would spare the people likewise describes Israel as God's "inheritance" (v. 1; Dt 9:26-29). Yahweh's people and place have been violated by pagan nations who worship false gods.

79:5-8 The people of Judah deserved their punishment, but the psalmist urges Yahweh to respond to the gross criminality of the nations during the fall of Jerusalem. The psalmist asks for forgiveness of sins and the swift expression of God's mercy. He stresses the great need in which the people find themselves.

79:9-13 Salvation is a physical and practical concept in the Psalter. Verse 10 implies that the best way to restore Yahweh's standing among the nations is through restoring Israel and bringing punishment on those nations who have mocked his character.

The people believe they have suffered enough and have learned their lesson—hence their reminder to God that they are his people. Their prayer is for permanent restoration and that renewed community will be marked by continual, grateful praise.

✣ **79:1-13** Why pray if God already knows what we're going to pray? Prayer is about more than "getting things done"—it is about building and maintaining a relationship with a God who loves us and whom we love.

80:1-2 This psalm renews the call for restoration by the Shepherd-King.

80:3, 7, 19 The three parts of this psalm are divided by a repeated chorus in vv. 3, 7, and 19. The essential content is a call for restoration followed by an appeal for blessing.

3 Restore[k] us,[l] O God;
make your face shine on us,
that we may be saved.

4 How long, LORD God Almighty,
will your anger smolder
against the prayers of your
people?
5 You have fed them with the bread of
tears;
you have made them drink tears
by the bowlful.[m]
6 You have made us an object of
derision[a] to our neighbors,
and our enemies mock us.[n]

7 Restore us, God Almighty;
make your face shine on us,
that we may be saved.

8 You transplanted a vine[o] from
Egypt;
you drove out[p] the nations and
planted it.
9 You cleared the ground for it,
and it took root and filled the
land.
10 The mountains were covered with
its shade,
the mighty cedars with its
branches.
11 Its branches reached as far as the
Sea,[b]
its shoots as far as the River.[c][q]

12 Why have you broken down its walls[r]
so that all who pass by pick its
grapes?
13 Boars from the forest ravage[s] it,
and insects from the fields feed
on it.
14 Return to us, God Almighty!
Look down from heaven and see![t]
Watch over this vine,
15 the root your right hand has planted,
the son[d] you have raised up for
yourself.

16 Your vine is cut down, it is burned
with fire;
at your rebuke[u] your people
perish.
17 Let your hand rest on the man at
your right hand,
the son of man you have raised up
for yourself.
18 Then we will not turn away from
you;
revive us, and we will call on your
name.

19 Restore us, LORD God Almighty;
make your face shine on us,
that we may be saved.

80:3 [k] Ps 85:4; La 5:21 [l] Nu 6:25
80:5 [m] Ps 42:3; Isa 30:20
80:6 [n] Ps 79:4
80:8 [o] Isa 5:1-2; Jer 2:21 [p] Jos 13:6; Ac 7:45
80:11 [q] Ps 72:8
80:12 [r] Ps 89:40; Isa 5:5
80:13 [s] Jer 5:6
80:14 [t] Isa 63:15
80:16 [u] Ps 39:11; 76:6
81:1 [v] Ps 66:1
81:2 [w] Ex 15:20 [x] Ps 92:3

Ps 80:19 ❖ What areas of our lives need to be restored to God? How does Christ pave a way for this to happen (see Col 1:19-20)?

Psalm 81[e]

For the director of music. According to gittith.[f] Of Asaph.

1 Sing for joy to God our strength;
shout aloud to the God of Jacob![v]
2 Begin the music, strike the timbrel,[w]
play the melodious harp[x] and lyre.

3 Sound the ram's horn at the New
Moon,
and when the moon is full, on the
day of our festival;

[a] 6 Probable reading of the original Hebrew text; Masoretic Text *contention* [b] *11* Probably the Mediterranean [c] *11* That is, the Euphrates [d] *15* Or *branch* [e] In Hebrew texts 81:1-16 is numbered 81:2-17. [f] Title: Probably a musical term

---

80:4-6 The psalmist's prayer is directed toward the God *who is the cause* of their present suffering. *His* anger smolders. *He* fed his people with "the bread of tears" (v. 5). *He* caused their enemies to mock them.

80:8-18 This passage recounts the exodus story using the vine metaphor for God's people. These verses show the care Yahweh took to ensure this vine takes root and bears fruit. Poetic imagery depicts Israel as a vineyard spoiled by foreign nations. The psalmist's implied willingness to endure God's scrutiny (v. 14) is explained in v. 16—they would rather endure fire that purifies than fire that simply destroys.

80:19 The psalm closes with the final rendering of the refrain, which seeks the blessing and practical help of Yahweh.

✚ **80:1-19** Jesus' description of himself as the "true vine" in Jn 15 encourages a healthy attitude of dependence. It is by remaining in him and relying on him that we are enabled to be fruitful. An attitude of dependence is realistic and drives us to prayer—dependence *has* to be a good thing.

81:1-5b Worship in the Psalms is wholehearted and full of enthusiasm. The praise command is a reminder that God remains unchanged even in the people's experience of distress.

4 this is a decree for Israel,
an ordinance of the God of Jacob.
5 When God went out against Egypt,[y]
he established it as a statute for Joseph.

I heard an unknown voice say:[z]

6 "I removed the burden from their shoulders;[a]
their hands were set free from the basket.
7 In your distress you called[b] and I rescued you,
I answered[c] you out of a thundercloud;
I tested you at the waters of Meribah.[a][d]
8 Hear me, my people,[e] and I will warn you—
if you would only listen to me, Israel!
9 You shall have no foreign god[f] among you;
you shall not worship any god other than me.
10 I am the LORD your God,
who brought you up out of Egypt.[g]
Open wide your mouth and I will fill[h] it.

11 "But my people would not listen to me;
Israel would not submit to me.[i]
12 So I gave them over[j] to their stubborn hearts
to follow their own devices.

13 "If my people would only listen to me,[k]
if Israel would only follow my ways,
14 how quickly I would subdue[l] their enemies
and turn my hand against[m] their foes!
15 Those who hate the LORD would cringe before him,
and their punishment would last forever.
16 But you would be fed with the finest of wheat;[n]
with honey from the rock I would satisfy you."

Psalm 82

A psalm of Asaph.

1 God presides in the great assembly;
he renders judgment[o] among the "gods":

2 "How long will you[b] defend the unjust
and show partiality[p] to the wicked?[a][q]
3 Defend the weak and the fatherless;[r]
uphold the cause of the poor[s] and the oppressed.
4 Rescue the weak and the needy;
deliver them from the hand of the wicked.

5 "The 'gods' know nothing, they understand nothing.[t]
They walk about in darkness;[u]
all the foundations[v] of the earth are shaken.

6 "I said, 'You are "gods";[w]
you are all sons of the Most High.'

81:5 [y] Ex 11:4 [z] Ps 114:1
81:6 [a] Isa 9:4
81:7 [b] Ex 2:23; Ps 50:15 [c] Ex 19:19 [d] Ex 17:7
81:8 [e] Ps 50:7
81:9 [f] Ex 20:3; Dt 32:12; Isa 43:12
81:10 [g] Ex 20:2 [h] Ps 107:9
81:11 [i] Ex 32:1-6
81:12 [j] Ac 7:42; Ro 1:24
81:13 [k] Dt 5:29; Isa 48:18
81:14 [l] Ps 47:3 [m] Am 1:8
81:16 [n] Dt 32:14
82:1 [o] Ps 58:11; Isa 3:13
82:2 [p] Dt 1:17 [q] Ps 58:1-2; Pr 18:5
82:3 [r] Dt 24:17 [s] Jer 22:16
82:5 [t] Ps 14:4; Mic 3:1 [u] Isa 59:9 [v] Ps 11:3
82:6 [w] Jn 10:34*

[a] 7,2 The Hebrew has *Selah* (a word of uncertain meaning) here. [b] 2 The Hebrew is plural.

Ps 81:4 ❖ Why does God command his people to celebrate? How does celebration benefit faith?

Ps 82:3 ❖ How can we help defend the needs of the weak and the poor?

81:5c–8 As well as reminding Israel of the exodus, God also reminds them he heard and answered their prayers. Inattentiveness is Israel's problem, not Yahweh's.
81:9–10 The reminder of the Shema (v. 8) draws the reader to thoughts of devotion to Yahweh alone, and that singular devotion becomes the express focus of these verses.
81:11–16 In Ps 80 the psalmist asks God "Why?" and "How long?" with regard to the exile. The second part of Yahweh's speech in this passage answers both questions. The exile occurred because Israel would not listen; if the people would finally *listen*, they would then see just how quickly Yahweh responds to their change of heart.

✣ **81:1–16** In praise we are reminded of who God is and how God works, so our praises can be important in shaping our perspective on our life and present experience.

82:1 Yahweh has called a meeting, and all the heavenly beings are obliged to attend.
82:2–4 Yahweh has delegated power to the "gods" to rule in accordance with his own standards. Since they have failed, he calls them to task.
82:5 These so-called deities do not even realize that social justice is the hallmark of a good society.
82:6–7 Yahweh reminds the "gods" (v. 6) that they owe their status to God in the first place. He confers status and can remove it just as quickly.

7 But you will die[x] like mere mortals;
you will fall like every other ruler."

8 Rise up,[y] O God, judge the earth,
for all the nations are your inheritance.[z]

Psalm 83[a]

A song. A psalm of Asaph.

1 O God, do not remain silent;[a]
do not turn a deaf ear,
do not stand aloof, O God.
2 See how your enemies growl,[b]
how your foes rear their heads.[c]
3 With cunning they conspire[d] against your people;
they plot against those you cherish.
4 "Come," they say, "let us destroy[e] them as a nation,
so that Israel's name is remembered[f] no more."

5 With one mind they plot together;[g]
they form an alliance against you —
6 the tents of Edom[h] and the Ishmaelites,
of Moab[i] and the Hagrites,[j]
7 Byblos,[k] Ammon and Amalek,
Philistia, with the people of Tyre.[l]
8 Even Assyria has joined them
to reinforce Lot's descendants.[b][m]

9 Do to them as you did to Midian,[n]
as you did to Sisera and Jabin at the river Kishon,[o]
10 who perished at Endor
and became like dung[p] on the ground.

82:7 [x] Ps 49:12; Eze 31:14
82:8 [y] Ps 12:5 [z] Ps 2:8; Rev 11:15
83:1 [a] Ps 28:1; 35:22
83:2 [b] Ps 2:1; Isa 17:12 [c] Jdg 8:28; Ps 81:15
83:3 [d] Ps 31:13
83:4 [e] Est 3:6 [f] Jer 11:19
83:5 [g] Ps 2:2
83:6 [h] Ps 137:7 [i] 2Ch 20:1 [j] Ge 25:16
83:7 [k] Jos 13:5 [l] Eze 27:3
83:8 [m] Dt 2:9
83:9 [n] Jdg 7:1-23 [o] Jdg 4:23-24
83:10 [p] Zep 1:17
83:11 [q] Jdg 7:25 [r] Jdg 8:12, 21
83:12 [s] 2Ch 20:11
83:13 [t] Ps 35:5; Isa 17:13
83:14 [u] Dt 32:22; Isa 9:18
83:15 [v] Job 9:17
83:16 [w] Ps 109:29; 132:18
83:17 [x] Ps 35:4
83:18 [y] Ps 59:13
84:1 [z] Ps 27:4; 43:3; 132:5

Ps 83:1-4 ❖ What evil or violence in the world around us can we raise up before God in prayer?

11 Make their nobles like Oreb and Zeeb,[q]
all their princes like Zebah and Zalmunna,[r]
12 who said, "Let us take possession[s]
of the pasturelands of God."

13 Make them like tumbleweed, my God,
like chaff[t] before the wind.
14 As fire consumes the forest
or a flame sets the mountains ablaze,[u]
15 so pursue them with your tempest
and terrify them with your storm.[v]
16 Cover their faces with shame,[w] LORD,
so that they will seek your name.

17 May they ever be ashamed and dismayed;
may they perish in disgrace.[x]
18 Let them know that you, whose name is the LORD —
that you alone are the Most High
over all the earth.[y]

Psalm 84[c]

For the director of music. According to gittith.[d] Of the Sons of Korah. A psalm.

1 How lovely is your dwelling place,[z]
LORD Almighty!

[a] In Hebrew texts 83:1-18 is numbered 83:2-19.
[b] 8 The Hebrew has *Selah* (a word of uncertain meaning) here.
[c] In Hebrew texts 84:1-12 is numbered 84:2-13.
[d] Title: Probably a musical term

82:8 The prayer is the logical conclusion that follows from the neutralizing of the gods by Yahweh's judgment on them (vv. 6–7). The psalmist cries out, asking Yahweh to reassume control over "all the nations," not just Israel, as his inheritance.

82:1-8 Social justice is basic to the nature of the God of the Bible.

83:1 This psalm begins with a threefold prayer that God will not be silent.
83:2-8 The psalmist moves to lament. The nations are in rebellion against God and his design for the world. The nations listed in vv. 6–8 are consciously rebelling against Yahweh by killing his people.
83:9-12 It seems that the psalmist is focusing particularly on the victories of God during the time of the judges.
83:13-15 These verses expand this prayer for divine deliverance from military persecution. The poet demands that these forces become insignificant before the power of Yahweh.
83:16-18 In some ways we naturally balk at the violent overtones of this prayer, yet the purpose of it is quite remarkable. The psalmist prays that Yahweh would make the enemies who had conspired to destroy the covenant community part of that same family of God's people.

83:1-18 Injustice and evil should be named for what they are, and our prayers should reflect the revulsion the Creator feels when his laws and his people are violated. Repentance and justice should be the focus of our prayers.

84:1-4 The psalmist describes the beauty and benefits of dwelling in the presence of God. The

[2]My soul yearns,[a] even faints,
for the courts of the LORD;
my heart and my flesh cry out
for the living God.
[3]Even the sparrow has found a home,
and the swallow a nest for herself,
where she may have her young—
a place near your altar,[b]
LORD Almighty, my King and my
God.[c]
[4]Blessed are those who dwell in your
house;
they are ever praising you.[a]

[5]Blessed are those whose strength[d] is
in you,
whose hearts are set on
pilgrimage.[e]
[6]As they pass through the Valley of
Baka,
they make it a place of springs;
the autumn[f] rains also cover it
with pools.[b]
[7]They go from strength to strength,[g]
till each appears[h] before God in
Zion.

[8]Hear my prayer, LORD God Almighty;
listen to me, God of Jacob.
[9]Look on our shield,[c][i] O God;
look with favor on your anointed
one.[j]

[10]Better is one day in your courts
than a thousand elsewhere;
I would rather be a doorkeeper[k] in
the house of my God
than dwell in the tents of the
wicked.
[11]For the LORD God is a sun[l] and
shield;[m]
the LORD bestows favor and
honor;
no good thing does he withhold[n]
from those whose walk is
blameless.

84:2 [a] Ps 42:1-2
84:3 [b] Ps 43:4 [c] Ps 5:2
84:5 [d] Ps 81:1 [e] Jer 31:6
84:6 [f] Joel 2:23
84:7 [g] Pr 4:18 [h] Dt 16:16
84:9 [i] Ps 59:11 [j] 1Sa 16:6; Ps 2:2; 132:17
84:10 [k] 1Ch 23:5
84:11 [l] Isa 60:19; Rev 21:23 [m] Ge 15:1 [n] Ps 34:10
84:12 [o] Ps 2:12
85:1 [p] Ps 14:7; Jer 30:18; Eze 39:25
85:2 [q] Nu 14:19 [r] Ps 78:38
85:3 [s] Ps 106:23 [t] Ex 32:12; Dt 13:17; Ps 78:38; Jnh 3:9
85:4 [u] Ps 80:3,7
85:5 [v] Ps 79:5
85:6 [w] Ps 80:18; Hab 3:2

Ps 84:1-4 ❖ What does it look like for Christians to "dwell" in the house of God? How can we live in this reality?

Ps 85:4-7 ❖ How does Christ provide security and hope in our prayers for forgiveness (see Jn 3:16)?

[12]LORD Almighty,
blessed[o] is the one who trusts in
you.

Psalm 85[d]

For the director of music. Of the Sons of Korah. A psalm.

[1]You, LORD, showed favor to your
land;
you restored the fortunes[p] of
Jacob.
[2]You forgave[q] the iniquity[r] of your
people
and covered all their sins.[e]
[3]You set aside all your wrath[s]
and turned from your fierce
anger.[t]

[4]Restore[u] us again, God our
Savior,
and put away your displeasure
toward us.
[5]Will you be angry with us forever?[v]
Will you prolong your anger
through all generations?
[6]Will you not revive[w] us again,
that your people may rejoice in
you?
[7]Show us your unfailing love, LORD,
and grant us your salvation.

[a] 4 The Hebrew has *Selah* (a word of uncertain meaning) here and at the end of verse 8.
[b] 6 Or *blessings*
[c] 9 Or *sovereign*
[d] In Hebrew texts 85:1-13 is numbered 85:2-14.
[e] 2 The Hebrew has *Selah* (a word of uncertain meaning) here.

---

language of the "soul" and "heart" and "flesh" (v. 2) is used to express completeness of desire.
84:5-7 The poet is fully aware that God's blessing and protection are everywhere. The pilgrims heading to Jerusalem transform the challenging landscape. They are equipped with divine strength.
84:8-9 The psalm moves from celebration to a prayer for protection of the king.
84:10-12 One day in the tangible presence of God in the Jerusalem temple is better than a thousand days spent anywhere else. The God who reigns is inclined to do good toward people. He is also capable of ordering all circumstances for their benefit.

84:1-12 There is great happiness to be found in coming together with other believers to worship God. Such fellowship is a source of great joy and provides believers in community with a reservoir of strength to keep going in the Christian faith (Heb 10:25).

85:1-3 Sin is a burden. Through forgiveness, God lifts that weight from the Israelite's shoulders and sets aside his righteous anger.
85:4-7 The psalmist is confident to pray because he knows that salvation is part of God's character. The questions of vv. 5-6 are rhetorical. Spiritual

8 I will listen to what God the LORD says;
he promises peace[x] to his people, his faithful servants —
but let them not turn to folly.
9 Surely his salvation[y] is near those who fear him,
that his glory[z] may dwell in our land.

10 Love and faithfulness[a] meet together;
righteousness[b] and peace kiss each other.
11 Faithfulness springs forth from the earth,
and righteousness[c] looks down from heaven.
12 The LORD will indeed give what is good,[d]
and our land will yield[e] its harvest.
13 Righteousness goes before him
and prepares the way for his steps.

Psalm 86

A prayer of David.

1 Hear me, LORD, and answer[f] me,
for I am poor and needy.
2 Guard my life, for I am faithful to you;
save your servant who trusts in you.[g]
You are my God; 3 have mercy[h] on me, Lord,
for I call[i] to you all day long.
4 Bring joy to your servant, Lord,
for I put my trust[j] in you.

5 You, Lord, are forgiving and good,
abounding in love[k] to all who call to you.

85:8 [x] Zec 9:10
85:9 [y] Isa 46:13 [z] Zec 2:5
85:10 [a] Ps 89:14; Pr 3:3 [b] Ps 72:2-3; Isa 32:17
85:11 [c] Isa 45:8
85:12 [d] Ps 84:11; Jas 1:17 [e] Lev 26:4; Ps 67:6; Zec 8:12
86:1 [f] Ps 17:6
86:2 [g] Ps 25:2; 31:14
86:3 [h] Ps 4:1; 57:1 [i] Ps 88:9
86:4 [j] Ps 25:1; 143:8
86:5 [k] Ex 34:6; Ne 9:17; Ps 103:8; 145:8; Joel 2:13; Jnh 4:2
86:7 [l] Ps 50:15
86:8 [m] Ex 15:11; Dt 3:24; Ps 89:6
86:9 [n] Ps 66:4; Rev 15:4 [o] Isa 43:7
86:10 [p] Ps 72:18 [q] Dt 6:4; Mk 12:29; 1Co 8:4
86:11 [r] Ps 25:5 [s] Jer 32:39
86:14 [t] Ps 54:3
86:15 [u] Ps 103:8

Ps 86:11 ❖ What kinds of things threaten to divide our hearts and our allegiance to God?

6 Hear my prayer, LORD;
listen to my cry for mercy.
7 When I am in distress,[l] I call to you,
because you answer me.

8 Among the gods there is none like you,[m] Lord;
no deeds can compare with yours.
9 All the nations you have made
will come and worship[n] before you, Lord;
they will bring glory[o] to your name.
10 For you are great and do marvelous deeds;[p]
you alone[q] are God.

11 Teach me your way,[r] LORD,
that I may rely on your faithfulness;
give me an undivided[s] heart,
that I may fear your name.
12 I will praise you, Lord my God, with all my heart;
I will glorify your name forever.
13 For great is your love toward me;
you have delivered me from the depths,
from the realm of the dead.

14 Arrogant foes are attacking me, O God;
ruthless people are trying to kill me —
they have no regard for you.[t]
15 But you, Lord, are a compassionate and gracious[u] God,

---

renewal results in people who are grateful and rejoice in their relationship with God.

85:8-9 God himself—by his spoken word—recreates the peace and wholeness of relationship. The psalmist urges his readers to turn away from behaviors that lead them to doubt God's love and acceptance.

85:10-13 The psalmist points the readers again to a God of grace and unmerited love. The psalm ends with a reminder of the righteousness of God.

✥ **85:1-13** Like the psalmist, we can struggle to accept that God still loves us and that his grace is sufficient to forgive all our sins (2Co 12:9). Yet the promises of our unchanging God remain the same regardless of our feelings at any particular moment.

86:1-7 In the face of great trouble, the psalmist calls out to God for mercy because prayer is his only source of hope. God will hear because of who *he* is.

86:8-10 God's incomparable greatness sets him apart from all the gods of the nations. The nations themselves will come to realize that Yahweh is far greater than the false gods they worship.

86:11-17 The poet now prays for God's help to live a life of commitment to Yahweh. The first aspect of this prayer for devotion is cognitive (v. 11a). The second element is holistic, heartfelt devotion to God (v. 11b). Verse 13 gives a clear reason for the exemplary devotion witnessed in the preceding verses.

86:15 The poet is aware that he need not fear the character of his enemies because he knows the character of God.

✥ **86:1-17** Missional activity that is biblically based reflects and speaks about our loving God and all of the wonderful promises he has made and things he has done for humanity.

CHARACTER OF GOD // GOD IS FORGIVING

Psalm 86:5: You, Lord, are forgiving and good, abounding in love to all who call to you.

God's forgiving nature is what leads him to pardon humans for their sins. God would be fully justified in destroying those who sin against him—after all, God's justice demands that sins be punished. How is the tension between God's mercy and God's justice resolved? It is resolved in the forgiveness God offers through Jesus Christ.

Even before the time of Christ, God's children recognized that God was a forgiving God. God gave Israel a system of ceremonies and sacrifices to remind them both that they were sinners and that with God they could find forgiveness. This was not cheap and easy forgiveness, however. It came at the cost of a sacrifice.

Those sacrifices pointed toward their fulfillment in Jesus Christ, the atoning sacrifice for the sins of the world. At the cross, he secured God's forgiveness for all God's children. This did not negate God's justice; on the contrary, God's justice was carried out against Christ so that God's mercy could be poured out upon people. One of the common Hebrew words translated "forgive" is *nasa'*, which literally means "carry" or "lift up." At the cross, Jesus carried human sin upon himself (1Pe 2:24).

Nothing compelled God to be a forgiving God. It is simply his nature. He does not extend forgiveness because humans deserve it. Quite the opposite: God extends forgiveness even though humans do not deserve it. God's forgiveness is where God's love intersects with human failure. Thanks be to God!

APPLICATION ✤ If not for God's forgiving nature, we would all be beyond hope. No person is without sin (Ro 3:23), and therefore each person is in need of forgiveness. The good news is that God is a forgiving God. He is not a begrudging forgiver; Ps 86:5 tells us that God is ready to forgive. In the parable of the lost son (Lk 15:11–32), we see a picture of the way God forgives. The father in the parable did not wait with crossed arms, listing demands before granting forgiveness when his son came home. Instead, the father ran to his son with open arms, eager to take back his child into his household. That's how God longs to forgive his children.

slow to anger, abounding in love
and faithfulness.[v]
16 Turn to me and have mercy
on me;
show your strength in behalf of
your servant;
save me, because I serve you
just as my mother did.[w]
17 Give me a sign of your goodness,
that my enemies may see it and
be put to shame,
for you, LORD, have helped me and
comforted me.

Psalm 87

Of the Sons of Korah. A psalm. A song.

1 He has founded his city on the holy
mountain.
2 The LORD loves the gates of Zion[x]

86:15 [v] Ex 34:6; Ne 9:17; Joel 2:13
86:16 [w] Ps 116:16
87:2 [x] Ps 78:68

Ps 87:4 ✤ God says he will declare that many of Israel's enemies were "born in Zion." What does this show us about the wideness of God's mercy, and how does it affect the way we look at those who we fear are far from God?

more than all the other dwellings
of Jacob.

3 Glorious things are said of you,
city of God:[a][y]
4 "I will record Rahab[b][z] and Babylon
among those who acknowledge
me—
Philistia too, and Tyre[a], along with
Cush[c]—

87:3 [y] Ps 46:4; Isa 60:1
87:4 [z] Job 9:13 [a] Ps 45:12

[a] *3* The Hebrew has *Selah* (a word of uncertain meaning) here and at the end of verse 6.
[b] *4* A poetic name for Egypt [c] *4* That is, the upper Nile region

87:1–3 Zion is founded by God as a place of special holiness.
87:4–7 God's proclamation of Zion's greatness begins with the inclusion of Israel's enemies among those who "acknowledge" or "know" (v. 4) him. "Rahab" is frequently used as a metaphor for Egypt.

In this psalm a sense of belonging is extended to nations outside Israel. God graciously enters these nations in his list of citizens; the psalmist points to a future reality in which these countries become part of God's people.

CHARACTER OF GOD // GOD IS JUST

Psalm 89:14: Righteousness and justice are the foundation of your throne; love and faithfulness go before you.

Justice and righteousness are the foundation of God's throne. This means all God's judgments are upright and fair. God judges people with equity (Ps 98:9).

In our modern world, we may find it an uncomfortable idea to have a cosmic judge watching all our actions. In a world that prioritizes privacy and worries that the state or companies are too invasive, we may struggle to praise God as a judge over all the earth.

But in fact God's justice is good news for all of us, particularly for the oppressed. If not for God's justice, the wicked would continue to do evil, treading on the weak and taking advantage of the poor. The fact that God's throne is established on justice and righteousness assures believers that the wicked will be held to account. The cries of the oppressed will be heard and vindicated when God judges the earth.

God's justice means that God does not play favorites. We see this in the Bible. Even King David, whom God had chosen as a man after his own heart to lead Israel, was not exempt from punishment when he fell into sin. The same was true for the Israelite nation. Though God had chosen them as his holy people to live as a light to others, when they repeatedly fell into sin, God punished them by handing them over to their enemies. God did not show favoritism by refusing to punish them for their sin; in fact, he held them to a higher standard, since he had revealed his will and instructions to them (Am 3:2).

APPLICATION ✤ God's justice is good news because it means the wicked will be held to account. However, if God were solely a God of justice, not one of us could stand before him. Thankfully, God also shows mercy to his children. This does not mean he abandons justice in the lives of believers—far from it. In an amazing act of love, God carried out his justice upon Jesus Christ on the cross in order that he might extend mercy to believers. Our only hope is to stand under God's amazing mercy through Jesus Christ.

I have raised up a young man
from among the people.
20 I have found David[w] my servant;[x]
with my sacred oil I have
anointed[y] him.
21 My hand will sustain him;
surely my arm will strengthen
him.[z]
22 The enemy will not get the better of
him;
the wicked will not oppress[a] him.
23 I will crush his foes before him[b]
and strike down his adversaries.[c]
24 My faithful love will be with him,[d]
and through my name his horn[a]
will be exalted.
25 I will set his hand over the sea,
his right hand over the rivers.[e]
26 He will call out to me, 'You are my
Father,[f]
my God, the Rock my Savior.'[g]
27 And I will appoint him to be my
firstborn,[h]
the most exalted[i] of the kings[j] of
the earth.
28 I will maintain my love to him
forever,
and my covenant with him will
never fail.[k]
29 I will establish his line forever,
his throne as long as the heavens
endure.[l]

30 "If his sons forsake my law
and do not follow my statutes,
31 if they violate my decrees
and fail to keep my commands,
32 I will punish their sin with the
rod,
their iniquity with flogging;[m]
33 but I will not take my love from
him,[n]
nor will I ever betray my
faithfulness.
34 I will not violate my covenant

89:20 [w] Ac 13:22 [x] Ps 78:70 [y] 1Sa 16:1,12
89:21 [z] Ps 18:35
89:22 [a] 2Sa 7:10
89:23 [b] Ps 18:40 [c] 2Sa 7:9
89:24 [d] 2Sa 7:15
89:25 [e] Ps 72:8
89:26 [f] 2Sa 7:14 [g] 2Sa 22:47
89:27 [h] Col 1:18 [i] Nu 24:7 [j] Rev 1:5; 19:16
89:28 [k] ver 33-34; Isa 55:3
89:29 [l] ver 4, 36; Dt 11:21; Jer 33:17
89:32 [m] 2Sa 7:14
89:33 [n] 2Sa 7:15

[a] 24 *Horn* here symbolizes strength.

89:24–29 The second aspect of the promise to David is that of a continuous line of successors to perpetuate his dynasty (vv. 27–29).

89:30–32 What happens if David's heirs do not love Yahweh in the manner that he did? Clearly, personal piety plays a critical role in continuing this covenant line.

89:33–37 The rest of this section focuses on God's continuing love for David, expressed by way of God's continuing grace toward his ancestral line.

or alter what my lips have uttered.[o]
35 Once for all, I have sworn by my
holiness —
and I will not lie to David —
36 that his line will continue forever
and his throne endure before me
like the sun;
37 it will be established forever like the
moon,
the faithful witness in the sky."

38 But you have rejected,[p] you have
spurned,
you have been very angry with
your anointed one.
39 You have renounced the covenant
with your servant
and have defiled his crown in the
dust.[q]
40 You have broken through all his walls[r]
and reduced his strongholds[s] to
ruins.
41 All who pass by have plundered him;
he has become the scorn of his
neighbors.[t]
42 You have exalted the right hand of
his foes;
you have made all his enemies
rejoice.[u]
43 Indeed, you have turned back the
edge of his sword
and have not supported him in
battle.[v]
44 You have put an end to his splendor
and cast his throne to the ground.
45 You have cut short the days of his
youth;
you have covered him with a
mantle of shame.[w]
46 How long, LORD? Will you hide
yourself forever?
How long will your wrath burn
like fire?[x]

89:34 [o] Nu 23:19
89:38 [p] Dt 32:19; 1Ch 28:9; Ps 44:9
89:39 [q] La 5:16
89:40 [r] Ps 80:12 [s] La 2:2
89:41 [t] Ps 44:13
89:42 [u] Ps 13:2; 80:6
89:43 [v] Ps 44:10
89:45 [w] Ps 44:15; 109:29
89:46 [x] Ps 79:5

Ps 89:32-37 ❖ Why would God bind himself in a covenant to sinful humanity? How does God keep his covenant after we sin against him (see Mt 26:28)?

47 Remember how fleeting is my life.[y]
For what futility you have created
all humanity!
48 Who can live and not see death,
or who can escape the power of
the grave?[z]
49 Lord, where is your former great
love,
which in your faithfulness you
swore to David?
50 Remember, Lord, how your servant
has[a] been mocked,[a]
how I bear in my heart the taunts
of all the nations,
51 the taunts with which your enemies,
LORD, have mocked,
with which they have mocked
every step of your anointed
one.[b]

52 Praise be to the LORD forever!
Amen and Amen.[c]

BOOK IV

Psalms 90 – 106

Psalm 90

A prayer of Moses the man of God.

1 Lord, you have been our dwelling
place[d]
throughout all generations.
2 Before the mountains were born[e]

89:47 [y] Job 7:7; Ps 39:5
89:48 [z] Ps 22:29; 49:9
89:50 [a] Ps 69:19
89:51 [b] Ps 74:10
89:52 [c] Ps 41:13; 72:19
90:1 [d] Dt 33:27; Eze 11:16
90:2 [e] Job 15:7; Pr 8:25

[a] *50 Or your servants have*

89:38-45 In confusion, the psalmist cries out. The promise of security (v. 22) has been dashed by military defeat (vv. 40-41). The promise of divine strength (v. 21) has been transferred to enemies (v. 42). The promise of an eternal line of descendants (vv. 27-29) has been brought to a crushing end (vv. 44-45). The once exalted status of the anointed one of Yahweh (v. 20) has been rejected and cast down (vv. 39, 44-45).

89:46-51 The exclamation "How long?" seeks an end to the conflict of faith and experience. It all boils down to the essential question in v. 49. With lack of understanding comes prayer. Only in relationship with Yahweh can one make sense of all the theological incongruities of life.

89:52 This verse has an influence on this psalm as well as concluding the book as a whole. There is no resolution implied here. It does not change or deny the paradox; it simply acknowledges the dichotomy. The doxology reminds the reader that God is worthy even when his people are conflicted in their experience of him.

89:1-52 It is as we learn the worship of God that we are equipped to deal with the complexities and incongruities of life. In worship, we are shaped and equipped to find our strength in God, even when we do not really understand what God is doing.

90:1-6 Yahweh is still—and is always—the "dwelling place" (v. 1) of his people. The essence of the people's

or you brought forth the whole
world,
from everlasting to everlasting
you are God.[f]

3 You turn people back to dust,
saying, "Return to dust, you
mortals."[g]
4 A thousand years in your sight
are like a day that has just
gone by,
or like a watch in the night.[h]
5 Yet you sweep people away[i] in the
sleep of death —
they are like the new grass of the
morning:
6 In the morning it springs up new,
but by evening it is dry and
withered.[j]

7 We are consumed by your anger
and terrified by your indignation.
8 You have set our iniquities before
you,
our secret sins[k] in the light of your
presence.
9 All our days pass away under your
wrath;
we finish our years with a moan.[l]
10 Our days may come to seventy years,
or eighty, if our strength endures;
yet the best of them are but trouble
and sorrow,
for they quickly pass, and we fly
away.[m]
11 If only we knew the power of your
anger!
Your wrath is as great as the fear
that is your due.[n]
12 Teach us to number our days,[o]
that we may gain a heart of
wisdom.[p]

90:2 [f] Ps 102:24-27
90:3 [g] Ge 3:19; Job 34:15
90:4 [h] 2Pe 3:8
90:5 [i] Ps 73:20; Isa 40:6
90:6 [j] Mt 6:30; Jas 1:10
90:8 [k] Ps 19:12
90:9 [l] Ps 78:33
90:10 [m] Job 20:8
90:11 [n] Ps 76:7
90:12 [o] Ps 39:4 [p] Dt 32:29

Ps 90:10–12 ❖ How does contemplating the brevity of life spur us toward God and his wisdom?

---

security is found in God's eternal and unchangeable nature. This focus contrasts strongly with the discussion of the brevity of *human* life in vv. 3–6.

90:7–11 Verse 8 gives the clear reason for the divine anger mentioned in the previous verse: Human sin has provoked a response from God. God's righteous anger should always provoke a response of repentance and faithfulness in his people.

90:12–17 This psalm recognizes human frailty and the importance of responding properly to that realization. The lament of this psalm centers on the mercy of God in response to sin. The supplication seeks a gracious response from God *despite* the people's sin. Only God's grace can maintain our relationship with him in his holiness.

CHARACTER OF GOD // GOD IS ETERNAL

Psalm 90:2: Before the mountains were born or you brought forth the whole world, from everlasting to everlasting you are God.

God existed before everything, and there was no time when God did not exist. Philosophers and theologians debate the finer points of God's being eternal versus everlasting—*eternal* meaning "God exists completely outside of time" and *everlasting* meaning "God exists continually in time." In this intellectual playground, the important point is the same: God preexists everything that is not himself, and everything that is not God came about through God's act of creation.

God's eternal nature confounds our minds. How can anything exist eternally without beginning? We struggle with this concept because everything we encounter in life—every person, every nation, every object, every idea—is contingent, meaning its existence depends on something else. There is only one entity that is properly noncontingent: God himself.

Since ancient times thinkers have reflected on the fact that, since everything we encounter is contingent, there must be a creator or "first cause" behind it all—something eternal. The Bible teaches us that this is true. God is the eternal perfect Creator, Lord over creation and time itself.

APPLICATION ✜ How does it benefit believers to understand that God is without beginning or end? God's eternal nature gives us comfort because we can be sure that God will never fail. No power came before him; no power can outlast him. When God makes an everlasting promise, he will keep it. The One who promises his people eternal life in Christ (Jn 3:16) is himself the everlasting source of that life.

13 Relent, LORD! How long[q] will it be?
Have compassion on your servants.[r]
14 Satisfy[s] us in the morning with your unfailing love,
that we may sing for joy[t] and be glad all our days.[u]
15 Make us glad for as many days as you have afflicted us,
for as many years as we have seen trouble.
16 May your deeds be shown to your servants,
your splendor to their children.[v]

17 May the favor[a] of the Lord our God rest on us;
establish the work of our hands for us —
yes, establish the work of our hands.[w]

Psalm 91

1 Whoever dwells in the shelter[x] of the Most High
will rest in the shadow[y] of the Almighty.[b]
2 I will say of the LORD, "He is my refuge[z] and my fortress,
my God, in whom I trust."

3 Surely he will save you
from the fowler's snare[a]
and from the deadly pestilence.[b]
4 He will cover you with his feathers,
and under his wings you will find refuge;[c]
his faithfulness will be your shield[d] and rampart.
5 You will not fear[e] the terror of night,
nor the arrow that flies by day,
6 nor the pestilence that stalks in the darkness,
nor the plague that destroys at midday.
7 A thousand may fall at your side,
ten thousand at your right hand,
but it will not come near you.
8 You will only observe with your eyes
and see the punishment of the wicked.[f]

9 If you say, "The LORD is my refuge,"
and you make the Most High your dwelling,
10 no harm[g] will overtake you,
no disaster will come near your tent.
11 For he will command his angels[h] concerning you
to guard you in all your ways;[i]
12 they will lift you up in their hands,
so that you will not strike your foot against a stone.[j]
13 You will tread on the lion and the cobra;
you will trample the great lion and the serpent.[k]

14 "Because he[c] loves me," says the LORD, "I will rescue him;
I will protect him, for he acknowledges my name.
15 He will call on me, and I will answer him;
I will be with him in trouble,
I will deliver him and honor him.[l]
16 With long life[m] I will satisfy him
and show him my salvation.[n]"

90:13 [q] Ps 6:3 [r] Dt 32:36; Ps 135:14
90:14 [s] Ps 103:5 [t] Ps 85:6 [u] Ps 31:7
90:16 [v] Ps 44:1; Hab 3:2
90:17 [w] Isa 26:12
91:1 [x] Ps 31:20 [y] Ps 17:8
91:2 [z] Ps 142:5
91:3 [a] Ps 124:7; Pr 6:5 [b] 1Ki 8:37
91:4 [c] Ps 17:8 [d] Ps 35:2
91:5 [e] Job 5:21
91:8 [f] Ps 37:34; 58:10; Mal 1:5
91:10 [g] Pr 12:21
91:11 [h] Heb 1:14 [i] Ps 34:7
91:12 [j] Mt 4:6*; Lk 4:10-11*
91:13 [k] Da 6:22; Lk 10:19
91:15 [l] 1Sa 2:30; Ps 50:15; Jn 12:26
91:16 [m] Dt 6:2; Ps 21:4 [n] Ps 50:23

[a] 17 Or *beauty* [b] 1 Hebrew *Shaddai*
[c] 14 That is, probably the king

Ps 91:9–13 ❖ How has God been like a refuge for believers?

✣ 90:1–17 Our lives are brief and we are frail. Without that realization, we will never adopt the right attitude of dependence on God that should characterize our every day.

91:1–2 This psalm paints a detailed picture of the individual who chooses to trust in Yahweh above all else. Faith is not an abstract entity. For these faithful believers, it is the object of their trust that is important: God himself, and nothing less.
91:3–13 The poet depicts a world full of dangers. Each of the two stanzas ends by describing the believer's status in the thick of surrounding turmoil. God must be a dwelling place for his people—a refuge and place of security even in dark and troubled times.
91:14–16 It is one thing to be encouraged by the poet to believe these things; it is quite another experience to hear this promised protection in the form of a prophetic word directly from God. The covenantal God is *never* absent from those who take refuge in him—especially not in their times of greatest distress.

✣ 91:1–16 Psalm 91's promise is not that life will be easy but rather that God will always be present. The psalm details the promise of deliverance and salvation that can come to those who place their trust in him.

Psalm 92[a]

A psalm. A song. For the Sabbath day.

1 It is good to praise the LORD
and make music to your name,[o]
O Most High,[p]
2 proclaiming your love in the morning[q]
and your faithfulness at night,
3 to the music of the ten-stringed lyre
and the melody of the harp.[r]

4 For you make me glad by your deeds, LORD;
I sing for joy at what your hands have done.[s]
5 How great are your works,[t] LORD,
how profound your thoughts![u]
6 Senseless people[v] do not know,
fools do not understand,
7 that though the wicked spring up like grass
and all evildoers flourish,
they will be destroyed forever.

8 But you, LORD, are forever exalted.

9 For surely your enemies, LORD,
surely your enemies will perish;
all evildoers will be scattered.[w]
10 You have exalted my horn[b][x] like that of a wild ox;
fine oils[y] have been poured on me.
11 My eyes have seen the defeat of my adversaries;
my ears have heard the rout of my wicked foes.[z]

12 The righteous will flourish like a palm tree,
they will grow like a cedar of Lebanon;[a]
13 planted in the house of the LORD,
they will flourish in the courts of our God.[b]
14 They will still bear fruit[c] in old age,
they will stay fresh and green,
15 proclaiming, "The LORD is upright;
he is my Rock, and there is no wickedness in him.[d]"

92:1 [o] Ps 147:1 [p] Ps 135:3
92:2 [q] Ps 89:1
92:3 [r] 1Sa 10:5; Ne 12:27; Ps 33:2
92:4 [s] Ps 8:6; 143:5
92:5 [t] Rev 15:3 [u] Ps 40:5; 139:17; Isa 28:29; Ro 11:33
92:6 [v] Ps 73:22
92:9 [w] Ps 68:1; 89:10
92:10 [x] Ps 89:17 [y] Ps 23:5
92:11 [z] Ps 54:7; 91:8
92:12 [a] Ps 1:3; 52:8; Jer 17:8; Hos 14:6
92:13 [b] Ps 100:4
92:14 [c] Jn 15:2
92:15 [d] Job 34:10
93:1 [e] Ps 97:1 [f] Ps 104:1 [g] Ps 65:6 [h] Ps 96:10
93:2 [i] Ps 45:6
93:3 [j] Ps 96:11
93:4 [k] Ps 65:7
93:5 [l] Ps 29:2

Ps 92:1-4 ❖ What role does music play in our faith? What is the most meaningful way for you to worship God?

Ps 93 ❖ How can this short psalm inspire us as believers today? What does it mean that our good God is eternally on his throne?

Psalm 93

1 The LORD reigns,[e] he is robed in majesty;[f]
the LORD is robed in majesty and armed with strength;[g]
indeed, the world is established, firm and secure.[h]
2 Your throne was established long ago;
you are from all eternity.[i]

3 The seas[j] have lifted up, LORD,
the seas have lifted up their voice;
the seas have lifted up their pounding waves.
4 Mightier than the thunder[k] of the great waters,
mightier than the breakers of the sea—
the LORD on high is mighty.

5 Your statutes, LORD, stand firm;
holiness[l] adorns your house
for endless days.

[a] In Hebrew texts 92:1-15 is numbered 92:2-16.
[b] 10 *Horn* here symbolizes strength.

92:1-3 In the ancient Near East it was common to praise gods for fear they might turn nasty. But it is good to praise God because he himself is good.
92:4-8 Not only are the Lord's works a great encouragement, so are his thoughts. Anyone who fails to realize this truth is a fool (vv. 5–6). Whatever exaltation oppressors enjoy is brief. The eternal Creator, on the other hand, is praised forever.
92:9-11 The blessing and stability of the righteous come from divine intervention in the events of this world. The imagery describes the strength and restoration of the believer at the hand of Yahweh.
92:12-15 Those rejecting Yahweh are like grass (v. 7). The righteous, however, are like the palm tree and the cedar (v. 12). These images communicate perpetual growth and fruitfulness. By remaining close to Yahweh, the believer lives under his blessing, protection, and providential care.

✚ **92:1-15** We pray "your kingdom come, your will be done" (Mt 6:10), and we rejoice when that kingdom does come little by little, and more and more fully in our day.

93:1 Yahweh has such glory and power that there is no mistaking his high office within the created order.
93:2 God's kingship becomes a visible reality in the creation of the universe.
93:3-4 "The seas" could refer to the power of the sea, the surrounding nations, or the mythical forces of chaos.
93:5 There is no doubt as to God's power. Equally, *his character* is beyond question.

✚ **93:1-5** Many things in life *are* entirely beyond our control. That is why the psalmist reminds

Psalm 94

1 The LORD is a God who avenges.[m]
O God who avenges, shine forth.[n]
2 Rise up, Judge[o] of the earth;
pay back[p] to the proud what they deserve.
3 How long, LORD, will the wicked,
how long will the wicked be jubilant?

4 They pour out arrogant[q] words;
all the evildoers are full of boasting.[r]
5 They crush your people,[s] LORD;
they oppress your inheritance.
6 They slay the widow and the foreigner;
they murder the fatherless.
7 They say, "The LORD does not see;[t]
the God of Jacob takes no notice."
8 Take notice, you senseless ones[u]
among the people;
you fools, when will you become wise?
9 Does he who fashioned the ear not hear?
Does he who formed the eye not see?[v]
10 Does he who disciplines nations not punish?
Does he who teaches[w] mankind lack knowledge?
11 The LORD knows all human plans;
he knows that they are futile.[x]

12 Blessed is the one you discipline,[y] LORD,
the one you teach[z] from your law;
13 you grant them relief from days of trouble,
till a pit[a] is dug for the wicked.
14 For the LORD will not reject his people;[b]
he will never forsake his inheritance.
15 Judgment will again be founded on righteousness,[c]
and all the upright in heart will follow it.

16 Who will rise up[d] for me against the wicked?
Who will take a stand for me against evildoers?[e]
17 Unless the LORD had given me help,[f]
I would soon have dwelt in the silence of death.
18 When I said, "My foot is slipping,[g]"
your unfailing love, LORD, supported me.
19 When anxiety was great within me,
your consolation brought me joy.

20 Can a corrupt throne be allied with you—
a throne that brings on misery by its decrees?[h]
21 The wicked band together[i] against the righteous
and condemn the innocent[j] to death.
22 But the LORD has become my fortress,
and my God the rock in whom I take refuge.[k]
23 He will repay[l] them for their sins

94:1 [m] Na 1:2; Ro 12:19 [n] Ps 80:1
94:2 [o] Ge 18:25 [p] Ps 31:23
94:4 [q] Ps 31:18 [r] Ps 52:1
94:5 [s] Isa 3:15
94:7 [t] Job 22:14; Ps 10:11
94:8 [u] Ps 92:6
94:9 [v] Ex 4:11; Pr 20:12
94:10 [w] Job 35:11; Isa 28:26
94:11 [x] 1Co 3:20*
94:12 [y] Job 5:17; Heb 12:5 [z] Dt 8:3
94:13 [a] Ps 55:23
94:14 [b] 1Sa 12:22; Ps 37:28; Ro 11:2
94:15 [c] Ps 97:2
94:16 [d] Nu 10:35; Ps 17:13 [e] Ps 59:2
94:17 [f] Ps 124:2
94:18 [g] Ps 38:16
94:20 [h] Ps 58:2
94:21 [i] Ps 56:6 [j] Ps 106:38; Pr 17:15,26
94:22 [k] Ps 18:2; 59:9
94:23 [l] Ps 7:16

Ps 94:1–3 ❖ Are we ever tempted to take revenge into our own hands? Why should judgment be left to God (see Dt 32:35)?

---

us not only of the power of God but also of his character.

94:1–3 The psalmist's plea is not based on an understanding of God as a wrathful vigilante; rather, his appeal is to the ultimate Judge of humanity.
94:4–7 The poet voices indignation at the arrogance of evil people in society. Their pride is vocal as well as behavioral. Such flagrant self-glorification rubs salt into the wounds of the oppressed.
94:8–11 The foolish wicked show disdain for God in the words of v. 7, but God has nothing but disdain for them. Verse 11 affirms that the intentions of the wicked will come to nothing.
94:12–15 Verse 12 points to the link between discipline and teaching. There is a lesson that can be learned *before* God brings his punishment. True happiness is to be found in *walking in God's paths,* not rejecting them.
94:16–19 Yahweh will respond by standing against the evildoers. The questions in v. 16 also challenge the readers to take a stand against social wrongs.
94:20–23 Security goes far beyond the reach of those who hold temporal office. Yahweh himself is the psalmist's fortress and refuge. The poet is certain of the ultimate arrival of divine judgment. Effectively, the speaker is making his stand alongside the poor and voiceless of society.

✜ **94:1–23** Our task is to associate actively with the voiceless and to declare God's justice in our societies before he comes again in vengeance to judge the earth.

and destroy them for their
wickedness;
the LORD our God will destroy
them.

Psalm 95

1 Come, let us sing for joy to the LORD;
let us shout aloud[m] to the Rock[n] of
our salvation.
2 Let us come before him[o] with
thanksgiving
and extol him with music[p] and
song.

3 For the LORD is the great God,[q]
the great King above all gods.[r]
4 In his hand are the depths of the
earth,
and the mountain peaks belong to
him.
5 The sea is his, for he made it,
and his hands formed the dry
land.[s]

6 Come, let us bow down[t] in worship,
let us kneel[u] before the LORD our
Maker;[v]
7 for he is our God
and we are the people of his
pasture,[w]
the flock under his care.

Today, if only you would hear his
voice,
8 "Do not harden your hearts as you
did at Meribah,[a][x]
as you did that day at Massah[b] in
the wilderness,
9 where your ancestors tested[y] me;
they tried me, though they had
seen what I did.
10 For forty years[z] I was angry with that
generation;

95:1 [m] Ps 81:1 [n] 2Sa 22:47
95:2 [o] Mic 6:6 [p] Ps 81:2; Eph 5:19
95:3 [q] Ps 48:1; 145:3 [r] Ps 96:4; 97:9
95:5 [s] Ge 1:9; Ps 146:6
95:6 [t] Php 2:10 [u] 2Ch 6:13 [v] Ps 100:3; 149:2; Isa 17:7; Da 6:10-11; Hos 8:14
95:7 [w] Ps 74:1; 79:13
95:8 [x] Ex 17:7
95:9 [y] Nu 14:22; Ps 78:18; 1Co 10:9
95:10 [z] Ac 7:36; Heb 3:17
95:11 [a] Nu 14:23 [b] Dt 1:35; Heb 4:3*
96:1 [c] 1Ch 16:23
96:2 [d] Ps 71:15
96:4 [e] Ps 18:3; 145:3 [f] Ps 89:7 [g] Ps 95:3
96:5 [h] Ps 115:15
96:6 [i] Ps 29:1
96:7 [j] Ps 29:1 [k] Ps 22:27

Ps 95:7 ❖ Where and how do we hear God's voice today? How can we heed that voice?

I said, 'They are a people whose
hearts go astray,
and they have not known my
ways.'
11 So I declared on oath[a] in my anger,
'They shall never enter my rest.' "[b]

Psalm 96

96:1–13pp // 1Ch 16:23–33

1 Sing to the LORD[c] a new song;
sing to the LORD, all the earth.
2 Sing to the LORD, praise his name;
proclaim his salvation[d] day after
day.
3 Declare his glory among the nations,
his marvelous deeds among all
peoples.

4 For great is the LORD and most
worthy of praise;[e]
he is to be feared[f] above all gods.[g]
5 For all the gods of the nations are
idols,
but the LORD made the heavens.[h]
6 Splendor and majesty are before
him;
strength and glory[i] are in his
sanctuary.

7 Ascribe to the LORD,[j] all you families
of nations,[k]
ascribe to the LORD glory and
strength.
8 Ascribe to the LORD the glory due his
name;

[a] 8 *Meribah* means *quarreling.* [b] 8 *Massah* means *testing.*

95:1–5 Why should the people worship Yahweh as opposed to any other god? Because he is the "great God" and "great King" (v. 3).
95:6–7c As a community, the worshipers celebrate their God loudly because he is Creator, but they also bow before him because he is King.
95:7d–11 The worshiping community should be careful to *listen* to his voice when they "hear" it (v. 7d). The verb takes on an implication of *obedience*. It was because the desert generation explicitly and continually denied God's good character that they were excluded from entering the promised land as a place of rest.

✚ **95:1–11** The need for identity is basic to human existence, so Israel responds in joyous worship *because* they know to whom they belong. There is a wonderful sense of certainty that surrounds this joyful response.

96:1–3 The call to worship includes commands of proclamation and declaration. The *whole earth* is called to praise.
96:4–6 The psalmist encourages the nations to compare the insignificance of their gods with the significance of Yahweh. The worthless gods may (or may not) live in the heavens, but Yahweh created that dwelling space.
96:7–10 Yahweh reigns, and if this statement is true, then it requires a response.

bring an offering[l] and come into
his courts.
9 Worship the LORD in the splendor of
his[a] holiness;[m]
tremble[n] before him, all the earth.[o]
10 Say among the nations, "The LORD
reigns.[p]"
The world is firmly established, it
cannot be moved;[q]
he will judge the peoples with
equity.[r]

11 Let the heavens rejoice, let the earth
be glad;[s]
let the sea resound, and all that is
in it.
12 Let the fields be jubilant, and
everything in them;
let all the trees of the forest[t] sing
for joy.[u]
13 Let all creation rejoice before the
LORD, for he comes,
he comes to judge[v] the earth.
He will judge the world in
righteousness
and the peoples in his
faithfulness.

Psalm 97

1 The LORD reigns,[w] let the earth be
glad;[x]
let the distant shores rejoice.
2 Clouds and thick darkness[y] surround
him;
righteousness and justice are the
foundation of his throne.[z]
3 Fire[a] goes before[b] him
and consumes[c] his foes on every
side.
4 His lightning lights up the world;
the earth sees and trembles.[d]

5 The mountains melt[e] like wax
before the LORD,
before the Lord of all the earth.[f]
6 The heavens proclaim his
righteousness,[g]
and all peoples see his glory.[h]

7 All who worship images[i] are put to
shame,[j]
those who boast in idols —
worship him,[k] all you gods!

8 Zion hears and rejoices
and the villages of Judah are glad
because of your judgments,[l] LORD.
9 For you, LORD, are the Most High
over all the earth;[m]
you are exalted[n] far above all
gods.
10 Let those who love the LORD hate
evil,[o]
for he guards the lives of his
faithful ones[p]
and delivers[q] them from the hand
of the wicked.[r]
11 Light shines[b][s] on the righteous
and joy on the upright in heart.
12 Rejoice in the LORD, you who are
righteous,
and praise his holy name.[t]

96:8 [l] Ps 45:12; 72:10
96:9 [m] Ps 29:2 [n] Ps 114:7 [o] Ps 33:8
96:10 [p] Ps 97:1 [q] Ps 93:1 [r] Ps 67:4
96:11 [s] Ps 97:1; 98:7; Isa 49:13
96:12 [t] Isa 44:23 [u] Ps 65:13
96:13 [v] Rev 19:11
97:1 [w] Ps 96:10 [x] Ps 96:11
97:2 [y] Ex 19:9; Ps 18:11 [z] Ps 89:14
97:3 [a] Da 7:10 [b] Hab 3:5 [c] Ps 18:8
97:4 [d] Ps 104:32
97:5 [e] Ps 46:2, 6; Mic 1:4 [f] Jos 3:11
97:6 [g] Ps 50:6 [h] Ps 19:1
97:7 [i] Lev 26:1 [j] Jer 10:14 [k] Heb 1:6
97:8 [l] Ps 48:11
97:9 [m] Ps 83:18; 95:3 [n] Ex 18:11
97:10 [o] Ps 34:14; Am 5:15; Ro 12:9 [p] Pr 2:8 [q] Da 3:28 [r] Ps 37:40; Jer 15:21
97:11 [s] Job 22:28
97:12 [t] Ps 30:4

[a] 9 Or *LORD with the splendor of* [b] 11 One Hebrew manuscript and ancient versions (see also 112:4); most Hebrew manuscripts *Light is sown*

Ps 96:11–13 ❖ How does creation praise God? How do powerful moments in nature make us feel God's glory?

Ps 97:10 ❖ What does it mean for us to "hate evil"? How can we do this while still loving people and speaking the truth in love (see Eph 4:15)?

96:11–13 The environmental response here shows the significance of the natural world in God's grand design for humankind.

96:1–13 Any song of praise and worship to God that truly reflects his identity will speak of the way he has and still does reach out to restore and renew sinful humanity. It will also speak of how he draws us into a new relationship with him. Our songs should be acts of worship to God that declare his character as a missionary God (v. 10).

97:1 The poet again extends the benefits of Yahweh's rule to the whole created order, including foreign nations.
97:2–6 We see similar language used to describe God's appearance before Israel at Mount Sinai in Ex 19–20. There is, of course, irony in the fact that clouds and thick darkness actually bring the light of revelation (Ps 97:11). The psalmist foresees a day when all peoples will acknowledge his true character (v. 6b).
97:7–10 Whose God/god is actually worth worshiping? The answer is clear: Whether or not the gods of the nations exist, they are false and are subject to Yahweh's lordship. So they too are called to worship him.
97:11–12 Whoever responds to God in righteousness and uprightness of heart receives light and joy.

97:1–12 God is King and Judge. The standards and priorities that he sets should govern our daily living. The dictates of his kingdom and his rule should be our habitual practice.

Ps 98:1-3 ❖ How can the global perspective of this passage fire our passion for supporting missions around the world?

Ps 99:8 ❖ How does Jesus bring together God's forgiveness and justice (see 1Pe 3:18)? How does this fill us with hope as we worship the Lord?

Psalm 98

A psalm.

1 Sing to the LORD a new song,[u]
for he has done marvelous things;[v]
his right hand[w] and his holy arm[x]
have worked salvation for him.
2 The LORD has made his salvation known[y]
and revealed his righteousness to the nations.
3 He has remembered[z] his love
and his faithfulness to Israel;
all the ends of the earth have seen
the salvation of our God.

4 Shout for joy[a] to the LORD, all the earth,
burst into jubilant song with music;
5 make music to the LORD with the harp,[b]
with the harp and the sound of singing,[c]
6 with trumpets[d] and the blast of the ram's horn —
shout for joy before the LORD, the King.[e]

7 Let the sea resound, and everything in it,
the world, and all who live in it.[f]
8 Let the rivers clap their hands,
let the mountains[g] sing together for joy;
9 let them sing before the LORD,
for he comes to judge the earth.
He will judge the world in righteousness
and the peoples with equity.[h]

Psalm 99

1 The LORD reigns,[i]
let the nations tremble;
he sits enthroned between the cherubim,[j]
let the earth shake.
2 Great is the LORD[k] in Zion;
he is exalted[l] over all the nations.
3 Let them praise your great and awesome name[m] —
he is holy.

4 The King is mighty, he loves justice[n] —
you have established equity;[o]
in Jacob you have done
what is just and right.
5 Exalt[p] the LORD our God
and worship at his footstool;
he is holy.

6 Moses[q] and Aaron were among his priests,
Samuel[r] was among those who called on his name;
they called on the LORD
and he answered[s] them.
7 He spoke to them from the pillar of cloud;[t]
they kept his statutes and the decrees he gave them.

8 LORD our God,
you answered them;
you were to Israel a forgiving God,[u]

98:1 [u] Ps 96:1 [v] Ps 96:3 [w] Ex 15:6 [x] Isa 52:10
98:2 [y] Isa 52:10
98:3 [z] Lk 1:54
98:4 [a] Isa 44:23
98:5 [b] Ps 92:3 [c] Isa 51:3
98:6 [d] Nu 10:10 [e] Ps 47:7
98:7 [f] Ps 24:1
98:8 [g] Isa 55:12
98:9 [h] Ps 96:10
99:1 [i] Ps 97:1 [j] Ex 25:22
99:2 [k] Ps 48:1 [l] Ps 97:9; 113:4
99:3 [m] Ps 76:1
99:4 [n] Ps 11:7 [o] Ps 98:9
99:5 [p] Ps 132:7
99:6 [q] Ex 24:6 [r] Jer 15:1 [s] 1Sa 7:9
99:7 [t] Ex 33:9
99:8 [u] Nu 14:20

98:1-3 God's activity in human history stands as a testimony to the nations.

98:4-6 The establishment of God's authority, given his nature, gives the whole earth good cause to rejoice.

98:7-9 The created realm confirms Yahweh's right to judge. It emphasizes the unquestionable nature of that right.

✜ **98:1-9** As God's steadfast love and faithfulness are displayed in his creation and worked out in the people who make up the church, others are drawn to join that community of faith. As the collective church experiences the blessings of God openly and without embarrassment, others are drawn to know and love this God who does great things.

99:1-3 God reigns absolutely, and the whole world should respond accordingly. His presence in Jerusalem has a significance that goes far beyond Zion, Judah, and Israel.

99:4-5 Verse 4a can be rendered, "And the might of a King, he loves justice." Another option is "And a King's might is his love of justice."

99:6-9 The psalmist highlights the intercessory ministry of three OT figures of faith. They prayed to Yahweh and he responded to their petitions. The poet draws attention to God's grace, but his mercy should never be abused.

though you punished their
misdeeds.[a]
9 Exalt the LORD our God
and worship at his holy
mountain,
for the LORD our God is holy.

Psalm 100

A psalm. For giving grateful praise.

1 Shout for joy[v] to the LORD, all the
earth.
2 Worship the LORD with gladness;
come before him[w] with joyful
songs.
3 Know that the LORD is God.[x]
It is he who made us,[y] and we are
his[b];
we are his people, the sheep of his
pasture.[z]

4 Enter his gates with thanksgiving
and his courts with praise;
give thanks to him and praise his
name.[a]
5 For the LORD is good[b] and his love
endures forever;[c]
his faithfulness[d] continues
through all generations.

Psalm 101

Of David. A psalm.

1 I will sing of your love[e] and
justice;
to you, LORD, I will sing praise.
2 I will be careful to lead a blameless
life —
when will you come to me?

I will conduct the affairs of my
house
with a blameless heart.
3 I will not look with approval
on anything that is vile.[f]

I hate what faithless people do;[g]
I will have no part in it.
4 The perverse of heart[h] shall be far
from me;
I will have nothing to do with
what is evil.

5 Whoever slanders their neighbor[i] in
secret,
I will put to silence;
whoever has haughty eyes[j] and a
proud heart,
I will not tolerate.

6 My eyes will be on the faithful in the
land,
that they may dwell with me;
the one whose walk is blameless[k]
will minister to me.

7 No one who practices deceit
will dwell in my house;

100:1 [v] Ps 98:4
100:2 [w] Ps 95:2
100:3 [x] Ps 46:10 [y] Job 10:3 [z] Ps 74:1; Eze 34:31
100:4 [a] Ps 116:17
100:5 [b] 1Ch 16:34; Ps 25:8 [c] Ezr 3:11; Ps 106:1 [d] Ps 119:90
101:1 [e] Ps 51:14; 89:1; 145:7
101:3 [f] Dt 15:9 [g] Ps 40:4
101:4 [h] Pr 11:20
101:5 [i] Ps 50:20 [j] Ps 10:5; Pr 6:17
101:6 [k] Ps 119:1

[a] 8 Or *God, / an avenger of the wrongs done to them* [b] 3 Or *and not we ourselves*

Ps 100:1-5 ❖ How can we integrate our "grateful praise" toward God into our lives today?

Ps 101:3 ❖ How can we follow the Holy Spirit's sanctifying work by removing evil and temptations from our lives? What steps can we take to do that today?

✚ 99:1-9 Our God is a holy God, and therefore he is absolutely consistent in his response to his people in that he answers all people in accordance with his divine will. When God's people cry to him for mercy, he hears and answers their prayer.

100:1-3 The invitation to draw near with confidence is premised on the realization that God is the one true God, Creator, and King over the universe.
100:4-5 Normally, non-Israelites would have been excluded from the inner court of the temple, but in v. 4 they are encouraged not only to "enter his gates with thanksgiving" but also to enter "his courts" (i.e., enter the inner court) with praise, joining the voices of believers from around the world.

✚ 100:1-5 As a church, we need to consider more carefully our public praise of God as a form of outreach.

101:1-2 The theological point of these opening verses seems to be that the poet-king will reflect the ways of Yahweh's rule in his own human and political kingship.
101:3-8 The poet-king rejects the behavioral consequences of a wicked worldview. Surely the wrong attitude of heart will ultimately lead to wrong moral actions.

✚ 101:1-8 The contemporary Western church has an unnatural focus on "being nice." We see being noncontroversial as an essential part of our witness. Yet our emphasis on "niceness" can lead to the absolute denial of the church's prophetic office. Those who vehemently oppose God's ways in this world need to be called to account with an eye toward helping them realize the error of their ways (2Pe 3:9). Believers play a critical role in that task.

no one who speaks falsely
will stand in my presence.

8 Every morning[l] I will put to silence
all the wicked[m] in the land;
I will cut off every evildoer[n]
from the city of the LORD.[o]

Psalm 102[a]

A prayer of an afflicted person who has grown weak and pours out a lament before the LORD.

1 Hear my prayer, LORD;
let my cry for help[p] come to you.
2 Do not hide your face[q] from me
when I am in distress.
Turn your ear to me;
when I call, answer me quickly.

3 For my days vanish like smoke;[r]
my bones burn like glowing
embers.
4 My heart is blighted and withered
like grass;[s]
I forget to eat my food.
5 In my distress I groan aloud
and am reduced to skin and
bones.
6 I am like a desert owl,[t]
like an owl among the ruins.
7 I lie awake;[u] I have become
like a bird alone[v] on a roof.
8 All day long my enemies taunt me;
those who rail against me use my
name as a curse.
9 For I eat ashes as my food
and mingle my drink with tears[w]
10 because of your great wrath,[x]
for you have taken me up and
thrown me aside.
11 My days are like the evening
shadow;[y]
I wither away like grass.

12 But you, LORD, sit enthroned
forever;[z]
your renown endures[a] through all
generations.

101:8 [l] Jer 21:12 [m] Ps 75:10 [n] Ps 118:10-12 [o] Ps 46:4
102:1 [p] Ex 2:23
102:2 [q] Ps 69:17
102:3 [r] Jas 4:14
102:4 [s] Ps 37:2
102:6 [t] Job 30:29; Isa 34:11
102:7 [u] Ps 77:4 [v] Ps 38:11
102:9 [w] Ps 42:3
102:10 [x] Ps 38:3
102:11 [y] Job 14:2
102:12 [z] Ps 9:7 [a] Ps 135:13

Ps 102:27–28 ❖ How is God's immutability, or unchanging nature, a source of comfort and hope?

13 You will arise and have compassion[b]
on Zion,
for it is time to show favor to her;
the appointed time has come.
14 For her stones are dear to your
servants;
her very dust moves them to pity.
15 The nations will fear[c] the name of
the LORD,
all the kings[d] of the earth will
revere your glory.
16 For the LORD will rebuild Zion
and appear in his glory.[e]
17 He will respond to the prayer[f] of the
destitute;
he will not despise their plea.

18 Let this be written[g] for a future
generation,
that a people not yet created[h] may
praise the LORD:
19 "The LORD looked down[i] from his
sanctuary on high,
from heaven he viewed the earth,
20 to hear the groans of the prisoners[j]
and release those condemned to
death."
21 So the name of the LORD will be
declared[k] in Zion
and his praise in Jerusalem
22 when the peoples and the kingdoms
assemble to worship the LORD.

23 In the course of my life[b] he broke my
strength;
he cut short my days.
24 So I said:
"Do not take me away, my God, in
the midst of my days;
your years go on[l] through all
generations.

102:13 [b] Isa 60:10
102:15 [c] 1Ki 8:43 [d] Ps 138:4
102:16 [e] Isa 60:1-2
102:17 [f] Ne 1:6
102:18 [g] Ro 15:4 [h] Ps 22:31
102:19 [i] Dt 26:15
102:20 [j] Ps 79:11
102:21 [k] Ps 22:22
102:24 [l] Ps 90:2; Isa 38:10

[a] In Hebrew texts 102:1-28 is numbered 102:2-29.
[b] *23 Or By his power*

102:1–11 The graphic images in this passage imply suffering. The reader is drawn to feel the despair of the poet, whose body is failing him. The second aspect of lament is focused on the opposition of enemies and expressed in terms of loneliness and social isolation. The third element focuses on God as the ultimate cause of the psalmist's torment.
102:12–22 The movement from the individual to Zion is a surprising one, but such a transition is not altogether uncommon. Nevertheless, there is hope! Israel's God still reigns, despite all appearances to the contrary. He pays attention to the realities of his people. He hears the needs of his people *and* frees those who are imprisoned *so that* his name will be declared in the midst of his people.
102:23–28 The fleeting brevity of human life, particularly a life apparently being cut short by illness, is contrasted with the eternal reign of God. The psalmist declares that even though his days may be shortened, there is hope for the future because of God's covenantal promises to his people. God is a God of restoration (v. 16).

25 In the beginning[m] you laid the
foundations of the earth,
and the heavens are the work of
your hands.
26 They will perish,[n] but you remain;
they will all wear out like a
garment.
Like clothing you will change them
and they will be discarded.
27 But you remain the same,[o]
and your years will never end.
28 The children of your servants[p] will
live in your presence;
their descendants[q] will be
established before you."

Psalm 103

Of David.

1 Praise the LORD, my soul;[r]
all my inmost being, praise his
holy name.
2 Praise the LORD, my soul,
and forget not all his benefits—
3 who forgives all your sins[s]
and heals[t] all your diseases,
4 who redeems your life from the pit
and crowns you with love and
compassion,
5 who satisfies your desires with good
things
so that your youth is renewed like
the eagle's.[u]

6 The LORD works righteousness
and justice for all the oppressed.

7 He made known[v] his ways[w] to Moses,
his deeds[x] to the people of Israel:
8 The LORD is compassionate and
gracious,[y]
slow to anger, abounding in love.
9 He will not always accuse,
nor will he harbor his anger
forever;[z]

102:25 [m] Ge 1:1; Heb 1:10-12*
102:26 [n] Isa 34:4; Mt 24:35; 2Pe 3:7-10; Rev 20:11
102:27 [o] Mal 3:6; Heb 13:8; Jas 1:17
102:28 [p] Ps 69:36 [q] Ps 89:4
103:1 [r] Ps 104:1
103:3 [s] Ps 130:8 [t] Ex 15:26
103:5 [u] Isa 40:31
103:7 [v] Ps 99:7; 147:19 [w] Ex 33:13 [x] Ps 106:22
103:8 [y] Ex 34:6; Ps 86:15; Jas 5:11
103:9 [z] Ps 30:5; Isa 57:16; Jer 3:5,12; Mic 7:18
103:10 [a] Ezr 9:13
103:11 [b] Ps 57:10
103:12 [c] 2Sa 12:13
103:13 [d] Mal 3:17
103:14 [e] Isa 29:16
103:15 [f] Ps 90:5 [g] Job 14:2; Jas 1:10; 1Pe 1:24
103:16 [h] Isa 40:7 [i] Job 7:10
103:18 [j] Dt 7:9
103:19 [k] Ps 47:2
103:20 [l] Ps 148:2; Heb 1:14 [m] Ps 29:1

Ps 103:2 ❖ What are some benefits of being a child of God? How can we keep them on our minds and hearts so that we always remember them?

10 he does not treat us as our sins
deserve[a]
or repay us according to our
iniquities.
11 For as high as the heavens are above
the earth,
so great is his love[b] for those who
fear him;
12 as far as the east is from the west,
so far has he removed our
transgressions[c] from us.

13 As a father has compassion[d] on his
children,
so the LORD has compassion on
those who fear him;
14 for he knows how we are formed,[e]
he remembers that we are dust.
15 The life of mortals is like grass,[f]
they flourish like a flower[g] of the
field;
16 the wind blows[h] over it and it is gone,
and its place[i] remembers it no
more.
17 But from everlasting to everlasting
the LORD's love is with those who
fear him,
and his righteousness with their
children's children—
18 with those who keep his covenant
and remember to obey his
precepts.[j]

19 The LORD has established his throne
in heaven,
and his kingdom rules[k] over all.

20 Praise the LORD, you his angels,[l]
you mighty ones[m] who do his
bidding,

102:1–28 Remembering God's faithful work in the world brings hope to even the darkest of personal circumstances. Prayer is a deeply personal matter, but Ps 102 models an attitude to prayer that goes beyond the solely personal, pointing to the glory of God shown in his past, present, and future faithfulness. We should follow its example.

103:1–2 The poet addresses his very inner being with the call to praise the Lord. The command not to forget affirms the implication in the opening verse: It is easy to forget in our inner being the many reasons we have to praise God.

103:3–6 The second section outlines the character of God, listing five actions that typify that character; the first focuses on the forgiveness of sins. Often in the Hebrew Bible, first place in a list indicates the priority of the author's emphasis.

103:7–19 A direct quotation from Ex 34:6 (see Ps 103:8) continues the poet's focus on God's grace, compassion, and forgiveness. The compassionate love of a father for his children is the only human experience that can approximate God's love for his children. God's people respond to his grace by a commitment to love him through remembering and applying his teaching.

103:20–22 This call to worship addressed to the

CHARACTER OF GOD // GOD IS COMPASSIONATE

Psalm 103:13: As a father has compassion on his children, so the LORD has compassion on those who fear him.

God's compassionate nature is often connected to his merciful willingness to forgive. Psalm 77:9 laments, "Has God forgotten to be merciful? Has he in anger withheld his compassion?" The writer goes on to find hope in remembering God's mighty acts and deeds of mercy in the past (Ps 77:10–11).

David also connects God's compassion to his forgiveness in Ps 51:1b: "According to your great compassion blot out my transgressions." This aspect of God's compassion is closely tied to his gracious and forgiving nature. God's compassion makes him a forgiving God.

But there is another meaningful aspect of God's compassion. God says that he hears the cries of people who are oppressed because he is compassionate (Ex 22:27). Here God's compassion reveals itself as a passion for justice. Because of God's compassion, he shows mercy and comfort to those who are oppressed and marginalized.

Christ demonstrated this compassionate nature of God when he reached out to marginalized individuals, such as lepers (Mt 8:1–4) and Samaritans (Jn 4:1–26). God watches over people who are downtrodden and lonely. He hears the cries of the oppressed and upholds their cause by his righteous judgments.

APPLICATION God's children can take tremendous comfort in God's compassion. It moves God to forgive sin and welcome his children to him through Christ. However, we cannot be satisfied to receive God's compassion for ourselves without extending that same compassion into the world. God calls us to be people of compassion and justice who care for and protect people who are on the margins (see Lk 10:25–37). God's compassion is a wonderful gift. Our response of gratitude needs to include demonstrating God's compassion for others in a hurting world. We show our love for God through loving others well.

who obey his word.
21 Praise the LORD, all his heavenly hosts,[n]
you his servants who do his will.
22 Praise the LORD, all his works[o]
everywhere in his dominion.

Praise the LORD, my soul.

Psalm 104

1 Praise the LORD, my soul.[p]

LORD my God, you are very great;
you are clothed with splendor and majesty.

2 The LORD wraps[q] himself in light as with a garment;
he stretches out the heavens[r] like a tent
3 and lays the beams[s] of his upper chambers on their waters.
He makes the clouds[t] his chariot
and rides on the wings of the wind.[u]
4 He makes winds his messengers,[a][v]
flames of fire[w] his servants.

5 He set the earth[x] on its foundations;
it can never be moved.
6 You covered it[y] with the watery depths[z] as with a garment;
the waters stood above the mountains.
7 But at your rebuke[a] the waters fled,

103:21 [n] 1Ki 22:19
103:22 [o] Ps 145:10
104:1 [p] Ps 103:22
104:2 [q] Da 7:9 [r] Isa 40:22
104:3 [s] Am 9:6 [t] Isa 19:1 [u] Ps 18:10
104:4 [v] Ps 148:8; Heb 1:7* [w] 2Ki 2:11
104:5 [x] Job 26:7; Ps 24:1-2
104:6 [y] Ge 7:19 [z] Ge 1:2
104:7 [a] Ps 18:15

[a] 4 Or *angels*

angelic armies of the Lord is the natural response to his cosmic reign. The emphasis remains on *doing* the word of God. The angels do his word to heed the sound of his word, providing an example for everyone who wants to worship God with their lives (v. 18).

103:1–22 Together with the psalmist, we must remind ourselves of God's eternal love for us (v. 17)—a love that will not be tempered by our human weakness (vv. 13–16).

104:1–4 Why praise? Because God is *very* great! The poet provides himself with an immediate justification for praise based on God's nature.

104:5–18 The earth is established because it was created and set in place by Yahweh, who again is "very great" (v. 1). Far from being a chaotic threat

at the sound of your thunder they
took to flight;
8 they flowed over the mountains,
they went down into the valleys,
to the place you assigned[b] for
them.
9 You set a boundary they cannot cross;
never again will they cover the
earth.

10 He makes springs[c] pour water into
the ravines;
it flows between the mountains.
11 They give water to all the beasts of
the field;
the wild donkeys quench their
thirst.
12 The birds of the sky[d] nest by the
waters;
they sing among the branches.
13 He waters the mountains[e] from his
upper chambers;
the land is satisfied by the fruit of
his work.
14 He makes grass grow[f] for the cattle,
and plants for people to
cultivate—
bringing forth food[g] from the
earth:
15 wine[h] that gladdens human hearts,
oil[i] to make their faces shine,
and bread that sustains their
hearts.
16 The trees of the LORD are well
watered,
the cedars of Lebanon that he
planted.
17 There the birds[j] make their nests;
the stork has its home in the
junipers.
18 The high mountains belong to the
wild goats;
the crags are a refuge for the
hyrax.[k]

19 He made the moon to mark the
seasons,[l]
and the sun[m] knows when to go
down.
20 You bring darkness,[n] it becomes
night,[o]
and all the beasts of the forest[p]
prowl.
21 The lions roar for their prey
and seek their food from God.[q]
22 The sun rises, and they steal away;
they return and lie down in their
dens.[r]
23 Then people go out to their work,[s]
to their labor until evening.

24 How many are your works,[t] LORD!
In wisdom you made[u] them all;
the earth is full of your creatures.
25 There is the sea,[v] vast and spacious,
teeming with creatures beyond
number—
living things both large and small.
26 There the ships[w] go to and fro,
and Leviathan,[x] which you formed
to frolic there.

27 All creatures look to you
to give them their food[y] at the
proper time.
28 When you give it to them,
they gather it up;
when you open your hand,
they are satisfied[z] with good
things.
29 When you hide your face,[a]
they are terrified;
when you take away their breath,
they die and return to the dust.[b]
30 When you send your Spirit,
they are created,
and you renew the face of the
ground.

Ps 104:27-30 ❖ How does remembering God's loving care over all creatures, not just humans, fill us with a Job-like sense of wonder and awe?

104:8 [b] Ps 33:7
104:10 [c] Ps 107:33; Isa 41:18
104:12 [d] Mt 8:20
104:13 [e] Ps 147:8; Jer 10:13
104:14 [f] Job 38:27; Ps 147:8 [g] Ge 1:30; Job 28:5
104:15 [h] Jdg 9:13 [i] Ps 23:5; 92:10; Lk 7:46
104:17 [j] ver 12
104:18 [k] Pr 30:26
104:19 [l] Ge 1:14 [m] Ps 19:6
104:20 [n] Isa 45:7 [o] Ps 74:16 [p] Ps 50:10
104:21 [q] Job 38:39; Ps 145:15; Joel 1:20
104:22 [r] Job 37:8
104:23 [s] Ge 3:19
104:24 [t] Ps 40:5 [u] Pr 3:19
104:25 [v] Ps 69:34
104:26 [w] Ps 107:23; Eze 27:9 [x] Job 41:1
104:27 [y] Job 36:31; Ps 136:25; 145:15; 147:9
104:28 [z] Ps 145:16
104:29 [a] Dt 31:17 [b] Job 34:14; Ecc 12:7

---

that is barely held in check, the waters have a vital role to play in God's provision for all the living creatures (vv. 10–18).

104:19–23 From right places, the psalmist moves on to consider appropriate times and seasons. This sense of right and appropriate order continues throughout the ensuing verses of this section. As God has worked in the creation of the universe, work and rest are both ingrained within that natural rhythm of the day.

104:24 The association between God's wisdom and his works of creation is a common one in the poetic texts of the OT (see Pr 8; Job 28; 38–41). The creation-wisdom link implies that God's ways are somehow deeply ingrained in the natural order.

104:25–26 The psalmist presents the oceans as a playground for ships and sea monsters. It really is a delightful image that continues the sense of purposefulness from the previous stanza. The psalmist projects a glorious sense of delight in the way in which God made the seas.

104:27–30 The message is simple: All living beings, be they animals or people, are completely dependent on their Creator every moment of life. We cannot demand our next breath: It is a gift. This dependence is cause for praise.

Psalm 106

106:1,47–48pp // 1Ch 16:34–36

1 Praise the LORD.[a]

Give thanks to the LORD, for he is good;[k]
his love endures forever.

2 Who can proclaim the mighty acts[l] of the LORD
or fully declare his praise?
3 Blessed are those who act justly,
who always do what is right.[m]

4 Remember me,[n] LORD, when you show favor to your people,
come to my aid when you save them,
5 that I may enjoy the prosperity[o] of your chosen ones,
that I may share in the joy[p] of your nation
and join your inheritance in giving praise.

6 We have sinned,[q] even as our ancestors did;
we have done wrong and acted wickedly.
7 When our ancestors were in Egypt,
they gave no thought to your miracles;
they did not remember[r] your many kindnesses,
and they rebelled by the sea,[s] the Red Sea.[b]
8 Yet he saved them for his name's sake,[t]
to make his mighty power known.
9 He rebuked[u] the Red Sea, and it dried up;[v]
he led them through[w] the depths as through a desert.
10 He saved them[x] from the hand of the foe;
from the hand of the enemy he redeemed them.[y]

106:1 [k] Ps 100:5; 105:1
106:2 [l] Ps 145:4, 12
106:3 [m] Ps 15:2
106:4 [n] Ps 119:132
106:5 [o] Ps 1:3 [p] Ps 118:15
106:6 [q] Da 9:5
106:7 [r] Ps 78:11, 42 [s] Ex 14:11-12
106:8 [t] Ex 9:16
106:9 [u] Ps 18:15 [v] Ex 14:21; Na 1:4 [w] Isa 63:11-14
106:10 [x] Ex 14:30 [y] Ps 107:2
106:11 [z] Ex 14:28; 15:5
106:12 [a] Ex 15:1-21
106:13 [b] Ex 15:24
106:14 [c] 1Co 10:9
106:15 [d] Nu 11:31 [e] Isa 10:16
106:16 [f] Nu 16:1-3
106:17 [g] Dt 11:6
106:18 [h] Nu 16:35
106:19 [i] Ex 32:4
106:20 [j] Jer 2:11; Ro 1:23
106:21 [k] Ps 78:11 [l] Dt 10:21
106:22 [m] Ps 105:27

Ps 106:13–15 ❖ Why is it sometimes so easy to forget God and backslide in our faith practice? Where can we find hope in such times?

11 The waters covered[z] their adversaries;
not one of them survived.
12 Then they believed his promises
and sang his praise.[a]

13 But they soon forgot[b] what he had done
and did not wait for his plan to unfold.
14 In the desert they gave in to their craving;
in the wilderness they put God to the test.[c]
15 So he gave them[d] what they asked for,
but sent a wasting disease[e] among them.

16 In the camp they grew envious[f] of Moses
and of Aaron, who was consecrated to the LORD.
17 The earth opened[g] up and swallowed Dathan;
it buried the company of Abiram.
18 Fire blazed[h] among their followers;
a flame consumed the wicked.
19 At Horeb they made a calf[i]
and worshiped an idol cast from metal.
20 They exchanged their glorious God[j]
for an image of a bull, which eats grass.
21 They forgot the God[k] who saved them,
who had done great things[l] in Egypt,
22 miracles in the land of Ham[m]

[a] 1 Hebrew *Hallelu Yah*; also in verse 48 [b] 7 Or *the Sea of Reeds*; also in verses 9 and 22

106:1–5 The history of the nation would never have continued for as long as it did apart from God's steadfast love. Just as it is impossible to express fully or even adequately God's worth in praise, so also it is impossible to give an account of all God's activity in human history.
106:6–12 Failure to reflect on the *many* kindnesses God had shown to Israel led to rebellion in a time of stress. Yahweh saved Israel because he was true to himself, not because the people responded well to the threat they faced.
106:13–18 All too soon after God's mighty deliverance, the people's selective amnesia returns, and they rebel. Verses 14–15 probably refer to Nu 11:4–35, where the people complain about the lack of meat. The second desert rebellion recorded by the psalmist (Ps 106:16–18) is found in Nu 16. The rebellions called into question the goodness of God's character and his design for the people.
106:19–23 Making an idol from metal and declaring that inanimate thing to be the living God is ridiculous enough. Doing so at Sinai, the place where God revealed his love and commands for his people, makes the sin and betrayal just that more heinous.

and awesome deeds by the Red Sea.
23 So he said he would destroy[n] them —
had not Moses, his chosen one,
stood in the breach[o] before him
to keep his wrath from destroying
them.

24 Then they despised the pleasant
land;[p]
they did not believe[q] his promise.
25 They grumbled[r] in their tents
and did not obey the LORD.
26 So he swore[s] to them with uplifted
hand
that he would make them fall in
the wilderness,[t]
27 make their descendants fall among
the nations
and scatter[u] them throughout the
lands.

28 They yoked themselves to the Baal
of Peor[v]
and ate sacrifices offered to
lifeless gods;
29 they aroused the LORD's anger by
their wicked deeds,
and a plague broke out among
them.
30 But Phinehas stood up and
intervened,
and the plague was checked.[w]
31 This was credited to him[x] as
righteousness
for endless generations to come.
32 By the waters of Meribah[y] they
angered the LORD,
and trouble came to Moses
because of them;
33 for they rebelled against the Spirit of
God,
and rash words came from Moses'
lips.[a][z]

34 They did not destroy[a] the peoples
as the LORD had commanded[b]
them,

106:23 [n] Ex 32:10 [o] Ex 32:11-14
106:24 [p] Dt 8:7; Eze 20:6 [q] Heb 3:18-19
106:25 [r] Nu 14:2
106:26 [s] Eze 20:15; Heb 3:11 [t] Nu 14:28-35
106:27 [u] Lev 26:33; Ps 44:11
106:28 [v] Nu 25:2-3; Hos 9:10
106:30 [w] Nu 25:8
106:31 [x] Nu 25:11-13
106:32 [y] Nu 20:2-13; Ps 81:7
106:33 [z] Nu 20:8-12
106:34 [a] Jdg 1:21 [b] Dt 7:16
106:35 [c] Jdg 3:5-6
106:36 [d] Jdg 2:12
106:37 [e] 2Ki 16:3; 17:17
106:38 [f] Nu 35:33
106:39 [g] Eze 20:18 [h] Lev 17:7; Nu 15:39
106:40 [i] Jdg 2:14; Ps 78:59 [j] Dt 9:29
106:41 [k] Jdg 2:14; Ne 9:27
106:43 [l] Jdg 2:16-19
106:44 [m] Jdg 3:9; 10:10
106:45 [n] Lev 26:42; Ps 105:8 [o] Jdg 2:18
106:46 [p] Ezr 9:9; Jer 42:12
106:47 [q] Ps 147:2

35 but they mingled[c] with the nations
and adopted their customs.
36 They worshiped their idols,[d]
which became a snare to them.
37 They sacrificed their sons[e]
and their daughters to false gods.
38 They shed innocent blood,
the blood of their sons[f] and
daughters,
whom they sacrificed to the idols of
Canaan,
and the land was desecrated by
their blood.
39 They defiled themselves[g] by what
they did;
by their deeds they prostituted[h]
themselves.

40 Therefore the LORD was angry[i] with
his people
and abhorred his inheritance.[j]
41 He gave them into the hands[k] of the
nations,
and their foes ruled over them.
42 Their enemies oppressed them
and subjected them to their
power.
43 Many times he delivered them,
but they were bent on rebellion[l]
and they wasted away in their sin.
44 Yet he took note of their distress
when he heard their cry;[m]
45 for their sake he remembered his
covenant[n]
and out of his great love[o] he
relented.
46 He caused all who held them captive
to show them mercy.[p]

47 Save us, LORD our God,
and gather us[q] from the nations,
that we may give thanks to your
holy name
and glory in your praise.

[a] *33* Or *against his spirit, / and rash words came from his lips*

106:24–27 The next failing highlighted by the psalmist is the people's response to the report of the ten spies (Nu 13–14). Faithlessness has a cross-generational impact that resonates through the ages from exodus to exile.
106:28–33 Their "yoking" (v. 28) leads to a string of events that shows the ups and downs of a community's unraveling and veering away from its true identity. The events of Nu 25 describe an idolatrous orgy of cultic prostitution quelled only by the radical intervention of Phineas. The action for which Moses is punished is rooted in the constant, vexing rebellion of the people.
106:34–39 The command that Israel root out their enemies from the promised land was a moral imperative to prevent pagan worship through the sacrifice of children. The people of Israel were meant to be distinctive from all the other tribes and nations. God's people proved themselves unworthy of their calling, so the punishments of Dt 28 were bound to unfold as promised by God.
106:40–46 The exile was the inevitable consequence of the nation's action. Despite this image of decay and decline, grace triumphs over rebellion.
106:47–48 The prayer for salvation places the psalmist with the people in the exile. The concluding

48 Praise be to the LORD, the God of
Israel,
from everlasting to everlasting.
Let all the people say, "Amen!"[r]
Praise the LORD.

BOOK V

Psalms 107–150

Psalm 107

1 Give thanks to the LORD,[s] for he is
good;
his love endures forever.

2 Let the redeemed[t] of the LORD tell
their story—
those he redeemed from the hand
of the foe,
3 those he gathered[u] from the lands,
from east and west, from north
and south.[a]

4 Some wandered in desert[v]
wastelands,
finding no way to a city where
they could settle.
5 They were hungry and thirsty,
and their lives ebbed away.
6 Then they cried out[w] to the LORD in
their trouble,
and he delivered them from their
distress.
7 He led them by a straight way[x]
to a city where they could settle.
8 Let them give thanks to the LORD for
his unfailing love
and his wonderful deeds for
mankind,

106:48 [r] Ps 41:13
107:1 [s] Ps 106:1
107:2 [t] Ps 106:10
107:3 [u] Ps 106:47; Isa 43:5-6
107:4 [v] Nu 14:33; 32:13
107:6 [w] Ps 50:15
107:7 [x] Ezr 8:21

Ps 107:2 ❖ What is *your* story? Whom can you tell about what God has done for you?

9 for he satisfies[y] the thirsty
and fills the hungry with good
things.[z]

10 Some sat in darkness,[a] in utter
darkness,
prisoners suffering in iron
chains,[b]
11 because they rebelled[c] against God's
commands
and despised the plans[d] of the
Most High.
12 So he subjected them to bitter labor;
they stumbled, and there was no
one to help.[e]
13 Then they cried to the LORD in their
trouble,
and he saved them from their
distress.
14 He brought them out of darkness,
the utter darkness,
and broke away their chains.[f]
15 Let them give thanks to the LORD for
his unfailing love
and his wonderful deeds for
mankind,
16 for he breaks down gates of bronze
and cuts through bars of iron.

17 Some became fools through their
rebellious ways
and suffered affliction[g] because of
their iniquities.
18 They loathed all food[h]
and drew near the gates of death.[i]

107:9 [y] Ps 22:26; Lk 1:53 [z] Ps 34:10
107:10 [a] Lk 1:79 [b] Job 36:8
107:11 [c] Ps 106:7; La 3:42 [d] 2Ch 36:16
107:12 [e] Ps 22:11
107:14 [f] Ps 116:16; Lk 13:16; Ac 12:7
107:17 [g] Isa 65:6-7; La 3:39
107:18 [h] Job 33:20 [i] Job 33:22; Ps 9:13; 88:3

[a] 3 Hebrew *north and the sea*

---

call to praise serves as a doxology that indicates the close of Book 4 of the Psalter as well as the logical conclusion of the psalm.

✣ **106:1-48** Most Christians, at some point, feel condemned and dismayed by the repeating pattern of seeking forgiveness followed by sudden relapse. The poet was able to believe that God's grace was bigger and more determined than the often-repeated sins of the people. How much more should we, having seen what he has done for us in Jesus, be able to trust in God's great love? Therefore we denounce sin in our lives and strive to please him through our actions out of gratitude for his saving work on our behalf.

107:1-3 The commitment of Yahweh to his people may not be fully captured with the word "love" (v. 1). The Hebrew term reminds the community of the foundational hope for deliverance, past and future. The people are to give thanks to the Lord because he has gathered them from the lands, but also because he has delivered them from places that threatened to unleash chaos into the lives of God's people.

107:4-9 In each scene of deliverance, the psalmist recounts how the people cried out to God and how they were delivered (vv. 6, 13, 19, 28). Because of the Lord's steadfast love and his "wonderful deeds" (v. 8), the people are delivered from "their trouble" and "their distress" (v. 6). They are given a city to live in, and their appetites are satisfied.

107:10-16 Those in prison make a connection between their dire circumstances and their lack of faithfulness to God. The people cried out to Yahweh, and he delivered them.

107:17-22 Later in this section, the gates of death are referred to as "the grave" (v. 20). In other words, the people's sins have led to their pit. Nonetheless,

[19]Then they cried to the LORD in their
trouble,
and he saved them from their
distress.
[20]He sent out his word[j] and healed
them;[k]
he rescued[l] them from the grave.[m]
[21]Let them give thanks to the LORD for
his unfailing love
and his wonderful deeds for
mankind.
[22]Let them sacrifice thank offerings[n]
and tell of his works[o] with songs
of joy.

[23]Some went out on the sea in ships;
they were merchants on the
mighty waters.
[24]They saw the works of the LORD,
his wonderful deeds in the deep.
[25]For he spoke[p] and stirred up a
tempest[q]
that lifted high the waves.[r]
[26]They mounted up to the heavens
and went down to the depths;
in their peril their courage
melted[s] away.
[27]They reeled and staggered like
drunkards;
they were at their wits' end.
[28]Then they cried out to the LORD in
their trouble,
and he brought them out of their
distress.
[29]He stilled the storm[t] to a whisper;
the waves[u] of the sea[a] were
hushed.
[30]They were glad when it grew calm,
and he guided them to their
desired haven.
[31]Let them give thanks to the LORD for
his unfailing love
and his wonderful deeds for
mankind.
[32]Let them exalt him in the assembly[v]
of the people
and praise him in the council of
the elders.

[33]He turned rivers into a desert,[w]
flowing springs into thirsty ground,
[34]and fruitful land into a salt waste,[x]
because of the wickedness of
those who lived there.
[35]He turned the desert into pools of
water[y]
and the parched ground into
flowing springs;
[36]there he brought the hungry to live,
and they founded a city where
they could settle.
[37]They sowed fields and planted
vineyards[z]
that yielded a fruitful harvest;
[38]he blessed them, and their numbers
greatly increased,[a]
and he did not let their herds
diminish.

[39]Then their numbers decreased,[b] and
they were humbled
by oppression, calamity and
sorrow;
[40]he who pours contempt on nobles[c]
made them wander in a trackless
waste.[d]
[41]But he lifted the needy[e] out of their
affliction
and increased their families like
flocks.
[42]The upright see and rejoice,[f]
but all the wicked shut their
mouths.[g]

107:20 [j]Mt 8:8 [k]Ps 103:3 [l]Job 33:28 [m]Ps 30:3; 49:15
107:22 [n]Lev 7:12; Ps 50:14; 116:17 [o]Ps 9:11; 73:28; 118:17
107:25 [p]Ps 105:31 [q]Jnh 1:4 [r]Ps 93:3
107:26 [s]Ps 22:14
107:29 [t]Mt 8:26 [u]Ps 89:9
107:32 [v]Ps 22:22, 25; 35:18
107:33 [w]1Ki 17:1; Ps 74:15
107:34 [x]Ge 13:10; 14:3; 19:25
107:35 [y]Ps 114:8; Isa 41:18
107:37 [z]Isa 65:21
107:38 [a]Ge 12:2; 17:16, 20; Ex 1:7
107:39 [b]2Ki 10:32; Eze 5:12
107:40 [c]Job 12:21 [d]Job 12:24
107:41 [e]1Sa 2:8; Ps 113:7-9
107:42 [f]Job 22:19 [g]Job 5:16; Ps 63:11; Ro 3:19

[a] *29* Dead Sea Scrolls; Masoretic Text / *their waves*

---

those sick under the weight of sin cry to Yahweh for deliverance, and he delivers them from their oppression or distress.

107:23–32 Three times the psalmist refers to the sea in terms that are metaphorically rich in meaning (vv. 23b, 24b, 26a). Frequently these terms connote chaos and the threat of death (cf. 69:1, 2, 15).

107:33–41 Verses 33–34 open the final hymn with a stark reminder of Yahweh's power. This exercise of Yahweh's power is a response to the wickedness of those who dwell in the land. The theology of the poor plays a significant role in vv. 39–41. Yahweh lifted them out of their affliction and blessed them by increasing their families.

107:42–43 The upright are instructed to "see" (v. 42) and learn from the stories of deliverance and the testimonies of Yahweh's transforming work in the world. Should they do so, they will be led to rejoicing, while those engaged in wickedness will have their mouths shut in the light of Yahweh's power.

107:1–43 In our technological age, people are falling into exile in new and more sophisticated ways. When circumstances become challenging or conversations become difficult, people resort to social media as a means of escape. Rather than engaging others, people withdraw into a modern form of isolationism (aptly described in vv. 1–16). Ironically, for many people, deliverance is associated with being exiled from others—a concept foreign to the psalmist and to the church. God calls

43 Let the one who is wise[h] heed these
things
and ponder the loving deeds[i] of
the LORD.

Psalm 108[a]

108:1–5pp // Ps 57:7–11
108:6–13pp // Ps 60:5–12

A song. A psalm of David.

1 My heart, O God, is steadfast;
I will sing and make music with
all my soul.
2 Awake, harp and lyre!
I will awaken the dawn.
3 I will praise you, LORD, among the
nations;
I will sing of you among the
peoples.
4 For great is your love, higher than
the heavens;
your faithfulness reaches to the
skies.
5 Be exalted, O God, above the
heavens;
let your glory be over all the earth.[j]

6 Save us and help us with your right
hand,
that those you love may be
delivered.
7 God has spoken from his sanctuary:
"In triumph I will parcel out
Shechem
and measure off the Valley of
Sukkoth.
8 Gilead is mine, Manasseh is mine;
Ephraim is my helmet,
Judah[k] is my scepter.
9 Moab is my washbasin,
on Edom I toss my sandal;
over Philistia I shout in triumph."

10 Who will bring me to the fortified
city?
Who will lead me to Edom?
11 Is it not you, God, you who have
rejected us
and no longer go out with our
armies?[l]
12 Give us aid against the enemy,
for human help is worthless.
13 With God we will gain the victory,
and he will trample down our
enemies.

107:43 [h] Jer 9:12; Hos 14:9 [i] Ps 64:9
108:5 [j] Ps 57:5
108:8 [k] Ge 49:10
108:11 [l] Ps 44:9
109:1 [m] Ps 83:1
109:2 [n] Ps 52:4; 120:2
109:3 [o] Ps 69:4 [p] Ps 35:7; Jn 15:25
109:4 [q] Ps 69:13
109:5 [r] Ps 35:12; 38:20
109:6 [s] Zec 3:1

Ps 108:6 ❖ What trials are you praying for God to bring you through or save you from right now?

Ps 109:1–5 ❖ What do we do when people turn against us? How do we find strength in God?

Psalm 109

For the director of music. Of David. A psalm.

1 My God, whom I praise,
do not remain silent,[m]
2 for people who are wicked and
deceitful
have opened their mouths
against me;
they have spoken against me with
lying tongues.[n]
3 With words of hatred[o] they
surround me;
they attack me without cause.[p]
4 In return for my friendship they
accuse me,
but I am a man of prayer.[q]
5 They repay me evil for good,[r]
and hatred for my friendship.

6 Appoint someone evil to oppose my
enemy;
let an accuser[s] stand at his right
hand.

[a] In Hebrew texts 108:1-13 is numbered 108:2-14.

all believers back to fellowship with himself and others.

108:1–4 The psalmist announces that he will make a confession concerning all that God has done on behalf of his people. The psalmist provides a specific rationale in v. 4.
108:5–6 Because Yahweh has assumed his rightful place over the heavens as Sovereign over the created world, the psalmist has confidence that God will deliver his people.
108:7–9 This divine oracle suggests God's intent to act on behalf of his people by bringing deliverance.
108:10–13 The psalmist concludes with a plea that God will come to the aid of his people followed by a confession that God and God alone can tread down Israel's foes.

108:1–13 The psalmist refuses to believe in a secondhand god because he refuses to allow the circumstances that surround him to define God. That's sound wisdom for believers today as well.

109:1–5 In v. 1 the psalmist announces that he praises God. In vv. 2–5 the psalmist rehearses the situation that has prompted this prayer: Loyalty and friendship have given way to accusation and hatred.
109:6–7 As he has been charged by a wicked

[7]When he is tried, let him be found
guilty,
and may his prayers condemn[t]
him.
[8]May his days be few;
may another take his place[u] of
leadership.
[9]May his children be fatherless
and his wife a widow.[v]
[10]May his children be wandering
beggars;
may they be driven[a] from their
ruined homes.
[11]May a creditor seize all he has;
may strangers plunder the fruits
of his labor.[w]
[12]May no one extend kindness to him
or take pity[x] on his fatherless
children.
[13]May his descendants be cut off,[y]
their names blotted out[z] from the
next generation.
[14]May the iniquity of his fathers[a] be
remembered before the LORD;
may the sin of his mother never
be blotted out.
[15]May their sins always remain before
the LORD,
that he may blot out their name[b]
from the earth.

[16]For he never thought of doing a
kindness,
but hounded to death the poor
and the needy[c] and the
brokenhearted.[d]
[17]He loved to pronounce a curse —
may it come back on him.[e]
He found no pleasure in blessing —
may it be far from him.
[18]He wore cursing[f] as his garment;
it entered into his body like
water,[g]
into his bones like oil.
[19]May it be like a cloak wrapped about
him,
like a belt tied forever around
him.
[20]May this be the LORD's payment[h] to
my accusers,
to those who speak evil[i] of me.

[21]But you, Sovereign LORD,
help me for your name's sake;[j]
out of the goodness of your love,[k]
deliver me.
[22]For I am poor and needy,
and my heart is wounded
within me.
[23]I fade away like an evening
shadow;[l]
I am shaken off like a locust.
[24]My knees give[m] way from fasting;
my body is thin and gaunt.
[25]I am an object of scorn[n] to my
accusers;
when they see me, they shake
their heads.[o]

[26]Help me,[p] LORD my God;
save me according to your
unfailing love.
[27]Let them know[q] that it is your hand,
that you, LORD, have done it.
[28]While they curse,[r] may you bless;
may those who attack me be put
to shame,
but may your servant rejoice.[s]
[29]May my accusers be clothed with
disgrace
and wrapped in shame[t] as in a
cloak.

[30]With my mouth I will greatly extol
the LORD;
in the great throng[u] of worshipers
I will praise him.

109:7 [t]Pr 28:9
109:8 [u]Ac 1:20*
109:9 [v]Ex 22:24
109:11 [w]Job 5:5
109:12 [x]Isa 9:17
109:13 [y]Job 18:19; Ps 37:28 [z]Pr 10:7
109:14 [a]Ex 20:5; Ne 4:5; Jer 18:23
109:15 [b]Job 18:17; Ps 34:16
109:16 [c]Ps 37:14,32 [d]Ps 34:18
109:17 [e]Pr 14:14; Eze 35:6
109:18 [f]Ps 73:6 [g]Nu 5:22
109:20 [h]Ps 94:23; 2Ti 4:14 [i]Ps 71:10
109:21 [j]Ps 79:9 [k]Ps 69:16
109:23 [l]Ps 102:11
109:24 [m]Heb 12:12
109:25 [n]Ps 22:6 [o]Mt 27:39; Mk 15:29
109:26 [p]Ps 119:86
109:27 [q]Job 37:7
109:28 [r]2Sa 16:12 [s]Isa 65:14
109:29 [t]Ps 35:26; 132:18
109:30 [u]Ps 35:18; 111:1

[a] *10* Septuagint; Hebrew *sought*

---

person (v. 2), the psalmist requests that a wicked person be appointed over those who have made false claims. Even if the enemy offers up a plea to Yahweh, the psalmist requests that such a prayer would "condemn him" (v. 7) or better yet that such a prayer would simply "miss the mark."

109:8–19 The apparent viciousness in vv. 8–15 may best be understood if the reader considers the psalmist's claim in vv. 16–19. The Hebrew in v. 17 can also be rendered, "He loved cursing and it entered him."

109:20–25 The psalmist pleads with Yahweh for the sake of Yahweh's reputation. The psalmist then requests that Yahweh deliver him "out of the goodness of [his] love" (v. 21). Yahweh is depicted as the Master, capable of delivering the psalmist, and the psalmist describes himself as the servant.

109:26–29 The psalmist requests that Yahweh bless him while clothing the accusers in shame. At first glance such a request may appear retaliatory, but in a culture dominated by honor and shame, if Yahweh delivers the psalmist and clears the psalmist of any wrong, then the enemies have lost face.

109:30–31 By declaring in the final verse that Yahweh stands "at the right hand of the needy," the psalmist asserts his belief that God must be standing alongside him as well.

✣ **109:1–31** The language of this psalm strips away any veneer, exposing the inhumanity

[31]For he stands at the right hand[v] of
the needy,
to save their lives from those who
would condemn them.

Psalm 110

Of David. A psalm.

[1]The LORD says[w] to my lord:[a]

"Sit at my right hand
until I make your enemies
a footstool for your feet."[x]

[2]The LORD will extend your mighty
scepter[y] from Zion, saying,
"Rule in the midst of your
enemies!"
[3]Your troops will be willing
on your day of battle.
Arrayed in holy splendor,[z]
your young men will come to you
like dew from the morning's
womb.[b]

[4]The LORD has sworn
and will not change his mind:[a]
"You are a priest forever,[b]
in the order of Melchizedek.[c]"

[5]The Lord is at your right hand[c];[d]
he will crush kings[e] on the day of
his wrath.[f]

109:31 [v]Ps 16:8; 73:23; 121:5
110:1 [w]Mt 22:44*; Mk 12:36*; Lk 20:42*; Ac 2:34* [x]1Co 15:25
110:2 [y]Ps 45:6
110:3 [z]Jdg 5:2; Ps 96:9
110:4 [a]Nu 23:19 [b]Heb 5:6*; 7:21* [c]Heb 7:15-17*
110:5 [d]Ps 16:8 [e]Ps 2:12 [f]Ps 2:5; Ro 2:5

[a] *1* Or *Lord* [b] *3* The meaning of the Hebrew for this sentence is uncertain. [c] *5* Or *My lord is at your right hand, LORD*

Ps 110:4 ❖ How does Heb 7:11-28 deepen our understanding of the way Christ is our priest "in the order of Melchizedek"? Why is it important to have such a high priest?

---

experienced by one trapped by injustice. This psalm asks us to acknowledge injustice but then to declare that injustice does not have the final word. Our prayers are meant to be joined with all those seeking justice so together we might proclaim that the God we serve is indeed a God of justice.

110:1–3 The term "my lord" in v. 1 suggests a hierarchical relationship between the person speaking and the one being addressed. The king being addressed is invited to sit at the right hand of Yahweh, implying a position of honor.
110:4–7 In 2Sa 7 the Lord swore to David that he would establish a kingdom for David, and Yahweh affirms that he will not change his mind. Yahweh's

PEOPLE TO KNOW // MELCHIZEDEK

PSALM 110:4: Melchizedek was a mysterious king of Salem who appeared to Abraham after Abraham's battle with Kedorlaomer. Melchizedek is called a priest of God Most High. He blessed Abraham and gave Abraham bread and wine. In response, Abraham gave Melchizedek a tenth of his possessions (Ge 14:18–20).

The psalmist recalls the story of Melchizedek in Ps 110:4, where God makes a divine promise: "You are a priest forever, in the order of Melchizedek."

The author of Hebrews understood this psalm to be about Jesus, who, like Melchizedek, was both priest and king. As priest, he accomplished the forgiveness of sins; as king, he is Lord over all. The fact that Jesus filled the role of priest despite not being from the priestly tribe of Levi was made possible, according to Hebrews, by the fact that Jesus was "a high priest forever, in the order of Melchizedek" (Heb 6:20).

Some speculate that Melchizedek's appearance to Abraham may have been a Christophany, an appearance by the preincarnate Christ. After all, he blessed Abraham, gave him wine and bread (prefiguring the Eucharist), and then Abraham offered Melchizedek a tithe of his possessions, which the Law of Moses later stipulated as the proper offering to God. Furthermore, Hebrews describes Melchizedek as being "without father or mother, without genealogy, without beginning of days or end of life" (Heb 7:3).

Others contend that Melchizedek was not the preincarnate Christ but rather a "type of Christ," pointing toward Christ in the same way other OT characters such as David point to Christ.

APPLICATION ✣ Melchizedek means "king of righteousness." As a priest, he bestowed God's blessing on Abraham. The fact that Melchizedek's origin is unclear reminds us that God is at work in all areas of life, even in places where we think he may be absent. Melchizedek also reminds us that Christ is both Priest and King, the One who forgives our sins and is Lord over our lives.

[6]He will judge the nations,[g] heaping
up the dead[h]
and crushing the rulers[i] of the
whole earth.
[7]He will drink from a brook along the
way,[a]
and so he will lift his head high.[j]

Psalm 111[b]

[1]Praise the LORD.[c]

I will extol the LORD with all my
heart
in the council of the upright and
in the assembly.

[2]Great are the works[k] of the LORD;
they are pondered by all who
delight in them.
[3]Glorious and majestic are his deeds,
and his righteousness endures
forever.
[4]He has caused his wonders to be
remembered;
the LORD is gracious and
compassionate.[l]
[5]He provides food[m] for those who fear
him;
he remembers his covenant
forever.

[6]He has shown his people the power
of his works,
giving them the lands of other
nations.
[7]The works of his hands are faithful
and just;
all his precepts are trustworthy.[n]
[8]They are established for ever[o] and
ever,
enacted in faithfulness and
uprightness.
[9]He provided redemption[p] for his
people;
he ordained his covenant
forever —
holy and awesome[q] is his name.

[10]The fear of the LORD is the
beginning of wisdom;[r]
all who follow his precepts have
good understanding.[s]
To him belongs eternal praise.[t]

Psalm 112[b]

[1]Praise the LORD.[c]

Blessed are those who fear the LORD,[u]
who find great delight[v] in his
commands.

[2]Their children will be mighty in the
land;
the generation of the upright will
be blessed.
[3]Wealth and riches are in their
houses,
and their righteousness endures
forever.
[4]Even in darkness light dawns[w] for
the upright,
for those who are gracious
and compassionate and
righteous.[x]
[5]Good will come to those who are
generous and lend freely,[y]

110:6 [g]Isa 2:4 [h]Isa 66:24 [i]Ps 68:21
110:7 [j]Ps 27:6
111:2 [k]Ps 92:5; 143:5
111:4 [l]Ps 103:8
111:5 [m]Mt 6:26, 31-33
111:7 [n]Ps 19:7; Rev 15:3
111:8 [o]Isa 40:8; Mt 5:18
111:9 [p]Lk 1:68 [q]Ps 99:3; Lk 1:49
111:10 [r]Pr 9:10 [s]Ecc 12:13 [t]Ps 145:2
112:1 [u]Ps 128:1 [v]Ps 119:14, 16, 47, 92
112:4 [w]Job 11:17 [x]Ps 97:11
112:5 [y]Ps 37:21, 26

Ps 111:10 ❖ How can we integrate the truths of this verse into our lives today?

Ps 112:5 ❖ What are three ways we might be more generous with what God has given to us?

[a] *7* The meaning of the Hebrew for this clause is uncertain. [b] This psalm is an acrostic poem, the lines of which begin with the successive letters of the Hebrew alphabet. [c] *1,1* Hebrew *Hallelu Yah*

appearance at the right hand of the king implies protection and support.

✣ **110:1–7** Those who stand in opposition to the work of God and who appear to have power are not our source of hope. God knows all and sees all, so we must trust in him when our circumstances lead us to believe that God is not in control.

111:1–2 The verb "extol" (v. 1) can mean to praise, but it can also mean "confess" or "proclaim." This poem is spoken *about* God *to* the congregation.
111:3–6 Verse 3 invokes the image of Yahweh as divine King, while vv. 4–6 describe the life-sustaining world established by God.
111:7–10 The precepts of God are reliable because they introduce a world filled with faithfulness and justice. If one carries out the precepts of God, then there will be a reward.

✣ **111:1–10** The works of God call us, even now, to root our lives in the story of God *and* in the values and commitments expressed in his word.

112:1 In Ps 111 the psalmist calls people to delight in the *works* of God, while here in Ps 112 the emphasis shifts to the *words* of God.
112:2–5 "Mighty" offspring (v. 2) are not a *reward* for faithful living; rather, they are the *result* of faithful living. Those who have wealth and riches

who conduct their affairs with justice.

6 Surely the righteous will never be shaken;
they will be remembered[z] forever.
7 They will have no fear of bad news;
their hearts are steadfast,[a]
trusting in the LORD.
8 Their hearts are secure, they will have no fear;
in the end they will look in triumph on their foes.[b]
9 They have freely scattered their gifts to the poor,[c]
their righteousness endures forever;
their horn[a] will be lifted[d] high in honor.

10 The wicked will see[e] and be vexed,
they will gnash their teeth[f] and waste away;[g]
the longings of the wicked will come to nothing.[h]

Psalm 113

1 Praise the LORD.[b]

Praise the LORD, you his servants;[i]
praise the name of the LORD.
2 Let the name of the LORD be praised,
both now and forevermore.[j]
3 From the rising of the sun[k] to the place where it sets,
the name of the LORD is to be praised.

4 The LORD is exalted[l] over all the nations,
his glory above the heavens.[m]
5 Who is like the LORD our God,[n]
the One who sits enthroned[o] on high,
6 who stoops down to look[p]
on the heavens and the earth?

7 He raises the poor[q] from the dust
and lifts the needy[r] from the ash heap;
8 he seats them[s] with princes,
with the princes of his people.
9 He settles the childless[t] woman in her home
as a happy mother of children.

Praise the LORD.

Psalm 114

1 When Israel came out of Egypt,[u]
Jacob from a people of foreign tongue,
2 Judah became God's sanctuary,
Israel his dominion.

3 The sea looked and fled,[v]
the Jordan turned back;[w]
4 the mountains leaped like rams,
the hills like lambs.

Ps 113:7 ❖ Where have we seen God's care for people who are poor and in humble circumstances? How can we be the hands of Christ in showing love to people who are poor?

Ps 114:2 ❖ How can we fulfill our sacred identity as God's temple (see 1Co 3:16)?

112:6 [z] Pr 10:7
112:7 [a] Ps 57:7; Pr 1:33
112:8 [b] Ps 59:10
112:9 [c] 2Co 9:9* [d] Ps 75:10
112:10 [e] Ps 86:17 [f] Ps 37:12 [g] Ps 58:7-8 [h] Pr 11:7
113:1 [i] Ps 135:1
113:2 [j] Da 2:20
113:3 [k] Isa 59:19; Mal 1:11
113:4 [l] Ps 99:2 [m] Ps 8:1; 97:9
113:5 [n] Ps 89:6 [o] Ps 103:19
113:6 [p] Ps 11:4; 138:6; Isa 57:15
113:7 [q] 1Sa 2:8 [r] Ps 107:41
113:8 [s] Job 36:7
113:9 [t] 1Sa 2:5; Ps 68:6; Isa 54:1
114:1 [u] Ex 13:3
114:3 [v] Ex 14:21; Ps 77:16 [w] Jos 3:16

[a] 9 *Horn* here symbolizes dignity. [b] 1 Hebrew *Hallelu Yah*; also in verse 9

---

have received them *from God*, but they are to be used *for the community.*

112:6–9 Verses 7–8 address two issues that likely would have produced anxiety and fear: bad news and enemies. Those who fear and trust in God possess hearts that are firmly established.

112:10 According to Ps 112, while the wicked may gnash their teeth, ultimately they will melt away. The fate of the wicked mirrors the fate of the wicked in 1:6—both will come to an end.

✣ **112:1–10** According to the psalmist, this blessed life is one that lives in relationship with God and one that finds "great delight" in the purposes of God in the world (v. 1).

113:1–3 The praise of the Lord's name should fill the entire earth, from horizon to horizon.

113:4–6 Yahweh's exaltation above the heavens does not suggest that he has abandoned his people. It ensures the faithful oversight of God and his capacity to deliver.

113:7–9 Yahweh is worthy of Israel's praise because he is enthroned on high, but also because he delivers the most vulnerable from their plight.

✣ **113:1–9** Although God reigns on high, he has come to be with us and remains among us. Praise the Lord—hallelujah!

114:1–2 The psalmist recounts the decisive moment in Israel's history—the exodus—and draws theological conclusions from that event.

114:3–4 These verses build on the images associated with the exodus and the entry into the promised land.

[5]Why was it, sea, that you fled?
Why, Jordan, did you turn back?
[6]Why, mountains, did you leap like rams,
you hills, like lambs?

[7]Tremble, earth,[x] at the presence of the Lord,
at the presence of the God of Jacob,
[8]who turned the rock into a pool,
the hard rock into springs of water.[y]

Psalm 115

115:4–11pp // Ps 135:15–20

[1]Not to us, LORD, not to us
but to your name be the glory,[z]
because of your love and faithfulness.

114:7 [x] Ps 96:9
114:8 [y] Ex 17:6; Nu 20:11; Ps 107:35
115:1 [z] Ps 96:8; Isa 48:11; Eze 36:32
115:2 [a] Ps 42:3; 79:10
115:3 [b] Ps 103:19 [c] Ps 135:6; Da 4:35
115:4 [d] Dt 4:28; Jer 10:3-5
115:5 [e] Jer 10:5

[2]Why do the nations say,
"Where is their God?"[a]
[3]Our God is in heaven;[b]
he does whatever pleases him.[c]
[4]But their idols are silver and gold,
made by human hands.[d]
[5]They have mouths, but cannot speak,[e]
eyes, but cannot see.
[6]They have ears, but cannot hear,
noses, but cannot smell.
[7]They have hands, but cannot feel,
feet, but cannot walk,
nor can they utter a sound with their throats.
[8]Those who make them will be like them,
and so will all who trust in them.

[9]All you Israelites, trust in the LORD—
he is their help and shield.

114:5–6 The psalmist has modified the narrative in vv. 3–4 so that the same information now reads as rhetorical questions.
114:7–8 The psalmist calls all creation to acknowledge God as the divine King. Even as he can turn rocks into pools of water, so also can God turn a people into his sanctuary.

✜ **114:1–8** In unison with the psalmist, we echo, "Tremble, earth" (v. 7)—tremble indeed. God's power, his love, and his righteous deeds in history fill his followers with awe.

115:1–2 This confession functions like a thesis statement by presenting the community's primary response to the crisis articulated in v. 2.
115:3–8 The psalmist invites a comparison between "our God" (v. 3) and "their idols" (v. 4). The juxtaposition reinforces Israel's monotheistic claim.
115:9–11 These verses are a threefold call for each group to trust in the Lord. Those who trust in

CHARACTER OF GOD // GOD IS SOVEREIGN

Psalm 115:3: Our God is in heaven; he does whatever pleases him.

God's sovereignty is that aspect of his nature that teaches he is in complete control. Nothing happens outside of what God allows. Jesus said that not even a sparrow can fall to the ground outside of God's care (Mt 10:29).

This truth raises a difficult question: Why do bad things happen? The Bible explains that humans were given a choice. And when they fell into sin, creation came under a curse. Relationships became broken. Yet even this did not happen outside of God's knowledge. And when sin entered the world, God had a plan to bring redemption to all people through Jesus Christ. At the time of the fall, when all seemed lost, God made that promise (Ge 3:15).

Not even Satan himself can act beyond where God allows (Job 1-2). God has evil on a leash. Yes, with sin comes brokenness, pain and tragedy. And yes, powers of evil continue to press and destroy in the world. But none of this is beyond God's control.

God's sovereignty is closely connected to his lordship. When Abraham called God "Sovereign LORD" (Ge 15:2), he used the Hebrew word *adonai* to expand on the name of God (Yahweh). God is Lord over all creation. There is no corner of the universe—and no corner of our lives—that does not belong fully to God.

APPLICATION ✜ Because God is sovereign, we do not need to be fearful or uncertain about the events of this world. Instead, we know that God is in control. God's sovereignty holds everything together; we do not need to be anxious. We can be confident and certain that reality is not governed by chance. Evil does not have free reign. God's plans will never fail. God holds everything—including the future—in his loving hands.

10 House of Aaron,[f] trust in the LORD—
he is their help and shield.
11 You who fear him, trust in the
LORD—
he is their help and shield.

12 The LORD remembers us and will
bless us:
He will bless his people Israel,
he will bless the house of Aaron,
13 he will bless those who fear[g] the
LORD—
small and great alike.

14 May the LORD cause you to flourish,[h]
both you and your children.
15 May you be blessed by the LORD,
the Maker of heaven[i] and earth.

16 The highest heavens belong to the
LORD,[j]
but the earth he has given[k] to
mankind.
17 It is not the dead[l] who praise the
LORD,
those who go down to the place of
silence;
18 it is we who extol the LORD,
both now and forevermore.[m]

Praise the LORD.[a]

Psalm 116

1 I love the LORD,[n] for he heard my
voice;
he heard my cry[o] for mercy.
2 Because he turned his ear[p] to me,
I will call on him as long as I live.

3 The cords of death[q] entangled me,
the anguish of the grave came
over me;
I was overcome by distress and
sorrow.

115:10 [f] Ps 118:3
115:13 [g] Ps 128:1,4
115:14 [h] Dt 1:11
115:15 [i] Ge 1:1; 14:19; Ps 96:5
115:16 [j] Ps 89:11 [k] Ps 8:6-8
115:17 [l] Ps 6:5; 88:10-12; Isa 38:18
115:18 [m] Ps 113:2; Da 2:20
116:1 [n] Ps 18:1 [o] Ps 66:19
116:2 [p] Ps 40:1
116:3 [q] Ps 18:4-5
116:4 [r] Ps 118:5 [s] Ps 22:20
116:5 [t] Ezr 9:15; Ne 9:8; Ps 103:8; 145:17
116:6 [u] Ps 19:7; 79:8
116:7 [v] Jer 6:16; Mt 11:29 [w] Ps 13:6
116:8 [x] Ps 56:13
116:9 [y] Ps 27:13
116:10 [z] 2Co 4:13*
116:11 [a] Ro 3:4
116:13 [b] Ps 16:5; 80:18
116:14 [c] Ps 22:25; Jnh 2:9
116:15 [d] Ps 72:14

Ps 115:8 ❖ Why do people become more and more like what they worship? How can this truth benefit us?

Ps 116:1-6 ❖ When has God heard our cry for mercy and shown us his love and compassion?

4 Then I called on the name[r] of the
LORD:
"LORD, save me![s]"

5 The LORD is gracious and righteous;[t]
our God is full of compassion.
6 The LORD protects the unwary;
when I was brought low,[u] he
saved me.

7 Return to your rest,[v] my soul,
for the LORD has been good[w] to
you.

8 For you, LORD, have delivered me[x]
from death,
my eyes from tears,
my feet from stumbling,
9 that I may walk before the LORD
in the land of the living.[y]

10 I trusted[z] in the LORD when I said,
"I am greatly afflicted";
11 in my alarm I said,
"Everyone is a liar."[a]

12 What shall I return to the LORD
for all his goodness to me?

13 I will lift up the cup of salvation
and call on the name[b] of the LORD.
14 I will fulfill my vows[c] to the LORD
in the presence of all his people.

15 Precious in the sight[d] of the LORD

[a] 18 Hebrew *Hallelu Yah*

lifeless idols have no hope, but those who trust in Yahweh have a deliverer and a protector.
115:12–13 The circumstances are such that the nations are questioning the presence of Israel's God. The assertion that God has remembered his people signals that deliverance is on the way.
115:14–15 The speaker (priest) replies to the people's confession with a prayer that God would increase his people and that the present generation and those to follow would be the beneficiaries.
115:16–18 The twofold confession returns to the theme of God as the Creator to whom belongs all creation while also introducing a new theme: While we live, praise is our occupation.

✣ **115:1–18** Our way forward in this life and the next is through God and with God.

116:1–2 God has heard the psalmist's prayer. Yahweh's faithful action in the past will prompt the psalmist to turn to him in the future.
116:3–6 The psalmist recounts the deliverance that prompted his thanksgiving. He recounts the depths of his plight in vv. 3 and 6b.
116:7–9 The psalmist turns to reflect on his own condition in the present. Oppressive, life-threatening conditions have been replaced by conditions of hope.
116:10–11 Verses 10–11 serve as a summary of the reasons for thanksgiving.
116:12–14 The poet considers his response to God and participates in a sacrificial thanksgiving meal. His praise is manifested in action before the people of God.
116:15–16 As part of the act of thanksgiving, the psalmist offers up the third confession of trust in these verses.

CHARACTER OF GOD // GOD IS GRACIOUS

Psalm 116:5: The LORD is gracious and righteous; our God is full of compassion.

To be gracious means to have a giving nature. God describes himself as gracious to Moses (Ex 34:6), and this aspect of God's nature is consistently repeated throughout Scripture. As God's people experienced God's goodness and forgiveness, they were reminded time and again that God is indeed a gracious God.

God's gracious character means that he does not treat certain persons as their sins deserve. While we all are sinners and deserve punishment (Ro 3:23), God's grace moves him to withhold that punishment for those who accept his gift of salvation through Jesus Christ. God's grace is the merciful counterpoint to God's justice. God's justice demands punishment; God's grace extends salvation and forgiveness instead.

This does not mean God fails to uphold justice. Instead, God directed his justice toward Christ on the cross in the place of every sinner. Those who believe in and accept the salvation Jesus offers receive grace instead of punishment. This is not because believers have ever done anything to deserve this salvation—grace is given, not earned. There could hardly be better news than to learn that the God of the universe, a God of justice, is also "compassionate and gracious [and] abounding in love" (Ex 34:6).

APPLICATION ✣ The only reason people can receive salvation is through God's grace. God's gracious character should evoke deep gratitude within those who have accepted his salvation. No one can boast of earning God's love. For each person, salvation is a gift of God (Eph 2:8–10). God's gracious nature should also lead his followers to be people of grace themselves. As Jesus directed his disciples, "Freely you have received; freely give" (Mt 10:8b).

is the death of his faithful
servants.
16 Truly I am your servant, LORD;[e]
I serve you just as my mother did;[f]
you have freed me from my chains.

17 I will sacrifice a thank offering[g] to
you
and call on the name of the LORD.
18 I will fulfill my vows to the LORD
in the presence of all his people,
19 in the courts[h] of the house of the
LORD—
in your midst, Jerusalem.

Praise the LORD.[a]

Psalm 117

1 Praise the LORD, all you nations;[i]
extol him, all you peoples.

Ps 117 ✣ Let the words of this psalm sink into your life today. Consider memorizing it, or write it on a piece of paper and place it in a location where you'll see it every day.

2 For great is his love toward us,
and the faithfulness of the LORD[j]
endures forever.

Praise the LORD.[a]

Psalm 118

1 Give thanks to the LORD,[k] for he is
good;
his love endures forever.[l]
2 Let Israel say:[m]

116:16 [e] Ps 119:125; 143:12 [f] Ps 86:16
116:17 [g] Lev 7:12; Ps 50:14
116:19 [h] Ps 96:8; 135:2
117:1 [i] Ro 15:11*
117:2 [j] Ps 100:5
118:1 [k] 1Ch 16:8 [l] Ps 106:1; 136:1
118:2 [m] Ps 115:9

[a] 19,2 Hebrew *Hallelu Yah*

116:17–19 The poem concludes with the psalmist's promise to give a thanksgiving offering while once again calling on the name of the Lord. Then his deliverance will be full and complete.

✣ **116:1–19** There are others who need to know these same truths about *our God*. And while ministers can climb into the pulpit weekly to make that proclamation, what many people really want to hear is a testimony grounded in pure and enthusiastic thanksgiving.

117:1–2 The psalmist contends that the very fact of Yahweh's love and faithfulness will elicit praise from the nations.

✣ **117:1–2** This God is the hope of us all (Ro 15:12).

118:1–4 Giving thanks carries with it the sense of giving testimony about Yahweh's goodness and steadfast love. Verses 2–4 invite Israel, the house of Aaron, and those who fear God to make a communal confession.

"His love endures forever."
3 Let the house of Aaron say:
"His love endures forever."
4 Let those who fear the LORD say:
"His love endures forever."

5 When hard pressed,[n] I cried to the LORD;
he brought me into a spacious place.[o]
6 The LORD is with me;[p] I will not be afraid.
What can mere mortals do to me?[q]
7 The LORD is with me; he is my helper.[r]
I look in triumph on my enemies.[s]

8 It is better to take refuge in the LORD[t]
than to trust in humans.[u]
9 It is better to take refuge in the LORD
than to trust in princes.[v]
10 All the nations surrounded me,
but in the name of the LORD I cut them down.[w]
11 They surrounded me[x] on every side,[y]
but in the name of the LORD I cut them down.
12 They swarmed around me like bees,[z]
but they were consumed as quickly as burning thorns;[a]
in the name of the LORD I cut them down.
13 I was pushed back and about to fall,
but the LORD helped me.[b]
14 The LORD is my strength[c] and my defense[a];
he has become my salvation.[d]

15 Shouts of joy[e] and victory
resound in the tents of the righteous:
"The LORD's right hand[f] has done mighty things!
16 The LORD's right hand is lifted high;
the LORD's right hand has done mighty things!"
17 I will not die[g] but live,
and will proclaim[h] what the LORD has done.
18 The LORD has chastened me severely,
but he has not given me over to death.[i]
19 Open for me the gates[j] of the righteous;
I will enter and give thanks to the LORD.
20 This is the gate of the LORD
through which the righteous may enter.[k]
21 I will give you thanks, for you answered me;[l]
you have become my salvation.

22 The stone the builders rejected
has become the cornerstone;[m]
23 the LORD has done this,
and it is marvelous in our eyes.
24 The LORD has done it this very day;
let us rejoice today and be glad.

25 LORD, save us!
LORD, grant us success!

26 Blessed is he who comes[n] in the name of the LORD.
From the house of the LORD we bless you.[b]
27 The LORD is God,
and he has made his light shine[o] on us.
With boughs in hand, join in the festal procession
up[c] to the horns of the altar.

Ps 118:6–7 ❖ How does having a deep relationship with God relieve us from fearing those around us?

118:5 [n] Ps 120:1 [o] Ps 18:19
118:6 [p] Heb 13:6* [q] Ps 27:1; 56:4
118:7 [r] Ps 54:4 [s] Ps 59:10
118:8 [t] Ps 40:4 [u] Jer 17:5
118:9 [v] Ps 146:3
118:10 [w] Ps 18:40
118:11 [x] Ps 88:17 [y] Ps 3:6
118:12 [z] Dt 1:44 [a] Ps 58:9
118:13 [b] Ps 86:17; 140:4
118:14 [c] Ex 15:2 [d] Isa 12:2
118:15 [e] Ps 68:3 [f] Ps 89:13
118:17 [g] Ps 6:5; Hab 1:12 [h] Ex 15:6; Ps 73:28
118:18 [i] 2Co 6:9
118:19 [j] Isa 26:2
118:20 [k] Ps 24:7; Isa 35:8; Rev 22:14
118:21 [l] Ps 116:1
118:22 [m] Mt 21:42; Mk 12:10; Lk 20:17*; Ac 4:11*; 1Pe 2:7*
118:26 [n] Mt 21:9*; Mk 11:9*; Lk 13:35*; 19:38*; Jn 12:13*
118:27 [o] 1Pe 2:9

[a] 14 Or *song* [b] 26 The Hebrew is plural. [c] 27 Or *Bind the festal sacrifice with ropes / and take it*

118:5–18 The psalmist recounts how "all the nations" (v. 10) had surrounded him, but Yahweh delivered him. Within this section there are two interludes (vv. 8–9, 15–16); both play a critical role in the theology of the section. The first interlude makes use of language from the wisdom tradition, while the second one invokes imagery associated with the exodus.

118:19–28 The final section of the psalm rehearses a thanksgiving ceremony that would have probably taken place near or within the temple precinct. The participants in this liturgy likely included the individual psalmist (vv. 19, 21, 28), the temple priests or ministers (vv. 20, 26–27), and the worshiping community (vv. 22–25). Following the declaration by the priests in v. 27 that Yahweh is God, the psalmist speaks again in affirming not only that Yahweh is God but also that Yahweh is *his* God (v. 28).

[28]You are my God, and I will praise
you;
you are my God,[p] and I will exalt[q]
you.
[29]Give thanks to the LORD, for he is
good;
his love endures forever.

Psalm 119[a]

א Aleph

[1]Blessed are those whose ways are
blameless,
who walk[r] according to the law of
the LORD.
[2]Blessed are those who keep his
statutes
and seek him with all their
heart —[s]
[3]they do no wrong[t]
but follow his ways.
[4]You have laid down precepts
that are to be fully obeyed.
[5]Oh, that my ways were steadfast
in obeying your decrees!
[6]Then I would not be put to shame
when I consider all your
commands.
[7]I will praise you with an upright
heart
as I learn your righteous laws.
[8]I will obey your decrees;
do not utterly forsake me.

ב Beth

[9]How can a young person stay on the
path of purity?
By living according to your word.[u]
[10]I seek you with all my heart;[v]
do not let me stray from your
commands.[w]
[11]I have hidden your word in my
heart[x]
that I might not sin against you.
[12]Praise be to you, LORD;
teach me your decrees.[y]
[13]With my lips I recount
all the laws that come from your
mouth.[z]
[14]I rejoice in following your statutes
as one rejoices in great riches.
[15]I meditate on your precepts[a]
and consider your ways.
[16]I delight[b] in your decrees;
I will not neglect your word.

ג Gimel

[17]Be good to your servant[c] while I live,
that I may obey your word.
[18]Open my eyes that I may see
wonderful things in your law.
[19]I am a stranger on earth;[d]
do not hide your commands
from me.
[20]My soul is consumed[e] with longing
for your laws[f] at all times.
[21]You rebuke the arrogant, who are
accursed,
those who stray[g] from your
commands.

118:28 [p] Isa 25:1 [q] Ex 15:2
119:1 [r] Ps 128:1
119:2 [s] Dt 6:5
119:3 [t] 1Jn 3:9; 5:18
119:9 [u] 2Ch 6:16
119:10 [v] 2Ch 15:15
[w] ver 21,118
119:11 [x] Ps 37:31; Lk 2:19,51
119:12 [y] ver 26
119:13 [z] Ps 40:9
119:15 [a] Ps 1:2
119:16 [b] Ps 1:2
119:17 [c] Ps 13:6; 116:7
119:19 [d] 1Ch 29:15; Ps 39:12; 2Co 5:6; Heb 11:13
119:20 [e] Ps 42:2; 84:2 [f] Ps 63:1
119:21 [g] ver 10

[a] This psalm is an acrostic poem, the stanzas of which begin with successive letters of the Hebrew alphabet; moreover, the verses of each stanza begin with the same letter of the Hebrew alphabet.

Ps 119:9 ❖ Young or old, how can we more fully pursue purity by conforming our lives to God's Word?

118:29 The psalm opens with this affirmation, but the deliverance recounted in vv. 5–18 and the events of the thanksgiving celebration in vv. 19–28 give new reasons for the call to give thanks.

118:1–29 The lengthy narration in vv. 5–18 can serve as a model for our thanksgiving. Rather than simply offering a hasty "thank you" to God, we also might do well to describe the depths of our own trouble and the reality of our own helplessness. As we make this recitation-turned-confession, we are also reminded of the greatness of God's deliverance. It is in these moments that we may find ourselves overwhelmed with a sense of true thanksgiving.

119:1–8 In this psalm the poet acknowledges that the ways of the "blessed" are blameless because they walk in the ways of the Torah and seek instruction with their heart. In vv. 1–4 the psalmist describes the blessed life as one rooted in the Torah of Yahweh. In vv. 5–8, he refers to troubled circumstances. The psalmist holds the desire to live a blessed life along with the reality of a threatened existence. The reader needs to root life in the instruction of God amid such challenging circumstances.

119:9–16 The psalmist explains that a person must live according to God's "word." The term can refer to the written revelation or to God's direct communication. The pure path is reached by choosing to live according to God's Word; in v. 11, the heart of the blessed person becomes a storehouse of God's words.

119:17–24 The psalmist makes clear the impact threats have had upon him as he refers to those who plague him. Over against the threatening group, the psalmist self-identifies as "your servant" in vv. 17, 23. Although the psalmist feels pressure from his enemies, he longs for God's laws (v. 20), for they provide guidance amid the challenges he confronts.

22 Remove from me their scorn[h] and
contempt,
for I keep your statutes.
23 Though rulers sit together and
slander me,
your servant will meditate on
your decrees.
24 Your statutes are my delight;
they are my counselors.

ד Daleth

25 I am laid low in the dust;[i]
preserve my life[j] according to your
word.
26 I gave an account of my ways and
you answered me;
teach me your decrees.[k]
27 Cause me to understand the way of
your precepts,
that I may meditate on your
wonderful deeds.[l]
28 My soul is weary with sorrow;[m]
strengthen me[n] according to your
word.
29 Keep me from deceitful ways;
be gracious to me and teach me
your law.
30 I have chosen the way of
faithfulness;
I have set my heart on your
laws.
31 I hold fast[o] to your statutes, LORD;
do not let me be put to shame.
32 I run in the path of your commands,
for you have broadened my
understanding.

ה He

33 Teach me,[p] LORD, the way of your
decrees,
that I may follow it to the end.[a]
34 Give me understanding, so that I
may keep your law
and obey it with all my heart.
35 Direct me in the path of your
commands,
for there I find delight.
36 Turn my heart[q] toward your statutes
and not toward selfish gain.[r]
37 Turn my eyes away from worthless
things;
preserve my life[s] according to
your word.[b]
38 Fulfill your promise[t] to your
servant,
so that you may be feared.
39 Take away the disgrace I dread,
for your laws are good.
40 How I long[u] for your precepts!
In your righteousness preserve
my life.

ו Waw

41 May your unfailing love come to me,
LORD,
your salvation, according to your
promise;
42 then I can answer[v] anyone who
taunts me,
for I trust in your word.
43 Never take your word of truth from
my mouth,
for I have put my hope in your
laws.
44 I will always obey your law,
for ever and ever.
45 I will walk about in freedom,
for I have sought out your
precepts.
46 I will speak of your statutes before
kings[w]
and will not be put to shame,
47 for I delight in your commands
because I love them.
48 I reach out for your commands,
which I love,
that I may meditate on your
decrees.

119:22 [h] Ps 39:8
119:25 [i] Ps 44:25 [j] Ps 143:11
119:26 [k] Ps 25:4; 27:11; 86:11
119:27 [l] Ps 145:5
119:28 [m] Ps 107:26 [n] Ps 20:2; 1Pe 5:10
119:31 [o] Dt 11:22
119:33 [p] ver 12
119:36 [q] 1Ki 8:58 [r] Eze 33:31; Mk 7:21-22; Lk 12:15; Heb 13:5
119:37 [s] Ps 71:20; Isa 33:15
119:38 [t] 2Sa 7:25
119:40 [u] ver 20
119:42 [v] Pr 27:11
119:46 [w] Mt 10:18; Ac 26:1-2

[a] 33 Or *follow it for its reward* [b] 37 Two manuscripts of the Masoretic Text and Dead Sea Scrolls; most manuscripts of the Masoretic Text *life in your way*

119:25–32 The psalmist's plight is compared with his confession in v. 31. Although his life *clings* to the dust (v. 25), he confesses that he *clings* (NIV "hold fast," v. 31) to the statutes of God. On the one hand, by following the paths of Yahweh's instruction, his understanding will be enlarged. On the other hand, the reference to paths and open spaces suggests deliverance.

119:33–40 Every line in this passage begins with an imperative addressed to Yahweh. Yahweh is depicted as the teacher for his pupil, the psalmist. The psalmist asks God to remove distractions: "selfish gain" (v. 36) and "worthless things" (v. 37). The value of Yahweh's Torah surpasses all things. In v. 38 the psalmist refers to the covenantal relationship that defines his life with Yahweh.

119:41–48 The psalmist requests that Yahweh's "unfailing love" and "salvation" (v. 41) come to him. The taunting of the enemies has prompted this plea. Because the psalmist trusts in God's "word" (v. 42), he can "walk about in freedom" (v. 45). The section draws to a close with the psalmist's confessing his loyal love to the ways of Yahweh.

ז Zayin

49 Remember your word to your
servant,
for you have given me hope.
50 My comfort in my suffering is this:
Your promise preserves my life.[x]
51 The arrogant mock me[y]
unmercifully,
but I do not turn[z] from your law.
52 I remember,[a] LORD, your ancient
laws,
and I find comfort in them.
53 Indignation grips me[b] because of the
wicked,
who have forsaken your law.[c]
54 Your decrees are the theme of my
song
wherever I lodge.
55 In the night, LORD, I remember[d] your
name,
that I may keep your law.
56 This has been my practice:
I obey your precepts.

ח Heth

57 You are my portion,[e] LORD;
I have promised to obey your
words.
58 I have sought your face with all my
heart;
be gracious to me[f] according to
your promise.[g]
59 I have considered my ways[h]
and have turned my steps to your
statutes.
60 I will hasten and not delay
to obey your commands.
61 Though the wicked bind me with
ropes,
I will not forget[i] your law.
62 At midnight[j] I rise to give you
thanks
for your righteous laws.
63 I am a friend to all who fear you,[k]
to all who follow your precepts.

119:50 [x] Ro 15:4
119:51 [y] Jer 20:7 [z] ver 157; Job 23:11; Ps 44:18
119:52 [a] Ps 103:18
119:53 [b] Ezr 9:3 [c] Ps 89:30
119:55 [d] Ps 63:6
119:57 [e] Ps 16:5; La 3:24
119:58 [f] 1Ki 13:6 [g] ver 41
119:59 [h] Lk 15:17-18
119:61 [i] Ps 140:5
119:62 [j] Ac 16:25
119:63 [k] Ps 101:6-7
119:64 [l] Ps 33:5
119:67 [m] Jer 31:18-19; Heb 12:11
119:68 [n] Ps 106:1; 107:1; Mt 19:17 [o] ver 12
119:69 [p] Job 13:4; Ps 109:2
119:70 [q] Ps 17:10; Isa 6:10; Ac 28:27
119:72 [r] Ps 19:10; Pr 8:10-11, 19
119:73 [s] Job 10:8; Ps 100:3; 138:8; 139:13-16
119:74 [t] Ps 34:2

Ps 119:71 ❖ How can affliction bring us closer to God and his decrees?

64 The earth is filled with your love,[l]
LORD;
teach me your decrees.

ט Teth

65 Do good to your servant
according to your word, LORD.
66 Teach me knowledge and good
judgment,
for I trust your commands.
67 Before I was afflicted I went astray,[m]
but now I obey your word.
68 You are good,[n] and what you do is
good;
teach me your decrees.[o]
69 Though the arrogant have smeared
me with lies,[p]
I keep your precepts with all my
heart.
70 Their hearts are callous[q] and
unfeeling,
but I delight in your law.
71 It was good for me to be afflicted
so that I might learn your
decrees.
72 The law from your mouth is more
precious to me
than thousands of pieces of silver
and gold.[r]

י Yodh

73 Your hands made me[s] and
formed me;
give me understanding to learn
your commands.
74 May those who fear you rejoice[t]
when they see me,
for I have put my hope in your
word.
75 I know, LORD, that your laws are
righteous,

119:49–56 The focus of this section is the word "to remember." The psalmist implores Yahweh to remember his "word" (cf. vv. 17, 25). He "remembers" Yahweh's ancient laws (v. 52). The psalmist confesses that at night he remembers the name of Yahweh (v. 55). The psalmist holds in tension the reality of his world with his tenacious commitment to the Torah of Yahweh.

119:57–64 While the psalmist feels like an alien, he is not without a home: Yahweh will be his portion. The psalmist also has a community. The wicked remain a present danger, but that threat is not faced in isolation.

119:65–72 In this section, the operative word is "good." In Deuteronomy, this term represents the life-sustaining gifts or blessings of Yahweh (cf. Dt 10:13). Like his enemies, the psalmist had gone astray. Whatever gain he may have achieved, the psalmist now concludes that the only source of value is the law (Ps 119:72).

119:73–80 The psalmist declares that he was fashioned by God and consequently designed to live out God's commandments. Human life and faithful obedience are intertwined in this passage with the larger truth that true life, as fashioned by God, includes faithfulness to God's instruction.

and that in faithfulness[u] you have
afflicted me.
76 May your unfailing love be my
comfort,
according to your promise to your
servant.
77 Let your compassion[v] come to me
that I may live,
for your law is my delight.
78 May the arrogant[w] be put to shame
for wronging me without
cause;[x]
but I will meditate on your
precepts.
79 May those who fear you turn to me,
those who understand your
statutes.
80 May I wholeheartedly follow your
decrees,
that I may not be put to shame.

כ Kaph

81 My soul faints[y] with longing for your
salvation,
but I have put my hope in your
word.
82 My eyes fail,[z] looking for your
promise;
I say, "When will you
comfort me?"
83 Though I am like a wineskin in the
smoke,
I do not forget your decrees.
84 How long[a] must your servant wait?
When will you punish my
persecutors?
85 The arrogant dig pits[b] to trap me,
contrary to your law.
86 All your commands are
trustworthy;[c]
help me,[d] for I am being
persecuted without cause.[e]
87 They almost wiped me from the
earth,
but I have not forsaken[f] your
precepts.
88 In your unfailing love preserve my
life,
that I may obey the statutes of
your mouth.

ל Lamedh

89 Your word, LORD, is eternal;[g]
it stands firm in the heavens.
90 Your faithfulness[h] continues
through all generations;
you established the earth, and it
endures.[i]
91 Your laws endure[j] to this day,
for all things serve you.
92 If your law had not been my delight,
I would have perished in my
affliction.
93 I will never forget your precepts,
for by them you have preserved
my life.
94 Save me, for I am yours;
I have sought out your precepts.
95 The wicked are waiting to
destroy me,
but I will ponder your statutes.
96 To all perfection I see a limit,
but your commands are
boundless.

מ Mem

97 Oh, how I love your law!
I meditate[k] on it all day long.
98 Your commands are always with me
and make me wiser[l] than my
enemies.
99 I have more insight than all my
teachers,
for I meditate on your statutes.
100 I have more understanding than the
elders,
for I obey your precepts.[m]
101 I have kept my feet[n] from every evil
path
so that I might obey your word.
102 I have not departed from your laws,
for you yourself have taught me.
103 How sweet are your words to my
taste,
sweeter than honey[o] to my
mouth![p]

119:75 [u] Heb 12:5-11
119:77 [v] ver 41
119:78 [w] Jer 50:32 [x] ver 86,161
119:81 [y] Ps 84:2
119:82 [z] Ps 69:3; La 2:11
119:84 [a] Ps 39:4; Rev 6:10
119:85 [b] Ps 35:7; Jer 18:20,22
119:86 [c] Ps 35:19 [d] Ps 109:26 [e] ver 78
119:87 [f] Isa 58:2
119:89 [g] Mt 24:34-35; 1Pe 1:25
119:90 [h] Ps 36:5 [i] Ps 148:6; Ecc 1:4
119:91 [j] Jer 33:25
119:97 [k] Ps 1:2
119:98 [l] Dt 4:6
119:100 [m] Job 32:7-9
119:101 [n] Pr 1:15
119:103 [o] Ps 19:10; Pr 8:11 [p] Pr 24:13-14

119:81–88 This section functions as the center of Ps 119, both literally and figuratively. It provides the most specific account of the psalmist's plight and serves to anchor the lament element of the psalm. The psalmist can do nothing other than to petition Yahweh for help (v. 86).
119:89–96 This section emphasizes the psalmist's cause for hope: the faithfulness of Yahweh and the strength of his Torah. Yahweh's enthronement in the heavens secures his rightful place as King over all creation. Similarly, Yahweh's word stands firm in the heavens. Because of that enduring power, the psalmist confesses, "I am yours" (v. 94).
119:97–104 The psalmist confesses that he meditates on Yahweh's laws all day long. He has received instruction from Yahweh himself. Like honey, Yahweh's instruction has been life-giving and life-sustaining. It is because of all these things that the psalmist begins the passage with his declaration, "Oh, how I love your law!"

104 I gain understanding from your
precepts;
therefore I hate every wrong path.[q]

נ Nun

105 Your word is a lamp for my feet,
a light[r] on my path.
106 I have taken an oath[s] and
confirmed it,
that I will follow your righteous
laws.
107 I have suffered much;
preserve my life, LORD, according
to your word.
108 Accept, LORD, the willing praise of
my mouth,[t]
and teach me your laws.
109 Though I constantly take my life in
my hands,[u]
I will not forget your law.
110 The wicked have set a snare[v] for me,
but I have not strayed[w] from your
precepts.
111 Your statutes are my heritage
forever;
they are the joy of my heart.
112 My heart is set on keeping your
decrees
to the very end.[a][x]

ס Samekh

113 I hate double-minded people,[y]
but I love your law.
114 You are my refuge and my shield;[z]
I have put my hope[a] in your word.
115 Away from me,[b] you evildoers,
that I may keep the commands of
my God!
116 Sustain me,[c] my God, according to
your promise, and I will live;
do not let my hopes be dashed.[d]
117 Uphold me, and I will be delivered;
I will always have regard for your
decrees.
118 You reject all who stray from your
decrees,
for their delusions come to
nothing.
119 All the wicked of the earth you
discard like dross;[e]
therefore I love your statutes.
120 My flesh trembles[f] in fear of you;
I stand in awe of your laws.

ע Ayin

121 I have done what is righteous and
just;
do not leave me to my oppressors.
122 Ensure your servant's well-being;[g]
do not let the arrogant
oppress me.
123 My eyes fail, looking for your
salvation,
looking for your righteous
promise.[h]
124 Deal with your servant according to
your love
and teach me your decrees.[i]
125 I am your servant;[j] give me
discernment
that I may understand your
statutes.
126 It is time for you to act, LORD;
your law is being broken.
127 Because I love your commands
more than gold,[k] more than pure
gold,
128 and because I consider all your
precepts right,
I hate every wrong path.[l]

פ Pe

129 Your statutes are wonderful;
therefore I obey them.
130 The unfolding of your words gives
light;[m]

Ps 119:105 ❖ When the path of our life is unclear, how can God's Word be our guide?

119:104 [q] ver 128
119:105 [r] Pr 6:23
119:106 [s] Ne 10:29
119:108 [t] Hos 14:2; Heb 13:15
119:109 [u] Jdg 12:3; Job 13:14
119:110 [v] Ps 140:5; 141:9 [w] ver 10
119:112 [x] ver 33
119:113 [y] Jas 1:8
119:114 [z] Ps 32:7; 91:1 [a] ver 74
119:115 [b] Ps 6:8; 139:19; Mt 7:23
119:116 [c] Ps 54:4 [d] Ps 25:2; Ro 5:5; 9:33
119:119 [e] Eze 22:18,19
119:120 [f] Hab 3:16
119:122 [g] Job 17:3
119:123 [h] ver 82
119:124 [i] ver 12
119:125 [j] Ps 116:16
119:127 [k] Ps 19:10
119:128 [l] ver 104, 163
119:130 [m] Pr 6:23

[a] 112 Or *decrees / for their enduring reward*

119:105–112 The psalmist needs a lamp to light his way because of the darkness that threatens the path. This darkness is the result of the affliction he is enduring and the traps being set by the wicked to snare him. The light of God's word will enable the psalmist to see such snares and avoid them altogether.
119:113–120 The psalmist announces his hostility toward people with divided loyalties. He remains single-minded in his commitment to Yahweh. Yahweh will reject those who remain double-minded (v. 118a); they will be ultimately cast aside like dross. The passage concludes with his confession, "I stand in awe of your laws."
119:121–128 The first two verses refer to the oppression the psalmist is experiencing at the hands of the arrogant. The entire situation leads the psalmist to register his formal complaint in v. 126a: The Torah has been abolished. As a result, the poet announces, "It is time for you to act, LORD."
119:129–136 This section highlights the "wonder-working" power of the Torah. Yahweh's instruction provides light in the darkness, satisfies the thirsty, and directs the paths of God's people. In the concluding

it gives understanding to the
simple.[n]
131 I open my mouth and pant,[o]
longing for your commands.[p]
132 Turn to me and have mercy[q] on me,
as you always do to those who
love your name.
133 Direct my footsteps according to
your word;[r]
let no sin rule[s] over me.
134 Redeem me from human
oppression,[t]
that I may obey your precepts.
135 Make your face shine[u] on your
servant
and teach me your decrees.
136 Streams of tears[v] flow from my eyes,
for your law is not obeyed.[w]

צ Tsadhe

137 You are righteous,[x] LORD,
and your laws are right.[y]
138 The statutes you have laid down are
righteous;[z]
they are fully trustworthy.
139 My zeal wears me out,[a]
for my enemies ignore your
words.
140 Your promises have been
thoroughly tested,[b]
and your servant loves them.
141 Though I am lowly and despised,[c]
I do not forget your precepts.
142 Your righteousness is everlasting
and your law is true.[d]
143 Trouble and distress have come
upon me,
but your commands give me
delight.
144 Your statutes are always righteous;
give me understanding[e] that I
may live.

ק Qoph

145 I call with all my heart; answer me,
LORD,
and I will obey your decrees.
146 I call out to you; save me
and I will keep your statutes.
147 I rise before dawn[f] and cry for help;
I have put my hope in your word.
148 My eyes stay open through the
watches of the night,[g]
that I may meditate on your
promises.
149 Hear my voice in accordance with
your love;
preserve my life, LORD, according
to your laws.
150 Those who devise wicked schemes
are near,
but they are far from your law.
151 Yet you are near,[h] LORD,
and all your commands are true.[i]
152 Long ago I learned from your
statutes
that you established them to last
forever.[j]

ר Resh

153 Look on my suffering[k] and
deliver me,
for I have not forgotten[l] your law.
154 Defend my cause[m] and redeem me;[n]
preserve my life according to your
promise.
155 Salvation is far from the wicked,
for they do not seek out[o] your
decrees.
156 Your compassion, LORD, is great;
preserve my life[p] according to
your laws.
157 Many are the foes who
persecute me,[q]
but I have not turned from your
statutes.
158 I look on the faithless with
loathing,[r]
for they do not obey your word.
159 See how I love your precepts;
preserve my life, LORD, in
accordance with your love.
160 All your words are true;
all your righteous laws are eternal.

119:130 [n] Ps 19:7
119:131 [o] Ps 42:1 [p] ver 20
119:132 [q] Ps 25:16; 106:4
119:133 [r] Ps 17:5 [s] Ps 19:13; Ro 6:12
119:134 [t] Ps 142:6; Lk 1:74
119:135 [u] Nu 6:25; Ps 4:6
119:136 [v] Jer 9:1, 18 [w] Eze 9:4
119:137 [x] Ezr 9:15; Jer 12:1 [y] Ne 9:13
119:138 [z] Ps 19:7
119:139 [a] Ps 69:9; Jn 2:17
119:140 [b] Ps 12:6
119:141 [c] Ps 22:6
119:142 [d] Ps 19:7
119:144 [e] Ps 19:9
119:147 [f] Ps 5:3; 57:8; 108:2
119:148 [g] Ps 63:6
119:151 [h] Ps 34:18; 145:18 [i] ver 142
119:152 [j] Lk 21:33
119:153 [k] La 5:1 [l] Pr 3:1
119:154 [m] Mic 7:9 [n] 1Sa 24:15
119:155 [o] Job 5:4
119:156 [p] 2Sa 24:14
119:157 [q] Ps 7:1
119:158 [r] Ps 139:21

---

verse, the psalmist weeps because of the rampant disobedience that characterizes his society.

119:137–144 This section opens with the declaration that God is "righteous" and repeatedly contends that Yahweh's instruction is righteous. Although the enemies ignore God's words (v. 139), the psalmist confesses his love for those words (v. 140). They are the psalmist's source of life.

119:145–152 The psalmist longs for the coming deliverance of Yahweh: He declares that through the watches of night he meditates on God's promises. While in the present moment, the psalmist is harassed by the enemy, he takes heart that the justice of God has been from "long ago" and is meant to "last forever" (v. 152).

119:153–160 Three times the psalmist recounts his faithfulness to God's law (vv. 153, 157, 159). Twice the psalmist observes the insolence of the enemies against God's law (vv. 155, 158). Three times he asks for Yahweh to "preserve [his] life" (vv. 154, 156, 159). The psalmist's faithfulness and his claim to deliverance are linked.

ש Sin and Shin

161 Rulers persecute me[s] without cause,
but my heart trembles at your word.
162 I rejoice in your promise
like one who finds great spoil.[t]
163 I hate and detest falsehood
but I love your law.
164 Seven times a day I praise you
for your righteous laws.
165 Great peace[u] have those who love your law,
and nothing can make them stumble.
166 I wait for your salvation,[v] LORD,
and I follow your commands.
167 I obey your statutes,
for I love them greatly.
168 I obey your precepts and your statutes,
for all my ways are known[w] to you.

ת Taw

169 May my cry come[x] before you, LORD;
give me understanding according to your word.
170 May my supplication come[y] before you;
deliver me[z] according to your promise.
171 May my lips overflow with praise,[a]
for you teach me[b] your decrees.
172 May my tongue sing of your word,
for all your commands are righteous.
173 May your hand be ready to help[c] me,
for I have chosen[d] your precepts.
174 I long for your salvation,[e] LORD,
and your law gives me delight.
175 Let me live[f] that I may praise you,
and may your laws sustain me.
176 I have strayed like a lost sheep.[g]
Seek your servant,
for I have not forgotten your commands.

119:161 [s] 1Sa 24:11
119:162 [t] 1Sa 30:16
119:165 [u] Pr 3:2; Isa 26:3,12; 32:17
119:166 [v] Ge 49:18
119:168 [w] Pr 5:21
119:169 [x] Ps 18:6
119:170 [y] Ps 28:2 [z] Ps 31:2
119:171 [a] Ps 51:15 [b] Ps 94:12
119:173 [c] Ps 37:24 [d] Jos 24:22
119:174 [e] ver 166
119:175 [f] Isa 55:3
119:176 [g] Isa 53:6
120:1 [h] Ps 102:2; Jnh 2:2
120:2 [i] Pr 12:22 [j] Ps 52:4
120:4 [k] Ps 45:5
120:5 [l] Ge 25:13; Jer 49:28

Ps 119:164 ❖ How can we make praising God a more active and regular part of our daily routine?

Psalm 120

A song of ascents.

1 I call on the LORD in my distress,[h]
and he answers me.
2 Save me, LORD,
from lying lips[i]
and from deceitful tongues.[j]

3 What will he do to you,
and what more besides,
you deceitful tongue?
4 He will punish you with a warrior's sharp arrows,[k]
with burning coals of the broom bush.

5 Woe to me that I dwell in Meshek,
that I live among the tents of Kedar![l]
6 Too long have I lived
among those who hate peace.

119:161–168 While one could shudder or be in fear of worldly powers, the psalmist confesses that his heart "trembles" (v. 161) before the word of Yahweh. Military victors may collect the spoils of war, but the psalmist has found a "great spoil" (v. 162) in the instruction of God. Those who are victorious in battle may find temporary rest, but the psalmist announces that "great peace" (v. 165) awaits those who love the law of God. His love of the law is so great, in fact, that he praises God seven times a day. **119:169–176** What binds the sections of this passage together is the relationship between being faithful to the Torah of Yahweh and the sheer gift of life that it brings. The poet concludes the psalm by confessing that, while he has not forgotten the commandments of God, he is a frail creature of dust, a "lost sheep" (v. 176) who stands in need of the mercy of God. The psalmist remains committed to God in the certainty that God is committed to him.

✣ **119:1–176** The beatitudes in Mt 5 and Ps 119 reflect the perilous circumstances faced by followers of God. The faithful encounter persecution (vv. 86, 157, 161; Mt 5:10, 11). They experience the derisive insults of the ungodly (Ps 119:23; Mt 5:11). Yet each of the beatitudes in Matthew begins with "Blessed," even as Ps 119:1–2 open with "Blessed." Both texts describe the life of the faithful as they await the fullness of God's work in the world.

120:1 God's deliverance of the psalmist from a previous threat provides assurance that God can redeem him again.
120:2 The nature of the distress appears in this verse.
120:3–4 The psalmist turns to address the enemy rhetorically: Their lives will be laid waste even as cities were laid waste by arrows and flames of fire.
120:5–7 The psalmist provides further explanation concerning the situation. These verses suggest that the one with a deceitful tongue threatens violence, presumably against the psalmist.

✣ **120:1–7** Psalm 120 invites us to give words to the human hunger for peace. The faithful follower of God will be careful to guard his tongue and speak for peace while others slander God's name.

[7]I am for peace;
but when I speak, they are for war.

Psalm 121

A song of ascents.

[1]I lift up my eyes to the mountains —
where does my help come from?
[2]My help comes from the LORD,
the Maker of heaven and earth.[m]

[3]He will not let your foot slip —
he who watches over you will not
slumber;
[4]indeed, he who watches over Israel
will neither slumber nor sleep.

[5]The LORD watches over[n] you —
the LORD is your shade at your
right hand;
[6]the sun[o] will not harm you by day,
nor the moon by night.

[7]The LORD will keep you from all
harm[p] —
he will watch over your life;
[8]the LORD will watch over your
coming and going
both now and forevermore.[q]

Psalm 122

A song of ascents. Of David.

[1]I rejoiced with those who said to me,
"Let us go to the house of the
LORD."
[2]Our feet are standing
in your gates, Jerusalem.

[3]Jerusalem is built like a city
that is closely compacted together.
[4]That is where the tribes go up —
the tribes of the LORD —
to praise the name of the LORD
according to the statute given to
Israel.
[5]There stand the thrones for
judgment,
the thrones of the house of David.

[6]Pray for the peace of Jerusalem:
"May those who love[r] you be
secure.
[7]May there be peace within your walls
and security within your citadels."
[8]For the sake of my family and friends,
I will say, "Peace be within you."
[9]For the sake of the house of the LORD
our God,
I will seek your prosperity.[s]

Psalm 123

A song of ascents.

[1]I lift up my eyes to you,
to you who sit enthroned[t] in
heaven.
[2]As the eyes of slaves look to the
hand of their master,
as the eyes of a female slave look
to the hand of her mistress,

121:2 [m] Ps 115:15; 124:8
121:5 [n] Isa 25:4
121:6 [o] Ps 91:5; Isa 49:10; Rev 7:16
121:7 [p] Ps 41:2; 91:10-12
121:8 [q] Dt 28:6
122:6 [r] Ps 51:18
122:9 [s] Ne 2:10
123:1 [t] Ps 11:4; 121:1; 141:8

Ps 120:7 ❖ How can God help us deal with people in our lives who always try to stir up conflict?

Ps 121:3-4 ❖ How can the truths in these two verses bring comfort to us and our families today?

Ps 122:1-2 ❖ What kind of joy and support do we find in gathering with fellow believers?

Ps 123:1 ❖ How does the phrase "I lift up my eyes to you" in v. 1 inspire our position toward God in prayer?

121:1–2 "Mountains" likely refers to Zion, the mountain of God.
121:3–4 Yahweh remains on watch to protect his people because God will not "slumber nor sleep" (v. 4).
121:5–6 Because the soldier carried his shield on his left arm, the right side of his body remained vulnerable. A friend at his "right hand" (v. 5) provided protection.
121:7–8 The phrase "coming and going" (v. 8) refers to the general activity of life.

✥ **121:1–8** Those who pray this psalm do not walk alone.

122:1–2 The psalmist's source of joy remains being in the presence of God himself. Verse 1 recounts the moment when the psalmist was invited to make the pilgrimage to Jerusalem; v. 2 records his arrival at the gates of the city.
122:3–5 Jerusalem is a refuge. From the thrones in Jerusalem go forth the decisions that can lead to peace for the land.
122:6–9 The name "Jerusalem" itself reinforces the theme of peace, given that the Hebrew root for "peace" comprises part of the city's name, "Jeru*salem*."

✥ **122:1–9** Like the pilgrims in Ps 122, we too may continue to celebrate a way of life rooted deeply in the presence of God.

123:1–2 Even as a servant would wait for any signal from the hand of the master, those enduring hardship look to the hand of Yahweh in the face of their current plight.

so our eyes look to the LORD[u] our God,
till he shows us his mercy.

3 Have mercy on us, LORD, have mercy on us,
for we have endured no end of contempt.
4 We have endured no end
of ridicule from the arrogant,
of contempt from the proud.

Psalm 124

A song of ascents. Of David.

1 If the LORD had not been on our side —
let Israel say[v] —
2 if the LORD had not been on our side
when people attacked us,
3 they would have swallowed us alive
when their anger flared against us;
4 the flood would have engulfed us,
the torrent would have swept over us,
5 the raging waters
would have swept us away.

6 Praise be to the LORD,
who has not let us be torn by their teeth.
7 We have escaped like a bird
from the fowler's snare;[w]
the snare has been broken,
and we have escaped.
8 Our help is in the name of the LORD,
the Maker of heaven[x] and earth.

Psalm 125

A song of ascents.

1 Those who trust in the LORD are like Mount Zion,
which cannot be shaken[y] but endures forever.
2 As the mountains surround Jerusalem,
so the LORD surrounds[z] his people
both now and forevermore.

3 The scepter of the wicked will not remain[a]
over the land allotted to the righteous,
for then the righteous might use
their hands to do evil.[b]

4 LORD, do good[c] to those who are good,
to those who are upright in heart.[d]
5 But those who turn[e] to crooked ways[f]
the LORD will banish with the evildoers.

Peace be on Israel.[g]

Psalm 126

A song of ascents.

1 When the LORD restored[h] the fortunes of[a] Zion,
we were like those who dreamed.[b]

123:2 [u] Ps 25:15
124:1 [v] Ps 129:1
124:7 [w] Ps 91:3; Pr 6:5
124:8 [x] Ge 1:1; Ps 121:2; 134:3
125:1 [y] Ps 46:5
125:2 [z] Ps 121:8; Zec 2:4-5
125:3 [a] Ps 89:22; Pr 22:8; Isa 14:5 [b] 1Sa 24:10; Ps 55:20
125:4 [c] Ps 119:68 [d] Ps 7:10; 36:10; 94:15
125:5 [e] Job 23:11 [f] Pr 2:15; Isa 59:8 [g] Ps 128:6
126:1 [h] Ps 85:1; Hos 6:11

[a] 1 Or LORD brought back the captives to *[b] 1 Or those restored to health*

Ps 124:7 ❖ How does God help believers through difficult situations? How can we ask for his help?

Ps 125:1-2 ❖ Think about these words tonight as you lie down to sleep.

Ps 126:1-2 ❖ Has there been a time in your life when God has moved so powerfully that it hasn't seemed real?

123:3-4 The language could signify a small group of the faithful who have been shamed or the people of Israel who have been humiliated by their conquerors.

✣ **123:1-4** When others ridicule our faith, we wait with certainty that the King will see our plight and reassure us of the wisdom of our decision to follow him.

124:1-5 Had not Yahweh been on the side of Israel, the people would have been wiped out.
124:6-7 The community celebrates their deliverance from a siege or some other foreign occupation.
124:8 No earthly threat is ever a match for the "Maker of heaven and earth."

✣ **124:1-8** Amid a world of swirling waters and fowlers' snares, the Maker of heaven and earth is for us.

125:1-3 Mount Zion encourages confidence on the part of those who pray the psalms. Yahweh will protect the people and remove the threat that is before them.
125:4-5 Individuals can either align themselves with those who choose to do good or with those who "turn to crooked ways" (v. 5). Toward each kind of person, Yahweh acts with justice.

✣ **125:1-5** God's presence and God's protection prove sufficient in a world that appears unruly and unstable.

126:1-3 A dream in the ancient Near East was understood as a medium for divine revelation. Thus, when the community declared that they were dreamers, they were announcing that Yahweh's work of restoration was at hand.

2 Our mouths were filled with
laughter,
our tongues with songs of joy.[i]
Then it was said among the nations,
"The LORD has done great things[j]
for them."
3 The LORD has done great things
for us,
and we are filled with joy.[k]

4 Restore our fortunes,[a] LORD,
like streams in the Negev.[l]
5 Those who sow with tears
will reap with songs of joy.[m]
6 Those who go out weeping,
carrying seed to sow,
will return with songs of joy,
carrying sheaves with them.

Psalm 127

A song of ascents. Of Solomon.

1 Unless the LORD builds[n] the house,
the builders labor in vain.
Unless the LORD watches[o] over the
city,
the guards stand watch in vain.
2 In vain you rise early
and stay up late,
toiling for food[p] to eat —
for he grants sleep[q] to[b] those he
loves.

3 Children are a heritage from the
LORD,
offspring a reward[r] from him.
4 Like arrows in the hands of a warrior
are children born in one's youth.
5 Blessed is the man
whose quiver is full of them.
They will not be put to shame
when they contend with their
opponents[s] in court.

126:2 [i] Job 8:21; Ps 51:14 [j] Ps 71:19
126:3 [k] Isa 25:9
126:4 [l] Isa 35:6; 43:19
126:5 [m] Isa 35:10
127:1 [n] Ps 78:69 [o] Ps 121:4
127:2 [p] Ge 3:17 [q] Job 11:18
127:3 [r] Ge 33:5

Ps 127:1 ❖ "Unless the LORD builds the house, the builders labor in vain." What does this mean for believers and their everyday work in the world?

Ps 128 ❖ Let this positive and peaceful psalm wash over you and your family today.

Psalm 128

A song of ascents.

1 Blessed are all who fear the LORD,[t]
who walk in obedience to him.[u]
2 You will eat the fruit of your labor;[v]
blessings and prosperity[w] will be
yours.
3 Your wife will be like a fruitful vine[x]
within your house;
your children will be like olive
shoots[y]
around your table.
4 Yes, this will be the blessing
for the man who fears the LORD.

5 May the LORD bless you from Zion;[z]
may you see the prosperity of
Jerusalem
all the days of your life.
6 May you live to see your children's
children —[a]
peace be on Israel.[b]

127:5 [s] Pr 27:11
128:1 [t] Ps 112:1 [u] Ps 119:1-3
128:2 [v] Isa 3:10 [w] Ecc 8:12
128:3 [x] Eze 19:10 [y] Ps 52:8; 144:12
128:5 [z] Ps 20:2; 134:3
128:6 [a] Ge 50:23; Job 42:16 [b] Ps 125:5

[a] 4 Or *Bring back our captives* [b] 2 Or *eat — / for while they sleep he provides for*

126:4–6 Simple agricultural images provide powerfully rich metaphors of hope.

✥ **126:1–6** The harvest will bring shouts of joy, but the harvest will come only if the seed has been planted—weeping and all. To plant anything is an act of faith. The end cannot be known, only trusted. Yet the farmer who follows the Lord perceives the reality of the One who makes the seed grow.

127:1–2 The psalmist explains the necessity of God's involvement in two spheres of life: the home and the city.
127:3–5 In the second half the poet turns to familial matters and considers the blessings associated with a larger family.

✥ **127:1–5** Those of us who live in the US are well acquainted with the rhetoric of the "American dream." Because we believe success is contingent upon effort, we are compelled to work harder and are essentially resigned to "toiling for food" (v. 2). Those who place their security in their own efforts will soon find all of those efforts are done "in vain" (v. 1).

128:1–4 The psalmist knows the blessed life is oriented toward God's purposes in the world. One should "fear the LORD" (v. 1) because of what he can bring—life in all its fullness.
128:5–6 This psalm closes with blessings upon the pilgrims making their journey from their homes to Mount Zion.

✥ **128:1–6** Those who seek to order their lives rightly will soon realize that the goal of life is not to *earn* divine blessing but to *receive* the simple elements of life *as* divine blessing.

Psalm 129

A song of ascents.

1 "They have greatly oppressed me
from my youth,"[c]
let Israel say;[d]
2 "they have greatly oppressed me
from my youth,
but they have not gained the
victory[e] over me.
3 Plowmen have plowed my back
and made their furrows long.
4 But the LORD is righteous;[f]
he has cut me free from the cords
of the wicked."

5 May all who hate Zion[g]
be turned back in shame.[h]
6 May they be like grass on the roof,
which withers[i] before it can grow;
7 a reaper cannot fill his hands with it,
nor one who gathers fill his arms.
8 May those who pass by not say to
them,
"The blessing of the LORD be on
you;
we bless you[j] in the name of the
LORD."

Psalm 130

A song of ascents.

1 Out of the depths[k] I cry to you, LORD;
2 Lord, hear my voice.[l]
Let your ears be attentive[m]
to my cry for mercy.

3 If you, LORD, kept a record of sins,
Lord, who could stand?[n]
4 But with you there is forgiveness,[o]
so that we can, with reverence,
serve you.[p]

5 I wait for the LORD,[q] my whole being
waits,
and in his word[r] I put my hope.
6 I wait for the Lord
more than watchmen[s] wait for the
morning,
more than watchmen wait for the
morning.[t]

7 Israel, put your hope[u] in the LORD,
for with the LORD is unfailing love
and with him is full redemption.
8 He himself will redeem[v] Israel
from all their sins.

Psalm 131

A song of ascents. Of David.

1 My heart is not proud,[w] LORD,
my eyes are not haughty;
I do not concern myself with great
matters
or things too wonderful for me.

129:1 [c] Ps 88:15; Hos 2:15 [d] Ps 124:1
129:2 [e] Mt 16:18
129:4 [f] Ps 119:137
129:5 [g] Mic 4:11 [h] Ps 71:13
129:6 [i] Ps 37:2
129:8 [j] Ru 2:4; Ps 118:26
130:1 [k] Ps 42:7; 69:2; La 3:55
130:2 [l] Ps 28:2 [m] 2Ch 6:40; Ps 64:1
130:3 [n] Ps 76:7; 143:2
130:4 [o] Ex 34:7; Isa 55:7; Jer 33:8
[p] 1Ki 8:40
130:5 [q] Ps 27:14; 33:20; Isa 8:17 [r] Ps 119:81
130:6 [s] Ps 63:6 [t] Ps 119:147
130:7 [u] Ps 131:3
130:8 [v] Lk 1:68
131:1 [w] Ps 101:5; Ro 12:16

Ps 129:4 ❖ How can we as believers testify to God's liberating work in our lives today?

Ps 130:3–4 ❖ How does God's forgiveness of sins, accomplished through Christ (see Ro 6:23), free us to serve him with our whole heart?

Ps 131:1–2 ❖ What does finding true contentment in God look like (see 1Ti 6:6)? How can we resist the desire to try to "know it all" and instead humbly leave the big questions in God's hands (see Dt 29:29)?

129:1–4 Despite repeated episodes of oppression, the community gives thanks because God has consistently delivered his people. First-person language might warrant interpreting the attacks as personal or individual attacks, but the context suggests Israel's history of oppression is in view.

129:5–8 The curses in vv. 5–8 suggest that a persistent threat remains—one that Yahweh must remedy.

129:1–8 We should acknowledge the true injustice in the world and long for God's redeeming and redemptive work to overturn this injustice. Such an approach can be heard in the teaching of Jesus: "Blessed are those who hunger and thirst for righteousness, for they will be filled" (Mt 5:6).

130:1–2 Although the psalmist highlights the distance between himself and God, Yahweh hears.

130:3–4 The relationship once broken by sin is restored—not by us but by God. Forgiveness results in faithful service.

130:5–6 In ancient cities, guards were stationed on the city walls to keep watch. Just as these guards awaited the morning, so, too, does the psalmist wait on God.

130:7–8 The psalmist exhorts the community to wait and hope as he does.

130:1–8 As we reflect on our own sinfulness we might be inclined to turn away from God. The psalmist turns to God and cries out, setting an example for us to do the same.

131:1–3 Like the infant child resting upon its mother, all Israel is called to trust in God with the assurance that its collective life will be cared for "both now and forevermore" (v. 3).

[2]But I have calmed and quieted myself,
I am like a weaned child with its mother;
like a weaned child I am content.[x]
[3]Israel, put your hope[y] in the LORD
both now and forevermore.

Psalm 132

132:8–10pp // 2Ch 6:41–42

A song of ascents.

[1]LORD, remember David
and all his self-denial.
[2]He swore an oath to the LORD,
he made a vow to the Mighty One of Jacob:[z]
[3]"I will not enter my house
or go to my bed,
[4]I will allow no sleep to my eyes
or slumber to my eyelids,
[5]till I find a place[a] for the LORD,
a dwelling for the Mighty One of Jacob."

[6]We heard it in Ephrathah,[b]
we came upon it in the fields of Jaar:[a c]
[7]"Let us go to his dwelling place,[d]
let us worship at his footstool,[e] saying,
[8]'Arise, LORD,[f] and come to your resting place,
you and the ark of your might.
[9]May your priests be clothed with your righteousness;[g]
may your faithful people sing for joy.' "

131:2 [x]Mt 18:3; 1Co 14:20
131:3 [y]Ps 130:7
132:2 [z]Ge 49:24
132:5 [a]Ac 7:46
132:6 [b]1Sa 17:12 [c]1Sa 7:2
132:7 [d]Ps 5:7 [e]Ps 99:5
132:8 [f]Nu 10:35; Ps 78:61
132:9 [g]Job 29:14; Isa 61:3,10

Ps 132:7 ❖ What does it mean for believers to "worship at [God's] footstool"?

[10]For the sake of your servant David,
do not reject your anointed one.

[11]The LORD swore an oath to David,[h]
a sure oath he will not revoke:
"One of your own descendants[i]
I will place on your throne.
[12]If your sons keep my covenant
and the statutes I teach them,
then their sons will sit
on your throne[j] for ever and ever."

[13]For the LORD has chosen Zion,[k]
he has desired it for his dwelling, saying,
[14]"This is my resting place for ever and ever;[l]
here I will sit enthroned, for I have desired it.
[15]I will bless her with abundant provisions;
her poor I will satisfy with food.[m]
[16]I will clothe her priests[n] with salvation,
and her faithful people will ever sing for joy.

[17]"Here I will make a horn[b] grow[o] for David
and set up a lamp[p] for my anointed one.
[18]I will clothe his enemies with shame,[q]
but his head will be adorned with a radiant crown."

132:11 [h]Ps 89:3-4,35 [i]2Sa 7:12
132:12 [j]Lk 1:32; Ac 2:30
132:13 [k]Ps 48:1-2
132:14 [l]Ps 68:16
132:15 [m]Ps 107:9; 147:14
132:16 [n]2Ch 6:41
132:17 [o]Eze 29:21; Lk 1:69 [p]1Ki 11:36; 2Ch 21:7
132:18 [q]Ps 35:26; 109:29

[a] 6 Or *heard of it in Ephrathah, / we found it in the fields of Jearim.* (See 1 Chron. 13:5,6) (And no quotation marks around verses 7-9) [b] 17 *Horn* here symbolizes strong one, that is, king.

✜ **131:1-3** As we approach God, we need to take the posture of a dependent child—the very model of the one who is invited into the kingdom of God (Mt 18:1–4).

132:1–5 The oath that David made to Yahweh anchors the first section by providing a rationale for God's remembrance. Second Samuel 6 recalls David's bringing the ark to Jerusalem, the site of his newly conquered capital, with the primary intent of finding a resting place for the ark.
132:6–10 The psalmist recounts the movement of the ark from Kiriath Jearim to Jerusalem (see 1Ch 13:5–6). The community places themselves in the story by using the first-person plural, "we."
132:11–12 David's name functions as a bookend of sorts. The second half of the psalm places the focus on Yahweh's fidelity both to the Davidic dynasty and to Zion, the place of Yahweh's dwelling (v. 13).
132:17–18 The first half of the psalm urged Yahweh not to turn from or reject the anointed one (v. 10). The final section answers this petition by confirming Yahweh's faithfulness to the line of David. The "horn" symbolizes royal power and suggests that it will "grow" (v. 17) or sprout up yet again.

✜ **132:1-18** Psalm 132 invites us to think more deliberately about how we cultivate memory and how we nurture hope. Both are necessary for those who seek to walk in the way of the Lord.

Psalm 133

A song of ascents. Of David.

1 How good and pleasant it is
when God's people live together[r]
in unity!
2 It is like precious oil poured on the
head,[s]
running down on the beard,
running down on Aaron's beard,
down on the collar of his robe.
3 It is as if the dew of Hermon[t]
were falling on Mount Zion.
For there the LORD bestows his
blessing,[u]
even life forevermore.[v]

Psalm 134

A song of ascents.

1 Praise the LORD, all you servants[w] of
the LORD
who minister by night[x] in the
house of the LORD.
2 Lift up your hands[y] in the sanctuary
and praise the LORD.
3 May the LORD bless you from Zion,[z]
he who is the Maker of heaven[a]
and earth.

Psalm 135

135:15–20pp // Ps 115:4–11

1 Praise the LORD.[a]

Praise the name of the LORD;
praise him, you servants[b] of the
LORD,
2 you who minister in the house[c] of
the LORD,
in the courts[d] of the house of our
God.

3 Praise the LORD, for the LORD is
good;[e]
sing praise to his name, for that is
pleasant.[f]
4 For the LORD has chosen Jacob[g] to be
his own,
Israel to be his treasured
possession.[h]

5 I know that the LORD is great,[i]
that our Lord is greater than all
gods.[j]
6 The LORD does whatever pleases him,[k]
in the heavens and on the earth,
in the seas and all their depths.
7 He makes clouds rise from the ends
of the earth;
he sends lightning with the rain[l]
and brings out the wind[m] from his
storehouses.[n]

8 He struck down the firstborn[o] of
Egypt,

133:1 [r] Ge 13:8; Heb 13:1
133:2 [s] Ex 30:25
133:3 [t] Dt 4:48 [u] Lev 25:21; Dt 28:8 [v] Ps 42:8
134:1 [w] Ps 135:1-2 [x] 1Ch 9:33
134:2 [y] Ps 28:2; 1Ti 2:8
134:3 [z] Ps 128:5 [a] Ps 124:8
135:1 [b] Ps 113:1; 134:1
135:2 [c] Lk 2:37 [d] Ps 116:19
135:3 [e] Ps 119:68 [f] Ps 147:1
135:4 [g] Dt 10:15; 1Pe 2:9 [h] Ex 19:5; Dt 7:6
135:5 [i] Ps 48:1 [j] Ps 97:9
135:6 [k] Ps 115:3
135:7 [l] Jer 10:13; Zec 10:1 [m] Job 28:25 [n] Job 38:22
135:8 [o] Ex 12:12; Ps 78:51

[a] *1* Hebrew *Hallelu Yah*; also in verses 3 and 21

Ps 133:1–3 ❖ Why is it so difficult for God's children to find unity? Why is it so important to strive for this goal (see Jn 17:21)?

Ps 134 ❖ Imagine the people of God singing this song on their way up to Jerusalem to worship in the temple. How might this have fueled their praise?

Ps 135:5–8 ❖ What are the idols we see people worshiping today, and how useful are they in bringing help to us and our problems? What might be a better place to put our trust?

133:1 Psalm 133 begins with a wisdom saying that clearly could stand alone (and perhaps did at some point in its history). The saying commends a particular way of life, namely, that of familial unity. **133:2–3b** Oil suggests a festive setting. Dew suggests a reference to the mountains of Zion. **133:3c–d** The blessings of God pour from Zion and are best received when God's people gather together in unity of purpose and worship.

✣ **133:1–3** Amid real threats and anticipated hopes, the pilgrims leaned into their identity as the people of God.

134:1–3 Within the framework of a covenant, or even a patron-client relationship, the master or lord would bestow favor on the servant. In return the servant would speak well of, or "bless" (v. 3), the master.

✣ **134:1–3** We lift our hands to God, the "Maker of heaven and earth" (v. 3), resting in the assurance that from him all blessings flow.

135:1–4 Following the repeated call to praise, the psalmist puts forth two reasons justifying this call. The reference to Yahweh's kingship in v. 4 foreshadows the explicit references to Yahweh's kingship in the following verses. **135:5–7** The mention of storm clouds, wind, and rain evoked the images of the Canaanite god of storms and weather—Baal. The point was not to compare Yahweh to Baal but to declare that Yahweh alone reigns over creation. **135:8–14** The psalmist considers God's power among the nations. The psalmist has no need to rehearse the entirety of this history, nor does he provide considerable detail.

the firstborn of people and
animals.
[9] He sent his signs[p] and wonders into
your midst, Egypt,
against Pharaoh and all his
servants.[q]
[10] He struck down many[r] nations
and killed mighty kings—
[11] Sihon[s] king of the Amorites,
Og king of Bashan,
and all the kings of Canaan[t]—
[12] and he gave their land as an
inheritance,[u]
an inheritance to his people Israel.

[13] Your name, LORD, endures forever,[v]
your renown,[w] LORD, through all
generations.
[14] For the LORD will vindicate his
people
and have compassion on his
servants.[x]

[15] The idols of the nations are silver
and gold,
made by human hands.
[16] They have mouths, but cannot
speak,
eyes, but cannot see.
[17] They have ears, but cannot hear,
nor is there breath in their
mouths.
[18] Those who make them will be like
them,
and so will all who trust in them.

[19] All you Israelites, praise the LORD;
house of Aaron, praise the LORD;
[20] house of Levi, praise the LORD;
you who fear him, praise the
LORD.
[21] Praise be to the LORD from Zion,[y]
to him who dwells in Jerusalem.

Praise the LORD.

135:9 [p] Dt 6:22 [q] Ps 136:10-15
135:10 [r] Nu 21:21-25; Ps 136:17-21
135:11 [s] Nu 21:21 [t] Jos 12:7-24
135:12 [u] Ps 78:55
135:13 [v] Ex 3:15 [w] Ps 102:12
135:14 [x] Dt 32:36
135:21 [y] Ps 134:3

136:1 [z] Ps 106:1 [a] 1Ch 16:34; 2Ch 20:21
136:2 [b] Dt 10:17
136:4 [c] Ps 72:18
136:5 [d] Pr 3:19; Jer 51:15 [e] Ge 1:1
136:6 [f] Ge 1:9; Jer 10:12 [g] Ps 24:2
136:7 [h] Ge 1:14, 16
136:8 [i] Ge 1:16
136:10 [j] Ex 12:29; Ps 135:8
136:11 [k] Ex 6:6; 12:51
136:12 [l] Dt 4:34; Ps 44:3
136:13 [m] Ex 14:21; Ps 78:13

Ps 136 ❖ Let the recurring refrain of this psalm encourage you today.

Psalm 136

[1] Give thanks to the LORD, for he is
good.[z]
His love endures forever.[a]
[2] Give thanks to the God of gods.[b]
His love endures forever.
[3] Give thanks to the Lord of lords:
His love endures forever.

[4] to him who alone does great
wonders,[c]
His love endures forever.
[5] who by his understanding[d] made
the heavens,[e]
His love endures forever.
[6] who spread out the earth[f] upon the
waters,[g]
His love endures forever.
[7] who made the great lights[h]—
His love endures forever.
[8] the sun to govern[i] the day,
His love endures forever.
[9] the moon and stars to govern the
night;
His love endures forever.

[10] to him who struck down the
firstborn[j] of Egypt
His love endures forever.
[11] and brought Israel out[k] from among
them
His love endures forever.
[12] with a mighty hand and
outstretched arm;[l]
His love endures forever.

[13] to him who divided the Red Sea[a][m]
asunder
His love endures forever.

[a] *13* Or *the Sea of Reeds*; also in verse 15

135:15–18 Verse 17 inserts a text from Jeremiah's critique of idols (see Jer 10:14). The lack of breath in their mouths suggests that there is no life in them (Ge 2:7). So, too, are "those who make them" and who rely on them (Ps 135:18).
135:19–21 The poet models the final section of Ps 135 after the language found in 115:9–11. The emphasis on Zion in the concluding verse serves to create an arc back to the Songs of Ascent (132:13; 133:3; 134:3).

✤ **135:1–21** The point of the hymn is to confess what we know about God, and what we know about God begins with election (v. 4). Because God has chosen us as his covenantal partners, he has acted on our behalf to secure our future.

136:1–3 Psalm 136 opens with a call for Israel to confess that Yahweh is good. The reference to the divine name in v. 1 is the only appearance of the term in the psalm.
136:4–9 The psalmist turns to consider Yahweh's work as Creator. The focus of the description is theological.
136:10–15 The psalmist turns to God's demonstration of power against the Egyptians. In Ps 136 the poet refers to the striking of the firstborn in Egypt, the coming out of Egypt, and the crossing of the Red Sea—key elements of the exodus story.

[14]and brought Israel through[n] the
midst of it,
His love endures forever.
[15]but swept Pharaoh and his army into
the Red Sea;[o]
His love endures forever.

[16]to him who led his people through
the wilderness;[p]
His love endures forever.

[17]to him who struck down great
kings,[q]
His love endures forever.
[18]and killed mighty kings[r] —
His love endures forever.
[19]Sihon king of the Amorites[s]
His love endures forever.
[20]and Og king of Bashan —
His love endures forever.
[21]and gave their land[t] as an
inheritance,
His love endures forever.
[22]an inheritance to his servant Israel.
His love endures forever.

[23]He remembered us[u] in our low
estate
His love endures forever.
[24]and freed us from our enemies.[v]
His love endures forever.
[25]He gives food[w] to every creature.
His love endures forever.

[26]Give thanks to the God of heaven.
His love endures forever.

Psalm 137

[1]By the rivers of Babylon[x] we sat and
wept[y]
when we remembered Zion.
[2]There on the poplars
we hung our harps,
[3]for there our captors asked us for
songs,
our tormentors demanded[z] songs
of joy;
they said, "Sing us one of the
songs of Zion!"

[4]How can we sing the songs of the
LORD
while in a foreign land?
[5]If I forget you, Jerusalem,
may my right hand forget its
skill.
[6]May my tongue cling to the roof[a] of
my mouth
if I do not remember you,
if I do not consider Jerusalem
my highest joy.

[7]Remember, LORD, what the
Edomites[b] did
on the day Jerusalem fell.[c]
"Tear it down," they cried,
"tear it down to its foundations!"
[8]Daughter Babylon, doomed to
destruction,[d]
happy is the one who repays you
according to what you have done
to us.
[9]Happy is the one who seizes your
infants
and dashes them[e] against the
rocks.

136:14 [n] Ex 14:22
136:15 [o] Ex 14:27; Ps 135:9
136:16 [p] Ex 13:18
136:17 [q] Ps 135:9-12
136:18 [r] Dt 29:7
136:19 [s] Nu 21:21-25
136:21 [t] Jos 12:1
136:23 [u] Ps 113:7
136:24 [v] Ps 107:2
136:25 [w] Ps 104:27; 145:15
137:1 [x] Eze 1:1, 3 [y] Ne 1:4
137:3 [z] Ps 80:6
137:6 [a] Eze 3:26
137:7 [b] Jer 49:7; La 4:21-22; Eze 25:12 [c] Ob 11
137:8 [d] Isa 13:1, 19; Jer 25:12, 26; Jer 50:15; Rev 18:6
137:9 [e] 2Ki 8:12; Isa 13:16

Ps 137:1-3 ❖ How can we find comfort in God through our grief?

136:16–22 This section begins with Israel's departure from Egypt and culminates in their arrival in the promised land. The focus is not on the journey but on the demonstration of Yahweh's power in defeating the kings who threatened Israel's entrance into the land.
136:23–25 The psalmist introduces first-person plural language (i.e., "our low estate," "our enemies"). The story is not merely of a generation dead and gone, but also of *us*.
136:26 Having recounted Yahweh's decisive acts on Israel's behalf, the community must praise this God.

136:1–26 When we read and study the Bible, we do more than simply recall a story—we confess a truth and lean into a vision. God's faithfulness to us in the past compels us to hope in a future in which God's vision of reality continues to unfold.

137:1–4 The image in v. 1 is of a community whose home was in exile.
137:5–6 This confession expresses the psalmist's commitment and invites the community to believe similarly.
137:7–9 This section calls on Yahweh to remember. In particular, the psalmist implores Yahweh to remember, or call to mind, the actions of the Edomites and the Babylonians. The disturbing language is rooted in the tactics of warfare as practiced in that cultural setting.

137:1–9 This psalm reminds us that we should be less concerned about how this psalm fits neatly into "our world" and more concerned about those who find themselves in difficult circumstances. The principles of God's oversight over our suffering and his care for us as his people, however, clearly come through.

Psalm 138

Of David.

[1]I will praise you, LORD, with all my heart;
before the "gods"[f] I will sing your praise.
[2]I will bow down toward your holy temple[g]
and will praise your name
for your unfailing love and your faithfulness,
for you have so exalted your solemn decree
that it surpasses your fame.[h]
[3]When I called, you answered me;
you greatly emboldened me.

[4]May all the kings of the earth[i] praise you, LORD,
when they hear what you have decreed.
[5]May they sing of the ways of the LORD,
for the glory of the LORD is great.

[6]Though the LORD is exalted, he looks kindly on the lowly;[j]
though lofty, he sees them[k] from afar.
[7]Though I walk[l] in the midst of trouble,
you preserve my life.
You stretch out your hand against the anger of my foes;[m]
with your right hand[n] you save me.[o]
[8]The LORD will vindicate[p] me;
your love, LORD, endures forever—
do not abandon the works of your hands.[q]

138:1 [f]Ps 95:3; 96:4
138:2 [g]1Ki 8:29; Ps 5:7; 28:2 [h]Isa 42:21
138:4 [i]Ps 102:15
138:6 [j]Ps 113:6; Isa 57:15 [k]Pr 3:34; Jas 4:6
138:7 [l]Ps 23:4 [m]Jer 51:25 [n]Ps 20:6 [o]Ps 71:20
138:8 [p]Ps 57:2; Php 1:6 [q]Job 10:3, 8; 14:15

Ps 138:1 ❖ What are the "gods" of today that we can praise God in front of?

Ps 139:1–8 ❖ How does God's complete knowledge of our thoughts and actions shape the way we live? How does it strengthen or comfort us?

Psalm 139

For the director of music.
Of David. A psalm.

[1]You have searched me,[r] LORD,
and you know[s] me.
[2]You know when I sit and when I rise;[t]
you perceive my thoughts[u] from afar.
[3]You discern my going out and my lying down;
you are familiar with all my ways.[v]
[4]Before a word is on my tongue
you, LORD, know it completely.[w]
[5]You hem me in[x] behind and before,
and you lay your hand upon me.
[6]Such knowledge is too wonderful for me,
too lofty[y] for me to attain.

[7]Where can I go from your Spirit?
Where can I flee[z] from your presence?
[8]If I go up to the heavens,[a] you are there;
if I make my bed[b] in the depths, you are there.
[9]If I rise on the wings of the dawn,
if I settle on the far side of the sea,
[10]even there your hand will guide me,[c]
your right hand will hold me fast.
[11]If I say, "Surely the darkness will hide me
and the light become night around me,"

139:1 [r]Ps 17:3 [s]Jer 12:3
139:2 [t]2Ki 19:27 [u]Mt 9:4; Jn 2:24
139:3 [v]Job 31:4
139:4 [w]Heb 4:13
139:5 [x]Ps 34:7
139:6 [y]Job 42:3; Ro 11:33
139:7 [z]Jer 23:24; Jnh 1:3
139:8 [a]Am 9:2-3 [b]Pr 15:11
139:10 [c]Ps 23:3

138:1–3 The act of confessing Yahweh "before the 'gods'" (v. 1) asserts Yahweh's supremacy over all other presumed deities.
138:4–6 The world powers, the "kings of the earth" (v. 4), will join with the psalmist in making a confession about Israel's God. The kings of the earth hear the words of Yahweh's mouth, thus leading them to acknowledge that he reigns.
138:7–8 The psalmist recounts Yahweh's commitment as divine King to lift up the lowly. That declaration serves as the ground of hope for the psalmist. Here the psalmist moves from a general claim about Yahweh to its significance for his predicament.

✣ **138:1–8** The transcendent God is capable of reaching into the present moment while also pointing to the divine future.

139:1–6 The poet captures the fullness of God's knowledge using several pairs of opposites. For example, "when I sit" and "when I rise" (v. 2), "my going out and my lying down" (v. 3), and "behind and before" (v. 5). Poetically speaking, these pairs of opposites replace more abstract concepts such as "all," "every," or "always." Yahweh surrounds the psalmist.
139:7–12 The psalmist quickly recognizes the fault in his own logic; darkness quickly ceases

CHARACTER OF GOD // GOD IS OMNIPRESENT

Psalm 139:7: Where can I go from your Spirit? Where can I flee from your presence?

God's omnipresence means that God is everywhere at all times. Psalm 139 expresses this truth with the questions, "Where can I go from your Spirit? Where can I flee from your presence?" The answer is: nowhere. God is all places at once.

During the time of the ancient Israelites, many of the surrounding nations viewed their gods as regional deities, tied to a specific area. Israel, however, understood that the God they worshiped was the Creator, the one and only true God. Their God was everywhere.

Even in the depths of the sea, from the belly of a fish, Jonah was able to pray to God (Jnh 2). Jonah actively tried to run away from God and God's call on his life but found out the hard way that he could not escape God. Psalm 139:8 affirms, "If I make my bed in the depths, you are there." We cannot run away from God's presence.

APPLICATION ✚ Far from being threatening, God's omnipresence is a great comfort and assurance. We are never far from God, no matter where we go. While sin can distance us from God spiritually, God's presence is always with us, and God is always ready to welcome his children back into full relationship with him. God promises to never leave nor forsake his children (Heb 13:5). Christ promised to be with his followers always (Mt 28:20). We can be confident knowing that God is always with us, no matter where we go and no matter what challenge we face.

12 even the darkness will not be dark[d]
to you;
the night will shine like the day,
for darkness is as light to you.

13 For you created my inmost being;[e]
you knit me together[f] in my
mother's womb.
14 I praise you because I am fearfully
and wonderfully made;
your works are wonderful,[g]
I know that full well.
15 My frame was not hidden from you
when I was made in the secret
place,
when I was woven together[h] in the
depths of the earth.[i]
16 Your eyes saw my unformed body;
all the days ordained for me were
written in your book
before one of them came to be.

17 How precious to me are your
thoughts,[a] God![j]
How vast is the sum of them!
18 Were I to count them,
they would outnumber the grains
of sand —
when I awake, I am still with you.

19 If only you, God, would slay the
wicked![k]
Away from me,[l] you who are
bloodthirsty!
20 They speak of you with evil intent;
your adversaries misuse your
name.[m]
21 Do I not hate those[n] who hate you,
LORD,
and abhor those who are in
rebellion against you?

139:12 [d]Job 34:22; Da 2:22
139:13 [e]Ps 119:73 [f]Job 10:11
139:14 [g]Ps 40:5
139:15 [h]Job 10:11 [i]Ps 63:9
139:17 [j]Ps 40:5
139:19 [k]Isa 11:4 [l]Ps 119:115
139:20 [m]Jude 15
139:21 [n]2Ch 19:2; Ps 31:6; 119:113; 119:158

[a] 17 Or *How amazing are your thoughts concerning me*

to be darkness because of the radiant light of God.

139:13–18 God has been involved in the life of the psalmist from his very beginning. The focus on his birth reinforces the claims made in the first two sections. The first concentrates on the comprehensive nature of God's knowing presence and the second highlights the psalmist's inability to escape the pervasive presence of God. These claims make sense "because" (v. 14) God has been with the psalmist from the beginning of his life.

139:19–24 In these six verses the psalmist utters a petition, a declaration of commitment, and a concluding plea. Through his petitions, the psalmist aligns himself with God and asks for God to redress his present circumstances.

✚ **139:1–24** Many of the great hymns of the Christian faith give considerable attention to the personal relationship between God and the individual. Hymns such as these tend to highlight the comfort the believer gains from God's presence. Rarely do hymns remind us of the kind of pervasive presence of God in our lives that might prompt a sense of holy awe and respect, but the awesome nature of Ps 139 can lead us to that conclusion.

Psalm 143

A psalm of David.

1 LORD, hear my prayer,
listen to my cry for mercy;[j]
in your faithfulness[k] and
righteousness[l]
come to my relief.
2 Do not bring your servant into
judgment,
for no one living is righteous[m]
before you.
3 The enemy pursues me,
he crushes me to the ground;
he makes me dwell in the darkness
like those long dead.
4 So my spirit grows faint within me;
my heart within me is dismayed.[n]
5 I remember[o] the days of long ago;
I meditate on all your works
and consider what your hands
have done.
6 I spread out my hands[p] to you;
I thirst for you like a parched
land.[a]

7 Answer me quickly,[q] LORD;
my spirit fails.
Do not hide your face[r] from me
or I will be like those who go
down to the pit.
8 Let the morning bring me word of
your unfailing love,[s]
for I have put my trust in you.
Show me the way[t] I should go,
for to you I entrust my life.[u]
9 Rescue me from my enemies,[v] LORD,
for I hide myself in you.
10 Teach me to do your will,
for you are my God;
may your good Spirit
lead[w] me on level ground.

143:1 [j] Ps 140:6 [k] Ps 89:1-2 [l] Ps 71:2
143:2 [m] Ps 14:3; Ecc 7:20; Ro 3:20
143:4 [n] Ps 142:3
143:5 [o] Ps 77:6
143:6 [p] Ps 63:1; 88:9
143:7 [q] Ps 69:17 [r] Ps 27:9; 28:1
143:8 [s] Ps 46:5; 90:14 [t] Ps 27:11 [u] Ps 25:1-2
143:9 [v] Ps 31:15
143:10 [w] Ne 9:20; Ps 23:3; 25:4-5

Ps 143:8 ❖ How does God direct us in the way we should go? How can we better follow his leading?

11 For your name's sake, LORD, preserve
my life;[x]
in your righteousness,[y] bring me
out of trouble.
12 In your unfailing love, silence my
enemies;
destroy all my foes,[z]
for I am your servant.[a]

Psalm 144

Of David.

1 Praise be to the LORD my Rock,[b]
who trains my hands for war,
my fingers for battle.
2 He is my loving God and my
fortress,[c]
my stronghold and my deliverer,
my shield,[d] in whom I take refuge,
who subdues peoples[b] under me.

3 LORD, what are human beings[e] that
you care for them,
mere mortals that you think of
them?
4 They are like a breath;
their days are like a fleeting
shadow.[f]

5 Part your heavens,[g] LORD, and come
down;
touch the mountains, so that they
smoke.[h]

143:11 [x] Ps 119:25 [y] Ps 31:1
143:12 [z] Ps 52:5; 54:5 [a] Ps 116:16
144:1 [b] Ps 18:2, 34
144:2 [c] Ps 59:9; 91:2 [d] Ps 84:9
144:3 [e] Ps 8:4; Heb 2:6
144:4 [f] Ps 39:11; 102:11
144:5 [g] Ps 18:9; Isa 64:1 [h] Ps 104:32

[a] 6 The Hebrew has *Selah* (a word of uncertain meaning) here. [b] 2 Many manuscripts of the Masoretic Text, Dead Sea Scrolls, Aquila, Jerome and Syriac; most manuscripts of the Masoretic Text *subdues my people*

143:1–2 The petitions both for action and inaction reflect the psalmist's longing for God's mercy. The psalmist implores Yahweh to withhold his judgment and instead deliver him from his enemies.
143:3–6 The language of threat involves metaphors and imagery associated with death. The rehearsal of the threats is followed by a recollection of the past and then a brief description of the psalmist's posture of prayer in the present.
143:7–12 The motif of God's attentive care in the morning serves as a cause for both hope and celebration. In the final line, the poet declares himself the servant of God, reinforcing the rationale for divine action—God's covenantal faithfulness.

✜ **143:1–12** Our only hope for true freedom is found in our willingness to enter into a relationship with God—a relationship that is both initiated and sustained by God. It is in this relationship that we discover a hopeful word for our troubling circumstances.

144:1–2 The relational nature of the comments is emphasized by the repeated use of first-person singular language. The psalmist draws much of his imagery from Ps 18.
144:3–4 The psalmist confesses that human life is like a "breath," a word that stresses the temporary nature of life.
144:5–8 The psalmist envisions Yahweh as the God of the heavens but seeks to close that distance.

6 Send forth lightning and scatter the enemy;
shoot your arrows[i] and rout them.
7 Reach down your hand from on high;
deliver me and rescue me
from the mighty waters,[j]
from the hands of foreigners[k]
8 whose mouths are full of lies,[l]
whose right hands are deceitful.

9 I will sing a new song to you, my God;
on the ten-stringed lyre[m] I will make music to you,
10 to the One who gives victory to kings,
who delivers his servant David.[n]

From the deadly sword 11 deliver me;
rescue me from the hands of foreigners
whose mouths are full of lies,
whose right hands are deceitful.[o]

12 Then our sons in their youth
will be like well-nurtured plants,[p]
and our daughters will be like pillars
carved to adorn a palace.
13 Our barns will be filled
with every kind of provision.
Our sheep will increase by thousands,
by tens of thousands in our fields;
14 our oxen will draw heavy loads.[a]
There will be no breaching of walls,
no going into captivity,
no cry of distress in our streets.
15 Blessed is the people[q] of whom this is true;
blessed is the people whose God is the LORD.

144:6 [i] Ps 7:12-13; 18:14
144:7 [j] Ps 69:2 [k] Ps 18:44
144:8 [l] Ps 12:2
144:9 [m] Ps 33:2-3
144:10 [n] Ps 18:50
144:11 [o] Ps 12:2; Isa 44:20
144:12 [p] Ps 128:3
144:15 [q] Ps 33:12

Ps 144:13 ❖ How has God blessed us with good things and granted us his protection?

Ps 145:4–5 ❖ Where has God given us opportunities to share about his love with the next generation? How can we glorify God by sharing his Word with others?

Psalm 145[b]

A psalm of praise. Of David.

1 I will exalt you,[r] my God the King;[s]
I will praise your name for ever and ever.
2 Every day I will praise[t] you
and extol your name for ever and ever.

3 Great is the LORD and most worthy of praise;
his greatness no one can fathom.[u]
4 One generation[v] commends your works to another;
they tell of your mighty acts.
5 They speak of the glorious splendor of your majesty—
and I will meditate on your wonderful works.[c][w]
6 They tell of the power of your awesome works—[x]
and I will proclaim[y] your great deeds.
7 They celebrate your abundant goodness[z]

145:1 [r] Ps 30:1; 34:1 [s] Ps 5:2
145:2 [t] Ps 71:6
145:3 [u] Job 5:9; Ps 147:5; Ro 11:33
145:4 [v] Isa 38:19
145:5 [w] Ps 119:27
145:6 [x] Ps 66:3 [y] Dt 32:3
145:7 [z] Isa 63:7

[a] 14 Or *our chieftains will be firmly established*
[b] This psalm is an acrostic poem, the verses of which (including verse 13b) begin with the successive letters of the Hebrew alphabet.
[c] 5 Dead Sea Scrolls and Syriac (see also Septuagint); Masoretic Text *On the glorious splendor of your majesty / and on your wonderful works I will meditate*

144:9–11 The reason Yahweh deserves praise (v. 10) provides the rationale for the request. Yahweh's faithfulness in the past provides the rationale for the requests that follow.
144:12–14 In these verses the community describes how their life will look once Yahweh has rid the land of their oppressive enemies.
144:15 The psalmist announces that "blessed" are the people whose lives reflect that which is described in vv. 12–14. The second beatitude suggests that such a "blessed" existence is possible because Yahweh is Israel's God.

✣ **144:1–15** In the Psalms and elsewhere in Scripture we are asked to renounce our sense of self-sufficiency. After all, we are but fleeting shadows. And because we're well aware of what *we are*, we must lean fully into who *he is*—the divine King (see Ps 145).

145:1–2 The psalmist confesses Yahweh as "my God the King" (v. 1). In the light of his confession, the psalmist commits to three actions: "exalt," "praise," and "extol."
145:3–7 The declaration that Yahweh is great in v. 3 complements the earlier confession that he is *the* King (v. 1). Yahweh's "awesome works" (v. 6) should inspire fear and awe in the beneficiaries of those works.

and joyfully sing of your
righteousness.[a]

8 The LORD is gracious and
compassionate,[b]
slow to anger and rich in love.[c]

9 The LORD is good[d] to all;
he has compassion on all he has
made.
10 All your works praise you,[e] LORD;
your faithful people extol you.[f]
11 They tell of the glory of your kingdom
and speak of your might,
12 so that all people may know of your
mighty acts[g]
and the glorious splendor of your
kingdom.
13 Your kingdom is an everlasting
kingdom,[h]
and your dominion endures
through all generations.

The LORD is trustworthy in all he
promises
and faithful in all he does.[a]
14 The LORD upholds[i] all who fall
and lifts up all[j] who are bowed
down.
15 The eyes of all look to you,
and you give them their food[k] at
the proper time.
16 You open your hand
and satisfy the desires[l] of every
living thing.

17 The LORD is righteous in all his ways
and faithful in all he does.
18 The LORD is near[m] to all who call on
him,[n]
to all who call on him in truth.
19 He fulfills the desires[o] of those who
fear him;
he hears their cry[p] and saves
them.

145:7 [a] Ps 51:14
145:8 [b] Ps 86:15 [c] Ex 34:6; Nu 14:18
145:9 [d] Ps 100:5
145:10 [e] Ps 19:1 [f] Ps 68:26
145:12 [g] Ps 105:1
145:13 [h] 1Ti 1:17; 2Pe 1:11
145:14 [i] Ps 37:24 [j] Ps 146:8
145:15 [k] Ps 104:27; 136:25
145:16 [l] Ps 104:28
145:18 [m] Dt 4:7 [n] Jn 4:24
145:19 [o] Ps 37:4 [p] Pr 15:29

[a] *13* One manuscript of the Masoretic Text, Dead Sea Scrolls and Syriac (see also Septuagint); most manuscripts of the Masoretic Text do not have the last two lines of verse 13.

145:8–9 In celebrating God's character, the poet references the "graciousness formula" of Ex 34:6–7, in which Yahweh describes himself. Psalm 145:8 quotes the Exodus text nearly verbatim.
145:10 All God's works bear witness to his identity as the One great God. God bestows blessings upon his people and his people, in return, speak well of God.
145:11–13 Within this short section of the psalm, the word for "kingdom" appears four times, each time referencing Yahweh, the divine King.
145:14–20 The psalmist confesses Yahweh's sovereign care over all creation and those who call on him. Yahweh watches over his people, but the way of the wicked he will destroy (cf. 1:6).

CHARACTER OF GOD // **GOD IS RIGHTEOUS**

Psalm 145:17: The LORD is righteous in all his ways and faithful in all he does.

The *righteousness of God* means that God always does what is right and always acts in keeping with his holy and just nature. God is never crooked or corrupt. God has never done and will never do anything evil or unrighteous.

In Psalm 11, David asks, where can the righteous go when the wicked shake the very foundations of the world with their evil (Ps 11:3)? The answer: Righteous people can look beyond themselves to their righteous God. God sits on his heavenly throne and sees everything that happens on earth. He examines the righteous and judges the wicked.

God's righteousness means that he will never assist the schemes of the wicked. God will not be manipulated by humans. God does not need human praise or offerings; he is an impartial and just judge. As Psalm 11 says, "[God] loves justice; the upright will see his face" (Ps 11:7).

Unfortunately, no human is righteous; all have sinned (Ro 3:23). How, then, can people find hope in the righteousness of God? The Good News of the gospel is that, in Christ, God removes our sin. Through Jesus' sacrifice on the cross, God's children become righteous, making it possible for them to stand before their righteous God (2Co 5:21).

APPLICATION ✜ Since our sin is taken away through Christ, we can live free and righteous lives by the power of God's Spirit living within us. God calls believers to live righteous lives so that we might point others to our righteous God. Just as God's righteousness means he will never willingly take part in promoting evil or participating in sin, the same must be true for those who believe in and follow him. Through the process of sanctification, we should prayerfully work to lead ever more righteous lives, giving glory to our heavenly Father.

CHARACTER OF GOD // GOD IS THE SUSTAINER

Psalm 146:9: The LORD watches over the foreigner and sustains the fatherless and the widow, but he frustrates the ways of the wicked.

God is the One who sustains all creatures, but most especially those who believe in him and follow him. When Elijah was depressed and despaired of life, God sent him food to sustain him for his journey (1Ki 19:5–8). God sustained the Israelites in the wilderness with miraculous provisions of food and water. Even their clothes did not wear out (Dt 29:5).

The Psalms frequently praise God for being the One who sustains. Psalm 3:5 says that the reason we wake up again after we fall asleep is because God sustains us. Psalm 121:3 reminds us that God never sleeps; even when we fall asleep, God is watching over us to sustain us. Psalm 55:22 promises that God will sustain those who cast their cares on him and that the righteous will never be shaken.

God's sustaining hand upholds those who are downtrodden, particularly people who are oppressed and marginalized. Psalm 146:9 says that God "watches over the foreigner and sustains the fatherless and the widow." These are the three groups of people whom God repeatedly instructs the Israelites to care for: foreigners, widows, and the fatherless. Even when Israel failed to care for those on the margins, God was watching over them. He heard their cries and sent his prophets to announce judgment against those who mistreated them (see Isa 1:23).

APPLICATION When we are weary, we can cast ourselves on God in the hope and knowledge that he is the One who sustains us. Christ said, "Come to me, all you who are weary and burdened, and I will give you rest" (Mt 11:28). Like Elijah in the wilderness, God will be our Sustainer and Provider. His mercy will carry us when our strength is gone.

Ps 146:3 ❖ How can we avoid pinning our hopes on political leaders or other leaders in society? Why are all such hopes in humans ultimately in vain?

20 The LORD watches over all who love him,[q]
but all the wicked he will destroy.[r]

21 My mouth will speak[s] in praise of the LORD.
Let every creature[t] praise his holy name
for ever and ever.

Psalm 146

1 Praise the LORD.[a]

Praise the LORD,[u] my soul.

2 I will praise the LORD all my life;[v]
I will sing praise to my God as long as I live.
3 Do not put your trust in princes,[w]
in human beings,[x] who cannot save.
4 When their spirit departs, they return to the ground;[y]
on that very day their plans come to nothing.[z]
5 Blessed are those[a] whose help[b] is the God of Jacob,
whose hope is in the LORD their God.

6 He is the Maker of heaven[c] and earth,
the sea, and everything in them—
he remains faithful[d] forever.
7 He upholds the cause of the oppressed[e]
and gives food to the hungry.[f]
The LORD sets prisoners free,[g]
8 the LORD gives sight to the blind,[h]
the LORD lifts up those who are bowed down,
the LORD loves the righteous.
9 The LORD watches over the foreigner

145:20 [q] Ps 31:23; 97:10 [r] Ps 9:5
145:21 [s] Ps 71:8 [t] Ps 65:2
146:1 [u] Ps 103:1
146:2 [v] Ps 104:33
146:3 [w] Ps 118:9 [x] Isa 2:22
146:4 [y] Ps 104:29; Ecc 12:7 [z] Ps 33:10; 1Co 2:6
146:5 [a] Ps 144:15; Jer 17:7 [b] Ps 71:5
146:6 [c] Ps 115:15; Ac 14:15; Rev 14:7 [d] Ps 117:2
146:7 [e] Ps 103:6 [f] Ps 107:9 [g] Ps 68:6
146:8 [h] Mt 9:30

[a] *1* Hebrew *Hallelu Yah*; also in verse 10

145:21 The psalm concludes by repeating three words from v. 1: "praise" twice, and "name." Here the psalmist expresses his desire for "every creature" to praise or bless God. Even as God's kingdom is "everlasting" (v. 13), so too must our praise be "for ever and ever" (v. 21).

145:1–21 The psalmist explains that a people of praise are those who remember and tell, recall and proclaim.

146:1–2 The psalm opens with a call to "Praise the LORD," an exhortation that repeats at the close of the psalm.

146:3–4 The psalmist emphasizes the fleeting nature of humans and human power.

146:5–9 Beginning with a beatitude, the psalmist recounts the activity of this God who merits our praise.

and sustains the fatherless and
the widow,[i]
but he frustrates the ways of the
wicked.

10 The LORD reigns[j] forever,
your God, O Zion, for all
generations.

Praise the LORD.

Psalm 147

1 Praise the LORD.[a]

How good it is to sing praises to our
God,
how pleasant[k] and fitting to praise
him![l]

2 The LORD builds up Jerusalem;[m]
he gathers the exiles[n] of Israel.
3 He heals the brokenhearted
and binds up their wounds.
4 He determines the number of the
stars[o]
and calls them each by name.
5 Great is our Lord[p] and mighty in
power;
his understanding has no
limit.[q]
6 The LORD sustains the humble[r]
but casts the wicked to the
ground.

7 Sing to the LORD[s] with grateful
praise;
make music to our God on the
harp.

8 He covers the sky with clouds;
he supplies the earth with rain[t]
and makes grass grow[u] on the
hills.

Ps 147:3 ❖ How have we experienced the healing power of God's love?

9 He provides food[v] for the cattle
and for the young ravens[w] when
they call.

10 His pleasure is not in the strength[x]
of the horse,[y]
nor his delight in the legs of the
warrior;
11 the LORD delights in those who fear
him,
who put their hope in his
unfailing love.

12 Extol the LORD, Jerusalem;
praise your God, Zion.

13 He strengthens the bars of your
gates
and blesses your people within
you.
14 He grants peace[z] to your borders
and satisfies you[a] with the finest
of wheat.

15 He sends his command[b] to the
earth;
his word runs swiftly.
16 He spreads the snow[c] like wool
and scatters the frost[d] like
ashes.
17 He hurls down his hail like pebbles.
Who can withstand his icy
blast?
18 He sends his word[e] and melts
them;
he stirs up his breezes, and the
waters flow.

146:9 [i] Ex 22:22; Dt 10:18; Ps 68:5
146:10 [j] Ex 15:18; Ps 10:16
147:1 [k] Ps 135:3 [l] Ps 33:1
147:2 [m] Ps 102:16 [n] Dt 30:3
147:4 [o] Isa 40:26
147:5 [p] Ps 48:1 [q] Isa 40:28
147:6 [r] Ps 146:8-9
147:7 [s] Ps 33:3
147:8 [t] Job 38:26 [u] Ps 104:14
147:9 [v] Ps 104:27-28; Mt 6:26 [w] Job 38:41
147:10 [x] 1Sa 16:7 [y] Ps 33:16-17
147:14 [z] Isa 60:17-18 [a] Ps 132:15
147:15 [b] Job 37:12
147:16 [c] Job 37:6 [d] Job 38:29
147:18 [e] Ps 33:9

[a] *1* Hebrew *Hallelu Yah;* also in verse 20

146:10 The hope for Zion rests fully with the divine King, who demonstrated his dominion in the exodus and stands poised to do so again.

✚ **146:1-10** We can spend our life singing praises because God "remains faithful forever" (v. 6). God indeed is our Maker and Defender, redeemer and friend, because he is the God who has and will reign forever.

147:1-6 The Great Shepherd heals the brokenhearted and the wounded. Those who have been scattered need to be lifted up. This image stands in contrast to the fate of the wicked, whom Yahweh "casts . . . to the ground" (v. 6).
147:7-9 The community is invited to sing in a spirit of thanksgiving. Verses 8-9 allude to Yahweh's providing food for his creation.
147:10-11 Despite the impressive power associated with military might, the psalmist confesses that Israel's God "delights in those who fear him . . . [and] hope in his unfailing love" (v. 11).
147:12-20 In vv. 13-14 the psalmist identifies four ways in which Yahweh demonstrates his concern for Jerusalem. The final two lines focus on the role of God's word in governing his people (vv. 19-20). God's "word" reminds them of the One with whom they are in covenant—namely, the divine King.

✚ **147:1-20** The God who sends his word to order and sustain creation is the God who continues to come to us in his word, and in the Word, so that we too might be ordered and sustained by the very power of God that is at work in the world. Because he comes to us, sustains us, and shapes us, we are invited to praise the Lord.

CHARACTER OF GOD // GOD IS OMNISCIENT

Psalm 147:5: Great is our Lord and mighty in power; his understanding has no limit.

Psalm 147:5 declares that God's "understanding has no limit." God is omniscient, or "all knowing." There are no mysteries God does not understand. The past and the future are known to him completely. From the smallest subatomic particles to the most distant reaches of the universe, God knows it all.

Through Isaiah the prophet God declares, "For my thoughts are not your thoughts, neither are your ways my ways" (Isa 55:8). This is wonderful news! There is so much that we do not understand, from politics to science to ethics to the workings of our own minds and hearts (Jer 17:9). Our omniscient God, however, knows and understands all. Indeed, he created the whole universe; nothing within it is too hard for God to grasp.

Sometimes we call our time in history the "information age." Yet our understanding of the universe keeps changing. Old paradigms give way to new ones. The truth is, we will never catch up to God in understanding how the world or the universe works. The One who made it is the One who understands it fully.

APPLICATION Understanding God's all-knowing nature should lead us to deeper trust in God. When Israel's king Hezekiah was threatened by the mighty power of Assyria, Hezekiah went straight to God (2Ki 19:14–19). Hezekiah trusted that God knew the whole situation, and he put his trust in the Lord rather than in his own strength. Trusting in God's omniscience should inspire the same faith in us.

Most precious about God's omniscience is the certain hope it offers that God's salvation plan is secure. Since God knows everything, including the future, we can be certain that nothing is outside his plan. While we only "know in part" (1Co 13:9), we can trust in the God who knows fully.

19 He has revealed his word to Jacob,
his laws and decrees[f] to Israel.
20 He has done this for no other
nation;[g]
they do not know his laws.[a]

Praise the LORD.

Psalm 148

1 Praise the LORD.[b]

Praise the LORD from the heavens;
praise him in the heights above.
2 Praise him, all his angels;[h]
praise him, all his heavenly hosts.
3 Praise him, sun and moon;
praise him, all you shining stars.
4 Praise him, you highest heavens
and you waters above the skies.[i]

5 Let them praise the name of the
LORD,
for at his command[j] they were
created,
6 and he established them for ever and
ever —
he issued a decree[k] that will never
pass away.

7 Praise the LORD from the earth,
you great sea creatures[l] and all
ocean depths,
8 lightning and hail, snow and clouds,
stormy winds that do his
bidding,[m]
9 you mountains and all hills,[n]
fruit trees and all cedars,
10 wild animals and all cattle,
small creatures and flying birds,
11 kings of the earth and all nations,
you princes and all rulers on
earth,
12 young men and women,
old men and children.

147:19 [f] Dt 33:4; Mal 4:4
147:20 [g] Dt 4:7-8,32-34
148:2 [h] Ps 103:20
148:4 [i] Ge 1:7; 1Ki 8:27
148:5 [j] Ge 1:1,6; Ps 33:6,9
148:6 [k] Job 38:33; Ps 89:37; Jer 33:25
148:7 [l] Ps 74:13-14
148:8 [m] Ps 147:15-18
148:9 [n] Isa 44:23; 49:13; 55:12

[a] 20 Masoretic Text; Dead Sea Scrolls and Septuagint *nation; / he has not made his laws known to them* [b] 1 Hebrew *Hallelu Yah*; also in verse 14

148:1–6 Verses 1–5 call on the heavens and all that inhabit them to praise Yahweh. No power on earth or in the heavens can thwart what Yahweh has created and established.
148:7–14 Verses 7–8 include three pairs of objects: sea creatures and ocean depths; lightning and hail; and snow and clouds. Verses 9–12a continue the pairing of terms, beginning with nature. Humans are not mentioned until vv. 11–12. Yahweh himself is assumed to be above the earth.

148:1–14 In this psalm we are asked to dispense with our own ideas about the nature of God and even ourselves. Instead, we are invited into a chorus with all creation as we

[13] Let them praise the name of the LORD,[o]
for his name alone is exalted;
his splendor is above the earth and the heavens.[p]
[14] And he has raised up for his people a horn,[a][q]
the praise of all his faithful servants,
of Israel, the people close to his heart.

Praise the LORD.

Psalm 149

[1] Praise the LORD.[b][r]

Sing to the LORD a new song,
his praise in the assembly[s] of his faithful people.

[2] Let Israel rejoice in their Maker;[t]
let the people of Zion be glad in their King.[u]
[3] Let them praise his name with dancing
and make music to him with timbrel and harp.[v]
[4] For the LORD takes delight[w] in his people;
he crowns the humble with victory.[x]
[5] Let his faithful people rejoice[y] in this honor
and sing for joy on their beds.[z]

[6] May the praise of God be in their mouths[a]
and a double-edged[b] sword in their hands,
[7] to inflict vengeance on the nations
and punishment on the peoples,
[8] to bind their kings with fetters,
their nobles with shackles of iron,
[9] to carry out the sentence written against them —[c]
this is the glory of all his faithful people.[d]

Praise the LORD.

Psalm 150

[1] Praise the LORD.[c]

Praise God in his sanctuary;[e]
praise him in his mighty heavens.[f]
[2] Praise him for his acts of power;[g]
praise him for his surpassing greatness.[h]
[3] Praise him with the sounding of the trumpet,
praise him with the harp and lyre,[i]
[4] praise him with timbrel and dancing,[j]
praise him with the strings[k] and pipe,
[5] praise him with the clash of cymbals,[l]
praise him with resounding cymbals.

[6] Let everything[m] that has breath praise the LORD.

Praise the LORD.

148:13 [o] Isa 12:4 [p] Ps 8:1; 113:4
148:14 [q] Ps 75:10
149:1 [r] Ps 33:2 [s] Ps 35:18
149:2 [t] Ps 95:6 [u] Ps 47:6; Zec 9:9
149:3 [v] Ps 81:2; 150:4
149:4 [w] Ps 35:27 [x] Ps 132:16
149:5 [y] Ps 132:16 [z] Job 35:10
149:6 [a] Ps 66:17 [b] Heb 4:12; Rev 1:16
149:9 [c] Dt 7:1; Eze 28:26 [d] Ps 148:14
150:1 [e] Ps 102:19 [f] Ps 19:1
150:2 [g] Dt 3:24 [h] Ps 145:5-6
150:3 [i] Ps 149:3
150:4 [j] Ex 15:20 [k] Isa 38:20
150:5 [l] 1Ch 13:8; 15:16
150:6 [m] Ps 145:21

[a] 14 *Horn* here symbolizes strength.
[b] 1 Hebrew *Hallelu Yah*; also in verse 9
[c] 1 Hebrew *Hallelu Yah*; also in verse 6

Ps 148:11-14 ❖ How can we make joyfully praising God a bigger part of our lives?

Ps 149:1-5 ❖ What does God's crown of victory look like in our lives (see Rev 2:10)? How can we give the Lord thanks and praise?

Ps 150 ❖ Take a few moments to read this psalm out loud. Does hearing it audibly deepen its meaning in any way?

lift our voices to the one true God who stands over earth and heaven.

149:1-4 The psalmist's "new song" (v. 1) has little to do with his song's being a "new" composition. These songs announce the coming of a new and just world.
149:5-9 The second passage resumes the call to praise. A series of statements concerning the demonstration of Yahweh's rule over the world follows in vv. 7-9.

149:1-9 God invites his people to join him in establishing his kingdom. As we pray the Psalter, we learn of God and his ways in the world, and *his* vision of the kingdom slowly becomes *our* vision of the kingdom.

150:1-2 The first two verses focus on God and his role as the Sovereign over all creation.
150:3-5 The praise of God as the great King begins in the context of celebratory worship.
150:6 With this final exhortation, the psalmist extends the summons beyond the temple, inviting all creation to praise God.

150:1-6 When we praise God, we are doing far more than simply listing all the good qualities God possesses; we are uttering a confession about the reality of our God. In so doing, we are declaring that the divine King is coming still.

Author: King Solomon and other wise men

Audience: The people of Israel

Date: Primarily during Solomon's reign (970–930 BC)

Theme: God has placed an order in creation to which we should pay attention in order to live wisely.

PERSPECTIVE

Wisdom is in short supply these days. Look around and one finds plenty of knowledgeable people. Look in other places and one finds plenty of good-hearted people. But we look hard to find people both good-hearted and knowledgeable—or, put a better way, people who have learned how to integrate their hard-won knowledge with their grace-imparted goodness. The book of Proverbs teaches applied knowledge—wisdom; this makes Proverbs an extremely important book.

We live in a culture that suffers from having separated knowledge from ethics. Because of the importance and influence of science and technology in our world, we live with the notion that one can know things without knowing how those same things should be used. Scientists working on the first atomic bomb, for example, might have pretended that they were extending the frontiers of knowledge, when in fact they were creating knowledge that could be used for horrific human ends. No wisdom there, for sure.

Wisdom is not an easy nut to crack, however. If it were so easy, it wouldn't be in such short supply. What makes it difficult? At least five things:

First, wisdom often seems cryptic. That is, it is often hard to understand—not because the content is so difficult, but because it is usually radical and subversive. That is, it usually goes against established cultural norms that are typically geared toward economic success or political power. It takes ears specially trained in the ways of the gospel to hear the wisdom of many proverbs. "Ears to hear," Jesus

Reading Proverbs

The book of Proverbs begins with a prologue, followed by nine chapters that contrast the way of wisdom with the way of folly. The next major section (chs. 10–22) contains primarily individual proverbs of Solomon in couplet form; there is no identifiable structure to this section, except for two or three proverbs occasionally being on the same theme. The last few

	1400 BC	1300	1200	1100	1000	900	800	700	600	500	400
David's reign (1010–970 BC)					■						
Solomon's reign (970–930 BC)					■						
Many proverbs written (c. 970–930 BC)					■						
Division of the kingdom (930 BC)					♦						
Exile of Israel (722 BC)								♦			
Hezekiah's reign (715–686 BC)								■			
Proverbs compiled and edited (715–686 BC)								■			
Fall of Jerusalem (586 BC)									♦		

chapters are proverbs attributed to people other than Solomon.

Key Verse

The fear of the LORD is the beginning of knowledge, but fools despise wisdom and instruction.

—Proverbs 1:7

called them (Mk 4:9, 23). Second, wisdom often seems ambiguous. Ambiguity is the very thing one would think wisdom is designed to do away with, but Proverbs teaches us that is not true. Wisdom is sometimes found in the interaction between two proverbs rather than the statement of just one:

> Do not answer a fool according to his folly,
> or you yourself will be just like him.
> Answer a fool according to his folly,
> or he will be wise in his own eyes. (26:4–5)

We have to read both, we have to understand both, and then we have to read both and understand them together before wisdom emerges.

Third, wisdom, like everything else human, is culture specific. Wisdom in one culture is not always wisdom in another. Thus, when we read in Proverbs 7 about the virtues of a good woman, one of the questions that results is, what are the virtues of a good man? The book of Proverbs contains some wisdom but not all wisdom. It is the product of a culture that didn't think to warn its daughters about men to avoid, as Proverbs 7 warns young men about women to avoid. It takes some effort to convert this message for the 21st century.

Fourth, wisdom takes courage to implement. It is not enough to see what action is required by the knowledge we attain. We have to do more than recognize and acknowledge the action wisdom requires; we have to *do it* as well. It is not enough to say that most basic and earliest Christian creed, "Jesus is Lord." We must also act in ways that acknowledge that Jesus is Lord—by obeying, loving, and relating to Jesus as Lord.

Finally, wisdom is broad-minded. It teaches us that not just any old actions implied by our knowledge will do. Our actions must be measured by the extent to which they contribute to God's plan: the building of the kingdom of God; human flourishing; the well-being of the whole creation. But trying to work out the future effects of today's causes is not so easy.

Perhaps the greatest of all the lessons of Proverbs is this—that the wisdom it extols is hard to find but most worthy of seeking.

TAKING THE NEXT STEPS

Most of the proverbs were written by Solomon (see Pr 1:1; 10:1; 25:1), though at least some of them were collected long after his death (see Pr 25:1). First Kings 4:32 claims that Solomon wrote at least three thousand proverbs. At the heart of the wisdom contained in this book is God, who is in control of all of life. Many of these gems are designed to help give direction in our day-to-day lives and to shape our attitudes toward God, toward our fellow humans, and toward ourselves. A certain number of proverbs, however, merely describe patterns that the author observes from daily life but which are not necessarily normative.

In addition to the advice of specific proverbs, several general principles stand out. (1) No true education can take place unless we have committed ourselves to the Lord. (2) Two of the areas of life that present the greatest danger, particularly to young people, are alcohol (or other substance abuse) and sex. (3) The home ought to be a haven of love, with proper lines of authority and the members of the family showing respect to one other. (4) In the daily work that we perform, honesty and industriousness are two key characteristics. (5) In our relations with other human beings, we ought to be kind, compassionate, generous and humble.

WHAT TO LOOK FOR IN PROVERBS

- The origin and benefits of wisdom (chs. 1–4; 9)
- Warnings against sexual sins (chs. 5; 7)
- Wisdom as a person (ch. 8)
- The wife of noble character (ch. 31)

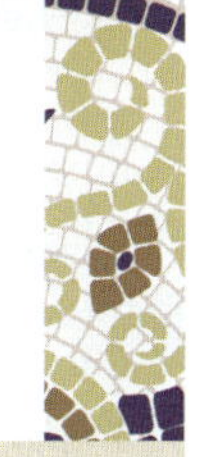

Purpose and Theme

1 The proverbs of Solomon[a] son of David, king of Israel:[b]

2 for gaining wisdom and instruction;
for understanding words of insight;
3 for receiving instruction in prudent behavior,
doing what is right and just and fair;
4 for giving prudence to those who are simple,[a][c]
knowledge and discretion[d] to the young—
5 let the wise listen and add to their learning,[e]
and let the discerning get guidance—
6 for understanding proverbs and parables,[f]
the sayings and riddles[g] of the wise.[b]

7 The fear of the LORD[h] is the beginning of knowledge,
but fools[c] despise wisdom and instruction.

1:1 [a] 1Ki 4:29-34 [b] Pr 10:1; 25:1; Ecc 1:1
1:4 [c] Pr 8:5 [d] Pr 2:10-11; 8:12
1:5 [e] Pr 9:9
1:6 [f] Ps 49:4; 78:2 [g] Nu 12:8
1:7 [h] Job 28:28; Ps 111:10; Pr 9:10; 15:33; Ecc 12:13

Pr 1:7 ❖ What does a life of pursuing Christian wisdom look like? What practices can we foster or habits can we form to pursue a life like this?

[a] 4 The Hebrew word rendered *simple* in Proverbs denotes a person who is gullible, without moral direction and inclined to evil.
[b] 6 Or *understanding a proverb, namely, a parable, / and the sayings of the wise, their riddles*
[c] 7 The Hebrew words rendered *fool* in Proverbs, and often elsewhere in the Old Testament, denote a person who is morally deficient.

1:1–7 We should always pay attention to beginnings and endings of literary works because writers tend to put their most important thoughts and images there. In this case, "fear of the LORD" not only concludes this prologue (v. 7), it also appears at the end of the book (31:30).

APPLICATION ✚ **1:1–7** Wisdom is not so much a goal to be attained as it is a posture of humility, a willingness to receive instruction. A wise person is a learning person, a person in process, not a finished product.

KEY THEMES IN PROVERBS

THEME	LESSONS	REFERENCES
Fear of the Lord	The "beginning of wisdom," to fear the Lord is to recognize God's authority in every aspect of our lives.	1:7, 29; 2:5; 3:7-8; 8:13; 9:10; 10:27; 14:26-27; 15:16, 33; 16:6; 19:23; 22:4; 23:17
Wisdom	Wisdom is the application of truth to our daily existence.	1-5; 7:4; 8; 9:1-13; 10:13, 23, 31; 11:2; 13:10; 14:6, 8, 33; 15:33; 16:16; 17:24; 18:4; 19:20; 21:30; 23:23; 24:3; 28:26; 29:3, 15
Folly	Folly is a rebellious departure from the life of wisdom.	1:21-22; 3:35; 5:22-23; 9:13-18; 10:14, 23; 12:15-16, 23; 13:16; 14:7-9, 16; 18:2; 19:10; 22:15; 26:1, 11; 27:3, 22; 29:9
Humility	More dangerous than folly is pride; Proverbs calls all who would be wise to remain humble.	3:34; 6:16-17a; 12:1; 14:1; 15:21, 33; 16:18-19; 17:12, 24; 18:2; 21:4, 24; 22:4; 25:6-7, 14; 26:1-12; 27:1-2, 21; 29:1, 23; 30:32
Friendship	Friends can influence us for good, bring joy and walk with us through life's challenges. Proverbs encourages us to choose them carefully.	13:20; 17:7; 18:24; 20:19; 22:24-25; 23:20-21; 24:21-22; 27:6, 17
Marriage	Marriage multiplies the implications of friendship, defining our lives like few other relationships.	5:15-19; 6:27-29, 32-33; 7:21-27; 12:4; 18:22; 19:13; 21:9, 19; 25:24; 27:8, 15-16; 31:9-31
Parenting	Parents are the primary teachers of wisdom and, sadly, folly. Proverbs presents parents with tools for raising children of understanding.	4:3-9; 10:1; 13:1; 15:20; 17:6, 21, 25; 19:13-14, 18, 26; 20:7; 22:15; 23:13-14, 24; 29:15, 17
Respect	Proverbs instructs us to respect others, both those in authority and those we are called to lead.	12:1; 13:1, 10, 13-14, 18; 15:5, 12, 31-32; 19:16, 20, 26-27; 22:17, 28; 23:22; 28:7, 9, 15-16, 24; 29:1, 3; 20:11, 17; 31:8-9
Speech	Our words have power beyond belief. As James would later write, "Those who consider themselves religious and yet do not keep a tight rein on their tongues deceive themselves" (1:26).	6:12-15, 16-17b, 19; 10:10-14, 18-21, 31-32; 11:9, 12-13, 24-28; 12:13-14, 17-19; 13:2-3, 5; 14:3, 5-6, 25; 15:4, 7, 23, 26, 28; 16:1, 13, 20, 23-24, 27-28, 30; 17:7, 9, 27-28; 18:2, 4, 6-8, 13, 20-21; 19:1, 5, 9; 20:3, 15-16, 19, 25; 21:6, 28; 22:11; 23:9, 15-16; 24:26, 28; 25:11-13, 15, 18, 20, 23; 26:20-28; 27:5, 14; 28:23; 29:5, 20
Finances	The "fear of the LORD" must be applied in this most practical of life spheres by honoring God with our resources.	3:9-10; 6:1-5, 10-11; 8:18; 10:2-5, 15-16, 22; 11:1, 4, 7, 15-16; 12:9; 13:7-8, 11, 22-23; 14:20-21; 15:6, 16-17, 27; 16:8; 18:11; 19:4, 17; 20:10, 21, 23; 21:6, 13, 17, 23; 22:7, 9, 16, 26-27; 23:4-5; 24:1-4, 27; 27:13, 23-27; 28:6, 11, 19-20, 22
Work	Proverbs promotes an ethic of diligent work, defined by excellence.	6:6-11; 10:2-5, 26; 12:10-11, 24, 27; 13:4; 14:23; 15:19; 17:1; 18:9; 19:15, 24; 20:14, 13; 21:5, 25-26; 22:29; 24:30-34; 26:13-16; 27:18
Moderation	In emotion, appetite and lifestyle, Proverbs commends a life of moderation.	14:16; 15:18; 16:32; 17:27; 19:11, 19; 20:1; 21:17; 22:24-25; 23:1-3, 20-21; 25:28; 27:4; 28:7; 29:22; 31:3-8

Prologue: Exhortations to Embrace Wisdom

Warning Against the Invitation of Sinful Men

8 Listen, my son,[i] to your father's
instruction
and do not forsake your mother's
teaching.[j]
9 They are a garland to grace your
head
and a chain to adorn your neck.[k]

10 My son, if sinful men entice[l] you,
do not give in[m] to them.[n]
11 If they say, "Come along with us;
let's lie in wait[o] for innocent
blood,
let's ambush some harmless soul;
12 let's swallow them alive, like the
grave,
and whole, like those who go
down to the pit;[p]
13 we will get all sorts of valuable
things
and fill our houses with plunder;
14 cast lots with us;
we will all share the loot" —
15 my son, do not go along with them,
do not set foot[q] on their paths;[r]
16 for their feet rush into evil,
they are swift to shed blood.[s]
17 How useless to spread a net
where every bird can see it!
18 These men lie in wait for their own
blood;
they ambush only themselves!
19 Such are the paths of all who go after
ill-gotten gain;
it takes away the life of those who
get it.[t]

1:8 [i] Pr 4:1 [j] Pr 6:20
1:9 [k] Pr 4:1-9
1:10 [l] Ge 39:7 [m] Dt 13:8 [n] Pr 16:29; Eph 5:11
1:11 [o] Ps 10:8
1:12 [p] Ps 28:1
1:15 [q] Ps 119:101 [r] Ps 1:1; Pr 4:14
1:16 [s] Pr 6:18; Isa 59:7
1:19 [t] Pr 15:27

Wisdom's Rebuke

20 Out in the open wisdom calls
aloud,[u]
she raises her voice in the public
square;
21 on top of the wall[a] she cries out,
at the city gate she makes her
speech:

22 "How long will you who are simple[v]
love your simple ways?
How long will mockers delight in
mockery
and fools hate knowledge?
23 Repent at my rebuke!
Then I will pour out my thoughts
to you,
I will make known to you my
teachings.
24 But since you refuse to listen when I
call[w]
and no one pays attention when I
stretch out my hand,
25 since you disregard all my advice
and do not accept my rebuke,
26 I in turn will laugh[x] when disaster
strikes you;
I will mock when calamity
overtakes you[y] —
27 when calamity overtakes you like a
storm,
when disaster sweeps over you
like a whirlwind,
when distress and trouble
overwhelm you.

28 "Then they will call to me but I will
not answer;[z]
they will look for me but will not
find me,[a]

1:20 [u] Pr 8:1; 9:1-3,13-15
1:22 [v] Pr 8:5; 9:4,16
1:24 [w] Isa 65:12; 66:4; Jer 7:13; Zec 7:11
1:26 [x] Ps 2:4 [y] Pr 6:15; 10:24
1:28 [z] 1Sa 8:18; Isa 1:15; Jer 11:11; Mic 3:4 [a] Job 27:9; Pr 8:17; Eze 8:18; Zec 7:13

[a] 21 Septuagint; Hebrew / *at noisy street corners*

1:8–19 The literary setting for the instruction in chs. 1–9 is the homeschooling of a young man coming of age. If the prologue of vv. 1–7 presents the purposes of the book, the sections that immediately follow offer two vivid examples of wisdom instruction. The invitation to join violent men (vv. 8–19) and the first speech of personified Wisdom (vv. 20–33) are lessons in learning how to discern true speech from false.

✜ **1:8–19** This first lesson in wisdom asks each of us to think about the messages we hear and our resulting actions. Wisdom offers to guide us, as we will see in the following section.

1:20–23 The "simple" (or naïve, v. 4) can learn if they leave their simple and misguided ways behind, but if they love those ways and "hate knowledge" (v. 22), they become fools who hate wisdom and discipline (v. 7). Mockers' rejection is active; they scoff and ridicule. Wisdom's rebuke is correction, an offer of instruction that is personal and direct.

1:24–27 Those who ignored Wisdom's rebuke will only receive her mocking.

1:28–33 Rejection of Wisdom is revealed for what it really is: a rejection of the Lord. Wisdom stresses this rejection is not done out of ignorance but choice. The final call also promises safety to those who will listen and turn from their wicked ways.

✜ **1:20–33** Wisdom's warning and correction tell us the truth about human nature. In a word, we can be easily led astray. We also learn that we are at a new crossroads every day, as the path that leads away from Jesus beckons. Every day we must choose to follow him again and again.

29 since they hated knowledge
and did not choose to fear the
LORD.[b]
30 Since they would not accept my
advice
and spurned my rebuke,[c]
31 they will eat the fruit of their ways
and be filled with the fruit of their
schemes.[d]
32 For the waywardness of the simple
will kill them,
and the complacency of fools will
destroy them;[e]
33 but whoever listens to me will live in
safety[f]
and be at ease, without fear of
harm."[g]

Moral Benefits of Wisdom

2 My son, if you accept my words
and store up my commands
within you,
2 turning your ear to wisdom
and applying your heart to
understanding[h] —
3 indeed, if you call out for insight
and cry aloud for understanding,
4 and if you look for it as for silver
and search for it as for hidden
treasure,[i]
5 then you will understand the fear of
the LORD
and find the knowledge of God.[j]
6 For the LORD gives wisdom;[k]
from his mouth come knowledge
and understanding.
7 He holds success in store for the
upright,
he is a shield[l] to those whose walk
is blameless,[m]
8 for he guards the course of the just
and protects the way of his
faithful ones.[n]

1:29 [b] Job 21:14
1:30 [c] ver 25; Ps 81:11
1:31 [d] Job 4:8; Pr 14:14; Isa 3:11; Jer 6:19
1:32 [e] Jer 2:19
1:33 [f] Ps 25:12; Pr 3:23 [g] Ps 112:8
2:2 [h] Pr 22:17
2:4 [i] Job 3:21; Pr 3:14; Mt 13:44
2:5 [j] Pr 1:7
2:6 [k] 1Ki 3:9,12; Jas 1:5
2:7 [l] Pr 30:5-6 [m] Ps 84:11
2:8 [n] 1Sa 2:9; Ps 66:9
2:10 [o] Pr 14:33
2:11 [p] Pr 4:6; 6:22
2:13 [q] Pr 4:19; Jn 3:19
2:14 [r] Pr 10:23; Jer 11:15
2:15 [s] Ps 125:5 [t] Pr 21:8
2:16 [u] Pr 5:1-6; 6:20-29; 7:5-27
2:17 [v] Mal 2:14
2:18 [w] Pr 7:27
2:19 [x] Ecc 7:26

Pr 2:12 ❖ How can wisdom protect us from wicked influences?

9 Then you will understand what is
right and just
and fair — every good path.
10 For wisdom will enter your heart,[o]
and knowledge will be pleasant to
your soul.
11 Discretion will protect you,
and understanding will guard
you.[p]

12 Wisdom will save you from the ways
of wicked men,
from men whose words are
perverse,
13 who have left the straight paths
to walk in dark ways,[q]
14 who delight in doing wrong
and rejoice in the perverseness of
evil,[r]
15 whose paths are crooked[s]
and who are devious in their
ways.[t]

16 Wisdom will save you also from the
adulterous woman,[u]
from the wayward woman with
her seductive words,
17 who has left the partner of her youth
and ignored the covenant she
made before God.[a][v]
18 Surely her house leads down to
death
and her paths to the spirits of the
dead.[w]
19 None who go to her return
or attain the paths of life.[x]

20 Thus you will walk in the ways of the
good

[a] 17 Or *covenant of her God*

2:1–4 The three "if you" phrases portray this search for wisdom as strenuous. The lifelong rewards of the search make the work worthwhile.

2:5–8 The first reward of diligence is not wisdom, but God. The quest for wisdom brings one to "the fear of the LORD" (v. 5), the beginning of knowledge (cf. 1:7)—here set in parallel with "the knowledge of God" (2:5). Wisdom is a gift of God (v. 6), but what a contrast that gift makes with the desperate work of study just described!

Four descriptions of the traveler in vv. 7–8 put the responsibility on following God's path toward right living. The search for wisdom brings gifts of knowledge and the protection one needs to walk on the way.

2:9–11 "Wisdom" and "knowledge" are internalized in v. 10, entering the heart and forming character. Discretion and understanding, thus internalized, offer protection from misguided decision-making.

2:12–15 The danger lies in the men's invitation to join them in their evil. The six descriptions of their way stress the fact that they choose to walk in "dark ways" (v. 13), and that they love doing it.

2:16–19 The wayward or adulterous woman appears four times in Pr 1–9. Each description highlights the false and seductive nature of her words and the deadly end of following her way.

2:20–22 For ancient Israel, land was not considered a possession as much as a privilege. Its inhabitants lived as stewards, enjoying the fruits of obedient

and keep to the paths of the
righteous.
21 For the upright will live in the
land,[y]
and the blameless will remain
in it;
22 but the wicked will be cut off from
the land,[z]
and the unfaithful will be torn
from it.[a]

Wisdom Bestows Well-Being

3 My son, do not forget my teaching,[b]
but keep my commands in your
heart,
2 for they will prolong your life many
years[c]
and bring you peace and
prosperity.

3 Let love and faithfulness never leave
you;
bind them around your neck,
write them on the tablet of your
heart.[d]
4 Then you will win favor and a good
name
in the sight of God and man.[e]

5 Trust in the LORD[f] with all your
heart
and lean not on your own
understanding;
6 in all your ways submit to him,
and he will make your paths[g]
straight.[ah]

7 Do not be wise in your own eyes;[i]
fear the LORD and shun evil.[j]
8 This will bring health to your body[k]
and nourishment to your bones.[l]

2:21 [y] Ps 37:29
2:22 [z] Job 18:17; Ps 37:38 [a] Dt 28:63; Pr 10:30
3:1 [b] Pr 4:5
3:2 [c] Pr 4:10
3:3 [d] Ex 13:9; Pr 6:21; 7:3; 2Co 3:3
3:4 [e] 1Sa 2:26; Lk 2:52
3:5 [f] Ps 37:3,5
3:6 [g] 1Ch 28:9 [h] Pr 16:3; Isa 45:13
3:7 [i] Ro 12:16 [j] Job 1:1; Pr 16:6
3:8 [k] Pr 4:22 [l] Job 21:24

Pr 3:5 ❖ How do we tell when we are leaning "on [our] own understanding"? What are ways we can direct ourselves toward trusting in God in these moments?

9 Honor the LORD with your wealth,
with the firstfruits[m] of all your
crops;
10 then your barns will be filled[n] to
overflowing,
and your vats will brim over with
new wine.[o]

11 My son, do not despise the LORD's
discipline,[p]
and do not resent his rebuke,
12 because the LORD disciplines those
he loves,[q]
as a father the son he delights in.[br]

13 Blessed are those who find wisdom,
those who gain understanding,
14 for she is more profitable than silver
and yields better returns than
gold.[s]
15 She is more precious than rubies;[t]
nothing you desire can compare
with her.[u]
16 Long life is in her right hand;
in her left hand are riches and
honor.[v]
17 Her ways are pleasant ways,
and all her paths are peace.[w]
18 She is a tree of life[x] to those who take
hold of her;

3:9 [m] Ex 22:29; 23:19; Dt 26:1-15
3:10 [n] Dt 28:8 [o] Joel 2:24
3:11 [p] Job 5:17
3:12 [q] Pr 13:24; Rev 3:19 [r] Dt 8:5; Heb 12:5-6*
3:14 [s] Job 28:15; Pr 8:19; 16:16
3:15 [t] Job 28:18 [u] Pr 8:11
3:16 [v] Pr 8:18
3:17 [w] Pr 16:7; Mt 11:28-30
3:18 [x] Ge 2:9; Pr 11:30; Rev 2:7

[a] 6 Or *will direct your paths* [b] 12 Hebrew; Septuagint *loves, / and he chastens everyone he accepts as his child*

---

relationship with God. This passage hearkens back to the blessings and curses narrative in Dt 28.

2:1-22 Families must give this instruction careful attention since parents are the primary teachers. Education is taking place all the time in the home, and so it seems reasonable to ensure that teaching in biblical wisdom be included in the process.

3:1-10 The three benefits of long life, prosperity, and good reputation appear at the very start of the first instruction (vv. 1-4). These objects come as the result of personal effort in learning wisdom and choosing to live wisely.

Descriptions of a good name (v. 4), straight paths (v. 6), bodily health (v. 8), and overflowing barns and wine vats (v. 10) are all variations on the theme of the good life. It is better to think of these benefits as the typical (but not guaranteed) results of a certain way of living rather than rewards.

The heart gives direction to life by making the primary choice between arrogant self-reliance and trust. The heart that trusts, fears, and honors Yahweh knows that life can only be found in paths that lead toward him, not away.

3:11-12 The "discipline" spoken of here is primarily that of teaching and correction (v. 11). It is not equivalent to punishment. Verbal discipline both teaches and corrects.

3:13-18 Wisdom makes her second appearance in Proverbs. Two sets of images follow the blessing of the one who finds wisdom and gains understanding. The first set compares her worth to the world's greatest wealth (vv. 14-15). A second series complements the offer of long life and prosperity from v. 2. The "tree of life" (v. 18) in Proverbs appears as a source of good life and health rather than of eternal life.

those who hold her fast will be
blessed.

19 By wisdom the LORD laid the earth's
foundations,[y]
by understanding he set the
heavens[z] in place;
20 by his knowledge the watery depths
were divided,
and the clouds let drop the dew.

21 My son, do not let wisdom and
understanding out of your
sight,[a]
preserve sound judgment and
discretion;
22 they will be life for you,
an ornament to grace your
neck.[b]
23 Then you will go on your way in
safety,
and your foot will not stumble.[c]
24 When you lie down,[d] you will not be
afraid;
when you lie down, your sleep[e]
will be sweet.
25 Have no fear of sudden disaster
or of the ruin that overtakes the
wicked,
26 for the LORD will be at your side
and will keep your foot[f] from
being snared.

27 Do not withhold good from those to
whom it is due,
when it is in your power to act.
28 Do not say to your neighbor,
"Come back tomorrow and I'll give
it to you" —
when you already have it with
you.[g]
29 Do not plot harm against your
neighbor,
who lives trustfully near you.
30 Do not accuse anyone for no
reason —
when they have done you no
harm.

31 Do not envy[h] the violent
or choose any of their ways.

32 For the LORD detests the perverse[i]
but takes the upright into his
confidence.[j]
33 The LORD's curse[k] is on the house of
the wicked,[l]
but he blesses the home of the
righteous.[m]
34 He mocks proud mockers
but shows favor to the humble[n]
and oppressed.
35 The wise inherit honor,
but fools get only shame.

Get Wisdom at Any Cost

4 Listen, my sons,[o] to a father's
instruction;
pay attention and gain
understanding.
2 I give you sound learning,
so do not forsake my teaching.
3 For I too was a son to my father,
still tender, and cherished by my
mother.
4 Then he taught me, and he said
to me,
"Take hold of my words with all
your heart;
keep my commands, and you will
live.[p]

3:19 [y] Ps 104:24 [z] Pr 8:27-29
3:21 [a] Pr 4:20-22
3:22 [b] Pr 1:8-9
3:23 [c] Ps 37:24; Pr 4:12
3:24 [d] Lev 26:6; Ps 3:5 [e] Job 11:18
3:26 [f] 1Sa 2:9
3:28 [g] Lev 19:13; Dt 24:15
3:31 [h] Ps 37:1; Pr 24:1-2
3:32 [i] Pr 11:20 [j] Job 29:4; Ps 25:14
3:33 [k] Dt 11:28; Mal 2:2 [l] Zec 5:4 [m] Ps 1:3
3:34 [n] Jas 4:6*; 1Pe 5:5*
4:1 [o] Pr 1:8
4:4 [p] Pr 7:2

3:19–20 A depiction similar to Ge 1 makes a surprising appearance, almost as if the tree of life triggers thoughts about creation. The same wisdom dividing the waters above from the waters below also sends enough water to allow life to flourish. **3:21–35** Yahweh will keep the wise son safe; he will also keep the son's foot from being snared. Safe passage by day is paired with peaceful rest at night. Yahweh protects all the time. The assurance that God will be the son's confidence comes again in vv. 31–32, restating the disaster of the wicked in v. 25. **3:27–32** The list of five prohibitions against bad treatment of neighbors stands in symmetry with the five admonitions to honor Yahweh in vv. 1–10. The structure indicates that right relationship with God motivates right dealings with neighbors. **3:33–35** The final three verses continue the series of contrasts that began in v. 32, each comparing Yahweh's dealings with the righteous and the wicked. Verse 35 reverses the order of the previous contrasts so that the wise come first and fools come in dead last.

3:1–35 There are two commands in this chapter. The first, said in many ways, is "find wisdom," learning the teachings so we can learn to love. The second is "keep a close watch on your hand," not holding back or grasping what is not ours in the first place. These are close to Jesus' command to love God and one's neighbor (Mt 22:34–40).

4:1–9 The connection between "a father's instruction" (v. 1) and the teaching of past generations comes through the father's quotation of words he first heard long ago. They are short and direct: "Get wisdom, get understanding" (v. 5). Many generations have proved the worth of wisdom. The son can ask if experience has proven the father's claims. Sons can observe their parents to see whether what they say is true.

[5]Get wisdom,[q] get understanding;
do not forget my words or turn away from them.
[6]Do not forsake wisdom, and she will protect you;[r]
love her, and she will watch over you.
[7]The beginning of wisdom is this:
Get[a] wisdom.
Though it cost all[s] you have,[b] get understanding.[t]
[8]Cherish her, and she will exalt you;
embrace her, and she will honor you.[u]
[9]She will give you a garland to grace your head
and present you with a glorious crown."[v]

[10]Listen, my son, accept what I say,
and the years of your life will be many.[w]
[11]I instruct[x] you in the way of wisdom
and lead you along straight paths.
[12]When you walk, your steps will not be hampered;
when you run, you will not stumble.[y]
[13]Hold on to instruction, do not let it go;
guard it well, for it is your life.[z]
[14]Do not set foot on the path of the wicked
or walk in the way of evildoers.[a]
[15]Avoid it, do not travel on it;
turn from it and go on your way.
[16]For they cannot rest until they do evil;[b]
they are robbed of sleep till they make someone stumble.
[17]They eat the bread of wickedness
and drink the wine of violence.

[18]The path of the righteous[c] is like the morning sun,
shining ever brighter till the full light of day.[d]
[19]But the way of the wicked is like deep darkness;[e]
they do not know what makes them stumble.

[20]My son, pay attention to what I say;
turn your ear to my words.[f]
[21]Do not let them out of your sight,[g]
keep them within your heart;
[22]for they are life to those who find them
and health to one's whole body.[h]
[23]Above all else, guard your heart,
for everything you do flows from it.[i]
[24]Keep your mouth free of perversity;
keep corrupt talk far from your lips.
[25]Let your eyes look straight ahead;
fix your gaze directly before you.
[26]Give careful thought to the[c] paths for your feet[j]
and be steadfast in all your ways.
[27]Do not turn to the right or the left;[k]
keep your foot from evil.

4:5 [q]Pr 16:16
4:6 [r]2Th 2:10
4:7 [s]Mt 13:44-46 [t]Pr 23:23
4:8 [u]1Sa 2:30; Pr 3:18
4:9 [v]Pr 1:8-9
4:10 [w]Pr 3:2
4:11 [x]1Sa 12:23
4:12 [y]Job 18:7; Pr 3:23
4:13 [z]Pr 3:22
4:14 [a]Ps 1:1; Pr 1:15
4:16 [b]Ps 36:4; Mic 2:1
4:18 [c]Isa 26:7 [d]2Sa 23:4; Da 12:3; Mt 5:14; Php 2:15
4:19 [e]Job 18:5; Pr 2:13; Isa 59:9-10; Jn 12:35
4:20 [f]Pr 5:1
4:21 [g]Pr 3:21; 7:1-2
4:22 [h]Pr 3:8; 12:18
4:23 [i]Mt 12:34; Lk 6:45
4:26 [j]Heb 12:13*
4:27 [k]Dt 5:32; 28:14

[a] 7 Or *Wisdom is supreme; therefore get* [b] 7 Or *wisdom. / Whatever else you get* [c] 26 Or *Make level*

Pr 4:13 ❖ What can we do not only to gain wisdom but also to hold on to it through all the ups and downs of life?

4:10–19 The repeated words "path" and "way" contrast the clear and well-lit path of the righteous with the dark and treacherous way of the wicked. The imagery shifts to guarding a treasure, portraying a traveler who closely guards his money. In summary, this section of instruction contrasts the benefits of the righteous and the woes of the wicked.
4:20–27 An anatomy of righteousness follows, urging the son to keep the father's words before his eyes and in his heart so they can direct him. The heart that holds on to teaching is a source of life, which is maintained by accepting good teachings and keeping them close (vv. 20–21). In the ancient world, the heart served as the control center for the rest of human anatomy.
4:23–24 A guarded heart and wisdom-informed speech go together.
4:24–26 The next set of body images shows the outflow of a heart that is guarded: Perversity and corrupt talk are placed far from the mouth and lips, eyes look straight ahead, and the feet do not turn right or left from level and sure paths.

The ethical life is not only an inheritance, but also a life work. For this reason, the father appeals to the son to take his teaching with him on the journey.

✣ **4:1–27** The images of wisdom as a life partner, a path for life, and a guard are symbols of lifelong commitments that direct everyday choices. In the ancient world, a person heading out on a long journey on foot would typically choose a good traveling companion. They would choose a well-traveled and safe path and would keep their eyes on the goal and feet on that path. That's the analogy for our lives that the writer wants us to see here.

Warning Against Adultery

5 My son, pay attention to my wisdom,
turn your ear to my words[l] of insight,
2 that you may maintain discretion
and your lips may preserve knowledge.
3 For the lips of the adulterous woman drip honey,
and her speech is smoother than oil;[m]
4 but in the end she is bitter as gall,[n]
sharp as a double-edged sword.
5 Her feet go down to death;
her steps lead straight to the grave.[o]
6 She gives no thought to the way of life;
her paths wander aimlessly, but she does not know it.[p]

7 Now then, my sons, listen[q] to me;
do not turn aside from what I say.
8 Keep to a path far from her,[r]
do not go near the door of her house,
9 lest you lose your honor to others
and your dignity[a] to one who is cruel,
10 lest strangers feast on your wealth
and your toil enrich the house of another.
11 At the end of your life you will groan,
when your flesh and body are spent.
12 You will say, "How I hated discipline!
How my heart spurned correction![s]
13 I would not obey my teachers
or turn my ear to my instructors.
14 And I was soon in serious trouble
in the assembly of God's people."

15 Drink water from your own cistern,
running water from your own well.
16 Should your springs overflow in the streets,
your streams of water in the public squares?
17 Let them be yours alone,
never to be shared with strangers.
18 May your fountain[t] be blessed,
and may you rejoice in the wife of your youth.[u]
19 A loving doe, a graceful deer[v]—
may her breasts satisfy you always,
may you ever be intoxicated with her love.
20 Why, my son, be intoxicated with another man's wife?
Why embrace the bosom of a wayward woman?

21 For your ways are in full view[w] of the LORD,
and he examines all your paths.[x]
22 The evil deeds of the wicked ensnare them;[y]
the cords of their sins hold them fast.[z]
23 For lack of discipline they will die,[a]
led astray by their own great folly.

5:1 [l] Pr 4:20; 22:17
5:3 [m] Ps 55:21; Pr 2:16; 7:5
5:4 [n] Ecc 7:26
5:5 [o] Pr 7:26-27
5:6 [p] Pr 30:20
5:7 [q] Pr 7:24
5:8 [r] Pr 7:1-27
5:12 [s] Pr 1:29; 12:1
5:18 [t] SS 4:12-15 [u] Ecc 9:9; Mal 2:14
5:19 [v] SS 2:9; 4:5
5:21 [w] Ps 119:168; Hos 7:2 [x] Job 14:16; Job 31:4; 34:21; Pr 15:3; Jer 16:17; 32:19; Heb 4:13
5:22 [y] Ps 9:16 [z] Nu 32:23; Ps 7:15-16; Pr 1:31-32
5:23 [a] Job 4:21; 36:12

Pr 5:21 ❖ Is God's omnipresence comforting or threatening? Why?

[a] 9 Or *years*

5:1–6 Years of single-minded faithfulness can be instantly compromised by adultery. The principal contrast is between the deceptive lips (v. 3) of the woman and the lips (v. 2) of the young man, which are tasked to preserve knowledge and wisdom. She represents the folly of adultery and all that is foreign to the way of wisdom.
5:7–14 The son is told to make his path *far* from the woman. The admonitions in vv. 9–14 are all negative. "Death" (vv. 5–6) is here defined as loss of strength, years, substance, and reputation, the reverse of wisdom's benefits of long life, riches, and honor.
5:11–14 The teacher fast-forwards to the end of the son's life. He tells the young man he "will groan" (v. 11). Perhaps the most potent source of regret is the shame that comes to light in the last few words of v. 14.
5:15–23 What do these various symbols of water and drinking stand for? The suggestions made by interpreters include the pleasures of physical love, the production of offspring, the squandered seed that does not produce offspring, or the wife herself. The verses direct the son to have physical relations with his wife alone. To take one's intimacy to strangers is to risk losing all to strangers; to drink from one's own well is to keep all that is one's own, including one's life.

✥ **5:1–23** The portrayal of adultery in this chapter highlights the lies that come before it happens and the losses that follow. It is no accident that the description of the other woman centers on her words, not her beauty, because she represents the lie that fleeting sexual pleasure can be corrupted in ways for which it was never designed.

Warnings Against Folly

6 My son, if you have put up security
for your neighbor,[b]
if you have shaken hands in
pledge[c] for a stranger,
2 you have been trapped by what you
said,
ensnared by the words of your
mouth.
3 So do this, my son, to free yourself,
since you have fallen into your
neighbor's hands:
Go — to the point of exhaustion —[a]
and give your neighbor no rest!
4 Allow no sleep to your eyes,
no slumber to your eyelids.[d]
5 Free yourself, like a gazelle from the
hand of the hunter,
like a bird from the snare of the
fowler.[e]

6 Go to the ant, you sluggard;[f]
consider its ways and be wise!
7 It has no commander,
no overseer or ruler,
8 yet it stores its provisions in summer
and gathers its food at harvest.[g]

9 How long will you lie there, you
sluggard?[h]
When will you get up from your
sleep?
10 A little sleep, a little slumber,
a little folding of the hands to
rest[i] —
11 and poverty[j] will come on you like a
thief
and scarcity like an armed man.

6:1 [b] Pr 17:18 [c] Pr 11:15; 22:26-27
6:4 [d] Ps 132:4
6:5 [e] Ps 91:3
6:6 [f] Pr 20:4
6:8 [g] Pr 10:4
6:9 [h] Pr 24:30-34
6:10 [i] Pr 24:33
6:11 [j] Pr 24:30-34

Pr 6:6-8 ❖ Where can we find or have we found lessons for wise living from the natural world?

12 A troublemaker and a villain,
who goes about with a corrupt
mouth,
13 who winks maliciously with his
eye,[k]
signals with his feet
and motions with his fingers,
14 who plots evil[l] with deceit in his
heart —
he always stirs up conflict.[m]
15 Therefore disaster will overtake him
in an instant;
he will suddenly be destroyed —
without remedy.[n]

16 There are six things the LORD hates,
seven that are detestable to him:
17 haughty eyes,
a lying tongue,[o]
hands that shed innocent blood,[p]
18 a heart that devises wicked schemes,
feet that are quick to rush into
evil,[q]
19 a false witness[r] who pours out lies
and a person who stirs up
conflict in the community.[s]

Warning Against Adultery

20 My son, keep your father's command
and do not forsake your mother's
teaching.[t]

6:13 [k] Ps 35:19
6:14 [l] Mic 2:1 [m] ver 16-19
6:15 [n] 2Ch 36:16
6:17 [o] Ps 120:2; Pr 12:22 [p] Dt 19:10; Isa 1:15; 59:7
6:18 [q] Ge 6:5
6:19 [r] Ps 27:12 [s] ver 12-15
6:20 [t] Pr 1:8

[a] 3 Or *Go and humble yourself,*

6:1–5 The teacher speaks against agreeing to become the guarantee of security for someone else's loan. Each mention of this practice in Proverbs warns against getting involved.

6:6–11 Having just used the analogy of the trapped bird (v. 5), this second warning depicts the ant's foresight and hard work (v. 6). Analogies taken from the animal kingdom were common in the ancient Near East.

The sluggard exemplifies folly (19:15; 21:24–26; 26:12–16), particularly in matters of food production. The example of the ant's diligence and planning challenges the idea of avoiding one's duties and responsibilities. It urges the young man to do all he can to prevent being caught in the position of needing a loan and a guarantor.

6:12–15 Mouth, eye, feet, and fingers are all used to secretly communicate false and damaging messages. They are outward expressions of internal plotting and deceit (v. 14). Disaster will come suddenly, making its appearance more frightening (v. 15).

6:16–19 The numerical pattern places emphasis on the final statement. The last two items in the list are not body parts but rather persons recognized by their actions: the "false witness" and the "person who stirs up conflict" (v. 19). Thus, the climax to this section intensifies the description of the scoundrel in vv. 12–15.

6:20–35 No one who touches another man's wife will go unpunished. The commands and corrections are likened to a lamp that keeps feet from stumbling in the dark and allows the traveler to stay on a path to life (v. 23).

6:1–35 The teachers of Proverbs see that both ill-advised pledges and laziness are forms of shirking responsibility for one's self and livelihood. Their message is deceptively simple: Take responsibility for what is yours, and do not take responsibility for what is not. The warning against pledges tells us to avoid bad commitments. The picture of the sluggard tells us to be proactive and keep commitments that are good. Godly wisdom helps us know which is which. The problem facing many Christians today is not idleness but overcommitment.

21 Bind them always on your heart;
fasten them around your neck.[u]
22 When you walk, they will guide you;
when you sleep, they will watch
over you;
when you awake, they will speak
to you.
23 For this command is a lamp,
this teaching is a light,[v]
and correction and instruction
are the way to life,
24 keeping you from your neighbor's
wife,
from the smooth talk of a
wayward woman.[w]

25 Do not lust in your heart after her
beauty
or let her captivate you with her
eyes.

26 For a prostitute can be had for a loaf
of bread,
but another man's wife preys on
your very life.[x]
27 Can a man scoop fire into his lap
without his clothes being burned?
28 Can a man walk on hot coals
without his feet being scorched?
29 So is he who sleeps[y] with another
man's wife;[z]
no one who touches her will go
unpunished.

30 People do not despise a thief if he
steals
to satisfy his hunger when he is
starving.
31 Yet if he is caught, he must pay
sevenfold,[a]
though it costs him all the wealth
of his house.
32 But a man who commits adultery[b]
has no sense;[c]
whoever does so destroys
himself.
33 Blows and disgrace are his lot,
and his shame will never[d] be
wiped away.
34 For jealousy[e] arouses a husband's
fury,[f]
and he will show no mercy when
he takes revenge.
35 He will not accept any compensation;
he will refuse a bribe, however
great it is.[g]

Warning Against the Adulterous Woman

7 My son,[h] keep my words
and store up my commands
within you.
2 Keep my commands and you will
live;[i]
guard my teachings as the apple
of your eye.
3 Bind them on your fingers;
write them on the tablet of your
heart.[j]
4 Say to wisdom, "You are my sister,"
and to insight, "You are my
relative."
5 They will keep you from the
adulterous woman,
from the wayward woman with
her seductive words.[k]

6 At the window of my house
I looked down through the lattice.
7 I saw among the simple,
I noticed among the young men,
a youth who had no sense.[l]
8 He was going down the street near
her corner,
walking along in the direction of
her house
9 at twilight,[m] as the day was fading,
as the dark of night set in.

10 Then out came a woman to meet
him,
dressed like a prostitute and with
crafty intent.
11 (She is unruly[n] and defiant,
her feet never stay at home;
12 now in the street, now in the
squares,
at every corner she lurks.)[o]

6:21 [u] Pr 3:3; 7:1-3
6:23 [v] Ps 19:8; 119:105
6:24 [w] Pr 2:16; 7:5
6:26 [x] Pr 7:22-23; 29:3
6:29 [y] Ex 20:14 [z] Pr 2:16-19; 5:8
6:31 [a] Ex 22:1-14
6:32 [b] Ex 20:14 [c] Pr 7:7; 9:4,16
6:33 [d] Pr 5:9-14
6:34 [e] Nu 5:14 [f] Ge 34:7
6:35 [g] Job 31:9-11; SS 8:7
7:1 [h] Pr 1:8; 2:1
7:2 [i] Pr 4:4
7:3 [j] Dt 6:8; Pr 3:3
7:5 [k] ver 21; Job 31:9; Pr 2:16; 6:24
7:7 [l] Pr 1:22; 6:32
7:9 [m] Job 24:15
7:11 [n] Pr 9:13; 1Ti 5:13
7:12 [o] Pr 8:1-36; 23:26-28

7:1–5 The whole person—eye, hand, and heart—is to be dedicated to learning. Keeping the teachings will keep the young man from the other woman and her seductive words (vv. 2, 5).
7:6–9 Watching those who are passing by, the speaker notes that among the "simple" and "young men" is one who "had no sense" (v. 7), a preview of the way the story will unfold.
7:10–20 A woman is heading in the direction of the young man to meet him. Before we hear her, we see her. She is "dressed like a prostitute" (v. 10): Her attire signals her intent. Her brazen face is literally made strong and hard as she pursues her prey.

Three enticements follow: The sacrifices offer the delicacy of meat (v. 14); the bed offers the pleasures of love (vv. 16–17); the husband *not* at home promises a sense of security (vv. 19–20). Having touched his lips with a kiss, all her other seductions come from her words. What the young man does not know is that these words are the bait of a trap.

13 She took hold of him[p] and kissed
him
and with a brazen face she said:[q]

14 "Today I fulfilled my vows,
and I have food from my
fellowship offering[r] at home.
15 So I came out to meet you;
I looked for you and have found
you!
16 I have covered my bed
with colored linens from Egypt.
17 I have perfumed my bed[s]
with myrrh,[t] aloes and
cinnamon.
18 Come, let's drink deeply of love till
morning;
let's enjoy ourselves with love![u]
19 My husband is not at home;
he has gone on a long journey.
20 He took his purse filled with money
and will not be home till full
moon."

21 With persuasive words she led him
astray;
she seduced him with her smooth
talk.[v]
22 All at once he followed her
like an ox going to the slaughter,
like a deer[a] stepping into a noose[b][w]
23 till an arrow pierces[x] his liver,
like a bird darting into a snare,
little knowing it will cost him his
life.[y]

24 Now then, my sons, listen[z] to me;
pay attention to what I say.
25 Do not let your heart turn to her
ways
or stray into her paths.[a]
26 Many are the victims she has
brought down;
her slain are a mighty throng.

7:13 [p] Ge 39:12 [q] Pr 1:20
7:14 [r] Lev 7:11-18
7:17 [s] Est 1:6; Isa 57:7; Eze 23:41; Am 6:4 [t] Ge 37:25
7:18 [u] Ge 39:7
7:21 [v] Pr 5:3
7:22 [w] Job 18:10
7:23 [x] Job 15:22; 16:13 [y] Pr 6:26; Ecc 7:26; 9:12
7:24 [z] Pr 1:8-9; 5:7; 8:32
7:25 [a] Pr 5:7-8
7:27 [b] Pr 2:18; 5:5; 9:18; Rev 22:15
8:1 [c] Pr 1:20; 9:3
8:3 [d] Job 29:7
8:5 [e] Pr 1:22 [f] Pr 1:4
8:7 [g] Ps 37:30; Jn 8:14

Pr 7:24–27 ❖ What temptations that initially seem alluring ultimately lead to misery and death?

27 Her house is a highway to the grave,
leading down to the chambers of
death.[b]

Wisdom's Call

8 Does not wisdom call out?[c]
Does not understanding raise her
voice?
2 At the highest point along the way,
where the paths meet, she takes
her stand;
3 beside the gate leading into the city,
at the entrance, she cries aloud:[d]
4 "To you, O people, I call out;
I raise my voice to all mankind.
5 You who are simple,[e] gain
prudence;[f]
you who are foolish, set your
hearts on it.[c]
6 Listen, for I have trustworthy things
to say;
I open my lips to speak what is
right.
7 My mouth speaks what is true,[g]
for my lips detest wickedness.
8 All the words of my mouth are just;
none of them is crooked or
perverse.
9 To the discerning all of them are
right;
they are upright to those who
have found knowledge.
10 Choose my instruction instead of
silver,

[a] *22* Syriac (see also Septuagint); Hebrew *fool*
[b] *22* The meaning of the Hebrew for this line is uncertain. [c] *5* Septuagint; Hebrew *foolish, instruct your minds*

7:21–23 "With persuasive words she led him astray" (v. 21). The persuasive words are literally "much teaching," which can indicate either taking or receiving teaching. These persuasive words and false teaching lead the young man astray to his death.
7:24–27 The final image the parental teachers wish to leave in their son's mind is that of the highway to the "grave" (v. 27). The woman's house and its awaiting pleasures seem so alluring, yet it becomes a home for the dead.

✣ **7:1–27** It is appropriate to use discretion in speaking about matters of sexual behavior, but our embarrassment should never promote silence. We must help young people and adults understand what Proverbs teaches about sexual desire and the need for faithfulness in life with their future spouses.

8:1–3 Wisdom calls out like a street preacher, seeking hearers and followers. Her words contribute not only to our understanding of creation but also to our understanding of the Word, who was with God in the beginning (Jn 1:1).
8:4–21 The speech of Wisdom in ch. 8 stands alone as a work of art. It also provides a strategic answer to all that has come to the reader's attention since her last appearance. Unlike the wayward woman, Wisdom offers good teaching in vv. 1–21. (1) Wisdom speaks to all humankind (vv. 1–5); (2) Wisdom speaks what is noble and precious (vv. 6–11); (3) Wisdom gives righteous

knowledge rather than choice
gold,[h]
11 for wisdom is more precious[i] than
rubies,
and nothing you desire can
compare with her.[j]

12 "I, wisdom, dwell together with
prudence;
I possess knowledge and
discretion.[k]
13 To fear the LORD is to hate evil;[l]
I hate[m] pride and arrogance,
evil behavior and perverse speech.
14 Counsel and sound judgment are
mine;
I have insight, I have power.[n]
15 By me kings reign
and rulers[o] issue decrees that are
just;
16 by me princes govern,
and nobles — all who rule on
earth.[a]
17 I love those who love me,[p]
and those who seek me find me.[q]
18 With me are riches and honor,[r]
enduring wealth and prosperity.[s]
19 My fruit is better than fine gold;
what I yield surpasses choice
silver.[t]
20 I walk in the way of righteousness,
along the paths of justice,
21 bestowing a rich inheritance on
those who love me
and making their treasuries full.[u]

22 "The LORD brought me forth as the
first of his works,[b,c]
before his deeds of old;
23 I was formed long ages ago,
at the very beginning, when the
world came to be.
24 When there were no watery depths, I
was given birth,
when there were no springs
overflowing with water;[v]
25 before the mountains were settled in
place,
before the hills, I was given birth,[w]
26 before he made the world or its
fields
or any of the dust of the earth.[x]
27 I was there when he set the heavens
in place,[y]
when he marked out the horizon
on the face of the deep,
28 when he established the clouds
above
and fixed securely the fountains
of the deep,
29 when he gave the sea its boundary[z]
so the waters would not overstep
his command,[a]
and when he marked out the
foundations of the earth.[b]
30 Then I was constantly[d] at his side.[c]
I was filled with delight day after
day,

8:10 [h] Pr 3:14-15
8:11 [i] Job 28:17-19 [j] Pr 3:13-15
8:12 [k] Pr 1:4
8:13 [l] Pr 16:6 [m] Jer 44:4
8:14 [n] Pr 21:22; Ecc 7:19
8:15 [o] Da 2:21; Ro 13:1
8:17 [p] 1Sa 2:30; Ps 91:14; Jn 14:21-24 [q] Pr 1:28; Jas 1:5
8:18 [r] Pr 3:16 [s] Dt 8:18; Mt 6:33
8:19 [t] Pr 3:13-14; 10:20
8:21 [u] Pr 24:4
8:24 [v] Ge 7:11
8:25 [w] Job 15:7
8:26 [x] Ps 90:2
8:27 [y] Pr 3:19
8:29 [z] Ge 1:9; Job 38:10; Ps 16:6 [a] Ps 104:9 [b] Job 38:5
8:30 [c] Jn 1:1-3

Pr 8:10-11 ❖ Do our lives show that we value wisdom more highly than wealth? Why or why not?

[a] 16 Some Hebrew manuscripts and Septuagint; other Hebrew manuscripts *all righteous rulers* [b] 22 Or *way*; or *dominion* [c] 22 Or *The LORD possessed me at the beginning of his work*; or *The LORD brought me forth at the beginning of his work* [d] 30 Or *was the artisan*; or *was a little child*

counsel to rulers (vv. 12–16); (4) Wisdom gives love, honor, and wealth to those who love her (vv. 17–21).
8:22–36 Even the most casual reader will notice a shift in topic that marks the second half of Wisdom's speech in v. 22. (1) It is the only verse in the whole speech to begin with "the LORD," who is the main actor in all that follows. Wisdom is happy to say that only *she was there* when Yahweh made the heavens and the earth. (2) Following v. 22, Wisdom takes her listeners back to the dawn of creation to claim that she was a witness to God's great work. In asserting that she was there first, Wisdom continues to establish her authority to speak on God's behalf.

Wisdom speaks about her role in the founding and administration of the world *so that* she can make a claim that sounds like Jesus' words: "No one comes to the Father except through me" (Jn 14:6).

The second half of Wisdom's speech in vv. 22–36 is organized chronologically: (1) Wisdom was there *before* anything else (vv. 22–26); (2) Wisdom was present *when* the orders of creation were set in place (vv. 27–31); (3) Wisdom is *now* the one to whom we must listen (vv. 32–36).

This structure highlights the authority of her ways and words (vv. 32–33). To ignore them is to hate them, and to hate her is to love death (v. 36). Both chs. 7 and 8 end with the word "death," a bitter frame surrounding the images of creation and life.

8:1-36 Americans who have become cynical after learning that their presidents and other government officials have lied about war, wiretapping, and womanizing now listen with a critical ear. They will not tolerate speech that distorts or traffics in half-truths, presenting only what serves the speaker's purposes. Therefore, righteous speech is ethical; it speaks the truth out of concern for others and rejects self-serving distortions.

rejoicing always in his presence,
31 rejoicing in his whole world
and delighting in mankind.[d]

32 "Now then, my children, listen to me;
blessed are[e] those who keep my ways.[f]
33 Listen to my instruction and be wise;
do not disregard it.
34 Blessed are those who listen[g] to me,
watching daily at my doors,
waiting at my doorway.
35 For those who find me[h] find life
and receive favor from the LORD.[i]
36 But those who fail to find me harm themselves;[j]
all who hate me love death."

Invitations of Wisdom and Folly

9 Wisdom has built[k] her house;
she has set up[a] its seven pillars.
2 She has prepared her meat and mixed her wine;
she has also set her table.[l]
3 She has sent out her servants, and she calls[m]
from the highest point of the city,[n]
4 "Let all who are simple come to my house!"
To those who have no sense[o] she says,
5 "Come, eat my food
and drink the wine I have mixed.[p]
6 Leave your simple ways and you will live;[q]
walk in the way of insight."

7 Whoever corrects a mocker invites insults;
whoever rebukes the wicked incurs abuse.[r]

8:31 [d] Ps 16:3; 104:1-30
8:32 [e] Lk 11:28 [f] Ps 119:1-2
8:34 [g] Pr 3:13,18
8:35 [h] Pr 3:13-18 [i] Pr 12:2
8:36 [j] Pr 15:32
9:1 [k] Eph 2:20-22; 1Pe 2:5
9:2 [l] Lk 14:16-23
9:3 [m] Pr 8:1-3 [n] ver 14
9:4 [o] Pr 6:32
9:5 [p] Isa 55:1
9:6 [q] Pr 8:35
9:7 [r] Pr 23:9

Pr 9:12 ❖ How is godly wisdom its own reward?

8 Do not rebuke mockers[s] or they will hate you;
rebuke the wise and they will love you.[t]
9 Instruct the wise and they will be wiser still;
teach the righteous and they will add to their learning.[u]

10 The fear of the LORD[v] is the beginning of wisdom,
and knowledge of the Holy One is understanding.
11 For through wisdom[b] your days will be many,
and years will be added to your life.[w]
12 If you are wise, your wisdom will reward you;
if you are a mocker, you alone will suffer.

13 Folly is an unruly woman;[x]
she is simple and knows nothing.[y]
14 She sits at the door of her house,
on a seat at the highest point of the city,[z]
15 calling out to those who pass by,
who go straight on their way,
16 "Let all who are simple come to my house!"
To those who have no sense she says,
17 "Stolen water is sweet;
food eaten in secret is delicious!"[a]

a *1* Septuagint, Syriac and Targum; Hebrew *has hewn out* *b* *11* Septuagint, Syriac and Targum; Hebrew *me*

9:8 [s] Pr 15:12 [t] Ps 141:5
9:9 [u] Pr 1:5,7
9:10 [v] Job 28:28; Pr 1:7
9:11 [w] Pr 3:16; 10:27
9:13 [x] Pr 7:11 [y] Pr 5:6
9:14 [z] ver 3
9:17 [a] Pr 20:17

9:1–6 The speaker sets the location of Wisdom's speech at the highest place in the city. From this visible and central location, she invites her hearers. Wisdom offers her teaching, symbolized in the lavish banquet. In contrast to the wayward woman of ch. 7, her meat and drink will bring life, not death. The number seven (v. 1) is often associated with seven days of creation and completion. If Wisdom has built her house, it is finished and it is good—nothing else is needed.

Wisdom's invitation means leaving simple ways behind and walking in the way of understanding.

9:7–12 This section appears to interrupt the contrast between the invitations of Wisdom and Folly. It begins with the responses of the mocker and the wise person (vv. 7–9) and ends with their rewards (vv. 11–12). In the central position, "the fear of the LORD" (v. 10) explains the different outcomes of each.

9:13–18 Whereas Wisdom is portrayed as hardworking and generous, Folly is loud and boisterous. Just as Wisdom calls from the highest places, Folly takes a seat at the high places and calls to those who pass by. She calls away those who want to walk a straight path.

✣ **9:1–18** Knowing the fear of the Lord helps us to discern good influences from bad. Wisdom recognizes that we're impacted by both positive and negative influences, but instead of attempting to shut negative messages out, she tries to help the reader learn to discern and decide which path to follow.

18 But little do they know that the dead
are there,
that her guests are deep in the
realm of the dead.[b]

Proverbs of Solomon

10 The proverbs of Solomon:[c]

A wise son brings joy to his father,[d]
but a foolish son brings grief to
his mother.

2 Ill-gotten treasures have no lasting
value,[e]
but righteousness delivers from
death.[f]

3 The LORD does not let the righteous
go hungry,[g]
but he thwarts the craving of the
wicked.

4 Lazy hands make for poverty,[h]
but diligent hands bring wealth.[i]

5 He who gathers crops in summer is a
prudent son,
but he who sleeps during harvest
is a disgraceful son.

6 Blessings crown the head of the
righteous,
but violence overwhelms the
mouth of the wicked.[a][j]

7 The name of the righteous[k] is used
in blessings,[b]
but the name of the wicked[l] will
rot.[m]

8 The wise in heart accept
commands,
but a chattering fool comes to
ruin.[n]

9:18 [b] Pr 2:18; 7:26-27
10:1 [c] Pr 1:1 [d] Pr 15:20; 29:3
10:2 [e] Pr 21:6 [f] Pr 11:4,19
10:3 [g] Mt 6:25-34
10:4 [h] Pr 19:15 [i] Pr 12:24; 13:4; 21:5
10:6 [j] ver 8,11,14
10:7 [k] Ps 112:6 [l] Ps 109:13 [m] Ps 9:6
10:8 [n] Mt 7:24-27
10:9 [o] Isa 33:15 [p] Ps 23:4 [q] Pr 28:18
10:10 [r] Ps 35:19
10:11 [s] Ps 37:30; Pr 13:12,14,19 [t] ver 6
10:12 [u] Pr 17:9; 1Co 13:4-7; 1Pe 4:8
10:13 [v] ver 31 [w] Pr 26:3
10:14 [x] Pr 18:6,7
10:15 [y] Pr 18:11 [z] Pr 19:7
10:16 [a] Pr 11:18-19
10:17 [b] Pr 6:23

Pr 10:19 ❖ Why is controlling our speech such an important part of wisdom and godliness (see Jas 3:8–10)?

9 Whoever walks in integrity[o] walks
securely,[p]
but whoever takes crooked paths
will be found out.[q]

10 Whoever winks maliciously[r] causes
grief,
and a chattering fool comes to
ruin.

11 The mouth of the righteous is a
fountain of life,[s]
but the mouth of the wicked
conceals violence.[t]

12 Hatred stirs up conflict,
but love covers over all wrongs.[u]

13 Wisdom is found on the lips of the
discerning,[v]
but a rod is for the back of one
who has no sense.[w]

14 The wise store up knowledge,
but the mouth of a fool invites
ruin.[x]

15 The wealth of the rich is their
fortified city,[y]
but poverty is the ruin of the
poor.[z]

16 The wages of the righteous is life,
but the earnings of the wicked are
sin and death.[a]

17 Whoever heeds discipline shows the
way to life,[b]

[a] 6 Or *righteous, / but the mouth of the wicked conceals violence* [b] 7 See Gen. 48:20.

10:1 The intended contrast is between the honor or shame that comes to both parents based on their son's choices.
10:2 For anyone who takes moral shortcuts in acquiring wealth, their riches will not offer security.
10:3 Desire brings life or death, depending on the intention that guides it.
10:4 This is not a promise God must fulfill but a description of what generally happens.
10:5 Proactivity and hard work brings reward; laziness brings shame.
10:6 This is another example of a general principle that can be applied to life.
10:7 Like the body, reputations can putrefy.
10:8 The wise are silent and learn. The fool is too busy prattling to learn what will prevent ruin.
10:9 This contrast warns against loss of reputation, not the physical danger that a reader might expect.
10:10 This saying presents a twofold picture of wickedness.
10:11 Righteous speech refreshes and maintains life.
10:12 Hatred stirs up; love smooths over.
10:13 There are two contrasts, the first between the wisdom that is found on the lips and the punishment that falls on the back, the second between the person who has discernment and the one who lacks judgment.
10:14 The wise know when to share knowledge and when to keep it in reserve; fools, lacking discretion, speak words that will come back to harm them.
10:15 One must store knowledge for protection.
10:16 Only the wages of righteousness can give final security.
10:17 The contrast with "life" in v. 17 is similar to that in v. 16; one expects to read "death" but instead finds wandering or erring, a kind of "sin."

but whoever ignores correction
leads others astray.

18 Whoever conceals hatred with lying
lips
and spreads slander is a fool.

19 Sin is not ended by multiplying
words,
but the prudent hold their
tongues.[c]

20 The tongue of the righteous is
choice silver,
but the heart of the wicked is of
little value.

21 The lips of the righteous nourish
many,
but fools die for lack of sense.[d]

22 The blessing of the LORD brings
wealth,[e]
without painful toil for it.

23 A fool finds pleasure in wicked
schemes,[f]
but a person of understanding
delights in wisdom.

24 What the wicked dread[g] will
overtake them;
what the righteous desire will be
granted.[h]

25 When the storm has swept by, the
wicked are gone,
but the righteous stand firm[i]
forever.[j]

26 As vinegar to the teeth and smoke to
the eyes,
so are sluggards to those who send
them.[k]

27 The fear of the LORD adds length to
life,[l]
but the years of the wicked are cut
short.[m]

28 The prospect of the righteous is joy,
but the hopes of the wicked come
to nothing.[n]

29 The way of the LORD is a refuge for
the blameless,
but it is the ruin of those who do
evil.[o]

30 The righteous will never be
uprooted,
but the wicked will not remain in
the land.[p]

31 From the mouth of the righteous
comes the fruit of wisdom,[q]
but a perverse tongue will be
silenced.

32 The lips of the righteous know what
finds favor,[r]
but the mouth of the wicked only
what is perverse.

11 The LORD detests dishonest
scales,[s]
but accurate weights find favor
with him.[t]

2 When pride comes, then comes
disgrace,[u]
but with humility comes
wisdom.[v]

10:19 [c] Pr 17:28; Ecc 5:3; Jas 1:19; 3:2-12
10:21 [d] Pr 5:22-23; Hos 4:1, 6,14
10:22 [e] Ge 24:35; Ps 37:22
10:23 [f] Pr 2:14; 15:21
10:24 [g] Isa 66:4 [h] Ps 145:17-19; Mt 5:6; 1Jn 5:14-15
10:25 [i] Ps 15:5 [j] Pr 12:3,7; Mt 7:24-27
10:26 [k] Pr 26:6
10:27 [l] Pr 9:10-11 [m] Job 15:32
10:28 [n] Job 8:13; Pr 11:7
10:29 [o] Pr 21:15
10:30 [p] Ps 37:9, 28-29; Pr 2:20-22
10:31 [q] Ps 37:30
10:32 [r] Ecc 10:12
11:1 [s] Lev 19:36; Dt 25:13-16; Pr 20:10,23 [t] Pr 16:11
11:2 [u] Pr 16:18 [v] Pr 18:12; 29:23

10:18 The difference between hiding hatred and spreading it through slander is one of action, not intent; both deceptions can be destructive.
10:19 Words are like sheep; the more there are, the better the chances that some will go astray.
10:20 The contrast of worth ("choice silver" versus "little value") traces the outflow of the tongue to its source, the heart.
10:21 The wise speak in a way that benefits others; the fool speaks in a way that leads to his own ruin.
10:22 The blessing of Yahweh brings wealth that does not come with trouble.
10:23 The fool and wise person have different understandings of what brings pleasure.
10:24 Are you righteous? Are you wicked? Be careful what you wish for.
10:25 Read together, vv. 24 and 25 suggest that the righteous desire and are given long life.
10:26 The proverb reflects the difficulty of working with a sluggard.
10:27 The theme returns to the respective futures of the righteous and wicked, reminding the reader of v. 16.
10:28 The wicked fail to get what they desire (v. 28) and receive what they fear (v. 24).
10:29 Having considered the blessing and fear of Yahweh, the proverb now recommends the "way" of Yahweh.
10:30 The image is of the wicked being a plant pulled up by its roots.
10:31–32 This final proverb pair should be read together, since the second lines of both describe the tongue and speech.

10:1–32 The proverbs encourage the value of diligence. We are wise to review these verses with our children, giving them many examples from our own personal lives as to how these verses have applied to us. The teachings of this chapter encourage and model wise discussion.

11:1 Ancient merchants sometimes kept two sets of weighing stones, one for buying and one for selling. This verse speaks to baseline personal integrity.
11:2 Pride motivates those who believe they can abuse others and not be brought to account.

3 The integrity of the upright guides them,
but the unfaithful are destroyed by their duplicity.[w]

4 Wealth is worthless in the day of wrath,[x]
but righteousness delivers from death.[y]

5 The righteousness of the blameless makes their paths straight,
but the wicked are brought down by their own wickedness.[z]

6 The righteousness of the upright delivers them,
but the unfaithful are trapped by evil desires.

7 Hopes placed in mortals die with them;
all the promise of[a] their power comes to nothing.[a]

8 The righteous person is rescued from trouble,
and it falls on the wicked instead.[b]

9 With their mouths the godless destroy their neighbors,
but through knowledge the righteous escape.

10 When the righteous prosper, the city rejoices;[c]
when the wicked perish, there are shouts of joy.

11 Through the blessing of the upright a city is exalted,
but by the mouth of the wicked it is destroyed.[d]

11:3 [w] Pr 13:6
11:4 [x] Eze 7:19; Zep 1:18 [y] Ge 7:1; Pr 10:2
11:5 [z] Pr 5:21-23
11:7 [a] Pr 10:28
11:8 [b] Pr 21:18
11:10 [c] Pr 28:12
11:11 [d] Pr 29:8

Pr 11:4-10 ❖ How does righteousness benefit us during the course of our lives? How can we grow in righteousness?

12 Whoever derides their neighbor has no sense,[e]
but the one who has understanding holds their tongue.

13 A gossip betrays a confidence,[f]
but a trustworthy person keeps a secret.

14 For lack of guidance a nation falls,[g]
but victory is won through many advisers.[h]

15 Whoever puts up security[i] for a stranger will surely suffer,
but whoever refuses to shake hands in pledge is safe.

16 A kindhearted woman gains honor,[j]
but ruthless men gain only wealth.

17 Those who are kind benefit themselves,
but the cruel bring ruin on themselves.

18 A wicked person earns deceptive wages,
but the one who sows righteousness reaps a sure reward.[k]

11:12 [e] Pr 14:21
11:13 [f] Lev 19:16; Pr 20:19; 1Ti 5:13
11:14 [g] Pr 20:18 [h] Pr 15:22; 24:6
11:15 [i] Pr 6:1
11:16 [j] Pr 31:31
11:18 [k] Hos 10:12-13

[a] 7 Two Hebrew manuscripts; most Hebrew manuscripts, Vulgate, Syriac and Targum *When the wicked die, their hope perishes; / all they expected from*

11:3 This contrast imagines roads filled with dangers. One would be glad to have a wise guide in such situations.
11:4-10 The next seven verses present variations on the word for "righteousness" and its use in v. 4.
11:5 Verses 5–6 form a pair contrasting the fates of the righteous and the wicked.
11:6 Righteousness keeps its bearer safe and free while wickedness ensnares and destroys.
11:7 Because the wicked have no desire for wisdom, their hopes die with them.
11:8 The wicked bring their own trouble on themselves.
11:9 These next six proverbs are clustered around the theme of speech. We may not be protected from the verbal assaults of others, but we will be rescued from the backlash that uncontrolled speech brings on itself.
11:10 The sounds of rejoicing may come when outcomes are fitting; real-world experience tells us that too often they are not.
11:11 The life of the city is affected for better or worse by the character of its citizens.
11:12 The words of the wicked destroy by deriding others or by breaking confidence. The trustworthy person keeps silent.
11:13 This proverb applies to personal relationships and business practices.
11:14 Just as negative words can tear down, good counsel builds up and brings victory.
11:15 Admonition to neighbor love is qualified by this warning against getting involved with someone else's finances.
11:16 The kindheartedness of the woman wins her the favor of others; the term "only wealth" makes a value judgment on the ruthlessness or aggression of men.
11:17 Kindness and cruelty done to others turn back on the doer.
11:18 There is a wordplay on the Hebrew terms for "deceptive" in v. 18a and "reward" in v. 18b.

19 Truly the righteous attain life,
but whoever pursues evil finds death.

20 The LORD detests those whose hearts are perverse,
but he delights in those whose ways are blameless.[l]

21 Be sure of this: The wicked will not go unpunished,
but those who are righteous will go free.[m]

22 Like a gold ring in a pig's snout
is a beautiful woman who shows no discretion.

23 The desire of the righteous ends only in good,
but the hope of the wicked only in wrath.

24 One person gives freely, yet gains even more;
another withholds unduly, but comes to poverty.

25 A generous person will prosper;
whoever refreshes others will be refreshed.[n]

26 People curse the one who hoards grain,
but they pray God's blessing on the one who is willing to sell.

27 Whoever seeks good finds favor,
but evil comes to one who searches for it.[o]

28 Those who trust in their riches will fall,[p]
but the righteous will thrive like a green leaf.[q]

29 Whoever brings ruin on their family will inherit only wind,
and the fool will be servant to the wise.[r]

30 The fruit of the righteous is a tree of life,[s]
and the one who is wise saves lives.

31 If the righteous receive their due[t] on earth,
how much more the ungodly and the sinner!

12 Whoever loves discipline loves knowledge,
but whoever hates correction is stupid.[u]

2 Good people obtain favor from the LORD,
but he condemns those who devise wicked schemes.

3 No one can be established through wickedness,
but the righteous cannot be uprooted.[v]

4 A wife of noble character is her husband's crown,
but a disgraceful wife is like decay in his bones.[w]

11:20 [l] 1Ch 29:17; Ps 119:1; Pr 12:2, 22
11:21 [m] Pr 16:5
11:25 [n] Mt 5:7; 2Co 9:6-9
11:27 [o] Est 7:10; Ps 7:15-16
11:28 [p] Job 31:24-28; Ps 49:6; 52:7; Mk 10:25; 1Ti 6:17 [q] Ps 1:3; 92:12-14; Jer 17:8
11:29 [r] Pr 14:19
11:30 [s] Jas 5:20
11:31 [t] Pr 13:21; Jer 25:29; 1Pe 4:18
12:1 [u] Pr 9:7-9; 15:5,10,12,32
12:3 [v] Pr 10:25
12:4 [w] Pr 14:30

11:19 "Life" and "death" complete each line of this verse, which contrasts a person of true righteousness and one who pursues evil.
11:20 Like the dishonest scales of v. 1, perverse hearts are an abomination to the Lord.
11:21 The contrast is between sure punishment of the guilty and sure grace to the righteous.
11:22 This saying is less a put-down of beautiful and foolish women than it is of men who might prefer them.
11:23 This verse connects vv. 20–23, pitting good desires against wicked hope.
11:24 The theme of generosity versus withholding runs throughout this section.
11:25 The one who nurtures others will be nurtured in turn.
11:26 While honor is not the primary motivation for doing good, it is not discounted.
11:27 This verse compares two seekers: one who seeks good and finds goodwill, the other who pursues evil for others only to have it come to him.
11:28 Finding false security in possessions motivates evil behaviors.
11:29 The negative reward for evil even extends to one's family.
11:30 The wise promote life; they do not take it away.
11:31 A straightforward statement of just rewards summarizes the theme of the chapter and assures that Yahweh hates perversity and loves righteousness; therefore, rewards will be forthcoming.

✣ **11:1–31** Daily we are given countless opportunities to seek good instead of evil. In seeking good we are also seeking the kingdom of God and his righteousness (Mt 6:33).

12:1 This proverb contrasts loving discipline with hating correction.
12:2 Good people shape life according to unselfish values, while schemers only look to their own intentions.
12:3 Yahweh told Jeremiah he would pull up the roots of those who advance through wickedness (Jer 1:9–10).
12:4 The instruction of this proverb is to value character above beauty.

5 The plans of the righteous are just,
but the advice of the wicked is deceitful.

6 The words of the wicked lie in wait for blood,
but the speech of the upright rescues them.[x]

7 The wicked are overthrown and are no more,[y]
but the house of the righteous stands firm.[z]

8 A person is praised according to their prudence,
and one with a warped mind is despised.

9 Better to be a nobody and yet have a servant
than pretend to be somebody and have no food.

10 The righteous care for the needs of their animals,
but the kindest acts of the wicked are cruel.

11 Those who work their land will have abundant food,
but those who chase fantasies have no sense.[a]

12 The wicked desire the stronghold of evildoers,
but the root of the righteous endures.

13 Evildoers are trapped by their sinful talk,[b]
and so the innocent escape trouble.[c]

12:6 [x] Pr 14:3
12:7 [y] Ps 37:36 [z] Pr 10:25
12:11 [a] Pr 28:19
12:13 [b] Pr 18:7 [c] Pr 21:23; 2Pe 2:9

Pr 12:18 ❖ How can we bring healing to others through our words?

14 From the fruit of their lips people are filled with good things,[d]
and the work of their hands brings them reward.[e]

15 The way of fools seems right to them,[f]
but the wise listen to advice.

16 Fools show their annoyance at once,
but the prudent overlook an insult.[g]

17 An honest witness tells the truth,
but a false witness tells lies.[h]

18 The words of the reckless pierce like swords,[i]
but the tongue of the wise brings healing.[j]

19 Truthful lips endure forever,
but a lying tongue lasts only a moment.

20 Deceit is in the hearts of those who plot evil,
but those who promote peace have joy.

21 No harm overtakes the righteous,[k]
but the wicked have their fill of trouble.

22 The LORD detests lying lips,[l]
but he delights in people who are trustworthy.[m]

23 The prudent keep their knowledge to themselves,[n]
but a fool's heart blurts out folly.

12:14 [d] Pr 13:2; 15:23; 18:20 [e] Isa 3:10-11
12:15 [f] Pr 14:12; 16:2,25; Lk 18:11
12:16 [g] Pr 29:11
12:17 [h] Pr 14:5,25
12:18 [i] Ps 57:4 [j] Pr 15:4
12:21 [k] Ps 91:10
12:22 [l] Pr 6:17; Rev 22:15 [m] Pr 11:20
12:23 [n] Pr 10:14; 13:16

12:5 The contrast focuses attention on the intentions of persons.
12:6 The upright are delivered by the very means the wicked meant to do harm.
12:7 This verse echoes the theme of permanence introduced in v. 3.
12:8 This proverb reminds us of the importance of shame and honor as motivators for many cultures.
12:9 The "better . . . than" saying is a typical form of proverb.
12:10 This proverb hints toward hyperbole: Better to be the righteous person's horse than the wicked person's neighbor!
12:11 A proverb about the rewards of labor moves the imagery from the stable to the field.
12:12 This verse restates and summarizes the theme of the section.
12:13 "Oh, what a tangled web we weave, when we first practice to deceive" (Sir Walter Scott).
12:14 Just as speaking is a form of doing, so both hands and mouth can be put to purposes good or evil.
12:15 This first of two proverbs about fools contrasts two counselors.
12:16 The contrast in both vv. 15 and 16 is between the loud fool and the silent sage.
12:17 Sometimes an honest witness must counteract the lies of the false witness.
12:18 Words usually leave their mark for good or bad.
12:19 Lies build on a precarious branch. It sometimes takes time for truth to show itself strong.
12:20 The wise one absorbs what is heard so it can be offered to others and the joy shared.
12:21 The joy of peace brings freedom from fear.
12:22 That which Yahweh "detests" is an abomination.
12:23 This proverb provides a humorous explanation for why knowledge so often seems in short supply.

24 Diligent hands will rule,
but laziness ends in forced labor.[o]

25 Anxiety weighs down the heart,[p]
but a kind word cheers it up.

26 The righteous choose their friends carefully,
but the way of the wicked leads them astray.

27 The lazy do not roast[a] any game,
but the diligent feed on the riches of the hunt.

28 In the way of righteousness there is life;[q]
along that path is immortality.

13 A wise son heeds his father's instruction,
but a mocker does not respond to rebukes.[r]

2 From the fruit of their lips people enjoy good things,[s]
but the unfaithful have an appetite for violence.

3 Those who guard their lips[t] preserve their lives,[u]
but those who speak rashly will come to ruin.[v]

4 A sluggard's appetite is never filled,
but the desires of the diligent are fully satisfied.

5 The righteous hate what is false,
but the wicked make themselves a stench
and bring shame on themselves.

Pr 13:10 ❖ Why does pride lead to strife? How can we grow in humility?

6 Righteousness guards the person of integrity,
but wickedness overthrows the sinner.[w]

7 One person pretends to be rich, yet has nothing;
another pretends to be poor, yet has great wealth.[x]

8 A person's riches may ransom their life,
but the poor cannot respond to threatening rebukes.

9 The light of the righteous shines brightly,
but the lamp of the wicked is snuffed out.[y]

10 Where there is strife, there is pride,
but wisdom is found in those who take advice.

11 Dishonest money dwindles away,[z]
but whoever gathers money little by little makes it grow.

12 Hope deferred makes the heart sick,
but a longing fulfilled is a tree of life.

13 Whoever scorns instruction will pay for it,[a]

12:24 [o] Pr 10:4
12:25 [p] Pr 15:13; Isa 50:4
12:28 [q] Dt 30:15
13:1 [r] Pr 10:1
13:2 [s] Pr 12:14
13:3 [t] Jas 3:2 [u] Pr 21:23 [v] Pr 18:7, 20-21
13:6 [w] Pr 11:3, 5
13:7 [x] 2Co 6:10
13:9 [y] Job 18:5; Pr 4:18-19; 24:20
13:11 [z] Pr 10:2
13:13 [a] Nu 15:31; 2Ch 36:16

[a] *27* The meaning of the Hebrew for this word is uncertain.

12:24 Another take on the blessed life of one who refuses to be lazy.
12:25 Self-talk from an anxious heart is contrasted with the external word that brings joy.
12:26 The way of the wicked leads nowhere, and those who take it become lost.
12:27 Lazy people have nothing to give others, for they cannot even take care of themselves.
12:28 This last saying connects the themes of this chapter with the recurring motif of the two ways: life and death.

✣ **12:1–28** The proverbs of this chapter continue to encourage the reader to be open to instruction by reminding them that wisdom and folly will make themselves known. Neither remains hidden for long.

13:1 While responsibility to choose is set squarely on the learner, teaching is the parent's responsibility.
13:2–3 These sayings caution us to watch what our mouths put out as well as what they take in to satisfy our desires.
13:4 A proverb about the sluggard completes this cluster of sayings about appetite and desire.
13:5 The contrast pits falsehood against its result of disgrace.
13:6 This saying personifies righteousness as protector and wickedness as destroyer.
13:7 Riches are not as clear an indication of worth as we often believe.
13:8 Riches can get one out of trouble, but it is better to hear no threat of trouble at all.
13:9 The image of the lamp signifies a long and happy life.
13:10 Pride is here described as an unwillingness to listen and learn.
13:11 The first line can read "meaningless wealth" (alternate translation). The contrast with the second line suggests that it is wealth gained from no labor—perhaps by theft or speculation.
13:12 This proverb simply contrasts hope deferred and longing fulfilled, noting the effects of both.
13:13 The contrast between one who pays and one who is paid is in view here.

but whoever respects a command
is rewarded.

14 The teaching of the wise is a
fountain of life,[b]
turning a person from the snares
of death.[c]

15 Good judgment wins favor,
but the way of the unfaithful leads
to their destruction.[a]

16 All who are prudent act with[b]
knowledge,
but fools expose their folly.[d]

17 A wicked messenger falls into
trouble,
but a trustworthy envoy brings
healing.[e]

18 Whoever disregards discipline
comes to poverty and shame,
but whoever heeds correction is
honored.[f]

19 A longing fulfilled is sweet to the
soul,
but fools detest turning from evil.

20 Walk with the wise and become
wise,
for a companion of fools suffers
harm.[g]

21 Trouble pursues the sinner,
but the righteous[h] are rewarded
with good things.

22 A good person leaves an inheritance
for their children's children,
but a sinner's wealth is stored up
for the righteous.[i]

23 An unplowed field produces food for
the poor,
but injustice sweeps it away.

24 Whoever spares the rod hates their
children,
but the one who loves their
children is careful to
discipline them.[j]

25 The righteous eat to their hearts'
content,
but the stomach of the wicked
goes hungry.[k]

14 The wise woman builds her
house,[l]
but with her own hands the
foolish one tears hers down.

2 Whoever fears the LORD walks
uprightly,
but those who despise him are
devious in their ways.

3 A fool's mouth lashes out with
pride,
but the lips of the wise protect
them.[m]

4 Where there are no oxen, the
manger is empty,
but from the strength of an ox
come abundant harvests.

13:14 [b] Pr 10:11 [c] Pr 14:27
13:16 [d] Pr 12:23
13:17 [e] Pr 25:13
13:18 [f] Pr 15:5, 31-32
13:20 [g] Pr 15:31
13:21 [h] Ps 32:10
13:22 [i] Job 27:17; Ecc 2:26
13:24 [j] Pr 19:18; 22:15; 23:13-14; 29:15,17; Heb 12:7
13:25 [k] Ps 34:10; Pr 10:3
14:1 [l] Pr 24:3
14:3 [m] Pr 12:6

[a] *15* Septuagint and Syriac; the meaning of the Hebrew for this phrase is uncertain. [b] *16* Or *prudent protect themselves through*

13:14 The fountain of life is associated with righteous speech, the fear of Yahweh, and right understanding.
13:15 This saying compares "good judgment" with the actions of those who reject it.
13:16 Demonstration of learning, or lack of it, is at the heart of this proverb.
13:17 A person who sends someone into a conflict situation wants to send someone who will make it better, not worse.
13:18 The key word "discipline" appears, marking the beginning, middle, and end of this chapter.
13:19 Fools who refuse to turn from evil will not enjoy the sweetness of fulfilled desire; their actions will bear bitter fruit.
13:20 Fools refuse to turn from evil and fail to choose good company.
13:21 Fools and sinners not only find trouble; trouble seeks them.
13:22 The reward of v. 21 can be passed on to one's children and grandchildren.
13:23 God's blessings may favor the poor, but their gain can be taken by injustice.
13:24 Here the larger issue is one of instruction, not the means used to bring it about.
13:25 The contrast of this proverb suggests this hunger is a reward, but given what we have seen of the wicked and their undisciplined desires, it is a justified one.

13:1–25 The discipline of loving instruction makes the difference between "longing fulfilled" and "craving" that is not fulfilled. The benefits of the disciplined life are the legacy we leave to our children and grandchildren.

14:1 The sages speak here of our main direction in life.
14:2 The way of the wise contrasts with the fool who rejects Yahweh.
14:3 The contrast between a fool's "mouth" and a wise person's "lips" is linked to their rewards, punishment, or protection.
14:4 Invest in assets that bring a greater return. It costs money to keep an ox, but without investing in the ox, there is no harvest.

5 An honest witness does not deceive,
but a false witness pours out lies.[n]

6 The mocker seeks wisdom and finds none,
but knowledge comes easily to the discerning.

7 Stay away from a fool,
for you will not find knowledge on their lips.

8 The wisdom of the prudent is to give thought to their ways,
but the folly of fools is deception.[o]

9 Fools mock at making amends for sin,
but goodwill is found among the upright.

10 Each heart knows its own bitterness,
and no one else can share its joy.

11 The house of the wicked will be destroyed,
but the tent of the upright will flourish.[p]

12 There is a way that appears to be right,[q]
but in the end it leads to death.[r]

13 Even in laughter[s] the heart may ache,
and rejoicing may end in grief.

14 The faithless will be fully repaid for their ways,[t]
and the good rewarded for theirs.[u]

15 The simple believe anything,
but the prudent give thought to their steps.

16 The wise fear the LORD and shun evil,[v]
but a fool is hotheaded and yet feels secure.

17 A quick-tempered person does foolish things,[w]
and the one who devises evil schemes is hated.

18 The simple inherit folly,
but the prudent are crowned with knowledge.

19 Evildoers will bow down in the presence of the good,
and the wicked at the gates of the righteous.[x]

20 The poor are shunned even by their neighbors,
but the rich have many friends.[y]

21 It is a sin to despise one's neighbor,[z]
but blessed is the one who is kind to the needy.[a]

22 Do not those who plot evil go astray?
But those who plan what is good find[a] love and faithfulness.

14:5 [n] Pr 6:19; 12:17
14:8 [o] ver 24
14:11 [p] Pr 3:33; 12:7
14:12 [q] Pr 12:15 [r] Pr 16:25
14:13 [s] Ecc 2:2
14:14 [t] Pr 1:31 [u] Pr 12:14
14:16 [v] Pr 22:3
14:17 [w] ver 29
14:19 [x] Pr 11:29
14:20 [y] Pr 19:4,7
14:21 [z] Pr 11:12 [a] Ps 41:1; Pr 19:17

[a] 22 Or *show*

Pr 14:12 ❖ What are some of the "ways" that appear right but in fact lead to death? What lies does society peddle of this variety?

14:5 The false witness is a "lie breather" (alternate translation).
14:6 Knowledge comes quickly and easily to the one who has cultivated discernment.
14:7 If mockers have not found wisdom, neither will knowledge be found with the fool.
14:8 The contrast in this saying is between thoughtful consideration of the way one walks and deception.
14:9 The contrast here is between a scornful attitude toward reconciliation and a lifestyle that rarely needs it.
14:10 Even while our lives are shared with others, our deepest thoughts and feelings remain hidden. So we must be careful what we assume about other people.
14:11 The Hebrew word for "flourish" typically refers to plants that sprout or bud.
14:12 "Way" points to the choices that require foresight, while the "end" describes outcomes.
14:13 When read alongside v. 10, the first and second lines correspond—the first on the theme of inner hurt, the second on the word "joy."
14:14 The "faithless" are "those whose hearts have turned" (alternate translation).
14:15 These are the naive people that Wisdom tried so desperately to reach, but Folly was never far away.
14:16 Verses 16–17 are linked by images of hair-trigger temper and folly.
14:17 The comparison is between the impulsively foolish and premeditated evil, a product of scheming.
14:18 In both lines, the rewards not only correspond to the qualities of "folly" and prudence, they foster and nurture them.
14:19 The proverb offers hope to those who too often see the good bowing before the power of an evil person.
14:20 The main contrast is between the self-interested love shown to the rich and the selfless kindness shown to the poor.
14:21 The saying turns the focus away from the experience of the poor in v. 20 to the responsibility of those who help or fail them.
14:22 Those who plan evil are rewarded with going

23 All hard work brings a profit,
but mere talk leads only to poverty.

24 The wealth of the wise is their crown,
but the folly of fools yields folly.

25 A truthful witness saves lives,
but a false witness is deceitful.[b]

26 Whoever fears the LORD has a secure fortress,[c]
and for their children it will be a refuge.

27 The fear of the LORD is a fountain of life,
turning a person from the snares of death.[d]

28 A large population is a king's glory,
but without subjects a prince is ruined.

29 Whoever is patient has great understanding,
but one who is quick-tempered displays folly.[e]

30 A heart at peace gives life to the body,
but envy rots the bones.[f]

31 Whoever oppresses the poor shows contempt for their Maker,[g]
but whoever is kind to the needy honors God.

14:25 [b] ver 5
14:26 [c] Pr 18:10; 19:23; Isa 33:6
14:27 [d] Pr 13:14
14:29 [e] Ecc 7:8-9; Jas 1:19
14:30 [f] Pr 12:4
14:31 [g] Pr 17:5

32 When calamity comes, the wicked are brought down,[h]
but even in death the righteous seek refuge in God.[i]

33 Wisdom reposes in the heart of the discerning[j]
and even among fools she lets herself be known.[a]

34 Righteousness exalts a nation,[k]
but sin condemns any people.

35 A king delights in a wise servant,
but a shameful servant arouses his fury.[l]

15 A gentle answer turns away wrath,[m]
but a harsh word stirs up anger.

2 The tongue of the wise adorns knowledge,
but the mouth of the fool gushes folly.[n]

3 The eyes[o] of the LORD are everywhere,[p]
keeping watch on the wicked and the good.[q]

4 The soothing tongue is a tree of life,
but a perverse tongue crushes the spirit.

5 A fool spurns a parent's discipline,

14:32 [h] Pr 6:15 [i] Job 13:15; 2Ti 4:18
14:33 [j] Pr 2:6-10
14:34 [k] Pr 11:11
14:35 [l] Mt 24:45-51; 25:14-30
15:1 [m] Pr 25:15
15:2 [n] Pr 12:23
15:3 [o] 2Ch 16:9 [p] Job 31:4; Heb 4:13 [q] Job 34:21; Jer 16:17

[a] 33 Hebrew; Septuagint and Syriac *discerning / but in the heart of fools she is not known*

---

astray, so it is better to plan for good and enjoy its return in love and faithfulness.
14:23 The contrast of mere talk and effort is that of intention and follow through, emptiness and payoff.
14:24 Fools receive only the foolishness they began with.
14:25 In a court of law, we depend on the truthful witness to free innocent people.
14:26 The "fortress" is a confidence or reliance in which one trusts. Parents can influence their children to trust in the Lord.
14:27 To animals, the difference between a spring of water and a net is life and death, but the human capacity to worship turns us from one to the other.
14:28 The larger the kingdom, the larger the status, but even a ruler's power is dependent on the quality of relationships in the kingdom.
14:29 If it is hard to believe that one displays wisdom by holding one's temper, the reverse picture of uncontrolled anger is certainly convincing.
14:30 Jealousy, passion, and envy eat one from the inside out, rotting the bones.
14:31 The absence of the fear of Yahweh gives a person the audacity to oppress the poor whom God loves.
14:32 The righteous are protected from the "calamity" that brings down the wicked.
14:33 Wisdom is available to both the discerning and to fools, yet she only stays with the former.
14:34 Righteousness lifts a nation's reputation high, but sin brings it disgrace.
14:35 A good kingdom requires good citizens.

14:1-35 How can one person do anything about individual and corporate greed? While the answers are not simple, a commitment to exploring them makes a good start. Soaking in the wisdom of Proverbs helps us discern what is good and what is not, and from there we can act on what we learn.

15:1 The first saying turns the focus of this chapter toward speech that turns away wrath.
15:2 Another saying on speaking distinguishes the wise and foolish by what their mouths produce.
15:3 Human tongues speak, and heavenly eyes watch.
15:4 Speech that does damage is deceitful; speech that heals is truthful.
15:5 Wisdom to teach others is learned in listening.

but whoever heeds correction
shows prudence.[r]

6 The house of the righteous contains
great treasure,[s]
but the income of the wicked
brings ruin.

7 The lips of the wise spread
knowledge,
but the hearts of fools are not
upright.

8 The LORD detests the sacrifice of the
wicked,[t]
but the prayer of the upright
pleases him.[u]

9 The LORD detests the way of the
wicked,
but he loves those who pursue
righteousness.[v]

10 Stern discipline awaits anyone who
leaves the path;
the one who hates correction will
die.[w]

11 Death and Destruction[a] lie open
before the LORD[x] —
how much more do human hearts![y]

12 Mockers resent correction,[z]
so they avoid the wise.

13 A happy heart makes the face
cheerful,
but heartache crushes the spirit.[a]

14 The discerning heart seeks
knowledge,[b]
but the mouth of a fool feeds on
folly.

15:5 [r] Pr 13:1
15:6 [s] Pr 8:21
15:8 [t] Pr 21:27; Isa 1:11; Jer 6:20 [u] ver 29
15:9 [v] Pr 21:21; 1Ti 6:11
15:10 [w] Pr 1:31-32; 5:12
15:11 [x] Job 26:6; Ps 139:8 [y] 2Ch 6:30; Ps 44:21
15:12 [z] Am 5:10
15:13 [a] Pr 12:25; 17:22; 18:14
15:14 [b] Pr 18:15

15:15 [c] ver 13
15:16 [d] Ps 37:16-17; Pr 16:8; 1Ti 6:6
15:17 [e] Pr 17:1
15:18 [f] Pr 26:21 [g] Ge 13:8
15:19 [h] Pr 22:5
15:20 [i] Pr 10:1
15:21 [j] Pr 10:23
15:22 [k] Pr 11:14
15:23 [l] Pr 12:14 [m] Pr 25:11

15 All the days of the oppressed are
wretched,
but the cheerful heart has a
continual feast.[c]

16 Better a little with the fear of the
LORD
than great wealth with turmoil.[d]

17 Better a small serving of vegetables
with love
than a fattened calf with hatred.[e]

18 A hot-tempered person stirs up
conflict,[f]
but the one who is patient calms a
quarrel.[g]

19 The way of the sluggard is blocked
with thorns,[h]
but the path of the upright is a
highway.

20 A wise son brings joy to his father,[i]
but a foolish man despises his
mother.

21 Folly brings joy to one who has no
sense,[j]
but whoever has understanding
keeps a straight course.

22 Plans fail for lack of counsel,
but with many advisers they
succeed.[k]

23 A person finds joy in giving an apt
reply[l] —
and how good is a timely word![m]

24 The path of life leads upward for the
prudent

[a] 11 Hebrew *Abaddon*

15:6 Only the righteous receive rewards worth keeping and sharing.
15:7 A wise person desires to spread knowledge as an antidote to folly.
15:8 Worship must never be divorced from our day-to-day actions.
15:9 The proverb contrasts two paths, indicated by use of the words "way" and "pursue."
15:10 Whoever wishes to stay on the path had better prepare for correction or reproof.
15:11 "How much more" sayings take an accepted truth and apply it to a new situation.
15:12 The "mocker" appears in Wisdom's speeches and a number of individual sayings.
15:13 This proverb explores the wide range of our emotional states and their effects.
15:14 A heart that seeks knowledge will find it; folly, by contrast, is hardly gourmet fare.
15:15 This last of the heart sayings sets the stage for another pair of sayings on contentment in vv. 16–17.
15:16 Mitigating factors may make having little preferable to having much; by implication, the "fear of the LORD," like wisdom, is worth more than gold or jewels.
15:17 Taken together, vv. 15–17 redefine what is to be considered a good feast: namely, the cheerful heart.
15:18 One's response to a situation influences it for good or bad.
15:19 Thorns and briars slow the way and make traveling miserable; they may be a sign of folly, for who would choose such a route?
15:20 The second line implies the link between wisdom and love.
15:21 Folly has its delights, but the person of understanding is not misled.
15:22 A wise person listens to the advice of other trusted counselors.
15:23 Knowing how to speak the right word at the right time is worth celebrating.
15:24 Everyone wants "life," but too many pursue it in ways that lead to death.

to keep them from going down to
the realm of the dead.

25 The LORD tears down the house of
the proud,[n]
but he sets the widow's boundary
stones in place.[o]

26 The LORD detests the thoughts of the
wicked,[p]
but gracious words are pure in his
sight.

27 The greedy bring ruin to their
households,
but the one who hates bribes will
live.[q]

28 The heart of the righteous weighs its
answers,[r]
but the mouth of the wicked
gushes evil.

29 The LORD is far from the wicked,
but he hears the prayer of the
righteous.[s]

30 Light in a messenger's eyes brings
joy to the heart,
and good news gives health to the
bones.

31 Whoever heeds life-giving
correction
will be at home among the wise.[t]

32 Those who disregard discipline
despise themselves,[u]
but the one who heeds correction
gains understanding.

33 Wisdom's instruction is to fear the
LORD,[v]
and humility comes before
honor.[w]

16 To humans belong the plans of
the heart,
but from the LORD comes the
proper answer of the tongue.[x]

2 All a person's ways seem pure to
them,
but motives are weighed by the
LORD.[y]

3 Commit to the LORD whatever
you do,
and he will establish your plans.[z]

4 The LORD works out everything to
its proper end[a] —
even the wicked for a day of
disaster.[b]

5 The LORD detests all the proud of
heart.[c]
Be sure of this: They will not go
unpunished.[d]

6 Through love and faithfulness sin is
atoned for;
through the fear of the LORD evil
is avoided.[e]

7 When the LORD takes pleasure in
anyone's way,
he causes their enemies to make
peace with them.

15:25 [n] Pr 12:7 [o] Dt 19:14; Ps 68:5-6; Pr 23:10-11
15:26 [p] Pr 6:16
15:27 [q] Ex 23:8; Isa 33:15
15:28 [r] 1Pe 3:15
15:29 [s] Ps 145:18-19
15:31 [t] ver 5
15:32 [u] Pr 1:7
15:33 [v] Pr 1:7 [w] Pr 18:12
16:1 [x] Pr 19:21
16:2 [y] Pr 21:2
16:3 [z] Ps 37:5-6; Pr 3:5-6
16:4 [a] Isa 43:7 [b] Ro 9:22
16:5 [c] Pr 6:16 [d] Pr 11:20-21
16:6 [e] Pr 14:16

Pr 15:31 ❖ How can we learn to cherish the Lord's correction and discipline? Where might God want us to correct something in our lives right now?

15:25 Yahweh brings down the high and mighty and lifts up the lowly.
15:26 Yahweh looks at the intentions that motivate right and wrong behaviors.
15:27 The greedy person thinks only of gains, not consequences.
15:28 When this inner work is ignored, the mouth pours out folly and its close cousin, evil.
15:29 If we read vv. 28 and 29 together, the evil speech of the wicked is the counterpart to the prayers of the righteous.
15:30 Messages that come from a good heart bring health and life to those who receive them.
15:31 Rebuke brings life because it brings wisdom.
15:32 Those who ignore discipline disrespect the wise and hate themselves.
15:33 Fear of Yahweh, which includes walking away from self-rule, provides instruction in wisdom.

✤ **15:1–33** These sayings on speech commend gentleness and truthfulness. Such speech turns away wrath, brings healing, and calms quarrels. These proverbs translate easily into the concerns of our own day, and preachers and teachers may find examples of each of these in every walk of life.

16:1 Humans act according to their intentions, but God is somehow at work in those acts.
16:2 Yahweh discerns our motivations better than we can.
16:3 We might paraphrase: "Pray, plan, and then act."
16:4 Yahweh does what he purposes, even when we have other plans.
16:5 The wicked cannot undo God's intentions for the world by opposing them.
16:6 "Fear of the LORD" takes on new significance here as both motivation and means for avoiding moral evil.
16:7 We might paraphrase this proverb, "Peace with God, peace with others."

8 Better a little with righteousness
than much gain[f] with injustice.

9 In their hearts humans plan their
course,
but the LORD establishes their
steps.[g]

10 The lips of a king speak as an oracle,
and his mouth does not betray
justice.

11 Honest scales and balances belong to
the LORD;
all the weights in the bag are of
his making.[h]

12 Kings detest wrongdoing,
for a throne is established through
righteousness.[i]

13 Kings take pleasure in honest lips;
they value the one who speaks
what is right.[j]

14 A king's wrath is a messenger of
death,[k]
but the wise will appease it.

15 When a king's face brightens, it
means life;[l]
his favor is like a rain cloud in
spring.

16 How much better to get wisdom than
gold,
to get insight rather than silver![m]

17 The highway of the upright avoids
evil;
those who guard their ways
preserve their lives.

18 Pride goes before destruction,
a haughty spirit before a fall.[n]

19 Better to be lowly in spirit along with
the oppressed
than to share plunder with the
proud.

20 Whoever gives heed to instruction
prospers,[a]
and blessed is the one who trusts
in the LORD.[o]

21 The wise in heart are called
discerning,
and gracious words promote
instruction.[b][p]

22 Prudence is a fountain of life to the
prudent,[q]
but folly brings punishment to
fools.

23 The hearts of the wise make their
mouths prudent,
and their lips promote instruction.[c]

24 Gracious words are a honeycomb,
sweet to the soul and healing to
the bones.[r]

25 There is a way that appears to be
right,[s]
but in the end it leads to death.[t]

26 The appetite of laborers works for
them;
their hunger drives them on.

16:8 [f] Ps 37:16
16:9 [g] Jer 10:23
16:11 [h] Pr 11:1
16:12 [i] Pr 25:5
16:13 [j] Pr 14:35
16:14 [k] Pr 19:12
16:15 [l] Job 29:24
16:16 [m] Pr 8:10, 19
16:18 [n] Pr 11:2; 18:12
16:20 [o] Ps 2:12; 34:8; Pr 19:8; Jer 17:7
16:21 [p] ver 23
16:22 [q] Pr 13:14
16:24 [r] Pr 24:13-14
16:25 [s] Pr 12:15 [t] Pr 14:12

[a] 20 Or *whoever speaks prudently finds what is good* [b] 21 Or *words make a person persuasive* [c] 23 Or *prudent / and make their lips persuasive*

16:8 Because interests sometimes conflict, one should choose righteousness and justice over profit.
16:9 Human plans and God's oversight are in cooperation, not conflict.
16:10 "Lips" and "mouth" point to the king's responsibility to enact "justice."
16:11 Even when humans intend to deceive, God's justice will win out.
16:12 The throne is established when the king shares Yahweh's abhorrence of the wicked person's deeds.
16:13 Just as wise kings detest the wrong, they love those who do right.
16:14 Wise persons know how to calm anger and how to speak the truth without arousing it.
16:15 The juxtaposition of opposites—the sun and a dark rain cloud—surprise the reader with their similarity; both are welcome and necessary for a good crop.
16:16 Gain without the integrity of wisdom loses its value.
16:17 The straight way turns away from evil and watches over life.
16:18 The Hebrew could read, "Before destruction, pride, and before stumbling, a haughty spirit" (alternate translation).
16:19 Communities are contrasted here: one in which goods are divided, but with gloating and resentment; the other where there is no wealth to divide, only joyful sharing and company.
16:20 Trust believes that God's way is best and gladly follows it.
16:21 The charge to gain wisdom carries a second charge to pass it on through persuasive teaching.
16:22 The contrast is between "prudence" and "folly" along with each one's results, "life" and "punishment."
16:23 The second line could be translated "adds learning to the lips," perhaps a reference to the ongoing learning of the wise.
16:24 Honey is the symbol for the teaching that brings life.
16:25 We need a godly external reference point to set our course.
16:26 The repetition of the word "appetite" from

[27]A scoundrel plots evil,
and on their lips it is like a scorching fire.[u]

[28]A perverse person stirs up conflict,[v]
and a gossip separates close friends.[w]

[29]A violent person entices their neighbor
and leads them down a path that is not good.[x]

[30]Whoever winks with their eye is plotting perversity;
whoever purses their lips is bent on evil.

[31]Gray hair is a crown of splendor;[y]
it is attained in the way of righteousness.

[32]Better a patient person than a warrior,
one with self-control than one who takes a city.

[33]The lot is cast into the lap,
but its every decision is from the LORD.[z]

17 Better a dry crust with peace and quiet
than a house full of feasting, with strife.[a]

[2]A prudent servant will rule over a disgraceful son
and will share the inheritance as one of the family.

16:27 [u]Jas 3:6 16:28 [v]Pr 15:18 [w]Pr 17:9 16:29 [x]Pr 1:10; 12:26 16:31 [y]Pr 20:29 16:33 [z]Pr 18:18; 29:26 17:1 [a]Pr 15:16,17

17:3 [b]Pr 27:21 [c]1Ch 29:17; Ps 26:2; Jer 17:10 17:5 [d]Pr 14:31 [e]Job 31:29 [f]Ob 12 17:6 [g]Pr 13:22 17:9 [h]Pr 10:12 [i]Pr 16:28

Pr 16:32 ❖ Does patience come easily? Why are patience and self-control important for God's children (see Gal 5:22)?

[3]The crucible for silver and the furnace for gold,[b]
but the LORD tests the heart.[c]

[4]A wicked person listens to deceitful lips;
a liar pays attention to a destructive tongue.

[5]Whoever mocks the poor shows contempt for their Maker;[d]
whoever gloats over disaster[e] will not go unpunished.[f]

[6]Children's children[g] are a crown to the aged,
and parents are the pride of their children.

[7]Eloquent lips are unsuited to a godless fool —
how much worse lying lips to a ruler!

[8]A bribe is seen as a charm by the one who gives it;
they think success will come at every turn.

[9]Whoever would foster love covers over an offense,[h]
but whoever repeats the matter separates close friends.[i]

---

v. 24 (where it is translated "soul") suggests that we compare the sweetness of the honeycomb with the hunger that motivates a worker.

16:27 A "scorching fire" quickly spreads, destroying everything in its path as it burns out of control.

16:28 The similarity between the two lines is the absence of goodwill and unity. The difference is that one can create it loudly or quietly.

16:29 A strong contrast stands between the teacher who spreads health and peace and the "teacher" who spreads division and violence.

16:30 The image of pressing both the eyes and lips seems to be a common act of "perversity," linking this verse with the dissension and gossip of v. 28.

16:31 Long life is a reward for persevering in the righteous way.

16:32 Better to exhibit self-control than to control others.

16:33 Both lots and stones point to Yahweh's desire for decisions that reflect his will.

16:1–33 Servant leadership rejects pride in favor of humble identification with the lowly and oppressed, forgoes personal gains, and holds wisdom as more valuable than gold.

17:1 If the goal of harmony is not met, what good is a table filled with sumptuous food?

17:2 Status means little if it is not matched by wise character.

17:3 "Tests" parallels the crucible and furnace, which removes impurities and tempers the metal. The "LORD" is the tester, and the heart is tested.

17:4 Ironically, the liar can be taken in by the same sort of deception in others.

17:5 Attitude is an action waiting to happen, so the way we view others determines the way we will treat them.

17:6 Perhaps an encouragement to set a wise example is implied in this statement of the ideal.

17:7 The climax in the saying comes with the words "how much worse"; it is even worse to find lying lips with a leader or noble.

17:8 The saying is descriptive and does not commend paying bribes. Those who count on bribes to accomplish their work are only fooling themselves.

17:9 It is better to forgive and forget.

10 A rebuke impresses a discerning
person
more than a hundred lashes a fool.

11 Evildoers foster rebellion against
God;
the messenger of death will be
sent against them.

12 Better to meet a bear robbed of her
cubs
than a fool bent on folly.

13 Evil will never leave the house
of one who pays back evil[j] for
good.

14 Starting a quarrel is like breaching a
dam;
so drop the matter before a
dispute breaks out.[k]

15 Acquitting the guilty and
condemning the innocent[l] —
the LORD detests them both.[m]

16 Why should fools have money in
hand to buy wisdom,
when they are not able to
understand it?[n]

17 A friend loves at all times,
and a brother is born for a time of
adversity.

18 One who has no sense shakes hands
in pledge
and puts up security for a
neighbor.[o]

19 Whoever loves a quarrel loves sin;
whoever builds a high gate invites
destruction.

17:13 [j] Ps 109:4-5; Jer 18:20
17:14 [k] Pr 20:3
17:15 [l] Pr 18:5 [m] Ex 23:6-7; Isa 5:23
17:16 [n] Pr 23:23
17:18 [o] Pr 6:1-5; 11:15; 22:26-27

Pr 17:17 ❖ When have close friends carried you through a difficult time? In a similar way, how can believers do this today?

20 One whose heart is corrupt does not
prosper;
one whose tongue is perverse falls
into trouble.

21 To have a fool for a child brings
grief;
there is no joy for the parent of a
godless fool.[p]

22 A cheerful heart is good medicine,
but a crushed spirit dries up the
bones.[q]

23 The wicked accept bribes[r] in secret
to pervert the course of justice.

24 A discerning person keeps wisdom
in view,
but a fool's eyes[s] wander to the
ends of the earth.

25 A foolish son brings grief to his
father
and bitterness to the mother who
bore him.[t]

26 If imposing a fine on the innocent is
not good,[u]
surely to flog honest officials is
not right.

27 The one who has knowledge uses
words with restraint,
and whoever has understanding is
even-tempered.[v]

17:21 [p] Pr 10:1
17:22 [q] Ps 22:15; Pr 15:13
17:23 [r] Ex 23:8
17:24 [s] Ecc 2:14
17:25 [t] Pr 10:1
17:26 [u] Pr 18:5
17:27 [v] Pr 14:29; Jas 1:19

17:10 Blows won't work if words won't.
17:11 One can seek reconciliation, or one can seek rebellion; the choice is clear.
17:12 The proverb compares the danger of a bear *without* her cubs to fools whose folly goes *with* them wherever they go. The wise will steer clear of both.
17:13 Evil in its shortsightedness is just plain dumb.
17:14 As water cannot be brought back under control once released, a quarrel can escalate beyond expectation.
17:15 False judgments are detestable in Yahweh's eyes.
17:16 Wisdom is a gift of God and must be acquired through study. Even if wisdom could be bought, the fool would not know what to do with it.
17:17 The saying implicitly rebukes those who claim friendship but are absent when needed.
17:18 This proverb pair advises readers to avoid trouble, not a neighbor in need.
17:19 If holding on to an offense leads one to build a "high gate" (presumably to keep away neighbors), one trusts in a false hope.
17:20 This proverb links "heart" and "tongue" to represent the whole person's thoughts and actions.
17:21 This proverb reminds us that the effects of folly spread throughout the family and to others as well.
17:22 In Proverbs, the "crushed spirit" is brought on by heartache and is hard to bear.
17:23 A bribe given in secret does its damaging work.
17:24 This saying contrasts the person who keeps wisdom nearby and the fool who looks everywhere else for answers.
17:25 The second of the sayings about bearing a foolish son, this variation on the theme adds the "bitterness" of the mother to the father's "grief."
17:26 The proverb recommends fair judgment for all members of society.
17:27 This saying presents two signs of a person who has gathered "knowledge"—that one moderates both words and temper.

28 Even fools are thought wise if they keep silent,
and discerning if they hold their tongues.[w]

18 An unfriendly person pursues selfish ends
and against all sound judgment starts quarrels.

2 Fools find no pleasure in understanding
but delight in airing their own opinions.[x]

3 When wickedness comes, so does contempt,
and with shame comes reproach.

4 The words of the mouth are deep waters,
but the fountain of wisdom is a rushing stream.

5 It is not good to be partial to the wicked[y]
and so deprive the innocent of justice.[z]

6 The lips of fools bring them strife,
and their mouths invite a beating.

7 The mouths of fools are their undoing,
and their lips are a snare[a] to their very lives.[b]

8 The words of a gossip are like choice morsels;
they go down to the inmost parts.[c]

9 One who is slack in his work
is brother to one who destroys.[d]

10 The name of the LORD is a fortified tower;[e]
the righteous run to it and are safe.

11 The wealth of the rich is their fortified city;[f]
they imagine it a wall too high to scale.

12 Before a downfall the heart is haughty,
but humility comes before honor.[g]

13 To answer before listening—
that is folly and shame.[h]

14 The human spirit can endure in sickness,
but a crushed spirit who can bear?[i]

15 The heart of the discerning acquires knowledge,[j]
for the ears of the wise seek it out.

16 A gift[k] opens the way
and ushers the giver into the presence of the great.

17 In a lawsuit the first to speak seems right,
until someone comes forward and cross-examines.

18 Casting the lot settles disputes[l]
and keeps strong opponents apart.

Pr 18:6-8 ❖ Why do words have the power to undo a person's life and reputation?

17:28 [w] Job 13:5
18:2 [x] Pr 12:23
18:5 [y] Lev 19:15; Pr 24:23-25; 28:21 [z] Ps 82:2; Pr 17:15
18:7 [a] Ps 140:9 [b] Ps 64:8; Pr 10:14; 12:13; 13:3; Ecc 10:12
18:8 [c] Pr 26:22
18:9 [d] Pr 28:24
18:10 [e] 2Sa 22:3; Ps 61:3
18:11 [f] Pr 10:15
18:12 [g] Pr 11:2; 15:33; 16:18
18:13 [h] Pr 20:25; Jn 7:51
18:14 [i] Pr 15:13; 17:22
18:15 [j] Pr 15:14
18:16 [k] Ge 32:20
18:18 [l] Pr 16:33

17:28 Reserve and restraint are so powerfully communicative that even fools can appear wise.

✣ **17:1-28** No wonder Jesus prayed for the unity of the church—he knew what was coming. Conflict and its roots in inordinate desire have always been with us.

18:1 This picture of isolation and quarreling continues the theme of behaviors that bring strife.
18:2 Interested only in showing what he knows, the person in this verse accomplishes the opposite.
18:3 "Contempt" goes everywhere with the wicked.
18:4 Words, like deep waters, can mislead. The "fountain of wisdom" reminds readers of the fountain of life.
18:5 One should not clear the guilty and condemn the innocent.
18:6 It is not certain whether the blows here are the result of a fight or punishment.
18:7 Fools have no one to blame but themselves.
18:8 We do well to remember that tidbits of gossip may be stored for evil purposes. Our biting words can bite back.
18:9 "One who is slack" drops what is in the hands, but the destruction from such negligence is no accident.
18:10 The phrase "name of the LORD" occurs only here in Proverbs, but frequently in the Psalms it is a sign of refuge.
18:11 Wealth is only a strong city and high wall as the wealthy "imagine it."
18:12 It seems that either attitude leads inevitably to its opposite.
18:13 Fools only like to hear themselves talk.
18:14 The connection between spirit and body links the proverbs that mention the crushed spirit.
18:15 The ear of the wise searches for knowledge by sorting knowledge from folly.
18:16 This gift only seeks to buy access to power.
18:17 It is better to hear both sides before passing judgment.
18:18 Yahweh's decisions are compared with the lot. In a sense, the lot gives the decision over to God.

19 A brother wronged is more
unyielding than a fortified
city;
disputes are like the barred gates
of a citadel.

20 From the fruit of their mouth a
person's stomach is filled;
with the harvest of their lips they
are satisfied.[m]

21 The tongue has the power of life and
death,
and those who love it will eat its
fruit.[n]

22 He who finds a wife finds what is
good[o]
and receives favor from the LORD.[p]

23 The poor plead for mercy,
but the rich answer harshly.

24 One who has unreliable friends soon
comes to ruin,
but there is a friend who sticks
closer than a brother.[q]

19

Better the poor whose walk is
blameless
than a fool whose lips are perverse.[r]

2 Desire without knowledge is not
good —
how much more will hasty feet
miss the way![s]

3 A person's own folly leads to their
ruin,
yet their heart rages against the
LORD.

4 Wealth attracts many friends,
but even the closest friend of the
poor person deserts them.[t]

5 A false witness[u] will not go
unpunished,
and whoever pours out lies will
not go free.[v]

6 Many curry favor with a ruler,[w]
and everyone is the friend of one
who gives gifts.[x]

7 The poor are shunned by all their
relatives —
how much more do their friends
avoid them!
Though the poor pursue them with
pleading,
they are nowhere to be found.[a][y]

8 The one who gets wisdom loves
life;
the one who cherishes
understanding will soon
prosper.[z]

9 A false witness will not go
unpunished,
and whoever pours out lies will
perish.[a]

10 It is not fitting for a fool[b] to live in
luxury —
how much worse for a slave to rule
over princes![c]

11 A person's wisdom yields patience;[d]

18:20 [m] Pr 12:14
18:21 [n] Pr 13:2-3; Mt 12:37
18:22 [o] Pr 12:4 [p] Pr 19:14; 31:10
18:24 [q] Pr 17:17; Jn 15:13-15
19:1 [r] Pr 28:6
19:2 [s] Pr 29:20
19:4 [t] Pr 14:20
19:5 [u] Ex 23:1 [v] Dt 19:19; Pr 21:28
19:6 [w] Pr 29:26 [x] Pr 17:8; 18:16
19:7 [y] ver 4; Ps 38:11
19:8 [z] Pr 16:20
19:9 [a] ver 5
19:10 [b] Pr 26:1 [c] Pr 30:21-23; Ecc 10:5-7
19:11 [d] Pr 16:32

[a] 7 The meaning of the Hebrew for this sentence is uncertain.

18:19 One expects the brother to stand with, not against. Sibling conflict is the worst example of good relations distorted.
18:20 This saying might be paraphrased, "We'd better be able to stomach what we say."
18:21 The one who "love[s]" the tongue understands its power and uses it for good.
18:22 As Wisdom calls out and offers herself, so does Yahweh; yet humans must seek her and Yahweh diligently.
18:23 Often the poor must plead with someone who holds power over them, while the rich can answer harshly to those of lower status.
18:24 This saying compares many friends to one who loves and sticks close like a brother. At times, less is more.

18:1–24 All our speaking and listening end up in the "inmost parts" (v. 8), so make a conscious effort to reject gossip and other forms of put-downs.

19:1 The path of the feet and words of the mouth serve as expressions of either wisdom or folly.
19:2 This proverb holds out patience and caution as knowledgeable companions of desire.
19:3 The fool, having ruined his life, wants to blame God.
19:4 Tragically, most people would rather be a friend to the rich than to the poor.
19:5 If one gains wealth or courts friendship through falsehood, that perverse use of speech will eventually be repaid.
19:6 This kind of friendship is hollow for both parties, being based only on self-interest and personal gain.
19:7 The poor person is deserted even by relatives, so it is not unexpected that friends also keep their distance.
19:8 An upbeat saying intrudes on this unhappy series of proverbs, assuring the reader that those who acquire "wisdom" care for themselves.
19:9 Perjury is more than a preference for the rich over the poor; it is an outright attack.
19:10 Fools usually do not live in luxury, but sometimes exceptions disprove the rule.
19:11 When we protect our status by quarreling, we stand to lose it the most.

it is to one's glory to overlook an
offense.

12 A king's rage is like the roar of a lion,
but his favor is like dew[e] on the grass.[f]

13 A foolish child is a father's ruin,[g]
and a quarrelsome wife is like the constant dripping of a leaky roof.[h]

14 Houses and wealth are inherited from parents,[i]
but a prudent wife is from the LORD.[j]

15 Laziness brings on deep sleep,
and the shiftless go hungry.[k]

16 Whoever keeps commandments keeps their life,
but whoever shows contempt for their ways will die.[l]

17 Whoever is kind to the poor lends to the LORD,
and he will reward them for what they have done.[m]

18 Discipline your children, for in that there is hope;
do not be a willing party to their death.[n]

19 A hot-tempered person must pay the penalty;
rescue them, and you will have to do it again.

20 Listen to advice and accept discipline,[o]
and at the end you will be counted among the wise.[p]

19:12 [e] Ps 133:3 [f] Pr 16:14-15
19:13 [g] Pr 10:1 [h] Pr 21:9
19:14 [i] 2Co 12:14 [j] Pr 18:22
19:15 [k] Pr 6:9; 10:4
19:16 [l] Pr 16:17; Lk 10:28
19:17 [m] Mt 10:42; 2Co 9:6-8
19:18 [n] Pr 13:24; 23:13-14
19:20 [o] Pr 4:1 [p] Pr 12:15

Pr 19:17 ❖ How is our treatment of others a measure of our love for God (see Mt 25:40-45)?

21 Many are the plans in a person's heart,
but it is the LORD's purpose that prevails.[q]

22 What a person desires is unfailing love[a];
better to be poor than a liar.

23 The fear of the LORD leads to life;
then one rests content, untouched by trouble.[r]

24 A sluggard buries his hand in the dish;
he will not even bring it back to his mouth![s]

25 Flog a mocker, and the simple will learn prudence;
rebuke the discerning, and they will gain knowledge.[t]

26 Whoever robs their father and drives out their mother[u]
is a child who brings shame and disgrace.

27 Stop listening to instruction, my son,
and you will stray from the words of knowledge.

28 A corrupt witness mocks at justice,
and the mouth of the wicked gulps down evil.[v]

29 Penalties are prepared for mockers,

19:21 [q] Ps 33:11; Pr 16:9; Isa 14:24,27
19:23 [r] Ps 25:13; Pr 12:21; 1Ti 4:8
19:24 [s] Pr 26:15
19:25 [t] Pr 9:9; 21:11
19:26 [u] Pr 28:24
19:28 [v] Job 15:16

[a] 22 Or *Greed is a person's shame*

19:12 If it is wise to practice patience and restrain anger, it is also wise to do everything possible to keep from provoking anger in one more powerful. **19:13** The dripping roof is destructive and dangerous, a fitting parallel for the ruin of the foolish son. **19:14** The correspondence between decision and blessing is held up but not explained. **19:15** As laziness only brings sleep, the appetite of the idle goes hungry. **19:16** To refuse guidance is to be careless about where one walks. **19:17** While the poor often cannot repay, Yahweh always can. **19:18** The proverb urges parents to exercise such discipline "for in that there is hope," the possibility for a good outcome. **19:19** The saying offers advice on handling someone who has not cultivated patience. **19:20** Wisdom is a lifelong project, not a job order that one fulfills and moves on. **19:21** The proverb urges its readers to consider final outcomes and ends. **19:22** It is better to be poor and honest than to have great gain through lies. **19:23** To fear Yahweh is to fear nothing else. **19:24** The exaggeration shows that sloth will leave one hungry. **19:25** Discipline a mocker as an example to the simple because the mocker is beyond learning. **19:26** Failing to honor and care for parents is a dangerous possibility, especially when the son's foolishness has left the parents destitute. **19:27** A young learner can be led astray by another woman, a sign of one's own folly (5:20, 23), wine and beer (20:1), and evil men (28:10). **19:28** Desire without knowledge is not good, for one may swallow poison. **19:29** The beatings may not instruct the mockers

and beatings for the backs of
fools.[w]

20 Wine is a mocker and beer a
brawler;
whoever is led astray by them is
not wise.[x]

2 A king's wrath strikes terror like the
roar of a lion;[y]
those who anger him forfeit their
lives.[z]

3 It is to one's honor to avoid strife,
but every fool is quick to quarrel.[a]

4 Sluggards do not plow in season;
so at harvest time they look but
find nothing.

5 The purposes of a person's heart are
deep waters,
but one who has insight draws
them out.

6 Many claim to have unfailing love,
but a faithful person who can find?[b]

7 The righteous lead blameless lives;
blessed are their children after
them.[c]

8 When a king sits on his throne to
judge,
he winnows out all evil with his
eyes.[d]

9 Who can say, "I have kept my heart
pure;
I am clean and without sin"?[e]

10 Differing weights and differing
measures —
the LORD detests them both.[f]

11 Even small children are known by
their actions,
so is their conduct really pure[g]
and upright?

12 Ears that hear and eyes that see —
the LORD has made them both.[h]

13 Do not love sleep or you will grow
poor;[i]
stay awake and you will have food
to spare.

14 "It's no good, it's no good!" says the
buyer —
then goes off and boasts about the
purchase.

15 Gold there is, and rubies in
abundance,
but lips that speak knowledge are
a rare jewel.

16 Take the garment of one who puts
up security for a stranger;
hold it in pledge[j] if it is done for
an outsider.[k]

17 Food gained by fraud tastes sweet,[l]
but one ends up with a mouth full
of gravel.

18 Plans are established by seeking
advice;
so if you wage war, obtain
guidance.[m]

19:29 [w] Pr 26:3
20:1 [x] Pr 31:4
20:2 [y] Pr 19:12 [z] Pr 8:36
20:3 [a] Pr 17:14
20:6 [b] Ps 12:1
20:7 [c] Ps 37:25-26; 112:2
20:8 [d] ver 26; Pr 25:4-5
20:9 [e] 1Ki 8:46; Ecc 7:20; 1Jn 1:8
20:10 [f] ver 23; Pr 11:1
20:11 [g] Mt 7:16
20:12 [h] Ps 94:9
20:13 [i] Pr 6:11; 19:15
20:16 [j] Ex 22:26 [k] Pr 27:13
20:17 [l] Pr 9:17
20:18 [m] Pr 11:14; 24:6

---

or fools, but they will teach the willing student that God's justice is not mocked.

> **19:1–29** In our haste to fulfill our wants we can easily misstep. Proverbs would have us learn another way. Instead of worrying about how well we are doing, we can worry about how well those with less are doing. Seeing that what we have is a gift, we are free to give it again.

20:1 Alcohol's influence can change the demeanor of normally calm and rational people.
20:2 The wise take warning, but fools who provoke anger may pay with their lives.
20:3 Those who quarrel will lose standing.
20:4 This comic example of the sluggard recommends both foresight and activity. People who refuse to work shouldn't question why they don't have what they need.
20:5 Like water from the bottom of a well, human "purposes" can be drawn out if one has "insight."
20:6 This proverb on faithfulness recalls the friendship themes of the previous chapter.
20:7 Children can be the beneficiaries of a parent's faith (see 14:26).
20:8 The king's work of discernment is like Yahweh, who judges in righteousness.
20:9 The point is that there are more people who claim to have dealt with the sin in their lives than actually have.
20:10 False measures speak to one's personal integrity; they are an abomination to Yahweh.
20:11 Actions reveal character to those who have learned the art of discernment.
20:12 God made eyes and ears to perceive and understand, and he is pleased when they do.
20:13 The one who sleeps could lose the inheritance.
20:14 Here there are two kinds of speaking: one for negotiating and one for boasting. The two faces of the corrupt are highlighted here.
20:15 The proverb asks, "What do we value the most?"
20:16 Ironically, one who makes an unwise pledge may well have given his shirt, for he will surely lose it.
20:17 Speaking falsely has its own negative reward.
20:18 One should seek out advice from someone who speaks words of knowledge.

[19] A gossip betrays a confidence;[n]
so avoid anyone who talks too much.

[20] If someone curses their father or mother,[o]
their lamp will be snuffed out in pitch darkness.[p]

[21] An inheritance claimed too soon
will not be blessed at the end.

[22] Do not say, "I'll pay you back for this wrong!"[q]
Wait for the LORD, and he will avenge you.[r]

[23] The LORD detests differing weights,
and dishonest scales do not please him.[s]

[24] A person's steps are directed by the LORD.
How then can anyone understand their own way?[t]

[25] It is a trap to dedicate something rashly
and only later to consider one's vows.[u]

[26] A wise king winnows out the wicked;
he drives the threshing wheel over them.[v]

[27] The human spirit is[a] the lamp of the LORD
that sheds light on one's inmost being.

[28] Love and faithfulness keep a king safe;
through love his throne is made secure.[w]

[29] The glory of young men is their strength,
gray hair the splendor of the old.[x]

[30] Blows and wounds scrub[y] away evil,
and beatings purge the inmost being.

21 In the LORD's hand the king's heart is a stream of water
that he channels toward all who please him.

[2] A person may think their own ways are right,
but the LORD weighs the heart.[z]

[3] To do what is right and just
is more acceptable to the LORD than sacrifice.[a]

[4] Haughty eyes[b] and a proud heart —
the unplowed field of the wicked — produce sin.

[5] The plans of the diligent lead to profit[c]
as surely as haste leads to poverty.

[6] A fortune made by a lying tongue

20:19 [n] Pr 11:13
20:20 [o] Pr 30:11 [p] Ex 21:17; Job 18:5
20:22 [q] Pr 24:29 [r] Ro 12:19
20:23 [s] ver 10
20:24 [t] Jer 10:23
20:25 [u] Ecc 5:2, 4-5
20:26 [v] ver 8
20:28 [w] Pr 29:14
20:29 [x] Pr 16:31
20:30 [y] Pr 22:15
21:2 [z] Pr 16:2; 24:12; Lk 16:15
21:3 [a] 1Sa 15:22; Pr 15:8; Isa 1:11; Hos 6:6; Mic 6:6-8
21:4 [b] Pr 6:17
21:5 [c] Pr 10:4; 28:22

[a] 27 Or *A person's words are*

Pr 20:18 ❖ How can we find trusted Christian mentors to whom we can go for advice?

20:19 If you listen to a secret, someone else will probably hear yours.
20:20 The extinguished "lamp" can refer to losing light when it is most needed, but it may be a metaphor for losing one's life.
20:21 Inappropriate behavior at the start cannot lead to blessing, divine or human, at the end.
20:22 Just as wisdom teaches us to hold back our words in general, this proverb specifically warns against words of vengeance.
20:23 This proverb is a variation on v. 10.
20:24 This juxtaposition of human plans with God's sovereign action is not meant to discourage planning but rather to guide it.
20:25 The metaphor of the trap resonates with anyone who has made a promise only to regret it later.
20:26 To "winnow" is also to scatter the chaff to the winds; wisdom also gives the power of discernment.
20:27 The image of God's light searching human interior spaces fits in well with neighboring proverbs on the inner life.
20:28 The throne that winnows out evil (v. 26) is also protected by love.
20:29 If strength is spent wisely, the return is a long life, symbolized by the gray head.
20:30 One can either acquire discernment to discipline oneself or fail to learn discernment and suffer the discipline of someone who has.

✚ **20:1–30** The idolatry of sin is imagining we have the authority to make our own way, becoming a law unto ourselves.

21:1 As water is directed by irrigation ditches and dams, the righteous king's heart will follow Yahweh to establish justice.
21:2 Yahweh alone can determine what is known and what is hidden from a person's self-perceptions.
21:3 It is easier to have sacrifice without right living than to have right living without religious practice.
21:4 Haughty eyes and arrogant kings will be brought low, but kings who reject arrogance are more likely to govern rightly.
21:5 Here, "haste" is a form of laziness.
21:6 The "fleeting vapor" and "deadly snare" negate security.

is a fleeting vapor and a deadly
snare.[a][d]

7 The violence of the wicked will drag
them away,
for they refuse to do what is right.

8 The way of the guilty is devious,[e]
but the conduct of the innocent is
upright.

9 Better to live on a corner of the roof
than share a house with a
quarrelsome wife.[f]

10 The wicked crave evil;
their neighbors get no mercy from
them.

11 When a mocker is punished, the
simple gain wisdom;
by paying attention to the wise
they get knowledge.[g]

12 The Righteous One[b] takes note of
the house of the wicked
and brings the wicked to ruin.[h]

13 Whoever shuts their ears to the cry
of the poor
will also cry out and not be
answered.[i]

14 A gift given in secret soothes anger,
and a bribe concealed in the cloak
pacifies great wrath.[j]

15 When justice is done, it brings joy to
the righteous
but terror to evildoers.[k]

16 Whoever strays from the path of
prudence
comes to rest in the company of
the dead.[l]

17 Whoever loves pleasure will become
poor;
whoever loves wine and olive oil
will never be rich.[m]

18 The wicked become a ransom[n] for
the righteous,
and the unfaithful for the upright.

19 Better to live in a desert
than with a quarrelsome and
nagging wife.[o]

20 The wise store up choice food and
olive oil,
but fools gulp theirs down.

21 Whoever pursues righteousness and
love
finds life, prosperity[c] and honor.[p]

22 One who is wise can go up against
the city of the mighty[q]
and pull down the stronghold in
which they trust.

23 Those who guard their mouths[r] and
their tongues
keep themselves from calamity.[s]

24 The proud and arrogant person[t] —
"Mocker" is his name —
behaves with insolent fury.

25 The craving of a sluggard will be the
death of him,[u]

21:6 [d] 2Pe 2:3
21:8 [e] Pr 2:15
21:9 [f] Pr 25:24
21:11 [g] Pr 19:25
21:12 [h] Pr 14:11
21:13 [i] Mt 18:30-34; Jas 2:13
21:14 [j] Pr 18:16; 19:6
21:15 [k] Pr 10:29
21:16 [l] Ps 49:14
21:17 [m] Pr 23:20-21,29-35
21:18 [n] Pr 11:8; Isa 43:3
21:19 [o] ver 9
21:21 [p] Mt 5:6
21:22 [q] Ecc 9:15-16
21:23 [r] Jas 3:2 [s] Pr 12:13; 13:3
21:24 [t] Ps 1:1; Pr 1:22; Isa 16:6; Jer 48:29
21:25 [u] Pr 13:4

[a] 6 Some Hebrew manuscripts, Septuagint and Vulgate; most Hebrew manuscripts *vapor for those who seek death* [b] 12 Or *The righteous person* [c] 21 Or *righteousness*

21:7 Those who refuse to do justice for others will find themselves judged.
21:8 Character and deeds match more often than they do not.
21:9 The humor in this proverb breaks up the seriousness of the sayings on pride and injustice.
21:10 How can a self-centered person show mercy to a neighbor?
21:11 Even a naive person can learn from the example of one who gets punished.
21:12 God overthrows the wicked and frustrates the words of the unfaithful.
21:13 The "cry of the poor" here may be either their ever-present need or their response to a specific injustice.
21:14 Both lines of this saying emphasize the hiddenness of the bribe, a sign it is given to pervert justice.
21:15 Public justice is in view here as both the righteous and evil see the outcome.
21:16 The traveler who strays from the good path will not end up in a good place.
21:17 To love wine and oil and not the work that produces them is shortsighted.
21:18 The righteous are rescued from the trouble that impacts the wicked instead of them.
21:19 Better to be homeless in the desert than in a miserable domestic situation.
21:20 This saying contrasts one who practices moderation with the fool who swallows everything.
21:21 In seeking these virtues, one also finds the three primary desires of the proverbs: life, prosperity, and honor.
21:22 The last Hebrew word translated as "they trust" is key, pointing out the confidence placed in strength and numbers and contrasting it with the wise person's trust in God.
21:23 It is harder to guard one's speech than a city.
21:24 "Insolent fury" describes the rages of someone who exercises no control over mouth and tongue.
21:25 How often laziness and gluttony go together.

because his hands refuse to work.
26 All day long he craves for more,
but the righteous give without sparing.[v]

27 The sacrifice of the wicked is detestable[w] —
how much more so when brought with evil intent![x]

28 A false witness will perish,[y]
but a careful listener will testify successfully.

29 The wicked put up a bold front,
but the upright give thought to their ways.

30 There is no wisdom,[z] no insight, no plan
that can succeed against the LORD.[a]

31 The horse is made ready for the day of battle,
but victory rests with the LORD.[b]

22 A good name is more desirable than great riches;
to be esteemed is better than silver or gold.[c]

2 Rich and poor have this in common:
The LORD is the Maker of them all.[d]

3 The prudent see danger and take refuge,[e]
but the simple keep going and pay the penalty.[f]

4 Humility is the fear of the LORD;
its wages are riches and honor and life.

21:26 [v] Ps 37:26; Mt 5:42; Eph 4:28
21:27 [w] Isa 66:3; Jer 6:20; Am 5:22 [x] Pr 15:8
21:28 [y] Pr 19:5
21:30 [z] Jer 9:23 [a] Isa 8:10; Ac 5:39
21:31 [b] Ps 3:8; 33:12-19; Isa 31:1
22:1 [c] Ecc 7:1
22:2 [d] Job 31:15
22:3 [e] Pr 14:16 [f] Pr 27:12

Pr 21:25–26 ❖ How is our willingness to work a reflection of our character? What does laziness say about our life and faith?

Pr 22:9 ❖ When have you been blessed through blessing others?

5 In the paths of the wicked are snares and pitfalls,[g]
but those who would preserve their life stay far from them.

6 Start children off on the way they should go,[h]
and even when they are old they will not turn from it.

7 The rich rule over the poor,
and the borrower is slave to the lender.

8 Whoever sows injustice reaps calamity,[i]
and the rod they wield in fury will be broken.[j]

9 The generous will themselves be blessed,[k]
for they share their food with the poor.[l]

10 Drive out the mocker, and out goes strife;
quarrels and insults are ended.[m]

11 One who loves a pure heart and who speaks with grace
will have the king for a friend.[n]

22:5 [g] Pr 15:19
22:6 [h] Eph 6:4
22:8 [i] Job 4:8 [j] Ps 125:3
22:9 [k] 2Co 9:6 [l] Pr 19:17
22:10 [m] Pr 18:6; 26:20
22:11 [n] Pr 16:13; Mt 5:8

21:26 If the righteous give without sparing, the giving goes beyond what one has to spare.
21:27 The hypocritical sacrifices of a wicked person are despicable to Yahweh.
21:28 The discerning person will endure.
21:29 One is self-centered; the other lives in harmony with Yahweh's creation and community.
21:30 The terms "wisdom," "insight," and "plan" may have military connotations that are made more explicit in the next verse.
21:31 The two proverbs name related errors. The first is to go against God; the second is to forget to thank God and trust in one's own foresight and strength.

✚ **21:1–31** Most of us are vulnerable to sins of omission. Even if we do not actively take advantage of the poor, we do often fail to hear their cries and act on their behalf (v. 13).

22:1 Good character will make itself known around town.
22:2 Favoritism dishonors Yahweh, the "Maker of them all."
22:3 The prudent see evil coming and hide. The simple, not even knowing the danger, walk straight toward it.
22:4 "Riches and honor and life" come to those who seek higher ideals and lower status.
22:5 One who is vigilant guards "life."
22:6 This proverb illustrates a general truth rather than guaranteeing the success of any method of parenting.
22:7 Many commentators take this as a warning against borrowing, but it may be a more general observation about the responsibilities of those who have power.
22:8 This version of "you reap what you sow" extends the idea of responsibility from v. 7.
22:9 The attitude behind sharing with the poor has more in common with v. 2 than vv. 7, 16.
22:10 The proverb does not advocate suppressing conflict, only unnecessary arguing.
22:11 The person who practices wise and good speech is welcomed by all—even the king.

12 The eyes of the LORD keep watch
over knowledge,
but he frustrates the words of the
unfaithful.

13 The sluggard says, "There's a lion
outside![o]
I'll be killed in the public square!"

14 The mouth of an adulterous woman
is a deep pit;[p]
a man who is under the LORD's
wrath falls into it.[q]

15 Folly is bound up in the heart of a
child,
but the rod of discipline will drive
it far away.[r]

16 One who oppresses the poor to
increase his wealth
and one who gives gifts to the
rich — both come to poverty.

Thirty Sayings of the Wise

Saying 1

17 Pay attention and turn your ear to
the sayings of the wise;[s]
apply your heart to what I teach,
18 for it is pleasing when you keep
them in your heart
and have all of them ready on
your lips.
19 So that your trust may be in the
LORD,
I teach you today, even you.
20 Have I not written thirty sayings for
you,
sayings of counsel and knowledge,
21 teaching you to be honest and to
speak the truth,[t]
so that you bring back truthful
reports
to those you serve?

Saying 2

22 Do not exploit the poor[u] because
they are poor
and do not crush the needy in
court,[v]
23 for the LORD will take up their
case[w]
and will exact life for life.[x]

Saying 3

24 Do not make friends with a
hot-tempered person,
do not associate with one easily
angered,
25 or you may learn their ways
and get yourself ensnared.[y]

Saying 4

26 Do not be one who shakes hands in
pledge[z]
or puts up security for debts;
27 if you lack the means to pay,
your very bed will be snatched
from under you.[a]

Saying 5

28 Do not move an ancient boundary
stone[b]
set up by your ancestors.

22:13 [o] Pr 26:13
22:14 [p] Pr 2:16; 5:3-5; 7:5; 23:27 [q] Ecc 7:26
22:15 [r] Pr 13:24; 23:14
22:17 [s] Pr 5:1
22:21 [t] Lk 1:3-4; 1Pe 3:15
22:22 [u] Zec 7:10 [v] Ex 23:6; Mal 3:5
22:23 [w] Ps 12:5 [x] 1Sa 25:39; Pr 23:10-11
22:25 [y] 1Co 15:33
22:26 [z] Pr 11:15
22:27 [a] Pr 17:18
22:28 [b] Dt 19:14; Pr 23:10

22:12 Yahweh not only judges how "knowledge" leads one to live, but he also "frustrates" wicked persons.
22:13 Although few excuses are as transparent as this one, Yahweh can tell whenever one's words come from knowledge or deception.
22:14 We would expect the one who falls into the pit of her words to incur wrath, but here we get the reverse.
22:15 Better the rod used for discipline than a trap of sin and death—though this rod can also be symbolic of parents' teaching.
22:16 Oppressors wake up to find they have become one of the group they have oppressed.

✣ **22:1-16** Yahweh takes up the case of those who have been crushed and plundered. Therefore, to respond as God does is to become an advocate for the poor, using whatever resources and authority are available to offer mercy and work for justice.

22:17 A prologue of sorts includes a call to attention and motivations for learning, much like the prologue of 1:1–7.
22:18 This motivation envisions a synthesis of wisdom that is perhaps greater than the sum of the parts.
22:19 Knowledge and wisdom are not the source of one's confidence; teaching is to inspire trust in Yahweh, integrating intellectual study and faith.
22:20 For the first time in Proverbs, oral teaching has given way to teaching by means of the written word.
22:21 Verse 21 sets out a secondary goal—that is, to show how one might return reliable words in answer to one who sends.
22:22-23 Exploitation is one way to take what belongs to another. "Take up their case" (v. 23) echoes the voice of the prophets, who portray Yahweh as judge, prosecutor, and executor.
22:24-27 A number of the proverbs warn against a "hot-tempered" person (v. 24), but describing this person's influence as a snare is new. The "pledge" (v. 26) was compared with a trap in 6:1-5, but here the teacher warns against repossession.
22:28 To move a marker for financial gain is to defraud those who are most vulnerable.

Saying 6

29 Do you see someone skilled in their work?
They will serve[c] before kings;
they will not serve before officials of low rank.

Saying 7

23 When you sit to dine with a ruler,
note well what[a] is before you,
2 and put a knife to your throat
if you are given to gluttony.
3 Do not crave his delicacies,[d]
for that food is deceptive.

Saying 8

4 Do not wear yourself out to get rich;
do not trust your own cleverness.
5 Cast but a glance at riches, and they are gone,
for they will surely sprout wings
and fly off to the sky like an eagle.[e]

Saying 9

6 Do not eat the food of a begrudging host,
do not crave his delicacies;[f]
7 for he is the kind of person
who is always thinking about the cost.[b]
"Eat and drink," he says to you,
but his heart is not with you.
8 You will vomit up the little you have eaten
and will have wasted your compliments.

Saying 10

9 Do not speak to fools,
for they will scorn your prudent words.[g]

Saying 11

10 Do not move an ancient boundary stone[h]
or encroach on the fields of the fatherless,
11 for their Defender[i] is strong;
he will take up their case against you.[j]

Saying 12

12 Apply your heart to instruction
and your ears to words of knowledge.

Saying 13

13 Do not withhold discipline from a child;
if you punish them with the rod, they will not die.
14 Punish them with the rod
and save them from death.

Saying 14

15 My son, if your heart is wise,
then my heart will be glad indeed;
16 my inmost being will rejoice
when your lips speak what is right.[k]

Saying 15

17 Do not let your heart envy[l] sinners,
but always be zealous for the fear of the LORD.
18 There is surely a future hope for you,
and your hope will not be cut off.[m]

Saying 16

19 Listen, my son, and be wise,
and set your heart on the right path:

22:29 [c] Ge 41:46
23:3 [d] ver 6-8
23:5 [e] Pr 27:24
23:6 [f] Ps 141:4
23:9 [g] Pr 1:7; 9:7; Mt 7:6
23:10 [h] Dt 19:14; Pr 22:28
23:11 [i] Job 19:25 [j] Pr 22:22-23
23:16 [k] ver 24; Pr 27:11
23:17 [l] Ps 37:1; Pr 28:14
23:18 [m] Ps 9:18; Pr 24:14,19-20

[a] *1* Or *who* [b] *7* Or *for as he thinks within himself, / so he is*; or *for as he puts on a feast, / so he is*

22:29 If earlier proverbs about the king stressed his responsibilities for executing justice and his capacities for discerning evil intention, these instructions give advice about working for such a person.

23:1–3 "Put[ting] a knife to your throat" (v. 2) is not a threat of death but rather holding a knife to one's desire.

23:4–5 Riches are deceptive; therefore, one should have the wisdom to know when to stop pursuing them or show restraint (cf. v. 2).

23:6–8 Usually, a meal is a sign of hospitality and friendship to all who come by; yet there are other meals where motives other than friendship are present. Just as Wisdom offered a banquet of life and Folly a meal of death (9:1–18), so here food and appetite are used as metaphors for the attitude one brings to their possessions and wealth.

23:9–11 One should take care when speaking to a fool who will not listen to instruction. The poor have a defender in Yahweh.

23:12–14 A renewed call to attention comes with a call to "apply" oneself (v. 12). Verses 13–14 are a call to the responsibility of teaching and correcting.

23:15–18 Two conditional sayings work individually and as a pair in vv. 15, 16. The teacher's whole "inmost being" rejoices at this meeting of wise heart and upright speech (v. 16).

Wisdom first looks to Yahweh, then toward the prosperity of others with improved vision. Envy and zeal are intense feelings of love and desire.

23:19–21 The "drowsiness" (v. 21) may come from

20 Do not join those who drink too
much wine[n]
or gorge themselves on meat,
21 for drunkards and gluttons become
poor,[o]
and drowsiness clothes them in
rags.

Saying 17

22 Listen to your father, who gave you
life,
and do not despise your mother
when she is old.[p]
23 Buy the truth and do not sell it —
wisdom, instruction and insight
as well.[q]
24 The father of a righteous child has
great joy;
a man who fathers a wise son
rejoices in him.[r]
25 May your father and mother
rejoice;
may she who gave you birth be
joyful!

Saying 18

26 My son,[s] give me your heart
and let your eyes delight in my
ways,[t]
27 for an adulterous woman is a deep
pit,[u]
and a wayward wife is a narrow
well.
28 Like a bandit she lies in wait[v]
and multiplies the unfaithful
among men.

Saying 19

29 Who has woe? Who has sorrow?
Who has strife? Who has
complaints?
Who has needless bruises? Who
has bloodshot eyes?
30 Those who linger over wine,[w]
who go to sample bowls of mixed
wine.
31 Do not gaze at wine when it is red,
when it sparkles in the cup,
when it goes down smoothly!
32 In the end it bites like a snake
and poisons like a viper.
33 Your eyes will see strange sights,
and your mind will imagine
confusing things.
34 You will be like one sleeping on the
high seas,
lying on top of the rigging.
35 "They hit me," you will say, "but I'm
not hurt!
They beat me, but I don't feel it!
When will I wake up
so I can find another drink?"

Saying 20

24 Do not envy[x] the wicked,
do not desire their company;
2 for their hearts plot violence,
and their lips talk about making
trouble.[y]

Saying 21

3 By wisdom a house is built,[z]
and through understanding it is
established;
4 through knowledge its rooms are
filled
with rare and beautiful treasures.[a]

23:20 [n] Isa 5:11, 22; Ro 13:13; Eph 5:18
23:21 [o] Pr 21:17
23:22 [p] Lev 19:32; Pr 1:8; 30:17; Eph 6:1-2
23:23 [q] Pr 4:7
23:24 [r] ver 15-16; Pr 10:1; 15:20
23:26 [s] Pr 3:1; 5:1-6 [t] Ps 18:21; Pr 4:4
23:27 [u] Pr 22:14
23:28 [v] Pr 7:11-12; Ecc 7:26
23:30 [w] Ps 75:8; Isa 5:11; Eph 5:18
24:1 [x] Ps 37:1; 73:3; Pr 3:31-32; 23:17-18
24:2 [y] Ps 10:7
24:3 [z] Pr 14:1
24:4 [a] Pr 8:21

Pr 23:19–21 ❖ How careful are we about the company we keep? Do our closest friends help build up our faith?

wine or simply from love of sleep. This teaching calls for restraint as well as independent thinking in the face of peer pressure.
23:22–25 The parental teachers again speak of gladness at their son's wise choices. This young man honors his parents by honoring their teaching.
23:26–28 To give the heart is to entrust it to the one who will direct it through teaching. The motivation for this charge is the danger of the prostitute, whose promiscuous ways are a deep pit. Those who do not watch their ways can be targets for predators.
23:29–35 A series of rhetorical questions begins with general descriptions of woe and sorrow and ends with the hangover problem of eyes that are bloodshot. The person who has these problems is the one who lingers over wine (v. 20). The braggart claims he is not hurt, but in reality he leaves himself wide open to this form of self-abuse.

✜ **22:17—23:35** A first step in self-evaluation is taking an inventory of our pursuits and the satisfaction they bring. In our age of plenty, when many middle- and upper-class people do not struggle for basic needs, a pursuit that is not satisfying can be a sign that we are into something that's bad for us.

24:1–2 What kind of company can one have with people who constantly think and speak about trouble?
24:3–4 While warnings against greed have been associated with wealth in other proverbs, here the motivations are like those of Woman Wisdom, who holds life in one hand and wealth and honor in the other.

Saying 22

5 The wise prevail through great power,
and those who have knowledge muster their strength.
6 Surely you need guidance to wage war,
and victory is won through many advisers.[b]

Saying 23

7 Wisdom is too high for fools;
in the assembly at the gate they must not open their mouths.

Saying 24

8 Whoever plots evil
will be known as a schemer.
9 The schemes of folly are sin,
and people detest a mocker.

Saying 25

10 If you falter in a time of trouble,
how small is your strength![c]
11 Rescue those being led away to death;
hold back those staggering toward slaughter.[d]
12 If you say, "But we knew nothing about this,"
does not he who weighs[e] the heart perceive it?
Does not he who guards your life know it?
Will he not repay everyone according to what they have done?[f]

Saying 26

13 Eat honey, my son, for it is good;
honey from the comb is sweet to your taste.
14 Know also that wisdom is like honey for you:
If you find it, there is a future hope for you,
and your hope will not be cut off.[g]

Saying 27

15 Do not lurk like a thief near the house of the righteous,
do not plunder their dwelling place;
16 for though the righteous fall seven times, they rise again,
but the wicked stumble when calamity strikes.[h]

Saying 28

17 Do not gloat[i] when your enemy falls;
when they stumble, do not let your heart rejoice,[j]
18 or the LORD will see and disapprove
and turn his wrath away from them.

Saying 29

19 Do not fret[k] because of evildoers
or be envious of the wicked,
20 for the evildoer has no future hope,
and the lamp of the wicked will be snuffed out.[l]

Saying 30

21 Fear the LORD and the king,[m] my son,
and do not join with rebellious officials,
22 for those two will send sudden destruction on them,
and who knows what calamities they can bring?

Pr 24:17-18 ❖ How can we share the mind of Christ when we see the misfortune of others, rather than scornfully looking down on them?

24:6 [b] Pr 11:14; 20:18; Lk 14:31
24:10 [c] Job 4:5; Jer 51:46; Heb 12:3
24:11 [d] Ps 82:4; Isa 58:6-7
24:12 [e] Pr 21:2 [f] Job 34:11; Ps 62:12; Ro 2:6*
24:14 [g] Ps 119:103; Pr 16:24; 23:18
24:16 [h] Job 5:19; Ps 34:19; Mic 7:8
24:17 [i] Ob 12 [j] Job 31:29
24:19 [k] Ps 37:1
24:20 [l] Job 18:5; Pr 13:9; 23:17-18
24:21 [m] Ro 13:1-5; 1Pe 2:17

24:5–6 The might of the wise is gained through following the teaching of others who have experience.
24:7–10 If guidance and counsel help one win a battle, the fool has none to give.

Verses 8-9 are linked by the word "scheme." Strong language links this figure with the detested mocker. The one who falters in v. 10 has little reserve against trouble.
24:11–12 There are no valid excuses for standing idle when it is possible to help. Yahweh will pay back according to a person's deeds.
24:13–14 A pair of sayings compare the sweet taste of honey and its nourishment to the goodness of wisdom that builds, fills, and fortifies a house.
24:15–16 "Lurk like a thief" reminds readers of the violent men of 1:11. The righteous may fall, but they rise again—not like the wicked.
24:17–18 Yahweh would rather have us rejoice over rescues and leave matters of judgment to him.
24:19–20 Being righteous is one thing, but the next step is trusting in God's ultimate judgment when life does not move in predictable ways.
24:21–22 The dangers of bad association have been highlighted throughout the words of the wise; this final word assures us that there is no alliance that can withstand the wrath of God and king.

Further Sayings of the Wise

23 These also are sayings of the wise:[n]

To show partiality[o] in judging is not good:[p]

24 Whoever says to the guilty, "You are innocent,"[q]
will be cursed by peoples and denounced by nations.
25 But it will go well with those who convict the guilty,
and rich blessing will come on them.

26 An honest answer
is like a kiss on the lips.

27 Put your outdoor work in order
and get your fields ready;
after that, build your house.

28 Do not testify against your neighbor without cause[r] —
would you use your lips to mislead?
29 Do not say, "I'll do to them as they have done to me;
I'll pay them back for what they did."[s]

30 I went past the field of a sluggard,[t]
past the vineyard of someone who has no sense;
31 thorns had come up everywhere,
the ground was covered with weeds,
and the stone wall was in ruins.
32 I applied my heart to what I observed
and learned a lesson from what I saw:
33 A little sleep, a little slumber,
a little folding of the hands to rest[u] —
34 and poverty will come on you like a thief
and scarcity like an armed man.[v]

More Proverbs of Solomon

25 These are more proverbs[w] of Solomon, compiled by the men of Hezekiah king of Judah:[x]

2 It is the glory of God to conceal a matter;
to search out a matter is the glory of kings.[y]
3 As the heavens are high and the earth is deep,
so the hearts of kings are unsearchable.

4 Remove the dross from the silver,
and a silversmith can produce a vessel;
5 remove wicked officials from the king's presence,[z]
and his throne will be established[a] through righteousness.[b]

6 Do not exalt yourself in the king's presence,
and do not claim a place among his great men;
7 it is better for him to say to you,
"Come up here,"[c]
than for him to humiliate you before his nobles.

What you have seen with your eyes

24:23 [n] Pr 1:6 [o] Lev 19:15 [p] Pr 28:21
24:24 [q] Pr 17:15
24:28 [r] Ps 7:4; Pr 25:18; Eph 4:25
24:29 [s] Pr 20:22; Mt 5:38-41; Ro 12:17
24:30 [t] Pr 6:6-11; 26:13-16
24:33 [u] Pr 6:10
24:34 [v] Pr 10:4; Ecc 10:18
25:1 [w] 1Ki 4:32 [x] Pr 1:1
25:2 [y] Pr 16:10-15
25:5 [z] Pr 20:8 [a] 2Sa 7:13 [b] Pr 16:12; 29:14
25:7 [c] Lk 14:7-10

24:23–26 A case is not judged based on who is involved. Verse 24 expands this idea. Verses 25–26 present a picture of those who judge rightly. The "kiss" in the ancient world communicated loyalty as well as affection (v. 26).
24:27–28 The proverb recommends putting first things first. It is folly to have a house to live in but no provisions to live on. This direct imperative to work is framed with two sayings about lips that are honest and deceitful (vv. 26, 28).
24:29 Yahweh forbids any attempt to take vengeance into one's own hands.
24:30–34 Diligence demonstrates wisdom and is essential for successful living. Negligence exacts a high price.

24:1–34 These teachings remind us that in choosing wisdom we acquire a home and stores aplenty, that we have food that is delicious and nourishing, and that these come with the responsibility to watch over our fields and work them. In other words, we who preach and teach are charged to point toward the fullness and richness of a life lived in pursuit of God's way that so many pass by in their pursuit of things that don't last.

25:1 Hezekiah and Solomon are remembered for their leadership but also for leaving kingdoms that did not survive them.
25:2 It is a king's duty to search out matters of truth in human affairs.
25:3 Just as no one can fathom all there is to know of Yahweh, so the heart of the king is never fully known, even to himself.
25:4–5 No one prefers a corrupt government any more than anyone wants impure silver; it is in this sense that the throne is "established through righteousness" (v. 5).
25:6–7 If you claim honor for yourself, you will be put in your place (see Lk 14:7–11).

8 do not bring[a] hastily to court,
for what will you do in the end
if your neighbor puts you to shame?[d]

9 If you take your neighbor to court,
do not betray another's confidence,
10 or the one who hears it may shame you
and the charge against you will stand.

11 Like apples[b] of gold in settings of silver[e]
is a ruling rightly given.
12 Like an earring of gold or an ornament of fine gold
is the rebuke of a wise judge to a listening ear.[f]

13 Like a snow-cooled drink at harvest time
is a trustworthy messenger to the one who sends him;
he refreshes the spirit of his master.[g]
14 Like clouds and wind without rain
is one who boasts of gifts never given.

15 Through patience a ruler can be persuaded,[h]
and a gentle tongue can break a bone.[i]

16 If you find honey, eat just enough —
too much of it, and you will vomit.[j]
17 Seldom set foot in your neighbor's house —
too much of you, and they will hate you.

25:8 [d] Mt 5:25-26
25:11 [e] ver 12; Pr 15:23
25:12 [f] ver 11; Ps 141:5; Pr 13:18; 15:31
25:13 [g] Pr 10:26; 13:17
25:15 [h] Ecc 10:4 [i] Pr 15:1
25:16 [j] ver 27
25:18 [k] Ps 57:4; Pr 12:18
25:22 [l] Ps 18:8 [m] 2Sa 16:12; 2Ch 28:15; Mt 5:44; Ro 12:20*
25:24 [n] Pr 21:9
25:25 [o] Pr 15:30

Pr 25:21-22 ❖ Where do we have opportunities to love our "enemies" (see Mt 5:44)?

18 Like a club or a sword or a sharp arrow
is one who gives false testimony against a neighbor.[k]
19 Like a broken tooth or a lame foot
is reliance on the unfaithful in a time of trouble.
20 Like one who takes away a garment on a cold day,
or like vinegar poured on a wound,
is one who sings songs to a heavy heart.

21 If your enemy is hungry, give him food to eat;
if he is thirsty, give him water to drink.
22 In doing this, you will heap burning coals[l] on his head,
and the LORD will reward you.[m]

23 Like a north wind that brings unexpected rain
is a sly tongue — which provokes a horrified look.

24 Better to live on a corner of the roof
than share a house with a quarrelsome wife.[n]

25 Like cold water to a weary soul
is good news from a distant land.[o]
26 Like a muddied spring or a polluted well
are the righteous who give way to the wicked.

[a] 7,8 Or *nobles / on whom you had set your eyes. / [8]Do not go* [b] 11 Or possibly *apricots*

25:8 One should not move too quickly to a high position or be too quick to contend before a judge.
25:9-10 It is also possible to speak rashly when the time comes to argue a case, resulting in a bad reputation.
25:11-12 A word of reproof or correction must find a receptive listener. The sender must craft persuasive words and discern when it is best to speak.
25:13-15 All three proverbs show the difference between speaking faithfully and falsely. The soft tongue that persuades is not a sign of weakness but power.
25:16-17 Friends and neighbors are good as long as visits are not too frequent or too long.
25:18-20 This trio of sayings describes people who cannot be trusted or counted on. In each case, what is needed is lost or missing.
25:21-22 What does it mean to heap burning coals on the enemy's head? Ancient Near Eastern culture had a variety of practices: Coals placed in a tray were carried on the head as a gift to the poor or a sign of repentance; burning coals were placed on the head to punish or to heal wounds.
25:23-24 Secret words about others will be heard and will produce negative results.
25:25-26 Good and bad sources of drinking water are compared to the positive and negative experiences of life. Whether the "righteous who give way to the wicked" is a victim or someone who fails to stand (v. 26), the outcome for those who need clear water is the same.

[27]It is not good to eat too much honey,[p]
nor is it honorable to search out
matters that are too deep.[q]
[28]Like a city whose walls are broken
through
is a person who lacks self-control.

26 Like snow in summer or rain[r] in
harvest,
honor is not fitting for a fool.[s]
[2]Like a fluttering sparrow or a darting
swallow,
an undeserved curse does not
come to rest.[t]
[3]A whip for the horse, a bridle for the
donkey,[u]
and a rod for the backs of fools![v]
[4]Do not answer a fool according to his
folly,
or you yourself will be just like
him.[w]
[5]Answer a fool according to his folly,
or he will be wise in his own eyes.[x]
[6]Sending a message by the hands of a
fool[y]
is like cutting off one's feet or
drinking poison.
[7]Like the useless legs of one who is
lame
is a proverb in the mouth of a fool.[z]
[8]Like tying a stone in a sling
is the giving of honor to a fool.[a]
[9]Like a thornbush in a drunkard's
hand
is a proverb in the mouth of a fool.[b]
[10]Like an archer who wounds at
random
is one who hires a fool or any
passer-by.
[11]As a dog returns to its vomit,[c]
so fools repeat their folly.[d]
[12]Do you see a person wise in their
own eyes?[e]
There is more hope for a fool than
for them.[f]
[13]A sluggard says,[g] "There's a lion in
the road,
a fierce lion roaming the
streets!"[h]
[14]As a door turns on its hinges,
so a sluggard turns on his bed.[i]
[15]A sluggard buries his hand in the
dish;
he is too lazy to bring it back to
his mouth.[j]
[16]A sluggard is wiser in his own eyes
than seven people who answer
discreetly.
[17]Like one who grabs a stray dog by
the ears
is someone who rushes into a
quarrel not their own.
[18]Like a maniac shooting
flaming arrows of death
[19]is one who deceives their neighbor
and says, "I was only joking!"
[20]Without wood a fire goes out;

25:27 [p]ver 16 [q]Pr 27:2; Mt 23:12
26:1 [r]1Sa 12:17 [s]ver 8; Pr 19:10
26:2 [t]Nu 23:8; Dt 23:5
26:3 [u]Ps 32:9 [v]Pr 10:13
26:4 [w]ver 5; Isa 36:21
26:5 [x]ver 4; Pr 3:7
26:6 [y]Pr 10:26
26:7 [z]ver 9
26:8 [a]ver 1
26:9 [b]ver 7
26:11 [c]2Pe 2:22* [d]Ex 8:15; Ps 85:8
26:12 [e]Pr 3:7 [f]Pr 29:20
26:13 [g]Pr 6:6-11; 24:30-34 [h]Pr 22:13
26:14 [i]Pr 6:9
26:15 [j]Pr 19:24

Pr 26:4–5 ❖ How can we discern when it is best to answer a fool and when it is best to keep our mouths shut?

25:27–28 A person who does not know when to stop eating honey or to refrain from seeking accolades is a person who lacks self-control.

25:1–28 Restraint and reflection are the sages' remedies for self-centered and unwise living. Even loving actions can be taken as offensive, so we need to guard our actions and search out our motivations.

26:1 Snow does not come in summer, and rain is not welcome during harvest; similarly, glory should not come to a fool.
26:2 The metaphors depict birds one never sees at rest (23:5); so also an "undeserved curse" never lands.
26:3 If a rod is recommended, the fool is no smarter than beasts of burden.
26:4–5 This famous pair of contrasting sayings show that it is not always easy to know how to make a fitting response to a fool.
26:6 It is not clear whether the harm described is done to the sender or to others, but the former is more likely.
26:7 Anyone can memorize a collection of sayings and apply them inappropriately.
26:8 Giving honor to a fool is not only inappropriate but also dangerous.
26:9 When spoken by a fool, a proverb has little effect.
26:10 Sending a fool to teach creates danger for all.
26:11–12 The dog's actions make holding on to folly seem particularly distasteful. There is more chance that the fool will learn than will someone who is "wise in their own" eyes (v. 12).
26:13–16 These verses present a series of vignettes on the sluggard: three that demonstrate his laziness, and the fourth to show that like the fool, he is "wiser in his own eyes" (v. 16). Although the proverbs have associated the sluggard's behavior with folly, he does not see it that way, which is perhaps his greatest folly of all.
26:17–19 These extended sayings depict one who does not take seriously the ruinous effects of his words and actions.
26:20–22 Taken together, one can see the need to cut out both the behavior and the person who

without a gossip a quarrel dies
down.[k]
21 As charcoal to embers and as wood
to fire,
so is a quarrelsome person for
kindling strife.[l]
22 The words of a gossip are like choice
morsels;
they go down to the inmost
parts.[m]

23 Like a coating of silver dross on
earthenware
are fervent[a] lips with an evil
heart.
24 Enemies disguise themselves with
their lips,[n]
but in their hearts they harbor
deceit.[o]
25 Though their speech is charming,[p]
do not believe them,
for seven abominations fill their
hearts.[q]
26 Their malice may be concealed by
deception,
but their wickedness will be
exposed in the assembly.
27 Whoever digs a pit[r] will fall into it;[s]
if someone rolls a stone, it will roll
back on them.[t]
28 A lying tongue hates those it hurts,
and a flattering mouth[u] works
ruin.

27 Do not boast[v] about tomorrow,
for you do not know what a day
may bring.[w]

2 Let someone else praise you, and not
your own mouth;
an outsider, and not your own lips.[x]

3 Stone is heavy and sand[y] a burden,
but a fool's provocation is heavier
than both.

4 Anger is cruel and fury
overwhelming,
but who can stand before
jealousy?[z]

5 Better is open rebuke
than hidden love.

6 Wounds from a friend can be
trusted,
but an enemy multiplies kisses.[a]

7 One who is full loathes honey from
the comb,
but to the hungry even what is
bitter tastes sweet.

8 Like a bird that flees its nest[b]
is anyone who flees from home.

9 Perfume[c] and incense bring joy to
the heart,
and the pleasantness of a friend
springs from their heartfelt
advice.

10 Do not forsake your friend or a
friend of your family,
and do not go to your relative's
house when disaster[d] strikes
you —
better a neighbor nearby than a
relative far away.

11 Be wise, my son, and bring joy to my
heart;[e]
then I can answer anyone who
treats me with contempt.[f]

26:20 [k] Pr 22:10
26:21 [l] Pr 14:17; 15:18
26:22 [m] Pr 18:8
26:24 [n] Ps 31:18 [o] Ps 41:6; Pr 10:18; 12:20
26:25 [p] Ps 28:3 [q] Jer 9:4-8
26:27 [r] Ps 7:15 [s] Est 6:13 [t] Est 2:23; 7:9; Ps 35:8; 141:10; Pr 28:10; 29:6; Isa 50:11
26:28 [u] Ps 12:3; Pr 29:5
27:1 [v] 1Ki 20:11 [w] Mt 6:34; Lk 12:19-20; Jas 4:13-16
27:2 [x] Pr 25:27
27:3 [y] Job 6:3
27:4 [z] Nu 5:14
27:6 [a] Ps 141:5; Pr 28:23
27:8 [b] Isa 16:2
27:9 [c] Est 2:12; Ps 45:8
27:10 [d] Pr 17:17; 18:24
27:11 [e] Pr 10:1; 23:15-16 [f] Ge 24:60

[a] 23 Hebrew; Septuagint *smooth*

---

stirs up quarrels. Morsels of "gossip" (v. 20) have a negative influence on one's mind and heart.

26:23–25 Three proverbs develop the theme of deception, describing it as an attractive surface that hides the ugliness lying beneath.

26:26–28 Three examples of evil deeds that backfire begin with the ultimate end of deception. When malice is exposed, everyone will know. The false tongue not only hurts others, but it also hurts itself because it leads to its own ruin.

26:1–28 If we are to apply the principles of these proverbs to our own day, we may as well admit that at times we have all played the fool or the troublemaker to some degree. The problem is that we are messing with the basic chemistry of communication: We are in danger of blowing up the lab, hurting others as well as ourselves.

27:1 This famous proverb speaks about the capriciousness of life.

27:2 Lips were made for building up one another, not for building up ourselves.

27:3–4 We feel burdened by the folly of others, but who has not been knocked down by our own jealousy?

27:5–6 Reproof is painful but profitable. Friendship sometimes brings praise and sometimes wounds, but those wounds are also faithful.

27:7–8 One whose hunger is satisfied literally walks past or tramples honey, while someone who strays from home is like the bird that leaves the safety of the nest.

27:9–10 The sweet smells of incense cause the heart to rejoice, just as the sweetness of a friend and neighbor is better than one's own counsel.

27:11–12 A father is glad to see his son exercise prudence and follow a wise path.

[12]The prudent see danger and take refuge,
but the simple keep going and pay the penalty.[g]

[13]Take the garment of one who puts up security for a stranger;
hold it in pledge if it is done for an outsider.[h]

[14]If anyone loudly blesses their neighbor early in the morning,
it will be taken as a curse.

[15]A quarrelsome wife is like the dripping[i]
of a leaky roof in a rainstorm;
[16]restraining her is like restraining the wind
or grasping oil with the hand.

[17]As iron sharpens iron,
so one person sharpens another.

[18]The one who guards a fig tree will eat its fruit,[j]
and whoever protects their master will be honored.[k]

[19]As water reflects the face,
so one's life reflects the heart.[a]

[20]Death and Destruction[b] are never satisfied,[l]
and neither are human eyes.[m]

[21]The crucible for silver and the furnace for gold,[n]
but people are tested by their praise.

[22]Though you grind a fool in a mortar,
grinding them like grain with a pestle,
you will not remove their folly from them.

[23]Be sure you know the condition of your flocks,[o]
give careful attention to your herds;
[24]for riches do not endure forever,[p]
and a crown is not secure for all generations.
[25]When the hay is removed and new growth appears
and the grass from the hills is gathered in,
[26]the lambs will provide you with clothing,
and the goats with the price of a field.
[27]You will have plenty of goats' milk to feed your family
and to nourish your female servants.

28 The wicked flee[q] though no one pursues,[r]
but the righteous are as bold as a lion.[s]

[2]When a country is rebellious, it has many rulers,
but a ruler with discernment and knowledge maintains order.

[3]A ruler[c] who oppresses the poor
is like a driving rain that leaves no crops.

27:12 [g] Pr 22:3
27:13 [h] Pr 20:16
27:15 [i] Est 1:18; Pr 19:13
27:18 [j] 1Co 9:7 [k] Lk 19:12-27
27:20 [l] Pr 30:15-16; Hab 2:5 [m] Ecc 1:8; 6:7
27:21 [n] Pr 17:3
27:23 [o] Pr 12:10
27:24 [p] Pr 23:5
28:1 [q] 2Ki 7:7 [r] Lev 26:17; Ps 53:5 [s] Ps 138:3

[a] 19 Or *so others reflect your heart back to you*
[b] 20 Hebrew *Abaddon*
[c] 3 Or *A poor person*

Pr 27:17 ❖ How have our Christian friends shaped and sharpened us?

27:13–14 Treating strangers like neighbors and neighbors like enemies shows that excessive actions are inappropriate even if intended to be friendly.
27:15–16 Little can be done with a contentious person.
27:17–18 Two proverbs speak about good relations with neighbors and employers. By serving well *and* keeping the employer sharp, servants receive honor (v. 18).
27:19–20 If kind hearts can reflect one another in friendship, it is also true that greedy eyes can devour another's life.
27:21–22 The way we react to the praise of others reveals our motives, either honorable or dishonorable. Folly cannot be separated from the fool, for it is too deeply ingrained.
27:23–27 These last five verses make up an extended poem, notable for its pastoral imagery. The person is to know the "condition" (literally, "face," v. 23) of the flocks, just as the wise study and know the human heart. One never arrives at a place where work is not necessary, and vv. 26–27 describe the payoff for diligence.

✥ **27:1–27** It is hard to see when legitimate concern for well-being turns the corner into greed, the desire for possessions that makes them into gods. The proverbs and poem of this chapter help us to see that there is an approach to life and possessions that sets them in proper perspective.

28:1 Righteous confidence is contrasted with the fear of the wicked, always looking over their shoulders as they flee.
28:2 People will rebel unless led by a person of wisdom.
28:3 The natural image of torrential rain that flattens grain is clear.

4 Those who forsake instruction
praise the wicked,
but those who heed it resist them.

5 Evildoers do not understand what is
right,
but those who seek the LORD
understand it fully.

6 Better the poor whose walk is
blameless
than the rich whose ways are
perverse.[t]

7 A discerning son heeds instruction,
but a companion of gluttons
disgraces his father.[u]

8 Whoever increases wealth by taking
interest[v] or profit from the
poor
amasses it for another,[w] who will
be kind to the poor.[x]

9 If anyone turns a deaf ear to my
instruction,
even their prayers are detestable.[y]

10 Whoever leads the upright along an
evil path
will fall into their own trap,[z]
but the blameless will receive a
good inheritance.

11 The rich are wise in their own eyes;
one who is poor and discerning
sees how deluded they are.

12 When the righteous triumph, there
is great elation;[a]
but when the wicked rise to
power, people go into
hiding.[b]

Pr 28:11 ❖ How can wealth blind us to godly wisdom and discernment?

13 Whoever conceals their sins[c] does
not prosper,
but the one who confesses and
renounces them finds mercy.[d]

14 Blessed is the one who always
trembles before God,
but whoever hardens their heart
falls into trouble.

15 Like a roaring lion or a charging bear
is a wicked ruler over a helpless
people.

16 A tyrannical ruler practices
extortion,
but one who hates ill-gotten gain
will enjoy a long reign.

17 Anyone tormented by the guilt of
murder
will seek refuge[e] in the grave;
let no one hold them back.

18 The one whose walk is blameless is
kept safe,
but the one whose ways are
perverse will fall[f] into the pit.[a]

19 Those who work their land will have
abundant food,
but those who chase fantasies will
have their fill of poverty.[g]

20 A faithful person will be richly
blessed,
but one eager to get rich will not
go unpunished.[h]

28:6 [t] Pr 19:1
28:7 [u] Pr 23:19-21
28:8 [v] Ex 18:21 [w] Job 27:17; Pr 13:22 [x] Ps 112:9; Pr 14:31; Lk 14:12-14
28:9 [y] Ps 66:18; 109:7; Pr 15:8; Isa 1:13
28:10 [z] Pr 26:27
28:12 [a] 2Ki 11:20 [b] Pr 11:10; 29:2
28:13 [c] Job 31:33 [d] Ps 32:1-5; 1Jn 1:9
28:17 [e] Ge 9:6
28:18 [f] Pr 10:9
28:19 [g] Pr 12:11
28:20 [h] ver 22; Pr 10:6; 1Ti 6:9

[a] *18* Syriac (see Septuagint); Hebrew *into one*

28:4 The righteous keep their ways straight and ensure others do the same.
28:5 This saying contrasts those who "do not understand" with those who "understand all things" (alternate translation) because they seek Yahweh.
28:6 In both cases, the only essential possession is integrity.
28:7 A person can choose to be discerning or disgraceful.
28:8 Ill-gotten wealth goes to one who will give it back to the poor.
28:9 One who won't listen to God won't be heard by God.
28:10 This proverb presents an evil person leading another along a path strewn with his own traps, reminding readers of 1:17–18.
28:11 We would expect the contrasting poor person to be humble, with downcast eyes. Instead, this person has eyes that see through the bravado of a deluded wealthy person.
28:12 A leader's character will have consequences for everyone.
28:13 People may forgive a person who truly changes.
28:14 A hard heart will hide, not confess.
28:15 In Proverbs, the king's wrath is like the lion's roar (19:12; 20:2); here, the roar is like a wicked person ruling over the helpless poor.
28:16 This contrasts the tyrant who rules with "great oppression" (alternate translation) and the good ruler who "makes long the days" (alternate translation); that is, has a long life.
28:17 Sins of blood start a justice in motion that cannot be derailed.
28:18 The blameless are "kept safe" (or "saved"), although the protector is not named.
28:19 This saying is nearly identical to 12:11.
28:20 If one seeks the goal of possessions alone, even more will be lost.

21 To show partiality is not good[i]—
yet a person will do wrong for a piece of bread.[j]

22 The stingy are eager to get rich
and are unaware that poverty awaits them.[k]

23 Whoever rebukes a person will in the end gain favor
rather than one who has a flattering tongue.[l]

24 Whoever robs their father or mother[m]
and says, "It's not wrong,"
is partner to one who destroys.[n]

25 The greedy stir up conflict,
but those who trust in the LORD[o] will prosper.

26 Those who trust in themselves are fools,[p]
but those who walk in wisdom are kept safe.

27 Those who give to the poor will lack nothing,[q]
but those who close their eyes to them receive many curses.

28 When the wicked rise to power, people go into hiding;[r]
but when the wicked perish, the righteous thrive.

28:21 [i]Pr 18:5 [j]Eze 13:19
28:22 [k]ver 20; Pr 23:6
28:23 [l]Pr 27:5-6
28:24 [m]Pr 19:26 [n]Pr 18:9
28:25 [o]Pr 29:25
28:26 [p]Ps 4:5; Pr 3:5
28:27 [q]Dt 15:7; 24:19; Pr 19:17; 22:9
28:28 [r]ver 12

29 Whoever remains stiff-necked after many rebukes
will suddenly be destroyed—without remedy.[s]

2 When the righteous thrive, the people rejoice;[t]
when the wicked rule, the people groan.[u]

3 A man who loves wisdom brings joy to his father,[v]
but a companion of prostitutes squanders his wealth.[w]

4 By justice a king gives a country stability,[x]
but those who are greedy for[a] bribes tear it down.

5 Those who flatter their neighbors
are spreading nets for their feet.

6 Evildoers are snared by their own sin,[y]
but the righteous shout for joy and are glad.

7 The righteous care about justice for the poor,[z]
but the wicked have no such concern.

8 Mockers stir up a city,
but the wise turn away anger.[a]

29:1 [s]2Ch 36:16; Pr 6:15
29:2 [t]Est 8:15 [u]Pr 28:12
29:3 [v]Pr 10:1 [w]Pr 5:8-10; Lk 15:11-32
29:4 [x]Pr 8:15-16
29:6 [y]Ecc 9:12
29:7 [z]Job 29:16; Ps 41:1; Pr 31:8-9
29:8 [a]Pr 11:11; 16:14

[a] 4 Or *who give*

28:21 People will thoughtlessly risk great penalties for miniscule potential rewards.
28:22 Acquiring wealth just to hold on to it makes a poor goal for one's life.
28:23 The honest tongue, not a "flattering" one, earns favor.
28:24 Parents who have given their very selves to their children deserve care when they have needs in their later years.
28:25 Greed brings "conflict"; trust brings prosperity.
28:26 Although it seems logical that we know our needs and can look out for our own best interests, nothing is further from the truth.
28:27 The key is to be able to see need, but many shut their eyes.
28:28 The wicked will perish; after that, the righteous will thrive.

✣ **28:1–28** Christians are first called to live as an alternate community to the ways of the world, balancing radical identification and distinction. Christians are also called upon to vote and serve as community leaders. While the church exists as a model of what might be, challenging and inspiring the rest of the community, its members are also faced with the responsibility of presenting their views on social and political matters and of lending support to local civic bodies and service organizations.

29:1 The stubborn ox became a symbol of rebellious Israel.
29:2 The effects of wisdom and folly are especially pronounced when practiced by someone in authority.
29:3 This saying pits love of wisdom against prostitutes, similar to personifications of Wisdom and Folly throughout the book.
29:4 "Justice" is the highest responsibility of the king.
29:5 It is not clear whether "their feet" goes with the neighbor or the flatterer. If the first, the contrast is between the smooth words of flattery and the harsh capture of the net. If the latter, the proverb is like the saying "what goes around comes around."
29:6 The net spread out for others (v. 5) is also the sin that traps the trapper.
29:7 "A righteous one knows the rights of the poor; a wicked one does not understand such knowledge" (alternate translation).
29:8 This saying is the first of a series about speaking and listening (vv. 8–12).

9 If a wise person goes to court with a
fool,
the fool rages and scoffs, and
there is no peace.

10 The bloodthirsty hate a person of
integrity
and seek to kill the upright.[b]

11 Fools give full vent to their rage,
but the wise bring calm in the
end.[c]

12 If a ruler listens to lies,
all his officials become wicked.

13 The poor and the oppressor have
this in common:
The LORD gives sight to the eyes of
both.[d]

14 If a king judges the poor with
fairness,
his throne will be established
forever.[e]

15 A rod and a reprimand impart
wisdom,
but a child left undisciplined
disgraces its mother.[f]

16 When the wicked thrive, so does sin,
but the righteous will see their
downfall.[g]

17 Discipline your children, and they
will give you peace;
they will bring you the delights
you desire.[h]

18 Where there is no revelation, people
cast off restraint;

29:10 [b] 1Jn 3:12
29:11 [c] Pr 12:16; 19:11
29:13 [d] Pr 22:2; Mt 5:45
29:14 [e] Ps 72:1-5; Pr 16:12
29:15 [f] Pr 10:1; 13:24; 17:21,25
29:16 [g] Ps 37:35-36; 58:10; 91:8; 92:11
29:17 [h] ver 15; Pr 10:1

Pr 29:15 ❖ How has positive discipline benefited our character and faith?

but blessed is the one who heeds
wisdom's instruction.[i]

19 Servants cannot be corrected by
mere words;
though they understand, they will
not respond.

20 Do you see someone who speaks in
haste?
There is more hope for a fool than
for them.[j]

21 A servant pampered from youth
will turn out to be insolent.

22 An angry person stirs up conflict,
and a hot-tempered person
commits many sins.[k]

23 Pride brings a person low,
but the lowly in spirit gain honor.[l]

24 The accomplices of thieves are their
own enemies;
they are put under oath and dare
not testify.[m]

25 Fear of man will prove to be a snare,
but whoever trusts in the LORD[n] is
kept safe.

26 Many seek an audience with a ruler,[o]
but it is from the LORD that one
gets justice.

27 The righteous detest the dishonest;
the wicked detest the upright.[p]

29:18 [i] Ps 1:1-2; 119:1-2; Jn 13:17
29:20 [j] Pr 26:12; Jas 1:19
29:22 [k] Pr 14:17; 15:18; 26:21
29:23 [l] Pr 11:2; 15:33; 16:18; Isa 66:2; Mt 23:12
29:24 [m] Lev 5:1
29:25 [n] Pr 28:25
29:26 [o] Pr 19:6
29:27 [p] ver 10

29:9 The wise may calm someone's anger, but not the rage of a recalcitrant fool.
29:10 The evil intent of those who hate upright integrity contrasts with those who love it.
29:11 The wise give their words beauty and persuasiveness.
29:12 Those in authority must weed out the word of falsehood before it takes root.
29:13 The power imbalance between two people is restored with one look at the One who gives them both sight.
29:14 Yahweh, who judges the poor faithfully, is strong and stable.
29:15 The parent who neglects needed correction risks receiving unwanted shame.
29:16 This proverb on character is equally applicable to business, courts, and households.
29:17 This proverb stresses the positive aspect of discipline.
29:18 This proverb goes far beyond church programs and goal setting to our personal lives. In all things, we need to follow the godly way and work within its wise parameters.
29:19 Servants were expected to follow orders, and at times more than a verbal prodding was necessary.
29:20 To say that "there is more hope for a fool" is to use hyperbole to show how serious the matter is.
29:21 Discipline provided early on will lead to a happier life for the child and the parent.
29:22 As wrath goes uncontrolled, so does its damage.
29:23 Better to be called up higher than put lower.
29:24 To hold back testimony when it is called for is a crime of complicity.
29:25 One can show kindness without fear since Yahweh rewards.
29:26 The proverb lends assurance for those times when no justice from an earthly ruler can be obtained.
29:27 "Detest" communicates more than a feeling of mutual distaste; instead, it indicates that the two ways of life are totally incompatible.

✣ **29:1–27** Many believe that most decisions about behavior are a matter of personal choice.

Sayings of Agur

30 The sayings of Agur son of Jakeh — an inspired utterance.

This man's utterance to Ithiel:

"I am weary, God,
but I can prevail.[a]
2 Surely I am only a brute, not a man;
I do not have human understanding.
3 I have not learned wisdom,
nor have I attained to the knowledge of the Holy One.[q]
4 Who has gone up[r] to heaven and come down?
Whose hands[s] have gathered up the wind?
Who has wrapped up the waters[t] in a cloak?[u]
Who has established all the ends of the earth?
What is his name,[v] and what is the name of his son?
Surely you know!

5 "Every word of God is flawless;[w]
he is a shield[x] to those who take refuge in him.
6 Do not add[y] to his words,
or he will rebuke you and prove you a liar.

7 "Two things I ask of you, LORD;
do not refuse me before I die:
8 Keep falsehood and lies far from me;
give me neither poverty nor riches,
but give me only my daily bread.[z]
9 Otherwise, I may have too much and disown[a] you
and say, 'Who is the LORD?'[b]
Or I may become poor and steal,
and so dishonor the name of my God.[c]

10 "Do not slander a servant to their master,
or they will curse you, and you will pay for it.

11 "There are those who curse their fathers
and do not bless their mothers;[d]
12 those who are pure in their own eyes[e]
and yet are not cleansed of their filth;[f]
13 those whose eyes are ever so haughty,[g]
whose glances are so disdainful;
14 those whose teeth[h] are swords
and whose jaws are set with knives[i]
to devour[j] the poor[k] from the earth
and the needy from among mankind.[l]

15 "The leech has two daughters.
'Give! Give!' they cry.

"There are three things that are never satisfied,[m]
four that never say, 'Enough!':
16 the grave,[n] the barren womb,
land, which is never satisfied with water,
and fire, which never says, 'Enough!'

17 "The eye that mocks[o] a father,
that scorns an aged mother,

30:3 [q] Pr 9:10
30:4 [r] Ps 24:1-2; Jn 3:13; Eph 4:7-10 [s] Ps 104:3; Isa 40:12 [t] Job 26:8; 38:8-9 [u] Ge 1:2 [v] Rev 19:12
30:5 [w] Ps 12:6; 18:30 [x] Ge 15:1; Ps 84:11
30:6 [y] Dt 4:2; 12:32; Rev 22:18
30:8 [z] Mt 6:11
30:9 [a] Jos 24:27; Isa 1:4; 59:13 [b] Dt 6:12; 8:10-14; Hos 13:6 [c] Dt 8:12
30:11 [d] Pr 20:20
30:12 [e] Pr 16:2; Lk 18:11 [f] Jer 2:23,35
30:13 [g] 2Sa 22:28; Job 41:34; Ps 131:1; Pr 6:17
30:14 [h] Job 4:11; 29:17; Ps 3:7 [i] Ps 57:4 [j] Job 24:9; Ps 14:4 [k] Am 8:4; Mic 2:2 [l] Job 19:22
30:15 [m] Pr 27:20
30:16 [n] Pr 27:20; Isa 5:14; 14:9,11; Hab 2:5
30:17 [o] Dt 21:18-21; Pr 23:22

[a] *1* With a different word division of the Hebrew; Masoretic Text *utterance to Ithiel, / to Ithiel and Ukal:*

The faulty logic of this thinking was exposed by a series of antidrug ads. Young people looked into the camera and said, "I killed a drug runner"; "I bribed police"; "I helped so-and-so die of an overdose." By participating in the drug trade, people are complicit in all sorts of unspeakable crimes. Such are the unintended consequences of intentionally living a life far from God.

30:1–5 Agur's message begins with a confession of ignorance (v. 2). Humans uniquely perceive spiritual matters and have a relationship with their Creator. To lack such perception is to be like an animal.

Four questions in v. 4 initiate a series of "fours" that runs throughout the chapter. The questions imply that God acts to create and maintain a world, but God also speaks (v. 5). That pure word shows that God is a "shield" (v. 5) to those who take refuge in him.

30:6–10 Verses 5–6 are linked around the theme of God's words. Any additions to those faultless words will prove false. To talk when we should be listening is never wise.

The theme of falsehood continues into v. 10, for slandering a servant is probably to bring a false report. Such bad talk brings a curse.

30:11–14 Each of the next four verses describes "one of a generation" who rejects the way of wisdom, the opposite of God's intention for humankind.

30:15–17 The leech's twin daughters are repulsive and sobering metaphors for a greedy generation. The following sayings bring together four more leech-like consumers that will take all they can.

will be pecked out by the ravens of
the valley,
will be eaten by the vultures.[p]

18 "There are three things that are too
amazing for me,
four that I do not understand:
19 the way of an eagle in the sky,
the way of a snake on a rock,
the way of a ship on the high seas,
and the way of a man with a
young woman.

20 "This is the way of an adulterous
woman:
She eats and wipes her mouth
and says, 'I've done nothing
wrong.'[q]

21 "Under three things the earth
trembles,
under four it cannot bear up:
22 a servant who becomes king,[r]
a godless fool who gets plenty to
eat,
23 a contemptible woman who gets
married,
and a servant who displaces her
mistress.

24 "Four things on earth are small,
yet they are extremely wise:
25 Ants are creatures of little strength,
yet they store up their food in the
summer;[s]
26 hyraxes[t] are creatures of little power,
yet they make their home in the
crags;
27 locusts[u] have no king,
yet they advance together in
ranks;

30:17 [p] Job 15:23
30:20 [q] Pr 5:6
30:22 [r] Pr 19:10; 29:2
30:25 [s] Pr 6:6-8
30:26 [t] Ps 104:18
30:27 [u] Ex 10:4

Pr 30:24-28 ❖ Where do we find God's great wisdom in small things?

28 a lizard can be caught with the hand,
yet it is found in kings' palaces.

29 "There are three things that are
stately in their stride,
four that move with stately
bearing:
30 a lion, mighty among beasts,
who retreats before nothing;
31 a strutting rooster, a he-goat,
and a king secure against revolt.[a]

32 "If you play the fool and exalt
yourself,
or if you plan evil,
clap your hand over your mouth![v]
33 For as churning cream produces
butter,
and as twisting the nose produces
blood,
so stirring up anger produces
strife."

Sayings of King Lemuel

31 The sayings[w] of King Lemuel—
an inspired utterance his mother
taught him.

2 Listen, my son! Listen, son of my
womb!
Listen, my son, the answer to my
prayers![x]
3 Do not spend your strength[b] on
women,

30:32 [v] Job 21:5; 29:9
31:1 [w] Pr 22:17
31:2 [x] Jdg 11:30; Isa 49:15

[a] *31* The meaning of the Hebrew for this phrase is uncertain. [b] *3* Or *wealth*

30:18–20 The second of the "three-four" sayings brings together four phenomena about which the speaker says, "I do not understand" (v. 18). All four creatures know their part of the created order: Eagles don't try to swim, snakes don't try to fly, and ships that go on rocks are destroyed. Therefore, men or women who despise the mystery of love and sex and move outside of its boundaries are like those who step out of their place in created order.
30:21–23 The four items listed threaten to overturn the created order. In the view of the sages, there is an order to life, and if it is just and fair, it should not be disturbed.
30:24–28 These small creatures teach great lessons about being a people, asking ancient readers: "What kind of people do you want to be—strong, led by a king? You don't need that as much as you need wisdom."
30:29–31 The use of "king" in v. 31 brings together its occurrences in vv. 24–28, suggesting that we understand these brave and stately four in light of the small and wise four. Again, power comes not from strength or numbers alone but from wisdom.
30:32–33 Speech is for defending others, not for plotting and speaking evil. The three lines of v. 33 are linked by the repetition of the translation "produces."

30:1–33 Courage comes from having a healthy assessment of who we are—limitations, sins, and all—but also in being able to see who God is as well. Pride subverts both, driving us to gobble up all we can in our foolish and insatiable hunger and to speak in ways that churn up anger and violence.

31:1–2 These sayings are not really Lemuel's but his mother's, a reminder that women serve as teachers throughout the book.
31:3–5 The ideal king protects the poor and

your vigor on those who ruin
kings.[y]
4 It is not for kings, Lemuel —
it is not for kings to drink wine,[z]
not for rulers to crave beer,
5 lest they drink[a] and forget what has
been decreed,[b]
and deprive all the oppressed of
their rights.
6 Let beer be for those who are
perishing,
wine[c] for those who are in
anguish!
7 Let them drink[d] and forget their
poverty
and remember their misery no
more.
8 Speak[e] up for those who cannot
speak for themselves,
for the rights of all who are
destitute.
9 Speak up and judge fairly;
defend the rights of the poor and
needy.[f]

Epilogue: The Wife of Noble Character

10 [a]A wife of noble character[g] who can
find?[h]
She is worth far more than rubies.
11 Her husband[i] has full confidence in
her
and lacks nothing of value.[j]
12 She brings him good, not harm,
all the days of her life.
13 She selects wool and flax
and works with eager hands.[k]
14 She is like the merchant ships,
bringing her food from afar.
15 She gets up while it is still night;
she provides food for her family
and portions for her female
servants.
16 She considers a field and buys it;
out of her earnings she plants a
vineyard.
17 She sets about her work vigorously;
her arms are strong for her tasks.
18 She sees that her trading is profitable,
and her lamp does not go out at
night.
19 In her hand she holds the distaff
and grasps the spindle with her
fingers.
20 She opens her arms to the poor
and extends her hands to the
needy.[l]
21 When it snows, she has no fear for
her household;
for all of them are clothed in
scarlet.
22 She makes coverings for her bed;
she is clothed in fine linen and
purple.
23 Her husband is respected at the city
gate,
where he takes his seat among the
elders[m] of the land.
24 She makes linen garments and sells
them,
and supplies the merchants with
sashes.
25 She is clothed with strength and
dignity;
she can laugh at the days to come.

31:3 [y] Dt 17:17; 1Ki 11:3; Ne 13:26; Pr 5:1-14
31:4 [z] Pr 20:1; Ecc 10:16-17; Isa 5:22
31:5 [a] 1Ki 16:9 [b] Pr 16:12; Hos 4:11
31:6 [c] Ge 14:18
31:7 [d] Est 1:10
31:8 [e] 1Sa 19:4; Job 29:12-17
31:9 [f] Lev 19:15; Dt 1:16; Pr 24:23; 29:7; Isa 1:17; Jer 22:16
31:10 [g] Ru 3:11; Pr 12:4; 18:22 [h] Pr 8:35; 19:14
31:11 [i] Ge 2:18 [j] Pr 12:4
31:13 [k] 1Ti 2:9-10
31:20 [l] Dt 15:11; Eph 4:28; Heb 13:16
31:23 [m] Ex 3:16; Ru 4:1,11; Pr 12:4

Pr 31:8 ❖ How can we speak up for and defend the rights and needs of those who are often voiceless?

[a] *10* Verses 10-31 are an acrostic poem, the verses of which begin with the successive letters of the Hebrew alphabet.

---

defenseless, caring for them instead of amassing wealth and building great palaces.
31:6–9 Behind this recommendation to give drink is a concern for responsible execution of judgment and care. Moreover, the offer of drink is not the only solution; we would be more concerned about this counsel were it not followed by the call to compassionately speak out for the poor.
31:10–11 From the start we are given a clue that somehow this poem is a summary of all that has been said about wisdom in Proverbs. The first of the praises describes this woman's character as a treasure. Her husband recognizes her worth, for he "lacks nothing" (v. 11).
31:12–18 This woman works and trades night and day to provide for herself and her household; she is as wise as the evil characters of ch. 30 are foolish and self-centered.
31:19–20 The wordplay here creates a contrast between the hands that close on her tools of production but open to share her rewards with the poor.
31:21–29 The husband and household appear twice: first as beneficiaries, then as those who praise her.
31:25–26 The wordplay in v. 25 clothes this woman in "strength and dignity." The husband is not the only one who speaks wisely, for she "opens her mouth in wisdom" (alternate translation, v. 26a), just as Lemuel was instructed in vv. 8–9. The "faithful instruction" (v. 26b) is both true to the tradition and to the marginalized people it serves. If

[26] She speaks with wisdom,
and faithful instruction is on her tongue.[n]
[27] She watches over the affairs of her household
and does not eat the bread of idleness.
[28] Her children arise and call her blessed;
her husband also, and he praises her:
[29] "Many women do noble things,
but you surpass them all."
[30] Charm is deceptive, and beauty is fleeting;
but a woman who fears the LORD is to be praised.
[31] Honor her for all that her hands have done,
and let her works bring her praise[o] at the city gate.

31:26 [n] Pr 10:31
31:31 [o] Pr 11:16

---

the husband speaks for justice at the gates, she does the same in the home. If the start of the poem lauds the good she brings to her husband, the end rewards her with praise, from her children and her spouse.

31:30-31 More important than any beauty, charm, or even work is the fear of Yahweh, which shapes all that this woman is. What else can we readers do but join in giving her praise (v. 30) and "honor" (v. 31)?

31:1-31 Perhaps the most important aspect of the conclusion to the book of Proverbs is that both Lemuel's mother and the woman of noble character teach and model the orderly life of wisdom. Let us be taught not only to live sober and responsible lives but also to "speak up for those who cannot speak for themselves" (v. 8). Let us manage our affairs so as to provide well for family and stranger.

Ecclesiastes

Author: Possibly King Solomon

Audience: The people of Israel

Date: Unknown; possibly as early as the tenth century BC

Theme: This wisdom teacher reveals what he has discovered about the meaninglessness of every human endeavor without God at the center of one's life.

PERSPECTIVE

Ecclesiastes is a difficult book: The language is difficult, the book is filled with wordplays, the argument is complex, it doesn't mention other major biblical figures like Abraham, Isaac, and Jacob, and it doesn't refer to any of God's dealings with Israel. Its themes, other commentators have said, border on contradictions. It is a difficult book because when compared with the rest of the OT books, it is different.

So too with the Song of Songs. An erotic love song, even if its ultimate meaning is an extended metaphor of God's love for Israel and/or the church and vice versa, does not lend itself easily to division into easily manageable study extracts or word studies. On a human level, it seems almost too explicit for our sensitivities.

So what can we learn from these unusual pieces of writing? Because they fall into the category of wisdom literature, they reveal truth in ways different from historical and prophetic literature.

Consider the authorship of Ecclesiastes. In truth, we do not know who the author is. The book effectively veils the writer's identity so that we are forced to focus on the content. This pattern was typical of ancient Near Eastern literature, where it was commonplace to write anonymously. We therefore have difficulty digesting or paying attention to an idea unless it is personified in a personality. Perhaps one lesson we need to learn is that ideas don't always need personality.

Consider another example: The text of Ecclesiastes is filled with what appear to be contradictions. In one place pleasure is condemned ("What does pleasure accomplish?" 2:2) and in another place endorsed

Reading Ecclesiastes

Reading this book can be frustrating, for there is no formal structure to its content. It is perhaps best to see the author as taking several themes and presenting different snapshots of them, each from a different angle. By the time he is finished, however, we have grasped the overall impact of his message.

Event	Timeline (1400 BC – 400 BC)
Saul's reign (1050–1010 BC)	
David's reign (1010–970 BC)	
Solomon's reign (970–930 BC)	
Book of Ecclesiastes written (c. 970–930 BC)	
Building of the temple (966–959 BC)	
Division of the kingdom (930 BC)	
Exile of Israel (722 BC)	
Fall of Jerusalem (586 BC)	

Key Verse

Now all has been heard; here is the conclusion of the matter: Fear God and keep his commandments, for this is the duty of all mankind.

—Ecclesiastes 12:13

("I commend the enjoyment of life," 8:15). Two theories have regularly been put forth to try to explain these contradictions. According to the quotation theory, the author of Ecclesiastes quotes people he does not agree with in order to highlight his own view. The addition theory, by contrast, maintains that a later editor added material in order to "correct" the author's view. But an even better explanation is that by juxtaposing these simple though contrasting statements, the author reveals a deeper truth on the subject—revelation through comparison and paradox.

Or consider a third example: The tone of Ecclesiastes is often seen as gloomy. Perhaps the most well-known and oft-quoted verse in the whole text is 1:2 ("Everything is meaningless"), although 12:7 ("The dust returns to the ground it came from") will win no happy-face awards. It is true that death is a frequent topic in Ecclesiastes. Yet one does not come away from reading this book seeing death as victor. On the contrary, it is obvious that life is the theme—more specifically, the life we have in God. Such life, the author seems to say, can only be fully enjoyed in the context of human death and futility.

Finally, a fourth example: What better way to gain an appreciation for the inexhaustible love of God than by comparing it to human love? By telling a love story with explicit imagery of love, the author of the Song of Songs points us beyond human love to God's love. This can be dangerous because human love, like everything else human, is tainted by the fall, and as such is open to abuse. Yet one cannot come away from reading the Song of Songs without a deepened appreciation for God's passionate providence for us.

We live in a paradoxical age. It is a time of unparalleled discovery and knowledge. Science has made it possible for us to approach the distant stars and the microscopic atom. We know more than our ancestors could have ever dreamed. Yet somehow we don't seem to understand the many facts of our existence with any more clarity than our ancestors understood the far fewer number of facts they had at their fingertips. Nevertheless, when all is said and done, these two books encourage us to fall at the feet of God and find our meaning in life through him.

TAKING THE NEXT STEPS

Christians are called to live in this world that God has created and loves, even while anticipating a world to come. We are no less in need, therefore, of advice about living (as well as about waiting), about the pitfalls of wealth and wisdom, about the centrality of God to the good life, and about our response to puzzlement and pain. Ecclesiastes, as part of the Scripture that is given to us for shaping faith and life, offers us such advice, correlating as it does with extensive sections of the NT that also touch on such themes.

This book, possibly written by Solomon but probably not, describes a search that the author engaged in throughout his life to find the purpose of life. By and large, his conclusions stand in contrast to the book of Proverbs; whereas Proverbs discovers principles that apply to everyday life with general consistency, Ecclesiastes asserts that there is much in life that is meaningless—that simply does not make sense. This gives a pervasively gloomy tone to the book. In the most essential aspect, however, Proverbs and Ecclesiastes agree perfectly: With God, life is rich and meaningful; without him, all is hopeless.

Several important messages for our personal lives stand out. (1) All humans are searching for happiness in life. (2) We will never find true happiness if we leave the Lord out of our lives. Money and possessions will never bring the satisfaction we crave. (3) Even for those who love and serve the Lord, not everything in life will make sense. It is only on judgment day that we can be sure the righteous will be rewarded and the wicked punished.

WHAT TO LOOK FOR IN ECCLESIASTES

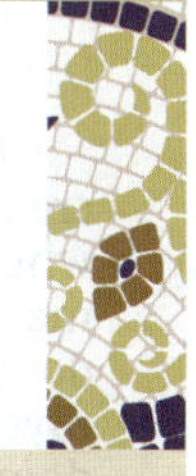

- The author's search for meaning in life (chs. 1–2)
- A time for everything (ch. 3)
- Money and possessions (chs. 5–6)
- Youth and old age in the light of God and his Word (ch. 12)

Everything Is Meaningless

1 The words of the Teacher,[a][a] son of David, king in Jerusalem:[b]

2 "Meaningless! Meaningless!"
says the Teacher.
"Utterly meaningless!
Everything is meaningless."[c]

3 What do people gain from all their labors
at which they toil under the sun?[d]
4 Generations come and generations go,
but the earth remains forever.[e]
5 The sun rises and the sun sets,
and hurries back to where it rises.[f]
6 The wind blows to the south
and turns to the north;
round and round it goes,
ever returning on its course.
7 All streams flow into the sea,
yet the sea is never full.
To the place the streams come from,
there they return again.[g]
8 All things are wearisome,
more than one can say.
The eye never has enough of seeing,[h]
nor the ear its fill of hearing.
9 What has been will be again,
what has been done will be done again;[i]

1:1 [a] ver 12; Ecc 7:27; 12:10 [b] Pr 1:1
1:2 [c] Ps 39:5-6; 62:9; 144:4; Ecc 12:8; Ro 8:20-21
1:3 [d] Ecc 2:11,22; 3:9; 5:15-16
1:4 [e] Ps 104:5; 119:90
1:5 [f] Ps 19:5-6
1:7 [g] Job 36:28
1:8 [h] Pr 27:20
1:9 [i] Ecc 2:12; 3:15

[a] *1* Or *the leader of the assembly*; also in verses 2 and 12

1:1 The Teacher himself is "presented" to the reader by still another person who makes himself known in 12:9–14.
1:2 The emphasis lies not on whether certain ways of living possess *meaning in themselves*, but on whether these ways of living succeed in *achieving the goals* that humans set before themselves.
1:4–9 The world is an essentially unchanging place. The human participants in the drama of creation are relatively insignificant when considered in this context.

there is nothing new under the
sun.
10 Is there anything of which one can
say,
"Look! This is something new"?
It was here already, long ago;
it was here before our time.
11 No one remembers the former
generations,
and even those yet to come
will not be remembered
by those who follow them.[j]

Wisdom Is Meaningless

12 I, the Teacher,[k] was king over Israel in
Jerusalem. 13 I applied my mind to study
and to explore by wisdom all that is done
under the heavens. What a heavy burden God has laid on mankind![l] 14 I have
seen all the things that are done under
the sun; all of them are meaningless, a
chasing after the wind.[m]

15 What is crooked cannot be
straightened;[n]
what is lacking cannot be counted.

16 I said to myself, "Look, I have increased in wisdom more than anyone
who has ruled over Jerusalem before
me;[o] I have experienced much of wisdom and knowledge." 17 Then I applied
myself to the understanding of wisdom,[p] and also of madness and folly,[q]
but I learned that this, too, is a chasing
after the wind.

18 For with much wisdom comes much
sorrow;
the more knowledge, the more
grief.[r]

Pleasures Are Meaningless

2 I said to myself, "Come now, I will
test you with pleasure[s] to find out
what is good." But that also proved to
be meaningless. 2 "Laughter,"[t] I said, "is
madness. And what does pleasure accomplish?" 3 I tried cheering myself with

1:11 [j] Ecc 2:16
1:12 [k] ver 1
1:13 [l] Ge 3:17; Ecc 3:10
1:14 [m] Ecc 2:11,17
1:15 [n] Ecc 7:13
1:16 [o] 1Ki 3:12; 4:30; Ecc 2:9
1:17 [p] Ecc 7:23 [q] Ecc 2:3,12; 7:25
1:18 [r] Ecc 2:23; 12:12
2:1 [s] Ecc 7:4; 8:15; Lk 12:19
2:2 [t] Pr 14:13; Ecc 7:6

Ecc 1:14 ❖ When has life felt like "chasing after the wind"? Why is this often
true "under the sun"?

Ecc 2:1-3 ❖ What results when we live
our lives in pursuit of pleasure? What
things bring us the most joy?

wine,[u] and embracing folly[v] — my mind
still guiding me with wisdom. I wanted
to see what was good for people to do
under the heavens during the few days
of their lives.
4 I undertook great projects: I built
houses for myself[w] and planted vineyards.[x] 5 I made gardens and parks and
planted all kinds of fruit trees in them.
6 I made reservoirs to water groves of
flourishing trees. 7 I bought male and
female slaves and had other slaves who
were born in my house. I also owned
more herds and flocks than anyone in
Jerusalem before me. 8 I amassed silver
and gold[y] for myself, and the treasure
of kings and provinces. I acquired male
and female singers,[z] and a harem[a] as
well — the delights of a man's heart. 9 I
became greater by far than anyone in
Jerusalem before me.[a] In all this my wisdom stayed with me.

10 I denied myself nothing my eyes
desired;
I refused my heart no pleasure.
My heart took delight in all my
labor,
and this was the reward for all my
toil.
11 Yet when I surveyed all that my
hands had done
and what I had toiled to achieve,
everything was meaningless, a
chasing after the wind;[b]
nothing was gained under the
sun.[c]

2:3 [u] ver 24-25; Ecc 3:12-13 [v] Ecc 1:17
2:4 [w] 1Ki 7:1-12 [x] SS 8:11
2:8 [y] 1Ki 9:28; 10:10,14,21 [z] 2Sa 19:35
2:9 [a] 1Ch 29:25; Ecc 1:16
2:11 [b] Ecc 1:14 [c] Ecc 1:3

[a] *8* The meaning of the Hebrew for this phrase is uncertain.

APPLICATION ✚ 1:1-11 The more things change, the more they stay the same (v. 9). This life on earth is intended to have as its center the God who created everything and who holds everything in his hand. He calls us to love him and our neighbor and to care for the world he has entrusted to us.

1:12-18 The passage comes to us in two sections (vv. 12-15 and vv. 16-18), each with its own purpose statement, discovery, and concluding proverb. Although wisdom and knowledge are good and useful, they paradoxically bring "sorrow" and "grief" (v. 18) because they clarify how evil the business of living can be.

2:1-11 The "king" set out to ambitiously transform his environment and thereby facilitate his enjoyment of life. While engaged in the experiment, he found joy; but considering it afterward, he pronounced it all a "chasing after the wind" (v. 11).

Wisdom and Folly Are Meaningless

12 Then I turned my thoughts to
consider wisdom,
and also madness and folly.[d]
What more can the king's
successor do
than what has already been
done?[e]
13 I saw that wisdom[f] is better than
folly,[g]
just as light is better than
darkness.
14 The wise have eyes in their heads,
while the fool walks in the
darkness;
but I came to realize
that the same fate overtakes them
both.[h]

15 Then I said to myself,

"The fate of the fool will overtake
me also.
What then do I gain by being
wise?"[i]
I said to myself,
"This too is meaningless."
16 For the wise, like the fool, will not be
long remembered;
the days have already come when
both have been forgotten.[j]
Like the fool, the wise too must die!

Toil Is Meaningless

17 So I hated life, because the work that
is done under the sun was grievous to
me. All of it is meaningless, a chasing
after the wind.[k] 18 I hated all the things I
had toiled for under the sun, because I
must leave them to the one who comes
after me.[l] 19 And who knows whether that
person will be wise or foolish? Yet they
will have control over all the fruit of my
toil into which I have poured my effort
and skill under the sun. This too is meaningless. 20 So my heart began to despair
over all my toilsome labor under the sun.
21 For a person may labor with wisdom,
knowledge and skill, and then they must
leave all they own to another who has not
toiled for it. This too is meaningless and
a great misfortune. 22 What do people get
for all the toil and anxious striving with
which they labor under the sun?[m] 23 All
their days their work is grief and pain;[n]
even at night their minds do not rest.
This too is meaningless.
24 A person can do nothing better than
to eat and drink[o] and find satisfaction in
their own toil.[p] This too, I see, is from
the hand of God,[q] 25 for without him, who
can eat or find enjoyment? 26 To the person who pleases him, God gives wisdom,
knowledge and happiness, but to the
sinner he gives the task of gathering and
storing up wealth[r] to hand it over to the
one who pleases God.[s] This too is meaningless, a chasing after the wind.

A Time for Everything

3 There is a time[t] for everything,
and a season for every activity
under the heavens:

2 a time to be born and a time to die,
a time to plant and a time to
uproot,
3 a time to kill and a time to heal,
a time to tear down and a time to
build,
4 a time to weep and a time to laugh,
a time to mourn and a time to
dance,
5 a time to scatter stones and a time to
gather them,
a time to embrace and a time to
refrain from embracing,

2:12 [d] Ecc 1:17 [e] Ecc 1:9; 7:25
2:13 [f] Ecc 7:19; 9:18 [g] Ecc 7:11-12
2:14 [h] Ps 49:10; Pr 17:24; Ecc 3:19; 6:6; 7:2; 9:3,11-12
2:15 [i] Ecc 6:8
2:16 [j] Ecc 1:11; 9:5
2:17 [k] Ecc 4:2
2:18 [l] Ps 39:6; 49:10
2:22 [m] Ecc 1:3; 3:9
2:23 [n] Job 5:7; 14:1; Ecc 1:18
2:24 [o] Ecc 8:15; 1Co 15:32 [p] Ecc 3:22 [q] Ecc 3:12-13; 5:17-19; 9:7-10
2:26 [r] Job 27:17 [s] Pr 13:22
3:1 [t] ver 11,17; Ecc 8:6

2:12–16 The question arises in the Teacher's mind: What does he "gain by being wise" (v. 15)? Wisdom does not offer mortal beings release from the "evil business" of living (see 1:12–18); it also cannot solve the problem of death.

2:17–26 Life lived from such a perspective is marked by pointlessness (vv. 17, 19, 21, 23); despair or hopelessness (v. 20); misfortune (v. 21); pain, grief, and restlessness (v. 23). Those who seek to control their life only and always attempt to run after what cannot be caught.

It is madness to seek profit from life, and the consequence is misery for those who fail to realize the pointlessness of it. Wisdom, by contrast, acknowledges God as the center of existence and gladly embraces human limitations.

1:12—2:26 It is not difficult to understand the application of 1:12—2:26 when we remember the reality of our modern culture that underlies its confident, abrasive tone and its stubborn desire to pretend to be God. The reality is the widespread sense of futility and weariness that the Teacher himself describes in his first-person testimony. It gives readers a perspective on worldly effort, success, and attaining possessions that provides a very different perspective on our culture.

3:1–8 The totality of life is represented here in a series of opposites.

6 a time to search and a time to
give up,
a time to keep and a time to throw
away,
7 a time to tear and a time to mend,
a time to be silent[u] and a time to
speak,
8 a time to love and a time to hate,
a time for war and a time for
peace.

9What do workers gain from their
toil?[v] 10I have seen the burden God has
laid on the human race.[w] 11He has made
everything beautiful in its time.[x] He has
also set eternity in the human heart; yet[a]
no one can fathom[y] what God has done
from beginning to end.[z] 12I know that
there is nothing better for people than
to be happy and to do good while they
live. 13That each of them may eat and
drink,[a] and find satisfaction[b] in all their
toil — this is the gift of God.[c] 14I know
that everything God does will endure
forever; nothing can be added to it and
nothing taken from it. God does it so that
people will fear him.[d]

15Whatever is has already been,[e]
and what will be has been
before;[f]
and God will call the past to
account.[b]

16And I saw something else under the
sun:

In the place of judgment —
wickedness was there,
in the place of justice —
wickedness was there.

3:7 [u]Am 5:13
3:9 [v]Ecc 1:3
3:10 [w]Ecc 1:13
3:11 [x]ver 1 [y]Job 11:7; Ecc 8:17 [z]Job 28:23; Ro 11:33
3:13 [a]Ecc 2:3 [b]Ps 34:12 [c]Dt 12:7,18; Ecc 2:24; 5:19
3:14 [d]Job 23:15; Ecc 5:7; 7:18; 8:12-13; Jas 1:17
3:15 [e]Ecc 6:10 [f]Ecc 1:9
3:17 [g]Job 19:29; Ecc 11:9; Mt 16:27; Ro 2:6-8; 2Th 1:6-7 [h]ver 1
3:18 [i]Ps 73:22
3:19 [j]Ecc 2:14
3:20 [k]Ge 2:7; 3:19; Job 34:15
3:21 [l]Ecc 12:7
3:22 [m]Ecc 2:24; 5:18 [n]Job 31:2
4:1 [o]Ps 12:5; Ecc 3:16

Ecc 3:11 ❖ How has God set eternity in our hearts? How does this draw us toward him?

17I said to myself,

"God will bring into judgment[g]
both the righteous and the
wicked,
for there will be a time for every
activity,
a time to judge every deed."[h]

18I also said to myself, "As for humans,
God tests them so that they may see that
they are like the animals.[i] 19Surely the
fate of human beings[j] is like that of the
animals; the same fate awaits them both:
As one dies, so dies the other. All have the
same breath[c]; humans have no advantage over animals. Everything is meaningless. 20All go to the same place; all
come from dust, and to dust all return.[k]
21Who knows if the human spirit rises
upward[l] and if the spirit of the animal
goes down into the earth?"
22So I saw that there is nothing better
for a person than to enjoy their work,[m]
because that is their lot.[n] For who can
bring them to see what will happen after them?

Oppression, Toil, Friendlessness

4 Again I looked and saw all the oppression[o] that was taking place under the sun:

[a] *11* Or *also placed ignorance in the human heart, so that* [b] *15* Or *God calls back the past*
[c] *19* Or *spirit*

3:9–15 What is "evil" about life from this point of view is that it cannot be controlled and manipulated to render the rewards one is seeking. The problem facing the human "actor" is that there is another "Actor" whose actions are decisive ones (v. 11). This Creator "has made everything beautiful in its time" (v. 11). There is an elegance about how life works, as one era succeeds the last.

Yet the Teacher's point is this: Humans cannot "fathom [or "find"] what God has done from beginning to end" (v. 11). Only God truly understands and controls the times. Therefore our human ideas of how to control our circumstances are insufficient; those who try will only know frustration. The alternative is to give up on our quest for profit and recognition and to reorient our lives toward the Creator. The only rational response to reality is to "fear [God]" (v. 14).

3:16–22 Verses 16–17 address the question of injustice in the world; vv. 18–22 return to the theme of death as an ultimate reality. The Teacher is agnostic about life after death. He advocates that the reader get on with life and not worry too much about the details, which lie with God.

✜ **3:1–22** We cannot truly understand or control "the times," and so we are cast back on God, who holds our times in his hands and who alone knows the span of our individual days. Yet the God on whom we are cast is good, and he is *for us* (Ro 8:31). Our response to his grace and blessing should be to seize the time that we have and live it well and joyfully to his glory and praise.

4:1–7 Envy is the fuel that feeds the fires of our human striving after gain. Chasing the neighbor above us on the ladder, we inevitably step on the head of the neighbor below us. As disastrous as this is for the people who are trampled on, it is also futile for the person who is upwardly mobile at others' expense. The life of striving is fundamentally anti-neighbor.

I saw the tears of the oppressed —
and they have no comforter;
power was on the side of their oppressors —
and they have no comforter.[p]
2 And I declared that the dead,[q]
who had already died,
are happier than the living,
who are still alive.[r]
3 But better than both
is the one who has never been born,[s]
who has not seen the evil
that is done under the sun.[t]

4 And I saw that all toil and all achievement spring from one person's envy of another. This too is meaningless, a chasing after the wind.[u]

5 Fools fold their hands[v]
and ruin themselves.
6 Better one handful with tranquillity
than two handfuls with toil[w]
and chasing after the wind.

7 Again I saw something meaningless under the sun:

8 There was a man all alone;
he had neither son nor brother.
There was no end to his toil,
yet his eyes were not content[x]
with his wealth.
"For whom am I toiling," he asked,
"and why am I depriving myself of enjoyment?"
This too is meaningless —
a miserable business!
9 Two are better than one,
because they have a good return
for their labor:
10 If either of them falls down,
one can help the other up.
But pity anyone who falls
and has no one to help them up.

4:1 [p] La 1:16
4:2 [q] Jer 20:17-18; 22:10 [r] Job 3:17; 10:18
4:3 [s] Job 3:16; Ecc 6:3 [t] Job 3:22
4:4 [u] Ecc 1:14
4:5 [v] Pr 6:10
4:6 [w] Pr 15:16-17; 16:8
4:8 [x] Pr 27:20

Ecc 4:9 ❖ How have human relationships blessed you? Think of three people who have been especially supportive to you, and thank God for them today. Then thank those three people.

11 Also, if two lie down together, they
will keep warm.
But how can one keep warm
alone?
12 Though one may be overpowered,
two can defend themselves.
A cord of three strands is not quickly
broken.

Advancement Is Meaningless

13 Better a poor but wise youth than an
old but foolish king who no longer knows
how to heed a warning. 14 The youth may
have come from prison to the kingship,
or he may have been born in poverty
within his kingdom. 15 I saw that all who
lived and walked under the sun followed
the youth, the king's successor. 16 There
was no end to all the people who were
before them. But those who came later were not pleased with the successor.
This too is meaningless, a chasing after
the wind.

Fulfill Your Vow to God

5 [a] Guard your steps when you go to
the house of God. Go near to listen
rather than to offer the sacrifice of fools,
who do not know that they do wrong.

2 Do not be quick with your mouth,
do not be hasty in your heart
to utter anything before God.[y]
God is in heaven
and you are on earth,
so let your words be few.[z]

5:2 [y] Jdg 11:35 [z] Job 6:24; Pr 10:19; 20:25

[a] In Hebrew texts 5:1 is numbered 4:17, and 5:2-20 is numbered 5:1-19.

4:8–12 Advancement all too often brings with it the loss of the self, as people lose touch with who they are where they have come from.

4:1–16 The religious individualism that lays great emphasis on a person's relationship with God but little emphasis on a person's social, economic, political, and religious relationships with other people has little, in the end, to do with the Bible. The proper goal of the Christian is to be found in right relationship with God, neighbor, and God's world *now* and in the future, which will include by God's grace a future beyond death.

5:1–7 Temple vows involved promises to consecrate such things as sacrifices or money to God in return for granting a prayer request.

5:1–7 Silence is undervalued in the noisy, intrusive world that most of us inhabit. Noise deafens us to reality. Silent reflection—including deliberate inactivity—is necessary if we are to regain perspective and remember who God really is, what that really means, and what, therefore, the church and a life lived in following God is *for*.

3 A dream[a] comes when there are
many cares,
and many words mark the speech
of a fool.[b]

4 When you make a vow to God, do not
delay to fulfill it.[c] He has no pleasure in
fools; fulfill your vow.[d] 5 It is better not
to make a vow than to make one and not
fulfill it.[e] 6 Do not let your mouth lead
you into sin. And do not protest to the
temple messenger, "My vow was a mistake." Why should God be angry at what
you say and destroy the work of your
hands? 7 Much dreaming and many words
are meaningless. Therefore fear God.[f]

Riches Are Meaningless

8 If you see the poor oppressed[g] in a
district, and justice and rights denied, do
not be surprised at such things; for one
official is eyed by a higher one, and over
them both are others higher still. 9 The
increase from the land is taken by all;
the king himself profits from the fields.

10 Whoever loves money never has
enough;
whoever loves wealth is never
satisfied with their income.
This too is meaningless.

11 As goods increase,
so do those who consume them.
And what benefit are they to the
owners
except to feast their eyes on them?

12 The sleep of a laborer is sweet,
whether they eat little or much,
but as for the rich, their abundance
permits them no sleep.[h]

13 I have seen a grievous evil under the
sun:[i]

wealth hoarded to the harm of its
owners,
14 or wealth lost through some
misfortune,
so that when they have children
there is nothing left for them to
inherit.
15 Everyone comes naked from their
mother's womb,
and as everyone comes, so they
depart.[j]
They take nothing from their toil[k]
that they can carry in their hands.[l]

16 This too is a grievous evil:

As everyone comes, so they depart,
and what do they gain,
since they toil for the wind?[m]
17 All their days they eat in darkness,
with great frustration, affliction
and anger.

18 This is what I have observed to be
good: that it is appropriate for a person
to eat, to drink[n] and to find satisfaction
in their toilsome labor[o] under the sun
during the few days of life God has given
them — for this is their lot. 19 Moreover,
when God gives someone wealth and
possessions,[p] and the ability to enjoy
them,[q] to accept their lot[r] and be happy
in their toil — this is a gift of God.[s] 20 They
seldom reflect on the days of their life,
because God keeps them occupied with
gladness of heart.[t]

6 I have seen another evil under the
sun, and it weighs heavily on mankind: 2 God gives some people wealth,
possessions and honor, so that they lack
nothing their hearts desire, but God
does not grant them the ability to enjoy
them,[u] and strangers enjoy them instead.
This is meaningless, a grievous evil.[v]
3 A man may have a hundred children

5:3 [a] Job 20:8 [b] Ecc 10:14
5:4 [c] Dt 23:21; Jdg 11:35; Ps 119:60 [d] Nu 30:2; Ps 66:13-14; 76:11
5:5 [e] Nu 30:2-4; Pr 20:25; Jnh 2:9; Ac 5:4
5:7 [f] Ecc 3:14; 12:13
5:8 [g] Ps 12:5; Ecc 4:1
5:12 [h] Job 20:20
5:13 [i] Ecc 6:1-2
5:15 [j] Job 1:21 [k] Ps 49:17; 1Ti 6:7 [l] Ecc 1:3
5:16 [m] Pr 11:29; Ecc 1:3
5:18 [n] Ecc 2:3 [o] Ecc 2:10,24
5:19 [p] 1Ch 29:12; 2Ch 1:12 [q] Ecc 6:2 [r] Job 31:2 [s] Ecc 2:24; 3:13
5:20 [t] Dt 12:7,18
6:2 [u] Ps 17:14; Ecc 5:19 [v] Ecc 5:13

Ecc 5:1-7 ❖ How good are we at controlling our speech? Why is it often better to speak less than we do?

Ecc 6:1-2 ❖ How does the passing nature of this life caution us against setting our hearts on possessions and wealth (see Ps 62:10)?

5:10 Like all false gods, money never fulfills those who pursue it; it only feeds the insatiable desire for more.
5:12 The life of a laborer may contain less consumption, but it provides peace that permits restful slumber.
5:13–14 For those who pursue gain and oppress the poor, there is only dissatisfaction, restlessness, frustration, affliction, and anger.
5:18–20 As we adjust ourselves to a more God-focused reality, it is possible to find peace of mind and joy during our lives. Yet the Teacher returns to reinforce what he has said in vv. 8–17: It is possible to have all that the heart desires (6:2) and yet to find no joy in it.
6:3 Long life and abundance of offspring are characteristic indicators of God's blessing in the Bible. Yet of what use are they if a person cannot "enjoy his prosperity"?

and live many years; yet no matter how
long he lives, if he cannot enjoy his prosperity and does not receive proper burial,
I say that a stillborn[w] child is better off
than he.[x] 4It comes without meaning, it
departs in darkness, and in darkness its
name is shrouded. 5Though it never saw
the sun or knew anything, it has more
rest than does that man— 6even if he
lives a thousand years twice over but
fails to enjoy his prosperity. Do not all
go to the same place?

7Everyone's toil is for their
mouth,
yet their appetite is never
satisfied.[y]
8What advantage have the wise over
fools?[z]
What do the poor gain
by knowing how to conduct
themselves before others?
9Better what the eye sees
than the roving of the appetite.
This too is meaningless,
a chasing after the wind.[a]

10Whatever exists has already been
named,
and what humanity is has been
known;
no one can contend
with someone who is stronger.
11The more the words,
the less the meaning,
and how does that profit
anyone?

12For who knows what is good for a
person in life, during the few and meaningless days[b] they pass through like a
shadow?[c] Who can tell them what will
happen under the sun after they are
gone?

6:3 [w] Job 3:16; Ecc 4:3 [x] Job 3:3
6:7 [y] Pr 16:26; 27:20
6:8 [z] Ecc 2:15
6:9 [a] Ecc 1:14
6:12 [b] Job 10:20 [c] Job 14:2; Ps 39:6; Jas 4:14

Wisdom

7 A good name is better than fine
perfume,[d]
and the day of death better than
the day of birth.
2It is better to go to a house of
mourning
than to go to a house of feasting,
for death[e] is the destiny[f] of
everyone;
the living should take this to
heart.
3Frustration is better than laughter,[g]
because a sad face is good for the
heart.
4The heart of the wise is in the house
of mourning,
but the heart of fools is in the
house of pleasure.[h]
5It is better to heed the rebuke[i] of a
wise person
than to listen to the song of fools.
6Like the crackling of thorns[j] under
the pot,
so is the laughter[k] of fools.
This too is meaningless.

7Extortion turns a wise person into a
fool,
and a bribe[l] corrupts the heart.

8The end of a matter is better than its
beginning,
and patience[m] is better than
pride.
9Do not be quickly provoked[n] in your
spirit,
for anger resides in the lap of
fools.

10Do not say, "Why were the old days
better than these?"
For it is not wise to ask such
questions.

7:1 [d] Pr 22:1; SS 1:3
7:2 [e] Pr 11:19 [f] Ps 90:12
7:3 [g] Pr 14:13
7:4 [h] Ecc 2:1; Jer 16:8
7:5 [i] Ps 141:5; Pr 13:18; 15:31-32
7:6 [j] Ps 58:9; 118:12 [k] Ecc 2:2
7:7 [l] Ex 18:21; 23:8; Dt 16:19
7:8 [m] Pr 14:29; Gal 5:22; Eph 4:2
7:9 [n] Mt 5:22; Pr 14:17; Jas 1:19

6:7–9 Consumption is powerless to fill the gaping void that is the human appetite. Verse 8 is best taken as the question to which v. 9 is the answer. We should rest content with what lies before us and resist the temptation to wander off in search of more.

6:10–12 As the Teacher brings this section of his reflections to a close, he underlines that these truths must be accepted rather than debated. It is irrational to seek anything from life other than harmony with creation as it really is and with God who makes it that way. Life lived in any other manner can only end in frustration and tears.

5:8—6:12 The words that often drown out the word of God are those of advertisers—those great prophets and evangelists of consumption. The first step toward defying rampant consumption among Christians is conscious resistance to their rhetoric and myth-making; yet we will not even realize that advertisers are telling us lies about reality if we do not take steps first to deal with the hold that the idols they worship also have on our hearts.

7:1–6 There is a way of living that is *centered* on feasting. This life pushes reality to the margins by flooding the senses with sensation and drowning out quiet contemplation with noise. People who live with endless distraction and consumption don't have the attention span required to consider the deeper and more important issues of life.

[11]Wisdom, like an inheritance, is a
good thing[o]
and benefits those who see the
sun.[p]
[12]Wisdom is a shelter
as money is a shelter,
but the advantage of knowledge is
this:
Wisdom preserves those who
have it.

[13]Consider what God has done:[q]

Who can straighten
what he has made crooked?[r]
[14]When times are good, be happy;
but when times are bad, consider
this:
God has made the one
as well as the other.
Therefore, no one can discover
anything about their future.

[15]In this meaningless life[s] of mine I
have seen both of these:

the righteous perishing in their
righteousness,
and the wicked living long in their
wickedness.[t]
[16]Do not be overrighteous,
neither be overwise —
why destroy yourself?
[17]Do not be overwicked,
and do not be a fool —
why die before your time?[u]
[18]It is good to grasp the one
and not let go of the other.
Whoever fears God[v] will avoid all
extremes.[a]

7:11 [o] Pr 8:10-11; Ecc 2:13 [p] Ecc 11:7
7:13 [q] Ecc 2:24 [r] Ecc 1:15
7:15 [s] Job 7:7 [t] Ecc 8:12-14; Jer 12:1
7:17 [u] Job 15:32; Ps 55:23
7:18 [v] Ecc 3:14
7:19 [w] Ecc 2:13 [x] Ecc 9:13-18
7:20 [y] Ps 14:3 [z] 1Ki 8:46; 2Ch 6:36; Pr 20:9; Ro 3:23
7:21 [a] Pr 30:10
7:23 [b] Ecc 1:17; Ro 1:22
7:24 [c] Job 28:12
7:25 [d] Job 28:3 [e] Ecc 1:17
7:26 [f] Ex 10:7; Jdg 14:15

Ecc 7:20 ❖ How does acknowledging the depravity of sin lead us to God's grace (see Ro 3:23–24)?

[19]Wisdom[w] makes one wise person
more powerful[x]
than ten rulers in a city.

[20]Indeed, there is no one on earth who
is righteous,[y]
no one who does what is right and
never sins.[z]

[21]Do not pay attention to every word
people say,
or you[a] may hear your servant
cursing you —
[22]for you know in your heart
that many times you yourself have
cursed others.

[23]All this I tested by wisdom and I said,

"I am determined to be wise"[b] —
but this was beyond me.
[24]Whatever exists is far off and most
profound —
who can discover it?[c]
[25]So I turned my mind to
understand,
to investigate and to search out
wisdom and the scheme of
things[d]
and to understand the stupidity of
wickedness
and the madness of folly.[e]

[26]I find more bitter than death
the woman who is a snare,[f]

[a] 18 Or *will follow them both*

7:11–12 To embrace wisdom is to embrace life itself, along with all the gifts that may be bestowed with life—length of days and riches and honor. But to embrace and pursue riches and honor as a goal in life is to head for inevitable disaster.

✣ **7:1–12** We live in an escapist culture. The materialist mansion that we as modern people have constructed for ourselves has become for many an unbearably oppressive prison whose spiritual emptiness is all too apparent. The only way to find purpose and heal our pain is to confront reality rather than to seek to escape from it. Only when we shift our emphasis to the way of following God can our priorities realign.

7:13–14 The wise person accepts the world as he or she finds it, receiving both good and bad from God.
7:16–18 Wisdom is attractive to many people because it appears to offer control over life. Yet this represents a profound misunderstanding of its purpose.
7:19–22 Wisdom may be pursued from selfish motives, but it is vastly superior to political or military power, which depends on wisdom for success. Yet the wise person will still be flawed because he or she is a human being.
7:23–29 Although a comprehensive grasp of reality is unattainable, some discoveries are possible. Verses 26–29 recount some such findings.

✣ **7:13–29** God is God and we are not. When we forget this, we make a foundational human mistake. The consequences are disastrous for other people, for creation more generally, and eventually for us. The only safe kind of human wisdom is wisdom that is rooted in God and centered in Jesus Christ, which thus knows its limitations and boundaries.

whose heart is a trap
and whose hands are chains.
The man who pleases God will
escape her,
but the sinner she will ensnare.[g]

27"Look," says the Teacher,[a][h] "this is
what I have discovered:

"Adding one thing to another to
discover the scheme of
things —
28 while I was still searching
but not finding —
I found one upright man among a
thousand,
but not one upright woman[i]
among them all.
29 This only have I found:
God created mankind upright,
but they have gone in search of
many schemes."

8

Who is like the wise?
Who knows the explanation of
things?
A person's wisdom brightens their
face
and changes its hard appearance.

Obey the King

2Obey the king's command, I say, because you took an oath before God. 3Do
not be in a hurry to leave the king's presence.[j] Do not stand up for a bad cause, for
he will do whatever he pleases. 4Since a
king's word is supreme, who can say to
him, "What are you doing?[k]"

5 Whoever obeys his command will
come to no harm,
and the wise heart will know the
proper time and procedure.
6 For there is a proper time and
procedure for every matter,[l]
though a person may be weighed
down by misery.

7 Since no one knows the future,
who can tell someone else what is
to come?
8 As no one has power over the wind
to contain it,
so[b] no one has power over the
time of their death.
As no one is discharged in time of
war,
so wickedness will not release
those who practice it.

9All this I saw, as I applied my mind
to everything done under the sun. There
is a time when a man lords it over others to his own[c] hurt. 10Then too, I saw
the wicked buried[m] — those who used
to come and go from the holy place and
receive praise[d] in the city where they did
this. This too is meaningless.
11When the sentence for a crime is not
quickly carried out, people's hearts are
filled with schemes to do wrong. 12Al-
though a wicked person who commits
a hundred crimes may live a long time,
I know that it will go better[n] with those
who fear God,[o] who are reverent before
him.[p] 13Yet because the wicked do not
fear God,[q] it will not go well with them,
and their days[r] will not lengthen like a
shadow.
14There is something else meaningless that occurs on earth: the righteous
who get what the wicked deserve, and
the wicked who get what the righteous
deserve.[s] This too, I say, is meaningless.[t]

7:26 [g] Pr 2:16-19; 5:3-5; 7:23; 22:14
7:27 [h] Ecc 1:1
7:28 [i] 1Ki 11:3
8:3 [j] Ecc 10:4
8:4 [k] Job 9:12; Est 1:19; Da 4:35
8:6 [l] Ecc 3:1
8:10 [m] Ecc 1:11
8:12 [n] Dt 12:28; Ps 37:11,18-19; Pr 1:32-33; Isa 3:10-11 [o] Ex 1:20 [p] Ecc 3:14
8:13 [q] Ecc 3:14; Isa 3:11 [r] Dt 4:40; Job 5:26; Ps 34:12; Isa 65:20
8:14 [s] Job 21:7; Ps 73:14; Mal 3:15 [t] Ecc 7:15

[a] *27 Or the leader of the assembly* [b] *8 Or over the human spirit to retain it, / and so* [c] *9 Or to their* [d] *10* Some Hebrew manuscripts and Septuagint (Aquila); most Hebrew manuscripts *and are forgotten*

8:2–3 The wise person will think more than twice before opposing the king. He will not foolishly rush to speech and action.
8:4–6 The truly wise person knows not to flaunt his wisdom when confronted by a foolish ruler, for there is a serious risk if he does so.
8:7–8 Humans do not have control over their lives. Various images are given in v. 8 to underline this point.
8:9 This statement is ambiguous (alternately, "there is a time when a man exercises power over a man for hurt to him"). Does the "hurt" fall only on the king's victims, or ultimately on the king himself?
8:11–17 One of the unfortunate results of divine patience with human sinfulness is that foolish hearts are consistently "filled with schemes to do wrong" (v. 11). The longer God delays his judgment, the more these will persist. Yet he waits patiently for people to turn to him (2Pe 3:9).

✥ **8:1–17** This chapter touches on governing authority. One of the most serious idolatries for people in the modern world is equating God's purposes with their own secular national purposes. The idolatry of "God and country" takes many forms, but it is only a short step to the form of idolatry in which God is enlisted in support of one's country, one's culture, and one's way of life. God will not be bound by any nation's priorities.

15 So I commend the enjoyment of life[u],
because there is nothing better for a person under the sun than to eat and drink[v]
and be glad.[w] Then joy will accompany
them in their toil all the days of the life
God has given them under the sun.
16 When I applied my mind to know
wisdom[x] and to observe the labor that
is done on earth[y] — people getting no
sleep day or night — 17 then I saw all that
God has done.[z] No one can comprehend
what goes on under the sun. Despite all
their efforts to search it out, no one can
discover its meaning. Even if the wise
claim they know, they cannot really comprehend it.[a]

A Common Destiny for All

9 So I reflected on all this and concluded that the righteous and the wise
and what they do are in God's hands,
but no one knows whether love or hate
awaits them.[b] 2 All share a common destiny — the righteous and the wicked, the
good and the bad,[a] the clean and the
unclean, those who offer sacrifices and
those who do not.

As it is with the good,
so with the sinful;
as it is with those who take oaths,
so with those who are afraid to
take them.[c]

3 This is the evil in everything that
happens under the sun: The same destiny overtakes all.[d] The hearts of people, moreover, are full of evil and there
is madness in their hearts while they
live,[e] and afterward they join the dead.[f]
4 Anyone who is among the living has
hope[b] — even a live dog is better off than
a dead lion!

5 For the living know that they will
die,
but the dead know nothing;[g]
they have no further reward,
and even their name[h] is
forgotten.[i]
6 Their love, their hate
and their jealousy have long since
vanished;
never again will they have a part
in anything that happens under
the sun.[j]

7 Go, eat your food with gladness, and
drink your wine[k] with a joyful heart,[l] for
God has already approved what you do.
8 Always be clothed in white,[m] and always
anoint your head with oil. 9 Enjoy life
with your wife,[n] whom you love, all the
days of this meaningless life that God
has given you under the sun — all your
meaningless days. For this is your lot[o]
in life and in your toilsome labor under
the sun. 10 Whatever[p] your hand finds to
do, do it with all your might,[q] for in the
realm of the dead,[r] where you are going,
there is neither working nor planning
nor knowledge nor wisdom.[s]

11 I have seen something else under
the sun:

The race is not to the swift
or the battle to the strong,[t]
nor does food come to the wise[u]

8:15 [u] Ps 42:8 [v] Ex 32:6; Ecc 2:3 [w] Ecc 2:24; 3:12-13; 5:18; 9:7
8:16 [x] Ecc 1:17 [y] Ecc 1:13
8:17 [z] Job 28:3 [a] Job 5:9; 28:23; Ecc 3:11; Ro 11:33
9:1 [b] Dt 33:3; Job 12:10; Ecc 10:14
9:2 [c] Job 9:22; Ecc 2:14; 6:6; 7:2
9:3 [d] Job 9:22; Ecc 2:14 [e] Jer 11:8; 13:10; 16:12; 17:9 [f] Job 21:26
9:5 [g] Job 14:21 [h] Ps 9:6 [i] Ecc 1:11; 2:16; Isa 26:14
9:6 [j] Job 21:21
9:7 [k] Nu 6:20 [l] Ecc 2:24; 8:15
9:8 [m] Ps 23:5; Rev 3:4
9:9 [n] Pr 5:18 [o] Job 31:2
9:10 [p] 1Sa 10:7 [q] Ecc 11:6; Ro 12:11; Col 3:23 [r] Nu 16:33 [s] Ecc 2:24
9:11 [t] Am 2:14-15 [u] Job 32:13; Isa 47:10; Jer 9:23

Ecc 8:14 ❖ Where have we observed the apparent reversal of fortunes for the righteous and the wicked? Why, then, choose to be righteous (see 2Co 5:10)?

Ecc 9:10 ❖ What work can we do to God's glory in the days of life he gives us? How can we be assured this work is meaningful (see 1Co 15:57-58)?

[a] 2 Septuagint (Aquila), Vulgate and Syriac; Hebrew does not have *and the bad.* [b] 4 Or *What then is to be chosen? With all who live, there is hope*

9:1-3 The righteous and the wise will experience in life both "love" and "hate" (v. 1), which may simply be another way of saying "good and evil." Their experience is in this respect no different from that of the wicked and the foolish.
9:4-5 The living know *something*, however, whereas the dead know nothing (v. 5). Life indicates hope.
9:7-10 Life is indeed a mixed bag; death awaits us all. What is the wise response? It is to seek joy where it may be found in positive action and right living.
9:11-12 Life's outcomes (other than death) are not predictable in their specifics; good and bad come to all.

✣ **9:1-12** We live in a world in which cause and effect are often visibly in connection with each other: Press a light switch, and the light comes on. This promise of control is a seductive one and lies at the heart of much of everyday advertising. We no longer need to be the victims of our frailty and mortality. The Teacher and other biblical writers remind us that the idea that we have any such control over cause and effect is a myth.

It is true that the universe is an ordered place

or wealth to the brilliant
or favor to the learned;
but time and chance[v] happen to
them all.[w]

12 Moreover, no one knows when their
hour will come:

As fish are caught in a cruel net,
or birds are taken in a snare,
so people are trapped by evil times[x]
that fall unexpectedly upon
them.[y]

Wisdom Better Than Folly

13 I also saw under the sun this example of wisdom[z] that greatly impressed
me: 14 There was once a small city with
only a few people in it. And a powerful
king came against it, surrounded it and
built huge siege works against it. 15 Now
there lived in that city a man poor but
wise, and he saved the city by his wisdom. But nobody remembered that poor
man.[a] 16 So I said, "Wisdom is better than
strength." But the poor man's wisdom is
despised, and his words are no longer
heeded.[b]

17 The quiet words of the wise are
more to be heeded
than the shouts of a ruler of fools.
18 Wisdom[c] is better than weapons of
war,
but one sinner destroys much
good.

10 As dead flies give perfume a bad
smell,
so a little folly[d] outweighs wisdom
and honor.
2 The heart of the wise inclines to the
right,
but the heart of the fool to the
left.
3 Even as fools walk along the road,
they lack sense
and show everyone[e] how stupid
they are.
4 If a ruler's anger rises against you,

9:11 [v] Ecc 2:14 [w] Dt 8:18
9:12 [x] Pr 29:6 [y] Ps 73:22; Ecc 2:14; 8:7
9:13 [z] 2Sa 20:22
9:15 [a] Ge 40:14; Ecc 1:11; 2:16; 4:13
9:16 [b] Pr 21:22; Ecc 7:19
9:18 [c] ver 16
10:1 [d] Pr 13:16; 18:2
10:3 [e] Pr 13:16; 18:2

10:4 [f] Ecc 8:3 [g] Pr 16:14; 25:15
10:6 [h] Pr 29:2
10:7 [i] Pr 19:10
10:8 [j] Ps 7:15; 57:6; Pr 26:27 [k] Est 2:23; Ps 9:16; Am 5:19
10:9 [l] Pr 26:27
10:11 [m] Ps 58:5; Isa 3:3
10:12 [n] Pr 10:32 [o] Pr 10:14; 14:3; 15:2; 18:7
10:14 [p] Pr 15:2; Ecc 5:3; 6:12; 8:7 [q] Ecc 9:1

Ecc 10:4 ❖ How can our calm demeanor prevent worsening conflict? How can we remain calm during contentious moments?

do not leave your post;[f]
calmness can lay great offenses to
rest.[g]

5 There is an evil I have seen under
the sun,
the sort of error that arises from a
ruler:
6 Fools are put in many high
positions,[h]
while the rich occupy the low
ones.
7 I have seen slaves on horseback,
while princes go on foot like
slaves.[i]

8 Whoever digs a pit may fall into it;[j]
whoever breaks through a wall
may be bitten by a snake.[k]
9 Whoever quarries stones may be
injured by them;
whoever splits logs may be
endangered by them.[l]

10 If the ax is dull
and its edge unsharpened,
more strength is needed,
but skill will bring success.

11 If a snake bites before it is charmed,
the charmer receives no fee.[m]

12 Words from the mouth of the wise
are gracious,[n]
but fools are consumed by their
own lips.[o]
13 At the beginning their words are
folly;
at the end they are wicked
madness—
14 and fools multiply words.[p]

No one knows what is coming—
who can tell someone else what
will happen after them?[q]

---

and that cause and effect are features of its reality. Yet the universe is not a machine; it is a personally created and governed space, whose Originator and Sustainer is the living God.

9:15–17 Wealth and social class are more impressive to people than wisdom.
10:2–3 People make bizarre choices in life. The inner lives of wise and foolish persons are set in completely different directions.
10:8–9 Unforeseen happenings can cause hurt. The completion of everyday tasks can result not in satisfaction and well-being but in injury. So it is with our words and actions; they can and often do result in unintended consequences.
10:12–14 The self-destructive words of the fool begin in folly and end in madness. The fool's words devour him.

[15]The toil of fools wearies them;
they do not know the way to town.

[16]Woe to the land whose king was a
servant[a][r]
and whose princes feast in the
morning.
[17]Blessed is the land whose king is of
noble birth
and whose princes eat at a proper
time —
for strength and not for
drunkenness.[s]

[18]Through laziness, the rafters sag;
because of idle hands, the house
leaks.[t]

[19]A feast is made for laughter,
wine[u] makes life merry,
and money is the answer for
everything.

[20]Do not revile the king[v] even in your
thoughts,
or curse the rich in your bedroom,
because a bird in the sky may carry
your words,
and a bird on the wing may report
what you say.

Invest in Many Ventures

11 Ship[w] your grain across the sea;
after many days you may receive a
return.[x]
[2]Invest in seven ventures, yes, in
eight;
you do not know what disaster
may come upon the land.

[3]If clouds are full of water,
they pour rain on the earth.
Whether a tree falls to the south or
to the north,
in the place where it falls, there it
will lie.
[4]Whoever watches the wind will not
plant;
whoever looks at the clouds will
not reap.

[5]As you do not know the path of the
wind,[y]
or how the body is formed[b] in a
mother's womb,[z]
so you cannot understand the work
of God,
the Maker of all things.
[6]Sow your seed in the morning,
and at evening let your hands not
be idle,[a]
for you do not know which will
succeed,
whether this or that,
or whether both will do equally
well.

Remember Your Creator While Young

[7]Light is sweet,
and it pleases the eyes to see the
sun.[b]

10:16 [r] Isa 3:4-5,12
10:17 [s] Dt 14:26; 1Sa 25:36; Pr 31:4
10:18 [t] Pr 20:4; 24:30-34
10:19 [u] Ge 14:18; Jdg 9:13
10:20 [v] Ex 22:28
11:1 [w] ver 6; Isa 32:20; Hos 10:12 [x] Dt 24:19; Pr 19:17; Mt 10:42
11:5 [y] Jn 3:8-10 [z] Ps 139:14-16
11:6 [a] Ecc 9:10
11:7 [b] Ecc 7:11

[a] *16 Or king is a child* [b] *5 Or know how life* (or *the spirit*) */ enters the body being formed*

Ecc 11:1-6 ❖ How can we find contentment in the work God has given us without being overly attached to results (see 1Co 3:6)?

10:16–17 The closing verses of ch. 10 envision two contrasting scenarios: a land whose king was previously a "servant" (v. 16) and a land whose king himself originates from the ruling classes. The intent is to describe what influences the experienced ruler responds to.

10:20 Giving in to the temptation to indulge in bad-mouthing is unwise. Thoughts can easily spill out into words that may find their way back to the rich and powerful, those with authority to influence our well-being.

9:13—10:20 We live in a world where information is widely privileged over wisdom. The truth is that we have never known so much and understood so little. We live in a world, in fact, in which biblical wisdom is routinely suspected, mocked, and despised. The Teacher advises that the ancient path of contemplating and submitting to God's power and oversight is the only path forward that makes any sense.

11:1–6 In the light of all that we do not know, the Teacher offers his advice. What these same readers should *not* do is described in v. 4. In v. 6 the Teacher advocates a course of action opposite to the one described in v. 4.

11:7–8 There is no reason one cannot "enjoy" life along the lines that the Teacher has described in this book. Yet one must never forget that dark days will come as well.

11:1–8 The Bible replaces the modern myth that humans are advancing and getting more and more like divinity with the harsh fact of human fallenness. The Bible recognizes technological progress, but also that it can coexist with barbarism.

Whereas those who tell the first story look ahead to boundless possibilities stretching into the future, the Bible knows of a sudden ending to everything, as God's sovereignty over his universe is displayed in an ultimate way. That

8 However many years anyone may
live,
let them enjoy them all.
But let them remember[c] the days of
darkness,
for there will be many.
Everything to come is
meaningless.

9 You who are young, be happy while
you are young,
and let your heart give you joy in
the days of your youth.
Follow the ways of your heart
and whatever your eyes see,
but know that for all these
things
God will bring you into
judgment.[d]
10 So then, banish anxiety[e] from your
heart
and cast off the troubles of your
body,
for youth and vigor are
meaningless.[f]

12 Remember[g] your Creator
in the days of your youth,
before the days of trouble[h] come
and the years approach when you
will say,
"I find no pleasure in them"—
2 before the sun and the light
and the moon and the stars grow
dark,
and the clouds return after the
rain;
3 when the keepers of the house
tremble,
and the strong men stoop,
when the grinders cease because
they are few,
and those looking through the
windows grow dim;
4 when the doors to the street are
closed

11:8 [c] Ecc 12:1
11:9 [d] Job 19:29; Ecc 2:24; 3:17; 12:14; Ro 14:10
11:10 [e] Ps 94:19 [f] Ecc 2:24
12:1 [g] Ecc 11:8 [h] 2Sa 19:35

12:4 [i] Jer 25:10
12:5 [j] Job 17:13; 10:21 [k] Jer 9:17; Am 5:16
12:7 [l] Ge 3:19; Job 34:15; Ps 146:4 [m] Ecc 3:21 [n] Job 20:8; Zec 12:1
12:8 [o] Ecc 1:2
12:9 [p] 1Ki 4:32

Ecc 12:1-8 ❖ Why should we build a strong faith and relationship with God before the days of trouble come? How are we building that today?

and the sound of grinding
fades;
when people rise up at the sound of
birds,
but all their songs grow faint;[i]
5 when people are afraid of
heights
and of dangers in the streets;
when the almond tree blossoms
and the grasshopper drags itself
along
and desire no longer is stirred.
Then people go to their eternal
home[j]
and mourners[k] go about the
streets.

6 Remember him—before the silver
cord is severed,
and the golden bowl is broken;
before the pitcher is shattered at the
spring,
and the wheel broken at the
well,
7 and the dust returns[l] to the ground
it came from,
and the spirit returns to God[m] who
gave it.[n]

8 "Meaningless! Meaningless!" says the
Teacher.[a]
"Everything is meaningless![o]"

The Conclusion of the Matter

9 Not only was the Teacher wise, but he
also imparted knowledge to the people.
He pondered and searched out and set
in order many proverbs.[p] 10 The Teacher

[a] 8 Or *the leader of the assembly*; also in verses 9 and 10

is the real truth, pointing to the reality that must be juxtaposed with our modern myths of innate human goodness.

11:9-10 These verses are not an invitation to hedonism. A life marked by brevity need not be a life of futility, if life is embraced for what it is and joy is rightly pursued.
12:1-8 This passage speaks of the fleeting nature of life and the decrease of ability that comes with age. God gives life, and then in due course takes it away.

12:9-14 The words of the Teacher are designed so that we may live well before God. We must always remember that the universe is a moral place. We are accountable for the ways we spend our days.

✜ **11:9—12:14** The biblical narrative—and all the texts that are bound up with it, reflect on it, and comment on it—provides us with the map we need both for our own journey through life and for helping others find the best path.

The Teacher paints a corner of the map. He

searched to find just the right words, and
what he wrote was upright and true.[q]
11 The words of the wise are like goads,
their collected sayings like firmly embedded nails[r] — given by one shepherd.[a]
12 Be warned, my son, of anything in addition to them.

Of making many books there is no end,
and much study wearies the body.[s]

13 Now all has been heard;
here is the conclusion of the
matter:
Fear God and keep his
commandments,[t]
for this is the duty of all mankind.[u]
14 For God will bring every deed into
judgment,[v]
including every hidden thing,[w]
whether it is good or evil.

12:10 [q] Pr 22:20-21
12:11 [r] Ezr 9:8
12:12 [s] Ecc 1:18
12:13 [t] Dt 4:2; 10:12 [u] Mic 6:8
12:14 [v] Ecc 3:17 [w] Mt 10:26; 1Co 4:5

[a] *11* Or *Shepherd*

suggests to us that the young person needs to be told about the reality of decay and death and what this signifies about God and ourselves. This is important because young people often think of themselves as indestructible. The young person also needs to be told, however, about the wisdom and goodness of God and be encouraged to live in response to that goodness. This involves virtue, of course, but it also involves joy. It is important to speak about both.

Song of Songs

Author: Unknown, though traditionally King Solomon

Audience: The people of Israel

Date: Unknown, possibly as early as the tenth century BC

Theme: God, through the wisdom writer, celebrates intimate human love as a gift and also as a key to understanding God's own love for his people.

PERSPECTIVE

It has been the common Jewish and Christian view up until modern times that Solomon wrote this song. Yet Solomon only appears in this book in third-person references. Moreover, when the essentially negative character of most of the material mentioning "the king" is recognized, the case for Solomonic authorship is further weakened.

The heading itself can signify that the song *concerns* Solomon. In Song of Songs, the focus of attention is on his famed possession of women. This feature allows the biblical author to explore love and sexual intimacy and to present to us a particular vision of the world for consideration.

For more perspective on this fascinating book, please turn to the Introduction to Ecclesiastes.

Reading Song of Songs

It is best to read this book in a single sitting, before looking at any individual parts. The translators of the NIV have aided the reader by identifying various speakers within the song. As a work of art, it builds up to its peak in SS 8:6–7.

TAKING THE NEXT STEPS

This love song concerns King Solomon, who wrote one thousand and five songs (1Ki 4:32). While interpretations vary immensely, most today recognize this book as an expression of deep love and intense feelings between a man and a woman, with different speakers sharing their thoughts throughout the poem.

This love poem gives direction to us in our lives. (1) The main message conveyed is that marital love, created by God already in the Garden of Eden, is good and pure. (2) Since the Bible elsewhere

Key Verses

Place me like a seal over your heart, like a seal on your arm; for love is as strong as death, its jealousy unyielding as the grave. It burns like blazing fire, like a mighty flame. Many waters cannot quench love; rivers cannot sweep it away. If one were to give all the wealth of one's house for love, it would be utterly scorned.

—Song of Songs 8:6–7

compares God's love for his people to love within marriage (see Eph 5:22–33), this book helps us to understand the intensity of Christ's love for the church.

WHAT TO LOOK FOR IN SONG OF SONGS

- The couple and their friends set the stage for the book (ch. 1)
- The terrors of the night: the woman searches for her beloved (ch. 3)
- The man compliments his intended, and she responds (ch. 4)
- Love is as strong as death (ch. 8)

1

Solomon's Song of Songs.[a]

She[a]

2 Let him kiss me with the kisses of his mouth—
for your love[b] is more delightful than wine.
3 Pleasing is the fragrance of your perfumes;[c]
your name[d] is like perfume poured out.
No wonder the young women[e] love you!
4 Take me away with you—let us hurry!
Let the king bring me into his chambers.[f]

Friends

We rejoice and delight in you[b];
we will praise your love more than wine.

She

How right they are to adore you!

5 Dark am I, yet lovely,[g]
daughters of Jerusalem,[h]
dark like the tents of Kedar,
like the tent curtains of Solomon.[c]
6 Do not stare at me because I am dark,
because I am darkened by the sun.
My mother's sons were angry with me
and made me take care of the vineyards;[i]
my own vineyard I had to neglect.
7 Tell me, you whom I love,
where you graze your flock
and where you rest your sheep[j] at midday.
Why should I be like a veiled woman
beside the flocks of your friends?

Friends

8 If you do not know, most beautiful of women,[k]
follow the tracks of the sheep
and graze your young goats
by the tents of the shepherds.

He

9 I liken you, my darling, to a mare
among Pharaoh's chariot horses.[l]
10 Your cheeks[m] are beautiful with earrings,
your neck with strings of jewels.[n]
11 We will make you earrings of gold,
studded with silver.

She

12 While the king was at his table,
my perfume spread its fragrance.[o]
13 My beloved is to me a sachet of myrrh
resting between my breasts.

1:1 [a] 1Ki 4:32
1:2 [b] SS 4:10
1:3 [c] SS 4:10 [d] Ecc 7:1 [e] Ps 45:14
1:4 [f] Ps 45:15
1:5 [g] SS 2:14; 4:3 [h] SS 2:7; 5:8; 5:16
1:6 [i] Ps 69:8; SS 8:12
1:7 [j] SS 3:1-4; Isa 13:20
1:8 [k] SS 5:9; 6:1
1:9 [l] 2Ch 1:17
1:10 [m] SS 5:13 [n] Isa 61:10
1:12 [o] SS 4:11-14

[a] The main male and female speakers (identified primarily on the basis of the gender of the relevant Hebrew forms) are indicated by the captions *He* and *She* respectively. The words of others are marked *Friends*. In some instances the divisions and their captions are debatable. [b] 4 The Hebrew is masculine singular. [c] 5 Or *Salma*

1:1–4 The second line of v. 4 can be also understood not as expressing a desire but as referring to a past action: "The king brought me into his chambers" (alternate translation; NIV "Let the king bring"). Evidence will accumulate as we move through this song that the king and the lover are certainly *not* to be identified as being together.
1:6–7 Our speaker's attention has moved from her beloved man to a wider circle of women and then back once again at the end of v. 6 to her beloved. She wishes to find him, for she fears otherwise that she will be mistaken for a prostitute.
1:9 Pharaoh's chariots were typically drawn by stallions hitched in pairs; a mare placed among them would have caused great disruption, as her scent or mere presence would distract the workhorses.

It seems that we have three main characters in this book rather than simply two. (1) There is the woman, who has come to the royal court yet longs to return to the outside, where her special friend is to be found. (2) There is the king, who inhabits the inside world of the court and knows the woman (perhaps sexually, although this is not explicit) as a member of his royal harem. (3) There is, finally, the man who is to be found in the outside world, the beloved, represented by grazing lands, vineyards, and forests. He is certainly romantically and sexually (although this is still only implicit) involved with the woman.

APPLICATION ✚ 1:1–17 The Song of Songs does not speak in favor of sexual repression. But neither does it speak in favor of sexual license and the kind of pursuit of "rights" (by men or women) that in the end destroys all humanity. The sexual intimacy of this song is intimacy in the context of commitment—the kind of commitment that in mutuality gives up "rights" in pursuit of relationship.

14 My beloved is to me a cluster of
henna[p] blossoms
from the vineyards of En Gedi.[q]

He

15 How beautiful[r] you are, my darling!
Oh, how beautiful!
Your eyes are doves.[s]

She

16 How handsome you are, my beloved!
Oh, how charming!
And our bed is verdant.

He

17 The beams of our house are cedars;[t]
our rafters are firs.

She[a]

2 I am a rose[b][u] of Sharon,[v]
a lily[w] of the valleys.

He

2 Like a lily among thorns
is my darling among the young
women.

She

3 Like an apple[c] tree among the trees
of the forest
is my beloved[x] among the young
men.
I delight[y] to sit in his shade,
and his fruit is sweet to my taste.[z]
4 Let him lead me to the banquet hall,[a]
and let his banner[b] over me be
love.
5 Strengthen me with raisins,
refresh me with apples,[c]
for I am faint with love.[d]
6 His left arm is under my head,
and his right arm embraces me.[e]
7 Daughters of Jerusalem, I charge
you[f]
by the gazelles and by the does of
the field:
Do not arouse or awaken love
until it so desires.[g]

1:14 [p] SS 4:13 [q] 1Sa 23:29
1:15 [r] SS 4:7 [s] SS 2:14; 4:1; 5:2,12; 6:9
1:17 [t] 1Ki 6:9
2:1 [u] Isa 35:1 [v] S 1Ch 27:29 [w] SS 5:13; Hos 14:5
2:3 [x] SS 1:14 [y] SS 1:4 [z] SS 4:16
2:4 [a] Est 1:11 [b] Nu 1:52
2:5 [c] SS 7:8 [d] SS 5:8
2:6 [e] SS 8:3
2:7 [f] SS 5:8 [g] SS 3:5; 8:4
2:8 [h] ver 17; SS 8:14
2:9 [i] 2Sa 2:18 [j] ver 17; SS 8:14
2:13 [k] Isa 28:4; Jer 24:2; Hos 9:10; Mic 7:1; Na 3:12 [l] SS 7:12
2:14 [m] Ge 8:8; SS 1:15 [n] SS 1:5; 8:13
2:15 [o] Jdg 15:4

SS 1:15–16 ❖ Why might God have put romantic love poetry in the Bible? What does God-honoring romance look like?

SS 2:7 ❖ Why is it important not to awaken love before its time? In a culture of instant pleasure, how can we follow God's instructions?

8 Listen! My beloved!
Look! Here he comes,
leaping across the mountains,
bounding over the hills.[h]
9 My beloved is like a gazelle[i] or a
young stag.[j]
Look! There he stands behind our
wall,
gazing through the windows,
peering through the lattice.
10 My beloved spoke and said to me,
"Arise, my darling,
my beautiful one, come with me.
11 See! The winter is past;
the rains are over and gone.
12 Flowers appear on the earth;
the season of singing has come,
the cooing of doves
is heard in our land.
13 The fig tree forms its early fruit;[k]
the blossoming[l] vines spread their
fragrance.
Arise, come, my darling;
my beautiful one, come with me."

He

14 My dove[m] in the clefts of the rock,
in the hiding places on the
mountainside,
show me your face,
let me hear your voice;
for your voice is sweet,
and your face is lovely.[n]
15 Catch for us the foxes,[o]
the little foxes

[a] Or *He* [b] *1* Probably a member of the crocus family [c] *3* Or possibly *apricot;* here and elsewhere in Song of Songs

2:1–2 The woman compares herself to two flowers, and her lover responds in by agreeing with her self-description, and possibly even praising her more highly than she herself does.
2:4 The banner that the man hangs is "love," indicating that love is the defining activity in which the man and the woman engage.
2:7 Because of the devastating and overpowering results of love, the pair should ensure that it is awakened only when the timing and circumstances are right.
2:8–10 The man, likened to a gazelle, is swift and athletic as well as beautiful, and he speeds across the mountains and hills toward the woman who waits for him. He desires her to come out and be seen.
2:15 The "vineyards" are the very women whom men would like to persuade to come outside,

that ruin the vineyards,[p]
our vineyards that are in bloom.[q]

She

16 My beloved is mine and I am his;[r]
he browses among the lilies.[s]
17 Until the day breaks
and the shadows flee,[t]
turn, my beloved,[u]
and be like a gazelle
or like a young stag[v]
on the rugged hills.[a][w]

3 All night long on my bed
I looked[x] for the one my heart
loves;
I looked for him but did not find
him.
2 I will get up now and go about the
city,
through its streets and squares;
I will search for the one my heart
loves.
So I looked for him but did not
find him.
3 The watchmen found me
as they made their rounds in the
city.[y]
"Have you seen the one my heart
loves?"
4 Scarcely had I passed them
when I found the one my heart
loves.
I held him and would not let him go
till I had brought him to my
mother's house,[z]
to the room of the one who
conceived me.[a]
5 Daughters of Jerusalem, I charge
you[b]
by the gazelles and by the does of
the field:
Do not arouse or awaken love
until it so desires.[c]

6 Who is this coming up from the
wilderness[d]
like a column of smoke,
perfumed with myrrh[e] and incense
made from all the spices[f] of the
merchant?
7 Look! It is Solomon's carriage,
escorted by sixty warriors,[g]
the noblest of Israel,
8 all of them wearing the sword,
all experienced in battle,
each with his sword at his side,
prepared for the terrors of the
night.[h]
9 King Solomon made for himself the
carriage;
he made it of wood from
Lebanon.
10 Its posts he made of silver,
its base of gold.
Its seat was upholstered with purple,

2:15 [p] SS 1:6 [q] SS 7:12
2:16 [r] SS 7:10 [s] SS 4:5; 6:3
2:17 [t] SS 4:6 [u] SS 1:14 [v] ver 9 [w] ver 8
3:1 [x] SS 5:6; Isa 26:9
3:3 [y] SS 5:7
3:4 [z] SS 8:2 [a] SS 6:9
3:5 [b] SS 2:7 [c] SS 8:4
3:6 [d] SS 8:5 [e] SS 1:13; 4:6,14 [f] Ex 30:34
3:7 [g] 1Sa 8:11
3:8 [h] Job 15:22; Ps 91:5

[a] 17 Or *the hills of Bether*

SS 3:1–5 ❖ Why did God create humans with such a strong desire for companionship (see Ge 2:18)?

---

and the "foxes" are presumably those men intent on sexual conquest. If the woman's lover and his friends really do wish women to come out into the countryside, then they are invited first to ensure their safety.

2:16–17 The lover's hopes have been realized, and he is invited in all his athletic beauty to leap over "the rugged hills" (v. 17)—hills cut by a deep valley. These are most naturally understood in the context as referring to the beloved's breasts. The lovers are together for an extended period and revel in each other's company.

2:1–17 Christians are the heirs of a long-standing tradition that has characterized a spiritual person as someone who disguises and/or trivializes his or her own beauty, and perhaps even comes to deny it or hate it. The Song of Songs, especially ch. 2, offers the church both challenge and healing. It challenges false dichotomies between the earthly and the heavenly, demanding that we give up all notions that beauty is somehow incompatible with godliness and even with God. It legitimates the enjoyment of and the mutual embrace of beauty as an aspect of the enjoyment and the embrace of God, and it encourages us to affirm each other in our beauty.

3:1–4 The dream signals her fear of loss, and even a longing to return to the safety and security of her youth.

3:6–11 A good case can be made for taking vv. 6–11 as a bitter satire concerning Solomon and his string of sacrificial female victims. Verse 6 is an allusion to a victim who lies on the "altar," which is Solomon's bed. To name the royal bed a "wilderness" (v. 6) is to contrast the lovemaking that happens there with the lovemaking that happens elsewhere in this song, which is so routinely associated with fertility and abundant vegetation.

The first part of our chapter concerns an individual woman who is in love with an individual man and initiates an anxious search for him. There is, by contrast, no true intimacy experienced in the desert. Her purpose is to offer a stark contrast between her relationships with the two men already introduced in chs. 1–2.

its interior inlaid with love.
Daughters of Jerusalem, [11]come out,
and look, you daughters of Zion.[i]
Look[a] on King Solomon wearing a crown,
the crown with which his mother crowned him
on the day of his wedding,
the day his heart rejoiced.[j]

He

4 How beautiful you are, my darling!
Oh, how beautiful!
Your eyes behind your veil are doves.[k]
Your hair is like a flock of goats
descending from the hills of Gilead.[l]
2 Your teeth are like a flock of sheep just shorn,
coming up from the washing.
Each has its twin;
not one of them is alone.[m]
3 Your lips are like a scarlet ribbon;
your mouth[n] is lovely.
Your temples behind your veil
are like the halves of a pomegranate.[o]
4 Your neck is like the tower[p] of David,
built with courses of stone[b];
on it hang a thousand shields,[q]
all of them shields of warriors.
5 Your breasts[r] are like two fawns,
like twin fawns of a gazelle[s]
that browse among the lilies.[t]
6 Until the day breaks
and the shadows flee,[u]
I will go to the mountain of myrrh[v]
and to the hill of incense.
7 You are altogether beautiful,[w] my darling;
there is no flaw in you.

3:11 [i] Isa 4:4 [j] Isa 62:5
4:1 [k] SS 1:15; 5:12 [l] SS 6:5; Mic 7:14
4:2 [m] SS 6:6
4:3 [n] SS 5:16 [o] SS 6:7
4:4 [p] SS 7:4 [q] Eze 27:10
4:5 [r] SS 7:3 [s] Pr 5:19 [t] SS 2:16; 6:2-3
4:6 [u] SS 2:17 [v] ver 14
4:7 [w] SS 1:15

SS 4:10-11 ❖ How can we appropriately delight in the good relationships God has put in our lives? How can we avoid seeing people only through the lens of how they can make us feel?

8 Come with me from Lebanon, my bride,[x]
come with me from Lebanon.
Descend from the crest of Amana,
from the top of Senir,[y] the summit of Hermon,[z]
from the lions' dens
and the mountain haunts of leopards.
9 You have stolen my heart, my sister, my bride;
you have stolen my heart
with one glance of your eyes,
with one jewel of your necklace.[a]
10 How delightful[b] is your love[c], my sister, my bride!
How much more pleasing is your love than wine,
and the fragrance of your perfume
more than any spice!
11 Your lips drop sweetness as the honeycomb, my bride;
milk and honey are under your tongue.[d]
The fragrance of your garments
is like the fragrance of Lebanon.[e]
12 You are a garden locked up, my sister, my bride;
you are a spring enclosed, a sealed fountain.[f]

4:8 [x] SS 5:1 [y] Dt 3:9 [z] 1Ch 5:23
4:9 [a] Ge 41:42
4:10 [b] SS 7:6 [c] SS 1:2
4:11 [d] Ps 19:10; SS 5:1 [e] Hos 14:6
4:12 [f] Pr 5:15-18

[a] 10,11 Or *interior lovingly inlaid / by the daughters of Jerusalem. /* [11]*Come out, you daughters of Zion, / and look* [b] 4 The meaning of the Hebrew for this phrase is uncertain.

✚ **3:1-11** In this troubled world, sex is often bound up with power and its abuse. It was gifted to us so that we could witness through it the Love that governs the universe, but it has come to symbolize everything that has gone wrong with human relationships in the world. The need that many appear to have to dominate and to conquer others sexually is still a marked feature of our world. The Song of Songs lauds romance while reminding us not to be romantic about a world in which coercion and violence all too often corrupt human affairs.

4:1 After the impersonal sexual activity implied in 3:6-11, the lover begins with his beloved's eyes; for to look into the eyes is to encounter the inner aspects of a person, not simply a body.
4:5-6 Only after he has surveyed this scene does he move on to still-familiar territory, an intimacy that lasts "until the day breaks and the shadows flee" (v. 6). She is the one and only woman for him, a person to be looked in the eyes and understood on a deep level.
4:7 The woman is to her lover an expansive and fertile landscape—magnificent, flawless. She is to be affirmed and enjoyed rather than controlled.
4:8-15 The woman's full participation in this relationship and her personal control over this participation is underlined. Both the garden itself and its water supply are described as "locked up" (v. 12). Entry can only be attained by those who possess permission or a key.

13 Your plants are an orchard of
pomegranates[g]
with choice fruits,
with henna[h] and nard,
14 nard and saffron,
calamus and cinnamon,[i]
with every kind of incense tree,
with myrrh[j] and aloes
and all the finest spices.[k]
15 You are[a] a garden fountain,
a well of flowing water
streaming down from Lebanon.

She

16 Awake, north wind,
and come, south wind!
Blow on my garden,
that its fragrance may spread
everywhere.
Let my beloved come into his
garden
and taste its choice fruits.[l]

He

5 I have come into my garden, my
sister, my bride;[m]
I have gathered my myrrh with
my spice.
I have eaten my honeycomb and my
honey;
I have drunk my wine and my
milk.[n]

Friends

Eat, friends, and drink;
drink your fill of love.

She

2 I slept but my heart was awake.
Listen! My beloved is knocking:
"Open to me, my sister, my darling,
my dove, my flawless[o] one.[p]
My head is drenched with dew,
my hair with the dampness of the
night."
3 I have taken off my robe —
must I put it on again?
I have washed my feet —
must I soil them again?
4 My beloved thrust his hand through
the latch-opening;
my heart began to pound for
him.
5 I arose to open for my beloved,
and my hands dripped with
myrrh,[q]
my fingers with flowing myrrh,
on the handles of the bolt.
6 I opened for my beloved,[r]
but my beloved had left; he was
gone.[s]
My heart sank at his departure.[b]
I looked[t] for him but did not find
him.
I called him but he did not
answer.
7 The watchmen found me
as they made their rounds in the
city.[u]
They beat me, they bruised me;
they took away my cloak,
those watchmen of the walls!
8 Daughters of Jerusalem, I charge
you[v] —
if you find my beloved,
what will you tell him?
Tell him I am faint with love.[w]

Friends

9 How is your beloved better than
others,
most beautiful of women?[x]

4:13 [g] SS 6:11; 7:12 [h] SS 1:14
4:14 [i] Ex 30:23 [j] SS 3:6 [k] SS 1:12
4:16 [l] SS 2:3; 5:1
5:1 [m] SS 4:8 [n] SS 4:11; Isa 55:1
5:2 [o] SS 4:7 [p] SS 6:9
5:5 [q] ver 13
5:6 [r] SS 6:1 [s] SS 6:2 [t] SS 3:1
5:7 [u] SS 3:3
5:8 [v] SS 2:7; 3:5 [w] SS 2:5
5:9 [x] SS 1:8; 6:1

[a] 15 Or *I am* (spoken by *She*) [b] 6 Or *heart had gone out to him when he spoke*

4:16—5:1 The hope is expressed that the wind will blow on the garden, sending its fragrance out into the countryside and guiding the lover to find it as he searches for his beloved. Song of Songs 5:1 reports the resolution of the whole situation: The man finds the garden and consumes what is within.

4:1—5:1 We live in a world saturated by sex while people remain desperate for love. True erotic love in the context of deep commitment is in short supply. Eros focuses on the particular woman, the particular man—the beloved himself or herself. In the midst of the sexualized and depersonalized world (represented in 3:6-11) in which men and women question their unique worth and beauty, endure assaults on their sense of self, and know deep alienation, eros calls us to mutual affirmation, respect, and intimacy—the antidote prescribed in 4:1—5:1.

5:2-4 The woman is asleep, even though her heart is "awake" (v. 2). When she hears her lover knocking at her door, the woman's initial resistance does not last long. She goes to the door and, finding him already gone, immediately goes out in search of him.
5:7 The city watchmen inflict violence on her and take away her cloak. The beating is followed only by a plea that others should help in bringing the lovers back together again.
5:8-9 She urges the daughters of Jerusalem to tell her lover that his beloved is lovesick.

let us spend the night in the
villages.[a]
12 Let us go early to the vineyards[r]
to see if the vines have budded,[s]
if their blossoms[t] have opened,
and if the pomegranates[u] are in
bloom[v] —
there I will give you my love.
13 The mandrakes[w] send out their
fragrance,
and at our door is every delicacy,
both new and old,
that I have stored up for you, my
beloved.[x]

8 If only you were to me like a
brother,
who was nursed at my mother's
breasts!
Then, if I found you outside,
I would kiss you,
and no one would despise me.
2 I would lead you
and bring you to my mother's
house[y] —
she who has taught me.
I would give you spiced wine to
drink,
the nectar of my pomegranates.
3 His left arm is under my head
and his right arm embraces me.[z]
4 Daughters of Jerusalem, I charge
you:
Do not arouse or awaken love
until it so desires.[a]

Friends

5 Who is this coming up from the
wilderness[b]
leaning on her beloved?

7:12 [r] SS 1:6 [s] SS 2:15 [t] SS 2:13 [u] SS 4:13 [v] SS 6:11
7:13 [w] Ge 30:14 [x] SS 4:16
8:2 [y] SS 3:4
8:3 [z] SS 2:6
8:4 [a] SS 2:7; 3:5
8:5 [b] SS 3:6 [c] SS 3:4
8:6 [d] SS 1:2 [e] Nu 5:14
8:7 [f] Pr 6:35

SS 8:6-7 ❖ Why is love the strongest and greatest human virtue (Col 3:12-14)?

She

Under the apple tree I roused you;
there your mother conceived[c]
you,
there she who was in labor gave
you birth.
6 Place me like a seal over your heart,
like a seal on your arm;
for love[d] is as strong as death,
its jealousy[b][e] unyielding as the
grave.
It burns like blazing fire,
like a mighty flame.[c]
7 Many waters cannot quench love;
rivers cannot sweep it away.
If one were to give
all the wealth of one's house for
love,
it[d] would be utterly scorned.[f]

Friends

8 We have a little sister,
and her breasts are not yet
grown.
What shall we do for our sister
on the day she is spoken for?
9 If she is a wall,
we will build towers of silver on
her.
If she is a door,
we will enclose her with panels of
cedar.

[a] *11* Or *the henna bushes* [b] *6* Or *ardor* [c] *6* Or *fire, / like the very flame of the* LORD [d] *7* Or *he*

---

fertile regions of the countryside where his own desire for her was first kindled. The "mandrakes" of v. 13 are plants thought to have aphrodisiac qualities; these are pictured as growing in the locale where lovemaking will take place. The "locale" is, of course, as much the woman herself as a "place" to which both lovers go. This is particularly clear in the remainder of v. 13, which speaks of a "door" giving access to "every delicacy" that has been stored up for the man—an opening already hinted at in the opening of the blossoms in v. 12.

✤ **6:11—7:13** Marriage today has become the target of bitter humor and the focus of widespread suspicion. It is a dark pit into which we will certainly fall unless we, like the prodigal son, come "to our senses" in sufficient time (Lk 15:17). Those of us who marry find that love has drawn us out of ourselves and enabled us, for a while and to an extent, to behave unselfishly. It has even led us to a place in which we find ourselves making promises to another person about lifelong commitment.

God never "comes to his senses" in his love affair with us; he never withdraws from us out of a desire for self-protection. The wounds that still mark Jesus' hands and side witness to the powerful, self-sacrificial, life-altering love that he demonstrates for those who believe and offers to those who have yet to believe and follow him.

8:1-5 Chapter 8 draws many threads together as the Song of Songs comes to its conclusion. The obstacles to the coveted relationship are implied already in vv. 1-5 in the references to those who would "despise" the woman for her kisses (v. 1) and in the allusion to the king's bed (v. 5a).

8:8-12 The woman's brothers speak in vv. 8-9, drawing a sharp retort from the woman in vv. 10-12,

She

10 I am a wall,
and my breasts are like towers.
Thus I have become in his eyes
like one bringing contentment.
11 Solomon had a vineyard[g] in Baal Hamon;
he let out his vineyard to tenants.
Each was to bring for its fruit
a thousand shekels[a][h] of silver.
12 But my own vineyard[i] is mine to give;
the thousand shekels are for you, Solomon,
and two hundred[b] are for those who tend its fruit.

He

13 You who dwell in the gardens
with friends in attendance,
let me hear your voice!

She

14 Come away, my beloved,
and be like a gazelle[j]
or like a young stag[k]
on the spice-laden mountains.[l]

8:11 [g] Ecc 2:4 [h] Isa 7:23
8:12 [i] SS 1:6
8:14 [j] Pr 5:19 [k] SS 2:9 [l] SS 2:8, 17

[a] *11* That is, about 25 pounds or about 12 kilograms; also in verse 12 [b] *12* That is, about 5 pounds or about 2.3 kilograms

---

which establishes her independence from both the brothers and Solomon. In response to Solomon's claim to ownership of her as "vineyard," she responds most forcibly: "My own vineyard is mine to give" (v. 12). She will not be possessed by any man other than the one she has chosen.

8:13–14 The song ends with the couple's words to each other as they transcend all obstacles and reaffirm their love.

✥ **8:1–14** The myth that "death cannot stop true love" is powerful; it continues to captivate our souls. We have an insatiable desire to have it told to us again and again. Hollywood regularly obliges, knowing that this myth will always sell. Against all sense, human beings have a deep need to believe fairy tales to be true, even as they have ceased to believe in any God who might reveal to them what truth is.

Our culture insists, against all the evidence, that good, in the end, defeats evil. Since it is at least a faith of some kind, romanticism is in the end much closer to the truth than pessimism, for it recognizes, however imperfectly, that Love lies at the heart of things. Only the gospel supplies the larger framework, however, in which its deficits can be made up and its errors corrected. For the gospel tells us of a God who calls us to himself and whose love makes sense of ours.

Author: The prophet Isaiah

Audience: The people of Judah and Jerusalem

Date: Between 740 and 680 BC

Theme: The Holy One of Israel, through Isaiah, challenges his people to rightly respond to his presence among them or face imminent judgment even though there will be eventual restoration.

Reading Isaiah

In the first 35 chapters, Isaiah prophesies to the people of his day concerning contemporary events, speaking words of judgment against Judah and the other nations. Chapters 36–39 form a historical interlude focusing on events in the life of King Hezekiah. The last 27 chapters relate to events more than 100 years after Isaiah's death: the Babylonian captiv-

PERSPECTIVE

Isaiah, son of Amoz, spends much of his writing time relating visions of destruction and visions of blessings about the divided nation of Israel and her surrounding neighbors. Admittedly this can make for exciting reading, particularly if you enjoy hearing about other people's problems. But it is difficult to see what the Lord-defying words and deeds of Israel have to do with us who live in the 21st century. Even though Isaiah seems to be warning a country that has an immoral domestic and foreign policy, at a deeper level the warnings and judgments are for us today. So how are we to read this book in a way that best communicates God's message to us?

First, we should expect to hear God's voice to us in Isaiah's words. This means bringing one's faith to a reading of the text. When Isaiah tells Israel to "go into the rocks, hide in the ground from the fearful presence of the LORD and the splendor of his majesty" (Isa 2:10), it may not be necessary to load up a backpack and head for the Colorado Rockies. But it is necessary to expect that in that admonition there is a message for us.

Second, we must recognize that the message is not in narrative prose but is embedded in visions, oracles, metaphors, and allusions. Isaiah was not a straight-talking prophet; he was a poetic prophet. Look at the way the type is laid out on the pages of your Bible. It looks like poetry. Only rarely in the pages of Isaiah do you see the blocks of type we associate with the narrative portions of the Bible or with other books we read.

	1200 BC	1100	1000	900	800	700	600	500	400
Division of the kingdom (930 BC)									
Ministries of Elijah and Elisha in Israel (c. 875–797 BC)									
Ministries of Amos and Hosea in Israel (c. 760–715 BC)									
Isaiah's ministry in Judah (c. 740–681 BC)									
Micah's ministry in Judah (c. 735–700 BC)									
Exile of Israel (722 BC)									
Book of Isaiah written (c. 700–681 BC)									
Fall of Jerusalem (586 BC)									

To understand this kind of writing we need to think about why someone chooses to write in poetic form. The most important reason is that poetry is best at communicating the sort of wisdom that our culture makes it difficult to hear.

Third, notice that a subtle shift takes place in Isaiah that moves us away from seeing these visions as oracles aimed directly, solely, at the nation of Israel. To see this shift, a little history reminder is in order. Most of the people of Isaiah's day (including the Israelites) were used to thinking of gods as tribal gods. Each tribe, each people group, had their own god. The question was not primarily whether those gods were real (the assumption was that they were). The real question was whose god was the most powerful.

Contrast that with the way we look at God today. Most of us today assume that God is strong; our focus is on God's relating to individuals, not to groups of people. As a result, many modern students of Isaiah think that the subtle shift apparent in Isaiah is from viewing the gods as tribal gods to viewing God as the God of individuals. Perhaps. There is no question that the image we end up with in taking the OT texts as a whole is monotheistic—they present a righteous God concerned about individual persons.

But the real shift in Isaiah is toward a view of God as the Lord not of just tribes, not of just individuals, but as the Lord of all: "This is what the LORD says:

> 'Heaven is my throne
> and the earth is my footstool....
> Has not my hand made all these things,
> and so they came into being?'" (Isa 66:1–2)

God reigns over all. Let the Lord be glorified.

ity and the hope of return under King Cyrus.

Key Verse

For to us a child is born, to us a son is given, and the government will be on his shoulders. And he will be called Wonderful Counselor, Mighty God, Everlasting Father, Prince of Peace. Of the greatness of his government and peace there will be no end. He will reign on David's throne and over his kingdom, establishing and upholding it with justice and righteousness from that time on and forever. The zeal of the LORD Almighty will accomplish this.

—Isa 9:6–7

TAKING THE NEXT STEPS

Isaiah began his work as a prophet in the year that King Uzziah died (see 2Ch 26:21–22; Isa 6:1) and prophesied during the reigns of Jotham, Ahaz, and Hezekiah.

The historical section recounting events in the life of King Hezekiah (Isa 36–39) is an almost exact duplicate of what is recorded in 2Ki 18–20. Isaiah spent most of his life in Jerusalem; during that time the city of Samaria was destroyed and the people of the nation of Israel scattered among the nations. But Isaiah saw the same sins among the people of

Judah and prophesied judgment against them; he foresaw the coming captivity in Babylon. But he also offered hope to the people by prophesying that they would return to the promised land. Isaiah has filled his book with powerful messages that apply to our day as well. (1) Reading God's list of the sins for which he judged Judah spurs us to examine our own lives to see if we are guilty of the same sins. (2) We can find courage and comfort in the faithfulness of God, who always keeps his promises—his promise to preserve a remnant who are faithful to him and his promise to send a Savior, the promised Messiah of the book of Isaiah. (3) Isaiah gives us a vision of God's salvation reaching to the ends of the earth and challenges us to proclaim his message everywhere. (4) God says there is a new age coming, ruled by the Messiah, when there will be perfect peace and joy for all the inhabitants of God's kingdom.

WHAT TO LOOK FOR IN ISAIAH

- God's offer to a rebellious nation (ch. 1)
- Isaiah's call from God (ch. 6)
- The sign of Immanuel (chs. 7–8)
- The coming of the son of David, the branch of Jesse (chs. 9; 11)
- Songs of joyful praise (chs. 12; 25–26)
- Comfort for God's people (chs. 40; 66)
- The promised deliverance (chs. 42; 45; 49; 51–52; 59)
- The suffering servant of the Lord (ch. 53)
- Invitation to seek the Lord (ch. 55)
- The glory of Zion (chs. 60; 62)

1 The vision[a] concerning Judah and Jerusalem[b] that Isaiah son of Amoz saw[c] during the reigns of Uzziah,[d] Jotham, Ahaz[e] and Hezekiah, kings of Judah.

A Rebellious Nation

2 Hear me, you heavens! Listen, earth!
  For the LORD has spoken:[f]
"I reared children and brought them up,
  but they have rebelled[g] against me.
3 The ox knows its master,
  the donkey its owner's manger,
but Israel does not know,[h]
  my people do not understand."

4 Woe to the sinful nation,
  a people whose guilt is great,
a brood of evildoers,[i]
  children given to corruption!
They have forsaken the LORD;
  they have spurned the Holy One[j] of Israel
  and turned their backs on him.

5 Why should you be beaten anymore?
  Why do you persist in rebellion?[k]
Your whole head is injured,
  your whole heart afflicted.[l]
6 From the sole of your foot to the top of your head
  there is no soundness[m] —
only wounds and welts
  and open sores,
not cleansed or bandaged[n]
  or soothed with olive oil.[o]

1:1 [a] Nu 12:6 [b] Isa 40:9 [c] Isa 2:1 [d] 2Ch 26:22 [e] 2Ki 16:1
1:2 [f] Mic 1:2 [g] Isa 30:1,9; 65:2
1:3 [h] Jer 8:7; 9:3,6
1:4 [i] Isa 14:20 [j] Isa 5:19,24
1:5 [k] Isa 31:6 [l] Isa 33:6,24
1:6 [m] Ps 38:3 [n] Isa 30:26; Jer 8:22 [o] Lk 10:34

1:1-9 These opening verses introduce the author, date, and charge against the people of Judah. Chapter 6 makes it plain that Isaiah's ministry began in the last year of King Uzziah's reign, about 740 BC.

The charges against Judah are those of rebellion (v. 2) and corruption (v. 4). Isaiah concludes that only because of the mercy of God does the land continue to exist at all (v. 9).

APPLICATION ✚ 1:1-9 The alternative to rebellion is not mechanical obedience. God has not prescribed every action for us. He has merely defined the outer limits beyond which we may not go without hurting ourselves. Just as the law of gravity does not render us mindless robots, neither does the law forbidding stealing.

7 Your country is desolate,[p]
your cities burned with fire;
your fields are being stripped by
foreigners
right before you,
laid waste as when overthrown by
strangers.
8 Daughter Zion is left
like a shelter in a vineyard,
like a hut[q] in a cucumber field,
like a city under siege.
9 Unless the LORD Almighty
had left us some survivors,[r]
we would have become like Sodom,
we would have been like
Gomorrah.[s]

10 Hear the word of the LORD,[t]
you rulers of Sodom;[u]
listen to the instruction[v] of our
God,
you people of Gomorrah!
11 "The multitude of your sacrifices —
what are they to me?" says the
LORD.
"I have more than enough of burnt
offerings,
of rams and the fat of fattened
animals;[w]
I have no pleasure
in the blood of bulls[x] and lambs
and goats.[y]
12 When you come to appear
before me,
who has asked this of you,[z]
this trampling of my courts?
13 Stop bringing meaningless
offerings![a]
Your incense[b] is detestable to me.
New Moons, Sabbaths and
convocations[c] —
I cannot bear your worthless
assemblies.

1:7 [p] Lev 26:34
1:8 [q] Job 27:18
1:9 [r] Isa 10:20-22; 37:4, 31-32 [s] Ge 19:24; Ro 9:29*
1:10 [t] Isa 28:14 [u] Isa 3:9; Eze 16:49; Ro 9:29; Rev 11:8 [v] Isa 8:20
1:11 [w] Ps 50:8 [x] Jer 6:20 [y] 1Sa 15:22; Mal 1:10
1:12 [z] Ex 23:17
1:13 [a] Isa 66:3 [b] Jer 7:9 [c] 1Ch 23:31
1:14 [d] Lev 23:1-44; Nu 28:11-29:39; Isa 29:1 [e] Isa 7:13; 43:22,24
1:15 [f] Isa 8:17; 59:2; Mic 3:4 [g] Isa 59:3
1:16 [h] Isa 52:11 [i] Isa 55:7; Jer 25:5
1:17 [j] Zep 2:3 [k] Ps 82:3
1:18 [l] Isa 41:1; 43:9,26 [m] Ps 51:7; Rev 7:14
1:19 [n] Dt 30:15-16; Isa 55:2
1:20 [o] Isa 3:25; 65:12 [p] Isa 34:16; 40:5; 58:14; Mic 4:4

Isa 1:13–17 ❖ Religious pageantry is meaningless without righteousness and justice. How are we demonstrating these virtues in our faith?

14 Your New Moon feasts and your
appointed festivals[d]
I hate with all my being.
They have become a burden to me;
I am weary[e] of bearing them.
15 When you spread out your hands in
prayer,
I hide[f] my eyes from you;
even when you offer many prayers,
I am not listening.

Your hands are full of blood![g]

16 Wash and make yourselves clean.
Take your evil deeds out of my
sight;[h]
stop doing wrong.[i]
17 Learn to do right; seek justice.[j]
Defend the oppressed.[a]
Take up the cause of the fatherless;[k]
plead the case of the widow.

18 "Come now, let us settle the matter,"[l]
says the LORD.
"Though your sins are like scarlet,
they shall be as white as snow;[m]
though they are red as crimson,
they shall be like wool.
19 If you are willing and obedient,
you will eat the good things of the
land;[n]
20 but if you resist and rebel,
you will be devoured by the
sword."[o]
For the mouth of the LORD
has spoken.[p]

[a] 17 Or *justice. / Correct the oppressor*

1:10–11 In v. 9, the author states that only because of God's mercy has Israel and Judah not been destroyed like Sodom and Gomorrah. In v. 10, he reinforces the comparison. If the Israelites are thinking that they simply need to perform all the rituals more carefully to secure God's blessings and avert judgment, they are sorely mistaken.
1:11–15 God responds to that idea with dripping scorn. The way of religiosity is a dead-end street. Their hands are full of the blood of sacrifice, but they are also full of the blood of the innocent. They want God to bless them, but they are the source of destruction for those around them.
1:16–17 What God wants is right and just behavior. Anyone can perform rituals, but the person who acts like God has entered into a life-changing relationship with him. That is what God wants.
1:18–20 Here God is challenging us to do our best thinking. If one way of acting brings destruction and another brings forgiveness and all the blessings of life, which choice is best?

✣ **1:10–20** How easy it is to think that when we go to church regularly, read the Bible, pray, tithe, and don't engage in substance abuse or other sins, God somehow owes us something. Moreover, how easy it is to think that when we have done all these things, God should be grateful to have such faithful servants as us. It is easy for these behaviors to become substitutes for real biblical faith.

21 See how the faithful city
has become a prostitute![q]
She once was full of justice;
righteousness used to dwell in her—
but now murderers!
22 Your silver has become dross,
your choice wine is diluted with water.
23 Your rulers are rebels,
partners with thieves;
they all love bribes[r]
and chase after gifts.
They do not defend the cause of the fatherless;
the widow's case does not come before them.[s]

24 Therefore the Lord, the LORD Almighty,
the Mighty One of Israel, declares:
"Ah! I will vent my wrath on my foes
and avenge[t] myself on my enemies.
25 I will turn my hand against you;[a]
I will thoroughly purge away your dross
and remove all your impurities.[u]
26 I will restore your leaders as in days of old,[v]
your rulers as at the beginning.
Afterward you will be called
the City of Righteousness,[w]
the Faithful City.[x]"

27 Zion will be delivered with justice,
her penitent ones with righteousness.[y]
28 But rebels and sinners will both be broken,
and those who forsake the LORD
will perish.[z]

29 "You will be ashamed because of the sacred oaks[a]
in which you have delighted;
you will be disgraced because of the gardens[b]
that you have chosen.
30 You will be like an oak with fading leaves,
like a garden without water.
31 The mighty man will become tinder
and his work a spark;
both will burn together,
with no one to quench the fire.[c]"

1:21 [q] Isa 57:3-9; Jer 2:20
1:23 [r] Ex 23:8 [s] Isa 10:2; Jer 5:28; Eze 22:6-7; Zec 7:10
1:24 [t] Isa 35:4; 59:17; 61:2; 63:4
1:25 [u] Eze 22:22; Mal 3:3
1:26 [v] Jer 33:7, 11 [w] Isa 33:5; 62:1; Zec 8:3 [x] Isa 60:14; 62:2
1:27 [y] Isa 35:10; 62:12; 63:4
1:28 [z] Ps 9:5; Isa 24:20; 66:24; 2Th 1:8-9
1:29 [a] Isa 57:5 [b] Isa 65:3; 66:17
1:31 [c] Isa 5:24; 9:18-19; 26:11; 33:14; 66:15-16,24
2:1 [d] Isa 1:1
2:2 [e] Isa 27:13; 56:7; 66:20; Mic 4:7
2:3 [f] Isa 51:4,7

The Mountain of the LORD

2:1–4pp // Mic 4:1–3

2 This is what Isaiah son of Amoz saw concerning Judah and Jerusalem:[d]

2 In the last days

the mountain[e] of the LORD's temple
will be established
as the highest of the mountains;
it will be exalted above the hills,
and all nations will stream to it.

3 Many peoples will come and say,

"Come, let us go up to the mountain of the LORD,
to the temple of the God of Jacob.
He will teach us his ways,
so that we may walk in his paths."
The law[f] will go out from Zion,

[a] *25* That is, against Jerusalem

1:21–23 The Lord intended faithfulness and got adultery; he intended righteousness and got murder. Instead of silver he got dross; instead of pure wine, tasteless dilution. Instead of rulers he got rebels; instead of defenders of the helpless, takers of bribes.

1:24–26 God's people assumed a position of privilege. How it must have stung when Isaiah said that they were *not* God's favorites but his enemies! God's judgment is never his last word. The fires of exile will be used to fulfill God's intentions.

1:27–31 God's justice and righteousness will redeem Zion. But that justice and righteousness are available because the people have repented and reaffirmed their willingness to imitate God's behavior.

In many ways Zion is seen to be the wife of Yahweh. The same imagery is to be found in Hosea and Ezekiel. Yahweh expects faithfulness and loyalty in return. Sadly, that is not the case. Yet in spite of that, God intends to find a way to call the nation back to himself (49:15–21; 66:7–11).

Characteristically, no matter how promising his messages of salvation may be, Isaiah never provides false comfort. The good news is for those who repent. Those who persist in rebellion *will* be destroyed.

1:21–31 We see the church increasingly marginalized as a force to change society. What should be our attitude? Isaiah would say we should not try to increase our power and influence. Rather, we should look inward at our own lives and outward at a lost and broken world. We must be confident God does not intend us harm and aware that he demands purity and selfless love in all our relationships.

2:1–3 Zion is the mountain where humanity should seek God. This is where God has given instructions (Torah) on how to walk in his ways. Thus, the nations come to Jerusalem to learn how the Creator intends his creations to live.

the word of the LORD from
Jerusalem.[g]
4 He will judge between the nations
and will settle disputes for many
peoples.
They will beat their swords into
plowshares
and their spears into pruning
hooks.[h]
Nation will not take up sword
against nation,[i]
nor will they train for war
anymore.

5 Come, descendants of Jacob,[j]
let us walk in the light[k] of the
LORD.

The Day of the LORD

6 You, LORD, have abandoned[l] your
people,
the descendants of Jacob.
They are full of superstitions from
the East;
they practice divination like the
Philistines[m]
and embrace[n] pagan customs.[o]
7 Their land is full of silver and gold;
there is no end to their treasures.
Their land is full of horses;[p]
there is no end to their chariots.[q]
8 Their land is full of idols;[r]
they bow down to the work of
their hands,
to what their fingers[s] have
made.
9 So people will be brought low[t]
and everyone humbled[u] —
do not forgive them.[a][v]

2:3 [g] Lk 24:47
2:4 [h] Joel 3:10 [i] Ps 46:9; Isa 9:5; 11:6-9; 32:18; Hos 2:18; Zec 9:10
2:5 [j] Isa 58:1 [k] Isa 60:1,19-20; 1Jn 1:5,7
2:6 [l] Dt 31:17 [m] 2Ki 1:2 [n] Pr 6:1 [o] 2Ki 16:7
2:7 [p] Dt 17:16 [q] Isa 31:1; Mic 5:10
2:8 [r] Isa 10:9-11 [s] Isa 17:8
2:9 [t] Ps 62:9 [u] Isa 5:15 [v] Ne 4:5
2:10 [w] 2Th 1:9; Rev 6:15-16
2:11 [x] Isa 5:15; 37:23
2:12 [y] Isa 24:4, 21; Mal 4:1 [z] Job 40:11
2:13 [a] Zec 11:2
2:14 [b] Isa 30:25; 40:4
2:15 [c] Isa 25:2,12
2:16 [d] 1Ki 10:22
2:17 [e] ver 11
2:18 [f] Isa 21:9

Isa 2:4 ❖ How can we be agents of God's coming peace today?

10 Go into the rocks, hide in the ground
from the fearful presence of the
LORD
and the splendor of his majesty![w]
11 The eyes of the arrogant will be
humbled
and human pride[x] brought low;
the LORD alone will be exalted in
that day.

12 The LORD Almighty has a day in
store
for all the proud and lofty,
for all that is exalted[y]
(and they will be humbled),[z]
13 for all the cedars of Lebanon, tall and
lofty,
and all the oaks of Bashan,[a]
14 for all the towering mountains
and all the high hills,[b]
15 for every lofty tower
and every fortified wall,[c]
16 for every trading ship[b][d]
and every stately vessel.
17 The arrogance of man will be
brought low
and human pride humbled;
the LORD alone will be exalted in
that day,[e]
18 and the idols will totally disappear.[f]

19 People will flee to caves in the rocks
and to holes in the ground

[a] 9 Or *not raise them up* [b] 16 Hebrew *every ship of Tarshish*

2:4–5 When the nations walk in God's ways, they will be submitting to his lordship. The concept of judgment involves the establishment of governmental order. Thus, the expected outcome of God's word among the nations is harmony.

The "God of Jacob" (v. 3) has become involved in their lives so the world may know him and be redeemed. If even the Gentiles will one day seek God's ways, surely God's chosen people should be walking in those ways now.

✜ **2:1–5** The danger of taking this passage too seriously is that we try to create utopian societies where conflicts cannot occur. These inevitably fail. The danger of not taking the passage seriously enough is that we simply relegate God's promises to an unknown future. We must reaffirm the truth of these promises: God is the God of the whole world. We must put God's ways into practice in our own lives. We must start reaching out to the poor and the helpless. We must give up our lust for riches and power.

2:6–11 God has abandoned the "descendants of Jacob" (v. 6) because instead of being filled with the ways of the true God, they are full of human wisdom. They have filled themselves with the world's values: wealth and power. In Isaiah's time "horses" and "chariots" (v. 7) represented the most powerful weapons of war available. Self-interest leads to self-worship, and the outcome is idolatry. Throughout the book, Isaiah mocks the practice of idolatry and questions how something made by humans can possibly take care of humans.

2:12–18 The Lord's glory is contrasted with every "high" thing in creation. That includes trees, mountains, fortifications, and beautiful, tall-masted ships. Nothing in all creation can compare to the Lord. How can mere humans hope to stand up to him?

2:19–22 Idols that humans created and called holy will be cast away to "the moles and bats" (v. 20),

from the fearful presence of the
LORD
and the splendor of his majesty,
when he rises to shake the earth.[g]
20 In that day people will throw away
to the moles and bats[h]
their idols of silver and idols of gold,
which they made to worship.
21 They will flee to caverns in the rocks
and to the overhanging crags
from the fearful presence of the
LORD
and the splendor of his majesty,
when he rises to shake the earth.[i]

22 Stop trusting in mere humans,[j]
who have but a breath in their
nostrils.
Why hold them in esteem?[k]

Judgment on Jerusalem and Judah

3 See now, the Lord,
the LORD Almighty,
is about to take from Jerusalem and
Judah
both supply and support:
all supplies of food[l] and all supplies
of water,[m]
2 the hero and the warrior,[n]
the judge and the prophet,
the diviner and the elder,[o]
3 the captain of fifty and the man of
rank,
the counselor, skilled craftsman
and clever enchanter.

4 "I will make mere youths their
officials;
children will rule over them."[p]

5 People will oppress each other —
man against man, neighbor
against neighbor.[q]
The young will rise up against the
old,
the nobody against the honored.

2:19 [g] Heb 12:26
2:20 [h] Lev 11:19
2:21 [i] ver 19
2:22 [j] Ps 146:3; Jer 17:5 [k] Ps 8:4; 144:3; Isa 40:15; Jas 4:14
3:1 [l] Lev 26:26 [m] Isa 5:13; Eze 4:16
3:2 [n] Eze 17:13 [o] 2Ki 24:14; Isa 9:14-15
3:4 [p] Ecc 10:16 *fn*
3:5 [q] Isa 9:19; Jer 9:8; Mic 7:2,6
3:7 [r] Eze 34:4; Hos 5:13
3:8 [s] Isa 1:7 [t] Isa 9:15,17 [u] Ps 73:9,11
3:9 [v] Ge 13:13 [w] Pr 8:36; Ro 6:23
3:10 [x] Dt 28:1-14 [y] Ps 128:2
3:11 [z] Dt 28:15-68
3:12 [a] ver 4 [b] Isa 9:16
3:13 [c] Mic 6:2

Isa 3:13-15 ❖ Where have we seen bad leadership corrupt church communities?

6 A man will seize one of his brothers
in his father's house, and say,
"You have a cloak, you be our leader;
take charge of this heap of ruins!"
7 But in that day he will cry out,
"I have no remedy.[r]
I have no food or clothing in my
house;
do not make me the leader of the
people."

8 Jerusalem staggers,
Judah is falling;[s]
their words[t] and deeds are against
the LORD,
defying[u] his glorious presence.
9 The look on their faces testifies
against them;
they parade their sin like Sodom;[v]
they do not hide it.
Woe to them!
They have brought disaster[w] upon
themselves.

10 Tell the righteous it will be well[x]
with them,
for they will enjoy the fruit of
their deeds.[y]
11 Woe to the wicked!
Disaster[z] is upon them!
They will be paid back
for what their hands have done.

12 Youths[a] oppress my people,
women rule over them.
My people, your guides lead you
astray;[b]
they turn you from the path.

13 The LORD takes his place in court;
he rises to judge[c] the people.

---

the most unclean of animals. Attempts to make humanity holy end up making us unclean. Attempts to give ourselves significance render us worthless.
3:1–5 God is going to deprive the people of their false security. Instead of great men, inexperienced "youths" (v. 4) will be their leaders. Anarchy and violence will remove the last vestiges of order.
3:6–7 Since no one with natural leadership skills is left to govern "this heap of ruins" (v. 6), even the possession of a cloak will qualify someone to assume leadership—but such a person will not take the job.
3:8–9 Judah's sin is arrogance. Ultimately, it is to commit the sin of Sodom and Gomorrah, the insistence of the residents that they had the right to determine right and wrong. The only result of such pride is "disaster" (v. 9).
3:10–11 These verses underline the cause-and-effect nature of relations with God. If we respect his parameters, we may expect positive results. If we choose not to, negative results follow.
3:12–15 These verses detail God's judgment on the leaders whom Judah has idolized. Their behavior demonstrates they are unqualified. They are "youths" and "women" (v. 12), two categories of society that had neither the training nor the status to give leadership. These elders oppress the poor. They have "ruined" (v. 14) the Lord's vineyard with their greed and lust for power.

14 The LORD enters into judgment[d]
against the elders and leaders of
his people:
"It is you who have ruined my
vineyard;
the plunder[e] from the poor is in
your houses.
15 What do you mean by crushing my
people[f]
and grinding the faces of the
poor?"
declares the Lord,
the LORD Almighty.

16 The LORD says,
"The women of Zion[g] are haughty,
walking along with outstretched
necks,
flirting with their eyes,
strutting along with swaying hips,
with ornaments jingling on their
ankles.
17 Therefore the Lord will bring sores
on the heads of the women of
Zion;
the LORD will make their scalps
bald."

18 In that day the Lord will snatch away
their finery: the bangles and headbands
and crescent necklaces,[h] 19 the earrings
and bracelets and veils, 20 the headdress-
es[i] and anklets and sashes, the perfume
bottles and charms, 21 the signet rings
and nose rings, 22 the fine robes and the
capes and cloaks, the purses 23 and mirrors, and the linen garments and tiaras
and shawls.

3:14 [d] Job 22:4 [e] Job 24:9; Jas 2:6
3:15 [f] Ps 94:5
3:16 [g] SS 3:11
3:18 [h] Jdg 8:21
3:20 [i] Ex 39:28
3:24 [j] Est 2:12 [k] Pr 31:24 [l] Isa 22:12 [m] La 2:10; Eze 27:30-31 [n] 1Pe 3:3
3:25 [o] Isa 1:20
3:26 [p] Jer 14:2 [q] La 2:10
4:1 [r] Isa 13:12 [s] 2Th 3:12 [t] Ge 30:23
4:2 [u] Isa 11:1-5; 53:2; Jer 23:5-6; Zec 3:8; 6:12 [v] Ps 72:16
4:3 [w] Ro 11:5 [x] Isa 52:1; 60:21 [y] Lk 10:20
4:4 [z] Isa 3:24 [a] Isa 1:15

Isa 4:4 ❖ How have we experienced the cleansing Spirit of God?

24 Instead of fragrance[j] there will be a
stench;
instead of a sash,[k] a rope;
instead of well-dressed hair,
baldness;[l]
instead of fine clothing,
sackcloth;[m]
instead of beauty,[n] branding.
25 Your men will fall by the sword,[o]
your warriors in battle.
26 The gates of Zion will lament and
mourn;[p]
destitute, she will sit on the
ground.[q]

4 1 In that day seven women
will take hold of one man[r]
and say, "We will eat our own food[s]
and provide our own clothes;
only let us be called by your name.
Take away our disgrace!"[t]

The Branch of the LORD

2 In that day the Branch of the LORD[u]
will be beautiful and glorious, and the
fruit[v] of the land will be the pride and
glory of the survivors in Israel. 3 Those
who are left in Zion, who remain[w] in Jerusalem, will be called holy,[x] all who are
recorded[y] among the living in Jerusalem.
4 The Lord will wash away the filth[z] of
the women of Zion; he will cleanse the
bloodstains[a] from Jerusalem by a spirit[a]

[a] 4 Or *the Spirit*

3:16—4:1 This third section on human arrogance is the most graphic of all and is being used to symbolize the nation as a whole. This conclusion is reinforced both by the use of "women [or daughters] of Zion" in 4:4 and by the way in which Zion is personified in 3:25–26.

3:17-24 Arrogant heads will be bowed in shame (v. 17). Beautiful clothing will be stripped off and replaced with a strip of burlap and a piece of rope (v. 24). The city will be reduced to utter destitution.

4:1 The prophet gives the final graphic illustration of humiliation. Isaiah foresees a day when so many of the men have died that there are not enough fathers and husbands to go around. In utter humiliation, seven women will beg one man to give them his name with no obligation on his part at all. Here is the final degradation of human pride.

✣ **2:6—4:1** We humans must live for something beyond ourselves. Modern philosophers argue that we must each create our own pattern of meaning, all the time knowing that there is no meaning. Tragically, this philosophy has come to rule the day.

4:2-6 The phrase "the Branch of the LORD" (v. 2) should be understood in light of messianic promises. The promises here are not in place of judgment but through it. The "survivors" (v. 2) are the remnant left after the "fire" (v. 4) of judgment has done its work. There are three results of that raging firestorm. (1) The people will belong to God alone and reflect his character (v. 3). (2) They will be cleansed of the accumulated guilt of all their sins (v. 4). (3) They will experience the presence of God not as a threat but as a blessing (v. 5).

✣ **4:2-6** In many cases, adversity is the judgment of God and the result of our sin. But it is not a cruel God who brings judgment. Rather, it is a loving God who sees no other way to bring us to the place where he can live in us.

of judgment[b] and a spirit[a] of fire.[c] 5Then
the LORD will create over all of Mount
Zion and over those who assemble there
a cloud of smoke by day and a glow of
flaming fire by night;[d] over everything
the glory[b][e] will be a canopy. 6It will be a
shelter[f] and shade from the heat of the
day, and a refuge[g] and hiding place from
the storm and rain.

The Song of the Vineyard

5 I will sing for the one I love
  a song about his vineyard:[h]
My loved one had a vineyard
  on a fertile hillside.
2 He dug it up and cleared it of stones
  and planted it with the choicest
    vines.[i]
He built a watchtower in it
  and cut out a winepress as well.
Then he looked for a crop of good
    grapes,
  but it yielded only bad fruit.[j]

3 "Now you dwellers in Jerusalem and
    people of Judah,
  judge between me and my
    vineyard.[k]
4 What more could have been done for
    my vineyard
  than I have done for it?[l]
When I looked for good grapes,
  why did it yield only bad?
5 Now I will tell you
  what I am going to do to my
    vineyard:
I will take away its hedge,
  and it will be destroyed;
I will break down its wall,[m]
  and it will be trampled.[n]
6 I will make it a wasteland,
  neither pruned nor cultivated,
  and briers and thorns[o] will grow
    there.

4:4 [b] Isa 28:6 [c] Isa 1:31; Mt 3:11
4:5 [d] Ex 13:21 [e] Isa 60:1
4:6 [f] Ps 27:5 [g] Isa 25:4
5:1 [h] Ps 80:8-9
5:2 [i] Jer 2:21 [j] Mt 21:19; Mk 11:13; Lk 13:6
5:3 [k] Mt 21:40
5:4 [l] 2Ch 36:15; Jer 2:5-7; Mic 6:3-4; Mt 23:37
5:5 [m] Ps 80:12 [n] Isa 28:3,18; La 1:15; Lk 21:24
5:6 [o] Isa 7:23, 24; Heb 6:8
5:7 [p] Ps 80:8 [q] Isa 59:15
5:8 [r] Jer 22:13 [s] Mic 2:2; Hab 2:9-12
5:9 [t] Isa 22:14 [u] Isa 6:11-12; Mt 23:38
5:10 [v] Lev 26:26
5:11 [w] Pr 23:29-30

Isa 5:8 ❖ Why does selfish ambition and accumulation ultimately lead to loneliness and isolation?

I will command the clouds
  not to rain on it."

7 The vineyard[p] of the LORD Almighty
  is the nation of Israel,
and the people of Judah
  are the vines he delighted in.
And he looked for justice,[q] but saw
    bloodshed;
  for righteousness, but heard cries
    of distress.

Woes and Judgments

8 Woe[r] to you who add house to
    house
  and join field to field[s]
till no space is left
  and you live alone in the land.

9 The LORD Almighty has declared in
my hearing:[t]

"Surely the great houses will become
    desolate,[u]
  the fine mansions left without
    occupants.
10 A ten-acre vineyard will produce
    only a bath[c] of wine;
  a homer[d] of seed will yield only an
    ephah[e] of grain."[v]

11 Woe to those who rise early in the
    morning
  to run after their drinks,
who stay up late at night
  till they are inflamed with wine.[w]

[a] *4* Or *the Spirit* [b] *5* Or *over all the glory there*
[c] *10* That is, about 6 gallons or about 22 liters
[d] *10* That is, probably about 360 pounds or about 160 kilograms [e] *10* That is, probably about 36 pounds or about 16 kilograms

5:1-6 Grapes is the crop that grows best in Judah. As the illustration makes plain, a grape crop demands a great deal of preparation and care. This is the work of an entire year. Then the finest vines that one can afford must be purchased and carefully set out. During that second year, the cleared rocks must be built into fences and watchtowers. Finally, in the third year, the fruit of all the previous labor is ready.

It is easy to imagine a vineyard owner's outrage when the outcome of all their labor is only bitter grapes (v. 2). When Isaiah announces that he is going to tear down the wall, let the wild animals in, and pray for the heavens to stop raining (vv. 5–6), we can imagine the hearers shouting, "Yes, do it!"
5:7–24 But the hearers suddenly realize Isaiah is talking about them. He begins with a general statement in v. 7 and then gives specific "woes" in vv. 8–24. This is a word associated with funerals. Just as the vineyard of bitter grapes will be destroyed because of what it produced, so will Israel.
5:8–10 The particular expression of greed addressed in v. 8 is greed for bigger houses and more land. In the covenant, God gave his land as grants for the respective families for all time. In vv. 9–10 God announces a punishment that fits the crime.
5:11–17 The "bitter grape" is self-indulgence, and much of the passage is the announcement of judgment on this behavior. Once again, the punishment fits the crime. As these wealthy and noble people have focused on what goes down their throats, the day will come when nothing goes down (v. 13).

12 They have harps and lyres at their
banquets,
pipes and timbrels and wine,
but they have no regard[x] for the
deeds of the LORD,
no respect for the work of his
hands.[y]
13 Therefore my people will go into
exile[z]
for lack of understanding;[a]
those of high rank will die of
hunger
and the common people will be
parched with thirst.
14 Therefore Death[b] expands its jaws,
opening wide its mouth;[c]
into it will descend their nobles and
masses
with all their brawlers and
revelers.
15 So people will be brought low[d]
and everyone humbled,[e]
the eyes of the arrogant[f] humbled.
16 But the LORD Almighty will be
exalted by his justice,[g]
and the holy God will be proved
holy[h] by his righteous acts.
17 Then sheep will graze as in their
own pasture;[i]
lambs will feed[a] among the ruins
of the rich.

18 Woe to those who draw sin along
with cords of deceit,
and wickedness[j] as with cart
ropes,
19 to those who say, "Let God hurry;
let him hasten his work
so we may see it.
The plan of the Holy One of Israel —
let it approach, let it come into
view,
so we may know it."[k]

20 Woe to those who call evil good
and good evil,
who put darkness for light
and light for darkness,[l]
who put bitter for sweet
and sweet for bitter.[m]

21 Woe to those who are wise in their
own eyes[n]
and clever in their own sight.

22 Woe to those who are heroes at
drinking wine[o]
and champions at mixing drinks,
23 who acquit the guilty for a bribe,[p]
but deny justice[q] to the innocent.[r]
24 Therefore, as tongues of fire lick up
straw
and as dry grass sinks down in the
flames,
so their roots will decay[s]
and their flowers blow away like
dust;
for they have rejected the law of the
LORD Almighty
and spurned the word[t] of the Holy
One of Israel.
25 Therefore the LORD's anger[u] burns
against his people;
his hand is raised and he strikes
them down.
The mountains shake,
and the dead bodies are like
refuse[v] in the streets.

Yet for all this, his anger is not
turned away,[w]
his hand is still upraised.[x]

26 He lifts up a banner for the distant
nations,
he whistles[y] for those at the ends
of the earth.[z]

5:12 [x] Job 34:27 [y] Ps 28:5; Am 6:5-6
5:13 [z] Hos 4:6 [a] Isa 1:3; Hos 4:6
5:14 [b] Pr 30:16 [c] Nu 16:30
5:15 [d] Isa 10:33 [e] Isa 2:9 [f] Isa 2:11
5:16 [g] Isa 28:17; 30:18; 33:5; 61:8 [h] Isa 29:23
5:17 [i] Isa 7:25; Zep 2:6,14
5:18 [j] Isa 59:4-8; Jer 23:14
5:19 [k] Jer 17:15; Eze 12:22; 2Pe 3:4
5:20 [l] Mt 6:22-23; Lk 11:34-35 [m] Am 5:7
5:21 [n] Pr 3:7; Ro 12:16; 1Co 3:18-20
5:22 [o] Pr 23:20
5:23 [p] Ex 23:8 [q] Isa 10:2 [r] Ps 94:21; Jas 5:6
5:24 [s] Job 18:16 [t] Isa 8:6; 30:9,12
5:25 [u] 2Ki 22:13 [v] 2Ki 9:37 [w] Jer 4:8; Da 9:16 [x] Isa 9:12,17,21; 10:4
5:26 [y] Isa 7:18; Zec 10:8 [z] Dt 28:49; Isa 13:5; 18:3

[a] 17 Septuagint; Hebrew / *strangers will eat*

5:18–19 The prophet describes underlying attitudes that precede and follow the sins of the flesh. The first is cynicism that dares God to take action. These are people who delight in sinning. They insist that if such a course of action is so bad, the great God will certainly take action against it. In the meantime, they intend to keep right on living for themselves at all costs.
5:20–21 The fourth woe takes the situation one step further. Now it is declaring that there is no such thing as sin. Such persons have revolted against any moral authority at all.
5:22–24 The final woe speaks ironically of those who are great at what does not matter (mixing drinks) and therefore neglect what does matter—justice.

The people have rejected the instruction of the only One in the universe who has the right to be called "Holy," who has given himself to Israel (v. 24). They have rejected the instruction of the One who is in a position to give such instructions.
5:25–30 The great powers of the world are instruments in the hands of God. They come in response to his signal. In vv. 27–29, short couplets create a sense of urgency.

5:1–30 The Christian church today faces a crisis of worldview. Our culture has lost the idea that we owe obedience to God. As a result, we are becoming lawless. We in the church need to push against denial of the fact that our Creator has built into his universe certain spiritual principles that are as unchangeable as any of the natural principles.

Here they come,
swiftly and speedily!
27 Not one of them grows tired or stumbles,
not one slumbers or sleeps;
not a belt is loosened at the waist,[a]
not a sandal strap is broken.[b]
28 Their arrows are sharp,[c]
all their bows[d] are strung;
their horses' hooves seem like flint,
their chariot wheels like a whirlwind.
29 Their roar is like that of the lion,[e]
they roar like young lions;
they growl as they seize[f] their prey
and carry it off with no one to rescue.[g]
30 In that day they will roar over it
like the roaring of the sea.[h]
And if one looks at the land,
there is only darkness and distress;[i]
even the sun will be darkened[j] by clouds.

5:27 [a] Job 12:18 [b] Joel 2:7-8
5:28 [c] Ps 45:5 [d] Ps 7:12
5:29 [e] Jer 51:38; Zep 3:3; Zec 11:3 [f] Isa 10:6; 49:24-25 [g] Isa 42:22; Mic 5:8
5:30 [h] Lk 21:25 [i] Isa 8:22; Jer 4:23-28 [j] Joel 2:10
6:1 [k] 2Ch 26:22, 23 [l] 2Ki 15:7 [m] Jn 12:41 [n] Rev 4:2
6:2 [o] Rev 4:8 [p] Eze 1:11
6:3 [q] Ps 72:19; Rev 4:8

Isaiah's Commission

6 In the year that King Uzziah[k] died,[l]
I saw the Lord,[m] high and exalted,
seated on a throne;[n] and the train of his
robe filled the temple. 2 Above him were
seraphim,[o] each with six wings: With two
wings they covered their faces, with two
they covered their feet,[p] and with two
they were flying. 3 And they were calling
to one another:

"Holy, holy, holy is the LORD Almighty;
the whole earth is full of his glory."[q]

4 At the sound of their voices the doorposts and thresholds shook and the temple was filled with smoke.

6:1–13 The Assyrian emperor Tiglath-Pileser III established himself as a military conqueror to be feared. But when the powerful Uzziah was on the throne, the immediacy of the threat was blurred. When Uzziah was removed, the danger could no longer be ignored.

6:3–4 In the ancient Near East the term "holy" was not used especially widely. For the Hebrews, the idea of what was "holy" was decidedly different. Throughout the entire OT, Israel learned that God's holy character set him apart from us humans.

PEOPLE TO KNOW // ISAIAH

ISAIAH 6:1-8: The prophet Isaiah ministered in Jerusalem during the fall of the northern kingdom of Israel. He had a dramatic prophetic call. One day he was confronted with the overwhelming glory of God: He saw a vision of angels surrounding God's throne. One angel touched Isaiah's lips with a burning coal, telling him his sin had been atoned for. God then called out, "Whom shall I send?" Isaiah replied, "Here am I. Send me!" (Isa 6:1-8).

Isaiah ministered in Jerusalem for many years, working closely with good kings and bad. When King Hezekiah was ill, God sent Isaiah to tell him he would soon die (Isa 38:1). When Hezekiah prayed fervently to God, God sent Isaiah back to tell the king he would live 15 more years. As a sign that this promise would come true, God caused a shadow to move backward.

Isaiah is best known for his prophetic messages. After Psalms, Isaiah is the most quoted book in the NT—for good reason. Many passages point clearly to the Messiah. When Philip met the Ethiopian eunuch, the eunuch was reading from Isaiah 53 (Ac 8:32-33). Beginning with this passage, Philip led the eunuch to Christ.

While Isaiah's prophecy contains judgment, it also bursts with beautiful and hopeful passages promising God's redemption through the Messiah and a renewed creation of peace and harmony. Isaiah foretells a great messianic banquet prepared for all peoples (Isa 25:6-8). Jesus read words from Isaiah 61 and declared these words were fulfilled in himself (Lk 4:16-21).

APPLICATION ✤ Isaiah's calling is instructive for every believer. Being confronted with God's glory brings into sharp relief how sinful we are, and yet God graciously calls and equips us for his mission. God provides a way for us to be in his presence through his grace in Jesus Christ. Isaiah was faithful in bringing God's message in both good times and bad. Our calling is the same: to speak God's truth and point to the hope of God's anointed Messiah, whether in good times or bad.

CHARACTER OF GOD // GOD IS HOLY

Isaiah 6:3: "Holy, holy, holy is the LORD Almighty; the whole earth is full of his glory."

Scripture teaches that God is holy, and God focused much of his instructions to the early Israelites on teaching them what holiness looked like in their lives. They were called to be a holy nation, and within their community the Levites were called to the special holy task of being priests. They observed holy space in God's tabernacle. On the holiest day of the year (the Day of Atonement), the holiest person (the high priest) went into the Most Holy Place (where God's ark resided) to seek atonement for the sins of the people (Lev 16). God wanted them to display his holiness in their conduct so that the other nations would see what God is like.

Holiness has the basic meaning of being "set apart." God's holiness is perfect; he is untainted by any sin. Because God is holy and we are not, we are unable to enter God's mighty presence on our own. This is why Isaiah's vision of God in Isaiah 6 filled the prophet with fear. The weight of God's holiness was overwhelming for him.

By God's grace, God has provided means of access into his presence. In the OT, God provided Israel with ceremonial instructions for the priests to intercede on behalf of the people. Priests were able to seek forgiveness for the sins of the people through offerings and sacrifices. These offerings and sacrifices themselves pointed forward to the full atoning work of Christ, whom the NT calls both our great high priest (Heb 4:14) and our atoning sacrifice (1Jn 2:2).

Through Christ, we can approach our holy God with confidence (Heb 4:16). Though God's holiness is completely pure, God graciously provides a way through Jesus Christ for us to come near.

APPLICATION ✣ Though we are not holy in the same way as God, God nonetheless calls us to be holy. First Peter 1:15 says, "But just as he who called you is holy, so be holy in all you do." God says in Leviticus 11:44, "Be holy, because I am holy." Through the atoning sacrifice of Christ, we become God's holy people, a royal priesthood, representing God's holiness and love to the world (1Pe 2:9).

Isa 6:8 ❖ If we've said yes to God's call on our lives, what is God calling us to do for his kingdom and glory?

5"Woe to me!" I cried. "I am ruined!
For I am a man of unclean lips, and I
live among a people of unclean lips,[r] and
my eyes have seen the King,[s] the LORD
Almighty."

6Then one of the seraphim flew to me
with a live coal in his hand, which he had
taken with tongs from the altar. 7With
it he touched my mouth and said, "See,
this has touched your lips;[t] your guilt is
taken away and your sin atoned for."[u]

8Then I heard the voice[v] of the Lord
saying, "Whom shall I send? And who
will go for us?"

And I said, "Here am I. Send me!"

9He said, "Go[w] and tell this people:
" 'Be ever hearing, but never
understanding;
be ever seeing, but never
perceiving.'[x]
10Make the heart of this people
calloused;[y]
make their ears dull
and close their eyes.[a]
Otherwise they might see with their
eyes,
hear with their ears,[z]
understand with their hearts,
and turn and be healed."[a]

6:5 [r] Jer 9:3-8 [s] Jer 51:57
6:7 [t] Jer 1:9 [u] 1Jn 1:7
6:8 [v] Ac 9:4
6:9 [w] Eze 3:11 [x] Mt 13:15*; Lk 8:10*
6:10 [y] Dt 32:15; Ps 119:70 [z] Jer 5:21 [a] Mt 13:13-15; Mk 4:12*; Ac 28:26-27*

[a] 9,10 Hebrew; Septuagint *'You will be ever hearing, but never understanding; / you will be ever seeing, but never perceiving.' / 10This people's heart has become calloused; / they hardly hear with their ears, / and they have closed their eyes*

6:5–7 Why does Isaiah say that his "lips" are unclean (v. 5)? Why not his heart? It may be that the lips are evidence of what is really in the heart. A related possibility is that having just heard the golden tones of the seraphim, Isaiah knows that his lips could never be used in such holy service.

Isaiah does not even bother to ask for cleansing or deliverance. But God has not given him this vision to annihilate him. Rather, he wants Isaiah to discover his true vocation.

6:8–13 Isaiah is called upon to preach a message that will only push Israel farther away from God. But some will turn, preserving his words until the fires of the exile fall and a generation is willing to listen.

11Then I said, "For how long, Lord?"[b]
And he answered:

"Until the cities lie ruined[c]
and without inhabitant,
until the houses are left deserted
and the fields ruined and ravaged,
12until the LORD has sent everyone far
away[d]
and the land is utterly forsaken.[e]
13And though a tenth remains[f] in the
land,
it will again be laid waste.
But as the terebinth and oak
leave stumps when they are cut
down,
so the holy seed will be the stump
in the land."[g]

The Sign of Immanuel

7 When Ahaz son of Jotham, the son
of Uzziah, was king of Judah, King
Rezin[h] of Aram[i] and Pekah[j] son of Remaliah king of Israel marched up to fight
against Jerusalem, but they could not
overpower it.
2Now the house of David[k] was told,
"Aram has allied itself with[a] Ephraim[l]";
so the hearts of Ahaz and his people
were shaken, as the trees of the forest
are shaken by the wind.
3Then the LORD said to Isaiah, "Go out,
you and your son Shear-Jashub,[b] to meet
Ahaz at the end of the aqueduct of the
Upper Pool, on the road to the Launderer's Field.[m] 4Say to him, 'Be careful, keep
calm[n] and don't be afraid.[o] Do not lose
heart[p] because of these two smoldering stubs[q] of firewood — because of the
fierce anger[r] of Rezin and Aram and of
the son of Remaliah. 5Aram, Ephraim
and Remaliah's son have plotted your
ruin, saying, 6"Let us invade Judah; let
us tear it apart and divide it among ourselves, and make the son of Tabeel king
over it." 7Yet this is what the Sovereign
LORD says:

"'It will not take place,
it will not happen,[s]
8for the head of Aram is Damascus,[t]
and the head of Damascus is only
Rezin.
Within sixty-five years
Ephraim will be too shattered[u] to
be a people.
9The head of Ephraim is Samaria,
and the head of Samaria is only
Remaliah's son.
If you do not stand firm in your
faith,[v]
you will not stand at all.'"[w]

10Again the LORD spoke to Ahaz, 11"Ask
the LORD your God for a sign, whether
in the deepest depths or in the highest
heights."
12But Ahaz said, "I will not ask; I will
not put the LORD to the test."
13Then Isaiah said, "Hear now, you
house of David! Is it not enough to try
the patience of humans? Will you try the

6:11 [b]Ps 79:5 [c]Lev 26:31
6:12 [d]Dt 28:64 [e]Jer 4:29
6:13 [f]Isa 1:9 [g]Job 14:7
7:1 [h]2Ki 15:37 [i]2Ch 28:5 [j]2Ki 15:25
7:2 [k]ver 13; Isa 22:22 [l]Isa 9:9
7:3 [m]2Ki 18:17; Isa 36:2
7:4 [n]Isa 30:15 [o]Isa 35:4 [p]Dt 20:3 [q]Zec 3:2 [r]Isa 10:24
7:7 [s]Isa 8:10; Ac 4:25
7:8 [t]Ge 14:15 [u]Isa 17:1-3
7:9 [v]2Ch 20:20 [w]Isa 8:6-8; 30:12-14

[a] 2 Or *has set up camp in* [b] 3 *Shear-Jashub* means *a remnant will return.*

6:1-13 We have all heard people tell stories about how they were dragged kicking and screaming into the Lord's service. Why is that? Perhaps it is because those of us who have been raised in the church, who still regularly participate, have never really felt the in-depth wonder of having been forgiven of our sins and given new life.

7:1-9 The events described in these verses probably occurred around 735 BC. Syria and Israel are attacking Judah, likely attempting to force them to join a coalition against the Assyrians. They seek to depose Ahaz and put the son of someone named Tabeel on the throne in his place (v. 6).

There were no fool-proof procedures for breaking into a well-defended, walled city. It was possible to force such a city to surrender by stopping its water supply. Ahaz wants to be sure that such a thing does not happen.

Throughout chs. 7-11, children are important figures. The first is presented here, accompanying his father to confront the king (v. 3). This child's name means "only a remnant will return."

The prophet tells the king that fear is not necessary (vv. 4-9). In the end, it does not matter what Rezin and Pekah say (vv. 5-6). In "sixty-five years" (v. 8), a way of saying within one person's lifetime, they would not even be a people. Isaiah concludes his appeal to trust God.

7:10-25 God offers Ahaz a sign to prompt faith. But Ahaz refuses the challenge (v. 12). He says that to ask for a sign would be to test God, something forbidden in the Torah (Dt 6:16). But the testing referred to in the Torah is not believing God's promises. To step out in faith is nothing like the rebellions in the desert. Ahaz's piety is only a mask for unbelief.

7:13-16 Isaiah recognizes Ahaz's hesitancy and responds with frustration. God says he will give Ahaz a sign anyway (v. 14). The sign seems to be that before a child conceived at the time of the prophecy is 12 years old, the two aggressor nations will be destroyed (v. 16).

patience of my God[x] also? 14Therefore the
Lord himself will give you[a] a sign: The
virgin[b] will conceive and give birth to a
son,[y] and[c] will call him Immanuel.[dz] 15He
will be eating curds and honey[a] when
he knows enough to reject the wrong
and choose the right, 16for before the
boy knows[b] enough to reject the wrong
and choose the right, the land of the two
kings you dread will be laid waste.[c] 17The
LORD will bring on you and on your people and on the house of your father a
time unlike any since Ephraim broke
away[d] from Judah — he will bring the
king of Assyria.[e]"

Assyria, the LORD's Instrument

18In that day the LORD will whistle[f] for
flies from the Nile delta in Egypt and for
bees from the land of Assyria.[g] 19They
will all come and settle in the steep ravines and in the crevices[h] in the rocks, on
all the thornbushes and at all the water
holes. 20In that day the Lord will use[i] a
razor hired from beyond the Euphrates
River — the king of Assyria[j] — to shave
your head and private parts, and to cut
off your beard also. 21In that day, a person will keep alive a young cow and two
goats. 22And because of the abundance of
the milk they give, there will be curds to
eat. All who remain in the land will eat
curds and honey. 23In that day, in every
place where there were a thousand vines
worth a thousand silver shekels,[e] there
will be only briers and thorns.[k] 24Hunt-
ers will go there with bow and arrow, for
the land will be covered with briers and
thorns. 25As for all the hills once cultivated by the hoe, you will no longer go
there for fear of the briers and thorns;
they will become places where cattle are
turned loose and where sheep run.[l]

Isaiah and His Children as Signs

8 The LORD said to me, "Take a large
scroll[m] and write on it with an ordinary pen: Maher-Shalal-Hash-Baz."[fn] 2So I
called in Uriah[o] the priest and Zechariah
son of Jeberekiah as reliable witnesses
for me. 3Then I made love to the prophetess, and she conceived and gave birth
to a son. And the LORD said to me, "Name
him Maher-Shalal-Hash-Baz. 4For before
the boy knows[p] how to say 'My father' or
'My mother,' the wealth of Damascus and
the plunder of Samaria will be carried off
by the king of Assyria.[q]"
5The LORD spoke to me again:

6"Because this people has rejected[r]
the gently flowing waters of
Shiloah[s]

7:13 [x] Isa 25:1
7:14 [y] Lk 1:31 [z] Isa 8:8,10; Mt 1:23*
7:15 [a] ver 22
7:16 [b] Isa 8:4 [c] Isa 17:3; Hos 5:9,13; Am 1:3-5
7:17 [d] 1Ki 12:16 [e] 2Ch 28:20
7:18 [f] Isa 5:26 [g] Isa 13:5
7:19 [h] Isa 2:19
7:20 [i] Isa 10:15 [j] Isa 8:7; 10:5
7:23 [k] Isa 5:6
7:25 [l] Isa 5:17
8:1 [m] Isa 30:8; Hab 2:2 [n] ver 3; Hab 2:2
8:2 [o] 2Ki 16:10
8:4 [p] Isa 7:16 [q] Isa 7:8
8:6 [r] Isa 5:24 [s] Jn 9:7

[a] 14 The Hebrew is plural. [b] 14 Or *young woman* [c] 14 Masoretic Text; Dead Sea Scrolls *son, and he* or *son, and they* [d] 14 *Immanuel* means *God with us.* [e] 23 That is, about 25 pounds or about 12 kilograms [f] 1 *Maher-Shalal-Hash-Baz* means *quick to the plunder, swift to the spoil*; also in verse 3.

Isa 7:14 ❖ How is Christ the ultimate sign of God's commitment and love to us (see Mt 1:21–23)?

However, three factors raise questions about this interpretation. (1) God himself urges Ahaz to ask for a remarkable sign (v. 11). Nothing seems remarkable about the sign God gives. (2) The second is that the Hebrew word for "virgin" (v. 14) is a relatively unusual one meaning "young woman of marriageable age." (3) Finally, the choice of a name for the child (v. 14) is strange since its relevance to the situation is not clear.

Taken together, these suggest that the sign is more than meets the eye. Matthew (1:23) has not merely appropriated the text for his own purposes. The sign had a single meaning but a double significance. Its meaning is that "God is with us." The first significance is for Ahaz's own day.

But is God *really* with us? The answer to the question is "yes." God has come to take up residence with us as one of us. How has that fact been accomplished? By giving this child a human mother but no human father.

The child is a sign that God is with Judah in two ways. Since God is with them, they need not fear their two small neighbors. But since Ahaz has doubted God, he will discover God who *is* with us, bringing the very thing he has trusted against him (vv. 18–19).

✣ **7:1-25** We need to seek God's word—something Ahaz did not do. We need to seek it in the Scriptures, in the counsel of godly leaders, in the nature of our circumstances, and in our own hearts. What we must avoid at all costs is what Ahaz did: deciding what we want and then asking God if he could please bless what we want.

8:1-5 Isaiah is to write down the child's name even before he is conceived as evidence of predictive prophecy. The language of 8:3 is similar to that of 7:14, which suggests that the two verses may refer to the same event. Maher-Shalal-Hash-Baz may be the first fulfillment of the Immanuel sign. If this is so, before the child learns to speak clearly, Damascus and Samaria will have been plundered.

8:6-10 These verses encapsulate Isaiah's (and God's) perspective on history. God is with Israel;

and rejoices over Rezin
and the son of Remaliah,[t]
7 therefore the Lord is about to bring
against them
the mighty floodwaters[u] of the
Euphrates —
the king of Assyria[v] with all his
pomp.
It will overflow all its channels,
run over all its banks
8 and sweep on into Judah, swirling
over it,
passing through it and reaching
up to the neck.
Its outspread wings will cover the
breadth of your land,
Immanuel[a]!"[w]

9 Raise the war cry,[b][x] you nations, and
be shattered!
Listen, all you distant lands.
Prepare[y] for battle, and be shattered!
Prepare for battle, and be
shattered!
10 Devise your strategy, but it will be
thwarted;[z]
propose your plan, but it will not
stand,[a]
for God is with us.[c][b]

11 This is what the LORD says to me with
his strong hand upon me,[c] warning me
not to follow[d] the way of this people:

12 "Do not call conspiracy[e]
everything this people calls a
conspiracy;
do not fear what they fear,
and do not dread it.[f]
13 The LORD Almighty is the one you
are to regard as holy,[g]
he is the one you are to fear,
he is the one you are to dread.[h]
14 He will be a holy place;[i]
for both Israel and Judah he
will be
a stone that causes people to
stumble
and a rock that makes them fall.[j]
And for the people of Jerusalem he
will be
a trap and a snare.[k]
15 Many of them will stumble;[l]
they will fall and be broken,
they will be snared and captured."

16 Bind up this testimony of warning
and seal[m] up God's instruction
among my disciples.
17 I will wait[n] for the LORD,
who is hiding[o] his face from the
descendants of Jacob.
I will put my trust in him.

18 Here am I, and the children the LORD
has given me.[p] We are signs[q] and symbols
in Israel from the LORD Almighty, who
dwells on Mount Zion.[r]

The Darkness Turns to Light

19 When someone tells you to consult[s]
mediums and spiritists, who whisper
and mutter,[t] should not a people inquire
of their God? Why consult the dead on
behalf of the living? 20 Consult God's instruction[u] and the testimony of warning.

[a] 8 *Immanuel* means *God with us.* [b] 9 Or *Do your worst* [c] 10 Hebrew *Immanuel*

8:6 [t] Isa 7:1
8:7 [u] Isa 17:12-13 [v] Isa 7:20
8:8 [w] Isa 7:14
8:9 [x] Isa 17:12-13 [y] Joel 3:9
8:10 [z] Job 5:12 [a] Isa 7:7 [b] Isa 7:14; Ro 8:31
8:11 [c] Eze 3:14 [d] Eze 2:8
8:12 [e] Isa 7:2; 30:1 [f] 1Pe 3:14*
8:13 [g] Nu 20:12 [h] Isa 29:23
8:14 [i] Isa 4:6; Eze 11:16 [j] Lk 2:34; Ro 9:33*; 1Pe 2:8* [k] Isa 24:17-18
8:15 [l] Isa 28:13; 59:10; Lk 20:18; Ro 9:32
8:16 [m] Isa 29:11-12
8:17 [n] Hab 2:3 [o] Dt 31:17; Isa 54:8
8:18 [p] Heb 2:13* [q] Lk 2:34 [r] Ps 9:11
8:19 [s] 1Sa 28:8 [t] Isa 29:4
8:20 [u] Isa 1:10; Lk 16:29

Isa 8:11 ❖ In what area of life is God telling us not to follow the ways of the people around us?

---

if Israel tries to live as if that were not so, there will be tragic consequences (vv. 6–8). At the same time, the nations must never forget that they are instruments in God's hand. They are mistaken if they think they can wipe out his people to achieve their own geopolitical goals. God *is* with his people and will achieve his goals through them (vv. 9–10).

8:11–22 In 735 BC Jerusalem was threatened by enemies all around. In that context, God comes to Isaiah with specific instructions. In the first place, the prophet is not to lose his focus on God. He should focus his attention on serving the God who determines all destinies.

8:12–13 The fear of the unknown is a defiling kind of fear, but the "fear of the LORD" is clean (Ps 19:9). This describes a way of life that pays primary attention to the ways of the "holy" one (Isa 8:13).

8:14 God will be a sanctuary for Isaiah. Those who refuse to give God that central place in their lives will find a "stone" in the road over which they will "stumble."

Here we come again to the dual significance of "God is with us." God's presence is the one inescapable fact of human life. We *will* encounter him in one way or another. Those who make a place for him find him to be the glue that holds everything together. Those who ignore him find their lives to be askew and cannot understand why.

8:16–17 Should Isaiah give up in frustration? Should he keep hammering away at a people who cannot understand him? The answer is the middle way. He should not give up declaring God's word, but he should do it with disciples who will "seal up" (i.e., "treasure") those words for another day (v. 16).

8:19–22 Here we read what happens when people refuse to trust and obey God. They prefer instead to consult the dead. They have trusted other things instead of God, and all of them have failed.

If anyone does not speak according to
this word, they have no light[v] of dawn.
21 Distressed and hungry, they will roam
through the land; when they are famished, they will become enraged and,
looking upward, will curse[w] their king
and their God. 22 Then they will look toward the earth and see only distress and
darkness and fearful gloom, and they
will be thrust into utter darkness.[x]

9[a] Nevertheless, there will be no more
gloom for those who were in distress. In the past he humbled the land
of Zebulun and the land of Naphtali,[y] but
in the future he will honor Galilee of the
nations, by the Way of the Sea, beyond
the Jordan —

2 The people walking in darkness
have seen a great light;[z]
on those living in the land of deep
darkness[a]
a light has dawned.[b]
3 You have enlarged the nation
and increased their joy;
they rejoice before you
as people rejoice at the harvest,
as warriors rejoice
when dividing the plunder.
4 For as in the day of Midian's defeat,[c]
you have shattered
the yoke[d] that burdens them,
the bar across their shoulders,[e]
the rod of their oppressor.[f]
5 Every warrior's boot used in battle
and every garment rolled in blood
will be destined for burning,[g]
will be fuel for the fire.
6 For to us a child is born,[h]
to us a son is given,[i]
and the government[j] will be on
his shoulders.
And he will be called
Wonderful Counselor,[k] Mighty
God,[l]
Everlasting Father, Prince of
Peace.[m]
7 Of the greatness of his government
and peace
there will be no end.[n]
He will reign on David's throne
and over his kingdom,
establishing and upholding it
with justice[o] and righteousness
from that time on and forever.
The zeal[p] of the LORD Almighty
will accomplish this.

The LORD's Anger Against Israel

8 The Lord has sent a message against
Jacob;
it will fall on Israel.
9 All the people will know it —
Ephraim and the inhabitants of
Samaria[q] —
who say with pride
and arrogance[r] of heart,
10 "The bricks have fallen down,
but we will rebuild with dressed
stone;
the fig trees have been felled,
but we will replace them with
cedars."
11 But the LORD has strengthened
Rezin's[s] foes against them
and has spurred their enemies on.
12 Arameans[t] from the east and
Philistines[u] from the west

8:20 [v] Mic 3:6
8:21 [w] Rev 16:11
8:22 [x] ver 20; Isa 5:30
9:1 [y] 2Ki 15:29
9:2 [z] Eph 5:8 [a] Lk 1:79 [b] Mt 4:15-16*
9:4 [c] Jdg 7:25 [d] Isa 14:25 [e] Isa 10:27 [f] Isa 14:4; 49:26; 51:13; 54:14
9:5 [g] Isa 2:4
9:6 [h] Isa 53:2; Lk 2:11 [i] Jn 3:16 [j] Mt 28:18
[k] Isa 28:29 [l] Isa 10:21; 11:2 [m] Isa 26:3,12; 66:12
9:7 [n] Da 2:44; Lk 1:33 [o] Isa 11:4; 16:5; 32:1,16 [p] Isa 37:32; 59:17
9:9 [q] Isa 7:9 [r] Isa 46:12
9:11 [s] Isa 7:8
9:12 [t] 2Ki 16:6 [u] 2Ch 28:18

[a] In Hebrew texts 9:1 is numbered 8:23, and 9:2-21 is numbered 9:1-20.

Isa 9:2 ❖ How does Christ bring light into darkness (see Jn 1:4-5)? How have we experienced this power of Christ in our own lives?

8:1-22 It is interesting to watch the fascination of modern people with so-called conspiracy theories. But Isaiah calls us to give up the fascination with "what really happened." He calls us to believe that God is at work in history and that we can trust him to work all things together for the good of those who are called according to his purpose (Ro 8:28).

9:1-5 The Assyrian conquests began in the tribal territory of Zebulun and Naphtali. This was a lush agricultural area and the main trade route from Mesopotamia to Egypt. God is greater than Assyria, and he promises these people will experience victory (vv. 3-5).

9:6-7 For the third time in as many chapters, the birth of a child is prophetically predicted. All three refer to the promised Messiah and point to the government and the social and personal integration he will produce, which will be eternal.

9:1-7 Have we allowed the Child-King to take over the "government" of our lives? Only then can we know the benefits of Immanuel, "God with us." We cannot have the light, the honor, the joy, the abundance, or the integration that he offers in any other way.

9:8-12 The charges God lodges against Israel all have to do with ethical behavior, with the Mosaic covenant providing the background.

have devoured[v] Israel with open
mouth.

Yet for all this, his anger is not
turned away,
his hand is still upraised.[w]

13 But the people have not returned to
him who struck[x] them,
nor have they sought[y] the LORD
Almighty.
14 So the LORD will cut off from Israel
both head and tail,
both palm branch and reed[z] in a
single day;[a]
15 the elders[b] and dignitaries are the
head,
the prophets who teach lies are
the tail.
16 Those who guide[c] this people
mislead them,
and those who are guided are led
astray.[d]
17 Therefore the Lord will take no
pleasure in the young men,[e]
nor will he pity[f] the fatherless and
widows,
for everyone is ungodly[g] and
wicked,[h]
every mouth speaks folly.[i]

Yet for all this, his anger is not
turned away,
his hand is still upraised.[j]

18 Surely wickedness burns like a
fire;[k]
it consumes briers and thorns,
it sets the forest thickets ablaze,[l]
so that it rolls upward in a column
of smoke.
19 By the wrath[m] of the LORD Almighty
the land will be scorched
and the people will be fuel for the
fire;[n]
they will not spare one another.[o]
20 On the right they will devour,
but still be hungry;[p]
on the left they will eat,[q]
but not be satisfied.
Each will feed on the flesh of their
own offspring[a]:
21 Manasseh will feed on Ephraim, and
Ephraim on Manasseh;
together they will turn against
Judah.[r]

Yet for all this, his anger is not
turned away,
his hand is still upraised.[s]

10 Woe to those who make unjust
laws,
to those who issue oppressive
decrees,[t]
2 to deprive[u] the poor of their rights
and withhold justice from the
oppressed of my people,[v]
making widows their prey
and robbing the fatherless.
3 What will you do on the day of
reckoning,[w]
when disaster[x] comes from afar?
To whom will you run for help?[y]
Where will you leave your riches?
4 Nothing will remain but to cringe
among the captives[z]
or fall among the slain.[a]

Yet for all this, his anger is not
turned away,[b]
his hand is still upraised.

God's Judgment on Assyria

5 "Woe to the Assyrian,[c] the rod of my
anger,
in whose hand is the club[d] of my
wrath![e]
6 I send him against a godless[f] nation,

9:12 [v] Ps 79:7 [w] Isa 5:25
9:13 [x] Jer 5:3 [y] Isa 31:1; Hos 7:7,10
9:14 [z] Isa 19:15 [a] Rev 18:8
9:15 [b] Isa 3:2-3
9:16 [c] Mt 15:14; 23:16,24 [d] Isa 3:12
9:17 [e] Jer 18:21 [f] Isa 27:11 [g] Isa 10:6 [h] Isa 1:4 [i] Mt 12:34 [j] Isa 5:25
9:18 [k] Mal 4:1 [l] Ps 83:14
9:19 [m] Isa 13:9,13 [n] Isa 1:31 [o] Mic 7:2,6
9:20 [p] Lev 26:26 [q] Isa 49:26
9:21 [r] 2Ch 28:6 [s] Isa 5:25
10:1 [t] Ps 58:2
10:2 [u] Isa 3:14 [v] Isa 5:23
10:3 [w] Job 31:14; Hos 9:7 [x] Lk 19:44 [y] Isa 20:6
10:4 [z] Isa 24:22 [a] Isa 22:2; 34:3; 66:16 [b] Isa 5:25
10:5 [c] Isa 14:25; Zep 2:13 [d] Jer 51:20 [e] Isa 13:3,5,13; 30:30; 66:14
10:6 [f] Isa 9:17

[a] *20* Or *arm*

9:13–17 When God is forsaken, the natural substitute for his leadership lies with human leaders. God will deprive Israel and Judah of all such false leaders. **9:18–21** The breakdown of social structure results because sin is burning up the land. God's righteous judgment adds tinder to the flame. As the final siege begins, the devouring of one's "own offspring" ceases to be metaphorical and becomes a horrible, literal fact (v. 20). In a world where the self reigns supreme, Israel turns on Judah, their brother tribe to the south. **10:1–4** In a world characterized by human arrogance, justice becomes a rare commodity. God's particular anger is reserved for those who consciously use the legal system to oppress the poor. There will not be enough "riches" (v. 3) to deliver them from captivity.

9:8—10:4 God's anger and love are found in both OT and NT. Jesus himself became terribly angry on several occasions. Does God get angry? Yes, but it is not the selfish anger of a fallen human. It is the heartbroken response of an Artist who watches his artistic creations doing things that violate not only his original dream but also their very natures.

10:5–6 Assyria is the "rod" (v. 5) in God's upraised hand that is raised up to punish "a godless nation" (v. 6). Surely the Assyrians are the ones who are "godless." The Israelites know better, yet they deny the truth.

I dispatch him against a people
who anger me,[g]
to seize loot and snatch plunder,[h]
and to trample them down like
mud in the streets.
7 But this is not what he intends,[i]
this is not what he has in mind;
his purpose is to destroy,
to put an end to many nations.
8 'Are not my commanders[j] all kings?'
he says.
9 'Has not Kalno[k] fared like
Carchemish?[l]
Is not Hamath like Arpad,
and Samaria[m] like Damascus?[n]
10 As my hand seized the kingdoms of
the idols,[o]
kingdoms whose images excelled
those of Jerusalem and
Samaria —
11 shall I not deal with Jerusalem and
her images
as I dealt with Samaria and her
idols?' "

12 When the Lord has finished all his
work[p] against Mount Zion[q] and Jerusalem, he will say, "I will punish the king of
Assyria[r] for the willful pride of his heart
and the haughty look in his eyes. 13 For
he says:

" 'By the strength of my hand I have
done this,[s]
and by my wisdom, because I have
understanding.
I removed the boundaries of
nations,
I plundered their treasures;[t]
like a mighty one I subdued[a] their
kings.
14 As one reaches into a nest,[u]
so my hand reached for the
wealth[v] of the nations;
as people gather abandoned
eggs,
so I gathered all the countries;
not one flapped a wing,
or opened its mouth to chirp.' "

15 Does the ax raise itself above the
person who swings it,
or the saw boast against the one
who uses it?[w]
As if a rod were to wield the person
who lifts it up,
or a club[x] brandish the one who is
not wood!
16 Therefore, the Lord, the LORD
Almighty,
will send a wasting disease[y] upon
his sturdy warriors;
under his pomp[z] a fire will be
kindled
like a blazing flame.
17 The Light of Israel will become a
fire,[a]
their Holy One[b] a flame;
in a single day it will burn and
consume
his thorns[c] and his briers.[d]
18 The splendor of his forests[e] and
fertile fields
it will completely destroy,
as when a sick person wastes
away.
19 And the remaining trees of his
forests will be so few[f]
that a child could write them
down.

The Remnant of Israel

20 In that day[g] the remnant of Israel,
the survivors of Jacob,
will no longer rely[h] on him
who struck them down[i]

10:6 [g] Isa 9:19 [h] Isa 5:29
10:7 [i] Ge 50:20; Ac 4:23-28
10:8 [j] 2Ki 18:24
10:9 [k] Ge 10:10 [l] 2Ch 35:20 [m] 2Ki 17:6 [n] 2Ki 16:9
10:10 [o] 2Ki 19:18
10:12 [p] Isa 28:21-22; 65:7 [q] 2Ki 19:31 [r] Jer 50:18
10:13 [s] Isa 37:24; Da 4:30 [t] Eze 28:4
10:14 [u] Jer 49:16; Ob 4 [v] Job 31:25
10:15 [w] Isa 45:9; Ro 9:20-21 [x] ver 5
10:16 [y] ver 18; Isa 17:4 [z] Isa 8:7
10:17 [a] Isa 31:9 [b] Isa 37:23 [c] Nu 11:1-3 [d] Isa 9:18
10:18 [e] 2Ki 19:23
10:19 [f] Isa 21:17
10:20 [g] Isa 11:10, 11 [h] 2Ki 16:7 [i] 2Ch 28:20

[a] 13 Or *treasures; / I subdued the mighty,*

10:7–11 Their "purpose" is to conquer and "destroy" as many nations as possible (v. 7). This idea is expressed in the quotation put in the mouth of the Assyrian king in vv. 8–11. The king says he is superior to everything on earth, including all gods. He is so great that even his "commanders" (v. 8) are the equivalent of the kings of other lands. He claims he is superior to God and will do to Jerusalem whatever he wants.

10:12–14 As Isaiah points out, when Jerusalem's punishment is complete, Assyria's will begin. That punishment will be because of Assyrian "pride" (v. 12), which is expressed in another quotation from their king (vv. 13–14). That king does not recognize that he is being moved by the hand of God.

10:15–16 God said he would cut down the "forests" (v. 18) of Judah's pride, and Assyria is the "ax" (v. 15) in God's hand to accomplish that task. God also said that he would punish his people for their sin (v. 25), and Assyria is the instrument of that punishment.

Because Assyria refuses to recognize the truth, God will turn them over to destruction. The "flame" (v. 16) of God's holiness will turn on those who refuse to admit that he is superior to them.

10:17–19 The metaphors of field and forest are used again to convey the idea of glory destroyed. The least in Assyria and the greatest will be consumed—and all "in a single day" (v. 17). This most likely refers to the destruction of the Assyrian army in 701 BC (see 37:36–37).

10:20–21 "In that day" speaks of that future time

but will truly rely[j] on the LORD,
the Holy One of Israel.
21 A remnant[k] will return,[a] a remnant of Jacob
will return to the Mighty God.[l]
22 Though your people be like the sand by the sea, Israel,
only a remnant will return.[m]
Destruction has been decreed,[n]
overwhelming and righteous.
23 The Lord, the LORD Almighty, will carry out
the destruction decreed upon the whole land.[o]

24 Therefore this is what the Lord, the LORD Almighty, says:

"My people who live in Zion,[p]
do not be afraid of the Assyrians,
who beat[q] you with a rod
and lift up a club against you, as Egypt did.
25 Very soon[r] my anger against you will end
and my wrath[s] will be directed to their destruction."

26 The LORD Almighty will lash[t] them with a whip,
as when he struck down Midian[u]
at the rock of Oreb;
and he will raise his staff over the waters,[v]
as he did in Egypt.
27 In that day their burden will be lifted from your shoulders,
their yoke[w] from your neck;[x]
the yoke will be broken
because you have grown so fat.[b]

10:20 [j] Isa 17:7
10:21 [k] Isa 6:13 [l] Isa 9:6
10:22 [m] Ro 9:27-28 [n] Isa 28:22; Da 9:27
10:23 [o] Isa 28:22; Ro 9:27-28*
10:24 [p] Ps 87:5-6 [q] Ex 5:14
10:25 [r] Isa 17:14 [s] ver 5; Da 11:36
10:26 [t] Isa 37:36-38 [u] Isa 9:4 [v] Ex 14:16
10:27 [w] Isa 9:4 [x] Isa 14:25
10:28 [y] 1Sa 14:2 [z] 1Sa 13:2
10:29 [a] Jos 18:25
10:30 [b] 1Sa 25:44 [c] Ne 11:32
10:32 [d] 1Sa 21:1 [e] Jer 6:23
10:33 [f] Am 2:9

Isa 10:24-34 ❖ Why is God's announcement of judgment on the wicked a cause for hope? What makes us cry out for God's justice on the wicked?

28 They enter Aiath;
they pass through Migron;[y]
they store supplies at Mikmash.[z]
29 They go over the pass, and say,
"We will camp overnight at Geba."
Ramah[a] trembles;
Gibeah of Saul flees.
30 Cry out, Daughter Gallim![b]
Listen, Laishah!
Poor Anathoth![c]
31 Madmenah is in flight;
the people of Gebim take cover.
32 This day they will halt at Nob;[d]
they will shake their fist
at the mount of Daughter Zion,[e]
at the hill of Jerusalem.

33 See, the Lord, the LORD Almighty,
will lop off the boughs with great power.
The lofty trees will be felled,
the tall[f] ones will be brought low.
34 He will cut down the forest thickets with an ax;
Lebanon will fall before the Mighty One.

[a] 21 Hebrew *shear-jashub* (see 7:3 and note); also in verse 22 [b] 27 Hebrew; Septuagint *broken / from your shoulders*

---

when all the punishment at the hands of the nations will be over and the purified "remnant" (v. 21) of God's people will be brought home.
10:22-23 Isaiah guards against false expectations. He insists to his hearers that even though the destruction will not be complete, it will be thorough. It has been so "decreed" (v. 22). But the remnant will no longer "rely on" (v. 20) their worst enemy. They will trust "the Holy One of Israel" (v. 20).
10:24-25 Because Assyria will be judged and a remnant will survive, the people of Judah should not live in fear. As Isaiah earlier said to Ahaz, no emergency action is necessary (v. 25).
10:26-27 Isaiah turns to two experiences from the past as confirmation of the Lord's power to protect.
10:28-32 These verses express the almost unstoppable approach of the enemy army. It does not matter that the route is rugged and filled with obstacles—on they come. This is a metaphor for Assyria. Nothing can stop them. Judah must come to terms with them or be destroyed.
10:33-34 Isaiah tells his hearers they should look at another reality. For at the moment when the Assyrians believe their ax will topple the Judean tree, Judah's God turns the ax upon the ax! Judah should be relying on the true Mighty One, not on the ax in the Mighty One's hand.

10:5-34 Any nation that attempts to put itself in the place of God cannot survive. Will the United States learn this lesson? Will we carry out our tasks in humility, recognizing the terrible risks of pride? The history of nations in the Christian West is not encouraging in this respect. One after another has come to power proclaiming its dependence on God, and one after another has exited the scene in disgrace, having come to believe that they were sufficient in themselves and ultimately in control of their own destinies.

The Branch From Jesse

11 A shoot will come up from the
stump of Jesse;[g]
from his roots a Branch[h] will bear
fruit.
2 The Spirit[i] of the LORD will rest on
him—
the Spirit of wisdom[j] and of
understanding,
the Spirit of counsel and of
might,[k]
the Spirit of the knowledge and
fear of the LORD—
3 and he will delight in the fear of the
LORD.

He will not judge by what he sees
with his eyes,[l]
or decide by what he hears with
his ears;[m]
4 but with righteousness[n] he will
judge the needy,
with justice[o] he will give decisions
for the poor[p] of the earth.
He will strike[q] the earth with the rod
of his mouth;
with the breath[r] of his lips he will
slay the wicked.
5 Righteousness will be his belt
and faithfulness[s] the sash around
his waist.[t]

6 The wolf will live with the lamb,[u]
the leopard will lie down with the
goat,
the calf and the lion and the
yearling[a] together;
and a little child will lead them.
7 The cow will feed with the bear,
their young will lie down
together,
and the lion will eat straw like
the ox.

11:1 [g] ver 10; Isa 9:7; Rev 5:5 [h] Isa 4:2
11:2 [i] Isa 42:1; 48:16; 61:1; Mt 3:16; Jn 1:32-33 [j] Eph 1:17 [k] 2Ti 1:7
11:3 [l] Jn 7:24 [m] Jn 2:25
11:4 [n] Ps 72:2 [o] Isa 9:7 [p] Isa 3:14 [q] Mal 4:6 [r] Job 4:9; 2Th 2:8
11:5 [s] Isa 25:1 [t] Eph 6:14
11:6 [u] Isa 65:25
11:9 [v] Job 5:23 [w] Ps 98:2-3; Isa 52:10 [x] Isa 45:6,14; Hab 2:14
11:10 [y] Jn 12:32 [z] Isa 49:23; Lk 2:32 [a] Ro 15:12* [b] Isa 14:3; 28:12; 32:17-18
11:11 [c] Isa 10:20 [d] Isa 19:24; Hos 11:11; Mic 7:12; Zec 10:10 [e] Ge 10:22 [f] Isa 42:4,10,12; 66:19
11:12 [g] Zep 3:10
11:13 [h] Jer 3:18; Eze 37:16-17,22; Hos 1:11

Isa 11:9 ❖ Is the knowledge of the Lord increasing in the world? How can we support efforts to spread the Good News of Christ?

8 The infant will play near the cobra's
den,
and the young child will put its
hand into the viper's nest.
9 They will neither harm nor destroy[v]
on all my holy mountain,
for the earth[w] will be filled with the
knowledge[x] of the LORD
as the waters cover the sea.

10 In that day the Root of Jesse will stand
as a banner[y] for the peoples; the nations[z]
will rally to him,[a] and his resting place[b]
will be glorious. 11 In that day[c] the Lord
will reach out his hand a second time to
reclaim the surviving remnant of his people from Assyria,[d] from Lower Egypt, from
Upper Egypt, from Cush,[b] from Elam,[e]
from Babylonia,[c] from Hamath and from
the islands[f] of the Mediterranean.

12 He will raise a banner for the nations
and gather the exiles of Israel;
he will assemble the scattered
people[g] of Judah
from the four quarters of the
earth.
13 Ephraim's jealousy will vanish,
and Judah's enemies[d] will be
destroyed;
Ephraim will not be jealous of
Judah,
nor Judah hostile toward
Ephraim.[h]

[a] 6 Hebrew; Septuagint *lion will feed* [b] 11 That is, the upper Nile region [c] 11 Hebrew *Shinar* [d] 13 Or *hostility*

11:1-3a The Messiah will spring from the very roots of David's dynasty. Although Israel's pride has been thoroughly cut down and burned, in this field of stumps there is still life in the original root—a life that resides finally in the faithfulness of God.
11:3b-4 This Messiah will not rule in the power and the motivation of the fallen human spirit, but by the life and breath of God himself. He will not be biased in favor of the rich and powerful. His words will be more powerful than the mightiest "rod," and the "breath" of his lips will not only pronounce the sentence of the "wicked" but will actually kill them (v. 4).
11:5-8 "Righteousness" and "faithfulness" (v. 5) will be at the very heart of this person's existence. The result of this kind of leadership will be peace—not merely the cessation of hostilities but unity within all of creation.
11:9 The means by which this restoration will be accomplished is described in global terms: "The earth will be filled with the knowledge of the LORD as the waters cover the sea." For the Hebrews, all true knowledge is based on experience. The Messiah, whom everyone will acknowledge, will make it possible for all people to know God intimately.
11:10-14 As God previously ran up a "banner" (5:26) to call the enemy nations, now the Messiah is a "banner" (11:10, 12) calling the nations to himself.

The prophet envisions a day when hostility, stretching back to the division after Solomon's death and even further, will be permanently healed. The division between Samaria and Judea at the time of Christ was one continuation of that hostility. When Christ drew some of the Samaritans to himself (Jn 4), he was beginning to bridge the gulf.

14 They will swoop down on the slopes
of Philistia to the west;
together they will plunder the
people to the east.
They will subdue Edom[i] and Moab,[j]
and the Ammonites will be subject
to them.
15 The LORD will dry up
the gulf of the Egyptian sea;
with a scorching wind he will sweep
his hand[k]
over the Euphrates River.[l]
He will break it up into seven
streams
so that anyone can cross over in
sandals.
16 There will be a highway[m] for the
remnant of his people
that is left from Assyria,
as there was for Israel
when they came up from Egypt.[n]

Songs of Praise

12 In that day you will say:

"I will praise[o] you, LORD.
Although you were angry with me,
your anger has turned away
and you have comforted me.
2 Surely God is my salvation;
I will trust[p] and not be afraid.
The LORD, the LORD himself, is my
strength and my defense[a];
he has become my salvation.[q]"
3 With joy you will draw water[r]
from the wells of salvation.

4 In that day you will say:

"Give praise to the LORD, proclaim
his name;[s]
make known among the nations
what he has done,
and proclaim that his name is
exalted.
5 Sing[t] to the LORD, for he has done
glorious things;[u]
let this be known to all the world.
6 Shout aloud and sing for joy, people
of Zion,
for great is the Holy One of Israel[v]
among you.[w]"

Isa 12:1 ❖ How has Christ turned away God's anger (see Ro 3:25)? How does this transform our relationship with God into one of comfort?

A Prophecy Against Babylon

13 A prophecy against Babylon that
Isaiah son of Amoz saw:

2 Raise a banner[x] on a bare hilltop,
shout to them;
beckon to them
to enter the gates of the nobles.
3 I have commanded those I prepared
for battle;
I have summoned my warriors[y] to
carry out my wrath —
those who rejoice[z] in my triumph.

4 Listen, a noise on the mountains,
like that of a great multitude![a]
Listen, an uproar among the
kingdoms,
like nations massing together!
The LORD Almighty is mustering
an army for war.
5 They come from faraway lands,

[a] 2 Or *song*

11:14 [i] Da 11:41; Joel 3:19 [j] Isa 16:14; 25:10
11:15 [k] Isa 19:16 [l] Isa 7:20
11:16 [m] Isa 19:23; 62:10 [n] Ex 14:26-31
12:1 [o] Isa 25:1
12:2 [p] Isa 26:3 [q] Ex 15:2; Ps 118:14
12:3 [r] Jn 4:10,14
12:4 [s] Ps 105:1; Isa 24:15
12:5 [t] Ex 15:1 [u] Ps 98:1
12:6 [v] Isa 49:26 [w] Zep 3:14-17
13:2 [x] Jer 50:2; 51:27
13:3 [y] Joel 3:11 [z] Ps 149:2
13:4 [a] Joel 3:14

11:15–16 It is unclear how literal the prophet intends these figures to be taken, but the point is clear: There will be no effective barrier to the return of his people either from the south ("the gulf of the Egyptian sea") or from the north ("the Euphrates River"; v. 15).

11:1–16 Just as there will be a literal return of Christ, there will also be a literal new heaven and new earth over which Christ will reign; this chapter looks forward to that kingdom. When that day comes, all of God's creatures will experience creation as it was originally meant to be.

12:1–3 God has turned his righteous anger to comfort (v. 1). He can and should be trusted. He is "strength," he is song, he is "salvation" (v. 2). Who would not trust such a God as this?

12:4–6 Verse 4 instructs the believer's response: thanks, prayer, and witness. God's wondrous works cannot be proclaimed with a long face. They must be sung "to all the world" (v. 5).

12:1–6 God reconciled us to himself through his own work on the cross. We were condemned sinners, but God found a way to satisfy his own justice in that Christ has died in our place. In place of judgment, God through Jesus offers us salvation and encouragement.

13:1 The first oracle, or prophetic message (chs. 13–14), begins with Babylon, which was not a world power in Isaiah's lifetime.

13:2–8 Isaiah emphasizes the terror of coming judgment. God's armies come from the "ends of the heavens" (v. 5). This is an apocalyptic judgment. Even the mightiest and most glorious of earth's nations are no match for God (vv. 7–8).

from the ends of the heavens[b] —
the LORD and the weapons of his wrath —
to destroy[c] the whole country.

6 Wail,[d] for the day[e] of the LORD is near;
it will come like destruction from the Almighty.[a]
7 Because of this, all hands will go limp,
every heart will melt with fear.[f]
8 Terror[g] will seize them,
pain and anguish will grip them;
they will writhe like a woman in labor.
They will look aghast at each other,
their faces aflame.[h]

9 See, the day of the LORD is coming
—a cruel day, with wrath and fierce anger—
to make the land desolate
and destroy the sinners within it.
10 The stars of heaven and their constellations
will not show their light.
The rising sun[i] will be darkened[j]
and the moon will not give its light.[k]
11 I will punish[l] the world for its evil,
the wicked for their sins.
I will put an end to the arrogance of the haughty
and will humble the pride of the ruthless.
12 I will make people[m] scarcer than pure gold,
more rare than the gold of Ophir.
13 Therefore I will make the heavens tremble;[n]
and the earth will shake from its place
at the wrath of the LORD Almighty,
in the day of his burning anger.

14 Like a hunted gazelle,
like sheep without a shepherd,[o]
they will all return to their own people,
they will flee to their native land.[p]
15 Whoever is captured will be thrust through;
all who are caught will fall[q] by the sword.[r]
16 Their infants[s] will be dashed to pieces before their eyes;
their houses will be looted and their wives violated.

17 See, I will stir up[t] against them the Medes,
who do not care for silver
and have no delight in gold.[u]
18 Their bows will strike down the young men;
they will have no mercy on infants,
nor will they look with compassion on children.
19 Babylon, the jewel of kingdoms,
the pride and glory[v] of the Babylonians,[b]
will be overthrown[w] by God
like Sodom and Gomorrah.[x]
20 She will never be inhabited[y]
or lived in through all generations;
there no nomads[z] will pitch their tents,
there no shepherds will rest their flocks.
21 But desert creatures[a] will lie there,
jackals will fill her houses;
there the owls will dwell,
and there the wild goats will leap about.

13:5 [b] Isa 5:26 [c] Isa 24:1
13:6 [d] Eze 30:2 [e] Isa 2:12; Joel 1:15
13:7 [f] Eze 21:7
13:8 [g] Isa 21:4 [h] Na 2:10
13:10 [i] Isa 24:23 [j] Isa 5:30; Rev 8:12 [k] Eze 32:7; Mt 24:29*; Mk 13:24*
13:11 [l] Isa 3:11; 11:4; 26:21
13:12 [m] Isa 4:1
13:13 [n] Isa 34:4; 51:6; Hag 2:6
13:14 [o] 1Ki 22:17 [p] Jer 50:16
13:15 [q] Jer 51:4 [r] Isa 14:19; Jer 50:25
13:16 [s] Ps 137:9
13:17 [t] Jer 51:1 [u] Pr 6:34-35
13:19 [v] Da 4:30 [w] Rev 14:8 [x] Ge 19:24
13:20 [y] Isa 14:23; 34:10-15 [z] 2Ch 17:11
13:21 [a] Rev 18:2

[a] 6 Hebrew *Shaddai* [b] 19 Or *Chaldeans*

Isa 13:19 ❖ How does God turn the fortunes of haughty nations? How should a nation conduct itself before God?

13:9-13 The greatest of all sins is pride. Oftentimes, pagans suggested that the stars were gods made in human form. In fact, says Isaiah, they are the servants of the Almighty (v. 10).
13:14-16 Verses 14-15 describe the breakup of the collection of city-states out of which every ancient empire was crafted. There would be no protection from the invaders.
13:17-22 The Medes were a warlike people from the Zagros Mountains east of the Tigris River (modern Iran). Isaiah predicts the Medes will undo Babylon (vv. 19-22).

The Medo-Persian conquest of Babylon signaled the beginning of the end of Babylon. In the eighteenth century AD, even its location was unknown. Isaiah's prophecy about its becoming a haunt of "hyenas" and "jackals" (v. 22) came true with a vengeance.

13:1-22 Physical things are all passing faster than we can imagine. So wisdom asks: What will survive the wreck of all human accomplishments? We should be looking to God's eternal realities, which will never pass away.

22 Hyenas will inhabit her strongholds,[b]
jackals[c] her luxurious palaces.
Her time is at hand,[d]
and her days will not be prolonged.

14

The LORD will have compassion[e]
on Jacob;
once again he will choose[f] Israel
and will settle them in their own
land.
Foreigners[g] will join them
and unite with the descendants of
Jacob.
2 Nations will take them
and bring[h] them to their own place.
And Israel will take possession of
the nations[i]
and make them male and female
servants in the LORD's land.
They will make captives of their
captors
and rule over their oppressors.[j]

3 On the day the LORD gives you relief[k] from your suffering and turmoil
and from the harsh labor forced on you,
4 you will take up this taunt[l] against the
king of Babylon:

How the oppressor[m] has come to an
end!
How his fury[a] has ended!
5 The LORD has broken the rod of the
wicked,[n]
the scepter of the rulers,
6 which in anger struck down peoples[o]
with unceasing blows,
and in fury subdued nations
with relentless aggression.[p]
7 All the lands are at rest and at peace;
they break into singing.[q]
8 Even the junipers[r] and the cedars of
Lebanon
gloat over you and say,
"Now that you have been laid low,
no one comes to cut us down."

9 The realm of the dead[s] below is all
astir

Isa 14:3 ❖ Where do we find relief from the suffering and turmoil in our lives (see Mt 11:28)?

to meet you at your coming;
it rouses the spirits of the departed
to greet you —
all those who were leaders in the
world;
it makes them rise from their
thrones —
all those who were kings over the
nations.
10 They will all respond,
they will say to you,
"You also have become weak, as we
are;
you have become like us."[t]
11 All your pomp has been brought
down to the grave,
along with the noise of your
harps;
maggots are spread out beneath you
and worms[u] cover you.

12 How you have fallen[v] from heaven,
morning star,[w] son of the dawn!
You have been cast down to the
earth,
you who once laid low the
nations!
13 You said in your heart,
"I will ascend[x] to the heavens;
I will raise my throne[y]
above the stars of God;
I will sit enthroned on the mount of
assembly,
on the utmost heights of Mount
Zaphon.[b]
14 I will ascend above the tops of the
clouds;
I will make myself like the Most
High."[z]

[a] 4 Dead Sea Scrolls, Septuagint and Syriac; the meaning of the word in the Masoretic Text is uncertain. [b] 13 Or *of the north;* Zaphon was the most sacred mountain of the Canaanites.

13:22 [b] Isa 25:2 [c] Isa 34:13 [d] Jer 51:33
14:1 [e] Ps 102:13; Isa 49:10, 13; 54:7-8, 10 [f] Isa 41:8; 44:1; 49:7; Zec 1:17; 2:12 [g] Eph 2:12-19
14:2 [h] Isa 60:9 [i] Isa 49:7, 23 [j] Isa 60:14; 61:5
14:3 [k] Isa 11:10
14:4 [l] Hab 2:6 [m] Isa 9:4
14:5 [n] Ps 125:3
14:6 [o] Isa 10:14 [p] Isa 47:6
14:7 [q] Ps 98:1; 126:1-3
14:8 [r] Eze 31:16
14:9 [s] Eze 32:21
14:10 [t] Eze 32:21
14:11 [u] Isa 51:8
14:12 [v] Isa 34:4; Lk 10:18 [w] 2Pe 1:19; Rev 2:28; 8:10; 9:1
14:13 [x] Da 5:23; 8:10; Mt 11:23 [y] Eze 28:2; 2Th 2:4
14:14 [z] Isa 47:8; 2Th 2:4

14:1–4a Once more the prophet affirms that the Mesopotamian powers are tools in God's hand. Once their work is finished, they will be judged and Israel restored.
14:4b–8 The poet anticipates how grateful the people on earth are to have "rest" (v. 7) from the repeated blows of the oppressor's weapons. The whole creation, including the trees, are glad.
14:9–11 Verse 11 is a masterpiece of sarcasm and irony. The beautiful grave and its coverings are a writhing mass of "maggots" (v. 11). Human pretension is no match for the grim reality of death and decay.
14:12–15 Isaiah has taken a number of themes familiar to his hearers and woven them together to make his unique theological point. This man, who thought to make himself equal to God, is mocked by death. He has been taken from the "heights" (v. 13) of his own pretensions to the "depths of the pit" (v. 15) in one terrible moment.

15 But you are brought down to the realm of the dead,
to the depths[a] of the pit.

16 Those who see you stare at you,
they ponder your fate:[b]
"Is this the man who shook the earth
and made kingdoms tremble,
17 the man who made the world a wilderness,[c]
who overthrew its cities
and would not let his captives go home?"

18 All the kings of the nations lie in state,
each in his own tomb.
19 But you are cast out[d] of your tomb
like a rejected branch;
you are covered with the slain,
with those pierced by the sword,
those who descend to the stones of the pit.[e]
Like a corpse trampled underfoot,
20 you will not join them in burial,
for you have destroyed your land
and killed your people.

Let the offspring[f] of the wicked[g]
never be mentioned[h] again.
21 Prepare a place to slaughter his children
for the sins of their ancestors;[i]
they are not to rise to inherit the land
and cover the earth with their cities.

22 "I will rise up against them,"
declares the LORD Almighty.
"I will wipe out Babylon's name and survivors,
her offspring and descendants,[j]"
declares the LORD.

23 "I will turn her into a place for owls[k]
and into swampland;
I will sweep her with the broom of destruction,"
declares the LORD Almighty.

24 The LORD Almighty has sworn,[l]

"Surely, as I have planned, so it will be,
and as I have purposed, so it will happen.[m]
25 I will crush the Assyrian[n] in my land;
on my mountains I will trample him down.
His yoke[o] will be taken from my people,
and his burden removed from their shoulders.[p]"

26 This is the plan[q] determined for the whole world;
this is the hand[r] stretched out over all nations.
27 For the LORD Almighty has purposed,
and who can thwart him?
His hand is stretched out, and who can turn it back?[s]

A Prophecy Against the Philistines

28 This prophecy[t] came in the year King Ahaz[u] died:

29 Do not rejoice, all you Philistines,[v]
that the rod that struck you is broken;
from the root of that snake will spring up a viper,[w]
its fruit will be a darting, venomous serpent.
30 The poorest of the poor will find pasture,

14:15 [a] Mt 11:23; Lk 10:15
14:16 [b] Jer 50:23
14:17 [c] Joel 2:3
14:19 [d] Isa 22:16-18 [e] Jer 41:7-9
14:20 [f] Job 18:19 [g] Isa 1:4 [h] Ps 21:10
14:21 [i] Ex 20:5; Lev 26:39
14:22 [j] 1Ki 14:10; Job 18:19
14:23 [k] Isa 34:11-15; Zep 2:14
14:24 [l] Isa 45:23 [m] Ac 4:28
14:25 [n] Isa 10:5, 12 [o] Isa 9:4 [p] Isa 10:27
14:26 [q] Isa 23:9 [r] Ex 15:12
14:27 [s] 2Ch 20:6; Isa 43:13; Da 4:35
14:28 [t] Isa 13:1 [u] 2Ki 16:20
14:29 [v] 2Ch 26:6 [w] Isa 11:8

14:16–19 No single individual is being addressed here. This "king of Babylon" (v. 4) is a blend of all the proud kings who have ruled on the earth. Verses 16–20 show people staring at the mangled corpse of the tyrant. Instead of a dignified death and an honorable burial, the corpse is abandoned in the field. Neither does he have any continuing dynasty.
14:20b–21 These verses express the hope that the oppressor will have no offspring to carry on his name. His destruction will thereby be complete.
14:22–23 Not only will the king of Babylon have no offspring and thus no living memorial, neither will Babylon itself.
14:24–27 Any person or nation that lifts itself up against the plan and purpose of God marks itself for destruction. Verse 25 seems to refer to the destruction of Sennacherib's army in Judah in 701 BC (as described in 37:36).

✣ **14:1–27** We have been made to reflect the glory of the only God. If a mirror says, "No, I will reflect only myself" and turns the lights off, it should not be surprised to discover there is nothing to reflect. When humans say, "I will live only for myself," they should not be surprised to discover that there is no life to be lived.

14:28–29 It is not clear what the significance of Ahaz's death is for the meaning of this oracle. Perhaps the Philistines were urging Hezekiah to join them because Assyria, "the rod that struck [them,] is broken" (v. 29a). If that is correct, Isaiah quickly disabuses them of such a false notion (v. 29b).
14:30–32 These verses strengthen the suggestion that the Philistines are inviting the Judeans to join

and the needy[x] will lie down in
safety.[y]
But your root I will destroy by
famine;[z]
it will slay[a] your survivors.

31 Wail, you gate![b] Howl, you city!
Melt away, all you Philistines!
A cloud of smoke comes from the
north,[c]
and there is not a straggler in its
ranks.
32 What answer shall be given
to the envoys[d] of that nation?
"The LORD has established Zion,[e]
and in her his afflicted people will
find refuge.[f]"

A Prophecy Against Moab

16:6–12pp // Jer 48:29–36

15 A prophecy against Moab:[g]

Ar in Moab is ruined,[h]
destroyed in a night!
Kir in Moab is ruined,
destroyed in a night!
2 Dibon goes up to its temple,
to its high places[i] to weep;
Moab wails over Nebo and
Medeba.
Every head is shaved[j]
and every beard cut off.
3 In the streets they wear sackcloth;
on the roofs and in the public
squares[k]
they all wail,
prostrate with weeping.[l]
4 Heshbon and Elealeh[m] cry out,
their voices are heard all the way
to Jahaz.
Therefore the armed men of Moab
cry out,
and their hearts are faint.

5 My heart cries out over Moab;[n]
her fugitives flee as far as Zoar,
as far as Eglath Shelishiyah.

14:30 [x] Isa 3:15 [y] Isa 7:21-22 [z] Isa 8:21; 9:20; 51:19 [a] Jer 25:16
14:31 [b] Isa 3:26 [c] Jer 1:14
14:32 [d] Isa 37:9 [e] Ps 87:2,5; Isa 44:28; 54:11 [f] Isa 4:6; Jas 2:5
15:1 [g] Isa 11:14 [h] Jer 48:24,41
15:2 [i] Jer 48:35 [j] Lev 21:5
15:3 [k] Jer 48:38 [l] Isa 22:4
15:4 [m] Nu 32:3
15:5 [n] Jer 48:31

Isa 15:5–9 ❖ Why does God announce judgment rather than only hope? When have God's warning words of judgment been a good thing in our lives?

They go up the hill to Luhith,
weeping as they go;
on the road to Horonaim[o]
they lament their destruction.[p]
6 The waters of Nimrim are dried up[q]
and the grass is withered;[r]
the vegetation is gone
and nothing green is left.
7 So the wealth they have acquired[s]
and stored up
they carry away over the Ravine of
the Poplars.
8 Their outcry echoes along the border
of Moab;
their wailing reaches as far as
Eglaim,
their lamentation as far as Beer
Elim.
9 The waters of Dimon[a] are full of
blood,
but I will bring still more upon
Dimon[a] —
a lion[t] upon the fugitives of Moab
and upon those who remain in the
land.

16 Send lambs[u] as tribute
to the ruler of the land,
from Sela,[v] across the desert,
to the mount of Daughter Zion.[w]
2 Like fluttering birds
pushed from the nest,[x]
so are the women of Moab
at the fords of the Arnon.[y]

3 "Make up your mind," Moab says.
"Render a decision.

[o] Jer 48:3,34 [p] Jer 4:20; 48:5
15:6 [q] Isa 19:5-7; Jer 48:34 [r] Joel 1:12
15:7 [s] Isa 30:6; Jer 48:36
15:9 [t] 2Ki 17:25
16:1 [u] 2Ki 3:4 [v] 2Ki 14:7 [w] Isa 10:32
16:2 [x] Pr 27:8 [y] Nu 21:13-14; Jer 48:20

[a] 9 *Dimon*, a wordplay on *Dibon* (see verse 2), sounds like the Hebrew for *blood*.

---

them in revolt. Isaiah answers that the Lord will take care of Judah without any help from the Philistines.

✜ **14:28–32** The church today is often in the position of Judah. When we feel beleaguered on every hand, we begin to look for allies. The history of the church's attempts to do this is a pretty sorry one. The Bible says, "Trust in the LORD with all your heart and lean not on your own understanding" (Pr 3:5). That is what Isaiah is saying in this passage as well.

15:1–4 Except for Kir (v. 1), the towns and villages mentioned here all are found in the northern part of Moab.
15:5–8 The known sites are in the southern part of Moab. This north-to-south movement would have been characteristic of the southward flight of the Moabites before an army heading south from Damascus.
16:1–5 The prophet knows that Moab's only hope is in the Lord and in the Messiah he has promised. Isaiah speaks about the ultimate trust not only for the Moabites but for the whole world.

Make your shadow like night —
at high noon.
Hide the fugitives,[z]
do not betray the refugees.
4 Let the Moabite fugitives stay with
you;
be their shelter from the
destroyer."

The oppressor[a] will come to an end,
and destruction will cease;
the aggressor will vanish from the
land.
5 In love a throne[b] will be established;
in faithfulness a man will sit on
it —
one from the house[a] of David[c] —
one who in judging seeks justice[d]
and speeds the cause of
righteousness.

6 We have heard of Moab's[e] pride[f] —
how great is her arrogance! —
of her conceit, her pride and her
insolence;
but her boasts are empty.
7 Therefore the Moabites wail,[g]
they wail together for Moab.
Lament and grieve
for the raisin cakes[h] of Kir
Hareseth.[i]
8 The fields of Heshbon wither,
the vines of Sibmah also.
The rulers of the nations
have trampled down the choicest
vines,
which once reached Jazer
and spread toward the desert.
Their shoots spread out
and went as far as the sea.[b]
9 So I weep,[j] as Jazer weeps,
for the vines of Sibmah.
Heshbon and Elealeh,
I drench you with tears!
The shouts of joy over your ripened
fruit
and over your harvests[k] have been
stilled.
10 Joy and gladness are taken away
from the orchards;[l]
no one sings or shouts in the
vineyards;
no one treads[m] out wine at the
presses,[n]
for I have put an end to the
shouting.
11 My heart laments for Moab[o] like a
harp,
my inmost being[p] for Kir
Hareseth.
12 When Moab appears at her high
place,
she only wears herself out;
when she goes to her shrine[q] to pray,
it is to no avail.[r]

13 This is the word the LORD has already spoken concerning Moab. 14 But
now the LORD says: "Within three years,
as a servant bound by contract would
count them, Moab's splendor and all her
many people will be despised,[s] and her
survivors will be very few and feeble."[t]

A Prophecy Against Damascus

17 A prophecy against Damascus:[u]

"See, Damascus will no longer be a
city
but will become a heap of ruins.[v]
2 The cities of Aroer will be deserted
and left to flocks,[w] which will lie
down,
with no one to make them afraid.[x]

16:3 [z] 1Ki 18:4
16:4 [a] Isa 9:4
16:5 [b] Da 7:14; Mic 4:7 [c] Lk 1:32 [d] Isa 9:7
16:6 [e] Am 2:1; Zep 2:8 [f] Ob 3; Zep 2:10
16:7 [g] Jer 48:20 [h] 1Ch 16:3 [i] 2Ki 3:25
16:9 [j] Isa 15:3
[k] Jer 40:12
16:10 [l] Isa 24:7-8 [m] Jdg 9:27 [n] Job 24:11
16:11 [o] Isa 15:5 [p] Isa 63:15; Hos 11:8; Php 2:1
16:12 [q] Isa 15:2 [r] 1Ki 18:29
16:14 [s] Isa 25:10; Jer 48:42 [t] Isa 21:17
17:1 [u] Ge 14:15; Jer 49:23; Ac 9:2 [v] Isa 25:2; Am 1:3; Zec 9:1
17:2 [w] Isa 7:21; Eze 25:5 [x] Jer 7:33; Mic 4:4

[a] 5 Hebrew *tent* [b] 8 Probably the Dead Sea

Isa 16:4-5 ❖ Where do we see oppression and destruction in the world? How can seeing these things energize our prayers?

16:6-13 After a glimpse of that future hope, which should give people the basis for living lives of trust in dark hours, the prophet swings back to the grim present realities.

16:14 Isaiah asserts that within three years, his predictions will be fulfilled. There was a major destruction of Moab by the Assyrians in 715 BC, so these words may have been first spoken in 718 BC. The prophet dares to stake both his reputation and God's on the fulfillment of what he says will happen.

✚ 15:1—16:14 None of our accomplishments can save us from the brutality of humans run amok. All our efforts to gain control over our environment, whether it be home or office or love of life, will only end in exhaustion. In the end, the only final hope is to be found in the "man . . . from the house of David" of 16:5—the man Jesus Christ. Only in his eternal kingdom is there true freedom and justice.

17:1-11 Verses 1–3 speak of the fall of Aram (Syria). The fading glory of Jacob then becomes the main topic in the rest of the segment.

3 The fortified city will disappear from
Ephraim,
and royal power from Damascus;
the remnant of Aram will be
like the glory[y] of the Israelites,"[z]
declares the LORD Almighty.

4 "In that day the glory of Jacob will
fade;
the fat of his body will waste[a] away.
5 It will be as when reapers harvest the
standing grain,
gathering[b] the grain in their
arms —
as when someone gleans heads of
grain
in the Valley of Rephaim.
6 Yet some gleanings will remain,[c]
as when an olive tree is beaten,[d]
leaving two or three olives on the
topmost branches,
four or five on the fruitful
boughs,"
declares the LORD, the God
of Israel.

7 In that day people will look[e] to their
Maker
and turn their eyes to the Holy
One[f] of Israel.
8 They will not look to the altars,
the work of their hands,[g]
and they will have no regard for the
Asherah poles[a]
and the incense altars their
fingers have made.

9 In that day their strong cities, which
they left because of the Israelites, will
be like places abandoned to thickets and
undergrowth. And all will be desolation.

10 You have forgotten[h] God your
Savior;[i]
you have not remembered the
Rock, your fortress.
Therefore, though you set out the
finest plants
and plant imported vines,
11 though on the day you set them out,
you make them grow,
and on the morning[j] when you
plant them, you bring them
to bud,
yet the harvest will be as
nothing[k]
in the day of disease and incurable
pain.[l]

12 Woe to the many nations that
rage —
they rage like the raging sea![m]
Woe to the peoples who roar —
they roar like the roaring of great
waters!
13 Although the peoples roar like the
roar of surging waters,
when he rebukes[n] them they flee[o]
far away,
driven before the wind like chaff[p] on
the hills,
like tumbleweed before a gale.[q]
14 In the evening, sudden terror!
Before the morning, they are
gone![r]
This is the portion of those who
loot us,
the lot of those who plunder us.

17:3 [y] ver 4; Hos 9:11 [z] Isa 7:8,16; 8:4
17:4 [a] Isa 10:16
17:5 [b] ver 11; Jer 51:33; Joel 3:13; Mt 13:30
17:6 [c] Dt 4:27; Isa 24:13 [d] Isa 27:12
17:7 [e] Isa 10:20 [f] Mic 7:7
17:8 [g] Isa 2:18, 20; 30:22
17:10 [h] Isa 51:13 [i] Ps 68:19; Isa 12:2
17:11 [j] Ps 90:6 [k] Hos 8:7 [l] Job 4:8
17:12 [m] Ps 18:4; Jer 6:23; Lk 21:25
17:13 [n] Ps 9:5 [o] Isa 13:14 [p] Isa 41:2,15-16 [q] Job 21:18
17:14 [r] 2Ki 19:35

[a] *8* That is, wooden symbols of the goddess Asherah

Isa 17:7-8 ❖ What things compete for our allegiance to the Lord? How can we completely turn away from them and toward God?

17:4-6 Hardly anything of the nation will remain, though there *will* be something left.
17:7-8 Isaiah speaks of the day when the Israelites will be purified by judgment and will reject their idols.
17:9-10a Isaiah once more demonstrates his familiar pattern. Yes, there is the hope for the future, but between then and the present, there is the awful reality of judgment. Why? Because the people have "forgotten God" (v. 10a).
17:10b-11 Isaiah expresses this in imagery that is familiar to these agricultural people. Judgment is coming and cannot be averted. The best of human effort is not enough to solve the basic human problem of sin. Someday the remnant of Israel will learn that fact.

17:1-11 The epidemics of pornography and drug addiction today are contemporary manifestations of an age-old problem. To paraphrase the prophet, we may be able to import the finest digital imaging and pain-management technology, but "the harvest will be as nothing in the day of disease and incurable pain" (v. 11). Instead of a society that is genuinely healthy and fruitful, because people are turned outward and can sublimate their desires to accomplish worthwhile goals, we will have a society that is wholly given over to pleasing itself and is ultimately barren.

17:12-14 The prophet compares the nations to the

A Prophecy Against Cush

18 Woe to the land of whirring wings[a]
along the rivers of Cush,[b][s]
2 which sends envoys by sea
in papyrus[t] boats over the water.

Go, swift messengers,
to a people tall and smooth-skinned,
to a people feared far and wide,
an aggressive[u] nation of strange speech,
whose land is divided by rivers.[v]

3 All you people of the world,
you who live on the earth,
when a banner[w] is raised on the mountains,
you will see it,
and when a trumpet sounds,
you will hear it.
4 This is what the LORD says to me:
"I will remain quiet and will look on from my dwelling place,[x]
like shimmering heat in the sunshine,
like a cloud of dew[y] in the heat of harvest."
5 For, before the harvest, when the blossom is gone
and the flower becomes a ripening grape,
he will cut off the shoots with pruning knives,
and cut down and take away the spreading branches.[z]
6 They will all be left to the mountain birds of prey
and to the wild animals;[a]
the birds will feed on them all summer,
the wild animals all winter.

18:1 [s] Isa 20:3-5; Eze 30:4-5,9; Zep 2:12; 3:10
18:2 [t] Ex 2:3 [u] Ge 10:8-9; 2Ch 12:3 [v] ver 7
18:3 [w] Isa 5:26
18:4 [x] Isa 26:21; Hos 5:15 [y] Isa 26:19; Hos 14:5
18:5 [z] Isa 17:10-11; Eze 17:6
18:6 [a] Isa 56:9; Jer 7:33; Eze 32:4; 39:17

Isa 18:7 ❖ What God-given gifts can we present back to God as an act of worship?

7 At that time gifts will be brought to the LORD Almighty

from a people tall and smooth-skinned,
from a people feared far and wide,
an aggressive nation of strange speech,
whose land is divided by rivers—

the gifts will be brought to Mount Zion, the place of the Name of the LORD Almighty.[b]

A Prophecy Against Egypt

19 A prophecy[c] against Egypt:[d]

See, the LORD rides on a swift cloud[e]
and is coming to Egypt.
The idols of Egypt tremble before him,
and the hearts of the Egyptians melt[f] with fear.

2 "I will stir up Egyptian against Egyptian—
brother will fight against brother,[g]
neighbor against neighbor,
city against city,
kingdom against kingdom.[h]
3 The Egyptians will lose heart,
and I will bring their plans to nothing;
they will consult the idols and the spirits of the dead,
the mediums and the spiritists.[i]

18:7 [b] Ps 68:31
19:1 [c] Isa 13:1; Jer 43:12 [d] Ex 12:12; Joel 3:19 [e] Ps 18:10; 104:3; Rev 1:7 [f] Jos 2:11
19:2 [g] Jdg 7:22; Mt 10:21,36 [h] 2Ch 20:23
19:3 [i] Isa 8:19; 47:13; Da 2:2,10

[a] 1 Or *of locusts* [b] 1 That is, the upper Nile region

---

raging sea: It appears as if they are the ultimate reality. But in fact, the One who sits in the heavens is the ultimate reality. Isaiah is attempting to get his people to focus beyond apparent realities and look toward the One who is reality in himself.
18:1-3 In about 740 BC the Ethiopian Piankhy (also known as Piye) took over Egypt. He along with his successor, Shabako (715-702 BC), brought a new energy to Egyptian affairs. Most likely both of them attempted to cement alliances with various surrounding countries in order to counter the Assyrian threat.
18:4-7 God's activity often seems unnoticeable. In his harvest, God will cut down the enemy nations like unproductive branches on a vine. Judeans should remember that the day will come when the Ethiopians will be giving gifts to the God of Jerusalem.

17:12—18:7 When we think of the prediction that the Ethiopians will come to Jerusalem bringing gifts to the Lord (v. 7), we remember the Ethiopian eunuch who became a believer (Ac 8:26-39).

19:1-4 In several places Israelite writers appropriate the imagery of Baal to say that the Lord rides upon the clouds (e.g., Ps 104:3). The "idols" (Isa 19:1, 3) of Egypt are utterly helpless. The Egyptians were an orderly people. As a result, when rapid change came, they tended to "lose heart" (v. 3), and order quickly gave way to disorder.

4 I will hand the Egyptians over
to the power of a cruel master,
and a fierce king[j] will rule over them,"
declares the Lord, the LORD
Almighty.

5 The waters of the river will dry up,[k]
and the riverbed will be parched
and dry.
6 The canals will stink;[l]
the streams of Egypt will dwindle
and dry up.[m]
The reeds and rushes will wither,[n]
7 also the plants along the Nile,
at the mouth of the river.
Every sown field[o] along the Nile
will become parched, will blow
away and be no more.
8 The fishermen[p] will groan and
lament,
all who cast hooks[q] into the Nile;
those who throw nets on the water
will pine away.
9 Those who work with combed flax
will despair,
the weavers of fine linen[r] will lose
hope.
10 The workers in cloth will be
dejected,
and all the wage earners will be
sick at heart.

11 The officials of Zoan[s] are nothing
but fools;
the wise counselors of Pharaoh
give senseless advice.
How can you say to Pharaoh,
"I am one of the wise men,[t]
a disciple of the ancient kings"?

12 Where are your wise men[u] now?
Let them show you and make
known
what the LORD Almighty
has planned[v] against Egypt.
13 The officials of Zoan have become
fools,
the leaders of Memphis[w] are
deceived;
the cornerstones of her peoples
have led Egypt astray.
14 The LORD has poured into them
a spirit of dizziness;[x]
they make Egypt stagger in all that
she does,
as a drunkard staggers around in
his vomit.
15 There is nothing Egypt can do —
head or tail, palm branch or reed.[y]

16 In that day the Egyptians will become weaklings.[z] They will shudder with
fear[a] at the uplifted hand[b] that the LORD
Almighty raises against them. 17 And the
land of Judah will bring terror to the
Egyptians; everyone to whom Judah is
mentioned will be terrified, because of
what the LORD Almighty is planning[c]
against them.
18 In that day five cities in Egypt will
speak the language of Canaan and swear
allegiance[d] to the LORD Almighty. One of
them will be called the City of the Sun.[a]
19 In that day there will be an altar[e]
to the LORD in the heart of Egypt, and
a monument[f] to the LORD at its border.
20 It will be a sign and witness to the LORD
Almighty in the land of Egypt. When they
cry out to the LORD because of their oppressors, he will send them a savior and
defender, and he will rescue[g] them. 21 So

[a] 18 Some manuscripts of the Masoretic Text, Dead Sea Scrolls, Symmachus and Vulgate; most manuscripts of the Masoretic Text *City of Destruction*

19:4 [j] Isa 20:4; Jer 46:26; Eze 29:19
19:5 [k] Jer 51:36
19:6 [l] Ex 7:18 [m] Isa 37:25; Eze 30:12 [n] Isa 15:6
19:7 [o] Isa 23:3
19:8 [p] Eze 47:10 [q] Hab 1:15
19:9 [r] Pr 7:16; Eze 27:7
19:11 [s] Nu 13:22 [t] 1Ki 4:30; Ac 7:22
19:12 [u] 1Co 1:20 [v] Isa 14:24; Ro 9:17
19:13 [w] Jer 2:16; Eze 30:13,16
19:14 [x] Mt 17:17
19:15 [y] Isa 9:14
19:16 [z] Jer 51:30; Na 3:13 [a] Heb 10:31 [b] Isa 11:15
19:17 [c] Isa 14:24
19:18 [d] Zep 3:9
19:19 [e] Jos 22:10 [f] Ge 28:18
19:20 [g] Isa 49:24-26

19:5–10 If not for the Nile River, Egypt would be an extension of the Sahara Desert. Isaiah envisions a day when the mighty river will run dry, along with all the activities dependent on it: agriculture, fisheries, and flax-making.
19:11–15 It is tempting to think that there is an allusion to Joseph's story in the inability of the Egyptian wise men to know what the Lord has "planned" for Egypt (v. 12). Egypt's entire collection of counselors is helpless to discern what Israel's God is going to do with them and their land.
19:16–25 There is also a positive reason why trusting in Egypt is foolish: The Egyptians will one day turn to Judah's God. Four different prose statements are made here, each headed by the phrase "in that day" (vv. 16, 18, 19, 23). A good English equivalent is "at that time."
19:16–17 The Egyptians will be plunged into terror when God acts. Because Judah's God is at work, the very name of Judah will frighten the people of Egypt.
19:18–25 This passage shows that God's ultimate purpose is to bring the people of Egypt to worship him together with Israel and Assyria. The ultimate vision of the Hebrew prophets is that Israel will be a blessing to the nations as it leads them to the one true God.

The hope of Egypt is expressed in three movements. (1) Several cities will speak Hebrew and swear allegiance to the Lord (v. 18). (2) The Lord will be worshiped in Egypt, with an "altar" in the center of the land and a "monument" to God on the border (v. 19). (3) God is not merely going to deliver Egypt and Israel from the Assyrian oppressors; he is going to join the three countries together in the common worship of the Lord (v. 25).

the LORD will make himself known to
the Egyptians, and in that day they will
acknowledge[h] the LORD. They will worship[i] with sacrifices and grain offerings;
they will make vows to the LORD and keep
them. 22The LORD will strike[j] Egypt with
a plague; he will strike them and heal
them. They will turn[k] to the LORD, and he
will respond to their pleas and heal[l] them.
23In that day there will be a highway[m]
from Egypt to Assyria. The Assyrians will
go to Egypt and the Egyptians to Assyria.
The Egyptians and Assyrians will worship[n] together. 24In that day Israel will be
the third, along with Egypt and Assyria,
a blessing[a] on the earth. 25The LORD Almighty will bless them, saying, "Blessed
be Egypt my people,[o] Assyria my handiwork,[p] and Israel my inheritance.[q]"

A Prophecy Against Egypt and Cush

20 In the year that the supreme commander,[r] sent by Sargon king of
Assyria, came to Ashdod and attacked
and captured it — 2at that time the LORD
spoke through Isaiah son of Amoz.[s] He
said to him, "Take off the sackcloth[t]
from your body and the sandals[u] from
your feet." And he did so, going around
stripped[v] and barefoot.[w]
3Then the LORD said, "Just as my servant Isaiah has gone stripped and barefoot for three years, as a sign[x] and portent
against Egypt and Cush,[b][y] 4so the king[z]
of Assyria will lead away stripped and
barefoot the Egyptian captives and Cushite exiles, young and old, with buttocks
bared — to Egypt's shame.[a] 5Those who
trusted in Cush and boasted in Egypt[b]
will be dismayed and put to shame. 6In
that day the people who live on this coast
will say, 'See what has happened to those

19:21 [h] Isa 11:9 [i] Isa 56:7; Mal 1:11
19:22 [j] Heb 12:11 [k] Isa 45:14; Hos 14:1 [l] Dt 32:39
19:23 [m] Isa 11:16 [n] Isa 27:13
19:25 [o] Ps 100:3 [p] Isa 29:23; 45:11; 60:21; 64:8; Eph 2:10 [q] Hos 2:23
20:1 [r] 2Ki 18:17
20:2 [s] Isa 13:1 [t] Zec 13:4; Mt 3:4 [u] Eze 24:17, 23 [v] 1Sa 19:24 [w] Mic 1:8
20:3 [x] Isa 8:18 [y] Isa 37:9; 43:3
20:4 [z] Isa 19:4 [a] Isa 47:3; Jer 13:22, 26
20:5 [b] 2Ki 18:21; Isa 30:5
20:6 [c] Isa 10:3 [d] Jer 30:15-17; Mt 23:33; 1Th 5:3; Heb 2:3
21:1 [e] Isa 13:21; Jer 51:43 [f] Zec 9:14
21:2 [g] Ps 60:3 [h] Isa 33:1 [i] Isa 22:6; Jer 49:34
21:3 [j] Ps 48:6; Isa 26:17
21:5 [k] Jer 51:39, 57; Da 5:2

Isa 19:18-25 ❖ Where have we seen enemies of God transformed into worshipers?

Isa 20:5 ❖ What are some things believers misplace their trust in today?

we relied on, those we fled to for help[c]
and deliverance from the king of Assyria!
How then can we escape?[d]' "

A Prophecy Against Babylon

21 A prophecy against the Desert[e] by
the Sea:

Like whirlwinds sweeping through
the southland,[f]
an invader comes from the desert,
from a land of terror.

2A dire[g] vision has been shown to me:
The traitor betrays,[h] the looter
takes loot.
Elam,[i] attack! Media, lay siege!
I will bring to an end all the
groaning she caused.

3At this my body is racked with pain,
pangs seize me, like those of a
woman in labor;[j]
I am staggered by what I hear,
I am bewildered by what I see.
4My heart falters,
fear makes me tremble;
the twilight I longed for
has become a horror to me.

5They set the tables,
they spread the rugs,
they eat, they drink![k]

[a] 24 Or *Assyria, whose names will be used in blessings* (see Gen. 48:20); or *Assyria, who will be seen by others as blessed* [b] 3 That is, the upper Nile region; also in verse 5

20:1-6 The Hebrew word for "stripped" (v. 2) can connote full or partial nudity, such as only wearing a loincloth, leaving the "buttocks bared" (v. 4). Isaiah is acting out what is going to happen when the Assyrians strip the Egyptians and march them off into captivity.

✣ **19:1—20:6** Will the promises recorded here be fulfilled? Yes, they will. In fact, from one point of view they already have been fulfilled. For the first half of the first millennium, Egypt was one of the major centers of Christian—that is, biblical—faith. But we should be careful to avoid two extremes. On the one hand we should not say that the only possible fulfillment is a literal one according to one person's, or one group's, definition of "literal." On the other hand, we should not say that the spiritual teaching of these predictions is all that is important. If God is God, then history is still his arena to act in as he chooses.

21:1-2 Like a whirlwind in the "southland" of Judah, destruction will suddenly sweep in (v. 1). Babylon's power will be built on betrayal and plunder, but the day will come when the tables will be turned. Both "Elam" and "Media" were occasionally allies of Babylon, and both will turn against it (v. 2).
21:3-4 Probably the best explanation for the grief that racks Isaiah is that he is lamenting for those who put their trust in Babylon and will be destroyed when that trust fails (v. 4).
21:5 Verse 5 reminds the reader of the scene in Da 5.

Get up, you officers,
oil the shields!

6This is what the Lord says to me:

"Go, post a lookout
and have him report what he sees.
7When he sees chariots[l]
with teams of horses,
riders on donkeys
or riders on camels,
let him be alert,
fully alert."

8And the lookout[a][m] shouted,

"Day after day, my lord, I stand on
the watchtower;
every night I stay at my post.
9Look, here comes a man in a
chariot
with a team of horses.
And he gives back the answer:
'Babylon[n] has fallen,[o] has fallen!
All the images of its gods[p]
lie shattered on the ground!'"

10My people who are crushed on the
threshing floor,[q]
I tell you what I have heard
from the LORD Almighty,
from the God of Israel.

A Prophecy Against Edom

11A prophecy against Dumah[b]:[r]

Someone calls to me from Seir,[s]
"Watchman, what is left of the
night?
Watchman, what is left of the
night?"
12The watchman replies,
"Morning is coming, but also the
night.
If you would ask, then ask;
and come back yet again."

21:7 [l] ver 9
21:8 [m] Hab 2:1
21:9 [n] Rev 14:8 [o] Jer 51:8; Rev 18:2 [p] Isa 46:1; Jer 50:2; 51:44
21:10 [q] Jer 51:33
21:11 [r] Ge 25:14 [s] Ge 32:3
21:13 [t] Isa 13:1
21:14 [u] Ge 25:15
21:15 [v] Isa 13:14
21:16 [w] Isa 16:14 [x] Isa 17:3 [y] Ps 120:5; Isa 60:7
21:17 [z] Isa 10:19
22:1 [a] Isa 13:1 [b] Ps 125:2; Jer 21:13; Joel 3:2,12,14
22:2 [c] Isa 32:13

Isa 21:9 ❖ What specific idols do we follow in the world today that need to be smashed?

A Prophecy Against Arabia

13A prophecy[t] against Arabia:

You caravans of Dedanites,
who camp in the thickets of
Arabia,
14 bring water for the thirsty;
you who live in Tema,[u]
bring food for the fugitives.
15They flee[v] from the sword,
from the drawn sword,
from the bent bow
and from the heat of battle.

16This is what the Lord says to me:
"Within one year, as a servant bound
by contract[w] would count it, all the splendor[x] of Kedar[y] will come to an end. 17The
survivors of the archers, the warriors of
Kedar, will be few.[z]" The LORD, the God
of Israel, has spoken.

A Prophecy About Jerusalem

22 A prophecy[a] against the Valley[b]
of Vision:

What troubles you now,
that you have all gone up on the
roofs,
2you town so full of commotion,
you city of tumult and revelry?[c]
Your slain were not killed by the
sword,
nor did they die in battle.
3All your leaders have fled
together;

[a] 8 Dead Sea Scrolls and Syriac; Masoretic Text *A lion* [b] 11 *Dumah*, a wordplay on *Edom*, means *silence* or *stillness*.

21:6–9 The overall sense here is clear enough—look for the message to come that "Babylon has fallen" (v. 9). The significance of the references to chariots and teams of horses is not as clear. Perhaps they are suggestive of the fleeing, defeated remnants of an army. The people of Judah had been crushed under the sled of Assyria, so it looks as if Babylon offers a ray of hope. But Isaiah, the watchman, sees that as a false hope.
21:11–12 Perhaps the thought is that even the Edomites turn to Isaiah, the Judean "watchman," to see what is happening in the east.
21:13–17 The oasis of "Tema" (v. 14) was located in an area of northwest Arabia known as Kedar (v. 16). Tema is significant because this was the headquarters of the last king of Babylon.
21:16–17 Isaiah makes it clear that Kedar itself will not escape the disaster.

✣ **21:1–17** These three oracles speak of the fickleness of human promises. Are people depending on us? Are we only interested in using them for our own advantage? These are serious questions because of the immense capacity for self-deception that human self-interest provokes.

22:1–7 The people are rejoicing over the short-term lifting of the Assyrian threat, but the prophet sees how this whole episode will end 125 years later and weeps "bitterly" (v. 4).

they have been captured without
using the bow.
All you who were caught were taken
prisoner together,
having fled while the enemy was
still far away.
4 Therefore I said, "Turn away
from me;
let me weep[d] bitterly.
Do not try to console me
over the destruction of my
people."[e]

5 The Lord, the LORD Almighty, has a
day
of tumult and trampling and
terror[f]
in the Valley of Vision,
a day of battering down walls
and of crying out to the mountains.
6 Elam[g] takes up the quiver,[h]
with her charioteers and horses;
Kir[i] uncovers the shield.
7 Your choicest valleys are full of
chariots,
and horsemen are posted at the
city gates.[j]

8 The Lord stripped away the defenses
of Judah,
and you looked in that day
to the weapons[k] in the Palace of
the Forest.[l]
9 You saw that the walls of the City of
David
were broken through in many
places;
you stored up water
in the Lower Pool.[m]
10 You counted the buildings in
Jerusalem
and tore down houses to
strengthen the wall.
11 You built a reservoir between the
two walls[n]
for the water of the Old Pool,[o]
but you did not look to the One who
made it,
or have regard for the One who
planned it long ago.

12 The Lord, the LORD Almighty,
called you on that day
to weep[p] and to wail,
to tear out your hair[q] and put on
sackcloth.[r]
13 But see, there is joy and revelry,
slaughtering of cattle and killing
of sheep,
eating of meat and drinking of
wine![s]
"Let us eat and drink," you say,
"for tomorrow we die!"[t]

14 The LORD Almighty has revealed this
in my hearing:[u] "Till your dying day this
sin will not be atoned[v] for," says the Lord,
the LORD Almighty.

15 This is what the Lord, the LORD Almighty, says:

"Go, say to this steward,
to Shebna[w] the palace
administrator:
16 What are you doing here and who
gave you permission
to cut out a grave[x] for yourself
here,
hewing your grave on the height
and chiseling your resting place in
the rock?
17 "Beware, the LORD is about to take
firm hold of you
and hurl you away, you mighty
man.
18 He will roll you up tightly like a ball
and throw[y] you into a large
country.
There you will die
and there the chariots you were so
proud of

22:4 [d] Isa 15:3; Lk 19:41 [e] Jer 9:1
22:5 [f] La 1:5
22:6 [g] Isa 21:2 [h] Jer 49:35 [i] 2Ki 16:9
22:7 [j] 2Ch 32:1-2
22:8 [k] 2Ch 32:5 [l] 1Ki 7:2
22:9 [m] 2Ch 32:4
22:11 [n] 2Ki 25:4; Jer 39:4 [o] 2Ch 32:4
22:12 [p] Joel 2:17 [q] Mic 1:16 [r] Joel 1:13
22:13 [s] Isa 5:22; 28:7-8; 56:12; Lk 17:26-29 [t] 1Co 15:32*
22:14 [u] Isa 5:9 [v] Isa 13:11; 26:21; 30:13-14; Eze 24:13
22:15 [w] 2Ki 18:18; Isa 36:3
22:16 [x] Mt 27:60
22:18 [y] Isa 17:13

22:8–11 The prophet makes his pronouncement against the Valley of Vision. Note the recurrence of verbs for "seeing" in vv. 8, 9, and 11. The repeated "you" is probably Hezekiah. We know he strengthened the walls of Jerusalem and had the famous tunnel dug to bring water from the spring of Gihon to the pool at the foot of the old city (2Ch 32:1–5).

Jerusalem exists as the capital city of Judah only because of the grace and power of God (Isa 22:11). The land is a covenant gift from their covenant Lord. Thus, the most important thing is to be sure that they are acting within the covenant Lord's will and that their relationship with him is intact. This will allow them to receive the promised blessings of the covenant. But they are not.

22:12–14 It is because of Judah's sin that God is calling for weeping and wailing (v. 12). Apart from confession, repentance, and the mercy of God, there is no possibility for the sins of the nation to be "atoned for" (v. 14).

22:15–19 Shebna carries great responsibility for the well-being of the country, but he is building himself a fine rock tomb. Instead of leading the living, he is making sure he will be remembered in death.

Isaiah tells Shebna that far from being significant, he is a "disgrace to [his] master's house"

will become a disgrace to your
master's house.
19 I will depose you from your office,
and you will be ousted from your
position.

20 "In that day I will summon my servant, Eliakim[z] son of Hilkiah. 21 I will
clothe him with your robe and fasten your
sash around him and hand your authority
over to him. He will be a father to those
who live in Jerusalem and to the people
of Judah. 22 I will place on his shoulder the
key[a] to the house of David;[b] what he opens
no one can shut, and what he shuts no one
can open.[c] 23 I will drive him like a peg[d]
into a firm place;[e] he will become a seat[a]
of honor[f] for the house of his father. 24 All
the glory of his family will hang on him:
its offspring and offshoots — all its lesser vessels, from the bowls to all the jars.

25 "In that day," declares the LORD Almighty, "the peg[g] driven into the firm
place will give way; it will be sheared off
and will fall, and the load hanging on it
will be cut down." The LORD has spoken.[h]

A Prophecy Against Tyre

23 A prophecy against Tyre:[i]

Wail, you ships[j] of Tarshish![k]
For Tyre is destroyed
and left without house or harbor.
From the land of Cyprus
word has come to them.

2 Be silent, you people of the island
and you merchants of Sidon,
whom the seafarers have enriched.
3 On the great waters
came the grain of the Shihor;
the harvest of the Nile[b][l] was the
revenue of Tyre,[m]
and she became the marketplace
of the nations.

4 Be ashamed, Sidon,[n] and you fortress
of the sea,
for the sea has spoken:
"I have neither been in labor nor
given birth;
I have neither reared sons nor
brought up daughters."
5 When word comes to Egypt,
they will be in anguish at the
report from Tyre.

6 Cross over to Tarshish;
wail, you people of the island.
7 Is this your city of revelry,[o]
the old, old city,
whose feet have taken her
to settle in far-off lands?
8 Who planned this against Tyre,
the bestower of crowns,
whose merchants are princes,
whose traders are renowned in
the earth?
9 The LORD Almighty planned it,
to bring down[p] her pride in all her
splendor

22:20 [z] 2Ki 18:18; Isa 36:3
22:22 [a] Rev 3:7 [b] Isa 7:2 [c] Job 12:14
22:23 [d] Zec 10:4 [e] Ezr 9:8 [f] 1Sa 2:7-8; Job 36:7
22:25 [g] ver 23 [h] Isa 46:11; Mic 4:4
23:1 [i] Jos 19:29; 1Ki 5:1; Jer 47:4; Eze 26,27,28; Joel 3:4-8; Am 1:9-10; Zec 9:2-4 [j] 1Ki 10:22 [k] Ge 10:4; Isa 2:16 *fn*
23:3 [l] Isa 19:7 [m] Eze 27:3
23:4 [n] Ge 10:15, 19
23:7 [o] Isa 22:2; 32:13
23:9 [p] Job 40:11

[a] 23 Or *throne* [b] 2,3 Masoretic Text; Dead Sea Scrolls *Sidon, / who cross over the sea; / your envoys* [3]*are on the great waters. / The grain of the Shihor, / the harvest of the Nile,*

Isa 22:15–19 ❖ Shebna was more interested in making himself an impressive tomb than in leading God's people. Where might pride or thoughts about our own legacy distract us from the tasks God calls us to?

(v. 18). Instead of being memorialized before all the people, he will be wadded up and thrown away like an old rag.

22:21–22 For a person like Shebna to have his official uniform taken from him and given to another will be terribly humiliating. The "key" in v. 22 represents the authority to grant access to the king. Unlike Shebna, Eliakim will be concerned for the people and will act as a "father" (v. 21) to them.

22:23–25 Eliakim's family will become a special burden. Eventually, he will crack under the strain, and all that has been dependent on him will come crashing down (v. 25).

✥ **22:1–25** We may choose to be Eliakim or Shebna. We may focus on the temporal or the eternal. If we focus on the temporal, we and all our works will perish with the temporal. If we choose the eternal, then none of our temporal works will ever be lost (Ro 8:13).

23:1–3 The reference to "the island" in v. 2 is a recognition that Tyre consisted of both a mainland city and an offshore island, with the harbor between the two. The Nile Valley produced much grain that was of no use to the Egyptians unless they sold it.

23:4–5 The Canaanite sea god Yam cries out, bereft of children. Tyre, his foremost child, is gone. When the word reaches Egypt, the Egyptians "will be in anguish" (v. 5).

23:7–8 Tyre was a "city of revelry" (v. 7), a place of wealth and pleasure. It was also an "old" city, a mother city that had given birth to Tarshish. Tyre's merchants had become so wealthy that they were no longer considered businessmen but rather were a part of the nobility.

23:9–12 Isaiah sees the day when all of this activity

and to humble[q] all who are
renowned[r] on the earth.

10 Till[a] your land as they do along the
Nile,
Daughter Tarshish,
for you no longer have a harbor.
11 The LORD has stretched out his
hand[s] over the sea
and made its kingdoms tremble.
He has given an order concerning
Phoenicia
that her fortresses be destroyed.[t]
12 He said, "No more of your
reveling,[u]
Virgin Daughter[v] Sidon, now
crushed!

"Up, cross over to Cyprus;
even there you will find no rest."
13 Look at the land of the Babylonians,[b]
this people that is now of no
account!
The Assyrians[w] have made it
a place for desert creatures;
they raised up their siege towers,
they stripped its fortresses bare
and turned it into a ruin.[x]

14 Wail, you ships of Tarshish;[y]
your fortress is destroyed!

15 At that time Tyre[z] will be forgotten
for seventy years, the span of a king's life.
But at the end of these seventy years, it
will happen to Tyre as in the song of the
prostitute:

16 "Take up a harp, walk through the
city,
you forgotten prostitute;
play the harp well, sing many a song,
so that you will be remembered."

17 At the end of seventy years, the LORD
will deal with Tyre. She will return to her
lucrative prostitution[a] and will ply her
trade with all the kingdoms on the face
of the earth. 18 Yet her profit and her earnings will be set apart for the LORD;[b] they
will not be stored up or hoarded. Her profits will go to those who live before the
LORD,[c] for abundant food and fine clothes.

23:9 [q] Isa 13:11 [r] Isa 5:13; 9:15
23:11 [s] Ex 14:21 [t] Isa 25:2; Zec 9:3-4
23:12 [u] Rev 18:22 [v] Isa 47:1
23:13 [w] Isa 10:5 [x] Isa 10:7
23:14 [y] Isa 2:16 *fn*
23:15 [z] Jer 25:22
23:17 [a] Eze 16:26; Na 3:4; Rev 17:1
23:18 [b] Ex 28:36; Ps 72:10 [c] Isa 60:5-9; Mic 4:13
24:1 [d] ver 20; Isa 2:19-21; 33:9
24:2 [e] Hos 4:9 [f] Eze 7:12 [g] Lev 25:35-37; Dt 23:19-20
24:3 [h] Isa 6:11-12

Isa 23:18 ❖ How can God use even what is evil in the world to benefit his people?

The LORD's Devastation of the Earth

24 See, the LORD is going to lay
waste the earth[d]
and devastate it;
he will ruin its face
and scatter its inhabitants—
2 it will be the same
for priest as for people,[e]
for the master as for his servant,
for the mistress as for her servant,
for seller as for buyer,[f]
for borrower as for lender,
for debtor as for creditor.[g]
3 The earth will be completely laid
waste
and totally plundered.[h]
The LORD has spoken
this word.

[a] *10* Dead Sea Scrolls and some Septuagint manuscripts; Masoretic Text *Go through*
[b] *13* Or *Chaldeans*

will come to a screeching halt. Tarshish will become self-sufficient since Egyptian grain will no longer be available (v. 10). Tyre will fall according to the eternal purposes of the Holy One of Israel. God's hand is extended against pride in all its forms.
23:13–14 The reader is invited to compare the fate of Babylon with that which is coming to Tyre. The two cities that begin and end the sequence of oracles are brought together here. Neither will escape the judgment planned by God.
23:15–18 It is not clear what the 70-year period in v. 15 refers to. Perhaps it is simply an indefinite time of punishment, with the number 70 referring to completeness. After this time the Lord will permit Tyre to regain some of its former prominence (v. 17).

✣ **23:1–18** Comfort, pleasure, and security—these are things humans have been looking for since the beginning of time. And what will give these to us? Money—and the more the better. In other words, we are just like the materialistic people of Tyre. We have forgotten or ignored Jesus' words: "Do not store up for yourselves treasures on earth, where moths and vermin destroy, and where thieves break in and steal. But store up for yourselves treasures in heaven, where moths and vermin do not destroy, and where thieves do not break in and steal. For where your treasure is, there your heart will be also" (Mt 6:19–21).

24:1–13 Why is this destruction coming? It is the result of the choices that earth's inhabitants have made. Verses 4–13 use one of the common images of this early part of the book to make this statement—the vine. Isaiah insists that there are laws that God the Creator has written on the human conscience. Thus, he will not admit any argument of ignorance as justification for sin.

4 The earth dries up and withers,
the world languishes and withers,
the heavens[i] languish with the
earth.
5 The earth is defiled[j] by its people;
they have disobeyed[k] the laws,
violated the statutes
and broken the everlasting
covenant.
6 Therefore a curse consumes the
earth;
its people must bear their guilt.
Therefore earth's inhabitants are
burned up,[l]
and very few are left.
7 The new wine dries up and the vine
withers;[m]
all the merrymakers groan.[n]
8 The joyful timbrels[o] are stilled,
the noise[p] of the revelers has
stopped,
the joyful harp[q] is silent.[r]
9 No longer do they drink wine[s] with a
song;
the beer is bitter[t] to its drinkers.
10 The ruined city lies desolate;
the entrance to every house is
barred.
11 In the streets they cry out for wine;
all joy turns to gloom,[u]
all joyful sounds are banished
from the earth.
12 The city is left in ruins,
its gate is battered to pieces.
13 So will it be on the earth
and among the nations,
as when an olive tree is beaten,[v]
or as when gleanings are left after
the grape harvest.

14 They raise their voices, they shout
for joy;[w]
from the west they acclaim the
LORD's majesty.

24:4 [i] Isa 2:12
24:5 [j] Ge 3:17; Nu 35:33 [k] Isa 10:6; 59:12
24:6 [l] Isa 1:31
24:7 [m] Joel 1:10-12 [n] Isa 16:8-10
24:8 [o] Isa 5:12 [p] Jer 7:34; 16:9; 25:10; Hos 2:11 [q] Rev 18:22 [r] Eze 26:13
24:9 [s] Isa 5:11, 22 [t] Isa 5:20
24:11 [u] Isa 16:10; 32:13; Jer 14:3
24:13 [v] Isa 17:6
24:14 [w] Isa 12:6
24:15 [x] Isa 66:19 [y] Isa 25:3; Mal 1:11
24:16 [z] Isa 28:5 [a] Isa 21:2; Jer 5:11
24:17 [b] Jer 48:43
24:18 [c] Ge 7:11 [d] Ps 18:7
24:19 [e] Dt 11:6
24:20 [f] Isa 19:14 [g] Isa 1:2, 28; 43:27
24:21 [h] Isa 10:12

Isa 24:21 ❖ What present-day powers and authorities will ultimately fall under the punishment of God (see Eph 1:21)?

15 Therefore in the east give glory[x] to
the LORD;
exalt[y] the name of the LORD, the
God of Israel,
in the islands of the sea.
16 From the ends of the earth we hear
singing:
"Glory[z] to the Righteous One."

But I said, "I waste away, I waste
away!
Woe to me!
The treacherous betray!
With treachery the treacherous
betray![a]"
17 Terror and pit and snare[b] await you,
people of the earth.
18 Whoever flees at the sound of terror
will fall into a pit;
whoever climbs out of the pit
will be caught in a snare.

The floodgates of the heavens[c] are
opened,
the foundations of the earth
shake.[d]
19 The earth is broken up,
the earth is split asunder,[e]
the earth is violently shaken.
20 The earth reels like a drunkard,[f]
it sways like a hut in the wind;
so heavy upon it is the guilt of its
rebellion[g]
that it falls — never to rise again.

21 In that day the LORD will punish[h]
the powers in the heavens above
and the kings on the earth below.
22 They will be herded together

24:5 The "covenant" in v. 5 may refer to the Noahic covenant of Ge 9:1–17 with its prohibition of bloodshed.
24:6 One of the features of covenants was the custom of the parties calling down curses on themselves should they fail to keep the covenant. Earth's inhabitants are under a "curse" and bear "guilt" for what they have done.
24:10–13 The "city" of earth (vv. 10, 12) lies silent and desolate. The forced and artificial cheerfulness induced by alcohol (vv. 7, 9, 11) vanishes like a vapor before the awful realities of judgment and destruction. As mighty and alluring as the city of earth is, a day of harvest is coming when all the fruit will be stripped off. Nothing will be left.
24:14–18a These verses are something of a riddle because of the dramatic contrast between vv. 14–16a and vv. 16b–18a. The first segment is likely the cry of joy from those who have been oppressed by the evil earth-city. They are looking joyously at the end of the story. But the prophet sees all the horrors that must take place before that final resolution, and he is stricken by them.
24:18b–23 The imagery is reminiscent of the flood in Ge 6. But the water is only an image. The real weight that crushes the earth is the "guilt of its rebellion" (v. 20). Again, the issue is clear: the human problem of rebellion against God.
24:21–23 People in the ancient world considered the "powers in the heavens" (v. 21)—that is, the

like prisoners[i] bound in a
dungeon;[j]
they will be shut up in prison
and be punished[a] after many days.[k]
23 The moon will be dismayed,
the sun[l] ashamed;
for the LORD Almighty will reign[m]
on Mount Zion[n] and in Jerusalem,
and before its elders — with great
glory.[o]

Praise to the LORD

25 LORD, you are my God;
I will exalt you and praise your
name,
for in perfect faithfulness
you have done wonderful things,[p]
things planned[q] long ago.
2 You have made the city a heap of
rubble,[r]
the fortified[s] town a ruin,
the foreigners' stronghold[t] a city no
more;
it will never be rebuilt.
3 Therefore strong peoples will honor
you;
cities of ruthless[u] nations will
revere you.
4 You have been a refuge[v] for the poor,
a refuge for the needy in their
distress,
a shelter from the storm
and a shade from the heat.
For the breath of the ruthless[w]
is like a storm driving against a
wall

24:22 [i] Isa 10:4 [j] Isa 42:7,22 [k] Eze 38:8
24:23 [l] Isa 13:10 [m] Rev 22:5 [n] Heb 12:22 [o] Isa 60:19
25:1 [p] Ps 98:1 [q] Nu 23:19
25:2 [r] Isa 17:1 [s] Isa 17:3 [t] Isa 13:22
25:3 [u] Isa 13:11
25:4 [v] Isa 4:6; 17:10; 27:5; 33:16 [w] Isa 29:5; 49:25
25:5 [x] Jer 51:55
25:6 [y] Isa 2:2 [z] Isa 1:19; Mt 8:11; 22:4 [a] Pr 9:2
25:7 [b] 2Co 3:15-16; Eph 4:18
25:8 [c] Hos 13:14; 1Co 15:54-55* [d] Isa 30:19; 35:10; 51:11; 65:19; Rev 7:17; 21:4 [e] Mt 5:11; 1Pe 4:14
25:9 [f] Isa 40:9 [g] Ps 20:5; Isa 33:22; 35:4; 49:25-26; 60:16

Isa 25:7–8 ❖ How does the victory of Christ over death fill us with hope and encouragement (see 1Co 15:54–57)?

5 and like the heat of the desert.
You silence[x] the uproar of
foreigners;
as heat is reduced by the shadow
of a cloud,
so the song of the ruthless is
stilled.

6 On this mountain[y] the LORD
Almighty will prepare
a feast[z] of rich food for all peoples,
a banquet of aged wine —
the best of meats and the finest of
wines.[a]
7 On this mountain he will destroy
the shroud[b] that enfolds all
peoples,
the sheet that covers all nations;
8 he will swallow up death[c] forever.
The Sovereign LORD will wipe away
the tears[d]
from all faces;
he will remove his people's disgrace[e]
from all the earth.
The LORD has spoken.

9 In that day they will say,

"Surely this is our God;[f]
we trusted in him, and he
saved[g] us.

[a] 22 Or *released*

---

stars, the sun, and the moon—to be deities. But the God of Israel insists they are not. If God chooses, he can turn off their light and shut them up in a dark "prison" (v. 22).

There is only One who has the right to be called King of the universe. Where will be the seat of his rule? He will rule on "Mount Zion," and the "elders" (v. 23) will be his attendants.

✣ **24:1–23** Only God is eternal, and he will one day bring down the curtain on earth's final stage. It will be too late to get ready for that day when it arrives. Either we are ready every day, or we are not ready at all. Consider how you can help those in your circle of influence to prepare for this final day, which is sure to come (see Zep 1:14–18; 3:8–10; 2Th 1:9–10; 2Pe 3:10).

25:1–12 Israel's Lord has been faithful and has "done wonderful things" (v. 1). Redemption and deliverance are not for Israel alone but for all peoples who turn to God in faith and humility. There is no sense in which God is pleased with the destruction of the wicked. He wants to invite "all peoples" (vv. 6–8) to his feast.

25:9–12 Verse 9 emphasizes the trustworthiness of God. God can be trusted when nothing and no one else on earth can. If we trust the nations of humanity instead of God, they will turn on us and destroy us. But the thought of this unit does not end on this glorious note. Yes, God is merciful. But no one dare presume on that grace. Sin *will* be punished.

✣ **25:1–12** This passage has one of the clearest teachings on resurrection in the OT. As such it speaks to the greatest issue in the modern world—the issue of death. Death takes away the possibility of individual human significance. The only alternative is to say that humanity will go on after we die and that therefore we have some significance as a part of the race. But that is our only significance, and a very small one. As Christians, however, we know that we have not been created for death but for life. Death has lost its sting, and the grave has been robbed of its victory (1Co 15:55).

This is the LORD, we trusted in him;
let us rejoice[h] and be glad in his salvation."

10 The hand of the LORD will rest on this mountain;
but Moab[i] will be trampled in their land
as straw is trampled down in the manure.
11 They will stretch out their hands in it,
as swimmers stretch out their hands to swim.
God will bring down[j] their pride[k]
despite the cleverness[a] of their hands.
12 He will bring down your high fortified walls
and lay them low;[l]
he will bring them down to the ground,
to the very dust.

A Song of Praise

26 In that day this song will be sung in the land of Judah:

We have a strong city;[m]
God makes salvation
its walls[n] and ramparts.
2 Open the gates
that the righteous[o] nation may enter,
the nation that keeps faith.
3 You will keep in perfect peace
those whose minds are steadfast,
because they trust in you.
4 Trust[p] in the LORD forever,
for the LORD, the LORD himself, is the Rock eternal.
5 He humbles those who dwell on high,
he lays the lofty city low;
he levels it to the ground[q]
and casts it down to the dust.
6 Feet trample it down—
the feet of the oppressed,
the footsteps of the poor.[r]

25:9 [h] Isa 35:2, 10
25:10 [i] Am 2:1-3
25:11 [j] Isa 5:25; 14:26; 16:14 [k] Job 40:12
25:12 [l] Isa 15:1
26:1 [m] Isa 14:32 [n] Isa 60:18
26:2 [o] Isa 54:14; 58:8; 62:2
26:4 [p] Isa 12:2; 50:10
26:5 [q] Isa 25:12
26:6 [r] Isa 3:15

Isa 26:1-4 ❖ How can we help "open the gates" for new people to join God's community (v. 2)?

7 The path of the righteous is level;
you, the Upright One, make the way of the righteous smooth.[s]
8 Yes, LORD, walking in the way of your laws,[b][t]
we wait for you;
your name[u] and renown
are the desire of our hearts.
9 My soul yearns for you in the night;
in the morning my spirit longs[v] for you.
When your judgments come upon the earth,
the people of the world learn righteousness.[w]
10 But when grace is shown to the wicked,
they do not learn righteousness;
even in a land of uprightness they go on doing evil[x]
and do not regard[y] the majesty of the LORD.
11 LORD, your hand is lifted high,
but they do not see[z] it.
Let them see your zeal for your people and be put to shame;
let the fire[a] reserved for your enemies consume them.

12 LORD, you establish peace for us;
all that we have accomplished you have done for us.
13 LORD our God, other lords[b] besides you have ruled over us,
but your name alone do we honor.[c]
14 They are now dead,[d] they live no more;
their spirits do not rise.
You punished them and brought them to ruin;[e]

26:7 [s] Isa 42:16
26:8 [t] Isa 56:1 [u] Isa 12:4
26:9 [v] Ps 63:1; 78:34; Isa 55:6 [w] Mt 6:33
26:10 [x] Isa 32:6 [y] Isa 22:12-13; Hos 11:7; Jn 5:37-38; Ro 2:4
26:11 [z] Isa 44:9, 18 [a] Heb 10:27
26:13 [b] Isa 2:8; 10:5,11 [c] Isa 63:7
26:14 [d] Dt 4:28 [e] Isa 10:3

[a] *11* The meaning of the Hebrew for this word is uncertain. [b] *8* Or *judgments*

26:1-6 The city of God, populated with the faithful, has the open gates of confidence. This comes from a complete inner integrity rooted in "trust" (v. 3). This trust is justified because the Lord is a "Rock" that is "eternal" (v. 4). He will bring the "lofty city" of earth down into the dust (vv. 5-6). **26:7-9** The prophet asks God to speed that day of retribution. God only asks them to live in the way for which they were made. The righteous do not say they trust God and then violate God's regulations for fruitful living. God's honor and reputation have become the believers' deepest desire (v. 8). **26:10-11** In the absence of repentance, "grace" may actually be counterproductive (v. 10). Unless the "wicked" (v. 10) experience God's "judgments" (v. 9), they will see no reason to change. **26:12-18** The people have been unable to accomplish God's work in the world, and they call on him to demonstrate his delivering power there. The people are helpless. Isaiah longs to see God's

you wiped out all memory of them.
15 You have enlarged the nation, LORD;
you have enlarged the nation.
You have gained glory for yourself;
you have extended all the borders[f]
of the land.

16 LORD, they came to you in their
distress;[g]
when you disciplined them,
they could barely whisper a
prayer.[a]
17 As a pregnant woman about to give
birth[h]
writhes and cries out in her pain,
so were we in your presence, LORD.
18 We were with child, we writhed in
labor,
but we gave birth[i] to wind.
We have not brought salvation[j] to
the earth,
and the people of the world have
not come to life.

19 But your dead[k] will live, LORD;
their bodies will rise —
let those who dwell in the dust
wake up and shout for joy —
your dew is like the dew of the
morning;
the earth will give birth to her
dead.[l]

20 Go, my people, enter your rooms
and shut the doors[m] behind you;
hide[n] yourselves for a little while
until his wrath has passed by.[o]
21 See, the LORD is coming[p] out of his
dwelling[q]
to punish[r] the people of the earth
for their sins.
The earth will disclose the blood[s]
shed on it;
the earth will conceal its slain no
longer.

Deliverance of Israel

27 In that day,

the LORD will punish with his
sword[t] —
his fierce, great and powerful
sword —
Leviathan[u] the gliding serpent,
Leviathan the coiling serpent;
he will slay the monster[v] of the sea.

2 In that day —

"Sing about a fruitful vineyard:[w]
3 I, the LORD, watch over it;
I water[x] it continually.
I guard it day and night
so that no one may harm it.
4 I am not angry.
If only there were briers and thorns
confronting me!
I would march against them in
battle;
I would set them all on fire.[y]
5 Or else let them come to me for
refuge;[z]
let them make peace[a] with me,
yes, let them make peace
with me."

6 In days to come Jacob will take
root,
Israel will bud and blossom[b]
and fill all the world with fruit.[c]

7 Has the LORD struck her
as he struck[d] down those who
struck her?

26:15 [f] Isa 33:17
26:16 [g] Hos 5:15
26:17 [h] Jn 16:21
26:18 [i] Isa 33:11; 59:4 [j] Ps 17:14
26:19 [k] Isa 25:8; Eph 5:14 [l] Eze 37:1-14; Da 12:2
26:20 [m] Ex 12:23 [n] Ps 91:1, 4 [o] Ps 30:5; Isa 54:7-8
26:21 [p] Jude 14 [q] Mic 1:3 [r] Isa 13:9, 11; 30:12-14 [s] Job 16:18; Lk 11:50-51
27:1 [t] Isa 34:6; 66:16 [u] Job 3:8 [v] Ps 74:13
27:2 [w] Jer 2:21
27:3 [x] Isa 58:11
27:4 [y] Isa 10:17; Mt 3:12; Heb 6:8
27:5 [z] Isa 25:4 [a] Job 22:21; Ro 5:1; 2Co 5:20
27:6 [b] Hos 14:5-6 [c] Isa 37:31
27:7 [d] Isa 37:36-38

[a] *16* The meaning of the Hebrew for this clause is uncertain.

---

justice (vv. 9–11), but he also wants to see God's salvation made available through Israel.
26:19 The prophet tells the people not to despair. Death does not have the last word; God does.
26:20—27:1 Canaanite mythology told of a sea serpent named Leviathan. Isaiah is simply making use of emotive images familiar to many in his audience to make his point: No enemy can defeat God's plan and purposes.

✣ **26:1—27:1** These verses in Isaiah are written for just such an ambiguous time as ours—when the lines between right and wrong are not clear. In our busy modern world the Scriptural admonition "Do not be anxious about anything" (Php 4:6) is hard to apply to our lives. We are anxious about *everything.*

What must we do? We must guard what we let into our minds. This begins at home. Many of our homes are places where cluttered minds, the distractions of social and other media, and misplaced priorities rule the day. Yet Christians are called to follow and apply the teaching in Philippians and make a stand against the prevailing culture. Jesus is our peace (Jn 14:27); he values devotion and calls us to focus on his kingdom priorities (see Lk 10:38–42).

27:2-6 In ch. 5, God called in the wild animals to destroy the vineyard of bitter grapes that his nation had become. Now the vineyard of "Jacob" is going to be so fruitful that it will fill "all the world with fruit" (v. 6).
27:7-11 What accounts for this radical shift? Yes, God had indeed driven Israel out (v. 8), but his purpose was not annihilation but cleansing (v. 9).

Has she been killed
as those were killed who killed
her?
8 By warfare[a] and exile[e] you contend
with her —
with his fierce blast he drives her
out,
as on a day the east wind blows.
9 By this, then, will Jacob's guilt be
atoned for,
and this will be the full fruit of the
removal of his sin:[f]
When he makes all the altar stones
to be like limestone crushed to
pieces,
no Asherah poles[b][g] or incense altars
will be left standing.
10 The fortified city stands desolate,[h]
an abandoned settlement,
forsaken like the wilderness;
there the calves graze,
there they lie down;[i]
they strip its branches bare.
11 When its twigs are dry, they are
broken off
and women come and make fires
with them.
For this is a people without
understanding;[j]
so their Maker has no compassion
on them,
and their Creator[k] shows them no
favor.[l]

12 In that day the LORD will thresh
from the flowing Euphrates to the Wadi
of Egypt,[m] and you, Israel, will be gathered[n] up one by one. 13 And in that day
a great trumpet[o] will sound. Those who
were perishing in Assyria and those who
were exiled in Egypt[p] will come and worship the LORD on the holy mountain in
Jerusalem.

Woe to the Leaders of Ephraim and Judah

28 Woe to that wreath, the pride of
Ephraim's[q] drunkards,

27:8 [e] Isa 50:1; 54:7
27:9 [f] Ro 11:27* [g] Ex 34:13
27:10 [h] Isa 32:14; Jer 26:6 [i] Isa 17:2
27:11 [j] Dt 32:28; Isa 1:3; Jer 8:7 [k] Dt 32:18; Isa 43:1,7,15; 44:1-2,21,24 [l] Isa 9:17
27:12 [m] Ge 15:18 [n] Dt 30:4; Isa 11:12; 17:6
27:13 [o] Lev 25:9; Mt 24:31 [p] Isa 19:21,25
28:1 [q] ver 3; Isa 9:9
[r] ver 4 [s] Hos 7:5
28:2 [t] Isa 40:10 [u] Isa 30:30; Eze 13:11 [v] Isa 29:6 [w] Isa 8:7
28:3 [x] ver 1
28:4 [y] ver 1 [z] Hos 9:10; Na 3:12
28:5 [a] Isa 62:3
28:6 [b] Isa 11:2-4; 32:1,16 [c] Jn 5:30 [d] 2Ch 32:8

Isa 27:9 ❖ How does Jesus' atonement for sin open the way for us to follow God's will (see Heb 13:15–16)?

Isa 28:5–6 ❖ Sometimes we worry about the judgment of other people. How can we instead focus on the justice of God?

to the fading flower, his glorious
beauty,
set on the head of a fertile
valley[r] —
to that city, the pride of those laid
low by wine![s]
2 See, the Lord has one who is
powerful[t] and strong.
Like a hailstorm[u] and a
destructive wind,[v]
like a driving rain and a flooding[w]
downpour,
he will throw it forcefully to the
ground.
3 That wreath, the pride of Ephraim's[x]
drunkards,
will be trampled underfoot.
4 That fading flower, his glorious
beauty,
set on the head of a fertile
valley,[y]
will be like figs[z] ripe before
harvest —
as soon as people see them and
take them in hand,
they swallow them.

5 In that day the LORD Almighty
will be a glorious crown,[a]
a beautiful wreath
for the remnant of his people.
6 He will be a spirit of justice[b]
to the one who sits in judgment,[c]
a source of strength
to those who turn back the battle[d]
at the gate.

[a] *8* See Septuagint; the meaning of the Hebrew for this word is uncertain. [b] *9* That is, wooden symbols of the goddess Asherah

27:12–13 The writer uses the metaphor of harvest. The same point is made with a different metaphor: the trumpet call of muster for battle. The exiles from north and south are called to "worship the LORD on the holy mountain" (v. 13).

✚ **27:2–13** God's actions in our lives today continue to be not for the purpose of destruction but for refinement. If trouble and adversity have come our way, our attitude about God's care and concern for us will make all the difference in how we receive them.

28:1–4 The drunken partygoers in Samaria wear these wreaths on their heads as they try to forget the terror facing them. Isaiah sees a day when all these wreaths will be thrown to the ground and trampled.

28:5–6 In contrast to the previous wreath image, there is another "wreath"—the Lord himself (v. 5).

7 And these also stagger from wine[e]
and reel[f] from beer:
Priests[g] and prophets[h] stagger from beer
and are befuddled with wine;
they reel from beer,
they stagger when seeing visions,[i]
they stumble when rendering decisions.
8 All the tables are covered with vomit[j]
and there is not a spot without filth.

9 "Who is it he is trying to teach?[k]
To whom is he explaining his message?
To children weaned[l] from their milk,[m]
to those just taken from the breast?
10 For it is:
Do this, do that,
a rule for this, a rule for that[a];
a little here, a little there."

11 Very well then, with foreign lips and strange tongues[n]
God will speak to this people,[o]
12 to whom he said,
"This is the resting place, let the weary rest";[p]
and, "This is the place of repose" —
but they would not listen.
13 So then, the word of the LORD to them will become:
Do this, do that,
a rule for this, a rule for that;
a little here, a little there —
so that as they go they will fall backward;
they will be injured[q] and snared and captured.[r]

14 Therefore hear the word of the LORD,[s] you scoffers
who rule this people in Jerusalem.
15 You boast, "We have entered into a covenant with death,
with the realm of the dead we have made an agreement.
When an overwhelming scourge sweeps by,[t]
it cannot touch us,
for we have made a lie[u] our refuge
and falsehood[b] our hiding place.[v]"

16 So this is what the Sovereign LORD says:

"See, I lay a stone in Zion, a tested stone,[w]
a precious cornerstone for a sure foundation;
the one who relies on it
will never be stricken with panic.[x]
17 I will make justice[y] the measuring line
and righteousness the plumb line;[z]
hail will sweep away your refuge, the lie,
and water will overflow your hiding place.
18 Your covenant with death will be annulled;
your agreement with the realm of the dead will not stand.[a]
When the overwhelming scourge sweeps by,[b]
you will be beaten down[c] by it.
19 As often as it comes it will carry you away;[d]
morning after morning, by day and by night,
it will sweep through."

28:7 [e] Isa 22:13 [f] Isa 56:10-12 [g] Isa 24:2 [h] Isa 9:15 [i] Isa 29:11; Hos 4:11
28:8 [j] Jer 48:26
28:9 [k] ver 26; Isa 30:20; 48:17; 50:4; 54:13 [l] Ps 131:2 [m] Heb 5:12-13
28:11 [n] Isa 33:19 [o] 1Co 14:21*
28:12 [p] Isa 11:10; Mt 11:28-29
28:13 [q] Mt 21:44 [r] Isa 8:15
28:14 [s] Isa 1:10
28:15 [t] ver 2, 18; Isa 8:7-8; 30:28; Da 11:22 [u] Isa 9:15 [v] Isa 29:15
28:16 [w] Ps 118:22; Isa 8:14-15; Mt 21:42; Ac 4:11; Eph 2:20 [x] Ro 9:33*; 10:11*; 1Pe 2:6*
28:17 [y] Isa 5:16 [z] 2Ki 21:13
28:18 [a] Isa 7:7 [b] ver 15 [c] Da 8:13
28:19 [d] 2Ki 24:2

[a] *10* Hebrew */ sav lasav sav lasav / kav lakav kav lakav* (probably meaningless sounds mimicking the prophet's words); also in verse 13 [b] *15* Or *false gods*

He will be the source of beauty and glory for those who submit to him. He will give "justice" to the judges and "strength" to the soldiers (v. 6).

28:7–8 The priests and prophets are no better off. Alcohol abuse is only a symptom of their deeper problem. They are unwilling to surrender their needs and desires to the Lord. The result is that those who should be giving clear guidance and teaching in that desperate hour are "befuddled" (v. 7) and staggering around in a stupor.

28:9–10 These verses express the mockery of these religious leaders from the true prophet.

28:11–13 The prophet responds. Since they refuse God's invitation to rest in him, they will learn his truth through "foreign lips and strange tongues" (v. 11). If the people will not learn the easy way of faith, then they must learn the hard way of experience.

28:14–15 A scoffer is someone who not only rejects the truth but also makes light of it. These Judean scoffers have laughed at the foolishness of trusting God and made cynical covenants "with death" (v. 15a), probably referring to an alliance with Egypt.

28:16 God asserts that he alone is trustworthy. The "stone" (v. 16) is probably to be understood as God's trustworthiness.

28:17–19 The "hiding place" the leaders have so built is going to be swept away like a hut in a windstorm (v. 17). The flood will come again and again.

The understanding of this message
will bring sheer terror.[e]
20 The bed is too short to stretch
out on,
the blanket too narrow to wrap
around you.[f]
21 The LORD will rise up as he did at
Mount Perazim,[g]
he will rouse himself as in the
Valley of Gibeon[h] —
to do his work,[i] his strange work,
and perform his task, his alien
task.
22 Now stop your mocking,
or your chains will become
heavier;
the Lord, the LORD Almighty, has
told me
of the destruction decreed[j] against
the whole land.[k]

23 Listen and hear my voice;
pay attention and hear what I say.
24 When a farmer plows for planting,
does he plow continually?
Does he keep on breaking up and
working the soil?
25 When he has leveled the surface,
does he not sow caraway and
scatter cumin?[l]
Does he not plant wheat in its
place,[a]
barley in its plot,[a]
and spelt[m] in its field?
26 His God instructs him
and teaches him the right way.
27 Caraway is not threshed with a
sledge,
nor is the wheel of a cart rolled
over cumin;
caraway is beaten out with a rod,
and cumin with a stick.
28 Grain must be ground to make
bread;
so one does not go on threshing it
forever.
The wheels of a threshing cart may
be rolled over it,
but one does not use horses to
grind grain.
29 All this also comes from the LORD
Almighty,
whose plan is wonderful,[n]
whose wisdom is magnificent.[o]

28:19 [e] Job 18:11
28:20 [f] Isa 59:6
28:21 [g] 1Ch 14:11 [h] Jos 10:10, 12; 1Ch 14:16 [i] Isa 10:12; Lk 19:41-44
28:22 [j] Isa 10:22 [k] Isa 10:23
28:25 [l] Mt 23:23 [m] Ex 9:32
28:29 [n] Isa 9:6 [o] Ro 11:33
29:1 [p] Isa 22:12-13 [q] 2Sa 5:9 [r] Isa 1:14
29:2 [s] Isa 3:26; La 2:5
29:3 [t] Lk 19:43-44

Woe to David's City

29 Woe[p] to you, Ariel, Ariel,[q]
the city where David settled!
Add year to year
and let your cycle of festivals[r]
go on.
2 Yet I will besiege Ariel;
she will mourn and lament,[s]
she will be to me like an altar
hearth.[b]
3 I will encamp against you on all
sides;
I will encircle[t] you with towers

[a] *25* The meaning of the Hebrew for this word is uncertain. [b] *2* The Hebrew for *altar hearth* sounds like the Hebrew for *Ariel.*

28:20-22 Just as the Lord struck down the Philistines with a flood at "Mount Perazim" and scattered the Canaanites with hail in the "Valley of Gibeon" (v. 21), so now he will treat his own people like those enemies. The scoffers had better start listening to what "the Lord, the LORD Almighty" (v. 22) is actually saying.

28:23-29 A farmer knows that there are certain appropriate ways to do things. In each of these illustrations from the world of agriculture, Isaiah says these peasants have learned these principles from God, the Creator. Why cannot these wise counselors be as intelligent as an uneducated peasant when it comes to understanding that God can be trusted and humans cannot?

28:1-29 Some spiritual principles are as simple and ironclad as physical ones. The pagans of Isaiah's day had observed these and had written them into their civil law codes. Even they knew that no human society could long survive where lying, stealing, murder, and adultery occurred with any regularity. The Creator is a God of truth, integrity, love, and faithfulness, and thus his creation reflects that character. Modern legal theory is deeply opposed to the idea of "natural law." Isaiah would merely shake his head and point to the farmer. "Are there 'natural laws' in nature?" he would ask. If so, why would we think there are none in the rest of the natural world—that is, the world of the spirit?

29:1-2 This second "woe" is addressed to Jerusalem (v. 1), also called "Ariel" (v. 2). One possible meaning of the word is "altar hearth" (v. 2), which is the most probable explanation.

Jerusalem's problem is that the people believe they have immunity from judgment because they have the true religion of Yahweh (vv. 1, 13). Isaiah says this worship is worthless because it is heartless (v. 13).

Verse 2 suggests all of Jerusalem will become an "altar hearth" on which the people themselves will become the sacrifice.

29:3-4 Verse 4 is perhaps an allusion to the worship of the dead and to spiritism.

and set up my siege works against
you.
4 Brought low, you will speak from the
ground;
your speech will mumble[u] out of
the dust.
Your voice will come ghostlike from
the earth;
out of the dust your speech will
whisper.

5 But your many enemies will become
like fine dust,
the ruthless hordes like blown
chaff.[v]
Suddenly,[w] in an instant,
6 the LORD Almighty will come
with thunder and earthquake[x] and
great noise,
with windstorm and tempest and
flames of a devouring fire.
7 Then the hordes of all the nations[y]
that fight against Ariel,
that attack her and her fortress
and besiege her,
will be as it is with a dream,[z]
with a vision in the night—
8 as when a hungry person dreams of
eating,
but awakens[a] hungry still;
as when a thirsty person dreams of
drinking,
but awakens faint and thirsty still.
So will it be with the hordes of all
the nations
that fight against Mount Zion.

9 Be stunned and amazed,
blind yourselves and be sightless;
be drunk,[b] but not from wine,[c]
stagger, but not from beer.
10 The LORD has brought over you a
deep sleep:
He has sealed your eyes[d] (the
prophets);[e]
he has covered your heads (the
seers).[f]

29:4 [u] Isa 8:19
29:5 [v] Isa 17:13 [w] Isa 17:14; 1Th 5:3
29:6 [x] Mt 24:7; Mk 13:8; Lk 21:11; Rev 11:19
29:7 [y] Mic 4:11-12; Zec 12:9 [z] Job 20:8
29:8 [a] Ps 73:20
29:9 [b] Isa 51:17 [c] Isa 51:21-22
29:10 [d] Ps 69:23; Isa 6:9-10; Ro 11:8* [e] Mic 3:6 [f] Isa 9:9
29:11 [g] Isa 8:16; Mt 13:11; Rev 5:1-2
29:13 [h] Eze 33:31 [i] Mt 15:8-9*; Mk 7:6-7*; Col 2:22
29:14 [j] Hab 1:5 [k] Jer 8:9; 49:7 [l] Isa 6:9-10; 1Co 1:19*
29:15 [m] Ps 10:11-13; 94:7; Isa 57:12 [n] Job 22:13
29:16 [o] Isa 45:9; 64:8; Ro 9:20-21*

Isa 29:13 ❖ Where do we see people honoring God with their words while their hearts are far from him? When might we have been guilty of this?

11 For you this whole vision is nothing
but words sealed[g] in a scroll. And if you
give the scroll to someone who can read,
and say, "Read this, please," they will answer, "I can't; it is sealed." 12 Or if you give
the scroll to someone who cannot read,
and say, "Read this, please," they will answer, "I don't know how to read."

13 The Lord says:

"These people come near to me with
their mouth
and honor me with their lips,
but their hearts are far from me.[h]
Their worship of me
is based on merely human rules
they have been taught.[a][i]
14 Therefore once more I will astound
these people
with wonder upon wonder;[j]
the wisdom of the wise[k] will perish,
the intelligence of the intelligent
will vanish.[l]"
15 Woe to those who go to great
depths
to hide their plans from the
LORD,
who do their work in darkness and
think,
"Who sees us?[m] Who will know?"[n]
16 You turn things upside down,
as if the potter were thought to be
like the clay!
Shall what is formed say to the one
who formed it,
"You did not make me"?
Can the pot say to the potter,[o]
"You know nothing"?

[a] 13 Hebrew; Septuagint *They worship me in vain; / their teachings are merely human rules*

29:5-8 Because God, not Assyria, puts his people into the dust, God can make Jerusalem's enemies as insubstantial as "fine dust" (v. 5). They appear so weighty, but before God they are as thin and as vaporous as a "dream" (vv. 7, 8).
29:9-12 The people have blinded themselves, yet at the same time, God has made the prophets unable to see the truth. As a result, the word of God is a closed book to the people.
29:13-14 Jerusalem's religion has become a performance with its inhabitants themselves as both actors and audience. They go through the motions with no expectation of any real encounter with the living God.

✤ **29:1-14** The pagans believed that when certain human activities had been performed, the gods were compelled to respond. Their activity had more to do with manipulation than worship. Again and again, the OT speaks out against such an idea. God cannot be manipulated through anything done in this world. He forgives through his grace alone.

29:15-24 This third "woe" is composed of both judgment (vv. 15-16) and hope (vv. 17-24).
29:15-16 The counselors have made their "plans"

17 In a very short time, will not
Lebanon be turned into a
fertile field[p]
and the fertile field seem like a
forest?[q]
18 In that day the deaf[r] will hear the
words of the scroll,
and out of gloom and darkness
the eyes of the blind will see.[s]
19 Once more the humble[t] will rejoice
in the LORD;
the needy[u] will rejoice in the Holy
One of Israel.
20 The ruthless will vanish,
the mockers[v] will disappear,
and all who have an eye for evil[w]
will be cut down—
21 those who with a word make
someone out to be guilty,
who ensnare the defender in
court[x]
and with false testimony deprive
the innocent of justice.[y]

22 Therefore this is what the LORD, who
redeemed Abraham,[z] says to the descendants of Jacob:

"No longer will Jacob be ashamed;[a]
no longer will their faces grow
pale.
23 When they see among them their
children,[b]
the work of my hands,[c]
they will keep my name holy;
they will acknowledge the
holiness of the Holy One of
Jacob,
and will stand in awe of the God of
Israel.
24 Those who are wayward[d] in spirit
will gain understanding;[e]
those who complain will accept
instruction."[f]

Woe to the Obstinate Nation

30 "Woe[g] to the obstinate
children,"[h]
declares the LORD,
"to those who carry out plans that
are not mine,
forming an alliance,[i] but not by
my Spirit,
heaping sin upon sin;
2 who go down to Egypt[j]
without consulting[k] me;
who look for help to Pharaoh's
protection,[l]
to Egypt's shade for refuge.
3 But Pharaoh's protection will be to
your shame,
Egypt's shade will bring you
disgrace.[m]
4 Though they have officials in Zoan[n]
and their envoys have arrived in
Hanes,
5 everyone will be put to shame
because of a people[o] useless to
them,
who bring neither help nor
advantage,
but only shame and disgrace."

6 A prophecy concerning the animals
of the Negev:

Through a land of hardship and
distress,[p]
of lions and lionesses,
of adders and darting snakes,[q]

29:17 [p] Ps 84:6 [q] Isa 32:15
29:18 [r] Mk 7:37 [s] Isa 32:3; 35:5; Mt 11:5
29:19 [t] Isa 61:1; Mt 5:5; 11:29 [u] Isa 14:30; Mt 11:5; Jas 1:9; 2:5
29:20 [v] Isa 28:22 [w] Isa 59:4; Mic 2:1
29:21 [x] Am 5:10, 15 [y] Isa 5:23; 32:7
29:22 [z] Isa 41:8; 63:16 [a] Isa 49:23
29:23 [b] Isa 49:20-26 [c] Isa 19:25
29:24 [d] Isa 28:7; Heb 5:2 [e] Isa 41:20; 60:16 [f] Isa 30:21
30:1 [g] Isa 29:15 [h] Isa 1:2 [i] Isa 8:12
30:2 [j] Isa 31:1 [k] Nu 27:21 [l] Isa 36:9
30:3 [m] Isa 20:4-5; 36:6
30:4 [n] Isa 19:11
30:5 [o] ver 7
30:6 [p] Ex 5:10, 21; Isa 8:22; Jer 11:4 [q] Dt 8:15

(v. 15) without consulting the Lord's prophet, foolishly hoping he will not find out. Isaiah says this is like the pot telling the potter how to do his work.

29:17–24 The promises made here are more far-reaching than for mere physical restoration. They deal primarily with the spiritual needs of the nation. They promise a day when the kinds of attitudes and behaviors that have brought the nation to this dark day will be radically changed.

Those who are in covenant with God are committed to replicating God's holy character, his "name" (v. 23), in their own behavior. No longer will the descendants of Jacob take "the Holy One" for granted (v. 23). Instead of the stubbornness, willfulness, and general hardheadedness that tend to characterize all humans (not just Israel), there will be a grasp of "understanding" and a genuine teachability (v. 24).

✚ **29:15–24** Here in Isaiah, God promises that the day will come when believers can fulfill the demands of the covenant. Through what Christ has done for us in forgiving the sin of the broken covenant and in giving us his Spirit, it is now possible for us to fulfill all the "righteous requirement[s] of the law" (Ro 8:3–4) in real life.

30:1–5 God has carefully reared these "children," but they do not consult their Father for advice (v. 1). Because they are "wayward in spirit" (29:24), they refuse to be led by God's Spirit.

On the surface, Egypt is large enough and powerful enough to be like a large palm tree, whose fronds offer "shade" (30:2) from Assyria's blazing sun. But God sees things differently: Everyone who puts their trust in Egypt will be disgraced (v. 5).

30:6–7 This idea of Egypt's helplessness is illustrated in a two-verse "prophecy" (v. 6). The mention of "envoys" (v. 6) suggests that this is a diplomatic mission and that the caravan is carrying a large payment for the Egyptian "help" (v. 7).

the envoys carry their riches on
donkeys' backs,
their treasures[r] on the humps of
camels,
to that unprofitable nation,
7 to Egypt, whose help is utterly
useless.
Therefore I call her
Rahab the Do-Nothing.

8 Go now, write it on a tablet for them,
inscribe it on a scroll,[s]
that for the days to come
it may be an everlasting witness.
9 For these are rebellious people,
deceitful[t] children,
children unwilling to listen to the
LORD's instruction.[u]
10 They say to the seers,
"See no more visions[v]!"
and to the prophets,
"Give us no more visions of what
is right!
Tell us pleasant things,[w]
prophesy illusions.[x]
11 Leave this way,
get off this path,
and stop confronting[y] us
with the Holy One of Israel!"

12 Therefore this is what the Holy One
of Israel says:

"Because you have rejected this
message,[z]
relied on oppression[a]
and depended on deceit,
13 this sin will become for you
like a high wall,[b] cracked and
bulging,
that collapses[c] suddenly,[d] in an
instant.
14 It will break in pieces like pottery,[e]

30:6 [r]Isa 15:7
30:8 [s]Isa 8:1; Hab 2:2
30:9 [t]Isa 28:15; 59:3-4 [u]Isa 1:10
30:10 [v]Jer 11:21; Am 7:13 [w]1Ki 22:8 [x]Eze 13:7; Ro 16:18
30:11 [y]Job 21:14
30:12 [z]Isa 5:24 [a]Isa 5:7
30:13 [b]Ps 62:3 [c]1Ki 20:30 [d]Isa 29:5
30:14 [e]Ps 2:9; Jer 19:10-11
30:15 [f]Isa 32:17
30:16 [g]Isa 31:1,3
30:17 [h]Lev 26:8; Jos 23:10 [i]Lev 26:36; Dt 28:25
30:18 [j]Isa 42:14; 2Pe 3:9, 15 [k]Isa 5:16 [l]Isa 25:9
30:19 [m]Isa 60:20; 61:3

Isa 30:10–11 ❖ What causes people to want to silence the word of God and not listen to God's messengers?

shattered so mercilessly
that among its pieces not a fragment
will be found
for taking coals from a hearth
or scooping water out of a cistern."

15 This is what the Sovereign LORD, the
Holy One of Israel, says:

"In repentance and rest is your
salvation,
in quietness and trust[f] is your
strength,
but you would have none of it.
16 You said, 'No, we will flee on
horses.'[g]
Therefore you will flee!
You said, 'We will ride off on swift
horses.'
Therefore your pursuers will be
swift!
17 A thousand will flee
at the threat of one;
at the threat of five[h]
you will all flee[i] away,
till you are left
like a flagstaff on a mountaintop,
like a banner on a hill."

18 Yet the LORD longs[j] to be gracious to
you;
therefore he will rise up to show
you compassion.
For the LORD is a God of justice.[k]
Blessed are all who wait for him![l]

19 People of Zion, who live in Jerusalem,
you will weep no more.[m] How gracious he
will be when you cry for help! As soon as

30:8–11 Isaiah offers the purpose of writing down prophetic words, so that when the predictions come true, people will know it. The people do not want to hear "the LORD's instruction" (v. 9) or "what is right" (v. 10). Instead, they ask the prophets to say pleasant things to them. They may not literally ask for "illusions" (v. 10), but Isaiah says that is what they are actually asking for (v. 11).
30:12–14 Ironically, Isaiah's response is to tell them "what the Holy One of Israel says" (v. 12). They have rejected the truth that God alone can be trusted and instead have trusted in "oppression" (v. 12) and lies. As a result, their destruction will come as suddenly as a collapsing wall.
30:15 God has told them again and again the prescription for their condition. They must turn back to him in "repentance" and "rest" in him. In quietly trusting him, they will find both "salvation" and "strength."
30:16–17 Verse 16 offers a strong contrast with v. 15. Instead of quietness and trust, there will be rapid flight, and their "pursuers" will overtake them (v. 16). As a result, they will be as forlorn as a tattered flag whipping in the wind, with nothing but corpses surrounding it.
30:18 So, what is God's course of action in the face of this reality? Isaiah presents the picture of the Creator of the universe patiently standing, waiting for us to turn back to him to receive the grace and compassion that are in his fatherly heart.
30:19–22 This last section details what will happen when the Israelites finally come to their senses and turn back to God. Isaiah sees a day coming when the people will "cry" (v. 19) out to God, and

he hears, he will answer[n] you. 20Although
the Lord gives you the bread[o] of adversity
and the water of affliction, your teachers will be hidden[p] no more; with your
own eyes you will see them. 21Whether
you turn to the right or to the left, your
ears will hear a voice[q] behind you, saying,
"This is the way; walk in it." 22Then you
will desecrate your idols[r] overlaid with
silver and your images covered with gold;
you will throw them away like a menstrual cloth and say to them, "Away with you!"

23He will also send you rain[s] for the
seed you sow in the ground, and the food
that comes from the land will be rich
and plentiful. In that day your cattle will
graze in broad meadows.[t] 24The oxen and
donkeys that work the soil will eat fodder and mash, spread out with fork[u] and
shovel. 25In the day of great slaughter,
when the towers[v] fall, streams of water
will flow[w] on every high mountain and
every lofty hill. 26The moon will shine
like the sun,[x] and the sunlight will be
seven times brighter, like the light of
seven full days, when the LORD binds up
the bruises of his people and heals[y] the
wounds he inflicted.

27 See, the Name[z] of the LORD comes
 from afar,
 with burning anger[a] and dense
 clouds of smoke;
his lips are full of wrath,[b]
 and his tongue is a consuming
 fire.
28 His breath[c] is like a rushing torrent,
 rising up to the neck.[d]
He shakes the nations in the sieve[e]
 of destruction;
he places in the jaws of the
 peoples
 a bit[f] that leads them astray.
29 And you will sing
 as on the night you celebrate a
 holy festival;
your hearts will rejoice
 as when people playing pipes
 go up
to the mountain[g] of the LORD,
 to the Rock of Israel.
30 The LORD will cause people to hear
 his majestic voice
 and will make them see his arm
 coming down
with raging anger and consuming
 fire,
 with cloudburst, thunderstorm
 and hail.
31 The voice of the LORD will shatter
 Assyria;[h]
 with his rod he will strike[i] them
 down.
32 Every stroke the LORD lays on them
 with his punishing club
will be to the music of timbrels and
 harps,
 as he fights them in battle with
 the blows of his arm.[j]
33 Topheth[k] has long been prepared;
 it has been made ready for the
 king.
Its fire pit has been made deep and
 wide,
 with an abundance of fire and
 wood;
the breath of the LORD,
 like a stream of burning
 sulfur,[l]
 sets it ablaze.

30:19 [n] Ps 50:15; Isa 58:9; 65:24; Mt 7:7-11
30:20 [o] 1Ki 22:27 [p] Ps 74:9; Am 8:11
30:21 [q] Isa 29:24
30:22 [r] Ex 32:4
30:23 [s] Isa 65:21-22 [t] Ps 65:13
30:24 [u] Mt 3:12; Lk 3:17
30:25 [v] Isa 2:15 [w] Isa 41:18
30:26 [x] Isa 24:23; 60:19-20; Rev 21:23; 22:5 [y] Dt 32:39; Isa 1:5
30:27 [z] Isa 59:19 [a] Isa 66:14 [b] Isa 10:5
30:28 [c] Isa 11:4 [d] Isa 8:8 [e] Am 9:9 [f] 2Ki 19:28; Isa 37:29
30:29 [g] Ps 42:4
30:31 [h] Isa 10:5, 12 [i] Isa 11:4
30:32 [j] Isa 11:15; Eze 32:10
30:33 [k] 2Ki 23:10 [l] Ge 19:24

he will "answer" them with grace (v. 19). Their spiritual eyes will be open. Their spiritual ears will only need the merest whisper to turn them to the right or the left. As a result, they will despise all of their expensive idols.

30:23–26 When God's people are responsive and have stopped manipulating the physical, social, and spiritual world for their own advantage, God will bless freely.

30:25–26 The contrast here is between "slaughter" (v. 25) and healing. This may refer to earth's final battle (cf. Zec 14:1–4; Mal 4:1–2). It may also refer to the destruction of pride, because height, barrenness, and darkness are associated with pride elsewhere in the book (Isa 2:12–17; 8:21–22; 47:5).

30:27–33 In the final promise, the language has a certain "end of history" flavor. Yet v. 31 makes it clear that the ultimate subject of God's wrath here is Assyria. This should make us cautious about what passages we assign as "end-time" promises.

One recurring feature is a reference to the Lord's mouth, breath, and voice (vv. 27, 28, 30, 31, 33). Just as his word is life and health to those who respond to it, it is sudden, terrible death to those who reject it.

30:1–33 Just as the OT put the correct relationship with God within the context of absolute loyalty to a covenant king, the NT calls us to turn from loyalty to ourselves and become the glad subjects of heaven's King (1Pe 5:6). If we find real trust difficult, perhaps it is because there has never been a real change of king in our lives. The idea that we can have the benefits of the kingdom without turning away from our own attempts at personal kingship is a fallacy.

Woe to Those Who Rely on Egypt

31 Woe to those who go down to
Egypt[m] for help,
who rely on horses,
who trust in the multitude of their
chariots[n]
and in the great strength of their
horsemen,
but do not look to the Holy One of
Israel,
or seek help from the LORD.[o]
2 Yet he too is wise[p] and can bring
disaster;[q]
he does not take back his words.[r]
He will rise up against that wicked
nation,[s]
against those who help evildoers.
3 But the Egyptians[t] are mere mortals
and not God;[u]
their horses are flesh and not
spirit.
When the LORD stretches out his
hand,[v]
those who help will stumble,
those who are helped[w] will fall;
all will perish together.

4 This is what the LORD says to me:

"As a lion[x] growls,
a great lion over its prey—
and though a whole band of
shepherds
is called together against it,
it is not frightened by their shouts
or disturbed by their clamor—
so the LORD Almighty will come
down[y]
to do battle on Mount Zion and on
its heights.
5 Like birds hovering overhead,
the LORD Almighty will shield[z]
Jerusalem;
he will shield it and deliver[a] it,
he will 'pass over' it and will
rescue it."

6 Return, you Israelites, to the One you
have so greatly revolted against. 7 For in
that day every one of you will reject the
idols of silver and gold[b] your sinful hands
have made.

8 "Assyria[c] will fall by no human
sword;
a sword, not of mortals, will
devour[d] them.
They will flee before the sword
and their young men will be put
to forced labor.[e]
9 Their stronghold[f] will fall because of
terror;
at the sight of the battle standard
their commanders will panic,"
declares the LORD,
whose fire[g] is in Zion,
whose furnace is in Jerusalem.

The Kingdom of Righteousness

32 See, a king[h] will reign in
righteousness
and rulers will rule with justice.[i]
2 Each one will be like a shelter[j] from
the wind
and a refuge from the storm,
like streams of water in the desert
and the shadow of a great rock in
a thirsty land.

3 Then the eyes of those who see will
no longer be closed,[k]

31:1 [m] Dt 17:16; Isa 30:2, 5 [n] Isa 2:7 [o] Ps 20:7; Da 9:13
31:2 [p] Ro 16:27 [q] Isa 45:7 [r] Nu 23:19 [s] Isa 32:6
31:3 [t] Isa 36:9 [u] Eze 28:9; 2Th 2:4 [v] Isa 9:17, 21 [w] Isa 30:5-7
31:4 [x] Nu 24:9; Hos 11:10; Am 3:8 [y] Isa 42:13
31:5 [z] Ps 91:4 [a] Isa 37:35; 38:6
31:7 [b] Isa 2:20; 30:22
31:8 [c] Isa 10:12 [d] Isa 14:25; 37:7 [e] Ge 49:15
31:9 [f] Dt 32:31, 37 [g] Isa 10:17
32:1 [h] Eze 37:24 [i] Ps 72:1-4; Isa 9:7
32:2 [j] Isa 4:6
32:3 [k] Isa 29:18

Isa 31:1-3 ❖ When have we relied on human strength—our own or someone else's—rather than God's power? What happened when we did?

31:1-3 The present "woe" is specifically against "those who go down to Egypt for help" (v. 1). They have chosen to trust pagan armies and horses instead of "the Holy One of Israel" (v. 1). They have chosen to trust the creation rather than the Creator. This is foolish, as vv. 2-3 explains.

31:4-9 Isaiah has been counseling the Israelites not to trust Egypt because Egypt cannot help. Here he develops the other side of the argument: Trust the Lord because he is the only One who can deliver you.

Just as vv. 1-3 are the most specific in denouncing the counsel to trust Egypt, so vv. 8-9 are the most specific in promising deliverance from the Assyrian threat. Isaiah's main point is that it is much wiser to trust God than Egypt in the face of the Assyrians.

✜ **31:1-9** The Jews in Jesus' day read the prophecies of the Messiah and were almost completely unprepared for the way in which they were actually fulfilled. We need to be reading the text with faith and yet openness to the ways God works in the world; God loves to do things in new ways.

32:1-4 There seems to be good reason to see this material as God's promise of his Messiah in view of the failure of all the human messiahs. The blessing is described in four vivid similes in v. 2: a "shelter," a "refuge," "streams of water," and "shadow" (or shade) in the desert. In this new kingdom, "eyes" will see, and "ears" will hear (v. 3).

and the ears of those who hear
will listen.
4 The fearful heart will know and
understand,[l]
and the stammering tongue will
be fluent and clear.
5 No longer will the fool[m] be called
noble
nor the scoundrel be highly
respected.
6 For fools speak folly,[n]
their hearts are bent on evil:
They practice ungodliness[o]
and spread error[p] concerning the
LORD;
the hungry they leave empty[q]
and from the thirsty they
withhold water.
7 Scoundrels use wicked methods,[r]
they make up evil schemes[s]
to destroy the poor with lies,
even when the plea of the needy[t]
is just.
8 But the noble make noble plans,
and by noble deeds[u] they stand.

The Women of Jerusalem

9 You women who are so complacent,
rise up and listen[v] to me;
you daughters who feel secure,[w]
hear what I have to say!
10 In little more than a year
you who feel secure will tremble;
the grape harvest will fail,[x]
and the harvest of fruit will not
come.
11 Tremble, you complacent women;
shudder, you daughters who feel
secure!
Strip off your fine clothes[y]
and wrap yourselves in rags.

Isa 32:16-18 ❖ How does true righteousness bring peace and confidence into our lives?

12 Beat your breasts[z] for the pleasant
fields,
for the fruitful vines
13 and for the land of my people,
a land overgrown with thorns and
briers[a] —
yes, mourn for all houses of
merriment
and for this city of revelry.[b]
14 The fortress[c] will be abandoned,
the noisy city deserted;[d]
citadel and watchtower[e] will become
a wasteland forever,
the delight of donkeys,[f] a pasture
for flocks,
15 till the Spirit[g] is poured on us from
on high,
and the desert becomes a fertile
field,[h]
and the fertile field seems like a
forest.[i]
16 The LORD's justice will dwell in the
desert,
his righteousness live in the
fertile field.
17 The fruit of that righteousness will
be peace;[j]
its effect will be quietness and
confidence[k] forever.
18 My people will live in peaceful
dwelling places,
in secure homes,
in undisturbed places of rest.[l]
19 Though hail[m] flattens the forest[n]
and the city is leveled[o]
completely,

32:4 [l] Isa 29:24
32:5 [m] 1Sa 25:25
32:6 [n] Pr 19:3 [o] Isa 9:17 [p] Isa 9:16 [q] Isa 3:15
32:7 [r] Jer 5:26-28 [s] Mic 7:3 [t] Isa 61:1
32:8 [u] Pr 11:25
32:9 [v] Isa 28:23 [w] Isa 47:8; Am 6:1; Zep 2:15
32:10 [x] Isa 5:5-6; 24:7
32:11 [y] Isa 47:2
32:12 [z] Na 2:7
32:13 [a] Isa 5:6 [b] Isa 22:2
32:14 [c] Isa 13:22 [d] Isa 6:11; 27:10 [e] Isa 34:13 [f] Ps 104:11
32:15 [g] Isa 11:2; Joel 2:28 [h] Ps 107:35; Isa 35:1-2 [i] Isa 29:17
32:17 [j] Ps 119:165; Ro 14:17; Jas 3:18 [k] Isa 30:15
32:18 [l] Hos 2:18-23
32:19 [m] Isa 28:17; 30:30 [n] Isa 10:19; Zec 11:2 [o] Isa 24:10; 27:10

32:5-8 Here is a lengthy contrast between the "fool" and the "noble" (v. 5). Those who are "noble" have learned that God can be trusted to supply their needs. They no longer need to grasp but can give.

✚ **32:1-8** Money has no morality, but the people who make it and give it do. The "fool" who gives believes that their gifts entitle them to manipulate and control; those who give in a "noble" way do not give with ulterior motives.

32:9-11 These verses condemn "women" who are "complacent" and "secure" (v. 9), for in only one year, all that will be changed. They should start mourning now (vv. 11-12) because of the agricultural disaster about to come on them.
32:12-14 The land and nation will become barren and deserted. "Merriment" and "revelry" will cease (v. 13). All the places where strength could be expected will be abandoned.
32:15-20 But the warning of the previous passage will not mean God has failed. The prediction of tragedy is immediately followed by God's promise of hope. God has something in mind that will make possible true productivity and security—namely, his own "Spirit" (v. 15). In the messianic kingdom, the Spirit will fall on barren hearts. The things that the covenant required but could not produce—"justice" and "righteousness" (v. 16)—will spring up.

✚ **32:9-20** Just as Isaiah had promised, the Messiah, through the Holy Spirit he has given, makes it possible for Christians to live a life of true nobility. When we believe in Jesus

20 how blessed you will be,
sowing[p] your seed by every stream,
and letting your cattle and
donkeys range free.[q]

Distress and Help

33 Woe to you, destroyer,
you who have not been destroyed!
Woe to you, betrayer,
you who have not been betrayed!
When you stop destroying,
you will be destroyed;[r]
when you stop betraying,
you will be betrayed.[s]

2 LORD, be gracious to us;
we long for you.
Be our strength[t] every morning,
our salvation[u] in time of distress.
3 At the uproar of your army, the
peoples flee;
when you rise up,[v] the nations
scatter.
4 Your plunder, O nations, is harvested
as by young locusts;
like a swarm of locusts people
pounce on it.
5 The LORD is exalted,[w] for he dwells
on high;
he will fill Zion with his justice[x]
and righteousness.[y]
6 He will be the sure foundation for
your times,
a rich store of salvation[z] and
wisdom and knowledge;
the fear[a] of the LORD is the key to
this treasure.[a]

7 Look, their brave men cry aloud in
the streets;
the envoys[b] of peace weep bitterly.
8 The highways are deserted,
no travelers are on the roads.[c]
The treaty is broken,
its witnesses[b] are despised,
no one is respected.
9 The land dries up[d] and wastes away,
Lebanon[e] is ashamed and
withers;[f]
Sharon is like the Arabah,
and Bashan and Carmel drop their
leaves.

10 "Now will I arise,[g]" says the LORD.
"Now will I be exalted;
now will I be lifted up.
11 You conceive[h] chaff,
you give birth[i] to straw;
your breath is a fire[j] that
consumes you.
12 The peoples will be burned to ashes;
like cut thornbushes they will be
set ablaze.[k]"

13 You who are far away,[l] hear[m] what I
have done;
you who are near, acknowledge
my power!
14 The sinners in Zion are terrified;
trembling[n] grips the godless:
"Who of us can dwell with the
consuming fire?[o]
Who of us can dwell with
everlasting burning?"
15 Those who walk righteously[p]
and speak what is right,[q]
who reject gain from extortion
and keep their hands from
accepting bribes,

32:20 [p] Ecc 11:1 [q] Isa 30:24
33:1 [r] Hab 2:8; Mt 7:2 [s] Isa 21:2
33:2 [t] Isa 40:10; 51:9; 59:16 [u] Isa 25:9
33:3 [v] Isa 59:16-18
33:5 [w] Ps 97:9 [x] Isa 28:6 [y] Isa 1:26
33:6 [z] Isa 51:6 [a] Isa 11:2-3; Mt 6:33
33:7 [b] 2Ki 18:37
33:8 [c] Jdg 5:6; Isa 35:8
33:9 [d] Isa 3:26 [e] Isa 2:13; 35:2 [f] Isa 24:4
33:10 [g] Ps 12:5; Isa 2:21
33:11 [h] Ps 7:14; Isa 59:4; Jas 1:15 [i] Isa 26:18 [j] Isa 1:31
33:12 [k] Isa 10:17
33:13 [l] Ps 48:10; 49:1 [m] Isa 49:1
33:14 [n] Isa 32:11 [o] Isa 30:30; Heb 12:29
33:15 [p] Isa 58:8 [q] Ps 15:2; 24:4

[a] 6 Or *is a treasure from him* [b] 8 Dead Sea Scrolls; Masoretic Text / *the cities*

---

and trust him for our salvation, we take hold of inner resources with which we can meet everything that comes at us and can triumph over any circumstances.

33:1–4 The emphasis on betrayal in v. 1 is used as a foil to depict the radically different character of the biblical God and of the kingdom he will build. **33:5–6** The Lord is the only One who is truly "exalted" (v. 5). His character will provide a "foundation" on which people can live with confidence (v. 6). That foundation is "justice" and "righteousness" (v. 5), and on it can be erected "salvation and wisdom and knowledge" (v. 6). All of this is available to the person who acknowledges that God is the Lord and gives him reverent obedience. **33:7–14** Verses 7–9 paint a picture of hopelessness. But there *is* hope. Assyria started a fire, and one day God will bring that fire back on them. He is the "everlasting burning" (v. 14) with whom people must somehow come to terms. But how can mere humans "dwell" with him (v. 14)? It is not God's mystical essence that separates us from himself; rather, it is his character. Thus, what is required is a change of character on our part.
33:15–16 Here the specifics of "right" behavior are spelled out (v. 15). The behaviors are primarily relational. Such a person can "dwell" with God on the "heights" (v. 16). In that setting, they will be secure and have their needs supplied.

✤ **33:1–16** No one can earn a place with God by their righteous behavior. Rather, God gives us that place because Jesus Christ has died in our place. But God has not only given us eternal life; he has also given us his Spirit so that we can strive to reflect, in our daily lives, our only Savior.

who stop their ears against plots of murder
and shut their eyes[r] against contemplating evil—
16 they are the ones who will dwell on the heights,
whose refuge[s] will be the mountain fortress.[t]
Their bread will be supplied,
and water will not fail[u] them.

17 Your eyes will see the king[v] in his beauty
and view a land that stretches afar.[w]
18 In your thoughts you will ponder the former terror:[x]
"Where is that chief officer?
Where is the one who took the revenue?
Where is the officer in charge of the towers?"
19 You will see those arrogant people no more,
people whose speech is obscure,
whose language is strange and incomprehensible.[y]

20 Look on Zion, the city of our festivals;
your eyes will see Jerusalem,
a peaceful abode,[z] a tent that will not be moved;[a]
its stakes will never be pulled up,
nor any of its ropes broken.
21 There the LORD will be our Mighty One.
It will be like a place of broad rivers and streams.[b]
No galley with oars will ride them,
no mighty ship will sail them.

33:15 [r] Ps 119:37
33:16 [s] Isa 25:4 [t] Isa 26:1 [u] Isa 49:10
33:17 [v] Isa 6:5 [w] Isa 26:15
33:18 [x] Isa 17:14
33:19 [y] Isa 28:11; Jer 5:15
33:20 [z] Isa 32:18 [a] Ps 46:5; 125:1-2
33:21 [b] Isa 41:18; 48:18; 66:12

33:22 [c] Isa 11:4 [d] Isa 2:3; Jas 4:12 [e] Ps 89:18 [f] Isa 25:9
33:23 [g] 2Ki 7:8 [h] 2Ki 7:16
33:24 [i] Isa 30:26 [j] Jer 50:20; 1Jn 1:7-9
34:1 [k] Isa 41:1; 43:9 [l] Ps 49:1 [m] Dt 32:1
34:2 [n] Isa 13:5 [o] Isa 30:25
34:3 [p] Joel 2:20; Am 4:10 [q] ver 7; Eze 14:19; 35:6; 38:22

Isa 33:20–24 ❖ How have we experienced the safety and protection God promises his people?

22 For the LORD is our judge,[c]
the LORD is our lawgiver,[d]
the LORD is our king;[e]
it is he who will save[f] us.

23 Your rigging hangs loose:
The mast is not held secure,
the sail is not spread.
Then an abundance of spoils will be divided
and even the lame[g] will carry off plunder.[h]
24 No one living in Zion will say, "I am ill";[i]
and the sins of those who dwell there will be forgiven.[j]

Judgment Against the Nations

34 Come near, you nations, and listen;
pay attention, you peoples![k]
Let the earth[l] hear, and all that is in it,
the world, and all that comes out of it![m]
2 The LORD is angry with all nations;
his wrath is on all their armies.
He will totally destroy[a][n] them,
he will give them over to slaughter.[o]
3 Their slain will be thrown out,
their dead bodies will stink;[p]
the mountains will be soaked with their blood.[q]

[a] 2 The Hebrew term refers to the irrevocable giving over of things or persons to the LORD, often by totally destroying them; also in verse 5.

33:17–19 The "king" (v. 17) here is the One to whom Hezekiah goes in humble subjection (vv. 16–20) and who thereby removes the Assyrian siege "towers" (v. 18) from Jerusalem. This divine King makes it so that the alien Assyrian speech is not heard in Judah for a long time.

33:20–22 The city will have peaceful "rivers and streams" (v. 21) flowing through it, a symbol of peace and abundance. Why? Because of the righteous character of the Lord, who is Israel's "king" (v. 22).

33:23–24 It is not clear who is being addressed in the first half of v. 23. However, in the overall context, it is most likely the destroying, betraying nation with which the chapter began.

The final promise for the Zion ruled by the Messiah is that it will be a place of health, both physical and spiritual. All the effects of its inhabitants' "sins" (v. 24) will be done away with.

33:17–24 In Christ there are endless opportunities for growth and development. He does not press us into a mold to produce robots who will serve him. Rather, he calls us friends, allowing each of us to find our own place in his kingdom plans and purposes. His plans for us have been on his mind since before we were born (Ps 139:13–18), and he delights in leading us into following his way (Ro 8:29).

34:1–4 God calls the defendants to hear the decree pronounced against them. The judgment affects the entire cosmos. This is a conflict between the

4 All the stars in the sky will be
dissolved[r]
and the heavens rolled up[s] like a
scroll;
all the starry host will fall[t]
like withered leaves from the vine,
like shriveled figs from the fig
tree.

5 My sword[u] has drunk its fill in the
heavens;
see, it descends in judgment on
Edom,[v]
the people I have totally
destroyed.[w]
6 The sword of the LORD is bathed in
blood,
it is covered with fat—
the blood of lambs and goats,
fat from the kidneys of rams.
For the LORD has a sacrifice in
Bozrah
and a great slaughter in the land
of Edom.
7 And the wild oxen will fall with
them,
the bull calves and the great
bulls.[x]
Their land will be drenched with
blood,
and the dust will be soaked with
fat.

8 For the LORD has a day of
vengeance,[y]
a year of retribution, to uphold
Zion's cause.
9 Edom's streams will be turned into
pitch,
her dust into burning sulfur;
her land will become blazing
pitch!
10 It will not be quenched night or day;
its smoke will rise forever.[z]
From generation to generation it
will lie desolate;[a]
no one will ever pass through it
again.
11 The desert owl[a][b] and screech owl[a]
will possess it;
the great owl[a] and the raven will
nest there.
God will stretch out over Edom
the measuring line of chaos
and the plumb line[c] of desolation.
12 Her nobles will have nothing there
to be called a kingdom,
all her princes[d] will vanish[e] away.
13 Thorns will overrun her citadels,
nettles and brambles her
strongholds.[f]
She will become a haunt for jackals,[g]
a home for owls.
14 Desert creatures will meet with
hyenas,[h]
and wild goats will bleat to each
other;
there the night creatures will also lie
down
and find for themselves places of
rest.
15 The owl will nest there and lay eggs,

34:4 [r] Isa 13:13; 2Pe 3:10 [s] Eze 32:7-8 [t] Joel 2:31; Mt 24:29*; Rev 6:13
34:5 [u] Dt 32:41-42; Jer 46:10; Eze 21:5 [v] Am 1:11-12 [w] Isa 24:6; Mal 1:4
34:7 [x] Ps 68:30
34:8 [y] Isa 63:4
34:10 [z] Rev 14:10-11; 19:3 [a] Isa 13:20; 24:1; Eze 29:12; Mal 1:3
34:11 [b] Zep 2:14; Rev 18:2 [c] 2Ki 21:13; La 2:8
34:12 [d] Jer 27:20; 39:6 [e] Isa 41:11-12
34:13 [f] Isa 13:22; 32:13 [g] Ps 44:19; Jer 9:11; 10:22
34:14 [h] Isa 13:22

Isa 34:8–15 ❖ Where have we seen chaos and desolation beset the lives of those who reject God?

a *11* The precise identification of these birds is uncertain.

Creator and those who have rebelled against him; it is a conflict with cosmic consequences.

34:5–17 Why is Edom singled out to represent the nations of the earth? As early as the entry of Israel into the land of Canaan, Edom opposed God's plan (Nu 20:14–21). The section on Edom can be divided in two parts. The first (Isa 34:5–8) speaks of the bloody destruction that is going to fall on Edom for Zion's sake. The second part (vv. 9–17) speaks of the desert that Edom will become.

The description in vv. 9–17 goes into considerable detail to make its point. The language of vv. 9–10 is reminiscent of the destruction of Sodom and Gomorrah in Ge 19. This may be another reason why Edom is chosen to represent the destruction of the nations: Its territory is largely desert, which is nearly uninhabitable. Thus, it fits what Isaiah wants to say about the results of trusting human glory. The nations of the earth have chosen to flaunt their rebellion and must pay the price for doing so.

34:1–17 What are our churches trusting in? Large budgets, impressive buildings, powerful preaching? If so, we have put our trust in the creature. The place given to prayer in a local congregation is a good measure of where a church's trust really is. If its only focused praying is the Sunday morning pastoral prayer, that congregation is headed into the desert. By contrast, when a congregation makes real, earnest prayer a top priority, it is actually making a practice of trusting God and is headed into a flourishing garden. The pastor who teaches the congregation to pray and the congregation who teaches their pastor to pray has gone far toward a change of allegiance from the world to God.

she will hatch them, and care for
her young
under the shadow of her wings;
there also the falcons[i] will gather,
each with its mate.

16 Look in the scroll[j] of the LORD and
read:

None of these will be missing,
not one will lack her mate.
For it is his mouth[k] that has given
the order,
and his Spirit will gather them
together.
17 He allots their portions;[l]
his hand distributes them by
measure.
They will possess it forever
and dwell there from generation
to generation.[m]

Joy of the Redeemed

35 The desert[n] and the parched land
will be glad;
the wilderness will rejoice and
blossom.[o]
Like the crocus, 2 it will burst into
bloom;
it will rejoice greatly and shout for
joy.[p]
The glory of Lebanon[q] will be given
to it,
the splendor of Carmel[r] and
Sharon;
they will see the glory of the
LORD,
the splendor of our God.[s]

3 Strengthen the feeble hands,
steady the knees[t] that give way;
4 say to those with fearful hearts,
"Be strong, do not fear;
your God will come,
he will come with vengeance;[u]
with divine retribution
he will come to save you."

5 Then will the eyes of the blind be
opened[v]
and the ears of the deaf[w]
unstopped.
6 Then will the lame[x] leap like a deer,
and the mute tongue[y] shout for joy.
Water will gush forth in the
wilderness
and streams[z] in the desert.
7 The burning sand will become a pool,
the thirsty ground bubbling
springs.[a]
In the haunts where jackals[b] once lay,
grass and reeds and papyrus will
grow.

8 And a highway[c] will be there;
it will be called the Way of
Holiness;[d]
it will be for those who walk on
that Way.
The unclean[e] will not journey on it;
wicked fools will not go about
on it.
9 No lion[f] will be there,
nor any ravenous beast;[g]
they will not be found there.
But only the redeemed[h] will walk
there,
10 and those the LORD has rescued will
return.
They will enter Zion with singing;
everlasting joy[i] will crown their
heads.
Gladness and joy will overtake them,
and sorrow and sighing will flee
away.[j]

34:15 [i] Dt 14:13
34:16 [j] Isa 30:8 [k] Isa 1:20; 58:14
34:17 [l] Isa 17:14; Jer 13:25 [m] ver 10
35:1 [n] Isa 27:10; 41:18-19 [o] Isa 51:3
35:2 [p] Isa 25:9; 55:12 [q] Isa 32:15 [r] SS 7:5 [s] Isa 25:9
35:3 [t] Job 4:4; Heb 12:12
35:4 [u] Isa 1:24; 34:8
35:5 [v] Mt 11:5; Jn 9:6-7 [w] Isa 29:18; 50:4
35:6 [x] Mt 15:30; Jn 5:8-9; Ac 3:8 [y] Isa 32:4; Mt 9:32-33; 12:22; Lk 11:14 [z] Isa 41:18; Jn 7:38
35:7 [a] Isa 49:10 [b] Isa 13:22
35:8 [c] Isa 11:16; 33:8; Mt 7:13-14 [d] Isa 4:3; 1Pe 1:15 [e] Isa 52:1
35:9 [f] Isa 30:6 [g] Isa 34:14 [h] Isa 51:11; 62:12; 63:4
35:10 [i] Isa 25:9 [j] Isa 30:19; 51:11; Rev 7:17; 21:4

Isa 35:1-10 ❖ How have we seen lives dramatically changed by God's transforming love?

35:1-7 God will turn the "desert" into a garden (v. 1). The "burning sand will become a pool," and the places "where jackals once lay" (v. 7) will become grassy meadows. Verses 3–6a and 8 make it plain that this restoration is a spiritual one. Those who are discouraged and fearful will be given courage and strength.

35:8-10 This idea is furthered with an additional image—namely, that of a "highway" (v. 8). In the rugged highlands of Judah and Ephraim as well as in the desert east and south of Judah's central ridge, a straight and level highway would be a wonderful thing.

This highway is the way to God. It is the way of holiness on which the "redeemed" walk (v. 9). Verse 10 describes the end result of this journey to the city of God (cf. 25:7–8).

35:1-10 God has delivered us from our sins so that we can participate in his life and character. This is what Paul has in mind when he says that believers are to "work out your salvation with fear and trembling, for it is God who works in you to will and to act in order to fulfill his good purpose" (Php 2:12–13). God has come to us and through the work of the Holy Spirit makes it possible for us to walk with him in greater and greater likeness to him.

Sennacherib Threatens Jerusalem

36:1–22pp // 2Ki 18:13,17–37; 2Ch 32:9–19

36 In the fourteenth year of King Hezekiah's reign, Sennacherib[k] king of Assyria attacked all the fortified cities of Judah and captured them. 2Then the king of Assyria sent his field commander with a large army from Lachish to King Hezekiah at Jerusalem. When the commander stopped at the aqueduct of the Upper Pool, on the road to the Launderer's Field,[l] 3Eliakim[m] son of Hilkiah the palace administrator, Shebna[n] the secretary, and Joah son of Asaph the recorder went out to him.

4The field commander said to them, "Tell Hezekiah:

"'This is what the great king, the king of Assyria, says: On what are you basing this confidence of yours? 5You say you have counsel and might for war—but you speak only empty words. On whom are you depending, that you rebel[o] against me? 6Look, I know you are depending on Egypt,[p] that splintered reed[q] of a staff, which pierces the hand of anyone who leans on it! Such is Pharaoh king of Egypt to all who depend on him. 7But if you say to me, "We are depending on the LORD our God"—isn't he the one whose high places and altars Hezekiah removed,[r] saying to Judah and Jerusalem, "You must worship before this altar"?[s]

8"'Come now, make a bargain with my master, the king of Assyria: I will give you two thousand horses—if you can put riders on them! 9How then can you repulse one officer of the least of my master's officials, even though you are depending on Egypt[t] for chariots and horsemen[a]?[u] 10Furthermore, have I come to attack and destroy this land without the LORD? The LORD himself told[v] me to march against this country and destroy it.'"

11Then Eliakim, Shebna and Joah said to the field commander, "Please speak to your servants in Aramaic,[w] since we understand it. Don't speak to us in Hebrew in the hearing of the people on the wall."

12But the commander replied, "Was it only to your master and you that my master sent me to say these things, and not to the people sitting on the wall—who, like you, will have to eat their own excrement and drink their own urine?"

13Then the commander stood and called out in Hebrew,[x] "Hear the words of the great king, the king of Assyria! 14This is what the king says: Do not let Hezekiah deceive you. He cannot deliver you! 15Do not let Hezekiah persuade you to trust in the LORD when he says, 'The LORD will surely deliver us; this city will not be given into the hand of the king of Assyria.'[y]

36:1 [k]2Ch 32:1
36:2 [l]Isa 7:3
36:3 [m]Isa 22:20-21 [n]2Ki 18:18
36:5 [o]2Ki 18:7
36:6 [p]Isa 30:2, 5 [q]Eze 29:6-7
36:7 [r]2Ki 18:4 [s]Dt 12:2-5
36:9 [t]Isa 31:3 [u]Isa 30:2-5
36:10 [v]1Ki 13:18
36:11 [w]Ezr 4:7
36:13 [x]2Ch 32:18
36:15 [y]Isa 37:10

[a] 9 Or *charioteers*

36:1-4 The "field commander" (v. 2) is the third-highest-ranking officer in the Assyrian army, so this move against Jerusalem is a serious one. The main army is engaged in the siege of Lachish, the last remaining Judean walled city except Jerusalem; all the rest have fallen to the Assyrians.

It is significant that the field commander stands in exactly the same spot where Isaiah stood some 34 or 35 years earlier when he had confronted Ahaz (cf. 7:3). The warnings Isaiah gave over the foolishness of trusting Assyria instead of God are all coming true—with a vengeance.

36:5-7 The field commander's speech hammers the fearful Judeans with every possible argument that might undermine their trust—and trust is clearly what this conflict is about. He proceeds to demolish, from his point of view, each possible basis for hope that they could win a confrontation with Assyria. He belittles Egypt's military power: That "splintered reed" will break (v. 6).

36:7 The commander turns to another possible source of help: the Lord. He believes God is unhappy at the destruction of the high places outside of Jerusalem. The pagan Assyrian cannot understand that the unity of God is undermined by worship of him in places other than Jerusalem.

36:8-9 Assyria could afford to give two thousand horses to Judah and still win. Judah cannot muster two thousand trained horsemen to ride the horses. In that light, the help from Egypt is useless, because Judah cannot make good use of whatever military assistance they might receive.

36:10-20 The Assyrian field commander switches gears again, asserting that "the LORD," the God of Israel, has directed him to "destroy" the "land" (v. 10). The Assyrian foreign office may have discovered these were things the prophets of Israel were saying. Yet the field commander's assertion that his king can defeat Judah's God just as he has every other god (vv. 18-20) makes it clear that all he really believes in is earthly power.

It is interesting that the Assyrian refers to his master as "the king" on several occasions (vv. 8, 13, 14, 16, 18) but refers to the king of Judah only by his name. Here is one more part of the power play.

The real issue comes out in vv. 14-20: The Assyrian officer says in the bluntest of terms that Hezekiah "cannot deliver you" (v. 14), because "the

16“Do not listen to Hezekiah. This is what the king of Assyria says: Make peace with me and come out to me. Then each of you will eat fruit from your own vine and fig tree[z] and drink water from your own cistern,[a] 17until I come and take you to a land like your own—a land of grain and new wine, a land of bread and vineyards.

18“Do not let Hezekiah mislead you when he says, ‘The LORD will deliver us.’ Have the gods of any nations ever delivered their lands from the hand of the king of Assyria? 19Where are the gods of Hamath and Arpad? Where are the gods of Sepharvaim? Have they rescued Samaria from my hand? 20Who of all the gods[b] of these countries have been able to save their lands from me? How then can the LORD deliver Jerusalem from my hand?”

21But the people remained silent and said nothing in reply, because the king had commanded, “Do not answer him.”[c]

22Then Eliakim son of Hilkiah the palace administrator, Shebna the secretary and Joah son of Asaph the recorder went to Hezekiah, with their clothes torn, and told him what the field commander had said.

Jerusalem's Deliverance Foretold

37:1–13pp // 2Ki 19:1–13

37 When King Hezekiah heard this, he tore his clothes and put on sackcloth and went into the temple of the LORD. 2He sent Eliakim the palace administrator, Shebna the secretary, and the leading priests, all wearing sackcloth, to the prophet Isaiah son of Amoz.[d] 3They told him, “This is what Hezekiah says: This day is a day of distress and rebuke and disgrace, as when children come to the moment of birth[e] and there is no strength to deliver them. 4It may be that the LORD your God will hear the words of the field commander, whom his master, the king of Assyria, has sent to ridicule the living God, and that he will rebuke him for the words the LORD your God has heard.[f] Therefore pray for the remnant[g] that still survives.”

5When King Hezekiah's officials came to Isaiah, 6Isaiah said to them, “Tell your master, ‘This is what the LORD says: Do not be afraid[h] of what you have heard—those words with which the underlings of the king of Assyria have blasphemed me. 7Listen! When he hears a certain report,[i] I will make him want to return to his own country, and there I will have him cut down with the sword.’ ”

8When the field commander heard that the king of Assyria had left Lachish, he withdrew and found the king fighting against Libnah.[j]

9Now Sennacherib received a report[k] that Tirhakah, the king of Cush,[a] was marching out to fight against him. When he heard it, he sent messengers to Hezekiah with this word: 10“Say to Hezekiah king of Judah: Do not let the god you depend on deceive you when he says, ‘Jerusalem will not be given into the hands of the king of Assyria.’[l] 11Surely

36:16 [z] 1Ki 4:25; Zec 3:10 [a] Pr 5:15
36:20 [b] 1Ki 20:23
36:21 [c] Pr 9:7-8; 26:4
37:2 [d] Isa 1:1
37:3 [e] Isa 26:18; 66:9; Hos 13:13
37:4 [f] Isa 36:13, 18-20 [g] Isa 1:9
37:6 [h] Isa 7:4
37:7 [i] ver 9
37:8 [j] Nu 33:20
37:9 [k] ver 7
37:10 [l] Isa 36:15

[a] 9 That is, the upper Nile region

Isa 36:16-20 ❖ When someone discourages our faith and tries to make us doubt God, how do we respond?

LORD will [not] deliver” the inhabitants of the city (vv. 18–20).

37:1-4 Hezekiah's response to his advisers' report is instructive: Not only does Hezekiah himself turn to God, but he also sends an impressive delegation to consult with Isaiah. Hezekiah is particularly concerned about the disgrace that this situation brings on God and wonders if God will let that stand.

37:5-7 The response God gives to Isaiah makes it clear he does not intend to let the challenge pass unaddressed. The king may be terrified, but the God who speaks through Isaiah is not. He will not allow the Assyrian to succeed in his plans but will send him home. There, Sennacherib will be “cut down with the sword” (v. 7).

✤ **36:1—37:7** The decision that Hezekiah was faced with was dire and the outcome unsure; that is, until he sought the Lord and asked for help. Then he found out what the fate of the Assyrian army would be.

Who are the “field commanders” today who try to dissuade us from trusting fully in God? Their arguments are convincing, and sometimes our circumstances seem hopeless. These kinds of decisions are personal, between us and the Lord, but the real issue for all of us is: Do we really trust the Lord to supply all our needs, or does our behavior say that we're ultimately trusting in things other than God?

37:8-13 Sennacherib decides to challenge God himself: “Do not let the god you depend on deceive you” (v. 10). Sennacherib's fatal mistake is that he does not realize that Judah's God is not man-made, like all the rest.

you have heard what the kings of Assyria
have done to all the countries, destroying them completely. And will you be
delivered?[m] 12 Did the gods of the nations
that were destroyed by my predecessors[n]
deliver them — the gods of Gozan, Harran,[o] Rezeph and the people of Eden who
were in Tel Assar? 13 Where is the king
of Hamath or the king of Arpad? Where
are the kings of Lair, Sepharvaim, Hena
and Ivvah?"

Hezekiah's Prayer

37:14–20pp // 2Ki 19:14–19

14 Hezekiah received the letter from the
messengers and read it. Then he went
up to the temple of the LORD and spread
it out before the LORD. 15 And Hezekiah
prayed to the LORD: 16 "LORD Almighty,
the God of Israel, enthroned between the
cherubim, you alone are God[p] over all the
kingdoms of the earth. You have made
heaven and earth. 17 Give ear, LORD, and
hear;[q] open your eyes, LORD, and see;[r]
listen to all the words Sennacherib has
sent to ridicule the living God.

18 "It is true, LORD, that the Assyrian
kings have laid waste all these peoples
and their lands.[s] 19 They have thrown
their gods into the fire and destroyed
them,[t] for they were not gods[u] but only
wood and stone, fashioned by human
hands. 20 Now, LORD our God, deliver us
from his hand, so that all the kingdoms
of the earth may know that you, LORD,
are the only God.[a][v]"

Sennacherib's Fall

37:21–38pp // 2Ki 19:20–37; 2Ch 32:20–21

21 Then Isaiah son of Amoz[w] sent a message to Hezekiah: "This is what the LORD,
the God of Israel, says: Because you have

37:11 [m] Isa 36:18-20
37:12 [n] 2Ki 18:11 [o] Ge 11:31; 12:1-4; Ac 7:2
37:16 [p] Dt 10:17; Ps 86:10; 136:2-3
37:17 [q] 2Ch 6:40 [r] Da 9:18
37:18 [s] 2Ki 15:29; Na 2:11-12
37:19 [t] Isa 26:14 [u] Isa 41:24,29
37:20 [v] Ps 46:10
37:21 [w] ver 2

37:22 [x] Job 16:4
37:23 [y] ver 4 [z] Isa 2:11
37:24 [a] Isa 14:8
37:25 [b] Dt 11:10
37:26 [c] Ac 2:23; 4:27-28; 1Pe 2:8

> **Isa 37:14** ❖ How can we, like Hezekiah, lay our problems or fears before the Lord rather than seeking to solve them ourselves?

prayed to me concerning Sennacherib
king of Assyria, 22 this is the word the
LORD has spoken against him:

"Virgin Daughter Zion
despises and mocks you.
Daughter Jerusalem
tosses her head[x] as you flee.
23 Who is it you have ridiculed and
blasphemed?[y]
Against whom have you raised
your voice
and lifted your eyes in pride?[z]
Against the Holy One of Israel!
24 By your messengers
you have ridiculed the Lord.
And you have said,
'With my many chariots
I have ascended the heights of the
mountains,
the utmost heights of Lebanon.[a]
I have cut down its tallest cedars,
the choicest of its junipers.
I have reached its remotest heights,
the finest of its forests.
25 I have dug wells in foreign lands[b]
and drunk the water there.
With the soles of my feet
I have dried up all the streams of
Egypt.[b]'

26 "Have you not heard?
Long ago I ordained[c] it.

[a] 20 Dead Sea Scrolls (see also 2 Kings 19:19); Masoretic Text *you alone are the LORD*
[b] 25 Dead Sea Scrolls (see also 2 Kings 19:24); Masoretic Text does not have *in foreign lands.*

37:14–17 This time Hezekiah goes directly to God himself. His ascription of praise in v. 16 is a marvelous compendium of the attributes and character of God. Hezekiah's petition particularly stresses the fact that God is not an idol but is the "living God" (v. 17). Hezekiah prays with the confidence that his God not only can hear but wants to hear. Perhaps the most striking thing about this prayer is its focus on God's vindication rather than on the deliverance of the people.

Why does Hezekiah pray for the deliverance of his city? One reason alone is given: "so that all the kingdoms of the earth may know that you, LORD, are the only God" (v. 20). In many ways this is the climax of all the teaching found in chs. 7–35.

37:21–38 God's response to this prayer comes through Isaiah and is recorded in vv. 21–35. It appears in three parts, the first of which is addressed directly to Sennacherib (vv. 22–29); the second is addressed to Hezekiah (vv. 30–32), and the third is spoken of Sennacherib (vv. 33–35).

37:22–23 The opening phrase "Virgin Daughter Zion" suggests that the Assyrian attack on Jerusalem is comparable to a dominant male seeking to ravage a beautiful young girl (v. 22). But Assyria, the would-be rapist, has not taken into account "the Holy One of Israel" (v. 23).

37:24–29 These verses seem to extol Sennacherib. But what he does not know is that all of this has been "long ago . . . planned" (v. 26) by God. Assyria is a puppet being moved by Israel's God, and Sennacherib cannot hide from God. Just as God has brought him on the stage, he can take him off again.

In days of old I planned[d] it;
now I have brought it to pass,
that you have turned fortified cities
into piles of stone.[e]
27 Their people, drained of power,
are dismayed and put to shame.
They are like plants in the field,
like tender green shoots,
like grass sprouting on the roof,[f]
scorched[a] before it grows up.

28 "But I know where you are
and when you come and go[g]
and how you rage[h] against me.
29 Because you rage against me
and because your insolence[i] has
reached my ears,
I will put my hook in your nose[j]
and my bit in your mouth,
and I will make you return
by the way you came.[k]

30 "This will be the sign for you, Hezekiah:

"This year you will eat what grows
by itself,
and the second year what springs
from that.
But in the third year sow and reap,
plant vineyards and eat their fruit.
31 Once more a remnant of the
kingdom of Judah
will take root below and bear fruit[l]
above.
32 For out of Jerusalem will come a
remnant,
and out of Mount Zion a band of
survivors.

37:26 [d] Isa 10:6; 25:1 [e] Isa 25:2
37:27 [f] Ps 129:6
37:28 [g] Ps 139:1-3 [h] Ps 2:1
37:29 [i] Isa 10:12 [j] Isa 30:28; Eze 38:4 [k] ver 34
37:31 [l] Isa 27:6
37:32 [m] Isa 9:7
37:34 [n] ver 29
37:35 [o] Isa 31:5; 38:6 [p] Isa 43:25; 48:9,11 [q] 2Ki 20:6
37:36 [r] Isa 10:12
37:37 [s] Ge 10:11
37:38 [t] Ge 8:4; Jer 51:27

The zeal[m] of the LORD Almighty
will accomplish this.

33 "Therefore this is what the LORD says
concerning the king of Assyria:

"He will not enter this city
or shoot an arrow here.
He will not come before it with
shield
or build a siege ramp against it.
34 By the way that he came he will
return;[n]
he will not enter this city,"
declares the LORD.
35 "I will defend[o] this city and save it,
for my sake[p] and for the sake of
David[q] my servant!"

36 Then the angel of the LORD went
out and put to death a hundred and
eighty-five thousand in the Assyrian[r]
camp. When the people got up the next
morning — there were all the dead bodies! 37 So Sennacherib king of Assyria
broke camp and withdrew. He returned
to Nineveh[s] and stayed there.
38 One day, while he was worshiping
in the temple of his god Nisrok, his sons
Adrammelek and Sharezer killed him
with the sword, and they escaped to the
land of Ararat.[t] And Esarhaddon his son
succeeded him as king.

[a] 27 Some manuscripts of the Masoretic Text, Dead Sea Scrolls and some Septuagint manuscripts (see also 2 Kings 19:26); most manuscripts of the Masoretic Text *roof / and terraced fields*

37:30-32 These verses constitute a sign to Hezekiah that this is indeed a word from God. God has gone on record that he will do what he says and has given a means for checking the validity of what he has said. The three years described in v. 30 likely entail parts of three different calendar years. In God's mind, the more important point is that he will preserve a harvest for himself from among his people.

37:33-35 All God's promises are summed up here, where Isaiah makes two assertions about what will happen and gives a supporting reason for these assertions (v. 35). The Assyrian army will not mount any kind of an attack against the city. They will also not even "shoot an arrow" (v. 33) there. On the surface of it, this is amazing. Not only will the Assyrians not mount a siege against the city, but they will leave the area completely. The reason given for this amazing turn of events is that God "will defend" the city "and save it" (v. 35).

37:36-38 These verses are stunning in their terse, matter-of-fact reporting. This is definitely a "no contest" match. God simply sends the angel of death. And the angel is not finished on the Philistine plains. In later years, Sennacherib was at home in what should have been the safest place on earth for him; there his own sons "killed him with the sword" (v. 38). Despite all his boasts, Sennacherib could not stand against the living God.

37:8-38 This is maturity: having a correct estimate of your abilities and your liabilities, one that is not dependent on the opinions of others, and being secure in who you are and who you are becoming. But this is not really possible without the perspective of heaven. When we get ourselves "off our hands" and into God's hands, we no longer need to worry about what others think of us. Now it is God's reputation that matters to us, and we are freed from that debilitating self-concern that will otherwise eat us up. That is the picture we see in Hezekiah's prayer. Here is a man whose personal success and survival are no longer paramount. This is a free man.

Hezekiah's Illness

38:1–8pp // 2Ki 20:1–11; 2Ch 32:24–26

38 In those days Hezekiah became
ill and was at the point of death.
The prophet Isaiah son of Amoz[u] went
to him and said, "This is what the LORD
says: Put your house in order,[v] because
you are going to die; you will not recover."

2Hezekiah turned his face to the wall
and prayed to the LORD, 3"Remember,
LORD, how I have walked[w] before you
faithfully and with wholehearted devotion[x] and have done what is good in your
eyes.[y]" And Hezekiah wept[z] bitterly.

4Then the word of the LORD came to
Isaiah: 5"Go and tell Hezekiah, 'This is
what the LORD, the God of your father
David, says: I have heard your prayer and
seen your tears; I will add fifteen years[a]
to your life. 6And I will deliver you and
this city from the hand of the king of
Assyria. I will defend[b] this city.

7" 'This is the LORD's sign[c] to you that
the LORD will do what he has promised:
8I will make the shadow cast by the sun
go back the ten steps it has gone down
on the stairway of Ahaz.' " So the sunlight went back the ten steps it had gone
down.[d]

9A writing of Hezekiah king of Judah
after his illness and recovery:

10I said, "In the prime of my life[e]
must I go through the gates of
death[f]
and be robbed of the rest of my
years?[g]"

38:1 [u] Isa 37:2 [v] 2Sa 17:23
38:3 [w] Ne 13:14; Ps 26:3 [x] 1Ch 29:19 [y] Dt 6:18 [z] Ps 6:8
38:5 [a] 2Ki 18:2
38:6 [b] Isa 31:5; 37:35
38:7 [c] Isa 7:11,14
38:8 [d] Jos 10:13
38:10 [e] Ps 102:24 [f] Ps 107:18; 2Co 1:9 [g] Job 17:11

Isa 38:2–3 ❖ When have we pleaded with God for mercy?

38:1–8 Hezekiah does not actually ask for lengthened life. What he does is simply remind God that he has conducted his life with faithfulness and "wholehearted devotion" (v. 3). Hezekiah, who was only 39 years old at the time, is saying to God that he has met God's requirements for long life (cf. Ps 34:11–14) and is asking by implication if it is fair to cut his life short as though he were a wicked man (cf. Ps 37:35–36).

God responds to this argument and sends Isaiah back with a different word: one of 15 additional years. Like his father before him, Hezekiah is offered a sign to confirm God's gracious promise of deliverance.

38:9–20 Hezekiah's psalm seems to be largely a meditation on mortality.

38:10–14 Hezekiah speaks of the untimeliness of the announced death. Life is impermanent; but

CHARACTER OF GOD // GOD IS IMMUTABLE

Isaiah 38:1: "This is what the LORD says: Put your house in order, because you are going to die; you will not recover."

God's unchanging nature is called his immutability. While humans change over the course of their lives, preferring different foods or styles for a while and then finding something else they desire, God remains the same.

This is not to say that God does not at times appear to change his mind in the Bible. For example, God sent a prophet to tell King Hezekiah that his illness would not improve and would end in death (2Ki 20:1). When Hezekiah prayed fervently to God, God sent the prophet back to tell Hezekiah he would in fact be healed and would go on to live another 15 years.

But did God change? No. God knew from the beginning how this story would unfold. Hezekiah's response to the prophet's message was not a surprise that caused God to suddenly switch course. God knew the effect the prophet's words would have: Hezekiah would humble himself in prayer. God ordained the means for achieving his ends, and he knew the end from the beginning.

Therefore, even instances in Scripture that appear to show God changing his mind must be understood in light of the deeper truth of God's sovereignty and omniscience. Nothing surprises God. He knows each human word and thought before they occur (Ps 139:2–3).

APPLICATION ✣ God's immutability is a deep comfort. We do not need to fear that God will change his mind about us or that his promises will fail. In a world of uncertainty and fragile relationships, God remains rock solid. He will never abandon his children, and his love and truth will never change.

11 I said, "I will not again see the LORD himself
in the land of the living;[h]
no longer will I look on my fellow man,
or be with those who now dwell in this world.
12 Like a shepherd's tent[i] my house
has been pulled down[j] and taken from me.
Like a weaver I have rolled[k] up my life,
and he has cut me off from the loom;[l]
day and night[m] you made an end of me.
13 I waited patiently till dawn,
but like a lion he broke[n] all my bones;[o]
day and night you made an end of me.
14 I cried like a swift or thrush,
I moaned like a mourning dove.[p]
My eyes grew weak as I looked to the heavens.
I am being threatened; Lord, come to my aid!"[q]

15 But what can I say?
He has spoken to me, and he himself has done this.[r]
I will walk humbly[s] all my years
because of this anguish of my soul.[t]
16 Lord, by such things people live;
and my spirit finds life in them too.
You restored me to health
and let me live.[u]
17 Surely it was for my benefit
that I suffered such anguish.
In your love you kept me
from the pit[v] of destruction;
you have put all my sins[w]
behind your back.[x]
18 For the grave[y] cannot praise you,
death cannot sing your praise;[z]
those who go down to the pit[a]
cannot hope for your faithfulness.
19 The living, the living — they praise[b] you,
as I am doing today;
parents tell their children[c]
about your faithfulness.

20 The LORD will save me,
and we will sing[d] with stringed instruments[e]
all the days of our lives[f]
in the temple[g] of the LORD.

21 Isaiah had said, "Prepare a poultice
of figs and apply it to the boil, and he
will recover."
22 Hezekiah had asked, "What will be
the sign that I will go up to the temple
of the LORD?"

Envoys From Babylon

39:1–8pp // 2Ki 20:12–19

39 At that time Marduk-Baladan son
of Baladan king of Babylon[h] sent
Hezekiah letters and a gift, because he
had heard of his illness and recovery.
2 Hezekiah received the envoys[i] gladly

38:11 [h] Ps 27:13; 116:9
38:12 [i] 2Co 5:1, 4; 2Pe 1:13-14 [j] Job 4:21 [k] Heb 1:12 [l] Job 7:6 [m] Ps 73:14
38:13 [n] Ps 51:8 [o] Job 10:16; Da 6:24
38:14 [p] Isa 59:11 [q] Job 17:3
38:15 [r] Ps 39:9 [s] 1Ki 21:27 [t] Job 7:11
38:16 [u] Ps 119:25
38:17 [v] Ps 30:3 [w] Jer 31:34 [x] Isa 43:25; Mic 7:19
38:18 [y] Ecc 9:10 [z] Ps 6:5; 88:10-11; 115:17 [a] Ps 30:9
38:19 [b] Dt 6:7; Ps 118:17; 119:175 [c] Dt 11:19
38:20 [d] Ps 68:25 [e] Ps 33:2 [f] Ps 116:2 [g] Ps 116:17-19
39:1 [h] 2Ch 32:31
39:2 [i] 2Ch 32:31

---

just as death is from the Lord, so is life. If there is to be any hope, it is from "the heavens"; if any "aid" (v. 14), it is from the Lord.

38:15–17 It is unclear whether v. 15 is to be taken negatively or positively. The point seems to be that all of "this" (v. 15), both the disease and its subsequent removal, is the work of God. Hezekiah believes that the "anguish" he went through has been beneficial (v. 15). Perhaps one benefit is a new realization of God's "love" and mercy (v. 17).

38:18–19 These verses express the idea that it is to God's benefit to keep the faithful alive since those in the "grave cannot praise" God for his "faithfulness" (v. 18). Rather, it is "the living" (v. 19) who praise God and who pass along their testimony of his faithfulness to their children.

38:21–22 Verse 20 shows us that healing is from the Lord even if some intervening means is used to promote the healing. Verse 21 may explain why the sign involved the "stairway of Ahaz" (v. 8). As the sun moved up and down that stairway, so Hezekiah would once again move up and down the stairs of the "temple" (v. 20).

38:1–22 God does not change his mind concerning the basic nature of things. But God will gladly change what he has said about us if it can become a greater means to our blessing. God sees that his intervention will be a means of greater blessing for both Hezekiah and his people. Did God know that before? Of course he did. But the issue is whether Hezekiah will turn to God in faith at such a moment. If he will not, then there is little God can do for him and through him.

39:1–3 Marduk-Baladan was a Babylonian leader who was twice able to make himself king of Babylon in defiance of the Assyrians. Obviously, he was interested in encouraging any others in the Assyrian Empire who were potential allies or who would draw Assyrian attention away from him and onto themselves. There is something flattering when someone important pays attention to us. But there is also something dangerous as well— namely, that we try to convince the person their

and showed them what was in his storehouses — the silver, the gold,[j] the spices,
the fine olive oil — his entire armory and
everything found among his treasures.
There was nothing in his palace or in
all his kingdom that Hezekiah did not
show them.
³Then Isaiah the prophet went to King
Hezekiah and asked, "What did those
men say, and where did they come from?"
"From a distant land,[k]" Hezekiah replied. "They came to me from Babylon."
⁴The prophet asked, "What did they
see in your palace?"
"They saw everything in my palace,"
Hezekiah said. "There is nothing among
my treasures that I did not show them."
⁵Then Isaiah said to Hezekiah, "Hear
the word of the LORD Almighty: ⁶The
time will surely come when everything
in your palace, and all that your predecessors have stored up until this day, will
be carried off to Babylon.[l] Nothing will
be left, says the LORD. ⁷And some of your
descendants, your own flesh and blood
who will be born to you, will be taken
away, and they will become eunuchs in
the palace of the king of Babylon.[m]"
⁸"The word of the LORD you have spoken is good," Hezekiah replied. For he
thought, "There will be peace and security in my lifetime.[n]"

Comfort for God's People

40 Comfort, comfort[o] my people,
says your God.
²Speak tenderly[p] to Jerusalem,
and proclaim to her
that her hard service has been
completed,[q]
that her sin has been paid for,
that she has received from the
LORD's hand
double[r] for all her sins.

³A voice of one calling:
"In the wilderness prepare
the way[s] for the LORD[a];
make straight in the desert
a highway for our God.[b][t]
⁴Every valley shall be raised up,
every mountain and hill made
low;
the rough ground shall become
level,[u]
the rugged places a plain.
⁵And the glory of the LORD will be
revealed,
and all people will see it together.[v]
For the mouth of the LORD
has spoken."[w]

⁶A voice says, "Cry out."
And I said, "What shall I cry?"

"All people are like grass,[x]
and all their faithfulness is like
the flowers of the field.
⁷The grass withers and the flowers
fall,
because the breath[y] of the LORD
blows on them.

39:2 [j] 2Ki 18:15
39:3 [k] Dt 28:49
39:6 [l] 2Ki 24:13; Jer 20:5
39:7 [m] 2Ki 24:15; Da 1:1-7
39:8 [n] 2Ch 32:26
40:1 [o] Isa 12:1; 49:13; 51:3, 12; 52:9; 61:2; 66:13; Jer 31:13; Zep 3:14-17; 2Co 1:3
40:2 [p] Isa 35:4 [q] Isa 41:11-13; 49:25 [r] Isa 61:7; Jer 16:18; Zec 9:12; Rev 18:6
40:3 [s] Mal 3:1 [t] Mt 3:3*; Mk 1:3*; Jn 1:23*
40:4 [u] Isa 45:2, 13
40:5 [v] Isa 52:10; Lk 3:4-6* [w] Isa 1:20; 58:14
40:6 [x] Job 14:2
40:7 [y] Job 41:21

[a] 3 Or *A voice of one calling in the wilderness: / "Prepare the way for the LORD* [b] 3 Hebrew; Septuagint *make straight the paths of our God*

Isa 39:4 ❖ In a culture of consumerism, how can we avoid being prideful or ostentatious with our possessions?

Isa 40:3-5 ❖ How can we help prepare the way of the Lord so that others can see God's glory?

---

attention is justified. Sadly, that is the temptation into which Hezekiah falls.
39:4-8 This is not how we would like to remember such a good man. Yet this is how Isaiah has chosen for us to remember him. By showing that Hezekiah is both mortal and fallible, Isaiah shows that trust is intended to be a way of life, not a one-time experience. There is no final salvation in a human being, no matter how good he might be. Our hope is not in the perfectibility of humanity. The Messiah we look for is better than that.

39:1-8 The person who has cultivated a life of trust, who knows that everything he or she has is a gift from God, will be constantly deflecting the praise and honor from himself or herself to God. The ultimate test of our humility and submission to God comes when we answer this question: Who is getting the glory for our accomplishments?

40:1-11 No longer is the prophetic message to be primarily one of judgment. The message is to be one of hope.
40:1-2 Verses 1 and 2 provide an introduction and set the chapter's tone. Isaiah sees a day when God's servants will feel sure that all is lost. But the message to be proclaimed to them is that this is not so.
40:3-5 In the first stanza, God comes to helpless Zion to set her free. Nothing can prevent his swift coming to his people's aid, neither mountains nor valleys. There is no other hope.
40:6-8 That fact of the previous stanza is underlined in the second stanza: If the Judeans are to

Surely the people are grass.
8 The grass withers and the flowers fall,
but the word[z] of our God endures forever.[a]"

9 You who bring good news[b] to Zion,
go up on a high mountain.
You who bring good news to Jerusalem,[a]
lift up your voice with a shout,
lift it up, do not be afraid;
say to the towns of Judah,
"Here is your God!"[c]
10 See, the Sovereign LORD comes[d] with power,
and he rules[e] with a mighty arm.[f]
See, his reward[g] is with him,
and his recompense accompanies him.
11 He tends his flock like a shepherd:[h]
He gathers the lambs in his arms
and carries them close to his heart;
he gently leads those that have young.

12 Who has measured the waters[i] in the hollow of his hand,[j]
or with the breadth of his hand marked off the heavens?[k]
Who has held the dust of the earth in a basket,
or weighed the mountains on the scales
and the hills in a balance?
13 Who can fathom the Spirit[b] of the LORD,
or instruct the LORD as his counselor?[l]
14 Whom did the LORD consult to enlighten him,
and who taught him the right way?
Who was it that taught him knowledge,[m]
or showed him the path of understanding?

15 Surely the nations are like a drop in a bucket;
they are regarded as dust on the scales;
he weighs the islands as though they were fine dust.
16 Lebanon is not sufficient for altar fires,
nor its animals[n] enough for burnt offerings.
17 Before him all the nations[o] are as nothing;[p]
they are regarded by him as worthless
and less than nothing.[q]

18 With whom, then, will you compare God?[r]
To what image[s] will you liken him?
19 As for an idol,[t] a metalworker casts it,
and a goldsmith[u] overlays it with gold[v]
and fashions silver chains for it.
20 A person too poor to present such an offering
selects wood that will not rot;
they look for a skilled worker
to set up an idol that will not topple.[w]

40:8 [z] Isa 55:11; 59:21 [a] Mt 5:18; 1Pe 1:24-25*
40:9 [b] Isa 52:7-10; 61:1; Ro 10:15 [c] Isa 25:9
40:10 [d] Rev 22:7 [e] Isa 9:6-7 [f] Isa 59:16 [g] Isa 62:11; Rev 22:12
40:11 [h] Eze 34:23; Mic 5:4; Jn 10:11
40:12 [i] Job 38:10 [j] Pr 30:4 [k] Heb 1:10-12
40:13 [l] Ro 11:34*; 1Co 2:16*
40:14 [m] Job 21:22; Col 2:3
40:16 [n] Ps 50:9-11; Mic 6:7; Heb 10:5-9
40:17 [o] Isa 30:28 [p] Isa 29:7 [q] Da 4:35
40:18 [r] Ex 8:10; 1Sa 2:2; Isa 46:5 [s] Ac 17:29
40:19 [t] Ps 115:4 [u] Isa 41:7; Jer 10:3 [v] Isa 2:20
40:20 [w] 1Sa 5:3

[a] 9 Or *Zion, bringer of good news, / go up on a high mountain. / Jerusalem, bringer of good news*
[b] 13 Or *mind*

---

be delivered, God will have to do it. But if he *does* decide to do it, there is nothing the Babylonians will be able to do to prevent it. If God speaks a promise, that "word" will stand (v. 8).

40:9–11 Because God's word is sure, "Zion" (v. 9) is this messenger of good tidings. The good news is about the intervention of God in the world: He "comes" (v. 10). The Creator breaks into his world, both to break the power of evil with his strong "arm" (v. 10) and, "like a shepherd" (v. 11a), to gather up the broken in his gentle "arms" (v. 11b).

40:12–26 God is unique. He is able to deliver not because he is greater than the Babylonian gods; he is able to deliver because *he is the only God!*

40:12–14 The prophet employs a series of rhetorical questions intended to bring the reader to the point of saying that Yahweh is the sole Creator.

40:13–14 These verses seem particularly aimed at polytheistic religions, where a counselor/magician among the gods assists the other gods in realizing their purposes. Isaiah insists that "understanding" (v. 14) originated with God. To think otherwise is to give up transcendence. To give that up is to exist where life is only the outworking of a fatalistic cycle coming from nowhere and going nowhere.

40:16–17 Compared to the One who holds the oceans in his hand, the nations of the earth are "nothing" (v. 17). Verse 16 illustrates this point by saying that no earthly sacrifice is sufficient to manipulate him in favor of earthly concerns.

40:18–20 If the Lord is the sole Creator and the Lord of the nations, will we say that an idol is comparable to him? Certainly not! This diatribe against the idols is the first of several in this part of the book. The emphasis on making the idol is intentional. How can something made by humans possibly be the maker of the humans who made it?

21 Do you not know?
Have you not heard?
Has it not been told[x] you from the beginning?
Have you not understood[y] since the earth was founded?[z]
22 He sits enthroned above the circle of the earth,
and its people are like grasshoppers.[a]
He stretches out the heavens like a canopy,[b]
and spreads them out like a tent[c] to live in.
23 He brings princes[d] to naught
and reduces the rulers of this world to nothing.[e]
24 No sooner are they planted,
no sooner are they sown,
no sooner do they take root in the ground,
than he blows[f] on them and they wither,
and a whirlwind sweeps them away like chaff.

25 "To whom will you compare me?[g]
Or who is my equal?" says the Holy One.
26 Lift up your eyes and look to the heavens:[h]
Who created[i] all these?
He who brings out the starry host[j] one by one
and calls forth each of them by name.
Because of his great power and mighty strength,
not one of them is missing.[k]

40:21 [x] Ps 19:1; 50:6; Ac 14:17 [y] Ro 1:19 [z] Isa 48:13; 51:13
40:22 [a] Nu 13:33; Ps 104:2; Isa 42:5 [b] Job 22:14 [c] Job 36:29
40:23 [d] Isa 34:12 [e] Job 12:21; Ps 107:40
40:24 [f] Isa 41:16
40:25 [g] ver 18
40:26 [h] Isa 51:6 [i] Ps 89:11-13; Isa 42:5 [j] Ps 147:4 [k] Isa 34:16
40:27 [l] Job 27:2; Lk 18:7-8
40:28 [m] ver 21 [n] Ps 90:2 [o] Ps 147:5; Ro 11:33
40:29 [p] Isa 50:4; Jer 31:25
40:30 [q] Isa 9:17; Jer 6:11; 9:21
40:31 [r] Lk 18:1 [s] 2Co 4:16 [t] Ex 19:4; Ps 103:5 [u] 2Co 4:1; Heb 12:1-3
41:1 [v] Hab 2:20; Zec 2:13 [w] Isa 11:11 [x] Isa 48:16 [y] Isa 1:18; 34:1; 50:8
41:2 [z] Ezr 1:2 [a] ver 25; Isa 45:1,13

27 Why do you complain, Jacob?
Why do you say, Israel,
"My way is hidden from the LORD;
my cause is disregarded by my God"?[l]
28 Do you not know?
Have you not heard?[m]
The LORD is the everlasting[n] God,
the Creator of the ends of the earth.
He will not grow tired or weary,
and his understanding no one can fathom.[o]
29 He gives strength to the weary[p]
and increases the power of the weak.
30 Even youths grow tired and weary,
and young men[q] stumble and fall;
31 but those who hope[r] in the LORD
will renew their strength.[s]
They will soar on wings like eagles;[t]
they will run and not grow weary,
they will walk and not be faint.[u]

The Helper of Israel

41 "Be silent[v] before me, you islands![w]
Let the nations renew their strength!
Let them come forward[x] and speak;
let us meet together[y] at the place of judgment.

2 "Who has stirred[z] up one from the east,[a]
calling him in righteousness to his service[a]?

[a] 2 *Or east, / whom victory meets at every step*

40:21–24 The cycle begins again with v. 21, where the prophet asserts that God is not only other than the world but also other than the heavens, having stretched them out "like a tent" (v. 22). As a result, he is not overawed by the "rulers" (v. 23) of this earth. The tender plants of humanity are no match for the eternal judgments of God (v. 24).
40:25–26 Even the stars exist only because of God's "mighty strength" (v. 26).
40:27–31 The prophet speaks of both the being and the person of God. Thus, his question in v. 28 is rather incredulous: How could anyone who knows perfectly well who he is and what he is like say such things about God? Here we come back to the theme of trust. The God of all strength can give his people exactly what they need at the right time, whether to "soar," "run," or "walk" (v. 31).

40:1–31 The Bible is increasingly lost in Western society, and with it, the idea of transformation. So we fight for individual rights, and yet we increasingly deny any responsibility for our choices, arguing that we really do not have any choices since we are conditioned by society, our family, some tragedy, or even our genes. What has happened? We have kept the Bible's conclusion but denied its premises. We have accepted human worth while buying into deterministic evolution. But the Bible declares otherwise, giving us hope for transformation when we surrender our lives to God's purposes.

41:1 God will demonstrate to his fearful people that their captivity in Babylon in no way calls his power or lordship into question.
41:2–4 God begins with a rhetorical question in v. 2 and then repeats and answers it in v. 4. God has given the "nations" into Cyrus's hand (v. 2). Cyrus can subdue every nation he encounters with ease because this is in the God of Israel's plan.

He hands nations over to him
and subdues kings before him.
He turns them to dust[b] with his sword,
to windblown chaff[c] with his bow.
3 He pursues them and moves on unscathed,
by a path his feet have not traveled before.
4 Who has done this and carried it through,
calling forth the generations from the beginning?[d]
I, the LORD—with the first of them
and with the last[e]—I am he."

5 The islands[f] have seen it and fear;
the ends of the earth tremble.
They approach and come forward;
6 they help each other
and say to their companions, "Be strong!"
7 The metalworker encourages the goldsmith,[g]
and the one who smooths with the hammer
spurs on the one who strikes the anvil.
One says of the welding, "It is good."
The other nails down the idol so it will not topple.

8 "But you, Israel, my servant,
Jacob, whom I have chosen,
you descendants of Abraham[h] my friend,[i]
9 I took you from the ends of the earth,[j]
from its farthest corners I called you.
I said, 'You are my servant';
I have chosen[k] you and have not rejected you.
10 So do not fear, for I am with you;[l]
do not be dismayed, for I am your God.
I will strengthen you and help[m] you;
I will uphold you with my righteous right hand.

11 "All who rage[n] against you
will surely be ashamed and disgraced;[o]
those who oppose[p] you
will be as nothing and perish.[q]
12 Though you search for your enemies,
you will not find them.[r]
Those who wage war against you
will be as nothing[s] at all.
13 For I am the LORD your God
who takes hold of your right hand[t]
and says to you, Do not fear;
I will help[u] you.
14 Do not be afraid, you worm Jacob,
little Israel, do not fear,
for I myself will help you," declares the LORD,
your Redeemer, the Holy One of Israel.
15 "See, I will make you into a threshing sledge,[v]
new and sharp, with many teeth.
You will thresh the mountains and crush them,
and reduce the hills to chaff.
16 You will winnow[w] them, the wind will pick them up,
and a gale will blow them away.
But you will rejoice in the LORD
and glory[x] in the Holy One of Israel.

17 "The poor and needy search for water,[y]

41:2 [b] 2Sa 22:43 [c] Isa 40:24
41:4 [d] ver 26; Isa 46:10 [e] Isa 44:6; 48:12; Rev 1:8, 17; 22:13
41:5 [f] Eze 26:17-18
41:7 [g] Isa 40:19
41:8 [h] Isa 29:22; 51:2; 63:16 [i] 2Ch 20:7; Jas 2:23
41:9 [j] Isa 11:12 [k] Dt 7:6
41:10 [l] Jos 1:9; Isa 43:2,5; Ro 8:31 [m] ver 13-14; Isa 44:2; 49:8
41:11 [n] Isa 17:12 [o] Isa 45:24 [p] Ex 23:22 [q] Isa 29:8
41:12 [r] Ps 37:35-36 [s] Isa 17:14
41:13 [t] Isa 42:6; 45:1 [u] ver 10
41:15 [v] Mic 4:13
41:16 [w] Jer 51:2 [x] Isa 45:25
41:17 [y] Isa 43:20

Isa 41:8-11 ❖ When has God given us a special measure of his strength?

41:5-7 When the nations hear of Cyrus's conquests, they will be terrified. But what can they do? They do the only thing they can: make better idols. It is hard work to make your maker.
41:8-10 Unlike the nations around them, the Judean captives have nothing to fear. God is "with" them, to "strengthen," "help," and "uphold" them (v. 10b). God is personally present with his people, so they have nothing to "fear" (v. 10a).
41:11-14 God will protect his people, and their enemies will simply evaporate before the Lord. God will demonstrate his lordship by taking an active hand in their defense.
41:15-16 A "threshing sledge" was constructed from pieces of wood with sharp stones ("teeth") driven into them. This device was pulled around over a pile of cut grain so that the kernels of grain were separated from the husks. God will use Israel in his plan of world history.
41:17-20 These verses are a graphic summary of what has been said to this point.

✣ **41:1-20** With the help of the Creator of the entire universe at our backs, why should we be afraid? It is the almighty, independent Creator who freely comes to stand at our side and do through us what we cannot. God does not make us merely robots to speed his cause. What an unimaginable task, and yet what an incredible honor!

but there is none;
their tongues are parched with thirst.
But I the LORD will answer[z] them;
I, the God of Israel, will not forsake them.
18 I will make rivers flow[a] on barren heights,
and springs within the valleys.
I will turn the desert[b] into pools of water,
and the parched ground into springs.[c]
19 I will put in the desert
the cedar and the acacia, the myrtle and the olive.
I will set junipers in the wasteland,
the fir and the cypress together,[d]
20 so that people may see and know,
may consider and understand,
that the hand of the LORD has done this,
that the Holy One of Israel has created[e] it.

21 "Present your case," says the LORD.
"Set forth your arguments," says Jacob's King.[f]
22 "Tell us, you idols,
what is going to happen.[g]
Tell us what the former things were,
so that we may consider them
and know their final outcome.
Or declare to us the things to come,[h]
23 tell us what the future holds,
so we may know[i] that you are gods.
Do something, whether good or bad,[j]
so that we will be dismayed and filled with fear.
24 But you are less than nothing[k]
and your works are utterly worthless;
whoever chooses you is detestable.[l]

25 "I have stirred up one from the north,[m] and he comes —
one from the rising sun who calls on my name.
He treads[n] on rulers as if they were mortar,
as if he were a potter treading the clay.
26 Who told of this from the beginning,
so we could know,
or beforehand, so we could say,
'He was right'?
No one told of this,
no one foretold it,
no one heard any words[o] from you.
27 I was the first to tell[p] Zion, 'Look, here they are!'
I gave to Jerusalem a messenger of good news.[q]
28 I look but there is no one[r] —
no one among the gods to give counsel,[s]
no one to give answer when I ask them.
29 See, they are all false!
Their deeds amount to nothing;[t]
their images are but wind[u] and confusion.

The Servant of the LORD

42 "Here is my servant, whom I uphold,
my chosen one[v] in whom I delight;
I will put my Spirit[w] on him,
and he will bring justice to the nations.
2 He will not shout or cry out,
or raise his voice in the streets.

41:17 [z] Isa 30:19
41:18 [a] Isa 30:25 [b] Isa 43:19 [c] Isa 35:7
41:19 [d] Isa 60:13
41:20 [e] Job 12:9
41:21 [f] Isa 43:15
41:22 [g] Isa 43:9; 45:21 [h] Isa 46:10
41:23 [i] Isa 42:9; 44:7-8; 45:3 [j] Jer 10:5
41:24 [k] Isa 37:19; 44:9; 1Co 8:4 [l] Ps 115:8
41:25 [m] ver 2 [n] 2Sa 22:43
41:26 [o] Hab 2:18-19
41:27 [p] Isa 48:3, 16 [q] Isa 40:9
41:28 [r] Isa 50:2; 59:16; 63:5 [s] Isa 40:13-14
41:29 [t] ver 24 [u] Jer 5:13
42:1 [v] Isa 43:10; Lk 9:35; 1Pe 2:4, 6 [w] Isa 11:2; Mt 3:16-17; Jn 3:34

41:21–29 The prophet calls on the idolaters to give evidence that their idols have ever specifically predicted the future.

41:25–27 God responds to the challenge: He does have a plan for history. What unfolds before the exiles' eyes will prove it.

None of the idols predicted Cyrus's coming. The God of Israel did make such a prediction in advance (v. 27). In fact, that is exactly what he is doing through Isaiah, his "messenger of good news" in this very writing (v. 27).

41:28–29 This is a pronouncement of judgment on the idol worshipers. They are doomed to become like their gods: nothing, worthless, wind, and chaos. Their lives are doomed to become as meaningless as their gods are.

42:1–9 Just as God was able to bring down the Babylonian Empire through Cyrus, so he will bring "justice" (vv. 1, 3, 4) to the earth through his "servant" (v. 1). Verse 9 makes the connection clear by stating explicitly that the prediction concerning the servant is one of the "new things" that the gods could not declare in advance (v. 9). The Lord can do so with impunity.

42:1–3 The reiterated statement that this person is going to bring justice on the earth, that God's Spirit will be on him (v. 1), and that his accomplishment of this end will not be through oppression (v. 3) reminds us of the prophecies of the Messiah in chs. 9, 11, and 32. There we had the servant as King. Here we have the king as Servant.

3 A bruised reed he will not break,
and a smoldering wick he will not snuff out.
In faithfulness he will bring forth justice;[x]
4 he will not falter or be discouraged
till he establishes justice on earth.
In his teaching the islands will put their hope."[y]

5 This is what God the LORD says—
the Creator of the heavens, who stretches them out,
who spreads out the earth with all that springs from it,[z]
who gives breath[a] to its people,
and life to those who walk on it:
6 "I, the LORD, have called[b] you in righteousness;[c]
I will take hold of your hand.
I will keep[d] you and will make you
to be a covenant[e] for the people
and a light for the Gentiles,[f]
7 to open eyes that are blind,[g]
to free[h] captives from prison[i]
and to release from the dungeon
those who sit in darkness.

8 "I am the LORD; that is my name![j]
I will not yield my glory to another[k]
or my praise to idols.
9 See, the former things have taken place,
and new things I declare;
before they spring into being
I announce them to you."

Song of Praise to the LORD

10 Sing to the LORD a new song,[l]
his praise from the ends of the earth,[m]
you who go down to the sea, and all that is in it,[n]
you islands, and all who live in them.
11 Let the wilderness[o] and its towns
raise their voices;

42:3 [x] Ps 72:2
42:4 [y] Ge 49:10; Mt 12:18-21*
42:5 [z] Ps 24:2 [a] Ac 17:25
42:6 [b] Isa 43:1 [c] Jer 23:6 [d] Isa 26:3 [e] Isa 49:8 [f] Lk 2:32; Ac 13:47
42:7 [g] Isa 35:5 [h] Isa 49:9; 61:1 [i] Lk 4:19; 2Ti 2:26; Heb 2:14-15
42:8 [j] Ex 3:15 [k] Isa 48:11
42:10 [l] Ps 33:3; 40:3; 98:1 [m] Isa 49:6 [n] 1Ch 16:32; Ps 96:11
42:11 [o] Isa 32:16 [p] Isa 60:7 [q] Isa 52:7; Na 1:15
42:12 [r] Isa 24:15
42:13 [s] Isa 9:6 [t] Isa 26:11 [u] Hos 11:10 [v] Isa 66:14
42:15 [w] Eze 38:20 [x] Isa 50:2; Na 1:4-6
42:16 [y] Lk 1:78-79 [z] Isa 32:3 [a] Lk 3:5 [b] Heb 13:5
42:17 [c] Ps 97:7; Isa 1:29; 44:11; 45:16

Isa 42:8 ❖ How has God shown us his patience and mercy in times of distress?

let the settlements where Kedar[p] lives rejoice.
Let the people of Sela sing for joy;
let them shout from the mountaintops.[q]
12 Let them give glory[r] to the LORD
and proclaim his praise in the islands.
13 The LORD will march out like a champion,[s]
like a warrior he will stir up his zeal;[t]
with a shout[u] he will raise the battle cry
and will triumph over his enemies.[v]

14 "For a long time I have kept silent,
I have been quiet and held myself back.
But now, like a woman in childbirth,
I cry out, I gasp and pant.
15 I will lay waste[w] the mountains and hills
and dry up all their vegetation;
I will turn rivers into islands
and dry up[x] the pools.
16 I will lead[y] the blind[z] by ways they have not known,
along unfamiliar paths I will guide them;
I will turn the darkness into light before them
and make the rough places smooth.[a]
These are the things I will do;
I will not forsake[b] them.
17 But those who trust in idols,
who say to images, 'You are our gods,'
will be turned back in utter shame.[c]

✣ 41:21—42:9 The Servant brings God's right order into the world not from a position of strength but of weakness. He does not break an already-bent reed, nor does he quench a candle flame that is already flickering. Christ disarmed his enemies with love and grace and gentleness. We must minister in the same way.

42:10-13 Isaiah emphasizes that the Lord is the God of the whole world, and what he is going to do for Judah has joyous implications for the whole world.

42:14-17 If it seems God has "kept silent" (v. 14) as they endured the exile, that time is coming to a rapid close. Whatever obstacles may stand in the way will present no obstacle to God. Though they are "blind," he will give them "light" (v. 16). Their worst fears—that God has either abandoned them or is helpless—are groundless. By contrast, the Babylonian gods will be helpless to assist their people.

Israel Blind and Deaf

18 "Hear, you deaf;[d]
look, you blind, and see!
19 Who is blind[e] but my servant,[f]
and deaf like the messenger[g] I send?
Who is blind like the one in covenant[h] with me,
blind like the servant of the LORD?
20 You have seen many things, but you pay no attention;
your ears are open, but you do not listen."[i]
21 It pleased the LORD
for the sake of his righteousness
to make his law[j] great and glorious.
22 But this is a people plundered and looted,
all of them trapped in pits[k]
or hidden away in prisons.[l]
They have become plunder,
with no one to rescue them;
they have been made loot,
with no one to say, "Send them back."

23 Which of you will listen to this
or pay close attention[m] in time to come?
24 Who handed Jacob over to become loot,
and Israel to the plunderers?
Was it not the LORD,
against whom we have sinned?
For they would not follow[n] his ways;
they did not obey his law.
25 So he poured out on them his burning anger,
the violence of war.
It enveloped them in flames,[o] yet they did not understand;
it consumed them, but they did not take it to heart.[p]

42:18 [d]Isa 35:5
42:19 [e]Isa 43:8; Eze 12:2 [f]Isa 41:8-9 [g]Isa 44:26 [h]Isa 26:3
42:20 [i]Jer 6:10
42:21 [j]ver 4
42:22 [k]Isa 24:18 [l]Isa 24:22
42:23 [m]Isa 48:18
42:24 [n]Isa 30:15
42:25 [o]2Ki 25:9 [p]Isa 29:13; 47:7; 57:1,11; Hos 7:9

Isa 43:4-7 ❖ What community has God gathered around us? How is it comprised of different sorts of people? How can we be more involved in community life?

Israel's Only Savior

43 But now, this is what the LORD says—
he who created you, Jacob,
he who formed[q] you, Israel:[r]
"Do not fear, for I have redeemed[s] you;
I have summoned you by name;[t]
you are mine.
2 When you pass through the waters,[u]
I will be with you;[v]
and when you pass through the rivers,
they will not sweep over you.
When you walk through the fire,[w]
you will not be burned;
the flames will not set you ablaze.[x]
3 For I am the LORD your God,[y]
the Holy One of Israel, your Savior;
I give Egypt for your ransom,
Cush[a][z] and Seba in your stead.[a]
4 Since you are precious and honored in my sight,
and because I love[b] you,
I will give people in exchange for you,
nations in exchange for your life.
5 Do not be afraid,[c] for I am with you;[d]
I will bring your children[e] from the east
and gather you from the west.
6 I will say to the north, 'Give them up!'
and to the south,[f] 'Do not hold them back.'

43:1 [q]ver 7 [r]Ge 32:28; Isa 44:21 [s]Isa 44:2, 6 [t]Isa 42:6; 45:3-4
43:2 [u]Isa 8:7 [v]Dt 31:6,8 [w]Isa 29:6; 30:27 [x]Ps 66:12; Da 3:25-27
43:3 [y]Ex 20:2 [z]Isa 20:3 [a]Pr 21:18
43:4 [b]Isa 63:9
43:5 [c]Isa 44:2 [d]Jer 30:10-11 [e]Isa 41:8
43:6 [f]Ps 107:3

[a] *3* That is, the upper Nile region

42:18–24 The prophet commands the "deaf" to "hear" (v. 18). He calls on them to ask why they are in exile: God brought them down to destruction in punishment for their sin, but no one seemed to get the point.
42:25–43:1 The shift in tone from one verse to another is breathtaking. What God will now do is grace. God simply declares, as in 40:1–2, that he has "redeemed" his people (43:1). It is a completed fact.
43:2–7 The key to all of this is the personal relationship of God to his people. God will recover his people from all the lands where they have been taken. Even if the exiles themselves do not go home, their children will. God's promises will not fail.

42:10—43:7 One of the fundamental principles of the kingdom of God is that his grace precedes everything else. God calls his people to listen to and believe the promises he makes to deliver them. But his grace is declared before they are prepared to listen and believe. The most concise statement of this truth in the NT is found in Ro 5:8: God did everything necessary to deliver us from the consequences of our sin before there was any indication that we would respond to and accept that free act.

Bring my sons from afar
and my daughters[g] from the ends of the earth —
7 everyone who is called by my name,[h]
whom I created for my glory,
whom I formed and made.[i]"

8 Lead out those who have eyes but are blind,[j]
who have ears but are deaf.[k]
9 All the nations gather together[l]
and the peoples assemble.
Which of their gods foretold[m] this
and proclaimed to us the former things?
Let them bring in their witnesses to prove they were right,
so that others may hear and say, "It is true."
10 "You are my witnesses," declares the LORD,
"and my servant[n] whom I have chosen,
so that you may know and believe me
and understand that I am he.
Before me no god[o] was formed,
nor will there be one after me.
11 I, even I, am the LORD,
and apart from me there is no savior.[p]
12 I have revealed and saved and proclaimed —
I, and not some foreign god[q] among you.
You are my witnesses,[r]" declares the LORD, "that I am God.
13 Yes, and from ancient days[s] I am he.
No one can deliver out of my hand.
When I act, who can reverse it?"[t]

God's Mercy and Israel's Unfaithfulness

14 This is what the LORD says —
your Redeemer, the Holy One of Israel:
"For your sake I will send to Babylon
and bring down as fugitives[u] all the Babylonians,[a][v]
in the ships in which they took pride.
15 I am the LORD, your Holy One,
Israel's Creator, your King."

16 This is what the LORD says —
he who made a way through the sea,
a path through the mighty waters,[w]
17 who drew out[x] the chariots and horses,
the army and reinforcements together,[y]
and they lay there, never to rise again,
extinguished, snuffed out like a wick:
18 "Forget the former things;
do not dwell on the past.
19 See, I am doing a new thing![z]
Now it springs up; do you not perceive it?
I am making a way in the wilderness[a]
and streams in the wasteland.
20 The wild animals honor me,
the jackals[b] and the owls,
because I provide water[c] in the wilderness
and streams in the wasteland,
to give drink to my people, my chosen,
21 the people I formed for myself
that they may proclaim my praise.[d]

22 "Yet you have not called on me, Jacob,
you have not wearied yourselves for[b] me, Israel.[e]

[a] 14 Or *Chaldeans* [b] 22 Or *Jacob; / surely you have grown weary of*

43:6 [g] 2Co 6:18
43:7 [h] Isa 56:5; 63:19; Jas 2:7 [i] ver 1, 21; Ps 100:3; Eph 2:10
43:8 [j] Isa 6:9-10 [k] Isa 42:20; Eze 12:2
43:9 [l] Isa 41:1 [m] Isa 41:26
43:10 [n] Isa 41:8-9 [o] Isa 44:6, 8
43:11 [p] Isa 45:21
43:12 [q] Dt 32:12; Ps 81:9 [r] Isa 44:8
43:13 [s] Ps 90:2 [t] Job 9:12; Isa 14:27
43:14 [u] Isa 13:14-15 [v] Isa 23:13
43:16 [w] Ps 77:19; Isa 11:15; 51:10
43:17 [x] Ps 118:12; Isa 1:31 [y] Ex 14:9
43:19 [z] 2Co 5:17; Rev 21:5 [a] Ex 17:6; Nu 20:11
43:20 [b] Isa 13:22 [c] Isa 48:21
43:21 [d] Ps 102:18; 1Pe 2:9
43:22 [e] Isa 30:11

43:8–13 The One who is both judge and defendant turns to his blind and deaf servant and says, "You are my witnesses" (v. 10). God is going to do an amazing work on their behalf so that they can be the evidence he deserves.

Verses 10–13 relate that the people of Israel have been called into a relationship with God whereby they will "know" (affective) and "believe" (volitional) and "understand" (cognitive) that "I am he" (v. 10). This is God's ultimate statement of identity.

God has "revealed" himself, "saved" them, and "proclaimed" (v. 12) the meaning of what he has done. His revelation touches the whole of human personality.

43:14–17 God tells his people once again that he is going to deliver them from Babylon. But how is he going to deliver them? Verses 16–17 invite the people to remember what he did in the exodus.

43:18–21 After reminding them of his acts in the past, God tells them to "forget" all that (v. 18). What is going on? God loves doing things in "new" ways (v. 19). God promises to transform the desert created by arrogance and false trust into a place of "streams" where his "chosen" (v. 20) may have all their needs supplied. As a result, his people will "proclaim my praise" (v. 21).

43:22–28 The prophet steps back from that glorious future to talk about the present reality. Isaiah

23 You have not brought me sheep for
burnt offerings,
nor honored[f] me with your
sacrifices.[g]
I have not burdened you with grain
offerings
nor wearied you with demands[h]
for incense.[i]
24 You have not bought any fragrant
calamus[j] for me,
or lavished on me the fat of your
sacrifices.
But you have burdened me with
your sins
and wearied[k] me with your
offenses.[l]

25 "I, even I, am he who blots out
your transgressions,[m] for my own
sake,[n]
and remembers your sins no more.[o]
26 Review the past for me,
let us argue the matter together;[p]
state the case[q] for your innocence.
27 Your first father sinned;
those I sent to teach[r] you rebelled
against me.
28 So I disgraced the dignitaries of your
temple;
I consigned Jacob to destruction[a]
and Israel to scorn.[s]

Israel the Chosen

44 "But now listen, Jacob, my
servant,[t]
Israel, whom I have chosen.
2 This is what the LORD says—
he who made you, who formed
you in the womb,
and who will help[u] you:
Do not be afraid, Jacob, my servant,
Jeshurun,[b][v] whom I have chosen.
3 For I will pour water[w] on the thirsty
land,
and streams on the dry ground;
I will pour out my Spirit[x] on your
offspring,
and my blessing on your
descendants.[y]
4 They will spring up like grass in a
meadow,
like poplar trees[z] by flowing
streams.[a]
5 Some will say, 'I belong to the LORD';
others will call themselves by the
name of Jacob;
still others will write on their hand,[b]
'The LORD's,'[c]
and will take the name Israel.

The LORD, Not Idols

6 "This is what the LORD says—
Israel's King[d] and Redeemer,[e] the
LORD Almighty:
I am the first and I am the last;[f]
apart from me there is no God.
7 Who then is like me? Let him
proclaim it.
Let him declare and lay out
before me
what has happened since I
established my ancient
people,
and what is yet to come—

43:23 [f] Zec 7:5-6; Mal 1:6-8 [g] Am 5:25 [h] Jer 7:22 [i] Ex 30:35; Lev 2:1 **43:24** [j] Ex 30:23 [k] Isa 1:14; 7:13 [l] Mal 2:17 **43:25** [m] Ac 3:19 [n] Isa 37:35; Eze 36:22 [o] Isa 38:17; Jer 31:34 **43:26** [p] Isa 1:18 [q] Isa 41:1; 50:8 **43:27** [r] Isa 9:15; 28:7; Jer 5:31 **43:28** [s] Jer 24:9; Eze 5:15 **44:1** [t] ver 21; Jer 30:10; 46:27-28 **44:2** [u] Isa 41:10 [v] Dt 32:15 **44:3** [w] Joel 3:18 [x] Joel 2:28; Ac 2:17 [y] Isa 61:9; 65:23 **44:4** [z] Lev 23:40 [a] Job 40:22 **44:5** [b] Ex 13:9 [c] Zec 8:20-22 **44:6** [d] Isa 41:21 [e] Isa 43:1 [f] Isa 41:4; Rev 1:8,17; 22:13

[a] *28* The Hebrew term refers to the irrevocable giving over of things or persons to the LORD, often by totally destroying them. [b] *2 Jeshurun* means *the upright one,* that is, Israel.

---

points to the people's unbelief during the exile and in Isaiah's own day, for which judgment is still to come (v. 28). There is an implied charge that it seems unfair of God to have sent his people into exile in the first place.

43:22–24 God's answer to the people's charge reflects the kind of hyperbolic language that the prophets often use. God says that, in fact, they have not been calling on him at all; rather, they have wearied themselves with their sacrifices. They have piled up more and more sin until God could not bear it any longer.

43:25–28 God does not have to be manipulated into forgiving us. In fact, he cannot be so manipulated. What he has already done, he has done for his own sake; we have only to receive what he has done. The sacrifices were to be symbols of changed hearts and changed lives. Far from being unfair because of their careful ritual, the exile became necessary because of their empty rites.

44:1–5 God implores his people to "listen" (v. 1). Israel must not rely on mechanical rituals but enter into a relationship by listening to the One who speaks.

Just as God is strong enough to do something about their physical captivity, so he is great enough to do something about their persistent sinning. The means of that transformation is his Spirit (v. 3).

43:8—44:5 God simply declares a fact: "You are my witnesses" (43:10). Jesus says the same thing (Ac 1:8). Like it or not, we have been changed. We *are* evidence of his divine, delivering, transforming power. One's witness is the expression of one's experience. Like believers today, the exiles were not expected to make speeches, but to report what they knew to be true of God from their own experience.

44:6–8 Yahweh identifies himself inextricably with Israel. Although he is the only God, he has made himself known in relationship with a small,

CHARACTER OF GOD // GOD IS REDEEMER

Isaiah 44:6: This is what the LORD says—Israel's King and Redeemer, the LORD Almighty: I am the first and I am the last; apart from me there is no God.

In ancient Israel, a "redeemer" was someone who would buy back or rescue something or someone that had been taken in order to restore it to the family. When Lot was captured, Abraham rescued him (Ge 14:14-16). When Naomi's husband died and she lost everything, Boaz served as her redeemer (Ru 4:9-10).

The Bible calls God the Redeemer of his people. This is a powerful image, presenting God as the One who buys back his lost people. God will not let them slip away from him—even when they fall into sin, he is faithful and buys them back. Psalm 103:4 says that God redeems the lives of his children from the pit and crowns them with love and compassion. Psalm 130:8 says God will redeem Israel from all their sins.

Paul picks up the idea of God as Redeemer, teaching that God redeemed his children "from the curse of the law" (Gal 3:13). In Titus 2:14, Paul writes that Christ "gave himself for us to redeem us from all wickedness and to purify for himself a people that are his very own, eager to do what is good." Here we see that God redeems people for a purpose: to be his ambassadors of good in the world. Those whom God has redeemed are called to go out and redeem the world for God.

APPLICATION Understanding that God is our Redeemer reminds us that there is a cost for sin. Amazingly, however, God our Redeemer is the One who pays this cost (1Co 7:23). Like Abraham rescuing Lot (Ge 14), God rescues his children from the depths of their sin and from the punishment they would rightfully have received. We can never repay God for this gift—all we can do is worship and stand in awe of the One who has acted on our behalf to draw us to himself.

yes, let them foretell[g] what will
come.
8 Do not tremble, do not be afraid.
Did I not proclaim this and foretell
it long ago?
You are my witnesses. Is there any
God[h] besides me?
No, there is no other Rock;[i] I know
not one."

9 All who make idols are nothing,
and the things they treasure are
worthless.[j]
Those who would speak up for them
are blind;
they are ignorant, to their own
shame.
10 Who shapes a god and casts an idol,
which can profit nothing?[k]
11 People who do that will be put to
shame;[l]
such craftsmen are only human
beings.
Let them all come together and take
their stand;
they will be brought down to
terror and shame.[m]

12 The blacksmith[n] takes a tool
and works with it in the coals;
he shapes an idol with hammers,
he forges it with the might of his
arm.[o]
He gets hungry and loses his
strength;
he drinks no water and grows
faint.
13 The carpenter[p] measures with a line
and makes an outline with a
marker;
he roughs it out with chisels
and marks it with compasses.
He shapes it in human form,[q]

44:7 [g] Isa 41:22, 26
44:8 [h] Isa 43:10 [i] Dt 4:35; 1Sa 2:2
44:9 [j] Isa 41:24
44:10 [k] Isa 41:29; Jer 10:5; Ac 19:26
44:11 [l] Isa 1:29
[m] Isa 42:17
44:12 [n] Isa 40:19; 41:6-7 [o] Jer 10:3-5; Ac 17:29
44:13 [p] Isa 41:7 [q] Ps 115:4-7

Isa 44:12-20 Where do we see human-crafted gods today, whether physical or ideological? Why are gods made by humans such a foolish source of hope?

insignificant people. The people of Israel are "witnesses" (v. 8) to that fact.

44:9-11 The other peoples of earth "treasure" worthless things and have become "nothing" themselves (v. 9).

44:12-14 The prophet describes the process of making idols in great detail, showing how difficult it is to make one's own gods when the true God can be so easily found. Isaiah takes us backward through the complex process.

human form in all its glory,
that it may dwell in a shrine.[r]
14 He cut down cedars,
or perhaps took a cypress or oak.
He let it grow among the trees of the forest,
or planted a pine, and the rain made it grow.
15 It is used as fuel[s] for burning;
some of it he takes and warms himself,
he kindles a fire and bakes bread.
But he also fashions a god and worships it;
he makes an idol and bows[t] down to it.
16 Half of the wood he burns in the fire;
over it he prepares his meal,
he roasts his meat and eats his fill.
He also warms himself and says,
"Ah! I am warm; I see the fire."
17 From the rest he makes a god, his idol;
he bows down to it and worships.
He prays[u] to it and says,
"Save[v] me! You are my god!"
18 They know nothing, they understand[w] nothing;
their eyes[x] are plastered over so they cannot see,
and their minds closed so they cannot understand.
19 No one stops to think,
no one has the knowledge or understanding[y] to say,
"Half of it I used for fuel;
I even baked bread over its coals,
I roasted meat and I ate.
Shall I make a detestable[z] thing from what is left?
Shall I bow down to a block of wood?"
20 Such a person feeds on ashes;[a] a deluded[b] heart misleads him;
he cannot save himself, or say,
"Is not this thing in my right hand a lie?[c]"

21 "Remember[d] these things, Jacob,
for you, Israel, are my servant.
I have made you, you are my servant;[e]
Israel, I will not forget you.[f]
22 I have swept away[g] your offenses like a cloud,
your sins like the morning mist.
Return[h] to me,
for I have redeemed[i] you."
23 Sing for joy,[j] you heavens, for the LORD has done this;
shout aloud, you earth[k] beneath.
Burst into song, you mountains,[l]
you forests and all your trees,
for the LORD has redeemed Jacob,
he displays his glory[m] in Israel.

Jerusalem to Be Inhabited

24 "This is what the LORD says—
your Redeemer,[n] who formed you in the womb:

I am the LORD,
the Maker of all things,
who stretches out the heavens,[o]
who spreads out the earth by myself,
25 who foils[p] the signs of false prophets
and makes fools of diviners,[q]
who overthrows the learning of the wise[r]

44:13 [r] Jdg 17:4-5 44:15 [s] ver 19 [t] 2Ch 25:14 44:17 [u] 1Ki 18:26 [v] Isa 45:20 44:18 [w] Isa 1:3 [x] Isa 6:9-10 44:19 [y] Isa 5:13; 27:11; 45:20 [z] Dt 27:15 44:20 [a] Ps 102:9 [b] Job 15:31; Ro 1:21-23, 28; 2Th 2:11; 2Ti 3:13 [c] Isa 59:3, 4, 13; Ro 1:25 44:21 [d] Isa 46:8; Zec 10:9 [e] ver 1-2 [f] Isa 49:15 44:22 [g] Isa 43:25; Ac 3:19 [h] Isa 55:7 [i] 1Co 6:20 44:23 [j] Isa 42:10 [k] Ps 148:7 [l] Ps 98:8 [m] Isa 61:3 44:24 [n] Isa 43:14 [o] Isa 42:5 44:25 [p] Ps 33:10 [q] Isa 47:13 [r] 1Co 1:27

44:15–18 Isaiah comes to the heart of his argument. How in the world can a piece of wood, another part of which has been used to cook and heat, save a person? It cannot, and anyone who thinks it can has been mentally and spiritually blinded.

44:19–20 The ultimate seriousness of paganism and its consequences is seen here. In the OT, an "abomination" is to use a created thing in a way that violates its character. That is surely the case with idolatry.

44:21–22 These two verses give us God's appeal to his people based on what he has just said. They have not made God; he has "made" them (v. 21). If they will "remember," he will not "forget" (v. 21). He will find a way to forgive their "offenses" (v. 22) and to redeem them from their captivity.

44:6–22 The meaninglessness and pointlessness of life in a world where the transcendent God has been shut out is vividly portrayed in all the media today. We are already reaping the bitter fruits of the view that "this world is all there is" and the self-centered carelessness that comes along with it. Can things made with human hands save us from ourselves today any more than they could then? Not in the least. All the material things that distract us must all be rejected by Christians today as we seek the face of the one God more than anything else.

44:23 Nature is called to praise God for his greater redemptive "glory" that will be displayed "in Israel."

44:24–28 The "Redeemer" (v. 24) spells out his redemptive plans. These verses comprise a single sentence consisting of a succession of participles that define "I am the LORD" in v. 24. Here God identifies himself and demonstrates his lordship by what he does.

and turns it into nonsense,[s]
26 who carries out the words[t] of his servants
and fulfills[u] the predictions of his messengers,

who says of Jerusalem, 'It shall be inhabited,'
of the towns of Judah, 'They shall be rebuilt,'
and of their ruins, 'I will restore them,'[v]
27 who says to the watery deep, 'Be dry,
and I will dry up your streams,'
28 who says of Cyrus,[w] 'He is my shepherd
and will accomplish all that I please;
he will say of Jerusalem,[x] "Let it be rebuilt,"
and of the temple,[y] "Let its foundations be laid." '

45 "This is what the LORD says to his anointed,
to Cyrus, whose right hand I take hold[z] of
to subdue nations[a] before him
and to strip kings of their armor,
to open doors before him
so that gates will not be shut:
2 I will go before you
and will level[b] the mountains[a];
I will break down gates of bronze
and cut through bars of iron.[c]
3 I will give you hidden treasures,[d]
riches stored in secret places,[e]
so that you may know[f] that I am the LORD,
the God of Israel, who summons you by name.[g]
4 For the sake of Jacob my servant,[h]
of Israel my chosen,
I summon you by name
and bestow on you a title of honor,
though you do not acknowledge[i] me.
5 I am the LORD, and there is no other;[j]
apart from me there is no God.[k]
I will strengthen you,[l]
though you have not acknowledged me,
6 so that from the rising of the sun
to the place of its setting[m]
people may know there is none besides me.[n]
I am the LORD, and there is no other.
7 I form the light and create darkness,
I bring prosperity and create disaster;[o]
I, the LORD, do all these things.

8 "You heavens above, rain[p] down my righteousness;[q]
let the clouds shower it down.
Let the earth open wide,
let salvation[r] spring up,
let righteousness flourish with it;
I, the LORD, have created it.

9 "Woe to those who quarrel[s] with their Maker,
those who are nothing but potsherds
among the potsherds on the ground.
Does the clay say to the potter,[t]
'What are you making?'
Does your work say,
'The potter has no hands'?
10 Woe to the one who says to a father,
'What have you begotten?'
or to a mother,
'What have you brought to birth?'

11 "This is what the LORD says—

44:25 [s] 2Sa 15:31; 1Co 1:19-20
44:26 [t] Zec 1:6 [u] Isa 55:11; Mt 5:18 [v] Isa 49:8-21
44:28 [w] 2Ch 36:22 [x] Isa 14:32 [y] Ezr 1:2-4
45:1 [z] Ps 73:23; Isa 41:13; 42:6 [a] Jer 50:35
45:2 [b] Isa 40:4 [c] Ps 107:16; Jer 51:30
45:3 [d] Jer 50:37 [e] Jer 41:8 [f] Isa 41:23 [g] Ex 33:12; Isa 43:1
45:4 [h] Isa 41:8-9 [i] Ac 17:23
45:5 [j] Isa 44:8 [k] Ps 18:31 [l] Ps 18:39
45:6 [m] Isa 43:5; Mal 1:11 [n] ver 5, 18
45:7 [o] Isa 31:2; Am 3:6
45:8 [p] Ps 72:6; Joel 3:18 [q] Ps 85:11; Isa 60:21; 61:10, 11; Hos 10:12 [r] Isa 12:3
45:9 [s] Job 15:25 [t] Isa 29:16; Ro 9:20-21*

[a] 2 Dead Sea Scrolls and Septuagint; the meaning of the word in the Masoretic Text is uncertain.

45:1–3 Cyrus is specifically said to be God's "anointed" (v. 1). The victories that will come to him will be gifts from God's hand.

45:4–5 Twice is it said that God has called Cyrus "by name" (vv. 3, 4). This underlines the naming of Cyrus as an act of predictive prophecy. Isaiah has repeatedly insisted that God alone can tell the future. Attempts to do so by idolaters only make them look like "fools" (44:25).

One of the pieces of evidence of God's lordship is that he knows the name of one who does not know God's name. Even if Cyrus has never heard of Yahweh of Israel, Yahweh knows about Cyrus even before he is born. Cyrus's acknowledgment that he was called by the Lord to release his people (cf. Ezr 1:2) may be as much as this statement intends for him to do.

45:5–8 This segment ends much as the previous one (44:23–28) began: with a declaration of the absolute uniqueness of God.

45:9–13 Does God have the right to use someone who does not even know him to save his believing people? God pronounces doom ("woe," vv. 9–10) on those who challenge the rightness of his activity.

45:11–13 If the exiles will not let God deliver them in his own way, he is still their "God in a box" to do with as they choose. So in these verses God once more asserts that he is the Maker of the

the Holy One of Israel, and its
Maker:
Concerning things to come,
do you question me about my
children,
or give me orders about the work
of my hands?[u]
12 It is I who made the earth
and created mankind on it.
My own hands stretched out the
heavens;[v]
I marshaled their starry hosts.[w]
13 I will raise up Cyrus[a][x] in my
righteousness:
I will make all his ways straight.
He will rebuild my city
and set my exiles free,
but not for a price or reward,[y]
says the LORD Almighty."

14 This is what the LORD says:

"The products of Egypt and the
merchandise of Cush,[b]
and those tall Sabeans —
they will come over to you
and will be yours;
they will trudge behind you,
coming over to you in chains.[z]
They will bow down before you
and plead[a] with you, saying,
'Surely God is with you,[b] and there is
no other;
there is no other god.'"

15 Truly you are a God who has been
hiding[c] himself,
the God and Savior of Israel.
16 All the makers of idols will be put to
shame and disgraced;[d]
they will go off into disgrace
together.

45:11 [u] Isa 19:25
45:12 [v] Ge 2:1; Isa 42:5 [w] Ne 9:6
45:13 [x] 2Ch 36:22; Isa 41:2 [y] Isa 52:3
45:14 [z] Isa 14:1-2 [a] Jer 16:19; Zec 8:20-23 [b] 1Co 14:25
45:15 [c] Ps 44:24
45:16 [d] Isa 44:9, 11

Isa 45:13 ❖ God used pagan king Cyrus to free his people. When have we seen God use surprising means to accomplish his good purposes?

17 But Israel will be saved[e] by the LORD
with an everlasting salvation;[f]
you will never be put to shame or
disgraced,
to ages everlasting.

18 For this is what the LORD says —
he who created the heavens,
he is God;
he who fashioned and made the
earth,
he founded it;
he did not create it to be empty,[g]
but formed it to be inhabited[h] —
he says:
"I am the LORD,
and there is no other.[i]
19 I have not spoken in secret,[j]
from somewhere in a land of
darkness;
I have not said to Jacob's
descendants,[k]
'Seek me in vain.'
I, the LORD, speak the truth;
I declare what is right.[l]

20 "Gather together[m] and come;
assemble, you fugitives from the
nations.
Ignorant[n] are those who carry[o]
about idols of wood,
who pray to gods that cannot
save.[p]
21 Declare what is to be, present it —

45:17 [e] Ro 11:26 [f] Isa 26:4
45:18 [g] Ge 1:2 [h] Ge 1:26; Isa 42:5 [i] ver 5
45:19 [j] Isa 48:16 [k] Isa 41:8 [l] Dt 30:11
45:20 [m] Isa 43:9 [n] Isa 44:19 [o] Isa 46:1; Jer 10:5 [p] Isa 44:17; 46:6-7

[a] *13* Hebrew *him* [b] *14* That is, the upper Nile region

---

whole cosmos. If he does not have a right to set his "exiles free" (v. 13) as he chooses, who does?

✤ **44:23—45:13** People who zealously studied the Scriptures could not believe that Jesus could be the promised Messiah. People who had made a life's work of studying God's ways could not allow Jesus to deliver people in ways that seemed to violate how God was supposed to act. We may say that they had not studied the Scriptures well enough or that they were more concerned about justifying God's ways to themselves than they were about applying them to human hearts. But the question here is whether that behavior is descriptive of us and whether the strong words of Isaiah and Jesus might be directed at us.

45:14–17 This segment opens with a picture of people from the ends of the earth coming humbly to Israel, admitting that Israel's God is the only God (v. 14). The next three verses offer some reflection on this picture. God's people will not be "disgraced" (v. 16). They will be "saved" from captivity (v. 17).
45:18–19 Here is the reason why God's salvation can be affirmed: God created the universe for a purpose. He has revealed his desire for relationship as he has "spoken" to them again and again, inviting them to "seek" him (v. 19).
45:20–21 After this introduction, the idol makers are once more called to present themselves before God. But their description here is unusual. In v. 20, they are the "fugitives from the nations" (as in v. 14). The idols have failed, so they come carrying their useless images. The Lord affirmed he predicted this. Thus, he is the only God.

let them take counsel together.
Who foretold[q] this long ago,
who declared it from the distant past?
Was it not I, the LORD?
And there is no God apart from me,[r]
a righteous God and a Savior;
there is none but me.

22 "Turn[s] to me and be saved,[t]
all you ends of the earth;[u]
for I am God, and there is no other.
23 By myself I have sworn,[v]
my mouth has uttered in all integrity[w]
a word that will not be revoked:[x]
Before me every knee will bow;
by me every tongue will swear.[y]
24 They will say of me, 'In the LORD alone
are deliverance[z] and strength.' "
All who have raged against him
will come to him and be put to shame.[a]
25 But all the descendants of Israel
will find deliverance in the LORD
and will make their boast in him.[b]

Gods of Babylon

46 Bel[c] bows down, Nebo stoops low;
their idols are borne by beasts of burden.[a]
The images that are carried[d] about are burdensome,
a burden for the weary.
2 They stoop and bow down together;
unable to rescue the burden,
they themselves go off into captivity.[e]

3 "Listen[f] to me, you descendants of Jacob,
all the remnant of the people of Israel,
you whom I have upheld since your birth,
and have carried since you were born.
4 Even to your old age and gray hairs[g]
I am he,[h] I am he who will sustain you.
I have made you and I will carry you;
I will sustain you and I will rescue you.

5 "With whom will you compare me or count me equal?
To whom will you liken me that we may be compared?[i]
6 Some pour out gold from their bags
and weigh out silver on the scales;
they hire a goldsmith[j] to make it into a god,
and they bow down and worship it.[k]
7 They lift it to their shoulders and carry[l] it;
they set it up in its place, and there it stands.
From that spot it cannot move.
Even though someone cries out to it, it cannot answer;
it cannot save[m] them from their troubles.

8 "Remember[n] this, keep it in mind,
take it to heart, you rebels.
9 Remember the former things, those of long ago;[o]
I am God, and there is no other;
I am God, and there is none like me.[p]
10 I make known the end from the beginning,
from ancient times,[q] what is still to come.

45:21 [q] Isa 41:22 [r] ver 5
45:22 [s] Zec 12:10 [t] Nu 21:8-9; 2Ch 20:12 [u] Isa 49:6,12
45:23 [v] Ge 22:16 [w] Heb 6:13 [x] Isa 55:11 [y] Ps 63:11; Isa 19:18; Ro 14:11*; Php 2:10-11
45:24 [z] Jer 33:16 [a] Isa 41:11
45:25 [b] Isa 41:16
46:1 [c] Isa 21:9; Jer 50:2; 51:44 [d] Isa 45:20
46:2 [e] Jdg 18:17-18; 2Sa 5:21
46:3 [f] ver 12
46:4 [g] Ps 71:18 [h] Isa 43:13
46:5 [i] Isa 40:18, 25
46:6 [j] Isa 40:19 [k] Isa 44:17
46:7 [l] ver 1 [m] Isa 44:17; Isa 45:20
46:8 [n] Isa 44:21
46:9 [o] Dt 32:7 [p] Isa 45:5,21
46:10 [q] Isa 45:21

[a] 1 Or *are but beasts and cattle*

45:22–25 What follows next is surprising. We have an invitation to these people from the "ends of the earth" to "turn" to the Lord "and be saved" (v. 22). God does not want to destroy the idol makers but to save them.

46:1–4 The theme of God as the only Savior is now graphically illustrated. Those who have depended on the Babylonian gods "Bel" and "Nebo" load their idol gods onto oxcarts to be "carried" off "into captivity" (vv. 1–2). God reminds his people that he is the one who has "carried" (v. 3) them since their conception, and he promises to carry them through their "old age" (v. 4).

46:5–7 If people choose to make their own gods, they will have to carry what they have made.

46:8–13 These verses constitute the final summation and appeal in the disputation with the idols. The case has been presented; now God calls on his people to make their decision.

Cyrus, the "bird of prey" coming "from the east" (v. 11) will arrive in direct fulfillment of the prediction and purpose of God. The issue now is whether the exiles will keep their faith through 45 dark, uncertain years so that when Cyrus is revealed, there will still be a remnant who can reach out and take hold of God's hand.

CHARACTER OF GOD // GOD IS SOVEREIGN

Isaiah 46:9–10: "I am God, and there is no other; I am God, and there is none like me. I make known the end from the beginning, from ancient times, what is still to come. I say, 'My purpose will stand, and I will do all that I please.'"

There could hardly be a clearer proclamation of God's sovereignty than Isaiah 46:9-10. God declares that he knows the end from the beginning and he will accomplish all his purposes. No plan against God will stand, and no event will ever catch God off guard.

God's sovereignty refers to his complete control over all the universe. Everything besides God is his creation, whether physical or spiritual, and so all things exist completely under God's authority. Evil powers can never compete with God because they are only perversions of God's good creation. Furthermore, the enemy cannot act outside of what God allows. Although evil sometimes seems to run rampant in the world, God remains in complete control as Lord of the universe, and he is guiding the world toward a glorious future at Christ's return, when evil will be destroyed and there will be no more death or pain (Rev 21:4).

The fact that God is completely sovereign makes God's grace and mercy all the more remarkable. Rather than crushing those who oppose him and letting all sinners bear the consequences of their rebellion, God extends mercy in Jesus Christ. God's sovereign will for creation includes a plan of salvation for all people. This is a divine gift, based not on merit but on mercy.

APPLICATION ✚ God's sovereignty is a deep assurance for believers. God's salvation plan can never be undone, and God's people can never be torn from God's hand. No power against God will stand. God's sovereignty gives us confidence as we face the future, knowing that all things are in God's control. We are not slaves to fate or chance; our hope is secure in him. The Creator of all is also the Ruler of all, and he has known the end from the beginning.

I say, 'My purpose will stand,[r]
and I will do all that I please.'
11 From the east I summon a bird of
prey;
from a far-off land, a man to fulfill
my purpose.
What I have said, that I will bring
about;
what I have planned, that I
will do.
12 Listen[s] to me, you stubborn-
hearted,
you who are now far from my
righteousness.[t]
13 I am bringing my righteousness
near,
it is not far away;
and my salvation will not be
delayed.
I will grant salvation to Zion,
my splendor[u] to Israel.

46:10 [r] Pr 19:21; Ac 5:39
46:12 [s] ver 3 [t] Ps 119:150; Isa 48:1; Jer 2:5
46:13 [u] Isa 44:23

Isa 46:13 ✚ How has God brought his righteousness near (see 1Pe 1:10–12)? How can we lay hold of this righteousness?

The Fall of Babylon

47 "Go down, sit in the dust,
Virgin Daughter[v] Babylon;
sit on the ground without a throne,
queen city of the Babylonians.[a][w]
No more will you be called
tender or delicate.[x]
2 Take millstones[y] and grind[z] flour;
take off your veil.[a]
Lift up your skirts,[b] bare your legs,
and wade through the streams.
3 Your nakedness[c] will be exposed
and your shame[d] uncovered.

47:1 [v] Isa 23:12 [w] Ps 137:8; Jer 50:42; 51:33; Zec 2:7 [x] Dt 28:56
47:2 [y] Ex 11:5; Mt 24:41 [z] Jdg 16:21 [a] Ge 24:65 [b] Isa 32:11
47:3 [c] Eze 16:37; Na 3:5 [d] Isa 20:4

[a] *1* Or *Chaldeans*; also in verse 5

✚ **45:14—46:13** Only God can provide meaning, purpose, identity, and fulfillment. We truly begin to experience God's carrying of us when we take our hands off these things and relinquish them into God's hands. Until we are willing to release our survival into God's hands, we are allowing our fears to keep us from knowing God's care and deliverance.

47:1–4 Babylon was the queen of the world, the mightiest of the mighty. She will soon meet someone mightier, who says that she must leave her "throne" (v. 1). She will be humiliated. This language

I will take vengeance;[e]
I will spare no one."

4 Our Redeemer — the LORD Almighty
is his name[f] —
is the Holy One of Israel.

5 "Sit in silence, go into darkness,[g]
queen city of the Babylonians;
no more will you be called
queen of kingdoms.[h]
6 I was angry[i] with my people
and desecrated my inheritance;
I gave them into your hand,[j]
and you showed them no mercy.
Even on the aged
you laid a very heavy yoke.
7 You said, 'I am forever —
the eternal queen!'[k]
But you did not consider these
things
or reflect[l] on what might happen.[m]

8 "Now then, listen, you lover of
pleasure,
lounging in your security[n]
and saying to yourself,
'I am, and there is none besides
me.[o]
I will never be a widow[p]
or suffer the loss of children.'
9 Both of these will overtake you
in a moment,[q] on a single day:
loss of children[r] and widowhood.
They will come upon you in full
measure,
in spite of your many sorceries[s]
and all your potent spells.[t]
10 You have trusted[u] in your
wickedness
and have said, 'No one sees me.'[v]
Your wisdom[w] and knowledge
mislead[x] you
when you say to yourself,

47:3 [e] Isa 34:8
47:4 [f] Jer 50:34
47:5 [g] Isa 13:10 [h] Isa 13:19
47:6 [i] 2Ch 28:9 [j] Isa 10:13
47:7 [k] ver 5; Rev 18:7 [l] Isa 42:23,25 [m] Dt 32:29
47:8 [n] Isa 32:9 [o] Isa 45:6; Zep 2:15 [p] Rev 18:7
47:9 [q] Ps 73:19; 1Th 5:3; Rev 18:8-10 [r] Isa 13:18 [s] Na 3:4 [t] Rev 18:23
47:10 [u] Ps 52:7; 62:10 [v] Isa 29:15 [w] Isa 5:21 [x] Isa 44:20

Isa 47:12-15 ❖ When have we sought advice or guidance from an ungodly source? What was the result?

'I am, and there is none
besides me.'
11 Disaster will come upon you,
and you will not know how to
conjure it away.
A calamity will fall upon you
that you cannot ward off with a
ransom;
a catastrophe you cannot foresee
will suddenly[y] come upon you.

12 "Keep on, then, with your magic
spells
and with your many sorceries,[z]
which you have labored at since
childhood.
Perhaps you will succeed,
perhaps you will cause terror.
13 All the counsel you have received
has only worn you out![a]
Let your astrologers[b] come
forward,
those stargazers who make
predictions month by
month,
let them save[c] you from what is
coming upon you.
14 Surely they are like stubble;[d]
the fire will burn them up.
They cannot even save themselves
from the power of the flame.[e]
These are not coals for warmth;
this is not a fire to sit by.
15 That is all they are to you —
these you have dealt with
and labored[f] with since childhood.
All of them go on in their error;
there is not one that can save you.

47:11 [y] 1Th 5:3
47:12 [z] ver 9
47:13 [a] Isa 57:10; Jer 51:58 [b] Isa 44:25 [c] ver 15
47:14 [d] Isa 5:24; Na 1:10 [e] Isa 10:17; Jer 51:30,32,58
47:15 [f] Rev 18:11

---

is used elsewhere in the OT to describe being taken into exile (cf. 20:4).

47:5-11 The Babylonians made the fatal error of thinking that they were self-existent and self-perpetuating (vv. 8, 10). It never occurred to them that they might be agents of One who will hold them accountable.

Babylon is so convinced of her superiority that she cannot imagine herself as a widow bereft of children (vv. 8-9). The Babylonians were devoted to mastering magical arts, certain they could ward off any "calamity" (v. 11). They do not reckon with a God who is beyond all magical manipulation (cf. 65:11).

47:12-15 On a sarcastic note, the prophet tells Babylon to go ahead with her futile magic. Efforts to foretell and control events are wasted. The sorcerers lit a fire; it will only burn up those who started it.

47:1-15 Intelligence not surrendered to God can be a terrible curse for the human race. Our tremendous intelligence is, as it was for the Babylonians, aimed at making ourselves self-existent and self-perpetuating. How long will it be before the Redeemer, whose name is Yahweh of Heaven's Armies, the Holy One of Israel, tells us to get off our throne and to take our place in the dust? Personal humility before the God of all things brings reality into perspective (see Job 38-41).

Stubborn Israel

48 "Listen to this, you descendants of Jacob,
you who are called by the name of Israel
and come from the line of Judah,
you who take oaths in the name of the LORD
and invoke[g] the God of Israel —
but not in truth[h] or righteousness —
2 you who call yourselves citizens of the holy city[i]
and claim to rely[j] on the God of Israel —
the LORD Almighty is his name:
3 I foretold the former things[k] long ago,
my mouth announced[l] them and I made them known;
then suddenly I acted, and they came to pass.
4 For I knew how stubborn[m] you were;
your neck muscles[n] were iron,
your forehead[o] was bronze.
5 Therefore I told you these things long ago;
before they happened I announced them to you
so that you could not say,
'My images brought them about;[p]
my wooden image and metal god ordained them.'
6 You have heard these things; look at them all.
Will you not admit them?

"From now on I will tell you of new things,
of hidden things unknown to you.
7 They are created now, and not long ago;
you have not heard of them before today.
So you cannot say,
'Yes, I knew of them.'

48:1 [g] Isa 58:2 [h] Jer 4:2 48:2 [i] Isa 52:1 [j] Isa 10:20; Mic 3:11; Ro 2:17 48:3 [k] Isa 41:22 [l] Isa 45:21 48:4 [m] Dt 31:27 [n] Ex 32:9; Ac 7:51 [o] Eze 3:9 48:5 [p] Jer 44:15-18

48:8 [q] Dt 9:7, 24; Ps 58:3 48:9 [r] Ps 78:38; Isa 30:18 [s] Ne 9:31 48:10 [t] 1Ki 8:51 48:11 [u] 1Sa 12:22; Isa 37:35 [v] Dt 32:27; Jer 14:7, 21; Eze 20:9, 14, 22, 44 [w] Isa 42:8 48:12 [x] Isa 46:3 [y] Isa 41:4; Rev 1:17; 22:13 48:13 [z] Heb 1:10-12 [a] Ex 20:11 [b] Isa 40:26 48:14 [c] Isa 43:9 [d] Isa 46:10-11

Isa 48:10 ❖ When have you experienced God's refining work? What did God cleanse in your life?

8 You have neither heard nor understood;
from of old your ears have not been open.
Well do I know how treacherous you are;
you were called a rebel[q] from birth.
9 For my own name's sake I delay my wrath;[r]
for the sake of my praise I hold it back from you,
so as not to destroy you completely.[s]
10 See, I have refined you, though not as silver;
I have tested you in the furnace[t] of affliction.
11 For my own sake,[u] for my own sake, I do this.
How can I let myself be defamed?[v]
I will not yield my glory to another.[w]

Israel Freed

12 "Listen[x] to me, Jacob,
Israel, whom I have called:
I am he;
I am the first and I am the last.[y]
13 My own hand laid the foundations of the earth,[z]
and my right hand spread out the heavens;[a]
when I summon them,
they all stand up together.[b]

14 "Come together,[c] all of you, and listen:
Which of the idols has foretold these things?
The LORD's chosen ally
will carry out his purpose[d] against Babylon;

48:1–2 The people have a name, but their behavior has shown that they do not have a relationship.
48:3–6a The people have heard all the predictions God has made, and they know all his predictions have come true. He made the predictions precisely so that when the events occurred, it would be impossible to say an idol god performed the actions. In v. 6a, Isaiah calls the people to "admit" the truth of their experience and to draw the appropriate conclusions from that experience.
48:6b–11 Here the prophet turns to the future. The point is that God can say and do things that have never happened before. He is doing this precisely so that no idol may share his "glory" (v. 11).
48:12–22 These verses sharpen God's appeal to his people. Three times they are commanded to listen (vv. 12, 14, 16). As with a number of Hebrew words, "listen" does not permit a separation between perception and action. Thus, if you truly "hear" an admonition, you will obey it.
48:12–16 These verses recap the reasons why the people should listen to God. He is the sole Creator.

his arm will be against the
Babylonians.[a]
15 I, even I, have spoken;
yes, I have called[e] him.
I will bring him,
and he will succeed in his mission.

16 "Come near[f] me and listen to this:

"From the first announcement I
have not spoken in secret;[g]
at the time it happens, I am there."

And now the Sovereign LORD has
sent[h] me,
endowed with his Spirit.

17 This is what the LORD says —
your Redeemer,[i] the Holy One[j] of
Israel:
"I am the LORD your God,
who teaches you what is best for
you,
who directs[k] you in the way[l] you
should go.
18 If only you had paid attention[m] to
my commands,
your peace[n] would have been like
a river,
your well-being[o] like the waves of
the sea.
19 Your descendants would have been
like the sand,
your children like its numberless
grains;[p]
their name would never be blotted
out[q]
nor destroyed from before me."

20 Leave Babylon,
flee[r] from the Babylonians!
Announce this with shouts of joy[s]
and proclaim it.
Send it out to the ends of the earth;
say, "The LORD has redeemed[t] his
servant Jacob."
21 They did not thirst[u] when he led
them through the deserts;
he made water flow[v] for them
from the rock;
he split the rock
and water gushed out.[w]

22 "There is no peace," says the LORD,
"for the wicked."[x]

48:15 [e] Isa 45:1
48:16 [f] Isa 41:1 [g] Isa 45:19 [h] Zec 2:9,11
48:17 [i] Isa 49:7 [j] Isa 43:14 [k] Isa 49:10 [l] Ps 32:8
48:18 [m] Dt 32:29 [n] Ps 119:165; Isa 66:12 [o] Isa 45:8
48:19 [p] Ge 22:17 [q] Isa 56:5; 66:22
48:20 [r] Jer 50:8; 51:6, 45; Zec 2:6-7; Rev 18:4 [s] Isa 49:13 [t] Isa 52:9; 63:9
48:21 [u] Isa 41:17 [v] Isa 30:25 [w] Ex 17:6; Nu 20:11; Ps 105:41; Isa 35:6
48:22 [x] Isa 57:21
49:1 [y] Isa 44:24; 46:3; Mt 1:20 [z] Isa 7:14; 9:6; 44:2; Jer 1:5; Gal 1:15
49:2 [a] Isa 11:4; Rev 1:16
49:3 [b] Zec 3:8 [c] Isa 44:23

Isa 49:1-6 ❖ How is God displaying his splendor through believers' lives? What opportunities has he given us to be "a light" for others to know his love (v. 6)?

The Servant of the LORD

49 Listen to me, you islands;
hear this, you distant nations:
Before I was born[y] the LORD
called[z] me;
from my mother's womb he has
spoken my name.
2 He made my mouth like a sharpened
sword,[a]
in the shadow of his hand he
hid me;
he made me into a polished arrow
and concealed me in his quiver.
3 He said to me, "You are my servant,[b]
Israel, in whom I will display my
splendor.[c]"

[a] 14 Or *Chaldeans*; also in verse 20

He is the Lord of history. The challenge to hear is summed up in v. 16 with a reiteration of the claim that God is the speaking God.

48:17–22 These verses sum up everything that has been said in the chapter and, in some ways, in the entire subdivision (chs. 40–48). If Israel had "paid attention" in the past, none of the tragedies that are to befall them would have occurred (v. 18). Instead, all the promises that God had made to them would have been fulfilled (vv. 18–19).

But even if they will believe in God now, they can be delivered from Babylon. Just because no one had ever gone home from exile before does not mean it could not happen. The Creator can break in and make "water flow" (v. 21) from rocks if he chooses.

The allusion to the exodus is clear here. What God has done in the past shows that he can be equally creative to redeem his people again. "Announce this with shouts of joy" (v. 20). But joy is not the final note here. If the people persist in wickedness, none of these promises are for them. They must change if they are to have a part in the coming joy.

✣ **48:1–22** We can leave the "Babylons" that have enslaved us. We can be delivered from the guilt and shame of all our past sins. In Jesus Christ, God has made a way for us. If ever there was a "new thing" (43:19), the coming of Christ was it. God can do the impossible and bring about genuine change. He can do for us what we cannot do for ourselves.

49:1–6 The first revelation is one of call and confidence. The servant has no doubt of his call, his divine enablement, or his ultimate vindication. Like a "sharpened sword" or a "polished arrow" (v. 2), he will accomplish exactly what God wants at the appointed time. The Messiah will display the Lord's "splendor" (v. 3) and will "restore the tribes of Jacob" to the Lord. His work will include even "Gentiles" in its scope (v. 6).

4But I said, "I have labored in vain;[d]
I have spent my strength for nothing at all.
Yet what is due me is in the LORD's hand,
and my reward[e] is with my God."

5And now the LORD says—
he who formed me in the womb to be his servant
to bring Jacob back to him
and gather Israel[f] to himself,
for I am[a] honored[g] in the eyes of the LORD
and my God has been my strength—
6he says:
"It is too small a thing for you to be my servant
to restore the tribes of Jacob
and bring back those of Israel I have kept.
I will also make you a light for the Gentiles,[h]
that my salvation may reach to the ends of the earth."[i]

7This is what the LORD says—
the Redeemer and Holy One of Israel[j]—
to him who was despised[k] and abhorred by the nation,
to the servant of rulers:
"Kings[l] will see you and stand up,
princes will see and bow down,
because of the LORD, who is faithful,
the Holy One of Israel, who has chosen you."

Restoration of Israel

8This is what the LORD says:

"In the time of my favor[m] I will answer you,
and in the day of salvation I will help you;[n]
I will keep[o] you and will make you
to be a covenant for the people,[p]
to restore the land[q]
and to reassign its desolate inheritances,
9to say to the captives,[r] 'Come out,'
and to those in darkness, 'Be free!'

"They will feed beside the roads
and find pasture on every barren hill.[s]
10They will neither hunger nor thirst,[t]
nor will the desert heat or the sun beat down on them.[u]
He who has compassion[v] on them will guide them
and lead them beside springs[w] of water.
11I will turn all my mountains into roads,
and my highways[x] will be raised up.[y]
12See, they will come from afar[z]—
some from the north, some from the west,
some from the region of Aswan.[b]"

13Shout for joy, you heavens;
rejoice, you earth;
burst into song, you mountains![a]
For the LORD comforts[b] his people
and will have compassion on his afflicted ones.

14But Zion said, "The LORD has forsaken me,
the Lord has forgotten me."

15"Can a mother forget the baby at her breast
and have no compassion on the child she has borne?

49:4 [d]Isa 65:23 [e]Isa 35:4
49:5 [f]Isa 11:12 [g]Isa 43:4
49:6 [h]Lk 2:32 [i]Ac 13:47*
49:7 [j]Isa 48:17 [k]Ps 22:6; 69:7-9 [l]Isa 52:15
49:8 [m]Ps 69:13 [n]2Co 6:2* [o]Isa 26:3 [p]Isa 42:6 [q]Isa 44:26
49:9 [r]Isa 42:7; 61:1; Lk 4:19 [s]Isa 41:18
49:10 [t]Isa 33:16 [u]Ps 121:6; Rev 7:16 [v]Isa 14:1 [w]Isa 35:7
49:11 [x]Isa 11:16 [y]Isa 40:4
49:12 [z]Isa 43:5-6
49:13 [a]Isa 44:23 [b]Isa 40:1

[a] *5* Or *him, / but Israel would not be gathered; / yet I will be* [b] *12* Dead Sea Scrolls; Masoretic Text *Sinim*

49:7–12 Although the servant is "despised" (v. 7) a day will come when kings and princes will honor him. In particular, the servant's task is to be a representative of God's "covenant" (v. 8) to his people. Like a new Joshua he will settle the people in a land of abundance, where God will tend them as a shepherd. Verse 12 may be another indication of the worldwide scope of the servant's ministry.

49:13 As in vv. 10–17, the announcement of the work of the servant results in an outburst of praise. As there, nature is called on to sing the praise of its Creator and Redeemer.

49:1–13 As those who participate in the life of the Servant, we too can have that sense of enablement by God. We can be a "sharpened sword" or a "polished arrow" in his hand (v. 2). As we perform what may seem to be simple tasks, they may have more significance than we will ever know on this side of the grave. We can have that sense of having been divinely fitted for just what it is we are doing.

49:14–16 This passage consists of the people's negative response to the proclamation of the servant's redemptive work and God's extended

Though she may forget,
I will not forget you![c]
16 See, I have engraved[d] you on the palms of my hands;
your walls[e] are ever before me.
17 Your children hasten back,
and those who laid you waste[f] depart from you.
18 Lift up your eyes and look around;
all your children gather[g] and come to you.
As surely as I live,[h]" declares the LORD,
"you will wear[i] them all as ornaments;
you will put them on, like a bride.

19 "Though you were ruined and made desolate[j]
and your land laid waste,[k]
now you will be too small for your people,[l]
and those who devoured you will be far away.
20 The children born during your bereavement
will yet say in your hearing,
'This place is too small for us;
give us more space to live in.'[m]
21 Then you will say in your heart,
'Who bore me these?
I was bereaved and barren;
I was exiled and rejected.[n]
Who brought these up?
I was left[o] all alone,
but these — where have they come from?' "

22 This is what the Sovereign LORD says:

"See, I will beckon to the nations,
I will lift up my banner[p] to the peoples;
they will bring your sons in their arms
and carry your daughters on their hips.[q]
23 Kings[r] will be your foster fathers,
and their queens your nursing mothers.[s]
They will bow down before you with their faces to the ground;
they will lick the dust[t] at your feet.
Then you will know that I am the LORD;[u]
those who hope in me will not be disappointed."

24 Can plunder be taken from warriors,[v]
or captives be rescued from the fierce[a]?

25 But this is what the LORD says:

"Yes, captives[w] will be taken from warriors,[x]
and plunder retrieved from the fierce;
I will contend with those who contend with you,
and your children I will save.[y]
26 I will make your oppressors[z] eat[a] their own flesh;
they will be drunk on their own blood,[b] as with wine.
Then all mankind will know[c]
that I, the LORD, am your Savior,
your Redeemer, the Mighty One of Jacob."

Israel's Sin and the Servant's Obedience

50 This is what the LORD says:

"Where is your mother's certificate of divorce[d]
with which I sent her away?

49:15 [c] Isa 44:21
49:16 [d] SS 8:6 [e] Ps 48:12-13; Isa 62:6
49:17 [f] Isa 10:6
49:18 [g] Isa 43:5; 54:7; Isa 60:4 [h] Isa 45:23 [i] Isa 52:1
49:19 [j] Isa 54:1, 3 [k] Isa 5:6 [l] Zec 10:10
49:20 [m] Isa 54:1-3
49:21 [n] Isa 5:13 [o] Isa 1:8
49:22 [p] Isa 11:10 [q] Isa 60:4
49:23 [r] Isa 60:3, 10-11 [s] Isa 60:16 [t] Ps 72:9 [u] Mic 7:17
49:24 [v] Mt 12:29; Lk 11:21
49:25 [w] Isa 14:2 [x] Jer 50:33-34 [y] Isa 25:9; 35:4
49:26 [z] Isa 9:4 [a] Isa 9:20 [b] Rev 16:6 [c] Eze 39:7
50:1 [d] Dt 24:1; Jer 3:8; Hos 2:2

[a] 24 Dead Sea Scrolls, Vulgate and Syriac (see also Septuagint and verse 25); Masoretic Text *righteous*

---

reply (49:15—50:3). The people declare that "the Lord has forgotten" them (49:14). God replies he can no more forget them than a nursing mother can forget her baby.

49:17–23 God goes on to declare that the proof of his love for them will be seen in the abundance of descendants that will be born to Zion when she thought herself forever barren. God will cause the nations to bring the lost children home.

49:24–26 Who can break the grip of the captors? God responds that he can. But the astonishing thing is that he cannot do these things for his people if they will not put their trust in him. This passage is an expression of grace, reaching its climax in the passionate words of 50:1-3, where God insists that he has both the will and the power to redeem his people.

50:1–3 Just as no nation on earth can stand up to God, neither can sin. Do the people think he has divorced them? Where is the certificate? There is none. Do they think he was somehow forced to "sell" (v. 1) them against his will? Of course he has not. His "arm" is not "short" or weak (v. 2). If he can "dry up the sea" (v. 2) and turn off the sun, what is so difficult about defeating sin?

49:14—50:3 When we rush ahead to solve our problems in our own way without waiting

Or to which of my creditors
did I sell[e] you?
Because of your sins you were sold;[f]
because of your transgressions
your mother was sent away.
2 When I came, why was there no one?
When I called, why was there no
one to answer?[g]
Was my arm too short[h] to deliver
you?
Do I lack the strength[i] to rescue
you?
By a mere rebuke I dry up the sea,[j]
I turn rivers into a desert;
their fish rot for lack of water
and die of thirst.
3 I clothe the heavens with darkness
and make sackcloth[k] its covering."

4 The Sovereign LORD has given me a
well-instructed tongue,[l]
to know the word that sustains
the weary.[m]
He wakens me morning by
morning,[n]
wakens my ear to listen like one
being instructed.
5 The Sovereign LORD has opened my
ears;[o]
I have not been rebellious,[p]
I have not turned away.
6 I offered my back to those who
beat[q] me,
my cheeks to those who pulled
out my beard;
I did not hide my face
from mocking and spitting.[r]
7 Because the Sovereign LORD
helps[s] me,
I will not be disgraced.
Therefore have I set my face like
flint,[t]
and I know I will not be put to
shame.

50:1 [e] Ne 5:5; Mt 18:25 [f] Dt 32:30; Isa 52:3
50:2 [g] Isa 41:28 [h] Nu 11:23; Isa 59:1 [i] Ge 18:14 [j] Ex 14:22; Jos 3:16
50:3 [k] Rev 6:12
50:4 [l] Ex 4:12 [m] Mt 11:28 [n] Ps 5:3; 119:147; 143:8
50:5 [o] Isa 35:5 [p] Mt 26:39; Jn 8:29; 14:31; 15:10; Ac 26:19; Heb 5:8
50:6 [q] Isa 53:5; Mt 27:30; Mk 14:65; 15:19; Lk 22:63 [r] La 3:30; Mt 26:67
50:7 [s] Isa 42:1 [t] Eze 3:8-9
50:8 [u] Isa 43:26; Ro 8:32-34 [v] Isa 41:1
50:9 [w] Isa 41:10 [x] Job 13:28; Isa 51:8
50:10 [y] Isa 49:3 [z] Isa 26:4
50:11 [a] Pr 26:18 [b] Jas 3:6 [c] Isa 65:13-15
51:1 [d] Isa 46:3 [e] ver 7; Ps 94:15; Ro 9:30-31

Isa 50:6-9 ❖ When we experience ridicule for following God, how does God sustain and vindicate us?

8 He who vindicates me is near.
Who then will bring charges
against me?[u]
Let us face each other![v]
Who is my accuser?
Let him confront me!
9 It is the Sovereign LORD who
helps[w] me.
Who will condemn me?
They will all wear out like a
garment;
the moths[x] will eat them up.

10 Who among you fears the LORD
and obeys the word of his
servant?[y]
Let the one who walks in the
dark,
who has no light,
trust[z] in the name of the LORD
and rely on their God.
11 But now, all you who light fires
and provide yourselves with
flaming torches,[a]
go, walk in the light of your fires[b]
and of the torches you have set
ablaze.
This is what you shall receive from
my hand:
You will lie down in torment.[c]

Everlasting Salvation for Zion

51 "Listen[d] to me, you who pursue
righteousness[e]
and who seek the LORD:
Look to the rock from which you
were cut
and to the quarry from which you
were hewn;

on God to show us how he wants to deal with those problems, we have effectively said to him that we know better than he does. This is why Jesus required his disciples to wait in Jerusalem for him to fill them with his Holy Spirit (Ac 1:4–8). God was going to use them in dramatic ways to fulfill that purpose, but it was going to be in his way and through his power, not theirs.

50:4–9 The servant's obedience to the Lord will result in his suffering. If the message is declared, there is going to be abuse; the servant is willing to bear that abuse because he knows that God will vindicate him in the end (v. 9).

50:10–11 This brief introduction to the commentary on the servant's words highlights the emphasis on obedience to his message (51:1–9). It also contains a significant parallel between the Lord and the servant. To "fear the Lord" is synonymous with obeying "the word of his servant" (50:10) and vice versa.

Those who have "no light" (v. 10) can walk safely if they will entrust themselves to God. But those who reject God's revealed way will find "torment" (v. 11).

51:1–8 The commentary may be divided into three stanzas:

In vv. 1–3 God and the servant call on the righteous to remember God's dealings with Abraham and to recognize the creative power that brought

2 look to Abraham,[f] your father,
and to Sarah, who gave you birth.
When I called him he was only one
man,
and I blessed him and made him
many.[g]
3 The LORD will surely comfort[h] Zion
and will look with compassion on
all her ruins;[i]
he will make her deserts like Eden,[j]
her wastelands like the garden of
the LORD.
Joy and gladness[k] will be found in
her,
thanksgiving and the sound of
singing.

4 "Listen to me, my people;[l]
hear me, my nation:
Instruction will go out from me;
my justice[m] will become a light to
the nations.[n]
5 My righteousness draws near
speedily,
my salvation is on the way,[o]
and my arm[p] will bring justice to
the nations.
The islands will look to me
and wait in hope for my arm.
6 Lift up your eyes to the heavens,
look at the earth beneath;
the heavens will vanish like
smoke,[q]
the earth will wear out like a
garment[r]
and its inhabitants die like flies.
But my salvation will last forever,
my righteousness will never
fail.

51:2 [f] Isa 29:22; Ro 4:16; Heb 11:11 [g] Ge 12:2
51:3 [h] Isa 40:1 [i] Isa 52:9 [j] Ge 2:8 [k] Isa 25:9; 66:10
51:4 [l] Ps 50:7 [m] Isa 2:4 [n] Isa 42:4,6
51:5 [o] Isa 46:13 [p] Isa 40:10; 63:1,5
51:6 [q] Mt 24:35; 2Pe 3:10 [r] Ps 102:25-26
51:7 [s] ver 1 [t] Ps 37:31 [u] Mt 5:11; Ac 5:41
51:8 [v] Isa 50:9 [w] ver 6
51:9 [x] Isa 52:1 [y] Dt 4:34 [z] Ps 74:13
51:10 [a] Ex 14:22
51:11 [b] Isa 35:9

Isa 51:11 ❖ How has God's redeeming love filled us with praise and joy?

7 "Hear me, you who know what is
right,[s]
you people who have taken my
instruction to heart:[t]
Do not fear the reproach of mere
mortals
or be terrified by their insults.[u]
8 For the moth will eat them up like a
garment;[v]
the worm will devour them like
wool.
But my righteousness will last
forever,[w]
my salvation through all
generations."

9 Awake, awake, arm of the LORD,
clothe yourself with strength![x]
Awake, as in days gone by,
as in generations of old.[y]
Was it not you who cut Rahab to
pieces,
who pierced that monster[z]
through?
10 Was it not you who dried up the sea,[a]
the waters of the great deep,
who made a road in the depths of
the sea
so that the redeemed might cross
over?
11 Those the LORD has rescued[b] will
return.
They will enter Zion with singing;
everlasting joy will crown their
heads.

---

the world into existence in the first place. The emphasis in vv. 4-6 is the universal and eternal work of the servant. The servant brings the light to the "nations" (v. 4). Verses 7-8 assert that God has not abandoned Israel. Their commitments to know God and to do his will have not been in vain.

50:4—51:8 We can look back on the goodness of the Creator's intent and on the election love of Abraham's friend. But we can also look back on the coming of the promised Servant, the Son of the Father. With those things to look back on, we can look ahead to the future with confidence.

51:9-16 These verses deal with uncertainty over why God has not yet acted. Verses 9-11 present the question and vv. 12-16 give the Lord's answer. The opening verses have some of the characteristics of a community lament in that they express both doubt and hope.

At the same time, v. 11 looks forward to the day when the ransomed will return to "Zion with singing." The captives no longer doubt that God *will* act, but they wonder why he is waiting so long.

God responds by calling on the captives to focus on him and not their oppressors. There is no point in focusing on the "oppressor" (v. 13), because he will soon be gone. Far better to focus on the Comforter, to whom both the seen and the unseen worlds bow in obedience (v. 15). The servant's ministry is to reveal God. He will declare God's words, and nothing will be able to thwart those plans for him.

51:9-16 We are often told that if we entertain doubts, we do not have faith, and hope is impossible for us. As a result, there are people who never face their doubts and are forced to live lives of denial and superficiality. By contrast, there are those whose doubts are undeniable and who therefore conclude

Gladness and joy[c] will overtake
them,
and sorrow and sighing will flee
away.[d]

12"I, even I, am he who comforts[e]
you.
Who are you that you fear mere
mortals,[f]
human beings who are but grass,[g]
13that you forget[h] the LORD your
Maker,[i]
who stretches out the heavens[j]
and who lays the foundations of
the earth,
that you live in constant terror[k]
every day
because of the wrath of the
oppressor,
who is bent on destruction?
For where is the wrath of the
oppressor?
14 The cowering prisoners will soon
be set free;
they will not die in their dungeon,
nor will they lack bread.[l]
15For I am the LORD your God,
who stirs up the sea[m] so that its
waves roar —
the LORD Almighty is his name.
16I have put my words in your mouth[n]
and covered you with the shadow
of my hand[o] —
I who set the heavens in place,
who laid the foundations of the
earth,
and who say to Zion, 'You are my
people.'"

The Cup of the LORD's Wrath

17Awake, awake![p]
Rise up, Jerusalem,
you who have drunk from the hand
of the LORD
the cup of his wrath,[q]
you who have drained to its dregs
the goblet that makes people
stagger.[r]

51:11 [c]Jer 33:11 [d]Rev 7:17
51:12 [e]2Co 1:4 [f]Ps 118:6; Isa 2:22 [g]Isa 40:6-7; 1Pe 1:24
51:13 [h]Isa 17:10 [i]Isa 45:11 [j]Ps 104:2; Isa 48:13 [k]Isa 7:4
51:14 [l]Isa 49:10
51:15 [m]Jer 31:35
51:16 [n]Dt 18:18; Isa 59:21 [o]Ex 33:22
51:17 [p]Isa 52:1 [q]Job 21:20; Rev 14:10; 16:19 [r]Ps 60:3

18Among all the children[s] she bore
there was none to guide her;[t]
among all the children she reared
there was none to take her by the
hand.
19These double calamities[u] have come
upon you —
who can comfort you? —
ruin and destruction, famine[v] and
sword —
who can[a] console you?
20Your children have fainted;
they lie at every street corner,[w]
like antelope caught in a net.
They are filled with the wrath of the
LORD,
with the rebuke of your God.

21Therefore hear this, you afflicted
one,
made drunk,[x] but not with wine.
22This is what your Sovereign LORD
says,
your God, who defends[y] his
people:
"See, I have taken out of your hand
the cup[z] that made you stagger;
from that cup, the goblet of my
wrath,
you will never drink again.
23I will put it into the hands of your
tormentors,[a]
who said to you,
'Fall prostrate[b] that we may walk[c]
on you.'
And you made your back like the
ground,
like a street to be walked on."

52 Awake, awake,[d] Zion,
clothe yourself with strength![e]
Put on your garments of splendor,[f]
Jerusalem, the holy city.[g]
The uncircumcised and defiled
will not enter you again.[h]

51:18 [s]Ps 88:18 [t]Isa 49:21
51:19 [u]Isa 47:9 [v]Isa 14:30
51:20 [w]Isa 5:25; Jer 14:16
51:21 [x]ver 17; Isa 29:9
51:22 [y]Isa 49:25 [z]ver 17
51:23 [a]Isa 49:26; Jer 25:15-17, 26,28; 49:12 [b]Zec 12:2 [c]Jos 10:24
52:1 [d]Isa 51:17 [e]Isa 51:9 [f]Ex 28:2,40; Ps 110:3; Zec 3:4 [g]Ne 11:1; Mt 4:5; Rev 21:2 [h]Na 1:15; Rev 21:27

[a] *19* Dead Sea Scrolls, Septuagint, Vulgate and Syriac; Masoretic Text / *how can I*

---

that faith is impossible for them. Both kinds of persons need to look carefully at passages such as this and at the longer laments in the Psalms (e.g., Ps 6; Ps 22). God addresses the doubts of our modern minds as he did with his ancient people.

51:17 One of the recurring images of Scripture is the "cup of wrath," found from Psalms through Revelation.

51:18–23 With the destruction of the northern kingdom and then the southern kingdom, it looked as if the mother would die alone, her children dead and destroyed. But God says the cup of wrath is placed in the hands of the "tormentors" for them to drink (v. 23).

52:1–12 This passage falls naturally into two parts. In vv. 1–6, just as God demonstrated his unique deity in delivering his people from Egypt, so he will do again in delivering them from this new bondage.

2 Shake off your dust;[i]
rise up, sit enthroned, Jerusalem.
Free yourself from the chains on your neck,
Daughter Zion, now a captive.

3 For this is what the LORD says:

"You were sold for nothing,[j]
and without money[k] you will be redeemed."

4 For this is what the Sovereign LORD says:

"At first my people went down to Egypt[l] to live;
lately, Assyria has oppressed them.

5 "And now what do I have here?" declares the LORD.

"For my people have been taken away for nothing,
and those who rule them mock,[a]"
declares the LORD.
"And all day long
my name is constantly blasphemed.[m]
6 Therefore my people will know[n] my name;
therefore in that day they will know
that it is I who foretold it.
Yes, it is I."

7 How beautiful on the mountains
are the feet of those who bring good news,[o]
who proclaim peace,[p]
who bring good tidings,
who proclaim salvation,
who say to Zion,
"Your God reigns!"[q]

52:2 [i] Isa 29:4 52:3 [j] Ps 44:12 [k] Isa 45:13 52:4 [l] Ge 46:6 52:5 [m] Eze 36:20; Ro 2:24* 52:6 [n] Isa 49:23 52:7 [o] Isa 40:9; Ro 10:15* [p] Na 1:15; Eph 6:15 [q] Ps 93:1

Isa 52:7 ❖ Where can we bring the Good News of God's salvation?

8 Listen! Your watchmen[r] lift up their voices;
together they shout for joy.
When the LORD returns to Zion,
they will see it with their own eyes.
9 Burst into songs of joy[s] together,
you ruins[t] of Jerusalem,
for the LORD has comforted his people,
he has redeemed Jerusalem.[u]
10 The LORD will lay bare his holy arm
in the sight of all the nations,[v]
and all the ends of the earth will see
the salvation[w] of our God.

11 Depart,[x] depart, go out from there!
Touch no unclean thing![y]
Come out from it and be pure,[z]
you who carry the articles of the LORD's house.
12 But you will not leave in haste[a]
or go in flight;
for the LORD will go before you,[b]
the God of Israel will be your rear guard.[c]

The Suffering and Glory of the Servant

13 See, my servant[d] will act wisely[b];
he will be raised and lifted up and highly exalted.[e]
14 Just as there were many who were appalled at him[c]—
his appearance was so disfigured
beyond that of any human being

52:8 [r] Isa 62:6 52:9 [s] Ps 98:4 [t] Isa 51:3 [u] Isa 48:20 52:10 [v] Isa 66:18 [w] Ps 98:2-3; Lk 3:6 52:11 [x] Isa 48:20 [y] Isa 1:16; 2Co 6:17* [z] 2Ti 2:19 52:12 [a] Ex 12:11 [b] Mic 2:13 [c] Ex 14:19 52:13 [d] Isa 42:1 [e] Isa 57:15; Php 2:9

[a] 5 Dead Sea Scrolls and Vulgate; Masoretic Text *wail* [b] 13 Or *will prosper* [c] 14 Hebrew *you*

The second part (vv. 7–12) concludes all that has been said about redemption, not only since 49:1 but indeed since 40:1. Both the ability and the desire of God to restore his people to himself have been amply demonstrated; all that remains is for the songs to begin (52:9).

Suddenly, the watchmen on the walls of the city begin to "shout for joy" (v. 8). They have seen a messenger far away on the mountain, and he is signaling the "good news" (v. 7) of victory. God has laid bare "his holy arm" (v. 10), defeated the enemy, and "redeemed Jerusalem" (v. 9).

51:17—52:12 Why does God wait until we are helpless, or at least aware of our helplessness, before he acts? One of the main reasons is that we are usually unwilling to give up our control of the situation until we come to that point. As long as we think the solution to our problems is somehow in ourselves, we are liable to think of God as an assistant or as a fallback device. It is only when we admit that there is nothing we can do for ourselves to remove our sins and stop our sinning that we will turn to the Savior and receive the forgiveness, cleansing, and empowerment he has been wanting to give us the entire time.

52:13–15 The poem begins and closes on the same note of triumph. The spoils belong to the victor. That point opens and closes the poem because nothing in between seems like a victory.

The disfigurement of the servant is utterly shocking. He hardly appears to be human. The sense

and his form marred beyond
human likeness —
15 so he will sprinkle many nations,[a]
and kings will shut their mouths
because of him.
For what they were not told, they
will see,
and what they have not heard,
they will understand.[f]

53 Who has believed our message[g]
and to whom has the arm of the
LORD been revealed?[h]
2 He grew up before him like a tender
shoot,
and like a root out of dry ground.
He had no beauty or majesty to
attract us to him,
nothing in his appearance[i] that we
should desire him.
3 He was despised and rejected by
mankind,
a man of suffering, and familiar
with pain.[j]
Like one from whom people hide
their faces
he was despised,[k] and we held him
in low esteem.

4 Surely he took up our pain
and bore our suffering,[l]
yet we considered him punished by
God,[m]
stricken by him, and afflicted.
5 But he was pierced for our
transgressions,[n]
he was crushed for our iniquities;
the punishment that brought us
peace was on him,
and by his wounds we are healed.[o]

52:15 [f] Ro 15:21*; Eph 3:4-5
53:1 [g] Ro 10:16* [h] Jn 12:38*
53:2 [i] Isa 52:14
53:3 [j] ver 4, 10; Lk 18:31-33 [k] Ps 22:6; Jn 1:10-11
53:4 [l] Mt 8:17* [m] Jn 19:7
53:5 [n] Ro 4:25; 1Co 15:3; Heb 9:28 [o] 1Pe 2:24-25

Isa 53:5-12 ❖ How does this powerful prophecy point to Jesus (see Ac 8:30-35)? How do these words deepen our understanding of Christ's work on the cross on our behalf?

6 We all, like sheep, have gone astray,
each of us has turned to our own
way;
and the LORD has laid on him
the iniquity of us all.

7 He was oppressed and afflicted,
yet he did not open his mouth;[p]
he was led like a lamb to the
slaughter,
and as a sheep before its shearers
is silent,
so he did not open his mouth.
8 By oppression[b] and judgment he was
taken away.
Yet who of his generation
protested?
For he was cut off from the land of
the living;[q]
for the transgression[r] of my
people he was punished.[c]
9 He was assigned a grave with the
wicked,
and with the rich[s] in his death,
though he had done no violence,[t]
nor was any deceit in his mouth.[u]

10 Yet it was the LORD's will[v] to crush[w]
him and cause him to suffer,[x]

53:7 [p] Mk 14:61
53:8 [q] Da 9:26; Ac 8:32-33* [r] ver 12
53:9 [s] Mt 27:57-60 [t] Isa 42:1-3 [u] 1Pe 2:22*
53:10 [v] Isa 46:10 [w] ver 5 [x] ver 3

[a] 15 Or *so will many nations be amazed at him* (see also Septuagint) [b] 8 Or *From arrest*
[c] 8 Or *generation considered / that he was cut off from the land of the living, / that he was punished for the transgression of my people?*

---

of v. 15 is that the kings are struck dumb by the thought that the supposed conqueror has actually come to purify the nations by sprinkling something (Blood? Sacred water?) on them.

53:1-3 This servant is the promised "arm of the LORD" (v. 1). But that report is clearly disbelieved. Why? Three reasons are given. (1) He comes in a quiet and unassuming way (v. 2). (2) His "appearance" is quite ordinary (v. 2). (3) He takes on himself the pain and "suffering" of the world (v. 3).

We ignore suffering ("hide [our] faces") because it reminds us of our own vulnerability (v. 3). The servant has come to take away the sins of the world, but no one pays any attention to him.

53:4-6 Despite what "we" thought (v. 4), the servant is not suffering because God has inflicted deserved punishment on him. It is our suffering that he carried for "our transgressions" and "our iniquities" (v. 5). The servant has suffered in "our" place. "We" (v. 6), the blind, rebellious people of God (cf. 42:18-25), are the sheep who have gone astray, but he is the one who gets beaten for our willfulness.

53:7-9 Although his suffering is manifestly unjust, this servant accepts it without protest (v. 7). It is significant that the only extended metaphor in the poem deals with sheep, the animals of sacrifice.

The injustice of what the servant suffered is further underlined in vv. 8-9. He is "cut off" in the prime of life (v. 8). Isaiah's statement in 5:8 reflects the view of such prophets as Hosea and Amos (and Jesus). In their view, riches have all too often been amassed through violence and deceit. The servant is buried with the rich even "though" he did not do what they did (v. 9b).

53:10-12 What greater good could possibly justify the crushing of the servant? When the "life" (v. 10a) of the servant is offered as a sin offering, God's purpose in bringing him to this place is realized ("prosper," v. 10b). The servant did not come to tell people what God wants; rather, he

and though the LORD makes[a] his
life an offering for sin,
he will see his offspring[y] and
prolong his days,
and the will of the LORD will
prosper in his hand.
11 After he has suffered,[z]
he will see the light of life[b] and be
satisfied[c];
by his knowledge[d] my righteous
servant will justify[a] many,
and he will bear their iniquities.
12 Therefore I will give him a portion
among the great,[e][b]
and he will divide the spoils with
the strong,[f]
because he poured out his life unto
death,[c]
and was numbered with the
transgressors.[d]
For he bore the sin of many,
and made intercession for the
transgressors.

The Future Glory of Zion

54 "Sing, barren woman,
you who never bore a child;
burst into song, shout for joy,
you who were never in labor;
because more are the children[e] of
the desolate woman
than of her who has a husband,[f]"
says the LORD.

53:10 [y] Ps 22:30
53:11 [z] Jn 10:14-18 [a] Ro 5:18-19
53:12 [b] Php 2:9 [c] Mt 26:28, 38, 39, 42 [d] Mk 15:27*; Lk 22:37*; 23:32
54:1 [e] Isa 49:20 [f] 1Sa 2:5; Gal 4:27*
54:2 [g] Isa 49:19-20 [h] Ex 35:18; 39:40
54:3 [i] Isa 49:19
54:4 [j] Isa 51:7
54:5 [k] Jer 3:14

Isa 54:4–5 ❖ What shame from your past has God removed? How has God's healing power freed believers from the weight of shame and guilt?

2 "Enlarge the place of your tent,[g]
stretch your tent curtains wide,
do not hold back;
lengthen your cords,
strengthen your stakes.[h]
3 For you will spread out to the right
and to the left;
your descendants will dispossess
nations
and settle in their desolate[i] cities.

4 "Do not be afraid; you will not be put
to shame.
Do not fear disgrace; you will not
be humiliated.
You will forget the shame of your
youth
and remember no more the
reproach[j] of your widowhood.
5 For your Maker is your husband[k] —
the LORD Almighty is his name —

[a] 10 Hebrew *though you make* [b] 11 Dead Sea Scrolls (see also Septuagint); Masoretic Text does not have *the light of life.* [c] 11 Or (with Masoretic Text) *"He will see the fruit of his suffering / and will be satisfied* [d] 11 Or *by knowledge of him* [e] 12 Or *many* [f] 12 Or *numerous*

---

came to *be* what God wants *for* us. But how can someone who has been cut off from the land of the living without descendants ever have these things? It certainly looks as though resurrection is the only answer.

Verse 11 gives a more theological statement of what was accomplished in the servant's death. When his life has been offered up for others, he will "see" life again and be "satisfied." The hard struggle will have been worth it.

But what does that struggle accomplish for people who accept it on their own behalf? The second half of v. 11 answers that question in a tightly connected statement. Because the servant knows God in intimate relationship and indeed shares God's own righteousness (literally, "the righteous one, my servant"), he will in turn be able to make many people righteous. How? By bearing "their iniquities."

Why does God give his servant the victor's wreath? "Because" he was treated like one of the rebels when he was not and thus could bear their punishment and make "intercession" for them (v. 12).

✜ **52:13—53:12** Can humans thwart the will of God? Not in any ultimate sense. There *will* be a new heaven and a new earth, and all the redeemed *will* inhabit them. There *will* be a great crowd of the redeemed. But those who are invited first may choose not to come in (Lk 14:16–24). From God's side he has done everything necessary, and whoever will may come. But we must affirm and accept the offering made on our behalf.

54:1–10 In these ten verses God speaks to Israel in the image of a disgraced woman. She is the barren one, the widow, and the divorced one. To each of these, God promises restoration and hope, and the promises are brought to a climax in vv. 9–10.

In the ancient Near East, almost the worst fate that could befall a woman was to have no children. Here God says that those who have experienced his grace will no longer be fruitless but will have more descendants than they can account for.

Widowhood was also considered a disgrace in many parts of the ancient world. God says that Israel should no longer consider herself to be a widow. Her "Maker" is her "husband" (v. 5).

But there was an even worse disgrace than childlessness or widowhood: divorce. The divorced woman had been found wanting and was "rejected" (v. 6). This was Israel. But God has brought her back to himself. His "anger" was for a "moment," but his "compassion" is "everlasting" (vv. 7–8).

the Holy One of Israel is your
Redeemer;[l]
he is called the God of all the
earth.[m]
6 The LORD will call you back[n]
as if you were a wife deserted[o] and
distressed in spirit—
a wife who married young,
only to be rejected," says your God.
7 "For a brief moment[p] I abandoned
you,
but with deep compassion I will
bring you back.[q]
8 In a surge of anger[r]
I hid my face from you for a
moment,
but with everlasting kindness[s]
I will have compassion on you,"
says the LORD your Redeemer.

9 "To me this is like the days of Noah,
when I swore that the waters of
Noah would never again cover
the earth.[t]
So now I have sworn not to be
angry[u] with you,
never to rebuke you again.
10 Though the mountains be shaken[v]
and the hills be removed,
yet my unfailing love for you will
not be shaken[w]
nor my covenant[x] of peace be
removed,"
says the LORD, who has
compassion[y] on you.

11 "Afflicted[z] city, lashed by storms[a] and
not comforted,[b]
I will rebuild you with stones of
turquoise,[a][c]
your foundations[d] with lapis
lazuli.
12 I will make your battlements of
rubies,
your gates of sparkling jewels,
and all your walls of precious
stones.
13 All your children will be taught by
the LORD,[e]
and great will be their peace.[f]
14 In righteousness you will be
established:
Tyranny[g] will be far from you;
you will have nothing to fear.
Terror will be far removed;
it will not come near you.
15 If anyone does attack you, it will not
be my doing;
whoever attacks you will
surrender[h] to you.

16 "See, it is I who created the
blacksmith
who fans the coals into flame
and forges a weapon fit for its
work.
And it is I who have created the
destroyer to wreak havoc;
17 no weapon forged against you will
prevail,[i]
and you will refute[j] every tongue
that accuses you.
This is the heritage of the servants
of the LORD,
and this is their vindication
from me,"
declares the LORD.

Invitation to the Thirsty

55 "Come, all you who are thirsty,[k]
come to the waters;
and you who have no money,
come, buy[l] and eat!
Come, buy wine and milk[m]
without money and without cost.[n]

54:5 [l] Isa 48:17 [m] Isa 6:3
54:6 [n] Isa 49:14-21 [o] Isa 50:1-2; 62:4,12
54:7 [p] Isa 26:20 [q] Isa 49:18
54:8 [r] Isa 60:10 [s] ver 10
54:9 [t] Ge 8:21 [u] Isa 12:1
54:10 [v] Ps 46:2 [w] Isa 51:6 [x] Ps 89:34 [y] ver 8
54:11 [z] Isa 14:32 [a] Isa 28:2; 29:6 [b] Isa 51:19 [c] 1Ch 29:2; Rev 21:18 [d] Isa 28:16; Rev 21:19-20
54:13 [e] Jn 6:45* [f] Isa 48:18
54:14 [g] Isa 9:4
54:15 [h] Isa 41:11-16
54:17 [i] Isa 29:8 [j] Isa 45:24-25
55:1 [k] Jn 4:14; 7:37 [l] La 5:4; Mt 13:44; Rev 3:18 [m] SS 5:1 [n] Hos 14:4; Mt 10:8; Rev 21:6

[a] *11* The meaning of the Hebrew for this word is uncertain.

54:11–17 The people are like a city that has been "lashed by storms" (v. 11) and subjected to "tyranny" and "terror" (v. 14) and has experienced "havoc" (v. 16) within it. But since God is the one who brought all that to pass, he is the one who can change it all.

✜ **54:1–17** This passage shows us the heart of the gospel of Christ. God has reconciled his lost world to himself. He has not waited for us to find a way to bridge the gap between him and us. God gets no satisfaction from the richly deserved death of the sinner. Not even the death of the most heinous criminal brings a grim smile of satisfaction to the face of God. Rather, there is grief in his heart for those who refuse to accept his gracious offer of salvation.

55:1–5 God's invitation is not merely to find supplies to take care of bodily needs but to satisfy a person's whole being with true life. God promises another covenant, patterned after the unconditional one with "David" (v. 3).

In some sense, this "everlasting covenant" (v. 3) *is* the covenant with David. For what David was in part, "a witness to the peoples" (v. 4), the nation now will be able to bring to fulfillment. The nations of the world will flock to restored Israel because of their God. This is, of course, exactly what was predicted in Isa 2.

2 Why spend money on what is not bread,
and your labor on what does not satisfy?[o]
Listen, listen to me, and eat what is good,[p]
and you will delight in the richest of fare.
3 Give ear and come to me;
listen, that you may live.[q]
I will make an everlasting covenant[r] with you,
my faithful love[s] promised to David.[t]
4 See, I have made him a witness to the peoples,
a ruler and commander[u] of the peoples.
5 Surely you will summon nations[v] you know not,
and nations you do not know will come running to you,
because of the LORD your God,
the Holy One of Israel,
for he has endowed you with splendor."[w]

6 Seek the LORD while he may be found;[x]
call[y] on him while he is near.
7 Let the wicked forsake their ways
and the unrighteous their thoughts.[z]
Let them turn[a] to the LORD, and he will have mercy[b] on them,
and to our God, for he will freely pardon.[c]

8 "For my thoughts are not your thoughts,
neither are your ways my ways,"[d]
declares the LORD.
9 "As the heavens are higher than the earth,[e]
so are my ways higher than your ways
and my thoughts than your thoughts.
10 As the rain[f] and the snow
come down from heaven,
and do not return to it
without watering the earth
and making it bud and flourish,
so that it yields seed for the sower
and bread for the eater,[g]
11 so is my word that goes out from my mouth:
It will not return to me empty,[h]
but will accomplish what I desire
and achieve the purpose[i] for which I sent it.
12 You will go out in joy
and be led forth in peace;[j]
the mountains and hills
will burst into song before you,
and all the trees[k] of the field
will clap their hands.[l]
13 Instead of the thornbush will grow the juniper,
and instead of briers[m] the myrtle[n] will grow.
This will be for the LORD's renown,[o]
for an everlasting sign,
that will endure forever."

55:2 [o] Ps 22:26; Ecc 6:2; Hos 8:7 [p] Isa 1:19
55:3 [q] Lev 18:5; Ro 10:5 [r] Isa 61:8 [s] Isa 54:8 [t] Ac 13:34*
55:4 [u] Jer 30:9; Eze 34:23-24
55:5 [v] Isa 49:6 [w] Isa 60:9
55:6 [x] Ps 32:6; Isa 49:8; 2Co 6:1-2 [y] Isa 65:24
55:7 [z] Isa 32:7; 59:7 [a] Isa 44:22 [b] Isa 54:10 [c] Isa 1:18; 40:2
55:8 [d] Isa 53:6
55:9 [e] Ps 103:11
55:10 [f] Isa 30:23 [g] 2Co 9:10
55:11 [h] Isa 45:23 [i] Isa 44:26
55:12 [j] Isa 54:10, 13 [k] 1Ch 16:33 [l] Ps 98:8
55:13 [m] Isa 5:6 [n] Isa 41:19 [o] Isa 63:12
56:1 [p] Isa 1:17 [q] Ps 85:9

Isa 55:10-11 ❖ How is God's Word accomplishing its purpose in our lives?

Salvation for Others

56 This is what the LORD says:

"Maintain justice[p]
and do what is right,
for my salvation[q] is close at hand
and my righteousness will soon be revealed.

55:6-11 The people have a clear choice: to remain in unbelief or to proceed in uncertainty. For people in Isaiah's own day, and those who read these words in the exile, the message of what is now 52:13—53:12 was largely a mystery. Who is this person, and how can what he did *eternally* reconcile God and his people? God challenges them to exercise faith first and let understanding come afterward.
55:12-13 This summary says that all nature will rejoice in the redemption of humanity, and in place of sorrow and sighing there will be "joy" and "peace" (v. 12) as the captives return to their God.

55:1-13 Nothing has changed since the Garden of Eden: We do not wish to be told by our Creator that something is wrong for us when everything appears so delightful. Neither do we wish to be told that something is good for us when it looks as though it is going to take a lot of effort and may actually bring us some pain. We want to claim that we can direct our own lives and have God serve us, supplying our needs as we dictate. But doing so only leads to pain and frustration. Believers' faith always involves letting go of secure footholds and (apparent) certainties to do things God's way.

56:1-5 In chs. 1–39 the word "righteousness" is used for behavior that is in keeping with God's statutes. But in chs. 40–55, the term refers to God's

2 Blessed[r] is the one who does this—
the person who holds it fast,
who keeps the Sabbath[s] without
desecrating it,
and keeps their hands from doing
any evil."

3 Let no foreigner who is bound to the
LORD say,
"The LORD will surely exclude me
from his people."
And let no eunuch[t] complain,
"I am only a dry tree."

4 For this is what the LORD says:

"To the eunuchs who keep my
Sabbaths,
who choose what pleases me
and hold fast to my covenant—
5 to them I will give within my temple
and its walls[u]
a memorial and a name
better than sons and daughters;
I will give them an everlasting name
that will endure forever.[v]
6 And foreigners who bind themselves
to the LORD
to minister[w] to him,
to love the name of the LORD,
and to be his servants,
all who keep the Sabbath[x] without
desecrating it
and who hold fast to my
covenant—
7 these I will bring to my holy
mountain[y]
and give them joy in my house of
prayer.
Their burnt offerings and sacrifices[z]
will be accepted on my altar;
for my house will be called

56:2 [r] Ps 119:2 [s] Ex 20:8,10; Isa 58:13
56:3 [t] Jer 38:7 *fn*; Ac 8:27
56:5 [u] Isa 26:1; 60:18 [v] Isa 48:19; 55:13
56:6 [w] Isa 60:7, 10; 61:5 [x] ver 2,4
56:7 [y] Isa 2:2 [z] Ro 12:1; Heb 13:15

[a] Mt 21:13*; Lk 19:46* [b] Mk 11:17*
56:8 [c] Isa 11:12; 60:3-11; Jn 10:16
56:9 [d] Isa 18:6; Jer 12:9
56:10 [e] Eze 3:17 [f] Na 3:18
56:11 [g] Eze 34:2 [h] Isa 1:3 [i] Isa 57:17; Eze 13:19; Mic 3:11
56:12 [j] Ps 10:6; Lk 12:18-19
57:1 [k] Ps 12:1 [l] Isa 42:25

Isa 56:6-8 ❖ How can we extend God's love to outsiders so that through us God can "gather still others" (v. 8; see Lk 14:21-24)?

a house of prayer for all
nations."[a][b]
8 The Sovereign LORD declares—
he who gathers the exiles of
Israel:
"I will gather[c] still others to them
besides those already gathered."

God's Accusation Against the Wicked

9 Come, all you beasts of the field,[d]
come and devour, all you beasts of
the forest!
10 Israel's watchmen[e] are blind,
they all lack knowledge;
they are all mute dogs,
they cannot bark;
they lie around and dream,
they love to sleep.[f]
11 They are dogs with mighty
appetites;
they never have enough.
They are shepherds[g] who lack
understanding;[h]
they all turn to their own way,
they seek their own gain.[i]
12 "Come," each one cries, "let me get
wine!
Let us drink our fill of beer!
And tomorrow will be like today,
or even far better."[j]

57 The righteous perish,[k]
and no one takes it to heart;[l]
the devout are taken away,
and no one understands

"righteousness" in faithfully delivering his people despite their sin. Chapters 56–66 synthesize the two earlier sections, showing that righteous living is a requirement for the servants of God (i.e., chs. 1–39) but that such righteousness is only possible through the grace of God (i.e., chs. 40–55).

Verse 1 provides an immediate illustration. It calls on the reader to "maintain justice and do what is right" in language similar to that found repeatedly in chs. 1–39. But in the same breath it says we should do this because God's "righteousness"—that is, his "salvation"—is at hand (v. 1). We can only do righteousness because of God's righteousness made available to us.

56:6–8 The righteousness called for here is more than legalistic law-keeping. Verse 6 speaks in relational terms of binding oneself to God as an act of love, service, and worship. Those who do this will be brought into God's "house of prayer," there to participate in the worship of that place, because God's purpose is to gather "all nations" to himself (vv. 7–8).

✣ **56:1–8** Unless our adoption into a new family changes our behavior into the likeness of the head of that family, there is reason to doubt the reality of the adoption. Christians today must recover the understanding that while it is indeed by grace through faith, not our works, that we are saved (Eph 2:8–9), it is *for* good works that we have been saved (Eph 2:10).

56:9–12 This section begins with an attack on "Israel's watchmen" (v. 10) who are compared to "dogs" (v. 11) who do not bark because they are asleep with full stomachs. Clearly, this points to the religious leadership of the nation.

57:1–2 Return from captivity will not guarantee

that the righteous are taken away
to be spared from evil.[m]
2 Those who walk uprightly[n]
enter into peace;
they find rest as they lie in death.

3 "But you — come here, you children
of a sorceress,
you offspring of adulterers[o] and
prostitutes![p]
4 Who are you mocking?
At whom do you sneer
and stick out your tongue?
Are you not a brood of rebels,
the offspring of liars?
5 You burn with lust among the oaks
and under every spreading tree;[q]
you sacrifice your children[r] in the
ravines
and under the overhanging crags.
6 The idols[s] among the smooth stones
of the ravines are your portion;
indeed, they are your lot.
Yes, to them you have poured out
drink offerings[t]
and offered grain offerings.
In view of all this, should I
relent?[u]
7 You have made your bed on a high
and lofty hill;[v]
there you went up to offer your
sacrifices.
8 Behind your doors and your
doorposts
you have put your pagan symbols.
Forsaking me, you uncovered your
bed,
you climbed into it and opened it
wide;
you made a pact with those whose
beds you love,[w]
and you looked with lust on their
naked bodies.[x]
9 You went to Molek[a] with olive oil
and increased your perfumes.
You sent your ambassadors[b][y] far
away;
you descended to the very realm
of the dead!
10 You wearied yourself by such going
about,
but you would not say, 'It is
hopeless.'[z]
You found renewal of your strength,
and so you did not faint.

11 "Whom have you so dreaded and
feared[a]
that you have not been true to me,
and have neither remembered[b] me
nor taken this to heart?
Is it not because I have long been
silent[c]
that you do not fear me?
12 I will expose your righteousness and
your works,[d]
and they will not benefit you.
13 When you cry out[e] for help,
let your collection of idols save
you!
The wind will carry all of them off,
a mere breath will blow them
away.
But whoever takes refuge in me
will inherit the land[f]
and possess my holy mountain."[g]

57:1 [m] 2Ki 22:20
57:2 [n] Isa 26:7
57:3 [o] Mt 16:4 [p] Isa 1:21
57:5 [q] 2Ki 16:4 [r] Lev 18:21; Ps 106:37-38; Eze 16:20
57:6 [s] Jer 3:9 [t] Jer 7:18 [u] Jer 5:9,29; 9:9
57:7 [v] Jer 3:6; Eze 16:16
57:8 [w] Eze 16:26; 23:7 [x] Eze 23:18
57:9 [y] Eze 23:16, 40
57:10 [z] Jer 2:25; 18:12
57:11 [a] Pr 29:25 [b] Jer 2:32; 3:21 [c] Ps 50:21
57:12 [d] Isa 29:15; Mic 3:2-4,8
57:13 [e] Jer 22:20; 30:15 [f] Ps 37:9 [g] Isa 65:9-11

[a] 9 Or *to the king* [b] 9 Or *idols*

Isa 57:1-2 ❖ How is death, at times, a way God shows mercy to the righteous?

---

new behaviors for the people. If the leaders continue to be self-centered and power-hungry, the flock entrusted to them will continue to be overtaken by their spiritual enemies (56:9). But there is hope for the upright (57:2).

57:3–10 Now Isaiah turns directly to the people, addressing them as "you" (v. 3). Like those who worship rocks and trees (vv. 5–7), engage in ritual prostitution (v. 8), and sacrifice their children (vv. 5, 9), their only real desire is to manipulate divine power to their own advantage.

57:11–13 Following the description of the people's behavior, God pronounces his judgment. He begins with a question: This is the God who graciously delivered them; how could they not have "remembered" (v. 11) all this?

They would rather construct a religion that seems to give them control. But such a religion cannot stand up when the winds of adversity blow upon a life. It will collapse and blow away (57:13).

56:9—57:13 In so many ways, the satisfaction of supposed needs is all-important to us: We drink to excess, we eat to excess, we cannot get enough of self-gratification of all sorts, and we sacrifice our children, both the unborn and the living, to the satisfaction of these needs. What is the answer? The key is in self-surrender. Paul calls it "dying to oneself" (see Ro 6:11; Gal 2:20; Col 3:3–5). We surrender our needs to him, determined to be faithful to him and his ways above all else, leaving the fulfillment of our needs in his hand. Here there is freedom without excess, because we know that in the end it is God we want and that satisfying yet another craving will never satisfy that deeper longing.

Comfort for the Contrite

14And it will be said:

"Build up, build up, prepare the road!
Remove the obstacles out of the way of my people."[h]
15For this is what the high and exalted[i] One says —
he who lives forever,[j] whose name is holy:
"I live in a high and holy place,
but also with the one who is contrite[k] and lowly in spirit,[l]
to revive the spirit of the lowly
and to revive the heart of the contrite.[m]
16I will not accuse them forever,
nor will I always be angry,[n]
for then they would faint away because of me —
the very people I have created.
17I was enraged by their sinful greed;[o]
I punished them, and hid my face in anger,
yet they kept on in their willful ways.[p]
18I have seen their ways, but I will heal[q] them;
I will guide them and restore comfort[r] to Israel's mourners,
19 creating praise on their lips.[s]
Peace, peace,[t] to those far and near,"[u]
says the LORD. "And I will heal them."
20But the wicked[v] are like the tossing sea,
which cannot rest,

57:14 [h]Isa 62:10; Jer 18:15
57:15 [i]Isa 52:13 [j]Dt 33:27 [k]Ps 147:3 [l]Ps 34:18; 51:17; Isa 66:2 [m]Isa 61:1
57:16 [n]Ps 85:5; 103:9; Mic 7:18
57:17 [o]Isa 56:11 [p]Isa 1:4
57:18 [q]Isa 30:26 [r]Isa 61:1-3
57:19 [s]Isa 6:7; Heb 13:15 [t]Eph 2:17 [u]Ac 2:39
57:20 [v]Job 18:5-21

57:14–21 Once more, the highway imagery comes to the fore. But this is a highway on which the "contrite" (v. 15) can return to God. God's intention is not merely to punish but to go beyond that to giving his people a changed nature, where rebellion and pride will be replaced by "praise" and "peace" (v. 19).

These final verses emphasize once again that God's promises are not for the nation as a whole merely because they are the descendants of Jacob but specifically for those inside the nation—and outside—who recognize their need and turn to God with contrite hearts.

✣ **57:14–21** God is merciful. He wants to live with us and in us. He wants to heal us. The worst thing we can do is to return to the kind of legalistic righteousness of earlier generations. No, the message of these verses, and indeed of this entire last part of the book, is that while God expects real righteousness and justice in our lives, he also expects to do that in us and for us as a by-product of our loving relationship with him. We can only wonder at the indescribable generosity of that offer.

CHARACTER OF GOD // GOD IS ETERNAL

Isaiah 57:15: "For this is what the high and exalted One says—he who lives forever, whose name is holy . . ."

Isaiah 57:15 declares that God lives forever; he inhabits eternity. This does not mean that God exists only in time. God is the One who created time and he completely fills it, just as God fills space through his omnipresence.

To say that God inhabits eternity is to say that God exists above and outside of time. Though it is hard to comprehend, time itself is a product of creation. Without the universe, there could be no time—yet God would still exist self-sufficiently in eternity.

Nothing outside of God is eternal; all other realities find their source through God's work of creation. This shows the key distinction between God and creation. God is not part of the universe; rather, God stands outside of creation, and he spoke everything that is not himself into existence. Only God is without beginning or end.

Since God is eternal, he is not swayed by the whims of time. He is not limited to the present like his creation is. Since he stands outside of time, he can see his plan in its totality. He is able, by his sovereign hand, to lead creation toward its full redemption in Christ. Since God is eternal, creation can wait with hopeful certainty for that future.

APPLICATION ✣ God's eternal nature stretches our minds to consider the splendor and vastness of God. We cannot fully comprehend what it means to exist outside of time and to be without beginning or end. God's eternal nature should fill us with confidence that God sees the future as though it has already happened. God's promised redemption of creation, foretold in Scripture, cannot fail (Isa 14:24). We can rest our hope in the fact that the future itself is in God's all-powerful hands.

whose waves cast up mire and
mud.
21 "There is no peace,"[w] says my God,
"for the wicked."[x]

True Fasting

58 "Shout it aloud,[y] do not hold
back.
Raise your voice like a trumpet.
Declare to my people their rebellion[z]
and to the descendants of Jacob
their sins.
2 For day after day they seek[a] me out;
they seem eager to know my ways,
as if they were a nation that does
what is right
and has not forsaken the
commands of its God.
They ask me for just decisions
and seem eager for God to come
near[b] them.
3 'Why have we fasted,'[c] they say,
'and you have not seen it?
Why have we humbled ourselves,
and you have not noticed?'[d]

"Yet on the day of your fasting, you
do as you please[e]
and exploit all your workers.
4 Your fasting ends in quarreling and
strife,[f]
and in striking each other with
wicked fists.
You cannot fast as you do today
and expect your voice to be heard[g]
on high.
5 Is this the kind of fast[h] I have chosen,
only a day for people to humble[i]
themselves?
Is it only for bowing one's head like
a reed
and for lying in sackcloth and
ashes?[j]
Is that what you call a fast,
a day acceptable to the LORD?

6 "Is not this the kind of fasting I have
chosen:
to loose the chains of injustice[k]
and untie the cords of the yoke,

57:21 [w] Isa 59:8 [x] Isa 48:22
58:1 [y] Isa 40:6 [z] Isa 48:8
58:2 [a] Isa 48:1; Titus 1:16; Jas 4:8 [b] Isa 29:13
58:3 [c] Lev 16:29 [d] Mal 3:14 [e] Isa 22:13; Zec 7:5-6
58:4 [f] 1Ki 21:9-13; Isa 59:6 [g] Isa 59:2
58:5 [h] Zec 7:5 [i] 1Ki 21:27 [j] Job 2:8
58:6 [k] Ne 5:10-11 [l] Jer 34:9
58:7 [m] Eze 18:16; Lk 3:11 [n] Isa 16:4; Heb 13:2 [o] Job 31:19-20; Mt 25:36 [p] Ge 29:14; Lk 10:31-32
58:8 [q] Job 11:17 [r] Isa 30:26 [s] Ex 14:19
58:9 [t] Ps 50:15 [u] Pr 6:13 [v] Ps 12:2; Isa 59:13
58:10 [w] Dt 15:7-8 [x] Isa 42:16 [y] Job 11:17
58:11 [z] Ps 107:9 [a] SS 4:15 [b] Jn 4:14

Isa 58:6-9 ❖ How can we practice "the kind of fasting" God desires (v. 6)? Be specific.

to set the oppressed[l] free
and break every yoke?
7 Is it not to share your food with the
hungry[m]
and to provide the poor wanderer
with shelter[n] —
when you see the naked, to clothe[o]
them,
and not to turn away from your
own flesh and blood?[p]
8 Then your light will break forth like
the dawn,[q]
and your healing[r] will quickly
appear;
then your righteousness[a] will go
before you,
and the glory of the LORD will be
your rear guard.[s]
9 Then you will call,[t] and the LORD will
answer;
you will cry for help, and he will
say: Here am I.

"If you do away with the yoke of
oppression,
with the pointing finger[u] and
malicious talk,[v]
10 and if you spend yourselves in behalf
of the hungry
and satisfy the needs of the
oppressed,[w]
then your light[x] will rise in the
darkness,
and your night will become like
the noonday.[y]
11 The LORD will guide you always;
he will satisfy your needs[z] in a
sun-scorched land
and will strengthen your frame.
You will be like a well-watered
garden,[a]
like a spring[b] whose waters never
fail.

[a] 8 Or *your righteous One*

58:1–3 The people give every appearance of piety and genuine concern to know God's will. But in fact, says Isaiah, they are in a state of "rebellion" (v. 1). They are engaging in the behavior for the very same reasons the pagans do: to manipulate God to act in their favor.

58:4–12 God calls for behavior that is self-forgetful and outward-looking. Let acts of self-denial be for the sake of others and not for one's own sake. Eat less to have food to give to the "hungry" (v. 7). Wear less-expensive clothes to clothe the "naked" (vv. 7, 10). This is the kind of self-denial God has "chosen" (v. 6). Through God's people the blessings of his covenant light will be extended to the whole earth (vv. 8, 10).

12 Your people will rebuild the ancient ruins[c]
and will raise up the age-old foundations;[d]
you will be called Repairer of Broken Walls,
Restorer of Streets with Dwellings.

13 "If you keep your feet from breaking the Sabbath[e]
and from doing as you please on my holy day,
if you call the Sabbath a delight[f]
and the LORD's holy day honorable,
and if you honor it by not going your own way
and not doing as you please or speaking idle words,
14 then you will find your joy[g] in the LORD,
and I will cause you to ride in triumph on the heights[h] of the land
and to feast on the inheritance of your father Jacob."
For the mouth of the LORD has spoken.[i]

Sin, Confession and Redemption

59 Surely the arm of the LORD is not too short[j] to save,
nor his ear too dull to hear.[k]
2 But your iniquities have separated you from your God;
your sins have hidden his face from you,
so that he will not hear.[l]
3 For your hands are stained with blood,[m]
your fingers with guilt.

58:12 [c] Isa 49:8 [d] Isa 44:28
58:13 [e] Isa 56:2 [f] Ps 84:2,10
58:14 [g] Job 22:26 [h] Dt 32:13 [i] Isa 1:20
59:1 [j] Nu 11:23; Isa 50:2 [k] Isa 58:9; 65:24
59:2 [l] Isa 1:15; 58:4
59:3 [m] Isa 1:15

Isa 59:2-3 ❖ Why does sin distance us from God and numb us to his leading?

Your lips have spoken falsely,
and your tongue mutters wicked things.
4 No one calls for justice;
no one pleads a case with integrity.
They rely on empty arguments, they utter lies;
they conceive trouble and give birth to evil.[n]
5 They hatch the eggs of vipers
and spin a spider's web.[o]
Whoever eats their eggs will die,
and when one is broken, an adder is hatched.
6 Their cobwebs are useless for clothing;
they cannot cover themselves with what they make.[p]
Their deeds are evil deeds,
and acts of violence[q] are in their hands.
7 Their feet rush into sin;
they are swift to shed innocent blood.[r]
They pursue evil schemes;[s]
acts of violence mark their ways.[t]
8 The way of peace they do not know;
there is no justice in their paths.
They have turned them into crooked roads;
no one who walks along them will know peace.[u]
9 So justice is far from us,
and righteousness does not reach us.

59:4 [n] Job 15:35; Ps 7:14
59:5 [o] Job 8:14
59:6 [p] Isa 28:20 [q] Isa 58:4
59:7 [r] Pr 6:17 [s] Mk 7:21-22 [t] Ro 3:15-17*
59:8 [u] Isa 57:21; Lk 1:79

58:13–14 The Sabbath is commanded as one of the feast days and is to be considered as a time of delighting in the Lord and in all his blessings to us. It does not manipulate God. It is intended to develop and deepen our relationship with him.

✜ **58:1–14** We are still just as tempted to use religious behavior as a way of manipulating God. Other activities have replaced Israelite religious activities, such as church attendance, daily devotions, prayer, tithing, and so on, and these are all liable to the same dangers. The danger is that we engage in them to wring blessings from a God who we feel is disinclined to give blessings unless we manipulate him in some way. But what God desires is sincere surrender to his will and his way.

59:1–4 The lack of blessing is not God's fault but the people's. Their "iniquities" and "sins" (v. 2) have come between them and God. And as chs. 57–58 have shown, some of those sins are their very religiosity. Coupled with that are evidences of a broken social system: violence and injustice (vv. 3–4).

59:4–8 The things they produce are like the "eggs of vipers" and the webs of spiders (vv. 5–6). They are not only "useless" (v. 6) but worse: They are deadly. In contrast to the highway of holiness that God will prepare for his people (35:8), these "roads" are "crooked," and those who embark on them will find destruction and disintegration, not "peace" (59:8; see 52:7; 57:19).

59:9–15 Isaiah is speaking for all the faithful of the land. It would have been easy to consider himself above such things. But if the prophet was closely allied with God, he was also still inextricably part of his human community.

This confession is one of a person who has reflected deeply on the human condition. Isaiah is

We look for light, but all is darkness;[v]
for brightness, but we walk in
deep shadows.
10 Like the blind[w] we grope along the
wall,
feeling our way like people
without eyes.
At midday we stumble[x] as if it were
twilight;
among the strong, we are like the
dead.[y]
11 We all growl like bears;
we moan mournfully like doves.[z]
We look for justice, but find none;
for deliverance, but it is far away.

12 For our offenses[a] are many in your
sight,
and our sins testify[b] against us.
Our offenses are ever with us,
and we acknowledge our
iniquities:
13 rebellion and treachery against the
LORD,
turning our backs[c] on our God,
inciting revolt and oppression,[d]
uttering lies[e] our hearts have
conceived.
14 So justice is driven back,
and righteousness[f] stands at a
distance;
truth[g] has stumbled in the streets,
honesty cannot enter.
15 Truth is nowhere to be found,
and whoever shuns evil becomes a
prey.

The LORD looked and was displeased
that there was no justice.

59:9 [v] Isa 5:30; 8:20
59:10 [w] Dt 28:29 [x] Isa 8:15 [y] La 3:6
59:11 [z] Isa 38:14; Eze 7:16
59:12 [a] Ezr 9:6 [b] Isa 3:9
59:13 [c] Pr 30:9; Mt 10:33; Titus 1:16 [d] Isa 5:7 [e] Mk 7:21-22
59:14 [f] Isa 1:21 [g] Isa 48:1
59:16 [h] Isa 41:28 [i] Ps 98:1; Isa 63:5
59:17 [j] Eph 6:14 [k] Eph 6:17; 1Th 5:8 [l] Isa 63:3 [m] Isa 9:7
59:19 [n] Isa 49:12 [o] Ps 113:3
59:20 [p] Ac 2:38-39; Ro 11:26-27*
59:21 [q] Isa 11:2; 44:3

16 He saw that there was no one,[h]
he was appalled that there was no
one to intervene;
so his own arm achieved salvation[i]
for him,
and his own righteousness
sustained him.
17 He put on righteousness as his
breastplate,[j]
and the helmet[k] of salvation on
his head;
he put on the garments[l] of
vengeance
and wrapped himself in zeal[m] as
in a cloak.
18 According to what they have done,
so will he repay
wrath to his enemies
and retribution to his foes;
he will repay the islands their due.
19 From the west,[n] people will fear the
name of the LORD,
and from the rising of the sun,[o]
they will revere his glory.
For he will come like a pent-up flood
that the breath of the LORD drives
along.[a]

20 "The Redeemer will come to Zion,
to those in Jacob who repent of
their sins,"[p]
declares the LORD.

21 "As for me, this is my covenant with
them," says the LORD. "My Spirit,[q] who
is on you, will not depart from you, and
my words that I have put in your mouth

[a] 19 *Or When enemies come in like a flood, / the Spirit of the LORD will put them to flight*

---

showing the need for something other than stern discipline and good intentions if God's commands are to be fulfilled. What that something is will be uncovered in the next passage.

59:1–15a God created the universe as an expression of his own goodness. But he has permitted his creatures the possibility of choosing not to live within his purposes, and that choice on the part of our first parents was like introducing a virus into the body. It has infected the entire system, most especially the human system. Thus, just as cancer cells are able to capture the cells around them and turn them to their own destructive purposes, the Bible insists that there is a moral cancer let loose in the human system. Thankfully, he also offers us a remedy to that cancer (Mt 11:28; 1Pe 5:7).

59:15–19 In 52:13—53:12 the servant was submissive; now he is revealed as a conquering warrior (v. 17). He has come to defeat the power of evil in his people's lives. People all over the world will be affected by the witness of a righteous Israel. They will give God "glory" (v. 19) and turn to him in obedience.

59:20–21 Verses 20–21 conclude all that has been said in chs. 56–59. God will come to his repentant people, and his goal for them is for them to be witnesses that he, the only God, is indeed the only Savior. The "Spirit" of God (v. 21) can fill the lives and mouths of his people, making the witness promised in 2:1–5 not just a possibility but a reality. This is the fulfillment of the "covenant of peace" (54:10; see 55:3–5).

59:15b–21 Through the gift of the Holy Spirit, we can keep covenant with God, with no credit for the feat coming to us but with all glory being given to the conquering Christ. He enables us to live "blameless" lives (1Th 5:23), to walk in a "blameless" manner (Ge 17:1), and to keep us in that walk until the coming of Christ.

will always be on your lips, on the lips of your children and on the lips of their descendants — from this time on and forever," says the LORD.

The Glory of Zion

60 "Arise,[r] shine, for your light[s] has come,
and the glory of the LORD rises upon you.
2 See, darkness covers the earth
and thick darkness[t] is over the peoples,
but the LORD rises upon you
and his glory appears over you.
3 Nations[u] will come to your light,
and kings[v] to the brightness of your dawn.

4 "Lift up your eyes and look about you:
All assemble[w] and come to you;
your sons come from afar,
and your daughters[x] are carried on the hip.[y]
5 Then you will look and be radiant,
your heart will throb and swell with joy;
the wealth on the seas will be brought to you,
to you the riches of the nations will come.
6 Herds of camels will cover your land,
young camels of Midian[z] and Ephah.[a]
And all from Sheba[b] will come,
bearing gold and incense[c]
and proclaiming the praise[d] of the LORD.
7 All Kedar's[e] flocks will be gathered to you,
the rams of Nebaioth will serve you;
they will be accepted as offerings on my altar,
and I will adorn my glorious temple.[f]

8 "Who are these[g] that fly along like clouds,
like doves to their nests?
9 Surely the islands[h] look to me;
in the lead are the ships of Tarshish,[a][i]
bringing[j] your children from afar,
with their silver and gold,
to the honor of the LORD your God,
the Holy One of Israel,
for he has endowed you with splendor.[k]

10 "Foreigners[l] will rebuild your walls,
and their kings[m] will serve you.
Though in anger I struck you,
in favor I will show you compassion.[n]
11 Your gates[o] will always stand open,
they will never be shut, day or night,
so that people may bring you the wealth of the nations[p] —
their kings[q] led in triumphal procession.
12 For the nation or kingdom that will not serve[r] you will perish;
it will be utterly ruined.

13 "The glory of Lebanon[s] will come to you,
the juniper, the fir and the cypress together,[t]
to adorn my sanctuary;
and I will glorify the place for my feet.[u]
14 The children of your oppressors[v] will come bowing before you;
all who despise you will bow down[w] at your feet
and will call you the City of the LORD,
Zion[x] of the Holy One of Israel.

15 "Although you have been forsaken[y] and hated,
with no one traveling[z] through,

60:1 [r] Isa 52:2 [s] Eph 5:14
60:2 [t] Jer 13:16; Col 1:13
60:3 [u] Isa 45:14; Rev 21:24 [v] Isa 49:23
60:4 [w] Isa 11:12 [x] Isa 43:6 [y] Isa 49:20-22
60:6 [z] Ge 25:2 [a] Ge 25:4 [b] Ps 72:10 [c] Isa 43:23; Mt 2:11 [d] Isa 42:10
60:7 [e] Ge 25:13 [f] ver 13; Hag 2:3, 7,9
60:8 [g] Isa 49:21
60:9 [h] Isa 11:11 [i] Isa 2:16 *fn* [j] Isa 14:2; 43:6 [k] Isa 55:5
60:10 [l] Isa 14:1-2 [m] Isa 49:23; Rev 21:24 [n] Isa 54:8
60:11 [o] ver 18; Isa 62:10; Rev 21:25 [p] ver 5; Rev 21:26 [q] Ps 149:8
60:12 [r] Isa 14:2
60:13 [s] Isa 35:2 [t] Isa 41:19 [u] 1Ch 28:2; Ps 132:7
60:14 [v] Isa 14:2 [w] Isa 49:23; Rev 3:9 [x] Heb 12:22
60:15 [y] Isa 1:7-9; 6:12 [z] Isa 33:8

[a] 9 Or *the trading ships*

60:1–3 The emphasis on "light" in vv. 1–3 contrasts with 59:9. Where there was complete "darkness" (v. 2); there will now be "light" like that of the rising sun (v. 3). Israel has a mission: When the light of God dawns in Israel, the nations will recognize it for what it is and "come" (vv. 1, 3) flowing to it. Zion's light is not for itself but for others.
60:4–9 Here Isaiah emphasizes the worldwide nature of the pilgrimage of the nations. They will come with every kind of transportation, from camels to ships. Along with their wealth, the nations will also bring back Zion's "sons" and "daughters" (vv. 4, 9). All those who wished to return will be able to do so.
60:10–14 The nations will not only bring their wealth to Zion, but they will also come to serve her, and if not, their "kingdom . . . will be utterly ruined" (v. 12). If one does not choose to become a participant in worship with God's redeemed people, the only other option is to become their servant.
60:15–22 All of the benefits result from the gracious power of the Lord. Twice he asserts that "the

I will make you the everlasting
pride[a]
and the joy[b] of all generations.
16 You will drink the milk of nations
and be nursed[c] at royal breasts.
Then you will know that I, the LORD,
am your Savior,
your Redeemer,[d] the Mighty One
of Jacob.
17 Instead of bronze I will bring you
gold,
and silver in place of iron.
Instead of wood I will bring you
bronze,
and iron in place of stones.
I will make peace your governor
and well-being your ruler.
18 No longer will violence be heard in
your land,
nor ruin or destruction within
your borders,
but you will call your walls
Salvation[e]
and your gates Praise.
19 The sun will no more be your light
by day,
nor will the brightness of the
moon shine on you,
for the LORD will be your everlasting
light,[f]
and your God will be your glory.[g]
20 Your sun[h] will never set again,
and your moon will wane no
more;
the LORD will be your everlasting
light,
and your days of sorrow[i] will end.
21 Then all your people will be
righteous[j]
and they will possess[k] the land
forever.
They are the shoot I have planted,[l]
the work of my hands,[m]
for the display of my splendor.[n]

60:15 [a] Isa 4:2 [b] Isa 65:18
60:16 [c] Isa 49:23; 66:11,12 [d] Isa 59:20
60:18 [e] Isa 26:1
60:19 [f] Rev 22:5 [g] Zec 2:5; Rev 21:23
60:20 [h] Isa 30:26 [i] Isa 35:10
60:21 [j] Rev 21:27 [k] Ps 37:11, 22; Isa 57:13; 61:7 [l] Mt 15:13 [m] Isa 19:25; 29:23; Eph 2:10 [n] Isa 52:1

Isa 60:20-22 ❖ How can we live into this new creation vision today, living as a signpost of God's coming kingdom?

Isa 61:1-2 ❖ With God's Spirit upon us, how can we share in the work of Christ by doing these same things (see Lk 4:17-21)?

22 The least of you will become a
thousand,
the smallest a mighty nation.
I am the LORD;
in its time I will do this swiftly."

The Year of the LORD's Favor

61 The Spirit[o] of the Sovereign LORD
is on me,
because the LORD has
anointed[p] me
to proclaim good news to the
poor.[q]
He has sent me to bind up[r] the
brokenhearted,
to proclaim freedom for the
captives[s]
and release from darkness for the
prisoners,[a]
2 to proclaim the year of the LORD's
favor[t]
and the day of vengeance[u] of our
God,
to comfort[v] all who mourn,
3 and provide for those who grieve in
Zion—
to bestow on them a crown of
beauty
instead of ashes,
the oil of joy
instead of mourning,
and a garment of praise
instead of a spirit of despair.

61:1 [o] Isa 11:2 [p] Ps 45:7 [q] Mt 11:5; Lk 7:22 [r] Isa 57:15 [s] Isa 42:7; 49:9
61:2 [t] Isa 49:8; Lk 4:18-19* [u] Isa 34:8 [v] Isa 57:18; Mt 5:4

[a] 1 Hebrew; Septuagint *the blind*

LORD will be your everlasting light" (vv. 19, 20). It is he who will transform Zion from being "forsaken" and abandoned to being served by royalty (v. 15). It is he who will replace silver, iron, and stones with gold, silver, and bronze (v. 17).

60:18-21 It is God who will take away violence, ruin, and destruction and give peace and righteousness, salvation and praise in their place.

The ultimate transformation that the Savior produces is changing people who are helpless in sin into "righteous" people (v. 21).

60:1-22 Glory is never for oneself. It is always to be shared, given away, reflected. In Hebrew the word "glory" connotes what is weighty, significant, even real. This is what Christ has come to give us—the very reality of God. But just as he has given it to us from God, we are to give it back to him. As the light of his reality shines in us, no accolades should come to us but to the God who shines through us.

61:1-9 The results of the messiah's work are detailed, beginning with God's people becoming "oaks of righteousness" (v. 3). This is the opposite of what was said of them in 1:27-31, where they were an "oak with fading leaves" (1:30). The servant/messiah's work will not only deliver but also transform.

They will be called oaks of
righteousness,
a planting of the LORD
for the display of his splendor.[w]

4 They will rebuild the ancient ruins[x]
and restore the places long
devastated;
they will renew the ruined cities
that have been devastated for
generations.
5 Strangers[y] will shepherd your
flocks;
foreigners will work your fields
and vineyards.
6 And you will be called priests[z] of the
LORD,
you will be named ministers of
our God.
You will feed on the wealth[a] of
nations,
and in their riches you will boast.

7 Instead of your shame
you will receive a double[b] portion,
and instead of disgrace
you will rejoice in your
inheritance.
And so you will inherit a double
portion in your land,
and everlasting joy will be yours.

8 "For I, the LORD, love justice;[c]
I hate robbery and wrongdoing.
In my faithfulness I will reward my
people
and make an everlasting
covenant[d] with them.
9 Their descendants will be known
among the nations
and their offspring among the
peoples.
All who see them will acknowledge
that they are a people the LORD
has blessed."

61:3 [w] Isa 60:20-21
61:4 [x] Isa 49:8; Eze 36:33; Am 9:14
61:5 [y] Isa 14:1-2
61:6 [z] Ex 19:6; 1Pe 2:5 [a] Isa 60:11
61:7 [b] Isa 40:2; Zec 9:12
61:8 [c] Ps 11:7; Isa 5:16 [d] Isa 55:3

61:10 [e] Isa 25:9; Hab 3:18 [f] Ps 132:9; Isa 52:1 [g] Isa 49:18; Rev 21:2
61:11 [h] Ps 85:11
62:1 [i] Isa 1:26
62:2 [j] Isa 52:10; 60:3 [k] ver 4,12
62:3 [l] Isa 28:5; Zec 9:16; 1Th 2:19

Isa 62:1-5 ❖ Are we sometimes tempted to "keep silent" about our faith (v. 1)? How can we catch Isaiah's passion for proclaiming God's salvation to the world?

10 I delight greatly in the LORD;
my soul rejoices[e] in my God.
For he has clothed me with
garments of salvation
and arrayed me in a robe of his
righteousness,[f]
as a bridegroom adorns his head like
a priest,
and as a bride[g] adorns herself with
her jewels.
11 For as the soil makes the sprout
come up
and a garden causes seeds to
grow,
so the Sovereign LORD will make
righteousness[h]
and praise spring up before all
nations.

Zion's New Name

62 For Zion's sake I will not keep
silent,
for Jerusalem's sake I will not
remain quiet,
till her vindication[i] shines out like
the dawn,
her salvation like a blazing torch.
2 The nations[j] will see your
vindication,
and all kings your glory;
you will be called by a new name[k]
that the mouth of the LORD will
bestow.
3 You will be a crown[l] of splendor in
the LORD's hand,
a royal diadem in the hand of your
God.

61:10–11 As has happened before when the work of the servant/messiah is presented, the response is praise. Israel sees herself as a bride whom the groom has dressed in beautiful wedding garments of "salvation" and "righteousness" (v. 10). In v. 11, Israel sees herself as a fruitful field, flowering in "righteousness" and "praise." God will give his people the righteous behavior they have been unable to produce. He will do this for his own praise and glory before the nations.

❖ **61:1–11** As we give God the freedom to examine us and to remove what is killing us, we may enter into a painful process. But it is also a process that leads to wonderful freedom and joyous growth. Do we believe that Christ wants to deliver us from habitual sinning? Do we believe he can do that? Will *we*, personally and intentionally, believe him to do that in our lives? Will we keep on believing him to remake us into his image, despite setbacks and difficulties, right to the end of the road?

62:1–9 God has not cast off Zion (v. 4) but "rejoices" (v. 5) over her as a groom does a bride (cf. 61:10). "The nations will see" the "glory" that is their "vindication" (62:2). The nation will be a beautiful "crown" in God's "hand" (v. 3).

4 No longer will they call you
Deserted,[m]
or name your land Desolate.
But you will be called Hephzibah,[a]
and your land Beulah[b];
for the LORD will take delight[n] in you,
and your land will be married.[o]
5 As a young man marries a young
woman,
so will your Builder marry you;
as a bridegroom rejoices over his
bride,
so will your God rejoice[p] over you.

6 I have posted watchmen[q] on your
walls, Jerusalem;
they will never be silent day or
night.
You who call on the LORD,
give yourselves no rest,
7 and give him no rest[r] till he
establishes Jerusalem
and makes her the praise of the
earth.

8 The LORD has sworn by his right
hand
and by his mighty arm:
"Never again will I give your grain[s]
as food for your enemies,
and never again will foreigners
drink the new wine
for which you have toiled;
9 but those who harvest it will eat it
and praise the LORD,
and those who gather the grapes will
drink it
in the courts of my sanctuary."

10 Pass through, pass through the
gates!
Prepare the way for the people.
Build up, build up the highway![u]
Remove the stones.
Raise a banner[v] for the nations.

11 The LORD has made proclamation
to the ends of the earth:
"Say to Daughter Zion,[w]
'See, your Savior comes![x]
See, his reward is with him,
and his recompense accompanies
him.'"[y]
12 They will be called[z] the Holy People,[a]
the Redeemed[b] of the LORD;
and you will be called Sought After,
the City No Longer Deserted.[c]

God's Day of Vengeance and Redemption

63 Who is this coming from Edom,
from Bozrah,[d] with his garments
stained crimson?
Who is this, robed in splendor,
striding forward in the greatness
of his strength?

"It is I, proclaiming victory,
mighty to save."[e]

2 Why are your garments red,
like those of one treading the
winepress?

3 "I have trodden the winepress[f] alone;
from the nations no one was
with me.
I trampled them in my anger
and trod them down in my
wrath;[g]

62:4 [m] Isa 54:6 [n] Jer 32:41; Zep 3:17 [o] Jer 3:14; Hos 2:19
62:5 [p] Isa 65:19
62:6 [q] Isa 52:8; Eze 3:17
62:7 [r] Mt 15:21-28; Lk 18:1-8
62:8 [s] Dt 28:30-33; Isa 1:7; Jer 5:17
62:10 [t] Isa 60:11 [u] Isa 11:16; 57:14 [v] Isa 11:10
62:11 [w] Zec 9:9; Mt 21:5 [x] Rev 22:12 [y] Isa 40:10
62:12 [z] ver 4 [a] 1Pe 2:9 [b] Isa 35:9 [c] Isa 42:16
63:1 [d] Am 1:12 [e] Zep 3:17
63:3 [f] Rev 14:20; 19:15 [g] Isa 22:5

[a] 4 *Hephzibah* means *my delight is in her.*
[b] 4 *Beulah* means *married.*

62:10–12 Isaiah is drawing together strands from throughout his book to call the people to receive the promises God is making to them. They *can* be the righteous people of God, his "Holy People" (v. 12), who will draw all nations to him.

62:1–12 What causes feelings of self-worth? What enables people to go on living when problems seem to mount above eye level? Oddly enough, self-esteem outside of a positive complex of relationships is not a good thing but a bad one. Sociopaths often feel good about themselves and have nothing but contempt for others. In other words, at times we focus on the wrong thing. We should be helping people to find complex, stable webs of relationships in which they play a vital and necessary part. In such a setting they will know themselves to be of worth, but that worth will not be the most important thing to them. What will matter is that we find our "self" by giving it away to others and in leading others to God.

63:1–6 Israel is weak because it is sinful. In response, God does not say in 63:1—66:24 that he will destroy their physical enemies; rather, he will destroy the sinners *among his people.* God will vindicate those among his people who allow him to make them righteous, using these latter people to call the nations to worship the righteous God. They are his true servants (65:13–16; cf. 54:17).

Thus, the blood that stains the garments of the Victor (63:1, 3) is the blood of sinners from all nations, including his own nation, who have defied him. This is not destruction for its own sake. Rather, it is for the purpose of making redemption and "salvation" (vv. 4–5) available.

their blood spattered my garments,[h]
  and I stained all my clothing.
4 It was for me the day of vengeance;
  the year for me to redeem had come.
5 I looked, but there was no one[i] to help,
  I was appalled that no one gave support;
so my own arm[j] achieved salvation for me,
  and my own wrath sustained me.[k]
6 I trampled the nations in my anger;
  in my wrath I made them drunk[l]
  and poured their blood[m] on the ground."

Praise and Prayer

7 I will tell of the kindnesses[n] of the LORD,
  the deeds for which he is to be praised,
  according to all the LORD has done for us—
yes, the many good things
  he has done for Israel,
  according to his compassion[o] and many kindnesses.
8 He said, "Surely they are my people,[p]
  children who will be true to me";
  and so he became their Savior.
9 In all their distress he too was distressed,
  and the angel of his presence[q] saved them.[a]
In his love and mercy he redeemed[r] them;
  he lifted them up and carried[s] them
  all the days of old.
10 Yet they rebelled[t]
  and grieved his Holy Spirit.[u]

63:3 [h] Rev 19:13
63:5 [i] Isa 41:28 [j] Ps 44:3; 98:1 [k] Isa 59:16
63:6 [l] Isa 29:9 [m] Isa 34:3
63:7 [n] Isa 54:8 [o] Ps 51:1; Eph 2:4
63:8 [p] Isa 51:4
63:9 [q] Ex 33:14 [r] Dt 7:7-8 [s] Dt 1:31
63:10 [t] Ps 78:40 [u] Ps 51:11; Ac 7:51; Eph 4:30 [v] Ps 106:40
63:11 [w] Ex 14:22, 30 [x] Nu 11:17
63:12 [y] Ex 14:21-22; Isa 11:15
63:13 [z] Dt 32:12 [a] Jer 31:9
63:15 [b] Dt 26:15; Ps 80:14 [c] Ps 123:1 [d] Isa 9:7; 26:11

Isa 63:7-10 ❖ If you were to tell of God's kindness and "the deeds for which he is to be praised," what would you share about (v. 7)? Why?

So he turned and became their enemy[v]
  and he himself fought against them.

11 Then his people recalled[b] the days of old,
  the days of Moses and his people—
where is he who brought them through the sea,[w]
  with the shepherd of his flock?
Where is he who set
  his Holy Spirit[x] among them,
12 who sent his glorious arm of power
  to be at Moses' right hand,
who divided the waters[y] before them,
  to gain for himself everlasting renown,
13 who led[z] them through the depths?
Like a horse in open country,
  they did not stumble;[a]
14 like cattle that go down to the plain,
  they were given rest by the Spirit of the LORD.
This is how you guided your people
  to make for yourself a glorious name.

15 Look down from heaven[b] and see,
  from your lofty throne,[c] holy and glorious.
Where are your zeal[d] and your might?

[a] 9 Or *Savior* [9] *in their distress. / It was no envoy or angel / but his own presence that saved them*
[b] 11 Or *But may he recall*

63:1-6 If Christ is the divine Warrior who will eventually triumph over sin in the world at large, the time is now to let him defeat sin in our own lives.

63:7-14 Isaiah returns to a discussion of the human inability to do what is right (from 63:7 to 65:16). Here the prophet rehearses the theological significance of the exodus. The exodus events reveal the rebellious character of God's people. Isaiah does not say that they broke their covenant or they disobeyed their king. Rather, they "grieved [God's] Holy Spirit" (v. 10). That is the language of personal relationship.

This atmosphere is reinforced by such language as "lifted them up and carried them" (v. 9). A Father's love has been treated as worthless. The result is that their lover "became their enemy" (v. 10). Love and personal relationship do not invalidate the law of cause and effect.

In spite of the rebellion of the first generation in the desert, God did not abandon his people. Can he not also deliver them from their persistent rebellion and grieving of the Holy Spirit?

63:7-14 Isaiah calls us to return to our first love. It is not the stern Judge or the distant King who calls us, but the One who has carried us through all of our trials and over all of our years (cf. 46:3-4).

63:15-19 God has "withheld" his "might" and "compassion" from them (v. 15). This is not right

Your tenderness and compassion[e]
are withheld from us.
16 But you are our Father,
though Abraham does not know us
or Israel acknowledge[f] us;
you, LORD, are our Father,
our Redeemer[g] from of old is your
name.
17 Why, LORD, do you make us wander
from your ways
and harden our hearts so we do
not revere[h] you?
Return[i] for the sake of your servants,
the tribes that are your
inheritance.
18 For a little while your people
possessed your holy place,
but now our enemies have
trampled down your
sanctuary.[j]
19 We are yours from of old;
but you have not ruled over them,
they have not been called[a] by your
name.

64 [b] Oh, that you would rend the
heavens[k] and come down,[l]
that the mountains[m] would
tremble before you!
2 As when fire sets twigs ablaze
and causes water to boil,
come down to make your name
known to your enemies
and cause the nations to quake[n]
before you!
3 For when you did awesome[o] things
that we did not expect,
you came down, and the
mountains trembled before
you.
4 Since ancient times no one has
heard,

63:15 [e] Jer 31:20; Hos 11:8
63:16 [f] Job 14:21 [g] Isa 41:14; 44:6
63:17 [h] Isa 29:13 [i] Nu 10:36
63:18 [j] Ps 74:3-8
64:1 [k] Ps 18:9; 144:5 [l] Mic 1:3 [m] Ex 19:18
64:2 [n] Ps 99:1; Jer 5:22; 33:9
64:3 [o] Ps 65:5
64:4 [p] Isa 30:18; 1Co 2:9*
64:5 [q] Isa 26:8
64:6 [r] Isa 46:12; 48:1 [s] Ps 90:5-6
64:7 [t] Isa 59:4 [u] Dt 31:18; Isa 1:15; 54:8 [v] Isa 9:18
64:8 [w] Isa 63:16 [x] Isa 29:16
64:9 [y] Isa 57:17; 60:10 [z] Isa 43:25

Isa 64:4 ❖ What does it mean for us to "wait" for the Lord?

no ear has perceived,
no eye has seen any God besides you,
who acts on behalf of those who
wait for him.[p]
5 You come to the help of those who
gladly do right,[q]
who remember your ways.
But when we continued to sin
against them,
you were angry.
How then can we be saved?
6 All of us have become like one who
is unclean,
and all our righteous[r] acts are like
filthy rags;
we all shrivel up like a leaf,[s]
and like the wind our sins sweep
us away.
7 No one[t] calls on your name
or strives to lay hold of you;
for you have hidden[u] your face
from us
and have given us over[v] to[c] our
sins.

8 Yet you, LORD, are our Father.[w]
We are the clay, you are the
potter;[x]
we are all the work of your hand.
9 Do not be angry[y] beyond measure,
LORD;
do not remember our sins[z]
forever.

[a] 19 Or *We are like those you have never ruled, / like those never called* [b] In Hebrew texts 64:1 is numbered 63:19b, and 64:2-12 is numbered 64:1-11. [c] 7 Septuagint, Syriac and Targum; Hebrew *have made us melt because of*

because God is the true "Father" (v. 16) of Israel, much more so than "Abraham" and Jacob ("Israel"). Israel is not merely an ethnic group; they are first and foremost a spiritual group. They are who they are because of the covenant love of God. If that love should ever be withdrawn, their reason for existence would be called into question.

64:1–5 Isaiah moves from complaint to petition, calling on God to leave the "heavens" (v. 1) and to come to their aid. God's actions in the past demonstrate that this petition is not based in fantasy: Whenever God had manifested himself in the past, dramatic things occurred.

God acts on behalf of those who "wait for him" (v. 4); that is, those who put their trust in him. One evidence of such a trust is a life of godliness.

64:6–7 Trying to foster a relationship with a holy God while doing what is contrary to his character is a contradiction of terms. If the people tended to blame God for their hard-heartedness, at least they did not minimize the reality of their condition (v. 6). Here we are at the conundrum again: We are wasting away in our sins because we won't turn to God, and we won't turn to him because he has hidden his face from us. What is to be done?

64:8–12 Once again Isaiah asserts that the nation only exists because of God, the "Father" who brought them into existence, the "potter" who formed their "clay" on his wheel (v. 8). He should not allow the people's sins to make him forget that they are his creation, nor should he overlook the fact that all the sacred spaces that he presumably treasures are in ruins (vv. 10–11).

Oh, look on us, we pray,
for we are all your people.
10 Your sacred cities have become a wasteland;
even Zion is a wasteland,
Jerusalem a desolation.
11 Our holy and glorious temple,[a]
where our ancestors praised you,
has been burned with fire,
and all that we treasured[b] lies in ruins.
12 After all this, LORD, will you hold yourself back?[c]
Will you keep silent[d] and punish us beyond measure?

Judgment and Salvation

65 "I revealed myself to those who did not ask for me;
I was found by those who did not seek me.[e]
To a nation[f] that did not call on my name,
I said, 'Here am I, here am I.'
2 All day long I have held out my hands
to an obstinate people,[g]
who walk in ways not good,
pursuing their own imaginations[h]—
3 a people who continually provoke me
to my very face,[i]
offering sacrifices in gardens[j]
and burning incense on altars of brick;
4 who sit among the graves
and spend their nights keeping secret vigil;
who eat the flesh of pigs,[k]
and whose pots hold broth of impure meat;
5 who say, 'Keep away; don't come near me,
for I am too sacred[l] for you!'
Such people are smoke in my nostrils,
a fire that keeps burning all day.

6 "See, it stands written before me:
I will not keep silent[m] but will pay back[n] in full;
I will pay it back into their laps[o]—
7 both your sins[p] and the sins of your ancestors,"[q]
says the LORD.
"Because they burned sacrifices on the mountains
and defied me on the hills,[r]
I will measure into their laps
the full payment for their former deeds."

8 This is what the LORD says:

"As when juice is still found in a cluster of grapes
and people say, 'Don't destroy it,
there is still a blessing in it,'
so will I do in behalf of my servants;
I will not destroy them all.
9 I will bring forth descendants[s] from Jacob,
and from Judah those who will possess[t] my mountains;
my chosen people will inherit them,
and there will my servants live.[u]

64:11 [a] Ps 74:3-7 [b] La 1:7,10
64:12 [c] Ps 74:10-11; Isa 42:14 [d] Ps 83:1
65:1 [e] Hos 1:10; Ro 9:24-26; 10:20* [f] Eph 2:12
65:2 [g] Isa 1:2, 23; Ro 10:21* [h] Ps 81:11-12; Isa 66:18
65:3 [i] Job 1:11 [j] Isa 1:29
65:4 [k] Lev 11:7
65:5 [l] Mt 9:11; Lk 7:39; 18:9-12
65:6 [m] Ps 50:3 [n] Jer 16:18 [o] Ps 79:12
65:7 [p] Isa 22:14 [q] Ex 20:5 [r] Isa 57:7
65:9 [s] Isa 45:19 [t] Am 9:11-15 [u] Isa 32:18

Isa 65:1-5 ❖ How does God find us before we ever seek after him? What means does God use to lead us to his grace?

63:15—64:12 Paganism saw all of life as directed by the fates, where the position of the stars on the day of one's birth determined the possibilities for the rest of one's life. In a stunning contrast, the Bible declares that every person has real choices to make regarding the meaning and purpose of life and that every person will be held accountable for those choices.

65:1 In the previous section, 64:7 stated that "no one calls on [God's] name," because "you have hidden your face from us." This verse directly refutes that statement by saying that in fact God had "revealed" himself to people who did not call on his name.

65:2-3a So, what was their problem? Three ideas—obstinacy, devising one's own ways, and ways that are not good—describe in brief precisely what the human problem is. We have devised worship practices that we believe will manipulate God for our own ends.

65:3b-7 The worship practices described in these verses look like the preexilic Canaanite practices that were so attractive to the Israelites.

The people's claims to holiness produced by ritual magic are silly. The prophet says God "will not keep silent" (v. 6): God will fully repay them for all they have done.

65:8-11 God's punishment of sinners does not mean there is no remnant of the faithful. These are the ones God calls his "servants" (v. 8); these are the people who "seek" the Lord (v. 10). The servants of God stand in stark contrast with those who try to bypass a submissive relationship with God and seek to gain control of "Destiny" (v. 11) through religious behavior.

10 Sharon[v] will become a pasture for
flocks,
and the Valley of Achor[w] a resting
place for herds,
for my people who seek[x] me.

11 "But as for you who forsake[y] the
LORD
and forget my holy mountain,
who spread a table for Fortune
and fill bowls of mixed wine for
Destiny,
12 I will destine you for the sword,[z]
and all of you will fall in the
slaughter;
for I called but you did not answer,[a]
I spoke but you did not listen.[b]
You did evil in my sight
and chose what displeases me."

13 Therefore this is what the Sovereign
LORD says:

"My servants will eat,[c]
but you will go hungry;
my servants will drink,
but you will go thirsty;[d]
my servants will rejoice,
but you will be put to shame.[e]
14 My servants will sing
out of the joy of their hearts,
but you will cry out[f]
from anguish of heart
and wail in brokenness of spirit.
15 You will leave your name
for my chosen ones to use in their
curses;[g]
the Sovereign LORD will put you to
death,
but to his servants he will give
another name.
16 Whoever invokes a blessing in the
land
will do so by the one true God;[h]
whoever takes an oath in the land
will swear[i] by the one true God.
For the past troubles will be
forgotten
and hidden from my eyes.

New Heavens and a New Earth

17 "See, I will create
new heavens and a new earth.[j]
The former things will not be
remembered,[k]
nor will they come to mind.
18 But be glad and rejoice[l] forever
in what I will create,
for I will create Jerusalem to be a
delight
and its people a joy.
19 I will rejoice[m] over Jerusalem
and take delight in my people;
the sound of weeping and of crying[n]
will be heard in it no more.

20 "Never again will there be in it
an infant who lives but a few days,
or an old man who does not live
out his years;[o]
the one who dies at a hundred
will be thought a mere child;
the one who fails to reach[a] a
hundred
will be considered accursed.
21 They will build houses[p] and dwell in
them;
they will plant vineyards and eat
their fruit.[q]
22 No longer will they build houses and
others live in them,
or plant and others eat.
For as the days of a tree,[r]
so will be the days[s] of my people;
my chosen ones will long enjoy
the work of their hands.

[a] 20 *Or the sinner who reaches*

65:10 [v] Isa 35:2 [w] Jos 7:26 [x] Isa 51:1
65:11 [y] Dt 29:24-25; Isa 1:28
65:12 [z] Isa 27:1 [a] Pr 1:24-25; Isa 41:28; 66:4 [b] 2Ch 36:15-16; Jer 7:13
65:13 [c] Isa 1:19 [d] Isa 41:17 [e] Isa 44:9
65:14 [f] Mt 8:12; Lk 13:28
65:15 [g] Zec 8:13
65:16 [h] Ps 31:5 [i] Isa 19:18
65:17 [j] Isa 66:22; 2Pe 3:13 [k] Isa 43:18; Jer 3:16
65:18 [l] Ps 98:1-9; Isa 25:9
65:19 [m] Isa 35:10; 62:5 [n] Isa 25:8; Rev 7:17
65:20 [o] Ecc 8:13
65:21 [p] Isa 32:18 [q] Isa 37:30; Am 9:14
65:22 [r] Ps 92:12-14 [s] Ps 21:4; 91:16

65:12–16 "Jacob" will have "descendants," and "Judah" will possess the land of promise (v. 9), but not everyone called by the names of Jacob or Judah will share in the promise. Thus, vv. 13–16 detail the differences between "you" (i.e., those who have been trying to manipulate God for blessings) and "my servants" (i.e., those who seek God for himself with changed lives).

65:1–16 Unless we have come to the place where our service to God is growing out of a glad servant heart, it is all in vain. Can you imagine a bridegroom asking a minister how many hours a month he has to spend with his bride to keep the marriage in force? If he does ask this question, we know something is severely lacking in his devotion to his bride, and we also know the relationship is doomed.

65:17–23 God will "create" something that, while being in continuity with what had been, will yet be a completely new expression of that reality. Earthly realities give shape to the new realities. Because they are new, the tragic realities of this world need not be repeated. Thus, we may experience the reality of joy without the reality of weeping (vv. 18–19). Likewise, we may experience the delight of birth without the despair of death (v. 20). The satisfaction of building will not be accompanied by the fear of destruction and conquest (vv. 21–23).

23 They will not labor in vain,
nor will they bear children
doomed to misfortune;
for they will be a people blessed[t] by
the LORD,
they and their descendants[u] with
them.
24 Before they call[v] I will answer;
while they are still speaking[w] I
will hear.
25 The wolf and the lamb[x] will feed
together,
and the lion will eat straw like
the ox,
and dust will be the serpent's[y]
food.
They will neither harm nor destroy
on all my holy mountain,"
says the LORD.

Judgment and Hope

66 This is what the LORD says:
"Heaven is my throne,[z]
and the earth is my footstool.[a]
Where is the house[b] you will build
for me?
Where will my resting place be?
2 Has not my hand made all these
things,[c]
and so they came into being?"
declares the LORD.
"These are the ones I look on with
favor:
those who are humble and
contrite in spirit,[d]
and who tremble at my word.[e]
3 But whoever sacrifices a bull[f]
is like one who kills a person,
and whoever offers a lamb
is like one who breaks a dog's
neck;
whoever makes a grain offering
is like one who presents pig's
blood,
and whoever burns memorial
incense[g]
is like one who worships an idol.
They have chosen their own ways,[h]
and they delight in their
abominations;
4 so I also will choose harsh treatment
for them
and will bring on them what they
dread.[i]
For when I called, no one answered,[j]
when I spoke, no one listened.
They did evil[k] in my sight
and chose what displeases me."[l]

5 Hear the word of the LORD,
you who tremble at his word:
"Your own people who hate[m] you,
and exclude you because of my
name, have said,
'Let the LORD be glorified,
that we may see your joy!'
Yet they will be put to shame.[n]
6 Hear that uproar from the city,
hear that noise from the temple!
It is the sound of the LORD
repaying[o] his enemies all they
deserve.

7 "Before she goes into labor,[p]
she gives birth;
before the pains come upon her,
she delivers a son.[q]
8 Who has ever heard of such things?
Who has ever seen[r] such things like
this?
Can a country be born in a day

65:23 [t] Dt 28:3-12; Isa 61:9 [u] Ac 2:39
65:24 [v] Isa 55:6 [w] Da 9:20-23; 10:12
65:25 [x] Isa 11:6 [y] Ge 3:14; Mic 7:17
66:1 [z] Mt 23:22 [a] 1Ki 8:27; Mt 5:34-35 [b] 2Sa 7:7; Jn 4:20-21; Ac 7:49*; 17:24
66:2 [c] Isa 40:26; Ac 7:50* [d] Isa 57:15; Mt 5:3-4; Lk 18:13-14 [e] Ezr 9:4
66:3 [f] Isa 1:11 [g] Lev 2:2 [h] Isa 57:17
66:4 [i] Pr 10:24 [j] Pr 1:24; Jer 7:13 [k] 2Ki 21:2,4,6 [l] Isa 65:12
66:5 [m] Ps 38:20; Isa 60:15 [n] Lk 13:17
66:6 [o] Isa 65:6; Joel 3:7
66:7 [p] Isa 54:1 [q] Rev 12:5
66:8 [r] Isa 64:4

65:24–25 What we have here is not merely a poetic expression of the certainty of justice in some general sense but a prediction of real events in the age to come.

65:17–25 Our choices are of critical importance. Our actions are not predetermined. Instead, our actions will bear fruit from now on and forever. This ought to make us think a good deal more soberly about what we do. Far from living lives that are merely a duplicate of something that has always existed, we have the possibility of shaping the reality that is to come for the cause of Christ.

66:1–4 From the outset of the book and up to its very end, God has identified humanity's central problem as self-exaltation. We exalt ourselves and grasp at power to solve the problem of our extreme fragility, both physically and psychologically. When all is said and done, that is what ritualistic religion is about.

God esteems the "humble and contrite in spirit" (v. 2) who tremble at his word. To manipulate ritual is to do nothing other than to choose one's "own ways" (v. 3). Once again, God has not been silent when they called, as they had charged in 64:12. Instead, he has "called" (66:4). They are the ones who have been silent (v. 4).

66:5–6 God speaks once again to the remnant. These are the people of whom he spoke in v. 2, those "who tremble at his word" (v. 5). God will vindicate those who care more about what God says than whether their needs have been met.

66:7–11 This next unit describes Zion. Here the promise made in ch. 1 comes to its fruition. The

or a nation be brought forth in a moment?
Yet no sooner is Zion in labor
than she gives birth to her children.
9 Do I bring to the moment of birth[s]
and not give delivery?" says the LORD.
"Do I close up the womb
when I bring to delivery?" says your God.
10 "Rejoice[t] with Jerusalem and be glad for her,
all you who love[u] her;
rejoice greatly with her,
all you who mourn over her.
11 For you will nurse[v] and be satisfied
at her comforting breasts;
you will drink deeply
and delight in her overflowing abundance."

12 For this is what the LORD says:

"I will extend peace to her like a river,[w]
and the wealth[x] of nations like a flooding stream;
you will nurse and be carried[y] on her arm
and dandled on her knees.
13 As a mother comforts her child,
so will I comfort[z] you;
and you will be comforted over Jerusalem."

14 When you see this, your heart will rejoice
and you will flourish like grass;
the hand of the LORD will be made known to his servants,
but his fury[a] will be shown to his foes.
15 See, the LORD is coming with fire,
and his chariots[b] are like a whirlwind;
he will bring down his anger with fury,
and his rebuke[c] with flames of fire.
16 For with fire[d] and with his sword[e]
the LORD will execute judgment on all people,
and many will be those slain by the LORD.

17 "Those who consecrate and purify
themselves to go into the gardens,[f] following one who is among those who eat
the flesh of pigs,[g] rats and other unclean
things — they will meet their end[h] together with the one they follow," declares
the LORD.
18 "And I, because of what they have
planned and done, am about to come[a]
and gather the people of all nations and
languages, and they will come and see
my glory.
19 "I will set a sign[i] among them, and I
will send some of those who survive to

66:9 [s] Isa 37:3
66:10 [t] Dt 32:43; Ro 15:10 [u] Ps 26:8
66:11 [v] Isa 60:16
66:12 [w] Isa 48:18 [x] Ps 72:3; Isa 60:5; 61:6 [y] Isa 60:4
66:13 [z] Isa 40:1; 2Co 1:4
66:14 [a] Isa 10:5
66:15 [b] Ps 68:17 [c] Ps 9:5
66:16 [d] Isa 30:30 [e] Isa 27:1
66:17 [f] Isa 1:29 [g] Lev 11:7 [h] Ps 37:20; Isa 1:28
66:19 [i] Isa 11:10; 49:22

[a] *18* The meaning of the Hebrew for this clause is uncertain.

Isa 66:12–13 ❖ How has God sent his peace and comfort upon us? How has he been like a loving parent through difficult moments?

dross has been purged away, and instead of being adulterous, Zion has become the faithful city, the mother of nations (cf. 1:25–27).

God's gifts are out of all proportion to whatever we have done. He gives childbirth without labor (66:7–9). God's work meets our needs. This is the significance of nursing at the "breasts" of Zion (v. 11). A baby can be nothing other than absolutely dependent and receive what has been provided.

66:12–14 In such a vulnerable position, there is rest, rejoicing, and wholeness, or "peace" (v. 12). As in 12:1 and elsewhere, the idea behind the word "comfort" (66:13) is to encourage. Those who have come to God in penitent faith will find themselves encouraged just as a child does on its mother's lap.

Isaiah never wants his readers to be left in a position where they are so secure in God's election love that they forget the real possibility of judgment. The Lord's "hand" of deliverance, redemption, and power will be revealed to "his servants" (v. 14). His "fury will be shown to his foes" (v. 14). Once again, the question emerges: Am I among his servants or his foes?

66:15–24 This section concludes the book with an interplay of the twin themes of judgment and hope. Just as the two have been intertwined throughout the book, they are intertwined here. The beginning (vv. 15–17) and the end (v. 24) speak of the judgment that lies ahead for those who rebel against God and attempt to gain control of his power for themselves. A day will come when "fire" (vv. 15–16, 24) will be unleashed against an unrepentant world.

66:18–19 Judgment is not what God wants, and that is equally clear in this final section. These verses reveal God's desired way of bringing this sinful world to its close: universal redemption. God will use the very sins and schemes of the rebellious to reveal the glory of his salvation. The people of Zion who "survive" all the attempts of an evil world to destroy them will be sent to all the "nations" with a "sign" of God's "glory" (v. 19).

the nations — to Tarshish,[j] to the Libyans[a] and Lydians[k] (famous as archers),
to Tubal[l] and Greece, and to the distant
islands[m] that have not heard of my fame
or seen my glory.[n] They will proclaim my
glory among the nations. 20And they will
bring all your people, from all the nations, to my holy mountain in Jerusalem
as an offering to the LORD — on horses, in
chariots and wagons, and on mules and
camels," says the LORD. "They will bring
them, as the Israelites bring their grain
offerings, to the temple of the LORD in
ceremonially clean vessels.[o] 21And I will
select some of them also to be priests[p]
and Levites," says the LORD.

66:19 [j] Isa 2:16 [k] Eze 27:10 [l] Ge 10:2 [m] Isa 11:11 [n] 1Ch 16:24; Isa 24:15
66:20 [o] Isa 52:11
66:21 [p] Ex 19:6; Isa 61:6; 1Pe 2:5,9
66:22 [q] Isa 65:17; Heb 12:26-27; 2Pe 3:13; Rev 21:1 [r] Jn 10:27-29; 1Pe 1:4-5
66:23 [s] Eze 46:1-3 [t] Isa 19:21
66:24 [u] Isa 14:11 [v] Isa 1:31; Mk 9:48*

22"As the new heavens and the new
earth[q] that I make will endure before
me," declares the LORD, "so will your
name and descendants endure.[r] 23From
one New Moon to another and from one
Sabbath[s] to another, all mankind will
come and bow down[t] before me," says
the LORD. 24"And they will go out and
look on the dead bodies of those who
rebelled against me; the worms[u] that
eat them will not die, the fire that burns
them will not be quenched,[v] and they
will be loathsome to all mankind."

[a] *19* Some Septuagint manuscripts *Put* (Libyans); Hebrew *Pul*

66:20–23 The response of the nations to Israel's mission will be to restore the last remnants of the Israelites to Israel in a last great ingathering. Then comes the most stunning statement of all: "I will select some of them also to be priests and Levites" (v. 21). This is the strongest statement in the book that the election of Israel is not for Israel but for the world. That understanding is furthered by vv. 22–23, which speaks of the entire human race coming to worship God.

66:24 Why end the book on this grisly note? The wonderful promises of God have nothing to do with any who persist in rebellion. If the rebels are lulled into complacency by these good promises, they will be lost.

On the one hand, the promises of God are "Yes" and "Amen" (2Co 1:20). There *will* be a new heaven and a new earth (Isa 66:22), and those who rejoice to worship the one true God *will* participate in it. On the other hand, whether any of us participate in those promises is strictly up to us, and Isaiah never wants that to be forgotten.

66:1–24 God has delivered us from each of our Egypts by the blood of Jesus Christ. He has done this to write his covenant on our hearts through the power of the Holy Spirit and thus to take up residence in the tabernacle he desires most of all—the tabernacle of our hearts. He longs to fill that tabernacle with the glory that fills the earth. He wants to move each of us from that place where we cry out in horror, "Woe to me . . ." (6:5), to the place where we can "come and see [his] glory" (66:18)—and not merely to survive the experience but actually to have that glory reside in us. That is the goal of life for all who will believe.

Jeremiah

Author: Jeremiah

Audience: The people of Judah and Jerusalem during the reigns of their last five kings

Date: Between 626 and 586 BC

Theme: Through Jeremiah, God promises his people a new covenant beyond their exile.

Reading Jeremiah

Jeremiah is one of the most difficult prophetic books to follow since Jeremiah's prophecies do not follow each other in chronological order. Chapters 2–35 contain Jeremiah's warnings and exhortations to the nation of Judah, closing with promises of eventual restoration. The next three chapters describe the sufferings of Jeremiah himself. In chs. 39–45, the book describes the fall of

PERSPECTIVE

The theme of righteous kings, aided by powerful religious figures and reforming wayward people groups, is not an uncommon one in Middle Eastern and Asian history. One thinks, for example, of Asoka in Buddhist India, Constantine in Christian Rome, and Saladin in Islamic Palestine.

Typically, these righteous kings did not attempt to become religious leaders themselves by usurping power from bhikkhus, priests, and imams. Instead, they attempted to reform declining and/or wayward religious institutions. They rebuilt dilapidated religious buildings or built brand-new ones. They replaced immoral religious leaders with moral ones. They convened councils of religious leaders to articulate doctrine more fully in the face of new challenges. Often, they reemphasized religion's privileged place in the life of their cultures. In general, they acted as the consciences of drifting religious people.

The initial period of the book of Jeremiah is set in the context of such a king: Josiah. With the help of the prophet Jeremiah, Josiah attempted to restore not only the political but also the spiritual life of his nation, Judah. Unlike Asoka, Constantine, and Saladin, however, Josiah's reforms failed. To be sure, he did achieve some short-term successes. These successes, however, were temporary, as evidenced by the growing failures of Josiah's successors to maintain Israel's faithfulness to their agreement with God. That failure had disastrous effects; eventually Babylon conquered Judah and took thousands of Judeans into exile.

How are we to understand this unusual series of events? What

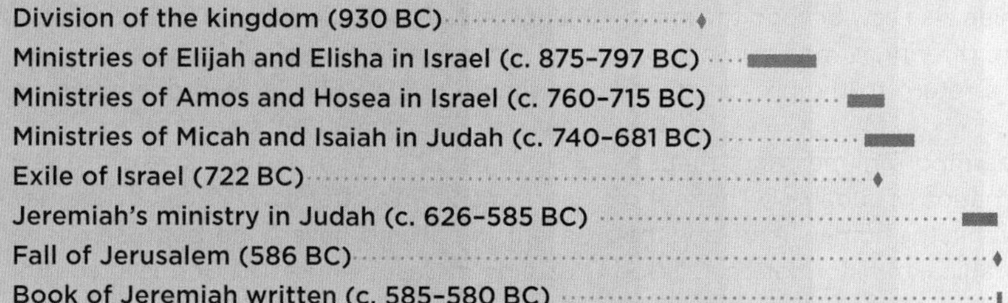

lessons do they teach us? Should we pray for a modern "king-prophet" tandem to rise up and cleanse us? What would make them successful?

The common wisdom in these stories is that spiritual faithfulness is more important than political good fortune. Although prophets frequently label political meltdowns as God's judgment and political successes as evidence of God's blessings, they also manage to elevate the importance of the spiritual over the political. Thus, even though Josiah's political strategies ultimately fail at the hands of his Egyptian killers, his attempts at moral reform earn him the label of ruler without equal (2Ki 23:25).

But to read the prophets — and Jeremiah is no exception — is to read over and over again that spiritual faithfulness and political good fortune go hand in hand in a cause-effect relationship (and vice versa—spiritual unfaithfulness leads to political calamities). The spiritual task of faithfully upholding one's end of the covenant leads to God's protection from political enemies and from economic ruin.

The broader understanding needed here must acknowledge two things before it becomes useful for us today. First, the identification between spiritual faithfulness and political success was much greater in Jeremiah's day than in ours. The Israelites were not too far from theocracy, rulership by God himself, as managed by priests. Even after they began to have kings, it was made clear that the kings ruled by God's choice and God's will. No political ruler today even comes close to having such a mandate.

Second, even after we realize this first difference, we must clearly prioritize the two factors: spirituality first, politics second. Or better, we should see politics as a fruit of spirituality, not its root or its equal. The Bible is clear that "politics" by any name is temporal while all the roads that lead to God usher us into the presence of eternity.

Jerusalem, and it ends with a series of judgments against the nations. Interspersed through the book are various chapters of historical narrative.

Key Verses

"This is the covenant I will make with the people of Israel after that time," declares the LORD. "I will put my law in their minds and write it on their hearts. I will be their God, and they will be my people . . . For I will forgive their wickedness and will remember their sins no more."

—Jeremiah 31:33–34

TAKING THE NEXT STEPS

Jeremiah prophesied in Jerusalem during the final years of the nation of Judah, beginning in the middle of the reign of King Josiah (2Ki 22:1—23:30). He saw the sin of the nation increasing, and he was appalled. Since he knew God controlled the affairs of the world and would not tolerate sin forever, Jeremiah predicted God's judgment of his people through the destruction of Jerusalem and the 70 years of exile in Babylon. Such prophecies were obviously unpopular and brought him a tremendous amount of suffering. But Jeremiah also saw beyond the immediate situation, offering a message of hope by predicting a return to the promised land after the exile.

Jeremiah has important messages for us as well as for the nation of Judah. (1) The root of sin lies deep within the human heart, and that heart needs a radical transformation. (2) God is patient with our sinfulness, but we must be realistic enough to know that eventually his patience will end, resulting in a time of severe judgment. (3) We can escape God's judgment only if we genuinely repent of our sins and turn to the Lord. (4) God's last word, however, is not one of judgment but one of mercy; in his faithfulness, he offers us a new covenant, a new agreement. No matter how difficult things may seem, we always have hope because of the coming of Jesus Christ. (5) God is in control of everything that happens, and he will work things out for our good.

WHAT TO LOOK FOR IN JEREMIAH

- The call of Jeremiah (ch. 1)
- Symbolic acts of Jeremiah (chs. 13; 16; 19; 27; 32; 43)
- A message from a potter's house (chs. 18–19)
- Prophecy of 70 years of captivity (ch. 25)
- Stories of Jeremiah's suffering (chs. 26; 37–38)
- A new covenant (ch. 31)
- The fall of Jerusalem (chs. 39; 52)
- Destruction prophesied against Babylon (chs. 50–51)

1 The words of Jeremiah son of Hilkiah, one of the priests at Anathoth[a] in
the territory of Benjamin. 2The word of
the LORD came to him in the thirteenth
year of the reign of Josiah son of Amon
king of Judah, 3and through the reign of
Jehoiakim[b] son of Josiah king of Judah,
down to the fifth month of the eleventh
year of Zedekiah[c] son of Josiah king of
Judah, when the people of Jerusalem
went into exile.[d]

The Call of Jeremiah

4The word of the LORD came to me,
saying,

5"Before I formed you in the womb I
knew[a][e] you,
before you were born[f] I set you
apart;
I appointed you as a prophet to
the nations.[g]"

6"Alas, Sovereign LORD," I said, "I
do not know how to speak;[h] I am too
young."[i]
7But the LORD said to me, "Do not say, 'I
am too young.' You must go to everyone
I send you to and say whatever I command you. 8Do not be afraid[j] of them,

1:1 [a]Jos 21:18; 1Ch 6:60; Jer 32:7-9
1:3 [b]2Ki 23:34 [c]2Ki 24:17; Jer 39:2 [d]Jer 52:15
1:5 [e]Ps 139:16 [f]Isa 49:1 [g]ver 10; Jer 25:15-26
1:6 [h]Ex 4:10; 6:12 [i]1Ki 3:7
1:8 [j]Eze 2:6

[a] 5 Or *chose*

1:1-3 The 40-plus years given for Jeremiah's ministry (c. 627–584 BC) cover some of the most tumultuous and tragic events of Judah's history. King Josiah attempted to free Judah from the control of Assyria and set Judah on the road to spiritual reform. His thirteenth year coincides with the demise of Assyria's last strong king, Ashurbanipal. In the eleventh year of Zedekiah, the Babylonian army captured and destroyed Jerusalem. Zedekiah was seized and blinded, and many Judeans were taken into exile by their captors.

APPLICATION 1:1-3 Jeremiah's words provide testimony that God uses both people and events to further his purposes and to instruct the faithful.

1:4-19 The rest of ch. 1 contains an account of Jeremiah's call and appointment to prophesy (vv. 4-10), followed by two divine oracles (vv. 11-12 and 13-19) assuring the prophet that God is with him as he delivers a judgmental word to Judah.
1:4-10 God decided to use Jeremiah prior to his birth. "Set apart" means "to be holy," a term reserved

for I am with you[k] and will rescue you,"
declares the LORD.
9Then the LORD reached out his hand
and touched[l] my mouth and said to me, "I
have put my words in your mouth.[m] 10See,
today I appoint you over nations and kingdoms to uproot and tear down, to destroy
and overthrow, to build and to plant."[n]
11The word of the LORD came to me:
"What do you see, Jeremiah?"[o]
"I see the branch of an almond tree,"
I replied.
12The LORD said to me, "You have seen
correctly, for I am watching[a] to see that
my word is fulfilled."
13The word of the LORD came to me
again: "What do you see?"[p]
"I see a pot that is boiling," I answered.
"It is tilting toward us from the north."
14The LORD said to me, "From the north
disaster will be poured out on all who live
in the land. 15I am about to summon all
the peoples of the northern kingdoms,"
declares the LORD.

"Their kings will come and set up
their thrones
in the entrance of the gates of
Jerusalem;
they will come against all her
surrounding walls
and against all the towns of Judah.[q]
16I will pronounce my judgments on
my people
because of their wickedness[r] in
forsaking me,[s]
in burning incense to other gods[t]
and in worshiping what their
hands have made.

17"Get yourself ready! Stand up and
say to them whatever I command you.

1:8 [k]Jos 1:5; Jer 15:20
1:9 [l]Isa 6:7 [m]Ex 4:12
1:10 [n]Jer 18:7-10; 24:6; 31:4,28
1:11 [o]Jer 24:3; Am 7:8
1:13 [p]Zec 4:2
1:15 [q]Jer 4:16; 9:11
1:16 [r]Dt 28:20 [s]Jer 17:13 [t]Jer 7:9; 19:4
1:17 [u]Eze 2:6
1:18 [v]Isa 50:7
1:19 [w]Jer 20:11 [x]ver 8
2:2 [y]Eze 16:8-14,60; Hos 2:15 [z]Dt 2:7
2:3 [a]Dt 7:6 [b]Ex 19:6 [c]Jas 1:18; Rev 14:4 [d]Isa 41:11; Jer 30:16 [e]Jer 50:7

Jer 1:7–8 ❖ What weaknesses do you think hinder our abilities to follow God's call? How has God shown us he can overcome these weaknesses?

Jer 2:2–3 ❖ Believers often backslide or lose their passion for faith. How can we better maintain our devotion to God?

Do not be terrified[u] by them, or I will
terrify you before them. 18Today I have
made you[v] a fortified city, an iron pillar
and a bronze wall to stand against the
whole land — against the kings of Judah,
its officials, its priests and the people of
the land. 19They will fight against you
but will not overcome you, for I am with
you[w] and will rescue[x] you," declares the
LORD.

Israel Forsakes God

2 The word of the LORD came to me:
2"Go and proclaim in the hearing of
Jerusalem:

"This is what the LORD says:

"'I remember the devotion of your
youth,[y]
how as a bride you loved me
and followed me through the
wilderness,[z]
through a land not sown.
3Israel was holy[a] to the LORD,[b]
the firstfruits[c] of his harvest;
all who devoured[d] her were held
guilty,[e]
and disaster overtook them,'"
declares the LORD.

[a] 12 The Hebrew for *watching* sounds like the Hebrew for *almond tree.*

---

for a particular task. God has appointed Jeremiah a "prophet to the nations" (v. 5). Jeremiah protests that he is too young and inexperienced. God provides assurances. Each of these assurances is a way to define a prophet. He or she is designated by God for a task and is granted his presence and guidance. The prophet speaks God's word for the occasion.

Verse 10 explains the phrase "prophet to the nations." Jeremiah's words will "tear down" much that his audience believes. After the terrible toll of Judah's failures has been reckoned, Jeremiah's positive words will begin to "build" up and "plant."

1:11–12 The Hebrew word for "almond tree" sounds like the Hebrew verb meaning "to watch." The almond tree becomes a sign to Jeremiah that God is watching over his word to bring it to fulfillment.

1:13–19 The pot is a metaphor for the threat to come on Jerusalem and Judah because of the people's disobedience. There is also an initial reference to those who will oppose Jeremiah (v. 19).

1:4–19 God does not call all believers to be prophets; some, however, are called to engage in prophetic activity, and all are called to trust the effectiveness of the prophetic word in Scripture. Two related elements in Jer 1 have continuing significance for understanding prophetic activity: Prophets depended on God for vindication rather than relying on their peers, and they also knew that their activity would result in opposition.

2:1–3 The combined imagery here recalls the exodus from Egypt, the covenant ceremony at Mount Sinai, and God's provision in the desert. This period of intimacy is contrasted with the estrangement from God of Jeremiah's contemporaries.

4 Hear the word of the LORD, you
descendants of Jacob,
all you clans of Israel.

5 This is what the LORD says:

"What fault did your ancestors find
in me,
that they strayed so far from me?
They followed worthless idols
and became worthless[f]
themselves.
6 They did not ask, 'Where is the LORD,
who brought us up out of Egypt[g]
and led us through the barren
wilderness,
through a land of deserts[h] and
ravines,[i]
a land of drought and utter
darkness,
a land where no one travels and
no one lives?'
7 I brought you into a fertile land
to eat its fruit and rich produce.[j]
But you came and defiled my land
and made my inheritance
detestable.[k]
8 The priests did not ask,
'Where is the LORD?'
Those who deal with the law did not
know me;[l]
the leaders rebelled against me.
The prophets prophesied by Baal,[m]
following worthless idols.[n]

9 "Therefore I bring charges[o] against
you again,"
declares the LORD.
"And I will bring charges against
your children's children.
10 Cross over to the coasts of Cyprus
and look,
send to Kedar[a] and observe
closely;
see if there has ever been
anything like this:
11 Has a nation ever changed its gods?
(Yet they are not gods[p] at all.)
But my people have exchanged their
glorious[q] God
for worthless idols.
12 Be appalled at this, you heavens,
and shudder with great horror,"
declares the LORD.
13 "My people have committed two
sins:
They have forsaken me,
the spring of living water,[r]
and have dug their own cisterns,
broken cisterns that cannot hold
water.
14 Is Israel a servant, a slave[s] by birth?
Why then has he become plunder?
15 Lions[t] have roared;
they have growled at him.
They have laid waste[u] his land;
his towns are burned and
deserted.
16 Also, the men of Memphis[v] and
Tahpanhes[w]
have cracked your skull.
17 Have you not brought this on
yourselves[x]
by forsaking the LORD your God
when he led you in the way?
18 Now why go to Egypt[y]
to drink water from the Nile[b]?[z]
And why go to Assyria
to drink water from the
Euphrates?
19 Your wickedness will punish you;
your backsliding[a] will rebuke[b]
you.
Consider then and realize
how evil and bitter[c] it is for you
when you forsake the LORD your God
and have no awe[d] of me,"
declares the Lord,
the LORD Almighty.

20 "Long ago you broke off your yoke[e]
and tore off your bonds;
you said, 'I will not serve you!'

[a] *10* In the Syro-Arabian desert [b] *18* Hebrew *Shihor;* that is, a branch of the Nile

2:5 [f] 2Ki 17:15
2:6 [g] Hos 13:4 [h] Dt 8:15 [i] Dt 32:10
2:7 [j] Nu 13:27; Dt 8:7-9; 11:10-12 [k] Ps 106:34-39; Jer 16:18
2:8 [l] Jer 4:22 [m] Jer 23:13 [n] Jer 16:19
2:9 [o] Eze 20:35-36; Mic 6:2
2:11 [p] Isa 37:19; Jer 16:20 [q] Ps 106:20; Ro 1:23
2:13 [r] Ps 36:9; Jn 4:14
2:14 [s] Ex 4:22
2:15 [t] Jer 4:7; 50:17 [u] Isa 1:7
2:16 [v] Isa 19:13 [w] Jer 43:7-9
2:17 [x] Jer 4:18
2:18 [y] Isa 30:2 [z] Jos 13:3
2:19 [a] Jer 3:11, 22 [b] Isa 3:9; Hos 5:5 [c] Job 20:14; Am 8:10 [d] Ps 36:1
2:20 [e] Lev 26:13

2:4–13 Israel is defined as "my people" (v. 13). Israel is accused of defecting from its first love to pursue "worthless idols" (v. 5). Baal, a popular Canaanite deity, is named specifically in v. 8.

Also, in v. 8, Jeremiah criticizes Judah's leadership (cf. v. 26). Priests had the sacred task of interpreting God's will and understanding Torah. God, the Great Shepherd, demands that the leadership of the people share in this shepherding role.

The Lord's faithfulness (vv. 6–7) is contrasted with the emptiness of idolatry. Succinctly stated: "My people have exchanged their glorious God for worthless idols" (v. 11) and have committed two evils: They have rejected the Lord and attempted unsuccessfully to support themselves (v. 13). Jeremiah compares the labor-intensive work of repairing cisterns with the idolatry of following other gods. The Lord, however, is a fountain of living water.

2:14–19 This indictment presupposes a close relationship between false worship and a disastrous political agenda. Just as Judah worships idols, so the state is also willing to make deals with Egypt and Assyria.

2:20–25 Because of their defection, the people

Indeed, on every high hill[f]
and under every spreading tree[g]
you lay down as a prostitute.
21 I had planted[h] you like a choice vine[i]
of sound and reliable stock.
How then did you turn against me
into a corrupt,[j] wild vine?
22 Although you wash yourself with soap
and use an abundance of cleansing powder,
the stain of your guilt is still before me,"
declares the Sovereign LORD.
23 "How can you say, 'I am not defiled;[k]
I have not run after the Baals'?[l]
See how you behaved in the valley;[m]
consider what you have done.
You are a swift she-camel
running[n] here and there,
24 a wild donkey[o] accustomed to the desert,
sniffing the wind in her craving—
in her heat who can restrain her?
Any males that pursue her need not tire themselves;
at mating time they will find her.
25 Do not run until your feet are bare
and your throat is dry.
But you said, 'It's no use!
I love foreign gods,[p]
and I must go after them.'
26 "As a thief is disgraced[q] when he is caught,
so the people of Israel are disgraced—
they, their kings and their officials,
their priests and their prophets.
27 They say to wood, 'You are my father,'
and to stone,[r] 'You gave me birth.'
They have turned their backs to me
and not their faces;[s]
yet when they are in trouble,[t] they say,
'Come and save us!'
28 Where then are the gods[u] you made for yourselves?
Let them come if they can save you
when you are in trouble![v]
For you, Judah, have as many gods
as you have towns.[w]

29 "Why do you bring charges against me?
You have all[x] rebelled against me,"
declares the LORD.
30 "In vain I punished your people;
they did not respond to correction.
Your sword has devoured your prophets[y]
like a ravenous lion.

31 "You of this generation, consider the
word of the LORD:

"Have I been a desert to Israel
or a land of great darkness?[z]
Why do my people say, 'We are free to roam;
we will come to you no more'?
32 Does a young woman forget her jewelry,
a bride her wedding ornaments?
Yet my people have forgotten me,
days without number.
33 How skilled you are at pursuing love!
Even the worst of women can learn from your ways.
34 On your clothes is found

2:20 [f] Isa 57:7; Jer 17:2 [g] Dt 12:2
2:21 [h] Ex 15:17 [i] Ps 80:8 [j] Isa 5:4
2:23 [k] Pr 30:12 [l] Jer 9:14 [m] Jer 7:31 [n] ver 33; Jer 31:22
2:24 [o] Jer 14:6
2:25 [p] Dt 32:16; Jer 3:13; 14:10
2:26 [q] Jer 48:27
2:27 [r] Jer 3:9 [s] Jer 18:17; 32:33 [t] Jdg 10:10; Isa 26:16
2:28 [u] Isa 45:20 [v] Dt 32:37 [w] 2Ki 17:29; Jer 11:13
2:29 [x] Jer 5:1; 6:13; Da 9:11
2:30 [y] Ne 9:26; Ac 7:52; 1Th 2:15
2:31 [z] Isa 45:19

---

are depicted as a prostitute or as animals in heat (v. 24). The location in v. 23 is likely the Valley of Hinnom, the probable site of child sacrifice to Molek or Baal.

2:26–32 In fertility cults, a tree is often the symbol of female fertility, and a stone pillar is the symbol of male fertility. The consequences are severe: The Lord has rejected those forces in which Judah has put its trust. In vv. 29–32, the prophet disputes the people. Apparently, some among them have accused God of negligence. God, through the prophets, has accused the people of defection. Forgetting is associated with not honoring God or with being disobedient, just as remembering is associated with doing what is expected.

2:33–37 "Prostitution" was more than a defection from the worship of the Lord. The image is that of blood spattered on a garment, blood from innocent people (v. 34). Injustice and unrighteousness flow from misunderstanding the Lord and what he desires from his covenant partner.

The final image is Jerusalem with her hands on her head. This is the posture of mourning, resignation, and captives being led away. Those entities (e.g., Assyria, Egypt) in whom the people have trusted will be unable to help them in their time of need.

2:1–37 In the US, churches are often invited (tempted?) to make alliances for gain or influence. Conservative churches may unite with a politically conservative figure. More liberal churches might ally with a more politically liberal figure. But who is using whom? Are not both parties using the other? Is it possible that there will be long-term pain for short-term gain in these alliances? The answer may

the lifeblood[a] of the innocent
poor,
though you did not catch them
breaking in.[b]
Yet in spite of all this
35 you say, 'I am innocent;
he is not angry with me.'
But I will pass judgment[c] on you
because you say, 'I have not
sinned.'[d]
36 Why do you go about so much,
changing[e] your ways?
You will be disappointed by Egypt[f]
as you were by Assyria.
37 You will also leave that place
with your hands on your head,[g]
for the LORD has rejected those you
trust;
you will not be helped[h] by them.

3 "If a man divorces[i] his wife
and she leaves him and marries
another man,
should he return to her again?
Would not the land be completely
defiled?
But you have lived as a prostitute
with many lovers[j] —
would you now return to me?"
declares the LORD.
2 "Look up to the barren heights and
see.
Is there any place where you have
not been ravished?
By the roadside[k] you sat waiting for
lovers,
sat like a nomad in the desert.
You have defiled the land[l]
with your prostitution and
wickedness.
3 Therefore the showers have been
withheld,[m]
and no spring rains[n] have fallen.
Yet you have the brazen look of a
prostitute;
you refuse to blush with shame.[o]
4 Have you not just called to me:

2:34 [a] 2Ki 21:16 [b] Ex 22:2
2:35 [c] Jer 25:31 [d] 1Jn 1:8,10
2:36 [e] Jer 31:22 [f] Isa 30:2,3,7
2:37 [g] 2Sa 13:19 [h] Jer 37:7
3:1 [i] Dt 24:1-4 [j] Jer 2:20,25; Eze 16:26,29
3:2 [k] Ge 38:14; Eze 16:25 [l] Jer 2:7
3:3 [m] Lev 26:19 [n] Jer 14:4 [o] Jer 6:15; 8:12; Zep 3:5
3:4 [p] ver 19 [q] Jer 2:2
3:5 [r] Ps 103:9; Isa 57:16
3:6 [s] Jer 17:2 [t] Jer 2:20
3:7 [u] Eze 16:46
3:8 [v] Eze 16:47; 23:11
3:9 [w] ver 2 [x] Isa 57:6 [y] Jer 2:27
3:10 [z] Jer 12:2
3:11 [a] Eze 16:52; 23:11 [b] ver 7
3:12 [c] 2Ki 17:3-6 [d] ver 14; Jer 31:21,22; Eze 33:11 [e] Ps 86:15
3:13 [f] Dt 30:1-3; Jer 14:20; 1Jn 1:9

Jer 3:6–7 ❖ How do the sins of one person infect the faith and righteousness of other believers? Where have we seen the ripple effects of abandoning God?

'My Father,[p] my friend from my
youth,[q]
5 will you always be angry?[r]
Will your wrath continue forever?'
This is how you talk,
but you do all the evil you can."

Unfaithful Israel

6 During the reign of King Josiah, the
LORD said to me, "Have you seen what
faithless Israel has done? She has gone
up on every high hill and under every
spreading tree[s] and has committed adultery[t] there. 7 I thought that after she had
done all this she would return to me but
she did not, and her unfaithful sister[u]
Judah saw it. 8 I gave faithless Israel her
certificate of divorce and sent her away
because of all her adulteries. Yet I saw
that her unfaithful sister Judah had no
fear;[v] she also went out and committed
adultery. 9 Because Israel's immorality mattered so little to her, she defiled
the land[w] and committed adultery with
stone[x] and wood.[y] 10 In spite of all this,
her unfaithful sister Judah did not return to me with all her heart, but only
in pretense,[z]" declares the LORD.
11 The LORD said to me, "Faithless Israel
is more righteous[a] than unfaithful[b] Judah. 12 Go, proclaim this message toward
the north:[c]

" 'Return,[d] faithless Israel,' declares
the LORD,
'I will frown on you no longer,
for I am faithful,' declares the LORD,
'I will not be angry[e] forever.
13 Only acknowledge[f] your guilt —
you have rebelled against the
LORD your God,

not be simple or obvious, but it is important to ask the questions of primary identity and covenant loyalty when considering affiliations or partnerships.

3:1–5 Jeremiah uses the relationship of a husband and his divorced wife as an analogy of the relationship between the Lord and his disobedient covenant people. Jerusalem is the spouse who has married many lovers, abandoning the Lord. As a result, she is defiled, estranged from her first husband, and incapable of mending the relationship. **3:6–10** The fate and infidelity of Israel are compared to the (worse) circumstances of Judah. Israel and Judah are described as sisters who have both committed adultery against their spouse. Surprisingly, Judah has learned nothing from the fall of Israel. **3:11–13** This oracle is intended for remnants of the former northern kingdom. God promises to be gracious and receptive, forgoing the anger proper to a spurned spouse. This oracle probably fits early

you have scattered your favors to
foreign gods[g]
under every spreading tree,[h]
and have not obeyed[i] me,'"
declares the LORD.

14"Return,[j] faithless people," declares
the LORD, "for I am your husband. I will
choose you—one from a town and two
from a clan—and bring you to Zion.
15Then I will give you shepherds[k] after
my own heart, who will lead you with
knowledge and understanding. 16In
those days, when your numbers have
increased greatly in the land," declares
the LORD, "people will no longer say, 'The
ark of the covenant of the LORD.' It will
never enter their minds or be remembered;[l] it will not be missed, nor will another one be made. 17At that time they
will call Jerusalem The Throne[m] of the
LORD, and all nations will gather in Jerusalem to honor[n] the name of the LORD.
No longer will they follow the stubbornness of their evil hearts.[o] 18In those days
the people of Judah will join the people
of Israel,[p] and together[q] they will come
from a northern[r] land to the land[s] I gave
your ancestors as an inheritance.
19"I myself said,

"'How gladly would I treat you like
my children
and give you a pleasant land,
the most beautiful inheritance of
any nation.'
I thought you would call me 'Father'[t]
and not turn away from
following me.
20But like a woman unfaithful to her
husband,
so you, Israel, have been
unfaithful to me,"
declares the LORD.

21A cry is heard on the barren
heights,[u]
the weeping and pleading of the
people of Israel,
because they have perverted their
ways
and have forgotten the LORD their
God.

22"Return,[v] faithless people;
I will cure[w] you of backsliding."

"Yes, we will come to you,
for you are the LORD our God.
23Surely the idolatrous commotion on
the hills
and mountains is a deception;
surely in the LORD our God
is the salvation[x] of Israel.
24From our youth shameful[y] gods have
consumed
the fruits of our ancestors'
labor—
their flocks and herds,
their sons and daughters.
25Let us lie down in our shame,[z]
and let our disgrace cover us.
We have sinned against the LORD
our God,
both we and our ancestors;
from our youth[a] till this day
we have not obeyed the LORD our
God."

4 "If you, Israel, will return,[b]
then return to me,"
declares the LORD.
"If you put your detestable idols[c] out
of my sight
and no longer go astray,
2and if in a truthful, just and
righteous way
you swear,[d] 'As surely as the LORD
lives,'[e]

3:13 [g] Jer 2:25 [h] Dt 12:2 [i] ver 25
3:14 [j] Hos 2:19
3:15 [k] Ac 20:28
3:16 [l] Isa 65:17
3:17 [m] Jer 17:12; Eze 43:7 [n] Isa 60:9 [o] Jer 11:8
3:18 [p] Hos 1:11 [q] Isa 11:13; Jer 50:4 [r] Jer 16:15; 31:8 [s] Am 9:15
3:19 [t] ver 4; Isa 63:16
3:21 [u] ver 2
3:22 [v] Hos 14:4 [w] Jer 33:6; Hos 6:1
3:23 [x] Ps 3:8; Jer 17:14
3:24 [y] Hos 9:10
3:25 [z] Ezr 9:6 [a] Jer 22:21
4:1 [b] Jer 3:1, 22; Joel 2:12 [c] Jer 35:15
4:2 [d] Dt 10:20; Isa 65:16 [e] Jer 12:16 [f] Ge 22:18; Gal 3:8

---

in Jeremiah's prophetic ministry, when King Josiah reached out to remnants of the covenant people in the former northern kingdom.

3:14–18 The Lord promises that he will bring back the prodigal children and establish them in their homeland. The ark of the covenant is portrayed as the throne (or royal footstool) of the cosmic Lord. In a renewed Jerusalem, no one will long for the lost ark because the whole city will be "The Throne of the LORD" (v. 17).

3:19–20 Both the marriage (unfaithful wife) and familial metaphors (children able to inherit) are again used to indicate Judah's sin.

3:21–25 Words of "returning" and of healing the people's "faithlessness" and "backsliding" (v. 22) are used in the promises of these verses. They offer confession of sin and repentance in vv. 22b–25.

4:1–2 When that time comes, God calls for a sincere "return" (v. 1) to him. The future restoration of God's people will lead other nations to find the Lord's blessing. This last element plays on the foundational promise of Ge 12:3.

✣ **3:1–4:2** Christians are the bride of Jesus Christ, God's Son (see Eph 5:22–33). Christ's disciples are bound to him through his resurrection, and the working of the Holy Spirit is present within them and the church, the corporate body of Christ. Disobedience ("sin") is

then the nations will invoke
blessings[f] by him
and in him they will boast."

[3]This is what the LORD says to the people of Judah and to Jerusalem:

"Break up your unplowed ground[g]
and do not sow among thorns.[h]
[4]Circumcise yourselves to the LORD,
circumcise your hearts,[i]
you people of Judah and
inhabitants of Jerusalem,
or my wrath[j] will flare up and burn
like fire
because of the evil you have
done —
burn with no one to quench[k] it.

Disaster From the North

[5]"Announce in Judah and proclaim in
Jerusalem and say:
'Sound the trumpet throughout
the land!'
Cry aloud and say:
'Gather together!
Let us flee to the fortified cities!'[l]
[6]Raise the signal to go to Zion!
Flee for safety without delay!
For I am bringing disaster from the
north,[m]
even terrible destruction."

[7]A lion[n] has come out of his lair;
a destroyer of nations has set out.
He has left his place
to lay waste[o] your land.

4:3 [g]Hos 10:12 [h]Mk 4:18
4:4 [i]Dt 10:16; Jer 9:26; Ro 2:28-29 [j]Zep 2:2 [k]Am 5:6
4:5 [l]Jos 10:20; Jer 8:14
4:6 [m]Jer 1:13-15; 50:3
4:7 [n]2Ki 24:1; Jer 2:15 [o]Isa 1:7 [p]Jer 25:9
4:8 [q]Isa 22:12; Jer 6:26 [r]Jer 30:24
4:9 [s]Isa 29:9
4:10 [t]2Th 2:11 [u]Jer 14:13
4:11 [v]Eze 17:10; Hos 13:15
4:12 [w]Jer 1:16
4:13 [x]Isa 19:1 [y]Isa 66:15 [z]Isa 5:28 [a]Dt 28:49; Hab 1:8
4:14 [b]Jas 4:8

Jer 4:4 ❖ How can we "circumcise [our] hearts" for God? What does this mean for the believer?

Your towns will lie in ruins[p]
without inhabitant.
[8]So put on sackcloth,[q]
lament and wail,
for the fierce anger[r] of the LORD
has not turned away from us.

[9]"In that day," declares the LORD,
"the king and the officials will lose
heart,
the priests will be horrified,
and the prophets will be appalled."[s]

[10]Then I said, "Alas, Sovereign LORD!
How completely you have deceived[t] this
people and Jerusalem by saying, 'You
will have peace,'[u] when the sword is at
our throats!"
[11]At that time this people and Jerusalem will be told, "A scorching wind[v] from
the barren heights in the desert blows
toward my people, but not to winnow
or cleanse; [12]a wind too strong for that
comes from me. Now I pronounce my
judgments[w] against them."

[13]Look! He advances like the clouds,[x]
his chariots[y] come like a whirlwind,[z]
his horses are swifter than eagles.[a]
Woe to us! We are ruined!
[14]Jerusalem, wash[b] the evil from your
heart and be saved.

---

not just failure to observe a norm or behavior; it is also the breaking of a bond and an affront to one's Lord. Adultery in theological terms is a crime against grace; it is infidelity against God who in Christ has called us into an intimate fellowship with himself and who has formed a church as the holy bride of Christ.

4:3–4 Removal of the foreskin from the male genitalia is a sign (Ge 17:11) of the covenant. Circumcision of the heart, the center of understanding and will, is a metaphor for wholehearted commitment to the Lord. This metaphor in Jeremiah leads us to understand that the act of circumcision is inadequate apart from personal commitment to follow the God who makes promises to us.

There are similar references elsewhere in Jeremiah and in Deuteronomy to the significance of both the terms "circumcision" and "heart." These various references assert that Israel must make a radical commitment to God and cannot fulfill that commitment unless God transforms them.

4:5–13 The Lord comes against the people like a lion whose blast of anger is like a searing wind. Verse 10 is an autobiographical comment. Possibly Jeremiah's own words about judgment to come have been proclaimed for several years but have not yet happened. The prophets and priests who have proclaimed peace have been right (so far). In frustration and alarm, Jeremiah wonders how God can allow these circumstances to exist.

4:14–22 The prophet pleads with Jerusalem to cleanse her heart and remove her wicked thoughts. God reminds Jerusalem of the dire consequences of her activity. Her own "conduct and actions" (v. 18) have brought these appalling circumstances to light.

In his own "heart" (note again the catchword) Jeremiah expresses horror at the realization of Jerusalem's impending doom (vv. 19–22). In striking fashion his emotional reaction to this doom is translated into physical reaction, with his writhing "in pain" (v. 19). The prophet lays the responsibility for failure with the people, who are described as "fools" and "senseless children" (v. 22).

This section begins with Jeremiah addressing Jerusalem in almost frantic fashion. The emotion fits that of the prophet, but the refrain of v. 17 ("declares the LORD") indicates that God is

How long will you harbor wicked
thoughts?
15 A voice is announcing from Dan,[c]
proclaiming disaster from the
hills of Ephraim.
16 "Tell this to the nations,
proclaim concerning Jerusalem:
'A besieging army is coming from a
distant land,
raising a war cry[d] against the cities
of Judah.
17 They surround[e] her like men
guarding a field,
because she has rebelled[f] against
me,'"
declares the LORD.
18 "Your own conduct and actions[g]
have brought this on you.[h]
This is your punishment.
How bitter[i] it is!
How it pierces to the heart!"

19 Oh, my anguish, my anguish![j]
I writhe in pain.
Oh, the agony of my heart!
My heart pounds within me,
I cannot keep silent.[k]
For I have heard the sound of the
trumpet;
I have heard the battle cry.[l]
20 Disaster follows disaster;[m]
the whole land lies in ruins.
In an instant my tents[n] are
destroyed,
my shelter in a moment.
21 How long must I see the battle
standard
and hear the sound of the
trumpet?

22 "My people are fools;[o]
they do not know me.[p]
They are senseless children;
they have no understanding.
They are skilled in doing evil;[q]
they know not how to do good."[r]

23 I looked at the earth,
and it was formless and empty;[s]
and at the heavens,
and their light was gone.
24 I looked at the mountains,
and they were quaking;[t]
all the hills were swaying.
25 I looked, and there were no people;
every bird in the sky had flown
away.[u]
26 I looked, and the fruitful land was a
desert;
all its towns lay in ruins
before the LORD, before his fierce
anger.

27 This is what the LORD says:

"The whole land will be ruined,
though I will not destroy[v] it
completely.
28 Therefore the earth will mourn[w]
and the heavens above grow
dark,[x]
because I have spoken and will not
relent,[y]
I have decided and will not turn
back.[z]"

29 At the sound of horsemen and
archers[a]
every town takes to flight.[b]
Some go into the thickets;
some climb up among the rocks.
All the towns are deserted;[c]
no one lives in them.

30 What are you doing,[d] you devastated
one?
Why dress yourself in scarlet
and put on jewels[e] of gold?
Why highlight your eyes with
makeup?[f]
You adorn yourself in vain.
Your lovers[g] despise you;
they want to kill you.

31 I hear a cry as of a woman in labor,[h]
a groan as of one bearing her first
child —
the cry of Daughter Zion gasping for
breath,[i]

4:15 [c] Jer 8:16
4:16 [d] Eze 21:22
4:17 [e] 2Ki 25:1, 4 [f] Jer 5:23
4:18 [g] Ps 107:17; Isa 50:1 [h] Jer 2:17 [i] Jer 2:19
4:19 [j] Isa 16:11; 22:4; Jer 9:10 [k] Jer 20:9 [l] Nu 10:9
4:20 [m] Ps 42:7; Eze 7:26 [n] Jer 10:20
4:22 [o] Jer 10:8 [p] Jer 2:8 [q] Jer 13:23; 1Co 14:20 [r] Ro 16:19
4:23 [s] Ge 1:2
4:24 [t] Isa 5:25; Eze 38:20
4:25 [u] Jer 9:10; 12:4; Zep 1:3
4:27 [v] Jer 5:10, 18; 12:12; 30:11; 46:28
4:28 [w] Jer 12:4, 11; 14:2; Hos 4:3 [x] Isa 5:30; 50:3 [y] Nu 23:19 [z] Jer 23:20; 30:24
4:29 [a] Jer 6:23 [b] 2Ki 25:4 [c] ver 7
4:30 [d] Isa 10:3-4 [e] Eze 23:40 [f] 2Ki 9:30 [g] La 1:2; Eze 23:9, 22
4:31 [h] Jer 13:21 [i] Isa 42:14

---

also concerned for the city. The writhing pain of vv. 19–20 may belong to Jerusalem, or perhaps it is the prophet who has begun to grasp the enormity of the coming tragedy.

The third party to this emotion-laden conversation is God himself. The sad comment in v. 22 that the people "do not know *me*" (emphasis added) can be no other than the voice of God himself. In the final analysis, no one—people, prophet, or God—remains aloof from the horror of it all.

4:23–26 In the visionary perspective of the prophet, the Judean landscape is transformed into something "formless and empty" (v. 23), the same two terms used in Ge 1:2 to describe the chaos of creation before God spoke order into existence.

4:27–31 God will speak and judgment will come just as God spoke and brought order out of chaos. In v. 31, the prophet depicts Jerusalem's cries like those of birth pangs. It is not, however, the joy of giving birth but the fear of death that is on this woman's lips. She is collapsing before murderers.

stretching out her hands[j] and
saying,
"Alas! I am fainting;
my life is given over to
murderers."

Not One Is Upright

5 "Go up and down[k] the streets of
Jerusalem,
look around and consider,
search through her squares.
If you can find but one person[l]
who deals honestly and seeks the
truth,
I will forgive[m] this city.
2 Although they say, 'As surely as the
LORD lives,'[n]
still they are swearing falsely."

3 LORD, do not your eyes[o] look for
truth?
You struck[p] them, but they felt no
pain;
you crushed them, but they
refused correction.[q]
They made their faces harder than
stone[r]
and refused to repent.
4 I thought, "These are only the poor;
they are foolish,
for they do not know[s] the way of the
LORD,
the requirements of their God.
5 So I will go to the leaders[t]
and speak to them;
surely they know the way of the
LORD,
the requirements of their God."
But with one accord they too had
broken off the yoke
and torn off the bonds.[u]
6 Therefore a lion from the forest will
attack them,
a wolf from the desert will ravage
them,
a leopard[v] will lie in wait near their
towns
to tear to pieces any who venture
out,

4:31 [j] Isa 1:15; La 1:17
5:1 [k] 2Ch 16:9; Eze 22:30 [l] Ge 18:32 [m] Ge 18:24
5:2 [n] Jer 4:2
5:3 [o] 2Ch 16:9 [p] Isa 9:13 [q] Jer 2:30; Zep 3:2 [r] Jer 7:26; 19:15; Eze 3:8-9
5:4 [s] Jer 8:7
5:5 [t] Mic 3:1, 9 [u] Ps 2:3; Jer 2:20
5:6 [v] Hos 13:7
[w] Jer 30:14
5:7 [x] Jos 23:7; Zep 1:5 [y] Dt 32:21; Jer 2:11; Gal 4:8 [z] Nu 25:1
5:8 [a] Jer 29:23; Eze 22:11
5:9 [b] ver 29; Jer 9:9
5:10 [c] Jer 4:27
5:11 [d] Jer 3:20
5:12 [e] Jer 23:17 [f] 2Ch 36:16; Jer 14:13
5:13 [g] Jer 14:15

Jer 5:3–5 ❖ What causes people to be obstinate and rebel against God's guidance and correction?

for their rebellion is great
and their backslidings many.[w]

7 "Why should I forgive you?
Your children have forsaken me
and sworn[x] by gods that are not
gods.[y]
I supplied all their needs,
yet they committed adultery[z]
and thronged to the houses of
prostitutes.
8 They are well-fed, lusty stallions,
each neighing for another man's
wife.[a]
9 Should I not punish them for this?"[b]
declares the LORD.
"Should I not avenge myself
on such a nation as this?

10 "Go through her vineyards and
ravage them,
but do not destroy them
completely.[c]
Strip off her branches,
for these people do not belong to
the LORD.
11 The people of Israel and the people
of Judah
have been utterly unfaithful[d]
to me,"
declares the LORD.

12 They have lied about the LORD;
they said, "He will do nothing!
No harm will come to us;[e]
we will never see sword or famine.[f]
13 The prophets[g] are but wind
and the word is not in them;
so let what they say be done to
them."

14 Therefore this is what the LORD God
Almighty says:

"Because the people have spoken
these words,

5:1–9 This section contains an interchange between God and the audience in Jerusalem. The passage begins with a challenge for people to search Jerusalem for anyone who "deals honestly and seeks the truth" (v. 1). Apparently, no one fits these requirements.
5:3–6 Jeremiah himself attempts a search, but "[the people's] rebellion is great" (v. 6). God's reply is that forgiveness is not presently an option (cf. vv. 9, 29).

5:10–17 Vines and branches symbolize people. Verse 12 places a quotation in their mouths to the effect that neither sword nor famine will strike them. Apparently, these sentiments are provoked by "prophets" since Jeremiah replies that these prophets "are but wind" (v. 13). Underlying a text like this is the assumption of a heated debate among prophets, all of whom claim to represent the will of God.

I will make my words in your mouth[h] a fire[i]
and these people the wood it consumes.
15 People of Israel," declares the LORD,
"I am bringing a distant nation[j] against you —
an ancient and enduring nation,
a people whose language[k] you do not know,
whose speech you do not understand.
16 Their quivers are like an open grave;
all of them are mighty warriors.
17 They will devour[l] your harvests and food,
devour[m] your sons and daughters;
they will devour[n] your flocks and herds,
devour your vines and fig trees.
With the sword they will destroy
the fortified cities in which you trust.[o]

18 "Yet even in those days," declares the
LORD, "I will not destroy[p] you completely.
19 And when the people ask,[q] 'Why has
the LORD our God done all this to us?'
you will tell them, 'As you have forsaken
me and served foreign gods[r] in your own
land, so now you will serve foreigners[s]
in a land not your own.'

20 "Announce this to the descendants of Jacob
and proclaim it in Judah:
21 Hear this, you foolish and senseless people,
who have eyes[t] but do not see,
who have ears but do not hear:[u]
22 Should you not fear[v] me?" declares the LORD.
"Should you not tremble in my presence?
I made the sand a boundary for the sea,
an everlasting barrier it cannot cross.
The waves may roll, but they cannot prevail;
they may roar, but they cannot cross it.
23 But these people have stubborn and rebellious[w] hearts;
they have turned aside and gone away.
24 They do not say to themselves,
'Let us fear the LORD our God,
who gives autumn and spring rains[x] in season,
who assures us of the regular weeks of harvest.'[y]
25 Your wrongdoings have kept these away;
your sins have deprived you of good.

26 "Among my people are the wicked
who lie in wait[z] like men who snare birds
and like those who set traps to catch people.
27 Like cages full of birds,
their houses are full of deceit;[a]
they have become rich[b] and powerful
28 and have grown fat[c] and sleek.
Their evil deeds have no limit;
they do not seek justice.
They do not promote the case of the fatherless;[d]
they do not defend the just cause of the poor.[e]
29 Should I not punish them for this?"
declares the LORD.
"Should I not avenge myself
on such a nation as this?

30 "A horrible[f] and shocking thing
has happened in the land:
31 The prophets prophesy lies,[g]
the priests rule by their own authority,
and my people love it this way.
But what will you do in the end?

5:14 [h] Jer 1:9; Hos 6:5 [i] Jer 23:29
5:15 [j] Dt 28:49; Isa 5:26; Jer 4:16 [k] Isa 28:11
5:17 [l] Lev 26:16; Jer 8:16 [m] Dt 28:32; Jer 50:7,17 [n] Dt 28:31 [o] Dt 28:33
5:18 [p] Jer 4:27
5:19 [q] Dt 29:24-26; 1Ki 9:9 [r] Jer 16:13 [s] Dt 28:48
5:21 [t] Isa 6:10; Eze 12:2 [u] Mt 13:15; Mk 8:18
5:22 [v] Dt 28:58
5:23 [w] Dt 21:18
5:24 [x] Ps 147:8; Joel 2:23 [y] Ge 8:22; Ac 14:17
5:26 [z] Ps 10:8; Pr 1:11
5:27 [a] Jer 9:6 [b] Jer 12:1
5:28 [c] Dt 32:15 [d] Zec 7:10 [e] Isa 1:23; Jer 7:6
5:30 [f] Jer 23:14; Hos 6:10
5:31 [g] Eze 13:6; Mic 2:11

5:15–17 The Lord makes Jeremiah's prophetic word of judgment like a fire consuming wood (v. 14). A foreign nation is coming to devastate the people. This depiction is one of the catchword topics used repeatedly in chs. 4–6. The people will be carried away and serve foreigners in a strange land (i.e., the exile).

5:18–19 Exile from the promised land does not bring an end to the existence of the people. The Lord also reinforces the exile as a just reward for the people's idolatry. In the exile they will serve foreigners.

5:20–31 Jeremiah describes the people as "senseless" (v. 21), possessing eyes that do not see and ears that do not hear. They refuse to "fear" (v. 22) the Lord; that is, they do not hold the Lord in awe and serve him with reverence.

5:26–28 A general breakdown of common decency,

Jerusalem Under Siege

6 "Flee for safety, people of Benjamin!
Flee from Jerusalem!
Sound the trumpet in Tekoa![h]
Raise the signal over Beth Hakkerem![i]
For disaster looms out of the north,[j]
even terrible destruction.
2 I will destroy Daughter Zion,
so beautiful and delicate.
3 Shepherds[k] with their flocks will come against her;
they will pitch their tents around[l] her,
each tending his own portion."

4 "Prepare for battle against her!
Arise, let us attack at noon![m]
But, alas, the daylight is fading,
and the shadows of evening grow long.
5 So arise, let us attack at night
and destroy her fortresses!"

6 This is what the LORD Almighty says:

"Cut down the trees[n]
and build siege ramps[o] against Jerusalem.
This city must be punished;
it is filled with oppression.
7 As a well pours out its water,
so she pours out her wickedness.
Violence[p] and destruction[q] resound in her;
her sickness and wounds are ever before me.
8 Take warning, Jerusalem,
or I will turn away[r] from you
and make your land desolate
so no one can live in it."

9 This is what the LORD Almighty says:

"Let them glean the remnant of Israel
as thoroughly as a vine;
pass your hand over the branches again,
like one gathering grapes."

6:1 [h] 2Ch 11:6 [i] Ne 3:14 [j] Jer 4:6
6:3 [k] Jer 12:10 [l] 2Ki 25:4; Lk 19:43
6:4 [m] Jer 15:8
6:6 [n] Dt 20:19-20 [o] Jer 32:24
6:7 [p] Ps 55:9; Eze 7:11,23 [q] Jer 20:8
6:8 [r] Eze 23:18; Hos 9:12
6:10 [s] Ac 7:51 [t] Jer 20:8
6:11 [u] Jer 7:20 [v] Job 32:20; Jer 20:9 [w] Jer 9:21
6:12 [x] Dt 28:30 [y] Jer 8:10; 38:22 [z] Isa 5:25
6:13 [a] Isa 56:11 [b] Jer 8:10
6:14 [c] Jer 4:10; 8:11; Eze 13:10

Jer 6:13–15 ❖ Have we heard believers preaching peace and comfort while ignoring the weighty matters of righteousness and justice? What tempts church leaders to preach weak messages like this?

10 To whom can I speak and give warning?
Who will listen to me?
Their ears are closed[a][s]
so they cannot hear.
The word[t] of the LORD is offensive to them;
they find no pleasure in it.
11 But I am full of the wrath[u] of the LORD,
and I cannot hold it in.[v]

"Pour it out on the children in the street
and on the young men[w] gathered together;
both husband and wife will be caught in it,
and the old, those weighed down with years.
12 Their houses will be turned over to others,[x]
together with their fields and their wives,[y]
when I stretch out my hand[z]
against those who live in the land,"
declares the LORD.
13 "From the least to the greatest,
all are greedy for gain;[a]
prophets and priests alike,
all practice deceit.[b]
14 They dress the wound of my people
as though it were not serious.
'Peace, peace,' they say,
when there is no peace.[c]
15 Are they ashamed of their detestable conduct?
No, they have no shame at all;

[a] 10 Hebrew *uncircumcised*

---

not to mention the covenant responsibilities of an elect nation, is described in here. Greed and violence go hand in hand.

6:1–9 Chapter 6 functions like a summary of chs. 4 and 5. It contains calls to flee from the enemy (v. 1) and to mourn the fall of the city (v. 26). Disaster is imminent for Judah and Jerusalem. The city is the "Daughter Zion" (v. 2), so beautiful and yet so tragic. Verse 6 depicts a siege. The enemy will glean the vineyard of the Lord (v. 9), making sure that even a surviving remnant feels the brunt of judgment.

6:10–15 Announcements about the coming judgment have fallen on deaf ears. Jeremiah confesses that he is wearied at holding in God's wrath, and he hears the command to pour it out on the city that has known no shame. The priests and prophets have led the people astray with their proclamations. The people are so shameless that they do not know how to blush.

they do not even know how to
blush.[d]
So they will fall among the fallen;
they will be brought down when I
punish them,"
says the LORD.

16This is what the LORD says:

"Stand at the crossroads and look;
ask for the ancient paths,[e]
ask where the good way[f] is, and walk
in it,
and you will find rest[g] for your
souls.
But you said, 'We will not walk
in it.'
17I appointed watchmen[h] over you and
said,
'Listen to the sound of the
trumpet!'
But you said, 'We will not listen.'[i]
18Therefore hear, you nations;
you who are witnesses,
observe what will happen to them.
19Hear, you earth:[j]
I am bringing disaster on this
people,
the fruit of their schemes,[k]
because they have not listened to
my words
and have rejected my law.[l]
20What do I care about incense from
Sheba
or sweet calamus[m] from a distant
land?
Your burnt offerings are not
acceptable;[n]
your sacrifices[o] do not please me."[p]

21Therefore this is what the LORD says:

"I will put obstacles before this
people.
Parents and children alike will
stumble[q] over them;
neighbors and friends will perish."

22This is what the LORD says:

"Look, an army is coming
from the land of the north;[r]
a great nation is being stirred up
from the ends of the earth.
23They are armed with bow and spear;
they are cruel and show no mercy.[s]
They sound like the roaring sea
as they ride on their horses;[t]
they come like men in battle
formation
to attack you, Daughter Zion."

24We have heard reports about them,
and our hands hang limp.
Anguish[u] has gripped us,
pain like that of a woman in
labor.[v]
25Do not go out to the fields
or walk on the roads,
for the enemy has a sword,
and there is terror on every side.[w]
26Put on sackcloth,[x] my people,
and roll in ashes;[y]
mourn with bitter wailing
as for an only son,[z]
for suddenly the destroyer
will come upon us.

27"I have made you a tester[a] of metals
and my people the ore,
that you may observe
and test their ways.
28They are all hardened rebels,[b]
going about to slander.[c]
They are bronze and iron;[d]
they all act corruptly.
29The bellows blow fiercely
to burn away the lead with fire,

6:15 [d] Jer 3:3; 8:10-12
6:16 [e] Jer 18:15 [f] Ps 119:3 [g] Mt 11:29
6:17 [h] Eze 3:17 [i] Jer 11:7-8; 25:4
6:19 [j] Isa 1:2; Jer 22:29 [k] Pr 1:31 [l] Jer 8:9
6:20 [m] Ex 30:23 [n] Am 5:22 [o] Ps 50:8-10; Jer 7:21; Mic 6:7-8 [p] Isa 1:11
6:21 [q] Isa 8:14
6:22 [r] Jer 1:15; 10:22
6:23 [s] Isa 13:18 [t] Jer 4:29
6:24 [u] Jer 4:19 [v] Jer 4:31; 50:41-43
6:25 [w] Jer 49:29
6:26 [x] Jer 4:8 [y] Jer 25:34; Mic 1:10 [z] Zec 12:10
6:27 [a] Jer 9:7
6:28 [b] Jer 5:23 [c] Jer 9:4 [d] Eze 22:18

6:16–26 Through his prophet, the Lord asks the people to (re-)consider the "good way," the "ancient paths" (v. 16) that lead to security. They are reminded that God raised up "watchmen" (v. 17) who warned the people—but to no avail. The people continue to reject God's "law" (v. 19). The fate to befall them is actually the "fruit of their [own] schemes" (v. 19).

God rejects the sacrifices of the people. They are inadequate in light of their disobedience. As part of their judgment, God will put "obstacles" (v. 21) in their way.

6:27–30 These verses describe God's refining process of calling for repentance. Judgment has confirmed that the people as a whole are corrupt. These verses also provide a definition of the prophetic office: Prophets are raised up by God as refiners.

4:3–6:30 Jeremiah's vision of chaos emerges spiritually from his deep involvement with people who refuse to obey divine standards and who are skeptical that God will actually judge them. Does this not sound familiar to Western ears? Is it not the case that Western society has essentially given in to the idea that moral and values-based judgments should be restricted to the private consideration so as not to intrude on public policy decisions? And does the rising perception that society is spinning out of moral control because of its spiritual bankruptcy not point to a future chaos? In this ever-deepening chaos-inducing reality, the members of the church of Jesus Christ are called to have and exercise their voice (Mk 16:15).

but the refining goes on in vain;
the wicked are not purged out.
30 They are called rejected silver,
because the LORD has rejected
them."[e]

False Religion Worthless

7 This is the word that came to Jeremiah from the LORD: 2"Stand[f] at the gate of the LORD's house and there proclaim this message:

"'Hear the word of the LORD, all you people of Judah who come through these gates to worship the LORD. 3This is what the LORD Almighty, the God of Israel, says: Reform your ways[g] and your actions, and I will let you live in this place. 4Do not trust in deceptive[h] words and say, "This is the temple of the LORD, the temple of the LORD, the temple of the LORD!" 5If you really change your ways and your actions and deal with each other justly,[i] 6if you do not oppress the foreigner, the fatherless or the widow and do not shed innocent blood[j] in this place, and if you do not follow other gods[k] to your own harm, 7then I will let you live in this place, in the land[l] I gave your ancestors for ever and ever. 8But look, you are trusting in deceptive words that are worthless.

9"'Will you steal and murder, commit adultery and perjury,[a] burn incense to Baal[m] and follow other gods[n] you have not known, 10and then come and stand before me in this house,[o] which bears my Name, and say, "We are safe" — safe to do all these detestable things? 11Has this house,[p] which bears my Name, become a den of robbers[q] to you? But I have been watching![r] declares the LORD.

12"'Go now to the place in Shiloh[s] where I first made a dwelling for my Name, and see what I did[t] to it because of the wickedness of my people Israel. 13While you were doing all these things, declares the LORD, I spoke to you again and again,[u] but you did not listen;[v] I called you, but you did not answer.[w] 14Therefore, what I did to Shiloh I will now do to the house that bears my Name,[x] the temple you trust in, the place I gave to you and your ancestors. 15I will thrust you from my presence, just as I did all your fellow Israelites, the people of Ephraim.'[y]

16"So do not pray for this people nor offer any plea[z] or petition for them; do not plead with me, for I will not listen to you. 17Do you not see what they are doing in the towns of Judah and in the streets of Jerusalem? 18The children gather wood, the fathers light the fire, and the women knead the dough and make cakes to offer to the Queen of Heaven.[a] They pour out drink offerings[b] to other gods to arouse[c] my anger. 19But am I the one they are provoking? declares the LORD. Are they not rather harming themselves, to their own shame?[d]

20"'Therefore this is what the Sovereign LORD says: My anger[e] and my wrath will be poured out on this place — on man and beast, on the trees of the field and on the crops of your land — and it will burn and not be quenched.

21"'This is what the LORD Almighty, the God of Israel, says: Go ahead, add your burnt offerings to your other sacrifices[f] and eat[g] the meat yourselves! 22For when I brought your ancestors out of Egypt and spoke to them, I did not just give them commands about burnt offerings and sacrifices,[h] 23but I gave them this command: Obey[i] me, and I will be your God

6:30 [e] Ps 119:119; Jer 7:29; Hos 9:17
7:2 [f] Jer 17:19
7:3 [g] Jer 18:11; 26:13
7:4 [h] Mic 3:11
7:5 [i] Jer 22:3
7:6 [j] Jer 2:34; 19:4 [k] Dt 8:19
7:7 [l] Dt 4:40
7:9 [m] Jer 11:13,17 [n] Ex 20:3
7:10 [o] Jer 32:34; Eze 23:38-39
7:11 [p] Isa 56:7 [q] Mt 21:13*; Mk 11:17*; Lk 19:46* [r] Jer 29:23
7:12 [s] Jos 18:1 [t] 1Sa 4:10-11,22; Ps 78:60-64
7:13 [u] 2Ch 36:15 [v] Isa 65:12 [w] Jer 35:17
7:14 [x] 1Ki 9:7
7:15 [y] Ps 78:67
7:16 [z] Ex 32:10; Dt 9:14; Jer 15:1
7:18 [a] Jer 44:17-19 [b] Jer 19:13 [c] 1Ki 14:9
7:19 [d] Jer 9:19
7:20 [e] Jer 42:18; La 2:3-5
7:21 [f] Isa 1:11; Am 5:21-22 [g] Hos 8:13
7:22 [h] 1Sa 15:22; Ps 51:16; Hos 6:6
7:23 [i] Ex 19:5

Jer 7:2-8 ❖ How is God calling us to reform our ways and actions? Where do we see the need for reform in our wider community? How can we be a part of that positive change?

[a] 9 *Or and swear by false gods*

7:1-15 Jeremiah warns worshipers not to trust in deceptive words that give them false hopes. The phrase "[this is] the temple of the LORD" (v. 4) seems to function like a mantra, as if simply repeating it makes it true. Just because the temple sits in Jerusalem, worshipers should not assume that they can break the covenant, come to the temple, and cry, "We are safe" (v. 10). The prophet points to the shrine during the time of Samuel (1Sa 1-4). God may send judgment even on a place of worship that bears his "Name" (Jer 7:10, 11).

Judah has oppressed the alien, the widow, and the orphan (v. 6). In v. 9, the Lord cites stealing, murder, adultery, and false witness. Those attending temple service love neither God nor neighbor. Instead, they grasp at the magical properties of the temple, hoping God will protect the city against the enemy.

7:16-34 Why should Jeremiah intercede for the people when some of them have turned to the worship of the Queen of Heaven and other deities? Their trust is misplaced. Sacrifices are not acceptable when the people are intentionally breaking the covenant.

and you will be my people.[j] Walk in obedience to all I command you, that it may go
well[k] with you. 24But they did not listen
or pay attention;[l] instead, they followed
the stubborn inclinations of their evil
hearts. They went backward and not forward. 25From the time your ancestors left
Egypt until now, day after day, again and
again I sent you my servants the prophets.[m] 26But they did not listen to me or
pay attention. They were stiff-necked and
did more evil than their ancestors.'[n]
27"When you tell[o] them all this, they
will not listen[p] to you; when you call to
them, they will not answer. 28Therefore
say to them, 'This is the nation that has
not obeyed the LORD its God or responded to correction. Truth has perished; it
has vanished from their lips.
29" 'Cut off[q] your hair and throw it
away; take up a lament on the barren
heights, for the LORD has rejected and
abandoned[r] this generation that is under his wrath.

The Valley of Slaughter

30" 'The people of Judah have done evil
in my eyes, declares the LORD. They have
set up their detestable idols[s] in the house
that bears my Name and have defiled[t]
it. 31They have built the high places of
Topheth[u] in the Valley of Ben Hinnom
to burn their sons and daughters[v] in the
fire—something I did not command, nor
did it enter my mind.[w] 32So beware, the
days are coming, declares the LORD, when
people will no longer call it Topheth or
the Valley of Ben Hinnom, but the Valley of Slaughter,[x] for they will bury[y] the
dead in Topheth until there is no more
room. 33Then the carcasses of this people
will become food[z] for the birds and the
wild animals, and there will be no one to
frighten them away. 34I will bring an end
to the sounds[a] of joy and gladness and to
the voices of bride and bridegroom[b] in the
towns of Judah and the streets of Jerusalem, for the land will become desolate.[c]
8 " 'At that time, declares the LORD, the
bones of the kings and officials of Judah, the bones of the priests and prophets, and the bones of the people of Jerusalem will be removed from their graves.
2They will be exposed to the sun and the
moon and all the stars of the heavens,
which they have loved and served[d] and
which they have followed and consulted
and worshiped. They will not be gathered
up or buried, but will be like dung lying
on the ground. 3Wherever I banish them,
all the survivors of this evil nation will
prefer death to life,[e] declares the LORD
Almighty.'

Jer 8:4-7 ❖ What causes human hearts to cling to deceit and resist repenting? Where is God calling you to let go of something and repent before him?

Sin and Punishment

4"Say to them, 'This is what the LORD
says:

" 'When people fall down, do they
not get up?[f]

7:23 [j] Lev 26:12 [k] Ex 15:26
7:24 [l] Ps 81:11-12; Jer 11:8
7:25 [m] Jer 25:4
7:26 [n] Jer 16:12
7:27 [o] Eze 2:7 [p] Eze 3:7
7:29 [q] Job 1:20; Isa 15:2; Mic 1:16 [r] Jer 6:30
7:30 [s] Eze 7:20-22 [t] Jer 32:34
7:31 [u] 2Ki 23:10 [v] Ps 106:38 [w] Jer 19:5
7:32 [x] Jer 19:6 [y] Jer 19:11
7:33 [z] Dt 28:26
7:34 [a] Isa 24:8; Eze 26:13 [b] Rev 18:23 [c] Lev 26:34
8:2 [d] 2Ki 23:5; Ac 7:42
8:3 [e] Job 3:22; Rev 9:6
8:4 [f] Pr 24:16

7:31–34 In a nearby valley nicknamed "Slaughter" (v. 32), the Judeans participated in the horrifying rites of child sacrifice (cf. 19:1–15). "Topheth" (7:31) is an uncertain term, but it refers to a place where human sacrificial and cremation rituals took place. Some Judeans must have believed that they appeased the Lord by participating in these rituals, since God protests through the prophet that he has not commanded such activities. Elsewhere these activities are associated with Baal and Molek (2Ki 23:10; Jer 19:5). Jerusalem itself will become a place of slaughter (like nearby Topheth) because of her rejection of the Lord.

8:1–3 These words may have been added to the sermon because they reflect the horror of manipulating and exposing human corpses. The Topheth rites in 7:30–34 apparently included sacrificial rites with corpses (of children). Without repentance, death will be the only future for Judah.

✣ **7:1—8:3** Theology matters, not because God insists on a rigid intellectual system but because unless we understand who God is, we will be in basic error about everything else that is ultimately important. The church will not save anyone (nor did the temple or animal sacrifice); it is a means to a goal, not the end itself. Understood correctly it is a means for people to know God and be rightly related to him.

Jeremiah's address means not only that theology matters, but that it matters in the practical applications of the Christian life. His condemnation of the immorality of the people illustrates the old adage that "I may not believe everything you say, but I believe everything you do." Behavior matters because it is a key to a person's allegiance. Christian ethics, like the social institutions and actions of Jeremiah's day, are a means to an end—to worship and serve the living God.

8:4–12 God's people are woefully and willfully ignorant of God's "requirements" (v. 7) of behavior,

When someone turns away, do
they not return?
5 Why then have these people turned
away?
Why does Jerusalem always turn
away?
They cling to deceit;[g]
they refuse to return.[h]
6 I have listened attentively,
but they do not say what is right.
None of them repent[i] of their
wickedness,
saying, "What have I done?"
Each pursues their own course[j]
like a horse charging into battle.
7 Even the stork in the sky
knows her appointed seasons,
and the dove, the swift and the
thrush
observe the time of their
migration.
But my people do not know[k]
the requirements of the LORD.

8 " 'How can you say, "We are wise,
for we have the law[l] of the LORD,"
when actually the lying pen of the
scribes
has handled it falsely?
9 The wise[m] will be put to shame;
they will be dismayed and
trapped.
Since they have rejected the word[n]
of the LORD,
what kind of wisdom do they
have?
10 Therefore I will give their wives to
other men
and their fields to new owners.[o]
From the least to the greatest,
all are greedy for gain;[p]
prophets and priests alike,
all practice deceit.
11 They dress the wound of my people
as though it were not serious.
"Peace, peace," they say,
when there is no peace.[q]
12 Are they ashamed of their detestable
conduct?
No, they have no shame[r] at all;
they do not even know how to
blush.
So they will fall among the fallen;
they will be brought down when
they are punished,[s]
says the LORD.[t]

13 " 'I will take away their harvest,
declares the LORD.
There will be no grapes on the
vine.[u]
There will be no figs[v] on the tree,
and their leaves will wither.[w]
What I have given them
will be taken[x] from them.[a]' "

14 Why are we sitting here?
Gather together!
Let us flee to the fortified cities[y]
and perish there!
For the LORD our God has doomed us
to perish
and given us poisoned water[z] to
drink,
because we have sinned[a] against
him.
15 We hoped for peace[b]
but no good has come,
for a time of healing
but there is only terror.[c]
16 The snorting of the enemy's
horses
is heard from Dan;[d]
at the neighing of their stallions
the whole land trembles.
They have come to devour
the land and everything in it,
the city and all who live there.

8:5 [g] Jer 5:27 [h] Jer 7:24; 9:6
8:6 [i] Rev 9:20 [j] Ps 14:1-3
8:7 [k] Isa 1:3; Jer 5:4-5
8:8 [l] Ro 2:17
8:9 [m] Jer 6:15 [n] Jer 6:19
8:10 [o] Jer 6:12 [p] Isa 56:11
8:11 [q] Jer 6:14
8:12 [r] Jer 3:3 [s] Ps 52:5-7; Isa 3:9 [t] Jer 6:15
8:13 [u] Joel 1:7 [v] Lk 13:6 [w] Mt 21:19 [x] Jer 5:17
8:14 [y] Jer 4:5; 35:11 [z] Dt 29:18; Jer 9:15; 23:15 [a] Jer 14:7,20
8:15 [b] ver 11 [c] Jer 14:19
8:16 [d] Jer 4:15

[a] *13* The meaning of the Hebrew for this sentence is uncertain.

---

which are designed to regulate life. To the reply from the people in v. 8, Jeremiah charges that human interpretation has made God's truth into a lie. The deceitful interpretation of God's instruction blunts its judgmental force against sin. Priest and prophet alike are proclaiming "peace" (v. 11) when all is not well.

Religious leaders might have dulled the sharp edge of Josiah's reforms (2Ki 22–23). Presumably, the priests' interpretations have kept God's word from challenging and instructing the people.

8:13–17 Jeremiah depicts the people as coming to the terrifying realization that the enemy is approaching. God is judging them for their transgressions. The reference to the enemy horses at Dan indicates that the enemy is approaching from the north.

The unrealistic hope of the people for peace is self-delusion, a rejection of God's law. "Poisoned water" (v. 14) more likely refers to the problems with water stored in cisterns than it might point to God's intentionally poisoning wells. Sieges typically resulted in heavy reliance on poor water resources stored in cisterns. Perhaps the term "venomous snakes" (v. 17) indicates the deadly work of the invaders.

17 "See, I will send venomous snakes[e]
among you,
vipers that cannot be charmed,[f]
and they will bite you,"
declares the LORD.

18 You who are my Comforter[a] in
sorrow,
my heart is faint[g] within me.
19 Listen to the cry of my people
from a land far away:[h]
"Is the LORD not in Zion?
Is her King no longer there?"

"Why have they aroused my anger
with their images,
with their worthless foreign
idols?"[i]

20 "The harvest is past,
the summer has ended,
and we are not saved."

21 Since my people are crushed, I am
crushed;
I mourn,[j] and horror grips me.
22 Is there no balm in Gilead?[k]
Is there no physician there?
Why then is there no healing[l]
for the wound of my people?
9[b] 1 Oh, that my head were a spring
of water
and my eyes a fountain of tears!
I would weep[m] day and night
for the slain of my people.[n]
2 Oh, that I had in the desert
a lodging place for travelers,
so that I might leave my people
and go away from them;
for they are all adulterers,[o]
a crowd of unfaithful people.
3 "They make ready their tongue
like a bow, to shoot lies;[p]
it is not by truth
that they triumph[c] in the land.
They go from one sin to another;
they do not acknowledge me,"
declares the LORD.
4 "Beware of your friends;
do not trust anyone in your clan.[q]
For every one of them is a deceiver,[d r]
and every friend a slanderer.

8:17 [e] Nu 21:6; Dt 32:24 [f] Ps 58:5
8:18 [g] La 5:17
8:19 [h] Jer 9:16 [i] Dt 32:21
8:21 [j] Jer 14:17
8:22 [k] Ge 37:25 [l] Jer 30:12
9:1 [m] Jer 13:17; La 2:11,18 [n] Isa 22:4
9:2 [o] Jer 5:7-8; 23:10; Hos 4:2
9:3 [p] Ps 64:3
9:4 [q] Mic 7:5-6 [r] Ge 27:35

Jer 9:4-6 ❖ Are there people near us, perhaps even family members, of whom we need to be spiritually wary? How can we protect ourselves from spiritually damaging relationships?

5 Friend deceives friend,
and no one speaks the truth.
They have taught their tongues to
lie;
they weary themselves with
sinning.
6 You[e] live in the midst of deception;[s]
in their deceit they refuse to
acknowledge me,"
declares the LORD.

7 Therefore this is what the LORD Almighty says:

"See, I will refine[t] and test[u] them,
for what else can I do
because of the sin of my people?
8 Their tongue[v] is a deadly arrow;
it speaks deceitfully.
With their mouths they all speak
cordially to their neighbors,
but in their hearts they set traps[w]
for them.
9 Should I not punish them for this?"
declares the LORD.
"Should I not avenge[x] myself
on such a nation as this?"

10 I will weep and wail for the
mountains
and take up a lament concerning
the wilderness grasslands.
They are desolate and untraveled,
and the lowing of cattle is not
heard.
The birds[y] have all fled
and the animals are gone.

11 "I will make Jerusalem a heap of
ruins,

9:6 [s] Jer 5:27
9:7 [t] Isa 1:25 [u] Jer 6:27
9:8 [v] ver 3 [w] Jer 5:26
9:9 [x] Jer 5:9,29
9:10 [y] Jer 4:25; 12:4; Hos 4:3

[a] *18* The meaning of the Hebrew for this word is uncertain. [b] In Hebrew texts 9:1 is numbered 8:23, and 9:2-26 is numbered 9:1-25. [c] *3* Or *lies; / they are not valiant for truth* [d] *4* Or *a deceiving Jacob* [e] *6* That is, Jeremiah (the Hebrew is singular)

8:18–22 Jeremiah's prophetic words demonstrate that he is not aloof or indifferent to the suffering of the people. Indeed, three times (vv. 19, 21–22) the people are called "my people," a phrase appropriate also in the mouth of God. This point should not be lost on the reader. The sorrow Jeremiah feels at the fate of his people is that felt by God as well. Prophetic person and prophetic message converge to reveal not only the God of righteous judgment but the God of sorrows as well.
9:1–11 As with the previous section, readers encounter a merging of Jeremiah and God's voices.
9:7–10 We have a conversation between God and the prophet in vv. 1–6 followed by an announcement

a haunt of jackals;[z]
and I will lay waste the towns of
Judah
so no one can live there."[a]

12Who is wise[b] enough to understand
this? Who has been instructed by the
LORD and can explain it? Why has the
land been ruined and laid waste like a
desert that no one can cross?
13The LORD said, "It is because they have
forsaken my law, which I set before them;
they have not obeyed me or followed my
law.[c] 14Instead, they have followed[d] the
stubbornness of their hearts;[e] they have
followed the Baals, as their ancestors
taught them." 15Therefore this is what
the LORD Almighty, the God of Israel, says:
"See, I will make this people eat bitter
food[f] and drink poisoned water.[g] 16I will
scatter them among nations[h] that neither
they nor their ancestors have known,[i] and
I will pursue them with the sword[j] until
I have made an end of them."[k]

17This is what the LORD Almighty says:

"Consider now! Call for the wailing
women[l] to come;
send for the most skillful of them.
18 Let them come quickly
and wail over us
till our eyes overflow with tears
and water streams from our
eyelids.[m]
19 The sound of wailing is heard from
Zion:
'How ruined[n] we are!
How great is our shame!
We must leave our land
because our houses are in ruins.'"
20 Now, you women, hear the word of
the LORD;
open your ears to the words of his
mouth.
Teach your daughters how to wail;
teach one another a lament.[o]
21 Death has climbed in through our
windows
and has entered our fortresses;
it has removed the children from
the streets
and the young men[p] from the
public squares.

22Say, "This is what the LORD declares:

"'Dead bodies will lie
like dung[q] on the open field,
like cut grain behind the reaper,
with no one to gather them.'"

23This is what the LORD says:

"Let not the wise boast of their
wisdom[r]
or the strong boast of their
strength[s]
or the rich boast of their riches,[t]
24 but let the one who boasts boast[u]
about this:
that they have the understanding
to know me,
that I am the LORD,[v] who exercises
kindness,[w]
justice and righteousness[x] on
earth,
for in these I delight,"
declares the LORD.

25"The days are coming," declares
the LORD, "when I will punish all who
are circumcised only in the flesh[y] —
26Egypt, Judah, Edom, Ammon, Moab
and all who live in the wilderness in
distant places.[a][z] For all these nations
are really uncircumcised, and even the
whole house of Israel is uncircumcised
in heart.[a]"

[a] 26 Or *wilderness and who clip the hair by their foreheads*

9:11 [z] Isa 34:13 [a] Isa 25:2; Jer 26:9
9:12 [b] Ps 107:43; Hos 14:9
9:13 [c] 2Ch 7:19; Ps 89:30-32
9:14 [d] Jer 2:8,23 [e] Jer 7:24
9:15 [f] La 3:15 [g] Jer 8:14
9:16 [h] Lev 26:33 [i] Dt 28:64 [j] Eze 5:2 [k] Jer 44:27; Eze 5:12
9:17 [l] 2Ch 35:25; Ecc 12:5; Am 5:16
9:18 [m] Jer 14:17
9:19 [n] Jer 4:13
9:20 [o] Isa 32:9-13
9:21 [p] 2Ch 36:17
9:22 [q] Jer 8:2
9:23 [r] Ecc 9:11 [s] 1Ki 20:11 [t] Eze 28:4-5
9:24 [u] 1Co 1:31*; Gal 6:14 [v] 2Co 10:17* [w] Ps 51:1; Mic 7:18 [x] Ps 36:6
9:25 [y] Ro 2:8-9
9:26 [z] Jer 25:23 [a] Lev 26:41; Ac 7:51; Ro 2:28

---

of judgment on the people in vv. 7–11. In v. 10, God weeps and wails (like Jeremiah) for the destruction to come.

9:12–22 Note the introductory formula for divine communication (e.g., "The LORD said") in vv. 13, 17, 22. Judgment has fallen on Judah for her sins. Following the Baals is a blatant example of the people's folly.

Mourning cries mark the demise of shameful Judah. Exile is upon them. Death is personified as climbing into homes and roaming the doomed cities of Judah. Verses 17 and 20 refer to wailing women; women played a leading role in funeral lamentation.

A precise context for these prophecies is not given. Perhaps they reflect the initial Babylonian constriction of Jerusalem under Nebuchadnezzar in 598/597 BC, or the devastating drought mentioned elsewhere in Jeremiah (14:1–6).

9:23–26 Verses 23–24 return again to the theme of wisdom in such a time as this. Verse 25 is the typical introduction to a prophetic depiction of the future. Note that indications of God's speaking are found in each of the verses in vv. 23–25.

Verses 23–24 are almost proverbial in form. True wisdom recognizes that God has sent judgment on Judah; above all, it is knowledge of the Lord and his character. God reveals himself as One who practices and takes delight in kindness, justice, and righteousness. As vv. 25–26 make clear, any nations who spurn God's integrity will see his judgment.

God and Idols

10:12–16pp // Jer 51:15–19

10 Hear what the LORD says to you, people of Israel. 2This is what the LORD says:

“Do not learn the ways of the
nations[b]
or be terrified by signs in the
heavens,
though the nations are terrified
by them.
3For the practices of the peoples are
worthless;
they cut a tree out of the forest,
and a craftsman[c] shapes it with his
chisel.
4They adorn it with silver and gold;
they fasten it with hammer and
nails
so it will not totter.[d]
5Like a scarecrow in a cucumber
field,
their idols cannot speak;[e]
they must be carried
because they cannot walk.[f]
Do not fear them;
they can do no harm
nor can they do any good.”[g]

6No one is like you, LORD;
you are great,[h]
and your name is mighty in
power.
7Who should not fear you,
King of the nations?[i]
This is your due.
Among all the wise leaders of the
nations
and in all their kingdoms,
there is no one like you.

8They are all senseless and foolish;[j]
they are taught by worthless
wooden idols.
9Hammered silver is brought from
Tarshish
and gold from Uphaz.
What the craftsman and goldsmith
have made[k]
is then dressed in blue and
purple—
all made by skilled workers.
10But the LORD is the true God;
he is the living God, the eternal
King.
When he is angry, the earth trembles;
the nations cannot endure his
wrath.[l]

11“Tell them this: ‘These gods, who did
not make the heavens and the earth, will
perish[m] from the earth and from under
the heavens.’ ”[a]

12But God made the earth by his
power;
he founded the world by his
wisdom
and stretched out the heavens[n] by
his understanding.
13When he thunders,[o] the waters in
the heavens roar;
he makes clouds rise from the
ends of the earth.
He sends lightning with the rain[p]
and brings out the wind from his
storehouses.

14Everyone is senseless and without
knowledge;
every goldsmith is shamed by his
idols.
The images he makes are a fraud;
they have no breath in them.
15They are worthless,[q] the objects of
mockery;
when their judgment comes, they
will perish.
16He who is the Portion[r] of Jacob is not
like these,
for he is the Maker of all things,[s]
including Israel, the people of his
inheritance[t]—
the LORD Almighty is his name.[u]

10:2 [b] Lev 20:23
10:3 [c] Isa 40:19
10:4 [d] Isa 41:7
10:5 [e] 1Co 12:2 [f] Ps 115:5,7 [g] Isa 41:24; 46:7
10:6 [h] Ps 48:1
10:7 [i] Ps 22:28; Rev 15:4
10:8 [j] Isa 40:19; Jer 4:22
10:9 [k] Ps 115:4; Isa 40:19
10:10 [l] Ps 76:7
10:11 [m] Ps 96:5; Isa 2:18
10:12 [n] Ge 1:1, 8; Job 9:8; Isa 40:22
10:13 [o] Job 36:29 [p] Ps 135:7
10:15 [q] Isa 41:24; Jer 14:22
10:16 [r] Dt 32:9; Ps 119:57 [s] ver 12 [t] Ps 74:2 [u] Jer 31:35; 32:18

[a] *11* The text of this verse is in Aramaic.

10:1–16 These verses contain an extended critique of idolatry and affirm that the Lord is Ruler over all. Verse 2 refers to looking to the stars to predict the future. Verses 3–5 criticize making and worshiping wooden images. Verses 9-10 note that an idol can be decorated but never divine. Verse 11 is a proverb written in Aramaic. Perhaps it is a traditional saying that the prophet adopts here for emphasis. Divine images are judged in v. 15 with the statement that they are “worthless, the objects of mockery.”

10:10–16 The lifeless images of idols are contrasted with the uniqueness of the “living God” (vv. 10–12). His cosmic kingship is affirmed twice (vv. 7, 10). This God, the “Maker of all things,” is also the “Portion of Jacob” (v. 16). Even the wisdom from other nations is foolishness compared to God’s truth.

The text is cast in a teaching mode rather than as a list of reasons why Israel is being judged. Assimilation to a dominant culture was a real issue for Israelites and Judeans among other nations.

Coming Destruction

17 Gather up your belongings[v] to leave
the land,
you who live under siege.
18 For this is what the LORD says:
"At this time I will hurl[w] out
those who live in this land;
I will bring distress on them
so that they may be captured."

19 Woe to me because of my injury!
My wound[x] is incurable!
Yet I said to myself,
"This is my sickness, and I must
endure[y] it."
20 My tent[z] is destroyed;
all its ropes are snapped.
My children are gone from me and
are no more;[a]
no one is left now to pitch my tent
or to set up my shelter.
21 The shepherds are senseless
and do not inquire of the LORD;
so they do not prosper
and all their flock is scattered.[b]
22 Listen! The report is coming—
a great commotion from the land
of the north!
It will make the towns of Judah
desolate,
a haunt of jackals.[c]

10:17 [v] Eze 12:3-12
10:18 [w] 1Sa 25:29
10:19 [x] Jer 14:17 [y] Mic 7:9
10:20 [z] Jer 4:20 [a] Jer 31:15; La 1:5
10:21 [b] Jer 23:2
10:22 [c] Jer 9:11

Jer 10:23-25 ❖ Why is it important we remember that our lives are not our own (see 1Co 6:19-20)? How does this shape our thinking and conduct?

Jeremiah's Prayer

23 LORD, I know that people's lives are
not their own;
it is not for them to direct their
steps.[d]
24 Discipline me, LORD, but only in due
measure—
not in your anger,[e]
or you will reduce me to nothing.[f]
25 Pour out your wrath on the nations[g]
that do not acknowledge you,
on the peoples who do not call on
your name.[h]
For they have devoured[i] Jacob;
they have devoured him
completely
and destroyed his homeland.[j]

The Covenant Is Broken

11 This is the word that came to Jeremiah from the LORD: 2 "Listen to the
terms of this covenant and tell them to
the people of Judah and to those who
live in Jerusalem. 3 Tell them that this is

10:23 [d] Pr 20:24
10:24 [e] Ps 6:1; 38:1 [f] Jer 30:11
10:25 [g] Zep 3:8 [h] Job 18:21; Ps 14:4 [i] Ps 79:7; Jer 8:16 [j] Ps 79:6-7

10:17–22 One may see the voices in this passage as follows:
[*prophet* to Jerusalem] vv. 17–18: "Gather up your belongings. . . ."
[*Jerusalem* to herself] vv. 19–20: "Woe to me because of my injury! . . ."
[*prophet* to Jerusalem] vv. 21–22: "The shepherds are senseless and do not inquire of the LORD. . . ."
10:23–25 The poetic collection of 8:4—10:25 concludes with the prayer of a punished individual. The speaker is almost certainly Jeremiah; the question is whether he speaks personally or as a member of a wounded and judged people.

There is more wisdom than resignation in the way the prayer begins. A person does not ultimately direct his or her own pathways; rather, they are in the hands of God. Recognizing this fact is a first step toward wisdom. Much of the prayer is about justice: Jeremiah pleads with God to judge the enemy who has devoured Jacob.

✜ **8:4—10:25** The role of Christians and the church in engaging the world requires a passionate identification with the foolishness of the world. Those who would offer a grave spiritual diagnosis must love the patients and not stand separate from them. This is a model of the church, which not only receives a judgmental word from Jeremiah, but also which, by God's grace, seeks to minister to hurting people and to rectify society's ills.

Jeremiah may be a prophetic reminder of the deep sorrow that should meet all Christians when they reflect on the circumstances of those who do not know God. The lost are, after all, estranged siblings of the Lord, who wept and died for them.

11:1–17 The chapter begins with an address from God to Jeremiah instructing the prophet about the people's failures to remain faithful to "this covenant" (vv. 2–3; cf. vv. 6, 8, 10). Verses 6–14 offer a second communication from God.

The Lord recognizes that Jeremiah's report will fall on deaf ears and hard hearts. As a result, the prophet is commanded not to pray for the people. Verse 14 assumes that intercession will do no good because the people will remain incorrigible. Verses 1–17 appear to be a summary of reflections on the failure of Judah and Jerusalem to keep God's covenant rather than a report of the prophet's actual presentation to the people.

Details in vv. 1–17 offer further perspective on the term "covenant," but they also leave a number of things assumed on the part of hearers/readers. This covenant is something God "commanded" the ancestors of Judah and Jerusalem (vv. 4, 8), who were slaves in Egypt, to follow. Obedience to God is expected since he redeemed Israel and they belong to him.

The covenant was established on God's gifts of deliverance and instruction. It contained curses for

what the LORD, the God of Israel, says:
'Cursed[k] is the one who does not obey
the terms of this covenant — 4the terms
I commanded your ancestors when I
brought them out of Egypt, out of the
iron-smelting furnace.[l] I said, 'Obey[m]
me and do everything I command you,
and you will be my people,[n] and I will be
your God. 5Then I will fulfill the oath I
swore[o] to your ancestors, to give them a
land flowing with milk and honey' — the
land you possess today."

I answered, "Amen, LORD."

6The LORD said to me, "Proclaim all
these words in the towns of Judah and
in the streets of Jerusalem: 'Listen to
the terms of this covenant and follow[p]
them. 7From the time I brought your
ancestors up from Egypt until today, I
warned them again and again,[q] saying,
"Obey me." 8But they did not listen or
pay attention;[r] instead, they followed
the stubbornness of their evil hearts.
So I brought on them all the curses[s] of
the covenant I had commanded them
to follow but that they did not keep.' "

9Then the LORD said to me, "There is a
conspiracy[t] among the people of Judah
and those who live in Jerusalem. 10They
have returned to the sins of their ancestors,[u] who refused to listen to my words.
They have followed other gods[v] to serve
them. Both Israel and Judah have broken
the covenant I made with their ancestors.
11Therefore this is what the LORD says: 'I
will bring on them a disaster[w] they cannot escape. Although they cry[x] out to me,
I will not listen[y] to them. 12The towns
of Judah and the people of Jerusalem
will go and cry out to the gods to whom
they burn incense,[z] but they will not help
them at all when disaster[a] strikes. 13You,
Judah, have as many gods as you have
towns; and the altars you have set up to
burn incense[b] to that shameful[c] god Baal
are as many as the streets of Jerusalem.'

14"Do not pray[d] for this people or offer
any plea or petition for them, because I
will not listen[e] when they call to me in
the time of their distress.

15"What is my beloved doing in my
temple
as she, with many others, works
out her evil schemes?
Can consecrated meat avert your
punishment?
When you engage in your
wickedness,
then you rejoice.[a]"

16The LORD called you a thriving olive
tree
with fruit beautiful in form.
But with the roar of a mighty
storm
he will set it on fire,[f]
and its branches will be broken.[g]

11:3 [k]Dt 27:26; Gal 3:10
11:4 [l]Dt 4:20; 1Ki 8:51 [m]Ex 24:8 [n]Jer 7:23; 31:33
11:5 [o]Ex 13:5; Dt 7:12; Ps 105:8-11
11:6 [p]Dt 15:5; Ro 2:13; Jas 1:22
11:7 [q]2Ch 36:15
11:8 [r]Jer 7:26 [s]Lev 26:14-43
11:9 [t]Eze 22:25
11:10 [u]Dt 9:7 [v]Jdg 2:12-13
11:11 [w]2Ki 22:16 [x]Jer 14:12; Eze 8:18 [y]ver 14; Pr 1:28; Isa 1:15; Zec 7:13
11:12 [z]Jer 44:17 [a]Dt 32:37
11:13 [b]Jer 7:9 [c]Jer 3:24
11:14 [d]Ex 32:10 [e]ver 11
11:16 [f]Jer 21:14 [g]Isa 27:11; Ro 11:17-24

[a] 15 Or *Could consecrated meat avert your punishment? / Then you would rejoice*

---

the people's disobedience to the covenant stipulations (vv. 3, 8, 11). Accusations in vv. 9–13 that Judah venerates other gods confirm a violation of the covenant God established with the people (Dt 5:7–10) and the reason for reminding them of the curses for disobedience.

The particulars of Jer 11:1–17 assume a historical and theological context that spans the promises to Abraham, the deliverance from Egypt, covenant-making at Mount Sinai, and guidance to the promised land. King Josiah had undertaken a movement for covenant renewal (2Ki 22–23) by calling Judah back to the fundamental principles of the Sinai/Horeb covenant. He read to the assembled people (probably the book of Deuteronomy) and officiated at a ceremony of covenant-making, and the people responded affirmatively (2Ki 23:1–3). His reforming efforts coincided with the call of the young Jeremiah.

Two elements about the role of Josiah's reforming activity may help in interpreting Jer 11:1–17. (1) The book of Deuteronomy is essentially a covenant-renewal document. Moses emphasized that it was time for the younger generation who came out of Egypt to respond affirmatively to the covenant claim that God had on them. Jeremiah, a prophet like Moses (cf. Dt 18:18), takes up a similar role of calling the people back to their first love and reminding them of the consequences. (2) Moses commanded that the words of God's Torah be read every seven years at the Festival of Tabernacles (Dt 31:9–13). It is possible that Jeremiah's "sermon" as summarized in Jer 11 is influenced by the prophet's support for the covenant reform measures instituted earlier by Josiah as well as by the opportunity to reflect on God's covenantal instructions as they were read periodically in Judah.

11:1–17 It is a mistake simply to assume that people who try harder will succeed in their commitments. There will be no lasting success apart from a lasting transformation. Such transformation as God in Christ supplies is a process that begins with a gracious acceptance of the claims of the gospel and continues to and beyond death. The prophet addresses God's people, and his message is profoundly theological. "Trying harder" in secular terms is a bandage on a mortal wound.

17The LORD Almighty, who planted[h] you,
has decreed disaster for you, because the
people of both Israel and Judah have
done evil and aroused my anger by burning incense to Baal.[i]

Plot Against Jeremiah

18Because the LORD revealed their
plot to me, I knew it, for at that time he
showed me what they were doing. 19I
had been like a gentle lamb led to the
slaughter; I did not realize that they had
plotted[j] against me, saying,

"Let us destroy the tree and its
fruit;
let us cut him off from the land of
the living,[k]
that his name be remembered[l] no
more."
20But you, LORD Almighty, who judge
righteously
and test the heart and mind,[m]
let me see your vengeance on them,
for to you I have committed my
cause.

21Therefore this is what the LORD says
about the people of Anathoth who are
threatening to kill you,[n] saying, "Do not
prophesy in the name of the LORD or you
will die[o] by our hands"— 22therefore this
is what the LORD Almighty says: "I will
punish them. Their young men[p] will die
by the sword, their sons and daughters
by famine. 23Not even a remnant[q] will be
left to them, because I will bring disaster
on the people of Anathoth in the year of
their punishment.[r]"

Jeremiah's Complaint

12 You are always righteous,[s] LORD,
when I bring a case before you.
Yet I would speak with you about
your justice:
Why does the way of the wicked
prosper?[t]
Why do all the faithless live at
ease?
2You have planted[u] them, and they
have taken root;
they grow and bear fruit.
You are always on their lips
but far from their hearts.[v]
3Yet you know me, LORD;
you see me and test[w] my thoughts
about you.
Drag them off like sheep to be
butchered!
Set them apart for the day of
slaughter![x]
4How long will the land lie parched[y]
and the grass in every field be
withered?[z]
Because those who live in it are
wicked,
the animals and birds have
perished.[a]
Moreover, the people are saying,
"He will not see what happens
to us."

God's Answer

5"If you have raced with men on foot
and they have worn you out,
how can you compete with
horses?
If you stumble[a] in safe country,
how will you manage in the
thickets[b] by[b] the Jordan?
6Your relatives, members of your
own family—
even they have betrayed you;

11:17 [h] Isa 5:2; Jer 12:2 [i] Jer 7:9
11:19 [j] Jer 18:18; 20:10 [k] Job 28:13; Isa 53:8 [l] Ps 83:4
11:20 [m] Ps 7:9
11:21 [n] Jer 12:6 [o] Jer 26:8, 11; 38:4
11:22 [p] Jer 18:21
11:23 [q] Jer 6:9 [r] Jer 23:12
12:1 [s] Ezr 9:15 [t] Jer 5:27-28
12:2 [u] Jer 11:17 [v] Isa 29:13; Jer 3:10; Mt 15:8; Titus 1:16
12:3 [w] Ps 7:9; 11:5; 139:1-4; Jer 11:20 [x] Jer 17:18
12:4 [y] Jer 4:28 [z] Joel 1:10-12 [a] Jer 4:25; 9:10
12:5 [b] Jer 49:19; 50:44

Jer 11:18-23 ❖ Where do we see people or groups trying to silence the word of God today?

Jer 12:1-4 ❖ Do you ever struggle with the way God appears to withhold justice in the world? Why or why not?

[a] 5 Or *you feel secure only* [b] 5 Or *the flooding of*

11:18-23 God reveals that Jeremiah's neighbors intend to humiliate him and bring his prophetic work to an end. Indeed, the phrase "cut him off from the land of the living" (v. 19) indicates murder, as does the threat of v. 21.

"A lamb led to the slaughter" (v. 19) carries with it the imagery of innocence on the part of the lamb. Jeremiah's predicament is not God's judgment on him but the plot of others who oppose his message and seek to harm him.

The short prayer of the prophet in v. 20 is based on the conviction that God is a righteous Judge. Jeremiah asks for deliverance and for God to judge those who persecute him unjustly. Verses 21-23 reveal a judgment on those who seek Jeremiah's life.

12:1-6 If God is so clearly opposed to the activity of the wicked, then why not judge them and be done with it? Readers can see why this passage follows that of the description of Jeremiah's persecution in 11:18-23.

God's reply (12:5-6) does not "take the bait" and offer a defense of his providence. He simply calls the prophet to keep on the task at hand.

they have raised a loud cry against
you.[c]
Do not trust them,
though they speak well of you.[d]

7"I will forsake my house,
abandon[e] my inheritance;
I will give the one I love
into the hands of her enemies.
8 My inheritance has become to me
like a lion in the forest.
She roars at me;
therefore I hate her.[f]
9 Has not my inheritance become
to me
like a speckled bird of prey
that other birds of prey surround
and attack?
Go and gather all the wild beasts;
bring them to devour.[g]
10 Many shepherds[h] will ruin my
vineyard
and trample down my field;
they will turn my pleasant field
into a desolate wasteland.[i]
11 It will be made a wasteland,
parched and desolate before me;[j]
the whole land will be laid waste
because there is no one who cares.
12 Over all the barren heights in the
desert
destroyers will swarm,
for the sword of the LORD[k] will
devour
from one end of the land to the
other;[l]
no one will be safe.
13 They will sow wheat but reap thorns;
they will wear themselves out but
gain nothing.[m]
They will bear the shame of their
harvest
because of the LORD's fierce
anger."[n]

12:6 [c] Pr 26:24-25; Jer 9:4 [d] Ps 12:2
12:7 [e] Jer 7:29
12:8 [f] Hos 9:15; Am 6:8
12:9 [g] Isa 56:9; Jer 15:3; Eze 23:25
12:10 [h] Jer 23:1 [i] Isa 5:1-7
12:11 [j] ver 4; Isa 42:25; Jer 23:10
12:12 [k] Jer 47:6 [l] Jer 3:2
12:13 [m] Lev 26:20; Dt 28:38; Mic 6:15; Hag 1:6 [n] Jer 4:26
12:14 [o] Zec 2:7-9
12:15 [p] Am 9:14-15
12:16 [q] Jer 4:2 [r] Jos 23:7 [s] Isa 49:6; Jer 3:17
12:17 [t] Isa 60:12
13:5 [u] Ex 40:16
13:9 [v] Lev 26:19

14This is what the LORD says: "As for
all my wicked neighbors who seize the
inheritance I gave my people Israel, I
will uproot[o] them from their lands and
I will uproot the people of Judah from
among them. 15But after I uproot them,
I will again have compassion and will
bring[p] each of them back to their own
inheritance and their own country. 16And
if they learn well the ways of my people
and swear by my name, saying, 'As surely
as the LORD lives'[q] — even as they once
taught my people to swear by Baal[r] —
then they will be established among my
people.[s] 17But if any nation does not listen, I will completely uproot and destroy[t]
it," declares the LORD.

A Linen Belt

13 This is what the LORD said to me:
"Go and buy a linen belt and put it
around your waist, but do not let it touch
water." 2So I bought a belt, as the LORD
directed, and put it around my waist.
3Then the word of the LORD came to
me a second time: 4"Take the belt you
bought and are wearing around your
waist, and go now to Perath[a] and hide
it there in a crevice in the rocks." 5So I
went and hid it at Perath, as the LORD
told me.[u]
6Many days later the LORD said to me,
"Go now to Perath and get the belt I told
you to hide there." 7So I went to Perath
and dug up the belt and took it from the
place where I had hidden it, but now it
was ruined and completely useless.
8Then the word of the LORD came to
me: 9"This is what the LORD says: 'In
the same way I will ruin the pride of Judah and the great pride[v] of Jerusalem.

[a] 4 Or possibly *to the Euphrates;* similarly in verses 5-7

12:7-13 Verse 7 describes Judah as God's house, the people whom God loves. As the head of his household, God experiences pain at its downfall and at the perversion of his inheritance. Hatred (v. 8) is not the opposite of love; that is indifference. Hatred is the sad effect of betrayed and wounded love.

12:14-17 This word about the neighboring states around Judah anticipates elements in the oracles concerning foreign nations in chs. 25; 46–51.

11:18–12:17 Family and friends alike apparently opposed Jeremiah's prophetic activity. His opposition, his despair, and even the threats to his life came not from his sinfulness but from the exercise of his faith in responding to God's call. This is a perennial issue for Christians—more likely in some cultures and settings than in others—but a perennial issue nevertheless.

13:1-11 The verb "be bound" in v. 11 is the same word used in Ge 2:24 to describe the man who leaves his parents to be "united" to his wife and to become "one flesh." The waistcloth became soiled because Jeremiah removed it and buried it near the bank of the water. Israel and Judah were formed for God's "renown and praise and honor" (Jer 13:11), but because of their unfaithfulness they are no better than dirty underwear.

10These wicked people, who refuse to
listen to my words, who follow the stubbornness of their hearts[w] and go after
other gods[x] to serve and worship them,
will be like this belt — completely useless! 11For as a belt is bound around the
waist, so I bound all the people of Israel
and all the people of Judah to me,' declares the LORD, 'to be my people for my
renown[y] and praise and honor.[z] But they
have not listened.'[a]

Wineskins

12"Say to them: 'This is what the LORD,
the God of Israel, says: Every wineskin
should be filled with wine.' And if they
say to you, 'Don't we know that every
wineskin should be filled with wine?'
13then tell them, 'This is what the LORD
says: I am going to fill with drunkenness[b] all who live in this land, including
the kings who sit on David's throne, the
priests, the prophets and all those living
in Jerusalem. 14I will smash them one
against the other, parents and children
alike, declares the LORD. I will allow no
pity or mercy or compassion[c] to keep me
from destroying[d] them.'"

Threat of Captivity

15 Hear and pay attention,
do not be arrogant,
for the LORD has spoken.
16 Give glory[e] to the LORD your God
before he brings the darkness,
before your feet stumble[f]
on the darkening hills.
You hope for light,
but he will turn it to utter darkness
and change it to deep gloom.[g]
17 If you do not listen,[h]
I will weep in secret
because of your pride;
my eyes will weep bitterly,
overflowing with tears,[i]
because the LORD's flock[j] will be
taken captive.[k]

13:10 [w] Jer 11:8; 16:12 [x] Jer 9:14
13:11 [y] Jer 32:20; 33:9 [z] Ex 19:5-6 [a] Jer 7:26
13:13 [b] Ps 60:3; 75:8; Isa 51:17; 63:6; Jer 51:57
13:14 [c] Jer 16:5 [d] Dt 29:20; Eze 5:10
13:16 [e] Jos 7:19 [f] Jer 23:12 [g] Isa 59:9
13:17 [h] Mal 2:2 [i] Jer 9:1 [j] Ps 80:1; Jer 23:1 [k] Jer 14:18
13:19 [l] Jer 20:4; 52:30
13:20 [m] Jer 6:22; Hab 1:6 [n] Jer 23:2
13:21 [o] Jer 38:22 [p] Jer 4:31
13:22 [q] Jer 9:2-6; 16:10-12 [r] Eze 16:37; Na 3:5-6
13:24 [s] Ps 1:4 [t] Lev 26:33
13:25 [u] Job 20:29; Mt 24:51

Jer 13:15–17 ❖ How can we share Jeremiah's passion for the spiritual health of the people around us?

18 Say to the king and to the queen
mother,
"Come down from your thrones,
for your glorious crowns
will fall from your heads."
19 The cities in the Negev will be
shut up,
and there will be no one to open
them.
All Judah[l] will be carried into exile,
carried completely away.

20 Look up and see
those who are coming from the
north.[m]
Where is the flock[n] that was
entrusted to you,
the sheep of which you boasted?
21 What will you say when the LORD
sets over you
those you cultivated as your
special allies?[o]
Will not pain grip you
like that of a woman in labor?[p]
22 And if you ask yourself,
"Why has this happened to
me?" —
it is because of your many sins[q]
that your skirts have been torn off
and your body mistreated.[r]
23 Can an Ethiopian[a] change his skin
or a leopard its spots?
Neither can you do good
who are accustomed to doing evil.

24 "I will scatter you like chaff[s]
driven by the desert wind.[t]
25 This is your lot,
the portion[u] I have decreed for
you,"
declares the LORD,

[a] *23* Hebrew *Cushite* (probably a person from the upper Nile region)

13:12–14 Neither waistcloth nor wine jars fulfill their intended functions and thus are failures.
13:15–17 Perhaps this command calls them to admit the justice of the judgment about to befall them. It is possible, however, that the call to "give glory to the LORD" (v. 16) is a way to avert the disaster to come. If so, then Jeremiah's message functions as a call for repentance and change on the part of the people.
13:18–19 These verses point to a particular source of pride, the king and queen mother. This short section is the only one in Jeremiah in which the role of the queen mother is taken up.
13:20–27 Just as neither Ethiopians (Africans) nor leopards can change the distinctive color of their skin, so the evil propensity of God's people cannot be removed by their own hand. Jerusalem is personified as a prostitute whose private parts are shamefully exposed.

The concluding question (v. 27) assumes that Jerusalem could at least seek the Lord, who alone could heal her failures.

"because you have forgotten me
and trusted in false gods.
26 I will pull up your skirts over your face
that your shame may be seen[v]—
27 your adulteries and lustful neighings,
your shameless prostitution![w]
I have seen your detestable acts
on the hills and in the fields.[x]
Woe to you, Jerusalem!
How long will you be unclean?"[y]

Drought, Famine, Sword

14 This is the word of the LORD that came to Jeremiah concerning the drought:

2 "Judah mourns,[z]
her cities languish;
they wail for the land,
and a cry goes up from Jerusalem.
3 The nobles send their servants for water;
they go to the cisterns
but find no water.[a]
They return with their jars unfilled;
dismayed and despairing,
they cover their heads.[b]
4 The ground is cracked
because there is no rain in the land;[c]
the farmers are dismayed
and cover their heads.
5 Even the doe in the field
deserts her newborn fawn
because there is no grass.[d]
6 Wild donkeys stand on the barren heights[e]
and pant like jackals;
their eyes fail
for lack of food."

7 Although our sins testify[f] against us,
do something, LORD, for the sake of your name.
For we have often rebelled;[g]
we have sinned[h] against you.
8 You who are the hope[i] of Israel,
its Savior in times of distress,
why are you like a stranger in the land,
like a traveler who stays only a night?
9 Why are you like a man taken by surprise,
like a warrior powerless to save?[j]
You are among[k] us, LORD,
and we bear your name;[l]
do not forsake us!

10 This is what the LORD says about this people:

"They greatly love to wander;
they do not restrain their feet.[m]
So the LORD does not accept[n] them;
he will now remember[o] their wickedness
and punish them for their sins."[p]

11 Then the LORD said to me, "Do not
pray[q] for the well-being of this people.
12 Although they fast, I will not listen to
their cry;[r] though they offer burnt offerings[s] and grain offerings, I will not
accept[t] them. Instead, I will destroy them
with the sword, famine and plague."
13 But I said, "Alas, Sovereign LORD! The
prophets keep telling them, 'You will not
see the sword or suffer famine.[u] Indeed, I
will give you lasting peace in this place.'"
14 Then the LORD said to me, "The
prophets are prophesying lies[v] in my
name. I have not sent[w] them or appointed them or spoken to them. They are
prophesying to you false visions,[x] divinations,[y] idolatries[a] and the delusions
of their own minds. 15 Therefore this is
what the LORD says about the prophets

13:26 [v] La 1:8; Eze 16:37; Hos 2:10
13:27 [w] Jer 2:20 [x] Eze 6:13 [y] Hos 8:5
14:2 [z] Isa 3:26; Jer 8:21
14:3 [a] 2Ki 18:31; Job 6:19-20 [b] 2Sa 15:30
14:4 [c] Jer 3:3
14:5 [d] Isa 15:6
14:6 [e] Job 39:5-6; Jer 2:24
14:7 [f] Hos 5:5 [g] Jer 5:6 [h] Jer 8:14
14:8 [i] Jer 17:13
14:9 [j] Isa 50:2 [k] Jer 8:19 [l] Isa 63:19; Jer 15:16
14:10 [m] Ps 119:101; Jer 2:25 [n] Jer 6:20; Am 5:22 [o] Hos 9:9 [p] Jer 44:21-23; Hos 8:13
14:11 [q] Ex 32:10
14:12 [r] Isa 1:15; Jer 11:11 [s] Jer 7:21 [t] Jer 6:20
14:13 [u] Jer 5:12
14:14 [v] Jer 27:14 [w] Jer 23:21, 32 [x] Jer 23:16 [y] Eze 12:24

[a] 14 Or *visions, worthless divinations*

✣ **13:1-27** Perhaps modern Christians should give more consideration to the impact of symbolic acts as part of their discipleship. Communication involves not just words but deeds. Is this not true on both an individual and a corporate scale? A church that refuses to move from a changing neighborhood is making a statement as surely as is the church that moves. A Christian who volunteers in the nursery program "speaks" as surely as the teacher of a class. The church that refuses to play the insidious games of nationalism or racism speaks as well.

14:1-6 Judah and Jerusalem mourn over the devastating effects of a drought.
14:7-9 The people confess their sin against God. In confessional terms God is described as Israel's hope and Savior in troubled times (v. 8). Verse 9 reflects the tradition of God as a valiant warrior who defends and delivers his people.
14:10-16 This mostly prose section records the "give and take" between God and the prophet. Verse 10 contains a poetic oracle that God does not accept the people. In vv. 11 and 14 come autobiographical introductions: "Then the LORD said to me." Jeremiah is told to not pray for the people. Prophets who have led the people astray are obviously making Jeremiah's life more difficult by

who are prophesying in my name: I did
not send them, yet they are saying, 'No
sword or famine will touch this land.'
Those same prophets will perish[z] by
sword and famine.[a] 16And the people
they are prophesying to will be thrown
out into the streets of Jerusalem because
of the famine and sword. There will be
no one to bury[b] them, their wives, their
sons and their daughters.[c] I will pour
out on them the calamity they deserve.[d]

17"Speak this word to them:

"'Let my eyes overflow with tears[e]
night and day without ceasing;
for the Virgin Daughter, my people,
has suffered a grievous wound,
a crushing blow.[f]
18If I go into the country,
I see those slain by the sword;
if I go into the city,
I see the ravages of famine.[g]
Both prophet and priest
have gone to a land they know
not.'"

19Have you rejected Judah
completely?[h]
Do you despise Zion?
Why have you afflicted us
so that we cannot be healed?[i]
We hoped for peace
but no good has come,
for a time of healing
but there is only terror.[j]
20We acknowledge our wickedness,
LORD,
and the guilt of our ancestors;
we have indeed sinned[k] against
you.
21For the sake of your name[l] do not
despise us;
do not dishonor your glorious
throne.[m]

14:15 [z]Eze 14:9 [a]Jer 5:12-13
14:16 [b]Ps 79:3 [c]Jer 7:33 [d]Pr 1:31
14:17 [e]Jer 9:1 [f]Jer 8:21
14:18 [g]Eze 7:15
14:19 [h]Jer 7:29 [i]Jer 30:12-13 [j]Jer 8:15
14:20 [k]Da 9:7-8
14:21 [l]ver 7 [m]Jer 3:17
14:22 [n]Ps 135:7
15:1 [o]Ex 32:11; Nu 14:13-20 [p]1Sa 7:9 [q]Jer 7:16; Eze 14:14,20 [r]2Ki 17:20
15:2 [s]Jer 43:11 [t]Jer 14:12 [u]Rev 13:10
15:3 [v]Lev 26:16 [w]Dt 28:26 [x]Lev 26:22; Eze 14:21
15:4 [y]Jer 24:9; 29:18 [z]Dt 28:25 [a]2Ki 21:2; 23:26-27
15:5 [b]Isa 51:19; Jer 13:14; 21:7; Na 3:7
15:6 [c]Jer 6:19; 7:24

Jer 14:14–16 ❖ How can we identify false prophets today (see Mt 7:16)?

Remember your covenant with us
and do not break it.
22Do any of the worthless idols of the
nations bring rain?[n]
Do the skies themselves send
down showers?
No, it is you, LORD our God.
Therefore our hope is in you,
for you are the one who does all
this.

15 Then the LORD said to me: "Even if
Moses[o] and Samuel[p] were to stand
before me, my heart would not go out
to this people.[q] Send them away from
my presence![r] Let them go! 2And if they
ask you, 'Where shall we go?' tell them,
'This is what the LORD says:

"'Those destined for death, to
death;
those for the sword, to the sword;[s]
those for starvation, to starvation;[t]
those for captivity, to captivity.'[u]

3"I will send four kinds of destroyers[v]
against them," declares the LORD, "the
sword to kill and the dogs to drag away
and the birds[w] and the wild animals to
devour and destroy.[x] 4I will make them
abhorrent[y] to all the kingdoms of the
earth[z] because of what Manasseh[a] son of
Hezekiah king of Judah did in Jerusalem.

5"Who will have pity[b] on you,
Jerusalem?
Who will mourn for you?
Who will stop to ask how you are?
6You have rejected[c] me," declares the
LORD.
"You keep on backsliding.

---

speaking in the Lord's name and contradicting his own prophecies of judgment.

14:17–18 These two verses offer an example of lament in which it is difficult to know who is speaking, Jeremiah or God. "The Virgin Daughter, my people" (v. 17) reflects more naturally on God as speaker than the prophet.

14:19–22 The second corporate confession/petition of the people asks plaintively if God has completely rejected Judah and Zion. With the confession of sin also comes the refrain, "For the sake of your name do not despise us" (v. 21; cf. vv. 7, 9), and a plea for God to remember his covenant with them and not to annul it.

15:1–9 The reference to Moses and Samuel as mediators and intercessors evokes the memory of past events in Israel's history (Ex 32:30–35; 34:1–27). In the work of Moses and Samuel, one finds models of God moving to preserve his people after intercessory prayers.

For God to dismiss the work of Moses and Samuel as valuable in the present moment of Judah's sin is, in effect, to say that judgment cannot be averted. Judgment to come is described graphically in Jer 15:2. Jeremiah cites the lingering effects of Manasseh's reign (v. 4) as reasons for the coming judgment. This accusation has parallels in 2Ki 21:1–18; 23:26; 24:3–4, where the judgment to come on Judah and Jerusalem in Jeremiah's day derives from the overflowing wickedness of Manasseh's reign.

So I will reach out[d] and destroy you;
I am tired of holding back.
7 I will winnow them with a winnowing fork
at the city gates of the land.
I will bring bereavement and destruction on my people,[e]
for they have not changed their ways.
8 I will make their widows more numerous
than the sand of the sea.
At midday I will bring a destroyer[f]
against the mothers of their young men;
suddenly I will bring down on them
anguish and terror.
9 The mother of seven will grow faint[g]
and breathe her last.
Her sun will set while it is still day;
she will be disgraced and humiliated.
I will put the survivors to the sword[h]
before their enemies,"
declares the LORD.

10 Alas, my mother, that you gave me birth,[i]
a man with whom the whole land strives and contends![j]
I have neither lent[k] nor borrowed,
yet everyone curses me.

11 The LORD said,

"Surely I will deliver you[l] for a good purpose;
surely I will make your enemies plead[m] with you
in times of disaster and times of distress.

12 "Can a man break iron —
iron from the north[n] — or bronze?

13 "Your wealth and your treasures
I will give as plunder, without charge,[o]
because of all your sins
throughout your country.[p]
14 I will enslave you to your enemies
in[a] a land you do not know,[q]
for my anger will kindle a fire[r]
that will burn against you."

15 LORD, you understand;
remember me and care for me.
Avenge me on my persecutors.[s]
You are long-suffering — do not take me away;
think of how I suffer reproach for your sake.[t]
16 When your words came, I ate[u] them;
they were my joy and my heart's delight,[v]
for I bear your name,[w]
LORD God Almighty.
17 I never sat[x] in the company of revelers,
never made merry with them;
I sat alone because your hand was on me
and you had filled me with indignation.

15:6 [d] Zep 1:4
15:7 [e] Jer 18:21
15:8 [f] Jer 6:4
15:9 [g] 1Sa 2:5 [h] Jer 21:7
15:10 [i] Job 3:1 [j] Jer 1:19 [k] Lev 25:36
15:11 [l] Jer 40:4 [m] Jer 21:1-2; 37:3; 42:1-3
15:12 [n] Jer 28:14
15:13 [o] Ps 44:12 [p] Jer 17:3
15:14 [q] Dt 28:36; Jer 16:13 [r] Dt 32:22; Ps 21:9
15:15 [s] Jer 12:3 [t] Ps 69:7-9
15:16 [u] Eze 3:3; Rev 10:10 [v] Ps 119:72,103 [w] Jer 14:9
15:17 [x] Ps 1:1; 26:4-5; Jer 16:8

[a] 14 Some Hebrew manuscripts, Septuagint and Syriac (see also 17:4); most Hebrew manuscripts *I will cause your enemies to bring you / into*

14:1—15:9 Many prayers for rain are heard frequently during months of drought. Dry conditions are an effective reminder of how easily life can get out of balance and how circumstances of drought can only be remedied from above. Nevertheless, when rain finally comes, drought conditions are quickly forgotten. Jeremiah 14 is a beneficial reminder of the true source of life and of the One who calls a people into existence for his glory and praise.

15:10 In this verse Jeremiah laments his birth and therefore is similar to Job (Job 3). His contemporaries curse him, and the pain of his isolation has made even God seem deceitful and unreliable to him. He feels as if there is no purpose for him to continue living. Such language is an indication of despair, not plans for suicide. Jeremiah describes the "curses" that have come to him.

15:11 God replies that he will deliver Jeremiah for a "good purpose" and will bring his enemies to a place where they will need to plead with him. This last comment perhaps leads to the further pronouncement of judgment on Judah in the next passage.

15:12–14 The text of v. 12 and the interpretation of these three verses is difficult. The best overall option is to see all three verses as a judgment speech on Judah. They repeat material found in 17:3–4, where the context is clearly judgment on the people.

15:15–18 Jeremiah turns once again to the Lord. As part of his complaint he notes that his enemies are also God's enemies. Jeremiah suffers his reproach because he represents God's word to the people. He describes encountering God's words with the surprising claim that he "ate" them, and they became his joy (v. 16).

Jeremiah confesses that he feels God's hand, that God is the source of the resentment he experiences. As his emotions boil over, the prophet asks God why his (Jeremiah's) pain is unending and why he (God) has become like failing water.

18 Why is my pain unending
 and my wound grievous and
  incurable?[y]
You are to me like a deceptive brook,
 like a spring that fails.[z]

19 Therefore this is what the LORD says:

"If you repent, I will restore you
 that you may serve[a] me;
if you utter worthy, not worthless,
  words,
 you will be my spokesman.
Let this people turn to you,
 but you must not turn to them.
20 I will make you a wall to this
  people,
 a fortified wall of bronze;
they will fight against you
 but will not overcome you,
for I am with you
 to rescue and save you,"[b]
   declares the LORD.
21 "I will save you from the hands of
  the wicked
 and deliver[c] you from the grasp of
  the cruel."[d]

Day of Disaster

16 Then the word of the LORD came
to me: 2"You must not marry[e] and
have sons or daughters in this place."
3For this is what the LORD says about
the sons and daughters born in this
land and about the women who are
their mothers and the men who are
their fathers:[f] 4"They will die of deadly
diseases. They will not be mourned or
buried[g] but will be like dung lying on
the ground.[h] They will perish by sword
and famine, and their dead bodies will
become food for the birds and the wild
animals."[i]
5For this is what the LORD says: "Do
not enter a house where there is a funeral meal; do not go to mourn or show
sympathy, because I have withdrawn
my blessing, my love and my pity from
this people," declares the LORD. 6"Both
high and low will die in this land.[j] They
will not be buried or mourned, and no
one will cut[k] themselves or shave[l] their
head for the dead. 7No one will offer food
to comfort those who mourn[m] for the
dead — not even for a father or a mother — nor will anyone give them a drink
to console them.
8"And do not enter a house where
there is feasting and sit down to eat
and drink.[n] 9For this is what the LORD
Almighty, the God of Israel, says: Before your eyes and in your days I will
bring an end to the sounds[o] of joy and
gladness and to the voices of bride and
bridegroom in this place.[p]
10"When you tell these people all this
and they ask you, 'Why has the LORD decreed such a great disaster against us?

15:18 [y] Jer 30:15; Mic 1:9 [z] Job 6:15
15:19 [a] Zec 3:7
15:20 [b] Jer 20:11; Eze 3:8
15:21 [c] Jer 50:34 [d] Ge 48:16
16:2 [e] 1Co 7:26-27
16:3 [f] Jer 6:21
16:4 [g] Jer 25:33 [h] Ps 83:10; Jer 9:22 [i] Ps 79:1-3; Jer 15:3; 34:20
16:6 [j] Eze 9:5-6 [k] Lev 19:28 [l] Jer 41:5; 47:5
16:7 [m] Eze 24:17; Hos 9:4
16:8 [n] Ecc 7:2-4; Jer 15:17
16:9 [o] Isa 24:8; Eze 26:13; Hos 2:11 [p] Rev 18:23

Jer 15:20 ❖ When have you felt God's protective hand at work in your life?

Jer 16:10-13 ❖ Are there "generational sins" in our families? Where have we seen sins passed down from parents that grow worse in the lives of their children?

15:19–21 God's reply is not to deal with the particulars of Jeremiah's anger but to remind him that the path of the faithful and obedient prophet is still open to him. God has called him to prophesy in this historical hour of judgment.

Verse 19 has two plays on the verb "turn/return." If Jeremiah will "repent" (i.e., change his tune and direction), then God will "restore" him (v. 19a). The same Hebrew word is used in both cases. Using the same verb, God states that the people should "turn" to Jeremiah but that Jeremiah should not "turn" to them (v. 19b). Verses 20–21 are reminiscent of Jeremiah's initial call in 1:18–19. He still has the same task ahead of him and the same assurance that God is with him.

✣ **15:10–21** Ministry can be painful and costly. Jeremiah's lament shows one of God's chosen vessels suffering because of his service to God. His life is an OT form of Jesus' call to discipleship: Take up your cross and follow me (Lk 9:23). Even when Jeremiah is stretched seemingly to the breaking point, God reminds him of his call to prophetic ministry. For the prophet there is no alternative but to turn (return) once again to the Lord, who called him and promised him protection.

16:1–9 God commands Jeremiah not to marry or have children, since judgment is coming soon. Jeremiah is not to enter a house for feasting or celebration either, for the joy of a bride and groom will also be silenced in the coming devastation. Here again he bears the mark of his ministry.

16:10–13 "Why such judgment?" the people ask (cf. v. 10). The answer is the crushing reply that both their ancestors and the current generation have forsaken the Lord. The current generation is particularly stubborn and motivated by an evil heart. The punishment for having "defiled" (v. 18) God's land is to be cast from the land and humiliated in exile by worshiping other deities.

What wrong have we done? What sin
have we committed against the LORD
our God?'[q] 11 then say to them, 'It is because your ancestors forsook me,' declares the LORD, 'and followed other gods
and served and worshiped them. They
forsook me and did not keep my law.[r]
12 But you have behaved more wickedly
than your ancestors.[s] See how all of you
are following the stubbornness of your
evil hearts[t] instead of obeying me. 13 So
I will throw you out of this land into a
land neither you nor your ancestors have
known,[u] and there you will serve other
gods[v] day and night, for I will show you
no favor.'[w]

14 "However, the days are coming," declares the LORD, "when it will no longer
be said, 'As surely as the LORD lives, who
brought the Israelites up out of Egypt,'[x]
15 but it will be said, 'As surely as the LORD
lives, who brought the Israelites up out
of the land of the north and out of all the
countries where he had banished them.'[y]
For I will restore[z] them to the land I gave
their ancestors.

16 "But now I will send for many fishermen," declares the LORD, "and they
will catch them.[a] After that I will send
for many hunters, and they will hunt[b]
them down on every mountain and hill
and from the crevices of the rocks.[c] 17 My
eyes are on all their ways; they are not
hidden[d] from me, nor is their sin concealed from my eyes.[e] 18 I will repay them
double[f] for their wickedness and their
sin, because they have defiled my land[g]
with the lifeless forms of their vile images and have filled my inheritance with
their detestable idols."

16:10 [q] Dt 29:24; Jer 5:19
16:11 [r] Dt 29:25-26; 1Ki 9:9; Ps 106:35-43; Jer 22:9
16:12 [s] Jer 7:26 [t] Ecc 9:3; Jer 13:10
16:13 [u] Dt 28:36; Jer 5:19 [v] Dt 4:28 [w] Jer 15:5
16:14 [x] Dt 15:15; Jer 23:7-8
16:15 [y] Isa 11:11; Jer 23:8 [z] Jer 24:6
16:16 [a] Am 4:2; Hab 1:14-15 [b] Am 9:3; Mic 7:2 [c] 1Sa 26:20
16:17 [d] 1Co 4:5; Heb 4:13 [e] Pr 15:3
16:18 [f] Isa 40:2; Rev 18:6 [g] Nu 35:34; Jer 2:7
16:19 [h] Isa 2:2; Jer 3:17 [i] Ps 4:2
16:20 [j] Ps 115:4-7; Isa 37:19; Jer 2:11
17:1 [k] Job 19:24 [l] Pr 3:3; 2Co 3:3
17:2 [m] 2Ch 24:18 [n] Jer 2:20
17:3 [o] 2Ki 24:13 [p] Jer 26:18; Mic 3:12 [q] Jer 15:13
17:4 [r] La 5:2 [s] Dt 28:48; Jer 12:7 [t] Jer 16:13

19 LORD, my strength and my fortress,
my refuge in time of distress,
to you the nations will come[h]
from the ends of the earth and
say,
"Our ancestors possessed nothing
but false gods,[i]
worthless idols that did them no
good.
20 Do people make their own gods?
Yes, but they are not gods!"[j]

21 "Therefore I will teach them —
this time I will teach them
my power and might.
Then they will know
that my name is the LORD.

17 "Judah's sin is engraved with an
iron tool,[k]
inscribed with a flint point,
on the tablets of their hearts[l]
and on the horns of their altars.
2 Even their children remember
their altars and Asherah poles[a][m]
beside the spreading trees
and on the high hills.[n]
3 My mountain in the land
and your[b] wealth and all your
treasures
I will give away as plunder,[o]
together with your high places,[p]
because of sin throughout your
country.[q]
4 Through your own fault you will lose
the inheritance[r] I gave you.
I will enslave you to your enemies[s]
in a land[t] you do not know,

[a] 2 That is, wooden symbols of the goddess Asherah [b] *2,3* Or *hills / 3and the mountains of the land. / Your*

16:14–15 God announces that the judgment of the exile will be matched by the saving exodus from foreign territory and back to the promised land.
16:16–18 The announcement of fishing and hunting for offenders in foreign lands is obscure. Perhaps these are a reply to the sarcasm of people who say that God will not judge them for their sins in exile. God is not limited by geography.
16:19–21 Along with the confession of the people's sinfulness is an affirmation that "the nations will come" to God (v. 19). God is the prophet's refuge and strength—characteristics that separate him from the foolishness of idols. This leads to the declaration that God has acted in history so that people may know that his name is Yahweh (cf. Ex 6:3).

✣ **16:1–21** Knowledge of God is not mere intellectual comprehension or understanding—even the devil and his demons believe that God exists (Jas 2:19). True knowledge of God is formed in relationship with him and in obedience to his claims of exclusive worship. God serves as a fortress and refuge to those who trust him and who humbly seek to follow his revealed will. God is also a righteous Judge whose timing in judging sin should not be confused with indifference.

17:1 Judah's sinfulness is described as "engraved with an iron tool . . . on the tablets of their hearts" (v. 1). This metaphor underscores the permanent nature of sin and its corrosive effects on the people.
17:2–4 "Asherah poles" are evidence for Judah's defection from the Lord, along with the people's embracing of false worship. Recovered inscriptions from ancient Judah contain references to "YHWH and his Asherah." These texts demonstrate a kind of unhealthy syncretism from the time of Jeremiah.

for you have kindled my anger,
and it will burn[u] forever."

5This is what the LORD says:

"Cursed is the one who trusts in man,[v]
who draws strength from mere flesh
and whose heart turns away from the LORD.
6That person will be like a bush in the wastelands;
they will not see prosperity when it comes.
They will dwell in the parched places of the desert,
in a salt[w] land where no one lives.

7"But blessed is the one who trusts[x] in the LORD,
whose confidence is in him.
8They will be like a tree planted by the water
that sends out its roots by the stream.
It does not fear when heat comes;
its leaves are always green.
It has no worries in a year of drought[y]
and never fails to bear fruit."[z]

9The heart[a] is deceitful above all things
and beyond cure.
Who can understand it?

10"I the LORD search the heart[b]
and examine the mind,[c]
to reward[d] each person according to their conduct,
according to what their deeds deserve."[e]

11Like a partridge that hatches eggs it did not lay

Jer 17:7-10 ❖ What do we think God sees when he examines our hearts? How does Christ give us hope despite God's full knowledge of our thoughts (see 2Co 5:17)?

are those who gain riches by unjust means.
When their lives are half gone, their riches will desert them,
and in the end they will prove to be fools.[f]

12A glorious throne,[g] exalted from the beginning,
is the place of our sanctuary.
13LORD, you are the hope[h] of Israel;
all who forsake[i] you will be put to shame.
Those who turn away from you will be written in the dust
because they have forsaken the LORD,
the spring of living water.

14Heal me, LORD, and I will be healed;
save me and I will be saved,
for you are the one I praise.[j]
15They keep saying to me,
"Where is the word of the LORD?
Let it now be fulfilled!"[k]
16I have not run away from being your shepherd;
you know I have not desired the day of despair.
What passes my lips is open before you.
17Do not be a terror[l] to me;
you are my refuge[m] in the day of disaster.
18Let my persecutors be put to shame,
but keep me from shame;
let them be terrified,
but keep me from terror.

17:4 [u] Jer 7:20; 15:14
17:5 [v] Isa 2:22; 30:1-3
17:6 [w] Dt 29:23; Job 39:6
17:7 [x] Ps 34:8; 40:4; Pr 16:20
17:8 [y] Jer 14:1-6 [z] Ps 1:3; 92:12-14
17:9 [a] Ecc 9:3; Mt 13:15; Mk 7:21-22
17:10 [b] 1Sa 16:7; Rev 2:23 [c] Ps 17:3; 139:23; Jer 11:20; 20:12; Ro 8:27 [d] Ps 62:12; Jer 32:19 [e] Ro 2:6
17:11 [f] Lk 12:20
17:12 [g] Jer 3:17
17:13 [h] Jer 14:8 [i] Isa 1:28; Jer 2:17
17:14 [j] Ps 109:1
17:15 [k] Isa 5:19; 2Pe 3:4
17:17 [l] Ps 88:15-16 [m] Jer 16:19; Na 1:7

17:5-8 This passage reads like a "play" on Ps 1. The contrast is between trust in human effort and reliance on God.

17:9-13 Verse 9 presents the heart as the source of deceitfulness. The depths of its potential depravity are difficult to measure. Part of what God does in overseeing blessings and curses is to connect the disposition of the human heart and the deeds that flow from it.

Verse 11 is another proverbial statement. Jeremiah's use of this proverb suggests a connection between Judah's "gains" from idolatry and the sad loss of its land and freedom. Only a fool would want such gains.

17:12-13 These two verses join the blessing of the sanctuary with God's presence as "the spring of living water" (cf. 2:13). That God is "the hope of Israel" (17:13) has been used by Jeremiah before (14:8).

17:14-18 "Healing" likely means the kind of restoration of emotional and physical well-being that only God can grant. Since Jeremiah has been the object of scorn and ridicule, his acceptance by God is crucial to his survival.

The prophet reminds God that he has walked the path of discipleship. He has taken no joy in announcing a day of despair. It is almost as if waiting for the prophecies of disaster to be fulfilled has made Jeremiah feel separated from God, so he prays that God will be his "refuge" (v. 17).

Bring on them the day of disaster;
destroy them with double
destruction.[n]

Keeping the Sabbath Day Holy

19This is what the LORD said to me:
"Go and stand at the Gate of the People,[a]
through which the kings of Judah go in
and out; stand also at all the other gates
of Jerusalem.[o] 20Say to them, 'Hear the
word of the LORD, you kings of Judah and
all people of Judah and everyone living
in Jerusalem[p] who come through these
gates.[q] 21This is what the LORD says: Be
careful not to carry a load on the Sabbath[r] day or bring it through the gates
of Jerusalem. 22Do not bring a load out
of your houses or do any work on the
Sabbath, but keep the Sabbath day holy,
as I commanded your ancestors.[s] 23Yet
they did not listen or pay attention;[t]
they were stiff-necked[u] and would not
listen or respond to discipline.[v] 24But
if you are careful to obey me, declares
the LORD, and bring no load through the
gates of this city on the Sabbath, but keep
the Sabbath day holy by not doing any
work on it, 25then kings who sit on David's throne[w] will come through the gates
of this city with their officials. They and
their officials will come riding in chariots
and on horses, accompanied by the men
of Judah and those living in Jerusalem,
and this city will be inhabited forever.
26People will come from the towns of Judah and the villages around Jerusalem,
from the territory of Benjamin and the
western foothills, from the hill country
and the Negev,[x] bringing burnt offerings and sacrifices, grain offerings and
incense, and bringing thank offerings
to the house of the LORD. 27But if you
do not obey[y] me to keep the Sabbath
day holy by not carrying any load as you
come through the gates of Jerusalem on
the Sabbath day, then I will kindle an
unquenchable fire[z] in the gates of Jerusalem that will consume her fortresses.' "[a]

17:18 [n] Ps 35:1-8
17:19 [o] Jer 7:2; 26:2
17:20 [p] Jer 19:3 [q] Jer 22:2
17:21 [r] Nu 15:32-36; Ne 13:15-21; Jn 5:10
17:22 [s] Ex 20:8; 31:13; Isa 56:2-6; Eze 20:12
17:23 [t] Jer 7:26 [u] Jer 19:15 [v] Jer 7:28
17:25 [w] 2Sa 7:13; Isa 9:7; Jer 22:2, 4; Lk 1:32
17:26 [x] Jer 32:44; 33:13; Zec 7:7
17:27 [y] Jer 22:5 [z] Jer 7:20 [a] 2Ki 25:9; Am 2:5
18:6 [b] Isa 45:9; Ro 9:20-21
18:7 [c] Jer 1:10
18:8 [d] Jer 26:13; Jnh 3:8-10 [e] Eze 18:21; Hos 11:8-9
18:9 [f] Jer 1:10; 31:28

Jer 18:6 ❖ How is God shaping us, like clay in the hands of a potter?

At the Potter's House

18 This is the word that came to Jeremiah from the LORD: 2"Go down to
the potter's house, and there I will give
you my message." 3So I went down to the
potter's house, and I saw him working at
the wheel. 4But the pot he was shaping
from the clay was marred in his hands;
so the potter formed it into another pot,
shaping it as seemed best to him.
5Then the word of the LORD came to
me. 6He said, "Can I not do with you,
Israel, as this potter does?" declares the
LORD. "Like clay[b] in the hand of the potter, so are you in my hand, Israel. 7If at
any time I announce that a nation or
kingdom is to be uprooted,[c] torn down
and destroyed, 8and if that nation I
warned repents of its evil, then I will
relent[d] and not inflict on it the disaster[e]
I had planned. 9And if at another time I
announce that a nation or kingdom is to
be built[f] up and planted, 10and if it does

[a] 19 Or *Army*

17:19–27 In his temple sermon, Jeremiah charged the people with several failures, including theft, murder, and perjury (7:9). These terms come from the Ten Commandments.

Note that Jeremiah's specific accusation in these verses concerns carrying loads on the Sabbath (i.e., working rather than refraining from labor). Resting from work helped make the Sabbath day holy. If God's people honor him by keeping the Sabbath, then not only Jerusalem but the various regions of Judah will be inhabited, and right worship will be offered to the Lord. This is the one place in the chapter that suggests a role for repentance and renewed obedience to God's law.

✣ **17:1–27** To proclaim that God has spoken decisively to the world in Jesus Christ, we must recover the doctrine of the corporate nature of sin. In the modern West, places to start a conversation are the prevalence of addictive behavior, racism, random violence, and other evils. All of these phenomena in Western societies are symptomatic of larger issues of human existence, and they stand under the judgment of God's Word. Nevertheless, they defy easy explanation or cure. They are irrational, and they lead to more of the same in spirals of self-destruction.

18:1–11 Jeremiah's visit to the workshop is what might be termed a "parable in action." The meaning of this illustration is clear: Just as the potter may form and reform the same clay until he is either satisfied or decides to dump the clay completely, so God can form and reform the house of Israel (v. 6). If God announces judgment on a nation and that nation repents, then that judgment can be reversed or simply canceled. Correspondingly, if God has announced goodness for a kingdom and it acts faithlessly, then that good can also be reversed.

evil[g] in my sight and does not obey me,
then I will reconsider[h] the good I had
intended to do for it.
11"Now therefore say to the people of
Judah and those living in Jerusalem,
'This is what the LORD says: Look! I am
preparing a disaster[i] for you and devising
a plan against you. So turn[j] from your
evil ways,[k] each one of you, and reform
your ways and your actions.' 12But they
will reply, 'It's no use.[l] We will continue
with our own plans; we will all follow the
stubbornness of our evil hearts.'"

13Therefore this is what the LORD says:

"Inquire among the nations:
Who has ever heard anything like
this?[m]
A most horrible[n] thing has been
done
by Virgin Israel.
14 Does the snow of Lebanon
ever vanish from its rocky slopes?
Do its cool waters from distant
sources
ever stop flowing?[a]
15 Yet my people have forgotten me;
they burn incense to worthless
idols,[o]
which made them stumble in their
ways,
in the ancient paths.[p]
They made them walk in byways,
on roads not built up.[q]
16 Their land will be an object of
horror[r]
and of lasting scorn;[s]
all who pass by will be appalled
and will shake their heads.[t]
17 Like a wind[u] from the east,
I will scatter them before their
enemies;
I will show them my back and not
my face[v]
in the day of their disaster."

18They said, "Come, let's make plans[w]
against Jeremiah; for the teaching of the
law by the priest[x] will not cease, nor will
counsel from the wise, nor the word from
the prophets.[y] So come, let's attack him
with our tongues[z] and pay no attention
to anything he says."

19 Listen to me, LORD;
hear what my accusers are saying!
20 Should good be repaid with evil?
Yet they have dug a pit[a] for me.
Remember that I stood before you
and spoke in their behalf[b]
to turn your wrath away from
them.
21 So give their children over to
famine;[c]
hand them over to the power of
the sword.
Let their wives be made childless
and widows;[d]
let their men be put to death,
their young men slain by the
sword in battle.
22 Let a cry[e] be heard from their houses
when you suddenly bring invaders
against them,
for they have dug a pit to capture me
and have hidden snares[f] for my
feet.
23 But you, LORD, know
all their plots to kill[g] me.
Do not forgive[h] their crimes
or blot out their sins from your
sight.
Let them be overthrown before you;
deal with them in the time of your
anger.

19 This is what the LORD says: "Go
and buy a clay jar from a potter.[i]
Take along some of the elders[j] of the
people and of the priests 2and go out to

[a] 14 The meaning of the Hebrew for this sentence is uncertain.

18:10 [g] Eze 33:18 [h] 1Sa 2:29-30
18:11 [i] Jer 4:6 [j] 2Ki 17:13; Isa 1:16-19 [k] Jer 7:3
18:12 [l] Isa 57:10; Jer 2:25
18:13 [m] Isa 66:8; Jer 2:10 [n] Jer 5:30
18:15 [o] Jer 10:15 [p] Jer 6:16 [q] Isa 57:14; 62:10
18:16 [r] Jer 25:9 [s] Jer 19:8 [t] Ps 22:7
18:17 [u] Jer 13:24 [v] Jer 2:27
18:18 [w] Jer 11:19 [x] Mal 2:7 [y] Jer 5:13 [z] Ps 52:2
18:20 [a] Ps 35:7; 57:6 [b] Ps 106:23
18:21 [c] Jer 11:22 [d] Ps 109:9
18:22 [e] Jer 6:26 [f] Ps 140:5
18:23 [g] Jer 11:21 [h] Ps 109:14
19:1 [i] Jer 18:2 [j] Nu 11:17

18:12 This verse puts a quote in the mouth of the people to the effect that they will follow their own stubborn heart.
18:13–17 God does not take "no" for an answer easily. This poetic reply begins with an indignant question. An appalling thing has happened; God's people have forgotten him and worshiped worthless idols.
18:18–23 Jeremiah's opponents intend to attack and ignore him. Jeremiah prays that his enemies may fall into the pit they have dug.
19:1–13 With the breaking of the jar, Jeremiah indicates the irrevocable judgment to come. Just as the smashed earthenware cannot be repaired, so Judah cannot be reformed. For original hearers and readers, there is likely added significance to the earthenware pot. Topheth likely contained a section where earthenware jars with the charred remains of sacrificial victims were collected.

Jeremiah understands Topheth as a place of defilement and its earthenware jars as symbolic of slaughter. Indeed, he gives the valley a devastating nickname: "Valley of Slaughter" (v. 6; cf. 7:32). Judgment will come on Jerusalem in such a way that there will be no other place to bury the dead except in Topheth, the place of ritual slaughter and cultic defilement.

the Valley of Ben Hinnom,[k] near the entrance of the Potsherd Gate. There proclaim the words I tell you, 3and say, 'Hear
the word of the LORD, you kings[l] of Judah
and people of Jerusalem. This is what the
LORD Almighty, the God of Israel, says:
Listen! I am going to bring a disaster[m]
on this place that will make the ears of
everyone who hears of it tingle.[n] 4For
they have forsaken[o] me and made this a
place of foreign gods; they have burned
incense[p] in it to gods that neither they
nor their ancestors nor the kings of Judah
ever knew, and they have filled this place
with the blood of the innocent.[q] 5They
have built the high places of Baal to burn
their children[r] in the fire as offerings to
Baal — something I did not command or
mention, nor did it enter my mind.[s] 6So
beware, the days are coming, declares
the LORD, when people will no longer call
this place Topheth or the Valley of Ben
Hinnom,[t] but the Valley of Slaughter.[u]
7" 'In this place I will ruin[a] the plans of
Judah and Jerusalem. I will make them
fall by the sword before their enemies,[v]
at the hands of those who want to kill
them, and I will give their carcasses[w] as
food[x] to the birds and the wild animals.
8I will devastate this city and make it an
object of horror and scorn;[y] all who pass
by will be appalled and will scoff because
of all its wounds. 9I will make them eat[z]
the flesh of their sons and daughters,
and they will eat one another's flesh because their enemies[a] will press the siege
so hard against them to destroy them.'
10"Then break the jar[b] while those who
go with you are watching, 11and say to
them, 'This is what the LORD Almighty

19:2 [k]Jos 15:8
19:3 [l]Jer 17:20 [m]Jer 6:19 [n]1Sa 3:11
19:4 [o]Dt 28:20; Isa 65:11 [p]Lev 18:21 [q]2Ki 21:16; Jer 2:34
19:5 [r]Lev 18:21; Ps 106:37-38 [s]Jer 7:31; 32:35
19:6 [t]Jos 15:8 [u]Jer 7:32
19:7 [v]Lev 26:17; Dt 28:25 [w]Jer 16:4; 34:20 [x]Ps 79:2
19:8 [y]Jer 18:16
19:9 [z]Lev 26:29; Dt 28:49-57; La 4:10 [a]Isa 9:20
19:10 [b]ver 1
19:11 [c]Ps 2:9; Isa 30:14 [d]Jer 7:32
19:13 [e]Jer 32:29; 52:13 [f]Dt 4:19; Ac 7:42 [g]Jer 7:18; Eze 20:28
19:14 [h]2Ch 20:5; Jer 26:2
19:15 [i]Ne 9:16; Jer 7:26; 17:23
20:1 [j]1Ch 24:14 [k]2Ki 25:18
20:2 [l]Jer 1:19

Jer 19:10-13 ❖ How can we find the courage, like Jeremiah, to proclaim God's hard words of judgment against wickedness and hypocrisy?

says: I will smash[c] this nation and this
city just as this potter's jar is smashed
and cannot be repaired. They will bury[d]
the dead in Topheth until there is no
more room. 12This is what I will do to
this place and to those who live here,
declares the LORD. I will make this city
like Topheth. 13The houses[e] in Jerusalem and those of the kings of Judah will
be defiled like this place, Topheth — all
the houses where they burned incense
on the roofs to all the starry hosts[f] and
poured out drink offerings[g] to other
gods.' "
14Jeremiah then returned from Topheth, where the LORD had sent him to
prophesy, and stood in the court[h] of the
LORD's temple and said to all the people, 15"This is what the LORD Almighty,
the God of Israel, says: 'Listen! I am
going to bring on this city and all the
villages around it every disaster I pronounced against them, because they
were stiff-necked[i] and would not listen
to my words.' "

Jeremiah and Pashhur

20 When the priest Pashhur son of
Immer,[j] the official[k] in charge of
the temple of the LORD, heard Jeremiah
prophesying these things, 2he had Jeremiah the prophet beaten[l] and put in the

[a] 7 The Hebrew for *ruin* sounds like the Hebrew for *jar* (see verses 1 and 10).

19:14–15 Jeremiah leaves Topheth and goes to the courtyard of the temple to proclaim that God will "bring on this city and all the villages around it every disaster [he] pronounced against them, because they were stiff-necked and would not listen to [his] words" (v. 15). His presence in the temple courtyard is tantamount to bringing the defilement of Topheth into the temple (entering a cemetery or touching a corpse rendered a person ceremonially unclean). Furthermore, the reference to "stiff-necked" people points to the failure of the people to recognize the possibility of repentance that was announced in 18:7-11.

✣ **18:1—19:15** In authentic discussions about God's purpose and goodness, there is an inherent reference to a future entrusted to God; it is a future we finite humans cannot completely understand. We are called to trust in the work of the Potter, to walk by faith and not by sight, and to accept God's judgment in the present in the hope that the Potter will reshape the future.

20:1–3 Pashhur represents the religious establishment, especially the priests who care for and officiate at the temple. In fact, he is described as the chief officer at the temple.

Pashhur is from a segment of the population who prove to be some of Jeremiah's most persistent persecutors. With the temple looming in the background, Jeremiah's treatment is portrayed as God's judgment on him, carried out by the priests who care for God's house. Upon his release, Jeremiah gives Pashhur a new name, "Terror on Every Side" (v. 3). The Hebrew expression occurs elsewhere in Jeremiah to describe the plight of Judah when the foe from the north comes against the state and its capital city.

stocks[m] at the Upper Gate of Benjamin[n] at
the LORD's temple. 3The next day, when
Pashhur released him from the stocks,
Jeremiah said to him, "The LORD's name
for you is not Pashhur, but Terror on Every Side.[o] 4For this is what the LORD says:
'I will make you a terror to yourself and to
all your friends; with your own eyes[p] you
will see them fall by the sword of their enemies. I will give[q] all Judah into the hands
of the king of Babylon, who will carry[r]
them away to Babylon or put them to the
sword. 5I will deliver all the wealth[s] of this
city into the hands of their enemies — all
its products, all its valuables and all the
treasures of the kings of Judah. They will
take it away[t] as plunder and carry it off
to Babylon. 6And you, Pashhur, and all
who live in your house will go into exile to Babylon. There you will die and be
buried, you and all your friends to whom
you have prophesied[u] lies.' "

Jeremiah's Complaint

7You deceived[a] me, LORD, and I was
deceived[a];
you overpowered me and
prevailed.
I am ridiculed all day long;
everyone mocks me.
8Whenever I speak, I cry out
proclaiming violence and
destruction.[v]
So the word of the LORD has
brought me
insult and reproach[w] all day long.
9But if I say, "I will not mention his
word
or speak anymore in his name,"
his word is in my heart like a fire,[x]
a fire shut up in my bones.

Jer 20:7-10 ❖ When have you struggled with what God put you through? How have you voiced your complaints to God?

I am weary of holding it in;[y]
indeed, I cannot.
10I hear many whispering,
"Terror[z] on every side!
Denounce[a] him! Let's denounce
him!"
All my friends[b]
are waiting for me to slip,[c] saying,
"Perhaps he will be deceived;
then we will prevail[d] over him
and take our revenge on him."

11But the LORD[e] is with me like a
mighty warrior;
so my persecutors[f] will stumble
and not prevail.[g]
They will fail and be thoroughly
disgraced;[h]
their dishonor will never be
forgotten.
12LORD Almighty, you who examine
the righteous
and probe the heart and mind,[i]
let me see your vengeance[j] on them,
for to you I have committed[k] my
cause.

13Sing to the LORD!
Give praise to the LORD!
He rescues[l] the life of the needy
from the hands of the wicked.

14Cursed be the day I was born![m]
May the day my mother bore me
not be blessed!

[a] 7 Or *persuaded*

20:2 [m] Job 13:27 [n] Jer 37:13; 38:7; Zec 14:10
20:3 [o] ver 10
20:4 [p] Jer 29:21 [q] Jer 21:10 [r] Jer 52:27
20:5 [s] Jer 17:3 [t] 2Ki 20:17
20:6 [u] Jer 14:15; La 2:14
20:8 [v] Jer 6:7 [w] 2Ch 36:16; Jer 6:10
20:9 [x] Ps 39:3
[y] Job 32:18-20; Ac 4:20
20:10 [z] Ps 31:13; Jer 6:25 [a] Isa 29:21 [b] Ps 41:9 [c] Lk 11:53-54 [d] 1Ki 19:2
20:11 [e] Jer 1:8; Ro 8:31 [f] Jer 17:18 [g] Jer 15:20 [h] Jer 23:40
20:12 [i] Jer 17:10 [j] Ps 54:7; 59:10 [k] Ps 62:8; Jer 11:20
20:13 [l] Ps 35:10
20:14 [m] Job 3:3; Jer 15:10

20:4–6 Jeremiah announces in the name of the Lord that Pashhur has "prophesied lies" (v. 6) and that he will enter Babylon as a captive. Jeremiah's prophetic witness in the temple may have prompted his arrest and thrashing. As a priest, however, Pashhur almost certainly took the opportunity to speak a word of judgment in public about Jeremiah and his actions. These would have taken the form of rejecting Jeremiah's words and actions and claiming divine judgment on him.
20:7–10 The prophet is persecuted because of "the word of the LORD" (v. 8). His persecutors lie in wait to ambush him and ridicule him with his own phrase, "terror on every side" (v. 10), as if to say that Jeremiah is a deluded madman who speaks incessantly about terror to come. In his frustration and bitterness Jeremiah accuses God of "deceiving" him (v. 7), a strong term that can also refer to seduction.
20:11–13 Verse 11 affirms that God is strong to save. In context this means that the prophet's persecutors will fail.
20:14–18 The prophet regrets the day he was born (cf. 15:10), as he, like Job, suffers unjustly. It is difficult to know whether the complaint of 20:7–18 should be read sequentially, as if the movement of the prayer/complaint is significant. If so, it suggests that Jeremiah goes back and forth in his resolve to carry out his prophetic work.

✚ **20:1–18** There is much to learn from the honest expression of Jeremiah's human limitations. One may—with Christ's help—bear innocent suffering with a certain grace. Jeremiah feels

PEOPLE TO KNOW // **JEREMIAH**

JEREMIAH 20:7–18: Jeremiah's ministry spanned Judah's highest highs and lowest lows. On the positive side, he ministered during the religious reforms of King Josiah. Eventually, however, he saw God's judgment enacted against Jerusalem when Babylon burned the city of Jerusalem and dragged its occupants into exile in 586 BC (2Ki 25:8–21).

God appointed Jeremiah to his prophetic task before he was born (Jer 1:5). From a young age, God gave Jeremiah difficult messages to proclaim and warned him these messages would not be warmly accepted. Nonetheless, God promised to be with Jeremiah, telling him his oppressors would not overcome him.

Jeremiah is often called the "weeping prophet." He bore the weight of God's messages of judgment, which he had no choice but to speak. God's word was like fire in his bones. His reward for speaking God's word was that his people plotted to kill him (Jer 11:18–19; 26:8). Other times, Jeremiah was beaten and put in stocks (Jer 20:2–3), his scroll of God's messages was burned by the king (Jer 36:23), and he was thrown in a cistern and left to die (Jer 38:6–10). Fortunately, God moved Ebed-Melek to save Jeremiah from this muddy fate.

While Jeremiah's messages described judgment and destruction, they also foretold God's future grace through a new covenant. Jeremiah also promised that God would be with the exiles even in their dark moments, assuring them of hope and a future (Jer 29:11).

Jeremiah himself was dragged to Egypt by some Jews fleeing from the Babylonian destruction (Jer 43:5–7). He most likely died in Egypt.

APPLICATION Jeremiah sets an example for speaking God's Word even in the darkest of circumstances and in the face of angry rejection and persecution. Like Jeremiah, we can be honest with God about our anguish and struggles, but we should also be obedient to God. As it was for Jeremiah, God's message should be like fire in our bones: uncontainable. We need to point the world to Jesus.

15 Cursed be the man who brought my
father the news,
who made him very glad, saying,
"A child is born to you — a son!"
16 May that man be like the towns[n]
the LORD overthrew without pity.
May he hear wailing in the morning,
a battle cry at noon.
17 For he did not kill me in the womb,[o]
with my mother as my grave,
her womb enlarged forever.
18 Why did I ever come out of the
womb
to see trouble and sorrow
and to end my days in shame?[p]

20:16 [n] Ge 19:25
20:17 [o] Job 10:18-19
20:18 [p] Ps 90:9
21:1 [q] 2Ki 24:18; Jer 52:1 [r] Jer 38:1 [s] 2Ki 25:18; Jer 29:25; 37:3
21:2 [t] Jer 37:3, 7 [u] 2Ki 25:1 [v] Ps 44:1-4; Jer 32:17

God Rejects Zedekiah's Request

21 The word came to Jeremiah from
the LORD when King Zedekiah[q] sent
to him Pashhur[r] son of Malkijah and the
priest Zephaniah[s] son of Maaseiah. They
said: 2"Inquire[t] now of the LORD for us
because Nebuchadnezzar[a][u] king of Babylon is attacking us. Perhaps the LORD
will perform wonders[v] for us as in times
past so that he will withdraw from us."
3But Jeremiah answered them, "Tell
Zedekiah, 4'This is what the LORD, the

[a] 2 Hebrew *Nebuchadrezzar,* of which *Nebuchadnezzar* is a variant; here and often in Jeremiah and Ezekiel

crushed by the burdens of the prophetic office. He experiences the sinking feeling that not only is all lost but that God seems involved in his pain. It will take the humiliation of Christ for the redemptive element of suffering to emerge, but in his own way Jeremiah suffers on our behalf. He demonstrates what it is like to feel the burdens of human failure and personal frustration as a part of his calling, and he does so to instruct us about the cost of discipleship, but also as a testimony that God is faithful still—beyond our finite understanding and in spite of our complaints.

21:1–2 Zedekiah is king—the first reference to the last king of Judah since the superscription to the book of Jeremiah—and the date is c. 588 BC. The name Pashhur is the same as that of the priest in ch. 20, although they are two different people.

Pashhur and Zephaniah ask Jeremiah to inquire of the Lord and to intercede for the nation.

21:3–7 The Lord's reply is full of the judgmental language seen in virtually every previous chapter. What is new is a specific reference to Nebuchadnezzar, king of Babylon, and the specifics of the siege of Jerusalem. Babylon itself is mentioned specifically for the first time only in the previous chapter (20:4–6).

God of Israel, says: I am about to turn[w]
against you the weapons of war that are
in your hands, which you are using to
fight the king of Babylon and the Babylonians[a] who are outside the wall besieging[x] you. And I will gather them inside
this city. 5 I myself will fight against you
with an outstretched hand[y] and a mighty
arm in furious anger and in great wrath.
6 I will strike down those who live in this
city — both man and beast — and they
will die of a terrible plague.[z] 7 After that,
declares the LORD, I will give Zedekiah[a]
king of Judah, his officials and the people
in this city who survive the plague, sword
and famine, into the hands of Nebuchadnezzar king of Babylon[b] and to their enemies who want to kill them. He will put
them to the sword; he will show them no
mercy or pity or compassion.'[c]
8 "Furthermore, tell the people, 'This
is what the LORD says: See, I am setting
before you the way of life and the way
of death. 9 Whoever stays in this city will
die by the sword, famine or plague.[d] But
whoever goes out and surrenders to the
Babylonians who are besieging you will
live; they will escape with their lives.[e] 10 I
have determined to do this city harm[f]
and not good, declares the LORD. It will
be given into the hands[g] of the king of
Babylon, and he will destroy it with fire.'[h]
11 "Moreover, say to the royal house[i] of
Judah, 'Hear the word of the LORD. 12 This
is what the LORD says to you, house of
David:

21:4 [w] Jer 32:5 [x] Jer 37:8-10
21:5 [y] Jer 6:12
21:6 [z] Jer 14:12
21:7 [a] 2Ki 25:7; Jer 52:9 [b] Jer 37:17; 39:5 [c] 2Ch 36:17; Eze 7:9; Hab 1:6
21:9 [d] Jer 14:12 [e] Jer 38:2,17; 39:18; 45:5
21:10 [f] Jer 44:11, 27; Am 9:4 [g] Jer 32:28; 38:2-3 [h] Jer 52:13
21:11 [i] Jer 13:18

Jer 21:8 ❖ How can we lay hold of the path of life God offers (see Jn 11:25)?

" 'Administer justice[j] every morning;
rescue from the hand of the
oppressor
the one who has been robbed,
or my wrath will break out and burn
like fire
because of the evil you have
done —
burn with no one to quench[k] it.
13 I am against[l] you, Jerusalem,
you who live above this valley[m]
on the rocky plateau, declares the
LORD —
you who say, "Who can come
against us?
Who can enter our refuge?"[n]
14 I will punish you as your deeds[o]
deserve,
declares the LORD.
I will kindle a fire[p] in your forests[q]
that will consume everything
around you.' "

Judgment Against Wicked Kings

22 This is what the LORD says: "Go
down to the palace of the king
of Judah and proclaim this message
there: 2 'Hear the word of the LORD to
you, king of Judah, you who sit on David's throne[r] — you, your officials and
your people who come through these

21:12 [j] Jer 22:3 [k] Isa 1:31
21:13 [l] Eze 13:8 [m] Ps 125:2 [n] Jer 49:4; Ob 3-4
21:14 [o] Isa 3:10-11 [p] 2Ch 36:19; Jer 52:13 [q] Eze 20:47
22:2 [r] Jer 17:25; Lk 1:32

[a] 4 Or *Chaldeans*; also in verse 9

God is a valiant warrior, but the enemy at the moment is Judah, not Babylon. The fall of the city, therefore, is certain.

21:8–10 Jeremiah mediates part of God's reply to the state officials in language reminiscent of Dt 30:11–20. Death is the fate of those who stay in the city; those who leave and are taken captive by the Babylonians will escape with their lives. The best that can be done for the Judeans is to convince them to submit to the Babylonians and thereby save their lives. God's resolve to judge the city is described in Hebrew as "the setting of his face" ("determined to do"), an expression for single-minded determination (Jer 21:10).

✤ **21:1–10** Christians may see in Jeremiah's hard words here an example of the "razor's edge" of biblical theism. God fights against the powers of evil and corruption—and as with every fight, the results are not pretty. God will fight the powers of evil when they oppress his people, but God can also use the powers of evil in this world to judge his people. God is not indifferent to the sins of his people, and his holiness demands punishment for unrepentant sin.

21:11–14 These verses can be read as further commentary on Jeremiah's word to Zedekiah in vv. 1–10. Early morning was the time when people in towns and villages rose and met one another on their way to perform daily tasks. When they met at the gate of the city or village, they also worked out the city's administrative and judicial affairs and witnessed agreements. Jeremiah's charge to the royal house, therefore, is to be a court of appeal for the oppressed "every morning" (v. 11).

22:1–9 Readers should not overlook the verb "go down" (v. 1). About the only place from which Jeremiah can "go down" is from the temple mount. This incidental comment tells us much about one important place where Jeremiah receives his prompting from God.

The shedding of "innocent blood" (v. 3) required ceremonies for penance; otherwise, responsibility fell on the whole community.

gates.[s] 3This is what the LORD says: Do
what is just[t] and right. Rescue from the
hand of the oppressor[u] the one who has
been robbed. Do no wrong or violence to
the foreigner, the fatherless or the widow,[v] and do not shed innocent blood in
this place. 4For if you are careful to carry
out these commands, then kings[w] who
sit on David's throne will come through
the gates of this palace, riding in chariots and on horses, accompanied by their
officials and their people. 5But if you do
not obey[x] these commands, declares the
LORD, I swear[y] by myself that this palace
will become a ruin.'"

6For this is what the LORD says about
the palace of the king of Judah:

"Though you are like Gilead to me,
like the summit of Lebanon,
I will surely make you like a
wasteland,[z]
like towns not inhabited.
7I will send destroyers[a] against you,
each man with his weapons,
and they will cut[b] up your fine cedar
beams
and throw them into the fire.

8"People from many nations will pass
by this city and will ask one another,
'Why has the LORD done such a thing to
this great city?'[c] 9And the answer will
be: 'Because they have forsaken the covenant of the LORD their God and have
worshiped and served other gods.[d]'"

10Do not weep for the dead[e] king or
mourn[f] his loss;
rather, weep bitterly for him who
is exiled,
because he will never return
nor see his native land again.

11For this is what the LORD says about
Shallum[a][g] son of Josiah, who succeeded
his father as king of Judah but has gone
from this place: "He will never return.

[s] Jer 17:20
22:3 [t] Mic 6:8; Zec 7:9 [u] Ps 72:4; Jer 21:12 [v] Ex 22:22
22:4 [w] Jer 17:25
22:5 [x] Jer 17:27 [y] Heb 6:13
22:6 [z] Mic 3:12
22:7 [a] Jer 4:7 [b] Isa 10:34
22:8 [c] Dt 29:25-26; 1Ki 9:8-9; Jer 16:10-11
22:9 [d] 2Ki 22:17; 2Ch 34:25
22:10 [e] Ecc 4:2 [f] ver 18
22:11 [g] 2Ki 23:31
22:12 [h] 2Ki 23:34
22:13 [i] Mic 3:10; Hab 2:9 [j] Lev 19:13; Jas 5:4
22:14 [k] Isa 5:8-9 [l] 2Sa 7:2
22:15 [m] 2Ki 23:25 [n] Ps 128:2; Isa 3:10
22:16 [o] Ps 72:1-4,12-13
22:17 [p] 2Ki 24:4

Jer 22:15–17 ❖ Who are people of righteousness and justice we can imitate? How do their actions point to God's love?

12He will die[h] in the place where they
have led him captive; he will not see this
land again."

13"Woe to him who builds[i] his palace
by unrighteousness,
his upper rooms by injustice,
making his own people work for
nothing,
not paying[j] them for their labor.
14He says, 'I will build myself a great
palace[k]
with spacious upper rooms.'
So he makes large windows in it,
panels it with cedar[l]
and decorates it in red.

15"Does it make you a king
to have more and more cedar?
Did not your father have food and
drink?
He did what was right and just,[m]
so all went well[n] with him.
16He defended the cause of the poor
and needy,[o]
and so all went well.
Is that not what it means to
know me?"
declares the LORD.
17"But your eyes and your heart
are set only on dishonest gain,
on shedding innocent blood[p]
and on oppression and extortion."

18Therefore this is what the LORD says
about Jehoiakim son of Josiah king of
Judah:

"They will not mourn for him:
'Alas, my brother! Alas, my sister!'
They will not mourn for him:

[a] *11* Also called *Jehoahaz*

22:10–12 Of the three kings addressed directly, the briefest prophecy concerns Shallum, that is, Jehoahaz, the son of and immediate successor to Josiah. He was placed on the throne after the death of his father but subsequently removed by the Egyptian pharaoh after a brief reign. The fate of this king foreshadows that of the people.

22:13–23 Jeremiah pronounces a judgmental "woe" (v. 13) on Jehoiakim, the older brother of Jehoahaz, who succeeded his younger brother on the throne. Verse 13 describes Jehoiakim's activities as unrighteous and as examples of "injustice." Jehoiakim's arrogant building project is described as "his palace." Almost certainly this is not a primary residence since the royal palace in Jerusalem had been in existence as long as the temple.

22:15–16 Josiah is described as one who lived the life of a king (he ate and drank) but who also did what was "right and just" (v. 15), defending "the cause of the poor and needy" (v. 16). Jeremiah describes this activity as an example of "what it means to know" (v. 16) the Lord. Josiah is the only king from his day whom Jeremiah praises.

'Alas, my master! Alas, his
splendor!'
19 He will have the burial of a donkey —
dragged away and thrown[q]
outside the gates of Jerusalem."

20 "Go up to Lebanon and cry out,
let your voice be heard in Bashan,
cry out from Abarim,[r]
for all your allies are crushed.
21 I warned you when you felt secure,
but you said, 'I will not listen!'
This has been your way from your
youth;[s]
you have not obeyed[t] me.
22 The wind will drive all your
shepherds away,
and your allies will go into exile.
Then you will be ashamed and
disgraced
because of all your wickedness.
23 You who live in 'Lebanon,[a]'
who are nestled in cedar
buildings,
how you will groan when pangs
come upon you,
pain[u] like that of a woman in
labor!

24 "As surely as I live," declares the
LORD, "even if you, Jehoiachin[b][v] son of
Jehoiakim king of Judah, were a signet ring on my right hand, I would still
pull you off. 25 I will deliver[w] you into
the hands of those who want to kill you,
those you fear — Nebuchadnezzar king
of Babylon and the Babylonians.[c] 26 I will
hurl[x] you and the mother who gave you
birth into another country, where neither
of you was born, and there you both will
die. 27 You will never come back to the
land you long to return to."

28 Is this man Jehoiachin a despised,
broken pot,[y]
an object no one wants?
Why will he and his children be
hurled[z] out,
cast into a land[a] they do not
know?
29 O land,[b] land, land,
hear the word of the LORD!
30 This is what the LORD says:
"Record this man as if childless,[c]
a man who will not prosper[d] in his
lifetime,
for none of his offspring will
prosper,
none will sit on the throne[e] of
David
or rule anymore in Judah."

Jer 23:1-4 ❖ How do bad church leaders hurt God's "flock"?

The Righteous Branch

23 "Woe to the shepherds[f] who are
destroying and scattering[g] the
sheep of my pasture!"[h] declares the LORD.
2 Therefore this is what the LORD, the God
of Israel, says to the shepherds who tend
my people: "Because you have scattered
my flock and driven them away and have
not bestowed care on them, I will bestow
punishment on you for the evil[i] you have
done," declares the LORD. 3 "I myself will
gather the remnant[j] of my flock out of all
the countries where I have driven them
and will bring them back to their pasture,
where they will be fruitful and increase
in number. 4 I will place shepherds[k] over
them who will tend them, and they will
no longer be afraid[l] or terrified, nor will
any be missing,[m]" declares the LORD.

22:19 [q] Jer 36:30
22:20 [r] Nu 27:12
22:21 [s] Jer 3:25; 32:30 [t] Jer 7:23-28
22:23 [u] Jer 4:31
22:24 [v] 2Ki 24:6, 8; Jer 37:1
22:25 [w] 2Ki 24:16; Jer 34:20
22:26 [x] 2Ki 24:8; 2Ch 36:10
22:28 [y] Ps 31:12; Jer 48:38; Hos 8:8 [z] Jer 15:1 [a] Jer 17:4
22:29 [b] Jer 6:19; Mic 1:2
22:30 [c] 1Ch 3:18; Mt 1:12 [d] Jer 10:21 [e] Ps 94:20
23:1 [f] Jer 10:21; Eze 34:1-10; Zec 11:15-17 [g] Isa 56:11 [h] Eze 34:31
23:2 [i] Jer 21:12
23:3 [j] Isa 11:10-12; Jer 32:37; Eze 34:11-16
23:4 [k] Jer 3:15; 31:10; Eze 34:23 [l] Jer 30:10; 46:27-28 [m] Jn 6:39

[a] *23* That is, the palace in Jerusalem (see 1 Kings 7:2) [b] *24* Hebrew *Koniah,* a variant of *Jehoiachin;* also in verse 28 [c] *25* Or *Chaldeans*

22:24–30 This address to Jehoiachin has several grammatical complexities. The gist of the message is that he falls under the present judgment. More precisely, he and his family will go into Babylonian exile, and the young king will be reckoned as childless—although he has descendants—since his sons will not sit on the throne of David and rule as kings in Judah.

✣ **21:11—22:30** The harsh word to Jehoiakim also contains an affirmation of what it means to know God. In his case, the contrast with his father, Josiah, is telling. The test of knowing God is a commitment to the things of God—justice and righteousness for God's people. To know God is to be committed to his revealed will in the places of responsibility (ministry) where one lives and works. Of course, to know God means also to be rightly and personally in relationship with him.

23:1–4 Punishment and crime are linked for the shepherds in this brief prose text. The scattered flock is identified as the exiled remnant of God's people, who will be brought back to their homeland (vv. 3, 7–8). This passage, therefore, probably originated after the first wave of exiles was taken away to Babylon in 597 BC.

5 "The days are coming," declares the
 LORD,
"when I will raise up for David[a] a
 righteous Branch,[n]
a King who will reign[o] wisely
 and do what is just and right[p] in
 the land.
6 In his days Judah will be saved
 and Israel will live in safety.
This is the name[q] by which he will
 be called:
 The LORD Our Righteous Savior.[r]

7 "So then, the days are coming," declares
the LORD, "when people will no longer say,
'As surely as the LORD lives, who brought
the Israelites up out of Egypt,'[s] 8 but they
will say, 'As surely as the LORD lives, who
brought the descendants of Israel up out
of the land of the north and out of all the
countries where he had banished them.'
Then they will live in their own land."[t]

Lying Prophets

9 Concerning the prophets:

My heart is broken within me;
 all my bones tremble.
I am like a drunken man,
 like a strong man overcome by
 wine,
because of the LORD
 and his holy words.[u]
10 The land is full of adulterers;[v]
 because of the curse[b] the land lies
 parched
 and the pastures[w] in the
 wilderness are withered.[x]
The prophets follow an evil course
 and use their power unjustly.
11 "Both prophet and priest are godless;[y]
 even in my temple[z] I find their
 wickedness,"
 declares the LORD.
12 "Therefore their path will become
 slippery;[a]
 they will be banished to darkness
 and there they will fall.
I will bring disaster on them
 in the year they are punished,[b]"
 declares the LORD.

13 "Among the prophets of Samaria
 I saw this repulsive thing:
They prophesied by Baal[c]
 and led my people Israel astray.
14 And among the prophets of
 Jerusalem
 I have seen something horrible:[d]
 They commit adultery and live a
 lie.[e]
They strengthen the hands of
 evildoers,[f]
 so that not one of them turns
 from their wickedness.
They are all like Sodom[g] to me;
 the people of Jerusalem are like
 Gomorrah."[h]

15 Therefore this is what the LORD Almighty says concerning the prophets:

"I will make them eat bitter food
 and drink poisoned water,[i]
because from the prophets of
 Jerusalem
 ungodliness has spread
 throughout the land."

23:5 [n] Isa 4:2 [o] Isa 9:7 [p] Isa 11:1; Zec 6:12
23:6 [q] Jer 33:16; Mt 1:21-23 [r] Ro 3:21-22; 1Co 1:30
23:7 [s] Jer 16:14
23:8 [t] Isa 43:5-6; Am 9:14-15
23:9 [u] Jer 20:8-9
23:10 [v] Jer 9:2 [w] Ps 107:34; Jer 9:10 [x] Hos 4:2-3
23:11 [y] Jer 6:13; 8:10; Zep 3:4 [z] Jer 7:10
23:12 [a] Ps 35:6; Jer 13:16 [b] Jer 11:23
23:13 [c] Jer 2:8
23:14 [d] Jer 5:30 [e] Jer 29:23 [f] Eze 13:22 [g] Ge 18:20 [h] Isa 1:9-10; Jer 20:16
23:15 [i] Jer 8:14; 9:15

[a] 5 *Or up from David's line* [b] 10 *Or because of these things*

23:5–6 God will raise up a king from David's line. His wonderful name, "The LORD Our Righteous Savior" (v. 6), is a pun on the name Zedekiah (= Righteous is Yahweh), the last king of Judah (who reigned from 597–587/586 BC). For the generation of Jeremiah, the symbolic name of this "righteous Branch" (v. 5) is probably a sarcastic judgment on Zedekiah. It points to God's resolve to restore his people and fulfill his promises to the Davidic line.

The name of the king represents significant claims about the work of God. In his days Judah and Israel "will be saved" (v. 6) and will dwell securely. The righteousness indicated in his name is for the people, even though it is not fully their own.

23:7–8 Just as something new and wonderful will emerge from David's line, so a second exodus will occur, and the exiled people will return to their land.

23:9–10 Jeremiah reacts to the dire straits of his people and the power of his prophetic opponents to mislead them. He mentions drought conditions as one element of his horror (cf. ch. 14). God's words have made the prophet like a drunken man. It is not clear whether this is metaphorical language or if he has actual physical symptoms.

23:11–12 These verses confirm that the prophets and priests who serve there are also offering messages of assurance that the nation will not fall.

23:13–14 Prophets of Samaria prophesied by Baal and led God's people astray (cf. v. 27). This historical comment interprets the fall of Israel and Samaria in 722/721 BC. Something equally heinous is then reported with respect to the prophets in Jerusalem: They are adulterers and are living a lie.

23:15–24 The command "Do not listen to . . . the prophets" (v. 16) is addressed to the people. There will be no peace or security for a people who despise God.

The oracle about judgment on the prophets notes that the people will better understand this matter in "days to come" (v. 20). It is the function of a book like Jeremiah, published after Judah's demise, to make clear that the people had trusted in lies.

16This is what the LORD Almighty says:

"Do not listen[j] to what the prophets
are prophesying to you;
they fill you with false hopes.
They speak visions[k] from their own
minds,
not from the mouth[l] of the LORD.
17They keep saying to those who
despise me,
'The LORD says: You will have
peace.'[m]
And to all who follow the
stubbornness[n] of their hearts
they say, 'No harm[o] will come to
you.'
18But which of them has stood in the
council of the LORD
to see or to hear his word?
Who has listened and heard his
word?
19See, the storm[p] of the LORD
will burst out in wrath,
a whirlwind swirling down
on the heads of the wicked.
20The anger[q] of the LORD will not turn
back[r]
until he fully accomplishes
the purposes of his heart.
In days to come
you will understand it clearly.
21I did not send[s] these prophets,
yet they have run with their
message;
I did not speak to them,
yet they have prophesied.
22But if they had stood in my council,
they would have proclaimed my
words to my people
and would have turned[t] them from
their evil ways
and from their evil deeds.

23"Am I only a God nearby,[u]"
declares the LORD,
"and not a God far away?
24Who can hide[v] in secret places
so that I cannot see them?"
declares the LORD.
"Do not I fill heaven and earth?"[w]
declares the LORD.

25"I have heard what the prophets say
who prophesy lies[x] in my name. They say,
'I had a dream![y] I had a dream!' 26How
long will this continue in the hearts of
these lying prophets, who prophesy the
delusions[z] of their own minds? 27They
think the dreams they tell one another
will make my people forget[a] my name,
just as their ancestors forgot[b] my name
through Baal worship. 28Let the prophet who has a dream recount the dream,
but let the one who has my word speak it
faithfully. For what has straw to do with
grain?" declares the LORD. 29"Is not my
word like fire,"[c] declares the LORD, "and
like a hammer that breaks a rock in pieces?
30"Therefore," declares the LORD, "I am
against[d] the prophets[e] who steal from
one another words supposedly from me.
31Yes," declares the LORD, "I am against
the prophets who wag their own tongues
and yet declare, 'The LORD declares.'[f] 32In-
deed, I am against those who prophesy
false dreams,[g]" declares the LORD. "They
tell them and lead my people astray with
their reckless lies, yet I did not send or
appoint them. They do not benefit[h] these
people in the least," declares the LORD.

False Prophecy

33"When these people, or a prophet
or a priest, ask you, 'What is the message[i] from the LORD?' say to them, 'What
message? I will forsake[j] you, declares the
LORD.' 34If a prophet or a priest or anyone
else claims, 'This is a message[k] from the
LORD,' I will punish[l] them and their

23:16 [j] Jer 27:9-10,14; Mt 7:15 [k] Jer 14:14 [l] Jer 9:20
23:17 [m] Jer 8:11 [n] Jer 13:10 [o] Jer 5:12; Am 9:10; Mic 3:11
23:19 [p] Jer 25:32; 30:23
23:20 [q] 2Ki 23:26 [r] Jer 30:24
23:21 [s] Jer 14:14; 27:15
23:22 [t] Jer 25:5; Zec 1:4
23:23 [u] Ps 139:1-10
23:24 [v] Job 22:12-14 [w] 1Ki 8:27
23:25 [x] Jer 14:14 [y] ver 28,32; Jer 29:8
23:26 [z] 1Ti 4:1-2
23:27 [a] Dt 13:1-3; Jer 29:8 [b] Jdg 3:7; 8:33-34
23:29 [c] Jer 5:14
23:30 [d] Ps 34:16 [e] Dt 18:20; Jer 14:15
23:31 [f] ver 17
23:32 [g] ver 25 [h] Jer 7:8; La 2:14
23:33 [i] Mal 1:1 [j] ver 39
23:34 [k] La 2:14 [l] Zec 13:3

23:18 God denies sending these prophets. If they had been in God's council, then they would have proclaimed the evil deeds of the people and attempted to turn them from their acts and the consequences.

23:23–24 The rhetorical questions here are also intended for the people's hearing. Whether near or far, the people and their deeds are known to God, who fills heaven and earth (with his presence).

23:25–32 The prose comments continue the criticism of Jerusalem's prophets. One of their modes of communicating is dream reports. Verse 28 makes a distinction between the faithful reporting of God's word and the reporting of a dream. The implication is that the reception of the word is a different form of experience, but it is not further defined. In effect, it is like the hammer that shatters rock.

23:33–40 These verses begin with a play on one of the words for "message," which can also be translated as "burden." In all the criticism of the prophets, the expression "false prophet" is not used. Some of these prophets probably deserved the description. Some, however, might not have deserved such a description. Perhaps they had been of service in the cause of the Lord in times past, and they sincerely hoped that their message of peace and security had its origin with the Lord.

CHARACTER OF GOD // GOD IS OMNIPRESENT

Jeremiah 23:24: "Who can hide in secret places so that I cannot see them?" declares the LORD. "Do not I fill heaven and earth?" declares the LORD.

God is omnipresent, meaning he is present everywhere all the time. There is no place in creation where a person can hide from God. As God said through the prophet Jeremiah, he fills the heaven and earth and there are no secret places that God cannot see (Jer 23:24).

Think of a writer writing a book. Everything that happens on each page is known by the author. Nothing happens in the book that the author does not know completely, for the author wrote each part. In a way, the author's presence pervades the book. While God does not meticulously control every human word and action, as Creator of the universe God knows every part of his creation and oversees every part of it simultaneously.

For those who live opposed to God's will, this is bad news. There is nowhere to hide from God, and he sees everything that people try to do in secret. Try as they may, they cannot run from God. For those who fear God, however, his omnipresence is a deep comfort. Wherever they go, they know God is with them. They are never alone, for they know God's presence is everywhere.

APPLICATION ✤ God's omnipresence may seem like an abstract concept, but it reminds us of the close communion we have with God. God is not like some distant watchmaker who set the world in motion and stands far off from his creation, as some believe. Instead, God fills his creation with his presence. We are never far from God. In a world of many uncertainties, this is a deep comfort.

household. 35This is what each of you
keeps saying to your friends and other
Israelites: 'What is the LORD's answer?'[m]
or 'What has the LORD spoken?' 36But you
must not mention 'a message from the
LORD' again, because each one's word becomes their own message. So you distort[n]
the words of the living God, the LORD Almighty, our God. 37This is what you keep
saying to a prophet: 'What is the LORD's
answer to you?' or 'What has the LORD
spoken?' 38Although you claim, 'This is a
message from the LORD,' this is what the
LORD says: You used the words, 'This is a
message from the LORD,' even though I
told you that you must not claim, 'This is
a message from the LORD.' 39Therefore, I
will surely forget you and cast[o] you out of
my presence along with the city I gave to
you and your ancestors. 40I will bring on
you everlasting disgrace[p] — everlasting
shame that will not be forgotten."

Two Baskets of Figs

24 After Jehoiachin[a][q] son of Jehoiakim king of Judah and the officials, the skilled workers and the artisans
of Judah were carried into exile from
Jerusalem to Babylon by Nebuchadnezzar king of Babylon, the LORD showed
me two baskets of figs[r] placed in front
of the temple of the LORD. 2One basket

23:35 [m] Jer 33:3; 42:4
23:36 [n] Gal 1:7-8; 2Pe 3:16
23:39 [o] Jer 7:15
23:40 [p] Jer 20:11; Eze 5:14-15
24:1 [q] 2Ki 24:16; 2Ch 36:9; Jer 29:2 [r] Am 8:1-2

[a] *1* Hebrew *Jeconiah,* a variant of *Jehoiachin*

These judgments against the religious leaders of the people are related to other passages in Jeremiah. Various narratives and oracles make it clear that Jehoiakim and Zedekiah failed as shepherds of the nation. Some members of the priesthood were hostile to Jeremiah (20:1-6). Jeremiah's prayers of lament are derived, in part, from his experiences of ridicule and humiliation at the hands of these leaders.

✤ **23:1-40** With the life of the people in crisis, Jeremiah announced that Judah had to change or judgment would come. Eventually he understood that any repentance would be too little and too late. Those prophets who disagreed with him were wrong historically and theologically. Their words diverted the people's attention from seeking the Lord to a false assurance that he would protect them.

Is this not like the turmoil over Jesus' public ministry, where he continually called people to a life of commitment and spiritual discernment in counting the cost of discipleship? Discipleship (i.e., following Christ) is also a form of leadership, and vice versa. Christ came not to be served but to serve (Mk 10:45). That is the point of Christology; it is the point for all shepherds in the church.

24:1-10 Jeremiah observes two baskets of figs left as offerings at the temple, one of which contains ripe figs and the other rotten figs. The Lord tells

had very good figs, like those that ripen
early; the other basket had very bad[s] figs,
so bad they could not be eaten.
3Then the LORD asked me, "What do
you see,[t] Jeremiah?"
"Figs," I answered. "The good ones are
very good, but the bad ones are so bad
they cannot be eaten."
4Then the word of the LORD came to
me: 5"This is what the LORD, the God
of Israel, says: 'Like these good figs, I
regard as good the exiles from Judah,
whom I sent away from this place to the
land of the Babylonians.[a] 6My eyes will
watch over them for their good, and I
will bring them back[u] to this land. I will
build[v] them up and not tear them down;
I will plant them and not uproot them. 7I
will give them a heart to know me, that
I am the LORD. They will be my people,[w]
and I will be their God, for they will return[x] to me with all their heart.[y]
8" 'But like the bad[z] figs, which are so
bad they cannot be eaten,' says the LORD,
'so will I deal with Zedekiah king of Judah, his officials[a] and the survivors[b] from
Jerusalem, whether they remain in this
land or live in Egypt.[c] 9I will make them
abhorrent[d] and an offense to all the kingdoms of the earth, a reproach and a byword,[e] a curse[b][f] and an object of ridicule,
wherever I banish[g] them. 10I will send
the sword,[h] famine and plague[i] against
them until they are destroyed from the
land I gave to them and their ancestors.' "

Seventy Years of Captivity

25 The word came to Jeremiah concerning all the people of Judah in
the fourth year of Jehoiakim[j] son of Josiah king of Judah, which was the first year
of Nebuchadnezzar[k] king of Babylon.
2So Jeremiah the prophet said to all the
people of Judah[l] and to all those living
in Jerusalem: 3For twenty-three years—
from the thirteenth year of Josiah[m] son
of Amon king of Judah until this very
day—the word of the LORD has come
to me and I have spoken to you again
and again,[n] but you have not listened.[o]
4And though the LORD has sent all his
servants the prophets[p] to you again and
again, you have not listened or paid any
attention. 5They said, "Turn now, each of
you, from your evil ways and your evil
practices, and you can stay in the land
the LORD gave to you and your ancestors
for ever and ever. 6Do not follow other
gods[q] to serve and worship them; do not
arouse my anger with what your hands
have made. Then I will not harm you."
7"But you did not listen to me," declares the LORD, "and you have aroused
my anger with what your hands have
made,[r] and you have brought harm[s] to
yourselves."
8Therefore the LORD Almighty says
this: "Because you have not listened to
my words, 9I will summon[t] all the peoples of the north[u] and my servant[v] Nebuchadnezzar king of Babylon," declares
the LORD, "and I will bring them against

Jer 24:4-7 ❖ When have we felt God's loving promises and care in the midst of a difficult time?

24:2 [s] Isa 5:4
24:3 [t] Jer 1:11; Am 8:2
24:6 [u] Jer 29:10; Eze 11:17 [v] Jer 33:7; 42:10
24:7 [w] Isa 51:16; Jer 31:33; Heb 8:10 [x] Jer 32:40 [y] Eze 11:19
24:8 [z] Jer 29:17 [a] Jer 39:6 [b] Jer 39:9 [c] Jer 44:1, 26
24:9 [d] Jer 15:4; 34:17 [e] Dt 28:25; 1Ki 9:7 [f] Jer 29:18 [g] Dt 28:37
24:10 [h] Isa 51:19 [i] Jer 27:8
25:1 [j] 2Ki 24:2; Jer 36:1 [k] 2Ki 24:1
25:2 [l] Jer 18:11
25:3 [m] Jer 1:2 [n] Jer 11:7; 26:5 [o] Jer 7:26
25:4 [p] Jer 7:25
25:6 [q] Dt 8:19
25:7 [r] Dt 32:21 [s] 2Ki 21:15
25:9 [t] Isa 13:3-5 [u] Jer 1:15 [v] Jer 27:6

[a] 5 Or *Chaldeans* [b] 9 That is, their names will be used in cursing (see 29:22); or, others will see that they are cursed.

the prophet that the good figs are like the Judeans taken into exile, while the rotten figs represent Zedekiah and those who remain in Jerusalem and Judah. The Lord promises to do good to the exilic community, to bring them back from exile, and to give them a heart to know him. Concerning those remaining in Judah, however, the Lord promises judgment.

One finds in this autobiographic prophetic report a shorthand version of what the larger book of Jeremiah intends to accomplish. For those on whom the judgment of the exile has fallen, God announces that he intends to "build them up" and to "plant" (v. 6) them again in the promised land. Return to the land is not all that God intends, although the return is a sign of something more fundamental—a wholehearted return to the Lord. Thus, there is also the promise of a heart prepared by God to know him as well as the reinstitution of the covenant relationship (v. 7).

✣ **24:1–10** God is just in judgment and yet One who justifies (accepts as righteous) those who trust him for their salvation. This is a paraphrase of Ro 3:26; it also captures the intent of Jer 24. God brings judgment on those who spurn him and reject his covenant. But he also seeks to save that which is lost and to give a new heart to those whom he calls into fellowship. The divided fate of the two communities in Jeremiah's day illustrates God's use of the historical process for judgment and restoration.

25:1–7 The refusal of the people to heed Jeremiah's warnings and earlier calls for repentance (cf. v. 5) has now led to the brink of judgment. The judgment to come on Judah and Jerusalem is only part of what Nebuchadnezzar will do. Other nations will also come under his domination.

25:8–10 Shockingly, v. 9 describes Nebuchadnezzar

this land and its inhabitants and against
all the surrounding nations. I will completely destroy[a] them and make them
an object of horror and scorn,[w] and an
everlasting ruin. 10 I will banish from
them the sounds[x] of joy and gladness,
the voices of bride and bridegroom,[y] the
sound of millstones[z] and the light of the
lamp.[a] 11 This whole country will become
a desolate wasteland,[b] and these nations
will serve the king of Babylon seventy
years.[c]
12 "But when the seventy years[d] are fulfilled, I will punish the king of Babylon
and his nation, the land of the Babylonians,[b] for their guilt," declares the LORD,
"and will make it desolate[e] forever. 13 I
will bring on that land all the things I
have spoken against it, all that are written in this book and prophesied by Jeremiah against all the nations. 14 They
themselves will be enslaved[f] by many
nations[g] and great kings; I will repay[h]
them according to their deeds and the
work of their hands."

The Cup of God's Wrath

15 This is what the LORD, the God of Israel, said to me: "Take from my hand
this cup[i] filled with the wine of my wrath
and make all the nations to whom I send
you drink it. 16 When they drink it, they
will stagger[j] and go mad[k] because of the
sword I will send among them."
17 So I took the cup from the LORD's
hand and made all the nations to whom
he sent[l] me drink it: 18 Jerusalem and the
towns of Judah, its kings and officials,
to make them a ruin and an object of
horror and scorn, a curse[c][m] — as they are
today;[n] 19 Pharaoh king of Egypt, his attendants, his officials and all his people,
20 and all the foreign people there; all the
kings of Uz;[o] all the kings of the Philistines (those of Ashkelon,[p] Gaza, Ekron,
and the people left at Ashdod); 21 Edom,
Moab and Ammon;[q] 22 all the kings of
Tyre and Sidon;[r] the kings of the coastlands[s] across the sea; 23 Dedan, Tema, Buz
and all who are in distant places[d];[t] 24 all
the kings of Arabia[u] and all the kings of
the foreign people who live in the wilderness; 25 all the kings of Zimri, Elam[v] and
Media; 26 and all the kings of the north,[w]
near and far, one after the other — all the
kingdoms on the face of the earth. And
after all of them, the king of Sheshak[e][x]
will drink it too.
27 "Then tell them, 'This is what the
LORD Almighty, the God of Israel, says:
Drink, get drunk[y] and vomit, and fall
to rise no more because of the sword[z]
I will send among you.' 28 But if they
refuse to take the cup from your hand
and drink, tell them, 'This is what the
LORD Almighty says: You must drink it!
29 See, I am beginning to bring disaster[a]

25:9 [w] Jer 18:16
25:10 [x] Isa 24:8; Eze 26:13 [y] Jer 7:34 [z] Ecc 12:3-4 [a] Rev 18:22-23
25:11 [b] Jer 4:26-27; 12:11-12 [c] 2Ch 36:21
25:12 [d] Jer 29:10 [e] Isa 13:19-22; 14:22-23
25:14 [f] Jer 27:7 [g] Jer 50:9; 51:27-28 [h] Jer 51:6
25:15 [i] Isa 51:17; Ps 75:8; Rev 14:10
25:16 [j] Na 3:11 [k] Jer 51:7
25:17 [l] Jer 1:10
25:18 [m] Jer 24:9 [n] Jer 44:22
25:20 [o] Job 1:1 [p] Jer 47:5
25:21 [q] Jer 49:1
25:22 [r] Jer 47:4 [s] Jer 31:10
25:23 [t] Jer 9:26; 49:32
25:24 [u] 2Ch 9:14
25:25 [v] Ge 10:22
25:26 [w] Jer 50:3, 9 [x] Jer 51:41
25:27 [y] ver 16, 28; Hab 2:16 [z] Eze 21:4
25:29 [a] Jer 13:12-14

[a] 9 The Hebrew term refers to the irrevocable giving over of things or persons to the LORD, often by totally destroying them. [b] 12 Or *Chaldeans* [c] 18 That is, their names to be used in cursing (see 29:22); or, to be seen by others as cursed [d] 23 *Or who clip the hair by their foreheads* [e] 26 *Sheshak* is a cryptogram for Babylon.

Jer 25:15-29 ❖ Why would someone need to drink the cup of God's wrath? How does Christ provide hope (see Mt 26:39)?

as God's "servant." The historical judgment to come on Judah is God's work against his sinful people. The king's servanthood does not grant him saving knowledge of God. One may compare the language of "anointed" used to describe Cyrus (Isa 45:1–7).

25:11–14 The judgment against Judah predicts that they will serve Babylon "seventy years." The actual period was about 66 years, starting from the first year of Nebuchadnezzar's kingship in 605 BC to the fall of Babylon in 539. It is 70 years almost exactly starting from the destruction of the temple in 586 BC to its rededication in 516 BC (cf. Ezr 6:15). More likely, 70 is a round number representing the fulfillment of an extended period.

25:15–38 The cup is a metaphor for the turmoil to come among the nations, when God's sword of judgment is unleashed.

All the nations are caught up in the description of the judgment to come. It is not just Jerusalem, "the city that bears [God's] Name" (v. 29), who will bear judgment. God is depicted as cosmic judge. The imagery suggests that the face of the earth is strewn about with the effects of destruction. This prophetic proclamation is like that in Daniel and Zechariah, which depict catastrophic change in apocalyptic form.

✣ **25:1–38** Christians cannot assume that the misfortune of every nation is God's judgment and that a period of relative peace is evidence of his favor. God's work through the historical process is more complicated than that. There is no time in world history when this reality doesn't apply. The larger pattern can only be glimpsed by faith, and that faith must allow for a broader meaning that cannot be fully grasped at any one point in history.

on the city that bears my Name,[b] and will
you indeed go unpunished?[c] You will not
go unpunished, for I am calling down a
sword on all[d] who live on the earth, declares the LORD Almighty.'

30 "Now prophesy all these words
against them and say to them:

" 'The LORD will roar[e] from on high;
he will thunder[f] from his holy
dwelling
and roar mightily against his land.
He will shout like those who tread
the grapes,
shout against all who live on the
earth.
31 The tumult will resound to the ends
of the earth,
for the LORD will bring charges[g]
against the nations;
he will bring judgment on all
mankind
and put the wicked to the sword,' "
declares the LORD.

32 This is what the LORD Almighty says:

"Look! Disaster is spreading
from nation to nation;[h]
a mighty storm[i] is rising
from the ends of the earth."

33 At that time those slain[j] by the LORD
will be everywhere—from one end of
the earth to the other. They will not be
mourned or gathered[k] up or buried,[l] but
will be like dung lying on the ground.

34 Weep and wail, you shepherds;
roll[m] in the dust, you leaders of
the flock.
For your time to be slaughtered[n] has
come;
you will fall like the best of the
rams.[a]
35 The shepherds will have nowhere to
flee,
the leaders of the flock no place to
escape.[o]
36 Hear the cry of the shepherds,
the wailing of the leaders of the
flock,
for the LORD is destroying their
pasture.
37 The peaceful meadows will be laid
waste
because of the fierce anger of the
LORD.
38 Like a lion[p] he will leave his lair,
and their land will become
desolate
because of the sword[b] of the
oppressor
and because of the LORD's fierce
anger.

Jeremiah Threatened With Death

26 Early in the reign of Jehoiakim[q]
son of Josiah king of Judah, this
word came from the LORD: 2 "This is what
the LORD says: Stand in the courtyard[r]
of the LORD's house and speak to all the
people of the towns of Judah who come
to worship in the house of the LORD. Tell[s]
them everything I command you; do
not omit[t] a word. 3 Perhaps they will listen and each will turn[u] from their evil
ways. Then I will relent[v] and not inflict
on them the disaster I was planning because of the evil they have done. 4 Say to
them, 'This is what the LORD says: If you
do not listen[w] to me and follow my law,[x]
which I have set before you, 5 and if you
do not listen to the words of my servants
the prophets, whom I have sent to you
again and again (though you have not
listened[y]), 6 then I will make this house
like Shiloh[z] and this city a curse[c][a] among
all the nations of the earth.' "
7 The priests, the prophets and all

25:29 [b] 1Pe 4:17 [c] Pr 11:31 [d] ver 30-31
25:30 [e] Isa 16:10; 42:13 [f] Joel 3:16; Am 1:2
25:31 [g] Hos 4:1; Joel 3:2; Mic 6:2
25:32 [h] Isa 34:2 [i] Jer 23:19
25:33 [j] Isa 66:16; Eze 39:17-20 [k] Jer 16:4 [l] Ps 79:3
25:34 [m] Jer 6:26 [n] Isa 34:6; Jer 50:27
25:35 [o] Job 11:20
25:38 [p] Jer 4:7
26:1 [q] 2Ki 23:36
26:2 [r] Jer 19:14 [s] Jer 1:17; Mt 28:20; Ac 20:27 [t] Dt 4:2
26:3 [u] Jer 36:7 [v] Jer 18:8
26:4 [w] Lev 26:14 [x] 1Ki 9:6
26:5 [y] Jer 25:4
26:6 [z] Jos 18:1 [a] 2Ki 22:19

[a] *34* Septuagint; Hebrew *fall and be shattered like fine pottery* [b] *38* Some Hebrew manuscripts and Septuagint (see also 46:16 and 50:16); most Hebrew manuscripts *anger* [c] *6* That is, its name will be used in cursing (see 29:22); or, others will see that it is cursed.

26:1–6 The assumption of many in the audience is that God will protect the temple no matter what. To speak against the temple is tantamount to speaking against God himself. This is blasphemy. **26:7–19** Priests, prophets and others propose the death sentence for blasphemy and treason. The essentials of a public trial ensue when certain officials take their seat in the "New Gate" of the temple complex (v. 10). This location lends gravity to the situation and the charges against the prophet.

Jeremiah defends himself as one in the line of prophets (cf. v. 5). He recognizes that he is "in [their] hands" (v. 14). Still, he warns them that if they execute him, they will incur the judgment of bringing "innocent blood on [themselves]" (v. 15).

Jeremiah has spoken to them in the name of the Lord. He meets, therefore, at least one of Deuteronomy's criteria for judging prophecy (Dt 18). Some elders of the land add that Jeremiah is no different from Micah, who prophesied in Hezekiah's reign that Jerusalem would be destroyed (cf. Jer 26:18 with Mic 3:12). King Hezekiah did not execute

the people heard Jeremiah speak these
words in the house of the LORD. 8But
as soon as Jeremiah finished telling
all the people everything the LORD had
commanded him to say, the priests, the
prophets and all the people seized him
and said, "You must die! 9Why do you
prophesy in the LORD's name that this
house will be like Shiloh and this city
will be desolate and deserted?"[b] And all
the people crowded around Jeremiah in
the house of the LORD.

10When the officials of Judah heard
about these things, they went up from
the royal palace to the house of the LORD
and took their places at the entrance of
the New Gate of the LORD's house. 11Then
the priests and the prophets said to the
officials and all the people, "This man
should be sentenced to death[c] because
he has prophesied against this city. You
have heard it with your own ears!"

12Then Jeremiah said to all the officials[d] and all the people: "The LORD sent
me to prophesy[e] against this house and
this city all the things you have heard.[f]
13Now reform[g] your ways and your actions and obey the LORD your God. Then
the LORD will relent and not bring the
disaster he has pronounced against you.
14As for me, I am in your hands;[h] do with
me whatever you think is good and right.
15Be assured, however, that if you put
me to death, you will bring the guilt of
innocent blood on yourselves and on
this city and on those who live in it, for
in truth the LORD has sent me to you to
speak all these words in your hearing."

16Then the officials[i] and all the people said to the priests and the prophets,
"This man should not be sentenced to
death![j] He has spoken to us in the name
of the LORD our God."

26:9 [b] Jer 9:11
26:11 [c] Dt 18:20; Jer 18:23; 38:4; Mt 26:66; Ac 6:11
26:12 [d] Jer 1:18 [e] Am 7:15; Ac 4:18-20; 5:29 [f] ver 2,15
26:13 [g] Jer 7:5; Joel 2:12-14
26:14 [h] Jer 38:5
26:16 [i] Ac 23:9 [j] Ac 5:34-39; 23:29
26:18 [k] Mic 1:1 [l] Isa 2:3 [m] Ne 4:2; Jer 9:11 [n] Mic 4:1; Zec 8:3 [o] Jer 17:3
26:19 [p] 2Ch 32:24-26; Isa 37:14-20 [q] Ex 32:14; 2Sa 24:16 [r] Jer 44:7 [s] Hab 2:10
26:20 [t] Jos 9:17
26:21 [u] 1Ki 19:2 [v] Mt 10:23
26:22 [w] Jer 36:12,25

Jer 26:7-11 ❖ How can proclaiming God's truth to hostile listeners be dangerous business still today?

17Some of the elders of the land
stepped forward and said to the entire
assembly of people, 18"Micah[k] of Moresheth prophesied in the days of Hezekiah
king of Judah. He told all the people of
Judah, 'This is what the LORD Almighty
says:

"'Zion[l] will be plowed like a field,
Jerusalem will become a heap of
rubble,[m]
the temple hill[n] a mound
overgrown with thickets.'[a][o]

19"Did Hezekiah king of Judah or anyone else in Judah put him to death? Did
not Hezekiah[p] fear the LORD and seek
his favor? And did not the LORD relent,[q]
so that he did not bring the disaster[r] he
pronounced against them? We are about
to bring a terrible disaster[s] on ourselves!"

20(Now Uriah son of Shemaiah from
Kiriath Jearim[t] was another man who
prophesied in the name of the LORD;
he prophesied the same things against
this city and this land as Jeremiah did.
21When King Jehoiakim[u] and all his
officers and officials heard his words,
the king was determined to put him to
death. But Uriah heard of it and fled[v]
in fear to Egypt. 22King Jehoiakim,
however, sent Elnathan[w] son of Akbor
to Egypt, along with some other men.
23They brought Uriah out of Egypt and
took him to King Jehoiakim, who had
him struck down with a sword and his
body thrown into the burial place of the
common people.)

[a] *18* Micah 3:12

Micah; instead, he feared the Lord, and the Lord relented concerning the announced judgment. This is an implied recognition of Jeremiah's claim.

The people understand that Hezekiah's reaction to the prophecy was genuine repentance and that God used the unconditional prophecy to move the king and people toward change.

26:20–24 A prophet named Uriah, however, was not given the reprieve given to Jeremiah. King Jehoiakim's execution of Uriah thereby brings the judgment of "innocent blood" on himself and his administration. Jeremiah might have been executed except that an important official, Ahikam son of Shaphan, stood on his side. With Ahikam one gets a glimpse of someone who sympathized with Jeremiah and his prophetic task. His brother later lends to Baruch, Jeremiah's scribe, his office overlooking the temple complex (36:10).

✣ **26:1–24** Judgmental prophecy does not reach its final goal when (or even if) a predicted disaster occurs. While God may vindicate his righteousness through judgment of the wicked (and thereby instruct others), such judgment (enacted in history or simply announced) may also serve the larger ends of renewing his people. Both righteousness and renewal are goals of God according to the broader Scriptural teaching. Attaining these goals through improvement is a consistent pattern of God's dealings with his people.

24 Furthermore, Ahikam[x] son of Shaphan supported Jeremiah, and so he was not handed over to the people to be put to death.

Judah to Serve Nebuchadnezzar

27 Early in the reign of Zedekiah[a][y] son of Josiah king of Judah, this word came to Jeremiah from the LORD: 2 This is what the LORD said to me: "Make a yoke[z] out of straps and crossbars and put it on your neck. 3 Then send word to the kings of Edom, Moab, Ammon,[a] Tyre and Sidon through the envoys who have come to Jerusalem to Zedekiah king of Judah. 4 Give them a message for their masters and say, 'This is what the LORD Almighty, the God of Israel, says: "Tell this to your masters: 5 With my great power and outstretched arm[b] I made the earth and its people and the animals that are on it, and I give[c] it to anyone I please. 6 Now I will give all your countries into the hands of my servant[d] Nebuchadnezzar[e] king of Babylon; I will make even the wild animals subject to him.[f] 7 All nations will serve[g] him and his son and his grandson until the time[h] for his land comes; then many nations and great kings will subjugate[i] him.

8 " ' "If, however, any nation or kingdom will not serve Nebuchadnezzar king of Babylon or bow its neck under his yoke, I will punish that nation with the sword, famine and plague, declares the LORD, until I destroy it by his hand. 9 So do not listen to your prophets, your diviners, your interpreters of dreams, your mediums[j] or your sorcerers who tell you, 'You will not serve the king of Babylon.' 10 They prophesy lies[k] to you that will only serve to remove you far from your lands; I will banish you and you will perish. 11 But if any nation will bow its neck under the yoke[l] of the king of Babylon and serve him, I will let that nation remain in its own land to till it and to live there, declares the LORD." ' "

12 I gave the same message to Zedekiah king of Judah. I said, "Bow your neck under the yoke of the king of Babylon; serve him and his people, and you will live. 13 Why will you and your people die[m] by the sword, famine and plague with which the LORD has threatened any nation that will not serve the king of Babylon? 14 Do not listen to the words of the prophets who say to you, 'You will not serve the king of Babylon,' for they are prophesying lies[n] to you. 15 'I have not sent[o] them,' declares the LORD. 'They are prophesying lies in my name.[p] Therefore, I will banish you and you will perish,[q] both you and the prophets who prophesy to you.' "

16 Then I said to the priests and all these people, "This is what the LORD says: Do not listen to the prophets who say, 'Very soon now the articles[r] from the LORD's house will be brought back from Babylon.' They are prophesying lies to you. 17 Do not listen to them. Serve the king of Babylon, and you will live. Why should this city become a ruin? 18 If they are

26:24 [x]2Ki 22:12
27:1 [y]2Ch 36:11
27:2 [z]Jer 28:10, 13
27:3 [a]Jer 25:21
27:5 [b]Dt 9:29 [c]Ps 115:16
27:6 [d]Jer 25:9 [e]Jer 21:7; Eze 29:18-20 [f]Jer 28:14; Da 2:37-38
27:7 [g]2Ch 36:20 [h]Jer 25:12 [i]Jer 25:14; Da 5:28
27:9 [j]Dt 18:11
27:10 [k]Jer 23:25
27:11 [l]Jer 21:9
27:13 [m]Eze 18:31
27:14 [n]Jer 14:14
27:15 [o]Jer 23:21 [p]Jer 29:9 [q]Jer 6:15
27:16 [r]2Ki 24:13; 2Ch 36:7,10; Jer 28:3; Da 1:2

Jer 27:16–22 ❖ Imagine hearing these words from a trusted leader. How should we respond when called by God to do hard things that may not make sense in the moment?

[a] *1* A few Hebrew manuscripts and Syriac (see also 27:3,12 and 28:1); most Hebrew manuscripts *Jehoiakim* (Most Septuagint manuscripts do not have this verse.)

27:1–22 God has given limited historical reign to Babylon and Nebuchadnezzar. To oppose Babylon at this time is to oppose God's will as Creator and Lord.

In keeping with prophecies made elsewhere, the end of Babylonian dominance is also acknowledged. Babylon's end is noted (v. 7), as is God's intent to restore the temple vessels taken by Nebuchadnezzar and those of his people now in exile (v. 22).

The majority of ch. 27 concerns the work of other prophets who oppose the message of Jeremiah (vv. 9, 14–18). Jeremiah's years of proclaiming an assault on Jerusalem have proved true, but the city itself has survived. Those who prophesied "peace" have been proved wrong, but the Judean state and its capital are still intact.

27:16–22 The concluding verses point to a time when God will bring back temple vessels from Babylon to Jerusalem. Babylon did not take them away because God was powerless—Nebuchadnezzar is God's servant, not his conqueror. The vessels will be returned when God is ready.

✣ **27:1–22** This chapter is concerned with God's timing and the larger design of his historical purposes in forming a people for himself. It is simply true that God's timing is often not *our* timing and God's ways are not our ways (Isa 55:8). What Jeremiah calls his contemporaries to believe is that their first impulse is wrong. They have yet to see the error of their ways, and until God has dealt with that, they will not be liberated from political oppression or anything else.

prophets and have the word of the LORD,
let them plead[s] with the LORD Almighty
that the articles remaining in the house
of the LORD and in the palace of the king
of Judah and in Jerusalem not be taken
to Babylon. 19For this is what the LORD Almighty says about the pillars, the bronze
Sea,[t] the movable stands and the other
articles[u] that are left in this city, 20which
Nebuchadnezzar king of Babylon did not
take away when he carried[v] Jehoiachin[aw]
son of Jehoiakim king of Judah into exile
from Jerusalem to Babylon, along with
all the nobles of Judah and Jerusalem —
21yes, this is what the LORD Almighty, the
God of Israel, says about the things that
are left in the house of the LORD and in
the palace of the king of Judah and in
Jerusalem: 22'They will be taken[x] to Babylon and there they will remain until the
day[y] I come for them,' declares the LORD.
'Then I will bring[z] them back and restore
them to this place.'"

The False Prophet Hananiah

28 In the fifth month of that same
year, the fourth year, early in the
reign of Zedekiah[a] king of Judah, the
prophet Hananiah son of Azzur, who was
from Gibeon,[b] said to me in the house of
the LORD in the presence of the priests
and all the people: 2"This is what the
LORD Almighty, the God of Israel, says:
'I will break the yoke[c] of the king of
Babylon. 3Within two years I will bring
back to this place all the articles[d] of the
LORD's house that Nebuchadnezzar king
of Babylon removed from here and took
to Babylon. 4I will also bring back to this
place Jehoiachin[ae] son of Jehoiakim king
of Judah and all the other exiles from
Judah who went to Babylon,' declares
the LORD, 'for I will break the yoke of
the king of Babylon.'"
5Then the prophet Jeremiah replied to
the prophet Hananiah before the priests
and all the people who were standing in
the house of the LORD. 6He said, "Amen!
May the LORD do so! May the LORD fulfill the words you have prophesied by
bringing the articles of the LORD's house
and all the exiles back to this place from
Babylon. 7Nevertheless, listen to what I
have to say in your hearing and in the
hearing of all the people: 8From early
times the prophets who preceded you
and me have prophesied war, disaster
and plague[f] against many countries and
great kingdoms. 9But the prophet who
prophesies peace will be recognized as
one truly sent by the LORD only if his
prediction comes true.[g]"
10Then the prophet Hananiah took the
yoke[h] off the neck of the prophet Jeremiah and broke it, 11and he said[i] before all
the people, "This is what the LORD says:
'In the same way I will break the yoke
of Nebuchadnezzar king of Babylon off
the neck of all the nations within two
years.'" At this, the prophet Jeremiah
went on his way.
12After the prophet Hananiah had broken the yoke off the neck of the prophet
Jeremiah, the word of the LORD came to

Jer 28:5-9 ❖ How can we test the words of those who claim to speak for God (see 1Jn 4:1)?

27:18 [s] 1Sa 7:8
27:19 [t] 2Ki 25:13 [u] Jer 52:17-23
27:20 [v] 2Ch 36:10; Jer 24:1 [w] Jer 22:24
27:22 [x] 2Ki 25:13 [y] 2Ch 36:21 [z] Ezr 1:7; 7:19
28:1 [a] Jer 27:1,3 [b] Jos 9:3
28:2 [c] Jer 27:12
28:3 [d] 2Ki 24:13
28:4 [e] Jer 22:24-27
28:8 [f] Lev 26:14-17; Isa 5:5-7
28:9 [g] Dt 18:22
28:10 [h] Jer 27:2
28:11 [i] Jer 14:14; 27:10

[a] *20,4* Hebrew *Jeconiah,* a variant of *Jehoiachin*

28:1–4 Hananiah's name means "The LORD is [*or* has been] gracious." Hananiah prophesies that God will restore to Jerusalem the temple vessels taken by the Babylonians in 597 BC and the exiled Judean king. Hananiah represents the unnamed prophets who are leading the people astray.

Hananiah performs a prophetic symbolic act in breaking the wooden yoke that Jeremiah is wearing. Throughout the chapter Hananiah is described as "the prophet." Both the terminology and the form of his public address indicate that he is a prophet of God, perhaps even one who has served God faithfully on previous occasions. Now, however, the content of his oracle is wrong.

Hananiah makes his announcement in the courtyard of the temple complex (vv. 2–4). Jeremiah's encounter with Hananiah in the temple symbolizes their differing viewpoints on what it means that God dwells in the midst of his people. Hananiah seems to think that God's presence means that God's defense of the house and the people is always near at hand.

28:5–11 Jeremiah's first reaction ("Amen!" v. 6) seems to indicate agreement. Jeremiah is open to hearing God speak through Hananiah. By way of first response, Jeremiah reminds Hananiah and their audience in the temple that prophets of the Lord have habitually announced disaster and judgment—the prophet who predicts peace will be proven correct only when that word comes to pass (vv. 8–9). A prophecy of disaster or judgment, however, is evaluated differently. It is intended to induce alarm and provoke people to action.

28:12–17 The word of the Lord comes to Jeremiah, and he confronts Hananiah with the message that Babylon rules with God's clear approval and that Hananiah has made the people believe a "lie" (v. 15).

Jeremiah: 13“Go and tell Hananiah, ‘This
is what the LORD says: You have broken
a wooden yoke, but in its place you will
get a yoke of iron. 14This is what the LORD
Almighty, the God of Israel, says: I will
put an iron yoke[j] on the necks of all these
nations to make them serve[k] Nebuchadnezzar king of Babylon, and they will
serve him. I will even give him control
over the wild animals.[l]’ ”
15Then the prophet Jeremiah said to
Hananiah the prophet, “Listen, Hananiah! The LORD has not sent[m] you, yet you
have persuaded this nation to trust in
lies.[n] 16Therefore this is what the LORD
says: ‘I am about to remove you from the
face of the earth.[o] This very year you are
going to die, because you have preached
rebellion[p] against the LORD.’ ”
17In the seventh month of that same
year, Hananiah the prophet died.

A Letter to the Exiles

29 This is the text of the letter that
the prophet Jeremiah sent from
Jerusalem to the surviving elders among
the exiles and to the priests, the prophets
and all the other people Nebuchadnezzar
had carried into exile from Jerusalem
to Babylon.[q] 2(This was after King Jehoiachin[a][r] and the queen mother, the
court officials and the leaders of Judah
and Jerusalem, the skilled workers and
the artisans had gone into exile from
Jerusalem.) 3He entrusted the letter to
Elasah son of Shaphan and to Gemariah
son of Hilkiah, whom Zedekiah king of
Judah sent to King Nebuchadnezzar in
Babylon. It said:

Jer 29:10-14 ❖ What do we believe are God’s good plans for the future? How do they fill us with hope?

4This is what the LORD Almighty,
the God of Israel, says to all those I
carried[s] into exile from Jerusalem
to Babylon: 5“Build[t] houses and
settle down; plant gardens and eat
what they produce. 6Marry and have
sons and daughters; find wives for
your sons and give your daughters
in marriage, so that they too may
have sons and daughters. Increase
in number there; do not decrease.
7Also, seek the peace and prosperity
of the city to which I have carried
you into exile. Pray[u] to the LORD for
it, because if it prospers, you too will
prosper.” 8Yes, this is what the LORD
Almighty, the God of Israel, says:
“Do not let the prophets and diviners among you deceive[v] you. Do not
listen to the dreams you encourage
them to have.[w] 9They are prophesying lies[x] to you in my name. I have
not sent them,” declares the LORD.
10This is what the LORD says:
“When seventy years[y] are completed
for Babylon, I will come to you and
fulfill my good promise to bring you
back[z] to this place. 11For I know the
plans[a] I have for you,” declares the
LORD, “plans to prosper you and not
to harm you, plans to give you hope
and a future. 12Then you will call on

28:14 [j] Dt 28:48 [k] Jer 25:11 [l] Jer 27:6
28:15 [m] Jer 29:31 [n] Jer 20:6; 29:21; La 2:14; Eze 13:6
28:16 [o] Ge 7:4 [p] Dt 13:5; Jer 29:32
29:1 [q] 2Ch 36:10
29:2 [r] 2Ki 24:12; Jer 22:24-28
29:4 [s] Jer 24:5
29:5 [t] ver 28
29:7 [u] Ezr 6:10; 1Ti 2:1-2
29:8 [v] Jer 37:9 [w] Jer 23:27
29:9 [x] Jer 14:14; 27:15
29:10 [y] 2Ch 36:21; Jer 25:12; Da 9:2 [z] Jer 21:22
29:11 [a] Ps 40:5

[a] 2 Hebrew *Jeconiah,* a variant of *Jehoiachin*

Jeremiah proclaims that God will now have the people serve Babylon through an iron yoke. In a somber word, Jeremiah announces that Hananiah will die within the year (vv. 12–17). That death is interpreted as judgment on the prophet and his word.

✣ **28:1–17** An authentic prophet cannot overlook the barriers between what God has called his people to be and what they in their human weakness actually represent. Wherever there is an automatic reliance on God’s will to save without accepting his refining judgments as a process of sanctification, there is the real possibility of misrepresenting God to any generation.

29:1–3 Jeremiah writes a letter to the Judean community in Babylon, taken into exile with Jehoiachin in 597 BC. Several prophets among the exiles have announced the imminent decline of Babylon and a return of the exiles to Judah (vv. 8–9, 15, 21–28). Some of the agitators are named (vv. 21–22, 24). These figures demonstrate that Jeremiah’s prophecies are known in Babylon.

Chapter 29 contains the same charges made against Hananiah in ch. 28. The prophets cause the people to trust in a lie (29:9, 21, 23, 31), and their words are, in effect, rebellion against the Lord (vv. 31–32).

29:4–9 Nebuchadnezzar was the historical agent who took the people into exile, but in v. 4 the theological point is made that it is actually the work of God himself. The people are to seek the prosperity of Babylon because it will affect them as well. Most important, they are to pray for their captors.

29:10–14 These hopeful verses help prepare readers for the section known to interpreters as the Book of Consolation (chs. 30–31). Jeremiah notes that the future of the people in exile rests on God’s “good promise” (29:10). In v. 11 the gracious promise is described as plans God has for the people. The restoration, however, is based on their seeking God with their whole heart.

me and come and pray to me, and
I will listen[b] to you. 13 You will seek[c]
me and find me when you seek me
with all your heart.[d] 14 I will be found
by you," declares the LORD, "and will
bring you back[e] from captivity.[a] I
will gather you from all the nations
and places where I have banished
you," declares the LORD, "and will
bring you back to the place from
which I carried you into exile."[f]
15 You may say, "The LORD has
raised up prophets for us in Babylon," 16 but this is what the LORD
says about the king who sits on
David's throne and all the people
who remain in this city, your fellow citizens who did not go with you
into exile— 17 yes, this is what the
LORD Almighty says: "I will send the
sword, famine and plague[g] against
them and I will make them like figs[h]
that are so bad they cannot be eaten.
18 I will pursue them with the sword,
famine and plague and will make
them abhorrent[i] to all the kingdoms
of the earth, a curse[b] and an object
of horror,[j] of scorn and reproach,
among all the nations where I drive
them. 19 For they have not listened
to my words,"[k] declares the LORD,
"words that I sent to them again and
again by my servants the prophets.[l]
And you exiles have not listened either," declares the LORD.
20 Therefore, hear the word of the
LORD, all you exiles whom I have
sent[m] away from Jerusalem to Babylon. 21 This is what the LORD Almighty, the God of Israel, says about
Ahab son of Kolaiah and Zedekiah
son of Maaseiah, who are prophesying lies[n] to you in my name: "I
will deliver them into the hands of
Nebuchadnezzar king of Babylon,
and he will put them to death before
your very eyes. 22 Because of them,
all the exiles from Judah who are
in Babylon will use this curse: 'May
the LORD treat you like Zedekiah
and Ahab, whom the king of Babylon burned[o] in the fire.' 23 For they
have done outrageous things in Israel; they have committed adultery[p]
with their neighbors' wives, and in
my name they have uttered lies—
which I did not authorize. I know[q]
it and am a witness to it," declares
the LORD.

Message to Shemaiah

24 Tell Shemaiah the Nehelamite,
25 "This is what the LORD Almighty, the
God of Israel, says: You sent letters in
your own name to all the people in Jerusalem, to the priest Zephaniah[r] son of
Maaseiah, and to all the other priests.
You said to Zephaniah, 26 'The LORD has
appointed you priest in place of Jehoiada to be in charge of the house of the
LORD; you should put any maniac[s] who
acts like a prophet into the stocks[t] and
neck-irons. 27 So why have you not reprimanded Jeremiah from Anathoth, who
poses as a prophet among you? 28 He has
sent this message[u] to us in Babylon: It
will be a long time.[v] Therefore build[w]
houses and settle down; plant gardens
and eat what they produce.'"
29 Zephaniah the priest, however,
read the letter to Jeremiah the prophet.
30 Then the word of the LORD came to
Jeremiah: 31 "Send this message to all
the exiles: 'This is what the LORD says
about Shemaiah[x] the Nehelamite: Because Shemaiah has prophesied to you,
even though I did not send[y] him, and has
persuaded you to trust in lies, 32 this is
what the LORD says: I will surely punish

29:12 [b] Ps 145:19
29:13 [c] Mt 7:7 [d] Dt 4:29; Jer 24:7
29:14 [e] Dt 30:3; Jer 30:3 [f] Jer 23:3-4
29:17 [g] Jer 27:8 [h] Jer 24:8-10
29:18 [i] Jer 15:4 [j] Dt 28:25; Jer 42:18
29:19 [k] Jer 6:19 [l] Jer 25:4
29:20 [m] Jer 24:5
29:21 [n] ver 9; Jer 14:14
29:22 [o] Da 3:6
29:23 [p] Jer 23:14 [q] Heb 4:13
29:25 [r] 2Ki 25:18; Jer 21:1
29:26 [s] 2Ki 9:11; Hos 9:7; Jn 10:20 [t] Jer 20:2
29:28 [u] ver 1 [v] ver 10 [w] ver 5
29:31 [x] ver 24 [y] Jer 14:14; 28:15

[a] 14 Or *will restore your fortunes* [b] 18 That is, their names will be used in cursing (see verse 22); or, others will see that they are cursed.

29:15–23 Jeremiah describes God as making King Zedekiah and the people in Jerusalem like poor "figs that . . . cannot be eaten" (v. 17). Because the king in Jerusalem and his people refuse to acknowledge God's judgment and refuse to embrace his covenant stipulations, they will be given over to the disasters of the sword and plague. The last part of this section warns the exiles not to listen to these prophetic agitators.

29:24–32 A particular opponent of Jeremiah, Shemaiah the Nehelamite, is singled out for criticism and judgment.

29:1–32 Prayer is a form of applied theology. Prayer is not for the benefit of God, although both praise and petition belong in a relationship with God. Prayer changes both the perceptions of those who pray and their actions. Through prayer one can look at opponents or problems as more than someone or something to be overcome. They can become a means of education and sanctification, the means through which one finds growth in relationship with God.

Shemaiah the Nehelamite and his descendants.[z] He will have no one left
among this people, nor will he see the
good[a] things I will do for my people, declares the LORD, because he has preached
rebellion[b] against me.' "

Restoration of Israel

30 This is the word that came to Jeremiah from the LORD: 2"This is
what the LORD, the God of Israel, says:
'Write[c] in a book all the words I have
spoken to you. 3The days are coming,'
declares the LORD, 'when I will bring[d]
my people Israel and Judah back from
captivity[a] and restore[e] them to the land
I gave their ancestors to possess,' says
the LORD."

4These are the words the LORD spoke
concerning Israel and Judah: 5"This is
what the LORD says:

" 'Cries of fear[f] are heard —
terror, not peace.
6 Ask and see:
Can a man bear children?
Then why do I see every strong man
with his hands on his stomach like
a woman in labor,[g]
every face turned deathly pale?
7 How awful that day[h] will be!
No other will be like it.
It will be a time of trouble[i] for Jacob,
but he will be saved[j] out of it.

8 " 'In that day,' declares the LORD
Almighty,
'I will break the yoke[k] off their
necks
and will tear off their bonds;
no longer will foreigners enslave
them.[l]
9 Instead, they will serve the LORD
their God
and David[m] their king,[n]
whom I will raise up for them.

10 " 'So do not be afraid,[o] Jacob my
servant;[p]
do not be dismayed, Israel,'
declares the LORD.
'I will surely save[q] you out of a
distant place,
your descendants from the land of
their exile.
Jacob will again have peace and
security,[r]
and no one will make him afraid.
11 I am with you and will save you,'
declares the LORD.
'Though I completely destroy all the
nations
among which I scatter you,
I will not completely destroy[s] you.
I will discipline[t] you but only in due
measure;
I will not let you go entirely
unpunished.'[u]

12"This is what the LORD says:

" 'Your wound is incurable,
your injury beyond healing.[v]
13 There is no one to plead your cause,
no remedy for your sore,
no healing[w] for you.
14 All your allies[x] have forgotten you;
they care nothing for you.
I have struck you as an enemy[y]
would
and punished you as would the
cruel,[z]
because your guilt is so great
and your sins[a] so many.
15 Why do you cry out over your
wound,
your pain that has no cure?
Because of your great guilt and
many sins
I have done these things to you.

16 " 'But all who devour[b] you will be
devoured;
all your enemies will go into
exile.[c]

[a] 3 Or *will restore the fortunes of my people Israel and Judah*

29:32 [z] 1Sa 2:30-33 [a] ver 10 [b] Jer 28:16
30:2 [c] Isa 30:8
30:3 [d] Jer 29:14 [e] Jer 16:15
30:5 [f] Jer 6:25
30:6 [g] Jer 4:31
30:7 [h] Isa 2:12; Joel 2:11 [i] Zep 1:15 [j] ver 10
30:8 [k] Isa 9:4 [l] Eze 34:27
30:9 [m] Isa 55:3-4; Lk 1:69; Ac 2:30; 13:23 [n] Eze 34:23-24; 37:24; Hos 3:5
30:10 [o] Isa 43:5; Jer 46:27-28 [p] Isa 44:2 [q] Jer 29:14 [r] Isa 35:9
30:11 [s] Jer 4:27; 46:28 [t] Jer 10:24 [u] Am 9:8
30:12 [v] Jer 15:18
30:13 [w] Jer 8:22; 14:19; 46:11
30:14 [x] Jer 22:20; La 1:2 [y] Job 13:24 [z] Job 30:21 [a] Jer 5:6
30:16 [b] Isa 33:1; Jer 2:3; 10:25 [c] Isa 14:2; Joel 3:4-8

30:1–3 The primary claim about the future is that the affliction of "Jacob" (vv. 7, 10, 18) will be removed and the people will be restored to their land and to a better relationship with God. Jeremiah announces a restoration of the covenant relationship between God and his people (v. 22).
30:4–7 This portion of ch. 30 is a bit cryptic with respect to the future turmoil it points toward. Jacob will be saved from a time of trouble.
30:8–11 Yokes and bonds will be removed from Jacob, and the people will no longer be enslaved by foreigners. The expression "David their king" in v. 9 likely means someone from David's line. This hope finds its ultimate fulfillment in the NT proclamation that Jesus is David's greater Son. The injunction, "do not be afraid," addressed to Jacob as God's "servant" (v. 10), reminds the reader of the prophecies in the book of Isaiah.
30:12–17 Jerusalem is addressed. The description of its guilt and helplessness reminds the reader/hearer of the book of Lamentations. Zion's enemies will be destroyed, and the city will be restored.

Those who plunder[d] you will be
plundered;
all who make spoil of you I will
despoil.
17 But I will restore you to health
and heal your wounds,'
declares the LORD,
'because you are called an outcast,[e]
Zion for whom no one cares.'

18 "This is what the LORD says:

" 'I will restore the fortunes[f] of
Jacob's tents
and have compassion[g] on his
dwellings;
the city will be rebuilt[h] on her ruins,
and the palace will stand in its
proper place.
19 From them will come songs[i] of
thanksgiving[j]
and the sound of rejoicing.[k]
I will add to their numbers,[l]
and they will not be decreased;
I will bring them honor,[m]
and they will not be disdained.
20 Their children[n] will be as in days of
old,
and their community will be
established[o] before me;
I will punish all who oppress them.
21 Their leader[p] will be one of their
own;
their ruler will arise from among
them.
I will bring him near[q] and he will
come close to me —
for who is he who will devote
himself
to be close to me?'
declares the LORD.

30:16 [d] Jer 50:10
30:17 [e] Jer 33:24
30:18 [f] ver 3; Jer 31:23 [g] Ps 102:13 [h] Jer 31:4,24,38
30:19 [i] Isa 35:10; 51:11 [j] Isa 51:3 [k] Ps 126:1-2; Jer 31:4 [l] Jer 33:22 [m] Isa 60:9
30:20 [n] Isa 54:13; Jer 31:17 [o] Isa 54:14
30:21 [p] ver 9 [q] Nu 16:5
30:23 [r] Jer 23:19
30:24 [s] Jer 4:8 [t] Jer 4:28 [u] Jer 23:19-20
31:1 [v] Jer 30:22
31:2 [w] Nu 14:20 [x] Ex 33:14
31:3 [y] Dt 4:37 [z] Hos 11:4
31:4 [a] Jer 30:19

Jer 30:18–22 ❖ When has God restored your life to joy and praise after a season of trials?

22 " 'So you will be my people,
and I will be your God.' "

23 See, the storm[r] of the LORD
will burst out in wrath,
a driving wind swirling down
on the heads of the wicked.
24 The fierce anger[s] of the LORD will
not turn back[t]
until he fully accomplishes
the purposes of his heart.
In days to come
you will understand[u] this.

31 "At that time," declares the LORD, "I
will be the God[v] of all the families
of Israel, and they will be my people."
2 This is what the LORD says:

"The people who survive the sword
will find favor[w] in the wilderness;
I will come to give rest[x] to Israel."

3 The LORD appeared to us in the past,[a]
saying:

"I have loved[y] you with an
everlasting love;
I have drawn[z] you with unfailing
kindness.
4 I will build you up again,
and you, Virgin Israel, will be
rebuilt.
Again you will take up your timbrels
and go out to dance with the
joyful.[a]

[a] 3 Or *LORD has appeared to us from afar*

30:18–22 There is an allusion to future leadership that will spring up from among the people (v. 21). The concluding verse reiterates the covenant formula (cf. 24:7).

30:23–24 This surprising section puts the future under the claim of God's righteous judgment. The final verse is cryptic. Only the future ("in days to come") will reveal the extent of God's purposes. Thus, the full significance of these prophecies will only be realized in the distant future.

✚ **30:1–24** A glance at biblical prophecy confirms that God has been faithful to his promises, but his faithfulness comes in surprising ways. Oftentimes it is at some distance that people of faith can see more clearly what God has done. Perhaps what is more important for people of faith today is to concentrate on the "constants" in the prophecy of the Bible rather than on a blueprint mentality that believes it can predict the future.

What are some of those constants? One is certainly that God is the Judge of all people. In addition, God has called people into fellowship and has promised to be their God. These two things will not change.

31:1 "That time" is a reference to a decisive period of divine activity and the resulting changes.

31:2–6 God reminds his people that they can find his favor even in the desert. The future rebuilding of "Virgin Israel" (v. 4) indicates that God has loved them with an "everlasting love" and drawn them back to himself with "unfailing kindness" (v. 3).

Those in Ephraim will call to one another with the request to "go up to Zion" (v. 6). This is pilgrimage language.

5 Again you will plant vineyards
on the hills of Samaria;[b]
the farmers will plant them
and enjoy their fruit.[c]
6 There will be a day when watchmen cry out
on the hills of Ephraim,
'Come, let us go up to Zion,
to the LORD our God.'"[d]

7 This is what the LORD says:

"Sing with joy for Jacob;
shout for the foremost[e] of the nations.
Make your praises heard, and say,
'LORD, save[f] your people,
the remnant[g] of Israel.'
8 See, I will bring them from the land of the north[h]
and gather[i] them from the ends of the earth.
Among them will be the blind[j] and the lame,[k]
expectant mothers and women in labor;
a great throng will return.
9 They will come with weeping;[l]
they will pray as I bring them back.
I will lead[m] them beside streams of water
on a level[n] path where they will not stumble,
because I am Israel's father,[o]
and Ephraim is my firstborn son.
10 "Hear the word of the LORD, you nations;
proclaim it in distant coastlands:[p]
'He who scattered Israel will gather[q] them
and will watch over his flock like a shepherd.'[r]
11 For the LORD will deliver Jacob
and redeem[s] them from the hand
of those stronger[t] than they.

31:5 [b] Jer 50:19 [c] Isa 65:21; Am 9:14
31:6 [d] Isa 2:3; Jer 50:4-5; Mic 4:2
31:7 [e] Dt 28:13; Isa 61:9 [f] Ps 14:7; 28:9 [g] Isa 37:31
31:8 [h] Jer 3:18; 23:8 [i] Dt 30:4; Eze 34:12-14 [j] Isa 42:16 [k] Eze 34:16; Mic 4:6
31:9 [l] Ps 126:5 [m] Isa 63:13 [n] Isa 49:11 [o] Ex 4:22; Jer 3:4
31:10 [p] Isa 66:19; Jer 25:22 [q] Jer 50:19 [r] Isa 40:11; Eze 34:12
31:11 [s] Isa 44:23; 48:20 [t] Ps 142:6
31:12 [u] Eze 17:23; Mic 4:1 [v] Joel 3:18 [w] Hos 2:21-22 [x] Isa 58:11 [y] Isa 65:19; Jn 16:22; Rev 7:17
31:13 [z] Isa 61:3 [a] Ps 30:11; Isa 51:11
31:14 [b] ver 25
31:15 [c] Jos 18:25 [d] Ge 37:35 [e] Jer 10:20; Mt 2:17-18*
31:16 [f] Isa 25:8; 30:19 [g] Ru 2:12 [h] Jer 30:3; Eze 11:17

12 They will come and shout for joy on the heights[u] of Zion;
they will rejoice in the bounty[v] of the LORD—
the grain, the new wine and the olive oil,[w]
the young of the flocks and herds.
They will be like a well-watered garden,[x]
and they will sorrow[y] no more.
13 Then young women will dance and be glad,
young men and old as well.
I will turn their mourning[z] into gladness;
I will give them comfort and joy[a]
instead of sorrow.
14 I will satisfy[b] the priests with abundance,
and my people will be filled with my bounty,"
declares the LORD.

15 This is what the LORD says:

"A voice is heard in Ramah,[c]
mourning and great weeping,
Rachel weeping for her children
and refusing to be comforted,[d]
because they are no more."[e]

16 This is what the LORD says:

"Restrain your voice from weeping
and your eyes from tears,[f]
for your work will be rewarded,[g]"
declares the LORD.
"They will return[h] from the land of the enemy.
17 So there is hope for your descendants,"
declares the LORD.
"Your children will return to their own land.

18 "I have surely heard Ephraim's moaning:

31:7–9 The Lord proposes a song of praise for a saved remnant. Readers should take note of the term "Israel" in context. Verse 9 uses the term to refer specifically to the former northern kingdom.
31:10–14 The poetry of v. 11 links two terms to describe God's reclaiming his people. The NIV translates the first verb "deliver." The term is used also for the ransom of a slave (Ex 21:8). The second verb is translated by the NIV as "redeem." The word has its roots in family custom, where a relative frees other family members from debts or other social obligations.

In its primary sense the passage refers to the new exodus. The language of joy and delight in Jer 31:12–14 is every bit as extravagant as the thorough language of judgment used elsewhere in Jeremiah. "Mourning" will be turned into "gladness" (v. 13).
31:15–17 Rachel died soon after her son Benjamin was born; she was buried between Bethel and Bethlehem (Ge 35:16–26). A monument was built to mark her tomb. Jeremiah's reference to "weeping" in Ramah (meaning "hill" in Hebrew) apparently refers to the place of this monument. Rachel's children are coming home.
31:18–20 The Israelites who have sinned and been cast from their land are personified in Ephraim. God tenderly accepts his repentance, describing Ephraim as his "dear son" (v. 20; cf. v. 9).

'You disciplined[i] me like an
unruly calf,[j]
and I have been disciplined.
Restore[k] me, and I will return,
because you are the LORD my God.
19 After I strayed,[l]
I repented;
after I came to understand,
I beat[m] my breast.
I was ashamed and humiliated
because I bore the disgrace of my
youth.'
20 Is not Ephraim my dear son,
the child in whom I delight?
Though I often speak against him,
I still remember[n] him.
Therefore my heart yearns for him;
I have great compassion[o] for him,"
declares the LORD.

21 "Set up road signs;
put up guideposts.
Take note of the highway,[p]
the road that you take.
Return,[q] Virgin[r] Israel,
return to your towns.
22 How long will you wander,[s]
unfaithful[t] Daughter Israel?
The LORD will create a new thing on
earth —
the woman will return to[a] the
man."

23 This is what the LORD Almighty, the
God of Israel, says: "When I bring them
back from captivity,[b][u] the people in the
land of Judah and in its towns will once
again use these words: 'The LORD bless
you, you prosperous city,[v] you sacred
mountain.'[w]
24 People will live[x] together
in Judah and all its towns — farmers and
those who move about with their flocks.
25 I will refresh the weary and satisfy the
faint."[y]

26 At this I awoke[z] and looked around.
My sleep had been pleasant to me.
27 "The days are coming," declares
the LORD, "when I will plant[a] the king-

31:18 [i] Job 5:17
[j] Hos 4:16
[k] Ps 80:3
31:19 [l] Eze 36:31
[m] Eze 21:12; Lk 18:13
31:20 [n] Hos 4:4; 11:8 [o] Isa 55:7; 63:15; Mic 7:18
31:21 [p] Jer 50:5
[q] Isa 52:11 [r] ver 4
31:22 [s] Jer 2:23
[t] Jer 3:6
31:23 [u] Jer 30:18
[v] Isa 1:26
[w] Ps 48:1; Zec 8:3
31:24 [x] Zec 8:4-8
31:25 [y] Jn 4:14
31:26 [z] Zec 4:1
31:27 [a] Eze 36:9-11; Hos 2:23
31:28 [b] Jer 18:8; 44:27 [c] Jer 1:10
31:29 [d] La 5:7
[e] Eze 18:2
31:30 [f] Isa 3:11; Gal 6:7
31:31 [g] Jer 32:40; Eze 37:26; Lk 22:20; Heb 8:8-12*; 10:16-17
31:32 [h] Ex 24:8
[i] Dt 5:3
31:33 [j] 2Co 3:3
[k] Jer 24:7; Heb 10:16

Jer 31:31-34 ❖ How does God's new covenant bring us into a relationship with him (see Lk 22:20)?

doms of Israel and Judah with the offspring of people and of animals.
28 Just
as I watched over them to uproot and
tear down, and to overthrow, destroy
and bring disaster,[b] so I will watch over
them to build and to plant,"[c] declares
the LORD.
29 "In those days people will
no longer say,

'The parents[d] have eaten sour
grapes,
and the children's teeth are set on
edge.'[e]

30 Instead, everyone will die for their own
sin;[f] whoever eats sour grapes — their
own teeth will be set on edge.

31 "The days are coming," declares the
LORD,
"when I will make a new
covenant[g]
with the people of Israel
and with the people of Judah.
32 It will not be like the covenant[h]
I made with their ancestors[i]
when I took them by the hand
to lead them out of Egypt,
because they broke my covenant,
though I was a husband to[c]
them,[d]"
declares the LORD.
33 "This is the covenant I will make
with the people of Israel
after that time," declares the LORD.
"I will put my law in their minds
and write it on their hearts.[j]
I will be their God,
and they will be my people.[k]

[a] *22* *Or will protect* [b] *23* Or *I restore their fortunes* [c] *32* Hebrew; Septuagint and Syriac */ and I turned away from* [d] *32* Or *was their master*

31:21–22 The poetry calls for highway markers to be erected so that "Virgin Israel" (v. 21) can find her way home. The text describes her return to her homeland as a new thing that God will create (v. 22).
31:23–25 Restoration is the theme here. While this theme is familiar in the immediate context, it is still important to note that God is the chief actor in the drama of the return.
31:27–30 God will build and plant Israel and Judah. The use of both names conveys totality (cf. v. 31). The form of their life together is not stated. Furthermore, the future will bring an end to the complaints that shared judgment is unjust (vv. 29–30).
31:31–34 This well-known passage, with its proclamation of a new covenant, is a summary of Jeremiah's message. God's Torah ("law," the verbal expression of his will) will become a part of a person/people when God writes it on their hearts. Knowledge of God, therefore, is internalized. Sin's power is made obsolete by the astounding announcement that God will not remember their sins.

34 No longer will they teach[l] their
neighbor,
or say to one another, 'Know the
LORD,'
because they will all know[m] me,
from the least of them to the
greatest,"
declares the LORD.
"For I will forgive[n] their wickedness
and will remember their sins[o] no
more."

35 This is what the LORD says,

he who appoints[p] the sun
to shine by day,
who decrees the moon and stars
to shine by night,[q]
who stirs up the sea
so that its waves roar—
the LORD Almighty is his name:[r]
36 "Only if these decrees[s] vanish from
my sight,"
declares the LORD,
"will Israel[t] ever cease
being a nation before me."

37 This is what the LORD says:

"Only if the heavens above can be
measured[u]
and the foundations of the earth
below be searched out
will I reject[v] all the descendants of
Israel
because of all they have done,"
declares the LORD.

38 "The days are coming," declares the
LORD, "when this city will be rebuilt[w] for
me from the Tower of Hananel[x] to the
Corner Gate.[y] 39 The measuring line will
stretch from there straight to the hill
of Gareb and then turn to Goah. 40 The
whole valley[z] where dead bodies[a] and
ashes are thrown, and all the terraces
out to the Kidron Valley[b] on the east as
far as the corner of the Horse Gate,[c] will
be holy[d] to the LORD. The city will never
again be uprooted or demolished."

31:34 [l] 1Jn 2:27 [m] Jn 6:45 [n] Isa 54:13; Jer 33:8; 50:20 [o] Mic 7:19; Ro 11:27; Heb 10:17* 31:35 [p] Ps 136:7-9 [q] Ge 1:16 [r] Jer 10:16 31:36 [s] Isa 54:9-10; Jer 33:20-26 [t] Ps 89:36-37 31:37 [u] Jer 33:22 [v] Jer 33:24-26; Ro 11:1-5 31:38 [w] Jer 30:18 [x] Ne 3:1 [y] 2Ki 14:13; Zec 14:10 31:40 [z] Jer 7:31-32 [a] Jer 8:2 [b] 2Sa 15:23; Jn 18:1 [c] 2Ki 11:16 [d] Joel 3:17; Zec 14:21 32:1 [e] 2Ki 25:1 [f] Jer 25:1; 39:1 32:2 [g] Ne 3:25; Jer 37:21 32:3 [h] Jer 26:8-9 [i] ver 28; Jer 34:2-3 32:4 [j] Jer 38:18, 23; 39:5-7; 52:9 32:5 [k] Jer 39:7; Eze 12:13 [l] Jer 21:4 32:7 [m] Lev 25:24-25; Ru 4:3-4; Mt 27:10*

Jeremiah Buys a Field

32 This is the word that came to Jeremiah from the LORD in the tenth[e]
year of Zedekiah king of Judah, which was
the eighteenth[f] year of Nebuchadnezzar.
2 The army of the king of Babylon was
then besieging Jerusalem, and Jeremiah
the prophet was confined in the courtyard
of the guard[g] in the royal palace of Judah.
3 Now Zedekiah king of Judah had imprisoned him there, saying, "Why do you
prophesy[h] as you do? You say, 'This is
what the LORD says: I am about to give
this city into the hands of the king of
Babylon, and he will capture[i] it. 4 Zedekiah king of Judah will not escape[j] the
Babylonians[a] but will certainly be given
into the hands of the king of Babylon,
and will speak with him face to face and
see him with his own eyes. 5 He will take[k]
Zedekiah to Babylon, where he will remain until I deal with him, declares the
LORD. If you fight against the Babylonians, you will not succeed.' "[l]
6 Jeremiah said, "The word of the LORD
came to me: 7 Hanamel son of Shallum
your uncle is going to come to you and
say, 'Buy my field at Anathoth, because
as nearest relative it is your right and
duty[m] to buy it.'

[a] 4 Or *Chaldeans*; also in verses 5, 24, 25, 28, 29 and 43

31:35–40 Just as the order of the cosmos is sure, so is God's commitment to his people. Jerusalem is to be transformed and will never again be overthrown.

✣ **31:1–40** Jeremiah 31 is the voice of an inspired spiritual ancestor who spoke to his contemporaries about God's action in their lives and that of their descendants. Perhaps in the present, we can think of things in our lives that are "signs" of God at work—things whose shape and function portray the work of God. These things may be personal; they may concern the family; they may be part of the life of fellowship one enjoys among friends and in the activities of a congregation. Signs of redemption should point not only to what has already been accomplished in Christ but also to what still lies ahead. There is always a future tense to the life of believers.

32:1–15 Babylon has besieged Jerusalem for a second time, and Jeremiah is confined in the city by a royal guard. Apparently, the Babylonians began the siege late in the year 588 BC.

32:3–5 Jeremiah's prophecies about Babylon have been perceived as treasonous. As a result, he is confined on several occasions. His announcement to Zedekiah here that Jerusalem and the king will be handed over to Babylon is essentially repeated in 34:2–3.

32:6–15 Jeremiah purchases some family property. A particularly significant element of what defined most families was its patrimony or its inheritance. This property, unlike other things the family possessed, was not to be sold to those outside of the extended family.

32:7–11 According to v. 7, the prophet has the right of redemption to the property owned by Hanamel. A time of siege is not the time to be buying prop-

8"Then, just as the LORD had said, my
cousin Hanamel came to me in the courtyard of the guard and said, 'Buy my field
at Anathoth in the territory of Benjamin.
Since it is your right to redeem it and
possess it, buy it for yourself.'

"I knew that this was the word of the
LORD; 9so I bought the field at Anathoth
from my cousin Hanamel and weighed
out for him seventeen shekels[a] of silver.[n]
10I signed and sealed the deed, had it
witnessed,[o] and weighed out the silver
on the scales. 11I took the deed of purchase — the sealed copy containing the
terms and conditions, as well as the unsealed copy — 12and I gave this deed to
Baruch[p] son of Neriah,[q] the son of Mahseiah, in the presence of my cousin Hanamel and of the witnesses who had signed
the deed and of all the Jews sitting in the
courtyard of the guard.

13"In their presence I gave Baruch
these instructions: 14'This is what the
LORD Almighty, the God of Israel, says:
Take these documents, both the sealed
and unsealed copies of the deed of purchase, and put them in a clay jar so they
will last a long time. 15For this is what the
LORD Almighty, the God of Israel, says:
Houses, fields and vineyards will again
be bought in this land.'[r]

16"After I had given the deed of purchase to Baruch son of Neriah, I prayed
to the LORD:

> 17"Ah, Sovereign LORD,[s] you have
> made the heavens and the earth by
> your great power and outstretched
> arm.[t] Nothing is too hard[u] for you.
> 18You show love[v] to thousands
> but bring the punishment for the

32:9 [n] Ge 23:16
32:10 [o] Ru 4:9
32:12 [p] ver 16; Jer 36:4; 43:3, 6; 45:1 [q] Jer 51:59
32:15 [r] ver 43-44; Jer 30:18; Am 9:14-15
32:17 [s] Jer 1:6 [t] 2Ki 19:15; Ps 102:25 [u] Mt 19:26
32:18 [v] Dt 5:10

[a] 9 That is, about 7 ounces or about 200 grams

---

erty; such a request reflects a time of desperation as families seek whatever means they can to keep life and limb together.

When the Babylonian victory and the siege of Jerusalem seem merely a matter of time, Jeremiah purchases the property because God has declared there will be a future restoration (v. 15).

32:12–15 Baruch is a scribe (36:32); the preparation, reading, and preservation of documents are skills of his profession. Baruch will assist Jeremiah in preparing a scroll of prophecies in ch. 36. The preservation of the purchase documents is described in some detail. Later, they will verify Jeremiah's prophecy that land and fields will again be bought.

32:16–25 Jeremiah praises God as Creator, as merciful and righteous Judge, and as the true God who chose Israel as his own. Also, he acknowledges that the Babylonian siege is God's work. This prayer ends abruptly with the statement that God has commanded Jeremiah to go and buy the field.

CHARACTER OF GOD // GOD IS OMNIPOTENT

Jeremiah 32:17: "Ah, Sovereign LORD, you have made the heavens and the earth by your great power and outstretched arm. Nothing is too hard for you."

Omnipotent simply means "all powerful." Jeremiah praises God's omnipotent nature in Jer 32:17: "Nothing is too hard for you." God's power is not limited by anything. He spoke all of creation, visible and invisible, into being, and God's power is supreme over all.

God's omnipotence is clearly shown in his act of creation. Who but God could speak galaxies into existence out of nothing? The universe is a testimony of God's power. God also shows his omnipotence through his providential hand, which upholds and sustains creation (Col 1:17). The cycle of seasons, growth and harvests, birth and death, all occur according to God's providential care. Finally, God's omnipotence is shown through his redemption plan. Through Jesus Christ, God has defeated and judged evil. No power can stand against God.

While it may appear from our vantage point that forces of evil pose a threat to God, the reality is that God is completely without equal. No creature, even the devil, could ever threaten the Creator.

APPLICATION ✚ God's omnipotence is a mighty comfort for believers. When we look at the chaos around us, we can remain confident that God is the all-powerful One who spoke creation into being and who continues to hold it in his hand. No power can defeat God or undo the good plans he has for redeeming his creation. As we eagerly await the fullness of God's redemption plan, evil may still lash out—but make no mistake about it: Evil is on borrowed time. Our hope is firmly built on God's victory through Christ, which cannot be undone by any other power or authority.

parents' sins into the laps of their
children[w] after them. Great and
mighty God, whose name is the
LORD Almighty,[x] 19great are your purposes and mighty are your deeds.[y]
Your eyes are open to the ways of
all mankind;[z] you reward each person according to their conduct and
as their deeds deserve.[a] 20You performed signs and wonders in Egypt[b]
and have continued them to this day,
in Israel and among all mankind,
and have gained the renown that is
still yours. 21You brought your people Israel out of Egypt with signs and
wonders, by a mighty hand[c] and an
outstretched arm and with great terror.[d] 22You gave them this land you
had sworn to give their ancestors, a
land flowing with milk and honey.[e]
23They came in and took possession[f]
of it, but they did not obey you or follow your law;[g] they did not do what
you commanded them to do. So you
brought all this disaster[h] on them.

24"See how the siege ramps are
built up to take the city. Because of
the sword, famine and plague,[i] the
city will be given into the hands of
the Babylonians who are attacking
it. What you said[j] has happened, as
you now see. 25And though the city
will be given into the hands of the
Babylonians, you, Sovereign LORD,
say to me, 'Buy the field with silver and have the transaction witnessed.'"

26Then the word of the LORD came to
Jeremiah: 27"I am the LORD, the God of all
mankind.[k] Is anything too hard for me?
28Therefore this is what the LORD says: I
am about to give this city into the hands
of the Babylonians and to Nebuchadnezzar[l] king of Babylon, who will capture
it.[m] 29The Babylonians who are attacking
this city will come in and set it on fire;

32:18 [w] Ex 20:5 [x] Jer 10:16
32:19 [y] Isa 28:29 [z] Pr 5:21; Jer 16:17 [a] Jer 17:10; Mt 16:27
32:20 [b] Ex 9:16
32:21 [c] Ex 6:6; 1Ch 17:21; Da 9:15 [d] Dt 26:8
32:22 [e] Ex 3:8; Jer 11:5
32:23 [f] Ps 44:2; 78:54-55 [g] Ne 9:26; Jer 11:8 [h] Da 9:14
32:24 [i] Jer 14:12 [j] Dt 4:25-26; Jos 23:15-16
32:27 [k] Nu 16:22
32:28 [l] 2Ch 36:17 [m] ver 3
32:29 [n] 2Ch 36:19; Jer 21:10; 37:8,10; 52:13 [o] Jer 19:13 [p] Jer 44:18
32:30 [q] Jer 22:21 [r] Jer 8:19 [s] Jer 25:7
32:31 [t] 2Ki 23:27; 24:3
32:32 [u] Isa 1:4-6; Da 9:8
32:33 [v] Jer 2:27; Eze 8:16 [w] Jer 7:13
32:34 [x] Jer 7:30
32:35 [y] Lev 18:21 [z] Jer 7:31; 19:5
32:36 [a] ver 24
32:37 [b] Jer 23:3, 6 [c] Dt 30:3; Eze 34:28
32:38 [d] Jer 24:7; 2Co 6:16*
32:39 [e] Eze 11:19

Jer 32:39-41 ❖ How can we demonstrate "singleness of heart and action" (v. 39) for God?

they will burn it down,[n] along with the
houses[o] where the people aroused my
anger by burning incense on the roofs to
Baal and by pouring out drink offerings[p]
to other gods.

30"The people of Israel and Judah have
done nothing but evil in my sight from
their youth;[q] indeed, the people of Israel
have done nothing but arouse my anger[r] with what their hands have made,[s]
declares the LORD. 31From the day it was
built until now, this city has so aroused
my anger and wrath that I must remove[t]
it from my sight. 32The people of Israel
and Judah have provoked me by all the
evil[u] they have done — they, their kings
and officials, their priests and prophets,
the people of Judah and those living in
Jerusalem. 33They turned their backs[v] to
me and not their faces; though I taught[w]
them again and again, they would not
listen or respond to discipline. 34They
set up their vile images in the house that
bears my Name and defiled[x] it. 35They
built high places for Baal in the Valley
of Ben Hinnom to sacrifice their sons
and daughters to Molek,[y] though I never commanded — nor did it enter my
mind[z] — that they should do such a detestable thing and so make Judah sin.

36"You are saying about this city, 'By
the sword, famine and plague[a] it will be
given into the hands of the king of Babylon'; but this is what the LORD, the God
of Israel, says: 37I will surely gather[b] them
from all the lands where I banish them
in my furious anger and great wrath; I
will bring them back to this place and let
them live in safety.[c] 38They will be my
people,[d] and I will be their God. 39I will
give them singleness[e] of heart and action, so that they will always fear me and

32:26–39 God speaks to Jeremiah after the prophet's prayer concludes. He summarizes what Jeremiah has proclaimed for years: that a righteous judgment will befall Judah and Jerusalem. It will proceed not from God's weakness but from his intention to discipline and purge his people.

In addition to declaring his wrath, God reiterates the significance of Jeremiah's land purchase as a sign of the Lord's resolve to restore and bless his people. Both current calamity and future blessing are the work of God.

32:39–44 God's announced future promises an "everlasting covenant" (v. 40), a changed heart for the people, and life again in the promised land.

✣ 32:1–44 The whole concept of redemption requires one party's giving to another party who has nothing to give: Those who have give to those who don't. It is usually easier to argue about the faults of those who don't have rather than to celebrate that God has

that all will then go well for them and for
their children after them. 40 I will make
an everlasting covenant[f] with them: I
will never stop doing good to them, and
I will inspire them to fear me, so that
they will never turn away from me.[g] 41 I
will rejoice in doing them good[h] and will
assuredly plant[i] them in this land with
all my heart and soul.
42 "This is what the LORD says: As I
have brought all this great calamity
on this people, so I will give them all
the prosperity I have promised[j] them.
43 Once more fields will be bought[k] in this
land of which you say, 'It is a desolate
waste, without people or animals, for
it has been given into the hands of the
Babylonians.' 44 Fields will be bought for
silver, and deeds[l] will be signed, sealed
and witnessed in the territory of Benjamin, in the villages around Jerusalem, in
the towns of Judah and in the towns of
the hill country, of the western foothills
and of the Negev,[m] because I will restore[n]
their fortunes,[a] declares the LORD."

Promise of Restoration

33 While Jeremiah was still confined
in the courtyard[o] of the guard,
the word of the LORD came to him a
second time: 2 "This is what the LORD
says, he who made the earth,[p] the LORD
who formed it and established it—the
LORD is his name:[q] 3 'Call[r] to me and I
will answer you and tell you great and
unsearchable things you do not know.'
4 For this is what the LORD, the God of
Israel, says about the houses in this
city and the royal palaces of Judah that
have been torn down to be used against
the siege[s] ramps[t] and the sword 5 in the
fight with the Babylonians[b]: 'They will be
filled with the dead bodies of the people
I will slay in my anger and wrath.[u] I will
hide my face[v] from this city because of
all its wickedness.

6 " 'Nevertheless, I will bring health
and healing to it; I will heal my people
and will let them enjoy abundant peace
and security. 7 I will bring Judah[w] and
Israel back from captivity[c][x] and will rebuild them as they were before.[y] 8 I will
cleanse[z] them from all the sin they have
committed against me and will forgive[a]
all their sins of rebellion against me.
9 Then this city will bring me renown,
joy, praise[b] and honor[c] before all nations
on earth that hear of all the good things
I do for it; and they will be in awe and
will tremble at the abundant prosperity
and peace I provide for it.'
10 "This is what the LORD says: 'You say
about this place, "It is a desolate waste,
without people or animals."[d] Yet in the
towns of Judah and the streets of Jerusalem that are deserted, inhabited by
neither people nor animals, there will
be heard once more 11 the sounds of joy
and gladness,[e] the voices of bride and
bridegroom, and the voices of those who
bring thank offerings[f] to the house of the
LORD, saying,

"Give thanks to the LORD Almighty,
for the LORD is good;[g]
his love endures forever."[h]

For I will restore the fortunes of the land
as they were before,' says the LORD.
12 "This is what the LORD Almighty says:
'In this place, desolate[i] and without people or animals—in all its towns there
will again be pastures for shepherds to
rest their flocks.[j] 13 In the towns of the hill
country, of the western foothills and of
the Negev,[k] in the territory of Benjamin,
in the villages around Jerusalem and in
the towns of Judah, flocks will again pass
under the hand[l] of the one who counts
them,' says the LORD.

[a] 44 Or *will bring them back from captivity*
[b] 5 Or *Chaldeans*
[c] 7 Or *will restore the fortunes of Judah and Israel*

32:40 [f] Isa 55:3 [g] Jer 24:7
32:41 [h] Dt 30:9 [i] Jer 24:6; 31:28; Am 9:15
32:42 [j] Jer 31:28
32:43 [k] ver 15
32:44 [l] ver 10 [m] Jer 17:26 [n] Jer 33:7, 11, 26
33:1 [o] Jer 32:2-3; 37:21; 38:28
33:2 [p] Jer 10:16 [q] Ex 3:15; 15:3
33:3 [r] Isa 55:6; Jer 29:12
33:4 [s] Eze 4:2 [t] Jer 32:24; Hab 1:10
33:5 [u] Jer 21:4-7 [v] Isa 8:17
33:7 [w] Jer 32:44 [x] Jer 30:3; Am 9:14 [y] Isa 1:26
33:8 [z] Heb 9:13-14 [a] Jer 31:34; Mic 7:18; Zec 13:1
33:9 [b] Jer 13:11 [c] Isa 62:7; Jer 3:17
33:10 [d] Jer 32:43
33:11 [e] Isa 51:3 [f] Lev 7:12 [g] 1Ch 16:8; Ps 136:1 [h] 1Ch 16:34; 2Ch 5:13; Ps 100:4-5
33:12 [i] Jer 32:43 [j] Isa 65:10; Eze 34:11-15
33:13 [k] Jer 17:26 [l] Lev 27:32

provided some with the opportunity to give so that others might live.

Evangelism and social ethics both work best when they follow the Scriptural pattern of joyful giving without concern for an accounting of merits. It is amazing what can be "redeemed" by the simple giving of time, talents and treasure that have been given by the Lord.

33:1–3 The emphasis in this chapter is on God's speaking (vv. 2, 10, 12, 17, 19, 23).

33:4–9 The turning fortunes of the people are here described as God's "healing" them (v. 6). Healing also includes forgiveness, resettlement, rebuilding Jerusalem, and security while living there.

33:10–13 Cities in Judah will again be inhabited. The temple will again host worship. Verse 11 contains a familiar refrain from the temple liturgy: "Give thanks to the LORD Almighty, for the LORD is good; his love endures forever." This is the characteristic phrase of the temple singers appointed by David (1Ch 16:41).

14“ ‘The days are coming,’ declares the
LORD, ‘when I will fulfill the good prom-
ise[m] I made to the people of Israel and
Judah.

15“ ‘In those days and at that time
I will make a righteous[n] Branch[o]
sprout from David’s line;
he will do what is just and right in
the land.
16In those days Judah will be saved[p]
and Jerusalem will live in safety.
This is the name by which it[a] will be
called:
The LORD Our Righteous Savior.’[q]

17For this is what the LORD says: ‘David
will never fail[r] to have a man to sit on the
throne of Israel, 18nor will the Levitical[s]
priests ever fail to have a man to stand
before me continually to offer burnt offerings, to burn grain offerings and to
present sacrifices.[t]’ ”
19The word of the LORD came to Jeremiah: 20“This is what the LORD says:
‘If you can break my covenant with the
day[u] and my covenant with the night,
so that day and night no longer come
at their appointed time, 21then my covenant[v] with David my servant — and
my covenant with the Levites who are
priests ministering before me — can be
broken and David will no longer have a
descendant to reign on his throne.[w] 22I
will make the descendants of David my
servant and the Levites who minister
before me as countless[x] as the stars in
the sky and as measureless as the sand
on the seashore.’ ”
23The word of the LORD came to Jeremiah: 24“Have you not noticed that these
people are saying, ‘The LORD has rejected
the two kingdoms[b][y] he chose’? So they
despise[z] my people and no longer regard
them as a nation.[a] 25This is what the LORD
says: ‘If I have not made my covenant
with day and night[b] and established the
laws of heaven and earth,[c] 26then I will
reject[d] the descendants of Jacob[e] and
David my servant and will not choose
one of his sons to rule over the descendants of Abraham, Isaac and Jacob. For
I will restore their fortunes[c][f] and have
compassion on them.’ ”

33:14 [m]Jer 29:10
33:15 [n]Ps 72:2 [o]Isa 4:2; 11:1; Jer 23:5
33:16 [p]Isa 45:17 [q]1Co 1:30
33:17 [r]2Sa 7:13; 1Ki 2:4; Ps 89:29-37; Lk 1:33
33:18 [s]Dt 18:1 [t]Heb 13:15
33:20 [u]Ps 89:36
33:21 [v]Ps 89:34 [w]2Ch 7:18
33:22 [x]Ge 15:5
33:24 [y]Eze 37:22 [z]Ne 4:4 [a]Jer 30:17
33:25 [b]Jer 31:35-36 [c]Ps 74:16-17
33:26 [d]Jer 31:37 [e]Isa 14:1 [f]ver 7
34:1 [g]Jer 27:7 [h]2Ki 25:1; Jer 39:1
34:2 [i]2Ch 36:11 [j]ver 22; Jer 32:29; 37:8
34:3 [k]2Ki 25:7; Jer 21:7; 32:4

Jer 33:14-16 ❖ Christ is the promised righteous Savior. How does his righteousness affect our actions (see 2Co 5:21)?

Warning to Zedekiah

34 While Nebuchadnezzar king of
Babylon and all his army and all
the kingdoms and peoples[g] in the empire
he ruled were fighting against Jerusalem[h] and all its surrounding towns, this
word came to Jeremiah from the LORD:
2“This is what the LORD, the God of Israel,
says: Go to Zedekiah[i] king of Judah and
tell him, ‘This is what the LORD says: I
am about to give this city into the hands
of the king of Babylon, and he will burn
it down.[j] 3You will not escape from his
grasp but will surely be captured and
given into his hands.[k] You will see the
king of Babylon with your own eyes, and
he will speak with you face to face. And
you will go to Babylon.
4“ ‘Yet hear the LORD’s promise to you,
Zedekiah king of Judah. This is what the

[a] 16 Or *he* [b] 24 Or *families* [c] 26 Or *will bring them back from captivity*

33:14-18 In addition to the restoration of the people, Jeremiah announces that “a righteous Branch . . . from David’s line” (v. 15) will arise and execute justice and righteousness. This promise is messianic, depending on the promises made by God to David’s family. Jerusalem will even receive a new symbolic name: “The LORD Our Righteous Savior” (v. 16).

33:19-22 God will permanently undergird two fundamental institutions of the people. First, someone from David’s line will be head of the people; second, descendants of Levi, the priestly tribe, will always be available to officiate in public worship.

33:23-26 Those who conclude that God has simply rejected them are wrong. God has not broken his covenant with day and night (cf. v. 20), nor has he rejected his people. God’s covenant with day and night expresses his sovereign resolve to maintain a generous order. Because of his mercy, the people still have a future.

✜ **33:1-26** God often finds an opportunity to redefine people’s perspectives when they are suddenly limited in their freedom. Many such people have turned their lives over to God’s control as they have spent their time in prison involved in prison ministries and have done much good for the kingdom of God while incarcerated. God’s promised future has the power to change the present circumstances of people as they yield themselves to the leading of the Holy Spirit.

34:1-5 The fate of Zedekiah and of the city and nation are bound together. Their present course of disaster will inevitably lead to a tragic conclusion.

LORD says concerning you: You will not
die by the sword; 5 you will die peacefully. As people make a funeral fire[l] in
honor of your predecessors, the kings
who ruled before you, so they will make
a fire in your honor and lament, "Alas,[m]
master!" I myself make this promise,
declares the LORD.'"
6 Then Jeremiah the prophet told all
this to Zedekiah king of Judah, in Jerusalem, 7 while the army of the king of
Babylon was fighting against Jerusalem
and the other cities of Judah that were
still holding out — Lachish[n] and Azekah.[o]
These were the only fortified cities left
in Judah.

Freedom for Slaves

8 The word came to Jeremiah from the
LORD after King Zedekiah had made a
covenant with all the people[p] in Jerusalem to proclaim freedom[q] for the slaves.
9 Everyone was to free their Hebrew
slaves, both male and female; no one
was to hold a fellow Hebrew in bondage.[r]
10 So all the officials and people who entered into this covenant agreed that they
would free their male and female slaves
and no longer hold them in bondage.
They agreed, and set them free. 11 But
afterward they changed their minds and
took back the slaves they had freed and
enslaved them again.
12 Then the word of the LORD came to
Jeremiah: 13 "This is what the LORD, the
God of Israel, says: I made a covenant
with your ancestors[s] when I brought
them out of Egypt, out of the land of
slavery. I said, 14 'Every seventh year each
of you must free any fellow Hebrews who
have sold themselves to you. After they
have served you six years, you must let
them go free.'[a][t] Your ancestors, however, did not listen to me or pay attention[u]
to me. 15 Recently you repented and did
what is right in my sight: Each of you
proclaimed freedom to your own people.[v] You even made a covenant before
me in the house that bears my Name.[w]
16 But now you have turned around[x] and
profaned[y] my name; each of you has tak-
en back the male and female slaves you
had set free to go where they wished.
You have forced them to become your
slaves again.
17 "Therefore this is what the LORD says:
You have not obeyed me; you have not
proclaimed freedom to your own people.
So I now proclaim 'freedom' for you,[z] declares the LORD — 'freedom' to fall by the
sword, plague and famine. I will make
you abhorrent to all the kingdoms of
the earth.[a] 18 Those who have violated
my covenant and have not fulfilled the
terms of the covenant they made before
me, I will treat like the calf they cut in
two and then walked between its pieces.[b]
19 The leaders of Judah and Jerusalem,
the court officials,[c] the priests and all the
people of the land who walked between

34:5 [l] 2Ch 16:14; 21:19 [m] Jer 22:18
34:7 [n] Jos 10:3 [o] Jos 10:10; 2Ch 11:9
34:8 [p] 2Ki 11:17 [q] Ex 21:2; Lev 25:10,39-41; Ne 5:5-8
34:9 [r] Lev 25:39-46
34:13 [s] Ex 24:8
34:14 [t] Ex 21:2 [u] Dt 15:12; 2Ki 17:14
34:15 [v] ver 8 [w] Jer 7:10-11; 32:34
34:16 [x] Eze 3:20; 18:24 [y] Ex 20:7; Lev 19:12
34:17 [z] Mt 7:2; Gal 6:7 [a] Dt 28:25,64; Jer 29:18
34:18 [b] Ge 15:10
34:19 [c] Zep 3:3-4

Jer 34:8–11 ❖ Sin can be like a prison. How can we help bring the freedom of Christ to those who are in various forms of bondage?

[a] *14* Deut. 15:12

These prophecies indicate the possible improvement of the king's threatening circumstances.

34:6–7 The two cities of Azekah and Lachish were still holding out against the Babylonian forces when Jeremiah made his prophecies to Zedekiah. During the 1930s an expedition excavated at the site of Lachish. Near the gate and interior fortress, the excavation team found several letters written on pottery shards dating from the time of Jeremiah. One of the letters states that the signal fires from Azekah, located a few kilometers to the north of Lachish, could no longer be seen.

34:8–22 King Zedekiah had initiated a covenant to set free Judean slaves. After the release of the slaves, circumstances improved enough that the solemn oath of the covenant was broken. The slaves were taken back by their owners. The people are also accused of breaking the covenant God made with their ancestors when he brought them out of Egypt.

34:14–15 The allusion to Dt 15 is important to understanding God's anger over the injustice done to the slaves. Justice toward slaves is linked with the content of the covenant stipulations given to the people's ancestors. God has not gone back on his good word and work, so neither should the slave owners in Judah.

34:17 God offers Judah and Jerusalem "freedom" to fall to Babylon. In this announcement of judgment, the punishment to come fits the crime.

34:18–19 The owners and officials who passed between the parts of the calf probably indicates an oath as part of the solemn covenant ceremony. In such ceremonies, those who walked between the parts of the slain animals enacted symbolically their passing through death and dismemberment as a pledge to keep their word (cf. Ge 15:7–21). "Walked between the pieces" (Jer 34:19) thus became a symbolic act. Since the Judeans passed between the parts of the calf when making an oath to free the slaves but subsequently did not keep their word, they themselves will be like the sacrificial animals.

the pieces of the calf, 20I will deliver[d] into
the hands of their enemies who want to
kill them.[e] Their dead bodies will become
food for the birds and the wild animals.[f]
21"I will deliver Zedekiah[g] king of Judah and his officials[h] into the hands of
their enemies who want to kill them, to
the army of the king of Babylon, which
has withdrawn[i] from you. 22I am going
to give the order, declares the LORD, and
I will bring them back to this city. They
will fight against it, take[j] it and burn[k] it
down. And I will lay waste the towns of
Judah so no one can live there."

The Rekabites

35 This is the word that came to Jeremiah from the LORD during the
reign of Jehoiakim[l] son of Josiah king
of Judah: 2"Go to the Rekabite[m] family
and invite them to come to one of the
side rooms[n] of the house of the LORD and
give them wine to drink."
3So I went to get Jaazaniah son of Jeremiah, the son of Habazziniah, and his
brothers and all his sons — the whole
family of the Rekabites. 4I brought them
into the house of the LORD, into the room
of the sons of Hanan son of Igdaliah the
man of God.[o] It was next to the room of
the officials, which was over that of Maaseiah son of Shallum[p] the doorkeeper.[q]
5Then I set bowls full of wine and some
cups before the Rekabites and said to
them, "Drink some wine."
6But they replied, "We do not drink

34:20 [d] Jer 21:7 [e] Jer 11:21 [f] Dt 28:26; Jer 7:33; 19:7
34:21 [g] Jer 32:4 [h] Jer 39:6; 52:24-27 [i] Jer 37:5
34:22 [j] Jer 39:1-2 [k] Jer 39:8
35:1 [l] 2Ch 36:5
35:2 [m] 2Ki 10:15; 1Ch 2:55 [n] 1Ki 6:5
35:4 [o] Dt 33:1 [p] 1Ch 9:19 [q] 2Ki 12:9

✣ **34:1-22** One wonders what later historians will say of the tumultuous social changes that have swept through much of the Western world. Surely the accelerated pace of change itself will be seen as one of the remarkable characteristics of the period. Perhaps future generations will be making the same necessary adaptations to cope with the pace of societal changes.

Change seems to dictate for many people that they keep their options open, that they try to remain flexible, and that they make no commitments unless they can identify an easy way to back out of whatever it is they're considering. Perhaps the Christians of the future will have the courage of conviction to point out that promises, divine and human, are the rock on which all relationships stand.

35:1-11 Some scholars have seen the Rekabites as an anti-Canaanite faction and conservative representatives of a nomadic ideal from Israel's past. Others have seen them more as an alternative community or commercial guild associated with the design and building of chariots. Jehonadab, the founder of the Rekabites, is described as the

PEOPLE TO KNOW // REKABITES

JEREMIAH 35:1-16: When God raised up Jehu to rid Jerusalem of Ahab's family and the Baal worship they promoted, Jehu received help from Jehonadab, son of Rekab, to destroy Baal's temple and priests (2Ki 10:23).

Much later, Jehonadab's descendants, the Rekabites, appear as an example of faithfulness to unfaithful Judah. God told Jeremiah to invite the Rekabites to the temple and offer them wine (Jer 35:2). Jeremiah obeyed, but the Rekabites refused the wine, citing the instruction of their forefather, Jehonadab. They told Jeremiah that, because of Jehonadab's command over 200 years earlier, they faithfully avoided drinking wine and building houses. They lived as nomads in obedience to Jehonadab's word.

God told Jeremiah that the people of Judah should learn a lesson from the Rekabites, who only needed to hear a command once to obey it forever (Jer 35:13). Judah, on the other hand, had received God's messages again and again, telling them to turn from evil and to do good. Despite God's constant reminding, Judah refused to obey God (Jer 35:16). Therefore, God announced that he would bring disaster on Jerusalem but that the Rekabites would never cease to have a descendant who served the Lord (Jer 35:19).

APPLICATION ✣ There's an old hymn that says we are "prone to wander." How true that is, both for OT people of Judah and for believers today. The Rekabites provide an amazing example of faithfulness to instruction. God desires the same kind of faithful obedience from all his children. God wants us to stay on the good path laid out in Scripture and not turn to the right or the left, which would lead to our destruction. God's instructions are not burdensome or petty; they are designed for our flourishing, and we are called to walk faithfully in them.

wine, because our forefather Jehonadab[a][r] son of Rekab gave us this command: 'Neither you nor your descendants must ever drink wine.[s] 7Also you
must never build houses, sow seed or
plant vineyards; you must never have
any of these things, but must always live
in tents.[t] Then you will live a long time
in the land[u] where you are nomads.' 8We
have obeyed everything our forefather[v]
Jehonadab son of Rekab commanded us.
Neither we nor our wives nor our sons
and daughters have ever drunk wine 9or
built houses to live in or had vineyards,
fields or crops.[w] 10We have lived in tents
and have fully obeyed everything our
forefather Jehonadab commanded us.
11But when Nebuchadnezzar king of Babylon invaded[x] this land, we said, 'Come,
we must go to Jerusalem[y] to escape the
Babylonian[b] and Aramean armies.' So we
have remained in Jerusalem."
12Then the word of the LORD came to
Jeremiah, saying: 13"This is what the
LORD Almighty, the God of Israel, says:
Go and tell the people of Judah and those
living in Jerusalem, 'Will you not learn
a lesson[z] and obey my words?' declares
the LORD. 14'Jehonadab son of Rekab
ordered his descendants not to drink
wine and this command has been kept.
To this day they do not drink wine, because they obey their forefather's command. But I have spoken to you again
and again,[a] yet you have not obeyed[b] me.
15Again and again I sent all my servants
the prophets[c] to you. They said, "Each of
you must turn[d] from your wicked ways
and reform[e] your actions; do not follow

35:6 [r]2Ki 10:15 [s]Lev 10:9; Nu 6:2-4; Lk 1:15
35:7 [t]Heb 11:9 [u]Ex 20:12; Eph 6:2-3
35:8 [v]Pr 1:8; Col 3:20
35:9 [w]1Ti 6:6
35:11 [x]2Ki 24:1 [y]Jer 8:14
35:13 [z]Jer 6:10; 32:33
35:14 [a]Jer 7:13; 25:3 [b]Isa 30:9
35:15 [c]Jer 7:25 [d]Jer 26:3 [e]Isa 1:16-17; Jer 4:1; 18:11; Eze 18:30

Jer 35:12-16 ❖ Where do we struggle to consistently follow God's instructions? What are ways to develop our discipleship endurance?

other gods to serve them. Then you will
live in the land[f] I have given to you and
your ancestors." But you have not paid
attention or listened[g] to me. 16The descendants of Jehonadab son of Rekab
have carried out the command their forefather[h] gave them, but these people have
not obeyed me.'
17"Therefore this is what the LORD God
Almighty, the God of Israel, says: 'Listen!
I am going to bring on Judah and on everyone living in Jerusalem every disaster[i] I pronounced against them. I spoke
to them, but they did not listen;[j] I called
to them, but they did not answer.'"[k]
18Then Jeremiah said to the family of
the Rekabites, "This is what the LORD Almighty, the God of Israel, says: 'You have
obeyed the command of your forefather
Jehonadab and have followed all his instructions and have done everything he
ordered.' 19Therefore this is what the
LORD Almighty, the God of Israel, says:
'Jehonadab son of Rekab will never fail[l]
to have a descendant to serve[m] me.'"

Jehoiakim Burns Jeremiah's Scroll

36 In the fourth year of Jehoiakim[n]
son of Josiah king of Judah, this
word came to Jeremiah from the LORD:
2"Take a scroll[o] and write on it all the

[f]Jer 25:5 [g]Jer 7:26
35:16 [h]Mal 1:6
35:17 [i]Jos 23:15; Jer 21:4-7 [j]Pr 1:24; Ro 10:21 [k]Isa 65:12; 66:4; Jer 7:13
35:19 [l]Jer 33:17 [m]Jer 15:19
36:1 [n]2Ch 36:5
36:2 [o]Ex 17:14; Jer 30:2; Hab 2:2

[a] 6 Hebrew *Jonadab,* a variant of *Jehonadab;* here and often in this chapter [b] 11 Or *Chaldean*

---

group's "forefather" in v. 8. Whatever the origin of the Rekabites, their faithful practice of their community's values becomes a prophetic sign against the lack of integrity in Judah and Jerusalem. The prophetic symbolism of this account is accentuated by the scene of wine cups set before the Rekabites in the chambers of Hanan's sons (v. 4). Their reply—that they do not drink wine—is narrated for the effect such a scene will have on the larger community of Judah and Jerusalem.

35:12-17 The fact that Jeremiah has invited the Rekabites to meet him at a room near the temple ensures that their responses are seen by other members of the community. The incident contrasts the Rekabites' obedience to their community standards with the Judeans' faithlessness to theirs. Judah has consistently disobeyed the word of God's servants, the prophets (v. 15).

35:18-19 The final word of the chapter is addressed to the Rekabites. God promises that they will always have someone to "serve" (v. 19) the Lord; that is, they will never be forgotten by God, and their place with him is secure.

35:1-19 Several things can be said about the nature of faithful witness on the basis of Jer 35 (and the book of Jeremiah as a whole). (1) Faith in God is expressed by living in community with other believers. The community of faith (i.e., the church) helps give shape not only to what one believes but how one lives responsibly as a result of faith. (2) God has called people to lead public lives of obedience to his revealed will. Obedience is not just pleasing to God; it can be an effective witness to the larger culture in which believers find themselves. (3) The exercise of the Christian faith may involve giving up certain practices common to a culture for the sake of the gospel.

36:1-3 Jehoiakim's fourth year was 605 BC. In that year, Nebuchadnezzar ascended the Babylonian

words I have spoken to you concerning Israel, Judah and all the other nations from the time I began speaking to you in the reign of Josiah[p] till now. 3 Perhaps[q] when the people of Judah hear[r] about every disaster I plan to inflict on them, they will each turn[s] from their wicked ways; then I will forgive[t] their wickedness and their sin."

4 So Jeremiah called Baruch[u] son of Neriah, and while Jeremiah dictated[v] all the words the LORD had spoken to him, Baruch wrote them on the scroll.[w] 5 Then Jeremiah told Baruch, "I am restricted; I am not allowed to go to the LORD's temple. 6 So you go to the house of the LORD on a day of fasting[x] and read to the people from the scroll the words of the LORD that you wrote as I dictated. Read them to all the people of Judah who come in from their towns. 7 Perhaps they will bring their petition before the LORD and will each turn[y] from their wicked ways, for the anger[z] and wrath pronounced against this people by the LORD are great."

8 Baruch son of Neriah did everything Jeremiah the prophet told him to do; at the LORD's temple he read the words of the LORD from the scroll. 9 In the ninth month[a] of the fifth year of Jehoiakim son of Josiah king of Judah, a time of fasting[b] before the LORD was proclaimed for all the people in Jerusalem and those who had come from the towns of Judah. 10 From the room of Gemariah son of Shaphan the secretary,[c] which was in the upper courtyard at the entrance of the New Gate[d] of the temple, Baruch read to all the people at the LORD's temple the words of Jeremiah from the scroll.

11 When Micaiah son of Gemariah, the son of Shaphan, heard all the words of the LORD from the scroll, 12 he went down to the secretary's room in the royal palace, where all the officials were sitting: Elishama the secretary, Delaiah son of Shemaiah, Elnathan[e] son of Akbor, Gemariah son of Shaphan, Zedekiah son of Hananiah, and all the other officials. 13 After Micaiah told them everything he had heard Baruch read to the people from the scroll, 14 all the officials sent Jehudi[f] son of Nethaniah, the son of Shelemiah, the son of Cushi, to say to Baruch, "Bring the scroll from which you have read to the people and come." So Baruch son of Neriah went to them with the scroll in his hand. 15 They said to him, "Sit down, please, and read it to us."

So Baruch read it to them. 16 When they heard all these words, they looked at each other in fear and said to Baruch, "We must report all these words to the king." 17 Then they asked Baruch, "Tell us, how did you come to write all this? Did Jeremiah dictate it?"

18 "Yes," Baruch replied, "he dictated[g] all these words to me, and I wrote them in ink on the scroll."

19 Then the officials said to Baruch, "You and Jeremiah, go and hide.[h] Don't let anyone know where you are."

20 After they put the scroll in the room of Elishama the secretary, they went to

36:2 [p] Jer 1:2; 25:3
36:3 [q] ver 7; Eze 12:3 [r] Mk 4:12 [s] Jer 26:3; Jnh 3:8; Ac 3:19 [t] Jer 18:8
36:4 [u] Jer 32:12 [v] ver 18 [w] Eze 2:9
36:6 [x] ver 9
36:7 [y] Jer 26:3 [z] Dt 31:17
36:9 [a] ver 22 [b] 2Ch 20:3
36:10 [c] Jer 52:25 [d] Jer 26:10
36:12 [e] Jer 26:22
36:14 [f] ver 21
36:18 [g] ver 4
36:19 [h] 1Ki 17:3

---

throne, and his forces defeated the Egyptians in battle at Carchemish. Since Jehoiakim had been placed on the throne in Judah by the Egyptians (2Ki 23:34–37), this defeat was potentially an ominous sign for him and the Judean leadership.

36:4–7 Just why Jeremiah had been banned from preaching in the temple is a mystery (v. 5). Possibly the temple sermon Jeremiah delivered at the beginning of Jehoiakim's reign (26:1; cf. ch. 7) led to his restriction from delivering oracles at that site. The influential family of Shaphan appears sympathetic to Jeremiah, and its members may be part of the largely anonymous group who have preserved the words of the prophet.

Here readers encounter another theme of the chapter. The written scroll of Jeremiah's prophecies is an adequate substitute for the living voice of the prophet. Jeremiah hopes that the hard words he delivers to the people will be a catalyst for repentance and change (36:7).

36:8–9 This is a year or so later than the chronological notice in v. 1. The solemn fast becomes the occasion for Baruch to deliver the prophetic message of Jeremiah.

36:10–13 The words of the scroll delivered orally by Baruch are given the same prophetic authority as that of Jeremiah. Baruch is asked in an initial interrogation whether these are the words from the mouth of Jeremiah; he replies that they are (vv. 17–18). The only one described as hearing anything at the temple is Micaiah, who "heard all the words of the LORD from the scroll" (v. 11). This detail is not coincidental. The chain of authority runs backward from Baruch to Jeremiah to the Lord. The prophetic word rejected by the people is ultimately that of the Lord.

36:11–19 The officials named here represent Judean leadership. Some of them represent people sympathetic to Jeremiah. Gemariah has taken a big risk in allowing Baruch to use his office as the location for preaching to the crowds in the temple courtyard. This suggests that he, like his sibling Ahikam (26:24), has heard something authentic in Jeremiah's preaching.

36:20–26 The callous rejection of Jeremiah's

the king in the courtyard and reported everything to him. 21The king sent Jehudi[i] to get the scroll, and Jehudi brought it from the room of Elishama the secretary and read it to the king[j] and all the officials standing beside him. 22It was the ninth month and the king was sitting in the winter apartment,[k] with a fire burning in the firepot in front of him. 23Whenever Jehudi had read three or four columns of the scroll, the king cut them off with a scribe's knife and threw them into the firepot, until the entire scroll was burned in the fire.[l] 24The king and all his attendants who heard all these words showed no fear,[m] nor did they tear their clothes.[n] 25Even though Elnathan, Delaiah and Gemariah urged the king not to burn the scroll, he would not listen to them. 26Instead, the king commanded Jerahmeel, a son of the king, Seraiah son of Azriel and Shelemiah son of Abdeel to arrest[o] Baruch the scribe and Jeremiah the prophet. But the LORD had hidden[p] them.

27After the king burned the scroll containing the words that Baruch had written at Jeremiah's dictation,[q] the word of the LORD came to Jeremiah: 28"Take another scroll and write on it all the words that were on the first scroll, which Jehoiakim king of Judah burned up. 29Also tell Jehoiakim king of Judah, 'This is what the LORD says: You burned that scroll and said, "Why did you write on it that the king of Babylon would certainly come and destroy this land and wipe from it[r] both man and beast?" 30Therefore this is what the LORD says about Jehoiakim king of Judah: He will have no one to sit on the throne of David; his body will be thrown out[s] and exposed to the heat by day and the frost by night. 31I will punish him and his children and his attendants for their wickedness; I will bring on them and those living in Jerusalem and the people of Judah every disaster[t] I pronounced against them, because they have not listened.'"

32So Jeremiah took another scroll and gave it to the scribe Baruch son of Neriah, and as Jeremiah dictated,[u] Baruch wrote[v] on it all the words of the scroll that Jehoiakim king of Judah had burned[w] in the fire. And many similar words were added to them.

36:21 [i] ver 14 [j] 2Ki 22:10
36:22 [k] Am 3:15
36:23 [l] 1Ki 22:8
36:24 [m] Ps 36:1 [n] Ge 37:29; 2Ki 22:11; Isa 37:1
36:26 [o] Mt 23:34 [p] Jer 15:21
36:27 [q] ver 4
36:29 [r] Isa 30:10
36:30 [s] Jer 22:19
36:31 [t] Pr 29:1
36:32 [u] ver 4 [v] Ex 34:1 [w] ver 23
37:1 [x] 2Ki 24:17 [y] Eze 17:13 [z] 2Ki 24:8,12; 2Ch 36:10; Jer 22:24
37:2 [a] 2Ki 24:19; 2Ch 36:12,14

Jer 36:20-26 ❖ Where have we seen God's Word openly disrespected and cast aside? How can we find courage to respond when we see this happen?

Jeremiah in Prison

37 Zedekiah[x] son of Josiah was made king[y] of Judah by Nebuchadnezzar king of Babylon; he reigned in place of Jehoiachin[a][z] son of Jehoiakim. 2Neither he nor his attendants nor the people of the land paid any attention[a] to the words the LORD had spoken through Jeremiah the prophet.

3King Zedekiah, however, sent Jehukal

[a] 1 Hebrew *Koniah,* a variant of *Jehoiachin*

---

words by Jehoiakim reminds readers of his father Josiah. When Josiah heard the words of the Torah, he tore his garments as a sign that he recognized the authority of the prophetic scroll to judge him and his nation (2Ki 22). In contemptuous fashion, Jehoiakim doesn't tear his garments; rather, he cuts the scroll in pieces and burns it.

36:27–32 Jehoiakim and Judah's fate is sealed by their indifference and even hostility to Jeremiah's prophetic word. Baruch's reading of Jeremiah's scroll is the second recorded time that the prophet's words have been given at the temple and create worry. The delegation to arrest Baruch and Jeremiah may not itself have been empowered to execute the two men. The narrator notes, almost in passing, that the Lord had hidden them.

The Lord's command to compile another scroll likely comes while Jeremiah and Baruch are hiding from the royal officials who are searching for them. Along with the command comes a revelation to Jeremiah that judgment will come on Jehoiakim and that it will be extended broadly to Judah and Jerusalem.

36:1–32 The account of the prophetic scroll in Jer 36 illustrates that neither people nor king were prepared to hear or obey the word of the Lord. Thus, at one level the account becomes a testimony to the consequences of that refusal. But at another level, there were those who did obey the word of the Lord. They preserved the account for posterity so that God's judging word from the past might become God's correcting and instructive word to future generations. It is the nature of God's Word: It always accomplishes its purpose (Isa 55:11). This question is valid for all of us today: Who among us recognizes the judging, correcting, and restorative nature of God's Word? Who among us can apply it to our own lives and tell others about what we've learned?

37:1–2 These two verses summarize Zedekiah's 11 years as king.

37:3–5 An Egyptian army is moving toward Judah to threaten the Babylonian army. Jeremiah was

son of Shelemiah with the priest
Zephaniah[b] son of Maaseiah to Jeremiah
the prophet with this message: "Please
pray[c] to the LORD our God for us."
4Now Jeremiah was free to come and
go among the people, for he had not yet
been put in prison.[d] 5Pharaoh's army had
marched out of Egypt,[e] and when the
Babylonians[a] who were besieging Jerusalem heard the report about them, they
withdrew[f] from Jerusalem.[g]
6Then the word of the LORD came to
Jeremiah the prophet: 7"This is what the
LORD, the God of Israel, says: Tell the king
of Judah, who sent you to inquire[h] of me,
'Pharaoh's army, which has marched out
to support you, will go back to its own
land, to Egypt.[i] 8Then the Babylonians
will return and attack this city; they will
capture it and burn[j] it down.'
9"This is what the LORD says: Do not
deceive[k] yourselves, thinking, 'The Babylonians will surely leave us.' They will
not! 10Even if you were to defeat the entire Babylonian[b] army that is attacking
you and only wounded men were left
in their tents, they would come out and
burn this city down."
11After the Babylonian army had withdrawn[l] from Jerusalem because of Pharaoh's army, 12Jeremiah started to leave
the city to go to the territory of Benjamin to get his share of the property[m]
among the people there. 13But when he
reached the Benjamin Gate, the captain

> **Jer 37:3** ❖ What prayers of interces-
> sion might we raise to God on behalf
> of our political leaders?

of the guard, whose name was Irijah son
of Shelemiah, the son of Hananiah, arrested him and said, "You are deserting
to the Babylonians!"
14"That's not true!" Jeremiah said. "I
am not deserting to the Babylonians."
But Irijah would not listen to him; instead, he arrested[n] Jeremiah and brought
him to the officials. 15They were angry
with Jeremiah and had him beaten[o] and
imprisoned in the house[p] of Jonathan
the secretary, which they had made into
a prison.
16Jeremiah was put into a vaulted
cell in a dungeon, where he remained a
long time. 17Then King Zedekiah sent for
him and had him brought to the palace,
where he asked[q] him privately,[r] "Is there
any word from the LORD?"
"Yes," Jeremiah replied, "you will be
delivered[s] into the hands of the king of
Babylon."
18Then Jeremiah said to King Zedekiah, "What crime[t] have I committed
against you or your attendants or this
people, that you have put me in prison?
19Where are your prophets who prophesied to you, 'The king of Babylon will

[a] *5* Or *Chaldeans*; also in verses 8, 9, 13 and 14
[b] *10* Or *Chaldean*; also in verse 11

37:3 [b] Jer 29:25; 52:24 [c] 1Ki 13:6; Jer 21:1-2; 42:2
37:4 [d] ver 15; Jer 32:2
37:5 [e] Eze 17:15 [f] Jer 34:21 [g] 2Ki 24:7
37:7 [h] 2Ki 22:18 [i] Jer 2:36; La 4:17
37:8 [j] Jer 34:22; 39:8
37:9 [k] Jer 29:8
37:11 [l] ver 5
37:12 [m] Jer 32:9
37:14 [n] Jer 40:4
37:15 [o] Jer 20:2 [p] Jer 38:26
37:17 [q] Jer 15:11 [r] Jer 38:16 [s] Jer 21:7
37:18 [t] 1Sa 26:18; Jn 10:32; Ac 25:8

---

confined in a variety of circumstances during Zedekiah's reign.

37:6–10 These verses report on a revelation given to Jeremiah for Zedekiah: Babylon will succeed in taking the city. The Egyptian army will not turn the tide.

37:11–15 The appearance of the Egyptian army causes a temporary lifting of the Babylonian siege. According to the summary statement in v. 12, Jeremiah wants to go to the Benjamite tribal area in order to get his share of the property. The guards of the city are suspicious that the prophet wants to leave the city in order to desert to the Babylonians. He is beaten and placed in confinement.

37:16–21 Zedekiah appears to be a classic case of a divided mind under pressure. On the one hand, he desperately seeks guidance, including his requests that Jeremiah pray to God (v. 3) and that Jeremiah mediate God's will to him (v. 17). On the other hand, the word of the Lord causes him anxiety and demands what his self-serving nature will not allow. So Zedekiah mistreats the very prophet he approaches for help.

Jeremiah is confined to a house belonging to a scribe (v. 15) and later to a place associated with a guardhouse (v. 21). He is beaten at the scribe's house and his rations in the guardhouse quarters are minimal, yet when the city is starving Jeremiah is assured at least some food by order of the king. In v. 18 Jeremiah asks what he has done to deserve this treatment; the implied point is that he has told the truth and that Zedekiah is persecuting him for it.

> ✜ **37:1–21** It is important to remember how easy it is to assault the messenger rather than to listen carefully and learn humbly from him or her. It is more convenient to reject an "unfriendly" assessment than it is to look in the mirror of God's Word.
>
> Paradoxically, there is also hope in this disquieting account. Even in judging Zedekiah and the people, God is still at work to keep his promises. Zedekiah's family (i.e., that of David) will still be privileged to play a crucial role in God's economy. Moreover, what most Judeans think is an awful tragedy—the fall of the state and the resulting exile—is also the seedbed of new beginnings.

not attack you or this land'? 20But now,
my lord the king, please listen. Let me
bring my petition before you: Do not
send me back to the house of Jonathan
the secretary, or I will die there."
21King Zedekiah then gave orders for
Jeremiah to be placed in the courtyard
of the guard and given a loaf of bread
from the street of the bakers each day
until all the bread[u] in the city was gone.[v]
So Jeremiah remained in the courtyard
of the guard.[w]

Jeremiah Thrown Into a Cistern

38 Shephatiah son of Mattan, Gedaliah son of Pashhur, Jehukal[a][x] son
of Shelemiah, and Pashhur son of Malkijah heard what Jeremiah was telling all
the people when he said, 2"This is what
the LORD says: 'Whoever stays in this city
will die by the sword, famine or plague,[y]
but whoever goes over to the Babylonians[b] will live. They will escape with their
lives; they will live.'[z] 3And this is what
the LORD says: 'This city will certainly be
given into the hands of the army of the
king of Babylon, who will capture it.'"[a]
4Then the officials[b] said to the king,
"This man should be put to death.[c] He is
discouraging the soldiers who are left in
this city, as well as all the people, by the
things he is saying to them. This man
is not seeking the good of these people
but their ruin."
5"He is in your hands," King Zedekiah
answered. "The king can do nothing to
oppose you."
6So they took Jeremiah and put him
into the cistern of Malkijah, the king's
son, which was in the courtyard of the
guard.[d] They lowered Jeremiah by ropes
into the cistern; it had no water in it,
only mud, and Jeremiah sank down into
the mud.
7But Ebed-Melek,[e] a Cushite,[c] an official[d][f] in the royal palace, heard that
they had put Jeremiah into the cistern.
While the king was sitting in the Benjamin Gate,[g] 8Ebed-Melek went out of
the palace and said to him, 9"My lord
the king, these men have acted wickedly in all they have done to Jeremiah the
prophet. They have thrown him into a
cistern, where he will starve to death
when there is no longer any bread[h] in
the city."
10Then the king commanded Ebed-
Melek the Cushite, "Take thirty men
from here with you and lift Jeremiah the
prophet out of the cistern before he dies."
11So Ebed-Melek took the men with
him and went to a room under the treasury in the palace. He took some old rags
and worn-out clothes from there and
let them down with ropes to Jeremiah
in the cistern. 12Ebed-Melek the Cushite
said to Jeremiah, "Put these old rags and
worn-out clothes under your arms to pad
the ropes." Jeremiah did so, 13and they
pulled him up with the ropes and lifted
him out of the cistern. And Jeremiah
remained in the courtyard of the guard.[i]

Zedekiah Questions Jeremiah Again

14Then King Zedekiah sent for Jeremiah the prophet and had him brought to
the third entrance to the temple of the
LORD. "I am going to ask you something,"
the king said to Jeremiah. "Do not hide[j]
anything from me."

37:21 [u] Isa 33:16; Jer 38:9 [v] 2Ki 25:3; Jer 52:6 [w] Jer 32:2; 38:6, 13,28
38:1 [x] Jer 37:3
38:2 [y] Jer 34:17 [z] Jer 21:9; 39:18; 45:5
38:3 [a] Jer 21:4, 10; 32:3
38:4 [b] Jer 36:12 [c] Jer 26:11
38:6 [d] Jer 37:21
38:7 [e] Jer 39:16 [f] Ac 8:27 [g] Job 29:7
38:9 [h] Jer 37:21
38:13 [i] Jer 37:21
38:14 [j] 1Sa 3:17

Jer 38:7-13 ❖ Ebed-Melek saved Jeremiah from death in a cistern. When has a servant of God been a special help to you? How did you show your gratitude for their kindness?

[a] 1 Hebrew *Jukal*, a variant of *Jehukal* [b] 2 Or *Chaldeans*; also in verses 18, 19 and 23 [c] 7 Probably from the upper Nile region [d] 7 Or *a eunuch*

38:1–6 These officials are angry with Jeremiah because his words about Babylonian supremacy are discouraging (v. 4). The officials lower Jeremiah into a cistern that has mud but no water. Indirectly this comment tells the reader about the desperate circumstances of the siege: An empty cistern indicates water scarcity.

38:7–13 One of the palace officials, a eunuch from Ethiopia, courageously approaches Zedekiah to overturn the order sending Jeremiah to a slow and painful death. He secures an agreement from the king and goes with 30 men to pull the weakened prophet from the muddy cistern.

One gains an idea of how weak the prophet has become from the description of Ebed-Melek's manner of rescuing him from the muck. The men provide some worn-out rags to place under Jeremiah's arms so that the rope harness will not injure him. Jeremiah is freed from his sentence of slow death, but he is still kept under confinement with Zedekiah's guards.

38:14–17 Zedekiah is not through with the prophet. As in earlier cases (21:1; 37:3), the king seeks spiritual advice from him. Initially, Jeremiah seeks assurance that he will not be killed, and the king swears not to hand the prophet over to those who want to kill him.

15 Jeremiah said to Zedekiah, "If I give
you an answer, will you not kill me? Even
if I did give you counsel, you would not
listen to me."
16 But King Zedekiah swore this oath
secretly[k] to Jeremiah: "As surely as the
LORD lives, who has given us breath,[l] I
will neither kill you nor hand you over
to those who want to kill you."[m]
17 Then Jeremiah said to Zedekiah,
"This is what the LORD God Almighty, the
God of Israel, says: 'If you surrender to
the officers of the king of Babylon, your
life will be spared and this city will not
be burned down; you and your family
will live.[n] 18 But if you will not surrender
to the officers of the king of Babylon,
this city will be given into the hands[o]
of the Babylonians and they will burn[p]
it down; you yourself will not escape[q]
from them.'"
19 King Zedekiah said to Jeremiah, "I
am afraid[r] of the Jews who have gone
over[s] to the Babylonians, for the Babylonians may hand me over to them and
they will mistreat me."
20 "They will not hand you over," Jeremiah replied. "Obey[t] the LORD by doing
what I tell you. Then it will go well with
you, and your life[u] will be spared. 21 But
if you refuse to surrender, this is what
the LORD has revealed to me: 22 All the
women[v] left in the palace of the king of
Judah will be brought out to the officials
of the king of Babylon. Those women
will say to you:

"'They misled you and overcame
you—
those trusted friends of yours.
Your feet are sunk in the mud;
your friends have deserted you.'

23 "All your wives and children[w] will
be brought out to the Babylonians. You
yourself will not escape from their hands
but will be captured[x] by the king of Babylon; and this city will[a] be burned down."
24 Then Zedekiah said to Jeremiah, "Do
not let anyone know about this conversation, or you may die. 25 If the officials hear
that I talked with you, and they come to
you and say, 'Tell us what you said to the
king and what the king said to you; do
not hide it from us or we will kill you,'
26 then tell them, 'I was pleading with the
king not to send me back to Jonathan's
house[y] to die there.'"
27 All the officials did come to Jeremiah and question him, and he told them
everything the king had ordered him
to say. So they said no more to him, for
no one had heard his conversation with
the king.
28 And Jeremiah remained in the courtyard of the guard[z] until the day Jerusalem was captured.

The Fall of Jerusalem

39:1–10pp // 2Ki 25:1–12; Jer 52:4–16

39 This is how Jerusalem was tak-
en: 1 In the ninth year of Zedekiah
king of Judah, in the tenth month, Nebuchadnezzar king of Babylon marched
against Jerusalem with his whole army
and laid siege[a] to it. 2 And on the ninth
day of the fourth month of Zedekiah's
eleventh year, the city wall was broken
through. 3 Then all the officials[b] of the
king of Babylon came and took seats
in the Middle Gate: Nergal-Sharezer of
Samgar, Nebo-Sarsekim a chief officer,
Nergal-Sharezer a high official and all

38:16 [k] Jer 37:17 [l] Isa 42:5; 57:16 [m] ver 4
38:17 [n] 2Ki 24:12; Jer 21:9
38:18 [o] ver 3; Jer 34:3 [p] Jer 37:8 [q] Jer 24:8; 32:4
38:19 [r] Isa 51:12; Jn 12:42 [s] Jer 39:9
38:20 [t] Jer 11:4 [u] Isa 55:3
38:22 [v] Jer 6:12
38:23 [w] 2Ki 25:6 [x] Jer 41:10
38:26 [y] Jer 37:15
38:28 [z] Jer 37:21; 39:14
39:1 [a] 2Ki 25:1; Jer 52:4; Eze 24:2
39:3 [b] Jer 21:4

[a] 23 Or *and you will cause this city to*

38:18–23 Zedekiah is as worried about his personal safety and future as he is about the city and the state. Jeremiah sets before the king the alternatives of surrendering and trusting the Lord for his safety or holding out and seeing the Babylonians victorious. The latter scenario includes the burning of the city (v. 23).

38:24–28 Zedekiah asks Jeremiah not to reveal their conversation. This is another indication of the king's divided mind. Both Jeremiah and Zedekiah are the subject of rumor and conspiracy. Zedekiah has precious few people whom he can trust.

38:1–28a In the case of Zedekiah, not to act decisively and obediently to Jeremiah's prophetic word means simply keeping on with the old and tired policies of failure. In his case, not to decide is actually to make a fateful decision.

God's providence is designed so people may inevitably face their fears and choose among difficult options. This is not necessarily "bad news." The issue is first discernment and then trusting God, who sends such matters our way. Jesus prayed for the cup of suffering to be taken away (Lk 22:39–44). Yet what remained most important for Jesus (and for us) is discerning God's will.

38:28b—39:7 Zedekiah's fate is essentially the same as that of the city and people (39:4–7). He attempts to escape the consequences of Jerusalem's fall by fleeing to the Jordan Valley. He is caught by the Babylonian army with gruesome results.

the other officials of the king of Babylon.
4When Zedekiah king of Judah and all
the soldiers saw them, they fled; they left
the city at night by way of the king's garden, through the gate between the two
walls, and headed toward the Arabah.[a]
5But the Babylonian[b] army pursued
them and overtook Zedekiah[c] in the
plains of Jericho. They captured him
and took him to Nebuchadnezzar king
of Babylon at Riblah[d] in the land of Hamath, where he pronounced sentence on
him. 6There at Riblah the king of Babylon slaughtered the sons of Zedekiah
before his eyes and also killed all the
nobles of Judah. 7Then he put out Zedekiah's eyes[e] and bound him with bronze
shackles to take him to Babylon.[f]
8The Babylonians[c] set fire[g] to the royal palace and the houses of the people
and broke down the walls[h] of Jerusalem.
9Nebuzaradan commander of the imperial guard carried into exile to Babylon
the people who remained in the city,
along with those who had gone over to
him, and the rest of the people.[i] 10But
Nebuzaradan the commander of the
guard left behind in the land of Judah
some of the poor people, who owned
nothing; and at that time he gave them
vineyards and fields.
11Now Nebuchadnezzar king of Babylon had given these orders about Jeremiah through Nebuzaradan commander
of the imperial guard: 12"Take him and
look after him; don't harm[j] him but do
for him whatever he asks." 13So Nebuzaradan the commander of the guard, Neb-

39:5 [c]Jer 32:4 [d]2Ki 23:33
39:7 [e]Eze 12:13 [f]Jer 32:5
39:8 [g]Jer 38:18 [h]Ne 1:3
39:9 [i]Jer 40:1
39:12 [j]Pr 16:7; 1Pe 3:13

39:14 [k]Jer 38:28 [l]2Ki 22:12 [m]Jer 40:5
39:16 [n]Jer 38:7 [o]Jer 21:10; Da 9:12
39:17 [p]Ps 41:1-2
39:18 [q]Jer 45:5 [r]Jer 21:9; 38:2 [s]Jer 17:7

Jer 39:17-18 ❖ How have believers experienced blessings from God through their trust in him? How have you personally experienced these blessings? Explain.

ushazban a chief officer, Nergal-Sharezer
a high official and all the other officers
of the king of Babylon 14sent and had
Jeremiah taken out of the courtyard of
the guard.[k] They turned him over to Gedaliah son of Ahikam,[l] the son of Shaphan,
to take him back to his home. So he remained among his own people.[m]
15While Jeremiah had been confined
in the courtyard of the guard, the word
of the LORD came to him: 16"Go and tell
Ebed-Melek[n] the Cushite, 'This is what
the LORD Almighty, the God of Israel, says: I am about to fulfill my words
against this city — words concerning disaster,[o] not prosperity. At that time they
will be fulfilled before your eyes. 17But
I will rescue[p] you on that day, declares
the LORD; you will not be given into the
hands of those you fear. 18I will save you;
you will not fall by the sword[q] but will
escape with your life,[r] because you trust[s]
in me, declares the LORD.'"

Jeremiah Freed

40 The word came to Jeremiah from
the LORD after Nebuzaradan commander of the imperial guard had released him at Ramah. He had found

[a] 4 Or *the Jordan Valley* [b] 5 Or *Chaldean* [c] 8 Or *Chaldeans*

39:8-10 These verses describe succinctly the actual burning of the city. Nebuzaradan, a high-ranking Babylonian official, organizes much of the surviving population into a group for exile. Some of the poorest people in Judah are left to tend the land. Thus Judah is not totally depopulated, and the Babylonians will be able to extract tribute from those who remain.

39:11-14 Jeremiah's confinement serves no Babylonian purpose, and perhaps Nebuchadnezzar has heard secondhand that a Judean prophet proclaimed his supremacy. The Babylonians turn him over to Gedaliah; in the next chapter we learn that Nebuchadnezzar will appoint Gedaliah as governor of Judah. Here we see again the illustrious family of Shaphan, whose members had been supportive of Jeremiah.

39:15-18 Ebed-Melek, the eunuch who saved Jeremiah's life, is granted life by God.

✣ **38:28b—39:18** A tragedy that is anticipated and yet comes to pass is, in some sense, doubly tragic, because if it is anticipated, there should be ways of easing its harshness. Tragedy suggests that an event or process does not have to turn out that way. In theological terms it suggests that God may have preferred it otherwise (cf. Eze 18:32). The circumstances of Judah's fall were both allowed and then used by God in the history of his people.

Yet there can be a personal word from God that comes amid tragedy or judgment. One sees it in the gift of life to Ebed-Melek. Grace happens, but it cannot be presumed upon. God is the God of new beginnings as well as the God of historical destiny. How judgment and new life work out in God's economy is what gives shape to the Christian life and confirms God as Lord of all circumstances.

40:1-6 Many people in ancient times believed in the power of a local deity in its sphere of influence. There is no reason to suspect sarcasm or insincerity on the part of Nebuzaradan.

Jeremiah bound in chains among all the captives from Jerusalem and Judah who were being carried into exile to Babylon. 2When the commander of the guard found Jeremiah, he said to him, "The LORD your God decreed this disaster for this place.[t] 3And now the LORD has brought it about; he has done just as he said he would. All this happened because you people sinned[u] against the LORD and did not obey[v] him. 4But today I am freeing you from the chains on your wrists. Come with me to Babylon, if you like, and I will look after you; but if you do not want to, then don't come. Look, the whole country lies before you; go wherever you please."[w] 5However, before Jeremiah turned to go,[a] Nebuzaradan added, "Go back to Gedaliah[x] son of Ahikam, the son of Shaphan, whom the king of Babylon has appointed over the towns of Judah, and live with him among the people, or go anywhere else you please."[y]

Then the commander gave him provisions and a present and let him go. 6So Jeremiah went to Gedaliah son of Ahikam at Mizpah[z] and stayed with him among the people who were left behind in the land.

Gedaliah Assassinated

40:7–9; 41:1–3pp // 2Ki 25:22–26

7When all the army officers and their men who were still in the open country heard that the king of Babylon had appointed Gedaliah son of Ahikam as governor over the land and had put him in charge of the men, women and children who were the poorest[a] in the land and who had not been carried into exile to Babylon, 8they came to Gedaliah at Mizpah[b] — Ishmael[c] son of Nethaniah, Johanan and Jonathan the sons of Kareah, Seraiah son of Tanhumeth, the sons of Ephai the Netophathite,[d] and Jaazaniah[b] the son of the Maakathite,[e] and their men. 9Gedaliah son of Ahikam, the son of Shaphan, took an oath to reassure them and their men. "Do not be afraid to serve[f] the Babylonians,[c]" he said. "Settle down in the land and serve the king of Babylon, and it will go well with you.[g] 10I myself will stay at Mizpah[h] to represent you before the Babylonians who come to us, but you are to harvest the wine, summer fruit and olive oil, and put them in your storage jars, and live in the towns you have taken over."[i]

11When all the Jews in Moab,[j] Ammon, Edom and all the other countries heard that the king of Babylon had left a remnant in Judah and had appointed Gedaliah son of Ahikam, the son of Shaphan, as governor over them, 12they all came back to the land of Judah, to Gedaliah at Mizpah, from all the countries where they had been scattered.[k] And they harvested an abundance of wine and summer fruit.

13Johanan son of Kareah and all the army officers still in the open country came to Gedaliah at Mizpah[l] 14and said to him, "Don't you know that Baalis king of the Ammonites[m] has sent Ishmael son of Nethaniah to take your life?" But Gedaliah son of Ahikam did not believe them.

15Then Johanan son of Kareah said privately to Gedaliah in Mizpah, "Let me go

40:2 [t] Jer 50:7
40:3 [u] Da 9:11 [v] Dt 29:24-28; Ro 2:5-9
40:4 [w] Ge 13:9; Jer 39:11-12
40:5 [x] 2Ki 25:22 [y] Jer 39:14
40:6 [z] Jdg 20:1; 1Sa 7:5-17
40:7 [a] Jer 39:10
40:8 [b] ver 13 [c] ver 14; Jer 41:1, 2
[d] 2Sa 23:28 [e] Dt 3:14
40:9 [f] Jer 27:11 [g] Jer 38:20
40:10 [h] ver 6 [i] Dt 1:39
40:11 [j] Nu 25:1
40:12 [k] Jer 43:5
40:13 [l] ver 8
40:14 [m] 2Sa 10:1-19; Jer 25:21; 41:10

Jer 40:1-6 ❖ When have you experienced surprising mercy and kindness from an unexpected source? How may God have been behind it?

[a] 5 Or *Jeremiah answered* [b] 8 Hebrew *Jezaniah*, a variant of *Jaazaniah* [c] 9 Or *Chaldeans*; also in verse 10

Jeremiah is also given a choice whether to go to Babylon or remain in the land with Gedaliah. From the point of view of personal security, it would likely be better for Jeremiah to accompany Nebuzaradan to Babylon, but he chooses to remain with the remnant in the land. That Jeremiah is given provisions and a "present" by the Babylonians (v. 5b) is recognition on their part that the prophet predicted their success.

40:7–16 A remnant of people from Judea begin to gather around Gedaliah at Mizpah, about five miles north of Jerusalem. Johanan is a member of the Judean army but also seemingly well-connected to the remaining officials in Judah. Ishmael is related to the royal family of Judah (41:1). Johanan discovers that Baalis, king of the Ammonites (40:14), has concocted a plot with Ishmael to assassinate Gedaliah. Indeed, Johanan informs Gedaliah about what he knows, but Gedaliah does not believe the report.

40:10–11 These verses remind us of the continuing impact of the Babylonian siege. Now that the Babylonians have completed their siege and the main elements of the army have returned to Babylon, many Judeans return to see what remains of their former property. Upon doing so, they also find that additional property needs tending.

40:12–16 All in all, it is a precarious time for those who remain in the land. They can be called the "remnant of Judah" (v. 15), and the tasks of bringing life back to a more even keel are overwhelming.

and kill Ishmael son of Nethaniah, and
no one will know it. Why should he take
your life and cause all the Jews who are
gathered around you to be scattered and
the remnant of Judah to perish?"
16But Gedaliah son of Ahikam said to
Johanan son of Kareah, "Don't do such
a thing! What you are saying about Ishmael is not true."

41 In the seventh month Ishmael[n] son
of Nethaniah, the son of Elishama,
who was of royal blood and had been one
of the king's officers, came with ten men
to Gedaliah son of Ahikam at Mizpah.
While they were eating together there,
2Ishmael[o] son of Nethaniah and the ten
men who were with him got up and
struck down Gedaliah son of Ahikam, the
son of Shaphan, with the sword, killing
the one whom the king of Babylon had
appointed[p] as governor over the land.[q]
3Ishmael also killed all the men of Judah who were with Gedaliah at Mizpah,
as well as the Babylonian[a] soldiers who
were there.
4The day after Gedaliah's assassination,
before anyone knew about it, 5eighty
men who had shaved off their beards,[r]
torn their clothes and cut themselves
came from Shechem,[s] Shiloh[t] and Samaria,[u] bringing grain offerings and
incense with them to the house of the
LORD.[v] 6Ishmael son of Nethaniah went
out from Mizpah to meet them, weeping[w] as he went. When he met them, he
said, "Come to Gedaliah son of Ahikam."
7When they went into the city, Ishmael
son of Nethaniah and the men who were
with him slaughtered them and threw
them into a cistern. 8But ten of them said
to Ishmael, "Don't kill us! We have wheat
and barley, olive oil and honey, hidden
in a field."[x] So he let them alone and did
not kill them with the others. 9Now the
cistern where he threw all the bodies of
the men he had killed along with Gedaliah was the one King Asa[y] had made as
part of his defense[z] against Baasha[a] king
of Israel. Ishmael son of Nethaniah filled
it with the dead.
10Ishmael made captives of all the rest
of the people[b] who were in Mizpah — the
king's daughters along with all the others
who were left there, over whom Nebuzaradan commander of the imperial
guard had appointed Gedaliah son of
Ahikam. Ishmael son of Nethaniah took
them captive and set out to cross over to
the Ammonites.[c]
11When Johanan[d] son of Kareah and
all the army officers who were with him
heard about all the crimes Ishmael son of
Nethaniah had committed, 12they took all
their men and went to fight Ishmael son
of Nethaniah. They caught up with him
near the great pool[e] in Gibeon. 13When
all the people[f] Ishmael had with him saw
Johanan son of Kareah and the army officers who were with him, they were glad.
14All the people Ishmael had taken captive
at Mizpah turned and went over to Johanan son of Kareah. 15But Ishmael son of
Nethaniah and eight of his men escaped[g]
from Johanan and fled to the Ammonites.

Flight to Egypt

16Then Johanan son of Kareah and all
the army officers who were with him led
away all the people of Mizpah who had
survived,[h] whom Johanan had recovered from Ishmael son of Nethaniah after
Ishmael had assassinated Gedaliah son of
Ahikam — the soldiers, women, children

41:1 [n]Jer 40:8
41:2 [o]Ps 41:9; 109:5 [p]Jer 40:5 [q]2Sa 3:27; 20:9-10
41:5 [r]Lev 19:27 [s]Ge 33:18; Jdg 9:1-57; 1Ki 12:1 [t]Jos 18:1 [u]1Ki 16:24 [v]2Ki 25:9
41:6 [w]2Sa 3:16
41:8 [x]Isa 45:3
41:9 [y]1Ki 15:22; 2Ch 16:6 [z]Jdg 6:2 [a]2Ch 16:1
41:10 [b]Jer 40:7, 12 [c]Jer 40:14
41:11 [d]Jer 40:8
41:12 [e]2Sa 2:13
41:13 [f]ver 10
41:15 [g]Job 21:30; Pr 28:17
41:16 [h]Jer 43:4

Jer 41:10 ❖ Why can difficult times lead to increased sin and corruption? How can we remain righteous even in devastating circumstances?

[a] 3 Or *Chaldean*

41:1-3 Chapter 41 narrates quickly Ishmael's treacherous murder of Gedaliah. The massacre is both a strike against the Babylonians and an attempt by Ishmael to seize power. In addition to Gedaliah, Ishmael murders "all the men of Judah" (v. 3), the Judean men who work with Gedaliah in administrative affairs. Verses 10 and 16 report the survival of some people from the town of Mizpah.

41:4-8 Here is unintended commentary on the importance of the temple for people who lived outside the territory of Judah. The people who return from the north want to present grain offerings and incense at the temple in Jerusalem.

Ishmael gains their confidence and brings them to Mizpah, only to murder most of them. A few are spared who offer him provisions they have hidden in a field.

41:9-10 Ishmael gathers the townspeople and sets out to cross over the Jordan River to the Ammonites. Among his captives are daughters of the king. Most likely these are daughters of Zedekiah from his marriages with women of prominent local families.

41:11-15 Johanan and his soldiers attempt to intercept Ishmael. The two groups meet near Gibeon, with the result that most of the captives taken by Ishmael are recovered by Johanan and his officers, but Ishmael and eight of his men escape.

41:16-18 The question faced by Johanan and his

and court officials he had recovered from
Gibeon. 17And they went on, stopping
at Geruth Kimham[i] near Bethlehem on
their way to Egypt[j] 18to escape the Babylonians.[a] They were afraid[k] of them
because Ishmael son of Nethaniah had
killed Gedaliah[l] son of Ahikam, whom
the king of Babylon had appointed as
governor over the land.

42 Then all the army officers, including Johanan[m] son of Kareah and
Jezaniah[b] son of Hoshaiah, and all the
people from the least to the greatest[n]
approached 2Jeremiah the prophet and
said to him, "Please hear our petition
and pray[o] to the LORD your God for this
entire remnant.[p] For as you now see,
though we were once many, now only
a few[q] are left. 3Pray that the LORD your
God will tell us where we should go and
what we should do."[r]

4"I have heard you," replied Jeremiah
the prophet. "I will certainly pray[s] to the
LORD your God as you have requested; I
will tell you everything the LORD says
and will keep nothing back from you."[t]

5Then they said to Jeremiah, "May
the LORD be a true and faithful witness[u]
against us if we do not act in accordance
with everything the LORD your God sends
you to tell us. 6Whether it is favorable or
unfavorable, we will obey the LORD our
God, to whom we are sending you, so that
it will go well[v] with us, for we will obey[w]
the LORD our God."

41:17 [i] 2Sa 19:37 [j] Jer 42:14
41:18 [k] Isa 51:12; Jer 42:16; Lk 12:4-5 [l] Jer 40:5
42:1 [m] Jer 40:13; 41:11 [n] Jer 6:13; 44:12
42:2 [o] Jer 36:7; Ac 8:24; Jas 5:16 [p] Isa 1:9 [q] Lev 26:22; La 1:1
42:3 [r] Ps 86:11; Pr 3:6
42:4 [s] Ex 8:29; 1Sa 12:23 [t] 1Ki 22:14; 1Sa 3:17
42:5 [u] Ge 31:50
42:6 [v] Dt 5:29; 6:3; Jer 7:23 [w] Ex 24:7; Jos 24:24
42:8 [x] ver 1
42:9 [y] 2Ki 22:15
42:10 [z] Jer 24:6 [a] Jer 31:28 [b] Eze 36:36 [c] Jer 18:8
42:11 [d] Jer 27:11 [e] Nu 14:9 [f] Isa 43:5 [g] Jer 1:8; Ro 8:31
42:12 [h] Ps 106:44-46
42:13 [i] Jer 44:16
42:14 [j] Nu 11:4-5

Jer 42:10-12 ❖ If we have fears, how can we find confidence in God in the face of those fears?

7Ten days later the word of the LORD
came to Jeremiah. 8So he called together
Johanan son of Kareah and all the army
officers[x] who were with him and all the
people from the least to the greatest. 9He
said to them, "This is what the LORD, the
God of Israel, to whom you sent me to
present your petition, says:[y] 10'If you stay
in this land, I will build[z] you up and not
tear you down; I will plant[a] you and not
uproot you,[b] for I have relented concerning the disaster I have inflicted on you.[c]
11Do not be afraid of the king of Babylon,[d]
whom you now fear.[e] Do not be afraid of
him, declares the LORD, for I am with you
and will save[f] you and deliver you from
his hands.[g] 12I will show you compassion
so that he will have compassion on you
and restore you to your land.'[h]

13"However, if you say, 'We will not stay
in this land,' and so disobey[i] the LORD
your God, 14and if you say, 'No, we will
go and live in Egypt,[j] where we will not
see war or hear the trumpet or be hungry for bread,' 15then hear the word of
the LORD, you remnant of Judah. This
is what the LORD Almighty, the God of
Israel, says: 'If you are determined to go

[a] *18* Or *Chaldeans* [b] *1* Hebrew; Septuagint (see also 43:2) *Azariah*

---

band is, "What now?" Their fear of Babylonian retaliation and the treachery of men like Ishmael lead them to flee the region. Their choice of venue is Egypt, where already a sizable group of Judeans live.

✣ **40:1—41:18** For North American readers, the depressing account of Gedaliah's murder and the continuing downward spiral in Judah may strike a chord in their historical memory. Abraham Lincoln announced that a "house divided against itself cannot stand." He knew he was quoting a biblical text (cf. Mk 3:24-25), and he believed that God would judge the United States for its folly in the slave trade and its continuing bitter conflict over ways to resolve the matter.

Lincoln (like Gedaliah and Jeremiah) is something of a tragic figure. None of these men atoned for the sins of others, but they did suffer as part of their calling. Their tragedy raises an interesting question. If God uses their tragic circumstances to instruct his people and to evoke measures of repentance and sympathy, then they serve a larger purpose. Moreover, failure can be the prelude to and even the beginning of new directions.

In the midst of a national humiliation, Gedaliah advises his contemporaries not to fear. Jeremiah chooses the more difficult road rather than setting off to Babylon. Do those who have tasted new life in the crucified and risen Lord have eyes to see and ears to hear what the Spirit is saying?

42:1-6 Should the remnant associated with Johanan (and until recently with Gedaliah) flee to Egypt or not? They seek the counsel of God through Jeremiah and promise to obey his word. There is an implied self-curse in v. 5, should the company of Judeans not heed the Lord's instruction. Jeremiah agrees to seek counsel from the Lord and to tell them everything the Lord reveals.

42:7-22 Jeremiah's reply to the request of Johanan takes two forms. After ten days he begins with the preface, "This is what the LORD . . . says" (v. 9), where the gist of the message is that God will preserve the remnant of Judeans if they stay in the land. Should they choose to disregard his word and to flee to Egypt, judgment will come on them there.

to Egypt and you do go to settle there, 16then the sword[k] you fear will overtake you there, and the famine you dread will follow you into Egypt, and there you will die. 17Indeed, all who are determined to go to Egypt to settle there will die by the sword, famine and plague;[l] not one of them will survive or escape the disaster I will bring on them.' 18This is what the LORD Almighty, the God of Israel, says: 'As my anger and wrath[m] have been poured out on those who lived in Jerusalem,[n] so will my wrath be poured out on you when you go to Egypt. You will be a curse[a] and an object of horror,[o] a curse[a] and an object of reproach; you will never see this place again.'[p]

19"Remnant of Judah, the LORD has told you, 'Do not go to Egypt.'[q] Be sure of this: I warn you today 20that you made a fatal mistake when you sent me to the LORD your God and said, 'Pray to the LORD our God for us; tell us everything he says and we will do it.'[r] 21I have told you today, but you still have not obeyed the LORD your God in all he sent me to tell you.[s] 22So now, be sure of this: You will die by the sword, famine and plague[t] in the place where you want to go to settle."[u]

43 When Jeremiah had finished telling the people all the words of the LORD their God—everything the LORD had sent him to tell them[v]— 2Azariah son of Hoshaiah and Johanan[w] son of Kareah and all the arrogant men said to Jeremiah, "You are lying! The LORD our God has not sent you to say, 'You must not go to Egypt to settle there.' 3But Baruch son of Neriah is inciting you against us to hand us over to the Babylonians,[b] so they may kill us or carry us into exile to Babylon."[x]

4So Johanan son of Kareah and all the army officers and all the people disobeyed the LORD's command[y] to stay in the land of Judah.[z] 5Instead, Johanan son of Kareah and all the army officers led away all the remnant of Judah who had come back to live in the land of Judah from all the nations where they had been scattered.[a] 6They also led away all those whom Nebuzaradan commander of the imperial guard had left with Gedaliah son of Ahikam, the son of Shaphan—the men, the women, the children and the king's daughters. And they took Jeremiah the prophet and Baruch son of Neriah along with them. 7So they entered Egypt in disobedience to the LORD and went as far as Tahpanhes.[b]

8In Tahpanhes[c] the word of the LORD came to Jeremiah: 9"While the Jews are watching, take some large stones with you and bury them in clay in the brick pavement at the entrance to Pharaoh's palace in Tahpanhes. 10Then say to them, 'This is what the LORD Almighty, the God of Israel, says: I will send for my servant[d] Nebuchadnezzar king of Babylon, and I will set his throne over these stones I have buried here; he will spread his royal canopy above them. 11He will come and

Jer 43:1-3 ❖ How do we respond when people reject what we say about God and make false accusations against us?

42:16 [k]Eze 11:8
42:17 [l]ver 22; Jer 44:13
42:18 [m]Dt 29:18-20; Jer 7:20 [n]2Ch 36:19; Jer 39:1-9 [o]Jer 29:18 [p]Jer 22:10
42:19 [q]Dt 17:16; Isa 30:7
42:20 [r]ver 2
42:21 [s]Eze 2:7; Zec 7:11-12
42:22 [t]ver 17; Eze 6:11 [u]Hos 9:6
43:1 [v]Jer 26:8; 42:9-22
43:2 [w]Jer 42:1
43:3 [x]Jer 38:4
43:4 [y]Jer 42:5-6 [z]Jer 42:10
43:5 [a]Jer 40:12
43:7 [b]Jer 2:16; 44:1
43:8 [c]Jer 2:16
43:10 [d]Isa 44:28; Jer 25:9; 27:6

[a] *18* That is, your name will be used in cursing (see 29:22); or, others will see that you are cursed.
[b] *3* Or *Chaldeans*

43:1-7 Their reaction to Jeremiah's prophetic message is similar to that of Zedekiah. The latter specifically asked Jeremiah for a word from the Lord, but when he didn't like what Jeremiah provided, he simply refused to obey.

Johanan leads the group to Tahpanhes in Egypt. Jeremiah and Baruch are taken with them, but not willingly. Tahpanhes (cf. 2:16) is in the eastern section of the Nile Delta. It is one of the first communities that a traveler from Palestine would encounter when approaching the Nile Delta from the east. As 44:1 makes clear, it was one of several cities in Egypt with a Judean population.

✣ **42:1—43:7** Christians should not understand obedience to God's revealed will as an irrelevant burden or needless constriction; obedience is the proper response needed to fulfill one's calling. In biblical terms obedience perfectly describes the path of discipleship. It is certainly easy to complain that we don't always know God's will and to offer that as a reason why we don't do something. One should not make light of the difficulties associated with discerning God's will, but it is more frequently the case that people ignore discipleship because of moral laziness and failure to trust God than from their inability to determine at least the basics of a proper course of action.

43:8-13 Jeremiah's prophetic depiction of Nebuchadnezzar's presence is an indication that Babylon will conquer Egypt. Moreover, judgment will come on those Judeans who think they have escaped the reach of the Babylonians by fleeing to Egypt.

attack Egypt,[e] bringing death to those
destined for death, captivity to those
destined for captivity, and the sword to
those destined for the sword.[f] 12He will
set fire to the temples of the gods[g] of
Egypt; he will burn their temples and
take their gods captive. As a shepherd
picks[h] his garment clean of lice, so he will
pick Egypt clean and depart. 13There in
the temple of the sun[a] in Egypt he will
demolish the sacred pillars and will burn
down the temples of the gods of Egypt.'"

Disaster Because of Idolatry

44 This word came to Jeremiah concerning all the Jews living in Lower Egypt — in Migdol,[i] Tahpanhes[j] and
Memphis[k] — and in Upper Egypt:[l] 2"This
is what the LORD Almighty, the God of
Israel, says: You saw the great disaster
I brought on Jerusalem and on all the
towns of Judah. Today they lie deserted
and in ruins[m] 3because of the evil they
have done. They aroused my anger by
burning incense to and worshiping other
gods[n] that neither they nor you nor your
ancestors[o] ever knew. 4Again and again[p]
I sent my servants the prophets,[q] who
said, 'Do not do this detestable thing that
I hate!' 5But they did not listen or pay
attention; they did not turn from their
wickedness or stop burning incense to
other gods.[r] 6Therefore, my fierce anger was poured out; it raged against the
towns of Judah and the streets of Jerusalem and made them the desolate ruins
they are today.
7"Now this is what the LORD God Almighty, the God of Israel, says: Why bring
such great disaster[s] on yourselves by cutting off from Judah the men and wom-
en,[t] the children and infants, and so leave
yourselves without a remnant? 8Why
arouse my anger with what your hands
have made,[u] burning incense to other
gods in Egypt, where you have come to
live?[v] You will destroy yourselves and
make yourselves a curse[b] and an object
of reproach[w] among all the nations on
earth. 9Have you forgotten the wickedness committed by your ancestors and
by the kings and queens of Judah and
the wickedness committed by you and
your wives in the land of Judah and the
streets of Jerusalem?[x] 10To this day they
have not humbled themselves or shown
reverence, nor have they followed my
law[y] and the decrees I set before you and
your ancestors.[z]
11"Therefore this is what the LORD Almighty, the God of Israel, says: I am determined to bring disaster[a] on you and
to destroy all Judah. 12I will take away the
remnant[b] of Judah who were determined
to go to Egypt to settle there. They will
all perish in Egypt; they will fall by the
sword or die from famine. From the least
to the greatest, they will die by sword or
famine.[c] They will become a curse and
an object of horror, a curse and an object
of reproach.[d] 13I will punish those who
live in Egypt with the sword, famine and
plague,[e] as I punished Jerusalem. 14None
of the remnant of Judah who have gone
to live in Egypt will escape or survive to
return to the land of Judah, to which they
long to return and live; none will return
except a few fugitives."[f]
15Then all the men who knew that their
wives were burning incense to other
gods, along with all the women who were
present — a large assembly — and all the
people living in Lower and Upper Egypt,
said to Jeremiah, 16"We will not listen[g]

43:11 [e] Jer 46:13-26; Eze 29:19-20 [f] Jer 15:2; 44:13; Zec 11:9
43:12 [g] Jer 46:25; Eze 30:13 [h] Ps 104:2; 109:18-19
44:1 [i] Ex 14:2 [j] Jer 43:7, 8 [k] Isa 19:13 [l] Isa 11:11; Jer 46:14
44:2 [m] Isa 6:11; Jer 9:11; 34:22
44:3 [n] ver 8; Dt 13:6-11; 29:26 [o] Dt 32:17; Jer 19:4
44:4 [p] Jer 7:13 [q] Jer 7:25; 25:4; 26:5
44:5 [r] Jer 11:8-10
44:7 [s] Jer 26:19 [t] Jer 51:22
44:8 [u] Jer 25:6-7 [v] 1Co 10:22 [w] Jer 42:18
44:9 [x] ver 17, 21
44:10 [y] Jos 1:7 [z] 1Ki 9:6-9
44:11 [a] Jer 21:10; Am 9:4
44:12 [b] ver 7 [c] Isa 1:28 [d] Jer 29:18; 42:15-18
44:13 [e] Jer 42:17
44:14 [f] ver 28; Jer 22:24-27; Ro 9:27
44:16 [g] Jer 11:8-10

[a] 13 Or *in Heliopolis*
[b] 8 That is, your name will be used in cursing (see 29:22); or, others will see that you are cursed; also in verse 12; similarly in verse 22.

44:1–6 The bitter exchange between prophet and people in ch. 44 underscores the deep cultural and religious divisions in the Judean community.
44:7–14 Verse 7 contains a rhetorical question: "Why bring such great disaster on yourselves?" Actions have consequences; the idolatry and unfaithfulness of Judeans in Egypt will have the same self-inflicted consequences as did idolatry and unfaithfulness in Judah. The Judeans in Egypt seem not to have associated the fall of Judah and Jerusalem with God's judgment on their faithlessness.
44:15–19 The people's testy reply to the prophet's judgment speech reflects two significant assumptions about religious practice on the part of Judeans. (1) Religion has the primary function of securing the health and safety of a group. (2) The worship of the Queen of Heaven was stopped earlier in Judah (by Josiah?) and subsequently resumed. The fortunes of the people, so they claim, have turned out better with her than with the Lord (v. 17). As a result, the Judeans in Egypt intend to maintain the worship of the Queen of Heaven as did their ancestors and their kings in Judah.

In particular, the Judean women reply that their worship of the Queen of Heaven was done with the agreement of their husbands (v. 19). Although Jeremiah's previous comments have not singled out either Judean women or worship of the Queen of Heaven, their role in her cult takes center stage as the example of idolatry and unfaithfulness.

to the message you have spoken to us in the name of the LORD! 17 We will certainly do everything we said we would:[h] We will burn incense to the Queen of Heaven[i] and will pour out drink offerings to her just as we and our ancestors, our kings and our officials did in the towns of Judah and in the streets of Jerusalem. At that time we had plenty of food and were well off and suffered no harm.[j] 18 But ever since we stopped burning incense to the Queen of Heaven and pouring out drink offerings to her, we have had nothing and have been perishing by sword and famine.[k]"

19 The women added, "When we burned incense to the Queen of Heaven[l] and poured out drink offerings to her, did not our husbands know that we were making cakes impressed with her image and pouring out drink offerings to her?"

20 Then Jeremiah said to all the people, both men and women, who were answering him, 21 "Did not the LORD remember[m] and call to mind the incense[n] burned in the towns of Judah and the streets of Jerusalem[o] by you and your ancestors,[p] your kings and your officials and the people of the land? 22 When the LORD could no longer endure your wicked actions and the detestable things you did, your land became a curse[q] and a desolate waste without inhabitants, as it is today.[r] 23 Because you have burned incense and have sinned against the LORD and have not obeyed him or followed his law or his decrees or his stipulations, this disaster[s] has come upon you, as you now see."[t]

24 Then Jeremiah said to all the people, including the women,[u] "Hear the word of the LORD, all you people of Judah in Egypt.[v] 25 This is what the LORD Almighty, the God of Israel, says: You and your wives have done what you said you

44:17 [h] Dt 23:23 [i] ver 25; Jer 7:18 [j] Hos 2:5-13
44:18 [k] Mal 3:13-15
44:19 [l] Jer 7:18
44:21 [m] Isa 64:9; Jer 14:10 [n] Jer 11:13 [o] ver 9 [p] Ps 79:8
44:22 [q] Jer 25:18 [r] Ge 19:13; Ps 107:33-34
44:23 [s] Jer 40:2 [t] 1Ki 9:9; Jer 7:13-15; Da 9:11-12
44:24 [u] ver 15 [v] Jer 43:7
44:25 [w] ver 17 [x] Eze 20:39
44:26 [y] Ge 22:16; Isa 48:1; Heb 6:13-17 [z] Dt 32:40; Ps 50:16
44:27 [a] Jer 31:28
44:28 [b] ver 13-14; Isa 10:19 [c] ver 17, 25-26
44:29 [d] Pr 19:21
44:30 [e] Jer 46:26; Eze 30:21 [f] 2Ki 25:1-7 [g] Jer 39:5
45:1 [h] Jer 32:12; 36:4,18,32 [i] 2Ch 36:5

Jer 44:15-18 ❖ As we read this passage, we find out that couples were complicit in their unfaithfulness to God. How might Mt 18:6 apply here?

would do when you promised, 'We will certainly carry out the vows we made to burn incense and pour out drink offerings to the Queen of Heaven.'[w]

"Go ahead then, do what you promised! Keep your vows![x] 26 But hear the word of the LORD, all you Jews living in Egypt: 'I swear[y] by my great name,' says the LORD, 'that no one from Judah living anywhere in Egypt will ever again invoke my name or swear, "As surely as the Sovereign LORD lives."[z] 27 For I am watching over them for harm,[a] not for good; the Jews in Egypt will perish by sword and famine until they are all destroyed. 28 Those who escape the sword and return to the land of Judah from Egypt will be very few.[b] Then the whole remnant of Judah who came to live in Egypt will know whose word will stand — mine or theirs.[c]

29 " 'This will be the sign to you that I will punish you in this place,' declares the LORD, 'so that you will know that my threats of harm against you will surely stand.'[d] 30 This is what the LORD says: 'I am going to deliver Pharaoh[e] Hophra king of Egypt into the hands of his enemies who want to kill him, just as I gave Zedekiah[f] king of Judah into the hands of Nebuchadnezzar king of Babylon, the enemy who wanted to kill him.' "[g]

A Message to Baruch

45 When Baruch[h] son of Neriah wrote on a scroll the words Jeremiah the prophet dictated in the fourth year of Jehoiakim[i] son of Josiah king

---

44:20–30 Jeremiah recognizes that his give-and-take with the crowd has set out both their resolve to remain worshipers of the Queen of Heaven and God's resolve that his word of judgment will come to pass. He predicts, therefore, that Pharaoh Hophra, the current ruler of Egypt, will be given over to the hands of his enemies as a sign of God's mastery of affairs, even in Egypt. In 569 BC Hophra was killed by one of his officials in a military coup.

43:8—44:30 "The fear of the LORD is the beginning of knowledge" (Pr 1:7). The pathway to life begins by acknowledging that every road leads to death except the one charted by God. Jeremiah's contemporaries in Egypt simply could not face the fact that they had been (and remained) part of a failed political and religious enterprise. Tragically, they were willing to do almost anything to hear from God: kidnap Jeremiah and Baruch, worship the Queen of Heaven, and so on. What they refused to do was to acknowledge their failure and depend on the God of grace, who can make all things new.

45:1–2 The prophecy concerning Baruch is out of place chronologically with the preceding chapters (chs. 37–44). Verse 1 provides a date in the fourth

PEOPLE TO KNOW // BARUCH

JEREMIAH 45:1-5: Baruch was the scribe of the "weeping prophet" Jeremiah, who prophesied in the nation of Judah. Baruch had the weighty task of copying down God's words of prophecy given to Jeremiah. The hope was that the people in the nation would hear God's words, turn from their wicked ways and return to following God. Jeremiah sent Baruch to read the words of the scroll at the temple. Bravely, Baruch obeyed.

When royal officials heard Baruch reading the scroll, they made him come and read it to them in a private audience. Learning the words had been given to Baruch by Jeremiah, they resolved to bring the scroll to the king—but they warned Baruch to hide with Jeremiah.

King Jehoiakim had his secretary read the scroll to him, and as it was read, the king cut off pieces of it and burned them (Jer 36:23). He ordered Baruch and Jeremiah arrested, but God protected them. Then, like Moses' copying down the Ten Commandments in stone a second time, Baruch wrote a second copy of God's message. Jehoiakim's fire could not silence the word of God.

Jeremiah's last word from God to Baruch is a promise that, though Baruch saw sorrow and woe, God would sustain him (Jer 45:1-5).

APPLICATION ✣ Supporting a prophet proved to be risky business for Baruch. Copying down God's message of judgment on Jerusalem was not well received by the king, and it made his boss, Jeremiah, a pariah. Yet Baruch obeyed his calling.

Today we are still called to deliver prophetic messages from Scripture. This involves speaking against evil and sin. Our words won't always be warmly accepted by those who hear them. Our task is not to win the favor of kings; it is to proclaim God's truth, like Baruch did.

of Judah, Jeremiah said this to Baruch:
2"This is what the LORD, the God of Israel, says to you, Baruch: 3You said, 'Woe
to me! The LORD has added sorrow to
my pain; I am worn out with groaning[j]
and find no rest.' 4But the LORD has
told me to say to you, 'This is what the
LORD says: I will overthrow what I have
built and uproot what I have planted,[k]
throughout the earth.[l] 5Should you then
seek great things for yourself? Do not
seek them.[m] For I will bring disaster on
all people, declares the LORD, but wherever you go I will let you escape with
your life.'"[n]

45:3 [j] Ps 69:3
45:4 [k] Jer 11:17 [l] Isa 5:5-7; Jer 18:7-10
45:5 [m] Mt 6:25-27,33 [n] Jer 21:9; 38:2; 39:18

Jer 45:5 ✣ When has God given you a special message or sign of reassurance, perhaps in the midst of a bleak time?

---

year of Jehoiakim (605 BC), which coincides with the command from the Lord in 36:1 for Jeremiah to prepare a scroll of his prophecies.

Why does this account come at the end of the description of the Egyptian journey of Jeremiah and Baruch? These words confirm that Baruch served God and would be enabled to perform his calling. Moreover, the placement of this prophecy reinforces the claim that Baruch's presence in Egypt is not the result of God's disfavor. Although neither prophet nor companion will escape the fate of the nation, God will vindicate them.

45:3-5 Baruch's "woe" (v. 3) is a counterpart to the laments of Jeremiah. There is a cost to serving the Lord in times such as these. The divine message to Baruch repeats the language of uprooting and tearing down used at Jeremiah's commission to the prophetic office (1:10). In the tragic affairs of Judah and Jerusalem, God has been at work to uproot and tear down. Baruch has no more "right" (to use modern Western language) than anyone else to expect that he will escape the consequences of judgment that have swept through the region.

God calls Baruch to be faithful. His personal safety resides with God. God promises him that his life has been granted to him "wherever" (45:5) he might go.

✣ **45:1-5** Christians who feel isolated or depressed over their circumstances are invited to measure their lives against a Scriptural pattern including saints such as Abraham, Joseph, Moses, Jeremiah, and Baruch. Abraham made mistakes in Egypt. Joseph was unjustly imprisoned there. Moses committed murder there and struggled against Pharaoh to mobilize his people to leave. Jeremiah and Baruch were kidnapped and brought to Egypt.

None of these saints, however, lacked the attention of God, who remained faithful to them in times of upheaval. This did not cause their pain to go away. Their lives were gifts in service to the Lord in and through these difficulties. And through their difficulties God formed disciples.

A Message About Egypt

46 This is the word of the LORD that came to Jeremiah the prophet concerning the nations:[o]

2Concerning Egypt:

This is the message against the army of Pharaoh Necho[p] king of Egypt, which was defeated at Carchemish[q] on the Euphrates River by Nebuchadnezzar king of Babylon in the fourth year of Jehoiakim[r] son of Josiah king of Judah:

3"Prepare your shields,[s] both large
and small,
and march out for battle!
4Harness the horses,
mount the steeds!
Take your positions
with helmets on!
Polish[t] your spears,
put on your armor![u]
5What do I see?
They are terrified,
they are retreating,
their warriors are defeated.
They flee[v] in haste
without looking back,
and there is terror[w] on every side,"
declares the LORD.
6"The swift cannot flee[x]
nor the strong escape.
In the north by the River Euphrates
they stumble and fall.[y]
7"Who is this that rises like the Nile,
like rivers of surging waters?[z]
8Egypt rises like the Nile,
like rivers of surging waters.
She says, 'I will rise and cover the
earth;
I will destroy cities and their
people.'
9Charge, you horses!
Drive furiously, you charioteers![a]
March on, you warriors — men of
Cush[a] and Put who carry
shields,
men of Lydia[b] who draw the bow.
10But that day[c] belongs to the Lord,
the LORD Almighty —
a day of vengeance, for vengeance
on his foes.
The sword will devour[d] till it is
satisfied,
till it has quenched its thirst with
blood.
For the Lord, the LORD Almighty, will
offer sacrifice[e]
in the land of the north by the
River Euphrates.
11"Go up to Gilead and get balm,[f]
Virgin[g] Daughter Egypt.
But you try many medicines in vain;
there is no healing[h] for you.
12The nations will hear of your shame;
your cries will fill the earth.
One warrior will stumble over
another;
both will fall[i] down together."

13This is the message the LORD spoke to Jeremiah the prophet about the coming of Nebuchadnezzar king of Babylon to attack Egypt:[j]

14"Announce this in Egypt, and
proclaim it in Migdol;
proclaim it also in Memphis and
Tahpanhes:[k]
'Take your positions and get ready,
for the sword devours those
around you.'

46:1 [o] Jer 1:10; 25:15-38
46:2 [p] 2Ki 23:29 [q] 2Ch 35:20 [r] Jer 45:1
46:3 [s] Isa 21:5; Jer 51:11-12
46:4 [t] Eze 21:9-11 [u] 1Sa 17:5, 38; 2Ch 26:14; Ne 4:16
46:5 [v] ver 21 [w] Jer 49:29
46:6 [x] Isa 30:16 [y] ver 12, 16; Da 11:19
46:7 [z] Jer 47:2
46:9 [a] Jer 47:3 [b] Isa 66:19
46:10 [c] Joel 1:15 [d] Dt 32:42 [e] Zep 1:7
46:11 [f] Jer 8:22 [g] Isa 47:1 [h] Jer 30:13; Mic 1:9
46:12 [i] Isa 19:4; Na 3:8-10
46:13 [j] Isa 19:1
46:14 [k] Jer 43:8

Jer 46:11-12 ❖ Why does looking for comfort and help away from God always ultimately fail?

[a] 9 That is, the upper Nile region

46:1 The fourth year of Jehoiakim was 605 BC, the year of the fateful battle between the Pharaoh Necho and Nebuchadnezzar (v. 26). The Egyptians were routed, which was predicted as part of the judgment in the historical process, but it was not the end of the Egyptians themselves.
46:2-12 This message is directed to the army of Pharaoh Necho. In 609 BC Pharaoh's army had marched to join the Assyrian army and oppose the emerging power of Babylon. At that time, Josiah had attempted to head off the Egyptian army at Megiddo and was mortally wounded in an unsuccessful effort to stop the Egyptian advance (2Ki 23:29-30; 2Ch 35:20-24). Jehoiakim was chosen by the Egyptian to succeed his father Josiah. The martial language of the message depicts elements of the Egyptian army preparing to fight and then fleeing in terror. The boastful pride of the Egyptians is described in imperialistic terms (Jer 46:8), only to be reversed by divine judgment on a day that "belongs to the Lord" (v. 10).

Egypt is also described in familial terms as "Virgin Daughter" (v. 11). She who seeks a balm in Gilead will find that there is no healing for her.
46:13-20 Unlike the companion message in vv. 2-12, this prophecy is undated. Essentially the prophecy announces that Babylon will bring God's judgment on Egypt.

15 Why will your warriors be laid low?
They cannot stand, for the LORD
will push them down.[l]
16 They will stumble[m] repeatedly;
they will fall[n] over each other.
They will say, 'Get up, let us go back
to our own people and our native
lands,
away from the sword of the
oppressor.'
17 There they will exclaim,
'Pharaoh king of Egypt is only a
loud noise;
he has missed his opportunity.[o]'

18 "As surely as I live," declares the
King,[p]
whose name is the LORD Almighty,
"one will come who is like Tabor[q]
among the mountains,
like Carmel[r] by the sea.
19 Pack your belongings for exile,[s]
you who live in Egypt,
for Memphis will be laid waste
and lie in ruins without
inhabitant.

20 "Egypt is a beautiful heifer,
but a gadfly is coming
against her from the north.[t]
21 The mercenaries[u] in her ranks
are like fattened calves.
They too will turn and flee[v] together,
they will not stand their ground,
for the day[w] of disaster is coming
upon them,
the time for them to be punished.
22 Egypt will hiss like a fleeing serpent
as the enemy advances in force;
they will come against her with axes,
like men who cut down trees.
23 They will chop down her forest,"
declares the LORD,
"dense though it be.

46:15 [l] Isa 66:15-16
46:16 [m] Lev 26:37 [n] ver 6
46:17 [o] Isa 19:11-16
46:18 [p] Jer 48:15 [q] Jos 19:22 [r] 1Ki 18:42
46:19 [s] Isa 20:4
46:20 [t] ver 24; Jer 47:2
46:21 [u] 2Ki 7:6 [v] ver 5 [w] Ps 37:13
46:23 [x] Jdg 7:12
46:24 [y] Jer 1:15
46:25 [z] Eze 30:14; Na 3:8 [a] Jer 43:12 [b] Isa 20:6
46:26 [c] Jer 44:30 [d] Eze 32:11 [e] Eze 29:11-16
46:27 [f] Isa 41:13; 43:5 [g] Isa 11:11; Jer 50:19
46:28 [h] Isa 8:9-10 [i] Jer 4:27
47:1 [j] Ge 10:19; Am 1:6; Zec 9:5-7

They are more numerous than
locusts,[x]
they cannot be counted.
24 Daughter Egypt will be put to shame,
given into the hands of the people
of the north.[y]"

25 The LORD Almighty, the God of Israel,
says: "I am about to bring punishment
on Amon god of Thebes,[z] on Pharaoh, on
Egypt and her gods[a] and her kings, and
on those who rely[b] on Pharaoh.
26 I will
give them into the hands[c] of those who
want to kill them — Nebuchadnezzar
king[d] of Babylon and his officers. Later,
however, Egypt will be inhabited[e] as in
times past," declares the LORD.

27 "Do not be afraid,[f] Jacob my servant;
do not be dismayed, Israel.
I will surely save you out of a distant
place,
your descendants from the land of
their exile.[g]
Jacob will again have peace and
security,
and no one will make him afraid.
28 Do not be afraid, Jacob my servant,
for I am with you,"[h] declares the
LORD.
"Though I completely destroy[i] all
the nations
among which I scatter you,
I will not completely destroy you.
I will discipline you but only in due
measure;
I will not let you go entirely
unpunished."

A Message About the Philistines

47 This is the word of the LORD that came to Jeremiah the prophet concerning the Philistines before Pharaoh attacked Gaza:[j]

46:21–26 The disastrous event is a day in the future. Egypt is personified as a female ("Daughter Egypt," v. 24) who will be put to shame by a people from the north. Part of the judgment to come is directed at Amon, one of the Egyptian deities. Judgment, however, is not the end of Egypt as a nation; it will again be inhabited.

46:27–28 Following the messages against Egypt is a prediction of the restoration of God's people. Those on whom God's judgment has fallen have been disciplined justly. In his mercy, God will not make an end of them. Those God used to discipline his people (such as the Egyptians) will suffer the fate of those whose pride, cruelty, and idolatry have kept them from acknowledging the work of God.

47:1–7 Two Philistine cities are named here: Gaza and Ashkelon. The message against the Philistines possibly comes with Nebuchadnezzar's preparations to attack Gaza (cf. v. 2). Gaza was a trading center. The assault in question could have been committed by the Egyptians between 609 BC, when Necho moved from Egypt to north Syria, and 605 BC, when the Egyptians were defeated at Carchemish. It is difficult to place this message in a specific historical context, but there are several plausible options because of frequent military actions in the region.

The message against the Philistines is similar to the messages against Egypt. The Philistines will be defeated on some future day (v. 4). People will mourn for Gaza and Ashkelon. God's historical judgment is personified through a poetic address to his sword (v. 6).

2This is what the LORD says:

"See how the waters are rising in the north;[k]
they will become an overflowing torrent.
They will overflow the land and everything in it,
the towns and those who live in them.
The people will cry out;
all who dwell in the land will wail
3at the sound of the hooves of galloping steeds,
at the noise of enemy chariots
and the rumble of their wheels.
Parents will not turn to help their children;
their hands will hang limp.
4For the day has come
to destroy all the Philistines
and to remove all survivors
who could help Tyre[l] and Sidon.[m]
The LORD is about to destroy the Philistines,[n]
the remnant from the coasts of Caphtor.[a][o]
5Gaza will shave[p] her head in mourning;
Ashkelon[q] will be silenced.
You remnant on the plain,
how long will you cut yourselves?

6"'Alas, sword[r] of the LORD,
how long till you rest?
Return to your sheath;
cease and be still.'
7But how can it rest
when the LORD has commanded it,
when he has ordered it
to attack Ashkelon and the coast?"

A Message About Moab

48:29–36pp // Isa 16:6–12

48 Concerning Moab:

This is what the LORD Almighty, the God of Israel, says:

47:2 [k]Isa 8:7; 14:31
47:4 [l]Am 1:9-10; Zec 9:2-4 [m]Jer 25:22 [n]Ge 10:14; Joel 3:4 [o]Dt 2:23
47:5 [p]Jer 41:5; Mic 1:16 [q]Jer 25:20
47:6 [r]Jer 12:12

Jer 47:4–7 ❖ Upon what violence or oppression in the world are we praying for God to bring his just judgment? Why does God wait to exact such judgment (see 2Pe 3:9)?

Jer 48:7 ❖ How can we avoid the temptation to trust in our own deeds or wealth? Why is this temptation so prevalent today?

"Woe to Nebo,[s] for it will be ruined.
Kiriathaim[t] will be disgraced and captured;
the stronghold[b] will be disgraced and shattered.
2Moab will be praised[u] no more;
in Heshbon[c][v] people will plot her downfall:
'Come, let us put an end to that nation.'
You, the people of Madmen,[d] will also be silenced;
the sword will pursue you.
3Cries of anguish arise from Horonaim,[w]
cries of great havoc and destruction.
4Moab will be broken;
her little ones will cry out.[e]
5They go up the hill to Luhith,[x]
weeping bitterly as they go;
on the road down to Horonaim
anguished cries over the destruction are heard.
6Flee! Run for your lives;
become like a bush[f] in the desert.[y]
7Since you trust in your deeds and riches,
you too will be taken captive,
and Chemosh[z] will go into exile,[a]
together with his priests and officials.

48:1 [s]Nu 32:38 [t]Nu 32:37
48:2 [u]Isa 16:14 [v]Nu 21:25
48:3 [w]Isa 15:5
48:5 [x]Isa 15:5
48:6 [y]Jer 17:6
48:7 [z]Nu 21:29 [a]Isa 46:1-2; Jer 49:3

[a] 4 That is, Crete [b] 1 Or *captured; / Misgab* [c] 2 The Hebrew for *Heshbon* sounds like the Hebrew for *plot.* [d] 2 The name of the Moabite town Madmen sounds like the Hebrew for *be silenced.* [e] 4 Hebrew; Septuagint / *proclaim it to Zoar* [f] 6 Or *like Aroer*

48:1–25 The Moabites receive an extensive address in vv. 1–47 that preserves a significant knowledge of geography. Over 20 different cities (settlements) are named in the poetic indictment against Judah's eastern neighbor. The Moabites and Israelites were distant relatives.

The repetition of a concluding prophetic formula ("declares the LORD") in vv. 25, 30, 35, 38, 43, 44, and 47 suggests that more than one prophetic announcement has been collected in Jer 48.

48:7–13 Verse 7 mentions Chemosh, the god of Moab. One way to refer to Moab was to call them the "people of Chemosh" (Nu 21:29). He, like his people, will suffer defeat and go into exile. In the future, Moab will be ashamed of Chemosh, just as Israel was ashamed when trusting Bethel (Jer 48:13). The name "Bethel" here likely refers to a deity rather than a place.

8 The destroyer will come against
every town,
and not a town will escape.
The valley will be ruined
and the plateau destroyed,
because the LORD has spoken.
9 Put salt on Moab,
for she will be laid waste[a];
her towns will become desolate,
with no one to live in them.

10 "A curse on anyone who is lax in
doing the LORD's work!
A curse on anyone who keeps their
sword[b] from bloodshed![c]

11 "Moab has been at rest[d] from youth,
like wine left on its dregs,[e]
not poured from one jar to
another —
she has not gone into exile.
So she tastes as she did,
and her aroma is unchanged.
12 But days are coming,"
declares the LORD,
"when I will send men who pour
from pitchers,
and they will pour her out;
they will empty her pitchers
and smash her jars.
13 Then Moab will be ashamed[f] of
Chemosh,
as Israel was ashamed
when they trusted in Bethel.

14 "How can you say, 'We are warriors,[g]
men valiant in battle'?
15 Moab will be destroyed and her
towns invaded;
her finest young men will go
down in the slaughter,[h]"
declares the King,[i] whose name is
the LORD Almighty.[j]
16 "The fall of Moab is at hand;[k]
her calamity will come quickly.
17 Mourn for her, all who live around
her,
all who know her fame;
say, 'How broken is the mighty
scepter,
how broken the glorious staff!'

18 "Come down from your glory
and sit on the parched ground,[l]
you inhabitants of Daughter
Dibon,[m]
for the one who destroys Moab
will come up against you
and ruin your fortified cities.[n]
19 Stand by the road and watch,
you who live in Aroer.[o]
Ask the man fleeing and the woman
escaping,
ask them, 'What has happened?'
20 Moab is disgraced, for she is
shattered.
Wail[p] and cry out!
Announce by the Arnon[q]
that Moab is destroyed.
21 Judgment has come to the plateau —
to Holon, Jahzah[r] and Mephaath,[s]
22 to Dibon,[t] Nebo and Beth
Diblathaim,
23 to Kiriathaim, Beth Gamul and Beth
Meon,[u]
24 to Kerioth[v] and Bozrah —
to all the towns of Moab, far and
near.
25 Moab's horn[b][w] is cut off;
her arm[x] is broken,"
declares the LORD.

26 "Make her drunk,[y]
for she has defied the LORD.
Let Moab wallow in her vomit;
let her be an object of ridicule.
27 Was not Israel the object of your
ridicule?[z]
Was she caught among thieves,
that you shake your head[a] in scorn[b]
whenever you speak of her?
28 Abandon your towns and dwell
among the rocks,
you who live in Moab.
Be like a dove[c] that makes its nest
at the mouth of a cave.[d]

29 "We have heard of Moab's pride[e] —
how great is her arrogance! —
of her insolence, her pride, her
conceit
and the haughtiness of her heart.
30 I know her insolence but it is futile,"
declares the LORD,

48:10 [b] Jer 47:6 [c] 1Ki 20:42; 2Ki 13:15-19
48:11 [d] Zec 1:15 [e] Zep 1:12
48:13 [f] Hos 10:6
48:14 [g] Ps 33:16
48:15 [h] Jer 50:27 [i] Jer 46:18 [j] Jer 51:57
48:16 [k] Isa 13:22
48:18 [l] Isa 47:1 [m] Nu 21:30; Jos 13:9 [n] ver 8
48:19 [o] Dt 2:36
48:20 [p] Isa 16:7 [q] Nu 21:13
48:21 [r] Nu 21:23; Isa 15:4 [s] Jos 13:18
48:22 [t] Jos 13:9, 17
48:23 [u] Jos 13:17
48:24 [v] Am 2:2
48:25 [w] Ps 75:10 [x] Ps 10:15; Eze 30:21
48:26 [y] Jer 25:16, 27
48:27 [z] Jer 2:26 [a] Job 16:4; Jer 18:16 [b] Mic 7:8-10
48:28 [c] Ps 55:6-7 [d] Jdg 6:2
48:29 [e] Job 40:12; Isa 16:6

[a] 9 Or *Give wings to Moab, / for she will fly away*
[b] 25 *Horn* here symbolizes strength.

48:14–25 As with Egypt and Judah, Jeremiah uses familial language for Moab. Her cities will be ruined, and she will wail a funeral lament. Even physical mutilation is mentioned. Moab's "horn" (v. 25), a metaphor for strength, will be cut off and her arm broken.

48:26–47 These prophecies continue the depiction of Moab's humiliation. As with the previous message, the language is graphic.

"and her boasts accomplish
nothing.
31 Therefore I wail[f] over Moab,
for all Moab I cry out,
I moan for the people of Kir
Hareseth.[g]
32 I weep for you, as Jazer weeps,
you vines of Sibmah.[h]
Your branches spread as far as the
sea[a];
they reached as far as[b] Jazer.
The destroyer has fallen
on your ripened fruit and
grapes.
33 Joy and gladness are gone
from the orchards and fields of
Moab.
I have stopped the flow of wine[i]
from the presses;
no one treads them with shouts of
joy.[j]
Although there are shouts,
they are not shouts of joy.

34 "The sound of their cry rises
from Heshbon to Elealeh[k] and
Jahaz,[l]
from Zoar[m] as far as Horonaim[n] and
Eglath Shelishiyah,
for even the waters of Nimrim are
dried up.[o]
35 In Moab I will put an end
to those who make offerings on
the high places[p]
and burn incense[q] to their gods,"
declares the LORD.
36 "So my heart laments[r] for Moab like
the music of a pipe;
it laments like a pipe for the
people of Kir Hareseth.
The wealth they acquired[s] is
gone.
37 Every head is shaved[t]
and every beard cut off;
every hand is slashed
and every waist is covered with
sackcloth.[u]
38 On all the roofs in Moab
and in the public squares
there is nothing but mourning,
for I have broken Moab
like a jar[v] that no one wants,"
declares the LORD.

48:31 [f] Isa 15:5-8 [g] 2Ki 3:25
48:32 [h] Isa 16:8-9
48:33 [i] Isa 16:10 [j] Joel 1:12
48:34 [k] Nu 32:3 [l] Isa 15:4 [m] Ge 13:10 [n] Isa 15:5 [o] Isa 15:6
48:35 [p] Isa 15:2; 16:12 [q] Jer 11:13
48:36 [r] Isa 16:11 [s] Isa 15:7
48:37 [t] Isa 15:2; Jer 41:5 [u] Ge 37:34
48:38 [v] Jer 22:28
48:40 [w] Dt 28:49; Hab 1:8 [x] Isa 8:8
48:41 [y] Isa 21:3
48:42 [z] Ps 83:4; Isa 16:14 [a] ver 2 [b] ver 26
48:43 [c] Isa 24:17
48:44 [d] 1Ki 19:17; Isa 24:18 [e] Jer 11:23
48:45 [f] Nu 21:21, 26-28 [g] Nu 24:17
48:46 [h] Nu 21:29
48:47 [i] Jer 12:15; 49:6,39

39 "How shattered she is! How they
wail!
How Moab turns her back in
shame!
Moab has become an object of
ridicule,
an object of horror to all those
around her."

40 This is what the LORD says:

"Look! An eagle is swooping[w]
down,
spreading its wings[x] over Moab.
41 Kerioth[c] will be captured
and the strongholds taken.
In that day the hearts of Moab's
warriors
will be like the heart of a woman
in labor.[y]
42 Moab will be destroyed[z] as a nation[a]
because she defied[b] the LORD.
43 Terror and pit and snare[c] await you,
you people of Moab,"
declares the LORD.
44 "Whoever flees[d] from the terror
will fall into a pit,
whoever climbs out of the pit
will be caught in a snare;
for I will bring on Moab
the year[e] of her punishment,"
declares the LORD.

45 "In the shadow of Heshbon
the fugitives stand helpless,
for a fire has gone out from
Heshbon,
a blaze from the midst of Sihon;[f]
it burns the foreheads of Moab,
the skulls[g] of the noisy boasters.
46 Woe to you, Moab![h]
The people of Chemosh are
destroyed;
your sons are taken into exile
and your daughters into captivity.

47 "Yet I will restore[i] the fortunes of
Moab
in days to come,"
declares the LORD.

Here ends the judgment on Moab.

[a] 32 Probably the Dead Sea [b] 32 Two Hebrew manuscripts and Septuagint; most Hebrew manuscripts *as far as the Sea of* [c] 41 Or *The cities*

48:31–32 Jeremiah is moved by the intensity of depicting Moab's downfall.
48:42 Moab will be judged because "she defied the LORD."
48:47 The last line of these intricate poetic prophecies is one of restoration. This is the same phrase God uses elsewhere in predicting the restoration of Israel.

A Message About Ammon

49 Concerning the Ammonites:[j]

This is what the LORD says:

"Has Israel no sons?
Has Israel no heir?
Why then has Molek[a] taken
possession of Gad?
Why do his people live in its towns?
2 But the days are coming,"
declares the LORD,
"when I will sound the battle cry[k]
against Rabbah[l] of the
Ammonites;
it will become a mound of ruins,
and its surrounding villages will
be set on fire.
Then Israel will drive out
those who drove her out,[m]"
says the LORD.
3 "Wail, Heshbon, for Ai[n] is destroyed!
Cry out, you inhabitants of
Rabbah!
Put on sackcloth and mourn;
rush here and there inside the
walls,
for Molek will go into exile,[o]
together with his priests and
officials.
4 Why do you boast of your valleys,
boast of your valleys so fruitful?
Unfaithful Daughter Ammon,
you trust in your riches[p] and say,
'Who will attack me?'[q]
5 I will bring terror on you
from all those around you,"
declares the Lord,
the LORD Almighty.
"Every one of you will be driven
away,
and no one will gather the
fugitives.

6 "Yet afterward, I will restore[r] the
fortunes of the Ammonites,"
declares the LORD.

A Message About Edom

49:9–10pp // Ob 5–6
49:14–16pp // Ob 1–4

7 Concerning Edom:[s]

This is what the LORD Almighty says:

"Is there no longer wisdom in
Teman?[t]
Has counsel perished from the
prudent?
Has their wisdom decayed?
8 Turn and flee, hide in deep caves,
you who live in Dedan,[u]
for I will bring disaster on Esau
at the time when I punish him.
9 If grape pickers came to you,
would they not leave a few
grapes?
If thieves came during the night,
would they not steal only as much
as they wanted?
10 But I will strip Esau bare;
I will uncover his hiding places,
so that he cannot conceal himself.
His armed men are destroyed,
also his allies and neighbors,
so there is no one[v] to say,
11 'Leave your fatherless children;[w] I
will keep them alive.
Your widows too can depend on
me.'"

12 This is what the LORD says: "If those
who do not deserve to drink the cup[x]
must drink it, why should you go unpunished?[y] You will not go unpunished,
but must drink it. 13 I swear[z] by myself,"

49:1 [j] Am 1:13; Zep 2:8-9
49:2 [k] Jer 4:19 [l] Dt 3:11 [m] Isa 14:2; Eze 21:28-32; 25:2-11
49:3 [n] Jos 8:28 [o] Jer 48:7
49:4 [p] Jer 9:23; 1Ti 6:17 [q] Jer 21:13
49:6 [r] ver 39; Jer 48:47
49:7 [s] Ge 25:30; Eze 25:12 [t] Ge 36:11,15,34
49:8 [u] Jer 25:23
49:10 [v] Mal 1:2-5
49:11 [w] Hos 14:3
49:12 [x] Jer 25:15 [y] Jer 25:28-29
49:13 [z] Ge 22:16

[a] 1 Or *their king*; also in verse 3

49:1–6 The message against the Ammonites is much briefer than the one against Moab. Ammon's chief deity was Molek. Solomon married an Ammonite princess and built a temple for Molek's worship on the hill east of the temple mount in Jerusalem (see 1Ki 11:7). Baalis, king of Ammon at the time of Jerusalem's fall, plotted with Ishmael to murder Gedaliah, the Judean governor appointed by the Babylonians (Jer 40–41).

Rabbah is the capital city of Ammon. Its remains form part of the impressive citadel at the heart of modern-day Amman, Jordan. The judgment to come on Ammon is depicted as defeat and exile.

49:7–22 Like Ammon and Moab, the Edomites are related to God's people—in their case, through Esau (Ge 36). Esau is mentioned explicitly in Jer 49:8, 10 as a synonym for Edom. The bitterness reflected in the relationship between Jacob and Esau was reflected later in the relationship between Judah and Edom in the days of Jeremiah and into the postexilic period.

Those who lived east of Palestine were celebrated as wise. Jeremiah's discourse against the Edomites depicts its day of judgment as the loss or failure of its wisdom. The region of Dedan (v. 8) is in the Arabian desert, but its inhabitants were linked with Edom through trade.

Bozrah (vv. 13, 22) is the capital city of Edom. Its ruins are located near the modern Jordanian village of Buseirah. Verse 19 depicts God as a lion coming upon Edom. His plan is to destroy them, which will come on a day that strikes fear into the heart of a warrior.

declares the LORD, "that Bozrah[a] will become a ruin and a curse,[a] an object of horror and reproach; and all its towns will be in ruins forever."

14 I have heard a message from the LORD;
an envoy was sent to the nations to say,
"Assemble yourselves to attack it!
Rise up for battle!"

15 "Now I will make you small among the nations,
despised by mankind.
16 The terror you inspire
and the pride of your heart have deceived you,
you who live in the clefts of the rocks,
who occupy the heights of the hill.
Though you build your nest[b] as high as the eagle's,
from there I will bring you down,"
declares the LORD.
17 "Edom will become an object of horror;[c]
all who pass by will be appalled and will scoff
because of all its wounds.[d]
18 As Sodom and Gomorrah[e] were overthrown,
along with their neighboring towns,"
says the LORD,
"so no one will live there;
no people will dwell[f] in it.

19 "Like a lion coming up from Jordan's thickets[g]
to a rich pastureland,
I will chase Edom from its land in an instant.
Who is the chosen one I will appoint for this?
Who is like me and who can challenge me?[h]
And what shepherd can stand against me?"

20 Therefore, hear what the LORD has planned against Edom,
what he has purposed[i] against those who live in Teman:
The young of the flock[j] will be dragged away;
their pasture will be appalled at their fate.
21 At the sound of their fall the earth will tremble;[k]
their cry[l] will resound to the Red Sea.[b]
22 Look! An eagle will soar and swoop[m] down,
spreading its wings over Bozrah.
In that day the hearts of Edom's warriors
will be like the heart of a woman in labor.[n]

A Message About Damascus

23 Concerning Damascus:[o]

"Hamath[p] and Arpad[q] are dismayed,
for they have heard bad news.
They are disheartened,
troubled like[c] the restless sea.[r]
24 Damascus has become feeble,
she has turned to flee
and panic has gripped her;
anguish and pain have seized her,
pain like that of a woman in labor.
25 Why has the city of renown not been abandoned,
the town in which I delight?
26 Surely, her young men will fall in the streets;
all her soldiers will be silenced[s] in that day,"
declares the LORD Almighty.
27 "I will set fire[t] to the walls of Damascus;
it will consume the fortresses of Ben-Hadad.[u]"

A Message About Kedar and Hazor

28 Concerning Kedar[v] and the kingdoms of Hazor, which Nebuchadnezzar king of Babylon attacked:

49:13 [a] Ge 36:33; Isa 34:6
49:16 [b] Job 39:27; Am 9:2
49:17 [c] ver 13 [d] Jer 50:13; Eze 35:7
49:18 [e] Ge 19:24; Dt 29:23 [f] ver 33
49:19 [g] Jer 12:5 [h] Jer 50:44
49:20 [i] Isa 14:27 [j] Jer 50:45
49:21 [k] Eze 26:15 [l] Jer 50:46; Eze 26:18
49:22 [m] Hos 8:1 [n] Isa 13:8; Jer 48:40-41
49:23 [o] Ge 14:15; 2Ch 16:2; Ac 9:2 [p] Isa 10:9; Am 6:2; Zec 9:2 [q] 2Ki 18:34 [r] Ge 49:4; Isa 57:20
49:26 [s] Jer 50:30
49:27 [t] Jer 43:12; Am 1:4 [u] 1Ki 15:18
49:28 [v] Ge 25:13

[a] 13 That is, its name will be used in cursing (see 29:22); or, others will see that it is cursed.
[b] 21 Or *the Sea of Reeds* [c] 23 Hebrew *on* or *by*

49:23–27 Perhaps Damascus is named here because of the Aramean raids reported in 2Ki 24:2. Damascus suffered devastating attacks from the Assyrians in the ninth and eighth centuries BC because it was a persistent location in the region for anti-Assyrian activities.

Damascus is personified as a weak woman having labor pains. Hadad is a well-known Aramean deity, and the name Ben-Hadad designates a king as the adopted "son" of the deity. Several kings from Damascus had this name/title.

49:28–33 Kedar and Hazor most likely refer to Arab tribesmen who were attacked by the Babylonians in Nebuchadnezzar's sixth year (winter of 599 BC).

17 "Israel is a scattered flock
that lions[m] have chased away.
The first to devour them
was the king[n] of Assyria;
the last to crush their bones
was Nebuchadnezzar[o] king[p] of Babylon."

18 Therefore this is what the LORD Almighty, the God of Israel, says:

"I will punish the king of Babylon and his land
as I punished the king[q] of Assyria.[r]
19 But I will bring[s] Israel back to their own pasture,
and they will graze on Carmel and Bashan;
their appetite will be satisfied
on the hills[t] of Ephraim and Gilead.
20 In those days, at that time,"
declares the LORD,
"search will be made for Israel's guilt,
but there will be none,
and for the sins[u] of Judah,
but none will be found,
for I will forgive[v] the remnant[w] I spare.

21 "Attack the land of Merathaim
and those who live in Pekod.[x]
Pursue, kill and completely destroy[a] them,"
declares the LORD.
"Do everything I have commanded you.
22 The noise[y] of battle is in the land,
the noise of great destruction!
23 How broken and shattered
is the hammer of the whole earth!
How desolate[z] is Babylon
among the nations!
24 I set a trap[a] for you, Babylon,
and you were caught before you knew it;
you were found and captured[b]
because you opposed[c] the LORD.
25 The LORD has opened his arsenal
and brought out the weapons[d] of his wrath,
for the Sovereign LORD Almighty has work to do
in the land of the Babylonians.[e]

50:17 [m] Jer 2:15 [n] 2Ki 17:6 [o] 2Ki 24:10, 14 [p] 2Ki 25:7
50:18 [q] Isa 10:12 [r] Eze 31:3
50:19 [s] Jer 31:10; Eze 34:13 [t] Jer 31:5; 33:12
50:20 [u] Mic 7:18, 19 [v] Jer 31:34 [w] Isa 1:9
50:21 [x] Eze 23:23
50:22 [y] Jer 4:19-21; 51:54
50:23 [z] Isa 14:16
50:24 [a] Da 5:30-31 [b] Jer 51:31 [c] Job 9:4
50:25 [d] Isa 13:5 [e] Jer 51:25, 55

Jer 50:20 ❖ How are we freed by the removal of our sins (see Jn 1:29)? How can we live for God's glory in this freedom?

26 Come against her from afar.
Break open her granaries;
pile her up like heaps of grain.
Completely destroy[f] her
and leave her no remnant.
27 Kill all her young bulls;
let them go down to the slaughter!
Woe to them! For their day has come,
the time for them to be punished.
28 Listen to the fugitives and refugees from Babylon
declaring in Zion[g]
how the LORD our God has taken vengeance,[h]
vengeance for his temple.

29 "Summon archers against Babylon,
all those who draw the bow.[i]
Encamp all around her;
let no one escape.
Repay[j] her for her deeds;[k]
do to her as she has done.
For she has defied[l] the LORD,
the Holy One of Israel.
30 Therefore, her young men[m] will fall in the streets;
all her soldiers will be silenced in that day,"
declares the LORD.
31 "See, I am against[n] you, you arrogant one,"
declares the Lord, the LORD Almighty,
"for your day has come,
the time for you to be punished.
32 The arrogant one will stumble and fall
and no one will help her up;
I will kindle a fire[o] in her towns
that will consume all who are around her."

33 This is what the LORD Almighty says:

"The people of Israel are oppressed,[p]
and the people of Judah as well.

50:26 [f] Isa 14:22-23
50:28 [g] Isa 48:20; Jer 51:10 [h] ver 15
50:29 [i] ver 14 [j] Rev 18:6 [k] Jer 51:56 [l] Isa 47:10
50:30 [m] Isa 13:18; Jer 49:26
50:31 [n] Jer 21:13
50:32 [o] Jer 21:14; 49:27
50:33 [p] Isa 58:6

[a] *21* The Hebrew term refers to the irrevocable giving over of things or persons to the LORD, often by totally destroying them; also in verse 26.

50:18–32 As with Assyria, so with Babylon: God will judge the oppressor. Vengeance on God's part is another motive for judgment (v. 28; cf. 51:11).
50:33–46 God is strong, not just as a judge of iniquity, but as the redeemer of his people. Verse 34 celebrates God as the One who supports his people's cause.

The overthrow of Babylon is compared to that of

All their captors hold them fast,
refusing to let them go.[q]
34 Yet their Redeemer is strong;
the LORD Almighty[r] is his name.
He will vigorously defend their cause[s]
so that he may bring rest[t] to their land,
but unrest to those who live in Babylon.

35 "A sword[u] against the Babylonians!"
declares the LORD—
"against those who live in Babylon
and against her officials and wise[v] men!
36 A sword against her false prophets!
They will become fools.
A sword against her warriors![w]
They will be filled with terror.
37 A sword against her horses and chariots[x]
and all the foreigners in her ranks!
They will become weaklings.[y]
A sword against her treasures!
They will be plundered.
38 A drought on[a] her waters!
They will dry[z] up.
For it is a land of idols,[a]
idols that will go mad with terror.

39 "So desert creatures and hyenas will live there,
and there the owl will dwell.
It will never again be inhabited
or lived in from generation to generation.[b]
40 As I overthrew Sodom and Gomorrah[c]
along with their neighboring towns,"
declares the LORD,
"so no one will live there;
no people will dwell in it.

41 "Look! An army is coming from the north;[d]
a great nation and many kings
are being stirred up from the ends of the earth.[e]
42 They are armed with bows[f] and spears;
they are cruel and without mercy.[g]
They sound like the roaring sea[h]
as they ride on their horses;
they come like men in battle formation
to attack you, Daughter Babylon.[i]
43 The king of Babylon has heard reports about them,
and his hands hang limp.
Anguish has gripped him,
pain like that of a woman in labor.
44 Like a lion coming up from Jordan's thickets
to a rich pastureland,
I will chase Babylon from its land in an instant.
Who is the chosen[j] one I will appoint for this?
Who is like me and who can challenge me?[k]
And what shepherd can stand against me?"

45 Therefore, hear what the LORD has planned against Babylon,
what he has purposed[l] against the land of the Babylonians:
The young of the flock will be dragged away;
their pasture will be appalled at their fate.
46 At the sound of Babylon's capture
the earth will tremble;
its cry[m] will resound among the nations.

51 This is what the LORD says:

"See, I will stir up the spirit of a destroyer
against Babylon and the people of Leb Kamai.[b]
2 I will send foreigners to Babylon
to winnow[n] her and to devastate her land;
they will oppose her on every side
in the day of her disaster.
3 Let not the archer string his bow,[o]
nor let him put on his armor.[p]

50:33 [q] Isa 14:17
50:34 [r] Jer 51:19 [s] Jer 15:21; 51:36 [t] Isa 14:7
50:35 [u] Jer 47:6 [v] Da 5:7
50:36 [w] Jer 49:22
50:37 [x] Jer 51:21 [y] Jer 51:30; Na 3:13
50:38 [z] Jer 51:36 [a] ver 2
50:39 [b] Isa 13:19-22; 34:13-15; Jer 51:37; Rev 18:2
50:40 [c] Ge 19:24
50:41 [d] Jer 6:22 [e] Isa 13:4; Jer 51:22-28
50:42 [f] ver 14 [g] Isa 13:18 [h] Isa 5:30 [i] Jer 6:23
50:44 [j] Nu 16:5 [k] Job 41:10; Isa 46:9; Jer 49:19
50:45 [l] Ps 33:11; Isa 14:24; Jer 51:11
50:46 [m] Rev 18:9-10
51:2 [n] Isa 41:16; Jer 15:7; Mt 3:12
51:3 [o] Jer 50:29 [p] Jer 46:4

[a] 38 Or *A sword against* [b] 1 *Leb Kamai* is a cryptogram for Chaldea, that is, Babylonia.

Sodom and Gomorrah (v. 40). As Jer 50:9; 51:27–28 indicate, God has summoned several groups against Babylon. These claims elaborate on the theme that an enemy from the north will attack Babylon.
51:1–23 Chapter 51 continues the contrast between the coming deliverance of Judean exiles and the judgment to befall Babylon. One of the poetic symbols Jeremiah uses is that of the "cup" (v. 7), a vessel that indicates the future when its contents are consumed: Babylon itself is depicted as a cup from which Judah and the nations drank, but now it is ready to be smashed.

Do not spare her young men;
completely destroy[a] her army.
4 They will fall[q] down slain in Babylon,[b]
fatally wounded in her streets.[r]
5 For Israel and Judah have not been forsaken[s]
by their God, the LORD Almighty,
though their land[c] is full of guilt[t]
before the Holy One of Israel.

6 "Flee[u] from Babylon!
Run for your lives!
Do not be destroyed because of her sins.[v]
It is time for the LORD's vengeance;[w]
he will repay[x] her what she deserves.
7 Babylon was a gold cup[y] in the LORD's hand;
she made the whole earth drunk.
The nations drank her wine;
therefore they have now gone mad.
8 Babylon will suddenly fall[z] and be broken.
Wail over her!
Get balm[a] for her pain;
perhaps she can be healed.

9 " 'We would have healed Babylon,
but she cannot be healed;
let us leave[b] her and each go to our own land,
for her judgment[c] reaches to the skies,
it rises as high as the heavens.'

10 " 'The LORD has vindicated[d] us;
come, let us tell in Zion
what the LORD our God has done.'[e]

11 "Sharpen the arrows,[f]
take up the shields![g]
The LORD has stirred up the kings of the Medes,[h]
because his purpose[i] is to destroy Babylon.
The LORD will take vengeance,
vengeance for his temple.[j]
12 Lift up a banner against the walls of Babylon!
Reinforce the guard,
station the watchmen,
prepare an ambush!
The LORD will carry out his purpose,
his decree against the people of Babylon.
13 You who live by many waters[k]
and are rich in treasures,[l]
your end has come,
the time for you to be destroyed.
14 The LORD Almighty has sworn by himself:[m]
I will surely fill you with troops, as with a swarm of locusts,[n]
and they will shout[o] in triumph over you.

15 "He made the earth by his power;
he founded the world by his wisdom
and stretched[p] out the heavens by his understanding.
16 When he thunders,[q] the waters in the heavens roar;
he makes clouds rise from the ends of the earth.
He sends lightning with the rain
and brings out the wind from his storehouses.[r]

17 "Everyone is senseless and without knowledge;
every goldsmith is shamed by his idols.
The images he makes are a fraud;[s]
they have no breath in them.
18 They are worthless,[t] the objects of mockery;
when their judgment comes, they will perish.
19 He who is the Portion of Jacob is not like these,
for he is the Maker of all things,
including the people of his inheritance —
the LORD Almighty is his name.

20 "You are my war club,[u]
my weapon for battle —
with you I shatter[v] nations,
with you I destroy kingdoms,
21 with you I shatter horse and rider,[w]
with you I shatter chariot and driver,
22 with you I shatter man and woman,

51:4 [q] Isa 13:15 [r] Jer 49:26; 50:30
51:5 [s] Isa 54:6-8 [t] Hos 4:1
51:6 [u] Jer 50:8 [v] Nu 16:26; Rev 18:4 [w] Jer 50:15 [x] Jer 25:14
51:7 [y] Jer 25:15-16; Rev 14:8-10; 17:4
51:8 [z] Isa 21:9; Rev 14:8 [a] Jer 46:11
51:9 [b] Isa 13:14; Jer 50:16 [c] Rev 18:4-5
51:10 [d] Mic 7:9 [e] Jer 50:28
51:11 [f] Jer 50:9 [g] Jer 46:4 [h] ver 28 [i] Jer 50:45 [j] Jer 50:28
51:13 [k] Rev 17:1, 15 [l] Isa 45:3; Hab 2:9
51:14 [m] Am 6:8 [n] ver 27; Na 3:15 [o] Jer 50:15
51:15 [p] Ge 1:1; Job 9:8; Ps 104:2
51:16 [q] Ps 18:11-13 [r] Ps 135:7; Jnh 1:4
51:17 [s] Isa 44:20; Hab 2:18-19
51:18 [t] Jer 18:15
51:20 [u] Isa 10:5 [v] Mic 4:13
51:21 [w] Ex 15:1

[a] 3 The Hebrew term refers to the irrevocable giving over of things or persons to the LORD, often by totally destroying them. [b] 4 Or *Chaldea* [c] 5 Or *Almighty, / and the land of the Babylonians*

51:15–19 These verses celebrate the creative power and wisdom of God. In contrast to human idol-makers, God is "the Maker of all things" (v. 19).

with you I shatter old man and
 youth,
with you I shatter young man and
 young woman,[x]
23 with you I shatter shepherd and
 flock,
with you I shatter farmer and
 oxen,
with you I shatter governors and
 officials.[y]

24 "Before your eyes I will repay[z] Babylon and all who live in Babylonia[a] for all the wrong they have done in Zion," declares the LORD.

25 "I am against you, you destroying
 mountain,
you who destroy the whole earth,"
 declares the LORD.
"I will stretch out my hand against
 you,
roll you off the cliffs,
and make you a burned-out
 mountain.[a]
26 No rock will be taken from you for a
 cornerstone,
nor any stone for a foundation,
for you will be desolate[b] forever,"
 declares the LORD.

27 "Lift up a banner[c] in the land!
Blow the trumpet among the
 nations!
Prepare the nations for battle
 against her;
summon against her these
 kingdoms:[d]
Ararat,[e] Minni and Ashkenaz.[f]
Appoint a commander against her;
send up horses like a swarm of
 locusts.
28 Prepare the nations for battle against
 her—
the kings of the Medes,[g]
their governors and all their
 officials,
and all the countries they rule.
29 The land trembles and writhes,
for the LORD's purposes against
 Babylon stand—
to lay waste the land of Babylon
 so that no one will live there.[h]
30 Babylon's warriors[i] have stopped
 fighting;
they remain in their strongholds.
Their strength is exhausted;
they have become weaklings.[j]
Her dwellings are set on fire;
the bars[k] of her gates are broken.
31 One courier[l] follows another
and messenger follows messenger
to announce to the king of Babylon
that his entire city is captured,
32 the river crossings seized,
the marshes set on fire,
and the soldiers terrified.[m]"

33 This is what the LORD Almighty, the God of Israel, says:

"Daughter Babylon is like a
 threshing floor[n]
at the time it is trampled;
the time to harvest[o] her will soon
 come."

34 "Nebuchadnezzar[p] king of Babylon
 has devoured us,
he has thrown us into confusion,
he has made us an empty jar.
Like a serpent he has swallowed us
and filled his stomach with our
 delicacies,
and then has spewed us out.
35 May the violence done to our flesh[b]
 be on Babylon,"
say the inhabitants of Zion.
"May our blood be on those who live
 in Babylonia,"
says Jerusalem.[q]

36 Therefore this is what the LORD says:

"See, I will defend your cause[r]
and avenge[s] you;
I will dry up[t] her sea
and make her springs dry.
37 Babylon will be a heap of ruins,
a haunt[u] of jackals,

51:22 [x] 2Ch 36:17; Isa 13:17-18
51:23 [y] ver 57
51:24 [z] Jer 50:15
51:25 [a] Zec 4:7
51:26 [b] ver 29; Isa 13:19-22; Jer 50:12
51:27 [c] Isa 13:2; Jer 50:2 [d] Jer 25:14 [e] Ge 8:4 [f] Ge 10:3
51:28 [g] ver 11
51:29 [h] ver 43; Isa 13:20
51:30 [i] Jer 50:36 [j] Isa 19:16 [k] Isa 45:2; La 2:9; Na 3:13
51:31 [l] 2Sa 18:19-31
51:32 [m] Jer 50:36
51:33 [n] Isa 21:10 [o] Isa 17:5; Hos 6:11
51:34 [p] Jer 50:17
51:35 [q] ver 24; Ps 137:8
51:36 [r] Ps 140:12; Jer 50:34; La 3:58 [s] ver 6; Ro 12:19 [t] Jer 50:38
51:37 [u] Isa 13:22; Rev 18:2

[a] 24 Or *Chaldea*; also in verse 35 [b] 35 Or *done to us and to our children*

51:24–58 These verses portray four of Babylon's neighbors as threats. The Medes are mentioned twice (vv. 11, 28). They were a people to the north and east of Babylon incorporated into the Persian state by Cyrus the Great. Ararat, Minni, and the Ashkenaz (vv. 27–28) were also peoples from the north and northeast of Babylon.

51:34–40 Personified Jerusalem speaks: Her first-person speech is similar to that found in the book of Lamentations.

The gods of Babylon are also judged in the fall of the city. Specifically mentioned is Bel (v. 44). The imagery of judgment against Babylon alludes to the tower of Babylon (Babel) in Ge 11:1–9. God will send destroyers against Babylon, even if the city reaches the sky (Jer 51:53).

an object of horror and scorn,
a place where no one lives.[v]
38 Her people all roar like young lions,
they growl like lion cubs.
39 But while they are aroused,
I will set out a feast for them
and make them drunk,
so that they shout with laughter —
then sleep forever and not awake,"
declares the LORD.[w]
40 "I will bring them down
like lambs to the slaughter,
like rams and goats.

41 "How Sheshak[a][x] will be captured,[y]
the boast of the whole earth
seized!
How desolate Babylon will be
among the nations!
42 The sea will rise over Babylon;
its roaring waves[z] will cover her.
43 Her towns will be desolate,
a dry and desert land,
a land where no one lives,
through which no one travels.[a]
44 I will punish Bel[b] in Babylon
and make him spew out[c] what he
has swallowed.
The nations will no longer stream to
him.
And the wall[d] of Babylon will
fall.

45 "Come out[e] of her, my people!
Run[f] for your lives!
Run from the fierce anger of the
LORD.
46 Do not lose heart or be afraid[g]
when rumors[h] are heard in the
land;
one rumor comes this year, another
the next,
rumors of violence in the land
and of ruler against ruler.
47 For the time will surely come
when I will punish the idols[i] of
Babylon;
her whole land will be disgraced[j]
and her slain will all lie fallen
within her.
48 Then heaven and earth and all that
is in them
will shout[k] for joy over Babylon,
for out of the north[l]
destroyers will attack her,"
declares the LORD.

49 "Babylon must fall because of Israel's
slain,
just as the slain in all the earth
have fallen because of Babylon.[m]
50 You who have escaped the sword,
leave[n] and do not linger!
Remember[o] the LORD in a distant
land,
and call to mind Jerusalem."

51 "We are disgraced,[p]
for we have been insulted
and shame covers our faces,
because foreigners have entered
the holy places of the LORD's
house."[q]

52 "But days are coming," declares the
LORD,
"when I will punish her idols,[r]
and throughout her land
the wounded will groan.
53 Even if Babylon ascends to the
heavens[s]
and fortifies her lofty stronghold,
I will send destroyers[t] against
her,"
declares the LORD.

54 "The sound of a cry comes from
Babylon,
the sound of great destruction[u]
from the land of the Babylonians.[b]
55 The LORD will destroy Babylon;
he will silence her noisy din.
Waves[v] of enemies will rage like
great waters;
the roar of their voices will
resound.
56 A destroyer[w] will come against
Babylon;
her warriors will be captured,
and their bows will be broken.[x]
For the LORD is a God of retribution;
he will repay[y] in full.
57 I will make her officials and wise
men drunk,
her governors, officers and
warriors as well;
they will sleep[z] forever and not
awake,"
declares the King,[a] whose name is
the LORD Almighty.

Jer 51:45-48 ❖ Are there areas of life in which we still need to flee from wicked influences? What can we do to remove ourselves from evil contexts?

51:37 [v] Jer 50:13, 39
51:39 [w] ver 57
51:41 [x] Jer 25:26 [y] Isa 13:19
51:42 [z] Isa 8:7
51:43 [a] ver 29, 62; Isa 13:20; Jer 2:6
51:44 [b] Isa 46:1 [c] ver 34 [d] ver 58; Jer 50:15
51:45 [e] Rev 18:4 [f] ver 6; Isa 48:20; Jer 50:8
51:46 [g] Jer 46:27 [h] 2Ki 19:7
51:47 [i] ver 52; Isa 46:1-2; Jer 50:2 [j] Jer 50:12
51:48 [k] Isa 44:23; Rev 18:20 [l] ver 11
51:49 [m] Ps 137:8; Jer 50:29
51:50 [n] ver 45 [o] Ps 137:6
51:51 [p] Ps 44:13-16; 79:4 [q] La 1:10
51:52 [r] ver 47
51:53 [s] Ge 11:4; Isa 14:13-14 [t] Jer 49:16
51:54 [u] Jer 50:22
51:55 [v] Ps 18:4
51:56 [w] ver 48 [x] Ps 46:9 [y] ver 6; Ps 94:1-2; Hab 2:8
51:57 [z] Ps 76:5; Jer 25:27 [a] Jer 46:18; 48:15

[a] 41 *Sheshak* is a cryptogram for Babylon.
[b] 54 Or *Chaldeans*

58 This is what the LORD Almighty says:

"Babylon's thick wall[b] will be leveled
  and her high gates set on fire;
the peoples[c] exhaust themselves for
    nothing,
  the nations' labor is only fuel for
    the flames."[d]

59 This is the message Jeremiah the prophet gave to the staff officer Seraiah son of Neriah,[e] the son of Mahseiah, when he went to Babylon with Zedekiah[f] king of Judah in the fourth[g] year of his reign. 60 Jeremiah had written on a scroll[h] about all the disasters that would come upon Babylon — all that had been recorded concerning Babylon. 61 He said to Seraiah, "When you get to Babylon, see that you read all these words aloud. 62 Then say, 'LORD, you have said you will destroy this place, so that neither people nor animals will live in it; it will be desolate[i] forever.' 63 When you finish reading this scroll, tie a stone to it and throw it into the Euphrates. 64 Then say, 'So will Babylon sink to rise no more because of the disaster I will bring on her. And her people[j] will fall.' "

The words of Jeremiah end[k] here.

The Fall of Jerusalem

52:1–3pp // 2Ki 24:18–20; 2Ch 36:11–16
52:4–16pp // Jer 39:1–10
52:4–21pp // 2Ki 25:1–21; 2Ch 36:17–20

52 Zedekiah[l] was twenty-one years old when he became king, and he reigned in Jerusalem eleven years. His mother's name was Hamutal daughter of Jeremiah; she was from Libnah.[m] 2 He did evil in the eyes of the LORD, just as Jehoiakim[n] had done. 3 It was because of the LORD's anger that all this happened to Jerusalem and Judah,[o] and in the end he thrust them from his presence.

Now Zedekiah rebelled[p] against the king of Babylon.

4 So in the ninth year of Zedekiah's reign, on the tenth[q] day of the tenth month, Nebuchadnezzar king of Babylon marched against Jerusalem[r] with his whole army. They encamped outside the city and built siege works all around it.[s] 5 The city was kept under siege until the eleventh year of King Zedekiah.

6 By the ninth day of the fourth month the famine in the city had become so severe that there was no food for the people to eat.[t] 7 Then the city wall was broken through, and the whole army fled. They left the city at night through the gate between the two walls near the king's garden, though the Babylonians[a] were surrounding the city. They fled toward the Arabah,[b] 8 but the Babylonian[c] army pursued King Zedekiah and overtook him in the plains of Jericho. All his soldiers were separated from him and scattered, 9 and he was captured.[u]

He was taken to the king of Babylon at Riblah[v] in the land of Hamath,[w] where he pronounced sentence on him. 10 There at Riblah the king of Babylon killed the sons[x] of Zedekiah before his eyes; he also killed all the officials of Judah. 11 Then he put out Zedekiah's eyes, bound him with bronze shackles and took him to Babylon, where he put him in prison till the day of his death.[y]

12 On the tenth day of the fifth[z] month,

51:58 [b] ver 44 [c] ver 64 [d] Hab 2:13
51:59 [e] Jer 36:4 [f] Jer 52:1 [g] Jer 28:1
51:60 [h] Jer 30:2; 36:2
51:62 [i] Isa 13:20; Jer 50:13, 39
51:64 [j] ver 58 [k] Job 31:40
52:1 [l] 2Ki 24:17 [m] Jos 10:29; 2Ki 8:22
52:2 [n] Jer 36:30
52:3 [o] Isa 3:1 [p] Eze 17:12-16
52:4 [q] Zec 8:19 [r] 2Ki 25:1-7; Jer 39:1 [s] Eze 24:1-2
52:6 [t] Isa 3:1
52:9 [u] Jer 32:4 [v] Nu 34:11 [w] Nu 13:21
52:10 [x] Jer 22:30
52:11 [y] Eze 12:13
52:12 [z] Zec 7:5; 8:19

[a] 7 Or *Chaldeans*; also in verse 17 [b] 7 Or *the Jordan Valley* [c] 8 Or *Chaldean*; also in verse 14

51:59–64 The chapter concludes with a prose account of Seraiah, brother of Baruch, who traveled to Babylon in Zedekiah's fourth year (594/593 BC). Seraiah performed a symbolic act to depict the judgment to come on Babylon. Just as the written scroll sank when Seraiah threw it into the river, so will Babylon sink and rise no more.

50:1—51:64 In pondering the judgments of history, perhaps no region is more strife-ridden and more difficult to understand than the Middle East. The Christian church finds itself caught up in debates about morality and the just exercise of force in that region. These debates are good when they remind Christians that God is not mocked, and that no nation or ethnic group will have the final say on judgment day. They can mislead if they allow people to think that it is only the "other side" that is wrong and sinful in God's assessment.

No group comes out unscathed in the book of Jeremiah. There is plenty of folly and failure to go around, whether in Judah or in Babylon. God's promise to rescue his people comes not because they are morally perfect but because of the grace of his promise to them. His standards of judgment are a stark reminder of how much grace is needed for the rescue of the saints in any generation.

52:1–11 The date of the ninth day and fourth month (v. 6) refers to the last year of Zedekiah's reign. The details of Zedekiah's capture should be compared with 39:1-7 and 2Ki 25:1-7.

52:12–16 This brief description of the city's fall should be compared with 39:8 and 2Ki 25:8-12.

in the nineteenth year of Nebuchadnezzar king of Babylon, Nebuzaradan[a]
commander of the imperial guard, who
served the king of Babylon, came to Jerusalem. 13He set fire[b] to the temple[c] of
the LORD, the royal palace and all the
houses of Jerusalem. Every important
building he burned down. 14The whole
Babylonian army, under the commander
of the imperial guard, broke down all the
walls[d] around Jerusalem. 15Nebuzaradan
the commander of the guard carried into
exile some of the poorest people and
those who remained in the city, along
with the rest of the craftsmen[a] and those
who had deserted to the king of Babylon.
16But Nebuzaradan left behind[e] the rest
of the poorest people of the land to work
the vineyards and fields.

17The Babylonians broke up the bronze
pillars,[f] the movable stands[g] and the
bronze Sea[h] that were at the temple of
the LORD and they carried all the bronze
to Babylon.[i] 18They also took away the
pots, shovels, wick trimmers, sprinkling
bowls, dishes and all the bronze articles
used in the temple service.[j] 19The commander of the imperial guard took away
the basins, censers,[k] sprinkling bowls,
pots, lampstands, dishes and bowls used
for drink offerings — all that were made
of pure gold or silver.

20The bronze from the two pillars, the
Sea and the twelve bronze bulls under
it, and the movable stands, which King
Solomon had made for the temple of the
LORD, was more than could be weighed.[l]
21Each pillar was eighteen cubits high
and twelve cubits in circumference[b];
each was four fingers thick, and hollow.[m]
22The bronze capital[n] on top of one pillar
was five cubits[c] high and was decorated
with a network and pomegranates of
bronze all around. The other pillar, with
its pomegranates, was similar. 23There
were ninety-six pomegranates on the
sides; the total number of pomegran-

52:12 [a] Jer 39:9
52:13 [b] 2Ch 36:19; Ps 74:8; La 2:6 [c] Ps 79:1; Mic 3:12
52:14 [d] Ne 1:3
52:16 [e] Jer 40:6
52:17 [f] 1Ki 7:15 [g] 1Ki 7:27-37 [h] 1Ki 7:23 [i] Jer 27:19-22
52:18 [j] Ex 27:3; 1Ki 7:45
52:19 [k] 1Ki 7:50
52:20 [l] 1Ki 7:47
52:21 [m] 1Ki 7:15
52:22 [n] 1Ki 7:16
52:23 [o] 1Ki 7:20
52:24 [p] 2Ki 25:18 [q] Jer 21:1; 37:3
52:26 [r] ver 12
52:27 [s] Jer 20:4
52:28 [t] 2Ki 24:14-16; 2Ch 36:20

Jer 52:12–30 ❖ How can devastating circumstances lead us closer to God? When have we seen people emerge from tragedy with a stronger faith?

ates[o] above the surrounding network
was a hundred.

24The commander of the guard took
as prisoners Seraiah[p] the chief priest,
Zephaniah[q] the priest next in rank
and the three doorkeepers. 25Of those
still in the city, he took the officer in
charge of the fighting men, and seven
royal advisers. He also took the secretary who was chief officer in charge
of conscripting the people of the land,
sixty of whom were found in the city.
26Nebuzaradan[r] the commander took
them all and brought them to the king
of Babylon at Riblah. 27There at Riblah,
in the land of Hamath, the king had
them executed.

So Judah went into captivity, away[s]
from her land. 28This is the number of
the people Nebuchadnezzar carried into
exile:[t]

in the seventh year, 3,023 Jews;
29in Nebuchadnezzar's eighteenth year,
832 people from Jerusalem;
30in his twenty-third year,
745 Jews taken into exile by Nebuzaradan the commander of the imperial guard.
There were 4,600 people in all.

Jehoiachin Released

52:31–34pp // 2Ki 25:27–30

31In the thirty-seventh year of the exile
of Jehoiachin king of Judah, in the year
Awel-Marduk became king of Babylon,

[a] *15* Or *the populace* [b] *21* That is, about 27 feet high and 18 feet in circumference or about 8.1 meters high and 5.4 meters in circumference [c] *22* That is, about 7 1/2 feet or about 2.3 meters

52:17–23 These verses include a brief report of the looting of the temple (see also 2Ki 25:13–17). A comparison of the account here and that in 2 Kings is fascinating. Each begins with a report that the Babylonians broke the bronze pillars, and there are similar details preserved between them. Nevertheless, each account preserves some distinctive elements.
52:24–27a These verses closely parallel 2Ki 25:18–21.
52:27b–30 These verses preserve references to two waves of exiles during the reign of Nebuchadnezzar. The first wave came during the reign of Jehoiachin (597 BC), and the second came in 582 BC.
52:31–34 This notice about Jehoiachin, which concludes Jeremiah, is paralleled in 2Ki 25:27–30, which also concludes 2 Kings. It is far more than a simple report about a minor monarch's being exiled. The report supports a type of muted but stubborn faith. Even when the land of Judah and the city of Jerusalem lie in ruins, one from David's line still lives.

on the twenty-fifth day of the twelfth
month, he released Jehoiachin king of
Judah and freed him from prison. 32He
spoke kindly to him and gave him a seat
of honor higher than those of the other
kings who were with him in Babylon.
33So Jehoiachin put aside his prison
clothes and for the rest of his life ate
regularly at the king's table.[u] 34Day by
day the king of Babylon gave Jehoiachin
a regular allowance[v] as long as he lived,
till the day of his death.

52:33 [u] 2Sa 9:7
52:34 [v] 2Sa 9:10

52:1–34 It is possible for those who "hope in the LORD" (Isa 40:31) to renew their strength. It is possible because God provides the strength we need in our times of need. It is possible because no matter how strong or resilient the enemy, the future belongs to God, who is faithful. How this happens is the mystery of grace. One cannot explain it by a formula; one can only point to the God of new beginnings as the faithful God and Lord of life and death.

Author: Unknown, but the work reflects the times and message of the prophet Jeremiah

Audience: Jews in Babylonian exile who are lamenting the destruction of Jerusalem

Date: Shortly after the fall of Jerusalem in 586 BC

Theme: God's people discerned his loving compassion and faithfulness even as they lamented the cataclysmic destruction of Jerusalem.

Reading Lamentations

Each one of the five chapters of Lamentations is a separate lament with a somewhat different theme, revolving around the middle chapter's exaltation of God's compassion and faithfulness.

PERSPECTIVE

No author is named in the Hebrew version of this book; it appears not in the prophetic section of the Hebrew Bible but in the last section, entitled "the Writings." Much of the book gives voice to the people's communal experience of judgment and exile.

Although it is unlikely that Jeremiah is the author of Lamentations, its association with him is one of several indications that the work fits into the broader context of the prophet's later life and times. The perspective of the voices in Lamentations is that of the Babylonian exile. At some point in the exile, Judeans began to lament corporately and publicly in order to remember Jerusalem, the capital city, the location of the temple, and the symbolic mother of the people.

The five poetic chapters do not have a narrative base or reflect a literary plot. It is not clear whether the five chapters were always joined in a collection or if one or more of them originated independently of the others. Thus, the effect of reading them sequentially is that of artful repetition, where the themes of suffering, judgment, confession of sin, and divine abandonment reappear.

Lamentations takes up the traditions of funeral poetry and prayers of anguish to drive home the uncomfortable truth that no one is finally exempt from God's searching judgments. To be sure, Lamentations confesses that God's mercies are new every morning (3:22–24), but the weight of the poems points toward human responsibility, anguish, and despair, and speaks about such experiences to the Lord. In the service of a greater revelation to come from God, Lamentations speaks

	1200 BC	1100	1000	900	800	700	600	500	400
Division of the kingdom (930 BC)				♦					
Ministries of Elijah and Elisha in Israel (c. 875–797 BC)				▬	▬				
Ministries of Amos and Hosea in Israel (c. 760–715 BC)						▬			
Ministries of Micah and Isaiah in Judah (c. 740–681 BC)						▬			
Exile of Israel (722 BC)						♦			
Jeremiah's ministry in Judah (c. 626–585 BC)							▬		
Fall of Jerusalem (586 BC)							♦		
Book of Lamentations written (c. 586–580 BC)							▮		

both for and to human suffering, which is how we should approach the book today.

For additional perspective on the background to the book of Lamentations, see the Introduction to the book of Jeremiah.

Key Verses

Because of the LORD's great love we are not consumed, for his compassions never fail. They are new every morning; great is your faithfulness.

—Lamentations 3:22–23

TAKING THE NEXT STEPS

These writings reflect the times and circumstances of Jeremiah as the weeping prophet. He and his people agonized over the awful devastation of Jerusalem and the terrible slaughter of human life that surrounded them. No book of the Bible is more intense in expressing grief than this one.

However, the author did not doubt that God was just in allowing these tragic events to happen. In fact, he went so far as to praise God's faithfulness. It may be difficult to see how these five laments apply to us today, but they do have practical significance. (1) It is appropriate for us, when we see the terrible consequences of sin in the human race, to burst into tears before God. (2) The ultimate reason for mourning ought to be what our sins did to the perfect Son of God, Jesus. (3) Even though we may begin with lament, we must always end with repentance, as this book does. (4) No matter how difficult our circumstances may be, we can always find reason to praise God for his faithfulness and love.

WHAT TO LOOK FOR IN LAMENTATIONS

- Jerusalem's misery (ch. 1)
- The Lord's anger (ch. 2)
- Judah's complaint and consolation (ch. 3)
- Contrast of the past and the present (ch. 4)
- Appeal for forgiveness (ch. 5)

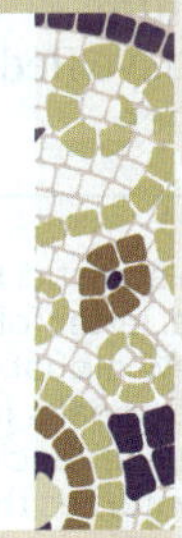

1[a] How deserted lies the city,
once so full of people!
How like a widow[a] is she,
who once was great[b] among the nations!
She who was queen among the provinces
has now become a slave.[c]

2 Bitterly she weeps[d] at night,
tears are on her cheeks.
Among all her lovers[e]
there is no one to comfort her.
All her friends have betrayed[f] her;
they have become her enemies.[g]

3 After affliction and harsh labor,
Judah has gone into exile.[h]
She dwells among the nations;
she finds no resting place.[i]
All who pursue her have overtaken her
in the midst of her distress.

4 The roads to Zion mourn,
for no one comes to her appointed festivals.
All her gateways are desolate,[j]
her priests groan,
her young women grieve,
and she is in bitter anguish.[k]

5 Her foes have become her masters;
her enemies are at ease.
The LORD has brought her grief[l]
because of her many sins.
Her children have gone into exile,[m]
captive before the foe.

6 All the splendor has departed
from Daughter Zion.[n]
Her princes are like deer
that find no pasture;
in weakness they have fled
before the pursuer.

7 In the days of her affliction and wandering
Jerusalem remembers all the treasures
that were hers in days of old.
When her people fell into enemy hands,
there was no one to help her.[o]
Her enemies looked at her
and laughed at her destruction.

8 Jerusalem has sinned[p] greatly
and so has become unclean.
All who honored her despise her,
for they have all seen her naked;[q]
she herself groans[r]
and turns away.

9 Her filthiness clung to her skirts;
she did not consider her future.[s]
Her fall[t] was astounding;
there was none to comfort[u] her.
"Look, LORD, on my affliction,[v]
for the enemy has triumphed."

10 The enemy laid hands
on all her treasures;[w]
she saw pagan nations
enter her sanctuary[x] —
those you had forbidden[y]
to enter your assembly.

11 All her people groan[z]
as they search for bread;[a]
they barter their treasures for food
to keep themselves alive.
"Look, LORD, and consider,
for I am despised."

12 "Is it nothing to you, all you who pass by?[b]
Look around and see.
Is any suffering like my suffering[c]

1:1 [a] Isa 47:8 [b] 1Ki 4:21 [c] Isa 3:26; Jer 40:9
1:2 [d] Ps 6:6 [e] Jer 3:1 [f] Jer 4:30; Mic 7:5 [g] ver 16
1:3 [h] Jer 13:19 [i] Dt 28:65
1:4 [j] Jer 9:11 [k] Joel 1:8-13
1:5 [l] Jer 30:15 [m] Jer 39:9; 52:28-30
1:6 [n] Jer 13:18
1:7 [o] Jer 37:7; La 4:17
1:8 [p] ver 20; Isa 59:2-13 [q] Jer 13:22,26 [r] ver 21,22
1:9 [s] Dt 32:28-29; Isa 47:7; Eze 24:13 [t] Jer 13:18 [u] Ecc 4:1; Jer 16:7 [v] Ps 25:18
1:10 [w] Isa 64:11 [x] Ps 74:7-8; Jer 51:51 [y] Dt 23:3
1:11 [z] Ps 38:8 [a] Jer 52:6
1:12 [b] Jer 18:16 [c] ver 18

[a] This chapter is an acrostic poem, the verses of which begin with the successive letters of the Hebrew alphabet.

1:1–22 This chapter is an acrostic. Each verse begins with a word whose initial letter follows the 22-letter sequence of the Hebrew alphabet.

More than one voice speaks in ch. 1. When the chapter is read as a unit, the "back and forth" of the two voices mutually reinforces the tragic dilemma of Jerusalem. The two voices alternate between the poet (vv. 1-9a, 10-11a, 17) and the personification of Jerusalem (vv. 9b, 11b-16, 18-22).

The language of chapter 1 refers to the sinfulness of Judah and to their resulting sorrow and suffering. The emphasis falls, however, on the grief, the suffering, and the pitiful nature of the city. She "weeps" (vv. 1-2, 16) and "groans" (vv. 8, 21-22) and is "in bitter anguish" (v. 4) and "distress" (vv. 20-21). Nothing here points to the relief of the city's woes.

1:1 Verse 1 indicates the theme of the chapter; it depicts the city of Jerusalem personified as a once-noble woman, now a widow and a slave.

1:2–5 The term "lovers" has a sexual overtone, referring either to other gods pursued or to stronger neighbors with whom Israel or Judah sought to ingratiate themselves. Because of her sinfulness, the Lord has judged her (v. 5; cf. vv. 16, 18).

1:7 The voice of the poet depicts Jerusalem in the posture of "remembering" her days of affliction. This posture of bringing to mind again captures much of the reason for the book of Lamentations as a whole.

that was inflicted on me,
that the LORD brought on me
in the day of his fierce anger?[d]

13 "From on high he sent fire,
sent it down into my bones.[e]
He spread a net for my feet
and turned me back.
He made me desolate,[f]
faint[g] all the day long.

14 "My sins have been bound into a
yoke[a];[h]
by his hands they were woven
together.
They have been hung on my neck,
and the Lord has sapped my
strength.
He has given me into the hands[i]
of those I cannot withstand.

15 "The Lord has rejected
all the warriors in my midst;[j]
he has summoned an army[k]
against me
to[b] crush my young men.[l]
In his winepress the Lord has
trampled
Virgin Daughter Judah.

16 "This is why I weep
and my eyes overflow with tears.[m]
No one is near to comfort[n] me,
no one to restore my spirit.
My children are destitute
because the enemy has
prevailed."[o]

17 Zion stretches out her hands,[p]
but there is no one to comfort her.
The LORD has decreed for Jacob
that his neighbors become his
foes;
Jerusalem has become
an unclean thing among them.

18 "The LORD is righteous,
yet I rebelled[q] against his
command.
Listen, all you peoples;
look on my suffering.[r]

1:12 [d] Isa 13:13; Jer 30:24
1:13 [e] Job 30:30 [f] Jer 44:6 [g] Hab 3:16
1:14 [h] Dt 28:48; Isa 47:6 [i] Jer 32:5
1:15 [j] Jer 37:10 [k] Isa 41:2 [l] Isa 28:18; Jer 18:21
1:16 [m] La 2:11, 18; 3:48-49 [n] Ps 69:20; Ecc 4:1 [o] ver 2; Jer 13:17; 14:17
1:17 [p] Jer 4:31
1:18 [q] 1Sa 12:14 [r] ver 12

La 1:14 ❖ When have we experienced the burden of our own sins? How can we find release from this burden?

My young men and young women
have gone into exile.[s]

19 "I called to my allies
but they betrayed me.
My priests and my elders
perished[t] in the city
while they searched for food
to keep themselves alive.

20 "See, LORD, how distressed[u] I am!
I am in torment[v] within,
and in my heart I am disturbed,
for I have been most rebellious.
Outside, the sword bereaves;
inside, there is only death.[w]

21 "People have heard my groaning,[x]
but there is no one to comfort me.[y]
All my enemies have heard of my
distress;
they rejoice[z] at what you have
done.
May you bring the day[a] you have
announced
so they may become like me.

22 "Let all their wickedness come
before you;
deal with them
as you have dealt with me
because of all my sins.[b]
My groans are many
and my heart is faint."

2[c] How the Lord has covered
Daughter Zion
with the cloud of his anger[d]![c]

[a] *14* Most Hebrew manuscripts; many Hebrew manuscripts and Septuagint *He kept watch over my sins* [b] *15* Or *has set a time for me / when he will* [c] This chapter is an acrostic poem, the verses of which begin with the successive letters of the Hebrew alphabet. [d] *1* Or *How the Lord in his anger / has treated Daughter Zion with contempt*

[s] Dt 28:32, 41
1:19 [t] Jer 14:15; La 2:20
1:20 [u] Jer 4:19 [v] La 2:11 [w] Dt 32:25; Eze 7:15
1:21 [x] ver 8 [y] ver 4 [z] La 2:15 [a] Isa 47:11; Jer 30:16
1:22 [b] Ne 4:5
2:1 [c] La 3:44

1:22 Personified Jerusalem asks that the evil done to her by her enemies be brought before God so that he can deal with them. An answer to this sentiment also lies largely outside the book.

APPLICATION ✚ **1:1–22** The poetry of Lamentations is one of the most articulate voices for confession of sin and lament over failure. The poems themselves point first to the consequences of failure; as tragedy they loom larger than life and seemingly out of proportion to the failure. But most important, they are directed to the only One who can hear them fully and adequately respond.

2:1–22 These verses describe, in the third person, the suffering and anguish of the city through what God has done to them. God has covered the city

He has hurled down the splendor of Israel
from heaven to earth;
he has not remembered his footstool[d]
in the day of his anger.

2 Without pity[e] the Lord has swallowed[f] up
all the dwellings of Jacob;
in his wrath he has torn down
the strongholds[g] of Daughter Judah.
He has brought her kingdom and its princes
down to the ground[h] in dishonor.

3 In fierce anger he has cut off
every horn[a,b][i] of Israel.
He has withdrawn his right hand[j]
at the approach of the enemy.
He has burned in Jacob like a flaming fire
that consumes everything around it.[k]

4 Like an enemy he has strung his bow;[l]
his right hand is ready.
Like a foe he has slain
all who were pleasing to the eye;[m]
he has poured out his wrath like fire[n]
on the tent of Daughter Zion.

5 The Lord is like an enemy;[o]
he has swallowed up Israel.
He has swallowed up all her palaces
and destroyed her strongholds.[p]
He has multiplied mourning and lamentation
for Daughter Judah.[q]

6 He has laid waste his dwelling like a garden;
he has destroyed his place of meeting.[r]
The LORD has made Zion forget
her appointed festivals and her Sabbaths;[s]
in his fierce anger he has spurned
both king and priest.[t]

7 The Lord has rejected his altar
and abandoned his sanctuary.
He has given the walls of her palaces[u]
into the hands of the enemy;
they have raised a shout in the house of the LORD
as on the day of an appointed festival.

8 The LORD determined to tear down
the wall around Daughter Zion.
He stretched out a measuring line[v]
and did not withhold his hand
from destroying.
He made ramparts and walls lament;
together they wasted away.[w]

9 Her gates[x] have sunk into the ground;
their bars he has broken and destroyed.
Her king and her princes are exiled[y]
among the nations,

2:1 [d] Ps 99:5; 132:7
2:2 [e] La 3:43 [f] Ps 21:9 [g] Ps 89:39-40; Mic 5:11 [h] Isa 25:12
2:3 [i] Ps 75:5, 10 [j] Ps 74:11 [k] Isa 42:25; Jer 21:4-5,14
2:4 [l] Job 16:13; La 3:12-13 [m] Eze 24:16, 25 [n] Isa 42:25; Jer 7:20
2:5 [o] Jer 30:14 [p] ver 2 [q] Jer 9:17-20
2:6 [r] Jer 52:13 [s] La 1:4; Zep 3:18 [t] La 4:16
2:7 [u] Ps 74:7-8; Isa 64:11; Jer 33:4-5
2:8 [v] 2Ki 21:13; Isa 34:11 [w] Isa 3:26
2:9 [x] Ne 1:3 [y] Dt 28:36; 2Ki 24:15

[a] 3 Or *off / all the strength*; or *every king*
[b] 3 *Horn* here symbolizes strength.

---

with "the cloud of his anger" (v. 1); he has "burned in Jacob like a flaming fire" (v. 3; cf. v. 5); God has "given the walls of her palaces into the hands of the enemy" (v. 7); and so on. Verses 9–10 describe Jerusalem in her pathetic state.

The chapter's voices are as follows:

Verses 1–10 are the poet's description of Jerusalem's anguish and humiliation.

Verses 11–13 are the poet's first-person response to Jerusalem's wretchedness.

Verses 14–17 are again the poet's description of Jerusalem.

Verses 18–19 are a call to Jerusalem's walls to cry out to God.

Verses 20–22 are addressed to God by Jerusalem (perhaps more specifically her "walls"; cf. v. 18).

2:3 The poet laments the fact that God has "cut off every horn of Israel." The term *horn* can be used as a metaphor for strength or honor, though it can also refer to the upraised corner of a sacrificial altar (Ex 29:12; Lev 4:7; Ps 118:27). Those who "grasped the horns of the altar" had asylum and would not be killed (cf. 1Ki 1:49–53). Thus, the comment can mean that God has destroyed the pride and nobility of the people. It can also mean that God has removed any means of seeking asylum.

2:6–8 God has "laid waste his dwelling" and "destroyed his place of meeting" (v. 6). Verse 7 elaborates on this matter: God has "rejected his altar and abandoned his sanctuary." The presence of the sacred temple in the midst of Jerusalem was no guarantee of God's benevolence or protection. Even parts of the city are personified to underscore the horror of what has befallen God's jewel. The walls of the city lament and weep over their destruction (vv. 8, 18).

2:9–20 The king is rejected and exiled (v. 9; see v. 6); the prophets failed (vv. 9, 14, 20). Priests are spurned, and Torah is gone (vv. 9, 20).

God used the enemy to judge his people and his city. In remarkably pointed and anguished language, the poet asks God whether he has ever treated anyone else like this (v. 20). It is as if God has become the enemy by using the enemy.

the law[z] is no more,
and her prophets no longer find
visions[a] from the LORD.

10 The elders of Daughter Zion
sit on the ground in silence;
they have sprinkled dust on their
heads[b]
and put on sackcloth.[c]
The young women of Jerusalem
have bowed their heads to the
ground.[d]

11 My eyes fail from weeping,[e]
I am in torment within[f];
my heart is poured out[g] on the
ground
because my people are destroyed,
because children and infants faint[h]
in the streets of the city.

12 They say to their mothers,
"Where is bread and wine?"
as they faint like the wounded
in the streets of the city,
as their lives ebb away
in their mothers' arms.[i]

13 What can I say for you?
With what can I compare you,
Daughter Jerusalem?
To what can I liken you,
that I may comfort you,
Virgin Daughter Zion?[j]
Your wound is as deep as the
sea.[k]
Who can heal you?

14 The visions of your prophets
were false and worthless;
they did not expose your sin
to ward off your captivity.[l]

2:9 [z] 2Ch 15:3 [a] Jer 14:14
2:10 [b] Job 2:12 [c] Isa 15:3 [d] Job 2:13; Isa 3:26
2:11 [e] La 1:16; 3:48-51 [f] La 1:20 [g] ver 19; Ps 22:14 [h] La 4:4
2:12 [i] La 4:4
2:13 [j] Isa 37:22 [k] Jer 14:17; La 1:12
2:14 [l] Isa 58:1 [m] Jer 2:8; 23:25-32,33-40; 29:9; Eze 13:3; 22:28
2:15 [n] Eze 25:6 [o] Jer 19:8 [p] Ps 50:2 [q] Ps 48:2
2:16 [r] Ps 56:2; La 3:46 [s] Job 16:9 [t] Ps 35:25
2:17 [u] Dt 28:15-45 [v] ver 2; Eze 5:11 [w] Ps 89:42
2:18 [x] Ps 119:145 [y] La 1:16 [z] Jer 9:1

La 2:17 ❖ How does God's devastating judgment upon Judah increase our gratitude for Christ's saving work?

The prophecies they gave you
were false and misleading.[m]

15 All who pass your way
clap their hands at you;[n]
they scoff[o] and shake their heads
at Daughter Jerusalem:
"Is this the city that was called
the perfection of beauty,[p]
the joy of the whole earth?"[q]

16 All your enemies open their
mouths
wide against you;[r]
they scoff and gnash their teeth[s]
and say, "We have swallowed her
up.[t]
This is the day we have waited for;
we have lived to see it."

17 The LORD has done what he planned;
he has fulfilled his word,
which he decreed long ago.[u]
He has overthrown you without
pity,[v]
he has let the enemy gloat over
you,
he has exalted the horn[a] of your
foes.[w]

18 The hearts of the people
cry out to the Lord.[x]
You walls of Daughter Zion,
let your tears[y] flow like a river
day and night;[z]

[a] 17 *Horn* here symbolizes strength.

2:11–12 The poet uses the first-person "I" to describe his weeping and torment with respect to the awful condition of "my people" (v. 11). It seems best overall to take v. 11 as also the voice of the poet. The fact that the voices alternate between description and first-person lament give perspective and depth to the circumstances of Jerusalem's humiliation.
2:13–22 First-person references come also in these verses. Verse 13 is the voice of the poet addressing Jerusalem, but vv. 20–22 is perhaps better taken as the voice of Jerusalem. Verse 22 refers to those whom the speaker has cared for and raised—verbs associated with child-rearing.

Since Jerusalem is frequently personified as a mother, it seems best to see her as the final speaker of ch. 2. In fact, vv. 18–19 seem to address the wall(s) of Jerusalem: They have the urge to cry out.
2:15 The great distinction of Zion's calling is reflected. She is the "splendor" (v. 1) of Israel. This word can be used of an ornament or jewel. The city was "the perfection of beauty, the joy of the whole earth" (v. 15; cf. Ps 48:2), until it came crashing down.

✤ **2:1–22** The frankness of the language in Lamentations should persuade people that God is open to them expressing their real feelings and their honest reactions to tragedy. There is no "answer" in the immediacy of overwhelming tragedy, and one's prayers ought to reflect that.

The great miracle of the gospel is that the One to whom despair and bitterness are directed is the One whose only Son suffered on the cross. God, who used powerful armies to fight against sinful Jerusalem and Judah, also engaged the principalities and powers of this world to gain an eternal victory for his people (Eph 6:12).

give yourself no relief,
your eyes no rest.[a]

19 Arise, cry out in the night,
as the watches of the night
begin;
pour out your heart[b] like water
in the presence of the Lord.[c]
Lift up your hands to him
for the lives of your children,
who faint[d] from hunger
at every street corner.

20 "Look, LORD, and consider:
Whom have you ever treated like
this?
Should women eat their offspring,[e]
the children they have cared for?[f]
Should priest and prophet be
killed[g]
in the sanctuary of the Lord?

21 "Young and old lie together
in the dust of the streets;
my young men and young women
have fallen by the sword.[h]
You have slain them in the day of
your anger;
you have slaughtered them
without pity.[i]

22 "As you summon to a feast day,
so you summoned against me
terrors[j] on every side.
In the day of the LORD's anger
no one escaped or survived;
those I cared for and reared[k]
my enemy has destroyed."

3[a] I am the man who has seen
affliction
by the rod of the LORD's wrath.[l]
2 He has driven me away and made
me walk
in darkness[m] rather than light;
3 indeed, he has turned his hand
against me[n]
again and again, all day long.

4 He has made my skin and my flesh
grow old
and has broken my bones.[o]
5 He has besieged me and
surrounded me
with bitterness[p] and hardship.[q]
6 He has made me dwell in darkness
like those long dead.[r]

7 He has walled me in so I cannot
escape;[s]
he has weighed me down with
chains.[t]
8 Even when I call out or cry for help,
he shuts out my prayer.[u]
9 He has barred my way with blocks of
stone;
he has made my paths crooked.[v]

10 Like a bear lying in wait,
like a lion in hiding,
11 he dragged me from the path and
mangled[w] me
and left me without help.
12 He drew his bow[x]
and made me the target[y] for his
arrows.[z]

13 He pierced my heart
with arrows from his quiver.[a]
14 I became the laughingstock[b] of all
my people;
they mock me in song[c] all day
long.
15 He has filled me with bitter herbs
and given me gall to drink.[d]

16 He has broken my teeth with
gravel;[e]
he has trampled me in the dust.
17 I have been deprived of peace;
I have forgotten what
prosperity is.
18 So I say, "My splendor is gone
and all that I had hoped from the
LORD."[f]

19 I remember my affliction and my
wandering,
the bitterness and the gall.
20 I well remember them,
and my soul is downcast[g] within
me.[h]
21 Yet this I call to mind
and therefore I have hope:

[a] This chapter is an acrostic poem; the verses of each stanza begin with the successive letters of the Hebrew alphabet, and the verses within each stanza begin with the same letter.

2:18 [a] La 3:49
2:19 [b] 1Sa 1:15; Ps 62:8 [c] Isa 26:9 [d] Isa 51:20
2:20 [e] Dt 28:53; Jer 19:9 [f] La 4:10 [g] Ps 78:64; Jer 14:15
2:21 [h] 2Ch 36:17; Ps 78:62-63; Jer 6:11 [i] Jer 13:14; La 3:43; Zec 11:6
2:22 [j] Ps 31:13; Jer 6:25 [k] Hos 9:13
3:1 [l] Job 19:21; Ps 88:7
3:2 [m] Jer 4:23
3:3 [n] Isa 5:25
3:4 [o] Ps 51:8; Isa 38:13; Jer 50:17
3:5 [p] ver 19 [q] Jer 23:15
3:6 [r] Ps 88:5-6
3:7 [s] Job 3:23 [t] Jer 40:4
3:8 [u] Job 30:20; Ps 22:2
3:9 [v] Isa 63:17; Hos 2:6
3:11 [w] Hos 6:1
3:12 [x] La 2:4 [y] Job 7:20 [z] Ps 7:12-13; 38:2
3:13 [a] Job 6:4
3:14 [b] Jer 20:7 [c] Job 30:9
3:15 [d] Jer 9:15
3:16 [e] Pr 20:17
3:18 [f] Job 17:15
3:20 [g] Ps 42:5 [h] Ps 42:11

3:1–12 The poet first sees God as the source of trouble. He has turned his rod and hand against the poet (vv. 1–3). God has besieged and walled him in (vv. 4–9). God is a lion or bear, or more menacingly, an archer taking aim at the poet (vv. 10–12). **3:19–24** Both suffering and redemption are part of the poet's experience, and he remembers God as being the source of both. Since he knows that God is strong to save, he says he has "hope" (vv. 21, 24). God, who has struck both Jerusalem and the poet, is the same One who can overturn the shame of public judgment and humiliation.

22 Because of the LORD's great love we
are not consumed,
for his compassions never fail.[i]
23 They are new every morning;
great is your faithfulness.[j]
24 I say to myself, "The LORD is my
portion;[k]
therefore I will wait for him."

25 The LORD is good to those whose
hope is in him,
to the one who seeks him;[l]
26 it is good to wait quietly
for the salvation of the LORD.[m]
27 It is good for a man to bear the
yoke
while he is young.

28 Let him sit alone in silence,[n]
for the LORD has laid it on him.
29 Let him bury his face in the dust —
there may yet be hope.[o]
30 Let him offer his cheek to one who
would strike him,[p]
and let him be filled with disgrace.

31 For no one is cast off
by the Lord forever.[q]

3:22 [i] Ps 78:38; Mal 3:6
3:23 [j] Zep 3:5
3:24 [k] Ps 16:5
3:25 [l] Isa 25:9; 30:18
3:26 [m] Ps 37:7; 40:1
3:28 [n] Jer 15:17
3:29 [o] Jer 31:17
3:30 [p] Job 16:10; Isa 50:6
3:31 [q] Ps 94:14; Isa 54:7

La 3:21-24 ❖ When has God shown you his never-failing compassion? How has it carried you through difficult times?

32 Though he brings grief, he will show
compassion,
so great is his unfailing love.[r]
33 For he does not willingly bring
affliction
or grief to anyone.[s]

34 To crush underfoot
all prisoners in the land,
35 to deny people their rights
before the Most High,
36 to deprive them of justice —
would not the Lord see such
things?[t]

37 Who can speak and have it
happen
if the Lord has not decreed it?[u]
38 Is it not from the mouth of the Most
High
that both calamities and good
things come?[v]

3:32 [r] Ps 78:38; Hos 11:8
3:33 [s] Eze 33:11
3:36 [t] Jer 22:3; Hab 1:13
3:37 [u] Ps 33:9-11
3:38 [v] Job 2:10; Isa 45:7; Jer 32:42

3:22-23 The word translated "love" also carries the meaning of kindness and loyalty. The poet confesses that God is great in faithfulness.

CHARACTER OF GOD // **GOD IS FAITHFUL**

Lamentations 3:22-23: "Because of the LORD's great love we are not consumed, for his compassions never fail. They are new every morning; great is your faithfulness."

Lamentations was written in one of the bleakest moments in Judah's history. The Babylonians destroyed Jerusalem and exiled the Jews in 586 BC. God's temple was torn down, and the temple articles were stolen. All hope seemed lost.

The writer of Lamentations records this tragedy and its aftermath with gut-wrenching detail. Yet right in the middle of this book comes a remarkable assurance: God's love and mercy never fail, and God's faithfulness is great (La 3:22-23).

How could the author say that, given what he had seen? The destruction around him was a clear reminder that placing one's hope in anything other than God is bound to fail. Kingdoms rise and fall. Rulers succeed and fail. Armies are a vain hope for deliverance. In the midst of all the shifting sands, one thing alone remains steadfast: God.

God gave the author of Lamentations eyes to see through his current darkness. Despite how things looked at the moment, God gave him hope that God had not abandoned his people. God's compassion and love would not fail. God would remain faithful even through and beyond disaster. And, indeed, that is what happened. When Cyrus of Persia rose to power and his kingdom defeated the Babylonians, Cyrus allowed the Jewish exiles to return home and rebuild their city in 539 BC.

APPLICATION ✤ When life seems chaotic and unpredictable, we need to be reminded of God's faithfulness. Storms may come and tragedy may strike, but God will always be faithful. God's faithfulness does not mean God will remove his children from the storms, but it does mean that whatever storm we find ourselves in, God is there with us. Christ promised always to be with those who follow him (Mt 28:20), including during the darkest seasons of our lives.

39 Why should the living complain
when punished for their sins?[w]

40 Let us examine our ways and test
them,[x]
and let us return to the LORD.[y]
41 Let us lift up our hearts and our
hands
to God in heaven,[z] and say:
42 "We have sinned and rebelled[a]
and you have not forgiven.[b]

43 "You have covered yourself with
anger and pursued us;
you have slain without pity.[c]
44 You have covered yourself with a
cloud[d]
so that no prayer[e] can get through.
45 You have made us scum[f] and refuse
among the nations.

46 "All our enemies have opened their
mouths
wide against us.[g]
47 We have suffered terror and pitfalls,[h]
ruin and destruction.[i]"
48 Streams of tears flow from my eyes[j]
because my people are destroyed.[k]

49 My eyes will flow unceasingly,
without relief,[l]
50 until the LORD looks down
from heaven and sees.[m]
51 What I see brings grief to my soul
because of all the women of my
city.

52 Those who were my enemies
without cause
hunted me like a bird.[n]
53 They tried to end my life in a pit[o]
and threw stones at me;
54 the waters closed over my head,[p]
and I thought I was about to
perish.

55 I called on your name, LORD,
from the depths of the pit.[q]
56 You heard my plea:[r] "Do not close
your ears
to my cry for relief."
57 You came near when I called you,
and you said, "Do not fear."[s]

58 You, Lord, took up my case;[t]
you redeemed my life.[u]
59 LORD, you have seen the wrong done
to me.[v]
Uphold my cause!
60 You have seen the depth of their
vengeance,
all their plots against me.[w]

61 LORD, you have heard their insults,
all their plots against me—
62 what my enemies whisper and
mutter
against me all day long.[x]

3:39 [w] Jer 30:15; Mic 7:9
3:40 [x] 2Co 13:5 [y] Ps 119:59; 139:23-24
3:41 [z] Ps 25:1; 28:2
3:42 [a] Da 9:5 [b] Jer 5:7-9
3:43 [c] La 2:2, 17, 21
3:44 [d] Ps 97:2 [e] ver 8
3:45 [f] 1Co 4:13
3:46 [g] La 2:16
3:47 [h] Jer 48:43 [i] Isa 24:17-18; 51:19
3:48 [j] La 1:16 [k] La 2:11
3:49 [l] Jer 14:17
3:50 [m] Isa 63:15
3:52 [n] Ps 35:7
3:53 [o] Jer 37:16
3:54 [p] Ps 69:2; Jnh 2:3-5
3:55 [q] Ps 130:1; Jnh 2:2
3:56 [r] Ps 55:1
3:57 [s] Isa 41:10
3:58 [t] Jer 51:36 [u] Ps 34:22; Jer 50:34
3:59 [v] Jer 18:19-20
3:60 [w] Jer 11:20; 18:18
3:62 [x] Eze 36:3

3:40–45 The poet is moved to speak about repentance. Significantly, the language is first-person plural: "Let us examine . . . let us return . . . let us lift" (vv. 40, 41). This indicates that the poet's experience is linked with that of his community. They become one before God. It also signifies the function or impact of Lamentations as a whole.
3:46–63 Using slightly different language, the poet recounts how the enemies of Zion have condemned and hunted him (vv. 46–54). They plot, insult, and mock him (vv. 58–63). He contains in his person the suffering endured by the city and its inhabitants. Because his experience is shared by his contemporaries, it is relatively easy to follow the shift in the language from "I" to "we."
3:52–58 As with psalms of lament/complaint, the poet speaks of the "pit," which seeks to claim his life (vv. 53, 55). In the stanzas of vv. 52–57, the poet prays like the writer of Ps 130: "Out of the depths I cry to you, LORD" (130:1). The poet then reminds God that he has seen and heard what the enemies have done. His own life is like a judicial case (La 3:58), where God the judge should rule in his favor.

The chapter concludes with the plea of the poet for God to judge his enemies. In this the poet is also reminiscent of Jeremiah, who sought judgment on his tormenters (Jer 11:20; 15:15; 17:18; 18:19–23; 20:12).

✤ **3:1–66** It is illuminating to set the language of La 3 in the context of the modern quest for spirituality, as it has several marks of authentic spirituality.

Judgment is consistent with the character of God revealed in Torah, prophecy, and the psalms.

The poet learns that prayer and confession directed toward God bring him into fellowship with God.

He finds that repentance is a tangible way of relating to God. Repentance is not a magical elixir, but a series of steps taken toward God in obedience to his will.

He seeks God for deliverance and healing. He is able to see that his circumstances are the occasion for fresh prayers and newfound vows.

It probably never occurs to him that his spirituality can be a private matter. His confession that God is faithful also includes affirmation that "we" are not consumed (v. 22). His call to repentance offers steps for "us" to return to the Lord.

For the poet, waiting on the Lord (v. 24) includes the practices of prayer and repentance; he does not assume that waiting is merely marking time.

63 Look at them! Sitting or standing,
they mock me in their songs.

64 Pay them back what they deserve, LORD,
for what their hands have done.[y]
65 Put a veil over their hearts,[z]
and may your curse be on them!
66 Pursue them in anger and destroy them
from under the heavens of the LORD.

4 [a] How the gold has lost its luster,
the fine gold become dull!
The sacred gems are scattered
at every street corner.[a]

2 How the precious children of Zion,
once worth their weight in gold,
are now considered as pots of clay,
the work of a potter's hands!

3 Even jackals offer their breasts
to nurse their young,
but my people have become heartless
like ostriches in the desert.[b]

4 Because of thirst the infant's tongue
sticks to the roof of its mouth;[c]
the children beg for bread,
but no one gives it to them.[d]

5 Those who once ate delicacies
are destitute in the streets.
Those brought up in royal purple[e]
now lie on ash heaps.[f]

6 The punishment of my people
is greater than that of Sodom,[g]
which was overthrown in a moment
without a hand turned to help her.

7 Their princes were brighter than snow
and whiter than milk,
their bodies more ruddy than rubies,
their appearance like lapis lazuli.

3:64 [y] Ps 28:4
3:65 [z] Isa 6:10
4:1 [a] Eze 7:19
4:3 [b] Job 39:16
4:4 [c] Ps 22:15 [d] La 2:11,12
4:5 [e] Jer 6:2 [f] Am 6:3-7
4:6 [g] Ge 19:25

La 4:3 ❖ How can we avoid becoming cold and heartless during times of trial? What are ways we can show generosity and love to those suffering through such times?

8 But now they are blacker[h] than soot;
they are not recognized in the streets.
Their skin has shriveled on their bones;[i]
it has become as dry as a stick.

9 Those killed by the sword are better off
than those who die of famine;
racked with hunger, they waste away
for lack of food from the field.[j]

10 With their own hands
compassionate women
have cooked their own children,[k]
who became their food
when my people were destroyed.

11 The LORD has given full vent to his wrath;
he has poured out his fierce anger.
He kindled a fire[l] in Zion
that consumed her foundations.[m]

12 The kings of the earth did not believe,
nor did any of the peoples of the world,
that enemies and foes could enter
the gates of Jerusalem.[n]

13 But it happened because of the sins
of her prophets
and the iniquities of her priests,[o]
who shed within her
the blood of the righteous.

14 Now they grope through the streets
as if they were blind.[p]

4:8 [h] Job 30:28 [i] Ps 102:3-5
4:9 [j] Jer 15:2; 16:4
4:10 [k] Lev 26:29; Dt 28:53-57; Jer 19:9; La 2:20; Eze 5:10
4:11 [l] Jer 17:27 [m] Dt 32:22; Jer 7:20; Eze 22:31
4:12 [n] 1Ki 9:9; Jer 21:13
4:13 [o] Jer 5:31; 6:13; Eze 22:28; Mic 3:11
4:14 [p] Isa 59:10

[a] This chapter is an acrostic poem, the verses of which begin with the successive letters of the Hebrew alphabet.

4:1-6 The poet of Lamentations underscores the pain and despair of his generation rhetorically by noting how much longer and more painful it is to starve than to die by the sword. Perhaps we should interpret similarly the comment about the punishment on Zion as being greater than that for Sodom (v. 6).

4:7-13 The leadership of the people shed "the blood of the righteous" (v. 13, i.e., innocent blood). Whether this means by active persecution or by allowing injustice is not stated.

The popular "theology of Zion" is reflected in v. 12: the belief that God would not allow Jerusalem to fall. The poet of Lamentations notes (perhaps rhetorically) that foreign kings were surprised at Zion's fall, as if everyone knew of Zion's special status.

4:14-19 Verse 17 picks up on another theme given in prophetic accounts: namely, that help from another state would not save Zion. Jeremiah notes that the Babylonian siege was temporarily lifted because of an approaching Egyptian army (Jer 34:21-22; 37:5-11). Hopes for relief, however, quickly died when the siege was reinstated.

They are so defiled with blood[q]
that no one dares to touch their garments.

15 "Go away! You are unclean!" people cry to them.
"Away! Away! Don't touch us!"
When they flee and wander about,
people among the nations say,
"They can stay here no longer."[r]

16 The LORD himself has scattered them;
he no longer watches over them.[s]
The priests are shown no honor,
the elders[t] no favor.

17 Moreover, our eyes failed,
looking in vain[u] for help;[v]
from our towers we watched
for a nation[w] that could not save us.

18 People stalked us at every step,
so we could not walk in our streets.
Our end was near, our days were numbered,
for our end had come.[x]

19 Our pursuers were swifter
than eagles[y] in the sky;
they chased us[z] over the mountains
and lay in wait for us in the desert.

20 The LORD's anointed,[a] our very life breath,
was caught in their traps.[b]
We thought that under his shadow
we would live among the nations.

21 Rejoice and be glad, Daughter Edom,
you who live in the land of Uz.
But to you also the cup[c] will be passed;
you will be drunk and stripped naked.[d]

22 Your punishment will end, Daughter Zion;[e]
he will not prolong your exile.
But he will punish your sin,
Daughter Edom,
and expose your wickedness.[f]

5 Remember, LORD, what has happened to us;
look, and see our disgrace.[g]
2 Our inheritance[h] has been turned over to strangers,
our homes[i] to foreigners.
3 We have become fatherless,
our mothers are widows.[j]
4 We must buy the water we drink;
our wood can be had only at a price.[k]
5 Those who pursue us are at our heels;
we are weary[l] and find no rest.
6 We submitted to Egypt and Assyria[m]
to get enough bread.
7 Our ancestors sinned and are no more,

4:14 [q] Jer 2:34; 19:4
4:15 [r] Lev 13:46
4:16 [s] Isa 9:14-16 [t] La 5:12
4:17 [u] Isa 20:5; Eze 29:16 [v] La 1:7 [w] Jer 37:7
4:18 [x] Eze 7:2-12; Am 8:2
4:19 [y] Dt 28:49 [z] Isa 5:26-28
4:20 [a] 2Sa 19:21 [b] Jer 39:5; Eze 12:12-13; 19:4, 8
4:21 [c] Jer 25:15 [d] Isa 34:6-10; Am 1:11-12; Ob 16
4:22 [e] Isa 40:2; Jer 33:8 [f] Ps 137:7; Mal 1:4
5:1 [g] Ps 44:13-16; 89:50
5:2 [h] Ps 79:1 [i] Zep 1:13
5:3 [j] Jer 15:8; 18:21
5:4 [k] Isa 3:1
5:5 [l] Ne 9:37
5:6 [m] Hos 9:3

4:20 The poet speaks movingly of Zedekiah, Zion's reigning monarch at the time of the city's fall. He uses a striking phrase to describe his royal role—that Zedekiah was the very "life breath" of the people. This verse reflects poignant appreciation for the royal office ("the LORD's anointed"). The royal messiah (i.e., "anointed one") represented and gave life to the people. Metaphorically his "shadow" provided security for the people like the shadow or wings of the Lord for the righteous (cf. Ru 2:12; Ps 17:8; 91:1, 4).

4:21–22 These verses refer to an end to Zion's punishment and the beginning of Edom's judgment from the Lord. Nothing is said directly about an Edomite role in the fall of Jerusalem, but the vicious language of Ps 137:7, Joel 3:19–21, and Ob 10–14 make it clear that Edom had committed treachery.

This oracle-like conclusion to La 4 has a strong ironic bite to it. Edom is actually called on to rejoice and be glad (in the present) because the cup is about to be passed. The content of the cup initially tastes good, but it contains the wrath of judgment soon to be dispensed.

The judgment that fell on Zion was severe, but it will have an end (v. 22a). In succinct fashion the two parts of this affirmation show the major function of Lamentations. On the one hand, judgment has fallen, and the resulting tragedies are everywhere in evidence. On the other hand, a confession on the part of the people helps prepare the way for the new thing God will do.

4:1–22 The past, present, and future alike come under the judging, refining, and transforming work of God. We are called to moral and spiritual accountability. All of us have a past as well as a future in which we are held morally and spiritually accountable. There will be harsh and tragic words in the future for those who think that freedom and pleasure are the goals of human existence. By God's grace they can be gifts in due season, but that is a far different matter than the goal of radical autonomy and living apart from God. The latter is a false god and leads ultimately to catastrophe.

5:1–22 The poet offers a catalog of characters whose lives have been shattered by the loss of Jerusalem: The joy is gone from the people's hearts (v. 15). The voices of the text sound weary, resigned, and accusatory.

and we bear their punishment.[n]
8 Slaves[o] rule over us,
and there is no one to free us from their hands.[p]
9 We get our bread at the risk of our lives
because of the sword in the desert.
10 Our skin is hot as an oven,
feverish from hunger.[q]
11 Women have been violated[r] in Zion,
and virgins in the towns of Judah.
12 Princes have been hung up by their hands;
elders are shown no respect.[s]
13 Young men toil at the millstones;
boys stagger under loads of wood.
14 The elders are gone from the city gate;
the young men have stopped their music.[t]
15 Joy is gone from our hearts;
our dancing has turned to mourning.[u]
16 The crown[v] has fallen from our head.
Woe to us, for we have sinned![w]
17 Because of this our hearts[x] are faint,
because of these things our eyes[y] grow dim
18 for Mount Zion, which lies desolate,[z]
with jackals prowling over it.

19 You, LORD, reign forever;
your throne endures[a] from generation to generation.
20 Why do you always forget us?[b]
Why do you forsake us so long?
21 Restore[c] us to yourself, LORD, that we may return;
renew our days as of old
22 unless you have utterly rejected us
and are angry with us beyond measure.[d]

5:7 [n] Jer 14:20; 16:12
5:8 [o] Ne 5:15 [p] Zec 11:6
5:10 [q] La 4:8-9
5:11 [r] Zec 14:2
5:12 [s] La 4:16
5:14 [t] Isa 24:8; Jer 7:34
5:15 [u] Jer 25:10
5:16 [v] Ps 89:39
[w] Isa 3:11
5:17 [x] Isa 1:5 [y] Ps 6:7
5:18 [z] Mic 3:12
5:19 [a] Ps 45:6; 102:12,24-27
5:20 [b] Ps 13:1; 44:24
5:21 [c] Ps 80:3
5:22 [d] Isa 64:9

La 5:15-22 ❖ What does true repentance with a contrite heart look like? What does Christ promise to those who come to him in this way (see Jn 6:37)?

5:22 The last verse both raises a question and provides an implied answer. There is no doubt in the mind of the poet that God has rejected and judged his people. But has God irrevocably and utterly rejected them? Is his anger without appeasement? An answer is hinted at in the confession of God's daily mercy (3:22–24), in the claim that Judah's exile will not last forever (4:22), and in the request for God to restore the people to himself (5:21).

✜ **5:1-22** Lamentations unmasks the hypocrisy of humankind in any generation. It pushes all who read its despairing poetry to reflect on the meaning and purpose of their own lives. Within the dominant despair of the book are indications that God has spoken a renewing and redeeming word. In the fullness of time, that Word took on flesh (Jn 1:14), was crucified (Jn 19:16–18), died (Jn 19:28–30), and rose again (Jn 20:1–2, 15–16).

God is not aloof toward despair. He has taken despair upon himself through the cross and resurrection of his Son, erasing its death-dealing curse and bringing healing and immortality to light.

Ezekiel

Author: Ezekiel

Audience: Jews who were taken captive to Babylonia

Date: After the Babylonian conquest of Israel in 597 BC

Theme: God's presence is the key to life.

Reading Ezekiel

The book of Ezekiel divides basically into two parts. The first thirty-two chapters concentrate primarily on judgment—of God's people and of the heathen nations—because of sin and disobedience. The last sixteen chapters offer hope and consolation to those who have already undergone God's judgment. Particularly noteworthy in this book are the spectacular visions that God gave Ezekiel and the many

PERSPECTIVE

Some think that Ezekiel is difficult to interpret because of its visions. They maintain that such books, by their nature, are not meant to communicate truth in a literal manner. These truths do not lend themselves to scientific language. They are heavy with a surplus of meaning that goes beyond the scientific.

Ezekiel's difficulty emerges not only from the visions but also from the fact that Ezekiel was written over a number of years that spanned a chaotic, confusing time. Ezekiel spoke to people at three different phases of a crisis situation: when they were about to be overrun by a desperately cruel foreign political power; when they were overrun and deported to an alien land; and when their restoration to their lost land was in view. Each phase elicited a distinct message from the prophet.

How should we understand the changing and sometimes irreconcilable passages of Ezekiel? Many principles come to bear. But one of them must be an awareness of the historical circumstances of Ezekiel's time. Once that background is in place, some coherence begins to emerge.

Even with all this help, however, a key ingredient is still missing. Where does the story come from, the story that holds all the changing pieces together? It doesn't come from the Assyrians. It doesn't come from the Egyptians. It doesn't come from the Babylonians. It doesn't even come from the changing fortunes of Judah, Israel, or Jerusalem. To fully understand Ezekiel we must fast-forward six hundred years to the life of Jesus of Nazareth. There we discover a story so inspiring, so unifying, so redemptive that the difficulties, dangers, and despairs of life begin to take on a slightly unreal cast, like the horrors of a bad movie.

	1200 BC	1100	1000	900	800	700	600	500	400
Division of the kingdom (930 BC)				♦					
Ministries of Micah and Isaiah in Judah (c. 740–681 BC)						▬			
Jeremiah's ministry in Judah (c. 626–585 BC)							▬		
Daniel's exile in Babylon (c. 605–536 BC)							▬		
Ezekiel's ministry (c. 593–571 BC)							▬		
Fall of Jerusalem (586 BC)							♦		
Book of Ezekiel written (c. 571 BC)							♦		
First return of exiles to Jerusalem (538 BC)								♦	

In their place what becomes increasingly, overwhelmingly real is the fact of our restoration in the hands of a loving God. The last act of our lives is so filled with God's love that everything else takes on additional meaning. In our darkest hours, the outstretched arms of God are there to catch us.

No matter what our circumstances, the Lord is in control. Thanks be to God!

TAKING THE NEXT STEPS

Ezekiel was carried into exile in the second wave of Jews brought to Babylon (see Jer 52:27–30; Eze 1:2–3). During the first part of his ministry, he prophesied that Jerusalem would fall because of its sin against the Lord. But after God's judgment in destroying Jerusalem and the temple, Ezekiel shifted to a message of hope and restoration. He assured the exiles in Babylon that God, as a universal God, was not confined to the land of Judah. And Ezekiel was careful to insist that God dealt not only with the nation as a whole, but also with individuals.

As we read the book of Ezekiel, we receive both warnings and instructions for our daily lives. (1) God takes sin seriously, and if we insist on a life of wickedness, God will come in judgment. (2) God calls us individually to account for our sins, and he offers each of us pardon through the name of Jesus. (3) The God of the Bible has the power to take we who are dead in sin and by his Spirit breathe new life into us. (4) God wants the whole world to know that he is the Lord. That reminds us of our responsibility to tell everyone of the wonderful acts of God. (5) The final chapters of Ezekiel, alluded to many times in the book of Revelation, sharpen our hope for the return of Christ and the kingdom he is going to establish.

actions that the prophet performed in order to symbolize his message. And running like a thread throughout the book is the phrase: "Then they will know that I am the LORD."

Key Verse

I will give you a new heart and put a new spirit in you; I will remove from you your heart of stone and give you a heart of flesh.

—Ezekiel 36:26

WHAT TO LOOK FOR IN EZEKIEL

- The call of Ezekiel (chs. 1–3)
- Ezekiel's symbolic acts (chs. 4–5; 12; 21)
- God's glory leaving Jerusalem and later returning (chs. 10; 43)
- Sins of Judah compared to prostitution and adultery (chs. 16; 23)
- The fall of Jerusalem (ch. 33)
- The failure of the shepherds; the Lord as the Shepherd (ch. 34)
- The vision of the dry bones (ch. 37)
- The battle of Gog and Magog (chs. 38–39)
- The vision of the restored temple and renewed worship (chs. 40–48)

Ezekiel's Inaugural Vision

1 In my thirtieth year, in the fourth
month on the fifth day, while I was
among the exiles[a] by the Kebar River,
the heavens were opened[b] and I saw visions[c] of God.
2 On the fifth of the month — it was
the fifth year of the exile of King Jehoiachin[d] — 3 the word of the LORD came
to Ezekiel the priest, the son of Buzi, by
the Kebar River in the land of the Babylonians.[a] There the hand of the LORD
was on him.[e]
4 I looked, and I saw a windstorm coming out of the north[f] — an immense
cloud with flashing lightning and surrounded by brilliant light. The center of
the fire looked like glowing metal,[g] 5 and
in the fire was what looked like four living creatures.[h] In appearance their form
was human,[i] 6 but each of them had four
faces[j] and four wings. 7 Their legs were
straight; their feet were like those of a
calf and gleamed like burnished bronze.[k]
8 Under their wings on their four sides
they had human hands.[l] All four of them
had faces and wings, 9 and the wings of
one touched the wings of another. Each
one went straight ahead; they did not
turn as they moved.[m]
10 Their faces looked like this: Each
of the four had the face of a human being, and on the right side each had the
face of a lion, and on the left the face of
an ox; each also had the face of an eagle.[n] 11 Such were their faces. They each
had two wings[o] spreading out upward,
each wing touching that of the creature
on either side; and each had two other wings covering its body. 12 Each one
went straight ahead. Wherever the spirit
would go, they would go, without turning as they went. 13 The appearance of the
living creatures was like burning coals
of fire or like torches. Fire moved back
and forth among the creatures; it was
bright, and lightning[p] flashed out of it.
14 The creatures sped back and forth like
flashes of lightning.[q]

1:1 [a] Eze 11:24-25 [b] Mt 3:16; Ac 7:56 [c] Ex 24:10
1:2 [d] 2Ki 24:15
1:3 [e] 2Ki 3:15; Eze 3:14, 22
1:4 [f] Jer 1:14 [g] Eze 8:2
1:5 [h] Rev 4:6 [i] ver 26
1:6 [j] Eze 10:14
1:7 [k] Da 10:6; Rev 1:15
1:8 [l] Eze 10:8
1:9 [m] Eze 10:22
1:10 [n] Eze 10:14; Rev 4:7
1:11 [o] Isa 6:2
1:13 [p] Rev 4:5
1:14 [q] Ps 29:7

[a] 3 Or *Chaldeans*

1:1–3 The opening vision of the prophet Ezekiel is placed in the fifth year of Jehoiachin's exile, that is, 593 BC. The prophet lived among the exiles of Babylonia. Historically and socially, therefore, Ezekiel's message was addressed to those in exile.

Ezekiel was confronted by a dramatic spectacle: The heavens were opened, and he saw "visions of God" (v. 1). The prophet was given a divine perspective on the events unfolding around him. This was evidence that God had been dramatically at work even in the apparently hopeless situation of the exiles, a work that the prophet is invited to "show and tell" to those around him.

APPLICATION ✣ 1:1–3 As exiles, we are not homeless and hopeless. We have a home—it is just not here. Why do we love to read the Scriptures daily? Because they speak to us of home. Why do we live differently from those around us? Because we remember that we are soon going home (1Pe 4:1–7).

1:4–24 Ezekiel's vision opens with the Lord in the midst of a motion-filled "windstorm" (v. 4). The living creatures it contains have legs and wings. Torches are moving back and forth between the creatures while alongside the creatures are various wheels, with each "wheel intersecting a wheel" (v. 16).

Ezekiel's vision draws on traditional ancient Near Eastern elements. The imagery of the Lord riding on the storm was a common way of describing the Divine Warrior. The Divine Warrior is here approaching to wage war against his own people, not to deliver them.

15As I looked at the living creatures, I
saw a wheel on the ground beside each
creature with its four faces. 16This was
the appearance and structure of the
wheels: They sparkled like topaz,[r] and
all four looked alike. Each appeared to be
made like a wheel intersecting a wheel.
17As they moved, they would go in any
one of the four directions the creatures
faced; the wheels did not change direction[s] as the creatures went. 18Their rims
were high and awesome, and all four
rims were full of eyes[t] all around.
19When the living creatures moved,
the wheels beside them moved; and
when the living creatures rose from the
ground, the wheels also rose. 20Wherev-
er the spirit would go, they would go,[u]
and the wheels would rise along with
them, because the spirit of the living
creatures was in the wheels. 21When the
creatures moved, they also moved; when
the creatures stood still, they also stood
still; and when the creatures rose from
the ground, the wheels rose along with
them, because the spirit of the living
creatures was in the wheels.[v]
22Spread out above the heads of the
living creatures was what looked something like a vault,[w] sparkling like crystal,
and awesome. 23Under the vault their
wings were stretched out one toward the
other, and each had two wings covering
its body. 24When the creatures moved, I
heard the sound of their wings, like the
roar of rushing waters, like the voice[x]
of the Almighty,[a] like the tumult of an
army.[y] When they stood still, they lowered their wings.
25Then there came a voice from above
the vault over their heads as they stood
with lowered wings. 26Above the vault
over their heads was what looked like
a throne of lapis lazuli,[z] and high above
on the throne was a figure like that of a
man.[a] 27I saw that from what appeared
to be his waist up he looked like glowing metal, as if full of fire, and that from
there down he looked like fire; and brilliant light surrounded him.[b] 28Like the
appearance of a rainbow[c] in the clouds
on a rainy day, so was the radiance
around him.[d]
This was the appearance of the likeness of the glory[e] of the LORD. When I
saw it, I fell facedown,[f] and I heard the
voice of one speaking.

Eze 1:28 ❖ When have you been overwhelmed by God's glory?

1:16 [r] Eze 10:9-11; Da 10:6
1:17 [s] ver 9
1:18 [t] Eze 10:12; Rev 4:6
1:20 [u] ver 12
1:21 [v] Eze 10:17
1:22 [w] Eze 10:1
1:24 [x] Eze 10:5; 43:2; Da 10:6; Rev 1:15; 19:6
[y] 2Ki 7:6
1:26 [z] Ex 24:10; Eze 10:1
[a] Rev 1:13
1:27 [b] Eze 8:2
1:28 [c] Ge 9:13; Rev 10:1
[d] Rev 4:2
[e] Eze 8:4
[f] Eze 3:23; Da 8:17; Rev 1:17
2:1 [g] Da 10:11

Ezekiel's Call to Be a Prophet

2 He said to me, "Son of man,[b] stand[g]
up on your feet and I will speak to
you." 2As he spoke, the Spirit came into

[a] 24 Hebrew *Shaddai* [b] 1 The Hebrew phrase *ben adam* means *human being*. The phrase *son of man* is retained as a form of address here and throughout Ezekiel because of its possible association with "Son of Man" in the New Testament.

1:25–27 The Lord's throne-chariot is supported by living creatures, which are recognizable as cherubim throne-bearers (cf. Ps 18:10) and are identified as such in Eze 10:1. The cherubim are also God's heavenly bodyguard. The threatening nature of their presence comes from their role as enforcers of divine judgment (see Ge 3:24).

1:28 Mention of the rainbow allows the possibility of a ray of hope even in the midst of the gloom. The message of the vision is that flight is useless. The throne-chariot can proceed easily to any of the four points of the compass, without even having to turn, symbolizing God's omnipresence (vv. 12, 17). The wheels are covered with eyes, symbolizing the omniscience of God. In the face of such an awesome, ominous appearing of God, it is small wonder that Ezekiel fell on his face.

✣ **1:4–28** God will achieve his purposes—with or without us. Given that truth, Christians need to adopt a balance between progressivism and traditionalism. On the one hand, not everything that is new is of God. On the other hand, neither is everything new automatically suspect. Our understanding of the Scriptures and how they are to be applied to our present times is constantly growing as new challenges drive us back to reread old passages and reevaluate the traditions we have received. In all these deliberations, discernment and wisdom come from God (Jas 1:5).

2:1–8 Ezekiel is being sent to the Israelites, who are a "rebellious nation" (v. 3). They have hardened themselves, externally and internally, becoming "obstinate" and "stubborn" (v. 4). Even though the people will not listen to his words, "they will know that a prophet has been among them" (v. 5). They will recognize that God had warned them of what was about to happen.

Ezekiel is the very picture of compliant obedience because of an infusion of divine Spirit (v. 2). Without God's power, Ezekiel can do nothing.

Addressing Ezekiel as "son of man" (v. 3) distinguishes him from the Sovereign God. But this expression may perhaps also mark him out from all his contemporaries. They are the sons of Israel.

me and raised me[h] to my feet, and I
heard him speaking to me.
3He said: "Son of man, I am sending
you to the Israelites, to a rebellious nation that has rebelled against me; they
and their ancestors have been in revolt
against me to this very day.[i] 4The people
to whom I am sending you are obstinate and stubborn.[j] Say to them, 'This
is what the Sovereign LORD says.' 5And
whether they listen or fail to listen[k] — for
they are a rebellious people[l] — they will
know that a prophet has been among
them.[m] 6And you, son of man, do not be
afraid[n] of them or their words. Do not be
afraid, though briers and thorns[o] are all
around you and you live among scorpions. Do not be afraid of what they say
or be terrified by them, though they are
a rebellious people.[p] 7You must speak
my words to them, whether they listen
or fail to listen, for they are rebellious.[q]
8But you, son of man, listen to what I say
to you. Do not rebel like that rebellious
people;[r] open your mouth and eat[s] what
I give you."
9Then I looked, and I saw a hand[t]
stretched out to me. In it was a scroll,
10which he unrolled before me. On both
sides of it were written words of lament
and mourning and woe.[u]

3 And he said to me, "Son of man, eat
what is before you, eat this scroll;
then go and speak to the people of Israel." 2So I opened my mouth, and he gave
me the scroll to eat.
3Then he said to me, "Son of man, eat
this scroll I am giving you and fill your
stomach with it." So I ate[v] it, and it tasted
as sweet as honey[w] in my mouth.
4He then said to me: "Son of man, go
now to the people of Israel and speak my
words to them. 5You are not being sent to
a people of obscure speech and strange
language,[x] but to the people of Israel —

2:2 [h] Eze 3:24; Da 8:18
2:3 [i] Jer 3:25; Eze 20:8-24
2:4 [j] Eze 3:7
2:5 [k] Eze 3:11 [l] Eze 3:27 [m] Eze 33:33
2:6 [n] Jer 1:8, 17 [o] Isa 9:18; Mic 7:4 [p] Eze 3:9
2:7 [q] Jer 1:7; Eze 3:10-11
2:8 [r] Isa 50:5 [s] Jer 15:16; Rev 10:9
2:9 [t] Eze 8:3
2:10 [u] Rev 8:13
3:3 [v] Jer 15:16 [w] Ps 19:10; Ps 119:103; Rev 10:9-10
3:5 [x] Isa 28:11; Jnh 1:2
3:6 [y] Mt 11:21-23
3:7 [z] Eze 2:4; Jn 15:20-23
3:8 [a] Jer 1:18
3:9 [b] Isa 50:7; Eze 2:6; Mic 3:8
3:11 [c] Eze 2:4-5,7
3:12 [d] Eze 8:3; Ac 8:39
3:13 [e] Eze 1:24; 10:5,16-17
3:15 [f] Ps 137:1

Eze 2:3-5 ❖ Whom is God sending us to, "whether they listen or fail to listen"?

Eze 3:1-3 ❖ How can we "eat" God's message so that it becomes part of who we are?

6not to many peoples of obscure speech
and strange language, whose words you
cannot understand. Surely if I had sent
you to them, they would have listened
to you.[y] 7But the people of Israel are not
willing to listen to you because they are
not willing to listen to me, for all the
Israelites are hardened and obstinate.[z]
8But I will make you as unyielding and
hardened as they are.[a] 9I will make your
forehead like the hardest stone, harder
than flint. Do not be afraid of them or
terrified by them, though they are a rebellious people.[b]"
10And he said to me, "Son of man, listen
carefully and take to heart all the words
I speak to you. 11Go now to your people
in exile and speak to them. Say to them,
'This is what the Sovereign LORD says,'
whether they listen or fail to listen.[c]"
12Then the Spirit lifted me up,[d] and I
heard behind me a loud rumbling sound
as the glory of the LORD rose from the
place where it was standing.[a] 13It was the
sound of the wings of the living creatures brushing against each other and
the sound of the wheels beside them, a
loud rumbling sound.[e] 14The Spirit then
lifted me up and took me away, and I
went in bitterness and in the anger of
my spirit, with the strong hand of the
LORD on me. 15I came to the exiles who
lived at Tel Aviv near the Kebar River.[f]
And there, where they were living, I sat

[a] 12 Probable reading of the original Hebrew text; Masoretic Text *sound — may the glory of the LORD be praised from his place*

2:9—3:3 God hands the scroll to Ezekiel and causes him to eat it.

3:4-15 The vision ends on what appears at first sight to be a discordant note (vv. 14-15). On one hand, the prophet remains under "the strong hand of the LORD" (v. 14) and shares the Lord's feelings—feelings of wrath and anger. On the other hand, he sits among the exiles and sees the forthcoming overwhelming devastation of his people (v. 15).

✚ **2:1—3:15** Some labor for Christ for many years in areas resistant to the Good News but see only a handful of converts. Are they operating in the wrong place? If the primary goal of missions is to see the world converted, then the answer to that question may be yes. But if the primary goal of missions is the same as the goal set before Ezekiel—faithfulness to the task, so that God may be glorified—then the answer is different. In biblical perspective, the primary goal of missions is to bring glory to God through faithful obedience and to trust him alone with the harvest.

among them for seven days[g] — deeply
distressed.

Ezekiel's Task as Watchman

16At the end of seven days the word of
the LORD came to me:[h] 17"Son of man, I
have made you a watchman[i] for the people of Israel; so hear the word I speak and
give them warning from me. 18When I
say to a wicked person, 'You will surely die,' and you do not warn them or
speak out to dissuade them from their
evil ways in order to save their life, that
wicked person will die for[a] their sin,
and I will hold you accountable for their
blood.[j] 19But if you do warn the wicked
person and they do not turn from their
wickedness or from their evil ways, they
will die for their sin; but you will have
saved yourself.[k]

20"Again, when a righteous person
turns from their righteousness and does
evil, and I put a stumbling block before
them, they will die. Since you did not
warn them, they will die for their sin.
The righteous things that person did will
not be remembered, and I will hold you
accountable for their blood.[l] 21But if you
do warn the righteous person not to sin
and they do not sin, they will surely live
because they took warning, and you will
have saved yourself.[m]"

22The hand of the LORD[n] was on me
there, and he said to me, "Get up and
go[o] out to the plain,[p] and there I will
speak to you." 23So I got up and went
out to the plain. And the glory of the
LORD was standing there, like the glory I had seen by the Kebar River,[q] and
I fell facedown.[r]

24Then the Spirit came into me and
raised me[s] to my feet. He spoke to me
and said: "Go, shut yourself inside your
house. 25And you, son of man, they will
tie with ropes; you will be bound so that
you cannot go out among the people.[t]
26I will make your tongue stick to the
roof of your mouth so that you will be
silent and unable to rebuke them, for
they are a rebellious people.[u] 27But when
I speak to you, I will open your mouth
and you shall say to them, 'This is what
the Sovereign LORD says.'[v] Whoever will
listen let them listen, and whoever will
refuse let them refuse; for they are a rebellious people.[w]

Siege of Jerusalem Symbolized

4 "Now, son of man, take a block of clay,
put it in front of you and draw the
city of Jerusalem on it. 2Then lay siege
to it: Erect siege works against it, build
a ramp[x] up to it, set up camps against it
and put battering rams around it.[y] 3Then
take an iron pan, place it as an iron wall
between you and the city and turn your
face toward it. It will be under siege, and
you shall besiege it. This will be a sign[z]
to the people of Israel.[a]

4"Then lie on your left side and put the
sin of the people of Israel upon yourself.[b]
You are to bear their sin for the number of days you lie on your side. 5I have

3:15 [g] Job 2:13
3:16 [h] Jer 42:7
3:17 [i] Isa 52:8; Jer 6:17; Eze 33:7-9
3:18 [j] ver 20; Eze 33:6
3:19 [k] 2Ki 17:13; Eze 14:14,20; Ac 18:6; 20:26; 1Ti 4:14-16
3:20 [l] Ps 125:5; Eze 18:24; 33:12,18
3:21 [m] Ac 20:31
3:22 [n] Eze 1:3 [o] Ac 9:6 [p] Eze 8:4
3:23 [q] Eze 1:1 [r] Eze 1:28
3:24 [s] Eze 2:2
3:25 [t] Eze 4:8
3:26 [u] Eze 2:5; 24:27; 33:22
3:27 [v] ver 11 [w] Eze 12:3; 24:27; 33:22
4:2 [x] Jer 6:6 [y] Eze 21:22
4:3 [z] Isa 8:18; 20:3; Eze 12:3-6; 24:24,27 [a] Jer 39:1

[a] 18 Or *in*; also in verses 19 and 20 [b] 4 Or *upon your side*

3:16-23 The idea of the prophet as a "watchman" (v. 17) is a familiar one in the OT. In this case, the "enemy" of whom the people have to beware is none other than God himself.

Just as a watchman has to warn everyone in the city, so also Ezekiel must address his message of judgment to all, whether they listen or not (cf. Eze 2:7). Those who respond faithfully to his proclamation will "live" (v. 21) in a relationship with the Sovereign Lord that flows from obedience. Death, on the other hand, means estrangement from God and the community.

3:24-27 Ezekiel is ordered to remain confined to his house and told that he will not be able to speak. The prophet's role, at least up until the fall of Jerusalem, is restricted to delivering the divine sentence of judgment (v. 27).

✣ **3:16-27** As Christians, we have a calling from God. The Spirit of God that inspired the prophets now indwells us; only instead of swallowing a scroll, as Ezekiel did, we take in a book—the Bible. Through this Book, God continues to speak. This is the message we have been given to communicate. Though we may be creative in the way we communicate the message, we are not free to be creative with the content of the message that we are to deliver.

4:1-3 Ezekiel is to set up a large iron plate between himself and the city (v. 3), symbolizing the cutting off of relationships between God and his people. There is now no channel by which the people can communicate with God. By his demonstration, Ezekiel is to make the invisible aggressor visible.

4:4-8 The sign changes to a new sign-act. Ezekiel is to lie on his left side for 390 days, representing 390 years, bearing the guilt of the entire covenant community of Israel. The sin of the community is placed on him (v. 4).

assigned you the same number of days as the years of their sin. So for 390 days you will bear the sin of the people of Israel.

6"After you have finished this, lie down again, this time on your right side, and bear the sin of the people of Judah. I have assigned you 40 days, a day for each year.[b] 7Turn your face toward the siege of Jerusalem and with bared arm prophesy against her. 8I will tie you up with ropes so that you cannot turn from one side to the other until you have finished the days of your siege.[c]

9"Take wheat and barley, beans and lentils, millet and spelt;[d] put them in a storage jar and use them to make bread for yourself. You are to eat it during the 390 days you lie on your side. 10Weigh out twenty shekels[a] of food to eat each day and eat it at set times. 11Also measure out a sixth of a hin[b] of water and drink it at set times. 12Eat the food as you would a loaf of barley bread; bake it in the sight of the people, using human excrement[e] for fuel." 13The LORD said, "In this way the people of Israel will eat defiled food among the nations where I will drive them."[f]

14Then I said, "Not so, Sovereign LORD![g] I have never defiled myself. From my youth until now I have never eaten anything found dead[h] or torn by wild animals. No impure meat has ever entered my mouth.[i]"

15"Very well," he said, "I will let you bake your bread over cow dung instead of human excrement."

16He then said to me: "Son of man, I am about to cut off[j] the food supply in Jerusalem. The people will eat rationed food in anxiety and drink rationed water in despair,[k] 17for food and water will be scarce. They will be appalled at the sight of each other and will waste away because of[c] their sin.[l]

4:6 [b] Nu 14:34; Da 9:24-26; 12:11-12
4:8 [c] Eze 3:25
4:9 [d] Isa 28:25
4:12 [e] Isa 36:12
4:13 [f] Hos 9:3
4:14 [g] Jer 1:6; Eze 9:8; 20:49 [h] Lev 11:39 [i] Ex 22:31; Dt 14:3; Ac 10:14
4:16 [j] Ps 105:16; Eze 5:16 [k] ver 10-11; Lev 26:26; Isa 3:1; Eze 12:19
4:17 [l] Lev 26:39; Eze 24:23; 33:10
5:1 [m] Isa 7:20 [n] Eze 44:20 [o] Lev 21:5
5:2 [p] ver 12; Lev 26:33
5:3 [q] Jer 39:10
5:6 [r] Jer 11:10; Eze 16:47-51; Zec 7:11

Eze 4:4-8 ❖ How does Ezekiel's task foreshadow the work of Christ (see 1Pe 2:24)? Why is it important that Christ bore our sins in his body?

Eze 5:5-7 ❖ How could God's people, given every advantage through receiving his law, actually become more evil than the nations around them? Where does evil still affect God's family?

God's Razor of Judgment

5 "Now, son of man, take a sharp sword and use it as a barber's razor[m] to shave[n] your head and your beard.[o] Then take a set of scales and divide up the hair. 2When the days of your siege come to an end, burn a third of the hair inside the city. Take a third and strike it with the sword all around the city. And scatter a third to the wind. For I will pursue them with drawn sword.[p] 3But take a few hairs and tuck them away in the folds of your garment.[q] 4Again, take a few of these and throw them into the fire and burn them up. A fire will spread from there to all Israel.

5"This is what the Sovereign LORD says: This is Jerusalem, which I have set in the center of the nations, with countries all around her. 6Yet in her wickedness she has rebelled against my laws and decrees more than the nations and countries around her. She has rejected my laws and has not followed my decrees.[r]

[a] *10* That is, about 8 ounces or about 230 grams
[b] *11* That is, about 2/3 quart or about 0.6 liter
[c] *17* Or *away in*

4:9-11 The siege and fall of Jerusalem are depicted by Ezekiel eating siege rations throughout the 390 days (v. 9).

4:12-13 Ezekiel's diet during this period has a twofold aspect: first, it symbolizes the siege diet that the people of Jerusalem will have to eat; second, Ezekiel is instructed to cook in a ceremonially unclean way, symbolizing the defiled food that the Israelites will eat in exile (v. 13). By this means, the twofold message of judgment is proclaimed on all Israel—both those who remain in Jerusalem and those who are in exile.

4:14-17 When Ezekiel asserts that he has never consumed anything defiled, the decree is promptly modified by the Lord to allow the prophet to maintain his ceremonial purity. Ezekiel thus stands as a picture of a righteous remnant.

✜ **4:1-17** The prophetic sign-acts Ezekiel executed were more than mere visual aids or attention-getting devices. They were delivered with divine authority and thus functioned as the divine word made visible and sure. In Ezekiel's case, the message took over the messenger in a life-dominating way.

5:1-4 Ezekiel is called upon to shave his head and his beard. He must use a "sharp sword" (v. 1). The sword links this image with the military nature of the coming disaster. The prophet's hair represents the different fates that will meet the inhabitants of Jerusalem.

5:5-6 The people have committed idolatry and thus defiled the sanctuary (vv. 9, 11). They have not followed the Lord's laws or decrees (v. 6; cf.

7“Therefore this is what the Sovereign
LORD says: You have been more unruly
than the nations around you and have
not followed my decrees or kept my laws.
You have not even[a] conformed to the
standards of the nations around you.[s]
8“Therefore this is what the Sovereign
LORD says: I myself am against you, Jerusalem, and I will inflict punishment
on you in the sight of the nations.[t] 9Be-
cause of all your detestable idols, I will
do to you what I have never done before
and will never do again.[u] 10Therefore in
your midst parents will eat their children, and children will eat their parents.[v]
I will inflict punishment on you and will
scatter all your survivors to the winds.[w]
11Therefore as surely as I live, declares
the Sovereign LORD, because you have
defiled my sanctuary with all your vile
images[x] and detestable practices,[y] I myself will shave you; I will not look on you
with pity or spare you.[z] 12A third of your
people will die of the plague or perish by
famine inside you; a third will fall by the
sword outside your walls; and a third I
will scatter to the winds and pursue with
drawn sword.[a]
13“Then my anger will cease and my
wrath[b] against them will subside, and I
will be avenged.[c] And when I have spent
my wrath on them, they will know that I
the LORD have spoken in my zeal.
14“I will make you a ruin and a reproach among the nations around you,
in the sight of all who pass by.[d] 15You will
be a reproach and a taunt, a warning and
an object of horror to the nations around
you when I inflict punishment on you
in anger and in wrath and with stinging rebuke.[e] I the LORD have spoken.[f]
16When I shoot at you with my deadly
and destructive arrows of famine, I will
shoot to destroy you. I will bring more
and more famine upon you and cut off
your supply of food.[g] 17I will send famine
and wild beasts against you, and they will
leave you childless. Plague and bloodshed[h] will sweep through you, and I will
bring the sword against you. I the LORD
have spoken.[i]”

5:7 [s] 2Ch 33:9; Jer 2:10-11; Eze 16:47
5:8 [t] Eze 15:7
5:9 [u] Da 9:12; Mt 24:21
5:10 [v] Lev 26:29; La 2:20 [w] Lev 26:33; Ps 44:11; Eze 12:14; Zec 2:6
5:11 [x] Eze 7:20 [y] 2Ch 36:14; Eze 8:6 [z] Eze 7:4,9
5:12 [a] ver 2,17; Jer 15:2; 21:9; Eze 6:11-12; 12:14
5:13 [b] Eze 21:17; 36:6 [c] Isa 1:24
5:14 [d] Lev 26:32; Ne 2:17; Ps 74:3-10; 79:1-4
5:15 [e] 1Ki 9:7; Jer 22:8-9; 24:9 [f] Eze 25:17
5:16 [g] Dt 32:24
5:17 [h] Eze 38:22 [i] Eze 14:21
6:2 [j] Eze 36:1
6:3 [k] Eze 36:4 [l] Lev 26:30
6:4 [m] 2Ch 14:5

Eze 6:1-7 ❖ High places were centers of idol worship. What “high places” might we need to destroy in our lives?

Doom for the Mountains of Israel

6 The word of the LORD came to me:
2“Son of man, set your face against
the mountains[j] of Israel; prophesy
against them 3and say: ‘You mountains
of Israel, hear the word of the Sovereign
LORD. This is what the Sovereign LORD
says to the mountains and hills, to the
ravines and valleys:[k] I am about to bring
a sword against you, and I will destroy
your high places.[l] 4Your altars will be demolished and your incense altars[m] will
be smashed; and I will slay your people in front of your idols. 5I will lay the
dead bodies of the Israelites in front of

[a] 7 Most Hebrew manuscripts; some Hebrew manuscripts and Syriac *You have*

Lev 26:14–15). As a result, the curses of Lev 26 will be operative in their midst.

5:7–12 Israel has not merely failed to live up to God’s standards; they have not even lived up to the standards of the nations around them (v. 7). Instead of being a light to the nations, they have led the nations further into the darkness. The Lord will not show pity or spare his beloved but rebellious people (vv. 11–12).

5:13–17 God’s anger and wrath must be poured out on Israel so that they may know the Lord is a jealous God (5:13; cf. Ex 20:5). He will not share the devotion of his people with another. For now, they will be a ruin and reproach in the sight of the nations (5:14). But God’s anger will cease, and his wrath will subside once it has been fully vented, for the Lord is merciful and gracious as well as jealous (Ex 34:6, 14).

✜ **5:1–17** How can God forgive the guilty and still be just? We who live this side of Christmas and Easter have a much clearer understanding. How can God be just and still forgive the guilty? How can the fire pass over us and not completely burn us alive? It is only because it has already passed over Jesus and poured out its heat on him.

6:1–7 Prior to the building of the Jerusalem temple, the people were permitted to use the high places as locations for offering sacrifices to the Lord (1Ki 3:2). Once the temple structure was completed, however, the worship of Israel was to be centralized in Jerusalem (Dt 12). These local high places became the entry points for Canaanite religious ideas and images.

God asserts that he will do what successive generations of kings failed to do and put an end to this abomination. When God acts decisively in this way, the result will be that Israel “will know that I am the LORD” (6:7). This so-called “recognition formula” stresses the fact that the knowledge of the Lord comes about as a direct result of God’s actions in history.

their idols, and I will scatter your bones[n]
around your altars. 6Wherever you live,
the towns will be laid waste and the high
places demolished, so that your altars
will be laid waste and devastated, your
idols[o] smashed and ruined, your incense
altars[p] broken down, and what you have
made wiped out.[q] 7Your people will fall
slain among you, and you will know that
I am the LORD.
8"'But I will spare some, for some of
you will escape[r] the sword when you
are scattered among the lands and nations.[s] 9Then in the nations where they
have been carried captive, those who
escape will remember me—how I have
been grieved[t] by their adulterous hearts,
which have turned away from me, and
by their eyes, which have lusted after
their idols.[u] They will loathe themselves
for the evil they have done and for all
their detestable practices.[v] 10And they
will know that I am the LORD; I did not
threaten in vain to bring this calamity
on them.
11"'This is what the Sovereign LORD
says: Strike your hands together and
stamp your feet and cry out "Alas!" because of all the wicked and detestable
practices of the people of Israel, for
they will fall by the sword, famine and
plague.[w] 12One who is far away will die of
the plague, and one who is near will fall
by the sword, and anyone who survives
and is spared will die of famine. So will I
pour out my wrath on them.[x] 13And they
will know that I am the LORD, when their
people lie slain among their idols around
their altars, on every high hill and on all
the mountaintops, under every spreading tree and every leafy oak[y]—places
where they offered fragrant incense to
all their idols.[z] 14And I will stretch out
my hand[a] against them and make the
land a desolate waste from the desert to
Diblah[a]—wherever they live. Then they
will know that I am the LORD.[b]'"

6:5 [n] Jer 8:1-2
6:6 [o] Mic 1:7; Zec 13:2 [p] Lev 26:30 [q] Isa 6:11; Eze 5:14
6:8 [r] Jer 44:28 [s] Isa 6:13; Jer 44:14; Eze 12:16; 14:22
6:9 [t] Ps 78:40; Isa 7:13 [u] Eze 20:7,24 [v] Eze 20:43; 36:31
6:11 [w] Eze 5:12; 21:14,17; 25:6
6:12 [x] Eze 5:12
6:13 [y] Isa 57:5 [z] 1Ki 14:23; Jer 2:20; Eze 20:28; Hos 4:13
6:14 [a] Isa 5:25 [b] Eze 14:13
7:2 [c] Am 8:2,10 [d] Rev 7:1; 20:8
7:4 [e] Eze 5:11
7:5 [f] 2Ki 21:12
7:7 [g] Eze 12:23; Zep 1:14

The End Has Come

7 The word of the LORD came to me:
2"Son of man, this is what the Sovereign LORD says to the land of Israel:

"'The end![c] The end has come
upon the four corners[d] of the land!
3The end is now upon you,
and I will unleash my anger
against you.
I will judge you according to your
conduct
and repay you for all your
detestable practices.
4I will not look on you with pity;[e]
I will not spare you.
I will surely repay you for your
conduct
and for the detestable practices
among you.

"'Then you will know that I am the LORD.'

5"This is what the Sovereign LORD says:

"'Disaster![f] Unheard-of[b] disaster!
See, it comes!
6The end has come!
The end has come!
It has roused itself against you.
See, it comes!
7Doom has come upon you,
upon you who dwell in the land.
The time has come! The day is near![g]

[a] 14 Most Hebrew manuscripts; a few Hebrew manuscripts *Riblah* [b] 5 Most Hebrew manuscripts; some Hebrew manuscripts and Syriac *Disaster after*

6:8–10 The people will remember the Lord's grief at their adulterous actions and experience self-loathing at their evil ways. Their sin of idolatry will become an object of horror in their eyes.

6:11–14 Ezekiel does not end his oracle on this "happy" thought. The threefold judgment of sword, famine, and plague is once again unleashed on the land. When the people are killed around their idolatrous altars and the entire land from south to north is turned into a desolate waste, the knowledge of the Lord will be established.

The oracles see two possibilities: repentance and return to the Lord (vv. 8–10) or total devastation (vv. 11–14). Both are indeed possible endings to Israel's story; in either event, the Lord's justice will be seen and known.

6:1–14 If in fact there is a God who designed the whole cosmic and human story with a purpose, then what we believe about this God becomes a matter of supreme and decisive importance.

7:1–4 Ezekiel's message is expanded geographically. The prophet widens his scope of attention to include judgment on the whole "land of Israel" (v. 2). Ezekiel insists repeatedly that doom is not merely imminent but has actually arrived.

7:5–9 The second oracle picks up from the first oracle the theme of the personal nature of divine judgment on the people's sin. A significantly modified version of the recognition formula appears, "Then you will know that it is I the LORD who strikes you" (v. 9).

There is panic, not joy, on the
mountains.
8 I am about to pour out my wrath[h] on
you
and spend my anger against you.
I will judge you according to your
conduct
and repay you for all your
detestable practices.[i]
9 I will not look on you with pity;
I will not spare you.
I will repay you for your conduct
and for the detestable practices
among you.

" 'Then you will know that it is I the LORD
who strikes you.

10 " 'See, the day!
See, it comes!
Doom has burst forth,
the rod[j] has budded,
arrogance has blossomed!
11 Violence has arisen,[a]
a rod to punish the wicked.
None of the people will be left,
none of that crowd —
none of their wealth,
nothing of value.[k]
12 The time has come!
The day has arrived!
Let not the buyer rejoice
nor the seller grieve,
for my wrath is on the whole
crowd.[l]
13 The seller will not recover
the property that was sold —
as long as both buyer and seller
live.
For the vision concerning the whole
crowd
will not be reversed.
Because of their sins, not one of
them
will preserve their life.[m]
14 " 'They have blown the trumpet,
they have made all things
ready,
but no one will go into battle,
for my wrath is on the whole
crowd.
15 Outside is the sword;
inside are plague and famine.
Those in the country
will die by the sword;
those in the city
will be devoured by famine and
plague.[n]
16 The fugitives who escape
will flee to the mountains.
Like doves[o] of the valleys,
they will all moan,
each for their own sins.[p]
17 Every hand will go limp;[q]
every leg will be wet with urine.
18 They will put on sackcloth
and be clothed with terror.[r]
Every face will be covered with
shame,
and every head will be shaved.[s]
19 " 'They will throw their silver into
the streets,
and their gold will be treated as a
thing unclean.
Their silver and gold
will not be able to deliver them
in the day of the LORD's wrath.[t]
It will not satisfy their hunger
or fill their stomachs,
for it has caused them to stumble[u]
into sin.[v]
20 They took pride in their beautiful
jewelry
and used it to make their
detestable idols.
They made it into vile images;[w]
therefore I will make it a thing
unclean for them.

Eze 7:8–9 ❖ How does the reality of God's wrath against sin deepen our wonder at God's grace (see Eph 2:1–10)?

7:8 [h] Isa 42:25; Eze 9:8; 14:19; Na 1:6 [i] Eze 20:8, 21; 36:19
7:10 [j] Ps 89:32; Isa 10:5
7:11 [k] Jer 16:6; Zep 1:18
7:12 [l] ver 7; Isa 5:13-14; Eze 30:3
7:13 [m] Lev 25:24-28
7:15 [n] Dt 32:25; Jer 14:18; La 1:20; Eze 5:12
7:16 [o] Isa 59:11 [p] Ezr 9:15; Eze 6:8
7:17 [q] Isa 13:7; Eze 21:7; 22:14
7:18 [r] Ps 55:5 [s] Isa 15:2-3; Eze 27:31; Am 8:10
7:19 [t] Eze 13:5; Zep 1:7,18 [u] Eze 14:3 [v] Pr 11:4
7:20 [w] Jer 7:30

[a] 11 Or *The violent one has become*

7:10–27 The third oracle begins with a brief introduction that draws out the organic connection between Judah's sin and her punishment. Israel's "doom has burst forth, the rod has budded, arrogance has blossomed! Violence has arisen, a rod to punish wickedness" (vv. 10–11) Alongside Israel's blossoming pride and violence, however, the rod of God's judgment has been growing: namely, Babylon (v. 21).
7:12 When the threatened judgment falls, commercial transactions will lose their meaning; there will be no such thing as a good deal or a bad deal, whether for the buyer or the seller.
7:17–18 Paralyzing fear will result in loss of control of bodily functions. The people will put on a show of mourning by means of their clothes and their shaven heads, yet no mercy or forgiveness will be found there.
7:20 Gold and silver will be worse than worthless; they will not simply be regarded as trash, because gold and silver furnished the materials for the people's idolatry.

21 I will give their wealth as plunder to
foreigners
and as loot to the wicked of the
earth,
who will defile it.[x]
22 I will turn my face[y] away from the
people,
and robbers will desecrate the
place I treasure.
They will enter it
and will defile it.

23 "'Prepare chains!
For the land is full of bloodshed,[z]
and the city is full of violence.
24 I will bring the most wicked of
nations
to take possession of their
houses.
I will put an end to the pride of the
mighty,
and their sanctuaries[a] will be
desecrated.[b]
25 When terror comes,
they will seek peace in vain.[c]
26 Calamity upon calamity[d] will come,
and rumor upon rumor.
They will go searching for a vision
from the prophet,
priestly instruction in the law will
cease,
the counsel of the elders will come
to an end.[e]
27 The king will mourn,
the prince will be clothed with
despair,[f]
and the hands of the people of the
land will tremble.
I will deal with them according to
their conduct,[g]
and by their own standards I will
judge them.

"'Then they will know that I am the
LORD.[h]'"

7:21 [x] 2Ki 24:13
7:22 [y] Eze 39:23-24
7:23 [z] 2Ki 21:16
7:24 [a] Eze 24:21 [b] 2Ch 7:20; Eze 28:7
7:25 [c] Eze 13:10, 16
7:26 [d] Jer 4:20 [e] Isa 47:11; Eze 20:1-3; Mic 3:6
7:27 [f] Ps 109:19; Eze 26:16 [g] Eze 18:20
[h] ver 4
8:1 [i] Eze 14:1 [j] Eze 33:31 [k] Eze 1:1-3
8:2 [l] Eze 1:4, 26-27
8:3 [m] Eze 3:12; 11:1 [n] Ex 20:5; Dt 32:16
8:4 [o] Eze 1:28 [p] Eze 3:22
8:5 [q] Ps 78:58; Jer 32:34
8:6 [r] Eze 5:11

Eze 8:1-13 ❖ Where does idolatry still creep into God's community? How can we identify and remove the modern-day "idols"?

Idolatry in the Temple

8 In the sixth year, in the sixth month
on the fifth day, while I was sitting
in my house and the elders[i] of Judah
were sitting before[j] me, the hand of the
Sovereign LORD came on me there.[k] 2 I
looked, and I saw a figure like that of
a man.[a] From what appeared to be his
waist down he was like fire, and from
there up his appearance was as bright as
glowing metal.[l] 3 He stretched out what
looked like a hand and took me by the
hair of my head. The Spirit lifted me up[m]
between earth and heaven and in visions
of God he took me to Jerusalem, to the
entrance of the north gate of the inner
court, where the idol that provokes to
jealousy[n] stood. 4 And there before me
was the glory[o] of the God of Israel, as in
the vision I had seen in the plain.[p]
5 Then he said to me, "Son of man, look
toward the north." So I looked, and in the
entrance north of the gate of the altar I
saw this idol[q] of jealousy.
6 And he said to me, "Son of man, do
you see what they are doing — the utterly
detestable[r] things the Israelites are doing

[a] 2 Or *saw a fiery figure*

7:21-24 Judah will be given over into the hand of her enemies, and all her possessions will be handed over as plunder. The Lord will turn away his face, allowing the wicked of the earth to pollute the land and even to desecrate "the place I treasure."

7:25-27 The people will seek peace and not find it, whether they seek it through the channel of religious leadership or political leadership.

7:1-27 Even believers will have to give an account for their actions, as the apostle Paul reminds us (2Co 5:10). We need to learn to see the end from the beginning, to visualize the future vividly here and now, and to let that vision dominate our lives.

8:1 The vision opens with a date: the fifth day of the sixth month of the sixth year (of Jehoiachin's exile); in our reckoning, that would be September 18, 592 BC. The vision of chs. 8-11 is intended for a specific audience, "the elders of Judah" (v. 1), who have gathered at Ezekiel's house.

8:2-18 Ezekiel is transported by the agency of the Spirit and shown the defiled City of Jerusalem.

In four brief scenes (vv. 3-6, 7-13, 14-15, 16) Ezekiel is shown the comprehensive nature of the sins of Jerusalem. The people's sin extends from outside the city gate to the inner courtyard of the temple itself. It involves both men and women—even the seventy elders, who are symbolic of the leadership of the whole people. It includes idolatry imported from all sorts of surrounding nations (Canaan, Egypt, and Babylon) and involving all kinds of gods (male and female human figures, animal figures, and stellar bodies).

This is a unified, universalized religion, the ultimate multifaith worship service. From the Lord's perspective, however, the picture is one of abomination piled on abomination.

here, things that will drive me far from
my sanctuary? But you will see things
that are even more detestable."
7Then he brought me to the entrance
to the court. I looked, and I saw a hole
in the wall. 8He said to me, "Son of man,
now dig into the wall." So I dug into the
wall and saw a doorway there.
9And he said to me, "Go in and see the
wicked and detestable things they are
doing here." 10So I went in and looked,
and I saw portrayed all over the walls
all kinds of crawling things and unclean
animals and all the idols of Israel.[s] 11In
front of them stood seventy elders of Israel, and Jaazaniah son of Shaphan was
standing among them. Each had a censer[t] in his hand, and a fragrant cloud of
incense[u] was rising.
12He said to me, "Son of man, have you
seen what the elders of Israel are doing
in the darkness, each at the shrine of his
own idol? They say, 'The LORD does not
see[v] us; the LORD has forsaken the land.'"
13Again, he said, "You will see them doing
things that are even more detestable."
14Then he brought me to the entrance
of the north gate of the house of the
LORD, and I saw women sitting there,
mourning the god Tammuz. 15He said to
me, "Do you see this, son of man? You
will see things that are even more detestable than this."
16He then brought me into the inner
court of the house of the LORD, and there
at the entrance to the temple, between
the portico and the altar,[w] were about
twenty-five men. With their backs toward the temple of the LORD and their
faces toward the east, they were bowing
down to the sun in the east.[x]
17He said to me, "Have you seen this,
son of man? Is it a trivial matter for
the people of Judah to do the detestable things they are doing here? Must

8:10 [s] Ex 20:4
8:11 [t] Nu 16:17 [u] Nu 16:35
8:12 [v] Ps 10:11; Isa 29:15; Eze 9:9
8:16 [w] Joel 2:17 [x] Dt 4:19; 17:3; Job 31:28; Jer 2:27; Eze 11:1,12
8:17 [y] Eze 9:9 [z] Eze 16:26
8:18 [a] Eze 9:10; 24:14 [b] Isa 1:15; Jer 11:11; Mic 3:4; Zec 7:13
9:2 [c] Lev 16:4; Eze 10:2; Rev 15:6
9:3 [d] Eze 10:4 [e] Eze 11:22
9:4 [f] Ex 12:7; 2Co 1:22; Rev 7:3; 9:4 [g] Ps 119:136; Jer 13:17; Eze 21:6 [h] Ps 119:53
9:5 [i] Eze 5:11
9:6 [j] Eze 8:11-13, 16 [k] 2Ch 36:17; Jer 25:29; 1Pe 4:17
9:8 [l] Jos 7:6

they also fill the land with violence[y] and
continually arouse my anger?[z] Look at
them putting the branch to their nose!
18Therefore I will deal with them in anger; I will not look on them with pity[a] or
spare them. Although they shout in my
ears, I will not listen[b] to them."

Judgment on the Idolaters

9 Then I heard him call out in a loud
voice, "Bring near those who are appointed to execute judgment on the city,
each with a weapon in his hand." 2And I
saw six men coming from the direction
of the upper gate, which faces north, each
with a deadly weapon in his hand. With
them was a man clothed in linen[c] who
had a writing kit at his side. They came
in and stood beside the bronze altar.
3Now the glory[d] of the God of Israel went up from above the cherubim,[e]
where it had been, and moved to the
threshold of the temple. Then the LORD
called to the man clothed in linen who
had the writing kit at his side 4and said
to him, "Go throughout the city of Jerusalem and put a mark[f] on the foreheads
of those who grieve and lament[g] over
all the detestable things that are done
in it.[h]"
5As I listened, he said to the others,
"Follow him through the city and kill,
without showing pity[i] or compassion.
6Slaughter the old men, the young men
and women, the mothers and children,
but do not touch anyone who has the
mark. Begin at my sanctuary." So they
began with the old men[j] who were in
front of the temple.[k]
7Then he said to them, "Defile the
temple and fill the courts with the slain.
Go!" So they went out and began killing
throughout the city. 8While they were
killing and I was left alone, I fell facedown,[l] crying out, "Alas, Sovereign LORD!

9:1–4 The Lord summons six "guards," each of whom appears armed with a club. These figures are normally interpreted as angelic beings because of their superhuman role in the vision and the symbolic nature of their total number (seven). There is also another figure, Ezekiel's alter ego, who is commanded to mark the faithful people in the city on their foreheads.

9:5–6a Hard on the heels of the scribe figure come the agents of destruction, who themselves take on the attitude of God toward the people. All those without the mark are to be killed—young and old, male and female. The categories listed demonstrate that even the defenseless, the frail, and the innocent are condemned to destruction.

9:6b–7 The slaughter is to begin at the temple with the chief idolaters: the twenty-five elders who were worshiping the sun (cf. 8:16). The killing takes place within the temple itself; it is already so contaminated by their idolatry that God himself has no reservations about defiling it further.

9:8 In the midst of the carnage, Ezekiel is left alone and he cries out. The Lord's answer points to the depth of the abominations of the house of Israel and Judah. They can expect no pity but rather just retribution for their actions, which is the final

Are you going to destroy the entire remnant of Israel in this outpouring of your
wrath on Jerusalem?[m]”
9He answered me, “The sin of the people of Israel and Judah is exceedingly
great; the land is full of bloodshed and
the city is full of injustice.[n] They say,
‘The LORD has forsaken the land; the
LORD does not see.’[o] 10So I will not look
on them with pity[p] or spare them, but I
will bring down on their own heads what
they have done.[q]”
11Then the man in linen with the writing kit at his side brought back word, saying, “I have done as you commanded.”

God's Glory Departs From the Temple

10 I looked, and I saw the likeness
of a throne[r] of lapis lazuli[s] above
the vault[t] that was over the heads of the
cherubim. 2The LORD said to the man
clothed in linen,[u] “Go in among the
wheels[v] beneath the cherubim. Fill[w] your
hands with burning coals from among
the cherubim and scatter them over the
city.” And as I watched, he went in.
3Now the cherubim were standing on
the south side of the temple when the
man went in, and a cloud filled the inner
court. 4Then the glory of the LORD[x] rose
from above the cherubim and moved to
the threshold of the temple. The cloud
filled the temple, and the court was full
of the radiance of the glory of the LORD.
5The sound of the wings of the cherubim
could be heard as far away as the outer
court, like the voice[y] of God Almighty[a]
when he speaks.
6When the LORD commanded the
man in linen, “Take fire from among the
wheels, from among the cherubim,” the
man went in and stood beside a wheel.
7Then one of the cherubim reached out
his hand to the fire that was among
them. He took up some of it and put it
into the hands of the man in linen, who
took it and went out. 8(Under the wings
of the cherubim could be seen what
looked like human hands.)[z]
9I looked, and I saw beside the cherubim four wheels, one beside each of
the cherubim; the wheels sparkled like
topaz.[a] 10As for their appearance, the
four of them looked alike; each was like
a wheel intersecting a wheel. 11As they
moved, they would go in any one of
the four directions the cherubim faced;
the wheels did not turn about[b] as the
cherubim went. The cherubim went in
whatever direction the head faced, without turning as they went. 12Their entire
bodies, including their backs, their hands
and their wings, were completely full
of eyes,[b] as were their four wheels.[c] 13I
heard the wheels being called “the whirl-
ing wheels.” 14Each of the cherubim[d] had
four faces:[e] One face was that of a cherub,
the second the face of a human being, the
third the face of a lion, and the fourth
the face of an eagle.[f]
15Then the cherubim rose upward.
These were the living creatures[g] I had
seen by the Kebar River. 16When the

Eze 9:9 ❖ What sins and wickedness around us can we grieve and lament today? What can we do today to help these evils to cease?

9:8 [m] Eze 11:13; Am 7:1-6
9:9 [n] Eze 22:29 [o] Job 22:13; Eze 8:12
9:10 [p] Eze 7:4; 8:18 [q] Isa 65:6; Eze 11:21
10:1 [r] Rev 4:2 [s] Ex 24:10 [t] Eze 1:22
10:2 [u] Eze 9:2 [v] Eze 1:15 [w] Rev 8:5
10:4 [x] Eze 1:28; 9:3
10:5 [y] Job 40:9; Eze 1:24
10:8 [z] Eze 1:8
10:9 [a] Eze 1:15-16; Rev 21:20
10:12 [b] Rev 4:6-8 [c] Eze 1:15-21
10:14 [d] 1Ki 7:36 [e] Eze 1:6 [f] Eze 1:10; Rev 4:7
10:15 [g] Eze 1:3,5

[a] 5 Hebrew *El-Shaddai* [b] 11 Or *aside*

proof that God has indeed seen everything that has happened in and around the city.

9:9-11 Yet when it appears that all hope is gone, suddenly the priestly figure with the writing kit reappears, saying, "I have done as you commanded" (v. 11). We are not told how many people he has marked—indeed, we are not even told that he has marked any—yet his presence acts to lessen slightly the awful severity of the judgment, just as the rainbow of 1:28 tempers slightly the coming windstorm of God's wrath.

8:1—9:11 We too face an abundance of idols all around us in our multicultural age. Frequently, people speak of our age as being one of pluralism, as if that somehow makes our time distinct from the past. This is nonsense, for at many times in the past, not least during the NT era and the time of the exile, God's people have found themselves placed in a melting pot of world religions.

The options available in the "marketplace of religions" have often been just as diverse in previous centuries as they are at present. The hallmark of any pluralistic age is that idolatry comes in all shapes and sizes, no matter what religious institution we choose to attend. The key for Christians is to pray for discernment and choose wisely, joining communities who submit to and worship the only One true God (Jn 4:24).

10:1-2 At the Lord's command, an angel takes burning coals from beneath the heavenly throne in order to burn the city to the ground.

10:3-5 The divine chariot is drawn up on the south side of the temple. Then Ezekiel sees a cloud filling the inner court and the glory of God on the move once more.

cherubim moved, the wheels beside them
moved; and when the cherubim spread
their wings to rise from the ground, the
wheels did not leave their side. 17When
the cherubim stood still, they also stood
still; and when the cherubim rose, they
rose with them, because the spirit of the
living creatures was in them.[h]
18Then the glory of the LORD departed from over the threshold of the temple and stopped above the cherubim.[i]
19While I watched, the cherubim spread
their wings and rose from the ground,
and as they went, the wheels went with
them.[j] They stopped at the entrance of
the east gate of the LORD's house, and
the glory of the God of Israel was above
them.
20These were the living creatures I had
seen beneath the God of Israel by the Kebar River,[k] and I realized that they were
cherubim. 21Each had four faces[l] and four
wings,[m] and under their wings was what
looked like human hands. 22Their faces
had the same appearance as those I had
seen by the Kebar River. Each one went
straight ahead.

God's Sure Judgment on Jerusalem

11 Then the Spirit lifted me up and
brought me to the gate of the house
of the LORD that faces east. There at the
entrance of the gate were twenty-five
men, and I saw among them Jaazaniah
son of Azzur and Pelatiah son of Benaiah,
leaders of the people.[n] 2The LORD said
to me, "Son of man, these are the men
who are plotting evil and giving wicked
advice in this city. 3They say, 'Haven't our
houses been recently rebuilt? This city is
a pot,[o] and we are the meat in it.'[p] 4There-
fore prophesy[q] against them; prophesy,
son of man."
5Then the Spirit of the LORD came on
me, and he told me to say: "This is what
the LORD says: That is what you are saying, you leaders in Israel, but I know
what is going through your mind.[r] 6You
have killed many people in this city and
filled its streets with the dead.[s]
7"Therefore this is what the Sovereign
LORD says: The bodies you have thrown
there are the meat and this city is the
pot, but I will drive you out of it.[t] 8You
fear the sword, and the sword is what I
will bring against you, declares the Sovereign LORD.[u] 9I will drive you out of the
city and deliver you into the hands[v] of
foreigners and inflict punishment on
you.[w] 10You will fall by the sword, and
I will execute judgment on you at the
borders of Israel.[x] Then you will know
that I am the LORD. 11This city will not be
a pot[y] for you, nor will you be the meat
in it; I will execute judgment on you at
the borders of Israel. 12And you will know
that I am the LORD, for you have not followed my decrees[z] or kept my laws but
have conformed to the standards of the
nations around you.[a]"
13Now as I was prophesying, Pelatiah[b]
son of Benaiah died. Then I fell facedown

10:17 [h]Eze 1:20-21
10:18 [i]Ps 18:10
10:19 [j]Eze 11:1, 22
10:20 [k]Eze 1:1
10:21 [l]Eze 41:18 [m]Eze 1:6
11:1 [n]Eze 8:16; 10:19; 43:4-5
11:3 [o]Jer 1:13; Eze 24:3 [p]ver 7,11
11:4 [q]Eze 3:4,17
11:5 [r]Jer 17:10
11:6 [s]Eze 7:23; 22:6
11:7 [t]Eze 24:3-13; Mic 3:2-3
11:8 [u]Pr 10:24
11:9 [v]Ps 106:41 [w]Dt 28:36; Eze 5:8
11:10 [x]2Ki 14:25
11:11 [y]ver 3
11:12 [z]Lev 18:4; Eze 18:9 [a]Eze 8:10
11:13 [b]ver 1

Eze 10:18–19 ❖ What causes God's glory to leave his people? How can we be confident that God's presence will not leave us (see 2Co 1:22)?

Eze 11:4–12 ❖ What or whom might God be calling us to speak against?

10:18–19 The city itself is now effectively doomed, cut off from divine aid from its true Protector, waiting for the axe to fall. The Lord has abandoned the city to the empty hope offered by the idols for which the people abandoned him.

11:1–2 At the entrance to the east gate, Ezekiel sees a group of men whose number (v. 1) and whose function (giving advice, v. 2) suggest they are elders. Ezekiel is told that these leaders have been "plotting evil" (v. 2). In opposition to the prophetic word of forthcoming judgment on Jerusalem, they have apparently been arrogantly asserting the security of their position.

11:3–4 "This city is a pot, and we are the meat" (v. 3) may be interpreted as a statement of the relative value of those who remain in Jerusalem and the exiles (the best part, the "meat," is put in the cooking pot while the undesired portion is thrown into the fire). The elders regard the current situation as an expression of God's favor on them (see v. 15). They think of themselves as the true remnant while those in exile are under God's judgment.

11:5–12 In the message that follows, the Lord rejects the elders' claim. The city will provide no protection for them. The sword that they fear will come on them and they will fall by it. The land will not be their possession; rather, the Lord will bring them out of the city to judge them at the very edge of the land, at the "borders of Israel" (v. 10).

11:13–15 In this prophecy, there is a challenge to the Jerusalemites' claim to possess the land. Far from the land of Canaan being their "possession" (v. 15; cf. Ex 6:8), the inhabitants of Jerusalem will die outside the land because of their failure to keep the Lord's decrees and laws. Ezekiel falls on his face and cries out, "Alas, Sovereign LORD! Will you completely destroy the remnant of Israel?" (v. 13; cf. 9:8).

and cried out in a loud voice, “Alas, Sovereign LORD! Will you completely destroy
the remnant of Israel?[c]”

The Promise of Israel's Return

14The word of the LORD came to me:
15“Son of man, the people of Jerusalem
have said of your fellow exiles and all
the other Israelites, ‘They are far away
from the LORD; this land was given to
us as our possession.’[d]
16“Therefore say: ‘This is what the
Sovereign LORD says: Although I sent
them far away among the nations and
scattered them among the countries, yet
for a little while I have been a sanctuary[e]
for them in the countries where they
have gone.’
17“Therefore say: ‘This is what the Sovereign LORD says: I will gather you from
the nations and bring you back from the
countries where you have been scattered,
and I will give you back the land of Israel again.’[f]
18“They will return to it and remove all
its vile images[g] and detestable idols.[h] 19I
will give them an undivided heart[i] and
put a new spirit in them; I will remove
from them their heart of stone[j] and give
them a heart of flesh.[k] 20Then they will
follow my decrees and be careful to keep
my laws.[l] They will be my people, and
I will be their God.[m] 21But as for those
whose hearts are devoted to their vile
images and detestable idols, I will bring
down on their own heads what they have
done, declares the Sovereign LORD.[n]”
22Then the cherubim, with the wheels
beside them, spread their wings, and
the glory of the God of Israel was above
them.[o] 23The glory[p] of the LORD went up
from within the city and stopped above
the mountain[q] east of it. 24The Spirit[r]
lifted me up and brought me to the exiles in Babylonia[a] in the vision[s] given by
the Spirit of God.
Then the vision I had seen went up
from me, 25and I told the exiles everything the LORD had shown me.[t]

11:13 [c]Eze 9:8
11:15 [d]Eze 33:24
11:16 [e]Ps 90:1; 91:9; Isa 8:14
11:17 [f]Jer 3:18; 24:5-6; Eze 28:25; 34:13
11:18 [g]Eze 5:11 [h]Eze 37:23
11:19 [i]Jer 32:39 [j]Zec 7:12 [k]Eze 18:31; 36:26; 2Co 3:3
11:20 [l]Ps 105:45 [m]Eze 14:11; 36:26-28
11:21 [n]Eze 9:10; 16:43
11:22 [o]Eze 10:19
11:23 [p]Eze 8:4; 10:4 [q]Zec 14:4
11:24 [r]Eze 8:3 [s]2Co 12:2-4
11:25 [t]Eze 3:4,11
12:2 [u]Isa 6:10; Eze 2:6-8; Mt 13:15
12:3 [v]Jer 36:3 [w]Jer 26:3 [x]2Ti 2:25-26

Eze 12:3-11 ❖ How can our lives be a living sign acting out God's message to the world around us?

The Exile Symbolized

12 The word of the LORD came to me:
2“Son of man, you are living among
a rebellious people. They have eyes to see
but do not see and ears to hear but do not
hear, for they are a rebellious people.[u]
3“Therefore, son of man, pack your
belongings for exile and in the daytime, as they watch, set out and go from
where you are to another place. Perhaps[v]
they will understand,[w] though they are
a rebellious people.[x] 4During the daytime, while they watch, bring out your
belongings packed for exile. Then in

[a] 24 Or *Chaldea*

11:16 The response to Ezekiel's cry is a glorious declaration that the future of Israel lies among the exiles. Yes, they have been sent far away from the land of Israel, but even there they have not been cast out of the Lord's presence. The Lord's movement is not simply a departure *from* Jerusalem, but also a departure *to* Babylon, to be a sanctuary for his true people there.
11:17-18 There will be a new exodus of the Lord's true people from all the nations to which they have been scattered (v. 17; cf. Ex 6:6); the land that Ezekiel cannot redeem for his redemption relatives (see v. 15) will be redeemed for them by the Lord (cf. Ex 6:6). The detestable idols and vile images with which the former inhabitants filled the land (7:20; 8:3-17) will be removed by the new inhabitants (v. 18).
11:19-20 The Lord will create in his new people “an undivided heart” (v. 19). His new people will observe both decrees and laws (v. 20). This is the first substantive indication in Ezekiel of a solid hope for the future for God's people in exile.
11:21 There is, however, no such promised hope for those who remain in the land. They will receive just judgment for their idolatry.

✣ **10:1–11:25** Most assume we can easily identify those on whom God's favor rests. But God's presence is not so easily discerned. In the Bible, he is most often found with the poor and the weak—the despised and rejected, those whom the world typically regards as castoffs. So, when Jesus comes, his primary ministry takes place in the open air. He is known as the friend of tax collectors and sinners (Mt 11:19). When he seeks twelve disciples, he goes not to the religious training schools but to the workplaces of ordinary men and women. The essence of his training program is not a rigorous course of book study, but three years of being in his presence. We also receive the benefits of this training in reading the NT.

12:1-2 The exiles do not see what the Lord shows them simply because they are rebellious. This saying of v. 2 underlies the sign-acts that follow it.
12:3-9 Ezekiel is first to put together an exile's pack. These preparations are to be made in the daytime, though the departure is delayed until evening, representing God's delaying of judgment until the proper time.

the evening, while they are watching,
go out like those who go into exile.[y]
5While they watch, dig through the wall
and take your belongings out through it.
6Put them on your shoulder as they are
watching and carry them out at dusk.
Cover your face so that you cannot see
the land, for I have made you a sign[z] to
the Israelites."

7So I did as I was commanded.[a] During
the day I brought out my things packed
for exile. Then in the evening I dug
through the wall with my hands. I took
my belongings out at dusk, carrying them
on my shoulders while they watched.

8In the morning the word of the LORD
came to me: 9"Son of man, did not the
Israelites, that rebellious people, ask you,
'What are you doing?'[b]

10"Say to them, 'This is what the Sovereign LORD says: This prophecy concerns
the prince in Jerusalem and all the Israelites who are there.' 11Say to them, 'I am
a sign to you.'

"As I have done, so it will be done to
them. They will go into exile as captives.[c]

12"The prince among them will put
his things on his shoulder at dusk[d] and
leave, and a hole will be dug in the wall
for him to go through. He will cover his
face so that he cannot see the land.[e] 13I
will spread my net[f] for him, and he will
be caught in my snare;[g] I will bring him to
Babylonia, the land of the Chaldeans, but
he will not see[h] it, and there he will die.[i] 14I
will scatter to the winds all those around
him — his staff and all his troops — and
I will pursue them with drawn sword.[j]

15"They will know that I am the LORD,
when I disperse them among the nations
and scatter them through the countries.
16But I will spare a few of them from the
sword, famine and plague, so that in the
nations where they go they may acknowledge all their detestable practices. Then
they will know that I am the LORD.[k]"

17The word of the LORD came to me:
18"Son of man, tremble as you eat your
food,[l] and shudder in fear as you drink
your water. 19Say to the people of the
land: 'This is what the Sovereign LORD
says about those living in Jerusalem and
in the land of Israel: They will eat their
food in anxiety and drink their water in
despair, for their land will be stripped of
everything[m] in it because of the violence
of all who live there.[n] 20The inhabited
towns will be laid waste and the land will
be desolate. Then you will know that I
am the LORD.[o]' "

There Will Be No Delay

21The word of the LORD came to me:
22"Son of man, what is this proverb you
have in the land of Israel: 'The days go
by and every vision comes to nothing'?[p]
23Say to them, 'This is what the Sovereign LORD says: I am going to put an end
to this proverb, and they will no longer
quote it in Israel.' Say to them, 'The days
are near when every vision will be fulfilled.[q] 24For there will be no more false
visions or flattering divinations[r] among
the people of Israel. 25But I the LORD will
speak what I will, and it shall be fulfilled
without delay. For in your days, you rebellious people, I will fulfill whatever I
say, declares the Sovereign LORD.[s]' "

26The word of the LORD came to me:
27"Son of man, the Israelites are saying,

12:4 [y] ver 12; Jer 39:4
12:6 [z] ver 12; Isa 8:18; 20:3; Eze 4:3; 24:24
12:7 [a] Eze 24:18; 37:10
12:9 [b] Eze 17:12; 20:49; 24:19
12:11 [c] 2Ki 25:7; Jer 15:2; 52:15
12:12 [d] Jer 39:4 [e] Jer 52:7
12:13 [f] Eze 17:20; 19:8; Hos 7:12 [g] Isa 24:17-18 [h] Jer 39:7 [i] Jer 52:11; Eze 17:16
12:14 [j] 2Ki 25:5; Eze 5:10,12
12:16 [k] Jer 22:8-9; Eze 6:8-10; 14:22
12:18 [l] La 5:9; Eze 4:16
12:19 [m] Eze 6:6-14; Mic 7:13; Zec 7:14 [n] Eze 4:16; 23:33
12:20 [o] Isa 7:23-24; Jer 4:7
12:22 [p] Eze 11:3; Am 6:3; 2Pe 3:4
12:23 [q] Ps 37:13; Joel 2:1; Zep 1:14
12:24 [r] Jer 14:14; Eze 13:23; Zec 13:2-4
12:25 [s] Isa 14:24; Hab 1:5

12:10–16 Though the imagery here is complex, the essential message seems reasonably straightforward. This anti-exodus will center on the person of the prince, Zedekiah.

The Lord is the one who will bring Zedekiah to Babylonia and will scatter his forces to the winds, pursuing him with drawn sword. The Lord is the one who will disperse his followers among the nations. Their defeat and dispersal are evidence of the Lord's wrath in action.

12:17–20 To this initial sign-act and interpretation, a further one is then added: Ezekiel is to eat and drink with trembling and shuddering, depicting the anxiety that the inhabitants of Jerusalem and Judah will feel (v. 19). The land of Judah and all who remain in it are doomed.

12:1–20 The word Ezekiel received was symbolized in his actions—actions that were uncomfortable and costly. How, though, does God's Word take flesh through us? Evangelicals have sometimes been accused of making the Word who became flesh (Jn 1:14) back into words again. We can talk a good talk but don't always have the walk to match it. A world with ears tightly closed against the truth needs to see the reality of our faith written in our own changed lives.

12:21–25 As he does on a number of other occasions, Ezekiel addresses these issues by presenting two current popular sayings or slogans. The first "proverb" of the people asserts the ineffectiveness of the prophetic word in general (v. 22). The Lord's response throws a slightly revised form of their saying back in their faces (v. 23).

12:26–28 Alongside these unbelievers was apparently a second party: the delayers. They simply hoped that this word of judgment would not take

‘The vision he sees is for many years
from now, and he prophesies about the
distant future.’[t]
28“Therefore say to them, ‘This is what
the Sovereign LORD says: None of my
words will be delayed any longer; whatever I say will be fulfilled, declares the
Sovereign LORD.’ ”

False Prophets Condemned

13 The word of the LORD came to me:
2“Son of man, prophesy against the
prophets of Israel who are now prophesying. Say to those who prophesy out of
their own imagination: ‘Hear the word
of the LORD![u] 3This is what the Sovereign
LORD says: Woe to the foolish[a] prophets[v]
who follow their own spirit and have
seen nothing![w] 4Your prophets, Israel,
are like jackals among ruins. 5You have
not gone up to the breaches in the wall to
repair[x] it for the people of Israel so that
it will stand firm in the battle on the day
of the LORD.[y] 6Their visions are false and
their divinations a lie. Even though the
LORD has not sent them, they say, “The
LORD declares,” and expect him to fulfill
their words.[z] 7Have you not seen false visions and uttered lying divinations when
you say, “The LORD declares,” though I
have not spoken?
8“ ‘Therefore this is what the Sovereign LORD says: Because of your false
words and lying visions, I am against
you, declares the Sovereign LORD. 9My
hand will be against the prophets who
see false visions and utter lying divinations. They will not belong to the council
of my people or be listed in the records[a]
of Israel, nor will they enter the land of
Israel. Then you will know that I am the
Sovereign LORD.[b]

12:27 [t] Da 10:14
13:2 [u] ver 17; Jer 23:16; 37:19
13:3 [v] La 2:14 [w] Jer 23:25-32
13:5 [x] Isa 58:12; Eze 22:30 [y] Eze 7:19
13:6 [z] Jer 28:15; Eze 22:28
13:9 [a] Jer 17:13 [b] Eze 20:38
13:10 [c] Jer 50:6 [d] Eze 7:25; 22:28
13:11 [e] Eze 38:22
13:13 [f] Rev 11:19; 16:21 [g] Ex 9:25; Isa 30:30
13:14 [h] Mic 1:6 [i] Jer 6:15
13:16 [j] Isa 57:21; Jer 6:14
13:17 [k] Rev 2:20 [l] ver 2

Eze 13:1–7 ❖ How can we be on our guard against false prophets and teachers today?

10“ ‘Because they lead my people
astray,[c] saying, “Peace,” when there is
no peace, and because, when a flimsy
wall is built, they cover it with whitewash,[d] 11therefore tell those who cover it with whitewash that it is going to
fall. Rain will come in torrents, and I will
send hailstones hurtling down, and violent winds will burst forth.[e] 12When the
wall collapses, will people not ask you,
“Where is the whitewash you covered
it with?”
13“ ‘Therefore this is what the Sovereign LORD says: In my wrath I will unleash a violent wind, and in my anger
hailstones[f] and torrents of rain will fall
with destructive fury.[g] 14I will tear down
the wall you have covered with whitewash and will level it to the ground so
that its foundation[h] will be laid bare.
When it[b] falls,[i] you will be destroyed in
it; and you will know that I am the LORD.
15So I will pour out my wrath against the
wall and against those who covered it
with whitewash. I will say to you, “The
wall is gone and so are those who whitewashed it, 16those prophets of Israel who
prophesied to Jerusalem and saw visions
of peace for her when there was no peace,
declares the Sovereign LORD.[j]” ’
17“Now, son of man, set your face
against the daughters[k] of your people
who prophesy out of their own imagination. Prophesy against them[l] 18and
say, ‘This is what the Sovereign LORD
says: Woe to the women who sew magic

[a] 3 Or *wicked* [b] 14 Or *the city*

---

effect until a future generation. This second group also receives a “no more” answer from the Lord: There will be no more delay; the Lord will fulfill whatever he has spoken.

13:1–16 The foundational difference between Ezekiel and “the prophets of Israel” (v. 2a) is the *origin* of their prophecy: The false prophets “prophesy out of their own imagination” (v. 2b), whereas Ezekiel declares the vision that the Sovereign Lord has revealed to him (cf. 11:25).

Ezekiel also criticizes the content of their messages. “Their visions are false and their divinations a lie” (v. 6). This criticism of the prophets is expressed in a series of pictures. (1) They have acted “like jackals among ruins” (v. 4). (2) Intent on pursuing their own prey, these skulking scavengers have failed to take on the dangerous but necessary task of standing in the gaps to build up a solid protection for Israel on the day of the Lord (v. 5).

Ezekiel then describes the “prophets of Israel” using the image of a wall. In vv. 10–16 the image is of a poorly constructed wall, which the prophets, rather than rebuilding properly, merely cover with “whitewash” (v. 10), thus giving it a misleadingly solid appearance. Its true nature will be exposed, however, by the coming of the storm (vv. 12–15).

13:17–19 It seems that the women were involved in tying magic bands of some kind, which may have been amulets worn around the neck. The prophetesses are also charged with making *veils* for their heads (v. 18). Whatever the precise form of their actions, this passage makes clear they are not those of a true prophet of the Lord.

The women are not criticized for dealing with

charms on all their wrists and make veils
of various lengths for their heads in order to ensnare people. Will you ensnare
the lives of my people but preserve your
own? 19 You have profaned[m] me among
my people for a few handfuls of barley
and scraps of bread. By lying to my people, who listen to lies, you have killed
those who should not have died and have
spared those who should not live.[n]
20 " 'Therefore this is what the Sovereign LORD says: I am against your magic
charms with which you ensnare people
like birds and I will tear them from your
arms; I will set free the people that you
ensnare like birds. 21 I will tear off your
veils and save my people from your
hands, and they will no longer fall prey
to your power. Then you will know that
I am the LORD.[o] 22 Because you disheartened the righteous with your lies, when I
had brought them no grief, and because
you encouraged the wicked not to turn
from their evil ways and so save their
lives,[p] 23 therefore you will no longer see
false visions or practice divination.[q] I will
save my people from your hands. And
then you will know that I am the LORD.[r]' "

Idolaters Condemned

14 Some of the elders of Israel came
to me and sat down in front of
me.[s] 2 Then the word of the LORD came
to me: 3 "Son of man, these men have set
up idols in their hearts and put wicked stumbling blocks[t] before their faces.
Should I let them inquire of me at all?[u]
4 Therefore speak to them and tell them,
'This is what the Sovereign LORD says:
When any of the Israelites set up idols
in their hearts and put a wicked stumbling block before their faces and then
go to a prophet, I the LORD will answer
them myself in keeping with their great
idolatry. 5 I will do this to recapture the
hearts of the people of Israel, who have
all deserted[v] me for their idols.'[w]
6 "Therefore say to the people of Israel, 'This is what the Sovereign LORD
says: Repent! Turn from your idols and
renounce all your detestable practices![x]
7 " 'When any of the Israelites or any
foreigner[y] residing in Israel separate
themselves from me and set up idols in
their hearts and put a wicked stumbling
block before their faces and then go to a
prophet to inquire of me, I the LORD will
answer them myself. 8 I will set my face
against[z] them and make them an example and a byword.[a] I will remove them
from my people. Then you will know that
I am the LORD.
9 " 'And if the prophet[b] is enticed[c] to
utter a prophecy, I the LORD have enticed

13:19 [m] Eze 20:39; 22:26 [n] Pr 28:21
13:21 [o] Ps 91:3
13:22 [p] Jer 23:14; Eze 33:14-16
13:23 [q] ver 6; Eze 12:24 [r] Mic 3:6
14:1 [s] Eze 8:1; 20:1
14:3 [t] ver 7; Eze 7:19 [u] Isa 1:15; Eze 20:31
14:5 [v] Zec 11:8 [w] Jer 2:11
14:6 [x] Isa 2:20; 30:22
14:7 [y] Ex 12:48; 20:10
14:8 [z] Eze 15:7 [a] Eze 5:15
14:9 [b] Jer 14:15 [c] Jer 4:10

Eze 14:2-5 ❖ What does it mean to set up idols in our hearts? How can we make sure our hearts are clear of any idols?

---

the wrong questions but for giving the wrong answers (v. 22). Their magically derived oracles are afflicting those who ought not to have been afflicted and comforting those who ought not to have been comforted.

It's clear that the prophesying women are motivated by pursuit of personal profit. The result of their activities is deadly, killing "those who should not have died" and sparing "those who should not live" (v. 19). The women's destructive work in this area prevents the wicked from becoming aware of their true state, putting both their lives and the women's own lives in jeopardy (v. 18).

13:20-23 The closing verses of the chapter, while still grammatically addressed to the women, pick up themes from the first section to round off the whole. The "prophets of Israel" (v. 2) are a stumbling block to the reception of Ezekiel's message of national judgment, while the "[women] who prophesy" (v. 17) undermine his calling to proclaim life to the righteous and to warn the wicked to turn from their ways.

✤ **12:21—13:23** Satan's strategy is to imitate God's means of self-revelation in order to confuse the message. We are therefore not automatically to believe those who claim to be speaking the word of God to us. As John instructs us, we are to test every spirit (1Jn 4:1). The urgent need to test those who claim to bring God's message to us did not come to an end in Ezekiel's day; it was true in NT times, and it is still true today.

14:1-4 The phrase "wicked stumbling block" (v. 3), which occurs six times in Ezekiel, is invariably linked to idolatry. Because the hearts of the exiled elders are divided between the Lord and idols, the Lord will give the elders no answer to their inquiry except an answer of judgment.

14:5-8 All of the exiles have deserted the Lord for their idols. The Lord will answer them himself. Do they want a word from the Lord? The Lord will demonstrate his attitude toward them. But there is still room for God's people to repent and return to God (v. 6).

14:9-11 The result of God's purifying judgment will be a faithful and undefiled people, cleansed from their transgressions. The goal of the covenant—God's dwelling in the midst of his people—will

that prophet, and I will stretch out my hand against him and destroy him from among my people Israel.[d] 10They will bear their guilt — the prophet will be as guilty as the one who consults him. 11Then the people of Israel will no longer stray[e] from me, nor will they defile themselves anymore with all their sins. They will be my people, and I will be their God, declares the Sovereign LORD.[f]' "

Jerusalem's Judgment Inescapable

12The word of the LORD came to me: 13"Son of man, if a country sins against me by being unfaithful and I stretch out my hand against it to cut off its food supply[g] and send famine upon it and kill its people and their animals,[h] 14even if these three men — Noah,[i] Daniel[a][j] and Job[k] — were in it, they could save only themselves by their righteousness,[l] declares the Sovereign LORD.

15"Or if I send wild beasts[m] through that country and they leave it childless and it becomes desolate so that no one can pass through it because of the beasts,[n] 16as surely as I live, declares the Sovereign LORD, even if these three men were in it, they could not save their own sons or daughters. They alone would be saved, but the land would be desolate.[o]

17"Or if I bring a sword[p] against that country and say, 'Let the sword pass throughout the land,' and I kill its people and their animals,[q] 18as surely as I live, declares the Sovereign LORD, even if these three men were in it, they could not save their own sons or daughters. They alone would be saved.

19"Or if I send a plague into that land and pour out my wrath[r] on it through bloodshed, killing its people and their animals,[s] 20as surely as I live, declares the Sovereign LORD, even if Noah, Daniel and Job were in it, they could save neither son nor daughter. They would save only themselves by their righteousness.[t]

21"For this is what the Sovereign LORD says: How much worse will it be when I send against Jerusalem my four dreadful judgments — sword and famine and wild beasts and plague — to kill its men and their animals![u] 22Yet there will be some survivors — sons and daughters who will be brought out of it.[v] They will come to you, and when you see their conduct[w] and their actions, you will be consoled regarding the disaster I have brought on Jerusalem — every disaster I have brought on it. 23You will be consoled when you see their conduct and their actions, for you will know that I have done nothing in it without cause, declares the Sovereign LORD.[x]"

Jerusalem as a Useless Vine

15 The word of the LORD came to me: 2"Son of man, how is the wood of a vine[y] different from that of a branch from any of the trees in the forest? 3Is wood ever taken from it to make anything useful? Do they make pegs from it

14:9 [d] 1Ki 22:23
14:11 [e] Eze 48:11 [f] Eze 11:19-20; 37:23
14:13 [g] Lev 26:26 [h] Eze 5:16; 6:14; 15:8
14:14 [i] Ge 6:8 [j] ver 20; Eze 28:3; Da 1:6; 6:13 [k] Job 1:1 [l] Job 42:9; Jer 15:1; Eze 18:20
14:15 [m] Eze 5:17 [n] Lev 26:22
14:16 [o] Eze 18:20
14:17 [p] Lev 26:25; Eze 5:12; 21:3-4 [q] Eze 25:13; Zep 1:3
14:19 [r] Eze 7:8 [s] Eze 38:22
14:20 [t] ver 14
14:21 [u] Jer 15:3; Eze 5:17; 33:27; Am 4:6-10; Rev 6:8
14:22 [v] Eze 12:16 [w] Eze 20:43
14:23 [x] Jer 22:8-9
15:2 [y] Isa 5:1-7; Jer 2:21; Hos 10:1

[a] 14 Or *Danel*, a man of renown in ancient literature; also in verse 20

---

certainly not be thwarted, not even by Israel's sin (v. 11).

> ✚ **14:1-11** All of us who claim the name of Christ have divided hearts. Outwardly, our appearance may "fit": We go to church regularly and appear to be decent, religious people. Yet when it comes to the tough decisions in life, there are standards operating other than God's Word, which demonstrates that our hearts are influenced by things other than the One true God.

14:12-20 The phrase "by being unfaithful" (v. 13) refers to a breach of a covenant relationship. This may be through marital infidelity (Nu 5:12, 27), misusing something that belongs to the Lord (Jos 7:1), or another covenant violation (e.g., Lev 26:40; Eze 17:20). Such a breach of the covenant brings the curses described in Lev 26.

These covenant curses are itemized individually in the form of four test cases (vv. 13-14, 15-16, 17-18, 19-20). Because of the people's sin, not even Noah, Daniel, or Job would be able to save anyone from the curses to come (14:14, 16, 18, 20); their righteousness would only be sufficient to save themselves.

14:21-23 Unexpectedly, some will survive the catastrophe to "console" (v. 22) the exiles by allowing them to see the extent of Jerusalem's depravity. When the exiles see the behavior of this "unspiritual remnant," they will know the Lord has not acted without cause.

> ✚ **14:12-23** The astonishing fact is not that God judged Jerusalem, but that God allows our contemporary society, with all its flagrant and secret sins, to continue to exist. However, we should not regard that patience as inability to act. God's "slowness" is patience in order to allow time for all of his chosen people to repent.

15:1-5 Ezekiel 15 is a brief parable, a pictorial story with a sting in the tail. The prunings cut from the vine were familiar objects, and it is immediately apparent to all that they serve no useful purpose.

Eze 15:7 ❖ How does God's righteous anger teach us about God's holiness and authority?

to hang things on? 4And after it is thrown
on the fire as fuel and the fire burns both
ends and chars the middle, is it then useful for anything?[z] 5If it was not useful for
anything when it was whole, how much
less can it be made into something useful when the fire has burned it and it is
charred?
6"Therefore this is what the Sovereign
LORD says: As I have given the wood of
the vine among the trees of the forest as
fuel for the fire, so will I treat the people
living in Jerusalem. 7I will set my face
against[a] them. Although they have come
out of the fire, the fire will yet consume
them. And when I set my face against
them, you will know that I am the LORD.[b]
8I will make the land desolate[c] because
they have been unfaithful,[d] declares the
Sovereign LORD."

Jerusalem as an Adulterous Wife

16 The word of the LORD came to me:
2"Son of man, confront Jerusalem
with her detestable practices[e] 3and say,
'This is what the Sovereign LORD says
to Jerusalem: Your ancestry[f] and birth
were in the land of the Canaanites; your
father was an Amorite and your mother a
Hittite.[g] 4On the day you were born[h] your
cord was not cut, nor were you washed
with water to make you clean, nor were
you rubbed with salt or wrapped in
cloths. 5No one looked on you with pity
or had compassion enough to do any of
these things for you. Rather, you were
thrown out into the open field, for on the
day you were born you were despised.
6" 'Then I passed by and saw you kicking about in your blood, and as you lay
there in your blood I said to you, "Live!"[a][i]
7I made you grow[j] like a plant of the field.
You grew and developed and entered
puberty. Your breasts had formed and
your hair had grown, yet you were stark
naked.[k]
8" 'Later I passed by, and when I looked
at you and saw that you were old enough
for love, I spread the corner of my garment[l] over you and covered your naked
body. I gave you my solemn oath and
entered into a covenant with you, declares the Sovereign LORD, and you became mine.[m]
9" 'I bathed you with water and
washed[n] the blood from you and put
ointments on you. 10I clothed you with
an embroidered[o] dress and put sandals
of fine leather on you. I dressed you in
fine linen[p] and covered you with costly
garments.[q] 11I adorned you with jewelry:[r] I put bracelets[s] on your arms and a
necklace[t] around your neck, 12and I put a
ring on your nose,[u] earrings on your ears
and a beautiful crown[v] on your head. 13So
you were adorned with gold and silver;
your clothes were of fine linen and costly
fabric and embroidered cloth. Your food
was honey, olive oil[w] and the finest flour.
You became very beautiful and rose to
be a queen.[x] 14And your fame[y] spread
among the nations on account of your

15:4 [z] Eze 19:14; Jn 15:6
15:7 [a] Ps 34:16; Eze 14:8 [b] Isa 24:18; Am 9:1-4
15:8 [c] Eze 14:13 [d] Eze 17:20
16:2 [e] Eze 20:4; 22:2
16:3 [f] Eze 21:30 [g] ver 45
16:4 [h] Hos 2:3
16:6 [i] Ex 19:4
16:7 [j] Dt 1:10 [k] Ex 1:7
16:8 [l] Ru 3:9 [m] Jer 2:2; Hos 2:7,19-20
16:9 [n] Ru 3:3
16:10 [o] Ex 26:36 [p] Eze 27:16 [q] ver 18
16:11 [r] Eze 23:40 [s] Isa 3:19; Eze 23:42 [t] Ge 41:42
16:12 [u] Isa 3:21 [v] Isa 28:5; Jer 13:18
16:13 [w] 1Sa 10:1 [x] Dt 32:13-14; 1Ki 4:21
16:14 [y] 1Ki 10:24

[a] 6 A few Hebrew manuscripts, Septuagint and Syriac; most Hebrew manuscripts repeat *and as you lay there in your blood I said to you, "Live!"*

15:6-8 Jerusalem is like that vine wood. It is fit for nothing but to be thrown back onto the fire and consumed completely. As in 14:12-23, the unfaithfulness of the land in pursuing idols will result in its being made desolate.

✣ **15:1-8** Fruitful branches are pruned just as much as fruitless ones are cast off (Jn 15:2, 6). For the Christian, suffering is a "fruitful" part of life (cf. Heb 12:11). As we suffer, we are further conformed to the likeness of Christ, the suffering servant. As we suffer, we are detached from our passionate absorption with ourselves and this present world. We are taught to refocus our attention on the glories that await us in the place where suffering will be no more.

16:1-5 Jerusalem's roots are entirely natural and pagan. Even before David captured it and made it his capital, it was an important (pagan) city.

16:6-7 The child Jerusalem was born to heartless parents who abandoned the newborn infant. Passing by this sorry spectacle, God spoke his life-giving word, causing her to live and thrive like a plant of the field. This period corresponds to the pre-Israelite period of Jerusalem's history, when she was not yet directly included in God's purposes.

16:8-13 At the end of this time, the Lord spread a corner of his robe over her, symbolically covering her nakedness (v. 8). In the terms of the metaphor, he married her. The Lord's choice of Jerusalem was a true love match on his part (vv. 8-9). He provided her with a wardrobe fit for a queen (v. 10). She is clothed in materials associated with the tabernacle, underlining her symbolic identity as the home of the temple.

16:14 Because of her natural beauty and the splendor with which the Lord had endowed her, Jerusalem's fame spread far and wide.

beauty,[z] because the splendor I had given
you made your beauty perfect, declares
the Sovereign LORD.
15“ ‘But you trusted in your beauty and
used your fame to become a prostitute.
You lavished your favors on anyone who
passed by[a] and your beauty became his.[b]
16You took some of your garments to
make gaudy high places, where you
carried on your prostitution.[c] You went
to him, and he possessed your beauty.[a]
17You also took the fine jewelry I gave
you, the jewelry made of my gold and
silver, and you made for yourself male
idols and engaged in prostitution with
them.[d] 18And you took your embroidered
clothes to put on them, and you offered
my oil and incense before them. 19Also
the food I provided for you — the flour,
olive oil and honey I gave you to eat —
you offered as fragrant incense before
them. That is what happened, declares
the Sovereign LORD.[e]
20“ ‘And you took your sons and daughters[f] whom you bore to me[g] and sacrificed them as food to the idols. Was your
prostitution not enough?[h] 21You slaughtered my children and sacrificed them to
the idols.[i] 22In all your detestable practices and your prostitution you did not
remember the days of your youth,[j] when
you were naked and bare, kicking about
in your blood.[k]
23“ ‘Woe! Woe to you, declares the Sovereign LORD. In addition to all your other wickedness, 24you built a mound for
yourself and made a lofty shrine[l] in every
public square.[m] 25At every street corner
you built your lofty shrines and degraded your beauty, spreading your legs with
increasing promiscuity to anyone who
passed by.[n] 26You engaged in prostitution
with the Egyptians, your neighbors with
large genitals, and aroused my anger[o]
with your increasing promiscuity.[p] 27So
I stretched out my hand[q] against you
and reduced your territory; I gave you
over to the greed of your enemies, the
daughters of the Philistines,[r] who were
shocked by your lewd conduct. 28You
engaged in prostitution with the Assyrians[s] too, because you were insatiable;
and even after that, you still were not
satisfied. 29Then you increased your promiscuity to include Babylonia,[b][t] a land of
merchants, but even with this you were
not satisfied.
30“ ‘I am filled with fury against you,[c]
declares the Sovereign LORD, when you
do all these things, acting like a brazen prostitute![u] 31When you built your
mounds at every street corner and
made your lofty shrines[v] in every public square, you were unlike a prostitute,
because you scorned payment.
32“ ‘You adulterous wife! You prefer
strangers to your own husband! 33All
prostitutes receive gifts, but you give
gifts[w] to all your lovers, bribing them to
come to you from everywhere for your
illicit favors.[x] 34So in your prostitution
you are the opposite of others; no one
runs after you for your favors. You are
the very opposite, for you give payment
and none is given to you.
35“ ‘Therefore, you prostitute, hear the
word of the LORD! 36This is what the Sovereign LORD says: Because you poured
out your lust and exposed your naked
body in your promiscuity with your lovers, and because of all your detestable
idols, and because you gave them your
children’s blood,[y] 37therefore I am going
to gather all your lovers, with whom you
found pleasure, those you loved as well
as those you hated. I will gather them

16:14 [z] La 2:15
16:15 [a] ver 25 [b] Isa 57:8; Jer 2:20; Eze 23:3; 27:3
16:16 [c] 2Ki 23:7
16:17 [d] Eze 7:20
16:19 [e] Hos 2:8
16:20 [f] Jer 7:31 [g] Ex 13:2 [h] Ps 106:37-38; Isa 57:5; Eze 23:37
16:21 [i] 2Ki 17:17; Jer 19:5
16:22 [j] Jer 2:2; Hos 11:1 [k] ver 6
16:24 [l] ver 31; Isa 57:7 [m] Ps 78:58; Jer 2:20; 3:2; Eze 20:28
16:25 [n] ver 15; Pr 9:14
16:26 [o] Eze 8:17 [p] Eze 20:8; 23:19-21
16:27 [q] Eze 20:33 [r] 2Ch 28:18
16:28 [s] 2Ki 16:7
16:29 [t] Eze 23:14-17
16:30 [u] Jer 3:3
16:31 [v] ver 24
16:33 [w] Isa 30:6; 57:9 [x] Hos 8:9-10
16:36 [y] Jer 19:5; Eze 23:10

Eze 16:19-50 ❖ How can we avoid the sins of Sodom and instead show humility, compassion, and mercy?

[a] *16* The meaning of the Hebrew for this sentence is uncertain. [b] *29* Or *Chaldea* [c] *30* Or *How feverish is your heart,*

16:15-22 Despite Jerusalem’s God-given advantages, she trusted in her beauty and prostituted her reputation. The beautiful clothes were used to adorn the high places. The gold and silver were used to manufacture the idols themselves; the flour, oil, and honey, which had been given to her for food, were offered instead to her idols. Even her children, those whom she had borne to the Lord, were not safe—they were sacrificed to the idols she had made for herself.

16:23-34 Jerusalem’s behavior descends to ever-deeper depths. Indeed, Jerusalem did not even act like a normal prostitute, for Jerusalem had been so perverse in her lust that she paid everyone to join in her depravity (v. 34).

16:35-43 For Jerusalem, the natural and inevitable consequence of an adulterous lifestyle was an adulteress’s death (v. 38). The normal practice was for adulteresses first to be exposed naked in public (cf. Na 3:5), followed by their stoning by the assembly (v. 40; Dt 22:22).

against you from all around and will strip you in front of them, and they will see you stark naked.[z] 38I will sentence you to the punishment of women who commit adultery and who shed blood;[a] I will bring on you the blood vengeance of my wrath and jealous anger.[b] 39Then I will deliver you into the hands of your lovers, and they will tear down your mounds and destroy your lofty shrines. They will strip you of your clothes and take your fine jewelry and leave you stark naked.[c] 40They will bring a mob against you, who will stone[d] you and hack you to pieces with their swords. 41They will burn down[e] your houses and inflict punishment on you in the sight of many women.[f] I will put a stop[g] to your prostitution, and you will no longer pay your lovers. 42Then my wrath against you will subside and my jealous anger will turn away from you; I will be calm and no longer angry.[h]

43" 'Because you did not remember[i] the days of your youth but enraged me with all these things, I will surely bring down[j] on your head what you have done, declares the Sovereign LORD. Did you not add lewdness to all your other detestable practices?[k]

44" 'Everyone who quotes proverbs will quote this proverb about you: "Like mother, like daughter." 45You are a true daughter of your mother, who despised her husband and her children; and you are a true sister of your sisters, who despised their husbands and their children. Your mother was a Hittite and your father an Amorite.[l] 46Your older sister was Samaria, who lived to the north of you with her daughters; and your younger sister, who lived to the south of you with her daughters, was Sodom.[m] 47You not only followed their ways and copied their detestable practices, but in all your ways you soon became more depraved than they.[n] 48As surely as I live, declares the Sovereign LORD, your sister Sodom and her daughters never did what you and your daughters have done.[o]

49" 'Now this was the sin of your sister Sodom:[p] She and her daughters were arrogant,[q] overfed and unconcerned; they did not help the poor and needy.[r] 50They were haughty and did detestable things before me. Therefore I did away with them as you have seen.[s] 51Samaria did not commit half the sins you did. You have done more detestable things than they, and have made your sisters seem righteous by all these things you have done.[t] 52Bear your disgrace, for you have furnished some justification for your sisters. Because your sins were more vile than theirs, they appear more righteous than you. So then, be ashamed and bear your disgrace, for you have made your sisters appear righteous.

53" 'However, I will restore[u] the fortunes of Sodom and her daughters and of Samaria and her daughters, and your fortunes along with them, 54so that you may bear your disgrace[v] and be ashamed of all you have done in giving them comfort. 55And your sisters, Sodom with her daughters and Samaria with her daughters, will return to what they were before; and you and your daughters will return to what you were before.[w] 56You would not even mention your sister Sodom in the day of your pride, 57before your wickedness was uncovered. Even so, you are now scorned by the daughters of Edom[a][x] and all her neighbors and the daughters of the Philistines—all those around you who despise you. 58You will bear the consequences of your lewdness and your detestable practices, declares the LORD.[y]

59" 'This is what the Sovereign LORD

16:37 [z] Jer 13:22
16:38 [a] Eze 23:45 [b] Lev 20:10; Eze 23:25
16:39 [c] Eze 23:26; Hos 2:3
16:40 [d] Jn 8:5,7
16:41 [e] Dt 13:16 [f] Eze 23:10 [g] Eze 23:27,48
16:42 [h] Isa 54:9; Eze 5:13; 39:29
16:43 [i] Ps 78:42 [j] Eze 22:31 [k] ver 22; Eze 11:21
16:45 [l] Eze 23:2
16:46 [m] Ge 13:10-13; Eze 23:4
16:47 [n] 2Ki 21:9; Eze 5:7
16:48 [o] Mt 10:15; 11:23-24
16:49 [p] Ge 13:13 [q] Ps 138:6 [r] Eze 18:7,12,16; Lk 12:16-20
16:50 [s] Ge 18:20-21; 19:5
16:51 [t] Jer 3:8-11
16:53 [u] Isa 19:24-25
16:54 [v] Jer 2:26; Eze 14:22
16:55 [w] Mal 3:4
16:57 [x] 2Ki 16:6
16:58 [y] Eze 23:49

[a] 57 Many Hebrew manuscripts and Syriac; most Hebrew manuscripts, Septuagint and Vulgate *Aram*

16:44–45 The imagery changes from the husband-wife relationship to mother and daughter. Jerusalem rejected her adoptive "family" and despised her husband and children. She is like her mother, the Hittite, who was married to an Amorite.

16:46–48 Jerusalem is like her natural sisters, Samaria and Sodom. Samaria, the former capital of the northern kingdom of Israel, is described as her older sister. Sodom, the "younger" (v. 46) sister, is physically smaller.

16:51–58 According to Ezekiel, Jerusalem did more detestable things than either Samaria or Sodom, making them seem (comparatively) righteous. This comparison is designed to evoke a sense of shame on Jerusalem's part (v. 52). Just as in her pride Jerusalem once scorned Sodom, Jerusalem's sin has been uncovered, and the surrounding nations now scorn her (v. 57).

16:59–61 Judgment is not God's last word. The Lord will remember the days of Jerusalem's youth and establish an everlasting covenant with her. On the one hand, she will be profoundly aware of having broken the covenant (v. 61). On the other, she can also look back to the days of her youth—the days

says: I will deal with you as you deserve,
because you have despised my oath by
breaking the covenant.[z] 60Yet I will remember the covenant I made with you in
the days of your youth, and I will establish an everlasting covenant[a] with you.
61Then you will remember your ways and
be ashamed[b] when you receive your sisters, both those who are older than you
and those who are younger. I will give
them to you as daughters, but not on the
basis of my covenant with you. 62So I will
establish my covenant with you, and you
will know that I am the LORD.[c] 63Then,
when I make atonement[d] for you for all
you have done, you will remember and
be ashamed and never again open your
mouth[e] because of your humiliation, declares the Sovereign LORD.[f]' "

Two Eagles and a Vine

17 The word of the LORD came to me:
2"Son of man, set forth an allegory
and tell it to the Israelites as a parable.[g]
3Say to them, 'This is what the Sovereign
LORD says: A great eagle[h] with powerful
wings, long feathers and full plumage of
varied colors came to Lebanon.[i] Taking
hold of the top of a cedar, 4he broke off
its topmost shoot and carried it away to
a land of merchants, where he planted
it in a city of traders.
5" 'He took one of the seedlings of the
land and put it in fertile soil. He planted
it like a willow by abundant water,[j] 6and
it sprouted and became a low, spreading
vine. Its branches turned toward him,
but its roots remained under it. So it became a vine and produced branches and
put out leafy boughs.
7" 'But there was another great eagle
with powerful wings and full plumage.
The vine now sent out its roots toward
him from the plot where it was planted
and stretched out its branches to him
for water.[k] 8It had been planted in good
soil by abundant water so that it would
produce branches, bear fruit and become
a splendid vine.'
9"Say to them, 'This is what the Sovereign LORD says: Will it thrive? Will it not
be uprooted and stripped of its fruit so
that it withers? All its new growth will
wither. It will not take a strong arm or
many people to pull it up by the roots.
10It has been planted,[l] but will it thrive?
Will it not wither completely when the
east wind strikes it — wither away in the
plot where it grew?' "
11Then the word of the LORD came to

16:59 [z] Eze 17:19
16:60 [a] Jer 32:40; Eze 37:26
16:61 [b] Eze 20:43
16:62 [c] Jer 24:7; Eze 20:37,43-44; Hos 2:19-20
16:63 [d] Ps 65:3; 79:9 [e] Ro 3:19 [f] Ps 39:9; Da 9:7-8
17:2 [g] Eze 20:49
17:3 [h] Hos 8:1 [i] Jer 22:23
17:5 [j] Dt 8:7-9; Isa 44:4
17:7 [k] Eze 31:4
17:10 [l] Hos 13:15

when she was similarly naked and bare before the Lord. If he chose her once, can he not do so again?

16:62–63 The nations will view Jerusalem as an object lesson of the wideness of God's mercy. On the day when the Lord "makes atonement" (v. 63) for Jerusalem, she will remember God's goodness to her and be ashamed; her tongue will be stilled and her pride humbled once and for all.

16:1–63 How can one explain the obscenity of the cross? What good God could permit such a death? What awful thing could be so bad that only such an atonement could pay for it?

The answer is *sin*. In the cross, we see sin revealed in its starkest, most abominable ugliness. There, if we sweep away for a second the prettification with which we sentimentalize that terrible moment, we see God's "R" rated answer to human sin. There is the "atonement" that God made (v. 63), the ransom that he paid for his people (cf. Mk 10:45). The cost of our salvation was not silver and gold but the precious blood of the Lord Jesus Christ (1Pe 1:18–19).

17:1–15 The political realities depicted in this allegory were obvious to the original audience. So there is a certain irony in Ezekiel saying to his audience: "Do you not know what these things mean?" (v. 12). His hearers could have supplied the interpretation: The first eagle is the king of Babylon, while the cedar sprig is Jehoiachin, whom Nebuchadnezzar carried off to Babylon, along with Ezekiel himself. The "seedlings of your land" (v. 5) is Zedekiah, Jehoiachin's uncle, whom Nebuchadnezzar installed in Jehoiachin's place. The second eagle is Egypt, from whom Zedekiah was seeking aid to break free from the Babylonian yoke.

The meaning of the parable is self-evident: Zedekiah's foreign policy is worse than foolish, it is suicidal. But the allegory is a riddle as well as a parable. It conceals a deeper truth as well as reveals an obvious lesson. For instance, Lebanon is not only the proverbial home of all cedars but also the name of one of Solomon's palaces (cf. 1Ki 7:2; Jer 22:23). So, the discerning reader is invited to consider who planted "the cedar in Lebanon" in the first place. Who established the Davidic dynasty in Jerusalem? Who brought them to the land of Canaan, just as Nebuchadnezzar brought Jehoiachin "to the land of merchants" (17:4)?

Moreover, the cultivated vine is a classic picture of the Lord's provision for Israel (Isa 5:1–7). Likewise, Ezekiel's address to Judah as "this rebellious people" (17:12) describes the history of their relationship with the Lord much better than their history (to date) with Babylon.

Taken together, these hints supply a deeper significance. If Zedekiah's abandoning of his situation in favor of the Egyptian option is a foolish breach of the covenant relationship, what may we say about Israel's abandonment of the Lord?

me: 12"Say to this rebellious people, 'Do
you not know what these things mean?[m]'
Say to them: 'The king of Babylon went
to Jerusalem and carried off her king
and her nobles,[n] bringing them back
with him to Babylon.[o] 13Then he took a
member of the royal family and made
a treaty with him, putting him under
oath.[p] He also carried away the leading
men of the land, 14so that the kingdom
would be brought low,[q] unable to rise
again, surviving only by keeping his treaty. 15But the king rebelled[r] against him by
sending his envoys to Egypt to get horses
and a large army.[s] Will he succeed? Will
he who does such things escape? Will he
break the treaty and yet escape?[t]
16" 'As surely as I live, declares the Sovereign LORD, he shall die[u] in Babylon,
in the land of the king who put him on
the throne, whose oath he despised and
whose treaty he broke.[v] 17Pharaoh[w] with
his mighty army and great horde will be
of no help to him in war, when ramps[x]
are built and siege works erected to destroy many lives.[y] 18He despised the oath
by breaking the covenant. Because he
had given his hand in pledge[z] and yet
did all these things, he shall not escape.
19" 'Therefore this is what the Sovereign LORD says: As surely as I live, I will
repay him for despising my oath and
breaking my covenant.[a] 20I will spread
my net[b] for him, and he will be caught
in my snare. I will bring him to Babylon
and execute judgment[c] on him there because he was unfaithful to me. 21All his
choice troops will fall by the sword,[d] and
the survivors[e] will be scattered to the
winds.[f] Then you will know that I the
LORD have spoken.
22" 'This is what the Sovereign LORD
says: I myself will take a shoot from the
very top of a cedar and plant it; I will break
off a tender sprig from its topmost shoots
and plant it on a high and lofty mountain.[g] 23On the mountain heights of Israel
I will plant it; it will produce branches and
bear fruit and become a splendid cedar.
Birds of every kind will nest in it; they will
find shelter in the shade of its branches.[h]
24All the trees of the forest[i] will know that
I the LORD bring down the tall tree and
make the low tree grow tall. I dry up the
green tree and make the dry tree flourish.
" 'I the LORD have spoken, and I will
do it.[j]' "

17:12 [m] Eze 12:9 [n] 2Ki 24:15 [o] Eze 24:19
17:13 [p] 2Ch 36:13
17:14 [q] Eze 29:14
17:15 [r] Jer 52:3 [s] Dt 17:16 [t] Jer 34:3; 38:18
17:16 [u] Jer 52:11; Eze 12:13 [v] 2Ki 24:17
17:17 [w] Jer 37:7 [x] Eze 4:2 [y] Isa 36:6; Jer 37:5; Eze 29:6-7
17:18 [z] 1Ch 29:24
17:19 [a] Eze 16:59
17:20 [b] Eze 12:13; 32:3 [c] Jer 2:35; Eze 20:36
17:21 [d] Eze 12:14 [e] 2Ki 25:11 [f] 2Ki 25:5
17:22 [g] Jer 23:5; Eze 20:40; 36:1, 36; 37:22
17:23 [h] Ps 92:12; Isa 2:2; Eze 31:6; Da 4:12; Hos 14:5-7; Mt 13:32
17:24 [i] Ps 96:12 [j] Eze 19:12; 21:26; 22:14; Am 9:11
18:2 [k] Isa 3:15; Jer 31:29; La 5:7
18:4 [l] ver 20; Isa 42:5; Ro 6:23

Eze 17:22-24 ❖ How has God provided us with a place of safety and rest?

Eze 18:3-18 ❖ What behaviors should you copy from your parents? What behaviors from them do you not want to carry on? Why?

The One Who Sins Will Die

18 The word of the LORD came to
me: 2"What do you people mean
by quoting this proverb about the land
of Israel:

" 'The parents eat sour grapes,
and the children's teeth are set on
edge'?[k]

3"As surely as I live, declares the Sovereign LORD, you will no longer quote this
proverb in Israel. 4For everyone belongs
to me, the parent as well as the child—
both alike belong to me. The one who
sins is the one who will die.[l]

5"Suppose there is a righteous man
who does what is just and right.

17:16-21 Thus, at just the moment when it seems that Ezekiel has unpacked the meaning of the fable, he launches into its *real* meaning with the word "therefore" (v. 19). The political leadership has despised and broken the Lord's covenant. The coming judgment is the judgment of God on a rebellious house.

17:22-24 At the same time, the latter part of this chapter reworks the fable in more positive terms. The Lord will take a new shoot from the cedar and plant it on a high and lofty mountain. It will grow into a lofty tree, providing shelter for birds of all kinds. All the trees of the field (the nations) will understand the Lord's sovereignty in history, seeing that the rise and fall of empires is entirely his doing. Against all logic, the Lord will reverse the failures of the past.

✤ **17:1-24** On a societal level, we think the problem with our world is essentially political. We should work for political change, and we should plan for the future. Yet we can be so busy doing the good things that we miss out on the one insight that is truly necessary—the best thing: maintaining our personal and corporate spiritual life with God.

18:1-4 The Lord's response to the people's proverb is a categorical denial of its applicability: Everyone belongs to him. There is no unfair punishment to the next generation for the sins of the fathers. Some may be tempted to question God's goodness, but Ezekiel affirms that God's ways are just.

18:5-9 The first part of this debate is a case study covering three successive generations. The first

6 He does not eat at the mountain[m] shrines
or look to the idols[n] of Israel.
He does not defile his neighbor's wife
or have sexual relations with a woman during her period.
7 He does not oppress[o] anyone,
but returns what he took in pledge[p] for a loan.
He does not commit robbery
but gives his food to the hungry
and provides clothing for the naked.[q]
8 He does not lend to them at interest
or take a profit from them.[r]
He withholds his hand from doing wrong
and judges fairly[s] between two parties.
9 He follows my decrees
and faithfully keeps my laws.
That man is righteous;[t]
he will surely live,[u]
declares the Sovereign LORD.

10 "Suppose he has a violent son, who
sheds blood[v] or does any of these other
things[a] 11 (though the father has done
none of them):

"He eats at the mountain shrines.
He defiles his neighbor's wife.
12 He oppresses the poor[w] and needy.
He commits robbery.
He does not return what he took in pledge.
He looks to the idols.
He does detestable things.[x]
13 He lends at interest and takes a profit.[y]

Will such a man live? He will not! Because he has done all these detestable things, he is to be put to death; his blood will be on his own head.[z]

18:6 [m] Eze 22:9 [n] Dt 4:19; Eze 6:13; 20:24 18:7 [o] Ex 22:21 [p] Ex 22:26; Dt 24:12 [q] Dt 15:11; Mt 25:36 18:8 [r] Ex 22:25; Lev 25:35-37; Dt 23:19-20 [s] Zec 8:16 18:9 [t] Hab 2:4 [u] Lev 18:5; Eze 20:11; Am 5:4 18:10 [v] Ex 21:12 18:12 [w] Am 4:1 [x] 2Ki 21:11; Isa 59:6-7; Jer 22:17; Eze 8:6,17 18:13 [y] Ex 22:25 [z] Eze 33:4-5
18:14 [a] 2Ch 34:21; Pr 23:24 18:16 [b] Ps 41:1; Isa 58:10 18:19 [c] Ex 20:5; Dt 5:9; Jer 15:4; Zec 1:3-6 18:20 [d] Dt 24:16; 1Ki 8:32; 2Ki 14:6; Isa 3:11; Mt 16:27; Ro 2:9

14 "But suppose this son has a son who
sees all the sins his father commits, and
though he sees them, he does not do
such things:[a]

15 "He does not eat at the mountain shrines
or look to the idols of Israel.
He does not defile his neighbor's wife.
16 He does not oppress anyone
or require a pledge for a loan.
He does not commit robbery
but gives his food to the hungry
and provides clothing for the naked.[b]
17 He withholds his hand from mistreating the poor
and takes no interest or profit from them.
He keeps my laws and follows my decrees.

He will not die for his father's sin; he
will surely live. 18 But his father will die
for his own sin, because he practiced extortion, robbed his brother and did what
was wrong among his people.
19 "Yet you ask, 'Why does the son not
share the guilt of his father?' Since the
son has done what is just and right and
has been careful to keep all my decrees,
he will surely live.[c] 20 The one who sins
is the one who will die. The child will not
share the guilt of the parent, nor will the
parent share the guilt of the child. The
righteousness of the righteous will be
credited to them, and the wickedness
of the wicked will be charged against
them.[d]
21 "But if a wicked person turns away
from all the sins they have committed
and keeps all my decrees and does what
is just and right, that person will surely

[a] 10 Or *things to a brother*

---

man mentioned is orthodox in his religious practice (see 6:3–7). This person "follows my decrees and faithfully keeps my laws" (v. 9a). What is the verdict on such a person? "That man is righteous; he will surely live" (v. 9b).

18:10–13 On the other hand, suppose this man's son is the antithesis of all his father stands for. "Will such a man live? He will not!" (v. 13). He will die, and his death will be no one's fault but his own.

18:14–18 But suppose this second man also has a son who swims against the tide. He sees what his father does and deliberately follows a different and better course. According to Ezekiel, "he will surely live" (v. 17).

18:19–20 No one can dispute the justice of Ezekiel's assertion. If this generation is experiencing the "death" of exile and if God deals justly with each generation, then they must also be guilty before God.

18:21–29 Since their death sentence is decreed, shouldn't they simply eat, drink, and try to be merry in the time that remains to them? Ezekiel addresses that question by proposing another pair of case studies. The first concerns a wicked person who turns from his sins and does what is right (v. 21). Grace is possible for the one who repents (vv. 22–23). By contrast, the righteous person who "repents" of righteousness and abandons God will not escape judgment.

live; they will not die.[e] 22None of the offenses they have committed will be remembered against them. Because of the
righteous things they have done, they
will live.[f] 23Do I take any pleasure in the
death of the wicked? declares the Sovereign LORD. Rather, am I not pleased[g]
when they turn from their ways and live?[h]
24"But if a righteous person turns
from their righteousness and commits
sin and does the same detestable things
the wicked person does, will they live?
None of the righteous things that person
has done will be remembered. Because
of the unfaithfulness they are guilty of
and because of the sins they have committed, they will die.[i]
25"Yet you say, 'The way of the Lord is
not just.' Hear, you Israelites: Is my way
unjust?[j] Is it not your ways that are unjust? 26If a righteous person turns from
their righteousness and commits sin,
they will die for it; because of the sin
they have committed they will die. 27But
if a wicked person turns away from the
wickedness they have committed and
does what is just and right, they will save
their life.[k] 28Because they consider all the
offenses they have committed and turn
away from them, that person will surely
live; they will not die. 29Yet the Israelites
say, 'The way of the Lord is not just.' Are
my ways unjust, people of Israel? Is it
not your ways that are unjust?
30"Therefore, you Israelites, I will
judge each of you according to your own
ways, declares the Sovereign LORD. Repent![l] Turn away from all your offenses;
then sin will not be your downfall.[m] 31Rid
yourselves of all the offenses you have
committed, and get a new heart[n] and a
new spirit. Why will you die, people of
Israel?[o] 32For I take no pleasure in the
death of anyone, declares the Sovereign
LORD. Repent and live![p]

18:21 [e] Eze 33:12,19
18:22 [f] Ps 18:20-24; Isa 43:25; Mic 7:19
18:23 [g] Ps 147:11 [h] Eze 33:11; 1Ti 2:4
18:24 [i] 1Sa 15:11; 2Ch 24:17-20; Eze 3:20; 20:27; 2Pe 2:20-22
18:25 [j] Ge 18:25; Jer 12:1; Eze 33:17; Zep 3:5; Mal 2:17; 3:13-15
18:27 [k] Isa 1:18
18:30 [l] Mt 3:2 [m] Eze 7:3; 33:20; Hos 12:6
18:31 [n] Ps 51:10 [o] Isa 1:16-17; Eze 11:19; 36:26
18:32 [p] Eze 33:11

Eze 19:1,14 ❖ What lament can we raise regarding wayward leaders of the church?

A Lament Over Israel's Princes

19 "Take up a lament[q] concerning the
princes[r] of Israel 2and say:

"'What a lioness was your mother
among the lions!
She lay down among them
and reared her cubs.
3She brought up one of her cubs,
and he became a strong lion.
He learned to tear the prey
and he became a man-eater.
4The nations heard about him,
and he was trapped in their pit.
They led him with hooks
to the land of Egypt.[s]

5"'When she saw her hope
unfulfilled,
her expectation gone,
she took another of her cubs
and made him a strong lion.[t]
6He prowled among the lions,
for he was now a strong lion.
He learned to tear the prey
and he became a man-eater.[u]
7He broke down[a] their strongholds
and devastated[v] their towns.
The land and all who were in it
were terrified by his roaring.
8Then the nations[w] came against
him,
those from regions round about.
They spread their net for him,
and he was trapped in their pit.[x]
9With hooks they pulled him into a
cage
and brought him to the king of
Babylon.[y]

19:1 [q] Eze 26:17; 27:2,32 [r] 2Ki 24:6
19:4 [s] 2Ki 23:33-34; 2Ch 36:4
19:5 [t] 2Ki 23:34
19:6 [u] 2Ki 24:9; 2Ch 36:9
19:7 [v] Eze 30:12
19:8 [w] 2Ki 24:2 [x] 2Ki 24:11
19:9 [y] 2Ch 36:6

[a] 7 Targum (see Septuagint); Hebrew *He knew*

18:30–32 The essential point the prophet is making is introduced by the word "therefore" (v. 30). Judgment is coming, but even now it is not too late.

✤ **18:1–32** Ezekiel's passion to convey the message of life for everyone who will repent fits the cost paid by Jesus to make it possible. The only appropriate response to the cross is to plead and exhort and pour out our lives to communicate the gospel of Jesus Christ. Like Ezekiel, we must confront men and women here and now with their desperate need to turn from their sins and to receive forgiveness and new life through Christ, and thus live forever with God and his people.

19:1–14 Ezekiel's lament is made up of two distinct images: a lioness and her cubs, and a vine and its branches. Both were familiar images for the royal tribe of Judah.

19:2–9 The first image is of a mother lioness who produces a number of cubs. Out of them, she chooses one to be the leader of the pack. He behaves in lionlike fashion, tearing the prey and even consuming people. The point is that the current rulers of Judah are simply the latest

They put him in prison,
so his roar was heard no longer
on the mountains of Israel.[z]

10 "'Your mother was like a vine in
your vineyard[a]
planted by the water;
it was fruitful and full of branches
because of abundant water.[a]
11 Its branches were strong,
fit for a ruler's scepter.
It towered high
above the thick foliage,
conspicuous for its height
and for its many branches.[b]
12 But it was uprooted[c] in fury
and thrown to the ground.
The east wind made it shrivel,
it was stripped of its fruit;
its strong branches withered
and fire consumed them.[d]
13 Now it is planted in the desert,[e]
in a dry and thirsty land.[f]
14 Fire spread from one of its main[b]
branches
and consumed[g] its fruit.
No strong branch is left on it
fit for a ruler's scepter.'[h]

"This is a lament and is to be used as a
lament."

Rebellious Israel Purged

20 In the seventh year, in the fifth
month on the tenth day, some of
the elders of Israel came to inquire of the
LORD, and they sat down in front of me.[i]
2 Then the word of the LORD came to
me: 3 "Son of man, speak to the elders of
Israel and say to them, 'This is what the
Sovereign LORD says: Have you come to
inquire[j] of me? As surely as I live, I will
not let you inquire of me, declares the
Sovereign LORD.[k]'
4 "Will you judge them? Will you judge
them, son of man? Then confront them
with the detestable practices of their ancestors[l] 5 and say to them: 'This is what
the Sovereign LORD says: On the day I
chose[m] Israel, I swore with uplifted hand
to the descendants of Jacob and revealed
myself to them in Egypt. With uplifted
hand I said to them, "I am the LORD your
God.[n]" 6 On that day I swore to them that
I would bring them out of Egypt into
a land I had searched out for them, a
land flowing with milk and honey,[o] the
most beautiful of all lands.[p] 7 And I said
to them, "Each of you, get rid of the vile
images[q] you have set your eyes on, and
do not defile yourselves with the idols of
Egypt. I am the LORD your God.[r]"
8 "'But they rebelled against me and
would not listen to me; they did not
get rid of the vile images they had set
their eyes on, nor did they forsake the
idols of Egypt.[s] So I said I would pour
out my wrath on them and spend my
anger against them in Egypt.[t] 9 But for
the sake of my name, I brought them
out of Egypt.[u] I did it to keep my name
from being profaned in the eyes of the
nations among whom they lived and in
whose sight I had revealed myself to the
Israelites. 10 Therefore I led them out of
Egypt and brought them into the wilderness.[v] 11 I gave them my decrees and
made known to them my laws, by which
the person who obeys them will live.[w]
12 Also I gave them my Sabbaths as a sign[x]

19:9 [z] 2Ki 24:15
19:10 [a] Ps 80:8-11
19:11 [b] Eze 31:3; Da 4:11
19:12 [c] Eze 17:10 [d] Isa 27:11; Eze 28:17; Hos 13:15
19:13 [e] Eze 20:35 [f] Hos 2:3
19:14 [g] Eze 20:47 [h] Eze 15:4
20:1 [i] Eze 8:1
20:3 [j] Eze 14:3 [k] Mic 3:7
20:4 [l] Eze 16:2; 22:2; Mt 23:32
20:5 [m] Dt 7:6 [n] Ex 6:7
20:6 [o] Ex 3:8; Jer 32:22 [p] Dt 8:7; Ps 48:2; Da 8:9
20:7 [q] Ex 20:4 [r] Ex 20:2; Lev 18:3; Dt 29:18
20:8 [s] Eze 7:8 [t] Isa 63:10
20:9 [u] Eze 36:22; 39:7
20:10 [v] Ex 13:18
20:11 [w] Lev 18:5; Dt 4:7-8; Ro 10:5
20:12 [x] Ex 31:13

[a] *10* Two Hebrew manuscripts; most Hebrew manuscripts *your blood* [b] *14* Or *from under its*

---

outcroppings of the rock of oppression and pride from which they were cut.

19:10–14 In the second image, a vine is planted in a vineyard beside abundant waters. The perfect conditions. The vine is Judah, planted by the Lord in perfect conditions which led to abundant growth. She produces many offspring capable of ruling, but pride is her downfall.

✣ **19:1–14** We make New Year's resolutions and plans to quit this bad habit, abandon that sin, start to do this good thing, and generally overhaul our lives. We think, "Next year, I'll be a little better than I was this year." Ezekiel's lament tells us that New Year's resolutions aren't enough, just as a new Davidic king wouldn't be enough. God will have to do something far more radical to save us. The Good News is that in Jesus Christ, God has done precisely such a radical new work.

20:1–3 The elders have assembled before Ezekiel in order to "inquire of the LORD" (v. 1). But seeking the Lord requires exclusive devotion. This is precisely where the elders fail the test.

20:4–23 Ezekiel chooses three generations: those who lived in Egypt at the time of the exodus (vv. 5–10), the desert generation (vv. 11–15), and their children (vv. 18–23). Each generation's history is presented as a six-stage cycle.

To each comes the gracious self-announcement "I the LORD" (vv. 12, 20; cf. v. 5). The basis for this self-revelation is a covenant oath sworn by God to bring the people to the promised land. But this decisive act required that Israel respond to God's covenant by being exclusively devoted to him.

between us, so they would know that I
the LORD made them holy.
13"'Yet the people of Israel rebelled[y]
against me in the wilderness. They did
not follow my decrees but rejected my
laws—by which the person who obeys
them will live—and they utterly desecrated my Sabbaths. So I said I would
pour out my wrath[z] on them and destroy
them in the wilderness.[a] 14But for the
sake of my name I did what would keep
it from being profaned in the eyes of the
nations in whose sight I had brought
them out.[b] 15Also with uplifted hand I
swore to them in the wilderness that I
would not bring them into the land I
had given them—a land flowing with
milk and honey, the most beautiful of
all lands[c]— 16because they rejected
my laws and did not follow my decrees
and desecrated my Sabbaths. For their
hearts[d] were devoted to their idols.[e] 17Yet
I looked on them with pity and did not
destroy them or put an end to them in
the wilderness. 18I said to their children
in the wilderness, "Do not follow the statutes of your parents[f] or keep their laws or
defile yourselves with their idols. 19I am
the LORD your God;[g] follow my decrees
and be careful to keep my laws.[h] 20Keep
my Sabbaths holy, that they may be a
sign between us. Then you will know
that I am the LORD your God.[i]"
21"'But the children rebelled against
me: They did not follow my decrees,
they were not careful to keep my laws,
of which I said, "The person who obeys
them will live by them," and they desecrated my Sabbaths. So I said I would
pour out my wrath on them and spend
my anger against them in the wilderness.
22But I withheld[j] my hand, and for the
sake of my name I did what would keep
it from being profaned in the eyes of the
nations in whose sight I had brought
them out. 23Also with uplifted hand I
swore to them in the wilderness that I
would disperse them among the nations
and scatter[k] them through the countries,
24because they had not obeyed my laws
but had rejected my decrees and desecrated my Sabbaths,[l] and their eyes
lusted after[m] their parents' idols.[n] 25So
I gave[o] them other statutes that were
not good and laws through which they
could not live;[p] 26I defiled them through
their gifts—the sacrifice of every firstborn—that I might fill them with horror
so they would know that I am the LORD.[q]'
27"Therefore, son of man, speak to the
people of Israel and say to them, 'This is
what the Sovereign LORD says: In this also
your ancestors blasphemed[r] me by being
unfaithful to me:[s] 28When I brought them
into the land[t] I had sworn to give them
and they saw any high hill or any leafy
tree, there they offered their sacrifices,
made offerings that aroused my anger,
presented their fragrant incense and
poured out their drink offerings.[u] 29Then
I said to them: What is this high place you
go to?'" (It is called Bamah[a] to this day.)

Rebellious Israel Renewed

30"Therefore say to the Israelites: 'This
is what the Sovereign LORD says: Will you
defile yourselves[v] the way your ancestors did and lust after their vile images?[w]
31When you offer your gifts—the sacrifice of your children[x] in the fire—you
continue to defile yourselves with all
your idols to this day. Am I to let you
inquire of me, you Israelites? As surely
as I live, declares the Sovereign LORD, I
will not let you inquire of me.[y]
32"'You say, "We want to be like the
nations, like the peoples of the world,

[a] 29 *Bamah* means *high place.*

20:13 [y] Ps 78:40 [z] Dt 9:8 [a] Nu 14:29; Ps 95:8-10; Isa 56:6
20:14 [b] Eze 36:23
20:15 [c] Ps 95:11; 106:26
20:16 [d] Nu 15:39 [e] Am 5:26
20:18 [f] Zec 1:4
20:19 [g] Ex 20:2 [h] Dt 5:32-33; 6:1-2; 8:1; 11:1; 12:1
20:20 [i] Jer 17:22
20:22 [j] Ps 78:38
20:23 [k] Lev 26:33; Dt 28:64
20:24 [l] ver 13 [m] Eze 6:9 [n] ver 16
20:25 [o] Ps 81:12 [p] 2Th 2:11
20:26 [q] 2Ki 17:17
20:27 [r] Ro 2:24 [s] Eze 18:24
20:28 [t] Ps 78:55,58 [u] Eze 6:13
20:30 [v] ver 43 [w] Jer 16:12
20:31 [x] Eze 16:20 [y] Ps 106:37-39; Jer 7:31

20:24–26 Israel's consistent response to this gracious self-revelation was rebellion. Three times the Lord threatened to destroy them. Yet each time he held back his hand (cf. Nu 14:15–16). Nonetheless, in each case, limited judgment does fall.

20:27–31 To this threefold cycle of gracious election, rebellion, and limited judgment, a conclusion is added. Israel's present is exactly the same as Israel's past: poisoned with vile images, child sacrifice, and idolatry (v. 31). Such people need not expect any reply to their attempts to inquire of the Lord.

20:32–38 But what should they expect from the Lord? The answer is given in this passage. God will establish a purified people to worship him (vv. 40–41). He will do this through a new exodus, not because of any merit on Israel's part but for the sake of his own name (v. 44).

God's people cannot be destroyed completely, not because they do not deserve it but because God has staked his reputation on the covenant promises made to them. His divine nature requires faithfulness to his promise.

Therefore, there must necessarily be a new act of salvation on God's part, a new exodus. Israel cannot be abandoned (v. 32). Whether that thought is one of desire or of despair is not really the issue; rather, the focus is on the impossibility of such a thing happening (cf. 36:22–23).

who serve wood and stone." But what
you have in mind will never happen.
33 As surely as I live, declares the Sovereign LORD, I will reign over you with a
mighty hand and an outstretched arm
and with outpoured wrath.[z] 34 I will bring
you from the nations[a] and gather you
from the countries where you have been
scattered—with a mighty hand and an
outstretched arm and with outpoured
wrath.[b] 35 I will bring you into the wilderness of the nations and there, face
to face, I will execute judgment[c] upon
you. 36 As I judged your ancestors in the
wilderness of the land of Egypt, so I will
judge you, declares the Sovereign LORD.[d]
37 I will take note of you as you pass under my rod,[e] and I will bring you into the
bond of the covenant.[f] 38 I will purge[g] you
of those who revolt and rebel against
me. Although I will bring them out of
the land where they are living, yet they
will not enter the land of Israel. Then you
will know that I am the LORD.[h]
39 " 'As for you, people of Israel, this is
what the Sovereign LORD says: Go and
serve your idols,[i] every one of you! But
afterward you will surely listen to me
and no longer profane my holy name
with your gifts and idols.[j] 40 For on my
holy mountain, the high mountain of
Israel, declares the Sovereign LORD, there
in the land all the people of Israel will
serve me, and there I will accept them.

20:33 [z] Jer 21:5
20:34 [a] 2Co 6:17* [b] Isa 27:12-13; Jer 44:6; La 2:4
20:35 [c] Jer 2:35
20:36 [d] Nu 11:1-35; 1Co 10:5-10
20:37 [e] Lev 27:32; Jer 33:13 [f] Eze 16:62
20:38 [g] Eze 34:17-22; Am 9:9-10 [h] Ps 95:11; Jer 44:14; Eze 13:9; Mal 3:3; Heb 4:3
20:39 [i] Jer 44:25 [j] Isa 1:13; Eze 43:7; Am 4:4
20:40 [k] Isa 60:7 [l] Isa 56:7; Mal 3:4
20:41 [m] Eze 28:25; 36:23 [n] Eze 11:17
20:42 [o] Eze 38:23 [p] Eze 34:13; 36:24
20:43 [q] Eze 6:9; 16:61; Hos 5:15
20:44 [r] Eze 36:22 [s] Eze 24:24
20:46 [t] Eze 21:2; Am 7:16

Eze 20:41 ❖ How can our lives be like fragrant incense to God? How can we show God's holiness to the watching world?

There I will require your offerings[k] and
your choice gifts,[a] along with all your
holy sacrifices.[l] 41 I will accept you as
fragrant incense when I bring you out
from the nations and gather you from
the countries where you have been scattered, and I will be proved holy[m] through
you in the sight of the nations.[n] 42 Then
you will know that I am the LORD,[o] when
I bring you into the land of Israel,[p] the
land I had sworn with uplifted hand to
give to your ancestors. 43 There you will
remember your conduct and all the actions by which you have defiled yourselves, and you will loathe yourselves
for all the evil you have done.[q] 44 You
will know that I am the LORD, when I
deal with you for my name's sake[r] and
not according to your evil ways and your
corrupt practices, you people of Israel,
declares the Sovereign LORD.[s]' "

Prophecy Against the South

45 The word of the LORD came to me:
46 "Son of man, set your face toward
the south; preach against the south
and prophesy against[t] the forest of the

[a] 40 Or *and the gifts of your firstfruits*

Divine election cannot be revoked; the Lord will reign over the people (v. 33). But the message of God's kingship is not necessarily good news. Just as the unfaithful Israelites were brought up out of Egypt only to die in the desert, so too the regathered Israel will be purged in the "wilderness of the nations." There God will meet with his people "face to face," just as he met with Moses "face to face" in the tent of meeting (v. 35; Ex 33:11).

But this face-to-face meeting will be a meeting of personal judgment. God will single out the transgressors from the faithful just as a shepherd counts and separates his sheep by passing them one by one under his rod (v. 37).

20:39–44 The application to the present generation comes here. The choice is theirs to make. They may go and serve their idols if they wish, but they must remember this: God's purpose in the election of Israel will stand (v. 40).

The new exodus will bring pure worship offered by a purified people, displaying the holy Lord to the nations. There the oath made in Egypt (v. 5) will be fulfilled (v. 42). The remnant who survived judgment will realize the immensity of their own sin and appreciate the faithfulness of God to his covenant promises (v. 44).

✣ **20:1–44** Rebellion is never simply against an abstract conception of God, but against the personal God of grace. Satan always seeks to persuade us, as he did our first parents, that God is a harsh taskmaster who will exploit us and abuse us if we allow him, and that he seeks to deny us things that are good (Ge 3:1). The reality is exactly the opposite, for them and for us.

God had made a perfect world for Adam and Eve to live in and placed them in the most perfect spot within it, a paradise. Their area of personal freedom was large; the restriction minuscule. Yet after being deceived into reading that minuscule restriction as bondage, they gave in to temptation, only to discover too late what true bondage was.

20:45–49 Ezekiel is commanded to face toward the south of Israel and preach against it; fire is coming on the southern forest, which will consume every tree, "both green and dry" (v. 47). This fire will be recognized as the work of the Lord and will not be extinguished. But the people's response to this message is apparently total lack of comprehension (v. 49).

southland.[u] 47Say to the southern forest:
'Hear the word of the LORD. This is what
the Sovereign LORD says: I am about to set
fire to you, and it will consume all your
trees, both green and dry. The blazing
flame will not be quenched, and every
face from south to north will be scorched
by it.[v] 48Everyone will see that I the LORD
have kindled it; it will not be quenched.[w]' "
49Then I said, "Sovereign LORD, they
are saying of me, 'Isn't he just telling
parables?[x]' "[a]

Babylon as God's Sword of Judgment

21 [b] The word of the LORD came to me:
2"Son of man, set your face against
Jerusalem and preach against the sanctuary. Prophesy against[y] the land of Israel 3and say to her: 'This is what the LORD
says: I am against you.[z] I will draw my
sword from its sheath and cut off from
you both the righteous and the wicked.[a]
4Because I am going to cut off the righteous and the wicked, my sword will be
unsheathed against everyone from south
to north.[b] 5Then all people will know that
I the LORD have drawn my sword from its
sheath; it will not return[c] again.'[d]
6"Therefore groan, son of man! Groan
before them with broken heart and bitter
grief.[e] 7And when they ask you, 'Why are
you groaning?' you shall say, 'Because of
the news that is coming. Every heart will
melt with fear and every hand go limp;[f]
every spirit will become faint and every
leg will be wet with urine.' It is coming!
It will surely take place, declares the Sovereign LORD."
8The word of the LORD came to me:
9"Son of man, prophesy and say, 'This
is what the Lord says:

" 'A sword, a sword,
sharpened and polished —
10sharpened for the slaughter,[g]
polished to flash like lightning!

" 'Shall we rejoice in the scepter of my
royal son? The sword despises every such
stick.

20:46 [u]Isa 30:6; Jer 13:19
20:47 [v]Isa 9:18-19; 13:8; Jer 21:14
20:48 [w]Jer 7:20
20:49 [x]Mt 13:13; Jn 16:25
21:2 [y]Eze 20:46
21:3 [z]Jer 21:13 [a]ver 9-11; Job 9:22
21:4 [b]Eze 20:47
21:5 [c]ver 30 [d]Na 1:9
21:6 [e]Isa 22:4
21:7 [f]Eze 22:14; 7:17
21:10 [g]Ps 110:5-6; Isa 34:5-6
21:11 [h]Jer 46:4
21:12 [i]Jer 31:19
21:14 [j]Nu 24:10 [k]Eze 6:11; 30:24
21:15 [l]2Sa 17:10 [m]Ps 22:14
21:17 [n]ver 14; Eze 22:13 [o]Eze 5:13

11" 'The sword is appointed to be
polished,[h]
to be grasped with the hand;
it is sharpened and polished,
made ready for the hand of the
slayer.
12Cry out and wail, son of man,
for it is against my people;
it is against all the princes of
Israel.
They are thrown to the sword
along with my people.
Therefore beat your breast.[i]

13" 'Testing will surely come. And what
if even the scepter, which the sword despises, does not continue? declares the
Sovereign LORD.'

14"So then, son of man, prophesy
and strike your hands[j] together.
Let the sword strike twice,
even three times.
It is a sword for slaughter —
a sword for great slaughter,
closing in on them from every
side.[k]
15So that hearts may melt with fear[l]
and the fallen be many,
I have stationed the sword for
slaughter[c]
at all their gates.
Look! It is forged to strike like
lightning,
it is grasped for slaughter.[m]
16Slash to the right, you sword,
then to the left,
wherever your blade is turned.
17I too will strike my hands[n] together,
and my wrath[o] will subside.
I the LORD have spoken."

18The word of the LORD came to me:
19"Son of man, mark out two roads for
the sword of the king of Babylon to take,
both starting from the same country.

[a] *49* In Hebrew texts 20:45-49 is numbered 21:1-5.
[b] In Hebrew texts 21:1-32 is numbered 21:6-37.
[c] *15* Septuagint; the meaning of the Hebrew for this word is uncertain.

21:1–5 Israel is the southland. The image of fire is linked with the sword of the Lord, which is coming to cut off both righteous (the green tree) and wicked (the dry tree), from the south to the north of the land. The sword has been drawn from its scabbard and will not return there.
21:6–17 The twin judgment images of cutting and burning are maintained in the twin actions of sharpening and burnishing (v. 10). These actions prepare the weapon for action. Israel will be surrounded, hemmed in on all sides, with no place to run or hide (vv. 14–16).
21:18–23 Here we are introduced to the sword of the king of Babylon. The prophet is instructed to perform a sign-act, marking out a three-way road junction with a signpost. Ezekiel is to act out the

Make a signpost where the road branches
off to the city. 20Mark out one road for
the sword to come against Rabbah of the
Ammonites[p] and another against Judah
and fortified Jerusalem. 21For the king of
Babylon will stop at the fork in the road,
at the junction of the two roads, to seek
an omen: He will cast lots[q] with arrows,
he will consult his idols, he will examine
the liver.[r] 22Into his right hand will come
the lot for Jerusalem, where he is to set
up battering rams, to give the command
to slaughter, to sound the battle cry, to
set battering rams against the gates, to
build a ramp and to erect siege works.[s]
23It will seem like a false omen to those
who have sworn allegiance to him, but
he will remind[t] them of their guilt and
take them captive.

24"Therefore this is what the Sovereign LORD says: 'Because you people have
brought to mind your guilt by your open
rebellion, revealing your sins in all that
you do—because you have done this,
you will be taken captive.

25" 'You profane and wicked prince of
Israel, whose day has come, whose time
of punishment has reached its climax,[u]
26this is what the Sovereign LORD says:
Take off the turban, remove the crown.[v]
It will not be as it was: The lowly will be
exalted and the exalted will be brought
low.[w] 27A ruin! A ruin! I will make it a
ruin! The crown will not be restored until he to whom it rightfully belongs shall
come; to him I will give it.'[x]

28"And you, son of man, prophesy and
say, 'This is what the Sovereign LORD says
about the Ammonites[y] and their insults:

" 'A sword,[z] a sword,
drawn for the slaughter,
polished to consume
and to flash like lightning!
29Despite false visions concerning you
and lying divinations about you,
it will be laid on the necks
of the wicked who are to be slain,
whose day has come,
whose time of punishment has
reached its climax.[a]

30" 'Let the sword return to its sheath.[b]
In the place where you were
created,
in the land of your ancestry,[c]
I will judge you.
31I will pour out my wrath on you
and breathe out my fiery anger[d]
against you;
I will deliver you into the hands of
brutal men,
men skilled in destruction.[e]
32You will be fuel for the fire,[f]

21:20 [p] Dt 3:11; Jer 49:2; Am 1:14
21:21 [q] Pr 16:33 [r] Nu 22:7; 23:23
21:22 [s] Eze 4:2; 26:9
21:23 [t] Nu 5:15
21:25 [u] Eze 35:5
21:26 [v] Jer 13:18 [w] Ps 75:7; Eze 17:24
21:27 [x] Ps 2:6; Jer 23:5-6; Eze 37:24; Hag 2:21-22
21:28 [y] Zep 2:8 [z] Jer 12:12
21:29 [a] ver 25; Eze 22:28; 35:5
21:30 [b] Jer 47:6 [c] Eze 16:3
21:31 [d] Eze 22:20-21 [e] Jer 51:20-23
21:32 [f] Mal 4:1

Eze 21:25-27 ❖ Where have we seen God exalt the lowly? Why does God do this?

---

forces of the king of Babylon coming to this parting of the ways and deciding which route to follow.

Ezekiel pictures the king using all the pagan means of decision making (v. 21). Ironically, the "lying divinations" that had found such favor with God's people (13:7) now become the very means through which judgment comes on them (21:23).

21:24-32 By introducing Zedekiah by title rather than by name, Ezekiel puts the focus of the judgment on the office, not the person. Zedekiah will be stripped of the insignia of royalty, the turban and the crown (v. 26). In him, the old order of things has reached a conclusion. A divine reordering of society is called for, in which the Lord will exalt the lowly and bring down the exalted (cf. 17:24).

Ezekiel has reshaped the traditional messianic oracle of Ge 49:10 into a threatening oracle of judgment. Now the scepter will not depart from Judah until the coming of the judge—Nebuchadnezzar. Heathen Nebuchadnezzar may be God's chosen instrument of judgment in Eze 21, yet the dominant reality in both cases is the plan and purpose of God.

The (pagan) oracle that directed Nebuchadnezzar toward Jerusalem is a stay of execution for Ammon. They too will feel the cutting edge of the sword of God's judgment (cf. v. 29 with v. 25).

20:45—21:32 The destruction of Jerusalem in 586 BC was terribly comprehensive when God handed over judgment to the sword of Babylon. However, it was merely a sideshow when compared to the comprehensive judgment of the world that awaits the coming of the One to whom judgment belongs. God's wrath is aroused at the rebellious thoughts, deeds, and words of those whom he has created. When the Judge of all the earth comes to settle final accounts, the sword will fall on unrepentant sinners to their eternal doom.

The doctrine of eternal torment in hell is not popular these days. In the modern world, it is rarely the topic of sermons. Far more often it is the subject of attempts to present the biblical teaching in a kinder, gentler light. Like the inhabitants of Jerusalem, we are convinced that the Judge will choose the other road and we will be spared. It's hard for us to believe that the Bible's teaching on eternal punishment should be taken literally, at least not with reference to ourselves. But it is precisely with reference to ourselves that we should consider this doctrine.

your blood will be shed in your
land,
you will be remembered[g] no more;
for I the LORD have spoken.'"

Judgment on Jerusalem's Sins

22 The word of the LORD came to me:
2"Son of man, will you judge her? Will
you judge this city of bloodshed?[h] Then
confront her with all her detestable practices[i] 3and say: 'This is what the Sovereign LORD says: You city that brings on
herself doom by shedding blood[j] in her
midst and defiles herself by making
idols, 4you have become guilty because
of the blood you have shed[k] and have become defiled by the idols you have made.
You have brought your days to a close,
and the end of your years has come.[l]
Therefore I will make you an object of
scorn to the nations and a laughingstock
to all the countries.[m] 5Those who are near
and those who are far away will mock
you, you infamous city, full of turmoil.
6" 'See how each of the princes of Israel
who are in you uses his power to shed
blood.[n] 7In you they have treated father
and mother with contempt;[o] in you they
have oppressed the foreigner and mistreated the fatherless and the widow.[p]
8You have despised my holy things and
desecrated my Sabbaths.[q] 9In you are
slanderers[r] who are bent on shedding
blood; in you are those who eat at the
mountain shrines[s] and commit lewd
acts.[t] 10In you are those who dishon-
or their father's bed; in you are those
who violate women during their period,
when they are ceremonially unclean.[u]
11In you one man commits a detestable
offense with his neighbor's wife, another
shamefully defiles his daughter-in-law,[v]
and another violates his sister,[w] his own
father's daughter. 12In you are people
who accept bribes[x] to shed blood; you
take interest and make a profit from the
poor. You extort unjust gain from your
neighbors.[y] And you have forgotten me,
declares the Sovereign LORD.
13" 'I will surely strike my hands[z] together at the unjust gain[a] you have made
and at the blood[b] you have shed in your
midst. 14Will your courage endure or
your hands be strong in the day I deal
with you? I the LORD have spoken,[c] and
I will do it.[d] 15I will disperse you among
the nations and scatter[e] you through the
countries; and I will put an end to your
uncleanness.[f] 16When you have been defiled[α] in the eyes of the nations, you will
know that I am the LORD.'"
17Then the word of the LORD came to
me: 18"Son of man, the people of Israel
have become dross[g] to me; all of them
are the copper, tin, iron and lead left inside a furnace. They are but the dross
of silver.[h] 19Therefore this is what the
Sovereign LORD says: 'Because you have
all become dross, I will gather you into
Jerusalem. 20As silver, copper, iron, lead
and tin are gathered into a furnace to be
melted with a fiery blast, so will I gather
you in my anger and my wrath and put
you inside the city and melt you.[i] 21I will
gather you and I will blow on you with
my fiery wrath, and you will be melted
inside her. 22As silver is melted[j] in a furnace, so you will be melted inside her,
and you will know that I the LORD have
poured out my wrath on you.'"[k]

[α] 16 Or *When I have allotted you your inheritance*

21:32 [g] Eze 25:10
22:2 [h] Eze 24:6, 9; Na 3:1 [i] Eze 16:2
22:3 [j] ver 6, 13, 27; Eze 23:37, 45
22:4 [k] 2Ki 21:16 [l] Eze 21:25 [m] Eze 5:14
22:6 [n] Isa 1:23
22:7 [o] Dt 5:16; 27:16 [p] Ex 22:21-22
22:8 [q] Eze 23:38-39
22:9 [r] Lev 19:16 [s] Eze 18:11 [t] Hos 4:10, 14
22:10 [u] Lev 18:8, 19
22:11 [v] Lev 18:15 [w] Lev 18:9; 2Sa 13:14
22:12 [x] Dt 27:25; Mic 7:3 [y] Lev 19:13
22:13 [z] Eze 21:17 [a] Isa 33:15 [b] ver 3
22:14 [c] Eze 24:14 [d] Eze 17:24; 21:7
22:15 [e] Dt 4:27; Zec 7:14 [f] Eze 23:27
22:18 [g] Ps 119:119; Isa 1:22 [h] Jer 6:28-30
22:20 [i] Mal 3:2
22:22 [j] Isa 1:25 [k] Eze 20:8, 33

Eze 22:6-12 ❖ How is today's culture still plagued by sexual sin? How might Christians address such sins in society?

22:1-5 Jerusalem's sins involve both social sins—that is, sins against humanity—and religious sins—that is, sins against God (e.g., manufacturing idols). Social sins lead to "guilt" (v. 4) deserving punishment. Religious sins lead to "defilement" (v. 4), unfitness for being in God's presence. Judgment will make Jerusalem into an "object of scorn" (vv. 4, 5) to the nations around her.
22:6-12 This is the first catalog of Jerusalem's crimes. The charges are directed against the "princes of Israel" (v. 6), designating the former kings of Judah. The sins listed here are an accusation of having violated the Holiness Code of Lev 18–20 and 25.
22:13-16 The next two sections (vv. 13-16, 17-22) deal with the Lord's response to his people's sin under the twin images of *judgment by scattering* and *judgment by gathering*. The Lord will now act, dispersing Judah among the nations. In this way, the Lord will bring an end to Judah's uncleanness (v. 15).
22:17-22 Paradoxically, there appears also a judgment by gathering. The house of Israel is gathered into Jerusalem to experience the destructive impact of the Lord's wrath. This is paradoxical not merely because "gathering" is the logical opposite of "scattering," but also because the terminology of gathering is normally used in a positive sense.

23Again the word of the LORD came to
me: 24"Son of man, say to the land, 'You
are a land that has not been cleansed or
rained on in the day of wrath.'[l] 25There
is a conspiracy[m] of her princes[a] within
her like a roaring lion tearing its prey;
they devour people,[n] take treasures and
precious things and make many widows[o]
within her. 26Her priests do violence to
my law[p] and profane my holy things;
they do not distinguish between the holy
and the common;[q] they teach that there
is no difference between the unclean
and the clean;[r] and they shut their eyes
to the keeping of my Sabbaths, so that
I am profaned among them.[s] 27Her officials within her are like wolves tearing
their prey; they shed blood and kill people to make unjust gain.[t] 28Her prophets
whitewash[u] these deeds for them by false
visions and lying divinations. They say,
'This is what the Sovereign LORD says'—
when the LORD has not spoken.[v] 29The
people of the land practice extortion and
commit robbery; they oppress the poor
and needy and mistreat the foreigner,[w]
denying them justice.[x]

30"I looked for someone among them
who would build up the wall[y] and stand
before me in the gap on behalf of the
land so I would not have to destroy it,
but I found no one.[z] 31So I will pour out
my wrath on them and consume them
with my fiery anger, bringing down[a] on
their own heads all they have done, declares the Sovereign LORD.[b]"

22:24 [l]Eze 24:13
22:25 [m]Jer 11:9 [n]Hos 6:9 [o]Jer 15:8
22:26 [p]Mal 2:7-8 [q]Eze 44:23 [r]Lev 10:10 [s]1Sa 2:12-17; Jer 2:8, 26; Hag 2:11-14
22:27 [t]Isa 1:23
22:28 [u]Eze 13:10 [v]Eze 13:2, 6-7
22:29 [w]Ex 22:21; 23:9 [x]Isa 5:7
22:30 [y]Eze 13:5 [z]Ps 106:23; Jer 5:1
22:31 [a]Eze 16:43 [b]Eze 7:8-9; 9:10; Ro 2:8
23:2 [c]Jer 3:7; Eze 16:45
23:3 [d]Jos 24:14 [e]Lev 17:7
23:5 [f]2Ki 16:7; Hos 5:13 [g]Hos 8:9
23:7 [h]Hos 5:3; 6:10
23:8 [i]Ex 32:4

Two Adulterous Sisters

23 The word of the LORD came to
me: 2"Son of man, there were two
women, daughters of the same mother.[c]
3They became prostitutes in Egypt,[d] engaging in prostitution[e] from their youth.
In that land their breasts were fondled
and their virgin bosoms caressed. 4The
older was named Oholah, and her sister
was Oholibah. They were mine and gave
birth to sons and daughters. Oholah is
Samaria, and Oholibah is Jerusalem.

5"Oholah engaged in prostitution while
she was still mine; and she lusted after
her lovers, the Assyrians[f]—warriors[g]
6clothed in blue, governors and commanders, all of them handsome young
men, and mounted horsemen. 7She gave
herself as a prostitute to all the elite of
the Assyrians and defiled herself with all
the idols of everyone she lusted after.[h]
8She did not give up the prostitution she
began in Egypt,[i] when during her youth

[a] 25 Septuagint; Hebrew *prophets*

22:23–25 The outpouring of God's wrath has not yet happened to Judah. She remains "a land that has not been cleansed" (v. 24). Because of this lack of cleansing in the past, the land remains full of oppression, which will lead to a final pouring out of indignation on the people.

The "princes" have wreaked havoc through a series of social sins (v. 25). The "officials," described as being "like wolves," have likewise misused their power for the purpose of "unjust gain" (v. 27).

22:26–28 The "priests" did "violence to my law and profane[d] my holy things" (v. 26). The "prophets" are unreliable whitewashers, telling people what they want to hear.

22:29 The "people of the land," a group of powerful men with close ties to the Davidic house, have been exploiting those unable to defend themselves.

22:30–31 We again read of the Lord's response. He sought "someone among them who would build up the wall and stand before me in the gap on behalf of the land" (v. 30). In other words, he sought a true prophet. But no one was found to deflect God's wrath. The last, ominous words of the Lord are the same in both cases: "[I will bring] down on their own heads all they have done" (v. 31; cf. 11:21).

✣ **22:1–31** Modern people are unconvinced of the reality of their sin. Even those who still talk about sins have frequently lost the sense of the comprehensive nature of sin. Preachers (and churches) tend to have a shortened list of actual sins that they preach against. Along with the loss of the sense of sin goes the loss of understanding of God's wrath. A knowledge of sin and the understanding of God's wrath go together. It should therefore be no surprise that in a society where sin is no longer believed in, the wrath of God against sin is not understood.

23:1–2 Two women are introduced in the opening verses as sisters sharing a common mother. This is intended to denote a shared heredity between the northern and southern kingdoms but a deeper commonality: Though they are two in number, they are one in nature, living parallel lives.

23:3–4 In Egypt, these women gave themselves over to prostitution. But in spite of that, the Lord married them. Israel's past unfaithfulness to the Lord was not news to those familiar with the events recounted in Exodus and Numbers.

23:5–10 In the next verses, however, Ezekiel sketches the history of the older sister, Oholah (i.e., Samaria, the northern kingdom; 23:5–10). She lusted after the Assyrians and their idols. The Lord gave her over into the hand of her lovers, the Assyrians. The very things that attracted her to them were exerted against her. They stripped her naked and killed her.

men slept with her, caressed her virgin bosom and poured out their lust on her.[j]

9 "Therefore I delivered her into the hands[k] of her lovers, the Assyrians, for whom she lusted.[l] 10 They stripped[m] her naked, took away her sons and daughters and killed her with the sword. She became a byword among women,[n] and punishment was inflicted on her.[o]

11 "Her sister Oholibah saw this, yet in her lust and prostitution she was more depraved than her sister.[p] 12 She too lusted after the Assyrians — governors and commanders, warriors in full dress, mounted horsemen, all handsome young men.[q] 13 I saw that she too defiled herself; both of them went the same way.

14 "But she carried her prostitution still further. She saw men portrayed on a wall,[r] figures of Chaldeans[a] portrayed in red,[s] 15 with belts around their waists and flowing turbans on their heads; all of them looked like Babylonian chariot officers, natives of Chaldea.[b] 16 As soon as she saw them, she lusted after them and sent messengers to them in Chaldea. 17 Then the Babylonians came to her, to the bed of love, and in their lust they defiled her. After she had been defiled by them, she turned away from them in disgust. 18 When she carried on her prostitution openly and exposed her naked body, I turned away[t] from her in disgust, just as I had turned away from her sister.[u] 19 Yet she became more and more promiscuous as she recalled the days of her youth, when she was a prostitute in Egypt. 20 There she lusted after her lovers, whose genitals were like those of donkeys and whose emission was like that of horses. 21 So you longed for the lewdness of your youth, when in Egypt your bosom was caressed and your young breasts fondled.[c][v]

23:8 [j] Eze 16:15
23:9 [k] 2Ki 18:11 [l] Hos 11:5
23:10 [m] Hos 2:10 [n] Eze 16:41 [o] Eze 16:36
23:11 [p] Jer 3:8-11; Eze 16:51
23:12 [q] 2Ki 16:7-15; 2Ch 28:16
23:14 [r] Eze 8:10 [s] Jer 22:14
23:18 [t] Ps 78:59; 106:40; Jer 6:8 [u] Jer 12:8; Am 5:21
23:21 [v] Eze 16:26
23:22 [w] Eze 16:37
23:23 [x] 2Ki 20:14-18 [y] Jer 50:21 [z] 2Ki 24:2
23:24 [a] Jer 47:3; Eze 26:7, 10; Na 2:4 [b] Jer 39:5-6
23:25 [c] ver 47 [d] Eze 20:47-48
23:26 [e] Jer 13:22 [f] Isa 3:18-23; Eze 16:39
23:27 [g] Eze 16:41
23:28 [h] Jer 34:20

22 "Therefore, Oholibah, this is what the Sovereign LORD says: I will stir up your lovers against you, those you turned away from in disgust, and I will bring them against you from every side[w] — 23 the Babylonians[x] and all the Chaldeans, the men of Pekod[y] and Shoa and Koa, and all the Assyrians with them, handsome young men, all of them governors and commanders, chariot officers and men of high rank, all mounted on horses.[z] 24 They will come against you with weapons,[d] chariots and wagons[a] and with a throng of people; they will take up positions against you on every side with large and small shields and with helmets. I will turn you over to them for punishment,[b] and they will punish you according to their standards. 25 I will direct my jealous anger against you, and they will deal with you in fury. They will cut off your noses and your ears, and those of you who are left will fall by the sword. They will take away your sons and daughters,[c] and those of you who are left will be consumed by fire.[d] 26 They will also strip[e] you of your clothes and take your fine jewelry.[f] 27 So I will put a stop[g] to the lewdness and prostitution you began in Egypt. You will not look on these things with longing or remember Egypt anymore.

28 "For this is what the Sovereign LORD says: I am about to deliver you into the hands[h] of those you hate, to those you turned away from in disgust. 29 They will deal with you in hatred and take away everything you have worked for. They will leave you stark naked, and the shame

[a] 14 Or *Babylonians* [b] 15 Or *Babylonia;* also in verse 16 [c] 21 Syriac (see also verse 3); Hebrew *caressed because of your young breasts*
[d] 24 The meaning of the Hebrew for this word is uncertain.

23:11–16 As the chapter unfolds, it is evident that Oholibah is not merely like her sister; she is *worse* than her sister. She "saw" and yet still became more depraved in her lust. She added the Babylonians to her little black book (v. 14). She was worse not merely in the number of her lovers (two instead of one) but in the nature of their relationship. She was not merely willing to be seduced but was herself the active seductress (v. 16).

23:17–18 Having been defiled by her lovers, she became disgusted with them and turned away from them. But she continued her prostitution openly so that the Lord turned away from her.

23:19–21 This sister was not even limited by natural relationships; instead, she sought those whose sexual capacities were not merely superhuman but positively bestial.

23:22–25 The result of such absolute depravity is predictable. As with Oholah, the things that attracted Oholibah to her lovers are now used against her. This combination of divine and human judgment is further developed in the following verses. As Jerusalem's sins were worse than her sister's, so also will her punishment be.

23:26–35 The goal of this judgment is forgetting the prostitution begun in Egypt. Her lovers have now become her enemies, those who will strip her and plunder her. As she followed in the pattern of her elder sister, so now she will share her elder sister's fate (vv. 32–35).

of your prostitution will be exposed.
Your lewdness and promiscuity[i] 30have
brought this on you, because you lusted
after the nations and defiled yourself
with their idols.[j] 31You have gone the
way of your sister; so I will put her cup[k]
into your hand.[l]
32"This is what the Sovereign LORD
says:

"You will drink your sister's cup,
a cup large and deep;
it will bring scorn and derision,
for it holds so much.[m]
33You will be filled with drunkenness
and sorrow,
the cup of ruin and desolation,
the cup of your sister Samaria.[n]
34You will drink it[o] and drain it dry
and chew on its pieces —
and you will tear your breasts.

I have spoken, declares the Sovereign
LORD.

35"Therefore this is what the Sovereign
LORD says: Since you have forgotten[p] me
and turned your back on me,[q] you must
bear the consequences of your lewdness
and prostitution."
36The LORD said to me: "Son of man,
will you judge Oholah and Oholibah?
Then confront[r] them with their detestable practices,[s] 37for they have committed adultery and blood is on their hands.
They committed adultery with their
idols; they even sacrificed their children,
whom they bore to me, as food for them.[t]
38They have also done this to me: At that
same time they defiled my sanctuary
and desecrated my Sabbaths. 39On the
very day they sacrificed their children
to their idols, they entered my sanctuary
and desecrated[u] it. That is what they did
in my house.[v]

23:29 [i] Dt 28:48
23:30 [j] Eze 6:9
23:31 [k] Jer 25:15 [l] 2Ki 21:13
23:32 [m] Ps 60:3; Isa 51:17; Jer 25:15
23:33 [n] Jer 25:15-16
23:34 [o] Ps 75:8; Isa 51:17
23:35 [p] Isa 17:10; Jer 3:21 [q] 1Ki 14:9
23:36 [r] Eze 16:2 [s] Isa 58:1; Eze 22:2; Mic 3:8
23:37 [t] Eze 16:36
23:39 [u] 2Ki 21:4 [v] Jer 7:10
23:40 [w] Isa 57:9 [x] 2Ki 9:30 [y] Jer 4:30; Eze 16:13-19
23:41 [z] Est 1:6; Pr 7:17; Am 6:4 [a] Isa 65:11; Eze 44:16
23:42 [b] Ge 24:30 [c] Eze 16:11-12
23:43 [d] ver 3
23:45 [e] Lev 20:10; Eze 16:38; Hos 6:5
23:46 [f] Eze 16:40
23:47 [g] 2Ch 36:19 [h] 2Ch 36:17; Eze 16:40-41
23:48 [i] 2Pe 2:6

Eze 23:35 ❖ Why are adultery or prostitution appropriate metaphors for unfaithfulness to God? Why does God deserve our undivided hearts and devotion?

40"They even sent messengers for men
who came from far away,[w] and when they
arrived you bathed yourself for them,
applied eye makeup[x] and put on your
jewelry.[y] 41You sat on an elegant couch,[z]
with a table[a] spread before it on which
you had placed the incense and olive oil
that belonged to me.
42"The noise of a carefree crowd was
around her; drunkards were brought
from the desert along with men from
the rabble, and they put bracelets[b] on
the wrists of the woman and her sister
and beautiful crowns on their heads.[c]
43Then I said about the one worn out
by adultery, 'Now let them use her as a
prostitute,[d] for that is all she is.' 44And
they slept with her. As men sleep with a
prostitute, so they slept with those lewd
women, Oholah and Oholibah. 45But
righteous judges will sentence them to
the punishment of women who commit adultery and shed blood, because
they are adulterous and blood is on their
hands.[e]
46"This is what the Sovereign LORD
says: Bring a mob[f] against them and
give them over to terror and plunder.
47The mob will stone them and cut them
down with their swords; they will kill
their sons and daughters and burn[g]
down their houses.[h]
48"So I will put an end to lewdness in
the land, that all women may take warning and not imitate you.[i] 49You will suffer
the penalty for your lewdness and bear
the consequences of your sins of idolatry.

23:36–43 In the remaining verses, Ezekiel is once more cast into the role of prosecuting attorney. Jerusalem is to be confronted with her adultery and bloodshed. Sanctuary and Sabbath have been defiled, and even their children have been sacrificed (vv. 38–39). Their true nature is becoming clear to all: they appear as an aging, worn-out prostitute (v. 43).

23:44–49 Once more, the conclusion of the sisters' activities is clearly stated: An army will come, plundering them, stoning them, and putting them to the sword. Their children will be slaughtered, their homes burned. Thus, the Lord will bring to an end all such adultery. This time the object lesson will be heeded, and "all women" (v. 48) will learn and not do likewise. The chapter closes with the recognition formula: "Then you will know that I am the Sovereign LORD" (23:49).

✤ **23:1–49** There is no message of hope in Eze 23. The stone is rolled away to reveal the gaping mouth of the tomb, which is ready to swallow up defiled Jerusalem. But from a NT perspective, the opened mouth of another tomb speaks a word of comfort. Because Christ has died in our place, and more than that has risen from the dead, there is now no condemnation for those of us who place our trust in Christ Jesus (Ro 8:1).

Then you will know that I am the Sovereign LORD.[j]"

Jerusalem as a Cooking Pot

24 In the ninth year, in the tenth
month on the tenth day, the word
of the LORD came to me:[k] 2"Son of man,
record this date, this very date, because
the king of Babylon has laid siege to Jerusalem this very day.[l] 3Tell this rebellious people[m] a parable[n] and say to them:
'This is what the Sovereign LORD says:

"'Put on the cooking pot;[o] put it on
and pour water into it.
4Put into it the pieces of meat,
all the choice pieces — the leg and
the shoulder.
Fill it with the best of these bones;
5 take the pick of the flock.[p]
Pile wood beneath it for the bones;
bring it to a boil
and cook the bones in it.[q]

6"'For this is what the Sovereign LORD
says:

"'Woe to the city of bloodshed,[r]
to the pot now encrusted,
whose deposit will not go away!
Take the meat out piece by piece
in whatever order[s] it comes.

7"'For the blood she shed is in her
midst:
She poured it on the bare rock;
she did not pour it on the ground,
where the dust would cover it.[t]
8To stir up wrath and take revenge
I put her blood on the bare rock,
so that it would not be covered.

9"'Therefore this is what the Sovereign
LORD says:

"'Woe to the city of bloodshed!
I, too, will pile the wood high.

23:49 [j]Eze 7:4; 9:10; 20:38
24:1 [k]Eze 8:1
24:2 [l]2Ki 25:1; Jer 39:1; 52:4
24:3 [m]Isa 1:2; Eze 2:3,6 [n]Eze 17:2; 20:49 [o]Jer 1:13; Eze 11:3
24:5 [p]Jer 52:10 [q]Jer 52:24-27
24:6 [r]Eze 22:2 [s]Ob 11; Na 3:10
24:7 [t]Lev 17:13
24:11 [u]Jer 21:10; Eze 22:15
24:13 [v]Jer 6:28-30; Eze 16:42; 22:24
24:14 [w]Eze 36:19 [x]Eze 18:30
24:16 [y]Jer 13:17; 16:5; 22:10
24:17 [z]Jer 16:7

Eze 24:13 ❖ Why might believers sometimes resist God's efforts to cleanse and sanctify them?

10So heap on the wood
and kindle the fire.
Cook the meat well,
mixing in the spices;
and let the bones be charred.
11Then set the empty pot on the
coals
till it becomes hot and its copper
glows,
so that its impurities may be
melted
and its deposit burned away.[u]
12It has frustrated all efforts;
its heavy deposit has not been
removed,
not even by fire.

13"'Now your impurity is lewdness.
Because I tried to cleanse you but you
would not be cleansed from your impurity, you will not be clean again until my
wrath against you has subsided.[v]

14"'I the LORD have spoken. The time
has come for me to act. I will not hold
back; I will not have pity, nor will I relent. You will be judged according to your
conduct and your actions,[w] declares the
Sovereign LORD.[x]'"

Ezekiel's Wife Dies

15The word of the LORD came to me:
16"Son of man, with one blow I am about
to take away from you the delight of your
eyes. Yet do not lament or weep or shed
any tears.[y] 17Groan quietly; do not mourn
for the dead. Keep your turban fastened
and your sandals on your feet; do not
cover your mustache and beard or eat
the customary food of mourners.[z]"

24:1–5 Nebuchadnezzar is depicted as designating Jerusalem as the sacrificial lamb. This sacrificial language leads into a parable in which Jerusalem is compared to a cooking pot (v. 3). The sacrificial animal has been cut up and all of its pieces "gathered" to be boiled, presumably as a fellowship offering.
24:6 What ought to be a tasty sacred meal is, in fact, a foul, profane mess. This filth that is inside her will not "go away." The filth that will not come out of the pot reflects the frustration of a burned-on mess that cannot be removed. Yet, metaphorically, Jerusalem's inhabitants hope to emerge unscathed at the end of the siege. But their only exit from the pot will be for judgment. There will be no escape.
24:7–8 The blood Jerusalem has shed in her midst is left uncovered, poured out on a bare rock rather than on the ground. Blood left exposed would provoke the wrath of God, so their action is nothing less than a deliberate act of sacrilege.
24:9–14 The empty pot is now transformed into a kind of refiner's furnace in a final attempt to try to melt away the impurities (v. 11). But all efforts have proved ineffective. God's wrath must be satisfied (vv. 13–14), and it is time for that definitive final action to begin.
24:15–18 The sword first strikes the prophet himself in the most painful and personal of his prophetic sign-acts. His own wife, the delight of his eyes, is suddenly taken from him (v. 16). This is a sudden

18So I spoke to the people in the morning, and in the evening my wife died.
The next morning I did as I had been
commanded.
19Then the people asked me, "Won't
you tell us what these things have to do
with us?[a] Why are you acting like this?"
20So I said to them, "The word of the
LORD came to me: 21Say to the people of
Israel, 'This is what the Sovereign LORD
says: I am about to desecrate my sanctuary — the stronghold in which you
take pride, the delight of your eyes,[b]
the object of your affection. The sons
and daughters[c] you left behind will fall
by the sword.[d] 22And you will do as I
have done. You will not cover your mustache and beard or eat the customary
food of mourners.[e] 23You will keep your
turbans on your heads and your sandals on your feet. You will not mourn[f]
or weep but will waste away because
of[a] your sins and groan among yourselves.[g] 24Ezekiel will be a sign[h] to you;
you will do just as he has done. When
this happens, you will know that I am
the Sovereign LORD.'
25"And you, son of man, on the day
I take away their stronghold, their joy
and glory, the delight of their eyes, their
heart's desire, and their sons and daughters[i] as well — 26on that day a fugitive
will come to tell you[j] the news. 27At that
time your mouth will be opened; you
will speak with him and will no longer
be silent. So you will be a sign to them,
and they will know that I am the LORD.[k]"

24:19 [a] Eze 12:9; 37:18
24:21 [b] Ps 27:4 [c] Eze 23:25 [d] Jer 7:14,15; Eze 23:47
24:22 [e] Jer 16:7
24:23 [f] Job 27:15 [g] Ps 78:64
24:24 [h] Isa 20:3; Eze 4:3; 12:11
24:25 [i] Jer 11:22
24:26 [j] 1Sa 4:12; Job 1:15-19
24:27 [k] Eze 3:26; 33:22

25:2 [l] Eze 21:28; Zep 2:8-9 [m] Jer 49:1-6
25:3 [n] Eze 26:2; 36:2 [o] Pr 17:5
25:4 [p] Jdg 6:3 [q] Dt 28:33,51; Jdg 6:33
25:5 [r] Dt 3:11; Eze 21:20 [s] Isa 17:2
25:6 [t] Ob 12; Zep 2:8
25:7 [u] Zep 1:4 [v] Eze 21:31 [w] Am 1:14-15

Eze 25:6-7 ❖ When have we seen people gloat over the misfortunes of God's people? How will God bring ultimate justice upon such pride?

A Prophecy Against Ammon

25 The word of the LORD came to
me: 2"Son of man, set your face
against the Ammonites[l] and prophesy
against them.[m] 3Say to them, 'Hear the
word of the Sovereign LORD. This is what
the Sovereign LORD says: Because you
said "Aha![n]" over my sanctuary when it
was desecrated and over the land of Israel when it was laid waste and over the
people of Judah when they went into
exile,[o] 4therefore I am going to give you
to the people of the East[p] as a possession.
They will set up their camps and pitch
their tents among you; they will eat your
fruit and drink your milk.[q] 5I will turn
Rabbah[r] into a pasture for camels and
Ammon into a resting place for sheep.[s]
Then you will know that I am the LORD.
6For this is what the Sovereign LORD says:
Because you have clapped your hands
and stamped your feet, rejoicing with
all the malice of your heart against the
land of Israel,[t] 7therefore I will stretch
out my hand[u] against you and give you
as plunder to the nations. I will wipe you
out from among the nations and exterminate you from the countries. I will
destroy[v] you, and you will know that I
am the LORD.[w]'"

[a] *23* Or *away in*

---

stroke directly from God. Yet Ezekiel is not permitted to mourn publicly (v. 17).

24:19–25 This strange behavior is to be a sign to the people of the significance of what is to come (v. 24). The temple in Jerusalem, their pride and joy and the delight of their eyes, will be desecrated by God. Yet the people will not mourn publicly for the temple (v. 22). Only inward grief will be possible.

24:26–27 When the news of the fall of Jerusalem is confirmed, Ezekiel's lips will be opened, and he will finally be able to speak. With the destruction of Jerusalem, his words of judgment for the city will come to an end; their time will be complete.

✣ **24:1–27** Just as the deepest night for Jerusalem is the beginning of the end of God's wrath on his people and the turning point to hope in Ezekiel's message, so also the death of Jesus Christ on the cross is the turning point in the history of redemption. The blackness of Good Friday causes the light of Easter Sunday to break out with fresh power for Christ's disciples. The taking away of their Lord, the delight of their eyes, to lay him in a tomb, is paradoxically the means by which they may be enabled to enjoy him forever.

Sometimes God actually takes from us that which is most precious to us. In those moments, as we are enabled by his grace to say, "Not my will, but yours be done, Lord," we become living signs to the world around us of God's grace and glory. Moreover, we do not mourn as the world mourns, for in the midst of our sadness and real sense of painful loss, we have the assurance that just as our Lord has risen, so also will all his people (1Th 4:13).

25:1–7 The Lord tells the prophet to set his face toward the Ammonites and prophesy against them. They exulted in noisy triumph when Judah fell (v. 3). Because of that attitude, the Ammonites too will experience judgment. Their produce will be eaten by others and their people exterminated. As a result of this judgment the Ammonites "will know that I am the LORD" (v. 7).

A Prophecy Against Moab

8“This is what the Sovereign LORD says: ‘Because Moab[x] and Seir said, “Look, Judah has become like all the other nations,” 9therefore I will expose the flank of Moab, beginning at its frontier towns — Beth Jeshimoth[y], Baal Meon[z] and Kiriathaim[a] — the glory of that land. 10I will give Moab along with the Ammonites to the people of the East as a possession, so that the Ammonites will not be remembered[b] among the nations; 11and I will inflict punishment on Moab. Then they will know that I am the LORD.’ ”

A Prophecy Against Edom

12“This is what the Sovereign LORD says: ‘Because Edom[c] took revenge on Judah and became very guilty by doing so, 13therefore this is what the Sovereign LORD says: I will stretch out my hand against Edom and kill both man and beast.[d] I will lay it waste, and from Teman to Dedan[e] they will fall by the sword. 14I will take vengeance on Edom by the hand of my people Israel, and they will deal with Edom in accordance with my anger[f] and my wrath; they will know my vengeance, declares the Sovereign LORD.’ ”

A Prophecy Against Philistia

15“This is what the Sovereign LORD says: ‘Because the Philistines[g] acted in vengeance and took revenge with malice in their hearts, and with ancient hostility sought to destroy Judah, 16therefore this is what the Sovereign LORD says: I am about to stretch out my hand against the Philistines,[h] and I will wipe out the Kerethites[i] and destroy those remaining along the coast. 17I will carry out great vengeance on them and punish them in my wrath. Then they will know that I am the LORD, when I take vengeance on them.’ ”

25:8 [x] Jer 48:1; Am 2:1
25:9 [y] Nu 33:49 [z] Nu 32:3; Jos 13:17 [a] Nu 32:37; Jos 13:19
25:10 [b] Eze 21:32
25:12 [c] 2Ch 28:17
25:13 [d] Eze 29:8 [e] Jer 25:23
25:14 [f] Eze 35:11
25:15 [g] 2Ch 28:18
25:16 [h] Jer 47:1-7 [i] 1Sa 30:14; Zep 2:4-5

A Prophecy Against Tyre

26 In the eleventh month of the twelfth[a] year, on the first day of the month, the word of the LORD came to me: 2“Son of man, because Tyre[j] has said of Jerusalem, ‘Aha![k] The gate to the nations is broken, and its doors have swung open to me; now that she lies in ruins I will prosper,’ 3therefore this is what the Sovereign LORD says: I am against you, Tyre, and I will bring many nations against you, like the sea[l] casting up its waves. 4They will destroy[m] the walls of Tyre[n] and pull down her towers; I will scrape away her rubble and make her a bare rock. 5Out in the sea[o] she will become a place to spread fishnets, for I have spoken, declares the Sovereign LORD. She will become plunder[p] for the nations, 6and her settlements on the mainland will be ravaged by the sword. Then they will know that I am the LORD.

7“For this is what the Sovereign LORD says: From the north I am going to bring against Tyre Nebuchadnezzar[b][q] king of

26:2 [j] 2Sa 5:11; Isa 23 [k] Eze 25:3
26:3 [l] Isa 5:30; Jer 50:42; 51:42
26:4 [m] Isa 23:1, 11 [n] Am 1:10
26:5 [o] Eze 27:32 [p] Eze 29:19
26:7 [q] Jer 27:6

[a] *1* Probable reading of the original Hebrew text; Masoretic Text does not have *month of the twelfth.* [b] *7* Hebrew *Nebuchadrezzar,* of which *Nebuchadnezzar* is a variant; here and often in Ezekiel and Jeremiah

---

25:8–11 The oracle against Moab charges them with saying, “Look, Judah has become like all the other nations” (v. 8). Judah had indeed become like the nations. But not in the sense in which Moab intended. They are the ones who will be left unremembered on the stage of world history (v. 10).

25:12–14 The Edomites seem to have actively participated in Judah’s downfall. Although they were close kin of the Israelites, they had no compassion on their brothers. The result will be God’s execution of vengeance on them, using his own people to do so (v. 14).

25:15–17 The Philistines are likewise charged with trying to settle old scores, seeking to work out their “ancient hostility” toward Israel in the destruction of the chosen people. They too will experience the vengeance of God (v. 17).

✣ **25:1–17** We would do well to remember the words of Jesus that the measure we use in judging others will be the same one used on us (Lk 6:38). Trembling before the awful reality of the judgment of God, we should seek to persuade all people to flee the wrath to come (2Co 5:10–11).

26:1–6 The charge against Tyre is similar to that raised against Judah’s other neighbors: She rejoiced when Jerusalem fell, seeing in that event the opportunity for personal gain.

Ezekiel is quick to point out that the God who brought judgment on Jerusalem is also against Tyre. The Lord will bring many nations against her. Her walls will be destroyed, and her towers torn down. She will become plunder for the nations.

The general expression “many nations” (v. 3) resolves into the specific figure of Nebuchadnezzar, king of Babylon.

26:7–14 The assault and destruction of Tyre is described in great, if rather stereotypical, detail. Her former glory will never be regained.

Babylon, king of kings,[r] with horses and
chariots,[s] with horsemen and a great
army. 8He will ravage your settlements
on the mainland with the sword; he will
set up siege works[t] against you, build
a ramp[u] up to your walls and raise his
shields against you. 9He will direct the
blows of his battering rams against your
walls and demolish your towers with his
weapons. 10His horses will be so many
that they will cover you with dust. Your
walls will tremble at the noise of the
warhorses, wagons and chariots[v] when
he enters your gates as men enter a city
whose walls have been broken through.
11The hooves[w] of his horses will trample
all your streets; he will kill your people
with the sword, and your strong pillars[x]
will fall to the ground.[y] 12They will plunder your wealth and loot your merchandise; they will break down your walls and
demolish your fine houses and throw
your stones, timber and rubble into the
sea.[z] 13I will put an end[a] to your noisy
songs, and the music of your harps[b] will
be heard no more.[c] 14I will make you a
bare rock, and you will become a place
to spread fishnets. You will never be rebuilt,[d] for I the LORD have spoken, declares the Sovereign LORD.

15"This is what the Sovereign LORD says
to Tyre: Will not the coastlands[e] tremble[f] at the sound of your fall, when the
wounded groan and the slaughter takes
place in you? 16Then all the princes of the
coast will step down from their thrones
and lay aside their robes and take off
their embroidered garments. Clothed[g]
with terror, they will sit on the ground,
trembling[h] every moment, appalled[i] at
you. 17Then they will take up a lament[j]
concerning you and say to you:

"'How you are destroyed, city of
renown,
peopled by men of the sea!
You were a power on the seas,
you and your citizens;
you put your terror
on all who lived there.[k]

18Now the coastlands tremble
on the day of your fall;
the islands in the sea
are terrified at your collapse.'[l]

19"This is what the Sovereign LORD
says: When I make you a desolate city,
like cities no longer inhabited, and
when I bring the ocean depths over you
and its vast waters cover you,[m] 20then
I will bring you down with those who
go down to the pit,[n] to the people of
long ago. I will make you dwell in the
earth below, as in ancient ruins, with
those who go down to the pit, and you
will not return or take your place[a] in
the land of the living.[o] 21I will bring
you to a horrible end and you will be
no more. You will be sought, but you
will never again be found, declares the
Sovereign LORD."[p]

26:7 [r] Ezr 7:12; Da 2:37 [s] Eze 23:24; Na 2:3-4
26:8 [t] Jer 6:6 [u] Eze 21:22
26:10 [v] Jer 4:13
26:11 [w] Isa 5:28 [x] Jer 43:13 [y] Isa 26:5
26:12 [z] Isa 23:8; Eze 27:3-27; 28:8
26:13 [a] Jer 7:34 [b] Isa 14:11 [c] Jer 25:10; Rev 18:22
26:14 [d] Job 12:14; Mal 1:4
26:15 [e] Eze 27:35 [f] Jer 49:21
26:16 [g] Job 8:22 [h] Hos 11:10 [i] Eze 32:10
26:17 [j] Eze 19:1; 27:32 [k] Isa 14:12
26:18 [l] Isa 23:5; 41:5; Eze 27:35
26:19 [m] Isa 8:7-8
26:20 [n] Eze 32:18; Am 9:2; Jnh 2:2,6 [o] Eze 32:24,30
26:21 [p] Eze 27:36; 28:19; Rev 18:21
27:3 [q] ver 33 [r] Eze 28:2
27:5 [s] Dt 3:9

Eze 26:19-21 ❖ When does a society become so corrupt and sinful that God wipes it out (see Ge 18:32)?

Eze 27:2 ❖ Why would God tell the prophet to sing a lament over a sinful city? What might God be calling us to lament in the world around us?

A Lament Over Tyre

27 The word of the LORD came to me:
2"Son of man, take up a lament
concerning Tyre. 3Say to Tyre, situated
at the gateway to the sea,[q] merchant of
peoples on many coasts, 'This is what
the Sovereign LORD says:

"'You say, Tyre,
"I am perfect in beauty.[r]"
4Your domain was on the high seas;
your builders brought your beauty
to perfection.
5They made all your timbers
of juniper from Senir[b];[s]
they took a cedar from Lebanon
to make a mast for you.

[a] 20 Septuagint; Hebrew *return, and I will give glory*   [b] 5 That is, Mount Hermon

26:15-21 The terrible fall of Tyre will have an impact on her maritime trading partners, the "coastlands" or islands (v. 15). It will be as if the island city has sunk into the heart of the chaotic "ocean depths" (v. 19), its inhabitants condemned to "the pit" (v. 20), never to return. Though people look for Tyre, she will have utterly vanished, wiped out completely by God, never again to be found (v. 21).

27:1-11 Ezekiel describes in great detail the glory of Tyre using the metaphor of a majestic ship. She was a legend in her own mind—beautiful to the point of perfection. She was fitted out with prime timbers for her construction, fine cloth for her sails and awnings. Her crew had been recruited from the best available, bringing her beauty to perfection. Could there ever have been a more perfect "ship"?

6 Of oaks[t] from Bashan
they made your oars;
of cypress wood[a] from the coasts of
Cyprus[u]
they made your deck, adorned
with ivory.
7 Fine embroidered linen from Egypt
was your sail
and served as your banner;
your awnings were of blue and
purple[v]
from the coasts of Elishah.
8 Men of Sidon and Arvad[w] were your
oarsmen;
your skilled men, Tyre, were
aboard as your sailors.[x]
9 Veteran craftsmen of Byblos[y] were
on board
as shipwrights to caulk your
seams.
All the ships of the sea and their
sailors
came alongside to trade for your
wares.

10 " 'Men of Persia,[z] Lydia and Put[a]
served as soldiers in your army.
They hung their shields and helmets
on your walls,
bringing you splendor.
11 Men of Arvad and Helek
guarded your walls on every side;
men of Gammad
were in your towers.
They hung their shields around your
walls;
they brought your beauty to
perfection.

12 " 'Tarshish[b] did business with you
because of your great wealth of goods;[c]
they exchanged silver, iron, tin and lead
for your merchandise.
13 " 'Greece, Tubal and Meshek[d] did
business with you; they traded human
beings[e] and articles of bronze for your
wares.
14 " 'Men of Beth Togarmah[f] exchanged
chariot horses, cavalry horses and mules
for your merchandise.
15 " 'The men of Rhodes[b][g] traded with
you, and many coastlands[h] were your
customers; they paid you with ivory[i]
tusks and ebony.
16 " 'Aram[c][j] did business with you because of your many products; they exchanged turquoise,[k] purple fabric, embroidered work, fine linen, coral and
rubies for your merchandise.
17 " 'Judah and Israel traded with you;
they exchanged wheat from Minnith[l] and
confections,[d] honey, olive oil and balm
for your wares.
18 " 'Damascus[m] did business with you
because of your many products and great
wealth of goods. They offered wine from
Helbon, wool from Zahar 19 and casks of
wine from Izal in exchange for your
wares: wrought iron, cassia and calamus.
20 " 'Dedan traded in saddle blankets
with you.
21 " 'Arabia and all the princes of Kedar[n]
were your customers; they did business
with you in lambs, rams and goats.
22 " 'The merchants of Sheba[o] and Raamah traded with you; for your merchandise they exchanged the finest of
all kinds of spices[p] and precious stones,
and gold.
23 " 'Harran,[q] Kanneh and Eden[r] and
merchants of Sheba, Ashur and Kilmad
traded with you. 24 In your marketplace
they traded with you beautiful garments,
blue fabric, embroidered work and mul-
ticolored rugs with cords twisted and
tightly knotted.

25 " 'The ships of Tarshish[s] serve
as carriers for your wares.
You are filled with heavy cargo
as you sail the sea.
26 Your oarsmen take you
out to the high seas.
But the east wind[t] will break you to
pieces
far out at sea.

27:6 [t] Nu 21:33; Jer 22:20; Zec 11:2 [u] Ge 10:4; Isa 23:12
27:7 [v] Ex 25:4; Jer 10:9
27:8 [w] Ge 10:18 [x] 1Ki 9:27
27:9 [y] Jos 13:5; 1Ki 5:18
27:10 [z] Eze 38:5 [a] Eze 30:5
27:12 [b] Ge 10:4 [c] ver 18, 33
27:13 [d] Ge 10:2; Isa 66:19; Eze 38:2 [e] Rev 18:13
27:14 [f] Ge 10:3; Eze 38:6
27:15 [g] Ge 10:7 [h] Jer 25:22 [i] 1Ki 10:22; Rev 18:12
27:16 [j] Jdg 10:6; Isa 7:1-8 [k] Eze 28:13
27:17 [l] Jdg 11:33
27:18 [m] Ge 14:15; Eze 47:16-18
27:21 [n] Ge 25:13; Isa 60:7
27:22 [o] Ge 10:7, 28; 1Ki 10:1-2; Isa 60:6 [p] Ge 43:11
27:23 [q] 2Ki 19:12 [r] Isa 37:12
27:25 [s] Isa 2:16 *fn*
27:26 [t] Ps 48:7; Jer 18:17

[a] 6 Targum; the Masoretic Text has a different division of the consonants. [b] 15 Septuagint; Hebrew *Dedan* [c] 16 Most Hebrew manuscripts; some Hebrew manuscripts and Syriac *Edom* [d] 17 The meaning of the Hebrew for this word is uncertain.

27:12–24 The cargo list seems to be organized by geographic areas, starting with the Mediterranean and moving on through Palestinian regions from south to north, to Syria, Arabia, and finally Mesopotamia. The picture is established of Tyre as the commercial crossroads of the world.
27:25–27 Her apparent invincibility contains the seeds of her own downfall. She is "filled with heavy cargo" (v. 25), a description that fits the city of Tyre literally as well as the ship Tyre metaphorically. An east wind (from Babylon) will start to blow, and the mighty vessel will founder with the loss of all hands. Her beauty and security will count for nothing when the storm strikes.

27 Your wealth,[u] merchandise and
wares,
your mariners, sailors and
shipwrights,
your merchants and all your
soldiers,
and everyone else on board
will sink into the heart of the sea
on the day of your shipwreck.
28 The shorelands will quake[v]
when your sailors cry out.
29 All who handle the oars
will abandon their ships;
the mariners and all the sailors
will stand on the shore.
30 They will raise their voice
and cry bitterly over you;
they will sprinkle dust[w] on their
heads
and roll[x] in ashes.[y]
31 They will shave their heads because
of you
and will put on sackcloth.
They will weep[z] over you with
anguish of soul
and with bitter mourning.[a]
32 As they wail and mourn over you,
they will take up a lament[b]
concerning you:
"Who was ever silenced like
Tyre,
surrounded by the sea?"
33 When your merchandise went out
on the seas,
you satisfied many nations;
with your great wealth[c] and your
wares
you enriched the kings of the
earth.

27:27 [u] Pr 11:4
27:28 [v] Eze 26:15
27:30 [w] 2Sa 1:2 [x] Jer 6:26 [y] Rev 18:18-19
27:31 [z] Isa 16:9 [a] Isa 22:12; Eze 7:18
27:32 [b] Eze 26:17
27:33 [c] ver 12; Eze 28:4-5

Eze 28:1-5 ❖ Why is God so opposed to the sin of pride? How can we fight against the sin of pride in our lives?

34 Now you are shattered by the sea
in the depths of the waters;
your wares and all your company
have gone down with you.[d]
35 All who live in the coastlands[e]
are appalled at you;
their kings shudder with horror
and their faces are distorted with
fear.
36 The merchants among the nations
scoff at you;[f]
you have come to a horrible end
and will be no more.[g]' "

A Prophecy Against the King of Tyre

28 The word of the LORD came to me:
2 "Son of man, say to the ruler of
Tyre, 'This is what the Sovereign LORD
says:

" 'In the pride of your heart
you say, "I am a god;
I sit on the throne[h] of a god
in the heart of the seas."
But you are a mere mortal and not a
god,
though you think you are as wise
as a god.[i]
3 Are you wiser than Daniel[a]?[j]
Is no secret hidden from you?
4 By your wisdom and understanding
you have gained wealth for
yourself

27:34 [d] Zec 9:4
27:35 [e] Eze 26:15
27:36 [f] Jer 18:16; 19:8; 49:17; 50:13; Zep 2:15 [g] Ps 37:10,36; Eze 26:21
28:2 [h] Isa 14:13 [i] Ps 9:20; 82:6-7; Isa 31:3; 2Th 2:4
28:3 [j] Da 1:20; 5:11-12

[a] 3 Or *Danel*, a man of renown in ancient literature

27:28-36 Once again those who watch from the sidelines tremble, and a lament is raised for the doomed city. The one who judged Jerusalem will also judge Tyre, the marketplace of the "nations" (vv. 33, 36).

26:1–27:36 The true answer to seduction is to open people's eyes to the shallowness of the "beauty" on offer. Today seduction lives in materialistic excess, drawing the world away from God and proclaiming its name more widely than the Good News of Jesus Christ. Consumerism is making disciples in all nations through its seductive charms.

At the heart of seduction, however, is a lie that what you see is what you get. And Satan, the eternal liar, is skilled at making us see things from their most attractive perspective. How does God wean our hearts from the seductiveness of this world? The way for us to learn to resist the attractiveness of Satan's seduction is to learn to fix our eyes on the truth, on Jesus.

If Jerusalem's beauty was not spiritually discerned even during its prosperous days, then it was not surprising that many would be seduced away by the apparent beauty of its rival during her humiliation at the time of the exile. So also, there are many today who are unable to discern the beauty of Christ crucified. Their eyes are blinded to the truth. The world still seems to offer far more attractive alternatives than the Son of Man.

28:1-2 The ruler of Tyre acts as a kind of personification of the city. He is accused of extreme pride. He claims to exercise the divine authority that comes from sitting on the throne of the gods.
28:3-5 This ruler claims to be as wise as a god—wiser than the ancient hero Daniel (v. 3). His skill in trading has brought him gold and silver, and along with his wealth his pride has grown enormously (v. 5).

and amassed gold and silver
in your treasuries.[k]
5 By your great skill in trading
you have increased your wealth,
and because of your wealth
your heart has grown proud.[l]

6 " 'Therefore this is what the Sovereign LORD says:

" 'Because you think you are wise,
as wise as a god,
7 I am going to bring foreigners
against you,
the most ruthless of nations;[m]
they will draw their swords against
your beauty and wisdom
and pierce your shining splendor.
8 They will bring you down to the
pit,[n]
and you will die a violent death
in the heart of the seas.[o]
9 Will you then say, "I am a god,"
in the presence of those who kill
you?
You will be but a mortal, not a god,
in the hands of those who slay
you.
10 You will die the death of the
uncircumcised[p]
at the hands of foreigners.

I have spoken, declares the Sovereign LORD.' "

11 The word of the LORD came to me:
12 "Son of man, take up a lament[q] concerning the king of Tyre and say to him:
'This is what the Sovereign LORD says:

" 'You were the seal of perfection,
full of wisdom and perfect in
beauty.[r]
13 You were in Eden,[s]
the garden of God;[t]
every precious stone adorned you:
carnelian, chrysolite and emerald,
topaz, onyx and jasper,
lapis lazuli, turquoise[u] and beryl.[a]
Your settings and mountings[b] were
made of gold;
on the day you were created they
were prepared.
14 You were anointed[v] as a guardian
cherub,[w]
for so I ordained you.
You were on the holy mount of God;
you walked among the fiery
stones.
15 You were blameless in your ways
from the day you were created
till wickedness was found in you.
16 Through your widespread trade
you were filled with violence,[x]
and you sinned.
So I drove you in disgrace from the
mount of God,
and I expelled you, guardian
cherub,[y]
from among the fiery stones.
17 Your heart became proud[z]
on account of your beauty,
and you corrupted your wisdom
because of your splendor.
So I threw you to the earth;
I made a spectacle of you before
kings.
18 By your many sins and dishonest
trade
you have desecrated your
sanctuaries.
So I made a fire come out from you,
and it consumed you,
and I reduced you to ashes[a] on the
ground
in the sight of all who were
watching.
19 All the nations who knew you
are appalled at you;
you have come to a horrible end
and will be no more.[b]' "

28:4 [k] Zec 9:3
28:5 [l] Job 31:25; Ps 52:7; 62:10; Hos 12:8; 13:6
28:7 [m] Eze 30:11; 31:12; 32:12; Hab 1:6
28:8 [n] Eze 32:30 [o] Eze 27:27
28:10 [p] Eze 31:18; 32:19,24
28:12 [q] Eze 19:1 [r] Eze 27:2-4
28:13 [s] Ge 2:8 [t] Eze 31:8-9 [u] Eze 27:16
28:14 [v] Ex 30:26; 40:9 [w] Ex 25:17-20
28:16 [x] Hab 2:17 [y] Ge 3:24
28:17 [z] Eze 31:10
28:18 [a] Mal 4:3
28:19 [b] Jer 51:64; Eze 26:21; 27:36

[a] *13* The precise identification of some of these precious stones is uncertain. [b] *13* The meaning of the Hebrew for this phrase is uncertain.

28:6–10 His wisdom will not help him when God brings the nations against him. He will be helpless when his captors put him to death. Far from being a god, he will go down to "the pit," (v. 8), dying in the chaotic heart of the seas.
28:11–15 The king's eulogy (with perhaps more than a hint of sarcasm?) appears to take his claims of divinity seriously. The king is described as having been present in Eden. He was anointed as a "guardian cherub" (v. 14). He had access to the center of the divine presence.
28:16–17 The abundance of this king's trade brought with it not merely riches but also violence and pride; his "wisdom" became corrupt and led him into wickedness.
28:18–19 Far from being a god, the king of Tyre's very presence defiled sanctuaries. He was made a public spectacle before the kings of the earth and consumed by fire from within. The end result of this judgment is that the king of Tyre, like his city, will come to a horrible end; in other words, the captain will go down with the ship (26:19).

A Prophecy Against Sidon

20The word of the LORD came to me:
21"Son of man, set your face against[c] Sidon;[d] prophesy against her 22and say:
'This is what the Sovereign LORD says:

"'I am against you, Sidon,
and among you I will display my
glory.[e]
You will know that I am the LORD,
when I inflict punishment[f] on you
and within you am proved to be
holy.
23I will send a plague upon you
and make blood flow in your
streets.
The slain will fall within you,
with the sword against you on
every side.
Then you will know that I am the
LORD.[g]

24"'No longer will the people of Israel
have malicious neighbors who are painful briers and sharp thorns.[h] Then they
will know that I am the Sovereign LORD.
25"'This is what the Sovereign LORD
says: When I gather[i] the people of Israel
from the nations where they have been
scattered,[j] I will be proved holy[k] through
them in the sight of the nations. Then
they will live in their own land, which I
gave to my servant Jacob.[l] 26They will
live there in safety[m] and will build houses and plant vineyards; they will live in
safety when I inflict punishment on all
their neighbors who maligned them.
Then they will know that I am the LORD
their God.[n]'"

28:21 [c]Eze 6:2 [d]Ge 10:15; Jer 25:22
28:22 [e]Eze 39:13 [f]Eze 30:19
28:23 [g]Eze 38:22
28:24 [h]Nu 33:55; Jos 23:13; Eze 2:6
28:25 [i]Ps 106:47; Jer 32:37 [j]Isa 11:12 [k]Eze 20:41 [l]Jer 23:8; Eze 11:17; 34:27; 37:25
28:26 [m]Jer 23:6 [n]Isa 65:21; Jer 32:15; Eze 38:8; Am 9:14-15
29:1 [o]ver 17; Eze 26:1
29:2 [p]Jer 25:19 [q]Isa 19:1-17; Jer 46:2; Eze 30:1-26; 31:1-18; 32:1-32
29:3 [r]Jer 44:30 [s]Ps 74:13; Isa 27:1; Eze 32:2
29:4 [t]2Ki 19:28 [u]Eze 38:4
29:5 [v]Jer 7:33; 34:20; Eze 32:4-6; 39:4

A Prophecy Against Egypt

Judgment on Pharaoh

29 In the tenth year, in the tenth
month on the twelfth day, the
word of the LORD came to me:[o] 2"Son of
man, set your face against Pharaoh king
of Egypt[p] and prophesy against him and
against all Egypt.[q] 3Speak to him and say:
'This is what the Sovereign LORD says:

"'I am against you, Pharaoh[r] king of
Egypt,
you great monster[s] lying among
your streams.
You say, "The Nile belongs to me;
I made it for myself."
4But I will put hooks[t] in your jaws
and make the fish of your streams
stick to your scales.
I will pull you out from among your
streams,
with all the fish sticking to your
scales.[u]
5I will leave you in the desert,
you and all the fish of your
streams.
You will fall on the open field
and not be gathered or picked up.
I will give you as food
to the beasts of the earth and the
birds of the sky.[v]

6Then all who live in Egypt will know
that I am the LORD.

28:20–23 The Lord will gain glory for himself by executing judgments on Sidon.

28:24–26 These words build hope in Ezekiel's immediate audience. The judgments on the nations are ultimately for Israel's own good. When the full regathering of the nation takes place, she will dwell in safety.

God will demonstrate his holiness by once again gathering his own people to the promised land. The people will be able to build houses and plant vineyards (v. 26), long-term projects that speak of settled security. Instead of the usual "then they will know that I am the LORD," the oracle closes with, "Then they will know that I am the LORD their God" (v. 26), personalizing the relationship. Paradise, which the king of Tyre claimed and lost, may still be regained by God's own people.

28:1–26 The wisdom of the world may offer a godlike ability to succeed in everything we attempt while living lives free of pain and sickness. It offers a seductively attractive path to those who are suffering physically or otherwise lacking in some area of their lives. The wisdom of the world, however, is foolishness to God (1Co 1:20).

For the Christian, wisdom consists in consulting God and in living according to his Word. To be a sincere Christian is to know and trust that God is the only One who understands the destiny of history—and of our own individual lives. To those who have surrendered their lives to God's loving direction, that realization brings comfort rather than dread.

29:1–5 The sea monster was a well-known element of ancient Near Eastern mythology. In Ezekiel, the mythical picture blends with the geographically appropriate image of Pharaoh as a great crocodile, depicting the ruler of Egypt as a supernatural force of destruction.

For all Pharaoh's boasts of divine power, he will be trapped with hooks (v. 4). He will be brought into the desert and executed along with "all the fish of your streams" (v. 5), either his allies or the members of his armed forces.

29:6–7 The reason for this act of judgment becomes clear. Egypt has been an unstable support to Judah.

"'You have been a staff of reed[w] for
the people of Israel. 7When they grasped
you with their hands, you splintered[x]
and you tore open their shoulders; when
they leaned on you, you broke and their
backs were wrenched.[a][y]

8"'Therefore this is what the Sovereign
LORD says: I will bring a sword against
you and kill both man and beast.[z] 9Egypt
will become a desolate wasteland. Then
they will know that I am the LORD.

"'Because you said, "The Nile is mine;
I made it,[a]" 10therefore I am against you
and against your streams, and I will make
the land of Egypt a ruin and a desolate
waste from Migdol to Aswan,[b] as far as the
border of Cush.[b] 11The foot of neither man
nor beast will pass through it; no one will
live there for forty years.[c] 12I will make the
land of Egypt desolate among devastated
lands, and her cities will lie desolate forty
years among ruined cities. And I will disperse the Egyptians among the nations
and scatter them through the countries.[d]

13"'Yet this is what the Sovereign LORD
says: At the end of forty years I will gather the Egyptians from the nations where
they were scattered. 14I will bring them
back from captivity and return them to
Upper Egypt,[e] the land of their ancestry.
There they will be a lowly[f] kingdom. 15It
will be the lowliest of kingdoms and will
never again exalt itself above the other
nations.[g] I will make it so weak that it
will never again rule over the nations.
16Egypt will no longer be a source of confidence[h] for the people of Israel but will
be a reminder of their sin in turning to
her for help. Then they will know that I
am the Sovereign LORD.[i]'"

Nebuchadnezzar's Reward

17In the twenty-seventh year, in the
first month on the first day, the word

29:6 [w] 2Ki 18:21; Isa 36:6
29:7 [x] Isa 36:6 [y] Eze 17:15-17
29:8 [z] Eze 14:17; 32:11-13
29:9 [a] Eze 30:7-8,13-19
29:10 [b] Eze 30:6
29:11 [c] Eze 32:13
29:12 [d] Jer 46:19; Eze 30:7,23,26
29:14 [e] Eze 30:14 [f] Eze 17:14
29:15 [g] Zec 10:11
29:16 [h] Isa 36:4,6 [i] Isa 30:2; Hos 8:13
29:17 [j] Eze 24:1
29:18 [k] Jer 27:6; Eze 26:7-8 [l] Jer 48:37
29:19 [m] Jer 43:10-13; Eze 30:4,10,24-25
29:20 [n] Isa 10:6-7; 45:1; Jer 25:9
29:21 [o] Ps 132:17 [p] Eze 33:22 [q] Eze 24:27
30:2 [r] Isa 13:6
30:3 [s] Eze 7:7; Joel 2:1,11; Ob 15 [t] ver 18; Eze 7:12,19

Eze 29:9-10 ❖ How can we be careful not to take credit for God's work? Why is this sometimes tempting?

of the LORD came to me:[j] 18"Son of man,
Nebuchadnezzar[k] king of Babylon drove
his army in a hard campaign against
Tyre; every head was rubbed bare[l] and
every shoulder made raw. Yet he and his
army got no reward from the campaign
he led against Tyre. 19Therefore this is
what the Sovereign LORD says: I am going to give Egypt to Nebuchadnezzar
king of Babylon, and he will carry off
its wealth. He will loot and plunder the
land as pay for his army.[m] 20I have giv-
en him Egypt as a reward for his efforts
because he and his army did it for me,
declares the Sovereign LORD.[n]

21"On that day I will make a horn[c][o]
grow for the Israelites, and I will open
your mouth[p] among them. Then they
will know that I am the LORD.[q]"

A Lament Over Egypt

30 The word of the LORD came to me:
2"Son of man, prophesy and say:
'This is what the Sovereign LORD says:

"'Wail[r] and say,
"Alas for that day!"
3For the day is near,[s]
the day of the LORD[t] is near —
a day of clouds,
a time of doom for the nations.
4A sword will come against Egypt,
and anguish will come upon
Cush.[d]
When the slain fall in Egypt,

[a] *7* Syriac (see also Septuagint and Vulgate); Hebrew *and you caused their backs to stand*
[b] *10* That is, the upper Nile region
[c] *21* *Horn* here symbolizes strength.
[d] *4* That is, the upper Nile region; also in verses 5 and 9

29:8–11 God's people should have known better than to trust in Egypt. Still, Egypt is guilty of proving untrustworthy. Egypt's arrogant claims to creator status contribute to Judah's sin. As a result, she too will be judged by God and turned into an utter devastation (v. 10). The whole of Egypt will be uninhabited for forty years.

29:12–16 Egypt will be scattered among the nations and dispersed among the peoples, just like Judah. Even more strikingly, they will be returned to the land from which they originated (v. 14). But Egypt will not be fully restored (v. 16).

29:17–21 Though the effort expended was great, the plunder achieved at the end of Nebuchadnezzar's campaign was minimal (v. 18). In compensation, since they were working for the Lord (v. 20), the Lord will give Egypt's wealth as plunder for Nebuchadnezzar's army.

30:1–19 The prophet is instructed to wail and mourn for the coming of the day of the Lord's judgment on Egypt. Egypt's allies will fall along with Egypt. The entire confederacy will be reduced to a shattered and burned ruin at the hand of Nebuchadnezzar and his ruthless army (vv. 10–12). The cities of Egypt will be destroyed.

In the imagery of the cosmic day of the Lord, the light will be turned to darkness and the proud strength of Egypt brought to an end (v. 18). By

her wealth will be carried away
and her foundations torn
down.[u]

5 Cush and Libya,[v] Lydia and all Arabia,
Kub and the people[w] of the covenant
land will fall by the sword along with
Egypt.
6 " 'This is what the LORD says:

" 'The allies of Egypt will fall
and her proud strength will fail.
From Migdol to Aswan[x]
they will fall by the sword within
her,
declares the Sovereign LORD.
7 " 'They will be desolate
among desolate lands,
and their cities will lie
among ruined cities.[y]
8 Then they will know that I am the
LORD,
when I set fire to Egypt
and all her helpers are crushed.

9 " 'On that day messengers will go out
from me in ships to frighten Cush[z] out
of her complacency. Anguish[a] will take
hold of them on the day of Egypt's doom,
for it is sure to come.[b]

10 " 'This is what the Sovereign LORD
says:

" 'I will put an end to the hordes of
Egypt
by the hand of Nebuchadnezzar
king of Babylon.[c]
11 He and his army — the most ruthless
of nations[d] —
will be brought in to destroy the
land.
They will draw their swords against
Egypt
and fill the land with the slain.
12 I will dry up[e] the waters of the
Nile[f]
and sell the land to an evil nation;
by the hand of foreigners
I will lay waste the land and
everything in it.

I the LORD have spoken.

13 " 'This is what the Sovereign LORD
says:

" 'I will destroy the idols[g]
and put an end to the images in
Memphis.[h]
No longer will there be a prince in
Egypt,[i]
and I will spread fear throughout
the land.
14 I will lay[j] waste Upper Egypt,
set fire to Zoan[k]
and inflict punishment on
Thebes.[l]
15 I will pour out my wrath on
Pelusium,
the stronghold of Egypt,
and wipe out the hordes of
Thebes.
16 I will set fire to Egypt;
Pelusium will writhe in agony.
Thebes will be taken by storm;
Memphis will be in constant
distress.
17 The young men of Heliopolis[m] and
Bubastis
will fall by the sword,
and the cities themselves will go
into captivity.
18 Dark will be the day at Tahpanhes
when I break the yoke of
Egypt;[n]
there her proud strength will
come to an end.
She will be covered with clouds,
and her villages will go into
captivity.[o]
19 So I will inflict punishment on
Egypt,
and they will know that I am the
LORD.' "

30:4 [u] Eze 29:19
30:5 [v] Eze 27:10 [w] Jer 25:20
30:6 [x] Eze 29:10
30:7 [y] Eze 29:12
30:9 [z] Isa 18:1-2 [a] Isa 23:5 [b] Eze 32:9-10
30:10 [c] Eze 29:19
30:11 [d] Eze 28:7
30:12 [e] Isa 19:6 [f] Eze 29:9
30:13 [g] Jer 43:12 [h] Isa 19:13 [i] Zec 10:11
30:14 [j] Eze 29:14 [k] Ps 78:12,43 [l] Jer 46:25
30:17 [m] Ge 41:45
30:18 [n] Lev 26:13 [o] ver 3

---

this means, God will demonstrate conclusively his existence and power in front of a watching world.

✣ **29:1—30:19** Like Israel before him, Jesus faced the allure of the ways of the world. Whereas Israel failed, Jesus endured faithfully. He did so because he was not deceived by Satan (Mt 4:1-11). He saw clearly that things are not always as they appear. Satan offers a solution for our felt needs—immediate relief for the blister points of life. However, our felt needs are not always our real needs. Sometimes what offers temporary relief causes long-term problems.

Jesus rejected Satan's quick-fix solutions in favor of a life lived in obedience to God's call, a hard path that led all the way to the cross. Why did he do so? Because he saw the ultimate reality of life: that men and women would be eternally lost without a Savior, someone who lived the life of perfect obedience in their place and who died the death their sins deserved.

Pharaoh's Arms Are Broken

[20]In the eleventh year, in the first
month on the seventh day, the word of
the LORD came to me:[p] [21]"Son of man, I
have broken the arm[q] of Pharaoh king
of Egypt. It has not been bound up to
be healed[r] or put in a splint so that it
may become strong enough to hold a
sword. [22]Therefore this is what the Sovereign LORD says: I am against Pharaoh
king of Egypt.[s] I will break both his arms,
the good arm as well as the broken one,
and make the sword fall from his hand.[t]
[23]I will disperse the Egyptians among
the nations and scatter them through
the countries.[u] [24]I will strengthen[v] the
arms of the king of Babylon and put my
sword[w] in his hand, but I will break the
arms of Pharaoh, and he will groan before him like a mortally wounded man.
[25]I will strengthen the arms of the king of
Babylon, but the arms of Pharaoh will fall
limp. Then they will know that I am the
LORD, when I put my sword into the hand
of the king of Babylon and he brandish-
es it against Egypt. [26]I will disperse the
Egyptians among the nations and scatter
them through the countries. Then they
will know that I am the LORD.[x]"

Pharaoh as a Felled Cedar of Lebanon

31 In the eleventh year,[y] in the third
month on the first day, the word of
the LORD came to me:[z] [2]"Son of man, say to
Pharaoh king of Egypt and to his hordes:

"'Who can be compared with you in
majesty?
[3]Consider Assyria, once a cedar in
Lebanon,
with beautiful branches
overshadowing the forest;
it towered on high,
its top above the thick foliage.[a]
[4]The waters nourished it,
deep springs made it grow tall;
their streams flowed
all around its base
and sent their channels
to all the trees of the field.
[5]So it towered higher
than all the trees of the field;
its boughs increased
and its branches grew long,
spreading because of abundant
waters.[b]
[6]All the birds of the sky
nested in its boughs,
all the animals of the wild
gave birth under its branches;
all the great nations
lived in its shade.[c]
[7]It was majestic in beauty,
with its spreading boughs,
for its roots went down
to abundant waters.
[8]The cedars[d] in the garden of God
could not rival it,
nor could the junipers
equal its boughs,
nor could the plane trees
compare with its branches —
no tree in the garden of God
could match its beauty.[e]
[9]I made it beautiful
with abundant branches,
the envy of all the trees of Eden[f]
in the garden of God.[g]

[10]"'Therefore this is what the Sovereign LORD says: Because the great cedar towered over the thick foliage, and

30:20 [p] Eze 26:1; 29:17; 31:1
30:21 [q] Jer 48:25 [r] Jer 30:13; 46:11
30:22 [s] Jer 46:25 [t] Ps 37:17
30:23 [u] Eze 29:12
30:24 [v] Zec 10:6,12 [w] Eze 21:14; Zep 2:12
30:26 [x] Eze 29:12
31:1 [y] Jer 52:5 [z] Eze 30:20
31:3 [a] Isa 10:34
31:5 [b] Eze 17:5
31:6 [c] Eze 17:23; Mt 13:32
31:8 [d] Ps 80:10 [e] Ge 2:8-9
31:9 [f] Ge 2:8 [g] Ge 13:10; Eze 28:13

Eze 30:20-26 ❖ How does it comfort us to know that nations rise and fall by God's will? How might this also be challenging?

30:20-26 The defeat of Egypt is described in terms of breaking Pharaoh's arm, his source of strength. The fundamental contrast is between the broken arms of Pharaoh and the arms of Nebuchadnezzar strengthened by the Lord (v. 25). This bout is clearly not an equal contest.

The arm of the Lord is not directly referenced, but the Lord's action is evident everywhere. He is the one who will break Pharaoh's arms and strengthen Nebuchadnezzar's (vv. 22, 25). Nebuchadnezzar will draw the Lord's sword against Egypt, and the Lord will scatter the Egyptians among the nations (v. 26).

31:1-6 Pharaoh is like a cypress or a mighty cedar in Lebanon, a tree of supernatural proportions. Egypt's roots were fed by the deep springs under the earth (v. 4). She grew higher than all the other trees of the earth, providing shelter for all the birds of the air and the beasts of the field.

31:7-15 It was the Lord who had raised Egypt to her elevated status (v. 9), but she considered her attainments something of which to be proud. The Lord can just as easily cast her down. The source of execution is human (v. 11), but the instructions come from on high. The tree no longer provides shade and protection; instead, its fallen branches are merely a convenient resting place for them (v. 13). All the dominant nations that come after her are bound for the underworld (vv. 14-15).

because it was proud[h] of its height, 11I
gave it into the hands of the ruler of the
nations, for him to deal with according
to its wickedness. I cast it aside,[i] 12and
the most ruthless of foreign nations[j]
cut it down and left it. Its boughs fell
on the mountains and in all the valleys;[k] its branches lay broken in all the
ravines of the land. All the nations of
the earth came out from under its shade
and left it.[l] 13All the birds settled on the
fallen tree, and all the wild animals
lived among its branches.[m] 14Therefore
no other trees by the waters are ever to
tower proudly on high, lifting their tops
above the thick foliage. No other trees
so well-watered are ever to reach such a
height; they are all destined for death,[n]
for the earth below, among mortals who
go down to the realm of the dead.[o]
15" 'This is what the Sovereign LORD
says: On the day it was brought down
to the realm of the dead I covered the
deep springs with mourning for it; I held
back its streams, and its abundant waters
were restrained. Because of it I clothed
Lebanon with gloom, and all the trees
of the field withered away. 16I made the
nations tremble[p] at the sound of its fall
when I brought it down to the realm of
the dead to be with those who go down
to the pit. Then all the trees[q] of Eden,
the choicest and best of Lebanon, the
well-watered trees, were consoled[r] in the
earth below.[s] 17They too, like the great
cedar, had gone down to the realm of
the dead, to those killed by the sword,[t]
along with the armed men who lived in
its shade among the nations.
18" 'Which of the trees of Eden can be
compared with you in splendor and majesty? Yet you, too, will be brought down
with the trees of Eden to the earth below;
you will lie among the uncircumcised,[u]
with those killed by the sword.
" 'This is Pharaoh and all his hordes,
declares the Sovereign LORD.' "

31:10 [h] Isa 14:13-14; Eze 28:17
31:11 [i] Da 5:20
31:12 [j] Eze 28:7 [k] Eze 32:5; 35:8 [l] Eze 32:11-12; Da 4:14
31:13 [m] Isa 18:6; Eze 29:5; 32:4
31:14 [n] Ps 82:7 [o] Ps 63:9; Eze 26:20; 32:24
31:16 [p] Eze 26:15 [q] Isa 14:8 [r] Eze 14:22; 32:31 [s] Isa 14:15; Eze 32:18
31:17 [t] Ps 9:17
31:18 [u] Jer 9:26; Eze 32:19, 21
32:1 [v] Eze 31:1; 33:21
32:2 [w] Eze 19:1; 27:2 [x] Eze 19:3, 6; Na 2:11-13 [y] Eze 29:3; 34:18
32:3 [z] Eze 12:13
32:4 [a] Isa 18:6; Eze 31:12-13
32:5 [b] Eze 31:12
32:6 [c] Isa 34:3

Eze 31:10-14 ❖ Why do the wicked and proud often look more impressive than everyone else? How are their fortunes reversed in the end?

Eze 32:1-15 ❖ How does Pharaoh serve as a cautionary example against pride and selfishness?

A Lament Over Pharaoh

32 In the twelfth year, in the twelfth
month on the first day, the word
of the LORD came to me:[v] 2"Son of man,
take up a lament[w] concerning Pharaoh
king of Egypt and say to him:

" 'You are like a lion[x] among the nations;
you are like a monster in the seas
thrashing about in your streams,
churning the water with your feet
and muddying the streams.[y]

3" 'This is what the Sovereign LORD
says:

" 'With a great throng of people
I will cast my net over you,
and they will haul you up in my net.[z]
4I will throw you on the land
and hurl you on the open field.
I will let all the birds of the sky settle on you
and all the animals of the wild
gorge themselves on you.[a]
5I will spread your flesh on the mountains
and fill the valleys[b] with your remains.
6I will drench the land with your flowing blood[c]
all the way to the mountains,
and the ravines will be filled with your flesh.
7When I snuff you out, I will cover the heavens
and darken their stars;

31:16–18 The predecessors who had envied the beautiful tree were gratified to see its demise, while those who had allied themselves to it went down with it to Sheol (v. 17). Ezekiel brings out the point of the word picture explicitly in v. 18: Though Egypt's splendor and majesty were unrivaled in all the powerful nations who went before, she too will share their fate in the underworld.

32:1–6 The lion and crocodile are two mighty beasts who appear all-powerful, yet once more the Lord will cast his net over Pharaoh. His corpse will be thrown to the ground to provide a home and food for the birds of the air and beasts of the field. His body is big enough to be spread on the mountains and fill the valleys, his blood enough to water the land and fill the ravines (vv. 5–6).

32:7–10 When Egypt falls, the heavens will be darkened, and sun, moon, and stars will fail to give light. The peoples will be appalled, and their kings will shudder because of the scale of Egypt's devastation, fearing for their own lives.

I will cover the sun with a cloud,
and the moon will not give its light.[d]
8 All the shining lights in the heavens
I will darken over you;
I will bring darkness over your land,
declares the Sovereign LORD.
9 I will trouble the hearts of many peoples
when I bring about your destruction among the nations,
among[a] lands you have not known.
10 I will cause many peoples to be appalled at you,
and their kings will shudder with horror because of you
when I brandish my sword before them.
On the day[e] of your downfall
each of them will tremble
every moment for his life.[f]

11 " 'For this is what the Sovereign LORD says:

" 'The sword of the king of Babylon[g]
will come against you.
12 I will cause your hordes to fall
by the swords of mighty men —
the most ruthless of all nations.[h]
They will shatter the pride of Egypt,
and all her hordes will be overthrown.[i]
13 I will destroy all her cattle
from beside abundant waters
no longer to be stirred by the foot of man
or muddied by the hooves of cattle.[j]
14 Then I will let her waters settle
and make her streams flow like oil,
declares the Sovereign LORD.
15 When I make Egypt desolate
and strip the land of everything in it,
when I strike down all who live there,
then they will know that I am the LORD.[k]'

16 "This is the lament[l] they will chant
for her. The daughters of the nations will
chant it; for Egypt and all her hordes
they will chant it, declares the Sovereign LORD."

Egypt's Descent Into the Realm of the Dead

17 In the twelfth year, on the fifteenth
day of the month, the word of the LORD
came to me:[m] 18 "Son of man, wail for

32:7 [d] Isa 13:10; 34:4; Eze 30:3; Joel 2:2,31; 3:15; Mt 24:29; Rev 8:12
32:10 [e] Jer 46:10 [f] Eze 26:16; 27:35
32:11 [g] Jer 46:26
32:12 [h] Eze 28:7 [i] Eze 31:11-12
32:13 [j] Eze 29:8, 11
32:15 [k] Ex 7:5; 14:4,18; Ps 107:33-34; Eze 6:7
32:16 [l] 2Sa 1:17; 2Ch 35:25; Eze 26:17
32:17 [m] ver 1

[a] 9 Hebrew; Septuagint *bring you into captivity among the nations, / to*

32:11–16 In this final onslaught against Egypt, the king of Babylon will shatter her pride. All people and animals will be cut off from the land. The waters of Egypt will flow as clear and smooth as oil, untroubled by any disturbance (v. 14). Egypt will once again recognize the sovereign power of the Lord; all that waits is the execution of the divine decree (v. 16).

32:17–32 The final oracle draws out and expands an idea present in an earlier pronouncement: Egypt's future home will be among the unquiet dead and those who fell by the sword (v. 21). A place of punishment is prepared, and Pharaoh qualifies to join the club (v. 28). Pharaoh, like the kings of the other nations, spreads terror in the land of the living, but soon he will become merely a part of the terror that inhabits the land of the dead. The sovereign Lord has spoken (v. 32).

30:20—32:32 The declaration on US bank notes is unequivocal: "In God we trust." Unfortunately, it is a single-mindedness that few of us, even as Christians, live out in practice. The temptation to trust in the paper on which the slogan is written rather than in the God of whom the slogan speaks is real.

Consider the power of the myth of career. How many people have devoted their lives to finding a fulfilling and rewarding job? In the process, they may sacrifice precious relationships and outside interests on the altar of success, which they have defined as career progress. How many find, if they finally reach the top of the ladder, that they wish they had climbed a different one?

But perhaps these two idols are too obvious. Perhaps we have instead sacrificed everything on the altar of family. What could be more noble than laying down our lives for the sake of our loved ones? Yet if we only trust in family to provide meaning and value in our lives, then we too are headed for disappointment sooner or later.

The ultimate dissolution of all earthly relationships is a fact that cannot be overstated. Relationships by blood or marriage may serve to gain us citizenship in earthly kingdoms, but like money and career, they will do us no good when it comes to citizenship in the kingdom of heaven. This is why Christians hope in and point the way to a better kingdom beyond this world (Mt 6:19–24).

the hordes of Egypt and consign[n] to the earth below both her and the daughters of mighty nations, along with those who go down to the pit.[o] 19Say to them, 'Are you more favored than others? Go down and be laid among the uncircumcised.'[p] 20They will fall among those killed by the sword. The sword is drawn; let her be dragged[q] off with all her hordes. 21From within the realm of the dead[r] the mighty leaders will say of Egypt and her allies, 'They have come down and they lie with the uncircumcised, with those killed by the sword.'

22"Assyria is there with her whole army; she is surrounded by the graves of all her slain, all who have fallen by the sword. 23Their graves are in the depths of the pit[s] and her army lies around her grave. All who had spread terror in the land of the living are slain, fallen by the sword.

24"Elam[t] is there, with all her hordes around her grave. All of them are slain, fallen by the sword.[u] All who had spread terror in the land of the living[v] went down uncircumcised to the earth below. They bear their shame with those who go down to the pit.[w] 25A bed is made for her among the slain, with all her hordes around her grave. All of them are uncircumcised, killed by the sword. Because their terror had spread in the land of the living, they bear their shame with those who go down to the pit; they are laid among the slain.

26"Meshek and Tubal[x] are there, with all their hordes around their graves. All of them are uncircumcised, killed by the sword because they spread their terror in the land of the living. 27But they do not lie with the fallen warriors of old,[a] who went down to the realm of the dead with their weapons of war — their swords placed under their heads and their shields[b] resting on their bones — though these warriors also had terrorized the land of the living.

28"You too, Pharaoh, will be broken and will lie among the uncircumcised, with those killed by the sword.

29"Edom[y] is there, her kings and all her princes; despite their power, they are laid with those killed by the sword. They lie with the uncircumcised, with those who go down to the pit.[z]

30"All the princes of the north[a] and all the Sidonians[b] are there; they went down with the slain in disgrace despite the terror caused by their power. They lie uncircumcised with those killed by the sword and bear their shame with those who go down to the pit.

31"Pharaoh — he and all his army — will see them and he will be consoled[c] for all his hordes that were killed by the sword, declares the Sovereign LORD. 32Although I had him spread terror in the land of the living, Pharaoh and all his hordes will be laid among the uncircumcised, with those killed by the sword, declares the Sovereign LORD."

Renewal of Ezekiel's Call as Watchman

33 The word of the LORD came to me: 2"Son of man, speak to your people and say to them: 'When I bring the sword[d] against a land, and the people of the land choose one of their men and make him their watchman,[e] 3and he sees the sword coming against the land and blows the trumpet[f] to warn the people, 4then if anyone hears the trumpet but does not heed the warning[g] and the sword comes and takes their life, their blood will be on their own head.[h] 5Since they heard the sound of the trumpet but did not heed the warning, their blood will be on their own head. If they had heeded the warning, they would have saved themselves. 6But if the watchman sees the sword coming and does not blow the trumpet to warn the people and the sword comes and takes someone's life, that person's life will be taken because of their sin, but I will hold the watchman accountable for their blood.'[i]

7"Son of man, I have made you a watchman for the people of Israel; so hear the word I speak and give them warning from me.[j] 8When I say to the

32:18 [n]Jer 1:10 [o]Eze 31:14,16; Mic 1:8
32:19 [p]ver 29-30; Eze 28:10; 31:18
32:20 [q]Ps 28:3
32:21 [r]Isa 14:9
32:23 [s]Isa 14:15
32:24 [t]Ge 10:22 [u]Jer 49:37 [v]Job 28:13 [w]Eze 26:20
32:26 [x]Ge 10:2; Eze 27:13
32:29 [y]Isa 34:5-15; Jer 49:7; Eze 35:15; Ob 1 [z]Eze 25:12-14
32:30 [a]Jer 25:26; Eze 38:6; 39:2 [b]Jer 25:22; Eze 28:21
32:31 [c]Eze 14:22; 31:16
33:2 [d]Jer 12:12 [e]Eze 3:11
33:3 [f]Hos 8:1
33:4 [g]2Ch 25:16 [h]Jer 6:17; Eze 18:13; Zec 1:4; Ac 18:6
33:6 [i]Eze 3:18
33:7 [j]Jer 26:2; Eze 3:17

[a] 27 Septuagint; Hebrew *warriors who were uncircumcised* [b] 27 Probable reading of the original Hebrew text; Masoretic Text *punishment*

33:1-10 The watchman was responsible for the consequences of what came to the city only if he did not warn the people (vv. 2-6). From this general principle, Ezekiel moves to the specific case facing the people in vv. 7-9: Clearly, he is free from any culpability in the death of the wicked.

But does this mean that there is now no hope for God's rebellious people? This seems to have been the thought among at least some of the exiles (v. 10).

wicked, 'You wicked person, you will
surely die,[k]' and you do not speak out
to dissuade them from their ways, that
wicked person will die for[a] their sin,
and I will hold you accountable for their
blood.[l] 9But if you do warn the wicked
person to turn from their ways and they
do not do so, they will die for their sin,
though you yourself will be saved.[m]
10"Son of man, say to the Israelites,
'This is what you are saying: "Our offenses and sins weigh us down, and we are
wasting away[n] because of[b] them. How
then can we live?[o]"' 11Say to them, 'As
surely as I live, declares the Sovereign
LORD, I take no pleasure in the death
of the wicked, but rather that they turn
from their ways and live.[p] Turn! Turn
from your evil ways! Why will you die,
people of Israel?'[q]
12"Therefore, son of man, say to your
people, 'If someone who is righteous
disobeys, that person's former righteousness will count for nothing. And
if someone who is wicked repents, that
person's former wickedness will not
bring condemnation. The righteous person who sins will not be allowed to live
even though they were formerly righteous.'[r] 13If I tell a righteous person that
they will surely live, but then they trust
in their righteousness and do evil, none
of the righteous things that person has
done will be remembered; they will die
for the evil they have done.[s] 14And if I say
to a wicked person, 'You will surely die,'
but they then turn away from their sin
and do what is just[t] and right — 15if they
give back what they took in pledge for a
loan, return what they have stolen,[u] follow the decrees that give life, and do no
evil — that person will surely live; they

33:8 [k]ver 14 [l]Eze 18:4
33:9 [m]Eze 3:17-19
33:10 [n]Eze 24:23 [o]Lev 26:39; Eze 4:17
33:11 [p]Eze 18:32; 2Pe 3:9 [q]Eze 18:23
33:12 [r]2Ch 7:14; Eze 3:20
33:13 [s]Eze 18:24; Heb 10:38; 2Pe 2:20-21
33:14 [t]Eze 18:27
33:15 [u]Ex 22:1-4; Lev 6:2-5
[v]Eze 20:11; Lk 19:8
33:16 [w]Isa 43:25; Eze 18:22
33:18 [x]Eze 3:20; Eze 18:26
33:21 [y]Eze 24:26 [z]2Ki 25:4,10; Jer 39:1-2; Eze 32:1
33:22 [a]Eze 1:3 [b]Lk 1:64 [c]Eze 3:26-27; 24:27
33:24 [d]Eze 36:4 [e]Isa 51:2; Jer 40:7; Eze 11:15; Ac 7:5
33:25 [f]Ge 9:4; Dt 12:16

Eze 33:12-16 ❖ Humans are fickle, wavering between righteous and unrighteous acts. What hope, then, is there for finding salvation (see Ro 5:8)?

will not die.[v] 16None of the sins that person has committed will be remembered
against them. They have done what is
just and right; they will surely live.[w]
17"Yet your people say, 'The way of the
Lord is not just.' But it is their way that
is not just. 18If a righteous person turns
from their righteousness and does evil,
they will die for it.[x] 19And if a wicked person turns away from their wickedness
and does what is just and right, they will
live by doing so. 20Yet you Israelites say,
'The way of the Lord is not just.' But I
will judge each of you according to your
own ways."

Jerusalem's Fall Explained

21In the twelfth year of our exile, in the
tenth month on the fifth day, a man who
had escaped[y] from Jerusalem came to me
and said, "The city has fallen![z]" 22Now
the evening before the man arrived, the
hand of the LORD was on me,[a] and he
opened my mouth[b] before the man came
to me in the morning. So my mouth was
opened and I was no longer silent.[c]
23Then the word of the LORD came to
me: 24"Son of man, the people living in
those ruins[d] in the land of Israel are saying, 'Abraham was only one man, yet he
possessed the land. But we are many;
surely the land has been given to us as
our possession.'[e] 25Therefore say to them,
'This is what the Sovereign LORD says:
Since you eat meat with the blood[f] still in

[a] *8* Or *in*; also in verse 9 [b] *10* Or *away in*

33:11-16 Ezekiel's answer to that question is that the living God takes no pleasure in the death of the wicked but rather seeks their repentance that they may live (v. 11). Even now, it is not too late to turn and be saved. The fundamental covenant choice of life or death is still open to the people.

The prophet appeals to two case studies. In the first case, someone trusts in their former righteousness (v. 13) and does evil; they will surely die and not live. In the second, a wicked man turns from his sins and does what is right; he will surely live and not die. Neither judgment nor salvation is an automatic process. Each works itself out through a life lived in accordance with the terms of the covenant.

33:17-20 The problem is with the people's lack of righteousness. They have consistently chosen the path to death over the path to life. That is what makes it bad news that God will judge each according to their own ways (v. 20).

33:21-22 This is the context in which Ezekiel places the news of Jerusalem's destruction. Ezekiel's lack of ability to speak (3:26-27) is now removed. The possibility of a new beginning for God's people similarly exists. But which will they choose: life or death?

33:23-24 Both back home in Judah and among the exiles it is business as usual. Those who remain behind in Judah see the situation as an opportunity for economic gain. They interpret God's covenant promise of the land to Abraham as an inalienable right, an unconditional covenant (v. 24).

33:25-29 The prophet describes the people's disobedience in stereotypical terms. These

it and look to your idols and shed blood,
should you then possess the land?[g] 26You
rely on your sword, you do detestable
things, and each of you defiles his neighbor's wife.[h] Should you then possess the
land?'
27"Say this to them: 'This is what the
Sovereign LORD says: As surely as I live,
those who are left in the ruins will fall by
the sword, those out in the country I will
give to the wild animals to be devoured,
and those in strongholds and caves will
die of a plague.[i] 28I will make the land a
desolate waste, and her proud strength
will come to an end, and the mountains
of Israel will become desolate so that
no one will cross them. 29Then they will
know that I am the LORD, when I have
made the land a desolate waste because
of all the detestable things they have
done.'
30"As for you, son of man, your people are talking together about you by
the walls and at the doors of the houses,
saying to each other, 'Come and hear the
message that has come from the LORD.'
31My people come to you, as they usually do, and sit before[j] you to hear your
words, but they do not put them into
practice. Their mouths speak of love, but
their hearts are greedy for unjust gain.[k]
32Indeed, to them you are nothing more
than one who sings love songs with a
beautiful voice and plays an instrument
well, for they hear your words but do not
put them into practice.[l]
33"When all this comes true — and it
surely will — then they will know that a
prophet has been among them.[m]"

33:25 [g] Jer 7:9-10; Eze 22:6,27
33:26 [h] Eze 22:11
33:27 [i] 1Sa 13:6; Isa 2:19; Jer 42:22; Eze 39:4
33:31 [j] Eze 8:1 [k] Ps 78:36-37; Isa 29:13; Eze 22:27; Mt 13:22; 1Jn 3:18
33:32 [l] Mk 6:20
33:33 [m] 1Sa 3:20; Jer 28:9; Eze 2:5
34:2 [n] Ps 78:70-72; Isa 40:11; Jer 3:15; 23:1; Mic 3:11; Jn 10:11; 21:15-17
34:3 [o] Isa 56:11; Eze 22:27; Zec 11:16
34:4 [p] Zec 11:15-17
34:5 [q] Nu 27:17 [r] ver 28; Isa 56:9
34:6 [s] Ps 142:4; 1Pe 2:25

Eze 34:1-6 ❖ God has called us to be shepherds for part of his flock in that we all have influence in the lives of others. How can we live up to God's will for his shepherds as described in these verses?

The LORD Will Be Israel's Shepherd

34 The word of the LORD came to me:
2"Son of man, prophesy against the
shepherds of Israel; prophesy and say to
them: 'This is what the Sovereign LORD
says: Woe to you shepherds of Israel who
only take care of yourselves! Should not
shepherds take care of the flock?[n] 3You eat
the curds, clothe yourselves with the wool
and slaughter the choice animals, but you
do not take care of the flock.[o] 4You have
not strengthened the weak or healed the
sick or bound up the injured. You have
not brought back the strays or searched
for the lost. You have ruled them harshly and brutally.[p] 5So they were scattered
because there was no shepherd,[q] and
when they were scattered they became
food for all the wild animals.[r] 6My sheep
wandered over all the mountains and on
every high hill. They were scattered over
the whole earth, and no one searched or
looked for them.[s]
7"'Therefore, you shepherds, hear the
word of the LORD: 8As surely as I live,
declares the Sovereign LORD, because
my flock lacks a shepherd and so has
been plundered and has become food
for all the wild animals, and because my
shepherds did not search for my flock but
cared for themselves rather than for my

---

covenant-breakers will inherit the three curses of the covenant: the sword, wild animals, and plague (v. 27; cf. Lev 26:22, 25). The land will continue to suffer God's judgment until it becomes a desolate wasteland (cf. Lev 26:32–33).

33:30–33 The matters just described are no better among the exiles. The news of Jerusalem's fall appears to have given Ezekiel's message a certain popularity (v. 30). His declarations on spiritual matters may arouse curiosity but are scarcely taken as authoritative. Time, however, will prove the power of the word of the Lord through Ezekiel.

33:1–33 For some, a major life crisis may cause them to attend church, but only as superficial hearers. Like Ezekiel's audience, they may find the form of the message interesting and stimulating, but they never feel its power in their hearts as a life-changing reality. In our day, there is a focus on "seeker-sensitive" services that will present the gospel in a way that will be attractive to such people. The end task of the church, however, is first to assemble seekers and then to make disciples.

34:1–16 This chapter opens with an oracle against "the shepherds of Israel."

34:1–6 Ezekiel's oracle of judgment declares that the Lord is coming *against* his shepherds—the former kings of Judah—because they have failed to fulfill their role of shepherd properly. These shepherds have viewed their position as an opportunity for personal gain.

34:7–16 Judgment is coming on these failed shepherds. In the absence of a true shepherd, the flock has been scattered and plundered. But now their shepherding will be ended as the Lord rescues his sheep (v. 10). The Lord will himself search out and care for the flock, gathering them from all the places where they were scattered.

flock, 9therefore, you shepherds, hear
the word of the LORD: 10This is what the
Sovereign LORD says: I am against[t] the
shepherds and will hold them accountable for my flock. I will remove them
from tending the flock so that the shepherds can no longer feed themselves. I
will rescue[u] my flock from their mouths,
and it will no longer be food for them.[v]
11" 'For this is what the Sovereign LORD
says: I myself will search for my sheep
and look after them. 12As a shepherd[w]
looks after his scattered flock when he is
with them, so will I look after my sheep.
I will rescue them from all the places
where they were scattered on a day of
clouds and darkness.[x] 13I will bring them
out from the nations and gather them
from the countries, and I will bring
them into their own land. I will pasture
them on the mountains of Israel, in the
ravines and in all the settlements in the
land.[y] 14I will tend them in a good pasture, and the mountain heights of Israel[z]
will be their grazing land. There they
will lie down in good grazing land, and
there they will feed in a rich pasture[a]
on the mountains of Israel.[b] 15I myself
will tend my sheep and have them lie
down, declares the Sovereign LORD.[c] 16I
will search for the lost and bring back
the strays. I will bind up the injured and
strengthen the weak,[d] but the sleek and
the strong I will destroy. I will shepherd
the flock with justice.[e]
17" 'As for you, my flock, this is what
the Sovereign LORD says: I will judge between one sheep and another, and between rams and goats.[f] 18Is it not enough
for you to feed on the good pasture? Must
you also trample the rest of your pasture with your feet? Is it not enough for
you to drink clear water? Must you also
muddy the rest with your feet? 19Must
my flock feed on what you have trampled and drink what you have muddied
with your feet?
20" 'Therefore this is what the Sovereign LORD says to them: See, I myself
will judge between the fat sheep and
the lean sheep. 21Because you shove
with flank and shoulder, butting all the
weak sheep with your horns[g] until you
have driven them away, 22I will save my
flock, and they will no longer be plundered. I will judge between one sheep
and another.[h] 23I will place over them
one shepherd, my servant David, and he
will tend[i] them; he will tend them and be
their shepherd. 24I the LORD will be their
God,[j] and my servant David will be prince
among them. I the LORD have spoken.[k]
25" 'I will make a covenant of peace
with them and rid the land of savage
beasts[l] so that they may live in the wilderness and sleep in the forests in safety.[m] 26I will make them and the places
surrounding my hill a blessing.[a][n] I will
send down showers in season;[o] there
will be showers of blessing.[p] 27The trees
will yield their fruit and the ground will
yield its crops; the people will be secure

34:10 [t]Jer 21:13 [u]Ps 72:14 [v]1Sa 2:29-30; Zec 10:3
34:12 [w]Isa 40:11; Jer 31:10; Lk 19:10 [x]Eze 30:3
34:13 [y]Jer 23:3
34:14 [z]Eze 20:40 [a]Ps 23:2 [b]Eze 36:29-30
34:15 [c]Ps 23:1-2
34:16 [d]Mic 4:6 [e]Isa 10:16; Lk 5:32
34:17 [f]Mt 25:32-33
34:21 [g]Dt 33:17
34:22 [h]Ps 72:12-14; Jer 23:2-3
34:23 [i]Isa 40:11
34:24 [j]Eze 36:28 [k]Jer 30:9
34:25 [l]Lev 26:6 [m]Isa 11:6-9; Hos 2:18
34:26 [n]Ge 12:2 [o]Ps 68:9 [p]Dt 11:13-15; Isa 44:3

[a] 26 Or *I will cause them and the places surrounding my hill to be named in blessings* (see Gen. 48:20); or *I will cause them and the places surrounding my hill to be seen as blessed*

34:17–21 The image of God as the Good Shepherd leads into a further oracle of judgment against the "rams and goats" (v. 17) or the "fat sheep" (v. 20). These are the broader class of leaders of the community: those who had oppressed the weak.

34:22–24 The Lord will intervene to execute judgment within his flock, setting up over them "one shepherd, my servant David," who will act as their "prince" (vv. 23–24). This future ruler is nothing less than the fulfillment of the covenant with David. That covenant promise will be fulfilled with the raising up of a new David (v. 23), who will be the Lord's servant and his people's shepherd.

34:25–31 In addition, the Lord will make "a covenant of peace" (v. 25) with his flock. In place of the curses of the Sinai covenant (Lev 26:14–35), they will now experience the blessings of the covenant (Lev 26:4–13). The state of experiencing the blessings that flow from a harmonious relationship with God is what makes this distinctively a "covenant of peace." This covenant is thus not so much a "new" covenant as it is the experience of the blessings promised in the original covenant. The people will be his sheep and he will be their God.

34:1–31 What does it mean for a Christian leader to be a shepherd? It is a unique combination of afflicting the comfortable and comforting the afflicted. The bad shepherds of Eze 34 were criticized because they ignored the fat sheep who were oppressing the other sheep, while they lived comfortably off the products of the flock. In contrast, the good shepherd will both confront the fat sheep and tenderly care for the weak sheep (v. 16).

Taking care of the weak sheep is hard, painful, time-consuming work. As a result, some shepherds gradually turn into mere managers of the flock, and as long as the flock is growing in numbers, no one complains. God is against such shepherds, however. He is the one to whom every shepherd is ultimately accountable.

in their land. They will know that I am the LORD, when I break the bars of their yoke[q] and rescue them from the hands of those who enslaved them.[r] 28They will no longer be plundered by the nations, nor will wild animals devour them. They will live in safety, and no one will make them afraid.[s] 29I will provide for them a land renowned[t] for its crops, and they will no longer be victims of famine[u] in the land or bear the scorn[v] of the nations.[w] 30Then they will know that I, the LORD their God, am with them and that they, the Israelites, are my people, declares the Sovereign LORD.[x] 31You are my sheep, the sheep of my pasture,[y] and I am your God, declares the Sovereign LORD.' "

A Prophecy Against Edom

35 The word of the LORD came to me: 2"Son of man, set your face against Mount Seir; prophesy against it 3and say: 'This is what the Sovereign LORD says: I am against you, Mount Seir, and I will stretch out my hand[z] against you and make you a desolate waste.[a] 4I will turn your towns into ruins and you will be desolate. Then you will know that I am the LORD.[b]

5" 'Because you harbored an ancient hostility and delivered the Israelites over to the sword at the time of their calamity, the time their punishment reached its climax,[c] 6therefore as surely as I live, declares the Sovereign LORD, I will give you over to bloodshed and it will pursue you.[d] Since you did not hate bloodshed, bloodshed will pursue you. 7I will make Mount Seir a desolate waste and cut off from it all who come and go. 8I will fill your mountains with the slain; those killed by the sword will fall on your hills and in your valleys and in all your ravines.[e] 9I will make you desolate forever;

> **Eze 35:6** ❖ When we fail to hate sin, we invite it into our lives. From which particular sins or evil do we need to distance ourselves?

your towns will not be inhabited. Then you will know that I am the LORD.[f]

10" 'Because you have said, "These two nations and countries will be ours and we will take possession[g] of them," even though I the LORD was there, 11therefore as surely as I live, declares the Sovereign LORD, I will treat you in accordance with the anger[h] and jealousy you showed in your hatred of them and I will make myself known among them when I judge you.[i] 12Then you will know that I the LORD have heard all the contemptible things you have said against the mountains of Israel. You said, "They have been laid waste and have been given over to us to devour.[j]" 13You boasted against me and spoke against me without restraint, and I heard it.[k] 14This is what the Sovereign LORD says: While the whole earth rejoices, I will make you desolate.[l] 15Because you rejoiced[m] when the inheritance of Israel became desolate, that is how I will treat you. You will be desolate, Mount Seir,[n] you and all of Edom.[o] Then they will know that I am the LORD.' "

Hope for the Mountains of Israel

36 "Son of man, prophesy to the mountains of Israel and say, 'Mountains of Israel, hear the word of the LORD. 2This is what the Sovereign LORD says: The enemy said of you, "Aha![p] The ancient heights[q] have become our possession.[r]" ' 3Therefore prophesy and say, 'This is what the Sovereign LORD says: Because they ravaged and crushed you from every side so that you became the possession of the rest of the nations

34:27 [q]Lev 26:13 [r]Jer 30:8
34:28 [s]Jer 30:10; Eze 39:26
34:29 [t]Isa 4:2 [u]Eze 36:29 [v]Eze 36:6 [w]Eze 36:15
34:30 [x]Eze 14:11; 37:27
34:31 [y]Ps 100:3; Jer 23:1
35:3 [z]Jer 6:12 [a]Eze 25:12-14
35:4 [b]ver 9
35:5 [c]Ps 137:7; Eze 21:29
35:6 [d]Isa 63:2-6
35:8 [e]Eze 31:12
35:9 [f]Jer 49:13
35:10 [g]Ps 83:12; Eze 36:2,5
35:11 [h]Eze 25:14 [i]Ps 9:16; Mt 7:2
35:12 [j]Jer 50:7
35:13 [k]Da 11:36
35:14 [l]Jer 51:48
35:15 [m]Ob 12 [n]ver 3 [o]Isa 34:5-6,11; Jer 50:11-13; La 4:21
36:2 [p]Eze 25:3 [q]Dt 32:13 [r]Eze 35:10

35:1–4 The chapter opens with an address against Mount Seir, the symbol of Edom. Edom, the nation to the southeast of Judah, had apparently taken advantage of the destruction of Jerusalem to move into Judean territory and take it over. The Lord declared that because of this, judgment would come on Mount Seir.

35:5–9 The reason for God's judgment is given: Because the Edomites gave the Israelites over to the sword in their time of judgment. This hostility reached all the way back to the time of Jacob and Esau (Esau was also known as "Edom"), as recorded in Ge 27–28. Because Edom saw an opportunity to reclaim Esau's stolen birthright by helping the Babylonians, now they will become "desolate forever" (v. 9).

35:10–15 The source of Edom's constant hostility toward God's people becomes clear (v. 10). This ambition will be thwarted by the Lord's intervention. Just as Edom rejoiced at Israel's downfall, so many nations will rejoice at theirs (v. 15).

36:1–15 If ch. 35 gives the dark side of the future, this passage gives the bright side: the return of God's people to the land of promise. Edom will be brought down to the depths; Israel will return to possess the land that is now in the hands of many nations.

and the object of people's malicious talk
and slander,[s] 4therefore, mountains of
Israel, hear the word of the Sovereign
LORD: This is what the Sovereign LORD
says to the mountains and hills, to the
ravines and valleys,[t] to the desolate ruins
and the deserted towns that have been
plundered and ridiculed by the rest of
the nations around you[u]— 5this is what
the Sovereign LORD says: In my burning
zeal I have spoken against the rest of the
nations, and against all Edom, for with
glee and with malice in their hearts they
made my land their own possession so
that they might plunder its pastureland.'[v]
6Therefore prophesy concerning the land
of Israel and say to the mountains and
hills, to the ravines and valleys: 'This is
what the Sovereign LORD says: I speak in
my jealous wrath because you have suffered the scorn of the nations.[w] 7There-
fore this is what the Sovereign LORD says:
I swear with uplifted hand that the nations around you will also suffer scorn.
8" 'But you, mountains of Israel, will
produce branches and fruit[x] for my people Israel, for they will soon come home.
9I am concerned for you and will look on
you with favor; you will be plowed and
sown, 10and I will cause many people to
live on you—yes, all of Israel. The towns
will be inhabited and the ruins rebuilt.[y]
11I will increase the number of people
and animals living on you, and they will
be fruitful and become numerous. I will
settle people on you as in the past[z] and
will make you prosper more than before.[a] Then you will know that I am the
LORD. 12I will cause people, my people
Israel, to live on you. They will possess
you, and you will be their inheritance;[b]
you will never again deprive them of
their children.
13" 'This is what the Sovereign LORD
says: Because some say to you, "You devour people[c] and deprive your nation
of its children," 14therefore you will no
longer devour people or make your nation childless, declares the Sovereign
LORD. 15No longer will I make you hear
the taunts of the nations, and no longer
will you suffer the scorn of the peoples
or cause your nation to fall, declares the
Sovereign LORD.[d]' "

Israel's Restoration Assured

16Again the word of the LORD came to
me: 17"Son of man, when the people of
Israel were living in their own land, they
defiled it by their conduct and their actions. Their conduct was like a woman's
monthly uncleanness in my sight.[e] 18So
I poured out[f] my wrath on them because
they had shed blood in the land and because they had defiled it with their idols.
19I dispersed them among the nations,
and they were scattered[g] through the
countries; I judged them according to
their conduct and their actions.[h] 20And
wherever they went among the nations
they profaned[i] my holy name, for it was
said of them, 'These are the LORD's people, and yet they had to leave his land.'[j]
21I had concern for my holy name, which

36:3 [s] Ps 44:13-14
36:4 [t] Eze 6:3 [u] Dt 11:11; Ps 79:4; Eze 34:28
36:5 [v] Jer 50:11; Eze 25:12-14; 35:10,15
36:6 [w] Ps 123:3-4; Eze 34:29
36:8 [x] Isa 27:6
36:10 [y] ver 33; Isa 49:17-23
36:11 [z] Mic 7:14 [a] Jer 31:28; Eze 16:55
36:12 [b] Eze 47:14,22
36:13 [c] Nu 13:32
36:15 [d] Ps 89:50-51; Eze 34:29
36:17 [e] Jer 2:7
36:18 [f] 2Ch 34:21
36:19 [g] Dt 28:64 [h] Eze 39:24
36:20 [i] Ro 2:24 [j] Isa 52:5; Jer 33:24; Eze 12:16

36:5–15 Edom's fate represents all who seek to benefit from Israel's misfortune. They will meet the same end at the hands of Israel's jealous God. Israel has once again become "my people" (v. 8). The mountains of Israel will burst forth with a primeval fruitfulness as the Lord turns his face toward them in blessing. People and animals will multiply and be fruitful for the Israelites (v. 11), an echo of the creation mandate in Ge 1:28. This re-creation will not merely be a return to the former status quo but will be something even better than their original state.

35:1—36:15 Despite Israel's sin and rebellion against God, the honor of his name required him to preserve for himself a people. Astonishingly, the way in which he has chosen to do so is by grafting the Gentiles into a new nonethnic entity: the true Israel of God (Ro 11:17, 26; Gal 6:16). We were grafted into the vine because he chose us to bear lasting fruit for him (Jn 15:16). All is of grace, even our fruitfulness, so that no one can boast in the presence of God.

36:16–18 The people, while they lived in their own land, polluted it by their actions. As a result, they could not remain in God's presence, and he could not remain in their midst. Communication with God through the OT means of grace was impossible when one was in a state of impurity as a result of contact with death.

Israel had turned the land into a permanent place of death, unfit for divine habitation (v. 18). God had no choice but to bring the curses of the covenant, just as he had threatened when they first entered the land (Dt 29:22–28).

36:19–21 This action, however, created a new problem for God. He had established a relationship between himself, his people, and the land. Yet now the nations could see that the Lord's people were absent from his land. That three-way relationship had been broken. While Israel was scattered among the nations, they continually profaned the divine name (vv. 20–21) simply by being in exile instead of in the land of promise.

36:22–23 Because of the sovereign, irrevocable

the people of Israel profaned among the nations where they had gone.[k]

22 "Therefore say to the Israelites, 'This is what the Sovereign LORD says: It is not for your sake, people of Israel, that I am going to do these things, but for the sake of my holy name, which you have profaned[l] among the nations where you have gone.[m] 23 I will show the holiness of my great name, which has been profaned among the nations, the name you have profaned among them. Then the nations will know that I am the LORD, declares the Sovereign LORD, when I am proved holy[n] through you before their eyes.[o]

24 " 'For I will take you out of the nations; I will gather you from all the countries and bring you back into your own land.[p] 25 I will sprinkle[q] clean water on you, and you will be clean; I will cleanse[r] you from all your impurities and from all your idols.[s] 26 I will give you a new heart[t] and put a new spirit in you; I will remove from you your heart of stone and give you a heart of flesh.[u] 27 And I will put my Spirit[v] in you and move you to follow my decrees and be careful to keep my laws. 28 Then you will live in the land I gave your ancestors; you will be my people,[w] and I will be your God.[x] 29 I will save you from all your uncleanness. I will call for the grain and make it plentiful and will not bring famine[y] upon you. 30 I will increase the fruit of the trees and the crops of the field, so that you will no longer suffer disgrace among the nations because of famine.[z]

36:21 [k] Ps 74:18; Isa 48:9
36:22 [l] Ro 2:24* [m] Ps 106:8
36:23 [n] Eze 20:41 [o] Ps 126:2; Isa 5:16
36:24 [p] Eze 34:13; 37:21
36:25 [q] Heb 9:13; 10:22 [r] Ps 51:2,7 [s] Zec 13:2
36:26 [t] Jer 24:7 [u] Ps 51:10; Eze 11:19
36:27 [v] Eze 37:14
36:28 [w] Jer 30:22 [x] Eze 14:11; 37:14,27
36:29 [y] Eze 34:29
36:30 [z] Lev 26:4-5; Eze 34:27; Hos 2:21-22

36:31 [a] Eze 6:9; 20:43
36:32 [b] Dt 9:5
36:35 [c] Joel 2:3 [d] Isa 51:3
36:36 [e] Eze 17:22; 22:14; 37:14; 39:27-28
36:38 [f] 1Ki 8:63; 2Ch 35:7-9

Eze 36:24–32 ❖ How can we know God has given us new hearts and his Spirit? What is the evidence in our lives of these things?

31 Then you will remember your evil ways and wicked deeds, and you will loathe yourselves for your sins and detestable practices.[a] 32 I want you to know that I am not doing this for your sake, declares the Sovereign LORD. Be ashamed and disgraced for your conduct, people of Israel![b]

33 " 'This is what the Sovereign LORD says: On the day I cleanse you from all your sins, I will resettle your towns, and the ruins will be rebuilt. 34 The desolate land will be cultivated instead of lying desolate in the sight of all who pass through it. 35 They will say, "This land that was laid waste has become like the garden of Eden;[c] the cities that were lying in ruins, desolate and destroyed, are now fortified and inhabited.[d]" 36 Then the nations around you that remain will know that I the LORD have rebuilt what was destroyed and have replanted what was desolate. I the LORD have spoken, and I will do it.'[e]

37 "This is what the Sovereign LORD says: Once again I will yield to Israel's plea and do this for them: I will make their people as numerous as sheep, 38 as numerous as the flocks for offerings[f] at Jerusalem during her appointed festivals. So will the ruined cities be filled with flocks of people. Then they will know that I am the LORD."

---

covenant, mercy not only *may* but *must* be shown to Israel. The honor of God's name will be vindicated by a show of power among the nations when he brings Israel back to her land. The Lord will act, not for Israel's sake, but for the sake of his own name.

36:24–25 This act involves a total change in Israel's nature. When Israel is gathered and returned from the nations to its own land, she will be cleansed from all her past impurities and idolatries (v. 25).

36:26–30 Israel's heart and spirit will be made new. Unresponsive, unyielding stone will be replaced by warm, living, responsive flesh (v. 26). The Spirit of God will indwell them and create in them both the will and the ability to obey God and dwell with him in blessing (vv. 27–30).

36:31–38 God will also restore the land, making it "like the garden of Eden" (v. 35). Places that were torn down will be inhabited and fortified. Numerous "people" (vv. 37–38) will fill the cities to overflowing. The chief blessing, however, will be that God permits himself to be sought by them to act on their behalf (v. 37).

✣ **36:16–38** The work of God in believers is a two-stage process, just as it is depicted in Eze 36. First there is an initial work of *purification*, which corresponds to the outward sprinkling of water on the restored Israel (v. 25). Then there is an ongoing work of internal *renovation*, which Ezekiel describes under the figure of receiving the new heart and new spirit through the internal work of the divine Spirit (vv. 26–27). These two stages are both necessary to being a Christian, and this passage may well be the one that lies behind Jesus' statement to the teacher Nicodemus in Jn 3:5.

The Valley of Dry Bones

37 The hand of the LORD was on me,[g]
and he brought me out by the Spirit[h] of the LORD and set me in the middle
of a valley;[i] it was full of bones.[j] 2He led
me back and forth among them, and I
saw a great many bones on the floor of
the valley, bones that were very dry. 3He
asked me, "Son of man, can these bones
live?"
I said, "Sovereign LORD, you alone
know.[k]"
4Then he said to me, "Prophesy to
these bones and say to them, 'Dry bones,
hear the word of the LORD![l] 5This is what
the Sovereign LORD says to these bones: I
will make breath[a] enter you, and you will
come to life.[m] 6I will attach tendons to
you and make flesh come upon you and
cover you with skin; I will put breath in
you, and you will come to life. Then you
will know that I am the LORD.[n]' "
7So I prophesied as I was commanded.
And as I was prophesying, there was a
noise, a rattling sound, and the bones
came together, bone to bone. 8I looked,
and tendons and flesh appeared on them
and skin covered them, but there was no
breath in them.
9Then he said to me, "Prophesy to the

37:1 [g] Eze 1:3; 8:3 [h] Eze 11:24; Lk 4:1; Ac 8:39 [i] Jer 7:32 [j] Jer 8:2; Eze 40:1
37:3 [k] Dt 32:39; 1Sa 2:6; Isa 26:19
37:4 [l] Jer 22:29
37:5 [m] Ge 2:7; Ps 104:29-30
37:6 [n] Eze 38:23; Joel 2:27; 3:17

Eze 37:7-10 ❖ How does the breath of God give us new life (see Jn 20:22)?

[a] 5 The Hebrew for this word can also mean *wind* or *spirit* (see verses 6-14).

37:1-4 The Lord's question to the prophet, "Son of man, can these bones live?" (v. 3a) seems redundant. It seems as if God's people have been utterly destroyed for their sin. End of story.

Recognizing the sovereign power of God, however, the prophet turns the question back to God (v. 3b). God has the power to bring the dry bones back to life; the question is whether his will is to do so. That question is swiftly answered in the affirmative.

37:5-6 Ezekiel is told to prophesy to the bones and require them to listen to the word of the Lord; in response, the Lord will make breath enter them and bring them back to life.

37:7-10 The prophet obediently speaks the word and sees the power of God instantly unleashed. While he is prophesying, the bones come together—but still without life. Then Ezekiel speaks to the wind. Like the creation of Adam in Ge 2, the recreation of this mighty army is a two-stage process of forming and filling.

PEOPLE TO KNOW // EZEKIEL

EZEKIEL 37:1-6: Ezekiel was taken from Jerusalem to Babylon as a captive about ten years before Jerusalem was destroyed under Nebuchadnezzar in 586 BC. Ezekiel came from a priestly line.

God called Ezekiel to be a prophet and filled him with his Spirit, commissioning him to deliver divine messages of judgment to the Israelites (Eze 2:1-8). God instructed Ezekiel to perform many dramatic sign-acts, including eating a scroll, (Eze 3:1), staging an attack on a miniature clay Jerusalem (Eze 4:1-3), and eating food cooked over dried animal dung (Eze 4:15). Ezekiel also received a vision of God's presence leaving the temple, showing the dire extent of Israel's failure (Eze 10).

God's characterization of Israel's sins through Ezekiel is particularly vivid. As a picture of the spiritual death of Israel, God showed Ezekiel a valley filled with human bones (Eze 37:1-3). Then God did a remarkable thing: he commanded Ezekiel to prophesy, and the bones took on flesh and returned to life. God sent the message that he intended to restore his people from their exile and spiritual death.

Ezekiel's prophecy ends with a prolonged vision of a new temple and restored Israel (Eze 40-48). Ezekiel sees the glory of God, which had departed, returning once again to Jerusalem. This vision is echoed in Revelation 21-22, where John shares his vision of God's new heaven and new earth. But in John's vision there is no temple—God himself is the temple (Rev 21:22).

APPLICATION ✚ Ezekiel prophesied during the dark years of the Israelites' captivity and exile, and he had to bravely share the bad news and face the angry response of the people to whom he ministered. God's people today are still called to speak against evil and unrighteousness. While it may not make us popular, speaking God's truth in the world is a task entrusted to us for God's glory. Like Ezekiel, our message is not only one of judgment. It is also a message of restoration and beautiful hope in the promise of God's coming kingdom.

breath;[o] prophesy, son of man, and say
to it, 'This is what the Sovereign LORD
says: Come, breath, from the four winds
and breathe into these slain, that they
may live.'" 10So I prophesied as he commanded me, and breath entered them;
they came to life and stood up on their
feet—a vast army.[p]

11Then he said to me: "Son of man,
these bones are the people of Israel.
They say, 'Our bones are dried up and our
hope is gone; we are cut off.'[q] 12Therefore
prophesy and say to them: 'This is what
the Sovereign LORD says: My people, I am
going to open your graves and bring you
up from them; I will bring you back to
the land of Israel.[r] 13Then you, my people, will know that I am the LORD, when I
open your graves and bring you up from
them. 14I will put my Spirit[s] in you and
you will live, and I will settle you in your
own land. Then you will know that I the
LORD have spoken, and I have done it,
declares the LORD.[t]'"

One Nation Under One King

15The word of the LORD came to me:
16"Son of man, take a stick of wood and
write on it, 'Belonging to Judah and the
Israelites[u] associated with him.'[v] Then
take another stick of wood, and write
on it, 'Belonging to Joseph (that is, to
Ephraim) and all the Israelites associated with him.' 17Join them together into
one stick so that they will become one
in your hand.[w]

18"When your people ask you, 'Won't
you tell us what you mean by this?'[x]
19say to them, 'This is what the Sovereign LORD says: I am going to take the
stick of Joseph—which is in Ephraim's
hand—and of the Israelite tribes associated with him, and join it to Judah's
stick. I will make them into a single stick
of wood, and they will become one in
my hand.'[y] 20Hold before their eyes the
sticks you have written on 21and say to
them, 'This is what the Sovereign LORD
says: I will take the Israelites out of the
nations where they have gone. I will
gather them from all around and bring
them back into their own land.[z] 22I will
make them one nation in the land, on
the mountains of Israel. There will be
one king over all of them and they will
never again be two nations or be divided
into two kingdoms.[a] 23They will no longer defile[b] themselves with their idols
and vile images or with any of their offenses, for I will save them from all their
sinful backsliding,[a] and I will cleanse
them. They will be my people, and I will
be their God.[c]

24"'My servant David[d] will be king over
them, and they will all have one shepherd.[e] They will follow my laws and be
careful to keep my decrees.[f] 25They will
live in the land I gave to my servant Jacob, the land where your ancestors lived.[g]

37:9 [o] Ps 104:30
37:10 [p] Rev 11:11
37:11 [q] La 3:54
37:12 [r] Dt 32:39; 1Sa 2:6; Isa 26:19; Hos 13:14; Am 9:14-15
37:14 [s] Joel 2:28-29 [t] Eze 36:27-28,36
37:16 [u] 1Ki 12:20; 2Ch 10:17-19 [v] Nu 17:2-3; 2Ch 15:9
37:17 [w] ver 24; Isa 11:13; Jer 50:4; Hos 1:11
37:18 [x] Eze 24:19
37:19 [y] Zec 10:6
37:21 [z] Isa 43:5-6; Eze 36:24; 39:27
37:22 [a] Isa 11:13; Jer 3:18; Hos 1:11
37:23 [b] Eze 36:25; 43:7 [c] Eze 11:18; 36:28
37:24 [d] Hos 3:5 [e] Isa 40:11; Eze 34:23 [f] Ps 78:70-71
37:25 [g] Eze 28:25

[a] *23* Many Hebrew manuscripts (see also Septuagint); most Hebrew manuscripts *all their dwelling places where they sinned*

37:11–14 The oracle that follows the vision makes explicit what the vision has already recounted: The dry bones are the whole house of Israel, cut off from God's life-giving presence (v. 11). Without contradicting this self-perception that their present situation is hopeless, the Lord affirms there is hope for the future. The promises of a new spirit and a return to the land made in 36:27–36 will indeed be fulfilled.

> ✣ **37:1–14** Just as the dry bones in Ezekiel did not remain dead, so also Christ did not remain in the tomb. If believers have been truly buried with him in baptism, we also are made similarly alive in Christ. Our sins are forgiven; the hold of the law over us is broken, nailed to the cross (Col 2:14). We are not dry bones any longer but rather living, breathing, Spirit-infused children of God (Ro 8:16). What Ezekiel saw in visionary form has now become a reality.

37:16–17 A sign-act involves the prophet's taking two sticks, each of which he is to inscribe with a name. Strictly speaking, the two rivals for first place among Jacob's sons are Judah and Joseph; hence the proper designation of the sticks as "Belonging to Judah . . . belonging to Joseph" (v. 16). Historically, however, the rivalry had become essentially a struggle between (the tribes of) Judah and Ephraim. Ezekiel is then instructed to join the sticks together in his hand so that they become one stick (v. 17).

37:18–23 Clearly, this action anticipates the reunification of northern and southern kingdoms. Because the action itself is so transparent, the expected question from the audience is about the deeper significance of the sign. The Lord's reply emphasizes that "I" (v. 22) will accomplish all this, a divine act of reuniting his people.

37:24–27 The reunion will happen by the Lord's providing a single servant-leader (v. 24). It will result in a return to a single, divinely approved sanctuary in their midst.

The covenant relationship between God and his people will be restored. Enduring blessings will flow. The covenant will be "an everlasting covenant"; the sanctuary will be restored to their midst "forever" (v. 26).

They and their children and their children's children will live there forever,[h] and David my servant will be their prince forever.[i] 26 I will make a covenant of peace[j] with them; it will be an everlasting covenant. I will establish them and increase their numbers,[k] and I will put my sanctuary among them forever.[l] 27 My dwelling place[m] will be with them; I will be their God, and they will be my people.[n] 28 Then the nations will know that I the LORD make Israel holy,[o] when my sanctuary is among them forever.' "

The LORD's Great Victory Over the Nations

38 The word of the LORD came to me: 2 "Son of man, set your face against Gog, of the land of Magog,[p] the chief prince of[a] Meshek and Tubal;[q] prophesy against him 3 and say: 'This is what the Sovereign LORD says: I am against you, Gog, chief prince of[b] Meshek and Tubal.[r] 4 I will turn you around, put hooks[s] in your jaws and bring you out with your whole army—your horses, your horsemen fully armed, and a great horde with large and small shields, all of them brandishing their swords.[t] 5 Persia, Cush[c][u] and Put[v] will be with them, all with shields and helmets, 6 also Gomer[w] with all its troops, and Beth Togarmah[x] from the far north with all its troops—the many nations with you.

7 " 'Get ready; be prepared,[y] you and all the hordes gathered about you, and take command of them. 8 After many days[z] you will be called to arms. In future years you will invade a land that has recovered from war, whose people were gathered from many nations[a] to the mountains of Israel, which had long been desolate. They had been brought out from the nations, and now all of them live in safety.[b] 9 You and all your troops and the many nations with you will go up, advancing like a storm;[c] you will be like a cloud[d] covering the land.

10 " 'This is what the Sovereign LORD says: On that day thoughts will come into your mind and you will devise an evil scheme.[e] 11 You will say, "I will invade a land of unwalled villages; I will attack a peaceful and unsuspecting people—all of them living without walls and without gates and bars.[f] 12 I will plunder and loot and turn my hand against the resettled ruins and the people gathered from the nations, rich in livestock and goods, living at the center of the land.[d]" 13 Sheba[g] and Dedan and the merchants of Tarshish and all her villages[e] will say to you, "Have you come to plunder? Have you gathered your hordes to loot, to carry

> **Eze 38:10-13** ❖ Where are the vulnerable and innocent still oppressed today? How can we support and pray for them?

37:25 [h]Am 9:15 [i]Isa 11:1
37:26 [j]Isa 55:3 [k]Jer 30:19 [l]Eze 16:62
37:27 [m]Lev 26:11; Jn 1:14 [n]2Co 6:16*
37:28 [o]Ex 31:13; Eze 20:12
38:2 [p]Ge 10:2 [q]Rev 20:8
38:3 [r]Eze 39:1
38:4 [s]2Ki 19:28 [t]Eze 29:4; Da 11:40
38:5 [u]Ge 10:6 [v]Eze 27:10
38:6 [w]Ge 10:2 [x]Eze 27:14
38:7 [y]Isa 8:9
38:8 [z]Isa 24:22 [a]Isa 11:11 [b]Jer 23:6
38:9 [c]Isa 28:2 [d]Jer 4:13; Joel 2:2
38:10 [e]Ps 36:4; Mic 2:1
38:11 [f]Jer 49:31; Zec 2:4
38:13 [g]Eze 27:22

[a] 2 Or *the prince of Rosh,* [b] 3 Or *Gog, prince of Rosh,* [c] 5 That is, the upper Nile region
[d] 12 The Hebrew for this phrase means *the navel of the earth.* [e] 13 Or *her strong lions*

37:28 The nations will recognize that the Lord has endowed his people with a new level of holiness. The temple's restoration is objective evidence of the Lord's purpose to make a holy people.

> ✣ **37:15-28** Christ himself is our true temple because he accomplished in himself everything to which the tabernacle and temple of the OT pointed. Because Jesus is our temple, he himself is what unites his people together in worship.
>
> When Jesus met with the woman of Samaria, he prophesied an end to the divisions between Jews and Samaritans founded on their separate temples (Jn 4:21-24). This marked a radical change in the old order of things, which anticipated the nations' coming to worship God at Mount Zion.
>
> With the coming of Christ, the old division between Jew and Samaritan in worship is broken down—not by Samaritans coming to the temple in Jerusalem but by Jew and Samaritan alike being incorporated into Christ himself as the final temple (Gal 3:28).

38:1-10 The biblical Gog is a fear-inducing figure of cosmic proportions. To make matters worse, he is not alone. He is the commander-in-chief of a coalition of forces gathered from the ends of the earth. Though Gog and his allies are far from unwilling participants in the coming conflict, the controlling force in all this is the Lord who directs them.
38:11-12 Israel is dwelling "at the center of the land [earth]" (v. 12), a description that is theological rather than geographical. This position at the center of God's favor, which Jerusalem had forfeited through her sin, has now been restored to the land.
38:13-16 The ungodly will cast greedy eyes in Israel's direction and will advance against them like an overshadowing cloud (vv. 9, 16). But Gog has fundamentally misread the match-up. It is not a matter of his vast and well-equipped army against a defenseless nation. Rather, by tangling with Israel, Gog is taking on Israel's God. The only reason Gog is permitted to come is so the Lord may demonstrate his greatness and his holiness in defeating this monstrous alliance (v. 16).

off silver and gold, to take away livestock and goods and to seize much plunder?[h]" '

14"Therefore, son of man, prophesy and say to Gog: 'This is what the Sovereign LORD says: In that day, when my people Israel are living in safety,[i] will you not take notice of it? 15You will come from your place in the far north, you and many nations with you, all of them riding on horses, a great horde, a mighty army.[j] 16You will advance against my people Israel like a cloud[k] that covers the land. In days to come, Gog, I will bring you against my land, so that the nations may know me when I am proved holy through you before their eyes.[l]

17" 'This is what the Sovereign LORD says: You are the one I spoke of in former days by my servants the prophets of Israel. At that time they prophesied for years that I would bring you against them. 18This is what will happen in that day: When Gog attacks the land of Israel, my hot anger will be aroused, declares the Sovereign LORD. 19In my zeal and fiery wrath I declare that at that time there shall be a great earthquake in the land of Israel.[m] 20The fish in the sea, the birds in the sky, the beasts of the field, every creature that moves along the ground, and all the people on the face of the earth will tremble at my presence. The mountains will be overturned, the cliffs will crumble and every wall will fall to the ground.[n] 21I will summon a sword[o] against Gog on all my mountains, declares the Sovereign LORD. Every man's sword will be against his brother.[p] 22I will execute judgment[q] on him with plague and bloodshed; I will pour down torrents of rain, hailstones[r] and burning sulfur on him and on his troops and on the many nations with him. 23And so I will show my greatness and my holiness, and I will make myself known in the sight of many nations. Then they will know that I am the LORD.[s]'

39 "Son of man, prophesy against Gog and say: 'This is what the Sovereign LORD says: I am against you, Gog, chief prince of[a] Meshek and Tubal.[t] 2I will turn you around and drag you along. I will bring you from the far north and send you against the mountains of Israel. 3Then I will strike your bow[u] from your left hand and make your arrows[v] drop from your right hand. 4On the mountains of Israel you will fall, you and all your troops and the nations with you. I will give you as food to all kinds of carrion birds and to the wild animals.[w] 5You will fall in the open field, for I have spoken, declares the Sovereign LORD. 6I will send fire[x] on Magog and on those who live in safety in the coastlands,[y] and they will know that I am the LORD.

7" 'I will make known my holy name among my people Israel. I will no longer let my holy name be profaned,[z] and the nations will know that I the LORD am the Holy One in Israel.[a] 8It is coming! It will surely take place, declares the Sovereign LORD. This is the day I have spoken of.

9" 'Then those who live in the towns of Israel will go out and use the weapons for fuel and burn them up—the small and large shields, the bows and arrows, the war clubs and spears. For seven years they will use them for fuel.[b] 10They will not need to gather wood from the fields or cut it from the forests, because they will use the weapons for fuel. And they will plunder those who plundered them and loot those who looted them, declares the Sovereign LORD.[c]

11" 'On that day I will give Gog a burial place in Israel, in the valley of those who travel east of the Sea. It will block the way of travelers, because Gog and all his hordes will be buried there. So it will be called the Valley of Hamon Gog.[bd]

12" 'For seven months the Israelites will be burying them in order to cleanse the land.[e] 13All the people of the land will bury them, and the day I display my glory[f] will be a memorable day for them,

[a] 1 Or *Gog, prince of Rosh,* [b] 11 *Hamon Gog* means *hordes of Gog.*

38:13 [h] Isa 10:6; Jer 15:13
38:14 [i] ver 8; Zec 2:5
38:15 [j] Eze 39:2
38:16 [k] ver 9 [l] Isa 29:23; Eze 39:21
38:19 [m] Ps 18:7; Eze 5:13; Hag 2:6,21
38:20 [n] Hos 4:3; Na 1:5
38:21 [o] Eze 14:17 [p] 1Sa 14:20; 2Ch 20:23; Hag 2:22
38:22 [q] Isa 66:16; Jer 25:31 [r] Ps 18:12; Rev 16:21
38:23 [s] Eze 36:23
39:1 [t] Eze 38:2,3
39:3 [u] Hos 1:5 [v] Ps 76:3
39:4 [w] ver 17-20; Eze 29:5; 33:27
39:6 [x] Eze 30:8; Am 1:4 [y] Jer 25:22
39:7 [z] Ex 20:7 [a] Isa 12:6; Eze 36:16,23
39:9 [b] Ps 46:9
39:10 [c] Isa 14:2; 33:1; Hab 2:8
39:11 [d] Eze 38:2
39:12 [e] Dt 21:23
39:13 [f] Eze 28:22

38:17–23 Therefore, God's judgment falls on Gog. Israel has felt God's hot anger, zeal, and fiery wrath; these are now turned against Gog. God will reveal his power and holiness to the nations not by destroying his unholy people but by protecting his restored people (v. 23).

39:1–8 Ezekiel begins in ch. 39 by announcing the slaughter of Gog.

39:9–11 Once God has decisively dealt with Gog as a threat, Israel is called to act. She merely carries out the mopping-up operation after the battle. The troops who came to plunder are now plundered.

39:12–16 Israel will also be active in purifying the land by burying the corpses. The whole house of Israel will be engaged in this burial process.

declares the Sovereign LORD. 14People will be continually employed in cleansing the land. They will spread out across the land and, along with others, they will bury any bodies that are lying on the ground.

"'After the seven months they will carry out a more detailed search. 15As they go through the land, anyone who sees a human bone will leave a marker beside it until the gravediggers bury it in the Valley of Hamon Gog, 16near a town called Hamonah.[a] And so they will cleanse the land.'

17"Son of man, this is what the Sovereign LORD says: Call out to every kind of bird[g] and all the wild animals: 'Assemble and come together from all around to the sacrifice I am preparing for you, the great sacrifice on the mountains of Israel. There you will eat flesh and drink blood. 18You will eat the flesh of mighty men and drink the blood of the princes of the earth as if they were rams and lambs, goats and bulls — all of them fattened animals from Bashan.[h] 19At the sacrifice I am preparing for you, you will eat fat till you are glutted and drink blood till you are drunk. 20At my table you will eat your fill of horses and riders, mighty men and soldiers of every kind,' declares the Sovereign LORD.[i]

21"I will display my glory among the nations, and all the nations will see the punishment I inflict and the hand I lay on them.[j] 22From that day forward the people of Israel will know that I am the LORD their God. 23And the nations will know that the people of Israel went into exile for their sin, because they were unfaithful to me. So I hid my face from them and handed them over to their enemies, and they all fell by the sword.[k] 24I dealt with them according to their uncleanness and their offenses, and I hid my face from them.[l]

25"Therefore this is what the Sovereign LORD says: I will now restore the fortunes of Jacob[b][m] and will have compassion[n] on all the people of Israel, and I will be zealous for my holy name.[o] 26They will forget their shame and all the unfaithfulness they showed toward me when they lived in safety[p] in their land with no one to make them afraid.[q] 27When I have brought them back from the nations and have gathered them from the countries of their enemies, I will be proved holy through them in the sight of many nations.[r] 28Then they will know that I am the LORD their God, for though I sent them into exile among the nations, I will gather them to their own land, not leaving any behind. 29I will no longer hide my face from them, for I will pour out my Spirit[s] on the people of Israel, declares the Sovereign LORD."

39:17 [g] Rev 19:17
39:18 [h] Ps 22:12; Jer 51:40
39:20 [i] Rev 19:17-18
39:21 [j] Ex 9:16; Isa 37:20; Eze 38:16
39:23 [k] Isa 1:15; 59:2; Jer 22:8-9; 44:23
39:24 [l] Jer 2:17, 19; 4:18; Eze 36:19
39:25 [m] Jer 33:7; Eze 34:13 [n] Jer 30:18 [o] Isa 27:12-13
39:26 [p] 1Ki 4:25 [q] Isa 17:2; Eze 34:28; Mic 4:4
39:27 [r] Eze 36:23-24; 37:21; 38:16
39:29 [s] Joel 2:28; Ac 2:17

Eze 39:27 ❖ How is God being "proved holy" through us in the sight of those around us?

[a] *16 Hamonah* means *horde*. [b] *25* Or *now bring Jacob back from captivity*

39:17–20 Here the birds and the beasts are invited to join in a kind of gruesome "messianic banquet." The humans have been killed to feed the animals from all around.

39:21–29 The lesson Israel is to draw from these chapters is explicitly laid out for them here. The Lord's sovereignty is displayed before the nations in two separate movements.

In the first, God demonstrated his sovereignty by sending his own people into exile because of their sin and unfaithfulness (v. 23).

In the days to come, a new period in Israel's history is beginning. God's people will return from exile; he will have compassion on them. They will know the Lord their God, the One who sent them into exile, is the same Lord who returns them from exile (v. 28). The covenant-keeping God will pour out his Spirit on his people, as he once poured out his wrath on them, and he will never again hide his face from them (v. 29).

✚ **38:1—39:29** Many contemporary Christians treat these passages as checklists on the road to Armageddon, providing a countdown on the road to the end of the world. However, this is not how the passage was intended to be read. Rather, it is a dramatic statement of a central truth: No matter what the forces of evil may throw at God's people, God's purpose and victory stands secure.

In the end, God is going to win. This may seem a simple (even simplistic) point, but it is central to the thrust of the Gog narrative. It does not matter how big the opposition, how well-organized they are, how powerful their weaponry, or how paltry the resources of God's people; ultimately, the enemy's plans will come to nothing.

Christians take comfort in the fact that no matter what Satan throws against the church, the full number of the elect from the north and south and east and west will be brought in and will sit down together at God's table to share in the heavenly feast (Rev 19:6–9).

The Temple Area Restored

40 In the twenty-fifth year of our exile, at the beginning of the year,
on the tenth of the month, in the fourteenth year after the fall of the city[t] — on
that very day the hand of the LORD was
on me[u] and he took me there. 2In visions[v]
of God he took me to the land of Israel
and set me on a very high mountain,[w] on
whose south side were some buildings
that looked like a city. 3He took me there,
and I saw a man whose appearance was
like bronze;[x] he was standing in the gateway with a linen cord and a measuring
rod[y] in his hand. 4The man said to me,
"Son of man, look carefully and listen
closely and pay attention to everything
I am going to show you, for that is why
you have been brought here. Tell[z] the
people of Israel everything you see.[a]"

The East Gate to the Outer Court

5I saw a wall completely surrounding
the temple area. The length of the measuring rod in the man's hand was six long
cubits,[a] each of which was a cubit and a
handbreadth. He measured[b] the wall; it
was one measuring rod thick and one
rod high.
6Then he went to the east gate.[c] He
climbed its steps and measured the
threshold of the gate; it was one rod
deep. 7The alcoves[d] for the guards were
one rod long and one rod wide, and the
projecting walls between the alcoves
were five cubits[b] thick. And the threshold of the gate next to the portico facing
the temple was one rod deep.
8Then he measured the portico of the
gateway; 9it[c] was eight cubits[d] deep and
its jambs were two cubits[e] thick. The portico of the gateway faced the temple.
10Inside the east gate were three alcoves on each side; the three had the
same measurements, and the faces of
the projecting walls on each side had the
same measurements. 11Then he measured the width of the entrance of the
gateway; it was ten cubits and its length
was thirteen cubits.[f] 12In front of each
alcove was a wall one cubit high, and the
alcoves were six cubits square. 13Then
he measured the gateway from the top
of the rear wall of one alcove to the top
of the opposite one; the distance was
twenty-five cubits[g] from one parapet
opening to the opposite one. 14He measured along the faces of the projecting
walls all around the inside of the gateway — sixty cubits.[h] The measurement
was up to the portico[i] facing the courtyard.[j][e] 15The distance from the entrance
of the gateway to the far end of its portico
was fifty cubits.[k] 16The alcoves and the
projecting walls inside the gateway were
surmounted by narrow parapet openings
all around, as was the portico; the openings all around faced inward. The faces
of the projecting walls were decorated
with palm trees.[f]

The Outer Court

17Then he brought me into the outer court.[g] There I saw some rooms and

40:1 [t] 2Ki 25:7; Jer 39:1-10; 52:4-11; Eze 33:21 [u] Eze 1:3
40:2 [v] Da 7:1, 7 [w] Eze 17:22; Rev 21:10
40:3 [x] Eze 1:7; Da 10:6; Rev 1:15 [y] Eze 47:3; Zec 2:1-2; Rev 11:1; 21:15
40:4 [z] Jer 26:2 [a] Eze 44:5
40:5 [b] Eze 42:20
40:6 [c] Eze 8:16
40:7 [d] ver 36
40:14 [e] Ex 27:9
40:16 [f] ver 21-22; 2Ch 3:5; Eze 41:26
40:17 [g] Rev 11:2

[a] *5* That is, about 11 feet or about 3.2 meters; also in verse 12. The long cubit of about 21 inches or about 53 centimeters is the basic unit of measurement of length throughout chapters 40 – 48. [b] *7* That is, about 8 3/4 feet or about 2.7 meters; also in verse 48 [c] *8,9* Many Hebrew manuscripts, Septuagint, Vulgate and Syriac; most Hebrew manuscripts *gateway facing the temple; it was one rod deep. 9Then he measured the portico of the gateway; it* [d] *9* That is, about 14 feet or about 4.2 meters [e] *9* That is, about 3 1/2 feet or about 1 meter [f] *11* That is, about 18 feet wide and 23 feet long or about 5.3 meters wide and 6.9 meters long [g] *13* That is, about 44 feet or about 13 meters; also in verses 21, 25, 29, 30, 33 and 36 [h] *14* That is, about 105 feet or about 32 meters [i] *14* Septuagint; Hebrew *projecting wall* [j] *14* The meaning of the Hebrew for this verse is uncertain. [k] *15* That is, about 88 feet or about 27 meters; also in verses 21, 25, 29, 33 and 36

40:1–4 This vision of the heavenly city is dated from the destruction of Jerusalem. Fourteen years have passed since that earth-shattering event. It was on this very day that Ezekiel saw his "visions of God" (v. 2). This journey is equivalent to Moses' ascent up Mount Sinai to receive the law. Moses also received on the mountaintop a detailed design for building the tabernacle.

Ezekiel is met by an angelic figure who will be his tour guide around the temple. The angel is equipped with a linen cord and a measuring rod to enable him to measure the various parts of the temple.

40:5–16 It is highly significant that the first thing the prophet sees on his tour is a wall surrounding the whole temple area (v. 5). This wall is 10.5 feet tall and 10.5 feet thick. The three sides that permit access are dominated by massive fortress-style gatehouses, almost 45 feet wide and 90 feet deep (vv. 13, 15). There is no doubt as to the initial impression that Ezekiel's temple is intended to have: It is a mighty fortress that clearly separates the sacred from the profane.

40:17–19 The single key measurement in the outer court is its breadth, roughly 175 feet from the outer gateway to the inner gateway (v. 19). This substantial

a pavement that had been constructed
all around the court; there were thirty
rooms[h] along the pavement.[i] 18It abut-
ted the sides of the gateways and was
as wide as they were long; this was the
lower pavement. 19Then he measured
the distance from the inside of the lower gateway to the outside of the inner
court;[j] it was a hundred cubits[ak] on the
east side as well as on the north.

The North Gate

20Then he measured the length and
width of the north gate, leading into the
outer court. 21Its alcoves[l] — three on each
side — its projecting walls and its portico
had the same measurements as those
of the first gateway. It was fifty cubits
long and twenty-five cubits wide. 22Its
openings, its portico[m] and its palm tree
decorations had the same measurements
as those of the gate facing east. Seven
steps led up to it, with its portico opposite them. 23There was a gate to the
inner court facing the north gate, just
as there was on the east. He measured
from one gate to the opposite one; it was
a hundred cubits.[n]

The South Gate

24Then he led me to the south side
and I saw the south gate. He measured
its jambs and its portico, and they had
the same measurements as the others.
25The gateway and its portico had narrow
openings all around, like the openings
of the others. It was fifty cubits long and
twenty-five cubits wide.[o] 26Seven steps
led up to it, with its portico opposite
them; it had palm tree decorations on
the faces of the projecting walls on each
side.[p] 27The inner court[q] also had a gate
facing south, and he measured from this
gate to the outer gate on the south side;
it was a hundred cubits.

The Gates to the Inner Court

28Then he brought me into the inner court through the south gate, and
he measured the south gate; it had the
same measurements[r] as the others. 29Its
alcoves, its projecting walls and its portico had the same measurements as the
others. The gateway and its portico had
openings all around. It was fifty cubits
long and twenty-five cubits wide. 30(The
porticoes[s] of the gateways around the
inner court were twenty-five cubits wide
and five cubits deep.) 31Its portico[t] faced
the outer court; palm trees decorated its
jambs, and eight steps led up to it.

32Then he brought me to the inner
court on the east side, and he measured
the gateway; it had the same measurements as the others. 33Its alcoves, its
projecting walls and its portico had the
same measurements as the others. The
gateway and its portico had openings
all around. It was fifty cubits long and
twenty-five cubits wide. 34Its portico[u]
faced the outer court; palm trees decorated the jambs on either side, and eight
steps led up to it.

35Then he brought me to the north
gate[v] and measured it. It had the same
measurements as the others, 36as did
its alcoves,[w] its projecting walls and its
portico, and it had openings all around.
It was fifty cubits long and twenty-five
cubits wide. 37Its portico[b] faced the outer
court; palm trees decorated the jambs on
either side, and eight steps led up to it.

The Rooms for Preparing Sacrifices

38A room with a doorway was by the
portico in each of the inner gateways,
where the burnt offerings[x] were washed.
39In the portico of the gateway were two
tables on each side, on which the burnt
offerings,[y] sin offerings[cz] and guilt offerings[a] were slaughtered. 40By the outside
wall of the portico of the gateway, near
the steps at the entrance of the north
gateway were two tables, and on the other side of the steps were two tables. 41So
there were four tables on one side of the
gateway and four on the other — eight
tables in all — on which the sacrifices

40:17 [h] Eze 41:6 [i] Eze 42:1
40:19 [j] Eze 46:1 [k] ver 23,27
40:21 [l] ver 7
40:22 [m] ver 49
40:23 [n] ver 19
40:25 [o] ver 33
40:26 [p] ver 22
40:27 [q] ver 32
40:28 [r] ver 35
40:30 [s] ver 21
40:31 [t] ver 22
40:34 [u] ver 22
40:35 [v] Eze 44:4; 47:2
40:36 [w] ver 7
40:38 [x] 2Ch 4:6; Eze 42:13
40:39 [y] Eze 46:2 [z] Lev 4:3,28 [a] Lev 7:1

[a] *19* That is, about 175 feet or about 53 meters; also in verses 23, 27 and 47 [b] *37* Septuagint (see also verses 31 and 34); Hebrew *jambs* [c] *39* Or *purification offerings*

dimension provides a buffer zone around the holy things in the inner courtyard.

40:28–37 The inner courtyard is defended by gates identical to those of the outer court. It is elevated by about 8 feet, with the gates being approached by a flight of eight steps (vv. 31, 34, 37).

40:38–43 There are rooms for washing the sacrifices, while the porticoes were used for slaughtering the sacrifices. The primary function of this temple is as a place of sacrifice.

were slaughtered. 42 There were also four tables of dressed stone[b] for the burnt offerings, each a cubit and a half long, a cubit and a half wide and a cubit high.[a] On them were placed the utensils for slaughtering the burnt offerings and the other sacrifices.[c] 43 And double-pronged hooks, each a handbreadth[b] long, were attached to the wall all around. The tables were for the flesh of the offerings.

The Rooms for the Priests

44 Outside the inner gate, within the inner court, were two rooms, one[c] at the side of the north gate and facing south, and another at the side of the south[d] gate and facing north. 45 He said to me, "The room facing south is for the priests who guard the temple,[d] 46 and the room facing north[e] is for the priests who guard the altar.[f] These are the sons of Zadok,[g] who are the only Levites who may draw near to the LORD to minister before him.[h]"

47 Then he measured the court: It was square—a hundred cubits long and a hundred cubits wide. And the altar was in front of the temple.

The New Temple

48 He brought me to the portico of the temple[i] and measured the jambs of the portico; they were five cubits wide on either side. The width of the entrance was fourteen cubits[e] and its projecting walls were[f] three cubits[g] wide on either side. 49 The portico[j] was twenty cubits[h] wide, and twelve[i] cubits[j] from front to back. It was reached by a flight of stairs,[k] and there were pillars[k] on each side of the jambs.

41 Then the man brought me to the main hall[l] and measured the jambs; the width of the jambs was six cubits[l] on each side.[m] 2 The entrance was ten cubits[n] wide, and the projecting walls on each side of it were five cubits[o] wide. He also measured the main hall; it was forty cubits long and twenty cubits wide.[p][m]

3 Then he went into the inner sanctuary and measured the jambs of the entrance; each was two cubits[q] wide. The entrance was six cubits wide, and the projecting walls on each side of it were seven cubits[r] wide. 4 And he measured the length of the inner sanctuary; it was twenty cubits, and its width was twenty cubits across the end of the main hall.[n] He said to me, "This is the Most Holy Place.[o]"

5 Then he measured the wall of the temple; it was six cubits thick, and each side room around the temple was four cubits[s] wide. 6 The side rooms were on three levels, one above another, thirty[p] on each level. There were ledges all around the wall of the temple to serve as supports for the side rooms, so that

40:42 [b] Ex 20:25 [c] ver 39
40:45 [d] 1Ch 9:23
40:46 [e] Eze 42:13 [f] Nu 18:5 [g] 1Ki 2:35 [h] Nu 16:5; Eze 43:19; 44:15; 45:4; 48:11
40:48 [i] 1Ki 6:2
40:49 [j] ver 22; 1Ki 6:3 [k] 1Ki 7:15
41:1 [l] ver 23
41:2 [m] 2Ch 3:3
41:4 [n] 1Ki 6:20 [o] Ex 26:33; Heb 9:3-8
41:6 [p] Eze 40:17

Eze 40:45-46 ❖ How can we protect and promote God's house, the church?

[a] *42* That is, about 2 2/3 feet long and wide and 21 inches high or about 80 centimeters long and wide and 53 centimeters high [b] *43* That is, about 3 1/2 inches or about 9 centimeters [c] *44* Septuagint; Hebrew *were rooms for singers, which were* [d] *44* Septuagint; Hebrew *east* [e] *48* That is, about 25 feet or about 7.4 meters [f] *48* Septuagint; Hebrew *entrance was* [g] *48* That is, about 5 1/4 feet or about 1.6 meters [h] *49* That is, about 35 feet or about 11 meters [i] *49* Septuagint; Hebrew *eleven* [j] *49* That is, about 21 feet or about 6.4 meters [k] *49* Hebrew; Septuagint *Ten steps led up to it* [l] *1* That is, about 11 feet or about 3.2 meters; also in verses 3, 5 and 8 [m] *1* One Hebrew manuscript and Septuagint; most Hebrew manuscripts *side, the width of the tent* [n] *2* That is, about 18 feet or about 5.3 meters [o] *2* That is, about 8 3/4 feet or about 2.7 meters; also in verses 9, 11 and 12 [p] *2* That is, about 70 feet long and 35 feet wide or about 21 meters long and 11 meters wide [q] *3* That is, about 3 1/2 feet or about 1.1 meters; also in verse 22 [r] *3* That is, about 12 feet or about 3.7 meters [s] *5* That is, about 7 feet or about 2.1 meters

40:44-47 The prophet also sees two rooms for the Zadokite priests. Both sets of spaces separate access to a restricted space, which is reserved for the priests, so that proper sacrifices may be offered.
40:48-49 Ezekiel is led on to the temple structure itself. It is located as the protected center at the heart of the complex. It is the highest point of an edifice that is itself on top of the high mountain. It is the space of the temple complex that is described in most detail and with the most precise measurements.
41:1-4 The temple is a three-part structure: portico, outer sanctuary, and inner sanctuary. Its architecture focuses attention on "the Most Holy Place" (v. 4). This is the only square space within the temple building, and it is reached by passing through three openings of increasing narrowness. This design feature emphasizes the sanctity of the Most Holy Place, a sanctity so great that Ezekiel himself is not permitted to enter it.
41:5-12 All around the temple building are no fewer than ninety rooms on three levels. Behind the temple is a "building" of unspecified purpose (vv. 10, 12). It may simply have functioned to protect the rear approach to the temple building.

the supports were not inserted into the wall of the temple.[q] 7The side rooms all around the temple were wider at each successive level. The structure surrounding the temple was built in ascending stages, so that the rooms widened as one went upward. A stairway[r] went up from the lowest floor to the top floor through the middle floor.

8I saw that the temple had a raised base all around it, forming the foundation of the side rooms. It was the length of the rod, six long cubits. 9The outer wall of the side rooms was five cubits thick. The open area between the side rooms of the temple 10and the priests' rooms was twenty cubits wide all around the temple. 11There were entrances to the side rooms from the open area, one on the north and another on the south; and the base adjoining the open area was five cubits wide all around.

12The building facing the temple courtyard on the west side was seventy cubits[a] wide. The wall of the building was five cubits thick all around, and its length was ninety cubits.[b]

13Then he measured the temple; it was a hundred cubits[c] long, and the temple courtyard and the building with its walls were also a hundred cubits long. 14The width of the temple courtyard on the east, including the front of the temple, was a hundred cubits.[s]

15Then he measured the length of the building facing the courtyard at the rear of the temple, including its galleries[t] on each side; it was a hundred cubits.

The main hall, the inner sanctuary and the portico facing the court, 16as well as the thresholds and the narrow windows[u] and galleries around the three of them — everything beyond and including the threshold was covered with wood. The floor, the wall up to the windows, and the windows were covered.[v] 17In the space above the outside of the entrance to the inner sanctuary and on the walls at regular intervals all around the inner and outer sanctuary 18were carved[w] cherubim[x] and palm trees.[y] Palm trees alternated with cherubim. Each cherub had two faces:[z] 19the face of a human being toward the palm tree on one side and the face of a lion toward the palm tree on the other. They were carved all around the whole temple.[a] 20From the floor to the area above the entrance, cherubim and palm trees were carved on the wall of the main hall.

21The main hall[b] had a rectangular doorframe, and the one at the front of the Most Holy Place was similar. 22There was a wooden altar[c] three cubits[d] high and two cubits square[e]; its corners, its base[f] and its sides were of wood. The man said to me, "This is the table[d] that is before the LORD." 23Both the main hall[e] and the Most Holy Place had double doors.[f] 24Each door had two leaves — two hinged leaves[g] for each door. 25And on the doors of the main hall were carved cherubim and palm trees like those carved on the walls, and there was a wooden overhang on the front of the portico. 26On the sidewalls of the portico were narrow windows with palm trees carved on each side. The side rooms of the temple also had overhangs.[h]

Eze 41:15-20 ❖ In the worship spaces we frequent, what do the furnishing show about God?

The Rooms for the Priests

42 Then the man led me northward into the outer court and brought me to the rooms[i] opposite the temple courtyard[j] and opposite the outer wall

41:6 [q] 1Ki 6:5
41:7 [r] 1Ki 6:8
41:14 [s] Eze 40:47
41:15 [t] Eze 42:3
41:16 [u] 1Ki 6:4 [v] ver 25-26; 1Ki 6:15; Eze 42:3
41:18 [w] 1Ki 6:18 [x] Ex 37:7; 2Ch 3:7 [y] 1Ki 6:29; 7:36 [z] Eze 10:21
41:19 [a] Eze 10:14
41:21 [b] ver 1
41:22 [c] Ex 30:1 [d] Ex 25:23; Eze 23:41; 44:16; Mal 1:7,12
41:23 [e] ver 1 [f] 1Ki 6:32
41:24 [g] 1Ki 6:34
41:26 [h] ver 15-16; Eze 40:16
42:1 [i] ver 13 [j] Eze 41:12-14

[a] *12* That is, about 123 feet or about 37 meters
[b] *12* That is, about 158 feet or about 48 meters
[c] *13* That is, about 175 feet or about 53 meters; also in verses 14 and 15
[d] *22* That is, about 5 1/4 feet or about 1.5 meters
[e] *22* Septuagint; Hebrew *long*
[f] *22* Septuagint; Hebrew *length*

41:16-22 The temple is described as completely paneled with wood and decorated with images of palm trees and cherubim. The furniture within the temple building is an "altar" of wood which is designated "the table that is before the LORD" (v. 22). This is presumably the table on which the "bread of the Presence" was laid out before the Lord (1Ki 7:48).

42:1-14 Ezekiel heads outward once more in his description of the complex. His attention is first drawn to a series of rooms for the priests. The rooms are built on three levels, and it appears that the priests could enter at the top from the inner court (v. 12) and emerge from the bottom into the outer court (v. 9). This serves to underline the status of the rooms as boundary areas for activities that, if not properly contained, might violate the gradation of holiness.

In addition to eating the sacred offerings here, the priests were also required to leave behind the

on the north side.[k] 2The building whose door faced north was a hundred cubits long and fifty cubits wide.[a] 3Both in the section twenty cubits[b] from the inner court and in the section opposite the pavement of the outer court, gallery[l] faced gallery at the three levels.[m] 4In front of the rooms was an inner passageway ten cubits wide and a hundred cubits[c] long.[d] Their doors were on the north.[n] 5Now the upper rooms were narrower, for the galleries took more space from them than from the rooms on the lower and middle floors of the building. 6The rooms on the top floor had no pillars, as the courts had; so they were smaller in floor space than those on the lower and middle floors. 7There was an outer wall parallel to the rooms and the outer court; it extended in front of the rooms for fifty cubits. 8While the row of rooms on the side next to the outer court was fifty cubits long, the row on the side nearest the sanctuary was a hundred cubits long. 9The lower rooms had an entrance[o] on the east side as one enters them from the outer court.

10On the south side[e] along the length of the wall of the outer court, adjoining the temple courtyard and opposite the outer wall, were rooms[p] 11with a passageway in front of them. These were like the rooms on the north; they had the same length and width, with similar exits and dimensions. Similar to the doorways on the north 12were the doorways of the rooms on the south. There was a doorway at the beginning of the passageway that was parallel to the corresponding wall extending eastward, by which one enters the rooms.

13Then he said to me, "The north[q] and south rooms facing the temple courtyard are the priests' rooms, where the priests who approach the LORD will eat the most holy offerings. There they will put the most holy offerings — the grain offerings, the sin offerings[f][r] and the guilt offerings[s] — for the place is holy.[t] 14Once the priests enter the holy precincts, they are not to go into the outer court until they leave behind the garments[u] in which they minister, for these are holy. They are to put on other clothes before they go near the places that are for the people.[v]"

15When he had finished measuring what was inside the temple area, he led me out by the east gate[w] and measured the area all around: 16He measured the east side with the measuring rod; it was five hundred cubits.[g,h] 17He measured the

42:1 [k]Eze 40:17
42:3 [l]Eze 41:15 [m]Eze 41:16
42:4 [n]Eze 46:19
42:9 [o]Eze 44:5; 46:19
42:10 [p]ver 1
42:13 [q]Eze 40:46 [r]Lev 10:17; 6:25 [s]Lev 14:13 [t]Ex 29:31; Lev 6:29; 7:6; 10:12-13; Nu 18:9-10
42:14 [u]Eze 44:19 [v]Ex 29:9; Lev 8:7-9
42:15 [w]Eze 43:1

Eze 42:4 ❖ What are ways we can "dress" ourselves for God's holy service (see Col 3:12–14)?

[a] *2* That is, about 175 feet long and 88 feet wide or about 53 meters long and 27 meters wide
[b] *3* That is, about 35 feet or about 11 meters
[c] *4* Septuagint and Syriac; Hebrew *and one cubit*
[d] *4* That is, about 18 feet wide and 175 feet long or about 5.3 meters wide and 53 meters long
[e] *10* Septuagint; Hebrew *Eastward*
[f] *13* Or *purification offerings*
[g] *16* See Septuagint of verse 17; Hebrew *rods*; also in verses 18 and 19.
[h] *16* Five hundred cubits equal about 875 feet or about 265 meters; also in verses 17, 18 and 19.

sacred clothes in which they had ministered in these rooms so they might not bring that which was holy into dangerous contact with the profane (v. 14).

42:15–20 Ezekiel is brought back out to survey the temple from the outside. Its overall dimensions are square, 500 cubits by 500 cubits (vv. 16–20). In the tabernacle, only the Most Holy Place is square. In Ezekiel's temple, the entire structure bears an increased level of sanctity that is expressed in its overall shape. The final note highlights the wall and its function: It serves "to separate the holy from the common" (v. 20). Never again will the profane intrude on the realm of the holy as it did in the past.

✣ **40:1—42:20** There are no walls that keep us out of God's presence. This is not because we are more holy than Ezekiel and his hearers but because we have been credited with the perfect righteousness of Christ in place of our filthy rags (Isa 64:6). Jesus' once-for-all sacrifice has turned us from aliens and strangers to insiders who are able to "approach God's throne . . . with confidence" (Heb 4:16).

We should remember that one wall still remains and that many are still outsiders to God's grace. Some live beyond the message of the gospel proclamation. Others have heard the gospel proclaimed over and over again yet have repeatedly rejected it. Nothing and no one impure can ever enter God's heavenly holy city. Even the most moral person, if they do not believe and trust in Christ, is outside the wall; left to themselves, such people must perish utterly.

Our calling as priests of the new temple is to teach these people the one way to holiness through trusting in Christ—seeking to draw them into the new world we have been given, where paradise once more stands open to God's people and the tree of life is freely accessible to all.

north side; it was five hundred cubits[a] by
the measuring rod. 18He measured the
south side; it was five hundred cubits
by the measuring rod. 19Then he turned
to the west side and measured; it was
five hundred cubits by the measuring
rod. 20So he measured[x] the area on all
four sides. It had a wall around it,[y] five
hundred cubits long and five hundred
cubits wide,[z] to separate the holy from
the common.[a]

God's Glory Returns to the Temple

43 Then the man brought me to the
gate facing east,[b] 2and I saw the
glory of the God of Israel coming from
the east. His voice was like the roar of
rushing waters,[c] and the land was radiant with his glory.[d] 3The vision I saw
was like the vision I had seen when he[b]
came to destroy the city and like the visions I had seen by the Kebar River, and
I fell facedown. 4The glory[e] of the LORD
entered the temple through the gate facing east.[f] 5Then the Spirit[g] lifted me up[h]
and brought me into the inner court, and
the glory of the LORD filled the temple.
6While the man was standing beside
me, I heard someone speaking to me
from inside the temple. 7He said: "Son of
man, this is the place of my throne and
the place for the soles of my feet. This
is where I will live among the Israelites
forever. The people of Israel will never again defile my holy name — neither
they nor their kings — by their prostitution and the funeral offerings[c] for their
kings at their death.[d][i] 8When they placed
their threshold next to my threshold and
their doorposts beside my doorposts,
with only a wall between me and them,
they defiled my holy name by their detestable practices. So I destroyed them in
my anger. 9Now let them put away from
me their prostitution and the funeral
offerings for their kings, and I will live
among them forever.[j]
10"Son of man, describe the temple to
the people of Israel, that they may be
ashamed[k] of their sins. Let them consider
its perfection, 11and if they are ashamed
of all they have done, make known to
them the design of the temple — its arrangement, its exits and entrances — its
whole design and all its regulations[e] and
laws. Write these down before them so
that they may be faithful to its design
and follow all its regulations.[l]
12"This is the law of the temple: All the
surrounding area[m] on top of the mountain will be most holy. Such is the law
of the temple.

The Great Altar Restored

13"These are the measurements of the
altar[n] in long cubits,[f] that cubit being a
cubit and a handbreadth: Its gutter is a
cubit deep and a cubit wide, with a rim
of one span[g] around the edge. And this

42:20 [x]Eze 40:5 [y]Zec 2:5 [z]Eze 45:2; Rev 21:16 [a]Eze 22:26
43:1 [b]Eze 10:19; 42:15; 44:1; 46:1
43:2 [c]Rev 1:15 [d]Isa 6:3; Eze 11:23; Rev 18:1
43:4 [e]Eze 1:28 [f]Eze 10:19
43:5 [g]Eze 11:24 [h]Eze 3:12; 8:3
43:7 [i]Lev 26:30
43:9 [j]Eze 37:26-28
43:10 [k]Eze 16:61
43:11 [l]Eze 44:5
43:12 [m]Eze 40:2
43:13 [n]2Ch 4:1

Eze 43:4-5 ❖ As the temple of God (see 1Co 6:19), how can we let the glory of God enter and fill us? How will this glory within us affect the way we live?

[a] *17* Septuagint; Hebrew *rods* [b] *3* Some Hebrew manuscripts and Vulgate; most Hebrew manuscripts *I* [c] *7* Or *the memorial monuments;* also in verse 9 [d] *7* Or *their high places* [e] *11* Some Hebrew manuscripts and Septuagint; most Hebrew manuscripts *regulations and its whole design* [f] *13* That is, about 21 inches or about 53 centimeters; also in verses 14 and 17. The long cubit is the basic unit for linear measurement throughout Ezekiel 40 – 48. [g] *13* That is, about 11 inches or about 27 centimeters

43:1–4 God's glory returns to the temple through the east gate, from the same direction in which it had earlier left (10:18–19). On its return, the glory of God fills the temple (1Ki 8:10–11). It even causes the land itself to shine.
43:5–6 The prophet is picked up by the Spirit and dropped in the inner court to hear the word of the Lord. What is new is not the Lord's claim to kingship or the area over which he makes that claim, it is the assertion that his kingship will be exercised there *forever*.
43:7–9 In the past, the house of Israel and their kings had defiled the Lord's name.
43:10–12 Ezekiel is being shown these things so that he can relay them to his own generation. The temple vision is a teaching tool. Its dimensions and regulations all serve a single purpose: that the whole area all around the temple may be most holy (v. 12).
43:13–17 The importance of this altar to Ezekiel's plan is evident from its detailed description. Additionally, it is the center of the temple complex. The dimensions of the altar are 18 cubits by 18 cubits (31.5 feet square) at the lowest level and 14 cubits by 14 cubits (24.5 feet square) at the highest. At each corner of the top level there are projections, or "horns" (v. 20), to which blood is applied during some aspects of the ritual. The whole structure stands 9 cubits (about 15 feet) high and is approached by a flight of steps from the east. In Ezekiel's temple, the priest faces west, toward the Most Holy Place. This avoids any suggestion of a repetition of the sun worship of 8:16.

is the height of the altar: 14From the gutter on the ground up to the lower ledge
that goes around the altar it is two cubits high, and the ledge is a cubit wide.[a]
From this lower ledge to the upper ledge
that goes around the altar it is four cubits high, and that ledge is also a cubit
wide.[b] 15Above that, the altar hearth is
four cubits high, and four horns[o] project upward from the hearth. 16The altar
hearth is square, twelve cubits[c] long and
twelve cubits wide. 17The upper ledge
also is square, fourteen cubits[d] long and
fourteen cubits wide. All around the altar
is a gutter of one cubit with a rim of half
a cubit.[e] The steps[p] of the altar face east."
18Then he said to me, "Son of man, this
is what the Sovereign LORD says: These
will be the regulations for sacrificing
burnt offerings[q] and splashing blood[r]
against the altar when it is built: 19You
are to give a young bull[s] as a sin offering[f] to the Levitical priests of the family
of Zadok,[t] who come near[u] to minister
before me, declares the Sovereign LORD.
20You are to take some of its blood and
put it on the four horns of the altar and
on the four corners of the upper ledge[v]
and all around the rim, and so purify the
altar[w] and make atonement for it. 21You
are to take the bull for the sin offering
and burn it in the designated part of the
temple area outside the sanctuary.[x]
22"On the second day you are to offer
a male goat without defect for a sin offering, and the altar is to be purified as
it was purified with the bull. 23When you
have finished purifying it, you are to offer a young bull and a ram from the flock,
both without defect.[y] 24You are to offer
them before the LORD, and the priests are
to sprinkle salt[z] on them and sacrifice
them as a burnt offering to the LORD.
25"For seven days[a] you are to provide
a male goat daily for a sin offering; you
are also to provide a young bull and a
ram from the flock, both without defect.[b] 26For seven days they are to make
atonement for the altar and cleanse it;
thus they will dedicate it. 27At the end
of these days, from the eighth day[c] on,
the priests are to present your burnt offerings and fellowship offerings[d] on the
altar. Then I will accept you, declares the
Sovereign LORD."

The Priesthood Restored

44 Then the man brought me back
to the outer gate of the sanctuary,
the one facing east,[e] and it was shut. 2The
LORD said to me, "This gate is to remain
shut. It must not be opened; no one may
enter through it.[f] It is to remain shut
because the LORD, the God of Israel, has
entered through it. 3The prince himself is
the only one who may sit inside the gateway to eat in the presence[g] of the LORD.
He is to enter by way of the portico of
the gateway and go out the same way.[h]"
4Then the man brought me by way of

43:15 [o] Ex 27:2
43:17 [p] Ex 20:26
43:18 [q] Ex 40:29 [r] Lev 1:5,11; Heb 9:21-22
43:19 [s] Lev 4:3; Eze 45:18-19 [t] Eze 44:15 [u] Nu 16:40; Eze 40:46
43:20 [v] ver 17 [w] Lev 16:19
43:21 [x] Ex 29:14; Heb 13:11
43:23 [y] Ex 29:1
43:24 [z] Lev 2:13; Mk 9:49-50
43:25 [a] Lev 8:33 [b] Ex 29:37
43:27 [c] Lev 9:1 [d] Lev 17:5
44:1 [e] Eze 43:1
44:2 [f] Eze 43:4-5
44:3 [g] Ex 24:9-11 [h] Eze 46:2, 8

[a] 14 That is, about 3 1/2 feet high and 1 3/4 feet wide or about 105 centimeters high and 53 centimeters wide [b] 14 That is, about 7 feet high and 1 3/4 feet wide or about 2.1 meters high and 53 centimeters wide [c] 16 That is, about 21 feet or about 6.4 meters [d] 17 That is, about 25 feet or about 7.4 meters [e] 17 That is, about 11 inches or about 27 centimeters [f] 19 Or *purification offering*; also in verses 21, 22 and 25

43:18–27 Ezekiel is assigned a key role in the consecration process. The body of the purification sacrifice is disposed of by burning it outside the sanctuary. The burnt offerings are also to be offered with salt (v. 24). Salt was the main preservative used in the ancient Near East and seems to have featured prominently in covenant ceremonies.

The purpose of this ritual is to "purify the altar and make atonement for it" (v. 20) so that the holy space can be used for the regular ministry of offering sacrifices. The concept of making atonement (or expiation) expresses the idea of ritually wiping away the impurities and sins that adhere to a person or object. Once Ezekiel has completed his inaugural ministry (v. 19), the priests will offer burnt offerings and fellowship offerings on the altar. They will once more be acceptable to God (v. 27).

43:1–27 When Christ comes into our lives, he does so in only one role: as King. One of the problems that existed in Judah was confusion over who was sovereign. This confusion was illustrated in the memorials glorifying earthly kings in a building intended to glorify the heavenly King. That may seem a foreign problem to us until we start to examine our own hearts and ask how much of our lives are lived to our own glory and how much to God's glory. Although we may confess with our mouths that our bodies are temples of the Holy Spirit, all too often our lives tell a different story.

44:1–4 The outer east gate will forever remain closed because the Lord entered through it on his return to the Most Holy Place. However, the space within the gate may be used by the prince for his sacred meals (v. 3). The royal figure has a limited, though still honorable, position.

EZEKIEL AND JOHN THE REVELATOR

More than any other book in the NT, Revelation draws on OT themes and images. Ezekiel provides the backdrop for many of these.

EZEKIEL	THEMES AND IMAGES	REVELATION
Eze 1; 10; 11:22-23	Living Creatures; Throne; Bow; Crystal	Rev 4
Eze 1:24-28; 8:4; 40:3; 43:1-3	Description of "a figure like that of a man"—appearance and voice	Rev 1:12-17; 2:18; 14:2
Eze 2:2; 3:12-14; 8:3-4; 11:1, 24; 37; 40:1-2; 43:3	The Holy Spirit acts, revealing and transporting	Rev 1:10; 17:3; 21:10
Eze 2:9—3:3	The scroll, inscribed on both sides; eating the scroll	Rev 5:1-4, 10:9-11
Eze 9:3-6	Sealing of the faithful; judgment	Rev 7:1-4
Eze 13:11-14; 38:22	Judgment from the sky—hail, wind, fire	Rev 8:7
Eze 14:12-18; 15:8	Judgment on the land—famine	Rev 6:5-8
Eze 16; 23	The great prostitute	Rev 17
Eze 26-27	Lament over fallen city; a trading list	Rev 18
Eze 38-39	Gog and Magog	Rev 20:7-10
Eze 37	Revival and reign with the Messiah	Rev 20:1-6
Eze 40-48	The New Jerusalem	Rev 3:12; 21
Eze 47:1-12	The river and leaves of healing	Rev 22

the north gate to the front of the temple.
I looked and saw the glory of the LORD
filling the temple[i] of the LORD, and I fell
facedown.[j]
5The LORD said to me, "Son of man,
look carefully, listen closely and give attention to everything I tell you concerning all the regulations and instructions
regarding the temple of the LORD. Give
attention to the entrance to the temple
and all the exits of the sanctuary.[k] 6Say
to rebellious Israel,[l] 'This is what the
Sovereign LORD says: Enough of your
detestable practices, people of Israel!
7In addition to all your other detestable
practices, you brought foreigners uncircumcised in heart[m] and flesh into my
sanctuary, desecrating my temple while
you offered me food, fat and blood, and
you broke my covenant.[n] 8Instead of carrying out your duty in regard to my holy
things, you put others in charge of my
sanctuary.[o] 9This is what the Sovereign
LORD says: No foreigner uncircumcised
in heart and flesh is to enter my sanctuary, not even the foreigners who live
among the Israelites.[p]
10" 'The Levites who went far from
me when Israel went astray[q] and who
wandered from me after their idols
must bear the consequences of their
sin.[r] 11They may serve in my sanctuary,
having charge of the gates of the temple
and serving in it; they may slaughter
the burnt offerings[s] and sacrifices for
the people and stand before the people and serve them.[t] 12But because they
served them in the presence of their
idols and made the people of Israel fall
into sin, therefore I have sworn with
uplifted hand[u] that they must bear the
consequences of their sin, declares the
Sovereign LORD.[v] 13They are not to come
near to serve me as priests or come near

44:4 [i]Isa 6:4; Rev 15:8 [j]Eze 1:28; 3:23
44:5 [k]Eze 40:4; 43:10-11
44:6 [l]Eze 3:9
44:7 [m]Lev 26:41 [n]Ge 17:14; Ex 12:48; Lev 22:25
44:8 [o]Lev 22:2; Nu 18:7
44:9 [p]Joel 3:17; Zec 14:21
44:10 [q]2Ki 23:8 [r]Nu 18:23
44:11 [s]2Ch 29:34 [t]Nu 3:5-37; 16:9; 1Ch 26:12-19
44:12 [u]Ps 106:26 [v]2Ki 16:10-16

44:5-9 The sin of the past lay in bringing "foreigners uncircumcised in heart and flesh into my sanctuary" (v. 7). This probably refers to the well-attested practice of employing foreign guards in the temple (2Ki 11:14-19).
44:10-14 Verse 10 identifies the legitimate temple guards: the Levites. The sin of the Levites, whatever its precise form, has consequences in terms of restrictions on access and service. The purpose of these regulations is to induce shame as they consider their detestable practices (v. 13).

any of my holy things or my most holy
offerings; they must bear the shame[w] of
their detestable practices.[x] 14And I will
appoint them to guard the temple for all
the work that is to be done in it.[y]
15" 'But the Levitical priests, who are
descendants of Zadok and who guarded
my sanctuary when the Israelites went
astray from me, are to come near to minister before me; they are to stand before
me to offer sacrifices of fat and blood, declares the Sovereign LORD.[z] 16They alone
are to enter my sanctuary; they alone
are to come near my table[a] to minister
before me and serve me as guards.[b]
17" 'When they enter the gates of the inner court, they are to wear linen clothes;[c]
they must not wear any woolen garment
while ministering at the gates of the inner court or inside the temple. 18They are
to wear linen turbans[d] on their heads
and linen undergarments[e] around their
waists. They must not wear anything that
makes them perspire.[f] 19When they go
out into the outer court where the people are, they are to take off the clothes
they have been ministering in and are
to leave them in the sacred rooms, and
put on other clothes, so that the people
are not consecrated[g] through contact
with their garments.[h]
20" 'They must not shave their heads
or let their hair grow long, but they are
to keep the hair of their heads trimmed.[i]
21No priest is to drink wine when he enters the inner court.[j] 22They must not
marry widows or divorced women; they
may marry only virgins of Israelite descent or widows of priests.[k] 23They are
to teach my people the difference between the holy and the common[l] and
show them how to distinguish between
the unclean and the clean.[m]
24" 'In any dispute, the priests are to
serve as judges[n] and decide it according
to my ordinances. They are to keep my
laws and my decrees for all my appointed
festivals, and they are to keep my Sabbaths holy.[o]
25" 'A priest must not defile himself by
going near a dead person; however, if the
dead person was his father or mother,
son or daughter, brother or unmarried
sister, then he may defile himself.[p] 26Af-
ter he is cleansed, he must wait seven
days.[q] 27On the day he goes into the inner
court of the sanctuary to minister in the
sanctuary, he is to offer a sin offering[a]
for himself, declares the Sovereign LORD.
28" 'I am to be the only inheritance[r] the
priests have. You are to give them no possession in Israel; I will be their possession. 29They will eat the grain offerings,

[a] 27 Or *purification offering*; also in verse 29

44:13 [w] Eze 16:61 [x] Nu 18:3
44:14 [y] Nu 18:4; 1Ch 23:28-32
44:15 [z] Jer 33:18; Eze 40:46; Zec 3:7
44:16 [a] Eze 41:22 [b] Nu 18:5
44:17 [c] Ex 39:27-28; Rev 19:8
44:18 [d] Ex 28:39; Isa 3:20 [e] Ex 28:42 [f] Lev 16:4
44:19 [g] Lev 6:27; Eze 46:20 [h] Lev 6:10-11; Eze 42:14
44:20 [i] Lev 21:5; Nu 6:5
44:21 [j] Lev 10:9
44:22 [k] Lev 21:7
44:23 [l] Eze 22:26 [m] Mal 2:7
44:24 [n] Dt 17:8-9; 1Ch 23:4 [o] 2Ch 19:8
44:25 [p] Lev 21:1-4
44:26 [q] Nu 19:14
44:28 [r] Nu 18:20; Dt 10:9; 18:1-2; Jos 13:33

Eze 44:28 ❖ What does it mean to have God himself as our inheritance? Why is this better than inheriting land or possessions?

44:15–16 Zadokite priests receive the privilege of sole access to the inner court and the offering of all sacrifices at the altar and the service at the table inside the sanctuary itself. This privilege is explained as being due to their faithful service in the time of Israel's apostasy.

44:17–19 Because the Zadokite priests operate closer to the Most Holy Place than any others, they face additional restrictions on their behavior. They must wear linen rather than woolen clothing when they minister so that they do not defile the inner court with their sweat. Moreover, they are to distinguish between the "sacred" clothes they wear for ministry and the "other clothes" (v. 19) they wear for the rest of life.

44:20–27 Of particular danger was the contamination associated with contact with death, either through contact with a corpse (v. 25) or through the ritual mourning practices (v. 20). The possibility of potentially fatal errors induced by consuming alcoholic beverages is also taken into account (v. 21). The need for pure priestly stock also requires the restriction of priestly marriage (v. 22).

44:28–31 Since the priests belong to the Lord, they are to have the Lord alone as their inheritance. Unlike the other tribes, they are to be allotted no territory of their own in the new promised land. Instead, they are to be provided for through the sacrificial system.

44:1–31 The privilege of close access to God is a reward we do not have to wait for eternity to begin to experience. We get to sample the firstfruits of that closeness ahead of time. Even now, we can approach the throne of God with boldness, presenting our praises and our petitions, basking in the glory of his love. But if we expect to experience the full blessing of communion with God, our behavior must reflect his holiness.

For the Zadokites, access to God's presence meant heavy restrictions on their lifestyle. There were things they could not touch, places they could not go, food they could not eat, and clothes they could not wear if they were to minister in the presence of the holy God. So too for us, if we hope to experience the blessing of God's presence with us, then our lifestyle will be (from the world's perspective) restricted.

the sin offerings and the guilt offerings;
and everything in Israel devoted[a] to the
LORD[s] will belong to them.[t] 30 The best of
all the firstfruits[u] and of all your special
gifts will belong to the priests. You are
to give them the first portion of your
ground meal[v] so that a blessing[w] may
rest on your household.[x] 31 The priests
must not eat anything, whether bird or
animal, found dead or torn by wild animals.[y]

Israel Fully Restored

45 "'When you allot the land as an
inheritance,[z] you are to present to
the LORD a portion of the land as a sacred
district, 25,000 cubits[b] long and 20,000[c]
cubits[d] wide; the entire area will be holy.[a]
2 Of this, a section 500 cubits[e] square[b] is
to be for the sanctuary, with 50 cubits[f]
around it for open land. 3 In the sacred
district, measure off a section 25,000
cubits long and 10,000 cubits[g] wide. In
it will be the sanctuary, the Most Holy
Place. 4 It will be the sacred portion of the
land for the priests,[c] who minister in the
sanctuary and who draw near to minister before the LORD. It will be a place for
their houses as well as a holy place for
the sanctuary.[d] 5 An area 25,000 cubits
long and 10,000 cubits wide will belong
to the Levites, who serve in the temple,
as their possession for towns to live in.[h][e]
6 "'You are to give the city as its property an area 5,000 cubits[i] wide and 25,000
cubits long, adjoining the sacred portion;
it will belong to all Israel.[f]
7 "'The prince will have the land bordering each side of the area formed by
the sacred district and the property of
the city. It will extend westward from
the west side and eastward from the east
side, running lengthwise from the western to the eastern border parallel to one
of the tribal portions.[g] 8 This land will be
his possession in Israel. And my princes
will no longer oppress my people but will
allow the people of Israel to possess the
land according to their tribes.[h]
9 "'This is what the Sovereign LORD
says: You have gone far enough, princes of Israel! Give up your violence and
oppression and do what is just and right.[i]
Stop dispossessing my people, declares
the Sovereign LORD. 10 You are to use accurate scales,[j] an accurate ephah[j][k] and
an accurate bath.[k] 11 The ephah[l] and the
bath are to be the same size, the bath
containing a tenth of a homer and the
ephah a tenth of a homer; the homer is to
be the standard measure for both. 12 The
shekel[l] is to consist of twenty gerahs.[m]
Twenty shekels plus twenty-five shekels
plus fifteen shekels equal one mina.[m]
13 "'This is the special gift you are
to offer: a sixth of an ephah[n] from
each homer of wheat and a sixth of an
ephah[o] from each homer of barley. 14 The

Eze 45:9–12 ❖ How do we see political leaders today dispossessing their people and practicing injustice? What does God think of such practices?

44:29 [s] Lev 27:21 [t] Nu 18:9,14
44:30 [u] Nu 18:12-13 [v] Nu 15:18-21 [w] Mal 3:10 [x] Ne 10:35-37
44:31 [y] Ex 22:31; Lev 22:8
45:1 [z] Eze 47:21-22 [a] Eze 48:8-9, 29
45:2 [b] Eze 42:20
45:4 [c] Eze 40:46 [d] Eze 48:10-11
45:5 [e] Eze 48:13
45:6 [f] Eze 48:15-18
45:7 [g] Eze 48:21
45:8 [h] Nu 26:53; Eze 46:18
45:9 [i] Jer 22:3; Zec 7:9-10; 8:16
45:10 [j] Dt 25:15; Pr 11:1; Am 8:4-6; Mic 6:10-11 [k] Lev 19:36
45:11 [l] Isa 5:10
45:12 [m] Ex 30:13; Lev 27:25; Nu 3:47

[a] *29* The Hebrew term refers to the irrevocable giving over of things or persons to the LORD.
[b] *1* That is, about 8 miles or about 13 kilometers; also in verses 3, 5 and 6
[c] *1* Septuagint (see also verses 3 and 5 and 48:9); Hebrew *10,000*
[d] *1* That is, about 6 1/2 miles or about 11 kilometers
[e] *2* That is, about 875 feet or about 265 meters
[f] *2* That is, about 88 feet or about 27 meters
[g] *3* That is, about 3 1/3 miles or about 5.3 kilometers; also in verse 5
[h] *5* Septuagint; Hebrew *temple; they will have as their possession 20 rooms*
[i] *6* That is, about 1 2/3 miles or about 2.7 kilometers
[j] *10* An ephah was a dry measure having the capacity of about 3/5 bushel or about 22 liters.
[k] *10* A bath was a liquid measure equaling about 6 gallons or about 22 liters.
[l] *12* A shekel weighed about 2/5 ounce or about 12 grams.
[m] *12* That is, 60 shekels; the common mina was 50 shekels. Sixty shekels were about 1 1/2 pounds or about 690 grams.
[n] *13* That is, probably about 6 pounds or about 2.7 kilograms
[o] *13* That is, probably about 5 pounds or about 2.3 kilograms

45:1–6 The primary focus of the division of the land is asserting divine sovereignty and safeguarding the divine presence in their midst. The primary purpose of the sacred district is to provide a zone of graded holiness outside the temple like that inside the temple. The same principles of graded access that applied within the temple complex have thus been applied to the land itself. The temple—not the city or the king—stands at the center of this Holy Land.

45:7–9 These princes in Ezekiel have no active part to play in distributing the land. The divine king has already allocated it.

45:10–17 The primary focus of the prince's duties is temple-centered. The prince ensures that accurate weights and measures are used in gathering up the offerings and gifts of the people. It is also the prince's responsibility to provide from his own resources the offerings for the special occasions. In both the regular and the special offerings, the prince has a central role as the representative of the people (v. 17).

prescribed portion of olive oil, measured
by the bath, is a tenth of a bath[a] from
each cor (which consists of ten baths or
one homer, for ten baths are equivalent
to a homer). 15Also one sheep is to be
taken from every flock of two hundred
from the well-watered pastures of Israel.
These will be used for the grain offerings,
burnt offerings[n] and fellowship offerings to make atonement[o] for the people,
declares the Sovereign LORD. 16All the
people of the land will be required to
give this special offering to the prince in
Israel. 17It will be the duty of the prince to
provide the burnt offerings, grain offerings and drink offerings at the festivals,
the New Moons and the Sabbaths[p]—at
all the appointed festivals of Israel. He
will provide the sin offerings,[b] grain offerings, burnt offerings and fellowship
offerings to make atonement for the Israelites.[q]
18" 'This is what the Sovereign LORD
says: In the first month[r] on the first day
you are to take a young bull without
defect[s] and purify the sanctuary.[t] 19The
priest is to take some of the blood of
the sin offering and put it on the doorposts of the temple, on the four corners
of the upper ledge[u] of the altar[v] and on
the gateposts of the inner court. 20You
are to do the same on the seventh day of
the month for anyone who sins unintentionally[w] or through ignorance; so you
are to make atonement for the temple.
21" 'In the first month on the fourteenth day you are to observe the Passover,[x] a festival lasting seven days,
during which you shall eat bread made
without yeast. 22On that day the prince is
to provide a bull as a sin offering for himself and for all the people of the land.[y]
23Every day during the seven days of the
festival he is to provide seven bulls and
seven rams[z] without defect as a burnt
offering to the LORD, and a male goat
for a sin offering.[a] 24He is to provide as
a grain offering[b] an ephah for each bull
and an ephah for each ram, along with a
hin[c] of olive oil for each ephah.[c]
25" 'During the seven days of the festival,[d] which begins in the seventh month
on the fifteenth day, he is to make the
same provision for sin offerings, burnt
offerings, grain offerings and oil.[e]

46 " 'This is what the Sovereign LORD
says: The gate of the inner court[f]
facing east[g] is to be shut on the six working days, but on the Sabbath day and
on the day of the New Moon[h] it is to be
opened. 2The prince is to enter from
the outside through the portico[i] of the
gateway and stand by the gatepost. The
priests are to sacrifice his burnt offering and his fellowship offerings. He is
to bow down in worship at the threshold of the gateway and then go out, but
the gate will not be shut until evening.[j]
3On the Sabbaths and New Moons the
people of the land are to worship in the
presence of the LORD at the entrance of
that gateway.[k] 4The burnt offering the
prince brings to the LORD on the Sabbath
day is to be six male lambs and a ram,
all without defect. 5The grain offering
given with the ram is to be an ephah,[d]
and the grain offering with the lambs is
to be as much as he pleases, along with
a hin[e] of olive oil for each ephah.[l] 6On
the day of the New Moon[m] he is to offer a young bull, six lambs and a ram,
all without defect. 7He is to provide as a

45:15 [n] Lev 1:4 [o] Lev 6:30
45:17 [p] Lev 23:38; Isa 66:23 [q] 1Ki 8:62; 2Ch 31:3; Eze 46:4-12
45:18 [r] Ex 12:2 [s] Lev 22:20; Heb 9:14 [t] Lev 16:16, 33
45:19 [u] Eze 43:17 [v] Lev 16:18-19; Eze 43:20
45:20 [w] Lev 4:27
45:21 [x] Ex 12:11; Lev 23:5-6
45:22 [y] Lev 4:14
45:23 [z] Job 42:8 [a] Nu 28:16-25
45:24 [b] Nu 28:12-13 [c] Eze 46:5-7
45:25 [d] Dt 16:13 [e] Lev 23:34-43; Nu 29:12-38
46:1 [f] Eze 40:19 [g] 1Ch 9:18 [h] ver 6; Isa 66:23
46:2 [i] ver 8 [j] ver 12; Eze 44:3
46:3 [k] Lk 1:10
46:5 [l] ver 11; Eze 45:24
46:6 [m] ver 1; Nu 10:10

[a] *14* That is, about 2 1/2 quarts or about 2.2 liters
[b] *17* Or *purification offerings;* also in verses 19, 22, 23 and 25
[c] *24* That is, about 1 gallon or about 3.8 liters
[d] *5* That is, probably about 35 pounds or about 16 kilograms; also in verses 7 and 11
[e] *5* That is, about 1 gallon or about 3.8 liters; also in verses 7 and 11

45:18–25 Ezekiel's calendar appears to be a stripped-down, focused edition of what had previously been in force. There is no mention of the Festival of Weeks, the third annual festival, and the remaining two festivals (Passover and Tabernacles) have become virtually symmetrical festivals of purification. Of the two, the festival of Passover retains more of its distinctive features.

The Passover offerings, provided by the prince, represent a substantial increase from the sacrifices demanded for the Passover in the Mosaic legislation of Nu 28.

The Festival of Tabernacles has lost all its original distinctiveness. It lacks any name or description, except for the fact that the prince is to provide the same offerings for it as at the Passover (v. 25). Ezekiel's special interest in purification remains clear in the prominent place given to the sin offerings in the list of v. 25. Both festivals thereby come to share the same interest in atonement for sin.

46:1–8 The prince is also required to provide the offerings for the Sabbath and New Moon festivals. He has the unique privilege, as a layman, of approaching the threshold of the inner east gate and prostrating himself there before the Lord. In Ezekiel's program, the laity are being kept at a "safe" distance from the holy things.

grain offering one ephah with the bull,
one ephah with the ram, and with the
lambs as much as he wants to give, along
with a hin of oil for each ephah.[n] 8When
the prince enters, he is to go in through
the portico[o] of the gateway, and he is to
come out the same way.[p]
9“ ‘When the people of the land come
before the LORD at the appointed festivals,[q] whoever enters by the north gate to
worship is to go out the south gate; and
whoever enters by the south gate is to go
out the north gate. No one is to return
through the gate by which they entered,
but each is to go out the opposite gate.
10The prince is to be among them, going
in when they go in and going out when
they go out.[r] 11At the feasts and the appointed festivals, the grain offering is to
be an ephah with a bull, an ephah with
a ram, and with the lambs as much as
he pleases, along with a hin of oil for
each ephah.[s]
12“ ‘When the prince provides[t] a freewill offering[u] to the LORD—whether a
burnt offering or fellowship offerings—
the gate facing east is to be opened for
him. He shall offer his burnt offering or
his fellowship offerings as he does on the
Sabbath day. Then he shall go out, and after he has gone out, the gate will be shut.[v]
13“ ‘Every day you are to provide a year-
old lamb without defect for a burnt offering to the LORD; morning by morning
you shall provide it.[w] 14You are also to
provide with it morning by morning a
grain offering, consisting of a sixth of
an ephah[a] with a third of a hin[b] of oil
to moisten the flour. The presenting of
this grain offering to the LORD is a lasting
ordinance.[x] 15So the lamb and the grain
offering and the oil shall be provided
morning by morning for a regular[y] burnt
offering.[z]

46:7 [n] Eze 45:24
46:8 [o] ver 2 [p] Eze 44:3
46:9 [q] Ex 23:14; 34:20
46:10 [r] 2Sa 6:14-15; Ps 42:4
46:11 [s] ver 5
46:12 [t] Eze 45:17 [u] Lev 7:16 [v] ver 2
46:13 [w] Ex 29:38; Nu 28:3
46:14 [x] Da 8:11
46:15 [y] Ex 29:42 [z] Ex 29:38; Nu 28:5-6

Eze 46:12 ❖ What freewill offering can we give to the Lord? How is offering what we have to God a fitting act of praise and devotion?

16“ ‘This is what the Sovereign LORD
says: If the prince makes a gift from his
inheritance to one of his sons, it will also
belong to his descendants; it is to be their
property by inheritance.[a] 17If, however,
he makes a gift from his inheritance to
one of his servants, the servant may keep
it until the year of freedom;[b] then it will
revert to the prince. His inheritance belongs to his sons only; it is theirs. 18The
prince must not take any of the inheritance[c] of the people, driving them off
their property. He is to give his sons their
inheritance out of his own property, so
that not one of my people will be separated from their property.’ ”
19Then the man brought me through
the entrance[d] at the side of the gate to
the sacred rooms facing north, which
belonged to the priests, and showed me
a place at the western end. 20He said to
me, “This is the place where the priests
are to cook the guilt offering and the sin
offering[c] and bake the grain offering, to
avoid bringing them into the outer court
and consecrating[e] the people.”[f]
21He then brought me to the outer
court and led me around to its four corners, and I saw in each corner another
court. 22In the four corners of the outer
court were enclosed[d] courts, forty cubits
long and thirty cubits wide;[e] each of the

46:16 [a] 2Ch 21:3
46:17 [b] Lev 25:10
46:18 [c] Lev 25:23; Eze 45:8; Mic 2:1-2
46:19 [d] Eze 42:9
46:20 [e] Lev 6:27 [f] Zec 14:20

[a] *14* That is, probably about 6 pounds or about 2.7 kilograms [b] *14* That is, about 1 1/2 quarts or about 1.3 liters [c] *20* Or *purification offering* [d] *22* The meaning of the Hebrew for this word is uncertain. [e] *22* That is, about 70 feet long and 53 feet wide or about 21 meters long and 16 meters wide

46:9–12 At the annual festivals, God's people are required to prostrate themselves before the Lord. The community at large is assigned no other tasks. Though the people are clearly expected to offer sacrifices of their own (cf. v. 24), these are relegated to footnote status.

The prince is chief worshiper (v. 10). But his privileged position is clear also from his access to the east gate of the inner court, which is opened for him whenever he wishes to offer a freewill sacrifice (v. 12).

46:13–15 The section on the sacrifices closes with the requirements for the daily sacrifice.

46:16–18 In an economy where the king typically rewarded loyal service by gifts of land, there would have been a perpetual temptation for the king to acquire ever more land with which to reward his followers. But the land is the Lord's, and he divides it. The prince is thereby continually reminded that he is a servant of the great king and must behave as such.

46:19–24 The entire section of 44:1—46:24 is rounded off by a return to the beginning. The heavenly messenger, inactive since 44:4, returns to guide the prophet out of the inner court. Together they arrive back at the outer court. The tour of the temple is thus neatly completed, having gone from the outside to the center (40:5—41:4) and back out again twice.

courts in the four corners was the same
size. 23Around the inside of each of the
four courts was a ledge of stone, with
places for fire built all around under the
ledge. 24He said to me, "These are the
kitchens where those who minister at
the temple are to cook the sacrifices of
the people."

The River From the Temple

47 The man brought me back to the
entrance to the temple, and I
saw water[g] coming out from under the
threshold of the temple toward the east
(for the temple faced east). The water was
coming down from under the south side
of the temple, south of the altar.[h] 2He
then brought me out through the north
gate and led me around the outside to
the outer gate facing east, and the water
was trickling from the south side.

3As the man went eastward with a
measuring line[i] in his hand, he measured
off a thousand cubits[a] and then led me
through water that was ankle-deep. 4He
measured off another thousand cubits
and led me through water that was knee-
deep. He measured off another thousand
and led me through water that was up
to the waist. 5He measured off another
thousand, but now it was a river that I
could not cross, because the water had
risen and was deep enough to swim in—
a river that no one could cross.[j] 6He asked
me, "Son of man, do you see this?"

Then he led me back to the bank of
the river. 7When I arrived there, I saw
a great number of trees on each side of
the river.[k] 8He said to me, "This water
flows toward the eastern region and goes
down into the Arabah,[b][l] where it enters
the Dead Sea. When it empties into the
sea, the salty water there becomes fresh.[m]
9Swarms of living creatures will live
wherever the river flows. There will be
large numbers of fish, because this water flows there and makes the salt water
fresh; so where the river flows everything will live.[n] 10Fishermen[o] will stand
along the shore; from En Gedi[p] to En
Eglaim there will be places for spreading
nets.[q] The fish will be of many kinds[r]—
like the fish of the Mediterranean Sea.[s]
11But the swamps and marshes will not
become fresh; they will be left for salt.[t]
12Fruit trees of all kinds will grow on both

47:1 [g] Isa 55:1 [h] Ps 46:4; Joel 3:18; Rev 22:1
47:3 [i] Eze 40:3
47:5 [j] Isa 11:9; Hab 2:14
47:7 [k] ver 12; Rev 22:2
47:8 [l] Dt 3:17; Jos 3:16 [m] Isa 41:18
47:9 [n] Isa 12:3; 55:1; Jn 4:14; 7:37-38
47:10 [o] Mt 4:19 [p] Jos 15:62 [q] Eze 26:5 [r] Ps 104:25; Mt 13:47 [s] Nu 34:6
47:11 [t] Dt 29:23

[a] 3 That is, about 1,700 feet or about 530 meters
[b] 8 Or *the Jordan Valley*

Eze 47:3-12 ❖ When have we experienced the living water of God (see Jn 4:14)? How can we move deeper into that water?

45:1—46:24 In order to appreciate the Good News of the gospel we need to confront ourselves again with the reality of God's perfect Law, which condemns our own sin and points us to Jesus as our sinless substitute. Without a deep appreciation of our sinfulness and impurity, real worship is not a possibility. In that worship, all God's people now have a central part to play. We need no human priests to stand between us and the holy God to conduct our worship on our behalf, for we have a great high priest, Jesus, who has perfectly met all our needs (Heb 10:19–22).

In light of that incredible privilege, let us indeed count it a great blessing to draw near to God in worship and adoration. Let us hold unswervingly to the hope we profess, and let us stir one another on to love and good deeds and lives of purified holiness, until the approaching day comes when Christ our King will return and we will be exiles no more (Heb 10:22-25).

47:1-2 The source of the living water is the temple itself. This was the site of the "Sea" in Solomon's temple (1Ki 7:23, 39). The "Sea" now becomes the source of a life-giving river that flows out from the temple, like the river of Eden (Ge 2:10–14).

47:3-6 The stream that starts out so pitifully small miraculously becomes progressively larger the farther he journeys along it. At first, it is a trickle; after 1,000 cubits (1,500 feet), it is ankle-deep; after another 1,000 cubits, it is knee-deep, then waist-deep, and finally an uncrossable torrent (v. 5). The guiding angel asks him to pause here and ponder its significance.

47:7-9 This river is also a transforming force wherever it flows. It brings fertility to the ground surrounding it and transforms the Dead Sea: "Where the river flows everything will live" (v. 9).

47:10-12 The numerous trees of v. 7 are now more closely defined as "fruit trees" (v. 12). They will be so full of life that they will bear new fruit every month to feed the population, and their leaves will be for healing. All of this happens because the trees are fed from the stream that flows from the temple.

47:1-12 Jesus used a different approach to sharing the gospel with the Samaritan woman (Jn 4:1-42). His focus was on bondage or emptiness, not guilt, as humanity's basic problem. Our basic need is freedom from slavery to sin. The gospel provides the freedom for us to be what we were created to be—God-centered worshipers. This is Paul's approach to the

banks of the river.[u] Their leaves will not
wither, nor will their fruit[v] fail. Every
month they will bear fruit, because the
water from the sanctuary flows to them.
Their fruit will serve for food and their
leaves for healing.[w]"

The Boundaries of the Land

13 This is what the Sovereign LORD says:
"These are the boundaries[x] of the land
that you will divide among the twelve
tribes of Israel as their inheritance, with
two portions for Joseph.[y] 14 You are to
divide it equally among them. Because
I swore with uplifted hand to give it to
your ancestors, this land will become
your inheritance.[z]

15 "This is to be the boundary of the
land:

"On the north side it will run from the
Mediterranean Sea by the Hethlon
road[a] past Lebo Hamath to Zedad,
16 Berothah[ab] and Sibraim (which
lies on the border between Damascus and Hamath),[c] as far as Hazer
Hattikon, which is on the border of
Hauran. 17 The boundary will extend
from the sea to Hazar Enan,[b] along
the northern border of Damascus,
with the border of Hamath to the
north. This will be the northern
boundary.[d]
18 "On the east side the boundary will
run between Hauran and Damascus,
along the Jordan between Gilead
and the land of Israel, to the Dead
Sea and as far as Tamar.[c] This will
be the eastern boundary.
19 "On the south side it will run from
Tamar as far as the waters of Meribah Kadesh,[e] then along the Wadi
of Egypt[f] to the Mediterranean Sea.[g]
This will be the southern boundary.
20 "On the west side, the Mediterranean
Sea will be the boundary to a point
opposite Lebo Hamath.[h] This will be
the western boundary.[i]

21 "You are to distribute this land
among yourselves according to the
tribes of Israel. 22 You are to allot it as
an inheritance for yourselves and for the
foreigners[j] residing among you and who
have children. You are to consider them
as native-born Israelites; along with you
they are to be allotted an inheritance
among the tribes of Israel.[k] 23 In whatever
tribe a foreigner resides, there you are
to give them their inheritance," declares
the Sovereign LORD.

The Division of the Land

48 "These are the tribes, listed by
name: At the northern frontier,
Dan[l] will have one portion; it will follow the Hethlon road[m] to Lebo Hamath;[n]
Hazar Enan and the northern border of
Damascus next to Hamath will be part
of its border from the east side to the
west side.
2 "Asher[o] will have one portion; it will
border the territory of Dan from east
to west.
3 "Naphtali[p] will have one portion; it
will border the territory of Asher from
east to west.

[a] *15,16* See Septuagint and 48:1; Hebrew *road to go into Zedad, 16Hamath, Berothah.* [b] *17* Hebrew *Enon,* a variant of *Enan* [c] *18* See Syriac; Hebrew *Israel. You will measure to the Dead Sea.*

47:12 [u] ver 7; Rev 22:2 [v] Ps 1:3 [w] Ge 2:9; Jer 17:8
47:13 [x] Nu 34:2-12 [y] Ge 48:5
47:14 [z] Ge 12:7; Dt 1:8; Eze 20:5-6
47:15 [a] Eze 48:1
47:16 [b] 2Sa 8:8 [c] Nu 13:21; Eze 48:1
47:17 [d] Eze 48:1
47:19 [e] Dt 32:51 [f] Isa 27:12 [g] Eze 48:28
47:20 [h] Eze 48:1 [i] Nu 34:6
47:22 [j] Isa 14:1 [k] Nu 26:55-56; Isa 56:6-7; Ro 10:12; Eph 2:12-16; 3:6; Col 3:11
48:1 [l] Ge 30:6 [m] Eze 47:15-17 [n] Eze 47:20
48:2 [o] Jos 19:24-31
48:3 [p] Jos 19:32-39

gospel in Galatians: You were in bondage to a futile, empty lifestyle, but Christ came to set you free (see Gal 5:1–12).

47:13–20 This is a larger area of territory than was ever controlled by Israel, even at the height of the Davidic empire. It is the same land that God promised to Moses. In receiving this land, the people receive the fulfillment of the covenant promise.

The Transjordan, historically the home of Reuben, Gad, and half of the tribe of Manasseh, is no longer considered part of the promised land. It was not part of the original promise.

47:21–23 The land is to be distributed "according to the tribes of Israel" (v. 21), which represents a return to the state of affairs before the kings. The reunited people receive the land as twelve tribes. There is to be an inheritance in the land not merely for the native-born Israelites but also for the foreigners who live there. Given the significance of the land in Eze 40–48, this is a high privilege indeed.

48:1–7 In ch. 48 the prophet moves on to the division of the land itself among the tribes. The entire land is oriented along the sacred east-west axis of the temple. The arrangement of the tribes within the land is not a random process. The number twelve is maintained by treating Ephraim and Manasseh as tribes in their own right. The four tribes most distant from the sacred zone, and therefore in the position of least honor, are Dan, Asher, Naphtali, and Gad. These were the sons of Jacob's concubines Zilpah and Bilhah (vv. 1–3, 27–28). The eight sons of Jacob's wives, Rachel and Leah, take the four strips immediately to the north and south of the sacred zone (vv. 4–7, 23–26).

4"Manasseh[q] will have one portion; it will border the territory of Naphtali from east to west.

5"Ephraim[r] will have one portion; it will border the territory of Manasseh[s] from east to west.[t]

6"Reuben[u] will have one portion; it will border the territory of Ephraim from east to west.

7"Judah[v] will have one portion; it will border the territory of Reuben from east to west.

8"Bordering the territory of Judah from east to west will be the portion you are to present as a special gift. It will be 25,000 cubits[a] wide, and its length from east to west will equal one of the tribal portions; the sanctuary will be in the center of it.[w]

9"The special portion you are to offer to the LORD will be 25,000 cubits long and 10,000 cubits[b] wide.[x] 10This will be the sacred portion for the priests. It will be 25,000 cubits long on the north side, 10,000 cubits wide on the west side, 10,000 cubits wide on the east side and 25,000 cubits long on the south side. In the center of it will be the sanctuary of the LORD.[y] 11This will be for the consecrated priests, the Zadokites,[z] who were faithful in serving me[a] and did not go astray as the Levites did when the Israelites went astray.[b] 12It will be a special gift to them from the sacred portion of the land, a most holy portion, bordering the territory of the Levites.

13"Alongside the territory of the priests, the Levites will have an allotment 25,000 cubits long and 10,000 cubits wide. Its total length will be 25,000 cubits and its width 10,000 cubits.[c] 14They must not sell or exchange any of it. This is the best of the land and must not pass into other hands, because it is holy to the LORD.[d]

15"The remaining area, 5,000 cubits[c] wide and 25,000 cubits long, will be for the common use of the city, for houses and for pastureland. The city will be in the center of it 16and will have these measurements: the north side 4,500 cubits,[d] the south side 4,500 cubits, the east side 4,500 cubits, and the west side 4,500 cubits.[e] 17The pastureland for the city will be 250 cubits[e] on the north, 250 cubits on the south, 250 cubits on the east, and 250 cubits on the west. 18What remains of the area, bordering on the sacred portion and running the length of it, will be 10,000 cubits on the east side and 10,000 cubits on the west side. Its produce will supply food for the workers of the city.[f] 19The workers from the city who farm it will come from all the tribes of Israel. 20The entire portion will be a square, 25,000 cubits on each side. As a special gift you will set aside the sacred portion, along with the property of the city.

21"What remains on both sides of the area formed by the sacred portion and the property of the city will belong to the prince. It will extend eastward from the 25,000 cubits of the sacred portion to the eastern border, and westward from the 25,000 cubits to the western border. Both these areas running the length of the tribal portions will belong to the prince, and the sacred portion with the temple sanctuary will be in the center of them.[g] 22So the property of the Levites and the property of the city will lie in the center of the area that belongs to the prince. The area belonging to the prince will lie between the border of Judah and the border of Benjamin.

23"As for the rest of the tribes: Benjamin[h] will have one portion; it will extend from the east side to the west side.

48:4 [q] Jos 17:1-11
48:5 [r] Jos 16:5-9 [s] Jos 17:7-10 [t] Jos 17:17
48:6 [u] Jos 13:15-21
48:7 [v] Jos 15:1-63
48:8 [w] ver 21
48:9 [x] Eze 45:1
48:10 [y] ver 21; Eze 45:3-4
48:11 [z] 2Sa 8:17 [a] Lev 8:35 [b] Eze 14:11; 44:15
48:13 [c] Eze 45:5
48:14 [d] Lev 25:34; 27:10,28
48:16 [e] Rev 21:16
48:18 [f] Eze 45:6
48:21 [g] ver 8,10; Eze 45:7
48:23 [h] Jos 18:11-28

[a] *8* That is, about 8 miles or about 13 kilometers; also in verses 9, 10, 13, 15, 20 and 21 [b] *9* That is, about 3 1/3 miles or about 5.3 kilometers; also in verses 10, 13 and 18 [c] *15* That is, about 1 2/3 miles or about 2.7 kilometers [d] *16* That is, about 1 1/2 miles or about 2.4 kilometers; also in verses 30, 32, 33 and 34 [e] *17* That is, about 440 feet or about 135 meters

48:8–9 The sacred portion is certainly the spiritual center of the land. The sacred strip is 25,000 cubits (almost eight miles) wide and extends across the breadth of the land. At its heart is a 25,000-cubit square which is itself comprised of three east-west strips, two of 10,000 cubits (2.8 miles) breadth and one of 5,000 cubits (1.4 miles).

48:10–14 The first of these 10,000-cubit strips is assigned to the Zadokite priests. It is a kind of Holy of Holies for the land. The second 10,000-cubit strip is allocated to the Levites.

48:15–20 The remaining 5,000-cubit strip along the southern edge of the sacred portion is the location of "the city." The city functions as a visible symbol and focus of the unity of the tribes.

48:21–22 Flanking the square sacred portion on both sides and occupying the remainder of the sacred strip is the land belonging to the prince. It is part of the sacred strip but not part of the central square. In this context it serves to indicate the prince's status: He ranks above the ordinary lay members of the tribes of Israel, yet below the priests and Levites.

24“Simeon[i] will have one portion; it
will border the territory of Benjamin
from east to west.
25“Issachar[j] will have one portion; it
will border the territory of Simeon from
east to west.
26“Zebulun[k] will have one portion; it
will border the territory of Issachar from
east to west.
27“Gad[l] will have one portion; it will
border the territory of Zebulun from
east to west.
28“The southern boundary of Gad will
run south from Tamar[m] to the waters of
Meribah Kadesh, then along the Wadi of
Egypt to the Mediterranean Sea.[n]
29“This is the land you are to allot as
an inheritance to the tribes of Israel, and
these will be their portions,” declares the
Sovereign LORD.

The Gates of the New City

30“These will be the exits of the city:
Beginning on the north side, which is
4,500 cubits long, 31the gates of the city
will be named after the tribes of Israel.
The three gates on the north side will
be the gate of Reuben, the gate of Judah
and the gate of Levi.
32“On the east side, which is 4,500 cubits long, will be three gates: the gate
of Joseph, the gate of Benjamin and the
gate of Dan.
33“On the south side, which measures
4,500 cubits, will be three gates: the gate
of Simeon, the gate of Issachar and the
gate of Zebulun.
34“On the west side, which is 4,500 cubits long, will be three gates: the gate
of Gad, the gate of Asher and the gate
of Naphtali.
35“The distance all around will be
18,000 cubits.[a]

“And the name of the city from that time on will be:

THE LORD IS THERE.[o]”

48:24 [i] Ge 29:33; Jos 19:1-9 **48:25** [j] Jos 19:17-23 **48:26** [k] Jos 19:10-16 **48:27** [l] Jos 13:24-28 **48:28** [m] Ge 14:7 [n] Eze 47:19 **48:35** [o] Isa 12:6; 24:23; Jer 3:17; 14:9; 33:16; Joel 3:21; Zec 2:10; Rev 21:3

[a] *35* That is, about 6 miles or about 9.5 kilometers

Eze 48:35 ❖ How does the name on the gates of the city give believers reassurance of God’s care for us both now and in the future?

48:30–35 The closing verses of the book bring us back to contemplate the city and some of the major themes of the vision of chs. 40–48. Yet the city is not an end in itself: It faces north, toward the temple, the center of the renewed land. The city is given a new name, reflecting the focus of the entire temple vision: “THE LORD IS THERE” (v. 35). The language of God’s dual presence is necessary in order to communicate both God’s transcendence and his immanence.

Temple and city are where chs. 40–48 started out (40:2), and they are where the vision ends. Both are transformed versions of the defiled and destroyed earthly institutions. In place of the earthly temple, contaminated by the sins of the people and abandoned by the presence of God (chs. 8–11), Ezekiel has seen an undefiled temple, refilled by God’s glory (chs. 40–43). In place of an adulterous city named Jerusalem, Ezekiel has seen a holy city named “THE LORD IS THERE” (v. 35). In place of a devastated land, Ezekiel has seen a land of peace and prosperity, watered by the river of life. In short, Ezekiel’s entire temple vision is the unfolding of his earlier prophecy (37:26–27).

✣ **47:13—48:35** We are to live lives completely centered on the new covenant temple: Jesus himself (Heb 12:22–28). Such lives revolve around the powerful worship of the awe-inspiring God, the living presence in our hearts of Jesus Christ our King, and the life-giving activity of his Spirit in our lives. So encouraged, we are empowered to take the gospel out to all the nations of the earth. The inheritance that is ours in Christ is offered not simply to the twelve historic tribes of Israel, nor even to those who are resident aliens in their midst, but to all to whom the word of God comes. As Peter put it on the day of Pentecost: “The promise is for you and your children and for all who are far off—for all whom the Lord our God will call” (Ac 2:39).

Thus, the nations will be brought in from the north and south and east and west and will sit down to feast with one another in the heavenly city, and the Lord of hosts and the Lamb will be there in their midst. Then indeed the heavenly city, the new Jerusalem, will fittingly bear the name that Ezekiel ascribed to it, “THE LORD IS THERE” (48:35).

Daniel

Author: Daniel
Audience: The Jewish exiles in Babylonia
Date: About 530 BC

Theme: The Most High God is sovereign over all human kingdoms.

Reading Daniel

Daniel divides into two clear sections. The first six chapters are the best known, for they contain the stories of the dreams of Nebuchadnezzar, the fiery furnace, the handwriting on the wall and the lion's den. The last six chapters contain several visions of the future that God gave Daniel.

PERSPECTIVE

"In spite of present appearances, God is in control." That is the core message of Daniel. What an appropriate message for Daniel's original audience. In exile in Babylon, it must have appeared to them that the great powers of the world—the Babylonians, the Medes, the Persians—were in control. By writing about his experiences as a captive Israelite who gained power in Babylon through his ability to interpret King Nebuchadnezzar's dreams, Daniel tells his compatriots that God, not a human king, is ultimately in control.

What an appropriate message for today also. When we look at our society and find overwhelming evidences of cultural decay and anti-Christian sentiment, it is tempting to question whether God really is in control. Perhaps we are sophisticated enough to know that human kingdoms are not in control. History witnesses to the reality that nations and states rise and fall. Still, we tend to see behind such misfortune powers that are anything but godlike—impersonal forces of fate, theories of deterministic science, Satan the master of evil. Can God possibly be in control?

Daniel said—and would say today if he were with us—yes. In spite of present appearances, God is in control: This is the universal message of this book, one that bridges the sixth-century BC and the AD twenty-first century contexts. It is worth our while to see how Daniel goes about convincing suffering readers of this hope-giving truth. He uses a two-pronged approach. He tells us six gripping stories of God's providence, then gives us five mystical visions that together blast our senses with impressions of God's great power. Why this combination of literal historical stories and mystical visions?

1200 BC 1100 1000 900 800 700 600 500 400

- Jeremiah's ministry in Judah (c. 626–585 BC)
- Daniel's exile in Babylon (c. 605–536 BC)
- Fall of Jerusalem (586 BC)
- Persia's conquest of Babylon (539 BC)
- Daniel in the lions' den (c. 539 BC)
- First return of exiles to Jerusalem (538 BC)
- Book of Daniel written (c. 536–530 BC)
- End of Daniel's ministry (c. 536 BC)

The historical stories of how God took care of the prophet Daniel as he navigated the tricky waters of Babylonian court politics are necessary to show us that God really does take care of his own. God is in control. Not in some meaningless, abstract, pie-in-the-sky way, but in the here and now.

But stories like this have their limitations. God's providence does not always show itself in "success" stories. Sometimes, as the book of Job attests, God is in control in cases where his children suffer mightily. "Success" stories are necessary to give us hope, but alone they tend to lead readers to misplace their focus—as in, Daniel succeeded because he was a vegetarian, so if we all become vegetarians, we will succeed too. Or, Daniel succeeded because he prayed in an upper room in full view of all the people of Babylon, so if we all pray in that manner we will succeed too. Not really. These stories are not irrelevant; they teach us important lessons. In order for these to be fully understood, we must know that a great deal is happening under the surface.

Enter the apocalyptic visions, which communicate to us that a great deal is happening in the course of history. God's greatness can be illustrated through everyday stories but cannot be captured by them. We need something further to show us that God encompasses the ordinary and the everyday but also goes beyond it. Daniel's visions can be understood up to a point, but cannot be completely understood in all details. They are specifically designed to communicate mystery. They leave us uncertain about specifics even though they clearly tell us that God is in control.

Daniel's message about God's control requires both the stories of the first six chapters and the visions of the last six. The stories give us comfort, the visions a sense of our finite nature. Without the latter, the stories could lead us to believe in a false relationship between human works and God's grace—if we do certain things, God must provide. Without the stories, the visions could lead us to an impractical, disembodied mysticism. With both, this book offers a hopeful confidence that God is indeed in control.

Key Verses

His dominion is an eternal dominion; his kingdom endures from generation to generation. All the peoples of the earth are regarded as nothing. He does as he pleases with the powers of heaven and the peoples of the earth. No one can hold back his hand or say to him: "What have you done?"

—Daniel 4:34b-35

TAKING THE NEXT STEPS

The prophet Daniel was among the first exiles carried away into the land of Babylon (see Jer 52:27–30; Da 1:1–2). As a promising young member of the Jewish nobility, he was ordered to serve in the palace of the king of Babylon. This was indeed an opportunity for political advancement for him and his friends, but obedience to the Lord was far more important to them. They knew that, even in this faraway land, God was in control, and, regardless of how discouraging things seemed at the present, the final victory belonged to the Lord and to his chosen people.

Readers of the Bible have always loved the book of Daniel because of its powerful messages. (1) It is important, even when we are away from family and church, to remain obedient to the Lord. (2) We can be sure that in the spiritual battles we fight, God will help us come out on top if we remain committed to him. (3) Though it may not always be evident, God controls the events that happen in our lives, and he will have his way. (4) The day is coming when Christ will return to establish his kingdom, destroying all his enemies and ours.

WHAT TO LOOK FOR IN DANIEL

- Daniel and his friends refuse the king's food (ch. 1)
- Nebuchadnezzar's dreams interpreted by Daniel (chs. 2; 4)
- Three men in the fiery furnace (ch. 3)
- Daniel's interpretation of the handwriting on the wall (ch. 5)
- Daniel and the lions' den (ch. 6)
- Daniel's intense prayer (ch. 9)

Daniel's Training in Babylon

1 In the third year of the reign of Jehoiakim king of Judah, Nebuchadnezzar[a] king of Babylon came to Jerusalem and besieged it.[b] 2 And the Lord delivered Jehoiakim king of Judah into his hand, along with some of the articles from the temple of God. These he carried off to the temple of his god in Babylonia[a] and put in the treasure house of his god.[c]

3 Then the king ordered Ashpenaz, chief of his court officials, to bring into the king's service some of the Israelites from the royal family and the nobility[d]— 4 young men without any physical defect, handsome, showing aptitude for every kind of learning, well informed, quick to understand, and qualified to serve in the king's palace. He was to teach them the language and literature of the Babylonians.[b] 5 The king assigned them a daily amount of food and wine[e] from the king's table. They were to be trained for three years, and after that they were to enter the king's service.[f]

1:1 [a] 2Ki 24:1 [b] 2Ch 36:6
1:2 [c] 2Ch 36:7; Jer 27:19-20; Zec 5:5-11
1:3 [d] 2Ki 20:18; 24:15; Isa 39:7
1:5 [e] ver 8, 10 [f] ver 19

Da 1:8 ❖ What choices would we make if we resolved not to defile ourselves with things that are opposed to God's will?

6 Among those who were chosen were some from Judah: Daniel,[g] Hananiah, Mishael and Azariah. 7 The chief official gave them new names: to Daniel, the name Belteshazzar;[h] to Hananiah, Shadrach; to Mishael, Meshach; and to Azariah, Abednego.[i]

8 But Daniel resolved not to defile[j] himself with the royal food and wine, and he asked the chief official for permission not to defile himself this way. 9 Now God had caused the official to show favor[k] and compassion[l] to Daniel, 10 but the official told Daniel, "I am afraid of my lord the king, who has assigned your[c] food and drink. Why should he see you looking worse than the other young men your

1:6 [g] Eze 14:14
1:7 [h] Da 4:8; 5:12 [i] Da 2:49; 3:12
1:8 [j] Eze 4:13-14
1:9 [k] Ge 39:21; Pr 16:7 [l] 1Ki 8:50; Ps 106:46

[a] 2 Hebrew *Shinar* [b] 4 Or *Chaldeans* [c] 10 The Hebrew for *your* and *you* in this verse is plural.

1:1–2 In 605 BC, Nebuchadnezzar defeated Jerusalem. He took away some of the temple vessels and a few of the noble youth.

1:3–7 Nebuchadnezzar's purpose with Daniel and the others was to train them in Babylonian ways for political and propaganda purposes. In the ancient Near East, a person's name was integrally connected with their identity. Thus, the Babylonians began the process of reeducation by giving their captives new names.

1:8–16 Daniel and his three friends refuse to be fed by the Babylonians. By doing so, they will be able to demonstrate that God alone is responsible for their success.

PEOPLE TO KNOW // DANIEL

DANIEL 1:6-21: Daniel was taken as a captive from Jerusalem and brought to Babylon under King Nebuchadnezzar. Being a promising young man of noble birth, he was brought into the service of the king. For three years, Daniel was taught the language and the literature of Babylon (Da 1:3-5).

When God enabled Daniel to interpret Nebuchadnezzar's dream, the king placed Daniel above all his other wise men and lavished him with gifts. When Daniel interpreted another of the king's dreams, the fulfillment of that dream—involving the king living like a wild animal—led Nebuchadnezzar to praise God (Da 4).

During the reign of King Darius, Daniel experienced a situation that would be remembered throughout time. Framed by treacherous officials, Daniel was thrown into a den filled with lions as punishment. God, however, protected Daniel and shut the lions' mouths. The next day Daniel was released, and the men who conspired against him, along with their families, were thrown to their deaths. Darius praised God and decreed that everyone else in all the world must worship God as well (Da 6:25-27), proving that God powerfully works in history to reveal his will in surprising ways.

APPLICATION ✣ Daniel was a man of faithful prayer. He was torn from his homeland at a young age and forced into the service of a foreign king. Perhaps because of these traumatic experiences, he found his strength and hope in God alone. While we will probably not experience such dramatic events as Daniel, his story shows that even in the most difficult scenarios, including losing everything, God is our strength. We can turn to him no matter what we are facing. God never abandoned Daniel, and God also promises his presence and care for us through his Holy Spirit.

age? The king would then have my head
because of you."
11 Daniel then said to the guard whom
the chief official had appointed over
Daniel, Hananiah, Mishael and Azariah,
12 "Please test your servants for ten days:
Give us nothing but vegetables to eat
and water to drink. 13 Then compare our
appearance with that of the young men
who eat the royal food, and treat your
servants in accordance with what you
see." 14 So he agreed to this and tested
them for ten days.
15 At the end of the ten days they looked
healthier and better nourished than
any of the young men who ate the royal
food.[m] 16 So the guard took away their
choice food and the wine they were to
drink and gave them vegetables instead.[n]
17 To these four young men God gave
knowledge and understanding[o] of all
kinds of literature and learning.[p] And
Daniel could understand visions and
dreams of all kinds.[q]
18 At the end of the time[r] set by the king
to bring them into his service, the chief
official presented them to Nebuchadnezzar. 19 The king talked with them, and he
found none equal to Daniel, Hananiah,
Mishael and Azariah; so they entered the
king's service.[s] 20 In every matter of wisdom and understanding about which the
king questioned them, he found them
ten times better than all the magicians
and enchanters in his whole kingdom.[t]
21 And Daniel remained there until the
first year of King Cyrus.[u]

Nebuchadnezzar's Dream

2 In the second year of his reign, Nebuchadnezzar had dreams;[v] his mind
was troubled[w] and he could not sleep.[x]

1:15 [m] Ex 23:25
1:16 [n] ver 12-13
1:17 [o] 1Ki 3:12
[p] Da 2:23; Jas 1:5 [q] Da 2:19, 30; 7:1; 8:1
1:18 [r] ver 5
1:19 [s] Ge 41:46
1:20 [t] 1Ki 4:30; Da 2:13,28
1:21 [u] Da 6:28; 10:1
2:1 [v] Job 33:15, 18; Da 4:5 [w] Ge 41:8 [x] Est 6:1; Da 6:18

1:17-20 God blessed Daniel with the ability to interpret dreams in a style that even this pagan monarch could recognize.

1:21 This message provided both encouragement and hope to those who had been taken from their land. It communicated that success without compromise was possible even in the midst of captivity.

APPLICATION ✣ **1:1-21** The contemporary church finds itself in a situation like Daniel's. We too live in a strange land. The god of modern culture is not the God of the Bible but is ultimately the self. Many Christians have a sense of oppression as they live their lives in the world today. Daniel asserts the liberating news that there are multiple effective ways to be a believer in an unbelieving world.

2:1-13 Babylonian religion encouraged looking for signs of the future in dreams. Nebuchadnezzar's

2So the king summoned the magicians,[y]
enchanters, sorcerers[z] and astrologers[a][a]
to tell him what he had dreamed.[b] When
they came in and stood before the king,
3he said to them, "I have had a dream
that troubles[c] me and I want to know
what it means.[b]"
4Then the astrologers answered the
king,[c][d] "May the king live forever![e] Tell
your servants the dream, and we will
interpret it."
5The king replied to the astrologers,
"This is what I have firmly decided: If
you do not tell me what my dream was
and interpret it, I will have you cut into
pieces[f] and your houses turned into
piles of rubble.[g] 6But if you tell me the
dream and explain it, you will receive
from me gifts and rewards and great
honor.[h] So tell me the dream and interpret it for me."
7Once more they replied, "Let the king
tell his servants the dream, and we will
interpret it."
8Then the king answered, "I am certain that you are trying to gain time,
because you realize that this is what I
have firmly decided: 9If you do not tell
me the dream, there is only one penalty[i]
for you. You have conspired to tell me
misleading and wicked things, hoping
the situation will change. So then, tell
me the dream, and I will know that you
can interpret it for me."[j]
10The astrologers answered the king,
"There is no one on earth who can do
what the king asks! No king, however
great and mighty, has ever asked such
a thing of any magician or enchanter
or astrologer.[k] 11What the king asks is
too difficult. No one can reveal it to the
king except the gods,[l] and they do not
live among humans."
12This made the king so angry and

2:2 [y]Ge 41:8 [z]Ex 7:11 [a]ver 10; Da 5:7 [b]Da 4:6
2:3 [c]Da 4:5
2:4 [d]Ezr 4:7 [e]Da 3:9; 5:10
2:5 [f]ver 12 [g]Ezr 6:11; Da 3:29
2:6 [h]ver 48; Da 5:7,16
2:9 [i]Est 4:11 [j]Isa 41:22-24
2:10 [k]ver 27
2:11 [l]Da 5:11

[a] 2 Or *Chaldeans*; also in verses 4, 5 and 10
[b] 3 Or *was*
[c] 4 At this point the Hebrew text has *in Aramaic*, indicating that the text from here through the end of chapter 7 is in Aramaic.

reaction to the diviners indicates that he is testing their integrity. Their response sets up the main lesson of the chapter: "No one can reveal it to the king except the gods, and they do not live among humans" (v. 11).

THE ANCIENT NEO-BABYLONIAN EMPIRE

EMPIRES AND KINGDOMS

(All dates BC; rulers important in Daniel in bold type.)

BABYLONIAN OR CHALDEAN	
Nabopolassar	625-605
Nebuchadnezzar	604-562 son
Evil-Merodach	561-560 son
Neriglissar	559-556
Labashi-Marduk	556 son
Nabonidus (Belshazzar)	555-539 (son)
PERSIAN OR ACHAEMENID	
Cyrus II	538-530
Cambyses II	529-522 son
Smerdis	522
Darius I	521-486
Xerxes I	485-465 son
Artaxerxes I	464-424 son
Darius II	423-405 son
Artaxerxes II	404-359 son
Artaxerxes III	358-338 son
Arses	337-336 son
Darius III	335-331
MACEDONIAN OR GREEK	
Alexander III	336-323
Philip Arrhidaeus	323-316 half-brother
Alexander IV	316-310 son of Alexander

PTOLEMAIC (EGYPT)	
Ptolemy I	323-285 (king from 305)
Ptolemy II	285-245 son
Ptolemy III	247-221 son
Ptolemy IV	221-203 son
Ptolemy V	203-181 son, married d. of Antiochus III, Cleopatra
Ptolemy VI	181-145 son
Ptolemy VII	145
Ptolemy VIII	169-164, 145-116 brother of P. VI
SELEUCID (SYRIA)	
Seleucus I	312-281
Antiochus I	281-260 son
Antiochus II	260-246 son, married d. of Ptolemy II, Berenice
Seleucus II	245-226 son
Seleucus III	225-223 son
Antiochus III	227-187 brother
Seleucus IV	187-175 son
Antiochus IV	175-164 Epiphanes, brother
Antiochus V	164-162 son
Demetrius I	162-150 cousin

furious[m] that he ordered the execution[n]
of all the wise men of Babylon. 13So the
decree was issued to put the wise men to
death, and men were sent to look for Daniel and his friends to put them to death.[o]
14When Arioch, the commander of the
king's guard, had gone out to put to death
the wise men of Babylon, Daniel spoke to
him with wisdom and tact. 15He asked the
king's officer, "Why did the king issue such
a harsh decree?" Arioch then explained
the matter to Daniel. 16At this, Daniel went
in to the king and asked for time, so that
he might interpret the dream for him.

2:12 [m]Da 3:13,19 [n]ver 5
2:13 [o]Da 1:20
2:17 [p]Da 1:6
2:18 [q]Isa 37:4 [r]Jer 33:3
2:19 [s]ver 28 [t]Job 33:15; Da 1:17

Da 2:17-18 ❖ When have we urged our friends to join us in prayer for God to solve a certain problem?

17Then Daniel returned to his house
and explained the matter to his friends
Hananiah, Mishael and Azariah.[p] 18He
urged them to plead for mercy[q] from the
God of heaven concerning this mystery,[r]
so that he and his friends might not be
executed with the rest of the wise men
of Babylon. 19During the night the mystery[s] was revealed to Daniel in a vision.[t]

2:14–18 Daniel hears of the king's dream and the aftermath. He and his friends have only one recourse: prayer. They understand that only God can supply the information they will need to answer the king's demands. In contrast to the beliefs of the Babylonians (v. 11), they know there is one God who lives among people: Daniel's God.

2:19–23 In his prayer, Daniel highlights two aspects

Then Daniel praised the God of heaven
20and said:

"Praise be to the name of God for
ever and ever;[u]
wisdom and power[v] are his.
21He changes times and seasons;[w]
he deposes[x] kings and raises up
others.
He gives wisdom[y] to the wise
and knowledge to the discerning.
22He reveals deep and hidden things;[z]
he knows what lies in darkness,[a]
and light[b] dwells with him.
23I thank and praise you, God of my
ancestors:[c]
You have given me wisdom[d] and
power,
you have made known to me what
we asked of you,
you have made known to us the
dream of the king."

Daniel Interprets the Dream

24Then Daniel went to Arioch,[e] whom
the king had appointed to execute the
wise men of Babylon, and said to him,
"Do not execute the wise men of Babylon. Take me to the king, and I will interpret his dream for him."
25Arioch took Daniel to the king at
once and said, "I have found a man
among the exiles from Judah[f] who can
tell the king what his dream means."
26The king asked Daniel (also called
Belteshazzar),[g] "Are you able to tell me
what I saw in my dream and interpret it?"
27Daniel replied, "No wise man, enchanter, magician or diviner can explain
to the king the mystery he has asked
about,[h] 28but there is a God in heaven
who reveals mysteries.[i] He has shown
King Nebuchadnezzar what will happen
in days to come.[j] Your dream and the visions that passed through your mind[k] as
you were lying in bed are these:
29"As Your Majesty was lying there,
your mind turned to things to come,
and the revealer of mysteries showed
you what is going to happen. 30As for
me, this mystery has been revealed[l] to
me, not because I have greater wisdom
than anyone else alive, but so that Your
Majesty may know the interpretation
and that you may understand what went
through your mind.
31"Your Majesty looked, and there before you stood a large statue — an enormous, dazzling statue,[m] awesome in appearance. 32The head of the statue was
made of pure gold, its chest and arms of
silver, its belly and thighs of bronze, 33its
legs of iron, its feet partly of iron and
partly of baked clay. 34While you were
watching, a rock was cut out, but not by
human hands.[n] It struck the statue on its
feet of iron and clay and smashed them.[o]
35Then the iron, the clay, the bronze, the
silver and the gold were all broken to
pieces and became like chaff on a threshing floor in the summer. The wind swept
them away[p] without leaving a trace. But
the rock that struck the statue became
a huge mountain[q] and filled the whole
earth.
36"This was the dream, and now we
will interpret it to the king. 37Your Majesty, you are the king of kings.[r] The God
of heaven has given you dominion[s] and
power and might and glory; 38in your
hands he has placed all mankind and
the beasts of the field and the birds in
the sky. Wherever they live, he has made
you ruler over them all.[t] You are that
head of gold.
39"After you, another kingdom will
arise, inferior to yours. Next, a third
kingdom, one of bronze, will rule over

2:20 [u] Ps 113:2; 145:1-2 [v] Jer 32:19
2:21 [w] Da 7:25 [x] Job 12:19; Ps 75:6-7 [y] Jas 1:5
2:22 [z] Job 12:22; Ps 25:14; Da 5:11 [a] Ps 139:11-12; Jer 23:24; Heb 4:13 [b] Isa 45:7; Jas 1:17
2:23 [c] Ex 3:15 [d] Da 1:17
2:24 [e] ver 14
2:25 [f] Da 1:6; 5:13; 6:13
2:26 [g] Da 1:7
2:27 [h] ver 10
2:28 [i] Ge 40:8; Am 4:13 [j] Ge 49:1; Da 10:14
[k] Da 4:5
2:30 [l] Isa 45:3; Da 1:17; Am 4:13
2:31 [m] Hab 1:7
2:34 [n] Zec 4:6 [o] ver 44-45; Ps 2:9; Isa 60:12; Da 8:25
2:35 [p] Ps 1:4; 37:10; Isa 17:13 [q] Isa 2:3; Mic 4:1
2:37 [r] Eze 26:7 [s] Jer 27:7
2:38 [t] Jer 27:6; Da 4:21-22

of God's character that play a pivotal role in this chapter and throughout the book: God is powerful, and God is wise. He is the one who "reveals deep and hidden things" (v. 22).

2:24–26 Arioch brings Daniel to Nebuchadnezzar. The king gets right to the point: "Are you able to tell me what I saw in my dream and interpret it?" (v. 26).

2:27–30 Daniel puts the focus directly on God. He is the "God in heaven who reveals mysteries" (v. 28). He then describes the content of the king's vision.

2:31–33 Besides its size, the statue is striking by virtue of its staged composition.

2:34–35 The statue is not the only character in the vision. Daniel also describes a rock made "not by human hands" (v. 34). The rock smashes into the feet of the statue and becomes a huge mountain, filling the whole world.

2:36–38 Daniel moves from dream report to dream interpretation, and we begin on solid interpretive ground. Speaking to Nebuchadnezzar, Daniel says, "You are that head of gold" (v. 38). Nebuchadnezzar must have rejoiced at this news. After all, in the scheme of "things to come" he was at the top, represented by the most precious of all metals.

2:39–43 Daniel interprets the remaining metals as symbolic of nations rather than individual kings. The identity of the following kingdoms has been much debated over the centuries.

In the light of interpretive confusion, it may be a

the whole earth. 40Finally, there will be a
fourth kingdom, strong as iron — for iron
breaks and smashes everything — and
as iron breaks things to pieces, so it will
crush and break all the others.[u] 41Just
as you saw that the feet and toes were
partly of baked clay and partly of iron,
so this will be a divided kingdom; yet it
will have some of the strength of iron
in it, even as you saw iron mixed with
clay. 42As the toes were partly iron and
partly clay, so this kingdom will be partly
strong and partly brittle. 43And just as
you saw the iron mixed with baked clay,
so the people will be a mixture and will
not remain united, any more than iron
mixes with clay.
44"In the time of those kings, the God
of heaven will set up a kingdom that will
never be destroyed, nor will it be left to
another people. It will crush[v] all those
kingdoms[w] and bring them to an end,
but it will itself endure forever.[x] 45This
is the meaning of the vision of the rock[y]
cut out of a mountain, but not by human
hands[z] — a rock that broke the iron, the
bronze, the clay, the silver and the gold
to pieces.

"The great God has shown the king
what will take place in the future. The
dream is true and its interpretation is
trustworthy."
46Then King Nebuchadnezzar fell prostrate[a] before Daniel and paid him honor
and ordered that an offering[b] and incense be presented to him. 47The king
said to Daniel, "Surely your God is the
God of gods[c] and the Lord of kings[d] and
a revealer of mysteries,[e] for you were
able to reveal this mystery."
48Then the king placed Daniel in a
high position and lavished many gifts
on him. He made him ruler over the entire province of Babylon and placed him
in charge of all its wise men.[f] 49Moreover,
at Daniel's request the king appointed
Shadrach, Meshach and Abednego administrators over the province of Babylon,[g] while Daniel himself remained
at the royal court.

2:40 [u] Da 7:7,23
2:44 [v] Ps 2:9; 1Co 15:24 [w] Isa 60:12 [x] Ps 145:13; Isa 9:7; Da 4:34; 6:26; 7:14,27; Mic 4:7,13; Lk 1:33
2:45 [y] Isa 28:16 [z] Da 8:25
2:46 [a] Da 8:17; Ac 10:25 [b] Ac 14:13
2:47 [c] Da 11:36 [d] Da 4:25 [e] ver 22,28
2:48 [f] ver 6; Da 4:9; 5:11
2:49 [g] Da 1:7
3:1 [h] Isa 46:6; Jer 16:20; Hab 2:19
3:2 [i] ver 27; Da 6:7
3:4 [j] Da 4:1; 6:25
3:5 [k] ver 10,15
3:6 [l] ver 11,15, 21; Jer 29:22; Da 6:7; Mt 13:42,50; Rev 13:15

The Image of Gold and the Blazing Furnace

3 King Nebuchadnezzar made an image[h] of gold, sixty cubits high and six
cubits wide,[a] and set it up on the plain of
Dura in the province of Babylon. 2He then
summoned the satraps, prefects, governors, advisers, treasurers, judges, magistrates and all the other provincial officials[i]
to come to the dedication of the image
he had set up. 3So the satraps, prefects,
governors, advisers, treasurers, judges,
magistrates and all the other provincial
officials assembled for the dedication of
the image that King Nebuchadnezzar had
set up, and they stood before it.
4Then the herald loudly proclaimed,
"Nations and peoples of every language,[j]
this is what you are commanded to do:
5As soon as you hear the sound of the
horn, flute, zither, lyre, harp, pipe and
all kinds of music, you must fall down
and worship the image of gold that King
Nebuchadnezzar has set up.[k] 6Whoever does not fall down and worship will
immediately be thrown into a blazing
furnace."[l]

[a] *1* That is, about 90 feet high and 9 feet wide or about 27 meters high and 2.7 meters wide

---

wrong strategy to associate the different stages of the statue with particular empires. The vision communicates something more general but also more vital: God is in control despite present conditions.

2:44–45 Note some crucial theological principles in the dream. First, a statue made by human hands starts out in grandeur and beauty but ends in weakness. Second, a statue is made with human ingenuity; the rock is explicitly said not to be the result of human intention or energy. Third, Daniel identifies the rock as God's kingdom. It is that rock that obliterates these human kingdoms. So God's kingdom will expand and take over the world, just as the rock becomes a huge mountain.

2:46–49 The concluding scene gives us a powerful picture that reinforces the theme of our book: The most powerful pagan in the world lies prostrate before an exiled Jew. Hope will rise in the hearts of those who identify with Daniel and his God.

2:1–49 From Daniel we learn that wisdom is a divinely given ability to have insight into the best way to live life. What does this mean in practical terms? It means that even though we live life in a troubled and confusing world, we also live it in relationship with Christ. We gain our wisdom in conversation with him. And how do we converse with Christ? Through prayer and through reading his Word.

3:1–7 The gold of this statue links the story with Nebuchadnezzar's recently described dream in which he was the head of gold. Nebuchadnezzar not only built the statue; he demanded a public demonstration of adoration.

With this rather imposing list of officials, we encounter a lengthy list that is repeated several times in the chapter. These lists appear repetitive to us, but their literary effect is to heighten the

7 Therefore, as soon as they heard the
sound of the horn, flute, zither, lyre, harp
and all kinds of music, all the nations
and peoples of every language fell down
and worshiped the image of gold that
King Nebuchadnezzar had set up.[m]
8 At this time some astrologers[a][n] came
forward and denounced the Jews. 9 They
said to King Nebuchadnezzar, "May the
king live forever![o] 10 Your Majesty has issued a decree[p] that everyone who hears
the sound of the horn, flute, zither, lyre,
harp, pipe and all kinds of music must
fall down and worship the image of
gold,[q] 11 and that whoever does not fall
down and worship will be thrown into
a blazing furnace. 12 But there are some
Jews whom you have set over the affairs
of the province of Babylon — Shadrach,
Meshach and Abednego[r] — who pay no
attention[s] to you, Your Majesty. They neither serve your gods nor worship the image of gold you have set up."[t]
13 Furious[u] with rage, Nebuchadnezzar
summoned Shadrach, Meshach and Abednego. So these men were brought before
the king, 14 and Nebuchadnezzar said to
them, "Is it true, Shadrach, Meshach and
Abednego, that you do not serve my gods[v]
or worship the image[w] of gold I have set
up? 15 Now when you hear the sound of
the horn, flute, zither, lyre, harp, pipe
and all kinds of music, if you are ready to
fall down and worship the image I made,
very good. But if you do not worship it,
you will be thrown immediately into a
blazing furnace. Then what god[x] will be
able to rescue[y] you from my hand?"
16 Shadrach, Meshach and Abednego[z]
replied to him, "King Nebuchadnezzar,
we do not need to defend ourselves before you in this matter. 17 If we are thrown
into the blazing furnace, the God we
serve is able to deliver[a] us from it, and

3:7 [m] ver 5
3:8 [n] Da 2:10
3:9 [o] Ne 2:3; Da 5:10; 6:6
3:10 [p] Da 6:12 [q] ver 4-6
3:12 [r] Da 2:49 [s] Da 6:13 [t] Est 3:3
3:13 [u] Da 2:12
3:14 [v] Isa 46:1; Jer 50:2 [w] ver 1
3:15 [x] Isa 36:18-20 [y] Ex 5:2; 2Ch 32:15
3:16 [z] Da 1:7
3:17 [a] Ps 27:1-2

Da 3:25 ❖ How does God make known his presence to us when we are in the midst of a threatening situation?

he will deliver[b] us[b] from Your Majesty's
hand. 18 But even if he does not, we want
you to know, Your Majesty, that we will
not serve your gods or worship the image
of gold you have set up.[c]"
19 Then Nebuchadnezzar was furious
with Shadrach, Meshach and Abednego,
and his attitude toward them changed.
He ordered the furnace heated seven[d]
times hotter than usual 20 and commanded some of the strongest soldiers
in his army to tie up Shadrach, Meshach
and Abednego and throw them into the
blazing furnace. 21 So these men, wearing
their robes, trousers, turbans and other
clothes, were bound and thrown into
the blazing furnace. 22 The king's command was so urgent and the furnace so
hot that the flames of the fire killed the
soldiers who took up Shadrach, Meshach
and Abednego,[e] 23 and these three men,
firmly tied, fell into the blazing furnace.
24 Then King Nebuchadnezzar leaped
to his feet in amazement and asked his
advisers, "Weren't there three men that
we tied up and threw into the fire?"
They replied, "Certainly, Your Majesty."
25 He said, "Look! I see four men walking around in the fire, unbound and unharmed, and the fourth looks like a son
of the gods."
26 Nebuchadnezzar then approached
the opening of the blazing furnace and
shouted, "Shadrach, Meshach and Abednego, servants of the Most High God,[f]
come out! Come here!"

[b] Job 5:19; Jer 1:8
3:18 [c] ver 28; Jos 24:15
3:19 [d] Lev 26:18-28
3:22 [e] Da 1:7
3:26 [f] Da 4:2,34

[a] 8 Or *Chaldeans* [b] 17 Or *If the God we serve is able to deliver us, then he will deliver us from the blazing furnace and*

---

feeling of danger toward the three friends who will be singled out of the group. The list of musical instruments heightens the tension, focusing on the moment of obedience or disobedience.

3:8–12 These men appear to be motivated out of professional jealousy. Close attention to the words of the astrologers reveals their strategy. In a phrase, they appeal to Nebuchadnezzar's sense of vanity.

3:13–15 The premise of this chapter is the enforced worship of Nebuchadnezzar's golden statue, which is a way of compelling loyalty. The report of the three friends' disloyal action angers the king. He immediately has them brought for a personal loyalty test.

3:16–18 The three friends acknowledge God's ability to save them, but they envision the possibility that God may also choose not to do so. No matter the result—deliverance or death—they will remain faithful to God.

3:19–23 Hearing their testimony, the king grows even more furious. He orders the furnace to be superheated, reflecting perhaps the heat of his own anger. Is there "a god" who can rescue them from the hands of such a powerful ruler?

3:24–27 Nebuchadnezzar himself gives us the answer (v. 25). The king quickly gets the message and orders the three out. Then Nebuchadnezzar and all the others, including the accusers, witness the extent of the miracle of deliverance. It was as if they had never been in the fire. God is showing Nebuchadnezzar who is in charge.

So Shadrach, Meshach and Abednego
came out of the fire, 27and the satraps,
prefects, governors and royal advisers[g]
crowded around them.[h] They saw that
the fire[i] had not harmed their bodies,
nor was a hair of their heads singed; their
robes were not scorched, and there was
no smell of fire on them.
28Then Nebuchadnezzar said, "Praise
be to the God of Shadrach, Meshach and
Abednego, who has sent his angel[j] and
rescued his servants! They trusted[k] in
him and defied the king's command and
were willing to give up their lives rather
than serve or worship any god except
their own God.[l] 29Therefore I decree[m]
that the people of any nation or language
who say anything against the God of Shadrach, Meshach and Abednego be cut
into pieces and their houses be turned
into piles of rubble,[n] for no other god
can save[o] in this way."
30Then the king promoted Shadrach,
Meshach and Abednego in the province
of Babylon.[p]

Nebuchadnezzar's Dream of a Tree

4 [a] King Nebuchadnezzar,

To the nations and peoples of every
language,[q] who live in all the earth:

May you prosper greatly![r]

2It is my pleasure to tell you about
the miraculous signs[s] and wonders
that the Most High God[t] has performed for me.

3How great are his signs,
how mighty his wonders![u]
His kingdom is an eternal
kingdom;
his dominion endures[v] from
generation to generation.

4I, Nebuchadnezzar, was at home
in my palace, contented[w] and prosperous. 5I had a dream[x] that made
me afraid. As I was lying in bed,
the images and visions that passed
through my mind[y] terrified me.
6So I commanded that all the wise
men of Babylon be brought before
me to interpret[z] the dream for me.
7When the magicians,[a] enchanters,
astrologers[b] and diviners[b] came, I
told them the dream, but they could
not interpret it for me.[c] 8Finally,
Daniel came into my presence and
I told him the dream. (He is called
Belteshazzar,[d] after the name of my
god, and the spirit of the holy gods[e]
is in him.)
9I said, "Belteshazzar, chief[f] of the
magicians, I know that the spirit
of the holy gods[g] is in you, and no
mystery is too difficult for you. Here
is my dream; interpret it for me.
10These are the visions I saw while
lying in bed:[h] I looked, and there before me stood a tree in the middle of
the land. Its height was enormous.[i]
11The tree grew large and strong and

3:27 [g] ver 2 [h] Isa 43:2; Heb 11:32-34 [i] Da 6:23
3:28 [j] Ps 34:7; Da 6:22; Ac 5:19 [k] Job 13:15; Ps 26:1; 84:12; Jer 17:7 [l] ver 18
3:29 [m] Da 6:26 [n] Ezr 6:11 [o] Da 6:27
3:30 [p] Da 2:49
4:1 [q] Da 3:4 [r] Da 6:25
4:2 [s] Ps 74:9 [t] Da 3:26
4:3 [u] Ps 105:27; Da 6:27 [v] Da 2:44
4:4 [w] Ps 30:6
4:5 [x] Da 2:1 [y] Da 2:28
4:6 [z] Da 2:2
4:7 [a] Ge 41:8 [b] Isa 44:25; Da 2:2 [c] Da 2:10
4:8 [d] Da 1:7 [e] Da 5:11,14
4:9 [f] Da 2:48 [g] Da 5:11-12
4:10 [h] ver 5 [i] Eze 31:3-4

[a] In Aramaic texts 4:1-3 is numbered 3:31-33, and 4:4-37 is numbered 4:1-34. [b] 7 Or *Chaldeans*

3:28–30 In his concluding speech in the present chapter, Nebuchadnezzar mentions the mysterious fourth person. Was this God himself, as the phrase "a son of the gods" (v. 25) might lead us to believe, or was it an angel? Even if the fourth figure was an angel, it was *God's* angel; God is still the redeemer.

The king then issues a command that will not allow anyone in his kingdom to show such a powerful deity any disrespect. Furthermore, Shadrach, Meshach, and Abednego get a further promotion, thwarting their accusers' intentions.

3:1–30 There is a constant threat to dilute the worship of the true God by elevating anything or anyone else to a comparable place of importance in our lives. Even as Christians, we are constantly in a struggle with this temptation. Whatever those societal idols are in our lives, whatever it is that distracts us and pulls our attention away from things that matter, we can learn from the example of these godly young men about the miraculous change that can come when we make a courageous stand for our commitment to God's way.

4:1–3 The content of Nebuchadnezzar's praise highlights God's sovereignty and the wonderful nature of his interaction with the world.
4:4–5 A dream intrudes into the king's peaceful mind, tormenting him with doubt and fear.
4:6–8 That Nebuchadnezzar still really hasn't "gotten it" is indicated by the parenthetical comment at the end of v. 8. He refers to Daniel by his Babylonian name, which connects him to the king's native god. He speaks of Daniel as the one in whom is the "spirit of the holy gods" (v. 8). Being polytheistic, Nebuchadnezzar has the intellectual framework to integrate Daniel's God into his existing, multi-god theology.
4:9–12 The king then relates the contents of his dream. Its main feature is a huge tree in the middle of the land. Nebuchadnezzar's dream shows that he identifies himself with the cosmic tree; he is the keeper of the cosmos, the true image of God, the perfect man.

its top touched the sky; it was visible
to the ends of the earth. 12Its leaves
were beautiful, its fruit abundant,
and on it was food for all. Under it
the wild animals found shelter, and
the birds lived in its branches;[j] from
it every creature was fed.
13"In the visions I saw while lying
in bed,[k] I looked, and there before
me was a holy one,[l] a messenger,[a]
coming down from heaven. 14He
called in a loud voice: 'Cut down the
tree and trim off its branches; strip
off its leaves and scatter its fruit. Let
the animals flee from under it and
the birds from its branches.[m] 15But
let the stump and its roots, bound
with iron and bronze, remain in the
ground, in the grass of the field.
"'Let him be drenched with the
dew of heaven, and let him live with
the animals among the plants of the
earth. 16Let his mind be changed
from that of a man and let him be
given the mind of an animal, till sev-
en times[b] pass by for him.[n]
17"'The decision is announced by
messengers, the holy ones declare
the verdict, so that the living may
know that the Most High[o] is sovereign[p] over all kingdoms on earth
and gives them to anyone he wishes
and sets over them the lowliest[q] of
people.'
18"This is the dream that I, King
Nebuchadnezzar, had. Now, Belteshazzar, tell me what it means, for
none of the wise men in my kingdom can interpret it for me.[r] But you
can,[s] because the spirit of the holy
gods is in you."[t]

Daniel Interprets the Dream

19Then Daniel (also called Belteshazzar) was greatly perplexed for
a time, and his thoughts terrified[u]
him. So the king said, "Belteshazzar,
do not let the dream or its meaning
alarm you."
Belteshazzar answered, "My lord,
if only the dream applied to your
enemies and its meaning to your
adversaries! 20The tree you saw,
which grew large and strong, with
its top touching the sky, visible to
the whole earth, 21with beautiful
leaves and abundant fruit, providing food for all, giving shelter to the
wild animals, and having nesting
places in its branches for the birds —
22Your Majesty, you are that tree![v]
You have become great and strong;
your greatness has grown until it
reaches the sky, and your dominion extends to distant parts of the
earth.[w]
23"Your Majesty saw a holy one,[x]
a messenger, coming down from
heaven and saying, 'Cut down the
tree and destroy it, but leave the
stump, bound with iron and bronze,
in the grass of the field, while its
roots remain in the ground. Let him
be drenched with the dew of heaven;
let him live with the wild animals,
until seven times pass by for him.'[y]
24"This is the interpretation, Your
Majesty, and this is the decree[z] the
Most High has issued against my
lord the king: 25You will be driven
away from people and will live with
the wild animals; you will eat grass
like the ox and be drenched with
the dew of heaven. Seven times will
pass by for you until you acknowledge that the Most High[a] is sovereign over all kingdoms on earth and
gives them to anyone he wishes.[b]
26The command to leave the stump
of the tree with its roots[c] means that
your kingdom will be restored to
you when you acknowledge that
Heaven rules.[d] 27Therefore, Your
Majesty, be pleased to accept my advice: Renounce your sins by doing
what is right, and your wickedness
by being kind to the oppressed.[e] It
may be that then your prosperity
will continue.[f]"

4:12 [j] Eze 17:23; Mt 13:32
4:13 [k] Da 7:1 [l] ver 23; Dt 33:2; Da 8:13
4:14 [m] Eze 31:12; Mt 3:10
4:16 [n] ver 23,32
4:17 [o] ver 2, 25; Ps 83:18 [p] Jer 27:5-7; Da 2:21; 5:18-21 [q] Da 11:21
4:18 [r] Ge 41:8; Da 5:8,15 [s] Ge 41:15 [t] ver 7-9
4:19 [u] Da 7:15, 28; 8:27; 10:16-17
4:22 [v] 2Sa 12:7 [w] Jer 27:7; Da 2:37-38; 5:18-19
4:23 [x] ver 13 [y] Da 5:21
4:24 [z] Job 40:12; Ps 107:40
4:25 [a] ver 17; Ps 83:18 [b] Jer 27:5; Da 5:21
4:26 [c] ver 15 [d] Da 2:37
4:27 [e] Isa 55:6-7 [f] 1Ki 21:29; Ps 41:3; Eze 18:22

[a] *13* Or *watchman;* also in verses 17 and 23
[b] *16* Or *years;* also in verses 23, 25 and 32

4:13–18 After the description of the tree, the king narrates the plot. It begins with the appearance of a "messenger." No doubt a supernatural being is meant. The watcher barks orders to dismantle the cosmic tree.
4:19–26 God's prophet is not vindictive; he shows concern for the well-being of the king. Since Nebuchadnezzar is the tree, he is also the subject of the coming judgment. As the tree will be knocked down, so will the king.
4:27 This message of judgment is conditional. Despite his greatness, Nebuchadnezzar must remain humble.

The Dream Is Fulfilled

28 All this happened[g] to King Nebuchadnezzar. 29 Twelve months later,
as the king was walking on the roof
of the royal palace of Babylon, 30 he
said, "Is not this the great Babylon I
have built as the royal residence, by
my mighty power and for the glory
of my majesty?"[h]
31 Even as the words were on his
lips, a voice came from heaven, "This
is what is decreed for you, King Nebuchadnezzar: Your royal authority
has been taken from you. 32 You
will be driven away from people
and will live with the wild animals;
you will eat grass like the ox. Seven
times will pass by for you until you
acknowledge that the Most High is
sovereign over all kingdoms on earth
and gives them to anyone he wishes."
33 Immediately what had been
said about Nebuchadnezzar was
fulfilled. He was driven away from
people and ate grass like the ox. His
body was drenched with the dew of
heaven until his hair grew like the
feathers of an eagle and his nails
like the claws of a bird.[i]

34 At the end of that time, I, Nebuchadnezzar, raised my eyes toward
heaven, and my sanity was restored.
Then I praised the Most High; I honored and glorified him who lives
forever.[j]

His dominion is an eternal
dominion;

4:28 [g] Nu 23:19
4:30 [h] Isa 37:24-25; Da 5:20; Hab 2:4
4:33 [i] Da 5:20-21
4:34 [j] Da 12:7; Rev 4:10

Da 4:34-35 ❖ Where have we seen God display his power in transforming a person from showing prideful arrogance to offering humble praise?

4:28-33 A period of twelve months passed before the crucial moment. Perhaps the dream frightened Nebuchadnezzar into temporary compliance. Or perhaps God waited until this moment of monumental pride to exercise his judgment. We cannot be sure.

Nebuchadnezzar had much to do with the greatness of Babylon. From biblical and ancient Near Eastern records, we know he had great wealth and was an accomplished builder. However, his power led to a pride that blinded him to broader realities.

4:34-37 Here we get little insight into Nebuchadnezzar's mental processes as he experiences this time of humbling. But we are told that the divine prescription works. The lesson is learned and the moral of the story is the last word (v. 37).

PEOPLE TO KNOW // NEBUCHADNEZZAR

DANIEL 4:34-37: Nebuchadnezzar was the king of Babylon who destroyed Jerusalem in 586 BC. God used him as an instrument of judgment upon Judah for their sins. The book of Daniel recounts events in Babylon under Nebuchadnezzar. Select exiles from Jerusalem of noble birth and good health were brought into the king's service, and he found none equal to Daniel, Hananiah, Mishael and Azariah (Da 1:19). Daniel in particular won Nebuchadnezzar's favor when he was able to interpret Nebuchadnezzar's dream through the power of God. Nebuchadnezzar made Daniel a high official in his kingdom.

Nebuchadnezzar experienced the power of God again when he witnessed another miracle. He had sentenced Shadrach, Meshach, and Abednego (Hananiah, Mishael and Azariah) to be burned for not bowing to a towering idol he had built (Da 3:19-20). In the furnace, the three Jewish exiles were unharmed, and an angel appeared along with them. After this, Nebuchadnezzar praised the God of Israel.

Daniel 4 is a first-person account told by Nebuchadnezzar of yet another dream Daniel interpreted for him, this one involving a truly bizarre fulfillment. Daniel told Nebuchadnezzar that the king would live as a wild animal for seven periods of time (possibly years), eating grass like an ox. A year later, as Nebuchadnezzar was bragging about his accomplishments (Da 4:30), his dream was fulfilled. He lived as a wild animal until God restored his sanity, and he again praised God.

APPLICATION ✣ In Jeremiah, God calls Nebuchadnezzar his "servant" (Jer 25:9). God can use anyone, whether they make good or bad choices, to accomplish his plans. God used Nebuchadnezzar as his weapon to strike Judah for their sin, but Nebuchadnezzar was never able to do more than God allowed. God holds the powers of evil on a leash; he controls the nations of the world, and he uses even the most unlikely people to achieve his sovereign will.

his kingdom endures from
generation to generation.[k]
35 All the peoples of the earth
are regarded as nothing.[l]
He does as he pleases[m]
with the powers of heaven
and the peoples of the earth.
No one can hold back his hand
or say to him: "What have you
done?"[n]

36 At the same time that my sanity was restored, my honor and splendor were returned to me for the glory of my kingdom.[o] My advisers and nobles sought me out, and I was restored to my throne and became even greater than before. 37 Now I, Nebuchadnezzar, praise and exalt and glorify the King of heaven, because everything he does is right and all his ways are just.[p] And those who walk in pride he is able to humble.[q]

The Writing on the Wall

5 King Belshazzar gave a great banquet[r] for a thousand of his nobles and drank wine with them. 2 While Belshazzar was drinking his wine, he gave orders to bring in the gold and silver goblets[s] that Nebuchadnezzar his father[a] had taken from the temple in Jerusalem, so that the king and his nobles, his wives and his concubines might drink from them.[t] 3 So they brought in the gold goblets that had been taken from the temple of God in Jerusalem, and the king and his nobles, his wives and his concubines drank from them. 4 As they drank the wine, they praised the gods of gold and silver, of bronze, iron, wood and stone.[u]

5 Suddenly the fingers of a human hand appeared and wrote on the plaster of the wall, near the lampstand in the royal palace. The king watched the hand as it wrote. 6 His face turned pale and he was so frightened[v] that his legs became weak[w] and his knees were knocking.

7 The king summoned the enchanters, astrologers[b] and diviners.[x] Then he said to these wise[y] men of Babylon, "Whoever reads this writing and tells me what it means will be clothed in purple and have a gold chain placed around his neck,[z] and he will be made the third highest ruler in the kingdom."[a]

8 Then all the king's wise men came in, but they could not read the writing or tell the king what it meant.[b] 9 So King Belshazzar became even more terrified[c] and his face grew more pale. His nobles were baffled.

10 The queen,[c] hearing the voices of the king and his nobles, came into the banquet hall. "May the king live forever!"[d] she said. "Don't be alarmed! Don't look so pale! 11 There is a man in your kingdom who has the spirit of the holy gods[e] in him. In the time of your father he was found to have insight and intelligence and wisdom[f] like that of the

4:34 [k] Ps 145:13; Da 2:44; 5:21; 6:26; Lk 1:33
4:35 [l] Isa 40:17 [m] Ps 115:3; 135:6 [n] Isa 45:9; Ro 9:20
4:36 [o] Pr 22:4
4:37 [p] Dt 32:4; Ps 33:4-5 [q] Ex 18:11; Job 40:11-12; Da 5:20,23
5:1 [r] Est 1:3
5:2 [s] 2Ki 24:13; Jer 52:19 [t] Est 1:7; Da 1:2
5:4 [u] Ps 135:15-18; Hab 2:19; Rev 9:20
5:6 [v] Da 4:5 [w] Eze 7:17
5:7 [x] Isa 44:25 [y] Da 4:6-7 [z] Ge 41:42 [a] Da 2:5-6,48; 6:2-3
5:8 [b] Da 2:10,27
5:9 [c] Isa 21:4
5:10 [d] Da 3:9
5:11 [e] Da 4:8-9, 19 [f] ver 14; Da 1:17

[a] 2 Or *ancestor*; or *predecessor*; also in verses 11, 13 and 18 [b] 7 Or *Chaldeans*; also in verse 11
[c] 10 Or *queen mother*

4:1-37 God humbles the proud. This divine work began in the Garden of Eden and continued with the account of the tower of Babel in Ge 11. In all these cases, pride led to rebellion; even an assault on heaven itself. The humble faithful can find comfort in these accounts, when God turned the arrogant pride of the ungodly into shame.

The NT makes it even more clear that God is in control. He has won a victory over an enemy even more powerful than Nebuchadnezzar, over a kingdom even more deadly and oppressive than the Babylonian Empire. He has defeated Satan and death itself (Jn 11:25-26; 1Co 15:55-57; Heb 2:14-15).

5:1-2 Belshazzar must have known the Persians would attack sooner or later. The banquet took place in this context. Was it to rally and encourage the leaders? To give them a diversion in the face of the onslaught? To "feast today, for tomorrow we die"? Perhaps a bit of all three.

5:3-4 The focus shifts to the holy goblets that Nebuchadnezzar had removed from the temple. These precious temple vessels are about to be profaned by being pressed into common use.

Belshazzar may have been making claims to power by comparing himself to his "father" (v. 2), Nebuchadnezzar. In the final analysis, it does not matter what was in Belshazzar's mind; in these actions he was virtually spitting in God's eye. Belshazzar combines blasphemy with idolatry, using God's holy goblets to toast the lifeless idols of his own religion.

5:5-6 Without explanation, a hand suddenly appears and starts writing strange words on the wall.

5:7-9 Terrified, Belshazzar calls for the wise men to make sense of the writing. The wise men, similarly, are unable to interpret the significance of the message.

5:10-12 Whoever the queen is, she has the solution to Belshazzar's problem: "Call for Daniel" (v. 12).

gods. Your father, King Nebuchadnezzar,
appointed him chief of the magicians,
enchanters, astrologers and diviners.[g]
12He did this because Daniel, whom the
king called Belteshazzar,[h] was found to
have a keen mind and knowledge and
understanding, and also the ability to interpret dreams, explain riddles and solve
difficult problems.[i] Call for Daniel, and
he will tell you what the writing means."
13So Daniel was brought before the
king, and the king said to him, "Are you
Daniel, one of the exiles my father the
king brought from Judah?[j] 14I have heard
that the spirit of the gods is in you and
that you have insight, intelligence and
outstanding wisdom. 15The wise men
and enchanters were brought before me
to read this writing and tell me what it
means, but they could not explain it.
16Now I have heard that you are able to
give interpretations and to solve difficult
problems. If you can read this writing and
tell me what it means, you will be clothed
in purple and have a gold chain placed
around your neck, and you will be made
the third highest ruler in the kingdom."
17Then Daniel answered the king, "You
may keep your gifts for yourself and give
your rewards to someone else.[k] Nevertheless, I will read the writing for the
king and tell him what it means.
18"Your Majesty, the Most High God
gave your father Nebuchadnezzar sovereignty and greatness and glory and
splendor.[l] 19Because of the high position
he gave him, all the nations and peoples
of every language dreaded and feared
him. Those the king wanted to put to
death, he put to death;[m] those he wanted to spare, he spared; those he wanted
to promote, he promoted; and those he
wanted to humble, he humbled. 20But
when his heart became arrogant and
hardened with pride,[n] he was deposed
from his royal throne and stripped[o] of

5:11 [g] Da 2:47-48
5:12 [h] Da 1:7 [i] ver 14-16; Da 6:3
5:13 [j] Da 6:13
5:17 [k] 2Ki 5:16
5:18 [l] Jer 27:7; Da 2:37-38
5:19 [m] Da 2:12-13; 3:6
5:20 [n] Da 4:30 [o] Jer 13:18
[p] Job 40:12; Isa 14:13-15
5:21 [q] Eze 17:24 [r] Da 4:16-17,35
5:22 [s] Ex 10:3; 2Ch 33:23
5:23 [t] Jer 50:29 [u] Ps 115:4-8; Hab 2:19 [v] Job 12:10 [w] Job 31:4; Jer 10:23
5:26 [x] Jer 27:7 [y] Isa 13:6
5:27 [z] Ps 62:9
5:28 [a] Isa 13:17 [b] Da 6:28

Da 5:21–23 ❖ In what good and bad ways do we follow in the ways our parents have taught us?

his glory.[p] 21He was driven away from
people and given the mind of an animal; he lived with the wild donkeys and
ate grass like the ox; and his body was
drenched with the dew of heaven, until
he acknowledged that the Most High God
is sovereign[q] over all kingdoms on earth
and sets over them anyone he wishes.[r]
22"But you, Belshazzar, his son,[a] have
not humbled[s] yourself, though you knew
all this. 23Instead, you have set yourself
up against[t] the Lord of heaven. You had
the goblets from his temple brought to
you, and you and your nobles, your wives
and your concubines drank wine from
them. You praised the gods of silver and
gold, of bronze, iron, wood and stone,
which cannot see or hear or understand.[u]
But you did not honor the God who holds
in his hand your life[v] and all your ways.[w]
24Therefore he sent the hand that wrote
the inscription.
25"This is the inscription that was written:

MENE, MENE, TEKEL, PARSIN

26"Here is what these words mean:

Mene[b]: God has numbered the
days[x] of your reign and
brought it to an end.[y]
27 *Tekel*[c]: You have been weighed
on the scales and found
wanting.[z]
28 *Peres*[d]: Your kingdom is divided and given to the Medes[a]
and Persians."[b]

[a] 22 Or *descendant*; or *successor* [b] 26 *Mene* can mean *numbered* or *mina* (a unit of money). [c] 27 *Tekel* can mean *weighed* or *shekel*. [d] 28 *Peres* (the singular of *Parsin*) can mean *divided* or *Persia* or *a half mina* or *a half shekel*.

5:13–16 The king first reminds Daniel of his place: Belshazzar is king; Daniel is his captive. Belshazzar then launches off a series of honorifics, but a close reading of the speech shows that the king himself does not endorse the reports: Twice he begins his words with "I have heard."

5:17–24 Daniel begins by refusing the offered gifts. He will interpret the writing on the wall free of charge. Before actually giving the interpretation, Daniel delivers a stinging rebuke to the king. Nebuchadnezzar was great, but when God confronted him, he ultimately acknowledged his position as God's inferior. Belshazzar has not learned that lesson.

5:25–28 Three different nouns are units of money and may also be translated: "Mina, mina, shekel, and a half." Daniel's interpretation takes these nouns and interprets them as verbal forms. The three verbal roots in order may be translated "numbered," "weighed," and "divided." Belshazzar and the Babylonians have not measured up, and so now another power will come to the throne. It is one dominated by Persia, which includes the Medes. The message is clear, and it spells doom.

29Then at Belshazzar's command, Daniel was clothed in purple, a gold chain
was placed around his neck, and he was
proclaimed the third highest ruler in
the kingdom.
30That very night Belshazzar,[c] king of
the Babylonians,[a] was slain,[d] 31and Darius[e] the Mede took over the kingdom,
at the age of sixty-two.[b]

Daniel in the Den of Lions

6[c] It pleased Darius[f] to appoint 120
satraps[g] to rule throughout the
kingdom, 2with three administrators
over them, one of whom was Daniel.[h]
The satraps were made accountable[i] to
them so that the king might not suffer loss. 3Now Daniel so distinguished
himself among the administrators and
the satraps by his exceptional qualities
that the king planned to set him over
the whole kingdom.[j] 4At this, the administrators and the satraps tried to
find grounds for charges against Daniel
in his conduct of government affairs,
but they were unable to do so. They
could find no corruption in him, because he was trustworthy and neither
corrupt nor negligent. 5Finally these
men said, "We will never find any basis for charges against this man Daniel
unless it has something to do with the
law of his God."[k]

5:30 [c] ver 1 [d] Isa 21:9; Jer 51:31
5:31 [e] Da 6:1; 9:1
6:1 [f] Da 5:31 [g] Est 1:1
6:2 [h] Da 2:48-49 [i] Ezr 4:22
6:3 [j] Ge 41:41; Est 10:3; Da 5:12-14
6:5 [k] Ac 24:13-16
6:6 [l] Ne 2:3; Da 2:4
6:7 [m] Da 3:2 [n] Ps 59:3; 64:2-6; Da 3:6
6:8 [o] Est 1:19
6:10 [p] 1Ki 8:48-49 [q] Ps 95:6 [r] Ac 5:29

Da 6:10–11 ❖ How can we imitate Daniel's courage to continue worshiping and serving God no matter what, even in the face of danger? Where did Daniel get this strength?

6So these administrators and satraps
went as a group to the king and said:
"May King Darius live forever![l] 7The royal
administrators, prefects, satraps, advisers and governors[m] have all agreed that
the king should issue an edict and enforce the decree that anyone who prays
to any god or human being during the
next thirty days, except to you, Your Majesty, shall be thrown into the lions' den.[n]
8Now, Your Majesty, issue the decree and
put it in writing so that it cannot be altered — in accordance with the law of
the Medes and Persians, which cannot
be repealed."[o] 9So King Darius put the
decree in writing.
10Now when Daniel learned that the
decree had been published, he went
home to his upstairs room where the
windows opened toward[p] Jerusalem.
Three times a day he got down on his
knees[q] and prayed, giving thanks to his
God, just as he had done before.[r] 11Then

[a] 30 Or *Chaldeans* [b] 31 In Aramaic texts this verse (5:31) is numbered 6:1. [c] In Aramaic texts 6:1-28 is numbered 6:2-29.

5:29–31 Belshazzar bestows the promised rewards on godly Daniel. While the text does not give us a window to Daniel's motivation, the scene shows us that the godly may ultimately receive their reward even from hostile and reluctant oppressors. The chapter ends by narrating the consequences of Belshazzar's ungodly acts. In seeing the prophecy fulfilled, we witness the reward given to displaced pride, idolatry, and blasphemy.

✣ **5:1–31** The NT teaches that God, in Jesus, judges evil and condemns the wicked (Jn 8:26; 12:31). God is still judge in the NT (2Ti 4:8), but there is also clear and strong teaching that God's followers are not in a position to judge others. Perhaps the most well-known teaching in this regard is found in Mt 7:1–2. God certainly judges, but we cannot know for certain when suffering and death is God's judgment and when it is not. Therefore we must never assume that a person who is suffering is under God's judgment.

6:1–9 The schemers' approach to the king is a masterpiece of political deception. These "administrators and satraps" claim their proposal has been unanimously approved by all of his subordinates. Of course, Daniel, the king's favorite, whom he is on the brink of promoting, does not even know about it. The proposal appeals to the vanity of the king. Perhaps this explains his ready acceptance of such a bizarre suggestion.

Daniel will find himself in an impossible situation from a human point of view, for the decree may not be repealed according to the custom of the Persians and Medes.

6:10 Daniel's response to this decree is simple: He goes upstairs and prays with the windows open toward Jerusalem. Daniel demonstrates unflinching obedience. He does not question, doubt, or worry; he acts.

Daniel's bowing toward Jerusalem is likely motivated by 1Ki 8:35–36. Of course, at the time of Daniel's prayer the temple was in ruins. Nonetheless, Judeans in exile, such as Daniel, turned regularly toward the city with longing in their hearts and hope for the future.

The mention of the "three times a day" indicates that Daniel's prayer is part of his regular habit. He is neither flaunting nor hiding his religious practice.

6:11 Those who plotted against Daniel knew that his behavior would conform to his spotless reputation. They knew that Daniel's religion was the fundamental guiding principle of his life, so they knew this plot would succeed.

these men went as a group and found
Daniel praying and asking God for help.
12So they went to the king and spoke to
him about his royal decree: "Did you
not publish a decree that during the
next thirty days anyone who prays to
any god or human being except to you,
Your Majesty, would be thrown into the
lions' den?"
The king answered, "The decree
stands — in accordance with the law of
the Medes and Persians, which cannot
be repealed."[s]
13Then they said to the king, "Daniel,
who is one of the exiles from Judah,[t]
pays no attention[u] to you, Your Majesty, or to the decree you put in writing.
He still prays three times a day." 14When
the king heard this, he was greatly distressed;[v] he was determined to rescue
Daniel and made every effort until sundown to save him.
15Then the men went as a group to
King Darius and said to him, "Remember, Your Majesty, that according to the
law of the Medes and Persians no decree or edict that the king issues can be
changed."[w]
16So the king gave the order, and they
brought Daniel and threw him into the
lions' den.[x] The king said to Daniel, "May
your God, whom you serve continually,
rescue[y] you!"
17A stone was brought and placed
over the mouth of the den, and the
king sealed[z] it with his own signet ring
and with the rings of his nobles, so that
Daniel's situation might not be changed.
18Then the king returned to his palace
and spent the night without eating[a]
and without any entertainment being
brought to him. And he could not sleep.[b]
19At the first light of dawn, the king got
up and hurried to the lions' den. 20When
he came near the den, he called to Daniel
in an anguished voice, "Daniel, servant
of the living God, has your God, whom
you serve continually, been able to rescue you from the lions?"[c]
21Daniel answered, "May the king live
forever![d] 22My God sent his angel,[e] and he
shut the mouths of the lions.[f] They have
not hurt me, because I was found innocent in his sight.[g] Nor have I ever done
any wrong before you, Your Majesty."
23The king was overjoyed and gave
orders to lift Daniel out of the den. And
when Daniel was lifted from the den, no
wound[h] was found on him, because he
had trusted[i] in his God.
24At the king's command, the men who
had falsely accused Daniel were brought
in and thrown into the lions' den,[j] along
with their wives and children.[k] And before they reached the floor of the den,
the lions overpowered them and crushed
all their bones.[l]
25Then King Darius wrote to all the
nations and peoples of every language
in all the earth:

6:12 [s] Est 1:19; Da 3:8-12
6:13 [t] Da 2:25; 5:13 [u] Est 3:8; Da 3:12
6:14 [v] Mk 6:26
6:15 [w] Est 8:8
6:16 [x] ver 7 [y] Job 5:19; Ps 37:39-40
6:17 [z] Mt 27:66
6:18 [a] 2Sa 12:17 [b] Est 6:1; Da 2:1
6:20 [c] Da 3:17
6:21 [d] Da 2:4
6:22 [e] Da 3:28 [f] Ps 91:11-13; Heb 11:33 [g] Ac 12:11; 2Ti 4:17
6:23 [h] Da 3:27 [i] 1Ch 5:20
6:24 [j] Dt 19:18-19; Est 7:9-10; Ps 54:5 [k] Dt 24:16; 2Ki 14:6 [l] Isa 38:13

6:12–15 The conspirators know where the king's sympathies lie, so before they accuse Daniel, they remind the king of his earlier decision and its binding character. They then confront the king with the news that indicts Daniel. The king reacts with extreme dismay. However, he is trapped by his own unchangeable words and must carry out the punishment.
6:16–18 As decreed, Daniel is thrown into the lions' den. The king commends Daniel into the hands of the prophet's God, then suffers a restless night of concern for Daniel.
6:19–20 Darius must have had at least a glimmer of hope that Daniel would survive the night. As day dawns, the king himself rushes to inquire about Daniel's condition.
6:21–22 Daniel's survival attests to his innocence and God's care.
6:23–24 How did Daniel survive? Had the lions been fed or drugged before Daniel was thrown to them? The answer comes when the king commands that Daniel's accusers and their families be thrown into the den. The viciousness and hunger of the lions are vividly displayed by the fact these people were attacked and killed "before they reached the floor of the den" (v. 24).
6:25–28 The chapter ends with the king issuing a second decree, this time promoting Daniel's God throughout his vast empire. Darius proclaims the God of Daniel "the living God" (v. 26). This indicates that the king believes that he not only exists but is active in the world. God's rescue of Daniel from the lions' den demonstrates that "he rescues and he saves" (v. 27).

✣ **6:1–28** At times, Western Christians misapply the example of Daniel. Some have pointed to such things as the lack of prayer in public schools, fights over Christmas displays in public places, and the removal of the Ten Commandments from courtrooms as evidence of oppression toward Christian belief and practice. But are these situations really similar to Da 6? Likely not. Daniel was not prohibited from praying in a certain location; he was forbidden to pray to God at all, even in private.

The confusion in the United States and other Western democracies probably arises because some Christians insist that their country is the modern equivalent of ancient Israel. However, there are not and can never be any modern

PEOPLE TO KNOW // DARIUS

DANIEL 6:25–28: Ezra and Daniel both mention a king named Darius. It is almost certain, however, that these are two different kings. Darius from Ezra (also named in Nehemiah, Haggai and Zechariah) reigned later and protected the Jews when they rebuilt the temple (Ezr 6:1–12). A different King Darius is named in Daniel 6.

Daniel had been taken to Babylon from Jerusalem as an exile under King Nebuchadnezzar (Da 1:1–3). He was put into the king's service, and the king elevated him to a high rank. Daniel maintained this high position during the reign of Darius; in fact, Darius intended to set him over the whole kingdom.

When Darius's officials framed Daniel out of envy, Darius was forced to have Daniel thrown into a pit filled with lions. Distressed, he cried out to Daniel, "May your God, whom you serve continually, rescue you!" (6:16).

That's exactly what happened. God shut the mouths of the lions, keeping Daniel safe. The next day Darius released Daniel and had the officials who had plotted against him thrown to the lions instead. Darius's decree, recorded in Daniel 6:26–27, stands as an amazing testament to the power of God revealed in the book of Proverbs: "In the LORD's hand the king's heart is a stream of water that he channels toward all who please him" (Pr 21:1).

APPLICATION Darius was foolish to issue a decree forcing everyone to only worship him, but ego can get the better of any of us. Once he realized Daniel might be killed, Darius regretted his actions. This was all part of God's plan to show Darius God's power. When confronted with the power of God, Darius shifted from selfishness to praising God. God calls each of us to make the same change in our own hearts: to shift from selfish motivations and to direct our praise and service to God.

"May you prosper greatly![m]

26 "I issue a decree that in every part of my kingdom people must fear and reverence the God of Daniel.[n]

"For he is the living God
and he endures forever;
his kingdom will not be destroyed,
his dominion will never end.[o]
27 He rescues and he saves;
he performs signs and wonders[p]
in the heavens and on the earth.
He has rescued Daniel
from the power of the lions."[q]

6:25 [m] Da 4:1
6:26 [n] Ps 99:1-3; Da 3:29 [o] Da 2:44; 4:34
6:27 [p] Da 4:3 [q] ver 22
6:28 [r] 2Ch 36:22; Da 1:21
7:1 [s] Da 5:1 [t] Da 1:17 [u] Jer 36:4
7:2 [v] Rev 7:1

28 So Daniel prospered during the reign of Darius and the reign of Cyrus[a][r] the Persian.

Daniel's Dream of Four Beasts

7 In the first year of Belshazzar[s] king of Babylon, Daniel had a dream, and visions passed through his mind[t] as he was lying in bed. He wrote[u] down the substance of his dream.

2 Daniel said: "In my vision at night I looked, and there before me were the four winds of heaven[v] churning up the great

[a] 28 Or *Darius, that is, the reign of Cyrus*

equivalents of ancient Israel. There is no such thing as a "Christian nation," except in the sense of a nation where most of the inhabitants happen to be Christian at that particular historical moment. The kingdom of God can never be limited to one geographical or political sphere. It will eventually fill all the earth (see 2:35 and note on 2:44–45).

7:1–14 Chapter 7 changes the tone of the book of Daniel and can be considered apocalyptic literature, which is a metaphor-rich genre. In this kind of material, metaphors and similes shed light on difficult concepts by relating them to something readers know from common experience. As such, these images speak truly and accurately, but not precisely, so we need to be cautious about how we interpret these images. God speaks to Daniel through a dream or through a mediator (e.g., 12:5–13). He is not commissioned to speak to the people, but rather to write it down. This is what distinguishes apocalyptic literature from the genre of prophecy.

This passage presents the reader with two image clusters. On the one hand, we have four beasts and horns, which represent depraved human kingdoms; on the other hand, we see two human-like figures, the Ancient of Days and one like a son of man, who show us an image of the divine realm.

7:1–2 Daniel's report of the vision begins on the coast of the sea, where the winds are whipping the waves into a frenzy. In the ancient Near East,

sea. 3Four great beasts,[w] each different
from the others, came up out of the sea.
4"The first was like a lion,[x] and it had
the wings of an eagle.[y] I watched until
its wings were torn off and it was lifted
from the ground so that it stood on two
feet like a human being, and the mind
of a human was given to it.
5"And there before me was a second
beast, which looked like a bear. It was
raised up on one of its sides, and it had
three ribs in its mouth between its teeth. It
was told, 'Get up and eat your fill of flesh!'[z]
6"After that, I looked, and there before
me was another beast, one that looked
like a leopard.[a] And on its back it had
four wings like those of a bird. This beast
had four heads, and it was given authority to rule.
7"After that, in my vision at night I
looked, and there before me was a fourth
beast — terrifying and frightening and
very powerful. It had large iron[b] teeth;
it crushed and devoured its victims and
trampled underfoot whatever was left. It
was different from all the former beasts,
and it had ten horns.[c]
8"While I was thinking about the
horns, there before me was another
horn, a little[d] one, which came up among
them; and three of the first horns were
uprooted before it. This horn had eyes
like the eyes of a human being[e] and a
mouth that spoke boastfully.[f]
9"As I looked,

"thrones were set in place,
and the Ancient of Days took his
seat.
His clothing was as white as snow;
the hair of his head was white like
wool.[g]
His throne was flaming with fire,
and its wheels[h] were all ablaze.
10A river of fire[i] was flowing,
coming out from before him.[j]
Thousands upon thousands
attended him;
ten thousand times ten thousand
stood before him.
The court was seated,
and the books[k] were opened.

11"Then I continued to watch because of the boastful words the horn
was speaking. I kept looking until the
beast was slain and its body destroyed
and thrown into the blazing fire.[l] 12(The
other beasts had been stripped of their
authority, but were allowed to live for a
period of time.)
13"In my vision at night I looked, and
there before me was one like a son of
man,[a][m] coming with the clouds of heav-
en.[n] He approached the Ancient of Days
and was led into his presence. 14He was
given authority,[o] glory and sovereign

7:3 [w] Rev 13:1
7:4 [x] Jer 4:7 [y] Eze 17:3
7:5 [z] Da 2:39
7:6 [a] Rev 13:2
7:7 [b] Da 2:40 [c] Rev 12:3
7:8 [d] Da 8:9 [e] Rev 9:7 [f] Ps 12:3; Rev 13:5-6
7:9 [g] Rev 1:14 [h] Eze 1:15; 10:6
7:10 [i] Ps 50:3; 97:3; Isa 30:27 [j] Dt 33:2; Ps 68:17; Rev 5:11 [k] Rev 20:11-15
7:11 [l] Rev 19:20
7:13 [m] Mt 8:20*; Rev 1:13* [n] Mt 24:30; Rev 1:7
7:14 [o] Mt 28:18

Da 7:13–14 ❖ How can we support the ministry of bringing the gospel to people from every nation, so that people of every language might worship Christ?

[a] *13* The Aramaic phrase *bar enash* means *human being*. The phrase *son of man* is retained here because of its use in the New Testament as a title of Jesus, probably based largely on this verse.

the sea was more than a dangerous place; it was seen as a threatening force that stood against the beneficial forces of creation.

7:3 Out of the chaotic sea arise four great beasts—symbols of forces allied against God and his creation order. These beasts are mutants, perversions of what God intended for his creation. As such, they evoke not only horror in the original reader but also revulsion.

7:4 The first is described as "like a lion, and it had the wings of an eagle." The most natural interpretation of the symbolism is that it stands for Babylonia.

Note that we find ourselves on slippery ground when it comes to specific and concrete historical identifications of the imagery of the four beasts. The purpose is not to write history in advance but to make a theological statement about the conflict between human evil and God.

7:5 The second beast, the bear, rises out of the sea. This beast is not a hybrid, but it is still a ferocious animal of prey.

7:6 Intentional ambiguity continues with the third beast. Leopards are fast cats, and with the addition of wings, we are to imagine blazing speed. Does it signify the blazing speed of the Persian army, or does it point to Alexander's lightning advance through the Near East and the four generals who divided his vast empire after his early death?

7:7 The fourth kingdom is the most puzzling of all. It appears to be only vaguely animal-like. The metallic composition of its weapons (teeth and claws) highlights its destructive power and ruthlessness. If one has already identified the first three as Babylon, Media, and Persia, then the fourth must be Greece. If, on the other hand, one has combined Media and Persia and identified the third as Greece, then the fourth kingdom must be Rome.

7:9–14 The first figure in this next vision is called the "Ancient of Days" (v. 9). He is God as judge. The second figure, "one like a son of man" (v. 13), is more startling. He is riding the cloud chariot, which God alone can do. Cloud imagery is associated with the Lord's appearance throughout the OT (Ex 13:21; 19:16; Lev 16:2; Ps 68:4; 104:3–4; Isa 19:1; Na 1:3).

power; all nations and peoples of every
language worshiped him.[p] His dominion
is an everlasting dominion that will not
pass away, and his kingdom is one that
will never be destroyed.[q]

The Interpretation of the Dream

15“I, Daniel, was troubled in spirit,
and the visions that passed through my
mind disturbed me.[r] 16I approached one
of those standing there and asked him
the meaning of all this.

“So he told me and gave me the interpretation[s] of these things: 17‘The four
great beasts are four kings that will rise
from the earth. 18But the holy people of
the Most High will receive the kingdom
and will possess it forever—yes, for ever
and ever.’[t]

19“Then I wanted to know the meaning
of the fourth beast, which was different
from all the others and most terrifying,
with its iron teeth and bronze claws—
the beast that crushed and devoured its
victims and trampled underfoot whatever was left. 20I also wanted to know about
the ten horns on its head and about the
other horn that came up, before which
three of them fell—the horn that looked
more imposing than the others and
that had eyes and a mouth that spoke
boastfully. 21As I watched, this horn was
waging war against the holy people and
defeating them,[u] 22until the Ancient of
Days came and pronounced judgment in
favor of the holy people of the Most High,
and the time came when they possessed
the kingdom.

23“He gave me this explanation: ‘The
fourth beast is a fourth kingdom that will
appear on earth. It will be different from
all the other kingdoms and will devour
the whole earth, trampling it down and
crushing it.[v] 24The ten horns[w] are ten
kings who will come from this kingdom.
After them another king will arise, different from the earlier ones; he will subdue
three kings. 25He will speak against the
Most High[x] and oppress his holy people
and try to change the set times[y] and the
laws. The holy people will be delivered
into his hands for a time, times and half
a time.[a][z]

26“‘But the court will sit, and his power
will be taken away and completely destroyed forever. 27Then the sovereignty,
power and greatness of all the kingdoms
under heaven will be handed over to the
holy people of the Most High. His kingdom will be an everlasting[a] kingdom,
and all rulers will worship[b] and obey
him.’

28“This is the end of the matter. I, Daniel, was deeply troubled[c] by my thoughts,
and my face turned pale, but I kept the
matter to myself.”

Daniel’s Vision of a Ram and a Goat

8 In the third year of King Belshazzar’s
reign, I, Daniel, had a vision, after
the one that had already appeared to
me. 2In my vision I saw myself in the
citadel of Susa[d] in the province of Elam;[e]
in the vision I was beside the Ulai Canal.
3I looked up,[f] and there before me was
a ram with two horns, standing beside
the canal, and the horns were long. One
of the horns was longer than the other
but grew up later. 4I watched the ram
as it charged toward the west and the
north and the south. No animal could
stand against it, and none could rescue
from its power. It did as it pleased[g] and
became great.

7:14 [p] Ps 72:11; 102:22; 1Co 15:27; Eph 1:22 [q] Da 2:44; Heb 12:28; Rev 11:15
7:15 [r] Da 4:19
7:16 [s] Da 8:16; 9:22; Zec 1:9
7:18 [t] Isa 60:12-14; Rev 2:26; 20:4
7:21 [u] Rev 13:7
7:23 [v] Da 2:40
7:24 [w] Rev 17:12
7:25 [x] Isa 37:23; Da 11:36 [y] Da 2:21 [z] Da 8:24; 12:7; Rev 12:14
7:27 [a] Da 2:44; 4:34; Lk 1:33; Rev 11:15; 22:5 [b] Ps 22:27; 72:11; 86:9
7:28 [c] Da 4:19
8:2 [d] Est 1:2 [e] Ge 10:22
8:3 [f] Da 10:5
8:4 [g] Da 11:3,16

[a] 25 *Or for a year, two years and half a year*

7:15-24 A strong case can be made that the fourth beast is Greece and the ten horns are the kings that followed Alexander, with the climactic horn being associated with Antiochus IV Epiphanes.

Other scholars have argued that the fourth kingdom must be Rome, and the ten horns should be identified as ten kingdoms that arise from that political entity, to be followed by a climactic rebel to be identified as the antichrist in the NT.

7:25-28 The puzzling phrase “a time, times and half a time” (v. 25) is often taken to mean three and a half years. It is better to understand this reference to be as vague as it sounds on first reading. The bigger lesson is that the rebellion of the little horn, which gets off to a fast start and seems like it is going to last forever, will suddenly be cut off.

7:1-28 Daniel 7 paints a horrifying picture of human evil. The picture of the beasts is consistent with the lesson we learn throughout the Bible—every man and woman is at heart a self-seeking rebel against God. When we see ourselves as being in this kind of open rebellion against God, the words of Ro 5:8 come into sharp focus: “God demonstrates his own love for us in this: While we were still sinners, Christ died for us.”

8:1-9 The symbol of the horn points to a king or a kingdom. This small horn takes on large proportions as it grows toward the “Beautiful Land” (v. 9), Israel.

5 As I was thinking about this, suddenly
a goat with a prominent horn between
its eyes came from the west, crossing
the whole earth without touching the
ground. 6 It came toward the two-horned
ram I had seen standing beside the canal
and charged at it in great rage. 7 I saw
it attack the ram furiously, striking the
ram and shattering its two horns. The
ram was powerless to stand against it;
the goat knocked it to the ground and
trampled on it,[h] and none could rescue
the ram from its power. 8 The goat became very great, but at the height of its
power the large horn was broken off,[i] and
in its place four prominent horns grew
up toward the four winds of heaven.[j]
9 Out of one of them came another
horn, which started small but grew in
power to the south and to the east and toward the Beautiful Land.[k] 10 It grew until
it reached[l] the host of the heavens, and
it threw some of the starry host down to
the earth[m] and trampled[n] on them. 11 It
set itself up to be as great as the commander of the army of the LORD;[o] it took
away the daily sacrifice[p] from the LORD,
and his sanctuary was thrown down.[q]
12 Because of rebellion, the LORD's people[a]
and the daily sacrifice were given over to
it. It prospered in everything it did, and
truth was thrown to the ground.
13 Then I heard a holy one[r] speaking,
and another holy one said to him, "How
long will it take for the vision to be fulfilled[s] — the vision concerning the daily
sacrifice, the rebellion that causes desolation, the surrender of the sanctuary
and the trampling underfoot[t] of the
LORD's people?"

Da 8:12 ❖ How do we see truth "thrown to the ground" today? How might this be a signal of things to come?

14 He said to me, "It will take 2,300 evenings and mornings; then the sanctuary
will be reconsecrated."[u]

The Interpretation of the Vision

15 While I, Daniel, was watching the vision[v] and trying to understand it, there
before me stood one who looked like a
man.[w] 16 And I heard a man's voice from
the Ulai calling, "Gabriel,[x] tell this man
the meaning of the vision."
17 As he came near the place where I
was standing, I was terrified and fell
prostrate.[y] "Son of man,"[b] he said to me,
"understand that the vision concerns the
time of the end."[z]
18 While he was speaking to me, I was in
a deep sleep, with my face to the ground.[a]
Then he touched me and raised me to
my feet.[b]
19 He said: "I am going to tell you what
will happen later in the time of wrath,
because the vision concerns the appointed time of the end.[c] 20 The two-horned
ram that you saw represents the kings
of Media and Persia. 21 The shaggy goat
is the king of Greece,[d] and the large horn
between its eyes is the first king.[e] 22 The
four horns that replaced the one that was

8:7 [h] Da 7:7
8:8 [i] 2Ch 26:16-21; Da 5:20 [j] Da 7:2; Rev 7:1
8:9 [k] Da 11:16
8:10 [l] Isa 14:13 [m] Rev 12:4 [n] Da 7:7
8:11 [o] Da 11:36-37 [p] Eze 46:13-14 [q] Da 11:31; 12:11
8:13 [r] Da 4:23 [s] Da 12:6 [t] Lk 21:24; Rev 11:2
8:14 [u] Da 12:11-12
8:15 [v] ver 1 [w] Da 10:16-18
8:16 [x] Da 9:21; Lk 1:19
8:17 [y] Eze 1:28; Da 2:46; Rev 1:17 [z] Hab 2:3
8:18 [a] Da 10:9 [b] Eze 2:2; Da 10:16-18
8:19 [c] Hab 2:3
8:21 [d] Da 10:20 [e] Da 11:3

[a] 12 Or *rebellion, the armies* [b] 17 The Hebrew phrase *ben adam* means *human being.* The phrase *son of man* is retained as a form of address here because of its possible association with "Son of Man" in the New Testament. [c] 19 Or *because the end will be at the appointed time*

8:10–11 The horn grows until it reaches the "host of the heavens" (v. 10) and enters a conflict with this heavenly army. Then the horn challenges "the commander of the army of the LORD" (v. 11). Its incursion is described as harm to the worship of Israel.

8:12–13 Verse 12 is difficult and its interpretation uncertain. In a word, it is clear that God's side will take some blows during the struggle "because of rebellion" (v. 12). How long will the sanctuary and its ritual be disrupted? The answer is addressed to Daniel in v. 14.

8:14 Even in historical retrospect, we cannot be dogmatic about the meaning of the 2,300 evenings and mornings. The number is given to assure Daniel's readers that God has things under control. This number is typical of chronological numbers throughout the book of Daniel.

8:15–16 Gabriel (meaning "God's hero"), a leading angel in God's heavenly army, appears before Daniel. The voice of God himself commands this powerful angelic being to reveal the meaning of the vision.

8:17–18 The first words from Gabriel might lead us to believe that the vision concerns the end of history, but the clear interpretation of the context places it squarely in the middle of the second century BC.

8:19–20 The animals are identified with particular and well-known political entities. The ram with the two horns represents the "kings of Media and Persia" (v. 20). In the vision itself, one horn grew larger than the other, a reference to the fact that the Persian part of this empire soon swallowed the Median part and assumed dominance.

8:21–22 The goat with the single horn that speedily devastated the ram is Greece, the single horn being its first king—Alexander the Great. After his sons were murdered, his conquered territory was

broken off represent four kingdoms that will emerge from his nation but will not have the same power.

23“In the latter part of their reign, when rebels have become completely wicked, a fierce-looking king, a master of intrigue, will arise. 24He will become very strong, but not by his own power. He will cause astounding devastation and will succeed in whatever he does. He will destroy those who are mighty, the holy people.[f] 25He will cause deceit to prosper, and he will consider himself superior. When they feel secure, he will destroy many and take his stand against the Prince of princes.[g] Yet he will be destroyed, but not by human power.[h]

26“The vision of the evenings and mornings that has been given you is true,[i] but seal[j] up the vision, for it concerns the distant future.”[k]

27I, Daniel, was worn out. I lay exhausted for several days. Then I got up and went about the king's business.[l] I was appalled[m] by the vision; it was beyond understanding.

Daniel's Prayer

9 In the first year of Darius[n] son of Xerxes[a] (a Mede by descent), who was made ruler over the Babylonian[b] kingdom — 2in the first year of his reign, I, Daniel, understood from the Scriptures, according to the word of the LORD given to Jeremiah the prophet, that the desolation of Jerusalem would last seventy[o] years. 3So I turned to the Lord God and pleaded with him in prayer and petition, in fasting, and in sackcloth and ashes.[p]

4I prayed to the LORD my God and confessed:

> “Lord, the great and awesome God,[q] who keeps his covenant of love[r] with those who love him and keep his commandments, 5we have sinned and done wrong.[s] We have been wicked and have rebelled; we have turned away[t] from your commands and laws.[u] 6We have not listened to your servants the prophets,[v] who spoke in your name to our kings, our princes and our ancestors, and to all the people of the land.
>
> 7“Lord, you are righteous, but this day we are covered with shame[w] — the people of Judah and the inhabitants of Jerusalem and all Israel, both near and far, in all the countries where you have scattered[x] us because of our unfaithfulness to you.[y] 8We and our kings, our princes and our ancestors are covered with shame, LORD, because

8:24 [f] Da 7:25; 11:36
8:25 [g] Da 11:36 [h] Da 2:34; 11:21
8:26 [i] Da 10:1 [j] Rev 22:10 [k] Da 10:14
8:27 [l] Da 2:48 [m] Da 7:28
9:1 [n] Da 5:31
9:2 [o] 2Ch 36:21; Jer 29:10; Zec 7:5
9:3 [p] Ne 1:4; Jer 29:12
9:4 [q] Dt 7:21 [r] Dt 7:9
9:5 [s] Ps 106:6 [t] Isa 53:6 [u] ver 11; La 1:20
9:6 [v] 2Ch 36:16; Jer 44:5
9:7 [w] Ps 44:15 [x] Dt 4:27; Am 9:9 [y] Jer 3:25

[a] 1 Hebrew *Ahasuerus* [b] 1 Or *Chaldean*

Da 9:4-14 ❖ How often in our prayers do we confess the sins of our community or society? Why would we do so? What might be the impact on our community if we do?

---

carved up between Alexander's powerful generals, the “four prominent horns” (v. 8; cf. v. 22).

8:23-25 The vision then skips over about two centuries of history. Scholars almost universally agree that the horn that grew out of one of the four is the second-century BC Seleucid ruler, Antiochus IV Epiphanes. Antiochus IV ordered the end of temple sacrifice in 167 BC and profaned the temple by introducing a holy object sacred to the god Zeus, to which he sacrificed a pig. Some have suggested that this holy object was a meteorite; it became a cult object that the Jews referred to as “an abomination that causes desolation” (9:27).

Such arrogance as has been reported about Antiochus IV Epiphanes can only lead to one conclusion: utter defeat.

✚ **8:1-27** Every generation has seen the “signs of the times.” This is why we are tempted, particularly when we have not listened to Jesus' clear teaching about not knowing the precise time of his return (Mk 13:32), to think that our time is indicated in these texts and that the end of the world is near.

The misuse of apocalyptic dates is an attempt to take control from God and place it firmly in our own sinful grasp. Such useless speculation leads to a complete disregard for past and present realities. God calls us to learn from the past while we live for him and his kingdom in the present. Then, of course, we can wait with hope for the future, knowing that all of history is in his loving hands.

9:1-4a Daniel's witness to the fall of Babylon (539 BC) may have caused him to turn to the Scriptures with new eyes. Daniel likely had passages like Jer 25:11-12; 29:10 in mind as he prayed. These passages teach that the king of Babylon will dominate the ancient Near East (including Judah) for seventy years. In the first year of Darius, Babylon has been replaced by Persia. Daniel recognizes this as the time when the exile may come to an end.

9:4b-10 Daniel's prayer paints a powerful picture of the Lord, especially in contrast to his people. God's people have not obeyed his commands but have rebelled against the covenant God made with them through Moses; this is why they are in exile.

we have sinned against you. 9 The
Lord our God is merciful and forgiving,[z] even though we have rebelled against him;[a] 10 we have not
obeyed the LORD our God or kept the
laws he gave us through his servants
the prophets.[b] 11 All Israel has transgressed your law and turned away,
refusing to obey you.

"Therefore the curses and sworn
judgments written in the Law of Moses, the servant of God, have been
poured out on us, because we have
sinned[c] against you. 12 You have
fulfilled[d] the words spoken against
us and against our rulers by bringing on us great disaster. Under the
whole heaven nothing has ever been
done like what has been done to Jerusalem.[e] 13 Just as it is written in the
Law of Moses, all this disaster has
come on us, yet we have not sought
the favor of the LORD our God by
turning from our sins and giving
attention to your truth.[f] 14 The LORD
did not hesitate to bring the disaster[g] on us, for the LORD our God is
righteous in everything he does; yet
we have not obeyed him.[h]

15 "Now, Lord our God, who
brought your people out of Egypt
with a mighty hand[i] and who made
for yourself a name[j] that endures to
this day, we have sinned, we have
done wrong. 16 Lord, in keeping with
all your righteous acts,[k] turn away
your anger and your wrath from Jerusalem,[l] your city, your holy hill.[m]
Our sins and the iniquities of our
ancestors have made Jerusalem and
your people an object of scorn[n] to all
those around us.

17 "Now, our God, hear the prayers
and petitions of your servant. For
your sake, Lord, look with favor[o] on
your desolate sanctuary. 18 Give ear,
our God, and hear; open your eyes
and see[p] the desolation of the city
that bears your Name.[q] We do not
make requests of you because we are
righteous, but because of your great
mercy. 19 Lord, listen! Lord, forgive![r]
Lord, hear and act! For your sake, my
God, do not delay, because your city
and your people bear your Name."

The Seventy "Sevens"

20 While I was speaking and praying,
confessing my sin and the sin of my people Israel and making my request to the
LORD my God for his holy hill[s]— 21 while
I was still in prayer, Gabriel,[t] the man I
had seen in the earlier vision, came to
me in swift flight about the time of the
evening sacrifice.[u] 22 He instructed me
and said to me, "Daniel, I have now come
to give you insight and understanding.
23 As soon as you began to pray, a word
went out, which I have come to tell you,
for you are highly esteemed.[v] Therefore,
consider the word and understand the
vision:[w]

24 "Seventy 'sevens'[a] are decreed for
your people and your holy city to finish[b]
transgression, to put an end to sin, to
atone[x] for wickedness, to bring in everlasting righteousness,[y] to seal up vision
and prophecy and to anoint the Most
Holy Place.[c]

25 "Know and understand this: From
the time the word goes out to restore
and rebuild[z] Jerusalem until the Anointed One,[d][a] the ruler, comes, there will be
seven 'sevens,' and sixty-two 'sevens.' It
will be rebuilt with streets and a trench,

9:9 [z] Ps 130:4 [a] Ne 9:17; Jer 14:7
9:10 [b] 2Ki 17:13-15; 18:12
9:11 [c] Isa 1:4-6; Jer 8:5-10
9:12 [d] Isa 44:26; Zec 1:6 [e] Jer 44:2-6; Eze 5:9
9:13 [f] Isa 9:13; Jer 2:30
9:14 [g] Jer 44:27 [h] Ne 9:33
9:15 [i] Jer 32:21 [j] Ne 9:10
9:16 [k] Ps 31:1 [l] Jer 32:32 [m] Zec 8:3 [n] Eze 5:14
9:17 [o] Nu 6:24-26; Ps 80:19
9:18 [p] Ps 80:14 [q] Isa 37:17; Jer 7:10-12; 25:29
9:19 [r] Ps 44:23
9:20 [s] ver 3; Ps 145:18; Isa 58:9
9:21 [t] Da 8:16; Lk 1:19 [u] Ex 29:39
9:23 [v] Da 10:19; Lk 1:28 [w] Da 10:11-12; Mt 24:15
9:24 [x] Isa 53:10 [y] Isa 56:1
9:25 [z] Ezr 4:24 [a] Jn 4:25

[a] 24 Or *'weeks'*; also in verses 25 and 26
[b] 24 Or *restrain* [c] 24 Or *the most holy One*
[d] 25 Or *an anointed one*; also in verse 26

9:11–14 In the next section of his prayer, Daniel draws a direct connection between the sin of the people and their present suffering. God's people had no excuse. The destruction of Jerusalem and the exile of Judah were not acts of an arbitrary God, but the consequences of the sinful actions of God's people, about which they were repeatedly warned.
9:15–19 The exodus was a pivotal event in the life of God's people. It defined them as a nation. In essence, the return from exile would be a sort of second exodus.

The plea for God's mercy is not the basis of God's restoration. If there is any hope, it is in God's righteousness and not their own (vv. 16, 18). Daniel's appeal is ultimately based not on the people's plight but on the reputation of God himself.
9:20–24 Daniel has prayed for forgiveness and restoration, and Gabriel now communicates the heavenly answer by reinterpreting the seventy years as seventy "sevens" (v. 24). During this period six actions will be completed. These six actions describe the eradication of evil and the establishment of righteousness.
9:25–27 Gabriel continues. Why exactly are the first seven "sevens" separated from the next sixty-two (vv. 25–26)? Apparently, we are to think of that shorter period as having a kind of integrity of its own.

The actions of the seventieth week are the work of a destructive force. The period of the prophecy ends with the end of this disruptive person.

but in times of trouble. 26After the sixty-
two 'sevens,' the Anointed One will be
put to death[b] and will have nothing.[a]
The people of the ruler who will come
will destroy the city and the sanctuary.
The end will come like a flood:[c] War will
continue until the end, and desolations
have been decreed. 27He will confirm a
covenant with many for one 'seven.'[b] In
the middle of the 'seven'[b] he will put an
end to sacrifice and offering. And at the
temple[c] he will set up an abomination
that causes desolation, until the end that
is decreed[d] is poured out on him.[d]"[e]

Daniel's Vision of a Man

10 In the third year of Cyrus[e] king of
Persia, a revelation was given to
Daniel (who was called Belteshazzar).[f]
Its message was true[g] and it concerned
a great war.[f] The understanding of the
message came to him in a vision.

2At that time I, Daniel, mourned[h] for
three weeks. 3I ate no choice food; no
meat or wine touched my lips; and I used
no lotions at all until the three weeks
were over.

4On the twenty-fourth day of the first
month, as I was standing on the bank of
the great river, the Tigris,[i] 5I looked up
and there before me was a man dressed
in linen,[j] with a belt of fine gold[k] from
Uphaz around his waist. 6His body was
like topaz, his face like lightning,[l] his
eyes like flaming torches,[m] his arms and
legs like the gleam of burnished bronze,[n]
and his voice like the sound of a multitude.

7I, Daniel, was the only one who saw
the vision; those who were with me did
not see it,[o] but such terror overwhelmed
them that they fled and hid themselves.
8So I was left alone,[p] gazing at this great
vision; I had no strength left,[q] my face
turned deathly pale and I was helpless.[r]
9Then I heard him speaking, and as I
listened to him, I fell into a deep sleep,
my face to the ground.[s]

10A hand touched me[t] and set me trembling on my hands and knees.[u] 11He said,
"Daniel, you who are highly esteemed,[v]
consider carefully the words I am about
to speak to you, and stand up,[w] for I have
now been sent to you." And when he said
this to me, I stood up trembling.

12Then he continued, "Do not be afraid,
Daniel. Since the first day that you set your
mind to gain understanding and to humble[x] yourself before your God, your words
were heard, and I have come in response
to them.[y] 13But the prince of the Persian
kingdom resisted me twenty-one days.
Then Michael,[z] one of the chief princes,
came to help me, because I was detained
there with the king of Persia. 14Now I have
come to explain[a] to you what will happen
to your people in the future, for the vision
concerns a time yet to come.[b]"

15While he was saying this to me, I
bowed with my face toward the ground
and was speechless.[c] 16Then one who
looked like a man[g] touched my lips, and

9:26 [b]Isa 53:8 [c]Na 1:8
9:27 [d]Isa 10:22
10:1 [e]Da 1:21 [f]Da 1:7 [g]Da 8:26
10:2 [h]Ezr 9:4
10:4 [i]Ge 2:14
10:5 [j]Eze 9:2; Rev 15:6 [k]Jer 10:9
10:6 [l]Mt 17:2 [m]Rev 19:12 [n]Rev 1:15
10:7 [o]2Ki 6:17-20; Ac 9:7
10:8 [p]Ge 32:24 [q]Da 8:27 [r]Hab 3:16
10:9 [s]Da 8:18
10:10 [t]Jer 1:9 [u]Rev 1:17
10:11 [v]Da 9:23 [w]Eze 2:1
10:12 [x]Da 9:3 [y]Da 9:20
10:13 [z]ver 21; Da 12:1; Jude 9
10:14 [a]Da 9:22 [b]Da 2:28; 8:26; Hab 2:3
10:15 [c]Eze 24:27; Lk 1:20

[a] 26 Or *death and will have no one*; or *death, but not for himself* [b] 27 Or *'week'* [c] 27 Septuagint and Theodotion; Hebrew *wing* [d] 27 Or *it* [e] 27 Or *And one who causes desolation will come upon the wing of the abominable temple, until the end that is decreed is poured out on the desolated city* [f] 1 Or *true and burdensome* [g] 16 Most manuscripts of the Masoretic Text; one manuscript of the Masoretic Text, Dead Sea Scrolls and Septuagint *Then something that looked like a human hand*

9:1–27 Daniel turned to the writings of Jeremiah to hear the voice of God. God then spoke to him further through Gabriel, an angel. Where do we go to hear God speak today? The opening verses of the book of Hebrews (1:1–4) point us in the right direction: Jesus is God's fullest revelation of himself to us. He is God in human form.

Where do we meet God in Jesus today? Most directly in the Bible.

10:1–3 For three weeks up to this moment, Daniel has been in mourning. From the later words of the supernatural being, we understand this period of mourning was accompanied by prayer for understanding (see v. 12). Daniel was in a state of prayerful turmoil.

10:4–9 On the twenty-fourth day of the first month, Daniel receives a vision of a heavenly being that terrifies him. He is dressed like a priest in linen and wearing a belt of gold. His physical description looks more like a statue than an actual human being. His voice booms (v. 6). Those around Daniel somehow sense some great power because they immediately flee the scene and hide.

10:10–11 As the supernatural figure speaks with Daniel, he encourages the prophet.

10:12–14 The picture that emerges here is of a heavenly conflict. The speaker—an unnamed angelic power—and Michael fight on God's side. On the other side stands "the prince of the Persian kingdom" (v. 13) who is powerful but evil as well. The heavenly messenger announces the substance of his message (v. 14).

10:15–17 Daniel is overwhelmed by the vision and

I opened my mouth and began to speak.[d]
I said to the one standing before me, "I
am overcome with anguish[e] because of
the vision, my lord, and I feel very weak.
17How can I, your servant, talk with you,
my lord? My strength is gone and I can
hardly breathe."[f]
18Again the one who looked like a
man touched[g] me and gave me strength.
19"Do not be afraid, you who are highly
esteemed," he said. "Peace![h] Be strong
now; be strong."[i]
When he spoke to me, I was strengthened and said, "Speak, my lord, since you
have given me strength."[j]
20So he said, "Do you know why I have
come to you? Soon I will return to fight
against the prince of Persia, and when
I go, the prince of Greece[k] will come;
21but first I will tell you what is written
in the Book of Truth.[l] (No one supports
me against them except Michael,[m] your
11 prince. 1And in the first year of Darius[n] the Mede, I took my stand to
support and protect him.)

The Kings of the South and the North

2"Now then, I tell you the truth:[o] Three
more kings will arise in Persia, and then
a fourth, who will be far richer than all
the others. When he has gained power
by his wealth, he will stir up everyone
against the kingdom of Greece.[p] 3Then
a mighty king will arise, who will rule
with great power and do as he pleases.[q]
4After he has arisen, his empire will be
broken up and parceled out toward the
four winds of heaven.[r] It will not go to his
descendants, nor will it have the power
he exercised, because his empire will be
uprooted and given to others.
5"The king of the South will become
strong, but one of his commanders will
become even stronger than he and will
rule his own kingdom with great power. 6After some years, they will become
allies. The daughter of the king of the
South will go to the king of the North to
make an alliance, but she will not retain
her power, and he and his power[a] will not
last. In those days she will be betrayed,
together with her royal escort and her
father[b] and the one who supported her.
7"One from her family line will arise to
take her place. He will attack the forces
of the king of the North[s] and enter his
fortress; he will fight against them and
be victorious. 8He will also seize their
gods,[t] their metal images and their valuable articles of silver and gold and carry
them off to Egypt.[u] For some years he
will leave the king of the North alone.
9Then the king of the North will invade
the realm of the king of the South but
will retreat to his own country. 10His sons
will prepare for war and assemble a great
army, which will sweep on like an irresistible flood[v] and carry the battle as far
as his fortress.

Da 10:20 ❖ When has God's Word strengthened you in a specific way?

10:16 [d] Isa 6:7; Jer 1:9; Da 8:15-18 [e] Isa 21:3
10:17 [f] Da 4:19
10:18 [g] ver 16
10:19 [h] Jdg 6:23; Isa 35:4 [i] Jos 1:9 [j] Isa 6:1-8
10:20 [k] Da 8:21; 11:2
10:21 [l] Da 11:2 [m] ver 13; Jude 9
11:1 [n] Da 5:31
11:2 [o] Da 10:21 [p] Da 10:20
11:3 [q] Da 8:4,21
11:4 [r] Da 7:2; 8:22
11:7 [s] ver 6
11:8 [t] Isa 37:19; 46:1-2 [u] Jer 43:12
11:10 [v] Isa 8:8; Jer 46:8; Da 9:26

[a] 6 Or *offspring* [b] 6 Or *child* (see Vulgate and Syriac)

---

bows to the ground, unable to speak. Thanks to supernatural support, the prophet announces that he is ready to receive the vision.

10:18–11:1 An angel is going to tell Daniel "what is written in the Book of Truth" (v. 21). The fact that God has scripted history and that the rescue of his people is the culmination is cause for great optimism and celebration.

✣ **10:1—11:1** In Da 10 the veil is pulled back slightly, and we see the divine realities behind human conflict. We are to fight, but we need to recognize that we will have victory only as we allow God to use us. We are not to be passive; we are to stand firm. But our strength to do this comes only as we put on the armor of God.

We must not underestimate our enemy's strength. Fighting against Satan in our own strength will lead to our quick and easy defeat. When we realize that we have no power in ourselves to fight the battles of life, we will be driven to Jesus, our Divine Warrior.

11:2–4 We are not certain who the fourth king is (v. 2). To be frank, we cannot be sure how to understand the mind of the author at this stage. We know the identity of the "mighty king" of v. 3—none other than Alexander, whom we call "the Great." But shortly after he came on the global scene he disappeared from it, and power passed into the hands of Alexander's four leading generals.

11:5–6 The king of the south was Ptolemy I. The king of the north was Seleucus I. When Ptolemy and Seleucus defeated Antigonus in Gaza in 312 BC, Syria-Palestine was assigned to Seleucus. Seleucus and his successors never gave up claim to this area.

11:7–9 Here we have an allusion to the fact that Ptolemy III came to the throne in 246 BC and waged war against Seleucus II, who had inherited the northern throne.

11:10–17 The sons of Seleucus II, alluded to in v. 10,

11"Then the king of the South will
march out in a rage and fight against the
king of the North, who will raise a large
army, but it will be defeated.[w] 12When
the army is carried off, the king of the
South will be filled with pride and will
slaughter many thousands, yet he will
not remain triumphant. 13For the king
of the North will muster another army,
larger than the first; and after several
years, he will advance with a huge army
fully equipped.

14"In those times many will rise
against the king of the South. Those
who are violent among your own people will rebel in fulfillment of the vision,
but without success. 15Then the king of
the North will come and build up siege
ramps[x] and will capture a fortified city.
The forces of the South will be powerless
to resist; even their best troops will not
have the strength to stand. 16The invader
will do as he pleases;[y] no one will be able
to stand against him.[z] He will establish
himself in the Beautiful Land and will
have the power to destroy it.[a] 17He will
determine to come with the might of
his entire kingdom and will make an
alliance with the king of the South. And
he will give him a daughter in marriage
in order to overthrow the kingdom, but
his plans[a] will not succeed[b] or help him.
18Then he will turn his attention to the
coastlands[c] and will take many of them,
but a commander will put an end to his
insolence and will turn his insolence
back on him.[d] 19After this, he will turn
back toward the fortresses of his own
country but will stumble and fall,[e] to be
seen no more.[f]

20"His successor will send out a tax
collector to maintain the royal splendor.[g] In a few years, however, he will be
destroyed, yet not in anger or in battle.

21"He will be succeeded by a contemptible[h] person who has not been given the
honor of royalty.[i] He will invade the kingdom when its people feel secure, and
he will seize it through intrigue. 22Then
an overwhelming army will be swept
away before him; both it and a prince of
the covenant will be destroyed.[j] 23After
coming to an agreement with him, he
will act deceitfully,[k] and with only a few
people he will rise to power. 24When the
richest provinces feel secure, he will invade them and will achieve what neither
his fathers nor his forefathers did. He
will distribute plunder, loot and wealth
among his followers.[l] He will plot the
overthrow of fortresses — but only for
a time.

25"With a large army he will stir up his
strength and courage against the king
of the South. The king of the South will
wage war with a large and very powerful
army, but he will not be able to stand
because of the plots devised against
him. 26Those who eat from the king's
provisions will try to destroy him; his
army will be swept away, and many will
fall in battle. 27The two kings, with their
hearts bent on evil,[m] will sit at the same
table and lie[n] to each other, but to no
avail, because an end will still come at
the appointed time.[o] 28The king of the
North will return to his own country with
great wealth, but his heart will be set
against the holy covenant. He will take
action against it and then return to his
own country.

29"At the appointed time he will invade the South again, but this time the
outcome will be different from what it
was before. 30Ships of the western coastlands[p] will oppose him, and he will lose
heart. Then he will turn back and vent
his fury against the holy covenant. He
will return and show favor to those who
forsake the holy covenant.

11:11 [w] Da 8:7-8
11:15 [x] Eze 4:2
11:16 [y] Da 8:4 [z] Jos 1:5; Da 8:7 [a] Da 8:9
11:17 [b] Ps 20:4
11:18 [c] Isa 66:19; Jer 25:22 [d] Hos 12:14
11:19 [e] Ps 27:2 [f] Ps 37:36; Eze 26:21
11:20 [g] Isa 60:17
11:21 [h] Da 4:17 [i] Da 8:25
11:22 [j] Da 8:10-11
11:23 [k] Da 8:25
11:24 [l] Ne 9:25
11:27 [m] Ps 64:6 [n] Ps 12:2; Jer 9:5 [o] Hab 2:3
11:30 [p] Ge 10:4

[a] 17 Or *but she*

---

are Seleucus III, who ruled from 227–223 BC, and one of the most famous of all the Seleucid rulers, Antiochus III the Great, who had a long reign from 223–187 BC. The story of Antiochus III the Great's reign continues through v. 19.

11:18–20 Antiochus never tired of ambition, and in accordance with the prophecy of v. 18 started annexing parts of Asia Minor as well as some Greek islands. His son Seleucus IV Philopator (187–175 BC) succeeded him. Seleucus IV died under mysterious circumstances just as his younger brother was returning to his homeland. That younger brother's name was Antiochus IV, who got the nickname Epiphanes ("god manifest"). The attention of the text turns now to this highly significant figure.

11:21–31 For our purposes, it is only important to point out that Antiochus took increasingly aggressive steps against proper worship of God. Most distressing was his stopping the daily sacrifice and placing in the temple an idolatrous object, probably a meteorite representing Baal Shamem (the Syrian version of Zeus). This object is called the "abomination that causes desolation" (v. 31) in the book of Daniel.

31“His armed forces will rise up to
desecrate the temple fortress and will
abolish the daily sacrifice. Then they will
set up the abomination that causes desolation.[q] 32With flattery he will corrupt
those who have violated the covenant,
but the people who know their God will
firmly resist[r] him.
33“Those who are wise will instruct[s]
many, though for a time they will fall by
the sword or be burned or captured or
plundered.[t] 34When they fall, they will
receive a little help, and many who are
not sincere[u] will join them. 35Some of
the wise will stumble, so that they may
be refined,[v] purified and made spotless
until the time of the end, for it will still
come at the appointed time.

The King Who Exalts Himself

36“The king will do as he pleases. He
will exalt and magnify himself above every god and will say unheard-of things[w]
against the God of gods.[x] He will be successful until the time of wrath[y] is completed, for what has been determined
must take place. 37He will show no regard
for the gods of his ancestors or for the
one desired by women, nor will he regard
any god, but will exalt himself above
them all. 38Instead of them, he will hon-
or a god of fortresses; a god unknown to
his ancestors he will honor with gold and
silver, with precious stones and costly
gifts. 39He will attack the mightiest fortresses with the help of a foreign god and
will greatly honor those who acknowledge him. He will make them rulers over
many people and will distribute the land
at a price.[a]
40“At the time of the end the king of
the South[z] will engage him in battle,
and the king of the North will storm[a]
out against him with chariots and cavalry and a great fleet of ships. He will invade many countries and sweep through
them like a flood.[b] 41He will also invade
the Beautiful Land. Many countries will
fall, but Edom,[c] Moab[d] and the leaders
of Ammon will be delivered from his
hand. 42He will extend his power over
many countries; Egypt will not escape.
43He will gain control of the treasures
of gold and silver and all the riches of
Egypt,[e] with the Libyans[f] and Cushites[b]
in submission. 44But reports from the
east and the north will alarm him, and he
will set out in a great rage to destroy and
annihilate many. 45He will pitch his royal
tents between the seas at[c] the beautiful
holy mountain. Yet he will come to his
end, and no one will help him.

The End Times

12 “At that time Michael,[g] the great
prince who protects your people,
will arise. There will be a time of distress[h] such as has not happened from the
beginning of nations until then. But at
that time your people—everyone whose

11:31 [q] Da 8:11-13; 9:27; Mt 24:15*; Mk 13:14*
11:32 [r] Mic 5:7-9
11:33 [s] Mal 2:7 [t] Mt 24:9; Jn 16:2; Heb 11:32-38
11:34 [u] Mt 7:15; Ro 16:18
11:35 [v] Ps 78:38; Da 12:10; Zec 13:9; Jn 15:2
11:36 [w] Rev 13:5-6 [x] Dt 10:17; Isa 14:13-14; Da 7:25; 8:11-12, 25; 2Th 2:4 [y] Isa 10:25; 26:20
11:40 [z] Isa 21:1 [a] Isa 5:28 [b] Eze 38:4
11:41 [c] Isa 11:14 [d] Jer 48:47
11:43 [e] Eze 30:4 [f] 2Ch 12:3; Na 3:9
12:1 [g] Da 10:13 [h] Da 9:12; Mt 24:21; Mk 13:19; Rev 16:18

Da 11:36-45 ❖ Why does God work out his plans for history and redemption through wars and turmoil? How can we find God in the midst of the chaos?

Da 12:1-3 ❖ How does Daniel's vision of the future resurrection shape our understanding of the importance of how we live today?

[a] *39* Or *land for a reward* [b] *43* That is, people from the upper Nile region [c] *45* Or *the sea and*

11:32–35 The people of God were split into two parties: those who supported Antiochus and those who did not. Jason had earlier been removed from the high priesthood and replaced by a person named Menelaus, who was not even a member of the right family to be a priest. Jason, the deposed high priest, heard a rumor that Antiochus had been killed, so he moved against Menelaus. However, Antiochus was far from dead. Upon his return, he had many massacred and sold as slaves.

11:36–45 Who is in mind in this passage? It is conceivable that Daniel thought he was still describing the climactic king of the north, but the divine intention may have been much broader. Biblical prophecy was often presented as one event, but as we witness its fulfillment, we see that it was really more complex than that.

11:36–39 The pride of this king will be enormous. He will exalt himself not only above every other human being but above the gods themselves.

11:40–45 At this stage of biblical revelation, we are getting some of the earliest glimpses of final things. The NT will provide much more information on the final judgment.

We should be extremely cautious in our treatment of these truths. All that can be said is that these six verses look forward to a violent end to history.

12:1–3 The wicked king at the end of Daniel represents and anticipates the horror of the antichrist. Here we deal with the definitive end of Antiochus's persecution of God's people as well as their final struggle.

We must not develop a whole doctrine of the afterlife from one verse (v. 2), but we can confidently affirm that it celebrates the vindication for

JERUSALEM DURING THE TIME OF THE PROPHETS

C. 750–586 BC

Refugees arrived in Jerusalem about the time of the fall of the northern kingdom (722 BC). Settlement spread to the western hill, and a new wall was added for protection. King Hezekiah's engineers carved an underground aqueduct out of solid rock to bring an ample water supply inside the city walls, enabling Jerusalem to survive the siege of Sennacherib in 701.

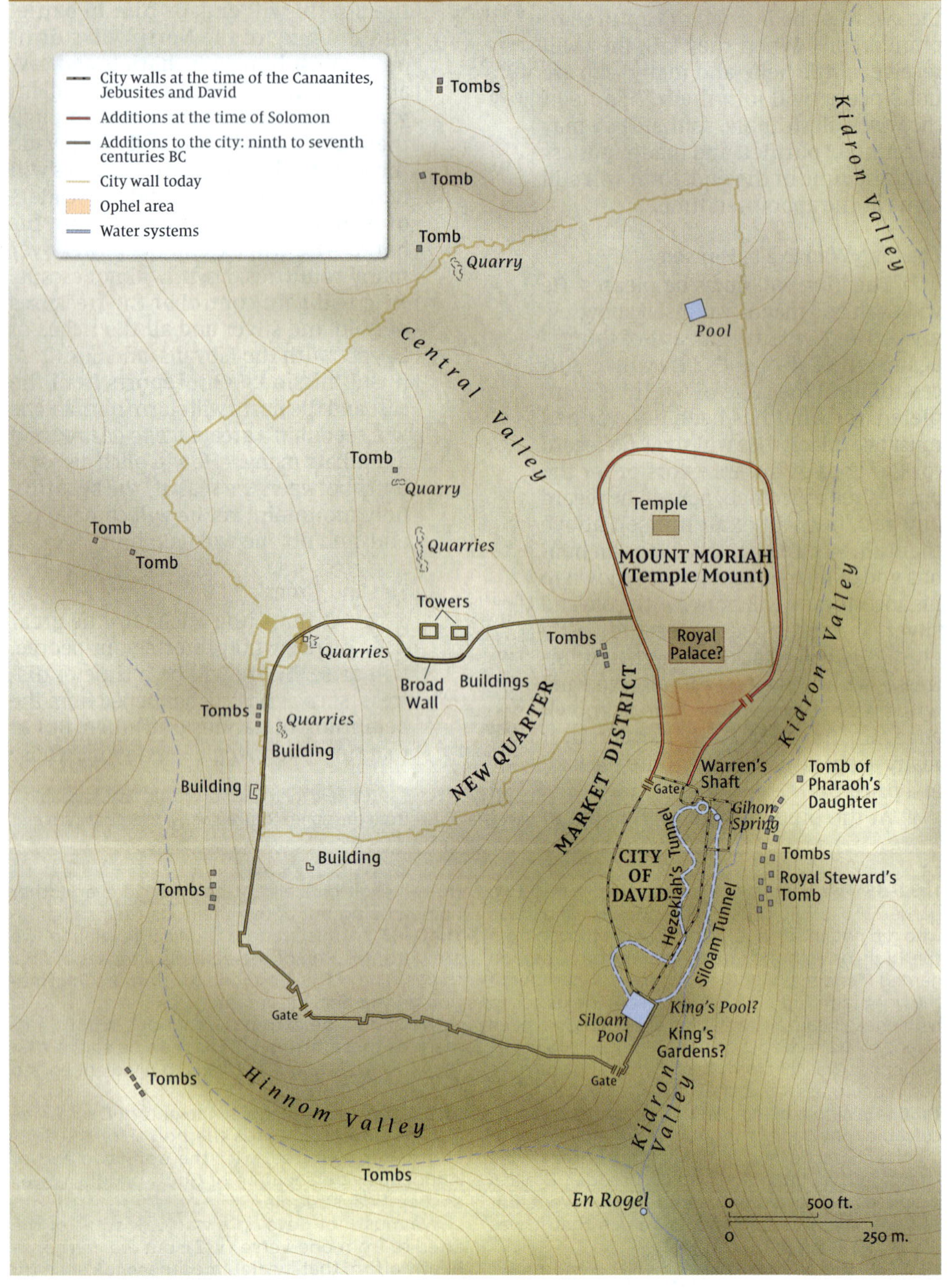

name is found written in the book[i]—will
be delivered.[j] 2Multitudes who sleep in
the dust of the earth will awake: some
to everlasting life, others to shame and
everlasting contempt.[k] 3Those who are
wise[a][l] will shine[m] like the brightness of
the heavens, and those who lead many to
righteousness, like the stars for ever and
ever.[n] 4But you, Daniel, roll up and seal[o]
the words of the scroll until the time of
the end.[p] Many will go here and there to
increase knowledge."

5Then I, Daniel, looked, and there before
me stood two others, one on this bank of
the river and one on the opposite bank.[q]
6One of them said to the man clothed in
linen,[r] who was above the waters of the
river, "How long will it be before these
astonishing things are fulfilled?"[s]
7The man clothed in linen, who was
above the waters of the river, lifted his
right hand and his left hand toward
heaven, and I heard him swear by him
who lives forever,[t] saying, "It will be for
a time, times and half a time.[b][u] When
the power of the holy people[v] has been
finally broken, all these things will be
completed.[w]"
8I heard, but I did not understand. So
I asked, "My lord, what will the outcome
of all this be?"
9He replied, "Go your way, Daniel, because the words are rolled up and sealed
until the time of the end.[x] 10Many will
be purified, made spotless and refined,[y]
but the wicked will continue to be wicked.[z] None of the wicked will understand,
but those who are wise will understand.[a]
11"From the time that the daily sacrifice is abolished and the abomination
that causes desolation[b] is set up, there
will be 1,290 days. 12Blessed is the one
who waits[c] for and reaches the end of
the 1,335 days.[d]
13"As for you, go your way till the end.
You will rest,[e] and then at the end of the
days you will rise to receive your allotted
inheritance.[f]"

12:1 [i] Ex 32:32; Ps 56:8 [j] Jer 30:7
12:2 [k] Isa 26:19; Mt 25:46; Jn 5:28-29
12:3 [l] Da 11:33 [m] Mt 13:43; Jn 5:35 [n] 1Co 15:42
12:4 [o] Isa 8:16 [p] ver 9,13; Rev 22:10
12:5 [q] Da 10:4
12:6 [r] Eze 9:2 [s] Da 8:13
12:7 [t] Rev 10:5-6 [u] Da 7:25 [v] Da 8:24 [w] Lk 21:24; Rev 10:7
12:9 [x] ver 4
12:10 [y] Da 11:35 [z] Isa 32:7; Rev 22:11 [a] Hos 14:9
12:11 [b] Da 8:11; 9:27; Mt 24:15*; Mk 13:14*
12:12 [c] Isa 30:18 [d] Da 8:14
12:13 [e] Isa 57:2 [f] Ps 16:5; Rev 14:13

[a] 3 Or *who impart wisdom* [b] 7 Or *a year, two years and half a year*

God's people that will come as the righteous are rewarded and the wicked are punished.

12:4 The best understanding of the "many will go here and there to increase knowledge" is a negative one (cf. Am 8:12): People will desperately try to find knowledge but fail in their attempt.

12:5–6 Daniel again finds himself in the position of overhearing a conversation between celestial beings. One of the angels on the bank addresses a climactic question to the other one.

12:7 Before answering, the hovering figure lifts both hands toward heaven and swears "by him who lives forever." The gesture suggests a solemn atmosphere around what is to follow. This figure then delivers a puzzling answer.

12:8–9 Daniel wants more information. The reply comes, not harshly but clearly, that now is not the time.

12:10 Nonetheless, the being does expand his earlier comments on the period to follow. We are likely to take them as words that describe the period from Daniel's time to the end.

12:11–13 The puzzling concepts continue in these verses. Two more time periods are specified. God alone knows—and that seems to be the point. "Leave it to God," the angel says to Daniel, and through him he speaks to us. This is a fitting conclusion for Daniel and for the book: We may suffer now, but God has given us a glimpse of the coming glory.

✣ **11:2—12:13** God is no less in control today than he was in antiquity. To hear some modern Christian leaders talk, we might not believe this is the case. With a note of panic in their voice, they tell us that things have gotten out of control in the seat of our government. If we do not act immediately (often by sending in a check!), our whole society will be turned over to the devil.

There is no need to give in to panic based around human rhetoric, no matter which political or denominational party it comes from. But Christians also must resist the temptation to disengage and refuse to stand for Christ in our modern world. No matter what the political or cultural climate, God expects us to work for righteousness' sake. So we move ahead in faith, standing for what's right, firm in the conviction that God *is* in control and that his plans will be enacted.

Hosea

Author: Probably Hosea

Audience: Primarily the northern kingdom of Israel

Date: Probably after the fall of the northern capital, Samaria (722–721 BC)

Theme: Hosea proclaims and demonstrates how a faithful God contends with his unfaithful people.

Reading Hosea

The first three chapters of Hosea describe his family life—especially the adultery of his wife, which was a symbol of the adultery of God's people. God's command to Hosea to continue loving his wife symbolized God's continuing love for his people and his intense longing to have them return. The rest of the book contains various messages of Hosea on the sins of the children of Israel and God's offer for them to return.

PERSPECTIVE

Prophecy has an important role to play today. It prepares us to face an unjust world.

How so? By telling us beforehand what God will do if we persist in our evil ways. Our standard way of dealing with evil and injustice is to attempt explanations after the fact. We try to explain how a good God, all-powerful in every way, can possibly allow the existence of evil. This problem is called "theodicy." It is one of the most difficult points in all of Christian theology. Biblical prophecy, by contrast, explains what God will do before he does it. When a prophetic explanation is used, God's action is seen as a response to our actions. Responsibility for evil and injustice is focused on our less-than-adequate actions rather than God's. Evil, at least in historical time, is seen as a problem of human nature, not God's nature.

Of course, this explanation does not solve all the problems. Theodicy persists when we ask the metaphysical question: Where did evil come from in the first place? But to the extent that we see Christianity as a life to be lived in response to God's gracious activity toward us, the prophetic approach to injustice is indispensable. Good, balanced Christian theology demands both theodicy and prophecy.

Unfortunately, prophecy, for reasons mentioned above, has fallen on hard times. Too often seen as the work of radicals and kooks, the scientific approach has chipped away at the prophets' pedestal, suggesting that if it cannot be measured after the fact, we have no right to pronounce its truth. Although science does not deliberately avoid

	1200 BC	1100	1000	900	800	700	600	500	400
Division of the kingdom (930 BC)									
Ministries of Elijah and Elisha in Israel (c. 875–797 BC)									
Amos's ministry in Israel (c. 760–750 BC)									
Hosea's ministry in Israel (c. 753–715 BC)									
Ministries of Micah and Isaiah in Judah (c. 740–681 BC)									
Exile of Israel (722 BC)									
Book of Hosea written (c. 715 BC)									
Fall of Jerusalem (586 BC)									

prediction, prediction must be based on observable facts—God's nature cannot be broken down in a test tube.

Furthermore, prophecy sounds so "preachy." The prophet, then and now, sounds exactly like our moralizing parents, warning us of the dire consequences of our too-hasty, instinct-motivated actions. Make no mistake, prophecy does have an indispensable moral element to it. If we do evil, if we support injustice, God will punish us. That is a message our feel-good culture seems to think we can best do without.

So what are we to do? We must learn from these great prophets. Listen to and repeat God's prophetic word—and do it in the most persuasive way we can. Hosea, Amos, and Micah all used powerful rhetorical techniques, self-disclosure, and hope to make sure their listeners had the best chance of comprehending the messages God sent in a way that changed behavior.

The rhetorical techniques ranged from puns to poetry, from repetition to parallel structure, from quips to quotes. Who among us can forget the memorable Micah 6:8: "He has shown you, O mortal, what is good. And what does the LORD require of you? To act justly and to love mercy and to walk humbly with your God." The rhythm and common sense of this wisdom make it unforgettable.

Perhaps we can reclaim the prophetic voice by expressing it in the language of today. It must be both challenging and winsome. It must be couched in language that does not minimize the importance of the words but connects it to the needs of the day.

We live in a day that requires the prophetic voice. We must not shirk our duty to deliver it. We can begin by reading these three great prophetic models in Hosea, Amos, and Micah. Then, one would hope, we can hear and repeat the word of the Lord clearly given.

Key Verses

"In that day," declares the LORD, "you will call me 'my husband'; you will no longer call me 'my master' . . . I will betroth you to me forever; I will betroth you in righteousness and justice, in love and compassion. I will betroth you in faithfulness, and you will acknowledge the LORD."

—Hosea 2:16, 19-20

TAKING THE NEXT STEPS

Hosea, the only prophet to come from the northern kingdom of Israel, ministered during the final years of that kingdom until Samaria was destroyed by the Assyrians (see 2Ki 14:23–29; 15:8–31; 17:1–23; Hos 1:1). He was appalled at the idolatry of God's people, an idolatry that he called adultery. He knew that because of their sin, God would soon respond in judgment, using the Assyrians as his agents. But Hosea went on to assure the Israelites that God's love for them would never die, and that God would rescue them if they returned to him.

Several important messages come through when we read the book of Hosea. (1) Just as God compares his relationship with the Israelites to a marriage, so we as Christians are in a marriage relationship with Christ, our bridegroom (see Eph 5:22–33). (2) Any time we flirt with the devil, we are just as guilty as the Israelites of practicing spiritual adultery. (3) As any husband becomes justifiably jealous and angry at the infidelity of his wife, so God will not stand for flirtation with the devil. (4) The basic sin that we commit is a failure to acknowledge God as Lord of all. (5) God loves us dearly, and as long as the return of Christ is delayed, he invites us to return to him.

WHAT TO LOOK FOR IN HOSEA

- Hosea's relationship with his adulterous wife (chs. 1; 3)
- The basic sins of the children of Israel (chs. 4; 12)
- God's threatened punishment (chs. 9–10)
- God's continual love for his children (chs. 11; 14)

1 The word of the LORD that came to
Hosea son of Beeri during the reigns
of Uzziah, Jotham, Ahaz and Hezekiah,
kings of Judah,[a] and during the reign
of Jeroboam[b] son of Jehoash[a] king of
Israel:[c]

Hosea's Wife and Children

2When the LORD began to speak
through Hosea, the LORD said to him,
"Go, marry a promiscuous[d] woman and
have children with her, for like an adulterous wife this land is guilty of unfaithfulness[e] to the LORD." 3So he married
Gomer daughter of Diblaim, and she
conceived and bore him a son.
4Then the LORD said to Hosea, "Call
him Jezreel,[f] because I will soon punish
the house of Jehu for the massacre at Jezreel, and I will put an end to the kingdom
of Israel. 5In that day I will break Israel's
bow in the Valley of Jezreel.[g]"
6Gomer[h] conceived again and gave
birth to a daughter. Then the LORD said
to Hosea, "Call her Lo-Ruhamah (which
means "not loved"), for I will no longer
show love to Israel,[i] that I should at all
forgive them. 7Yet I will show love to
Judah; and I will save them — not by
bow,[j] sword or battle, or by horses and
horsemen, but I, the LORD their God,[k]
will save them."
8After she had weaned Lo-Ruhamah,
Gomer had another son. 9Then the LORD
said, "Call him Lo-Ammi (which means
"not my people"), for you are not my people, and I am not your God.[b]
10"Yet the Israelites will be like the

1:1 [a] Isa 1:1; Mic 1:1 [b] 2Ki 13:13 [c] Am 1:1
1:2 [d] Jer 3:1; Hos 2:2,5; 3:1 [e] Dt 31:16; Jer 3:14; Eze 23:3-21; Hos 5:3
1:4 [f] 2Ki 10:1-14; Hos 2:22
1:5 [g] 2Ki 15:29
1:6 [h] ver 3 [i] Hos 2:4
1:7 [j] Ps 44:6 [k] Zec 4:6

Hos 1:2 ❖ How are God's children often like an adulterous spouse? When we are unfaithful to God, what are his promises to us if we repent (1 Jn 1:9)?

[a] 1 Hebrew *Joash*, a variant of *Jehoash* [b] 9 Or *your I AM*

1:1–3 These events date to the prosperous days of King Jeroboam II of Israel.

God instructed Hosea to marry an "adulterous wife" (v. 2). In accepting God's plan for his life, Hosea set himself up to feel some of the bitterness of God's pain, as well as the depth of his love for his unfaithful and undeserving people.

1:4–9 If Gomer represents the nation, the children represent the individual Israelites (2:2, 4).

1:4–5 The first child was named Jezreel to remind Hosea's audience of what had happened in the Valley of Jezreel, where King Jehu poured out the blood of innocent lives (2Ki 9–10). Violence at the beginning of Jehu's reign will parallel violence that will end Jehu's dynasty.

1:6–7 The second child born was a girl named "Lo-Ruhamah." This child's name reveals that God will end his tender feelings of deep affection that were foundational to his covenant relationship with his people. God's compassionate mercy will no longer be extended to them.

1:8–9 God gives the third child the name "Lo-Ammi . . . not my people." Now it is official; the covenant connection is broken.

1:10—2:1 This section ends by reversing the meaning of the children's names. At one moment, God rejects his people. In the next, he accepts them back. The covenant promises two possible destinies for Israel (curses and blessings); their unfaithfulness will result in their judgment, but

sand on the seashore, which cannot be
measured or counted.[l] In the place where
it was said to them, 'You are not my people,' they will be called 'children of the
living God.'[m] 11 The people of Judah and
the people of Israel will come together;[n]
they will appoint one leader[o] and will
come up out of the land,[p] for great will
be the day of Jezreel.[a]

2 [b] "Say of your brothers, 'My people,'
and of your sisters, 'My loved one.'[q]

Israel Punished and Restored

2 "Rebuke your mother,[r] rebuke her,
for she is not my wife,
and I am not her husband.
Let her remove the adulterous[s] look
from her face
and the unfaithfulness from
between her breasts.
3 Otherwise I will strip her naked
and make her as bare as on the
day she was born;[t]
I will make her like a desert,[u]
turn her into a parched land,
and slay her with thirst.
4 I will not show my love to her
children,[v]
because they are the children of
adultery.
5 Their mother has been unfaithful
and has conceived them in
disgrace.
She said, 'I will go after my lovers,[w]
who give me my food and my
water,
my wool and my linen, my olive
oil and my drink.'[x]
6 Therefore I will block her path with
thornbushes;
I will wall her in so that she
cannot find her way.[y]
7 She will chase after her lovers but
not catch them;
she will look for them but not find
them.[z]
Then she will say,
'I will go back to my husband as at
first,[a]
for then I was better off[b] than
now.'
8 She has not acknowledged[c] that I
was the one
who gave her the grain, the new
wine and oil,
who lavished on her the silver and
gold —
which they used for Baal.[d]

9 "Therefore I will take away my grain[e]
when it ripens,
and my new wine[f] when it is
ready.
I will take back my wool and my
linen,
intended to cover her naked body.
10 So now I will expose her lewdness
before the eyes of her lovers;
no one will take her out of my
hands.[g]
11 I will stop[h] all her celebrations:
her yearly festivals, her New
Moons,
her Sabbath days — all her
appointed festivals.[i]
12 I will ruin her vines[j] and her fig
trees,
which she said were her pay from
her lovers;

1:10 [l] Ge 22:17; Jer 33:22 [m] ver 9; Ro 9:26* 1:11 [n] Isa 11:12, 13 [o] Jer 23:5-8 [p] Eze 37:15-28 2:1 [q] ver 23 2:2 [r] ver 5; Isa 50:1; Hos 1:2 [s] Eze 23:45 2:3 [t] Eze 16:4,22 [u] Isa 32:13-14 2:4 [v] Eze 8:18 2:5 [w] Jer 3:6 [x] Jer 44:17-18 2:6 [y] Job 3:23; 19:8; La 3:9 2:7 [z] Hos 5:13 [a] Jer 2:2; 3:1 [b] Eze 16:8 2:8 [c] Isa 1:3 [d] Eze 16:15-19; Hos 8:4 2:9 [e] Hos 8:7 [f] Hos 9:2 2:10 [g] Eze 16:37 2:11 [h] Jer 7:34 [i] Isa 1:14; Jer 16:9; Hos 3:4; Am 8:10 2:12 [j] Isa 7:23; Jer 8:13

[a] *11* In Hebrew texts 1:10,11 is numbered 2:1,2.
[b] In Hebrew texts 2:1-23 is numbered 2:3-25.

God will bless his faithful people after a period of judgment.

APPLICATION ✚ 1:1—2:1 Just as he was displeased with Gomer and the rebellious people of Israel, God is not pleased with believers today who do not maintain a loyal commitment to him. He still looks at sin as prostitution—a serious and disgusting breach of a love relationship.

However, the theology of Hos 1 is not limited to the negative implications of sin in a person's life. Because of God's grace, people can be assured that his eternal plans and promises will be accomplished.

2:2–4 The Lord instructs the children to "rebuke" their mother, but God does the talking. The reference to breasts suggests the sexual nature of the nation's unfaithfulness. God is persuading Israel to remove the pagan culture of Canaan and its sexual fertility cult from the land.

God threatens to dry up the land. Since Baal was the god of rain and fertility, this would be a sign of Baal's powerlessness before the one true God and the consequences of the people's unfaithfulness.

2:5 Like a bold, strutting prostitute hunting down customers, the people of Israel pursued the Baal fertility religion.

2:6–8 God plans to win back his unfaithful people. He will symbolically hedge in his wife (v. 6); this is for her own good and for the good of their relationship (cf. 3:3). It will protect her from straying and returning to love other gods. God will discredit Baal's power (v. 7).

2:9–13 God will transform the people's thinking by not allowing the land to be fertile. God will strip her naked by stripping the land of any agricultural produce.

I will make them a thicket,[k]
and wild animals will devour them.[l]
13 I will punish her for the days
she burned incense to the Baals;[m]
she decked herself with rings and jewelry,[n]
and went after her lovers,[o]
but me she forgot,[p]"
declares the LORD.

14 "Therefore I am now going to allure her;
I will lead her into the wilderness
and speak tenderly to her.
15 There I will give her back her vineyards,
and will make the Valley of Achor[a][q] a door of hope.
There she will respond[b][r] as in the days of her youth,[s]
as in the day she came up out of Egypt.[t]

16 "In that day," declares the LORD,
"you will call me 'my husband';
you will no longer call me 'my master.[c]'
17 I will remove the names of the Baals from her lips;[u]
no longer will their names be invoked.[v]
18 In that day I will make a covenant for them
with the beasts of the field, the birds in the sky
and the creatures that move along the ground.[w]
Bow and sword and battle
I will abolish[x] from the land,
so that all may lie down in safety.[y]
19 I will betroth[z] you to me forever;
I will betroth you in[d] righteousness and justice,[a]
in[d] love and compassion.
20 I will betroth you in[d] faithfulness,
and you will acknowledge[b] the LORD.

21 "In that day I will respond,"
declares the LORD—
"I will respond[c] to the skies,
and they will respond to the earth;
22 and the earth will respond to the grain,
the new wine and the olive oil,[d]
and they will respond to Jezreel.[e]
23 I will plant[e] her for myself in the land;
I will show my love to the one I called 'Not my loved one.[f]'
I will say to those called 'Not my people,[g]' 'You are my people';[g]
and they will say, 'You are my God.[h]'"

2:12 [k] Isa 5:6 [l] Hos 13:8 2:13 [m] Hos 11:2 [n] Eze 16:17 [o] Hos 4:13 [p] Hos 4:6; 8:14; 13:6 2:15 [q] Jos 7:24, 26 [r] Ex 15:1-18 [s] Jer 2:2 [t] Hos 12:9 2:17 [u] Ex 23:13; Ps 16:4 [v] Jos 23:7 2:18 [w] Job 5:22 [x] Isa 2:4 [y] Jer 23:6; Eze 34:25 2:19 [z] Isa 62:4 [a] Isa 1:27 2:20 [b] Jer 31:34; Hos 6:6; 13:4 2:21 [c] Isa 55:10; Zec 8:12 2:22 [d] Jer 31:12; Joel 2:19 2:23 [e] Jer 31:27 [f] Hos 1:6 [g] Hos 1:10 [h] Ro 9:25*; 1Pe 2:10

[a] 15 *Achor* means *trouble.* [b] 15 Or *sing* [c] 16 Hebrew *baal* [d] 19,20 Or *with* [e] 22 *Jezreel* means *God plants.* [f] 23 Hebrew *Lo-Ruhamah* (see 1:6) [g] 23 Hebrew *Lo-Ammi* (see 1:9)

Hos 2:23 ❖ How does this verse instruct us as to the depth of God's compassion for his wayward people?

2:14–15 Hosea uses sexual terminology, stating that God will "allure" (v. 14) Israel back to himself. He will speak the tender love language that the people understand. The reversal of God's attitude and Israel's rejoicing indicate that this meeting in the desert will renew the covenant love between God and Israel.

2:16–23 The second half of this oracle is structured around three "in that day" promises, which refer to events at some unknown time in the future (vv. 16, 18, 21).

2:16–17 This period will begin with the reaffirmation of Israel's covenant commitment. God will be "my husband," not "my master" (v. 16); the people will no longer confuse the difference between God and Baal.

2:18–20 The second thing God will do "in that day" will be to reestablish a covenant relationship with his people and with nature.

2:21–23 The final "in that day" promises describe the effects of this new relationship on life in this world. Once God's people know and love him (vv. 15, 20), he can respond to their love by restoring the natural bounty and beauty of the created universe. The sowing of God will not be limited to just planting crops; he will also "plant" (v. 23) his people in their promised land. God's beautiful plan for this world will be accomplished through his grace.

2:2–23 Like Hosea, we must challenge ourselves and those in our sphere of influence to evaluate what our trust is based on. Do we actually see God as the final source of all economic blessing (Dt 8:17–18)? Or is prosperity just the result of fortunately being at the right place at the right time, of smart farming procedures with the latest chemicals and fertilizers, of great investment advice, or of having the right genes to produce a high IQ?

A central theme of Hos 2 is that God is the only Source who can meet people's needs. Any attempt to replace his proper role is seen as a prostitution of loyalties.

Hosea's Reconciliation With His Wife

3 The LORD said to me, "Go, show your
love to your wife again, though she
is loved by another man and is an adulteress.[i] Love her as the LORD loves the
Israelites, though they turn to other gods
and love the sacred raisin cakes.[j]"
2So I bought her for fifteen shekels[a] of
silver and about a homer and a lethek[b]
of barley. 3Then I told her, "You are to
live with me many days; you must not
be a prostitute or be intimate with any
man, and I will behave the same way
toward you."
4For the Israelites will live many days
without king or prince,[k] without sacrifice[l] or sacred stones, without ephod
or household gods.[m] 5Afterward the Israelites will return and seek the LORD
their God and David their king.[n] They
will come trembling to the LORD and to
his blessings in the last days.[o]

3:1 [i] Hos 1:2 [j] 2Sa 6:19
3:4 [k] Hos 13:11 [l] Da 11:31; Hos 2:11 [m] Jdg 17:5-6; Zec 10:2
3:5 [n] Eze 34:23-24 [o] Jer 50:4-5

Hos 3:2–3 ❖ How does Hosea's experience foreshadow the work of Christ, who buys back sinners to himself (see 1Co 6:20)? What does it mean for us to know that Christ "paid" for us with his blood?

The Charge Against Israel

4 Hear the word of the LORD, you
Israelites,

[a] 2 That is, about 6 ounces or about 170 grams
[b] 2 A homer and a lethek possibly weighed about 430 pounds or about 195 kilograms.

3:1–2 Hosea's love is demonstrated by his action of buying his wife. Some compare the price to the price of a slave, but we have no idea what a female slave cost in the time of Hosea. It is likely better to suppose that Hosea is simply paying off Gomer's debts as he takes her back into his home.
3:3–5 Just as Hosea cut Gomer off from the men who led her into adultery, so God will remove the factors that have caused Israel to destroy their relationship with him. Then, "in the last days" (v. 5), the covenant relationship between God and Israel will be restored. Both Hosea and God will love their wives and give them the blessings of their renewed covenant.

✤ **3:1–5** No one should ever question the availability of God's love. The question, rather, is this: Will people respond to God's love? Scripture assures us that God loves everyone in the whole world and does not want any to perish (2Pe 3:9). Paul also reassures his readers in the church at Rome that nothing can separate them from God's love (Ro 8:38–39).

4:1–3 This breakdown of covenant relationship results in the cursing of Israel's land. Hosea does not say how this will happen; what is important is that morality influences the economic and political

PEOPLE TO KNOW // HOSEA

HOSEA 3:1–5: Hosea proclaimed God's message with both his words and his life—in a heartbreaking way. God told Hosea to marry a promiscuous woman named Gomer. Then God told Hosea to give shocking names to their children. Their daughter's name meant "not loved" and their son's name meant "not my people."

God told Hosea to do all this to illustrate that Israel was acting like an unfaithful wife to God. God was faithful to his people, but they were not following him with their whole hearts; they were worshiping idols. So God wanted his people to know that he would no longer show love to them; they were no longer his people.

When Gomer was unfaithful to Hosea and left him, God told Hosea to do the unthinkable: Go pay the price to bring her back home (Hos 3:2–3). In this, too, Hosea mirrored God, paying a price to win back his unfaithful bride.

Hosea's prophecy of judgment ends with a promise of repentance and blessing (Hos 11:4). In loving conviction, God declares, "all my compassion is aroused. I will not carry out my fierce anger" (Hos 11:8–9).

Hosea's own life became a picture of God's pain for his wayward people and of God's enduring love and forgiveness for those he has chosen.

APPLICATION ✤ We are often unfaithful to God, and this grieves him. Like an unfaithful spouse, we allow other things to take our attention and commitment away from our first love instead of being faithful to him. Hosea assures us, however, that with God there is forgiveness. God does not punish us as our sins deserve, but instead welcomes us as his beloved children. How is this possible? Like Hosea paying the price to bring Gomer back, God paid the price for our sins through the sacrifice of Jesus Christ on the cross. Through Christ, God makes us his beloved children whom he will never leave nor forsake.

because the LORD has a charge to bring
against you who live in the land:
"There is no faithfulness, no love,
no acknowledgment[p] of God in the land.
2 There is only cursing,[a] lying[q] and murder,[r]
stealing[s] and adultery;
they break all bounds,
and bloodshed follows bloodshed.
3 Because of this the land dries up,[t]
and all who live in it waste away;[u]
the beasts of the field, the birds in the sky
and the fish in the sea are swept away.[v]

4 "But let no one bring a charge,
let no one accuse another,
for your people are like those
who bring charges against a priest.[w]
5 You stumble[x] day and night,
and the prophets stumble with you.
So I will destroy your mother[y] —
6 my people are destroyed from lack of knowledge.[z]

"Because you have rejected knowledge,
I also reject you as my priests;
because you have ignored the law[a] of your God,
I also will ignore your children.
7 The more priests there were,
the more they sinned against me;
they exchanged their glorious God[b][b] for something disgraceful.[c]
8 They feed on the sins of my people
and relish their wickedness.[d]
9 And it will be: Like people, like priests.[e]

4:1 [p] Jer 7:28
4:2 [q] Hos 7:3; 10:4 [r] Hos 6:9 [s] Hos 7:1
4:3 [t] Jer 4:28 [u] Isa 33:9 [v] Jer 4:25; Zep 1:3
4:4 [w] Dt 17:12; Eze 3:26
4:5 [x] Eze 14:7 [y] Hos 2:2
4:6 [z] Hos 2:13; Mal 2:7-8 [a] Hos 8:1,12
4:7 [b] Hab 2:16 [c] Hos 10:1,6; 13:6
4:8 [d] Isa 56:11; Mic 3:11
4:9 [e] Isa 24:2

[f] Jer 5:31; Hos 8:13; 9:9,15
4:10 [g] Lev 26:26; Mic 6:14 [h] Hos 7:14; 9:17
4:11 [i] Hos 5:4 [j] Pr 20:1
4:12 [k] Jer 2:27 [l] Hab 2:19 [m] Isa 44:20
4:13 [n] Isa 1:29 [o] Jer 3:6; Hos 11:2 [p] Jer 2:20; Am 7:17 [q] Hos 2:13
4:14 [r] ver 11

Hos 4:10–13 ❖ Why does a life of deserting God always lead to emptiness (see Jn 10:10)? How have people experienced this truth throughout history?

I will punish both of them for their ways
and repay them for their deeds.[f]

10 "They will eat but not have enough;[g]
they will engage in prostitution but not flourish,
because they have deserted[h] the LORD
to give themselves 11 to prostitution;[i]
old wine and new wine
take away their understanding.[j]
12 My people consult a wooden idol,[k]
and a diviner's rod speaks to them.[l]
A spirit of prostitution leads them astray;[m]
they are unfaithful to their God.
13 They sacrifice on the mountaintops
and burn offerings on the hills,
under oak,[n] poplar and terebinth,
where the shade is pleasant.[o]
Therefore your daughters turn to prostitution[p]
and your daughters-in-law to adultery.[q]

14 "I will not punish your daughters
when they turn to prostitution,
nor your daughters-in-law
when they commit adultery,
because the men themselves consort with harlots[r]

[a] *2* That is, to pronounce a curse on [b] *7* Syriac (see also an ancient Hebrew scribal tradition); Masoretic Text *me; / I will exchange their glory*

status of the nation. God has inserted a reciprocal relationship between obeying God and blessing the land into the fabric of covenantal theology. Hosea warns that all who live on the land will feel the consequences of their sins.

4:4–10 In this passage the prophet is encouraging the people to listen to what God has to say and not to dispute his charges. The prophets (v. 5) and even the mothers and children of the priests will suffer under God's punishment. This comes about because the priests have destroyed the people by failing to properly teach God's revelation in the Torah. The priests revel in their evil lifestyle (v. 8). They have even embraced the drinking and prostitution going on at these temples.

4:11–14 What is going on at the temples is astonishing: prostitution, drunkenness, idol worship, divination, and all the perversions that go with them. These practices lead people astray into unfaithful acts against God. Without proper teaching from Israel's priests, the population of Israel is filled with the "spirit of prostitution" (v. 12) and is blindly led away into a sensuous and selfish worldview that promotes debauchery rather than godliness.

God decides not to cast the primary blame on the participants in this debauchery (v. 14). Instead, God will punish the men who demand this perverse sexual activity.

and sacrifice with shrine
prostitutes —
a people without understanding
will come to ruin!

15 "Though you, Israel, commit
adultery,
do not let Judah become guilty.

"Do not go to Gilgal;[s]
do not go up to Beth Aven.[a]
And do not swear, 'As surely as the
LORD lives!'
16 The Israelites are stubborn,
like a stubborn heifer.
How then can the LORD pasture them
like lambs[t] in a meadow?
17 Ephraim is joined to idols;
leave him alone!
18 Even when their drinks are gone,
they continue their prostitution;
their rulers dearly love shameful
ways.
19 A whirlwind[u] will sweep them away,
and their sacrifices will bring
them shame.[v]

Judgment Against Israel

5 "Hear this, you priests!
Pay attention, you Israelites!
Listen, royal house!
This judgment is against you:
You have been a snare[w] at Mizpah,
a net spread out on Tabor.
2 The rebels are knee-deep in
slaughter.[x]
I will discipline all of them.[y]
3 I know all about Ephraim;
Israel is not hidden from me.
Ephraim, you have now turned to
prostitution;
Israel is corrupt.[z]

4:15 [s] Hos 9:15; 12:11; Am 4:4
4:16 [t] Isa 5:17; 7:25
4:19 [u] Hos 12:1; 13:15 [v] Isa 1:29
5:1 [w] Hos 6:9; 9:8
5:2 [x] Hos 4:2 [y] Hos 9:15
5:3 [z] Hos 6:10

Hos 5:5 ❖ Judah often followed in the sins of Israel, their neighbor to the north. How can we be especially careful about the people with whom we spend time and who influence us? Why is this so important?

4 "Their deeds do not permit them
to return to their God.
A spirit of prostitution[a] is in their
heart;
they do not acknowledge[b] the
LORD.
5 Israel's arrogance testifies[c] against
them;
the Israelites, even Ephraim,
stumble in their sin;
Judah also stumbles with them.
6 When they go with their flocks and
herds
to seek the LORD,[d]
they will not find him;
he has withdrawn[e] himself from
them.
7 They are unfaithful[f] to the LORD;
they give birth to illegitimate[g]
children.
When they celebrate their New
Moon feasts,
he will devour[b][h] their fields.

8 "Sound the trumpet in Gibeah,[i]
the horn in Ramah.[j]
Raise the battle cry in Beth Aven[a];[k]
lead on, Benjamin.
9 Ephraim will be laid waste
on the day of reckoning.[l]

5:4 [a] Hos 4:11 [b] Hos 4:6
5:5 [c] Hos 7:10
5:6 [d] Mic 6:6-7 [e] Pr 1:28; Isa 1:15; Eze 8:6
5:7 [f] Hos 6:7 [g] Hos 2:4 [h] Hos 2:11-12
5:8 [i] Hos 9:9; 10:9 [j] Isa 10:29 [k] Hos 4:15
5:9 [l] Isa 37:3; Hos 9:11-17

[a] *15,8* Beth Aven means *house of wickedness* (a derogatory name for Bethel, which means *house of God*). [b] *7* Or *Now their New Moon feasts / will devour them and*

4:15-16 God warns the Israelites not to influence the people of Judah with this unfaithful behavior. The people think God and Baal are the same divine being. Because of this confusion, it is almost impossible for the stubborn people of Israel to change (v. 16).
4:17-19 When people are this hardened, all one can do is let them wallow in their shameful ways. They will wake up soon and realize the shamefulness of what they are doing. They have given themselves over to such a depraved way of thinking that there is not much Hosea or God can do.

✤ **4:1-19** The blame for Israel's spiritual decline is put at the feet of its spiritual leaders. It is always dangerous to oversimplify the complexities of life, but the failure of spiritual leadership is one of the top reasons why people in the church fail to acknowledge God and be faithful and true to him.

5:1-7 The verdict in v. 1 ("judgment") comes for several reasons. First, hunting images suggest an atmosphere of deception and violence as people try to control the political scene. Next, the priests have encouraged religious prostitution (v. 3). A third problem is the nation's "arrogance" (v. 5). Finally, God has abandoned the people (v. 6).
5:8-11 Trumpet blasts bring a terrorizing announcement of impending war. Israel's warning is interrupted by Judah's condemnation because she is "like those who move boundary stones" (v. 10a). God will pour out his wrath on Judah for their sins and will destroy their land like a flood.

Among the tribes of Israel
I proclaim what is certain.[m]
10 Judah's leaders are like those
who move boundary stones.[n]
I will pour out my wrath[o] on them
like a flood of water.
11 Ephraim is oppressed,
trampled in judgment,
intent on pursuing idols.[a][p]
12 I am like a moth[q] to Ephraim,
like rot to the people of Judah.

13 "When Ephraim saw his sickness,
and Judah his sores,
then Ephraim turned to Assyria,[r]
and sent to the great king for help.[s]
But he is not able to cure[t] you,
not able to heal your sores.[u]
14 For I will be like a lion[v] to Ephraim,
like a great lion to Judah.
I will tear them to pieces and go away;
I will carry them off, with no one to rescue them.[w]
15 Then I will return to my lair
until they have borne their guilt
and seek my face[x] —
in their misery[y]
they will earnestly seek me.[z]"

Israel Unrepentant

6 "Come, let us return to the LORD.
He has torn us to pieces[a]
but he will heal us;
he has injured us
but he will bind up our wounds.[b]
2 After two days he will revive us;[c]
on the third day he will restore us,
that we may live in his presence.
3 Let us acknowledge the LORD;
let us press on to acknowledge him.
As surely as the sun rises,
he will appear;
he will come to us like the winter rains,[d]
like the spring rains that water the earth.[e]"

4 "What can I do with you, Ephraim?[f]
What can I do with you, Judah?
Your love is like the morning mist,
like the early dew that disappears.[g]
5 Therefore I cut you in pieces with my prophets,
I killed you with the words of my mouth[h] —
then my judgments go forth like the sun.[b][i]
6 For I desire mercy, not sacrifice,[j]
and acknowledgment[k] of God
rather than burnt offerings.

5:9 [m] Isa 46:10; Zec 1:6
5:10 [n] Dt 19:14 [o] Eze 7:8
5:11 [p] Hos 9:16; Mic 6:16
5:12 [q] Isa 51:8
5:13 [r] Hos 7:11; 8:9 [s] Hos 10:6 [t] Hos 14:3 [u] Jer 30:12
5:14 [v] Am 3:4 [w] Mic 5:8
5:15 [x] Hos 3:5 [y] Jer 2:27 [z] Isa 64:9
6:1 [a] Hos 5:14 [b] Dt 32:39; Jer 30:17; Hos 14:4
6:2 [c] Ps 30:5
6:3 [d] Joel 2:23 [e] Ps 72:6
6:4 [f] Hos 11:8 [g] Hos 7:1; 13:3
6:5 [h] Jer 1:9-10; 23:29 [i] Heb 4:12
6:6 [j] Isa 1:11; Mt 9:13*; 12:7* [k] Hos 2:20

[a] *11* The meaning of the Hebrew for this word is uncertain. [b] *5* The meaning of the Hebrew for this line is uncertain.

Hos 6:4-6 ❖ How has our devotion to God at times been like "morning mist"? What can we do to nurture a more consistent discipleship?

5:12–13 God, Israel's loving covenant partner, will be like a destructive "moth" and a "rot" (v. 12) to these people. Israel and Judah will be like an injured soldier whose wounds are festering with infection.
5:14 The second image pictures God as a destructive lion.

5:1-14 We face all kinds of decisions, troubles, and trials in this world. When God is excluded from the solution process, he may actually choose to exacerbate the problem rather than heal the situation. In fact, what people sometimes interpret as an earthly problem among humans may actually be a divine fight in which God himself is working against us to reveal the error of our ways or to direct us down another path. The ultimate resolution to this kind of problem is to reject sin, seek God, and humbly plead for restoration.

5:15—6:3 The prophet hopes his audience will accept his intercessory confession as their own decision to seek God. Hosea is confident that God will respond quickly to the people's turning back to him (6:2) and promises that God will be faithful to his promises.
6:4–6 God's dissatisfaction with his people is based on the fleeting nature of their love for him (v. 4b). The people must have a living relationship with God in order to know him, love him, fear him, worship only him, serve him, and obey him (Dt 10:12). Going through the religious motions will not cut it with God.

5:15—6:6 Revival is not an optional course of action for a church. It needs to be a vital part of every church calendar and a prayer concern of every believer. Revival is about living for God and glorifying his name. It encourages people to be restored from a cold, deadened condition to a living state of joy and peace. Spiritual leaders in the church need to encourage people to return to God, to look to him for restoration, and to desire to live in his marvelous presence. If a spiritual leader rejects the path of revival, the church will die.

7 As at Adam,[a] they have broken the
covenant;[l]
they were unfaithful[m] to me there.
8 Gilead is a city of evildoers,
stained with footprints of blood.
9 As marauders lie in ambush for a
victim,
so do bands of priests;
they murder on the road to
Shechem,
carrying out their wicked
schemes.[n]
10 I have seen a horrible[o] thing in
Israel:
There Ephraim is given to
prostitution,
Israel is defiled.[p]

11 "Also for you, Judah,
a harvest[q] is appointed.

"Whenever I would restore the
fortunes of my people,

7

1 whenever I would heal Israel,
the sins of Ephraim are exposed
and the crimes of Samaria
revealed.[r]
They practice deceit,[s]
thieves break into houses,[t]
bandits rob in the streets;
2 but they do not realize
that I remember[u] all their evil
deeds.
Their sins engulf them;[v]
they are always before me.

3 "They delight the king with their
wickedness,
the princes with their lies.[w]
4 They are all adulterers,[x]
burning like an oven
whose fire the baker need not stir
from the kneading of the dough
till it rises.
5 On the day of the festival of our king
the princes become inflamed with
wine,[y]
and he joins hands with the
mockers.
6 Their hearts are like an oven;[z]
they approach him with intrigue.
Their passion smolders all night;
in the morning it blazes like a
flaming fire.
7 All of them are hot as an oven;
they devour their rulers.
All their kings fall,
and none of them calls[a] on me.

8 "Ephraim mixes[b] with the nations;
Ephraim is a flat loaf not turned
over.
9 Foreigners sap his strength,[c]
but he does not realize it.
His hair is sprinkled with gray,
but he does not notice.
10 Israel's arrogance testifies against
him,[d]
but despite all this
he does not return to the LORD his
God
or search[e] for him.

11 "Ephraim is like a dove,[f]
easily deceived and senseless—
now calling to Egypt,
now turning to Assyria.[g]
12 When they go, I will throw my net[h]
over them;
I will pull them down like the
birds in the sky.
When I hear them flocking together,
I will catch them.
13 Woe[i] to them,
because they have strayed[j]
from me!

Hos 7:1-2 ❖ Here God through Hosea points out persistent, unrepented sin. Which of these can we root out of our own lives?

6:7 [l]Hos 8:1 [m]Hos 5:7
6:9 [n]Jer 7:9-10; Eze 22:9; Hos 7:1
6:10 [o]Jer 5:30 [p]Hos 5:3
6:11 [q]Jer 51:33; Joel 3:13
7:1 [r]Hos 6:4 [s]ver 13 [t]Hos 4:2
7:2 [u]Jer 14:10; Hos 8:13 [v]Jer 2:19
7:3 [w]Hos 4:2; Mic 7:3
7:4 [x]Jer 9:2
7:5 [y]Isa 28:1,7
7:6 [z]Ps 21:9
7:7 [a]ver 16
7:8 [b]ver 11; Ps 106:35; Hos 5:13
7:9 [c]Isa 1:7; Hos 8:7
7:10 [d]Hos 5:5 [e]Isa 9:13
7:11 [f]Hos 11:11 [g]Hos 5:13; 12:1
7:12 [h]Eze 12:13
7:13 [i]Hos 9:12 [j]Jer 14:10; Eze 34:4-6; Hos 9:17

[a] 7 Or *Like Adam*; or *Like human beings*

6:7–10 The priests' violent action is a betrayal that violates the agreement between God and Israel. A second sin implicating the priests is cultic prostitution throughout the land. God sees this "horrible thing" (v. 10); he will not overlook it.
6:11–7:2 Just as Israel's sins will be exposed when God comes to heal his people (7:1), so Judah's judgment will be necessary (6:11). Hosea lists some of the sins that God will expose. Perhaps most surprising is the utter callousness of the people toward these sinful acts.
7:3–7 Hosea describes these rulers as "adulterers" (v. 4). Like a hot oven, these people burn in their passion for political power. Instead of protecting the king, they are in on the plot.
7:8–9 Instead of depending on God to protect them and guide their political decisions, the new kings form alliances with other nations. These alliances require payment of heavy tribute and encourage cultural and religious compromises to keep the peace with the Assyrians. This drains the nation of its financial resources, its independence, and its moral strength.
7:10–12 Surprisingly, the people do not see how this creeping compromise is gradually undermining their identity. Like a foolish dove, Israel's foreign

Destruction to them,
because they have rebelled against me!
I long to redeem them
but they speak about me[k] falsely.
14 They do not cry out to me from their hearts[l]
but wail on their beds.
They slash themselves,[a] appealing to their gods
for grain and new wine,[m]
but they turn away from me.[n]
15 I trained them and strengthened their arms,
but they plot evil[o] against me.
16 They do not turn to the Most High;
they are like a faulty bow.[p]
Their leaders will fall by the sword
because of their insolent words.
For this they will be ridiculed[q]
in the land of Egypt.[r]

Israel to Reap the Whirlwind

8 "Put the trumpet to your lips!
An eagle[s] is over the house of the LORD
because the people have broken my covenant
and rebelled against my law.[t]
2 Israel cries out to me,
'Our God, we acknowledge you!'
3 But Israel has rejected what is good;
an enemy will pursue him.
4 They set up kings without my consent;
they choose princes without my approval.[u]
With their silver and gold
they make idols[v] for themselves
to their own destruction.
5 Samaria, throw out your calf-idol![w]
My anger burns against them.
How long will they be incapable of purity?[x]
6 They are from Israel!
This calf — a metalworker has made it;
it is not God.
It will be broken in pieces,
that calf of Samaria.

7 "They sow the wind
and reap the whirlwind.[y]
The stalk has no head;
it will produce no flour.
Were it to yield grain,
foreigners would swallow it up.[z]
8 Israel is swallowed up;[a]
now she is among the nations
like something no one wants.[b]
9 For they have gone up to Assyria
like a wild donkey wandering alone.
Ephraim has sold herself to lovers.
10 Although they have sold themselves among the nations,
I will now gather them together.[c]
They will begin to waste away[d]
under the oppression of the mighty king.

7:13 [k] ver 1; Mt 23:37
7:14 [l] Jer 3:10 [m] Am 2:8 [n] Hos 13:16
7:15 [o] Na 1:9,11
7:16 [p] Ps 78:9, 57 [q] Eze 23:32 [r] Hos 9:3
8:1 [s] Dt 28:49; Jer 4:13 [t] Hos 4:6; 6:7
8:4 [u] Hos 13:10 [v] Hos 2:8
8:5 [w] Hos 10:5 [x] Jer 13:27
8:7 [y] Pr 22:8; Isa 66:15; Hos 10:12-13; Na 1:3 [z] Hos 2:9
8:8 [a] Jer 51:34 [b] Jer 22:28
8:10 [c] Eze 16:37; 22:20 [d] Jer 42:2

Hos 8:2-6 ❖ What "idols" do we see people worshiping today, perhaps even while giving lip service to the God of the Bible? How does God view such behavior?

[a] *14* Some Hebrew manuscripts and Septuagint; most Hebrew manuscripts *They gather together*

policy flips and flops back and forth. God responds by capturing these senseless birds in his net.

7:13-16 God's people have rebelled against his authority, strayed from his instruction, and lied about their love and loyalty to him. When they bring sacrifices to the temple, they worship other gods. Israel will get what it deserves from God and will receive no sympathy from its former political partners.

✣ **6:7—7:16** God still hates sin, and the result of sin is still death. Christians are called to faithfully persuade their unbelieving friends and neighbors that after death there will be a court of justice where all people must give an account of their deeds (Ro 14:10-12). The great hope for redemption from the penalty for sin has been provided through the death of Jesus Christ.

8:1-3 The theme of destruction in vv. 1-3 is implicit in Hosea's charge to sound the trumpet to warn the people about an approaching military threat. Their rebellion against God's instructions is a willful rejection of God's authority and a denial of the relationship that has set them apart from all the other nations of the world.

8:4-6 These verses describe Israel's rebellion against God in the area of politics and worship. They have removed one king and appointed another without asking God for direction. The people have made idols—particularly the golden calves at Dan and Bethel (see 1Ki 12). These bull images were quickly confused with the Canaanite god Baal. God rejects this calf and will have it cut to pieces (vv. 4b, 6b).

8:7-10 Hosea laments because Israel's sowing of friendly alliances with other nations reaps the whirlwind of destruction. The nation sold herself like a prostitute through her alliance with the Assyrians.

11 "Though Ephraim built many altars
for sin offerings,
these have become altars for
sinning.[e]
12 I wrote for them the many things of
my law,
but they regarded them as
something foreign.
13 Though they offer sacrifices as gifts
to me,
and though they eat[f] the meat,
the LORD is not pleased with them.
Now he will remember[g] their
wickedness
and punish their sins:[h]
They will return to Egypt.[i]
14 Israel has forgotten[j] their Maker
and built palaces;
Judah has fortified many towns.
But I will send fire on their cities
that will consume their
fortresses."[k]

Punishment for Israel

9 Do not rejoice, Israel;
do not be jubilant[l] like the other
nations.
For you have been unfaithful[m] to
your God;
you love the wages of a prostitute
at every threshing floor.
2 Threshing floors and winepresses
will not feed the people;
the new wine[n] will fail them.
3 They will not remain[o] in the LORD's
land;
Ephraim will return to Egypt[p]
and eat unclean food in Assyria.[q]
4 They will not pour out wine
offerings to the LORD,
nor will their sacrifices please[r]
him.
Such sacrifices will be to them like
the bread of mourners;
all who eat them will be unclean.[s]
This food will be for themselves;
it will not come into the temple of
the LORD.

5 What will you do[t] on the day of your
appointed festivals,[u]
on the feast days of the LORD?
6 Even if they escape from destruction,
Egypt will gather them,
and Memphis[v] will bury them.
Their treasures of silver will be
taken over by briers,
and thorns[w] will overrun their
tents.
7 The days of punishment[x] are
coming,
the days of reckoning are at hand.
Let Israel know this.
Because your sins[y] are so many
and your hostility so great,
the prophet is considered a fool,[z]
the inspired person a maniac.
8 The prophet, along with my God,
is the watchman over Ephraim,[a]
yet snares[a] await him on all his
paths,
and hostility in the house of his
God.
9 They have sunk deep into
corruption,
as in the days of Gibeah.[b]
God will remember[c] their
wickedness
and punish them for their sins.

10 "When I found Israel,
it was like finding grapes in the
desert;
when I saw your ancestors,

8:11 [e] Hos 10:1; 12:11
8:13 [f] Jer 7:21 [g] Hos 7:2 [h] Hos 4:9 [i] Hos 9:3,6
8:14 [j] Dt 32:18; Hos 2:13 [k] Jer 17:27
9:1 [l] Isa 22:12-13 [m] Hos 10:5
9:2 [n] Hos 2:9
9:3 [o] Lev 25:23 [p] Hos 8:13 [q] Eze 4:13; Hos 7:11
9:4 [r] Jer 6:20; Hos 8:13 [s] Hag 2:13-14
9:5 [t] Isa 10:3; Jer 5:31 [u] Hos 2:11
9:6 [v] Isa 19:13 [w] Isa 5:6; Hos 10:8
9:7 [x] Isa 34:8; Jer 10:15; Mic 7:4 [y] Jer 16:18 [z] Isa 44:25; La 2:14; Eze 14:9-10
9:8 [a] Hos 5:1
9:9 [b] Jdg 19:16-30; Hos 5:8; 10:9 [c] Hos 8:13

[a] 8 Or *The prophet is the watchman over Ephraim, / the people of my God*

Hos 9:1-4 ❖ When is it wrong to rejoice? When should we instead lament because of what is going on in our lives or because of what we have done?

8:11-14 The people's "sacrifices" (v. 13) on the many pagan altars around the nation have brought greater sinning instead of cleansing of sin and divine approval. Therefore, in the near future, God will destroy these proud cities and the homes in them.
9:1-6 Apparently this festival changed over the years into a pagan celebration by adding activities common in Baal festivals. In response, God will reverse the people's false theology and remove the land's fertility (v. 2). He will also reverse their security by exiling them to foreign lands. There the Israelites will be unable to offer Levitical sacrifices (Lev 1-5; 23:13), so it will be impossible to please him.
9:7-9 In a final summary statement Hosea declares that the days of final reckoning and divine vengeance are close at hand. This statement draws a strong reaction from Hosea's audience. Since they do not see their own action as sinful, Hosea is branded a radical reactionary. But Hosea sees himself differently: He is God's "watchman" who warns the people of approaching danger to help them avoid destruction.
9:10 The story of Israel starts with positive images

it was like seeing the early fruit on
the fig tree.
But when they came to Baal Peor,[d]
they consecrated themselves to
that shameful idol[e]
and became as vile as the thing
they loved.
11 Ephraim's glory will fly away like a
bird[f] —
no birth, no pregnancy, no
conception.[g]
12 Even if they rear children,
I will bereave them of every one.
Woe[h] to them
when I turn away from them![i]
13 I have seen Ephraim, like Tyre,
planted in a pleasant place.[j]
But Ephraim will bring out
their children to the slayer."

14 Give them, LORD —
what will you give them?
Give them wombs that miscarry
and breasts that are dry.[k]

15 "Because of all their wickedness in
Gilgal,[l]
I hated them there.
Because of their sinful deeds,[m]
I will drive them out of my house.
I will no longer love them;
all their leaders are rebellious.[n]
16 Ephraim[o] is blighted,
their root is withered,
they yield no fruit.[p]
Even if they bear children,
I will slay[q] their cherished
offspring."

17 My God will reject them
because they have not obeyed[r]
him;
they will be wanderers among the
nations.[s]

10 Israel was a spreading vine;[t]
he brought forth fruit for
himself.
As his fruit increased,
he built more altars;[u]
as his land prospered,
he adorned his sacred stones.[v]
2 Their heart is deceitful,[w]
and now they must bear their
guilt.[x]
The LORD will demolish their altars[y]
and destroy their sacred stones.[z]

3 Then they will say, "We have no king
because we did not revere the
LORD.
But even if we had a king,
what could he do for us?"
4 They make many promises,
take false oaths[a]
and make agreements;[b]
therefore lawsuits spring up
like poisonous weeds in a plowed
field.
5 The people who live in Samaria fear

9:10 [d] Nu 25:1-5; Ps 106:28-29 [e] Jer 11:13; Hos 4:14
9:11 [f] Hos 4:7; 10:5 [g] ver 14
9:12 [h] Hos 7:13 [i] Dt 31:17
9:13 [j] Eze 27:3
9:14 [k] ver 11; Lk 23:29
9:15 [l] Hos 4:15 [m] Hos 7:2 [n] Isa 1:23; Hos 4:9; 5:2
9:16 [o] Hos 5:11 [p] Hos 8:7 [q] ver 12
9:17 [r] Hos 4:10 [s] Dt 28:65; Hos 7:13
10:1 [t] Eze 15:2 [u] 1Ki 14:23 [v] Hos 8:11; 12:11
10:2 [w] 1Ki 18:21 [x] Hos 13:16 [y] ver 8 [z] Mic 5:13
10:4 [a] Hos 4:2 [b] Eze 17:19; Am 5:7

of God's joy and excitement when he first entered a covenant relationship with them. But this joy was abruptly turned into something shameful when the people worshiped an idol at Baal Peor (v. 10b; see Nu 25:1–5).

9:11–14 God's curse on the nation for these detestable acts is described here. Hosea interrupts this dire prediction of slaughter with a brief prayer in v. 14. Hosea is sorrowfully agreeing with God's earlier statements: God should remove the fertility of the nation and curse their offspring (see Dt 28:4, 11).

9:15–16 The final subparagraph recalls Israel's sins at Gilgal. There was a pagan temple there, the place where Israel's first king was inaugurated (1Sa 11:15). God hated the political system that sprang from this initial event and the worship practices that spread from Gilgal. As a result, he will drive his unfaithful people out of his land.

9:17 Once again Hosea interrupts this prediction of judgment with a prayer that agrees with God's conclusion. This truly is a depressing ending—without hope, without divine love, and without a prophet to intercede.

8:1—9:17 If people do not please God with their worship and political leaders do not allow God to guide their decisions, how can God bless them with prosperity and children? Eventually these nations will end up like Israel. God will stand against them because of their sinful deeds; he will no longer love them because of their rebellious leaders (v. 15); he will reject them because they have rejected him.

It's a simple equation: If we and others do not make pleasing God a priority, God will not be pleased with us. What's called for here is sincere repentance and a commitment to follow God no matter what our outside influences encourage.

10:1–2 Israel is like a destroyed vine because she has selfishly used its fruit for herself. God will hold the people accountable.

10:3–4 One way of understanding the quotation here is that the people reject God as their divine king. They do not fear or call on him for help because they do not think he can do anything to change their situation. Instead of humbly confessing their failure to fear God, the people are unfaithful to their covenant with him.

10:5–8 Verse 5 describes the people's deep commitment to the golden calf at Bethel. When the

for the calf-idol of Beth Aven.[a][c]
Its people will mourn over it,
and so will its idolatrous priests,[d]
those who had rejoiced over its
splendor,
because it is taken from them into
exile.[e]
6 It will be carried to Assyria[f]
as tribute for the great king.[g]
Ephraim will be disgraced;[h]
Israel will be ashamed of its
foreign alliances.
7 Samaria's king will be destroyed,[i]
swept away like a twig on the
surface of the waters.
8 The high places of wickedness[b][j] will
be destroyed—
it is the sin of Israel.
Thorns[k] and thistles will grow up
and cover their altars.[l]
Then they will say to the mountains,
"Cover us!"
and to the hills, "Fall on us!"[m]

9 "Since the days of Gibeah,[n] you have
sinned, Israel,
and there you have remained.[c]
Will not war again overtake
the evildoers in Gibeah?
10 When I please, I will punish[o] them;
nations will be gathered against
them
to put them in bonds for their
double sin.
11 Ephraim is a trained heifer
that loves to thresh;
so I will put a yoke
on her fair neck.
I will drive Ephraim,
Judah must plow,
and Jacob must break up the
ground.

10:5 [c] Hos 5:8 [d] 2Ki 23:5 [e] Hos 8:5; 9:1, 3,11
10:6 [f] Hos 11:5 [g] Hos 5:13 [h] Isa 30:3; Hos 4:7
10:7 [i] Hos 13:11
10:8 [j] 1Ki 12:28-30; Hos 4:13 [k] Hos 9:6 [l] ver 2; Isa 32:13 [m] Lk 23:30*; Rev 6:16
10:9 [n] Hos 5:8
10:10 [o] Eze 5:13; Hos 4:9
10:12 [p] Pr 11:18 [q] Jer 4:3 [r] Hos 12:6 [s] Isa 45:8
10:13 [t] Job 4:8; Hos 7:3; 11:12; Gal 6:7-8 [u] Ps 33:16
10:14 [v] Isa 17:3 [w] Hos 13:16
10:15 [x] ver 7

Hos 10:12 ❖ How can we practice sowing righteousness and seeking the Lord "until he comes"?

12 Sow righteousness[p] for yourselves,
reap the fruit of unfailing love,
and break up your unplowed
ground;[q]
for it is time to seek[r] the LORD,
until he comes
and showers his righteousness[s] on
you.
13 But you have planted wickedness,
you have reaped evil,[t]
you have eaten the fruit of
deception.
Because you have depended on your
own strength
and on your many warriors,[u]
14 the roar of battle will rise against
your people,
so that all your fortresses will be
devastated[v]—
as Shalman devastated Beth Arbel
on the day of battle,
when mothers were dashed to the
ground with their children.[w]
15 So will it happen to you, Bethel,
because your wickedness is great.
When that day dawns,
the king of Israel will be
completely destroyed.[x]

God's Love for Israel

11 "When Israel was a child, I loved
him,

[a] *5 Beth Aven* means *house of wickedness* (a derogatory name for Bethel, which means *house of God*). [b] *8* Hebrew *aven*, a reference to Beth Aven (a derogatory name for Bethel); see verse 5. [c] *9* Or *there a stand was taken*

---

captive people finally see the impotence of Baal and the uselessness of having faith in this idol, they will be filled with overwhelming regret and want to die (v. 8b).

10:9–10 Hosea is removing any false hopes his audience may have. They will be chastened through military defeat and go into captivity for two sins (v. 10). Perhaps Hosea is referring to the two calves at Dan and Bethel, to the two times the people sinned at Gibeah, or to idol worship and trust in their army.

10:11–13 Hosea compares Israel to a well-trained, hard-working heifer whom God wanted to make his own (symbolic of a covenant relationship). He put his willing heifer to work plowing for him—an analogy that suggests God's election of his people. Israel instead planted unrighteous seeds and will now reap a harvest of evil (v. 13).

10:14–15 Because of Israel's trust in their army, God will destroy their military establishment and the fortifications that are designed to protect the army from attackers. God will use this enemy to completely destroy them.

✣ **10:1–15** The most serious self-deceptions in the church today are theological. This happens when people give absolute divine authority and status to humanly created perceptions that do not fully represent what God has said or what he desires. For example, to elevate one cultural method of expressing praise to God into a universal standard is the wrong way to approach the spirit of true worship.

11:1–4 The exodus established the father-son relationship and gave the Israelites a unique identity

and out of Egypt I called my son.[y]
2 But the more they were called,
the more they went away
from me.[a]
They sacrificed to the Baals[z]
and they burned incense to
images.[a]
3 It was I who taught Ephraim to walk,
taking them by the arms;[b]
but they did not realize
it was I who healed[c] them.
4 I led them with cords of human
kindness,
with ties of love.[d]
To them I was like one who lifts
a little child to the cheek,
and I bent down to feed[e] them.

5 "Will they not return to Egypt[f]
and will not Assyria[g] rule over
them
because they refuse to repent?
6 A sword[h] will flash in their cities;
it will devour their false prophets
and put an end to their plans.
7 My people are determined to turn
from me.[i]
Even though they call me God
Most High,
I will by no means exalt them.

8 "How can I give you up, Ephraim?[j]
How can I hand you over, Israel?
How can I treat you like Admah?
How can I make you like
Zeboyim?[k]
My heart is changed within me;
all my compassion is aroused.
9 I will not carry out my fierce anger,[l]
nor will I devastate[m] Ephraim
again.
For I am God, and not a man[n] —
the Holy One among you.
I will not come against their
cities.
10 They will follow the LORD;
he will roar like a lion.
When he roars,
his children will come trembling
from the west.[o]
11 They will come from Egypt,
trembling like sparrows,
from Assyria,[p] fluttering like
doves.
I will settle them in their homes,"[q]
declares the LORD.

Israel's Sin

12 Ephraim has surrounded me with
lies,[r]
Israel with deceit.
And Judah is unruly against God,
even against the faithful Holy
One.[b]

12[c] 1 Ephraim feeds on the wind;[s]
he pursues the east wind all day
and multiplies lies and violence.
He makes a treaty with Assyria
and sends olive oil to Egypt.[t]
2 The LORD has a charge[u] to bring
against Judah;
he will punish Jacob[d] according to
his ways

11:1 [y] Ex 4:22; Hos 12:9,13; 13:4; Mt 2:15* 11:2 [z] Hos 2:13 [a] 2Ki 17:15; Isa 65:7; Jer 18:15 11:3 [b] Dt 1:31; Hos 7:15 [c] Jer 30:17 11:4 [d] Jer 31:2-3 [e] Ex 16:32; Ps 78:25 11:5 [f] Hos 7:16 [g] Hos 10:6 11:6 [h] Hos 13:16 11:7 [i] Jer 3:6-7; 8:5 11:8 [j] Hos 6:4 [k] Ge 14:8 11:9 [l] Dt 13:17; Jer 30:11 [m] Mal 3:6 [n] Nu 23:19 11:10 [o] Hos 6:1-3 11:11 [p] Isa 11:11 [q] Eze 28:26 11:12 [r] Hos 4:2 12:1 [s] Eze 17:10 [t] 2Ki 17:4 12:2 [u] Mic 6:2

[a] 2 Septuagint; Hebrew *them* [b] 12 In Hebrew texts this verse (11:12) is numbered 12:1. [c] In Hebrew texts 12:1-14 is numbered 12:2-15. [d] 2 *Jacob* means *he grasps the heel,* a Hebrew idiom for *he takes advantage of* or *he deceives.*

Hos 11:4 ❖ How has God led us with his kindness and been like a loving parent to us? What is a fitting response to such gentle love?

as "my son" (v. 1). The nation quickly fell into apostasy, but God did not immediately give up on his son. The metaphors of "cords of human kindness, with ties of love" (v. 4) depict gentle leading rather than forced labor.
11:5-7 The Israelites refuse to repent and turn back to the worship of God alone; instead, they stubbornly turn away from following him (v. 7a). Eventually his patience will run out and his rebellious children will be judged.
11:8-9 The husband-wife or father-son relationships help humans understand—in an imperfect way—the personal, caring involvement that a holy, mysterious God has with his people. In compassion, God declares that he cannot totally give up on his people.
11:10-11 At some point in the future God will act like a lion and roar, calling his people to come back to their land in a new exodus and dwell in their own homes. God's love will accomplish his plan; human sinfulness will not triumph over his compassion.

11:1-11 If evangelism is a sign that believers have God's love in them and its transformational power compels them to tell others, one must wonder why there is such a small amount of the love of God (in the form of evangelistic activity) exhibited in the life of so many church members. Is it fair to say that a person who does not evangelize has never experienced the full power of the glories of God's love?

11:12—12:2 Israel is trying to find help from gods who cannot fulfill its desires. Because of these deceptive actions, God is bringing another charge in his lawsuit against his people.

and repay him according to his
deeds.[v]
3 In the womb he grasped his brother's
heel;[w]
as a man he struggled[x] with God.
4 He struggled with the angel and
overcame him;
he wept and begged for his favor.
He found him at Bethel[y]
and talked with him there —
5 the LORD God Almighty,
the LORD is his name![z]
6 But you must return to your God;
maintain love and justice,[a]
and wait for your God always.[b]

7 The merchant uses dishonest scales[c]
and loves to defraud.
8 Ephraim boasts,
"I am very rich; I have become
wealthy.[d]
With all my wealth they will not find
in me
any iniquity or sin."

9 "I have been the LORD your God
ever since you came out of Egypt;[e]
I will make you live in tents[f] again,
as in the days of your appointed
festivals.
10 I spoke to the prophets,
gave them many visions
and told parables[g] through
them."[h]

11 Is Gilead wicked?[i]
Its people are worthless!
Do they sacrifice bulls in Gilgal?[j]
Their altars will be like piles of
stones
on a plowed field.[k]
12 Jacob fled to the country of Aram[a];[l]
Israel served to get a wife,
and to pay for her he tended
sheep.[m]
13 The LORD used a prophet to bring
Israel up from Egypt,
by a prophet he cared for him.[n]
14 But Ephraim has aroused his bitter
anger;
his Lord will leave on him the
guilt of his bloodshed[o]
and will repay him for his
contempt.[p]

The LORD's Anger Against Israel

13 When Ephraim spoke, people
trembled;[q]
he was exalted[r] in Israel.
But he became guilty of Baal
worship[s] and died.
2 Now they sin more and more;
they make idols for themselves
from their silver,[t]
cleverly fashioned images,
all of them the work of craftsmen.
It is said of these people,
"They offer human sacrifices!
They kiss[b] calf-idols![u]"
3 Therefore they will be like the
morning mist,
like the early dew that disappears,[v]
like chaff[w] swirling from a
threshing floor,[x]
like smoke[y] escaping through a
window.

[a] 12 That is, Northwest Mesopotamia [b] 2 Or "Men who sacrifice / kiss

12:2 [v] Hos 4:9
12:3 [w] Ge 25:26 [x] Ge 32:24-29
12:4 [y] Ge 28:12-15; 35:15
12:5 [z] Ex 3:15
12:6 [a] Mic 6:8 [b] Hos 6:1-3; 10:12; Mic 7:7
12:7 [c] Am 8:5
12:8 [d] Ps 62:10; Rev 3:17
12:9 [e] Lev 23:43; Hos 11:1 [f] Ne 8:17
12:10 [g] Eze 20:49 [h] 2Ki 17:13; Jer 7:25
12:11 [i] Hos 6:8 [j] Hos 4:15 [k] Hos 8:11
12:12 [l] Ge 28:5 [m] Ge 29:18
12:13 [n] Ex 13:3; Isa 63:11-14
12:14 [o] Eze 18:13 [p] Da 11:18
13:1 [q] Jdg 12:1 [r] Jdg 8:1 [s] Hos 11:2
13:2 [t] Isa 46:6; Jer 10:4 [u] Isa 44:17-20
13:3 [v] Hos 6:4 [w] Isa 17:13 [x] Da 2:35 [y] Ps 68:2

Hos 12:6 ❖ This call to return to the Lord is similar to many others in the OT. What does that say to us about how God feels about our relationship with him?

12:3–6 Hosea tries to persuade his audience to "return to your God" (v. 6) as Jacob did, to have steadfast covenantal love for God, to follow the just practices in the Torah, and to earnestly wait for God in difficult times.
12:7–10 Those in the upper class boast about their illegally gained wealth. Their wealth will not protect them from God's conclusion that they are guilty.
12:11–14 Gilgal was a well-known place where people worshiped other gods (see 4:15; 9:15). As punishment, Gilead will be reduced to a "worthless" thing (v. 11).

Through Jacob's own efforts, he worked for a wife (Ge 29), but the nation of Israel was freed from slavery by God's grace. Hosea's audience should not follow the patterns of Jacob (self-effort and deception) but should allow God to care for them and bring them freedom.

13:1–3 The contrasts between Israel's past, present, and future continue to provide additional evidence of the nation's guilt and deception. Although Israel had many things going for it at the time of Jeroboam II, the people turned away from God. The consequence of this deceptive idolatry is stated in another verdict: Israel will disappear.

✜ **11:12—13:3** One way church members can ensure a proper relationship with God and avoid his condemnation is to always remember what God has done for them. Values and beliefs are cemented in the minds of people by repeatedly reemphasizing them. Transformation comes when people's hearts are so touched by the past work of Christ that they are willing to take up their cross and follow him (Mt 16:24).

4"But I have been the LORD your God
ever since you came out of Egypt.[z]
You shall acknowledge no God but
me,[a]
no Savior[b] except me.
5I cared for you in the wilderness,
in the land of burning heat.
6When I fed them, they were satisfied;
when they were satisfied, they
became proud;
then they forgot me.[c]
7So I will be like a lion to them,
like a leopard I will lurk by the
path.
8Like a bear robbed of her cubs,[d]
I will attack them and rip them
open;
like a lion I will devour them —
a wild animal will tear them
apart.[e]

9"You are destroyed, Israel,
because you are against me,[f]
against your helper.[g]
10Where is your king,[h] that he may
save you?
Where are your rulers in all your
towns,
of whom you said,
'Give me a king and princes'?[i]
11So in my anger I gave you a king,
and in my wrath I took him
away.[j]
12The guilt of Ephraim is stored up,
his sins are kept on record.[k]
13Pains as of a woman in childbirth[l]
come to him,
but he is a child without wisdom;
when the time arrives,
he doesn't have the sense to come
out of the womb.[m]

13:4 [z] Hos 12:9 [a] Ex 20:3 [b] Isa 43:11; 45:21-22
13:6 [c] Dt 32:12-15; Hos 2:13
13:8 [d] 2Sa 17:8 [e] Ps 50:22
13:9 [f] Jer 2:17-19 [g] Dt 33:29
13:10 [h] 2Ki 17:4 [i] 1Sa 8:6; Hos 8:4
13:11 [j] 1Ki 14:10; Hos 10:7
13:12 [k] Dt 32:34
13:13 [l] Isa 13:8; Mic 4:9-10 [m] Isa 66:9
13:14 [n] Ps 49:15; Eze 37:12-13 [o] 1Co 15:55*
13:15 [p] Hos 10:1 [q] Eze 19:12 [r] Jer 51:36 [s] Jer 20:5
13:16 [t] Hos 10:2 [u] Hos 7:14 [v] Hos 11:6 [w] 2Ki 8:12; Hos 10:14 [x] 2Ki 15:16; Isa 13:16
14:1 [y] Hos 5:5

Hos 13:14 ❖ How does Christ give us victory even over the power of death itself (see 1Co 15:10-57)?

14"I will deliver this people from the
power of the grave;[n]
I will redeem them from
death.
Where, O death, are your plagues?
Where, O grave, is your
destruction?[o]

"I will have no compassion,
15 even though he thrives[p] among his
brothers.
An east wind[q] from the LORD will
come,
blowing in from the desert;
his spring will fail
and his well dry up.[r]
His storehouse will be plundered[s]
of all its treasures.
16The people of Samaria must bear
their guilt,[t]
because they have rebelled[u]
against their God.
They will fall by the sword;[v]
their little ones will be dashed[w] to
the ground,
their pregnant women[x] ripped
open."[a]

Repentance to Bring Blessing

14 [b] Return, Israel, to the LORD your
God.
Your sins have been your
downfall![y]

[a] 16 In Hebrew texts this verse (13:16) is numbered 14:1. [b] In Hebrew texts 14:1-9 is numbered 14:2-10.

13:4-8 God is the covenant-making God who cared enough to deliver his people from Egyptian slavery. God provided for the nation while they were traveling for forty years in Sinai. If God had not cared, they would not have survived. Finally, God abundantly blessed them in the promised land. This brief historical background sets the stage for the verdict of the lawsuit in the rest of this chapter.

13:9-11 The people know what God desires, but still they reject him. Verses 10-11 take the form of a taunting explanation of where the nation went wrong.

13:12-16 A caveat comes in the middle of an announcement of judgment. God is overcome with love and refuses to totally destroy his people. He asserts his redemptive power to overcome the curse of death (v. 14a).

The final clause in v. 14 abruptly returns to the theme of judgment. How can God say they will die (vv. 12-13), then they will not die (v. 14a-b), and then that he will have no compassion on them and they will indeed die (vv. 14c-16)?

Hosea is not deceiving the people by telling them that God will not judge them. No, God will bring death on the nation soon, but death will not have final victory over God or his plans.

✣ **13:4-16** Through his provision of salvation and forgiveness of sins in Jesus, the sting of death is removed and eternal life with God is possible. This is just one more example of God's care. In light of God's past, present, and future care for us, how should we act today? Can we forget what God has done and proudly act as if we can run our own lives and make our own decisions? Why would we?

14:1-3 The first step in renewing any relationship is a humble admission of one's mistakes.

2 Take words with you
and return to the LORD.
Say to him:
"Forgive all our sins
and receive us graciously,[z]
that we may offer the fruit of our lips.[a][a]
3 Assyria cannot save us;
we will not mount warhorses.[b]
We will never again say 'Our gods'[c]
to what our own hands have made,
for in you the fatherless[d] find compassion."

4 "I will heal[e] their waywardness
and love them freely,[f]
for my anger has turned away from them.
5 I will be like the dew to Israel;
he will blossom like a lily.[g]
Like a cedar of Lebanon[h]
he will send down his roots;[i]
6 his young shoots will grow.
His splendor will be like an olive tree,[j]
his fragrance like a cedar of Lebanon.[k]
7 People will dwell again in his shade;[l]
they will flourish like the grain,
they will blossom like the vine—
Israel's fame will be like the wine[m] of Lebanon.[n]
8 Ephraim, what more have I[b] to do with idols?[o]
I will answer him and care for him.
I am like a flourishing juniper;
your fruitfulness comes from me."

9 Who is wise?[p] Let them realize these things.
Who is discerning? Let them understand.[q]
The ways of the LORD are right;[r]
the righteous walk[s] in them,
but the rebellious stumble in them.

14:2 [z] Mic 7:18-19 [a] Heb 13:15
14:3 [b] Ps 33:17; Isa 31:1 [c] Hos 8:6 [d] Ps 10:14; 68:5
14:4 [e] Hos 6:1 [f] Zep 3:17
14:5 [g] SS 2:1 [h] Isa 35:2 [i] Job 29:19
14:6 [j] Ps 52:8; Jer 11:16 [k] SS 4:11
14:7 [l] Ps 91:1-4 [m] Hos 2:22 [n] Eze 17:23
14:8 [o] ver 3
14:9 [p] Ps 107:43 [q] Pr 10:29; Isa 1:28 [r] Ps 111:7-8; Zep 3:5; Ac 13:10 [s] Isa 26:7

[a] 2 Or *offer our lips as sacrifices of bulls* [b] 8 Or Hebrew; Septuagint *What more has Ephraim*

Hos 14:1-2 ❖ "Confession is good for the soul" is a common saying. How does this passage reinforce that idea?

14:4-8 Hosea reveals how God will respond: He will heal their sinful waywardness. People need a miraculous act of God's healing grace to respond to him.

The fruitfulness of the nation is compared to a bountiful grain field, a blossoming grapevine, and the famous wine from Lebanon. These are all pictures of God's rich blessing.

14:9 If we want to be considered an upright or "righteous" people in God's eyes, we must follow what he has said. We cannot continue to refuse to submit to God's will and be considered wise.

14:1-9 Leading ourselves and others toward repentance is necessary since there is no other way to begin a relationship with God. Repentance is not just a negative theme of rejecting or "turning from"; it also has a positive theme of "turning toward."

If the abundance, joy, and hope of Hosea's presentation of repentance are contrasted with the hopelessness of the status quo, then suddenly repentance becomes appealing as a positive change for the better.

Joel

Author: Joel

Audience: The people of Judah

Date: Probably between the late seventh and early fifth centuries BC

Theme: The day of the Lord is coming in which God will bring restoration and blessing to the people of Judah only after judgment and repentance occur.

Reading Joel

This book is short enough to read in one sitting, though it does have two parts. The first part talks about the locust invasion and the response of God's people to this disaster. The second part, beginning at Joel 2:28, looks ahead to the more distant future, the new life in Christ and the outpouring of the Spirit. The prophecies of Joel are directed toward Judah and Jerusalem.

PERSPECTIVE

Prophets don't get to be prophets by being rays of sunshine. It is almost mandatory for prophets to be harbingers of doom. They sound morose and are generally irritable and cranky.

In the case of the biblical prophets, the context and nature of the doom that drove them to prophesy varies. Sometimes it is threats from outside Israel, sometimes internal dissention, and almost always a failure of holiness. The cause of the doom, however, never varies. It is always due to God's wrath falling on sin and sinner alike.

Joel, Obadiah, and Malachi (see the introductions for Obadiah and Malachi for more perspective) are three concise examples of the prophetic genre. Judgment drips like blood from the pages of these three books. God's wrath challenges Israelites in almost every paragraph. None of these books is long, but they make up for their concise nature with their pointed accusations and warnings.

We should not equate shortness with simplicity, however. It does not take much reading of this material to see that the judgment being communicated is a complicated affair. Each of the elements of these books—sin leads to judgment leads to repentance leads to restoration—needs to be nuanced in order to have practical meaning. Joel, Obadiah, and Malachi are all about judgment, but three different settings for that judgment emerge. Consider, for example, just one simple question: On whom does God's judgment fall? On Israel? On Israel's enemies? On us all? It is clear that for Joel, the locust invasion is a metaphor for what will happen on the day of the Lord, when all righteousness accounts will be settled. Joel's point is that the scope of

	1200 BC	1100	1000	900	800	700	600	500	400
Division of the kingdom (930 BC)									
Ministries of Elijah and Elisha in Israel (c. 875–797 BC)									
Joel's ministry in Judah (c. 835–796 BC?)									
Jonah's ministry in Nineveh (c. 800–750 BC)									
Amos's ministry in Israel (c. 760–750 BC)									
Hosea's ministry in Israel (c. 753–715 BC)									
Exile of Israel (722 BC)									
Fall of Jerusalem (586 BC)									

God's judgment exceeds them all. The scope is so wide that it drives us either to despair at ever measuring up or to submission to God's power.

The recognition that God's judgment falls on us all—on our enemies and on us—is a primary message of these three brief books taken together. Such a recognition helps us handle the more difficult questions those of us in the twenty-first century have about the questions of judgment:

First, can a loving God at the same time be a judge? The obvious answer for Joel, Obadiah, and Malachi is yes.

Second, are we God's instruments of judgment? Only in the most indirect sense. Since we ourselves are often judged, we cannot really claim the authority of being God's judges. The collective effect of Joel's, Obadiah's, and Malachi's messages is to anticipate Matthew 7:1: "Do not judge, or you too will be judged." The most we can do is call attention to the fact that God hates sin and will judge sinners. The day of the Lord will come.

Third, how clearly can we identify and differentiate between God's wrath and Satan's evil? Not clearly at all. In biblical times it took God's specially anointed prophets to make those calls. Today we must recognize that we are equally ignorant of God's righteous ways.

Joel tells us that God does judge righteousness. He tells us that God chooses the time, place, and method of judgment, but doesn't usually let us in on what he decides. While discharging his messages of doom and destruction, he leaves us all with a feeling not of hopelessness but of hopefulness. Joel does it with his promise of the outpouring of God's Holy Spirit on all people. "Return to the LORD your God, for he is gracious and compassionate, slow to anger and abounding in love, and he relents from sending calamity" (2:13).

Judgment for judgment's sake is not judgment but revenge. That is not what Joel, Obadiah, and Malachi are about. Theirs is a hard message, but it is a message that has repentance and restoration as its goal.

An unidentified army threatens Judah (2:1–11), while other peoples are explicitly identified in 3:4–8, raising the prophecies onto the world stage.

Key Verses

"Even now," declares the LORD, "return to me with all your heart, with fasting and weeping and mourning." Rend your heart and not your garments. Return to the LORD your God, for he is gracious and compassionate, slow to anger and abounding in love, and he relents from sending calamity.

—Joel 2:12–13

TAKING THE NEXT STEPS

We have no way of knowing when the prophet Joel lived, for no dates are given in his prophecy. But we do know that it was a time of great devastation, caused by a plague of locusts. Joel used this event to call the people to repentance; he went on to envision a time of restoration, both in the immediate future and in the more distant future.

Reading this prophecy ought to make us think about our own lives. (1) Whenever any natural disaster strikes, perhaps God is speaking to us and calling us to a renewed relationship with him. (2) When we bring our requests to the Lord in prayer, we should always accompany them with confession of sin and humility of heart. (3) God is a compassionate God, who will hear and answer the prayers of his people. (4) The sign that the messianic age is here is the Spirit of God living in our hearts and working his power within us.

WHAT TO LOOK FOR IN JOEL

- Devastation from a locust plague (ch. 1)
- Call to repentance (ch. 2)
- Promise of restoration (ch. 3)

1 The word of the LORD that came[a] to Joel[b] son of Pethuel.

An Invasion of Locusts

2 Hear this,[c] you elders;
listen, all who live in the land.[d]
Has anything like this ever
happened in your days
or in the days of your ancestors?[e]
3 Tell it to your children,[f]
and let your children tell it to their
children,
and their children to the next
generation.
4 What the locust swarm has left
the great locusts have eaten;
what the great locusts have left
the young locusts have eaten;
what the young locusts have left
other locusts[a] have eaten.[g]

5 Wake up, you drunkards, and weep!
Wail, all you drinkers of wine;[h]
wail because of the new wine,
for it has been snatched from your
lips.
6 A nation has invaded my land,
a mighty army without number;[i]
it has the teeth[j] of a lion,
the fangs of a lioness.
7 It has laid waste[k] my vines
and ruined my fig trees.[l]
It has stripped off their bark
and thrown it away,
leaving their branches white.

8 Mourn like a virgin in sackcloth[m]
grieving for the betrothed of her
youth.
9 Grain offerings and drink offerings[n]
are cut off from the house of the
LORD.
The priests are in mourning,
those who minister before the
LORD.
10 The fields are ruined,
the ground is dried up;[o]
the grain is destroyed,
the new wine[p] is dried up,
the olive oil fails.

11 Despair, you farmers,[q]
wail, you vine growers;
grieve for the wheat and the barley,
because the harvest of the field is
destroyed.[r]
12 The vine is dried up
and the fig tree is withered;

1:1 [a] Jer 1:2 [b] Ac 2:16
1:2 [c] Hos 5:1 [d] Hos 4:1 [e] Joel 2:2
1:3 [f] Ex 10:2; Ps 78:4
1:4 [g] Dt 28:39; Na 3:15
1:5 [h] Joel 3:3
1:6 [i] Joel 2:2,11,25 [j] Rev 9:8
1:7 [k] Isa 5:6 [l] Am 4:9
1:8 [m] ver 13; Isa 22:12; Am 8:10
1:9 [n] Hos 9:4; Joel 2:14,17
1:10 [o] Isa 24:4 [p] Hos 9:2
1:11 [q] Jer 14:3-4; Am 5:16 [r] Isa 17:11

[a] 4 The precise meaning of the four Hebrew words used here for locusts is uncertain.

1:1 Joel's prophecies are headed by two elements in addition to his name. First is the designation "the word of the LORD," referencing the personal name of Israel's God. Joel's father is Pethuel. His name means "a youth of/belonging to El," which reflects his parents' understanding of the divine source of offspring.
1:2–4 Rhetorical questions draw the audience into Joel's message, seeking a response rather than asking for actual information. Verse 4 reveals the subject of the message: the devastation that will result from swarms of locusts.
1:5–9 The second audience must lament for the wine that is newly pressed at this time of devastation. Wine serves to lessen the hardships of daily life.
1:10–14 Earth and field fail to produce three staples of life: grain, wine and oil. Food and drink make the heart glad; without them, joy dissipates.

the pomegranate, the palm and the
apple[a] tree —
all the trees of the field — are
dried up.[s]
Surely the people's joy
is withered away.

A Call to Lamentation

13 Put on sackcloth,[t] you priests, and
mourn;
wail, you who minister[u] before the
altar.
Come, spend the night in sackcloth,
you who minister before my God;
for the grain offerings and drink
offerings[v]
are withheld from the house of
your God.
14 Declare a holy fast;[w]
call a sacred assembly.
Summon the elders
and all who live in the land
to the house of the LORD your God,
and cry out[x] to the LORD.

15 Alas for that[y] day!
For the day of the LORD[z] is near;
it will come like destruction from
the Almighty.[b]

16 Has not the food been cut off[a]
before our very eyes —
joy and gladness
from the house of our God?[b]
17 The seeds are shriveled
beneath the clods.[c][c]
The storehouses are in ruins,
the granaries have been broken
down,
for the grain has dried up.

1:12 [s] Hag 2:19
1:13 [t] Jer 4:8 [u] Joel 2:17 [v] ver 9
1:14 [w] 2Ch 20:3 [x] Jnh 3:8
1:15 [y] Jer 30:7 [z] Isa 13:6, 9; Joel 2:1, 11, 31
1:16 [a] Isa 3:7 [b] Dt 12:7
1:17 [c] Isa 17:10-11
1:19 [d] Ps 50:15 [e] Am 7:4 [f] Jer 9:10
1:20 [g] Ps 104:21 [h] 1Ki 17:7
2:1 [i] Jer 4:5 [j] ver 15 [k] Joel 1:15; Zep 1:14-16 [l] Ob 15
2:2 [m] Am 5:18 [n] Da 9:12 [o] Joel 1:6 [p] Joel 1:2

Joel 1:13–14 ❖ What is God calling us to lament in the world? Why is lament an important task for God's children?

18 How the cattle moan!
The herds mill about
because they have no pasture;
even the flocks of sheep are
suffering.

19 To you, LORD, I call,[d]
for fire[e] has devoured the
pastures[f] in the wilderness
and flames have burned up all the
trees of the field.
20 Even the wild animals pant for
you;[g]
the streams of water have dried
up[h]
and fire has devoured the pastures
in the wilderness.

An Army of Locusts

2 Blow the trumpet[i] in Zion;[j]
sound the alarm on my holy hill.

Let all who live in the land tremble,
for the day of the LORD[k] is coming.
It is close at hand[l] —
2 a day of darkness[m] and gloom,[n]
a day of clouds and blackness.
Like dawn spreading across the
mountains
a large and mighty army[o] comes,
such as never was in ancient times[p]
nor ever will be in ages to come.

[a] *12* Or possibly *apricot* [b] *15* Hebrew *Shaddai*
[c] *17* The meaning of the Hebrew for this word is uncertain.

1:15–20 The cry for lament begins with an interjection of woe, "Alas," and concerns the nearness of "the day of the LORD" (v. 15), a statement familiar from other prophecies. Some anticipate the day as positive. Joel quickly corrects their misconception.
1:16–18 Both "food" and "joy and gladness" are denied to the temple. The domesticated animals, important for the Israelite household and religious economy, also feel the negative effects.
1:19–20 The writer turns to Yahweh himself, to whom he now calls. The destroying locusts are like an all-consuming fire and flame. This may be an indication that all of nature works together at one time against these poor folks, hitting them with locust, drought, and fire.

APPLICATION ✚ **1:1–20** While it does no good to speak hope to those heading for destruction unless they alter their path, it is also unhelpful to speak despair to those who are defeated and beaten down. Great prophets like Joel, Jonah, and even Jesus read the times and spoke elements of God's truth that were relevant to those times.
Which of Joel's messages can we connect with our day and age? How do we integrate these warnings into our lives, all the while looking with hope toward the restored heaven and earth of Rev 21:1–5?

2:1–2a The section begins with an urgent series of commands. The place where the alarm is raised is called "Zion" and "my holy hill." The reason for this alarm is again the coming of "the day of the LORD."
2:2b–3 This day is like a "mighty army" (v. 2b). The coming insect army follows a "scorched-earth policy." Previously there was land "like the garden of Eden" (v. 3). After the locusts' passing, it is a desert.

3 Before them fire devours,
behind them a flame blazes.
Before them the land is like the
garden of Eden,[q]
behind them, a desert waste[r]—
nothing escapes them.
4 They have the appearance of horses;[s]
they gallop along like cavalry.
5 With a noise like that of chariots[t]
they leap over the mountaintops,
like a crackling fire[u] consuming
stubble,
like a mighty army drawn up for
battle.

6 At the sight of them, nations are in
anguish;[v]
every face turns pale.[w]
7 They charge like warriors;
they scale walls like soldiers.
They all march in line,
not swerving[x] from their course.
8 They do not jostle each other;
each marches straight ahead.
They plunge through defenses
without breaking ranks.
9 They rush upon the city;
they run along the wall.
They climb into the houses;
like thieves they enter through
the windows.[y]

10 Before them the earth shakes,[z]
the heavens tremble,
the sun and moon are darkened,[a]
and the stars no longer shine.[b]
11 The LORD[c] thunders
at the head of his army;
his forces are beyond number,
and mighty is the army that obeys
his command.
The day of the LORD is great;[d]
it is dreadful.
Who can endure it?[e]

Rend Your Heart

12 "Even now," declares the LORD,
"return[f] to me with all your heart,
with fasting and weeping and
mourning."

13 Rend your heart[g]
and not your garments.[h]
Return to the LORD your God,
for he is gracious and
compassionate,
slow to anger and abounding in
love,[i]
and he relents from sending
calamity.[j]
14 Who knows? He may turn[k] and
relent
and leave behind a blessing[l]—
grain offerings and drink offerings[m]
for the LORD your God.

15 Blow the trumpet[n] in Zion,
declare a holy fast,[o]

2:3 [q] Ge 2:8 [r] Ps 105:34-35
2:4 [s] Rev 9:7
2:5 [t] Rev 9:9 [u] Isa 5:24; 30:30
2:6 [v] Isa 13:8 [w] Na 2:10
2:7 [x] Isa 5:27
2:9 [y] Jer 9:21
2:10 [z] Ps 18:7 [a] Mt 24:29 [b] Isa 13:10; Eze 32:8
2:11 [c] Joel 1:15 [d] Zep 1:14; Rev 18:8 [e] Eze 22:14
2:12 [f] Jer 4:1; Hos 12:6
2:13 [g] Ps 34:18; Isa 57:15 [h] Job 1:20 [i] Ex 34:6 [j] Jer 18:8
2:14 [k] Jer 26:3 [l] Hag 2:19 [m] Joel 1:13
2:15 [n] Nu 10:2 [o] Jer 36:9

2:4–8 These verses provide different but terrifying images and descriptions of the locust horde.
2:9–10 This passage describes the actual progression of events that the marauding forces will follow: ranging around the city, attacking the walls, and climbing up to and into the house windows. Even the sun, moon, and stars will lose their light as God removes his favor from his wayward people.
2:11 The terrifying description reaches its peak. The focus moves from humans to the earth and heavens, and now specifically to Yahweh, Israel's own covenant God. The locust swarm is a force brought and controlled by God himself. The "day of the LORD" (v. 11) is not just approaching; it is already here, and it is overwhelmingly unbearable.

2:1–11 While this passage describes a bleak and chilling picture, it is bracketed by rays of hope—acknowledgment that God hears and that he can turn back to the people in grace if they respond to him in an appropriate way. Though the darkness is rising, it will be overcome by the light. In reality, that light has already dawned (e.g., Isa 9:2; Mt 4:16).

2:12–13 The only appropriate response to the coming devastation is repentance. It must be total—not only demonstrated by outward signs but also with true, inner sorrow.

Repentance is to be based on who God is. The whole section expresses God's characteristics: He is not only a judge but also someone who wishes to temper his judgment if the correct response is heard.
2:14 It is theologically vital to note the hesitant question, "Who knows?" God is not obligated to show compassion and forgiveness.
2:15–17 The people are called to assemble for "sacred" (v. 15) purposes. The priests request that God's own be spared. Their claim to be God's people and inheritance would become a lie if they were destroyed.

The people realize this disaster is from God. God desires to restore the relationship and commands his people to approach him for restoration. Their attention is now directed away from the calamities and toward the possibility of restoration.

2:12–17 In an experience of personal crisis, there seems to be much more practical assurance of hope in knowing that we are in the hands of a God who loves us and cares for every aspect of our lives than in fearing that we worship a God who is emotionless and cold. Indeed, "God is love" (1Jn 4:8) and can be trusted with our anxiety and emotion (1Pe 5:7).

PEOPLE TO KNOW // **JOEL**

JOEL 2:12–14: The prophet Joel does not offer any autobiographical information in his book aside from the name of his father, Pethuel (Joel 1:1), a man named nowhere else in Scripture. Even determining a general date for when Joel prophesied is impossible since the book contains no concrete contextual details.

Joel opens his prophecy by describing a plague of locusts. Locust swarms were a common problem in the ancient Near East and are still a problem today. A swarm of locusts could destroy harvests and devastate food supplies. Joel uses locusts to paint a picture of impending destruction and calls on people to repent.

Joel envisions battles and chaos accompanying the coming "day of the LORD" (Joel 1:15). The plea of God through the prophet is for the people to return to the Lord with all their hearts. Joel 2 bursts with hope for God's people, promising prosperity and God's Spirit if they turn back to him.

Part of Joel's vision takes center stage on the day of Pentecost described in the NT. The outpouring of the Holy Spirit was anticipated in Joel 2:28–32, words that Peter quotes to the crowd in his powerful Pentecost sermon (Ac 2:14–21).

APPLICATION Most of Joel's prophecy does not make for easy reading. We may be left wondering what to do with the language of violent judgment. But Joel's focus on the day of the Lord should inspire us to live with God's future and God's justice in mind. It should point us to Jesus, who gives us victory over the sin and evil of the world. God's justice will rule in the end; through Christ, we can be on God's side when that great day comes. For those who are in Christ, it will not be a day to fear but instead a day to rejoice.

call a sacred assembly.[p]
16 Gather the people,
consecrate[q] the assembly;
bring together the elders,
gather the children,
those nursing at the breast.
Let the bridegroom[r] leave his room
and the bride her chamber.
17 Let the priests, who minister before the LORD,
weep between the portico and the altar.[s]
Let them say, "Spare your people, LORD.
Do not make your inheritance an object of scorn,[t]
a byword among the nations.
Why should they say among the peoples,
'Where is their God?[u]'"

The LORD's Answer

18 Then the LORD was jealous[v] for his land
and took pity on his people.

19 The LORD replied[a] to them:

"I am sending you grain, new wine and olive oil,[w]
enough to satisfy you fully;
never again will I make you
an object of scorn[x] to the nations.

20 "I will drive the northern horde[y] far from you,
pushing it into a parched and barren land;
its eastern ranks will drown in the Dead Sea
and its western ranks in the Mediterranean Sea.
And its stench[z] will go up;
its smell will rise."

Surely he has done great things!
21 Do not be afraid,[a] land of Judah;
be glad and rejoice.
Surely the LORD has done great things![b]
22 Do not be afraid, you wild animals,
for the pastures in the wilderness are becoming green.[c]
The trees are bearing their fruit;

2:15 [p] Joel 1:14
2:16 [q] Ex 19:10, 22 [r] Ps 19:5
2:17 [s] Eze 8:16; Mt 23:35 [t] Dt 9:26-29; Ps 44:13 [u] Ps 42:3
2:18 [v] Zec 1:14
2:19 [w] Jer 31:12 [x] Eze 34:29
2:20 [y] Jer 1:14-15 [z] Isa 34:3
2:21 [a] Isa 54:4; Zep 3:16-17 [b] Ps 126:3
2:22 [c] Ps 65:12

[a] 18,19 *Or LORD will be jealous . . . / and take pity . . . / 19The LORD will reply*

2:18–20 Until now, the problem has been presented and the response of the people has been called for. Now God's response unfolds.
2:21–23 The verbs in vv. 21–22 call the people to praise. Those previously summoned to fear, weep, and pray in Zion are now asked to join the rest of creation in celebration.

the fig tree and the vine yield
their riches.[d]
23 Be glad, people of Zion,
rejoice[e] in the LORD your God,
for he has given you the autumn
rains
because he is faithful.
He sends you abundant showers,
both autumn and spring rains,[f] as
before.
24 The threshing floors will be filled
with grain;
the vats will overflow[g] with new
wine[h] and oil.

25 "I will repay you for the years the
locusts have eaten —
the great locust and the young
locust,
the other locusts and the locust
swarm[a] —
my great army that I sent among you.
26 You will have plenty to eat, until you
are full,[i]
and you will praise[j] the name of
the LORD your God,
who has worked wonders[k] for you;
never again will my people be
shamed.
27 Then you will know that I am in
Israel,
that I am the LORD[l] your God,
and that there is no other;
never again will my people be
shamed.

The Day of the LORD

28 "And afterward,
I will pour out my Spirit[m] on all
people.

2:22 [d] Joel 1:18-20
2:23 [e] Ps 149:2; Isa 12:6; 41:16; Hab 3:18; Zec 10:7 [f] Lev 26:4
2:24 [g] Lev 26:10; Mal 3:10 [h] Am 9:13
2:26 [i] Lev 26:5 [j] Isa 62:9 [k] Ps 126:3; Isa 25:1
2:27 [l] Joel 3:17
2:28 [m] Eze 39:29
2:29 [n] 1Co 12:13; Gal 3:28
2:30 [o] Lk 21:11 [p] Mk 13:24-25
2:31 [q] Mt 24:29 [r] Isa 13:9-10; Mal 4:1,5
2:32 [s] Ac 2:17-21*; Ro 10:13* [t] Isa 46:13 [u] Ob 17 [v] Isa 11:11; Mic 4:7; Ro 9:27
3:1 [w] Jer 16:15

Joel 2:28–32 ❖ We live in the age of the Holy Spirit's outpouring (see Ac 2:14–21). How do we sense God's Spirit empowering, teaching and leading us?

Your sons and daughters will
prophesy,
your old men will dream dreams,
your young men will see visions.
29 Even on my servants,[n] both men and
women,
I will pour out my Spirit in those
days.
30 I will show wonders in the heavens[o]
and on the earth,[p]
blood and fire and billows of
smoke.
31 The sun will be turned to darkness[q]
and the moon to blood
before the coming of the great
and dreadful day of the LORD.[r]
32 And everyone who calls
on the name of the LORD will be
saved;[s]
for on Mount Zion[t] and in Jerusalem
there will be deliverance,[u]
as the LORD has said,
even among the survivors[v]
whom the LORD calls.[b]

The Nations Judged

3 [c] "In those days and at that time,
when I restore the fortunes[w] of
Judah and Jerusalem,

[a] *25* The precise meaning of the four Hebrew words used here for locusts is uncertain.
[b] *32* In Hebrew texts 2:28-32 is numbered 3:1-5.
[c] In Hebrew texts 3:1-21 is numbered 4:1-21.

2:24 The final stage of restoration follows. The locusts previously destroyed the land, but God graciously restores abundance.

2:25–27 This is a theological pivot point of the book: Yahweh exists, Yahweh is present with them, and only Yahweh—not any natural phenomenon of force—has divine power over them.

2:28–29 The recipients of the outpouring are clear from the text: "all people" (v. 28). Moses's prayer that all might be prophets (Nu 11:29) is fulfilled at this time.

This all happens "in those days" (cf. v. 29b; 3:1). Sometimes this phrase describes events fulfilled within the period of the OT. Sometimes, however, there are elements that are not ever fulfilled in this way. There can be, therefore, a future implication with this phrase, referring to a much later Pentecost (Ac 2:1–21) and beyond (Rev 9:6).

2:30–31 Displays in space ("the heavens") and on land ("the earth") accompany the Spirit's outpouring (v. 30). All of these phenomena call to mind the "day of the LORD." This time, the day is not described by its closeness but by its character.

2:32 Calling on God's name means praying for his help and even expressing allegiance and belonging to him. Unfortunately there are casualties, since those making the request of God are "among the survivors" (v. 32). This implies that there are also some who have perished.

✣ **2:18–32** God's desire is to shower his people with all good blessings, wanting to raise them to the heights rather than continuing to watch them despair. He desires all of our allegiance and love to be directed toward him, since our loyalty is limited and should never be squandered on another deity of any kind. His infinite blessing, however, is completely available to those who worship "in spirit and in truth" (Jn 4:24).

3:1–4 God directs his attention away from his own people to speak judgment and restoration on the

[2]I will gather all nations
and bring them down to the Valley
of Jehoshaphat.[a]
There I will put them on trial[x]
for what they did to my
inheritance, my people Israel,
because they scattered my people
among the nations
and divided up my land.
[3]They cast lots for my people
and traded boys for prostitutes;
they sold girls for wine[y] to drink.

[4]"Now what have you against me, Tyre
and Sidon[z] and all you regions of Philistia? Are you repaying me for something
I have done? If you are paying me back, I
will swiftly and speedily return on your
own heads what you have done.[a] [5]For you
took my silver and my gold and carried
off my finest treasures to your temples.[bb]
[6]You sold the people of Judah and Jerusalem to the Greeks, that you might send
them far from their homeland.
[7]"See, I am going to rouse them out of
the places to which you sold them,[c] and
I will return on your own heads what
you have done. [8]I will sell your sons[d]
and daughters to the people of Judah,[e]
and they will sell them to the Sabeans, a
nation far away." The LORD has spoken.

[9]Proclaim this among the nations:
Prepare for war![f]
Rouse the warriors![g]
Let all the fighting men draw near
and attack.
[10]Beat your plowshares into swords
and your pruning hooks[h] into
spears.

3:2 [x]Eze 36:5
3:3 [y]Am 2:6
3:4 [z]Mt 11:21 [a]Isa 34:8
3:5 [b]2Ch 21:16-17
3:7 [c]Isa 43:5-6; Jer 23:8
3:8 [d]Isa 60:14 [e]Isa 14:2
3:9 [f]Isa 8:9 [g]Jer 46:4
3:10 [h]Isa 2:4; Mic 4:3
[i]Zec 12:8
3:11 [j]Eze 38:15-16; Zep 3:8 [k]Isa 13:3
3:12 [l]Isa 2:4
3:13 [m]Hos 6:11; Mt 13:39; Rev 14:15-19 [n]Rev 14:20
3:14 [o]Isa 34:2-8; Joel 1:15
3:16 [p]Am 1:2 [q]Eze 38:19 [r]Jer 16:19

Joel 3:16 ❖ How can we make God our refuge and stronghold?

Let the weakling[i] say,
"I am strong!"
[11]Come quickly, all you nations from
every side,
and assemble[j] there.

Bring down your warriors,[k] LORD!

[12]"Let the nations be roused;
let them advance into the Valley
of Jehoshaphat,
for there I will sit
to judge[l] all the nations on every
side.
[13]Swing the sickle,
for the harvest[m] is ripe.
Come, trample the grapes,
for the winepress[n] is full
and the vats overflow—
so great is their wickedness!"

[14]Multitudes, multitudes
in the valley of decision!
For the day of the LORD[o] is near
in the valley of decision.
[15]The sun and moon will be darkened,
and the stars no longer shine.
[16]The LORD will roar from Zion
and thunder from Jerusalem;[p]
the earth and the heavens will
tremble.[q]
But the LORD will be a refuge for his
people,
a stronghold[r] for the people of
Israel.

[a] 2 *Jehoshaphat* means *the LORD judges*; also in verse 12. [b] 5 Or *palaces*

nations. These nations scatter God's people (v. 2). They misuse both male and female children as the means of barter, selling them so they can pursue all kinds of vice.
3:5–8 These verses detail some of the wrongs for which the nations are to be repaid. The slave traders will receive the same treatment they inflicted on Judah: They too will be sold.
3:9–12 Verse 11 shows an impatient prophet who is almost saying, "Enough talk, God. Please get moving!" Yahweh's directions resume in 3:12; he sits as a mighty, enthroned king or judge.

✣ **3:1–12** Every year tens of thousands of women and children are trafficked as sex workers—either as prostitutes or in the pornography industry. There are members of our churches who are supporting this slave trade through their participation, and this must be addressed. Each of us needs to evaluate our complicity in these industries, repent, and take a stand. On this and on many other vital ethical issues, theology cannot stay just in our heads but must also live through our hearts and in our actions.

3:13 God promised agricultural abundance for his people (2:24), and now this is applied metaphorically to the wickedness of the nations. They are cut down like grain.
3:14–15 Once again the approaching "day of the LORD" (v. 14) is mentioned, this time as it affects the nations rather than God's people. Nations will experience the same upset of earth and heavens as Judah suffered, with the exact clauses of 2:10 repeated.
3:16–17 The tabernacle and temple are called holy places, and this sanctity extends to the entire city. Foreign forces are to be kept away permanently, for they will "never again . . . invade her" (v. 17).

Blessings for God's People

17 "Then you will know that I, the LORD your God,[s]
dwell in Zion,[t] my holy hill.
Jerusalem will be holy;
never again will foreigners invade her.

18 "In that day the mountains will drip new wine,
and the hills will flow with milk;[u]
all the ravines of Judah will run with water.[v]
A fountain will flow out of the LORD's house[w]
and will water the valley of acacias.[a][x]

19 But Egypt will be desolate,
Edom a desert waste,
because of violence[y] done to the people of Judah,
in whose land they shed innocent blood.
20 Judah will be inhabited forever[z]
and Jerusalem through all generations.
21 Shall I leave their innocent blood unavenged?
No, I will not.[a]"

The LORD dwells in Zion!

3:17 [s] Joel 2:27 [t] Isa 4:3
3:18 [u] Ex 3:8 [v] Isa 30:25; 35:6 [w] Rev 22:1-2 [x] Eze 47:1; Am 9:13
3:19 [y] Ob 10
3:20 [z] Am 9:15
3:21 [a] Eze 36:25

[a] 18 Or *Valley of Shittim*

3:18 The new wine will be restored in abundance. The "hills will flow with milk." Not only will there be sufficient water for her needs, but its "fountain" will be a source of fresh water for others.
3:19–21 The nations, in contrast, receive no blessing but rather the devastation that once was Judah's. The entire prophecy comes to a close with these two positive sentiments to God's people: I will forgive you, and I am with you.

3:13–21 Being a member of or participating in church is not an end in itself; rather, it is a means to a greater end: developing an intimate relationship with God. The aim of the church should not be to get people to know *about* God, but rather to get to *know* God.

God is one party in the relationship, and he knows and loves those who are in relationship with him. But we are the other party and therefore must spend time with him—not only talking to him in prayer, but also listening to him, reading Scripture, and spending time with others in the Christian community in worship.

Each of us needs to return to a realization that we very much need to know God so that we do not wither and fade in our Christian walk (Jn 15:1-8).

Amos

Author: Amos

Audience: Primarily the idolatrous and indulgent people of the northern kingdom of Israel

Date: About 760–750 BC

Theme: God speaks through the prophet Amos to call for social justice as the indispensable expression of true piety and announces judgment for Israel's injustice.

PERSPECTIVE

How does one break the news to religious people that their good lives, deeds, behavior, and theology do not please God? How does one tell others that God will judge them for behavior they see as ethical? What is the right way of exposing deceptive theology or of undermining someone's security in useless acts of worship?

The prophet Amos faced some of these issues when he was called to warn the Israelites about a great punishment God was going to bring on them because of their failures. This prosperous and strong nation would soon be defeated and sent into exile. Amos called the nation back to their ancient religious traditions in the Torah and introduced new ideas that called for a transformation of the way his audience thought about God and their relationship to him.

Amos's words included criticisms of inadequate worship, misguided priorities, oppressive acts against the weak, and a lack of holiness. His messages were not given to degrade or ostracize the listeners, but to help people understand God's view of reality, to warn them of the judgment God would bring on the nation, and to cause a remnant of the people to change their behavior and turn to God. Amos wanted people to love God with all their hearts and to live like God's people in his chosen land, but they would not be able to do this if they continued in their sinful ways.

Amos's message was a call to recognize the deceptive nature of some of the people's failures. The prophet earnestly prayed for his listeners, lamented, and wept over what he saw coming on the land of Israel. He tried to motivate his brothers and sisters to transform their

Reading Amos

The book of Amos never states the purpose for writing down the prophecies Amos spoke in Israel; in fact, the book never clearly states who actually wrote down the oracles. Amos's ministry covers less than two years (1:1), somewhere between 765–760 BC, and his sermons are given at two key cities: Samaria, the capital and center of Israelite government, and Bethel, a center of Israelite religion.

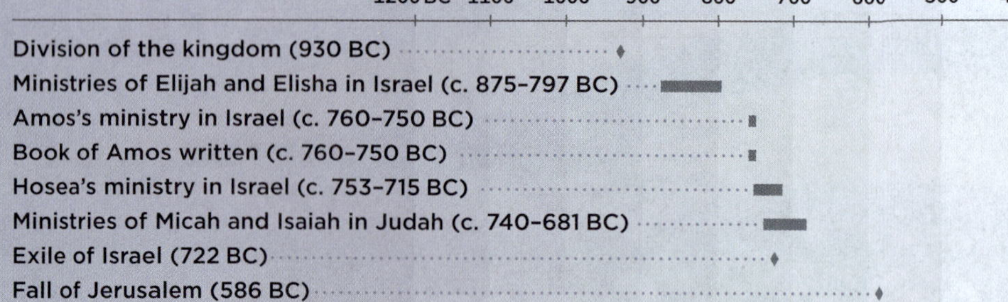

The book of Amos has three main sections. The first two chapters form a unit of God's judgment on the nations, including Judah and Israel. The next four chapters contain messages from God, beginning with "Hear" or "Woe." The last three chapters contain five visions of judgment, though Amos closes on a note of hope. Throughout this book, be aware that Amos sometimes uses rather blunt language.

Key Verse

Seek good, not evil, that you may live. Then the LORD God Almighty will be with you, just as you say he is.

—Amos 5:14

theology and personal behavior to avoid God's hand of punishment.

In revisiting the world of the prophets we must try to imagine their setting so that we can relate the principles in the prophet's message to our culture and our own personal lives. What can we learn from the failures of the Israelites during these years? Do the sermons of the prophet address basic issues that people still struggle with today? Does the spiritual life of the prophet and his view of ministry set an example for us in some area of our personal ministry? What areas of thinking is God trying to transform in our lives? These are the questions we are invited and challenged to consider as we read the words of prophets such as Amos.

TAKING THE NEXT STEPS

Amos, a prophet from southern Judah who lived at the same time as Hosea, was called by God to prophesy against the northern kingdom of Israel during the time of King Jeroboam II (2Ki 14:23–29). This was the time of Israel's greatest prosperity, but what Amos saw was idolatry, immorality, and far too many rich people getting richer at the expense of the poor. He cried out for social justice, prophesying judgment against his hearers if they continued in their present ways. But Amos spoke more than judgment; he also offered hope to those who would truly seek the Lord.

The book of Amos has a contemporary ring that is applicable to our daily lives. (1) In the affluence of the Western world, the dangers of materialism are as great today as they were in Amos's day. This book addresses those in our society who use whatever means they can, just or unjust, to increase their wealth at the expense of the poor. (2) We ought also to be aware of the severe judgment that the Lord has for those enslaved to religious formalism and hypocrisy. (3) One of the most important responsibilities God has given us is to show concern for the poor and the oppressed. (4) God is always ready to forgive those who repent of their sins and seek him as the Lord of their life.

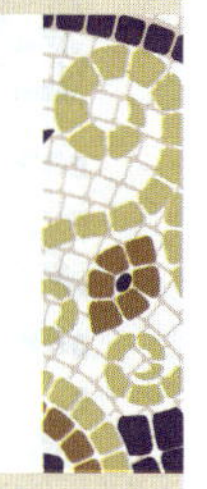

WHAT TO LOOK FOR IN AMOS

- Listing of the sins of Israel (ch. 4)
- Amos's call to repentance (ch. 5)
- Amos's confrontation with the ruling authorities in Israel (ch. 7)
- Destruction and restoration (ch. 9)

1 The words of Amos, one of the shepherds of Tekoa[a] — the vision he saw concerning Israel two years before the earthquake,[b] when Uzziah[c] was king of Judah and Jeroboam[d] son of Jehoash[a] was king of Israel.[e]

2 He said:

"The LORD roars[f] from Zion
and thunders from Jerusalem;[g]
the pastures of the shepherds
dry up,
and the top of Carmel[h] withers."[i]

Judgment on Israel's Neighbors

3 This is what the LORD says:

"For three sins of Damascus,[j]
even for four, I will not relent.[k]
Because she threshed Gilead
with sledges having iron teeth,
4 I will send fire[l] on the house of
Hazael
that will consume the fortresses[m]
of Ben-Hadad.[n]
5 I will break down the gate[o] of
Damascus;
I will destroy the king who is in[b]
the Valley of Aven[c]
and the one who holds the scepter in
Beth Eden.
The people of Aram will go into
exile to Kir,[p]"
says the LORD.

1:1 [a]2Sa 14:2 [b]Zec 14:5 [c]2Ch 26:23 [d]2Ki 14:23 [e]Hos 1:1
1:2 [f]Isa 42:13 [g]Joel 3:16 [h]Am 9:3 [i]Jer 12:4
1:3 [j]Isa 8:4; 17:1-3 [k]Am 2:6
1:4 [l]Jer 49:27 [m]Jer 17:27 [n]1Ki 20:1; 2Ki 6:24
1:5 [o]Jer 51:30 [p]2Ki 16:9
1:6 [q]1Sa 6:17; Zep 2:4 [r]Ob 11
1:8 [s]2Ch 26:6 [t]Ps 81:14 [u]Eze 25:16 [v]Isa 14:28-32; Zep 2:4-7
1:9 [w]1Ki 5:1; 9:11-14; Isa 23:1-18; Jer 25:22; Joel 3:4; Mt 11:21
1:10 [x]Zec 9:1-4
1:11 [y]Nu 20:14-21; 2Ch 28:17; Jer 49:7-22

6 This is what the LORD says:

"For three sins of Gaza,[q]
even for four, I will not relent.
Because she took captive whole
communities
and sold them to Edom,[r]
7 I will send fire on the walls of Gaza
that will consume her fortresses.
8 I will destroy the king[d] of Ashdod[s]
and the one who holds the scepter
in Ashkelon.
I will turn my hand[t] against Ekron,
till the last of the Philistines[u] are
dead,"
says the Sovereign LORD.[v]

9 This is what the LORD says:

"For three sins of Tyre,[w]
even for four, I will not relent.
Because she sold whole communities
of captives to Edom,
disregarding a treaty of
brotherhood,
10 I will send fire on the walls of Tyre
that will consume her fortresses.[x]"

11 This is what the LORD says:

"For three sins of Edom,[y]
even for four, I will not relent.

[a] *1* Hebrew *Joash*, a variant of *Jehoash* [b] *5* Or *the inhabitants of* [c] *5* *Aven* means *wickedness.* [d] *8* Or *inhabitants*

1:1 The text says nothing about Amos' family. He comes from Tekoa, a small rural Judean village about ten miles south of Jerusalem.
1:2 This hymn emphasizes God's roaring voice, his thunderous appeal from Zion.

APPLICATION ✣ 1:1-2 Many of the great men and women of God in our time started out much like Amos: They were common people who had no special status and perhaps had limited potential in the eyes of their friends and family. Yet God chose them to demonstrate his power through their weakness (1Co 1:27).

1:3-5 The rebellious act of the Syrians that Amos mentions is undated, but it likely happened years earlier. The punishment Amos announces involves the destruction of the king's house and military fortresses that have provided him security.
1:6-8 The Philistines' rebellious acts involve capturing whole communities. This is a wholesale kidnapping of peaceful people for the purpose of turning a profit. Philistia's punishment is similar to Syria's.
1:9-10 Tyre, the leading city of Phoenicia, has rebelled many times. God will act in wrath against them, bring down the thick walls of the city, and cause its strongly fortified palace fortresses to go up in flames.
1:11-12 Scripture describes years of animosity between Israel and Edom (descendants of the two brothers Jacob and Esau). The punishment clauses announce God's intention to end the terror that Edom has unleashed on its neighbors.

PEOPLE TO KNOW // AMOS

AMOS 1:1: Amos prophesied during the mid-eighth century BC. He was from Tekoa in Judah, but he spent most of his time prophesying in the northern kingdom of Israel. His message was generally addressed to both Israel and Judah.

Amos was a farmer, both a shepherd and a keeper of sycamore-fig trees (Am 7:14). He lived during a time of great affluence and material prosperity. But it was also a time of spiritual failure. The people engaged in idolatry and mistreated the poor and the vulnerable. Comfort and wealth led to lax moral and spiritual values.

Through Amos, God called Israel and Judah back to proper concern for others, the promotion of social justice, and personal righteous living. Amos decried the injustices he saw around him. He was a gifted speaker who used words creatively and powerfully to announce God's message: God expects righteousness and justice from his people (Am 5:24). Amos warned the people against empty religious routines, reminding them that God expected true commitment and full obedience. He prepared his nation for the destruction that was to come because of their complacency.

Judgment did not have the last word, however. Amos saw beyond the coming devastation. His book closes with a promise that God will preserve a remnant who will one day enjoy the bounty of God's mercy (Am 9:11–15).

APPLICATION ✤ Amos's cutting message rings as true today as it did in his lifetime. Today, we also witness how wealth and comfort can lead to moral and spiritual decay. Much of the world is more prosperous in the twenty-first century than at any prior time in human history. Still today, there are those whose religion consists only of empty routines void of any true commitment or faith. The challenge for God's people is to be a voice for righteousness and justice in the face of indifference and misplaced priorities. We need to care for people who are oppressed, defend those who are vulnerable, and stand against corruption and evil. When we do, we point forward to the beautiful reality of God's coming kingdom.

Because he pursued his brother with a sword
and slaughtered the women of the land,
because his anger raged continually
and his fury flamed unchecked,[z]
12 I will send fire on Teman[a]
that will consume the fortresses of Bozrah."

13 This is what the LORD says:

"For three sins of Ammon,[b]
even for four, I will not relent.
Because he ripped open the pregnant women[c] of Gilead
in order to extend his borders,
14 I will set fire to the walls of Rabbah[d]
that will consume her fortresses
amid war cries[e] on the day of battle,
amid violent winds on a stormy day.

1:11 [z] Eze 25:12-14
1:12 [a] Ob 9-10
1:13 [b] Jer 49:1-6; Eze 21:28; 25:2-7 [c] Hos 13:16
1:14 [d] Dt 3:11 [e] Am 2:2

Am 1:13–15 ✤ How does reading about the sins the people committed help us grapple with this challenging topic of God's punishment? How should Christians teach about God's judgment today?

15 Her king[a] will go into exile,
he and his officials together,"
says the LORD.

2 This is what the LORD says:

"For three sins of Moab,
even for four, I will not relent.
Because he burned to ashes
the bones of Edom's king,
2 I will send fire on Moab
that will consume the fortresses of Kerioth.[b]
Moab will go down in great tumult

[a] 15 Or */ Molek* [b] 2 Or *of her cities*

1:13–15 God's judgment on Ammon involves the destruction of their capital, Rabbah (modern Amman, Jordan), and the military fortresses in it.
2:1–3 The last foreign nation mentioned is Moab, the sister nation of Ammon. Their willful rebellious act has been to burn the bones of the king of Edom, but the Moabites may have gone one step further by using the king's ashes as lime, possibly to plaster the walls of a house. God's judgment of Moab is similar to what will happen to Ammon.

amid war cries and the blast of the
trumpet.
3 I will destroy her ruler[f]
and kill all her officials with him,"[g]
says the LORD.

4 This is what the LORD says:

"For three sins of Judah,[h]
even for four, I will not relent.
Because they have rejected the law[i]
of the LORD
and have not kept his decrees,[j]
because they have been led astray[k]
by false gods,[a][l]
the gods[b] their ancestors
followed,[m]
5 I will send fire on Judah
that will consume the fortresses of
Jerusalem.[n]"

Judgment on Israel

6 This is what the LORD says:

"For three sins of Israel,
even for four, I will not relent.
They sell the innocent for silver,
and the needy for a pair of
sandals.[o]
7 They trample on the heads of the
poor
as on the dust of the ground
and deny justice to the oppressed.
Father and son use the same girl
and so profane my holy name.[p]
8 They lie down beside every altar
on garments taken in pledge.[q]
In the house of their god
they drink wine[r] taken as fines.

2:3 [f] Ps 2:10 [g] Isa 40:23 2:4 [h] 2Ki 17:19; Hos 12:2 [i] Jer 6:19 [j] Eze 20:24 [k] Isa 9:16 [l] Isa 28:15 [m] 2Ki 22:13; Jer 16:12 2:5 [n] Jer 17:27; Hos 8:14 2:6 [o] Joel 3:3; Am 8:6 2:7 [p] Am 5:11-12; 8:4 2:8 [q] Ex 22:26 [r] Am 4:1; 6:6

Am 2:4-16 ❖ Why is it significant that God's longest words of judgment in this section are for his chosen people, Judah and Israel? What does this show about what it means to be the people of God?

9 "Yet I destroyed the Amorites[s] before
them,
though they were tall as the cedars
and strong as the oaks.
I destroyed their fruit above
and their roots[t] below.
10 I brought you up out of Egypt[u]
and led you forty years in the
wilderness[v]
to give you the land of the
Amorites.[w]

11 "I also raised up prophets[x] from
among your children
and Nazirites[y] from among your
youths.
Is this not true, people of Israel?"
declares the LORD.
12 "But you made the Nazirites drink
wine
and commanded the prophets not
to prophesy.[z]

13 "Now then, I will crush you
as a cart crushes when loaded with
grain.
14 The swift will not escape,
the strong[a] will not muster their
strength,

2:9 [s] Nu 21:23-26; Jos 10:12 [t] Eze 17:9; Mal 4:1 2:10 [u] Ex 20:2; Am 3:1 [v] Dt 2:7 [w] Ex 3:8; Am 9:7 2:11 [x] Dt 18:18; Jer 7:25 [y] Nu 6:2-3; Jdg 13:5 2:12 [z] Isa 30:10; Jer 11:21; Am 7:12-13; Mic 2:6 2:14 [a] Jer 9:23

[a] 4 Or *by lies* [b] 4 Or *lies*

1:3—2:3 Suppose one is looking for situations to apply the principle that God holds every nation accountable for its acts of inhumanity against people. In that case, one can look for atrocities in peaceful foreign nations that have a poor record on human rights, discover how military personnel treat innocent civilians in wartime, or move away from the national focus to examine the way individual people use their power to abuse others.

In all this, we must look at the same questions in our own lives. At our core, who are we? Is God pleased with the way we treat others?

2:4–5 The willful sin of Judah is a direct refusal to follow God's instructions in the Torah. Because of this direct refusal to accept what God has said, God will treat Judah just like every other nation.
2:6–8 The first accusations involve the unnecessary foreclosure on small loans by money lenders. The second accusations emphasize the physical abuse of the helpless and weak. The third rebellious act is the sexual abuse of a servant woman by both a father and son. The final accusations of oppression chronicle additional ways the powerful exploit the destitute.
2:9–11 Amos emphasizes what God did for Israel in the past by rescuing them when they were oppressed by stronger nations. One would expect Israel to be thankful and obey God's covenant conditions because of his grace. One would also assume that the Israelites would understand from their history that God fights for the oppressed.
2:12 The prophet reports that Israelites coerce people who have taken a Nazirite vow into drinking wine, breaking their vows of abstinence. This is in direct conflict with what God required and is a blatant attempt to substitute their own cultural rules for God's expectations.
2:13–16 The punishment statement focuses on the utter annihilation of Israel's army. This will be an awesome demonstration of God's power. As Amos's audience in Samaria heard these words, they must have been astonished and petrified.

and the warrior will not save his
life.[b]
15 The archer[c] will not stand his ground,
the fleet-footed soldier will not
get away,
and the horseman will not save
his life.
16 Even the bravest warriors[d]
will flee naked on that day,"
declares the LORD.

Witnesses Summoned Against Israel

3 Hear this word, people of Israel, the
word the LORD has spoken against
you — against the whole family I brought
up out of Egypt:[e]

2 "You only have I chosen[f]
of all the families of the earth;
therefore I will punish you
for all your sins.[g]"

3 Do two walk together
unless they have agreed to do so?
4 Does a lion roar in the thicket
when it has no prey?[h]
Does it growl in its den
when it has caught nothing?
5 Does a bird swoop down to a trap on
the ground
when no bait is there?
Does a trap spring up from the
ground
if it has not caught anything?
6 When a trumpet sounds in a city,
do not the people tremble?
When disaster comes to a city,
has not the LORD caused it?[i]

7 Surely the Sovereign LORD does
nothing
without revealing his plan[j]
to his servants the prophets.[k]

8 The lion has roared —
who will not fear?
The Sovereign LORD has spoken —
who can but prophesy?[l]

9 Proclaim to the fortresses of
Ashdod
and to the fortresses of Egypt:
"Assemble yourselves on the
mountains of Samaria;[m]
see the great unrest within her
and the oppression among her
people."

10 "They do not know how to do
right,[n]" declares the LORD,
"who store up in their fortresses[o]
what they have plundered[p] and
looted."

11 Therefore this is what the Sovereign
LORD says:

"An enemy will overrun your land,
pull down your strongholds
and plunder your fortresses.[q]"

12 This is what the LORD says:

"As a shepherd rescues from the
lion's[r] mouth
only two leg bones or a piece of an
ear,

2:14 [b] Ps 33:16; Isa 30:16-17
2:15 [c] Eze 39:3
2:16 [d] Jer 48:41
3:1 [e] Am 2:10
3:2 [f] Dt 7:6; Lk 12:47 [g] Jer 14:10
3:4 [h] Ps 104:21; Hos 5:14
3:6 [i] Isa 14:24-27; 45:7
3:7 [j] Ge 18:17; Da 9:22; Jn 15:15; Rev 10:7 [k] Jer 23:22
3:8 [l] Jer 20:9; Jnh 1:1-3; 3:1-3; Ac 4:20
3:9 [m] Am 4:1; 6:1
3:10 [n] Jer 4:22; Am 5:7; 6:12 [o] Zep 1:9 [p] Hab 2:8
3:11 [q] Am 2:5; 6:14
3:12 [r] 1Sa 17:34

Am 3:2 ❖ Why does being chosen by God merit more direct punishment for breaking God's commands? How does this reality point us to the ministry of Christ?

2:4–16 In a sense, Amos is living in two worlds. First, he's addressing the unfaithful people of Judah and Israel who have ignored God's covenant. Second, he's speaking about a pre-covenant situation for the pagan population in and around Israel.

If one looks at the cultures around the world today, one could suggest that some countries (especially Western) appear to be in a post-Christian era. We in the church should be less concerned about our loss of status in influencing the general values of society and concentrate more on getting our own house in order. True change comes in surrendering to God's purposes in our hearts as we rededicate ourselves, day after day, to his plans for our lives and for his creation.

3:1–2 The people were led out of Egypt to be God's people. If the Israelites forget what God did for them and do not live as his people, the curses of the covenant are inevitable (Dt 27–28).

3:3–6 Each question in this passage anticipates the answer "no." Most Israelites would agree that cities are destroyed by divine action. But if this is true, God is also the one who has the power to cause the destruction of Samaria.

3:7–8 The flow of this long series of questions is broken in v. 7. God does not just destroy cities or nations on a whim. Why has Amos revealed this news about God's plan to destroy Israel? God has revealed his plans to the prophet because he intends to act soon. He desires to have a servant warn those he will judge so that they will fear God (v. 8) and turn from their wickedness.

3:9–12 God will bring an unnamed enemy nation to oppress the royal and noble inhabitants of Samaria, and they will receive the same treatment they have given to others.

so will the Israelites living in
Samaria be rescued,
with only the head of a bed
and a piece of fabric[a] from a
couch.[bs]"

13"Hear this and testify[t] against the
descendants of Jacob," declares the Lord,
the LORD God Almighty.

14"On the day I punish Israel for her
sins,
I will destroy the altars of Bethel;[u]
the horns of the altar will be cut off
and fall to the ground.
15I will tear down the winter house[v]
along with the summer house;[w]
the houses adorned with ivory[x] will
be destroyed
and the mansions will be
demolished,"
declares the LORD.

Israel Has Not Returned to God

4 Hear this word, you cows of
Bashan[y] on Mount Samaria,[z]
you women who oppress the poor
and crush the needy
and say to your husbands, "Bring
us some drinks![a]"
2The Sovereign LORD has sworn by
his holiness:
"The time will surely come
when you will be taken away[b] with
hooks,
the last of you with fishhooks.[c]
3You will each go straight out
through breaches in the wall,[c]
and you will be cast out toward
Harmon,[d]"
declares the LORD.
4"Go to Bethel and sin;
go to Gilgal[d] and sin yet more.
Bring your sacrifices every
morning,[e]
your tithes[f] every three years.[eg]
5Burn leavened bread[h] as a thank
offering
and brag about your freewill
offerings[i] —
boast about them, you Israelites,
for this is what you love to do,"
declares the Sovereign LORD.

6"I gave you empty stomachs in every
city
and lack of bread in every town,
yet you have not returned to me,"
declares the LORD.[j]

7"I also withheld rain from you
when the harvest was still three
months away.
I sent rain on one town,

3:12 [s]Am 6:4
3:13 [t]Eze 2:7
3:14 [u]Am 5:5-6
3:15 [v]Jer 36:22 [w]Jdg 3:20 [x]1Ki 22:39
4:1 [y]Ps 22:12; Eze 39:18 [z]Am 3:9 [a]Am 2:8; 5:11; 8:6
4:2 [b]Am 6:8
4:3 [c]Eze 12:5
4:4 [d]Hos 4:15 [e]Nu 28:3 [f]Dt 14:28 [g]Eze 20:39; Am 5:21-22
4:5 [h]Lev 7:13 [i]Lev 22:18-21
4:6 [j]Isa 3:1; Jer 5:3; Hag 2:17

[a] 12 The meaning of the Hebrew for this phrase is uncertain. [b] 12 Or *Israelites be rescued, / those who sit in Samaria / on the edge of their beds / and in Damascus on their couches.* [c] 2 Or *away in baskets, / the last of you in fish baskets* [d] 3 Masoretic Text; with a different word division of the Hebrew (see Septuagint) *out, you mountain of oppression* [e] 4 Or *days*

Am 4:6-11 ❖ How can we tell when calamities or trials may be God's way of summoning us to return to him?

3:13–15 Amos describes the removal of two of Israel's sources of security: the altars where they worship and their fortified mansions. The altars of Bethel include those in the king's state temple (v. 13), where the golden calf was located (see 1Ki 12:28–32). God will also remove the royal court and the wealthy people's social status, financial security, and physical protection (v. 15) when he tears down their homes.
4:1–3 This imagery is a cutting reference to the rich women in Samaria. These pampered, self-indulgent, and bossy ladies maintain their lifestyle by exploiting the poor.

3:1–4:3 Are possessions and wealth evils that God hates, or can people have possessions if they do not let them become a source of security? Those without abundance are called to be content, and those with abundance must be content and generous with what they have (Php 4:12; 1Ti 6:17–18). The way we handle our possessions—holding them tightly and wanting for more, or holding them loosely and being generous toward others—says a lot about the condition of our hearts (Mt 6:21–24).

4:4–5 Amos does not just encourage people to go to the temples in Bethel and Gilgal; he sarcastically insists that they multiply their rebellious acts of worship. This statement reveals that their sacrifices only add to the people's sinfulness before God.

Amos's second encouragement (4:4b) mocks the people's overemphasis on repeatedly bringing sacrifices and tithes. The prophet wants his audience to ask themselves whether God is primarily impressed with religious acts, or if he's looking for something else within his worshiping people.

The Levitical regulations did allow for thank offerings of leavened bread (v. 5; cf. Lev 7:13), but there is no instruction to burn this bread. Thus, the problem Amos is pinpointing here relates to the pious person's bragging about his or her gifts that only honor themselves.
4:6–11 This passage is divided into five short sections by the concluding phrase, "'yet you have

but withheld it from another.[k]
One field had rain;
another had none and dried up.
8 People staggered from town to town
for water[l]
but did not get enough to drink,
yet you have not returned[m]
to me,"
declares the LORD.[n]

9 "Many times I struck your gardens
and vineyards,
destroying them with blight and
mildew.[o]
Locusts devoured your fig and olive
trees,[p]
yet you have not returned[q] to me,"
declares the LORD.

10 "I sent plagues[r] among you
as I did to Egypt.
I killed your young men with the
sword,
along with your captured horses.
I filled your nostrils with the stench
of your camps,
yet you have not returned to me,"
declares the LORD.[s]

11 "I overthrew some of you
as I overthrew Sodom and
Gomorrah.[t]
You were like a burning stick
snatched from the fire,
yet you have not returned to me,"
declares the LORD.

12 "Therefore this is what I will do to
you, Israel,
and because I will do this to you,
Israel,
prepare to meet your God."

13 He who forms the mountains,[u]
who creates the wind,
and who reveals his thoughts[v] to
mankind,
who turns dawn to darkness,
and treads on the heights of the
earth[w] —
the LORD God Almighty is his
name.[x]

A Lament and Call to Repentance

5 Hear this word, Israel, this lament[y] I
take up concerning you:

2 "Fallen is Virgin[z] Israel,
never to rise again,
deserted in her own land,
with no one to lift her up.[a]"

3 This is what the Sovereign LORD says
to Israel:

"Your city that marches out a
thousand strong
will have only a hundred left;
your town that marches out a
hundred strong
will have only ten left.[b]"

4 This is what the LORD says to Israel:

"Seek me and live;[c]
5 do not seek Bethel,
do not go to Gilgal,[d]
do not journey to Beersheba.[e]
For Gilgal will surely go into exile,

4:7 [k] Ex 9:4, 26; Dt 11:17; 2Ch 7:13
4:8 [l] Eze 4:16-17 [m] Jer 3:7 [n] Jer 14:4
4:9 [o] Dt 28:22 [p] Joel 1:7 [q] Jer 3:10; Hag 2:17
4:10 [r] Ex 9:3; Dt 28:27 [s] Isa 9:13
4:11 [t] Ge 19:24; Jer 23:14
4:13 [u] Ps 65:6 [v] Da 2:28 [w] Mic 1:3 [x] Isa 47:4; Am 5:8, 27; 9:6
5:1 [y] Eze 19:1
5:2 [z] Jer 14:17 [a] Jer 50:32; Am 8:14
5:3 [b] Isa 6:13; Am 6:9
5:4 [c] Isa 55:3; Jer 29:13
5:5 [d] 1Sa 11:14; Am 4:4 [e] Am 8:14

---

not returned to me,' declares the LORD" (vv. 6, 8, 9, 10, 11). By repeating this phrase, Amos hammers home his central message: The Israelites do not have a proper relationship with God.

4:12–13 The prophet's sermon comes to a peak with a final warning that the people of Israel must "prepare to meet your God" (v. 12). They can no longer avoid God because he is coming to meet them. His patience has ended.

The statement in v. 13 may have quoted a popular hymn that the people regularly sang but never thought much about. Indeed, it is a fearful thing to fall into the hands of an angry God.

4:4–13 We no longer offer burnt offerings or thank offerings with leavened bread in churches today, but we do have a variety of symbolic rituals that represent spiritual truths. If we are only concerned with impressing others in the church and making ourselves look good, our prayers, songs, liturgies, and repeated acts can become just as dead as the meaningless offerings that some offered in Israel.

Pride is insidious; it looks good on the outside, yet it's first on the list of the sins that God hates (Pr 8:13; 11:2; 16:5). We do well to check our internal motivation when we engage in selfless acts for God. Are they truly selfless?

5:1–3, 16–17 The nation of Israel, a once vibrant virgin, now lies totally helpless without hope of revival. The bitterness of the prophet's grief is evident, and the finality of Israel's destruction is clear.

Verse 3 points out why the nation has no hope: Its army has been decimated (90 percent of the troops have been killed), exactly as Amos predicted in 2:13–16. Everyone will mourn because death will touch every family.

5:4–6, 14–15 Next to these devastating laments is what appears to be a prophetic call of hope. It seems to function in two ways: first, as a partial explanation for why God is judging the wicked; second, as an encouragement to a small "remnant" (v. 15) of seekers.

and Bethel will be reduced to
nothing.[a][f]"
6 Seek[g] the LORD and live,[h]
or he will sweep through the
tribes of Joseph like a fire;[i]
it will devour them,
and Bethel[j] will have no one to
quench it.

7 There are those who turn justice
into bitterness[k]
and cast righteousness to the
ground.

8 He who made the Pleiades and Orion,[l]
who turns midnight into dawn[m]
and darkens day into night,[n]
who calls for the waters of the sea
and pours them out over the face
of the land —
the LORD is his name.[o]
9 With a blinding flash he destroys the
stronghold
and brings the fortified city to
ruin.[p]

10 There are those who hate the one
who upholds justice in court[q]
and detest the one who tells the
truth.[r]

11 You levy a straw tax on the poor[s]
and impose a tax on their grain.
Therefore, though you have built
stone mansions,[t]
you will not live in them;
though you have planted lush
vineyards,
you will not drink their wine.[u]
12 For I know how many are your
offenses
and how great your sins.

There are those who oppress the
innocent and take bribes
and deprive the poor of justice in
the courts.[v]
13 Therefore the prudent keep quiet in
such times,
for the times are evil.

14 Seek good, not evil,
that you may live.
Then the LORD God Almighty will be
with you,
just as you say he is.
15 Hate evil,[w] love good;
maintain justice in the courts.
Perhaps the LORD God Almighty will
have mercy[x]
on the remnant[y] of Joseph.

16 Therefore this is what the Lord, the
LORD God Almighty, says:

"There will be wailing[z] in all the
streets
and cries of anguish in every
public square.
The farmers[a] will be summoned to
weep
and the mourners to wail.
17 There will be wailing in all the
vineyards,
for I will pass through[b] your
midst,"
says the LORD.[c]

The Day of the LORD

18 Woe to you who long
for the day of the LORD![d]
Why do you long for the day of the
LORD?
That day will be darkness,[e] not
light.[f]
19 It will be as though a man fled from
a lion

5:5 [f] 1Sa 7:16
5:6 [g] Isa 55:6 [h] ver 14 [i] Dt 4:24 [j] Am 3:14
5:7 [k] Am 6:12
5:8 [l] Job 9:9 [m] Isa 42:16 [n] Ps 104:20; Am 8:9 [o] Ps 104:6-9; Am 4:13
5:9 [p] Mic 5:11
5:10 [q] Isa 29:21 [r] 1Ki 22:8
5:11 [s] Am 8:6 [t] Am 3:15 [u] Mic 6:15
5:12 [v] Isa 5:23; Am 2:6-7
5:15 [w] Ps 97:10; Ro 12:9 [x] Joel 2:14 [y] Mic 5:7,8
5:16 [z] Jer 9:17 [a] Joel 1:11
5:17 [b] Ex 12:12 [c] Isa 16:10; Jer 48:33
5:18 [d] Joel 1:15 [e] Joel 2:2 [f] Isa 5:19,30; Jer 30:7

[a] 5 Hebrew *aven*, a reference to Beth Aven (a derogatory name for Bethel); see Hosea 4:15.

5:7, 10–13 This series of accusations functions as another reason for God's plan to destroy Israel. We may wonder why God would want to destroy his people, but the straightforward answer goes back to the way these people treat others. Their moral values are not governed by relationships of justice (vv. 10, 12).

5:8–9 In this speech against paganism, Yahweh is seen as the one who created the magnificent spectacle of nature that people see every night in the heavens. The prophet is using positive traditions to support his view of God.

5:1–17 Amos, Job, and the psalmists allow us to face our deepest fears and sorrows simply because they voice their grief. These authors do not face their pain alone; they bring it to God, who can do something about it. Underlying their sorrow is a faith that believes God is trustworthy and understanding; he is a resource who can change our laments into assurance and praise (Ps 30:11–12).

5:18–20 Why would anyone not look forward to the time when God will bless his people and defeat their enemies? Amos's answer to his rhetorical "why" question reveals that Israel will suffer God's judgment, just like the foreign nations.

only to meet a bear,
as though he entered his house
and rested his hand on the wall
only to have a snake bite him.[g]
20 Will not the day of the LORD be
darkness, not light—
pitch-dark, without a ray of
brightness?[h]

21 "I hate, I despise your religious
festivals;[i]
your assemblies[j] are a stench to me.
22 Even though you bring me burnt
offerings and grain offerings,
I will not accept them.
Though you bring choice fellowship
offerings,
I will have no regard for them.[k]
23 Away with the noise of your songs!
I will not listen to the music of
your harps.[l]
24 But let justice[m] roll on like a river,
righteousness like a never-failing
stream![n]

25 "Did you bring me sacrifices[o] and
offerings
forty years[p] in the wilderness,
people of Israel?
26 You have lifted up the shrine of your
king,
the pedestal of your idols,
the star of your god[a]—
which you made for yourselves.
27 Therefore I will send you into exile
beyond Damascus,"
says the LORD, whose name is God
Almighty.[q]

Woe to the Complacent

6 Woe to you[r] who are complacent in
Zion,
and to you who feel secure on
Mount Samaria,
you notable men of the foremost
nation,
to whom the people of Israel
come![s]
2 Go to Kalneh[t] and look at it;
go from there to great Hamath,[u]
and then go down to Gath[v] in
Philistia.
Are they better off than[w] your two
kingdoms?
Is their land larger than yours?
3 You put off the day of disaster
and bring near a reign of terror.[x]
4 You lie on beds adorned with
ivory
and lounge on your couches.
You dine on choice lambs
and fattened calves.[y]
5 You strum away on your harps[z] like
David
and improvise on musical
instruments.[a]
6 You drink wine[b] by the bowlful
and use the finest lotions,
but you do not grieve[c] over the
ruin of Joseph.

5:19 [g] Job 20:24; Isa 24:17-18; Jer 15:2-3; 48:44
5:20 [h] Isa 13:10; Zep 1:15
5:21 [i] Lev 26:31 [j] Isa 1:11-16
5:22 [k] Isa 66:3; Am 4:4; Mic 6:6-7
5:23 [l] Am 6:5
5:24 [m] Jer 22:3 [n] Mic 6:8
5:25 [o] Isa 43:23 [p] Dt 32:17
5:27 [q] Am 4:13; Ac 7:42-43*
6:1 [r] Lk 6:24 [s] Isa 32:9-11
6:2 [t] Ge 10:10 [u] 2Ki 18:34 [v] 2Ch 26:6 [w] Na 3:8
6:3 [x] Isa 56:12; Am 9:10
6:4 [y] Eze 34:2-3; Am 3:12
6:5 [z] Isa 5:12; Am 5:23 [a] 1Ch 15:16
6:6 [b] Am 2:8 [c] Eze 9:4

[a] 26 Or *lifted up Sakkuth your king / and Kaiwan your idols, / your star-gods*; Septuagint *lifted up the shrine of Molek / and the star of your god Rephan, / their idols*

Am 5:21–24 ❖ How can we make justice and righteousness, rather than empty ceremonies and routines, the anchor of our Christian faith?

Am 6:1 ❖ When have we been complacent in our faith? Why is spiritual complacency so dangerous?

5:21–24 Amos reintroduces his critique of the nation's sacrifices. Verse 24 urges the people to pay close attention to the implications of what it means to worship God. If worship does not further the development of spiritual character, it may just be empty emotion.
5:25–27 God will exile the Israelites into some nation far away, into an unknown land beyond Damascus. Later records in 2Ki 17:23–24 verify that God did send these people into Assyria about forty years after Amos's prophecy (721 BC).

5:18–27 Although many churches are struggling with people's preferences for different styles of worship formats (seeker, contemporary, or traditional), a much deeper and more serious issue is the lifestyle people follow after the worship service is over. True and acceptable worship is not so much about issues of the style adopted by a particular congregation, but the extent to which the worshiper's life is transformed by being in the presence of a holy God.

6:1–3 The people in Zion, the capital of Judah, as well as the people in Samaria, the capital of Israel, have a deceptive feeling of well-being and security. Because Israel is not seeing the reality of its political situation, there is a real possibility that they may be defeated.
6:4–7 The second half of the woe laments the people's careless ease that comes from their wealth. With their money and power, they have everything they want. Amos announces that these people—the citizens of the "foremost" (v. 1) nation in the Near East—will be the "first" (v. 7) to go into captivity.

7Therefore you will be among the
first to go into exile;
your feasting and lounging will
end.

The LORD Abhors the Pride of Israel

8The Sovereign LORD has sworn by
himself[d] — the LORD God Almighty declares:

"I abhor[e] the pride of Jacob[f]
and detest his fortresses;
I will deliver up[g] the city
and everything in it.[h]"

9If ten[i] people are left in one house,
they too will die. 10And if the relative
who comes to carry the bodies out of
the house to burn them[a][j] asks anyone
who might be hiding there, "Is anyone
else with you?" and he says, "No," then
he will go on to say, "Hush![k] We must not
mention the name of the LORD."

11For the LORD has given the
command,
and he will smash the great house[l]
into pieces
and the small house into bits.[m]
12Do horses run on the rocky crags?
Does one plow the sea[b] with oxen?
But you have turned justice into
poison[n]
and the fruit of righteousness into
bitterness[o] —
13you who rejoice in the conquest of
Lo Debar[c]
and say, "Did we not take
Karnaim[d] by our own
strength?[p]"
14For the LORD God Almighty
declares,
"I will stir up a nation[q] against
you, Israel,
that will oppress you all the way
from Lebo Hamath[r] to the valley
of the Arabah.[s]"

Locusts, Fire and a Plumb Line

7 This is what the Sovereign LORD
showed me:[t] He was preparing
swarms of locusts[u] after the king's share
had been harvested and just as the late
crops were coming up. 2When they had
stripped the land clean,[v] I cried out, "Sovereign LORD, forgive! How can Jacob survive?[w] He is so small![x]"
3So the LORD relented.[y]
"This will not happen," the LORD said.[z]
4This is what the Sovereign LORD
showed me: The Sovereign LORD was
calling for judgment by fire;[a] it dried up
the great deep and devoured[b] the land.
5Then I cried out, "Sovereign LORD, I beg
you, stop! How can Jacob survive? He is
so small![c]"
6So the LORD relented.[d]

6:8 [d] Ge 22:16; Heb 6:13 [e] Lev 26:30 [f] Ps 47:4 [g] Am 4:2 [h] Dt 32:19 6:9 [i] Am 5:3 6:10 [j] 1Sa 31:12 [k] Am 8:3 6:11 [l] Am 3:15 [m] Isa 55:11 6:12 [n] Hos 10:4 [o] Am 5:7 6:13 [p] Job 8:15; Isa 28:14-15 6:14 [q] Jer 5:15 [r] 1Ki 8:65 [s] Am 3:11 7:1 [t] Am 8:1 [u] Joel 1:4 7:2 [v] Ex 10:15 [w] Isa 37:4 [x] Eze 11:13 7:3 [y] Dt 32:36; Jer 26:19; Jnh 3:10 [z] Hos 11:8 7:4 [a] Isa 66:16 [b] Dt 32:22 7:5 [c] ver 1-2; Joel 2:17 7:6 [d] Jnh 3:10

[a] 10 *Or to make a funeral fire in honor of the dead* [b] 12 With a different word division of the Hebrew; Masoretic Text *plow there* [c] 13 *Lo Debar* means *nothing.* [d] 13 *Karnaim* means *horns; horn* here symbolizes strength.

6:8–10 This paragraph contains two parts: vv. 8–11 detail God's oath, while vv. 12–14 describe the absurdity of Israel's military pride. The oath expresses God's hatred for Israel's trust in her fortified cities (vv. 8, 11). In vv. 9–10 Amos illustrates what will happen to the people who live in these fortresses.
6:12–14 The final subsection abruptly begins with a series of absurd questions. By using these ridiculous rhetorical questions, Amos makes it easier for his hearers to see the absurdity of their own action of turning righteousness into something vile, bitter, or poisonous.

6:1–14 Amos saw how riches and wealth caused the upper-class people to base their security in having the best that money could buy. Does this mean that believers today must buy old furniture instead of new pieces, or that at a wedding party, only crackers and cheese should be served with the wedding cake?

No one would want to suggest that it is wrong to have money, or that money always corrupts, or that people do not need money. Money is not the problem; we are (1Ti 6:10).

7:1–3 The locusts are being formed after the king's share of the crop has been harvested. This suggests that the royal needs have been met but that the average peasant farmer will be in serious trouble. The prophet prays for compassion, which reveals the depth of God's patience and his openness to hearing the prayers of righteous intercessors (see Jas 5:13–18).
7:4–6 Whatever the source of the fire, Amos intercedes with a prayer for God to stop the fire before it destroys the land of Israel. God stops the fire and gives the Israelites more time to respond.

7:1–6 Do we in the church still realize that God takes no pleasure in the punishment of the wicked (Eze 18:23) and that he desires that no one should perish but that all will come to a knowledge of the truth (2Pe 3:9)? Is the problem more related to the fact that we have not taken the time to get personally involved with unbelievers? What happens if we are one day asked, "Who were the lost people you prayed for?"

"This will not happen either," the Sovereign LORD said.

7This is what he showed me: The Lord
was standing by a wall that had been
built true to plumb,[a] with a plumb line[b]
in his hand. 8And the LORD asked me,
"What do you see,[e] Amos?[f]"
"A plumb line,[g]" I replied.
Then the Lord said, "Look, I am setting
a plumb line among my people Israel; I
will spare them no longer.[h]

9"The high places of Isaac will be
destroyed
and the sanctuaries[i] of Israel will
be ruined;
with my sword I will rise against
the house of Jeroboam.[j]"

Amos and Amaziah

10Then Amaziah the priest of Bethel[k]
sent a message to Jeroboam[l] king of Israel: "Amos is raising a conspiracy[m] against
you in the very heart of Israel. The land
cannot bear all his words.[n] 11For this is
what Amos is saying:

" 'Jeroboam will die by the sword,
and Israel will surely go into exile,
away from their native land.' "

12Then Amaziah said to Amos, "Get
out, you seer! Go back to the land of Judah. Earn your bread there and do your
prophesying there.[o] 13Don't prophesy
anymore at Bethel, because this is the
king's sanctuary and the temple of the
kingdom.[p]"
14Amos answered Amaziah, "I was neither a prophet[q] nor the son of a prophet,
but I was a shepherd, and I also took care
of sycamore-fig trees. 15But the LORD took
me from tending the flock[r] and said to
me, 'Go, prophesy to my people Israel.'[s]
16Now then, hear the word of the LORD.
You say,

" 'Do not prophesy against[t] Israel,
and stop preaching against the
descendants of Isaac.'

17"Therefore this is what the LORD says:

" 'Your wife will become a prostitute[u]
in the city,
and your sons and daughters will
fall by the sword.
Your land will be measured and
divided up,
and you yourself will die in a
pagan[c] country.
And Israel will surely go into exile,
away from their native land.[v]' "

A Basket of Ripe Fruit

8 This is what the Sovereign LORD
showed me: a basket of ripe fruit.
2"What do you see,[w] Amos?[x]" he asked.
"A basket of ripe fruit," I answered.
Then the LORD said to me, "The time
is ripe for my people Israel; I will spare
them no longer.[y]

7:8 [e] Jer 1:11, 13 [f] Isa 28:17; La 2:8; Am 8:2 [g] 2Ki 21:13 [h] Jer 15:6; Eze 7:2-9
7:9 [i] Lev 26:31 [j] 2Ki 15:9; Isa 63:18; Hos 10:8
7:10 [k] 1Ki 12:32 [l] 2Ki 14:23 [m] Jer 38:4 [n] Jer 26:8-11
7:12 [o] Mt 8:34
7:13 [p] Am 2:12; Ac 4:18
7:14 [q] 2Ki 2:5; 4:38
7:15 [r] 2Sa 7:8 [s] Jer 7:1-2; Eze 2:3-4
7:16 [t] Eze 20:46; Mic 2:6
7:17 [u] Hos 4:13 [v] 2Ki 17:6; Eze 4:13; Hos 9:3
8:2 [w] Jer 24:3 [x] Am 7:8 [y] Eze 7:2-9

[a] 7 The meaning of the Hebrew for this phrase is uncertain. [b] 7 The meaning of the Hebrew for this phrase is uncertain; also in verse 8. [c] 17 Hebrew *an unclean*

Am 7:14-15 ❖ How has God called you from your own specific background to serve him and speak his words?

7:7-9 Just as a builder tests the straightness of a wall with a plumb line, so God exposes the true state of his people's moral character and covenant faithfulness with his own plumb line. Will his people meet his holy standard? Verse 8 gives us our answer: God's patience has been exhausted; his punishment will not be delayed. God will destroy both the religious places of false worship and the dynasty of the king of Israel.

7:10 Amaziah's strong accusations that Amos's words are a "conspiracy" (v. 10) suggest an accusation that Amos is participating in an organized plot to overthrow the government.

7:11 Amaziah's quotation of Amos (v. 11) is not exact. Amaziah seems to reinvent Amos as a dangerous dissident.

7:12-13 This is not just an argument about where Amos can speak; this is a spiritual battle about accepting the message of the Lord or rejecting it. This conflict demonstrates Amaziah's guilt before God and his unworthiness to be the priestly spiritual leader of the nation of Israel.

7:7-17 There are times when people must take a strong stand against those who reject true doctrine and who oppose what God is trying to accomplish. Each person should be aware that such confrontations (like confronting an alcoholic sibling or parent) may be difficult emotional experiences, but people should not let fear prevent them from taking responsibility to oppose the spiritual forces of evil in this world. Taking a stand in this manner may not reduce persecution or conflict, but it will establish the truthfulness and authority of what God has said. This is the foundation of our faith, and it is worth fighting for.

8:1-3 Not only will the king and temple be destroyed (7:9), but God's own special covenant people will

3"In that day," declares the Sovereign
LORD, "the songs in the temple will turn
to wailing.[a][z] Many, many bodies — flung
everywhere! Silence![a]"

4Hear this, you who trample the
needy
and do away with the poor[b] of the
land,[c]

5saying,

"When will the New Moon be over
that we may sell grain,
and the Sabbath be ended
that we may market wheat?" —
skimping on the measure,
boosting the price
and cheating with dishonest
scales,[d]
6buying the poor with silver
and the needy for a pair of
sandals,
selling even the sweepings with
the wheat.[e]

7The LORD has sworn by himself, the
Pride of Jacob:[f] "I will never forget[g] anything they have done.

8"Will not the land tremble[h] for this,
and all who live in it mourn?
The whole land will rise like the
Nile;
it will be stirred up and then sink
like the river of Egypt.[i]

9"In that day," declares the Sovereign
LORD,

"I will make the sun go down at
noon
and darken the earth in broad
daylight.[j]

10I will turn your religious festivals
into mourning
and all your singing into weeping.
I will make all of you wear sackcloth[k]
and shave your heads.
I will make that time like mourning
for an only son[l]
and the end of it like a bitter day.[m]

11"The days are coming," declares the
Sovereign LORD,
"when I will send a famine
through the land —
not a famine of food or a thirst for
water,
but a famine of hearing the words
of the LORD.[n]
12People will stagger from sea to sea
and wander from north to east,
searching for the word of the LORD,
but they will not find it.[o]

13"In that day

"the lovely young women and
strong young men
will faint because of thirst.[p]
14Those who swear by the sin of
Samaria —
who say, 'As surely as your god
lives, Dan,'[q]
or, 'As surely as the god[b] of
Beersheba[r] lives' —
they will fall, never to rise again.[s]"

8:3 [z]Am 5:16 [a]Am 5:23; 6:10
8:4 [b]Pr 30:14 [c]Ps 14:4; Am 2:7
8:5 [d]2Ki 4:23; Ne 13:15-16; Hos 12:7; Mic 6:10-11
8:6 [e]Am 2:6
8:7 [f]Am 6:8 [g]Hos 8:13
8:8 [h]Hos 4:3 [i]Ps 18:7; Jer 46:8; Am 9:5
8:9 [j]Job 5:14; Isa 59:9-10; Jer 15:9; Am 5:8; Mic 3:6
8:10 [k]Jer 48:37 [l]Jer 6:26; Zec 12:10 [m]Eze 7:18
8:11 [n]1Sa 3:1; 2Ch 15:3; Eze 7:26
8:12 [o]Eze 20:3, 31
8:13 [p]Isa 41:17; Hos 2:3
8:14 [q]1Ki 12:29 [r]Am 5:5 [s]Am 5:2

[a] 3 Or *"the temple singers will wail* [b] 14 Hebrew *the way*

Am 8:4-6 ❖ How can we help serve and protect people who are poor and needy in our area?

cease to exist in the near future. The Bethel temple will not protect the worshipers, for God will bring mass destruction.

8:4-6 Amos focuses on the acts of the oppressors in v. 4 and their motives and methods in vv. 5-6. Those with the economic ability to help refuse to assist others and actually manipulate others to their own advantage.

8:7 God is angry over this greed, so he swears an oath that he "will never forget" (v. 7). By this oath God binds himself to a specific, unalterable course of action.

8:8-12 Amos describes how the land will tremble and mourn. In addition, there will be unusual signs of God's power over the heavens. Amos is not predicting the end of the world; rather, he is predicting the approaching day of the Lord for Israel (fulfilled in 722 BC, when the Assyrians captured Samaria). Like a desperate and confused traveler who does not know where to find water, these confused people will be unable to find any message from God.

8:13-14 These final verses deepen the hopelessness of "that day" by noting that the strongest members of society will grow faint and end up resorting to seeking assistance from other gods.

✣ **8:1-14** Part of any discussion on business ethics must deal with the attitudes and motivations people have toward their business activities. Sincere Christians who operate in the business world must be willing to accept responsibility for their choices and must be motivated by basic convictions of honesty and truthfulness, by the challenge of fulfilling their God-given purpose in life, and by a desire to honor God in all things.

Israel to Be Destroyed

9 I saw the Lord standing by the altar,
and he said:

"Strike the tops of the pillars
so that the thresholds shake.
Bring them down on the heads[t] of
all the people;
those who are left I will kill with
the sword.
Not one will get away,
none will escape.
2 Though they dig down to the depths
below,[u]
from there my hand will take them.
Though they climb up to the
heavens above,[v]
from there I will bring them
down.[w]
3 Though they hide themselves on the
top of Carmel,[x]
there I will hunt them down and
seize them.[y]
Though they hide from my eyes at
the bottom of the sea,
there I will command the serpent
to bite them.[z]
4 Though they are driven into exile by
their enemies,
there I will command the sword[a]
to slay them.

"I will keep my eye on them
for harm[b] and not for good.[c]"[d]

5 The Lord, the LORD Almighty —
he touches the earth and it melts,[e]
and all who live in it mourn;
the whole land rises like the Nile,
then sinks like the river of Egypt;[f]
6 he builds his lofty palace[a] in the
heavens
and sets its foundation[b] on the
earth;
he calls for the waters of the sea
and pours them out over the face
of the land —
the LORD is his name.[g]

7 "Are not you Israelites
the same to me as the Cushites[c]?"[h]
declares the LORD.
"Did I not bring Israel up from Egypt,
the Philistines from Caphtor[d][i]
and the Arameans from Kir?[j]

8 "Surely the eyes of the Sovereign
LORD
are on the sinful kingdom.
I will destroy it
from the face of the earth.
Yet I will not totally destroy
the descendants of Jacob,"
declares the LORD.[k]
9 "For I will give the command,
and I will shake the people of
Israel
among all the nations
as grain[l] is shaken in a sieve,[m]
and not a pebble will reach the
ground.
10 All the sinners among my people
will die by the sword,
all those who say,
'Disaster will not overtake or meet
us.'[n]

9:1 [t] Ps 68:21
9:2 [u] Ps 139:8 [v] Jer 51:53 [w] Ob 4
9:3 [x] Am 1:2 [y] Ps 139:8-10 [z] Jer 16:16-17
9:4 [a] Lev 26:33; Eze 5:12 [b] Jer 21:10 [c] Jer 39:16 [d] Jer 44:11
9:5 [e] Ps 46:2; Mic 1:4 [f] Am 8:8
9:6 [g] Ps 104:1-3, 5-6, 13; Am 5:8
9:7 [h] Isa 20:4; 43:3 [i] Dt 2:23; Jer 47:4 [j] 2Ki 16:9; Isa 22:6; Am 1:5; 2:10
9:8 [k] Jer 44:27
9:9 [l] Lk 22:31 [m] Isa 30:28
9:10 [n] Am 6:3

[a] 6 The meaning of the Hebrew for this phrase is uncertain. [b] 6 The meaning of the Hebrew for this word is uncertain. [c] 7 That is, people from the upper Nile region [d] 7 That is, Crete

---

9:1–4 To convince the audience of the impossibility of any hope of survival, Amos presents a series of five conditional clauses (vv. 2–4). Each clause gives a possible way one might try to escape from God's mighty hand of judgment. Each is a useless waste of effort.
9:5–6 Amos uses this hymn of praise to God to support his claim that this omnipotent God will judge Israel. There is no way to avoid God or to escape his wrath.
9:7–10 The audience questions Amos's conclusion that God will actually destroy Israel. They argue instead that "disaster will not overtake . . . us" (v. 10), basing their confidence in God on what he has done in the past and the promises he made to their ancestors. How can God now reject his own people?

The covenant conditions state that if God's people do not follow him or maintain their covenant relationship with him, he will not automatically bless them. Past election (3:1–2) and past acts of divine grace (2:9–10) do not rule out the possibility of future punishment.

9:1–10 People who have grown up in the church may think that they have the right to God's protection and blessing because of their past experience with God. No one should mistakenly think that all God requires is for us to be baptized or to join the church, though some do believe this because the truth of Scripture has not been adequately explained.

Strong Bible teaching is necessary to ground people firmly so that they are not led astray with deceptions: God wants all who follow him to be focused on his calling on our lives every day. He requires that we act; he expects us to be a force for him and a force for good in our spheres of influence and in the wider world (Jn 13:17; Jas 2:18).

Israel's Restoration

11"In that day

"I will restore David's fallen
shelter —
I will repair its broken walls
and restore its ruins —
and will rebuild it as it used to be,[o]
12 so that they may possess the
remnant of Edom[p]
and all the nations that bear my
name,[a][q]"
declares the LORD,
who will do these things.[r]

13"The days are coming," declares the
LORD,

"when the reaper will be overtaken
by the plowman[s]
and the planter by the one
treading grapes.
New wine will drip from the
mountains
and flow from all the hills,[t]
14 and I will bring my people Israel
back from exile.[b]

"They will rebuild the ruined cities[u]
and live in them.
They will plant vineyards and
drink their wine;
they will make gardens and eat
their fruit.[v]
15 I will plant[w] Israel in their own land,
never again to be uprooted
from the land I have given them,"

says the LORD your God.[x]

9:11 [o] Ps 80:12
9:12 [p] Nu 24:18 [q] Isa 43:7 [r] Ac 15:16-17*
9:13 [s] Lev 26:5 [t] Joel 3:18
9:14 [u] Isa 61:4 [v] Jer 30:18; 31:28; Eze 28:25-26
9:15 [w] Isa 60:21 [x] Jer 24:6; Eze 34:25-28; 37:12,25

Am 9:11-15 ❖ Why is it significant that even a cutting message like that of Amos does not end on a note of judgment but instead a note of hope? How can we live in the midst of chaos and injustice with such a posture of hope?

[a] 12 Hebrew; Septuagint *so that the remnant of people / and all the nations that bear my name may seek me* [b] 14 Or *will restore the fortunes of my people Israel*

9:11–12 These verses do not explain how this Davidic rule will be restored or clarify details about the ruler; they merely state that God himself will bring it about. The consequences of this Davidic revival will impact other nations so that they may also be included in this future kingdom.

9:13–15 The abundance of the crops will surpass everyone's imagination and exceed human ability to collect them. The grapes that are harvested around August and September will be so numerous that they will still not be finished at planting time in November. This salvation message ends with an open-ended promise that God will eternally give the land to his people (v. 15). At long last, they will be deeply rooted in the place God has given them.

9:11–15 The final word of Amos offers hope to the faithful remnant who will suffer with the wicked when God brings destruction on the nation of Israel. It also challenges unbelievers with the choice they can make: Reject God and suffer his curse or turn to God and accept this offer of hope.

Everyone needs to have some hope in his or her life. Hope is not based on an end-times chart or eliminated by difficult circumstances. It endures because God is the one who offers hope to those who will believe in him. Therefore, God must be at the center of all teaching about future events.

Author: Obadiah

Audience: The people of Judah suffering the treachery of the Edomites, descendants of Esau

Date: Probably the time of the Babylonian attacks on Jerusalem (605–586 BC)

Theme: God through Obadiah announces his judgment against the Edomites, who are gloating over Jerusalem's devastation by foreign powers.

Reading Obadiah

Since this book is only one chapter, it should be read in one sitting. It prophesies what God will do to Edom because of her violence against Israel.

PERSPECTIVE

The short prophecy of Obadiah, just twenty-one verses, finds Judah facing a difficult situation: Her next-door neighbor, Edom, whose inhabitants are related to the Judeans by blood, not only stood by when the Babylonian world power moved against Judah, they actively collaborated in that aggression.

What Judah needs to be reminded of is that neither geographical nor military advantage is the sole deciding factor of international relations, especially when these involve the very people of God. While Obadiah's message is a promise of hope to Judah, the message primarily presents itself as a threat to Edom and to all others who mistreat God's people.

Obadiah drives home the message that Israel's mortal enemy Edom will be brought low by God's consuming fire. God's judgment, it becomes clear, inevitably falls on any and all of Israel's enemies. "The day of the Lord is near for all nations. As you have done, it will be done to you; your deeds will return upon your own head" (v. 15). Obadiah's prediction that God will punish Edom for standing by as her kinsmen in Judah were overrun by Babylon could lead to a kind of nationalistic triumphalism ("We're number one and God will protect us") or to a humble recognition that God must not be trifled with.

At the end of his short message, Obadiah describes restoration in concrete material terms: "But on Mount Zion will be deliverance; it will be holy, and Jacob will possess his inheritance" (v. 17).

	1200 BC	1100	1000	900	800	700	600	500	400
Division of the kingdom (930 BC)									
Ministries of Elijah and Elisha in Israel (c. 875–797 BC)									
Joel's ministry in Judah (c. 835–796 BC?)									
Jonah's ministry in Nineveh (c. 800–750 BC)									
Amos's ministry in Israel (c. 760–750 BC)									
Hosea's ministry in Israel (c. 753–715 BC)									
Exile of Israel (722 BC)									
Obadiah's ministry (c. 605–585 BC?)									
Fall of Jerusalem (586 BC)									

Judgment for judgment's sake is not judgment but revenge. Obadiah's is a hard message, but it is a message that has repentance and restoration as its goal.

See the Introduction to Joel for more perspective on this book.

Key Verse

Deliverers will go up on Mount Zion to govern the mountains of Esau. And the kingdom will be the LORD's.

—Obadiah 21

TAKING THE NEXT STEPS

Although we do not know exactly when Obadiah lived, he probably prophesied either during the reign of Jehoram (2Ki 8:20–22) or during the twenty years preceding the fall of Jerusalem (2Ki 24–25). His main message is one of judgment against the nation of Edom. Through his message we learn that God loves his people and that he will never allow their enemies to remain unpunished. We still need to hear that message today.

WHAT TO LOOK FOR IN OBADIAH

- The Lord's First Message (vv. 1–4)
- The Lord's Second Message (vv. 5–7)
- The Lord's Third Message (vv. 8–18)
- Home Again (vv. 19–21)

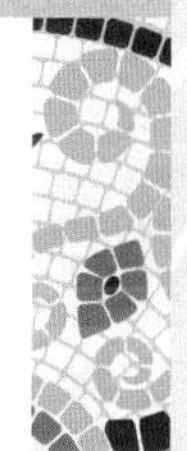

Obadiah's Vision

1–4pp // Jer 49:14–16
5–6pp // Jer 49:9–10

1 The vision of Obadiah.

This is what the Sovereign LORD says about Edom[a] —

We have heard a message from the
 LORD:
 An envoy[b] was sent to the nations
 to say,
"Rise, let us go against her for
 battle"[c] —

2 "See, I will make you small among
 the nations;
 you will be utterly despised.
3 The pride[d] of your heart has
 deceived you,
 you who live in the clefts of the
 rocks[a]
 and make your home on the
 heights,
you who say to yourself,
 'Who can bring me down to the
 ground?'[e]
4 Though you soar like the eagle
 and make your nest[f] among the
 stars,
 from there I will bring you
 down,"[g]
 declares the LORD.[h]

5 "If thieves came to you,
 if robbers in the night —
oh, what a disaster awaits you! —
 would they not steal only as much
 as they wanted?
If grape pickers came to you,
 would they not leave a few
 grapes?[i]
6 But how Esau will be ransacked,
 his hidden treasures pillaged!
7 All your allies[j] will force you to the
 border;
 your friends will deceive and
 overpower you;
those who eat your bread[k] will set a
 trap for you,[b]
 but you will not detect it.

8 "In that day," declares the LORD,
 "will I not destroy[l] the wise men
 of Edom,
 those of understanding in the
 mountains of Esau?
9 Your warriors, Teman,[m] will be
 terrified,
 and everyone in Esau's
 mountains
 will be cut down in the
 slaughter.
10 Because of the violence[n] against your
 brother Jacob,[o]

1 [a] Isa 63:1-6; Jer 49:7-22; Eze 25:12-14; Am 1:11-12 [b] Isa 18:2 [c] Jer 6:4-5
3 [d] Isa 16:6 [e] Isa 14:13-15; Rev 18:7
4 [f] Hab 2:9 [g] Isa 14:13 [h] Job 20:6
5 [i] Dt 24:21
7 [j] Jer 30:14 [k] Ps 41:9
8 [l] Job 5:12; Isa 29:14
9 [m] Ge 36:11,34
10 [n] Joel 3:19 [o] Ps 137:7; Am 1:11-12

[a] 3 Or *of Sela* [b] 7 The meaning of the Hebrew for this clause is uncertain.

1–4 Edom is confident because of her strategic advantage. Unfortunately, her assessment of herself does not look heavenward. It is not a human army who will bring Edom down, but the Warrior God himself.

APPLICATION ✜ 1–4 There is a fine line between self-confidence, self-reliance, and pride. Pride, an inflated self-perception, characterizes our age. "I did it my way," boasts a popular song of years ago. Unfortunately, in some areas, the same attitude invades the church. As we do God's work in the world, we do well to check our motivations and remember what God says about pride—he hates it (Pr 8:13; 11:2; 16:15).

5–7 Edom's former friends and allies turn against her. Rather than receiving the support expected from friends, Edom finds them to be her enemies. The Edomites are forcefully expelled from their dwellings and driven to the outskirts of their land.

✜ 5–7 Many people find themselves in situations where they face the threat of financial and medical loss. While the government might be of some help, the church should also provide care in these instances, much like the church did in the NT through generous distribution of wealth (e.g., Ac 2:44-45).

8–9 Yahweh promises that he will not only deprive Edom of tactical strength obtained from either wealth or allies, but he will also deny Edom two means of national support: the wise and the strong.

The "wise men" (v. 8) are important figures in the court, providing intellectual insight, good sense, and practical skill. In the face of these losses the trained soldiers of Edom, who are called upon to act with courage, are terrified.

✜ 8–9 The fact that neither today's society nor the church seems to be bothered about the loss of both moral vision and the ability to accomplish good in leading society is a concern. Where are today's leaders who will base decisions on biblical principles and godly integrity rather than on what fits their own moral or political leanings?

God calls us to make a stand and live by our convictions as committed Christians. That is how believers can effect real change.

10–15 Edom will receive back on her own head what she had done to her own "family." The most

you will be covered with shame;
you will be destroyed forever.[p]
11 On the day you stood aloof
while strangers carried off his wealth
and foreigners entered his gates
and cast lots[q] for Jerusalem,
you were like one of them.
12 You should not gloat over your brother
in the day of his misfortune,
nor rejoice[r] over the people of Judah
in the day of their destruction,[s]
nor boast so much
in the day of their trouble.[t]
13 You should not march through the gates of my people
in the day of their disaster,
nor gloat over them in their calamity[u]
in the day of their disaster,
nor seize their wealth
in the day of their disaster.
14 You should not wait at the crossroads
to cut down their fugitives,
nor hand over their survivors
in the day of their trouble.

15 "The day of the LORD is near[v]
for all nations.
As you have done, it will be done to you;
your deeds[w] will return upon your own head.

10 [p] Eze 35:9
11 [q] Na 3:10
12 [r] Eze 35:15 [s] Pr 17:5 [t] Mic 4:11
13 [u] Eze 35:5
15 [v] Eze 30:3 [w] Jer 50:29; Hab 2:8

Ob 12–14 ❖ Why should we not gloat over the misfortune of others? How can we instead practice the way of Christ (see Lk 6:27–31)?

---

despicable acts are those described in v. 14: Edom assists in the exile of a defeated people by turning over the defeated survivors. As a result, Edom will receive as she has given. As she exploited Judah's days of calamity (vv. 11–14), so a similar day will cause her distress.

10–15 Christian leaders must educate people within the church as to what constitutes violence and abuse, what its results are, and what the logical consequences of it should be. Often the behavior is not recognized as being hurtful, so discussion and teaching need to start addressing the issue. The state has taken some initial strides in this area through setting legal precedents and standards; current culture has also risen up to call the perpetrators to account. It is a shame if the church lags behind when we address abuse within our own precincts.

PEOPLE TO KNOW // OBADIAH

OBADIAH 1–21: The prophet Obadiah delivered God's message of judgment against Israel's neighbor, Edom. The Edomites were descendants of Jacob's brother, Esau. Family connection did not equal affection, however. Obadiah's message is one of impending doom.

Almost nothing is known about Obadiah. His book, the shortest in the OT, provides no biographical information. Some interpreters believe the prophet is the same Obadiah who served in King Ahab's court (1Ki 18). While possible, this claim cannot be proven.

Like Nahum, Obadiah's entire prophecy is focused on a foreign nation. Obadiah decried the pride and violence of Edom and warned them destruction was coming. The prophet accused Edom of gloating over Judah, "your brother," on the day of Judah's destruction (Ob 12). Apparently, Edom had taken advantage of Judah's military misfortune, even going so far as to loot the defeated cities (Ob 13).

Obadiah promised Edom that "as you have done, it will be done to you" (Ob 15). He prophesied the day of the Lord, a day of judgment, which is coming for all nations. The prophet also foretold deliverance coming from Zion, God's holy hill of Jerusalem

APPLICATION Obadiah's name means "servant of the Lord." As God's servant, he proclaimed a message of judgment on those who turn against God's children. It is important for Christians today to continue to proclaim the truth of God's justice and claim God's Word as our guide. Our hope is in a God who will not let wickedness stand forever; he will root it out and cast it down on the day of the Lord. This is what Obadiah prophesied and what he points us toward today.

[16] Just as you drank on my holy hill,
so all the nations will drink[x]
continually;
they will drink and drink
and be as if they had never been.
[17] But on Mount Zion will be
deliverance;[y]
it will be holy,[z]
and Jacob will possess his
inheritance.
[18] Jacob will be a fire
and Joseph a flame;
Esau will be stubble,
and they will set him on fire and
destroy[a] him.
There will be no survivors
from Esau."
The LORD has spoken.

[19] People from the Negev will occupy
the mountains of Esau,
and people from the foothills will
possess
the land of the Philistines.[b]
They will occupy the fields of
Ephraim and Samaria,[c]
and Benjamin will possess Gilead.
[20] This company of Israelite exiles who
are in Canaan
will possess the land as far as
Zarephath;[d]
the exiles from Jerusalem who are
in Sepharad
will possess the towns of the
Negev.[e]
[21] Deliverers will go up on[a] Mount
Zion
to govern the mountains of Esau.
And the kingdom will be the
LORD's.[f]

16 [x] Jer 25:15; 49:12
17 [y] Am 9:11-15 [z] Isa 4:3
18 [a] Zec 12:6
19 [b] Isa 11:14 [c] Jer 31:5
20 [d] 1Ki 17:9-10 [e] Jer 33:13
21 [f] Ps 22:28; Zec 14:9,16; Rev 11:15

[a] 21 Or *from*

16–18 Attention now turns to the people of Judah themselves. God's holy city will be restored and so will be his people. Edom will suffer what Judah has suffered at Edom's hand. Unlike Judah, which has survivors, Edom herself will have none.

16–18 As the US Constitution calls for a system of checks and balances between the branches of government, so the church needs to be ready and willing to bring a theological perspective to bear on secular enterprises. Decision-makers in office must be held accountable to standards derived from biblical concepts of equity and justice rather than simply national economic well-being. And we as individuals need to operate according to those same standards in our own lives.

19–21 Returnees come back to the inherited holdings of Israel. Freedom is won for oppressed Israel, and Edom is conquered. While Israel is still in exile, her King promises that he is on his way back to his throne (v. 21).

19–21 Both the OT and NT affirm that "the earth is the LORD's" (Ex 9:29; Ps 24:1; 1Co 10:26), all things and everyone included. Humanity has been mandated to look after creation and the people in it, supporting the helpless, widow, orphan, and alien (Jas 1:27). If they do not, Yahweh himself will be their support (Ps 68:5). Yahweh looks after and rescues his exiled people in the book of Obadiah. Will he not do the same for his oppressed people today?

As believers, we have the privilege of joining with God to assist those in need around us. As the Spirit leads, let us be courageous in bringing the love and provision of Jesus to a hurting world.

Jonah

Author: Unknown

Audience: The northern kingdom of Israel

Date: Jonah prophesied during the reign of Jeroboam II (793–753 BC); the date of the writing of the book was perhaps between 750 and 725

Theme: The Sovereign Lord uses Jonah's actions and words to communicate the fact that his compassion extends beyond Israel.

PERSPECTIVE

The prophet Jonah, son of Amittai, is mentioned just twice in the OT (2Ki 14:25; Jnh 1:1). The dating of the final form of the composition is widely disputed and includes a vast array of suggestions, ranging between the eighth and fourth centuries BC.

The book of Jonah contains only fifty-eight verses, but those few verses include quite a bit of excitement: a call from God refused, a storm at sea, the conversion of sailors, a miraculous rescue, a song of praise, the repentance of Israel's archenemy, and an intensely honest dialogue between Yahweh and Israel's most reluctant prophet. The book reveals the nature of Yahweh's relationship to the Gentile sailors, to Israel's enemy Nineveh, to nonhuman creation (the wind, a fish, a vine, a worm, and cattle), as well as to his messenger Jonah. The book is, in many ways, a microcosm of God's relationship to his whole creation in history.

For more perspective on this book, see the Introduction to Nahum.

Reading Jonah

The story of Jonah is short enough to read in one sitting. It begins with God's command to Jonah to preach to the Ninevites and Jonah's decision to run in the opposite direction. After God had punished Jonah, he called him a second time, and Jonah went. Much to the prophet's dismay, God forgave the repentant people of Nineveh.

TAKING THE NEXT STEPS

The prophet Jonah, mentioned in 2Ki 14:25, lived during the reign of Jeroboam II, a king who had restored Israel to a time of wealth and prosperity. Jonah was therefore a contemporary of Hosea and Amos. But in contrast to their ministries, his task was to demonstrate that God was a universal God, who extended his grace not only to the

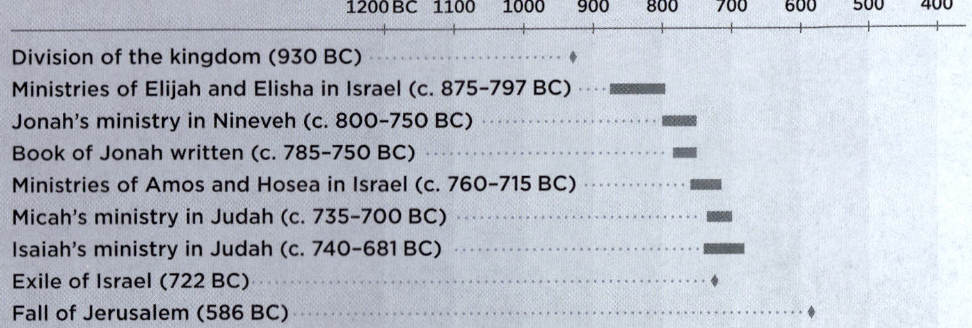

Key Verses

"Let everyone call urgently on God. Let them give up their evil ways and their violence. Who knows? God may yet relent and with compassion turn from his fierce anger so that we will not perish." When God saw what they did and how they turned from their evil ways, he relented and did not bring on them the destruction he had threatened.

—Jonah 3:8b–10

Israelites but to all nations, even to the wicked Assyrians. Therefore, Jonah must preach the message of the Lord to the city of Nineveh.

The story of Jonah directs our attention to some important insights for our daily lives. (1) God loves the human race everywhere, and he wants everyone to hear the message of his saving grace. (2) We cannot hide from God, for he sees wherever we go and whatever we do. (3) If we decide not to do what God wants us to do, he will judge us. (4) God is always ready to give us a second opportunity to respond to his will for our lives.

WHAT TO LOOK FOR IN JONAH

- Jonah's disobedience and the great storm at sea (ch. 1)
- Jonah's prayer from the belly of the great fish (ch. 2)
- Jonah's trip to Nineveh and the repentance of the people (ch. 3)
- God's lesson to Jonah about grace (ch. 4)

Jonah Flees From the LORD

1 The word of the LORD came to Jonah[a]
son of Amittai:[b] 2“Go to the great city
of Nineveh[c] and preach against it, because its wickedness has come up before me.”
3But Jonah ran[d] away from the LORD
and headed for Tarshish. He went down
to Joppa,[e] where he found a ship bound
for that port. After paying the fare, he
went aboard and sailed for Tarshish to
flee from the LORD.
4Then the LORD sent a great wind on
the sea, and such a violent storm arose
that the ship threatened to break up.[f]
5All the sailors were afraid and each
cried out to his own god. And they
threw the cargo into the sea to lighten
the ship.[g]
But Jonah had gone below deck, where
he lay down and fell into a deep sleep.
6The captain went to him and said, “How
can you sleep? Get up and call[h] on your
god! Maybe he will take notice of us so
that we will not perish.”[i]
7Then the sailors said to each other,
“Come, let us cast lots to find out who is
responsible for this calamity.”[j] They cast
lots and the lot fell on Jonah. 8So they
asked him, “Tell us, who is responsible
for making all this trouble for us? What
kind of work do you do? Where do you
come from? What is your country? From
what people are you?”
9He answered, “I am a Hebrew and I
worship the LORD, the God of heaven,[k]
who made the sea and the dry land.[l]”
10This terrified them and they asked,
“What have you done?” (They knew he
was running away from the LORD, because he had already told them so.)
11The sea was getting rougher and
rougher. So they asked him, “What
should we do to you to make the sea
calm down for us?”
12“Pick me up and throw me into the
sea,” he replied, “and it will become calm.
I know that it is my fault that this great
storm has come upon you.”[m]
13Instead, the men did their best to row
back to land. But they could not, for the
sea grew even wilder than before.[n] 14Then
they cried out to the LORD, “Please, LORD,
do not let us die for taking this man's life.
Do not hold us accountable for killing
an innocent man,[o] for you, LORD, have
done as you pleased.”[p] 15Then they took
Jonah and threw him overboard, and
the raging sea grew calm.[q] 16At this the
men greatly feared[r] the LORD, and they
offered a sacrifice to the LORD and made
vows to him.

Jonah's Prayer

17Now the LORD provided a huge fish
to swallow Jonah,[s] and Jonah was in the

Jnh 1:3 ❖ In what big and small ways do we run from God's will or command?

1:1 [a] Mt 12:39-41 [b] 2Ki 14:25
1:2 [c] Ge 10:11
1:3 [d] Ps 139:7 [e] Jos 19:46; Ac 9:36, 43
1:4 [f] Ps 107:23-26
1:5 [g] Ac 27:18-19
1:6 [h] Jnh 3:8 [i] Ps 107:28
1:7 [j] Jos 7:10-18; 1Sa 14:42
1:9 [k] Ac 17:24 [l] Ps 146:6
1:12 [m] 2Sa 24:17; 1Ch 21:17
1:13 [n] Pr 21:30
1:14 [o] Dt 21:8 [p] Ps 115:3
1:15 [q] Ps 107:29; Lk 8:24
1:16 [r] Mk 4:41
1:17 [s] Mt 12:40; 16:4; Lk 11:30

1:1–3 Yahweh tells Jonah to preach against the wicked city of Nineveh. Jonah runs in the opposite direction, heading for Tarshish. He goes down to Joppa, finds a ship, pays the fare, goes aboard, and sets sail.

The name “Jonah” means “dove.” In Ge 8:10–11 the dove Noah sent out from the ark returned with the branch of an olive tree—an enduring symbol of peace and compassion. The “dove” (Jonah) of peace will be Yahweh's agent, however reluctant at first.

1:4–5a Verse 4 turns our attention to the sailors and captain of the storm-bound ship. They are afraid because of the storm and cry out to their gods and throw their cargo overboard. The captain wakes Jonah to enlist him to pray, and the men cast lots and discover Jonah's sin.

1:5b–7 Jonah is passive in these verses. Exhausted from his struggle and decision to flee, he sleeps despite the chaos around him. He has temporarily escaped the pressure of God's word, but by fleeing he has also turned from the possibility of calling on his God.

The irony is that Jonah will die in either case. If he says nothing, the storm will kill them all. If he confesses, he knows he alone will die. God has reduced his decision to the question, “Will your life/death save the lives of others, or will it be an ordinary death at sea in a storm with pagan sailors?”

1:8–12 Jonah does not seem to be capable of simple repentance. He could have sought forgiveness during the storm and committed himself to go to Nineveh. Yet Jonah does have compassion on the innocent sailors. He will accept death for them—not in obedience to God but, nonetheless, in their place.

1:13–16 The actions of sacrifice and vows are precisely the actions of worship later declared by Jonah for *his* deliverance (2:9). The change in the sailors' relationship to Yahweh, evident in v. 16, is later paralleled in the Ninevites' repentance in ch. 3. Even in Jonah's disobedience, Yahweh has made Jonah effective in his prophetic call, bringing people to faith in Yahweh.

1:17 Jonah's rescue from drowning via a “great fish” may have caused even an ancient reader to stop and question whether this was a legend or a miraculous account. Yet Jesus refers to this account multiple times (Mt 12:40, Lk 11:30),

belly of the fish three days and three
2[a] nights. [1]From inside the fish Jonah
prayed to the LORD his God. [2]He said:

"In my distress I called to the LORD,[t]
and he answered me.
From deep in the realm of the dead I
called for help,
and you listened to my cry.
[3]You hurled me into the depths,[u]
into the very heart of the seas,
and the currents swirled
about me;
all your waves and breakers
swept over me.[v]
[4]I said, 'I have been banished
from your sight;[w]
yet I will look again
toward your holy temple.'

2:2 [t] Ps 18:6; 120:1
2:3 [u] Ps 88:6 [v] Ps 42:7
2:4 [w] Ps 31:22
2:5 [x] Ps 69:1-2

Jnh 2:1-9 ❖ How can Jonah's prayer in these verses help us as we face our own trials?

[5]The engulfing waters threatened me,[b]
the deep surrounded me;
seaweed was wrapped around my
head.[x]
[6]To the roots of the mountains I sank
down;
the earth beneath barred me in
forever.
But you, LORD my God,
brought my life up from the pit.

[a] In Hebrew texts 2:1 is numbered 1:17, and 2:1-10 is numbered 2:2-11. [b] 5 Or *waters were at my throat*

lending weight to the idea that this story actually happened.

APPLICATION ✚ **1:1–17** We should not run from God, but we do. Even our personal religious beliefs can cause us to run. Case in point, Jonah ran because he felt righteously indignant about God's mercy toward the cruel Ninevites. Why would he proclaim God's mercy to a people who had so cruelly decimated his own nation? Yet Jonah had to face the fact that he was in the wrong.

Until we admit we are on the run, we are lost. But when, with Jonah, we admit our true situation (v. 10), we have real hope.

2:1–9 Jonah's psalm of thanks primarily recounts his distress in the water and gives thanks to God for his amazing rescue. It begins with a summary of his cry for help (v. 2) and continues with four more stanzas describing Jonah's sinking in the water (vv. 3–6). In the refrain (vv. 7–9), Jonah summarizes his cry for rescue and declares Yahweh the source of salvation.

PEOPLE TO KNOW // JONAH

JONAH 2:1–10: The prophet Jonah didn't want to obey God. God told Jonah go up to preach to the people of Nineveh, the capital of Assyria—a nation known for viciously conquering and destroying other nations. Instead, Jonah went down to Joppa, down into a ship, down into the stormy sea, and even down into the belly of a great fish.

From the fish's belly, Jonah offered God a prayer of lament and praise (Jnh 2:1–9). God commanded the fish to spit Jonah up on dry land (the fish was more obedient than Jonah), and God recommissioned Jonah to preach to Nineveh. This time Jonah obeyed, but he became angry when the people actually responded to his message. Because of their repentance, God did not bring the destruction Jonah had preached. Jonah accused God of being too merciful, and in his spite he even asked God to end his life (Jnh 4:3).

God chastised Jonah for his anger. His book closes with God's rhetorical question, pointing out that it was right for God to show his concern for the inhabitants (and even the animals) of Nineveh. Jonah's story depicts the wide circle of God's compassion.

Jesus said that just as Jonah was in the belly of the fish for three days, so the Son of Man would spend three days and nights buried. Jesus also appealed to Nineveh's repentance as a witness against the hard hearts of those who refused to respond to his message: "Nineveh . . . repented at the preaching of Jonah, and now something greater than Jonah is here" (Mt 12:41).

APPLICATION ✚ We often want to claim God's mercy and love for ourselves while denying God has the same love for those whom we dislike. The Assyrians were known for violent and wicked deeds, but they were not outside the circle of God's concern and compassion. The message of Jonah for today is that God's compassion extends far beyond where we expect. Who knows who might respond to God's call for repentance.

7"When my life was ebbing away,
I remembered[y] you, LORD,
and my prayer[z] rose to you,
to your holy temple.[a]

8"Those who cling to worthless
idols[b]
turn away from God's love for
them.
9But I, with shouts of grateful
praise,
will sacrifice[c] to you.
What I have vowed[d] I will make
good.
I will say, 'Salvation[e] comes from
the LORD.'"

10And the LORD commanded the fish,
and it vomited Jonah onto dry land.

Jonah Goes to Nineveh

3 Then the word of the LORD came to
Jonah[f] a second time: 2"Go to the
great city of Nineveh and proclaim to it
the message I give you."
3Jonah obeyed the word of the LORD
and went to Nineveh. Now Nineveh was
a very large city; it took three days to
go through it. 4Jonah began by going a
day's journey into the city, proclaiming,
"Forty more days and Nineveh will be
overthrown." 5The Ninevites believed
God. A fast was proclaimed, and all of
them, from the greatest to the least, put
on sackcloth.[g]
6When Jonah's warning reached the
king of Nineveh, he rose from his throne,
took off his royal robes, covered himself
with sackcloth and sat down in the dust.[h]
7This is the proclamation he issued in
Nineveh:

"By the decree of the king and his nobles:

Do not let people or animals,
herds or flocks, taste anything;
do not let them eat or drink.[i] 8But
let people and animals be covered
with sackcloth. Let everyone call[j]
urgently on God. Let them give up
their evil ways and their violence.
9Who knows?[k] God may yet relent
and with compassion turn[l] from
his fierce anger so that we will not
perish."

10When God saw what they did and
how they turned from their evil ways, he
relented[m] and did not bring on them the
destruction[n] he had threatened.[o]

2:7 [y] Ps 77:11-12 [z] 2Ch 30:27 [a] Ps 11:4; 18:6
2:8 [b] 2Ki 17:15; Jer 10:8
2:9 [c] Ps 50:14, 23; Hos 14:2 [d] Ecc 5:4-5 [e] Ps 3:8
3:1 [f] Jnh 1:1
3:5 [g] Da 9:3; Lk 11:32
3:6 [h] Job 2:8,13; Eze 27:30-31
3:7 [i] 2Ch 20:3
3:8 [j] Ps 130:1; Jnh 1:6
3:9 [k] 2Sa 12:22 [l] Joel 2:14
3:10 [m] Am 7:6 [n] Jer 18:8 [o] Ex 32:14

Jnh 3:6–9 ❖ Note how one person—even one who reluctantly agrees to do the work of God—can have an enormous impact in the world.

2:10 The narrator tells us Yahweh talked to the fish, and "it vomited Jonah onto dry land."

The amazing context of the poetic prayer in this chapter is Jonah's gratitude *while inside* the fish. Jonah fully expected to die in the water. His thanksgiving within the belly of a fish is a joyful outburst, as he realizes that God has delivered him despite his running. Though not yet on dry land, his faith reaches a new level of understanding. He has no doubt that, as he was delivered from drowning, he will also eventually be delivered safely to the shore.

✣ **2:1–10** Jonah's song of thanksgiving demonstrates the power of praise and thanksgiving in any circumstance for the one who turns to Yahweh (vv. 4, 7). This prayer is far more than a poetic break in the narrative. Although Jonah's song is not full of repentance, it is enough in this situation that he turns toward Yahweh in worship. Jonah, like all believers called by Yahweh, must be reborn by God's grace.

3:1–10 Jonah's preaching, the Ninevites' repentance, and Yahweh's compassion make up the primary action of ch. 3.

3:1–5 This chapter begins with Jonah's obedience in proclaiming Yahweh's message. This time Jonah immediately goes to the "very large city" (v. 3) and begins proclaiming the "overthrowing" (v. 4) of the city within forty days. On the first day of the three-day job, the Ninevites believe, and the rest of the chapter continues with the Ninevites' dramatic public repentance from their evil and violence.

3:6–10 When the king hears Jonah's message, he issues a proclamation of fasting and sackcloth, even for the animals (vv. 6–8). He says in humility, "Who knows? God may yet relent . . . so that we will not perish" (v. 9). The chapter concludes with Yahweh's compassion and forgiveness. This is a great miracle. Even Israel's worst enemies believe, repent, and receive God's compassion and forgiveness.

✣ **3:1–10** Assyria was a long way from Jerusalem (about 500 miles). It dominated the ancient Near East for about 270 years, including a harsh domination of Israel and Judah. Yet the OT records God's concern for this distant and wicked people. This surprising fact has led interpreters to consider the Creator's "mission to the world" as a key theme of Jonah. The Creator seeks reconciliation with the whole creation (Ac 17:30; Col 1:19–20).

Jonah's Anger at the LORD's Compassion

4 But to Jonah this seemed very wrong,
and he became angry.[p] 2 He prayed to
the LORD, "Isn't this what I said, LORD,
when I was still at home? That is what I
tried to forestall by fleeing to Tarshish.
I knew[q] that you are a gracious and
compassionate God, slow to anger and
abounding in love,[r] a God who relents
from sending calamity.[s] 3 Now, LORD, take
away my life,[t] for it is better for me to
die[u] than to live."
4 But the LORD replied, "Is it right for
you to be angry?"[v]
5 Jonah had gone out and sat down at
a place east of the city. There he made
himself a shelter, sat in its shade and
waited to see what would happen to the
city. 6 Then the LORD God provided a leafy
plant[a] and made it grow up over Jonah
to give shade for his head to ease his
discomfort, and Jonah was very happy
about the plant. 7 But at dawn the next
day God provided a worm, which chewed
the plant so that it withered.[w] 8 When the
sun rose, God provided a scorching east
wind, and the sun blazed on Jonah's head
so that he grew faint. He wanted to die,
and said, "It would be better for me to
die than to live."
9 But God said to Jonah, "Is it right for
you to be angry about the plant?"
"It is," he said. "And I'm so angry I wish
I were dead."
10 But the LORD said, "You have been
concerned about this plant, though you
did not tend it or make it grow. It sprang
up overnight and died overnight. 11 And
should I not have concern[x] for the great
city of Nineveh,[y] in which there are more
than a hundred and twenty thousand
people who cannot tell their right hand
from their left—and also many animals?"

4:1 [p] ver 4; Lk 15:28
4:2 [q] Jer 20:7-8 [r] Ex 34:6; Ps 86:5,15 [s] Joel 2:13
4:3 [t] 1Ki 19:4 [u] Job 7:15
4:4 [v] Mt 20:11-15
4:7 [w] Joel 1:12
4:11 [x] Jnh 3:10 [y] Jnh 1:2; 3:2

Jnh 4:1-4 ❖ Do we, like Jonah, ever get upset when we see God's grace to certain others? How can we learn to see others through God's eyes rather than our own?

[a] 6 The precise identification of this plant is uncertain; also in verses 7, 9 and 10.

4:1–11 This chapter again focuses on the prophet's relationship with God as they dialogue about Jonah's anger over the ways of Yahweh. God argues his preference for compassion, even in horrible circumstances and with sinful people. God has compassion for what and whom he has made, no matter how ignorant, abusive, or violent the culture.
4:5–6 But Jonah is still angry about God's compassion, so God gives Jonah an object lesson in the form of a vine that provides Jonah some relief from the hot sun. He attempts to convince Jonah (and the reader) that compassion for all living things is more important than strict justice.
4:7–11 Jonah objects to the loss of the vine. God's primary question in the face of Jonah's frustration is creational: "If you are moved to pity over the destruction of a vine you did not create, shouldn't I have pity over the destruction of people and animals I did create?" (cf. vv. 10–11). God loves all his creation, for he is "gracious and compassionate" (v. 2).

4:1–11 We will make two applications of Jnh 4. (1) So many of our actions to protect ourselves from life are vain attempts to ward off catastrophe or trouble. Only God can save. Seeking protection apart from God leads to false security because life is unpredictable. Jonah constantly searches for shelter, and each shelter (ship, hut, plant) fails him in the end. Jonah even seeks shelter inside his narrow worldview and narrow theology, both of which God deconstructs for him. (2) "Should I not have concern . . . ?" (4:11). The answer to God's question is left open for us, but the answer God seeks from Jonah and from us is clearly, "Yes." God's intention is for all to know his love, both insiders and outsiders alike. We are called to affirm his intention and to participate in communicating his concern and love to a world that so desperately needs it.

Author: Micah

Audience: The people of Israel and Judah, especially the oppressive land-grabbers who supported Israel's corrupt political and religious leaders

Date: Probably between 700 and 650 BC

Theme: Micah proclaimed that God would judge Israel for covenant breaking by sending them into exile, yet he would restore a remnant of his people.

PERSPECTIVE

In every age God's people need to encourage and support civic, military, social, religious, political, and family leaders who are bold enough to lead them in just ways that please God. Israel needed this kind of capable leadership in the time of Micah, and the church needs people in all walks of life to stand up and challenge others to let principles of justice influence all their relationships. Since the Creator's dealings with his created world are based on people's loving God and their neighbors (the two great commandments in Dt 6:5 and Lev 19:18, respectively, which Jesus repeated in Mt 22:37 – 39), there is no other way to please God.

In a similar manner, Micah summarizes what God requires of people into three basic principles: to act justly toward others, to love mercy, and to walk humbly and circumspectly with him (6:8). These are essential qualities that should stand out as bright lights for everyone to see. Without spiritual development in these areas there is little hope of pleasing God in worship, of fulfilling one's leadership responsibilities, of becoming a transformational influence in society, or of being a role model in family life.

The challenge that Micah faced is not so different from the context of our modern world. Believers must be in the forefront of guiding their communities toward eliminating the injustices that so seriously plague the social, economic, and political life of cultures in every corner of the world. That kind of biblical leadership starts with the transformation of each person's own desires and actions. Then it can

Reading Micah

The book of Micah is a series of short speeches alternating between words of judgment and words of hope. The different sections do not necessarily follow each other in logical sequence, so each section can be read as an independent unit.

Micah's role as a preacher is to speak God's words with courage and to emphasize the theme of God's justice (3:8). Micah's theology works

	1200 BC	1100	1000	900	800	700	600	500	400
Division of the kingdom (930 BC)									
Ministries of Elijah and Elisha in Israel (c. 875–797 BC)									
Ministries of Amos and Hosea in Israel (c. 760–715 BC)									
Isaiah's ministry in Judah (c. 740–681 BC)									
Micah's ministry in Judah (c. 735–700 BC)									
Exile of Israel (722 BC)									
Book of Micah written (c. 700–650 BC)									
Fall of Jerusalem (586 BC)									

itself out into a practical appeal for people in Judah to recognize what God will do to those who reject him. This possibility causes him to lament at the thought of such a disaster (1:8–16).

Key Verse

He has shown you, O mortal, what is good. And what does the LORD require of you? To act justly and to love mercy and to walk humbly with your God.

—Micah 6:8

infiltrate into the very fiber of the relationships people have in their homes, their churches, their work, and their play. Acting justly, loving mercy, and walking closely with God are not just possible options that a person may want to think about; they are the heart and soul of pleasing or displeasing God.

TAKING THE NEXT STEPS

Micah, who came from a town in southern Judah, prophesied during the reigns of Jotham, Ahaz and Hezekiah (2Ki 15:32—16:20; 18:1—20:21). These were the last days of the northern kingdom of Israel, and he predicted the fall of Samaria (see Mic 1:6). His primary concern, however, was the growing wickedness in the southern kingdom of Judah prior to Hezekiah's reforms. His message combined judgment for sin and hope for the future.

As we did with the other prophets, we hear God's message for us through Micah. (1) God calls us to a life of justice, mercy and humility; he wants to root out of our lives all idolatry, greed, exploitation of others and religious hypocrisy. (2) Though God is patient with us and always holds out his offer of forgiveness, he will not tolerate unrepentant sinners forever but will come in judgment. (3) When God does forgive, his forgiveness is total and complete. He holds no grudges. (4) The wonderful future envisioned by Micah is already being enjoyed now because of Jesus, the promised ruler from Bethlehem, and will be fully and eternally enjoyed in God's new world of perfect love and justice.

WHAT TO LOOK FOR IN MICAH

- God's indictment of Israel's religious leaders (ch. 3)
- God's plans for the immediate and the more distant future (ch. 4)
- A ruler to come from Bethlehem (ch. 5)
- What the Lord requires (6:8)

1 The word of the LORD that came to Micah of Moresheth[a] during the reigns of Jotham,[b] Ahaz[c] and Hezekiah, kings of Judah[d] — the vision[e] he saw concerning Samaria and Jerusalem.

2 Hear, you peoples, all of you,[f]
listen, earth[g] and all who live in it,
that the Sovereign LORD may bear witness[h] against you,
the Lord from his holy temple.[i]

Judgment Against Samaria and Jerusalem

3 Look! The LORD is coming from his dwelling[j] place;
he comes down and treads on the heights of the earth.[k]
4 The mountains melt[l] beneath him
and the valleys split apart,[m]
like wax before the fire,
like water rushing down a slope.
5 All this is because of Jacob's transgression,
because of the sins of the people of Israel.
What is Jacob's transgression?
Is it not Samaria?[n]
What is Judah's high place?
Is it not Jerusalem?

6 "Therefore I will make Samaria a heap of rubble,
a place for planting vineyards.
I will pour her stones[o] into the valley
and lay bare her foundations.[p]
7 All her idols[q] will be broken to pieces;
all her temple gifts will be burned with fire;
I will destroy all her images.[r]
Since she gathered her gifts from the wages of prostitutes,[s]
as the wages of prostitutes they will again be used."

1:1 [a] Jer 26:18 [b] 1Ch 3:12 [c] 1Ch 3:13 [d] Hos 1:1 [e] Isa 1:1
1:2 [f] Ps 50:7 [g] Jer 6:19 [h] Ge 31:50; Dt 4:26; Isa 1:2 [i] Ps 11:4
1:3 [j] Isa 18:4 [k] Am 4:13
1:4 [l] Ps 46:2, 6 [m] Nu 16:31; Na 1:5
1:5 [n] Am 8:14
1:6 [o] Am 5:11 [p] Eze 13:14
1:7 [q] Eze 6:6 [r] Dt 9:21 [s] Dt 23:17-18
1:8 [t] Isa 15:3
1:9 [u] Jer 46:11 [v] 2Ki 18:13 [w] Isa 3:26
1:11 [x] Eze 23:29
1:12 [y] Jer 14:19

Mic 1:8–9 ❖ How can we mourn and lament the sins of God's people? Why is it instructive to do so?

Weeping and Mourning

8 Because of this I will weep[t] and wail;
I will go about barefoot and naked.
I will howl like a jackal
and moan like an owl.
9 For Samaria's plague[u] is incurable;
it has spread to Judah.[v]
It has reached the very gate[w] of my people,
even to Jerusalem itself.
10 Tell it not in Gath[a];
weep not at all.
In Beth Ophrah[b]
roll in the dust.
11 Pass by naked[x] and in shame,
you who live in Shaphir.[c]
Those who live in Zaanan[d]
will not come out.
Beth Ezel is in mourning;
it no longer protects you.
12 Those who live in Maroth[e] writhe in pain,
waiting for relief,[y]
because disaster has come from the LORD,
even to the gate of Jerusalem.

[a] 10 *Gath* sounds like the Hebrew for *tell.*
[b] 10 *Beth Ophrah* means *house of dust.*
[c] 11 *Shaphir* means *pleasant.*
[d] 11 *Zaanan* sounds like the Hebrew for *come out.*
[e] 12 *Maroth* sounds like the Hebrew for *bitter.*

1:1 The prophetic book of Micah begins in the usual manner: announcement of the divine source of the words that follow, identification of the prophet and the time periods when he preaches, and a brief comment about the subject of the prophecies.
1:2–4 The Lord's appearance evokes not only a sense of awe and fear but also a sense of joy. The awe and fear arise because of the power and glory of God's majesty. The joy arises because the people believe God is coming to defeat their enemies.
1:5–7 God accuses the northern nation of Israel of insurrection or rebellion against himself. The Judean audience in Jerusalem readily supports this idea. God predicts the destruction of the northern nation of Israel.

APPLICATION ✣ **1:1–7** No power can stand in the presence of a holy God when judgment is determined. If mountains melt like wax before his power, we should all consider what we will say when we meet him in judgment. The only hope is to turn from the sin that enrages God and rest in the power of God's grace, which brings forgiveness.

1:8–9 Micah's symbolic action is meant as a sign-act of things to come. Micah is behaving as the people will behave when this terrible disaster finally reaches Judah.
1:10–12 These towns seem to be chosen because puns can be made with their names. The puns are like saying: "Watertown will be covered with water," or "Washington will be washed away." Each town will suffer an evil end related to the meaning of its name. The God of Judah is sending it on them.

13 You who live in Lachish,[z]
harness fast horses to the chariot.
You are where the sin of Daughter
Zion began,
for the transgressions of Israel
were found in you.
14 Therefore you will give parting gifts[a]
to Moresheth Gath.
The town of Akzib[ab] will prove
deceptive[c]
to the kings of Israel.
15 I will bring a conqueror against you
who live in Mareshah.[bd]
The nobles of Israel
will flee to Adullam.[e]
16 Shave[f] your head in mourning
for the children in whom you
delight;
make yourself as bald as the vulture,
for they will go from you into
exile.

Human Plans and God's Plans

2 Woe to those who plan iniquity,
to those who plot evil on their
beds![g]
At morning's light they carry it out
because it is in their power to
do it.
2 They covet fields[h] and seize them,
and houses, and take them.
They defraud[i] people of their homes,
they rob them of their
inheritance.

3 Therefore, the LORD says:

"I am planning disaster[j] against this
people,
from which you cannot save
yourselves.

1:13 [z] Jos 10:3
1:14 [a] 2Ki 16:8 [b] Jos 15:44 [c] Jer 15:18
1:15 [d] Jos 15:44 [e] Jos 12:15
1:16 [f] Job 1:20
2:1 [g] Ps 36:4
2:2 [h] Isa 5:8 [i] Jer 22:17
2:3 [j] Jer 18:11; Am 3:1-2 [k] Isa 2:12
2:4 [l] Jer 4:13
2:5 [m] Jos 18:4
2:6 [n] Mic 6:16 [o] Am 2:12
2:7 [p] Ps 119:65 [q] Ps 15:2; 84:11

Mic 2:6 ❖ Where do we see God's people wanting to silence messages of judgment from God's Word? Why?

You will no longer walk proudly,[k]
for it will be a time of calamity.
4 In that day people will ridicule you;
they will taunt you with this
mournful song:
'We are utterly ruined;[l]
my people's possession is
divided up.
He takes it from me!
He assigns our fields to traitors.'"

5 Therefore you will have no one in
the assembly of the LORD
to divide the land[m] by lot.

False Prophets

6 "Do not prophesy," their prophets
say.
"Do not prophesy about these
things;
disgrace[n] will not overtake us.[o]"
7 You descendants of Jacob, should it
be said,
"Does the LORD become[c]
impatient?
Does he do such things?"

"Do not my words do good[p]
to the one whose ways are
upright?[q]
8 Lately my people have risen up
like an enemy.
You strip off the rich robe

[a] *14 Akzib* means *deception.* [b] *15 Mareshah* sounds like the Hebrew for *conqueror.* [c] *7* Or *Is the Spirit of the LORD*

1:13–16 The friends Micah grew up with and his parents and relatives who live in these towns will have to face this terrible day of disaster. This makes the coming attack personal for Micah.

❖ **1:8–16** Unfortunately, there seems to be little talk in the church today about lamenting the lost of this world—those who will suffer the punishment of eternal death. Moses, Amos, Micah, Jeremiah, Jesus, and Paul found grieving a fitting way to communicate their deep sorrow for those who will die without a relationship with God.

The change starts with us. Who can we pray for today? Who are the people that we know and love and feel concern for regarding their eternal destiny? The Holy Spirit can position us for critical discussions with these individuals. Pray that the God who constantly seeks the lost (Lk 15:4–7; 19:10) will allow you to work with him to make a difference in the lives of others for their eternal sake.

2:1–5 Most thieves work at night when no one can see them; ironically, the powerful thieves described here operate in broad daylight. The messenger formula in v. 3, "the LORD says," and the direct first-person address by God ("I am planning") emphasize the authority and certainty of what will happen. Micah sings a brief sarcastic lament (v. 4b). Today one might mockingly say: "Isn't it too bad! These poor rich people. What they coveted and stole is now being coveted and taken from them."
2:6–11 Micah's audience disputes his theological perspective and tries to stop him from prophesying. Micah weighs in with additional evidence to support his claim that these military and political leaders are oppressing God's people (vv. 8–10) and

from those who pass by without a care,
like men returning from battle.
9 You drive the women of my people
from their pleasant homes.[r]
You take away my blessing
from their children forever.
10 Get up, go away!
For this is not your resting place,[s]
because it is defiled,[t]
it is ruined, beyond all remedy.
11 If a liar and deceiver[u] comes and says,
'I will prophesy for you plenty of wine and beer,'
that would be just the prophet for this people![v]

Deliverance Promised

12 "I will surely gather all of you, Jacob;
I will surely bring together the remnant[w] of Israel.
I will bring them together like sheep in a pen,
like a flock in its pasture;
the place will throng with people.
13 The One who breaks open the way
will go up before[x] them;
they will break through the gate
and go out.
Their King will pass through before them,
the LORD at their head."

Leaders and Prophets Rebuked

3 Then I said,

"Listen, you leaders[y] of Jacob,
you rulers of Israel.
Should you not embrace justice,
2 you who hate good and love evil;
who tear the skin from my people
and the flesh from their bones;[z]

2:9 [r]Jer 10:20
2:10 [s]Dt 12:9 [t]Lev 18:25-29; Ps 106:38-39
2:11 [u]Jer 5:31 [v]Isa 30:10
2:12 [w]Mic 4:7; 5:7; 7:18
2:13 [x]Isa 52:12
3:1 [y]Jer 5:5
3:2 [z]Ps 53:4; Eze 22:27
3:3 [a]Ps 14:4 [b]Zep 3:3 [c]Eze 11:7
3:4 [d]Ps 18:41; Isa 1:15 [e]Dt 31:17
3:5 [f]Isa 3:12; 9:16
3:6 [g]Isa 8:19-22 [h]Isa 29:10
3:7 [i]Mic 7:16 [j]Isa 44:25
3:8 [k]Isa 58:1

Mic 3:8 ❖ How have we experienced God's power and Spirit strengthening us? How has God used these to embolden us for a task or calling?

3 who eat my people's flesh,[a]
strip off their skin
and break their bones in pieces;[b]
who chop them up like meat for the pan,
like flesh for the pot?[c]"

4 Then they will cry out to the LORD,
but he will not answer them.[d]
At that time he will hide his face[e] from them
because of the evil they have done.

5 This is what the LORD says:

"As for the prophets
who lead my people astray,[f]
they proclaim 'peace'
if they have something to eat,
but prepare to wage war against anyone
who refuses to feed them.
6 Therefore night will come over you,
without visions,
and darkness, without divination.[g]
The sun will set for the prophets,[h]
and the day will go dark for them.
7 The seers will be ashamed[i]
and the diviners disgraced.[j]
They will all cover their faces
because there is no answer from God."
8 But as for me, I am filled with power,
with the Spirit of the LORD,
and with justice and might,
to declare to Jacob his transgression,
to Israel his sin.[k]

---

deserve his judgment. But these leaders would rather have a discussion about the best wine produced in the land last year.

2:12–13 Verse 13 focuses on the sovereign King who will bring about this great event, not on how it will happen. God's people do not need all the details spelled out; they act in faith, trusting that God will do what he has promised.

✤ **2:1–13** The character of God has not changed. His actions on behalf of his people will continue. These facts bring assurance and hope and cause God's people to trust him as they struggle through trials. Although no one can predict what God will do in any specific situation, Scripture contains promises (Eze 36–39; Dan 7–8) that assure people today that God knows what will happen and that he will ultimately have victory over all the forces of evil.

3:1–4 This message is given to the political and civic leaders. Micah's analogy refers to the leaders treating the people like animals. The institutions meant to protect justice use pressure and violence to get what they want.

3:5–8 Unprincipled prophets love money and show favoritism for bribes (v. 5). Micah is filled by the Spirit. These false prophets are abandoned by God.

[9]Hear this, you leaders of Jacob,
you rulers of Israel,
who despise justice
and distort all that is right;[l]
[10]who build[m] Zion with bloodshed,[n]
and Jerusalem with wickedness.[o]
[11]Her leaders judge for a bribe,
her priests teach for a price,
and her prophets tell fortunes for money.[p]
Yet they look for the LORD's support and say,
"Is not the LORD among us?
No disaster will come upon us."[q]
[12]Therefore because of you,
Zion will be plowed like a field,
Jerusalem will become a heap of rubble,[r]
the temple hill a mound overgrown with thickets.

The Mountain of the LORD

4:1–3pp // Isa 2:1–4

4 In the last days

the mountain[s] of the LORD's temple will be established
as the highest of the mountains;
it will be exalted above the hills,[t]
and peoples will stream to it.[u]

[2]Many nations will come and say,

"Come, let us go up to the mountain of the LORD,[v]
to the temple of the God of Jacob.[w]
He will teach us his ways,[x]
so that we may walk in his paths."
The law will go out from Zion,
the word of the LORD from Jerusalem.

3:9 [l]Ps 58:1-2; Isa 1:23
3:10 [m]Jer 22:13 [n]Hab 2:12 [o]Eze 22:27
3:11 [p]Isa 1:23; Jer 6:13; Hos 4:8,18 [q]Jer 7:4
3:12 [r]Jer 26:18
4:1 [s]Zec 8:3 [t]Eze 17:22 [u]Ps 22:27; 86:9; Jer 3:17
4:2 [v]Jer 31:6 [w]Zec 2:11; 14:16 [x]Ps 25:8-9; Isa 54:13
4:3 [y]Isa 11:4 [z]Joel 3:10 [a]Isa 2:4
4:4 [b]1Ki 4:25 [c]Lev 26:6 [d]Isa 1:20; Zec 3:10
4:5 [e]2Ki 17:29 [f]Jos 24:14-15; Isa 26:8; Zec 10:12
4:6 [g]Ps 147:2 [h]Eze 34:13,16; 37:21; Zep 3:19
4:7 [i]Mic 2:12 [j]Da 7:14; Lk 1:33; Rev 11:15

Mic 4:2–5 ❖ How do we see the prophet's vision of "many nations" coming to God being fulfilled today? How can we support this mission of outreach for Christ?

[3]He will judge between many peoples
and will settle disputes for strong nations far and wide.[y]
They will beat their swords into plowshares
and their spears into pruning hooks.[z]
Nation will not take up sword against nation,
nor will they train for war anymore.[a]
[4]Everyone will sit under their own vine
and under their own fig tree,[b]
and no one will make them afraid,[c]
for the LORD Almighty has spoken.[d]
[5]All the nations may walk
in the name of their gods,[e]
but we will walk in the name of the LORD
our God for ever and ever.[f]

The LORD's Plan

[6]"In that day," declares the LORD,

"I will gather the lame;
I will assemble the exiles[g]
and those I have brought to grief.[h]
[7]I will make the lame my remnant,[i]
those driven away a strong nation.
The LORD will rule over them in Mount Zion
from that day and forever.[j]

3:9–12 Jer 26:17–19 recalls Micah's word for Hezekiah and the people of Judah. They responded by fearing the Lord and praying for mercy. Because they turned to God, God graciously decided not to destroy Judah at that time. The response by Hezekiah (see Isa 36–37) changes the course of history for Judah, but it happens only because Micah is willing to declare the sins of Judah.

✣ **3:1–12** If leaders cannot be trusted to do the right thing, how can one respect their decisions and follow them? Too often a leader's selfish desires are given a higher value than justice (vv. 5, 11). God sees when any leaders treat others unjustly and will hold each of them accountable for acts of injustice and selfish attitudes toward money.

4:1–5 Mic 4:1b–2 pictures people streaming to Jerusalem from many nations to hear the words of God and understand the "law" (v. 2) from God himself. When they come, every individual will have plenty to eat, be free of anxiety, and have a peaceful sense of security.

4:6–8 Here Micah assures his listeners that God has not forgotten them. God's promise that "the former dominion will be restored to you" (v. 8) emphasizes this return to Judah's ideal state. These promises give hope for the future to people who have little to look forward to.

✣ **4:1–8** Since God plans to establish his kingdom, believers should commit themselves to walk in God's ways and trust his leadership. He is the only basis for hope (v. 5). If this principle were actually practiced by every believer, the church would be transformed with the removal of petty politics and weak faith.

8 As for you, watchtower of the flock,
stronghold[a] of Daughter Zion,
the former dominion will be
restored[k] to you;
kingship will come to Daughter
Jerusalem."

9 Why do you now cry aloud —
have you no king[b][l]?
Has your ruler[c] perished,
that pain seizes you like that of a
woman in labor?[m]
10 Writhe in agony, Daughter Zion,
like a woman in labor,
for now you must leave the city
to camp in the open field.
You will go to Babylon;[n]
there you will be rescued.
There the LORD will redeem[o] you
out of the hand of your enemies.

11 But now many nations
are gathered against you.
They say, "Let her be defiled,
let our eyes gloat[p] over Zion!"
12 But they do not know
the thoughts of the LORD;
they do not understand his plan,[q]
that he has gathered them like
sheaves to the threshing
floor.
13 "Rise and thresh, Daughter Zion,
for I will give you horns of iron;
I will give you hooves of bronze,
and you will break to pieces many
nations."[r]
You will devote their ill-gotten gains
to the LORD,
their wealth to the Lord of all the
earth.

A Promised Ruler From Bethlehem

5 [d] Marshal your troops now, city of
troops,
for a siege is laid against us.
They will strike Israel's ruler
on the cheek[s] with a rod.

4:8 [k] Isa 1:26
4:9 [l] Jer 8:19 [m] Jer 30:6
4:10 [n] 2Ki 20:18; Isa 43:14 [o] Isa 48:20
4:11 [p] La 2:16; Ob 12
4:12 [q] Isa 55:8; Ro 11:33-34
4:13 [r] Da 2:44
5:1 [s] La 3:30
5:2 [t] Jn 7:42 [u] Ge 48:7 [v] Ps 102:25 [w] Mt 2:6*
5:4 [x] Isa 40:11; 49:9; Eze 34:11-15,23; Mic 7:14 [y] Isa 52:13; Lk 1:32
5:5 [z] Isa 9:6; Lk 2:14; Col 1:19-20 [a] Isa 8:7 [b] Isa 10:24-27
5:6 [c] Ge 10:8 [d] Zep 2:13 [e] Na 2:11-13

Mic 5:2-6 ❖ How is the son who came from Bethlehem, Jesus Christ, the peace for all God's people? How is Christ establishing that peace between us and those around us?

2 "But you, Bethlehem[t] Ephrathah,[u]
though you are small among the
clans[e] of Judah,
out of you will come for me
one who will be ruler over Israel,
whose origins are from of old,[v]
from ancient times."[w]

3 Therefore Israel will be abandoned
until the time when she who is in
labor bears a son,
and the rest of his brothers return
to join the Israelites.

4 He will stand and shepherd his
flock[x]
in the strength of the LORD,
in the majesty of the name of the
LORD his God.
And they will live securely, for then
his greatness[y]
will reach to the ends of the earth.

5 And he will be our peace[z]
when the Assyrians invade[a] our
land
and march through our fortresses.
We will raise against them seven
shepherds,
even eight commanders,[b]
6 who will rule[f] the land of Assyria
with the sword,
the land of Nimrod[c] with drawn
sword.[g][d]
He will deliver us from the Assyrians
when they invade our land
and march across our borders.[e]

[a] 8 Or *hill* [b] 9 Or *King* [c] 9 Or *Ruler* [d] In Hebrew texts 5:1 is numbered 4:14, and 5:2-15 is numbered 5:1-14. [e] 2 Or *rulers* [f] 6 Or *crush* [g] 6 Or *Nimrod in its gates*

4:9–10 Micah sees a near future that will cause the people to writhe in agony. The concluding good news of hope should have caused Micah's audience to face their present danger and cry out to God, putting their problems in the framework of God's ultimate plan for his people.
4:11–13 Micah contrasts the attacker's ideas with God's thoughts. Some time later God miraculously destroyed 185,000 Assyrian troops.
5:1–4 This passage encourages the people to prepare for the approaching siege in 701 BC. The positive message of hope in vv. 2–4 reminds the people of the messianic promise of the eternal reign of David's Son. Verse 3 clarifies that this ruler will not come immediately to prevent the present disaster. Micah describes the reign of this new messianic ruler in v. 4.
5:5–8 The expressions in vv. 5–6 contrast what God will do through the Messiah and what the audience is confidently saying about what "we" will do through "our" military strength. Verses 7–9 persuade his listeners not to count on their own strength; all they can do is trust the sovereign plan of God and wait for him to act.

[7]The remnant[f] of Jacob will be
in the midst of many peoples
like dew from the LORD,
like showers on the grass,[g]
which do not wait for anyone
or depend on man.
[8]The remnant of Jacob will be among
the nations,
in the midst of many peoples,
like a lion among the beasts of the
forest,[h]
like a young lion among flocks of
sheep,
which mauls and mangles[i] as it goes,
and no one can rescue.[j]
[9]Your hand will be lifted up[k] in
triumph over your enemies,
and all your foes will be destroyed.

[10]"In that day," declares the LORD,

"I will destroy your horses from
among you
and demolish your chariots.[l]
[11]I will destroy the cities[m] of your land
and tear down all your
strongholds.[n]
[12]I will destroy your witchcraft
and you will no longer cast spells.[o]
[13]I will destroy your idols
and your sacred stones from
among you;
you will no longer bow down
to the work of your hands.[p]
[14]I will uproot from among you your
Asherah poles[a][q]
when I demolish your cities.
[15]I will take vengeance[r] in anger and
wrath
on the nations that have not
obeyed me."

The LORD's Case Against Israel

6 Listen to what the LORD says:

"Stand up, plead my case before the
mountains;[s]
let the hills hear what you have to
say.

[2]"Hear,[t] you mountains, the LORD's
accusation;[u]
listen, you everlasting
foundations of the earth.
For the LORD has a case against his
people;
he is lodging a charge[v] against
Israel.

[3]"My people, what have I done to
you?
How have I burdened[w] you?
Answer me.
[4]I brought you up out of Egypt
and redeemed you from the land
of slavery.[x]

5:7 [f]Mic 2:12 [g]Isa 44:4
5:8 [h]Ge 49:9 [i]Mic 4:13; Zec 10:5 [j]Ps 50:22; Hos 5:14
5:9 [k]Ps 10:12
5:10 [l]Hos 14:3; Zec 9:10
5:11 [m]Isa 6:11 [n]Hos 10:14; Am 5:9
5:12 [o]Dt 18:10-12; Isa 2:6; 8:19
5:13 [p]Eze 6:9; Zec 13:2
5:14 [q]Ex 34:13
5:15 [r]Isa 65:12
6:1 [s]Ps 50:1; Eze 6:2
6:2 [t]Dt 32:1 [u]Hos 12:2 [v]Ps 50:7
6:3 [w]Jer 2:5
6:4 [x]Dt 7:8

[a] *14* That is, wooden symbols of the goddess Asherah

5:9 This oracle ends with a statement of victory over Judah's foes. Micah hopes those who hear this prayer will follow his example and commit their lives to God's care and protection.

✣ **4:9—5:9** Those who recognize that God is the sovereign King of this world will be more likely to bring their problems to him. If, however, we live around self-reliant and independent people who proudly struggle through problems in their own strength, then calling on God is less likely. Looking at this idea from the positive side, we can encourage those we know who are in crisis not to follow the mistakes of the past, but to seek God's help in all things.

5:10–11 Micah is reacting against the nationalistic fervor of war that optimistically imagines that military might is the key to the success of a nation. Although massive buildings and huge walls appear to provide hope to the nation, God's removal of them will leave the people with nothing to depend on but God.

5:12–14 Isa 2:6 and 8:19 describe some of the witchcraft and sorcery that gradually infiltrated into Judah. The final purging of the land will remove this stumbling. God will help the people focus on their true source of hope.

5:15 The Hebrew word translated "vengeance" refers to the just execution of divine control over the affairs of the world. Some who have ignored God's ways and disobeyed will reap their just reward.

✣ **5:10–15** Idols present a false hope to the worshiper, and most would concede that con artists in the religious world provide no real hope to those who are deluded by a lot of fast talk. Equally serious are the deceptive false hopes that are more realistic imitations of the truth, especially the hope offered by cults that make some use of the Bible.

False teachers are as much a problem today as they were in antiquity. This is why we are called to prayer and discernment as we read and study the Bible and listen to our Christian leaders (1Ki 3:9; Ps 119:125; Ro 12:1-2; 1Co 2:7-12).

6:1–2 The mountains (personified) know about the people's false worship of other gods. Verse 2 reveals that God has serious accusations of covenant unfaithfulness to bring against them.

6:3–5 God defends his past behavior by reciting his great acts of grace on behalf of his people. The fault of this situation does not lie with God.

I sent Moses[y] to lead you,
also Aaron[z] and Miriam.[a]
5 My people, remember
what Balak[b] king of Moab plotted
and what Balaam son of Beor answered.
Remember your journey from Shittim[c] to Gilgal,[d]
that you may know the righteous acts[e] of the LORD."

6 With what shall I come before the LORD
and bow down before the exalted God?
Shall I come before him with burnt offerings,
with calves a year old?[f]
7 Will the LORD be pleased with thousands of rams,[g]
with ten thousand rivers of olive oil?[h]
Shall I offer my firstborn[i] for my transgression,
the fruit of my body for the sin of my soul?[j]
8 He has shown you, O mortal, what is good.
And what does the LORD require of you?
To act justly[k] and to love mercy
and to walk humbly[a][l] with your God.[m]

Israel's Guilt and Punishment

9 Listen! The LORD is calling to the city—
and to fear your name is wisdom—
"Heed the rod and the One who appointed it.[b]
10 Am I still to forget your ill-gotten treasures, you wicked house,
and the short ephah,[c] which is accursed?[n]
11 Shall I acquit someone with dishonest scales,[o]
with a bag of false weights?
12 Your rich people are violent;[p]
your inhabitants are liars[q]
and their tongues speak deceitfully.[r]
13 Therefore, I have begun to destroy[s] you,
to ruin[d] you because of your sins.
14 You will eat but not be satisfied;[t]
your stomach will still be empty.[e]
You will store up but save nothing,[u]
because what you save[f] I will give to the sword.
15 You will plant but not harvest;[v]
you will press olives but not use the oil,

6:4 [y] Ex 4:16 [z] Ps 77:20 [a] Ex 15:20
6:5 [b] Nu 22:5-6 [c] Nu 25:1 [d] Jos 5:9-10 [e] Jdg 5:11; 1Sa 12:7
6:6 [f] Ps 40:6-8; 51:16-17
6:7 [g] Isa 40:16 [h] Ps 50:8-10 [i] Lev 18:21 [j] 2Ki 16:3
6:8 [k] Isa 1:17; Jer 22:3 [l] Isa 57:15 [m] Dt 10:12-13; 1Sa 15:22; Hos 6:6
6:10 [n] Eze 45:9-10; Am 3:10; 8:4-6
6:11 [o] Lev 19:36; Hos 12:7
6:12 [p] Isa 1:23 [q] Isa 3:8 [r] Jer 9:3
6:13 [s] Isa 1:7; 6:11
6:14 [t] Isa 9:20 [u] Isa 30:6
6:15 [v] Dt 28:38; Jer 12:13

[a] 8 Or *prudently* [b] 9 The meaning of the Hebrew for this line is uncertain. [c] 10 An ephah was a dry measure. [d] 13 Or *Therefore, I will make you ill and destroy you; / I will ruin* [e] 14 The meaning of the Hebrew for this word is uncertain. [f] 14 Or *You will press toward birth but not give birth, / and what you bring to birth*

Mic 6:6-8 ❖ Based on their actions, what do many Christians seem to think God requires of them? How can we live out what God actually requires, based on Micah 6:8?

6:6-7 The people try to defend themselves in a series of rhetorical statements. Were their gifts just a means of bribing God? No, they were much different. Gifts were an outward sign of the inner attitude of a broken and contrite heart.

6:8 Micah is not attempting to reveal some new standard of conduct or give an expanded or secret list of requirements that were previously unknown. God has already communicated that he wants these three basic things. Micah's description of God's requirements includes no negative statements about what is forbidden to the Israelites: It clearly and positively presents the keys to a full life within the covenant.

6:9-12 God now raises specific examples of covenant disloyalty. Among the people there has been no justice for others and no attempt to walk attentively with God.

6:13-16 Because of Israel's unfaithfulness, the only possible verdict is "guilty as charged." Micah hopes to convince his audience that their sins are serious. Because of sin, God will allow Jerusalem to be ruined and the people annihilated by their enemies. The nations will scornfully mock them. Micah warns them that this will certainly be God's verdict if there is no immediate turning from their evil ways.

✜ **6:1-16** One way church members today can ensure a proper relationship to God and avoid his condemnation is to always remember what he has done for them. This is why Paul encourages the church at Corinth to celebrate the Lord's Supper, basing it on the memory of what Jesus did at his last Passover and on the cross. When we make it a habit to remember and wonder at Jesus' great love for us in dying for us "while we were still sinners" (Ro 5:8), his gracious actions on our behalf can transform our daily attitudes and actions.

PEOPLE TO KNOW // MICAH

MICAH 6:8: Micah ministered in Judah at the same time as the prophet Isaiah. During this tumultuous time the Assyrians destroyed the northern kingdom of Israel and tried to carry out the same fate against Judah.

Micah's concerns, however, were not so much with geopolitics as they were with the moral and spiritual decay within his own community. Micah lamented the lack of justice and righteousness around him. He decried the greed and oppression practiced by wealthy leaders. Micah warned that because of the people's evil God would not answer when they cried out to him for help.

Micah had to contend with false prophets who wanted him to keep his mouth shut (Mic 2:6). Still, he boldly proclaimed a counter-cultural message of justice. Micah declared God's holy expectation: that his people act justly, love mercy and walk humbly before the Lord (Mic 6:8). Micah announced God's coming judgment on those who failed to apply this message to their own lives.

Judgment, however, does not have the last word in Micah. The prophet ends with hope and promise, praising God for pardoning sin and delighting to show mercy (Mic 7:18). Though judgment is certain, Micah ends with a vision of God's compassionate redemption.

APPLICATION The world desperately needs people who speak for justice for the oppressed and vulnerable and who speak against systems that take life instead of nurture it. Micah reminds us that in our humble walk before God, we need to act justly and love mercy. We need to share God's heart for people who are poor and for the marginalized. Perhaps, like Micah, we will find there are people who want us to remain silent, but like the prophet we should continue to speak God's justice and point to God's coming redemption.

you will crush grapes but not
drink the wine.[w]
16 You have observed the statutes of
Omri[x]
and all the practices of Ahab's[y]
house;
you have followed their
traditions.[z]
Therefore I will give you over to
ruin[a]
and your people to derision;
you will bear the scorn[b] of the
nations.[a]"

Israel's Misery

7 What misery is mine!
I am like one who gathers summer
fruit
at the gleaning of the vineyard;
there is no cluster of grapes to eat,
none of the early figs that I
crave.
2 The faithful have been swept from
the land;[c]
not one upright person
remains.
Everyone lies in wait to shed
blood;[d]
they hunt each other with
nets.[e]
3 Both hands are skilled in doing
evil;[f]
the ruler demands gifts,
the judge accepts bribes,
the powerful dictate what they
desire —
they all conspire together.
4 The best of them is like a brier,[g]
the most upright worse than a
thorn hedge.
The day God visits you has come,
the day your watchmen sound the
alarm.
Now is the time of your
confusion.[h]
5 Do not trust a neighbor;

6:15 [w] Am 5:11; Zep 1:13
6:16 [x] 1Ki 16:25 [y] 1Ki 16:29-33 [z] Jer 7:24 [a] Jer 25:9 [b] Jer 51:51
7:2 [c] Ps 12:1 [d] Mic 3:10 [e] Jer 5:26
7:3 [f] Pr 4:16
7:4 [g] Eze 2:6 [h] Isa 22:5; Hos 9:7

[a] 16 Septuagint; Hebrew *scorn due my people*

7:1–6 At the end of his life, Micah continues to weep over the corrupt social situation (vv. 3–4). Having wept over the problems in Judah, Micah gives a brief prophetic prayer of confidence. After this confident statement of divine retribution, Micah returns to lament how the present social upheaval has destroyed the normal peaceful and trusting relationship within the family and neighborhood (vv. 5–6).

put no confidence in a friend.[i]
Even with the woman who lies in your embrace
guard the words of your lips.
6 For a son dishonors his father,
a daughter rises up against her mother,[j]
a daughter-in-law against her mother-in-law—
a man's enemies are the members of his own household.[k]

7 But as for me, I watch in hope[l] for the LORD,
I wait for God my Savior;
my God will hear[m] me.

Israel Will Rise

8 Do not gloat over me,[n] my enemy!
Though I have fallen, I will rise.[o]
Though I sit in darkness,
the LORD will be my light.[p]
9 Because I have sinned against him,
I will bear the LORD's wrath,[q]
until he pleads my case
and upholds my cause.
He will bring me out into the light;
I will see his righteousness.[r]
10 Then my enemy will see it
and will be covered with shame,[s]
she who said to me,
"Where is the LORD your God?"
My eyes will see her downfall;[t]
even now she will be trampled[u] underfoot
like mire in the streets.

11 The day for building your walls[v] will come,
the day for extending your boundaries.
12 In that day people will come to you
from Assyria and the cities of Egypt,
even from Egypt to the Euphrates
and from sea to sea
and from mountain to mountain.[w]
13 The earth will become desolate
because of its inhabitants,
as the result of their deeds.[x]

7:5 [i] Jer 9:4
7:6 [j] Eze 22:7 [k] Mt 10:35-36*
7:7 [l] Ps 130:5; Isa 25:9 [m] Ps 4:3
7:8 [n] Pr 24:17 [o] Ps 37:24; Am 9:11 [p] Isa 9:2
7:9 [q] La 3:39-40 [r] Isa 46:13
7:10 [s] Ps 35:26 [t] Isa 51:23 [u] Zec 10:5
7:11 [v] Isa 54:11
7:12 [w] Isa 19:23-25
7:13 [x] Isa 3:10-11
7:14 [y] Mic 5:4 [z] Ps 23:4 [a] Jer 50:19
7:15 [b] Ex 3:20; Ps 78:12
7:16 [c] Isa 26:11
7:17 [d] Isa 25:3; 49:23; 59:19
7:18 [e] Isa 43:25; Jer 50:20 [f] Ps 103:8-13

Mic 7:18–20 ❖ How does God's amazing grace free us to live wholeheartedly for him? What does such wholehearted living look like?

Prayer and Praise

14 Shepherd[y] your people with your staff,[z]
the flock of your inheritance,
which lives by itself in a forest,
in fertile pasturelands.[a]
Let them feed in Bashan and Gilead[a]
as in days long ago.

15 "As in the days when you came out of Egypt,
I will show them my wonders.[b]"

16 Nations will see and be ashamed,[c]
deprived of all their power.
They will put their hands over their mouths
and their ears will become deaf.
17 They will lick dust like a snake,
like creatures that crawl on the ground.
They will come trembling out of their dens;
they will turn in fear[d] to the LORD our God
and will be afraid of you.
18 Who is a God like you,
who pardons sin[e] and forgives[f] the transgression

[a] 14 Or *in the middle of Carmel*

7:7–10 Micah's concentration on God rather than on his problems enables him to see a ray of hope for the future. Micah immediately expresses confidence that God will deliver the people from their fallen state (v. 8), forgive them of their sins (v. 9), and shame those who have mocked God (v. 10). In faith, Micah believes that the nation will rise again.
7:11–13 These promises confirm the expectations of the prophet (vv. 8–10). God has not forgotten his promises; he is not impotent, and his purposes have not changed.
7:14 Micah requests that God, as Shepherd-King of his people, take charge of his own flock by graciously ruling over them.
7:15–17 God recalls his marvelous deeds in the ancient past at the time of the exodus from Egypt. When God intervenes, the nations that oppress his people will be ashamed of their own puny strength and will bow in submission (vv. 16–17).
7:18–20 Micah's time of prayer ends with words of praise to God. This hymn is made up of two parts: a celebration of God and what he has done (v. 18), and praise for what God will do (vv. 19–20). God has one eternal plan: to use the descendants of Abraham to bless all the nations of the earth and to make of them a great nation. For Micah and his audience, that plan may seem like a lost cause, but through God's love and forgiveness

of the remnant[g] of his
inheritance?[h]
You do not stay angry[i] forever
but delight to show mercy.[j]
19 You will again have compassion
on us;
you will tread our sins underfoot
and hurl all our iniquities[k] into
the depths of the sea.[l]
20 You will be faithful to Jacob,
and show love to Abraham,
as you pledged on oath to our
ancestors[m]
in days long ago.

7:18 [g] Mic 2:12 [h] Ex 34:9 [i] Ps 103:9 [j] Jer 32:41
7:19 [k] Isa 43:25 [l] Jer 31:34
7:20 [m] Dt 7:8; Lk 1:72

---

he will miraculously accomplish his will on earth. Micah's bold hymn of faith in God's victory over sin provides real hope for the future.

7:1-20 For Micah, the depression of hopelessness turned not only to the possibility of hope but also to the confidence that victory over sin is certain because of our promise-keeping God. Like Micah, we can gain some semblance of hope by focusing not on the terrible plight of our world but on God, his past promises, and his ability and willingness to deal with the source of human hopelessness—sin itself (1Pe 2:24).

Nahum

Author: Nahum
Audience: The people of Judah
Date: Shortly before 612 BC

Theme: Nahum declares the universal sovereignty of God, who will judge Nineveh for its endless cruelty.

PERSPECTIVE

The book of Nahum darkly promises Judah's release from the oppression and cruelty of Nineveh. Nahum's prophecy celebrates the fall of the sadistic empire and is a word of judgment against it. The book of Jonah is similar in its prophecy of doom to the Assyrian Empire (Jonah 3:4; Nah 1:1–2), and both books end with questions from God, one of hope and one of despair (Jonah 4:11; Nah 3:19). Both books also deal with God's reputation as a just judge *and* a forgiving God (as revealed in the golden calf incident in Ex 34:5–6). Nahum focuses on judgment for the wicked, and Jonah focuses on grace to the repentant. Nahum ends without repentance, and history records Nineveh's fall to Babylon in 612 BC.

For more perspective on this book, see the Introduction to Jonah.

Reading Nahum

Nahum is different from other books of the OT in that most of it is addressed to the city of Nineveh rather than to God's people. Most of it prophesies the destruction of the city; the last few verses describe Nineveh's fall.

TAKING THE NEXT STEPS

Nahum (whose name means "comfort") prophesied during the time of King Josiah (2Ki 22–23), about a century after the northern kingdom of Israel had been annihilated by the Assyrians. His goal was to bring comfort to God's people in the southern kingdom by pronouncing judgment against the wicked and cruel city of Nineveh, capital of Assyria, which was threatening Judah.

Several messages stand out in this prophetic book. (1) God is the Lord of history and of all the nations of the world; he is in control of what happens to them. (2) Though God allows sin and evil in the world, he is well aware of it and will eventually come in swift judgment against

Ministries of Micah and Isaiah in Judah	(c. 740–681 BC)
Exile of Israel	(722 BC)
Nahum's ministry	(c. 645–620 BC)
Book of Nahum written	(c. 645–620 BC)
Zephaniah's ministry in Judah	(c. 640–627 BC)
Jeremiah's ministry in Judah	(c. 626–585 BC)
Habakkuk's ministry in Judah	(c. 605–588 BC)
Fall of Jerusalem	(586 BC)
Ministries of Haggai and Zechariah	(c. 520–480 BC)

Timeline scale: 1200 BC, 1100, 1000, 900, 800, 700, 600, 500, 400

those who champion wickedness and cruelty. (3) God comforts his people, not primarily by destroying their enemies but by demonstrating that he is the God who upholds justice. (4) God is calling us to a life of justice and fairness in our dealings with our fellow human beings.

Key Verse

The LORD is good, a refuge in times of trouble. He cares for those who trust in him.

—Nahum 1:7

WHAT TO LOOK FOR IN NAHUM

- The Lord's power over all the earth (ch. 1)
- The destruction of the destroyers (ch. 2)
- The end to Nineveh's endless cruelty (ch. 3)

1 A prophecy[a] concerning Nineveh.[b]
The book of the vision of Nahum the
Elkoshite.

The LORD's Anger Against Nineveh

2 The LORD is a jealous[c] and avenging God;
the LORD takes vengeance[d] and is filled with wrath.
The LORD takes vengeance on his foes
and vents his wrath against his enemies.
3 The LORD is slow to anger[e] but great in power;
the LORD will not leave the guilty unpunished.[f]
His way is in the whirlwind and the storm,
and clouds[g] are the dust of his feet.
4 He rebukes the sea and dries it up;
he makes all the rivers run dry.
Bashan and Carmel[h] wither
and the blossoms of Lebanon fade.
5 The mountains quake[i] before him
and the hills melt away.[j]
The earth trembles at his presence,
the world and all who live in it.
6 Who can withstand his indignation?
Who can endure[k] his fierce anger?
His wrath is poured out like fire;[l]
the rocks are shattered[m] before him.

7 The LORD is good,[n]
a refuge in times of trouble.

1:1 [a] Isa 13:1; 19:1; Jer 23:33-34 [b] Jnh 1:2; Na 2:8; Zep 2:13
1:2 [c] Ex 20:5 [d] Dt 32:41; Ps 94:1
1:3 [e] Ne 9:17 [f] Ex 34:7 [g] Ps 104:3
1:4 [h] Isa 33:9
1:5 [i] Ex 19:18 [j] Mic 1:4
1:6 [k] Mal 3:2 [l] Jer 10:10 [m] 1Ki 19:11
1:7 [n] Jer 33:11

1:1 This verse provides the reader with brief introductory information. The "prophecy" refers to Nahum's message, which was brought before the people. Oracles were often concerning nations that threatened Judah. This written document communicates the oracle that Nahum received as a "vision." **1:2–15** The theme of ch. 1 is Yahweh's wrath against cruelty. A longer section (vv. 1–10) and a shorter section (vv. 11–15) are its basic rhetorical parts. **1:2–10** This passage describes the strength of Yahweh's opposition to the Ninevite kingdom. Three subtitles present its subject matter. "Vengeance" (vv. 1–3a) describes Yahweh's anger against those "guilty" of violence. The "way" of the Creator (vv. 3b–6) describes Yahweh's use of the creation (in this case, the Babylonian army) to accomplish his purposes. The "good" and the "trouble" (vv. 7–10) declare that Yahweh is a "refuge" for those who trust in him but an "overwhelming flood" for those who plot against him.

He cares for[o] those who trust in him,
8 but with an overwhelming flood
he will make an end of Nineveh;
he will pursue his foes into the realm of darkness.

9 Whatever they plot against the LORD
he will bring[a] to an end;
trouble will not come a second time.
10 They will be entangled among thorns[p]
and drunk from their wine;
they will be consumed like dry stubble.[b][q]
11 From you, Nineveh, has one come forth
who plots evil against the LORD
and devises wicked plans.

12 This is what the LORD says:

"Although they have allies and are numerous,
they will be destroyed[r] and pass away.
Although I have afflicted you, Judah,
I will afflict you no more.[s]
13 Now I will break their yoke[t] from your neck
and tear your shackles away."

14 The LORD has given a command concerning you, Nineveh:
"You will have no descendants to bear your name.[u]
I will destroy the images[v] and idols
that are in the temple of your gods.
I will prepare your grave,[w]
for you are vile."

1:7 [o] Ps 1:6
1:10 [p] 2Sa 23:6 [q] Isa 5:24; Mal 4:1
1:12 [r] Isa 10:34 [s] Isa 54:6-8; La 3:31-32
1:13 [t] Isa 9:4
1:14 [u] Isa 14:22 [v] Mic 5:13 [w] Eze 32:22-23

Na 1:7-13 ❖ Why is God's judgment against the wicked good news for God's people? Where do we see God's people oppressed by evil powers today?

[a] 9 Or *What do you foes plot against the LORD? / He will bring it* [b] 10 The meaning of the Hebrew for this verse is uncertain.

1:11-15 The shorter rhetorical section ends with a "word" (v. 13a) concerning the reversal of Judah's situation. Nineveh's reversal will be from plotting "evil" (v. 11) to being in the "grave" (v. 14).

PEOPLE TO KNOW // NAHUM

NAHUM 1:1: The prophet Nahum is mentioned nowhere in the Bible outside of his short prophetic book, and no biographical details are given that offer a concrete picture of who he was. All we know of Nahum are his prophecies from God.

Nahum prophesied the destruction of Nineveh, the capital of Assyria. This destruction occurred in 612 BC. To illustrate Nineveh's coming destruction, Nahum refers to the past destruction of the Egyptian city of Thebes (Na 3:8), which was destroyed in 663 BC. Therefore, it is reasonable to believe Nahum ministered between those two events.

Nahum naturally pairs with Jonah, since both books deal with Nineveh. While Jonah depicts Nineveh's humble repentance, Nahum shows that any such repentance was short-lived, and judgment was coming. Interestingly, the books of Jonah and Nahum both end with a question, and they are the only two books in the Bible that do (Na 3:19).

Nahum prophesied a watery and fiery destruction for Nineveh, and ancient accounts as well as archaeology confirm this happened. In his prophecy, Nahum shows his literary genius. He employs wordplays and rich metaphors. Particularly striking is Nahum's choppy description of the horrific chaos of battle in Nahum 3:1-3. Nahum's message is clear: God will judge the people of Nineveh for their sins.

APPLICATION ✜ The message of Nahum may make readers uncomfortable (many lectionaries contain no readings from Nahum). After all, it is a book that promises destruction and devastation. Yet Nahum's name means "comfort." For those who are oppressed by wicked powers, it is comforting to hear that God will hold evildoers to account. God promised through Nahum that those who turn their backs on God will face judgment.

We don't delight in destruction, but when God carries out just judgment, it should bring us hope that there will ultimately be justice in the world. God promises to make all things new (Rev 21:5), and his redemption plan includes destroying evil and restoring those who suffer.

15 Look, there on the mountains,
the feet of one who brings good news,[x]
who proclaims peace![y]
Celebrate your festivals,[z] Judah,
and fulfill your vows.
No more will the wicked invade you;[a]
they will be completely destroyed.[a]

Nineveh to Fall

2 [b] An attacker[b] advances against you, Nineveh.
Guard the fortress,
watch the road,
brace yourselves,
marshal all your strength!

2 The LORD will restore[c] the splendor[d] of Jacob
like the splendor of Israel,
though destroyers have laid them waste
and have ruined their vines.

3 The shields of the soldiers are red;
the warriors are clad in scarlet.[e]
The metal on the chariots flashes
on the day they are made ready;
the spears of juniper are brandished.[c]
4 The chariots[f] storm through the streets,
rushing back and forth through the squares.
They look like flaming torches;
they dart about like lightning.

5 Nineveh summons her picked troops,
yet they stumble[g] on their way.
They dash to the city wall;
the protective shield is put in place.
6 The river gates[h] are thrown open
and the palace collapses.
7 It is decreed[d] that Nineveh
be exiled and carried away.
Her female slaves moan[i] like doves
and beat on their breasts.[j]
8 Nineveh is like a pool
whose water is draining away.
"Stop! Stop!" they cry,
but no one turns back.
9 Plunder the silver!
Plunder the gold!
The supply is endless,
the wealth from all its treasures!
10 She is pillaged, plundered, stripped!
Hearts melt, knees give way,
bodies tremble, every face grows pale.[k]

11 Where now is the lions' den,[l]
the place where they fed their young,
where the lion and lioness went,
and the cubs, with nothing to fear?
12 The lion killed[m] enough for his cubs
and strangled the prey for his mate,
filling his lairs with the kill
and his dens with the prey.

13 "I am against[n] you,"
declares the LORD Almighty.
"I will burn up your chariots in smoke,[o]
and the sword will devour your young lions.

1:15 [x] Isa 40:9; Ro 10:15 [y] Isa 52:7 [z] Lev 23:2-4 [a] Isa 52:1
2:1 [b] Jer 51:20
2:2 [c] Eze 37:23 [d] Isa 60:15
2:3 [e] Eze 23:14-15
2:4 [f] Jer 4:13
2:5 [g] Jer 46:12
2:6 [h] Na 3:13
2:7 [i] Isa 59:11 [j] Isa 32:12
2:10 [k] Isa 29:22
2:11 [l] Isa 5:29
2:12 [m] Jer 51:34
2:13 [n] Jer 21:13; Na 3:5 [o] Ps 46:9

[a] *15* In Hebrew texts this verse (1:15) is numbered 2:1. [b] In Hebrew texts 2:1-13 is numbered 2:2-14. [c] *3* Hebrew; Septuagint and Syriac *ready; / the horsemen rush to and fro.* [d] *7* The meaning of the Hebrew for this word is uncertain.

Na 2:11-13 ❖ Where have we seen God turn the fortunes of the proud and wicked?

APPLICATION ✣ 1:1-15 Those who have suffered violence may find that God's vengeance brings them comfort. Others may be horrified at God's wrath and the violence of his judgments. Life experience deeply influences how these verses are heard and interpreted.

2:1-13 Nahum 2 begins with the final battle inside Nineveh (vv. 1-10). Nineveh's preparations for battle are described in detail, followed by its unexpected fall (v. 6). The chapter concludes with a short mock lament over the end of the torturous "lions' den" (a term for Nineveh's walled city, vv. 11-12). It ends with Yahweh's direct curse against Nineveh (v. 13).

✣ 2:1-13 Christians have used warfare imagery to describe the advance of the gospel. Mark presents Jesus' confrontations with the spiritual enemy in his healing ministry (Mk 9:14-29). Paul describes how warfare against enemies is to be carried out: by heaping fiery coals of kindness on their heads (Ro 12:14-21). The early church martyrs took hope in these verses—that they would one day experience victory over their enemies: death and Satan, the opponents of life.

I will leave you no prey on the earth.
The voices of your messengers will no longer be heard."

Woe to Nineveh

3 Woe to the city of blood,[p]
full of lies,
full of plunder,
never without victims!
2 The crack of whips,
the clatter of wheels,
galloping horses
and jolting chariots!
3 Charging cavalry,
flashing swords
and glittering spears!
Many casualties,
piles of dead,
bodies without number,
people stumbling over the corpses[q] —
4 all because of the wanton lust of a prostitute,
alluring, the mistress of sorceries,[r]
who enslaved nations by her prostitution[s]
and peoples by her witchcraft.

5 "I am against[t] you," declares the LORD Almighty.
"I will lift your skirts[u] over your face.
I will show the nations your nakedness[v]
and the kingdoms your shame.
6 I will pelt you with filth,[w]
I will treat you with contempt[x]
and make you a spectacle.[y]
7 All who see you will flee from you and say,
'Nineveh[z] is in ruins — who will mourn for her?'[a]
Where can I find anyone to comfort[b] you?"

8 Are you better than[c] Thebes,[d]
situated on the Nile,[e]
with water around her?
The river was her defense,
the waters her wall.
9 Cush[a][f] and Egypt were her boundless strength;
Put[g] and Libya[h] were among her allies.
10 Yet she was taken captive[i]
and went into exile.
Her infants were dashed[j] to pieces
at every street corner.
Lots were cast for her nobles,
and all her great men were put in chains.
11 You too will become drunk;[k]
you will go into hiding[l]
and seek refuge from the enemy.

12 All your fortresses are like fig trees
with their first ripe fruit;
when they are shaken,
the figs[m] fall into the mouth of the eater.
13 Look at your troops —
they are all weaklings.[n]
The gates[o] of your land
are wide open to your enemies;
fire has consumed the bars of your gates.[p]

14 Draw water for the siege,[q]
strengthen your defenses![r]
Work the clay,
tread the mortar,
repair the brickwork!
15 There the fire will consume you;
the sword will cut you down —
they will devour you like a swarm of locusts.
Multiply like grasshoppers,
multiply like locusts![s]

3:1 p Eze 22:2; Mic 3:10
3:3 q 2Ki 19:35; Isa 34:3
3:4 r Isa 47:9 s Isa 23:17; Eze 16:25-29
3:5 t Na 2:13 u Jer 13:22 v Isa 47:3
3:6 w Job 9:31 x 1Sa 2:30; Jer 51:37 y Isa 14:16
3:7 z Na 1:1 a Jer 15:5 b Isa 51:19
3:8 c Am 6:2 d Jer 46:25 e Isa 19:6-9
3:9 f 2Ch 12:3 g Eze 27:10 h Eze 30:5
3:10 i Isa 20:4 j Isa 13:16; Hos 13:16
3:11 k Isa 49:26 l Isa 2:10
3:12 m Isa 28:4
3:13 n Isa 19:16; Jer 50:37 o Na 2:6 p Isa 45:2
3:14 q 2Ch 32:4 r Na 2:1
3:15 s Joel 1:4

[a] 9 That is, the upper Nile region

3:1–19 The graphic description of Nineveh's coming woe is presented in three parts.
3:1–7 A section on Nineveh's cruelty and exposure begins with a vivid description of Nineveh's bloody war-making (vv. 1–3; cf. 2:3–6) and with a strong sorceress metaphor for its deep offenses (v. 4; cf. 2:11–12). It continues with "the Lord Almighty's" second declaration, "I am against you" (v. 5), and with a description of Nineveh's coming exposure (vv. 5–6; cf. 2:13). Human response to the judgment follows (v. 7; cf. 2:7–10).
3:8–13 A unit on Nineveh's vulnerability compares Nineveh to the stronger cities of Egypt that have already fallen. Two metaphors tauntingly compare their fortresses to ripe fig trees and their troops to peace-loving women (vv. 12–13).
3:14–19 The final section on Nineveh's corruption—and celebration at its fall—mocks Nineveh's futile battle preparations and corrupt leadership. With the final metaphor of locusts, Nahum indicates that Nineveh's fall will be completed through its self-serving leaders who will plunder what they can and flee. The last word concerning the end of Nineveh's cruelty is to the king of Assyria. He will be abandoned by all his people as well as by his fearful allies.

16 You have increased the number of
your merchants
till they are more numerous than
the stars in the sky,
but like locusts they strip the land
and then fly away.
17 Your guards are like locusts,[t]
your officials like swarms of
locusts
that settle in the walls on a cold
day—
but when the sun appears they fly
away,
and no one knows where.

18 King of Assyria, your shepherds[a]
slumber;[u]
your nobles lie down to rest.[v]
Your people are scattered[w] on the
mountains
with no one to gather them.
19 Nothing can heal you;[x]
your wound is fatal.
All who hear the news about you
clap their hands[y] at your fall,
for who has not felt
your endless cruelty?

3:17 [t] Jer 51:27
3:18 [u] Ps 76:5-6
[v] Isa 56:10
[w] 1Ki 22:17
3:19 [x] Jer 30:13; Mic 1:9
[y] Job 27:23; La 2:15; Zep 2:15

Na 3:18-19 ❖ How might God's words of judgment lead those who listen to repent and turn to him?

[a] *18* That is, rulers

3:1-19 The descriptions of warfare in this chapter are especially disturbing. Avoiding these passages of Scripture is the most obvious way to avoid contemporary discomfort. At the other end of the spectrum, the book may be applied as an excuse for *human* violence against evil.

Between these two extremes, Christians have used a wide range of strategies for understanding Nahum. Those who have taken Nahum's words to heart may be prepared to speak and to act in accordance with the gospel. On that occasion Christians will have the opportunity to stand with the suffering and earn credibility as witnesses to God's power to punish sin and to execute justice in the world. Believers, like Nahum, can stand sure in their faith in a good God and his certain plan and ultimate protection for those who love and follow him (1:7).

Habakkuk

Author: Habakkuk

Audience: The people of Judah, struggling to comprehend the ways of God

Date: About 605 BC

Theme: In response to Habakkuk's questioning, God shows Habakkuk that in the midst of the evil that exists within both Judah and their enemies, Habakkuk's strength and joy are found in God alone.

PERSPECTIVE

The book of Habakkuk is a dialogue between Habakkuk and Yahweh during a vision Habakkuk receives from Yahweh. It begins with Habakkuk's complaint against local corruption and leads to a prophecy that spans ninety years as he is drawn into a progressively more difficult understanding of faith. It begins with the persistent question, "Why . . . ?" (1:3, 13) and ends with a sung prayer ("In wrath remember mercy," 3:2) and a confession of faith ("Though the fig tree does not bud . . . yet I will rejoice in the LORD," 3:17–18).

The prophet Habakkuk was probably an official temple musician-prophet (1 Chr 25:1). He was a contemporary of Nahum, Zephaniah, and Jeremiah and prophesied the fall of Judah to Babylon in the year of the Babylonians' victory over the Egyptians at Carchemish in northern Syria (605 BC).

TAKING THE NEXT STEPS

Habakkuk probably spoke his words during the reign of King Jehoiakim (2Ki 23:36—24:7), when the threat of the Babylonian invasion of Judah was increasing. As he reflected on what was about to happen, he complained to God about the rampant and unpunished evil in Judah and about God's declared means of dealing with that evil through the ruthless Babylonians. Habakkuk received an answer that God was indeed in control of the situation.

Reading Habakkuk

Habakkuk is unique in that he addresses God rather than the nation of Judah. The book focuses on his complaints and his prayer.

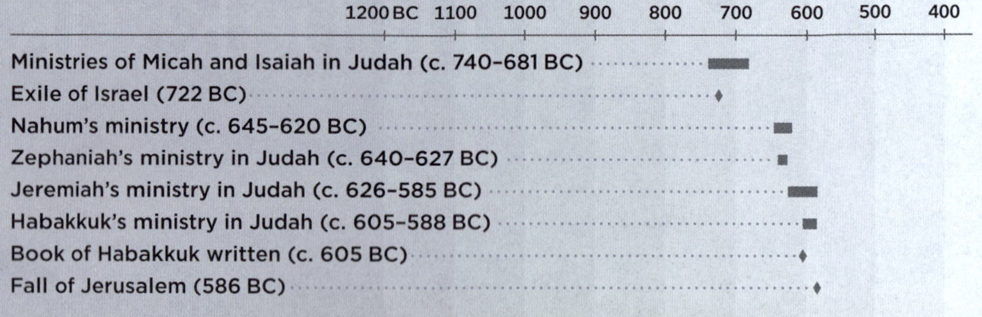

Key Verses

Though the fig tree does not bud and there are no grapes on the vines, though the olive crop fails and the fields produce no food, though there are no sheep in the pen and no cattle in the stalls, yet I will rejoice in the LORD, I will be joyful in God my Savior.

—Habakkuk 3:17–18

This short book of the Bible helps us to see God's perspective on some of the problems we face. (1) God is in control of the world; he knows what he is doing, and in his own time he will make what seems senseless to us fit into his plan. (2) God expects us to trust him and to believe that he has the power over all that happens. (3) As we reflect on God's glory and majesty, we must stand in silent awe.

WHAT TO LOOK FOR IN HABAKKUK

- Habakkuk's two complaints (ch. 1)
- God's revelation to Habakkuk (ch. 2)
- Habakkuk's prayer (ch. 3)

1 The prophecy[a] that Habakkuk the prophet received.

Habakkuk's Complaint

2 How long, LORD, must I call for
help,
but you do not listen?[b]
Or cry out to you, "Violence!"
but you do not save?[c]
3 Why do you make me look at
injustice?
Why do you tolerate[d] wrongdoing?
Destruction and violence[e] are
before me;
there is strife,[f] and conflict
abounds.
4 Therefore the law[g] is paralyzed,
and justice never prevails.
The wicked hem in the righteous,
so that justice is perverted.[h]

The LORD's Answer

5 "Look at the nations and watch —
and be utterly amazed.[i]
For I am going to do something in
your days
that you would not believe,
even if you were told.[j]

1:1 [a] Na 1:1
1:2 [b] Ps 13:1-2; 22:1-2 [c] Jer 14:9
1:3 [d] ver 13 [e] Jer 20:8 [f] Ps 55:9
1:4 [g] Ps 119:126 [h] Job 19:7; Isa 1:23; 5:20; Eze 9:9
1:5 [i] Isa 29:9 [j] Ac 13:41*

Hab 1:2–4 ❖ When have you cried out to God and felt as if he was not listening or answering? How can believers today relate to Habakkuk's lament?

1:1–17 The entire book of Habakkuk is an oracle given as a dialogue between Habakkuk and Yahweh. Chapter 1 records the prophet's first set of questions (vv. 2–4), Yahweh's first response (vv. 5–11), and the prophet's second set of questions (vv. 12–17).

6 I am raising up the Babylonians,[a][k]
that ruthless and impetuous
people,
who sweep across the whole earth
to seize dwellings not their
own.[l]
7 They are a feared and dreaded
people;[m]
they are a law to themselves
and promote their own honor.
8 Their horses are swifter[n] than
leopards,
fiercer than wolves at dusk.
Their cavalry gallops headlong;
their horsemen come from
afar.
They fly like an eagle swooping to
devour;
9 they all come intent on violence.
Their hordes[b] advance like a desert
wind
and gather prisoners[o] like sand.
10 They mock kings
and scoff at rulers.[p]
They laugh at all fortified cities;
by building earthen ramps they
capture them.
11 Then they sweep past like the wind[q]
and go on —
guilty people, whose own strength
is their god."[r]

Habakkuk's Second Complaint

12 LORD, are you not from everlasting?
My God, my Holy One,[s] you[c] will
never die.
You, LORD, have appointed[t] them to
execute judgment;
you, my Rock, have ordained
them to punish.
13 Your eyes are too pure to look on
evil;
you cannot tolerate
wrongdoing.[u]
Why then do you tolerate the
treacherous?
Why are you silent while the
wicked
swallow up those more righteous
than themselves?
14 You have made people like the fish
in the sea,
like the sea creatures that have no
ruler.
15 The wicked foe pulls all of them up
with hooks,[v]
he catches them in his net,[w]
he gathers them up in his dragnet;
and so he rejoices and is glad.
16 Therefore he sacrifices to his net
and burns incense[x] to his dragnet,
for by his net he lives in luxury
and enjoys the choicest food.
17 Is he to keep on emptying his net,
destroying nations without
mercy?[y]

2 I will stand at my watch[z]
and station myself on the
ramparts;[a]
I will look to see what he will say[b]
to me,
and what answer I am to give to
this complaint.[d][c]

The LORD's Answer

2 Then the LORD replied:

"Write[d] down the revelation
and make it plain on tablets

1:6 [k] 2Ki 24:2 [l] Jer 13:20
1:7 [m] Isa 18:7; Jer 39:5-9
1:8 [n] Jer 4:13
1:9 [o] Hab 2:5
1:10 [p] 2Ch 36:6
1:11 [q] Jer 4:11-12 [r] Da 4:30
1:12 [s] Isa 31:1 [t] Isa 10:6
1:13 [u] La 3:34-36
1:15 [v] Isa 19:8 [w] Jer 16:16
1:16 [x] Jer 44:8
1:17 [y] Isa 14:6; 19:8
2:1 [z] Isa 21:8 [a] Ps 48:13 [b] Ps 85:8 [c] Ps 5:3
2:2 [d] Rev 1:19

[a] 6 Or *Chaldeans* [b] 9 The meaning of the Hebrew for this word is uncertain. [c] 12 An ancient Hebrew scribal tradition; Masoretic Text *we* [d] 1 Or *and what to answer when I am rebuked*

1:12–17 Habakkuk's second set of questions intensifies and expands the original question in light of the new information given in Yahweh's response. The key question is asked in both sets: "Why do you tolerate wrongdoing?" (v. 3b), and "You cannot tolerate wrongdoing. Why then do you tolerate the treacherous?" (v. 13b).

APPLICATION ✣ 1:1–17 Habakkuk is a difficult book, especially in the modern context. Why does God give us a book with the death of Habakkuk's community as the basic plot?

For anyone who has experienced or may experience the loss of a good way of life, cultural displacement, or an abrupt change in cultural security, the message of Habakkuk is both relevant and timely. It does not sugarcoat reality. Within just a few years of this conversation, Jerusalem was completely destroyed.

God's fundamental message is that soon the internal corruption that Habakkuk dislikes will give way to a much worse external enemy. Habakkuk's response gives us an opportunity to see how a believer may deal faithfully with news of impending upheaval and destruction. Habakkuk responds like a person who has just heard that someone he loves has terminal cancer: with critical questions about God's plan and a plea for understanding.

2:1–20 Yahweh tells the prophet to take notes (v. 2) on the future.

so that a herald[a] may run with it.
3 For the revelation awaits an appointed time;
it speaks of the end[e]
and will not prove false.
Though it linger, wait[f] for it;
it[b] will certainly come
and will not delay.[g]

4 "See, the enemy is puffed up;
his desires are not upright —
but the righteous person will live by his faithfulness[c][h] —
5 indeed, wine[i] betrays him;
he is arrogant and never at rest.
Because he is as greedy as the grave
and like death is never satisfied,[j]
he gathers to himself all the nations
and takes captive all the peoples.

6 "Will not all of them taunt[k] him with ridicule and scorn, saying,

"'Woe to him who piles up stolen goods
and makes himself wealthy by extortion![l]
How long must this go on?'
7 Will not your creditors suddenly arise?
Will they not wake up and make you tremble?
Then you will become their prey.[m]
8 Because you have plundered many nations,
the peoples who are left will plunder you.[n]
For you have shed human blood;[o]
you have destroyed lands and cities and everyone in them.

9 "Woe to him who builds[p] his house by unjust gain,
setting his nest on high
to escape the clutches of ruin!
10 You have plotted the ruin[q] of many peoples,
shaming[r] your own house and forfeiting your life.
11 The stones[s] of the wall will cry out,
and the beams of the woodwork will echo it.

12 "Woe to him who builds a city with bloodshed[t]
and establishes a town by injustice!

2:3 [e] Da 8:17; 10:14 [f] Ps 27:14 [g] Eze 12:25; Heb 10:37-38
2:4 [h] Ro 1:17*; Gal 3:11*; Heb 10:37-38*
2:5 [i] Pr 20:1 [j] Pr 27:20; 30:15-16
2:6 [k] Isa 14:4 [l] Am 2:8
2:7 [m] Pr 29:1
2:8 [n] Isa 33:1; Zec 2:8-9 [o] ver 17
2:9 [p] Jer 22:13
2:10 [q] Jer 26:19 [r] ver 16
2:11 [s] Jos 24:27; Lk 19:40
2:12 [t] Mic 3:10

[a] 2 Or *so that whoever reads it* [b] 3 Or *Though he linger, wait for him; / he* [c] 4 Or *faith*

2:4–6a God tells him to write down and publish two paths in the world: puffed-up desire and faithfulness (v. 4). The way of puffed-up desire leads to five "woes" from the mouths of the Babylonians' captives in the rest of the chapter.
2:6b–20 The question about God's tolerance (1:13b) is addressed succinctly in v. 4b. This half verse may be the best-known verse of the book: "The righteous person will live by his faithfulness." The second question has a much more lengthy answer (vv. 6–20). Together these responses form Yahweh's "plain" truth for dealing with the situation and the persistence of wickedness in the world.

Several important points of God's reputation are at stake in this conversation. Three issues emerge. (1) How can the faithful believe if Jerusalem falls? This question is addressed in v. 4b. (2) How can God's reputation stand if the wicked prosper? This question is answered in the prophecy of Babylon's end (2:7–8, 10b, 16). (3) How does Yahweh's reputation stand up to Babylon's idolatry? This question is answered between the lines in vv. 11, 14, and 20.

2:1–20 Habakkuk 2 provides practical help for times when our foundations are shaken. When we receive bad news—for example, that someone we love will soon die, that peace and security are quickly moving toward war and destruction, or that our religious leadership has fallen from grace through corruption—our personal world can be shaken to the core.

Like us in these situations, Habakkuk is seeking a word of good news from Yahweh. Like the prophets, we may be racked with pain and fear, but the message is announced for all to hear: Death and its oppression have been defeated. Scripture gives us the freedom to grieve along with the faithful prophets when we experience severe loss, but it also sends us up onto the heights to look for the word of victory from the Lord.

Yahweh's message through Habakkuk does not promise a quick and false solution to suffering. He wants his hearers (and us) to understand that future reality, from an earthly standpoint, can look grim. But the message we can hear through this dialogue is that God is with his people in our suffering and dying and will deliver us in time. This message can be trusted: The righteous will live by faith in God's Word.

13 Has not the LORD Almighty
determined
that the people's labor is only fuel
for the fire,[u]
that the nations exhaust
themselves for nothing?[v]
14 For the earth will be filled with the
knowledge of the glory[w] of
the LORD
as the waters cover the sea.[x]

15 "Woe to him who gives drink to his
neighbors,
pouring it from the wineskin till
they are drunk,
so that he can gaze on their naked
bodies!
16 You will be filled with shame[y]
instead of glory.
Now it is your turn! Drink and
let your nakedness be
exposed[a]![z]
The cup[a] from the LORD's right hand
is coming around to you,
and disgrace will cover your
glory.
17 The violence[b] you have done to
Lebanon will overwhelm
you,
and your destruction of animals
will terrify you.[c]
For you have shed human blood;[d]
you have destroyed lands and
cities and everyone in
them.

18 "Of what value is an idol[e] carved by a
craftsman?
Or an image that teaches lies?
For the one who makes it trusts in
his own creation;
he makes idols that cannot
speak.[f]
19 Woe to him who says to wood, 'Come
to life!'
Or to lifeless stone, 'Wake up!'[g]
Can it give guidance?
It is covered with gold and
silver;[h]
there is no breath in it."

20 The LORD is in his holy temple;[i]
let all the earth be silent[j] before
him.

2:13 [u] Isa 50:11 [v] Isa 47:13
2:14 [w] Nu 14:21 [x] Isa 11:9
2:16 [y] ver 10 [z] La 4:21 [a] Isa 51:22
2:17 [b] Jer 51:35 [c] Jer 50:15 [d] ver 8
2:18 [e] Jer 5:21 [f] Ps 115:4-5; Jer 10:14
2:19 [g] 1Ki 18:27 [h] Jer 10:4
2:20 [i] Ps 11:4 [j] Isa 41:1

Hab 2:14 ❖ If, ultimately, the earth will be filled with the glory of the Lord, how can we live today in light of that final chapter of redemptive history?

Habakkuk's Prayer

3 A prayer of Habakkuk the prophet.
On *shigionoth*.[b]

2 LORD, I have heard[k] of your fame;
I stand in awe[l] of your deeds,
LORD.
Repeat[m] them in our day,
in our time make them known;
in wrath remember mercy.[n]

3 God came from Teman,
the Holy One from Mount
Paran.[c]
His glory covered the heavens
and his praise filled the earth.[o]
4 His splendor was like the sunrise;
rays flashed from his hand,
where his power was hidden.
5 Plague went before him;
pestilence followed his steps.
6 He stood, and shook the earth;
he looked, and made the nations
tremble.
The ancient mountains crumbled
and the age-old hills
collapsed[p] —
but he marches on forever.
7 I saw the tents of Cushan in distress,
the dwellings of Midian[q] in
anguish.[r]

8 Were you angry with the rivers,[s]
LORD?
Was your wrath against the
streams?
Did you rage against the sea
when you rode your horses
and your chariots to victory?[t]
9 You uncovered your bow,
you called for many arrows.[u]
You split the earth with rivers;
10 the mountains saw you and writhed.

3:2 [k] Ps 44:1 [l] Ps 119:120 [m] Ps 85:6 [n] Isa 54:8
3:3 [o] Ps 48:10
3:6 [p] Ps 114:1-6
3:7 [q] Jdg 7:24-25 [r] Ex 15:14
3:8 [s] Ex 7:20 [t] Ps 68:17
3:9 [u] Ps 7:12-13

[a] *16* Masoretic Text; Dead Sea Scrolls, Aquila, Vulgate and Syriac (see also Septuagint) *and stagger* [b] *1* Probably a literary or musical term [c] *3* The Hebrew has *Selah* (a word of uncertain meaning) here and at the middle of verse 9 and at the end of verse 13.

3:1–19 Habakkuk 3 is a song to Yahweh about his power and way in the world. The concluding verses (vv. 16–19) enclose the song into the whole revelation. The song is an integral conclusion of the entire oracle. The words of the prophet, even those spoken *to God* in ch. 3, are a gift *from God*. This circle of inspiration is a legacy of biblical prophecy in general.

Torrents of water swept by;
the deep roared[v]
and lifted its waves[w] on high.

11 Sun and moon stood still[x] in the heavens
at the glint of your flying arrows,[y]
at the lightning of your flashing spear.
12 In wrath you strode through the earth
and in anger you threshed[z] the nations.
13 You came out to deliver[a] your people,
to save your anointed one.
You crushed[b] the leader of the land of wickedness,
you stripped him from head to foot.
14 With his own spear you pierced his head
when his warriors stormed out to scatter us,[c]
gloating as though about to devour
the wretched[d] who were in hiding.
15 You trampled the sea with your horses,
churning the great waters.[e]

16 I heard and my heart pounded,
my lips quivered at the sound;
decay crept into my bones,
and my legs trembled.
Yet I will wait patiently for the day of calamity
to come on the nation invading us.
17 Though the fig tree does not bud

3:10 [v] Ps 98:7 [w] Ps 93:3
3:11 [x] Jos 10:13 [y] Ps 18:14
3:12 [z] Isa 41:15
3:13 [a] Ps 20:6; 28:8 [b] Ps 68:21; 110:6
3:14 [c] Jdg 7:22 [d] Ps 64:2-5
3:15 [e] Ex 15:8; Ps 77:19

3:16–19 As Habakkuk's song comes to its conclusion, the form and content change. In musical terms this is called a "bridge" that introduces a new musical theme and sometimes a change in key or tempo. The lyrics often offer a counterpoint to the previous theme of the song.

This counterpoint is powerful. In vv. 2–15, the prophet sang of the visible power of Yahweh. In vv. 16–19, he will sing of his persistent joy, even when the simplest sign of Yahweh's favor (food on the table) is absent.

Even though Habakkuk believes that Babylon will eventually fall (ch. 2), he knows that what is to come will be horrible. He goes on to describe the experience of oppression and poverty that will settle on the conquered. These are the conditions the prophet expects and anticipates overcoming in patience. He will not be a victim; he will be a survivor.

In this passage, Habakkuk rejoices despite the lack of goods and protection. He shows he is prepared to live by faith in unseen promises, even in suffering. Habakkuk's faith has found its sure footing *as faith*. He does not hope or believe in what he sees, but in what he has heard in the promises from Yahweh. His feet are established on the path by Yahweh, even on the difficult and rocky heights.

PEOPLE TO KNOW // HABAKKUK

HABAKKUK 3:17–19: Habakkuk was a prophet about whom nearly nothing is known. His book does not say where he was from or what family he was part of.

Habakkuk draws readers into the shock and dismay that the prophet experienced when he received a message from God. Habakkuk brought before God a complaint about the violence and injustice he saw around him in Judah. God responded that he was about to do something unbelievable: send an even more evil nation, Babylon, to destroy Judah.

Incredulous, Habakkuk questioned God's means of meting out justice. God's reply makes it clear: The violence and idolatry of his people needed to be punished. While it was puzzling for God to use an even more wicked nation to judge his wayward people, this was God's sovereign design.

Habakkuk's book ends with a beautiful promise and assurance that even when the world around seems dark and hopeless, God is still the strength and Savior of his people (Hab 3:17–19).

In Romans 1:17, Paul quotes Habakkuk 2:4, "The righteous will live by faith." Paul understood this statement to be a proclamation of the Good News that, through Christ, our righteousness comes by faith and is a gift from God.

APPLICATION Habakkuk models an open and honest prayer life. The book consists of a conversation between the prophet and God, and Habakkuk's frankness with God might be surprising. Is it okay to be that direct with God? Yes! God invites us to openly process our struggles with him in prayer. The book also invites us to trust, even in the darkest moments, that God is our strength and salvation. In the storms of life, we find peace and hope in God alone.

Hab 3:17–19 ❖ How can we praise God even when the world around us seems bleak and chaotic?

and there are no grapes on the vines,
though the olive crop fails
and the fields produce no food,[f]
though there are no sheep in the pen
and no cattle in the stalls,[g]
18 yet I will rejoice in the LORD,[h]
I will be joyful in God my Savior.

19 The Sovereign LORD is my strength;[i]
he makes my feet like the feet of a deer,
he enables me to tread on the heights.[j]

For the director of music. On my stringed instruments.

3:17 [f] Joel 1:10-12,18 [g] Jer 5:17 3:18 [h] Isa 61:10; Php 4:4 3:19 [i] Dt 33:29; Ps 46:1-5 [j] Dt 32:13; 2Sa 22:34; Ps 18:33

3:1–19 This chapter demonstrates the process of struggling with previously held conceptions of God as we grow into a better understanding of God's revelation. Through the centuries, people of faith have used vv. 16–19 more often than vv. 1–15. The last four verses represent a more seasoned, deepened, and stalwart faith than is presented earlier. They reflect the necessary maturation of a lasting faith that is free of illusions.

Nevertheless, vv. 1–15 do not reflect an immature "stage" or process that must be left behind. The strength of these verses is given by Yahweh to Habakkuk as a necessary memory of God's power. They offer depth and weight to the prophet's confessions of faith in vv. 16–19.

May we all be able to stand as firmly on our own rocky pathway as the prophet Habakkuk, convinced of God's faithfulness and choosing to be joyful no matter our circumstances.

Author: Zephaniah
Audience: The people of Judah
Date: Between 640 and 612 BC

Theme: God speaks through the prophet Zephaniah to announce the coming of the day of the Lord, when God will severely punish the nations, including apostate Judah, but will yet be merciful to his people.

Reading Zephaniah

The beginning of Zephaniah makes for frightening reading as the prophet speaks words of gloom and doom. But he ends his words on a positive note.

PERSPECTIVE

Zephaniah is a book of judgment against Judah and its capital city, Jerusalem (chs. 1 and 3). In the midst of this judgment comes God's call for a faithful remnant, who will be sheltered when Jerusalem and its enemies are destroyed. God's promise of joy returning to Jerusalem concludes the book.

Yahweh's zeal for the worship of his people is the unifying theme of this prophecy. This zeal is expressed in the devastating and jealous judgment of Yahweh against his wayward people, as well as in the promise that a remnant of worshipers will survive the day of the Lord's jealous wrath. His people's sins are many and varied, but all point to one reality: They no longer trust in Yahweh or worship him. Rather, they worship Baal and permit idolatrous priests (1:4). They worship the starry host and swear by Yahweh and by Molech (1:5). They turn back from Yahweh (1:6), engage in violence and fraud (1:9), are complacent and unbelieving (1:12), trust in wealth (1:8–10, 13, 18), and do not seek Yahweh (1:6; 2:1). The unrighteous know no shame (3:5a), rejoicing in pride and haughtiness (3:11). Twelve more sins are listed at the start of chapter 3. In these descriptions, we find the connection to our present situation.

Idolatry is the first problem Zephaniah mentions (1:4–6, 9), but he quickly moves to the problem behind the external idolatry: the focus of the human heart's trust and worship. They are proud and arrogant; they trust in themselves and in their wealth. Jerusalem is no different from her unbelieving neighbors, Moab and Assyria. Moab insulted and

	1200 BC	1100	1000	900	800	700	600	500	400
Ministries of Micah and Isaiah in Judah (c. 740–681 BC)									
Exile of Israel (722 BC)									
Nahum's ministry (c. 645–620 BC)									
Zephaniah's ministry in Judah (c. 640–627 BC)									
Book of Zephaniah written (c. 640–612 BC)									
Jeremiah's ministry in Judah (c. 626–585 BC)									
Habakkuk's ministry in Judah (c. 605–588 BC)									
Fall of Jerusalem (586 BC)									

threatened Yahweh's people (2:8). Assyria was guilty of blasphemy and pride (2:15). When we look at our own lives, are we as believers any different from the neighbors who surround us? Does our belief and hope for eternity stand out? When the weight and consequences of sin bring the unbelieving to despair, can they look to us for help and hope as they long to find the inner peace that comes from having a close relationship with Jesus?

Key Verse

"The LORD your God is with you, the Mighty Warrior who saves. He will take great delight in you; in his love he will no longer rebuke you, but will rejoice over you with singing."

—Zephaniah 3:17

TAKING THE NEXT STEPS

Zephaniah, a descendant of King Hezekiah, prophesied during the early reign of King Josiah, shortly after the wicked reign of Manasseh and Amon (2Ki 21–22). He saw the judgment of God, the day of the Lord, coming because of the sins of the nation of Judah. But he also made it clear that God would show mercy toward his people, thus ending on a note of hope.

Through the message of Zephaniah, we too receive important messages. (1) The prophecy of the coming day of the Lord warns us of the terror of God's final day, a day that will see worldwide judgment. (2) Those who humbly seek the Lord will be sheltered from the coming calamity. Therefore, we ought to turn to the Lord before it is too late. (3) God's deliverance ought to cause us to break forth into songs of joy and thanksgiving.

WHAT TO LOOK FOR IN ZEPHANIAH

- God's judgment against various nations (chs. 1–2)
- A remnant sheltered (ch. 2)
- Hope for the people of Judah (ch. 3)

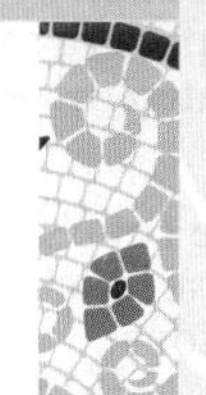

1 The word of the LORD that came to Zephaniah son of Cushi, the son of Gedaliah, the son of Amariah, the son of Hezekiah, during the reign of Josiah[a] son of Amon king of Judah:

Judgment on the Whole Earth in the Day of the LORD

2 "I will sweep away everything
from the face of the earth,"[b]
declares the LORD.
3 "I will sweep away both man and beast;
I will sweep away the birds in the sky[c]
and the fish in the sea—
and the idols that cause the wicked to stumble."[a]

"When I destroy all mankind
on the face of the earth,"[d]
declares the LORD,
4 "I will stretch out my hand[e] against Judah
and against all who live in Jerusalem.
I will destroy every remnant of Baal worship in this place,[f]
the very names of the idolatrous priests[g]—
5 those who bow down on the roofs
to worship the starry host,
those who bow down and swear by the LORD
and who also swear by Molek,[b][h]
6 those who turn back from following[i] the LORD
and neither seek[j] the LORD nor inquire[k] of him."

7 Be silent[l] before the Sovereign LORD,
for the day of the LORD[m] is near.
The LORD has prepared a sacrifice;[n]
he has consecrated those he has invited.

8 "On the day of the LORD's sacrifice
I will punish[o] the officials
and the king's sons[p]
and all those clad
in foreign clothes.
9 On that day I will punish
all who avoid stepping on the threshold,[c]
who fill the temple of their gods
with violence and deceit.[q]

10 "On that day,"
declares the LORD,
"a cry will go up from the Fish Gate,[r]
wailing from the New Quarter,
and a loud crash from the hills.
11 Wail,[s] you who live in the market district[d];
all your merchants will be wiped out,
all who trade with[e] silver will be destroyed.[t]
12 At that time I will search Jerusalem with lamps
and punish those who are complacent,[u]
who are like wine left on its dregs,[v]
who think, 'The LORD will do nothing,[w]
either good or bad.'
13 Their wealth will be plundered,[x]
their houses demolished.
Though they build houses,
they will not live in them;
though they plant vineyards,
they will not drink the wine."[y]

14 The great day of the LORD[z] is near[a]—
near and coming quickly.
The cry on the day of the LORD is bitter;
the Mighty Warrior shouts his battle cry.
15 That day will be a day of wrath—
a day of distress and anguish,
a day of trouble and ruin,
a day of darkness and gloom,
a day of clouds and blackness[b]—

1:1 [a] 2Ki 22:1; 2Ch 34:1-35:25
1:2 [b] Ge 6:7
1:3 [c] Jer 4:25 [d] Hos 4:3
1:4 [e] Jer 6:12 [f] Mic 5:13 [g] Hos 10:5
1:5 [h] Jer 5:7
1:6 [i] Isa 1:4; Jer 2:13 [j] Isa 9:13 [k] Hos 7:7
1:7 [l] Hab 2:20; Zec 2:13 [m] ver 14; Isa 13:6 [n] Isa 34:6; Jer 46:10
1:8 [o] Isa 24:21 [p] Jer 39:6
1:9 [q] Am 3:10
1:10 [r] 2Ch 33:14
1:11 [s] Jas 5:1 [t] Hos 9:6
1:12 [u] Am 6:1 [v] Jer 48:11 [w] Eze 8:12
1:13 [x] Jer 15:13 [y] Dt 28:30, 39; Am 5:11; Mic 6:15
1:14 [z] ver 7; Joel 1:15 [a] Eze 7:7
1:15 [b] Isa 22:5; Joel 2:2

[a] 3 The meaning of the Hebrew for this line is uncertain. [b] 5 Hebrew *Malkam* [c] 9 See 1 Samuel 5:5. [d] 11 Or *the Mortar* [e] 11 Or *in*

Zep 1:12–13 ❖ Sometimes believers grow complacent in their faith because God seems distant. Why is this an incorrect way of thinking and behaving?

1:1–17 Chapter 1 begins and ends without compromise: The offenses that demand this harsh judgment are listed as indictments against the people of Judah. Corrupt worship is at the top of the list (vv. 4–6). The wealthy leaders will become the consecrated sacrifice on the day of Yahweh (vv. 7–9). Believers who trust in commerce and wealth are also indicted (vv. 10–13). Finally, the prophet describes a great "day of darkness" (v. 15) and graphic death in Jerusalem.

16 a day of trumpet and battle cry[c]
against the fortified cities
and against the corner towers.[d]

17 "I will bring such distress on all people
that they will grope about like those who are blind,[e]
because they have sinned against the LORD.
Their blood will be poured out[f] like dust
and their entrails like dung.[g]
18 Neither their silver nor their gold
will be able to save them
on the day of the LORD's wrath."[h]

In the fire of his jealousy
the whole earth will be consumed,[i]
for he will make a sudden end
of all who live on the earth.[j]

Judah and Jerusalem Judged Along With the Nations

Judah Summoned to Repent

2 Gather together,[k] gather yourselves together,
you shameful[l] nation,
2 before the decree takes effect
and that day passes like windblown chaff,[m]
before the LORD's fierce anger[n]
comes upon you,
before the day of the LORD's wrath
comes upon you.
3 Seek[o] the LORD, all you humble of the land,
you who do what he commands.
Seek righteousness, seek humility;[p]
perhaps you will be sheltered[q]
on the day of the LORD's anger.

Philistia

4 Gaza[r] will be abandoned
and Ashkelon left in ruins.
At midday Ashdod will be emptied
and Ekron uprooted.
5 Woe to you who live by the sea,
you Kerethite[s] people;
the word of the LORD is against you,[t]
Canaan, land of the Philistines.
He says, "I will destroy you,
and none will be left."[u]
6 The land by the sea will become pastures
having wells for shepherds
and pens for flocks.[v]
7 That land will belong
to the remnant of the people of Judah;

1:16 [c] Jer 4:19 [d] Isa 2:15
1:17 [e] Isa 59:10 [f] Ps 79:3 [g] Jer 9:22
1:18 [h] Eze 7:19 [i] ver 2-3; Zep 3:8 [j] Ge 6:7
2:1 [k] 2Ch 20:4; Joel 1:14 [l] Jer 3:3; 6:15
2:2 [m] Isa 17:13; Hos 13:3 [n] La 4:11
2:3 [o] Am 5:6 [p] Ps 45:4; Am 5:14-15 [q] Ps 57:1
2:4 [r] Am 1:6, 7-8; Zec 9:5-7
2:5 [s] Eze 25:16 [t] Am 3:1 [u] Isa 14:30
2:6 [v] Isa 5:17

Zep 2:3 ❖ How can we seek the Lord as Zephaniah instructs? What might seeking after God look like in our everyday lives?

1:18 God's jealousy is easily misunderstood. God is "jealous" not because he is lacking in himself but because he is zealous for his creation that is in danger of corruption and death. God's "jealousy" is a prejudice *toward life* for his created and delivered people.

God's deep desire is to establish a remnant and preserve his faithful people. God's "jealousy" for a future of freedom, innocence, and justice in the world as he intended required a catastrophic act against his own sinful people. The only hope for their rescue as a faithful people was in the suffering of exile and captivity (Isa 37:32).

APPLICATION ✣ 1:1–18 Zephaniah 1 is perhaps the most graphic description of God's anger in the Bible. The intensity of that anger is a measure of how much he cares about the human subject. In Zephaniah we encounter God's ultimate concern for us.

What makes God this angry? The source of that anger is the same today as it was then. It is God's response when people who have prospered under his care turn away. It is God's response to people who are consumed with self-interest, who oppress others for their own personal gain, and who withhold their resources from the Lord's work. The language of this first chapter is clear: God's holiness demands that sin be eradicated and that unrepentant, sin-loving people be punished.

2:1–15 The theme of this chapter is the cleansing of other nations from the land so that it may be possessed in the future by the humble remnant of Judah.
2:1–3 This chapter begins with a call to the surviving remnant. It then declares that they will live again in the land (vv. 6–7, 9b, 11). The prophet calls on the humble and obedient to seek Yahweh, trusting in his protection on the day of the Lord's wrath.
2:4–15 The clearing and cleansing of the land is described in the remainder of the chapter. The violent "day of the LORD" (a judgment against Judah in ch. 1) is against the others living in that land in ch. 2. The Philistine cities will be completely destroyed (vv. 4–7). Because of their pride, Moab and Ammon will be plundered and possessed (vv. 8–11). Ethiopia (Cush) and Assyria will be turned into wild lands (vv. 12–15).

In the midst of the emptied land, we see a future with the survivors in the pastures and meadows (vv. 6–7). In the north will be domestic herds, wild animals, and birds (v. 14). God will renew the land, its animals, and a humble remnant of the people.

there they will find pasture.
In the evening they will lie down
in the houses of Ashkelon.
The LORD their God will care for
them;
he will restore their fortunes.[a][w]

Moab and Ammon

8 "I have heard the insults[x] of Moab
and the taunts of the Ammonites,
who insulted[y] my people
and made threats against their
land.
9 Therefore, as surely as I live,"
declares the LORD Almighty,
the God of Israel,
"surely Moab[z] will become like
Sodom,[a]
the Ammonites[b] like Gomorrah —
a place of weeds and salt pits,
a wasteland forever.
The remnant of my people will
plunder[c] them;
the survivors of my nation will
inherit their land.[d]"

10 This is what they will get in return
for their pride,[e]
for insulting[f] and mocking
the people of the LORD Almighty.
11 The LORD will be awesome[g] to them
when he destroys all the gods[h] of
the earth.
Distant nations will bow down to
him,[i]
all of them in their own lands.

Cush

12 "You Cushites,[b][j] too,
will be slain by my sword.[k]"

Assyria

13 He will stretch out his hand against
the north
and destroy Assyria,
leaving Nineveh[l] utterly desolate
and dry as the desert.[m]
14 Flocks and herds will lie down
there,
creatures of every kind.
The desert owl[n] and the screech owl
will roost on her columns.
Their hooting will echo through the
windows,
rubble will fill the doorways,
the beams of cedar will be
exposed.
15 This is the city of revelry[o]
that lived in safety.[p]
She said to herself,
"I am the one! And there is none
besides me."[q]
What a ruin she has become,
a lair for wild beasts!
All who pass by her scoff[r]
and shake their fists.

Jerusalem

3 Woe to the city of oppressors,[s]
rebellious and defiled![t]
2 She obeys[u] no one,
she accepts no correction.[v]
She does not trust in the LORD,
she does not draw near[w] to her
God.
3 Her officials within her
are roaring lions;
her rulers are evening wolves,[x]

[a] 7 Or *will bring back their captives* [b] 12 That is, people from the upper Nile region

2:7 [w] Ps 126:4; Jer 32:44
2:8 [x] Jer 48:27 [y] Eze 25:3
2:9 [z] Isa 15:1-16:14; Jer 48:1-47 [a] Dt 29:23 [b] Jer 49:1-6; Eze 25:1-7 [c] Isa 11:14 [d] Am 2:1-3
2:10 [e] Isa 16:6 [f] Jer 48:27
2:11 [g] Joel 2:11 [h] Zep 1:4 [i] Zep 3:9
2:12 [j] Isa 18:1; 20:4 [k] Jer 46:10
2:13 [l] Na 1:1 [m] Mic 5:6
2:14 [n] Isa 14:23
2:15 [o] Isa 32:9 [p] Isa 47:8 [q] Eze 28:2 [r] Na 3:19
3:1 [s] Jer 6:6 [t] Eze 23:30
3:2 [u] Jer 22:21 [v] Jer 7:28 [w] Ps 73:28; Jer 5:3
3:3 [x] Eze 22:27

2:10–11 These may be the most revealing expression of both Yahweh's complaint and desire for the nations. In place of pride, Yahweh will be "awesome to them," and "distant nations" (v. 11) will bow down in worship before the Lord.

2:1–15 God's opposition to arrogance is clear. Biblical humility does not, however, simply involve a life of personal religious devotion. The purpose of humility is societal justice and service toward those in need. Humility is relational and brings saving help.

The great example of Christ's humility calls us to have a similar attitude (Php 2:3–8). Christ did not cling to his equality with God; rather, he gave it up to become a servant in human form. His humility was not abstract; it led to the salvation of those who were (and are) desperately in need of it. He calls us to walk with him in the miraculous "rest" of this kind of humility (Mt 11:29).

3:1–20 This chapter begins with Jerusalem's judgment (vv. 1–8) and ends with her joy (vv. 9–20). The central verses form a bridge, with v. 8 speaking judgment and v. 9 announcing joy's beginning.

This chapter contains many changes in voice. Verses 1–10 are words of judgment spoken to the entire city of Jerusalem ("them"). Verses 11–20 are a word of hope spoken to the remnant ("you"). This combination of the "I" and the "you" makes this last chapter of Zephaniah powerfully personal.

3:1–8 The judgment of Jerusalem is divided into two parts. First, the city's sins of arrogance and corruption are described (vv. 1–5). Second, Yahweh describes the warnings he has given (vv. 6–8), but Jerusalem will not accept correction.

who leave nothing for the morning.
4 Her prophets are unprincipled;
they are treacherous people.[y]
Her priests profane the sanctuary
and do violence to the law.[z]
5 The LORD within her is righteous;
he does no wrong.[a]
Morning by morning he dispenses
his justice,
and every new day he does not fail,
yet the unrighteous know no
shame.

Jerusalem Remains Unrepentant

6 "I have destroyed nations;
their strongholds are demolished.
I have left their streets deserted,
with no one passing through.
Their cities are laid waste;[b]
they are deserted and empty.
7 Of Jerusalem I thought,
'Surely you will fear me
and accept correction!'
Then her place of refuge[a] would not
be destroyed,
nor all my punishments come
upon[b] her.
But they were still eager
to act corruptly[c] in all they did.
8 Therefore wait[d] for me,"
declares the LORD,
"for the day I will stand up to
testify.[c]
I have decided to assemble the
nations,[e]
to gather the kingdoms
and to pour out my wrath on
them —
all my fierce anger.
The whole world will be consumed[f]
by the fire of my jealous anger.

Restoration of Israel's Remnant

9 "Then I will purify the lips of the
peoples,
that all of them may call[g] on the
name of the LORD

3:4 [y] Jer 9:4 [z] Eze 22:26 3:5 [a] Dt 32:4 3:6 [b] Lev 26:31 3:7 [c] Hos 9:9 3:8 [d] Ps 27:14 [e] Joel 3:2 [f] Zep 1:18 3:9 [g] Zep 2:11

[a] 7 Or *her sanctuary* [b] 7 Or *all those I appointed over* [c] 8 Septuagint and Syriac; Hebrew *will rise up to plunder*

3:9–20 The joy of Jerusalem may also be read in two parts. In vv. 9–13 God makes promises for the remnant. The last verses (vv. 14–20) describe part of the day of joy in Jerusalem.

PEOPLE TO KNOW // ZEPHANIAH

ZEPHANIAH 3:9–20: Zephaniah was a prophet. He lived around the same time as Jeremiah, during the reign of King Josiah, who brought about spectacular religious reforms in Judah. Zephaniah ministered during a spiritually active time in the life of Israel.

Zephaniah described himself as the great-great-grandson of Hezekiah (Zec 1:1), and many believe this is the same Hezekiah who was king of Judah. If so, Zephaniah was closely related to the kings of Judah.

Despite the positive spiritual reforms enacted by King Josiah, Zephaniah's prophecy predicted total devastation. He began with a jarring message from God: "I will sweep away everything from the face of the earth" (Zep 1:2). Like the prophet Joel, Zephaniah foresaw the impending and frightful day of the Lord.

Clearly not everyone in Judah shared the devout heart of King Josiah. Zephaniah decried idolatry and spiritual complacency in the people. He chastised those who held to the vain hope that their wealth would keep them secure. Zephaniah extended his message of judgment beyond Israel's borders, but his longest prophecies pointed at the city of Jerusalem itself (Zep 3:1–8).

Shockingly, Zephaniah closed his message with God's beautiful promise to restore a faithful remnant. The prophet envisioned God taking delight in his beloved people, even rejoicing over them with singing (Zep 3:17).

APPLICATION Zephaniah warns us against becoming complacent in our faith. He describes certain people around him who think that God is inactive, never doing anything at all (Zep 1:12). Similarly, 2 Peter 3:4 speaks of those who think the world keeps turning with no sign that God will do anything—so people may as well do whatever they want.

Not so, Zephaniah warns. God is not asleep, and God will hold evil accountable. Zephaniah's message should encourage us to nurture our faith, not let it languish. It should anchor us upon the hopeful future promised by a God who delights so much in his people that he rejoices over them with singing.

and serve[h] him shoulder to
shoulder.
10 From beyond the rivers of Cush[a][i]
my worshipers, my scattered
people,
will bring me offerings.[j]
11 On that day you, Jerusalem, will not
be put to shame[k]
for all the wrongs you have done
to me,
because I will remove from you
your arrogant boasters.
Never again will you be haughty
on my holy hill.
12 But I will leave within you
the meek[l] and humble.
The remnant of Israel
will trust[m] in the name of the LORD.
13 They[n] will do no wrong;[o]
they will tell no lies.[p]
A deceitful tongue
will not be found in their mouths.
They will eat and lie down[q]
and no one will make them
afraid.[r]"

14 Sing, Daughter Zion;[s]
shout aloud,[t] Israel!
Be glad and rejoice with all your
heart,
Daughter Jerusalem!
15 The LORD has taken away your
punishment,
he has turned back your enemy.
The LORD, the King of Israel, is with
you;[u]
never again will you fear[v] any
harm.
16 On that day
they will say to Jerusalem,

3:9 [h] Isa 19:18
3:10 [i] Ps 68:31 [j] Isa 60:7
3:11 [k] Joel 2:26-27
3:12 [l] Isa 14:32 [m] Na 1:7
3:13 [n] Isa 10:21; Mic 4:7 [o] Ps 119:3 [p] Rev 14:5 [q] Eze 34:15; Zep 2:7 [r] Eze 34:25-28
3:14 [s] Zec 2:10 [t] Isa 12:6
3:15 [u] Eze 37:26-28 [v] Isa 54:14
3:16 [w] Job 4:3; Isa 35:3-4; Heb 12:12
3:17 [x] Isa 63:1 [y] Isa 62:4
3:19 [z] Eze 34:16; Mic 4:6 [a] Isa 60:18
3:20 [b] Jer 29:14; Eze 37:12 [c] Isa 56:5; 66:22 [d] Joel 3:1

Zep 3:12-13 ❖ If God's remnant of righteous children are those who are meek and humble, how can we nurture such attitudes in our own lives (see Mt 5:5)?

"Do not fear, Zion;
do not let your hands hang limp.[w]
17 The LORD your God is with you,
the Mighty Warrior who saves.[x]
He will take great delight[y] in you;
in his love he will no longer
rebuke you,
but will rejoice over you with
singing."

18 "I will remove from you
all who mourn over the loss of
your appointed festivals,
which is a burden and reproach
for you.
19 At that time I will deal
with all who oppressed you.
I will rescue the lame;
I will gather the exiles.[z]
I will give them praise[a] and honor
in every land where they have
suffered shame.
20 At that time I will gather you;
at that time I will bring[b] you
home.
I will give you honor[c] and praise
among all the peoples of the
earth
when I restore your fortunes[b][d]
before your very eyes,"
says the LORD.

[a] 10 That is, the upper Nile region [b] 20 Or *I bring back your captives*

3:20 This last verse fills out the last four of the seven promises. For exiled people, no set of promises carries more hope (see Ps 137). To be gathered home, to have what was lost restored, and to be honored by other peoples of the earth are things for which every culture longs. Hearing the promise before any of the loss occurred revealed the greater good God desired for them.

✜ **3:1-20** The world experiences God's judgment against sin daily, especially sins of human arrogance against God and his good creation: the violence of war maims children; human pollution destroys soil and drinking water; famine emaciates; corruption at the highest levels of government is discovered and prosecuted; criminals face indictment and prison.

God's judgment on corruption in the world's societies is reported as news every day. These judgments are not the final judgment, but they are, nonetheless, real judgments in the tradition of the book of Zephaniah. In the world today, actions have consequences, and God oversees the judgments on those actions.

Many societies since Zephaniah's oracle have suffered Jerusalem's fate. Some people in ancient Judah understood the prophet's warning and turned to Yahweh. They heard and saw the judgment before it arrived. As a result, they also heard and saw the hope that God offered.

We feel the same effects of sin in our own lives. Ignoring it doesn't make it go away; justifying it will only bring more judgment. Admitting that we are sinful, recognizing God's wrath on our personal sin, and honestly repenting with the help of the Holy Spirit is the beginning of our only hope to avoid the terrible consequences of our sin—certainly for our own lives, but also for the lives of our families and communities.

Haggai

Author: Haggai

Audience: The postexilic Jews living in Judah

Date: 520 BC

Theme: God, through the prophet Haggai, calls the complacent people of Judah to resume the rebuilding of the temple and in that way give priority to God and experience his blessing.

PERSPECTIVE

Being a prophet is counterintuitive. It means demonstrating unquestioning obedience to God by saying unpopular things that usually lead to persecution from powerful people. Consider Haggai. On September 1, 520 BC, God told him to go and confront his fellow Jews with their sluggishness in rebuilding the temple after returning from captivity. He went to the prince, Zerubbabel, and the high priest, Joshua. His compatriot, Zechariah, perhaps inspired by Haggai's courage, joined in the prophetic task two months later. Their basic message was: "You seem to have all the energy you need to build your own houses, but the temple, Yahweh's house, still lies in blackened ruins. Let's get busy."

Intriguingly, these confrontational messages didn't sow discord. They brought comfort. The overall response of the leaders and the people to the prophets' calls to get busy and get connected with God again was action and renewed relationships. The temple was built, and the people were restored—personally, communally, and spiritually.

If both being a prophet and the results of prophetic work are counterintuitive, perhaps the problem is with our intuition. Perhaps we are not reading the signs right. Perhaps we do not have ears to hear. Perhaps we are not speaking the word of the Lord but are spouting conventional wisdom. Perhaps.

It may just be possible, however, that prophetic work and the results of prophecy are supposed to be counterintuitive. After all, not everyone is called to be a prophet. If the sociology of the OT is any indication, it appears that prophets are odd ducks, a rare breed of religious fanatics who appear in certain times in certain places, do their thing,

Reading Haggai

The book of Haggai, containing four very brief prophecies, should be read in a single sitting. The prophets Haggai and Zechariah complement each other (see Introduction to Zechariah). Both prophets announce an imminent restoration inaugurated by the return of God that is dependent on repentance of the people. For Haggai, repentance can be shown in the rebuilding of the temple. The

	1200 BC	1100	1000	900	800	700	600	500	400
Fall of Jerusalem (586 BC)							♦		
First return of exiles to Jerusalem (c. 538 BC)								♦	
Ministries of Haggai and Zechariah (c. 520–480 BC)								▬	
Book of Haggai written (c. 520 BC)								♦	
Completion of temple (516 BC)								♦	
Second return to Jerusalem under Ezra (458 BC)								♦	
Third return to Jerusalem under Nehemiah (444 BC)								♦	
Malachi's ministry (c. 440–430 BC)								■	

prophet's message is summarized with Yahweh's message to the people in 1:8b, "Build my house, so that I may take pleasure in it and be honored." For both Haggai and Zechariah, the ultimate goal is the return of the presence and blessing of God to his people in order to transform the cosmos.

Key Verse

This is what the LORD Almighty says: "Give careful thought to your ways. Go up into the mountains and bring down timber and build my house, so that I may take pleasure in it and be honored," says the LORD.

—Haggai 1:7-8

and then disappear again. We are all called to be missionaries of the Word, but how long has it been since you met someone who was sure his or her calling was to be a prophet?

There is more to being a prophet than doing what a group of people thinks is good. Prophets must do what God thinks is good—and what God calls them to do. Prophets aren't just doers of the Word—they must first be hearers of the Word. Like Haggai and Zechariah.

For more perspective on this book, see the Introduction to Zechariah.

TAKING THE NEXT STEPS

Haggai prophesied to the Jews who had returned to the promised land after the exile in Babylon (see Ezr 1:1–8; 5:1–2; 6:13–18). Because the people did not have their priorities straight, they were spending too much time on their own houses instead of rebuilding the house of the Lord. Haggai, along with the prophet Zechariah, renewed their enthusiasm for this project and restored their hope for the future.

Although this book is short, it has important messages for us today. (1) Haggai clearly shows the consequences of obedience and disobedience to the Lord. (2) He challenges us to put our priorities in the right place, to seek first the kingdom of God. (3) He reminds us that God's concern is with the human race all over the world; we ought to be spreading everywhere the Good News of reconciliation in Christ.

WHAT TO LOOK FOR IN HAGGAI

- Encouragement to build God's house (ch. 1)
- The promised glory of God's house (ch. 2)
- Prophetic message on the day the foundation is laid (ch. 2)

A Call to Build the House of the LORD

1 In the second year of King Darius,[a]
on the first day of the sixth month,
the word of the LORD came through the
prophet Haggai[b] to Zerubbabel[c] son of
Shealtiel, governor[d] of Judah, and to
Joshua[e] son of Jozadak,[af] the high priest:
2This is what the LORD Almighty says:
"These people say, 'The time has not yet
come to rebuild the LORD's house.'"
3Then the word of the LORD came
through the prophet Haggai:[g] 4"Is it a
time for you yourselves to be living in
your paneled houses,[h] while this house
remains a ruin?[i]"
5Now this is what the LORD Almighty
says: "Give careful thought[j] to your ways.
6You have planted much, but harvested
little.[k] You eat, but never have enough.
You drink, but never have your fill. You
put on clothes, but are not warm. You
earn wages,[l] only to put them in a purse
with holes in it."

1:1 [a] Ezr 4:24 [b] Ezr 5:1 [c] Mt 1:12-13 [d] Ezr 5:3 [e] Ezr 2:2 [f] 1Ch 6:15; Ezr 3:2
1:3 [g] Ezr 5:1
1:4 [h] 2Sa 7:2 [i] ver 9; Jer 33:12
1:5 [j] La 3:40
1:6 [k] Dt 28:38 [l] Hag 2:16; Zec 8:10
1:8 [m] Ps 132:13-14
1:9 [n] ver 4
1:10 [o] Lev 26:19; Dt 28:23

Hag 1:3-11 ❖ Why does life lack satisfaction when we do not give God the proper central place in it? How can we give God the priority in our lives that he deserves?

7This is what the LORD Almighty
says: "Give careful thought to your
ways. 8Go up into the mountains and
bring down timber and build my house,
so that I may take pleasure[m] in it and
be honored," says the LORD. 9"You expected much, but see, it turned out
to be little. What you brought home,
I blew away. Why?" declares the LORD
Almighty. "Because of my house, which
remains a ruin,[n] while each of you is
busy with your own house. 10Therefore,
because of you the heavens have withheld their dew and the earth its crops.[o]

[a] *1* Hebrew *Jehozadak*, a variant of *Jozadak*; also in verses 12 and 14

1:1-11 Haggai's message comes at a significant time in the history of the Persian Empire and in the annual rhythm of the Jewish people. It is a call for action, followed by two responses by Yahweh (v. 8). On each side is a dialogue in which God's speeches anticipate and voice the people's thoughts and hearts (vv. 2-7, 9-11). In both dialogues, there is a connection between two basic issues: the house of the Lord and the poverty of the people.

At first the connection is made subtly through the use of questions (v. 4), but as we move into vv. 9-11, the connection is made directly and abrasively: "Why? . . . Because . . ." (v. 9). There is a clear correlation between these two things (v. 11).

Yahweh is displeased with the people's lack of attention to rebuilding the temple. The prophet calls them to action and warns that inaction will mean further curses. The ultimate purpose of this project is not relief from the curse, but the pleasure and glory of God.

PEOPLE TO KNOW // HAGGAI

HAGGAI 1:3: Cyrus of Persia decreed in 539 BC that the Jewish exiles could return home to Jerusalem. The Jews departed from Babylon and arrived in Jerusalem to find the city in shambles. The books of Ezra and Nehemiah describe the conditions and the rebuilding efforts. Haggai was the first prophet to minister during this time.

Haggai's prophecy focused on the importance of rebuilding God's temple. Haggai announced God's dismay that the people were living in paneled houses while God's temple lay in ruins (Hag 1:4). After laying the temple foundations, the people had become distracted with other things. Sixteen years had passed without any progress on rebuilding.

Haggai told the people that the reason they were leading unfulfilled lives was because they had abandoned God's house. Haggai promised the people that God was with them and encouraged them to get back to work. Haggai even made the stunning claim that the glory of the new temple would surpass the glory of Solomon's temple, which had been destroyed by the Babylonians in 586 BC. Later Haggai encouraged Zerubbabel, governor of the returned exiles (Hag 2:20-23). Zerubbabel was a descendant of David and is listed in the lineage of Jesus (Lk 3:27).

APPLICATION ✜ It can be so easy for us to focus on our busy lives and ignore our relationship with God. Our lives get filled with other demands. Haggai reminds us that our lives will always be unsatisfying until we give God priority and return to proper worship. Like the returned exiles, we have a building project: We need to build our lives around our Lord and Savior so that, by God's grace, we can be the temple of God's presence in the world (1Pe 2:5).

11 I called for a drought[p] on the fields
and the mountains, on the grain, the
new wine, the olive oil and everything
else the ground produces, on people
and livestock, and on all the labor of
your hands.[q]"

12 Then Zerubbabel[r] son of Shealtiel,
Joshua son of Jozadak, the high priest,
and the whole remnant[s] of the people
obeyed[t] the voice of the LORD their God
and the message of the prophet Haggai,
because the LORD their God had sent him.
And the people feared[u] the LORD.
13 Then Haggai, the LORD's messenger,
gave this message of the LORD to the
people: "I am with[v] you," declares the
LORD. 14 So the LORD stirred up the spirit
of Zerubbabel[w] son of Shealtiel, governor of Judah, and the spirit of Joshua
son of Jozadak, the high priest, and the
spirit of the whole remnant[x] of the people. They came and began to work on
the house of the LORD Almighty, their
God, 15 on the twenty-fourth day of the
sixth month.[y]

The Promised Glory of the New House

2 In the second year of King Darius,
1 on the twenty-first day of the seventh month, the word of the LORD came
through the prophet Haggai: 2 "Speak to
Zerubbabel son of Shealtiel, governor of
Judah, to Joshua son of Jozadak,[a] the
high priest, and to the remnant of the
people. Ask them, 3 'Who of you is left
who saw this house[z] in its former glory?
How does it look to you now? Does it not
seem to you like nothing?[a] 4 But now be
strong, Zerubbabel,' declares the LORD.
'Be strong,[b] Joshua son of Jozadak, the
high priest. Be strong, all you people of
the land,' declares the LORD, 'and work.
For I am with[c] you,' declares the LORD
Almighty. 5 'This is what I covenanted
with you when you came out of Egypt.[d]
And my Spirit[e] remains among you. Do
not fear.'
6 "This is what the LORD Almighty
says: 'In a little while[f] I will once more
shake the heavens and the earth,[g] the
sea and the dry land. 7 I will shake all nations, and what is desired by all nations
will come, and I will fill this house[h] with
glory,' says the LORD Almighty. 8 'The
silver is mine and the gold is mine,' declares the LORD Almighty. 9 'The glory[i] of
this present house will be greater than
the glory of the former house,' says
the LORD Almighty. 'And in this place
I will grant peace,' declares the LORD
Almighty."

1:11 [p] Dt 28:22; 1Ki 17:1 [q] Hag 2:17
1:12 [r] ver 1 [s] ver 14; Isa 1:9; Hag 2:2 [t] Isa 50:10 [u] Dt 31:12
1:13 [v] Mt 28:20; Ro 8:31
1:14 [w] Ezr 5:2 [x] ver 12
1:15 [y] ver 1
2:3 [z] Ezr 3:12 [a] Zec 4:10
2:4 [b] 1Ch 28:20; Zec 8:9; Eph 6:10 [c] 2Sa 5:10; Ac 7:9
2:5 [d] Ex 29:46 [e] Ne 9:20; Isa 63:11
2:6 [f] Isa 10:25 [g] Heb 12:26*
2:7 [h] Isa 60:7
2:9 [i] Ps 85:9

[a] 2 Hebrew *Jehozadak*, a variant of *Jozadak*; also in verse 4

APPLICATION ✣ 1:1-11 Read in light of the NT's redefinition of the temple as the Christian community, this passage challenges us to release our resources for God's kingdom work. Haggai also moves us to see our world from God's perspective, to make his priorities our priorities and to realize the consequences of not sharing these priorities. It places at its center not the human predicament (that is only a means to an end) but rather divine desire: a desire defined as God's pleasure and glorification.

1:12-15 These verses describe the people's response to Haggai's message. This response represents a massive step of faith. Nearly two decades prior to this, an earlier group of Jews—under their governor Sheshbazzar—had responded to the invitation of Persia's King Cyrus and begun to work on the same temple site, yet with little success (see Ezr 1; 5:15-16). Now a different generation begins the temple project again. The message of God's promised presence is essential to bolster the faith of these underdogs.

✣ 1:12-15 God graciously grants us the resources to fulfill his priorities. In the new covenant, God accompanies the call with his empowerment (see Jer 31:31-34). He provides the spiritual resources, especially through his Holy Spirit, to fulfill his mandate within our own generation as we respond to his call and move ahead in faith.

2:1-9 This oracle came on day 21 of this seventh month, which was the busiest month in the Israelite festival calendar. The lack of progress on the project coupled with the enormity of the task may have been heightened by celebrating a festival in the unsightly ruins.

Haggai calls a disgruntled and discouraged community to work with renewed strength and without paralyzing fear.

✣ 2:1-9 It is possible to focus so intently on the experiences of past giants of the faith that we begin to live vicariously through these stories. This can impact our own experience with God. Reflecting on the past is not entirely negative; there is much to learn, and good comes as we long for God to work in us as he has in the past. However, when such reflection on the past intimidates us or stops us from moving ahead in faith, we need to hear the message of Hag 2:1-9.

Blessings for a Defiled People

10On the twenty-fourth day of the ninth month,[j] in the second year of Darius, the word of the LORD came to the prophet Haggai: 11"This is what the LORD Almighty says: 'Ask the priests[k] what the law says: 12If someone carries consecrated meat in the fold of their garment, and that fold touches some bread or stew, some wine, olive oil or other food, does it become consecrated?[l]' "

The priests answered, "No."

13Then Haggai said, "If a person defiled by contact with a dead body touches one of these things, does it become defiled?"

"Yes," the priests replied, "it becomes defiled.[m]"

14Then Haggai said, " 'So it is with this people and this nation in my sight,' declares the LORD. 'Whatever they do and whatever they offer[n] there is defiled.

15" 'Now give careful thought[o] to this from this day on[a] — consider how things were before one stone was laid[p] on another in the LORD's temple.[q] 16When anyone came to a heap of twenty measures, there were only ten. When anyone went to a wine vat to draw fifty measures, there were only twenty.[r] 17I struck all the work of your hands[s] with blight,[t] mildew and hail, yet you did not return to me,' declares the LORD.[u] 18'From this day on, from this twenty-fourth day of the ninth month, give careful thought to the day when the foundation[v] of the LORD's temple was laid. Give careful thought: 19Is there yet any seed left in the barn? Until now, the vine and the fig tree, the pomegranate and the olive tree have not borne fruit.

" 'From this day on I will bless you.' "

2:10 [j]ver 1
2:11 [k]Lev 10:10-11; Dt 17:8-11; Mal 2:7
2:12 [l]Lev 6:27; Mt 23:19
2:13 [m]Lev 22:4-6
2:14 [n]Isa 1:13
2:15 [o]Hag 1:5 [p]Ezr 3:10 [q]Ezr 4:24
2:16 [r]Hag 1:6
2:17 [s]Hag 1:11 [t]Dt 28:22; 1Ki 8:37; Am 4:9 [u]Am 4:6
2:18 [v]Zec 8:9
2:21 [w]Ezr 5:2
2:22 [x]Da 2:44 [y]Mic 5:10 [z]Jdg 7:22
2:23 [a]Isa 43:10

Hag 2:9 ❖ Sometimes we think the past was better than the present. How might God be showing us that what he is building now is even greater than what he did before (see Jn 14:12)?

Zerubbabel the LORD's Signet Ring

20The word of the LORD came to Haggai a second time on the twenty-fourth day of the month: 21"Tell Zerubbabel[w] governor of Judah that I am going to shake the heavens and the earth. 22I will overturn royal thrones and shatter the power of the foreign kingdoms.[x] I will overthrow chariots[y] and their drivers; horses and their riders will fall, each by the sword of his brother.[z]

23" 'On that day,' declares the LORD Almighty, 'I will take you, my servant[a] Zerubbabel son of Shealtiel,' declares the LORD, 'and I will make you like my signet ring, for I have chosen you,' declares the LORD Almighty."

[a] 15 Or *to the days past*

2:10–23 The book of Haggai records the date of the prophet's prophecies to provide a historical backdrop for reading the text. This third section is connected to a significant celebration related to the temple rebuilding.

The date coincides with the three-month anniversary of the beginning of the rebuilding project and, more importantly, with "the day when the foundation of the LORD's temple was laid" (v. 18). On this day, Haggai addresses not only the people on the topic of blessing (vv. 15–19) but also the priests on the topic of purity (vv. 10–14) and Zerubbabel on the topic of royal power (vv. 20–23). Haggai's message is once again linked to a ritual celebration, but this time with a ceremony connected with rebuilding the temple.

This passage functions as a positive encouragement for the people, affirming their decision to move forward in the rebuilding project and to lay the foundation of the temple. Haggai encourages the people by comparing the dismal past with the promised future. This future blessing is ultimately linked to the reestablishment of the royal house represented by Zerubbabel, who becomes a symbol of hope for the community of God.

✣ **2:10–23** Only through Jesus, the One who transforms our fallen state through his death and resurrection, can our actions and sacrifices be acceptable before God. Those who are redeemed by Jesus can now walk in obedience by the Holy Spirit. However, even this new covenant community can become trapped in the meaningless practice of sacrifice without obedience. Within the church today it is easy to bring our sacrifice—whether our verbal worship, material contributions, or gifts and abilities—and yet be walking in disobedience, either because of a heart that is disengaged from the God of covenant or because of a pattern of life lived contrary to God's standards.

The coming of Christ means that we can live with far more hope than those who lived in Haggai's time. Jesus has come, fulfilling the prophetic hope of the OT. This grants to us far more closure and certainty than those who longed for the coming messianic age. We continue to live, though, in faith as did Haggai's audience. We wait for God to overthrow all earthly power through the arrival of the Divine Warrior in the last days (Rev 19).

Zechariah

Author: Zechariah
Audience: The postexilic Jews living in Judah
Date: 520 to about 480 BC

Theme: God, through the prophet Zechariah, encourages his people to complete the rebuilding of the temple. He then uses visions and symbols to foreshadow their glorious future.

Reading Zechariah

After a brief introductory call to repentance, the first six chapters contain prophetic visions that stress the power and control of God. The next two chapters stress the responsibilities and blessings of God's people. The last six chapters are a series of prophetic messages that picture the glorious future God has in store for us. Much of Zechariah is difficult to understand, since so much use is made of symbols.

PERSPECTIVE

The prophets Haggai and Zechariah complement each other. Both announce an imminent restoration inaugurated by the return of God that is dependent on the repentance of the people. For Zechariah, repentance is demonstrated in the people's purity in their covenant relationship to Yahweh. The prophet's message is encapsulated in Yahweh's plea in 1:3, "Return to me . . . and I will return to you." For both Zechariah and Haggai, the ultimate goal is the return of the presence and blessing of God to his people in order to transform the cosmos.

For more perspective on this book, see the Introduction to Haggai.

TAKING THE NEXT STEPS

Zechariah (like Haggai) prophesied to the Jews who had returned to the promised land after the exile in Babylon (see Ezr 1:1–8; 5:1–2; 6:13–18). He joined Haggai in stirring up the people to start working once again on the temple, but his primary call was for spiritual renewal through repentance. Because of the insecurities the small band of Jews must have felt in this hostile environment, Zechariah took it on himself to encourage them, primarily by giving them a number of pictures of God in control.

Through Zechariah, God is also speaking to us. (1) God wants us to confess and turn from our sin too. If we do repent, he will respond to us with blessing. (2) We can be sure, in the court of heaven, that those who have Jesus as their lawyer will win out over the prosecutor

Event	1200 BC – 400 BC
Fall of Jerusalem (586 BC)	♦
First return of exiles to Jerusalem (538 BC)	♦
Ministries of Haggai and Zechariah (c. 520–480 BC)	▬
Book of Zechariah written (c. 520–480 BC)	▬
Completion of temple (516 BC)	♦
Second return to Jerusalem under Ezra (458 BC)	♦
Third return to Jerusalem under Nehemiah (444 BC)	♦
Malachi's ministry (c. 440–430 BC)	▪

Timeline scale: 1200 BC, 1100, 1000, 900, 800, 700, 600, 500, 400

Satan. (3) More important than observing religious rituals is helping others in justice and compassion. (4) Regardless of what happens in our lives, we can take comfort from knowing that God is in control and that he will have his way. (5) Since God plans to have people from all nations come to him, we ought to spread the gospel of his grace throughout the world.

Key Verses

"Therefore tell the people: This is what the LORD Almighty says: 'Return to me,' declares the LORD Almighty, 'and I will return to you,' says the LORD Almighty. Do not be like your ancestors . . . they would not listen or pay attention to me, declares the LORD."

—Zechariah 1:3-4

WHAT TO LOOK FOR IN ZECHARIAH

- The vision of the heavenly courtroom (ch. 3)
- The truth that compassion is more important than religious ritual (ch. 7)
- The coming of the humble king of Zion (ch. 9)
- The final victory of the Lord (ch. 14)

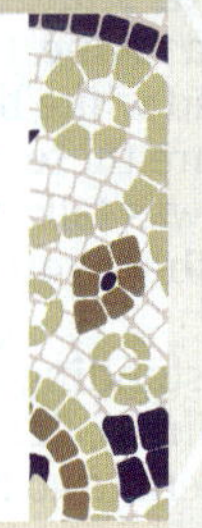

A Call to Return to the LORD

1 In the eighth month of the second
year of Darius,[a] the word of the LORD
came to the prophet Zechariah[b] son of
Berekiah,[c] the son of Iddo:[d]
2"The LORD was very angry[e] with your
ancestors. 3Therefore tell the people:
This is what the LORD Almighty says: 'Return to me,' declares the LORD Almighty,
'and I will return to you,'[f] says the LORD
Almighty. 4Do not be like your ancestors,[g] to whom the earlier prophets proclaimed: This is what the LORD Almighty

1:1 [a] Ezr 4:24; 6:15 [b] Ezr 5:1 [c] Mt 23:35; Lk 11:51 [d] ver 7; Ne 12:4
1:2 [e] 2Ch 36:16
1:3 [f] Mal 3:7; Jas 4:8
1:4 [g] 2Ch 36:15

Zec 1:3 ❖ In what areas of life might God be calling us to "return" to him? What could this return look like?

1:1-6 Zechariah, arising from the priesthood as a prophetic voice, is a good candidate to set the agenda for the true repentance called for in these first verses. God speaks to Zechariah and tells him to declare to the present generation a message that echoes former prophets. Verse 6b reports the reaction of the people to Zechariah's initial message and picks up the narrative thread from 1:1. Verse 2 looks to the past, expressing God's anger toward the former generation. This is explained in more detail in vv. 4-6a as a negative example to avoid. Verse 3 identifies the goal of this prophetic message, which has both a human (v. 6b) and divine (1:7—2:13) element.

APPLICATION ✚ **1:1-6** Biblical repentance is a matter of turning *to* as well as turning *from*. As such, it is focused not only on behavioral patterns, but more importantly and more fundamentally on relational patterns. In other words, repentance involves someone to *love*, not just some way to *act*. By reorienting our perspective on sin and repentance in this way, we do not reduce but enhance the call to purity and holiness. Set in this context we are encouraged to live faithfully before God in all areas of life, not just in areas centered around our limited lists of vices and virtues.

says: 'Turn from your evil ways[h] and your evil practices.' But they would not listen or pay attention to me,[i] declares the LORD. 5Where are your ancestors now? And the prophets, do they live forever? 6But did not my words and my decrees, which I commanded my servants the prophets, overtake your ancestors?

"Then they repented and said, 'The LORD Almighty has done to us what our ways and practices deserve,[j] just as he determined to do.'"

The Man Among the Myrtle Trees

7On the twenty-fourth day of the eleventh month, the month of Shebat, in the second year of Darius, the word of the LORD came to the prophet Zechariah son of Berekiah, the son of Iddo.

8During the night I had a vision, and there before me was a man mounted on a red[k] horse. He was standing among the myrtle trees in a ravine. Behind him were red, brown and white horses.[l]

9I asked, "What are these, my lord?"

The angel[m] who was talking with me answered, "I will show you what they are."

10Then the man standing among the myrtle trees explained, "They are the ones the LORD has sent to go throughout the earth."[n]

11And they reported to the angel of the LORD who was standing among the myrtle trees, "We have gone throughout the earth and found the whole world at rest and in peace."[o]

12Then the angel of the LORD said, "LORD Almighty, how long will you withhold mercy from Jerusalem and from the towns of Judah, which you have been angry with these seventy[p] years?" 13So the LORD spoke kind and comforting words to the angel who talked with me.[q]

14Then the angel who was speaking to me said, "Proclaim this word: This is what the LORD Almighty says: 'I am very jealous[r] for Jerusalem and Zion, 15and I am very angry with the nations that feel secure.[s] I was only a little angry, but they went too far with the punishment.'[t]

16"Therefore this is what the LORD says: 'I will return[u] to Jerusalem with mercy, and there my house will be rebuilt. And the measuring line[v] will be stretched out over Jerusalem,' declares the LORD Almighty.

17"Proclaim further: This is what the LORD Almighty says: 'My towns will again overflow with prosperity, and the LORD will again comfort[w] Zion and choose[x] Jerusalem.'"[y]

Four Horns and Four Craftsmen

18Then I looked up, and there before me were four horns. 19I asked the angel who was speaking to me, "What are these?"

He answered me, "These are the horns[z] that scattered Judah, Israel and Jerusalem."

20Then the LORD showed me four craftsmen. 21I asked, "What are these coming to do?"

1:4 [h] Ps 106:6 [i] 2Ch 24:19; Ps 78:8; Jer 6:17
1:6 [j] Jer 12:14-17; La 2:17
1:8 [k] Rev 6:4 [l] Zec 6:2-7
1:9 [m] Zec 4:1, 4-5
1:10 [n] Zec 6:5-8
1:11 [o] Isa 14:7
1:12 [p] Da 9:2
1:13 [q] Zec 4:1
1:14 [r] Joel 2:18; Zec 8:2
1:15 [s] Jer 48:11 [t] Ps 123:3-4; Am 1:11
1:16 [u] Zec 8:3 [v] Zec 2:1-2
1:17 [w] Isa 51:3 [x] Isa 14:1 [y] Zec 2:12
1:19 [z] Am 6:13

1:7-17 These visions in 1:7—6:15 are often referred to as the "night visions." This first vision is drawn from a military context. A worldwide reconnaissance team is reporting back to the commanding officer in a secret location. This scene reminds readers that the Lord is in control of history.

1:11-12 The report appears at first to be positive: The angels have found "the whole world at rest and in peace" (v. 11). The angel of the Lord appears to be looking for evidence of an upheaval that will usher in a new day for God's people. He cries out to Yahweh: "How long?" The allusion to "seventy years" (v. 12) clearly refers to the exile, the purpose of which was to discipline God's people.

1:13-15 God speaks "kind and comforting words" (v. 13) to the angel in highly emotive terms. God's promise flows out of his character and reflects his intense loyalty to his people. This passion is linked with God's anger toward the nations (v. 15).

1:16-17 After describing the present situation, the message transitions to the announcement of salvation. Yahweh promises to "return to Jerusalem with mercy" (v. 16). Not only will God rebuild his house and his city, but he will also make them prosperous as he comforts and chooses them.

1:7-17 The visionary scene displays God's sovereignty over the affairs of the world. Faith in God's sovereignty is essential to the faithful Christian walk as we await the return of Christ.

The words of the apostles in Acts powerfully express such faith for us as Christians. Fresh from persecution, the believers "raised their voices together in prayer to God" and began with the simple cry: "Sovereign Lord" (Ac 4:23-30). May that also be our cry as the people of God.

1:18-20 In this second vision, Zechariah sees four horns and individuals who are identified as four craftsmen. The angel tells Zechariah that these horns are those that have "scattered Judah, Israel and Jerusalem" (v. 19). The horn is a common image of national military might.

He answered, "These are the horns
that scattered Judah so that no one could
raise their head, but the craftsmen have
come to terrify them and throw down
these horns of the nations who lifted up
their horns[a] against the land of Judah to
scatter its people."[ab]

A Man With a Measuring Line

2[b] Then I looked up, and there before
me was a man with a measuring
line in his hand. 2I asked, "Where are
you going?"
He answered me, "To measure Jerusalem, to find out how wide and how
long it is."[c]
3While the angel who was speaking to
me was leaving, another angel came to
meet him 4and said to him: "Run, tell that
young man, 'Jerusalem will be a city without walls[d] because of the great number[e]
of people and animals in it. 5And I myself
will be a wall[f] of fire around it,' declares
the LORD, 'and I will be its glory[g] within.'
6"Come! Come! Flee from the land of
the north," declares the LORD, "for I have
scattered you to the four winds of heav-
en,"[h] declares the LORD.

> **Zec 2:4-5** ❖ How has God surrounded us like a wall? At what times do we experience his special protection?

7"Come, Zion! Escape, you who live
in Daughter Babylon!"[i] 8For this is
what the LORD Almighty says: "After
the Glorious One has sent me against
the nations that have plundered you —
for whoever touches you touches the
apple of his eye[j] — 9I will surely raise
my hand against them so that their
slaves will plunder them.[ck] Then you
will know that the LORD Almighty has
sent me.[l]
10"Shout and be glad, Daughter Zion.[m]
For I am coming,[n] and I will live among
you,"[o] declares the LORD. 11"Many nations
will be joined with the LORD in that day
and will become my people. I will live
among you and you will know that the
LORD Almighty has sent me to you. 12The
LORD will inherit[p] Judah as his portion
in the holy land and will again choose[q]

[a] *21* In Hebrew texts 1:18-21 is numbered 2:1-4.
[b] In Hebrew texts 2:1-13 is numbered 2:5-17.
[c] *8,9* Or *says after . . . eye: 9"I . . . plunder them."*

1:21 [a]Ps 75:4 [b]Ps 75:10
2:2 [c]Eze 40:3; Rev 21:15
2:4 [d]Eze 38:11 [e]Isa 49:20; Jer 30:19; 33:22
2:5 [f]Isa 26:1 [g]Rev 21:23
2:6 [h]Eze 17:21
2:7 [i]Isa 48:20
2:8 [j]Dt 32:10
2:9 [k]Isa 14:2 [l]Zec 4:9
2:10 [m]Zep 3:14 [n]Zec 9:9 [o]Lev 26:12; Zec 8:3
2:12 [p]Dt 32:9; Ps 33:12; Jer 10:16 [q]Zec 1:17

1:21 The devastation of Israel and Judah's exile is summed up in the statement "no one could raise their head." But Zechariah sees a scene that offers hope to his community: The nations that have scattered Israel will be powerless to abuse the Jewish community any longer. Before the rebuilding project described in the next chapters, the power of the nations must be smashed. God's passion for his people is expressed in his punishment of Babylon.

> ✜ **1:18-21** Christ came to earth in a helpless state and conquered sin and death through the helplessness of the cross. This is the basis for our humble walk of faith, and it is an example to those who take up their cross and follow him (Mk 8:34). The weak things of the world conquer sin and evil, not because of their weakness but because we weak believers have to rely on God to work through us.
>
> When we realize that we are helpless in the face of sin and evil in this world, we are forced to trust in the only One who can rescue us from our predicament. As we surrender to God in faith, we find empowerment to defeat sin in our own lives and to move forward to build his kingdom. Humans are weak; God is strong. The Holy Spirit fuels us with confidence that no matter what we are called to build for the Lord, we are accompanied by the most powerful ally in the universe.

2:1-5 This encounter with an individual holding surveying equipment fits the historical context. The people had returned to the land and were restoring the temple in Jerusalem. The vision of this passage unpacks the promises of the initial vision in 1:8-17: in particular, the promise that God will return, rebuild the temple and city (1:16), and restore prosperity (1:17). This continues the tone of comfort that began in 1:13 in response to the initial repentance of the people (1:1-6).

> ✜ **2:1-5** The glorious message of the NT is that God has graced us with his presence through his Holy Spirit. Yet as communities of faith, we are often unaware of God's absence in our midst and need to cry to him to pour out his Spirit.

2:6-13 This oracle calls the people to respond to God's promise by returning to his land and city, where he promises his presence. Verse 11 introduces a surprise by declaring that foreigners will enter the community of the Lord. This universal vision will be realized as Judah and Jerusalem are reinstated as God's special possession. God's return to his land, city, and temple has implications for all humanity.

> ✜ **2:6-13** This oracle calls God's community to escape "the corruption in the world caused by evil desires" (2Pe 1:4), but also to embrace God's redemptive plan for the world. God's passion for the nations has existed from the outset of redemptive history and peaked in the revelation of Jesus Christ. Through him all people have access to a renewed relationship with their Creator.

Jerusalem. 13 Be still[r] before the LORD, all
mankind, because he has roused himself
from his holy dwelling."

Clean Garments for the High Priest

3 Then he showed me Joshua[s] the high
priest standing before the angel of
the LORD, and Satan[a][t] standing at his
right side to accuse him. 2 The LORD said
to Satan, "The LORD rebuke you,[u] Satan!
The LORD, who has chosen[v] Jerusalem,
rebuke you! Is not this man a burning
stick snatched from the fire?"[w]
3 Now Joshua was dressed in filthy
clothes as he stood before the angel. 4 The
angel said to those who were standing
before him, "Take off his filthy clothes."
Then he said to Joshua, "See, I have
taken away your sin,[x] and I will put fine
garments[y] on you."
5 Then I said, "Put a clean turban[z] on
his head." So they put a clean turban on
his head and clothed him, while the angel of the LORD stood by.
6 The angel of the LORD gave this
charge to Joshua: 7 "This is what the LORD
Almighty says: 'If you will walk in obedience to me and keep my requirements,
then you will govern my house[a] and have
charge of my courts, and I will give you a
place among these standing here.
8 " 'Listen, High Priest Joshua, you and
your associates seated before you, who
are men symbolic[b] of things to come:
I am going to bring my servant, the
Branch.[c] 9 See, the stone I have set in
front of Joshua! There are seven eyes[b]
on that one stone,[d] and I will engrave an
inscription on it,' says the LORD Almighty,

2:13 [r] Hab 2:20
3:1 [s] Hag 1:1; Zec 6:11 [t] Ps 109:6
3:2 [u] Jude 9 [v] Isa 14:1 [w] Am 4:11; Jude 23
3:4 [x] Eze 36:25; Mic 7:18 [y] Isa 52:1; Rev 19:8
3:5 [z] Ex 29:6
3:7 [a] Dt 17:8-11; Eze 44:15-16
3:8 [b] Eze 12:11 [c] Isa 4:2
3:9 [d] Isa 28:16 [e] Jer 50:20
3:10 [f] 1Ki 4:25; Mic 4:4
4:1 [g] Da 8:18 [h] Jer 31:26
4:2 [i] Jer 1:13 [j] Ex 25:31; Rev 1:12 [k] Rev 4:5
4:3 [l] ver 11; Rev 11:4
4:5 [m] Zec 1:9
4:6 [n] Ezr 5:2 [o] Isa 11:2-4; Hos 1:7

Zec 3:3-4 ❖ What are practical ways we can "take off" sin and clothe ourselves in righteousness (see Eph 4:22-24)?

Zec 4:6 ❖ How can we rely on God's Spirit rather than our own might or power? Where do we struggle to do this, and why is it challenging?

'and I will remove the sin[e] of this land
in a single day.
10 " 'In that day each of you will invite
your neighbor to sit under your vine and
fig tree,[f]' declares the LORD Almighty."

The Gold Lampstand and the Two Olive Trees

4 Then the angel who talked with
me returned and woke[g] me up, like
someone awakened from sleep.[h] 2 He
asked me, "What do you see?"[i]
I answered, "I see a solid gold lampstand[j] with a bowl at the top and seven
lamps[k] on it, with seven channels to the
lamps. 3 Also there are two olive trees[l] by
it, one on the right of the bowl and the
other on its left."
4 I asked the angel who talked with me,
"What are these, my lord?"
5 He answered, "Do you not know what
these are?"
"No, my lord," I replied.[m]
6 So he said to me, "This is the word of
the LORD to Zerubbabel:[n] 'Not by might
nor by power, but by my Spirit,'[o] says the
LORD Almighty.

[a] 1 Hebrew *satan* means *adversary.* [b] 9 Or *facets*

3:1–10 The Lord shows Zechariah a scene that features Joshua, a priestly figure. Joshua is the focus of a meeting of the heavenly council in which the Lord is surrounded by his angelic messengers.

On the right side of Joshua stands "Satan" (v. 1), who brings an accusation and seeks a guilty verdict. Rather than deny the accusations, the Lord rebukes the accuser and moves to change the condition of the high priest, represented by the change from "filthy clothes" to "fine garments" (v. 4). The removal of sin "in a single day" (v. 9) alludes to the high priest's role as representative of Israel. Through the rituals of the Day of Atonement, he made atonement for the sins of the people.

This chapter uses Joshua's rank as high priest for two purposes. First, it assures the high priest Joshua of God's blessing and calls him to faithfulness. Second, it speaks to Joshua as representative of his priestly line. This points to something far greater—a new era that will culminate in the coming of a royal Davidic ruler.

✣ **3:1–10** God's sovereign choice and gracious provision ultimately undermines the arguments of the accuser, a fact that can be applied to our ultimate spiritual adversary. Before we fall into sin, he whispers in our ear that sin is of no great consequence. Then he turns on us and reminds us that the same sin has made us eternally unworthy of God's kingdom. This chapter reminds us that God's sovereign election and free grace silences both accuser and accusation.

4:1–14 The lampstand, signifying God's presence and sovereignty, is fueled by oil supplied by the prophets. These oracles are messages of encouragement and hope for Zerubbabel (vv. 6–8), who undertakes the temple building project in the first oracle. Surely the "oil" of prophecy fueled the building project, bringing God's presence on earth in the form of the promised Spirit (v. 6).

7"What are you, mighty mountain?
Before Zerubbabel you will become level ground.[p] Then he will bring out the
capstone[q] to shouts of 'God bless it! God
bless it!' "
8Then the word of the LORD came to
me: 9"The hands of Zerubbabel have
laid the foundation[r] of this temple; his
hands will also complete it.[s] Then you
will know that the LORD Almighty has
sent me[t] to you.
10"Who dares despise the day of small
things,[u] since the seven eyes[v] of the LORD
that range throughout the earth will rejoice when they see the chosen capstone[a]
in the hand of Zerubbabel?"
11Then I asked the angel, "What are
these two olive trees[w] on the right and
the left of the lampstand?"
12Again I asked him, "What are these
two olive branches beside the two gold
pipes that pour out golden oil?"
13He replied, "Do you not know what
these are?"
"No, my lord," I said.
14So he said, "These are the two who
are anointed[x] to[b] serve the Lord of all
the earth."

The Flying Scroll

5 I looked again, and there before me
was a flying scroll.[y]
2He asked me, "What do you see?"
I answered, "I see a flying scroll, twenty cubits long and ten cubits wide.[c]"

4:7 [p] Jer 51:25 [q] Ps 118:22
4:9 [r] Ezr 3:11 [s] Ezr 3:8; 6:15; Zec 6:12 [t] Zec 2:9
4:10 [u] Hag 2:3 [v] Zec 3:9; Rev 5:6
4:11 [w] ver 3; Rev 11:4
4:14 [x] Ex 29:7; 40:15; Da 9:24-26; Zec 3:1-7
5:1 [y] Eze 2:9; Rev 5:1
5:3 [z] Isa 24:6; 43:28; Mal 3:9;
4:6 [a] Ex 20:15; Mal 3:8 [b] Isa 48:1
5:4 [c] Lev 14:34-45; Hab 2:9-11; Mal 3:5

Zec 5:6-8 ❖ Why do we need God to take care of our sin for us? Why can't we deal with it on our own (see Ro 8:3-4)?

3And he said to me, "This is the curse[z]
that is going out over the whole land;
for according to what it says on one
side, every thief[a] will be banished, and
according to what it says on the other,
everyone who swears falsely[b] will be
banished. 4The LORD Almighty declares,
'I will send it out, and it will enter the
house of the thief and the house of anyone who swears falsely by my name. It
will remain in that house and destroy
it completely, both its timbers and its
stones.[c]' "

The Woman in a Basket

5Then the angel who was speaking to
me came forward and said to me, "Look
up and see what is appearing."
6I asked, "What is it?"
He replied, "It is a basket." And he added, "This is the iniquity[d] of the people
throughout the land."
7Then the cover of lead was raised, and
there in the basket sat a woman! 8He
said, "This is wickedness," and he pushed

[a] 10 Or *the plumb line* [b] 14 Or *two who bring oil and* [c] 2 That is, about 30 feet long and 15 feet wide or about 9 meters long and 4.5 meters wide [d] 6 Or *appearance*

✣ **4:1-14** This chapter calls the church back to the empowerment for its life and mission by God's Spirit, which provides us with the courage to overcome the incredible challenges that stand in our way. God's word through Zechariah came at the right time, reminding Zerubbabel of his need for the Spirit's empowerment to accomplish the task of rebuilding the temple. As communities of faith, we also face formidable tasks that remind us of our desperate need for God's empowerment. Prayer for the Spirit's help should always be our first action; claiming the promise of the Spirit's presence in our work must be the foundation of all of our efforts.

5:1-4 The scroll in v. 1 has several unusual features. The fact that it can fly points to the speed with which it can execute judgment. The fact that it is double-sided links the scroll to the covenant document delivered to Moses on Mount Sinai. That it is so large most likely signifies a scroll that displays a section of the law that is equivalent to the size of both transgression and territory. This vision raises the profile of the law as the guide to life in covenant relationship.

✣ **5:1-4** This message has enduring significance for the Christian community as we seek to embody the values of this ancient law. With the confidence that Christians now live in the new era of the Spirit, we must be a community preoccupied by the law of Christ, which is continually being written on our hearts (Heb 8:10).

5:5-11 The prophet is commanded to observe a measuring "basket" (v. 6) exiting the sanctuary. This container is "the iniquity of the people" (v. 6). Inside the basket is a goddess or her idol, representing the people's unfaithfulness through idolatry. The "one" woman in the basket is distinguished from the "two women" who lift it (v. 9).

Zechariah asks the obvious question: "Where are they taking the basket?" The destination is "the country of Babylonia" (see NIV text note; literally, "Shinar"). The Tower of Babel was located in Shinar, a story that expresses humanity's attempt to overthrow God's rule.

The measuring basket with its dangerous contents will be placed in a temple built specially for it. This new structure will function as a shrine for the pagan goddess inside.

her back into the basket and pushed its
lead cover down on it.[d]
9 Then I looked up — and there before
me were two women, with the wind in
their wings! They had wings like those
of a stork,[e] and they lifted up the basket
between heaven and earth.
10 "Where are they taking the basket?" I
asked the angel who was speaking to me.
11 He replied, "To the country of Babylonia[a][f] to build a house[g] for it. When
the house is ready, the basket will be set
there in its place."[h]

Four Chariots

6 I looked up again, and there before
me were four chariots[i] coming out
from between two mountains — mountains of bronze. 2 The first chariot had
red horses, the second black,[j] 3 the third
white,[k] and the fourth dappled — all of
them powerful. 4 I asked the angel who
was speaking to me, "What are these,
my lord?"
5 The angel answered me, "These are
the four spirits[b][l] of heaven, going out
from standing in the presence of the Lord
of the whole world. 6 The one with the
black horses is going toward the north
country, the one with the white horses
toward the west,[c] and the one with the
dappled horses toward the south."
7 When the powerful horses went out,
they were straining to go throughout
the earth.[m] And he said, "Go throughout the earth!" So they went throughout
the earth.

5:8 [d] Mic 6:11
5:9 [e] Lev 11:19
5:11 [f] Ge 10:10 [g] Jer 29:5,28 [h] Da 1:2
6:1 [i] ver 5
6:2 [j] Rev 6:5
6:3 [k] Rev 6:2
6:5 [l] Eze 37:9; Mt 24:31; Rev 7:1
6:7 [m] Zec 1:10

Zec 6:11–13 ❖ Why is it important that Christ is not only King but also Priest (see Heb 4:14–16)? How is Christ the Branch building his temple through his people?

8 Then he called to me, "Look, those going toward the north country have given
my Spirit[d] rest[n] in the land of the north."

A Crown for Joshua

9 The word of the LORD came to me:
10 "Take silver and gold from the exiles
Heldai, Tobijah and Jedaiah, who have
arrived from Babylon.[o] Go the same day
to the house of Josiah son of Zephaniah. 11 Take the silver and gold and make
a crown,[p] and set it on the head of the
high priest, Joshua[q] son of Jozadak.[e][r]
12 Tell him this is what the LORD Almighty
says: 'Here is the man whose name is the
Branch,[s] and he will branch out from his
place and build the temple of the LORD.[t]
13 It is he who will build the temple of the
LORD, and he will be clothed with majesty and will sit and rule on his throne.
And he[f] will be a priest[u] on his throne.
And there will be harmony between the
two.' 14 The crown will be given to Heldai,[g] Tobijah, Jedaiah and Hen[h] son of
Zephaniah as a memorial in the temple
of the LORD. 15 Those who are far away

6:8 [n] Eze 5:13; 24:13
6:10 [o] Ezr 7:14-16; Jer 28:6
6:11 [p] Ps 21:3 [q] Zec 3:1 [r] Ezr 3:2
6:12 [s] Isa 4:2; Zec 3:8 [t] Ezr 3:8-10; Zec 4:6-9
6:13 [u] Ps 110:4

[a] 11 Hebrew *Shinar* [b] 5 Or *winds* [c] 6 Or *horses after them* [d] 8 Or *spirit* [e] 11 Hebrew *Jehozadak*, a variant of *Jozadak* [f] 13 Or *there* [g] 14 Syriac; Hebrew *Helem* [h] 14 Or *and the gracious one, the*

✣ **5:5–11** The two women in this scene may perhaps be equated to individuals who guard the worship of God in our church services. Such talented individuals desire to "put a lid on" distraction and wickedness as they lead people into worship of God. Worship is not a "preliminary event" that happens before the "main event"—the sermon. Being a worship leader today demands a high level of theological and spiritual training. Worship teams urgently need to be mentored in their study and experience of God so that they may help lead others into relationship with God.

6:1–8 The four winds of heaven, God's agents for judgment, are depicted as four chariots drawn by different colored horses. When these powerful beasts are finally released, they bring judgment on "the land of the north" (v. 8), venting God's wrath on the nation that exiled his people. God's comforting words have become reality as he unleashes his might on the helpless Babylonians.

✣ **6:1–8** These words declared to believers living in the early Persian period that God had made good on his promise to break the oppression of Babylon. But this message has continued to speak throughout the history of redemption as God has consistently rescued his people. This redemption peaked in the work of God in Christ. Through these passages God speaks to us, a community also longing for release from exile, and wages divine war on our behalf.

6:9–15 Zechariah is to oversee the manufacture of two crowns from the silver and gold of the people who have returned to the land. One is to be placed on the head of the high priest Joshua, who then receives a special message from God.

This message concerns a figure who will fulfill Jeremiah's promise of a descendant of David ("Branch," v. 12) and who will rebuild the temple. The priest will have a major role to play when this individual arrives, and they will work together.

will come and help to build the temple
of the LORD,[v] and you will know that the
LORD Almighty has sent me to you.[w] This
will happen if you diligently obey[x] the
LORD your God."

Justice and Mercy, Not Fasting

7 In the fourth year of King Darius, the
word of the LORD came to Zechariah
on the fourth day of the ninth month,
the month of Kislev.[y] 2The people of
Bethel had sent Sharezer and Regem-
Melek, together with their men, to entreat[z] the LORD 3by asking the priests of
the house of the LORD Almighty and the
prophets, "Should I mourn[a] and fast in
the fifth[b] month, as I have done for so
many years?"
4Then the word of the LORD Almighty
came to me: 5"Ask all the people of the
land and the priests, 'When you fasted[c]
and mourned in the fifth and seventh
months for the past seventy years, was
it really for me that you fasted? 6And
when you were eating and drinking,
were you not just feasting for yourselves? 7Are these not the words the
LORD proclaimed through the earlier
prophets[d] when Jerusalem and its surrounding towns were at rest[e] and prosperous, and the Negev and the western
foothills[f] were settled?'"
8And the word of the LORD came again
to Zechariah: 9"This is what the LORD
Almighty said: 'Administer true justice;[g]
show mercy and compassion to one another. 10Do not oppress the widow or the
fatherless, the foreigner[h] or the poor. Do
not plot evil against each other.'[i]
11"But they refused to pay attention;
stubbornly they turned their backs and
covered their ears.[j] 12They made their
hearts as hard as flint[k] and would not
listen to the law or to the words that
the LORD Almighty had sent by his Spirit through the earlier prophets.[l] So the
LORD Almighty was very angry.[m]
13" 'When I called, they did not listen;[n]
so when they called, I would not listen,'[o]
says the LORD Almighty.[p] 14'I scattered[q]
them with a whirlwind[r] among all the
nations, where they were strangers. The
land they left behind them was so desolate that no one traveled through it.
This is how they made the pleasant land
desolate.[s]'"

The LORD Promises to Bless Jerusalem

8 The word of the LORD Almighty came
to me.
2This is what the LORD Almighty says:
"I am very jealous for Zion; I am burning
with jealousy for her."

6:15 [v] Isa 60:10 [w] Zec 2:9-11 [x] Isa 58:12; Jer 7:23; Zec 3:7
7:1 [y] Ne 1:1
7:2 [z] Jer 26:19; Zec 8:21
7:3 [a] Zec 12:12-14 [b] Jer 52:12-14; Zec 8:19
7:5 [c] Isa 58:5
7:7 [d] Zec 1:4 [e] Jer 22:21 [f] Jer 17:26
7:9 [g] Zec 8:16
7:10 [h] Ex 22:21 [i] Ex 22:22; Isa 1:17
7:11 [j] Jer 8:5; 11:10; 17:23
7:12 [k] Jer 17:1; Eze 11:19 [l] Ne 9:29 [m] Da 9:12
7:13 [n] Pr 1:24 [o] Isa 1:15; Jer 11:11; 14:12; Mic 3:4 [p] Pr 1:28
7:14 [q] Dt 4:27; 28:64-67 [r] Jer 23:19 [s] Jer 44:6

Zec 7:4-7 ❖ How can we tell when we are worshiping in a selfish way, more concerned about enjoying the worship style than about obeying God's will?

6:9-15 The main purpose of the church is to participate in the restoration of God's rule in this world. Christ came proclaiming this rule of God ("kingdom of God"; Mk 1:15) and inaugurated it through his death, resurrection, and ascension. As the church proclaims the gospel, it is fulfilling this purpose by announcing the kingdom. As the church worships the Lord, it witnesses to his rule on earth. As the church serves its community, it extends the kingdom to those who desperately need to hear about it. As the church equips the saints by teaching them obedience to Christ, it is expanding the rule of God more deeply into the life of a community of faith.

7:1-14 People from Bethel approach the temple officials for a decision on a liturgical matter. Zechariah offers a history lesson in the consequences of ignoring or rejecting God's message.

The prophet is not on a tangent unrelated to the original question of the delegation. Zechariah is using the very liturgy from the days of fasting in order to drive home his point about the people's lack of repentance.

7:1-14 The revelation of Jesus Christ and his grace was preceded by the call to repentance through John the Baptist. God was serious about a covenant relationship with his people—a relationship based on extending his grace to a sinful people. But such grace required sincere repentance. This principle is reflected in the hope of chs. 7 and 8 and needs to inform our own experience with God today.

In a rush to get people to pray a prayer of faith to God, Christians often present a truncated view of conversion—that is, one that involves turning to God but not necessarily turning from sin. God demands faithfulness in relationship and calls us to repentance as he extends grace to us through Christ's death and resurrection. As people are invited to respond to God in faith, they must reflect deeply over the condition of their hearts and lives, renounce their past life of sin, and humbly ask for the Spirit to enable their new life in Christ.

8:1-2 After having just encountered 7:4-14 with its description of God's discipline of the former generation, we might expect an oracle of judgment directed

3 This is what the LORD says: "I will return[t] to Zion and dwell in Jerusalem.[u]
Then Jerusalem will be called the Faithful City, and the mountain of the LORD
Almighty will be called the Holy Mountain."
4 This is what the LORD Almighty says:
"Once again men and women of ripe old
age will sit in the streets of Jerusalem,[v]
each of them with cane in hand because
of their age. 5 The city streets will be filled
with boys and girls playing there.[w]"
6 This is what the LORD Almighty says:
"It may seem marvelous to the remnant
of this people at that time,[x] but will it
seem marvelous to me?[y]" declares the
LORD Almighty.
7 This is what the LORD Almighty says:
"I will save my people from the countries
of the east and the west.[z] 8 I will bring
them back[a] to live in Jerusalem; they will
be my people,[b] and I will be faithful and
righteous to them as their God."
9 This is what the LORD Almighty says:
"Now hear these words, 'Let your hands
be strong[c] so that the temple may be
built.' This is also what the prophets[d] said
who were present when the foundation
was laid for the house of the LORD Almighty. 10 Before that time there were no
wages[e] for people or hire for animals. No
one could go about their business safely because of their enemies, since I had
turned everyone against their neighbor.
11 But now I will not deal with the remnant of this people as I did in the past,"[f]
declares the LORD Almighty.
12 "The seed will grow well, the vine
will yield its fruit,[g] the ground will produce its crops,[h] and the heavens will drop
their dew.[i] I will give all these things as
an inheritance[j] to the remnant of this
people. 13 Just as you, Judah and Israel,
have been a curse[a][k] among the nations,
so I will save you, and you will be a blessing.[b][l] Do not be afraid, but let your hands
be strong."
14 This is what the LORD Almighty says:
"Just as I had determined to bring disaster[m] on you and showed no pity when your
ancestors angered me," says the LORD Almighty, 15 "so now I have determined to do
good[n] again to Jerusalem and Judah. Do
not be afraid. 16 These are the things you
are to do: Speak the truth[o] to each other,
and render true and sound judgment in
your courts;[p] 17 do not plot evil[q] against
each other, and do not love to swear falsely.[r] I hate all this," declares the LORD.
18 The word of the LORD Almighty came
to me.
19 This is what the LORD Almighty says:
"The fasts of the fourth,[s] fifth,[t] seventh[u]
and tenth[v] months will become joyful[w]
and glad occasions and happy festivals

8:3 [t] Zec 1:16 [u] Zec 2:10
8:4 [v] Isa 65:20
8:5 [w] Jer 30:20; 31:13
8:6 [x] Ps 118:23; 126:1-3 [y] Jer 32:17, 27
8:7 [z] Ps 107:3; Isa 11:11; 43:5
8:8 [a] Zec 10:10 [b] Eze 11:19-20; 36:28; Zec 2:11
8:9 [c] Hag 2:4 [d] Ezr 5:1
8:10 [e] Hag 1:6
8:11 [f] Isa 12:1
8:12 [g] Joel 2:22 [h] Ps 67:6 [i] Ge 27:28 [j] Ob 17
8:13 [k] Jer 42:18 [l] Ge 12:2
8:14 [m] Jer 31:28; Eze 24:14
8:15 [n] ver 13; Jer 29:11; Mic 7:18-20
8:16 [o] Ps 15:2; Eph 4:25 [p] Zec 7:9
8:17 [q] Pr 3:29 [r] Pr 6:16-19
8:19 [s] Jer 39:2 [t] Jer 52:12 [u] 2Ki 25:25 [v] Jer 52:4 [w] Ps 30:11

[a] *13* That is, your name has been used in cursing (see Jer. 29:22); or, you have been regarded as under a curse. [b] *13* Or *and your name will be used in blessings* (see Gen. 48:20); or *and you will be seen as blessed*

---

at Judah. The surprise, however, is that Zechariah speaks of Israel's deliverance as God's wrath is directed toward the nations who abused Israel.

8:3 Zechariah's description of God's return to Jerusalem is closely linked to Ex 25:8, which uses the same Hebrew phrase to describe God's dwelling in the tabernacle.

8:4 The prophet uses two images that represent life at its two extremes (childhood and old age), the periods of people's greatest vulnerability. These images reveal a life blessed with abundance of provisions and protection from harm.

8:5 Yahweh's passionate zeal transforms Jerusalem into a city with the qualities of his character and with a renewed life of prosperity and peace.

8:6–8 Zechariah now proclaims the means by which this miraculous God will fill his city: He will rescue his people from their exile and return them to Jerusalem.

8:9–13 Here we return to the style familiar from the book of Haggai with its regular use of the phrases "let your hands be strong" (vv. 9, 13), "do not be afraid" (v. 13), and an emphasis on rebuilding the temple. The message here is designed to encourage those involved in the rebuilding project.

God's new stance toward the community will be expressed through renewed blessing of the land. The final verse repeats themes of blessing and cursing. Zechariah contrasts the people's experience in exile with their future experience in the coming era when they become a conduit for God's blessing to the nations.

8:1–13 In his passionate zeal for his people, Yahweh's intention moves from discipline to deliverance. God is the one who must enact salvation for his people. He eagerly desires to save and know his people. This revelation of God's heart is the greatest source of hope for every generation.

8:14–15 Zechariah plays on the term "determined" to signal a new era of redemptive history. The use of this term emphasizes divine intentionality and is only used elsewhere in the Hebrew Bible in reference to Yahweh's discipline. Now instead of disaster, the people will experience good.

8:16–17 The comforting words in v. 13 bring closure to this oracle of salvation. The prophet, however, is not finished. Now he identifies the people's part in redemptive history. These verses offer a list of admonitions to follow and prohibitions to avoid.

for Judah. Therefore love truth[x] and
peace."
20This is what the LORD Almighty says:
"Many peoples and the inhabitants of
many cities will yet come, 21and the inhabitants of one city will go to another and
say, 'Let us go at once to entreat[y] the LORD
and seek the LORD Almighty. I myself am
going.' 22And many peoples and powerful
nations will come to Jerusalem to seek
the LORD Almighty and to entreat him."[z]
23This is what the LORD Almighty says:
"In those days ten people from all languages and nations will take firm hold
of one Jew by the hem of his robe and
say, 'Let us go with you, because we have
heard that God is with you.' "[a]

Judgment on Israel's Enemies

9 A prophecy:

The word of the LORD is against the
land of Hadrak
and will come to rest on
Damascus[b] —
for the eyes of all people and all the
tribes of Israel
are on the LORD —[a]
2and on Hamath[c] too, which borders
on it,
and on Tyre[d] and Sidon, though
they are very skillful.
3Tyre has built herself a stronghold;
she has heaped up silver like dust,
and gold like the dirt of the
streets.[e]
4But the Lord will take away her
possessions
and destroy her power on the sea,
and she will be consumed by fire.[f]
5Ashkelon will see it and fear;
Gaza will writhe in agony,
and Ekron too, for her hope will
wither.
Gaza will lose her king
and Ashkelon will be deserted.
6A mongrel people will occupy
Ashdod,
and I will put an end to the pride
of the Philistines.
7I will take the blood from their
mouths,
the forbidden food from between
their teeth.
Those who are left will belong to our
God
and become a clan in Judah,
and Ekron will be like the
Jebusites.
8But I will encamp at my temple
to guard it against marauding
forces.
Never again will an oppressor
overrun my people,
for now I am keeping watch.[g]

The Coming of Zion's King

9Rejoice greatly, Daughter Zion!
Shout, Daughter Jerusalem!

8:19 [x] ver 16
8:21 [y] Zec 7:2
8:22 [z] Ps 117:1; Isa 60:3; Zec 2:11
8:23 [a] Isa 45:14; 1Co 14:25
9:1 [b] Isa 17:1
9:2 [c] Jer 49:23 [d] Eze 28:1-19
9:3 [e] Job 27:16; Eze 28:4
9:4 [f] Isa 23:1; Eze 26:3-5; 28:18
9:8 [g] Isa 52:1; 54:14

Zec 8:23 ❖ How can we put God on display in such a way that others will say "God is with you"?

[a] 1 Or *Damascus. / For the eye of the LORD is on all people, / as well as on the tribes of Israel,*

8:18-19 The people have been called to proper fasting: an expression of repentance and a commitment to obedience. The new era will not arrive unless the people obey the ethical demands urged by the earlier prophets.

8:20-23 The first oracle (vv. 20-22) reflects a strong tradition in the prophetic movement in which the nations are drawn to Jerusalem to seek Yahweh. The second oracle (v. 23) highlights the role of the Jewish community returning from exile. Their obedience will usher in the new era in which all nations will bend their knee—either in glad adoration or in broken submission.

❖ **8:14-23** Zechariah looks to the future with hope. He envisions a day of restoration when repentant people will rejoice in the presence of their God. This reminds us that fasting has covenant relationship as its goal.

Churches and individuals should take opportunities to enjoy fellowship meals together during their yearly rhythm of life as a congregation. These meals can become opportunities to share God's goodness with one another in word and deed. Communal celebrations on Easter Sunday and Christmas are important to the life of our faith communities.

9:1-8 Since the focus is on "all the tribes of Israel" (v. 1), traditional enemies of both the northern and southern tribes are mentioned. The sacking and burning of Tyre sends shock waves down the coast in vv. 5-8. To the south along the great coastal highway lie the city-states traditionally associated with the Philistines; they realize that they are next in the path of this Divine Warrior. If invincible Tyre is no match for this Warrior, they have little hope. In v. 8 the Divine Warrior reaches his destination at the temple in Jerusalem. There God promises that there will never again be a return to the conditions of the exile.

9:9-10 The presence of a human king in Jerusalem/

PEOPLE TO KNOW // ZECHARIAH

ZECHARIAH 9:9–13: As did Haggai, Zechariah ministered in Jerusalem to the returned exiles from Babylon, encouraging them to rebuild God's temple. His prophecy is full of vivid and at times strange imagery. The book that bears his name is the longest of the minor prophets, and the NT contains more allusions to Zechariah than to any other minor prophet.

Zechariah's prophecy begins with eight bizarre visions, all of which the prophet received on a single night (Zec 1:8—6:8). Zechariah goes on to deliver prophetic messages oriented to the coming of God's anointed Messiah. For example, God told Zechariah to place a crown on the head of the high priest, Joshua, pointing to one who would combine the offices of king and priest (as Melchizedek had): Jesus Christ (Zec 6:11).

Later passages also point clearly to the story of Jesus. Zechariah 9:9–13 foretells of a righteous and humble king who rides on a donkey. This prophecy was fulfilled in Jesus' entry into Jerusalem the Sunday before his crucifixion (Mk 11:1–11). The thirty pieces of silver used to pay a potter in Zechariah 11:13 are echoed in the price Judas was paid to betray Jesus (Mt 27:6–11).

Zechariah's book of colorful prophecies ends with a vision of the Lord coming to earth and living water flowing from Jerusalem. The Lord will reign over the whole earth (Zec 14:8–9).

APPLICATION ✣ Zechariah ministered in Jerusalem during a very difficult time. The returned exiles wondered whether God had abandoned them. Still today, communities of believers go through seasons where God's promises seem distant. Like Zechariah, we need to point others to Christ and to the sure hope of God's salvation. In dry times, it is all the more important to repent and turn back to God, to proclaim the hope of God's redemptive plan found in Jesus Christ.

See, your king comes to you,
righteous and victorious,[h]
lowly and riding on a donkey,
on a colt, the foal of a donkey.[i]
10 I will take away the chariots from Ephraim
and the warhorses from Jerusalem,
and the battle bow will be broken.[j]
He will proclaim peace to the nations.
His rule will extend from sea to sea
and from the River[a] to the ends of the earth.[k]
11 As for you, because of the blood of my covenant[l] with you,
I will free your prisoners[m] from the waterless pit.
12 Return to your fortress,[n] you prisoners of hope;
even now I announce that I will restore twice as much to you.
13 I will bend Judah as I bend my bow
and fill it with Ephraim.[o]
I will rouse your sons, Zion,
against your sons, Greece,[p]
and make you like a warrior's sword.[q]

The LORD Will Appear

14 Then the LORD will appear over them;[r]
his arrow will flash like lightning.[s]

9:9 [h] Isa 9:6-7; 43:3-11; Jer 23:5-6; Zep 3:14-15; Zec 2:10 [i] Mt 21:5*; Jn 12:15*
9:10 [j] Hos 1:7; 2:18; Mic 4:3; 5:10; Zec 10:4 [k] Ps 72:8
9:11 [l] Ex 24:8 [m] Isa 42:7
9:12 [n] Joel 3:16
9:13 [o] Isa 49:2 [p] Joel 3:6 [q] Jer 51:20
9:14 [r] Isa 31:5 [s] Ps 18:14; Hab 3:11

Zec 9:9–12 ✣ Why is it significant that Christ, the victorious king, comes to his people in humility and lowliness (see Mt 21:1–9)?

[a] *10* That is, the Euphrates

Zion is an essential component in God's rule over the nations of the earth (Ps 2). This king is not portrayed as a triumphant figure but as an individual faithful to the covenant and reliant on God for salvation. He enters the city on a lowly donkey, an image that has prophetic and messianic significance (Mt 21:1–11).

The "chariot," "horse," and "battle bow" (9:10a) are essential for advanced warfare in the ancient Near East. They will be unnecessary for this king who relies on the Divine Warrior. Peace will be proclaimed to the "nations" (v. 10b).

9:11–17 The time has come for the people's return. The basis of this promised liberation is the "blood of my covenant" (v. 11). On the basis of this ancient covenant agreement, God promises salvation for his exiled people. The return of these prisoners will be accompanied by incredible blessing. They will become weapons in God's hands.

9:14 The focus is on the military action of the

The Sovereign LORD will sound the
trumpet;
he will march in the storms[t] of the
south,
15 and the LORD Almighty will shield[u]
them.
They will destroy
and overcome with slingstones.
They will drink and roar as with
wine;
they will be full like a bowl
used for sprinkling[a] the corners[v]
of the altar.
16 The LORD their God will save his
people on that day
as a shepherd saves his flock.
They will sparkle in his land
like jewels in a crown.[w]
17 How attractive and beautiful they
will be!
Grain will make the young men
thrive,
and new wine the young women.

The LORD Will Care for Judah

10 Ask the LORD for rain in the
springtime;
it is the LORD who sends the
thunderstorms.
He gives showers of rain to all
people,
and plants of the field to
everyone.
2 The idols[x] speak deceitfully,
diviners see visions that lie;
they tell dreams that are false,
they give comfort in vain.
Therefore the people wander like
sheep
oppressed for lack of a shepherd.[y]

3 "My anger burns against the
shepherds,
and I will punish the leaders;[z]
for the LORD Almighty will care
for his flock, the people of Judah,
and make them like a proud horse
in battle.
4 From Judah will come the
cornerstone,
from him the tent peg,[a]
from him the battle bow,[b]
from him every ruler.
5 Together they[b] will be like warriors
in battle
trampling their enemy into the
mud of the streets.[c]
They will fight because the LORD is
with them,
and they will put the enemy
horsemen to shame.[d]

6 "I will strengthen Judah
and save the tribes of Joseph.
I will restore them
because I have compassion on
them.[e]
They will be as though
I had not rejected them,
for I am the LORD their God
and I will answer[f] them.
7 The Ephraimites will become like
warriors,
and their hearts will be glad as
with wine.[g]
Their children will see it and be
joyful;
their hearts will rejoice in the
LORD.

9:14 [t] Isa 21:1; 66:15
9:15 [u] Isa 37:35; Zec 12:8 [v] Ex 27:2
9:16 [w] Isa 62:3; Jer 31:11
10:2 [x] Eze 21:21 [y] Eze 34:5; Hos 3:4; Mt 9:36
10:3 [z] Jer 25:34
10:4 [a] Isa 22:23 [b] Zec 9:10
10:5 [c] 2Sa 22:43 [d] Am 2:15; Hag 2:22
10:6 [e] Zec 8:7-8 [f] Zec 13:9
10:7 [g] Zec 9:15

[a] 15 *Or bowl, / like* [b] 4,5 *Or ruler, all of them together. / [5]They*

Divine Warrior. There is also a minor role for God's people in this battle. Protected by God, the people gain victory—not with sophisticated weapons but with the lowly sling, an allusion to David's victory over Goliath.

9:1–17 God is in control, and his past record and future promise reveal that he has no patience for the material splendor and military power of the nations. God's sovereign plan, however, should not be interpreted in an exclusively negative manner.

God envisions a community that transcends Israel's borders and ethnicity. The same is true for Christians today. In our pursuit of truth, justice, and redemption, we can villainize enemies of the faith to the point that we revel in their condemnation. As Christ associated with those considered far less than holy, so we need to reach out in love to those who are lost. We cannot lose sight of God's desire to bring blessing through us to all people.

10:1–2 The temptation to serve other gods was especially strong in matters related to agricultural activity. This connection between rain and idolatry is made explicit in v. 2.
10:3 God's desire is to shepherd his flock, but they have abandoned his leadership. God thus addresses the human shepherds who have led the community astray.
10:4–5 Verse 5 confirms that the previous verse refers to a group of leaders. The identity of this new leadership caste from Judah is not specified. It most likely involves royal leadership, which has led many to see here a reference to a future messianic figure.
10:6–8 The phrase "tribes of Joseph" (v. 6) refers

8 I will signal[h] for them
and gather them in.
Surely I will redeem them;
they will be as numerous[i] as before.
9 Though I scatter them among the peoples,
yet in distant lands they will remember me.[j]
They and their children will survive,
and they will return.
10 I will bring them back from Egypt
and gather them from Assyria.[k]
I will bring them to Gilead[l] and Lebanon,
and there will not be room[m] enough for them.
11 They will pass through the sea of trouble;
the surging sea will be subdued
and all the depths of the Nile will dry up.[n]
Assyria's pride[o] will be brought down
and Egypt's scepter[p] will pass away.
12 I will strengthen them in the LORD
and in his name they will live securely,[q]"
declares the LORD.

11 Open your doors, Lebanon,[r]
so that fire may devour your cedars!
2 Wail, you juniper, for the cedar has fallen;
the stately trees are ruined!
Wail, oaks of Bashan;
the dense forest[s] has been cut down!

10:8 [h] Isa 5:26 [i] Jer 33:22; Eze 36:11
10:9 [j] Eze 6:9
10:10 [k] Isa 11:11 [l] Jer 50:19 [m] Isa 49:19
10:11 [n] Isa 19:5-7; 51:10 [o] Zep 2:13 [p] Eze 30:13
10:12 [q] Mic 4:5
11:1 [r] Eze 31:3
11:2 [s] Isa 32:19
11:3 [t] Jer 2:15; 50:44
11:5 [u] Jer 50:7; Eze 34:2-3
11:6 [v] Zec 14:13 [w] Isa 9:19-21; Jer 13:14; Mic 5:8; 7:2-6

Zec 10:11-12 ❖ How has God led his people through the "sea of trouble"? When have we felt God still the chaos around us or strengthen us in the midst of it?

Zec 11:7-17 ❖ How do God's people show disregard for the Good Shepherd today? What causes the flock to—implicitly or explicitly—detest its Shepherd?

3 Listen to the wail of the shepherds;
their rich pastures are destroyed!
Listen to the roar of the lions;
the lush thicket of the Jordan is ruined![t]

Two Shepherds

4 This is what the LORD my God says:
"Shepherd the flock marked for slaughter. 5 Their buyers slaughter them and go
unpunished. Those who sell them say,
'Praise the LORD, I am rich!' Their own
shepherds do not spare them.[u] 6 For I will
no longer have pity on the people of the
land," declares the LORD. "I will give everyone into the hands of their neighbors[v]
and their king. They will devastate the
land, and I will not rescue anyone from
their hands."[w]
7 So I shepherded the flock marked for
slaughter, particularly the oppressed of
the flock. Then I took two staffs and
called one Favor and the other Union,
and I shepherded the flock. 8 In one
month I got rid of the three shepherds.
The flock detested me, and I grew

to tribes taken into exile when Samaria, their capital, fell to the Assyrians in the late eighth century BC. God promises to "save" this community and "restore" them to their former state. This promise links God's answer to an assumed cry from the exilic community: "I will answer them" (v. 6).
10:9-11 In v. 9 we are told that "in distant lands they will remember me." This kind of remembering involves the religious affections of the community.
God's restorative action is based on his compassion and his covenant. These defeated, depressed, and decimated people will become skilled warriors.
10:12 God now promises the same benefits the house of Judah enjoyed: to be strengthened by God. This strength will enable them to walk in his name. The restored community will regain control over their land.

✥ **10:1-12** As we face challenges and decisions in life, the one to whom we turn for wisdom and direction and the way in which we process that enlightenment are indicators of whom we ultimately trust. Whether those challenges are uncertain working conditions as the community in Zec 10 experienced, or fluctuating fortunes of financial markets and unpredictable changes in our physical condition, we must trust God's perspective on these issues, seek counsel from mature Christians, and reflect deeply on God's Word.

11:1-3 Verse 1 mixes metaphors by envisioning a fiery conflagration of great cedars that are protected within a city called Lebanon. Verse 2 picks up on the cedar of Lebanon but changes the imagery to cutting as the cedars are felled. The addressee in v. 3 is uncertain as the imagery shifts once again.
11:4-7 This exhortation makes the prophet a shepherd. The flock is destined for complete destruction. The positive intention of this shepherd is confirmed by the fact that he takes two staffs, called "Favor" and "Union" (v. 7).
11:8-9 Verse 8 signals the beginning of trouble for God's appointed shepherd. He must rid the flock

weary of them 9and said, "I will not be
your shepherd. Let the dying die, and the
perishing perish.[x] Let those who are left
eat one another's flesh."
10Then I took my staff called Favor[y]
and broke it, revoking[z] the covenant I
had made with all the nations. 11It was revoked on that day, and so the oppressed
of the flock who were watching me knew
it was the word of the LORD.
12I told them, "If you think it best, give
me my pay; but if not, keep it." So they
paid me thirty pieces of silver.[a]
13And the LORD said to me, "Throw it
to the potter" — the handsome price at
which they valued me! So I took the thirty pieces of silver and threw them to the
potter at the house of the LORD.[b]
14Then I broke my second staff called
Union, breaking the family bond between Judah and Israel.
15Then the LORD said to me, "Take
again the equipment of a foolish shepherd. 16For I am going to raise up a shepherd over the land who will not care for
the lost, or seek the young, or heal the
injured, or feed the healthy, but will eat
the meat of the choice sheep, tearing off
their hooves.

17"Woe to the worthless shepherd,[c]
who deserts the flock!
May the sword strike his arm[d] and
his right eye!
May his arm be completely
withered,
his right eye totally blinded!"[e]

11:9 [x]Jer 15:2; 43:11
11:10 [y]ver 7 [z]Ps 89:39; Jer 14:21
11:12 [a]Ex 21:32; Mt 26:15
11:13 [b]Mt 27:9-10*; Ac 1:18-19
11:17 [c]Jer 23:1 [d]Eze 30:21-22 [e]Jer 23:1

12:1 [f]Isa 42:5; Jer 51:15 [g]Ps 102:25; Heb 1:10 [h]Isa 57:16
12:2 [i]Ps 75:8 [j]Isa 51:23 [k]Zec 14:14
12:3 [l]Zec 14:2 [m]Da 2:34-35 [n]Mt 21:44
12:4 [o]Ps 76:6
12:6 [p]Isa 10:17-18; Zec 11:1 [q]Ob 18
12:7 [r]Jer 30:18; Am 9:11
12:8 [s]Joel 3:16; Zec 9:15

Jerusalem's Enemies to Be Destroyed

12 A prophecy: The word of the LORD
concerning Israel.

The LORD, who stretches out the heavens,[f] who lays the foundation of the
earth,[g] and who forms the human spirit
within a person,[h] declares: 2"I am going
to make Jerusalem a cup[i] that sends all
the surrounding peoples reeling.[j] Judah[k]
will be besieged as well as Jerusalem.
3On that day, when all the nations[l] of
the earth are gathered against her, I will
make Jerusalem an immovable rock[m]
for all the nations. All who try to move
it will injure[n] themselves. 4On that day I
will strike every horse with panic and its
rider with madness," declares the LORD.
"I will keep a watchful eye over Judah,
but I will blind all the horses of the nations.[o] 5Then the clans of Judah will say
in their hearts, 'The people of Jerusalem
are strong, because the LORD Almighty
is their God.'
6"On that day I will make the clans of
Judah like a firepot[p] in a woodpile, like a
flaming torch among sheaves. They will
consume[q] all the surrounding peoples
right and left, but Jerusalem will remain
intact in her place.
7"The LORD will save the dwellings
of Judah first, so that the honor of the
house of David and of Jerusalem's inhabitants may not be greater than that
of Judah.[r] 8On that day the LORD will
shield[s] those who live in Jerusalem, so
that the feeblest among them will be

---

of the uncaring shepherds of v. 5. The removal of these shepherds appears to cause a mutual rejection with serious results.

11:10–12 Before breaking the second staff in v. 14, the prophet reports his request that his wages be paid. The "them" of v. 12 most likely refers to the "nations" of v. 10, who are the buyers of v. 5. Having terminated his contract with these nations, the shepherd now requests his wages, but he gives them the option to refuse.

11:13–14 The prophet reports a second sign-act (v. 13). God instructs the shepherd to throw the payment to the "potter" in "the house of the LORD" (v. 13). The tone here is one of strong rejection of payment, highlighting the broken relationship with the nations. This signals an end to the covenant with the nations. The shepherd breaks the staff called "Union" (v. 14), an action that represents the shattering of the brotherhood between Judah and Israel.

11:15–16 Verse 15 introduces the final sign-act, where the Lord instructs the prophet to "take the equipment of a foolish shepherd." The folly of this shepherd is explained in v. 16. In stark contrast to the good shepherd, the foolish shepherd will turn on the remaining sheep and devour all edible meat.

11:17 The prophet pronounces judgment on shepherds who are compared with the inadequate shepherds of Ezekiel's day.

11:1–17 This chapter addresses serious leadership issues and is useful for addressing similar concerns in God's community today. One of the priorities of church leadership, whether clergy or laity, must be honest examination of motivations. The leader who is transparent in his direction and decisions and who invites honest examination displays strength, not weakness, and secures long-term vitality in ministry.

12:1 These snippets of praise establish Yahweh's right to proclaim the message and his ability to act against or for the recipients.

12:2–8 Taken together, four images emphasize God's victory over the surrounding nations through Jerusalem and Judah.

like David, and the house of David will
be like God,[t] like the angel of the LORD
going before[u] them. 9On that day I will
set out to destroy all the nations that
attack Jerusalem.[v]

Mourning for the One They Pierced

10"And I will pour out on the house
of David and the inhabitants of Jerusalem a spirit[a] of grace and supplication.[w]
They will look on[b] me, the one they have
pierced,[x] and they will mourn for him as
one mourns for an only child, and grieve
bitterly for him as one grieves for a firstborn son. 11On that day the weeping in
Jerusalem will be as great as the weeping
of Hadad Rimmon in the plain of Megiddo.[y] 12The land will mourn,[z] each clan by
itself, with their wives by themselves:
the clan of the house of David and their
wives, the clan of the house of Nathan
and their wives, 13the clan of the house of
Levi and their wives, the clan of Shimei
and their wives, 14and all the rest of the
clans and their wives.

Cleansing From Sin

13 "On that day a fountain[a] will be
opened to the house of David and
the inhabitants of Jerusalem, to cleanse[b]
them from sin and impurity.
2"On that day, I will banish the names
of the idols[c] from the land, and they will
be remembered no more," declares the
LORD Almighty. "I will remove both the
prophets[d] and the spirit of impurity from
the land. 3And if anyone still prophesies,
their father and mother, to whom they
were born, will say to them, 'You must
die, because you have told lies in the
LORD's name.' Then their own parents
will stab the one who prophesies.[e]
4"On that day every prophet will be
ashamed[f] of their prophetic vision. They
will not put on a prophet's garment[g] of
hair[h] in order to deceive. 5Each will say,
'I am not a prophet. I am a farmer; the
land has been my livelihood since my
youth.[c]'[i] 6If someone asks, 'What are
these wounds on your body[d]?' they will
answer, 'The wounds I was given at the
house of my friends.'

The Shepherd Struck, the Sheep Scattered

7"Awake, sword,[j] against my
shepherd,[k]
against the man who is close
to me!"

12:8 [t] Ps 82:6 [u] Mic 7:8
12:9 [v] Zec 14:2-3
12:10 [w] Isa 44:3; Eze 39:29; Joel 2:28-29 [x] Jn 19:34,37*; Rev 1:7
12:11 [y] 2Ki 23:29
12:12 [z] Mt 24:30; Rev 1:7
13:1 [a] Jer 17:13 [b] Ps 51:2; Heb 9:14
13:2 [c] Ex 23:13; Eze 36:25; Hos 2:17 [d] 1Ki 22:22; Jer 23:14-15
13:3 [e] Dt 13:6-11; 18:20; Jer 23:34; Eze 14:9
13:4 [f] Jer 6:15; Mic 3:6-7 [g] Mt 3:4 [h] 2Ki 1:8; Isa 20:2
13:5 [i] Am 7:14
13:7 [j] Jer 47:6 [k] Isa 40:11; 53:4; Eze 37:24

[a] 10 Or *the Spirit* [b] 10 Or *to* [c] 5 Or *farmer; a man sold me in my youth* [d] 6 Or *wounds between your hands*

Zec 12:10 ❖ How can this messianic prophecy inspire believers today?

12:9—13:1 Accompanying salvation from external forces will be an internal renewal. God's pouring out his Spirit declares his unique and manifest presence upon his people.

12:10-14 This passage describes the impact of God's Spirit (see NIV text note) on the community. The people mourn over the fact that they had "pierced" (v. 10) someone. Some see here an allusion to the suffering servant of Isa 53, a representative (often messianic) figure.

13:1 The term "fountain" here speaks of a spring that brings forth fresh water. The community has received the "spirit of grace and supplication" (12:10) in order to mourn their actions and be ritually cleansed.

13:2-5 We know that this metaphorical slaying has brought defilement, but what is the nature of this slaying? The people have rejected their God by turning to idolatry. In v. 2, impurity is clearly defined as idolatry and divination. The idols and their prophets will be removed from the land. The people will be so transformed that parents will enact the Torah's judgment against their own child—a hyperbolic image symbolizing passionate zeal for God.

13:6 This verse brings this section on false prophecy to a close. What should not be missed in all this is that God initiates these various aspects of renewal.

✣ **12:1—13:6** Sometimes guilt is used to motivate repentance, but 12:10 declares that it is the Spirit "of grace and supplication" that stimulates such response. This means that it is an operation of God within the heart of his community, which in the NT perspective means the work of the Holy Spirit within the life of believers. We do not conjure up this response to God; rather, it is *his* work. This is an important truth for the teacher as well as the hearer of the gospel, both of whom must rely on God for this divine work.

13:7-9 The sword is an image of death and judgment. The phrase "awake . . . against" (v. 7) is used for wielding a weapon in battle as well as for raising up an army. This sword is instructed to "strike" (v. 7). Because the image of the sword is connected with God's judgment, this shepherd is apparently someone who is struck as a result of some offense. This is not surprising in light of the many negative depictions of shepherds elsewhere in chs. 9-14.

Because of the loss of the shepherd, the flock will be scattered. This scattering leaves the "little ones" (v. 7) vulnerable to attack, which comes from God. This indicates that God will discipline the flock to purify them.

declares the LORD Almighty.
"Strike the shepherd,
and the sheep will be scattered,[l]
and I will turn my hand against
the little ones.
8 In the whole land," declares the
LORD,
"two-thirds will be struck down
and perish;
yet one-third will be left in it.[m]
9 This third I will put into the fire;[n]
I will refine them like silver[o]
and test them like gold.
They will call[p] on my name
and I will answer[q] them;
I will say, 'They are my people,'[r]
and they will say, 'The LORD is our
God.[s]' "

The LORD Comes and Reigns

14 A day of the LORD[t] is coming, Jerusalem, when your possessions
will be plundered and divided up within
your very walls.
2 I will gather all the nations to Jerusalem to fight against it; the city will
be captured, the houses ransacked, and
the women raped. Half of the city will
go into exile, but the rest of the people
will not be taken from the city.[u] 3 Then
the LORD will go out and fight[v] against
those nations, as he fights on a day of
battle. 4 On that day his feet will stand on
the Mount of Olives,[w] east of Jerusalem,
and the Mount of Olives will be split in
two from east to west, forming a great
valley, with half of the mountain moving north and half moving south. 5 You
will flee by my mountain valley, for it
will extend to Azel. You will flee as you
fled from the earthquake[a][x] in the days
of Uzziah king of Judah. Then the LORD
my God will come,[y] and all the holy ones
with him.[z]
6 On that day there will be neither sunlight[a] nor cold, frosty darkness. 7 It will
be a unique[b] day—a day known only to
the LORD—with no distinction between
day and night.[c] When evening comes,
there will be light.[d]
8 On that day living water[e] will flow
out from Jerusalem, half of it east[f] to the
Dead Sea and half of it west to the Mediterranean Sea, in summer and in winter.
9 The LORD will be king over the whole
earth.[g] On that day there will be one
LORD, and his name the only name.[h]

13:7 [l] Mt 26:31*; Mk 14:27*
13:8 [m] Eze 5:2-4,12
13:9 [n] Mal 3:2 [o] Isa 48:10; 1Pe 1:6-7 [p] Ps 50:15 [q] Zec 10:6 [r] Jer 30:22 [s] Jer 29:12
14:1 [t] Isa 13:9; Mal 4:1
14:2 [u] Isa 13:6; Zec 13:8
14:3 [v] Zec 9:14-15
14:4 [w] Eze 11:23
14:5 [x] Am 1:1 [y] Isa 29:6; 66:15-16 [z] Mt 16:27; 25:31
14:6 [a] Isa 13:10; Jer 4:23
14:7 [b] Jer 30:7 [c] Rev 21:23-25; 22:5 [d] Isa 30:26
14:8 [e] Eze 47:1-12; Jn 7:38; Rev 22:1-2 [f] Joel 2:20
14:9 [g] Dt 6:4; Isa 45:24; Rev 11:15 [h] Eph 4:5-6

[a] 5 Or *5My mountain valley will be blocked and will extend to Azel. It will be blocked as it was blocked because of the earthquake*

Zec 13:9 ❖ How does the refining work of God affect our lives? What things in our lives might still need to be "burned off" through God's refining fire?

Zec 14:8-9 ❖ How is God's living water flowing into the world today (see Jn 7:37-38)? How can we be part of this life-giving flow?

13:8-9 The process of purification is described in vv. 8-9 as the community is divided into thirds: a third struck with the sword (those who fall outside the city) and a third scattered to the wind (those who are exiled). The final third survives but then undergoes further discipline.

The second half of v. 9 reveals the result of this refining process: The covenant relationship between God and his people will be restored. God will declare them "my people" while they affirm that he is "our God" (v. 9).

✚ **13:7-9** A key theme throughout biblical theology is that of the remnant. God forms a holy community from sinful humanity. The gospel challenges the "health and wealth gospel" that promises physical well-being in exchange for accepting God's salvation and giving of time and money. In the NT account, when people devote their lives to Christ they are greeted more often with suffering rather than success. We should not be surprised, then, at suffering but rather should embrace it as part of God's purification of his remnant community (Ro 8:18-39; 1Pe 4:17).

14:1-2 The phrase "a day of the LORD is coming" (v. 1) emphasizes the doom about to strike the city. No reason is offered for this action, but one must assume that it is linked to the misdeeds of the people in the city.

14:3-5 While vv. 1-2 envision disaster for Jerusalem and its inhabitants, v. 3 signals a reversal of fortunes. The Lord enters the fight and marches out against the same nations that he previously sent against Jerusalem.

God's descent on the Mount of Olives wreaks havoc in the natural order. A newly created valley will be an escape route for those who have remained behind in Jerusalem. The valley will serve another purpose: to provide a path for the triumphal return of Yahweh to his seat of rule. The "holy ones" (v. 5) are the remnant who have fled from danger and now return under the protection of their Almighty God.

14:6-7 The vocabulary of v. 7 is reminiscent of the account of creation in Ge 1. This image of a future era with perpetual light is a regular feature of apocalyptic literature.

14:8-9 The transformation of the cosmos continues in v. 8. A flow of water from within Jerusalem will

10The whole land, from Geba[i] to Rimmon, south of Jerusalem, will become
like the Arabah. But Jerusalem will be
raised up[j] high from the Benjamin Gate
to the site of the First Gate, to the Corner
Gate, and from the Tower of Hananel to
the royal winepresses, and will remain
in its place.[k] 11It will be inhabited; never again will it be destroyed. Jerusalem
will be secure.[l]

12This is the plague with which the
LORD will strike all the nations that fought
against Jerusalem: Their flesh will rot
while they are still standing on their feet,
their eyes will rot in their sockets, and
their tongues will rot in their mouths.[m]
13On that day people will be stricken by
the LORD with great panic. They will seize
each other by the hand and attack one
another.[n] 14Judah[o] too will fight at Jerusalem. The wealth of all the surrounding
nations will be collected[p]—great quantities of gold and silver and clothing. 15A
similar plague[q] will strike the horses and
mules, the camels and donkeys, and all
the animals in those camps.

16Then the survivors from all the nations that have attacked Jerusalem will
go up year after year to worship the King,
the LORD Almighty, and to celebrate the
Festival of Tabernacles.[r] 17If any of the
peoples of the earth do not go up to Jerusalem to worship the King, the LORD
Almighty, they will have no rain.[s] 18If
the Egyptian people do not go up and
take part, they will have no rain. The
LORD[a] will bring on them the plague he
inflicts on the nations that do not go up
to celebrate the Festival of Tabernacles.[t]
19This will be the punishment of Egypt
and the punishment of all the nations
that do not go up to celebrate the Festival of Tabernacles.

20On that day HOLY TO THE LORD will be
inscribed on the bells of the horses, and
the cooking pots[u] in the LORD's house
will be like the sacred bowls[v] in front
of the altar. 21Every pot in Jerusalem
and Judah will be holy[w] to the LORD Almighty, and all who come to sacrifice will
take some of the pots and cook in them.
And on that day[x] there will no longer be
a Canaanite[b][y] in the house of the LORD
Almighty.[z]

14:10 [i] 1Ki 15:22 [j] Jer 30:18; Am 9:11 [k] Zec 12:6
14:11 [l] Eze 34:25-28
14:12 [m] Lev 26:16; Dt 28:22
14:13 [n] Zec 11:6
14:14 [o] Zec 12:2 [p] Isa 23:18
14:15 [q] ver 12
14:16 [r] Isa 60:6-9
14:17 [s] Jer 14:4; Am 4:7
14:18 [t] ver 12
14:20 [u] Eze 46:20 [v] Zec 9:15
14:21 [w] Ro 14:6-7; 1Co 10:31 [x] Ne 8:10 [y] Zec 9:8 [z] Eze 44:9

[a] *18* Or *part, then the LORD* [b] *21* Or *merchant*

---

exceed the needs of the city, running throughout the land and emptying into the Dead Sea and the Mediterranean Sea.

14:10–11 God's right to rule is linked to his power over the cosmos and nations. As Divine Warrior, he takes his legitimate place as king of the earth. Verse 10 envisions further transformation: Jerusalem will tower over the land to which all nations stream. According to v. 11, this elevated and spacious city will be filled with inhabitants who will enjoy security.

14:12–15 God strikes his opponents with a horrific plague that generates overwhelming panic among the nations. The defeat of the armies is confirmed by the collection of plunder. The animals suffer the same plague as the soldiers.

14:16–21 The fact that the nations participate in the celebration is not the only surprising feature of the final section of this chapter. There is a significant shift in perspective on ritual holiness in vv. 20–21. In this new Jerusalem, that which was unclean will be made clean.

This new ritual condition of Jerusalem and Judah will eliminate the need for merchants in the temple precincts. The term "Canaanite" in v. 21 can denote the merchant class that bought and sold goods. This verse indicates that there will be no more room for such merchants.

This final oracle brings not only chs. 9–14 but also the entire book of Zechariah to a climactic end. Its cosmic vision of the establishment of the kingship involves the appearance of the Divine Warrior. His very presence shakes the cosmos. It stirs the submission of both creation and culture to his mighty rule from his place where his presence resides: the temple in Jerusalem. God's people will be cleansed, and the nations will bend their knees. They will express their allegiance through worship at the place of his holy presence.

14:1–21 Zechariah 14 was written to a community with little reason for hope to raise their vision beyond their present circumstances, that they might see the world from God's eternal perspective and live accordingly. As Christians we need to hear this message of triumphant hope—not so that we can vindictively anticipate the downfall of our enemies, but so that we may be encouraged to live by faith in the present age, confident in the transforming message that we carry to others. We long for the arrival of Christ, who has come and will come again. Zechariah 14 grants us hope that our lives are not lived in vain, and that God will someday transform the cosmic and political structures of our world as he renews his creation.

Author: Malachi
Audience: The postexilic Jews living in Judah
Date: About 430 BC

Theme: Malachi, speaking for God, assures the postexilic Jewish community that when the Lord comes to judge, he will spare those who serve him.

PERSPECTIVE

Though the date when Malachi preached is somewhat uncertain, it seems most likely that he ministered between Nehemiah's first and second term as governor of Judah (see Introduction to Nehemiah). The sins he condemns bear similarity to the sins that Nehemiah had to deal with in his second term (Ne 13:4–31). But Malachi does more than merely point out these sins; Malachi pulls no punches. He calls the negligent priesthood to account, and he chastises the callous commoners who are ignoring their families. He also calls the people to renew their commitment to the Lord and his ways; only then will they begin to receive blessings from him.

Malachi's prophecy ends in a way fitting for the last book of the OT. He predicts the coming of a Messiah who will lead the people to the realization of all their dreams and hopes, a Messiah who would be announced by a prophet (who turned out to be John the Baptist).

For more perspective on this book, see the Introduction to Joel.

TAKING THE NEXT STEPS

Through the voice of Malachi, we receive some powerful practical messages. (1) The sins that Malachi unmasked and for which he condemned the people have a contemporary ring: materialism, hypocrisy, complacency, and divorce. (2) We must make tithes and offerings a priority in our lives for God to give us blessings. (3) Our God is a God of both love and justice, and he does not change. Therefore, we can

Reading Malachi

Malachi is the last of the twelve Minor Prophets, closing the collection of the Prophets—and, in the Protestant canon, the entire OT. The book itself is unique in the OT because of its form—a dispute or dialogue between God and those of his people who have become apathetic or even antagonistic to him. The prophecy closes with a look forward to the day of the Lord, a time of judg-

	1200 BC	1100	1000	900	800	700	600	500	400
Fall of Jerusalem (586 BC)									
First return of exiles to Jerusalem (538 BC)									
Ministries of Haggai and Zechariah (c. 520–480 BC)									
Completion of temple (516 BC)									
Second return to Jerusalem under Ezra (458 BC)									
Third return to Jerusalem under Nehemiah (444 BC)									
Malachi's ministry (c. 440–430 BC)									
Book of Malachi written (c. 430 BC)									

ment for those who refuse to follow God's ways.

A unique feature of Malachi's style is the dialogue between God and his people, through which God pointed out their sins and called them to repent and return to him. The people, on the other hand, responded with fruitless and impotent arguments.

Key Verses

"See, I will send the prophet Elijah to you before that great and dreadful day of the LORD comes. He will turn the hearts of the parents to their children, and the hearts of the children to their parents; or else I will come and strike the land with total destruction."

—Malachi 4:5-6

be sure that he will take away our guilt if we repent and turn to him, but he will judge us if we do not. (4) As a loving father, God pleads with us to recommit our lives to him and his ways.

WHAT TO LOOK FOR IN MALACHI

- A perspective on hypocritical worship (ch. 1)
- The coming of the Messiah (chs. 3–4)

1 A prophecy:[a] The word[b] of the LORD
to Israel through Malachi.[a]

Israel Doubts God's Love

2"I have loved[c] you," says the LORD.
"But you ask, 'How have you loved us?'
"Was not Esau Jacob's brother?" declares the LORD. "Yet I have loved Jacob,[d]
3but Esau I have hated, and I have turned
his hill country into a wasteland[e] and left
his inheritance to the desert jackals.[f]"
4Edom may say, "Though we have been
crushed, we will rebuild[g] the ruins."
But this is what the LORD Almighty
says: "They may build, but I will demolish. They will be called the Wicked Land,
a people always under the wrath of the
LORD.[h] 5You will see it with your own
eyes and say, 'Great[i] is the LORD—even
beyond the borders of Israel!'[j]

Breaking Covenant Through Blemished Sacrifices

6"A son honors his father, and a slave
his master. If I am a father, where is the
honor due me? If I am a master, where
is the respect[k] due me?" says the LORD
Almighty.[l]
"It is you priests who show contempt
for my name.
"But you ask, 'How have we shown
contempt for your name?'
7"By offering defiled food[m] on my
altar.

1:1 [a]Na 1:1 [b]1Pe 4:11
1:2 [c]Dt 4:37 [d]Ro 9:13*
1:3 [e]Isa 34:10 [f]Eze 35:3-9
1:4 [g]Isa 9:10 [h]Eze 25:12-14
1:5 [i]Ps 35:27; Mic 5:4 [j]Am 1:11-12
1:6 [k]Isa 1:2 [l]Job 5:17
1:7 [m]ver 12; Lev 21:6

[a] 1 *Malachi* means *my messenger.*

1:1–2 Verses 1–5 recall the strained relationship between Jacob and his brother, Esau. The first statement God makes is that he loves them (v. 2).
1:2–3 This statement pair (love-hate) concerns election rather than emotions: Jacob (and his line) is chosen by God while Esau (and his line) is peripheral to the story of God's continued activity in the Bible. God's "hate" for Esau is expressed in geographic terms. Rather than a place of refuge, it will be a "wasteland" ruined by warfare.
1:4–5 Judah, who questions God's love, will experience it (v. 5). They are loved, even if they do not respond in kind.

APPLICATION ✚ 1:1–5 God maintains covenant love with his chosen people even though they regularly "un-chose" him. This kind of covenantal, committed love must serve as a model to all believers, since we are to love each other as God, in the person of Jesus his Son, loves us (Jn 13:34).

1:6–7 God expected sacrifices and offerings to be taken from his good gifts and returned to him. They represented one's love, loyalty, honor, and sometimes sorrow for sin and wrongdoing. However, instead of respect, God receives "contempt" (v. 6).

PEOPLE TO KNOW // MALACHI

MALACHI 1:1: Malachi ministered after the Jews had returned from exile and rebuilt Jerusalem. While they were glad to once again have a temple and their land, they wondered whether God would do great things again or if God had somehow forgotten about them. They began to doubt God's love.

As the people's experience of God began to feel less vibrant, their lifestyles and morals became emptier. They worshiped only in the most token way, not with sincerity or much care. They stopped giving God the best they had to offer. The priests failed to teach and demonstrate righteousness. The people stopped caring for one another. Men started freely divorcing their wives instead of committing to their safety and protection.

Malachi lamented the people's apathy and sinful actions. He foresaw God sending a mighty messenger to prepare the way for the Lord, who would come to purify and to judge. Malachi calls that messenger Elijah (Mal 4:5), the great prophet who confronted the evil of Ahab and Jezebel (1Ki 18). This "Elijah" would turn the hearts of parents back toward their children and the hearts of children back to their parents, restoring justice in the land. Jesus told his disciples that Malachi's prophecy about Elijah was fulfilled through John the Baptist (Mt 11:14).

APPLICATION ✚ It is easy to relate to the conditions in which Malachi ministered. Still today our worship of God can become empty routine and our lifestyles might reflect the world's values more than God's. Malachi's message should wake us up from our spiritual slumbers. God takes our worship and our treatment of one another seriously. It's important to give God our best and to show love and justice in this world. For those who follow Malachi's message through John the Baptist and place their trust in Jesus, the day of Christ's return will not be a day of sorrow but a day of joy.

"But you ask, 'How have we defiled you?'

"By saying that the LORD's table is contemptible. 8 When you offer blind animals for sacrifice, is that not wrong? When you sacrifice lame or diseased animals,[n] is that not wrong? Try offering them to your governor! Would he be pleased with you? Would he accept you?" says the LORD Almighty.[o]

9 "Now plead with God to be gracious to us. With such offerings[p] from your hands, will he accept you?"—says the LORD Almighty.

10 "Oh, that one of you would shut the temple doors, so that you would not light useless fires on my altar! I am not pleased[q] with you," says the LORD Almighty, "and I will accept no offering[r] from your hands. 11 My name will be great among the nations, from where the sun rises to where it sets. In every place incense[s] and pure offerings will be brought to me, because my name will be great among the nations," says the LORD Almighty.

12 "But you profane it by saying, 'The Lord's table is defiled,' and, 'Its food[t] is contemptible.' 13 And you say, 'What a burden!'[u] and you sniff at it contemptuously," says the LORD Almighty.

"When you bring injured, lame or diseased animals and offer them as sacrifices, should I accept them from your hands?" says the LORD. 14 "Cursed is the cheat who has an acceptable male in his flock and vows to give it, but then sacrifices a blemished animal[v] to the Lord. For I am a great king,[w]" says the LORD Almighty, "and my name is to be feared among the nations.

1:8 [n] Lev 22:22; Dt 15:21 [o] Isa 43:23
1:9 [p] Lev 23:33-44
1:10 [q] Hos 5:6 [r] Isa 1:11-14; Jer 14:12
1:11 [s] Isa 60:6-7; Rev 8:3
1:12 [t] ver 7
1:13 [u] Isa 43:22-24
1:14 [v] Lev 22:18-21 [w] 1Ti 6:15
2:1 [x] ver 7
2:2 [y] Dt 28:20
2:3 [z] Ex 29:14 [a] 1Ki 14:10
2:4 [b] Nu 3:12
2:5 [c] Dt 33:9 [d] Nu 25:12
2:6 [e] Dt 33:10 [f] Jer 23:22; Jas 5:19-20
2:7 [g] Jer 18:18 [h] Nu 27:21 [i] Lev 10:11

Mal 1:6-9 ❖ When have we offered God less than our best? What does offering God the best of what we have mean for us today?

Additional Warning to the Priests

2 "And now, you priests, this warning is for you.[x] 2 If you do not listen, and if you do not resolve to honor my name," says the LORD Almighty, "I will send a curse[y] on you, and I will curse your blessings. Yes, I have already cursed them, because you have not resolved to honor me.

3 "Because of you I will rebuke your descendants[a]; I will smear on your faces the dung[z] from your festival sacrifices, and you will be carried off with it.[a] 4 And you will know that I have sent you this warning so that my covenant with Levi[b] may continue," says the LORD Almighty. 5 "My covenant was with him, a covenant[c] of life and peace,[d] and I gave them to him; this called for reverence and he revered me and stood in awe of my name. 6 True instruction[e] was in his mouth and nothing false was found on his lips. He walked with me in peace and uprightness, and turned many from sin.[f]

7 "For the lips of a priest[g] ought to preserve knowledge, because he is the messenger[h] of the LORD Almighty and people seek instruction from his mouth.[i]

[a] 3 Or *will blight your grain*

1:8-10 The priests know that what they are doing is "wrong" (v. 8). God is calling for the temple doors to close to protect the priests themselves from doing further unacceptable acts. Any such offerings are "useless" (v. 10), having no effect.
1:11-13 God's name extends "among the nations" (v. 11). In emphatic contrast with the rest of the world who worship God correctly, the author returns to the priests who do not do so. Inner contempt is exemplified by outward actions: bringing unacceptable sacrifices.
1:14 Yahweh is the only true Lord and should be treated as such.

1:6-14 We offer God our second best, thinking what we are able to do is good enough. Try offering that to a boss (cf. "the governor," v. 8), suggesting that he or she pay for forty hours of work a week when we really only work thirty. That would not be good enough for an earthly boss, so why should we think half-hearted worship is good enough for God? Should we expect him to accept our second-best offerings? "Good enough" seldom is.

2:1-3 Yahweh strongly warns the priests. Now no longer able to perform their functions, which require ritual purity, the priests are expelled from the camp like unclean animal remains.
2:4-5 From the human perspective of the priests, the admonition/covenant involves ritual purity and ministry. In contrast, from the perspective of Yahweh Almighty, it involves the blessings spelled out in the next verse. The priests are again reminded that while the covenant is with Levi, it originates with God alone ("*my* covenant," v. 5).
2:6-9 The ideal established by Levi is that his descendants, the priests, should live what they speak (v. 7). The priests stand in stark contrast to this ideal, however. They are humiliated "before all the people" (v. 9). Those in whose presence the humiliation occurs are most likely the same as the "many" of vv. 6 and 8.

8But you have turned from the way and
by your teaching have caused many to
stumble;[j] you have violated the covenant
with Levi," says the LORD Almighty. 9"So
I have caused you to be despised[k] and
humiliated before all the people, because
you have not followed my ways but have
shown partiality in matters of the law."

Breaking Covenant Through Divorce

10Do we not all have one Father[a]?[l] Did
not one God create us? Why do we profane the covenant[m] of our ancestors by
being unfaithful to one another?

11Judah has been unfaithful. A detestable thing has been committed in Israel
and in Jerusalem: Judah has desecrated
the sanctuary the LORD loves by marrying[n] women who worship a foreign god.[o]
12As for the man who does this, whoever
he may be, may the LORD remove[p] him
from the tents of Jacob[b]—even though
he brings an offering[q] to the LORD Almighty.

13Another thing you do: You flood the
LORD's altar with tears. You weep and
wail because he no longer looks with favor[r] on your offerings or accepts them
with pleasure from your hands. 14You
ask, "Why?" It is because the LORD is the
witness between you and the wife of your
youth.[s] You have been unfaithful to her,
though she is your partner, the wife of
your marriage covenant.

2:8 [j] Jer 18:15
2:9 [k] 1Sa 2:30
2:10 [l] 1Co 8:6 [m] Ex 19:5
2:11 [n] Ne 13:23 [o] Ezr 9:1; Jer 3:7-9
2:12 [p] Eze 24:21 [q] Mal 1:10
2:13 [r] Jer 14:12
2:14 [s] Pr 5:18
2:15 [t] Ge 2:24; Mt 19:4-6 [u] 1Co 7:14
2:16 [v] Dt 24:1; Mt 5:31-32; 19:4-9
2:17 [w] Isa 43:24
3:1 [x] Isa 40:3; Mt 11:10*; Mk 1:2*; Lk 7:27*

Mal 2:13-16 ❖ How can Christians protect and promote strong, God-honoring marriages?

15Has not the one God made you?[t] You
belong to him in body and spirit. And
what does the one God seek? Godly offspring.[c][u] So be on your guard, and do not
be unfaithful to the wife of your youth.

16"The man who hates and divorces his
wife,[v]" says the LORD, the God of Israel,
"does violence to the one he should protect,"[d] says the LORD Almighty.

So be on your guard, and do not be
unfaithful.

Breaking Covenant Through Injustice

17You have wearied[w] the LORD with
your words.

"How have we wearied him?" you ask.

By saying, "All who do evil are good in
the eyes of the LORD, and he is pleased
with them" or "Where is the God of justice?"

3 "I will send my messenger, who will
prepare the way before me.[x] Then

[a] *10* Or *father* [b] *12* Or *[12]May the LORD remove from the tents of Jacob anyone who gives testimony in behalf of the man who does this* [c] *15* The meaning of the Hebrew for the first part of this verse is uncertain. [d] *16* Or *"I hate divorce," says the LORD, the God of Israel, "because the man who divorces his wife covers his garment with violence,"*

❖ **2:1-9** We teach by our words, but we also teach by our lives. This is the definition of "integrity"—an unbroken wholeness where there is no gap between words and deeds in the matter under discussion. This integrity must characterize the life of the Israelite priest as well as that of each Christian as a member of a kingdom of priests (Ex 19:6; Rev 1:6).

2:10-13 These wrongdoers attempt to cover their continuing sin by surface religiosity. The use of three terms of emotional distress ("tears," "weep," "wail"; v. 13) denotes extreme agitation. All three arise from a break in the relationship between Israel and their covenant God. As long as Yahweh no longer acknowledges the value of their ritual, the relationship is severed.

2:14-16 The passage ends with a human picture of broken relationship (in marriage) that exemplifies the breach in the divine-human relationship.

❖ **2:10-16** Domestic abuse among its members is one area in which the church should hang its head in shame. Based on an incorrect reading of 2:16, spouses who have asked for help have been callously sent back into this abuse. This is coupled with a misunderstanding of another passage about submission (Eph 5:22).

How should we address this problem in the light of both Malachi and Paul? A valid reading is to see domestic violence as being like a divorce: If a spouse has done this, they have de facto broken the covenant relationship, initiating a divorce in a hateful way. Malachi's image leaves no doubt as to the seriousness of this offense.

2:17 Israel questions God's personal character. The disturbing claim is that evil is in fact "good." In a second statement, they question God's "justice."

3:1-5 Yahweh strongly refutes the accusations against his character, indicating his action is imminent. The people are facing "the day of his coming" (v. 2), referred to in other prophecies as the "day of the LORD" (see 4:1, 3). He comes first as a "refiner's fire" (3:3). The prophets use this process to signify eliminating sinful behavior through the fire of God's judgment and wrath. Yahweh serves as a witness to "testify" (v. 5) against an array of evildoers.

suddenly the Lord you are seeking will
come to his temple; the messenger of the
covenant, whom you desire, will come,"
says the LORD Almighty.
2But who can endure[y] the day of his
coming? Who can stand when he appears? For he will be like a refiner's fire[z]
or a launderer's soap. 3He will sit as a refiner and purifier of silver;[a] he will purify[b] the Levites and refine them like gold
and silver. Then the LORD will have men
who will bring offerings in righteousness, 4and the offerings[c] of Judah and
Jerusalem will be acceptable to the LORD,
as in days gone by, as in former years.[d]
5"So I will come to put you on trial. I
will be quick to testify against sorcerers,
adulterers and perjurers,[e] against those
who defraud laborers of their wages,[f]
who oppress the widows[g] and the fatherless, and deprive the foreigners among
you of justice, but do not fear me," says
the LORD Almighty.

Breaking Covenant by Withholding Tithes

6"I the LORD do not change.[h] So you,
the descendants of Jacob, are not destroyed. 7Ever since the time of your ancestors you have turned away[i] from my
decrees and have not kept them. Return
to me, and I will return to you,"[j] says the
LORD Almighty.
"But you ask, 'How are we to return?'

3:2 [y] Eze 22:14; Rev 6:17 [z] Zec 13:9; Mt 3:10-12
3:3 [a] Da 12:10 [b] Isa 1:25
3:4 [c] 2Ch 7:12; Ps 51:19; Mal 1:11 [d] 2Ch 7:3
3:5 [e] Jer 7:9 [f] Lev 19:13; Jas 5:4 [g] Ex 22:22
3:6 [h] Nu 23:19; Jas 1:17
3:7 [i] Jer 7:26; Ac 7:51 [j] Zec 1:3

Mal 3:6-7 ❖ How does God's unchanging nature guarantee salvation for his children? What comfort do we take in the unchanging nature of God?

✣ **2:17—3:5** Too many Christians today believe and act like one part of life is religious and the rest is secular. Healing from this harmful spiritual idea is much needed. We need to open our eyes to eliminate this artificial and unbiblical separation. Every act believers do has religious significance in this world; when we acknowledge that, we acknowledge that every inch of this world and of our lives belongs only to God.

3:6 Yahweh has not changed. Because God is steadfast, Israel is "not destroyed" even though she deserves it. Hope is not lost, however, since God makes an offer to his people: Mutual restoration is possible if only they return to him.
3:7 The people dispute with God again. While this could be interpreted as an honest act of repentance, it is more likely a sarcastic protest of innocence.

CHARACTER OF GOD // GOD IS IMMUTABLE

Malachi 3:6: "I the LORD do not change."

The Bible teaches that God does not change. This characteristic of God is called "immutability." As an old Christian hymn declares, there is "no shadow"—not even a hint or a suggestion—"of turning" with God. James says the same thing: God "does not change like shifting shadows" (Jas 1:17).

The fact that God is unchanging is a necessary result of God's other attributes, especially God's perfect knowledge, power, and omnipresence. Since God knows the future and is all-powerful in accomplishing the future he desires, God will *never* change. God established his plans before creation itself, including his plan of salvation (see Eph 1:4). Since God is all-powerful and all-knowing, no surprise could ever catch God off guard and cause him to change.

Far from making God static and inert, James sees God's immutability as a cause for joy. God's unchanging nature means God's goodness will never stop. God will continue to pour out his blessings and mercy upon his people. Since God will never change, he will never cease to be loving and compassionate.

APPLICATION ✣ Few things are more frustrating than unpredictable behavior in others. If we work for someone who is inconsistent and volatile, we will never feel settled or safe. Fortunately, God is not unpredictable. God will not love us one day and turn from us the next. God's immutability assures us that we can always be confident in him, knowing that our hope in him will never be disappointed. God's love and mercy will always be upon us, because God will never change.

8“Will a mere mortal rob God? Yet you
rob me.
“But you ask, ‘How are we robbing
you?’
“In tithes[k] and offerings. 9You are under a curse—your whole nation—because you are robbing me. 10Bring the
whole tithe into the storehouse,[l] that
there may be food in my house. Test me
in this,” says the LORD Almighty, “and see
if I will not throw open the floodgates[m]
of heaven and pour out so much blessing
that there will not be room enough to
store it. 11I will prevent pests from devouring your crops, and the vines in your
fields will not drop their fruit before it
is ripe,” says the LORD Almighty. 12“Then
all the nations will call you blessed,[n] for
yours will be a delightful land,”[o] says the
LORD Almighty.

Israel Speaks Arrogantly Against God

13“You have spoken arrogantly[p] against
me,” says the LORD.
“Yet you ask, ‘What have we said
against you?’
14“You have said, ‘It is futile[q] to serve
God. What do we gain by carrying out
his requirements and going about like
mourners[r] before the LORD Almighty?
15But now we call the arrogant blessed.
Certainly evildoers[s] prosper, and even
when they put God to the test, they get
away with it.’”

3:8 [k]Ne 13:10-12
3:10 [l]Ne 13:12 [m]2Ki 7:2
3:12 [n]Isa 61:9 [o]Isa 62:4
3:13 [p]Mal 2:17
3:14 [q]Ps 73:13 [r]Isa 58:3
3:15 [s]Jer 7:10
3:16 [t]Ps 34:15 [u]Ps 56:8
3:17 [v]Dt 7:6 [w]Ps 103:13; Isa 26:20
3:18 [x]Ge 18:25
4:1 [y]Joel 2:31 [z]Isa 5:24; Ob 18
4:2 [a]Lk 1:78; Eph 5:14 [b]Isa 30:26 [c]Isa 35:6
4:3 [d]Job 40:12 [e]Eze 28:18

The Faithful Remnant

16Then those who feared the LORD
talked with each other, and the LORD
listened and heard.[t] A scroll[u] of remembrance was written in his presence concerning those who feared the LORD and
honored his name.
17“On the day when I act,” says the
LORD Almighty, “they will be my treasured possession.[v] I will spare[w] them,
just as a father has compassion and
spares his son who serves him. 18And
you will again see the distinction between the righteous[x] and the wicked,
between those who serve God and those
who do not.

Judgment and Covenant Renewal

4 [a] “Surely the day is coming;[y] it will
burn like a furnace. All the arrogant and every evildoer will be stubble,[z]
and the day that is coming will set them
on fire,” says the LORD Almighty. “Not
a root or a branch will be left to them.
2But for you who revere my name, the
sun of righteousness[a] will rise with healing[b] in its rays. And you will go out and
frolic[c] like well-fed calves. 3Then you
will trample[d] on the wicked; they will
be ashes[e] under the soles of your feet
on the day when I act,” says the LORD
Almighty.

[a] In Hebrew texts 4:1-6 is numbered 3:19-24.

3:8–9 God asserts that the people are robbers, and the results of repeatedly robbing God are severe: They are “cursed” (v. 9). This refers to the hardships faced by the postexilic Hebrew community.
3:10 The prophet provides a remedy for Israelite wrongdoings: Present the tithe. The purpose of bringing the tithes is providing food and other items for the house of God.
3:11–12 God promises to open the heavenly floodgates. Rather than drought, water pours out. Judah will become a “delightful land” (v. 12). Where previously God was not delighted with useless sacrifices, now that the correct covenant relationship is restored, delight and acceptance are restored as well.

> ✣ **3:6–12** There is a wider issue beyond this particular passage. God’s promises do not change, but neither do their recipients. God pledges blessings, but they are conditional. The recipients of God’s blessings are those who obey the Lord. When we act like redeemed children of God, we will be treated as such.

3:13–15 For the last time, Malachi’s hearers dispute a divine claim. They are questioning the worth of following and serving God.
3:16–18 Verse 16 shows the more acceptable response of others in the prophet’s audience. This group is made up of God-fearers who show appropriate awe and reverence for God and his ways. Yahweh’s “scroll of remembrance” (v. 16) is like the Persian record kept for royal consultation. God continues to declare his actions in his pity, compassion, and grace sparing the people from the punishment that they deserve.
4:1 The coming day is now more clearly defined. A characteristic of this day is indicated by how it comes: with burning. God’s fiery judgment is so fierce that nothing remains. Judgment is not the final word for all of Judah, however—only for the wicked. Since evildoers are to be destroyed, the remaining faithful who revere God’s name are blessed.
4:2–3 The “sun of righteousness” (v. 2) has been understood as referring to God himself, a divine title with messianic overtones. This is a fitting image to show evidence of a new day dawning.

4"Remember the law[f] of my servant
Moses, the decrees and laws I gave him
at Horeb for all Israel.
5"See, I will send the prophet Elijah[g] to
you before that great and dreadful day of
the LORD comes.[h] 6He will turn the hearts
of the parents to their children,[i] and the
hearts of the children to their parents;
or else I will come and strike[j] the land
with total destruction."[k]

4:4 [f] Ps 147:19
4:5 [g] Mt 11:14; Lk 1:17 [h] Joel 2:31
4:6 [i] Lk 1:17 [j] Isa 11:4; Rev 19:15 [k] Zec 5:3

Mal 4:5–6 ❖ How do Malachi's observations about the relationships between parents and children resonate in our minds as they form the last words of the OT?

4:4 The audience is commanded to "remember" and act upon the Mosaic Law, just as God himself remembers his covenant. The biblical notion of remembering also requires faithful obedience. **4:5–6** Before the new day arrives, another event will precede it. God is about to send a messenger in the person of Elijah. Elijah's mysterious disappearance—with no mention of his death (2Ki 2:11–12)—leaves open the possibility of his reappearing and continuing his prophetic ministry. In Malachi, this ministry becomes associated with the coming day of Yahweh. Elijah's ministry will be one of restoration and repentance, something God desires.

3:13—4:6 Christian communion is a reminder of the great sacrificial work of Christ on the cross. In eating and drinking the meal we make a covenant commitment to God, symbolically and sacrificially offering ourselves. Remembering also has future ramifications. It directs us to the initial, close relationship between God and humanity as established in creation, pointing to the coming day when the human-divine relationship will be restored not by human effort but by divine sacrifice.

THE NEW TESTAMENT

New Testament Chronology

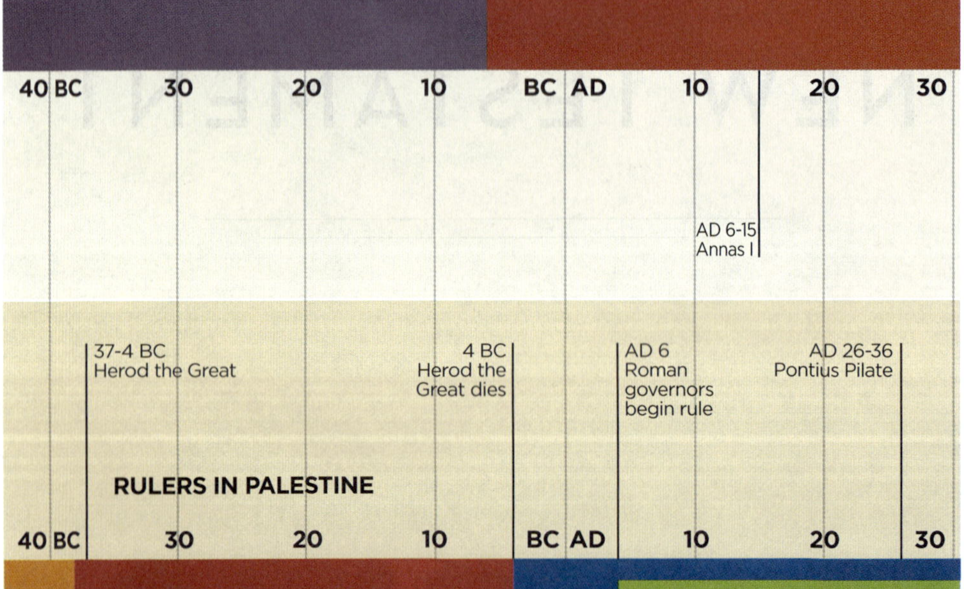

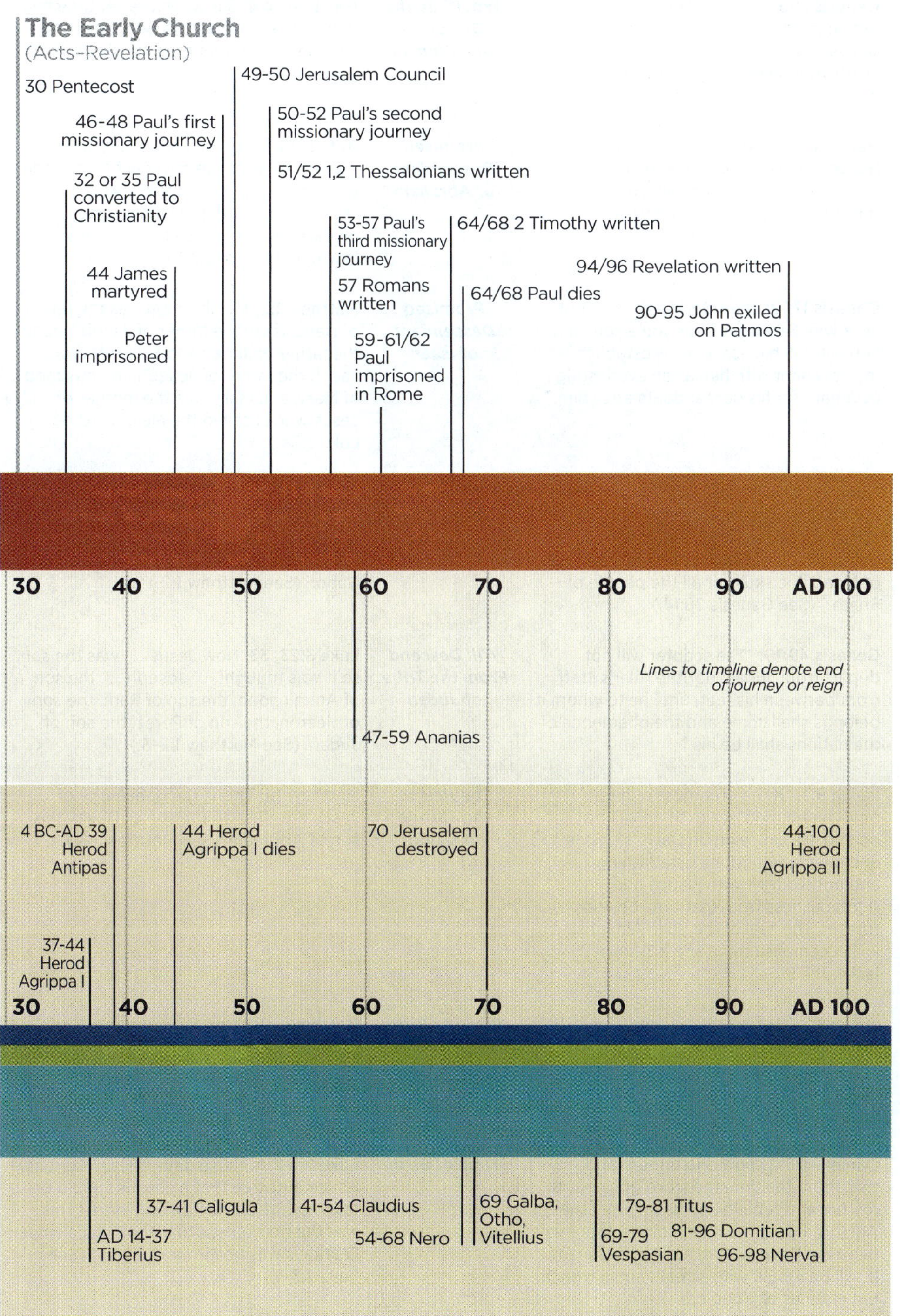
The Early Church
(Acts–Revelation)
30 Pentecost
46-48 Paul's first missionary journey
32 or 35 Paul converted to Christianity
44 James martyred
Peter imprisoned
49-50 Jerusalem Council
50-52 Paul's second missionary journey
51/52 1,2 Thessalonians written
53-57 Paul's third missionary journey
57 Romans written
59-61/62 Paul imprisoned in Rome
64/68 2 Timothy written
64/68 Paul dies
94/96 Revelation written
90-95 John exiled on Patmos
30
40
50
60
70
80
90
AD 100
Lines to timeline denote end of journey or reign
47-59 Ananias
4 BC-AD 39 Herod Antipas
37-44 Herod Agrippa I
44 Herod Agrippa I dies
70 Jerusalem destroyed
44-100 Herod Agrippa II
30
40
50
60
70
80
90
AD 100
AD 14-37 Tiberius
37-41 Caligula
41-54 Claudius
54-68 Nero
69 Galba, Otho, Vitellius
69-79 Vespasian
79-81 Titus
81-96 Domitian
96-98 Nerva

MESSIANIC PROPHECIES AND THEIR FULFILLMENT ARRANGED CHRONOLOGICALLY

PROPHECIES	SUMMARY	FULFILLMENT
Genesis 3:15: "And I will put enmity between you and the woman, and between your offspring and hers; he will crush your head, and you will strike his heel."	***Would Be the "Offspring" of a Woman***	**Galatians 4:4:** But when the set time had fully come, God sent his Son, born of a woman, born under the law. (See Luke 2:7; Revelation 12:5.)
Genesis 18:18: Abraham will surely become a great and powerful nation, and all nations on earth will be blessed through him. (See also Genesis 12:3.)	***Promised Descendant of Abraham***	**Acts 3:25:** "And you are heirs of the prophets and of the covenant God made with your fathers. He said to Abraham, 'Through your offspring all peoples on earth will be blessed.'" (See also Matthew 1:1; Luke 3:34.)
Genesis 17:19: Then God said, "Yes, but your wife Sarah will bear you a son, and you will call him Isaac. I will establish my covenant with him as an everlasting covenant for his descendants after him."	***Promised Descendant of Isaac***	**Matthew 1:2, 16:** Abraham was the father of Isaac, Isaac the father of Jacob, Jacob the father of Judah and his brothers . . . Jacob the father of Joseph, the husband of Mary, and Mary was the mother of Jesus who is called the Messiah. (See Luke 3:34.)
Numbers 24:17: "I see him, but not now; I behold him, but not near. A star will come out of Jacob; a scepter will rise out of Israel. He will crush the foreheads of Moab, the skulls of all the people of Sheth." (See Genesis 28:14.)	***Promised Descendant of Jacob***	**Luke 3:23, 34:** Now Jesus himself . . . was the son, so it was thought, of Joseph . . . the son of Jacob, the son of Isaac, the son of Abraham, the son of Terah, the son of Nahor. (See Matthew 1:2.)
Genesis 49:10: "The scepter will not depart from Judah, nor the ruler's staff from between his feet, until he to whom it belongs shall come and the obedience of the nations shall be his."	***Will Descend From the Tribe of Judah***	**Luke 3:23, 33:** Now Jesus . . . was the son, so it was thought, of Joseph . . . the son of Amminadab, the son of Ram, the son of Hezron, the son of Perez, the son of Judah. (See Matthew 1:2–3.)
Isaiah 9:7: Of the greatness of his government and peace there will be no end. He will reign on David's throne and over his kingdom, establishing and upholding it with justice and righteousness from that time on and forever. The zeal of the LORD Almighty will accomplish this. (See 2 Samuel 7:13; Isaiah 11:1–5.)	***The Heir to the Throne of David***	**Matthew 1:1:** This is the genealogy of Jesus the Messiah the son of David, the son of Abraham. (See Matthew 1:6.)
Micah 5:2: "But you, Bethlehem Ephrathah, though you are small among the clans of Judah, out of you will come for me one who will be ruler over Israel, whose origins are from of old, from ancient times."	***Place of Birth***	**Matthew 2:1:** After Jesus was born in Bethlehem in Judea, during the time of King Herod, Magi from the east came to Jerusalem. (See Luke 2:4–7.)
Daniel 9:25: "Know and understand this: From the time the word goes out to restore and rebuild Jerusalem until the Anointed One, the ruler, comes, there will be seven 'sevens,' and sixty-two 'sevens.' It will be rebuilt with streets and a trench, but in times of trouble."	***Time of Birth***	**Luke 2:1–2:** In those days Caesar Augustus issued a decree that a census should be taken of the entire Roman world. (This was the first census that took place while Quirinius was governor of Syria.) (See Luke 2:3–7.)

PROPHECIES	SUMMARY	FULFILLMENT
Isaiah 7:14: "Therefore the Lord himself will give you a sign: The virgin will conceive and give birth to a son, and will call him Immanuel."	***Born of a Virgin***	**Matthew 1:18:** This is how the birth of Jesus the Messiah came about: His mother Mary was pledged to be married to Joseph, but before they came together, she was found to be pregnant through the Holy Spirit. (See Luke 1:26-35.)
Jeremiah 31:15: This is what the LORD says: "A voice is heard in Ramah, mourning and great weeping, Rachel weeping for her children and refusing to be comforted, because they are no more."	***Massacre of Infants***	**Matthew 2:16:** When Herod realized that he had been outwitted by the Magi, he was furious, and he gave orders to kill all the boys in Bethlehem and its vicinity who were two years old and under, in accordance with the time he had learned from the Magi. (See Matthew 2:17, 18.)
Hosea 11:1: When Israel was a child, I loved him, and out of Egypt I called my son.	***Flight Into Egypt***	**Matthew 2:14:** So he got up, took the child and his mother during the night and left for Egypt. (See Matthew 2:15.)
Isaiah 9:1-2: Nevertheless, there will be no more gloom for those who were in distress. In the past he humbled the land of Zebulun and the land of Naphtali, but in the future he will honor Galilee of the nations, by the Way of the Sea, beyond the Jordan—The people walking in darkness have seen a great light; on those living in the land of deep darkness a light has dawned.	***Ministry in Galilee***	**Matthew 4:12-16:** When Jesus heard that John had been put in prison, he withdrew to Galilee. Leaving Nazareth, he went and lived in Capernaum, which was by the lake in the area of Zebulun and Naphtali—to fulfill what was said through the prophet Isaiah: "Land of Zebulun and land of Naphtali, the Way of the Sea, beyond the Jordan, Galilee of the Gentiles—the people living in darkness have seen a great light; on those living in the land of the shadow of death a light has dawned."
Deuteronomy 18:15: The LORD your God will raise up for you a prophet like me from among you, from your fellow Israelites. You must listen to him.	***As a Prophet***	**John 6:14:** After the people saw the sign Jesus performed, they began to say, "Surely this is the Prophet who is to come into the world." (See John 1:45; Acts 3:19-26.)
Psalm 110:4: The LORD has sworn and will not change his mind: "You are a priest forever, in the order of Melchizedek."	***As a Priest, Like Melchizedek,***	**Hebrews 6:20:** Jesus . . . has become a high priest forever, in the order of Melchizedek. (See Hebrews 5:5-6; 7:15-17.)
Isaiah 53:3: He was despised and rejected by mankind, a man of suffering, and familiar with pain. Like one from whom people hide their faces he was despised, and we held him in low esteem. (See Psalm 2:2.)	***His Rejection by Jews***	**John 1:11:** He came to that which was his own, but his own did not receive him. (See Luke 4:29; 17:25; 23:18; John 5:43.)
Isaiah 11:2: The Spirit of the LORD will rest on him—the Spirit of wisdom and of understanding, the Spirit of counsel and of might, the Spirit of the knowledge and fear of the LORD. (See Psalm 45:7; Isaiah 11:3-4.)	***Some of His Characteristics***	**Luke 2:52:** And Jesus grew in wisdom and stature, and in favor with God and man. (See Luke 4:18.)
Zechariah 9:9: Rejoice greatly, Daughter Zion! Shout, Daughter Jerusalem! See, your king comes to you, righteous and victorious, lowly and riding on a donkey, on a colt, the foal of a donkey. (See Isaiah 62:11.)	***His Triumphal Entry***	**John 12:13-14:** They took palm branches and went out to meet him, shouting, "Hosanna!" "Blessed is he who comes in the name of the Lord!" "Blessed is the king of Israel!" Jesus found a young donkey and sat on it, as it is written. (See Matthew 21:1-11; John 12:12.)

PROPHECIES	SUMMARY	FULFILLMENT
Psalm 41:9: Even my close friend, someone I trusted, one who shared my bread, has turned against me.	***Betrayed by a Friend***	**Mark 14:10:** Then Judas Iscariot, one of the Twelve, went to the chief priests to betray Jesus to them. (See Matthew 26:14-16; Mark 14:43-45.)
Zechariah 11:12: I told them, "If you think it best, give me my pay; but if not, keep it." So they paid me thirty pieces of silver. (See Zechariah 11:13.)	***Sold for Thirty Pieces of Silver***	**Matthew 26:14, 15:** Judas Iscariot . . . asked, "What are you willing to give me if I deliver him over to you?" So they counted out for him thirty pieces of silver. (See Matthew 27:3-10.)
Zechariah 11:13: And the LORD said to me, "Throw it to the potter"—the handsome price at which they valued me! So I took the thirty pieces of silver and threw them to the potter at the house of the LORD.	***Money to Be Returned for a Potter's Field***	**Matthew 27:6-7:** The chief priests picked up the coins and said, "It is against the law to put this into the treasury, since it is blood money." So they decided to use the money to buy the potter's field as a burial place for foreigners. (See Matthew 27:3-5, 8-10.)
Psalm 109:7-8: When he is tried, let him be found guilty, and may his prayers condemn him. May his days be few; may another take his place of leadership.	***Judas' Office to Be Taken by Another***	**Acts 1:18-20:** (With the payment he received for his wickedness, Judas bought a field; there he fell headlong, his body burst open and all his intestines spilled out. Everyone in Jerusalem heard about this, so they called that field in their language Akeldama, that is, Field of Blood.) "For," said Peter, "it is written in the Book of Psalms: "'May his place be deserted; let there be no one to dwell in it,' and, 'May another take his place of leadership.'" (See Acts 1:16, 17.)
Psalm 27:12: Do not turn me over to the desire of my foes, for false witnesses rise up against me, spouting malicious accusations. (See Psalm 35:11.)	***False Witnesses Accuse Him***	**Matthew 26:60-61:** But they did not find any, though many false witnesses came forward. Finally two came forward and declared, "This fellow said, 'I am able to destroy the temple of God and rebuild it in three days.'"
Isaiah 53:7: He was oppressed and afflicted, yet he did not open his mouth; he was led like a lamb to the slaughter, and as a sheep before its shearers is silent, so he did not open his mouth. (See Psalm 38:13-14.)	***Silent When Accused***	**Matthew 26:62-63:** Then the high priest stood up and said to Jesus, "Are you not going to answer? What is this testimony that these men are bringing against you?" But Jesus remained silent. The high priest said to him, "I charge you under oath by the living God: Tell us if you are the Messiah, the Son of God." (See Matthew 27:12-14.)
Isaiah 50:6: I offered my back to those who beat me, my cheeks to those who pulled out my beard; I did not hide my face from mocking and spitting.	***Beaten and Spit Upon***	**Mark 14:65:** Then some began to spit at him; they blindfolded him, struck him with their fists, and said, "Prophesy!" And the guards took him and beat him. (See Mark 15:17; John 18:22; 19:1-3.)
Psalm 69:4: Those who hate me without reason outnumber the hairs of my head; many are my enemies without cause, those who seek to destroy me. I am forced to restore what I did not steal. (See Psalm 109:3-5.)	***Hated Without a Reason***	**John 15:23-25:** "Whoever hates me hates my Father as well. If I had not done among them the works no one else did, they would not be guilty of sin. As it is, they have seen, and yet they have hated both me and my Father. But this is to fulfill what is written in their Law: 'They hated me without reason.'"

PROPHECIES	SUMMARY	FULFILLMENT
Isaiah 53:4–5: Surely he took up our pain and bore our suffering, yet we considered him punished by God, stricken by him, and afflicted. But he was pierced for our transgressions, he was crushed for our iniquities; the punishment that brought us peace was on him, and by his wounds we are healed. (See Isaiah 53:6, 12.)	***Suffered Vicariously***	**Matthew 8:16–17:** When evening came, many who were demon-possessed were brought to him, and he drove out the spirits with a word and healed all the sick. This was to fulfill what was spoken through the prophet Isaiah: "He took up our infirmities and bore our diseases." (See Romans 4:25; 1 Corinthians 15:3.)
Isaiah 53:12: Therefore I will give him a portion among the great, and he will divide the spoils with the strong, because he poured out his life unto death, and was numbered with the transgressors. For he bore the sin of many, and made intercession for the transgressors.	***Crucified With Sinners***	**Matthew 27:38:** Two rebels were crucified with him, one on his right and one on his left. (See Mark 15:27, 28; Luke 23:33.)
Psalm 22:16: Dogs surround me, a pack of villains encircles me; they pierce my hands and my feet. (See Zechariah 12:10.)	***Hands and Feet Pierced***	**John 20:27:** Then he said to Thomas, "Put your finger here; see my hands. Reach out your hand and put it into my side. Stop doubting and believe." (See John 19:37; 20:25, 26.)
Psalm 22:6–8: But I am a worm and not a man, scorned by everyone, despised by the people. All who see me mock me; they hurl insults, shaking their heads. "He trusts in the LORD," they say, "let the LORD rescue him. Let him deliver him, since he delights in him."	***Mocked and Insulted***	**Matthew 27:39–40:** Those who passed by hurled insults at him, shaking their heads and saying, "You who are going to destroy the temple and build it in three days, save yourself! Come down from the cross, if you are the Son of God!" (See Matthew 27:41–44; Mark 15:29–32.)
Psalm 69:21: They put gall in my food and gave me vinegar for my thirst.	***Given Gall (Sour Wine) and Vinegar***	**John 19:29:** A jar of wine vinegar was there, so they soaked a sponge in it, put the sponge on a stalk of the hyssop plant, and lifted it to Jesus' lips. (See Matthew 27:34, 48.)
Psalm 22:8: "He trusts in the LORD," they say, "let the LORD rescue him. Let him deliver him, since he delights in him."	***Hears Prophetic Words Repeated in Mockery***	**Matthew 27:43:** "He trusts in God. Let God rescue him now if he wants him, for he said, 'I am the Son of God.'"
Psalm 109:4: In return for my friendship they accuse me, but I am a man of prayer. (See Isaiah 53:12.)	***Prays for His Enemies***	**Luke 23:34:** Jesus said, "Father, forgive them, for they do not know what they are doing." And they divided up his clothes by casting lots.
Zechariah 12:10: And I will pour out on the house of David and the inhabitants of Jerusalem a spirit of grace and supplication. They will look on me, the one they have pierced, and they will mourn for him as one mourns for an only child, and grieve bitterly for him as one grieves for a firstborn son.	***His Side to Be Pierced***	**John 19:34:** Instead, one of the soldiers pierced Jesus' side with a spear, bringing a sudden flow of blood and water.
Psalm 22:18: They divide my clothes among them and cast lots for my garment.	***Soldiers Cast Lots for His Clothes***	**Mark 15:24:** And they crucified him. Dividing up his clothes, they cast lots to see what each would get. (See John 19:24.)
Psalm 34:19, 20: The LORD . . . protects all his bones, not one of them will be broken. (See Exodus 12:46.)	***Not a Bone to Be Broken***	**John 19:33:** But when they came to Jesus and found that he was already dead, they did not break his legs.

PROPHECIES	SUMMARY	FULFILLMENT
Isaiah 53:9: He was assigned a grave with the wicked, and with the rich in his death, though he had done no violence, nor was any deceit in his mouth.	***To Be Buried With the Rich***	**Matthew 27:57–60:** As evening approached, there came a rich man from Arimathea, named Joseph, who had himself become a disciple of Jesus. Going to Pilate, he asked for Jesus' body, and Pilate ordered that it be given to him. Joseph took the body, wrapped it in a clean linen cloth, and placed it in his own new tomb that he had cut out of the rock. He rolled a big stone in front of the entrance to the tomb and went away.
Psalm 16:10: You will not abandon me to the realm of the dead, nor will you let your faithful one see decay. (See Matthew 16:21.)	***His Resurrection***	**Matthew 28:9:** Suddenly Jesus met them. "Greetings," he said. They came to him, clasped his feet and worshiped him. (See Luke 24:36–48.)
Psalm 68:18: When you ascended on high, you took many captives; you received gifts from people, even from the rebellious—that you, LORD God, might dwell there.	***His Ascension***	**Luke 24:50–51:** When he had led them out to the vicinity of Bethany, he lifted up his hands and blessed them. While he was blessing them, he left them and was taken up into heaven. (See Acts 1:9.)

Author: Matthew, also called Levi
Audience: Greek-speaking Jewish Christians
Date: Between AD 50 and 70

Theme: Matthew presents Jesus as the Jewish Messiah sent by God to bring salvation to Israel and the nations in fulfillment of OT Scriptures.

PERSPECTIVE

It is probably safe to say that the most often read part of the Gospel of Matthew in our day is the Sermon on the Mount (chs. 5–7). It is easy to imagine why. We live in a moralistic, legalistic, individualistic age. The Sermon on the Mount can be read as a guidebook for ethical living, to be followed regardless of what you think of God, the Jewish community, or the Christian church. Unfortunately, this is the wrong way to read the Sermon on the Mount and the Gospel of Matthew as a whole.

Why? Because reading it this way assumes that the way we choose to behave determines who we are and determines our identity. And that's not true at all. What the Gospel of Matthew teaches us in general and what the Sermon on the Mount teaches us in particular is that who we are (or more precisely, *whose* we are, i.e., whom we choose to follow or identify with) determines how we behave. If we choose to follow Jesus as Messiah, Matthew tells us, then the Sermon on the Mount is a description of how we will behave.

Three important things happen, all of them bad, when we read the Sermon on the Mount incorrectly.

First, we overestimate our goodness. It is tempting to think of our characters as something we carefully craft, using a brick of honesty here, a two-by-four of generosity there, built on a cement foundation of discipline and energy. In such a scenario we choose the goal, and we choose the building methods and materials we need to achieve the goal. And it is up to us to make the grade. Matthew says we are not that good (e.g., 5:27–28; 12:34, 36; 15:11, 19).

Second, we underestimate our capacity for evil. The reason we cannot let our innate, God-created goodness dominate our personalities

Reading Matthew

This Gospel begins with a genealogy of Jesus and the story of his birth. Starting with ch. 3, it can be divided into five main sections, each telling first what Jesus did and then what Jesus said; each section closes the same way (see 7:28; 11:1; 13:53; 19:1; 26:1). The last three chapters tell the story of the death and resurrection of Jesus.

Herod the Great's reign	c. 37–4 BC
Jesus' birth	c. 6/5 BC
Jesus' flight to Egypt	c. 5/4 BC
Beginning of John the Baptist's ministry	c. AD 26
Beginning of Jesus' ministry	c. AD 26
Jesus' death, resurrection and ascension	c. AD 30
Paul's conversion	c. AD 35
Book of Matthew written	c. AD 60–70

Timeline scale: 10 BC, AD 1, 10, 20, 30, 40, 50, 60, 70, 80, 90, 100

Key Verses

Now when Jesus saw the crowds, he went up on a mountainside and sat down. His disciples came to him, and he began to teach them. He said: "Blessed are the poor in spirit, for theirs is the kingdom of heaven. Blessed are those who mourn, for they will be comforted. Blessed are the meek, for they will inherit the earth . . ."

—Matthew 5:1-5

is because we have been infected with a pervasive force that has radically impaired our ability to let our lights of goodness shine. We all feel this force and perhaps wish it weren't true. Matthew says we choose to identify with the Messiah because when it comes right down to it, we have no other choice. "Unless you change and become like little children, you will never enter the kingdom of heaven" (18:3).

Third, we rely less on God than we should. Because we are tempted not to choose to identify first with the Messiah, letting our characters emerge as a result of that choice, we instead decide to do a little remedial work to make ourselves a little more acceptable to God before we submit. When we make that choice, however, we make it impossible to rely on God as we should: that is, completely.

The Sermon on the Mount is an impossible ideal if read as an ethical treatise to which we need to measure up. It is a wonderful description of what we can become if we identify ourselves with Christ and allow his love to express itself through us. Read that way, it is a glorious promise of what we are and what we will become: the hope of Christian living that Matthew saw so clearly.

TAKING THE NEXT STEPS

This account of the life of Jesus has been attributed to Matthew, one of the disciples of Jesus. Matthew seemed to have primarily a Jewish audience in mind, for he presented Jesus as the promised Messiah who fulfilled the prophecies, sacrifices, commands, and teachings of the OT. He portrayed Jesus as the Son of God, who showed throughout his life that he had divine authority that was acknowledged by both humans and angels. Matthew carefully outlined for those who professed to be Christ's followers the instructions that Jesus gave on true discipleship and on proper pastoral care in the church. And he reminded his readers that Jesus was the Savior of all nations, who had sent his followers on a worldwide mission with the message of the gospel.

Several important messages stand out in this Gospel. (1) We can be sure that God's Word is true, for the OT prophecies about the coming of the Messiah came true in Jesus. (2) Jesus wants us to acknowledge him as the Christ, the Son of the living God, and to follow his instructions for our daily lives. (3) The Sermon on the Mount is one of the best summaries on how to serve God and love our fellow human beings. (4) We learn in the Gospel of Matthew how to relate to and care for fellow church members, particularly those who are experiencing difficulties. (5) Jesus wants us to tell our friends and neighbors, as well as people throughout the entire world, the Good News about salvation in his name.

WHAT TO LOOK FOR IN MATTHEW

- Jesus' birth and the visit of the Magi (chs. 1–2)
- The Sermon on the Mount (chs. 5–7)
- Some miracles of Jesus (chs. 8–9; 14–15)
- Jesus' sending out his disciples (ch. 10)
- Some parables of Jesus (chs. 13; 18; 20–21; 25)
- Peter's confession and Jesus' prediction of his own death (ch. 16)
- Judgment on the Pharisees (ch. 23)
- Jesus' prediction of the future (ch. 24)
- Jesus' passion, death, and resurrection (chs. 26–28)

The Genealogy of Jesus the Messiah

1:1–17pp // Lk 3:23–38
1:3–6pp // Ru 4:18–22
1:7–11pp // 1Ch 3:10–17

1 This is the genealogy[a] of Jesus the Messiah[b] the son of David,[a] the son of Abraham:[b]

2 Abraham was the father of Isaac,[c]
Isaac the father of Jacob,[d]
Jacob the father of Judah and his brothers,[e]
3 Judah the father of Perez and Zerah, whose mother was Tamar,[f]
Perez the father of Hezron,
Hezron the father of Ram,
4 Ram the father of Amminadab,
Amminadab the father of Nahshon,
Nahshon the father of Salmon,
5 Salmon the father of Boaz, whose mother was Rahab,
Boaz the father of Obed, whose mother was Ruth,
Obed the father of Jesse,
6 and Jesse the father of King David.[g]

David was the father of Solomon, whose mother had been Uriah's wife,[h]
7 Solomon the father of Rehoboam,
Rehoboam the father of Abijah,
Abijah the father of Asa,
8 Asa the father of Jehoshaphat,
Jehoshaphat the father of Jehoram,
Jehoram the father of Uzziah,
9 Uzziah the father of Jotham,
Jotham the father of Ahaz,
Ahaz the father of Hezekiah,
10 Hezekiah the father of Manasseh,[i]
Manasseh the father of Amon,
Amon the father of Josiah,
11 and Josiah the father of Jeconiah[c] and his brothers at the time of the exile to Babylon.[j]

12 After the exile to Babylon:
Jeconiah was the father of Shealtiel,[k]

1:1 [a] 2Sa 7:12-16; Isa 9:6,7; 11:1; Jer 23:5,6; Mt 9:27; Lk 1:32,69; Ro 1:3; Rev 22:16 [b] Ge 22:18; Gal 3:16
1:2 [c] Ge 21:3,12 [d] Ge 25:26 [e] Ge 29:35
1:3 [f] Ge 38:27-30
1:6 [g] 1Sa 16:1; 17:12 [h] 2Sa 12:24
1:10 [i] 2Ki 20:21
1:11 [j] 2Ki 24:14-16; Jer 27:20; Da 1:1,2
1:12 [k] 1Ch 3:17

[a] *1* Or *is an account of the origin* [b] *1* Or *Jesus Christ. Messiah* (Hebrew) and *Christ* (Greek) both mean *Anointed One*; also in verse 18. [c] *11* That is, Jehoiachin; also in verse 12

1:1 In tracing the ancestry to Abraham, Matthew holds a light of hope to the entire world. The covenant God made with Abraham was a promise of blessing to all the nations.
1:2–6a "Abraham was the father of Isaac." This expression emphasizes the human background of each generation, which paves the way for a dramatic change in v. 16, where Matthew points to the divine origin of Jesus.
1:6b–11 The alternating series of godly and wicked kings is striking.
1:12–16 After the return of Israel from the exile, the Davidic line continues through Jeconiah.

ISRAEL IN EARLY NEW TESTAMENT TIMES
Extent of Herod's kingdom
Herodian fortress city
Decapolis city (time of Herod)
Other city
ABILENE
Litani R.
ITUREA
Abana R.
Damascus
Sidon
PHOENICIA
Mediterranean Sea
Mt. Hermon
Pharpar R.
Leontes R.
Tyre
SYRIA
Caesarea Philippi
GAULANITIS
Lake Hula
TRACONITIS
Jebel Jarmak
GALILEE
TETRARCHY OF PHILIP
Chorazin
Capernaum
Bethsaida
Gennesaret
Sea of Galilee
Raphana
Ptolemais
Cana of Galilee
Magadan (Magdala)
Gergesa (Kursi)
Tiberias
Hippos
Mt. Carmel
Nazareth
Mt. Tabor
Gadara
Yarmuk R.
BATANEA
Kishon R.
Abila
AURANITIS
Dor
Nain
Mt. Moreh
Bethany on the other side of the Jordan?
Megiddo
Caesarea
Mt. Gilboa
Scythopolis
Pella
Dion
DECAPOLIS
SAMARIA
Salim?
Samaria
Gerasa
Jordan R.
Mt. Ebal
Sychar
Jabbok R.
Amathus
Yarkon R.
Mt. Gerizim
PEREA
Joppa
Antipatris
Alexandrium
Philadelphia
Jericho
Jamnia (Jabneel)
Emmaus
Cyprus
Bethany on the other side of the Jordan?
Mt. of Olives
Ashdod
Jerusalem
Bethany
Heshbon
Mt. Nebo
Bethlehem
Hyrcania
Medeba
Ashkelon
Herodium
JUDEA
Machaerus
Adora
Hebron
Dead Sea
Gaza
Besor Valley
Arnon R.
Masada
IDUMEA
NABATEA
Arad
Raphia
Beersheba
Malatha
0 20 km.
0 20 miles
Zered R.

Shealtiel the father of Zerubbabel,[l]
13 Zerubbabel the father of Abihud,
Abihud the father of Eliakim,
Eliakim the father of Azor,
14 Azor the father of Zadok,
Zadok the father of Akim,
Akim the father of Elihud,
15 Elihud the father of Eleazar,
Eleazar the father of Matthan,
Matthan the father of Jacob,
16 and Jacob the father of Joseph, the
husband of Mary,[m] and Mary
was the mother of Jesus who
is called the Messiah.[n]

17 Thus there were fourteen generations
in all from Abraham to David, fourteen
from David to the exile to Babylon, and
fourteen from the exile to the Messiah.

Joseph Accepts Jesus as His Son

18 This is how the birth of Jesus the
Messiah came about[a]: His mother Mary
was pledged to be married to Joseph,
but before they came together, she was
found to be pregnant through the Holy
Spirit.[o] 19 Because Joseph her husband
was faithful to the law, and yet[b] did not
want to expose her to public disgrace,
he had in mind to divorce[p] her quietly.
20 But after he had considered this, an
angel of the Lord appeared to him in a
dream and said, "Joseph son of David,
do not be afraid to take Mary home as
your wife, because what is conceived in
her is from the Holy Spirit. 21 She will give
birth to a son, and you are to give him
the name Jesus,[c][q] because he will save
his people from their sins."[r]
22 All this took place to fulfill what
the Lord had said through the prophet:
23 "The virgin will conceive and give birth
to a son, and they will call him Immanuel"[d][s] (which means "God with us").
24 When Joseph woke up, he did what
the angel of the Lord had commanded
him and took Mary home as his wife.
25 But he did not consummate their marriage until she gave birth to a son. And
he gave him the name Jesus.[t]

1:12 [l] 1Ch 3:19; Ezr 3:2
1:16 [m] Lk 1:27 [n] Mt 27:17
1:18 [o] Lk 1:35
1:19 [p] Dt 24:1
1:21 [q] Lk 1:31 [r] Lk 2:11; Ac 5:31; 13:23,28
1:23 [s] Isa 7:14; 8:8,10
1:25 [t] ver 21

[a] 18 Or *The origin of Jesus the Messiah was like this* [b] 19 Or *was a righteous man and* [c] 21 *Jesus* is the Greek form of *Joshua,* which means *the* LORD *saves.* [d] 23 Isaiah 7:14

1:16–17 The original Greek emphasizes that Mary is the biological parent, preparing the reader for the virgin birth.

APPLICATION ✣ 1:1–17 The covenantal promise includes all humanity. Matthew shows us that we have another set of roots—roots of faith. Once a person becomes a Christian, he or she is immediately adopted into a family of faith that has a long and well-documented genealogy.

1:18–19 The marriage customs of Jewish culture at that time usually included two basic stages of the relationship: the betrothal and the wedding. The betrothal stage involved a legally binding contract and could only be broken by a formal process of divorce. In a formal ceremony about a year after the betrothal, the wedding took place.
1:20–21 The angel dramatically announces to Joseph in a dream that the conception of the child is from the Holy Spirit. Here at the beginning of the NT age, the Holy Spirit plays a crucial role. Jesus Messiah is God incarnate, whose miraculous conception and origin are only explained through the work of God the Holy Spirit.

The name *Jesus* was popular in first-century Judaism and was given to sons as a symbolic hope for Yahweh's anticipated sending of salvation. Many expected a messiah who would save Israel from Roman oppression. The angel draws on a less popular theme: salvation from sin.
1:22–23 At the time of Ahaz (734 BC) Isaiah prophesied that a woman who was a virgin would bear a son named Immanuel. Since Isaiah's prophecy was first fulfilled in his time (Isa 7:16), this prophecy is fulfilled in a more incredible way with Jesus. In Isaiah the reference is to a woman who had yet to bear a child, but Matthew clarifies that not only had Mary not yet born a child, she had also never had a sexual experience. So Matthew declares that Jesus ultimately fulfills the prophecy of Isa 7:14.
1:24–25 When Joseph awakes from his sleep, he is obedient to the angel's directive and carries out the second phase of the marital process by engaging in the formal wedding ceremony. Matthew emphasizes Joseph's remarkable character. Not only is Mary seen as a godly woman, but Joseph takes the lead in carrying out the angel's instructions.

✣ **1:18–25** The explicit nature of the role of the Holy Spirit in this passage enables us to begin to see the unfolding revelation of God throughout Scripture. This activity of the Spirit is more plain in the expansion of the church in the book of Acts and in the teaching of later NT authors, but we begin to see it come into play with the conception and birth of Jesus Messiah.

What a privilege and responsibility we now have to live at this stage of history. In their obedience to the work of the Spirit, young Joseph and Mary give us a precursor of how godly relationships can be pure and characterized by serving one another. Today, that is the real basis on which we can pursue a godly marriage and family and, indeed, see the transformation of any of our relationships, both within and outside the church, through the transforming work of God's Spirit.

> **Mt 1:24** ❖ Sometimes God's commands are not easy. How can we better follow God's will when the calling seems difficult?

The Magi Visit the Messiah

2 After Jesus was born in Bethlehem
in Judea,[u] during the time of King
Herod,[v] Magi[a] from the east came to Jerusalem 2and asked, "Where is the one
who has been born king of the Jews?[w]
We saw his star[x] when it rose and have
come to worship him."
3When King Herod heard this he was
disturbed, and all Jerusalem with him.
4When he had called together all the people's chief priests and teachers of the
law, he asked them where the Messiah
was to be born. 5"In Bethlehem[y] in Judea," they replied, "for this is what the
prophet has written:

6" 'But you, Bethlehem, in the land of
Judah,
are by no means least among the
rulers of Judah;
for out of you will come a ruler
who will shepherd my people
Israel.'[b]"[z]

7Then Herod called the Magi secretly
and found out from them the exact time
the star had appeared. 8He sent them
to Bethlehem and said, "Go and search
carefully for the child. As soon as you

2:1 [u] Lk 2:4-7 [v] Lk 1:5
2:2 [w] Jer 23:5; Mt 27:11; Mk 15:2; Jn 1:49; 18:33-37 [x] Nu 24:17
2:5 [y] Jn 7:42
2:6 [z] 2Sa 5:2; Mic 5:2

[a] 1 Traditionally *wise men* [b] 6 Micah 5:2,4

2:1–2 Herod most likely died in March of 4 BC. Since Herod is still alive when the Magi arrive in Jerusalem, the dating of Jesus' birth is placed by most scholars somewhere between 6 and 4 BC.

The universal significance of the birth of the child Jesus is announced immediately because Magi from the east arrive in Jerusalem. The term "Magi" originally referred to a priestly caste in ancient Persia. The arrival of Gentile religious leaders from the east implies they had been regularly exposed to Hebrew Scriptures, prophecy, and teachers. The Magi may have become familiar with Balaam's prophecy of a messianic deliverer (Nu 24:17).

2:3–8 The word "Jerusalem" represents the religious and political leadership of Israel. The leadership know the consequences they might suffer if Herod were to fly into a rage at a perceived threat. They have aligned themselves politically with Herod, and if his power base is threatened, so is theirs.

The central leadership of the Jews was lodged in the "chief priests" and the "teachers of the law" (v. 4). The chief priests were members of the Sanhedrin, joining the high priest in giving oversight to the temple activities, treasury, and priestly orders.

PEOPLE TO KNOW // HERROD THE GREAT

MATTHEW 2:1–12: Herod the Great was a tyrannical and vengeful king, yet he was also an architectural genius. Some of his building achievements still stand today.

Herod's story in the Bible shows only his paranoid and vengeful side. When Magi from the east came to his palace asking about a new king born in the area, "he was disturbed, and all Jerusalem with him" (Mt 2:3). As king, his mental state affected his entire community.

Herod hid his wrath from the Magi and disguised it with interest. Learning from the religious leaders that the Messiah was to be born in Bethlehem nearby, Herod sent the Magi to find baby Jesus and to report back to him when they had done so, that he could also "go and worship him" (Mt 2:8). The Magi, however, were warned in a dream not to return to Herod. They went home by another route.

When Herod realized he had been duped, he flew into a rage. Like Pharaoh killing the baby Hebrew boys (Ex 1:22), Herod demanded that all the boys around Bethlehem under the age of two be put to death (Mt 2:16). He could not abide the thought of a challenger to his authority. An angel appeared to Joseph in a dream telling him to flee to Egypt; Joseph, Mary and Jesus escaped.

APPLICATION ✚ Herod's legacy is a warning about the danger of sin in the life of a person in the position of power. Herod was a brilliant man, but his pride, jealousy and anger made him a terrible and terrifying leader. While we may not wield the same power as Herod, our hearts are susceptible to the same danger. In any position of leadership or authority, we need to examine our motivations and calling. Instead of seeking to preserve our own control and authority, we need to humble ourselves to God's authority and allow him to guide us as we acknowledge that he is the true King and Leader of all.

Mt 2:11 ❖ What does it look like to give our best to Jesus?

find him, report to me, so that I too may
go and worship him."
9After they had heard the king, they
went on their way, and the star they had
seen when it rose went ahead of them
until it stopped over the place where
the child was. 10When they saw the star,
they were overjoyed. 11On coming to
the house, they saw the child with his
mother Mary, and they bowed down and
worshiped him.[a] Then they opened their
treasures and presented him with gifts[b]
of gold, frankincense and myrrh. 12And
having been warned[c] in a dream[d] not to
go back to Herod, they returned to their
country by another route.

The Escape to Egypt

13When they had gone, an angel[e] of
the Lord appeared to Joseph in a dream.[f]
"Get up," he said, "take the child and his
mother and escape to Egypt. Stay there
until I tell you, for Herod is going to
search for the child to kill him."
14So he got up, took the child and his
mother during the night and left for
Egypt, 15where he stayed until the death
of Herod. And so was fulfilled what the
Lord had said through the prophet: "Out
of Egypt I called my son."[a][g]
16When Herod realized that he had
been outwitted by the Magi, he was
furious, and he gave orders to kill all
the boys in Bethlehem and its vicinity
who were two years old and under, in
accordance with the time he had learned
from the Magi. 17Then what was said
through the prophet Jeremiah was fulfilled:

18"A voice is heard in Ramah,
weeping and great mourning,
Rachel weeping for her children
and refusing to be comforted,
because they are no more."[b][h]

The Return to Nazareth

19After Herod died, an angel of the
Lord appeared in a dream[i] to Joseph in
Egypt 20and said, "Get up, take the child
and his mother and go to the land of

2:11 [a] Isa 60:3 [b] Ps 72:10
2:12 [c] Heb 11:7 [d] ver 13,19,22; Mt 27:19
2:13 [e] Ac 5:19 [f] ver 12,19,22
2:15 [g] Ex 4:22, 23; Hos 11:1
2:18 [h] Jer 31:15
2:19 [i] ver 12, 13,22

[a] *15* Hosea 11:1 [b] *18* Jer. 31:15

2:9–12 The purpose of the Magi's pilgrimage to see the child is accomplished as they "bowed down and worshiped him" (v. 11). It is doubtful that at this time these quasi-pagan religious figures understand Jesus' divine nature. Their worship is far more than even they understand.

"Gold" is the most often mentioned valued metal in Scripture. "Incense" was used in Israel ceremonially as part of a recipe for the only incense permitted on the altar (Ex 30:9, 34–38). A dead body was prepared for burial by washing, dressing it in special garments, and packing it with fragrant "myrrh" and other spices to stifle the smell of a body as it decayed.

Joseph was visited in a dream by an angel (Mt 1:20). It seems plausible that the same angel appears in the Magi's warning dream (2:12). If so, the warning in a dream is consistent with the view that the star guiding them was an angel.

✣ **2:1–12** The very act of sacrificial giving defines what it means to love each other. The Magi did not know the full identity of Jesus as we are privileged to know, yet they demonstrated worship and gift-giving at the arrival of the king of the Jews. Our sacrificial worship and love of Jesus will produce true, sacrificial love for one another.

At this most fundamental level, Matthew teaches us that Jesus' arrival in history to initiate the salvation of his people from their sins surely requires that we give ourselves to him. When we do so, his life becomes the pattern for our own lives.

2:13–15 Once the Magi escape safely, the angel of the Lord again appears in a dream to warn Joseph about Herod's scheme to murder the child. Joseph is again immediately obedient, escaping to Egypt by night.

Matthew points to the flight and later return from Egypt as a fulfillment of Scripture. Matthew has a multifaceted perspective on the way that Jesus "fulfills" the OT Scriptures. (1) In some cases, "fulfill" can indicate the way in which the events of Jesus' earthly life and ministry enact what the prophets predicted. (2) In other cases, "fulfill" can indicate the way in which Jesus brings the entire OT Scripture to its full intended meaning. (3) In still other cases, Matthew's use of "fulfill" can indicate the way in which Jesus' earthly life and ministry mirror certain aspects of the national history of Israel.

2:16–18 No other historical records exist of this incident, which is not surprising since Bethlehem was a somewhat small, rural town at this time. The events of Jesus' earthly life repeat the pattern of earlier attempts by a foreign power to wipe out God's chosen people.

2:19a Herod died at the age of 69 in March, 4 BC. Herod divided his kingdom between his sons, Archelaus, Herod Antipas, and Herod Philip. Herod Antipas ruled the region of Jesus' primary ministry.

2:19b–23 The family probably stayed in Egypt no more than a year. When they discover that Archelaus is ruling over Judea, Joseph detours to Nazareth in the region of Galilee, a region governed by Herod Antipas.

Nazareth was originally settled by people from

HOUSE OF HEROD

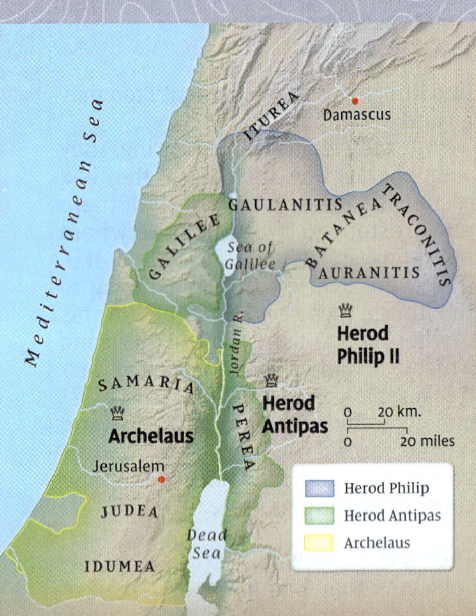

1ST GENERATION

♛ **Herod the Great** King of Judea, Galilee, Iturea, Traconitis (37–4 BC)

Birth of Jesus (Mt 2:1–19; Lk 1:5)

2ND GENERATION

♕ **Herod Philip II** *(MOTHER: CLEOPATRA)* Tetrarch of Iturea and Traconitis (4 BC–AD 34) (Lk 3:1)

♕ **Archelaus** *(MOTHER: MALTHACE)* Ethnarch of Judea, Idumea and Samaria (4 BC–AD 6); when Mary and Joseph left Egypt, they avoided Judea and settled in Nazareth (Mt 2:19–23)

Aristobulus *(MOTHER: MARIAMNE)* (died 10 BC)

♕ **Herod Antipas** *(MOTHER: MALTHACE)* Tetrarch of Galilee and Perea (4 BC–AD 39) (Lk 3:1); second husband of Herodias; he put John the Baptist to death (Mt 14:1–12; Mk 6:14–29); Pilate sent Jesus to him (Lk 23:7–12)

Herod Philip I *(MOTHER: MARIAMNE)* He did not rule; first husband of Herodias (Mt 14:3; Mk 6:17) (died c. AD 34)

Antipater *(MOTHER: DORIS)*

KEY:

♛	King
♕	Ethnarch/Tetrarch
BERNICE	italic capitals denote females
Antipater	bold type: bloodline of Herod the Great
Felix	light type: non-bloodline

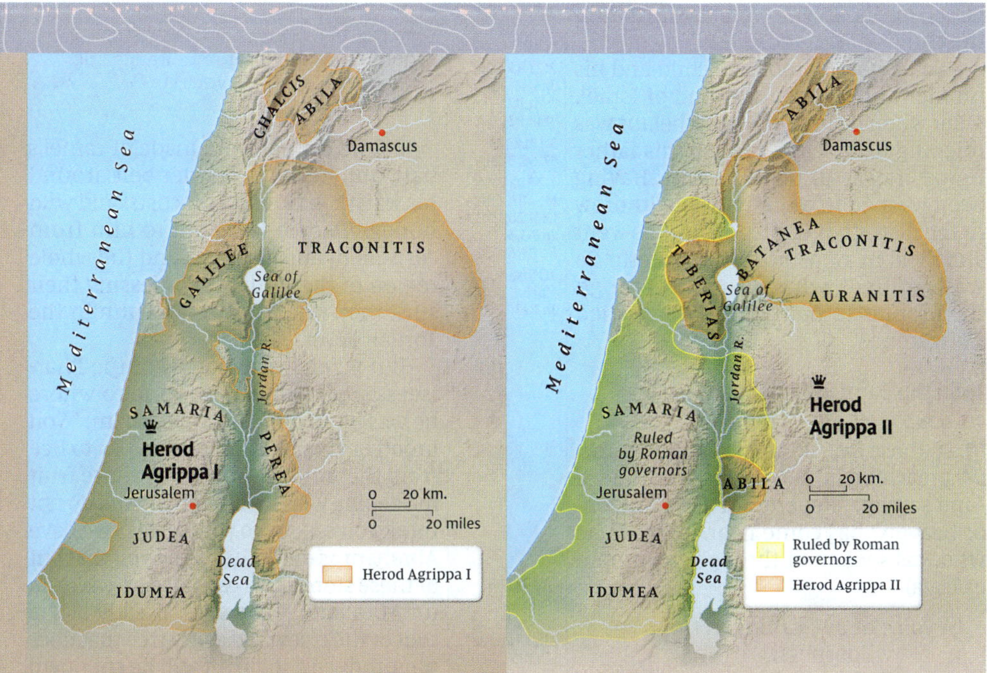

3RD GENERATION

Herod of Chalcis

♛ **Herod Agrippa I** King of Judea (AD 37–44); killed James; put Peter into prison; struck down by an angel (Ac 12:1–24)

HERODIAS Married her uncle Herod Philip I, and then a second uncle, Herod Antipas (Mt 14:3; Mk 6:17)

········· Denotes Herodias's marriage to Herod Antipas

– – – – Denotes Herodias's marriage to Herod Philip I and daughter of that marriage

4TH GENERATION

Felix (Governor of Judea)

DRUSILLA
Married Felix, governor of Judea (AD 52–59); Felix tried Paul (Ac 24:24)

♛ **Herod Agrippa II**
King of Judea; Paul makes a legal defense before him (Ac 25:13—26:32)

BERNICE
With her brother at the time of Paul's defense (Ac 25:13)

SALOME
Daughter of Herodias and Herod Philip I; danced in exchange for the head of John the Baptist (Mt 14:1–12; Mk 6:14–29)

Israel, for those who were trying to take
the child's life are dead."
21So he got up, took the child and his
mother and went to the land of Israel.
22But when he heard that Archelaus was
reigning in Judea in place of his father
Herod, he was afraid to go there. Having
been warned in a dream,[j] he withdrew
to the district of Galilee,[k] 23and he went
and lived in a town called Nazareth.[l] So
was fulfilled[m] what was said through
the prophets, that he would be called
a Nazarene.[n]

John the Baptist Prepares the Way

3:1–12pp // Mk 1:3–8; Lk 3:2–17

3 In those days John the Baptist[o] came,
preaching in the wilderness of Judea
2and saying, "Repent, for the kingdom
of heaven[p] has come near." 3This is he
who was spoken of through the prophet Isaiah:

"A voice of one calling in the
wilderness,
'Prepare the way for the Lord,
make straight paths for
him.'"[a][q]

2:22 [j] ver 12, 13,19; Mt 27:19 [k] Lk 2:39
2:23 [l] Lk 1:26; Jn 1:45,46 [m] Mt 1:22 [n] Mk 1:24
3:1 [o] Lk 1:13, 57-66; 3:2-19
3:2 [p] Da 2:44; Mt 4:17; 6:10; Lk 11:20; 21:31; Jn 3:3,5; Ac 1:3,6
3:3 [q] Isa 40:3; Mal 3:1; Lk 1:76; Jn 1:23
3:4 [r] 2Ki 1:8 [s] Lev 11:22
3:7 [t] Mt 12:34; 23:33 [u] Ro 1:18; 1Th 1:10
3:8 [v] Ac 26:20
3:10 [w] Mt 7:19; Lk 13:6-9; Jn 15:2,6

Mt 3:2 ❖ To *repent* means "to change our behavior." What repentance still needs to happen in your life?

4John's clothes were made of camel's
hair, and he had a leather belt around
his waist.[r] His food was locusts[s] and wild
honey. 5People went out to him from
Jerusalem and all Judea and the whole
region of the Jordan. 6Confessing their
sins, they were baptized by him in the
Jordan River.
7But when he saw many of the Pharisees and Sadducees coming to where
he was baptizing, he said to them: "You
brood of vipers![t] Who warned you to flee
from the coming wrath?[u] 8Produce fruit
in keeping with repentance.[v] 9And do not
think you can say to yourselves, 'We have
Abraham as our father.' I tell you that out
of these stones God can raise up children
for Abraham. 10The ax is already at the
root of the trees, and every tree that does
not produce good fruit will be cut down
and thrown into the fire.[w]

[a] *3* Isaiah 40:3

---

the line of David. Matthew also uses "Nazarene" to refer to an individual from a remote, despised area. To Jesus' followers, the expression "Jesus of Nazareth" marked him as the messianic deliverer (Ac 2:22; 3:6; 10:38). When used by his enemies, it was a title of scorn.

Matthew says nothing about Jesus' early years in Nazareth. Jesus' education would have also included learning the skills of his father—carpentry. Jesus grew up in a multicultural environment in which a number of languages were spoken by the common people—Aramaic, literary Hebrew, and some Latin, which was spoken especially by Roman military personnel.

✣ **2:13–23** As the name "Nazarene" was for Jesus, so the name "Christian" is a badge of honor, but it is also a badge of scorn and a designation for persecution. For many in the world today, wearing the name "Christian" is similar to what it was like for the early church. In places around the world, buildings are burned just because they are known to be "Christian" houses of worship. In many countries, people are placed in jail simply because they possess and distribute "Christian" literature. For Christians in many countries, persecution isn't just a historical fact but a current reality that is close to home.

Our walk with Jesus in this world will involve some kind of suffering for his name. Jesus suffered when doing the right and good thing. Persecution marked the fate of the church from its earliest days, yet it did not dim its passion for following Jesus, no matter what the cost.

3:1–3 John is the one foretold by Isaiah who would be designated to prepare the way for the Lord's arrival and kingdom (v. 3; cf. Isa 40:3).

3:4 John's appearance stirred up recollections of the prophecies of Elijah's return. John's diet and clothing embody in his lifestyle the message of repentance he preaches.

3:5–6 John's baptism was symbolic of purification. But in contrast to forms of baptism such as those at Qumran and by the Pharisees—both of which were highly structured and had regular, repeated washings—John's was a one-time baptism. His baptism called for a personal commitment to God's new activity within Israel.

3:7–10 The Pharisees were a lay fellowship, or brotherhood, connected with local synagogues and thus were popular with the common people. Their most-pronounced characteristic was their dedication to following oral tradition, which they obeyed rigorously to make the written law relevant to daily life. The Sadducees, by contrast, were a small group with aristocratic and priestly influence who took their authority from the activities of the temple.

The Pharisees and Sadducees are united in coming to where John is baptizing. John sees through their hypocrisy and has harsh words for them. Of all people, they should be the ones who prepare their hearts for the coming of the Messiah. Based on their intensive Scripture study, they should have been the first to prepare themselves to receive kingdom life. Instead, they will receive judgment.

11“I baptize you with[a] water for repentance. But after me comes one who is
more powerful than I, whose sandals I
am not worthy to carry. He will baptize
you with[a] the Holy Spirit[x] and fire.[y] 12His
winnowing fork is in his hand, and he
will clear his threshing floor, gathering
his wheat into the barn and burning up
the chaff with unquenchable fire.”[z]

The Baptism of Jesus

3:13–17pp // Mk 1:9–11; Lk 3:21,22; Jn 1:31–34

13Then Jesus came from Galilee to the
Jordan to be baptized by John.[a] 14But John
tried to deter him, saying, “I need to be
baptized by you, and do you come to me?”
15Jesus replied, “Let it be so now; it
is proper for us to do this to fulfill all
righteousness.” Then John consented.
16As soon as Jesus was baptized, he
went up out of the water. At that moment heaven was opened, and he saw
the Spirit of God[b] descending like a dove
and alighting on him. 17And a voice from
heaven[c] said, “This is my Son,[d] whom I
love; with him I am well pleased.”[e]

3:11 [x] Mk 1:8 [y] Isa 4:4; Ac 2:3,4
3:12 [z] Mt 13:30
3:13 [a] Mk 1:4
3:16 [b] Isa 11:2; 42:1
3:17 [c] Mt 17:5; Jn 12:28 [d] Ps 2:7; 2Pe 1:17,18 [e] Isa 42:1; Mt 12:18; 17:5; Mk 1:11; 9:7; Lk 9:35

[a] *11* Or *in*

3:11 John points ahead and beyond himself to another person. John especially emphasizes the contrast between himself and the coming One. (1) John himself knows clearly the identity of the One to come. John is the herald; the coming One is the messianic deliverer. (2) John’s baptism was only preparatory. The coming One will baptize with the blessing of the Holy Spirit. But the unrepentant he will baptize with the judgment of eternal fire.
3:12 At the end of a harvest, the farmer took a pitchfork and tossed the wheat into the air, where the wind blew the lighter chaff away. The wheat was then stored in the granary. The chaff was burned.
3:13–17 What does Jesus mean that in his baptism he and John will “fulfill all righteousness” (v. 15)? Jesus fulfills the hope of the Davidic king and righteous servant. But more important, he is also Immanuel, “God with us,” and Jesus, the One who will “save his people from their sins” (1:21, 23).

Jesus experiences a threefold revelation: (1) “Heaven was opened” (3:16). God himself is opening the gates to reveal something momentous. (2) Jesus’ anointing by the Spirit is both the coronation of Israel’s Messiah and the commissioning of God’s righteous servant for the work he will now carry out in the power and presence of the Spirit. (3) Jesus is heralded as the unique Son who is the triumphant messianic King (Ps 2) yet the humble servant (Isa 42).

✤ **3:1–17** We don’t like to offend. But John does warn us, as will Jesus later, of the coming

PEOPLE TO KNOW // JOHN THE BAPTIST

MATTHEW 3:13–17: John was the son of Elizabeth and her husband, Zechariah, who was a priest. When the angel Gabriel announced Elizabeth would have a child, he said the baby would be filled with the Holy Spirit even before he was born. Furthermore, he would bring the people back to God, have the spirit of Elijah the prophet and prepare the way for the Lord (Lk 1:15–17).

John became a fiery preacher. He lived in the wilderness, eating honey and locusts. His words of judgment were especially aimed at those who believed that they were God’s chosen and thus didn’t have to be righteous. He called them a “brood of vipers” and said they must change their ways (Lk 3:7–8). John attracted great crowds to the Jordan River where he taught and baptized. He instructed listeners to follow God and repent from their sin.

John said he came to prepare the way for One greater than himself who would baptize with the Holy Spirit (Lk 3:16). John was pointing to Jesus, and he had the honor of baptizing Jesus in the Jordan River. After this, John encouraged his disciples to follow Jesus instead of himself (Jn 1:35–37).

John was arrested by Herod Antipas after John had condemned Herod for marrying Herodias, the former wife of Philip, Herod’s own brother. Though Herod took an interest in John, Herodias plotted John’s death. Herod eventually had John beheaded (Mk 6:17–28).

APPLICATION ✤ John’s prophetic task was to prepare the way for Jesus. Crowds of people, from the most pious to the most sinful, came to hear John speak. Rather than enjoying the fame and trying to amass crowds and honor for himself, John always pointed away from himself and toward Christ. John is an example for how each believer should live and a model and guide for Christian leadership. Our lives should be focused on bringing others to Christ. John spoke God’s message shamelessly, even to the point of his own death. May we also be unashamed of the gospel (Ro 1:16).

Jesus Is Tested in the Wilderness

4:1–11pp // Mk 1:12,13; Lk 4:1–13

4 Then Jesus was led by the Spirit into
the wilderness to be tempted[a] by the
devil. 2After fasting forty days and forty nights,[f] he was hungry. 3The tempter[g]
came to him and said, "If you are the Son
of God,[h] tell these stones to become bread."
4Jesus answered, "It is written: 'Man
shall not live on bread alone, but on every word that comes from the mouth
of God.'[b]"[i]
5Then the devil took him to the holy
city[j] and had him stand on the highest
point of the temple. 6"If you are the Son
of God," he said, "throw yourself down.
For it is written:

"'He will command his angels
concerning you,
and they will lift you up in their
hands,
so that you will not strike your
foot against a stone.'[c]"[k]

7Jesus answered him, "It is also written:
'Do not put the Lord your God to the test.'[d]"[l]
8Again, the devil took him to a very
high mountain and showed him all the
kingdoms of the world and their splendor. 9"All this I will give you," he said,
"if you will bow down and worship me."
10Jesus said to him, "Away from me,
Satan![m] For it is written: 'Worship the
Lord your God, and serve him only.'[e]"[n]
11Then the devil left him, and angels
came and attended him.[o]

Jesus Begins to Preach

12When Jesus heard that John had
been put in prison,[p] he withdrew to Gal-

4:2 [f] Ex 34:28; 1Ki 19:8
4:3 [g] 1Th 3:5 [h] Mt 3:17; Jn 5:25; Ac 9:20
4:4 [i] Dt 8:3
4:5 [j] Ne 11:1; Da 9:24; Mt 27:53
4:6 [k] Ps 91:11,12
4:7 [l] Dt 6:16
4:10 [m] 1Ch 21:1 [n] Dt 6:13
4:11 [o] Mt 26:53; Lk 22:43; Heb 1:14
4:12 [p] Mt 14:3

Mt 4:11 ❖ How does God help us stand firm against temptation in our lives?

[a] *1* The Greek for *tempted* can also mean *tested.*
[b] *4* Deut. 8:3 [c] *6* Psalm 91:11,12 [d] *7* Deut. 6:16
[e] *10* Deut. 6:13

---

judgment for those who reject the message of the arriving kingdom of God. We can create a warped view of God and the gospel by overemphasizing the judgment to come, but we just as surely distort people's view if we minimize the reality of judgment.

John is inviting those who respond to his message to experience life, to escape from the wrath to come, and to await the baptism of the Holy Spirit that the coming One will bring. No message of judgment should ever be given without the accompanying message of promised life for those who respond.

Jesus laid aside both the glory and the independent exercise of his deity to live a life like ours on earth. That is why he is the very real, very tangible example of what our lives are being transformed into when we choose to follow him.

4:1–2 The Spirit that came on Jesus at his baptism leads him to the desert and empowers Jesus to withstand Satan's temptations. The Father uses Satan's evil intention to strengthen Jesus for his messianic role.

4:3–4 Satan does not doubt Jesus' identity as the Son of God, nor is he trying to get Jesus to doubt it. If Jesus turned the stones into bread he would be outside the Father's will for the Son's human experience. Temptations are one of the enemy's ways of trying to get a person to abandon God's will.

4:5–7 By intentionally putting himself in harm's way, Jesus would be inappropriately testing his Father's love, manipulating him to send a rescuing force of angels. Such a spectacular display would not honor the Father's pathway for Jesus: obediently proclaiming the gospel of the kingdom and suffering whatever consequences may come.

4:8–10 Satan tries to sidetrack Jesus by getting him to take a shortcut to gain the kingdom that will someday be his via the hard way of the cross. Jesus says, "Away from me, Satan!" (v. 10). In this response Jesus exerts his rightful authority over Satan by issuing his first command. He quotes for the third time the book of Deuteronomy.

4:11 Matthew adds a comforting comment: "And angels came and attended him." That is, angels attend to Jesus' physical needs after his long period of fasting. This comment indicates the cosmic significance of what has just happened. The Son has begun the invasion of Satan's domain.

✜ **4:1–11** A temptation is not always something inherently "evil" but rather consists of a good thing used for wrong purposes. Therefore, one of the most important considerations when addressing temptation is to understand the proper purpose for anything we face. Said in another way, what does God want for us in a situation? Being tempted is not a sin. Succumbing to the temptation is when it becomes sin.

4:12–17 Jesus makes Capernaum, located in the ancient region of Naphtali, his base of operations. Having moved there from Nazareth in what had been the ancient territory of Zebulun, Jesus fulfills another OT prophecy (v. 16). Here, these Jews are the first to see the great light of God's deliverance in Jesus.

The phrase "from that time on" (v. 17) marks a significant turning point. The preparations for Jesus' messianic ministry are complete. The prophesied miraculous birth and infancy of the Messiah have been established.

Matthew's summary of Jesus' message is the same as that of John the Baptist: "Repent, for the kingdom of heaven has come near" (v. 17). When

ilee.[q] 13Leaving Nazareth, he went and
lived in Capernaum,[r] which was by the
lake in the area of Zebulun and Naphtali — 14to fulfill what was said through
the prophet Isaiah:

15"Land of Zebulun and land of
Naphtali,
the Way of the Sea, beyond the
Jordan,
Galilee of the Gentiles —
16the people living in darkness
have seen a great light;
on those living in the land of the
shadow of death
a light has dawned."[a][s]

4:12 [q] Mk 1:14
4:13 [r] Mk 1:21; Lk 4:23,31; Jn 2:12; 4:46,47
4:16 [s] Isa 9:1,2; Lk 2:32
4:17 [t] Mt 3:2
4:18 [u] Mt 15:29; Mk 7:31; Jn 6:1 [v] Mt 16:17,18
4:19 [w] Mk 10:21, 28,52

17From that time on Jesus began to
preach, "Repent, for the kingdom of
heaven[t] has come near."

Jesus Calls His First Disciples

4:18–22pp // Mk 1:16–20; Lk 5:2–11; Jn 1:35–42

18As Jesus was walking beside the Sea
of Galilee,[u] he saw two brothers, Simon
called Peter[v] and his brother Andrew.
They were casting a net into the lake,
for they were fishermen. 19"Come,
follow me,"[w] Jesus said, "and I will
send you out to fish for people." 20At

[a] *16* Isaiah 9:1,2

---

people hear the kingdom of heaven is near, they expect Jesus to inaugurate the kind of kingdom consistent with their hopes.

Jesus will indeed fulfill the prophetic hope. But he will bring this hope to complete fulfillment only when he returns as the Son of Man in glory (cf. 24:29-31). This dual phenomenon is the "already but not yet" nature of the kingdom. Jesus has *already* inaugurated the kingdom, but it has *not yet* reached its final form.

4:18-22 Jesus approaches two men and calls out, "Come, follow me . . . and I will send you out to fish for people." They immediately leave their nets and follow him.

Next, Jesus sees two other brothers, James and John, the sons of Zebedee, who are mending their fishing nets. Caring for this equipment took up much of a morning after a night of fishing. Jesus interrupts their busy activities and calls them. By obeying Jesus' call, they are relinquishing

JESUS' BAPTISM AND TEMPTATION

Events surrounding Jesus' baptism reveal the intense religious excitement and social ferment of the early days of John the Baptist's ministry. Herod had been cruel and power-hungry; Roman military occupation was harsh. Some agitation centered around the change of governors from Gratus to Pilate in AD 26. Most of the people hoped for a religious solution to their intolerable political situation, and when they heard of a new prophet, they flocked out into the desert to hear him. The religious sect (Essenes) from Qumran professed similar doctrines of repentance and baptism. Jesus was baptized at Bethany on the other side of the Jordan (see Jn 1:28). John also baptized at "Aenon near Salim" (Jn 3:23).

Many interpreters place John's baptismal ministry at a point on the middle stretch of the Jordan River, where trade routes converge at a natural ford not far from the modern site of Tel Shalem.

once they left their nets and followed
him.
21Going on from there, he saw two
other brothers, James son of Zebedee
and his brother John.[x] They were in a
boat with their father Zebedee, preparing their nets. Jesus called them, 22and
immediately they left the boat and their
father and followed him.

Jesus Heals the Sick

23Jesus went throughout Galilee,[y]
teaching in their synagogues,[z] proclaiming the good news[a] of the kingdom,[b]
and healing every disease and sickness among the people.[c] 24News about
him spread all over Syria,[d] and people
brought to him all who were ill with various diseases, those suffering severe pain,
the demon-possessed,[e] those having seizures,[f] and the paralyzed;[g] and he healed
them. 25Large crowds from Galilee, the
Decapolis,[a] Jerusalem, Judea and the
region across the Jordan followed him.[h]

4:21 [x] Mt 20:20
4:23 [y] Mk 1:39; Lk 4:15, 44 [z] Mt 9:35; 13:54; Mk 1:21; Lk 4:15; Jn 6:59 [a] Mk 1:14 [b] Mt 3:2; Ac 20:25 [c] Mt 8:16; 15:30; Ac 10:38
4:24 [d] Lk 2:2 [e] Mt 8:16, 28; 9:32; 15:22; Mk 1:32; 5:15, 16, 18 [f] Mt 17:15 [g] Mt 8:6; 9:2; Mk 2:3
4:25 [h] Mk 3:7, 8; Lk 6:17
5:3 [i] ver 10, 19; Mt 25:34
5:4 [j] Isa 61:2, 3; Rev 7:17
5:5 [k] Ps 37:11; Ro 4:13
5:6 [l] Isa 55:1, 2

Introduction to the Sermon on the Mount

5 Now when Jesus saw the crowds, he
went up on a mountainside and sat
down. His disciples came to him, 2and
he began to teach them.

The Beatitudes

5:3–12pp // Lk 6:20–23

He said:

3"Blessed are the poor in spirit,
for theirs is the kingdom of
heaven.[i]
4Blessed are those who mourn,
for they will be comforted.[j]
5Blessed are the meek,
for they will inherit the earth.[k]
6Blessed are those who hunger and
thirst for righteousness,
for they will be filled.[l]
7Blessed are the merciful,
for they will be shown mercy.

[a] *25* That is, the Ten Cities

---

commitment to the family business, their assets, and their livelihood.

Discipleship to Jesus was going to be different from what many might have anticipated. It was not going to be simply an apprenticeship program. Discipleship was a life that began in relationship with the Master and moved into all areas of their experience. This is the beginning of kingdom life.

4:23–25 "Teaching" is often related to explaining truth to those already familiar with the content. "Proclaiming" or preaching is generally related to teaching truth to those unfamiliar with the content. This "good news" is also demonstrated through Jesus' "healing every disease and sickness among the people" (v. 23). Both teaching and miracles announce that Israel's hoped-for kingdom promise is at hand.

4:12–25 The darkness of our own world is real even when we, or those around us, don't notice it. To be away from Jesus is to be in darkness. We can't let the superficial appearances of people mask the real needs that even they might not recognize. To reach them most effectively we must take as our calling the joy of living in the light of Jesus and continually allow our lives to shine into theirs with the true kingdom life.

Whatever our profession, discipleship means that we prioritize joining with Jesus in reaching our daily world with the Good News of life in the kingdom of heaven. We follow Jesus' call to join him in advancing the kingdom of heaven.

5:1–2 Matthew specifies three primary groups of people around Jesus in his earthly ministry. The *disciples* are those who have made a commitment to Jesus as the Messiah. The *religious leaders* are Jesus' opponents for much of his ministry. The *crowd* is a curious group of people who have not yet made a commitment to him.

5:1–2 Jesus' Sermon on the Mount is not for a few highly-committed believers. The book of Matthew is a manual on discipleship, and throughout most of church history this Gospel has been used to provide the content of instruction for fully formed Christian living.

5:3 The "poor" persons who are spiritually and emotionally in need of God's help. These people will experience their most complete fulfillment as they draw on the resources of the kingdom of heaven to guide their lives.

5:4 Mourning characterizes life in the "already but not yet" presence of the kingdom. We mourn oppression, persecution, personal sin, and social evil because we mourn the things that God mourns. We can also become instruments of the Good News of the kingdom as we share with others the comfort of God.

5:5 The "meek" are people who do not assert themselves over others to advance their own causes. This does not imply weakness, however, for this same term is applied to Jesus.

5:6 Persons who "hunger and thirst" will die if they are not filled. Those who respond to Jesus' invitation to kingdom life will find he fills their deepest personal hunger and thirst for righteousness.

5:7 In God's great mercy he does not give humans what they deserve; rather, he gives to them what they need. True disciples have experienced God's merciful forgiveness that they can then demonstrate toward others.

8 Blessed are the pure in heart,[m]
for they will see God.[n]
9 Blessed are the peacemakers,
for they will be called children of
God.[o]
10 Blessed are those who are persecuted
because of righteousness,[p]
for theirs is the kingdom of
heaven.

11 "Blessed are you when people insult
you,[q] persecute you and falsely say all
kinds of evil against you because of me.
12 Rejoice and be glad,[r] because great is
your reward in heaven, for in the same
way they persecuted the prophets who
were before you.[s]

Salt and Light

13 "You are the salt of the earth. But if
the salt loses its saltiness, how can it be
made salty again? It is no longer good
for anything, except to be thrown out
and trampled underfoot.[t]
14 "You are the light of the world.[u] A
town built on a hill cannot be hidden.
15 Neither do people light a lamp and put
it under a bowl. Instead they put it on its
stand, and it gives light to everyone in
the house.[v] 16 In the same way, let your
light shine before others, that they may
see your good deeds and glorify[w] your
Father in heaven.

The Fulfillment of the Law

17 "Do not think that I have come to
abolish the Law or the Prophets; I have
not come to abolish them but to fulfill
them.[x] 18 For truly I tell you, until heaven
and earth disappear, not the smallest letter, not the least stroke of a pen, will by
any means disappear from the Law until
everything is accomplished.[y] 19 Therefore anyone who sets aside one of the
least of these commands[z] and teaches
others accordingly will be called least
in the kingdom of heaven, but whoever
practices and teaches these commands
will be called great in the kingdom of
heaven. 20 For I tell you that unless your
righteousness surpasses that of the Pharisees and the teachers of the law, you
will certainly not enter the kingdom of
heaven.

5:8 [m] Ps 24:3, 4 [n] Heb 12:14; Rev 22:4
5:9 [o] ver 44, 45; Ro 8:14
5:10 [p] 1Pe 3:14
5:11 [q] 1Pe 4:14
5:12 [r] Ac 5:41; 1Pe 4:13, 16 [s] Mt 23:31, 37; Ac 7:52; 1Th 2:15
5:13 [t] Mk 9:50; Lk 14:34, 35
5:14 [u] Jn 8:12
5:15 [v] Mk 4:21; Lk 8:16
5:16 [w] Mt 9:8
5:17 [x] Ro 3:31
5:18 [y] Lk 16:17
5:19 [z] Jas 2:10

Mt 5:16 ❖ How can we truly let our light shine and by our actions point others to God?

5:8 Jesus declares here that a pure heart is what produces external purity, not vice versa. Those who have set their heart on God will see God in the life and ministry of Jesus.

5:9 The theme of peace permeates the biblical record. Biblical peace is more than the absence of strife and conflict. It is a condition of human flourishing that indicates completeness and wholeness in every area of life, including one's relationship with God, neighbors, and others. The true peacemakers are those who wait and work for God.

5:10 Persecution especially points to the way that the religious leaders hounded the people and excluded any who did not embrace their particular brand of righteousness. Jesus says that the kingdom of God belongs to these oppressed people, not the religious leaders.

5:11–12 Jesus prepares his disciples for the time when persecution will indeed come to them. The kingdom is theirs, and in it they will truly rejoice.

5:13 The metaphor of salt and light indicates that the disciples of Jesus are themselves necessary for the welfare of the world. Imposter disciples, who simply attempt to put on the flavoring of the kingdom life, will be revealed.

5:14–16 Bearing the light of the gospel in both message and life will help others see that the kingdom of heaven is truly in the world, and they will glorify their heavenly Father.

✣ **5:3–16** The Beatitudes are expressions of Spirit-produced kingdom life, revealing to the entire world that a transformation of creation is beginning in Jesus' disciples. That is why we are blessed if we are his disciples.

5:17 Fulfilling the Law and the Prophets is more than obedience (i.e., keeping the law). Jesus has come to help his disciples have a deeper understanding of God's vision for kingdom living.

5:18: Jesus confirms the full authority of the OT as Scripture. His view of the divine authority of Scripture extends to the actual words, even letters and parts of letters. It entails what modern theologians refer to as verbal, plenary inspiration. Scripture does not simply contain the words of God; the words of Scripture are the very Word of God.

5:19 "Least" and "great" are ways to acknowledge those who have been faithful to the revealed will of God as it is taught by Jesus.

5:20 The arrival of the kingdom of heaven produces spiritual transformation in the disciple's heart, which will ultimately produce transformation in the disciple's external ethical life.

✣ **5:17–20** As the disciple continues to respond obediently to the word of God taught and preached by Jesus and energized by the Spirit, the newly transformed heart directs the transformation of the person from the inside to the outside. The indwelling Spirit directs the renewing of the mind, the disciplining of the

Murder

5:25,26pp // Lk 12:58,59

21"You have heard that it was said to
the people long ago, 'You shall not murder,[a][a] and anyone who murders will be
subject to judgment.' 22But I tell you that
anyone who is angry with a brother or
sister[b,c] will be subject to judgment.[b]
Again, anyone who says to a brother or
sister, 'Raca,'[d] is answerable to the court.[c]
And anyone who says, 'You fool!' will be
in danger of the fire of hell.[d]
23"Therefore, if you are offering your
gift at the altar and there remember that
your brother or sister has something
against you, 24leave your gift there in
front of the altar. First go and be reconciled to them; then come and offer
your gift.
25"Settle matters quickly with your adversary who is taking you to court. Do it
while you are still together on the way,
or your adversary may hand you over
to the judge, and the judge may hand
you over to the officer, and you may be
thrown into prison. 26Truly I tell you,
you will not get out until you have paid
the last penny.

Adultery

27"You have heard that it was said,
'You shall not commit adultery.'[e][e] 28But
I tell you that anyone who looks at a
woman lustfully has already committed
adultery with her in his heart.[f] 29If your
right eye causes you to stumble,[g] gouge
it out and throw it away. It is better for
you to lose one part of your body than
for your whole body to be thrown into
hell. 30And if your right hand causes you
to stumble, cut it off and throw it away.
It is better for you to lose one part of
your body than for your whole body to
go into hell.

Divorce

31"It has been said, 'Anyone who divorces his wife must give her a certificate
of divorce.'[f][h] 32But I tell you that anyone
who divorces his wife, except for sexual immorality, makes her the victim of
adultery, and anyone who marries a divorced woman commits adultery.[i]

Oaths

33"Again, you have heard that it was
said to the people long ago, 'Do not break
your oath,[j] but fulfill to the Lord the vows
you have made.'[k] 34But I tell you, do not

5:21 [a] Ex 20:13; Dt 5:17
5:22 [b] 1Jn 3:15 [c] Mt 26:59 [d] Jas 3:6
5:27 [e] Ex 20:14; Dt 5:18
5:28 [f] Pr 6:25
5:29 [g] Mt 18:6, 8,9; Mk 9:42-47
5:31 [h] Dt 24:1-4
5:32 [i] Lk 16:18
5:33 [j] Lev 19:12 [k] Nu 30:2; Dt 23:21; Mt 23:16-22

[a] *21* Exodus 20:13 [b] *22* The Greek word for *brother or sister* (*adelphos*) refers here to a fellow disciple, whether man or woman; also in verse 23. [c] *22* Some manuscripts *brother or sister without cause* [d] *22* An Aramaic term of contempt [e] *27* Exodus 20:14 [f] *31* Deut. 24:1

---

body, and the purifying of social relations so that the disciple says yes to God with his or her entire person. The disciple bears the fruit of the Spirit in a life given to God that is being transformed to be like Jesus.

5:21–26 The fact that men and women have been created in the image of God lies behind these teachings. Jesus' statement, "But I tell you," introduces three ways that a person's life can be injured, besides the physical act of murder: (1) by exhibiting anger toward a disciple, (2) by calling another disciple an Aramaic term that implies they are empty-headed, and (3) by saying "you fool" to a disciple (v. 22). To treat a person with such contempt is to strip away their personal identity.

The expression "fire of hell" (v. 22) is the English translation of *Gehenna*. It is from the Hebrew and means "valley of the son of Hinnom." This valley is where Ahaz and Manasseh sacrificed their sons to Molek (2Ki 23:10). Later, the valley was used to burn refuse from Jerusalem. The constant burning made the valley an appropriate reference to fires of punishment. By the time of Jesus, the term *Gehenna* was used to indicate the state of final punishment (cf. Mt 18:9).

5:27–30 It is not enough for spouses to only maintain physical purity. The purity of marriage includes exclusive devotion to one another in every aspect of each of their lives.

Jesus does not advocate physical self-mutilation in vv. 29–30. Through dramatic figures of speech, he indicates the kind of rigorous self-discipline that committed disciples must display.

5:31–32 Since divorce was a widespread phenomenon in the ancient world, God instituted a regulation through Moses. Jesus goes back to God's original intention both for marriage and the Mosaic regulation. God intended marriage to be a permanent union of a man and woman in a "one flesh" relationship (see Ge 2:24). One reason God hates divorce is because an illicit divorce turns the spouses into adulterers when they remarry.

However, as did Moses, Jesus allows for an exception—namely, when a person has committed any sinful sexual activity that intentionally divides the marital relationship. Jesus allows divorce in this case to protect the nonoffending partner.

5:33–37 Jesus goes to the heart of the law's intent regarding oaths when he says that his disciples are not to swear "at all" (v. 34). Jesus is telling his disciples they should be people of such integrity and truthfulness that whatever they say is absolutely believable and dependable.

swear an oath at all:[l] either by heaven,
for it is God's throne;[m] 35 or by the earth,
for it is his footstool; or by Jerusalem, for
it is the city of the Great King.[n] 36 And do
not swear by your head, for you cannot
make even one hair white or black. 37 All
you need to say is simply 'Yes' or 'No';[o]
anything beyond this comes from the
evil one.[a][p]

Eye for Eye

38 "You have heard that it was said, 'Eye
for eye, and tooth for tooth.'[b][q] 39 But I tell
you, do not resist an evil person. If anyone slaps you on the right cheek, turn to
them the other cheek also.[r] 40 And if anyone wants to sue you and take your shirt,
hand over your coat as well. 41 If anyone
forces you to go one mile, go with them
two miles. 42 Give to the one who asks
you, and do not turn away from the one
who wants to borrow from you.[s]

Love for Enemies

43 "You have heard that it was said,
'Love your neighbor[c][t] and hate your enemy.'[u] 44 But I tell you, love your enemies
and pray for those who persecute you,[v]
45 that you may be children[w] of your Father in heaven. He causes his sun to rise
on the evil and the good, and sends rain
on the righteous and the unrighteous.[x]
46 If you love those who love you, what
reward will you get?[y] Are not even the
tax collectors doing that? 47 And if you
greet only your own people, what are
you doing more than others? Do not even
pagans do that? 48 Be perfect, therefore,
as your heavenly Father is perfect.[z]

Giving to the Needy

6 "Be careful not to practice your righteousness in front of others to be
seen by them.[a] If you do, you will have
no reward from your Father in heaven.
2 "So when you give to the needy, do
not announce it with trumpets, as the
hypocrites do in the synagogues and
on the streets, to be honored by others.
Truly I tell you, they have received their
reward in full. 3 But when you give to the
needy, do not let your left hand know
what your right hand is doing, 4 so that
your giving may be in secret. Then your
Father, who sees what is done in secret,
will reward you.[b]

5:34 [l] Jas 5:12 [m] Isa 66:1; Mt 23:22
5:35 [n] Ps 48:2
5:37 [o] Jas 5:12 [p] Mt 6:13; 13:19, 38; Jn 17:15; 2Th 3:3; 1Jn 2:13,14; 3:12; 5:18,19
5:38 [q] Ex 21:24; Lev 24:20; Dt 19:21
5:39 [r] Lk 6:29; Ro 12:17,19; 1Co 6:7; 1Pe 3:9
5:42 [s] Dt 15:8; Lk 6:30
5:43 [t] Lev 19:18 [u] Dt 23:6
5:44 [v] Lk 6:27, 28; 23:34; Ac 7:60; Ro 12:14; 1Co 4:12; 1Pe 2:23
5:45 [w] ver 9 [x] Job 25:3
5:46 [y] Lk 6:32
5:48 [z] Lev 19:2; 1Pe 1:16
6:1 [a] Mt 23:5
6:4 [b] ver 6,18; Col 3:23,24

[a] *37* Or *from evil* [b] *38* Exodus 21:24; Lev. 24:20; Deut. 19:21 [c] *43* Lev. 19:18

5:38–42 The common person was at the mercy of the Romans everywhere. Within this oppressive atmosphere, Jesus points to the motivation of the individual disciple who has been taken advantage of and wronged. Even when they are being abused, they must think of ways to advance the kingdom of heaven and spread its influence on this earth. Jesus himself lived out this radical principle and became a vivid example for his followers.

5:43–47 Jesus takes the competing attitudes of love for neighbor and hate for enemy and brings them together in a way contrary to human nature and contrary to what was occurring in many areas in Israel. This teaching actually represents the love that God has for all humans. God loves all people and wants all to come to repentance. Jesus' disciples are to look at people in this world as God does and to love them enough to reach out to them with the message of reconciliation, even to the point that they "pray for those who persecute" (v. 44) them. This kind of love demonstrates a right relationship between God the Father and Jesus' disciples.

5:48 Jesus is the ultimate example for his disciples to follow as they hear the command, "Be perfect, therefore, as your heavenly Father is perfect." That statement implies a goal that Jesus' disciples are to pursue with restless dissatisfaction until they reach eternity.

5:21–48 Respecting the purity of marriage allows Jesus' disciples to understand God's original design for marriage and to be committed to its purity. We should be careful not to read into Jesus' statement about divorce what he did not imply. He did not declare the exception of *sexual infidelity* to require divorce; reconciliation and forgiveness are always the goal. Jesus also did not state that remarriage in the case of a legitimate divorce is invalid. Further, he did not state that illegitimate divorce and even illegitimate remarriage are unpardonable sins. While there are always consequences for going contrary to Jesus' intentions for us, we must be careful not to create oppressive burdens that cancel out God's grace and restoration.

6:1 The term translated "reward" can indicate payment of "wages" (20:8) or the compensation of a person's good deeds with a good prize.

6:2–4 The term translated "hypocrites" (v. 2) was originally used for actors on a Greek stage who put on various masks to play different roles. Jesus here criticizes the religious leaders for a particular form of hypocrisy: performing external acts of righteousness that mask, even from themselves, their own inner corruption. Jesus' disciples are to go to the opposite extreme and keep secret the work they do for Jesus. Human praise cannot be compared to the value of being recognized by God.

Prayer

6:9–13pp // Lk 11:2–4

5"And when you pray, do not be like the
hypocrites, for they love to pray standing[c] in the synagogues and on the street
corners to be seen by others. Truly I tell
you, they have received their reward in
full. 6But when you pray, go into your
room, close the door and pray to your
Father,[d] who is unseen. Then your Father, who sees what is done in secret, will
reward you. 7And when you pray, do not
keep on babbling[e] like pagans, for they
think they will be heard because of their
many words.[f] 8Do not be like them, for
your Father knows what you need[g] before you ask him.
9"This, then, is how you should pray:

"'Our Father in heaven,
hallowed be your name,
10 your kingdom[h] come,
your will be done,[i]
on earth as it is in heaven.
11 Give us today our daily
bread.[j]
12 And forgive us our debts,
as we also have forgiven our
debtors.[k]
13 And lead us not into temptation,[a][l]
but deliver us from the evil one.[b]'[m]

14For if you forgive other people when
they sin against you, your heavenly Father will also forgive you.[n] 15But if you do
not forgive others their sins, your Father
will not forgive your sins.[o]

Fasting

16"When you fast, do not look somber[p] as the hypocrites do, for they dis-
figure their faces to show others they
are fasting. Truly I tell you, they have
received their reward in full. 17But when
you fast, put oil on your head and wash
your face, 18so that it will not be obvious
to others that you are fasting, but only
to your Father, who is unseen; and your
Father, who sees what is done in secret,
will reward you.[q]

6:5 [c] Mk 11:25; Lk 18:10-14
6:6 [d] 2Ki 4:33
6:7 [e] Ecc 5:2 [f] 1Ki 18:26-29
6:8 [g] ver 32
6:10 [h] Mt 3:2 [i] Mt 26:39
6:11 [j] Pr 30:8
6:12 [k] Mt 18:21-35
6:13 [l] Jas 1:13 [m] Mt 5:37
6:14 [n] Mt 18:21-35; Mk 11:25, 26; Eph 4:32; Col 3:13
6:15 [o] Mt 18:35
6:16 [p] Isa 58:5
6:18 [q] ver 4, 6

[a] 13 The Greek for *temptation* can also mean *testing*. [b] 13 Or *from evil*; some late manuscripts *one, / for yours is the kingdom and the power and the glory forever. Amen.*

6:5–6 Prayer can be perverted into an act of hypocrisy when the external act masks an inner corrupt motive. Jesus directs his disciples to go to their inner "room." The focus is on intimacy with God in one's heart, which is at the center of all prayer, whether it happens to be given publicly or privately.
6:7–8 Long, continued prayer is not improper, because Jesus himself prayed through whole nights. Prayer is much about changing *us*, our character, our will, and our values, even while we seek God's response.
6:9–13 The way Jesus uses "*my* Father" (emphasis added) to address his heavenly Father is exceptional because Jesus is the unique Son (e.g., 7:21; 12:50). But God is also "*our* Father" (6:9, emphasis added), expressing the relationship we have with one another as disciples and with Jesus as our brother. Through this relationship, the disciples have entered into a relationship with Jesus' Father.
6:9 Jesus' disciples will honor God's name in their prayers but especially as they submit to his power and authority.
6:10 This petition is reflected in a prayer expressed in the early church's appeal, "Come, Lord!" This is the oldest recorded Christian prayer (1Co 16:22). In that cry, Paul applies the divine title "Lord" to Jesus the Messiah.

God reigns in heaven absolutely, so all of heaven experiences his perfect will. Jesus prays that earth will experience that same rule of God. Jesus' disciples, those who have submitted to God's will as Jesus did, are the living testimony to the world that God's will can be experienced today.
6:11 In the same way that manna was only given one day at a time, disciples are to rely on God for daily provisions. This helps them develop a conscious, daily dependence on him.
6:12 Sin creates an obligation or debt to God that we cannot possibly repay. Jesus' disciples are not simply to relish their own state of forgiveness; they are also to forgive others. Forgiveness of others is *proof* that the disciples' sins are forgiven and that they possesses salvation.
6:13 This petition indicates that the disciples should pray either for relief from testing or for their testing not to become an occasion for temptation. Disciples must rely on God for victory in all of the spiritual battles of life.
6:14–15 Once disciples have received forgiveness and salvation, they are to forgive with the same forgiveness they have received. This is the evidence they are indeed forgiven.
6:16–18 Jesus assumes his disciples will fast because he says simply, "When you fast" (v. 16). Disciples are to act as normal while fasting; other people do not need to know of their religious discipline. The reward for fasting is the continued development of inner righteousness to which all disciples are to aspire.

6:1–18 Throughout church history, the spiritual disciplines have been a key to spiritual growth. These disciplines are viewed from different perspectives. However we might view them, the important point is to remember that the righteousness of the kingdom of heaven is an inside-out process. Jesus provides this orientation to counteract the hypocritical practice of operating only on the surface.

Personal transformation begins in the inner person through the work of the Spirit of God,

Treasures in Heaven

6:22,23pp // Lk 11:34–36

19“Do not store up for yourselves treasures on earth,[r] where moths and vermin
destroy,[s] and where thieves break in and
steal. 20But store up for yourselves treasures in heaven,[t] where moths and vermin do not destroy, and where thieves do
not break in and steal.[u] 21For where your
treasure is, there your heart will be also.[v]
22“The eye is the lamp of the body. If
your eyes are healthy,[a] your whole body
will be full of light. 23But if your eyes are
unhealthy,[b] your whole body will be full
of darkness. If then the light within you
is darkness, how great is that darkness!
24“No one can serve two masters. Either you will hate the one and love the
other, or you will be devoted to the one
and despise the other. You cannot serve
both God and money.[w]

Do Not Worry

6:25–33pp // Lk 12:22–31

25“Therefore I tell you, do not worry[x] about your life, what you will eat
or drink; or about your body, what you
will wear. Is not life more than food, and
the body more than clothes? 26Look at
the birds of the air; they do not sow or
reap or store away in barns, and yet your
heavenly Father feeds them.[y] Are you not
much more valuable than they?[z] 27Can
any one of you by worrying add a single
hour to your life[c]?[a]
28“And why do you worry about clothes?
See how the flowers of the field grow.
They do not labor or spin. 29Yet I tell you
that not even Solomon in all his splendor[b] was dressed like one of these. 30If
that is how God clothes the grass of the
field, which is here today and tomorrow
is thrown into the fire, will he not much
more clothe you—you of little faith?[c] 31So
do not worry, saying, ‘What shall we eat?’
or ‘What shall we drink?’ or ‘What shall we
wear?’ 32For the pagans run after all these
things, and your heavenly Father knows
that you need them.[d] 33But seek first his
kingdom and his righteousness, and all
these things will be given to you as well.[e]
34Therefore do not worry about tomorrow,
for tomorrow will worry about itself. Each
day has enough trouble of its own.

6:19 [r] Pr 23:4; Heb 13:5 [s] Jas 5:2,3
6:20 [t] Mt 19:21; Lk 12:33; 18:22; 1Ti 6:19 [u] Lk 12:33
6:21 [v] Lk 12:34
6:24 [w] Lk 16:13
6:25 [x] ver 27, 28,31,34; Lk 10:41; 12:11, 22; Php 4:6; 1Pe 5:7
6:26 [y] Job 38:41; Ps 147:9 [z] Mt 10:29-31
6:27 [a] Ps 39:5
6:29 [b] 1Ki 10:4-7
6:30 [c] Mt 8:26; 14:31; 16:8
6:32 [d] ver 8
6:33 [e] Mt 19:29; Mk 10:29-30

Mt 6:21 ❖ Would someone looking at our lives conclude that our hearts are set on God? Why or why not?

[a] *22* The Greek for *healthy* here implies *generous.*
[b] *23* The Greek for *unhealthy* here implies *stingy.*
[c] *27* Or *single cubit to your height*

---

which produces change on the outside as we discipline ourselves to be more Christlike. That includes keeping our good works toward others secret so that we check our motivations. We do not do God’s work in the world to be praised by others. The same is true with prayer, fasting, and all the other spiritual disciplines.

6:19–21 Moth, rust, and thieves represent those forces that cause earthly treasures to diminish in value and finally be destroyed. Such things do not provide ultimate security. The contrast between “treasures on earth” and “treasures in heaven” implies a difference in values. Whatever the disciple has placed as his or her highest value is a gauge of the condition of the heart. The righteous value must be God himself for security and direction in life.
6:22–23 The eye becomes the conduit that fills the heart with what each person focuses on. If a disciple’s eyes are fixed on earthly treasure and earthly security, then the heart will likewise be full of darkness.
6:24 The term for “serve” indicates the work of a slave, not an employee. A slave is the property of one master, which implies exclusive service. One must completely reject anything that hinders attachment to Jesus and give oneself completely to him.
6:25 The principle about worry is expressed in the simple statement “Do not worry about your life.” Sometimes “worry” can be translated “concern.” Concern is inappropriate when it is misdirected, indicating a lack of trust in God.
6:26–27 Jesus’ disciples should not worry because the Father cares for his creatures. When Jesus’ disciples are responsible for carrying out the proper ways of life as ordained by God, God is faithful to carry out his end of the order.
6:28–30 “Little faith” is a favorite expression of Jesus, found mainly in this Gospel. It indicates not *absence* of faith but *deficiency* of faith.
6:31–32 Those with faith in God’s provision will not worry and will reject the pursuits and values of unbelievers.
6:33 The use of the imperative “seek” does not mean to look for something not present. Jesus has already announced the arrival of the kingdom. In this context, it means that his disciples are to make the kingdom of heaven the center of their priorities.
6:34 All the worry in the world today can do nothing about the cares and problems of tomorrow. As disciples learn to let God care for them today, they will become increasingly secure in his care for them tomorrow.

✜ **6:19–34** If we put Jesus at the center of our lives, we will avoid the modern idolatry of worry. We probably do not think of worry as a form of idolatry, but it is when we allow

CHARACTER OF GOD // GOD PROVIDES

Matthew 6:26: "Look at the birds of the air; they do not sow or reap or store away in barns, and yet your heavenly Father feeds them."

The created world is full of wonder. Generation after generation of animals survive in seemingly hostile conditions. From the smallest insects to the largest whales, the surviving and thriving of animals is a testimony to God, their heavenly provider.

God himself points this out to Job. God asked Job: Do you feed the lions? Do you feed the baby ravens? (Job 38:39–41). The point is that God alone provides for his creatures. Humorously, God points to the example of an ostrich mother: She's so foolish that she lays her eggs on the ground where they could get crushed, and then when they hatch, she is not even a good mother (Job 39:13–18). Despite that, the ostrich survives and puts even the horse and rider to shame when it runs.

When Jesus spoke about God providing for the needs of even the smallest birds, his point was that God will also supply the needs of his children. If God provides for little birds, how much more will God provide for his people who love him? Therefore, Jesus says, do not worry about what you will eat or what you will wear (Mt 6:25). God, your heavenly provider, knows what you need. The same God who provides for the lion, the raven and the ostrich will provide for you.

APPLICATION ✚ Jesus talks about God being our heavenly provider to teach us to trust in him. Sometimes we can get caught up in cycles of worry: Will we have enough? What if we don't? Our thoughts spiral into fear and fretting. Jesus wants to break us out of those unhealthy cycles. He reminds us that God already knows what we need, and God is our loving provider. Worry will not help us. We need to bring our hearts and minds back to God, our heavenly Father.

Judging Others

7:3–5pp // Lk 6:41,42

7 "Do not judge, or you too will be
judged.[f] 2 For in the same way you
judge others, you will be judged, and
with the measure you use, it will be measured to you.[g]
3 "Why do you look at the speck of
sawdust in your brother's eye and pay
no attention to the plank in your own
eye? 4 How can you say to your brother,
'Let me take the speck out of your eye,'
when all the time there is a plank in your
own eye? 5 You hypocrite, first take the
plank out of your own eye, and then you
will see clearly to remove the speck from
your brother's eye.
6 "Do not give dogs what is sacred; do
not throw your pearls to pigs. If you do,
they may trample them under their feet,
and turn and tear you to pieces.

Ask, Seek, Knock

7:7–11pp // Lk 11:9–13

7 "Ask and it will be given to you;[h] seek
and you will find; knock and the door

7:1 [f] Lk 6:37; Ro 14:4,10,13; 1Co 4:5; Jas 4:11,12
7:2 [g] Mk 4:24; Lk 6:38
7:7 [h] Mt 21:22; Mk 11:24; Jn 14:13,14; 15:7,16; 16:23,24; Jas 1:5-8; 4:2,3; 1Jn 3:22; 5:14,15

---

it to take our eyes off Jesus. We substitute despair, hopelessness, or fear in place of God and turn to our own efforts at trying to control our environment. This can be a harsh world, and worry can consume us. A way of reversing the trend toward anxiety is to look around at what we have and what God has done and then say, "Thank you." He is our Master and Provider, the One who has given us kingdom life, kingdom priorities, and kingdom values, by which we can truly say, "Thank you."

7:1-5 True disciples, those who have been impacted by the mercy of God in the arrival of the kingdom of heaven, will exhibit mercy toward one another, not judgment. The responsibility to help each other remove the "speck" of sin must come from a humble and self-examined life: one that has first removed the "plank" of self-righteous judgment.

7:6 In the ancient world, dogs lived in squalor, running in the streets and scavenging for food. The reference here includes all those who are hostile to Jesus' disciples. The gospel of the kingdom must not be defiled by those who are unreceptive to, or have rejected, Jesus' invitation.

Pigs, like dogs, were scavenging animals. "Pearls" symbolize the value of the message of the kingdom of heaven. Something so valuable should not be given to those who have no appreciation for such precious truths; their nature is demonstrated by their rejection of that message.

7:7-8 "Ask" indicates coming to God with humility. "Seek" links praying with action; for instance, praying for a job while at the same time checking out leads. "Knock" includes perseverance, as

will be opened to you. 8For everyone who asks receives; the one who seeks finds;[i] and to the one who knocks, the door will be opened.

9"Which of you, if your son asks for bread, will give him a stone? 10Or if he asks for a fish, will give him a snake? 11If you, then, though you are evil, know how to give good gifts to your children, how much more will your Father in heaven give good gifts to those who ask him! 12So in everything, do to others what you would have them do to you,[j] for this sums up the Law and the Prophets.[k]

The Narrow and Wide Gates

13"Enter through the narrow gate.[l] For wide is the gate and broad is the road that leads to destruction, and many enter through it. 14But small is the gate and narrow the road that leads to life, and only a few find it.

True and False Prophets

15"Watch out for false prophets.[m] They come to you in sheep's clothing, but inwardly they are ferocious wolves.[n] 16By their fruit you will recognize them.[o] Do people pick grapes from thornbushes, or figs from thistles?[p] 17Likewise, every good tree bears good fruit, but a bad tree bears bad fruit. 18A good tree cannot bear bad fruit, and a bad tree cannot bear good fruit. 19Every tree that does not bear good fruit is cut down and thrown into the fire.[q] 20Thus, by their fruit you will recognize them.

7:8 [i] Pr 8:17; Jer 29:12,13
7:12 [j] Lk 6:31 [k] Ro 13:8-10; Gal 5:14
7:13 [l] Lk 13:24
7:15 [m] Jer 23:16; Mt 24:24; Mk 13:22; Lk 6:26; 2Pe 2:1; 1Jn 4:1; Rev 16:13 [n] Ac 20:29
7:16 [o] Mt 12:33; Lk 6:44 [p] Jas 3:12
7:19 [q] Mt 3:10
7:21 [r] Hos 8:2; Mt 25:11 [s] Ro 2:13; Jas 1:22
7:22 [t] Mt 10:15 [u] 1Co 13:1-3
7:23 [v] Ps 6:8; Mt 25:12, 41; Lk 13:25-27
7:24 [w] Jas 1:22-25

Mt 7:24 ❖ How can we best put Jesus' words into practice today?

True and False Disciples

21"Not everyone who says to me, 'Lord, Lord,'[r] will enter the kingdom of heaven, but only the one who does the will of my Father who is in heaven.[s] 22Many will say to me on that day,[t] 'Lord, Lord, did we not prophesy in your name and in your name drive out demons and in your name perform many miracles?'[u] 23Then I will tell them plainly, 'I never knew you. Away from me, you evildoers!'[v]

The Wise and Foolish Builders

7:24–27pp // Lk 6:47–49

24"Therefore everyone who hears these words of mine and puts them into practice[w] is like a wise man who built his house on the rock. 25The rain came down, the streams rose, and the winds blew and beat against that house; yet it did not fall, because it had its foundation on the rock. 26But everyone who hears

---

when the disciple faithfully prays for unbelieving family members' salvation, shares the gospel, and demonstrates gospel values in their life.

7:9–11 The heavenly Father, who is absolutely trustworthy, will always give to the disciples what they really need.

7:12 Jesus' teaching on prayer and the Golden Rule brings to light two significant points about stability in one's discipleship. First, stability will come as disciples learn how to depend on their heavenly Father. Second, stability will come through a healthy commitment to live for the benefit of others.

✣ **7:1-12** The kind of balance advocated in this passage means to take two seemingly opposite truths and to live with them both at the same time, even though we may not be able to understand completely how they fit together. Doing so is demanding, because we are always thinking and weighing our actions and thoughts. We must recognize that in the Christian life, we are always in process. But our pursuit of the goal to understand and apply all of God's truth is what will help us to stay balanced.

7:13–14 One can travel comfortably on the roomy road. However, the comfort is deceiving, because it ends in "destruction" (v. 13), a common word for eternal punishment. The narrow gate and road are more restrictive because they are limited to Jesus and his manner of discipleship. The way of discipleship stretches throughout one's years on earth, ultimately leading to eternal life.

7:15–20 Jesus admonishes his disciples to be "fruit inspectors" of those passing themselves off as prophets. False prophets will lead people away from God or speak prophecies that are not fulfilled.

7:21–23 False disciples claim prophetic status and point to charismatic activity as a sign of discipleship (v. 22). False disciples gain power "in Jesus' name," but their activities are meaningless for their own eternal destiny. The ultimate authenticity of one's life will be proven at the end of time. Here Jesus claims the divine right to know the inner recesses of a person's heart.

7:24–27 The audience of the Sermon on the Mount would readily understand the surface meaning intended in the parable. But would they see Jesus' point? Would they reject the shifting sands of the religious leadership and choose instead Jesus' words as the foundation for their lives? The choice is no less stark in our own day. Wise men and women build their lives on Jesus, regardless of the current cultural or religious values or circumstances.

these words of mine and does not put them into practice is like a foolish man who built his house on sand. 27The rain came down, the streams rose, and the winds blew and beat against that house, and it fell with a great crash."

28When Jesus had finished saying these things,[x] the crowds were amazed at his teaching,[y] 29because he taught as one who had authority, and not as their teachers of the law.

Jesus Heals a Man With Leprosy

8:2–4pp // Mk 1:40–44; Lk 5:12–14

8 When Jesus came down from the mountainside, large crowds followed him. 2A man with leprosy[az] came and knelt before him[a] and said, "Lord, if you are willing, you can make me clean."

3Jesus reached out his hand and touched the man. "I am willing," he said. "Be clean!" Immediately he was cleansed of his leprosy. 4Then Jesus said to him, "See that you don't tell anyone.[b] But go, show yourself to the priest and offer the gift Moses commanded,[c] as a testimony to them."

The Faith of the Centurion

8:5–13pp // Lk 7:1–10

5When Jesus had entered Capernaum, a centurion came to him, asking for help. 6"Lord," he said, "my servant lies at home paralyzed, suffering terribly."

7Jesus said to him, "Shall I come and heal him?"

8The centurion replied, "Lord, I do not deserve to have you come under my roof. But just say the word, and my servant will be healed.[d] 9For I myself am a man under authority, with soldiers under me. I tell this one, 'Go,' and he goes; and that one, 'Come,' and he comes. I say to my servant, 'Do this,' and he does it."

10When Jesus heard this, he was amazed and said to those following him, "Truly I tell you, I have not found anyone in Israel with such great faith.[e] 11I say to you that many will come from the east and the west,[f] and will take their places at the feast with Abraham, Isaac and Jacob in the kingdom of heaven.[g] 12But the subjects of the kingdom[h] will be thrown outside, into the darkness, where there will be weeping and gnashing of teeth."[i]

13Then Jesus said to the centurion, "Go! Let it be done just as you believed it would."[j] And his servant was healed at that moment.

Jesus Heals Many

8:14–16pp // Mk 1:29–34; Lk 4:38–41

14When Jesus came into Peter's house, he saw Peter's mother-in-law lying in bed with a fever. 15He touched her hand and

7:28 [x] Mt 11:1; 13:53; 19:1; 26:1 [y] Mt 13:54; Mk 1:22; 6:2; Lk 4:32; Jn 7:46
8:2 [z] Lk 5:12 [a] Mt 9:18; 15:25; 18:26; 20:20
8:4 [b] Mt 9:30; Mk 5:43; 7:36; 8:30 [c] Lev 14:2-32
8:8 [d] Ps 107:20
8:10 [e] Mt 15:28
8:11 [f] Ps 107:3; Isa 49:12; 59:19; Mal 1:11 [g] Lk 13:29
8:12 [h] Mt 13:38 [i] Mt 13:42,50; 22:13; 24:51; 25:30; Lk 13:28
8:13 [j] Mt 9:22

[a] 2 The Greek word traditionally translated *leprosy* was used for various diseases affecting the skin.

7:28–29 Matthew's conclusion is ironic; it indicates a variety of emotional responses but not necessarily a commitment to Jesus' messianic ministry. Only when a person accepts Jesus' invitation and enters the kingdom of heaven do they become a disciple.

> **7:13–29** Jesus calls would-be disciples to carefully consider the alternative of life in the kingdom of heaven, as narrow and as difficult as it may be, against the popular road that leads to destruction.
>
> When we look closely at Jesus' saying in vv. 13-14, we see that the gate comes first. Jesus offers by grace the invitation to salvation and a life of walking with him. That decision determines our course in life. We must ask God for discernment and the wisdom of the Holy Spirit as we live all aspects of this life.

8:1–17 Matthew demonstrates how Jesus' messianic ministry breaks down barriers so that all may respond to his invitation to be a part of the kingdom of heaven.

8:1–4 As Jesus reaches out to touch the leper, instead of becoming unclean himself he cleanses the leper. By commanding the leper to perform the prescribed ritual of presenting himself to the priest, Jesus fulfills the law required of lepers for reentry into society (Lev 14:1–32).

8:5–13 The centurion of Capernaum must have been an able and responsible official who maintained good relations with the Jewish population. This centurion honors an even greater authority in Jesus, whose word alone, like God's word, can heal.

Jesus' statement in v. 10 both singles out the centurion for his exemplary faith and chastises Israel for its lack of faith. Those who do not turn to Jesus in faith as the messianic deliverer will receive just punishment, whether Jew or Gentile. The mission to the Gentiles has not yet been declared, but Jesus' reply to the centurion indicates that the door to the kingdom is open to whomever believes.

8:14–15 Matthew's expression "lying in bed with a fever" (v. 14) indicates that Peter's mother-in-law is in the throes of a severe illness, perhaps malaria. Matthew's use of "wait on" (v. 15) has significance beyond simple meal preparation. The woman's actions indicate gratitude for being healed, a strikingly significant motivation for all disciples of Jesus.

the fever left her, and she got up and
began to wait on him.
16When evening came, many who were
demon-possessed were brought to him,
and he drove out the spirits with a word
and healed all the sick.[k] 17This was to
fulfill[l] what was spoken through the
prophet Isaiah:

"He took up our infirmities
and bore our diseases."[a][m]

The Cost of Following Jesus

8:19–22pp // Lk 9:57–60

18When Jesus saw the crowd around
him, he gave orders to cross to the other
side of the lake.[n] 19Then a teacher of the
law came to him and said, "Teacher, I will
follow you wherever you go."
20Jesus replied, "Foxes have dens and
birds have nests, but the Son of Man[o] has
no place to lay his head."
21Another disciple said to him, "Lord,
first let me go and bury my father."
22But Jesus told him, "Follow me,[p] and
let the dead bury their own dead."

Jesus Calms the Storm

8:23–27pp // Mk 4:36–41; Lk 8:22–25
8:23–27Ref // Mt 14:22–33

23Then he got into the boat and his
disciples followed him. 24Suddenly a furious storm came up on the lake, so that
the waves swept over the boat. But Jesus
was sleeping. 25The disciples went and
woke him, saying, "Lord, save us! We're
going to drown!"
26He replied, "You of little faith,[q] why
are you so afraid?" Then he got up and
rebuked the winds and the waves, and
it was completely calm.[r]
27The men were amazed and asked,
"What kind of man is this? Even the
winds and the waves obey him!"

Jesus Restores Two Demon-Possessed Men

8:28–34pp // Mk 5:1–17; Lk 8:26–37

28When he arrived at the other side
in the region of the Gadarenes,[b] two
demon-possessed[s] men coming from
the tombs met him. They were so violent
that no one could pass that way. 29"What
do you want with us,[t] Son of God?" they

8:16 [k] Mt 4:23, 24
8:17 [l] Mt 1:22 [m] Isa 53:4
8:18 [n] Mk 4:35
8:20 [o] Da 7:13; Mt 12:8, 32, 40; 16:13, 27, 28; 17:9; 19:28; Mk 2:10; 8:31
8:22 [p] Mt 4:19
8:26 [q] Mt 6:30 [r] Ps 65:7; 89:9; 107:29
8:28 [s] Mt 4:24
8:29 [t] Jdg 11:12; 2Sa 16:10; 1Ki 17:18; Mk 1:24; Lk 4:34; Jn 2:4

Mt 8:10 ❖ Bold faith can show up in unexpected places. Where have you seen amazing faith displayed in your own life?

[a] *17* Isaiah 53:4 (see Septuagint) [b] *28* Some manuscripts *Gergesenes;* other manuscripts *Gerasenes*

8:16–17 Matthew specifies that Jesus' healing ministry fulfills the prophecy of Isa 53:4: "Surely he took up our pain and bore our suffering." Jesus does not himself become ill but takes and removes illness by his healing power. Jesus' entire ministry begins to reverse the cycle of suffering and death.
8:18–20 Jesus' form of discipleship is of a different sort from what the scribe has experienced in his prior training. The expression "no place to lay his head" (v. 20) indicates not a homeless philosopher but a ministry without comfortable benefits.

The expression "Son of Man" (v. 20) did not have popular associations attached to it. Jesus uses the expression to clarify who he is. First, the Son of Man is the humble Servant who has come to forgive the sins of common sinners (v. 20; 9:6; 11:19; 12:8, 32, 40). Second, the Son of Man is the suffering Servant whose atoning death and resurrection will redeem his people (16:13, 27–28; 17:9, 12, 22; 20:18, 28; 26:2, 24, 45). Finally, the Son of Man is the glorious King and Judge who will return to bring the kingdom of heaven to earth (10:23; 13:37, 41; 19:28; 24:27, 30, 37, 39, 44; 25:31; 26:64).
8:21–22 Jesus tests this disciple's commitment. He is elevating his call to "follow me" (v. 22) above all other allegiances. Anything that gets in the way of unqualified commitment to Jesus must be set aside.
8:23–27 Crossing the Sea of Galilee by night was a common experience for fishermen, who used nets throughout the night. This must have been a powerful storm for these disciples to be afraid. True faith will enable them to trust in God's care even when the circumstances do not look promising.

In the OT, God rebuked the sea (see Ex 14:21–29), as Jesus did here, demonstrating his sovereign control over all of nature. The reaction of the disciples says much about who they are beginning to understand Jesus to be.
8:28–34 Jesus is now in the predominantly Gentile region of the Decapolis, which explains why pigs are being raised. As Jesus arrives in what is called the Gadarenes, "two demon-possessed men coming from the tombs" meet him (v. 28). Gospel writers Mark and Luke single out a single spokesman and describe him in more detail, citing his name as "Legion." A Roman army legion had six thousand men.

The demons immediately recognize Jesus' true identity (v. 29a). The use of Jesus' title trumpets that another stronghold of Satan is being overpowered. These demons apparently know quite well an appointed "time" when Satan's forces will be judged (v. 29b). In Jesus' ministry, that "time" has already begun.

The request of the demons to enter the pigs is sinister. Demons are known to cause injury and pain to God's creatures. The destruction of the pigs leads the Gentiles of the region to ask Jesus to

shouted. "Have you come here to torture
us before the appointed time?"[u]
30Some distance from them a large
herd of pigs was feeding. 31The demons
begged Jesus, "If you drive us out, send
us into the herd of pigs."
32He said to them, "Go!" So they came
out and went into the pigs, and the whole
herd rushed down the steep bank into
the lake and died in the water. 33Those
tending the pigs ran off, went into the
town and reported all this, including what
had happened to the demon-possessed
men. 34Then the whole town went out to
meet Jesus. And when they saw him, they
pleaded with him to leave their region.[v]

Jesus Forgives and Heals a Paralyzed Man

9:2–8pp // Mk 2:3–12; Lk 5:18–26

9 Jesus stepped into a boat, crossed
over and came to his own town.[w]
2Some men brought to him a paralyzed
man,[x] lying on a mat. When Jesus saw
their faith,[y] he said to the man, "Take
heart,[z] son; your sins are forgiven."[a]
3At this, some of the teachers of the
law said to themselves, "This fellow is
blaspheming!"[b]
4Knowing their thoughts,[c] Jesus said,
"Why do you entertain evil thoughts in

8:29 [u] 2Pe 2:4
8:34 [v] Lk 5:8; Ac 16:39
9:1 [w] Mt 4:13
9:2 [x] Mt 4:24 [y] ver 22 [z] Jn 16:33 [a] Lk 7:48
9:3 [b] Mt 26:65; Jn 10:33
9:4 [c] Ps 94:11; Mt 12:25; Lk 6:8; 9:47; 11:17
9:6 [d] Mt 8:20
9:8 [e] Mt 5:16; 15:31; Lk 7:16; 13:13; 17:15; 23:47; Jn 15:8; Ac 4:21; 11:18; 21:20
9:11 [f] Mt 11:19; Lk 5:30; 15:2; Gal 2:15

Mt 9:11 ❖ How can we spread God's love among marginalized people near us?

your hearts? 5Which is easier: to say, 'Your
sins are forgiven,' or to say, 'Get up and
walk'? 6But I want you to know that the
Son of Man[d] has authority on earth to forgive sins." So he said to the paralyzed man,
"Get up, take your mat and go home."
7Then the man got up and went home.
8When the crowd saw this, they were filled
with awe; and they praised God,[e] who had
given such authority to man.

The Calling of Matthew

9:9–13pp // Mk 2:14–17; Lk 5:27–32

9As Jesus went on from there, he saw a
man named Matthew sitting at the tax collector's booth. "Follow me," he told him,
and Matthew got up and followed him.
10While Jesus was having dinner at
Matthew's house, many tax collectors
and sinners came and ate with him and
his disciples. 11When the Pharisees saw
this, they asked his disciples, "Why does
your teacher eat with tax collectors and
sinners?"[f]
12On hearing this, Jesus said, "It is not
the healthy who need a doctor, but the

---

leave. The scene implies that the legion of demons goes from the drowned swine looking for others to inhabit. This is an ominous thought for these people who have rejected Jesus.

9:1–8 Jesus connects sin and sickness explicitly. While individual sin may not directly cause a person's sickness, at the heart of humanity's problems is sin. Once sin is forgiven and redemption has occurred, all sickness and death will ultimately be abolished.

Jesus' rhetorical question to the teachers assumes it is easier to say one's sins are forgiven because there is no way of confirming whether or not it has happened. It is obviously much more difficult to declare a person healed because it can be immediately confirmed. The evidence of Jesus' authority is demonstrated as the man gets up and goes home.

✣ **8:1–9:8** For these veteran fishermen to express their fear and plea for help to a *carpenter* indicates that they know he can do what they cannot do for themselves. But what do they think he will do? After all, when he calms the storm they ask, "What kind of man is this?" (8:27). We can see they have faith, because they place as much confidence in Jesus as they think he can accomplish. A more complete knowledge of who he really is and what he is able to accomplish would allow them to trust him fully and without fear.

When we experience suffering in this life, we can rest secure in the knowledge that the Savior who suffered death on the cross for the forgiveness of our sins not only awaits us beyond this life but also, through his Holy Spirit, helps us as we endure the trials of this life.

9:9 Jesus' calling of a local tax collector, Matthew, is shocking. The expected tax revenue was a heavy toll to extract from the people of Galilee, who already had a hard life. Matthew is probably considered a traitor, selling out his own people to Roman occupation and rule.

Then Jesus shows up. Likely, this is the culmination of a prior relationship, similar to the call of the two sets of brothers—Peter and Andrew, and James and John. For Matthew, discipleship has an immediate cost. Collecting taxes meant a lucrative income for the tax collector; it was also a position that, once given up, could not be taken again. As a tax collector, Matthew would have been trained in secular scribal techniques. As a Galilean Jewish Christian, as he later wrote his Gospel he would have been able to interpret the life of Jesus from the perspective of OT expectations.

9:10–13 Matthew follows Jesus and arranges a dinner at his own home (see Lk 5:29). To the din-

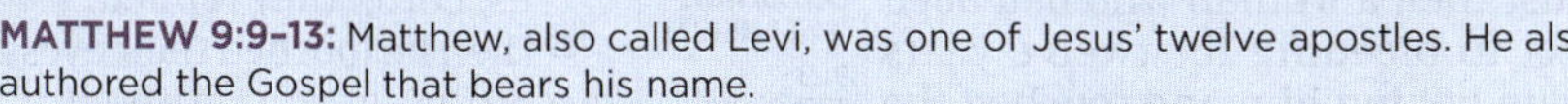

PEOPLE TO KNOW // **MATTHEW**

MATTHEW 9:9–13: Matthew, also called Levi, was one of Jesus' twelve apostles. He also authored the Gospel that bears his name.

Matthew was a tax collector. The Jews despised tax collectors since they took money from their own people on behalf of Rome. Tax collectors were known for extorting people, charging them extra money that they kept for themselves. Everyone knew tax collectors were not the sort of people that "good" Jews associated with.

But Jesus saw Matthew in his tax collector's booth and said, "Follow me" (Mt 9:9). Immediately Matthew left his old life behind and followed Jesus. Matthew then threw a large banquet for Jesus at his house (Lk 5:29), and many other tax collectors were there. The Pharisees grumbled about this to Jesus' disciples: "Why does your teacher eat with tax collectors and sinners?" (Mt 9:11). Jesus responded to the Pharisees, "It is not the healthy who need a doctor, but the sick" (Mt 9:12). Jesus showed his disregard for social boundaries and his compassion for all people, even those considered outcasts, including tax collectors like Matthew.

APPLICATION ✥ God cares about people on the margins—people who others might think are beyond hope. Matthew was open to following Jesus, immediately leaving his old life behind when Jesus called him, and even throwing a large banquet for him (Lk 5:28–29). When God asks us to move forward in faith, how do we respond? Do we think of excuses or act with fear? Or do we follow God's leading with faith, becoming a model for others of what it looks like to be a Christian? Matthew not only followed Jesus; he also invited many other tax collectors and sinners to the banquet to meet Jesus for themselves. No matter who we are or what we have done, we can follow Jesus and introduce others to him as well.

sick. 13But go and learn what this means: 'I
desire mercy, not sacrifice.'[a][g] For I have not
come to call the righteous, but sinners."[h]

Jesus Questioned About Fasting

9:14–17pp // Mk 2:18–22; Lk 5:33–39

14Then John's disciples came and asked
him, "How is it that we and the Pharisees fast often,[i] but your disciples do
not fast?"

15Jesus answered, "How can the guests
of the bridegroom mourn while he is
with them?[j] The time will come when
the bridegroom will be taken from them;
then they will fast.[k]

16"No one sews a patch of unshrunk
cloth on an old garment, for the patch
will pull away from the garment, making
the tear worse. 17Neither do people pour
new wine into old wineskins. If they do,
the skins will burst; the wine will run out
and the wineskins will be ruined. No,
they pour new wine into new wineskins,
and both are preserved."

Jesus Raises a Dead Girl and Heals a Sick Woman

9:18–26pp // Mk 5:22–43; Lk 8:41–56

18While he was saying this, a synagogue leader came and knelt before him[l]
and said, "My daughter has just died. But
come and put your hand on her,[m] and she

9:13 [g] Hos 6:6; Mic 6:6-8; Mt 12:7 [h] 1Ti 1:15
9:14 [i] Lk 18:12
9:15 [j] Jn 3:29 [k] Ac 13:2, 3; 14:23
9:18 [l] Mt 8:2 [m] Mk 5:23

[a] *13* Hosea 6:6

ner are invited "many tax collectors and sinners," most likely Matthew's closest companions up to this point. To the Pharisees, a sinner is a person who has violated the law according to the Pharisees' interpretations. But to Jesus, a sinner is any person who remains opposed to God's will.

The Pharisees are so caught up in their self-righteousness that they cannot see their own hard-hearted sinfulness. Jesus' merciful outreach demonstrates for us our own calling: to invite everyone to experience fellowship with and discipleship to Jesus.

9:14–17 Jesus' response to John the Baptist's disciples offers a proper perspective on spiritual growth and traditional practices. Spiritual growth is not automatically assured through rituals. Traditions are not commands from God. Jesus has not come just to patch up the old religious traditions; rather, he offers a new garment.

Wineskins were made from tanned and sometimes skinned animal hides. Over time they stretched to their limit and eventually became brittle. New wine that is still fermenting expands and will cause old skins to burst if new wine is poured into them. In other words, Jesus has not come to fill the old Jewish system of traditions with new life.

9:18–26 One of the leaders of the Jewish community comes forward with a pressing need.

will live." 19 Jesus got up and went with him, and so did his disciples.

20 Just then a woman who had been subject to bleeding for twelve years came up behind him and touched the edge of his cloak.[n] 21 She said to herself, "If I only touch his cloak, I will be healed."

22 Jesus turned and saw her. "Take heart, daughter," he said, "your faith has healed you."[o] And the woman was healed at that moment.[p]

23 When Jesus entered the synagogue leader's house and saw the noisy crowd and people playing pipes,[q] 24 he said, "Go away. The girl is not dead[r] but asleep."[s] But they laughed at him. 25 After the crowd had been put outside, he went in and took the girl by the hand, and she got up. 26 News of this spread through all that region.[t]

Jesus Heals the Blind and the Mute

27 As Jesus went on from there, two blind men followed him, calling out, "Have mercy on us, Son of David!"[u]

28 When he had gone indoors, the blind men came to him, and he asked them, "Do you believe that I am able to do this?"

"Yes, Lord," they replied.

29 Then he touched their eyes and said, "According to your faith let it be done to you";[v] 30 and their sight was restored. Jesus warned them sternly, "See that no one knows about this."[w] 31 But they went out and spread the news about him all over that region.[x]

32 While they were going out, a man who was demon-possessed[y] and could not talk[z] was brought to Jesus. 33 And when the demon was driven out, the man who had been mute spoke. The crowd was amazed and said, "Nothing like this has ever been seen in Israel."[a]

34 But the Pharisees said, "It is by the prince of demons that he drives out demons."[b]

The Workers Are Few

35 Jesus went through all the towns and villages, teaching in their synagogues, proclaiming the good news of the kingdom and healing every disease and sickness.[c] 36 When he saw the crowds, he had compassion on them,[d] because they were

9:20 [n] Mt 14:36; Mk 3:10
9:22 [o] Mk 10:52; Lk 7:50; 17:19; 18:42 [p] Mt 15:28
9:23 [q] 2Ch 35:25; Jer 9:17, 18
9:24 [r] Ac 20:10 [s] Jn 11:11-14
9:26 [t] Mt 4:24
9:27 [u] Mt 15:22; Mk 10:47; Lk 18:38-39
9:29 [v] ver 22
9:30 [w] Mt 8:4
9:31 [x] ver 26; Mk 7:36
9:32 [y] Mt 4:24 [z] Mt 12:22-24
9:33 [a] Mk 2:12
9:34 [b] Mt 12:24; Lk 11:15
9:35 [c] Mt 4:23
9:36 [d] Mt 14:14

Perhaps this man functions as both a community and synagogue leader. By kneeling before Jesus, he indicates extreme honor.

9:20–22 Jesus' emergency trip to Jairus's home is interrupted briefly by another dire need. This woman would be considered ritually unclean and excluded from normal social and religious relations. Contact with her would also render others unclean.

After 12 years of suffering and pursuing medical care, nothing has brought healing, so she approaches Jesus and touches "the edge of his cloak" (v. 20). On the four corners of a garment worn by men were "tassels" attached with a blue cord (Nu 15:37–41; Dt 22:12). These tassels reminded the wearer to obey God's commands and to be holy to God.

Jesus' expression, "Take heart, daughter," again underscores his compassion while his declaration "your faith has healed you" points to the source of healing (Mt 9:22). Faith itself does not heal; God does. This woman's faith brings her to the place where God can heal her. Jesus removes the public stigma of her physical condition and ushers her back into normal social and religious life.

9:23–26 Jesus then continues on to Jairus's home, where he encounters a typical Jewish mourning scene (v. 23). Many professional mourners would have joined the family and friends in expressing their grief. Jesus, however, indicates that the death of the little girl is merely sleep, at which the mourners laugh (v. 24). So he clears the house of the skeptics. Then Jesus takes the girl by the hand and brings her out of her sleep of death. This scene confirms for all believers that death is merely a state of sleep of one's body while awaiting the final resurrection.

9:27–31 Blindness was one of the worst conditions in the ancient world and considered only a little less serious than being dead. The messianic age promised to bring healing to people who were blind (Isa 29:18; 35:5; 42:7). Jesus' healing of people who were blind is one of his most frequently recorded miracles. These two men have connected Jesus with the prophecies concerning the son of David who would heal blindness, and they ask for that gift of messianic mercy.

The demand for secrecy is a regular aspect of Jesus' ministry. Jesus does not want crowds to clamor for the miracles alone or to think of him simply as a messianic wonder-worker. He is the Savior, the One who has come to bring salvation from sin.

9:32–34 Demon possession takes a variety of external forms. Here the phenomenon in some way prohibits the man from speaking (cf. 12:22). The exorcism of the demon and healing of muteness is a powerful demonstration that the kingdom of heaven has finally arrived.

Without eyes of faith, the Pharisees gather opposition to Jesus, protecting their religious domain and thinking they are protecting the people from Jesus. This sets Jesus' trajectory for the cross.

9:35–38 The verb "had compassion" (v. 36) describes Jesus' motivation to heal and feed the crowds and heal people who are blind (e.g., 14:14; 15:32).

9:36 The metaphor of sheep and shepherd was well-known in Israel's history. The job of the shepherd is to ensure that the sheep are led peacefully

harassed and helpless, like sheep without
a shepherd.[e] 37Then he said to his disciples, "The harvest[f] is plentiful but the
workers are few.[g] 38Ask the Lord of the
harvest, therefore, to send out workers
into his harvest field."

Jesus Sends Out the Twelve

10:2–4pp // Mk 3:16–19; Lk 6:14–16; Ac 1:13
10:9–15pp // Mk 6:8–11; Lk 9:3–5; 10:4–12
10:19–22pp // Mk 13:11–13; Lk 21:12–17
10:26–33pp // Lk 12:2–9
10:34,35pp // Lk 12:51–53

10 Jesus called his twelve disciples
to him and gave them authority
to drive out impure spirits[h] and to heal
every disease and sickness.
2These are the names of the twelve
apostles: first, Simon (who is called Peter) and his brother Andrew; James son
of Zebedee, and his brother John; 3Philip
and Bartholomew; Thomas and Matthew
the tax collector; James son of Alphaeus,
and Thaddaeus; 4Simon the Zealot and
Judas Iscariot, who betrayed him.[i]
5These twelve Jesus sent out with
the following instructions: "Do not go
among the Gentiles or enter any town
of the Samaritans.[j] 6Go rather to the lost
sheep of Israel.[k] 7As you go, proclaim this
message: 'The kingdom of heaven[l] has
come near.' 8Heal the sick, raise the dead,
cleanse those who have leprosy,[a] drive
out demons. Freely you have received;
freely give.
9"Do not get any gold or silver or copper to take with you in your belts[m] —
10no bag for the journey or extra shirt
or sandals or a staff, for the worker
is worth his keep.[n] 11Whatever town
or village you enter, search there for
some worthy person and stay at their
house until you leave. 12As you enter
the home, give it your greeting.[o] 13If the
home is deserving, let your peace rest
on it; if it is not, let your peace return to
you. 14If anyone will not welcome you or

9:36 [e] Nu 27:17; Eze 34:5, 6; Zec 10:2; Mk 6:34
9:37 [f] Jn 4:35 [g] Lk 10:2
10:1 [h] Mk 3:13-15; Lk 9:1
10:4 [i] Mt 26:14-16, 25, 47; Jn 13:2, 26, 27
10:5 [j] 2Ki 17:24; Lk 9:52; Jn 4:4-26, 39, 40; Ac 8:5, 25
10:6 [k] Jer 50:6; Mt 15:24
10:7 [l] Mt 3:2
10:9 [m] Lk 22:35
10:10 [n] 1Ti 5:18
10:12 [o] 1Sa 25:6

Mt 10:8 ✣ What would it look like for us to "freely give" in our everyday lives?

[a] *8* The Greek word traditionally translated *leprosy* was used for various diseases affecting the skin.

---

beside still waters and that they lack for nothing, but these leaders are harassing the helpless crowds.

9:37–38 Jesus is the promised suffering servant of Isa 53, who will take on himself not only the infirmities of his people but also their sins. The deeper illness of the man who was paralyzed and the spiritual sickness of tax collectors and Pharisees alike is their sin. Jesus sees deeply into the need of the crowds and has brought healing to both body and soul.

The "harvest" mission includes the immediate assignment of the Twelve to take the gospel message only to Israel but also the long-range mission of all disciples to take that message throughout the world until the Son of Man returns.

✣ **9:9–38** We observe scenes of evil on a daily basis. Whether enduring suffering with loved ones who are experiencing disease and death, watching the tragedy of those entrapped by a religious cult, or observing the incredible cruelty of gang violence, we know firsthand that evil is real in this world. But into these overwhelming scenes of evil, Jesus' messianic mission comes to offer hope. He healed the sick, cast out demons, and confronted religious hypocrisy in the first century, and he brings the same salvation to our sin-sick world. Today that includes sinners like you, me, and the raucous neighbor down the block. He has come with mercy and grace to save us from our own helpless state.

For Jesus, the message of the kingdom's saving power was primarily a ministry of spiritual healing. But this is not license for the church to neglect the role of ministering to the whole person. We should do all we can to alleviate suffering as a part of the message we bring to a lost and needy world.

10:1 In the gathering of the twelve disciples, we find the hint that Jesus is indeed the messianic king of Israel. The same authority that characterized Jesus' ministry in chs. 8–9 is now given to the Twelve.

10:2–4 "Apostle" has narrow and wide meanings in the NT. The narrow sense, as here, signifies the special representatives chosen to play a foundational role in the church. The wide sense of "apostle" can mean "messenger" or designate an individual missionary outside of the Twelve and Paul (1Co 12:28).

10:5–6 Jesus is dispelling any doubt as to whether he truly is the Messiah who fulfills the promises given to Israel and God's program of salvation history. But there is also a warning here: This is Israel's opportunity, and from here on, Israel will be fully responsible for its own decision.

10:7–8a The power of the Twelve is clearly an extension of Jesus' own power and is to be exercised in the same manner.

10:8b–10 The disciples were to undertake a relatively quick preaching tour through the Galilean countryside; extensive supplies were unnecessary. Jesus insists that "the worker is worth his keep" (v. 10), so they are to look to those to whom they minister to support their mission.

10:11–14 The word "worthy" (v. 11) indicates someone who responds positively to the disciples' message. Shaking the dust off of their feet when they

listen to your words, leave that home or
town and shake the dust off your feet.[p]
15 Truly I tell you, it will be more bearable for Sodom and Gomorrah[q] on the
day of judgment[r] than for that town.[s]
16 "I am sending you out like sheep
among wolves.[t] Therefore be as shrewd
as snakes and as innocent as doves.[u] 17 Be
on your guard; you will be handed over
to the local councils[v] and be flogged in
the synagogues.[w] 18 On my account you
will be brought before governors and
kings[x] as witnesses to them and to the
Gentiles. 19 But when they arrest you, do
not worry about what to say or how to say
it.[y] At that time you will be given what
to say, 20 for it will not be you speaking,
but the Spirit of your Father[z] speaking
through you.
21 "Brother will betray brother to death,
and a father his child; children will rebel
against their parents[a] and have them put
to death. 22 You will be hated by everyone
because of me, but the one who stands
firm to the end will be saved.[b] 23 When
you are persecuted in one place, flee to
another. Truly I tell you, you will not finish going through the towns of Israel
before the Son of Man comes.

24 "The student is not above the teacher, nor a servant above his master.[c] 25 It
is enough for students to be like their
teachers, and servants like their masters. If the head of the house has been
called Beelzebul,[d] how much more the
members of his household!
26 "So do not be afraid of them, for
there is nothing concealed that will not
be disclosed, or hidden that will not be
made known.[e] 27 What I tell you in the
dark, speak in the daylight; what is
whispered in your ear, proclaim from
the roofs. 28 Do not be afraid of those
who kill the body but cannot kill the
soul. Rather, be afraid of the One[f] who
can destroy both soul and body in hell.
29 Are not two sparrows sold for a penny? Yet not one of them will fall to the
ground outside your Father's care.[a]
30 And even the very hairs of your head
are all numbered.[g] 31 So don't be afraid;
you are worth more than many sparrows.[h]
32 "Whoever acknowledges me before
others,[i] I will also acknowledge before my
Father in heaven. 33 But whoever disowns

10:14 [p] Ne 5:13; Lk 10:11; Ac 13:51
10:15 [q] 2Pe 2:6 [r] Mt 12:36; 2Pe 2:9; 1Jn 4:17 [s] Mt 11:22,24
10:16 [t] Lk 10:3 [u] Ro 16:19
10:17 [v] Mt 5:22 [w] Mt 23:34; Mk 13:9; Ac 5:40; 26:11
10:18 [x] Ac 25:24-26
10:19 [y] Ex 4:12
10:20 [z] Ac 4:8
10:21 [a] ver 35, 36; Mic 7:6
10:22 [b] Mt 24:13; Mk 13:13
10:24 [c] Lk 6:40; Jn 13:16; 15:20
10:25 [d] Mk 3:22
10:26 [e] Mk 4:22; Lk 8:17
10:28 [f] Isa 8:12, 13; Heb 10:31
10:30 [g] 1Sa 14:45; 2Sa 14:11; Lk 21:18; Ac 27:34
10:31 [h] Mt 12:12
10:32 [i] Ro 10:9

[a] *29* Or *will*; or *knowledge*

---

leave is for the disciples a parable of judgment on those rejecting the message.

10:15 Increased light of God's revelation makes for increased responsibility. Those who have been exposed to Jesus' ministry and the witness of the disciples have greater responsibility for that privilege. The appeal is urgent: Jesus' earthly ministry is short, and both the blessings of the kingdom and the punishment of judgment are awaiting Israel's decision.

10:16a In the first part of the commissioning, Jesus gave instructions about the disciples' short-term mission. Now he is giving them instructions about their long-term mission throughout the world. The historical setting of Jesus' sending of the Twelve to the people of Israel has provided an occasion for him to teach about Christian missions to all nations.

10:17 Note that it is not "our" or "your" synagogues. The synagogue belongs to those opposed to Jesus' disciples.

10:18–20 The Spirit is the creative, empowering, guiding force in Jesus' own life. Through this same Spirit his disciples will find their own empowering and guidance to give their witness, no matter what trials come.

10:21–23 Some may think that the disciples are leading the people into idolatry with their call to worship Jesus; this will be a tragic misperception of Jesus' identity and message. As a result, the disciples will be delivered to persecution and death.

Along with family betrayal, Jesus' disciples will feel the hatred of "everyone because of [him]" (v. 22; cf. 24:9). An element of hyperbole may be included here, but this statement indicates something unavoidable that results from following Jesus and his message.

His *promise* is that the one who remains committed will not be consumed by the persecution but will experience the full blessing of the kingdom. The *reminder* is that the test of a disciple's real commitment to Jesus is whether he or she remains steadfast to the end.

10:23 What does "before the Son of Man comes" mean in this context? Some suggest that Jesus is promising the disciples that they will witness the final coming of the Son of Man while they are on their first Palestinian mission, or at his resurrection, or at Pentecost, or at the destruction of Jerusalem in AD 70. Others contend that this promise speaks to the coming of the Son of Man at the end of the age. The latter interpretation seems to fit the larger context here.

10:24–25 The Pharisees had accused Jesus of casting out demons by the "prince of demons" (9:34). The same accusation will naturally be lodged against his disciples as well.

10:26–31 Eventually, the opposition to Jesus' ministry will be revealed as false. If the disciples endure, they will be rewarded.

10:29–31 If the heavenly Father gives constant sovereign supervision to such insignificant creatures, surely he will do so for Jesus' disciples.

10:32–33 The easiest way to avoid persecution is to deny that one is Jesus' disciple. But the true

me before others, I will disown before my
Father in heaven.[j]
34"Do not suppose that I have come to
bring peace to the earth. I did not come
to bring peace, but a sword. 35For I have
come to turn

"'a man against his father,
a daughter against her mother,
a daughter-in-law against her
mother-in-law[k]—
36 a man's enemies will be the
members of his own
household.'[a][l]

37"Anyone who loves their father or
mother more than me is not worthy
of me; anyone who loves their son or
daughter more than me is not worthy of
me.[m] 38Whoever does not take up their
cross and follow me is not worthy of me.[n]
39Whoever finds their life will lose it, and
whoever loses their life for my sake will
find it.[o]
40"Anyone who welcomes you welcomes me,[p] and anyone who welcomes
me welcomes the one who sent me.[q]
41Whoever welcomes a prophet as a
prophet will receive a prophet's reward,
and whoever welcomes a righteous person as a righteous person will receive a
righteous person's reward. 42And if anyone gives even a cup of cold water to one
of these little ones who is my disciple,
truly I tell you, that person will certainly
not lose their reward."[r]

Jesus and John the Baptist

11:2–19pp // Lk 7:18–35

11 After Jesus had finished instructing his twelve disciples,[s] he went
on from there to teach and preach in the
towns of Galilee.[b]
2When John, who was in prison,[t] heard
about the deeds of the Messiah, he sent
his disciples 3to ask him, "Are you the
one who is to come,[u] or should we expect
someone else?"
4Jesus replied, "Go back and report to
John what you hear and see: 5The blind
receive sight, the lame walk, those who
have leprosy[c] are cleansed, the deaf hear,
the dead are raised, and the good news

10:33 [j] Mk 8:38; 2Ti 2:12
10:35 [k] ver 21
10:36 [l] Mic 7:6
10:37 [m] Lk 14:26
10:38 [n] Mt 16:24; Lk 14:27
10:39 [o] Lk 17:33; Jn 12:25
10:40 [p] Mt 18:5; Gal 4:14 [q] Lk 9:48; Jn 12:44; 13:20
10:42 [r] Mt 25:40; Mk 9:41; Heb 6:10
11:1 [s] Mt 7:28
11:2 [t] Mt 14:3
11:3 [u] Ps 118:26; Jn 11:27; Heb 10:37

[a] *36* Micah 7:6 [b] *1* Greek *in their towns*
[c] *5* The Greek word traditionally translated *leprosy* was used for various diseases affecting the skin.

---

disciple will publicly acknowledge and confess Jesus as Master and Savior.

10:34–36 The "sword" in v. 34 is metaphorical, as proven by Jesus' words for those who took up an actual sword to defend him in the garden of Gethsemane (26:52). The sword can be a metaphor for separation between those who believe and those who don't, even those in the same family.

10:37–39 Jesus indicates that his form of discipleship calls for giving him ultimate rule in one's life. This implies that he is God, because only God deserves higher place of honor than one's father and mother. Taking up God's will for one's life will result in gaining true life as Jesus' disciple.

10:40–42 Jesus' disciples go in the authority and with the message of Jesus himself. The "prophets" and the "righteous" refer to Christ-following prophets and righteous persons. To *welcome* means to welcome Jesus' gospel of the kingdom and so receive life's greatest reward—kingdom salvation and kingdom life.

10:1–42 When we read the story of Jesus' mission of the Twelve, we can also think of them as the greatest generation of the church. They were called out of the hardship of occupation by the Roman Empire, but they went on to fight a battle—not with swords and chariots but with the Good News of the kingdom of heaven and a message of transformation. They went on to lay the foundation of the church, and according to tradition most of them suffered martyrdom for the name of the Lord Jesus.

Scripture speaks of our own discipleship using the language of warfare, although it is not a war against flesh and blood (e.g., Eph 6:10-20; cf. 1Th 2:18). Christians are everyday people who have been called to advance the kingdom of God in an alien and hostile world. We are the church, the body of Jesus Christ, and we humbly serve God's purposes in the world. Some ministries are more visible than some others, but each individual is vitally necessary to the proper functioning of the church in this world. The story of the disciples' mission has immediate relevance for disciples in every era.

We must understand that we are called to an unwavering commitment to bring the gospel of the kingdom to our generation and to those who follow. Whether or not we take that call overseas, we need to support that mission with our prayers and our resources. That is the clear and urgent call of Jesus' mission discourse to every generation of the church.

11:1 The conclusion to the mission discourse, "After Jesus had finished," serves as a transition to the next section of narrative.

11:2–3 John rightly expected the Messiah to be a judging figure, so events are not unfolding as he anticipated. Jesus is not carrying out judgment; rather, he seems to be concentrating on healing and helping. John needs to have his understanding of the messianic program reconfirmed.

11:4–6 Jesus reiterates to John's disciples that the way his ministry has unfolded is in line with the

is proclaimed to the poor.[v] 6Blessed is
anyone who does not stumble on account of me."[w]

7As John's[x] disciples were leaving,
Jesus began to speak to the crowd about
John: "What did you go out into the wilderness to see? A reed swayed by the
wind? 8If not, what did you go out to
see? A man dressed in fine clothes? No,
those who wear fine clothes are in kings'
palaces. 9Then what did you go out to
see? A prophet?[y] Yes, I tell you, and more
than a prophet. 10This is the one about
whom it is written:

"'I will send my messenger ahead of
you,
who will prepare your way before
you.'[a][z]

11Truly I tell you, among those born of
women there has not risen anyone greater than John the Baptist; yet whoever is
least in the kingdom of heaven is greater
than he. 12From the days of John the Baptist until now, the kingdom of heaven has
been subjected to violence,[b] and violent
people have been raiding it. 13For all the
Prophets and the Law prophesied until
John. 14And if you are willing to accept it,
he is the Elijah who was to come.[a] 15Who-
ever has ears, let them hear.[b]

11:5 [v] Isa 35:4-6; 61:1; Lk 4:18,19
11:6 [w] Mt 13:21
11:7 [x] Mt 3:1
11:9 [y] Mt 21:26; Lk 1:76
11:10 [z] Mal 3:1; Mk 1:2
11:14 [a] Mal 4:5; Mt 17:10-13; Mk 9:11-13; Lk 1:17; Jn 1:21
11:15 [b] Mt 13:9, 43; Mk 4:23; Lk 14:35; Rev 2:7
11:18 [c] Mt 3:4 [d] Lk 1:15
11:19 [e] Mt 9:11
11:21 [f] Mk 6:45; Lk 9:10; Jn 12:21 [g] Mt 15:21; Lk 6:17; Ac 12:20 [h] Jnh 3:5-9

16"To what can I compare this generation? They are like children sitting
in the marketplaces and calling out to
others:

17"'We played the pipe for you,
and you did not dance;
we sang a dirge,
and you did not mourn.'

18For John came neither eating[c] nor
drinking,[d] and they say, 'He has a demon.'
19The Son of Man came eating and drinking, and they say, 'Here is a glutton and a
drunkard, a friend of tax collectors and
sinners.'[e] But wisdom is proved right by
her deeds."

Woe on Unrepentant Towns

11:21–23pp // Lk 10:13–15

20Then Jesus began to denounce the
towns in which most of his miracles had
been performed, because they did not
repent. 21"Woe to you, Chorazin! Woe
to you, Bethsaida![f] For if the miracles
that were performed in you had been
performed in Tyre and Sidon,[g] they
would have repented long ago in sackcloth and ashes.[h] 22But I tell you, it will
be more bearable for Tyre and Sidon on

[a] *10* Mal. 3:1 [b] *12* Or *been forcefully advancing*

---

prophetic promises, confirming for John that the blessings of the messianic age have arrived with Jesus' ministry. John and his disciples must use eyes of faith to recognize both blessing and judgment.

11:7–10 Through three rhetorical questions Jesus gives the crowds contrasting options about John, which will force them to acknowledge his identity and mission. (1) Was John a "reed swayed by the wind?" The metaphor suggests bending with the winds of circumstance. John, by contrast, went to prison rather than compromising the truth. (2) Was John "a man dressed in fine clothes?" Obviously, he was not. John was not motivated by greed. (3) Like OT prophets, John called the nation to repentance and declared God's program of salvation. Unlike them, he fulfilled the prophecy of a coming herald of the Messiah.

11:11 John is the greatest of those born during the OT era because of his crucial role in preparing the way for the Messiah and his kingdom. John's mission was great because of the greatness of the One he introduced. But those in the kingdom are greater because they have actually entered it.

11:12 Jesus points to the ongoing opposition that the kingdom of heaven has encountered since the days of John the Baptist. The saying foreshadows the gathering opposition to Jesus, which will come to a climax in his arrest, trial, and execution by the Jewish high priest, Caiaphas, and the Roman governor, Pontius Pilate.

11:13–15 Jesus' tribute to John peaks with a powerful testimony to the role John has played. Malachi prophesied that Elijah would prepare the way for the Messiah. John fulfilled Malachi's prophecy. From the moment he was conceived, John was designated as the one who would minister in the "spirit and power of Elijah" (Lk 1:17). Malachi prophesied that Elijah would prepare for the coming of the Lord himself. Jesus equates his ministry as Messiah with God's own arrival, another awe-inspiring revelation of his divine identity.

11:16–19 This is not a blanket condemnation of Israel, because Jesus' own disciples are Jews and large crowds of Jews still follow him around. It points sadly to the fact that only a small minority of the current generation will enter the narrow gate to the kingdom by accepting John's and Jesus' invitations.

Wisdom was often personified as a woman giving her children practical guidance. The personification illustrated how people guided by God's approach to life make the right decisions. The saying here appears to be proverbial. If this generation had seen John the Baptist and Jesus for who they said they were, their lives would have changed.

11:20–24 Jesus turns up the heat by denouncing the cities who have rejected his gospel message. The privilege of witnessing Jesus' miraculous ministry should have moved them to repent and accept the invitation to the kingdom of heaven.

the day of judgment than for you.[i] 23And
you, Capernaum,[j] will you be lifted to
the heavens? No, you will go down to
Hades.[a][k] For if the miracles that were
performed in you had been performed
in Sodom, it would have remained to
this day. 24But I tell you that it will be
more bearable for Sodom on the day of
judgment than for you."[l]

The Father Revealed in the Son

11:25–27pp // Lk 10:21,22

25At that time Jesus said, "I praise you,
Father,[m] Lord of heaven and earth, because you have hidden these things from
the wise and learned, and revealed them
to little children.[n] 26Yes, Father, for this
is what you were pleased to do.

27"All things have been committed
to me[o] by my Father.[p] No one knows
the Son except the Father, and no one
knows the Father except the Son and
those to whom the Son chooses to reveal him.[q]

28"Come to me,[r] all you who are weary
and burdened, and I will give you rest.
29Take my yoke upon you and learn
from me,[s] for I am gentle and humble
in heart, and you will find rest for your
souls.[t] 30For my yoke is easy and my burden is light."[u]

Mt 11:28 ❖ What burdens or worries can we take to Jesus to find true rest?

Jesus Is Lord of the Sabbath

12:1–8pp // Mk 2:23–28; Lk 6:1–5
12:9–14pp // Mk 3:1–6; Lk 6:6–11

12 At that time Jesus went through
the grainfields on the Sabbath.
His disciples were hungry and began to
pick some heads of grain[v] and eat them.
2When the Pharisees saw this, they said
to him, "Look! Your disciples are doing
what is unlawful on the Sabbath."[w]

3He answered, "Haven't you read what
David did when he and his companions
were hungry?[x] 4He entered the house
of God, and he and his companions ate
the consecrated bread—which was not
lawful for them to do, but only for the
priests.[y] 5Or haven't you read in the Law
that the priests on Sabbath duty in the

11:22 [i] ver 24; Mt 10:15
11:23 [j] Mt 4:13 [k] Isa 14:13-15
11:24 [l] Mt 10:15
11:25 [m] Lk 22:42; Jn 11:41 [n] 1Co 1:26-29
11:27 [o] Mt 28:18 [p] Jn 3:35; 13:3; 17:2 [q] Jn 10:15
11:28 [r] Jn 7:37
11:29 [s] Jn 13:15; Php 2:5; 1Pe 2:21; 1Jn 2:6
[t] Jer 6:16
11:30 [u] 1Jn 5:3
12:1 [v] Dt 23:25
12:2 [w] ver 10; Lk 13:14; 14:3; Jn 5:10; 7:23; 9:16
12:3 [x] 1Sa 21:6
12:4 [y] Lev 24:5,9

[a] 23 That is, the realm of the dead

11:25–26 Jesus contrasts people whose pride has caused them to reject Jesus' message with those whose humility allows them to be open to the arrival of the kingdom. The Father wants everyone to receive his care in the same way, as humble and repentant children.

11:27 Jesus has a profound divine self-consciousness. Jesus and the Father enjoy direct, intuitive, and immediate knowledge of each other. It is grounded in their divine relationship as Father and Son. Jesus' sonship involves an exclusive essential relationship with his Father. Jesus received from the Father the exclusive authority to reveal the Father; humans can know the Father only through the Son's revelation. God's program of salvation history comes from this unique, divine relationship.

11:28–30 Jesus' invitation starkly contrasts with the burdens of the Pharisees or Roman oppressors. His yoke—a metaphor for discipleship to him—promises rest because it is none other than a commitment to him. His disciples learn directly from him, and Jesus offers rest in himself for their souls through his authoritative understanding of God's truth.

The yoke of discipleship brings rest because Jesus has come gently, preaching and teaching the Good News of the kingdom. In humble human form, he has brought healing to sin-sick humanity. This is the true rest for which Israel has long hoped. Jesus' teaching is the true fulfillment of the law. Those who come to him will enter into a discipleship that produces rest for the soul (cf. Jer 6:16).

While discipleship to Jesus brings relief from the burden of Pharisaic regulations, it is not lawlessness. In fact, in Jesus' interpretation of the law, it is even more challenging. He calls his disciples to fulfill the law from the obedience of the heart, not simply through external obedience. His Spirit provides the strength to carry the load.

It is critical to remember that discipleship is not a religious obligation. Rather, it is an intimate relationship with the One who calls, "Come to me" and "Learn from me." As complicated as life may become, discipleship is at heart simply walking with Jesus in the real world and having him teach us moment by moment how to live life his way.

✥ **11:1–30** Of the many different types of people who gather in Christian worship each week, one group deserves special attention: those who come to the Lord with a questioning heart in need of rest. They need rest, the rest that only Jesus can ultimately give. The wise disciple leads people to Jesus and the spiritual rest only he can provide for the anxious and weary soul.

12:1–2 The Pharisees are now likely looking for opportunities to accuse Jesus and his disciples of crimes against the Law. The disciples could have been guilty of violating several rabbinic rules on this occasion, but not everyone shared the Pharisees' view of the Sabbath.

12:3–7 Jesus' reply puts the Pharisees on the defensive because he uses the OT itself, on which they prided themselves as experts, to combat

temple desecrate the Sabbath[z] and yet
are innocent? 6I tell you that something
greater than the temple is here.[a] 7If you
had known what these words mean, 'I
desire mercy, not sacrifice,'[ab] you would
not have condemned the innocent. 8For
the Son of Man[c] is Lord of the Sabbath."
9Going on from that place, he went
into their synagogue, 10and a man with
a shriveled hand was there. Looking for
a reason to bring charges against Jesus,
they asked him, "Is it lawful to heal on
the Sabbath?"[d]
11He said to them, "If any of you has a
sheep and it falls into a pit on the Sabbath, will you not take hold of it and lift
it out?[e] 12How much more valuable is a
person than a sheep![f] Therefore it is lawful to do good on the Sabbath."
13Then he said to the man, "Stretch out
your hand." So he stretched it out and it
was completely restored, just as sound as
the other. 14But the Pharisees went out
and plotted how they might kill Jesus.[g]

God's Chosen Servant

15Aware of this, Jesus withdrew from
that place. A large crowd followed him,
and he healed all who were ill.[h] 16He
warned them not to tell others about
him.[i] 17This was to fulfill what was spoken through the prophet Isaiah:

18"Here is my servant whom I have
chosen,
the one I love, in whom I
delight;[j]
I will put my Spirit on him,
and he will proclaim justice to the
nations.
19He will not quarrel or cry out;
no one will hear his voice in the
streets.
20A bruised reed he will not break,
and a smoldering wick he will not
snuff out,
till he has brought justice through to
victory.
21 In his name the nations will put
their hope."[bk]

Jesus and Beelzebul

12:25–29pp // Mk 3:23–27; Lk 11:17–22

22Then they brought him a demon-
possessed man who was blind and mute,
and Jesus healed him, so that he could
both talk and see.[l] 23All the people were
astonished and said, "Could this be the
Son of David?"[m]

12:5 [z] Nu 28:9, 10; Jn 7:22,23
12:6 [a] ver 41,42
12:7 [b] Hos 6:6; Mic 6:6-8; Mt 9:13
12:8 [c] Mt 8:20
12:10 [d] ver 2; Lk 13:14; 14:3; Jn 9:16
12:11 [e] Lk 14:5
12:12 [f] Mt 10:31
12:14 [g] Mt 26:4; 27:1; Mk 3:6; Lk 6:11; Jn 5:18; 11:53
12:15 [h] Mt 4:23
12:16 [i] Mt 8:4
12:18 [j] Mt 3:17
12:21 [k] Isa 42:1-4
12:22 [l] Mt 4:24; 9:32-33
12:23 [m] Mt 9:27

[a] *7* Hosea 6:6 [b] *21* Isaiah 42:1-4

---

their accusations. Jesus cites two OT examples to invalidate the Pharisees' charge. He then goes on to give a third response that clarifies his use of these examples.

First, Ahimelek the priest understood that David was serving God and was therefore entitled to the bread in his time of need. Ahimelek served God's purposes by feeding David (1Sa 21). The implication is that the intent of the law is to serve God's people, not for God's people to serve the law.

Second, Jesus emphasizes that if the priests were allowed to violate the Sabbath for the greater good of conducting the priestly rituals (Lev 24:5-8), how much more should Jesus and his disciples be allowed to do the work of God given to them? After all, he is someone greater than the temple.

Jesus' third response takes the argument one step further by quoting a second time from Hos 6:6. If they had understood the prophet, they would have extended mercy, not demanded more sacrifice. Jesus attacks the Pharisees' tendency to burden people's daily lives by their traditions.

12:8 Jesus concludes the argument with another remarkable clarification of his identity and authority. Jesus has revealed himself to Israel as their long-anticipated Messiah. The Sabbath is fulfilled not by the rigorous observance of the Pharisees but in living out the intent and motive of the Sabbath, which was designed to bring rest. As the Lord of the Sabbath, Jesus truly interprets its intent (cf. 11:28–30).

12:9–13 According to the Pharisees, this man is not a proper candidate for healing on the Sabbath since he could have waited until the next day.

Jesus counters with a question of his own which is not simply rhetorical. There was active debate in Judaism at the time on just such a point. Jesus contends that the higher principle is not simply abstaining from activity on the Sabbath but doing good on the Sabbath. The miracle confirms Jesus' authority to make these pronouncements about the Sabbath, once more validating his claim to be the messianic Son of Man.

12:14 In the Pharisees' eyes, Jesus' claim to messianic authority to interpret the Law is a heresy—a claim worthy of death. They are now convinced that Jesus is not God's agent.

12:15–21 Jesus is trying not to escape opposition but to keep it at bay until the time for his predicted betrayal, arrest, and death.

In this fulfillment quotation (Isa 42:1–4), Matthew gives one of the clearest declarations of Jesus' intent as Messiah: He is the gentle, Spirit-endowed, suffering servant who advances a mission of justice to the nations. The suffering servant's advance of justice will not break those who are abused, nor will it smother those who are nearly out of resources. He will provide ultimate victory for those who respond to the invitation to enter the kingdom.

12:22–24 In contrast to the reaction of the crowds, the Pharisees accuse Jesus of drawing on the

24But when the Pharisees heard this,
they said, "It is only by Beelzebul,[n] the
prince of demons, that this fellow drives
out demons."[o]
25Jesus knew their thoughts[p] and said
to them, "Every kingdom divided against
itself will be ruined, and every city or
household divided against itself will not
stand. 26If Satan[q] drives out Satan, he is
divided against himself. How then can
his kingdom stand? 27And if I drive out
demons by Beelzebul, by whom do your
people[r] drive them out? So then, they
will be your judges. 28But if it is by the
Spirit of God that I drive out demons,
then the kingdom of God has come upon
you.
29"Or again, how can anyone enter a
strong man's house and carry off his possessions unless he first ties up the strong
man? Then he can plunder his house.
30"Whoever is not with me is against
me, and whoever does not gather with
me scatters.[s] 31And so I tell you, every
kind of sin and slander can be forgiven,
but blasphemy against the Spirit will
not be forgiven.[t] 32Anyone who speaks
a word against the Son of Man will be
forgiven, but anyone who speaks against
the Holy Spirit will not be forgiven, either in this age[u] or in the age to come.[v]
33"Make a tree good and its fruit will
be good, or make a tree bad and its fruit
will be bad, for a tree is recognized by its
fruit.[w] 34You brood of vipers,[x] how can

12:24 [n]Mk 3:22 [o]Mt 9:34
12:25 [p]Mt 9:4
12:26 [q]Mt 4:10
12:27 [r]Ac 19:13
12:30 [s]Mk 9:40; Lk 11:23
12:31 [t]Mk 3:28, 29; Lk 12:10
12:32 [u]Titus 2:12 [v]Mk 10:30; Lk 20:34, 35; Eph 1:21; Heb 6:5
12:33 [w]Mt 7:16, 17; Lk 6:43, 44
12:34 [x]Mt 3:7; 23:33 [y]Mt 15:18; Lk 6:45
12:38 [z]Mt 16:1; Mk 8:11, 12; Lk 11:16; Jn 2:18; 6:30; 1Co 1:22
12:39 [a]Mt 16:4; Lk 11:29
12:40 [b]Jnh 1:17 [c]Mt 8:20 [d]Mt 16:21
12:41 [e]Jnh 1:2 [f]Jnh 3:5

Mt 12:33 ❖ Jesus said, "A tree is recognized by its fruit." What is the "fruit" of our lives, and what does it say about the condition of our hearts?

you who are evil say anything good? For
the mouth speaks[y] what the heart is full
of. 35A good man brings good things out
of the good stored up in him, and an evil
man brings evil things out of the evil
stored up in him. 36But I tell you that
everyone will have to give account on the
day of judgment for every empty word
they have spoken. 37For by your words
you will be acquitted, and by your words
you will be condemned."

The Sign of Jonah

12:39–42pp // Lk 11:29–32
12:43–45pp // Lk 11:24–26

38Then some of the Pharisees and
teachers of the law said to him, "Teacher, we want to see a sign from you."[z]
39He answered, "A wicked and adulterous generation asks for a sign! But
none will be given it except the sign of
the prophet Jonah.[a] 40For as Jonah was
three days and three nights in the belly
of a huge fish,[b] so the Son of Man[c] will
be three days and three nights in the
heart of the earth.[d] 41The men of Nineveh[e] will stand up at the judgment with
this generation and condemn it; for they
repented at the preaching of Jonah,[f] and

---

power of "Beelzebul." Practicing magic under the influence of Satan was a capital offense, punishable by stoning.

12:25–29 First, Jesus shows the illogical nature of the Pharisees' thinking. If Satan wanted to maintain rulership of this world, he would not work against himself. Second, Jesus alludes to his role of establishing the kingdom as entering a well-guarded house. Before Jesus can release those held captive, he must bind Satan. Jesus declares here that Satan's powers are now limited because of the arrival of the kingdom of God.

12:30–37 Jesus now goes on the offensive and declares two scathing accusations. (1) There is no middle ground with Jesus. He is Messiah, or he isn't. The OT regarded deliberate, defiant sin against God and his laws to be blasphemy, the guilt of which remained. Rejection of Jesus' ministry as validated by the Spirit is defiant, deliberate sin. As long as the Pharisees continue to reject that evidence, they cannot enter the kingdom and receive forgiveness.

This sin can be committed today only by unbelievers who reject the ministry of the Holy Spirit leading them to salvation. Ultimately, once a person has either hardened his or her heart to an irretrievable point in this life or has died without repenting, the chance for forgiveness has passed.

(2) The Pharisees attempt to hide their own wicked blasphemy by calling Jesus a blasphemer. But their slander is actually blasphemy against the Spirit of God. Since they refuse to repent, they will be held accountable for every word at the judgment.

12:38–42 The Pharisees are not asking for a sign in good faith. They are asking for a sign that they can use against Jesus. He recognizes their evil motive and refuses to fall into their trap. Because of their evil intention, the only other sign that Jesus will give to them is a sign of God's coming judgment on them. The Pharisees and their followers have had the greatest privilege. They will be condemned by the pagans of Nineveh, who repented when God's messenger, Jonah, arrived.

A second figure of condemnation against the Pharisees is another pagan—the queen of Sheba (1Ki 10:1–29). She too allowed God's revelation to penetrate her pagan heart.

The Gentiles see what the Pharisees and that fateful generation do not.

now something greater than Jonah is
here. 42The Queen of the South will rise
at the judgment with this generation and
condemn it; for she came[g] from the ends
of the earth to listen to Solomon's wisdom, and now something greater than
Solomon is here.
43"When an impure spirit comes out
of a person, it goes through arid places
seeking rest and does not find it. 44Then
it says, 'I will return to the house I left.'
When it arrives, it finds the house un-
occupied, swept clean and put in order.
45Then it goes and takes with it seven
other spirits more wicked than itself,
and they go in and live there. And the
final condition of that person is worse
than the first.[h] That is how it will be with
this wicked generation."

Jesus' Mother and Brothers

12:46–50pp // Mk 3:31–35; Lk 8:19–21

46While Jesus was still talking to
the crowd, his mother[i] and brothers[j]
stood outside, wanting to speak to him.
47Someone told him, "Your mother and
brothers are standing outside, wanting
to speak to you."
48He replied to him, "Who is my mother, and who are my brothers?" 49Pointing
to his disciples, he said, "Here are my
mother and my brothers. 50For whoever
does the will of my Father in heaven[k] is
my brother and sister and mother."

The Parable of the Sower

13:1–15pp // Mk 4:1–12; Lk 8:4–10
13:16,17pp // Lk 10:23,24
13:18–23pp // Mk 4:13–20; Lk 8:11–15

13 That same day Jesus went out of the
house[l] and sat by the lake. 2Such
large crowds gathered around him that
he got into a boat[m] and sat in it, while
all the people stood on the shore. 3Then
he told them many things in parables,
saying: "A farmer went out to sow his
seed. 4As he was scattering the seed,
some fell along the path, and the birds
came and ate it up. 5Some fell on rocky
places, where it did not have much soil.
It sprang up quickly, because the soil
was shallow. 6But when the sun came
up, the plants were scorched, and they
withered because they had no root. 7Oth-
er seed fell among thorns, which grew up
and choked the plants. 8Still other seed
fell on good soil, where it produced a
crop — a hundred,[n] sixty or thirty times

12:42 [g] 1Ki 10:1; 2Ch 9:1
12:45 [h] 2Pe 2:20
12:46 [i] Mt 1:18; 2:11,13,14,20; Lk 1:43; 2:33, 34,48,51; Jn 2:1,5; 19:25, 26 [j] Mt 13:55; Jn 2:12; 7:3,5; Ac 1:14; 1Co 9:5; Gal 1:19
12:50 [k] Jn 15:14
13:1 [l] ver 36; Mt 9:28
13:2 [m] Lk 5:3
13:8 [n] Ge 26:12

12:43-45 Jesus begins with a general statement of how demons operate. The verb "comes out" implies exorcism. The "rest" implies that although a demon can exist in a disembodied state, its evil purpose is best performed in an embodied state. Demons want to maintain ownership of a person.

The evil generation that Jesus addresses has experienced his powerful ministry, especially through his exorcisms. But Israel has not repented and turned to the kingdom of heaven. Therefore, they are more susceptible to the power of the evil one than ever before. But if they receive Jesus and the kingdom, Satan will flee from the presence of God in their lives.

12:46-50 Matthew 12:9–45 does not include any reference to the disciples. This indicates the topics discussed there are about entrance into the kingdom. However, as Jesus continues to address the crowd (v. 46), his mother and brothers stand outside, wanting to speak to him. Jesus now begins to require accountability of those to whom the invitation has been extended.

He has not come to abolish the family. Still, Jesus is here demonstrating the importance of singular commitment to him and to the kingdom of heaven, which places people in a new spiritual family. Jesus specifies the central feature that creates and characterizes this spiritual family. Each individual must respond to the will of the Father, obey Jesus' call to the kingdom, and become his disciple.

12:1-50 Encountering persecution while engaging in spiritual warfare are themes of this chapter. And all hinge on rightly obeying the Father's will as it is now revealed by Jesus Messiah. The opposition that we encounter will be of a variety of different types. In the increasingly secular society of the twenty-first century, we will encounter opposition to our faith from popular culture. As with Jesus, we may encounter opposition from our own family if they do not understand the way in which we want to serve God. On a more drastic level, Christians can expect opposition when we proclaim the message of the gospel.

13:1-3a Large crowds only heighten the animosity of the Pharisees, who up to now have been popular with the people and see their influence continuing to shift to Jesus.

13:4 Seed was sown "broadcast" style by scattering it in all directions while walking up and down the field.

13:5-6 The terrain in Israel was generally uneven and rocky in many places, with only thin layers of soil covering the rock.

13:7 The plants battled for nutrients from the soil, and as the thorny plants grew, they choked out the less hardy agricultural plants.

13:8 The straight meaning of the parable is that only seed sown on good earth yielded a crop. In fact, the seed sown on good soil yielded the

what was sown. 9 Whoever has ears, let
them hear."[o]
10 The disciples came to him and asked,
"Why do you speak to the people in parables?"
11 He replied, "Because the knowledge
of the secrets of the kingdom of heav-
en has been given to you,[p] but not to
them. 12 Whoever has will be given more,
and they will have an abundance. Whoever does not have, even what they have
will be taken from them.[q] 13 This is why I
speak to them in parables:

> "Though seeing, they do not see;
> though hearing, they do not hear
> or understand.[r]

14 In them is fulfilled the prophecy of
Isaiah:

> "'You will be ever hearing but never
> understanding;
> you will be ever seeing but never
> perceiving.
> 15 For this people's heart has become
> calloused;
> they hardly hear with their ears,
> and they have closed their
> eyes.
> Otherwise they might see with their
> eyes,
> hear with their ears,
> understand with their hearts
> and turn, and I would heal them.'[a][s]

16 But blessed are your eyes because they
see, and your ears because they hear.[t]
17 For truly I tell you, many prophets and
righteous people longed to see what you
see[u] but did not see it, and to hear what
you hear but did not hear it.
18 "Listen then to what the parable of the
sower means: 19 When anyone hears the
message about the kingdom[v] and does
not understand it, the evil one[w] comes
and snatches away what was sown in their
heart. This is the seed sown along the path.
20 The seed falling on rocky ground refers
to someone who hears the word and at
once receives it with joy. 21 But since they
have no root, they last only a short time.
When trouble or persecution comes because of the word, they quickly fall away.[x]
22 The seed falling among the thorns refers
to someone who hears the word, but the
worries of this life and the deceitfulness
of wealth[y] choke the word, making it unfruitful. 23 But the seed falling on good soil
refers to someone who hears the word
and understands it. This is the one who
produces a crop, yielding a hundred, sixty
or thirty times what was sown."[z]

13:9 [o] Mt 11:15
13:11 [p] Mt 11:25; 16:17; 19:11; Jn 6:65; 1Co 2:10, 14; Col 1:27; 1Jn 2:20, 27
13:12 [q] Mt 25:29; Lk 19:26
13:13 [r] Dt 29:4; Jer 5:21; Eze 12:2
13:15 [s] Isa 6:9, 10; Jn 12:40; Ac 28:26, 27; Ro 11:8
13:16 [t] Mt 16:17
13:17 [u] Jn 8:56; Heb 11:13; 1Pe 1:10-12
13:19 [v] Mt 4:23 [w] Mt 5:37
13:21 [x] Mt 11:6
13:22 [y] Mt 19:23; 1Ti 6:9, 10, 17
13:23 [z] ver 8

[a] *15* Isaiah 6:9,10 (see Septuagint)

Mt 13:22 ❖ How can we keep "worries" and the "deceitfulness of wealth" from choking out God's truth in our lives?

---

maximum of what it was created to produce, with varying amounts that reflected individual potential.
13:9 Those with spiritual ears can receive the spiritual message embedded in the parable.
13:10–17 The distinction between the disciples and the crowd is crucial to understand that Jesus uses the parables to cause the listener to decide about the kingdom of God.
13:11 The mystery is that the kingdom has arrived in a form different from what was anticipated. The initial understanding of the secrets of the kingdom of heaven that the disciples now have will grow into full understanding. But whatever understanding the crowd has, even that will be taken away.
13:12–13 God knows those who will harden their heart against Jesus' message, so the parables are used to harden the people's hearts to the point where eventually they will be unable to respond (v. 15). God also knows those who will respond to the message of the gospel, so the parables elicit a positive response (cf. v. 10). Both sayings balance God's divine sovereignty with each individual human's responsibility.
13:14–15 The crowd mirrors the people of Israel to whom the prophet Isaiah ministered. God does not force anyone to accept the message of the kingdom. The crowd's response is dictated by the nature of their heart.
13:16–17 Jesus' parables are designed to test his audience's spiritual "ears." Jesus accomplishes two important feats with the parables. First, the parables test the heart of the listener. Second, the parables give instruction to those who are responsive. They teach about how the kingdom operates very differently from that expected by the religious leaders and the crowds.
13:19 Some in the crowd have hardened their hearts against Jesus' message. That hardness of heart prevents the seed of the gospel from taking root, and they cannot understand its truth.
13:20–21 This type of heart exhibits a superficial reception of the gospel, but it does not take root. The seed of the gospel message is not able to penetrate to produce the change of regeneration in the person's heart.
13:22 The combined priorities of worry and wealth choke out the life of the message of the kingdom of heaven for a person with this type of heart so that it is unable to bear fruit.
13:23 The fruit of kingdom life proves that these kinds of people are truly children of the kingdom. Seed sown on good soil will yield the maximum it

The Parable of the Weeds

24Jesus told them another parable: "The kingdom of heaven is like[a] a man who sowed good seed in his field. 25But while everyone was sleeping, his enemy came and sowed weeds among the wheat, and went away. 26When the wheat sprouted and formed heads, then the weeds also appeared.

27"The owner's servants came to him and said, 'Sir, didn't you sow good seed in your field? Where then did the weeds come from?'

28" 'An enemy did this,' he replied.

"The servants asked him, 'Do you want us to go and pull them up?'

29" 'No,' he answered, 'because while you are pulling the weeds, you may uproot the wheat with them. 30Let both grow together until the harvest. At that time I will tell the harvesters: First collect the weeds and tie them in bundles to be burned; then gather the wheat and bring it into my barn.' "[b]

The Parables of the Mustard Seed and the Yeast

13:31,32pp // Mk 4:30–32
13:31–33pp // Lk 13:18–21

31He told them another parable: "The kingdom of heaven is like[c] a mustard seed,[d] which a man took and planted in his field. 32Though it is the smallest of all seeds, yet when it grows, it is the largest of garden plants and becomes a tree, so that the birds come and perch in its branches."[e]

33He told them still another parable: "The kingdom of heaven is like[f] yeast that a woman took and mixed into about sixty pounds[a] of flour[g] until it worked all through the dough."[h]

34Jesus spoke all these things to the crowd in parables; he did not say anything to them without using a parable.[i] 35So was fulfilled what was spoken through the prophet:

> "I will open my mouth in parables,
> I will utter things hidden since the creation of the world."[b][j]

The Parable of the Weeds Explained

36Then he left the crowd and went into the house. His disciples came to him and said, "Explain to us the parable[k] of the weeds in the field."

37He answered, "The one who sowed the good seed is the Son of Man.[l] 38The field is the world, and the good seed stands for the people of the kingdom. The weeds are the people of the evil one,[m] 39and the enemy who sows them is the devil. The harvest[n] is the end of the age,[o] and the harvesters are angels.[p]

40"As the weeds are pulled up and burned in the fire, so it will be at the end of the age. 41The Son of Man[q] will send out his angels,[r] and they will weed out of his kingdom everything that causes sin and all who do evil. 42They will throw them into the blazing furnace, where there will be weeping and gnashing of teeth.[s] 43Then the righteous will shine like the sun[t] in the kingdom of their Father. Whoever has ears, let them hear.[u]

The Parables of the Hidden Treasure and the Pearl

44"The kingdom of heaven is like[v] treasure hidden in a field. When a man found it, he hid it again, and then in his joy went and sold all he had and bought that field.[w]

13:24 [a] ver 31, 33, 45, 47; Mt 18:23; 20:1; 22:2; 25:1; Mk 4:26, 30
13:30 [b] Mt 3:12
13:31 [c] ver 24 [d] Mt 17:20; Lk 17:6
13:32 [e] Ps 104:12; Eze 17:23; 31:6; Da 4:12
13:33 [f] ver 24 [g] Ge 18:6 [h] Gal 5:9
13:34 [i] Mk 4:33; Jn 16:25
13:35 [j] Ps 78:2; Ro 16:25, 26; 1Co 2:7; Eph 3:9; Col 1:26
13:36 [k] Mt 15:15
13:37 [l] Mt 8:20
13:38 [m] Jn 8:44, 45; 1Jn 3:10
13:39 [n] Joel 3:13 [o] Mt 24:3; 28:20 [p] Rev 14:15
13:41 [q] Mt 8:20 [r] Mt 24:31
13:42 [s] ver 50; Mt 8:12
13:43 [t] Da 12:3 [u] Mt 11:15
13:44 [v] ver 24 [w] Isa 55:1; Php 3:7, 8

[a] *33* Or about 27 kilograms [b] *35* Psalm 78:2

is created to produce, with varying amounts that reflect individual potential.

13:24–30 The kingdom of heaven has indeed come into this world, but its advance does not mean that the enemy will be completely beaten during this age. That inevitable event awaits the final judgment, which is delayed.

13:31–32 The proverbial smallness of the mustard seed as a metaphor that describes the kingdom of God would have shocked the crowd. Israel always believed that God's kingdom would be powerful when established on the earth; they were not prepared for an insignificant beginning. The image of a large tree with birds alighting on its branches recalls several OT references to a great kingdom.

13:33 Scripture uses leaven almost exclusively as a negative metaphor, probably because fermentation implied disintegration and corruption. But here Jesus uses yeast to symbolize the positive, hidden permeation of the kingdom of heaven in this world. The kingdom of heaven is indeed active, although it is not at first fully observable, because it begins with an inner transformation of the heart.

13:34–35 The crowd must respond. They cannot stay in the middle ground forever.

13:36–43 The explanation of the parable of the wheat and weeds is unique in how Jesus identifies the story's main elements. Each of these elements is helpful for interpreting other parables.

13:44 The emphasis is on the supreme worth of the treasure that is unseen by others; it is worth

45"Again, the kingdom of heaven is
like[x] a merchant looking for fine pearls.
46When he found one of great value, he
went away and sold everything he had
and bought it.

The Parable of the Net

47"Once again, the kingdom of heav-
en is like[y] a net that was let down into
the lake and caught all kinds[z] of fish.
48When it was full, the fishermen pulled
it up on the shore. Then they sat down
and collected the good fish in baskets,
but threw the bad away. 49This is how it
will be at the end of the age. The angels
will come and separate the wicked from
the righteous[a] 50and throw them into
the blazing furnace, where there will be
weeping and gnashing of teeth.[b]
51"Have you understood all these
things?" Jesus asked.
"Yes," they replied.
52He said to them, "Therefore every
teacher of the law who has become a disciple in the kingdom of heaven is like the
owner of a house who brings out of his
storeroom new treasures as well as old."

A Prophet Without Honor

13:54–58pp // Mk 6:1–6

53When Jesus had finished these parables,[c] he moved on from there. 54Coming
to his hometown, he began teaching the
people in their synagogue,[d] and they were
amazed.[e] "Where did this man get this
wisdom and these miraculous powers?"
they asked. 55"Isn't this the carpenter's
son?[f] Isn't his mother's[g] name Mary, and
aren't his brothers James, Joseph, Simon
and Judas? 56Aren't all his sisters with us?
Where then did this man get all these
things?" 57And they took offense[h] at him.
But Jesus said to them, "A prophet is
not without honor except in his own
town and in his own home."[i]
58And he did not do many miracles
there because of their lack of faith.

John the Baptist Beheaded

14:1–12pp // Mk 6:14–29

14 At that time Herod[j] the tetrarch
heard the reports about Jesus,[k]
2and he said to his attendants, "This is
John the Baptist;[l] he has risen from the
dead! That is why miraculous powers are
at work in him."
3Now Herod had arrested John and
bound him and put him in prison[m] because of Herodias, his brother Philip's
wife,[n] 4for John had been saying to him:
"It is not lawful for you to have her."[o]
5Herod wanted to kill John, but he was
afraid of the people, because they considered John a prophet.[p]

13:45 [x] ver 24
13:47 [y] ver 24 [z] Mt 22:10
13:49 [a] Mt 25:32
13:50 [b] Mt 8:12
13:53 [c] Mt 7:28
13:54 [d] Mt 4:23 [e] Mt 7:28
13:55 [f] Lk 3:23; Jn 6:42 [g] Mt 12:46
13:57 [h] Jn 6:61 [i] Lk 4:24; Jn 4:44
14:1 [j] Mk 8:15; Lk 3:1,19; 13:31; 23:7,8; Ac 4:27; 12:1 [k] Lk 9:7-9
14:2 [l] Mt 3:1
14:3 [m] Mt 4:12; 11:2 [n] Lk 3:19,20
14:4 [o] Lev 18:16; 20:21
14:5 [p] Mt 11:9

---

far more than any sacrifice one might make to acquire it.

13:45–46 Instead of simply stumbling across a hidden treasure, a diligent search by one well-qualified to know its value ultimately leads to the kingdom. The point is not to buy one's way into the kingdom but to recognize its supreme value.

13:47–50 When Jesus comes in power, he will finish establishing his kingdom on the earth. The final arrival of the kingdom of heaven will then extend its net throughout the world.

13:51–52 Jesus likens the disciples to owners of a house. The householder brings new and old things from his treasure box to dispense them for the benefit of others.

All those who have become disciples of the kingdom of heaven have Jesus alone as their teacher. In the same way that Jesus has developed them, they are to make disciples of all the nations and teach these new disciples all that they have been taught by Jesus.

13:1–52 Just as Jesus had varied responses to his message, so will we. Faithfulness in sowing the gospel message is paramount, not the numbers of people who respond. The results are ultimately in the hands of God as well as in the choice of the individual. Our responsibility is to sow the seed, as did Jesus, trust God, and understand that there will inevitably be mixed responses. Nothing is comparable to the gospel message itself. It alone has potential power to produce life in dead soil. There are many stories of missionaries who labor for years in a foreign country before seeing even one conversion. Contentment in such situations comes through obedience and trusting God with the results.

13:53–58 Knowing his human roots, the townspeople conclude that since Jesus had no other training than that of a carpenter, he cannot be a proper source of wisdom, nor can he lay claim to supernatural powers.

Like the OT prophets who had consistently been rejected by the people of Israel, Jesus is likewise rejected. Because of the hardness of their hearts, they are not open to Jesus' ministry. Hard-heartedness and rejection prevent the ministry of the Spirit's healing, even as it prevents the forgiveness of sin.

14:1–12 Herod's guilty fear for having executed John combines with a confused notion of resurrection, probably based partly on Pharisaic beliefs and semi-pagan superstitious ideas of returning spirits.

Herodias's young daughter performs a dance for Herod. In this degraded setting, she dances

6 On Herod's birthday the daughter
of Herodias danced for the guests and
pleased Herod so much 7 that he promised with an oath to give her whatever
she asked. 8 Prompted by her mother,
she said, "Give me here on a platter the
head of John the Baptist." 9 The king was
distressed, but because of his oaths and
his dinner guests, he ordered that her request be granted 10 and had John beheaded[q] in the prison. 11 His head was brought
in on a platter and given to the girl, who
carried it to her mother. 12 John's disciples
came and took his body and buried it.[r]
Then they went and told Jesus.

Jesus Feeds the Five Thousand

14:13–21pp // Mk 6:32–44; Lk 9:10–17; Jn 6:1–13
14:13–21Ref // Mt 15:32–38

13 When Jesus heard what had happened, he withdrew by boat privately
to a solitary place. Hearing of this, the
crowds followed him on foot from the
towns. 14 When Jesus landed and saw
a large crowd, he had compassion on
them[s] and healed their sick.[t]
15 As evening approached, the disciples
came to him and said, "This is a remote
place, and it's already getting late. Send
the crowds away, so they can go to the
villages and buy themselves some food."
16 Jesus replied, "They do not need to
go away. You give them something to
eat."

14:10 [q] Mt 17:12
14:12 [r] Ac 8:2
14:14 [s] Mt 9:36 [t] Mt 4:23

Mt 14:16–17 ❖ Have you ever felt God ask you to do something you thought was impossible? What is the proper response in such situations?

17 "We have here only five loaves[u] of
bread and two fish," they answered.
18 "Bring them here to me," he said.
19 And he directed the people to sit down
on the grass. Taking the five loaves and
the two fish and looking up to heaven,
he gave thanks and broke the loaves.[v]
Then he gave them to the disciples, and
the disciples gave them to the people.
20 They all ate and were satisfied, and
the disciples picked up twelve basketfuls of broken pieces that were left over.
21 The number of those who ate was about
five thousand men, besides women and
children.

Jesus Walks on the Water

14:22–33pp // Mk 6:45–51; Jn 6:16–21
14:34–36pp // Mk 6:53–56

22 Immediately Jesus made the disciples get into the boat and go on ahead of
him to the other side, while he dismissed
the crowd. 23 After he had dismissed
them, he went up on a mountainside
by himself to pray.[w] Later that night, he
was there alone, 24 and the boat was already a considerable distance from land,
buffeted by the waves because the wind
was against it.

14:17 [u] Mt 16:9
14:19 [v] 1Sa 9:13; Mt 26:26; Mk 8:6; Lk 24:30; Ac 2:42; 27:35; 1Ti 4:4
14:23 [w] Lk 3:21

---

what is likely a highly sensual dance and, struck by her display, Herod makes an unwise promise. Her mother Herodias steps in immediately to eliminate another threat to her husband's reign. Herod Antipas knows that John is a prophet, popular with the people, and does not want to execute him. But he does not want to lose face in front of his guests.

14:13–14 A key to Jesus' ministry was the way he listened to and then obeyed his Father's will, which often took place through the discipline of solitude. As he prepares to make the final destined trip to Jerusalem and the cross, Jesus seeks his Father's fellowship. However, his popularity with the people has not diminished. Even though the crowd is fickle, Jesus has compassion for them. They have carried the sick to him from out of the towns, so Jesus heals them.

14:15–21 Such a large crowd might have presented problems because staple foods were not usually on hand. Jesus turns the problem back to the disciples. They scrounge around and come up with five loaves of bread and two fish. The season is spring, when the grass is lush and the streams are running full, so Jesus directs the crowd to sit down on the grass. He gives thanks, or offers a blessing, and breaks the loaves. Jesus does not bless the bread but blesses God for what will be the miraculous supply of bread.

Matthew narrates almost casually that the crowd eats until they are satisfied, and "the disciples picked up twelve basketfuls of broken pieces that were left over" (v. 20). The number twelve is significant for both the twelve tribes of Israel and the twelve disciples/apostles.

The crowd cannot get their eyes off their physical needs long enough to hear Jesus' message. Jesus leaves to focus on those who will accept his offer of salvation. But the miracle also has a lesson for the disciples: They must learn to see as Jesus sees.

14:22–27 After the crowd and disciples leave, Jesus is finally alone. Jesus is readying himself for the journey into Gentile regions, with the cross in Jerusalem looming ahead.

While Jesus is alone on the mountain in prayer, the disciples are having difficulty crossing the Sea of Galilee. They battle the waves for several hours. The disciples are afraid when they see Jesus walking on the water, thinking that he is a "ghost" (v. 26). In Greek literature this word is used for dream appearances or spirit appearances, but in the OT, it means a deception. The disciples may be thinking that some evil spirit is attempting to deceive them. Jesus gives

25Shortly before dawn Jesus went out
to them, walking on the lake. 26When the
disciples saw him walking on the lake,
they were terrified. "It's a ghost,"[x] they
said, and cried out in fear.
27But Jesus immediately said to them:
"Take courage![y] It is I. Don't be afraid."[z]
28"Lord, if it's you," Peter replied, "tell
me to come to you on the water."
29"Come," he said.
Then Peter got down out of the boat,
walked on the water and came toward
Jesus. 30But when he saw the wind, he
was afraid and, beginning to sink, cried
out, "Lord, save me!"
31Immediately Jesus reached out his
hand and caught him. "You of little
faith,"[a] he said, "why did you doubt?"
32And when they climbed into the
boat, the wind died down. 33Then those
who were in the boat worshiped him,
saying, "Truly you are the Son of God."[b]
34When they had crossed over, they
landed at Gennesaret. 35And when the
men of that place recognized Jesus, they
sent word to all the surrounding country.
People brought all their sick to him 36and
begged him to let the sick just touch the
edge of his cloak,[c] and all who touched
it were healed.

14:26 [x] Lk 24:37
14:27 [y] Mt 9:2; Ac 23:11 [z] Da 10:12; Mt 17:7; 28:10; Lk 1:13,30; 2:10; Ac 18:9; 23:11; Rev 1:17
14:31 [a] Mt 6:30
14:33 [b] Ps 2:7; Mt 4:3
14:36 [c] Mt 9:20
15:2 [d] Lk 11:38
15:4 [e] Ex 20:12; Dt 5:16; Eph 6:2 [f] Ex 21:17; Lev 20:9

That Which Defiles

15:1–20pp // Mk 7:1–23

15 Then some Pharisees and teachers
of the law came to Jesus from Jerusalem and asked, 2"Why do your disciples
break the tradition of the elders? They
don't wash their hands before they eat!"[d]
3Jesus replied, "And why do you break
the command of God for the sake of your
tradition? 4For God said, 'Honor your
father and mother'[a][e] and 'Anyone who
curses their father or mother is to be put
to death.'[b][f] 5But you say that if anyone
declares that what might have been used
to help their father or mother is 'devoted
to God,' 6they are not to 'honor their father or mother' with it. Thus you nullify
the word of God for the sake of your tradition. 7You hypocrites! Isaiah was right
when he prophesied about you:

[a] 4 Exodus 20:12; Deut. 5:16 [b] 4 Exodus 21:17; Lev. 20:9

them immediate assurance that he is no deceptive evil spirit but truly their master: The expression "It is I" (lit., "I am," v. 27) may allude to the voice of Yahweh from the burning bush (Ex 3:1–6).

14:28–32 The expression "Lord" was used elsewhere to address Jesus with a title of respect, but here it means far more. Jesus is walking on the water in the middle of wind and waves, something that elevates him above any other figure that Peter has ever known.

In reply to Peter's request, Jesus authoritatively says, "Come." After walking on water himself, Peter loses his focused faith in Jesus' divine identity and begins to sink beneath the seas. But then most importantly, Peter cries out, "Lord, save me!" The same Lord who could walk on the water is more than able to save Peter from sinking.

"Little faith" (v. 31) is not the same as the "no faith" of the hard-hearted townspeople of Nazareth. Peter's faith is like a burst of emotional energy; faith is not a commodity of which Peter needs more. Rather, Peter's faith is consistent trust in Jesus to accomplish what he has called Peter to do.

14:33 Worship is an action in Scripture reserved for God. The disciples are gripped with the reality that Jesus is much more than a mere teacher. He is the Son of God, so they worship him. They are understanding more clearly that Jesus is uniquely related to God the Father. Baffled as they must be, they give homage to him in a way that is only rightly given to God.

14:34–36 As on the occasion of the woman with the hemorrhage (9:20), "all who touched [his cloak] were healed" (14:36). This is a remarkable display of faith, in stark contrast to the Pharisees and teachers of the law.

13:53—14:36 Leadership under Jesus demands responding to him in effective faith in his divine power. We all face many circumstances for which we are unprepared. The difficulties we face change from day to day. But the one constant we have in this life is Jesus. As we go through life focused on an intimate walk with Jesus through every circumstance, we learn how to apply his teachings to our situations. We may never be in such a position as Peter was, but we can learn from him. When the Lord called him—whether to get out of the boat or later to become a leader in the early church—Jesus was always there to see him through.

15:1–2 The hands were a particular concern for cleanliness, as something unclean could be transmitted from oneself to others. The priests were required to wash their hands and feet prior to offering their service. The Pharisees adapted this concern for ceremonial cleanliness and applied it to common Israelites.

15:3–9 Jesus counters the Pharisees' charge. In his question, he goes to the heart of the problem, which is the relationship between the developing oral law and the written law. Jesus makes it clear that the OT came from God, while the Pharisees' and teachers' traditions are simply the rules of human elders.

The Pharisees and teachers of the law perform religious rituals externally. They have not been motivated to commit their entire inner person to God. Therefore, not only does their human tradition and teaching nullify God's Word, but their worship is empty of any real meaning.

8“‘These people honor me with their
lips,
but their hearts are far from me.
9They worship me in vain;
their teachings are merely human
rules.[g]’[a][h]”

10Jesus called the crowd to him and
said, “Listen and understand. 11What
goes into someone’s mouth does not defile them,[i] but what comes out of their
mouth, that is what defiles them.”[j]
12Then the disciples came to him and
asked, “Do you know that the Pharisees
were offended when they heard this?”
13He replied, “Every plant that my
heavenly Father has not planted[k] will
be pulled up by the roots. 14Leave them;
they are blind guides.[b][l] If the blind lead
the blind, both will fall into a pit.”[m]
15Peter said, “Explain the parable
to us.”[n]
16“Are you still so dull?”[o] Jesus asked
them. 17“Don’t you see that whatever enters the mouth goes into the stomach and
then out of the body? 18But the things that
come out of a person’s mouth come from
the heart,[p] and these defile them. 19For
out of the heart come evil thoughts—
murder, adultery, sexual immorality,
theft, false testimony, slander.[q] 20These
are what defile a person;[r] but eating with
unwashed hands does not defile them.”

15:9 [g] Col 2:20-22 [h] Isa 29:13; Mal 2:2
15:11 [i] Ac 10:14, 15 [j] ver 18
15:13 [k] Isa 60:21; 61:3; Jn 15:2
15:14 [l] Mt 23:16, 24; Ro 2:19 [m] Lk 6:39
15:15 [n] Mt 13:36
15:16 [o] Mt 16:9
15:18 [p] Mt 12:34; Lk 6:45; Jas 3:6
15:19 [q] Gal 5:19-21
15:20 [r] Ro 14:14
15:21 [s] Mt 11:21
15:22 [t] Mt 9:27 [u] Mt 4:24
15:24 [v] Mt 10:6, 23; Ro 15:8
15:25 [w] Mt 8:2

Mt 15:18 ❖ What do our words show about the condition of our hearts?

The Faith of a Canaanite Woman

15:21–28pp // Mk 7:24–30

21Leaving that place, Jesus withdrew
to the region of Tyre and Sidon.[s] 22A
Canaanite woman from that vicinity
came to him, crying out, “Lord, Son of
David,[t] have mercy on me! My daughter is
demon-possessed and suffering terribly.”[u]
23Jesus did not answer a word. So his
disciples came to him and urged him,
“Send her away, for she keeps crying out
after us.”
24He answered, “I was sent only to the
lost sheep of Israel.”[v]
25The woman came and knelt before
him.[w] “Lord, help me!” she said.
26He replied, “It is not right to take the
children’s bread and toss it to the dogs.”
27“Yes it is, Lord,” she said. “Even the

[a] 9 Isaiah 29:13 [b] 14 Some manuscripts *blind guides of the blind*

15:10–11 Ceremonial cleansing is not the key element in producing godliness. A hypocritical show of devotion to God can mask a heart more intent on gaining a religious reputation than seeking to do God’s will as revealed in the OT.

The Pharisees reveal that their inner life is unclean. They have not repented in the light of the arrival of the kingdom of heaven and received the righteousness that is Spirit-produced. They have deceived themselves and misled the people with their traditions, so Jesus gives due warning to the crowd.

15:12–14 Jesus has elevated himself as a critic of their entire religious tradition, which will undercut the religious leaders’ influence with the people.

Jesus replies to the disciples’ warning with two parables. First, he compares the fate of the Pharisees to that of a plant. The Pharisees have not been planted by the Father (v. 13). Jesus also likens the Pharisees to blind guides (v. 14). In their blindness, they lead the people astray because they cannot see the truth of God’s will in the OT.

15:15–16 Understanding Jesus’ parables and teaching is a key element of discipleship, because true disciples have spiritual ears to hear and spiritual eyes to see the truth of Jesus’ teaching, something the crowd does not have. As elsewhere in Matthew, Jesus explains the parable.

15:17–20 Jesus outlines to the disciples the central role that the heart plays in spiritual purity. God’s judgment concerns behavior that originates in the heart of a person. The spiritual heart is evil and must first be cleansed, producing a life that demonstrates righteous purity in word, thought, motivation, deed, and relationships. Kingdom righteousness is an inside-out transformation that begins with the heart and works throughout the process of the disciple’s life to produce external righteousness.

15:21 The Jews of Galilee have been privileged to hear and see Jesus’ message, but their lack of repentance condemns them, so Jesus “withdraws.” He and his disciples proceed to Gentile regions before heading to Judea and their final destination, Jerusalem.

15:22–28 This woman, a “Canaanite” (i.e., a pagan non-Jew), demonstrates familiarity with Jewish messianic tradition by calling Jesus “Son of David” (v. 22). She pleads for her suffering daughter.

Jesus does not reply to the woman’s cry for help. So she persists, a sign that she knows that Jesus can aid her. The “children’s bread” emphasizes the care that God promises to provide for his covenant children. As a metaphor, “dogs” is a humiliating label for those apart from, or enemies of, Israel’s covenant community (vv. 26–27).

This perceptive woman understands the program of God to go to Israel first, but she persists. In a sense, Jesus is testing her. Will she recognize that God ultimately desires to bring healing to all people? Jesus calls her response an exercise of “great faith,” which is rewarded by having her daughter healed that very hour (v. 28).

dogs eat the crumbs that fall from their
master's table."
28Then Jesus said to her, "Woman, you
have great faith![x] Your request is granted." And her daughter was healed at that
moment.

Jesus Feeds the Four Thousand

15:29–31pp // Mk 7:31–37
15:32–39pp // Mk 8:1–10
15:32–39Ref // Mt 14:13–21

29Jesus left there and went along
the Sea of Galilee. Then he went up on
a mountainside and sat down. 30Great
crowds came to him, bringing the lame,
the blind, the crippled, the mute and
many others, and laid them at his feet;
and he healed them.[y] 31The people were
amazed when they saw the mute speaking, the crippled made well, the lame
walking and the blind seeing. And they
praised the God of Israel.[z]
32Jesus called his disciples to him and
said, "I have compassion for these people;[a] they have already been with me
three days and have nothing to eat. I do
not want to send them away hungry, or
they may collapse on the way."
33His disciples answered, "Where could
we get enough bread in this remote place
to feed such a crowd?"
34"How many loaves do you have?"
Jesus asked.
"Seven," they replied, "and a few small
fish."
35He told the crowd to sit down on the
ground. 36Then he took the seven loaves
and the fish, and when he had given
thanks, he broke them[b] and gave them
to the disciples, and they in turn to the
people. 37They all ate and were satisfied.
Afterward the disciples picked up seven
basketfuls of broken pieces that were left
over.[c] 38The number of those who ate
was four thousand men, besides wom-
en and children. 39After Jesus had sent
the crowd away, he got into the boat and
went to the vicinity of Magadan.

The Demand for a Sign

16:1–12pp // Mk 8:11–21

16 The Pharisees and Sadducees[d] came
to Jesus and tested him by asking
him to show them a sign from heaven.[e]
2He replied, "When evening comes, you
say, 'It will be fair weather, for the sky is
red,' 3and in the morning, 'Today it will
be stormy, for the sky is red and overcast.'
You know how to interpret the appearance
of the sky, but you cannot interpret the
signs of the times.[a][f] 4A wicked and adulterous generation looks for a sign, but none
will be given it except the sign of Jonah."[g]
Jesus then left them and went away.

The Yeast of the Pharisees and Sadducees

5When they went across the lake,
the disciples forgot to take bread. 6"Be

15:28 [x] Mt 9:22
15:30 [y] Mt 4:23
15:31 [z] Mt 9:8
15:32 [a] Mt 9:36
15:36 [b] Mt 14:19
15:37 [c] Mt 16:10
16:1 [d] Ac 4:1 [e] Mt 12:38
16:3 [f] Lk 12:54-56
16:4 [g] Mt 12:39

[a] *2,3* Some early manuscripts do not have *When evening comes . . . of the times.*

15:29–31 Gentiles increasingly become the focus of Jesus' ministry. As Israel rejects the kingdom, Gentiles frequently come into view as recipients of his message and healing.

15:32–38 This is the second time that Jesus feeds a crowd of thousands, although this time he is in the Gentile region of the Decapolis. The disciples still have not fully grasped the magnitude of Jesus' identity because they question again where they will find supplies to feed such a massive group.

In this feeding, the number of small bread cakes is seven, and there are seven baskets left over. If the number of twelve baskets left over in feeding the five thousand is symbolic of Israel, then the number seven may symbolize the completion or fullness of God's meeting the needs of all peoples, including Gentiles.

15:39 This town was the center of Galilee's fish-processing industry, making it one of the most important fishing centers on the Sea of Galilee and the administrative seat of the surrounding region.

✣ **15:1–39** The word of God as revealed in Scripture must be understood as the sole authority that contains all that is necessary for salvation and the spiritual life. That word must be elevated above any human tradition. It is in God's Word that we have the clearest understanding of God's will for our daily lives and the life of our communities of faith. Teachers, preachers, and doctrinal formulations are helpful guides to individuals and churches, but Scripture must continually be upheld as the final authority.

16:1–4 Because the Jewish religious leaders are not seeking signs in good faith, the only validating sign Jesus will give them of his messianic authority will be his resurrection, like Jonah's appearance to the Ninevites after his time in the belly of the great fish. As with Jonah, Jesus' message of the kingdom is a message of repentance.

16:5–12 The prior use of yeast in the parable of the mystery of the kingdom of heaven should have prepared the disciples to understand that he was using it metaphorically again. Jesus patiently leads these fumbling disciples into the meaning that he intends them to understand.

careful," Jesus said to them. "Be on your
guard against the yeast of the Pharisees
and Sadducees."[h]
7 They discussed this among themselves and said, "It is because we didn't
bring any bread."
8 Aware of their discussion, Jesus
asked, "You of little faith,[i] why are you
talking among yourselves about having
no bread? 9 Do you still not understand?
Don't you remember the five loaves for
the five thousand, and how many basketfuls you gathered?[j] 10 Or the seven
loaves for the four thousand, and how
many basketfuls you gathered?[k] 11 How
is it you don't understand that I was
not talking to you about bread? But be
on your guard against the yeast of the
Pharisees and Sadducees." 12 Then they
understood that he was not telling them
to guard against the yeast used in bread,
but against the teaching of the Pharisees
and Sadducees.[l]

Peter Declares That Jesus Is the Messiah

16:13–16pp // Mk 8:27–29; Lk 9:18–20

13 When Jesus came to the region of
Caesarea Philippi, he asked his disciples,
"Who do people say the Son of Man is?"
14 They replied, "Some say John the
Baptist;[m] others say Elijah; and still oth-
ers, Jeremiah or one of the prophets."[n]

16:6 [h] Lk 12:1
16:8 [i] Mt 6:30
16:9 [j] Mt 14:17-21
16:10 [k] Mt 15:34-38
16:12 [l] Ac 4:1
16:14 [m] Mt 3:1; 14:2 [n] Mk 6:15; Jn 1:21
16:16 [o] Mt 4:3; Ps 42:2; Jn 11:27; Ac 14:15; 2Co 6:16; 1Th 1:9; 1Ti 3:15; Heb 10:31; 12:22
16:17 [p] 1Co 15:50; Gal 1:16; Eph 6:12; Heb 2:14
16:18 [q] Jn 1:42 [r] Eph 2:20
16:19 [s] Isa 22:22; Rev 3:7 [t] Mt 18:18; Jn 20:23
16:20 [u] Mk 8:30

Mt 16:15 ❖ Based on all you know about Jesus and how he has worked in your life, how would you personally answer Jesus' question, "Who do you say I am?"

15 "But what about you?" he asked.
"Who do you say I am?"
16 Simon Peter answered, "You are the
Messiah, the Son of the living God."[o]
17 Jesus replied, "Blessed are you, Simon son of Jonah, for this was not revealed to you by flesh and blood,[p] but by
my Father in heaven. 18 And I tell you that
you are Peter,[a][q] and on this rock I will
build my church,[r] and the gates of Hades[b]
will not overcome it. 19 I will give you the
keys[s] of the kingdom of heaven; whatever you bind on earth will be[c] bound in
heaven, and whatever you loose on earth
will be[c] loosed in heaven."[t] 20 Then he
ordered his disciples not to tell anyone[u]
that he was the Messiah.

Jesus Predicts His Death

16:21–28pp // Mk 8:31—9:1; Lk 9:22–27

21 From that time on Jesus began to
explain to his disciples that he must go

[a] 18 The Greek word for *Peter* means *rock.*
[b] 18 That is, the realm of the dead
[c] 19 Or *will have been*

16:13–14 This region, long a stronghold of pagan worship of Baal, the Greek god Pan, and Caesar, becomes the site where Jesus calls for a decision about his own identity. When Jesus asks, "Who do people say the Son of Man is?" the disciples' response is striking. Each response indicates that the people believe Jesus is a prophet, in line with one of the popular messianic expectations held in Israel.

16:15–16 Peter steps forward once again as a leader and spokesperson for the others. Prior to this, the expression "Messiah" has occurred only in Matthew's narrative; now it is used for the first time by a person to address Jesus directly. "Messiah" is a translation of the Hebrew term for "anointed." Peter further expresses Jesus' identity as "the Son of the living God." This expression has special significance in the area of Caesarea Philippi with its Baal, Pan, and Caesar worship. Jesus is the Son of the God who is living, not like those first two mythical, superstitious figures etched in stone or the obviously human and imperfect Caesar.

Peter confesses more than he really understands about Jesus' identity. He does not yet fully understand Jesus' mission, but his understanding is certainly increasing.

16:17–20 Jesus recognizes Peter for this statement but never places him above or apart from the other disciples. Peter is crucial for his role in the foundation of the church, but he is not the only part of the foundation. The expression "gates of Hades" referred to the realm and power of death (v. 18). Thus, Jesus promises that death will never overpower the church, his family of faith.

Peter opens the door of the kingdom to the Jews on Pentecost (Ac 2), to the Samaritans (Ac 8), and finally to the Gentiles (Ac 10). Once Peter used the keys to open the door to the kingdom of God, he passes from the scene. The door to the kingdom now stands open throughout the ages, so the keys are no longer needed.

Peter's authority is tied directly to his confession, which is a condensation of the gospel message. Through Peter's preaching of the gospel and the preaching of others who follow him, Jesus is presented as the only Messiah; those who believe have their sins forgiven and gain entrance to the kingdom.

16:20 Peter's confession is still subject to misunderstanding by the crowds and even by his own disciples. So Jesus warns his disciples not to further tell the crowds that he is the Messiah.

16:21 This is the first of four times in which Jesus predicts his arrest and crucifixion, but his disciples continually misunderstand its significance. By claiming the necessity of his coming death, Jesus begins to reveal the ultimate destiny and purpose for his life's ministry.

to Jerusalem and suffer many things[v] at
the hands of the elders, the chief priests
and the teachers of the law, and that he
must be killed and on the third day[w] be
raised to life.[x]
22Peter took him aside and began to
rebuke him. "Never, Lord!" he said. "This
shall never happen to you!"
23Jesus turned and said to Peter, "Get
behind me, Satan![y] You are a stumbling
block to me; you do not have in mind
the concerns of God, but merely human
concerns."
24Then Jesus said to his disciples,
"Whoever wants to be my disciple must
deny themselves and take up their cross
and follow me.[z] 25For whoever wants
to save their life[a] will lose it, but whoever loses their life for me will find it.[a]
26What good will it be for someone to
gain the whole world, yet forfeit their
soul? Or what can anyone give in exchange for their soul? 27For the Son of
Man[b] is going to come[c] in his Father's
glory with his angels, and then he will
reward each person according to what
they have done.[d]
28"Truly I tell you, some who are standing here will not taste death before they

16:21 [v] Mk 10:34; Lk 17:25 [w] Jn 2:19 [x] Mt 17:22, 23; 27:63; Mk 9:31; Lk 9:22; 18:31-33; 24:6, 7
16:23 [y] Mt 4:10
16:24 [z] Mt 10:38; Lk 14:27
16:25 [a] Jn 12:25
16:27 [b] Mt 8:20 [c] Ac 1:11 [d] Job 34:11; Ps 62:12; Jer 17:10; Ro 2:6; 2Co 5:10; Rev 22:12

Mt 17:4 ❖ How can we integrate the passion and memory of "mountain-top" experiences into our everyday lives?

see the Son of Man coming in his kingdom."

The Transfiguration

17:1–8pp // Lk 9:28–36
17:1–13pp // Mk 9:2–13

17 After six days Jesus took with him
Peter, James and John the brother
of James, and led them up a high mountain by themselves. 2There he was transfigured before them. His face shone like
the sun, and his clothes became as white
as the light. 3Just then there appeared
before them Moses and Elijah, talking
with Jesus.
4Peter said to Jesus, "Lord, it is good
for us to be here. If you wish, I will put
up three shelters — one for you, one for
Moses and one for Elijah."
5While he was still speaking, a bright
cloud covered them, and a voice from

[a] 25 The Greek word means either *life* or *soul*; also in verse 26.

16:22–23 Although Peter may appear to reflect appropriate concern, Jesus understands the source of Peter's admonition. Satan tried to tempt Jesus at the start of his earthly ministry (4:1-11). Now he uses a different strategy by trying to hinder Jesus' mission through Peter.

Peter here sets his mind on human ways, not on God's. He undoubtedly thinks he is protecting Jesus. Jesus will now show Peter that God's way is the way of the cross, for him and for all disciples.

16:24 The cross is for Jesus and for those who follow him in discipleship. This is an appropriate metaphor of the Father's will for a disciple's life.

16:25–28 Verses 25–28 give three related reasons why disciples must take up the cross of discipleship.

16:25 The person who tries to hang on to his own will and reject what God desires for him ultimately loses eternally all that he is attempting to protect in this life.

16:26 All of this world's physical riches, pleasures, and powers will do no one any ultimate good if one "forfeits" their spiritual existence to acquire them.

16:27–28 Whether at the end of one's life or at the unexpected time of the return of the Son of Man in glory, all must give account for the choices they have made.

Some of the Twelve standing with Jesus in Caesarea Philippi will remain alive until they see the Son of Man coming in his kingdom. Jesus points to the urgency of his disciples' taking up their cross. As they will see, Jesus will be transfigured in kingdom glory in just a few days. They must not delay to take up their cross because every day brings with it the possibility of impending reward or judgment.

✤ **16:1–28** We can each display a rocklike consistency in our lives if we know who we are as created and gifted and called by God (and no more!) and if we then commit ourselves to maximizing all God wants to do through us as his uniquely gifted vessels. To do so is to be motivated to know Jesus on his own terms, not ours, and to take his calling on our life with deadly seriousness—but not take ourselves too seriously in the process.

17:1 This mountain is not identified. Most scholars favor Mount Hermon.

17:2 Jesus' transformation is a reminder of Jesus' divine glory and a preview of his coming exaltation.

17:3 Both Moses and Elijah had visions of the glory of God on a mountain—Moses on Mount Sinai (Ex 19) and Elijah on Mount Horeb (1Ki 19:9-18). Both are mentioned together in Mal 4:4-6 at the end of the OT. The appearance on the mountain of these two saints with Jesus indicates the greatness of Jesus, who transcends them both as the One who will be declared the Son of God.

17:4 Perhaps Peter's suggestion is to make some sort of memorial fitting to the stature of these men. Peter here may still not fully grasp the stature of Jesus, for he is not just another OT figure like Moses and Elijah. Jesus is superior in every way.

17:5 A "bright cloud" appears, reminiscent of God's manifestation in the OT. God the Father

the cloud said, "This is my Son, whom I love; with him I am well pleased.[e] Listen to him!"[f]

6When the disciples heard this, they fell facedown to the ground, terrified. 7But Jesus came and touched them. "Get up," he said. "Don't be afraid."[g] 8When they looked up, they saw no one except Jesus.

9As they were coming down the mountain, Jesus instructed them, "Don't tell anyone[h] what you have seen, until the Son of Man[i] has been raised from the dead."[j]

10The disciples asked him, "Why then do the teachers of the law say that Elijah must come first?"

11Jesus replied, "To be sure, Elijah comes and will restore all things.[k] 12But I tell you, Elijah has already come,[l] and they did not recognize him, but have done to him everything they wished.[m] In the same way the Son of Man is going to suffer[n] at their hands." 13Then the disciples understood that he was talking to them about John the Baptist.

Jesus Heals a Demon-Possessed Boy

17:14–19pp // Mk 9:14–28; Lk 9:37–42

14When they came to the crowd, a man approached Jesus and knelt before him. 15"Lord, have mercy on my son," he said. "He has seizures[o] and is suffering greatly. He often falls into the fire or into the water. 16I brought him to your disciples, but they could not heal him."

17"You unbelieving and perverse generation," Jesus replied, "how long shall I stay with you? How long shall I put up with you? Bring the boy here to me." 18Jesus rebuked the demon, and it came out of the boy, and he was healed at that moment.

19Then the disciples came to Jesus in private and asked, "Why couldn't we drive it out?"

20He replied, "Because you have so little faith. Truly I tell you, if you have faith[p] as small as a mustard seed,[q] you can say to this mountain, 'Move from here to there,' and it will move.[r] Nothing will be impossible for you." [21][a]

Jesus Predicts His Death a Second Time

17:22–23pp // Mk 9:31–32; Lk 9:43b–45

22When they came together in Galilee, he said to them, "The Son of Man[s] is going to be delivered into the hands of men. 23They will kill him,[t] and on the third day[u] he will be raised to life."[v] And the disciples were filled with grief.

The Temple Tax

24After Jesus and his disciples arrived in Capernaum, the collectors of the two-drachma temple tax[w] came to Peter and

17:5 [e] Mt 3:17; 2Pe 1:17 [f] Ac 3:22,23
17:7 [g] Mt 14:27
17:9 [h] Mk 8:30 [i] Mt 8:20 [j] Mt 16:21
17:11 [k] Mal 4:6; Lk 1:16,17
17:12 [l] Mt 11:14 [m] Mt 14:3,10 [n] Mt 16:21
17:15 [o] Mt 4:24
17:20 [p] Mt 21:21 [q] Mt 13:31; Mk 11:23; Lk 17:6 [r] 1Co 13:2
17:22 [s] Mt 8:20
17:23 [t] Ac 2:23; 3:13 [u] Mt 16:21 [v] Mt 16:21
17:24 [w] Ex 30:13

[a] *21* Some manuscripts include here words similar to Mark 9:29.

---

audibly endorses Jesus, indicating that Jesus is both Son and suffering servant. Jesus tenderly tells his frightened disciples not to fear. This reassures them he is the same master that they have known, even though they have just experienced a stunning revelation of his divine nature.

17:8 When the disciples look up, they see no one except Jesus. Their focus is now exclusively on Jesus, the way Moses and Elijah would have desired. The disciples have received the most explicit revelation of Jesus' identity but still do not fully comprehend it.

17:9 Jesus tells the disciples that they may tell others about this experience only after he has been raised from the dead. Otherwise, the disciples and the crowd may think the time has come to begin Israel's military liberation. Jesus' message must be understood to focus on forgiveness of sins through his suffering on the cross.

17:10–12 Jesus clarifies Malachi's prophecy in the light of John the Baptist's ministry. John was the fulfillment of the arrival of the anticipated Elijah, but neither John's nor Jesus' ministry was accepted fully. Instead, John was executed, as Jesus will be. So the complete fulfillment of Malachi's promise of restoration and judgment cannot yet be accomplished. Another Elijah-type figure will have to come in the future.

17:13 Matthew emphasizes how Jesus and his teaching bring enlightenment in the path of discipleship.

17:14–16 The boy's father respects Jesus by calling him "Lord," but he goes beyond that. The father has such confidence in Jesus' ability to heal that he assumes that his disciples have this ability as well. But his confidence has been dashed.

17:17–18 "Unbelieving" indicates the current generation has not as a whole placed their faith in Jesus as the anticipated Messiah; "perverse" indicates that they have become distorted in their evaluation of Jesus, rejecting Jesus' demand for repentance. Demonstrating that he has ultimate authority over the satanic source of this illness, Jesus rebukes the demon, it comes out of the boy, and he is immediately healed.

17:19–20 The disciples do have faith in Jesus and his mission, but here it is not functioning properly; it is "little faith," or defective faith. Perhaps they were trying to put on a show for their own acclaim.

17:20 Jesus is getting the disciples to look at the real nature of faith. It is not the *amount* of faith that is in question but rather its *focus*. Faith is confidence that we can do what God calls us to do—it is "taking God at his word." Therefore, the disciples should not place confidence in what they have but have confidence that if God calls them to do something, they can do it in his strength.

17:22–23 This second prediction adds an ominous

asked, “Doesn’t your teacher pay the temple tax?”
25“Yes, he does,” he replied.
When Peter came into the house, Jesus
was the first to speak. “What do you
think, Simon?” he asked. “From whom
do the kings of the earth collect duty
and taxes[x] — from their own children
or from others?”
26“From others,” Peter answered.
“Then the children are exempt,” Jesus
said to him. 27“But so that we may not
cause offense,[y] go to the lake and throw
out your line. Take the first fish you
catch; open its mouth and you will find
a four-drachma coin. Take it and give it
to them for my tax and yours.”

The Greatest in the Kingdom of Heaven

18:1–5pp // Mk 9:33–37; Lk 9:46–48

18 At that time the disciples came
to Jesus and asked, “Who, then,
is the greatest in the kingdom of heav-
en?”
2He called a little child to him, and
placed the child among them. 3And he
said: “Truly I tell you, unless you change
and become like little children,[z] you will
never enter the kingdom of heaven.[a]
4Therefore, whoever takes the lowly
position of this child is the greatest in
the kingdom of heaven.[b] 5And whoever
welcomes one such child in my name
welcomes me.[c]

Causing to Stumble

6“If anyone causes one of these little
ones — those who believe in me — to
stumble, it would be better for them to
have a large millstone hung around their
neck and to be drowned in the depths of
the sea.[d] 7Woe to the world because of
the things that cause people to stumble! Such things must come, but woe to
the person through whom they come![e]
8If your hand or your foot causes you to
stumble,[f] cut it off and throw it away. It
is better for you to enter life maimed or
crippled than to have two hands or two
feet and be thrown into eternal fire. 9And
if your eye causes you to stumble,[g] gouge
it out and throw it away. It is better for
you to enter life with one eye than to
have two eyes and be thrown into the
fire of hell.[h]

17:25 [x] Mt 22:17-21; Ro 13:7
17:27 [y] Jn 6:61
18:3 [z] Mt 19:14; 1Pe 2:2 [a] Mt 3:2
18:4 [b] Mk 9:35
18:5 [c] Mt 10:40
18:6 [d] Mk 9:42; Lk 17:2
18:7 [e] Lk 17:1
18:8 [f] Mt 5:29; Mk 9:43,45
18:9 [g] Mt 5:29 [h] Mt 5:22

Mt 18:3 ❖ What might it look like to become like a little child in our faith? How could this be a desirable thing?

---

element: Jesus will be betrayed. Little do the disciples know that the traitor is one of them and that they themselves will abandon Jesus at his moment of greatest human need.

17:24–27 These representatives from the temple establishment may have been attempting, with deceit, to confirm charges of Jesus’ disloyalty to the temple. Peter knows of Jesus’ loyalty to the Law (5:17–19), so his answer is correct on one level. But once Jesus gets him alone in the house, he gives Peter a more profound insight. Rulers collect taxes from their subjects. The temple is his Father’s own house, so since Jesus is the Son of God his Father, he is exempt from the temple tax. And Jesus’ disciples, now part of the Father’s family, are likewise exempt.

So as not to offend the conscience of those Jews who have not yet experienced liberation through Jesus, they will both pay the tax. To make a striking impression on his disciples, Jesus instructs Peter to throw out a fishing line, where he will find the coin for paying the tax.

✣ **17:1–27** Jesus pointed to the *effectiveness* of faith. It is not the amount of our faith that works miracles. It is the focus of our faith on Jesus who will work miracles through us according to his will. Jesus’ point is that anyone with any amount of faith can do the most miraculous things, if that is what God has called us to do. Therefore, we should not place confidence in what we have; rather, we should be confident that if God calls us to do something, we can do it in his strength—even the things that seem absurdly impossible from the world’s point of view.

18:1–4 One of Jesus’ primary goals in this chapter is to revise the disciples’ understanding of “greatness” to the way God thinks about it. Jesus begins this process with a visual aid by calling a little child and celebrates the humility that comes from the child’s weakness, defenselessness, and vulnerability. Those who wish to enter the kingdom must turn away from their own power and call on God’s mercy to allow them to enter the kingdom of heaven.

18:5 Receiving a little child in the name of Christ means accepting and believing the witness of a Christian disciple.

18:6–7 To practice a lifestyle that regularly leads Jesus’ humble disciples into sin indicates that one is headed for eternal damnation, so it would be better to cut one’s life off quickly than to risk staying on that trajectory.

18:8–9 Jesus is not advocating physical self-mutilation, but through dramatic figures of speech he indicates the rigorous self-discipline that committed disciples need.

The Parable of the Wandering Sheep

18:12–14pp // Lk 15:4–7

10"See that you do not despise one of
these little ones. For I tell you that their
angels[i] in heaven always see the face of
my Father in heaven. [11][a]
12"What do you think? If a man owns
a hundred sheep, and one of them wanders away, will he not leave the ninety-
nine on the hills and go to look for the
one that wandered off? 13And if he finds
it, truly I tell you, he is happier about that
one sheep than about the ninety-nine
that did not wander off. 14In the same
way your Father in heaven is not willing that any of these little ones should
perish.

Dealing With Sin in the Church

15"If your brother or sister[b] sins,[c] go
and point out their fault,[j] just between
the two of you. If they listen to you,
you have won them over. 16But if they
will not listen, take one or two others
along, so that 'every matter may be established by the testimony of two or
three witnesses.'[d][k] 17If they still refuse
to listen, tell it to the church;[l] and if
they refuse to listen even to the church,
treat them as you would a pagan or a
tax collector.[m]
18"Truly I tell you, whatever you bind
on earth will be[e] bound in heaven, and
whatever you loose on earth will be[e]
loosed in heaven.[n]
19"Again, truly I tell you that if two
of you on earth agree about anything
they ask for, it will be done for them[o] by
my Father in heaven. 20For where two
or three gather in my name, there am
I with them."

The Parable of the Unmerciful Servant

21Then Peter came to Jesus and asked,
"Lord, how many times shall I forgive my
brother or sister who sins against me?[p]
Up to seven times?"[q]
22Jesus answered, "I tell you, not seven
times, but seventy-seven times.[f][r]
23"Therefore, the kingdom of heaven
is like[s] a king who wanted to settle accounts[t] with his servants. 24As he began
the settlement, a man who owed him ten
thousand bags of gold[g] was brought to
him. 25Since he was not able to pay,[u] the
master ordered that he and his wife and

18:10 [i] Ge 48:16; Ps 34:7; Ac 12:11, 15; Heb 1:14
18:15 [j] Lev 19:17; Lk 17:3; Gal 6:1; Jas 5:19,20
18:16 [k] Nu 35:30; Dt 17:6; 19:15; Jn 8:17; 2Co 13:1; 1Ti 5:19; Heb 10:28
18:17 [l] 1Co 6:1-6 [m] Ro 16:17; 2Th 3:6,14
18:18 [n] Mt 16:19; Jn 20:23
18:19 [o] Mt 7:7
18:21 [p] Mt 6:14 [q] Lk 17:4
18:22 [r] Ge 4:24
18:23 [s] Mt 13:24 [t] Mt 25:19
18:25 [u] Lk 7:42

[a] *11* Some manuscripts include here the words of Luke 19:10. [b] *15* The Greek word for *brother or sister* (*adelphos*) refers here to a fellow disciple, whether man or woman; also in verses 21 and 35. [c] *15* Some manuscripts *sins against you* [d] *16* Deut. 19:15 [e] *18* Or *will have been* [f] *22* Or *seventy times seven* [g] *24* Greek *ten thousand talents*; a talent was worth about 20 years of a day laborer's wages.

18:10 Whether or not Jesus' statement implies guardian angels who watch over individual believers on an ongoing basis, it does confirm that the heavenly Father uses angels to care for childlike disciples.

18:12–14 The joy of finding the lost sheep does not mean that it has more value than the others. Rather, the shepherd's joy demonstrates the depth of his concern, care, and love for all his sheep.

18:15–17 Jesus outlines four steps for dealing with a sinning member of the discipleship community, which has restoration as its intended goal.

Such an encounter must be undertaken with privacy so that if it is resolved, no undue attention will be given to the tragedy of sin committed by a member of the community.

If the first step does not result in repentance, one or two other members of the community should help mediate as witnesses.

The way in which this was carried out in the small house churches of the early church may be quite different than today. This may work most effectively when the church leaders are made aware of the situation and brought into the attempted restoration process rather than just making a public announcement.

Disciples who live with unconfessed sin indicate by their lives that they are not truly members of Jesus' spiritual family, so they should be treated as unbelievers with the same compassion and urgency needed to encourage them to repent.

18:18–19 The church is the instrument of God, who alone can grant forgiveness of sin or consign a person to judgment. Jesus' statement assures the church that God in heaven confirms its judgment on an unrepentant person. In this way, the church carries out the will of the heavenly Father on earth.

18:20 Jesus himself is with his disciples, guaranteeing that when they reach a consensus as they ask for guidance, his Father in heaven will guide them. A special emphasis of Matthew is that Jesus, who is Immanuel ("God with us," 1:23), gives his people his abiding presence even until the "end of the age" (28:20).

18:21–22 Peter's offer to forgive the person seven times, more than double the traditional expectations of his day, is generous, reflecting a desire for completeness that the number seven usually evokes. Jesus' response is that the number doesn't matter. Peter and the rest of the disciples are to continue to forgive without keeping count. Peter should go on forgiving because the reality of his own forgiveness is demonstrated in how God forgives others.

18:23–25 Some estimate that the amount the servant owed is the equivalent of hundreds of billions of dollars. The intention is to indicate an astronomical sum that can never be repaid.

his children and all that he had be sold[v]
to repay the debt.
26"At this the servant fell on his knees
before him.[w] 'Be patient with me,' he
begged, 'and I will pay back everything.'
27The servant's master took pity on him,
canceled the debt and let him go.
28"But when that servant went out,
he found one of his fellow servants who
owed him a hundred silver coins.[a] He
grabbed him and began to choke him.
'Pay back what you owe me!' he demanded.
29"His fellow servant fell to his knees
and begged him, 'Be patient with me,
and I will pay it back.'
30"But he refused. Instead, he went off
and had the man thrown into prison until he could pay the debt. 31When the other servants saw what had happened, they
were outraged and went and told their
master everything that had happened.
32"Then the master called the servant
in. 'You wicked servant,' he said, 'I canceled all that debt of yours because you
begged me to. 33Shouldn't you have had
mercy on your fellow servant just as I had
on you?' 34In anger his master handed
him over to the jailers to be tortured, until
he should pay back all he owed.
35"This is how my heavenly Father will
treat each of you unless you forgive your
brother or sister from your heart."[x]

18:25 [v]Lev 25:39; 2Ki 4:1; Ne 5:5,8
18:26 [w]Mt 8:2
18:35 [x]Mt 6:14; Jas 2:13
19:1 [y]Mt 7:28
19:2 [z]Mt 4:23
19:3 [a]Mt 5:31
19:4 [b]Ge 1:27; 5:2
19:5 [c]Ge 2:24; 1Co 6:16; Eph 5:31

Divorce

19:1–9pp // Mk 10:1–12

19 When Jesus had finished saying these things,[y] he left Galilee
and went into the region of Judea to
the other side of the Jordan. 2Large
crowds followed him, and he healed
them[z] there.
3Some Pharisees came to him to test
him. They asked, "Is it lawful for a man
to divorce his wife[a] for any and every
reason?"
4"Haven't you read," he replied, "that
at the beginning the Creator 'made them
male and female,'[b][b] 5and said, 'For this
reason a man will leave his father and
mother and be united to his wife, and the
two will become one flesh'[c]?[c] 6So they are

[a] *28* Greek *a hundred denarii;* a denarius was the usual daily wage of a day laborer (see 20:2).
[b] *4* Gen. 1:27 [c] *5* Gen. 2:24

18:26–27 The servant of the king makes a ridiculous petition, suggesting that with just a bit of patience, he can repay the debt. But his overwhelming trouble evokes pity from the king; the king cancels the debt and releases him. This first scene displays God's forgiveness toward those who have offended him.
18:28–30 The second servant pleads with almost identical words as the first servant. But instead of reacting with compassion and grace, the first servant delivers physical punishment by choking him. Instead of selling him into slavery, he throws him into the debtor's prison, an even more severe punishment than what the king threatened him with, making repaying the debt impossible.
18:31–34 The wicked servant has only taken selfish advantage of the master. Now he will receive the punishment that he deserved in the first place. He is handed over to the "torturers." Since it would be impossible for the servant to repay the vast amounts owed, the scene concludes with the grim certainty that he will experience that punishment forever, a harsh metaphorical reference to an eternal destiny of judgment.
18:35 A person who has truly experienced the mercy and grace of God by responding to the presence of his kingdom will be transformed into Jesus' disciple, which means experiencing a fundamentally transformed heart that produces a changed life that gives the same mercy and grace to others that one has received from God.

18:1–35 The key to forgiveness is to stop focusing on what others have done *to* us and focus instead on what Jesus has done *for* us.

An unspiritual community does not live in light of the cross and resurrection. Rather, it lives according to the prevailing cultural values. The kind of community that Jesus advances is based on receiving mercy and forgiveness, which in turn will urge us to demonstrate mercy and forgiveness.

True reconciliation is not simply a tolerant attitude toward one another in the same living space. It is a real, personal, loving connection between individuals that Jesus desires; without a heart attitude of forgiveness, this type of connection is impossible.

Another important facet to consider is that our forgiveness of others often points people toward God's forgiveness of them. Forgiveness not only sustains the intimacy of the community, but it is a powerful device that allows people to make changes in their own lives and to move on toward deeper intimacy with God.

19:1–2 Following Jesus' teaching concerning forgiveness, Matthew records events that reveal what life is to be like in Jesus' community of disciples.
19:3 A hotbed of discussion surrounded the interpretations of Moses' divorce regulation (Dt 24:1). The more conservative school of Shammai held to the letter of the Mosaic Law and said that the word "indecent" means "unchastity." The more liberal school of Hillel interpreted "indecent" to mean that "a man may divorce his wife for something as small as spoiling a dish for him."
19:4–6 Jesus goes back to the beginning of creation to demonstrate God's intention for the institution

no longer two, but one flesh. Therefore
what God has joined together, let no one
separate."
7"Why then," they asked, "did Moses
command that a man give his wife a certificate of divorce and send her away?"[d]
8Jesus replied, "Moses permitted you
to divorce your wives because your hearts
were hard. But it was not this way from
the beginning. 9I tell you that anyone
who divorces his wife, except for sexual
immorality, and marries another woman
commits adultery."[e]
10The disciples said to him, "If this is
the situation between a husband and
wife, it is better not to marry."
11Jesus replied, "Not everyone can accept this word, but only those to whom it
has been given.[f] 12For there are eunuchs
who were born that way, and there are
eunuchs who have been made eunuchs
by others — and there are those who
choose to live like eunuchs for the sake
of the kingdom of heaven. The one who
can accept this should accept it."

The Little Children and Jesus

19:13–15pp // Mk 10:13–16; Lk 18:15–17

13Then people brought little children
to Jesus for him to place his hands on
them[g] and pray for them. But the disciples rebuked them.
14Jesus said, "Let the little children
come to me, and do not hinder them,
for the kingdom of heaven belongs[h] to
such as these."[i] 15When he had placed his
hands on them, he went on from there.

The Rich and the Kingdom of God

19:16–29pp // Mk 10:17–30; Lk 18:18–30

16Just then a man came up to Jesus
and asked, "Teacher, what good thing
must I do to get eternal life[j]?"[k]
17"Why do you ask me about what is
good?" Jesus replied. "There is only One
who is good. If you want to enter life,
keep the commandments."[l]
18"Which ones?" he inquired.
Jesus replied, " 'You shall not murder,
you shall not commit adultery,[m] you shall
not steal, you shall not give false testimony, 19honor your father and mother,'[a][n]
and 'love your neighbor as yourself.'[b]"[o]
20"All these I have kept," the young
man said. "What do I still lack?"
21Jesus answered, "If you want to be
perfect,[p] go, sell your possessions and
give to the poor,[q] and you will have treasure in heaven.[r] Then come, follow me."
22When the young man heard this,
he went away sad, because he had great
wealth.
23Then Jesus said to his disciples, "Truly I
tell you, it is hard for someone who is rich[s]

19:7 [d] Dt 24:1-4; Mt 5:31
19:9 [e] Mt 5:32; Lk 16:18
19:11 [f] Mt 13:11; 1Co 7:7-9,17
19:13 [g] Mk 5:23
19:14 [h] Mt 25:34 [i] Mt 18:3; 1Pe 2:2
19:16 [j] Mt 25:46 [k] Lk 10:25
19:17 [l] Lev 18:5
19:18 [m] Jas 2:11
19:19 [n] Ex 20:12-16; Dt 5:16-20 [o] Lev 19:18; Mt 5:43
19:21 [p] Mt 5:48 [q] Lk 12:33; Ac 2:45; 4:34-35 [r] Mt 6:20
19:23 [s] Mt 13:22; 1Ti 6:9,10

[a] *19* Exodus 20:12-16; Deut. 5:16-20
[b] *19* Lev. 19:18

of marriage (Ge 2:24). God designed his human creatures as male and female, with marriage being a permanent bond of a man and woman into one new union that is consecrated by physical intercourse. God hates divorce, because it tears apart what should be considered a permanent union (cf. Mal 2:16).

19:7 But the Pharisees point to the Mosaic Law. Since sinful abuse of a marriage partner was a harsh reality in the ancient world, Moses instituted a regulation designed to do three things: protect the sanctity of marriage from something "indecent" defiling the relationship; protect the woman from being sent away without cause; and document her status as a legitimately divorced woman so that she would not be thought a prostitute or a runaway adulteress.

19:8–9 Jesus counters by once again going to God's original intention. Jesus emphasizes that divorce always evidences the presence of sin. The Pharisees look not at God's original intention but at Moses' statement.

Jesus allows for an exception to protect the nonoffending partner; he uses a word broader than "adultery." It includes whatever intentionally divides the marital relationship, possibly including, but not limited to, related sexual sins.

19:10–12 Singleness is an appropriate alternative for some. But nowhere in Scripture is celibacy seen as contributing to a higher form of spirituality than being married.

19:13–15 Jesus once again turns society's prevailing values on their head to show that childlikeness is required for entrance to the kingdom and is a necessary lifetime characteristic for Jesus' disciples.

19:16–22 Jesus takes the young man back to obeying the Law as an expression of faith in the truly good God. This is not to *earn* eternal life but to humbly obey the Law with childlike faith in God's goodness.

19:18–20 In v. 18 the young man responds to Jesus' directive to obey the commandments by asking, "Which ones?" Jesus replies by giving a representative listing of the Law. With unblinking confidence, the young man declares that he has kept them all. But he senses that he still lacks something. Jesus challenges him to see what his most cherished value actually is—in essence, the ruling god of his life. His wealth has become his god. Thus, Jesus calls him to exchange the god of wealth for following him as the one true God.

19:22 The man departs in distress, knowing deep in his heart that his decision has eternal consequences. He knew all along what he was lacking and rejects the invitation to life.

19:23–26 Wealth was often equated with the blessing of divine favor. Jesus knows that riches

to enter the kingdom of heaven. 24Again I
tell you, it is easier for a camel to go through
the eye of a needle than for someone who
is rich to enter the kingdom of God."
25When the disciples heard this, they
were greatly astonished and asked, "Who
then can be saved?"
26Jesus looked at them and said, "With
man this is impossible, but with God all
things are possible."[t]
27Peter answered him, "We have left
everything to follow you![u] What then
will there be for us?"
28Jesus said to them, "Truly I tell you,
at the renewal of all things, when the
Son of Man sits on his glorious throne,[v]
you who have followed me will also sit
on twelve thrones, judging the twelve
tribes of Israel.[w] 29And everyone who
has left houses or brothers or sisters or
father or mother or wife[a] or children or
fields for my sake will receive a hundred
times as much and will inherit eternal
life.[x] 30But many who are first will be
last, and many who are last will be first.[y]

The Parable of the Workers in the Vineyard

20 "For the kingdom of heaven is
like[z] a landowner who went out
early in the morning to hire workers for
his vineyard.[a] 2He agreed to pay them a
denarius[b] for the day and sent them into
his vineyard.

19:26 [t]Ge 18:14; Job 42:2; Jer 32:17; Zec 8:6; Lk 1:37; 18:27; Ro 4:21
19:27 [u]Mt 4:19
19:28 [v]Mt 20:21; 25:31 [w]Lk 22:28-30; Rev 3:21; 4:4; 20:4
19:29 [x]Mt 6:33; 25:46
19:30 [y]Mt 20:16; Mk 10:31; Lk 13:30
20:1 [z]Mt 13:24 [a]Mt 21:28, 33
20:8 [b]Lev 19:13; Dt 24:15

Mt 19:23-24 ❖ Why does material wealth pose such risk to true spiritual health?

3"About nine in the morning he went
out and saw others standing in the marketplace doing nothing. 4He told them,
'You also go and work in my vineyard,
and I will pay you whatever is right.' 5So
they went.
"He went out again about noon and
about three in the afternoon and did the
same thing. 6About five in the afternoon
he went out and found still others standing around. He asked them, 'Why have
you been standing here all day long doing nothing?'
7"'Because no one has hired us,' they
answered.
"He said to them, 'You also go and
work in my vineyard.'
8"When evening came,[b] the owner of
the vineyard said to his foreman, 'Call
the workers and pay them their wages,
beginning with the last ones hired and
going on to the first.'
9"The workers who were hired about
five in the afternoon came and each received a denarius. 10So when those came

[a] 29 Some manuscripts do not have *or wife*.
[b] 2 A denarius was the usual daily wage of a day laborer.

---

can keep people's eyes off of God. All we need to do is to acknowledge what rules our lives and exchange that treasure for the treasure of Jesus as one's God.

19:27-30 Peter rightly understands that the focus is not solely on the rich person but on all people. He and the others have left everything to follow Jesus. But Peter focuses on rewards. Jesus ends by showing that those who serve to gain rewards will be last, but those who are motivated by obedience will be first.

✜ **19:1-30** Even Christians can misplace their allegiance, so each person must be honest with themselves to know what the treasure of their heart truly is. To claim Jesus as Savior, each person must exchange the "god" of his or her life to have Jesus as God. The cost varies from person to person according to the god of each person's life, but it must be faced. So what rules our lives? What must be dethroned as that which is keeping us from experiencing freedom and fullness of life?

Salvation is not earned; it is received by faith through God's grace. But at the same time salvation is costly. It cost Jesus his life, and it costs us our lives as well. Being a disciple of Jesus is for those who have counted the cost and want real, eternal life received from a Savior who came to earth to seek and to save us and who lovingly and persistently transforms us into his image. These are tough words if we fear and resist him. But they are words of hope, promise, peace, and joy if we are tired of ruling our lives ourselves.

20:1-16 This parable is a lesson on gratitude and motivation in service; it is not about salvation or gaining eternal life, because salvation is not earned by works. Nor is the parable about rewards for service, because God will reward believers differently according to their service. Rather, this is a profound parable about what should be the disciple's motivation for service.

We should serve out of gratitude, because it is only through Jesus' work on our behalf that any disciple receives anything. Finding our purpose and understanding that our work is in the center of God's will provides a contentment that doesn't look for more. We already have the promise of eternal life, which is for every one of us who trusts in Jesus alone for our salvation.

PEOPLE TO KNOW // JAMES, SON OF ZEBEDEE

MATTHEW 20:20–28: James, son of Zebedee, was the brother of the Gospel writer John. Like Peter and Andrew, James and John were fishermen before Jesus called them to be disciples. Peter, James and John comprised Jesus' inner circle of followers.

Jesus called James to follow him when James was out fishing with his brother and father. James and John left their father and their boats and followed Christ (Mt 4:21–22).

James, along with Peter and John, witnessed Jesus' transfiguration, when Christ radiated with blinding light and a voice from heaven declared, "This is my Son, whom I love" (Mt 17:5). These three were also the only disciples present when Jesus raised Jairus's daughter from the dead (Mk 5:37–43).

James and John showed some presumption when they privately asked Jesus if they could sit on his left and right in his glorious kingdom—a request that earned them the consternation of their fellow apostles when they learned of the brothers' request. Jesus gave James and John the nickname "sons of thunder" (Mk 3:17), perhaps because of their zeal for judgment. They showed this side of their character when they asked Jesus if they could call down fire from heaven upon a Samaritan village that rejected Christ, but Jesus chastised them for this (Lk 9:54–55).

Aside from Judas Iscariot, James was the first apostle to die and the first to be martyred for his faith in Christ. Herod Agrippa had James put to death by the sword (Ac 12:2).

APPLICATION ✣ James had an up close view of Jesus' ministry, and what he saw instilled an unshakeable faith within him. James was the first apostle martyred, showing that he stood firm in his faith in Christ even when it meant losing his life. James's life is an example for us to also stay as close to Christ as we can, to get to know Jesus and to learn from him. With Jesus at the center of our life, there is nothing to fear, not even death. The apostle James anchors us in this deep hope and assurance.

who were hired first, they expected to receive more. But each one of them also received a denarius. 11When they received
it, they began to grumble[c] against the
landowner. 12'These who were hired last
worked only one hour,' they said, 'and
you have made them equal to us who
have borne the burden of the work and
the heat[d] of the day.'
13"But he answered one of them, 'I
am not being unfair to you, friend.[e]
Didn't you agree to work for a denarius?
14Take your pay and go. I want to give
the one who was hired last the same
as I gave you. 15Don't I have the right
to do what I want with my own money? Or are you envious because I am
generous?'[f]
16"So the last will be first, and the first
will be last."[g]

Jesus Predicts His Death a Third Time

20:17–19pp // Mk 10:32–34; Lk 18:31–33

17Now Jesus was going up to Jerusalem. On the way, he took the Twelve aside
and said to them, 18"We are going up to
Jerusalem,[h] and the Son of Man[i] will be
delivered over to the chief priests and the
teachers of the law.[j] They will condemn
him to death 19and will hand him over to
the Gentiles to be mocked and flogged[k]
and crucified.[l] On the third day[m] he will
be raised to life!"[n]

A Mother's Request

20:20–28pp // Mk 10:35–45

20Then the mother of Zebedee's sons[o]
came to Jesus with her sons and, kneeling down,[p] asked a favor of him.
21"What is it you want?" he asked.
She said, "Grant that one of these two

20:11 [c] Jnh 4:1
20:12 [d] Jnh 4:8; Lk 12:55; Jas 1:11
20:13 [e] Mt 22:12; 26:50
20:15 [f] Dt 15:9; Mk 7:22
20:16 [g] Mt 19:30
20:18 [h] Lk 9:51 [i] Mt 8:20 [j] Mt 16:21; 27:1,2
20:19 [k] Mt 16:21 [l] Ac 2:23 [m] Mt 16:21 [n] Mt 16:21
20:20 [o] Mt 4:21 [p] Mt 8:2

20:17–19 This is the third of Jesus' four predictions of his arrest and crucifixion. It is the first reference to Jerusalem, the religious leaders' role, and of the Gentiles as executioners.

20:20–22 Later identified as Salome, this woman is among those who attend Jesus at the cross and witness the empty tomb. She is likely the sister of Mary, Jesus' mother, and so she would be Jesus' aunt. Her sons, James and John, would be his cousins on his mother's side.

She is not pushing her sons into something they do not want, but together they are demonstrating their commitment to supporting Jesus in what lies ahead. The mother desires for her sons to have the highest positions of importance when Jesus inaugurates his future kingdom.

sons of mine may sit at your right and
the other at your left in your kingdom.”[q]
22“You don’t know what you are asking,” Jesus said to them. “Can you drink
the cup[r] I am going to drink?”
“We can,” they answered.
23Jesus said to them, “You will indeed
drink from my cup,[s] but to sit at my right
or left is not for me to grant. These places belong to those for whom they have
been prepared by my Father.”
24When the ten heard about this, they
were indignant[t] with the two brothers.
25Jesus called them together and said,
“You know that the rulers of the Gentiles
lord it over them, and their high officials
exercise authority over them. 26Not so
with you. Instead, whoever wants to become great among you must be your servant,[u] 27and whoever wants to be first must
be your slave— 28just as the Son of Man[v]
did not come to be served, but to serve,[w]
and to give his life as a ransom[x] for many.”

Two Blind Men Receive Sight

20:29–34pp // Mk 10:46–52; Lk 18:35–43

29As Jesus and his disciples were
leaving Jericho, a large crowd followed
him. 30Two blind men were sitting by
the roadside, and when they heard that
Jesus was going by, they shouted, “Lord,
Son of David,[y] have mercy on us!”
31The crowd rebuked them and told
them to be quiet, but they shouted all
the louder, “Lord, Son of David, have
mercy on us!”
32Jesus stopped and called them.
“What do you want me to do for you?”
he asked.
33“Lord,” they answered, “we want our
sight.”
34Jesus had compassion on them and
touched their eyes. Immediately they
received their sight and followed him.

Jesus Comes to Jerusalem as King

21:1–9pp // Mk 11:1–10; Lk 19:29–38
21:4–9pp // Jn 12:12–15

21 As they approached Jerusalem and
came to Bethphage on the Mount

20:21 [q] Mt 19:28
20:22 [r] Isa 51:17, 22; Jer 49:12; Mt 26:39, 42; Mk 14:36; Lk 22:42; Jn 18:11
20:23 [s] Ac 12:2; Rev 1:9
20:24 [t] Lk 22:24, 25
20:26 [u] Mt 23:11; Mk 9:35
20:28 [v] Mt 8:20 [w] Lk 22:27; Jn 13:13-16; 2Co 8:9; Php 2:7 [x] Isa 53:10; Mt 26:28; 1Ti 2:6; Titus 2:14; Heb 9:28; 1Pe 1:18,19
20:30 [y] Mt 9:27

Mt 20:24 ❖ Where have we seen envy or conflict among Jesus’ followers today? How can Christians learn to avoid such jealousies?

20:23 Jesus addresses the brothers directly. The “cup” refers figuratively to one’s divinely appointed destiny, whether blessing or wrath and disaster. Jesus is referring to his upcoming cup of suffering on the cross. The disciples will reaffirm their commitment to Jesus and his destiny, but they have little knowledge of what lies ahead.

20:24–28 The other disciples are probably indignant because of the brothers’ attempt to use their mother’s family relationship with Jesus as an unfair advantage. Jesus gathers all the disciples together to overturn their ambitions by making a contrast between what the world considers greatness and greatness in the kingdom of heaven.

20:29–34 This city was the new Jericho, a series of developments surrounding a huge palace complex first built by the Hasmoneans and greatly expanded by Herod the Great. The blind men ask for the gift of messianic mercy to heal their blindness. Although he has experienced increasing rejection, Jesus continues to have compassion on those in great need, so he touches their eyes and heals them, and they follow him.

20:31 The contrast in this incident is on the crowds who try to silence the two blind men. Yet the two men are the ones to whom Jesus directs his ministry; the crowds remain only spectators. Those without natural ability to follow Jesus are able, through his healing touch, to follow him.

✚ **20:1–34** Sacrifice is a concept that is readily understood when we think of it in terms of our own benefit. “No pain, no gain” is an old adage. It communicates a well-known and appreciated value—we must sacrifice present pleasure for personal future gain. That may mean the pain of physical exercise for the gain of a healthy heart or the pain of sacrificing to save enough to gain the benefits of education for a child. Jesus does not overturn that principle completely, but he does reverse the focus: “My pain, *others’* gain.”

But this does not mean that all ambition is bad. Ambition is bad when we are greedy, when we hurt and use people, when we exalt ourselves over others, when we are prideful. But the right kind of ambition involves hitching our goals to selfless servanthood. James’s and John’s strength was a weakness because it was greedy and selfish. But when ambition is selflessly directed toward service, God can use it in powerful ways. John’s ambitious drive guided and nurtured the early church in Jerusalem. James’s zeal resulted in his being the first apostle to suffer martyrdom, which became a turning point in the courageous story of the church. Disciples of Jesus are to be just as goal oriented as anyone in the world, but our ambition must be linked to selfless servanthood—giving our lives as a source of blessing to those for whom we have responsibility.

21:1–3 The term “Lord” can designate one’s earthly master or one’s deity. In this context, it is difficult to say what either the disciples or anyone else would have understood it to mean. Jesus plainly

of Olives,[z] Jesus sent two disciples, 2saying to them, "Go to the village ahead of
you, and at once you will find a donkey
tied there, with her colt by her. Untie
them and bring them to me. 3If anyone says anything to you, say that the
Lord needs them, and he will send them
right away."
4This took place to fulfill what was spoken through the prophet:

5"Say to Daughter Zion,
'See, your king comes to you,
gentle and riding on a donkey,
and on a colt, the foal of a
donkey.'"[aa]

6The disciples went and did as Jesus
had instructed them. 7They brought the
donkey and the colt and placed their
cloaks on them for Jesus to sit on. 8A
very large crowd spread their cloaks[b] on
the road, while others cut branches from
the trees and spread them on the road.
9The crowds that went ahead of him and
those that followed shouted,

"Hosanna[b] to the Son of David!"[c]

"Blessed is he who comes in the
name of the Lord!"[cd]

21:1 [z] Mt 24:3; 26:30; Mk 14:26; Lk 19:37; 21:37; 22:39; Jn 8:1; Ac 1:12
21:5 [a] Isa 62:11; Zec 9:9
21:8 [b] 2Ki 9:13
21:9 [c] ver 15; Mt 9:27
[d] Ps 118:26; Mt 23:39
[e] Lk 2:14
21:11 [f] Lk 7:16, 39; 24:19; Jn 1:21, 25; 6:14; 7:40
21:12 [g] Dt 14:26
[h] Ex 30:13
[i] Lev 1:14
21:13 [j] Isa 56:7
[k] Jer 7:11
21:14 [l] Mt 4:23

Mt 21:13 ❖ How can we protect and promote the integrity of God's house today?

"Hosanna[b] in the highest heaven!"[e]

10When Jesus entered Jerusalem, the
whole city was stirred and asked, "Who
is this?"
11The crowds answered, "This is Jesus,
the prophet[f] from Nazareth in Galilee."

Jesus at the Temple

21:12–16pp // Mk 11:15–18; Lk 19:45–47

12Jesus entered the temple courts and
drove out all who were buying[g] and selling there. He overturned the tables of
the money changers[h] and the benches of
those selling doves.[i] 13"It is written," he
said to them, "'My house will be called
a house of prayer,'[dj] but you are making
it 'a den of robbers.'[e]"[k]
14The blind and the lame came to him
at the temple, and he healed them.[l] 15But

[a] *5* Zech. 9:9 [b] *9* A Hebrew expression meaning "Save!" which became an exclamation of praise; also in verse 15 [c] *9* Psalm 118:25,26 [d] *13* Isaiah 56:7 [e] *13* Jer. 7:11

---

intends to refer to himself as the One who sovereignly oversees these events. At this climactic time of his earthly ministry, Jesus reveals himself with increasing clarity.

Jesus' descent from the Mount of Olives into Jerusalem evokes images of Zechariah's prophecy of the Lord's fighting against the nations (Zec 14:3-21). The crowds also would have seen Jesus' riding on a colt as fulfilling Zechariah's prophecy (Zec 9:9-13). The praise of the crowds comes from their own expectations of what they want Jesus to be. But for Jesus it is a self-disclosure to Israel. It will seal the fate of his people and be a testimony to his disciples once they reflect on these events with eyes of faith after his crucifixion and resurrection.

21:4-7 Matthew comments that Jesus' entrance into Jerusalem on a colt fulfills the prophecy of Zec 9:9. The time has now come for Jesus to declare openly that he is the righteous Davidic Messiah who offers salvation rather than a conquering military leader.

21:8 Many coins at the time of Jesus featured palms, indicating both Jewish and Roman nationalism.

Within the crowd are people with their own particular expectations that Jesus has come to liberate Jerusalem and the people of Israel from Roman oppression. Others are there out of curiosity and are caught up in the excitement.

21:9-10 The crowds shout out "Hosanna," the transliteration of the Hebrew expression "O save." The paranoid religious establishment wants an explanation of who Jesus intends to present himself to be.

21:11 The crowd generally says, "This is Jesus, the prophet from Nazareth in Galilee." Some in the crowd call him a prophet. Others who have called out "Hosanna" seem to expect Jesus to bring liberation, as had the kings of ancient Israel and the Maccabees of more recent times.

But Jesus has undertaken a different kind of Triumphal Entry from what many among the crowd expected. Jesus will triumph over the enemy of sin, bringing salvation to his people through his righteous sacrifice on the cross that looms ahead.

21:12-17 Matthew condenses some of the narrative of Jesus' activities during Holy Week, which is the case with his narrative here of the temple activities.

21:12 The money changers and merchants are making this a commercial operation, and the temptation for abuse is real since surplus tax was consigned to the temple fund. Doves were the sacrifice made by the poor and those making various personal offerings. Temple commerce was at times notorious for exploiting the needy.

21:13 The religious leaders are treating the temple as robbers do their dens—a place of storing their stolen wealth and for plotting future illegal activities. Jesus' action here has often been called a "cleansing" of the temple. Jesus goes beyond cleansing to perform a symbolic act of judgment against the religious leadership of Israel. This also demonstrates Jesus' authority over the sacrificial practices at the temple, which will be fulfilled with his upcoming crucifixion.

21:14-16 Jesus' actions in the temple should have caused the religious leaders to acknowledge his

when the chief priests and the teachers of the law saw the wonderful things
he did and the children shouting in the
temple courts, “Hosanna to the Son of
David,”[m] they were indignant.[n]
16“Do you hear what these children are
saying?” they asked him.
“Yes,” replied Jesus, “have you never
read,

“ ‘From the lips of children and
infants
you, Lord, have called forth your
praise’[a]?”[o]

17And he left them and went out of
the city to Bethany,[p] where he spent the
night.

Jesus Curses a Fig Tree

21:18–22pp // Mk 11:12–14,20–24

18Early in the morning, as Jesus was on
his way back to the city, he was hungry.
19Seeing a fig tree by the road, he went
up to it but found nothing on it except
leaves. Then he said to it, “May you never
bear fruit again!” Immediately the tree
withered.[q]
20When the disciples saw this, they
were amazed. “How did the fig tree wither so quickly?” they asked.
21Jesus replied, “Truly I tell you, if
you have faith and do not doubt,[r] not
only can you do what was done to the
fig tree, but also you can say to this
mountain, ‘Go, throw yourself into the
sea,’ and it will be done. 22If you believe,
you will receive whatever you ask for[s]
in prayer.”

The Authority of Jesus Questioned

21:23–27pp // Mk 11:27–33; Lk 20:1–8

23Jesus entered the temple courts, and,
while he was teaching, the chief priests
and the elders of the people came to him.
“By what authority[t] are you doing these
things?” they asked. “And who gave you
this authority?”
24Jesus replied, “I will also ask you one
question. If you answer me, I will tell
you by what authority I am doing these
things. 25John’s baptism—where did it
come from? Was it from heaven, or of
human origin?”
They discussed it among themselves
and said, “If we say, ‘From heaven,’ he
will ask, ‘Then why didn’t you believe
him?’ 26But if we say, ‘Of human origin’—
we are afraid of the people, for they all
hold that John was a prophet.”[u]
27So they answered Jesus, “We don’t
know.”
Then he said, “Neither will I tell you
by what authority I am doing these
things.

The Parable of the Two Sons

28“What do you think? There was a
man who had two sons. He went to the
first and said, ‘Son, go and work today
in the vineyard.’[v]

21:15 [m] ver 9; Mt 9:27 [n] Lk 19:39
21:16 [o] Ps 8:2
21:17 [p] Mt 26:6; Mk 11:1; Lk 24:50; Jn 11:1,18; 12:1
21:19 [q] Isa 34:4; Jer 8:13
21:21 [r] Mt 17:20; Lk 17:6; 1Co 13:2; Jas 1:6
21:22 [s] Mt 7:7
21:23 [t] Ac 4:7; 7:27
21:26 [u] Mt 11:9; Mk 6:20
21:28 [v] ver 33; Mt 20:1

[a] *16* Psalm 8:2 (see Septuagint)

---

authority. Instead, they become “indignant” at Jesus’ challenge to their authority (v. 15).

21:17 After the dramatic events of this Monday of Holy Week, Jesus leaves the religious leaders, most likely with their fury beginning to boil. He will return to the city and the temple the next day to engage them in extended debate. Most likely, Jesus stays at the home of Lazarus, whom he raised from the dead, and of his sisters, Mary and Martha.

21:18–22 Just as the fig tree’s fruitfulness was a sign of its health, so fruitfulness was a sign of Israel’s faithfulness to God’s covenantal standards. Now that Israel, especially represented by its religious leadership, has perverted the temple practices and has not repented at the appearance of Jesus Messiah, Israel is being judged by God.

Jesus’ cursing the fig tree is not a fit of temper but a symbolic act, demonstrating that God’s creatures must produce that for which they were created—to carry out God’s will.

Using the handy object of the Mount of Olives, or perhaps even the Temple Mount across the Kidron Valley, Jesus says that one with faith can throw a mountain into the sea. The point here is not the disciples’ amount of faith to do great things but rather their trust in accomplishing God’s will in God’s power.

21:23–27 Since Jesus had judged the religious leaders publicly, shaming them before the crowds, they respond by asking questions about Jesus’ authority. Instead of cowering before their challenge, Jesus engages the religious leaders in a series of rabbinic-type debates.

These religious leaders recognize the dilemma Jesus has put them in, so they refuse to answer. That refusal shows their dishonesty, and they must accept their fault. Therefore, Jesus feels no obligation to answer their question.

21:28–32 This parable and the next bring to mind the religious leaders, who have been called to serve God by serving the nation of Israel. The son that originally refused but then obeyed is like those in Israel who were disobedient to the Law, such as the tax collectors and prostitutes. When John arrived with the message of true righteousness, these people obeyed God’s call and were repentant. By contrast, the religious leaders are like the son who agreed but did nothing. They were

29"'I will not,' he answered, but later he changed his mind and went.

30"Then the father went to the other son and said the same thing. He answered, 'I will, sir,' but he did not go.

31"Which of the two did what his father wanted?"

"The first," they answered.

Jesus said to them, "Truly I tell you, the tax collectors[w] and the prostitutes[x] are entering the kingdom of God ahead of you. 32For John came to you to show you the way of righteousness,[y] and you did not believe him, but the tax collectors[z] and the prostitutes[a] did. And even after you saw this, you did not repent[b] and believe him.

The Parable of the Tenants

21:33–46pp // Mk 12:1–12; Lk 20:9–19

33"Listen to another parable: There was a landowner who planted[c] a vineyard. He put a wall around it, dug a winepress in it and built a watchtower.[d] Then he rented the vineyard to some farmers and moved to another place.[e] 34When the harvest time approached, he sent his servants[f] to the tenants to collect his fruit.

35"The tenants seized his servants; they beat one, killed another, and stoned a third.[g] 36Then he sent other servants[h] to them, more than the first time, and the tenants treated them the same way. 37Last of all, he sent his son to them. 'They will respect my son,' he said.

38"But when the tenants saw the son, they said to each other, 'This is the heir.[i] Come, let's kill him[j] and take his inheritance.'[k] 39So they took him and threw him out of the vineyard and killed him.

40"Therefore, when the owner of the vineyard comes, what will he do to those tenants?"

41"He will bring those wretches to a wretched end,"[l] they replied, "and he will rent the vineyard to other tenants,[m] who will give him his share of the crop at harvest time."

42Jesus said to them, "Have you never read in the Scriptures:

"'The stone the builders rejected
has become the cornerstone;
the Lord has done this,
and it is marvelous in our
eyes'*[a]*?[n]

43"Therefore I tell you that the kingdom of God will be taken away from you[o] and given to a people who will produce its fruit. 44Anyone who falls on this stone will be broken to pieces; anyone on whom it falls will be crushed."*[b]*[p]

45When the chief priests and the Pharisees heard Jesus' parables, they knew he was talking about them. 46They looked

21:31 [w] Lk 7:29 [x] Lk 7:50
21:32 [y] Mt 3:1-12 [z] Lk 3:12,13; 7:29 [a] Lk 7:36-50 [b] Lk 7:30
21:33 [c] Ps 80:8 [d] Isa 5:1-7 [e] Mt 25:14,15
21:34 [f] Mt 22:3
21:35 [g] 2Ch 24:21; Mt 23:34,37; Heb 11:36,37
21:36 [h] Mt 22:4
21:38 [i] Heb 1:2 [j] Mt 12:14 [k] Ps 2:8
21:41 [l] Mt 8:11,12 [m] Ac 13:46; 18:6; 28:28
21:42 [n] Ps 118:22,23; Ac 4:11; 1Pe 2:7
21:43 [o] Mt 8:12
21:44 [p] Lk 2:34

a 42 Psalm 118:22,23 *b* 44 Some manuscripts do not have verse 44.

---

externally obedient to the law but did not obey God's message through John.

21:33–46 Clearly alluding to Isa 5:1–7, Jesus intensifies his rebuke of the religious leadership by pronouncing God's judgment: The kingdom will be taken away from Israel and given to another people.

21:38–39 The landowner sending his own son to make a collection is an unmistakable allusion to God the Father's sending of his Son, Jesus. This is further evidence of Jesus' knowledge of his identity as God's unique Son. Through this parable, Jesus is publicly asserting his divine sonship to the religious leadership and the crowds.

The religious leaders have not acknowledged Jesus publicly as God's Son, nor have they publicly condemned Jesus out of fear of the crowds. But Jesus foretells what they will do to him.

21:41 The Jewish leaders cannot get away with their deception. Jesus concludes the parable by predicting their decline. Their privileged role is now being taken away. This also hints that Israel's privileged role will be taken away. The church will include both Jew and Gentile.

21:42–44 The two parts of the stone imagery are somewhat puzzling. The first half speaks of the personal accountability of individuals who stumble or fall into sin by not recognizing Jesus' identity. The second half of v. 44 emphasizes the absolute judgment that will fall on those who stumble over Jesus, probably drawing on the well-known stone imagery in Da 2:34–35, 44–45. At the end Jesus will come as Judge and fall on those who have rejected him.

✣ **21:1–46** The magnitude of the Holy Week events for the future of humanity must be understood correctly. We must understand what Jesus intended in Holy Week so that our own expectations and dreams are kept in line with his. Perhaps to help with this we might begin the practice of "walking" with Jesus through Holy Week. Try to visualize what Jesus was doing every day of that week, starting from the celebration with his disciples on the Saturday evening prior to Palm Sunday, all the way to the resurrection on Easter Sunday. We can be drawn into a more intimate relationship with Jesus after having walked with him through all of the events of this week.

for a way to arrest him, but they were
afraid of the crowd because the people
held that he was a prophet.[q]

The Parable of the Wedding Banquet

22:2–14Ref // Lk 14:16–24

22 Jesus spoke to them again in parables, saying: 2“The kingdom of
heaven is like[r] a king who prepared a
wedding banquet for his son. 3He sent his
servants[s] to those who had been invited
to the banquet to tell them to come, but
they refused to come.
4“Then he sent some more servants[t]
and said, ‘Tell those who have been invited that I have prepared my dinner:
My oxen and fattened cattle have been
butchered, and everything is ready.
Come to the wedding banquet.’
5“But they paid no attention and went
off — one to his field, another to his
business. 6The rest seized his servants,
mistreated them and killed them. 7The
king was enraged. He sent his army and
destroyed those murderers[u] and burned
their city.
8“Then he said to his servants, ‘The
wedding banquet is ready, but those I
invited did not deserve to come. 9So go to
the street corners[v] and invite to the banquet anyone you find.’ 10So the servants
went out into the streets and gathered
all the people they could find, the bad as
well as the good,[w] and the wedding hall
was filled with guests.
11“But when the king came in to see
the guests, he noticed a man there who
was not wearing wedding clothes. 12He
asked, ‘How did you get in here without
wedding clothes, friend[x]?’ The man was
speechless.
13“Then the king told the attendants,
‘Tie him hand and foot, and throw him
outside, into the darkness, where there
will be weeping and gnashing of teeth.’[y]
14“For many are invited, but few are
chosen.”[z]

Paying the Imperial Tax to Caesar

22:15–22pp // Mk 12:13–17; Lk 20:20–26

15Then the Pharisees went out and laid
plans to trap him in his words. 16They
sent their disciples to him along with
the Herodians.[a] “Teacher,” they said, “we
know that you are a man of integrity and
that you teach the way of God in accordance with the truth. You aren’t swayed
by others, because you pay no attention
to who they are. 17Tell us then, what is
your opinion? Is it right to pay the imperial tax[a][b] to Caesar or not?”
18But Jesus, knowing their evil intent, said, “You hypocrites, why are you
trying to trap me? 19Show me the coin
used for paying the tax.” They brought
him a denarius, 20and he asked them,
“Whose image is this? And whose inscription?”

21:46 [q] ver 11,26
22:2 [r] Mt 13:24
22:3 [s] Mt 21:34
22:4 [t] Mt 21:36
22:7 [u] Lk 19:27
22:9 [v] Eze 21:21
22:10 [w] Mt 13:47, 48
22:12 [x] Mt 20:13; 26:50
22:13 [y] Mt 8:12
22:14 [z] Rev 17:14
22:16 [a] Mk 3:6
22:17 [b] Mt 17:25

[a] 17 A special tax levied on subject peoples, not on Roman citizens

---

22:1-7 Some of the invitees still reject the king’s invitation—with trivial excuses. The rest actually abuse and kill the king’s messengers. This is an unbelievable insult to the king, who severely punishes his subjects with death and fire. This kind of punishment was used only in cases of the most serious treason and revolt against a king.

22:8-10 Only those who recognize their personal helplessness cast aside their self-reliance to accept the free gift of God’s grace. The wedding hall is filled with these undeserving guests who respond to the gracious invitation.

22:11-13 One of the guests has gained entrance to the wedding but does not have the appropriate wedding clothing. The implication is that the guest has proper clothing available but has declined to wear it. The man is bound and cast into the outer place of “weeping and gnashing of teeth,” language that commonly refers to eternal judgment (v. 13). Any who presume on God’s grace without honoring the Son will receive due judgment.

22:14 From a human perspective, only those who respond to the call appropriately are part of the banquet, a response which reveals God’s divine election.

22:15-17 Although the Herodians and the Pharisees would typically be at odds on many political and religious issues, here they combine to combat the common threat to their respective power bases. Calling Jesus “teacher” is a hypocritical attempt to disarm Jesus with their flattery.

Their question reveals a volatile issue in Israel. Some estimate that a Jewish family paid approximately 50 percent of its annual income to these various taxes. If Jesus answers that it is indeed right to pay taxes to Caesar, it will put him in league with Roman oppression. If Jesus answers that it is not right to pay taxes to Caesar, they can tell the Romans that Jesus is an insurrectionist. The Pharisees know that either answer will jeopardize Jesus’ mission—which is exactly their intent.

22:18-22 Jesus reverses the confrontation by taking the offensive. He is not merely attempting to wiggle out of one sticky, logical riddle by offering another. Rather, behind his answer is a profound statement of his role and the way those in the kingdom of God will operate in this world. He has not come as a military or political threat to the established rulers of this world. His kingdom is revolutionary, but until he returns in

21"Caesar's," they replied.
Then he said to them, "So give back
to Caesar what is Caesar's,[c] and to God
what is God's."
22When they heard this, they were
amazed. So they left him and went
away.[d]

Marriage at the Resurrection

22:23–33pp // Mk 12:18–27; Lk 20:27–40

23That same day the Sadducees,[e] who
say there is no resurrection,[f] came to him
with a question. 24"Teacher," they said,
"Moses told us that if a man dies without having children, his brother must
marry the widow and raise up offspring
for him.[g] 25Now there were seven brothers among us. The first one married and
died, and since he had no children, he
left his wife to his brother. 26The same
thing happened to the second and third
brother, right on down to the seventh.
27Finally, the woman died. 28Now then,
at the resurrection, whose wife will she
be of the seven, since all of them were
married to her?"
29Jesus replied, "You are in error because you do not know the Scriptures[h] or
the power of God. 30At the resurrection
people will neither marry nor be given in
marriage;[i] they will be like the angels in
heaven. 31But about the resurrection of
the dead — have you not read what God
said to you, 32'I am the God of Abraham,
the God of Isaac, and the God of Jacob'[a]?[j]
He is not the God of the dead but of the
living."
33When the crowds heard this, they
were astonished at his teaching.[k]

The Greatest Commandment

22:34–40pp // Mk 12:28–31

34Hearing that Jesus had silenced the
Sadducees,[l] the Pharisees got together.
35One of them, an expert in the law,[m]
tested him with this question: 36"Teacher, which is the greatest commandment
in the Law?"
37Jesus replied: " 'Love the Lord your
God with all your heart and with all your
soul and with all your mind.'[b][n] 38This is
the first and greatest commandment.
39And the second is like it: 'Love your
neighbor as yourself.'[c][o] 40All the Law and
the Prophets hang on these two commandments."[p]

Whose Son Is the Messiah?

22:41–46pp // Mk 12:35–37; Lk 20:41–44

41While the Pharisees were gathered
together, Jesus asked them, 42"What do
you think about the Messiah? Whose son
is he?"

22:21 [c] Ro 13:7
22:22 [d] Mk 12:12
22:23 [e] Ac 4:1 [f] Ac 23:8; 1Co 15:12
22:24 [g] Dt 25:5,6
22:29 [h] Jn 20:9
22:30 [i] Mt 24:38
22:32 [j] Ex 3:6; Ac 7:32
22:33 [k] Mt 7:28
22:34 [l] Ac 4:1
22:35 [m] Lk 7:30; 10:25; 11:45; 14:3
22:37 [n] Dt 6:5
22:39 [o] Lev 19:18; Mt 5:43; 19:19; Gal 5:14
22:40 [p] Mt 7:12

[a] *32* Exodus 3:6 [b] *37* Deut. 6:5
[c] *39* Lev. 19:18

Mt 22:21 ❖ What does it mean for Christians to "give back to Caesar what is Caesar's"?

---

glory, the kingdom will operate within the existing political order.

22:23–28 Like the Pharisees, the Sadducees try to create a theological trap to demonstrate that Jesus holds to biblically unsubstantiated doctrines. Since this group did not believe in the resurrection, their question reveals a hypocritical attempt to confound Jesus and others who believe in it.

22:29–30 Once again, Jesus turns the logic back on his questioners. He starts with their underlying foundational failure. They should recognize that the rest of the OT is also Scripture, where the doctrine of resurrection is clear.

Jesus does not suggest that humans become angels; rather, in the same way that angelic beings do not marry or procreate, the resurrected state ends the practice of marriage and ushers in entirely new relationships between resurrected humans.

22:31–32 Jesus develops a further clinching argument from the Pentateuch. Drawing on the present tense in Ex 3:6, Jesus states that if the patriarchs are still alive even though physically dead, and if the rest of Scripture points to the reality of resurrection, the Sadducees should believe God's power to raise the patriarchs.

22:33 The crowds express amazement at Jesus' profound responses to the Sadducees, but astonishment is not faith. Faith comes from conviction, not emotion.

22:34–36 A regular debate went on among rabbis to determine the weighty and light commandments. This legal expert is probably aware of this discussion.

22:37–40 Jesus' reply is not unexpected. He quotes Dt 6:5. These are the greatest commandments because they go to the essence of the way God has created humans to live. Jesus' inauguration of the kingdom enables this to be a concrete reality for his disciples.

22:41–42 Jesus goes on the offensive as he poses a question to the Pharisees: "What do you think about the Messiah? Whose son is he?"

This must have seemed like a simple question to the Pharisees, who answer: "The son of David." This is the automatic reply based on common knowledge.

22:43–45 But Jesus presses them further. The point that Jesus is making is taken from Ps 110:1, which he quotes—the most quoted OT passage in the NT. Jesus uses their own Scriptures to point out

"The son of David,"[q] they replied.
43He said to them, "How is it then that
David, speaking by the Spirit, calls him
'Lord'? For he says,

44" 'The Lord said to my Lord:
"Sit at my right hand
until I put your enemies
under your feet." '[a][r]

45If then David calls him 'Lord,' how can
he be his son?" 46No one could say a word
in reply, and from that day on no one
dared to ask him any more questions.[s]

A Warning Against Hypocrisy

23:1–7pp // Mk 12:38,39; Lk 20:45,46
23:37–39pp // Lk 13:34,35

23 Then Jesus said to the crowds and
to his disciples: 2"The teachers of
the law[t] and the Pharisees sit in Moses'
seat. 3So you must be careful to do everything they tell you. But do not do what
they do, for they do not practice what
they preach. 4They tie up heavy, cumber-
some loads and put them on other people's shoulders, but they themselves are
not willing to lift a finger to move them.[u]
5"Everything they do is done for people
to see:[v] They make their phylacteries[b][w]
wide and the tassels on their garments[x]
long; 6they love the place of honor at banquets and the most important seats in
the synagogues;[y] 7they love to be greeted
with respect in the marketplaces and to
be called 'Rabbi' by others.[z]
8"But you are not to be called 'Rabbi,'
for you have one Teacher, and you are all
brothers. 9And do not call anyone on earth
'father,' for you have one Father,[a] and he

22:42 [q] Mt 9:27
22:44 [r] Ps 110:1; Ac 2:34,35; 1Co 15:25; Heb 1:13; 10:13
22:46 [s] Mk 12:34; Lk 20:40
23:2 [t] Ezr 7:6, 25; Ne 8:4
23:4 [u] Lk 11:46; Ac 15:10; Gal 6:13
23:5 [v] Mt 6:1,2, 5,16 [w] Ex 13:9; Dt 6:8 [x] Nu 15:38; Dt 22:12
23:6 [y] Lk 11:43; 14:7; 20:46
23:7 [z] ver 8; Mk 9:5; 10:51; Jn 1:38,49
23:9 [a] Mal 1:6; Mt 7:11

Mt 23:5 ❖ Where do we see people practicing religion just for show and attention today?

[a] 44 Psalm 110:1 [b] 5 That is, boxes containing Scripture verses, worn on forehead and arm

---

the obvious implication of these combined points, which the Pharisees cannot avoid. "If then David calls him 'Lord,' how can he be his son?" (Mt 22:45). David says that the coming Messiah is not just his special human descendant but his "Lord."

22:46 Since the Pharisees do not adequately understand the OT prophecies regarding the Messiah, they do not understand the depth of the personal identity of the Messiah in relationship to Yahweh. Therefore they cannot understand the relationship of Jesus to Yahweh.

22:1–46 If we are to live lives of integrity before God, it is imperative that our beliefs be true and that our questions have intellectually satisfying answers. Jesus provided those for the first century, and he does so for us today. Without him, we are spiritually bankrupt and hopeless. The kind of Messiah envisioned by the Pharisees or by modern reinventions cannot offer eternal salvation or the power to live life as we know we should.

These truths lie at the center of Christian claims. If Jesus is truly the one whom he declares himself to be, we have a unique message to proclaim. Jesus is unlike any figure ever to walk the earth, for he is not simply a messenger but the Son of God. The religious leaders' silence is outspoken testimony that the implication of the text cannot be avoided: The Messiah has a special relationship to Yahweh, which Jesus claims for himself. Their silence is also outspoken testimony of their own avoidance of the implications of this reality for themselves. Jesus demands nothing less from all of us than to be accepted, served, and worshiped as our Lord.

23:1–4 Jesus' statement confirms the use of the seat of Moses as a place from which experts in the law teach. Jesus recognizes all accurate interpretation of Scripture is to be obeyed. Jesus does not condemn the pursuit of righteousness itself; rather, he points to specific issues in which the Pharisees preach one value but do not practice it themselves.

One of Jesus' core criticisms of these religious leaders throughout his ministry has been that they burden the people. "Heavy . . . loads . . . put . . . on . . . people's shoulders" (v. 4) points to the rabbinic oral tradition, a distinctive feature of the Pharisees.

23:5–7 The expression "for people to see" here focuses on two related practices: wearing religious garments and positioning oneself for religious prominence. Phylacteries were worn as an attempt to literally obey the admonition of Dt 11:18. The tassels reminded the people to obey God's commandment and to be holy to God (Nu 15:40). Jesus chides these religious leaders for extending the tassels to be admired by the people.

Sought-after religious positions of honor come in for a second criticism (Mt 23:6). Seating at special dinner occasions was set up according to a guest's rank or status. Jesus points out that positioning oneself for honor from anyone else goes against the command to be humble in service.

23:8–10 A disciple of Jesus will always and forever be only a disciple because Jesus alone is Teacher. Nor are Jesus' disciples to abuse the term "father."

Matthew uses a word found only here in the NT to describe the third title that Jesus' disciples are to avoid—"instructor." The term occurs in Greek literature to designate a private tutor, which may point to an instructor's authority over a student. Jesus' disciples are not to seek out personal authority as instructors over other disciples.

JEWISH SECTS

PHARISEES	
Their roots can be traced to the Hasidim of the second century BC (see note on Mk 2:16).	(1) Along with the Torah, they accepted as equally inspired and authoritative all the commands set forth in the oral traditions preserved by the rabbis.
	(2) On free will and determination, they held to a mediating view that did not allow either human free will or the sovereignty of God to cancel out the other.
	(3) They accepted a rather developed hierarchy of angels and demons.
	(4) They believed in the immortality of the soul and in reward and retribution after death.
	(5) They believed in the resurrection of the dead.
	(6) The main emphasis of their teaching was ethical rather than theological.
	(7) Their attentiveness to purity regulations arose in part from their concern to live as if they, like priests, were involved in temple service. This required a stricter code and attention to avoiding people who were currently in a state of ritual impurity.

SADDUCEES	
They probably had their beginning during the Hasmonean period (166–63 BC). Their demise occurred c. AD 70 with the fall of Jerusalem and the destruction of the temple.	(1) They considered only the books of Moses to be authoritative for proving doctrine, denying that the oral law was authoritative and binding.
	(2) They were very exacting in Levitical purity, given their regular temple involvement.
	(3) They attributed everything to free will.
	(4) They argued that there is neither resurrection of the dead nor a future life.
	(5) They rejected the idea of a spiritual world, including belief in angels and demons.

ESSENES	
They probably originated among the Hasidim, along with the Pharisees, from whom they later separated (1 Maccabees 2:42; 7:13). The Hasidim were a group of zealous Jews who took part with the Maccabeans in a revolt against the Syrians c. 165–155 BC. A group of Essenes probably moved to Qumran c. 150 BC, where they copied scrolls and deposited them in nearby caves.	(1) They strictly observed the purity laws of the Torah because they were performing temple rituals (though apart from the temple itself).
	(2) They practiced communal ownership of property.
	(3) They had a strong sense of mutual responsibility.
	(4) Daily worship was an important feature along with daily study of their sacred scriptures.
	(5) Solemn oaths of piety and obedience had to be taken.
	(6) Sacrifices were offered on holy days and during their sacred seasons, but not at the temple, which they considered to be corrupt.
	(7) Marriage was avoided by some but was not condemned in principle.
	(8) They attributed to predestination or fate everything that happened.

ZEALOTS	
They originated during the reign of Herod the Great c. 6 BC but were not an identifiable group until the AD 60s. A group of Zealots were among the last defenders against the Romans at Masada in AD 73.	(1) They opposed payment of taxes to a pagan emperor because they believed that allegiance was due to God alone.
	(2) They were fiercely loyal to Jewish tradition.
	(3) They endorsed the use of violence as long as it accomplished a good end.
	(4) They were opposed to the influence of Greek pagan culture in the Holy Land, including the Greek language.

is in heaven. 10Nor are you to be called instructors, for you have one Instructor, the Messiah. 11The greatest among you will be your servant.[b] 12For those who exalt themselves will be humbled, and those who humble themselves will be exalted.[c]

Seven Woes on the Teachers of the Law and the Pharisees

13"Woe to you, teachers of the law and Pharisees, you hypocrites![d] You shut the door of the kingdom of heaven in people's faces. You yourselves do not enter, nor will you let those enter who are trying to.[e] [14][a]

15"Woe to you, teachers of the law and Pharisees, you hypocrites! You travel over land and sea to win a single convert,[f] and when you have succeeded, you make them twice as much a child of hell[g] as you are.

16"Woe to you, blind guides![h] You say, 'If anyone swears by the temple, it means nothing; but anyone who swears by the gold of the temple is bound by that oath.'[i] 17You blind fools! Which is greater: the gold, or the temple that makes the gold sacred?[j] 18You also say, 'If anyone swears by the altar, it means nothing; but anyone who swears by the gift on the altar is bound by that oath.' 19You blind men! Which is greater: the gift, or the altar that makes the gift sacred?[k] 20Therefore, anyone who swears by the altar swears by it and by everything on it. 21And anyone who swears by the temple swears by it and by the one who dwells[l] in it. 22And anyone who swears by heaven swears by God's throne and by the one who sits on it.[m]

23"Woe to you, teachers of the law and Pharisees, you hypocrites! You give a tenth[n] of your spices—mint, dill and cumin. But you have neglected the more important matters of the law—justice, mercy and faithfulness.[o] You should have practiced the latter, without neglecting the former. 24You blind guides![p] You strain out a gnat but swallow a camel.

25"Woe to you, teachers of the law and Pharisees, you hypocrites! You clean the outside of the cup and dish,[q] but inside they are full of greed and self-indulgence.[r] 26Blind Pharisee! First clean the inside of the cup and dish, and then the outside also will be clean.

27"Woe to you, teachers of the law and Pharisees, you hypocrites! You are like whitewashed tombs,[s] which look beautiful on the outside but on the inside are full of the bones of the dead and everything unclean. 28In the same way, on the outside you appear to people as righteous but on the inside you are full of hypocrisy and wickedness.

29"Woe to you, teachers of the law and Pharisees, you hypocrites! You build tombs for the prophets[t] and decorate the graves of the righteous. 30And you say, 'If we had lived in the days of our ancestors, we would not have taken part with them in shedding the blood of the prophets.' 31So you testify against yourselves that you are the descendants of those who murdered the prophets.[u] 32Go ahead, then, and complete[v] what your ancestors started!

23:11 [b] Mt 20:26; Mk 9:35
23:12 [c] Lk 14:11
23:13 [d] ver 15, 23, 25, 27, 29 [e] Lk 11:52
23:15 [f] Ac 2:11; 6:5; 13:43 [g] Mt 5:22
23:16 [h] ver 24; Mt 15:14 [i] Mt 5:33-35
23:17 [j] Ex 30:29
23:19 [k] Ex 29:37
23:21 [l] 1Ki 8:13; Ps 26:8
23:22 [m] Ps 11:4; Mt 5:34
23:23 [n] Lev 27:30 [o] Mic 6:8; Lk 11:42
23:24 [p] ver 16
23:25 [q] Mk 7:4 [r] Lk 11:39
23:27 [s] Lk 11:44; Ac 23:3
23:29 [t] Lk 11:47, 48
23:31 [u] Ac 7:51-52
23:32 [v] 1Th 2:16

[a] *14* Some manuscripts include here words similar to Mark 12:40 and Luke 20:47.

23:11–12 Those who live out the humble role of servant will be exalted as true sons and daughters of the kingdom.
23:13–14 Jesus condemns these leaders for the type of hypocrisy in which they deceive the people through their false and deceptive leadership—that is, attempting to bring the people into a righteous relationship with God while at the same time not being in a genuine relationship with God themselves.
23:15 Jesus does not condemn spreading the word per se but criticizes the way that the Pharisees, zealous to win people to their own brand of Judaism, place them under their particularly burdensome code of conduct in the oral law.
23:16–22 Jesus now intentionally addresses the teachers of the law and the Pharisees, who develop ridiculous justifications for their own opinions, leading others astray.
23:23–24 The Pharisees' attention to ceremonial detail consumes so much of their time that they forget the more important matters.
23:25–26 The greed and self-indulgence of the Pharisees are inner motivations that impact external behavior. A root of hypocrisy is pride: the desire to have others see one as better than one actually is. Jesus accuses them of being clean on the outside but dirty on the inside; if the inside is clean, the outside will follow.
23:27–28 These religious leaders give the appearance of being righteous, but inwardly they are unrighteous. They have not opened themselves to the heart transformation that can come by responding to Jesus.
23:29–32 The religious leaders build beautiful monuments to the prophets, but they have the same motives as the people who killed those prophets. As they secretly prepare to have Jesus executed, they demonstrate their wicked, spiritually corrupt connection to the ancient murderers.

33"You snakes! You brood of vipers![w]
How will you escape being condemned
to hell?[x] 34Therefore I am sending you
prophets and sages and teachers. Some
of them you will kill and crucify;[y] others you will flog in your synagogues[z]
and pursue from town to town.[a] 35And
so upon you will come all the righteous
blood that has been shed on earth, from
the blood of righteous Abel[b] to the blood
of Zechariah son of Berekiah,[c] whom you
murdered between the temple and the
altar.[d] 36Truly I tell you, all this will come
on this generation.[e]
37"Jerusalem, Jerusalem, you who kill
the prophets and stone those sent to
you,[f] how often I have longed to gather
your children together, as a hen gathers her chicks under her wings, and you
were not willing. 38Look, your house
is left to you desolate.[g] 39For I tell you,
you will not see me again until you say,
'Blessed is he who comes in the name
of the Lord.'[a]"[h]

23:33 [w] Mt 3:7;
12:34 [x] Mt 5:22
23:34
[y] 2Ch 36:15,
16; Lk 11:49
[z] Mt 10:17
[a] Mt 10:23
23:35 [b] Ge 4:8;
Heb 11:4
[c] Zec 1:1
[d] 2Ch 24:21
23:36
[e] Mt 10:23;
24:34
23:37
[f] 2Ch 24:21;
Mt 5:12
23:38 [g] 1Ki 9:7,
8; Jer 22:5
23:39
[h] Ps 118:26;
Mt 21:9
24:2 [i] Lk 19:44
24:3 [j] Mt 21:1
24:5 [k] ver 11, 23,
24; 1Jn 2:18

The Destruction of the Temple and Signs of the End Times

24:1–51pp // Mk 13:1–37; Lk 21:5–36

24 Jesus left the temple and was
walking away when his disciples
came up to him to call his attention to its
buildings. 2"Do you see all these things?"
he asked. "Truly I tell you, not one stone
here will be left on another;[i] every one
will be thrown down."
3As Jesus was sitting on the Mount of
Olives,[j] the disciples came to him privately. "Tell us," they said, "when will
this happen, and what will be the sign of
your coming and of the end of the age?"
4Jesus answered: "Watch out that no
one deceives you. 5For many will come
in my name, claiming, 'I am the Messiah,' and will deceive many.[k] 6You will
hear of wars and rumors of wars, but
see to it that you are not alarmed. Such
things must happen, but the end is still

[a] 39 Psalm 118:26

23:33–36 "Snakes" and "brood of vipers" are synonyms used to heap up the guilt of these religious leaders. Jesus points ahead to the Christian era, when Israel will still be invited to Jesus through his messengers, but they will continue to reject that message.

The first righteous person in human history to be killed was Abel, slain by Cain in jealousy (Ge 4:1–16). The last murder recorded in the OT in the canonical order of the Hebrew Bible (Law, Prophets, Writings) is Zechariah, a son of the high priest, murdered in the courtyard of the temple (2Ch 24:20–22).

23:37–39 Jesus concludes his address to the people of Israel with a dramatic prophecy. This is the last time that Jesus addresses the crowds, who have had their opportunity to repent.

The implications of Jesus' quoting Ps 118:26 are profound. The same words were cited earlier in Mt 21:9 at Jesus' entrance to Jerusalem, shouted by those identifying him as the messianic son of David. Now as Jesus cites the same passage, he identifies himself with God's Messiah, Israel's Savior, the coming One, who will once again return to his people after a time of great judgment. At that time the people will have no other choice but to acknowledge him as Lord, either in great joy or in great sorrow.

23:1–39 As Christians we must listen to God's message through his other messengers and be careful when we see ourselves stifling every voice with which we disagree. Jesus rebukes the religious leaders because they are muffling God's righteous voice so that their own can be heard. God will avenge those who have lived righteously and have been abused by powerful leaders. There are other people out there who speak for God; we are not the only ones. We must examine those voices, but we will be wiser, more balanced, and better equipped when we learn from other sincere believers and join with them in advancing the kingdom of God.

24:1–3 The road from Jerusalem to Bethany crosses over the Mount of Olives, giving a spectacular view of the temple behind and below. In response to the disciples' statements about the temple, Jesus prophesies its destruction (which did occur in AD 70).

Jesus sits on the Mount of Olives when his disciples approach him to ask for his understanding of the events to which he has just alluded. Jesus' reply initiates an extended discussion. The disciples ask two questions: "When will this happen?" and "What will be the sign of your coming and of the end of the age?" (v. 3).

The way in which the disciples ask both questions may indicate that, to them, the destruction of the temple and the return are one event. In this discourse, Jesus prophesies both events in three parts. (1) Part one describes events, generally chronological, prior to the coming of Jesus (vv. 4–31). (2) Part two gives lessons on watching, waiting, and being prepared for the coming of Jesus (24:36—25:30). (3) Part three concludes the discourse with a warning of judgment and a promise of reward at the time of his coming (25:31–46).

24:4–8 Jesus explicitly outlines a number of conditions that must not be seen as indicators of the end of the age.

24:4–5 Prophetic figures and messianic deliverers had long attempted to provoke revolution. Jesus' disciples must not be deceived.

24:6–7 Wars will be a tragic part of this life until Jesus returns to redeem all creation.

to come. 7Nation will rise against nation,
and kingdom against kingdom.[l] There
will be famines[m] and earthquakes in various places. 8All these are the beginning
of birth pains.

9"Then you will be handed over to be
persecuted[n] and put to death,[o] and you
will be hated by all nations because of
me. 10At that time many will turn away
from the faith and will betray and hate
each other, 11and many false prophets[p]
will appear and deceive many people.
12Because of the increase of wickedness,
the love of most will grow cold, 13but the
one who stands firm to the end will be
saved.[q] 14And this gospel of the kingdom[r]
will be preached in the whole world[s] as
a testimony to all nations, and then the
end will come.

15"So when you see standing in the
holy place[t] 'the abomination that causes desolation,'[a][u] spoken of through the
prophet Daniel — let the reader understand — 16then let those who are
in Judea flee to the mountains. 17Let
no one on the housetop[v] go down to
take anything out of the house. 18Let
no one in the field go back to get their
cloak. 19How dreadful it will be in those
days for pregnant women and nursing
mothers![w] 20Pray that your flight will
not take place in winter or on the Sabbath. 21For then there will be great distress, unequaled from the beginning of
the world until now — and never to be
equaled again.[x]

22"If those days had not been cut
short, no one would survive, but for
the sake of the elect[y] those days will be
shortened. 23At that time if anyone says
to you, 'Look, here is the Messiah!' or,
'There he is!' do not believe it.[z] 24For
false messiahs and false prophets will
appear and perform great signs and
wonders[a] to deceive, if possible, even
the elect. 25See, I have told you ahead
of time.

24:7 [l] Isa 19:2 [m] Ac 11:28
24:9 [n] Mt 10:17 [o] Jn 16:2
24:11 [p] Mt 7:15
24:13 [q] Mt 10:22
24:14 [r] Mt 4:23 [s] Lk 2:1; 4:5; Ac 11:28; 17:6; Ro 10:18; Col 1:6, 23; Rev 3:10; 16:14
24:15 [t] Ac 6:13 [u] Da 9:27; 11:31; 12:11
24:17 [v] 1Sa 9:25; Mt 10:27; Lk 12:3; Ac 10:9
24:19 [w] Lk 23:29
24:21 [x] Da 12:1; Joel 2:2
24:22 [y] ver 24, 31
24:23 [z] Lk 17:23; 21:8
24:24 [a] 2Th 2:9-11; Rev 13:13

[a] *15* Daniel 9:27; 11:31; 12:11

24:8 Although the inauguration of the kingdom of heaven brings redemption to its citizens, the whole world continues to experience birth pains as it awaits final redemption. A baby does not typically come on the first pang, but once the pains begin, the birth process has started. So when we see these signs, we must remain on guard.

24:9–13 Jesus' disciples will have the privilege of carrying his name, but this activity also brings suffering because the antagonism and hatred that is directed toward Jesus will naturally fall on his followers.

24:10 Comfortable Christians will find it easier to turn away from Jesus and avoid suffering. They will not only seek their own escape; they will betray Jesus' followers, and love will be turned to hate as they utterly reject Jesus.

24:11 False prophets will surface and try to deceive Jesus' disciples.

24:12 All of the preceding phenomena are described as the increase of wickedness, which points to the spiritual death of those who fall away and those who have attempted to deceive the community.

24:13 "Saved" does not speak of rescue from physical death, because many true disciples have experienced martyrdom. The one who remains committed will experience the full blessing and peace of salvation with Jesus' arrival.

24:14 The only explicit condition to be met before Jesus returns is the proclamation of the gospel to all the nations. After that proclamation has occurred, the end will come. This future mission will be inaugurated with the risen Jesus' Great Commission (28:19–20), but it is prophesied here.

24:15 With the onset of the "abomination that causes desolation" as spoken of by Daniel, the period of "great distress" begins (v. 21). This event corresponds to Daniel's period of "seven," during which in the middle of the "seven" a ruler will set up "an abomination that causes desolation" (Da 9:27). When we look at Daniel (esp. 9:25–27) and the events of Revelation, this event marks the second half of the seven years of tribulation, the time of "great distress [tribulation]" (Mt 24:21). Apparently the first three and a half years is a time of relative peace and quiet.

Jesus predicts the destruction of Jerusalem and the temple in AD 70, but he also looks beyond to a future time when another "abomination that causes desolation" will arise.

24:16–20 Jesus accentuates the immediacy of danger that will accompany the abomination that causes desolation. First, when the abomination occurs, people are to flee Jerusalem with great haste. Second, the impending destruction means that there will be no time to gather provisions in the home. Third, the danger of travel in this perilous time will be greatest for pregnant mothers and their infants. Finally, flight in winter presents even more difficulty for those fleeing the horrors of approaching ruin.

24:21 While the time of the siege and destruction of Jerusalem were horrible, Matthew's description here indicates a time of tribulation that did not occur during the fall of Jerusalem. The vision Jesus paints points to the future.

24:22 If the wickedness of humanity and the wrath of God were allowed to run unchecked, there would be no end to the terror, and no one would survive. The expression "the elect" includes all who believe on Christ during this period.

24:23–28 The Son of Man will come in a spectacular manner, like lightning that is visible to all. Jesus makes a puzzling statement: "Wherever there is a carcass, there the vultures will gather" (v. 28). This proverb may indicate the visibility of Jesus' return when he comes to bring judgment on the deadness of this corrupt world.

26"So if anyone tells you, 'There he is,
out in the wilderness,' do not go out; or,
'Here he is, in the inner rooms,' do not
believe it. 27For as lightning[b] that comes
from the east is visible even in the west,
so will be the coming of the Son of Man.[c]
28Wherever there is a carcass, there the
vultures will gather.[d]
29"Immediately after the distress of
those days

"'the sun will be darkened,
and the moon will not give its
light;
the stars will fall from the sky,
and the heavenly bodies will be
shaken.'[a][e]

30"Then will appear the sign of the
Son of Man in heaven. And then all
the peoples of the earth[b] will mourn
when they see the Son of Man coming
on the clouds of heaven,[f] with power
and great glory.[c] 31And he will send his
angels[g] with a loud trumpet call,[h] and
they will gather his elect from the four
winds, from one end of the heavens to
the other.

24:27 [b] Lk 17:24 [c] Mt 8:20
24:28 [d] Lk 17:37
24:29 [e] Isa 13:10; 34:4; Eze 32:7; Joel 2:10, 31; Zep 1:15; Rev 6:12,13; 8:12
24:30 [f] Da 7:13; Rev 1:7
24:31 [g] Mt 13:41 [h] Isa 27:13; Zec 9:14; 1Co 15:52; 1Th 4:16; Rev 8:2; 10:7; 11:15
24:33 [i] Jas 5:9
24:34 [j] Mt 16:28; 23:36
24:35 [k] Mt 5:18
24:36 [l] Ac 1:7
24:37 [m] Ge 6:5; 7:6-23

Mt 24:36 ❖ Given Jesus' teaching here, why do so many people nonetheless try to predict the time of Christ's return?

32"Now learn this lesson from the fig
tree: As soon as its twigs get tender and
its leaves come out, you know that summer is near. 33Even so, when you see all
these things, you know that it[d] is near,
right at the door.[i] 34Truly I tell you, this
generation will certainly not pass away
until all these things have happened.[j]
35Heaven and earth will pass away, but
my words will never pass away.[k]

The Day and Hour Unknown

24:37–39pp // Lk 17:26,27
24:45–51pp // Lk 12:42–46

36"But about that day or hour no one
knows, not even the angels in heaven,
nor the Son,[e] but only the Father.[l] 37As it
was in the days of Noah,[m] so it will be at

[a] *29* Isaiah 13:10; 34:4 [b] *30* Or *the tribes of the land* [c] *30* See Daniel 7:13-14. [d] *33* Or *he*
[e] *36* Some manuscripts do not have *nor the Son.*

24:29-31 The celestial signs and the coming of Jesus will occur after the time of "great distress" (v. 21) just described in vv. 15–28. Once again, the mixture of prophecy referring to both the fall of Jerusalem and the end of the age should be acknowledged. Although the judgment that will be brought on Israel in AD 70 with the fall of Jerusalem does seem to be in Jesus' mind, the primary emphasis rests on the end of the age when he will come as the Son of Man in great universal power.
24:29 The darkness at Jesus' crucifixion was an indication that he had conquered the forces of evil on the cross, and the darkness during his second coming will be an indication that he will now exert his rule over all forces.
24:30-31 This language would hold special meaning to a Jewish audience, since the prophecy of Zec 12:10 speaks of the people of Israel mourning when they look on the One whom they have pierced. This kind of mourning produces repentance, or else it stems from recognition of their coming judgment. In the light of the place that Paul gives to Israel's future repentance and conversion (Ro 9–11; cf. Mt 23:39), repentance is more likely in view.
24:32-33 As the end grows closer, subtle increases of difficulty begin to mark the end. The budding tree can be overlooked; it is not spectacular and can even be unnoticed until too late. The point is that people must stay alert and must be forewarned by certain signs at the very end.
24:34-35 The identity of "this generation" (v. 34) has confused interpreters. Perhaps it is best to see a dual reference, as Jesus has done throughout the discourse. The saying is a word of warning that the arrival of the Son of Man will bring judgment. But the saying is also a word of encouragement to his followers that tribulation will not go on forever, as it may appear to those who are suffering in it. Summer is near.

In the final words of this section, Jesus gives a profound word of assurance to all those looking down the corridors of history. Jesus' rock-solid prophecy of his return to establish his kingdom on the earth provides the assurance needed by his disciples to maintain hope and determination.

✣ **24:1-35** The Bible does not record prophecy of end-time activity simply for curiosity's sake. The study of the future should spur us to godly living in the present. Jesus' statement, "See, I have told you ahead of time" (v. 25), stands in the middle of his prophecy of future events. He prophesies future events so that we will discipline ourselves to maintain and expand personal kingdom-righteousness in our daily lives regardless of our circumstances. He tells us these things not so that we will be obsessed with dates, events, and speculation about the insignificant details of his prophecy but rather to encourage us to godly living.

24:36 In Jesus' incarnation, he voluntarily limited the use of his divine attributes so that he could experience the full human life.
24:37-39 The people in the days of Noah did not heed the warnings of judgment that were given to them. Jesus' return will catch unaware all who do not listen to whatever warnings are given and who are spiritually unprepared.

the coming of the Son of Man. 38For in
the days before the flood, people were
eating and drinking, marrying and giving
in marriage,[n] up to the day Noah entered
the ark; 39and they knew nothing about
what would happen until the flood came
and took them all away. That is how it
will be at the coming of the Son of Man.
40Two men will be in the field; one will be
taken and the other left.[o] 41Two women
will be grinding with a hand mill; one
will be taken and the other left.[p]

42"Therefore keep watch, because you
do not know on what day your Lord will
come.[q] 43But understand this: If the owner of the house had known at what time
of night the thief was coming,[r] he would
have kept watch and would not have let his
house be broken into. 44So you also must be
ready,[s] because the Son of Man will come
at an hour when you do not expect him.

45"Who then is the faithful and wise servant,[t] whom the master has put in charge
of the servants in his household to give
them their food at the proper time? 46It
will be good for that servant whose master finds him doing so when he returns.[u]
47Truly I tell you, he will put him in charge
of all his possessions.[v] 48But suppose that
servant is wicked and says to himself, 'My
master is staying away a long time,' 49and
he then begins to beat his fellow servants
and to eat and drink with drunkards.[w]
50The master of that servant will come on
a day when he does not expect him and
at an hour he is not aware of. 51He will
cut him to pieces and assign him a place
with the hypocrites, where there will be
weeping and gnashing of teeth.[x]

24:38 [n] Mt 22:30
24:40 [o] Lk 17:34
24:41 [p] Lk 17:35
24:42 [q] Mt 25:13; Lk 12:40
24:43 [r] Lk 12:39
24:44 [s] 1Th 5:6
24:45 [t] Mt 25:21, 23
24:46 [u] Rev 16:15
24:47 [v] Mt 25:21, 23
24:49 [w] Lk 21:34
24:51 [x] Mt 8:12

25:1 [y] Mt 13:24 [z] Lk 12:35-38; Ac 20:8; Rev 4:5 [a] Rev 19:7; 21:2
25:2 [b] Mt 24:45
25:5 [c] 1Th 5:6
25:8 [d] Lk 12:35
25:10 [e] Rev 19:9
25:13 [f] Mt 24:42, 44; Mk 13:35; Lk 12:40
25:14 [g] Mt 21:33; Lk 19:12

The Parable of the Ten Virgins

25 "At that time the kingdom of heav-
en will be like[y] ten virgins who took
their lamps[z] and went out to meet the
bridegroom.[a] 2Five of them were foolish and five were wise.[b] 3The foolish ones
took their lamps but did not take any oil
with them. 4The wise ones, however,
took oil in jars along with their lamps.
5The bridegroom was a long time in coming, and they all became drowsy and fell
asleep.[c]

6"At midnight the cry rang out: 'Here's
the bridegroom! Come out to meet him!'

7"Then all the virgins woke up and
trimmed their lamps. 8The foolish ones
said to the wise, 'Give us some of your
oil; our lamps are going out.'[d]

9"'No,' they replied, 'there may not be
enough for both us and you. Instead, go
to those who sell oil and buy some for
yourselves.'

10"But while they were on their way
to buy the oil, the bridegroom arrived.
The virgins who were ready went in with
him to the wedding banquet.[e] And the
door was shut.

11"Later the others also came. 'Lord,
Lord,' they said, 'open the door for us!'

12"But he replied, 'Truly I tell you, I
don't know you.'

13"Therefore keep watch, because you
do not know the day or the hour.[f]

The Parable of the Bags of Gold

25:14–30Ref // Lk 19:12–27

14"Again, it will be like a man going
on a journey,[g] who called his servants
and entrusted his wealth to them. 15To

24:40–41 The "taking" and "leaving" are intriguing. These expressions may indicate that one is taken away to judgment and the other is left to enjoy the blessing of salvation. The point is that the Son of Man gathers his people at his return to enjoy the full appearance of the kingdom of God. Those left behind experience his judgment.
24:42–44 Jesus draws a comparison between his coming and the unexpectedness of a thief's activity, calling his disciples to recognize and know the lesson he is teaching. This parable stresses that watchfulness is necessary.
24:45–47 This man is the chief servant, head over the master's household affairs and staff. The test of his responsibility occurs when the master is absent: Will he faithfully carry out his tasks?
24:48–51 The long absence of his master allows the servant to abuse his authority. When the master does return, the slave is caught unaware. His place with hypocrites deserves the eternal condemnation of hell. The wicked servant is a false disciple.

Perhaps the servant thinks that the master will never return. This may be a subtle hint here that Jesus' return will be delayed, which will act as a test to the heart of each person.
25:1–13 After the wedding vows, the wedding party formed a processional to a wedding banquet, normally at the bridegroom's home. The lamp was a larger dome-shaped container with rags soaked in oil that a person carried to light the way while walking outside.

The reason for referring to the virgins as "wise" (v. 4) is because they are "ready" to go with the bridegroom to the wedding banquet (v. 10). The foolish virgins are not, which Jesus accentuates by stating, "And the door was shut" (v. 10).

As in the preceding parable, this is another distinction between two types of people—those who are truly disciples of Jesus and those who are not. Disciples of Jesus will be ready for the arrival of the Son of Man.
25:14–18 In terms of modern monetary value, the

one he gave five bags of gold, to another two bags, and to another one bag,[a]
each according to his ability.[h] Then he
went on his journey. 16 The man who had
received five bags of gold went at once
and put his money to work and gained
five bags more. 17 So also, the one with
two bags of gold gained two more. 18 But
the man who had received one bag went
off, dug a hole in the ground and hid his
master's money.

19 "After a long time the master of those
servants returned and settled accounts with
them.[i] 20 The man who had received five
bags of gold brought the other five. 'Master,' he said, 'you entrusted me with five
bags of gold. See, I have gained five more.'

21 "His master replied, 'Well done, good
and faithful servant! You have been
faithful with a few things; I will put you
in charge of many things.[j] Come and
share your master's happiness!'

22 "The man with two bags of gold also
came. 'Master,' he said, 'you entrusted
me with two bags of gold; see, I have
gained two more.'

23 "His master replied, 'Well done, good
and faithful servant! You have been
faithful with a few things; I will put you
in charge of many things.[k] Come and
share your master's happiness!'

24 "Then the man who had received
one bag of gold came. 'Master,' he said,
'I knew that you are a hard man, harvesting where you have not sown and
gathering where you have not scattered
seed. 25 So I was afraid and went out and
hid your gold in the ground. See, here is
what belongs to you.'

26 "His master replied, 'You wicked, lazy
servant! So you knew that I harvest where
I have not sown and gather where I have
not scattered seed? 27 Well then, you should
have put my money on deposit with the
bankers, so that when I returned I would
have received it back with interest.

28 " 'So take the bag of gold from him
and give it to the one who has ten bags.
29 For whoever has will be given more,
and they will have an abundance. Whoever does not have, even what they have
will be taken from them.[l] 30 And throw
that worthless servant outside, into the
darkness, where there will be weeping
and gnashing of teeth.'[m]

The Sheep and the Goats

31 "When the Son of Man comes[n] in his
glory, and all the angels with him, he
will sit on his glorious throne.[o] 32 All the
nations will be gathered before him, and
he will separate[p] the people one from another as a shepherd separates the sheep
from the goats.[q] 33 He will put the sheep
on his right and the goats on his left.

34 "Then the King will say to those on
his right, 'Come, you who are blessed by
my Father; take your inheritance, the
kingdom[r] prepared for you since the creation of the world.[s] 35 For I was hungry
and you gave me something to eat, I was
thirsty and you gave me something to
drink, I was a stranger and you invited me in,[t] 36 I needed clothes and you
clothed me,[u] I was sick and you looked
after me,[v] I was in prison and you came
to visit me.'[w]

37 "Then the righteous will answer him,
'Lord, when did we see you hungry and

25:15 [h] Mt 18:24, 25
25:19 [i] Mt 18:23
25:21 [j] ver 23; Mt 24:45, 47; Lk 16:10
25:23 [k] ver 21
25:29 [l] Mt 13:12; Mk 4:25; Lk 8:18; 19:26
25:30 [m] Mt 8:12
25:31 [n] Mt 16:27; Lk 17:30 [o] Mt 19:28
25:32 [p] Mal 3:18 [q] Eze 34:17, 20
25:34 [r] Mt 3:2; 5:3, 10, 19; 19:14; Ac 20:32; 1Co 15:50; Gal 5:21; Jas 2:5 [s] Heb 4:3; 9:26; Rev 13:8; 17:8
25:35 [t] Job 31:32; Isa 58:7; Eze 18:7; Heb 13:2
25:36 [u] Isa 58:7; Eze 18:7; Jas 2:15, 16 [v] Jas 1:27 [w] 2Ti 1:16

[a] 15 Greek *five talents . . . two talents . . . one talent*; also throughout this parable; a talent was worth about 20 years of a day laborer's wage.

---

landowner disperses perhaps approximately two million dollars to the three servants.

25:19–23 The sums dispersed by the homeowner apparently symbolize personal giftedness or abilities, but only generally: "each according to his ability" (v. 15). The identical statement of praise to both servants indicates that the point of the parable is not on the total amount earned but on faithful responsibility in living up to one's potential and giftedness. The reward of earnings bestowed may differ, but both servants received the identical joy in the presence of their master.

25:24–27 The wickedness of the third slave primarily stems from his attitude toward his master, which in turn has led to laziness and bad stewardship. Had he truly loved his master, he would not have attempted to place the blame on him but would have operated out of love.

25:28–30 The punishment is not simply taking away the talent. The master instructs that he should be thrown "outside, into the darkness, where there will be weeping and gnashing of teeth." As in the other parables, the contrast is between those whose eternal destiny is either salvation or eternal damnation.

25:31–33 The scene switches now to the glorious coming of the Son of Man. The nations as entities are not judged but rather the people within them are: "He will separate the people one from another as a shepherd separates the sheep from the goats" (v. 32).

25:34–40 The King represents the Son of Man sitting on the throne, bringing to mind Da 7:13–14. The King addresses the sheep on his right as "blessed by my Father" (Mt 25:34). The blessing consists of their inheritance, which is the kingdom they now receive. The sheep cared for Jesus when he was

Mt 25:40 ❖ Who are the "least of these" in our lives, and how can we extend love to them that displays our love for Christ?

feed you, or thirsty and give you something to drink? 38When did we see you
a stranger and invite you in, or needing
clothes and clothe you? 39When did we
see you sick or in prison and go to visit
you?'
40"The King will reply, 'Truly I tell you,
whatever you did for one of the least of
these brothers and sisters of mine, you
did for me.'[x]
41"Then he will say to those on his left,
'Depart from me,[y] you who are cursed,
into the eternal fire[z] prepared for the
devil and his angels.[a] 42For I was hungry and you gave me nothing to eat, I
was thirsty and you gave me nothing
to drink, 43I was a stranger and you did
not invite me in, I needed clothes and
you did not clothe me, I was sick and in
prison and you did not look after me.'
44"They also will answer, 'Lord, when
did we see you hungry or thirsty or a
stranger or needing clothes or sick or in
prison, and did not help you?'
45"He will reply, 'Truly I tell you, whatever you did not do for one of the least
of these, you did not do for me.'[b]
46"Then they will go away to eternal punishment, but the righteous to eternal life."[c][d]

The Plot Against Jesus

26:2–5pp // Mk 14:1,2; Lk 22:1,2

26 When Jesus had finished saying all
these things,[e] he said to his disciples, 2"As you know, the Passover[f] is two
days away—and the Son of Man will be
handed over to be crucified."
3Then the chief priests and the elders
of the people assembled[g] in the palace
of the high priest, whose name was Caiaphas,[h] 4and they schemed to arrest Jesus
secretly and kill him.[i] 5"But not during
the festival," they said, "or there may be
a riot[j] among the people."

Jesus Anointed at Bethany

26:6–13pp // Mk 14:3–9

26:6–13Ref // Lk 7:37,38; Jn 12:1–8

6While Jesus was in Bethany[k] in the
home of Simon the Leper, 7a woman came

25:40 [x] Pr 19:17; Mt 10:40,42; Heb 6:10; 13:2
25:41 [y] Mt 7:23 [z] Isa 66:24; Mt 3:12; 5:22; Mk 9:43,48; Lk 3:17; Jude 7 [a] 2Pe 2:4
25:45 [b] Pr 14:31; 17:5
25:46 [c] Mt 19:29; Jn 3:15,16,36; 17:2,3; Ro 2:7; Gal 6:8; 5:11, 13,20 [d] Da 12:2; Jn 5:29; Ac 24:15; Ro 2:7, 8; Gal 6:8
26:1 [e] Mt 7:28
26:2 [f] Jn 11:55; 13:1
26:3 [g] Ps 2:2 [h] ver 57; Jn 11:47-53; 18:13,14,24,28
26:4 [i] Mt 12:14
26:5 [j] Mt 27:24
26:6 [k] Mt 21:17

---

in need. These acts function as evidence that the sheep belong to the kingdom.

25:41–45 The goats are just as surprised as the sheep. Here, sins of omission are also worthy of eternal damnation because they are evidence that a person has not been made righteous by association with Jesus and the kingdom of God. Righteous acts spring from a heart sanctified by the Spirit of God. Persistently unrighteous acts, even of omission, indicate a heart lacking in the Spirit's work of transformation.

25:46 The important point throughout this scene is clear: judgment will come. Ultimately there are only two types of people: Those who have not followed Jesus are against him and will endure eternal punishment; Jesus' disciples are with him and will enjoy eternal life. This should produce the greatest joy in Jesus' disciples. But the fate of the wicked should also weigh heavily upon them, provoking the same kind of anguish that the apostle Paul experienced as he considered the eternal fate of his fellow Jews who had rejected Jesus (Ro 9:1-5).

✣ **24:36—25:46** The parable of the talents also demonstrates that disciples are prepared for the Lord's coming by their intentional *productivity*. It is vitally important to have a correct biblical perception of God's character, his activities, and his goals for us. This is the important role of solid Bible teaching and preaching, for our view of God determines our behavior. The parable reveals that the wicked servant distorted the image of his master, which then provided him with an excuse for his personal irresponsibility. The parable teaches us that a truthful understanding of God will bring about the productive investment of our lives.

26:1-2 This is the fourth and last time Jesus predicts his arrest and crucifixion. Jesus connects his death with the celebration of Passover.

26:3-4 As the conspiracy against Jesus proceeds in Matthew's narrative, the close cooperation between Caiaphas and the Roman government will be important in accounting for the way in which Jesus is so readily condemned and crucified.

For the first time in Matthew, the high priest is identified as "Caiaphas." Because the Roman governor appointed and deposed the high priest, the office was essentially political, and apparently, Caiaphas knew how to manipulate it well.

26:5 At this time of Passover, with thousands of pilgrims jamming Jerusalem and with nationalistic fervor running high, the people have been stirred by the rumors that Jesus is their expected Messiah. The religious leaders will bide their time until the best moment to arrest Jesus.

26:6-13 Matthew places Jesus' anointing in the context of the conspiracy to arrest Jesus. Placed in this context, the woman's act of honor stands out against the betrayal of Judas and the plotting of the high priest, Caiaphas.

26:6-7 Since Simon is hosting a meal in his own home, he has probably been healed of leprosy by Jesus, for lepers were required to live away from the common population. During the dinner,

to him with an alabaster jar of very expensive perfume, which she poured on
his head as he was reclining at the table.
8When the disciples saw this, they
were indignant. "Why this waste?" they
asked. 9"This perfume could have been
sold at a high price and the money given
to the poor."
10Aware of this, Jesus said to them,
"Why are you bothering this woman?
She has done a beautiful thing to me.
11The poor you will always have with
you,[a][l] but you will not always have me.
12When she poured this perfume on my
body, she did it to prepare me for burial.[m] 13Truly I tell you, wherever this gospel is preached throughout the world,
what she has done will also be told, in
memory of her."

Judas Agrees to Betray Jesus

26:14–16pp // Mk 14:10,11; Lk 22:3–6

14Then one of the Twelve — the one
called Judas Iscariot[n] — went to the chief
priests 15and asked, "What are you willing to give me if I deliver him over to
you?" So they counted out for him thirty
pieces of silver.[o] 16From then on Judas
watched for an opportunity to hand
him over.

26:11 [l] Dt 15:11
26:12 [m] Jn 19:40
26:14 [n] ver 25, 47; Mt 10:4
26:15 [o] Ex 21:32; Zec 11:12
26:17 [p] Ex 12:18-20
26:18 [q] Jn 7:6, 8, 30; 12:23; 13:1; 17:1
26:21 [r] Lk 22:21-23; Jn 13:21
26:23 [s] Ps 41:9; Jn 13:18

The Last Supper

26:17–19pp // Mk 14:12–16; Lk 22:7–13
26:20–24pp // Mk 14:17–21
26:26–29pp // Mk 14:22–25; Lk 22:17–20; 1Co 11:23–25

17On the first day of the Festival of Unleavened Bread,[p] the disciples came to
Jesus and asked, "Where do you want
us to make preparations for you to eat
the Passover?"
18He replied, "Go into the city to a certain man and tell him, 'The Teacher says:
My appointed time[q] is near. I am going to
celebrate the Passover with my disciples
at your house.'" 19So the disciples did as
Jesus had directed them and prepared
the Passover.
20When evening came, Jesus was reclining at the table with the Twelve.
21And while they were eating, he said,
"Truly I tell you, one of you will betray me."[r]
22They were very sad and began to say
to him one after the other, "Surely you
don't mean me, Lord?"
23Jesus replied, "The one who has
dipped his hand into the bowl with me
will betray me.[s] 24The Son of Man will

[a] *11* See Deut. 15:11.

---

a woman (identified in Jn 12:3 as Lazarus's sister Mary) approaches Jesus. The perfume is pure nard, an oil extracted from the root of a plant grown in India. By breaking the flask, Mary shows that she is not just pouring out a few drops to enhance the aroma of the feast but is performing the highest act of dedication to Jesus, even anointing his feet with the expensive oil.

26:8–9 The perfume costs at least three hundred denarii, equivalent to about a year's wages for the average worker in the time of Jesus. The other disciples do not know of Judas's thievery, but they also think this wastes precious funding. Poverty was a pervasive problem in Jerusalem and throughout Israel at this time in history.

26:10–13 Here Jesus is not relieving the disciples of caring for the poor. Jesus emphasizes that the woman is performing an act of tribute to him that can only be done at this time while he is with them. There are special circumstances that affect the disciples' practices while Jesus is still with them.

Jesus goes on to show the even more profound significance of Mary's deed. Whatever her actual motivation, Jesus tells his disciples she unknowingly has begun the preparations for his burial. She is memorializing his death for all generations to come.

26:14–16 Matthew's is the only Gospel that specifies the agreed-upon amount of 30 pieces of silver, a paltry amount.

26:17–30 There have been several attempted explanations of the differences between the Synoptics and the Gospel of John. Perhaps the passages in John use the expression "Passover" for the weeklong series of events, not just the Passover meal itself.

26:17–19 Either Jesus has made prearrangements for the room with friends in Jerusalem to avoid the Jewish authorities, or else these were divine arrangements.

26:20–22 During the Passover, Jesus' prediction of betrayal apparently comes as a surprise to all. Hence, they are "very sad" (v. 22) or distressed.

26:23 Jesus prolongs their dismay as he states, "The one who has dipped his hand into the bowl with me will betray me." Each of those around the room has dipped their bread into bowls that served the group, so this implies no more than one of those at the meal at that time will betray him, but no one knows who.

26:24–25 The betrayal points again to the profound interaction of God's sovereign control with each person's responsibility for their own decisions. Judas has sealed his own destiny by his personal choice, and he is now personally accountable.

Judas is never recorded to have addressed Jesus as "Lord." This is perhaps a clue to the fact that Jesus knew all along those who did not truly believe in him as their Lord and who would betray him.

THE LIFE OF CHRIST

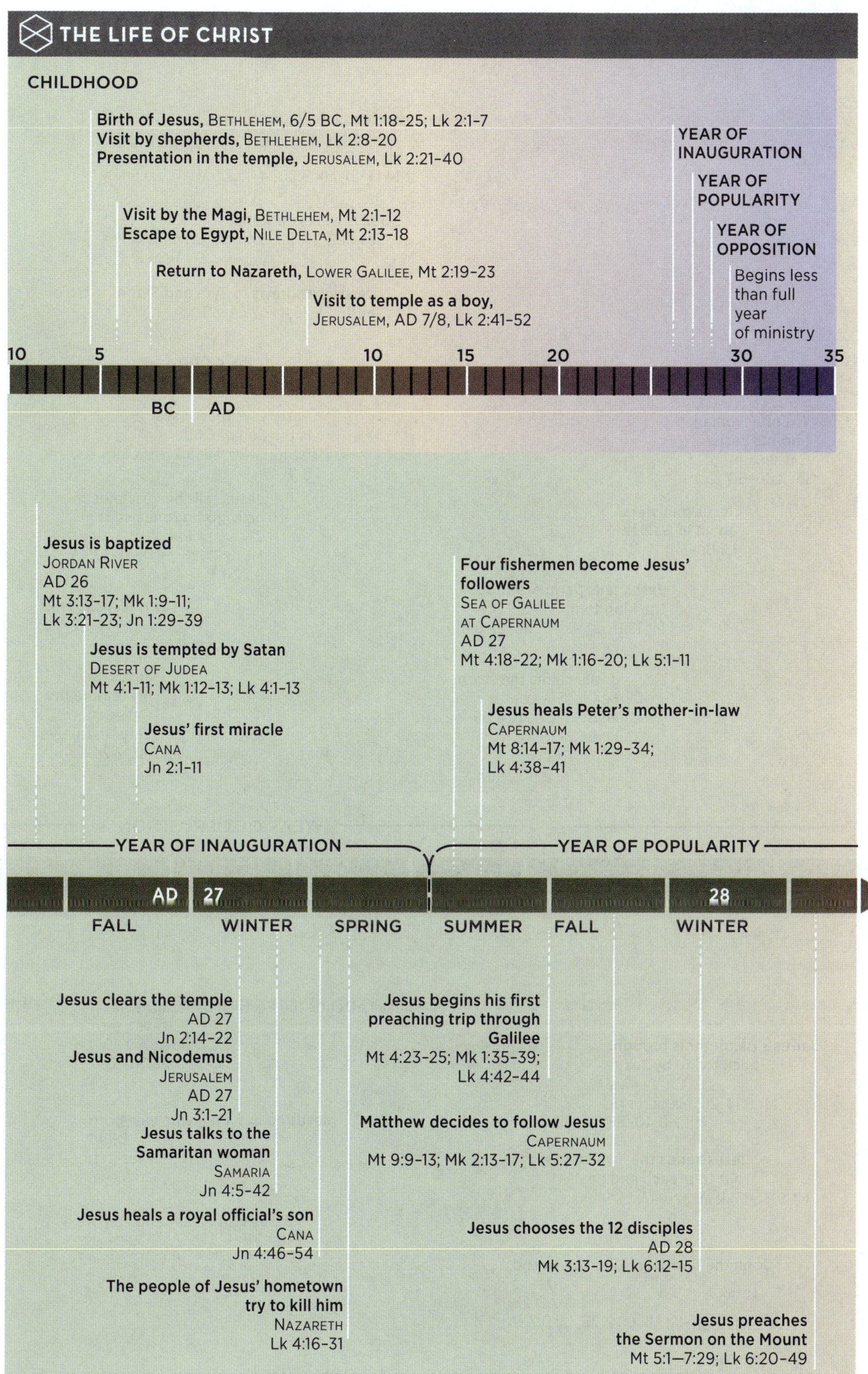

Dotted lines leading to the timeline are meant to define sequence of events only. All dates are approximate.

THE LIFE OF CHRIST *(continued)*

Jesus feeds the 5,000
NEAR BETHSAIDA
Spring, AD 29
Mt 14:13-21; Mk 6:30-44; Lk 9:10-17; Jn 6:1-14

Jesus walks on water
Mt 14:22-33; Mk 6:45-52; Jn 6:16-21

Jesus withdraws to Tyre and Sidon
Mt 15:21-28; Mk 7:24-30

Jesus feeds the 4,000
Mt 15:32-39; Mk 8:1-9

A sinful woman anoints Jesus
CAPERNAUM
Lk 7:36-50

Peter says that Jesus is the Son of God
Mt 16:13-20; Mk 8:27-30; Lk 9:18-21

Jesus ministers again in Galilee
Lk 8:1-3

Jesus tells his disciples he is going to die soon
CAESAREA PHILIPPI
Mt 16:21-26; Mk 8:31-37; Lk 9:22-25

Jesus tells parables about the kingdom
Mt 13:1-52; Mk 4:1-34; Lk 8:4-18

Jesus is transfigured
Mt 17:1-13; Mk 9:2-13; Lk 9:28-36

Jesus calms the storm
SEA OF GALILEE
Mt 8:23-27; Mk 4:35-41; Lk 8:22-25

Jesus pays his temple tax
CAPERNAUM
Later in that year
Mt 17:24-27

YEAR OF OPPOSITION

SPRING | SUMMER | FALL | 29 WINTER | SPRING | SUMMER | FALL

Jesus attends the Festival of Tabernacles
JERUSALEM
October, AD 29
Jn 7:11-52

Jairus's daughter is brought back to life by Jesus
CAPERNAUM
Mt 9:18-26; Mk 5:21-43; Lk 8:40-56

Jesus heals a man who was born blind
JERUSALEM
Jn 9:1-41

Jesus sends the Twelve out to preach and heal
Mt 9:35—11:1; Mk 6:6-13; Lk 9:1-6

Jesus visits Mary and Martha
BETHANY
Lk 10:38-42

John the Baptist is killed by Herod
MACHAERUS
AD 28
Mt 14:1-12; Mk 6:14-29; Lk 9:7-9

The most likely dates for Jesus' public ministry are AD 27-30; the next most likely option, however, is 30-33.

THE LIFE OF CHRIST *(continued)*

Jesus begins his last trip to Jerusalem
AD 30
Lk 17:11

Jesus blesses the little children
ACROSS THE JORDAN
Mt 19:13-15; Mk 10:13-16; Lk 18:15-17

Jesus talks to the rich young man
ACROSS THE JORDAN
Mt 19:16-30; Mk 10:17-31; Lk 18:18-30

Jesus again predicts his death and resurrection
NEAR THE JORDAN
Mt 20:17-19; Mk 10:32-34; Lk 18:31-34

Jesus heals blind Bartimaeus
JERICHO
Mt 20:29-34; Mk 10:46-52; Lk 18:35-43

Jesus talks to Zacchaeus
JERICHO
Lk 19:1-10

Jesus returns to Bethany to visit Mary and Martha
BETHANY
Jn 11:55—12:1

THE LAST WEEK
The "Triumphal" Entry, JERUSALEM, Sunday
Mt 21:1-11; Mk 11:1-10; Lk 19:29-44; Jn 12:12-19
Jesus curses the fig tree, Monday
Mt 21:18-19; Mk 11:12-14
Jesus clears the temple, Monday
Mt 21:12-13; Mk 11:15-18
The authority of Jesus questioned, Tuesday
Mt 21:23-27; Mk 11:27-33; Lk 20:1-8
Jesus teaches in the temple, Tuesday
Mt 21:28—23:39; Mk 12:1-44; Lk 20:9—21:4
Jesus anointed, BETHANY, Tuesday
Mt 26:6-13; Mk 14:3-9; Jn 12:2-11
The plot against Jesus, Wednesday
Mt 26:14-16; Mk 14:10-11; Lk 22:3-6
The Last Supper, Thursday
Mt 26:17-29; Mk 14:12-25; Lk 22:7-20; Jn 13:1-38
Jesus comforts the disciples, Thursday
Jn 14:1—16:33
Gethsemane, Thursday
Mt 26:36-46; Mk 14:32-42; Lk 22:40-46
Jesus' arrest and trial, Thursday night and Friday
Mt 26:47—27:26; Mk 14:43—15:15; Lk 22:47—23:25; Jn 18:2—19:16
Jesus' crucifixion and death, GOLGOTHA, Friday
Mt 27:27-56; Mk 15:16-41; Lk 23:26-49; Jn 19:17-30
The burial of Jesus, Joseph's Tomb, Friday
Mt 27:57-66; Mk 15:42-47; Lk 23:50-56; Jn 19:31-42

30 WINTER | SPRING | SUMMER | FALL | 31 WINTER | SPRING | SUMMER

AFTER THE RESURRECTION
The empty tomb
JERUSALEM, Sunday
Mt 28:1-10; Mk 16:1-8; Lk 24:1-12; Jn 20:1-10
Mary Magdalene sees Jesus in the garden
JERUSALEM, Sunday
Mt 16:9-11; Jn 20:11-18
Jesus appears to the two going to Emmaus
Sunday
Mk 16:12-13; Lk 24:13-35
Jesus appears to 10 disciples
JERUSALEM, Sunday
Mk 16:14; Lk 24:36-43; Jn 20:19-25
Jesus appears to the 11 disciples
JERUSALEM, One week later
Jn 20:26-31
Jesus talks with some of his disciples
SEA OF GALILEE, One week later
Jn 21:1-25
Jesus ascends to his Father in heaven
MOUNT OF OLIVES, 40 days later
Mt 28:16-20; Mk 16:19-20; Lk 24:44-53

Jesus raises Lazarus from the dead
BETHANY
Winter, AD 30
Jn 11:1-44

go just as it is written about him.[t] But
woe to that man who betrays the Son of
Man! It would be better for him if he had
not been born."
25 Then Judas, the one who would betray him, said, "Surely you don't mean
me, Rabbi?"[u]
Jesus answered, "You have said so."
26 While they were eating, Jesus took
bread, and when he had given thanks,
he broke it[v] and gave it to his disciples,
saying, "Take and eat; this is my body."
27 Then he took a cup, and when he
had given thanks, he gave it to them,
saying, "Drink from it, all of you. 28 This
is my blood of the[a] covenant,[w] which is
poured out for many for the forgiveness
of sins.[x] 29 I tell you, I will not drink from
this fruit of the vine from now on until
that day when I drink it new with you[y]
in my Father's kingdom."
30 When they had sung a hymn, they
went out to the Mount of Olives.[z]

Jesus Predicts Peter's Denial

26:31–35pp // Mk 14:27–31; Lk 22:31–34

31 Then Jesus told them, "This very
night you will all fall away on account
of me,[a] for it is written:

"'I will strike the shepherd,
and the sheep of the flock will be
scattered.'[bb]

32 But after I have risen, I will go ahead
of you into Galilee."[c]
33 Peter replied, "Even if all fall away
on account of you, I never will."
34 "Truly I tell you," Jesus answered,
"this very night, before the rooster crows,
you will disown me three times."[d]
35 But Peter declared, "Even if I have to
die with you,[e] I will never disown you."
And all the other disciples said the same.

Gethsemane

26:36–46pp // Mk 14:32–42; Lk 22:40–46

36 Then Jesus went with his disciples to
a place called Gethsemane, and he said to
them, "Sit here while I go over there and
pray." 37 He took Peter and the two sons of
Zebedee[f] along with him, and he began
to be sorrowful and troubled. 38 Then he
said to them, "My soul is overwhelmed
with sorrow[g] to the point of death. Stay
here and keep watch with me."[h]
39 Going a little farther, he fell with his
face to the ground and prayed, "My Father,

26:24 [t] Isa 53; Da 9:26; Mk 9:12; Lk 24:25-27, 46; Ac 17:2, 3; 26:22, 23
26:25 [u] Mt 23:7
26:26 [v] Mt 14:19; 1Co 10:16
26:28 [w] Ex 24:6-8; Heb 9:20 [x] Mt 20:28; Mk 1:4
26:29 [y] Ac 10:41
26:30 [z] Mt 21:1; Mk 14:26
26:31 [a] Mt 11:6 [b] Zec 13:7; Jn 16:32
26:32 [c] Mt 28:7, 10, 16
26:34 [d] ver 75; Jn 13:38
26:35 [e] Jn 13:37
26:37 [f] Mt 4:21
26:38 [g] Jn 12:27 [h] ver 40, 41

[a] 28 Some manuscripts *the new* [b] 31 Zech. 13:7

26:25 Judas has been carrying out his arrangements for the betrayal in secret. But Jesus' knowledge is divinely revealed: "You have said so." The NIV rendering of this phrase accurately reflects the literal Greek expression: "You yourself have said." Judas's own question has indicted him.

26:26–30 With the traitor gone, Jesus brings the symbolic significance of this meal to its intended fulfillment as he institutes what becomes known as the Lord's Supper.

26:26 Jesus becomes the sacrificial atonement for the "passing over" of the sins of the people. It is significant that Jesus uses bread, not the Passover lamb, to initiate the commemoration. Because of his death, the killing of a lamb will no longer be necessary. Later theological debates about the meaning of "body" and its relation to the presence of Jesus in the bread would not have even entered the minds of those hearing Jesus' words. They are having difficulty understanding the symbolism. But once the events of the cross transpire, they will recognize that the bread and the cup are profound memorials of the single most important event in history.

26:27–28 Continuing the symbolism, Jesus takes a cup, gives thanks, and asks all of them to join in drinking from it. Of the four cups of wine consumed at a Passover celebration, this is most likely the third cup. This third cup was often called the cup of redemption, corresponding to God's third promise in Ex 6:6. The shedding of Jesus' blood, which this cup foreshadows, opens the way for the redemption of all humanity.

26:29 Jesus gives a surprising twist to the occasion. Jesus' words hold out a poignant promise that his sacrificial death will bring forgiveness of sins and a sad indication that he will have to go away, but also an assurance that he will return to finally establish his kingdom of peace and redemption on earth.

26:31–35 After they sing together, Jesus goes with the Twelve to the Mount of Olives. Earlier, Jesus predicted that one of the Twelve would betray him. Now, he implies that all of them will lack courage. They will not stop being his disciples, but they will fail the test of courage to stand up for him. Their failure was also prophesied by Zechariah (Zec 13:7). This quotation demonstrates that even when God's actions are carried out by others, they are a result of his sovereign activity.

The difference between Judas and Peter is demonstrated by their behavior *after* their failures. Judas is satanically driven to accomplish his treachery because he never was a true believer (see Jn 17:12). Peter and the other disciples falter, but their repentance later brings them back to Jesus for restoration.

26:36–38 On their way out of Jerusalem, Jesus and his disciples stop at a place called Gethsemane. Once at Gethsemane, Jesus asks the inner group of three disciples (Peter, James, and John) to stay awake with him while he prays. Jesus asks them not to pray but to watch. This reveals the depth of Jesus' need for human relationship, which he feels is necessary to sustain him in his time of greatest need.

if it is possible, may this cup[i] be taken
from me. Yet not as I will, but as you will."[j]
40Then he returned to his disciples and
found them sleeping. "Couldn't you men
keep watch with me[k] for one hour?" he
asked Peter. 41"Watch and pray so that
you will not fall into temptation.[l] The
spirit is willing, but the flesh is weak."
42He went away a second time and
prayed, "My Father, if it is not possible
for this cup to be taken away unless I
drink it, may your will be done."
43When he came back, he again found
them sleeping, because their eyes were
heavy. 44So he left them and went away
once more and prayed the third time,
saying the same thing.
45Then he returned to the disciples
and said to them, "Are you still sleeping
and resting? Look, the hour[m] has come,
and the Son of Man is delivered into the
hands of sinners. 46Rise! Let us go! Here
comes my betrayer!"

Jesus Arrested

26:47–56pp // Mk 14:43–50; Lk 22:47–53

47While he was still speaking, Judas,
one of the Twelve, arrived. With him was
a large crowd armed with swords and
clubs, sent from the chief priests and the
elders of the people. 48Now the betrayer
had arranged a signal with them: "The
one I kiss is the man; arrest him." 49Go-
ing at once to Jesus, Judas said, "Greetings, Rabbi!"[n] and kissed him.
50Jesus replied, "Do what you came
for, friend."[a][o]
Then the men stepped forward, seized
Jesus and arrested him. 51With that,
one of Jesus' companions reached for
his sword,[p] drew it out and struck the
servant of the high priest, cutting off
his ear.[q]
52"Put your sword back in its place,"
Jesus said to him, "for all who draw the
sword will die by the sword.[r] 53Do you
think I cannot call on my Father, and he
will at once put at my disposal more than
twelve legions of angels?[s] 54But how then
would the Scriptures be fulfilled[t] that say
it must happen in this way?"

26:39 [i] Mt 20:22 [j] ver 42; Ps 40:6-8; Isa 50:5; Jn 5:30; 6:38
26:40 [k] ver 38
26:41 [l] Mt 6:13
26:45 [m] ver 18
26:49 [n] ver 25
26:50 [o] Mt 20:13; 22:12
26:51 [p] Lk 22:36, 38 [q] Jn 18:10
26:52 [r] Ge 9:6; Rev 13:10
26:53 [s] 2Ki 6:17; Da 7:10; Mt 4:11
26:54 [t] ver 24

Mt 26:39 ❖ How does this prayer show the fullness of Christ's humanity? How does the reality of Christ's humanity bring us comfort?

[a] 50 Or *"Why have you come, friend?"*

26:39 Matthew reveals one of the most profound insights into the intimacy between Father and Son. With harmless urgency and trustfulness, Jesus lays his life into his Father's hands. He started his ministry by being tempted in the desert; now, the temptation is intensified to its maximum. This is the devil's last-ditch effort to attempt to convince Jesus that the cross is unnecessary.

Although dreading the prospect of pain and death on the cross, the prospect of separation from the Father is a greater horror and a greater sorrow. But doing the will of the Father is Jesus' only motivation because he knows that hundreds of millions of people will be reconciled to the Father through his death.

26:40–41 After intensely wrestling in prayer, Jesus returns to find the trio of disciples sleeping. Jesus calls them to continue watching, yet now they must also pray about their own temptation. Jesus is not creating a proverbial expression to excuse human weakness but rather gives an example of how obedience to God's will is accomplished. The spiritual disciplines of watching and praying enable the heart to direct all aspects of a person's human nature so that the entire person is obedient to God.

26:42–44 Now there is the conscious recognition that it is not possible for the cup to be taken away and that Jesus must experience the depth of its wrath. He consciously submits to that destiny (see Heb 5:8). But the disciples have not yet learned this obedience. Again, Jesus goes back to find the trio sleeping. They have not learned the discipline of spirit over body.

26:45–46 The time for Jesus to accomplish his mission of salvation through the cross has arrived. Jesus has perhaps watched the troop of temple police being led by Judas cross the Kidron Valley and come to the garden with torches. Instead of fleeing, he calls his disciples to meet this challenge head-on.

✜ **26:1–46** Perhaps the most important lesson that we can learn from this section of Matthew's passion narrative is that God is in control. When we rest in God's will, we will find our peace. God is ultimately in control of all events around us. Human power structures, no matter how powerful they look, are not powerful enough to hinder God's intention to fulfill his ultimate desires and ends.

26:47 The most heavily armed of those coming with Judas would be a contingent of Roman soldiers. Levitical temple police and personal security guards of the chief priests and Sanhedrin probably make up another large detachment. They represent the highest authority of the Jewish people and are endorsed by the Roman governor's own forces.

26:48–49 Judas is forever known in biblical and historical infamy for his betrayal of Jesus.

26:50–51 Simon Peter tries to defend Jesus. Peter's use of force is not guided by kingdom priorities but by the human desire to retaliate.

26:52–54 Jesus points not to a particular prophetic passage here but to the Scriptures as a whole. As was the point in the prayers at Gethsemane, obedience to the Father's will for his life is Jesus' ultimate desire, not pursuing his own will.

55 In that hour Jesus said to the crowd,
"Am I leading a rebellion, that you have
come out with swords and clubs to capture
me? Every day I sat in the temple courts
teaching,[u] and you did not arrest me. 56 But
this has all taken place that the writings
of the prophets might be fulfilled."[v] Then
all the disciples deserted him and fled.

Jesus Before the Sanhedrin

26:57–68pp // Mk 14:53–65;
Jn 18:12,13,19–24

57 Those who had arrested Jesus took
him to Caiaphas[w] the high priest, where
the teachers of the law and the elders had
assembled. 58 But Peter followed him at
a distance, right up to the courtyard of
the high priest.[x] He entered and sat down
with the guards[y] to see the outcome.
59 The chief priests and the whole Sanhedrin[z] were looking for false evidence
against Jesus so that they could put him to
death. 60 But they did not find any, though
many false witnesses[a] came forward.
Finally two[b] came forward 61 and declared, "This fellow said, 'I am able to
destroy the temple of God and rebuild
it in three days.'"[c]
62 Then the high priest stood up and
said to Jesus, "Are you not going to answer? What is this testimony that these
men are bringing against you?" 63 But
Jesus remained silent.[d]
The high priest said to him, "I charge
you under oath[e] by the living God:[f] Tell
us if you are the Messiah, the Son of God."
64 "You have said so," Jesus replied.
"But I say to all of you: From now on
you will see the Son of Man sitting at
the right hand of the Mighty One[g] and
coming on the clouds of heaven."[a][h]
65 Then the high priest tore his clothes[i]
and said, "He has spoken blasphemy!
Why do we need any more witnesses?
Look, now you have heard the blasphemy. 66 What do you think?"
"He is worthy of death,"[j] they answered.
67 Then they spit in his face and struck
him with their fists.[k] Others slapped him
68 and said, "Prophesy to us, Messiah.
Who hit you?"[l]

Peter Disowns Jesus

26:69–75pp // Mk 14:66–72; Lk 22:55–62;
Jn 18:16–18,25–27

69 Now Peter was sitting out in the
courtyard, and a servant girl came to
him. "You also were with Jesus of Galilee," she said.
70 But he denied it before them all. "I

[a] 64 See Psalm 110:1; Daniel 7:13.

26:55 [u] Mk 12:35; Lk 21:37; Jn 7:14,28; 18:20
26:56 [v] ver 24
26:57 [w] ver 3
26:58 [x] Jn 18:15 [y] Jn 7:32,45,46
26:59 [z] Mt 5:22
26:60 [a] Ps 27:12; 35:11; Ac 6:13 [b] Dt 19:15
26:61 [c] Jn 2:19
26:63 [d] Mt 27:12,14 [e] Lev 5:1 [f] Mt 16:16
26:64 [g] Ps 110:1 [h] Da 7:13; Rev 1:7
26:65 [i] Mk 14:63
26:66 [j] Lev 24:16; Jn 19:7
26:67 [k] Mt 16:21; 27:30
26:68 [l] Lk 22:63-65

26:55–56a Jesus has been within their reach in the temple precincts teaching throughout the week. The question, "Am I leading a rebellion?" clearly rejects the idea that Jesus has any intention of leading an armed rebellion.
26:56b Jesus' prophetic word comes to pass: At the time of his greatest need for support, his closest followers desert him. He faces the cross alone.
26:57–68 Matthew highlights the illegality of Jesus' arrest and trial by pointing out that the teachers of the law and the elders have already assembled with the high priest. They are waiting to make a quick judgment of death. None of the Gospel writers gives a full account of the judicial process leading to Jesus' death, but the overall pattern that emerges is that the Jewish authorities first try Jesus and convict him of blasphemy, then they take him to Pilate and change the accusation to treason.
26:57–58 Peter demonstrates a personal courage that compels him to follow Jesus and the arresting delegation to the courtyard of the high priest, where he sits down among the guards. From there Peter can watch as Jesus is shuffled from hearing to hearing.
26:59–60 The Sanhedrin tries to find false witnesses who will testify against Jesus. The entire proceedings are a sham, for the Jewish leaders are manipulating the events to get Jesus out of the way as quickly as possible.
26:61–63a Finally, out of the pack of false witnesses are two who testify that Jesus said, "I am able to destroy the temple of God and rebuild it in three days" (v. 61). The high priest apparently views Jesus as exalting himself over the temple of God.
26:63a Throughout this long night, Jesus has spoken of the divine inevitability of these events. The theme of silence is noted at various times during the trials, fulfilling Isa 53:7 and placing the responsibility for his death back on his accusers.
26:63b The high priest is not thinking of Messiah in the Trinitarian sense that we know today to be true of Jesus. Rather, Caiaphas draws on the Jewish conception of Messiah as the Davidic king, God's anointed, who will rule his people forever.
26:64 Jesus declares that he is not just a human messianic deliverer; he is the divine Son of Man foretold in Da 7:13–14 and the object of the psalmist's reference to the divine figure who sits at the right hand of God (Ps 110:1–2), cited earlier in his debates with the Pharisees. Jesus is making himself to be equal with God.
26:65–68 From the standpoint of Jewish law, Jesus deserves death because he has claimed to be divine. From the standpoint of Roman law, however, blasphemy is not a capital crime. Therefore, the leaders will have to manipulate the charges and focus on Jesus as a common messianic pretender who is dangerous to Rome as an insurrectionist.
26:69–70 Peter has courageously stayed through the early morning hours in that hostile environment. But when his own personal safety is threatened by public exposure, Peter's courage deserts him.

don't know what you're talking about,"
he said.
71 Then he went out to the gateway,
where another servant girl saw him and
said to the people there, "This fellow was
with Jesus of Nazareth."
72 He denied it again, with an oath: "I
don't know the man!"
73 After a little while, those standing
there went up to Peter and said, "Surely
you are one of them; your accent gives
you away."
74 Then he began to call down curses,
and he swore to them, "I don't know
the man!"
Immediately a rooster crowed. 75 Then
Peter remembered the word Jesus had
spoken: "Before the rooster crows, you
will disown me three times."[m] And he
went outside and wept bitterly.

Judas Hangs Himself

27 Early in the morning, all the chief
priests and the elders of the people made their plans how to have Jesus
executed.[n] 2 So they bound him, led him
away and handed him over[o] to Pilate the
governor.[p]
3 When Judas, who had betrayed him,[q]
saw that Jesus was condemned, he was
seized with remorse and returned the
thirty pieces of silver[r] to the chief priests
and the elders. 4 "I have sinned," he
said, "for I have betrayed innocent
blood."
"What is that to us?" they replied.
"That's your responsibility."[s]
5 So Judas threw the money into the
temple[t] and left. Then he went away and
hanged himself.[u]
6 The chief priests picked up the coins
and said, "It is against the law to put this
into the treasury, since it is blood money." 7 So they decided to use the money to buy the potter's field as a burial
place for foreigners. 8 That is why it has
been called the Field of Blood[v] to this
day. 9 Then what was spoken by Jeremiah
the prophet was fulfilled:[w] "They took
the thirty pieces of silver, the price set
on him by the people of Israel, 10 and they
used them to buy the potter's field, as
the Lord commanded me."[a][x]

Jesus Before Pilate

27:11–26pp // Mk 15:2–15; Lk 23:2,3,18–25; Jn 18:29—19:16

11 Meanwhile Jesus stood before the
governor, and the governor asked him,
"Are you the king of the Jews?"[y]
"You have said so," Jesus replied.
12 When he was accused by the chief
priests and the elders, he gave no answer.[z] 13 Then Pilate asked him, "Don't
you hear the testimony they are bringing against you?"[a] 14 But Jesus made no
reply,[b] not even to a single charge — to
the great amazement of the governor.

26:75 [m] ver 34; Jn 13:38
27:1 [n] Mt 12:14; Mk 15:1; Lk 22:66
27:2 [o] Mt 20:19 [p] Mk 15:1; Lk 13:1; Ac 3:13; 1Ti 6:13
27:3 [q] Mt 10:4 [r] Mt 26:14,15
27:4 [s] ver 24
27:5 [t] Lk 1:9,21 [u] Ac 1:18
27:8 [v] Ac 1:19
27:9 [w] Mt 1:22
27:10 [x] Zec 11:12,13; Jer 32:6-9
27:11 [y] Mt 2:2
27:12 [z] Mt 26:63; Mk 14:61; Jn 19:9
27:13 [a] Mt 26:62
27:14 [b] Mk 14:61

[a] *10* See Zech. 11:12,13; Jer. 19:1-13; 32:6-9.

26:71–72 This second girl's confrontation escalates, and Peter's denial also escalates. The oath is not vulgar swearing but rather making a vow to something sacred to affirm the truth of his statement.

26:73–75 This third and final confrontation escalates the threat to Peter, so he intensifies his own denial by calling down curses on himself. His third and final denial takes the same form as the second, "I don't know the man!" (v. 74).

Peter's bitter weeping is recognition of his betrayal of Jesus; he has thrown away all that has given him a new identity as Jesus' disciple. But the weeping is perhaps also the first sign of his repentance.

27:1–2 When Pilate first became governor, he attempted to impose Roman superiority throughout Israel. He was exposed to increasing criticism from the Jews for such acts, which may have encouraged the religious leaders to capitalize on Pilate's vulnerability, leading them to align themselves with him in his attempt to maintain peace. Their demand for a legal death sentence on Jesus, a falsely accused rival to Caesar, would not have been an unwelcome way of putting down a popular uprising.

27:3–4 Matthew shows the magnitude of Judas's "remorse" but appears careful not to suggest that the betrayer repents of the sin. Had he truly repented, he would have sought forgiveness from God. Instead, he turns to the chief priests and the elders, who are just as guilty of Jesus' death.

27:5 Part of the structure on which he was hanging (perhaps the branch of a tree) broke, resulting in his falling and hitting some obstacle (perhaps rocks). Luke records the grisly result (Ac 1:18).

27:6–10 The irony is that the chief priests are careful not to defile the temple treasury with blood money, but they are the very ones who earlier schemed to provide the money that shed the blood of an innocent man.

27:11–14 Pilate's first question focuses on treason and insurrection. Jesus places the responsibility back on Pilate to discern properly what the question implies.

Pilate has certainly heard of Jesus prior to this encounter, but he is not prepared for the silence that Jesus maintains in the middle of these threatening circumstances. Jesus recognizes the trial is a sham, so he does not grace the charade with a reply. His refusal to speak may bring to mind among Matthew's readers the servant of Isa 53:7.

15 Now it was the governor's custom at
the festival to release a prisoner[c] chosen
by the crowd. 16 At that time they had a
well-known prisoner whose name was
Jesus[a] Barabbas. 17 So when the crowd
had gathered, Pilate asked them, "Which
one do you want me to release to you:
Jesus Barabbas, or Jesus who is called the
Messiah?"[d] 18 For he knew it was out of
self-interest that they had handed Jesus
over to him.
19 While Pilate was sitting on the
judge's seat,[e] his wife sent him this message: "Don't have anything to do with
that innocent[f] man, for I have suffered
a great deal today in a dream[g] because
of him."
20 But the chief priests and the elders
persuaded the crowd to ask for Barabbas
and to have Jesus executed.[h]
21 "Which of the two do you want me
to release to you?" asked the governor.
"Barabbas," they answered.
22 "What shall I do, then, with Jesus
who is called the Messiah?"[i] Pilate asked.
They all answered, "Crucify him!"
23 "Why? What crime has he committed?" asked Pilate.
But they shouted all the louder, "Crucify him!"
24 When Pilate saw that he was getting
nowhere, but that instead an uproar[j] was
starting, he took water and washed his
hands[k] in front of the crowd. "I am innocent of this man's blood,"[l] he said. "It
is your responsibility!"[m]
25 All the people answered, "His blood
is on us and on our children!"[n]
26 Then he released Barabbas to them.
But he had Jesus flogged,[o] and handed
him over to be crucified.

27:15 [c] Jn 18:39
27:17 [d] ver 22; Mt 1:16
27:19 [e] Jn 19:13 [f] ver 24 [g] Ge 20:6; Nu 12:6; 1Ki 3:5; Job 33:14-16; Mt 1:20; 2:12,13, 19,22
27:20 [h] Ac 3:14
27:22 [i] Mt 1:16
27:24 [j] Mt 26:5 [k] Ps 26:6 [l] Dt 21:6-8 [m] ver 4
27:25 [n] Jos 2:19; Ac 5:28
27:26 [o] Isa 53:5; Jn 19:1
27:27 [p] Jn 18:28, 33; 19:9
27:28 [q] Jn 19:2

The Soldiers Mock Jesus

27:27–31pp // Mk 15:16–20

27 Then the governor's soldiers took
Jesus into the Praetorium[p] and gathered the whole company of soldiers
around him. 28 They stripped him and
put a scarlet robe on him,[q] 29 and then

[a] *16* Many manuscripts do not have *Jesus;* also in verse 17.

27:15-18 Pilate's position as a senior official gave him the authority to acquit a prisoner. In an attempt to win the people's favor, he apparently initiated a custom in earlier years in which he released a prisoner at Passover whom the crowd favored. Barabbas was "well-known," evidently for his reputation as a freedom fighter who was regarded highly by the people.

Pilate knows that the high priest and Sanhedrin have indicted Jesus because they are envious of him. He is wise to their plotting, and he thinks that he has found a way to turn the crowds to himself while subtly putting the Sanhedrin back in their place.

27:19 Matthew alone records the incident of Pilate's wife attempting to deter him because of her dream. Pilate does not heed his wife's warning.

27:20 Throughout Jesus' ministry, the "crowd" has been offered salvation and discipleship. They have shouted with amazement and enthusiasm at his teaching, miracles, and Triumphal Entry to Jerusalem. But when something better is offered, they give up their shallow allegiance.

27:21-23 Pilate understands that Jesus has claimed the title "Messiah" as one who offers spiritual hope. That seems harmless enough to Pilate, so he tries to get the crowd to recall that many of them, even recently, have pinned their hopes on Jesus. But the crowd is unifying into a mob, and they "all" answer, "Crucify him!" (v. 22).

27:24 There is abundant background from Jewish as well as Hellenistic sources for the practice of washing one's hands as a way of showing public innocence.

27:25 Matthew emphasizes that the crowd and the religious leaders have had their opportunity. Now they must bear responsibility for not repenting and for asking for Jesus' death. The Jewish leaders and the crowds claim responsibility for Jesus' death. In their ignorance, they call down responsibility on their children, but this does not in any way excuse any form of anti-Semitism, then or now. Everyone is responsible for his or her own actions, but God's forgiveness awaits any who repent.

27:26 Roman flogging was different from Jewish flogging. Whereas flogging in the Jewish synagogue was limited to 40 lashes, no such restrictions limited Roman flogging. A condemned prisoner was tied to a post and brutally beaten with the cruel flagellum, a leather strap interwoven with pieces of bone and metal that cut through the prisoner's skin, leaving it hanging in sheds. The repeated flaying often exposed the bones and internal organs, and in many cases it was fatal. Flogging weakened the accused before crucifixion.

With the Sabbath approaching, the Romans flog Jesus nearly to death so he will not be left on the cross after sundown.

✤ **26:47—27:26** Those who reject Jesus, whether Jew or Gentile, will bear consequences. Only days after the crucifixion, thousands of Jews repent at Peter's preaching about Jesus, whom they put to death (Ac 2:23, 37-41), and even many of the priests will become believers (Ac 6:7). The responsibility of Christians today is to love the Jewish people as God does, to recognize the special place they enjoy in God's plan for the ages, and to share the gospel with them as we would any other people. No one can support racial bigotry toward Jews by appealing to Matthew's record.

27:27-31 Roman soldiers in Jerusalem at the time were known to play a cruel game with condemned

twisted together a crown of thorns and
set it on his head. They put a staff in his
right hand. Then they knelt in front of
him and mocked him. "Hail, king of the
Jews!" they said.[r] 30They spit on him,
and took the staff and struck him on the
head again and again.[s] 31After they had
mocked him, they took off the robe and
put his own clothes on him. Then they
led him away to crucify him.[t]

The Crucifixion of Jesus

27:33–44pp // Mk 15:22–32; Lk 23:33–43; Jn 19:17–24

32As they were going out,[u] they met
a man from Cyrene,[v] named Simon,
and they forced him to carry the cross.[w]
33They came to a place called Golgotha
(which means "the place of the skull").[x]
34There they offered Jesus wine to drink,
mixed with gall;[y] but after tasting it, he
refused to drink it. 35When they had crucified him, they divided up his clothes
by casting lots.[z] 36And sitting down, they
kept watch[a] over him there. 37Above his
head they placed the written charge
against him: THIS IS JESUS, THE KING OF
THE JEWS.
38Two rebels were crucified with him,[b]
one on his right and one on his left.
39Those who passed by hurled insults at
him, shaking their heads[c] 40and saying,

27:29 [r]Isa 53:3; Jn 19:2,3
27:30 [s]Mt 16:21; 26:67
27:31 [t]Isa 53:7
27:32 [u]Heb 13:12 [v]Ac 2:10; 6:9; 11:20; 13:1 [w]Mk 15:21; Lk 23:26
27:33 [x]Jn 19:17
27:34 [y]ver 48; Ps 69:21
27:35 [z]Ps 22:18
27:36 [a]ver 54
27:38 [b]Isa 53:12
27:39 [c]Ps 22:7; 109:25; La 2:15
27:40 [d]Mt 26:61; Jn 2:19 [e]ver 42 [f]Mt 4:3,6
27:42 [g]Jn 1:49; 12:13 [h]Jn 3:15
27:43 [i]Ps 22:8
27:45 [j]Am 8:9
27:46 [k]Ps 22:1

Mt 27:46 ❖ Why is it important that Christ can relate to our difficult moments, even when we feel abandoned by God (see Heb 4:15)?

"You who are going to destroy the temple
and build it in three days,[d] save yourself![e]
Come down from the cross, if you are the
Son of God!"[f] 41In the same way the chief
priests, the teachers of the law and the
elders mocked him. 42"He saved others,"
they said, "but he can't save himself! He's
the king of Israel![g] Let him come down
now from the cross, and we will believe[h]
in him. 43He trusts in God. Let God rescue
him[i] now if he wants him, for he said, 'I
am the Son of God.'" 44In the same way
the rebels who were crucified with him
also heaped insults on him.

The Death of Jesus

27:45–56pp // Mk 15:33–41; Lk 23:44–49; Jn 19:29–30

45From noon until three in the afternoon darkness[j] came over all the land.
46About three in the afternoon Jesus
cried out in a loud voice, *"Eli, Eli,[a] lema
sabachthani?"* (which means "My God,
my God, why have you forsaken me?").[bk]

[a] 46 Some manuscripts *Eloi, Eloi*
[b] 46 Psalm 22:1

prisoners. The charges against Jesus make him fair game for this torturous pastime. The soldiers dress him up and mock him as the "king of the Jews" (v. 29).

27:32–34 Criminals condemned to die were customarily required to carry the heavy wooden crosspiece on which they were to be nailed. It weighed more than 40 pounds and was strapped across the shoulders. The scourging and loss of blood had so weakened Jesus that he could hardly walk.

27:32 Simon is likely a Jew who has made a pilgrimage to Jerusalem for the Passover. Tradition tells us that this incident of carrying Jesus' cross so impacted Simon that he became a Christian, perhaps through Peter's preaching on Pentecost.

27:33 "Golgotha" is a transliteration of the Aramaic word for "skull." The common designation "Calvary" comes from the Latin word for skull, *calvaria*.

27:34 When Jesus tastes the bitter drink, he knows it will only intensify his parched thirst, so he refuses.

27:35–36 Matthew quotes nearly verbatim the Greek version of Ps 22:18. The lot is a form of gambling by the Roman guards as they divide up whatever is left of Jesus' clothes.

25:37 The soldiers place a placard above Jesus' head. Perhaps Jesus wore this placard strung around his neck as he walked to Golgotha. Ironically, however, this is an actual statement of truth about Jesus.

27:38 The mother of the two sons of Zebedee had requested the privilege of her sons being seated at Jesus' right- and left-hand side in his kingdom (20:21). With bitter irony, Matthew records that two rebel criminals form Jesus' right- and left-hand attendants on a cross, not a throne.

27:39–40 This derision mocks Jesus' claim of supernatural power. If he has such powers, he should be able to save himself. Matthew's readers will hear in these taunts from the passersby another allusion to Ps 22:6–7.

27:41–43 Matthew again alludes to Ps 22 as the religious leaders mock Jesus' supposed trust in God (Ps 22:8).

27:44 The two thieves join in the mockery by heaping insults on Jesus.

27:45 Darkness here displays a limitation on the power of Satan, God's displeasure on humanity for crucifying his Son, and God's judgment on the sins of the world.

27:46 Once again, the crucifixion scene recalls the lament of King David in Ps 22:1. Matthew gives us a singular focus on Jesus' feelings of being abandoned on the cross. He bears the divine retribution and punishment for sin, as the Father's cup of wrath is poured out on him in divine judgment.

Not only does Jesus bear the load of humanity's sin, but he becomes sin on our behalf. Jesus was not separated in his essence or substance from the Father as the second person of the Trinity. Rather, Jesus' divinely sustained humanity consciously experienced the full penalty of death for the sins of

47When some of those standing there
heard this, they said, "He's calling Elijah."
48Immediately one of them ran and
got a sponge. He filled it with wine vinegar,[l] put it on a staff, and offered it to
Jesus to drink. 49The rest said, "Now
leave him alone. Let's see if Elijah comes
to save him."
50And when Jesus had cried out again
in a loud voice, he gave up his spirit.[m]
51At that moment the curtain of the
temple[n] was torn in two from top to bottom. The earth shook, the rocks split[o] 52and
the tombs broke open. The bodies of many
holy people who had died were raised to
life. 53They came out of the tombs after
Jesus' resurrection and[a] went into the holy
city[p] and appeared to many people.
54When the centurion and those with
him who were guarding[q] Jesus saw the
earthquake and all that had happened,
they were terrified, and exclaimed,
"Surely he was the Son of God!"[r]
55Many women were there, watching
from a distance. They had followed
Jesus from Galilee to care for his needs.[s]
56Among them were Mary Magdalene,
Mary the mother of James and Joseph,[b]
and the mother of Zebedee's sons.[t]

The Burial of Jesus

27:57–61pp // Mk 15:42–47; Lk 23:50–56; Jn 19:38–42

57As evening approached, there came
a rich man from Arimathea, named Joseph, who had himself become a disciple
of Jesus. 58Going to Pilate, he asked for
Jesus' body, and Pilate ordered that it
be given to him. 59Joseph took the body,
wrapped it in a clean linen cloth, 60and
placed it in his own new tomb[u] that he
had cut out of the rock. He rolled a big
stone in front of the entrance to the tomb
and went away. 61Mary Magdalene and
the other Mary were sitting there opposite the tomb.

27:48 [l] ver 34; Ps 69:21
27:50 [m] Jn 19:30
27:51 [n] Ex 26:31-33; Heb 9:3,8 [o] ver 54
27:53 [p] Mt 4:5
27:54 [q] ver 36 [r] Mt 4:3; 17:5
27:55 [s] Lk 8:2,3
27:56 [t] Mk 15:47; Lk 24:10; Jn 19:25
27:60 [u] Mt 27:66; 28:2; Mk 16:4

[a] 53 Or *tombs, and after Jesus' resurrection they*
[b] 56 Greek *Joses*, a variant of *Joseph*

---

humanity. This lays the foundation for the theological doctrine of the atonement, in which Jesus' sacrifice on the cross is one of "vicarious atonement": Jesus suffers the punishment we deserve for our sin.

But Jesus still knows that this experience is not one of despair—he still calls his Father "my God, my God" (Mt 27:46). The relational separation he must endure while bearing the sins of humanity cannot separate him entirely from God.

27:47 Jesus' call to God in Aramaic (v. 46) sounds similar to the Hebrew name for Elijah, so the bystanders misunderstand him to be attempting to summon the prophet.

27:48-49 Someone in the crowd runs to get a sponge filled with the wine used by common people and soldiers as a daily drink with meals. Perhaps one of the bystanders is offering an act of kindness and mercy to Jesus. Or perhaps this person is continuing the earlier mockery.

27:50 Jesus cries out again in a loud voice. Then "he gave up his spirit." Matthew shows that to the very end, Jesus maintains control over his destiny. He approaches his death willingly.

27:51 The curtain was an elaborately woven fabric of 72 twisted braids of 24 threads each. The veil was 60 feet high and 30 feet wide. The tearing of the temple curtain testifies that Jesus' sacrifice on the cross has fulfilled the hopes expressed in Israel's years of temple sacrifice. Jesus is the permanently accessible new temple in whom all who turn to him are reconciled to the Father.

27:51b-53 Matthew emphasizes the victory over death that Jesus' sacrifice on the cross accomplishes. The supernatural raising of the bodies of these holy ones and their appearances in Jerusalem is a striking testimony to Jesus' accomplished work on the cross and, after that, his resurrection.

27:54 The centurion has probably been in attendance since Jesus' Roman trial and subsequent flogging and mocking by the soldiers. He has probably witnessed many crucifixions, but the cataclysmic events of the earthquake and opened tombs, plus the manner of Jesus' death, combine to draw out the statement, "Surely he was the Son of God!" As he watches the events unfold, he and his men are overwhelmed by the realization that Jesus is truly who he claimed to be.

27:55-56 As the women followed Jesus, they cared for his needs, called him Lord, and worshiped him after the resurrection. These descriptions not only designate the women to be disciples but also describe them as *exemplary* disciples of Jesus.

Since the women are present for Jesus' death and his burial by Joseph of Arimathea (v. 57), they can verify that Jesus is truly dead, not just unconscious. God is bestowing a special honor on them. They are examples of true discipleship to Jesus, and because of their faithfulness and courage, they are given the special honor of being eyewitnesses to these profound events.

27:57 Joseph is an example of a person who apparently did not follow Jesus around the countryside in his earthly ministry but who was still considered his disciple.

27:58 Joseph's action in initiating the burial of Jesus is both an act of obedience to Jewish law and an act of devotion to his Lord.

27:59 The Jews did not practice cremation or full embalming of corpses, but the body was prepared for burial by washing it, dressing it in special garments, and packing it in the linen cloth with fragrant spices.

27:60 Because the Sabbath is approaching, they cannot work with the dead and thus must return after the Sabbath to complete the preparations.

27:61 Matthew tells us that at least two of the women who witnessed Jesus' crucifixion stayed with Jesus even in death. It is even possible that

The Guard at the Tomb

62The next day, the one after Preparation
Day, the chief priests and the Pharisees
went to Pilate. 63"Sir," they said, "we remember that while he was still alive that
deceiver said, 'After three days I will rise
again.'[v] 64So give the order for the tomb to
be made secure until the third day. Otherwise, his disciples may come and steal the
body and tell the people that he has been
raised from the dead. This last deception
will be worse than the first."
65"Take a guard,"[w] Pilate answered.
"Go, make the tomb as secure as you
know how." 66So they went and made
the tomb secure by putting a seal[x] on the
stone[y] and posting the guard.[z]

Jesus Has Risen

28:1–8pp // Mk 16:1–8; Lk 24:1–10; Jn 20:1–8

28 After the Sabbath, at dawn on the
first day of the week, Mary Magdalene and the other Mary[a] went to look
at the tomb.
2There was a violent earthquake,[b] for
an angel[c] of the Lord came down from
heaven and, going to the tomb, rolled
back the stone and sat on it. 3His appearance was like lightning, and his clothes
were white as snow.[d] 4The guards were
so afraid of him that they shook and became like dead men.
5The angel said to the women, "Do not
be afraid,[e] for I know that you are looking for Jesus, who was crucified. 6He is
not here; he has risen, just as he said.[f]
Come and see the place where he lay.
7Then go quickly and tell his disciples:
'He has risen from the dead and is going
ahead of you into Galilee.[g] There you will
see him.' Now I have told you."
8So the women hurried away from the
tomb, afraid yet filled with joy, and ran
to tell his disciples. 9Suddenly Jesus met
them.[h] "Greetings," he said. They came

27:63 [v] Mt 16:21
27:65 [w] ver 66; Mt 28:11
27:66 [x] Da 6:17 [y] ver 60; Mt 28:2 [z] Mt 28:11
28:1 [a] Mt 27:56
28:2 [b] Mt 27:51 [c] Jn 20:12
28:3 [d] Da 10:6; Mk 9:3; Jn 20:12
28:5 [e] ver 10; Mt 14:27
28:6 [f] Mt 16:21
28:7 [g] ver 10,16; Mt 26:32
28:9 [h] Jn 20:14-18

---

these women worked with Joseph and Nicodemus to prepare Jesus' body for burial.

27:62-63 Because of Jesus' claims and his followers, the Jewish religious leaders sense that things may get out of control, so they enlist Pilate's aid in keeping the tomb secure.

27:64 Matthew makes it clear that the real deceivers are the religious leaders who actually deceive themselves.

27:65-66 After a family placed the body of one of its members in a burial recess in the tomb, a stone was placed over the entrance and was often sealed with clay. However, the "seal" here seems to be more of an official security device, with wax imprinted with the Roman seal anchoring both ends so that any tampering could be detected. While the religious leaders and Pilate have gone to extreme lengths to prevent a hoax about Jesus' resurrection, they provide another witness to the factual truth of the empty tomb.

✣ **27:27-66** Consider the little-known figures around the cross. Their diversity is remarkable, but the confession of their lips and life serve as examples for us. We may not ever accomplish great feats in the eyes of the world, but when we are gripped by the profound truths of what Jesus accomplished on the cross, we too will be energized by the Spirit of God to be men and women whose service to our master is a courageous witness that the gospel of the kingdom has triumphed. Jesus' amazing, divine, sacrificial love for us demands our soul, our life, our all, no matter what our position in life. That is the only proper response of a life that surveys the wondrous cross.

28:1 Matthew focuses his account on Mary Magdalene and the other Mary.

28:2-4 The brilliance of the angel of the Lord is often associated with descriptions of lightning, as is Jesus' own return. The white clothing symbolizes brilliant purity. These guards are battle-hardened veterans, used to facing fearful situations. But nothing has prepared them for this encounter.

28:5 For the first time, the angel speaks to the women. Jesus remains the Crucified One.

28:6 Jesus has indeed been raised from the dead, and God the Father is the One who raised Jesus from the dead. He has affirmed and declared the Son's identity and ministry by raising him. To complete the confirmation of the resurrection, the angel invites the women to enter the tomb to see the place where Jesus was laid. Jesus was not just raised spiritually but was resurrected physically; his body was no longer in the tomb.

28:7 God uses the women as witnesses not only to the central redemptive act of history—Jesus' death on the cross—but also to his resurrection.

Galilee was the central location of Jesus' earthly ministry. Now Galilee continues as a central place of his ascended ministry.

28:8 The women came to the tomb expecting to find death, but now everything is turned upside down. Their future now includes the risen Jesus, the long-anticipated and now fully realized Messiah of Israel and Savior of the world.

28:9 As the women go, the risen Jesus meets them to confirm the reality of their hopes. The presence of the risen Jesus turns their fear into worship. By mentioning that they "clasped his feet," Matthew subtly emphasizes that this is no mere spiritual vision but a physical resurrection.

It is unlikely that any Jew would have created such a story as fiction. First, there was disagreement among some of the rabbis as to the acceptability of a woman giving testimony in a court of law. Therefore it would seem unlikely that a Jew

to him, clasped his feet and worshiped him. 10Then Jesus said to them, "Do not be afraid. Go and tell my brothers[i] to go to Galilee; there they will see me."

The Guards' Report

11While the women were on their way, some of the guards[j] went into the city and reported to the chief priests everything that had happened. 12When the chief priests had met with the elders and devised a plan, they gave the soldiers a large sum of money, 13telling them, "You are to say, 'His disciples came during the night and stole him away while we were asleep.' 14If this report gets to the governor,[k] we will satisfy him and keep you out of trouble." 15So the soldiers took the money and did as they were instructed. And this story has been widely circulated among the Jews to this very day.

The Great Commission

16Then the eleven disciples went to Galilee, to the mountain where Jesus had told them to go.[l] 17When they saw him, they worshiped him; but some doubted. 18Then Jesus came to them and said, "All authority in heaven and on earth has been given to me.[m] 19There-

28:10 [i] Jn 20:17; Ro 8:29; Heb 2:11-13,17
28:11 [j] Mt 27:65, 66
28:14 [k] Mt 27:2
28:16 [l] ver 7,10; Mt 26:32
28:18 [m] Da 7:13, 14; Lk 10:22; Jn 3:35; 17:2; 1Co 15:27; Eph 1:20-22; Php 2:9,10

Mt 28:18-20 ❖ What does living out this "Great Commission" look like in our lives? How can we notice Christ's presence in every circumstance?

---

would fictionalize a woman's testimony in the case of Jesus' resurrection.

Second, the cowardly picture painted of the men hiding away in Jerusalem would offend the sensibilities of Jewish readers and doubtless would not have been recorded unless it were true.

Finally, the listing of the names of the women weighs against being fiction because these women were known in early Christian fellowship and would not have easily been associated with a false account.

28:10 Jesus' intention in directing these women to call for his brothers to meet him in Galilee marks an important turning point. This suggests that they should be regarded as equal in value to men and be restored as coworkers with men in the community of faith, a role they had been assigned from creation (see Ge 2:18–22).

The return to Galilee harks back to the region of "Galilee of the Gentiles" (cf. Mt 4:15–16), thus preparing the way for Jesus' commission to make disciples of all nations. Now the family of faith includes all who are Jesus' disciples no matter their gender, ethnicity, or religion.

28:11–15 Matthew is writing for a Jewish-Christian audience who have presumably heard about the charges circulating among the Jews that Jesus' body was stolen by his disciples.

28:11 They apparently did not see the risen Jesus, only the results of his resurrection. But they know that they have failed their orders to secure the burial scene, because the tomb is empty.

28:12 As soon as the chief priests hear the guards' report, they gather with the elders to immediately attempt damage control. One might wonder how these deliberations became known to the Christian community until we recall that some of Jesus' own followers, such as Nicodemus and Joseph of Arimathea, were part of the highest levels of the Jerusalem religious elite.

28:13 Why do the religious leaders make up this story? And why do the guards agree to be implicated for neglecting their duty? The religious leaders want to hide what really happened. The guards are likewise in a predicament. They cannot deny the tomb is empty, and they face possible execution for their failure to guard the tomb. Thus, with the backing of the Jewish leaders, they at least have a chance to escape punishment, and the religious leaders see in their proposal a crafty way of accounting for the empty tomb.

28:14–15 Matthew writes upwards of 30 years after these events, and yet he states, "And this story has been widely circulated among the Jews to this very day" (v. 15). This aside indicates an ongoing attempt by the Jewish leaders (over decades) to counteract the increasingly widespread belief that Jesus was indeed raised from the dead, proving his claim to be Messiah.

28:16–17 For the first time in Matthew's narrative, the disciples encounter the risen Jesus and worship him. Now that he has been raised they are prepared to give him the honor that is due him. "But," Matthew then notes, "some doubted." Perhaps other disciples from Judea and Galilee, who have not yet seen the risen Jesus, are the ones who doubt.

28:18 The commission captures Jesus' purpose for coming to earth, and its placement at the conclusion of this Gospel indicates Matthew's overall purpose for writing. Jesus has come to inaugurate the kingdom of God on earth by bringing men and women into a saving relationship with himself.

28:19–20 The Great Commission contains one primary, central command, the imperative "make disciples," with three subordinate participles: "go," "baptizing," and "teaching." The imperative explains the central thrust of the commission, while the participles describe aspects of the process.

Jesus' Great Commission implies more than securing salvation as his disciple. Implied in the imperative "make disciples" is both the call to, and the process of, becoming a disciple. Jesus spent a great deal of time guiding and instructing the disciples in their growth. He now sends them out to do the same.

Being a disciple of Jesus was primarily not an academic endeavor like being a Pharisee, nor even a commitment to a great prophet like John the Baptist. A disciple of Jesus comes to him and him alone for eternal life and will always be only a disciple of Jesus. The object of making disciples is "all the nations." People of every nation are to

fore go and make disciples of all nations,[n] baptizing them in the name of the Father and of the Son and of the Holy Spirit,[o] 20 and teaching[p] them to obey everything I have commanded you. And surely I am with you[q] always, to the very end of the age."[r]

28:19 [n] Mk 16:15, 16; Lk 24:47; Ac 1:8; 14:21 [o] Ac 2:38; 8:16; Ro 6:3, 4

28:20 [p] Ac 2:42 [q] Mt 18:20; Ac 18:10 [r] Mt 13:39

receive the opportunity to become Jesus' disciples. Jesus' ministry in Israel was the beginning point of a universal offer of salvation to all the peoples of the earth.

The participle "baptizing" describes the activity by which a new disciple identifies with Jesus and his community, and the participle "teaching" introduces the activities by which the new disciple grows in discipleship.

The final participial phrase in Jesus' Great Commission, "teaching," indicates the process by which disciples of Jesus are continually transformed through discipleship and the discipling process. *Discipleship* is the process by which a disciple is transformed, while *discipling* is the involvement of one disciple helping another to grow in his or her discipleship. What Jesus did in making disciples of his first followers, succeeding generations of the church will do in making new disciples of Jesus.

Jesus' entrance into history is captured in the name Immanuel, "God with us" (1:23), and his abiding presence with his disciples is evident in his concluding assurance, "I am with you always" (28:20). A true Israelite would proclaim only God to be eternal and omnipresent, so here Matthew records a concluding claim by Jesus to his deity. Thus, Jesus concludes the commission with the crucial element of discipleship: the presence of the Lord. Both those who obey the commission and those who respond are comforted by the awareness that the risen Jesus will continue to mold and shape all his disciples.

28:1-20 The wonderful promise of Jesus' continual presence (v. 20) invites us as readers into the story. This should not evoke fear or a guilty conscience; rather, it should spur all his disciples on to proclaim the Good News of the presence of the kingdom of God in our lives.

Our discipleship to the risen Jesus continues to be our greatest source of comfort, power, and security. As Matthew has demonstrated over and over, the arrival of Jesus began the greatest revolution that history has ever known. It begins in the heart, where Jesus enters and begins the transformation. But then it extends to every area of our lives so that our entire lives are impacted by the power of the kingdom of heaven.

We are the ongoing chapter of this story—walking receptacles of the presence of the risen Jesus and living demonstrations of the power of the kingdom of God. As we conclude our study of this magnificent Gospel, may our prayer be that our lives will be transformed by our Lord's abiding presence with us, and may we be faithful and obedient disciples of Jesus as we walk in closest intimacy with him and proclaim this Good News that he is with us "to the very end of the age" (v. 20).

Author: John Mark

Audience: Mostly Gentile Christians, probably in the church at Rome

Date: Between the mid-50s and late 60s AD

Theme: To encourage his readers to persevere through suffering and persecution, Mark presents Jesus as the Servant-Messiah and Son of God who died as a ransom for sinners.

Reading Mark

Mark reads like an action-packed drama. Most of his Gospel is a fast-paced story of what Jesus did, occasionally interspersed with some of Jesus' sayings. The only extended, uninterrupted speech of Jesus is found in ch. 13. After beginning his Gospel with the ministry of John the Baptist, Mark describes the Galilean ministry of Jesus, a period of time away from Galilee, and then

PERSPECTIVE

When it comes to living the Christian life, beginnings are better than endings. That may be one of the most important lessons that the Gospel of Mark, by its very structure, teaches us.

We live, unfortunately, in a society more interested in endings than in beginnings. Sporting contests, business profits, and personal résumés exalt final scores, bank accounts, and individual achievement. Endings are more important, it seems, than beginnings.

At first this seems right. Winning, money, and success make life a whole lot easier than losing, debt, and failure. Everyone concerned with raising a family and navigating through the difficult roadblocks of life needs to pay attention to endings. Although reasonable and attractive, placing too much emphasis on endings actually creates a climate in which it is impossible ever to be satisfied or whole. The "endings" turn out to be based on illusion. They are not really endings after all but merely secondary resting places that lead to new goals and more endings, stages, and levels that go on and on and never really get us to a satisfactory end. Is there another way?

Yes. The Gospel of Mark tells us the better way is focusing on beginnings rather than endings. Why? For one reason, it is a better way of describing reality. It gives answers, or hints at answers, to some of the more difficult problems of life. It gives meaning to suffering—although I suffer now, in the Christian life tomorrow is always a new beginning. It makes perseverance sensible: Why stick it out? Because life in Jesus Christ promises eternal life. It restores the virtue of hope to its rightful place in our lives.

	10 BC	AD 1	10	20	30	40	50	60	70	80	90	100
Herod the Great's reign (c. 37–4 BC)												
Jesus' birth (c. 6/5 BC)												
Jesus' flight to Egypt (c. 5/4 BC)												
Beginning of John the Baptist's ministry (c. AD 26)												
Beginning of Jesus' ministry (c. AD 26)												
Jesus' death, resurrection and ascension (c. AD 30)												
Paul's conversion (c. AD 35)												
Book of Mark written (c. AD 55–65)												

the trip to Judea and Jerusalem for the final days of his life (a story covering two-fifths of his Gospel). The word "immediately" is used 47 times, giving this whole account a sense of urgency.

Key Verse

"For even the Son of Man did not come to be served, but to serve, and to give his life as a ransom for many."

—Mark 10:45

This Gospel shows how the coming of Jesus Christ helps us focus on beginnings, leaving the endings to God. How? Primarily by showing that Jesus Christ is the New Beginning to end all new beginnings. In one sense, the whole story of the Bible is the story of God's giving first his chosen people and then the whole creation chance after chance to start over again and get their relationship right with God. Jesus Christ represents the culmination of that process, not by saving everyone once for all but by giving everyone the chance, forever and ever, to start over again at any time. We can never lose hope because there is always another chance, as offered by the life, death, and resurrection of Jesus Christ.

Mark's Gospel starts abruptly and really has no ending. Scholars speculate on the reason for this unique feature. Perhaps it was intentional on Mark's part—one more way of showing that Jesus, the New Beginning, did not end anything but made it possible for the story of God, working in human history and in the church, to go on and on. The story is never finished; we are living the salvation offered in Christ right now, and more and more people are beginning to experience the reality of this each and every day.

The ultimate new beginning, of course, is the resurrection. Death, the ultimate ending, has been defeated by Jesus Christ. Faith ceases to be faith when it is focused on endings. The resurrection symbolizes all the new beginnings of the Gospel of Mark as it teaches us that after Jesus Christ, there is no ending, only the hopeful promise of eternal life.

TAKING THE NEXT STEPS

This account of the life of Jesus has been attributed to John Mark, a disciple of Jesus first mentioned in Ac 12:12. The tradition behind this book suggests that Mark worked closely with Peter when he wrote it. Mark presents Jesus as the powerful Son of God who came to suffer and die to set us free from sin's bondage. In his earthly life, Jesus was a man of action, preaching the gospel and performing many miracles; Mark included far fewer of Jesus' parables and other teachings than either Matthew or Luke. At the same time, Mark showed how an air of mystery surrounded Jesus; neither his friends nor his enemies were able to determine who he really was.

As we study the picture Mark presents of Jesus, several important messages come to mind. (1) First and foremost, Mark challenges us to repent of our sins and turn to Jesus as God's Son sent to bring us back to God. (2) By devoting over one-third of his Gospel to Jesus' final week of suffering and death, Mark shows that to be the most important phase of Jesus' ministry. (3) Jesus was a man of intense emotions; God has created us with a full range of emotions, and he wants those emotions employed to serve him. (4) If (as Jesus himself predicted) we suffer for our faith, we are assured that our Savior knows what we are going through. (5) We must be on our guard against the hostile forces of evil, always and alertly watching for the return of Jesus on the clouds of heaven.

WHAT TO LOOK FOR IN MARK

- Miracles of Jesus (chs. 1; 5)
- Parables of Jesus (ch. 4)
- Jesus' last trip to Judea (ch. 11)
- Final controversies with the Jewish leaders (ch. 12)
- Predictions of the future (ch. 13)
- Jesus' final days (chs. 14–15)
- The resurrection (ch. 16)

John the Baptist Prepares the Way

1:2–8pp // Mt 3:1–11; Lk 3:2–16

1 The beginning of the good news about
Jesus the Messiah,[a] the Son of God,[b][a]
2 as it is written in Isaiah the prophet:

"I will send my messenger ahead of
you,
who will prepare your way"[c][b] —
3 "a voice of one calling in the
wilderness,
'Prepare the way for the Lord,
make straight paths for him.' "[d][c]

4 And so John the Baptist[d] appeared in
the wilderness, preaching a baptism of
repentance[e] for the forgiveness of sins.[f]
5 The whole Judean countryside and all
the people of Jerusalem went out to him.
Confessing their sins, they were baptized
by him in the Jordan River. 6 John wore
clothing made of camel's hair, with a
leather belt around his waist, and he
ate locusts[g] and wild honey. 7 And this
was his message: "After me comes the
one more powerful than I, the straps of
whose sandals I am not worthy to stoop
down and untie.[h] 8 I baptize you with[e]
water, but he will baptize you with[e] the
Holy Spirit."[i]

The Baptism and Testing of Jesus

1:9–11pp // Mt 3:13–17; Lk 3:21,22
1:12,13pp // Mt 4:1–11; Lk 4:1–13

9 At that time Jesus came from Nazareth[j] in Galilee and was baptized by John
in the Jordan. 10 Just as Jesus was coming
up out of the water, he saw heaven being
torn open and the Spirit descending on

1:1 [a] Mt 4:3
1:2 [b] Mal 3:1; Mt 11:10; Lk 7:27
1:3 [c] Isa 40:3; Jn 1:23
1:4 [d] Mt 3:1 [e] Ac 13:24 [f] Lk 1:77
1:6 [g] Lev 11:22
1:7 [h] Ac 13:25
1:8 [i] Isa 44:3; Joel 2:28; Ac 1:5; 2:4; 11:16; 19:4-6
1:9 [j] Mt 2:23

[a] *1* Or *Jesus Christ. Messiah* (Hebrew) and *Christ* (Greek) both mean *Anointed One.* [b] *1* Some manuscripts do not have *the Son of God.* [c] *2* Mal. 3:1 [d] *3* Isaiah 40:3 [e] *8* Or *in*

1:1 The first of Mark's Gospel functions as the title to the entire work. It contains three key terms that are vital for understanding what this work is about. The first term, "good news," refers to the whole story about Jesus—the words, deeds, death, and resurrection of Jesus and what this account means as God's act to save humanity.

Second, this work is about Jesus "Christ," or Jesus "the Messiah." For Jewish readers, "Messiah" was often a title of the coming deliverer anointed by God. Mark wants his readers to understand what it truly means for Jesus to be the Christ.

Finally, the title tells us that Mark's Gospel is about the "Son of God." For Mark, being the Messiah and the Son of God are one and the same thing.

1:2-3 By quoting these verses, Mark certifies that the OT confirms what he is about to tell.

1:4-8 Mark's interest in John is as the forerunner of Jesus. In Mark, he is simply John the Baptist, one who comes preaching and whose baptizing has to do with the forgiveness of sins. Mark is primarily interested in John's announcement that One who is more powerful than he is coming, who will baptize with the Spirit.

1:9 Jesus comes from a town that did not even rate a mention in the OT.

1:10a Mark describes that the heavens are "torn,"

him like a dove.[k] 11And a voice came from
heaven: "You are my Son,[l] whom I love;
with you I am well pleased."
12At once the Spirit sent him out into
the wilderness, 13and he was in the wilderness forty days, being tempted[a] by Satan.[m] He was with the wild animals, and angels attended him.

1:10 [k] Jn 1:32 1:11 [l] Mt 3:17 1:13 [m] Mt 4:10 1:14 [n] Mt 4:12 [o] Mt 4:23 1:15 [p] Gal 4:4; Eph 1:10 [q] Ac 20:21

Jesus Announces the Good News

1:16–20pp // Mt 4:18–22; Lk 5:2–11; Jn 1:35–42

14After John was put in prison, Jesus went into Galilee,[n] proclaiming the good news of God.[o] 15"The time has come,"[p] he said. "The kingdom of God has come near. Repent and believe the good news!"[q]

Jesus Calls His First Disciples

16As Jesus walked beside the Sea of Galilee, he saw Simon and his brother Andrew casting a net into the lake, for

1:21 [r] Mt 4:23; Mk 10:1

Mk 1:17 ❖ How is Jesus calling us to "fish for people"? What strategies can we use to better follow Christ's call?

they were fishermen. 17"Come, follow me," Jesus said, "and I will send you out to fish for people." 18At once they left their nets and followed him.
19When he had gone a little farther, he saw James son of Zebedee and his brother John in a boat, preparing their nets. 20Without delay he called them, and they left their father Zebedee in the boat with the hired men and followed him.

Jesus Drives Out an Impure Spirit

1:21–28pp // Lk 4:31–37

21They went to Capernaum, and when the Sabbath came, Jesus went into the synagogue and began to teach.[r] 22The

[a] 13 The Greek for *tempted* can also mean *tested.*

---

as one might imagine a bolt of lightning tearing through the clouds. What is opened may be closed; what is ripped cannot easily return to its former state. When Jesus comes out of the water, Mark tells us, all heaven breaks loose.

1:10b The same Spirit that once hovered over the waters in Ge 1 now descends on Jesus. This time, the Spirit hovers over a human being, not a formless void, which suggests that God intends to transform humanity.

1:11 In the OT, God is delighted in Israel when Israel is obedient. What the Scriptures ascribe to Israel, Mark transfers to Jesus (see Ps 2:7; Isa 42:1). This phrase may also allude to Isaac, whom Abraham offered up (Ge 22:2). One can interpret the voice at Jesus' baptism as God's announcement that Jesus has been chosen to rule over his people and that he assumes royal power as king.

1:12-13 The Spirit drives Jesus into the desert and Satan's clutches for 40 days. The beasts are evil and natural allies of evil powers. Satan must contend with a new Adam, one who has the power of heaven at his side.

APPLICATION ✜ **1:1-13** Mark shows no interest in listing Jesus' human credentials perhaps because those things might cause the reader to miss the divine dimension of who Jesus is. Jesus' status derives not from his family pedigree but from God. The narrator gives us access to this divine dimension in the prologue so that we know in advance the answers to the questions raised by a variety of characters in the story.

1:14a John's arrest sets the stage for the proclamation of the gospel. Herod Antipas may have thought he was getting his prophetic opponent out of the way, but this story is all part of preparing the way for the coming of the kingdom of God.

1:14b-15 The coming of the kingdom of God is the central theme in this Gospel. When God steps onto the stage of human history, it always comes as a surprise and as a scandal to those whose field of vision is limited.

The dominion of God has come near—so near that Mark believes people can touch it in Jesus. The divine story of Jesus requires immediate human decision and commitment: repentance, submission to God's reign, and trust that the incredible promises of Scripture are finding their fulfillment.

✜ **1:14-15** The preaching of repentance encounters at least four obstacles today. First, people tend to wince when they hear talk of repentance because that phrase has so often been used to lecture others. Jesus' call to repent is not a burning reprimand but an invitation to switch allegiances. Second, people tend to resent anyone who would dare to tell them they need to change. When we lose any sense of sin and responsibility, we also lose any burning desire for pardon. If we do not admit that we have a problem, then we do not get down on our knees and come to God for the solution.

Third, our contemporary culture has a shallow view of sin. Many have no sense that they have rebelled against God. Finally, our contemporary culture has a shallow view of repentance. Many have adopted religious rituals and believe that they have done their duty before God while countless unconfessed sins lurk within. But the call in the gospel to "repent and believe" indicates that repentance is not an end in itself; rather, it is the first step of faith.

1:16-20 The disciples are called to be agents who will bring a compelling message to others that will change their lives beyond recognition. Jesus' call has the same effect on them.

1:21-28 The crowds detect that this teacher speaks for God and not simply about God, as the scribes do. Jesus confronts demons with destruction

ANCIENT SITES MENTIONED IN THE NEW TESTAMENT

people were amazed at his teaching, because he taught them as one who had authority, not as the teachers of the law.[s]
23Just then a man in their synagogue who
was possessed by an impure spirit cried
out, 24"What do you want with us,[t] Jesus
of Nazareth?[u] Have you come to destroy us? I know who you are — the Holy One of God!"[v]
25"Be quiet!" said Jesus sternly. "Come
out of him!"[w] 26The impure spirit shook
the man violently and came out of him with a shriek.[x]

1:22 [s]Mt 7:28, 29 1:24 [t]Mt 8:29 [u]Mt 2:23; Lk 24:19; Ac 24:5 [v]Lk 1:35; Jn 6:69; Ac 3:14 1:25 [w]ver 34 1:26 [x]Mk 9:20 1:27 [y]Mk 10:24, 32 1:28 [z]Mt 9:26 1:29 [a]ver 21,23

27The people were all so amazed[y] that they asked each other, "What is this? A new teaching — and with authority! He even gives orders to impure spirits and they obey him."
28News about him spread quickly over the whole region[z] of Galilee.

Jesus Heals Many

1:29–31pp // Mt 8:14,15; Lk 4:38,39
1:32–34pp // Mt 8:16,17; Lk 4:40,41

29As soon as they left the synagogue,[a] they went with James and John to the

---

and Judaism with a new teaching. Consequently, both demons and the religious authorities will be threatened by him.

Most would take steps to remove the troublemaker from a place of worship, but Jesus moves to deliver the troubled man. The demons recognize that Jesus is not just another exorcist but the One God has anointed to break the rule of Satan.

One might think that Jesus would appreciate some free promotion before the synagogue crowd (v. 24). The unclean spirit is correct, but Jesus has no interest in demonic testimony.

1:29–31 An alternate rendering of v. 31, "the fever forsook her," suggests that the cause of the fever was supernatural. What is significant is Jesus' miraculous ability to extinguish an otherworldly fire—something that only God or God's agent could do.

home of Simon and Andrew. 30Simon's
mother-in-law was in bed with a fever,
and they immediately told Jesus about
her. 31So he went to her, took her hand
and helped her up.[b] The fever left her
and she began to wait on them.
32That evening after sunset the people
brought to Jesus all the sick and demon-
possessed.[c] 33The whole town gathered at
the door, 34and Jesus healed many who had
various diseases.[d] He also drove out many
demons, but he would not let the demons
speak because they knew who he was.[e]

Jesus Prays in a Solitary Place

1:35–38pp // Lk 4:42,43

35Very early in the morning, while it
was still dark, Jesus got up, left the house
and went off to a solitary place, where he
prayed.[f] 36Simon and his companions
went to look for him, 37and when they
found him, they exclaimed: "Everyone
is looking for you!"
38Jesus replied, "Let us go somewhere
else — to the nearby villages — so I can
preach there also. That is why I have
come."[g] 39So he traveled throughout
Galilee, preaching in their synagogues[h]
and driving out demons.[i]

Jesus Heals a Man With Leprosy

1:40–44pp // Mt 8:2–4; Lk 5:12–14

40A man with leprosy[a] came to him
and begged him on his knees,[j] "If you are
willing, you can make me clean."
41Jesus was indignant.[b] He reached
out his hand and touched the man. "I
am willing," he said. "Be clean!" 42Im-
mediately the leprosy left him and he
was cleansed.
43Jesus sent him away at once with a
strong warning: 44"See that you don't
tell this to anyone.[k] But go, show yourself to the priest[l] and offer the sacrifices
that Moses commanded for your cleansing,[m] as a testimony to them." 45Instead
he went out and began to talk freely,
spreading the news. As a result, Jesus
could no longer enter a town openly
but stayed outside in lonely places.[n]

1:31 [b] Lk 7:14
1:32 [c] Mt 4:24
1:34 [d] Mt 4:23 [e] Mk 3:12; Ac 16:17,18
1:35 [f] Lk 3:21
1:38 [g] Isa 61:1
1:39 [h] Mt 4:23 [i] Mt 4:24
1:40 [j] Mk 10:17
1:44 [k] Mt 8:4 [l] Lev 13:49 [m] Lev 14:1-32
1:45 [n] Lk 5:15,16

[a] *40* The Greek word traditionally translated *leprosy* was used for various diseases affecting the skin. [b] *41* Many manuscripts *Jesus was filled with compassion*

1:32–34 Jesus' healing miracles do not simply remedy human physical maladies; they represent a war against demonic forces.

1:35–37 Jesus' desire for secluded prayer makes it plain that Jesus is not a sorcerer working by magic independent of God's help. His authority, strength, and power come from God alone.

1:38–39 Jesus is not interested in the fleeting praise of crowds and refuses to go back to Capernaum because he needs to move on—he is to preach to all Israel. The Good News cannot be static: Jesus keeps his bags packed throughout the Gospel. He will not be distracted from his divine purpose, even by success, and will not remain in one place as a localized guru or healer.

1:40–42 Jesus is not annoyed at the man for breaking the ritual barriers that bar him from any contact with others. Jesus' being "indignant" may involve expressing the anger of God toward the ravages of the disease. His compassion for the man is expressed in his touch, probably the first time another "clean" human has touched this social outcast in a long time. He also commands him to "be clean." At Jesus' word, the leprosy leaves the man immediately.

1:43–45 Mark 1 records the first of Jesus' frequent commands to demons and to those whom he healed to keep silent (cf. vv. 25, 34). The command makes clear that Jesus has no interest in taking on the role of a celebrity healer. He knows that God's power is not revealed solely through miracles. That power will become clearest in his crucifixion and resurrection, but those who want only miracles can see virtually nothing of the true nature of Jesus' work.

Jesus also prefers to keep the news of his miracles quiet so that it will give him more time to plant the word of truth and put off his inevitable destruction by the powers that be. Whenever someone disobeys the command to be quiet, the next scene begins by mentioning the crush of the crowds. Ironically, Jesus' attempts to cloak himself in secrecy only serve to magnify his reputation.

Further, as far as Mark is concerned, Jesus' prioritizing secrecy makes it clear that any charges of rebellion made against Jesus are false. Consequently, Rome has no reason to fear him as a "king of the Jews," someone who is intent on inciting an uprising of the people.

Finally, the failure to hush those who are healed reveals that the news of his power to heal is not something that can be kept hidden. One cannot keep silent, and the Good News will spread to the ends of the earth.

1:16–45 The call and the instant response of these fishermen (vv. 16–20) reveal something of what discipleship to Jesus entails. This should shatter our comfortable world of middle-class discipleship. Few would make the radical commitment these first disciples made. Most wish Jesus offered an easier version of discipleship. But our calling today remains no less urgent. Around the world, Christians are abandoning position, wealth, and family for the cause of Christ; those of us in North America should act out of the same sense of sacrifice and commitment based on our gratitude to God for his forgiveness in Jesus.

Yet the people still came to him from
everywhere.[o]

Jesus Forgives and Heals a Paralyzed Man

2:3–12pp // Mt 9:2–8; Lk 5:18–26

2 A few days later, when Jesus again entered Capernaum, the people heard
that he had come home. 2They gathered
in such large numbers[p] that there was no
room left, not even outside the door, and
he preached the word to them. 3Some
men came, bringing to him a paralyzed
man,[q] carried by four of them. 4Since
they could not get him to Jesus because
of the crowd, they made an opening in
the roof above Jesus by digging through
it and then lowered the mat the man was
lying on. 5When Jesus saw their faith, he
said to the paralyzed man, "Son, your
sins are forgiven."[r]
6Now some teachers of the law were
sitting there, thinking to themselves,
7"Why does this fellow talk like that? He's
blaspheming! Who can forgive sins but
God alone?"[s]
8Immediately Jesus knew in his spirit
that this was what they were thinking in
their hearts, and he said to them, "Why
are you thinking these things? 9Which
is easier: to say to this paralyzed man,
'Your sins are forgiven,' or to say, 'Get up,
take your mat and walk'? 10But I want
you to know that the Son of Man[t] has
authority on earth to forgive sins." So
he said to the man, 11"I tell you, get up,
take your mat and go home." 12He got
up, took his mat and walked out in full
view of them all. This amazed everyone
and they praised God,[u] saying, "We have
never seen anything like this!"[v]

1:45 [o] Mk 2:13; Lk 5:17; Jn 6:2
2:2 [p] ver 13; Mk 1:45
2:3 [q] Mt 4:24
2:5 [r] Lk 7:48
2:7 [s] Isa 43:25
2:10 [t] Mt 8:20
2:12 [u] Mt 9:8 [v] Mt 9:33
2:13 [w] Mk 1:45; Lk 5:15; Jn 6:2
2:14 [x] Mt 4:19

Mk 2:3 ❖ To what lengths will we go to bring a friend to Jesus?

Jesus Calls Levi and Eats With Sinners

2:14–17pp // Mt 9:9–13; Lk 5:27–32

13Once again Jesus went out beside the
lake. A large crowd came to him,[w] and
he began to teach them. 14As he walked
along, he saw Levi son of Alphaeus sitting at the tax collector's booth. "Follow
me,"[x] Jesus told him, and Levi got up and
followed him.
15While Jesus was having dinner at
Levi's house, many tax collectors and
sinners were eating with him and his
disciples, for there were many who followed him. 16When the teachers of the

---

2:1–4 The crowd is only one of the obstacles that needs to be overcome for the man who is disabled to be healed. As the story progresses, the reader learns of two other obstacles: the suspicion of the teachers of the law and the potential hesitancy of the man to act on Jesus' command.

2:5 Jesus recognizes that only a tenacious faith would have led these men to go to so much trouble. The merciful granting of their request comes when Jesus announces to the disabled man, "Your sins are forgiven."

2:6–7 The teachers of the law, whose "sitting" contrasts with the active demonstration of faith of the men on the roof, ask themselves, "What possible redemptive authority can this man have?"

2:8–9 Jesus skirts the issue of blasphemy with a riddling question of his own.

2:10–11 Jesus commands the disabled man to get up and walk so all who see may know that the Son of Man has authority to forgive sins. The leaders' alarm is not misplaced; Jesus does presume to forgive sins on the basis of grace. How can Jesus speak for God in such startling and untraditional ways? The crucifixion will clarify this matter.

In Jesus' climactic announcement he refers to himself as "the Son of Man" (v. 10). In Mark, this title most adequately expresses who Jesus is. Although the term Son of Man is undefined, we do learn what he does: He has authority to forgive sins; he is Lord of the Sabbath; he will be betrayed, suffer humiliation and death, and be raised on the third day; he comes not to be served but to give his life as a ransom for many; he will be seated at the right hand of power, return on the clouds, and gather his elect.

2:12 The final obstacle to the man's healing is his own skepticism. It is overcome when the man displays the same faith as his friends by obeying Jesus' command and goes out before the whole crowd, his mat tucked under his arm.

✤ **2:1-12** Healing involves far more than the physical dimension; it also involves mental, social, and spiritual dimensions. Faith, prayer, and a deep sense of the forgiveness of sins are essential elements of discipleship to Jesus. He has come to inaugurate the kingdom of God and make his people whole—if not in the present age, then certainly in the resurrection and the age to come.

2:13–14 Jesus once again singles out a person and challenges him to follow. This time it is a tax official: Levi son of Alphaeus. Levi, also called Matthew, is stationed at an intersection of trade routes to collect tolls, tariffs, and customs, probably for Herod Antipas. Most Jews in Jesus' day would have called Matthew a traitor for selling out his people to one who supported the Roman government.

Matthew's obedience marks an even more radical break with his past than the other disciples. The others can always go back to fishing, but a toll collector who abandons his post can never return.

2:15–17 Jesus does more than preach repentance

PEOPLE TO KNOW // **FAITHFUL FRIENDS**

MARK 2:1-12: Jesus' healing and teaching ministry ensured there were always crowds pressing in to get near him. When people in Jesus' hometown of Capernaum heard he was in a house there, they filled the house and overflowed out the door. A group of men wanted to bring their paralyzed friend to see Jesus, hoping he would be healed, but there was simply no way to get close enough.

The men devised an ambitious plan. They made an opening in the roof of the house (the owner was probably not thrilled!) and lowered their paralyzed friend down to Jesus from above (Mk 2:4). Then the Bible says an amazing thing: "When Jesus saw their faith, he said to the paralyzed man, 'Son, your sins are forgiven'" (Mk 2:5). Whose faith did Jesus see? *Theirs*! The faith of the friends led Jesus to help the paralyzed man.

The religious leaders present were furious when Jesus claimed to forgive sins. In order to demonstrate his divine authority, Jesus also told the paralyzed man to get up and walk, which he did. The people praised God for witnessing this incredible event, and the tenacious friends received the miracle they had been hoping for.

APPLICATION ✜ How far would you go to bring someone to Jesus? We all know people who need to be introduced to Christ or who need to know Christ better. The faithful friends in this story offer an inspiring picture of godly determination to bring someone to Christ. They could have looked at the crowd and given up, but only one thing mattered: bringing their friend to Jesus. Jesus rewarded them for their faith, healing and even forgiving the sins of the paralyzed man. Is Christ eager to do the same when *you* bring someone to him? Yes!

law who were Pharisees[y] saw him eating with the sinners and tax collectors, they asked his disciples: "Why does he eat with tax collectors and sinners?"[z]
17On hearing this, Jesus said to them, "It is not the healthy who need a doctor, but the sick. I have not come to call the righteous, but sinners."[a]

Jesus Questioned About Fasting

2:18–22pp // Mt 9:14–17; Lk 5:33–38

18Now John's disciples and the Pharisees were fasting.[b] Some people came and asked Jesus, "How is it that John's disciples and the disciples of the Pharisees are fasting, but yours are not?"
19Jesus answered, "How can the guests of the bridegroom fast while he is with them? They cannot, so long as they have him with them. 20But the time will come when the bridegroom will be taken from them,[c] and on that day they will fast.
21"No one sews a patch of unshrunk cloth on an old garment. Otherwise, the new piece will pull away from the old, making the tear worse. 22And no one pours new wine into old wineskins. Otherwise, the wine will burst the skins, and both the wine and the wineskins will be ruined. No, they pour new wine into new wineskins."

Jesus Is Lord of the Sabbath

2:23–28pp // Mt 12:1–8; Lk 6:1–5
3:1–6pp // Mt 12:9–14; Lk 6:6–11

23One Sabbath Jesus was going through the grainfields, and as his disciples walked along, they began to pick some heads of grain.[d] 24The Pharisees said to him, "Look, why are they doing what is unlawful on the Sabbath?"[e]

2:16 [y] Ac 23:9 [z] Mt 9:11
2:17 [a] Lk 19:10; 1Ti 1:15
2:18 [b] Mt 6:16-18; Ac 13:2
2:20 [c] Lk 17:22
2:23 [d] Dt 23:25
2:24 [e] Mt 12:2

to sinners; he befriends them. This display of open acceptance of sinners appalls the Pharisees. No physician waits for the ill to recover fully before consulting with them. As their physician, Jesus offers the remedy that defeats the illness of these so-called sinners.

2:18–22 Jesus has not come to patch up an old system that does not match the revolutionary rule of God. The old, exemplified by the practice of fasting in this debate, cannot contain the new. Both will be ruined if they are combined.

2:23–26 Jesus' response to the Pharisees' question (v. 24) recalls when David violated the law by eating the bread of the Presence (1Sa 21:6). David's personal authority legitimized his actions. The strict regulations regarding the bread of the Presence could be set aside for David, who was fleeing for his life. How much more can holy regulations be set aside for Jesus, who is in a situation of far greater urgency in proclaiming the coming of the kingdom of God?

Jesus argues that it does not violate God's will for hungry people to have something to eat on the Sabbath, even if it infringes on the Pharisees' narrow interpretation of what is permitted.

25 He answered, "Have you never read what David did when he and his companions were hungry and in need? 26 In the days of Abiathar the high priest,[f] he entered the house of God and ate the consecrated bread, which is lawful only for priests to eat.[g] And he also gave some to his companions."[h]

27 Then he said to them, "The Sabbath was made for man,[i] not man for the Sabbath.[j] 28 So the Son of Man[k] is Lord even of the Sabbath."

Jesus Heals on the Sabbath

3 Another time Jesus went into the synagogue,[l] and a man with a shriveled hand was there. 2 Some of them were looking for a reason to accuse Jesus, so they watched him closely[m] to see if he would heal him on the Sabbath.[n] 3 Jesus said to the man with the shriveled hand, "Stand up in front of everyone."

4 Then Jesus asked them, "Which is lawful on the Sabbath: to do good or to do evil, to save life or to kill?" But they remained silent.

5 He looked around at them in anger and, deeply distressed at their stubborn hearts, said to the man, "Stretch out your hand." He stretched it out, and his hand was completely restored. 6 Then the Pharisees went out and began to plot with the Herodians[o] how they might kill Jesus.[p]

Crowds Follow Jesus

3:7–12pp // Mt 12:15,16; Lk 6:17–19

7 Jesus withdrew with his disciples to the lake, and a large crowd from Galilee followed.[q] 8 When they heard about all he was doing, many people came to him from Judea, Jerusalem, Idumea, and the regions across the Jordan and around Tyre and Sidon.[r] 9 Because of the crowd he told his disciples to have a small boat ready for him, to keep the people from crowding him. 10 For he had healed many,[s] so that those with diseases were pushing forward to touch him.[t] 11 Whenever the impure spirits saw him, they fell down before him and cried out, "You are the Son of God."[u] 12 But he gave them strict orders not to tell others about him.[v]

Jesus Appoints the Twelve

3:16–19pp // Mt 10:2–4; Lk 6:14–16; Ac 1:13

13 Jesus went up on a mountainside and called to him those he wanted,

2:26 [f] 1Ch 24:6; 2Sa 8:17 [g] Lev 24:5-9 [h] 1Sa 21:1-6
2:27 [i] Ex 23:12; Dt 5:14 [j] Col 2:16
2:28 [k] Mt 8:20
3:1 [l] Mt 4:23; Mk 1:21
3:2 [m] Mt 12:10 [n] Lk 14:1
3:6 [o] Mt 22:16; Mk 12:13 [p] Mt 12:14
3:7 [q] Mt 4:25
3:8 [r] Mt 11:21
3:10 [s] Mt 4:23 [t] Mt 9:20
3:11 [u] Mt 4:3; Mk 1:23,24
3:12 [v] Mt 8:4; Mk 1:24,25,34; Ac 16:17,18

2:27-28 The third part of the argument consists of the climactic announcement that the Son of Man is Lord of the Sabbath. This statement boldly affirms that the Son of Man is the One who decrees what is lawful and unlawful, permissible and impermissible. Any customs enforced by the Pharisees or their traditions are rendered null and void.
3:1-2 The second controversy over the Sabbath exposes the true nature of Jesus' opponents. It begins with the notice that they are treacherously inspecting his every move. The Pharisees want to see if he will heal on the Sabbath and violate their interpretation of the Law. A Sabbath violation, just like blasphemy, was punishable by death. The segment ends with the Pharisees joining forces with the Herodians to plot his death (v. 6).
3:3-4 With his defiant question, Jesus frames the issue around doing good or doing evil, saving life or destroying it. The question contains its own answer: doing good is not to be limited to certain days.
3:5 Healing by speaking is not a breach of the Sabbath. Jesus only violates the Pharisees' finespun interpretation of the Law.
3:6 These critics are so blindly cynical that they are furious when Jesus does good and saves a life on a holy day, but they have no qualms about doing harm and plotting a murder on that very same day with the secular powers that be.

✣ **2:13—3:6** Other religions are the result of a human search for God; the Christian faith presents itself as God's search for humans—even those the world considers the most unworthy. Many Christians today do not recognize that they harbor the very same attitude as these first-century Pharisees. We sing "Amazing grace . . . that saved a wretch like me," but we may have in mind only "our kind" of wretches. It may be too amazing for us that the same grace is extended to save those whom we believe truly deserve punishment.

It is one thing to go to them to witness to them; it is quite another to treat them as if they were in some way respectable and acceptable—persons whom God loves and extends forgiveness to. Yet this is precisely what Jesus did, and by so doing he makes it clear that one cannot win people with whom one is not willing to eat. The religiosity of the Pharisees is therefore something we must guard against in our own hearts.

3:7-10 Jesus' surging popularity threatens to undermine the Jewish leaders' leverage with the crowds.
3:11-12 The unclean spirits continue to know Jesus immediately, fall before him in surrender, and blurt out his identity. The translation, "He gave them strict orders," is frequently translated "rebuke." Jesus also "rebukes" the wind and sea to "be still" (4:39), and the muzzling of the demons, like the calming of the storm, is a sign that Jesus has authority over them.
3:13 Jesus' call creates a distinction between the

> **Mk 3:14–15** ❖ Jesus gives his followers power and authority to spread his message. How does the power of Christ work within us?

and they came to him.[w] 14He appointed twelve[a][x] that they might be with him and that he might send them out to preach 15and to have authority to drive out demons.[y] 16These are the twelve he appointed: Simon (to whom he gave the name Peter),[z] 17James son of Zebedee and his brother John (to them he gave the name Boanerges, which means "sons of thunder"), 18Andrew, Philip, Bartholomew, Matthew, Thomas, James son of Alphaeus, Thaddaeus, Simon the Zealot 19and Judas Iscariot, who betrayed him.

Jesus Accused by His Family and by Teachers of the Law

3:23–27pp // Mt 12:25–29; Lk 11:17–22
3:31–35pp // Mt 12:46–50; Lk 8:19–21

20Then Jesus entered a house, and again a crowd gathered,[a] so that he and his disciples were not even able to eat.[b] 21When his family[b] heard about this, they went to take charge of him, for they said, "He is out of his mind."[c]

22And the teachers of the law who came down from Jerusalem[d] said, "He is possessed by Beelzebul![e] By the prince of demons he is driving out demons."[f]

23So Jesus called them over to him and began to speak to them in parables:[g] "How can Satan[h] drive out Satan? 24If a kingdom is divided against itself, that kingdom cannot stand. 25If a house is divided against itself, that house cannot stand. 26And if Satan opposes himself and is divided, he cannot stand; his end has come. 27In fact, no one can enter a strong man's house without first tying him up. Then he can plunder the strong man's house.[i] 28Truly I tell you, people can be forgiven all their sins and every slander they utter, 29but whoever blasphemes against the Holy Spirit will never be forgiven; they are guilty of an eternal sin."[j]

30He said this because they were saying, "He has an impure spirit."

31Then Jesus' mother and brothers arrived.[k] Standing outside, they sent someone in to call him. 32A crowd was sitting around him, and they told him, "Your mother and brothers are outside looking for you."

3:13 [w] Mt 5:1
3:14 [x] Mk 6:30
3:15 [y] Mt 10:1
3:16 [z] Jn 1:42
3:20 [a] ver 7 [b] Mk 6:31
3:21 [c] Jn 10:20; Ac 26:24
3:22 [d] Mt 15:1 [e] Mt 10:25; 11:18; 12:24; Jn 7:20; 8:48,52; 10:20 [f] Mt 9:34
3:23 [g] Mk 4:2 [h] Mt 4:10
3:27 [i] Isa 49:24, 25
3:29 [j] Mt 12:31, 32; Lk 12:10
3:31 [k] ver 21

[a] 14 Some manuscripts *twelve — designating them apostles —* [b] 21 Or *his associates*

---

crowd and those who are summoned to follow after him as disciples with a particular task.

3:14–15 The Twelve have symbolic significance as a restoration of the twelve tribes of Israel, and Jesus stands over them as leader. Jesus' choosing the Twelve also implicitly renounces the leadership in Jerusalem.

The mission of the Twelve is twofold. Mark stresses the disciples' task of being "with [Jesus]." What does that mean? Most important, it denotes the Twelve as the witnesses to his ministry, who have learned from him and are qualified to pass on and verify what has been said about him. Their second task is to extend Jesus' work by preaching and casting out demons.

3:16–19 As he introduces the Twelve, Mark leaves no doubt as to the guilt of Judas (v. 19).

3:20–35 This segment is the first example of Mark's technique of bracketing (or "sandwiching"), where the narration begins with one story but is interrupted by another before it is concluded. This technique allows the two separate stories to make a similar point. Both Jesus' closest relations and the theological specialists from Jerusalem offer mistaken ideas about Jesus.

3:20–21, 31–35 Jesus' mother and his brothers are not making a friendly visit but want to "take charge of him" (v. 21). Jesus' response to the visit from his family would have been a shock to those who first heard it. One's family was one's life, and to reject family or to be cast out of the family was to lose one's life.

But Jesus affirms that life under God is not defined by relationships in a biological family. One's ultimate devotion is owed to God, who is head of a new divine family. Becoming a member of this new family has its costs. Devotion to him is likely to bring abuse and persecution.

3:22 The scene shifts to irate teachers of the law from Jerusalem. These teachers may have concluded that one who defies traditions and who does not bend to their authority could only be an undercover agent for Satan. On the other hand, they may be venomously attempting to undermine Jesus by branding him as being in league with the devil. The latter seems to be the case since Jesus warns them against blaspheming the Spirit (v. 29).

3:23–29 Jesus speaks to them in parables; these draw out the absurdity of their accusation and open the way to the truth. If their accusation is correct, Satan is irrationally trying to do himself in. If Jesus does not work by Satan's power, however, another explanation is at hand: A stronger one has bound the strong man and is pillaging his house.

This encounter with the teachers of the law from Jerusalem marks a shift in Jesus' approach to his religious antagonists. Although he withdraws, from now on he will show no mercy to his opponents whenever they confront him—he will expose their lies and assert his authority.

33"Who are my mother and my brothers?" he asked.
34Then he looked at those seated in
a circle around him and said, "Here are
my mother and my brothers! 35Whoever
does God's will is my brother and sister
and mother."

The Parable of the Sower

4:1–12pp // Mt 13:1–15; Lk 8:4–10
4:13–20pp // Mt 13:18–23; Lk 8:11–15

4 Again Jesus began to teach by the
lake.[l] The crowd that gathered around
him was so large that he got into a boat
and sat in it out on the lake, while all the
people were along the shore at the water's
edge. 2He taught them many things by
parables,[m] and in his teaching said: 3"Listen! A farmer went out to sow his seed.[n]
4As he was scattering the seed, some fell
along the path, and the birds came and ate
it up. 5Some fell on rocky places, where it
did not have much soil. It sprang up quickly, because the soil was shallow. 6But when
the sun came up, the plants were scorched,
and they withered because they had no
root. 7Other seed fell among thorns, which
grew up and choked the plants, so that
they did not bear grain. 8Still other seed
fell on good soil. It came up, grew and
produced a crop, some multiplying thirty, some sixty, some a hundred times."[o]
9Then Jesus said, "Whoever has ears
to hear, let them hear."[p]
10When he was alone, the Twelve and
the others around him asked him about
the parables. 11He told them, "The secret
of the kingdom of God[q] has been given to
you. But to those on the outside[r] everything is said in parables 12so that,

"'they may be ever seeing but never
perceiving,
and ever hearing but never
understanding;
otherwise they might turn and be
forgiven!'[a]"[s]

4:1 [l] Mk 2:13; 3:7
4:2 [m] ver 11; Mk 3:23
4:3 [n] ver 26
4:8 [o] Jn 15:5; Col 1:6
4:9 [p] ver 23; Mt 11:15
4:11 [q] Mt 3:2 [r] 1Co 5:12, 13; Col 4:5; 1Th 4:12; 1Ti 3:7
4:12 [s] Isa 6:9,10; Mt 13:13-15

[a] 12 Isaiah 6:9,10

3:7-35 Jesus' definition of the family may create problems for many individuals. The commitment to do the will of God may force some to make a wrenching choice between their biological family and their devotion God. While some may be forced to disengage from close family relationships that would strangle their commitment to God, we as Christians still need to be in relationships with people who are committed to us and we to them. We were created not to live alone but to live in families.

Jesus' words about the family can therefore become good news for everyone. If the church takes seriously Jesus' ideal of what the family is, this requires more than sharing a row of seats on Sunday morning and fellowship afterward. Instead, we as Christians are to invite other Christians to become our parents, our children, our siblings. The church is to take those who know the hurt of the world and bring them into the healing of community acceptance.

4:1-9 The farmer in this parable is cultivating marginal ground and laboring against challenging odds, so the rate of failure is not surprising. Given the nature of the land, the average farmer meets with frustration and failure, but in the end, they do receive a reward for their labors—a harvest where the seed has prospered in good soil. Jesus implies in the parable that he fully expects his Good News to meet with failure and success, but he focuses more attention on the reasons for the failure than the reasons for success.

Just as the field has different yields, the parable yields several points.

4:3 Jesus comes as the end-time farmer of God. The metaphor of planting takes on the greatest significance in that it implies that Jesus comes to renew Israel, and how one responds to his teaching decides whether one will be included or excluded.

4:4-7 The sower sows liberally even in unfruitful ground in hope of a harvest. Just as God sends rain on the righteous and the unrighteous (Mt 5:45), so also Jesus sows his word on good and bad soil. The parable therefore depicts a generous sower who excludes no one on principle.

4:8-9 The parable affirms that the farmer will have a harvest from good soil, and reveals that the kingdom of God does not come in one fell swoop, which instantly upends the old age. Evil does not vanish with the coming of the Messiah, and people do not universally respond.

The parable also makes clear that fruit bearing is an essential mark of the kingdom of God. The text mentions fruit bearing before the growth.

4:10-11 The term "secret" refers to a heavenly truth that is concealed from human understanding but is made known by God. Those who possess the secret of the kingdom will eventually be able to see what others cannot: The kingdom of God is advancing not just through miracles but also through suffering and persecution. Only in its final stage will it be publicly visible for all to see.

The phrase "in parables" in v. 11 takes on a different meaning from "by parables" in v. 2. It now means "bewildering puzzles." Jesus' revelation confuses the hardened, shallow, and indifferent mind; these persons suffer not from a thick skull but a hardened heart. Disciples are not more insightful than others: The mystery is something that is "given" to them. Their understanding comes by grace as Jesus' interpretation unlocks the mystery for them.

4:12 God told Isaiah the prophet to preach despite warning him in advance that it would only harden

JERUSALEM DURING THE MINISTRY OF JESUS

Herod the Great (reigned 37–4 BC) rebuilt the temple and its surrounding walls and also built a palace, a fortress, a theater and a hippodrome (stadium) for horse and chariot races. He brought the city to the zenith of its architectural beauty and Roman cultural expression. This became Jerusalem in the time of Jesus.

1 The "**FIRST WALL**," so named by Josephus, encircled the city during the Hasmonean period, which began in 167 BC. After the revolt led by Judas Maccabeus in 167, Jerusalem expanded steadily in a period of independence under its own Jewish kings.

2 The "**SECOND WALL**" was built by Herod the Great or by earlier Hasmonean kings. Precise location is difficult to determine. This wall was put up around a market area in a valley, protecting it from raiding and looting, but was of questionable military value. At its eastern end, however, Herod built a military barracks (Antonia Fortress).

3 The "**THIRD WALL**" (shown with red line) was begun by Herod Agrippa I between AD 41 and 44 to enclose the growing northern suburbs, but the work was apparently stopped. Its construction was resumed, in haste, only after the First Jewish Revolt broke out in AD 66.

4 House of Caiaphas the high priest,* identified here with today's Church of St. Peter in Gallicantu.

5 Deep valleys on the east, south and west permitted urban expansion only to the north.

6 Maximum city growth within walls by AD 70.

7 Archaeological excavations have revealed a monumental stairway and the continuation of Tyropoeon Street,*** which lies along the valley called "Valley of the Cheesemongers" by Josephus.

8 The Siloam aqueduct-tunnel, 1,749' long, was cut through solid bedrock, was 5'11" high (average) and followed an "S" shaped course made necessary by engineering difficulties. It was dug by order of King Hezekiah and provided water during King Sennacherib's threat to lay siege to the city in 701 BC (2Ch 32:30). Water flows through it to this very day.

* Location generally known, but style of architecture is unknown; artist's concept only, and Roman architecture is assumed.
** Location and architecture unknown, but referred to in written history; shown here for illustrative purposes.
*** Ancient feature has remained, or appearance has been determined from evidence.

13Then Jesus said to them, "Don't you
understand this parable? How then
will you understand any parable? 14The
farmer sows the word.[t] 15Some people
are like seed along the path, where the
word is sown. As soon as they hear it,
Satan[u] comes and takes away the word
that was sown in them. 16Others, like
seed sown on rocky places, hear the
word and at once receive it with joy. 17But
since they have no root, they last only a
short time. When trouble or persecution
comes because of the word, they quickly
fall away. 18Still others, like seed sown
among thorns, hear the word; 19but the
worries of this life, the deceitfulness of
wealth[v] and the desires for other things
come in and choke the word, making it
unfruitful. 20Others, like seed sown on
good soil, hear the word, accept it, and
produce a crop — some thirty, some sixty,
some a hundred times what was sown."

A Lamp on a Stand

21He said to them, "Do you bring in
a lamp to put it under a bowl or a bed?
Instead, don't you put it on its stand?[w]
22For whatever is hidden is meant to be
disclosed, and whatever is concealed is
meant to be brought out into the open.[x]
23If anyone has ears to hear, let them
hear."[y]

4:14 [t] Mk 16:20; Lk 1:2; Ac 4:31; 8:4; 16:6; 17:11; Php 1:14
4:15 [u] Mt 4:10
4:19 [v] Mt 19:23; 1Ti 6:9,10,17; 1Jn 2:15-17
4:21 [w] Mt 5:15
4:22 [x] Jer 16:17; Mt 10:26; Lk 8:17; 12:2
4:23 [y] ver 9; Mt 11:15
4:24 [z] Mt 7:2; Lk 6:38
4:25 [a] Mt 13:12; 25:29
4:26 [b] Mt 13:24
4:29 [c] Rev 14:15
4:30 [d] Mt 13:24

Mk 4:34 ❖ Parables are common stories that lead us to discover their deeper meaning. Why did Jesus favor this method of teaching?

24"Consider carefully what you hear,"
he continued. "With the measure you
use, it will be measured to you — and
even more.[z] 25Whoever has will be given
more; whoever does not have, even what
they have will be taken from them."[a]

The Parable of the Growing Seed

26He also said, "This is what the kingdom of God is like.[b] A man scatters seed
on the ground. 27Night and day, whether
he sleeps or gets up, the seed sprouts and
grows, though he does not know how.
28All by itself the soil produces grain —
first the stalk, then the head, then the
full kernel in the head. 29As soon as the
grain is ripe, he puts the sickle to it, because the harvest has come."[c]

The Parable of the Mustard Seed

4:30–32pp // Mt 13:31,32; Lk 13:18,19

30Again he said, "What shall we say the
kingdom of God is like,[d] or what parable
shall we use to describe it? 31It is like a
mustard seed, which is the smallest of
all seeds on earth. 32Yet when planted,

---

the hearts of the hearers. Jesus' explanation for the parables has the same ironic tone.

4:13 Disciples are no different from anyone else in needing explanations for the parables, but they are different from outsiders in that they choose to come to Jesus for explanations. However, insiders must watch how they listen. So-called insiders can become outsiders; otherwise there would be no reason to caution them to pay attention to how they listen so that they can discern what lies hidden beneath the surface.

4:14–20 The context in Mark assumes that there can be no understanding without interpretation, and Jesus provides one for those who ask. As the seed fails in three different ways in the bad soils, it succeeds in three different ways in good soil, but the parable and interpretation do not expand on the reasons for this varying success.

✣ **4:1–20** We can apply the parable to our own responsibility to receive the Word as good soil receives seed. Soil is unable to change its character, but humans can change theirs. Sometimes we can be like the hardened soil on the path: Nothing sinks in. Sometimes we are in danger of becoming like the shallow soil: Any hint of persecution or tribulation shrivels any faith we might have. Another danger is that of materialism, which cramps faith. We live in a narcissistic age that can trip us up at every turn, which is why believers must focus on carefully cultivating the seeds of God's Word in our hearts and lives.

4:21–23 The parable of the lamp affirms that God's purpose is not to shroud the light in darkness but to make it visible to all.

4:24–25 The parable of the measure refers to the ways people respond to the light. The one who snubs it has everything to lose; the one who risks faith in what now lies hidden has everything to gain.

4:26–29 The seed holds within itself the secret of its growth, and the earth is said to produce "all by itself." What has transpired under the ground will eventually become visible. This parable is linked closely to the parable of the mustard seed, and like the preceding parables of the lamp and measure, they help interpret one another. Both parables address the deceptive insignificance of the coming of the kingdom before its final manifestation.

4:30–32 The tiny seed has a power within itself to grow into something that one cannot ignore. The kingdom of God is already present in the work of Jesus but remains concealed and modest. Many would never guess that this inconspicuous presence will reach out to all the nations of the world.

it grows and becomes the largest of all
garden plants, with such big branches
that the birds can perch in its shade."
33With many similar parables Jesus
spoke the word to them, as much as they
could understand.[e] 34He did not say anything to them without using a parable.[f]
But when he was alone with his own disciples, he explained everything.

Jesus Calms the Storm

4:35–41pp // Mt 8:18,23–27; Lk 8:22–25

35That day when evening came, he said
to his disciples, "Let us go over to the
other side." 36Leaving the crowd behind,
they took him along, just as he was, in
the boat.[g] There were also other boats
with him. 37A furious squall came up, and
the waves broke over the boat, so that it
was nearly swamped. 38Jesus was in the
stern, sleeping on a cushion. The disciples woke him and said to him, "Teacher,
don't you care if we drown?"
39He got up, rebuked the wind and said
to the waves, "Quiet! Be still!" Then the
wind died down and it was completely
calm.
40He said to his disciples, "Why are you
so afraid? Do you still have no faith?"[h]
41They were terrified and asked each
other, "Who is this? Even the wind and
the waves obey him!"

Jesus Restores a Demon-Possessed Man

5:1–17pp // Mt 8:28–34; Lk 8:26–37
5:18–20pp // Lk 8:38,39

5 They went across the lake to the region of the Gerasenes.[a] 2When Jesus
got out of the boat,[i] a man with an impure spirit[j] came from the tombs to meet
him. 3This man lived in the tombs, and
no one could bind him anymore, not
even with a chain. 4For he had often been
chained hand and foot, but he tore the
chains apart and broke the irons on his
feet. No one was strong enough to subdue him. 5Night and day among the
tombs and in the hills he would cry out
and cut himself with stones.
6When he saw Jesus from a distance,
he ran and fell on his knees in front of

4:33 [e] Jn 16:12
4:34 [f] Jn 16:25
4:36 [g] ver 1; Mk 3:9; 5:2,21; 6:32,45
4:40 [h] Mt 14:31; Mk 16:14
5:2 [i] Mk 4:1 [j] Mk 1:23

[a] 1 Some manuscripts *Gadarenes*; other manuscripts *Gergesenes*

4:33–34 To understand the parables requires more than intellectual comprehension; it requires submitting to the Word in one's heart. Jesus uses parables to measure the spiritual perception of the audience because he knows that a Messiah who dies can only be perceived through a rare spiritual discernment.

> **4:21-34** These parables should instill confidence that overcomes despair. When we cannot see what transpires under the ground as the seed winters in the earth, we can become discouraged. Observers can easily write off this movement, particularly in our hurried, results-oriented age that demands immediate gratification. The slightest failure may drive us to a sense of hopelessness. The parables assure us that when we sow God's seed, it will accomplish its purpose. We may not be the ones who harvest the bounty, but it is not our harvest (1Co 3:6–9): It belongs to God.

4:35–38a The fishermen in the group are presumably expert mariners. Ironically, they are the ones who are terrified by the unexpected storm; Jesus, the carpenter, sleeps serenely. Jesus is physically exhausted. Those attuned to Scripture, however, catch a deeper significance behind his peaceful slumber. Jesus' sleep amid a raging storm is a sign of his trust in God, which contrasts with the terror of the disciples.
4:38b The disciples interpret Jesus' untroubled sleep as a sign of his indifference to their safety. They awaken him as if he were in some way responsible for their situation.

4:39 Jesus answers their anxious cries by rebuking the wind with a word. If the disciples only understood that they had set to sea with One who has such power, they would confess that all their fears were unfounded.
4:40–41 Faith is not something that is inborn; it can ebb and flow, depending on circumstances. Despite the disciples' fear and lack of faith, Jesus muzzles the storm and preserves their lives. The disciples' fear intensifies as it shifts to the person with them in the boat. The disciples' awe is appropriate, but they still have only the vaguest idea of who Jesus is and how he exercises such power.

> **4:35–41** Reading Mark helps us learn to trust in a Savior who does not deliver us *from* storms but *through* our storms. The Christian faith is not a refuge from the uncertainties and insecurities of the world; we can only find security with Jesus. Christians know that Jesus has beaten down the savage storms of life and carried us through, and the believer has no reason to fear anything from nature or the supernatural, from life or death (see Ro 8:31–39).

5:1–5 These demons do not cower in fear but rather cause the man to rush at Jesus. The Greek phrase used in v. 4 is used for taming a wild animal and could also be translated, "No one was able to tame him." People treat this man like a wild animal, and he acts like one. Evil spirits always deface humanity and destroy life.
5:6–8 In their desperate attempt to resist any exorcism, the demons are momentarily successful

him. 7He shouted at the top of his voice,
"What do you want with me,[k] Jesus, Son
of the Most High God?[l] In God's name
don't torture me!" 8For Jesus had said
to him, "Come out of this man, you impure spirit!"
9Then Jesus asked him, "What is your
name?"
"My name is Legion,"[m] he replied, "for
we are many." 10And he begged Jesus
again and again not to send them out
of the area.
11A large herd of pigs was feeding
on the nearby hillside. 12The demons
begged Jesus, "Send us among the pigs;
allow us to go into them." 13He gave them
permission, and the impure spirits came
out and went into the pigs. The herd,
about two thousand in number, rushed
down the steep bank into the lake and
were drowned.
14Those tending the pigs ran off and reported this in the town and countryside,
and the people went out to see what had
happened. 15When they came to Jesus,
they saw the man who had been possessed by the legion[n] of demons,[o] sitting
there, dressed and in his right mind; and
they were afraid. 16Those who had seen
it told the people what had happened to
the demon-possessed man — and told
about the pigs as well. 17Then the people began to plead with Jesus to leave
their region.
18As Jesus was getting into the boat,
the man who had been demon-possessed

5:7 [k]Mt 8:29 [l]Mt 4:3; Lk 1:32; 6:35; Ac 16:17; Heb 7:1
5:9 [m]ver 15
5:15 [n]ver 9 [o]ver 16,18; Mt 4:24
5:19 [p]Mt 8:4
5:20 [q]Mt 4:25; Mk 7:31
5:21 [r]Mt 9:1 [s]Mk 4:1
5:22 [t]ver 35, 36,38; Lk 13:14; Ac 13:15; 18:8,17
5:23 [u]Mt 19:13; Mk 6:5; 7:32; 8:23; 16:18; Lk 4:40; 13:13; Ac 6:6
5:25 [v]Lev 15:25-30

Mk 5:19 ❖ Jesus did not tell the healed demoniac to wait until he had a deeper understanding of God before he shared his story. What might keep us from telling people about how much God has done for us and how he has shown mercy to us?

begged to go with him. 19Jesus did not let
him, but said, "Go home to your own people and tell them[p] how much the Lord
has done for you, and how he has had
mercy on you." 20So the man went away
and began to tell in the Decapolis[a][q] how
much Jesus had done for him. And all
the people were amazed.

Jesus Raises a Dead Girl and Heals a Sick Woman

5:22–43pp // Mt 9:18–26; Lk 8:41–56

21When Jesus had again crossed over
by boat to the other side of the lake,[r] a
large crowd gathered around him while
he was by the lake.[s] 22Then one of the
synagogue leaders,[t] named Jairus, came,
and when he saw Jesus, he fell at his feet.
23He pleaded earnestly with him, "My
little daughter is dying. Please come
and put your hands on[u] her so that she
will be healed and live." 24So Jesus went
with him.
A large crowd followed and pressed
around him. 25And a woman was there
who had been subject to bleeding[v] for

[a] *20* That is, the Ten Cities

---

in creating a standoff. As an evasive tactic, the demonized man falls before Jesus as his possessing spirits use deception to persuade Jesus to leave them alone.

5:9-10 Jesus seems to block these diversionary tactics by asking for the demon's name. The evil spirits give a number for a name (v. 9), the number in a Roman regiment (consisting of six thousand foot soldiers and 120 horsemen).

5:11-13 The evil spirits request to be sent into an enormously large herd of pigs feeding on the hillside. Jesus seems all too gracious in granting the request, but it leads to a surprise ending. From a Jewish perspective, the scene is a joke: Unclean spirits and unclean animals are both wiped out in one fell swoop, and a human being is cleansed.

5:14-17 The demons had begged Jesus to let them stay in the region; the townspeople now beg Jesus to leave. This is another example of the outsiders who see but do not see, who hear but do not hear.

5:18-20 Jesus may grant the community's wishes for him to personally leave, but he leaves this disturbing evidence of his presence. The upshot is that the preaching of the gospel about Jesus expands into the Decapolis.

5:1-20 We may see a mirror of ourselves in this disturbed man—beaten down by others, divided against ourselves, a civil war raging inside, living among the gloomy tombs of life, and feeling all alone. If we can recognize ourselves in this tortured man, we can also see that deliverance is not something that someone else needs—no, the power of the gospel is also for us. We may be just as battered by life, though we may do a better job of hiding it behind our coherent words, our well-kept homes, and our smart clothes.

5:21-24 A synagogue official begs Jesus to heal his daughter. Jesus agrees.

5:25-28 Jesus' rush to the girl's side is interrupted by an anonymous woman. She is so desperate to be healed she sneaks up to touch Jesus' garments, hoping the touch will restore her to health.

This woman suffers physically, living every day with the signs of her mortality as the blood that

twelve years. 26She had suffered a great
deal under the care of many doctors and
had spent all she had, yet instead of getting better she grew worse. 27When she
heard about Jesus, she came up behind
him in the crowd and touched his cloak,
28because she thought, "If I just touch
his clothes,[w] I will be healed." 29Imme-
diately her bleeding stopped and she
felt in her body that she was freed from
her suffering.[x]

30At once Jesus realized that power[y] had gone out from him. He turned
around in the crowd and asked, "Who
touched my clothes?"

31"You see the people crowding against
you," his disciples answered, "and yet
you can ask, 'Who touched me?' "

32But Jesus kept looking around to
see who had done it. 33Then the woman, knowing what had happened to her,
came and fell at his feet and, trembling
with fear, told him the whole truth. 34He
said to her, "Daughter, your faith has
healed you.[z] Go in peace[a] and be freed
from your suffering."

35While Jesus was still speaking, some
people came from the house of Jairus,
the synagogue leader.[b] "Your daughter is
dead," they said. "Why bother the teacher
anymore?"

36Overhearing[a] what they said, Jesus
told him, "Don't be afraid; just believe."

37He did not let anyone follow him except Peter, James and John the brother of
James.[c] 38When they came to the home
of the synagogue leader,[d] Jesus saw a
commotion, with people crying and wailing loudly. 39He went in and said to them,
"Why all this commotion and wailing?
The child is not dead but asleep."[e] 40But
they laughed at him.

After he put them all out, he took the
child's father and mother and the disciples who were with him, and went in
where the child was. 41He took her by the
hand[f] and said to her, *"Talitha koum!"*
(which means "Little girl, I say to you,
get up!").[g] 42Immediately the girl stood
up and began to walk around (she was
twelve years old). At this they were completely astonished. 43He gave strict orders
not to let anyone know about this,[h] and
told them to give her something to eat.

5:28 [w] Mt 9:20
5:29 [x] ver 34
5:30 [y] Lk 5:17; 6:19
5:34 [z] Mt 9:22 [a] Ac 15:33
5:35 [b] ver 22
5:37 [c] Mt 4:21
5:38 [d] ver 22
5:39 [e] Mt 9:24
5:41 [f] Mk 1:31 [g] Lk 7:14; Ac 9:40
5:43 [h] Mt 8:4
6:1 [i] Mt 2:23
6:2 [j] Mk 1:21 [k] Mt 4:23 [l] Mt 7:28

A Prophet Without Honor

6:1–6pp // Mt 13:54–58

6 Jesus left there and went to his hometown,[i] accompanied by his disciples.
2When the Sabbath came,[j] he began to
teach in the synagogue,[k] and many who
heard him were amazed.[l]

"Where did this man get these things?"
they asked. "What's this wisdom that has
been given him? What are these remarkable miracles he is performing? 3Isn't this
the carpenter? Isn't this Mary's son and
the brother of James, Joseph,[b] Judas and

[a] 36 Or *Ignoring* [b] 3 Greek *Joses*, a variant of *Joseph*

is essential for life drains from her body. She suffers socially and psychologically, knowing that she is unclean in the eyes of her religious culture. Her trouble is intensified because she has exhausted her resources in pursuing treatments that haven't worked.
5:29 When she touches Jesus, her fountain of blood stops. But just as immediately, Jesus knows that power has gone out from him (v. 30).
5:30–34 Jesus asks this woman to step out in faith and be identified. When she does, he blesses her and announces that her faith has made her well.
5:35–36 One can only guess what the distraught father must be thinking about this delay. He must also demonstrate his trust in Jesus as the worst possible news comes. Both the woman and Jairus reveal that faith trusts regardless of how hopeless the situation may seem.
5:37–40 Jairus leads Jesus to his house, but his faith is again challenged by those already assembled to mourn the little girl's death. Their skepticism puts them outside.
5:41–43 In private, Jesus grasps the little girl's hand to raise her up. In so doing, Jesus utters an ordinary phrase. The offer of food (v. 43) shows that the child is really alive.

✣ **5:21–43** The healings in these two scenes show that faith opens the door to the power of God and transfers divine power to those who are utterly powerless. Faith can be imperfect; it can be bold; it can be halting; it can be brave; it can be laced with fear and trepidation. What counts for it to be effective is for it to be directed rightly to Jesus and God.

Faith is embodied in action. Faith is something that can be seen, like the men digging through a roof to bring their friend to Jesus. It kneels, begs, and reaches out to touch. It does not wait to see if the waters will divide before stepping out. It steps out, trusting God to do what is needed. Faith is spurred on by desperation, trusting that Jesus is sufficient to meet whatever need one has, standing firm in the belief of Jesus' resurrection power.

6:1–3 A "carpenter" (v. 3) could work with wood, metal, or stone. In Jesus' context, it probably denoted a woodworking handyman. Normally a man is identified as the son of his father. Some suggest they refer to Jesus in this way because his

> **Mk 6:4** ❖ Why might it be hard for ministry workers to be accepted in their own hometown or in the church in which they were raised?

Simon?[m] Aren't his sisters here with us?"
And they took offense at him.[n]
4Jesus said to them, "A prophet is not
without honor except in his own town,
among his relatives and in his own
home."[o] 5He could not do any miracles
there, except lay his hands on[p] a few sick
people and heal them. 6He was amazed
at their lack of faith.

Jesus Sends Out the Twelve

6:7–11pp // Mt 10:1,9–14; Lk 9:1,3–5

Then Jesus went around teaching from
village to village.[q] 7Calling the Twelve
to him,[r] he began to send them out two
by two[s] and gave them authority over
impure spirits.[t]
8These were his instructions: "Take
nothing for the journey except a staff—
no bread, no bag, no money in your belts.
9Wear sandals but not an extra shirt.
10Whenever you enter a house, stay
there until you leave that town. 11And
if any place will not welcome you or listen to you, leave that place and shake
the dust off your feet[u] as a testimony
against them."
12They went out and preached that
people should repent.[v] 13They drove out
many demons and anointed many sick
people with oil[w] and healed them.

John the Baptist Beheaded

6:14–29pp // Mt 14:1–12
6:14–16pp // Lk 9:7–9

14King Herod heard about this, for
Jesus' name had become well known.
Some were saying,[a] "John the Baptist[x]
has been raised from the dead, and that
is why miraculous powers are at work
in him."
15Others said, "He is Elijah."[y]
And still others claimed, "He is a
prophet,[z] like one of the prophets of
long ago."[a]
16But when Herod heard this, he said,
"John, whom I beheaded, has been raised
from the dead!"
17For Herod himself had given orders
to have John arrested, and he had him
bound and put in prison.[b] He did this
because of Herodias, his brother Philip's

6:3 [m] Mt 12:46 [n] Mt 11:6; Jn 6:61
6:4 [o] Lk 4:24; Jn 4:44
6:5 [p] Mk 5:23
6:6 [q] Mt 9:35; Mk 1:39; Lk 13:22
6:7 [r] Mk 3:13 [s] Dt 17:6; Lk 10:1 [t] Mt 10:1
6:11 [u] Mt 10:14
6:12 [v] Lk 9:6
6:13 [w] Jas 5:14
6:14 [x] Mt 3:1
6:15 [y] Mal 4:5 [z] Mt 21:11 [a] Mt 16:14; Mk 8:28
6:17 [b] Mt 4:12; 11:2; Lk 3:19,20

[a] 14 Some early manuscripts *He was saying*

---

father is no longer alive and thus are expressing their familiarity with his mother, who lives there. The references to his brothers and sisters emphasize that he is simply "a local boy." They refuse to believe any of his claims.

6:4–6a Jesus can do no miracles in Nazareth except heal a few people, and he marvels over the unbelief of the townspeople.

> ✥ **6:1–6a** When we judge others by appearances, we may be dead wrong. If Jesus were issued identity papers, his profession would list him as a carpenter, not Messiah. Those who evaluate Jesus by outward appearances will miss the truth about him. They are also likely to misjudge his followers.
>
> Mark tells us that Jesus' disciples accompanied him to Nazareth. Being with Jesus provides opportunities for learning. They perhaps learned from this indifferent response to Jesus' teaching and miracles that rejection will come sometimes when and where it is least expected. Rejection is not the end of the world, however. Failure is common to the experience of anyone who sows the seeds of the gospel. Christian missionaries perhaps can take comfort from this episode from Jesus' life when they too meet with skepticism.

6:6b–11 Jesus launched his public ministry by calling Israel to repentance; now he expands that mission by sending the Twelve to their unbelieving countrymen to preach repentance, to cast out demons, and to anoint the sick.

Jesus instructs them to stay in one home for the entirety of their visit to that town (v. 10). They are to be devoted first to the mission and not to their own comfort. Staying in one home also reduces the chance that they will create jealousy by moving to better quarters.

6:12–13 The disciples preach repentance, cast out demons, and anoint the sick with oil. This work is preparing them to take up their mission that will come after Jesus' death and resurrection. It introduces them to the requirement that they sacrifice their needs for the mission and opens them up to the rejection that will also come (vv. 8–11).

6:14–23 One of the things that must have troubled someone like "King Herod" (v. 14) is that Jesus and his disciples were proclaiming a simple message: God is king, and Herod is not.

The account of John's imprisonment and execution underscores the great wickedness of Herod. John reproaches him publicly for marrying Herodias, the wife of his half brother (v. 17). Herod's young stepdaughter captivates him with her presumably erotic dancing, which also hints of incestuous lust (v. 22).

6:14–29 The grisly detail of John's head brought to Herod on a platter caps off a banquet already polluted by excess. John dies because of the impulse of an evil woman and the weakness of her impotent and debauched husband.

wife, whom he had married. 18For John
had been saying to Herod, "It is not lawful for you to have your brother's wife."[c]
19So Herodias nursed a grudge against
John and wanted to kill him. But she was
not able to, 20because Herod feared John
and protected him, knowing him to be a
righteous and holy man.[d] When Herod
heard John, he was greatly puzzled[a]; yet
he liked to listen to him.
21Finally the opportune time came.
On his birthday Herod gave a banquet[e]
for his high officials and military commanders and the leading men of Galilee.[f]
22When the daughter of[b] Herodias came
in and danced, she pleased Herod and
his dinner guests.
The king said to the girl, "Ask me for
anything you want, and I'll give it to
you." 23And he promised her with an
oath, "Whatever you ask I will give you,
up to half my kingdom."[g]
24She went out and said to her mother,
"What shall I ask for?"
"The head of John the Baptist," she
answered.
25At once the girl hurried in to the king
with the request: "I want you to give me
right now the head of John the Baptist
on a platter."
26The king was greatly distressed,
but because of his oaths and his dinner
guests, he did not want to refuse her.
27So he immediately sent an execution-
er with orders to bring John's head. The
man went, beheaded John in the prison,
28and brought back his head on a platter.
He presented it to the girl, and she gave
it to her mother. 29On hearing of this,
John's disciples came and took his body
and laid it in a tomb.

Jesus Feeds the Five Thousand

6:32–44pp // Mt 14:13–21; Lk 9:10–17; Jn 6:5–13
6:32–44Ref // Mk 8:2–9

30The apostles[h] gathered around Jesus
and reported to him all they had done
and taught.[i] 31Then, because so many
people were coming and going that they
did not even have a chance to eat,[j] he said
to them, "Come with me by yourselves to
a quiet place and get some rest."
32So they went away by themselves in
a boat[k] to a solitary place. 33But many
who saw them leaving recognized them
and ran on foot from all the towns and
got there ahead of them. 34When Jesus
landed and saw a large crowd, he had
compassion on them, because they were
like sheep without a shepherd.[l] So he began teaching them many things.
35By this time it was late in the day,
so his disciples came to him. "This is a

6:18 [c] Lev 18:16; 20:21
6:20 [d] Mt 11:9; 21:26
6:21 [e] Est 1:3; 2:18 [f] Lk 3:1
6:23 [g] Est 5:3, 6; 7:2
6:30 [h] Mt 10:2; Lk 9:10; 17:5; 22:14; 24:10; Ac 1:2,26 [i] Lk 9:10
6:31 [j] Mk 3:20
6:32 [k] ver 45; Mk 4:36
6:34 [l] Mt 9:36

[a] 20 Some early manuscripts *he did many things*
[b] 22 Some early manuscripts *When his daughter*

6:30 The mission of the apostles brackets the account of the death of John. As we have seen before, recognizing this sandwich technique is crucial for unfolding Mark's theological purpose. The insertion interprets the flanking halves: What happens to John will happen to Jesus in his mission and to the disciples in theirs.

The world is filled with wicked people who will try to rub out the messengers of God and their disturbing message. But it will not work. The world will not easily be rid of prophets like John because of the God who raises the dead and enables disciples to remain faithful. The kingdom advances despite the murderous evil in the world.

6:6b–30 The disciples are to be so dedicated to the task of their mission that personal comforts become inconsequential. When Jesus sends them out, he expects them to concentrate more on getting the message out than getting the finest accommodations. He does not promise a successful career or protection from sickness, ordeals, or tyrants.

We do not always get to choose where we will go. It may be next door; it may be to death's door. Answering the call to serve others is risky business, but ignoring it or scorning it is even riskier.

6:31–34 Jesus does not show any irritation with the crowds for chasing him down. Instead, he has compassion on them because they are "like a sheep without a shepherd" (v. 34). His first response to their need is to teach them.

6:35–44 Instead of relating what Jesus taught, Mark describes the miraculous feeding of the crowd in the desert. The disciples stress that they are in a deserted place, and they ask in disbelief how they can possibly feed such a huge number of hungry people.

The feeding in the desert suggests several biblical themes. (1) It recalls God's miraculous provision of food in several stories of the OT. (2) It also foreshadows the messianic banquet and contrasts with the drunken debauchery of Herod's feast. (3) The feeding specifically recalls the Israelites' being fed in the desert. Jesus organizes the crowds and makes them sit in groups in rectangular sections, which makes it easier to feed them in an orderly fashion. (4) More suggestively, it counters the encampment of Israel. Moses had to contend with disgruntled people teetering on the edge of starvation. Those gathered around Jesus are all satisfied.

remote place," they said, "and it's already very late. 36Send the people away
so that they can go to the surrounding
countryside and villages and buy themselves something to eat."
37But he answered, "You give them
something to eat."[m]
They said to him, "That would take
more than half a year's wages[a]! Are we
to go and spend that much on bread and
give it to them to eat?"
38"How many loaves do you have?" he
asked. "Go and see."
When they found out, they said,
"Five—and two fish."[n]
39Then Jesus directed them to have
all the people sit down in groups on the
green grass. 40So they sat down in groups
of hundreds and fifties. 41Taking the five
loaves and the two fish and looking up
to heaven, he gave thanks and broke the
loaves.[o] Then he gave them to his disciples to distribute to the people. He also
divided the two fish among them all.
42They all ate and were satisfied, 43and
the disciples picked up twelve basketfuls
of broken pieces of bread and fish. 44The
number of the men who had eaten was
five thousand.

6:37 [m] 2Ki 4:42-44
6:38 [n] Mt 15:34; Mk 8:5
6:41 [o] Mt 14:19

Jesus Walks on the Water

6:45–51pp // Mt 14:22–32; Jn 6:15–21
6:53–56pp // Mt 14:34–36

45Immediately Jesus made his disciples get into the boat[p] and go on ahead
of him to Bethsaida,[q] while he dismissed
the crowd. 46After leaving them, he went
up on a mountainside to pray.[r]
47Later that night, the boat was in the
middle of the lake, and he was alone on
land. 48He saw the disciples straining at
the oars, because the wind was against
them. Shortly before dawn he went
out to them, walking on the lake. He
was about to pass by them, 49but when
they saw him walking on the lake, they
thought he was a ghost.[s] They cried out,
50because they all saw him and were terrified.
Immediately he spoke to them and
said, "Take courage! It is I. Don't be
afraid."[t] 51Then he climbed into the boat[u]

6:45 [p] ver 32 [q] Mt 11:21
6:46 [r] Lk 3:21
6:49 [s] Lk 24:37
6:50 [t] Mt 14:27
6:51 [u] ver 32

[a] 37 Greek *take two hundred denarii*

---

(5) Psalm 23 reverberates in the account of the feeding of the five thousand. Jesus' actions reflect the first line of the psalm, "The LORD is my shepherd." The barren desert has suddenly become fertile land as the shepherd finds good pasture for his flock beside the waters of the sea. Most importantly, however, Jesus restores their soul and guides them in right paths by teaching them.

(6) Elijah provided miraculously for the widow of Zarephath and raised her son from the dead. (7) Elisha fed a hundred prophets with 20 barley loaves; Jesus feeds five thousand people with five loaves. If we are meant to recall the works of these prophets of old, we see that in Jesus one greater than Elijah and Elisha is here.

(8) The action of Jesus' taking bread, giving thanks, breaking it, and giving it to the disciples matches Jesus' actions at the Last Supper. The abundance of food left over after feeding five thousand means that there is more to go around and much more where it came from. Those who come to hear the teaching of Jesus and to share in the broken bread will receive the same abundant blessing.

6:31–44 We have not done our duty if all we have done is point out the problems in society and lament them. The church cannot neglect either spiritual or physical hunger. Disciples are always servants of others—called to feed the sheep and not just themselves. The lesson from this account is clear: Through Jesus, we will always have enough to supply the needs of the church. The passage confirms that compassion combined with God's bounty and power can meet both the spiritual and physical needs of people around us.

6:45–47 Just as Jesus did not first feed the hungry multitudes but taught them, so he does not first rescue the disciples from their predicament but tries to teach them something by passing by them. They see only a ghost. The wind does not throw them into a panic, but the sight of Jesus passing by on the water does. When Jesus comes strolling across the waters, he shares in the unlimited power of the Creator.

6:48–50a Mark's explanation that Jesus "wanted to pass by them" (an alternate translation of v. 48) has caused confusion. Jesus' desire to pass by the disciples is not related to some ordinary purpose. The Greek verb for "to pass by," when connected to a divinity, refers to an epiphany.

6:50b–52 Mark offers a surprising explanation for the disciples' terror and amazement: "for they had not understood about the loaves; their hearts were hardened" (v. 52). The two incidents are somehow connected. What is it that they do not understand about the loaves? What does it have to do with walking on the water?

The disciples do not recognize that the blessing pronounced at the meal applies also to Jesus. The disciples are drawing closer to Jesus' opponents than to Jesus in their life stance. The difference between them and the opponents is significant, however: The disciples may be confused and blind, but they are not hostile to Jesus.

with them, and the wind died down.[v]
They were completely amazed, 52for they
had not understood about the loaves;
their hearts were hardened.[w]
53When they had crossed over, they
landed at Gennesaret and anchored
there.[x] 54As soon as they got out of the
boat, people recognized Jesus. 55They
ran throughout that whole region and
carried the sick on mats to wherever
they heard he was. 56And wherever he
went — into villages, towns or countryside — they placed the sick in the marketplaces. They begged him to let them
touch even the edge of his cloak,[y] and all
who touched it were healed.

That Which Defiles

7:1–23pp // Mt 15:1–20

7 The Pharisees and some of the teachers of the law who had come from
Jerusalem gathered around Jesus 2and
saw some of his disciples eating food
with hands that were defiled,[z] that is,
unwashed. 3(The Pharisees and all the
Jews do not eat unless they give their
hands a ceremonial washing, holding to
the tradition of the elders.[a] 4When they
come from the marketplace they do not
eat unless they wash. And they observe
many other traditions, such as the washing of cups, pitchers and kettles.[a])[b]
5So the Pharisees and teachers of the
law asked Jesus, "Why don't your disciples live according to the tradition of the

6:51 [v] Mk 4:39
6:52 [w] Mk 8:17-21
6:53 [x] Jn 6:24, 25
6:56 [y] Mt 9:20
7:2 [z] Ac 10:14, 28; 11:8; Ro 14:14
7:3 [a] ver 5, 8, 9, 13; Lk 11:38
7:4 [b] Mt 23:25; Lk 11:39
7:5 [c] ver 3; Gal 1:14; Col 2:8
7:7 [d] Isa 29:13
7:8 [e] ver 3
7:9 [f] ver 3
7:10 [g] Ex 20:12; Dt 5:16 [h] Ex 21:17; Lev 20:9
7:11 [i] Mt 23:16,18

Mk 7:6 ❖ How can we avoid the sin of honoring God with our words while at the same time having a heart that is far from God?

elders[c] instead of eating their food with
defiled hands?"
6He replied, "Isaiah was right when
he prophesied about you hypocrites; as
it is written:

> "'These people honor me with their
> lips,
> but their hearts are far from me.
> 7They worship me in vain;
> their teachings are merely human
> rules.'[bd]

8You have let go of the commands of
God and are holding on to human traditions."[e]
9And he continued, "You have a fine
way of setting aside the commands of
God in order to observe[c] your own traditions![f] 10For Moses said, 'Honor your
father and mother,'[dg] and, 'Anyone who
curses their father or mother is to be put
to death.'[eh] 11But you say[i] that if anyone
declares that what might have been used
to help their father or mother is Corban
(that is, devoted to God) — 12then you

[a] 4 Some early manuscripts *pitchers, kettles and dining couches* [b] 6,7 Isaiah 29:13 [c] 9 Some manuscripts *set up* [d] 10 Exodus 20:12; Deut. 5:16 [e] 10 Exodus 21:17; Lev. 20:9

6:53–56 Jesus sends the disciples off to Bethsaida, but they land in Gennesaret. Perhaps Mark wants the reader to see some significance in their going off course. They are unable to go to Bethsaida, just as they have been unable to understand about the loaves, and do not reach this destination until later (8:22). Meanwhile, the activities of Jesus involve a second series of mighty works intended to help the disciples to see. Jesus never gives up on the disciples despite their failures. He does not require his disciples to understand his message immediately.

✣ **6:45–56** Jesus' retreat shows that all humans need solitude, rest, and prayer (1:35; 6:31). In such moments we can meet ourselves face-to-face and hear God's speaking most clearly.

Note that Jesus does not rescue his disciples out of the sea but enables them to continue the voyage. Often Christ may pass by our lives in ways that we fail to see, and that might frighten us. How do we see him while we struggle in the dim hours of the night in this present age, overtaken by windy opposition? It may only become clear in retrospect, as it did for those first disciples. In this story, we are alerted that in the times of discouragement and fear Christ is passing by, showing his love and power and leading us across troubled waters.

7:1–9 The Levitical system regarded uncleanness as something transferable to persons, pots and other containers, clothes, and even houses by touch, lying, or sitting. To disregard such concerns means that Jesus redefines what it is that prevents fellowship with God.

7:10–13 God commands children to honor their parents, and that requires providing them with physical necessities. In this case, the Pharisees would allow a son to duck that responsibility to care for his parents by informing them that what support they might expect from him is "Corban," dedicated to God. Therefore, it cannot be used to help them.

From Jesus' point of view, the Pharisees' tradition turned the law on its head by insisting that the sanctity of the vow superseded the parents' right to support. One cannot elude God's commands by taking advantage of shrewd legal loopholes. Jesus exposes these sticklers for the law as more

no longer let them do anything for their
father or mother. 13 Thus you nullify the
word of God[j] by your tradition[k] that you
have handed down. And you do many
things like that."
14 Again Jesus called the crowd to him
and said, "Listen to me, everyone, and
understand this. 15 Nothing outside a person can defile them by going into them.
Rather, it is what comes out of a person
that defiles them." [16][a]
17 After he had left the crowd and entered the house, his disciples asked him[l]
about this parable. 18 "Are you so dull?"
he asked. "Don't you see that nothing
that enters a person from the outside
can defile them? 19 For it doesn't go into
their heart but into their stomach, and
then out of the body." (In saying this,
Jesus declared all foods[m] clean.)[n]
20 He went on: "What comes out of a
person is what defiles them. 21 For it is
from within, out of a person's heart, that
evil thoughts come—sexual immorality,
theft, murder, 22 adultery, greed,[o] malice, deceit, lewdness, envy, slander, arrogance and folly. 23 All these evils come
from inside and defile a person."

Jesus Honors a Syrophoenician Woman's Faith

7:24–30pp // Mt 15:21–28

24 Jesus left that place and went to the
vicinity of Tyre.[b][p] He entered a house and
did not want anyone to know it; yet he
could not keep his presence secret. 25 In
fact, as soon as she heard about him, a
woman whose little daughter was possessed by an impure spirit[q] came and fell
at his feet. 26 The woman was a Greek, born
in Syrian Phoenicia. She begged Jesus to
drive the demon out of her daughter.
27 "First let the children eat all they
want," he told her, "for it is not right to
take the children's bread and toss it to
the dogs."
28 "Lord," she replied, "even the
dogs under the table eat the children's
crumbs."

7:13 [j] Heb 4:12 [k] ver 3
7:17 [l] Mk 9:28
7:19 [m] Ro 14:1-12; Col 2:16; 1Ti 4:3-5 [n] Ac 10:15
7:22 [o] Mt 20:15
7:24 [p] Mt 11:21
7:25 [q] Mt 4:24

[a] *16* Some manuscripts include here the words of 4:23. [b] *24* Many early manuscripts *Tyre and Sidon*

interested in legal niceties than the requirement to love others.

7:14-23 Jesus does not differ with the Pharisees only over details such as washing hands; he rejects their whole approach to God's law. They are concerned about surface impurity and piety; Jesus is concerned about internal impurity that one cannot wash away by washing the hands.

The only defilement that the disciples need to worry about has to do with the heart, not the hands—with internal evil that leaks out from within a person, not food that ends up as waste. The list of vices that come from the heart deals with behavior that harms others. One needs more than a little water poured over cupped hands to cleanse this impurity.

7:1-23 Jesus' teaching had a direct impact on Christian missionary practice when Paul advised the Corinthians to eat whatever was set before them (1Co 8:1-13). We can imagine how we would respond if guests turned up their noses at the food we offered them because it somehow did not meet their religious standards. What if their rejection of our food also implied that we were somehow impure, somehow untouchable? It would hardly make us open to hear their message. In applying this passage, we should ask ourselves, "Are there subtle and not-so-subtle ways in which we communicate to others that they are 'dirty' and unfit for contact with us? How does it hinder our ability to lead them to Christ?"

Christians who concentrate on minor religiousness wind up with a religion that affects only the hands but that never touches the heart. Jesus tells us that goodness comes from inner purity—a life transformed from within—rather than from merely observing rules and doctrine.

7:24-26 A woman whose daughter is a victim of an unclean spirit asks for Jesus' help. She is a Gentile pagan. To the Jews, Gentiles were impure simply because they were not Jews. Will Jesus be as gracious to this lady from Tyre as he was to the unclean outcasts within Israel?

7:27 Jesus' response in this case may surprise us: He dismisses her appeal out of hand with what sounds like a sharp insult. Jesus comes as the Messiah of Israel, and this woman has no right as a Gentile to jump the queue to receive benefits from him.

7:28 Another surprise unfolds in the woman's unwillingness to be put off by this response. She recognizes that "the children" represent Israel and "the dogs" represent the Gentiles. She accepts the riddle's implications: Israel has precedence over Gentiles, and the time for the Gentiles to be influenced by Jesus' work has not yet come.

Instead of being bitter, she engages Jesus in a constructive exchange about his mission. She refuses to accept his dismissal and will not take no for an answer. She is not asking for a catered, full-course meal, just a little crumb of Jesus' power.

The woman's response reveals that she comprehends more about the bread that Jesus offers than even his disciples do. They have witnessed the feeding of the five thousand, but they still do not understand the bread that Jesus offers. She knows that she cannot insist on God's mercy and does not take offense when Jesus tells her

29 Then he told her, "For such a reply,
you may go; the demon has left your
daughter."
30 She went home and found her child
lying on the bed, and the demon gone.

Jesus Heals a Deaf and Mute Man

7:31–37pp // Mt 15:29–31

31 Then Jesus left the vicinity of Tyre[r]
and went through Sidon, down to the Sea
of Galilee[s] and into the region of the Decapolis.[a][t] 32 There some people brought
to him a man who was deaf and could
hardly talk,[u] and they begged Jesus to
place his hand on[v] him.
33 After he took him aside, away from
the crowd, Jesus put his fingers into the
man's ears. Then he spit[w] and touched
the man's tongue. 34 He looked up to
heaven[x] and with a deep sigh[y] said to
him, *"Ephphatha!"* (which means "Be
opened!"). 35 At this, the man's ears were
opened, his tongue was loosened and he
began to speak plainly.[z]
36 Jesus commanded them not to tell
anyone.[a] But the more he did so, the
more they kept talking about it. 37 People were overwhelmed with amazement.
"He has done everything well," they said.
"He even makes the deaf hear and the
mute speak."

Jesus Feeds the Four Thousand

8:1–9pp // Mt 15:32–39
8:1–9Ref // Mk 6:32–44
8:11–21pp // Mt 16:1–12

8 During those days another large
crowd gathered. Since they had nothing to eat, Jesus called his disciples to
him and said, 2 "I have compassion for
these people;[b] they have already been
with me three days and have nothing to
eat. 3 If I send them home hungry, they
will collapse on the way, because some of
them have come a long distance."
4 His disciples answered, "But where in
this remote place can anyone get enough
bread to feed them?"

7:31 [r] ver 24; Mt 11:21 [s] Mt 4:18 [t] Mt 4:25; Mk 5:20
7:32 [u] Mt 9:32; Lk 11:14 [v] Mk 5:23
7:33 [w] Mk 8:23
7:34 [x] Mk 6:41; Jn 11:41 [y] Mk 8:12
7:35 [z] Isa 35:5, 6
7:36 [a] Mt 8:4
8:2 [b] Mt 9:36

[a] *31* That is, the Ten Cities

so. She will gladly accept a lesser rank if it means getting fed.

7:29-30 Jesus relents and grants her request. Her witty comeback (v. 28) expresses sincere humility. This willingness to humble oneself is a key requirement for discipleship, something the disciples of Jesus at times have difficulty learning. When Jesus says that the demon has left her daughter, she does not insist that he go home with her to make sure. She goes in faith as she came in faith.

✣ **7:24-30** One can use this passage in an implicit assault on prejudice. This passage helps us to recognize that all humans share the same desperation when demonic powers and sickness corrupt our lives. We all stand in need of Jesus' help—high and low, rich and poor, urban and rural, Jew and Gentile. Jesus turns no one away who comes to him in humble faith.

Jesus' ministry reveals that God sent him not to reward the deserving but to serve the needy, whoever they are and wherever they may be found. We do well to notice in ourselves that pride can stiffen our knees so that they will not bow down, and it can muzzle our voice so that we do not plead with God in humility. We are all unworthy in the face of God's holiness, and we can take comfort in Jesus' gracious response to this woman's expressions of faith.

7:31-32 Just as the Jewish crowds in Galilee brought their sick to Jesus, a Gentile crowd brings a deaf and speechless man to him and begs Jesus to place his hand on him. Jesus ushers the man away from the crowd (v. 33).

7:33-35 In healing this deaf man, Jesus uses a sequence of actions, not just a spoken word. The vivid account creates an atmosphere of mystery and drama. He begins by putting his fingers in the man's ears, symbolic of opening them. Next, he spits and touches the man's tongue, symbolic of loosening his tongue. Then he looks up to heaven, the source of his power, and sighs deeply, a gesture of prayer. Immediately, the man can hear and speak.

7:36-37 The crowd's failure to obey Jesus' command for silence reveals that what Jesus does is so sensational that it is hopeless to try to hush it up. The chorus of Jesus' admirers proclaim the truth even if they do not fully understand it: Jesus does what only God can do. The Lord responded to Moses' excuses with these words: "Who gave human beings their mouths? Who makes them deaf or mute? Who gives them sight or makes them blind? Is it not I, the LORD?" (Ex 4:11). Jesus' actions in Mark show that he has that same divine power.

✣ **7:31-37** Jesus seeks to cure his disciples' blindness and deafness by taking them away from the pressing crowds and teaching them. Modern Christians need to act out the message of Good News for those who cannot understand in a language that is universally understood—through loving and kind deeds done for others. The church needs to love as Christ loved, to touch those who need assurance, and to pray visibly for healing.

8:1-3 Jesus is now offering a predominantly Gentile crowd the same opportunity to be fed that he offered to the Jewish crowd. The miracle signifies that Jesus is the Redeemer of the world, offering redemption to more than just the people of Israel.

8:4-10 The disciples were in on the feeding of five thousand, but this does not stop them from asking Jesus, "But where in this remote place can

5“How many loaves do you have?”
Jesus asked.
“Seven,” they replied.
6He told the crowd to sit down on the
ground. When he had taken the seven
loaves and given thanks, he broke them
and gave them to his disciples to distribute to the people, and they did so.
7They had a few small fish as well; he
gave thanks for them also and told the
disciples to distribute them.[c] 8The people
ate and were satisfied. Afterward the disciples picked up seven basketfuls of broken pieces that were left over.[d] 9About
four thousand were present. After he had
sent them away, 10he got into the boat
with his disciples and went to the region
of Dalmanutha.
11The Pharisees came and began to
question Jesus. To test him, they asked
him for a sign from heaven.[e] 12He sighed
deeply[f] and said, “Why does this generation ask for a sign? Truly I tell you, no
sign will be given to it.” 13Then he left
them, got back into the boat and crossed
to the other side.

The Yeast of the Pharisees and Herod

14The disciples had forgotten to bring
bread, except for one loaf they had with
them in the boat. 15“Be careful,” Jesus
warned them. “Watch out for the yeast[g]
of the Pharisees[h] and that of Herod.”[i]
16They discussed this with one another and said, “It is because we have no
bread.”

8:7 [c]Mt 14:19
8:8 [d]ver 20
8:11 [e]Mt 12:38
8:12 [f]Mk 7:34
8:15 [g]1Co 5:6-8 [h]Lk 12:1 [i]Mt 14:1; Mk 12:13
8:17 [j]Isa 6:9,10; Mk 6:52
8:19 [k]Mt 14:20; Mk 6:41-44; Lk 9:17; Jn 6:13
8:20 [l]ver 6-9; Mt 15:37
8:21 [m]Mk 6:52
8:22 [n]Mt 11:21 [o]Mk 10:46; Jn 9:1
8:23 [p]Mk 7:33 [q]Mk 5:23

17Aware of their discussion, Jesus
asked them: “Why are you talking about
having no bread? Do you still not see
or understand? Are your hearts hardened?[j] 18Do you have eyes but fail to
see, and ears but fail to hear? And don’t
you remember? 19When I broke the
five loaves for the five thousand, how
many basketfuls of pieces did you
pick up?”
“Twelve,”[k] they replied.
20“And when I broke the seven loaves
for the four thousand, how many basketfuls of pieces did you pick up?”
They answered, “Seven.”[l]
21He said to them, “Do you still not
understand?”[m]

Jesus Heals a Blind Man at Bethsaida

22They came to Bethsaida,[n] and some
people brought a blind man[o] and begged
Jesus to touch him. 23He took the blind
man by the hand and led him outside the
village. When he had spit[p] on the man’s
eyes and put his hands on[q] him, Jesus
asked, “Do you see anything?”
24He looked up and said, “I see people;
they look like trees walking around.”
25Once more Jesus put his hands
on the man’s eyes. Then his eyes were
opened, his sight was restored, and he
saw everything clearly. 26Jesus sent him
home, saying, “Don’t even go into[a] the
village.”

[a] 26 Some manuscripts *go and tell anyone in*

---

anyone get enough bread to feed them?” (v. 4). The answer to their question is obvious: from Jesus. They do not yet realize that even with their meager supplies, they have in Jesus enough to feed the entire world.

8:11-12 The reason Jesus balks at giving a sign here revolves around two issues: the meaning of the expression “a sign from heaven” and the defiant disposition of these opponents.

First, the Pharisees specifically ask for “a sign from heaven.” Jesus refuses to give the Pharisees a sign because God has sent him to give his life on the cross for all humanity, not to smash the enemies of Israel.

Second, the Pharisees have already received plenty of proof in chs. 1–2 of the source of Jesus’ power. Those who claim to know God and to teach God’s law to others do not recognize the signs that God has already displayed through Jesus because they are spiritually blind.

8:13-16 This last scene in the boat opens with an awkwardly phrased notice that the disciples forgot to bring bread, “except for one loaf they had with them in the boat” (v. 14). Why the contradiction between no loaves and one loaf? Mark wants the reader to recognize Jesus’ power to multiply one into an abundance of loaves to feed thousands.

8:17-21 Jesus believes that the miraculous feedings in the desert are the key events that should explain everything for the disciples. Jesus implies that it should point them on the way to recognizing Jesus as the Messiah, who works by the power of God.

8:22-26 The context, which portrays Jesus’ struggle to get his disciples to see anything, gives this unusual two-stage healing added significance. The blind man’s healing occurs between two examples of the disciples’ blindness. This physical healing of blindness serves as a model for the spiritual healing of the disciples’ sight, which also comes gradually and with difficulty.

✤ **8:1-26** These incidents show both Jesus’ opponents and disciples as being blind to what God is doing through Jesus. The blindness stems from many causes. Jesus has a vision of what the kingdom of God looks like; the disciples see nothing, no matter how

Peter Declares That Jesus Is the Messiah

8:27–29pp // Mt 16:13–16; Lk 9:18–20

27Jesus and his disciples went on to
the villages around Caesarea Philippi. On
the way he asked them, "Who do people
say I am?"
28They replied, "Some say John the
Baptist;[r] others say Elijah;[s] and still others, one of the prophets."
29"But what about you?" he asked.
"Who do you say I am?"
Peter answered, "You are the Messiah."[t]
30Jesus warned them not to tell anyone about him.[u]

Jesus Predicts His Death

8:31—9:1pp // Mt 16:21–28; Lk 9:22–27

31He then began to teach them that the
Son of Man[v] must suffer many things[w]
and be rejected by the elders, the chief
priests and the teachers of the law,[x] and
that he must be killed[y] and after three
days[z] rise again.[a] 32He spoke plainly[b]
about this, and Peter took him aside and
began to rebuke him.
33But when Jesus turned and looked
at his disciples, he rebuked Peter. "Get
behind me, Satan!"[c] he said. "You do not
have in mind the concerns of God, but
merely human concerns."

The Way of the Cross

34Then he called the crowd to him
along with his disciples and said: "Whoever wants to be my disciple must deny
themselves and take up their cross and
follow me.[d] 35For whoever wants to save
their life[a] will lose it, but whoever loses their life for me and for the gospel
will save it.[e] 36What good is it for someone to gain the whole world, yet forfeit
their soul? 37Or what can anyone give
in exchange for their soul? 38If anyone
is ashamed of me and my words in this

8:28 [r] Mt 3:1 [s] Mal 4:5
8:29 [t] Jn 6:69; 11:27
8:30 [u] Mt 8:4; 16:20; 17:9; Mk 9:9; Lk 9:21
8:31 [v] Mt 8:20 [w] Mt 16:21 [x] Mt 27:1, 2 [y] Ac 2:23; 3:13 [z] Mt 16:21 [a] Mt 16:21
8:32 [b] Jn 18:20
8:33 [c] Mt 4:10
8:34 [d] Mt 10:38; Lk 14:27
8:35 [e] Jn 12:25

[a] 35 The Greek word means either *life* or *soul;* also in verses 36 and 37.

Mk 8:35 ❖ What does it means to lose our lives for Christ and for the gospel in order to save our lives? How willing are we to follow this directive?

hard they strain their eyes. Everything looks to them like a barren landscape. They may remain in the dark temporarily, but Jesus calls them to trust his vision and reveals truth in increments.

8:27–28 This scene takes place in the unlikely location of Caesarea Philippi, which was famed for its cultic associations with the nature god, Pan. Jesus teaches his disciples by asking them probing questions. The first one is "Who do people say I am?" (v. 27). The disciples report Jesus' favorable ratings in the polls. These people have not hit on the truth, however. Jesus is more than just another in a long line of messengers from God.
8:29 Jesus probes further. Peter moves to the head of the class by giving the answer that makes sense of all that they have witnessed: "You are the Messiah" (v. 29). His confession occurs in the very center of the Gospel. The reader knows that Peter's answer is correct from the title of the Gospel (1:1). It seems a major breakthrough.
8:30 Jesus does not confirm Peter's confession or praise him for his insight. Instead, he warns him to tell no one. Peter's understanding of what "Messiah" means needs correction.
8:31 Jesus explains his mission to his disciples not simply to predict future events but to verify for his disciples that what is about to happen fulfills God's plan. The disciples can understand it only after the fact because this plan runs counter to everything they were conditioned to expect. For the disciples, Jesus' teaching about suffering and death flies in one ear and out the other.
8:32–33 Peter displays astonishing nerve by trying to set Jesus straight on what is and what is not necessary. Preconceived notions about the Messiah blur his vision, and he only considers the situation from a human perspective. He has begun to understand that Jesus must be the Messiah, but he does not have any understanding how Jesus' Passion ties into his identity.

Peter looks for a human ruler while Jesus tries to prepare the disciples for the reign of God. Peter thinks in human terms while Jesus seeks the divine will. The quest to uncover Jesus' identity does not end with the confession that he is the Messiah. The disciples cannot know who Jesus really is without accepting the necessity of his suffering and death. They cannot be his disciples unless they accept that fate for themselves.

As Jesus rebukes Peter, he looks at all the other disciples, which may suggest that Peter is not alone in his opinion about Jesus' suffering, just more daring in voicing it. So the rebuke is for all the disciples; they must all be made to see Jesus' work in the world differently.
8:34 Jesus insists that if the disciples want to follow him, they must learn to say, "Not my will but yours be done." Jesus also demands that his disciples take up a cross. This vivid imagery must have sounded strange but would have communicated danger and sacrifice. Finally, Jesus tells his disciples to follow the way he has chosen. Jesus does not want followers who marvel at his deeds but fail to follow his example.
8:35–37 Jesus appeals to the basic human desire to secure one's life as the rationale for making such a sacrifice.
8:38 Jesus uses the threat of judgment to induce his followers to be faithful.

adulterous and sinful generation, the Son of Man[f] will be ashamed of them[g] when he comes[h] in his Father's glory with the holy angels."

9 And he said to them, "Truly I tell you, some who are standing here will not taste death before they see that the kingdom of God has come[i] with power."[j]

The Transfiguration

9:2–8pp // Lk 9:28–36
9:2–13pp // Mt 17:1–13

2After six days Jesus took Peter, James and John[k] with him and led them up a high mountain, where they were all alone. There he was transfigured before them. 3His clothes became dazzling white,[l] whiter than anyone in the world could bleach them. 4And there appeared before them Elijah and Moses, who were talking with Jesus.

5Peter said to Jesus, "Rabbi,[m] it is good for us to be here. Let us put up three shelters—one for you, one for Moses and one for Elijah." 6(He did not know what to say, they were so frightened.)

7Then a cloud appeared and covered them, and a voice came from the cloud:[n] "This is my Son, whom I love. Listen to him!"[o]

8Suddenly, when they looked around, they no longer saw anyone with them except Jesus.

9As they were coming down the mountain, Jesus gave them orders not to tell anyone[p] what they had seen until the Son of Man[q] had risen from the dead. 10They kept the matter to themselves, discussing what "rising from the dead" meant.

11And they asked him, "Why do the teachers of the law say that Elijah must come first?"

12Jesus replied, "To be sure, Elijah does come first, and restores all things. Why then is it written that the Son of Man[r]

8:38 [f] Mt 8:20 [g] Mt 10:33; Lk 12:9 [h] 1Th 2:19
9:1 [i] Mk 13:30; Lk 22:18 [j] Mt 24:30; 25:31
9:2 [k] Mt 4:21
9:3 [l] Mt 28:3
9:5 [m] Mt 23:7
9:7 [n] Ex 24:16 [o] Mt 3:17
9:9 [p] Mk 8:30 [q] Mt 8:20
9:12 [r] Mt 8:20

9:1 Jesus concludes with a solemn promise that some of them "will not taste death before they see . . . the kingdom of God . . . [coming in] power." The best option assumes that the promise in this verse is somehow fulfilled within the story and in the events that take place after the resurrection.

Many will see nothing of what God is doing in the world and will be judged. Others will see the darkness at noon, the splitting of the temple veil, the empty tomb, and the reunion with the risen Lord as the kingdom of God coming in power.

> ✣ **8:27—9:1** Modern scholars tend to make Jesus over into their own image and, in the process, eliminate any eternal claim he might exert on their lives. Some present him as a revolutionary who gathered a band of desperadoes to bring about a social liberation of oppressed peasants. Others present him as an itinerant, nonviolent teacher spouting pithy truths; still others see him as a charismatic healer trying to reform Judaism. These speculations, all dressed up in the clothes of academic expertise, are no closer to the truth than the best guesses of Jesus' contemporaries, but the media will often seize on these opinions.
>
> We cannot allow contemporary "experts" to draw us away from what we know to be true about Jesus from these accounts in the Gospels: Jesus is the Messiah whom God sent to suffer and save his people through his death and resurrection.

9:2–3 The transfiguration account begins with a note that it happened "after six days." This specific logging of the time recalls Moses' six-day preparation before God appeared to him on the mountain (Ex 24:15–16). The transfiguration has echoes suggesting what happened to Moses on Sinai sheds light on the meaning of Jesus' transfiguration. Since Jewish traditions interpreted Moses' ascent of Sinai as God enthroning him, the parallels with Jesus' transfiguration cast Jesus as a king.

The transfiguration occurs on the seventh day after Peter's confession and connects Jesus' announcement of suffering with a glimpse of his promised resurrection glory. The transfiguration confirms that the suffering Jesus will endure will not be incompatible with his glory.

9:4 The presence of Elijah and Moses with Jesus on the high mountain rouses Jewish hopes about the final redemption of Israel and suggests that the time has been fulfilled. The kingdom of God has drawn near.

9:5–6 Another theme emerges in Peter's unthinking response to the presence of these saints. If the offer to build three shelters suggests some desire to honor them, he mistakenly puts Jesus on a par with Elijah and Moses. Elijah and Moses, as great as they were, do not share God's glory with Jesus.

9:7–8 Jesus' identity, bathed in divine glory, attended by the great saints of old, and confirmed by the voice of God, may take away the sting of his announcements about suffering for readers today. By assuring his disciples and us that he will ultimately win, he does not remove the necessity of suffering for himself and for all those who follow him.

9:9–10 As they walk back down the mountain, Jesus commands the three disciples to keep silent about what they saw and heard until the Son of Man should rise from the dead. The disciples are stumped because Jesus' teaching that he must suffer has not yet sunk in, which explains why Jesus orders them to keep quiet.

9:11–13 Jesus' statement about Elijah means that contrary to received opinion, Elijah's return does not signal the approach of messianic happy days. The disciples, however, question if Jesus has got it right. How can the Messiah be rejected and

must suffer much[s] and be rejected?[t] 13But
I tell you, Elijah has come,[u] and they have
done to him everything they wished, just
as it is written about him."

Jesus Heals a Boy Possessed by an Impure Spirit

9:14–28pp // Mt 17:14–19; Lk 9:37–43a

14When they came to the other disciples, they saw a large crowd around
them and the teachers of the law arguing
with them. 15As soon as all the people
saw Jesus, they were overwhelmed with
wonder and ran to greet him.
16"What are you arguing with them
about?" he asked.
17A man in the crowd answered,
"Teacher, I brought you my son, who is
possessed by a spirit that has robbed him
of speech. 18Whenever it seizes him, it
throws him to the ground. He foams at
the mouth, gnashes his teeth and becomes rigid. I asked your disciples to
drive out the spirit, but they could not."
19"You unbelieving generation," Jesus
replied, "how long shall I stay with you?
How long shall I put up with you? Bring
the boy to me."
20So they brought him. When the
spirit saw Jesus, it immediately threw
the boy into a convulsion. He fell to the
ground and rolled around, foaming at
the mouth.[v]

9:12 [s] Mt 16:21 [t] Lk 23:11
9:13 [u] Mt 11:14
9:20 [v] Mk 1:26
9:23 [w] Mt 21:21; Mk 11:23; Jn 11:40
9:25 [x] ver 15
9:28 [y] Mk 7:17

Mk 9:24 ❖ How can we overcome lingering unbelief?

21Jesus asked the boy's father, "How
long has he been like this?"
"From childhood," he answered. 22"It
has often thrown him into fire or water
to kill him. But if you can do anything,
take pity on us and help us."
23"'If you can'?" said Jesus. "Everything is possible for one who believes."[w]
24Immediately the boy's father exclaimed, "I do believe; help me overcome
my unbelief!"
25When Jesus saw that a crowd was
running to the scene,[x] he rebuked the
impure spirit. "You deaf and mute spirit," he said, "I command you, come out
of him and never enter him again."
26The spirit shrieked, convulsed him
violently and came out. The boy looked
so much like a corpse that many said,
"He's dead." 27But Jesus took him by the
hand and lifted him to his feet, and he
stood up.
28After Jesus had gone indoors, his
disciples asked him privately,[y] "Why
couldn't we drive it out?"
29He replied, "This kind can come out
only by prayer.[a]"

[a] 29 Some manuscripts *prayer and fasting*

---

suffer? Jesus answers that their expectations are all wrong. Elijah goes before the Messiah in the way of suffering and death.

✣ **9:2-13** Most readers would prefer to be with the disciples basking in the glory on the mountaintop rather than trudging along with them as they struggle and fail to understand Jesus' message. However, while we shuffle through our dark valleys, the words of our Lord remain constant. One must continue to listen to Jesus, whose words are able to sustain us after the spiritual highs of our lives, however dazzling they may have been, have grown dim.

9:14-20 When Jesus appears from the mountain, the crowds respond with fearful amazement and run to greet him. Immediately a crowd of people bring him a demon-possessed boy who is mute.
9:19 Jesus' question, "How long?" does not convey a wish to be rid of inept disciples but refers to how little time he has left to soften their hard-heartedness and teach them more fully about the power that can expel evil. Time is short.
9:20-22 At the heart of this exorcism is the struggle for faith, not the struggle with a demon. The disciples' failure to remove the demon has not taken away the father's hope.
9:23 The implied skepticism of his plea, "If you can," meets with a sharp comeback from Jesus. His capability is not at issue.

Whom does Jesus have in mind when he singles out "one who believes"? Does he refer to the miracle worker's faith or the faith of those who seek miracles? The answer is both. Unlike the disciples, Jesus possesses unlimited power because of his potent faith. He therefore chides the father for putting limits on what he can do to help him. As we've seen, aggressive faith has been a characteristic of all those who've asked Jesus for healing in this Gospel.
9:24 Unlike the people at Nazareth who refused to believe, the father repents of his unbelief. He pleads for help just as he is, a doubter.
9:24-27 Jesus' commands evoke a response from the demons, and this one defiantly throws his young victim around in one last gasp of harmful evil. Mark uses resurrection language of Jesus' actions: "he raised him" (he "lifted him to his feet" v. 27), and "he was raised" ("he stood up" v. 27). Jesus drives the evil spirit out and gives the boy new life.
9:28-29 In the final scene, the disciples want to review their failure in the privacy of the house. Jesus' response, "This kind can come out only by prayer," implies that they failed because they had not prayed.

Jesus Predicts His Death a Second Time

9:30–37pp // Mt 17:22–23; 18:1–5; Lk 9:43b–48

30They left that place and passed
through Galilee. Jesus did not want anyone to know where they were, 31because
he was teaching his disciples. He said to
them, "The Son of Man[z] is going to be
delivered into the hands of men. They
will kill him,[a] and after three days[b] he
will rise."[c] 32But they did not understand
what he meant[d] and were afraid to ask
him about it.

33They came to Capernaum.[e] When
he was in the house,[f] he asked them,
"What were you arguing about on the
road?" 34But they kept quiet because on
the way they had argued about who was
the greatest.[g]

35Sitting down, Jesus called the Twelve
and said, "Anyone who wants to be first
must be the very last, and the servant
of all."[h]

36He took a little child whom he placed
among them. Taking the child in his
arms,[i] he said to them, 37"Whoever welcomes one of these little children in my
name welcomes me; and whoever welcomes me does not welcome me but the
one who sent me."[j]

Whoever Is Not Against Us Is for Us

9:38–40pp // Lk 9:49,50

38"Teacher," said John, "we saw someone driving out demons in your name
and we told him to stop, because he was
not one of us."[k]

39"Do not stop him," Jesus said. "For no
one who does a miracle in my name can
in the next moment say anything bad
about me, 40for whoever is not against
us is for us.[l] 41Truly I tell you, anyone
who gives you a cup of water in my name
because you belong to the Messiah will
certainly not lose their reward.[m]

Causing to Stumble

42"If anyone causes one of these little ones — those who believe in me — to
stumble,[n] it would be better for them if a
large millstone were hung around their
neck and they were thrown into the sea.[o]
43If your hand causes you to stumble,[p]
cut it off. It is better for you to enter life
maimed than with two hands to go into
hell,[q] where the fire never goes out.[r] [44][a]
45And if your foot causes you to stumble,[s]
cut it off. It is better for you to enter life
crippled than to have two feet and be

9:31 [z] Mt 8:20 [a] ver 12; Ac 2:23; 3:13 [b] Mt 16:21 [c] Mt 16:21
9:32 [d] Lk 2:50; 9:45; 18:34; Jn 12:16
9:33 [e] Mt 4:13 [f] Mk 1:29
9:34 [g] Lk 22:24
9:35 [h] Mt 18:4; 20:26; Mk 10:43; Lk 22:26
9:36 [i] Mk 10:16
9:37 [j] Mt 10:40
9:38 [k] Nu 11:27-29
9:40 [l] Mt 12:30; Lk 11:23
9:41 [m] Mt 10:42
9:42 [n] Mt 5:29 [o] Mt 18:6; Lk 17:2
9:43 [p] Mt 5:29 [q] Mt 5:30; 18:8 [r] Mt 25:41
9:45 [s] Mt 5:29

[a] 44 Some manuscripts include here the words of verse 48.

9:14–29 The cause of the disciples' power failure becomes clear in the final scene: They had inadequate faith and insufficient prayer. Like the boy, their prayers were mute. A life of prayer goes hand in hand with effective ministry. It makes one receptive to the action of God. We cannot get ready for critical moments by quickly uttering a special prayer; we have to be ready to act through a prayerful life when the moment comes.

Dwight L. Moody said there were three kinds of faith: There is struggling faith, like a man in deep water desperately swimming; clinging faith, like a man hanging to the side of a boat; and resting faith, like a man safely within the boat who is able to reach out and help others get in. The Gospel of Mark intends to lead the reader to a resting faith, but it reveals that such faith can only come with divine help.

Faith requires humble trust. Jesus is not put off by the humble honesty of one who says, "I believe, but I am not certain." He grants what is asked to this desperate father. So we see that faith in Jesus comes as a gift and is sustained by Jesus' power. In Jesus' statement in v. 29 we learn that faith and prayer make a powerful combination. And through this entire account we also learn that faith is not just an inner entity; it has real impacts in the real world. Faith changes human reality.

9:30–32 The disciples do not comprehend what Jesus is talking about but are afraid to ask what he means. Either they are wary of being rebuked if they say anything, as Peter was earlier, or they prefer to live in a state of denial.

9:33–34 The picture Mark presents shows Jesus walking ahead of the disciples in silence on his way to his sacrificial death while his straggling followers self-promote.

9:35–37 The dispute opens the door for Jesus' teaching on selfless service. He presents them with a paradox: The one who wants to be first must become last of all and servant of all. As an example of what he means, Jesus places a little child in their midst. The child has no power, no status, and few rights. Jesus requires his "great" disciples to show humble service toward humble people like this child.

9:38–41 The disciples only recently failed to complete an exorcism, yet they do not hesitate to stop someone who is successful but who is not a member of their team. Jesus argues that the disciples cannot use his name to do mighty works and stop the work that is going on in other areas. Jesus then opens the doors wide to declare that all those who are not against him are actually for him.

9:42–48 Jesus promised a reward to outsiders who show his disciples a bare minimum of goodwill (v. 41), but he now threatens his disciples with dire judgment if they cause a little one who believes in him to slip. He uses hyperbole to make the point.

thrown into hell.[t] [46][a] [47]And if your eye
causes you to stumble,[u] pluck it out. It
is better for you to enter the kingdom of
God with one eye than to have two eyes
and be thrown into hell,[v] [48]where

"'the worms that eat them do not
die,
and the fire is not quenched.'[b][w]

[49]Everyone will be salted[x] with fire.
[50]"Salt is good, but if it loses its saltiness, how can you make it salty again?[y]
Have salt among yourselves,[z] and be at
peace with each other."[a]

Divorce

10:1–12pp // Mt 19:1–9

10 Jesus then left that place and went
into the region of Judea and across
the Jordan.[b] Again crowds of people
came to him, and as was his custom, he
taught them.[c]
[2]Some Pharisees[d] came and tested him
by asking, "Is it lawful for a man to divorce his wife?"
[3]"What did Moses command you?" he
replied.
[4]They said, "Moses permitted a man
to write a certificate of divorce and send
her away."[e]
[5]"It was because your hearts were
hard[f] that Moses wrote you this law,"
Jesus replied. [6]"But at the beginning
of creation God 'made them male and
female.'[c][g] [7]'For this reason a man will
leave his father and mother and be
united to his wife,[d] [8]and the two will
become one flesh.'[e][h] So they are no
longer two, but one flesh. [9]Therefore
what God has joined together, let no
one separate."
[10]When they were in the house again,
the disciples asked Jesus about this. [11]He
answered, "Anyone who divorces his wife
and marries another woman commits
adultery against her.[i] [12]And if she divorces

9:45 [t]Mt 18:8
9:47 [u]Mt 5:29 [v]Mt 5:29; 18:9
9:48 [w]Isa 66:24; Mt 25:41
9:49 [x]Lev 2:13
9:50 [y]Mt 5:13; Lk 14:34, 35 [z]Col 4:6 [a]Ro 12:18; 2Co 13:11; 1Th 5:13
10:1 [b]Mk 1:5; Jn 10:40; 11:7 [c]Mt 4:23; Mk 2:13; 4:2; 6:6,34
10:2 [d]Mk 2:16
10:4 [e]Dt 24:1-4; Mt 5:31
10:5 [f]Ps 95:8; Heb 3:15
10:6 [g]Ge 1:27; 5:2
10:8 [h]Ge 2:24; 1Co 6:16
10:11 [i]Mt 5:32; Lk 16:18

[a] 46 Some manuscripts include here the words of verse 48. [b] 48 Isaiah 66:24 [c] 6 Gen. 1:27 [d] 7 Some early manuscripts do not have *and be united to his wife.* [e] 8 Gen. 2:24

9:49–50 Jesus concludes his teaching in this section with two potentially puzzling sayings about salt. The first one appears only in Mark. Since salt was used for purification, this first statement tells the disciples that if they endure to the end, the suffering they undergo will not destroy them but will purify them for God.

The second salt saying divides into two halves. If salt fails to flavor or preserve food, it is not salt and is worthless. The same applies to the disciples. These statements are a reference to having meals together in the context of fellowship and peace; these concluding sayings present peaceful fellowship as the model for disciples' relationships.

✣ **9:30–50** One can use the text about the unfamiliar exorcist as being instructive for any community that believes that God can act only through them. The Christian world is becoming increasingly divided. So-called liberals afraid of so-called evangelicals criticize them, and vice versa. Each regards the other with deep suspicion and as somehow lesser Christians.

We must guard against the attitude of superiority that says, "You are different from me, and I despise you for being different." We can uncover this spirit by asking ourselves how we feel about the other churches in our neighborhoods. Would we pray that another church in the neighborhood succeed in its ministry even if it siphons off members from our church? Would we pray for that success if the church were of another denomination?

In the battle against evil, we must recognize that whatever particular group we belong to is not the only group of Christians in the world. We can then learn from others who worship the same Christ as Lord and Savior but who may use different language and emphasize different parts of Scripture than we do. As we link arms with our Christian brothers and sisters, our unity will be a sign of what God's power can do to drive out the evil and chaos infecting our world (see Jn 17:20–26).

10:1–3 The Pharisees are actually interested in something other than Jesus' legal opinion on this issue of divorce. But Jesus' response exposes a fatal flaw in the Pharisees' whole approach to the law. They come at the law asking, "What can I get away with?" This preoccupation with legal subtleties ultimately neglects love for neighbor. Jesus' question uncovers their sinful hearts hidden behind the mask of legal questioning.

10:4–5 The Pharisees respond by citing the Mosaic regulations covering the divorce process. Jesus' line of reasoning becomes clear. If the Mosaic legislation on this issue had its roots in people's hardness of heart, then it cannot reflect God's will. Divorce is sin in God's eyes because it originates in hard hearts in either one or both spouses.

10:6–9 The Pharisees need to remember what God has commanded about marriage rather than simply promoting what Moses has permitted. Jesus addresses marriage from the perspective of God's intention at the beginning of creation. One finds God's true intentions for marriage not in Dt 24:1–4 but earlier, in Ge 1–2, which is also a "book of Moses."

10:10–12 As has been his custom, Jesus gives his disciples additional instruction when they privately ask him for an explanation. Not only does he maintain that divorce is wrong, but Jesus brands remarriage to anyone after a divorce as adultery.

her husband and marries another man,
she commits adultery."[j]

The Little Children and Jesus

10:13–16pp // Mt 19:13–15; Lk 18:15–17

13People were bringing little children
to Jesus for him to place his hands on
them, but the disciples rebuked them.
14When Jesus saw this, he was indignant.
He said to them, "Let the little children
come to me, and do not hinder them,
for the kingdom of God belongs to such
as these.[k] 15Truly I tell you, anyone who
will not receive the kingdom of God like
a little child will never enter it."[l] 16And
he took the children in his arms,[m] placed
his hands on them and blessed them.

The Rich and the Kingdom of God

10:17–31pp // Mt 19:16–30; Lk 18:18–30

17As Jesus started on his way, a man
ran up to him and fell on his knees[n] before him. "Good teacher," he asked, "what
must I do to inherit eternal life?"[o]
18"Why do you call me good?" Jesus
answered. "No one is good—except God
alone. 19You know the commandments:
'You shall not murder, you shall not commit adultery, you shall not steal, you shall
not give false testimony, you shall not defraud, honor your father and mother.'[a]"[p]
20"Teacher," he declared, "all these I
have kept since I was a boy."
21Jesus looked at him and loved him.
"One thing you lack," he said. "Go, sell everything you have and give to the poor,[q]
and you will have treasure in heaven.[r]
Then come, follow me."[s]
22At this the man's face fell. He went
away sad, because he had great wealth.
23Jesus looked around and said to his
disciples, "How hard it is for the rich[t] to
enter the kingdom of God!"
24The disciples were amazed at his
words. But Jesus said again, "Children,
how hard it is[b] to enter the kingdom
of God![u] 25It is easier for a camel to go
through the eye of a needle than for

10:12 [j] Ro 7:3; 1Co 7:10,11
10:14 [k] Mt 25:34
10:15 [l] Mt 18:3
10:16 [m] Mk 9:36
10:17 [n] Mk 1:40 [o] Lk 10:25; Ac 20:32
10:19 [p] Ex 20:12-16; Dt 5:16-20
10:21 [q] Ac 2:45 [r] Mt 6:20; Lk 12:33 [s] Mt 4:19
10:23 [t] Ps 52:7; 62:10; 1Ti 6:9, 10,17
10:24 [u] Mt 7:13, 14

[a] *19* Exodus 20:12-16; Deut. 5:16-20 [b] *24* Some manuscripts *is for those who trust in riches*

Divorce stems from hardness of heart, which can lead to more hardness of heart.

10:13-16 Others have brought people who were paralyzed or blind to Jesus; now parents bring children to Jesus asking him to touch and bless them. The disciples want to be the gatekeepers who determine not only who can use Jesus' name (9:38) but also who can see him. So Jesus must indignantly intercede on behalf of the children and inform his disciples that the kingdom of God belongs to such as these.

In the ancient world, children had no status. Here the little ones are easily pushed aside because they are weak, but God works most powerfully in weakness. When one is appropriately little, like a child, or poor in spirit, one is more open to receiving the reign of God.

> **10:1-16** We must be sensitive not to beat people over the head with the Bible when they are already bruised and broken by a fractured relationship. While we in the church should proclaim God's original intention for marriage and announce God's judgment on sin, we must also proclaim God's forgiveness of sin and acceptance of sinners. The church must direct all sinners, regardless of marital status, to God's offer of forgiveness and provide a place for them to experience God's healing. For those who are experiencing the pain of separation or divorce, divorce recovery groups may provide an excellent opportunity to minister to people when they need help the most.

10:17-18 This faithful Jew who believed in the life to come must have been taken aback by Jesus' initial response, which gets to the core issue raised by this encounter. The man's initial question assumes that one can find goodness in human effort and accomplishments. As the scene develops, God's demands turn out to be far more costly than he bargained for.

10:19 Jesus directs this man to the Ten Commandments, which he already knows. Either the man is disappointed to learn nothing new from Jesus or pleased that his hunch about his good prospects in the age to come has been confirmed by a religious specialist.

10:20 Jesus does not sneer at his claims to have obeyed the law, but because he loves him, he directly challenges him. The command to sell everything sounds quite unreasonable to us, but most in the ancient world would have heard it as radical but sound advice for those who were seriously devout.

10:21-22 Jesus insists that the wisest investments accrue interest in the treasuries of heaven. In this man's case, it means giving all that he has to support the poor. He leaves "sad," revealing that he does not want to enter life under Jesus' guidance. He goes off, presumably in search of a second, more accommodating opinion. Jesus will not renegotiate the terms, however.

10:23-24 One can imagine the disciples standing with mouths wide open as they observe this exchange. Jesus lets a sincere, good man slip away, one whose deep pockets could help advance the kingdom cause—or at least their meager treasury. Jesus astounds them further by observing that the rich will have a hard time entering the kingdom of God.

10:24-26 Jesus resorts to colorful hyperbole to reinforce the point that those who are ruled by money cannot be ruled by God. The rich will find entering the kingdom of God (coming under God's rule) more

someone who is rich to enter the kingdom of God."[v]
26The disciples were even more
amazed, and said to each other, "Who
then can be saved?"
27Jesus looked at them and said, "With
man this is impossible, but not with God;
all things are possible with God."[w]
28Then Peter spoke up, "We have left
everything to follow you!"[x]
29"Truly I tell you," Jesus replied, "no
one who has left home or brothers or
sisters or mother or father or children
or fields for me and the gospel 30will fail
to receive a hundred times as much[y] in
this present age: homes, brothers, sisters,
mothers, children and fields — along
with persecutions — and in the age to
come[z] eternal life.[a] 31But many who are
first will be last, and the last first."[b]

Jesus Predicts His Death a Third Time

10:32–34pp // Mt 20:17–19; Lk 18:31–33

32They were on their way up to Jerusalem, with Jesus leading the way, and the
disciples were astonished, while those
who followed were afraid. Again he took
the Twelve[c] aside and told them what
was going to happen to him. 33"We are
going up to Jerusalem,"[d] he said, "and the
Son of Man[e] will be delivered over to the
chief priests and the teachers of the law.[f]
They will condemn him to death and will
hand him over to the Gentiles, 34who will
mock him and spit on him, flog him[g] and
kill him.[h] Three days later[i] he will rise."[j]

The Request of James and John

10:35–45pp // Mt 20:20–28

35Then James and John, the sons of
Zebedee, came to him. "Teacher," they
said, "we want you to do for us whatever we ask."
36"What do you want me to do for
you?" he asked.
37They replied, "Let one of us sit at
your right and the other at your left in
your glory."[k]
38"You don't know what you are asking,"[l] Jesus said. "Can you drink the cup[m]
I drink or be baptized with the baptism
I am baptized with?"[n]
39"We can," they answered.
Jesus said to them, "You will drink
the cup I drink and be baptized with the
baptism I am baptized with,[o] 40but to sit
at my right or left is not for me to grant.
These places belong to those for whom
they have been prepared."
41When the ten heard about this, they

10:25 [v] Lk 12:16-20
10:27 [w] Mt 19:26
10:28 [x] Mt 4:19
10:30 [y] Mt 6:33 [z] Mt 12:32 [a] Mt 25:46
10:31 [b] Mt 19:30
10:32 [c] Mk 3:16-19
10:33 [d] Lk 9:51 [e] Mt 8:20 [f] Mt 27:1,2
10:34 [g] Mt 16:21 [h] Ac 2:23; 3:13 [i] Mt 16:21 [j] Mt 16:21
10:37 [k] Mt 19:28
10:38 [l] Job 38:2 [m] Mt 20:22 [n] Lk 12:50
10:39 [o] Ac 12:2; Rev 1:9

---

difficult than trying to squeeze a camel through the eye of a needle. The disciples are shocked by this statement and assume that the prospects of entering the kingdom of God are hopeless for those who usually get whatever they want in this life. So they ask, "Who then can be saved?" (v. 26).

10:27 Jesus corrects the implicit assumption in the rich man's initial question. He assumed that one could attain eternal life by doing something. Since he wanted something he could do, Jesus obliged him by saying, "Sell everything you have and give to the poor" (v. 21). The disciples are to learn from this encounter that to enter the kingdom of God, one must submit to God's rule over every aspect of life.

10:28–31 Jesus is implying that his disciples must be prepared to give up everything for the cause. Peter quickly reminds Jesus that they have done exactly that, and Jesus promises that their sacrifice will be worthwhile.

10:17–31 The values of our materialistic culture seep in and can undermine the spirit proper to a follower of Jesus. We need to confront the materialism of our culture that has infiltrated the church.

Jesus said that the rich man in this story lacked one thing, though he did not specify what it was. In applying this passage to our contemporary situation, we can imagine that he lacked the very things that we ourselves may lack. He had too much to give up.

Wealth cannot make one holy or purchase eternal life. Entrance to the kingdom requires a radical change in priorities, personal sacrifice, trust in our new master for direction and provision, and compassion for others.

10:32–34 The disciples and Jesus are marching to Zion. Mark tells us that they are amazed and afraid. But each time Jesus speaks to them about his suffering, his words to his disciples go in one ear and out the other.

10:35–37 James and John are no different from Peter as they misinterpret what it means for Jesus to be the Messiah. Either Jesus' words about his suffering whistle right by them, or they must hope that he is only talking about a temporary setback that will be quickly reversed. James and John are as self-confident in their own abilities as the rich man was.

10:38–40 Jesus responds to their ill-timed and selfish request with grace. He informs them that the Father has not placed him in charge of the seating arrangements in the kingdom. The cup he talks about is a metaphor for suffering (Isa 51:17, 22), and baptism is a metaphor for being plunged into calamity (see Ps 42:7; 69:1). He will not be sprinkled with a bit of suffering; rather, he will be submerged in it.

10:41 The other disciples are angry because James and John beat them to the punch and may now have an edge over them for the available power

Mk 10:43–45 ❖ What are concrete ways we can better imitate the servant nature of Christ?

became indignant with James and John.
42Jesus called them together and said,
"You know that those who are regarded as rulers of the Gentiles lord it over them, and their high officials exercise authority over them.
43Not so with you. Instead, whoever wants to become great among you must be your servant,[p]
44and whoever wants to be first must be slave of all.
45For even the Son of Man did not come to be served, but to serve,[q] and to give his life as a ransom for many."[r]

Blind Bartimaeus Receives His Sight

10:46–52pp // Mt 20:29–34; Lk 18:35–43

46Then they came to Jericho. As Jesus and his disciples, together with a large crowd, were leaving the city, a blind man, Bartimaeus (which means "son of Timaeus"), was sitting by the roadside begging.
47When he heard that it was Jesus of Nazareth,[s] he began to shout, "Jesus, Son of David,[t] have mercy on me!"
48Many rebuked him and told him to be quiet, but he shouted all the more, "Son of David, have mercy on me!"
49Jesus stopped and said, "Call him."
So they called to the blind man, "Cheer up! On your feet! He's calling you."
50Throwing his cloak aside, he jumped to his feet and came to Jesus.
51"What do you want me to do for you?" Jesus asked him.
The blind man said, "Rabbi,[u] I want to see."
52"Go," said Jesus, "your faith has healed you."[v] Immediately he received his sight and followed[w] Jesus along the road.

Jesus Comes to Jerusalem as King

11:1–10pp // Mt 21:1–9; Lk 19:29–38
11:7–10pp // Jn 12:12–15

11 As they approached Jerusalem and came to Bethphage and Bethany[x] at the Mount of Olives,[y] Jesus sent two of

10:43 [p] Mk 9:35
10:45 [q] Mt 20:28 [r] Mt 20:28
10:47 [s] Mk 1:24 [t] Mt 9:27
10:51 [u] Mt 23:7
10:52 [v] Mt 9:22 [w] Mt 4:19
11:1 [x] Mt 21:17 [y] Mt 21:1

---

slots. Jealousy creates turmoil in the ranks. The disciples would rather bear a grudge than a cross.

10:42–44 Jesus tries to channel the disciples' desire to be great into humble service when he encourages them to be great servants of others. The disciples need to take Jesus as their model.

10:45 Jesus has told his disciples that he must die, but this is the only passage in Mark that tells us *why* he must die. The term "ransom" was used for compensation for personal injury or a crime, for purchasing the freedom of an enslaved relative, and for the price paid as an equivalent for the sacrifice of the firstborn. The concept of ransom, therefore, is connected to the idea of cost, substitution, and atonement. Jesus pays a price for others that they cannot pay themselves.

✜ **10:32–45** The church cannot thrive if its leaders are competing with one another for positions of power. Looking at James and John is like looking in the mirror. We can see our own selfishness, and Mark hopes that in doing so we can see how foolish we look.

10:46–48 Bartimaeus and others like him in the ancient world were totally dependent on others for charity, guidance, and protection. They were society's expendables.

That is exactly how the crowd treats Bartimaeus. When he cries out to Jesus as the "Son of David" (v. 47), they chide him for making a nuisance of himself. Jesus has reached the last stage of his journey to Jerusalem, but despite the shadow of the cross looming ever larger across his path, he can still hear the cries of others in distress.

10:49–51 The crowds tell Bartimaeus to keep quiet. Jesus, however, stops and says, "Call him" (v. 49)—further evidence that he came to serve. The man springs up to come to Jesus, who then asks him, "What do you want me to do for you?" (v. 51).

This question may seem an odd one to ask a blind man, but Jesus forces him to reflect on what he truly wants from him. Bartimaeus's answer demonstrates enough faith to transform him from a blind man begging along the way to a person who sees and follows Jesus on the way.

10:52 With his eyes now open, Bartimaeus decides to follow Jesus as every disciple is called to do. Like the first disciples Jesus called, he abandons his former way of life and leaves everything. The cloak he leaves behind (v. 50) is not much, but it is likely his sole worldly possession. Leaving just a garment may seem easier than selling all one has, but that is why Jesus indicated how hard it was for those with possessions to enter the kingdom.

✜ **10:46–52** If healing requires persistence, one must be intentional in coming to Jesus for relief. Bartimaeus does not simply want to meet the famous prophet from Nazareth in some misty-eyed, emotional way. He cries out specifically to Jesus because he believes that he will have mercy on him and can give him his sight.

"What do you want me to do for you?" is one of the most important questions God ever asks us, and the one to which we most frequently give the wrong answer. We ask for all the wrong things in life. Our answer to this question will reveal whether we want death or life—whether we want to be healed from our blindness or selfishly want to use God to do our bidding and fulfill our own desires.

11:1–10 Jesus enters Jerusalem as Israel's Messiah (cf. Zec 9:9). This deviates from Jesus' previous

his disciples, 2saying to them, "Go to the
village ahead of you, and just as you enter
it, you will find a colt tied there, which no
one has ever ridden.[z] Untie it and bring
it here. 3If anyone asks you, 'Why are you
doing this?' say, 'The Lord needs it and
will send it back here shortly.'"
4They went and found a colt outside
in the street, tied at a doorway.[a] As they
untied it, 5some people standing there
asked, "What are you doing, untying
that colt?" 6They answered as Jesus had
told them to, and the people let them
go. 7When they brought the colt to Jesus
and threw their cloaks over it, he sat on
it. 8Many people spread their cloaks on
the road, while others spread branches
they had cut in the fields. 9Those who
went ahead and those who followed
shouted,

"Hosanna!*a*"

"Blessed is he who comes in the
name of the Lord!"*b*[b]

10"Blessed is the coming kingdom of
our father David!"

"Hosanna in the highest heaven!"[c]

11Jesus entered Jerusalem and went into
the temple courts. He looked around at
everything, but since it was already late,
he went out to Bethany with the Twelve.[d]

Jesus Curses a Fig Tree and Clears the Temple Courts

11:12–14pp // Mt 21:18–22
11:15–18pp // Mt 21:12–16; Lk 19:45–47; Jn 2:13–16
11:20–24pp // Mt 21:19–22

12The next day as they were leaving
Bethany, Jesus was hungry. 13Seeing in
the distance a fig tree in leaf, he went
to find out if it had any fruit. When he
reached it, he found nothing but leaves,
because it was not the season for figs.[e]

11:2 [z] Nu 19:2; Dt 21:3; 1Sa 6:7
11:4 [a] Mk 14:16
11:9 [b] Ps 118:25, 26; Mt 23:39
11:10 [c] Lk 2:14
11:11 [d] Mt 21:12, 17
11:13 [e] Lk 13:6-9

a 9 A Hebrew expression meaning "Save!" which became an exclamation of praise; also in verse 10
b 9 Psalm 118:25,26

---

attempts to avoid calling attention to himself. What occurs now is a complete reversal: Jesus encourages public rejoicing by his entrance into the city.

11:11 The excitement generated by Jesus' arrival ends somewhat anticlimactically when he enters the temple, only to look around and leave. Mark raises the readers' expectations that something grand will happen, but nothing does. This colorless ending to Jesus' dramatic entry into Jerusalem shows more than meets the eye. Jesus enters the temple to inspect it, and the next day's events reveal that he comes not to restore it but to pronounce God's judgment on it.

✣ **11:1–11** The crowd shouts, "Hosanna!" Save us! thinking that Jesus has come to save them from their political enemies. But God wins by sending his Son to the cross, not by sending armies into bloody battles. As a king who gives his life for others, Jesus reigns with a kind of power that no earthly ruler can match.

We at times can be like that crowd, but Jesus knows that what we need most is for him to save us from ourselves. Human nature and aspirations change little over the years, and this incident reveals that we must be saved from inconsistent faith that abandons Jesus at the first sign of trouble. Jesus does not welcome cheers from throngs who will not pray with him in dark Gethsemane or go with him to an even darker Golgotha.

11:12–33 The fig-tree incident sandwiches the temple incident. Interpreting either in isolation from the other leads one in the wrong direction. We will first look at Jesus' actions in the temple and then see how the cursing of the fig tree helps explain what it means.

11:15–19 A key question to ask is why Jesus would purify something that he predicts will soon be destroyed (13:2). The best answer is that he does not intend to reform the temple.

11:15–17 Jesus appears in the temple as a charismatic prophet and acts out God's rejection of the temple practice and its coming destruction. Jesus' interpretation for his action is crucial for understanding what he intended. This teaching transforms a simple display of protest into an announcement of divine judgment (see 12:9).

The passage cited from Isa 56:7 in Mk 11:17 means that God did not plan for the temple to become a national shrine for Israel. Isaiah 56:1–8 contains God's promise of blessing for all who might think they are excluded from God's salvation: the foreigner, the eunuch, and the outcasts of Israel. Most assumed that Isa 56 spoke of some distant future, but Jesus expects it to be fulfilled in his day. The temple had become a nationalistic symbol that served only to divide Israel from the nations.

By quoting from Jer 7 (also in Mk 11:17), Jesus reminds the people that something holy can be perverted. The temple, God's house, has been made into "a den of robbers." One needs to read the context of Jer 7:1–15 to understand the allusion. The reference to the "den of robbers" has not only to do with the trade in the temple. It also denounces the false security that the Israelites' sacrificial practice breeds.

In other words, the robbers are not swindlers but bandits. The den is the place where robbers retreat after having committed their crimes. It is their hideout, a place of security and refuge. Jesus attacks the leaders for allowing the temple to degenerate into a safe hiding place where people think that they find forgiveness and fellowship with God no matter how they act on the outside.

11:12–14, 20–21 The fig-tree incident brackets the temple action and interprets it. It reveals more clearly that Jesus does not intend to cleanse the temple. Instead, his actions demonstrate that

14 Then he said to the tree, "May no one
ever eat fruit from you again." And his
disciples heard him say it.
15 On reaching Jerusalem, Jesus entered the temple courts and began
driving out those who were buying and
selling there. He overturned the tables
of the money changers and the benches of those selling doves, 16 and would
not allow anyone to carry merchandise
through the temple courts. 17 And as he
taught them, he said, "Is it not written:
'My house will be called a house of prayer
for all nations'[a]?[f] But you have made it
'a den of robbers.'[b]"[g]
18 The chief priests and the teachers of
the law heard this and began looking for
a way to kill him, for they feared him,[h]
because the whole crowd was amazed at
his teaching.[i]
19 When evening came, Jesus and his
disciples[c] went out of the city.[j]
20 In the morning, as they went along,
they saw the fig tree withered from the
roots. 21 Peter remembered and said to
Jesus, "Rabbi,[k] look! The fig tree you
cursed has withered!"
22 "Have faith in God," Jesus answered.
23 "Truly[d] I tell you, if anyone says to this
mountain, 'Go, throw yourself into the
sea,' and does not doubt in their heart
but believes that what they say will happen, it will be done for them.[l] 24 Therefore
I tell you, whatever you ask for in prayer,
believe that you have received it, and it
will be yours.[m] 25 And when you stand
praying, if you hold anything against
anyone, forgive them, so that your Father in heaven may forgive you your
sins."[n] [26][e]

11:17 [f] Isa 56:7 [g] Jer 7:11
11:18 [h] Mt 21:46; Mk 12:12; Lk 20:19 [i] Mt 7:28
11:19 [j] Lk 21:37
11:21 [k] Mt 23:7
11:23 [l] Mt 21:21
11:24 [m] Mt 7:7
11:25 [n] Mt 6:14

Mk 11:25 ❖ Are there people in our lives who we need to forgive? What is keeping us from offering them forgiveness?

The Authority of Jesus Questioned

11:27–33pp // Mt 21:23–27; Lk 20:1–8

27 They arrived again in Jerusalem, and
while Jesus was walking in the temple
courts, the chief priests, the teachers
of the law and the elders came to him.
28 "By what authority are you doing these
things?" they asked. "And who gave you
authority to do this?"
29 Jesus replied, "I will ask you one

[a] *17* Isaiah 56:7 [b] *17* Jer. 7:11 [c] *19* Some early manuscripts *came, Jesus* [d] *22,23* Some early manuscripts *"If you have faith in God," Jesus answered, 23"truly* [e] *26* Some manuscripts include here words similar to Matt. 6:15.

the fig tree that has not borne fruit is cursed, not reformed or cleansed.

Jesus surely knows it is not fig season. This detail is a clue for the reader to look beyond the surface meaning and to see its symbolic meaning. This action has to do with the temple. The word "season" (v. 13) is not the term for the growing season but rather the religious term found in 1:14-15 pointing to the time of the kingdom of God. Moreover, the tenants do not produce the fruits of the vineyard "at harvest time" (12:2; or "in season"). The barren fig tree represents the unfruitful temple Judaism that is unprepared to accept Jesus' messianic reign.

As the fig tree's time is barren (cf. Lk 13:6-9), so is the temple's. Time can run out for fruitless trees and prayerless temples. The center of salvation now shifts from the temple to Jesus and his death and resurrection. Faith in him will become the way to God, not the sacrifice of animals in the temple.

When Jesus and his disciples pass by the tree the next day, the fig tree is "withered from the roots" (Mk 11:20). For a fig tree in full leaf to shrivel so completely within a day is a miracle, and it conveys that the temple's condemnation is not a temporary measure. It is everlasting. The tree gave the impression that it might provide something to eat, just as the temple gives the impression that it is a place dedicated to the service of God. The temple only benefits the priestly hierarchy; it profits nothing for God.

11:22-23 Jesus does not say "mountains" but specifies "this mountain." He is most likely referring to the Temple Mount, Mount Zion. The temple would no longer be the focal point of God's presence. A holy place will be wherever disciples preach Jesus' gospel and wherever his people, Jews and Gentiles, gather to hear the message.

11:24-25 Jesus assures his disciples that the effectiveness of prayer has nothing to do with the temple or its sacrifices. When he dies on the cross, access to God is not closed off but rather opened up for all. His death creates a new house of prayer—a temple not made with hands, which will be without barriers or limitations.

Jesus concludes his explanation with a promise (v. 25). A relationship with God is based simply on faith and forgiveness. By the time Mark writes his Gospel, the temple is either besieged or already destroyed.

11:18, 27-28 The chief priests, the teachers of the law, and the elders are the very ones Jesus predicted would conspire to kill him. They challenge Jesus to present his qualifications for his actions.

11:29-30 Jesus refers back to the ministry of John the Baptist. John came preaching a baptism of repentance for the forgiveness of sins that bypassed the temple practice. It was free; no sacrifice was required except that of a repentant heart. Jesus implicitly aligns himself with the ministry of John, and if John's ministry was from heaven, then the temple has become irrelevant.

question. Answer me, and I will tell
you by what authority I am doing these
things. 30John's baptism — was it from
heaven, or of human origin? Tell me!"
31They discussed it among themselves
and said, "If we say, 'From heaven,' he
will ask, 'Then why didn't you believe
him?' 32But if we say, 'Of human origin' . . ." (They feared the people, for
everyone held that John really was a
prophet.)[o]
33So they answered Jesus, "We don't
know."

Jesus said, "Neither will I tell you by
what authority I am doing these things."

The Parable of the Tenants

12:1–12pp // Mt 21:33–46; Lk 20:9–19

12 Jesus then began to speak to them
in parables: "A man planted a vineyard.[p] He put a wall around it, dug a pit
for the winepress and built a watchtower.
Then he rented the vineyard to some
farmers and moved to another place.
2At harvest time he sent a servant to
the tenants to collect from them some
of the fruit of the vineyard. 3But they
seized him, beat him and sent him away
empty-handed. 4Then he sent another
servant to them; they struck this man
on the head and treated him shamefully. 5He sent still another, and that one
they killed. He sent many others; some
of them they beat, others they killed.
6"He had one left to send, a son, whom
he loved. He sent him last of all,[q] saying,
'They will respect my son.'
7"But the tenants said to one another,
'This is the heir. Come, let's kill him, and
the inheritance will be ours.' 8So they
took him and killed him, and threw him
out of the vineyard.
9"What then will the owner of the
vineyard do? He will come and kill those
tenants and give the vineyard to others. 10Haven't you read this passage of
Scripture:

"'The stone the builders rejected
has become the cornerstone;[r]
11the Lord has done this,
and it is marvelous in our
eyes'[a]?"[s]

11:32 [o] Mt 11:9
12:1 [p] Isa 5:1-7
12:6 [q] Heb 1:1-3
12:10 [r] Ac 4:11
12:11 [s] Ps 118:22, 23

[a] 11 Psalm 118:22,23

11:31–33 The authorities attempt to sidestep the challenge, but the damage is done. Mark's comment that "they feared the people" (v. 32) reveals that their authority derives from humans because they do not fear heaven.

> **11:12–33** In his actions and words in this chapter, it is clear that Jesus envisioned a future without a temple. But its downfall would not bring an end to effective prayer. What does prayer look like in his community?
>
> First, the community needs to pray *receptively*. Prayer is not imposing our will on God but opening up our lives to God's will. Second, people are to pray *confidently*. This text does not invite one to attempt magical miracles. When Christians pray in Jesus' name, they may be confident of God's response, but what they ask must be compatible with his teaching, life, and death. There are some things that Christians should not ask and some things that God will not give. Third, the new community is to pray *expectantly* and without discouragement. Our prayers should fix our attention on the long term and the large scale with God's kingdom in mind (Mt 6:33). Finally, the community is to pray *with a forgiving spirit*. We cannot make peace with God if we are holding grudges with others.

12:1–12 Jesus' story is an allegory of God's troubled relationship with Israel that is nearing its climax.
12:1–5 The word "servant" is a frequent designation in the OT for the prophets whom God sent to the people. The servants' treatment in the allegory surely called to mind the ill treatment that the prophets received.
12:6–8 The allegory reaches its finale after the servants fail to collect the fruit. The owner sends the son "last of all." He is identified as a "son, whom he loved" (v. 6), which recalls the voice from heaven identifying Jesus as "my Son, whom I love" (1:11; 9:7).

After the tenants assassinate the son, they throw his body outside and leave him unburied. To refuse to bury a corpse was an incredible offense in the ancient world.
12:9 The owner suddenly changes from one who is seemingly impotent to one who can exact revenge. He is now the lord of the vineyard who will destroy the tenants who killed his servants and son. But the lord is not through: He will also give the vineyard to others.
12:10–12 Jesus terminates this confrontation with a citation from Ps 118:22–23, the psalm that the crowd chanted when Jesus entered the city. The block of stone that the builders discarded becomes either the cornerstone or the capstone of a new structure. The image implies a new temple.

The final part of the quotation, "The Lord has done this, and it is marvelous in our eyes" (v. 11), attributes Jesus' condemnation of the temple to God's work. The tenants' destruction, the giving of the vineyard to others, and the transformation of a rejected stone into the cornerstone are marvelous to the ones who have eyes to see God's plan.

This allegory reflects that Jesus is claiming to be the Son of the Lord of the vineyard and that he is fully aware of his impending death at the hands of the authorities. Those who question the authenticity of the allegory tend to question both possibilities.

12Then the chief priests, the teachers of
the law and the elders looked for a way
to arrest him because they knew he had
spoken the parable against them. But
they were afraid of the crowd;[t] so they
left him and went away.[u]

Paying the Imperial Tax to Caesar

12:13–17pp // Mt 22:15–22; Lk 20:20–26

13Later they sent some of the Pharisees
and Herodians[v] to Jesus to catch him[w]
in his words. 14They came to him and
said, "Teacher, we know that you are a
man of integrity. You aren't swayed by
others, because you pay no attention to
who they are; but you teach the way of
God in accordance with the truth. Is it
right to pay the imperial tax[a] to Caesar
or not? 15Should we pay or shouldn't we?"
But Jesus knew their hypocrisy. "Why
are you trying to trap me?" he asked.
"Bring me a denarius and let me look
at it." 16They brought the coin, and he
asked them, "Whose image is this? And
whose inscription?"
"Caesar's," they replied.
17Then Jesus said to them, "Give back
to Caesar what is Caesar's and to God
what is God's."[x]
And they were amazed at him.

Marriage at the Resurrection

12:18–27pp // Mt 22:23–33; Lk 20:27–38

18Then the Sadducees,[y] who say there
is no resurrection,[z] came to him with a
question. 19"Teacher," they said, "Moses
wrote for us that if a man's brother dies
and leaves a wife but no children, the
man must marry the widow and raise
up offspring for his brother.[a] 20Now
there were seven brothers. The first one
married and died without leaving any
children. 21The second one married the
widow, but he also died, leaving no child.
It was the same with the third. 22In fact,
none of the seven left any children. Last
of all, the woman died too. 23At the resurrection[b] whose wife will she be, since
the seven were married to her?"
24Jesus replied, "Are you not in error
because you do not know the Scriptures[b]
or the power of God? 25When the dead rise,
they will neither marry nor be given in
marriage; they will be like the angels in
heaven.[c] 26Now about the dead rising —
have you not read in the Book of Moses, in
the account of the burning bush, how God
said to him, 'I am the God of Abraham,

12:12 [t]Mk 11:18 [u]Mt 22:22
12:13 [v]Mt 22:16; Mk 3:6 [w]Mt 12:10
12:17 [x]Ro 13:7
12:18 [y]Ac 4:1 [z]Ac 23:8; 1Co 15:12
12:19 [a]Dt 25:5
12:24 [b]2Ti 3:15-17
12:25 [c]1Co 15:42, 49,52

[a] 14 A special tax levied on subject peoples, not on Roman citizens [b] 23 Some manuscripts *resurrection, when people rise from the dead,*

12:1-12 The parable particularly applies to believers in the church today. God expects the vineyard, God's people, to be an accepting, prayerful, forgiving, devoted, and loving fellowship built around his Son, the one Stone that binds everything together. When we or the church become something other than this, we prompt God's judgment.

12:13-14 The chief priests, teachers of the law, and elders send Pharisees and the Herodians to snare Jesus in a carefully laid trap. His questioners bait the trap by asking a yes or no question about an explosive issue: taxes.

12:15-16 Jesus, knowing his questioners' motives, easily evades their ambush and sets a trap of his own. He asks the leaders to identify whose image is on the coin he asks for. When they answer, Jesus can now answer their question: Since they have no qualms about doing business with Caesar's money, they had better pay Caesar's taxes. And since they also have no problem bringing an image of Caesar and a symbol of his worldly power into God's temple, he makes them look impious and foolish.

12:17 Jesus does more than balance this statement when he tells them to give back to God what is God's. Exactly what we owe God becomes clear in Jesus' answer to a certain teacher of the law: We owe God love from all our heart, soul, mind, and strength (vv. 30, 33).

12:13-17 Jesus' response to his opponents in this section serves as a model for his followers. He speaks God's truth with such utter conviction that people listen. We as Christians may hold citizenship in heaven, but that does not exempt us from being exemplary citizens on earth.

12:18 The Sadducees rejected any theological innovations they believed came from anything other than the Pentateuch. The belief in the resurrection fell into this category, since the books of Moses never mention it.

12:19-23 The Sadducees bait Jesus with a teasing conundrum (based on their lack of belief in the resurrection).

12:24-27 Jesus answers these hostile questioners by going on the attack. The Sadducees are deceived because they are ignorant of Scripture and underestimate God's power. Jesus first corrects the Sadducees on their view of the resurrection. He then corrects the Sadducees' biblical ignorance by reminding them of the "bush" passage in the Torah that identifies God as the God of Abraham, Isaac, and Jacob (Ex 3:6). The living God would hardly identify himself as the God of corpses. Jesus' parting shot, "You are badly mistaken" (v. 27), affirms that some truths are not open to debate.

Mk 12:29–31 ❖ How can we keep love of God and neighbor at the forefront of our minds and actions?

the God of Isaac, and the God of Jacob'[a]?[d]
27He is not the God of the dead, but of the living. You are badly mistaken!"

The Greatest Commandment

12:28–34pp // Mt 22:34–40

28One of the teachers of the law[e] came and heard them debating. Noticing that Jesus had given them a good answer, he asked him, "Of all the commandments, which is the most important?"
29"The most important one," answered Jesus, "is this: 'Hear, O Israel: The Lord our God, the Lord is one.[b]
30Love the Lord your God with all your heart and with all your soul and with all your mind and with all your strength.'[c][f]
31The second is this: 'Love your neighbor as yourself.'[d][g] There is no commandment greater than these."
32"Well said, teacher," the man replied. "You are right in saying that God is one and there is no other but him.[h]
33To love him with all your heart, with all your understanding and with all your strength, and to love your neighbor as yourself is more important than all burnt offerings and sacrifices."[i]
34When Jesus saw that he had answered wisely, he said to him, "You are not far from the kingdom of God."[j] And from then on no one dared ask him any more questions.[k]

12:26 [d] Ex 3:6
12:28 [e] Lk 10:25-28; 20:39
12:30 [f] Dt 6:4,5
12:31 [g] Lev 19:18; Mt 5:43
12:32 [h] Dt 4:35, 39; Isa 45:6,14; 46:9
12:33 [i] 1Sa 15:22; Hos 6:6; Mic 6:6-8; Heb 10:8
12:34 [j] Mt 3:2 [k] Mt 22:46; Lk 20:40

Whose Son Is the Messiah?

12:35–37pp // Mt 22:41–46; Lk 20:41–44
12:38–40pp // Mt 23:1–7; Lk 20:45–47

35While Jesus was teaching in the temple courts,[l] he asked, "Why do the teachers of the law say that the Messiah is the son of David?[m]
36David himself, speaking by the Holy Spirit,[n] declared:

"'The Lord said to my Lord:
"Sit at my right hand
until I put your enemies
under your feet."'[e][o]

37David himself calls him 'Lord.' How then can he be his son?"
The large crowd[p] listened to him with delight.

Warning Against the Teachers of the Law

38As he taught, Jesus said, "Watch out for the teachers of the law. They like to walk around in flowing robes and be greeted with respect in the marketplaces,
39and have the most important seats in the synagogues and the places of honor at banquets.[q]
40They devour widows' houses and for a show make lengthy prayers. These men will be punished most severely."

The Widow's Offering

12:41–44pp // Lk 21:1–4

41Jesus sat down opposite the place where the offerings were put[r] and

12:35 [l] Mt 26:55 [m] Mt 9:27
12:36 [n] 2Sa 23:2 [o] Ps 110:1; Mt 22:44
12:37 [p] Jn 12:9
12:39 [q] Lk 11:43
12:41 [r] 2Ki 12:9; Jn 8:20

[a] 26 Exodus 3:6 [b] 29 Or *The Lord our God is one Lord* [c] 30 Deut. 6:4,5 [d] 31 Lev. 19:18 [e] 36 Psalm 110:1

✣ **12:18–27** The Sadducees pictured the resurrection in terms of what they were familiar with in earthly life, and it naturally made no sense. Jesus only tells them what is not there: no marriage or giving in marriage.

12:28–31 This teacher is asking, "What is the fundamental premise of the law on which all the individual commands depend?" Jesus gives an orthodox reply from the daily confession of Israel known as the *Shema*. The statement that no other command is greater than the two cited can mean that the other commands simply spell out different ways in which to apply these two primary ones.
12:32–34 The teacher of the law assumes a superior position from which he passes judgment on Jesus' teaching. But Jesus is the One who knows who is near or far from the kingdom of God.
12:35–37 Jesus cites Ps 110:1 to point out a conundrum: If the Messiah is the son of David, why does David address him "by the Holy Spirit" as "Lord"? It is hardly customary for fathers to address their sons in this way. One expects quite the reverse. How then can the Messiah be David's son?

Mark frequently challenges his readers to understand more of Jesus' full identity by posing questions. This one serves to correct the crowd's expectation of "the coming kingdom of [their] father David" (Mk 11:10). At this time, Jesus does not hold the earthly political and military authority of David, yet he is far greater than the great king of Israel, as is his kingdom: the kingdom of the Father.
12:38–40 First, Jesus chastises the teachers of the law for their desire to wear distinguished robes, which point to their desire to be honored by the people. Jesus accuses the teachers of the law of devouring widows' houses and criticizes their prayers. Their pride reveals their improper motives.
12:41–44 The rich in this scene give from their abundance, but they do not sacrifice their abundance. This poor widow gives all that she has to live on, which is next to nothing. She shows radical trust in God to provide for her in giving what she has to God.

watched the crowd putting their money into the temple treasury. Many rich people threw in large amounts. 42But a poor widow came and put in two very small copper coins, worth only a few cents.

43Calling his disciples to him, Jesus said, "Truly I tell you, this poor widow has put more into the treasury than all the others. 44They all gave out of their wealth; but she, out of her poverty, put in everything—all she had to live on."[s]

The Destruction of the Temple and Signs of the End Times

13:1–37pp // Mt 24:1–51; Lk 21:5–36

13 As Jesus was leaving the temple, one of his disciples said to him, "Look, Teacher! What massive stones! What magnificent buildings!"

2"Do you see all these great buildings?" replied Jesus. "Not one stone here will be left on another; every one will be thrown down."[t]

3As Jesus was sitting on the Mount of Olives[u] opposite the temple, Peter, James, John[v] and Andrew asked him privately, 4"Tell us, when will these things happen? And what will be the sign that they are all about to be fulfilled?"

5Jesus said to them: "Watch out that no one deceives you.[w] 6Many will come in my name, claiming, 'I am he,' and will deceive many. 7When you hear of wars and rumors of wars, do not be alarmed. Such things must happen, but the end is still to come. 8Nation will rise against nation, and kingdom against kingdom. There will be earthquakes in various places, and famines. These are the beginning of birth pains.

9"You must be on your guard. You will be handed over to the local councils and flogged in the synagogues.[x] On account of me you will stand before governors and kings as witnesses to them. 10And the gospel must first be preached to all nations. 11Whenever you are arrested and brought to trial, do not worry beforehand about what to say. Just say whatever is given you at the time, for it is not you speaking, but the Holy Spirit.[y]

12"Brother will betray brother to death, and a father his child. Children will rebel against their parents and have them put to death.[z] 13Everyone will hate you because of me,[a] but the one who stands firm to the end will be saved.[b]

14"When you see 'the abomination that causes desolation'[a][c] standing where it[b] does not belong—let the reader understand—then let those who are in Judea flee to the mountains. 15Let no one on the housetop go down or enter the house to take anything out. 16Let

12:44 [s] 2Co 8:12
13:2 [t] Lk 19:44
13:3 [u] Mt 21:1 [v] Mt 4:21
13:5 [w] ver 22; Jer 29:8; Eph 5:6; 2Th 2:3,10-12; 1Ti 4:1; 2Ti 3:13; 1Jn 4:6
13:9 [x] Mt 10:17
13:11 [y] Mt 10:19, 20; Lk 12:11,12
13:12 [z] Mic 7:6; Mt 10:21; Lk 12:51-53
13:13 [a] Jn 15:21 [b] Mt 10:22
13:14 [c] Da 9:27; 11:31; 12:11

[a] *14* Daniel 9:27; 11:31; 12:11 [b] *14* Or *he*

Mk 13:11 ❖ When have you experienced the Holy Spirit's help in a difficult moment when you were at a loss for words? How have you felt the Spirit assist you?

12:28–44 Our love for God is a response to God's love for us. Those who try to straddle the fence by allotting God only token love while maintaining a close friendship with the world are doomed to be frustrated in this world and doomed in the world to come. With God, it is all or nothing. Love cannot be tithed like money. Few can honestly sing, "All to Jesus I Surrender," but God requires nothing less.

13:1–4 As Jesus departs the temple, the disciples are impressed by its beauty. Jesus resets the disciples' attitude toward this building as he prophesies its complete destruction. When Jesus predicted his death and resurrection earlier, the disciples never asked when it would happen, but now they want to know exactly when this will occur and what the sign will be so that they can prepare themselves for what is to come.

13:5–6 The disciples will need uncommon spiritual insight to be able to withstand the deceivers and weather the storms of persecution. The deceivers lay claim to divine authority that rightfully belongs only to Jesus. The disciples must prepare themselves to see through these impostors and to maintain their focus on what Jesus has taught.

13:7–8 Jesus identifies these frightening things as the "beginning of birth pains" (v. 8)—a time of intense suffering. When the world is collapsing around them, Jesus-followers may hope for deliverance from their present distress, but Jesus says they must prepare themselves for the long haul.

13:9–13 These persecutors specifically target Christians because they are Christians. When these things happen, wise disciples will realize they are suffering precisely what Jesus predicted. The kingdom of God will silently advance as the disciples proclaim the gospel despite these trials.

It is necessary for the gospel to be preached first to the whole world (v. 10). The pre-Easter cowardice of the disciples will be transformed into bravery. The empty tomb is not the end of the gospel, only the beginning.

13:14–20 The warning in these verses applies specifically to the first and second generation of Jesus' disciples, those who will witness the war in Judea that will result in the destruction of the

no one in the field go back to get their
cloak. 17How dreadful it will be in those
days for pregnant women and nursing
mothers![d] 18Pray that this will not take
place in winter, 19because those will be
days of distress unequaled from the beginning, when God created the world,[e]
until now — and never to be equaled
again.[f]
20"If the Lord had not cut short those
days, no one would survive. But for the
sake of the elect, whom he has chosen,
he has shortened them. 21At that time
if anyone says to you, 'Look, here is the
Messiah!' or, 'Look, there he is!' do not
believe it.[g] 22For false messiahs and false
prophets[h] will appear and perform signs
and wonders[i] to deceive, if possible, even
the elect. 23So be on your guard;[j] I have
told you everything ahead of time.
24"But in those days, following that
distress,

"'the sun will be darkened,
and the moon will not give its light;
25the stars will fall from the sky,
and the heavenly bodies will be
shaken.'[a][k]

26"At that time people will see the Son
of Man coming in clouds[l] with great power and glory. 27And he will send his angels
and gather his elect from the four winds,
from the ends of the earth to the ends
of the heavens.[m]
28"Now learn this lesson from the
fig tree: As soon as its twigs get tender
and its leaves come out, you know that
summer is near. 29Even so, when you
see these things happening, you know
that it[b] is near, right at the door. 30Truly
I tell you, this generation[n] will certainly
not pass away until all these things have
happened.[o] 31Heaven and earth will pass
away, but my words will never pass away.[p]

The Day and Hour Unknown

32"But about that day or hour no one
knows, not even the angels in heaven,
nor the Son, but only the Father.[q] 33Be
on guard! Be alert[c]![r] You do not know
when that time will come. 34It's like a
man going away: He leaves his house
and puts his servants[s] in charge, each
with their assigned task, and tells the
one at the door to keep watch.
35"Therefore keep watch because you
do not know when the owner of the
house will come back — whether in
the evening, or at midnight, or when
the rooster crows, or at dawn. 36If he
comes suddenly, do not let him find you

13:17 [d] Lk 23:29
13:19 [e] Mk 10:6 [f] Da 9:26; 12:1; Joel 2:2
13:21 [g] Lk 17:23; 21:8
13:22 [h] Mt 7:15 [i] Jn 4:48; 2Th 2:9,10
13:23 [j] 2Pe 3:17
13:25 [k] Isa 13:10; 34:4; Mt 24:29
13:26 [l] Da 7:13; Mt 16:27; Rev 1:7
13:27 [m] Zec 2:6
13:30 [n] Lk 17:25 [o] Mk 9:1
13:31 [p] Mt 5:18
13:32 [q] Ac 1:7; 1Th 5:1,2
13:33 [r] 1Th 5:6
13:34 [s] Mt 25:14

[a] *25* Isaiah 13:10; 34:4 [b] *29* Or *he* [c] *33* Some manuscripts *alert and pray*

---

temple. The cue to take flight comes when they see the "abomination that causes desolation" (v. 14), which refers to what is detestable and rejected by God and causes horror and destruction among humankind. The term derives from Da 11:31. Whatever that abomination was, Mark intended the audience to understand it as another sign of the beginning of the birth pains.

The temple no longer symbolizes God's abiding favor and protection since God will allow it to be destroyed. To revere the temple means to reject trust in Jesus and his commands.

13:21–23 This unit about the war in Judea concludes as it began—with a warning about deceivers. However compelling these signs and however persuasive their interpretations, disciples must keep on their toes to resist their claims. Jesus urges them to hold fast to the certainty that God's Messiah has already come and is hidden in heaven, not on earth. He will not come to save the temple from its fate.

13:24–27 Two things are clear: The end of the temple must happen before the end of time, but it does not denote the end. Jesus is silent about what might lie between the two events. He simply says, "But in those days, following that distress" (v. 24).

How long following that distress? The uncertainty is deliberate, and Jesus does not intend for us to try to unravel it; otherwise, he would have given more definite clues. He expects his disciples to be ready for anything at any time.

Only in the return will the mystery of the Son of Man be completely visible for all to see. The clouds of his coming will reveal his glory as the One who shares in the majesty and power of God, who also comes in clouds.

The images of the sun darkening, the moon not giving its light, the stars falling, and the powers in the heaven shaking are woven together from the OT (Isa 13:10; Joel 2:10; 3:4, 20). Jesus' coming means salvation for the elect as angels are sent out to gather them. The elect are those who have faithfully responded to the gospel.

13:28–31 Many questions surround these verses. Yet it appears that the simplest explanation is to take the fig-tree parable and the statement that all these things will come on this generation as a reference to what will come before the destruction of the temple (vv. 5–23). Jesus' predictions about the temple's destruction will come true. Those things that humans believe are the center of the universe will disappear from the face of the earth. Only Jesus' words will stand forever.

13:32 Jesus must be obedient to the sovereign will of God, who determines the time for his return. No calculations done beforehand will be able to predict it: The end will come without any warning.

13:33–37 This parable applies to the coming of the Son of Man. Its key element is that the servants have no advance warning as to when the master of the house will return. Only those who are valiant

sleeping. 37What I say to you, I say to everyone: 'Watch!' "[t]

Jesus Anointed at Bethany

14:1–11pp // Mt 26:2–16
14:1,2,10,11pp // Lk 22:1–6
14:3–8Ref // Jn 12:1–8

14 Now the Passover[u] and the Festival
of Unleavened Bread were only two
days away, and the chief priests and the
teachers of the law were scheming to
arrest Jesus secretly and kill him.[v] 2"But
not during the festival," they said, "or the
people may riot."
3While he was in Bethany,[w] reclining
at the table in the home of Simon the
Leper, a woman came with an alabaster
jar of very expensive perfume, made of
pure nard. She broke the jar and poured
the perfume on his head.[x]
4Some of those present were saying
indignantly to one another, "Why this
waste of perfume? 5It could have been
sold for more than a year's wages[a] and
the money given to the poor." And they
rebuked her harshly.
6"Leave her alone," said Jesus. "Why
are you bothering her? She has done a
beautiful thing to me. 7The poor you will
always have with you,[b] and you can help
them any time you want.[y] But you will not
always have me. 8She did what she could.
She poured perfume on my body beforehand to prepare for my burial.[z] 9Truly I
tell you, wherever the gospel is preached
throughout the world,[a] what she has done
will also be told, in memory of her."
10Then Judas Iscariot, one of the
Twelve,[b] went to the chief priests to betray Jesus to them.[c] 11They were delighted to hear this and promised to give him
money. So he watched for an opportunity
to hand him over.

The Last Supper

14:12–26pp // Mt 26:17–30; Lk 22:7–23
14:22–25pp // 1Co 11:23–25

12On the first day of the Festival of Unleavened Bread, when it was customary
to sacrifice the Passover lamb,[d] Jesus'
disciples asked him, "Where do you want
us to go and make preparations for you
to eat the Passover?"
13So he sent two of his disciples, telling
them, "Go into the city, and a man carrying a jar of water will meet you. Follow
him. 14Say to the owner of the house he
enters, 'The Teacher asks: Where is my
guest room, where I may eat the Passover
with my disciples?' 15He will show you

13:37 [t]Lk 12:35-40
14:1 [u]Jn 11:55; 13:1 [v]Mt 12:14
14:3 [w]Mt 21:17 [x]Lk 7:37-39
14:7 [y]Dt 15:11
14:8 [z]Jn 19:40
14:9 [a]Mt 24:14; Mk 16:15
14:10 [b]Mk 3:16-19 [c]Mt 10:4
14:12 [d]Ex 12:1-11; Dt 16:1-4; 1Co 5:7

[a] 5 Greek *than three hundred denarii* [b] 7 See Deut. 15:11.

---

under fire and vigilant during the delay will be vindicated in the end.

13:1-37 The most important thing that Christians have been called to do in the face of Jesus' impending return is to preach the gospel to all the nations (v. 10). When the Son of Man comes, he will not quiz people to see whose predictions on the date were most accurate; rather, he will want to know what we were doing while we waited. Were we proclaiming the gospel to all the nations? Were we enduring suffering faithfully? Were we fulfilling our assigned tasks? That is why Jesus warns his disciples to be on their guard (v. 9).

14:1-11 During the Passover festival, tens of thousands of pilgrims flocked to Jerusalem. The population exploded to more than double its normal size. This was a particularly nervous time for the high priests and their police force since the chance for an outbreak of riots increased dramatically during this time.

14:3 The next scene finds Jesus dining at the home of Simon the leper. But Mark does not tell us who Simon is, why Jesus is there, or what the conversation is. Mark is only interested in what happens when an anonymous woman breaks into the company of men and pours precious perfume over Jesus' head. She breaks a costly jar containing pure nard, and the even more costly perfume streams out.

In the OT, kings were anointed in private, and this action sometimes signaled a revolt. Maybe this woman hopes it is time for God to intervene in the affairs of Israel with this king.

14:4-9 The bystanders complain about the waste of something so expensive. But Jesus cherishes this woman's devotion and defends her. The anointing reveals that Jesus knows about both his impending death and of his ultimate triumph. Good news pierces through the upcoming tragedy: Jesus announces that this woman's devotion will be remembered wherever the gospel is preached in the whole world.

14:1-11 Jesus' commending this anonymous woman reveals that we can never be fully aware of our own significance or role in God's kingdom. The woman had no idea of the worldwide significance of her action, nor did the high priests, Judas, or Pontius Pilate. It is a mistake for us to think that our sacrificial devotion is wasteful or insignificant. Who knows how God will use it?

14:12-16 Jesus gives the disciples directions that reflect either a miraculous event or a secret arrangement on Jesus' part. Either way, Jesus knows everything in advance and has total control of

a large room upstairs,[e] furnished and
ready. Make preparations for us there."
16The disciples left, went into the city
and found things just as Jesus had told
them. So they prepared the Passover.
17When evening came, Jesus arrived
with the Twelve. 18While they were reclining at the table eating, he said, "Truly
I tell you, one of you will betray me —
one who is eating with me."
19They were saddened, and one by
one they said to him, "Surely you don't
mean me?"
20"It is one of the Twelve," he replied,
"one who dips bread into the bowl with
me.[f] 21The Son of Man[g] will go just as it
is written about him. But woe to that
man who betrays the Son of Man! It
would be better for him if he had not
been born."
22While they were eating, Jesus took
bread, and when he had given thanks,
he broke it[h] and gave it to his disciples,
saying, "Take it; this is my body."
23Then he took a cup, and when he
had given thanks, he gave it to them,
and they all drank from it.[i]
24"This is my blood of the[a] covenant,[j]
which is poured out for many," he said to
them. 25"Truly I tell you, I will not drink
again from the fruit of the vine until that
day when I drink it new in the kingdom
of God."[k]
26When they had sung a hymn, they
went out to the Mount of Olives.[l]

14:15 [e] Ac 1:13
14:20 [f] Jn 13:18-27
14:21 [g] Mt 8:20
14:22 [h] Mt 14:19
14:23 [i] 1Co 10:16
14:24 [j] Mt 26:28
14:25 [k] Mt 3:2
14:26 [l] Mt 21:1
14:27 [m] Zec 13:7
14:28 [n] Mk 16:7
14:30 [o] ver 66-72; Lk 22:34; Jn 13:38
14:31 [p] Lk 22:33; Jn 13:37

Mk 14:29 ❖ When we get overconfident about our righteousness, what is the result?

Jesus Predicts Peter's Denial

14:27–31pp // Mt 26:31–35

27"You will all fall away," Jesus told
them, "for it is written:

"'I will strike the shepherd,
and the sheep will be scattered.'[b][m]

28But after I have risen, I will go ahead
of you into Galilee."[n]
29Peter declared, "Even if all fall away,
I will not."
30"Truly I tell you," Jesus answered,
"today — yes, tonight — before the rooster crows twice[c] you yourself will disown
me three times."[o]
31But Peter insisted emphatically, "Even
if I have to die with you,[p] I will never disown you." And all the others said the same.

[a] 24 Some manuscripts *the new* [b] 27 Zech. 13:7
[c] 30 Some early manuscripts do not have *twice.*

the situation. The emphasis falls on the statement: "The disciples . . . found things just as Jesus had told them" (v. 16).

14:17–21 The scene begins with Jesus' grave announcement that one of the Twelve will betray him. As the disciples ask him one by one, "Surely you don't mean me?" Jesus reassures no one but gives only a vague response (vv. 19–20). This statement confirms that the betrayer is in the room and is eating with him.

14:22 When Jesus breaks the bread and distributes it to the disciples, it means that what has happened to this bread will happen to him. What is significant is that Jesus uses an article of food so simple and so universal that the disciples can never again take bread, bless it, and break it without thinking of the last night that they were together with their Lord.

14:23–25 After the blessing of the cup, Jesus gives it to them. Mark reports that after they have all drunk from the cup, Jesus announces, "This is my blood of the covenant, which is poured out for many" (v. 24). Think of what this statement might have meant to a Jew in the first century. With everyone having drunk from the cup, the host says, "This is my blood."

What do Jesus' statements, "This is my body" and "This is my blood," imply? First, Jesus is saying that his death is a new sacrifice offered to God. No more sacrificial victims need to be killed; only bread broken and shared, wine poured out and shared. Second, Mark makes it clear that they all drank from one cup. Drinking the cup of someone meant entering into a communion of relationship with that person, to the point that one shared that person's destiny, whether good or bad. The disciples also had to follow in the way of their Lord and accept his destiny of suffering for themselves.

Finally, blood sealed or inaugurated a covenant. Jesus' sacrificial death is also a covenant-making event. It marks a new act of redemption and begins a new relationship between God and the people that supersedes the old.

14:26–27 Jesus' small band will be thrown into confusion and scattered in all directions. The citation from Zec 13:7 (Mk 14:27) reveals that what will happen is all in God's control.

14:28 Jesus again gives them a cheering promise, "After I have risen, I will go ahead of you into Galilee" (v. 28). For the fifth time in the Gospel, Jesus predicts his resurrection.

14:29–31 Peter insists that he will prove himself more trustworthy than the rest, who, he implies, probably will fall away. His competitive arrogance shows devotion to Jesus but also points to Peter's trust in his own strength and abilities. Consequently, Peter's failure at the crucial moment will be immortalized.

✣ **14:12–31** The Passover celebration was meant to place each generation in touch with that event and make it a present reality.

A HARMONISTIC OVERVIEW OF JESUS' TRIALS

PHASE	AUTHORITY/TIME/PLACE	EVENTS/JUDGMENT
THE JEWISH TRIAL		
1. First Jewish Phase (Jn 18:13–24)	Annas Thursday evening Annas's courtyard	Only John tells us that Jesus was originally sent to Annas, the former high priest and father-in-law of Caiaphas, for his initial questioning.
2. Second Jewish Phase (Mk 14:53–65; Mt 26:57–68; Lk 22:54)	Caiaphas and part of the Sanhedrin Thursday night Caiaphas's courtyard	False witnesses are brought against Jesus. When asked if he is the Christ, the Son of God, he responds positively but defines his role as that of the Son of Man. He is accused of blasphemy, mocked and beaten.
3. Third Jewish Phase (Mk 15:1a; Mt 27:1; Lk 22:66–71)	The full Sanhedrin Friday, early morning	While all three Synoptics mention this phase of the trial, Luke alone describes Jesus' confession in terms similar to those recorded by Mark and Matthew the evening before.
THE ROMAN TRIAL		
1. First Roman Phase (Mk 15:1b–5; Mt 27:2,11–14; Lk 23:1–5; Jn 18:28–38)	Pilate Friday, early morning at the Praetorium	The Sanhedrin leads Jesus away to the governor Pilate, who asks him if he is the king of the Jews. Jesus responds positively. In John's account, Jesus explains that his kingdom is not of this world.
2. Second Roman Phase (Lk 23:6–12)	Herod Antipas Friday morning at Herod's palace	Luke alone records that when Pilate learned that Jesus was from Galilee, he sent him to Herod, who was visiting Jerusalem. Herod questions Jesus without success, abuses him and returns him to Pilate.
3. Third Roman Phase (Mk 15:6–15; Mt 27:15–26; Lk 23:13–25)	Pilate Friday morning at the Praetorium	Holding to his custom to release a prisoner at Passover, Pilate attempts to free Jesus. Prompted by the chief priests, the crowds call for Barabbas's release and Jesus' crucifixion. Pilate scourges Jesus and turns him over for crucifixion.

Gethsemane

14:32–42pp // Mt 26:36–46; Lk 22:40–46

32They went to a place called Gethsemane, and Jesus said to his disciples,
"Sit here while I pray." 33He took Peter,
James and John[q] along with him, and
he began to be deeply distressed and
troubled. 34"My soul is overwhelmed
with sorrow to the point of death,"[r]
he said to them. "Stay here and keep
watch."
35Going a little farther, he fell to the
ground and prayed that if possible the
hour[s] might pass from him. 36*"Abba,*[a]
Father,"[t] he said, "everything is possible

14:33 [q] Mt 4:21
14:34 [r] Jn 12:27
14:35 [s] ver 41; Mt 26:18
14:36 [t] Ro 8:15; Gal 4:6

[a] 36 Aramaic for *father*

In the same way, the Lord's Supper is not a memorial of something past and gone; rather, it reminds us of what the Lord has done for us and makes his death and his presence a living reality.

14:32–35 Mark allows us to see Jesus suffering psychological anguish before his physical suffering. Jesus is in the grip of a shuddering horror as he faces the dreadful prospect before him.

14:36 Jesus' prayer of lament follows a well-known pattern of lament found in the Psalms. Jesus here expresses his intimacy with his Father as well as his confidence in God's nearness and loving care. His prayer does not try to run counter to the Father's purpose but explores the limits

for you. Take this cup[u] from me. Yet not
what I will, but what you will."[v]
37Then he returned to his disciples and
found them sleeping. "Simon," he said to
Peter, "are you asleep? Couldn't you keep
watch for one hour? 38Watch and pray so
that you will not fall into temptation.[w] The
spirit is willing, but the flesh is weak."[x]
39Once more he went away and prayed
the same thing. 40When he came back,
he again found them sleeping, because
their eyes were heavy. They did not know
what to say to him.
41Returning the third time, he said to
them, "Are you still sleeping and resting?
Enough! The hour[y] has come. Look, the
Son of Man is delivered into the hands
of sinners. 42Rise! Let us go! Here comes
my betrayer!"

Jesus Arrested

14:43–50pp // Mt 26:47–56; Lk 22:47–50; Jn 18:3–11

43Just as he was speaking, Judas,[z] one
of the Twelve, appeared. With him was
a crowd armed with swords and clubs,
sent from the chief priests, the teachers
of the law, and the elders.
44Now the betrayer had arranged a
signal with them: "The one I kiss is the
man; arrest him and lead him away
under guard." 45Going at once to Jesus,
Judas said, "Rabbi!"[a] and kissed him.
46The men seized Jesus and arrested him. 47Then one of those standing
near drew his sword and struck the
servant of the high priest, cutting off
his ear.
48"Am I leading a rebellion," said
Jesus, "that you have come out with
swords and clubs to capture me? 49Ev-
ery day I was with you, teaching in the
temple courts,[b] and you did not arrest
me. But the Scriptures must be fulfilled."[c] 50Then everyone deserted him
and fled.[d]
51A young man, wearing nothing but
a linen garment, was following Jesus.
When they seized him, 52he fled naked,
leaving his garment behind.

14:36 [u] Mt 20:22 [v] Mt 26:39
14:38 [w] Mt 6:13 [x] Ro 7:22,23
14:41 [y] ver 35; Mt 26:18
14:43 [z] Mt 10:4
14:45 [a] Mt 23:7
14:49 [b] Mt 26:55 [c] Isa 53:7-12; Mt 1:22
14:50 [d] ver 27

---

of the purpose without trying to go beyond its boundaries.

The "cup" may represent God's wrathful judgment—the awful consequences of God's judgment on sinful humanity. On the other hand, the "cup" may simply refer to Jesus' death and the brutal suffering he must endure. In Gethsemane, Jesus meets the dreadful silence of heaven. Jesus overcomes the silence, fights off the human temptation to do as he wills, and through prayer, yields to God's will.

14:37–42 On the one hand, Jesus returns to his disciples as the Good Shepherd, who, confronted with the threat of the destruction of the flock, returns repeatedly to look after it. On the other hand, Mark underscores the failure of the disciples at this most crucial point.

Jesus' prayer in Gethsemane ends when he senses that the hour has come. Jesus knows that he will not be delivered. He has accepted God's will for himself and, through prayer, has prepared himself for what lies ahead. By contrast, the disciples have squandered the opportunity for prayer by sleeping. Consequently, they will fold under pressure.

14:43 Jesus earlier rebuked the temple as a robbers' den instead of a house of prayer for all nations. Now, ironically, temple guards arrest him in the middle of his prayer as if he is a robber.

14:44–45 The sad performance of Jesus' disciples in this crucial moment dominates this scene. Judas turns him over to a certain death with a warm gesture of love and the customary greeting of respect. This sign of intimacy and goodwill now forever becomes a sign of infamy and death.

14:46–49 Whether accidentally or intentionally, the high priest's servant's ear is cut off. Jesus condemns the violence directed at the arresting party and then announces that the Scriptures are being fulfilled.

14:50 The disciples have awakened sufficiently by this time to make their shameless getaway. They all forsake Jesus and flee. Jesus' arrest sets in motion the fulfillment of a whole range of Scriptures.

14:51–52 Mark alone includes the account of the young man who runs away into the darkness naked. The fear of this young man who is seized and stripped and escapes into the darkness is set against the courage of Jesus, who is seized and stripped and does not escape but is crucified.

14:32–52 In his garden prayer, Jesus models what he means when he tells his disciples to "watch" in 13:37. Spiritual drowsiness is dangerous and will prove the Christian's undoing. First, spiritual drowsiness starts when we stop praying. We often do not pray because we are unaware that we are in the midst of trial. Second, spiritual drowsiness grows when we are unable to recognize the onset of a trial or to accept it as God's will. The disciples heard only what they wanted to hear and tuned out Jesus' teaching on their impending suffering and their need to take up a cross. Third, spiritual drowsiness presumes that our personal will or strength will get us through the trial. We must be ever mindful how close we are to falling; the good news, however, is that failure in times of crisis is not permanent. Finally, spiritual drowsiness happens when we assume that we have arrived. The sudden arrival of trials in our lives can be a cruel reminder that confidence in our past spiritual achievements gets us nowhere.

Jesus Before the Sanhedrin

14:53–65pp // Mt 26:57–68; Jn 18:12,13,19–24
14:61–63pp // Lk 22:67–71

53They took Jesus to the high priest,
and all the chief priests, the elders and
the teachers of the law came together.
54Peter followed him at a distance, right
into the courtyard of the high priest.[e]
There he sat with the guards and warmed
himself at the fire.[f]
55The chief priests and the whole
Sanhedrin[g] were looking for evidence
against Jesus so that they could put
him to death, but they did not find any.
56Many testified falsely against him, but
their statements did not agree.
57Then some stood up and gave this false
testimony against him: 58"We heard him
say, 'I will destroy this temple made with
human hands and in three days will build
another,[h] not made with hands.'" 59Yet
even then their testimony did not agree.
60Then the high priest stood up before
them and asked Jesus, "Are you not going
to answer? What is this testimony that
these men are bringing against you?"
61But Jesus remained silent and gave
no answer.[i]
Again the high priest asked him, "Are
you the Messiah, the Son of the Blessed
One?"[j]
62"I am," said Jesus. "And you will see
the Son of Man sitting at the right hand
of the Mighty One and coming on the
clouds of heaven."[k]
63The high priest tore his clothes.[l]
"Why do we need any more witnesses?"
he asked. 64"You have heard the blasphemy. What do you think?"
They all condemned him as worthy
of death.[m] 65Then some began to spit
at him; they blindfolded him, struck
him with their fists, and said, "Prophesy!" And the guards took him and beat
him.[n]

Peter Disowns Jesus

14:66–72pp // Mt 26:69–75; Lk 22:56–62; Jn 18:16–18,25–27

66While Peter was below in the courtyard,[o] one of the servant girls of the high
priest came by. 67When she saw Peter
warming himself,[p] she looked closely
at him.
"You also were with that Nazarene,
Jesus,"[q] she said.
68But he denied it. "I don't know or

14:54 [e] Mt 26:3 [f] Jn 18:18
14:55 [g] Mt 5:22
14:58 [h] Mk 15:29; Jn 2:19
14:61 [i] Isa 53:7; Mt 27:12, 14; Mk 15:5; Lk 23:9; Jn 19:9 [j] Mt 16:16; Jn 4:25,26
14:62 [k] Rev 1:7
14:63 [l] Lev 10:6; 21:10; Nu 14:6; Ac 14:14
14:64 [m] Lev 24:16
14:65 [n] Mt 16:21
14:66 [o] ver 54
14:67 [p] ver 54 [q] Mk 1:24

14:53–54 Mark's trial scene pins the primary responsibility and initiative for Jesus' death on the high priest and his Sanhedrin. A hearing in the middle of the night suggests the kangaroo justice of a lynch mob, but it also shows that these leaders are under time constraints.

14:55–56 The ruling priests want Jesus dead and disgraced before the crowds. They presume his guilt because he is a threat. The hearing will serve to convince anyone who has doubts that he is worthy of death.

14:57–59 The law allowed an accused person to be condemned only on the evidence of two or more witnesses who agreed. Mark relates that many volunteer testimony against Jesus.

Jesus has indeed made menacing statements against this man-made temple. Since what the witnesses say about Jesus' stance toward the temple seems close to the truth, and since this charge resurfaces when passersby taunt him with it while he hangs from the cross (15:29), how is their testimony false?

Most likely Mark emphasizes that the testimony of the witnesses is false primarily because of the second element in the charge. His first readers may have held out hopes that Jesus as the Messiah would build another temple. Mark makes it clear that Jesus never claimed he would build another earthly temple.

14:60–61 Like the suffering servant of Isa 53, Jesus remains silent before his false accusers. The high priest takes charge and asks Jesus directly, "Are you the Messiah, the Son of the Blessed One?" (Mk 14:61). He piously avoids God's name while using underhanded means to get rid of an enemy.

14:62 Jesus publicly accepts that he is the Messiah with his reply: "I am." Jesus here affirms his identity before the high priest and his council and continues with an image that confirms this claim. But Jesus claims to be more than the Messiah. His affirmation far surpasses any current conception about the Messiah because he implies that he has divine authority, and that they will one day see it.

Jesus' prophecies have been fulfilled or are being fulfilled at this very moment. Meanwhile Jesus has just uttered another prophecy in this scene that is of a greater magnitude: "[They] will see the Son of Man sitting at the right hand of the Mighty One and coming on the clouds of heaven" (v. 62). Jesus will be vindicated in his resurrection and will judge his oppressors.

14:63–64 To the high priest, the evidence is conclusive: Jesus has incriminated himself, and the council unanimously condemns him. They judge him to be worthy of death.

14:65 The hearing before the Sanhedrin, which has made a mockery of justice, concludes with callous mockery of Jesus. The reader can see the irony in all of this: The blindfolded Jesus is the only one who truly sees, while his tormentors are blinded by their hatred.

14:66–72 Peter's trial in the courtyard is a parody of his Lord's trial. As Jesus confesses under immense pressure and hostility that seals his fate, Peter caves under the gentlest of pressure and lies to save himself.

understand what you're talking about,"[r]
he said, and went out into the entryway.[a]
69When the servant girl saw him there,
she said again to those standing around,
"This fellow is one of them." 70Again he
denied it.[s]
After a little while, those standing
near said to Peter, "Surely you are one
of them, for you are a Galilean."[t]
71He began to call down curses, and he
swore to them, "I don't know this man
you're talking about."[u]
72Immediately the rooster crowed the
second time.[b] Then Peter remembered
the word Jesus had spoken to him: "Before the rooster crows twice[c] you will
disown me three times."[v] And he broke
down and wept.

Jesus Before Pilate

15:2–15pp // Mt 27:11–26; Lk 23:2,3,18–25; Jn 18:29—19:16

15 Very early in the morning, the chief
priests, with the elders, the teachers
of the law[w] and the whole Sanhedrin,[x]
made their plans. So they bound Jesus, led
him away and handed him over to Pilate.[y]
2"Are you the king of the Jews?"[z] asked
Pilate.
"You have said so," Jesus replied.
3The chief priests accused him of
many things. 4So again Pilate asked him,
"Aren't you going to answer? See how
many things they are accusing you of."
5But Jesus still made no reply,[a] and
Pilate was amazed.
6Now it was the custom at the festival
to release a prisoner whom the people
requested. 7A man called Barabbas was
in prison with the insurrectionists who
had committed murder in the uprising.
8The crowd came up and asked Pilate to
do for them what he usually did.
9"Do you want me to release to you
the king of the Jews?"[b] asked Pilate,
10knowing it was out of self-interest that
the chief priests had handed Jesus over
to him. 11But the chief priests stirred up
the crowd to have Pilate release Barabbas[c] instead.
12"What shall I do, then, with the one
you call the king of the Jews?" Pilate
asked them.
13"Crucify him!" they shouted.
14"Why? What crime has he committed?" asked Pilate.
But they shouted all the louder, "Crucify him!"

14:68 [r] ver 30, 72
14:70 [s] ver 30, 68, 72 [t] Ac 2:7
14:71 [u] ver 30, 72
14:72 [v] ver 30, 68
15:1 [w] Mt 27:1; Lk 22:66 [x] Mt 5:22 [y] Mt 27:2
15:2 [z] ver 9, 12, 18, 26; Mt 2:2
15:5 [a] Mk 14:61
15:9 [b] ver 2
15:11 [c] Ac 3:14

[a] *68* Some early manuscripts *entryway and the rooster crowed* [b] *72* Some early manuscripts do not have *the second time.* [c] *72* Some early manuscripts do not have *twice.*

14:53–72 Jesus was killed by self-serving religious leaders in control of the temple who were intent on preserving their power. They were embedded in a prosperous and mighty institution, and institutions can forget their original purpose and become concerned only with self-preservation. Even institutions dedicated to God can be overtaken by evil and can try to impede God's will rather than serving as an agent of God's will.

Jesus confronted a corrupt institution and threatened its existence. What happened next should not surprise us. Confront corruption that exists today and see what happens.

Many Christians today in the West do not face the fierce persecution that engulfed the first Christians. Few are forced to choose between Christ and imprisonment or execution. Consequently, our denials of Christ may take more subtle forms, such as timid silence.

We may not want to be identified as Christians. We do not speak out against those who sarcastically dismiss Christianity as a fantasy. We try to blend into the crowd of our Lord's enemies because we do not want to be jeered by others or to rock any boats. But if Peter could be restored after denying his Lord and even cursing him, then there is hope for others who might be guilty of the same or worse. Peter's tears of remorse mark the beginning of that restoration; when we realize how, in big and small ways, we deny the lordship of Jesus over our lives, that's what marks the beginning of ours.

15:1–4 A Roman governor would not have put a native Jew on trial for his life simply because he had violated Jewish religious regulations. The high priests assert that if Jesus claims to be a king, he is guilty of a crime against the sovereign power of Rome. Sending him to Pilate in tethers also suggests that he is a threat to public order.

15:5 Much to Pilate's frustration, Jesus chooses to answer the charge ambiguously and then to remain silent, which amazes Pilate. The governor cannot release someone who refuses to deny such a serious charge. Jesus leaves it to God to provide the answer to the charges and to the evil massed against him.

15:6–15a Pilate is perplexed that the crowd cries for the release of the murderous Barabbas instead of the harmless Jesus. The crowd the religious leaders so feared has now become their willing pawn, and things turn ugly.

The crowd's choice is ironic. Barabbas, essentially a thug guilty of murder, will go free because Jesus has taken his place on the cross intended for him. Pilate is indifferent to his responsibility to carry out actual justice.

> **Mk 15:15** ❖ We have all made bad decisions because of the influence of "the crowd." How can Christians stand against such group pressure?

15Wanting to satisfy the crowd, Pilate
released Barabbas to them. He had Jesus
flogged,[d] and handed him over to be crucified.

The Soldiers Mock Jesus

15:16–20pp // Mt 27:27–31

16The soldiers led Jesus away into the
palace[e] (that is, the Praetorium) and
called together the whole company of
soldiers. 17They put a purple robe on him,
then twisted together a crown of thorns
and set it on him. 18And they began to
call out to him, "Hail, king of the Jews!"[f]
19Again and again they struck him on the
head with a staff and spit on him. Falling
on their knees, they paid homage to him.
20And when they had mocked him, they
took off the purple robe and put his own
clothes on him. Then they led him out[g]
to crucify him.

The Crucifixion of Jesus

15:22–32pp // Mt 27:33–44; Lk 23:33–43; Jn 19:17–24

21A certain man from Cyrene,[h] Simon,
the father of Alexander and Rufus,[i] was
passing by on his way in from the country, and they forced him to carry the
cross.[j] 22They brought Jesus to the place
called Golgotha (which means "the place
of the skull"). 23Then they offered him
wine mixed with myrrh,[k] but he did not
take it. 24And they crucified him. Dividing up his clothes, they cast lots[l] to see
what each would get.
25It was nine in the morning when
they crucified him. 26The written notice of the charge against him read: THE
KING OF THE JEWS.[m]
27They crucified two rebels with him,
one on his right and one on his left. [28][a]

15:15 [d] Isa 53:6
15:16 [e] Jn 18:28, 33; 19:9
15:18 [f] ver 2
15:20 [g] Heb 13:12
15:21 [h] Mt 27:32 [i] Ro 16:13 [j] Mt 27:32; Lk 23:26
15:23 [k] ver 36; Ps 69:21; Pr 31:6
15:24 [l] Ps 22:18
15:26 [m] ver 2

[a] 28 Some manuscripts include here words similar to Luke 22:37.

15:15b Prisoners to be flogged were bound to a pillar or post and whipped with a flagellum. This lash consisted of leather straps embedded with pieces of bone, lead, or bronze. It was fittingly called a "scorpion," and it ripped the prisoner's skin into bloody ribbons. Significant blood loss typically occurred, critically weakening the victim.
15:16-20 Mark reports that the whole company of soldiers (possibly around six hundred) joins in the mockery of Jesus in the courtyard of Pilate's praetorium. The soldiers' mock homage tops the masquerade. They hail him as "king of the Jews" and bow down before him. Their ridicule probably expresses as much contempt for the Jews as it does for Jesus. The mockery implies that this pitiful, weak figure is the kind of king the Jews deserve.

The recognition of Jesus in Mark's passion narrative is almost complete. A woman had lovingly anointed him in the home of a leper, which he announced was for his burial. The high priest asked if he was the Messiah, and he responded with a yes. Pilate called him the king of the Jews, and the soldiers mockingly saluted him as a king. While on earth, Jesus was a different type of king, and now cruel pagans anoint him with spit, crown him with thorns, and prepare to enthrone him on a cross.

> ✣ **15:1-20** People with no moral compass and no moral backbone often cave in to satisfy the crowd. Many today are like Pilate. They prefer Jesus to the envious, malicious high priests and the violent Barabbas, but that is as far as it goes. They see no harm in him, but they don't understand who he really is either, so they see no reason to risk anything for him.
>
> Jesus took the place of a condemned man. He did not volunteer to die specifically for Barabbas, but he was chosen by God to die for all sinful humanity. He accepted the bitter cup of judgment and took the place of a murderous rebel—and all similarly guilty humans (Ro 3:10).
>
> As Jesus' murder approached, he stood silent, answering nothing, taking nothing—except the lashes from the soldiers' whips. From our suffering Savior we can learn how to endure suffering with peace and grace, trusting in God to meet us in the midst of that suffering and to deliver us.

15:21 Mark identifies Simon as from Cyrene in North Africa and as the father of Rufus and Alexander. Most likely his name is remembered because he later became a Christian. Mark mentions the names of his two sons because they were known to the first readers of this Gospel.
15:22 The procession ends at a place called Golgotha, which Mark interprets for his Greek-speaking readers as "the place of the skull" (v. 22). Mark does not completely describe the details of Jesus' crucifixion, but the details Mark does isolate have theological significance.
15:23 Wine mixed with myrrh had an enhanced narcotic property. Those offering it may only have wanted to give their exhausted victim a spurt of energy so that he would last longer and suffer more. Jesus rejects the offer; he had made a vow at the Last Supper not to drink from the fruit of the vine until he would drink it again in the kingdom of God.
15:24 It was customary for executioners to split up the minor personal belongings of the person

29Those who passed by hurled insults
at him, shaking their heads[n] and saying, "So! You who are going to destroy
the temple and build it in three days,[o]
30come down from the cross and save
yourself!" 31In the same way the chief
priests and the teachers of the law
mocked him[p] among themselves. "He
saved others," they said, "but he can't
save himself! 32Let this Messiah,[q] this
king of Israel,[r] come down now from
the cross, that we may see and believe."
Those crucified with him also heaped
insults on him.

The Death of Jesus

15:33–41pp // Mt 27:45–56; Lk 23:44–49; Jn 19:29–30

33At noon, darkness came over the
whole land until three in the afternoon.[s] 34And at three in the afternoon
Jesus cried out in a loud voice, *"Eloi,
Eloi, lema sabachthani?"* (which means
"My God, my God, why have you forsak-
en me?").[a][t]

35When some of those standing near
heard this, they said, "Listen, he's calling Elijah."
36Someone ran, filled a sponge with
wine vinegar,[u] put it on a staff, and offered it to Jesus to drink. "Now leave him
alone. Let's see if Elijah comes to take
him down," he said.
37With a loud cry, Jesus breathed his
last.[v]
38The curtain of the temple was torn in
two from top to bottom.[w] 39And when the
centurion,[x] who stood there in front of
Jesus, saw how he died,[b] he said, "Surely
this man was the Son of God!"[y]
40Some women were watching from a
distance.[z] Among them were Mary Magdalene, Mary the mother of James the
younger and of Joseph,[c] and Salome.[a]
41In Galilee these women had followed
him and cared for his needs. Many other

15:29 [n] Ps 22:7; 109:25 [o] Mk 14:58; Jn 2:19
15:31 [p] Ps 22:7
15:32 [q] Mk 14:61 [r] ver 2
15:33 [s] Am 8:9
15:34 [t] Ps 22:1
15:36 [u] ver 23; Ps 69:21
15:37 [v] Jn 19:30
15:38 [w] Heb 10:19,20
15:39 [x] ver 45 [y] Mk 1:1,11; 9:7; Mt 4:3
15:40 [z] Ps 38:11 [a] Mk 16:1; Lk 24:10; Jn 19:25

[a] 34 Psalm 22:1 [b] 39 Some manuscripts *saw that he died with such a cry* [c] 40 Greek *Joses,* a variant of *Joseph;* also in verse 47

---

being executed. Mark mentions this detail as it also appears in Ps 22:18. This moment of absolute humiliation for Jesus is fully consistent with God's will.

15:29–31 The scornful passersby "hurled insults at him" (v. 29). The scene drips with irony as these scoffers spew their hatred from their own blind point of view and unknowingly proclaim the truth about Jesus. Mark may have intended an ironic contrast with the blasphemy charge against Jesus at the end of his initial interrogation. The reader must decide who is the real blasphemer—Jesus or the spectators.

15:32 Because they cannot see, his accusers next demand a miracle: They want him to come down from the cross so that they can see and believe. But a miraculous rescue would not have proven that he was the Messiah, the Son of God. They ask for tangible, earthly proof of the divine presence outside of God's will; because they do, they will never truly see anything.

15:33 The Pharisees had earlier demanded a sign from heaven, and Jesus refused. Now the leaders receive a sign from heaven, but it is not the kind they want or can understand.

15:34 Jesus' ghastly cry, "My God, my God, why have you forsaken me?" continues to perplex Christians. Interpreters are divided whether to consider only the words written (which come from Ps 22:1) or to weigh them against the entire psalm, a lament that ends with a triumphant hope of vindication.

15:35–36 The scoffers either misunderstand Jesus' final prayer or deliberately distort his words as a final jab. They think he is calling for Elijah, presumably to rescue him from the cross. Someone in the crowd runs to fill a sponge with sharp wine. Others stop this man and mockingly wait for a miraculous deliverance from Elijah, who was himself taken up in a chariot of fire.

15:37 With this last taunt, Jesus shouts out and "breathed his last." The loud cry is unusual, since crucified victims normally died of exhaustion and lack of breath.

15:38 This closing scene of Jesus' life parallels the opening scene of his baptism (1:9–11).

In Jesus' baptism, John appears in the garb of Elijah. In the crucifixion, bystanders think that Jesus is calling for Elijah to rescue him.

Both incidents also record the tearing of a holy place (the verb "torn" appears only in these two scenes in Mark). When Jesus ascended from the waters at his baptism, he saw the heavens, which Isaiah likens to a canopy (Isa 40:22), "torn open" (Mk 1:10). The blue linens of the temple veil were also comparable to the heavens.

God's divine presence descends on Jesus like a dove at his baptism. A heavenly voice announces, "You are my Son, whom I love" (1:11). The centurion echoes that voice from heaven: "Surely this man was the Son of God" (15:39).

While the tearing of the fabric of the heavens at the baptism scene was a private revelation for Jesus—only "he saw" (1:10)—the crucifixion is a public revelation for all to see. For the first time human beings can fully see what God intends to reveal.

15:39 The confession from the leader of the death squad marks the beginning of the fulfillment of Ps 22:27, "All the families of the nations will bow down before him."

15:40–41 The stance of these observers parallels that of Peter, who followed Jesus "at a distance" so that he might disguise his discipleship (14:54). They witness his death but do not confess as the centurion does.

women who had come up with him to
Jerusalem were also there.[b]

The Burial of Jesus

15:42–47pp // Mt 27:57–61; Lk 23:50–56; Jn 19:38–42

42It was Preparation Day (that is, the
day before the Sabbath).[c] So as evening
approached, 43Joseph of Arimathea, a
prominent member of the Council,[d] who
was himself waiting for the kingdom of
God,[e] went boldly to Pilate and asked for
Jesus' body. 44Pilate was surprised to hear
that he was already dead. Summoning
the centurion, he asked him if Jesus had
already died. 45When he learned from
the centurion[f] that it was so, he gave
the body to Joseph. 46So Joseph bought
some linen cloth, took down the body,
wrapped it in the linen, and placed it in
a tomb cut out of rock. Then he rolled a
stone against the entrance of the tomb.[g]
47Mary Magdalene and Mary the mother
of Joseph[h] saw where he was laid.

15:41 [b] Mt 27:55,56; Lk 8:2,3
15:42 [c] Mt 27:62; Jn 19:31
15:43 [d] Mt 5:22 [e] Mt 3:2; Lk 2:25,38
15:45 [f] ver 39
15:46 [g] Mk 16:3
15:47 [h] ver 40
16:1 [i] Lk 23:56; Jn 19:39,40
16:3 [j] Mk 15:46
16:5 [k] Jn 20:12
16:6 [l] Mk 1:24
16:7 [m] Jn 21:1-23 [n] Mk 14:28

Jesus Has Risen

16:1–8pp // Mt 28:1–8; Lk 24:1–10

16 When the Sabbath was over, Mary
Magdalene, Mary the mother of
James, and Salome bought spices[i] so
that they might go to anoint Jesus' body.
2Very early on the first day of the week,
just after sunrise, they were on their way
to the tomb 3and they asked each other,
"Who will roll the stone away from the
entrance of the tomb?"[j]

4But when they looked up, they saw
that the stone, which was very large, had
been rolled away. 5As they entered the
tomb, they saw a young man dressed in
a white robe[k] sitting on the right side,
and they were alarmed.

6"Don't be alarmed," he said. "You are
looking for Jesus the Nazarene,[l] who was
crucified. He has risen! He is not here. See
the place where they laid him. 7But go,
tell his disciples and Peter, 'He is going
ahead of you into Galilee. There you will
see him,[m] just as he told you.' "[n]

15:42–43 To ask for the body of someone executed for high treason could be looked upon as sympathizing and could earn one the same fate. But as a member of the council who condemned Jesus to death, Joseph is above suspicion.

15:44–45 Pilate's only concern is to establish that Jesus is actually dead. The centurion who confessed Jesus as the Son of God affirms that Jesus is in fact dead.

15:46–47 The passion began in the evening when Jesus came with his disciples for his Last Supper; it now ends in the evening with his burial. Joseph wraps Jesus' body up in a new linen cloth and buries him in a tomb carved in rock.

15:21–47 The cross is the point at which the blind rage of humanity against God is unleashed with a horrible intensity and is shown for what it is. The gospel story depicts many of the sins that put Jesus on this cross: pride, envy, jealousy, betrayal, cruelty, greed, indifference, cowardice, and murder. We need only add our own many sins to complete the list.

The question in the old spiritual, "Were you there when they crucified my Lord?" must be answered, "Yes." We were not there as loyal supporters to sing hymns, however. As we watch Jesus gasp on the cross, we must see ourselves as Barabbas, watching our Savior take our place and bearing our punishment on himself. All human beings still need saving from evil's power.

The cross reveals many profound truths about Jesus' sacrifice and our need for it. First, it reveals our sin and God's incredible power to defeat it. Second, it reveals God's unspeakable love for us. Third, in the crucifixion we see that God is always present in our sufferings, even when he seems absent. Fourth, the words of the centurion show us that God's truth permeates even the most unlikely hearts. Fifth, the violence of the scene demonstrates the pain of the human condition and the violent opposition that Christians face in the world. Finally, the torn curtain in the temple reveals a new way of life for all who will believe—access to a relationship with God the Father through the death and resurrection of Jesus, God's Son.

16:1–4 The women come to the tomb wondering how the stone can be moved; they leave wondering how the stone could have been moved.

16:5–6 When the women arrive at the tomb, they find an angelic figure who gives a typical angelic reassurance (v. 6) followed by what must have been startling news: "He has risen!" Mark's Gospel began with God's messenger announcing what God was about to do (1:1–2); it closes with God's messenger announcing what God has done.

16:7–8 The women must go to the disciples, who must in turn go to Galilee. This command is the first time that Jesus' followers are told to tell something about him. The crucifixion and the resurrection, therefore, mark a turning point. There is no need for silence or secrets now.

The resurrection revokes death and destruction, and it also revokes sin. A special nod to Peter (v. 7) hints at his full restoration despite his extraordinary denials. Jesus does not give up on his disciples, no matter how great their failure or how many their faults.

The announcement that "he is going ahead of you" (v. 7) is as important as the word that "he is not here" (v. 6). Just as the earthly Jesus led his frightened disciples to Jerusalem by going before

Mk 16:8 ❖ When we place ourselves in the sandals of these women, how might we have reacted to this surprising occurrence? Would fear have kept us silent after this experience? Why or why not?

8 Trembling and bewildered, the wom-
en went out and fled from the tomb.
They said nothing to anyone, because
they were afraid.[a]

[The earliest manuscripts and some other ancient witnesses do not have verses 9 – 20.]

9 When Jesus rose early on the first day of the
week, he appeared first to Mary Magdalene,[o] out
of whom he had driven seven demons. 10 She went
and told those who had been with him and who
were mourning and weeping. 11 When they heard
that Jesus was alive and that she had seen him,
they did not believe it.[p]
12 Afterward Jesus appeared in a different form
to two of them while they were walking in the
country.[q] 13 These returned and reported it to the
rest; but they did not believe them either.
14 Later Jesus appeared to the Eleven as they
were eating; he rebuked them for their lack of
faith and their stubborn refusal to believe those
who had seen him after he had risen.[r]
15 He said to them, "Go into all the world and
preach the gospel to all creation.[s] 16 Whoever be-
lieves and is baptized will be saved, but whoever
does not believe will be condemned.[t] 17 And these
signs will accompany those who believe: In my
name they will drive out demons;[u] they will speak
in new tongues;[v] 18 they will pick up snakes[w] with
their hands; and when they drink deadly poison,
it will not hurt them at all; they will place their
hands on[x] sick people, and they will get well."
19 After the Lord Jesus had spoken to them, he was
taken up into heaven[y] and he sat at the right hand
of God.[z] 20 Then the disciples went out and preached
everywhere, and the Lord worked with them and
confirmed his word by the signs that accompanied it.

16:9 [o] Jn 20:11-18
16:11 [p] ver 13,14; Lk 24:11
16:12 [q] Lk 24:13-32
16:14 [r] Lk 24:36-43
16:15 [s] Mt 28:18-20; Lk 24:47,48
16:16 [t] Jn 3:16, 18,36; Ac 16:31
16:17 [u] Mk 9:38; Lk 10:17; Ac 5:16; 8:7; 16:18; 19:13-16 [v] Ac 2:4; 10:46; 19:6; 1Co 12:10, 28,30
16:18 [w] Lk 10:19; Ac 28:3-5 [x] Ac 6:6
16:19 [y] Lk 24:50, 51; Jn 6:62; Ac 1:9-11; 1Ti 3:16 [z] Ps 110:1; Ro 8:34; Col 3:1; Heb 1:3; 12:2

[a] 8 Some manuscripts have the following ending between verses 8 and 9, and one manuscript has it after verse 8 (omitting verses 9-20): *Then they quickly reported all these instructions to those around Peter. After this, Jesus himself also sent out through them from east to west the sacred and imperishable proclamation of eternal salvation. Amen.*

---

them, so now the risen Jesus goes ahead of them still, leading the church.

The command to go to Galilee does make one thing clear: Jerusalem is not the center of God's movement. The disciples' future lies elsewhere. By going back to Galilee, where Jesus will be, the disciples go back to the promising birth of their call to discipleship. There they can regroup and begin again the journey of discipleship.

16:8 In the earliest and most reliable manuscripts, Mark's Gospel ends with v. 8. Such an abrupt ending has perplexed readers for centuries, as it both surprises and creates suspense. Mark may have felt no need to relate resurrection appearances to readers who had heard them so often.

When presented with this ending, we must ask, "What has happened? What will happen?" We must also go to Jesus and not only tell about his resurrection, but we must also tell the entire story from the beginning.

It is not a closed-minded disbelief that quiets the women's voices; that would remove the power of the gospel. Rather, the cause is likely pure and simple fear. Fear surfaces among Jesus' followers both before the cross and after the resurrection.

The resurrection does not mean that now everything is set right and that everyone will live "happily ever after." The flesh is still weak. Many will suffer the same fear as the women and will try to take cover in silence. Disciples must learn to lose their lives to save them, which means losing their fear.

✣ **16:1–8** The ending of Mark's Gospel forces us to enter the story. We are part of the next chapter. What would we have done if we had been the first ones to see the angel and hear this tremendous news? The question then becomes not what will the women do—how long will they keep silent?—but what will *we* do now that we have heard this story? Will we flee in fear and become silent? Will the story die with us? Will we obediently follow Jesus to Galilee, or will we try to hunker down in our safe cocoons?

The Gospel of Mark leaves us with unfinished business to preach the gospel to the ends of the earth. The ending (which really is a beginning) becomes a new phase of an unfolding story as the baton passes to us to join in the race and spread the news.

Mark's stunning ending raises the question, "Who will tell the story?" His Gospel is the account of the beginning of the gospel; will we now join in its continuation?

Peter asks, "Who is going to harm you if you are eager to do good?" (1Pe 3:13). The answer in the first century was, "Plenty of people will." Enemies were everywhere, and their threats naturally elicited fear and inhibited the witness of believers. The kinds of people who killed Jesus are still out there, ready to kill his followers. No one enjoys being hated or hunted down; it is safer to remain silent, to treasure all these things in our hearts (Lk 2:51) rather than to bare our hearts to others.

One might understand why those facing persecution might be reticent to speak, but what excuse do we, who enjoy all the comforts of life and the freedom of worship, have? The ancient call to the disciples remains the same for those of us who are Jesus' disciples today (Mt 28:18–20).

Luke

Author: Luke, a Gentile physician and missionary companion of Paul

Audience: Addressed to Theophilus, but intended for his church as well and ultimately for all believers

Date: Between AD 60s and 80s

Theme: Luke presents Jesus as the Messiah and Lord whose life, death and resurrection make salvation available to all people everywhere, even to the least, the last and the lost.

Reading Luke

Luke begins with a personal address to "most excellent Theophilus," hoping to instruct this man (probably a government official) about Jesus. After telling the stories of the births of John the Baptist and Jesus, Luke tells the life of Jesus by dividing his account into three geographical units: events in Galilee (Lk 4:14–9:50), events on the way to Jerusalem (Lk 9:51–19:27) and

PERSPECTIVE

What does the Gospel of Luke have to teach us today? Plenty.

Read or watch the news almost any day of the week, and you cannot help but get the impression that our world suffers from a new intellectual virus: the problem of the many and the one. Many races, one humanity. Many species, one creation. Many nations, one world. Many rights, one truth. We can clearly see the diversity in the world. At the same time, however, we know that diversity can too quickly turn to divisiveness and death if some reason to be unified is not found.

The gospel truth that Luke describes has the best chance at delivering this elusive unity. Luke was concerned to show us that the whole world ran according to a single plan laid out by God. Thus, the first sections about Jesus as a baby and young child illustrate how God was already at work in Jesus' life; the stories of John the Baptist and Jesus' baptism and temptation define a call to ministry that was worked out in precise detail; Jesus' early ministry around the lake called Galilee reveals a minister of extraordinary power and authority; in his final journey to Jerusalem, Jesus met all kinds of resistance and showed us how people following God's plan are able to persevere; and the stories of Jesus' final days demonstrate with clarity how Jesus practiced a spiritual leadership that was qualitatively different from the political, economic, and religious leaders of the day. Luke shows us that this extraordinary life was not some arbitrary coming together of random factors; it was a life breathed by God.

It is precisely this life, the life of Jesus Christ our Lord and Savior,

	10 BC	AD 1	10	20	30	40	50	60	70	80	90	100
Herod the Great's reign (c. 37–4 BC)												
Jesus' birth (c. 6/5 BC)												
Jesus' family's flight to Egypt (c. 5/4 BC)												
Jesus' visit to the temple (c. AD 7/8)												
Beginning of John the Baptist's ministry (c. AD 26)												
Beginning of Jesus' ministry (c. AD 26)												
Jesus' death, resurrection and ascension (c. AD 30)												
Paul's conversion (c. AD 35)												
Book of Luke written (c. AD 59–63)												

that sets the pattern for everyone; it pulls the fragmented and divisive elements of the world together. Luke takes great pains to explain how this God-breathed life made useless the old distinctions between Jew and Gentile. It is the life of Jesus Christ that pulls together competing visions of life and work.

And it is precisely this truth that forms the central application of Luke's Gospel for our world today. Only God, through the incarnation of Jesus Christ, can pull a divided world together. The divisions of our day seem much more complicated than the biblical illustration of Jew and Gentile. But the principle is the same: God unites. He unites not by denying us our distinctiveness—our race, our nationality, our culture. God, after all, made us who and what we are. No, God unites by standing for something above and beyond anything we know, thus providing us with a reason to pull together even as we enjoy our unique, God-created identities.

What does Luke mean for us today? The answer is, in one word, plenty. We can live together in peace only if we focus beyond ourselves to our sovereign God and the Son sent to save us.

events of Jesus' final week in Jerusalem (Lk 19:28–24:53). Parables, miracles, discourses and other stories of Jesus are all interspersed throughout the Gospel.

Key Verses

[Jesus] said to them . . . "Did not the Messiah have to suffer these things and then enter his glory?" And beginning with Moses and all the Prophets, he explained to them what was said in all the Scriptures concerning himself.

—Luke 24:25-27

TAKING THE NEXT STEPS

This account of the life of Jesus was written by Luke, a physician and a travel companion of Paul; it is the first of two volumes that he wrote on what Jesus did and taught (the second is the book of Acts; see Ac 1:1). The themes in this Gospel also appear in the book of Acts. Luke presents God's overall plan, beginning with Adam. At the center of this plan is Jesus Christ, Savior of the whole world, Jew and Gentile alike. In looking at the life of Christ, Luke stressed the compassion and social concern of Jesus for the "underdogs" of society, as well as the role of prayer in the life of Jesus. In addition, Luke filled his Gospel with elements of joy and praise to God.

There are many practical implications that stand out in reading this book. (1) Since Jesus is the only way to salvation, each of us must acknowledge him as our personal Savior and Lord. (2) Nothing great can ever be done for the Lord without intense prayer and dependence on the Holy Spirit. (3) We ought to be as concerned as Jesus was for those treated unjustly in society. (4) The Good News of the incredible benefits God gives us in Christ is cause for great rejoicing. (5) Because of Christ's victory over Satan and the powers of darkness, we too can live victoriously over sin.

WHAT TO LOOK FOR IN LUKE

- Birth of John the Baptist (ch. 1)
- Birth and childhood of Jesus (ch. 2)
- Ministry of John the Baptist (ch. 3)
- Temptation and early ministry of Jesus (ch. 4)
- Jesus' Sermon on the Plain (ch. 6)
- Significant discourses of Jesus (chs. 10–19)
- Jesus' final discussion with the Jews (ch. 20)
- The future predicted by Jesus (ch. 21)
- Jesus' final days and his death (chs. 22–23)
- Jesus' resurrection and appearances (ch. 24)

Introduction

1:1–4Ref // Ac 1:1

1 Many have undertaken to draw up an
account of the things that have been
fulfilled[a] among us, 2 just as they were
handed down to us by those who from
the first[a] were eyewitnesses[b] and servants of the word.[c] 3 With this in mind,
since I myself have carefully investigated
everything from the beginning, I too
decided to write an orderly account[d] for
you, most excellent[e] Theophilus,[f] 4 so that
you may know the certainty of the things
you have been taught.[g]

The Birth of John the Baptist Foretold

5 In the time of Herod king of Judea[h]
there was a priest named Zechariah,
who belonged to the priestly division
of Abijah;[i] his wife Elizabeth was also a
descendant of Aaron. 6 Both of them were
righteous in the sight of God, observing
all the Lord's commands and decrees
blamelessly.[j] 7 But they were childless because Elizabeth was not able to conceive,
and they were both very old.
8 Once when Zechariah's division was
on duty and he was serving as priest
before God,[k] 9 he was chosen by lot, according to the custom of the priesthood, to go into the temple of the Lord
and burn incense.[l] 10 And when the time
for the burning of incense came, all the
assembled worshipers were praying
outside.[m]

1:2 [a] Mk 1:1; Jn 15:27; Ac 1:21, 22 [b] Heb 2:3; 1Pe 5:1; 2Pe 1:16; 1Jn 1:1 [c] Mk 4:14
1:3 [d] Ac 11:4 [e] Ac 24:3; 26:25 [f] Ac 1:1
1:4 [g] Jn 20:31
1:5 [h] Mt 2:1 [i] 1Ch 24:10
1:6 [j] Ge 7:1; 1Ki 9:4
1:8 [k] 1Ch 24:19; 2Ch 8:14
1:9 [l] Ex 30:7, 8; 1Ch 23:13; 2Ch 29:11
1:10 [m] Lev 16:17

[a] *1* Or *been surely believed*

1:1–4 Luke tells us four things about his work before he tells us why he writes. First, he has "investigated" the story. He has taken a long and careful look at what he is about to tell us. Second, he went back to "the beginning." This is why he starts his story with John the Baptist, the forerunner, who points to Jesus. Third, Luke was thorough, having studied "everything." This is undoubtedly why there is so much fresh material in his account. About 30 percent of this Gospel is not found elsewhere. Finally, Luke worked "carefully," taking great care to develop his orderly account in a way that told the story clearly. Luke wants to reassure Theophilus, in order that he "may know the certainty of the things [he has] been taught" (v. 4).

APPLICATION ✥ 1:1–4 | Luke tells us of God's acts in history *through Jesus*. This main character is not a Savior made up in the image of a person's imagination. After all, who on his or her own would create a Savior who makes us all responsible for our sin and then chooses to pay the penalty for that sin by offering himself? The unusual nature of the story is a testimony to its authenticity. Its reality is the basis for the assurance Luke wishes to give his readers.

1:5–7 Luke begins his story by placing it in an established historical setting—the reign of Herod the Great (37–4 BC). When the angel appears to Zechariah, we are near the end of Herod's reign.
1:8–10 In his goodness, God picks an important moment in the career of Zechariah to make his divine move. A priest only officiated at the sacrifice once in his life, having been selected by lot. The angel appears in a moment of worship at a time when people recognized their need for cleansing from sin.

11Then an angel[n] of the Lord appeared
to him, standing at the right side of the
altar of incense.[o] 12When Zechariah saw
him, he was startled and was gripped with
fear.[p] 13But the angel said to him: "Do not
be afraid,[q] Zechariah; your prayer has been
heard. Your wife Elizabeth will bear you
a son, and you are to call him John.[r] 14He
will be a joy and delight to you, and many
will rejoice because of his birth,[s] 15for he
will be great in the sight of the Lord. He
is never to take wine or other fermented
drink,[t] and he will be filled with the Holy
Spirit even before he is born.[u] 16He will
bring back many of the people of Israel
to the Lord their God. 17And he will go on
before the Lord,[v] in the spirit and power of
Elijah,[w] to turn the hearts of the parents to
their children[x] and the disobedient to the
wisdom of the righteous — to make ready
a people prepared for the Lord."
18Zechariah asked the angel, "How can
I be sure of this? I am an old man and
my wife is well along in years."[y]
19The angel said to him, "I am Gabriel.[z]
I stand in the presence of God, and I have
been sent to speak to you and to tell you
this good news. 20And now you will be
silent and not able to speak[a] until the
day this happens, because you did not
believe my words, which will come true
at their appointed time."
21Meanwhile, the people were waiting
for Zechariah and wondering why he
stayed so long in the temple. 22When
he came out, he could not speak to
them. They realized he had seen a vision in the temple, for he kept making
signs[b] to them but remained unable to
speak.
23When his time of service was completed, he returned home. 24After this
his wife Elizabeth became pregnant and
for five months remained in seclusion.
25"The Lord has done this for me," she
said. "In these days he has shown his favor and taken away my disgrace[c] among
the people."

The Birth of Jesus Foretold

26In the sixth month of Elizabeth's
pregnancy, God sent the angel Gabriel[d]
to Nazareth,[e] a town in Galilee, 27to a
virgin pledged to be married to a man
named Joseph,[f] a descendant of David.
The virgin's name was Mary. 28The angel went to her and said, "Greetings,
you who are highly favored! The Lord
is with you."
29Mary was greatly troubled at his
words and wondered what kind of greeting this might be. 30But the angel said to
her, "Do not be afraid,[g] Mary; you have
found favor with God. 31You will conceive

1:11 [n] Ac 5:19 [o] Ex 30:1-10
1:12 [p] Jdg 6:22, 23; 13:22
1:13 [q] ver 30; Mt 14:27 [r] ver 60, 63
1:14 [s] ver 58
1:15 [t] Nu 6:3; Jdg 13:4; Lk 7:33 [u] Jer 1:5; Gal 1:15
1:17 [v] ver 76 [w] Mt 11:14 [x] Mal 4:5, 6
1:18 [y] ver 34; Ge 17:17
1:19 [z] ver 26; Da 8:16; 9:21; Mt 18:10
1:20 [a] Eze 3:26
1:22 [b] ver 62
1:25 [c] Ge 30:23; Isa 4:1
1:26 [d] ver 19 [e] Mt 2:23
1:27 [f] Mt 1:16, 18, 20; Lk 2:4
1:30 [g] ver 13; Mt 14:27

1:11–12 After comforting Zechariah, the angel announces why he has come. His name, Gabriel (v. 19), probably means "God is my hero," though Luke makes nothing of the name.
1:13–14 The birth of this child is like other births to formerly barren wives or other announcements of the birth of a special child. God has renewed his work among his people.
1:15–16 John will live an ascetic lifestyle. He may drink no strong drink. This is likely not a Nazirite vow, however, since there is no mention of not cutting his hair.
1:17 The declaration that he will "go on before the Lord" describes John as a prophet of the period of restoration of the promise. John's preparation for the Lord refers to God's powerful coming through his agent, Jesus. "To turn the hearts" and "make ready a people" reflects John's call for repentance.
1:18–22 Zechariah raises doubts about the angel's message (v. 18). Sometimes even sincere people have doubts about God's promise. After Gabriel confirms his message, he chides Zechariah for his unbelief.
1:23–25 Elizabeth does not react as a victim who has been bitter at God for her lack of a child. In fact, she seems to have accepted this fate and served God faithfully anyway. Thus, when the burden is removed, she rejoices that she is the object of God's personal concern.

1:5–25 The application of this text will be a refrain through the entire Gospel: Are we prepared for God, and do we respond to his work through the one he sent to lead us to him? John will point the way. In this passage, Zechariah and Elizabeth teach us to take our questions and our disappointments to God, and to be sure to take our rejoicing to him as well. We see from their lives that sometimes we are deprived of something because God has better things awaiting us down the road. When we wait patiently on the Lord, he often gives us more than we imagined possible. Zechariah and Elizabeth wanted a child; what they got was a prophet. God's ways are set to his clock, and they are often filled with things that cause us to wonder as we rejoice at his surprises.

1:26–27 The announcement in Nazareth shows that Mary came from humble, agrarian roots. Luke identifies Mary as a virgin, engaged to Joseph. A Jewish betrothal involved two steps: the formal engagement, including a contract and exchange of a bridal price, and then about a year later, a wedding.
1:28–37 Mary is "highly favored," receiving God's grace based on his sovereign action. She is honored

PEOPLE TO KNOW // MARY, MOTHER OF JESUS

LUKE 1:26–38: Mary's life changed dramatically when the angel Gabriel appeared to her. She was pledged to be married to Joseph when Gabriel told her she would conceive and give birth to a son through the Holy Spirit—a child who would reign on David's throne forever. Mary humbly replied that she was God's servant and that God's word should be fulfilled (Lk 1:26–38). The rest of this beloved and miraculous story is recorded in Luke chs. 1–2.

When Jesus was twelve years old, Mary and Joseph discovered he was missing as they returned home from celebrating Passover in Jerusalem. They went back and found Jesus in the temple courts, talking with religious teachers. Mary chastised Jesus for scaring her and Joseph, but Jesus responded that it was right for him to be in his father's house. Luke tells us that Mary pondered this in her heart (Lk 2:41–51).

Mary encouraged Jesus to perform his first public miracle at a wedding feast, helping the host who had run out of wine (Jn 2:1–5). Though Jesus said his time had not yet come, he miraculously turned water into wine. Mary was confident that Jesus would be able and willing to help.

Mary stayed near Jesus for much of his ministry, but she did not always understand him. At one point in his early ministry his family thought he was out of his mind (Mk 3:21); this may have included Mary, but the text is not clear.

Mary remained with Jesus to the time of his death. From the cross Jesus spoke to her, putting her in the care of his beloved disciple, John (Jn 19:26–27). After that, a prediction that had been made about Mary came to pass: "And a sword will pierce your own soul too" (Lk 2:35).

APPLICATION ✣ Mary was given a monumental task: to give birth to the Son of God and raise him to adulthood. She humbly accepted this calling. Mary sets an example for all of Jesus' followers who continue to bring the presence of Christ into the world through his Holy Spirit with acts of obedience and love. Mary was not only a devoted mother, but she was also a devoted follower of Christ and a faithful example throughout all of history of what it looks like to say yes to God's call.

and give birth to a son, and you are to
call him Jesus.[h] 32He will be great and will
be called the Son of the Most High.[i] The
Lord God will give him the throne of his
father David, 33and he will reign over Jacob's descendants forever; his kingdom[j]
will never end."[k]
34"How will this be," Mary asked the
angel, "since I am a virgin?"
35The angel answered, "The Holy
Spirit will come on you,[l] and the power of the Most High[m] will overshadow
you. So the holy one[n] to be born will be
called[a] the Son of God.[o] 36Even Elizabeth
your relative is going to have a child
in her old age, and she who was said
to be unable to conceive is in her sixth
month. 37For no word from God will ever
fail."[p]
38"I am the Lord's servant," Mary answered. "May your word to me be fulfilled." Then the angel left her.

1:31 [h] Isa 7:14; Mt 1:21,25; Lk 2:21
1:32 [i] ver 35,76; Mk 5:7
1:33 [j] Mt 28:18 [k] Da 2:44; 7:14, 27; Mic 4:7; Heb 1:8
1:35 [l] Mt 1:18 [m] ver 32,76 [n] Mk 1:24 [o] Mt 4:3
1:37 [p] Mt 19:26

[a] 35 Or *So the child to be born will be called holy,*

by God not because of anything she has done but simply because she is the chosen vessel for this demonstration of God's grace.

1:38 Mary's humble response reveals her character. This was no simple matter; she was being asked to bear a child as a virgin without being married. In standing up for God and his power, she will probably become the object of much doubt and ridicule.

Luke has not only explained how the plan of God is advanced by telling the details of the birth announcement, but he has also revealed the character of those surrounding the births of Jesus and John the Baptist. Woven throughout this cosmic story are human stories: All the figures involved are examples of spirituality as they respond to what God is doing among them.

✣ **1:26–38** God shows his greatness by working with anyone who is willing to be used by him, no matter how unassuming. Spiritual greatness is not a matter of social class, monetary influence, or degrees; it is rather a function of the heart. God can do great things through those who entrust the journey with him to his care. That means when God leads, the believer must simply reply, "May it be according to your will."

PEOPLE TO KNOW // **ELIZABETH**

LUKE 1:41–45: Elizabeth was the cousin of Jesus' mother, Mary. She was childless and unable to conceive. Yet God had plans for her. He sent the angel Gabriel to speak to her husband, the priest Zechariah, while he was in the temple. Gabriel told him that Elizabeth would have a child and said to name the child John, describing the child with words echoing Malachi's prophecy of a future Elijah (Mal 4:5–6; see Lk 1:17).

Elizabeth's story as recorded in Luke 1 recalls the experiences of OT women such as Sarah and Hannah. Elizabeth was unable to conceive until a divine announcement and a miracle changed her future. Elizabeth became the mother of John the Baptist, the prophetic messenger who prepared the way for Christ.

APPLICATION Elizabeth experienced the sorrow of longing for a child but being unable to have one until God brought about a joyous miracle. We all experience seasons of longing and waiting. Like Elizabeth, we can face years of disappointment and sorrow while we learn to accept our situation or wait on the next steps in God's plan. God sees our pain, and he has a fulfilling future planned for us. It may not include a miracle where we suddenly get our heart's desire. But it does include a wonderful inheritance for us in his kingdom. Like Elizabeth, we should be people who marvel at God's grace in the honor of knowing the Savior of the world, Jesus Christ.

Lk 1:38 Would you be able to accept God's astounding plan with as much grace and humility as Mary? Why or why not?

Mary Visits Elizabeth

39At that time Mary got ready and
hurried to a town in the hill country of
Judea,[q] 40where she entered Zechariah's
home and greeted Elizabeth. 41When Elizabeth heard Mary's greeting, the baby
leaped in her womb, and Elizabeth was
filled with the Holy Spirit. 42In a loud
voice she exclaimed: "Blessed are you
among women,[r] and blessed is the child
you will bear! 43But why am I so favored,
that the mother of my Lord should come
to me? 44As soon as the sound of your
greeting reached my ears, the baby in my
womb leaped for joy. 45Blessed is she who
has believed that the Lord would fulfill
his promises to her!"

Mary's Song

1:46–53pp // 1Sa 2:1–10

46And Mary said:

"My soul glorifies the Lord[s]
47 and my spirit rejoices in God my
Savior,[t]
48 for he has been mindful
of the humble state of his
servant.[u]
From now on all generations will
call me blessed,[v]
49 for the Mighty One has done great
things[w] for me —
holy is his name.[x]
50 His mercy extends to those who fear
him,
from generation to generation.[y]

1:39 [q] ver 65
1:42 [r] Jdg 5:24
1:46 [s] Ps 34:2,3
1:47 [t] 1Ti 1:1; 2:3
1:48 [u] Ps 138:6 [v] Lk 11:27
1:49 [w] Ps 71:19 [x] Ps 111:9
1:50 [y] Ex 20:6; Ps 103:17

1:39–41 The remark about the Spirit's filling Elizabeth is crucial, for it indicates that her remarks and emotions are directed by God. Elizabeth knows God does not owe her such a central role, and she is amazed at God's involvement with her.

1:42–45 Alongside Elizabeth's amazement is the lesson of Mary's blessing. We should not miss the significance of the testimony about these children that comes through this grateful mother-to-be. Three points are central: First, Mary's child is especially blessed, being at the center of God's fresh activity; second, there is amazement at being any part of these astounding events; and third, joy and blessing come to those who believe that God does what he says.

1:46–48 Mary's thanksgiving psalm comes in two parts. It is a praise psalm similar to Hannah's praise to God (1Sa 2:1). Verses 46–49 give Mary's personal praise for her specific situation while the rest of the hymn praises God's activity in more general terms. A shift in tense from present (vv. 46b–47) to past (v. 48a) to future (v. 48b) shows the broadening scope of her basis for praise.

1:49–52 The idea that all generations will praise her (v. 48b) leads to the idea of how God treats other God-fearers (vv. 49–53). Mary's feelings are clear. God owes her nothing, while she has received everything from him. But her story illustrates how God treats others, so she goes on to indicate that her story could be repeated a thousand times over (v. 50).

51 He has performed mighty deeds
with his arm;[z]
he has scattered those who
are proud in their inmost
thoughts.
52 He has brought down rulers from
their thrones
but has lifted up the humble.
53 He has filled the hungry with good
things[a]
but has sent the rich away empty.
54 He has helped his servant Israel,
remembering to be merciful[b]
55 to Abraham and his descendants[c]
forever,
just as he promised our ancestors."

56 Mary stayed with Elizabeth for about
three months and then returned home.

The Birth of John the Baptist

57 When it was time for Elizabeth to
have her baby, she gave birth to a son.
58 Her neighbors and relatives heard that
the Lord had shown her great mercy, and
they shared her joy.
59 On the eighth day they came to circumcise[d] the child, and they were going
to name him after his father Zechariah,
60 but his mother spoke up and said, "No!
He is to be called John."[e]
61 They said to her, "There is no one
among your relatives who has that name."
62 Then they made signs[f] to his father,
to find out what he would like to name
the child. 63 He asked for a writing tablet,
and to everyone's astonishment he wrote,
"His name is John."[g] 64 Immediately his
mouth was opened and his tongue set
free, and he began to speak,[h] praising
God. 65 All the neighbors were filled with
awe, and throughout the hill country of
Judea[i] people were talking about all these
things. 66 Everyone who heard this wondered about it, asking, "What then is this
child going to be?" For the Lord's hand
was with him.[j]

Zechariah's Song

67 His father Zechariah was filled with
the Holy Spirit and prophesied:[k]

68 "Praise be to the Lord, the God of
Israel,[l]
because he has come to his people
and redeemed them.[m]
69 He has raised up a horn[a][n] of
salvation for us
in the house of his servant
David[o]

1:51 [z] Ps 98:1; Isa 40:10
1:53 [a] Ps 107:9
1:54 [b] Ps 98:3
1:55 [c] Ge 17:19; Ps 132:11; Gal 3:16
1:59 [d] Ge 17:12; Lev 12:3; Lk 2:21; Php 3:5
1:60 [e] ver 13, 63
1:62 [f] ver 22
1:63 [g] ver 13, 60
1:64 [h] ver 20
1:65 [i] ver 39
1:66 [j] Ge 39:2; Ac 11:21
1:67 [k] Joel 2:28
1:68 [l] Ps 72:18 [m] Ps 111:9; Lk 7:16
1:69 [n] 1Sa 2:1, 10; Ps 18:2; 89:17; 132:17; Eze 29:21 [o] Mt 1:1

[a] 69 *Horn* here symbolizes a strong king.

1:53 The "hungry" Mary elevates are the "pious poor." They recognize their need and are more inclined to turn to God.
1:54–55 Though Israel is clearly in view in the psalm, the implication of the general praise in v. 50 opens the possibility that others outside the nation may also be blessed.

Mary expresses hope for Israel's vindication before her enemies. God will deliver this and more through Jesus. God does so because he "remembers" his promises (v. 54).

1:39–56 Luke aims at the heart with these texts. Believers must take God at his word and be amazed at his involvement with the details of their lives. God owes us nothing; we who have trusted Christ owe him everything. As the child leaped in Elizabeth's womb, so should our hearts leap in our chests when we consider the many blessings of God that we experience. God does what he says, and he has said much on behalf of the believer. The key is to expect a reversal of fortune and a deliverance in the future. Whatever our lot in this sinful and fallen world now, those who fear God can expect vindication.

Also note what causes Mary to be grateful. In an age where we expect so much as a matter of personal or human rights, we can develop an attitude of entitlement. Yet in Mary's humble example we see her recognize the honor given her to have God actively involved in her life. Her sense of gratitude for this privilege, lacking any hint of pride at her personal merit, spills over into a waterfall of praise and thankfulness—praise that is refreshing for its passion and sense of wonder.

1:57–60 Events like this are filled with tradition. Perhaps given Zechariah's recent debilitating condition, the crowd expects the child to be named Zechariah Junior. But Elizabeth gives her son the name "John."
1:61–63 The neighbors are so convinced an error has been made that they ask the father about this decision. Zechariah writes the name the angel had given him for the child.
1:64–66 Immediately Zechariah's tongue is freed, and he speaks in praise to God. His long silence has allowed him to reflect on what God called for him to do, and he is now prepared to do it.
1:67–79 With his lips freed to speak, Zechariah now praises God for what he is doing. This hymn of praise anticipates and overviews the careers of the two children whom divine destiny has brought together. As is often the case in Luke, the Spirit leads to bold testimony and praise.
1:68–70 The psalm's main theme appears in these verses, while its elaboration is the remainder of the psalm.

70 (as he said through his holy prophets
of long ago),[p]
71 salvation from our enemies
and from the hand of all who hate
us —
72 to show mercy to our ancestors[q]
and to remember his holy
covenant,[r]
73 the oath he swore to our father
Abraham:[s]
74 to rescue us from the hand of our
enemies,
and to enable us to serve him[t]
without fear
75 in holiness and righteousness[u]
before him all our days.

76 And you, my child, will be called a
prophet[v] of the Most High;[w]
for you will go on before the Lord
to prepare the way for him,[x]
77 to give his people the knowledge of
salvation
through the forgiveness of their
sins,[y]
78 because of the tender mercy of our
God,
by which the rising sun[z] will come
to us from heaven
79 to shine on those living in darkness
and in the shadow of death,[a]
to guide our feet into the path of
peace."

80 And the child grew and became
strong in spirit[a];[b] and he lived in the
wilderness until he appeared publicly
to Israel.

The Birth of Jesus

2 In those days Caesar Augustus[c] issued a decree that a census should
be taken of the entire Roman world.[d]
2 (This was the first census that took place
while[b] Quirinius was governor of Syria.)[e]
3 And everyone went to their own town
to register.
4 So Joseph also went up from the town
of Nazareth in Galilee to Judea, to Bethlehem[f] the town of David, because he
belonged to the house and line of David.
5 He went there to register with Mary, who
was pledged to be married to him and
was expecting a child. 6 While they were
there, the time came for the baby to be
born, 7 and she gave birth to her firstborn,
a son. She wrapped him in cloths and
placed him in a manger, because there
was no guest room available for them.
8 And there were shepherds living out

1:70 [p] Jer 23:5
1:72 [q] Mic 7:20 [r] Ps 105:8, 9; 106:45; Eze 16:60
1:73 [s] Ge 22:16-18
1:74 [t] Heb 9:14
1:75 [u] Eph 4:24
1:76 [v] Mt 11:9 [w] ver 32,35 [x] ver 17; Mal 3:1
1:77 [y] Jer 31:34; Mk 1:4
1:78 [z] Mal 4:2
1:79 [a] Isa 9:2; 59:9; Mt 4:16; Ac 26:18
1:80 [b] Lk 2:40, 52
2:1 [c] Mt 22:17; Lk 3:1 [d] Mt 24:14
2:2 [e] Mt 4:24
2:4 [f] Jn 7:42

[a] 80 Or *in the Spirit* [b] 2 Or *This census took place before*

1:71–75 What Zechariah desires most is to be rescued from his enemies so that he can serve God his whole life without fear and in righteousness and holiness.

Zechariah longs for the nation's vindication, possibly from Rome and the forces that direct it. In Luke's story, however, the scope of the hymn's hope may even be broader. He will show how the Promised One from David's line has power that extends beyond the political forces that sit over Israel. The son of David will take on the cosmic forces that bring pain and suffering into the world and oppress humanity.

1:76–77 Zechariah indicates that his own son will be a prophet for the Most High God, preparing a people for this coming visit of the Lord by telling them about "salvation through the forgiveness of their sins" (v. 77).

1:78–79 God will not only work through John. He will send "the rising sun" (v. 78; alternately "the morning star"), a likely allusion to Nu 24:17 and Isa 11:1–10. The Son, who serves as a bright morning light, comes from heaven and shines on those in darkness and death, guiding them into the path of peace. Significantly, Zechariah places himself among those who are in darkness.

1:57–80 The lesson that pious Zechariah learns is important, especially to those who have a rich spiritual heritage. He was a man of lifelong faith who still needed to grow. It is all too easy to view one's spiritual life as something that can be mastered rather than something to be actively maintained.

The only road to righteousness and peace, even for a righteous man like Zechariah, is to be prepared to see the light and follow it. The text raises the question and answers it with notes of praise: See the morning star, Jesus, and follow the light in the way of peace. What precisely that pathway involves is the rest of this Gospel's story, for which this hymn serves as a guiding introduction.

2:1–5 The journeying of everyone "to their own town to register" appears to be a sensitive decision by the Romans that allowed the Jews to follow their own custom of going to one's ancestral home. So Joseph and Mary go to Bethlehem, a place identified as "the town of David," because of Joseph's lineage in the royal family.

2:6–7 Jesus enters the world in as mundane a way as possible. Luke tells the story with exceptional brevity.

2:8–10 The testimony to Jesus' birth from the angelic host to shepherds is significant in scope. The announcement indicates that God desires to speak to every person about the coming

in the fields nearby, keeping watch over their flocks at night. 9An angel[g] of the Lord appeared to them, and the glory of the Lord shone around them, and they were terrified. 10But the angel said to them, "Do not be afraid.[h] I bring you good news that will cause great joy for all the people. 11Today in the town of David a Savior[i] has been born to you; he is the Messiah,[j] the Lord. 12This will be a sign[k] to you: You will find a baby wrapped in cloths and lying in a manger."

13Suddenly a great company of the heavenly host appeared with the angel, praising God and saying,

14"Glory to God in the highest heaven,
and on earth peace[l] to those on
whom his favor rests."

15When the angels had left them and gone into heaven, the shepherds said to one another, "Let's go to Bethlehem and see this thing that has happened, which the Lord has told us about."

16So they hurried off and found Mary and Joseph, and the baby, who was lying in the manger. 17When they had seen him, they spread the word concerning what had been told them about

2:9 [g] Lk 1:11; Ac 5:19
2:10 [h] Mt 14:27
2:11 [i] Mt 1:21; Jn 4:42; Ac 5:31 [j] Mt 1:16; 16:16, 20; Jn 11:27; Ac 2:36
2:12 [k] 1Sa 2:34; 2Ki 19:29; Isa 7:14
2:14 [l] Lk 1:79; Ro 5:1; Eph 2:14,17
2:19 [m] ver 51
2:20 [n] Mt 9:8
2:21 [o] Lk 1:59 [p] Lk 1:31
2:22 [q] Lev 12:2-8
2:23 [r] Ex 13:2,12, 15; Nu 3:13

Lk 2:17-18 ❖ Are we as eager as the shepherds were to tell others about our encounters with Christ? What could we tell people who ask?

this child, 18and all who heard it were amazed at what the shepherds said to them. 19But Mary treasured up all these things and pondered them in her heart.[m] 20The shepherds returned, glorifying and praising God[n] for all the things they had heard and seen, which were just as they had been told.

21On the eighth day, when it was time to circumcise the child,[o] he was named Jesus, the name the angel had given him before he was conceived.[p]

Jesus Presented in the Temple

22When the time came for the purification rites required by the Law of Moses,[q] Joseph and Mary took him to Jerusalem to present him to the Lord 23(as it is written in the Law of the Lord, "Every firstborn male is to be consecrated to the Lord"[a]),[r] 24and to offer a sacrifice in

[a] *23* Exodus 13:2,12

---

of Jesus, since all humanity is impacted by his coming.

2:11 The titles the angel uses for the newborn child are significant. "Savior" is rich in OT roots, especially as a figure for divine deliverance. "Messiah" (Hebrew for "anointed one") is a rare term in the OT; Ps 2:2 is the main technical regal use. What about "Lord"? One could argue that the rest of this Gospel and the book of Acts serve to explain the nature of Jesus' lordship.

2:12 The angelic revelation of a sign implies that the angel wanted the shepherds to go and see the child for themselves. This is the third sign in the infancy account (1:19–20, 36).

2:13–14 As if the announcement were not enough, the heavenly choir strikes up in praise to God, giving him honor for what is taking place. The picture of being a person of God's "favor" was a Jewish way of saying that someone was numbered among God's chosen people.

2:15–17 The shepherds find the child in the manger, just as the angel said. They respond obediently and cannot contain themselves from testifying to what God has done.

2:18–20 As is often the case when God's work is reported, those who hear the shepherds' testimony are amazed, while Mary simply ponders it all. God will surely do exactly what he has promised (v. 20).

✣ **2:1–21** The most humble birth for the most exalted figure ever born shows that the key values of life are found in the life itself, not in the trappings that come with life.

The birth of Jesus shows that greatness is not a function of the size of one's bank account or of one's social résumé. Status does not make the person, for God recognizes the quality of the inner person.

God shows his greatness by walking with us as we are where we are, not in elitist isolation and insulation, which is often the way the powerful live in the world. What the angels announced to the shepherds that night is announced on behalf of all humanity. Their journey to see these things should be every person's journey: to examine for themselves how Jesus fulfills all the promises God has made to us in the Scriptures.

Our rejoicing starts with Jesus in the story of his birth, but it does not stop there. He is involved in our lives even now. By the Spirit his presence continues to express itself in us. One day in heaven, face to face with men and women of every generation and nation, we will offer thanks before him. There is nothing wrong with getting in a little practice now.

2:22–24 The journey of Jesus' parents to the temple combines three separate ceremonies as recorded in God's law: the purification of a woman forty days after the birth of a child (Lev 12:1–5), the presentation of the firstborn to God (Ex 13:2,

keeping with what is said in the Law of
the Lord: "a pair of doves or two young
pigeons."[a][s]
25 Now there was a man in Jerusalem
called Simeon, who was righteous and
devout.[t] He was waiting for the consolation of Israel,[u] and the Holy Spirit was
on him. 26 It had been revealed to him
by the Holy Spirit that he would not die
before he had seen the Lord's Messiah.
27 Moved by the Spirit, he went into the
temple courts. When the parents brought
in the child Jesus to do for him what the
custom of the Law required,[v] 28 Simeon
took him in his arms and praised God,
saying:

29 "Sovereign Lord, as you have
promised,[w]
you may now dismiss[b] your
servant in peace.[x]
30 For my eyes have seen your
salvation,[y]
31 which you have prepared in the
sight of all nations:
32 a light for revelation to the Gentiles,
and the glory of your people
Israel."[z]

33 The child's father and mother marveled at what was said about him. 34 Then
Simeon blessed them and said to Mary,
his mother:[a] "This child is destined to
cause the falling[b] and rising of many
in Israel, and to be a sign that will be
spoken against, 35 so that the thoughts
of many hearts will be revealed. And a
sword will pierce your own soul too."
36 There was also a prophet,[c] Anna, the
daughter of Penuel, of the tribe of Asher.
She was very old; she had lived with her
husband seven years after her marriage,
37 and then was a widow until she was
eighty-four.[c][d] She never left the temple
but worshiped night and day, fasting and
praying.[e] 38 Coming up to them at that
very moment, she gave thanks to God
and spoke about the child to all who were
looking forward to the redemption of
Jerusalem.[f]
39 When Joseph and Mary had done
everything required by the Law of the
Lord, they returned to Galilee to their
own town of Nazareth.[g] 40 And the child
grew and became strong; he was filled
with wisdom, and the grace of God was
on him.[h]

The Boy Jesus at the Temple

41 Every year Jesus' parents went to
Jerusalem for the Festival of the Passover.[i] 42 When he was twelve years old,
they went up to the festival, according
to the custom. 43 After the festival was

2:24 [s] Lev 12:8
2:25 [t] Lk 1:6 [u] ver 38; Isa 52:9; Lk 23:51
2:27 [v] ver 22
2:29 [w] ver 26 [x] Ac 2:24
2:30 [y] Isa 52:10; Lk 3:6
2:32 [z] Isa 42:6; 49:6; Ac 13:47; 26:23
2:34 [a] Mt 12:46 [b] Isa 8:14; Mt 21:44; 1Co 1:23; 2Co 2:16; 1Pe 2:7,8
2:36 [c] Ac 21:9
2:37 [d] 1Ti 5:9 [e] Ac 13:3; 14:23; 1Ti 5:5
2:38 [f] ver 25; Isa 40:2; Lk 1:68; 24:21
2:39 [g] ver 51; Mt 2:23
2:40 [h] ver 52; Lk 1:80
2:41 [i] Ex 23:15; Dt 16:1-8

[a] 24 Lev. 12:8 [b] 29 Or *promised, / now dismiss*
[c] 37 Or *then had been a widow for eighty-four years.*

---

12), and the dedication of the firstborn into the Lord's service (Nu 3:13).

The rite of purification involved the offering of a burnt sacrifice and sin offering. The mention of turtledoves indicates that Joseph and Mary utilized the offering of the poor, though middle classes likely made such sacrifices as well.

2:25–27 As Joseph and Mary proceed, they meet Simeon, who represents the testimony of a wise elder who has walked with God. Part of his wisdom is seen in that he is looking for the hope of the nation. Those in touch with God's heart often wait expectantly for the completion of God's promises.

2:28–31 The prophet is testifying to Jesus in the nation's most sacred locale, the temple. Simeon begins by saying that God can take him now, for he has fulfilled his call of seeing the child who is the Christ. Once again, Luke has emphasized how God has performed his word.

2:32 Jesus is light, a theme already noted in 1:78–79. Simeon's remarks recall Isa 60:1–3, where the light of salvation comes with revelation and glory as the result. Jesus is a "revelation" to Gentiles, for they will be brought into blessing through his coming. Jesus is "glory" to Israel, for through him they will perform their service of ministry to the world.

2:33–35 Simeon prophesies that Jesus will split the nation in two. Some will see him as someone to be opposed. But his ministry reveals the condition of the heart: A person's reaction to Jesus reveals their reaction to God. Mary's pain will emerge from the intense rejection the child will experience.

2:36–40 Anna is introduced and her career summarized. In all likelihood she is over a hundred years old, having served God faithfully for decades in worship, prayer, and fasting. While her words are not recorded in Luke, her testimony makes everyone aware that God is doing something special in this child.

2:22–40 To see Jesus is to see God and his way revealed. Jesus is no longer visibly around so that we can look him in the face, but he is in the world in our hearts, which house the promised Holy Spirit (Jn 14:26), and Jesus is in his body, the church.

Simeon's story is instructive as an example of identifying with doing God's will and then surrendering to the timing of one's own death. Having seen Jesus and understanding that God's promises were fulfilled in him, Simeon is at peace. Everything else in his life—whatever trauma came before and whatever is to come as he faces death—pales in comparison. May the same be true in the life of every believer.

over, while his parents were returning
home, the boy Jesus stayed behind in
Jerusalem, but they were unaware of
it. 44Thinking he was in their company, they traveled on for a day. Then they
began looking for him among their relatives and friends. 45When they did not
find him, they went back to Jerusalem
to look for him. 46After three days they
found him in the temple courts, sitting
among the teachers, listening to them
and asking them questions. 47Everyone
who heard him was amazed[j] at his understanding and his answers. 48When his
parents saw him, they were astonished.
His mother[k] said to him, "Son, why have
you treated us like this? Your father[l] and
I have been anxiously searching for you."
49"Why were you searching for me?"
he asked. "Didn't you know I had to be in
my Father's house?"[a][m] 50But they did not
understand what he was saying to them.[n]
51Then he went down to Nazareth with
them[o] and was obedient to them. But his
mother treasured all these things in her
heart.[p] 52And Jesus grew in wisdom and
stature, and in favor with God and man.[q]

John the Baptist Prepares the Way

3:2–10pp // Mt 3:1–10; Mk 1:3–5
3:16,17pp // Mt 3:11,12; Mk 1:7,8

3 In the fifteenth year of the reign of Tiberius Caesar—when Pontius Pilate[r]
was governor of Judea, Herod[s] tetrarch of
Galilee, his brother Philip tetrarch of Iturea and Traconitis, and Lysanias tetrarch
of Abilene— 2during the high-priest-
hood of Annas and Caiaphas,[t] the word
of God came to John[u] son of Zechariah[v]
in the wilderness. 3He went into all the
country around the Jordan, preaching a
baptism of repentance for the forgiveness of sins.[w] 4As it is written in the book
of the words of Isaiah the prophet:

"A voice of one calling in the
wilderness,
'Prepare the way for the Lord,
make straight paths for him.
5Every valley shall be filled in,
every mountain and hill made
low.
The crooked roads shall become
straight,
the rough ways smooth.
6And all people will see God's
salvation.'"[b][x]

7John said to the crowds coming out
to be baptized by him, "You brood of vipers![y] Who warned you to flee from the
coming wrath?[z] 8Produce fruit in keeping with repentance. And do not begin
to say to yourselves, 'We have Abraham

2:47 [j] Mt 7:28
2:48 [k] Mt 12:46 [l] Lk 3:23; 4:22
2:49 [m] Jn 2:16
2:50 [n] Mk 9:32
2:51 [o] ver 39; Mt 2:23 [p] ver 19
2:52 [q] ver 40; 1Sa 2:26; Lk 1:80
3:1 [r] Mt 27:2 [s] Mt 14:1
3:2 [t] Mt 26:3; Jn 18:13; Ac 4:6 [u] Mt 3:1 [v] Lk 1:13
3:3 [w] ver 16; Mk 1:4
3:6 [x] Ps 98:2; Isa 40:3-5; 42:16; 52:10; Lk 2:30
3:7 [y] Mt 12:34; 23:33 [z] Ro 1:18

[a] 49 Or *be about my Father's business*
[b] 6 Isaiah 40:3-5

2:41–46 Passover was one of three annual festivals that were celebrated in the capital. On this particular occasion, Jesus remained behind in Jerusalem. His parents undoubtedly assumed Jesus was somewhere in the group traveling with them, but eventually they return to discover Jesus among the teachers in the temple.
2:47 Even at this young age Jesus has amazing knowledge of the things of God. In fact, those listening to him are astonished at his understanding.
2:48–49 A frustrated mother asks her budding adolescent how he could have behaved this way. Jesus' reply is just as direct.
2:51–52 Jesus has a call to instruct the nation. Though he is twelve now, a day is coming when this will be his priority. All Mary can do is ponder such events in her heart, something Luke's reader is also invited to do.

2:41–52 The questions of this passage still apply today: Who is Jesus, and is his authority such that even the most basic human relationships, like the parent-child relationship, are transcended? As with many texts in this Gospel, the basic question is: What do we think of Jesus' authority? Will we accept or reject his claims? Our relationship to God is determined by our response.

3:1–3 Luke portrays John's ministry as a call to repentance. His ministry of baptism is unprecedented. Judaism knew of repeated baptisms for temporary cleansing, but this was a call to submit to a one-time baptism in honor of the arrival of the era of salvation.
The concept of repentance has OT roots in the idea of turning away from sin and toward God. To be prepared for God's salvation, one's heart must be open to his message.
The possibility of salvation also implies a coming judgment. Thus, opportunity will become tragedy if a hearer does not respond. Salvation is not by family inheritance but by faith, by turning in trust to the living God.
3:4–6 Luke leaves no doubt as to the prophetic basis for John's ministry.
3:7 The Good News of repentance and forgiveness has a flip side—the threat of judgment for failing to respond to God. In effect, John is asking if his hearers understand what his baptism is really about and what is at stake. The people are to produce fruit worthy of repentance. If a person turns to God, their life should look different.
3:8–9 John's audience may have assumed that because they were Jews, they were guaranteed salvation as part of the elect family of God. John warns that such a heritage means nothing to

Lk 3:8 ❖ What might "fruit in keeping with repentance" look like in our lives? How would it show in our words, thoughts, and actions?

as our father.'[a] For I tell you that out of
these stones God can raise up children
for Abraham. 9The ax is already at the
root of the trees, and every tree that does
not produce good fruit will be cut down
and thrown into the fire."[b]
10"What should we do then?"[c] the
crowd asked.
11John answered, "Anyone who has two
shirts should share with the one who has
none, and anyone who has food should
do the same."[d]
12Even tax collectors came to be baptized.[e] "Teacher," they asked, "what
should we do?"
13"Don't collect any more than you are
required to,"[f] he told them.
14Then some soldiers asked him, "And
what should we do?"
He replied, "Don't extort money and
don't accuse people falsely[g] — be content
with your pay."
15The people were waiting expectantly
and were all wondering in their hearts
if John[h] might possibly be the Messiah.[i]
16John answered them all, "I baptize you
with[a] water.[j] But one who is more powerful than I will come, the straps of whose
sandals I am not worthy to untie. He will
baptize you with[a] the Holy Spirit and
fire.[k] 17His winnowing fork[l] is in his hand
to clear his threshing floor and to gather
the wheat into his barn, but he will burn
up the chaff with unquenchable fire."[m]
18And with many other words John exhorted the people and proclaimed the
good news to them.
19But when John rebuked Herod[n] the
tetrarch because of his marriage to Herodias, his brother's wife, and all the other
evil things he had done, 20Herod added
this to them all: He locked John up in
prison.[o]

The Baptism and Genealogy of Jesus

3:21,22pp // Mt 3:13–17; Mk 1:9–11
3:23–38pp // Mt 1:1–17

21When all the people were being baptized, Jesus was baptized too. And as he
was praying,[p] heaven was opened 22and
the Holy Spirit descended on him[q] in
bodily form like a dove. And a voice came
from heaven: "You are my Son,[r] whom I
love; with you I am well pleased."[s]

3:8 [a]Isa 51:2; Lk 19:9; Jn 8:33, 39; Ac 13:26; Ro 4:1,11,12,16, 17; Gal 3:7
3:9 [b]Mt 3:10
3:10 [c]ver 12,14; Ac 2:37; 16:30
3:11 [d]Isa 58:7
3:12 [e]Lk 7:29
3:13 [f]Lk 19:8
3:14 [g]Ex 23:1; Lev 19:11
3:15 [h]Mt 3:1 [i]Jn 1:19,20; Ac 13:25
3:16 [j]ver 3; Mk 1:4 [k]Jn 1:26, 33; Ac 1:5; 11:16; 19:4
3:17 [l]Isa 30:24 [m]Mt 13:30; 25:41
3:19 [n]ver 1
3:20 [o]Mt 14:3, 4; Mk 6:17-18
3:21 [p]Mt 14:23; Mk 1:35; 6:46; Lk 5:16; 6:12; 9:18,28; 11:1
3:22 [q]Isa 42:1; Jn 1:32,33; Ac 10:38 [r]Mt 3:17 [s]Mt 3:17

[a] 16 Or *in*

---

an individual who does not personally turn to God.

3:10 The crowd asks what they can do to avoid the wrath to come. At least some in the crowd understand that the important issue is not getting baptized but responding to God with a certain kind of heart and life.

3:11–14 John tells the crowd to be generous and honest in their daily dealings.

3:15 John denies that he is the Messiah and explains how they may know that the Christ has come.

3:16–17 Baptism with the Spirit and fire represents a presence and a purging that divides. That presence and purging are in view is made clear by v. 17, where the "winnowing fork" is said to be ready to clear the threshing floor.

3:18–20 John's message reaches the upper echelon of society; no one escapes his penetrating call to repent. He takes Herod to task for his marriage to Herodias, as they both left marriages to marry each other. Given the choice of repenting or denying sin, the ruler tries to remove the source of accountability.

3:21–22 Few moments are as important as when heaven speaks. Jesus' baptism has three significant points. First, when Jesus submits to this washing, he is declaring that John's message is true and that people must get prepared to receive salvation. Next, Jesus is praying when the Spirit descends, and Luke loves to mention how Jesus bathes his life in prayer. Finally, this is probably a private experience of Jesus. Luke does not record any reaction from the crowd, as in other cases when such events occur.

Here an "anointing" takes place. The Spirit descends like a dove on Jesus. The Spirit is associated with the presence of God in his creative work and in the presence of his grace. God vocally identifies Jesus as his Son as he anoints him for ministry.

God's statement weaves together three possible OT allusions: First, Jesus is identified in Ps 2:7 as the messianic Son. Second, the next allusion comes from Isa 42:1, a servant passage. Whether a third allusion appears in "whom I love" is debated. A likely option is to see an allusion to Isa 41:8, where the ideas of a chosen servant and a beloved person line up.

✜ **3:1–22** Sometimes doing God's will is not popular; it may involve personal risk. John speaks up and has to suffer the consequences of his public stand. He describes what sin is and calls people to account for it before God, but he also shows the way out of its sinister grip. The church today, and the believers who make up the church, need to do the same in calling wayward people back to Jesus.

When we are forgiven after turning to God, such forgiveness should yield a transformed

PEOPLE TO KNOW // JOSEPH, MARY'S HUSBAND

LUKE 4:22: Joseph was a righteous and selfless man. When Mary, to whom he was engaged, was found to be pregnant, he thought he needed to break off the engagement. This entailed divorcing her, since they were already legally bound. Yet instead of doing it publicly and humiliating her, Joseph endeavored to take care of this matter as quietly as possible (Mt 1:18–19). Even before he knew Mary's pregnancy was from God, he sought to treat her kindly.

When an angel told Joseph in a dream that Mary's baby was conceived through the Holy Spirit, Joseph obediently accepted his responsibility to stay with Mary, despite what others might have thought.

Jesus was born in Bethlehem, where Joseph and Mary had to travel due to a census. Mary and Joseph must have been shocked by the kind of visitors who came to see the baby: shepherds (Lk 2:16) and, sometime later, Magi from afar (Mt 2:1–2). Their awe and wonder turned to worry, however, when an angel appeared to Joseph once again in a dream, this time telling him to flee with his family to Egypt to save baby Jesus from the wrath of Herod (Mt 2:13). Once again, Joseph obeyed. After this, Joseph had two more divine dreams, telling him first to move back to Israel and then specifically to Nazareth (Mt 1:19–23).

APPLICATION Joseph never speaks a word in Scripture, yet his story is an example of obedience to God. God asked Joseph to do difficult things, and Joseph obeyed humbly. Joseph offers a superb example of humility and trust, and he was quick to follow God's instructions. He also demonstrates care and compassion through his treatment of Mary. Joseph is an example of what an honorable man of God looks like.

19 to proclaim the year of the Lord's
favor."[a][u]

20Then he rolled up the scroll, gave it
back to the attendant and sat down.[v] The
eyes of everyone in the synagogue were
fastened on him. 21He began by saying
to them, "Today this scripture is fulfilled
in your hearing."

22All spoke well of him and were
amazed at the gracious words that came
from his lips. "Isn't this Joseph's son?"
they asked.[w]

23Jesus said to them, "Surely you will
quote this proverb to me: 'Physician, heal
yourself!' And you will tell me, 'Do here
in your hometown[x] what we have heard
that you did in Capernaum.'"[y]

24"Truly I tell you," he continued, "no
prophet is accepted in his hometown.[z]
25I assure you that there were many widows in Israel in Elijah's time, when the
sky was shut for three and a half years
and there was a severe famine throughout the land.[a]
26Yet Elijah was not sent
to any of them, but to a widow in Zarephath in the region of Sidon.[b]
27And
there were many in Israel with leprosy[b]
in the time of Elisha the prophet, yet
not one of them was cleansed — only
Naaman the Syrian."[c]

28All the people in the synagogue
were furious when they heard this.
29They got up, drove him out of the
town,[d] and took him to the brow of the
hill on which the town was built, in or-

4:19 [u] Lev 25:10; Isa 61:1,2
4:20 [v] ver 17; Mt 26:55
4:22 [w] Mt 13:54, 55; Jn 6:42; 7:15
4:23 [x] ver 16 [y] Mk 1:21-28; 2:1-12
4:24 [z] Mt 13:57; Jn 4:44
4:25 [a] 1Ki 17:1; 18:1; Jas 5:17,18
4:26 [b] 1Ki 17:8-16; Mt 11:21
4:27 [c] 2Ki 5:1-14
4:29 [d] Nu 15:35; Ac 7:58; Heb 13:12

[a] *19* Isaiah 61:1,2 (see Septuagint); Isaiah 58:6
[b] *27* The Greek word traditionally translated *leprosy* was used for various diseases affecting the skin.

4:21 Jesus concludes his remarks by telling his audience that they are seeing the fulfillment of these words of Isaiah. Isa 61 was associated with the decisive end-time salvation of God, which Jesus has begun to introduce.

4:22 The crowd reacts with marvel and is overwhelmed by the content of his message. Despite their amazement, they are skeptical of his claims.

4:23–27 Jesus notes how a prophet is without honor in his own land. Jesus then singles out the period of Elijah and Elisha, one of the lowest, most apostate periods of the nation's history, warning his audience that their reaction recalls some of the lowest years in Israel's past.

4:28–30 Jesus' remark angers the crowd, and they want to remove him and cast him over the cliff—possibly alluding to their rejecting him as a false prophet worthy of complete rejection. Instead, Jesus walks away.

4:14–30 It is important to appreciate how central good teaching is to ministry. In an era

der to throw him off the cliff. 30But he walked right through the crowd and went on his way.[e]

Jesus Drives Out an Impure Spirit

4:31–37pp // Mk 1:21–28

31Then he went down to Capernaum,[f] a town in Galilee, and on the Sabbath he taught the people. 32They were amazed at his teaching,[g] because his words had authority.[h]

33In the synagogue there was a man possessed by a demon, an impure spirit. He cried out at the top of his voice, 34"Go away! What do you want with us,[i] Jesus of Nazareth?[j] Have you come to destroy us? I know who you are[k] — the Holy One of God!"[l]

35"Be quiet!" Jesus said sternly.[m] "Come out of him!" Then the demon threw the man down before them all and came out without injuring him.

36All the people were amazed[n] and said to each other, "What words these are! With authority[o] and power he gives orders to impure spirits and they come out!" 37And the news about him spread throughout the surrounding area.[p]

4:30 [e] Jn 8:59; 10:39
4:31 [f] ver 23; Mt 4:13
4:32 [g] Mt 7:28 [h] ver 36; Mt 7:29
4:34 [i] Mt 8:29 [j] Mk 1:24 [k] Jas 2:19 [l] ver 41; Mk 1:24
4:35 [m] ver 39, 41; Mt 8:26; Lk 8:24
4:36 [n] Mt 7:28 [o] ver 32; Mt 7:29; Mt 10:1
4:37 [p] ver 14; Mt 9:26
4:39 [q] ver 35, 41
4:40 [r] Mk 5:23 [s] Mt 4:23
4:41 [t] Mt 4:3 [u] ver 35 [v] Mt 8:4
4:43 [w] Mt 3:2
4:44 [x] Mt 4:23

Jesus Heals Many

4:38–41pp // Mt 8:14–17
4:38–43pp // Mk 1:29–38

38Jesus left the synagogue and went to the home of Simon. Now Simon's mother-in-law was suffering from a high fever, and they asked Jesus to help her. 39So he bent over her and rebuked[q] the fever, and it left her. She got up at once and began to wait on them.

40At sunset, the people brought to Jesus all who had various kinds of sickness, and laying his hands on each one,[r] he healed them.[s] 41Moreover, demons came out of many people, shouting, "You are the Son of God!"[t] But he rebuked[u] them and would not allow them to speak,[v] because they knew he was the Messiah.

42At daybreak, Jesus went out to a solitary place. The people were looking for him and when they came to where he was, they tried to keep him from leaving them. 43But he said, "I must proclaim the good news of the kingdom of God[w] to the other towns also, because that is why I was sent." 44And he kept on preaching in the synagogues of Judea.[x]

---

when feelings and interpersonal relationships are high on the agenda, it is wise to reflect on why Jesus spent so much time instructing people. One of the fundamental biblical assumptions is that human cultures distort reality. Our minds need reshaping and renewing so that our feelings and reactions will be more like what God desires. It takes careful cultural discernment to know how to respond to the subtleties our culture feeds us.

The major application emerging from this scene involves the nature of his mission. The believer's call is an extension of Jesus' mission. The fulfillment he points to is part of the fulfillment that the church proclaims. Values reflected in this mission should be reflected in our personal approach to others and in the church's outreach.

4:31-32 All of Jesus' miracles reflect a visual representation of some significant spiritual reality—often the depth of the cosmic struggle associated with his ministry. Since his work represents the powerful arrival of the force of righteousness into God's world, is it any wonder that Jesus must engage in hand-to-hand combat with the forces of evil? In a real sense, the miracles pull back a veil on the cosmic forces at work within creation.

The major feature in these verses is the recognition of the authority inherent in Jesus' teaching. Most rabbinic arguments set out various opinions on a matter. Truth was often a matter of establishing a precedent for an idea. Jesus does *not* teach this way. He declares God's will directly, even keeping his direct use of Scripture to a few limited situations. The crowds recognize his distinct approach to teaching and are astonished by it.

4:33-36 The first miracle of this Gospel is an exorcism. Followers of Judaism believed that in messianic times demonic power would be crushed. Jesus has already met with Satan; now he is facing off against Satan's cohorts.

Jesus' presence makes the demon nervous. Jesus rebukes the evil spirit, and immediately the man is restored. He also silences it. Apparently, Jesus wants nothing to do with demonic confession of him in public.

4:38-39 The next healing is less dramatic but just as significant. Jesus encounters Peter's mother-in-law at Peter's home, sick with a high fever. Jesus acts against another distinct threat to life. He rebukes the illness, and the woman is restored to health and begins serving them. This remark not only testifies to her recovery but also reflects her gratitude.

4:40-41 Word spreads quickly, and Jesus finds himself dealing with people who come to him with all kinds of maladies. Healings continue without interruption. His authority flows constantly. The Anointed One is showing the evidence of his unique calling.

4:42-44 Jesus withdraws for a private time of prayer, but the people look for him. Those in Capernaum want him to stay, but Jesus has been called to preach the kingdom of God elsewhere.

✚ **4:31-44** Many missionary organizations and churches in recent history have organized benevolent ministries and hospitals as expressions

Jesus Calls His First Disciples

5:1–11pp // Mt 4:18–22; Mk 1:16–20; Jn 1:40–42

5 One day as Jesus was standing by the Lake of Gennesaret,[a] the people were crowding around him and listening to the word of God.[y] 2He saw at the water's edge two boats, left there by the fishermen, who were washing their nets. 3He got into one of the boats, the one belonging to Simon, and asked him to put out a little from shore. Then he sat down and taught the people from the boat.[z]

4When he had finished speaking, he said to Simon, "Put out into deep water, and let down the nets for a catch."[a]

5Simon answered, "Master,[b] we've worked hard all night and haven't caught anything.[c] But because you say so, I will let down the nets."

6When they had done so, they caught such a large number of fish that their nets began to break.[d] 7So they signaled their partners in the other boat to come and help them, and they came and filled both boats so full that they began to sink.

8When Simon Peter saw this, he fell at Jesus' knees and said, "Go away from me, Lord; I am a sinful man!"[e] 9For he and all his companions were astonished at the catch of fish they had taken, 10and so were James and John, the sons of Zebedee, Simon's partners.

5:1 [y] Mk 4:14; Heb 4:12
5:3 [z] Mt 13:2
5:4 [a] Jn 21:6
5:5 [b] Lk 8:24, 45; 9:33, 49; 17:13 [c] Jn 21:3
5:6 [d] Jn 21:11
5:8 [e] Ge 18:27; Job 42:6; Isa 6:5
5:10 [f] Mt 14:27
5:11 [g] ver 28; Mt 4:19
5:12 [h] Mt 8:2
5:14 [i] Mt 8:4 [j] Lev 14:2-32
5:15 [k] Mt 9:26

Lk 5:13 ❖ Do you ever feel as if Christ might not be willing to help you? How does this verse bring comfort?

Then Jesus said to Simon, "Don't be afraid;[f] from now on you will fish for people." 11So they pulled their boats up on shore, left everything and followed him.[g]

Jesus Heals a Man With Leprosy

5:12–14pp // Mt 8:2–4; Mk 1:40–44

12While Jesus was in one of the towns, a man came along who was covered with leprosy.[b][h] When he saw Jesus, he fell with his face to the ground and begged him, "Lord, if you are willing, you can make me clean."

13Jesus reached out his hand and touched the man. "I am willing," he said. "Be clean!" And immediately the leprosy left him.

14Then Jesus ordered him, "Don't tell anyone,[i] but go, show yourself to the priest and offer the sacrifices that Moses commanded[j] for your cleansing, as a testimony to them."

15Yet the news about him spread all the more,[k] so that crowds of people came to hear him and to be healed of their

[a] *1* That is, the Sea of Galilee [b] *12* The Greek word traditionally translated *leprosy* was used for various diseases affecting the skin.

---

of the type of compassionate service Jesus performs here. Such a connection is justified. What the healings and exorcisms show is God's power and concern for humanity. Believers in the church should show no less compassion today. When we deal with the ravages of disease or show concern to those who are hurting, we are reflecting the kind of love God has for people who live in a fallen world.

5:1-5 Sometimes service for Jesus starts out rather innocently. Just ask Peter. The entire episode is both surprising and revealing. After teaching, Jesus tells Peter to head out and go fishing. Although Peter notes that conditions are not right, he agrees to cast the nets. This indicates potential in Peter, for he responds to Jesus' leading.

5:6-10a When the effort is overwhelmingly successful, Peter realizes that what has taken place is no accident; only an agent of God could have produced such a catch in the middle of the day. The other disciples are also "astonished."

In words full of respect and awe, he asks Jesus to depart. The premise behind this remark is that a man of God surely would want to have nothing to do with an everyday sinner. Peter's confession becomes his résumé for service. Humility is the elevator to spiritual greatness.

5:10b-11 Jesus issues a call to Peter to enter into the process of gathering people and rescuing them from the danger of a fallen world. Unlike fish, which are caught to be flayed and devoured, Peter will catch people and bring them into life. Jesus' prophetic leading and insight powerfully illustrate his call, indicating graphically the mission Peter has before him.

5:12-13 After this initial call, Luke relates two miracles that present further details about Jesus' authority and compassion. Luke introduces the first healing by mentioning that Jesus is venturing to other parts of Galilee, as he said he must do.

A man with leprosy approaches Jesus with humility, bowing before him. His request raises the question of Jesus' willingness to heal, not his capability. The picture of redemption should not be missed. Those who turn to Jesus for cleansing receive it from him because he willingly gives it.

5:14-15 Jesus sends the man to follow the Mosaic Law; the testimony before the priest will take a week. The ritual pictured the cleansing and removal of sin, so even the follow-up program for the formerly leprous man reinforces the message of what

sicknesses. 16But Jesus often withdrew
to lonely places and prayed.[l]

Jesus Forgives and Heals a Paralyzed Man

5:18–26pp // Mt 9:2–8; Mk 2:3–12

17One day Jesus was teaching, and
Pharisees and teachers of the law[m] were
sitting there. They had come from every
village of Galilee and from Judea and Jerusalem. And the power of the Lord was
with Jesus to heal the sick.[n] 18Some men
came carrying a paralyzed man on a mat
and tried to take him into the house to
lay him before Jesus. 19When they could
not find a way to do this because of the
crowd, they went up on the roof and lowered him on his mat through the tiles
into the middle of the crowd, right in
front of Jesus.
20When Jesus saw their faith, he said,
"Friend, your sins are forgiven."[o]
21The Pharisees and the teachers of
the law began thinking to themselves,
"Who is this fellow who speaks blasphemy? Who can forgive sins but God
alone?"[p]
22Jesus knew what they were thinking
and asked, "Why are you thinking these
things in your hearts? 23Which is easier:
to say, 'Your sins are forgiven,' or to say,
'Get up and walk'? 24But I want you to
know that the Son of Man[q] has authority
on earth to forgive sins." So he said to the
paralyzed man, "I tell you, get up, take
your mat and go home." 25Immediately
he stood up in front of them, took what
he had been lying on and went home
praising God. 26Everyone was amazed
and gave praise to God.[r] They were filled
with awe and said, "We have seen remarkable things today."

Jesus Calls Levi and Eats With Sinners

5:27–32pp // Mt 9:9–13; Mk 2:14–17

27After this, Jesus went out and saw a
tax collector by the name of Levi sitting
at his tax booth. "Follow me,"[s] Jesus said
to him, 28and Levi got up, left everything
and followed him.[t]
29Then Levi held a great banquet for
Jesus at his house, and a large crowd of
tax collectors[u] and others were eating
with them. 30But the Pharisees and the
teachers of the law who belonged to their
sect[v] complained to his disciples, "Why
do you eat and drink with tax collectors
and sinners?"[w]
31Jesus answered them, "It is not the
healthy who need a doctor, but the sick.
32I have not come to call the righteous,
but sinners to repentance."[x]

5:16 [l] Mt 14:23; Lk 3:21
5:17 [m] Mt 15:1; Lk 2:46 [n] Mk 5:30; Lk 6:19
5:20 [o] Lk 7:48, 49
5:21 [p] Isa 43:25
5:24 [q] Mt 8:20
5:26 [r] Mt 9:8
5:27 [s] Mt 4:19
5:28 [t] ver 11; Mt 4:19
5:29 [u] Lk 15:1
5:30 [v] Ac 23:9 [w] Mt 9:11
5:32 [x] Jn 3:17

Jesus has done. The fact that the testimony is for the priests is not surprising, given their need to understand what Jesus represents.

5:16 Luke bridges the two miracle stories and the hectic pace Jesus is leading by noting that he stops for prayer. Luke regularly notes such commitments to prayer.

5:17 The Pharisees were one of four religious parties in Judaism (Sadducees, Zealots, and Essenes are the others). They were a lay movement that developed many traditions and oral rulings to establish how the Mosaic Law should be applied in their generation.

5:18–20 As Jesus is teaching, a group of men bring a man who is paralyzed to him for healing. Jesus sees "their faith," a remark that is easy to move past. Faith in this context must mean the visible expression of faith, not a mere attitude, since Jesus sees it in the actions of the men. As a result, Jesus acts, giving the man much more than he was seeking: He forgives the man's sins.

5:21 A chain reaction follows. The Pharisees and scribes react to the theological implications of what Jesus just said. They know that only God forgives sin, so to claim to do what God does is blasphemy, a slander against God.

5:22–26 Logic tells us that it is easier to say one's sins are forgiven, since that cannot be seen; but in fact that is more difficult, since one must have the authority to forgive. Jesus links the two issues of forgiveness and healing together. He acts so that the audience can know the Son of Man has authority to forgive sins.

5:27–28 Just as sinners can enter into an intimate relationship with God, so can tax collectors. In other words, *anyone* who responds to Jesus can receive a blessing. Levi responds to the invitation, leaving his vocation and financial security behind to follow Jesus.

5:29–30 Levi then throws Jesus "a great banquet" (v. 29). The associations Jesus makes causes other religious figures to raise questions. In ancient culture, to share a meal with someone communicated acceptance.

5:31–32 Jesus then gives the rationale for his actions. Jesus' call goes out to those who realize they need help. If they desire to know God, the Lord will not reject them but will begin the process that will make them well.

✣ **5:1–32** The most significant lesson from the cleansing of the man with leprosy is that even outsiders can experience God's healing grace. The church is called by this example to reach out to those on the fringes of society. The leper's healing pictures Jesus making someone clean from sin; the story of the man who was paralyzed reinforces this verbally. This text warns us not to take any sin lightly, for it makes

Jesus Questioned About Fasting

5:33–39pp // Mt 9:14–17; Mk 2:18–22

33 They said to him, "John's disciples[y]
often fast and pray, and so do the disciples of the Pharisees, but yours go on
eating and drinking."
34 Jesus answered, "Can you make the
friends of the bridegroom[z] fast while he
is with them? 35 But the time will come
when the bridegroom will be taken from
them;[a] in those days they will fast."
36 He told them this parable: "No one
tears a piece out of a new garment to
patch an old one. Otherwise, they will
have torn the new garment, and the
patch from the new will not match the
old. 37 And no one pours new wine into
old wineskins. Otherwise, the new wine
will burst the skins; the wine will run
out and the wineskins will be ruined.
38 No, new wine must be poured into new
wineskins. 39 And no one after drinking
old wine wants the new, for they say, 'The
old is better.'"

Jesus Is Lord of the Sabbath

6:1–11pp // Mt 12:1–14; Mk 2:23—3:6

6 One Sabbath Jesus was going through
the grainfields, and his disciples began to pick some heads of grain, rub
them in their hands and eat the kernels.[b]
2 Some of the Pharisees asked, "Why are
you doing what is unlawful on the Sabbath?"[c]
3 Jesus answered them, "Have you never read what David did when he and his
companions were hungry?[d] 4 He entered
the house of God, and taking the consecrated bread, he ate what is lawful only
for priests to eat.[e] And he also gave some
to his companions." 5 Then Jesus said to
them, "The Son of Man[f] is Lord of the
Sabbath."
6 On another Sabbath[g] he went into the
synagogue and was teaching, and a man
was there whose right hand was shriveled. 7 The Pharisees and the teachers of
the law were looking for a reason to accuse Jesus, so they watched him closely[h]
to see if he would heal on the Sabbath.[i]
8 But Jesus knew what they were thinking[j] and said to the man with the shriveled hand, "Get up and stand in front of
everyone." So he got up and stood there.
9 Then Jesus said to them, "I ask you,
which is lawful on the Sabbath: to do
good or to do evil, to save life or to destroy it?"

5:33 [y] Lk 7:18; Jn 1:35; 3:25,26
5:34 [z] Jn 3:29
5:35 [a] Lk 9:22; 17:22; Jn 16:5-7
6:1 [b] Dt 23:25
6:2 [c] Mt 12:2
6:3 [d] 1Sa 21:6
6:4 [e] Lev 24:5,9
6:5 [f] Mt 8:20
6:6 [g] ver 1
6:7 [h] Mt 12:10 [i] Mt 12:2
6:8 [j] Mt 9:4

---

us unclean. God took sin so seriously that he gave his own Son to purify us from its stain.

And yet, Jesus' initiative in this passage is also revealing. He seeks sinners, keeping his eye out for them, and makes reaching out to them a priority. For evangelism to be effective, the unsaved must be engaged.

5:33 Fasting in Judaism was a major display of holiness. In the Judaism of Jesus' time, fasting was regarded as a virtue. The failure of Jesus' disciples to fast could be read as reflecting a lack of respect for God, a severe absence of piety.
5:34–35 Jesus not only explains why they do not fast but also explains the deep significance of the refusal. The picture he uses is of a wedding—a symbol often used to describe God's relationship with his people. When the groom is taken from them, fasting will be appropriate. Here is the first hint of Jesus' approaching suffering. It is no accident that Jesus makes this point as the opposition is rising.
5:36–39 Jesus declares that a new era with new perspectives has arrived. One cannot mix what Jesus brings with the old ways without blowing something up. Jesus is more than a reformer of Judaism; he has come to refashion it into something fresh. Those who like old wine do not try the new, for their minds are already made up: "The old is good." So Jesus expects many not to respond to his new way.
6:1–2 Luke moves immediately into the next event. The Mishnah (an ancient Jewish rule book) contained a list of thirty-nine prohibited activities. According to that list, the disciples in this scene are guilty of reaping, threshing, winnowing, and preparing food on the Sabbath.
6:3–4 Jesus defends their actions by citing Scripture. He knows the Pharisees have read 1Sa 21:1–7 and 22:8–9, but he argues they have misunderstood it. Jesus' reply has the Pharisees in a dilemma. In effect, if they condemn him on this issue, they criticize David as well.
6:5 The fact that Jesus is the Son of Man means that he has the right to regulate what takes place on the Sabbath. This remark underlines his unique position. His actions are not the issue; his authority is.

5:33—6:5 In the end, the correctness of what Jesus does with his disciples rests on his claims. Does he have authority as the Son of Man, so that his analysis of the OT and the present situation are authoritative over the law? If so, who then is Jesus? This is the fundamental question in this text. The Pharisees do not believe Jesus has the authority to say what he is teaching. Today many still challenge Jesus' authority. But if he is the Son of Man, he must be heard, for he reveals the way to God.

6:6–8 The scribes and Pharisees want to level a charge against Jesus. The Greek word for "watched" (v. 7) means "to spy on" or "to watch out of the corner of one's eye."
6:9 Jesus raises a fundamental question (v. 9). He is looking at the Sabbath from a relational angle.

10He looked around at them all, and then said to the man, "Stretch out your hand." He did so, and his hand was completely restored. 11But the Pharisees and the teachers of the law were furious[k] and began to discuss with one another what they might do to Jesus.

The Twelve Apostles

6:13–16pp // Mt 10:2–4; Mk 3:16–19; Ac 1:13

12One of those days Jesus went out to a mountainside to pray, and spent the night praying to God.[l] 13When morning came, he called his disciples to him and chose twelve of them, whom he also designated apostles:[m] 14Simon (whom he named Peter), his brother Andrew, James, John, Philip, Bartholomew, 15Matthew,[n] Thomas, James son of Alphaeus, Simon who was called the Zealot, 16Judas son of James, and Judas Iscariot, who became a traitor.

Blessings and Woes

6:20–23pp // Mt 5:3–12

17He went down with them and stood on a level place. A large crowd of his disciples was there and a great number of people from all over Judea, from Jerusalem, and from the coastal region around Tyre and Sidon,[o] 18who had come to hear him and to be healed of their diseases. Those troubled by impure spirits were cured, 19and the people all tried to touch him,[p] because power was coming from him and healing them all.[q]

20Looking at his disciples, he said:

"Blessed are you who are poor,
for yours is the kingdom of God.[r]
21 Blessed are you who hunger now,
for you will be satisfied.[s]
Blessed are you who weep now,
for you will laugh.[t]
22 Blessed are you when people hate you,
when they exclude you[u] and insult you[v]
and reject your name as evil,
because of the Son of Man.[w]

23"Rejoice in that day and leap for joy,[x] because great is your reward in heaven. For that is how their ancestors treated the prophets.[y]

24 "But woe to you who are rich,[z]
for you have already received your comfort.[a]

6:11 [k] Jn 5:18
6:12 [l] Lk 3:21
6:13 [m] Mk 6:30
6:15 [n] Mt 9:9
6:17 [o] Mt 4:25; 11:21; Mk 3:7,8
6:19 [p] Mt 9:20 [q] Mt 14:36; Mk 5:30; Lk 5:17
6:20 [r] Mt 25:34
6:21 [s] Isa 55:1,2; Mt 5:6 [t] Isa 61:2,3; Mt 5:4; Rev 7:17
6:22 [u] Jn 9:22; 16:2 [v] Isa 51:7 [w] Jn 15:21
6:23 [x] Mt 5:12 [y] Mt 5:12
6:24 [z] Jas 5:1 [a] Lk 16:25

Lk 6:22 ❖ Have you struggled with how others treat you because of your faith? Have you ever lost anything because of it? What assurance do Jesus' words provide?

The way he pursues the question almost suggests that a failure to act here would be to do evil. Will God vindicate Jesus and reveal the answer to his question?

6:10–11 Rather than rejoicing at his restoration, the leaders become angry at Jesus' success. The word for "anger" describes irrational anger, even pathological rage. A turning point has come. Refusing to accept the evidence Jesus has laid before them, they cast their vote against him.

6:12–16 Jesus' selection of the Twelve is preparation for the missions to come and an anticipation of his future departure through death. His selection is set in a context of communion with God. The number is designed to suggest a parallel to Israel's twelve tribes. Luke calls the group "apostles" (v. 13), indicating their role as commissioned representatives of Jesus.

❖ **6:6–16** This passage demonstrates the priority that showing mercy has in the mind of God. He is compassionate and wants us to help others whenever possible. Even a day of rest, like the Sabbath, is no reason to opt out of doing good. Jesus goes out of his way to show his opponents that this is how God desires others to be treated.

While on earth, he dedicated himself to serving others, especially others in need. He acted at the first opportunity. Our rapid response should match his.

6:17–19 Jesus declares God's grace of blessing to those who identify with him. In contrast, the woes, unique to Luke's Gospel, show God's displeasure with those who oppose the blessing Jesus gives and who persecute his disciples.

6:20 The pious poor are blessed because they have a position in the kingdom of God. Such people understand that they must depend on God, because their life is beyond their control.

6:21 Hunger is a result of harsh treatment by powerful people who take advantage of others. The blessing they will receive transcends any lack they have now.

Those who weep have paid the price of painful rejection for lining up with God. God sees their tears, which will be transformed into smiles.

6:22–23 The last unit is the key remark of the blessing sequence because it shows the religious dimensions of those who are blessed. A choice to follow Jesus meant the loss of family fellowship, dismissal from the synagogue, and removal from social contact. The call to "rejoice" is the one command among the blessings (v. 23); everything else is promise. God's grace will help them overcome their suffering for their faith.

6:24 The "rich" are singled out in the first woe because they often take advantage of the poor. The

25 Woe to you who are well fed now,
for you will go hungry.[b]
Woe to you who laugh now,
for you will mourn and weep.[c]
26 Woe to you when everyone speaks
well of you,
for that is how their ancestors
treated the false prophets.[d]

Love for Enemies

6:29,30pp // Mt 5:39–42

27 "But to you who are listening I say:
Love your enemies, do good to those
who hate you,[e] 28 bless those who curse
you, pray for those who mistreat you.[f]
29 If someone slaps you on one cheek,
turn to them the other also. If someone
takes your coat, do not withhold your
shirt from them. 30 Give to everyone who
asks you, and if anyone takes what belongs to you, do not demand it back.[g]
31 Do to others as you would have them
do to you.[h]
32 "If you love those who love you, what
credit is that to you?[i] Even sinners love
those who love them. 33 And if you do
good to those who are good to you, what
credit is that to you? Even sinners do
that. 34 And if you lend to those from
whom you expect repayment, what credit is that to you?[j] Even sinners lend to sinners, expecting to be repaid in full. 35 But
love your enemies, do good to them,[k]
and lend to them without expecting to
get anything back. Then your reward will
be great, and you will be children[l] of the
Most High,[m] because he is kind to the
ungrateful and wicked. 36 Be merciful,[n]
just as your Father[o] is merciful.

Judging Others

6:37–42pp // Mt 7:1–5

37 "Do not judge, and you will not be
judged.[p] Do not condemn, and you will
not be condemned. Forgive, and you will
be forgiven.[q] 38 Give, and it will be given
to you. A good measure, pressed down,
shaken together and running over, will be
poured into your lap.[r] For with the measure you use, it will be measured to you."[s]
39 He also told them this parable: "Can
the blind lead the blind? Will they not
both fall into a pit?[t] 40 The student is not
above the teacher, but everyone who is
fully trained will be like their teacher.[u]
41 "Why do you look at the speck of sawdust in your brother's eye and pay no
attention to the plank in your own eye?
42 How can you say to your brother, 'Brother, let me take the speck out of your eye,'
when you yourself fail to see the plank in
your own eye? You hypocrite, first take

6:25 [b] Isa 65:13 [c] Pr 14:13
6:26 [d] Mt 7:15
6:27 [e] ver 35; Mt 5:44; Ro 12:20
6:28 [f] Mt 5:44
6:30 [g] Dt 15:7,8,10; Pr 21:26
6:31 [h] Mt 7:12
6:32 [i] Mt 5:46
6:34 [j] Mt 5:42
6:35 [k] ver 27 [l] Ro 8:14 [m] Mk 5:7
6:36 [n] Jas 2:13 [o] Mt 5:48; 6:1; Lk 11:2; 12:32; Ro 8:15; Eph 4:6; 1Pe 1:17; 1Jn 1:3; 3:1
6:37 [p] Mt 7:1 [q] Mt 6:14
6:38 [r] Ps 79:12; Isa 65:6,7 [s] Mt 7:2; Mk 4:24
6:39 [t] Mt 15:14
6:40 [u] Mt 10:24; Jn 13:16

---

remark is a generalization since some people who are wealthy do respond to the gospel. But wealth can create a sense of independence that can result in distance from God and callousness toward others.

6:25 The next woe is against those "who are well fed now." Those who ignore God and place their hopes solely on the good life here have little comfort for the future.

6:26 The final woe reveals the spiritual depravity of these people. They wrongly see themselves as unaccountable to God.

6:27-28 Fundamental to kingdom ethics is love—a love that endures. People who have experienced the love of the Father are more hesitant to judge and ready to forgive. Four exhortations in vv. 27 and 28 make the key point: The special objects of love are one's enemies. The love Jesus commands demonstrates itself in concrete action. In the context of rejection, Jesus calls for extraordinary trust in God. Disciples should constantly reflect such love.

6:29 The early church consistently turned the other cheek by continuing to share the gospel with those who rejected them. Those who take the outer garment should also be allowed to have the undershirt. Jesus' point here is not to stand on a street corner and allow oneself to be robbed, but rather that ministry in the context of rejection requires being vulnerable again and again.

6:30-31 The disciple should also be compassionate and generous and should thus give to the needy. Such compassion represents a fundamental expression of love.

It is better to be defrauded than to bring reproach on Jesus' name. Those who strike against the disciples should not be treated differently by the disciples.

The disciple understands that God is watching over their situation, so any vindication should be left in his hands. The greatest vindication of all is to transform an enemy into a friend of God through the example of love.

6:32-36 It takes no effort to love those who are kind to us; even lost people love that way. The call of the disciple is to a greater love—a distinct love, a love that is unique in the world. Such love is rewarded because it distinguishes the presence of the children of God, who reflect the character of God. In other words, the standard of the disciple's behavior is the merciful character of God.

6:37-38 In imitation of God, the disciple should also be slow to judge (v. 37). The measure we use toward others is the measure God will use toward us. God honors a compassionate spirit.

6:39-40 Physical blindness is a common representation of spiritual blindness; thus, Jesus is warning here about religious leadership. One should follow the right teacher and not apply too much authority to oneself.

6:41-42 Jesus continues to attack a critical spirit. The way to deal with it is by paying attention to

the plank out of your eye, and then you
will see clearly to remove the speck from
your brother's eye.

A Tree and Its Fruit

6:43,44pp // Mt 7:16,18,20

43“No good tree bears bad fruit, nor
does a bad tree bear good fruit. 44Each
tree is recognized by its own fruit.[v] People do not pick figs from thornbushes, or
grapes from briers. 45A good man brings
good things out of the good stored up in
his heart, and an evil man brings evil
things out of the evil stored up in his
heart. For the mouth speaks what the
heart is full of.[w]

The Wise and Foolish Builders

6:47–49pp // Mt 7:24–27

46“Why do you call me, ‘Lord, Lord,’[x]
and do not do what I say?[y] 47As for everyone who comes to me and hears my
words and puts them into practice,[z] I
will show you what they are like. 48They
are like a man building a house, who
dug down deep and laid the foundation
on rock. When a flood came, the torrent
struck that house but could not shake it,
because it was well built. 49But the one
who hears my words and does not put
them into practice is like a man who built
a house on the ground without a foundation. The moment the torrent struck that
house, it collapsed and its destruction
was complete.”

6:44 [v] Mt 12:33
6:45 [w] Pr 4:23; Mt 12:34,35; Mk 7:20
6:46 [x] Jn 13:13 [y] Mal 1:6; Mt 7:21
6:47 [z] Lk 8:21; 11:28; Jas 1:22-25

The Faith of the Centurion

7:1–10pp // Mt 8:5–13

7 When Jesus had finished saying all
this[a] to the people who were listening, he entered Capernaum. 2There a
centurion's servant, whom his master
valued highly, was sick and about to
die. 3The centurion heard of Jesus and
sent some elders of the Jews to him,
asking him to come and heal his servant. 4When they came to Jesus, they
pleaded earnestly with him, “This
man deserves to have you do this, 5be-
cause he loves our nation and has built
our synagogue.” 6So Jesus went with
them.

He was not far from the house when
the centurion sent friends to say to him:
“Lord, don't trouble yourself, for I do not
deserve to have you come under my roof.
7That is why I did not even consider myself worthy to come to you. But say the
word, and my servant will be healed.[b]
8For I myself am a man under authority,
with soldiers under me. I tell this one,
‘Go,’ and he goes; and that one, ‘Come,’
and he comes. I say to my servant, ‘Do
this,’ and he does it.”

9When Jesus heard this, he was
amazed at him, and turning to the crowd
following him, he said, “I tell you, I have
not found such great faith even in Israel.” 10Then the men who had been sent
returned to the house and found the
servant well.

7:1 [a] Mt 7:28
7:7 [b] Ps 107:20

---

our own faults first and dealing fully with them before turning our attention to the treatment of the little faults of others.

6:43–45 How can one know the character of a person? Jesus says to check the fruit. The tongue is a litmus test of the soul, and the product of one's life is a litmus test of the heart. Each one should examine one's own self in this regard, not make assumptions about others.

6:46–49 To hear Jesus and do what he says is like building a home with a solid foundation. Such a home can stand up against the floods of life.

6:17–49 These blessings and woes possess two central points. First, God is aware of what we are going through, and he promises to vindicate the faithful. Second, to love in a way that is unlike the world risks being misunderstood. Only those who rest in God's care and have assurance of his blessing can endure that hard path. Acceptance comes from the Father, whom we seek to imitate. As a result, acceptance from others matters less.

To exemplify love in a hostile world is difficult. It takes a supernatural perspective and a change of thinking. We often have a hard time showing that love in the way we communicate with those who possess values different from our own. The connection between God's blessing and our ability to love should not be missed. Because of his blessing to us and our appreciation for him, we are able to love others. Because he gave, we can give. Because we know the joy of receiving from him, we are motivated to give to others. The actions Jesus calls for in his sermon apply to others what he has already applied to us. The deeper our understanding and appreciation of what God has done, the better prepared we will be to reflect his character to others.

7:1–5 The question raised in this story is significant at two levels: Will Jesus minister to someone from outside Israel, and will he minister to a wealthy man?

7:6–8 The centurion understands Jesus' authority and knows that if he just issues the order, the healing will occur. These remarks amaze Jesus. One can argue that the essence of faith is humility: recognizing God's power while trusting in God's care.

Jesus Raises a Widow's Son

7:11–16Ref // 1Ki 17:17–24; 2Ki 4:32–37; Mk 5:21–24,35–43; Jn 11:1–44

11 Soon afterward, Jesus went to a town
called Nain, and his disciples and a large
crowd went along with him. 12 As he approached the town gate, a dead person
was being carried out — the only son of
his mother, and she was a widow. And
a large crowd from the town was with
her. 13 When the Lord[c] saw her, his heart
went out to her and he said, "Don't cry."
14 Then he went up and touched the
bier they were carrying him on, and the
bearers stood still. He said, "Young man,
I say to you, get up!"[d] 15 The dead man sat
up and began to talk, and Jesus gave him
back to his mother.
16 They were all filled with awe[e] and
praised God.[f] "A great prophet[g] has appeared among us," they said. "God has
come to help his people."[h] 17 This news
about Jesus spread throughout Judea
and the surrounding country.[i]

Jesus and John the Baptist

7:18–35pp // Mt 11:2–19

18 John's[j] disciples[k] told him about all
these things. Calling two of them, 19 he
sent them to the Lord to ask, "Are you
the one who is to come, or should we
expect someone else?"
20 When the men came to Jesus, they
said, "John the Baptist sent us to you to
ask, 'Are you the one who is to come, or
should we expect someone else?'"
21 At that very time Jesus cured many
who had diseases, sicknesses[l] and evil
spirits, and gave sight to many who were
blind. 22 So he replied to the messengers,
"Go back and report to John what you
have seen and heard: The blind receive
sight, the lame walk, those who have
leprosy[a] are cleansed, the deaf hear, the
dead are raised, and the good news is proclaimed to the poor.[m] 23 Blessed is anyone
who does not stumble on account of me."
24 After John's messengers left, Jesus
began to speak to the crowd about John:
"What did you go out into the wilderness
to see? A reed swayed by the wind? 25 If
not, what did you go out to see? A man
dressed in fine clothes? No, those who
wear expensive clothes and indulge in
luxury are in palaces. 26 But what did you
go out to see? A prophet?[n] Yes, I tell you,
and more than a prophet. 27 This is the
one about whom it is written:

> "'I will send my messenger ahead of
> you,

7:13 [c] ver 19; Lk 10:1; 13:15; 17:5; 22:61; 24:34; Jn 11:2
7:14 [d] Mt 9:25; Mk 1:31; Lk 8:54; Jn 11:43; Ac 9:40
7:16 [e] Lk 1:65 [f] Mt 9:8 [g] ver 39; Mt 21:11 [h] Lk 1:68
7:17 [i] Mt 9:26
7:18 [j] Mt 3:1 [k] Lk 5:33
7:21 [l] Mt 4:23
7:22 [m] Isa 29:18,19; 35:5,6; 61:1,2; Lk 4:18
7:26 [n] Mt 11:9

[a] *22* The Greek word traditionally translated *leprosy* was used for various diseases affecting the skin.

7:11-15 In the next story Jesus simply tells the corpse to arise, and the formerly dead man sits up. Jesus restores the previously broken relationship between mother and son with renewed life.
7:16-17 Two basic questions about Jesus emerge from this story: What kind of understanding does the Israelite public have of Jesus, and why do they think of him this way?

The crowd concludes that Jesus is "a great prophet" (v. 16). Luke will show that granting Jesus prophetic status is not enough. The ancients often recognized that unusual events signaled that God was in their midst. The crowd here sees a connection between God and Jesus.

✣ **7:1-17** The first point of application regarding the centurion is that he, even as an outsider, had developed a good reputation with people from other backgrounds. In our country, as we become more diverse, Christians will need to develop cultural sensitivity if we hope to share the gospel in all possible contexts. The Bible communicates a respect for "God-fearers" like Cornelius (Ac 10) and this centurion. With such openness we can build new bridges for the gospel where we might have formerly isolated ourselves through fear or ignorance.

From the story of the widow's son we learn that death is not the end for those who know Christ. While this miracle reminds us of our frailty and mortality, it also shouts out to us about God's power to raise and transform. No wonder the crowd who saw this miracle was filled with awe. We should be also, as we contemplate Jesus' creative power and compassion.

7:18-20 John's question emerges because his disciples report to him what Jesus is doing. John does not wonder whether Jesus has been sent from God; he simply wants confirmation that his is the promised ministry of deliverance. Even the best of God's servants need reassurance from time to time.
7:21-23 Before recording Jesus' reply, Luke interjects a reminder about the scope of Jesus' ministry; it has involved healings, exorcisms, and even sight given to the blind. Jesus' ministry "graced" many with restoration. The envoys are simply to report what they have seen, using a collage of OT phrases from Isaiah, all of which refer to the coming period of decisive deliverance. Jesus' ministry signals fulfillment of these prophecies.
7:24-27 Jesus then raises the question about John for the crowd. People came to see John because he was a prophet. In fact, John was more than a prophet. At the time of his birth, he was the greatest man yet born. He represented the end of an era and pointed to the dawn of a new era of realization in God's plan.

who will prepare your way before
you.'[a][o]

28I tell you, among those born of women
there is no one greater than John; yet the
one who is least in the kingdom of God[p]
is greater than he."

29(All the people, even the tax collectors, when they heard Jesus' words, acknowledged that God's way was right, because they had been baptized by John.[q]
30But the Pharisees and the experts in
the law[r] rejected God's purpose for themselves, because they had not been baptized by John.)

31Jesus went on to say, "To what, then,
can I compare the people of this generation? What are they like? 32They are like
children sitting in the marketplace and
calling out to each other:

"'We played the pipe for you,
and you did not dance;
we sang a dirge,
and you did not cry.'

33For John the Baptist came neither
eating bread nor drinking wine,[s] and
you say, 'He has a demon.' 34The Son of
Man came eating and drinking, and you
say, 'Here is a glutton and a drunkard,
a friend of tax collectors and sinners.'[t]
35But wisdom is proved right by all her
children."

7:27 [o] Mal 3:1; Mt 11:10; Mk 1:2
7:28 [p] Mt 3:2
7:29 [q] Mt 21:32; Mk 1:5; Lk 3:12
7:30 [r] Mt 22:35
7:33 [s] Lk 1:15
7:34 [t] Lk 5:29, 30; 15:1, 2
7:39 [u] ver 16; Mt 21:11

Jesus Anointed by a Sinful Woman

7:37–39Ref // Mt 26:6–13; Mk 14:3–9; Jn 12:1–8

7:41,42Ref // Mt 18:23–34

36When one of the Pharisees invited
Jesus to have dinner with him, he went
to the Pharisee's house and reclined at
the table. 37A woman in that town who
lived a sinful life learned that Jesus was
eating at the Pharisee's house, so she
came there with an alabaster jar of perfume. 38As she stood behind him at his
feet weeping, she began to wet his feet
with her tears. Then she wiped them with
her hair, kissed them and poured perfume on them.

39When the Pharisee who had invited
him saw this, he said to himself, "If this
man were a prophet,[u] he would know
who is touching him and what kind of
woman she is — that she is a sinner."

40Jesus answered him, "Simon, I have
something to tell you."

"Tell me, teacher," he said.

41"Two people owed money to a certain moneylender. One owed him five

[a] *27* Mal. 3:1

7:28 John's greatness is nothing compared to those who participate in the new era's blessings and benefits. Jesus' remark here is one of the greatest affirmations of the believer's status in Scripture. To belong to the kingdom is a great privilege.

7:29–35 Jesus warns the current generation of religious leaders about their response to John through a parable. We might call it "the parable of the brats." They are the children who are seated and refuse to play, complaining that John and Jesus do not dance to their tune. Jesus' open effort to reach sinners represents a rejection of the leadership's more separatist approach.

The rebuke through the parable is another way to say that the leadership is hard-hearted in its rejection of God's way.

7:18–35 Often, we feel that the prophets of old had all the advantages. We think how great it would have been to be with Moses, Isaiah, or John the Baptist; how wonderful it would be to see God "really" work. But this passage indicates that anyone who truly knows Jesus has greater blessings. Just think, we have the Spirit of God within us and within our communities. We possess a forgiveness that is complete because of Jesus' finished work on the cross. These things are greater than the more temporary, imperfect gifts of the old era. God has given the church all the gifts we need to be effective in ministry, provided everyone does their part.

7:36 Even though the Pharisees oppose him, Jesus accepts the opportunity to visit with some of them. Since Jesus is a public figure, the door to this meal likely remains open so that interested people can enter, sit on the edge of the room, and hear the discussion.

7:37–38 The woman says nothing in this narrative, but her actions produce a wide range of discussion. Her sin is not identified. Her bold action of entering the room and anointing Jesus' feet with a jar of expensive perfume reflects great sacrifice, for such perfume was very costly. Moved by the moment, she weeps as she anoints Jesus and kisses his feet. The action reflects her humility.

7:39–40 The woman's action is shocking to Jesus' host. The rebuke is not because the woman has come to the meal, but because she did not stay on the sidelines. Because this woman has been branded a sinner, the leader clearly doubts Jesus' prophetic credentials. Ironically, Jesus reads his mind and tells a parable that explains his actions.

7:41–47 The parable pictures two debtors. Unlike most debt collectors, who would typically dial up the pressure for these people to pay their debts, the creditor forgives each debt.

The heart of Jesus' relational ethic is that, unlike

Lk 7:44-47 ❖ Where have we seen people with messy lives and difficult histories display beautiful acts of faith?

hundred denarii,[a] and the other fifty.
42Neither of them had the money to
pay him back, so he forgave the debts
of both. Now which of them will love
him more?"
43Simon replied, "I suppose the one
who had the bigger debt forgiven."
"You have judged correctly," Jesus said.
44Then he turned toward the woman and said to Simon, "Do you see this
woman? I came into your house. You
did not give me any water for my feet,[v]
but she wet my feet with her tears and
wiped them with her hair. 45You did not
give me a kiss,[w] but this woman, from
the time I entered, has not stopped kissing my feet. 46You did not put oil on my
head,[x] but she has poured perfume on
my feet. 47Therefore, I tell you, her many
sins have been forgiven — as her great
love has shown. But whoever has been
forgiven little loves little."
48Then Jesus said to her, "Your sins
are forgiven."[y]
49The other guests began to say among
themselves, "Who is this who even forgives sins?"
50Jesus said to the woman, "Your faith
has saved you;[z] go in peace."[a]

7:44 [v] Ge 18:4; 19:2; 43:24; Jdg 19:21; Jn 13:4-14; 1Ti 5:10
7:45 [w] Lk 22:47, 48; Ro 16:16
7:46 [x] Ps 23:5; Ecc 9:8
7:48 [y] Mt 9:2
7:50 [z] Mt 9:22; Mk 5:34; Lk 8:48 [a] Ac 15:33
8:1 [b] Mt 4:23
8:2 [c] Mt 27:55, 56
8:3 [d] Mt 14:1

The Parable of the Sower

8:4–15pp // Mt 13:2–23; Mk 4:1–20

8 After this, Jesus traveled about from
one town and village to another, proclaiming the good news of the kingdom
of God.[b] The Twelve were with him, 2and
also some women who had been cured
of evil spirits and diseases: Mary (called
Magdalene)[c] from whom seven demons
had come out; 3Joanna the wife of Chuza, the manager of Herod's[d] household;
Susanna; and many others. These wom-
en were helping to support them out of
their own means.
4While a large crowd was gathering
and people were coming to Jesus from
town after town, he told this parable:
5"A farmer went out to sow his seed. As
he was scattering the seed, some fell
along the path; it was trampled on, and
the birds ate it up. 6Some fell on rocky
ground, and when it came up, the plants
withered because they had no moisture.

[a] *41* A denarius was the usual daily wage of a day laborer (see Matt. 20:2).

---

the Pharisee, who can only dwell on the sinner's past record, Jesus prefers to see the potential that love and forgiveness possess for changing a person's heart. So he points out how the woman cared for him in a way his host has not.

7:48 But there is a reason for her love—her many sins are now forgiven. The one who is forgiven little, on the other hand, loves little. There is also an implied warning from Jesus to the Pharisee: "Your love may not be as great because you have not appreciated the depth of forgiveness God has made available to you." Jesus challenges such a way of looking at sin.

7:49-50 Jesus' words of forgiveness are also significant. Forgiving sins is an act limited to God, as the Pharisees well know. They know that Jesus is appropriating to himself the ultimate level of authority.

Jesus' final comment reveals a crucial theological sequence: first comes an offer of forgiveness from God, then the faith that saves. Such faith shows itself in the acts of love that this woman has performed for Jesus. Such is the fundamental cycle of relationship that exists between God and a believer.

8:1-3 Unique to Luke's Gospel, the evangelist here notes the work of three women of faith. When these women come to faith, they immediately give of their resources to enable Jesus' ministry to continue. This note is important, since the passage makes clear that those contributing to Jesus' ministry span both gender diversity and the social scale.

7:36—8:3 The woman who anoints Jesus' feet illustrates some basic truths. In terms of faith, she demonstrates an ability to overcome barriers, such as the popular perceptions about her. As a woman, to even contemplate publicly coming close Jesus was a risk, because women did not do such things in that culture. The fact that she was a sinner only heightened the risk, since a religious figure like Jesus might reject her. Yet her gratitude and humility were so great that getting close to Jesus was all she cared about.

She counted the cost and believed that Jesus would respond to her humble approach toward him. Jesus honored her faith. How many of us today would be so bold as to come forward and identify with Jesus in the face of the possible public rejection we would experience if we approached him?

8:4-8 As the parable explains, just because Jesus is God's chosen agent does not mean people respond to him automatically. The imagery draws on standard Middle Eastern farming practices. Jesus specifies four different types of soil on which the seed falls, calling on his audience to "hear" what is said in the parable.

PEOPLE TO KNOW // JOANNA AND OTHER WOMEN WHO SUPPORTED JESUS

LUKE 8:2-3: Luke 8:2-3 mentions a group of women whom Jesus had healed of diseases and demons. The most famous of these is Mary Magdalene. Luke also names Susanna "and many others." Most surprising, however, is the mention of Joanna the wife of Chuza, the manager of Herod's household. This was Herod Antipas, who was responsible for beheading John the Baptist (Mt 14:1-12). Joanna and these other women traveled with Jesus and his apostles, helping to support them out of their own means.

The fact that Jesus healed someone so close to Herod is intriguing. This connection may be partly responsible for word reaching Herod about Jesus (Mk 6:14-16). It may also be part of what interested Herod in Jesus when he hoped to see him perform a miracle (Lk 23:8). After all, the wife of Herod's manager had been miraculously healed and had left her old life to follow this remarkable teacher.

The women who supported Jesus were there when Jesus was buried, and they prepared spices and perfumes to anoint his body. On Easter morning, they found the tomb empty and ran back to tell the apostles. Luke specifically names Joanna among this group of women who brought news of the empty tomb to the others, showing that she continued to follow Jesus all the way to his death (Lk 24:10). The male disciples doubted the words of the women until they saw for themselves that the women were speaking the truth. It was the greatest truth in human history: the resurrection of the Son of God.

APPLICATION ✣ Jesus broke cultural social boundaries by welcoming women among his followers. Joanna and the others show Christ's radical invitation. At a time when women were not allowed to study with rabbis, they were welcomed by Jesus. These women also supported Jesus, giving their resources to his ministry. They walked with Jesus and listened to him. And when his tomb was empty, they proclaimed his resurrection. Joanna and the other women demonstrate true discipleship, devotion and faith—an example for all believers to follow today.

7Other seed fell among thorns, which
grew up with it and choked the plants.
8Still other seed fell on good soil. It came
up and yielded a crop, a hundred times
more than was sown."

When he said this, he called out, "Whoever has ears to hear, let them hear."[e]

9His disciples asked him what this
parable meant. 10He said, "The knowledge of the secrets of the kingdom of
God has been given to you,[f] but to others
I speak in parables, so that,

"'though seeing, they may not see;
though hearing, they may not
understand.'[a][g]

11"This is the meaning of the parable:
The seed is the word of God.[h] 12Those
along the path are the ones who hear,
and then the devil comes and takes away
the word from their hearts, so that they
may not believe and be saved. 13Those
on the rocky ground are the ones who

8:8 [e] Mt 11:15
8:10 [f] Mt 13:11
[g] Isa 6:9; Mt 13:13,14
8:11 [h] Heb 4:12

[a] *10* Isaiah 6:9

8:9-10 The disciples then ask Jesus why he speaks in parables without comments. His answer reveals a twofold reason. First, the disciples benefit from instruction because they are receiving the revelation of the kingdom's mysteries. The concept of mystery describes making a divine revelation clear. The disciples receive parables as a gift that reveals different aspects of God's grace. Second, to outsiders, the presence of parables is a form of judgment, concealing truths to prevent understanding by hardened hearts.

8:11-15 The major topic of Jesus' parables is the kingdom of God. The kingdom refers to the display of God's promised rule. In Jesus' ministry this era has arrived, though in the NT it arrives in phases. Jesus prepares for its coming through his ministry and by his work on the cross, which enables the new-covenant promise of forgiveness of sins to be put into place and allows the disciples to begin preaching its offer to everyone. The sign of the coming of the kingdom is the arrival of the Spirit. The parables deal with life in the kingdom both now and in the era to come.

Jesus explains to his disciples that the seed is the word of God, that is, the revelatory message about the kingdom. The focus of the parable is on the soils, not the seed since the seed gets four different reactions.

Fruit takes nurturing. Thus, Jesus' teaching does not look at the reaction to God's word in a

Lk 8:15 ❖ How can we nurture our hearts to be good soil that receives God's words and produces an abundant harvest?

receive the word with joy when they hear
it, but they have no root. They believe
for a while, but in the time of testing
they fall away.[i] 14The seed that fell among
thorns stands for those who hear, but
as they go on their way they are choked
by life's worries, riches[j] and pleasures,
and they do not mature. 15But the seed
on good soil stands for those with a noble and good heart, who hear the word,
retain it, and by persevering produce
a crop.

A Lamp on a Stand

16"No one lights a lamp and hides it in
a clay jar or puts it under a bed. Instead,
they put it on a stand, so that those who
come in can see the light.[k] 17For there
is nothing hidden that will not be disclosed, and nothing concealed that will
not be known or brought out into the
open.[l] 18Therefore consider carefully how
you listen. Whoever has will be given
more; whoever does not have, even what
they think they have will be taken from
them."[m]

8:13 [i] Mt 11:6
8:14 [j] Mt 19:23; 1Ti 6:9,10,17
8:16 [k] Mt 5:15; Mk 4:21; Lk 11:33
8:17 [l] Mt 10:26; Mk 4:22; Lk 12:2
8:18 [m] Mt 13:12; 25:29; Lk 19:26

Jesus' Mother and Brothers

8:19–21pp // Mt 12:46–50; Mk 3:31–35

19Now Jesus' mother and brothers came
to see him, but they were not able to get
near him because of the crowd. 20Some-
one told him, "Your mother and brothers[n]
are standing outside, wanting to see you."
21He replied, "My mother and brothers
are those who hear God's word and put
it into practice."[o]

Jesus Calms the Storm

8:22–25pp // Mt 8:23–27; Mk 4:36–41
8:22–25Ref // Mk 6:47–52; Jn 6:16–21

22One day Jesus said to his disciples,
"Let us go over to the other side of the
lake." So they got into a boat and set out.
23As they sailed, he fell asleep. A squall
came down on the lake, so that the boat
was being swamped, and they were in
great danger.
24The disciples went and woke him,
saying, "Master, Master,[p] we're going to
drown!"
He got up and rebuked[q] the wind and
the raging waters; the storm subsided,
and all was calm.[r] 25"Where is your faith?"
he asked his disciples.
In fear and amazement they asked
one another, "Who is this? He commands
even the winds and the water, and they
obey him."

8:20 [n] Jn 7:5
8:21 [o] Lk 6:47; 11:28; Jn 14:21
8:24 [p] Lk 5:5 [q] Lk 4:35,39,41 [r] Ps 107:29; Jnh 1:15

---

single moment but over a period of time, which may be why the planting analogy is used. Jesus' point deals with how response to the word is a product of a process.

Clearly those represented by the first soil are not saved, while the fourth are clearly among the redeemed. The debate stems from the second and third soils, where the parable is deliberately ambiguous. The literary thrust of the image of the second soil questions its healthy status. The same can be said for the third, where faith is not mentioned.

8:16–18 These verses call people to respond to the light because of the dire consequences of not doing so. The function of light is to make visible that which was previously hidden in darkness. So it will be with Jesus' message. There is much at stake, for whoever responds to revelation will get more. On the other hand, those who do not respond will end up with nothing.

8:19–21 These verses also highlight the importance of responding to God's word. When Jesus is told his family is seeking him, he replies with a proverbial-style remark that indicates where his family can be found: Jesus' family consists of those who hear the word of God and do it.

✣ **8:4–21** Many things can get in the way of responding to Jesus. The difference seems to be the condition of the heart. A healthy heart clings to God's Word; it beats fast for him and responds to him. Fruitfulness takes patience. As we labor to sow the seed of the kingdom, we must remember that different responses to our message of hope are inevitable. All of us are accountable to God, especially for how we respond to his revelation. He has put that revelation on a lampstand, where it is visible. Thus we all need to pay attention to what his truth reveals about where we are and what we are doing.

8:22–24 The Sea of Galilee is notorious for its changing and sometimes dangerous weather patterns. As Jesus rests in the boat, such a weather cycle occurs. Waves sweep over the edge and threaten to capsize them. Terrified, the disciples cry out to Jesus, who rebukes the wind. Immediately there is calm. Then Jesus asks a crucial question: "Where is your faith?" The dialogue stops here, so that we as readers can reflect on the event.

8:25 Luke goes on to record the disciples' reactions of fear and amazement. Their question is crucial because the OT makes it clear who has authority over nature: only God does. The disciples are beginning to appreciate just how powerful Jesus is.

✣ **8:22–25** This passage is a call for a deeper, trusting faith, even amid circumstances beyond

JESUS ANOINTED: LK 7:36-50

	LUKE	MARK/ MATTHEW	JOHN
Person	a sinner	a woman	Mary of Bethany
Place	Capernaum (?) at the house of Simon the Pharisee	Bethany, at the house of Simon the Leper	Bethany, apparently at Lazarus' house
Time	during the Galilean ministry	Holy Week two days before the Passover	six days before the Passover
Objection	not a real prophet	waste of money	waste of money
Made by	Simon	some of those present	Judas Iscariot

Jesus Restores a Demon-Possessed Man

8:26–37pp // Mt 8:28–34
8:26–39pp // Mk 5:1–20

26They sailed to the region of the Gerasenes,[a] which is across the lake from
Galilee. 27When Jesus stepped ashore,
he was met by a demon-possessed man
from the town. For a long time this man
had not worn clothes or lived in a house,
but had lived in the tombs. 28When he
saw Jesus, he cried out and fell at his feet,
shouting at the top of his voice, "What
do you want with me,[s] Jesus, Son of the
Most High God?[t] I beg you, don't torture
me!" 29For Jesus had commanded the impure spirit to come out of the man. Many
times it had seized him, and though he
was chained hand and foot and kept under guard, he had broken his chains and
had been driven by the demon into solitary places.

30Jesus asked him, "What is your
name?"

"Legion," he replied, because many
demons had gone into him. 31And they
begged Jesus repeatedly not to order
them to go into the Abyss.[u]

32A large herd of pigs was feeding there
on the hillside. The demons begged Jesus
to let them go into the pigs, and he gave
them permission. 33When the demons
came out of the man, they went into the
pigs, and the herd rushed down the steep
bank into the lake[v] and was drowned.

34When those tending the pigs saw
what had happened, they ran off and reported this in the town and countryside,
35and the people went out to see what
had happened. When they came to Jesus,
they found the man from whom the

8:28 [s] Mt 8:29 [t] Mk 5:7
8:31 [u] Rev 9:1, 2, 11; 11:7; 17:8; 20:1, 3
8:33 [v] ver 22, 23

[a] *26* Some manuscripts *Gadarenes*; other manuscripts *Gergesenes*; also in verse 37

our control. There is no telling how often some of the disciples, as former fishermen, had been involved in storms on this lake. Yet it was clear that they were powerless to deal with such forces on this trip.

Though their faith was weak, they did the right thing in turning to Jesus for help. Only their statement that they were at risk of death was in error. Had they understood God's care, they would have realized that divine care never takes a break, even when it leads into rough waters. Jesus' call for bold faith is also a call to reassurance that God is aware of whatever storms we are going through and is watching over us.

Luke has the disciples ask here, "Who is this?" and the rest of his Gospel shows the answer to this question. That answer is a central issue of life: Jesus is the unique Son of God.

8:26–30 In the Roman world, *legion* referred to a company of thousands of soldiers. In other words, Jesus is engaging in a major battle here. He is outnumbered, but not overmatched.

8:31–33 The demons' request has produced much speculation, none of which is answered by the text. What the incident involving the pigs does indicate is the real impact of demonic presence and influence—namely, the destruction of life.

8:34–37 When many people go out to see what happened, they see the formerly possessed man. He is seated calmly at the feet of Jesus, restored, clothed, and of sound mind. Jesus has rescued him from life among the tombs and brought him into the civilized world again. The scene is a picture of new life.

The local people do not care for Jesus' work, however. Mk 5:16 makes it clear that Jesus has had a negative economic impact on the region. The people do not want to lose more livestock;

demons had gone out, sitting at Jesus'
feet,[w] dressed and in his right mind; and
they were afraid. 36Those who had seen
it told the people how the demon-possessed[x] man had been cured. 37Then all
the people of the region of the Gerasenes
asked Jesus to leave them,[y] because they
were overcome with fear. So he got into
the boat and left.
38The man from whom the demons
had gone out begged to go with him, but
Jesus sent him away, saying, 39"Return
home and tell how much God has done
for you." So the man went away and told
all over town how much Jesus had done
for him.

Jesus Raises a Dead Girl and Heals a Sick Woman

8:40–56pp // Mt 9:18–26; Mk 5:22–43

40Now when Jesus returned, a crowd
welcomed him, for they were all expecting him. 41Then a man named Jairus,
a synagogue leader,[z] came and fell at
Jesus' feet, pleading with him to come to
his house 42because his only daughter, a
girl of about twelve, was dying.
As Jesus was on his way, the crowds
almost crushed him. 43And a woman was
there who had been subject to bleeding[a] for twelve years,[a] but no one could
heal her. 44She came up behind him and
touched the edge of his cloak,[b] and immediately her bleeding stopped.
45"Who touched me?" Jesus asked.
When they all denied it, Peter said,
"Master,[c] the people are crowding and
pressing against you."
46But Jesus said, "Someone touched
me;[d] I know that power has gone out
from me."[e]
47Then the woman, seeing that she
could not go unnoticed, came trembling
and fell at his feet. In the presence of all
the people, she told why she had touched
him and how she had been instantly
healed. 48Then he said to her, "Daughter,
your faith has healed you.[f] Go in peace."[g]
49While Jesus was still speaking, someone came from the house of Jairus, the
synagogue leader.[h] "Your daughter is
dead," he said. "Don't bother the teacher
anymore."
50Hearing this, Jesus said to Jairus,
"Don't be afraid; just believe, and she
will be healed."
51When he arrived at the house of Jairus, he did not let anyone go in with him
except Peter, John and James,[i] and the
child's father and mother. 52Meanwhile,

8:35 [w] Lk 10:39
8:36 [x] Mt 4:24
8:37 [y] Ac 16:39
8:41 [z] ver 49; Mk 5:22
8:43 [a] Lev 15:25-30
8:44 [b] Mt 9:20
8:45 [c] Lk 5:5
8:46 [d] Mt 14:36; Mk 3:10 [e] Lk 5:17; 6:19
8:48 [f] Mt 9:22 [g] Ac 15:33
8:49 [h] ver 41
8:51 [i] Mt 4:21

[a] 43 Many manuscripts *years, and she had spent all she had on doctors*

their fear has turned into rejection and a desire to have nothing more to do with the presence of divine authority.

8:38–39 The healed man wants to join Jesus' traveling group of disciples, but Jesus has another calling in mind. Someone must be left behind to share what God has done in the area. That is the man's task.

8:26–39 The exorcism in Lk 8 is but one picture of the dangerous character of such activity. Encounter with demons is not a neutral undertaking.

An attitude of "the devil made me do it" can turn sinners into victims who have no control over whom they decide to ally themselves with. Jesus' power over such forces should deliver us from any tendency to attribute too much to demonic power (Eph 1:15–23).

The delivered man gives us a final point of application. This newly healed and transformed man did not need to raise support to find his mission field; he simply needed to start sharing—which, in fact, he did. He could not tell the story of God's work in his life without discussing Jesus.

8:40–42 Jairus was a man in charge of arranging the service and the progress of worship. As Jesus approaches, the leader falls before Jesus and asks him to come to his house where his only daughter, a twelve-year-old, is near death.

8:43–45 Jesus starts heading for his house, but along the way another person also needs Jesus. A woman who has suffered from internal bleeding for twelve years wants Jesus to heal her. This condition renders her constantly ceremonially unclean, isolating her from Jewish religious life. Getting herself into position, she touches him as he walks by, and immediately she is healed.

8:46–47 Jesus stops to find out what has just happened. The touch he asks about is not just a physical touch but a touch that has answered a sincere cry for help. The silent faith of the woman needs exposure and recognition.

8:48 Jesus commends her, noting that her faith has saved her. There is nothing in Jesus' treatment of her that indicates rebuke. What the woman needs is reassurance and confidence that her actions need not remain secretive.

8:49–50 One can only imagine the desperate frustration Jairus feels at this delay. Then things get worse. When someone from Jairus's house appears to tell him it is too late, Jesus speaks comforting words to the synagogue ruler. Whereas the woman's faith needed bolstering because it was shy, Jairus's faith needs calming.

8:51–53 Amid community sorrow, Jesus calls on the mourners to stop, for the girl "is not dead but asleep" (v. 52).

all the people were wailing and mourning[j] for her. "Stop wailing," Jesus said.
"She is not dead but asleep."[k]
53They laughed at him, knowing that
she was dead. 54But he took her by the
hand and said, "My child, get up!"[l] 55Her
spirit returned, and at once she stood up.
Then Jesus told them to give her something to eat. 56Her parents were astonished, but he ordered them not to tell
anyone what had happened.[m]

Jesus Sends Out the Twelve

9:3–5pp // Mt 10:9–15; Mk 6:8–11
9:7–9pp // Mt 14:1,2; Mk 6:14–16

9 When Jesus had called the Twelve
together, he gave them power and
authority to drive out all demons[n] and
to cure diseases,[o] 2and he sent them out
to proclaim the kingdom of God[p] and to
heal the sick. 3He told them: "Take nothing for the journey—no staff, no bag, no
bread, no money, no extra shirt.[q] 4What-
ever house you enter, stay there until you
leave that town. 5If people do not welcome you, leave their town and shake the
dust off your feet as a testimony against
them."[r] 6So they set out and went from
village to village, proclaiming the good
news and healing people everywhere.
7Now Herod[s] the tetrarch heard about
all that was going on. And he was perplexed because some were saying that
John[t] had been raised from the dead,[u]
8others that Elijah had appeared,[v] and
still others that one of the prophets of
long ago had come back to life.[w] 9But
Herod said, "I beheaded John. Who, then,
is this I hear such things about?" And he
tried to see him.[x]

Jesus Feeds the Five Thousand

9:10–17pp // Mt 14:13–21; Mk 6:32–44; Jn 6:5–13
9:13–17Ref // 2Ki 4:42–44

10When the apostles[y] returned, they
reported to Jesus what they had done.
Then he took them with him and they
withdrew by themselves to a town called
Bethsaida,[z] 11but the crowds learned
about it and followed him. He welcomed
them and spoke to them about the kingdom of God,[a] and healed those who needed healing.
12Late in the afternoon the Twelve
came to him and said, "Send the crowd
away so they can go to the surrounding
villages and countryside and find food
and lodging, because we are in a remote
place here."
13He replied, "You give them something to eat."
They answered, "We have only five
loaves of bread and two fish—unless

8:52 [j] Lk 23:27 [k] Mt 9:24; Jn 11:11,13
8:54 [l] Lk 7:14
8:56 [m] Mt 8:4
9:1 [n] Mt 10:1 [o] Mt 4:23; Lk 5:17
9:2 [p] Mt 3:2
9:3 [q] Lk 10:4; 22:35
9:5 [r] Mt 10:14
9:7 [s] Mt 14:1 [t] Mt 3:1 [u] ver 19
9:8 [v] Mt 11:14 [w] ver 19; Jn 1:21
9:9 [x] Lk 23:8
9:10 [y] Mk 6:30 [z] Mt 11:21
9:11 [a] ver 2; Mt 3:2

8:54-56 Once inside, Jesus grasps the girl's hand and tells her to get up. The girl sits up, her spirit revived within her. The call to faith that Jesus made to Jairus has now received its answer. Jesus urges that the parents keep this miracle secret; broadcasting news of this healing far and wide will turn Jesus into a wonder-worker, with all the public attention focused on that ministry. Jesus wants the people's attention focused on his central teachings; he wants to major on the major issues.

✜ **8:40-56** It is often the case that what we think God ought to do right now, God chooses to act on later, while what we would put off, he chooses to handle right away. The most fundamental lesson in this passage is the combination of characteristics tied to faith. Faith should seize the initiative to act in dependence on God and speak about him, yet sometimes it must be patient. In one sense faith is "full speed ahead," while in another it is waiting patiently on the Lord. The Father does know best.

9:1 Jesus commissions the Twelve to minister for him in the towns and villages of the nation. They are to preach the kingdom and heal the sick. This combination reflects Jesus' ministry of word and deed.

9:2-6 In v. 2 the disciples are assigned to "proclaim the kingdom of God," while in v. 6 they are "proclaiming the good news." The gospel announces the arrival of blessing through Jesus in conjunction with the kingdom of God. The deeds of healing testify to the rule of God; his power and concern have been put on public display.

9:7-9 These verses continue to ask a basic question in this Gospel: "Who is Jesus?" This time it surfaces in Herod's court.

✜ **9:1-9** Evangelism requires engagement. Engagement-oriented ministries such as food kitchens or shelters for those without homes that are established to answer basic needs are often the hardest to sustain because they require a great deal of labor to make them effective. Nonetheless, such ministries have the potential of speaking the gospel more clearly than words alone do. Acts of care reinforce the claim that God cares about the real needs of people, putting flesh and blood on that truth.

9:10-13 This miracle of provision obviously indicates how Jesus meets needs. But there is a second key to the miracle, in that this provision comes through the disciples. Luke is indicating the importance Jesus gives to the concept that he will minister through his servants. In the future, they will do great things through Jesus' enabling power.

Lk 9:23 ❖ What does it mean for us to take up our cross daily and follow Christ? What is your "cross"?

we go and buy food for all this crowd."
14(About five thousand men were there.)
But he said to his disciples, "Have them
sit down in groups of about fifty each."
15The disciples did so, and everyone sat
down. 16Taking the five loaves and the two
fish and looking up to heaven, he gave
thanks and broke them.[b] Then he gave
them to the disciples to distribute to the
people. 17They all ate and were satisfied,
and the disciples picked up twelve basketfuls of broken pieces that were left over.

Peter Declares That Jesus Is the Messiah

9:18–20pp // Mt 16:13–16; Mk 8:27–29

18Once when Jesus was praying[c] in private and his disciples were with him,
he asked them, "Who do the crowds say
I am?"
19They replied, "Some say John the
Baptist;[d] others say Elijah; and still others, that one of the prophets of long ago
has come back to life."[e]
20"But what about you?" he asked.
"Who do you say I am?"
Peter answered, "God's Messiah."[f]

Jesus Predicts His Death

9:22–27pp // Mt 16:21–28; Mk 8:31—9:1

21Jesus strictly warned them not to
tell this to anyone.[g] 22And he said, "The
Son of Man[h] must suffer many things[i]
and be rejected by the elders, the chief
priests and the teachers of the law,[j] and
he must be killed[k] and on the third day[l]
be raised to life."[m]
23Then he said to them all: "Whoever
wants to be my disciple must deny themselves and take up their cross daily and follow me.[n] 24For whoever wants to save their
life will lose it, but whoever loses their life
for me will save it.[o] 25What good is it for
someone to gain the whole world, and yet

9:16 [b] Mt 14:19
9:18 [c] Lk 3:21
9:19 [d] Mt 3:1 [e] ver 7,8
9:20 [f] Jn 1:49; 6:66-69; 11:27
9:21 [g] Mt 16:20; Mk 8:30
9:22 [h] Mt 8:20 [i] Mt 16:21 [j] Mt 27:1, 2 [k] Ac 2:23; 3:13 [l] Mt 16:21 [m] Mt 16:21
9:23 [n] Mt 10:38; Lk 14:27
9:24 [o] Jn 12:25

9:14–17 Jesus asks for the disciples' assistance to group the crowd into units of fifty. Then taking the five loaves and two fish, he invokes God's blessing, breaks the bread, and hands the food to the disciples to distribute. Through their connection to Jesus, the disciples provide enough food for all present, with twelve baskets left over.

Luke does not detail how the multiplication of loaves and fish takes place. Rather, he stresses the provision itself. Jesus has a ministry that can meet our most fundamental needs. Additionally, the disciples can do all the things that are necessary for ministry through Christ who enables them (Php 4:13). In a sense Jesus in this miracle is preparing to pass the torch of ministry to them. So both those who provide the food and those who receive it can learn lessons from this miracle.

✣ 9:10–17 There is no one way to reach people. The ministry of provision takes many forms. But one dynamic is a constant: to be effective, the one who leads in setting out the provision must be Jesus. We who seek to provide what Jesus offers bring a picture of God's compassion to those we serve.

Jesus' later establishment of the Lord's Supper reflects this large-scale miracle. The meal of fellowship we enjoy at Jesus' feet means we are all seated at the same table. We should minister with the awareness that the table is his, and that the food he has provided is also his. We all partake of one loaf and one cup, and in that meal we all declare our allegiance to Jesus.

9:18–20 The crowd believes that Jesus is a prophet of some kind; perhaps the reappearance of John the Baptist. In contrast, Peter confesses Jesus as the Messiah, though this statement is short of a full confession of deity.

9:21–22 Peter's confession can lead to misunderstanding about what is ahead for Jesus. The disciples anticipate a direct route to glory. Jesus predicts the suffering of the Son of Man in rejection, death, and resurrection. This surprising route to glory causes Jesus to call for silence about the earlier confessions of him as Messiah, for the Messiah was traditionally seen as a triumphant figure who would not suffer at all.

Despite the need for more instruction, Peter's confession is a crucial turning point. In recognizing Jesus as the promised Messiah of God, he declares that Jesus is unique. Such a building block is fundamental to understanding God's plan of redemption and how it is accomplished through Jesus.

✣ 9:18–22 Blessing through commitment to Christ often requires great cost and pain, and we must be prepared to face the same sort of opposition Jesus faced. Some parts of the world have an inherently better understanding of this part of the walk with Christ than what exists in the West. For those of us who live in a society where sharing Jesus is not outlawed, testimonies from the persecuted church should encourage us to be bold.

9:23–24 Discipleship involves the fundamental commitment to self-denial and bearing one's cross. The call to follow Jesus is constant, growing out of those basic commitments. Discipleship therefore requires a fundamental shift of orientation as we align ourselves with God's will through humbly renouncing our own agenda. If we try to save our lives by preserving ourselves from the opposition of the world and/or by accommodating ourselves to the world, we lose real life.

9:25 Jesus' rhetorical question drives the point home. "To gain the whole world" means that we

lose or forfeit their very self? 26 Whoever is ashamed of me and my words, the Son of Man will be ashamed of them[p] when he comes in his glory and in the glory of the Father and of the holy angels.[q]

27 "Truly I tell you, some who are standing here will not taste death before they see the kingdom of God."

The Transfiguration

9:28–36pp // Mt 17:1–8; Mk 9:2–8

28 About eight days after Jesus said this, he took Peter, John and James[r] with him and went up onto a mountain to pray.[s] 29 As he was praying, the appearance of his face changed, and his clothes became as bright as a flash of lightning. 30 Two men, Moses and Elijah, appeared in glorious splendor, talking with Jesus. 31 They spoke about his departure,[a][t] which he was about to bring to fulfillment at Jerusalem. 32 Peter and his companions were very sleepy,[u] but when they became fully awake, they saw his glory and the two men standing with him. 33 As the men were leaving Jesus, Peter said to him, "Master,[v] it is good for us to be here. Let us put up three shelters—one for you, one for Moses and one for Elijah." (He did not know what he was saying.)

34 While he was speaking, a cloud appeared and covered them, and they were afraid as they entered the cloud. 35 A voice came from the cloud, saying, "This is my Son, whom I have chosen;[w] listen to him."[x] 36 When the voice had spoken, they found that Jesus was alone. The disciples kept this to themselves and did not tell anyone at that time what they had seen.[y]

Jesus Heals a Demon-Possessed Boy

9:37–42pp // Mt 17:14–18; Mk 9:14–27

37 The next day, when they came down from the mountain, a large crowd met him. 38 A man in the crowd called out, "Teacher, I beg you to look at my son, for he is my only child. 39 A spirit seizes him and he suddenly screams; it throws him into convulsions so that he foams at the mouth. It scarcely ever leaves him and is destroying him. 40 I begged your disciples to drive it out, but they could not."

9:26 [p] Mt 10:33; Lk 12:9; 2Ti 2:12 [q] Mt 16:27
9:28 [r] Mt 4:21 [s] Lk 3:21
9:31 [t] 2Pe 1:15
9:32 [u] Mt 26:43
9:33 [v] Lk 5:5
9:35 [w] Isa 42:1 [x] Mt 3:17
9:36 [y] Mt 17:9

[a] 31 Greek *exodos*

---

can choose to spend our time trying to gain all the provision, power, and property the world can provide. To Jesus, it makes no sense to live this way, for it makes one a loser at real life. Jesus faced a similar choice when he was tempted in the wilderness, but he knew that attempting to gain the world at the expense of one's soul is a bad investment and a losing proposition.

9:26 Those ashamed or afraid to confess the Son of Man will get what they have chosen: separation from him. On the other hand, by implication, those who ally themselves to Jesus will experience the kingdom of God.

9:27 Jesus' concluding remark appears to have two points of reference. First, some will experience the transfiguration, a preview of Jesus' coming glory. Second, the reference may anticipate Pentecost, when the power of the risen Jesus will manifest itself in the distribution of the Spirit.

> ✣ **9:23–27** Jesus saved us for discipleship. There is more to salvation than heaven. He saved us to change us, to make us different than we were before we came to know him. So discipleship is a full-time job, not a weekend hobby. As a lifestyle and commitment, it never takes a holiday. That is why Jesus calls us to bear our cross daily.

9:28 Jesus opts to go to a mountain to pray and takes Peter, John, and James with him.

9:29–31 During his time of prayer, Jesus is transformed. His glory recalls the description of Moses on the mountain in Ex 34:29–34. Jesus is not alone, as he is joined by Moses and Elijah, who span the early and late periods of OT history. Moses and Elijah are discussing Jesus' "departure," which alludes to the journey Jesus is taking, with its turning point being his death in Jerusalem.

9:32–33 Peter, in his excitement, asks Jesus if three booths should be built—an allusion to the Festival of Tabernacles. Peter correctly understands that Moses and Elijah represent hope and fulfillment, but he wants to set up three booths in a way that ranks the three figures equally. Luke signals that Peter speaks with ignorance.

9:34–35 The presence of the cloud recalls the presence of God in the exodus. The description "whom I have chosen" (v. 35) elaborates on the "whom I love" of the baptism scene (3:22). The addition of "listen to him" marks out the disciples' responsibility. They must pay attention to what Jesus is saying, for they have much to learn.

> ✣ **9:28–36** At the transfiguration, the disciples hear vocally what the mission and message of Jesus is, as well as how they are to respond to it. They are called to a new way of looking at Jesus. In the same way, a new heart leads us to sit at Jesus' feet, ready to learn and listen. This requires a reflective interaction with Scripture in our daily walk with God. This dynamic between God's Word and life enables us to interact wisely with the culture and with the people whom God brings into our lives.

9:37–40 The disciples still have much to learn from Jesus. This is the first of a series of passages where the disciples need serious correction. As the voice in the cloud said, the disciples must listen to Jesus.

9:41–43 Jesus' reply to the man's request for healing indicates that something is wrong, for

THE WOMEN IN LUKE'S GOSPEL

NAME	REFERENCE	SIGNIFICANCE
Mary, mother of Jesus	1-2; 8:19-20	The model of faithful obedience; "Blessed among women"; parented and supported Jesus
Elizabeth, mother of John	1:1-80	Shown great mercy by the Lord; had a child in old age; welcomed Mary in her pregnancy; recognized Mary as the "mother of [her] Lord"
Anna the prophetess	2:36-38	A holy woman who encouraged Mary and Joseph in the temple as they came to sacrifice
The widow of Nain	7:11-17	Jesus recognized her destitute circumstances and raised her son from the dead
The sinful woman who anointed Jesus at Simon's house	7:36-49	Showing much love, she was shown much grace as Jesus publicly pronounced her sins forgiven
Mary Magdalene	8:1-3; 24:1-11	Delivered of seven demons; a disciple who traveled with Jesus' coterie; present at the empty tomb
Susanna	8:1-3	A disciple who traveled with Jesus' coterie; provided financially for Jesus and disciples
Woman with the discharge of blood	8:43-48	Sought healing from Jesus despite social conventions
Mary of Bethany	10:38-42	Sat at Jesus' feet for instruction
Martha	10:38-42	In her zeal to provide Jesus hospitality, missed an opportunity for fellowship
Woman bound by a disabling spirit	13:10-17	Healed by Jesus on the Sabbath
The generous widow	21:1-4	Lauded by Jesus for giving much out of her little
Women at the cross	23:26-49	Faithfully followed Jesus, even to the cross
Joanna	8:1-3; 24:1-11	A disciple who traveled with Jesus' coterie; provided financially for Jesus and disciples; present at the empty tomb
Mary, mother of James	24:1-11	Present at the empty tomb

41"You unbelieving and perverse generation,"[z] Jesus replied, "how long shall I
stay with you and put up with you? Bring
your son here."
42Even while the boy was coming, the
demon threw him to the ground in a convulsion. But Jesus rebuked the impure
spirit, healed the boy and gave him back
to his father. 43And they were all amazed
at the greatness of God.

9:41 [z] Dt 32:5
9:44 [a] ver 22

Jesus Predicts His Death a Second Time

9:43b–45pp // Mt 17:22–23; Mk 9:31–32

While everyone was marveling at all
that Jesus did, he said to his disciples,
44"Listen carefully to what I am about
to tell you: The Son of Man is going to
be delivered into the hands of men."[a]
45But they did not understand what
this meant. It was hidden from them,

---

he describes the current generation as "unbelieving and perverse" (v. 41). While the spirit tries to further harm the boy, Jesus' protection is total.

9:44–45 Jesus again predicts his coming passion, including his betrayal. The disciples do not understand. The text is vague on who has "hidden" the truth from them. Is it God, or is Satan at work? By the end of the Gospel, the blinders will be removed. God certainly is most active in that removal, as the Emmaus scene in 24:13–35 shows.

so that they did not grasp it,[b] and they
were afraid to ask him about it.
46 An argument started among the
disciples as to which of them would be
the greatest.[c] 47 Jesus, knowing their
thoughts,[d] took a little child and had
him stand beside him. 48 Then he said
to them, "Whoever welcomes this little child in my name welcomes me; and
whoever welcomes me welcomes the one
who sent me.[e] For it is the one who is
least among you all who is the greatest."[f]
49 "Master,"[g] said John, "we saw someone driving out demons in your name
and we tried to stop him, because he is
not one of us."
50 "Do not stop him," Jesus said, "for
whoever is not against you is for you."[h]

Samaritan Opposition

51 As the time approached for him to
be taken up to heaven,[i] Jesus resolutely set out for Jerusalem.[j] 52 And he sent
messengers on ahead, who went into a
Samaritan[k] village to get things ready for
him; 53 but the people there did not welcome him, because he was heading for
Jerusalem. 54 When the disciples James
and John[l] saw this, they asked, "Lord,
do you want us to call fire down from
heaven to destroy them[a]?"[m] 55 But Jesus
turned and rebuked them. 56 Then he
and his disciples went to another village.

The Cost of Following Jesus

9:57–60pp // Mt 8:19–22

57 As they were walking along the road,[n]
a man said to him, "I will follow you
wherever you go."
58 Jesus replied, "Foxes have dens and
birds have nests, but the Son of Man[o] has
no place to lay his head."
59 He said to another man, "Follow me."[p]
But he replied, "Lord, first let me go
and bury my father."
60 Jesus said to him, "Let the dead bury
their own dead, but you go and proclaim
the kingdom of God."[q]
61 Still another said, "I will follow you,
Lord; but first let me go back and say
goodbye to my family."[r]
62 Jesus replied, "No one who puts a
hand to the plow and looks back is fit for
service in the kingdom of God."

9:45 [b] Mk 9:32
9:46 [c] Lk 22:24
9:47 [d] Mt 9:4
9:48 [e] Mt 10:40 [f] Mk 9:35
9:49 [g] Lk 5:5
9:50 [h] Mt 12:30; Lk 11:23
9:51 [i] Mk 16:19 [j] Lk 13:22; 17:11; 18:31; 19:28
9:52 [k] Mt 10:5
9:54 [l] Mt 4:21 [m] 2Ki 1:10,12
9:57 [n] ver 51
9:58 [o] Mt 8:20
9:59 [p] Mt 4:19
9:60 [q] Mt 3:2
9:61 [r] 1Ki 19:20

[a] 54 Some manuscripts *them, just as Elijah did*

9:46-50 Two brief incidents close Luke's report on the Galilean ministry. In the first, the disciples are haggling over who has the greatest position in the "Disciples' Hall of Fame." Jesus knows of their petty dispute, so he takes a child and points out to them the value of receiving such a child. Second, he tells them that ministry is not a copyrighted monopoly: Jesus wants all willing people to serve and encourages everyone to do so. All who serve the Lord faithfully deserve our support.

> **9:37-50** A potential time of struggle in our Christian walk is when God takes us on a journey using a path marked "unknown." We may feel unprepared and untrained, but God is saying, "Trust me for the direction I am taking you." He takes us to our destination and wants us to trust that walking with him does not always mean we understand him. He has his reasons, though it may be that the only result we discover is that we know him better. Here the disciples are on such a journey, as Jesus leads them further into the realization of what he is about to experience.

9:51-53 Luke describes a journey of destiny, which has as its destination Israel's capital. The journey starts with Jesus expanding his ministry into Samaritan territory. By Jews, this ethnic group was derided as made up of traitors and considered a collection of half-breeds. The fact that Jesus reaches out to these people indicates that he wants to broaden his ministry, but they reject him.

9:54-56 The disciples are not pleased with the lack of response in Samaria. They ask Jesus if fiery judgment should be called down from heaven, but Jesus rebukes them.

9:57-58 In a series of three encounters, Jesus shows the high priority he places on discipleship. The first exchange begins with a confident statement by a man that he will follow Jesus wherever he goes. This remark requires reflection, so Jesus warns the man precisely what that will require.

9:59-60 In the second case, a prospective follower wishes to bury his father before joining the group. Preaching the offer of life is more important than caring for the dead. Disciples must move forward, not memorialize what is past.

9:61-62 Again, Jesus issues what seems a harsh warning on the surface: Those who commit to follow and then look back are not fit for the kingdom. Plowing required a focused eye on what lay ahead. Similarly, discipleship demands attention to the rough road before us. Looking back risks being knocked off course.

> **9:51-62** Discipleship has an urgency to it that should have first place in our lives. And once we commit, we should not look back. God does not issue his call for a season but for a lifetime. Service for the kingdom begins at the moment we receive Jesus and continues until the Father calls us home. While the details of that commitment will be different for each person, the call to discipleship should have priority over everything else in our lives.

Jesus Sends Out the Seventy-Two

10:4–12pp // Lk 9:3–5
10:13–15,21,22pp // Mt 11:21–23,25–27
10:23,24pp // Mt 13:16,17

10 After this the Lord[s] appointed seventy-two[a] others[t] and sent them two by two[u] ahead of him to every town and place where he was about to go.[v] 2 He told them, "The harvest is plentiful, but the workers are few. Ask the Lord of the harvest, therefore, to send out workers into his harvest field.[w] 3 Go! I am sending you out like lambs among wolves.[x] 4 Do not take a purse or bag or sandals; and do not greet anyone on the road.

5 "When you enter a house, first say, 'Peace to this house.' 6 If someone who promotes peace is there, your peace will rest on them; if not, it will return to you. 7 Stay there, eating and drinking whatever they give you, for the worker deserves his wages.[y] Do not move around from house to house.

8 "When you enter a town and are welcomed, eat what is offered to you.[z] 9 Heal the sick who are there and tell them, 'The kingdom of God[a] has come near to you.' 10 But when you enter a town and are not welcomed, go into its streets and say, 11 'Even the dust of your town we wipe from our feet as a warning to you.[b] Yet be sure of this: The kingdom of God has come near.'[c] 12 I tell you, it will be more bearable on that day for Sodom[d] than for that town.[e]

13 "Woe to you,[f] Chorazin! Woe to you, Bethsaida! For if the miracles that were performed in you had been performed in Tyre and Sidon, they would have repented long ago, sitting in sackcloth[g] and ashes. 14 But it will be more bearable for Tyre and Sidon at the judgment than for you. 15 And you, Capernaum,[h] will you be lifted to the heavens? No, you will go down to Hades.[b]

16 "Whoever listens to you listens to me; whoever rejects you rejects me; but whoever rejects me rejects him who sent me."[i]

17 The seventy-two[j] returned with joy and said, "Lord, even the demons submit to us in your name."[k]

18 He replied, "I saw Satan[l] fall like lightning from heaven.[m] 19 I have given you authority to trample on snakes[n] and scorpions and to overcome all the power of the enemy; nothing will harm you. 20 However, do not rejoice that the spirits submit to you, but rejoice that your names are written in heaven."[o]

21 At that time Jesus, full of joy through the Holy Spirit, said, "I praise you, Father, Lord of heaven and earth, because you have hidden these things from the wise and learned, and revealed them to little children.[p] Yes, Father, for this is what you were pleased to do.

22 "All things have been committed to me by my Father.[q] No one knows who the Son is except the Father, and no one knows who the Father is except the Son and those to whom the Son chooses to reveal him."[r]

23 Then he turned to his disciples and

10:1 [s] Lk 7:13 [t] Lk 9:1,2,51,52 [u] Mk 6:7 [v] Mt 10:1
10:2 [w] Mt 9:37,38; Jn 4:35
10:3 [x] Mt 10:16
10:7 [y] Mt 10:10; 1Co 9:14; 1Ti 5:18
10:8 [z] 1Co 10:27
10:9 [a] Mt 3:2; 10:7
10:11 [b] Mt 10:14; Mk 6:11 [c] ver 9
10:12 [d] Mt 10:15 [e] Mt 11:24
10:13 [f] Lk 6:24-26 [g] Rev 11:3
10:15 [h] Mt 4:13
10:16 [i] Mt 10:40; Jn 13:20
10:17 [j] ver 1 [k] Mk 16:17
10:18 [l] Mt 4:10 [m] Isa 14:12; Rev 9:1; 12:8,9
10:19 [n] Mk 16:18; Ac 28:3-5
10:20 [o] Ex 32:32; Ps 69:28; Da 12:1; Php 4:3; Heb 12:23; Rev 13:8; 20:12; 21:27
10:21 [p] 1Co 1:26-29
10:22 [q] Mt 28:18 [r] Jn 1:18

[a] *1* Some manuscripts *seventy;* also in verse 17
[b] *15* That is, the realm of the dead

10:1–2 Jesus sends out another mission, this time involving seventy-two followers. What they do is only a start since they are to pray for more workers for the harvest. God is Lord of the harvest: He leads the mission, and he is responsible for "sending out" workers into the field.

10:3–4 The workers are "like lambs among wolves" (v. 3). There is danger and hostile rejection on all sides. As they go, they are to rest in the knowledge that God will provide for them. Their main responsibility is to heal the sick and declare the arrival of God's kingdom.

10:5–9 To announce the kingdom is not to say that everything associated with Jesus' authority is now active; rather, it is to say that the rule of God through Jesus has begun. The acts of this ministry support that claim by showing that evil forces and the presence of death cannot resist Jesus' authority.

10:10–15 If the disciples are rejected, then they must shake the dust from their feet and move on. This act declares a separation between God and the rejecting city and reflects their accountability to him for their decision. Rejecting such a gracious invitation is dangerous, with risks that lead into eternity.

10:16 Jesus places an unbreakable link between himself and his messengers. They are commissioned in such a way that they represent him. For people to hear them is to hear Jesus; for people to reject them is to reject Jesus.

10:17–20 The mission is a success, and the disciples return filled with excitement at the power they possess. In Jesus' name, even demons have submitted to them. But the submission of evil spirits to them is nothing compared to the fact that they are registered among the saved in heaven. True and eternal life with the everlasting God is the essence of blessing.

10:21–22 Jesus intercedes with a note of praise to God. Those of simple faith, not those who rest in their own wisdom, have come to see the blessing of God. He honors those who rely on him.

10:23–24 There is a blessing of divine approval in

PEOPLE TO KNOW // MARY OF BETHANY

LUKE 10:38–42: Mary of Bethany is probably best known for her commitment to learn from Jesus even when other priorities were vying for her attention. Mary was the sister of Martha and Lazarus; they were all good friends of Jesus.

One time when Jesus visited them, Martha was upset when Mary did not help her with the work necessary to host the guests. Exasperated, Martha confronted Jesus and asked why he didn't care that Mary had left her to do all the work. Jesus responded gently but told Martha that Mary had "chosen what is better, and it will not be taken away from her" (Lk 10:42). Jesus honored Mary for sitting at his feet and learning from him, for taking the position of a disciple.

Later, Jesus visited Mary and Martha when their brother, Lazarus, died. Jesus spoke to Martha, and then asked to see Mary. Mary went quickly to him. Jesus asked Mary to lead him to the place where Lazarus had been laid, and then he miraculously raised Lazarus back to life (Jn 11:43–44). Many of the Jews who had come to visit Mary saw and believed in Jesus.

The week of his death, Jesus was eating again at the home of Mary and Martha. Mary poured expensive perfume on Jesus' feet and lovingly wiped them with her hair (Jn 12:3) as a symbol of her devotion to her Lord. Jesus told those gathered that Mary was anointing him for his burial, a sign of love and honor.

APPLICATION ✣ Like Mary, we need to be people who sit at Jesus' feet and learn from him, taking the humble position of a disciple. There are many things in our lives that feel important and necessary, but we need to be able to discern the most important things. Like Mary, we need to be sure that we aren't distracted from our pursuit of knowing Jesus.

We should also give our best to Jesus, as did Mary when she poured costly perfume upon his feet. When we give Jesus our best and honor him with our lives, we show the world our devotion to Christ and glorify God.

said privately, "Blessed are the eyes that
see what you see. 24For I tell you that
many prophets and kings wanted to see
what you see but did not see it, and to
hear what you hear but did not hear it."[s]

The Parable of the Good Samaritan

10:25–28pp // Mt 22:34–40; Mk 12:28 31

25On one occasion an expert in the law
stood up to test Jesus. "Teacher," he asked,
"what must I do to inherit eternal life?"[t]

26"What is written in the Law?" he replied. "How do you read it?"

27He answered, "'Love the Lord your
God with all your heart and with all your
soul and with all your strength and with
all your mind'[a];[u] and, 'Love your neighbor as yourself.'[b]"[v]

28"You have answered correctly," Jesus
replied. "Do this and you will live."[w]

10:24 [s] 1Pe 1:10-12
10:25 [t] Mt 19:16; Lk 18:18
10:27 [u] Dt 6:5 [v] Lev 19:18; Mt 5:43
10:28 [w] Lev 18:5; Ro 7:10

[a] 27 Deut. 6:5 [b] 27 Lev. 19:18

---

sharing in the task of the Son. Jesus concludes with a beatitude for those who see what the seventy-two have seen. Kings and prophets longed to experience what they are experiencing but did not get this special honor. In short, what is happening now has never happened before in all of history. Those who have longed for this day are long gone, and the disciples must realize the privilege of hearing this brand-new kingdom message.

✣ **10:1–24** The gospel, so simple in this basic element of turning to God for forgiveness in Christ, is often too hard for many to comprehend, much less accept. Yet it is this very simplicity that caused Jesus to compare those who see and embrace it to little children. The insights into the kingdom that Jesus offers are things that prophets and kings longed to experience. We too are as privileged as the disciples who first heard this kingdom message.

10:25–27 When an expert in Jewish tradition asks Jesus what he must do to inherit eternal life, Jesus responds with a question of his own. He turns to the law, asking the lawyer what he sees it saying. The scribe replies from Dt 6:5, that portion of the law that a Jew recited daily and that calls on the nation to love God fully. He also cites the portion of Lev 19:18 that calls for the love of one's neighbor. This combination was known as the "Great Commandment."

10:28–29 Jesus commends the answer, but the lawyer's follow-up question attempts to create a distinction, arguing that some people are neighbors and others are not. In his story, Jesus responds to the suggestion that some people are "non-neighbors."

Lk 10:29-37 ❖ An enemy might be a neighbor. Who are the neighbors we struggle to love, and why should we love them anyway?

29But he wanted to justify himself,[x] so he asked Jesus, "And who is my neighbor?"

30In reply Jesus said: "A man was going down from Jerusalem to Jericho, when he was attacked by robbers. They stripped him of his clothes, beat him and went away, leaving him half dead. 31A priest happened to be going down the same road, and when he saw the man, he passed by on the other side.[y] 32So too, a Levite, when he came to the place and saw him, passed by on the other side. 33But a Samaritan,[z] as he traveled, came where the man was; and when he saw him, he took pity on him. 34He went to him and bandaged his wounds, pouring on oil and wine. Then he put the man on his own donkey, brought him to an inn and took care of him. 35The next day he took out two denarii[a] and gave them to the innkeeper. 'Look after him,' he said, 'and when I return, I will reimburse you for any extra expense you may have.'

36"Which of these three do you think was a neighbor to the man who fell into the hands of robbers?"

37The expert in the law replied, "The one who had mercy on him."

Jesus told him, "Go and do likewise."

At the Home of Martha and Mary

38As Jesus and his disciples were on their way, he came to a village where a woman named Martha[a] opened her home to him. 39She had a sister called Mary,[b] who sat at the Lord's feet[c] listening to what he said. 40But Martha was distracted by all the preparations that had to be made. She came to him and asked, "Lord, don't you care[d] that my sister has left me to do the work by myself? Tell her to help me!"

41"Martha, Martha," the Lord answered, "you are worried[e] and upset about many things, 42but few things are needed—or indeed only one.[b][f] Mary has chosen what is better, and it will not be taken away from her."

Jesus' Teaching on Prayer

11:2–4pp // Mt 6:9–13
11:9–13pp // Mt 7:7–11

11 One day Jesus was praying[g] in a certain place. When he finished, one of

10:29 [x] Lk 16:15
10:31 [y] Lev 21:1-3
10:33 [z] Mt 10:5
10:38 [a] Jn 11:1; 12:2
10:39 [b] Jn 11:1; 12:3 [c] Lk 8:35
10:40 [d] Mk 4:38
10:41 [e] Mt 6:25-34; Lk 12:11,22
10:42 [f] Ps 27:4
11:1 [g] Lk 3:21

[a] *35* A denarius was the usual daily wage of a day laborer (see Matt. 20:2). [b] *42* Some manuscripts *but only one thing is needed*

10:30 Jesus picks a Samaritan as the highlight of the story because such a person is a "non-neighbor" in the lawyer's eyes. Jesus visualizes the treacherous road from Jericho to Jerusalem as the site of the incident. This seventeen-mile journey was well known for its danger.

10:31–32 Why do the priest and Levite pass by? Perhaps they fear becoming "unclean" from touching what looks like a dead corpse. But the text makes no mention of any motive, and it is best not to speculate.

10:33–35 Next comes a Samaritan. This is surprising since one might expect a Jewish layperson to appear here, not this "half-breed." But the Samaritan has pity on the wounded traveler. He underwrites the victim's recovery from start to finish.

10:36–37 Jesus asks a simple question: "Which of these three . . . was a neighbor to the man?" (v. 36). The scribe cannot bring himself to identify the man by his ethnicity. Jesus tells the man to "go and do likewise." The point is obvious. Rather than worrying whether or not someone else is a neighbor, Jesus' call is to serve everyone who is in need.

✣ **10:25–37** One often hears that the task of dealing with pain in the world is so vast that we do not know where to begin or how we can even hope to make a dent in what needs to be done. Such thinking can become an excuse for inaction. A better attitude is to be proactive and pitch in where we see a need and understand that we have the ability to help.

10:38–40 This short passage is unique to Luke, and its story can be considered from two angles. One involves the perspective of Martha. Jesus does not criticize her for what she is doing but for being concerned about others' activities.

10:41–42 From the standpoint of Mary emerges the example of someone willing to sit at Jesus' feet and fellowship with him as his disciple. Discipleship sometimes requires that tasks be suspended while fellowship is maintained. Jesus actually calls this choice "better."

✣ **10:38–42** Mary's sitting at the feet of Jesus portrays a person willing to learn from him, while Martha's busyness pictures someone serving him. Disciples need to do both. In other words, discipleship is a balanced combination of two things: service and reflection. Jesus' remark to Martha points out our temptation to serve at the expense of being fed spiritually. But in the Christian life, some activities can wait. There is a time to work and a time to listen and learn.

11:1–2 The prayer opens with an address to the "Father." Disciples are called to childlike trust, not to a shallow, childish intimacy.

his disciples said to him, "Lord,[h] teach us
to pray, just as John taught his disciples."
2He said to them, "When you pray, say:

"'Father,[a]
hallowed be your name,
your kingdom[i] come.[b]
3Give us each day our daily bread.
4Forgive us our sins,
for we also forgive everyone who
sins against us.[c][j]
And lead us not into temptation.[d]'"[k]

5Then Jesus said to them, "Suppose
you have a friend, and you go to him at
midnight and say, 'Friend, lend me three
loaves of bread; 6a friend of mine on a
journey has come to me, and I have no
food to offer him.' 7And suppose the one
inside answers, 'Don't bother me. The
door is already locked, and my children
and I are in bed. I can't get up and give
you anything.' 8I tell you, even though he
will not get up and give you the bread because of friendship, yet because of your
shameless audacity[e] he will surely get
up and give you as much as you need.[l]
9"So I say to you: Ask and it will be
given to you;[m] seek and you will find;
knock and the door will be opened to
you. 10For everyone who asks receives;

11:1 [h] Jn 13:13
11:2 [i] Mt 3:2
11:4 [j] Mt 18:35; Mk 11:25 [k] Mt 26:41; Jas 1:13
11:8 [l] Lk 18:1-6
11:9 [m] Mt 7:7

Lk 11:13 ❖ What good gifts have we received from God? How have we expressed our gratitude?

the one who seeks finds; and to the one
who knocks, the door will be opened.
11"Which of you fathers, if your son
asks for[f] a fish, will give him a snake instead? 12Or if he asks for an egg, will give
him a scorpion? 13If you then, though you
are evil, know how to give good gifts to
your children, how much more will your
Father in heaven give the Holy Spirit to
those who ask him!"

Jesus and Beelzebul

11:14,15,17–22,24–26pp // Mt 12:22,24–29,43–45
11:17–22pp // Mk 3:23–27

14Jesus was driving out a demon that
was mute. When the demon left, the man
who had been mute spoke, and the crowd

[a] 2 Some manuscripts *Our Father in heaven*
[b] 2 Some manuscripts *come. May your will be done on earth as it is in heaven.*
[c] 4 Greek *everyone who is indebted to us*
[d] 4 Some manuscripts *temptation, but deliver us from the evil one*
[e] 8 Or *yet to preserve his good name*
[f] 11 Some manuscripts *for bread, will give him a stone? Or if he asks for*

Access that develops into close relationship need not destroy respect. So the first address to the Father is the statement that his name be kept holy. God is unique and set apart in his holy character. Next is the request for his kingdom to come: We pray that God's just rule be displayed on the earth.

11:3 The third remark contains a request for God to provide food for each succeeding day. This indicates our recognition that God is our provider, right down to the food that sustains us each day. Praying this prayer, the disciple acknowledges God's care at this basic level.

11:4 The disciple also seeks forgiveness of sin but does so recognizing that he or she must give in return what is asked for. It is wrong to ask from God what we are not willing to give to others.

The final request is for spiritual protection. Why should we ask God not to "lead us . . . into temptation"? The request reflects a depth of spiritual sensitivity, since it understands just how prone to sin we are if we do not seek God's face.

11:5–7 Jesus has told us what to pray, but the question remains: How should we come to the throne of grace? Jesus presents a parable that puts the prayer in context, emphasizing that God is approachable, gracious, generous, and ready to hear our requests.

Jesus poses the dilemma and then asks, "Which of you would have the nerve to go wake up his friend in the middle of the night to ask for bread?" The request for three loaves would meet the need. The answer shows the tension in the story.

11:8–10 Jesus comes to his main point: The neighbor responds because the petitioner has "shameless audacity." This Greek term combines two qualities: boldness and shamelessness.

11:11–13 Then Jesus provides another illustration. If a child asks for a basic meal—fish or eggs—will a father give him something dangerous instead, like a snake or scorpion? The Father delights in giving the basic spiritual provisions that the disciple needs to negotiate his or her way through life. If one needs strength or insight from God, he will provide good and beneficial things if we just ask.

✣ **11:1–13** God loves and cares for us. He wants what is best for us, and shows the extent of his commitment to us in the sacrifice of Jesus. Nothing can separate us from a close connection with him but ourselves and our failure to accept the care, provision, and access that come from his hands. We are to come to the Father knowing that his arms are open for us. We can be bold because we have Jesus' assurance that God cares for us. We can seek his face because we know he is there, waiting to hear and embrace our physical and spiritual needs when we ask humbly and in submission to his will.

11:14–15 The issue here is Jesus' authority. Some assign his work to Beelzebul. This name, probably originally referring to a pagan god, was applied to Satan, designating him as "lord of the flies."

THE HOLY SPIRIT IN LUKE-ACTS

ACTION	REFERENCES: LUKE	REFERENCES: ACTS
Anoints and empowers people for ministry and special circumstances	1:13-17; 3:21-22; 4:14; 4:18; 12:8-12	1:8; 2:17; 4:5-12; 4:31; 6:1-6; 8:14-17; 10:34-38; 20:28
Acts in Jesus' divine conception	1:35	
Provides supernatural knowledge, direction, gifts and revelation	1:41-45; 1:67-79; 2:25-35; 4:1; 12:12	1:2; 1:16; 2:1-4; 2:17; 4:25; 6:8-10; 7:55; 8:26-40; 10:19-20; 11:12; 11:28; 13:1-4; 15:28; 16:6-7; 19:1-6; 20:22-23; 21:4-14; 28:25
Given in the "baptism" of the Holy Spirit	3:16	1:4-5; 2:1-4; 8:14-17; 10:44—11:18; 15:6-8
Promised and given as a "gift" from the Father; evidences true faith	11:13	1:4-5; 2:33, 38; 15:6-8; 19:1-6

was amazed.[n] 15But some of them said,
"By Beelzebul,[o] the prince of demons, he
is driving out demons."[p] 16Others tested
him by asking for a sign from heaven.[q]
17Jesus knew their thoughts[r] and said
to them: "Any kingdom divided against
itself will be ruined, and a house divided
against itself will fall. 18If Satan[s] is divided against himself, how can his kingdom
stand? I say this because you claim that
I drive out demons by Beelzebul. 19Now
if I drive out demons by Beelzebul, by
whom do your followers drive them out?
So then, they will be your judges. 20But
if I drive out demons by the finger of
God,[t] then the kingdom of God[u] has come
upon you.
21"When a strong man, fully armed,
guards his own house, his possessions
are safe. 22But when someone stronger
attacks and overpowers him, he takes
away the armor in which the man trusted
and divides up his plunder.
23"Whoever is not with me is against
me, and whoever does not gather with
me scatters.[v]
24"When an impure spirit comes out
of a person, it goes through arid places

11:14 [n] Mt 9:32, 33
11:15 [o] Mk 3:22 [p] Mt 9:34
11:16 [q] Mt 12:38
11:17 [r] Mt 9:4
11:18 [s] Mt 4:10
11:20 [t] Ex 8:19 [u] Mt 3:2
11:23 [v] Mt 12:30; Mk 9:40; Lk 9:50

11:16 Others prefer to sit on the fence and wait for something more from Jesus.

11:17–18 Jesus rejects the connection to Satan on a simple premise. If Satan's goal is to destroy and Jesus is reversing the effects of destruction by healing, then how can one tie Jesus' work to the archdemon?

11:19 Jesus adds one more point to his assessment. Is Jesus pointing to all Jewish exorcists here, asking how they manage to do their work? This seems unlikely. More likely the allusion is to Jesus' disciples, who are also Jewish but who do their work through Jesus' commission.

11:20 Jesus outlines two possibilities: Either he works by satanic power or through divine connection. There is no third option, no neutral ground.

Jesus claims that his miracles are evidence of the presence of God's victorious rule. He is exhibiting his authority over Satan, establishing the earth as a place where righteousness can and does triumph over destruction.

11:21–23 Jesus summarizes his main point with a parable, illustrating his superior strength over Satan. This also implies that Jesus does not work with Satan but against him. There are only two sides, and the choice of allies in this cosmic battle is crucial.

11:14–23 This text has significant applications concerning the nature of the kingdom of God and the meaning of Jesus' victory. Christ's rule is designed to establish the presence of righteousness on the earth through establishing a people who reflect his character before others. The power Jesus gives enables his followers to display love and reconciliation in the context of renewed relationship, regardless of what obstacles may come. We have the potential as Jesus' disciples to live righteously as we walk with and respond to God's Spirit. To share in the kingdom is to share in the empowerment, peace, and other benefits that give us new life—not just in heaven but here and now on earth.

11:24–26 Refusing to respond to God's grace is not a matter of being neutral but of remaining in destructive hands.

seeking rest and does not find it. Then
it says, 'I will return to the house I left.'
25When it arrives, it finds the house
swept clean and put in order. 26Then it
goes and takes seven other spirits more
wicked than itself, and they go in and
live there. And the final condition of that
person is worse than the first."[w]

27As Jesus was saying these things, a
woman in the crowd called out, "Blessed
is the mother who gave you birth and
nursed you."[x]

28He replied, "Blessed rather are those
who hear the word of God[y] and obey it."[z]

The Sign of Jonah

11:29–32pp // Mt 12:39–42

29As the crowds increased, Jesus said,
"This is a wicked generation. It asks for a
sign,[a] but none will be given it except the
sign of Jonah.[b] 30For as Jonah was a sign to
the Ninevites, so also will the Son of Man
be to this generation. 31The Queen of the
South will rise at the judgment with the
people of this generation and condemn
them, for she came from the ends of the
earth to listen to Solomon's wisdom;[c] and
now something greater than Solomon is
here. 32The men of Nineveh will stand
up at the judgment with this generation
and condemn it, for they repented at the
preaching of Jonah;[d] and now something
greater than Jonah is here.

The Lamp of the Body

11:34,35pp // Mt 6:22,23

33"No one lights a lamp and puts it in
a place where it will be hidden, or under
a bowl. Instead they put it on its stand,
so that those who come in may see the
light.[e] 34Your eye is the lamp of your body.
When your eyes are healthy,[a] your whole
body also is full of light. But when they
are unhealthy,[b] your body also is full of
darkness. 35See to it, then, that the light
within you is not darkness. 36Therefore,
if your whole body is full of light, and no
part of it dark, it will be just as full of light
as when a lamp shines its light on you."

Woes on the Pharisees and the Experts in the Law

37When Jesus had finished speaking,
a Pharisee invited him to eat with him;
so he went in and reclined at the table.[f]
38But the Pharisee was surprised when
he noticed that Jesus did not first wash
before the meal.[g]

39Then the Lord[h] said to him, "Now
then, you Pharisees clean the outside of
the cup and dish, but inside you are full
of greed and wickedness.[i] 40You foolish
people![j] Did not the one who made the
outside make the inside also? 41But now
as for what is inside you—be generous
to the poor,[k] and everything will be clean
for you.[l]

42"Woe to you Pharisees, because you
give God a tenth[m] of your mint, rue and
all other kinds of garden herbs, but you
neglect justice and the love of God.[n] You
should have practiced the latter without
leaving the former undone.[o]

11:26 [w] 2Pe 2:20
11:27 [x] Lk 23:29
11:28 [y] Heb 4:12 [z] Pr 8:32; Lk 6:47; 8:21; Jn 14:21
11:29 [a] ver 16; Mt 12:38 [b] Jnh 1:17; Mt 16:4
11:31 [c] 1Ki 10:1; 2Ch 9:1
11:32 [d] Jnh 3:5
11:33 [e] Mt 5:15; Mk 4:21; Lk 8:16
11:37 [f] Lk 7:36; 14:1
11:38 [g] Mk 7:3,4
11:39 [h] Lk 7:13 [i] Mt 23:25,26; Mk 7:20-23
11:40 [j] Lk 12:20; 1Co 15:36
11:41 [k] Lk 12:33 [l] Ac 10:15
11:42 [m] Lk 18:12 [n] Dt 6:5; Mic 6:8 [o] Mt 23:23

[a] 34 The Greek for *healthy* here implies *generous*.
[b] 34 The Greek for *unhealthy* here implies *stingy*.

11:27–28 The next short exchange concludes with a beatitude. It was not unusual to honor a mother in that culture by the accomplishments of her sons. But Jesus transforms the remark into another opportunity to declare where real blessing in life lives—in those who hear and obey God's Word.

11:29–32 Jesus warns about the endless pursuit of signs. Jesus' miracles and signs point to what is more important—his teaching. To refuse Jesus is to face rejection in judgment and the condemnation of previous generations who understand the unique opportunity that Jesus' preaching provides.

11:33–36 Light not only has to be lit, it has to be received by the eye. The eye is a lamp in the sense that it is a doorkeeper. What the eye lets into the mind makes up the person. Of course, what is let in reflects where our heart is.

✣ **11:24–36** Pursuing every other avenue of life with diligence and energy while ignoring the soul produces people whose souls are empty shells, waiting to be filled with something. Hollow people often live shallow lives. If any discussion should engage the masses, it is the one that considers Jesus' true identity and then makes a decision of belief or unbelief. There is simply no more important answer to a question and no greater decision to be made. Will we recognize and follow the light, inviting others to do so, or will we remain in darkness?

11:37–41 Jesus knows what his host is thinking, so he begins with a rebuke. The general complaint is that the Pharisees clean the outside of the cup and dish, but inside there is the filth of extortion and greed. God is concerned with both inside and outside; in fact, the inside is of special concern to him.

11:42 Jesus then addresses tithing done while ignoring justice and love. These leaders must be sensitive both to tithing and to their character.

43"Woe to you Pharisees, because you
love the most important seats in the synagogues and respectful greetings in the
marketplaces.[p]
44"Woe to you, because you are like
unmarked graves,[q] which people walk
over without knowing it."
45One of the experts in the law[r] answered him, "Teacher, when you say
these things, you insult us also."
46Jesus replied, "And you experts in
the law, woe to you, because you load
people down with burdens they can
hardly carry, and you yourselves will not
lift one finger to help them.[s]
47"Woe to you, because you build
tombs for the prophets, and it was your
ancestors who killed them. 48So you
testify that you approve of what your
ancestors did; they killed the prophets,
and you build their tombs.[t] 49Because of
this, God in his wisdom[u] said, 'I will send
them prophets and apostles, some of
whom they will kill and others they will
persecute.'[v] 50Therefore this generation
will be held responsible for the blood of
all the prophets that has been shed since
the beginning of the world, 51from the
blood of Abel[w] to the blood of Zechariah,[x]
who was killed between the altar and the
sanctuary. Yes, I tell you, this generation
will be held responsible for it all.[y]

11:43 [p] Mt 23:6, 7; Mk 12:38-39; Lk 14:7; 20:46
11:44 [q] Mt 23:27
11:45 [r] Mt 22:35
11:46 [s] Mt 23:4
11:48 [t] Mt 23:29-32; Ac 7:51-53
11:49 [u] 1Co 1:24, 30; Col 2:3 [v] Mt 23:34
11:51 [w] Ge 4:8 [x] 2Ch 24:20, 21 [y] Mt 23:35, 36
11:52 [z] Mt 23:13
11:54 [a] Mt 12:10; Mk 12:13
12:1 [b] Mt 16:6, 11, 12; Mk 8:15
12:2 [c] Mk 4:22; Lk 8:17
12:4 [d] Jn 15:14, 15

52"Woe to you experts in the law, because you have taken away the key to
knowledge. You yourselves have not entered, and you have hindered those who
were entering."[z]
53When Jesus went outside, the Pharisees and the teachers of the law began to
oppose him fiercely and to besiege him
with questions, 54waiting to catch him
in something he might say.[a]

Warnings and Encouragements

12:2–9pp // Mt 10:26–33

12 Meanwhile, when a crowd of many
thousands had gathered, so that
they were trampling on one another,
Jesus began to speak first to his disciples,
saying: "Be[a] on your guard against the
yeast of the Pharisees, which is hypocrisy.[b] 2There is nothing concealed that will
not be disclosed, or hidden that will not
be made known.[c] 3What you have said
in the dark will be heard in the daylight,
and what you have whispered in the ear
in the inner rooms will be proclaimed
from the roofs.
4"I tell you, my friends,[d] do not be
afraid of those who kill the body and
after that can do no more. 5But I will
show you whom you should fear: Fear

[a] 1 *Or speak to his disciples, saying: "First of all, be*

11:43-44 Jesus also addresses the issue of pride. The Pharisees love the front seats in the synagogue. They are like an unmarked grave over which people walk without knowing; they are conductors of spiritual uncleanness, because they do not model real spirituality.
11:45-46 A scribe notes that if Jesus insists on condemning the Pharisees, he must include the scribes also. So Jesus issues more rebukes, this time with the scribes in view. The first rebuke is about showing lack of compassion: They call on others to bear the weight of tradition on their back, but they do nothing to help them carry the load.
11:47-51 Jesus declares these people are like their ancestors, those who killed the prophets. The scribes honor the tombs they created.
11:52 In the strongest remark of all, Jesus condemns the scribes for being the exact opposite of what they think. They believe they possess the key to knowledge, but they are an obstacle to truth.
11:53-54 The reaction is immediate. The scribes and Pharisees begin to "lie in wait" for Jesus, or, as the NIV says, "besiege him." The woes Jesus pronounces do not lead to repentance but to hardness of heart.

✥ **11:37-54** Legalists major in minors and ignore the major relational requirements God asks of his followers. Jesus is not criticizing tithing or watching out for one's spiritual walk. He condemns being so self-focused on spiritual matters that we ignore the condition of the heart and fail to notice those who are truly hurting.
Finally, Jesus' pronouncement of woes means that everyone, including those who claim an association with God, are accountable for their choices. Our culture loves to claim the right to choose. We must also embrace the responsibility that comes with the choice. So our job is to choose wisely and encourage others to do so as well.

12:1-12 Jesus turns his attention to the disciples as they deal with the huge crowds pressing around them. Their press raises an issue that becomes a temptation to the disciples: An effort to maintain popularity easily leads to hypocrisy.
12:2-3 To enhance the warning, Jesus emphasizes that everything will be disclosed before God when our lives are evaluated. On that coming day, disciples will have their stewardship examined and will be rewarded accordingly. Those who do not know the Lord will have their actions condemned.
12:4-7 In fearing God, we have nothing to fear from anyone else, for we are worth far more than the sparrows.

Lk 12:8–9 ❖ What are some ways we can acknowledge Christ before others? Why is this sometimes difficult?

him who, after your body has been killed,
has authority to throw you into hell. Yes,
I tell you, fear him.[e] 6Are not five sparrows sold for two pennies? Yet not one
of them is forgotten by God. 7Indeed,
the very hairs of your head are all numbered.[f] Don't be afraid; you are worth
more than many sparrows.[g]
8"I tell you, whoever publicly acknowledges me before others, the Son of Man
will also acknowledge before the angels
of God.[h] 9But whoever disowns me before
others will be disowned[i] before the angels of God. 10And everyone who speaks
a word against the Son of Man[j] will be
forgiven, but anyone who blasphemes
against the Holy Spirit will not be forgiven.[k]
11"When you are brought before synagogues, rulers and authorities, do not
worry about how you will defend yourselves or what you will say,[l] 12for the Holy
Spirit will teach you at that time what
you should say."[m]

12:5 [e] Heb 10:31
12:7 [f] Mt 10:30 [g] Mt 12:12
12:8 [h] Lk 15:10
12:9 [i] Mk 8:38; 2Ti 2:12
12:10 [j] Mt 8:20 [k] Mt 12:31,32; Mk 3:28-29; 1Jn 5:16
12:11 [l] Mt 10:17, 19; Mk 13:11; Lk 21:12,14
12:12 [m] Ex 4:12; Mt 10:20; Mk 13:11; Lk 21:15
12:15 [n] Job 20:20; 31:24; Ps 62:10
12:20 [o] Jer 17:11; Lk 11:40 [p] Job 27:8 [q] Ps 39:6; 49:10
12:21 [r] ver 33

The Parable of the Rich Fool

13Someone in the crowd said to him,
"Teacher, tell my brother to divide the
inheritance with me."
14Jesus replied, "Man, who appointed
me a judge or an arbiter between you?"
15Then he said to them, "Watch out! Be
on your guard against all kinds of greed;
life does not consist in an abundance of
possessions."[n]
16And he told them this parable: "The
ground of a certain rich man yielded an
abundant harvest. 17He thought to himself, 'What shall I do? I have no place to
store my crops.'
18"Then he said, 'This is what I'll do.
I will tear down my barns and build
bigger ones, and there I will store my
surplus grain. 19And I'll say to myself,
"You have plenty of grain laid up for
many years. Take life easy; eat, drink
and be merry." '
20"But God said to him, 'You fool![o] This
very night your life will be demanded
from you.[p] Then who will get what you
have prepared for yourself?'[q]
21"This is how it will be with whoever
stores up things for themselves but is
not rich toward God."[r]

12:8–9 This message about fearing God is reinforced in remarks about Jesus as the Son of Man. This juxtaposition of the fear of God with the Son of Man again shows the close connection between Christ's ministry and God's call.
12:10 Speaking a word against the Son of Man refers to a specific act of rejection, while rejecting the testimony of the Spirit refers to a permanent rejection of the message of salvation. This decision about the testimony the Spirit gives is the key issue for Jesus.
12:11–12 The Holy Spirit will teach his people what to say whenever they are challenged or presented with an opportunity to profess their faith. They can trust that their message will be his message. By fearing God, disciples have nothing to fear from people.

✜ **12:1–12** As Christians we often must face people who do not understand us, who reject the principles we live for, or who may even be hostile to our beliefs about God. In sharing about him we must risk the possibility of being rejected. However, the serious nature of the choice of rejecting the testimony of the Spirit about Jesus moves his disciples to tell the story about Jesus' gracious gift.

The unforgivable sin is rejecting what God has offered in the forgiveness present in Jesus. Texts like Rev 20:10–15 and 22:15 suggest that the unrighteous continue to exist outside the presence of God. In what are surely among the most tragic texts of the Bible, these passages teach that to reject God and to come into judgment is one of the most crushing experiences possible. That is why the teaching about judgment is so important, and that is why it is so crucial to share Jesus with those who need to know him.

12:13–16 The main issue in this parable is not wealth. Rather, it is one's attitude toward wealth as it deals with finding security in life. The man in the story did not acquire his harvest immorally; he simply had a good year. His error comes in how he views what has become his.
12:17–19 Five times in these verses the farmer speaks of what "I" will do, as if he owns it all. His goal is to ease back and withdraw from life. He feels no concern or responsibility for anyone else. The essence of greed is keeping God's gifts for yourself.
12:20–21 This is the ultimate "you can't take it with you" parable. Jesus concludes that this is how it will be for any who pile up treasures for themselves but are not rich toward God. Richness toward God means responding to life and blessing in a way that he desires, a way that honors him. The conclusion condemns greed as the attitude that hoards resources simply for one's own use.

✜ **12:13–21** This text calls for self-examination. How do I feel about what God has given to me? Is it mine? Am I a faithful steward of what has

Do Not Worry

12:22–31pp // Mt 6:25–33

22Then Jesus said to his disciples:
"Therefore I tell you, do not worry about
your life, what you will eat; or about
your body, what you will wear. 23For life
is more than food, and the body more
than clothes. 24Consider the ravens: They
do not sow or reap, they have no storeroom or barn; yet God feeds them.[s] And
how much more valuable you are than
birds! 25Who of you by worrying can add
a single hour to your life[a]? 26Since you
cannot do this very little thing, why do
you worry about the rest?

27"Consider how the wild flowers grow.
They do not labor or spin. Yet I tell you,
not even Solomon in all his splendor[t] was
dressed like one of these. 28If that is how
God clothes the grass of the field, which is
here today, and tomorrow is thrown into
the fire, how much more will he clothe
you—you of little faith![u] 29And do not set
your heart on what you will eat or drink;
do not worry about it. 30For the pagan
world runs after all such things, and your
Father[v] knows that you need them.[w] 31But
seek his kingdom,[x] and these things will
be given to you as well.[y]

32"Do not be afraid,[z] little flock, for
your Father has been pleased to give you
the kingdom.[a] 33Sell your possessions
and give to the poor.[b] Provide purses
for yourselves that will not wear out, a
treasure in heaven[c] that will never fail,
where no thief comes near and no moth
destroys.[d] 34For where your treasure is,
there your heart will be also.[e]

Watchfulness

12:35,36pp // Mt 25:1–13; Mk 13:33–37
12:39,40,42–46pp // Mt 24:43–51

35"Be dressed ready for service and
keep your lamps burning, 36like servants waiting for their master to return
from a wedding banquet, so that when he
comes and knocks they can immediately
open the door for him. 37It will be good
for those servants whose master finds
them watching when he comes.[f] Truly I
tell you, he will dress himself to serve,
will have them recline at the table and
will come and wait on them.[g] 38It will be
good for those servants whose master
finds them ready, even if he comes in the
middle of the night or toward daybreak.
39But understand this: If the owner of
the house had known at what hour the

12:24 [s] Job 38:41; Ps 147:9
12:27 [t] 1Ki 10:4-7
12:28 [u] Mt 6:30
12:30 [v] Lk 6:36 [w] Mt 6:8
12:31 [x] Mt 3:2 [y] Mt 19:29
12:32 [z] Mt 14:27 [a] Mt 25:34
12:33 [b] Mt 19:21; Ac 2:45 [c] Mt 6:20 [d] Jas 5:2
12:34 [e] Mt 6:21
12:37 [f] Mt 24:42, 46; 25:13 [g] Mt 20:28

[a] 25 Or *single cubit to your height*

---

come my way? Both the wise use of resources and the absence of greed are addressed here, since one attitude is the cause of the other.

12:22-26 The Greek verb used here implies that we should be constantly free of anxiety. Ravens were among the lower rank of living creatures, yet God is aware of even their needs. If he cares for them, how much more will he care for us.

From this illustration Jesus takes up some practical considerations about anxiety. What does worry contribute? Does it add any length to one's life? Anxiety, though perhaps a natural response to events that seem beyond our control, doesn't gain us anything.

12:27-30 Worry casts doubt on God's care. So Jesus addresses his listeners as people "of little faith." The essence of trust is to recognize that God will take care of what is in his hands.

12:31 To "seek [God's] kingdom" means to live as his representatives. We must represent him and reflect his righteousness in a world unconcerned about knowing God. That is the constant call of the disciple.

12:32 Sheep can be skittish and tend to frighten easily. Jesus casts God as a compassionate shepherd who cares for his own and gives them what they need in order to do what he has called them to do.

12:33-34 If we do not need to worry about the provisions of life, then we can be generous with what God has given us. God honors such generosity; in return, he gives us "treasure in heaven." A life attached to possessions becomes a stumbling block because it leads to high anxiety. Jesus indicates that one way in which disciples can be different in their testimony is to prioritize people over possessions.

12:22-34 A major obstacle to pursuing God's call is to think that we need to get security in other areas of our lives before we can be freed to serve as he wishes. In the process we can short-circuit what God calls us to do and get distracted with personal security issues. The spiritual life as Jesus sees it is not a life of comfort but of risk, exposure, weakness, and vulnerability.

The call of God will never take us to a place where the grace of God cannot sustain us. When we come to that realization (which we need to do over and over again in the Christian life), then we finally realize the practical reality of Jesus' call to not worry.

12:35-38 Disciples must be on constant watch, even during the darkness of the night. Disciples should be like servants who do not know exactly when the master will return. They should be ready to open the door when he arrives. Blessing awaits those whom the master finds ready and waiting at his return, even if he comes at a time when others might not be ready.

12:39-40 Jesus then uses the picture of the thief to illustrate his point: The reality of the master's

thief[h] was coming, he would not have
let his house be broken into. 40You also
must be ready,[i] because the Son of Man
will come at an hour when you do not
expect him."
41Peter asked, "Lord, are you telling
this parable to us, or to everyone?"
42The Lord[j] answered, "Who then is
the faithful and wise manager, whom
the master puts in charge of his servants
to give them their food allowance at the
proper time? 43It will be good for that
servant whom the master finds doing
so when he returns. 44Truly I tell you,
he will put him in charge of all his possessions. 45But suppose the servant says
to himself, 'My master is taking a long
time in coming,' and he then begins to
beat the other servants, both men and
women, and to eat and drink and get
drunk. 46The master of that servant will
come on a day when he does not expect
him and at an hour he is not aware of.[k]
He will cut him to pieces and assign him
a place with the unbelievers.
47"The servant who knows the master's
will and does not get ready or does not
do what the master wants will be beat-
en with many blows.[l] 48But the one who
does not know and does things deserving punishment will be beaten with few
blows.[m] From everyone who has been
given much, much will be demanded;
and from the one who has been entrusted with much, much more will be asked.

12:39 [h] Mt 6:19; 1Th 5:2; 2Pe 3:10; Rev 3:3; 16:15
12:40 [i] Mk 13:33; Lk 21:36
12:42 [j] Lk 7:13
12:46 [k] ver 40
12:47 [l] Dt 25:2
12:48 [m] Lev 5:17; Nu 15:27-30
12:50 [n] Mk 10:38 [o] Jn 19:30
12:53 [p] Mic 7:6; Mt 10:21
12:54 [q] Mt 16:2
12:56 [r] Mt 16:3
12:58 [s] Mt 5:25

Not Peace but Division

12:51–53pp // Mt 10:34–36

49"I have come to bring fire on the
earth, and how I wish it were already
kindled! 50But I have a baptism[n] to undergo, and what constraint I am under
until it is completed![o] 51Do you think I
came to bring peace on earth? No, I tell
you, but division. 52From now on there
will be five in one family divided against
each other, three against two and two
against three. 53They will be divided, father against son and son against father,
mother against daughter and daughter
against mother, mother-in-law against
daughter-in-law and daughter-in-law
against mother-in-law."[p]

Interpreting the Times

54He said to the crowd: "When you see
a cloud rising in the west, immediately
you say, 'It's going to rain,' and it does.[q]
55And when the south wind blows, you
say, 'It's going to be hot,' and it is. 56Hyp-
ocrites! You know how to interpret the
appearance of the earth and the sky. How
is it that you don't know how to interpret
this present time?[r]
57"Why don't you judge for yourselves
what is right? 58As you are going with your
adversary to the magistrate, try hard to
be reconciled on the way, or your adversary may drag you off to the judge, and
the judge turn you over to the officer, and
the officer throw you into prison.[s] 59I tell

---

return coupled with its uncertain timing demands watchfulness. Accountability to the Lord is a major NT theme. God's immense grace does not end our personal accountability.

12:41–48 Peter asks if the Lord is only speaking to the leaders or to everyone. Jesus then tells another parable about the benefits of watchfulness. Jesus pictures an accountability here that varies depending on what we know and what we do. Personal action makes a difference; we are accountable for our action as well as our inaction (v. 48).

12:35–48 We will be held accountable to the Lord at his return. This concept is frightening only if we have something to fear because we are unfaithful. With his return comes the hope of casting off our sinful humanity for a glorified and purified existence forever with God. These texts encourage us to live like what we shall become. If we live righteously, we will have nothing to fear when the Lord returns.

Not everything in this passage warns of judgment. At the heart of the Lord's return is a reminder of where our relationship with God should take us—namely, to make us more like him. In all the speculation about when and how he might come, we should certainly pay more attention to who we will be when he comes.

12:49–51 Jesus' "I have come" statements reveal his ministry's judging and purging work: to provide the way for people to make decisions about where they stand and to offer them the opportunity to be healed. But before he can exercise such judgment and authority, he must undergo his own "baptism," a reference to his approaching death.

12:52–53 Jesus knows that he forces choices, so he does not bring peace "but division." The choices are real, and people will choose differently.

12:54–56 Jesus calls on the crowd to reflect: They can read and anticipate the weather just by looking around, yet they are unable to discern the nature of current events that surround Jesus. In calling them "hypocrites," Jesus is trying to shock them into reflection. Their poor judgment leaves them at great risk.

12:57–59 The magistrate is like a sheriff in charge of a debtor's prison. The central idea is not that

you, you will not get out until you have paid the last penny."[t]

Repent or Perish

13 Now there were some present at that time who told Jesus about the Galileans whose blood Pilate[u] had mixed with their sacrifices. 2Jesus answered, "Do you think that these Galileans were worse sinners than all the other Galileans because they suffered this way?[v] 3I tell you, no! But unless you repent, you too will all perish. 4Or those eighteen who died when the tower in Siloam[w] fell on them — do you think they were more guilty than all the others living in Jerusalem? 5I tell you, no! But unless you repent,[x] you too will all perish."

6Then he told this parable: "A man had a fig tree growing in his vineyard, and he went to look for fruit on it but did not find any.[y] 7So he said to the man who took care of the vineyard, 'For three years now I've been coming to look for fruit on this fig tree and haven't found any. Cut it down![z] Why should it use up the soil?'

8"'Sir,' the man replied, 'leave it alone for one more year, and I'll dig around it and fertilize it. 9If it bears fruit next year, fine! If not, then cut it down.'"

12:59 [t] Mt 5:26; Mk 12:42
13:1 [u] Mt 27:2
13:2 [v] Jn 9:2,3
13:4 [w] Jn 9:7,11
13:5 [x] Mt 3:2; Ac 2:38
13:6 [y] Isa 5:2; Jer 8:13; Mt 21:19
13:7 [z] Mt 3:10

Lk 13:6-9 ❖ What does this parable teach us about God's patience when it seems to take a long time for the fruit of faith to appear?

Jesus Heals a Crippled Woman on the Sabbath

10On a Sabbath Jesus was teaching in one of the synagogues,[a] 11and a woman was there who had been crippled by a spirit for eighteen years.[b] She was bent over and could not straighten up at all. 12When Jesus saw her, he called her forward and said to her, "Woman, you are set free from your infirmity." 13Then he put his hands on her,[c] and immediately she straightened up and praised God.

14Indignant because Jesus had healed on the Sabbath,[d] the synagogue leader[e] said to the people, "There are six days for work.[f] So come and be healed on those days, not on the Sabbath."

15The Lord answered him, "You hypocrites! Doesn't each of you on the Sabbath untie your ox or donkey from the stall and lead it out to give it water?[g] 16Then should not this woman, a daughter of Abraham,[h] whom Satan[i] has kept

13:10 [a] Mt 4:23
13:11 [b] ver 16
13:13 [c] Mk 5:23
13:14 [d] Mt 12:2; Lk 14:3 [e] Mk 5:22 [f] Ex 20:9
13:15 [g] Lk 14:5
13:16 [h] Lk 3:8; 19:9 [i] Mt 4:10

---

one can get out of hell; it is that one will be held accountable for every sin one commits.

13:1–5 In the discussion of the two tragedies in these verses, the question emerges whether a worse level of sin causes a person to suffer a special judgment. Jesus deflects the question about the degree of sin because it distracts from the real issue: the presence of sin, no matter what its form.

The call to repent is a fundamental theme in Luke. Jesus has in mind the change of direction that can come after hearing God's message. With repentance comes a change of mind that brings a change of direction: a repentant person's orientation of life is directed in faith to God.

13:6–9 The closing parable discusses the nation, using a variation on a standard metaphor for Israel—a vineyard or an orchard. The image describes the unfruitful state of the nation of Israel and indicates that the time for the nation to respond is limited. The judgment came on Israel in AD 70.

✜ **12:49—13:9** This text calls each reader to consider where they stand before God. The Jesus of popular culture does not force such choices, but we may not manipulate the biblical Jesus into our own image. The Gospels are clear that many reacted against him because of the challenging nature of his prophetic call. But we are accountable for the debt of sin that we carry before God. Repentance is not an emotion or the act of agreeing to an idea; it is a reorientation to new life.

God is patient, but there does come a time when it is too late to repent. As we share Jesus, we can get the idea that there is much time for people to decide. Although ultimately the Spirit causes people to respond to Jesus, if we take a laid-back attitude we may not be as sensitive to opportunities to share as we could be.

13:10–13 In this culture, being a woman and suffering from such a malady makes this individual an outsider on two counts. Jesus notices her, lays hands on her, and she straightens up immediately. This would have been cause for immediate rejoicing except for one fact: it was the Sabbath.

13:14 The synagogue leader argues that Jesus has violated laws of working on the Sabbath. It is not clear precisely which rule Jesus has violated; all he has done is to address the woman and touch her.

13:15–16 Jesus responds sternly, calling those who agree with the synagogue ruler "hypocrites" (v. 15). If people show compassion to animals on the Sabbath, how much more compassion should a human receive?

What more appropriate day to defeat Satan and release people from his bonds than the day of rest when people should be contemplating God's goodness? The Sabbath is a day to remember God and celebrate the goodness of his healing grace. Jesus' approach to the issue is the exact opposite of the Jewish leadership's view.

bound for eighteen long years, be set free
on the Sabbath day from what bound
her?"
17When he said this, all his opponents
were humiliated,[j] but the people were
delighted with all the wonderful things
he was doing.

The Parables of the Mustard Seed and the Yeast

13:18,19pp // Mk 4:30–32
13:18–21pp // Mt 13:31–33

18Then Jesus asked, "What is the kingdom of God[k] like?[l] What shall I compare
it to? 19It is like a mustard seed, which a
man took and planted in his garden. It
grew and became a tree,[m] and the birds
perched in its branches."[n]
20Again he asked, "What shall I compare the kingdom of God to? 21It is like
yeast that a woman took and mixed
into about sixty pounds[a] of flour until
it worked all through the dough."[o]

The Narrow Door

22Then Jesus went through the towns
and villages, teaching as he made his
way to Jerusalem.[p] 23Someone asked
him, "Lord, are only a few people going
to be saved?"
He said to them, 24"Make every effort
to enter through the narrow door,[q] because many, I tell you, will try to enter
and will not be able to. 25Once the owner of the house gets up and closes the
door, you will stand outside knocking
and pleading, 'Sir, open the door for us.'
"But he will answer, 'I don't know you
or where you come from.'[r]
26"Then you will say, 'We ate and
drank with you, and you taught in our
streets.'
27"But he will reply, 'I don't know you
or where you come from. Away from me,
all you evildoers!'[s]
28"There will be weeping there, and
gnashing of teeth,[t] when you see Abraham, Isaac and Jacob and all the prophets in the kingdom of God, but you yourselves thrown out. 29People will come
from east and west[u] and north and south,
and will take their places at the feast in
the kingdom of God. 30Indeed there are
those who are last who will be first, and
first who will be last."[v]

Jesus' Sorrow for Jerusalem

13:34,35pp // Mt 23:37–39
13:34,35Ref // Lk 19:41

31At that time some Pharisees came to
Jesus and said to him, "Leave this place
and go somewhere else. Herod[w] wants
to kill you."
32He replied, "Go tell that fox, 'I will
keep on driving out demons and healing people today and tomorrow, and

[a] *21* Or about 27 kilograms

13:17 [j] Isa 66:5
13:18 [k] Mt 3:2 [l] Mt 13:24
13:19 [m] Lk 17:6 [n] Mt 13:32
13:21 [o] 1Co 5:6
13:22 [p] Lk 9:51
13:24 [q] Mt 7:13
13:25 [r] Mt 7:23; 25:10-12
13:27 [s] Mt 7:23; 25:41
13:28 [t] Mt 8:12
13:29 [u] Mt 8:11
13:30 [v] Mt 19:30
13:31 [w] Mt 14:1

13:17 The reaction is instantaneous: The leadership stands humiliated, while the crowd is delighted with what Jesus has done. In the cosmic battle over the woman, a ministry of compassion has emerged. Jesus rebukes those who want to apply the rules improperly. Legalism stands condemned.

✣ **13:10-17** The picture of physical deliverance here serves notice that deliverance is possible through Jesus. Establishing a relationship with God and accessing the power of God's presence in his Spirit empowers us with resources to renew our lives. Anytime is appropriate for such a move toward restoration. It is what Jesus' ministry—and the church's ministry today—are all about.

13:18-21 The parable of the mustard seed and the yeast make fundamentally the same point—that the kingdom starts out small but will eventually cover the whole earth. What the Jews expected to come all at once will grow gradually into greatness.

Jesus tells these parables to call for trust. He is building the kingdom, and people should trust God that it will come, even though the movement starts out looking so insignificant.

13:22-30 The next parable serves as a warning to Israel. Since the kingdom is coming, people should respond now, before the door closes. Nothing is more tragic than being close to God's blessing and missing out.

13:23-25 Someone asks Jesus if only a few are going to be saved. Jesus' reply makes it clear that this man's suspicion is correct. The verb "make every effort" (v. 24) speaks of laboring to get in. This implies that there is a specific route by which to enter; that is why Jesus mentions a *narrow* door and describes what that door is.

13:26-30 The banquet image looks at the time after Jesus returns, when those who trust in him are gathered to share in the celebration of salvation. There are no *ex post facto* opportunities. Entry comes through the means Jesus provides or not at all.

The end result for those who are outside is "weeping" and "gnashing of teeth," a sense of pain and frustration at having missed the moment (v. 28). The question, "Will the saved be few?" has become, "Will the saved be you?"

13:31-33 Here Jesus warns the nation by mentioning the city that represents it: Jerusalem. Verse 31 opens with the Pharisees warning Jesus that Herod is looking to kill him. While their statement looks like one of concern, it is not.

PEOPLE TO KNOW // HEROD ANTIPAS

LUKE 13:31–33: Herod Antipas was a son of Herod the Great, the tyrant who sought to have Jesus killed as a baby (Mt 2:16). After Herod the Great died, his territory was split among his sons. Herod Antipas did not have the title of "king" like his father. Instead, he was a tetrarch, ruler of one-quarter of his father's domain (Lk 3:1).

The night of Jesus' arrest, Pilate sent Jesus to Herod Antipas since Jesus was from the region he ruled. Herod Antipas was excited to see Jesus and hoped for a spectacular miracle (Lk 23:8). He was sorely disappointed: Jesus would not even answer his questions. Herod Antipas sent Jesus back to Pilate after his men had mocked Jesus and put a purple robe and crown of thorns upon his head—a cruel parody of royalty. Interestingly, this act of passing Jesus back and forth forged a friendship between Herod Antipas and Pilate.

Herod Antipas was an ineffective leader. He was afraid to kill John the Baptist because of the prophet's popularity, yet he was also too weak to defend John's life (Mt 14:1–12). He was interested in Jesus—but only because he wanted to see some dazzling miracle. When that didn't happen, he let Pilate make the final decision about Jesus' fate.

APPLICATION ✤ Herod Antipas's story is a warning against selfish and shallow living. He was interested in listening to the words of John the Baptist and wanted to meet Jesus, but he didn't let those encounters change his life. He met two of the most influential people in the Bible, and he went away unchanged. But what would we do if we had met Jesus or John face to face? We have their words recorded in the Bible; do we want to know Jesus only because we are interested in what he can do for us? Or will we let Jesus' words change our lives?

on the third day I will reach my goal.'[x]
33In any case, I must press on today and
tomorrow and the next day — for surely
no prophet[y] can die outside Jerusalem!
34"Jerusalem, Jerusalem, you who kill
the prophets and stone those sent to
you, how often I have longed to gather
your children together, as a hen gathers
her chicks under her wings,[z] and you
were not willing. 35Look, your house is
left to you desolate.[a] I tell you, you will
not see me again until you say, 'Blessed
is he who comes in the name of the
Lord.'[a]"[b]

13:32 [x] Heb 2:10
13:33 [y] Mt 21:11
13:34 [z] Mt 23:37
13:35 [a] Jer 12:17; 22:5 [b] Ps 118:26; Mt 21:9; Lk 19:38

Jesus at a Pharisee's House

14:8–10Ref // Pr 25:6,7

14 One Sabbath, when Jesus went
to eat in the house of a prominent Pharisee,[c] he was being carefully
watched.[d] 2There in front of him was a
man suffering from abnormal swelling of
his body. 3Jesus asked the Pharisees and
experts in the law,[e] "Is it lawful to heal
on the Sabbath or not?"[f] 4But they remained silent. So taking hold of the man,
he healed him and sent him on his way.

14:1 [c] Lk 7:36; 11:37 [d] Mt 12:10
14:3 [e] Mt 22:35 [f] Mt 12:2

[a] 35 Psalm 118:26

Jesus replies by stating that he will complete his mission: Nothing will stop him. So they are to tell the one who wants to destroy Jesus that he will continue to exorcise demons and heal people, and then he will complete his task. Death is the pivot point in his ministry. Jesus' presenting himself as a prophet underscores his function as the One who reveals God's will.

13:34–35 Then comes Jesus' lament. He speaks in the first person for God, as is typical of a prophet, and explains how he has longed to care for and protect Jerusalem as a hen cares for her chicks. Is there a more tender image than this? One of the tragedies of rejecting God's will is that people get what they ask for, including the dire consequences of an eternity separated from God.

✤ **13:18–35** The program of God's coming kingdom gives us hope. In the meantime, the kingdom is present in a more hidden form today. It does not display the fullness of power it will demonstrate one day, nor is its call to any single nation, party, or human institution. Rather, the kingdom is found wherever God's people are found.

14:1–6 As Jesus enters the house for the meal, a man suffering from dropsy (a condition of retaining bodily fluids) is there. Many see the condition as a result of God's judgment. So Jesus takes the initiative and asks the Pharisees and scribes if it is lawful to heal such a person on the Sabbath. They remain silent. Despite numerous opportunities, the leadership fails to see what God is doing.

5 Then he asked them, "If one of you has
a child[a] or an ox that falls into a well on
the Sabbath day, will you not immediately
pull it out?"[g] 6 And they had nothing to say.
7 When he noticed how the guests
picked the places of honor at the table,[h]
he told them this parable: 8 "When someone invites you to a wedding feast, do
not take the place of honor, for a person
more distinguished than you may have
been invited. 9 If so, the host who invited
both of you will come and say to you, 'Give
this person your seat.' Then, humiliated,
you will have to take the least important
place. 10 But when you are invited, take
the lowest place, so that when your host
comes, he will say to you, 'Friend, move
up to a better place.' Then you will be
honored in the presence of all the other
guests. 11 For all those who exalt themselves will be humbled, and those who
humble themselves will be exalted."[i]
12 Then Jesus said to his host, "When
you give a luncheon or dinner, do not invite your friends, your brothers or sisters,
your relatives, or your rich neighbors; if
you do, they may invite you back and so
you will be repaid. 13 But when you give
a banquet, invite the poor, the crippled,
the lame, the blind,[j] 14 and you will be
blessed. Although they cannot repay you,
you will be repaid at the resurrection of
the righteous."[k]

The Parable of the Great Banquet

14:16–24Ref // Mt 22:2–14

15 When one of those at the table with
him heard this, he said to Jesus, "Blessed
is the one who will eat at the feast[l] in the
kingdom of God."[m]
16 Jesus replied: "A certain man was
preparing a great banquet and invited
many guests. 17 At the time of the banquet he sent his servant to tell those who
had been invited, 'Come, for everything
is now ready.'
18 "But they all alike began to make excuses. The first said, 'I have just bought
a field, and I must go and see it. Please
excuse me.'
19 "Another said, 'I have just bought
five yoke of oxen, and I'm on my way to
try them out. Please excuse me.'
20 "Still another said, 'I just got married, so I can't come.'
21 "The servant came back and reported this to his master. Then the owner of
the house became angry and ordered his
servant, 'Go out quickly into the streets
and alleys of the town and bring in the
poor, the crippled, the blind and the
lame.'[n]
22 " 'Sir,' the servant said, 'what you ordered has been done, but there is still
room.'
23 "Then the master told his servant,
'Go out to the roads and country lanes
and compel them to come in, so that my
house will be full. 24 I tell you, not one of

Lk 14:13–14 ❖ How can we show Christ's love and hospitality to people who are poor and marginalized? What reward does Christ promise?

14:5 [g] Lk 13:15
14:7 [h] Lk 11:43
14:11 [i] Mt 23:12; Lk 18:14
14:13 [j] ver 21
14:14 [k] Ac 24:15
14:15 [l] Isa 25:6; Mt 26:29; Lk 13:29; Rev 19:9 [m] Mt 3:2
14:21 [n] ver 13

[a] 5 Some manuscripts *donkey*

14:7–11 This passage highlights the importance of genuine humility. The mention of shame is important because, in that ancient culture, honor and shame were key issues of a person's identity, worth, and character. God will exalt those who humble themselves. On the other hand, those who exalt themselves will be humbled by God.

14:12–14 Jesus expands the call as he challenges us to serve those who cannot repay our kindness. The best hospitality is that which is given, not exchanged. Then divine approval will come. True righteousness does not look for a payback but is offered free of charge, graciously, just as God in Christ has forgiven us.

14:15 This final portion of the meal scene summarizes all that Jesus has warned the nation about in these last few chapters. A guest remarks about the blessedness of sitting at the banquet table in the kingdom. Jesus challenges some of the assumptions in that remark with a parable.

14:16–24 The original invitees represent Israel. Although the nation is not responding, the time for the kingdom to arrive has come, and the initial celebration of its blessings will proceed. Others previously thought excluded from the celebration will get invitations. These people represent the spread of God's blessing beyond the bounds of the needy of Israel. Israel, though first in line, is missing her present chance to sit at the table. The first have indeed become last.

✣ **14:1–24** The Pharisees were not ready for any surprises; they wanted to define the limits of God's work. We sometimes risk missing what God is doing because we think we know how he will act. Those who wish to see God at work must be careful not to dictate to him. He acts as he wills and has revealed some aspects of his will to us, but that does not mean that he cannot sovereignly choose to manifest his grace in new ways not yet revealed to us. God will accomplish his plan, and we can expect that it will come in surprising ways.

PARABLES OF JESUS

PARABLE	MATTHEW	MARK	LUKE	PARABLE	MATTHEW	MARK	LUKE
Lamp under a bowl	5:14-15	4:21-22	8:16; 11:33	Ten virgins	25:1-13		
Wise and foolish builders	7:24-27		6:47-49	Bags of gold (minas)	25:14-30		19:12-27
New cloth on an old coat	9:16	2:21	5:36	Sheep and goats	25:31-46		
New wine in old wineskins	9:17	2:22	5:37-38	Growing seed		4:26-29	
Sower and the soils	13:3-8, 18-23	4:3-8, 14-20	8:5-8, 11-15	Watchful servants		13:35-37	12:35-40
Weeds	13:24-30, 36-43			Moneylender			7:41-43
Mustard seed	13:31-32	4:30-32	13:18-19	Good Samaritan			10:30-37
Yeast	13:33		13:20-21	Friend in need			11:5-8
Hidden treasure	13:44			Rich fool			12:16-21
Valuable pearl	13:45-46			Unfruitful fig tree			13:6-9
Net	13:47-50			Seats and invitations			14:7-14
Owner of a house	13:52			Great banquet			14:16-24
Lost sheep	18:12-14		15:4-7	Cost of discipleship			14:28-33
Unmerciful servant	18:23-34			Lost coin			15:8-10
Workers in the vineyard	20:1-16			Lost (prodigal) son			15:11-32
Two sons	21:28-32			Shrewd manager			16:1-8
Tenants	21:33-44	12:1-11	20:9-18	Rich man and Lazarus			16:19-31
Wedding banquet	22:2-14			Master and his servant			17:7-10
Fig tree	24:32-35	13:28-29	21:29-31	Persistent widow			18:2-8
Faithful and wise servant	24:45-51		12:42-48	Pharisee and tax collector			18:10-14

those who were invited will get a taste of my banquet.'"[o]

The Cost of Being a Disciple

25Large crowds were traveling with
Jesus, and turning to them he said: 26"If
anyone comes to me and does not hate
father and mother, wife and children,
brothers and sisters — yes, even their
own life — such a person cannot be my
disciple.[p] 27And whoever does not carry
their cross and follow me cannot be my
disciple.[q]
28"Suppose one of you wants to build a

14:24 [o] Mt 21:43; Ac 13:46
14:26 [p] Mt 10:37; Jn 12:25
14:27 [q] Mt 10:38; Lk 9:23

14:25-27 Jesus' attention turns here to his followers, asking them to assess what discipleship requires. He gets right to the point. The meaning of "hate" carries a comparative force here. The idea is that if we are forced to choose between Jesus and other priorities, the winner in that choice must be Jesus. In a first-century context, those who loved family more would not even consider Jesus. Those who loved their own lives more also would not consider Jesus, since trusting him might eventually mean martyrdom. His followers must understand the cost of discipleship.

14:28-30 To get his point across clearly, Jesus uses two illustrations. The first is of a man who

tower. Won't you first sit down and estimate the cost to see if you have enough
money to complete it? 29For if you lay the
foundation and are not able to finish it,
everyone who sees it will ridicule you,
30saying, 'This person began to build and
wasn't able to finish.'

31"Or suppose a king is about to go to
war against another king. Won't he first sit
down and consider whether he is able with
ten thousand men to oppose the one coming against him with twenty thousand? 32If
he is not able, he will send a delegation
while the other is still a long way off and
will ask for terms of peace. 33In the same
way, those of you who do not give up everything you have cannot be my disciples.[r]

34"Salt is good, but if it loses its saltiness, how can it be made salty again?[s]
35It is fit neither for the soil nor for the
manure pile; it is thrown out.[t]

"Whoever has ears to hear, let them
hear."[u]

The Parable of the Lost Sheep

15:4–7pp // Mt 18:12–14

15 Now the tax collectors[v] and sinners were all gathering around to
hear Jesus. 2But the Pharisees and the
teachers of the law muttered, "This man
welcomes sinners and eats with them."[w]

3Then Jesus told them this parable:[x]
4"Suppose one of you has a hundred
sheep and loses one of them. Doesn't he
leave the ninety-nine in the open country
and go after the lost sheep until he finds
it?[y] 5And when he finds it, he joyfully puts
it on his shoulders 6and goes home. Then
he calls his friends and neighbors together and says, 'Rejoice with me; I have found
my lost sheep.'[z] 7I tell you that in the same
way there will be more rejoicing in heav-
en over one sinner who repents than over
ninety-nine righteous persons who do not
need to repent.[a]

The Parable of the Lost Coin

8"Or suppose a woman has ten silver
coins[a] and loses one. Doesn't she light a

14:33 [r] Php 3:7,8
14:34 [s] Mk 9:50
14:35 [t] Mt 5:13 [u] Mt 11:15
15:1 [v] Lk 5:29
15:2 [w] Mt 9:11
15:3 [x] Mt 13:3
15:4 [y] Ps 23; 119:176; Jer 31:10; Eze 34:11-16; Lk 5:32; 19:10
15:6 [z] ver 9
15:7 [a] ver 10

> **Lk 15:1** ❖ Why were these outcasts attracted to Jesus? What draws us you to Jesus and his words?

[a] 8 Greek *ten drachmas*, each worth about a day's wages

---

builds a watchtower over his land or over a city (vv. 28-30). How sad to start construction and not have the money to finish. In other words, moving toward successful discipleship takes reflection; it is not an automatic exercise.

14:31-33 The second parable pictures a king assessing his strength in preparation for war. If he realizes he cannot win, he will send a delegation and negotiate peace. Similarly, says Jesus, those who want to be his disciples must make such an assessment (v. 33). No one can know everything involved at the start of the journey, but one can enter the journey with an understanding that God has access to all that we are.

14:34-35 In this part of the ancient world, salt could maintain its potency for up to fifteen years. Whether used as a type of seasoning, or as a preservative, or as a catalyst for a fire, it was only useful when it was salty. If it ceased to function as salt, it was thrown away. The remark notes that God can dispense with disciples who do not complete their call. God disciplines those who are not faithful to their call; that is why he calls us to hear what he says. Discipleship takes dedication and focus, and God is concerned with how his disciples walk. Jesus wants everyone on the journey to bring to it an understanding of what it requires and to resolve to stay on the path every step of the way.

> ✤ **14:25-35** Jesus calls us not just to a decision, but into a relationship. As a learner, a disciple enters into a relationship with Jesus and embarks on a lifetime journey of learning. Grace brings a relationship with God as a gift, but included is the journey of walking by God's grace.
>
> Another application of this text requires serious self-reflection. Do I yield to the Lord in every area of my life—my possessions, my family, even my own life? Do I really trust him to care for me? Have I counted the cost of discipleship? And do I trust him to empower me to represent Jesus to a needy world?

15:1-2 In a series of three parables in ch. 15, Jesus defends his involvement with the lost. (The third is related in vv. 11-32.) Jesus once again chooses the scribes and Pharisees as the foil for his comparison. They cannot believe that he is spending so much time receiving sinners and eating with them. Jesus argues, however, that the call of God demands they spend time seeking the lost.

15:3-7 A shepherd counting a hundred sheep comes up one short and goes to look for the lost animal. We are not told if he leaves the rest of his flock with neighbors, though that is likely. He would hardly put the ninety-nine at risk for one sheep. The hunt is successful when he finds the lost animal alive and well, so the shepherd calls his friends and neighbors to celebrate the recovery of his animal. Here is a picture of God's heart and his joy at the turning of one sinner back to him. Jesus searches for sinners because heaven rejoices at their recovery.

15:8-10 The second image is similar. The "silver coin" that is in view here is equal to a denarius, or a day's wage for an average worker. It is a modest sum. The woman's search takes time and

lamp, sweep the house and search carefully until she finds it? 9And when she
finds it, she calls her friends and neighbors together and says, 'Rejoice with me;
I have found my lost coin.'[b] 10In the same
way, I tell you, there is rejoicing in the
presence of the angels of God over one
sinner who repents."[c]

The Parable of the Lost Son

11Jesus continued: "There was a man
who had two sons.[d] 12The younger one
said to his father, 'Father, give me my
share of the estate.'[e] So he divided his
property[f] between them.
13"Not long after that, the younger
son got together all he had, set off for a
distant country and there squandered
his wealth[g] in wild living. 14After he had
spent everything, there was a severe
famine in that whole country, and he began to be in need. 15So he went and hired
himself out to a citizen of that country,
who sent him to his fields to feed pigs.[h]
16He longed to fill his stomach with the
pods that the pigs were eating, but no
one gave him anything.
17"When he came to his senses, he said,
'How many of my father's hired servants
have food to spare, and here I am starving to death! 18I will set out and go back
to my father and say to him: Father, I
have sinned[i] against heaven and against
you. 19I am no longer worthy to be called
your son; make me like one of your hired
servants.' 20So he got up and went to his
father.
"But while he was still a long way off, his
father saw him and was filled with compassion for him; he ran to his son, threw
his arms around him and kissed him.[j]
21"The son said to him, 'Father, I have
sinned against heaven and against you.[k]
I am no longer worthy to be called your
son.'
22"But the father said to his servants,
'Quick! Bring the best robe[l] and put it
on him. Put a ring on his finger[m] and
sandals on his feet. 23Bring the fattened
calf and kill it. Let's have a feast and celebrate. 24For this son of mine was dead
and is alive again;[n] he was lost and is
found.' So they began to celebrate.[o]
25"Meanwhile, the older son was in the
field. When he came near the house, he
heard music and dancing. 26So he called
one of the servants and asked him what
was going on. 27'Your brother has come,'
he replied, 'and your father has killed the
fattened calf because he has him back
safe and sound.'
28"The older brother became angry[p]
and refused to go in. So his father went
out and pleaded with him. 29But he answered his father, 'Look! All these years
I've been slaving for you and never disobeyed your orders. Yet you never gave
me even a young goat so I could celebrate with my friends. 30But when this
son of yours who has squandered your

15:9 [b] ver 6
15:10 [c] ver 7
15:11 [d] Mt 21:28
15:12 [e] Dt 21:17 [f] ver 30
15:13 [g] ver 30; Lk 16:1
15:15 [h] Lev 11:7
15:18 [i] Lev 26:40; Mt 3:2
15:20 [j] Ge 45:14, 15; 46:29; Ac 20:37
15:21 [k] Ps 51:4
15:22 [l] Zec 3:4; Rev 6:11 [m] Ge 41:42
15:24 [n] Eph 2:1, 5; 5:14; 1Ti 5:6 [o] ver 32
15:28 [p] Jnh 4:1

---

effort. When she does find it, she is as excited as the shepherd was. She also calls her neighbors to celebrate with her. Again, this is a picture of heaven's joy at a sinner's repentance.

These two parables are among the simplest stories of Jesus, communicating both truth and emotion. God wants servants who understand his heart to restore sinners. In both cases, the search takes work. In both cases, what is searched for seems to be a modest object. In both cases, the recovery of what was lost leads to rejoicing with others. This imagery underscores God's desire for disciples to share the goal of winning the lost back to him.

15:1-10 This passage says much about the heart of God for engaging those who are not interested in him. He cares enough for them to go looking for them, even when they have consciously stayed away. We should be like raiders in search of great treasure—only the treasures we seek are the lost souls of vulnerable sheep. The search is not always easy, but the joy at the end makes the effort worth the cost.

15:11–12 In what would have been a shocking move to Jesus' listeners, the father in the parable grants the request of his younger son. This detail pictures a father who is letting a sinner make his own decisions and go his own way.

15:13–16 This part of the story pictures the dire circumstances that sin produces: With no one to help him, the younger son is living a tragedy.

15:17–19 The wayward son finally comes "to his senses" (v. 17). Jesus pictures the resolve and humility of one who comes and places his spiritual welfare in God's hands, asking nothing but his grace. He will rest in the father's mercy.

15:20 This part of the story is another cultural surprise. Normally a father would have waited to receive some indication of respect before responding. But God's compassion is exceptional.

15:21–24 The son is not deterred. He begins to confess, but he is cut short as he is graciously received back into the family with full honor, as if nothing has happened.

15:25–30 Learning of the situation, the older brother is angry and refuses to go in. He wants nothing to do with his lost and wayward brother. To drive

property[q] with prostitutes[r] comes home,
you kill the fattened calf for him!'
31"'My son,' the father said, 'you are
always with me, and everything I have
is yours. 32But we had to celebrate and
be glad, because this brother of yours
was dead and is alive again; he was lost
and is found.'"[s]

The Parable of the Shrewd Manager

16 Jesus told his disciples: "There was
a rich man whose manager was accused of wasting his possessions.[t] 2So he
called him in and asked him, 'What is
this I hear about you? Give an account of
your management, because you cannot
be manager any longer.'
3"The manager said to himself, 'What
shall I do now? My master is taking away
my job. I'm not strong enough to dig, and
I'm ashamed to beg — 4I know what I'll
do so that, when I lose my job here, people will welcome me into their houses.'
5"So he called in each one of his master's debtors. He asked the first, 'How
much do you owe my master?'
6"'Nine hundred gallons[a] of olive oil,'
he replied.
"The manager told him, 'Take your
bill, sit down quickly, and make it four
hundred and fifty.'
7"Then he asked the second, 'And how
much do you owe?'
"'A thousand bushels[b] of wheat,' he
replied.
"He told him, 'Take your bill and make
it eight hundred.'
8"The master commended the dishonest manager because he had acted shrewdly. For the people of this world[u] are more
shrewd[v] in dealing with their own kind
than are the people of the light.[w] 9I tell
you, use worldly wealth[x] to gain friends
for yourselves, so that when it is gone, you
will be welcomed into eternal dwellings.[y]
10"Whoever can be trusted with very
little can also be trusted with much,[z] and
whoever is dishonest with very little will
also be dishonest with much. 11So if you
have not been trustworthy in handling
worldly wealth,[a] who will trust you with
true riches? 12And if you have not been
trustworthy with someone else's property,
who will give you property of your own?
13"No one can serve two masters. Either you will hate the one and love the

15:30 [q] ver 12,13 [r] Pr 29:3
15:32 [s] ver 24; Mal 3:17
16:1 [t] Lk 15:13,30
16:8 [u] Ps 17:14 [v] Ps 18:26 [w] Jn 12:36; Eph 5:8; 1Th 5:5
16:9 [x] ver 11, 13 [y] Mt 19:21; Lk 12:33
16:10 [z] Mt 25:21, 23; Lk 19:17
16:11 [a] ver 9,13

[a] 6 Or about 3,000 liters [b] 7 Or about 30 tons

---

the point home, the older brother notes the sin of "this son of yours" (v. 30; note: not "my brother").

15:31–32 The father responds without defensiveness, noting that the older son already has access to everything the father has. Given that the older son represents the Pharisees, this detail suggests that the full rights of sonship are the older son's as well, if he asks for them. But the celebration for the sibling ("this brother of yours"; v. 32) is necessary, since he is back from the dead. A sinner found is a cause to celebrate.

The story ends here. The parable pictures reversal: The son who was out of the house is now very much in, while the older son sits on the outside. The story also concludes with a point to ponder in that we are not told how the older son responds to the father.

> **15:11–32** The attitude of the father is at the center of the parable. We can be assured that God approaches with open arms sinners who turn to him. Even more, God maintains an active search for sinners, taking the initiative with them, for he sent the Son of Man "to seek and to save the lost" (19:10). He rejoices to bring the lost into his family, and he celebrates all who turn to him.

16:1–4 Facing a future on the streets, this fired manager contemplates his options. He develops a plan: His goal is simply to curry favor with his master's debtors so that they will help him. He is a prudent planner; having lost the protection of his former master, he looks for help elsewhere.

16:5–7 The manager takes inventory of those who owe his boss. In each case, he lowers the creditor's bill by sacrificing his own commission.

16:8–9 Jesus notes that the master commends "the dishonest manager" (v. 8) for his foresight. The manager has acted in light of what the future may bring and is ready for it now.

Jesus notes that people in the world give more thought to their physical well-being than the righteous do to their spiritual well-being. When the end comes and no more money is available, the one who has seen into the future and acted prudently will have been wise with the resources and stewardship God has given.

16:10–11 Who can entrust people with significant things of real value if they cannot handle worldly wealth? Jesus drives for a character in his disciples that reflects God's integrity, generosity, and grace.

16:13 A person in this world is faced with a fundamental choice of allegiance. No servant can serve two masters. If the resources we receive are a stewardship from God to be used in service to him and to others, then to serve God is to give our resources to meet the needs of those around us. Someday God will evaluate whether we have handled our resources in a way that anticipates his desires and values; if we have, we will receive his commendation.

> **16:1–13** How conscious are we that what we own is not really ours but has been loaned to us from the Lord, who wishes to see how faithfully we use his resources to serve those

> **Lk 16:15** ❖ In today's world, what do people "value highly"? Is this detestable to God, as Jesus says? Why or why not?

other, or you will be devoted to the one
and despise the other. You cannot serve
both God and money."[b]
14 The Pharisees, who loved money,[c]
heard all this and were sneering at
Jesus.[d] 15 He said to them, "You are the
ones who justify yourselves[e] in the eyes
of others, but God knows your hearts.[f]
What people value highly is detestable
in God's sight.

Additional Teachings

16 "The Law and the Prophets were proclaimed until John.[g] Since that time, the
good news of the kingdom of God is being preached,[h] and everyone is forcing
their way into it. 17 It is easier for heaven
and earth to disappear than for the least
stroke of a pen to drop out of the Law.[i]

16:13 [b] ver 9,11; Mt 6:24
16:14 [c] 1Ti 3:3 [d] Lk 23:35
16:15 [e] Lk 10:29 [f] 1Sa 16:7; Rev 2:23
16:16 [g] Mt 11:12, 13 [h] Mt 4:23
16:17 [i] Mt 5:18
16:18 [j] Mt 5:31, 32; 19:9; Mk 10:11; Ro 7:2,3; 1Co 7:10,11
16:19 [k] Eze 16:49
16:20 [l] Ac 3:2
16:21 [m] Mt 15:27
16:24 [n] ver 30; Lk 3:8 [o] Mt 5:22

18 "Anyone who divorces his wife and
marries another woman commits adultery, and the man who marries a divorced woman commits adultery.[j]

The Rich Man and Lazarus

19 "There was a rich man who was
dressed in purple and fine linen and
lived in luxury every day.[k] 20 At his gate
was laid a beggar[l] named Lazarus, covered with sores 21 and longing to eat what
fell from the rich man's table.[m] Even the
dogs came and licked his sores.
22 "The time came when the beggar
died and the angels carried him to Abraham's side. The rich man also died and
was buried. 23 In Hades, where he was in
torment, he looked up and saw Abraham
far away, with Lazarus by his side. 24 So he
called to him, 'Father Abraham,[n] have pity
on me and send Lazarus to dip the tip of
his finger in water and cool my tongue,
because I am in agony in this fire.'[o]
25 "But Abraham replied, 'Son, remember that in your lifetime you received

---

> in need? Jesus will soon reinforce such questions in 16:19–31, where he raises the question of how a poor, needy man named Lazarus was treated by a rich man.

16:14–15 The Pharisees' love for money has put them out of touch with Jesus' message. Jesus can hardly use a stronger word than what the NIV translates as "detestable" (v. 15). On the continuum that measure values, God and the Pharisees are on opposite ends.

16:16–17 God's plan divides into two periods: Law and Prophets, and kingdom. The boundary line is John the Baptist's ministry. The call of Jesus begins the realization of that promise. Now the kingdom is being proclaimed.

The last part of v. 16 is disputed. The word "is forcing" can be read differently. Many prefer to translate it, "Everyone is urged insistently to enter in." With this reading, the emphasis is on the preached word, which is what Jesus gives here.

16:18 Jesus closes with a note about divorce to illustrate that the ethical call of the kingdom is rooted in an integrity that matches the integrity of the period of the Law and the Prophets. If anyone makes a commitment before God in marriage and then divorces, this represents adultery, not only because it is an act of unfaithfulness but also because it is a violation of an original vow made before God. To break that commitment and remarry is to commit adultery.

> ✣ **16:14–18** The Christian community should be a place where integrity, transformation, and growth are evident. God has brought us into relationship with him to renew us as his image bearers. The essence of the community is that its dynamic will change us so that we become more like Christ. We must think through how to keep this fundamental dynamic of the Christian life vibrant and not be shaped by the values of our fallen world.

16:19–31 This story does not recount a historical interchange between two specific men. The details of the discussion in the afterlife, including the rich man's ability to engage Abraham in discussion, show its symbolic character. Yet it shows in a very real way the realities of our accountability before God.

16:19–21 The first portion of the account contrasts the condition of the rich man with that of Lazarus. The man is very wealthy; in contrast, Lazarus lies at his gate, begging and having his sores licked by wild dogs. This licking is significant since it makes Lazarus ceremonially unclean. His situation is as tragic as the rich man's is sumptuous.

16:22 Death is the great equalizer. Possessions and status symbols are left behind. Lazarus is in; the rich man is out. The standards of the afterlife are different from those of the appearances of this world.

16:23–24 The rich man looks up and sees Abraham and Lazarus together. Several points are worth noting here. First, the heat of torment may well depict the intense agony of being confined to the underworld, knowing that God exists and that one is not in heaven. Second, the rich man knew the poor man was out there, had needs, and even knew his name. Finally, the rich man's view of Lazarus has not changed since his death. He still views him as beneath him, as someone who might to be sent to give him relief.

16:25–26 What the rich man enacted in the past in refusing to help Lazarus is now being turned

your good things, while Lazarus received
bad things,[p] but now he is comforted
here and you are in agony.[q] 26And besides all this, between us and you a great
chasm has been set in place, so that those
who want to go from here to you cannot,
nor can anyone cross over from there
to us.'
27"He answered, 'Then I beg you, father, send Lazarus to my family, 28for I
have five brothers. Let him warn them,[r]
so that they will not also come to this
place of torment.'
29"Abraham replied, 'They have Moses[s] and the Prophets;[t] let them listen
to them.'
30" 'No, father Abraham,'[u] he said, 'but
if someone from the dead goes to them,
they will repent.'
31"He said to him, 'If they do not listen
to Moses and the Prophets, they will not
be convinced even if someone rises from
the dead.' "

16:25 [p] Ps 17:14 [q] Lk 6:21,24,25
16:28 [r] Ac 2:40; 20:23; 1Th 4:6
16:29 [s] Lk 24:27, 44; Jn 5:45-47; Ac 15:21 [t] Lk 4:17; Jn 1:45
16:30 [u] ver 24; Lk 3:8
17:1 [v] Mt 5:29 [w] Mt 18:7
17:2 [x] Mk 10:24; Lk 10:21 [y] Mt 5:29

Sin, Faith, Duty

17 Jesus said to his disciples: "Things
that cause people to stumble[v] are
bound to come, but woe to anyone
through whom they come.[w] 2It would be
better for them to be thrown into the sea
with a millstone tied around their neck
than to cause one of these little ones[x] to
stumble.[y] 3So watch yourselves.
"If your brother or sister[a] sins against
you, rebuke them;[z] and if they repent,
forgive them.[a] 4Even if they sin against
you seven times in a day and seven times
come back to you saying 'I repent,' you
must forgive them."[b]
5The apostles[c] said to the Lord,[d] "Increase our faith!"
6He replied, "If you have faith as small
as a mustard seed,[e] you can say to this
mulberry tree, 'Be uprooted and planted
in the sea,' and it will obey you.[f]
7"Suppose one of you has a servant
plowing or looking after the sheep. Will
he say to the servant when he comes in
from the field, 'Come along now and
sit down to eat'? 8Won't he rather say,
'Prepare my supper, get yourself ready
and wait on me[g] while I eat and drink;
after that you may eat and drink'? 9Will
he thank the servant because he did
what he was told to do? 10So you also,
when you have done everything you
were told to do, should say, 'We are unworthy servants; we have only done our
duty.' "[h]

17:3 [z] Mt 18:15 [a] Eph 4:32; Col 3:13
17:4 [b] Mt 18:21, 22
17:5 [c] Mk 6:30 [d] Lk 7:13
17:6 [e] Mt 13:31; 17:20; Lk 13:19 [f] Mt 21:21; Mk 9:23
17:8 [g] Lk 12:37
17:10 [h] 1Co 9:16

Lk 17:5-6 ❖ What does "mustard seed" faith looks like? How does its promise and potential affect life in the world today?

[a] 3 The Greek word for *brother or sister* (*adelphos*) refers here to a fellow disciple, whether man or woman.

on him, with one crucial difference: The current setup is permanent.

16:27–28 Abraham's reply to the rich man's plea is that God's word has made clear what he desires: Our devotion to him is seen in our care for others.

16:29–31 The rich man persists. He insists something spectacular and supernatural will change his family's minds. Those reading the parable in the Gospel, knowing the story of Jesus, are aware of the truth of this remark: Jesus' resurrection convinced only some that God was working through him. The parable closes with a dark and tragic note about how humanity often misses the opportunities God makes available.

✣ **16:19–31** The parable is designed to have us reflect on how we respond to people like Lazarus. A compassionate heart sees need and moves to help. If we find it difficult to help someone in need, then this parable exposes the hard quality in our hearts that God desires to soften (see Mic 6:8).

17:1–2 Jesus takes very seriously the offense of causing others to sin.

17:3–4 Equally important is the need to forgive. A sinner's repentance should produce the church's and a family's forgiveness. Both are to be supportive environments where forgiveness is central. The possibility of forgiveness raises the question of how often forgiveness should follow repentance. Jesus answers that seven times a day is required—a figurative way of saying that forgiveness should be given as often as repentance occurs.

17:5–6 Another key characteristic of discipleship is having faith. The issue for Jesus is not the amount of faith but its presence.

17:7–10 A final image in the passage is a short parable about service. As we live the Christian life and work to expand the kingdom, our attitude should be that we have only done our duty. Obedience is not a matter of merit (though God does honor it), but of duty.

✣ **17:1–10** This passage requires us to reflect on why communities are so slow to forgive. It is too easy to want to make people pay in full for their failures rather than to create an environment where restoration is possible. We must consider how to make our communities sensitive to sin but not closed to grace.

PEOPLE TO KNOW // MAN WITH LEPROSY WHO RETURNED

LUKE 17:11–19: Luke more than any other Gospel writer includes the stories of marginalized people. This may be because Luke himself was a Gentile and therefore a relative outsider to the Jewish-Christian story. In Luke 17, the evangelist shares the story of one of the most marginalized characters of all: a Samaritan leper.

Lepers were relegated to the outskirts of town, unable to return to village life until their skin disease had healed. Samaritans were hated by the Jews, regarded as half-breeds. Though Jews needed to cross through Samaritan territory to travel from Galilee to Jerusalem, some elected to cross the Jordan and take the long route simply to avoid Samaritan contact.

In Luke 17, Jesus was on his way to Jerusalem and was near the border of Galilee and Samaria. Ten lepers called out to him from a distance, asking Jesus to take pity on them. Jesus said to them, "Go, show yourselves to the priests" (Lk 17:14). They did so and they were cleansed.

One of the ten, a Samaritan man, returned to Jesus, praising God in a loud voice. He fell at Jesus' feet and thanked him. Jesus marveled that no one had returned to praise God except this Samaritan, to whom he then said, "Your faith has made you well."

APPLICATION Jesus praises the faith of the most hated kind of person in his community—not only a leper but a Samaritan leper. Clearly, Jesus does not judge people the way the world judges people. This should fill us with joy, knowing that what matters is not how the world sees us but how God sees us. Further, the Samaritan's story should remind us to be people of gratitude, thankful to God for all he has given us, and never neglecting to bring our thanks and praise to him for all the wonders he has performed in offering us salvation.

Jesus Heals Ten Men With Leprosy

11Now on his way to Jerusalem,[i] Jesus
traveled along the border between Samaria and Galilee.[j] 12As he was going
into a village, ten men who had leprosy[a][k] met him. They stood at a distance[l]
13and called out in a loud voice, "Jesus,
Master,[m] have pity on us!"

14When he saw them, he said, "Go, show yourselves to the priests."[n] And as they went, they were cleansed.

15One of them, when he saw he was healed, came back, praising God[o] in a loud
voice. 16He threw himself at Jesus' feet and thanked him—and he was a Samaritan.[p]

17Jesus asked, "Were not all ten cleansed? Where are the other nine?
18Has no one returned to give praise to God except this foreigner?" 19Then he
said to him, "Rise and go; your faith has made you well."[q]

17:11 [i] Lk 9:51 [j] Lk 9:51,52; Jn 4:3,4
17:12 [k] Mt 8:2 [l] Lev 13:45,46
17:13 [m] Lk 5:5
17:14 [n] Lev 14:2; Mt 8:4
17:15 [o] Mt 9:8
17:16 [p] Mt 10:5
17:19 [q] Mt 9:22

[a] 12 The Greek word traditionally translated *leprosy* was used for various diseases affecting the skin.

17:11–14 This miracle contains a double level of cultural tension since the main figure is both a leper and a Samaritan. Lepers were culturally isolated, and Samaritans were detested by Jews. The fact that these ten lepers draw near to Jesus says a lot, since lepers were expected to isolate themselves from people.

The lepers ask for mercy. This is a cry for compassion, a request that comes frequently to Jesus. Jesus immediately removes any doubt about his desire to show compassion. If they believe Jesus, they will obey what he tells them to do next. As the lepers turn, they are healed. This event pictures God's grace.

17:15–16 One of the men breaks from the group, falls at Jesus' feet, and offers thanksgiving for his healing. Luke notes that the man is a Samaritan. In some cases, those most sensitive to the gospel come from outside the community of faith.

17:17–19 Jesus then issues a final encouraging commendation. Jesus is probably saying that although ten have experienced the blessing of healing, only one has experienced salvation. Faith and salvation again merge.

17:11–19 The reaction of the nine in not returning thanks to Jesus shows how often we tend to take God's gracious actions for granted. When we realize that our blessings are a result of God's grace, it makes us into gentler, more grateful people. Such an attitude prevents us from assessing life in terms of what we are "owed," an attitude that can sow seeds of anger and bitterness.

The Coming of the Kingdom of God

17:26,27pp // Mt 24:37–39

20Once, on being asked by the Pharisees when the kingdom of God would
come,[r] Jesus replied, "The coming of the
kingdom of God is not something that
can be observed, 21nor will people say,
'Here it is,' or 'There it is,'[s] because the
kingdom of God is in your midst."[a]
22Then he said to his disciples, "The
time is coming when you will long to
see one of the days of the Son of Man,[t]
but you will not see it.[u] 23People will tell
you, 'There he is!' or 'Here he is!' Do not
go running off after them.[v] 24For the Son
of Man in his day[b] will be like the lightning,[w] which flashes and lights up the
sky from one end to the other. 25But first
he must suffer many things[x] and be rejected[y] by this generation.[z]
26"Just as it was in the days of Noah,[a]
so also will it be in the days of the Son
of Man. 27People were eating, drinking,
marrying and being given in marriage
up to the day Noah entered the ark. Then
the flood came and destroyed them all.
28"It was the same in the days of Lot.[b]
People were eating and drinking, buying
and selling, planting and building. 29But
the day Lot left Sodom, fire and sulfur
rained down from heaven and destroyed
them all.
30"It will be just like this on the day the
Son of Man is revealed.[c] 31On that day no
one who is on the housetop, with possessions inside, should go down to get them.
Likewise, no one in the field should go

17:20 [r] Mt 3:2
17:21 [s] ver 23
17:22 [t] Mt 8:20 [u] Mt 9:15; Lk 5:35
17:23 [v] Mt 24:23; Mk 13:21; Lk 21:8
17:24 [w] Mt 24:27
17:25 [x] Mt 16:21 [y] Lk 9:22; 18:32 [z] Mk 13:30; Lk 21:32
17:26 [a] Ge 7:6-24
17:28 [b] Ge 19:1-28
17:30 [c] Mt 10:23; 16:27; 24:3, 27,37,39; 25:31; 1Co 1:7; 1Th 2:19; 2Th 1:7; 2:8; 2Pe 3:4; Rev 1:7
17:31 [d] Mt 24:17, 18; Mk 13:15-16
17:32 [e] Ge 19:26
17:33 [f] Jn 12:25
17:35 [g] Mt 24:41
17:37 [h] Mt 24:28
18:1 [i] Isa 40:31; Lk 11:5-8; Ac 1:14; Ro 12:12; Eph 6:18; Col 4:2; 1Th 5:17
18:3 [j] Isa 1:17
18:5 [k] Lk 11:8
18:6 [l] Lk 7:13
18:7 [m] Ex 22:23; Ps 88:1; Rev 6:10

back for anything.[d] 32Remember Lot's
wife![e] 33Whoever tries to keep their life
will lose it, and whoever loses their life
will preserve it.[f] 34I tell you, on that night
two people will be in one bed; one will be
taken and the other left. 35Two women
will be grinding grain together; one will
be taken and the other left."[g] [36][c]
37"Where, Lord?" they asked.
He replied, "Where there is a dead
body, there the vultures will gather."[h]

The Parable of the Persistent Widow

18 Then Jesus told his disciples a parable to show them that they should
always pray and not give up.[i] 2He said:
"In a certain town there was a judge who
neither feared God nor cared what people thought. 3And there was a widow in
that town who kept coming to him with
the plea, 'Grant me justice[j] against my
adversary.'
4"For some time he refused. But finally
he said to himself, 'Even though I don't
fear God or care what people think, 5yet
because this widow keeps bothering me,
I will see that she gets justice, so that she
won't eventually come and attack me!'"[k]
6And the Lord[l] said, "Listen to what
the unjust judge says. 7And will not God
bring about justice for his chosen ones,
who cry out[m] to him day and night? Will
he keep putting them off? 8I tell you, he
will see that they get justice, and quickly.

[a] 21 Or *is within you* [b] 24 Some manuscripts do not have *in his day.* [c] 36 Some manuscripts include here words similar to Matt. 24:40.

17:20 Jews expected that the kingdom would come at once and with cosmic signs. Jesus begins his reply by noting that the kingdom does not come with signs to be observed.

17:21 This is one of the key kingdom verses in the NT. It is best to take this verse as teaching that the initial display of the kingdom has come with Jesus' ministry. The Pharisees are looking for the wrong things.

17:22–25 Jesus indicates that the expected day of the Son of Man's coming in power is a day they will long for but will not see. That is, the powerful display of that day is still coming. One crucial event must precede all of this: the suffering of the Son of Man.

17:26–29 Jesus compares the nature of the messianic judgment to two great periods of judgment against humanity. Both comparisons picture the absolute finality of God's judgment. The idea that there is a second chance on the judgment day is a myth as far as the Bible is concerned.

17:30–33 Such misplaced allegiance is why Jesus says that the person who seeks to save their life will lose it. Deciding to honor God may mean suffering now, but it means eternal glory later. We must be faithful until he comes.

17:34–37 Jesus' words that "one will be taken and the other left" involve the separation of the righteous from the unrighteous. The disciples' question "Where?" (v. 37) asks about the location of such judgment. Jesus deflects the question by pointing to the mood and reality of what he is saying: The day of the Son of Man will be a day of judgment. When he is done, only vultures will remain for those left in judgment.

18:1–8a What makes this parable so effective are its two characters, with whom we can easily identify. Jesus' argument goes that if a judge who is no respecter of persons hears the cry of the widow, how much more will a compassionate God hear the cries of his people?

The Lord asks us to reflect on the judge's reaction to the persistent requests of the woman. God will vindicate his people who constantly cry out to him and will judge those who persecute the righteous (v. 8a).

However, when the Son of Man[n] comes,[o]
will he find faith on the earth?"

The Parable of the Pharisee and the Tax Collector

9 To some who were confident of their
own righteousness[p] and looked down on
everyone else,[q] Jesus told this parable:
10 "Two men went up to the temple to pray,[r]
one a Pharisee and the other a tax collector. 11 The Pharisee stood by himself[s] and
prayed: 'God, I thank you that I am not like
other people — robbers, evildoers, adulterers — or even like this tax collector. 12 I fast[t]
twice a week and give a tenth[u] of all I get.'
13 "But the tax collector stood at a distance. He would not even look up to
heaven, but beat his breast[v] and said,
'God, have mercy on me, a sinner.'[w]
14 "I tell you that this man, rather than
the other, went home justified before
God. For all those who exalt themselves
will be humbled, and those who humble
themselves will be exalted."[x]

The Little Children and Jesus

18:15–17pp // Mt 19:13–15; Mk 10:13–16

15 People were also bringing babies
to Jesus for him to place his hands on

Lk 18:14 ❖ How can we humble ourselves like the tax collector did in Jesus' parable? Why should we?

them. When the disciples saw this, they
rebuked them. 16 But Jesus called the
children to him and said, "Let the little children come to me, and do not
hinder them, for the kingdom of God
belongs to such as these. 17 Truly I tell
you, anyone who will not receive the
kingdom of God like a little child[y] will
never enter it."

The Rich and the Kingdom of God

18:18–30pp // Mt 19:16–29; Mk 10:17–30

18 A certain ruler asked him, "Good
teacher, what must I do to inherit eternal life?"[z]
19 "Why do you call me good?" Jesus
answered. "No one is good — except God
alone. 20 You know the commandments:
'You shall not commit adultery, you shall
not murder, you shall not steal, you shall
not give false testimony, honor your father and mother.'[a]"[a]

[a] 20 Exodus 20:12-16; Deut. 5:16-20

18:8 [n] Mt 8:20 [o] Mt 16:27
18:9 [p] Lk 16:15 [q] Isa 65:5
18:10 [r] Ac 3:1
18:11 [s] Mt 6:5; Mk 11:25
18:12 [t] Isa 58:3; Mt 9:14 [u] Mal 3:8; Lk 11:42
18:13 [v] Isa 66:2; Jer 31:19; Lk 23:48 [w] Lk 5:32; 1Ti 1:15
18:14 [x] Mt 23:12; Lk 14:11
18:17 [y] Mt 11:25; 18:3
18:18 [z] Lk 10:25
18:20 [a] Ex 20:12-16; Dt 5:16-20; Ro 13:9

18:8b One final thought remains. When total vindication comes, will the Son of Man "find faith on the earth?" (v. 8b). In other words, will the delay, which is to some degree assumed in the parable, affect the faith of some, since Jesus calls us not to give up? The question is not answered.

❖ **17:20—18:8** Jesus talks about the end in grim terms and gruesome detail to make clear how serious the issue of judgment is for God. Judgment means accountability. In a society that tends to view adults as accountable only to themselves and their own consciences, it is a critical reminder that God holds us responsible for our actions. This text urges every person to choose wisely when it comes to the things of God: There is too much at stake to make the wrong choice.

Furthermore, every moment until the Lord returns is an opportunity to be God's instrument in changing the destiny of someone who does not yet know him, keeping our eyes focused on what is yet to come.

18:9–14 This parable is really the parable of the two prayers. The text is explicit about its audience (v. 9).
18:10–12 The Pharisee is grateful that he is not like other people. When the Pharisee is done, his prayer in effect is, "I thank you, God, that I am so great!" In fact, one gets the impression that God should be honored that this "faithful" Pharisee is on his team.
18:13 The tax collector does not stand up but approaches God with a sense of distance. He does not look up to heaven but beats his chest, a sign of contrition, fully aware that he approaches God as a sinner. He comes to God desiring only to improve his relationship to God.
18:14 Jesus' comment closes the passage: Those who exalt themselves will be humbled, while the humbled will be lifted up. What counts is a heart that appreciates what God can give.
18:15–17 Jesus invites the children to come to him because they are important people. One must trust God with the simple faith and humility of a dependent child. Entrance into the kingdom is a matter of humility that recognizes a need for God.

❖ **18:9–17** In our assertive society, pride often gets the accolades despite what it does to relationships and character. Pride makes the task more important than the people. The objective becomes the obstacle to human relationships. Jesus condemned pride because it is so insidiously destructive.

Humility is harder to discuss because it does not discuss itself. It simply gets out there and serves, often with sacrifice. It does not claim rights; it tries to do what is right. It does not brag about integrity; it displays it. Sometimes it is easy to miss what does not point to itself. But God sees the humble heart and lifts it up in honor. That is Jesus' challenge to us.

18:18–20 The ruler addresses Jesus as "Good

21“All these I have kept since I was a
boy,” he said.
22When Jesus heard this, he said to
him, “You still lack one thing. Sell everything you have and give to the poor,[b] and
you will have treasure in heaven.[c] Then
come, follow me.”
23When he heard this, he became very
sad, because he was very wealthy. 24Jesus
looked at him and said, “How hard it is
for the rich to enter the kingdom of God![d]
25Indeed, it is easier for a camel to go
through the eye of a needle than for
someone who is rich to enter the kingdom of God.”
26Those who heard this asked, “Who
then can be saved?”
27Jesus replied, “What is impossible
with man is possible with God.”[e]
28Peter said to him, “We have left all
we had to follow you!”[f]
29“Truly I tell you,” Jesus said to them,
“no one who has left home or wife or
brothers or sisters or parents or children
for the sake of the kingdom of God 30will
fail to receive many times as much in this
age, and in the age to come[g] eternal life.”[h]

18:22 [b] Ac 2:45 [c] Mt 6:20
18:24 [d] Pr 11:28
18:27 [e] Mt 19:26
18:28 [f] Mt 4:19
18:30 [g] Mt 12:32 [h] Mt 25:46
18:31 [i] Lk 9:51 [j] Ps 22; Isa 53 [k] Mt 8:20
18:32 [l] Lk 23:1
18:33 [m] Mt 16:21 [n] Ac 2:23 [o] Mt 16:21 [p] Mt 16:21
18:34 [q] Mk 9:32; Lk 9:45
18:35 [r] Lk 19:1
18:37 [s] Lk 19:4
18:38 [t] ver 39; Mt 9:27 [u] Mt 17:15; Lk 18:13

Jesus Predicts His Death a Third Time

18:31–33pp // Mt 20:17–19; Mk 10:32–34

31Jesus took the Twelve aside and told
them, “We are going up to Jerusalem,[i]
and everything that is written by the
prophets[j] about the Son of Man[k] will be
fulfilled. 32He will be delivered over to
the Gentiles.[l] They will mock him, insult him and spit on him; 33they will flog
him[m] and kill him.[n] On the third day[o] he
will rise again.”[p]
34The disciples did not understand any
of this. Its meaning was hidden from
them, and they did not know what he
was talking about.[q]

A Blind Beggar Receives His Sight

18:35–43pp // Mt 20:29–34; Mk 10:46–52

35As Jesus approached Jericho,[r] a blind
man was sitting by the roadside begging.
36When he heard the crowd going by, he
asked what was happening. 37They told
him, “Jesus of Nazareth is passing by.”[s]
38He called out, “Jesus, Son of David,[t]
have mercy[u] on me!”
39Those who led the way rebuked him
and told him to be quiet, but he shouted

---

teacher,” perhaps in an attempt to gain a good hearing. But Jesus puts the ruler on notice at the start that he will not be won over with a flattering greeting, warning the man that only God is good.

The issue of goodness raises the question of honoring God. Loving God first from the heart means not being drawn away into various expressions of idolatry that the world offers. One of the key dangers of wealth is that possessions come first, while people slip down the priority list.

18:21–22 The ruler replies that he has been obedient to the commands since his youth, and Jesus' charge is that he walk away from his great wealth and give it all away, instead investing in a more permanent treasure. The combination is crucial to understanding the nature of Jesus' reply. Will this man prefer what earth can give him or what heaven offers? This is not a test of works but a probing of his heart.

18:23 The man reacts with sadness. He is wealthy and would have to give up much. Jesus implies that the personal identity of a rich person is so bound up with the things of this earth that it is all but impossible for him to turn everything over to God's care.

18:24–28 Jesus' remarks to the rich man have traumatized the disciples. The rich were often seen as blessed. Have they done what Jesus is asking the ruler to do? Jesus' reply responds favorably to Peter.

18:29–30 The passage ends with the same topic that began it: “eternal life” (v. 30). Jesus is saying to Peter that God has made possible what would have otherwise been impossible.

18:18–30 This passage challenges us to ask where our fundamental anchors of identity lie. Possessions can be one such anchor. They can distract our sight from what is ultimately important and chain our hearts to the wrong point of identity. What is really frightening is how easy it is for all of us to choose earth over heaven. We do not, of course, have to be perfect to be saved, but God's people must recognize just how important trust in him is. Through hearts focused on the Lord, we receive eternal life and come to know him more fully.

18:31–33 Jesus announces they are heading to Jerusalem to fulfill all the prophets have written, emphasizing that the events to come are part of a divine design. Nothing catches Jesus off guard. Jesus will be given over to the Gentiles, who will mock, insult, spit on, flog, and then kill him. On the third day, he will rise again. After suffering will be glory and vindication.

Jesus' life fulfills Jewish prophecy, yet it is full of surprises as to how that fulfillment comes. Even those who most closely follow Jesus find these events incomprehensible.

18:34 It is often difficult to appreciate just how surprising Jesus' words in vv. 31–33 were for the original disciples.

18:35–38 Ironically, while many struggle to see who Jesus is, a blind man has full clarity of vision. In calling Jesus the “Son of David,” the blind man recognizes that Jesus is the promised Messiah of God. The blind man wants Jesus to exercise the power he has heard about on his behalf.

18:39–43 The popular perception is that this blind man is too insignificant to warrant Jesus' attention. The crowd is wrong. Even on his way to Jerusalem

all the more, "Son of David, have mercy on me!"[v]

40Jesus stopped and ordered the man to be brought to him. When he came near, Jesus asked him, 41"What do you want me to do for you?"

"Lord, I want to see," he replied.

42Jesus said to him, "Receive your sight; your faith has healed you."[w] 43Immediately he received his sight and followed Jesus, praising God. When all the people saw it, they also praised God.[x]

Zacchaeus the Tax Collector

19 Jesus entered Jericho[y] and was passing through. 2A man was there by the name of Zacchaeus; he was a chief tax collector and was wealthy. 3He wanted to see who Jesus was, but because he was short he could not see over the crowd. 4So he ran ahead and climbed a sycamore-fig[z] tree to see him, since Jesus was coming that way.[a]

5When Jesus reached the spot, he looked up and said to him, "Zacchaeus, come down immediately. I must stay at your house today." 6So he came down at once and welcomed him gladly.

7All the people saw this and began to mutter, "He has gone to be the guest of a sinner."[b]

18:39 [v]ver 38
18:42 [w]Mt 9:22
18:43 [x]Mt 9:8; Lk 13:17
19:1 [y]Lk 18:35
19:4 [z]1Ki 10:27; 1Ch 27:28; Isa 9:10 [a]Lk 18:37
19:7 [b]Mt 9:11

---

and his eventual death, Jesus is concerned about people like this blind man. Jesus asks the man what he wants—probably to draw out his faith—grants his request and notes that his faith has delivered him.

Jesus not only opens this man's eyes but also affirms that the blind man can now walk on the road with his eyes on God. His faith has brought deliverance and sight.

May this man's answer to Jesus' question in v. 41 be the answer that all believers give to their Savior's crucial question. Those who approach God confident that he can make them see are given spiritual sight.

✣ **18:31–43** The disciples' failure to see God's ways challenges us to ask ourselves whether we miss God's direction in our lives because we do not want to see the hard parts of his call. Such questions are answered in silent moments of private reflection or through interaction with those who know us well. Are we hesitant to step out in faith because we cannot guarantee the results? The road God wants us to travel is not always the most comfortable one.

Of course, recognizing Jesus as the Son of David is the basis of everything pictured in this passage. Luke never stops making the identity of Jesus the issue of this Gospel. This passage asks the questions in visual terms: Do you see who Jesus is, or are you blind? Blindness becomes sight when we turn to him.

19:1–5 Jesus' stay with the tax collector is necessary because it pictures what his ministry is all about—to lead the "hopeless cases" to God.

19:6–7 One who has simply sought to get a glimpse of the teacher now gets to meet him face to face,

PEOPLE TO KNOW // ZACCHAEUS

LUKE 19:1–10: Zacchaeus was a wealthy chief tax collector in Jericho. Tax collectors in Jesus' day were despised by the Jews. They were viewed as traitors who took money from their own people on behalf of Rome—and who skimmed off some of it for themselves too.

When Jesus passed through Jericho on his way to Jerusalem, Zacchaeus wanted to see him (Lk 19:3). However, Zacchaeus had a practical problem: He was short in stature and could not see over the crowd. Coming up with a creative solution, Zacchaeus climbed up a sycamore-fig tree to secure a good vantage point.

His life took a turn when Jesus stopped at the foot of the tree and said to Zacchaeus, "I must stay at your house today" (Lk 19:5). Zacchaeus gladly welcomed Jesus. He never expected that he, a tax collector, would play host to a religious teacher like Jesus.

Onlookers scoffed at Jesus for entering a tax collector's home; they considered Zacchaeus a sinner and traitor. But Zacchaeus penitently proclaimed his change of heart, vowing to give half his wealth to the poor and promising to pay back anyone he had cheated. Jesus declared that salvation had come to Zacchaeus's house and that Zacchaeus, too, was a son of Abraham. The outcast was welcomed back into the fold.

APPLICATION ✣ Zacchaeus shows us Christ's compassionate heart for people who are outcasts. Jesus disregarded the judgments of others when he went to Zacchaeus's house. Still today, God's heart goes out to the lost and the outcast, the hated and the rejected. Our task is to show the heart of Jesus to such people. As Jesus himself said to Zacchaeus, "The Son of Man came to seek and to save the lost" (Lk 19:10).

8But Zacchaeus stood up and said to the
Lord,[c] "Look, Lord! Here and now I give
half of my possessions to the poor, and if
I have cheated anybody out of anything,[d]
I will pay back four times the amount."[e]
9Jesus said to him, "Today salvation
has come to this house, because this man,
too, is a son of Abraham.[f] 10For the Son of
Man came to seek and to save the lost."[g]

The Parable of the Ten Minas

19:12–27Ref // Mt 25:14–30

11While they were listening to this, he
went on to tell them a parable, because
he was near Jerusalem and the people
thought that the kingdom of God[h] was
going to appear at once.[i] 12He said: "A man
of noble birth went to a distant country to
have himself appointed king and then to
return. 13So he called ten of his servants[j]
and gave them ten minas.[a] 'Put this money to work,' he said, 'until I come back.'
14"But his subjects hated him and sent
a delegation after him to say, 'We don't
want this man to be our king.'
15"He was made king, however, and
returned home. Then he sent for the servants to whom he had given the money,
in order to find out what they had gained
with it.
16"The first one came and said, 'Sir,
your mina has earned ten more.'
17" 'Well done, my good servant!'[k] his
master replied. 'Because you have been
trustworthy in a very small matter, take
charge of ten cities.'[l]
18"The second came and said, 'Sir, your
mina has earned five more.'
19"His master answered, 'You take
charge of five cities.'
20"Then another servant came and
said, 'Sir, here is your mina; I have kept it
laid away in a piece of cloth. 21I was afraid
of you, because you are a hard man. You
take out what you did not put in and reap
what you did not sow.'[m]
22"His master replied, 'I will judge
you by your own words,[n] you wicked

Lk 19:20-21 ❖ Should we be afraid of God in the same way the servant in the parable feared his master? Why or why not?

19:8 [c] Lk 7:13 [d] Lk 3:12, 13 [e] Ex 22:1; Lev 6:4,5; Nu 5:7; 2Sa 12:6
19:9 [f] Lk 3:8; 13:16; Ro 4:16; Gal 3:7
19:10 [g] Eze 34:12,16; Jn 3:17
19:11 [h] Mt 3:2 [i] Lk 17:20; Ac 1:6
19:13 [j] Mk 13:34
19:17 [k] Pr 27:18 [l] Lk 16:10
19:21 [m] Mt 25:24
19:22 [n] 2Sa 1:16; Job 15:6

[a] *13* A mina was about three months' wages.

---

but Jesus' choice of a host for the day is widely criticized. Zacchaeus is indeed a sinner, but Jesus does not write off those who remain open to God.
19:8 Zacchaeus expresses his appreciation of Jesus' acceptance by declaring his intent to be a different man. In Zacchaeus's changed heart, love for God expresses itself in love for others.

Giving away half of one's possessions serves as a rhetorical way of stating that one should place their possessions under God's stewardship. The resources we possess are the Lord's, and he guides us in how we are to use them.
19:9-10 Jesus endorses the response fully, noting that Zacchaeus's actions testify to a heart changed by the presence of God.

✣ **19:1-10** One of the errors sincere Christians can make is to separate themselves from the world in such a way that they lose contact with sinners. Usually two factors feed such isolation: a healthy desire not to succumb to standards of living that destroy moral integrity, and a subtle but deadly feeling of superiority that we are inherently better than others. This second element in the equation can squeeze out our ability to empathize with the sinner's plight. It forgets that our blessing is the result of God's gracious work, not anything about our character.

Another key application in this passage comes in the portrait of faith. Faith transforms people. Admitting wrong, asking for forgiveness, and trying to make restitution are like a spring shower that can open up the possibility of a fresh start. Finally, we can also see something of ourselves in the story of Zacchaeus. How often do we lose sight of the coming of Jesus? The moment we forget our continual need for renewal, we risk slipping into the self-delusion that we are somehow spiritually independent.

19:11-27 Luke is clear about why Jesus tells this parable. Jesus must inform his disciples that the full expression of kingdom authority will not come until his return, and he must explain what he expects of them in the interim.
19:12-13 A man of noble birth goes to a far country "to have himself appointed king and then to return" (v. 12). The Greek expression literally refers to his "receiving a kingdom"—a remark that pictures Jesus' reception of the kingdom after his resurrection and ascension. The servants represent anyone following Jesus.
19:14 The subjects who hate the ruler and do not want him as king represent Israel's rejection of Jesus.
19:15-21 Returning home, the newly appointed king requests an accounting by his servants. The main exchange takes place between the master and the third servant, one who has no sense of loyalty to his master. Although he is associated with the master, there is nothing that indicates that he trusts the master.
19:22-23 The master's reaction to the servant is strong and clear: This wicked servant will be condemned

servant! You knew, did you, that I am
a hard man, taking out what I did not
put in, and reaping what I did not sow?[o]
23Why then didn't you put my money on
deposit, so that when I came back, I could
have collected it with interest?'
24"Then he said to those standing by,
'Take his mina away from him and give
it to the one who has ten minas.'
25"'Sir,' they said, 'he already has ten!'
26"He replied, 'I tell you that to everyone who has, more will be given, but as
for the one who has nothing, even what
they have will be taken away.[p] 27But those
enemies of mine who did not want me
to be king over them — bring them here
and kill them in front of me.'"

Jesus Comes to Jerusalem as King

19:29–38pp // Mt 21:1–9; Mk 11:1–10
19:35–38pp // Jn 12:12–15

28After Jesus had said this, he went on
ahead, going up to Jerusalem.[q] 29As he
approached Bethphage and Bethany[r] at
the hill called the Mount of Olives,[s] he
sent two of his disciples, saying to them,
30"Go to the village ahead of you, and
as you enter it, you will find a colt tied
there, which no one has ever ridden. Untie it and bring it here. 31If anyone asks
you, 'Why are you untying it?' say, 'The
Lord needs it.'"

19:22 [o] Mt 25:26
19:26 [p] Mt 13:12; 25:29; Lk 8:18
19:28 [q] Mk 10:32; Lk 9:51
19:29 [r] Mt 21:17 [s] Mt 21:1
19:32 [t] Lk 22:13
19:36 [u] 2Ki 9:13
19:37 [v] Mt 21:1
19:38 [w] Ps 118:26; Lk 13:35 [x] Lk 2:14
19:39 [y] Mt 21:15, 16
19:40 [z] Hab 2:11
19:41 [a] Isa 22:4; Lk 13:34,35

32Those who were sent ahead went and
found it just as he had told them.[t] 33As
they were untying the colt, its owners
asked them, "Why are you untying the
colt?"
34They replied, "The Lord needs it."
35They brought it to Jesus, threw their
cloaks on the colt and put Jesus on it.
36As he went along, people spread their
cloaks[u] on the road.
37When he came near the place where
the road goes down the Mount of Olives,[v]
the whole crowd of disciples began joyfully to praise God in loud voices for all
the miracles they had seen:

38"Blessed is the king who comes in
the name of the Lord!"[a][w]

"Peace in heaven and glory in the
highest!"[x]

39Some of the Pharisees in the crowd
said to Jesus, "Teacher, rebuke your disciples!"[y]
40"I tell you," he replied, "if they keep
quiet, the stones will cry out."[z]
41As he approached Jerusalem and
saw the city, he wept over it[a] 42and said,
"If you, even you, had only known on
this day what would bring you peace —
but now it is hidden from your eyes.

[a] *38* Psalm 118:26

---

on his own testimony. The master's remarks are not his confession that he is a hard taskmaster; rather, they condemn the third servant's failure to follow through on how he viewed the master.

19:24-26 Jesus then makes the application: The one who has been trustworthy gets more, but the one who was not loses even what he has. Jesus applies a mathematical warning to the third servant: Nothing from nothing leaves nothing. Mere association with the community counts for nothing; what counts is personal relationship with Jesus.

19:27 Jesus deals with one more group in the parable—the subjects who did not want the nobleman to be king. These enemies are killed. This represents the fate of those who reject Jesus outright.

> **19:11-27** As our culture grows more independent from God, many claim they are not his subjects, or they try to create God in their image and form him in the frame of their expectations. Yet we all are accountable to God. Our lives last only a short time in this world, and they will be subject to examination by the God who is the source of all life and breath.

19:28-34 As Jesus approaches Jerusalem, he tells his disciples to get an animal so he can enter the capital. If anyone asks what they are doing, they are simply to say that the Lord needs it. In this culture, a dignitary could gain use of property for personal reasons. This right extended to people like rabbis.

19:35-36 Jesus is directing the sequence of events that leads to his death. The disciples throw their cloaks on the colt and put Jesus on it. As he proceeds, people spread their cloaks in front of him as well, much as a red carpet functions today. While the background is royal, the ride on a humble animal denotes not a Messiah of raw power but of humility and service.

19:37-38 Luke stays focused on the person of Jesus. In praising God, the disciples also praise Jesus. They proclaim the hope of Ps 118:26, where blessing falls on "the king who comes in the name of the Lord" (v. 38). For disciples, this is a great moment; the crowds also join in.

19:39-40 When the Pharisees come and ask Jesus to reject the claim and rebuke his disciples, he responds that if the disciples do not speak, creation will. This remark contains an inherent rebuke in that even stones know more about what is taking place than the religious leaders do.

19:41-42 Despite the fanfare, the entry is not a pleasant one for Jesus. He knows what lies ahead and that the pain he will suffer will not be limited to himself. The nation has made a frightful choice, with dire consequences for itself. What Jesus predicts is the consequence for covenant unfaithfulness.

43The days will come upon you when
your enemies will build an embankment
against you and encircle you and hem
you in on every side.[b] 44They will dash
you to the ground, you and the children
within your walls.[c] They will not leave
one stone on another,[d] because you did
not recognize the time of God's coming[e]
to you."

Jesus at the Temple

19:45,46pp // Mt 21:12–16; Mk 11:15–18; Jn 2:13–16

45When Jesus entered the temple
courts, he began to drive out those who
were selling. 46"It is written," he said
to them, "'My house will be a house of
prayer'[a];[f] but you have made it 'a den of
robbers.'[b]"[g]

47Every day he was teaching at the
temple.[h] But the chief priests, the teachers of the law and the leaders among the
people were trying to kill him.[i] 48Yet they
could not find any way to do it, because
all the people hung on his words.

The Authority of Jesus Questioned

20:1–8pp // Mt 21:23–27; Mk 11:27–33

20 One day as Jesus was teaching the
people in the temple courts[j] and
proclaiming the good news,[k] the chief
priests and the teachers of the law, together with the elders, came up to him.
2"Tell us by what authority you are doing
these things," they said. "Who gave you
this authority?"[l]

3He replied, "I will also ask you a question. Tell me: 4John's baptism[m] — was it
from heaven, or of human origin?"

5They discussed it among themselves
and said, "If we say, 'From heaven,' he
will ask, 'Why didn't you believe him?'
6But if we say, 'Of human origin,' all the
people[n] will stone us, because they are
persuaded that John was a prophet."[o]

7So they answered, "We don't know
where it was from."

8Jesus said, "Neither will I tell you by
what authority I am doing these things."

19:43 [b] Isa 29:3; Jer 6:6; Eze 4:2; 26:8; Lk 21:20
19:44 [c] Ps 137:9 [d] Mt 24:2; Mk 13:2; Lk 21:6 [e] 1Pe 2:12
19:46 [f] Isa 56:7 [g] Jer 7:11
19:47 [h] Mt 26:55 [i] Mt 12:14; Mk 11:18
20:1 [j] Mt 26:55 [k] Lk 8:1
20:2 [l] Jn 2:18; Ac 4:7; 7:27
20:4 [m] Mk 1:4
20:6 [n] Lk 7:29 [o] Mt 11:9

[a] 46 Isaiah 56:7 [b] 46 Jer. 7:11

19:43-44 Jesus' reference to "the days will come" indicates a prophetic message of doom. When the enemy finally enters the city, everyone will be slaughtered and there will be total destruction. Jesus knows what he is talking about—the decision to reject Jesus is a fundamental violation of covenant trust.

19:28-44 Jesus infuses his evangelism with a humility that is represented even in the way he enters Jerusalem as king. Like the Messiah, the church needs to be a community not just of testimony and words but of presence and service among those whom it seeks to reach. The touch of God's presence reveals his mercy. Proclaiming and revealing Jesus are more than a matter for the head.

The importance of making a wise decision about Jesus is a constant theme in this Gospel. Accepting Jesus leads to great blessing, while rejection leads to great pain. A time will come when we will each have to own up to our decision. Making the right decision will determine the character of that meeting.

19:45-46 Luke succinctly tells the story of the temple incident. Jesus drives out the merchants and quotes a composite OT citation.

19:47-48 Jesus' action strengthens the resolve of the Jewish leadership to deal with him. He cannot be allowed to dictate how worship will be conducted at the temple and thus blatantly challenge priestly practices. But his popularity makes them hesitant.

20:1-2 Here Luke returns to one of the central issues of his Gospel: Where does Jesus' authority come from? Such concerns motivate the priests and teachers of the law to probe Jesus as he teaches in the temple courts and shares the Good News of the kingdom.

20:3-4 Jesus responds with his own question: He asks them to assess John the Baptist's ministry. The question is brilliant because John's roots were as obscure as those of Jesus. John has already been accepted by the people as a prophet, so the leaders don't know what to say. Jesus has painted them into a corner.

20:5-8 The character of the leaders emerges as they deliberate among themselves. The issue they discuss is not the truth but appearances. The Jews decide to take a safe route and punt, claiming they do not know the answer to his question. They refused to recognize John, and now they are maintaining their distance from Jesus. The time for debate is past. The leadership has made their decision, and they should own up to it. Their failure to do so is an indictment on their inaction.

19:45—20:8 No doubt the leadership would have said that their resistance to Jesus was a response to someone creating havoc at the temple. But failure to engage in serious self-examination led to further sin. Sins, like lies, tend to travel in packs and devour like wolves. Untreated, sin becomes a thoroughly destructive force.

The negative character lesson of the Jewish leaders' deliberations has been noted above. But do we do the same things? Do we hesitate to speak up for our association with Jesus in contexts where it might not be popular? Do we use evasive tactics to hide previous actions that we now know were wrong? Do we tell people in public debate we are searching for truth when our mind is already made up?

The Parable of the Tenants

20:9–19pp // Mt 21:33–46; Mk 12:1–12

9He went on to tell the people this parable: "A man planted a vineyard,[p] rented it to some farmers and went away for a long time.[q] 10At harvest time he sent a servant to the tenants so they would give him some of the fruit of the vineyard. But the tenants beat him and sent him away empty-handed. 11He sent another servant, but that one also they beat and treated shamefully and sent away empty-handed. 12He sent still a third, and they wounded him and threw him out.

13"Then the owner of the vineyard said, 'What shall I do? I will send my son, whom I love;[r] perhaps they will respect him.'

14"But when the tenants saw him, they talked the matter over. 'This is the heir,' they said. 'Let's kill him, and the inheritance will be ours.' 15So they threw him out of the vineyard and killed him.

"What then will the owner of the vineyard do to them? 16He will come and kill those tenants[s] and give the vineyard to others."

When the people heard this, they said, "God forbid!"

17Jesus looked directly at them and asked, "Then what is the meaning of that which is written:

"'The stone the builders rejected
has become the cornerstone'[a]?[t]

18Everyone who falls on that stone will be broken to pieces; anyone on whom it falls will be crushed."[u]

19The teachers of the law and the chief priests looked for a way to arrest him[v] immediately, because they knew he had spoken this parable against them. But they were afraid of the people.[w]

Paying Taxes to Caesar

20:20–26pp // Mt 22:15–22; Mk 12:13–17

20Keeping a close watch on him, they sent spies, who pretended to be sincere. They hoped to catch Jesus in something he said,[x] so that they might hand him over to the power and authority of the governor.[y] 21So the spies questioned him: "Teacher, we know that you speak and teach what is right, and that you do not show partiality but teach the way of God in accordance with the truth.[z] 22Is it right for us to pay taxes to Caesar or not?"

23He saw through their duplicity and said to them, 24"Show me a denarius. Whose image and inscription are on it?"

"Caesar's," they replied.

25He said to them, "Then give back to Caesar what is Caesar's,[a] and to God what is God's."

20:9 [p] Isa 5:1-7 [q] Mt 25:14
20:13 [r] Mt 3:17
20:16 [s] Lk 19:27
20:17 [t] Ps 118:22; Ac 4:11
20:18 [u] Isa 8:14, 15
20:19 [v] Lk 19:47 [w] Mk 11:18
20:20 [x] Mt 12:10 [y] Mt 27:2
20:21 [z] Jn 3:2
20:25 [a] Lk 23:2; Ro 13:7

[a] *17* Psalm 118:22

20:9-12 It was not unusual in Jesus' day for land to be owned by one person and farmed by others. When a man plants a vineyard and rents it out to tenants, he expects to collect proceeds from the profit on the crops.

20:13 All the owner's efforts to collect his share are snubbed. So the owner decides to send "my son, whom I love," assuming they will treat his son with respect.

20:14-15 When the tenants see the son arrive, they see an opportunity. How will killing the heir reap benefits for them? The allusion here is to Jesus' approaching execution by the Jewish leadership: Jesus knows exactly what they are about, even though it makes no logical sense.

20:16 The crowd gets the point about the shift in who gets to tend the vineyard and exclaims, "God forbid!" Surely Israel and her leadership could never be guilty of such reckless disobedience.

20:17-18 Jesus cites Scripture and a popular proverb to drive home his point. Ps 118:22 teaches that the righteous one rejected by others is exalted by God as a key figure. OT Jews would have thought of their king in these terms; the rejectors would have been the Gentile nations. Jesus turns the image upside down, noting that now the king is rejected by his own people.

20:19 The leaders' opposition to Jesus grows more intense, for they know Jesus is challenging them. They want to arrest him, but the people remain an obstacle; Jesus is still too popular with the crowds. He will have to be discredited first, so that is where they turn their attention.

20:9-19 Though this text seems harsh in portraying God's casting aside of Israel, it is important to look at how patient and long-suffering God was. He rejects people only after a long effort of trying to gain a response from them. Jesus weeps as he enters Jerusalem because judgment is not what God desires to bring on anyone. Judgment comes only because we fail to respond to God's compassion and mercy.

20:20-21 The leadership is looking for anything Jesus might say that would allow them to hand him over to the governor on a political charge. In Roman custody, Jesus could be subject to the death penalty for treason.

20:22 These infiltrators have a brilliant plan to question Jesus about taxes. If Jesus supports Rome, his allegiance to Israel will be questioned. If he sides with the Jews, then he can be implicated in a crime under Roman law.

20:23-25 Jesus, aware of their craftiness, calls for a coin and asks who is responsible for its

26They were unable to trap him in
what he had said there in public. And
astonished by his answer, they became
silent.

The Resurrection and Marriage

20:27–40pp // Mt 22:23–33; Mk 12:18–27

27Some of the Sadducees,[b] who say
there is no resurrection,[c] came to Jesus
with a question. 28"Teacher," they said,
"Moses wrote for us that if a man's brother dies and leaves a wife but no children,
the man must marry the widow and raise
up offspring for his brother.[d] 29Now there
were seven brothers. The first one married a woman and died childless. 30The
second 31and then the third married her,
and in the same way the seven died, leaving no children. 32Finally, the woman
died too. 33Now then, at the resurrection
whose wife will she be, since the seven
were married to her?"
34Jesus replied, "The people of this age
marry and are given in marriage. 35But
those who are considered worthy of taking
part in the age to come[e] and in the resurrection from the dead will neither marry
nor be given in marriage, 36and they can
no longer die; for they are like the angels.
They are God's children,[f] since they are
children of the resurrection. 37But in the
account of the burning bush, even Moses
showed that the dead rise, for he calls the
Lord 'the God of Abraham, and the God of
Isaac, and the God of Jacob.'[a][g] 38He is not
the God of the dead, but of the living, for
to him all are alive."
39Some of the teachers of the law responded, "Well said, teacher!" 40And no
one dared to ask him any more questions.[h]

Whose Son Is the Messiah?

20:41–47pp // Mt 22:41—23:7; Mk 12:35–40

41Then Jesus said to them, "Why is it
said that the Messiah is the son of David?[i]
42David himself declares in the Book of
Psalms:

20:27 [b] Ac 4:1 [c] Ac 23:8; 1Co 15:12
20:28 [d] Dt 25:5
20:35 [e] Mt 12:32
20:36 [f] Jn 1:12; 1Jn 3:1-2
20:37 [g] Ex 3:6
20:40 [h] Mt 22:46; Mk 12:34
20:41 [i] Mt 1:1

[a] *37* Exodus 3:6

---

inscription. The Jews were carrying such coins in their pockets, proof that they already lived under Rome's sovereignty and accepted it by participating in its commerce.

20:26 Jesus turns the tables. Government has the right to exist and function, but its presence does not destroy one's allegiance to God. Jesus is not a political revolutionary who rails against Rome, nor is he a zealous nationalist. The leadership, embarrassed into silence, recognizes their effort has failed.

✣ **20:20-26** Though we can seek it, the church's call is not to reform culture, because reformation cannot take place by changing structures alone. Hearts must be changed. The church should be able to show the world what healthy relationships look like, how the needs of the poor can be met with compassion, what absence of racism looks like, how people can engage in business with integrity, how reconciliation takes place when people have failed one another, and so forth.

What does this perspective mean for our involvement in politics? The church as an alternative to culture must stay above culture in its critique of how government or any other institution does business. Government exists to protect the people, administer law and order, collect taxes, and serve the common good as a principle of justice; the church exists to nurture hearts and souls.

20:27-33 The Sadducees raise the issue of the resurrection, which they denied. The Sadducees had a standard question they liked to pose on the resurrection to try to show how ludicrous it was. They do not really want an answer, for they are convinced that the dilemma shows the lack of logic concerning resurrection. They also assume that the afterlife is like this life.

20:34-38 Jesus' reply takes two forms. This marriage dilemma misunderstands the afterlife, since marriage does not occur there. Thus, the problem the Sadducees pose is a trick question. Additionally, Jesus points out that Scripture does teach resurrection in the Torah in its mention of the patriarchs. If God makes promises to them and the afterlife is known, then resurrection seems an appropriate assumption. This is a fundamental doctrine of hope.

20:39-40 Jesus silences his opponents so that they do not want to ask him any more questions. He knows more about God's will and where he is going than his opponents do. He may be outnumbered a few thousand to one, but he can be trusted to teach the way of God.

✣ **20:27-40** That "we only go around once in life" is good theology. The proper response to that reality is vastly different than the view of advertisers. Rather than grabbing for all the riches this life offers, the uniqueness of our Christian journey means that we should pay careful attention to our one chance to walk with God.

20:41 One favorite identification of the Messiah among the Jews was to mark him as "son of David." Jesus wants to provide an expanded view of this title. At the center of the discussion is Ps 110:1, the most popular OT text used by Jesus and the early church.

20:42-43 This psalm articulates the hope of what Israel's ideal king will be. Jesus notes that David is the one speaking about this promise. If David is the speaker of this psalm and addresses the royal, messianic figure as his "Lord," how can the

Lk 20:45-47 ❖ Where do we see hypocrisy and injustice in the church? How can we take a stand against it?

"'The Lord said to my Lord:
"Sit at my right hand
43 until I make your enemies
a footstool for your feet."'[a][j]

44 David calls him 'Lord.' How then can
he be his son?"

Warning Against the Teachers of the Law

45 While all the people were listening,
Jesus said to his disciples, 46 "Beware of
the teachers of the law. They like to walk
around in flowing robes and love to be
greeted with respect in the marketplaces
and have the most important seats in the
synagogues and the places of honor at banquets.[k] 47 They devour widows' houses and
for a show make lengthy prayers. These
men will be punished most severely."

The Widow's Offering

21:1–4pp // Mk 12:41–44

21 As Jesus looked up, he saw the rich
putting their gifts into the temple
treasury.[l] 2 He also saw a poor widow put
in two very small copper coins. 3 "Truly I tell you," he said, "this poor widow
has put in more than all the others. 4 All
these people gave their gifts out of their
wealth; but she out of her poverty put in
all she had to live on."[m]

The Destruction of the Temple and Signs of the End Times

21:5–36pp // Mt 24; Mk 13
21:12–17pp // Mt 10:17–22

5 Some of his disciples were remarking
about how the temple was adorned with
beautiful stones and with gifts dedicated
to God. But Jesus said, 6 "As for what you
see here, the time will come when not
one stone will be left on another;[n] every
one of them will be thrown down."
7 "Teacher," they asked, "when will
these things happen? And what will
be the sign that they are about to take
place?"
8 He replied: "Watch out that you are not
deceived. For many will come in my name,
claiming, 'I am he,' and, 'The time is near.'
Do not follow them.[o] 9 When you hear of

20:43 [j] Ps 110:1; Mt 22:44
20:46 [k] Lk 11:43
21:1 [l] Mt 27:6; Jn 8:20
21:4 [m] 2Co 8:12
21:6 [n] Lk 19:44
21:8 [o] Lk 17:23

[a] *43* Psalm 110:1

title "son of David" be the best title for Messiah? A father normally did not bow to a son.

20:44 The text ends here with no answer. The question is posed for reflection, and that is precisely how Luke uses it. The issue of Jesus' identity will be the central point of debate as he goes to the cross. The implication that emerges from Jesus' being seated at God's right hand is that Jesus is both Lord and Christ.

✣ **20:41-44** This text functions as yet another call for reflection and decision about Jesus. As One who is both son of David and his Lord, Jesus should be honored with an allegiance worthy of a king.

20:45-47 Jesus warns of the pride of the teachers of the law, revealed in their long robes and the special greetings in the marketplace that they so love. Jesus also condemns their misuse of widows' funds. Apparently in managing widows' affairs, the teachers of the law took a large cut for themselves. Their pretentious long prayers for others in the face of such inconsideration made matters worse. They claimed to lead the people and to be examples of God's will, but their callousness showed through.

21:1-4 In contrast to the Pharisees and the rich who shower gifts into the treasury, a poor widow comes with two copper coins, which she readily gives away. This widow is not looking for credit, but only at how she can humbly serve God.

✣ **20:45—21:4** What we give to God deserves priority. He should not receive our leftovers. As is all too common, the leftovers mysteriously shrink in size to take care of things that are not necessities. On the other hand, giving to God what is set aside from the first inevitably limits what we use for ourselves, increasing our reliance on and trust in God.

21:5-38 While prophetic remarks dominate vv. 7-24, apocalyptic elements appear in vv. 25-28. What is the difference between these two? *Prophetic promise* frames itself in terms of everyday history where God works through agents already present, while *apocalyptic* speaks explicitly of God's breaking into history in a marvelous way.

21:5-7 The discourse begins with an observation about the temple in Jerusalem. Jesus and his disciples have just been at the temple, watching the widow make her offering, and some of the disciples comment on the temple's beauty. Jesus notes immediately that the building will not be permanent. With these words he predicts the destruction of Jerusalem in AD 70. Jesus' remark is devastating, since the temple was the heart and soul of Israel's worship.

The events tied to Jerusalem's fall mirror events that will bring the Son of Man's return. Jesus' discourse in this passage characterizes an entire period from the time of Jesus' remarks through the destruction of Jerusalem and into the period of the Lord's return.

21:9-11 The presence of wars and rumors of wars should not startle the disciples. Great calamities, like those that engulfed Jerusalem in AD 66-70, should not take them by surprise.

wars and uprisings, do not be frightened.
These things must happen first, but the
end will not come right away."
10Then he said to them: "Nation will
rise against nation, and kingdom against
kingdom.[p] 11There will be great earthquakes, famines and pestilences in various places, and fearful events and great
signs from heaven.[q]
12"But before all this, they will seize
you and persecute you. They will hand
you over to synagogues and put you in
prison, and you will be brought before
kings and governors, and all on account
of my name. 13And so you will bear testimony to me.[r] 14But make up your mind
not to worry beforehand how you will
defend yourselves.[s] 15For I will give you[t]
words and wisdom that none of your
adversaries will be able to resist or contradict. 16You will be betrayed even by
parents, brothers and sisters, relatives
and friends,[u] and they will put some of
you to death. 17Everyone will hate you
because of me.[v] 18But not a hair of your
head will perish.[w] 19Stand firm, and you
will win life.[x]
20"When you see Jerusalem being surrounded by armies,[y] you will know that
its desolation is near. 21Then let those
who are in Judea flee to the mountains,
let those in the city get out, and let those
in the country not enter the city.[z] 22For
this is the time of punishment[a] in fulfillment[b] of all that has been written.
23How dreadful it will be in those days for
pregnant women and nursing mothers!
There will be great distress in the land
and wrath against this people. 24They
will fall by the sword and will be taken
as prisoners to all the nations. Jerusalem
will be trampled[c] on by the Gentiles until
the times of the Gentiles are fulfilled.
25"There will be signs in the sun, moon
and stars. On the earth, nations will be
in anguish and perplexity at the roaring and tossing of the sea.[d] 26People will
faint from terror, apprehensive of what
is coming on the world, for the heavenly bodies will be shaken.[e] 27At that time
they will see the Son of Man[f] coming
in a cloud[g] with power and great glory.
28When these things begin to take place,
stand up and lift up your heads, because
your redemption is drawing near."[h]
29He told them this parable: "Look at
the fig tree and all the trees. 30When they
sprout leaves, you can see for yourselves
and know that summer is near. 31Even
so, when you see these things happening, you know that the kingdom of God[i]
is near.

21:10 [p] 2Ch 15:6; Isa 19:2
21:11 [q] Isa 29:6; Joel 2:30
21:13 [r] Php 1:12
21:14 [s] Lk 12:11
21:15 [t] Lk 12:12
21:16 [u] Lk 12:52, 53
21:17 [v] Jn 15:21
21:18 [w] Mt 10:30
21:19 [x] Mt 10:22
21:20 [y] Lk 19:43
21:21 [z] Lk 17:31
21:22 [a] Isa 63:4; Da 9:24-27; Hos 9:7 [b] Mt 1:22
21:24 [c] Isa 5:5; 63:18; Da 8:13; Rev 11:2
21:25 [d] 2Pe 3:10, 12
21:26 [e] Mt 24:29
21:27 [f] Mt 8:20 [g] Rev 1:7
21:28 [h] Lk 18:7
21:31 [i] Mt 3:2

21:12 Persecution comes first. This actually starts almost immediately after the crucifixion, and large portions of the book of Acts can be read as initial fulfillments of this prophecy. Jesus wants them to understand that, before the end arrives, believers will endure many difficult experiences.

21:13–15 Through these opportunities, the disciples will "bear testimony" to Jesus (v. 13). The theme of witness is a major one in Acts, beginning with Jesus' instruction and promise of the Holy Spirit in Ac 1:8.

21:16–17 Luke remains focused on what is going to happen soon as the gospel goes out to the Jewish community. Jesus says he will give them the words to say, while in 12:11–12 it was the Spirit. This statement indicates how closely together Jesus and the Spirit work. He is the one who sends the Spirit, who in turn enables his people to stand for him. No matter the situation, Jesus will give them answers to silence their opponents.

21:18–19 Jesus goes on to give a word about ultimate protection (v. 18; cf. 12:1–5). Though death may come, not a hair on any believer's head will perish. When it comes to life that counts—eternal life—believers can know that God will welcome them. To stand with Jesus is to have salvation.

21:20–23 These verses review predictions already made in 19:43–44. Jerusalem will be surrounded by armies, so its desolation is near. The Jewish historian Josephus, a contemporary of Luke, tells us that a million Jews were killed and nearly a hundred thousand taken captive. The judgment on Jerusalem was absolutely horrific.

Jerusalem should be avoided at all costs during this time. Those in Judea should flee to the mountains, while those in the city should try to get out. The language of "desolation" is important. Mt 24:15 and Mk 13:14 allude to the desecration of the temple. Luke appeals to the term as a general reference to judgment (v. 20). All these events take place "in fulfillment of all that has been written" (v. 22). There are no surprises in God's plan.

21:24 Gentiles will have a role in the city until "the times of the Gentiles are fulfilled." This phrase, which marks out an era, suggests that a time will again come when Israel will be prominent in God's plan.

21:25–26 Here Jesus addresses "the end" that begins with his return. Accompanying that return will be great cosmic signs that will be obvious to everyone. Jesus' description is of major and repeated catastrophe.

21:27–28 At such a moment of insecurity, the Son of Man will appear riding on the clouds. Jesus' return will mean that vindication has come near. God's people present at that time will be able to lift their heads, knowing that their redemption is near. In place of the fear (vv. 25–26) comes hope.

21:29–31 This short parable encourages his disciples to keep their eyes open for what God is doing.

Lk 21:34-36 ❖ How can we stay prepared for the Lord's return in a world full of distraction, entertainment, and anxiety?

32"Truly I tell you, this generation[j] will
certainly not pass away until all these
things have happened. 33Heaven and
earth will pass away, but my words will
never pass away.[k]
34"Be careful, or your hearts will be
weighed down with carousing, drunkenness and the anxieties of life,[l] and that
day will close on you suddenly[m] like a
trap. 35For it will come on all those who
live on the face of the whole earth. 36Be
always on the watch, and pray[n] that you
may be able to escape all that is about
to happen, and that you may be able to
stand before the Son of Man."
37Each day Jesus was teaching at the
temple,[o] and each evening he went out[p]
to spend the night on the hill called the
Mount of Olives,[q] 38and all the people
came early in the morning to hear him
at the temple.[r]

21:32 [j] Lk 11:50; 17:25
21:33 [k] Mt 5:18
21:34 [l] Mk 4:19 [m] Lk 12:40,46; 1Th 5:2-7
21:36 [n] Mt 26:41
21:37 [o] Mt 26:55 [p] Mk 11:19 [q] Mt 21:1
21:38 [r] Jn 8:2

22:1 [s] Jn 11:55
22:2 [t] Mt 12:14
22:3 [u] Mt 4:10; Jn 13:2 [v] Mt 10:4
22:4 [w] ver 52; Ac 4:1; 5:24
22:5 [x] Zec 11:12

Judas Agrees to Betray Jesus

22:1,2pp // Mt 26:2–5; Mk 14:1,2,10,11

22 Now the Festival of Unleavened
Bread, called the Passover, was approaching,[s] 2and the chief priests and the
teachers of the law were looking for some
way to get rid of Jesus,[t] for they were
afraid of the people. 3Then Satan[u] entered
Judas, called Iscariot,[v] one of the Twelve.
4And Judas went to the chief priests and
the officers of the temple guard[w] and discussed with them how he might betray
Jesus. 5They were delighted and agreed
to give him money.[x] 6He consented, and
watched for an opportunity to hand Jesus
over to them when no crowd was present.

The Last Supper

22:7–13pp // Mt 26:17–19; Mk 14:12–16
22:17–20pp // Mt 26:26–29; Mk 14:22–25; 1Co 11:23–25
22:21–23pp // Mt 26:21–24; Mk 14:18–21; Jn 13:21–30
22:25–27pp // Mt 20:25–28; Mk 10:42–45
22:33,34pp // Mt 26:33–35; Mk 14:29–31; Jn 13:37,38

7Then came the day of Unleavened
Bread on which the Passover lamb had

21:32 "This generation" appears to set a specific time frame for these events, none of which took place in the lifetime of the disciples (v. 32). It seems clear that whatever "generation" means, it did not refer to the generation of Jesus' time or that of Luke's readers. The view preferred here is that the "generation" that sees all these things refers to the generation present in v. 25. In other words, those who see the beginning of the end in the cosmic signs will see the arrival of the decisive era in the Son of Man's return. Once the events of the final act commence, they will take place rather quickly.
21:33 Jesus is so certain that what he is saying is true that he argues that creation will pass away but not his words (v. 33). The discourse is designed to inform and encourage faithfulness. To do so, what he declares about vindication must take place. Jesus' disciples can count on that fact.
21:34-36 Jesus then continues to warn the disciples to be sure that the day does not take them unaware like a trap. When the Lord does come back, everyone will be faced with the reality of his return and his powerful presence. Some will be ready for it, while others will be surprised. The ultimate goal is to "stand before the Son of Man" (v. 36).

✚ **21:5-38** Like the psalmists, we sometimes complain that God does not hear the cries of his people and that evil seems to be victorious in our world. Jesus in this discourse asserts God does control the direction of history. He calls us to be patient and to use our time in presenting the gospel of God's grace to others.
We must keep watch, stand fast, and trust God's timing with the reassurance that one day our deliverance will surely come. Even though we cannot see it, we can see Jesus, the Author and Defender of our faith, who promises that one day he will return for us in great power and glory. So, looking to him, we serve and wait with great expectation.

22:1-2 The Jewish leadership has been powerless to do anything about Jesus because of his popularity. All of that changes when Judas goes to the leadership to discuss how he might hand Jesus over to them. The chief priests' presence shows that the decision is being made at the highest levels.
22:3-6 It is hard to appreciate just how perfect Judas's offer is for the Jewish leaders. Now they can figure out Jesus' private whereabouts, and they have in-house testimony against him. All that is needed is to find an appropriate time to arrest the teacher. It must be a time when crowds are not present; Judas will determine that time. Sinister forces are behind Jesus' death.

✚ **22:1-6** If Satan directly opposed Jesus here, he will also directly oppose believers and the church. Defection from within is one of the most effective means he has to discredit the church. Faithfulness to God's will and commands, along with constantly seeking to be more Christlike through the power of the Spirit, prevents Satan from getting such a foothold in a believer's life.

22:7-13 Jesus sends his disciples to prepare to celebrate the Passover at a house that is ready

to be sacrificed.[y] 8Jesus sent Peter and
John,[z] saying, "Go and make preparations for us to eat the Passover."
9"Where do you want us to prepare for
it?" they asked.
10He replied, "As you enter the city,
a man carrying a jar of water will meet
you. Follow him to the house that he enters, 11and say to the owner of the house,
'The Teacher asks: Where is the guest
room, where I may eat the Passover with
my disciples?' 12He will show you a large
room upstairs, all furnished. Make preparations there."
13They left and found things just as
Jesus had told them.[a] So they prepared
the Passover.
14When the hour came, Jesus and his
apostles[b] reclined at the table.[c] 15And he
said to them, "I have eagerly desired to
eat this Passover with you before I suffer.[d] 16For I tell you, I will not eat it again
until it finds fulfillment in the kingdom
of God."[e]
17After taking the cup, he gave thanks
and said, "Take this and divide it among
you. 18For I tell you I will not drink again
from the fruit of the vine until the kingdom of God comes."
19And he took bread, gave thanks and
broke it,[f] and gave it to them, saying,
"This is my body given for you; do this
in remembrance of me."
20In the same way, after the supper he
took the cup, saying, "This cup is the new
covenant[g] in my blood, which is poured
out for you.[a] 21But the hand of him who
is going to betray me is with mine on
the table.[h] 22The Son of Man[i] will go as it
has been decreed.[j] But woe to that man
who betrays him!" 23They began to question among themselves which of them
it might be who would do this.
24A dispute also arose among them as
to which of them was considered to be
greatest.[k] 25Jesus said to them, "The kings
of the Gentiles lord it over them; and
those who exercise authority over them
call themselves Benefactors. 26But you are
not to be like that. Instead, the greatest
among you should be like the youngest,[l]
and the one who rules like the one who
serves.[m] 27For who is greater, the one who
is at the table or the one who serves? Is it
not the one who is at the table? But I am
among you as one who serves.[n] 28You are
those who have stood by me in my trials.

22:7 [y] Ex 12:18-20; Dt 16:5-8; Mk 14:12
22:8 [z] Ac 3:1,11; 4:13,19; 8:14
22:13 [a] Lk 19:32
22:14 [b] Mk 6:30 [c] Mt 26:20; Mk 14:17,18
22:15 [d] Mt 16:21
22:16 [e] Lk 14:15; Rev 19:9
22:19 [f] Mt 14:19
22:20 [g] Ex 24:8; Isa 42:6; Jer 31:31-34; Zec 9:11; 2Co 3:6; Heb 8:6; 9:15
22:21 [h] Ps 41:9
22:22 [i] Mt 8:20 [j] Ac 2:23; 4:28
22:24 [k] Mk 9:34; Lk 9:46
22:26 [l] 1Pe 5:5 [m] Mk 9:35; Lk 9:48
22:27 [n] Mt 20:28; Lk 12:37

[a] 19,20 Some manuscripts do not have *given for you . . . poured out for you.*

---

to host them. The details given may reflect that some type of prearrangement is in place, since Mt 26:18 suggests that the host knows who this "Teacher" is. The disciples go and find things just as Jesus has told them. This meal is also known as the Last Supper, and it forms the basis of the Lord's Supper. The background of the meal is likely a Passover meal.

22:14–18 Jesus notes how he has "eagerly desired" to celebrate this meal with his disciples. The mention of approaching suffering adds sorrow to what follows. Jesus will not celebrate this meal again until "it finds fulfillment in the kingdom of God" (v. 16). Jesus has in mind here the fulfillment of the kingdom when he returns to earth again.

22:19 The bread Jesus takes is a part of the third course of the meal, eaten along with the lamb and bitter herbs. Jesus takes the bread, gives thanks, breaks it, and passes it around the table. In that moment, the Jewish meal becomes Christianized. The bread symbolizes the broken body of Jesus offered on behalf of his community. It gives them a chance, as one body, to reaffirm what God has done for them. This meal is like a new start.

Thanksgiving to God for the bread is also thanksgiving for the offering that clears the way for a relationship to God. Exactly how Jesus' body is offered for them is not specified here. The Passover was a time when judgment came to the Egyptians in the death of their firstborn. Israel's firstborn were spared the judgment because the blood of a lamb was placed on the doors of their homes (see Ex 12). Jesus now becomes the symbol of such protection.

22:20 Jesus refers to the cup as "the new covenant in my blood" (v. 20). Jesus' blood opens up a new era of God's blessing (see Jer 31:31–34).

✚ **22:7–20** In the Lord's Supper, we acknowledge the presence of our Lord, his death, and his coming again. Sharing in the bread and wine together, we affirm our oneness before him and our submission to him, and we recall how we came to receive such grace. The ultimate commemoration of the Lord's table is a righteous life.

22:21–22 It is hard to imagine what Judas must have felt when Jesus revealed that he knew about Judas's betrayal.

22:23–30 Ironically, as Jesus faces his death and Judas engages in betrayal, the disciples worry about their status before Jesus. Jesus' reply is like his remarks in the other Gospels: Elitism and debate about status are out. Better to be a servant than to be served.

Jesus is not uninterested in their status question. He just does not want them to compare themselves to each other. Their constancy is noted and rewarded. The eleven will receive what Judas misses.

29And I confer on you a kingdom,[o] just as
my Father conferred one on me, 30so that
you may eat and drink at my table in my
kingdom[p] and sit on thrones, judging the
twelve tribes of Israel.[q]
31"Simon, Simon, Satan has asked[r]
to sift all of you as wheat.[s] 32But I have
prayed for you,[t] Simon, that your faith
may not fail. And when you have turned
back, strengthen your brothers."[u]
33But he replied, "Lord, I am ready to
go with you to prison and to death."[v]
34Jesus answered, "I tell you, Peter,
before the rooster crows today, you will
deny three times that you know me."
35Then Jesus asked them, "When I sent
you without purse, bag or sandals,[w] did
you lack anything?"
"Nothing," they answered.
36He said to them, "But now if you
have a purse, take it, and also a bag;
and if you don't have a sword, sell your
cloak and buy one. 37It is written: 'And he
was numbered with the transgressors'[a];[x]
and I tell you that this must be fulfilled
in me. Yes, what is written about me is
reaching its fulfillment."

22:29 [o] Mt 25:34; 2Ti 2:12
22:30 [p] Lk 14:15 [q] Mt 19:28
22:31 [r] Job 1:6-12 [s] Am 9:9
22:32 [t] Jn 17:9, 15; Ro 8:34 [u] Jn 21:15-17
22:33 [v] Jn 11:16
22:35 [w] Mt 10:9, 10; Lk 9:3; 10:4
22:37 [x] Isa 53:12
22:39 [y] Lk 21:37 [z] Mt 21:1
22:40 [a] Mt 6:13
22:41 [b] Lk 18:11
22:42 [c] Mt 20:22 [d] Mt 26:39
22:43 [e] Mt 4:11; Mk 1:13

38The disciples said, "See, Lord, here
are two swords."
"That's enough!" he replied.

Jesus Prays on the Mount of Olives

22:40–46pp // Mt 26:36–46; Mk 14:32–42

39Jesus went out as usual[y] to the
Mount of Olives,[z] and his disciples followed him. 40On reaching the place, he
said to them, "Pray that you will not fall
into temptation."[a] 41He withdrew about a
stone's throw beyond them, knelt down[b]
and prayed, 42"Father, if you are willing,
take this cup[c] from me; yet not my will,
but yours be done."[d] 43An angel from
heaven appeared to him and strengthened him.[e] 44And being in anguish, he
prayed more earnestly, and his sweat
was like drops of blood falling to the
ground.[b]
45When he rose from prayer and went
back to the disciples, he found them
asleep, exhausted from sorrow. 46"Why
are you sleeping?" he asked them. "Get

[a] *37* Isaiah 53:12 [b] *43,44* Many early manuscripts do not have verses 43 and 44.

22:31–32 Jesus singles out Peter for special attention because Satan has asked to take him through the sieve. Peter does not face this alone; Jesus intercedes for him and for his faith. Jesus goes on to note that when Peter has "turned back," he will be called on to strengthen the people (v. 32). This implies there will be a temporary failure followed by restoration and continued leadership.

22:33–34 Peter obviously comprehends by this time that death awaits Jesus, and he is confident Jesus need not face it alone. But Jesus knows Peter better than Peter does.

22:35–37 Jesus must prepare the disciples to face future realities. Earlier, when Jesus sent them out, God provided for them through people. But now it will be necessary to take money, a bag, and even a sword. They are now going to minister in a world that may well be hostile to them.

22:38 The disciples misunderstand Jesus' rhetorical remarks about defending themselves in the face of opposition. The sword inventory they really need is an inner one. Jesus thus closes the discussion with a dismissive remark.

✣ **22:21–38** In our world, leaders get all the perks and receive service. They wield power and authority with a recognition that their rank gives them the right to direct and coerce others into action. Jesus' approach to leadership is the exact opposite. Leadership is a responsibility and a trust to exercise one's skills and energies to serve those who are led.

Christian leadership is not the raw exercise of power but rather a sensitive and servant-like display of compassion, care, and service. It is the sharing of spiritual resources and energy in a way that leads by example. God exalts those who humble themselves, even as they lead by serving.

22:39–40 Before he goes to pray, Jesus tells his chosen disciples to pray so as to not fall into temptation. One almost has the sense that he is exemplifying what he calls for from them. Prayer is important since it brings us into communion with God and allows us to draw on his presence with us.

22:41–44 Jesus kneels down and intercedes, asking his Father if there might be some other way to accomplish what lies ahead. Jesus has bracketed his request on each end with a commitment to do God's will. The angelic appearance shows heaven's willingness to stand beside Jesus as he faces his calling.

22:45–46 When Jesus gets up and returns to his disciples, he finds them "exhausted from sorrow" and asleep (v. 45). They have begun to understand that rejection for Jesus lies just ahead and it has wiped them out emotionally.

✣ **22:39–46** As committed to God as Jesus is, heaven is just as committed to him. The remark about angelic strength should reassure us that as we turn to him, he will strengthen us. Other texts are clear about how God provides "the way out" for us if, as we face temptation, we recognize our need for him (e.g., 1Co 10:13).

up and pray so that you will not fall into
temptation."[f]

Jesus Arrested

22:47–53pp // Mt 26:47–56; Mk 14:43–50; Jn 18:3–11

47 While he was still speaking a crowd
came up, and the man who was called
Judas, one of the Twelve, was leading
them. He approached Jesus to kiss him,
48 but Jesus asked him, "Judas, are you
betraying the Son of Man with a kiss?"
49 When Jesus' followers saw what was
going to happen, they said, "Lord, should
we strike with our swords?"[g] 50 And one
of them struck the servant of the high
priest, cutting off his right ear.
51 But Jesus answered, "No more of
this!" And he touched the man's ear and
healed him.
52 Then Jesus said to the chief priests,
the officers of the temple guard,[h] and
the elders, who had come for him, "Am I
leading a rebellion, that you have come
with swords and clubs? 53 Every day I
was with you in the temple courts,[i]
and you did not lay a hand on me. But
this is your hour[j]—when darkness
reigns."[k]

Peter Disowns Jesus

22:55–62pp // Mt 26:69–75; Mk 14:66–72; Jn 18:16–18,25–27

54 Then seizing him, they led him away
and took him into the house of the high
priest.[l] Peter followed at a distance.[m]

22:46 [f] ver 40
22:49 [g] ver 38
22:52 [h] ver 4
22:53 [i] Mt 26:55 [j] Jn 12:27 [k] Mt 8:12; Jn 1:5; 3:20
22:54 [l] Mt 26:57; Mk 14:53 [m] Mt 26:58; Mk 14:54; Jn 18:15
22:59 [n] Lk 23:6
22:61 [o] Lk 7:13 [p] ver 34

Lk 22:56–62 ❖ Have we ever denied Jesus publicly? If so, how did or can we renew our commitment?

55 And when some there had kindled a fire
in the middle of the courtyard and had
sat down together, Peter sat down with
them. 56 A servant girl saw him seated
there in the firelight. She looked closely at him and said, "This man was with
him."
57 But he denied it. "Woman, I don't
know him," he said.
58 A little later someone else saw him
and said, "You also are one of them."
"Man, I am not!" Peter replied.
59 About an hour later another asserted, "Certainly this fellow was with him,
for he is a Galilean."[n]
60 Peter replied, "Man, I don't know
what you're talking about!" Just as he
was speaking, the rooster crowed. 61 The
Lord[o] turned and looked straight at Peter. Then Peter remembered the word
the Lord had spoken to him: "Before the
rooster crows today, you will disown me
three times."[p] 62 And he went outside and
wept bitterly.

The Guards Mock Jesus

22:63–65pp // Mt 26:67,68; Mk 14:65; Jn 18:22,23

63 The men who were guarding Jesus
began mocking and beating him. 64 They
blindfolded him and demanded,

22:47–48 The betrayal comes as a crowd approaches and Judas comes forward to give Jesus a kiss. The kiss, a sign of affection, has become a sign of defection and betrayal.

22:49–51 The disciples recall Jesus' remarks about swords. One of them (Peter, according to Jn 18:10), strikes at the servant of the high priest, severing his right ear. We do not know what effect this miracle may have had on the temple guards, but it does not stop them from carrying out their duty.

22:52–53 Jesus complains that they act as if he is a common criminal. There is only one explanation for what is happening: Satan's attempt to stop Jesus is underway.

✣ **22:47–53** There is a subtle strength in facing persecution as Jesus did, passively resting in the active defense of his God. The power of such a defense can be seen in our own time with those who have taken a similar approach to ethical issues in the public square. The church today has all the resources it needs to be as bold for Jesus as the early church was.

22:54–57 One of the maidservants recognizes Peter as one of Jesus' followers and says so. But Peter denies that he even knows Jesus.

22:58 Sometime later, someone else repeats the claim. Peter's denial here is not only of knowing Jesus but also of having any association with his fellow disciples.

22:59–61 The last denial follows about an hour later. Peter's accent identifies him as a man from the northern region of Israel, and he responds. He claims they have the wrong person. The "rock man" (which is the meaning of Peter's name) has been crushed to pieces by the pressure.

With the third denial the rooster crows, just as Jesus predicted. In an additional touch of drama, Luke records that the Lord looks straight at Peter, an act that indicates he knows what Peter has just done. Peter departs, weeping bitterly. Truly, Jesus knew Peter better than Peter knew himself.

22:63–65 Meanwhile, the soldiers mock Jesus mercilessly, identifying him as a prophet, the most popular conception of Jesus. But Rome worried about would-be kings, not about prophets.

"Prophesy! Who hit you?" 65And they said many other insulting things to him.[q]

Jesus Before Pilate and Herod

22:67–71pp // Mt 26:63–66; Mk 14:61–63; Jn 18:19–21
23:2,3pp // Mt 27:11–14; Mk 15:2–5; Jn 18:29–37
23:18–25pp // Mt 27:15–26; Mk 15:6–15; Jn 18:39—19:16

66At daybreak the council[r] of the elders of the people, both the chief priests and the teachers of the law, met together,[s] and Jesus was led before them. 67"If you are the Messiah," they said, "tell us."

Jesus answered, "If I tell you, you will not believe me, 68and if I asked you, you would not answer.[t] 69But from now on, the Son of Man will be seated at the right hand of the mighty God."[u]

70They all asked, "Are you then the Son of God?"[v]

He replied, "You say that I am."[w]

71Then they said, "Why do we need any more testimony? We have heard it from his own lips."

23 Then the whole assembly rose and led him off to Pilate.[x] 2And they began to accuse him, saying, "We have found this man subverting our nation.[y] He opposes payment of taxes to Caesar[z] and claims to be Messiah, a king."[a]

3So Pilate asked Jesus, "Are you the king of the Jews?"

"You have said so," Jesus replied.

4Then Pilate announced to the chief priests and the crowd, "I find no basis for a charge against this man."[b]

5But they insisted, "He stirs up the people all over Judea by his teaching. He started in Galilee[c] and has come all the way here."

6On hearing this, Pilate asked if the man was a Galilean.[d] 7When he learned that Jesus was under Herod's jurisdiction, he sent him to Herod,[e] who was also in Jerusalem at that time.

8When Herod saw Jesus, he was greatly pleased, because for a long time he had

22:65 [q] Mt 16:21
22:66 [r] Mt 5:22 [s] Mt 27:1; Mk 15:1
22:68 [t] Lk 20:3-8
22:69 [u] Mk 16:19
22:70 [v] Mt 4:3 [w] Mt 27:11; Lk 23:3
23:1 [x] Mt 27:2; Mk 15:1; Jn 18:28
23:2 [y] ver 14 [z] Lk 20:22 [a] Jn 19:12
23:4 [b] ver 14, 22, 41; Mt 27:23; Jn 18:38; 1Ti 6:13; 2Co 5:21
23:5 [c] Mk 1:14
23:6 [d] Lk 22:59
23:7 [e] Mt 14:1; Lk 3:1

22:66–71 The account of the trial has several irregularities according to the Mishnah. (1) The proceedings did not take place at the temple. (2) Jesus is allowed no defense. (3) Jesus does not blaspheme in the technical sense of the term by using the divine name. (4) The verdict comes on the same day as the trial, when two days were required to try capital crimes. (5) Jesus is being tried on a feast day, which is normally prohibited. (6) Contradictory testimony is supposed to clear the defendant. (7) The high priest is not supposed to issue the guilty verdict.
22:66–67 With chief priests and teachers of the law gathered together, Jesus is examined.
22:68–69 Jesus makes three claims here. First, he predicts that he will eventually be seated at God's right hand in heaven. Second, he claims to have authority from God, an authority he will exercise from this moment on. Finally, he has authority over them. They may run this trial, but he is the one who will ultimately judge.
22:70 Note how Luke is weaving titles together here: Messiah, Son of Man, and Son of God. Jesus replies to the Son of God question with, "You say that I am." The audience takes it positively: They have their man. Jesus is the witness the leadership sought and sends himself to the cross. Jesus spoke as he did because his claim is true.
22:71 Just what did Jesus say that was so condemning in Jewish eyes? The key remark appears to be his claim to be Son of God, not merely in a royal sense, but *as it is tied to the claim of being the Son of Man of Da 7:13–14.* Jesus in effect is claiming the right to go directly into God's presence and be seated with him in heaven. To Jewish ears this is highly offensive—worse than claiming the right to permanently reside in the Holy of Holies at the temple.

✣ **22:54–71** Christianity is a historically grounded faith. Without a cross, the Christian faith is of no more value than many other religious ethical systems or forms of psychology. Throughout this Gospel we have seen Jesus make himself the issue; reducing Christianity to moral teaching eliminates the unique person of the Christ from Christianity. Without him and what he accomplished in his death and resurrection, there is not much sense to the faith. Luke wants us to ponder whose side we are on.

23:1–2 After the Jewish trial, the entourage heads for Pilate. No doubt the meeting is quickly arranged. The heart of the case is a threefold accusation: (1) Jesus subverts the nation; (2) he opposes payment of taxes to Caesar; and (3) he claims to be Christ, a king.

An internal religious dispute is of no interest to Pilate, so more concrete political charges are needed. Since Pilate is responsible to keep the peace and collect taxes, the taxation charges challenge his ability to do his job faithfully. This second charge is blatantly false, as readers of Luke recognize from 20:20–26.
23:3–5 The third charge is the one Pilate pursues with a simple question, to which Jesus responds with a mild affirmative. Pilate's conclusion that there is "no basis for a charge" against Jesus should have been the end of the matter, but the Jewish leaders continue their protest.
23:6–7 Pilate thinks up a brilliant solution. He will send Jesus to Herod, since Herod has authority over Galilee. Now any decision Pilate makes will have Herod's consultation, and Pilate will be protected either way.
23:8–12 Herod is excited about meeting Jesus. He has heard about him and wants to see the Galilean

THE HERODS

NAME	DATES OF REIGN	TITLE	TERRITORY	NT PERIOD
Herod the Great	37–4 BC	King	Judea, Samaria, Galilee, Perea, Idumea, Traconitis	Time of Jesus' birth
Herod Philip II	4 BC–AD 34	Tetrarch	Iturea, Traconitis	Jesus' infancy till after his death and resurrection
Herod Antipas	4 BC–AD 39	Tetrarch	Galilee and Perea	Jesus' infancy till after his death and resurrection
Herod Archelaus	4 BC–AD 6	Ethnarch	Judea, Idumea, Samaria	Jesus' infancy till his early childhood
Herod Agrippa	AD 37–44	King	Judea, Samaria, Galilee, Perea, Idumea, northeast Palestine	Early years after Pentecost
Herod Agrippa II	AD 50–70	Tetrarch	Tiberias, Batanea, Traconitis, Auranitis, Abila	During the spread of Christianity to the Gentiles

From Robert L. Thomas, *Charts of the Gospels and the Life of Christ* (Grand Rapids: Zondervan, 2000), 74.

been wanting to see him.[f] From what
he had heard about him, he hoped to
see him perform a sign of some sort.
9He plied him with many questions,
but Jesus gave him no answer.[g] 10The
chief priests and the teachers of the law
were standing there, vehemently accusing him. 11Then Herod and his soldiers
ridiculed and mocked him. Dressing him
in an elegant robe,[h] they sent him back
to Pilate. 12That day Herod and Pilate
became friends[i]—before this they had
been enemies.

13Pilate called together the chief
priests, the rulers and the people, 14and
said to them, "You brought me this man
as one who was inciting the people to
rebellion. I have examined him in your
presence and have found no basis for
your charges against him.[j] 15Neither has
Herod, for he sent him back to us; as you
can see, he has done nothing to deserve
death. 16Therefore, I will punish him[k]
and then release him." [17][a]

18But the whole crowd shouted, "Away
with this man! Release Barabbas to us!"[l]
19(Barabbas had been thrown into prison for an insurrection in the city, and
for murder.)

20Wanting to release Jesus, Pilate

23:8 [f] Lk 9:9
23:9 [g] Mk 14:61
23:11 [h] Mk 15:17-19; Jn 19:2,3
23:12 [i] Ac 4:27
23:14 [j] ver 4
23:16 [k] ver 22; Mt 27:26; Jn 19:1; Ac 16:37; 2Co 11:23,24
23:18 [l] Ac 3:13,14

[a] *17* Some manuscripts include here words similar to Matt. 27:15 and Mark 15:6.

---

perform miracles. But he is disappointed by Jesus' lack of response to his questions. In the face of Jesus' silence, Herod and others react with more mocking. Then they send him back to Pilate.

✣ **23:1–12** When we engage in sharing about Jesus, we can expect a wide array of responses to him. Some will be decidedly hostile, while others will be more disinterested, just as in the trial scenes. But both constitute rejection. Evangelism often requires patience. Our primary responsibility before the Lord is to continue to share his story and the eternal hope it provides.

23:13–15 Pilate makes his clearest statement yet on how he sees the matter. Pilate concludes that "he has done nothing to deserve death" (v. 15), the same verdict Herod reached. It sounds like Jesus' release is coming.

23:16–19 Pilate knows he can't simply release Jesus and expect the crowd to remain peaceful, so he compromises by offering to flog Jesus before he releases him. This judgment receives a public reaction: "Away with this man! Release Barabbas to us!" (v. 18). The response must have caught Pilate off guard; Barabbas was incarcerated for leading an uprising and for murder. The crowd desires the release of a man who is clearly more dangerous than Jesus.

23:20–21 Crucifixion was designed to deter criminals. That is why the executions were public. The crowd wants Jesus not just to die but to experience this most gruesome form of execution. He is counted among the worst of criminals.

Lk 23:34 ❖ How do these words from the cross show the depth of Christ's love?

appealed to them again. 21But they kept
shouting, "Crucify him! Crucify him!"
22For the third time he spoke to them:
"Why? What crime has this man committed? I have found in him no grounds for
the death penalty. Therefore I will have
him punished and then release him."[m]
23But with loud shouts they insistently demanded that he be crucified, and
their shouts prevailed. 24So Pilate decided to grant their demand. 25He released
the man who had been thrown into prison for insurrection and murder, the one
they asked for, and surrendered Jesus to
their will.

The Crucifixion of Jesus

23:33–43pp // Mt 27:33–44; Mk 15:22–32; Jn 19:17–24

26As the soldiers led him away, they
seized Simon from Cyrene,[n] who was
on his way in from the country, and put
the cross on him and made him carry it
behind Jesus.[o] 27A large number of people followed him, including women who
mourned and wailed[p] for him. 28Jesus
turned and said to them, "Daughters of
Jerusalem, do not weep for me; weep for
yourselves and for your children.[q] 29For
the time will come when you will say,
'Blessed are the childless women, the
wombs that never bore and the breasts
that never nursed!'[r] 30Then

"'they will say to the mountains,
"Fall on us!"
and to the hills, "Cover us!"'[a][s]

31For if people do these things when the
tree is green, what will happen when it
is dry?"[t]
32Two other men, both criminals, were
also led out with him to be executed.[u]
33When they came to the place called
the Skull, they crucified him there, along
with the criminals—one on his right, the
other on his left. 34Jesus said, "Father,[v]
forgive them, for they do not know what
they are doing."[b][w] And they divided up
his clothes by casting lots.[x]
35The people stood watching, and the
rulers even sneered at him.[y] They said,
"He saved others; let him save himself
if he is God's Messiah, the Chosen One."[z]
36The soldiers also came up and
mocked him.[a] They offered him wine
vinegar[b] 37and said, "If you are the king
of the Jews,[c] save yourself."

23:22 [m] ver 16
23:26 [n] Mt 27:32 [o] Mk 15:21; Jn 19:17
23:27 [p] Lk 8:52
23:28 [q] Lk 19:41-44; 21:23,24
23:29 [r] Mt 24:19
23:30 [s] Isa 2:19; Hos 10:8; Rev 6:16
23:31 [t] Eze 20:47
23:32 [u] Isa 53:12; Mt 27:38; Mk 15:27; Jn 19:18
23:34 [v] Mt 11:25 [w] Mt 5:44 [x] Ps 22:18
23:35 [y] Ps 22:17 [z] Isa 42:1
23:36 [a] Ps 22:7 [b] Ps 69:21; Mt 27:48
23:37 [c] Lk 4:3,9

[a] *30* Hosea 10:8 [b] *34* Some early manuscripts do not have this sentence.

23:22-25 Pilate finally relents. Barabbas is released, while Jesus is surrendered to the will of the people. It is not justice that sends Jesus to the cross, but a hostile mass of humanity.

✜ **23:13-25** Barabbas's story is our story. Jesus freed us by his death, just as Barabbas was freed. One who saves a life is owed a life. The Christian walk is a statement of gratitude to the One who has taken our place. Jesus did not complain as he bore the cross for the murderer and for us. Those of us who have been rescued from the penalty of sin understand that Barabbas's freedom paints a picture of our escape from death through the gracious work of Jesus.

23:26 Without sleep and after a scourging, Jesus needs help in bearing the cross. Simon from Cyrene is drafted to carry the cross. As Jesus goes to the cross, another person, just like us, shares in his journey there.

23:27-31 The crowds that urged his execution have stayed on to see it carried out. With them is a group of women, wailing in mourning. Jesus urges them not to weep for him. The real issue is what his death means for those who reject him. Hard days lie ahead for the nation, in which "barren women" will be blessed. The judgment to come on the nation will be harsh.

23:32-33 The hill where executions take place protrudes out of the ground like a skull. Jesus' cross is situated between the two criminals. This is revealing, since in the debate between the criminals one of them will soon confess him and be saved. Jesus is the bridge by which the unrighteous can become the righteous.

23:34 Jesus turns again to the Father in prayer, asking that the actions of his enemies be forgiven. By praying for his enemies, Jesus has fulfilled his own instructions to pray for one's enemies. Jesus proves his love and compassion.

The soldiers divide up his clothes among them by casting lots. This remark alludes to Ps 22:18. Another part of that psalm shows up in Jesus' cry from the cross about being forsaken by God (Mt 27:46, Mk 15:34), which Luke does not record. Jesus is hanging on the cross as an innocent man, willingly dying for those who do not understand his death and who mock it.

23:35 This execution fits the pattern of public crucifixion known in the ancient world. The people "watch" what is taking place, and the leaders "sneer" (v. 35; both verbs appear in Ps 22:7). Their sarcasm shows just how much confidence and passion there is in Jesus' enemies.

23:36-38 The soldiers add to the mocking. They offer a dry "wine vinegar" that was used among the poor. Luke records the notice of the crime:

PEOPLE TO KNOW // THIEF ON THE CROSS

LUKE 23:39–43: Jesus was crucified between two common criminals. From one side, he was mocked and ridiculed. The criminal crucified next to him said contemptuously, "Aren't you the Messiah? Save yourself and us!" (Lk 23:39).

The criminal on the other side of Jesus, however, rebuked the first criminal. He said the two of them were receiving what they deserved for the crimes they committed; they were both guilty as charged. The man between them, though, had done nothing wrong. This criminal acknowledged that Jesus was innocent.

Then the man addressed Jesus directly, asking, "Jesus, remember me when you come into your kingdom" (Lk 23:42). With these words, he professed his faith that Jesus was the Messiah who would inaugurate the kingdom of God. Despite what his eyes saw—Jesus hanging on a cross to die—God opened the eyes of his heart to put his faith in Christ and humbly ask for salvation.

Christ responded mercifully with a promise to which desperate people through the ages have clung in hope: "Today you will be with me in paradise" (Lk 23:43).

APPLICATION ✚ It is never too late to put our faith in Christ. In the waning hours of his life, God softened the heart of the criminal next to Jesus, leading him to acknowledge his own sin and seek salvation.

Sometimes people don't want to ask God for forgiveness of their sins; they feel like they have failed too much and strayed from God too long. Jesus' words to the repentant criminal, however, show that God's mercy is always available when we turn to him in faith. It does not matter how far or how long we have strayed from God. Christ is ready to welcome us in. It is not too late!

38 There was a written notice above
him, which read: THIS IS THE KING OF
THE JEWS.[d]
39 One of the criminals who hung there
hurled insults at him: "Aren't you the
Messiah? Save yourself and us!"[e]
40 But the other criminal rebuked him.
"Don't you fear God," he said, "since you
are under the same sentence? 41 We are
punished justly, for we are getting what
our deeds deserve. But this man has
done nothing wrong."[f]
42 Then he said, "Jesus, remember me
when you come into your kingdom.[a]"[g]
43 Jesus answered him, "Truly I tell
you, today you will be with me in paradise."[h]

23:38 [d] Mt 2:2
23:39 [e] ver 35, 37
23:41 [f] ver 4
23:42 [g] Mt 16:27
23:43 [h] 2Co 12:3, 4; Rev 2:7
23:44 [i] Am 8:9
23:45 [j] Ex 26:31-33; Heb 9:3,8 [k] Heb 10:19,20
23:46 [l] Mt 27:50 [m] Ps 31:5; 1Pe 2:23 [n] Jn 19:30
23:47 [o] Mt 9:8

The Death of Jesus

23:44–49pp // Mt 27:45–56; Mk 15:33–41; Jn 19:29–30

44 It was now about noon, and darkness
came over the whole land until three
in the afternoon,[i] 45 for the sun stopped
shining. And the curtain of the temple[j]
was torn in two.[k] 46 Jesus called out with
a loud voice,[l] "Father, into your hands I
commit my spirit."[b][m] When he had said
this, he breathed his last.[n]
47 The centurion, seeing what had happened, praised God[o] and said, "Surely
this was a righteous man." 48 When all

[a] 42 Some manuscripts *come with your kingly power* [b] 46 Psalm 31:5

"THIS IS THE KING OF THE JEWS" (v. 38). He consistently shows how it is Jesus as the Christ who goes to the cross.

23:39–43 The scene turns back to the criminals. One of them accepts the claim that Jesus is a king, and declares he wants to share in his coming rule and to be among the righteous in the judgment. Jesus' reply indicates that an answer to his request will come sooner than the criminal hopes.

23:44–45 At midday it becomes dark for three hours. Now even the heavens testify to the nature of the hour. In the OT darkness often indicates judgment. Next, the curtain at the temple is torn in two. A time of judgment has come, and the temple is included in that judgment. The curtain shielded access to God; ripping it open demonstrates that access is no longer restricted.

23:46 Jesus' final words come from Ps 31:5. This psalm describes a righteous sufferer, just as Jesus is, and Jesus trusts his Father to care for him. What happens from this point on is up to God.

23:47 A Roman centurion declares that Jesus is surely "righteous." The centurion thus becomes a second witness to affirm Jesus' legal innocence as he is dying.

23:48 The crowds also react. They depart, beating their chests. Perhaps these terrifying cosmic signs convicted them of their guilt in condemning an innocent man.

the people who had gathered to witness
this sight saw what took place, they beat
their breasts[p] and went away. 49But all
those who knew him, including the
women who had followed him from
Galilee,[q] stood at a distance,[r] watching
these things.

The Burial of Jesus

23:50–56pp // Mt 27:57–61; Mk 15:42–47; Jn 19:38–42

50Now there was a man named Joseph,
a member of the Council, a good and upright man, 51who had not consented to
their decision and action. He came from
the Judean town of Arimathea, and he
himself was waiting for the kingdom
of God.[s] 52Going to Pilate, he asked for
Jesus' body. 53Then he took it down,
wrapped it in linen cloth and placed it
in a tomb cut in the rock, one in which
no one had yet been laid. 54It was Preparation Day,[t] and the Sabbath was about
to begin.
55The women who had come with
Jesus from Galilee[u] followed Joseph and
saw the tomb and how his body was laid
in it. 56Then they went home and prepared spices and perfumes.[v] But they
rested on the Sabbath in obedience to
the commandment.[w]

Jesus Has Risen

24:1–10pp // Mt 28:1–8; Mk 16:1–8; Jn 20:1–8

24 On the first day of the week, very
early in the morning, the wom-
en took the spices they had prepared[x]
and went to the tomb. 2They found the
stone rolled away from the tomb, 3but
when they entered, they did not find
the body of the Lord Jesus.[y] 4While
they were wondering about this, suddenly two men in clothes that gleamed
like lightning[z] stood beside them. 5In
their fright the women bowed down
with their faces to the ground, but the
men said to them, "Why do you look for
the living among the dead? 6He is not
here; he has risen! Remember how he
told you, while he was still with you in
Galilee:[a] 7'The Son of Man[b] must be delivered over to the hands of sinners, be
crucified and on the third day be raised

23:48 [p] Lk 18:13
23:49 [q] Lk 8:2 [r] Ps 38:11
23:51 [s] Lk 2:25, 38
23:54 [t] Mt 27:62
23:55 [u] ver 49
23:56 [v] Mk 16:1; Lk 24:1 [w] Ex 12:16; 20:10
24:1 [x] Lk 23:56
24:3 [y] ver 23, 24
24:4 [z] Jn 20:12
24:6 [a] Mt 17:22, 23; Mk 9:30-31; Lk 9:22; 24:44
24:7 [b] Mt 8:20

23:49 The disciples see all these things from a distance. The one thing this death has is numerous witnesses. Among them is a group of women who have been with Jesus from the start of his ministry in Galilee.

23:26–49 The cross is, at its heart, the offer of God's gracious forgiveness to those who embrace it. To embrace the cross means to renounce our own works as the basis of our salvation. Our relationship with God comes through trusting in Jesus and in his finished work. Our spiritual well-being rests solidly and securely in the hands of a caring heavenly Father.

23:50–54 Joseph of Arimathea takes possession of the body, brings it down from the cross, and wraps it in linen. Joseph then places the body in a previously unused tomb. Such tombs were present just north of the city. Jesus receives an honorable burial.

23:55–56 As the women prepare for the Sabbath, they also prepare spices and perfumes. These reduced the stench that surrounded a body's decomposition. The women fully intend to return to the tomb to honor their Lord. There is no indication they expect a resurrection that involves Jesus' physical body.

23:50–56 One of the charges some make today is that the resurrection was an event created by the early church to allow Jesus' memory and teaching to continue. If that were the case, the authors of the Gospels have certainly found an unusual way to describe the preparation for it. Their testimony is that the resurrection caught the disciples by surprise. When Jesus died, they figured he had departed. Even though Jesus prophesied his resurrection, it did not sink in. If the resurrection were a fabrication, would its creators portray the disciples as being so much at a loss to understand what Jesus was predicting? The implications of this contrast lead directly to a decision for the resurrection and to Jesus' claims about who he is.

24:1–3 The first hint that something unusual has taken place is that the stone is rolled away at the entrance of the tomb. The women enter the tomb only to find that "the body of the Lord" (v. 3) is missing. The predominant title for Jesus in this chapter is "Lord." Jesus' resurrection reveals his lordship and points to his exaltation and vindication by God.
24:4 At this point "two men" appear. The women know that they are in the presence of some type of supernatural beings, so they bow before them in respect.
24:5 The "men" speak to them by asking a simple question. In other words, Jesus is alive! The tomb could not hold him.
24:6–8 "Remember how he told you . . ." This remark is both a call to remember and a rebuke. When God speaks, we must listen with hearts that recognize who is speaking the promise. The angels' remark leads the women to recall Jesus' words, which are indeed coming to pass.

THE RESURRECTION

What are the implications of the Resurrection?

IF IT HAPPENED ...	IF IT DIDN'T ...
Jesus' death was "according to the Scriptures"—an atoning sacrifice and fulfillment of prophecy.	Jesus' death was, at best, an injustice perpetrated by Jewish authorities in collusion with Rome.
Jesus' identity as the prophesied Messiah is authenticated by his foretold resurrection.	Jesus did not fulfill prophecies regarding the resurrection and was not the promised Messiah.
The apostles' stories of encountering the risen Christ are trustworthy accounts of eyewitnesses.	The apostolic witness is, at best, a mistake, and at worst, a fabrication.
The preaching of the gospel is indeed "Good News," providing hope and forgiveness.	The preaching of the gospel is "useless."
Faith in the gospel is well-placed.	Faith in the gospel is foolish.
Those who have faith in Jesus have a sure hope that they too will be raised.	There is no promise of personal resurrection.
Sacrifice and suffering for the gospel is worthwhile for those who anticipate resurrection and reward.	Sacrifice and suffering are meaningless.
Those who believe in and accept the saving work of Jesus will be raised to eternal life.	"Those who have fallen asleep in Christ are lost . . . we are of all people most to be pitied" (1Co 15:12-19).

again.' "[c] 8Then they remembered his
words.[d]
9When they came back from the tomb,
they told all these things to the Elev-
en and to all the others. 10It was Mary
Magdalene, Joanna, Mary the mother of
James, and the others with them[e] who
told this to the apostles.[f] 11But they did
not believe[g] the women, because their
words seemed to them like nonsense.
12Peter, however, got up and ran to the
tomb. Bending over, he saw the strips
of linen lying by themselves,[h] and he
went away,[i] wondering to himself what
had happened.

On the Road to Emmaus

13Now that same day two of them were
going to a village called Emmaus, about
seven miles[a] from Jerusalem.[j] 14They
were talking with each other about everything that had happened. 15As they
talked and discussed these things with
each other, Jesus himself came up and

24:7 [c] Mt 16:21
24:8 [d] Jn 2:22
24:10 [e] Lk 8:1-3 [f] Mk 6:30
24:11 [g] Mk 16:11
24:12 [h] Jn 20:3-7 [i] Jn 20:10
24:13 [j] Mk 16:12

[a] 13 Or about 11 kilometers

24:9-10 The women journey back to where the disciples and others are gathered and tell their story. Culturally, such a story coming from women would be viewed with suspicion. One of the main proofs that the resurrection story is credible is the realization that the first-century church would never have created a story whose main first witnesses were women.
24:11 The first skeptics Jesus faces are his disciples.
24:12 Peter knows better than to doubt the Lord's word. He runs to the tomb and sees the grave clothes but no body. He leaves the tomb "wondering to himself what had happened."

24:1-12 Perhaps we should be less surprised when people initially stumble over the reality of the resurrection. After all, the disciples hurdle it only after much persuasion. The Bible is real as it tells its story. The doubt of the disciples is set forth with crystal clarity. Their slowness to believe is instructive: Resurrection is a doctrine that is hard to believe. For that reason, the Spirit needs to work in hearts as the gospel is shared.

Resurrection changes everything. Luke wants us to ponder the "so what" of Jesus' resurrection—that Jesus is alive and offers forgiveness, so that we can have a new relationship with God through him. For believers, resurrection is a reminder that new life is a gift from God that calls us to a life of gratitude. To those who do not know him, Scripture calls them to embrace what the resurrection means.

24:13-16 The two men traveling to Emmaus find themselves discussing what has taken place. Perhaps they are disputing the meaning of the empty tomb. Jesus' first post-resurrection appearance in Luke is both normal and mysterious at the same time. This description adds to the drama and the mystery of the resurrection.

PEOPLE TO KNOW // DISCIPLES ON THE ROAD TO EMMAUS

LUKE 24:13–35: Walking home from the terrible events of Jesus' crucifixion and death were two disciples, Cleopas and a companion. They were traumatized by what they had witnessed; they had put their hope in Jesus as God's Messiah. Dejected, they walked along the road back to their village of Emmaus.

A man walked up to them and asked what they were discussing. Voicing their dashed hope, Cleopas said, "We had hoped that he was the one who was going to redeem Israel" (Lk 24:21). He went on to say that some women claimed to have encountered an angel that morning who said Jesus was alive.

The stranger walking with them chided them for being foolish and slow to understand what the Scriptures taught: that the Messiah had to suffer these things. He gave them a Bible lesson to prove it (Lk 24:25–27).

When they came to the village, Cleopas and his friend prevailed on the man to stay and eat with them. As they sat down, the man took bread, gave thanks, broke it and gave it to them. Immediately their eyes were opened to the fact that the man was Jesus. Then he disappeared.

APPLICATION Cleopas and his friend placed their hope in the right place: Jesus the Messiah. However, they lacked vision to see the whole picture and thus became discouraged in their faith. Jesus was patient with them, just as Jesus is patient with us in our slow moments of misunderstanding. We, too, need our eyes opened to see Jesus. The words of the Bible reveal God and his plan. The Holy Spirit opens our eyes to see and our minds to understand. Our journey of faith echoes with the steps of Jesus, who walks with us, sharing our burdens and pointing us to the Father.

walked along with them;[k] 16but they were
kept from recognizing him.[l]
17He asked them, "What are you discussing together as you walk along?"

They stood still, their faces downcast. 18One of them, named Cleopas,[m]
asked him, "Are you the only one visiting Jerusalem who does not know the things that have happened there in these days?"
19"What things?" he asked.

"About Jesus of Nazareth,"[n] they replied. "He was a prophet,[o] powerful in word and deed before God and all the
people. 20The chief priests and our rulers[p] handed him over to be sentenced to death, and they crucified him; 21but
we had hoped that he was the one who was going to redeem Israel.[q] And what is more, it is the third day[r] since all this
took place. 22In addition, some of our women amazed us.[s] They went to the tomb early this morning 23but didn't find
his body. They came and told us that they had seen a vision of angels, who said he
was alive. 24Then some of our companions went to the tomb and found it just as the women had said, but they did not see Jesus."[t]
25He said to them, "How foolish you are, and how slow to believe all that the
prophets have spoken! 26Did not the Messiah have to suffer these things and
then enter his glory?"[u] 27And beginning
with Moses[v] and all the Prophets,[w] he explained to them what was said in all the Scriptures concerning himself.[x]
28As they approached the village to

24:15 [k] ver 36
24:16 [l] Jn 20:14; 21:4
24:18 [m] Jn 19:25
24:19 [n] Mk 1:24 [o] Mt 21:11
24:20 [p] Lk 23:13
24:21 [q] Lk 1:68; 2:38; 21:28 [r] Mt 16:21
24:22 [s] ver 1-10
24:24 [t] ver 12
24:26 [u] Heb 2:10; 1Pe 1:11
24:27 [v] Ge 3:15; Nu 21:9; Dt 18:15 [w] Isa 7:14; 9:6; 40:10, 11; 53; Eze 34:23; Da 9:24; Mic 7:20; Mal 3:1 [x] Jn 1:45

24:17–21 Of course, Jesus knows exactly what has happened, since it happened to him. Nonetheless, Jesus asks, "What things?" The disciples answer immediately, "About Jesus of Nazareth," and note his prophetic work. The disciples hoped Jesus would be the one to redeem Israel. That was the hope they saw nailed to a cross in the capital city.
24:22–24 But there is more to tell. Three days later, some of the women went to the tomb only to find it empty. They also reported angels telling them that Jesus was alive. Other companions went to the tomb and found it empty. The two disciples are baffled by what has taken place. The last thing they expect is a resurrection.
24:25–27 Jesus then launches into a rebuke, whose rationale becomes clearer as events move on. They must believe the messianic promises of the ancient Scriptures. Imagine listening to Jesus explain his work in the world "beginning with Moses and all the Prophets." What a discourse that must have been!
24:28–32 As the three near their stop at the village, it appears as if Jesus will journey on. But the two men persuade him to stay with them. In a move reminiscent of the Last Supper, Jesus takes

which they were going, Jesus continued
on as if he were going farther. 29But they
urged him strongly, "Stay with us, for it is
nearly evening; the day is almost over."
So he went in to stay with them.
30When he was at the table with them,
he took bread, gave thanks, broke it[y] and
began to give it to them. 31Then their
eyes were opened and they recognized
him,[z] and he disappeared from their
sight. 32They asked each other, "Were
not our hearts burning within us[a] while
he talked with us on the road and opened
the Scriptures[b] to us?"
33They got up and returned at once to
Jerusalem. There they found the Elev-
en and those with them, assembled
together 34and saying, "It is true! The
Lord has risen and has appeared to Simon."[c] 35Then the two told what had
happened on the way, and how Jesus
was recognized by them when he broke
the bread.[d]

Jesus Appears to the Disciples

36While they were still talking about
this, Jesus himself stood among them
and said to them, "Peace be with you."[e]
37They were startled and frightened,
thinking they saw a ghost.[f] 38He said to
them, "Why are you troubled, and why do
doubts rise in your minds? 39Look at my
hands and my feet. It is I myself! Touch
me and see;[g] a ghost does not have flesh
and bones, as you see I have."
40When he had said this, he showed
them his hands and feet. 41And while
they still did not believe it because of joy
and amazement, he asked them, "Do you
have anything here to eat?" 42They gave
him a piece of broiled fish, 43and he took
it and ate it in their presence.[h]
44He said to them, "This is what I told
you while I was still with you:[i] Everything must be fulfilled[j] that is written
about me in the Law of Moses,[k] the
Prophets and the Psalms."[l]
45Then he opened their minds so
they could understand the Scriptures.
46He told them, "This is what is written:
The Messiah will suffer and rise from
the dead on the third day, 47and repentance for the forgiveness of sins will be
preached in his name[m] to all nations,[n]
beginning at Jerusalem. 48You are witnesses[o] of these things. 49I am going to
send you what my Father has promised;[p]
but stay in the city until you have been
clothed with power from on high."

Lk 24:49 ❖ How has Christ clothed his followers with power? What does this power look like?

24:30 [y] Mt 14:19
24:31 [z] ver 16
24:32 [a] Ps 39:3 [b] ver 27,45
24:34 [c] 1Co 15:5
24:35 [d] ver 30, 31
24:36 [e] Jn 20:19,21, 26; 14:27
24:37 [f] Mk 6:49
24:39 [g] Jn 20:27; 1Jn 1:1
24:43 [h] Ac 10:41
24:44 [i] Lk 9:45; 18:34 [j] Mt 16:21; Lk 9:22,44; 18:31-33; 22:37 [k] ver 27 [l] Ps 2; 16; 22; 69; 72; 110; 118
24:47 [m] Ac 5:31; 10:43; 13:38 [n] Mt 28:19
24:48 [o] Ac 1:8; 2:32; 5:32; 13:31; 1Pe 5:1
24:49 [p] Jn 14:16; Ac 1:4

---

the bread, gives thanks, breaks it, and gives it to them. Suddenly, their eyes are opened.

24:33–35 Cleopas and his friend return at once to Jerusalem. There the Eleven and the others are still gathered and quite excited. Despair becomes delight as the truth about Jesus' resurrection begins to sink in.

✜ **24:13-35** Jesus' place at the right hand of God means that he possesses authority over all those forces that stand opposed to humanity. Such authority stands behind his ability to give us new birth into eternal life. We have access to the one who enables us to overcome whatever obstacles Satan places in our path. Everything that we have in Christ ultimately is made possible through the resurrection.

24:36–37 As the disciples are sharing reports, Jesus himself stands among them and gives them a beatitude that sums up his ministry in triumph: "Peace be with you." It is a greeting of comfort. The group is frightened by his appearance, since they think Jesus is a spirit (v. 37).

24:38–43 Jesus' remarks suggest some are still doubting even after the appearances. So he invites them to look at and touch his hands and feet. The resurrection body is both the same as and different from the physical body, retaining aspects of physicality while existing in a glorified condition. Jesus does everything he can to reassure his disciples that he is truly alive.

24:44 Jesus then explains what has taken place: The disciples are experiencing what Scripture promised and what the saints of old longed to see.

24:45–47 As Jesus instructs the disciples in the Scriptures, we must note that the church has developed its understanding of the OT from Jesus. In the same sense, Jesus has "opened [our] minds" so we can understand as the disciples did: Jesus, the Christ, the Messiah, was to suffer and die and to be raised. His disciples must now engage in preaching to the nations.

To repent is to change direction. This change of perspective embraces Jesus and the forgiveness he offers. This message of salvation extends to all the nations.

24:48–49 The disciples saw Jesus hang on the cross and have now seen him in his resurrection. Their calling is to share that what they know has taken place according to the Scriptures. Jesus will send them out, but not before he has equipped them. To this end he will send to them the Spirit from his Father. Until the Spirit comes, they must remain in Jerusalem.

The Ascension of Jesus

50When he had led them out to the vicinity of Bethany,[q] he lifted up his hands and
blessed them. 51While he was blessing them,
he left them and was taken up into heaven.[r]
52Then they worshiped him and returned to
Jerusalem with great joy. 53And they stayed
continually at the temple,[s] praising God.

24:50 [q] Mt 21:17
24:51 [r] 2Ki 2:11
24:53 [s] Ac 2:46

24:50–52 Luke's Gospel closes with Jesus' taking the disciples out to Bethany, lifting up his hands, blessing them, and departing into heaven. Jesus blesses the disciples as he departs to continue his work from God's side. What follows for them are worship and joy. They return to the temple, where Luke's story began with Zechariah, to praise God for all that has taken place.

24:36–53 Lest we get too nervous about evangelism, let's remember that we do not share Jesus by ourselves. Jesus has provided his Spirit, who indwells us to help us make sense of our testimony. The disciples waited for the Spirit to empower and enable them to share with conviction. To see how effective the Spirit can be, we need only contrast the Peter of the three denials with the Peter of the speeches recorded in the book of Acts.

We have an opportunity to share in that march of faith throughout history. God is at work in it all, fulfilling what he promised centuries ago in the OT. He is as present in our own sharing as he was in the commission Jesus issued to a small group of mostly Galilean followers in the first century. The march of faith moves one era at a time, one person at a time, one testimony at a time. Centuries ago, Luke wrote to reassure Theophilus that he belonged in that honored line (Lk 1:1-4). Fortunately for us, God made sure that Theophilus was not the only one to be reassured about the grace of Jesus.

Author: The apostle John

Audience: Primarily Gentile believers and seeking unbelievers

Date: Either the AD 60s or more likely the 80s or early 90s

Theme: John presents Jesus as the Word, the Messiah and the incarnate Son of God, who has come to reveal the Father and bring eternal life to all who believe in him.

PERSPECTIVE

The Gospel of John narrates the life of Jesus and teaches what that life meant to those who knew him or had heard about him.

One of the principal emphases of the book of John is Christology, which is the doctrine that studies the person and work of Christ. Needless to say, "Christology" was not a "doctrine" in John's day. Jesus had come among the disciples and the people, performing signs that revealed God's plan of redemption to them in public settings around Galilee and Jerusalem. He taught those who chose to follow him, and they were with him when he encountered resistance and was crucified. He was raised from the dead.

Yet in spite of the miraculous signs, pointed teachings, and resurrection (the raw data out of which Christology was shaped), it took hundreds of years for the church to come to some agreement about Jesus' incarnation—his humanity and divinity. The Gospel of John is in many ways the first reflection on his incarnate nature.

Little wonder, then, that the Gospel of John has been used to support the misplaced emphases that such a difficult teaching can fall prey to—and that it is still used to support mistaken impressions of who Jesus was. The present book is valuable today because in talking about who Jesus was, it resonates so clearly with spiritual needs common to our twenty-first century world.

For example, one of those needs is to be assured that Jesus was indeed the Son of God. Our faith rests on it. Although some suggest that we could better identify with a purely human Jesus, such a teaching would result in a much different religion that would do little

Reading John

John begins with an eighteen-verse prologue telling us who Jesus is. From John 1:19 to 12:50, often using a conversational style, he records various events in the life of Jesus; most of these stories have no parallel in the Gospels of Matthew, Mark or Luke. The next five chapters recount Jesus' last discourse with his disciples in the upper room. John closes his Gospel with an account of Jesus' death and resurrection.

Event	Dates
Herod the Great's reign (c. 37–4 BC)	
Jesus' birth (c. 6/5 BC)	
Jesus' family flees to Egypt (c. 5/4 BC)	
Beginning of John the Baptist's ministry (c. AD 26)	
Beginning of Jesus' ministry (c. AD 26)	
Jesus' death, resurrection and ascension (c. AD 30)	
Paul's conversion (c. AD 35)	
Book of John written (c. AD 60–95)	
John's exile on Patmos (c. AD 90–95)	

Timeline scale: 10 BC, AD 1, 10, 20, 30, 40, 50, 60, 70, 80, 90, 100

Key Verse

For God so loved the world that he gave his one and only Son, that whoever believes in him shall not perish but have eternal life.

—John 3:16

to meet our needs for God. True, Christ's divinity can be overemphasized if one ignores his humanity. Some early Christians did precisely that, saying that Christ was only divine and that his fleshly body was an illusion. That position, however, overlooks a more balanced teaching in John regarding Christ's humanity. We need a human Jesus with whom to identify. But such a Jesus can only help us if he also has the power of God as part of his make-up. Jesus Christ needs to be both human and divine.

Jesus' power to help us comes through another teaching of the book, the power of the Holy Spirit. The author makes clear that Jesus was filled with Holy Spirit power and that when he left the earth, the power of that Holy Spirit remained with us, accessible to us all to enable us to reach out to God.

An adequate Christology needs all of these elements today: a human Christ to redeem us, a divine Christ to reveal God's nature, and a powerful, Spirit-filled Christ to help us lead holy lives. The Gospel/letter of John provides all three—and it does so in a mysterious, literate way that calls to us and reveals more about Jesus as it pulls us deeper and deeper into the mystery of who God is.

TAKING THE NEXT STEPS

This account of the life of Jesus was almost certainly written by John, the disciple whom Jesus loved. John's stated purpose in his Gospel was that people might believe that Jesus was the Christ and so find life in his name (Jn 20:30–31). To those who were already believers in Christ, John emphasized how much they must love one another. At the same time, John was interested in demonstrating Jesus' power and authority, an authority that was greater than any other recognized authority in Jewish society. Finally, more clearly than the other Gospel writers, John presented Jesus as fully God and fully human.

The practical implications of this Gospel stand out clearly. (1) John wants us to believe that Jesus is the Christ and to experience rich, full, free lives as a result. (2) We must use the love that God has shown us as a pattern for our love for our fellow human beings. (3) Just as Jesus came to do his Father's will, so we should be doing what God wants us to do in our lives. (4) No one has more power and authority than Jesus Christ; the more we unite ourselves to him, the more we can be assured of victory over sin and the devil.

WHAT TO LOOK FOR IN JOHN

- Jesus and John the Baptist (ch. 1)
- Jesus' conversation with Nicodemus (ch. 3)
- Jesus' conversation with the woman of Samaria (ch. 4)
- Jesus feeds the multitude and discusses the bread of life (ch. 6)
- Jesus' healing of a man born blind (ch. 9)
- Jesus, the Good Shepherd (ch. 10)
- Jesus' resurrection of Lazarus (ch. 11)
- Jesus with his disciples in the upper room (chs. 14–16)
- Jesus' final prayer for his disciples (ch. 17)
- Jesus' trial and death (chs. 18–19)
- Jesus' resurrection and appearances to his disciples (chs. 20–21)

The Word Became Flesh

1 In the beginning was the Word,[a]
and the Word was with God,[b] and
the Word was God.[c] 2He was with God
in the beginning.[d] 3Through him all
things were made; without him nothing
was made that has been made.[e] 4In him
was life,[f] and that life was the light[g] of
all mankind. 5The light shines in the
darkness, and the darkness has not
overcome[a] it.[h]
6There was a man sent from God
whose name was John.[i] 7He came as a
witness to testify[j] concerning that light,
so that through him all might believe.[k]
8He himself was not the light; he came
only as a witness to the light.
9The true light[l] that gives light to everyone[m] was coming into the world. 10He
was in the world, and though the world
was made through him,[n] the world did
not recognize him. 11He came to that
which was his own, but his own did not
receive him. 12Yet to all who did receive

1:1 [a] Rev 19:13 [b] Jn 17:5; 1Jn 1:2 [c] Php 2:6
1:2 [d] Ge 1:1
1:3 [e] 1Co 8:6; Col 1:16; Heb 1:2
1:4 [f] Jn 5:26; 11:25; 14:6 [g] Jn 8:12
1:5 [h] Jn 3:19
1:6 [i] Mt 3:1
1:7 [j] ver 15,19,32 [k] ver 12
1:9 [l] 1Jn 2:8 [m] Isa 49:6
1:10 [n] Heb 1:2

[a] 5 Or *understood*

1:1–2 The initial allusion to Ge 1 cannot be missed. This is a Gospel that will record the re-creation of men and women, the giving of life in darkness where there is no hope. John begins by introducing Jesus as "the Word." He is building on contemporary Jewish thought, where the word of God took on personal creative attributes. John identifies this Word as Jesus Christ.

But John goes further: "And the Word *was* God." John is making an absolute affirmation about the eternal existence of the Word. Whatever we can say about God, we can and must say about the Word.

John is introducing deep theology about Jesus' true nature and about the Trinity. John expands our picture of Jesus with increasingly profound images. Jesus is the greatest person to ever walk the earth. He is the Messiah for whom the Jewish people have been waiting for centuries. He is the Son of God, the divine Messenger from the Father. Jesus is God himself.

1:3–4 John's language here is careful and specific: The Logos (the Word) has always existed; he was never created. Furthermore, *nothing* came into being without him. John stresses that the Logos does whatever God does. Therefore, whatever Jesus does is divine activity.

1:5 The entry of the Logos into the world (his incarnation) is described as light shining in the hostile darkness. The struggle between light and darkness will sound throughout the Gospel; the opposition to Jesus will be severe.

1:6 John the Baptist came as a witness to Jesus. This theme is clear in the other sections of the Gospel that refer to this forerunner.

1:7–8 This is the first time we see the word group for "witness" in the Gospel. Evidence and witnesses will come forward to verify the truth of Jesus' case, just as in a courtroom. John the Baptist is the first of these witnesses. John's main role is simply to identify and glorify Jesus.

1:9 John the Baptist was bearing witness to a reality, not simply to an idea. The "true light" was coming. This divine entry reaches all people, particularly those who are hostile to God. In John's vocabulary, the "world" is an important theological term, appearing seventy-eight times in this Gospel alone. The world is not the created environment. It is the sphere of creation that lives in rebellion against God.

But if the world is hostile, how can the true light enlighten *everyone*? Perhaps John is thinking of the accessibility everyone has to this one source of illumination. The light shines on every person, exposing them for who they are.

1:10–11 Despite the presence of the Logos in the world, despite the evidence of creation, the world failed to recognize him. Even though the focus of revelation has been in Israel, the Word has come for the entire world, not merely for the Jews.

1:12–13 John indicates that the light has its followers; Jesus has his disciples. Those who receive him become God's children. Those who follow the

LOCATIONS OF EVENTS IN THE LIFE OF JESUS

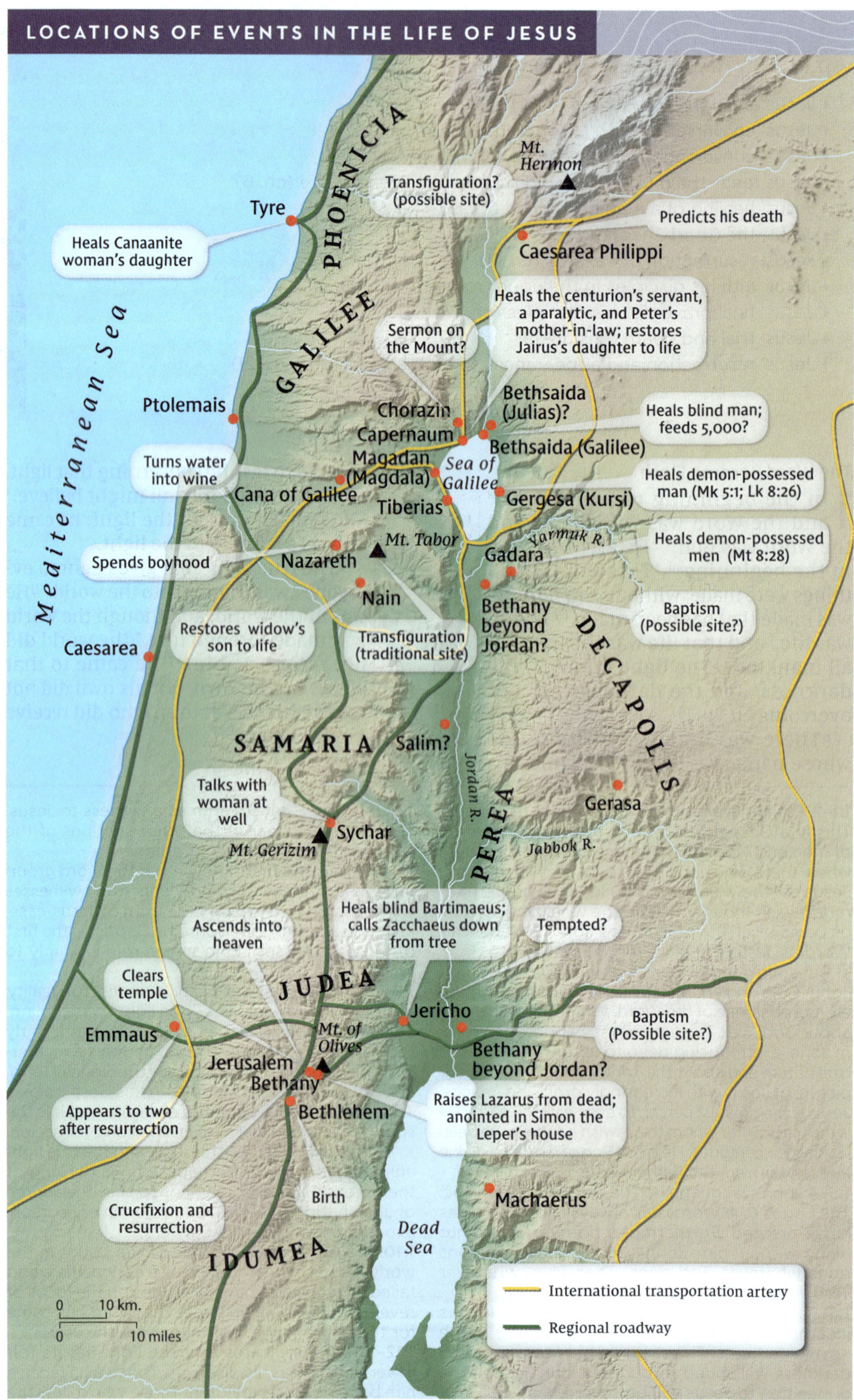

Jn 1:14 ❖ How does God show the world his glory through Christ?

him, to those who believed[o] in his name,[p]
he gave the right to become children of
God[q]— 13 children born not of natural
descent, nor of human decision or a husband's will, but born of God.[r]
14 The Word became flesh[s] and made
his dwelling among us. We have seen
his glory, the glory of the one and only
Son, who came from the Father, full of
grace and truth.[t]
15 (John testified[u] concerning him. He
cried out, saying, "This is the one I spoke
about when I said, 'He who comes after
me has surpassed me because he was
before me.'")[v] 16 Out of his fullness[w] we
have all received grace in place of grace
already given. 17 For the law was given
through Moses;[x] grace and truth came
through Jesus Christ.[y] 18 No one has ever
seen God,[z] but the one and only Son, who
is himself God and[aa] is in closest relationship with the Father, has made him
known.

1:12 [o] ver 7 [p] 1Jn 3:23 [q] Gal 3:26
1:13 [r] Jn 3:6; Jas 1:18; 1Pe 1:23; 1Jn 3:9
1:14 [s] Gal 4:4; Php 2:7, 8; 1Ti 3:16; Heb 2:14 [t] Jn 14:6
1:15 [u] ver 7 [v] ver 30; Mt 3:11
1:16 [w] Eph 1:23; Col 1:19
1:17 [x] Jn 7:19 [y] ver 14
1:18 [z] Ex 33:20; Jn 6:46; Col 1:15; 1Ti 6:16 [a] Jn 3:16,18; 1Jn 4:9
1:19 [b] Jn 2:18; 5:10,16; 6:41,52
1:20 [c] Jn 3:28; Lk 3:15,16
1:21 [d] Mt 11:14 [e] Dt 18:15
1:23 [f] Mt 3:1 [g] Isa 40:3

John the Baptist Denies Being the Messiah

19 Now this was John's testimony when
the Jewish leaders[bb] in Jerusalem sent
priests and Levites to ask him who he
was. 20 He did not fail to confess, but confessed freely, "I am not the Messiah."[c]
21 They asked him, "Then who are you?
Are you Elijah?"[d]
He said, "I am not."
"Are you the Prophet?"[e]
He answered, "No."
22 Finally they said, "Who are you?
Give us an answer to take back to those
who sent us. What do you say about
yourself?"
23 John replied in the words of Isaiah
the prophet, "I am the voice of one calling in the wilderness,[f] 'Make straight the
way for the Lord.'"[cg]
24 Now the Pharisees who had been

[a] 18 Some manuscripts *but the only Son, who* [b] 19 The Greek term traditionally translated *the Jews* (*hoi Ioudaioi*) refers here and elsewhere in John's Gospel to those Jewish leaders who opposed Jesus; also in 5:10,15,16; 7:1,11,13; 9:22; 18:14,28,36; 19:7,12,31,38; 20:19. [c] 23 Isaiah 40:3

Word will share in divine rebirth. This is John's understanding of conversion: deliberate faith joined with divine transformation.

1:14 This verse is one of the most important verses in the Bible. The Word did not just appear to be human; *the Word became flesh*. This Word "made his dwelling" among us and revealed his "glory." This verb for dwelling is employed in the Greek OT for the tabernacle of God. The glory of God, once restricted to the tabernacle, is now visible in tangible form in Christ.

1:15–16 It is curious that the word "grace," so common in the rest of the NT, appears only here in the prologue (four times) and then disappears. Grace is found in God's coming and working *despite* the hostility and rejection of the world. John emphasizes our experience and reception of this grace as its chief merit.

The more important word for John, however, is "truth" (vv. 14, 16). Most simply, truth is the opposite of falsehood, but John sees truth as penetrating far deeper. Truth is the self-disclosure that alone comes from God; truth is not just what is right but what is divine—*and this is right*.

1:17 Throughout this Gospel, it is clear that the apostle John and his community are struggling with opposition from the Jewish synagogue. John does not intend to show that the grace of Christ stands at odds with the revelation of Moses. The law likewise contains the grace of God and is an earlier display of it.

1:18 This verse joins v. 1 as the closing frame of the prologue, offering a summary statement about the divine origin of the Son. Christ's identity, his being, the essence of who he is makes his words God's words. Christ is fully God, who in his incarnation is revealing *himself* to the world.

APPLICATION ✚ 1:1–18 The natural eye cannot see the glory of God since it is dimmed by sin. So it was necessary for God to work, to self-disclose, to send his Son, who alone exposed God's heart. When God took this initiative, new possibilities were born—and still are today. Divine power is released into the broken world and its broken lives so that new life is possible. Transformation is not an inspired human work; it is a divine work through and through.

1:19–20 People from Jerusalem and the surrounding regions of Judea came out to be baptized or to investigate John. The term "the Jews" in John's Gospel generally represents the Jewish leadership in Jerusalem who are hostile to Jesus.

1:21–22 Here we have an interrogation by delegates from "official Judaism," from the temple and its interests. They ask John about his identity using three names, each of which probes John's intentions regarding Israel. First, John first denies that he is "the Christ." "Christ" is a Greek translation of the Hebrew word for "Messiah." Hope in a coming Messiah was widespread and filled with political implications. Second, they asked if he was Elijah. Jewish speculation proposed that Elijah was mysteriously alive and would return at the end of time. But John denies he is Elijah. Third, "The Prophet" is likely a reference to Dt 18:15–19, where a prophet "like Moses" would return to Israel sometime in the future. John's answer is succinct: I am not.

1:23–28 John identifies himself as "a voice" and

sent 25 questioned him, "Why then do
you baptize if you are not the Messiah,
nor Elijah, nor the Prophet?"
26 "I baptize with[a] water," John replied,
"but among you stands one you do not
know. 27 He is the one who comes after
me,[h] the straps of whose sandals I am
not worthy to untie."
28 This all happened at Bethany on the
other side of the Jordan,[i] where John
was baptizing.

John Testifies About Jesus

29 The next day John saw Jesus coming
toward him and said, "Look, the Lamb of
God,[j] who takes away the sin of the world!
30 This is the one I meant when I said, 'A
man who comes after me has surpassed
me because he was before me.'[k] 31 I myself
did not know him, but the reason I came
baptizing with water was that he might
be revealed to Israel."
32 Then John gave this testimony: "I saw
the Spirit come down from heaven as a
dove and remain on him.[l] 33 And I myself
did not know him, but the one who sent
me to baptize with water[m] told me, 'The
man on whom you see the Spirit come
down and remain is the one who will baptize with the Holy Spirit.'[n] 34 I have seen and
I testify that this is God's Chosen One."[b][o]

John's Disciples Follow Jesus

1:40–42pp // Mt 4:18–22; Mk 1:16–20; Lk 5:2–11

35 The next day John[p] was there again
with two of his disciples. 36 When he saw
Jesus passing by, he said, "Look, the
Lamb of God!"[q]
37 When the two disciples heard him
say this, they followed Jesus. 38 Turning
around, Jesus saw them following and
asked, "What do you want?"
They said, "Rabbi"[r] (which means
"Teacher"), "where are you staying?"
39 "Come," he replied, "and you will
see."
So they went and saw where he was
staying, and they spent that day with
him. It was about four in the afternoon.
40 Andrew, Simon Peter's brother, was
one of the two who heard what John had
said and who had followed Jesus. 41 The
first thing Andrew did was to find his
brother Simon and tell him, "We have
found the Messiah" (that is, the Christ).[s]
42 And he brought him to Jesus.
Jesus looked at him and said, "You are
Simon son of John. You will be called[t] Cephas" (which, when translated, is Peter[c]).[u]

Jesus Calls Philip and Nathanael

43 The next day Jesus decided to leave
for Galilee. Finding Philip,[v] he said to
him, "Follow me."[w]
44 Philip, like Andrew and Peter, was
from the town of Bethsaida.[x] 45 Philip
found Nathanael[y] and told him, "We
have found the one Moses wrote about
in the Law,[z] and about whom the prophets also wrote[a] — Jesus of Nazareth,[b] the
son of Joseph."[c]
46 "Nazareth! Can anything good come
from there?"[d] Nathanael asked.

1:27 [h] ver 15,30
1:28 [i] Jn 3:26; 10:40
1:29 [j] ver 36; Isa 53:7; 1Pe 1:19; Rev 5:6
1:30 [k] ver 15,27
1:32 [l] Mt 3:16; Mk 1:10
1:33 [m] Mk 1:4 [n] Mt 3:11; Mk 1:8
1:34 [o] ver 49; Mt 4:3
1:35 [p] Mt 3:1
1:36 [q] ver 29
1:38 [r] ver 49; Mt 23:7
1:41 [s] Jn 4:25
1:42 [t] Ge 17:5,15 [u] Mt 16:18
1:43 [v] Mt 10:3; Jn 6:5-7; 12:21, 22; 14:8,9 [w] Mt 4:19
1:44 [x] Mt 11:21; Jn 12:21
1:45 [y] Jn 21:2 [z] Lk 24:27 [a] Lk 24:27 [b] Mt 2:23; Mk 1:24 [c] Lk 3:23
1:46 [d] Jn 7:41, 42,52

[a] 26 Or *in*; also in verses 31 and 33 (twice)
[b] 34 See Isaiah 42:1; many manuscripts *is the Son of God.*
[c] 42 *Cephas* (Aramaic) and *Peter* (Greek) both mean *rock.*

---

quotes Isa 40:3 to identify his role in Jesus' mission (v. 23). He is a tool in God's hand, pointing to the dawn of the messianic era, which is now at hand.

1:29-34 John's certain knowledge of Jesus had come to him through revelation—when the Spirit descended on Jesus (v. 32).

1:29-31 John identifies Jesus as "the Lamb of God . . ." Here we see Jesus as a gift provided *by God* to take away sin. As a lamb he becomes a sacrificial animal whose death "carries away" sin.

1:32-33 John's second testimony is that he saw the Spirit descend and *remain* on Jesus. This is a permanent anointing unlike anything witnessed before in Judaism. Here John testifies that he has witnessed the dawning of the messianic era.

1:34 The final testimony given by John the Baptist here on this day is that Jesus "is God's Chosen One." "Chosen" likely comes from Isa 42:1, which emphasizes the Spirit-anointing of the Messiah and uses this title for him.

1:35-39 Two disciples hear John the Baptist testify to Jesus' identity. One is Andrew, Simon Peter's brother. The other is not named in v. 37. This unnamed disciple may be our first hidden reference to John, likely the "Beloved Disciple."

We are told that these events occur "about four in the afternoon" (v. 39). Jesus has invited them to spend the *entire* day with him. This visit becomes a teaching session, in which Jesus discloses his messianic identity and mastery over these new followers.

1:40-42 In Jewish culture, renaming indicates the authority of one person over another. Jesus is here asserting his authority over Peter and telling him that he is a different man. Despite Peter's frailty, which we will learn about later, this name signals Jesus' vision for what Peter will become.

1:43-47 Philip appears only rarely in the Gospels. Nathanael is not listed among the apostles; some speculate he is Matthew or Bartholomew. In all

PEOPLE TO KNOW // ANDREW

JOHN 1:41: Andrew was the brother of Peter and one of the twelve apostles of Jesus. Andrew and Peter were fishermen from the town of Bethsaida. Andrew was a disciple of John the Baptist and became the first named disciple of Jesus. The first thing Andrew did when he began following Jesus was to introduce his brother Peter to the Lord (Jn 1:40–42).

Jesus called Andrew and Peter to leave their fishing business behind and follow him (Mt 4:19; Mk 1:17). He said that when they followed him, they would learn to fish for people. Immediately they dropped everything and followed Christ.

Though less well known than his brother Peter, Andrew was someone who brought others to Jesus. Andrew brought his brother, Peter, to meet Jesus. He brought the boy with the fish and loaves to Jesus (Jn 6:9). And when some Greeks approached Philip, hoping to meet Jesus, Philip first went to Andrew before the two went together to Jesus (Jn 12:21–22). Andrew was a man passionate about introducing others to the Lord.

APPLICATION ✚ It can be hard to know how to introduce others to Jesus. We may feel awkward or unqualified to share our faith. Andrew serves as an encouragement. We do not need to be a bold preacher or a have all the right answers. We just need to be aware of those around us and then lovingly introduce them to the Christ we follow.

"Come and see," said Philip.
47When Jesus saw Nathanael approaching, he said of him, "Here truly is an Israelite[e] in whom there is no deceit."[f]
48"How do you know me?" Nathanael
asked.
Jesus answered, "I saw you while you
were still under the fig tree before Philip
called you."
49Then Nathanael declared, "Rabbi,[g]
you are the Son of God;[h] you are the king
of Israel."[i]
50Jesus said, "You believe[a] because I
told you I saw you under the fig tree. You
will see greater things than that." 51He
then added, "Very truly I tell you,[b] you[b]
will see 'heaven open,[j] and the angels of
God ascending and descending[k] on'[c] the
Son of Man."[l]

Jesus Changes Water Into Wine

2 On the third day a wedding took
place at Cana in Galilee.[m] Jesus'
mother[n] was there, 2and Jesus and his
disciples had also been invited to the
wedding. 3When the wine was gone,
Jesus' mother said to him, "They have
no more wine."

1:47 [e] Ro 9:4,6 [f] Ps 32:2 1:49 [g] ver 38; Mt 23:7 [h] ver 34; Mt 4:3 [i] Mt 2:2; 27:42; Jn 12:13 1:51 [j] Mt 3:16 [k] Ge 28:12 [l] Mt 8:20 2:1 [m] Jn 4:46; 21:2 [n] Mt 12:46

[a] *50* Or *Do you believe . . . ?* [b] *51* The Greek is plural. [c] *51* Gen. 28:12

three Synoptic stories Bartholomew is listed with Philip. But we cannot be sure.

1:48–49 Much to Nathanael's surprise, Jesus refers to seeing him "under the fig tree" (v. 48) at an earlier time. Jesus has a capacity for knowing that which is more than humanly possible. At once Nathanael, who now has experienced Jesus for himself, addresses him with a litany of titles. This man recognizes the true identity of Jesus.

1:50–51 This chapter has one more surprise: Verse 51 introduces Jesus' first use of the "very truly" formula (alternately "*amen, amen*"). Jesus describes angels ascending and descending on the Son of Man. This image springs from the patriarch Jacob's life (Ge 28:10–22).

Verse 51 also introduces us for the first time to the curious phrase "Son of Man." In Da 7:13–14 it appears as the title of a heavenly figure who is given ultimate authority by God. Jesus likely picks up this term and uses it extensively to avoid titles that would be loaded with political ideas.

✚ **1:19–51** Today churches are filled with men and women whose love for God is strong, yet whose understanding of the context of their faith is diminishing. When challenged, they struggle to defend it or self-consciously claim ignorance. But the claims about Jesus that John records in this first chapter form the bedrock for Christian belief in the identity of Christ as God. This is the firm foundation that all believers can stand on and to which they can confidently testify. It is the anchor that will keep disciples committed with their minds as well as their hearts when the going gets tough.

2:1–3 In the village culture of Palestine, weddings were important events. Gift-giving was carefully considered, not as a simple gesture of goodwill but as a means of bringing honor on the couple and their families. This practice gives us an interesting insight into the concern of the servants when the feast suddenly runs out of wine. This is

PEOPLE TO KNOW // BARTHOLOMEW (NATHANAEL)

JOHN 1:49: Bartholomew is mentioned in the lists of Jesus' disciples and nowhere else. We don't know how he met Jesus or what he contributed to the ministry.

Many scholars believe that the disciple named Nathanael in John's Gospel is the same person as Bartholomew. This claim is supported by three observations: (1) Nathanael is mentioned in John while Bartholomew is never mentioned in John; (2) Bartholomew appears to be a last name meaning "son of Talmai," and (3) the Synoptic Gospels always pair Bartholomew with Philip; and in John's Gospel, Nathanael appears with Philip (Jn 1:45).

If Bartholomew and Nathanael refer to the same person, we are offered a little more information about this follower of Christ. In the book of John, Jesus calls Philip as one of his disciples; Philip then seeks out Nathanael and says he had found the Messiah. Nathanael was incredulous of this claim when he learned Jesus was from Nazareth. Upon meeting Nathanael, Jesus declares him to be "an Israelite in whom there is no deceit" (Jn 1:47). Jesus tells Nathanael that he saw him sitting under a fig tree when Philip called him—a miraculous piece of knowledge that causes Nathanael to profess, "Rabbi, you are the Son of God; you are the king of Israel" (Jn 1:49). He is the first follower of Jesus to make such a bold profession of faith.

APPLICATION Bartholomew's fateful encounter with Christ changed his life forever. Bartholomew left his old life behind and followed Jesus faithfully throughout Christ's earthly ministry. While we cannot be certain of the accuracy, church tradition says that Bartholomew was martyred on a cross for his faith in Christ. Though much about him remains unknown, what we should learn from Bartholomew is simple: The best life is one that follows Jesus.

4"Woman,[a][o] why do you involve me?"[p]
Jesus replied. "My hour[q] has not yet
come."
5His mother said to the servants, "Do
whatever he tells you."[r]
6Nearby stood six stone water jars, the
kind used by the Jews for ceremonial
washing,[s] each holding from twenty to
thirty gallons.[b]
7Jesus said to the servants, "Fill the
jars with water"; so they filled them to
the brim.
8Then he told them, "Now draw some
out and take it to the master of the banquet."
They did so, 9and the master of the
banquet tasted the water that had
been turned into wine.[t] He did not realize
where it had come from, though
the servants who had drawn the water
knew. Then he called the bridegroom
aside 10and said, "Everyone brings out
the choice wine first and then the cheaper
wine after the guests have had too
much to drink; but you have saved the
best till now."
11What Jesus did here in Cana of Galilee
was the first of the signs[u] through which
he revealed his glory;[v] and his disciples
believed in him.[w]
12After this he went down to Capernaum[x]
with his mother and brothers[y]
and his disciples. There they stayed for
a few days.

2:4 [o] Jn 19:26 [p] Mt 8:29 [q] Mt 26:18; Jn 7:6
2:5 [r] Ge 41:55
2:6 [s] Mk 7:3, 4; Jn 3:25
2:9 [t] Jn 4:46
2:11 [u] ver 23; Jn 3:2; 4:48; 6:2, 14, 26, 30; 12:37; 20:30 [v] Jn 1:14 [w] Ex 14:31
2:12 [x] Mt 4:13 [y] Mt 12:46

[a] 4 The Greek for *Woman* does not denote any disrespect. [b] 6 Or from about 75 to about 115 liters

not merely an embarrassing situation; it is a dishonoring crisis for the host.

2:4–5 Mary's statement prompts Jesus to respond in an unexpected way. Translated into English the tone of this response seems harsh, but it is simply formal. Jesus must follow the course that has been determined for him by God. The important Greek word "hour" is used throughout this Gospel to look forward to Jesus' important work on the cross.

2:6–7 The note that the six jars are stone is a signal they are for Jewish purification washings. Each can hold over twenty gallons.

2:8–10 Jesus tells the stewards to take some of the water that is now wine and bring it to the head steward. The head steward makes a significant pronouncement: In most banquets, the best wine is served first, but Jesus is delivering something superior to anything the banquet has witnessed before. John emphasizes the quality of this wine and its timing: Drinks served before this wine are inferior.

2:11–12 John consistently refers to Jesus' mighty works as "signs." The signs are not merely acts of power and might, but they unveil that God is at work in Jesus.

THE SEVEN SIGNS OF JOHN'S GOSPEL

SIGN	VERSES
(1) Changing water into wine	2:1-11
(2) Healing an official's son	4:43-54
(3) Healing a disabled man at the Bethesda pool	5:1-15
(4) Feeding the 5,000	6:1-14
(5) Walking on water	6:16-21
(6) Healing the man born blind	9:1-12
(7) Raising Lazarus from the dead	11:1-44
Epilogue sign: the miraculous catch of fish	21:1-14

Adapted from *Four Portraits, One Jesus* by Mark L. Strauss, p. 302. Copyright © 2007 by Mark L. Strauss. Used by permission of Zondervan.

Jesus Clears the Temple Courts

2:14–16pp // Mt 21:12,13; Mk 11:15–17; Lk 19:45,46

13When it was almost time for the
Jewish Passover,[z] Jesus went up to Jerusalem.[a] 14In the temple courts he found
people selling cattle, sheep and doves,
and others sitting at tables exchang-
ing money. 15So he made a whip out of
cords, and drove all from the temple
courts, both sheep and cattle; he scattered the coins of the money changers
and overturned their tables. 16To those
who sold doves he said, "Get these out
of here! Stop turning my Father's house[b]
into a market!" 17His disciples remembered that it is written: "Zeal for your
house will consume me."[ac]
18The Jews then responded to him,
"What sign can you show us to prove
your authority to do all this?"[d]
19Jesus answered them, "Destroy this
temple, and I will raise it again in three
days."[e]
20They replied, "It has taken forty-six
years to build this temple, and you are
going to raise it in three days?" 21But the
temple he had spoken of was his body.[f]
22After he was raised from the dead, his
disciples recalled what he had said.[g] Then
they believed the scripture and the words
that Jesus had spoken.
23Now while he was in Jerusalem at the
Passover Festival,[h] many people saw the
signs he was performing and believed in
his name.[b] 24But Jesus would not entrust
himself to them, for he knew all people.
25He did not need any testimony about
mankind, for he knew what was in each
person.[i]

2:13 [z] Jn 11:55 [a] Dt 16:1-6; Lk 2:41
2:16 [b] Lk 2:49
2:17 [c] Ps 69:9
2:18 [d] Mt 12:38
2:19 [e] Mt 26:61; 27:40; Mk 14:58; 15:29
2:21 [f] 1Co 6:19
2:22 [g] Lk 24:5-8; Jn 12:16; 14:26
2:23 [h] ver 13
2:25 [i] Mt 9:4; Jn 6:61,64; 13:11

Jn 2:17 ❖ What might showing zeal for God's house look like in our lives?

[a] *17* Psalm 69:9 [b] *23* Or *in him*

2:13 Jesus comes to Jerusalem for a major festival in the city. He enters the temple (a place of sacrificial purification) and does a likewise symbolic work, demonstrating that it also will experience replacement and fulfillment (just as the stone water vessels in Cana were filled with new wine).
2:14–16 Matthew, Mark, and Luke place the temple cleansing at the end of the ministry of Jesus, while John introduces it at the beginning. In doing so, John is creating a theological portrait of Jesus' display of signs in the context of Judaism. Jesus is the fulfillment and replacement of Judaism's festivals and institutions.

Passover was celebrated each spring. Since pilgrims would need approved animals for sacrifice, a considerable animal selling business grew in the city at this time of year. Jesus is attacking the financial machinery of the festival system, which puts him at odds with Caiaphas and the temple leadership.
2:17 His disciples recall Ps 69:9. Here John is indicating two things. First, Jesus is driven to defend and promote his Father's interests in the world. Second, he is working out the purposes of God—purposes already outlined in the OT.
2:18–22 His critics demand that Jesus show some sign to demonstrate his authority to cause such upheaval. Curiously, Jesus refers to his *own* destruction and resurrection. Jesus' audience misunderstands him and thinks he is referring (ironically) to the Jerusalem temple.

In Judaism of this period, many spiritual leaders expected a new temple to be built, replacing the present temple in Jerusalem. Jesus' deeper meaning referred to his body, which would serve the same function as the temple—even replacing it. Jesus' death and resurrection will create a new covenant with God and make the services of the Jerusalem temple obsolete.
2:23–25 John is making a sweeping theological affirmation. God alone knows the hearts of men and women—and now Jesus has this same capacity.

✣ **2:1–25** The Cana story forces us to probe the relation of faith and miracle. The disciples saw the sign and believed in Jesus. The main problem with faith anchored to the miraculous is that miracles can become an end in themselves. People begin to seek bread rather than the bread of life. Yet, having sounded this note of caution, we still need to note that Jesus

Jesus Teaches Nicodemus

3 Now there was a Pharisee, a man named Nicodemus[j] who was a member of the Jewish ruling council.[k] 2He came to Jesus at night and said, "Rabbi, we know that you are a teacher who has come from God. For no one could perform the signs[l] you are doing if God were not with him."[m]

3:1 [j] Jn 7:50; 19:39 [k] Lk 23:13
3:2 [l] Jn 9:16, 33 [m] Ac 2:22; 10:38
3:3 [n] Jn 1:13; 1Pe 1:23

3Jesus replied, "Very truly I tell you, no one can see the kingdom of God unless they are born again.[a]"[n]

4"How can someone be born when they are old?" Nicodemus asked. "Surely they cannot enter a second time into their mother's womb to be born!"

[a] 3 The Greek for *again* also means *from above*; also in verse 7.

---

worked wonders and through these displayed his glory. Miraculous signs may become a powerful means to discover or strengthen faith.

Also consider Jesus' temple experience in this passage. He came to the center of Jewish life, and he acted there in what was considered an outrageous way by those who witnessed it. In that day the temple was a civic center where politics, religion, and law were virtually inseparable; to this place Jesus came as an agent of profound change. We are also called to be participants in our society; to respect it, yes, but also to be a witness for God's interests. To be salt and light. To be a light on a hill that cannot be missed. Evangelical Christianity is not often outrageous, but Jesus was outrageous in this instance. We need to be agents of change who not only speak the gospel to the world but who are also angered by the things that anger God.

3:1–2 Nicodemus was a member of the Jewish ruling council and a Pharisee. When this rabbi comes to Jesus at night, it may simply refer to his desire for privacy stemming from fear. But "night" is also likely a theological symbol expressing Nicodemus's spiritual relation to the truth. Nicodemus is a man of the darkness, while Jesus is the light.

3:3 Although the OT does not use the phrase "kingdom of God" in full, the notion is implicit throughout Scripture. Judaism taught it would be a future kingdom, and all Jews who faithfully kept the law would be admitted to it freely. Jesus however asserts that there is a new prerequisite to see or enter this kingdom: "No one can see the kingdom of God unless he is born *again*." Jesus is driving at something comprehensive: a complete renewal of the whole person.

3:4–5 Nicodemus's question shows that he is outside the kingdom and that he cannot penetrate its deeper truths, so Jesus must explain more fully. Divine birth is "of water and the Spirit" (v. 5). This is likely a reference to John the Baptist's baptism, which the Gospel has already introduced in the narrative. Nicodemus (by this reading) must submit to the baptism of repentance offered by John

PEOPLE TO KNOW // NICODEMUS

JOHN 3:1–21: Nicodemus was a Pharisee who took an interest in Jesus. He came to Jesus under cover of night to speak to him, saying he believed Jesus to be a teacher from God based on his wondrous signs (Jn 3:2). Jesus told Nicodemus that anyone desiring to enter God's kingdom needed to be born again, a metaphor that Nicodemus did not understand. Jesus explained that he needed to be born of the Spirit and not only born of flesh. Jesus went on to tell Nicodemus that Jesus himself would be lifted up, and that everyone who believed in him would have eternal life (Jn 3:14–15).

This conversation ends without resolution. Did Nicodemus respond and believe in Jesus as the Messiah? The story does not say. However, Nicodemus next appears in John's Gospel when other Pharisees try to have Jesus arrested. Nicodemus defended Jesus, saying that a man should not be condemned without first having a fair hearing, and was basically shouted down by his fellow Pharisees (Jn 7:50–52).

After Jesus' crucifixion, Joseph of Arimathea asked Pilate for Jesus' body. Joseph was a secret follower of Jesus because he feared the Jewish leaders. Nicodemus helped Joseph prepare Jesus' body for burial. Nicodemus supplied 75 pounds of myrrh and aloes and helped Joseph wrap Jesus' body in strips of linen. Together, the two men laid Jesus in Joseph's tomb (Jn 19:38–42).

APPLICATION ✣ Nicodemus started out curious about Jesus, and he ended up burying the crucified Lord. God uses our interest in Christ to reveal more of himself to us, and if we allow him, he can fan that spark into a vibrant faith. Even if we, like Nicodemus, take some time on our spiritual journey, drawing near to Jesus has the power to change the whole course of our lives. God can transform a passing curiosity into a life-changing faith in the crucified and risen Lord.

MIRACLES OF JESUS

HEALING MIRACLES	MATTHEW	MARK	LUKE	JOHN
Man with leprosy	8:2-4	1:40-42	5:12-13	
Roman centurion's servant	8:5-13		7:1-10	
Peter's mother-in-law	8:14-15	1:30-31	4:38-39	
Two men from Gadara	8:28-34	5:1-15	8:27-35	
Paralyzed man	9:2-7	2:3-12	5:18-25	
Woman with bleeding	9:20-22	5:25-29	8:43-48	
Two blind men	9:27-31			
Mute, demon-possessed man	9:32-33			
Man with a shriveled hand	12:10-13	3:1-5	6:6-10	
Blind, mute, demon-possessed man	12:22		11:14	
Canaanite woman's daughter	15:21-28	7:24-30		
Demon-possessed boy	17:14-18	9:17-29	9:38-43	
Two blind men (including Bartimaeus)	20:29-34	10:46-52	18:35-43	
Deaf mute		7:31-37		
Demon-possessed man in synagogue		1:23-26	4:33-35	
Blind man at Bethsaida		8:22-26		
Disabled woman			13:11-13	
Man with abnormal swelling			14:1-4	
Ten men with leprosy			17:11-19	
The high priest's servant			22:50-51	
Official's son at Capernaum				4:46-54
Sick man at pool of Bethesda				5:1-9
Man born blind				9:1-7
MIRACLES SHOWING POWER OVER NATURE				
Calming the storm	8:23-27	4:37-41	8:22-25	
Walking on water	14:25	6:48-51		6:19-21
Feeding the 5,000	14:15-21	6:35-44	9:12-17	6:6-13
Feeding the 4,000	15:32-38	8:1-9		
Coin in fish's mouth	17:24-27			
Fig tree withered	21:18-22	11:12-14, 20-25		
Large catch of fish			5:4-11	
Water turned into wine				2:1-11
Another large catch of fish				21:1-11
MIRACLES OF RAISING THE DEAD				
Jairus's daughter	9:18-19, 23-25	5:22-24, 38-42	8:41-42, 49-56	
Widow's son at Nain			7:11-15	
Lazarus				11:1-44

5 Jesus answered, "Very truly I tell you,
no one can enter the kingdom of God
unless they are born of water and the
Spirit.[o] 6 Flesh gives birth to flesh, but the
Spirit[a] gives birth to spirit.[p] 7 You should
not be surprised at my saying, 'You[b]
must be born again.' 8 The wind blows
wherever it pleases. You hear its sound,
but you cannot tell where it comes from
or where it is going. So it is with everyone
born of the Spirit."[c]
9 "How can this be?"[q] Nicodemus asked.
10 "You are Israel's teacher,"[r] said
Jesus, "and do you not understand these
things? 11 Very truly I tell you, we speak
of what we know,[s] and we testify to what
we have seen, but still you people do not
accept our testimony.[t] 12 I have spoken to
you of earthly things and you do not believe; how then will you believe if I speak
of heavenly things? 13 No one has ever
gone into heaven[u] except the one who
came from heaven[v]—the Son of Man.[d]
14 Just as Moses lifted up the snake in the
wilderness,[w] so the Son of Man must be
lifted up,[ex] 15 that everyone who believes[y]
may have eternal life in him."[f]
16 For God so loved[z] the world that he
gave his one and only Son, that whoever
believes in him shall not perish but have
eternal life.[a] 17 For God did not send his Son
into the world[b] to condemn the world, but
to save the world through him.[c] 18 Whoever believes in him is not condemned,[d]
but whoever does not believe stands condemned already because they have not
believed in the name of God's one and
only Son.[e] 19 This is the verdict: Light[f] has
come into the world, but people loved
darkness instead of light because their
deeds were evil. 20 Everyone who does
evil hates the light, and will not come
into the light for fear that their deeds will
be exposed.[g] 21 But whoever lives by the
truth comes into the light, so that it may
be seen plainly that what they have done
has been done in the sight of God.

John Testifies Again About Jesus

22 After this, Jesus and his disciples
went out into the Judean countryside,
where he spent some time with them,
and baptized.[h] 23 Now John also was baptizing at Aenon near Salim, because there
was plenty of water, and people were
coming and being baptized. 24 (This was

3:5 [o] Titus 3:5
3:6 [p] Jn 1:13; 1Co 15:50
3:9 [q] Jn 6:52, 60
3:10 [r] Lk 2:46
3:11 [s] Jn 1:18; 7:16, 17 [t] ver 32
3:13 [u] Pr 30:4; Ac 2:34; Eph 4:8-10 [v] Jn 6:38, 42
3:14 [w] Nu 21:8, 9 [x] Jn 8:28; 12:32
3:15 [y] ver 16, 36
3:16 [z] Ro 5:8; Eph 2:4; 1Jn 4:9, 10 [a] ver 36; Jn 6:29, 40; 11:25, 26
3:17 [b] Jn 6:29, 57; 10:36; 11:42; 17:8, 21; 20:21 [c] Jn 12:47; 1Jn 4:14
3:18 [d] Jn 5:24 [e] 1Jn 4:9
3:19 [f] Jn 1:4; 8:12
3:20 [g] Eph 5:11, 13
3:22 [h] Jn 4:2

[a] 6 Or *but spirit* [b] 7 The Greek is plural. [c] 8 The Greek for *Spirit* is the same as that for *wind.* [d] 13 Some manuscripts *Man, who is in heaven* [e] 14 The Greek for *lifted up* also means *exalted.* [f] 15 Some interpreters end the quotation with verse 21.

---

the Baptist at the Jordan. Following this he can experience the Spirit and transformation.

3:6-8 Jesus is pointing to the dawning of a new era which John the Baptist has inaugurated. Water baptism is expected, but Jesus now is one who baptizes "with the Holy Spirit" (1:33), and he will complete the dawning of this time. Above all, Nicodemus must understand that this era will be one in which the Spirit of God moves among humanity. Jesus compares the Spirit with the "wind": Its origin and movements are mysterious and cannot be contained by the human religious systems Jesus has already challenged.

3:9-10 Nicodemus is a man standing on the frontier, looking at a new country and wondering how such momentous events will unfold.

3:11-13 Jesus begins answering his question with "Very truly I tell you," as if to underscore the importance of what he is about to say. The irony is that he refers to Nicodemus as a rabbi, but now we see that this teacher does not know the answers. Only Jesus can explain the deeper mysteries of God. People who stumble on the elemental teachings of Jesus cannot hope to grasp the deeper realities. Jesus is the only One who has actually entered heaven's realms. Human teachers do not have access to this sort of revelation.

3:14-15 Jesus refers to a story from Nu 21 in which Moses is commanded to build a serpent of bronze to bring healing. In the same manner, Jesus says he must be "lifted up" in order to become the source of eternal life for all who believe (v. 14). John has in mind that the cross will not simply be a place of sacrifice and suffering but a place of departure and of return, when Jesus resumes his life with the Father. Jesus *ascends* to the cross. As we will see later in this Gospel, the cross will actually be a place of glorification.

3:16 The statement that God loves "*the world*" is surprising. The Son did not come to the world to save a select few; rather, he came to extend his saving grace to *the world*, namely, the all-encompassing circle of men and women who inhabit this planet.

3:17-18 The Son's entry into the darkness of this world is an act of judgment (v. 19; cf. 9:39) since divine light has unveiled the darkness for what it is. Those who see this light and recognize the tragedy of their situation have one responsibility—to believe.

Evil and darkness wage war against the light, trying to bring it down. However, its defeat is inevitable.

3:19-21 By contrast to the note above, those who love the light come to it and yearn for its truth. John is describing what happens when those in the world make a choice to believe—they are transformed into children of God.

3:22-24 This is our only record that Jesus had a baptizing ministry. But we must remain clear that at this point Jesus is conducting a baptism of repentance since the Spirit has not yet been given.

Jn 3:30 ❖ How can we practice becoming less while making Christ's name greater?

before John was put in prison.)[i] 25An
argument developed between some of
John's disciples and a certain Jew over
the matter of ceremonial washing.[j]
26They came to John and said to him,
"Rabbi,[k] that man who was with you on
the other side of the Jordan — the one
you testified[l] about — look, he is baptizing, and everyone is going to him."
27To this John replied, "A person can
receive only what is given them from
heaven. 28You yourselves can testify that
I said, 'I am not the Messiah but am sent
ahead of him.'[m] 29The bride belongs to
the bridegroom.[n] The friend who attends
the bridegroom waits and listens for him,
and is full of joy when he hears the bridegroom's voice. That joy is mine, and it is
now complete.[o] 30He must become greater; I must become less."[a]
31The one who comes from above[p] is
above all; the one who is from the earth
belongs to the earth, and speaks as one
from the earth.[q] The one who comes
from heaven is above all. 32He testifies
to what he has seen and heard,[r] but no
one accepts his testimony.[s] 33Whoever
has accepted it has certified that God is
truthful. 34For the one whom God has
sent[t] speaks the words of God, for God[b]
gives the Spirit[u] without limit. 35The Father loves the Son and has placed everything in his hands.[v] 36Whoever believes
in the Son has eternal life,[w] but whoever
rejects the Son will not see life, for God's
wrath remains on them.

3:24 [i] Mt 4:12; 14:3
3:25 [j] Jn 2:6
3:26 [k] Mt 23:7 [l] Jn 1:7
3:28 [m] Jn 1:20, 23
3:29 [n] Mt 9:15 [o] Jn 16:24; 17:13; Php 2:2; 1Jn 1:4; 2Jn 12
3:31 [p] ver 13 [q] Jn 8:23; 1Jn 4:5
3:32 [r] Jn 8:26; 15:15 [s] ver 11
3:34 [t] ver 17 [u] Mt 12:18; Lk 4:18; Ac 10:38
3:35 [v] Mt 28:18; Jn 5:20,22; 17:2
3:36 [w] ver 15; Jn 5:24; 6:47
4:1 [x] Jn 3:22,26
4:3 [y] Jn 3:22

Jesus Talks With a Samaritan Woman

4 Now Jesus learned that the Pharisees had heard that he was gaining and baptizing more disciples than
John[x] — 2although in fact it was not
Jesus who baptized, but his disciples.
3So he left Judea[y] and went back once
more to Galilee.
4Now he had to go through Samaria.
5So he came to a town in Samaria called
Sychar, near the plot of ground Jacob

[a] *30* Some interpreters end the quotation with verse 36. [b] *34* Greek *he*

3:25–30 The dispute described in vv. 25–26 is the root of the problem that John the Baptist's subsequent speech in vv. 27–30 will address. John's followers seem unhappy that Jesus is becoming a celebrated leader. The Baptist's answer corrects the rivalry. John affirms that he is not the Christ but his forerunner. Jesus is superior because of his heavenly origins.
3:31–33 In antiquity, wax seals were used to authenticate letters and possessions. John uses this image to testify that to embrace Jesus is to set a seal ("has certified," v. 33), to confirm, and to defend an entire constellation of beliefs that are central to God and the Christian faith.
3:32–36a God's love for the Son is so complete that *nothing* is beyond the Son's reach. The Father has commissioned the Son and has provided the Son with the Holy Spirit. Verse 34 does not refer to Jesus' giving the Spirit to us, but to God's giving the Spirit to his Son. The gift of life and Spirit that the Son will distribute comes from what he already enjoys. This gift will be distributed once the Son of God is glorified.
3:36b John looks at salvation from the other point of view. The world of darkness and unbelief stands under the judgment of God, and those who reject Jesus remain in the darkness, continuing to live under that divine judgment.

✣ **3:1–36** As with Nicodemus, there is a link between spiritual receptivity and the degree to which we are "settled" into a system of life and belief. The greater our comfort, the possibility of fewer opportunities to receive a new, transforming word from God. This is probably why the possibility of conversion to Christianity tends to decrease as people age.

Our degree of comfort also has to do with the scope of our religious knowledge. Nicodemus was a man skilled in religious rhetoric. He knew Scripture and had no doubt built his own "systematic theology" that explained God, his world, and his relation to both. His problem was not a lack of knowledge. Our religious knowledge can become a shield, a defense with which we protect ourselves from the very God we claim to know.

The profound message of Jn 3:16 that Jesus posed to Nicodemus is that "God so loved the world . . ." The work of Christ is *God* at work, *God* saving the world, *God* extending himself into the condition of our humanity and bringing about reconciliation. God himself is on our side. God himself is at work on our behalf. He did not send a messenger (Jesus) to do the dirty work; rather, God himself came to the cross and suffered to bring his beloved creation back to himself. We will discover more about this reality as we continue through this Gospel.

4:1–5 By Jesus' day, a smoldering tension existed between the regions of Judea and Samaria. A first-century reader would hardly expect Jesus and the woman to acknowledge each other's presence, much less to speak.

had given to his son Joseph.[z] 6Jacob's
well was there, and Jesus, tired as he was
from the journey, sat down by the well.
It was about noon.
7When a Samaritan woman came to
draw water, Jesus said to her, "Will you
give me a drink?" 8(His disciples had
gone into the town[a] to buy food.)
9The Samaritan woman said to him,
"You are a Jew and I am a Samaritan[b]
woman. How can you ask me for a
drink?" (For Jews do not associate with
Samaritans.[a])
10Jesus answered her, "If you knew the
gift of God and who it is that asks you for
a drink, you would have asked him and
he would have given you living water."[c]
11"Sir," the woman said, "you have
nothing to draw with and the well is
deep. Where can you get this living water? 12Are you greater than our father
Jacob, who gave us the well[d] and drank
from it himself, as did also his sons and
his livestock?"
13Jesus answered, "Everyone who
drinks this water will be thirsty again,
14but whoever drinks the water I give
them will never thirst.[e] Indeed, the water
I give them will become in them a spring
of water[f] welling up to eternal life."[g]
15The woman said to him, "Sir, give me
this water so that I won't get thirsty[h] and
have to keep coming here to draw water."
16He told her, "Go, call your husband
and come back."
17"I have no husband," she replied.
Jesus said to her, "You are right when
you say you have no husband. 18The fact
is, you have had five husbands, and the
man you now have is not your husband.
What you have just said is quite true."
19"Sir," the woman said, "I can see that
you are a prophet.[i] 20Our ancestors worshiped on this mountain,[j] but you Jews
claim that the place where we must worship is in Jerusalem."[k]
21"Woman," Jesus replied, "believe me,
a time is coming[l] when you will worship
the Father neither on this mountain nor
in Jerusalem.[m] 22You Samaritans worship
what you do not know;[n] we worship what
we do know, for salvation is from the
Jews.[o] 23Yet a time is coming and has
now come[p] when the true worshipers will

4:5 [z] Ge 33:19; 48:22; Jos 24:32
4:8 [a] ver 5,39
4:9 [b] Mt 10:5; Lk 9:52,53
4:10 [c] Isa 44:3; Jer 2:13; Zec 14:8; Jn 7:37,38; Rev 21:6; 22:1,17
4:12 [d] ver 6
4:14 [e] Jn 6:35 [f] Jn 7:38 [g] Mt 25:46
4:15 [h] Jn 6:34
4:19 [i] Mt 21:11
4:20 [j] Dt 11:29; Jos 8:33 [k] Lk 9:53
4:21 [l] Jn 5:28; 16:2 [m] Mal 1:11; 1Ti 2:8
4:22 [n] 2Ki 17:28-41 [o] Isa 2:3; Ro 3:1,2; 9:4,5
4:23 [p] Jn 5:25; 16:32

[a] 9 Or *do not use dishes Samaritans have used*

4:6 Here the Greek word for "well" refers to a "spring," a free-flowing water source or fountain. In this culture, water collection was the responsibility of women. In a world that isolated women socially, the task became an opportunity for women to meet and talk. This task took place either at early morning or dusk to avoid the Middle Eastern heat. This woman draws water when other women are absent. The implication is that she is a social outcast.

4:7 In this world men rarely spoke to women in public. Single men were *never* to speak to or touch women in public at any time. Above all, a rabbi would observe these ideals scrupulously.

4:9–10 The conversation between Jesus and the woman is a delightful, dramatic play. Woven through are two questions launched by Jesus in 4:10: Will this woman comprehend the gift of God and its giver? Will she ask for a drink?

4:11–12 "Living water" refers to *moving* water. Living water was precious and was the only water that could be used in ritual washings to make pure unclean worshipers. Shechem had no rivers or streams. How could a Jewish outsider who barely knew the terrain offer water that no one else had found? The woman is curious about the possibility of a nearby stream or spring, but Jesus wants her to look to the spiritual significance of what this water means. Living water is life nourished by God.

4:13–15 Jesus is talking about a new life that is available through the Spirit of God. But Jesus takes this promise a step further. He offers a dynamic experience that makes a life as living as the water itself. The water (or Spirit) will transform a life into water that "wells up" (v. 14), one that does not require reaching and dipping, but which gurgles with water until it spills over.

4:16–18 No doubt Jesus' request that this woman summon her husband was a shock. She has sinned, and the reputation that has dogged her and made her an outcast now has surfaced again. But Jesus is not simply judging her. She sees that this knowledge could only come from a messenger from God, so she looks for a way to deflect the moral investigation of this stranger.

4:19 The Samaritans understood the expectation of Dt 18:18, which said a great prophet would follow Moses. But this was to be the messianic figure of the final day. With her statement, the woman has opened the subject of messianism for Jesus.

4:20–24 Here the woman refers to the historic religious division between Jews and Samaritans. Both groups had serious disagreements about the proper location for worship. The Samaritans rejected the traditional location in Jerusalem that had been established by King David. In the Pentateuch, Abraham had built an altar at Shechem beneath Mount Gerizim. Jesus is being invited to enter this historical-religious dilemma and comment. But once again, Jesus deflects her question.

Jesus comments on the inadequacy of Samaritan worship, stating that Judaism is the religious history through which God has been at work. Jesus then indicates that the debate between Gerizim and Jerusalem will soon be obsolete. A cataclysmic change will occur *in worship* when Jesus goes to the cross. Worship in "spirit and truth" is the key

JESUS IN JUDEA AND SAMARIA

1 The most important port in the Holy Land in NT times.

2 The birthplace of Jesus (Mt 2:1; Lk 2:4).

3 John the Baptist baptized here (Jn 3:23). Aenon was also the probable location of John's ministry.

4 Here Jesus talked with a Samaritan woman at Jacob's well (Jn 4:5).

5 The mountain referred to by the Samaritan woman at the well as the worship center for the Samaritans (Jn 4:20–23).

6 Jesus raised Lazarus from the dead (Jn 11:43–44). Here at Bethany Jesus was anointed in the house of Simon the Leper (Mt 26:6). It was also the scene of the ascension (Lk 24:50–51).

7 Jesus healed a blind man here at Jericho (Mt 20:29) and called Zacchaeus down from a tree (Lk 19:1).

8 Most important biblical city. Jesus was crucified at Jerusalem as predicted (Mt 16:21; Mk 10:33; Lk 18:31).

9 The resurrected Jesus appeared to two people walking to Emmaus, and he ate with them there (Lk 24:13).

worship the Father in the Spirit[q] and in
truth, for they are the kind of worshipers
the Father seeks. 24God is spirit,[r] and his
worshipers must worship in the Spirit
and in truth."
25The woman said, "I know that Messiah" (called Christ)[s] "is coming. When he
comes, he will explain everything to us."
26Then Jesus declared, "I, the one
speaking to you—I am he."[t]

The Disciples Rejoin Jesus

27Just then his disciples returned[u] and
were surprised to find him talking with
a woman. But no one asked, "What do
you want?" or "Why are you talking with
her?"
28Then, leaving her water jar, the woman went back to the town and said to the
people, 29"Come, see a man who told me
everything I ever did.[v] Could this be the
Messiah?"[w] 30They came out of the town
and made their way toward him.
31Meanwhile his disciples urged him,
"Rabbi,[x] eat something."
32But he said to them, "I have food to
eat[y] that you know nothing about."
33Then his disciples said to each other, "Could someone have brought him
food?"
34"My food," said Jesus, "is to do the
will[z] of him who sent me and to finish
his work.[a] 35Don't you have a saying,
'It's still four months until harvest'? I
tell you, open your eyes and look at the
fields! They are ripe for harvest.[b] 36Even
now the one who reaps draws a wage and
harvests[c] a crop for eternal life,[d] so that
the sower and the reaper may be glad
together. 37Thus the saying 'One sows
and another reaps'[e] is true. 38I sent you
to reap what you have not worked for.
Others have done the hard work, and you
have reaped the benefits of their labor."

4:23 [q] Php 3:3
4:24 [r] Php 3:3
4:25 [s] Mt 1:16
4:26 [t] Jn 8:24; 9:35-37
4:27 [u] ver 8
4:29 [v] ver 17, 18 [w] Mt 12:23; Jn 7:26, 31
4:31 [x] Mt 23:7
4:32 [y] Job 23:12; Mt 4:4; Jn 6:27
4:34 [z] Mt 26:39; Jn 6:38; 17:4; 19:30 [a] Jn 19:30
4:35 [b] Mt 9:37; Lk 10:2
4:36 [c] Ro 1:13 [d] Mt 25:46
4:37 [e] Job 31:8; Mic 6:15
4:39 [f] ver 5 [g] ver 29
4:42 [h] Lk 2:11; 1Jn 4:14
4:43 [i] ver 40
4:44 [j] Mt 13:57; Lk 4:24

Jn 4:39 ❖ How can we share our own testimony about Jesus with those around us? What factors keep us from sharing more about Christ?

Many Samaritans Believe

39Many of the Samaritans from that
town[f] believed in him because of the
woman's testimony, "He told me everything I ever did."[g] 40So when the Samaritans came to him, they urged him to
stay with them, and he stayed two days.
41And because of his words many more
became believers.
42They said to the woman, "We no longer believe just because of what you said;
now we have heard for ourselves, and we
know that this man really is the Savior
of the world."[h]

Jesus Heals an Official's Son

43After the two days[i] he left for Galilee.
44(Now Jesus himself had pointed out
that a prophet has no honor in his own
country.)[j] 45When he arrived in Galilee,
the Galileans welcomed him. They had

---

phrase that controls what Jesus means. It is tied to Jesus' affirmation that "God is spirit" (v. 24). Jesus is describing something of the dynamic and life-giving character of God.

Worship in spirit is dynamically animated by God's Holy Spirit. But it is more. This is worship empowered by God but also informed by the revelation of God and provided to humans by the One who is the truth, Jesus Christ. This is worship not tied to holy places but impacted by a holy person who will inaugurate the era in which the Holy Spirit will change everything.

4:25–26 The Samaritans believed the coming Messiah would explain everything to them. But the woman implies that both she and Jesus will have to wait. With simple dignity, Jesus accepts that title for himself.

4:27 Jesus' disciples return and express amazement. They are likely thinking about the prohibitions forbidding a man to talk casually with a woman. But they may also have been intrigued that Jesus would engage a woman *theologically*. The rabbis taught that theological education was for men alone.

4:28–30 Much has been made of the woman leaving her jar behind to report to her neighbors. In her enthusiasm to share her discovery, she left anything that would hinder her.

4:31–34 Jesus' claim to possess food baffles the disciples, since their assignment was to purchase food. Their misunderstanding enables Jesus to press their thinking to another level. Obeying the Father is Jesus' more deeply satisfying task.

4:35–38 Jesus reminds his disciples of a farming proverb to point them to obedience. The fields are *now* ready for gathering. Jesus is in the world, God has planted the field with seed, and it is bearing fruit already.

4:39–42 The Samaritans reenter the scene, and the harvest is at hand. Their faith is based on the woman's testimony, which underscores the value of human witness to the work of God.

4:43–54 This story provides a closing "frame" to the section of the Gospel that outlines Jesus and four institutions of Judaism (purification, temple, rabbi, a well).

4:44–45 John is writing with genuine irony in v. 45 when he talks about the Galileans' welcome. As the next section in Galilee makes clear, they do not

PEOPLE TO KNOW // SAMARITAN WOMAN AT THE WELL

JOHN 4:1–42: Samaritans inhabited the area between two prominent Jewish territories, Galilee and Judea. Jews and Samaritans hated one another, and Jews traveling through Samaritan territory did all they could to minimize contact with the residents.

Jesus broke this pattern. Traveling north through Samaria, Jesus stopped in the town of Sychar and sat down by a well. When his disciples left him to go buy food, a Samaritan woman came out to draw water.

She came at noon rather than in the morning, hoping no one would be there, for she had a bad reputation. She'd had a string of husbands and was now living with a man to whom she was not married. She was shocked when Jesus, a Jewish man, asked her for some water from the well. When she said as much, Jesus told her he was able to give her "living water" (Jn 4:10).

In the course of conversation, she declared that Jesus must be a prophet because he knew so much about her. To deflect the conversation away from her personal life, she brought up a debate over where to worship God. Jesus said that true worshipers worship in "Spirit and in truth" (Jn 4:24). The woman said that when the Messiah came, he would explain everything, and Jesus said, "I am he" (Jn 4:26).

Transformed by her encounter with Jesus, the woman called the people of the town to come and meet him. Many Samaritans from the town believed in Jesus because of her witness (Jn 4:39).

APPLICATION ✣ No matter what lies in your past—embarrassing moments, sinful actions, tragic events—you will be safe coming to Jesus. He already knows everything about you, and he will give you the living water of his Holy Spirit. Don't be too ashamed to come to Christ. The woman at the well shows Christ's love and God's ability to use anyone—even those with stories of shame—to bring more people to himself.

seen all that he had done in Jerusalem
at the Passover Festival,[k] for they also
had been there.
46Once more he visited Cana in Galilee, where he had turned the water into
wine.[l] And there was a certain royal official whose son lay sick at Capernaum.
47When this man heard that Jesus had
arrived in Galilee from Judea,[m] he went
to him and begged him to come and heal
his son, who was close to death.
48"Unless you people see signs and
wonders,"[n] Jesus told him, "you will
never believe."
49The royal official said, "Sir, come
down before my child dies."
50"Go," Jesus replied, "your son will
live."
The man took Jesus at his word and
departed. 51While he was still on the way,
his servants met him with the news that
his boy was living. 52When he inquired
as to the time when his son got better,
they said to him, "Yesterday, at one in
the afternoon, the fever left him."
53Then the father realized that this was
the exact time at which Jesus had said to
him, "Your son will live." So he and his
whole household[o] believed.
54This was the second sign[p] Jesus performed after coming from Judea to Galilee.

4:45 [k] Jn 2:23
4:46 [l] Jn 2:1-11
4:47 [m] ver 3,54
4:48 [n] Da 4:2,3; Jn 2:11; Ac 2:43; 14:3; Ro 15:19; 2Co 12:12; Heb 2:4
4:53 [o] Ac 11:14
4:54 [p] ver 48; Jn 2:11

understand him. As a Jew, Jesus is commenting on his home culture, Judaism, which cannot provide one of its own prophets with honor.

4:46–54 A man asks Jesus persistently if he will come down to Capernaum to heal his son. Jesus heals the boy at a distance instead of traveling to Capernaum. A critical sentence in the story is v. 48. The attitude of the Galileans is the issue here. They want to see miracles; they do not want to try to discern what God is doing among them.

✣ **4:1–54** Not every Christian is comfortable with Jesus' evangelistic strategy here. It is not until Jesus utters a word of prophecy that suddenly the woman's eyes are opened in a new way. Jesus exhibits the power of the Spirit at work for her and thereby models the power of the Spirit that may someday be within her.

Jesus affirms that our abilities will imitate his (14:12), explaining that the gift of the Spirit given to the disciples following his glorification will equip them with abilities similar to his. But what does this mean for evangelism? Is a convincing testimony merely a presentation of belief or a persuasive presentation of the facts?

The Healing at the Pool

5 Some time later, Jesus went up to Jerusalem for one of the Jewish festivals. 2Now there is in Jerusalem near the
Sheep Gate[q] a pool, which in Aramaic[r] is
called Bethesda[a] and which is surrounded by five covered colonnades. 3Here a
great number of disabled people used
to lie — the blind, the lame, the paralyzed. [4][b] 5One who was there had been
an invalid for thirty-eight years. 6When
Jesus saw him lying there and learned
that he had been in this condition for a
long time, he asked him, "Do you want
to get well?"
7"Sir," the invalid replied, "I have no
one to help me into the pool when the
water is stirred. While I am trying to
get in, someone else goes down ahead
of me."
8Then Jesus said to him, "Get up! Pick
up your mat and walk."[s] 9At once the
man was cured; he picked up his mat
and walked.
The day on which this took place was
a Sabbath,[t] 10and so the Jewish leaders[u]
said to the man who had been healed,
"It is the Sabbath; the law forbids you
to carry your mat."[v]
11But he replied, "The man who made
me well said to me, 'Pick up your mat
and walk.' "
12So they asked him, "Who is this fellow who told you to pick it up and walk?"
13The man who was healed had no idea
who it was, for Jesus had slipped away
into the crowd that was there.
14Later Jesus found him at the temple and said to him, "See, you are well
again. Stop sinning[w] or something
worse may happen to you." 15The man
went away and told the Jewish leaders[x] that it was Jesus who had made
him well.

The Authority of the Son

16So, because Jesus was doing these
things on the Sabbath, the Jewish leaders
began to persecute him. 17In his defense
Jesus said to them, "My Father is always
at his work[y] to this very day, and I too am
working." 18For this reason they tried all
the more to kill him;[z] not only was he
breaking the Sabbath, but he was even
calling God his own Father, making himself equal with God.[a]

5:2 [q] Ne 3:1; 12:39 [r] Jn 19:13, 17,20; 20:16; Ac 21:40; 22:2; 26:14
5:8 [s] Mt 9:5,6; Mk 2:11; Lk 5:24
5:9 [t] Jn 9:14
5:10 [u] ver 16 [v] Ne 13:15-22; Jer 17:21; Mt 12:2
5:14 [w] Mk 2:5; Jn 8:11
5:15 [x] Jn 1:19
5:17 [y] Jn 9:4; 14:10
5:18 [z] Jn 7:1 [a] Jn 10:30,33; 19:7

[a] 2 Some manuscripts *Bethzatha*; other manuscripts *Bethsaida* [b] 3,4 Some manuscripts include here, wholly or in part, *paralyzed — and they waited for the moving of the waters. 4From time to time an angel of the Lord would come down and stir up the waters. The first one into the pool after each such disturbance would be cured of whatever disease they had.*

It must be more. Those outside the kingdom deserve to see signs of the Holy Spirit in us before they will step closer to faith themselves.

5:1–2 Today, this pool is located adjacent to the Church of St. Anne inside Jerusalem's Old City.
5:3–4 We learn in the story that the people believed that occasionally an angel would descend and stir the water of the pool, and the first one to touch the water would be healed. (See NIV text note on v. 4.)
5:5–7 Jesus meets a man who had been ill for thirty-eight years. This area was likely a regular place for him to spend the day. Here he could beg from people coming to the pool and take his chances at being healed.

Jesus takes the initiative, using words with implications beyond the miracle at hand: "Do you want to get well?" (v. 6). The man then appeals to his dilemma.
5:8–9a Jesus ignores both the superstition surrounding the pool and the man's complaint: "Get up! Pick up your mat and walk" (v. 8). The healing is immediate. The man simply obeys and is healed.
5:9b–13 The day when Jesus heals the man is the Sabbath, and immediately the story takes an abrupt and unsettling turn. A self-appointed enforcer of Sabbath law confronts the man who has been healed. Jesus' opponents show themselves in all their hostility for the first time in this Gospel. Their question shifts rapidly to the identity of the healer.
5:14–15 When Jesus sees this man who was healed, he says two things. "See, you are well" is no doubt a recognition that his cure was not short-lived, as many supposed cures were (v. 14a). But then Jesus remarks, "Stop sinning or something worse may happen to you" (v. 14b).

Is Jesus making some link between sin and physical ills? The man's sin and his condition are linked. Scripture indicates that some tragedies may be the result of specific sins, but people who have infirmities have not *necessarily* sinned. John 9:3 provides Jesus' correction of that idea.
5:16–18 We dare not miss the pivotal importance of these three verses. The Jewish leadership has uncovered two crimes that deserve the death penalty. First, Jesus was viewed as indifferent to divine Sabbath law as mediated through Jewish tradition.

The second charge against Jesus has to do with blasphemy. Jesus defends his Sabbath activity in v. 17. If God (who made the Sabbath) can continue to work positively while commanding rest, then Jesus' works on the Sabbath are defensible. Jesus is assuming divine rights (v. 19).

If the defense is true, Jesus is making a breathtaking claim: equality with God. If it is false, a serious crime against Judaism has been committed.

19Jesus gave them this answer: "Very
truly I tell you, the Son can do nothing
by himself;[b] he can do only what he sees
his Father doing, because whatever the
Father does the Son also does. 20For the
Father loves the Son[c] and shows him all
he does. Yes, and he will show him even
greater works than these,[d] so that you
will be amazed. 21For just as the Father
raises the dead and gives them life,[e]
even so the Son gives life[f] to whom he
is pleased to give it. 22Moreover, the Father judges no one, but has entrusted all
judgment to the Son,[g] 23that all may hon-
or the Son just as they honor the Father.
Whoever does not honor the Son does
not honor the Father, who sent him.[h]
24"Very truly I tell you, whoever hears
my word and believes him who sent me
has eternal life and will not be judged[i]
but has crossed over from death to life.[j]
25Very truly I tell you, a time is coming
and has now come[k] when the dead will
hear[l] the voice of the Son of God and
those who hear will live. 26For as the Father has life in himself, so he has granted
the Son also to have life in himself. 27And
he has given him authority to judge[m]
because he is the Son of Man.
28"Do not be amazed at this, for a time
is coming[n] when all who are in their
graves will hear his voice 29and come
out — those who have done what is good
will rise to live, and those who have done
what is evil will rise to be condemned.[o]
30By myself I can do nothing;[p] I judge
only as I hear, and my judgment is just,[q]
for I seek not to please myself but him
who sent me.[r]

5:19 [b] ver 30; Jn 8:28
5:20 [c] Jn 3:35 [d] Jn 14:12
5:21 [e] Ro 4:17; 8:11 [f] Jn 11:25
5:22 [g] ver 27; Jn 9:39; Ac 10:42; 17:31
5:23 [h] Lk 10:16; 1Jn 2:23
5:24 [i] Jn 3:18 [j] 1Jn 3:14
5:25 [k] Jn 4:23 [l] Jn 8:43,47
5:27 [m] ver 22; Ac 10:42; 17:31
5:28 [n] Jn 4:21
5:29 [o] Da 12:2; Mt 25:46
5:30 [p] ver 19 [q] Jn 8:16 [r] Mt 26:39; Jn 4:34; 6:38
5:31 [s] Jn 8:14
5:32 [t] ver 37; Jn 8:18
5:33 [u] Jn 1:7
5:34 [v] 1Jn 5:9
5:35 [w] 2Pe 1:19
5:36 [x] 1Jn 5:9 [y] Jn 14:11; 15:24 [z] Jn 3:17; 10:25
5:37 [a] Jn 8:18 [b] Dt 4:12; 1Ti 1:17; Jn 1:18
5:38 [c] 1Jn 2:14 [d] Jn 3:17
5:39 [e] Ro 2:17, 18 [f] Lk 24:27,44; Ac 13:27

Jn 5:39-40 ❖ When might religious practice and even study of Scripture get in the way of coming to Christ and finding true life?

Testimonies About Jesus

31"If I testify about myself, my testimony is not true.[s] 32There is another who
testifies in my favor,[t] and I know that his
testimony about me is true.
33"You have sent to John and he has
testified[u] to the truth. 34Not that I accept
human testimony;[v] but I mention it that
you may be saved. 35John was a lamp that
burned and gave light,[w] and you chose
for a time to enjoy his light.
36"I have testimony weightier than that
of John.[x] For the works that the Father has
given me to finish — the very works that
I am doing[y] — testify that the Father has
sent me.[z] 37And the Father who sent me
has himself testified concerning me.[a] You
have never heard his voice nor seen his
form,[b] 38nor does his word dwell in you,[c]
for you do not believe the one he sent.[d]
39You study[a] the Scriptures[e] diligently
because you think that in them you have
eternal life. These are the very Scriptures
that testify about me,[f] 40yet you refuse to
come to me to have life.

[a] 39 Or *39Study*

5:19 The Son does not simply draw inspiration from the Father but imitates him tirelessly and successfully. What makes this possible? John provides three answers in vv. 20–23.
5:20 The most important affirmation is that the Father loves the Son. The Greek present tense suggests ongoing, continuous affection here, which leads to complete disclosure of the deeper mysteries of the Father.
5:21-22 This love spills into two tasks entrusted to the Son that belong exclusively to the Father. God alone has power over life and can raise people from death. That Jesus can do it too sets him apart. Jesus also becomes the catalyst of divine judgment. Those who love darkness find themselves under judgment already. Whoever believes in the Son has life already. This makes Jesus God's premier agent in the world.
5:23 Jesus claims that whoever wishes to honor the Father must likewise honor the Son who represents him. And whoever dishonors the Son offends the Father whose presence stands behind him.
5:24-30 Now that the groundwork has been laid, Jesus expands and interprets what life and judgment really mean. To hear the words of Jesus is to believe God. God's word and Jesus' word are one and the same; to embrace one is to embrace the other. Jesus is expanding his divine claim. His authority over the Sabbath leads now to authority over eternal life. Because of *who* he is, Jesus can do what God does.
5:31-40 In OT law, more than one witness was needed in order to condemn someone. Jesus' claims are extraordinary. If the claims are corroborated, they stand. Jesus therefore identifies five witnesses to back up his claims. (1) The first witness is God (vv. 31-32). God's word and power are within Jesus, pointing to the truth of who he is. (2) The next witness is John the Baptist (vv. 33-35). John directed his followers to become Jesus' disciples. (3) Next Jesus points to his own works, enabled by the Father (v. 36). (4) Jesus adds the Scriptures to his list of witnesses (vv. 37-38). Jesus fulfills the Scripture. (5) The final witness is Moses (vv. 39-40), who is represented in Scripture, but whose words about the Messiah are unequivocal (Dt 18:15).

41“I do not accept glory from human
beings,[g] 42but I know you. I know that
you do not have the love of God in your
hearts. 43I have come in my Father’s
name, and you do not accept me; but if
someone else comes in his own name,
you will accept him. 44How can you believe since you accept glory from one
another but do not seek the glory that
comes from the only God[a]?[h]
45“But do not think I will accuse you
before the Father. Your accuser is Moses,[i]
on whom your hopes are set.[j] 46If you
believed Moses, you would believe me,
for he wrote about me.[k] 47But since you
do not believe what he wrote, how are
you going to believe what I say?”[l]

Jesus Feeds the Five Thousand

6:1–13pp // Mt 14:13–21; Mk 6:32–44; Lk 9:10–17

6 Some time after this, Jesus crossed
to the far shore of the Sea of Galilee
(that is, the Sea of Tiberias), 2and a great
crowd of people followed him because
they saw the signs[m] he had performed
by healing the sick. 3Then Jesus went up
on a mountainside[n] and sat down with
his disciples. 4The Jewish Passover Festival[o] was near.
5When Jesus looked up and saw a great
crowd coming toward him, he said to
Philip,[p] “Where shall we buy bread for
these people to eat?” 6He asked this only
to test him, for he already had in mind
what he was going to do.
7Philip answered him, “It would take
more than half a year’s wages[b] to buy
enough bread for each one to have a bite!”
8Another of his disciples, Andrew, Simon Peter’s brother,[q] spoke up, 9“Here
is a boy with five small barley loaves and
two small fish, but how far will they go
among so many?”[r]
10Jesus said, “Have the people sit
down.” There was plenty of grass in
that place, and they sat down (about
five thousand men were there). 11Jesus
then took the loaves, gave thanks,[s] and
distributed to those who were seated as
much as they wanted. He did the same
with the fish.
12When they had all had enough to
eat, he said to his disciples, “Gather the
pieces that are left over. Let nothing be
wasted.” 13So they gathered them and
filled twelve baskets with the pieces of
the five barley loaves left over by those
who had eaten.

5:41 [g] ver 44
5:44 [h] Ro 2:29
5:45 [i] Jn 9:28 [j] Ro 2:17
5:46 [k] Ge 3:15; Lk 24:27, 44; Ac 26:22
5:47 [l] Lk 16:29, 31
6:2 [m] Jn 2:11
6:3 [n] ver 15
6:4 [o] Jn 2:13; 11:55
6:5 [p] Jn 1:43
6:8 [q] Jn 1:40
6:9 [r] 2Ki 4:43
6:11 [s] ver 23; Mt 14:19

Jn 6:9 ❖ No matter how little we have, God can use it for great things. What can we offer to God today?

[a] 44 Some early manuscripts *the Only One*
[b] 7 Greek *take two hundred denarii*

5:41–44 Jesus turns the tables and moves from defense to prosecution. If these people cannot see the Father’s work in their midst, something must be profoundly wrong. Their disbelief is deliberate and the diagnosis severe: They love the religious life but have forgotten how to love God.
5:45–47 Jesus’ final reference to Moses points not only to Moses’ role as a witness (cf. above), but also to his role as judge. The very words of Moses will come back to judge the unbelieving. To know the Scriptures but not know God is extremely dangerous.

✣ **5:1–47** Jesus’ inquisitors represent the religious establishment. For them, the vigorous preservation of religious tradition counts more highly than the openness of faith. These people know their Scriptures but use them to defend all the wrong things.

On a national level, some conservative Christian groups unsheathe their religious swords over obscure doctrinal matters. On local levels, many of us have likely seen church members viciously lash out because they perceive their power and influence diminishing. Others lash out at their fellow members because they are “stuck in their old ways” and don’t have “true faith.” All of this bickering, this chapter suggests, is empty religion that seeks its own glory. In the end, it is religion that would condemn and crucify Jesus as a *religious* duty. Jesus calls us, as brothers and sisters in God’s family of the redeemed, to a better way.

6:1–15 Among the many miracles God performed through Moses in Egypt, two stand out as particularly remarkable: his deliverance of Israel through the sea (Ex 14), and his miraculous feeding of the people with manna for forty years in the desert.

In Jn 6, Jesus appears at Passover, repeating many of these themes. Jesus feeds a multitude with “heavenly” bread. Following the feeding, Jesus comes to the disciples walking on water.

These parallels provide a growing impression that Moses, the hero of Passover, has been superseded by Jesus. Jesus not only provides “bread from heaven” but is himself “the bread of life” (v. 35).
6:5–7 Jesus not only wants to provide food, he also wishes to test the developing faith of Philip, who does not yet grasp Jesus’ miraculous ability.
6:8–13 Andrew, Peter’s brother, locates a young boy carrying five barley loaves and two salted fish. In 2Ki 4:42–44 Elisha feeds a hundred men with twenty barley loaves and is assisted by a young servant. Elisha also had baskets of food left over.

I AM

STATEMENT AND REFERENCE	SIGNIFICANCE	OLD TESTAMENT BACKGROUND
"I, the one speaking to you—I am he" (4:26).	Jesus reveals his identity as the Messiah to the Samaritan woman.	Dt 18:15-22; Isa 9:6-7; 11:1-10; 28:16; 53; Jer 23:5-6; Mal 4
"I am the bread of life" (6:25-59).	Jesus identifies the divine origin and life-giving power of the wilderness manna with himself.	Ex 16:31-36; Dt 8:3; Ne 9:16-21; Ps 78:21-25
"I am the light of the world" (8:12-20; 9:1-7).	Throughout the OT, light is a symbol not only of truth and righteousness, but also of the Lord's presence.	Ge 1:3-5; Ex 13:21-22; 2Sa 23:1-5a; Ps 4:6; 27:1; 89:15; 90:8; 118:27; Isa 9:2
"Before Abraham was born, I am" (8:52-59).	Jesus indicates his preexistence as a member of the Trinity.	Ge 14:18-20; 21:12; Ex 3:13-14
"I am the gate for the sheep" (10:1-10).	The sheepfold gate both allowed entrance and prevented trespass; Jesus will be a gate for his sheep.	Jer 23:1-3
"I am the good shepherd" (10:11-18).	Running through Israel's historical, prophetic, wisdom and poetic literature is a powerful image: God as Shepherd. He is prefigured imperfectly in David's reign. His unfaithful representatives—prophets, priests and kings—are forever superseded when he comes himself in Jesus.	Ge 48:14-15; Nu 27:15-17; 2Sa 5:1-3; Ps 23:1-6; 80:1; Isa 40:10-11; Jer 31:10-11; Eze 34:22-24; 37:24; Mic 5:1-4
"I am God's Son" (10:32-36).	In Jewish culture, sons followed in their fathers' footsteps; sonship indicated representation; the Father is shown forth in the face of the Son.	Ps 82:6
"the Father is in me, and I in the Father" (10:32-38; 14:10-11).	Jesus indicates his intimate relationship with God the Father can be shared with his followers, far surpassing the OT experience.	Ps 82:6
"I am the resurrection and the life" (11:21-27).	Though only hinted at in the OT, Jesus explicitly holds out the promise of resurrection, first in raising Lazarus and ultimately on Easter morning.	Ps 16:10-11; Eze 37:11-14
"I am the way and the truth and the life" (14:5-6).	Throughout the OT, the "way of righteousness" is commended to Israel. Jesus himself became our pathway to a new, abundant and everlasting life.	Jos 24:16-18; Ps 16:11; Isa 30:19-24; 40:3; Jer 21:8-10; 50:5; Mal 3:1
"I am the true vine" (15:1-5).	The vine Israel was meant to be, Jesus is; he holds out the offer for each of us to join with him in representing the Father's intentions to the world around us.	Ps 80:8-19; Isa 5:1-7; Jer 2:21; 12:7-10; Eze 19:10-14; Hos 10:1; Joel 1:7

14After the people saw the sign[t] Jesus
performed, they began to say, "Surely
this is the Prophet who is to come into
the world."[u] 15Jesus, knowing that they
intended to come and make him king[v]
by force, withdrew again to a mountain
by himself.[w]

6:14 [t] Jn 2:11 [u] Dt 18:15,18; Mt 11:3; 21:11
6:15 [v] Jn 18:36 [w] Mt 14:23; Mk 6:46

Jesus Walks on the Water

6:16–21pp // Mt 14:22–33; Mk 6:47–51

16When evening came, his disciples
went down to the lake, 17where they got
into a boat and set off across the lake for
Capernaum. By now it was dark, and Jesus
had not yet joined them. 18A strong wind

6:14–15 Through this miracle, Jesus is fulfilling and re-creating images from Israel's sacred past. The crowd interprets Jesus' miracle as messianic. *He has just re-created the miracle of Moses!* Then they attempt to force kingship upon him. The crowd wants to *force* Jesus to define his mission and work politically, but Jesus wants no part of such a kingship.

6:16–19 While Jesus leaves for the mountains of upper Galilee, the disciples set sail, heading for the

was blowing and the waters grew rough.
19 When they had rowed about three or
four miles,[a] they saw Jesus approaching
the boat, walking on the water;[x] and they
were frightened. 20 But he said to them,
"It is I; don't be afraid."[y] 21 Then they were
willing to take him into the boat, and
immediately the boat reached the shore
where they were heading.
22 The next day the crowd that had
stayed on the opposite shore of the lake[z]
realized that only one boat had been
there, and that Jesus had not entered
it with his disciples, but that they had
gone away alone.[a] 23 Then some boats
from Tiberias[b] landed near the place
where the people had eaten the bread
after the Lord had given thanks.[c] 24 Once
the crowd realized that neither Jesus
nor his disciples were there, they got
into the boats and went to Capernaum
in search of Jesus.

Jesus the Bread of Life

25 When they found him on the other
side of the lake, they asked him, "Rabbi,[d]
when did you get here?"
26 Jesus answered, "Very truly I tell
you, you are looking for me,[e] not because
you saw the signs[f] I performed but because you ate the loaves and had your
fill. 27 Do not work for food that spoils,
but for food that endures[g] to eternal life,[h]
which the Son of Man[i] will give you. For
on him God the Father has placed his
seal[j] of approval."
28 Then they asked him, "What must
we do to do the works God requires?"
29 Jesus answered, "The work of God is
this: to believe[k] in the one he has sent."[l]
30 So they asked him, "What sign[m] then
will you give that we may see it and believe you?[n] What will you do? 31 Our ancestors ate the manna[o] in the wilderness; as
it is written: 'He gave them bread from
heaven to eat.'[b]"[p]
32 Jesus said to them, "Very truly I tell
you, it is not Moses who has given you
the bread from heaven, but it is my Father who gives you the true bread from
heaven. 33 For the bread of God is the
bread that comes down from heaven[q]
and gives life to the world."
34 "Sir," they said, "always give us this
bread."[r]
35 Then Jesus declared, "I am the bread
of life.[s] Whoever comes to me will never
go hungry, and whoever believes in me
will never be thirsty.[t] 36 But as I told you,
you have seen me and still you do not
believe. 37 All those the Father gives me[u]

6:19 [x] Job 9:8
6:20 [y] Mt 14:27
6:22 [z] ver 2 [a] ver 15-21
6:23 [b] ver 1 [c] ver 11
6:25 [d] Mt 23:7
6:26 [e] ver 24 [f] ver 30; Jn 2:11
6:27 [g] Isa 55:2 [h] ver 54; Mt 25:46; Jn 4:14 [i] Mt 8:20 [j] Ro 4:11; 1Co 9:2; 2Co 1:22; Eph 1:13; 4:30; 2Ti 2:19; Rev 7:3
6:29 [k] 1Jn 3:23 [l] Jn 3:17
6:30 [m] Jn 2:11 [n] Mt 12:38
6:31 [o] Nu 11:7-9 [p] Ex 16:4, 15; Ne 9:15; Ps 78:24; 105:40
6:33 [q] ver 50
6:34 [r] Jn 4:15
6:35 [s] ver 48,51 [t] Jn 4:14
6:37 [u] ver 39; Jn 17:2,6,9,24

[a] *19* Or about 5 or 6 kilometers
[b] *31* Exodus 16:4; Neh. 9:15; Psalm 78:24,25

---

lake's northeast shore. East-west winds are common on this sea, and fishermen watched for them carefully. The disciples' fear of the rough water, however, was surpassed by their terror at seeing Jesus walking to them on the water. Again, another motif reminds us of the moment when Moses led Israel through the water. Psalm 77 describes this moment in Israel's life and explains that it was in fact God who led them (Ps 77:20).

6:20-21 When Jesus arrives at the boat, he identifies himself with a term that was sure to suggest further images of the exodus story: "It is I" (v. 20). The verb "to be" reflects God's divine name given to Moses on Mount Sinai: "I AM WHO I AM" (Ex 3:14). The disciples' fear echoes Moses' response on the mountain when he learned God's name and saw the burning bush (Ex 3:2-6). Jesus' words indicate the disciples need not fear.

Jesus is barely in the boat when suddenly it arrives at its destination. Many interpreters suspect that we are witnessing yet another miracle here, as Jesus leads his disciples to their port.

6:22-24 The arrival of the crowd in the village of Capernaum introduces Jesus' major "bread of life" discourse (vv. 25-58), in which he carefully defines his relationship to the miracle and its deeper meaning.

6:25-31 As Jesus teaches in the synagogue, he wants to lift his hearers above a material understanding of his miracle. He argues they should not focus on the loaves and fish but on the greater food that lasts forever. But the synagogue audience offers a challenge. What sort of sign can Jesus give to validate his word?

6:32-34 Jesus' interpretation of the manna follows rabbinic lines perfectly. First, the true source of the manna was not Moses but God. If God is truly the source and if Jesus has been sent by God, the shocking turn in v. 33 should come as no surprise: The bread of God is a person who gives life to the world. With a stroke of genius, Jesus exploits a feature of Jewish belief and reinterprets it to refer to himself.

6:35 This famous saying heads the list of what we call the "'I am' sayings" in John. In each of these sayings, Jesus takes a motif from Judaism and reinterprets it for himself.

6:36 With remarkable candor, Jesus announces his disappointment with the crowd. Jesus says that their first step must be belief, but they refuse to take it. Such belief is not a leap into the darkness, for they have had the opportunity to see. Their decision is a willful refusal to act on what God has set before them.

6:37-40 Jesus next speaks confidently about the success of his work and the fulfillment of his mission. Jesus keeps people whom the Father has given into his care. He will not lose a single one of those who have come to him.

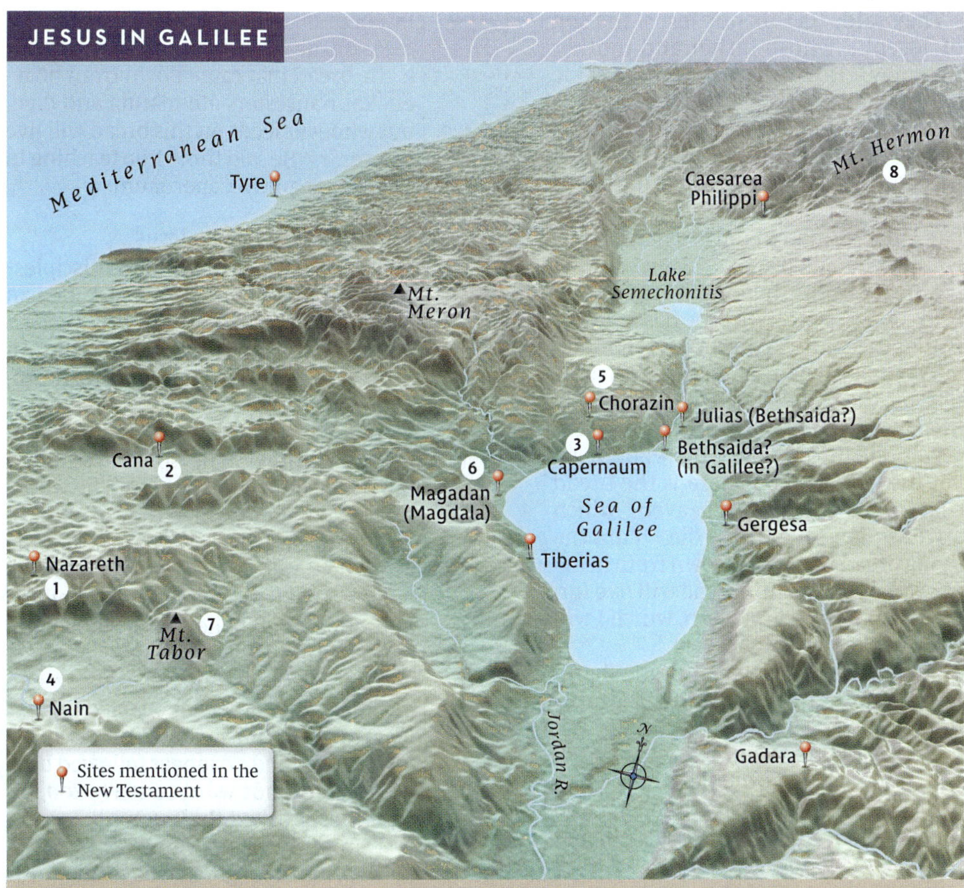

1 Town where Jesus grew up. He was rejected in the synagogue here and people sought to kill him (Lk 4:16).

2 Here at Cana Jesus performed his first miracle by turning water into wine at a wedding feast (Jn 2:1, 11). Home of Nathanael (Jn 21:2).

3 Site of many miracles of Jesus (Mt 8:5; Mk 2:1 and Lk 7:1; Mt 17:24; Mk 1:21 and Lk 4:31; Jn 4:46; 6:17). Jesus taught in the synagogue here at Capernaum (Jn 6:59).

4 Here at Nain Jesus raised a widow's son from the dead (Lk 7:11).

5 One of the cities against which Jesus pronounced a woe (Mt 11:21; Lk 10:13).

6 Fishing town and home of Mary Magdalene (Mt 15:39; Mk 8:10).

7 Mount Tabor, the traditional Mount of Transfiguration (Mt 17:1–8; Mk 9:2–8; Lk 9:28–36). However, many scholars identify Mount Hermon as the most likely site of the transfiguration (see Lk 9:28).

8 Mount Hermon is perhaps the more likely site of the transfiguration (see Lk 9:28).

will come to me, and whoever comes to
me I will never drive away. 38For I have
come down from heaven not to do my
will but to do the will of him who sent
me.[v] 39And this is the will of him who
sent me, that I shall lose none of all those
he has given me,[w] but raise them up at
the last day.[x] 40For my Father's will is
that everyone who looks to the Son and
believes in him shall have eternal life,[y]
and I will raise them up at the last day."
41At this the Jews there began to grumble about him because he said, "I am the
bread that came down from heaven."

6:38 [v] Jn 4:34; 5:30
6:39 [w] Jn 10:28; 17:12; 18:9 [x] ver 40, 44, 54
6:40 [y] Jn 3:15, 16

The sayings that began at v. 35 are part of the "bread of life" discourse because they state what Jesus has been saying in parable form. The "bread of life" is actually Jesus, just as the object of faith now should be Jesus.
6:41–42 It is one thing to say that we should be fed

42They said, "Is this not Jesus, the son
of Joseph,[z] whose father and mother
we know?[a] How can he now say, 'I came
down from heaven'?"[b]
43"Stop grumbling among yourselves,"
Jesus answered. 44"No one can come to
me unless the Father who sent me draws
them,[c] and I will raise them up at the last
day. 45It is written in the Prophets: 'They
will all be taught by God.'[a][d] Everyone who
has heard the Father and learned from
him comes to me. 46No one has seen the
Father except the one who is from God;[e]
only he has seen the Father. 47Very truly I
tell you, the one who believes has eternal
life. 48I am the bread of life.[f] 49Your ancestors ate the manna in the wilderness,
yet they died.[g] 50But here is the bread
that comes down from heaven,[h] which
anyone may eat and not die. 51I am the
living bread that came down from heav-
en. Whoever eats this bread will live forever. This bread is my flesh, which I will
give for the life of the world."[i]
52Then the Jews began to argue sharply among themselves,[j] "How can this
man give us his flesh to eat?"
53Jesus said to them, "Very truly I tell
you, unless you eat the flesh of the Son
of Man[k] and drink his blood, you have no
life in you. 54Whoever eats my flesh and
drinks my blood has eternal life, and I
will raise them up at the last day.[l] 55For
my flesh is real food and my blood is real
drink. 56Whoever eats my flesh and drinks
my blood remains in me, and I in them.[m]
57Just as the living Father sent me[n] and I
live because of the Father, so the one who
feeds on me will live because of me. 58This
is the bread that came down from heav-
en. Your ancestors ate manna and died,
but whoever feeds on this bread will live
forever."[o] 59He said this while teaching in
the synagogue in Capernaum.

Many Disciples Desert Jesus

60On hearing it, many of his disciples[p]
said, "This is a hard teaching. Who can
accept it?"
61Aware that his disciples were grumbling about this, Jesus said to them,
"Does this offend you?[q] 62Then what if
you see the Son of Man ascend to where
he was before![r] 63The Spirit gives life;[s]
the flesh counts for nothing. The words
I have spoken to you—they are full of
the Spirit[b] and life. 64Yet there are some
of you who do not believe." For Jesus
had known[t] from the beginning which
of them did not believe and who would
betray him. 65He went on to say, "This is
why I told you that no one can come to
me unless the Father has enabled them."[u]
66From this time many of his disciples[v]
turned back and no longer followed him.
67"You do not want to leave too, do
you?" Jesus asked the Twelve.[w]
68Simon Peter answered him,[x] "Lord,
to whom shall we go? You have the words
of eternal life. 69We have come to believe
and to know that you are the Holy One
of God."[y]

[a] *45* Isaiah 54:13 [b] *63* Or *are Spirit*; or *are spirit*

6:42 [z] Lk 4:22 [a] Jn 7:27,28 [b] ver 38,62
6:44 [c] ver 65; Jer 31:3; Jn 12:32
6:45 [d] Isa 54:13; Jer 31:33,34; Heb 8:10,11; 10:16
6:46 [e] Jn 1:18; 5:37; 7:29
6:48 [f] ver 35,51
6:49 [g] ver 31,58
6:50 [h] ver 33
6:51 [i] Heb 10:10
6:52 [j] Jn 7:43; 9:16; 10:19
6:53 [k] Mt 8:20
6:54 [l] ver 39
6:56 [m] Jn 15:4-7; 1Jn 3:24; 4:15
6:57 [n] Jn 3:17
6:58 [o] ver 49-51; Jn 3:36
6:60 [p] ver 66
6:61 [q] Mt 11:6
6:62 [r] Mk 16:19; Jn 3:13; 17:5
6:63 [s] 2Co 3:6
6:64 [t] Jn 2:25
6:65 [u] ver 37,44
6:66 [v] ver 60
6:67 [w] Mt 10:2
6:68 [x] Mt 16:16
6:69 [y] Mk 8:29; Lk 9:20

---

by God. It is quite another for Jesus to say that he is the source of that meal. The "grumbling" described in vv. 41, 43 (and 52) is reminiscent of the "murmuring" of the Israelites against Moses in the desert.

6:43–50 Jesus does not defend himself but instead returns to the problem of their spiritual receptivity. The idea of Jesus' divine origin is impossible to believe unless God gives them insight.

6:51 Jesus makes a pivotal statement, "This bread is my flesh, which I will give for the life of the world." When Jesus refers to his "flesh," we are at once reminded of 1:14, where *"flesh"* was used to describe the comprehensive life of the Son. The gift of Jesus is nothing other than a temple sacrifice that will benefit the world.

6:52 It is all too much for the crowd. Of course, Jesus is not proposing cannibalism for religious purposes. Earthly symbols must be converted into spiritual truths. What deeper spiritual truth needs to be uncovered?

6:53–58 Jesus' answer has proven difficult for almost every commentator. The only Judeo-Christian setting where such words make good sense is the Christian Eucharist—the Lord's Supper. Significantly, John does *not* record the words of institution later in Jesus' upper-room discourse. His language here echoes Luke's language at the supper: "This is my body given for you" (Lk 22:19).

6:59–62 Jesus points to yet one more feature of this coming hour. Not only will he die, but Jesus says he will return to heaven. It is through this complete work of Christ that life can be given to the world.

6:63–65 The "flesh" that "counts for nothing" in v. 63 recalls the literal flesh of v. 53. Jesus clarifies that taking his words literally is not the point. The life-giving gift is the Holy Spirit.

6:66–69 This is clearly a turning point for Jesus. The mystery of his person and work has now been laid out in full, and some of his followers decide to leave. For Peter this difficult exchange and exit provides an opportunity to give a courageous confession (vv. 68–69).

Jesus recognizes the confession as evidence of God's supernatural movement in Peter's life. These deeper things cannot be embraced by just anyone, but only by those whom God has enabled.

70 Then Jesus replied, "Have I not chosen you,[z] the Twelve? Yet one of you is
a devil!"[a] 71 (He meant Judas, the son of
Simon Iscariot, who, though one of the
Twelve, was later to betray him.)

Jesus Goes to the Festival of Tabernacles

7 After this, Jesus went around in Galilee. He did not want[a] to go about in
Judea because the Jewish leaders[b] there
were looking for a way to kill him.[c] 2 But
when the Jewish Festival of Tabernacles[d]
was near, 3 Jesus' brothers[e] said to him,
"Leave Galilee and go to Judea, so that
your disciples there may see the works
you do. 4 No one who wants to become
a public figure acts in secret. Since you
are doing these things, show yourself to
the world." 5 For even his own brothers
did not believe in him.[f]
6 Therefore Jesus told them, "My time[g]
is not yet here; for you any time will do.
7 The world cannot hate you, but it hates
me[h] because I testify that its works are
evil.[i] 8 You go to the festival. I am not[b] going up to this festival, because my time[j]
has not yet fully come." 9 After he had
said this, he stayed in Galilee.
10 However, after his brothers had left
for the festival, he went also, not publicly, but in secret. 11 Now at the festival the
Jewish leaders were watching for Jesus[k]
and asking, "Where is he?"
12 Among the crowds there was widespread whispering about him. Some said,
"He is a good man."
Others replied, "No, he deceives the
people."[l] 13 But no one would say anything
publicly about him for fear of the leaders.[m]

Jesus Teaches at the Festival

14 Not until halfway through the festival did Jesus go up to the temple courts
and begin to teach.[n] 15 The Jews[o] there
were amazed and asked, "How did this
man get such learning[p] without having
been taught?"[q]
16 Jesus answered, "My teaching is not
my own. It comes from the one who sent
me.[r] 17 Anyone who chooses to do the will
of God will find out[s] whether my teaching comes from God or whether I speak
on my own. 18 Whoever speaks on their
own does so to gain personal glory,[t] but
he who seeks the glory of the one who
sent him is a man of truth; there is nothing false about him. 19 Has not Moses giv-
en you the law?[u] Yet not one of you keeps
the law. Why are you trying to kill me?"[v]

6:70 [z] Jn 15:16, 19 [a] Jn 13:27
7:1 [b] Jn 1:19 [c] Jn 5:18
7:2 [d] Lev 23:34; Dt 16:16
7:3 [e] Mt 12:46
7:5 [f] Mk 3:21
7:6 [g] Mt 26:18
7:7 [h] Jn 15:18, 19 [i] Jn 3:19, 20
7:8 [j] ver 6
7:11 [k] Jn 11:56
7:12 [l] ver 40, 43
7:13 [m] Jn 9:22; 12:42; 19:38
7:14 [n] ver 28; Mt 26:55
7:15 [o] Jn 1:19 [p] Ac 26:24 [q] Mt 13:54
7:16 [r] Jn 3:11; 14:24
7:17 [s] Ps 25:14; Jn 8:43
7:18 [t] Jn 5:41; 8:50, 54
7:19 [u] Jn 1:17 [v] ver 1; Mt 12:14

[a] *1* Some manuscripts *not have authority*
[b] *8* Some manuscripts *not yet*

6:70–71 John introduces us to the disciple who will eventually betray Jesus. In Judas we can see an example of one who is close to Jesus and yet remains far from him and his kingdom priorities.

> ✜ **6:1–71** Being fed by God is such a simple concept that it has become hard to understand in a world congested with busyness. Like the pursuit of joy, the more we run after it with strategies and plans, the farther away it seems to flee from us. It is not gained by ministry accomplishments, righteous efforts, or the intellectual mastery of the Bible. Being fed by God requires a conversion of thinking, a discovery that God is eager to give life and renewal to anyone who can listen in simplicity and trust in his gracious provision. God himself enables those who come to him and believe to understand what that belief truly means (6:65).

7:1–5 Jesus has been avoiding Judea because he knows the depth of hostility waiting for him there. Jesus' brothers may be reminding him of his religious obligation or even pushing him to go public with his messianic identity. Either way, they do not believe in him (v. 5).

7:6–10 When Jesus says that he will not "go up" at the festival, he explains that he cannot because it is not yet his time (v. 8). Jesus intends no deception and attends the feast on his own, keeping his identity as quiet as possible to avoid his adversaries.

7:11–13 Jesus' arrival brings controversy and division. In their search for Jesus, some describe him as "good" while others describe him as a fraud. The Jewish leaders have decided to kill Jesus but are afraid of the crowd.

7:14–36 Jesus' listeners launch questions at him that permit Jesus to describe his identity and mission more completely. But the questions disclose how little his audience really understands.

7:14–17 Jesus posesses no official educational credentials. The Jewish leaders, in effect, wish to see these. Jesus complies by saying that his diplomas are divine: God has taught and commissioned him. Moreover, Jesus explains that if the leaders' lives are in harmony with God, they will recognize the character and source of his teaching.

In Jewish thought, authority was conferred from rabbi to rabbi through ordination. Jesus' problem in the eyes of the Jewish leadership is that he is not ordained. What is the source of his authority? Jesus' answer is clear: His authority stems directly from God.

7:18–19 It is clear from v. 19 that the Sabbath debate of ch. 5 still dominates Jesus' dialogue with these authorities. Jesus here returns to his previous line of argument: Those who do not keep the law of Moses should be reluctant to judge others.

20"You are demon-possessed,"[w] the
crowd answered. "Who is trying to kill
you?"
21Jesus said to them, "I did one miracle,
and you are all amazed. 22Yet, because Moses gave you circumcision[x] (though actually it did not come from Moses, but from
the patriarchs),[y] you circumcise a boy on
the Sabbath. 23Now if a boy can be circumcised on the Sabbath so that the law of Moses may not be broken, why are you angry
with me for healing a man's whole body
on the Sabbath? 24Stop judging by mere
appearances, but instead judge correctly."[z]

Division Over Who Jesus Is

25At that point some of the people of
Jerusalem began to ask, "Isn't this the
man they are trying to kill? 26Here he is,
speaking publicly, and they are not saying a word to him. Have the authorities[a]
really concluded that he is the Messiah?
27But we know where this man is from;[b]
when the Messiah comes, no one will
know where he is from."
28Then Jesus, still teaching in the temple courts,[c] cried out, "Yes, you know me,
and you know where I am from.[d] I am
not here on my own authority, but he
who sent me is true.[e] You do not know
him, 29but I know him[f] because I am
from him and he sent me."

7:20 [w] Jn 8:48; 10:20
7:22 [x] Lev 12:3 [y] Ge 17:10-14
7:24 [z] Isa 11:3, 4; Jn 8:15
7:26 [a] ver 48
7:27 [b] Mt 13:55; Lk 4:22
7:28 [c] ver 14 [d] Jn 8:14 [e] Jn 8:26, 42
7:29 [f] Mt 11:27

7:30 [g] ver 32, 44; Jn 10:39
7:31 [h] Jn 8:30 [i] Jn 2:11
7:33 [j] Jn 13:33; 16:16 [k] Jn 16:5, 10, 17, 28
7:34 [l] Jn 8:21; 13:33
7:35 [m] Jas 1:1 [n] Jn 12:20; 1Pe 1:1
7:37 [o] Lev 23:36

Jn 7:37-38 ❖ How has Christ helped you when you were thirsty? What do you think the rivers of living water flowing out of Christ's followers represent?

30At this they tried to seize him, but
no one laid a hand on him,[g] because his
hour had not yet come. 31Still, many in
the crowd believed in him.[h] They said,
"When the Messiah comes, will he perform more signs[i] than this man?"
32The Pharisees heard the crowd whispering such things about him. Then the
chief priests and the Pharisees sent temple guards to arrest him.
33Jesus said, "I am with you for only a
short time,[j] and then I am going to the
one who sent me.[k] 34You will look for
me, but you will not find me; and where
I am, you cannot come."[l]
35The Jews said to one another, "Where
does this man intend to go that we cannot find him? Will he go where our people live scattered[m] among the Greeks,[n]
and teach the Greeks? 36What did he
mean when he said, 'You will look for
me, but you will not find me,' and 'Where
I am, you cannot come'?"
37On the last and greatest day of the
festival,[o] Jesus stood and said in a loud

7:20 Jesus has to be cautious, protecting himself from those who want to assassinate him. Their statement accusing Jesus of being "demon-possessed" likely carries no theological weight and can simply be translated, "You're crazy!"

7:21-24 Jesus now expands his line of reasoning. If a boy can be *partially* healed on the Sabbath in this context, why should not a man be *completely* healed on the Sabbath? Jesus is fulfilling what the law was meant to do—bring renewal and redemption to God's people.

7:25-27 Once again the ironic misunderstanding of the crowd is displayed by their question in v. 27. The people think that he is disqualified from messianic status since they can trace Jesus' human origins.

7:28-29 Jesus simply makes a more astounding claim: He has come from God, whom he knows with unparalleled intimacy. This is paramount to a divine claim that radically breaks with all the principles of Judaism.

7:30-31 Some in the crowd try to arrest him for making divine claims, but their efforts are frustrated. Jesus will choose when his time has come.

7:32-36 The chief priests and Pharisees enlist police from the temple to arrest Jesus. No doubt, it leads Jesus to think about his death at their hands. As in the previous scenes, Jesus' statement inspires earthly misunderstanding. The Jewish leadership speculate that Jesus is simply talking about leaving Israel. But Jesus is talking about where they *cannot* go—heaven.

7:37-38 Each day of the feast witnessed a water ceremony in which a procession of priests descended to the south border of the city to the Gihon Spring. In the desert, God brought water from a rock, and here water was flowing from the sacrificial rock altar of the temple. Ezekiel and Zechariah had visions of rivers flowing from the temple in a miraculous display of God's blessing (Eze 47; Zec 14:8). In a drought-stricken land, it was a spectacular vision of life-giving water flowing from God's life-giving temple.

On this final day of celebration, Jesus steps into public view and makes his most stunning pronouncement of the feast, which parallels symbolically what Jesus did in Jn 6 at Passover. Just as earthly bread led to memories of heavenly bread (manna), which concluded with Jesus offering himself as the bread of life (6:35), so now Jesus is doing the same.

At the Festival of Tabernacles, Jesus is saying he is not only the new temple and source of living water but also the rock that, when struck, will yield life-giving water. Is it any surprise that when Jesus is struck on the cross with a spear, his side yields blood *and water* (19:34)?

voice, "Let anyone who is thirsty come
to me and drink.[p] 38Whoever believes in
me, as Scripture has said,[q] rivers of living water[r] will flow from within them."[a][s]
39By this he meant the Spirit,[t] whom
those who believed in him were later to
receive.[u] Up to that time the Spirit had
not been given, since Jesus had not yet
been glorified.[v]
40On hearing his words, some of the
people said, "Surely this man is the
Prophet."[w]
41Others said, "He is the Messiah."
Still others asked, "How can the Messiah come from Galilee?[x] 42Does not Scripture say that the Messiah will come from
David's descendants[y] and from Bethlehem,[z] the town where David lived?"
43Thus the people were divided[a] because
of Jesus. 44Some wanted to seize him, but
no one laid a hand on him.[b]

Unbelief of the Jewish Leaders

45Finally the temple guards went back
to the chief priests and the Pharisees,
who asked them, "Why didn't you bring
him in?"
46"No one ever spoke the way this man
does,"[c] the guards replied.
47"You mean he has deceived you
also?"[d] the Pharisees retorted. 48"Have
any of the rulers or of the Pharisees believed in him?[e] 49No! But this mob that
knows nothing of the law—there is a
curse on them."
50Nicodemus,[f] who had gone to Jesus
earlier and who was one of their own
number, asked, 51"Does our law condemn
a man without first hearing him to find
out what he has been doing?"
52They replied, "Are you from Galilee,
too? Look into it, and you will find that
a prophet does not come out of Galilee."[g]

[The earliest manuscripts and many other ancient witnesses do not have John 7:53—8:11. A few manuscripts include these verses, wholly or in part, after John 7:36, John 21:25, Luke 21:38 or Luke 24:53.]

8 *53Then they all went home, 1but Jesus went
to the Mount of Olives.*[h]
*2At dawn he appeared again in the temple
courts, where all the people gathered around him,
and he sat down to teach them.*[i] *3The teachers of
the law and the Pharisees brought in a woman
caught in adultery. They made her stand before the
group 4and said to Jesus, "Teacher, this woman was
caught in the act of adultery. 5In the Law Moses
commanded us to stone such women.*[j] *Now what
do you say?" 6They were using this question as a
trap,*[k] *in order to have a basis for accusing him.*[l]
But Jesus bent down and started to write on

7:37 [p] Isa 55:1; Rev 22:17
7:38 [q] Isa 58:11 [r] Jn 4:10 [s] Jn 4:14
7:39 [t] Joel 2:28; Ac 2:17,33 [u] Jn 20:22 [v] Jn 12:23; 13:31,32
7:40 [w] Mt 21:11; Jn 1:21
7:41 [x] ver 52; Jn 1:46
7:42 [y] Mt 1:1 [z] Mic 5:2; Mt 2:5,6; Lk 2:4
7:43 [a] Jn 9:16; 10:19
7:44 [b] ver 30
7:46 [c] Mt 7:28
7:47 [d] ver 12
7:48 [e] Jn 12:42
7:50 [f] Jn 3:1; 19:39
7:52 [g] ver 41
8:1 [h] Mt 21:1
8:2 [i] ver 20; Mt 26:55
8:5 [j] Lev 20:10; Dt 22:22
8:6 [k] Mt 22:15, 18 [l] Mt 12:10

[a] *37,38 Or me. And let anyone drink 38who believes in me." As Scripture has said, "Out of him* (or *them*) *will flow rivers of living water."*

7:39 John explains that Jesus was referring to the Holy Spirit in this pronouncement. This gift must await Jesus' "glorification" to be distributed. As we watch the Passion story unfold, we will do well to observe how the Spirit becomes a signal feature of Jesus' departure from the world and return to the Father.
7:40–52 The complete frustration of the Sanhedrin becomes clear. Even the temple police are impressed with Jesus. Nicodemus speaks up, urging caution and fair play. The Sanhedrin's objection that Jesus cannot be a prophet since he has come from Galilee is unfounded; the prophets Jonah and Nahum came from that very place.

7:1–52 Just as there is a worldly opposition to Jesus, there is likewise a religious opposition to Jesus. What does this opposition mean? Does a religious reflex ever arise in the church? Jesus is offering a spiritual mysticism and encounter with God that *always* makes the caretakers of traditional religion nervous. This can be especially true in those tightly drawn circles of conservative theology that sometimes seem impenetrable. To propose new freedom, new spontaneity, new thought—that is, to step outside the seemingly iron-clad precepts of traditional religious behavior or thinking—is to experience what Jesus proclaimed at the Festival of Tabernacles.

7:53—8:6a The religious leaders are making a legal claim: They possess strong testimony from two witnesses who saw the adulterous couple in a sexual context. The two witnesses had to see these things at the same time and place so that their testimonies would be identical. Such evidence virtually required the witnesses to set a trap. The law also expected that if a person witnessed another about to commit a sin, compassion required them to speak up. These witnesses stand silently, wanting to catch her and use her. Where is her lover? The accusers have permitted him to get away clean.

These witnesses bring the woman to Jesus and heap public shame on her. Their approach to the problem indicates that they wish to trap Jesus; her personal life is incidental. They have no interest in a trial.
8:6b–8 It is impossible to know what Jesus wrote in the dust. Jesus responds with his often-quoted statement, "Let any one of you who is without sin be the first to throw a stone at her." This is a direct reference to Dt 13:9 or 17:7, which says that those who witness a crime and bring home a successful accusation must be the first to stone the victim.

PEOPLE TO KNOW // WOMAN CAUGHT IN SIN

JOHN 8:1–11: Some religious leaders brought a woman before Jesus to test him. They humiliated her and put her on display to make a point. Would Jesus hold to the straightforward teaching of the Mosaic Law or would he have compassion on the woman?

When the leaders questioned Jesus, he did not respond. Instead, he bent down and began writing in the sand. Some speculate Jesus was listing sins the onlookers had committed. Others suggest that Jesus may have been writing down the names of the woman's accusers. Scripture does not clarify what he was doing.

When Jesus did speak, however, he did not fall into their trap. He simply said that the person to start the execution process should be guiltless: "Let any one of you who is without sin be the first to throw a stone at her" (Jn 8:7).

Starting with the oldest, the crowd dispersed. Jesus graciously said that he did not condemn her, and he told her to go and leave her life of sin.

APPLICATION ✣ Was Jesus unjust or unfaithful to God's Word by allowing the woman to go free? No. He knew, of course, that she had sinned. But Jesus came to earth to become sin for us, so that "we might become the righteousness of God" (2Co 5:21). Jesus does not ignore the consequences of sin. He bore them himself so that we would never have to. As was true with this woman, those who are in Christ face no condemnation (Ro 8:1). Christ invites us to walk in the power of his Spirit and leave our sinful lives behind.

the ground with his finger. 7When they kept on
questioning him, he straightened up and said to
them, "Let any one of you who is without sin be
the first to throw a stone[m] at her."[n] 8Again he
stooped down and wrote on the ground.
9At this, those who heard began to go away one
at a time, the older ones first, until only Jesus was
left, with the woman still standing there. 10Jesus
straightened up and asked her, "Woman, where
are they? Has no one condemned you?"
11"No one, sir," she said.

8:7 [m] Dt 17:7 [n] Ro 2:1,22
8:11 [o] Jn 3:17 [p] Jn 5:14
8:12 [q] Jn 6:35 [r] Jn 1:4; 12:35 [s] Pr 4:18; Mt 5:14

"Then neither do I condemn you,"[o] Jesus declared. "Go now and leave your life of sin."[p]

Dispute Over Jesus' Testimony

12When Jesus spoke again to the peo-
ple, he said, "I am[q] the light of the world.[r]
Whoever follows me will never walk in
darkness, but will have the light of life."[s]

In the world of antiquity, women who engaged in sexual sin could often find themselves in jeopardy much more quickly than their partners. Jesus may be cutting through the double standard to force the men who accuse the woman to test Jesus and to reflect on their own hypocrisy.

8:8–11 Jesus resumes his writing, and the religious leaders begin departing one by one. In the end, Jesus and the woman are left alone. Because Jesus must have been sitting and the woman standing, he now straightens up (v. 10) and speaks to her for the first time. His questions do not imply that the woman is innocent, since in v. 11 he warns her to leave a sinful life that has been her habit. He simply points to the absence of accusers. They have disappeared. The woman's response shows considerable respect for Jesus, who has likely literally saved her life.

✣ 7:53—8:11 The motive among these men is to trap Jesus; their strategy includes trapping the woman. Perhaps entrapment characterizes a good portion of their religious effort. They are religious police, although people with religious obsessions like this rarely see themselves this way. Christians who take godly righteousness seriously rarely see themselves this way either. Are we religious police? Does our healthy commitment to righteousness ever lapse into an obsessive preoccupation with the details of people's personal lives?

Sin is sin, and sexual sin is sin. Yet as we look at the contemporary church, it is fascinating to observe how we do not share the same reaction as Jesus to this woman and her sin. Is our reflex to judge and expel or to forgive and heal? We are not compromising the seriousness of sexual sin when we raise this question. Neither was Jesus. But Jesus had different reflexes.

8:12 This verse records Jesus' second "I am" saying. The Festival of Tabernacles occurred in the late autumn and celebrated the harvest. The autumnal equinox (where night and day are of equal length) provided the context for a light ceremony that was popular in Jerusalem and was orchestrated during Tabernacles.

Four large stands each held four golden bowls; these were placed in the heavily used court of women. These sixteen golden bowls (reached by ladders) were filled with oil. When they were lit

13 The Pharisees challenged him, "Here
you are, appearing as your own witness;
your testimony is not valid."[t]
14 Jesus answered, "Even if I testify
on my own behalf, my testimony is valid, for I know where I came from and
where I am going.[u] But you have no idea
where I come from[v] or where I am going.
15 You judge by human standards;[w] I pass
judgment on no one.[x] 16 But if I do judge,
my decisions are true, because I am not
alone. I stand with the Father, who sent
me.[y] 17 In your own Law it is written that
the testimony of two witnesses is true.[z] 18 I
am one who testifies for myself; my other witness is the Father, who sent me."[a]
19 Then they asked him, "Where is your
father?"
"You do not know me or my Fa-
ther,"[b] Jesus replied. "If you knew me,
you would know my Father also."[c] 20 He
spoke these words while teaching[d] in the
temple courts near the place where the
offerings were put.[e] Yet no one seized
him, because his hour had not yet come.[f]

Dispute Over Who Jesus Is

21 Once more Jesus said to them, "I am
going away, and you will look for me, and
you will die[g] in your sin. Where I go, you
cannot come."[h]
22 This made the Jews ask, "Will he kill
himself? Is that why he says, 'Where I go,
you cannot come'?"
23 But he continued, "You are from below; I am from above. You are of this
world; I am not of this world.[i] 24 I told
you that you would die in your sins; if
you do not believe that I am he,[j] you will
indeed die in your sins."
25 "Who are you?" they asked.
"Just what I have been telling you
from the beginning," Jesus replied. 26 "I
have much to say in judgment of you.
But he who sent me is trustworthy,[k] and
what I have heard from him I tell the
world."[l]
27 They did not understand that he was
telling them about his Father. 28 So Jesus
said, "When you have lifted up[a] the Son
of Man,[m] then you will know that I am
he and that I do nothing on my own but
speak just what the Father has taught
me. 29 The one who sent me is with me;
he has not left me alone,[n] for I always do
what pleases him."[o] 30 Even as he spoke,
many believed in him.[p]

Dispute Over Whose Children Jesus' Opponents Are

31 To the Jews who had believed him,
Jesus said, "If you hold to my teaching,[q]
you are really my disciples. 32 Then you
will know the truth, and the truth will
set you free."[r]
33 They answered him, "We are Abraham's

8:13 [t] Jn 5:31
8:14 [u] Jn 13:3; 16:28 [v] Jn 7:28; 9:29
8:15 [w] Jn 7:24 [x] Jn 3:17
8:16 [y] Jn 5:30
8:17 [z] Dt 17:6; Mt 18:16
8:18 [a] Jn 5:37
8:19 [b] Jn 16:3 [c] Jn 14:7; 1Jn 2:23
8:20 [d] Mt 26:55 [e] Mk 12:41 [f] Mt 26:18; Jn 7:30
8:21 [g] Eze 3:18 [h] Jn 7:34; 13:33
8:23 [i] Jn 3:31; 17:14
8:24 [j] Jn 4:26; 13:19
8:26 [k] Jn 7:28 [l] Jn 3:32; 15:15
8:28 [m] Jn 3:14; 5:19; 12:32
8:29 [n] ver 16; Jn 16:32 [o] Jn 4:34; 5:30; 6:38
8:30 [p] Jn 7:31
8:31 [q] Jn 15:7; 2Jn 9
8:32 [r] Ro 8:2; Jas 2:12

[a] *28* The Greek for *lifted up* also means *exalted.*

---

at night, all Jerusalem was illumined. In the very court where the lighting ceremony takes place, Jesus says that he is the true light of Jerusalem and the whole world.

8:13–18 Jesus' reference to himself as the light that guides people through darkness (as the pillar of light guided the Israelites in the desert) is quickly challenged. The Pharisees' argument echoes what occurred in ch. 5. Unfortunately, his opponents have forgotten that in the earlier Jerusalem debate, Jesus demonstrated he had ample witnesses to verify his claim. Now Jesus must repeat again that his Father is a second witness (v. 18).

But something important has now been added. Jesus' states that his judgment is true and his words are true because of their *origins*. This is a new and unexpected authority behind Jesus' testimony.

8:19–20 The root problem with Jesus' opponents is that they do not know the Father. Without a deep knowledge of God and his love, it is impossible to recognize his Son.

8:21–24 When Jesus says that he is leaving them, the crowd concludes that Jesus must be going to his death. Jesus will indeed die, and this departure will be a return to his Father in heaven.

8:25–28 Once the opportunity to hear and believe in Jesus is gone, the world is lost. But the crowd misses the point altogether. He is not a man with religious insight (from below), but God's Son (from above). This prompts his audience to ask its most important question. Not "What do you mean?" but "Who are you?"

The supreme moment of revelation is when Jesus is "lifted up," which is not merely the cross but the series of events that lead to his glorification: betrayal, trial, crucifixion, resurrection, and ascension. Through these events, the world will see *not* that Jesus is simply telling the truth but that he is the bearer of God's divine name ("I am").

8:30 The faith of some of the Jews in his audience provides an interesting counterpoint to what we learned in v. 20. Some completely oppose him, while others are receptive and welcoming.

8:31–35 With their history of slavery and bondage, Jews viewed freedom as a precious treasure. But here Jesus claims religious heritage does not bring true freedom: truth does (v. 32). Indeed, "the truth will set you free." But to be set free implies that there is a bondage from which one needs to be freed. The Jews consider themselves to be free (sons of Abraham), but Jesus insists they are slaves (of sin).

> **Jn 8:36** ❖ What does it look like to be set free by Christ? How does it affect our lives today?

descendants[s] and have never been slaves
of anyone. How can you say that we shall
be set free?"
34Jesus replied, "Very truly I tell you,
everyone who sins is a slave to sin.[t] 35Now
a slave has no permanent place in the
family, but a son belongs to it forever.[u]
36So if the Son sets you free, you will be
free indeed. 37I know that you are Abraham's descendants. Yet you are looking
for a way to kill me,[v] because you have
no room for my word. 38I am telling you
what I have seen in the Father's presence,[w] and you are doing what you have
heard from your father.[a]"
39"Abraham is our father," they answered.
"If you were Abraham's children,"[x] said
Jesus, "then you would[b] do what Abraham did. 40As it is, you are looking for a
way to kill me, a man who has told you
the truth that I heard from God.[y] Abraham did not do such things. 41You are
doing the works of your own father."[z]
"We are not illegitimate children," they
protested. "The only Father we have is
God himself."[a]
42Jesus said to them, "If God were your
Father, you would love me,[b] for I have
come here from God.[c] I have not come
on my own;[d] God sent me.[e] 43Why is my
language not clear to you? Because you
are unable to hear what I say. 44You belong to your father, the devil,[f] and you
want to carry out your father's desires.[g]
He was a murderer from the beginning,
not holding to the truth, for there is no
truth in him. When he lies, he speaks
his native language, for he is a liar and
the father of lies.[h] 45Yet because I tell the
truth,[i] you do not believe me! 46Can any
of you prove me guilty of sin? If I am telling the truth, why don't you believe me?
47Whoever belongs to God hears what
God says.[j] The reason you do not hear is
that you do not belong to God."

Jesus' Claims About Himself

48The Jews answered him, "Aren't we
right in saying that you are a Samaritan[k]
and demon-possessed?"[l]
49"I am not possessed by a demon,"
said Jesus, "but I honor my Father and
you dishonor me. 50I am not seeking
glory for myself;[m] but there is one who
seeks it, and he is the judge. 51Very truly
I tell you, whoever obeys my word will
never see death."[n]
52At this they exclaimed, "Now we
know that you are demon-possessed!
Abraham died and so did the prophets,
yet you say that whoever obeys your
word will never taste death. 53Are you

8:33 [s]ver 37,39; Mt 3:9 8:34 [t]Ro 6:16; 2Pe 2:19 8:35 [u]Gal 4:30 8:37 [v]ver 39,40 8:38 [w]Jn 5:19, 30; 14:10,24 8:39 [x]ver 37; Ro 9:7; Gal 3:7 8:40 [y]ver 26 8:41 [z]ver 38, 44 [a]Isa 63:16; 64:8 8:42 [b]1Jn 5:1 [c]Jn 16:27; 17:8 [d]Jn 7:28 [e]Jn 3:17 8:44 [f]1Jn 3:8 [g]ver 38,41 [h]Ge 3:4 8:45 [i]Jn 18:37 8:47 [j]Jn 18:37; 1Jn 4:6 8:48 [k]Mt 10:5 [l]ver 52; Jn 7:20 8:50 [m]ver 54; Jn 5:41 8:51 [n]Jn 11:26

[a] 38 *Or presence. Therefore do what you have heard from the Father.* [b] 39 Some early manuscripts *"If you are Abraham's children," said Jesus, "then*

8:36-38 Lineage from Abraham is a matter of faith. Any claim to blood heritage that brings spiritual privilege always stands in question. The "Son" who is secure and permanent is likely Jesus himself. If the son in such a large household sets a slave free, he will be free indeed (v. 36). Imagine, then, if the Son of God sets a slave free. The freedom enjoyed would be indescribable.

Jesus acknowledges the leaders descend from Abraham, but their desire to kill him proves that their lives are not guided by the Father. Jesus implies that their activity points to another spiritual father.

8:39-41a As the argument unfolds, Jesus' opponents see clearly where he is leading. Without Abraham, they cannot belong to God's people. "We are not illegitimate children" (v. 41) is now a defense and an attack. "We" is emphatic and implies comparison: *We* are not illegitimate (but *you* certainly are).

8:41b-42 If Jesus will not permit them Abraham, certainly (they think) he cannot forbid them an appeal to God. But Jesus rejects this as well. Since Jesus himself has come from God the Father, he declares that if their parentage also stemmed from God the Father, they would love the things of Jesus. The problem is not intellectual, but spiritual.

8:43-47 The climax of these implications is finally given in v. 44. His opponents' desire to kill Jesus unmasks the true nature of their spiritual ancestry: Satan. The murder the devil promoted "from the beginning" refers to Cain and Abel or to Satan's work that brought death into the world. This is contrasted with Jesus, the architect of truth and life.

8:48-50 The opponents of Jesus now turn back accusations on him (v. 48). This is a radical dishonoring, as the hostility between Jews and Samaritans was intense. This slur likely had become a curse, much like *heretic* or *unbeliever*, so Jesus does not even take the time to refute it.

8:51-55 Next, Jesus makes a claim about life and death. Jesus can promise life eternal to those who obey him, which sets him apart from every spiritual luminary in Judaism, Abraham included. At this the leaders answer aggressively. But Jesus' defense is that he is *not* glorifying himself; instead, he is faithfully witnessing to his relationship with the Father.

greater than our father Abraham?[o] He
died, and so did the prophets. Who do
you think you are?"
54Jesus replied, "If I glorify myself,[p]
my glory means nothing. My Father,
whom you claim as your God, is the one
who glorifies me.[q] 55Though you do not
know him,[r] I know him.[s] If I said I did
not, I would be a liar like you, but I do
know him and obey his word.[t] 56Your father Abraham[u] rejoiced at the thought of
seeing my day; he saw it[v] and was glad."
57"You are not yet fifty years old," they
said to him, "and you have seen Abraham!"
58"Very truly I tell you," Jesus answered, "before Abraham was born,[w] I
am!"[x] 59At this, they picked up stones
to stone him,[y] but Jesus hid himself,[z]
slipping away from the temple grounds.

Jesus Heals a Man Born Blind

9 As he went along, he saw a man blind
from birth. 2His disciples asked him,
"Rabbi,[a] who sinned,[b] this man[c] or his
parents,[d] that he was born blind?"
3"Neither this man nor his parents
sinned," said Jesus, "but this happened
so that the works of God might be displayed in him.[e] 4As long as it is day,[f] we
must do the works of him who sent me.
Night is coming, when no one can work.
5While I am in the world, I am the light
of the world."[g]
6After saying this, he spit[h] on the
ground, made some mud with the saliva, and put it on the man's eyes. 7"Go,"
he told him, "wash in the Pool of Siloam"[i] (this word means "Sent"). So the
man went and washed, and came home
seeing.[j]
8His neighbors and those who had formerly seen him begging asked, "Isn't this
the same man who used to sit and beg?"[k]
9Some claimed that he was.
Others said, "No, he only looks like
him."
But he himself insisted, "I am the man."
10"How then were your eyes opened?"
they asked.
11He replied, "The man they call Jesus
made some mud and put it on my eyes.
He told me to go to Siloam and wash. So I
went and washed, and then I could see."[l]
12"Where is this man?" they asked him.
"I don't know," he said.

8:53 [o] Jn 4:12
8:54 [p] ver 50 [q] Jn 16:14; 17:1,5
8:55 [r] ver 19 [s] Jn 7:28,29 [t] Jn 15:10
8:56 [u] ver 37, 39 [v] Mt 13:17; Heb 11:13
8:58 [w] Jn 1:2; 17:5,24 [x] Ex 3:14
8:59 [y] Lev 24:16; Jn 10:31; 11:8 [z] Jn 12:36
9:2 [a] Mt 23:7 [b] ver 34; Lk 13:2; Ac 28:4 [c] Eze 18:20 [d] Ex 20:5; Job 21:19
9:3 [e] Jn 11:4
9:4 [f] Jn 11:9; 12:35
9:5 [g] Jn 1:4; 8:12; 12:46
9:6 [h] Mk 7:33; 8:23
9:7 [i] ver 11; 2Ki 5:10; Lk 13:4 [j] Isa 35:5; Jn 11:37
9:8 [k] Ac 3:2,10
9:11 [l] ver 7

8:56–57 No rabbi would object to Jesus' claim that Abraham saw the messianic era. But Jesus does not say this. Instead, he says: "Your father Abraham rejoiced at the thought of seeing *my day*; he saw it and was glad" (emphasis added). But how can Jesus and Abraham know each other since Jesus is not even fifty years old?

8:58 The climax of the entire chapter arrives in this verse. "I am" echoes the Greek translation of God's divine name given in Ex 3:14. To exist before the birth of Abraham—and yet to stand here today—is the boldest claim Jesus has yet made. It recalls John's affirmation in the prologue (1:1–18) that the Word existed even at the beginning of time.

8:59 Jesus' audience interprets his words as a divine claim; they are furious because they believe they have heard blasphemy, for which stoning is the legal punishment. Yet Jesus slips away because God has appointed an hour when his death will be necessary. There is a divine plan, and no mob action will interrupt it.

8:12–59 If Jesus walked into our evangelical churches, if he picked up a religious symbol and challenged the symbol's original meaning, would we cheer or would we fight? Suddenly we might find ourselves defending *Christendom* instead of the Christian faith. The reflex that cannot see God in the prophetic voice of Jesus, that rebels and fights and attacks, is the work of Satan among *religious* people. It is a work that appeared within Judaism and that also appears within the Christian church. It is the work of darkness that is commonplace to the human heart. Above all, it is an evil work that makes a human voice louder than the voice of God.

John 8:12–59 is a severe call to Judaism that it must repent. But it is a call for us too, for those of us who have taken up the mantle worn by the temple leadership of Jerusalem.

9:1–7 Blindness was a common problem in antiquity, far more common than in modern experience. Eye disease had few cures, and unsanitary conditions considerably increased risks. The man whom Jesus meets at the Festival of Tabernacles has been blind from birth, which leads his disciples to ask about the origin of his suffering. They assume a connection between sin and suffering, but Jesus rejects this entire line of questioning. A summary of Jesus' response indicates that here is a man with a disability whose pain will now display the work of God in his life.

Jesus must work *so that* God's work may be displayed in this man's life. God has not made the man blind to show his glory; rather, God sent Jesus to do works of healing to show his glory.

9:8–34 The dramatic healing of this man must have made a significant stir among his immediate friends and family. The community's investigation of this man's experience is given to us in abbreviated form in the following verses.

9:8–13 The neighbors interrogate the man and in disbelief work to verify that he is indeed the man they knew as being blind. They do not reject the miracle but look to the Pharisees for counsel.

The Pharisees Investigate the Healing

13They brought to the Pharisees the
man who had been blind. 14Now the day
on which Jesus had made the mud and
opened the man's eyes was a Sabbath.[m]
15Therefore the Pharisees also asked him
how he had received his sight.[n] "He put
mud on my eyes," the man replied, "and
I washed, and now I see."

16Some of the Pharisees said, "This
man is not from God, for he does not
keep the Sabbath."[o]

But others asked, "How can a sinner perform such signs?" So they were divided.[p]
17Then they turned again to the blind
man, "What have you to say about him?
It was your eyes he opened."

The man replied, "He is a prophet."[q]
18They[r] still did not believe that he had
been blind and had received his sight
until they sent for the man's parents.
19"Is this your son?" they asked. "Is this
the one you say was born blind? How is
it that now he can see?"
20"We know he is our son," the parents
answered, "and we know he was born
blind. 21But how he can see now, or who
opened his eyes, we don't know. Ask him.
He is of age; he will speak for himself."
22His parents said this because they were
afraid of the Jewish leaders,[s] who already
had decided that anyone who acknowledged that Jesus was the Messiah would be
put out[t] of the synagogue.[u] 23That was why
his parents said, "He is of age; ask him."[v]
24A second time they summoned the
man who had been blind. "Give glory to
God by telling the truth,"[w] they said. "We
know this man is a sinner."[x]
25He replied, "Whether he is a sinner or
not, I don't know. One thing I do know.
I was blind but now I see!"
26Then they asked him, "What did he
do to you? How did he open your eyes?"

9:14 [m] Jn 5:9
9:15 [n] ver 10
9:16 [o] Mt 12:2 [p] Jn 6:52; 7:43; 10:19
9:17 [q] Mt 21:11
9:18 [r] Jn 1:19
9:22 [s] Jn 7:13 [t] ver 34; Lk 6:22 [u] Jn 12:42; 16:2
9:23 [v] ver 21
9:24 [w] Jos 7:19 [x] ver 16

9:27 [y] ver 15
9:28 [z] Jn 5:45
9:29 [a] Jn 8:14
9:31 [b] Ge 18:23-32; Ps 34:15,16; 66:18; 145:19, 20; Pr 15:29; Isa 1:15; 59:1, 2; Jn 15:7; Jas 5:16-18; 1Jn 5:14,15
9:33 [c] ver 16; Jn 3:2
9:34 [d] ver 2 [e] ver 22,35; Isa 66:5
9:36 [f] Ro 10:14
9:37 [g] Jn 4:26
9:38 [h] Mt 28:9
9:39 [i] Jn 5:22 [j] Jn 3:19

Jn 9:34 ❖ What might cause self-righteous people to react so strongly against genuine encounters with Christ?

27He answered, "I have told you already[y] and you did not listen. Why do
you want to hear it again? Do you want
to become his disciples too?"
28Then they hurled insults at him and
said, "You are this fellow's disciple! We
are disciples of Moses![z] 29We know that
God spoke to Moses, but as for this fellow, we don't even know where he comes
from."[a]
30The man answered, "Now that is
remarkable! You don't know where he
comes from, yet he opened my eyes.
31We know that God does not listen to
sinners. He listens to the godly person
who does his will.[b] 32Nobody has ever
heard of opening the eyes of a man born
blind. 33If this man were not from God,[c]
he could do nothing."
34To this they replied, "You were
steeped in sin at birth;[d] how dare you
lecture us!" And they threw him out.[e]

Spiritual Blindness

35Jesus heard that they had thrown
him out, and when he found him, he
said, "Do you believe in the Son of Man?"
36"Who is he, sir?" the man asked. "Tell
me so that I may believe in him."[f]
37Jesus said, "You have now seen
him; in fact, he is the one speaking
with you."[g]
38Then the man said, "Lord, I believe,"
and he worshiped him.[h]
39Jesus said,[a] "For judgment[i] I have
come into this world,[j] so that the blind

[a] 38,39 Some early manuscripts do not have *Then the man said . . . 39Jesus said.*

9:14–17 The Pharisees question the man about the healing, but their chief worry is about a violation of the Sabbath.
9:18–23 The Pharisees turn next to the man's parents to confirm a miracle has occurred. The parents deflect their questions and direct them back to their son, and John recounts the reasons for their response.
9:24–34 In exasperation, the man presses the Pharisees boldly, and the tension of the story mounts. Since God does not listen to sinners—and God has listened to Jesus—Jesus cannot be a sinner. Here we have the sharpest division between the man (who supports Jesus) and the leaders (who do not).

As the story progresses, Jesus is more closely revealed by name: he is "Jesus" (v. 10), then he is called a "prophet" (v. 17), then "the Messiah" (v. 22), and finally he is declared to be "from God" (v. 33). Jesus' identity is clarified as the story develops.
9:35–38 Jesus meets with the blind man privately to unveil the true depth of what he experienced. His confession of faith ("Lord, I believe," v. 38) and his worship indicate that he no longer lives in "darkness" in any sense.
9:39–41 The Pharisees, by contrast, have come forward to judge both the man and Jesus. But in the end, Jesus judges them. Jesus' opponents are physically sighted, but in reality they are spiritually blind.

will see[k] and those who see will become
blind."[l]
40 Some Pharisees who were with him
heard him say this and asked, "What? Are
we blind too?"[m]
41 Jesus said, "If you were blind, you
would not be guilty of sin; but now that
you claim you can see, your guilt remains.[n]

The Good Shepherd and His Sheep

10 "Very truly I tell you Pharisees, anyone who does not enter the sheep
pen by the gate, but climbs in by some
other way, is a thief and a robber. 2 The one
who enters by the gate is the shepherd
of the sheep.[o] 3 The gatekeeper opens the
gate for him, and the sheep listen to his
voice.[p] He calls his own sheep by name
and leads them out. 4 When he has brought
out all his own, he goes on ahead of them,
and his sheep follow him because they
know his voice. 5 But they will never follow a stranger; in fact, they will run away
from him because they do not recognize
a stranger's voice." 6 Jesus used this figure
of speech,[q] but the Pharisees did not understand what he was telling them.
7 Therefore Jesus said again, "Very truly
I tell you, I am the gate for the sheep. 8 All
who have come before me[r] are thieves
and robbers, but the sheep have not listened to them. 9 I am the gate; whoever
enters through me will be saved.[a] They
will come in and go out, and find pasture.
10 The thief comes only to steal and kill
and destroy; I have come that they may
have life, and have it to the full.
11 "I am the good shepherd.[s] The good
shepherd lays down his life for the sheep.[t]

9:39 [k] Lk 4:18 [l] Mt 13:13
9:40 [m] Ro 2:19
9:41 [n] Jn 15:22, 24
10:2 [o] ver 11,14
10:3 [p] ver 4,5, 14,16,27
10:6 [q] Jn 16:25
10:8 [r] Jer 23:1,2
10:11 [s] ver 14; Isa 40:11; Eze 34:11-16, 23; Heb 13:20; 1Pe 5:4; Rev 7:17 [t] Jn 15:13; 1Jn 3:16

Jn 10:11 ❖ How is being a sheep led by a good Shepherd a helpful metaphor for the Christian life?

[a] 9 Or *kept safe*

But the most serious condition these opponents possess (v. 41) is their insistence that they are innocent, that they understand fully the theological point Jesus is making, and that they reject it. Because they *claim* that they can see, their guilt is underscored since they are self-affirming in their religious position against Jesus.

9:1–41 This man's life should be depicted as a hopeless tragedy. He sat at the roadside and begged. No employment, no prospects for marriage, no social honor. He was at the bottom of the social ladder. His future was bleak, and he knew it. This hopelessness and darkness provide us with a potent image because John describes men and women without Christ to be in a crisis no less desperate. Jesus refers to those who "walk in darkness," and this is precisely the condition of people who are blind. Jesus lifts this image above the commonplace in order to make it a spiritual metaphor for the condition of the world that he has come to remedy.

The model of this man's conversion, however, is not simply about desperation and healing. He is courageous. He valiantly holds fast to what he cannot deny. His intellectual courage is matched by his personal fearlessness as he suffers persecution for his courage. This drama is also a part of John's conversion model. The man's faith is not in the miracle-working ability of Jesus. This is only the springboard. His faith quickly connects with the true identity of who Jesus is.

John contrasts the healed man's vigorous faith with the others who knowingly, willfully reject Jesus on religious grounds.

10:1–18 In the OT, God is the Shepherd of Israel (Ps 23:1). Moses and David were also shepherds by occupation. Impious kings in Israel were commonly understood to be false or bad shepherds.

John reminds us the occasion for this discourse is the Festival of Dedication (modern Hanukkah; v. 22). This is the only reference to this minor, intertestamental festival in the Bible. In the 160s BC, the Maccabean War pitted conservative Jewish fighters against Greeks and Hellenized Jews. Hanukkah was a season that asked hard questions about failed leadership and false shepherds.

10:1–5 At night, sheep were often herded into walled enclosures. Legitimate shepherds entered these enclosures through the main gate. Sheep recognized the voice of their shepherd (v. 4).

10:6 It is not surprising that Jesus' audience does not grasp the spiritual point he is making. In John the theme is consistently Jesus' identity; stories unveil who he is. But in each case, the problem is not necessarily intellectual. The problem is often an unwillingness to respond to the challenge of the saying.

10:7–10 Jesus' explanation turns the story creatively. In his interpretation, Jesus shifts some of the images. He becomes *the gate*. He stands in the gateway, and anyone who enters without his permission is not trustworthy. This image implies a warning that there are illegitimate shepherds whose entry he prohibits. The most likely target of Jesus' criticism is the Pharisees.

Jesus is the gate for the sheep; only those sheep who know him will enter the sheepfold and find safety. Jesus' image is that of well-fed sheep whose shepherd knows how to lead them to pasture and water daily and how to give them safe rest in the sturdy walls of the sheepfold each night.

10:11–13 At the final level of his interpretation, Jesus claims that he is the "good shepherd" (v. 11). The shepherd's job was severe, tiring, and hazardous. The hired hand is distinguished by his lack of commitment to the sheep. The good shepherd, by

12 The hired hand is not the shepherd and
does not own the sheep. So when he sees
the wolf coming, he abandons the sheep
and runs away.[u] Then the wolf attacks
the flock and scatters it. 13 The man runs
away because he is a hired hand and cares
nothing for the sheep.
14 "I am the good shepherd;[v] I know
my sheep[w] and my sheep know me —
15 just as the Father knows me and I know
the Father[x] — and I lay down my life for
the sheep. 16 I have other sheep[y] that are
not of this sheep pen. I must bring them
also. They too will listen to my voice, and
there shall be one flock[z] and one shepherd.[a] 17 The reason my Father loves me is
that I lay down my life[b] — only to take it
up again. 18 No one takes it from me, but
I lay it down of my own accord.[c] I have
authority to lay it down and authority
to take it up again. This command I received from my Father."[d]
19 The Jews who heard these words
were again divided.[e] 20 Many of them
said, "He is demon-possessed[f] and raving mad.[g] Why listen to him?"

10:12 [u] Zec 11:16, 17
10:14 [v] ver 11 [w] ver 27
10:15 [x] Mt 11:27
10:16 [y] Isa 56:8 [z] Jn 11:52; Eph 2:11-19 [a] Eze 37:24; 1Pe 2:25
10:17 [b] ver 11, 15,18
10:18 [c] Mt 26:53 [d] Jn 15:10; Php 2:8; Heb 5:8
10:19 [e] Jn 7:43; 9:16
10:20 [f] Jn 7:20 [g] Mk 3:21
10:21 [h] Mt 4:24 [i] Ex 4:11; Jn 9:32, 33
10:23 [j] Ac 3:11; 5:12
10:24 [k] Jn 1:19 [l] Jn 16:25, 29
10:25 [m] Jn 8:58 [n] Jn 5:36
10:26 [o] Jn 8:47
10:27 [p] ver 14 [q] ver 4
10:28 [r] Jn 6:39
10:29 [s] Jn 17:2, 6, 24 [t] Jn 14:28

21 But others said, "These are not the
sayings of a man possessed by a demon.[h] Can a demon open the eyes of
the blind?"[i]

Further Conflict Over Jesus' Claims

22 Then came the Festival of Dedication[a] at Jerusalem. It was winter, 23 and
Jesus was in the temple courts walking in
Solomon's Colonnade.[j] 24 The Jews[k] who
were there gathered around him, saying,
"How long will you keep us in suspense?
If you are the Messiah, tell us plainly."[l]
25 Jesus answered, "I did tell you,[m] but
you do not believe. The works I do in my
Father's name testify about me,[n] 26 but
you do not believe because you are not
my sheep.[o] 27 My sheep listen to my voice;
I know them,[p] and they follow me.[q] 28 I
give them eternal life, and they shall
never perish; no one will snatch them
out of my hand.[r] 29 My Father, who has
given them to me,[s] is greater than all[b];[t]

[a] *22* That is, Hanukkah [b] *29* Many early manuscripts *What my Father has given me is greater than all*

---

contrast, "owns the sheep" (see v. 12), which speaks to his unique, passionate commitment to them.

10:14–15 The most important feature of Jesus' role as shepherd is that he lays down his life for the sheep. He cares for them so much that he is willing to come between his flock and danger. He is *willing to die* for them. Jesus is pointing to the depth of his love for the flock of God and his own commitment to die for them in obedience to God's will.

10:16 Jesus further says there are "other sheep" (v. 16) that do not come from this sheepfold. If they come from a different fold, they come from outside of Judaism, which no doubt refers to Gentiles. This is Jesus' vision for the unity of the church: Jewish and Gentile believers living together under Christ's leadership.

10:17–18 Jesus next probes the deeper meaning of the Father's love for him. The fundamental element in this relationship is Jesus' dependence on and obedience to God's will. This is exemplified by his willingness to die on the cross.

The love and unity that Jesus and the Father share is underscored at the beginning of v. 18. Jesus was not a victim of human conspiracies. He was not a martyr whose life was tragically ended. Rather, he obediently participated in the plan of God. The early Christians who interpreted Jesus' death reinforced this view.

The final aspect of Jesus' uniqueness as the Good Shepherd is the authority he holds to die and retake his life in resurrection (vv. 17b–18). The resurrection, therefore, is not an afterthought in which God rescues his Son from an unexpected tragedy.

Jesus' authoritative, powerful activity from Good Friday to Easter Sunday operates in harmony with God, who has authorized and directed it.

10:19–21 John's chief interest here is in the opposite reactions now forming. Some believe that Jesus is "demon-possessed and raving mad" (v. 20). The reaction is antagonistic. Still others in the audience are impressed with Jesus, though they fail to identify Jesus accurately or exhibit belief. Nevertheless, they are open to new possibilities and unwilling to judge Jesus outright.

10:22–42 This is Jesus' final public disclosure of himself to his people. It will be an ultimate disclosure of his complete identity. The account ends with his returning to where it all began—the Jordan River, where John had baptized him.

10:24 The crowd is looking for an unambiguous statement about Jesus' identity. "How long will you keep us in suspense?" can also be translated "How long will you annoy us?" They want an open, clear statement from Jesus about his Messiahship, and no doubt they are poised to judge him if his answer is not to their liking.

10:25–27 Given the explosive, highly politicized views of the Messiah in this period, it is not surprising that Jesus has used restraint so far. Now his audience wants a "plain" statement. Even if Jesus were to speak plainly, only his "sheep" would recognize his voice (v. 26). The root problem is unbelief. The character of Jesus' life and his works or miracles wrought by God's power indicate his true identity. But only those who are Jesus' sheep can understand. The "other sheep" cannot understand his voice; he does not know them, and they do not follow.

10:28–29 Jesus' assignment has been to gather up "all those the Father gives" him (6:37–40). There-

no one can snatch them out of my Father's hand. 30 I and the Father are one."[u]
31 Again his Jewish opponents picked
up stones to stone him,[v] 32 but Jesus said
to them, "I have shown you many good
works from the Father. For which of these
do you stone me?"
33 "We are not stoning you for any good
work," they replied, "but for blasphemy,
because you, a mere man, claim to be
God."[w]
34 Jesus answered them, "Is it not
written in your Law,[x] 'I have said you
are "gods"'[a]?[y] 35 If he called them 'gods,'
to whom the word of God came — and
Scripture cannot be set aside — 36 what
about the one whom the Father set
apart[z] as his very own[a] and sent into
the world?[b] Why then do you accuse me
of blasphemy because I said, 'I am God's
Son'?[c] 37 Do not believe me unless I do
the works of my Father.[d] 38 But if I do
them, even though you do not believe
me, believe the works, that you may
know and understand that the Father
is in me, and I in the Father."[e] 39 Again
they tried to seize him,[f] but he escaped
their grasp.[g]
40 Then Jesus went back across the
Jordan[h] to the place where John had
been baptizing in the early days. There
he stayed, 41 and many people came to
him. They said, "Though John never performed a sign,[i] all that John said about
this man was true."[j] 42 And in that place
many believed in Jesus.[k]

The Death of Lazarus

11 Now a man named Lazarus was sick.
He was from Bethany,[l] the village
of Mary and her sister Martha.[m] 2 (This
Mary, whose brother Lazarus now lay
sick, was the same one who poured perfume on the Lord and wiped his feet

10:30 [u] Jn 17:21-23
10:31 [v] Jn 8:59
10:33 [w] Lev 24:16; Jn 5:18
10:34 [x] Jn 8:17; Ro 3:19 [y] Ps 82:6
10:36 [z] Jer 1:5 [a] Jn 6:69 [b] Jn 3:17 [c] Jn 5:17,18
10:37 [d] ver 25; Jn 15:24
10:38 [e] Jn 14:10, 11,20; 17:21
10:39 [f] Jn 7:30 [g] Lk 4:30; Jn 8:59
10:40 [h] Jn 1:28
10:41 [i] Jn 2:11; 3:30 [j] Jn 1:26,27, 30,34
10:42 [k] Jn 7:31
11:1 [l] Mt 21:17 [m] Lk 10:38
11:2 [n] Mk 14:3; Lk 7:38; Jn 12:3

[a] 34 Psalm 82:6

---

fore, his skill as the Good Shepherd secures them against all predators and thieves (v. 29).

10:30 The astounding affirmation given in v. 30 serves as a high point in the chapter. The sheep belong to the Father and the Son, and enjoy fellowship with both simultaneously. The sheep's protection results from the Father and Son's joint work.

10:31–33 This formulation of oneness is stronger than what we see elsewhere, and the response of the crowd (vv. 31, 33) suggests that they hear something different too. To the crowd, this is not a man who is saying he has joined his efforts with God; this is a man who is saying something blasphemous. His opponents believe he is claiming to be God.

10:34–39 Jesus' defense is carefully nuanced and takes advantage of Hanukkah's symbolism. He defends himself by citing Ps 82:6. If the word "god" can be applied to those other than God himself in the Scriptures, why are Jesus' words blasphemy?

Moreover, Jesus is the one whom God "sanctified" and sent into the world. The Greek verb for "set apart" means to consecrate or make something holy; this points to the meaning of Hanukkah itself. Judas Maccabeus had reclaimed the temple after he conquered his Greek oppressors. In 1 Maccabees 4:48 we read, "They also rebuilt the sanctuary and the interior of the temple, and consecrated ["sanctified"] the courts." Jesus, then, is the object of Hanukkah's interest. He is the "sanctified place," the "holy place," the "temple" of God celebrated in this season.

10:40–41 Jesus' departure from Judea is as much a theological statement as it is geographical. He is moving away from the area of conflict in Jerusalem and returning to where John the Baptist had worked. Jesus has come full circle.

For the last time, John the Baptist's role is affirmed. Echoing the words of 3:22–30, his ministry is placed in perspective. He was a trustworthy and reliable witness to the truth about Jesus.

10:42 Ironically, the evangelist adds, "And in that place many believed in Jesus" (v. 42). Jesus finds faith not among the ranks of the religious in the holy city of Jerusalem. Rather, he finds it when he moves to the desert. "Many people" made the effort to travel, "came to him" in the desert by the Jordan and believed in him, recognizing that this was God's hand behind Jesus' works and God's voice within his words.

10:1–42 The desert in Israel is tremendously important in order to understand the Bible. During the bulk of the year, the desert is inhospitable to life. It takes little convincing to show that the environment of the world is as treacherous as a Judean desert: It is hostile at every turn. We do live in a modern desert. Amid this moral chaos, in this threatening desert, whose voice—which shepherd—do we follow?

Every communicator of biblical truth needs to sound the alarm and point the audience to their need of a true shepherd who can genuinely lead them from the desert. John has given us a direct and simple solution. Jesus is the true Shepherd, and he is the only one who can endorse others who will lead the sheep. The final test of a shepherd's credentials is his or her fidelity to the leadership of Jesus.

11:1–5 When he was in Jerusalem, Jesus used Bethany as his base. Here in this small Judean community lived a family extremely dear to Jesus. Mary, Martha, and Lazarus may have become something like an extended family for Jesus.

When Jesus hears the report about Lazarus's illness, his response parallels his comments about the man born blind (9:1–5). The tragedy of this

with her hair.)[n] 3So the sisters sent word
to Jesus, "Lord, the one you love[o] is sick."
4When he heard this, Jesus said, "This
sickness will not end in death. No, it is
for God's glory[p] so that God's Son may be
glorified through it." 5Now Jesus loved
Martha and her sister and Lazarus. 6So
when he heard that Lazarus was sick, he
stayed where he was two more days, 7and
then he said to his disciples, "Let us go
back to Judea."[q]
8"But Rabbi,"[r] they said, "a short while
ago the Jews there tried to stone you,[s]
and yet you are going back?"
9Jesus answered, "Are there not twelve
hours of daylight? Anyone who walks in
the daytime will not stumble, for they
see by this world's light.[t] 10It is when a
person walks at night that they stumble,
for they have no light."
11After he had said this, he went on
to tell them, "Our friend[u] Lazarus has
fallen asleep;[v] but I am going there to
wake him up."
12His disciples replied, "Lord, if he
sleeps, he will get better." 13Jesus had
been speaking of his death, but his disciples thought he meant natural sleep.[w]
14So then he told them plainly, "Lazarus is dead, 15and for your sake I am glad
I was not there, so that you may believe.
But let us go to him."

11:3 [o]ver 5,36
11:4 [p]ver 40; Jn 9:3
11:7 [q]Jn 10:40
11:8 [r]Mt 23:7 [s]Jn 8:59; 10:31
11:9 [t]Jn 9:4; 12:35
11:11 [u]ver 3 [v]Ac 7:60
11:13 [w]Mt 9:24
11:16 [x]Mt 10:3; Jn 14:5; 20:24-28; 21:2; Ac 1:13
11:17 [y]ver 6,39
11:18 [z]ver 1
11:19 [a]ver 31; Job 2:11
11:20 [b]Lk 10:38-42
11:21 [c]ver 32,37
11:22 [d]ver 41, 42; Jn 9:31
11:24 [e]Da 12:2; Jn 5:28,29; Ac 24:15
11:25 [f]Jn 1:4

Jn 11:25–26 ❖ How can belief in Christ shape the way we live every day?

16Then Thomas[x] (also known as Didymus[a]) said to the rest of the disciples, "Let
us also go, that we may die with him."

Jesus Comforts the Sisters of Lazarus

17On his arrival, Jesus found that Lazarus had already been in the tomb for
four days.[y] 18Now Bethany[z] was less than
two miles[b] from Jerusalem, 19and many
Jews had come to Martha and Mary to
comfort them in the loss of their brother.[a] 20When Martha heard that Jesus was
coming, she went out to meet him, but
Mary stayed at home.[b]
21"Lord," Martha said to Jesus, "if you
had been here, my brother would not
have died.[c] 22But I know that even now
God will give you whatever you ask."[d]
23Jesus said to her, "Your brother will
rise again."
24Martha answered, "I know he will rise
again in the resurrection[e] at the last day."
25Jesus said to her, "I am the resurrection and the life.[f] The one who believes
in me will live, even though they die;

[a] 16 *Thomas* (Aramaic) and *Didymus* (Greek) both mean *twin*. [b] 18 Or about 3 kilometers

---

man's illness is not by God's design, but God will use it for an opportunity to glorify his Son.

11:6–7 Jesus does not respond immediately and come to Bethany. He waits two days. Jesus' delay is not the cause of Lazarus's death. When Jesus arrives in Bethany, Lazarus has been dead for four days, so Lazarus likely died right after the departure of the messengers. When the sisters meet Jesus, Lazarus is already buried. Jesus' delay serves not to promote the death but to heighten the significance of his own miraculous work. His aim is to reveal the glory of God's work in him and thereby to promote the faith of his followers.

11:8–16 The decision finally to go up to Judea must have been frightening to Jesus' disciples. During the previous autumn celebration at the Festival of Tabernacles, the authorities tried to arrest him, and the rumor was that they wanted to kill him. The threat is not simply to Jesus but to his disciples as well (v. 16). Being a disciple will pose dangers, even martyrdom, for anyone who follows Jesus.

11:17 There was a well-known Jewish belief that the soul of a dead person remained in the vicinity of the body for three days. Once decomposition set in, the soul departed. John wants us to know clearly that Lazarus is truly dead. The miracle of Jesus cannot be interpreted as a resuscitation.

11:18–19 Lazarus's death was not a private period of mourning for his family. Formal mourning lasted for seven days, and it commenced immediately on the day of burial, which took place on the same day as death. The extent and passion of mourning that occurs reflects how honored and esteemed Lazarus was in the village. Friends and family from far off came to join the scene. In this public atmosphere, Jesus' presence in Bethany would certainly become known to his enemies in Jerusalem.

11:20–37 The story follows the two sisters as each makes contact with Jesus. First Martha, then Mary, talks with Jesus; this is followed by the miracle itself. The sorrowful complaints of both women (vv. 21, 32) are virtually the same.

11:22 Despite what Martha says in v. 22, she likely does not expect Jesus to raise Lazarus from death, since in v. 39 she objects when Jesus wants to roll open the tomb. Instead, she is expressing faith. Martha's words can be paraphrased: "If you had been here, you could have healed Lazarus. Nevertheless, I still believe in you, that God works through you mightily."

11:23–27 But Jesus pushes Martha to a second, deeper level of discussion. His correction leads to one of the most famous and significant "I am" sayings in John's Gospel. Jesus says that *he is* resurrection and life (v. 25). Eternal life and rescue from death are not merely gifts obtained by appeal to God; they are aspects of a life associated with Jesus. If Jesus is life, then those who believe in him will enjoy the confidence and power over death that he does.

PEOPLE TO KNOW // MARTHA

JOHN 11:17–27: The Gospels share two stories about Martha, the sister of Mary and Lazarus. The three were dear friends of Jesus (Jn 11:5).

The first story comes from Luke 10:38–42. Jesus was at the house of Mary and Martha, which Martha had generously opened to him. While Martha was occupied with hosting duties, Mary simply sat at Jesus' feet and listened to him teach. Annoyed, Martha confronted Jesus, asking why he didn't care that Mary had left Martha to do all the work herself. Jesus tenderly corrected Martha, telling her that Mary had chosen the most important thing: to learn from him.

The second story has a tragic backdrop. Martha's brother, Lazarus, became sick and died. Jesus knew he was sick, but purposefully waited to come and visit until it was too late. When Jesus finally arrived, Martha spoke to him in her grief: "If you had been here, my brother would not have died. But I know that even now God will give you whatever you ask" (Jn 11:21–22). Jesus assured her that her brother would rise again. She replied that she believed he would rise at the final resurrection. Jesus told her that he himself was "the resurrection and the life" (Jn 11:25). Martha responded with a bold profession of faith: "I believe that you are the Messiah, the Son of God, who is come into the world" (Jn 11:27). Moments later, Jesus raised Lazarus from death.

APPLICATION ✣ Each of us can become so preoccupied with the necessities of the moment that we forget that our main priority is always our relationship with God. Like Martha, we need Jesus' gentle reminder about the most important thing: Christ himself. Fortunately, we are not defined by our mistakes. Martha showed the depth of her faith in Christ even in the dark moments of her brother's death. Her strong faith is an ongoing witness for believers. Indeed, she makes one of the clearest professions of faith recorded in the Gospels: "You are the Messiah, the Son of God." May her profession of faith also be ours.

26and whoever lives by believing in me
will never die. Do you believe this?"
27"Yes, Lord," she replied, "I believe
that you are the Messiah,[g] the Son of
God,[h] who is to come into the world."[i]
28After she had said this, she went back
and called her sister Mary aside. "The
Teacher[j] is here," she said, "and is asking
for you." 29When Mary heard this, she got
up quickly and went to him. 30Now Jesus
had not yet entered the village, but was
still at the place where Martha had met
him.[k] 31When the Jews who had been
with Mary in the house, comforting her,[l]
noticed how quickly she got up and went
out, they followed her, supposing she
was going to the tomb to mourn there.
32When Mary reached the place where
Jesus was and saw him, she fell at his feet
and said, "Lord, if you had been here, my
brother would not have died."[m]
33When Jesus saw her weeping, and
the Jews who had come along with her
also weeping, he was deeply moved[n] in
spirit and troubled.[o] 34"Where have you
laid him?" he asked.
"Come and see, Lord," they replied.
35Jesus wept.[p]
36Then the Jews said, "See how he
loved him!"[q]

11:27 [g] Lk 2:11 [h] Mt 16:16 [i] Jn 6:14
11:28 [j] Mt 26:18; Jn 13:13
11:30 [k] ver 20
11:31 [l] ver 19
11:32 [m] ver 21
11:33 [n] ver 38 [o] Jn 12:27
11:35 [p] Lk 19:41
11:36 [q] ver 3

11:26 Jesus' question to Martha, "Do you believe this?" is asking if her faith can embrace a belief in Jesus' lordship over death itself. Lazarus's resurrection becomes a proof of Jesus' statement.

11:27 Martha says yes; undoubtedly the implications of this yes are beyond her comprehension. If he has this sort of authority, he must also be "the Messiah, the Son of God."

11:28–33a Mary (like her sister) explains in dismay their sorrow over Jesus' absence while Lazarus was alive, and then is overcome with grief. The term "weeping" in the Greek describes loud wailing and crying, echoed by the people standing around Mary (v. 33a).

11:33b–37 When Jesus sees and hears their wailing, he is powerfully moved. The Greek verb describes outrage, fury, or anger. This is seen in John's explanation: Jesus was "troubled." Jesus is angry at death itself and at the devastation it brings.

Jesus' tears should be connected to the anger he is feeling so deeply. The public chaos surrounding him, the loud wailing and crying, and the scene of a cemetery and its devastating reminders—all the result of sin and death—together produce outrage in the Son of God as he works to reverse such damage.

37But some of them said, "Could not he who opened the eyes of the blind man[r] have kept this man from dying?"[s]

Jesus Raises Lazarus From the Dead

38Jesus, once more deeply moved,[t] came to the tomb. It was a cave with a stone laid across the entrance.[u] 39"Take away the stone," he said.

"But, Lord," said Martha, the sister of the dead man, "by this time there is a bad odor, for he has been there four days."[v]

40Then Jesus said, "Did I not tell you that if you believe,[w] you will see the glory of God?"[x]

41So they took away the stone. Then Jesus looked up[y] and said, "Father,[z] I thank you that you have heard me. 42I knew that you always hear me, but I said this for the benefit of the people standing here,[a] that they may believe that you sent me."[b]

43When he had said this, Jesus called in a loud voice, "Lazarus, come out!"[c] 44The dead man came out, his hands and feet wrapped with strips of linen,[d] and a cloth around his face.[e]

Jesus said to them, "Take off the grave clothes and let him go."

The Plot to Kill Jesus

45Therefore many of the Jews who had come to visit Mary,[f] and had seen what Jesus did,[g] believed in him.[h] 46But some of them went to the Pharisees and told them what Jesus had done. 47Then the chief priests and the Pharisees[i] called a meeting[j] of the Sanhedrin.[k]

"What are we accomplishing?" they asked. "Here is this man performing many signs.[l] 48If we let him go on like this, everyone will believe in him, and then the Romans will come and take away both our temple and our nation."

49Then one of them, named Caiaphas,[m] who was high priest that year,[n] spoke up, "You know nothing at all! 50You do not realize that it is better for you that one man die for the people than that the whole nation perish."[o]

51He did not say this on his own, but as high priest that year he prophesied that Jesus would die for the Jewish nation, 52and not only for that nation but also for the scattered children of God, to bring them together and make them one.[p] 53So from that day on they plotted to take his life.[q]

54Therefore Jesus no longer moved

11:37 [r] Jn 9:6,7 [s] ver 21,32
11:38 [t] ver 33 [u] Mt 27:60; Lk 24:2; Jn 20:1
11:39 [v] ver 17
11:40 [w] ver 23-25 [x] ver 4
11:41 [y] Jn 17:1 [z] Mt 11:25
11:42 [a] Jn 12:30 [b] Jn 3:17
11:43 [c] Lk 7:14
11:44 [d] Jn 19:40 [e] Jn 20:7
11:45 [f] ver 19 [g] Jn 2:23 [h] Ex 14:31; Jn 7:31
11:47 [i] ver 57 [j] Mt 26:3 [k] Mt 5:22 [l] Jn 2:11
11:49 [m] Mt 26:3 [n] ver 51; Jn 18:13,14
11:50 [o] Jn 18:14
11:52 [p] Isa 49:6; Jn 10:16
11:53 [q] Mt 12:14

11:38–39 As Jesus steps to the tomb itself, he is "once more deeply moved" (v. 38). The verb used here is the same one as in v. 33. The Lord of life is now directly confronting his opponent, death, symbolized in the cave-tomb before him.

Martha's response in v. 39 is critical for John's report of the scene. It reminds us that Lazarus is truly dead. Jesus does not simply resuscitate his friend. Lazarus must be "awakened" *from death.*

11:41–42 Jesus' prayer is interesting on several counts. First, it implies that Jesus had prayed *already* for Lazarus and that he is now coming to this great miracle fully prepared for what will take place. Second, Jesus prays publicly and does so "looking up" (v. 41). This was a common posture for Jewish prayer. Jesus is aware that his prayer is also for the benefit of these bystanders. Finally, Jesus addresses God as "Father" (not "our" father) and shows his personal intimacy with him.

11:43–44 The story drama peaks when Jesus calls for Lazarus to come out. This is not a whisper or a firm request; it is a shout of raw authority. When Lazarus emerges from the tomb, he is bound in grave wrappings—strips of fabric wrapped around his limbs and filled with burial spices. Jewish burial practices likewise tied the jaw closed and covered the face with a linen cloth.

Lazarus's coming from the grave is an amazing spectacle witnessed by a growing crowd of people, many of whom carry news of this miracle back to Jerusalem. Lazarus stands before Jesus wrapped tightly. Jesus loves Lazarus, and it is not hard to imagine him being the first to embrace his friend. Jesus remains in command and orders that someone unbind him.

11:45–46 Many of the Jews in Bethany who witnessed the events of that day "believed in him" (v. 45). John's sharp contrast with the "others," who go directly to the Pharisees, suggests they do not believe (v. 46).

11:47–48 The Sanhedrin's deliberations are noteworthy. They exhibit a paralyzing concern that if a messiah is embraced by the city, the Roman armies will suppress it. The Romans had shown their intolerance in the past (viewing it as a political challenge), and Jerusalem's leadership knows the seriousness of the threat now.

11:49–50 John summarizes the view of Caiaphas, the ruling high priest. For Caiaphas, political expediency is the key: If there must be a sacrifice, better to lose one man than the entire nation. The high council begins planning how they can kill Jesus.

These voices say more than even they expected. John knows this and tips us off to look beneath the surface: Jesus will indeed die for the salvation of the nation. An unwitting prophecy here points to the cross.

11:51–53 John knows that the death of Christ will perform a work that is far more profound than anyone imagines. It is not simply for the city of Jerusalem but for the "scattered children of God" (v. 52). John is no doubt referring to Gentiles, who likewise need to come into the family of God.

11:54–57 Jesus cannot risk being a public figure in

about publicly among the people of Judea.[r] Instead he withdrew to a region near
the wilderness, to a village called Ephraim, where he stayed with his disciples.
55When it was almost time for the Jewish Passover,[s] many went up from the
country to Jerusalem for their ceremonial cleansing[t] before the Passover. 56They
kept looking for Jesus,[u] and as they stood
in the temple courts they asked one another, "What do you think? Isn't he coming to the festival at all?" 57But the chief
priests and the Pharisees had given orders that anyone who found out where
Jesus was should report it so that they
might arrest him.

Jesus Anointed at Bethany

12:1–8Ref // Mt 26:6–13; Mk 14:3–9; Lk 7:37–39

12 Six days before the Passover,[v] Jesus
came to Bethany,[w] where Lazarus
lived, whom Jesus had raised from the
dead. 2Here a dinner was given in Jesus'
honor. Martha served,[x] while Lazarus was
among those reclining at the table with
him. 3Then Mary took about a pint[a] of
pure nard, an expensive perfume;[y] she
poured it on Jesus' feet and wiped his
feet with her hair.[z] And the house was
filled with the fragrance of the perfume.
4But one of his disciples, Judas Iscariot, who was later to betray him,[a] objected, 5"Why wasn't this perfume sold
and the money given to the poor? It was
worth a year's wages.[b]" 6He did not say
this because he cared about the poor but
because he was a thief; as keeper of the
money bag,[b] he used to help himself to
what was put into it.
7"Leave her alone," Jesus replied. "It
was intended that she should save this

11:54 [r] Jn 7:1
11:55 [s] Ex 12:13, 23, 27; Mt 26:1, 2; Mk 14:1; Jn 13:1 [t] 2Ch 30:17, 18
11:56 [u] Jn 7:11
12:1 [v] Jn 11:55 [w] Mt 21:17
12:2 [x] Lk 10:38-42
12:3 [y] Mk 14:3 [z] Jn 11:2
12:4 [a] Mt 10:4
12:6 [b] Jn 13:29

[a] 3 Or about 0.5 liter [b] 5 Greek *three hundred denarii*

the same manner any longer. He knows the hour of his glorification and will not permit anyone or anything to interrupt his mission. With characteristic geographical precision, John says that Jesus moves to the village of Ephraim (v. 54). Here Jesus is safe from the Sanhedrin, but he is also close enough to attend the upcoming Passover in Jerusalem.

From Jesus' point of view, his public ministry among his own people is completed. No longer will he provide any miraculous signs for them. He will now spend concentrated private time with those families (e.g., Martha, Mary, Lazarus), friends, and followers who know, trust, and believe in him. Jesus will indeed return to the public square once more during the Passover feast following his Triumphal Entry, but only to give an impassioned plea for belief (12:44). After this, the next time he appears in public, he will be a prisoner.

11:1–57 Every age struggles with the finality of the grave and the incomprehensibility of death. In some respects, we also live in an age that does its best to deny death. Today this process has been sanitized, taken over by professional hospitals, hospices, and morticians. All of this is cultural, springing from the heartfelt wish to make death less visceral, but it masks a profound anxiety that even the most well-conceived funeral service cannot disguise. Perhaps this is why, in the work of the church, funeral services become such potent opportunities for ministry.

There were many standing among the mourners of Bethany that day who had been friends with Lazarus. They knew he was dead; they had participated in his burial. But when he stepped from the grave, they refused to believe in Jesus. This is proof that signs alone cannot provoke faith.

This understanding of the limited success of the miracle is at the root of John's link between sign and explanation (or miracle and discourse). A sheer experience of the power of God is insufficient to persuade the human heart. Therefore, in the activity of believers in the church, words must accompany deeds. The raising of Lazarus thus provides us with theological revelation. It points us elsewhere, reminding us that Jesus' own work is greater even than this. Jesus is not demonstrating that death has a limited grip over humanity: for the moment, it does not. But *his own death and resurrection* affect the reality of death permanently for those who believe in him.

12:1–2 This is an important meal attended by many who want to honor Jesus publicly and memorialize this great event of Lazarus's life.

12:3 It goes without saying that Mary's dramatic gesture is astonishing. Nard was a rare and precious oil imported from northern India. Note that Mary's gift is called "pure" nard (v. 3), meaning it had no additives. Its value of three hundred denarii represents one year's wage for a day laborer.

Mary anoints Jesus generously, not simply on his feet, but also on his head; the oil no doubt runs down and perfumes his garments. The quantity is so great that the entire house is filled with its fragrance. John emphasizes Jesus' feet to show the sheer act of humble devotion on Mary's part and to provide a companion story for the foot washing of the next chapter. That she uses her hair to dry his feet indicates that Mary is acting with extravagant abandon, hoping that the close circle of friends will understand.

12:4–6 Judas's objection comes as no surprise. The legitimacy of Judas's complaint is tarnished by his own reputation.

12:7–8 Jesus' defense of Mary (vv. 7–8) is difficult to translate. The idea is no doubt that she had kept

perfume for the day of my burial.[c] 8 You will always have the poor among you,[a,d] but you will not always have me."

9 Meanwhile a large crowd of Jews found out that Jesus was there and came, not only because of him but also to see Lazarus, whom he had raised from the dead.[e] 10 So the chief priests made plans to kill Lazarus as well, 11 for on account of him[f] many of the Jews were going over to Jesus and believing in him.[g]

Jesus Comes to Jerusalem as King

12:12–15pp // Mt 21:4–9; Mk 11:7–10; Lk 19:35–38

12 The next day the great crowd that had come for the festival heard that Jesus was on his way to Jerusalem. 13 They took palm branches and went out to meet him, shouting,

"Hosanna![b]"

"Blessed is he who comes in the
name of the Lord!"[c,h]

"Blessed is the king of Israel!"[i]

14 Jesus found a young donkey and sat on it, as it is written:

15 "Do not be afraid, Daughter Zion;
see, your king is coming,
seated on a donkey's colt."[d,j]

16 At first his disciples did not understand all this.[k] Only after Jesus was glorified[l] did they realize that these things had been written about him and that these things had been done to him.

17 Now the crowd that was with him[m] when he called Lazarus from the tomb and raised him from the dead continued to spread the word. 18 Many people, because they had heard that he had performed this sign,[n] went out to meet him. 19 So the Pharisees said to one another, "See, this is getting us nowhere. Look how the whole world has gone after him!"[o]

Jesus Predicts His Death

20 Now there were some Greeks[p] among those who went up to worship at the festival. 21 They came to Philip, who was from Bethsaida[q] in Galilee, with a request. "Sir," they said, "we would like to see Jesus." 22 Philip went to tell Andrew; Andrew and Philip in turn told Jesus.

23 Jesus replied, "The hour has come for the Son of Man to be glorified.[r] 24 Very truly I tell you, unless a kernel of wheat falls to the ground and dies,[s] it remains

12:7 [c] Jn 19:40
12:8 [d] Dt 15:11
12:9 [e] Jn 11:43, 44
12:11 [f] ver 17, 18; Jn 11:45 [g] Jn 7:31
12:13 [h] Ps 118:25, 26 [i] Jn 1:49
12:15 [j] Zec 9:9
12:16 [k] Mk 9:32 [l] Jn 2:22; 7:39; 14:26
12:17 [m] Jn 11:42
12:18 [n] ver 11
12:19 [o] Jn 11:47, 48
12:20 [p] Jn 7:35; Ac 11:20
12:21 [q] Mt 11:21; Jn 1:44
12:23 [r] Jn 13:32; 17:1
12:24 [s] 1Co 15:36

[a] *8* See Deut. 15:11. [b] *13* A Hebrew expression meaning "Save!" which became an exclamation of praise [c] *13* Psalm 118:25,26 [d] *15* Zech. 9:9

---

this perfume for some later use, but now (unknowingly) has expended it for Jesus' embalming. Jesus has now been (figuratively) prepared for burial as he heads toward the day of his death and glorification.

Jesus' final words in v. 8 place personal adoration and social responsibility in tension. This is not to deny our responsibility to the poor, but to alert us to the wonder of who Mary and Martha are hosting that day.

12:9–15 It is important to keep in mind the significance of these crowds. Many scholars believe that the regular population of Jerusalem in this period was about fifty thousand. During Passover, it grew to perhaps between one hundred and one hundred twenty thousand. The crowds brought tension to the leadership of the city, who knew that any social disruption could explode violently.

The branches from date palms were abundant in Israel and had become a symbol of Jewish nationalism. This act of celebration is by no means neutral. It symbolizes Israel's national hopes—now focused on Jesus, being hailed as he enters the city.

The cry of "Hosanna!" (v. 13a) is an Aramaic phrase meaning "save us now!" The people then quote from Ps 118:26. What comes next ("blessed is the king of Israel!") is not in the psalm. The crowds are greeting a national liberator.

This scene is awash in Jewish political fervor. After Jesus fed the five thousand, the crowd attempted to take him "by force" and "make him king" (6:15). Jesus was misunderstood then; now he is misunderstood again.

Jesus' use of a young donkey is an attempt to calm the enthusiasm of the crowd. The triumphant king is not a man of war horses (Zec 9:10) but is one who will bring peace to all nations. He brings a gift of life, not conquest through war.

12:16 Not only do the crowds fail to understand the true nature of Jesus' kingship, but the disciples likewise misunderstand "all this" (v. 16).

12:17–19 We are reminded that the Pharisees have begun to despair at Jesus' popularity. When the Pharisees say "the whole world" (v. 19) has gone after him, the deeper irony is that these words point to the fulfillment of Jesus' primary mission.

12:20–22 The word "Greeks" (v. 20) was a label for anyone who was not Jewish. They are likely "God-fearers," Gentiles who admire the Jewish faith and respect its traditions. Such Gentiles were invited to the festivals but were permitted to go no further than the Court of the Gentiles within the temple precincts.

They approach Philip, probably because he has a Hellenistic name and comes from a Greek region (Bethsaida, 1:44). These God-fearers represent the "scattered children of God" of 11:52. They are the "other sheep" of 10:16. They want to "see" Jesus (12:21). These are foreigners who now stand ready to join the flock of Christ.

12:23 Curiously, the arrival of these God-fearers triggers "the hour" we have been hearing about

PEOPLE TO KNOW // PHILIP

JOHN 12:21–22: Philip was one of Jesus' twelve disciples. He was from the town of Bethsaida, as were Andrew and Peter. Throughout the Gospels we see Philip leading others to Jesus. After being called by Jesus, Philip found his friend Nathanael to tell him about Jesus. When Nathanael dismissively questioned Jesus' hometown of Nazareth, Philip answered him gently: "Come and see" (Jn 1:46).

In John 6 we read Philip's surprised, doubt-filled exclamation when Jesus tested him, asking him to feed a large crowd of people: "It would take more than half a year's wages to buy enough bread for each one to have a bite!" (Jn 6:7). Along with the other disciples, he learned that day Jesus' true definition of abundance and provision.

Later in the book of John, Philip leads the way to the Savior when some Greeks who had come to celebrate Passover ask for access to Jesus (Jn 12:21–22). After Jesus' death and resurrection, Philip had a role to play in the early church as an eyewitness to Jesus' saving actions. Notably, faithful Philip shared the Good News to a curious Ethiopian eunuch who was reading the book of Isaiah. He explained to this man how Isaiah's prophecy was fulfilled in Jesus. The official gratefully received the news of Jesus' salvation and was baptized on the spot.

APPLICATION ✤ People who are initially eager to follow Jesus go through a process of spiritual growth as the Holy Spirit reveals himself and the truth about God and Jesus the Messiah. We may share with others our excitement of our faith, but there will be times of stumbling and doubt. That is completely normal. It is encouraging for us to read about Philip and see him grow in his faith through his interactions with Jesus. Like Philip, we can be people who invite others to encounter Jesus. When we do, God will use us in his mission to further his kingdom on earth.

only a single seed. But if it dies, it produces many seeds. 25 Anyone who loves
their life will lose it, while anyone who
hates their life in this world will keep
it[t] for eternal life. 26 Whoever serves me
must follow me; and where I am, my servant also will be.[u] My Father will honor
the one who serves me.
27 "Now my soul is troubled,[v] and what
shall I say? 'Father,[w] save me from this
hour'?[x] No, it was for this very reason I
came to this hour. 28 Father, glorify your
name!"
Then a voice came from heaven,[y]
"I have glorified it, and will glorify it
again." 29 The crowd that was there and
heard it said it had thundered; others
said an angel had spoken to him.
30 Jesus said, "This voice was for your
benefit,[z] not mine. 31 Now is the time for
judgment on this world;[a] now the prince

12:25 [t] Mt 10:39; Mk 8:35; Lk 14:26
12:26 [u] Jn 14:3; 17:24; 2Co 5:8; 1Th 4:17
12:27 [v] Mt 26:38,39; Jn 11:33,38; 13:21 [w] Mt 11:25 [x] ver 23
12:28 [y] Mt 3:17
12:30 [z] Jn 11:42
12:31 [a] Jn 16:11

throughout the Gospel. Something has changed; the Greeks signal the closing of a chapter for Jesus. His ministry in Judaism is finished, and he now belongs to the wider world.

12:24–25 Jesus then offers an extended discourse that gives insight into the meaning of this hour. Just as a seed must "die" to give life (v. 24), so Jesus must die in order to give life to the world. This same law applies to disciples.

12:26 Jesus' sacrifice brings about life for others, but his disciples must practice this discipline so that they can gain life for themselves. Following Jesus involves self-sacrifice (v. 26a)—an echo of similar Synoptic sayings about bearing one's cross. John's version adds a promise: "Where I am, my servant also will be." This promise points to a unity of purpose between Jesus and his servants; it also guarantees that such servants will be with Jesus in heaven.

12:27–28a Jesus' turmoil (v. 27) recalls his agitation and anger when he stood before Lazarus's tomb. This turmoil should not be minimized. It can be read as a statement in the following manner: "What should I say? [pause] Father, save me from this hour—but no! It was for this very reason that I came to this hour."

Here we are listening to Jesus' genuine anguish and the strength of his obedience to his Father's will. In this sense, the prayer is similar to Jesus' words in Gethsemane, which are followed with a word of obedience. Jesus' conclusion reveals his commitment: "Father, glorify your name!" (v. 28a).

12:28b–29 God audibly affirms that he has *already* glorified himself in his Son, referring to the incarnation and work of Jesus. But he says he will glorify His name again; this will be the final act of glory, the cross. Some think the voice is only thunder. Others assign it to an angel.

12:30 This voice, Jesus says, is for those listening, not for him. God is continuing to supply the world with evidence of himself.

12:31–33 The "now" of this verse must be underscored and taken seriously. The cross of Christ

of this world[b] will be driven out. 32And
I, when I am lifted up[a] from the earth,[c]
will draw all people to myself."[d] 33He said
this to show the kind of death he was
going to die.[e]
34The crowd spoke up, "We have heard
from the Law that the Messiah will remain forever,[f] so how can you say, 'The
Son of Man[g] must be lifted up'?[h] Who is
this 'Son of Man'?"
35Then Jesus told them, "You are going to have the light[i] just a little while
longer. Walk while you have the light,[j]
before darkness overtakes you.[k] Whoever walks in the dark does not know
where they are going. 36Believe in the
light while you have the light, so that you
may become children of light."[l] When he
had finished speaking, Jesus left and hid
himself from them.[m]

Belief and Unbelief Among the Jews

37Even after Jesus had performed so
many signs[n] in their presence, they still
would not believe in him. 38This was to
fulfill the word of Isaiah the prophet:

> "Lord, who has believed our message
> and to whom has the arm of the
> Lord been revealed?"[b][o]

39For this reason they could not believe, because, as Isaiah says elsewhere:

> 40"He has blinded their eyes
> and hardened their hearts,
> so they can neither see with their
> eyes,
> nor understand with their
> hearts,
> nor turn — and I would heal
> them."[c][p]

41Isaiah said this because he saw Jesus'
glory[q] and spoke about him.[r]
42Yet at the same time many even
among the leaders believed in him.[s] But
because of the Pharisees[t] they would not
openly acknowledge their faith for fear
they would be put out of the synagogue;[u]
43for they loved human praise more than
praise from God.[v]
44Then Jesus cried out, "Whoever believes in me does not believe in me only,
but in the one who sent me.[w] 45The one
who looks at me is seeing the one who
sent me.[x] 46I have come into the world
as a light,[y] so that no one who believes
in me should stay in darkness.
47"If anyone hears my words but does
not keep them, I do not judge that person. For I did not come to judge the
world, but to save the world.[z] 48There
is a judge for the one who rejects me
and does not accept my words; the very
words I have spoken will condemn

Jn 12:46 ❖ What does it look like to "stay in darkness"? How does the light of Christ pull us away from such darkness?

12:31 [b] Jn 14:30; 16:11; 2Co 4:4; Eph 2:2; 1Jn 4:4
12:32 [c] ver 34; Jn 3:14; 8:28 [d] Jn 6:44
12:33 [e] Jn 18:32
12:34 [f] Ps 110:4; Isa 9:7; Eze 37:25; Da 7:14 [g] Mt 8:20 [h] Jn 3:14
12:35 [i] ver 46 [j] Eph 5:8 [k] 1Jn 2:11
12:36 [l] Lk 16:8 [m] Jn 8:59
12:37 [n] Jn 2:11
12:38 [o] Isa 53:1; Ro 10:16
12:40 [p] Isa 6:10; Mt 13:13,15
12:41 [q] Isa 6:1-4 [r] Lk 24:27
12:42 [s] ver 11; Jn 7:48 [t] Jn 7:13 [u] Jn 9:22
12:43 [v] Jn 5:44
12:44 [w] Mt 10:40; Jn 5:24
12:45 [x] Jn 14:9
12:46 [y] Jn 1:4; 3:19; 8:12; 9:5
12:47 [z] Jn 3:17

[a] *32* The Greek for *lifted up* also means *exalted.*
[b] *38* Isaiah 53:1
[c] *40* Isaiah 6:10

---

inaugurates judgment. It unmasks those opposed to God and aligned with Satan, who will crucify the Son. Like light shining in darkness, now every hidden darkness will be exposed.

12:34–36 What sort of Son of Man or Messiah is this who finds glory in death? Jesus denies them an answer, refusing to enter into speculation about the theological role of the Messiah in popular thought. Instead, he appeals to them to believe. The crowd must make a choice and *make it quickly* before the light disappears.

12:37–41 Jesus' public work is completed; his signs have been displayed in the world; his discourses have been delivered. *And yet, the signs have been rejected.* The theological message of these verses is anchored to Isaiah's experience. God called Isaiah to speak to Israel but forewarned him that his words would find no acceptance.

John is describing what we might call a "judicial" hardening that settles on people who are already guilty. When revelation comes and we refuse to believe, the light disappears (vv. 35–36), and when God's light departs from the world, the darkness (which is the default state of the world) closes over unbelieving hearts.

It is also important to see that rejection is hopeful in the plan of God. In John's understanding, the hardness of Israel is purposeful: Through their rejection, salvation through Christ will be won for all. Through their refusal to believe, the gospel will go out to the rest of the world.

12:42–43 The struggle for belief in the world has now entered its final stage. John introduces us to leaders in Judaism, such as Nicodemus, who are keenly interested in Jesus and some of whom have decided to believe in him. But they refuse to make this faith public, so that many of their colleagues do not even know about their interest. John is harshly critical of them, and the stinging rebuke is given in v. 43.

12:44–49 For John, this is no doubt a final theological summary, comprising the main motifs revealed in the ministry of Jesus. But we also have a warning: Jesus' word will remain as a deposit of revelation by which human lives may be judged.

them[a] at the last day. 49For I did not
speak on my own, but the Father who
sent me commanded me[b] to say all that
I have spoken. 50I know that his command leads to eternal life. So whatever
I say is just what the Father has told me
to say."

Jesus Washes His Disciples' Feet

13 It was just before the Passover Festival.[c] Jesus knew that the hour had
come[d] for him to leave this world and
go to the Father.[e] Having loved his own
who were in the world, he loved them
to the end.
2The evening meal was in progress,
and the devil had already prompted Judas, the son of Simon Iscariot, to betray
Jesus. 3Jesus knew that the Father had
put all things under his power,[f] and that
he had come from God[g] and was returning to God; 4so he got up from the meal,
took off his outer clothing, and wrapped
a towel around his waist. 5After that, he
poured water into a basin and began to
wash his disciples' feet,[h] drying them
with the towel that was wrapped around
him.
6He came to Simon Peter, who said to
him, "Lord, are you going to wash my
feet?"
7Jesus replied, "You do not realize now
what I am doing, but later you will understand."[i]
8"No," said Peter, "you shall never
wash my feet."
Jesus answered, "Unless I wash you,
you have no part with me."
9"Then, Lord," Simon Peter replied,
"not just my feet but my hands and my
head as well!"
10Jesus answered, "Those who have
had a bath need only to wash their feet;
their whole body is clean. And you are
clean,[j] though not every one of you." 11For
he knew who was going to betray him,

12:48 [a] Jn 5:45
12:49 [b] Jn 14:31
13:1 [c] Jn 11:55 [d] Jn 12:23 [e] Jn 16:28
13:3 [f] Mt 28:18 [g] Jn 8:42; 16:27, 28,30
13:5 [h] Lk 7:44
13:7 [i] ver 12
13:10 [j] Jn 15:3

12:50 The seriousness of Jesus' revelation is reinforced in the end when he returns to his first subject: the Father. Without doubt, the presence of the Father in the life and work of Jesus is the theme John does not want us to miss. When the world makes a decision about Jesus, it is really making a decision about God.

12:1-50 The crowd in Jerusalem assumed that Jesus and his movement would serve their cause. Their vision for society and Jesus' presence could together make changes they dearly desired. Jesus' failure to satisfy those visions (religious, political, and social) leads to a cry for crucifixion one week later.

In what ways do we also use Jesus to fuel our own visions for social and political change? Believers can be passionate about their agendas for social change, which they sometimes tie to their religious convictions. Jesus wants our personal devotion along with our praise and celebration. But too often we only see him through the issues of the day.

Our focus in this passage should help us understand what kingdom values emphasize: John's story honors Mary's personal devotion to her Lord before Jesus corrects the political misgivings of the crowd. Jesus' clear and unwavering description of his coming crucifixion and the God-directed purpose of the same has a special urgency (vv. 35-36). This is what should fuel believers' passion to expand God's kingdom on a daily basis.

13:1-38 The focus of the first half of John is on *the signs* of Jesus—evidences of his identity borne by miraculous works. The focus of the second half of John is on *the hour*. Jesus now must say farewell to his followers and begin his return to the Father through his arrest, crucifixion, resurrection, and ascension. In v. 1 Jesus recognizes that "his hour" has come to depart out of the world, and he focuses his attention on "his own," whom he has loved.

13:1-5 As the meal is being served, Jesus demonstrates the depth of his love for his followers. The task of foot washing was so menial that Jewish slaves were exempt, and the job was kept for Gentile slaves. We never find those with a higher status washing the feet of those beneath them. When Jesus takes off "his outer clothing" and wraps a towel around himself (v. 4), he is adopting the posture of a slave.

13:6-9 Peter reflects how shocking the deed must have seemed. Jesus is not simply giving them a lesson in humble service; he is doing something that symbolizes his greater act of sacrifice on the cross. Peter continues to object in the most strenuous way, and Jesus' rebuke is carefully worded. "If *I* do not wash you . . ." means that the question is not simply one of washing, but a question of *who* does the washing. Peter must participate in the work of Jesus (vv. 8-9). He lacks a cleansing that only Jesus can supply.

The foot washing symbolizes something more than a gesture of fellowship. Only the death of Jesus (and its acceptance by the believer) brings eternal life.

13:9-11 Peter concludes that if foot washing gains an inheritance with Jesus, what would a thoroughgoing "washing" gain? The cleansing work of Jesus—foot washing, symbolizing spiritual cleansing on the cross—is complete in itself; therefore, Peter does not need to pursue more.

The curious return to the subject of Judas in vv. 10b-11 indicates that Jesus' work of foot washing has not changed Judas's heart. The fact alone that Jesus washed Judas' feet is stunning and is a testimony to Jesus' patience and love for his followers (even for the man who betrays him).

and that was why he said not every one
was clean.
12 When he had finished washing their
feet, he put on his clothes and returned
to his place. "Do you understand what
I have done for you?" he asked them.
13 "You call me 'Teacher'[k] and 'Lord,'[l]
and rightly so, for that is what I am.
14 Now that I, your Lord and Teacher,
have washed your feet, you also should
wash one another's feet.[m] 15 I have set
you an example that you should do as
I have done for you.[n] 16 Very truly I tell
you, no servant is greater than his master,[o] nor is a messenger greater than the
one who sent him. 17 Now that you know
these things, you will be blessed if you
do them.[p]

Jesus Predicts His Betrayal

18 "I am not referring to all of you;[q] I
know those I have chosen.[r] But this is to
fulfill this passage of Scripture: 'He who
shared my bread[s] has turned[a][t] against
me.'[b][u]
19 "I am telling you now before it happens, so that when it does happen you
will believe[v] that I am who I am.[w] 20 Very
truly I tell you, whoever accepts anyone
I send accepts me; and whoever accepts
me accepts the one who sent me."[x]

13:13 [k] Jn 11:28 [l] Lk 6:46; 1Co 12:3; Php 2:11
13:14 [m] 1Pe 5:5
13:15 [n] Mt 11:29
13:16 [o] Mt 10:24; Lk 6:40; Jn 15:20
13:17 [p] Mt 7:24, 25; Lk 11:28; Jas 1:25
13:18 [q] ver 10 [r] Jn 15:16, 19 [s] Mt 26:23 [t] Jn 6:70 [u] Ps 41:9
13:19 [v] Jn 14:29; 16:4 [w] Jn 8:24
13:20 [x] Mt 10:40; Lk 10:16
13:21 [y] Jn 12:27 [z] Mt 26:21
13:23 [a] Jn 19:26; 20:2; 21:7, 20
13:25 [b] Jn 21:20
13:27 [c] Lk 22:3
13:29 [d] Jn 12:6
13:30 [e] Lk 22:53

21 After he had said this, Jesus was
troubled in spirit[y] and testified, "Very
truly I tell you, one of you is going to
betray me."[z]
22 His disciples stared at one another, at a loss to know which of them
he meant. 23 One of them, the disciple
whom Jesus loved,[a] was reclining next
to him. 24 Simon Peter motioned to this
disciple and said, "Ask him which one
he means."
25 Leaning back against Jesus, he asked
him, "Lord, who is it?"[b]
26 Jesus answered, "It is the one to
whom I will give this piece of bread when
I have dipped it in the dish." Then, dipping the piece of bread, he gave it to Judas, the son of Simon Iscariot. 27 As soon
as Judas took the bread, Satan entered
into him.[c]
So Jesus told him, "What you are about
to do, do quickly." 28 But no one at the
meal understood why Jesus said this
to him. 29 Since Judas had charge of the
money,[d] some thought Jesus was telling
him to buy what was needed for the festival, or to give something to the poor.
30 As soon as Judas had taken the bread,
he went out. And it was night.[e]

a 18 Greek *has lifted up his heel*   *b* 18 Psalm 41:9

13:12–15 Jesus provides a discourse explaining what he has just done. Jesus' sacrifice will be the supreme token of his overwhelming love for the world. Jesus now wants his followers to exemplify that same love to one another.

13:16–17 Jesus' proverb in v. 16 echoes well-known words from the Synoptic Gospels. Servants should not consider themselves to be greater than their masters; if this is so, what is applicable to the master (sacrifice) is likewise applicable to the servant.

13:18–19 Jesus' interpretation returns to thoughts of Judas (vv. 18–19). This builds the impression that Judas's betrayal weighs heavily on Jesus. Jesus knows each of these men now with him in the room. There have been no surprises after so many years together in ministry. Jesus wants *each* of them. Jesus' citation of Ps 41:9 (v. 18) underscores the personal affront that this betrayal meant. To "eat bread" is a cultural symbol that refers to personal intimacy, and to expose the bottom of the foot is another symbol of personal contempt.

13:20 Jesus returns to his subject of the servant and the master. As servants are obligated to reflect the work of their masters in every respect, so too such servants enjoy the respect and the authority that comes from working in their master's name.

13:21 This is the third and final time we read that Jesus is "deeply troubled." His words predicting his betrayal were firmly fixed in the Gospel tradition. John records a story unlike any other.

13:22–25 Since the disciples are eating a traditional Passover meal, it is necessary for them to recline. The Beloved Disciple enjoys a place of honor, seated on Jesus' right. This explains how he can easily lean back and place his head near Jesus' chest and speak to him privately. Peter is not as near and so must call to the Beloved Disciple. Judas likewise has a place of honor near Jesus because Jesus can dip bread into a common dish and serve the morsel to him.

13:26–29 Jesus promptly serves Judas, which the other disciples could have taken as a simple honoring gesture for Judas. If so, it is particularly ironic since this gesture of respect is the last thing Jesus can do for Judas, and it compares with Judas's last gesture of betrayal in the garden.

At this point, Satan controls Judas's fate, and Jesus dispatches him to pursue the course he has set for himself. The story implies that John understands everything going on in the room, though the other disciples may not have (v. 28).

13:30 The departure of Judas is at "night." The darkness of night represents the antithesis of Jesus, who is the light. Therefore, Judas represents a person John described in 3:19.

PEOPLE TO KNOW // **JUDAS**

JOHN 13:27: Judas was one of Jesus' twelve disciples. He likely started out following Jesus wholeheartedly, but we learn from Scripture that while Judas was initially trusted enough to be put in charge of the money bag, later he began to help himself to what was put into it (Jn 12:6).

During Passover week, a disillusioned Judas met with the religious leaders about handing Jesus over to them for thirty pieces of silver (Mt 26:15). They agreed this should be done when Jesus was not with a crowd. Satan had entered Judas (Jn 13:27), prompting Judas to scheme with the religious leaders.

At the Last Supper, Jesus identified Judas as the one who would betray him (Jn 13:26). Judas then left the table to get those who would arrest Jesus. When Jesus was praying in Gethsemane, Judas returned with soldiers and some Jewish religious leaders. He identified Jesus for the soldiers by walking up to him and giving him a kiss. Jesus was arrested, tried and crucified.

Judas was filled with remorse when he saw Jesus condemned (Mt 27:3). He tried to return the thirty pieces of silver, throwing the money before the priests at the temple court. Judas then went away and took his own life (see Ac 1:15–19).

APPLICATION ✣ Judas had a front-row seat to the miracles and love of Christ, yet his heart was hard. He chose to betray the One he had followed for years, seen perform miracle after miracle, and heard teach about love and God's kingdom. Judas's story warns us that it is possible to know a lot about Jesus but remain lost, living only for misplaced desires. We may know about Jesus and act right on the outside, but to truly change, we need God's Spirit to give us a new heart and to kindle love and faith within us. Watching Jesus is not enough. We need to follow him as Lord.

Jesus Predicts Peter's Denial

13:37,38pp // Mt 26:33–35; Mk 14:29–31; Lk 22:33,34

31When he was gone, Jesus said, "Now
the Son of Man is glorified[f] and God is
glorified in him.[g] 32If God is glorified in
him,[a] God will glorify the Son in himself,[h] and will glorify him at once.
33"My children, I will be with you only
a little longer. You will look for me, and
just as I told the Jews, so I tell you now:
Where I am going, you cannot come.[i]
34"A new command[j] I give you: Love
one another.[k] As I have loved you, so you
must love one another.[l] 35By this everyone will know that you are my disciples,
if you love one another."[m]
36Simon Peter asked him, "Lord, where
are you going?"

13:31 [f] Jn 7:39 [g] Jn 14:13; 17:4; 1Pe 4:11
13:32 [h] Jn 17:1
13:33 [i] Jn 7:33,34
13:34 [j] 1Jn 2:7-11; 3:11 [k] Lev 19:18; 1Th 4:9; 1Pe 1:22 [l] Jn 15:12; Eph 5:2; 1Jn 4:10,11
13:35 [m] 1Jn 3:14; 4:20

Jn 13:34–35 ❖ How can we love others as Christ has loved us? Are there any limits on that kind of love?

[a] 32 Many early manuscripts do not have *If God is glorified in him.*

13:31–38 Jesus is now left with "his own" to give them his final instructions. He encourages his disciples and comforts them. He also urges them to be obedient. Moreover, Jesus promises that his Spirit will indwell and empower his followers following his death.

13:31–32 With the departure of Judas Iscariot, Jesus speaks directly of his glorification. Throughout Jesus' life of perfect obedience, God has been honored. Jesus' glory occurs when God's glory radiates through him.

The supreme place where this divine radiance will be visible will be on the cross. This future glorification is not some distant event at the end of time or in heaven. The series of events will unfold at the end of this momentous week: Jesus' death, resurrection, and ascension.

13:33 This verse is a crucial thought for the farewell discourse. He is departing so that he can prepare for their arrival. His desire is not to abandon them but to enjoy their fellowship forever.

13:34–35 Jesus' statement in these verses is dramatic. Disciples are to reflect a love expressed through committed obedience.

But the word "new" may mean something more (v. 34). This "new command" may be a signal that Jesus is talking about life in a new era—a messianic era. In that era, love must characterize his followers: a love patterned on the generous, loving act of God that saves his people.

13:36–38 Peter is eager to be with Jesus even if it costs him his life, and his words echo the language of the Good Shepherd. Jesus goes on to prophesy that Peter's nerve will fail at the last moment. His good intentions to lay down his life, uttered so bravely, will not hold when confronted with genuine danger. Peter's eventual death ("but you will follow later," v. 36) will come up again in 21:18–19.

Jesus replied, "Where I am going, you cannot follow now,[n] but you will follow later."[o]

37 Peter asked, "Lord, why can't I follow you now? I will lay down my life for you."

38 Then Jesus answered, "Will you really lay down your life for me? Very truly I tell you, before the rooster crows, you will disown me three times![p]

Jesus Comforts His Disciples

14 "Do not let your hearts be troubled.[q] You believe in God[a]; believe also in me. 2 My Father's house has many rooms; if that were not so, would I have told you that I am going there[r] to prepare a place for you? 3 And if I go and prepare a place for you, I will come back and take you to be with me that you also may be where I am.[s] 4 You know the way to the place where I am going."

Jesus the Way to the Father

5 Thomas[t] said to him, "Lord, we don't know where you are going, so how can we know the way?"

6 Jesus answered, "I am the way[u] and the truth and the life.[v] No one comes to the Father except through me. 7 If you really know me, you will know[b] my Father as well.[w] From now on, you do know him and have seen him."

8 Philip said, "Lord, show us the Father and that will be enough for us."

9 Jesus answered: "Don't you know me, Philip, even after I have been among you such a long time? Anyone who has seen me has seen the Father.[x] How can you say, 'Show us the Father'? 10 Don't you believe that I am in the Father, and that the Father is in me?[y] The words I say to you I do not speak on my own authority.[z] Rather, it is the Father, living in me, who is doing his work. 11 Believe me when I say that I am in the Father and the Father is in me; or at least believe on the evidence of the works themselves.[a] 12 Very truly I tell you, whoever believes[b] in me will do the works I have been doing,[c] and they

13:36 [n] ver 33; Jn 14:2 [o] Jn 21:18,19; 2Pe 1:14
13:38 [p] Jn 18:27
14:1 [q] ver 27
14:2 [r] Jn 13:33, 36
14:3 [s] Jn 12:26
14:5 [t] Jn 11:16
14:6 [u] Jn 10:9 [v] Jn 11:25
14:7 [w] Jn 8:19
14:9 [x] Jn 12:45; Col 1:15; Heb 1:3
14:10 [y] Jn 10:38 [z] Jn 5:19
14:11 [a] Jn 5:36; 10:38
14:12 [b] Mt 21:21 [c] Lk 10:17

[a] 1 Or *Believe in God* [b] 7 Some manuscripts *If you really knew me, you would know*

13:1-38 Communicating Jesus' command to love was one of John's foremost concerns. The problem with this verse is that it may be impossible to order someone to love. Unless one has a profound experience of being loved, expressing profound love for another is virtually impossible.

Nothing so astonishes a fractured world as a community in which radical, faithful, genuine love is shared among its members. There are many places we can go to find communities of shared interest, people just like ourselves who enjoy sports or music or gardening or politics. But it is the mandate of the church to become a community of love, a circle of Christ's followers who invest in one another because Christ has invested in them. Believers are to exhibit love not based on the mutuality and attractiveness of its members but on the model of Christ, who washed the feet of everyone (including Judas).

14:1-11 On three previous occasions, John wrote of Jesus' deeply troubled feelings (11:33; 12:27; 13:21). Here, the disciples face the same feelings. Jesus is charging his disciples to hold fast, considering the upcoming crisis.

14:1-3 In his departure, Jesus will be working on the disciples' behalf, preparing a place for them. God's "house" is a place with many "rooms" (v. 2). This latter word is related to the verb repeated in this Gospel, to "remain" or "abide." Jesus promises that death will not interrupt the relationship they have enjoyed with him.

To have a place in heaven reserved for us is one thing; confidence in getting there is quite another. But Jesus promises that he "will come back" (v. 3). When will this "coming" occur? The best view takes vv. 2-3 as a plain promise of the second coming.

14:4-7 Thomas speaks up and presses for more clarification. Jesus' answer in v. 6 is the premier expression of the theology of this entire Gospel. Access to the Father's presence in heaven will only be through Jesus and no other.

Jesus is *the truth*. He is the authoritative representative and revealer of God. He discloses God exhaustively, unlike anyone else can, because he has seen God. Those who follow Jesus, who come to the Father through his "way," will be the ones who gain eternal "life."

Jesus has disclosed more than anyone expected. Instead of simply defining his destination, Jesus takes the next inevitable step: only the Father can lead us to himself. If his followers know Jesus, they will know the Father as well. Since they have known him, there is more to come, and they will discover the Father who is present in him. Moreover, they have seen the Father *already*.

14:8-11 Philip does not understand that *no one* has ever seen God (1:18a). It is beyond human capacity. But in Christ, Philip sees the full embodiment of God. Jesus is not simply a religious teacher or guide. He is the one in whom God can be found.

Jesus is God's envoy. Jesus is authorized both to work for and to speak for his sender. The Father is in Jesus, and he is in the Father. This is the unity of the Trinity.

14:12 Once Jesus departs, two promises will be realized in the community of faith: Great works will accompany those who believe, and prayer will be answered. Jesus has been performing deeds of humility, service, and love as well as miraculous signs. Jesus promises that his followers will do works that are "greater" even than these.

CHARACTER OF GOD // GOD IS TRUTH

John 14:6: "I am the way and the truth and the life. No one comes to the Father except through me."

Scripture teaches that God is truth. When the Son of God became a human in Jesus, he came "full of grace and truth" (Jn 1:14). Speaking to Thomas at the Last Supper, Jesus announced that he was "the way and the truth and the life" (Jn 14:6).

Everything Jesus spoke was the truth. His words were not only his own; he spoke what the Father desired (Jn 12:49). Therefore, because we know that God is trustworthy and that God and Jesus are full of truth, we can be assured that no word of Christ will fail. In the same way, we can trust the words in the Bible. If God is truth, then his words in the Bible are true. There are no lies, mistakes or guesses in God's Word. Scripture is founded in God's supreme wisdom and knowledge.

The completely truthful nature of God means that God is in fact the very foundation of truth. Nothing outside of God's design is true, and there is nowhere else truth can be found. Saint Augustine wrote that wherever truth is found, it belongs to God: All truth is God's truth. This means that all things in creation that humans discover as facts belong to God. Nothing is outside of God's domain.

APPLICATION In today's world, it can be difficult to know what is true. So many voices clamor for our attention and claim to have the right answer, the true answer. Truth is so important in society and in relationships. It is necessary for trust. It is necessary for justice. So how do we pick through the lies and find the truth? In order to know truth, we must know God. When we immerse ourselves in his Word and cultivate a relationship with him through prayer, we will find that we can discern the truth from lies because we will become transformed into a person more and more like Jesus (Ro 12:2). As we remain in him, we will know the truth and the truth will set us free (Jn 8:31-32).

will do even greater things than these,
because I am going to the Father. 13And
I will do whatever you ask[d] in my name,
so that the Father may be glorified in the
Son. 14You may ask me for anything in
my name, and I will do it.

Jesus Promises the Holy Spirit

15"If you love me, keep my commands.[e]
16And I will ask the Father, and he will
give you another advocate[f] to help you
and be with you forever— 17the Spirit of
truth.[g] The world cannot accept him,[h] because it neither sees him nor knows him.
But you know him, for he lives with you
and will be[a] in you. 18I will not leave you
as orphans; I will come to you.[i] 19Before

14:13 [d] Mt 7:7
14:15 [e] ver 21, 23; Jn 15:10; 1Jn 5:3
14:16 [f] Jn 15:26; 16:7
14:17 [g] Jn 15:26; 16:13; 1Jn 4:6 [h] 1Co 2:14
14:18 [i] ver 3, 28

[a] 17 Some early manuscripts *and is*

These works will be "greater" because regular people will do them. The Holy Spirit will inaugurate a new, never-before-seen reality.

14:13–14 Jesus and his disciples will hear one another's voice. This theme that Jesus will do what his disciples ask (in prayer) is frequent both in the farewell discourse and in John's letters. Such prayer is given in Jesus' "name" and directed to Jesus. This promise of answered prayer is really a continuation of what is given in v. 13. Such answered prayer is another "great work" that Jesus will accomplish among them.

14:15–16 Next, as Jesus anticipates his departure, he describes the Spirit that is coming. This gift is an outgrowth of the loving relationship between Jesus and his disciples.

Jesus uses an unusual term in v. 16 for the Spirit ("advocate"). It occurs in secular Greek literature for an advocate in a court of law, someone who comes alongside a person to speak in his or her defense and provide counsel. Jesus is an "Advocate" who is now sending a second "Advocate." This means that the ongoing work of the Spirit will be a continuation of the work of Jesus during the disciples' lifetime.

14:17 It is no surprise that the Holy Spirit is also called "the Spirit of truth" (v. 17). He communicates the truth about God. We know that Jesus is "the truth," and since the Spirit sustains Jesus' work, he will also continue to defend the truth of Jesus.

In John's Gospel, the "world" refers to the human environment that is in rebellion against God and in need of salvation. Jesus recognizes that such people cannot perceive the deeper things of God, such as the mystery of the Holy Spirit. The disciples, however, can know the Spirit of truth because Jesus has been with them all along, and he will be in them in the future through the Spirit.

14:18–20 "I will come to you" means that Jesus will not leave his followers desolate. But does this refer to the coming of the Spirit (vv. 16–17)? Subtle clues suggest that this indicates Jesus' coming after his resurrection on Easter. The time frame is specific

Jn 14:27 ❖ How have we experienced the peace of Christ in times we were troubled or afraid?

long, the world will not see me anymore,
but you will see me.[j] Because I live, you
also will live.[k] 20On that day you will realize that I am in my Father,[l] and you are
in me, and I am in you. 21Whoever has
my commands and keeps them is the
one who loves me.[m] The one who loves
me will be loved by my Father,[n] and I too
will love them and show myself to them."
22Then Judas[o] (not Judas Iscariot) said,
"But, Lord, why do you intend to show
yourself to us and not to the world?"[p]
23Jesus replied, "Anyone who loves me
will obey my teaching.[q] My Father will love
them, and we will come to them and make
our home with them.[r] 24Anyone who does
not love me will not obey my teaching.
These words you hear are not my own;
they belong to the Father who sent me.[s]
25"All this I have spoken while still with
you. 26But the Advocate,[t] the Holy Spirit,
whom the Father will send in my name,[u]
will teach you all things[v] and will remind
you of everything I have said to you.[w]
27Peace I leave with you; my peace I give
you.[x] I do not give to you as the world
gives. Do not let your hearts be troubled
and do not be afraid.
28"You heard me say, 'I am going away
and I am coming back to you.'[y] If you
loved me, you would be glad that I am
going to the Father,[z] for the Father is
greater than I.[a] 29I have told you now
before it happens, so that when it does
happen you will believe.[b] 30I will not say
much more to you, for the prince of this
world[c] is coming. He has no hold over
me, 31but he comes so that the world may
learn that I love the Father and do exactly what my Father has commanded me.[d]
"Come now; let us leave.

The Vine and the Branches

15 "I am the true vine,[e] and my Father is the gardener. 2He cuts off

14:19 [j]Jn 7:33, 34; 16:16 [k]Jn 6:57
14:20 [l]Jn 10:38
14:21 [m]1Jn 5:3 [n]1Jn 2:5
14:22 [o]Lk 6:16; Ac 1:13 [p]Ac 10:41
14:23 [q]ver 15 [r]1Jn 2:24; Rev 3:20
14:24 [s]Jn 7:16
14:26 [t]Jn 15:26; 16:7 [u]Ac 2:33 [v]Jn 16:13; 1Jn 2:20,27 [w]Jn 2:22
14:27 [x]Jn 16:33; Php 4:7; Col 3:15
14:28 [y]ver 2-4, 18 [z]Jn 5:18 [a]Jn 10:29; Php 2:6
14:29 [b]Jn 13:19; 16:4
14:30 [c]Jn 12:31
14:31 [d]Jn 10:18; 12:49
15:1 [e]Isa 5:1-7

("before long," v. 19), and the disciples are to look for "that day" (v. 20). In his resurrection, Jesus will return to them and validate that the power of the Father has been with him all along.

But the coming of Jesus on Easter will mean more than a mere return of Jesus to life. His aim is to establish the sort of intimacy and unity he has promised throughout the discourse. The oneness he enjoys with the Father parallels the oneness the disciples will enjoy with him. Thus the Easter return will be the bridge that will inaugurate the spiritual union Jesus wants with them.

14:21–24 Again, Jesus talks about obedience as a key to what is planned: those who love Jesus show it by their fidelity to his word. But those who fail to love and obey him are not connected to Jesus or the Father and cannot share in this divine union.

14:25–31 The Trinitarian implications of vv. 25–26 are inescapable: the Father will send the Spirit in the name of Jesus.

14:26 Jesus then emphasizes the conserving and teaching roles of the Spirit. During the earthly ministry of Jesus, understanding was difficult. But now, Jesus promises, the Spirit will help his followers remember and understand.

14:27–28a The discourse of ch. 14 closes with words of reassurance similar to those offered at the beginning. "Peace" in v. 27 refers to the restoration of humanity's relationship with God. Nothing in the world can offer such peace.

Jesus mentions again that his disciples are troubled. Jesus points to himself. Their love for him should lead to celebration because he is returning to where he began: He is returning to the Father.

14:28b Few verses have caused more controversy than this verse. The Father's greatness springs from his role as the origin and sender of Jesus, just as a ray of light might refer to the sun from which it came. The word picture Jesus often uses to describe his life is the agent sent on a mission. Within this agent-sender relationship, the originator of the mission has greater authority.

14:28–31 Not only should the disciples take comfort and rejoice because Jesus is returning to his origin, but they should realize that the events unfolding in Jerusalem for him are not controlled by Satan. When they occur, the disciples will recall his words and see his predictions fulfilled. Moreover, Jesus' obedience to God's plan should be seen as an example of his love for the Father.

✣ **14:1–31** Possessing an anticipation for heaven builds in us an eternal vantage point. We live in a world that continually keeps our eyes on the near horizon of the present and denies the limitations of our own mortality. Jesus offers a more positive incentive. Our true home, our complete security, has already been built for us by him in heaven. Once we embrace the significance of this notion, our attitudes toward this world completely change.

15:1 The vine represented the covenant people of God. In his final "I am" saying in this Gospel, Jesus declares that *he* is the true vine. The new concept is that God's vineyard holds *one vine*, and Israel must inquire if it is attached to him. No longer is Israel automatically seen as a vine growing in God's vineyard. Men and women are now branches growing from one stalk.

The key word is "remaining" or "abiding." Discipleship is not just a matter of acknowledging who Jesus is; it is being connected to Jesus spiritually in our inner lives.

15:2–3 That connection also means being "pruned." Those who remain in the vine are being readied

Jn 15:4 ❖ What happens when we try to bear fruit on our own? How can we remain in Christ?

every branch in me that bears no fruit,
while every branch that does bear fruit
he prunes[a] so that it will be even more
fruitful. 3You are already clean because
of the word I have spoken to you.[f] 4Re-
main in me, as I also remain in you.[g] No
branch can bear fruit by itself; it must
remain in the vine. Neither can you bear
fruit unless you remain in me.
5"I am the vine; you are the branches.
If you remain in me and I in you, you will
bear much fruit;[h] apart from me you can
do nothing. 6If you do not remain in me,
you are like a branch that is thrown away
and withers; such branches are picked
up, thrown into the fire and burned.[i] 7If
you remain in me and my words remain
in you, ask whatever you wish, and it will
be done for you.[j] 8This is to my Father's
glory,[k] that you bear much fruit, showing
yourselves to be my disciples.[l]
9"As the Father has loved me,[m] so have
I loved you. Now remain in my love. 10If
you keep my commands,[n] you will remain in my love, just as I have kept my
Father's commands and remain in his
love. 11I have told you this so that my joy
may be in you and that your joy may be
complete.[o] 12My command is this: Love
each other as I have loved you.[p] 13Greater
love has no one than this: to lay down
one's life for one's friends.[q] 14You are my
friends[r] if you do what I command.[s] 15I
no longer call you servants, because a
servant does not know his master's business. Instead, I have called you friends,
for everything that I learned from my
Father I have made known to you.[t] 16You
did not choose me, but I chose you and
appointed you[u] so that you might go and
bear fruit — fruit that will last — and so
that whatever you ask in my name the
Father will give you. 17This is my command: Love each other.[v]

The World Hates the Disciples

18"If the world hates you,[w] keep in
mind that it hated me first. 19If you belonged to the world, it would love you as
its own. As it is, you do not belong to the
world, but I have chosen you[x] out of the
world. That is why the world hates you.[y]
20Remember what I told you: 'A servant
is not greater than his master.'[b][z] If they
persecuted me, they will persecute you
also.[a] If they obeyed my teaching, they
will obey yours also. 21They will treat you
this way because of my name,[b] for they
do not know the one who sent me.[c] 22If I
had not come and spoken to them, they
would not be guilty of sin; but now they

15:3 [f] Jn 13:10; 17:17; Eph 5:26
15:4 [g] Jn 6:56; 1Jn 2:6
15:5 [h] ver 16
15:6 [i] ver 2
15:7 [j] Mt 7:7
15:8 [k] Mt 5:16 [l] Jn 8:31
15:9 [m] Jn 17:23, 24,26
15:10 [n] Jn 14:15
15:11 [o] Jn 17:13
15:12 [p] Jn 13:34
15:13 [q] Jn 10:11; Ro 5:7,8
15:14 [r] Lk 12:4 [s] Mt 12:50
15:15 [t] Jn 8:26
15:16 [u] Jn 6:70; 13:18
15:17 [v] ver 12
15:18 [w] 1Jn 3:13
15:19 [x] ver 16 [y] Jn 17:14
15:20 [z] Jn 13:16 [a] 2Ti 3:12
15:21 [b] Mt 10:22 [c] Jn 16:3

[a] *2* The Greek for *he prunes* also means *he cleans.*
[b] *20* John 13:16

---

for more fruit-bearing by the word Jesus is giving them.

15:4-6 To fail to "remain" in Christ risks separation from the vineyard and consequent destruction. There is only one evidence that a branch is truly alive: Does it produce clusters of grapes? Fruit-bearing is not a test; rather, fruit-bearing is a byproduct. Fruitfulness will be the inevitable outcome of an interior spiritual life connected with Jesus.

15:7-11 Jesus concludes the metaphor by drawing out some of the implications that come from "remaining" in him. Verse 7 compares remaining in Jesus and remaining in his word. Those whose lives are so in harmony with Jesus will find their prayers controlled by his word, and such prayers will be answered.

Jesus desires "that *my joy* may be in you" (v. 11, emphasis added). The Spirit makes this joy supernatural and substantial. Jesus' joy has come through his reliance on God and his obedience to his Father's will. We inherit the capacity given through the Spirit to enjoy God in the same manner.

15:12-13 Jesus moves on to describe life among the branches. This is the second time that Jesus has commanded his followers to love one another (also in 13:34). Such love for one another is a fulfillment of God's love for us; it requires that we also love God with our entire heart, soul, and strength.

15:14-17 Jesus then calls his disciples "friends" to distinguish them from servants who do not know the deeper thoughts of their masters. This title speaks of the highest relationship possible between God and a human being. Jesus chooses us as friends, which gives us tremendous security that his affection for us will not disappear.

Where true friendship exists, true disclosure accompanies it. Disciples possess the word of Jesus and will receive ongoing revelations of Jesus. Disciples thus know "God's heart." When they pray, their desires and God's will harmonize, making them participants in God's efforts in the world.

15:18-19 Jesus explains the hatred of the world as a continuation of the hatred he personally witnessed throughout his public ministry. Because the disciples are now separated from the world by virtue of their faith in Jesus, they qualify for similar treatment. Christians have passed from death to life and so should not expect the world's affections.

15:20-25 Jesus repeats the proverb about servants and masters—not to compromise his disciples' status as friends, but to teach that they now

have no excuse for their sin.[d] 23Whoever
hates me hates my Father as well. 24If I
had not done among them the works no
one else did,[e] they would not be guilty of
sin. As it is, they have seen, and yet they
have hated both me and my Father. 25But
this is to fulfill what is written in their
Law: 'They hated me without reason.'[a][f]

The Work of the Holy Spirit

26"When the Advocate[g] comes, whom
I will send to you from the Father[h] — the
Spirit of truth[i] who goes out from the
Father — he will testify about me.[j] 27And
you also must testify,[k] for you have been
with me from the beginning.[l]

16 "All this[m] I have told you so that you
will not fall away.[n] 2They will put
you out of the synagogue;[o] in fact, the
time is coming when anyone who kills
you will think they are offering a service
to God.[p] 3They will do such things because they have not known the Father or
me.[q] 4I have told you this, so that when
their time comes you will remember[r]
that I warned you about them. I did not
tell you this from the beginning because
I was with you, 5but now I am going to
him who sent me.[s] None of you asks me,
'Where are you going?'[t] 6Rather, you are
filled with grief because I have said these
things. 7But very truly I tell you, it is for
your good that I am going away. Unless
I go away, the Advocate[u] will not come to
you; but if I go, I will send him to you.[v]
8When he comes, he will prove the world
to be in the wrong about sin and righteousness and judgment: 9about sin,[w]
because people do not believe in me;
10about righteousness,[x] because I am
going to the Father, where you can see
me no longer; 11and about judgment,
because the prince of this world[y] now
stands condemned.

[a] 25 Psalms 35:19; 69:4

15:22 [d] Jn 9:41; Ro 1:20
15:24 [e] Jn 5:36
15:25 [f] Ps 35:19; 69:4
15:26 [g] Jn 14:16 [h] Jn 14:26 [i] Jn 14:17 [j] 1Jn 5:7
15:27 [k] Lk 24:48; 1Jn 1:2; 4:14 [l] Lk 1:2
16:1 [m] Jn 15:18-27 [n] Mt 11:6
16:2 [o] Jn 9:22 [p] Isa 66:5; Ac 26:9,10; Rev 6:9
16:3 [q] Jn 15:21; 17:25; 1Jn 3:1
16:4 [r] Jn 13:19
16:5 [s] Jn 7:33 [t] Jn 13:36; 14:5
16:7 [u] Jn 14:16, 26; 15:26 [v] Jn 7:39
16:9 [w] Jn 15:22
16:10 [x] Ac 3:14; 7:52; 1Pe 3:18
16:11 [y] Jn 12:31

---

share his status as persons no longer welcome in this fallen world.

The world is accountable before the revelation of God. Jesus' ministry provided both words and works that pointed to God. Now that they have seen and heard him, their guilt is irrefutable.

15:26–27 The Spirit will not only live in the disciples, enabling them to recall the words of Jesus; now he will become a witness. The disciples are witnesses and will be empowered as they deliver that message to the world.

The disciples will be forced to witness about Jesus as they are confronted. But the words they utter will be "the truth" because they are speaking about the work of God in Christ through the power of the Holy Spirit.

16:1–3 Jesus has taught his followers "all this" so that they will not "fall away." This word refers to someone who trips because of darkness. The greatest thing that the disciples have to fear, therefore, is that they will be unfaithful to the message of Jesus; or worse, renounce their faith.

16:4a To know in advance is to be equipped. To step into suffering and recognize that it follows the pattern of Jesus' life and fulfills his word may strengthen men and women for whom faith comes at a severe cost.

✣ **15:1–16:4a** Jesus is here revising Israel's theological assumptions about territory and religion. He is changing the place of rootedness for the people of God. Jesus here says God's vineyard has one vine, he is that vine, and attachment to God comes through attachment to him. It is no longer a matter of possessing the vineyard; it is now a matter of knowing the one true vine.

The Christian faith is not simply about believing the right things (though this is important). Nor is it simply a matter of living a Christlike life (though this is important too). Christian experience must necessarily have a mystical, spiritual dimension. To be a disciple means having the Father, Son, and Holy Spirit living in us (14:23–26).

What are the outcomes of this sort of life? The fruit Jesus expects from the branches is first and foremost love. As Jesus enjoyed the Father's love and reflected it to his followers, so now his love should fill their lives. Fruit then becomes a sign of spiritual life and vitality; fruit is not evidence by which we demonstrate that we belong in the vineyard.

16:4b–5 Jesus' candor about their coming sufferings stems from his awareness that he will not be with his disciples. In the future, they will have to bear the brunt of persecution. Jesus returns to the subject of his going away.

16:6–7 Sorrow has so swamped the disciples' lives that they have forgotten that Jesus' death is not the end of everything; it is rather the beginning. The point is the goal of his glorification—namely, his return to the Father's presence. If he does not go away, then the Spirit cannot come. In some fashion, then, it is mutually exclusive to have both this Spirit and Jesus on earth. The Spirit is a gift that must await the trigger of Jesus' departure.

16:8–11 Jesus gives another description of what the Spirit will do. The fundamental idea is that the world has already conducted its "trial" of Jesus and found him guilty and deserving of death. But in fact Jesus is innocent, and the world stands accused of error and sin. Its guilt will be exposed. It cannot deny that the verdict has been given any more than a criminal can miss the judgment passed on the final day of their trial. Since the world cannot receive the Spirit, this operation

Jn 16:13 ❖ How have you felt the guiding power of the Holy Spirit in your life?

12"I have much more to say to you,
more than you can now bear.[z] 13But
when he, the Spirit of truth,[a] comes, he
will guide you into all the truth.[b] He will
not speak on his own; he will speak only
what he hears, and he will tell you what
is yet to come. 14He will glorify me because it is from me that he will receive
what he will make known to you. 15All
that belongs to the Father is mine.[c] That
is why I said the Spirit will receive from
me what he will make known to you."

The Disciples' Grief Will Turn to Joy

16Jesus went on to say, "In a little
while[d] you will see me no more, and
then after a little while you will see me."[e]
17At this, some of his disciples said to
one another, "What does he mean by
saying, 'In a little while you will see me
no more, and then after a little while you
will see me,'[f] and 'Because I am going to
the Father'?"[g] 18They kept asking, "What
does he mean by 'a little while'? We don't
understand what he is saying."
19Jesus saw that they wanted to ask
him about this, so he said to them, "Are
you asking one another what I meant
when I said, 'In a little while you will
see me no more, and then after a little
while you will see me'? 20Very truly I tell
you, you will weep and mourn[h] while
the world rejoices. You will grieve, but
your grief will turn to joy.[i] 21A woman
giving birth to a child has pain[j] because
her time has come; but when her baby
is born she forgets the anguish because
of her joy that a child is born into the
world. 22So with you: Now is your time
of grief,[k] but I will see you again[l] and you
will rejoice, and no one will take away
your joy. 23In that day you will no longer
ask me anything. Very truly I tell you,
my Father will give you whatever you
ask in my name.[m] 24Until now you have
not asked for anything in my name. Ask
and you will receive, and your joy will
be complete.[n]
25"Though I have been speaking figuratively,[o] a time is coming[p] when I will
no longer use this kind of language but
will tell you plainly about my Father.
26In that day you will ask in my name.[q]
I am not saying that I will ask the Father
on your behalf. 27No, the Father himself
loves you because you have loved me[r]
and have believed that I came from God.
28I came from the Father and entered the
world; now I am leaving the world and
going back to the Father."[s]
29Then Jesus' disciples said, "Now you
are speaking clearly and without figures
of speech.[t] 30Now we can see that you

16:12 [z] Mk 4:33
16:13 [a] Jn 14:17 [b] Jn 14:26
16:15 [c] Jn 17:10
16:16 [d] Jn 7:33 [e] Jn 14:18-24
16:17 [f] ver 16 [g] ver 5
16:20 [h] Lk 23:27 [i] Jn 20:20
16:21 [j] Isa 26:17; 1Th 5:3
16:22 [k] ver 6 [l] ver 16
16:23 [m] Mt 7:7; Jn 15:16
16:24 [n] Jn 3:29; 15:11
16:25 [o] Mt 13:34; Jn 10:6 [p] ver 2
16:26 [q] ver 23, 24
16:27 [r] Jn 14:21, 23
16:28 [s] Jn 13:3
16:29 [t] ver 25

---

will be effected through the work of the church, which has the Spirit and which provides a bold testimony to the truth.

16:12–15 The Spirit will provide added revelations that the disciples have not yet heard. Jesus speaks of a future time when new things will be disclosed. The historical Jesus and his ministry stand alongside the ongoing living Jesus-in-Spirit, who is continuously experienced in the church.

The revelation of Jesus will continue in the community, and the Spirit will be the authoritative channel through which he is heard. Yet these revelations may not depart from what Jesus uttered in his historical ministry; that must always be the measure by which new revelations are tested.

16:16–22 Seven times in this chapter Jesus refers to "a little while," which prompts the central question of the section: "What does he mean by saying, 'In a little while'?" The confusion of the disciples is understandable.

This is not intentional ambiguity on Jesus' part. Rather, he is simply referring to his return in resurrection. He is departing from the world in his glorification, and the world will no longer have access to him. When he returns in resurrection, it will be his followers' final opportunity to see him as he has always been.

16:23–24 This joy at seeing Jesus will not only result in a renewed relationship with him, but it will have two notable effects: the joy of understanding and the joy of effective prayer. At last, they will understand. The momentous event of the resurrection will at once remove their fearfulness.

16:25–27 Jesus had taught "figuratively" (v. 25), but the Greek word used here does not simply mean illustrative speech or the use of metaphor and parable; rather, it is speech that is mysterious. The "hour" (v. 25; NIV "time") is the "hour of glorification" when Jesus returns to the Father and sends to his disciples the Holy Spirit. A new circle of fellowship is possible, which now includes Jesus, the disciple, *and the Father*.

16:28 One might call v. 28 a summary of John's doctrine of Christ. His origins are divine, and he comes from God. He was sent on a mission to the world; he will return to the Father after completing his work. This is the essence of the Gospel and the Christian faith, distilled to its most essential form.

16:29–30 The disciples immediately celebrate and feel confident that they understand. But this is one more example of tragic misunderstanding, such as we have seen in every other discourse. The time of complete understanding will come when the Spirit is given.

know all things and that you do not even
need to have anyone ask you questions.
This makes us believe that you came
from God."
31"Do you now believe?" Jesus replied. 32"A time is coming[u] and in fact
has come when you will be scattered,[v]
each to your own home. You will leave
me all alone. Yet I am not alone, for my
Father is with me.[w]
33"I have told you these things, so that
in me you may have peace.[x] In this world
you will have trouble.[y] But take heart! I
have overcome[z] the world."

Jesus Prays to Be Glorified

17 After Jesus said this, he looked toward heaven[a] and prayed:

"Father, the hour has come. Glorify your Son, that your Son may glorify you.[b] 2For you granted him authority over all people that he might
give eternal life to all those you have
given him.[c] 3Now this is eternal life:
that they know you, the only true
God, and Jesus Christ, whom you
have sent.[d] 4I have brought you glory[e] on earth by finishing the work
you gave me to do.[f] 5And now, Father, glorify me in your presence
with the glory I had with you[g] before
the world began.[h]

Jesus Prays for His Disciples

6"I have revealed you[a][i] to those
whom you gave me[j] out of the
world. They were yours; you gave
them to me and they have obeyed
your word. 7Now they know that
everything you have given me
comes from you. 8For I gave them
the words you gave me[k] and they
accepted them. They knew with certainty that I came from you,[l] and
they believed that you sent me.[m]
9I pray for them.[n] I am not praying
for the world, but for those you have
given me, for they are yours. 10All
I have is yours, and all you have is

16:32 [u]ver 2, 25 [v]Mt 26:31 [w]Jn 8:16, 29
16:33 [x]Jn 14:27 [y]Jn 15:18-21 [z]Ro 8:37; 1Jn 4:4
17:1 [a]Jn 11:41 [b]Jn 12:23; 13:31, 32
17:2 [c]ver 6, 9, 24; Da 7:14; Jn 6:37, 39
17:3 [d]ver 8, 18, 21, 23, 25; Jn 3:17
17:4 [e]Jn 13:31 [f]Jn 4:34
17:5 [g]Php 2:6 [h]Jn 1:2
17:6 [i]ver 26 [j]ver 2; Jn 6:37, 39
17:8 [k]ver 14, 26 [l]Jn 16:27 [m]ver 3, 18, 21, 23, 25; Jn 3:17
17:9 [n]Lk 22:32

[a] 6 Greek *your name*

16:31–33 Verse 33 records Jesus' final words to his disciples before his arrest. Jesus supplies comfort and reassurance. His exhortation is for their benefit since the days to come will be difficult for each of them. The solution is "courage" (16:33b; NIV "take heart!"). Despite the circumstances, the victory of Jesus ("I have overcome the world") outweighs the jeopardy of the present crisis.

16:4b–33 As we look at the work of the Spirit today, we see that not only does the Spirit recall, authenticate, and enliven the teaching of Jesus for each generation, but *also* the Spirit works creatively in the church, bringing a new prophetic word. This word never contradicts the historical word of Jesus and never deflects glory away from Jesus, but it may faithfully bring the church to see its message and mission in a new way. To restrict the Spirit's voice to the work of historical recitation—that is, to the application of the biblical text—is to restrict the Spirit's effort to speak to contemporary issues. The Spirit both equips those who guide the church into the deeper meaning of Scripture (teachers) and those who have a contemporary word for the church in its world today (prophets).

The great departure of the Christian faith from every other religious faith is that it does not simply set out an ideal or a moral code; it offers a means of achieving it. It is the offer of God to live in his followers and achieve in them the victory demonstrated in his Son Jesus Christ. And in that indwelling of the Spirit, an indescribable peace will be ours no matter what is happening in the world around us.

17:1–2 This section of the prayer finds Jesus talking to his Father about his efforts on earth to glorify him and to be obedient to his will. Now, with the work of the incarnation complete, Jesus anticipates his return to the glory he had before creation.

Addressing God as "Father" was a hallmark of Jesus' spirituality. For Jesus, the cross is not a place of shame but a place of honor. His oneness with the Father means that as he is glorified, so too is the Father glorified.

17:3 Eternal life comes through knowing God. The Hebrew notion of *knowing* encompasses experience and intimacy. For Christians, this means obedience to and love for God. Moreover, such knowledge *must include* a commitment to Jesus Christ, God's Son.

17:4–5 The first accomplishment of the incarnation was Jesus' display of God's glory for the world. Now Jesus says that he has accomplished this task God has given him to do. But does Jesus say that he is *finished* at this point in his life? No, because his work includes his death, resurrection, and return to the Father.

17:6 What has Jesus finished? Jesus has revealed God's "name" (v. 6, see NIV footnote). Throughout the Gospel, Jesus refers to his work as empowered by God's name. Jesus bears the name of God. Thus, in revealing himself, he has disclosed God's personhood (his name) to the entire world.

17:7–8 Those who have faith have truly understood what was happening in this divine revelation. They know that Jesus has come from God and his words are divine. Jesus' disciples can be described as followers who belonged to God—a remnant whom God delivered to Jesus.

17:9 The thought of this leads Jesus to pray for them specifically. They are precious because they

mine.[o] And glory has come to me
through them. 11I will remain in the
world no longer, but they are still
in the world,[p] and I am coming to
you.[q] Holy Father, protect them by
the power of[a] your name, the name
you gave me, so that they may be
one[r] as we are one.[s] 12While I was
with them, I protected them and
kept them safe by[b] that name you
gave me. None has been lost[t] except
the one doomed to destruction[u] so
that Scripture would be fulfilled.

13"I am coming to you now, but I
say these things while I am still in
the world, so that they may have
the full measure of my joy[v] within
them. 14I have given them your word
and the world has hated them,[w] for
they are not of the world any more
than I am of the world.[x] 15My prayer
is not that you take them out of the
world but that you protect them
from the evil one.[y] 16They are not
of the world, even as I am not of
it.[z] 17Sanctify them by[c] the truth;
your word is truth.[a] 18As you sent
me into the world,[b] I have sent them
into the world.[c] 19For them I sanctify
myself, that they too may be truly
sanctified.

17:10 [o] Jn 16:15
17:11 [p] Jn 13:1 [q] Jn 7:33 [r] ver 21-23 [s] Jn 10:30
17:12 [t] Jn 6:39 [u] Jn 6:70
17:13 [v] Jn 3:29
17:14 [w] Jn 15:19 [x] Jn 8:23
17:15 [y] Mt 5:37
17:16 [z] ver 14
17:17 [a] Jn 15:3
17:18 [b] ver 3, 8, 21, 23, 25 [c] Jn 20:21
17:21 [d] Jn 10:38 [e] ver 3, 8, 18, 23, 25; Jn 3:17

Jn 17:22-23 ❖ How well have Christ's followers done at demonstrating the unity he prayed for? How can we do better?

Jesus Prays for All Believers

20"My prayer is not for them
alone. I pray also for those who will
believe in me through their message, 21that all of them may be one,
Father, just as you are in me and I
am in you.[d] May they also be in us so
that the world may believe that you
have sent me.[e] 22I have given them

[a] 11 Or *Father, keep them faithful to* [b] 12 Or *kept them faithful to* [c] 17 Or *them to live in accordance with*

---

belong to the Father. The failure to read these verses in the wider context of John's theology has led many to misrepresent them. God loves the world and entered the world in his Son for the sake of the world. Now Jesus' work in the world is near completion, and he is praying exclusively for his immediate followers who will be left behind as he departs. Like a shepherd about to lay down his life for his sheep, he prays for his flock whom he has led and who now must persevere in the wilderness.

17:10 Note the similarity between Jesus' prayer in v. 10 and that in v. 1. God is glorified through his Son, and the Son is glorified through his disciples. Therefore, those features of Jesus' life that brought glory to God may likewise be the characteristics of discipleship that bring glory to Jesus. When a disciple's life bears fruit, God himself is glorified directly.

17:11-12 Jesus' first petition for his followers is that they remain united. Remarkably he desires that his disciples enjoy a oneness that is like the oneness he shares with the Father.

His disciples, however, remain in the world. This is an environment of hostility. The mission of the church is to challenge this world, drawing closer to those who love the truth and bringing them into the flock.

17:13-15 Jesus' next point concerns his disciples' strength in the world. Their assignment is dangerous, and so he prays for their protection. Jesus has given them his word; the Spirit will recall it and keep it secure. This divine revelation will become essential equipment in their survival.

Jesus also prays for their protection. He recognizes the power of evil, for he lost one of his disciples to Satan. He understands that representing God in this world is an invitation to genuine battle. His disciples must contend with these powers since they remain in this world. God's "name" will be a refuge.

17:16 Jesus' next concern has to do with holiness. The disciples live in the world, and yet Jesus can say that they are not "of the world" (vv. 14, 16). This points not to their location geographically but to their position spiritually.

17:17-18 Jesus prays that his disciples might be "sanctified" in the truth. This word refers to something made holy ("set apart"). To be holy is not a description of perfection (though this is included). It refers to a life that is so aligned with God that it reflects God's passions completely.

Jesus was "set apart" for a divine mission. The disciples also have a mission like Jesus. Their purpose for living is shaped by the mission God has for them.

17:19 When Jesus says that he *sanctifies* himself, what does he mean? Jesus is recommitting himself to the mission assigned by the Father. This priestly mission of service involves his sacrifice. Through his death on the cross, the disciples will experience something never known before. His death will enable them to experience a new holiness in a deep attachment with God.

17:20-21 Jesus next turns to pray for followers whom he has not yet met, which includes believers all throughout time and in the church today. He first prays that they will have a unity like that of his first disciples. This unity must be visibly based on love. When the world sees them, it will know they represent Jesus. This love is an outgrowth of the union Christians will enjoy with Jesus himself, a union modeled on the oneness of the Father and the Son.

17:22-24 Jesus was the bearer of God's glory, and now the church bears that glory. The thought is of the glory of God passing to Jesus' followers,

the glory that you gave me, that they may be one as we are one[f]— 23 I in them and you in me—so that they may be brought to complete unity. Then the world will know that you sent me[g] and have loved them[h] even as you have loved me.

24 "Father, I want those you have given me to be with me where I am,[i] and to see my glory,[j] the glory you have given me because you loved me before the creation of the world.[k]

25 "Righteous Father, though the world does not know you,[l] I know you, and they know that you have sent me.[m] 26 I have made you[a] known to them,[n] and will continue to make you known in order that the love you have for me may be in them[o] and that I myself may be in them."

Jesus Arrested

18:3–11pp // Mt 26:47–56; Mk 14:43–50; Lk 22:47–53

18 When he had finished praying, Jesus left with his disciples and crossed the Kidron Valley.[p] On the other side there was a garden,[q] and he and his disciples went into it.[r]

2 Now Judas, who betrayed him, knew the place, because Jesus had often met there with his disciples.[s] 3 So Judas came to the garden, guiding[t] a detachment of soldiers and some officials from the chief priests and the Pharisees.[u] They were carrying torches, lanterns and weapons.

4 Jesus, knowing all that was going to happen to him,[v] went out and asked them, "Who is it you want?"[w]

5 "Jesus of Nazareth," they replied.

"I am he," Jesus said. (And Judas the traitor was standing there with them.) 6 When Jesus said, "I am he," they drew back and fell to the ground.

7 Again he asked them, "Who is it you want?"[x]

"Jesus of Nazareth," they said.

8 Jesus answered, "I told you that I am he. If you are looking for me, then let these men go." 9 This happened so that the words he had spoken would be fulfilled: "I have not lost one of those you gave me."[b][y]

10 Then Simon Peter, who had a sword, drew it and struck the high priest's servant, cutting off his right ear. (The servant's name was Malchus.)

11 Jesus commanded Peter, "Put your sword away! Shall I not drink the cup[z] the Father has given me?"

17:22 [f] Jn 14:20
17:23 [g] Jn 3:17 [h] Jn 16:27
17:24 [i] Jn 12:26 [j] Jn 1:14 [k] ver 5; Mt 25:34
17:25 [l] Jn 15:21; 16:3 [m] ver 3, 8, 18, 21, 23; Jn 3:17; 7:29; 16:27
17:26 [n] ver 6 [o] Jn 15:9
18:1 [p] 2Sa 15:23 [q] ver 26 [r] Mt 26:36
18:2 [s] Lk 21:37; 22:39
18:3 [t] Ac 1:16 [u] ver 12
18:4 [v] Jn 6:64; 13:1, 11 [w] ver 7
18:7 [x] ver 4
18:9 [y] Jn 17:12
18:11 [z] Mt 20:22

[a] 26 Greek *your name* [b] 9 John 6:39

---

indwelling them. The confidence of the church's mission rests here: If it lives in the Spirit, if it reflects God's glory and love, if it demonstrates unity, then its testimony will astonish the world. Jesus prays that his followers will see the true glory that has existed in heaven since the beginning of time.

17:25–26 This anticipated glory, however, finds its counterpoint in the prayer's last sentences. Jesus addresses God as "righteous Father" (v. 25), reminding us that it is God's righteousness that has led to his justified judgment of the world. Yet all those who accept the Son will experience the love known only between Father and Son. These are the last words Jesus prays before his arrest: "that I myself may be in them" (v. 26). His last desire is to love his followers and indwell them.

17:1–26 We should see ourselves as the subjects of this prayer. Jesus is *our* Lord and Shepherd as much as he was the shepherd of this small circle of men. Therefore, when he prays he invites us to listen, to hear the quality of the love and honor shared between himself and God. He invites us to listen as he prays for all believers throughout time. We are the church, the body of believers built on the apostles' word.

18:1 Jesus leads his disciples out of the city to an olive grove, which grew along the west shoulder of the Mount of Olives.

18:2–3 A Roman "detachment" was large enough to warrant bringing along their commander and to be equipped with weapons. During festival seasons the Romans were aware of the explosive atmosphere in the city, and reinforcements routinely came to Jerusalem. At the beginning of the Passion story, then, we have a signal of Roman interest in Jesus and a hint that Pilate may already be participating. The presence of chief priests and Pharisees recalls their appearances elsewhere in the Gospel. The entire world—both Jew and Gentile—has come together against Jesus.

18:4–7 Jesus' foreknowledge gives him the ability to see the arrest before it unfolds. He steps forward and asks the first question: "Who is it you want?" (v. 4). The answer is surprising: "Jesus of Nazareth" (v. 5). Jesus then uses the "I am" formula we have seen elsewhere in the Gospel, which no doubt recalls God's divine name (v. 6).

Jesus' words provoke a response that even those who hear it likely do not understand. This is the biblical response of holy fear before the Lord, and the only response is to fall prostrate.

18:8–9 Jesus protects his followers from capture and so fulfills what he said in 17:12: He has lost not one of those whom God has given to him.

18:10–11 Peter's clumsy use of the sword he brought shows something of the chaos of the scene. We

12Then the detachment of soldiers
with its commander and the Jewish officials[a] arrested Jesus. They bound him
13and brought him first to Annas, who
was the father-in-law of Caiaphas,[b] the
high priest that year. 14Caiaphas was the
one who had advised the Jewish leaders
that it would be good if one man died
for the people.[c]

Peter's First Denial

18:16–18pp // Mt 26:69,70; Mk 14:66–68; Lk 22:55–57

15Simon Peter and another disciple
were following Jesus. Because this disciple was known to the high priest,[d] he
went with Jesus into the high priest's
courtyard,[e] 16but Peter had to wait outside at the door. The other disciple, who
was known to the high priest, came back,
spoke to the servant girl on duty there
and brought Peter in.
17"You aren't one of this man's disciples too, are you?" she asked Peter.
He replied, "I am not."[f]
18It was cold, and the servants and officials stood around a fire[g] they had made
to keep warm. Peter also was standing
with them, warming himself.[h]

The High Priest Questions Jesus

18:19–24pp // Mt 26:59–68; Mk 14:55–65; Lk 22:63–71

19Meanwhile, the high priest questioned Jesus about his disciples and his
teaching.

18:12 [a] ver 3
18:13 [b] ver 24; Mt 26:3
18:14 [c] Jn 11:49-51
18:15 [d] Mt 26:3 [e] Mt 26:58; Mk 14:54; Lk 22:54
18:17 [f] ver 25
18:18 [g] Jn 21:9 [h] Mk 14:54,67
18:20 [i] Mt 4:23 [j] Mt 26:55 [k] Jn 7:26
18:22 [l] ver 3 [m] Mt 16:21; Jn 19:3
18:23 [n] Mt 5:39; Ac 23:2-5
18:24 [o] ver 13; Mt 26:3
18:25 [p] ver 18 [q] ver 17
18:26 [r] ver 10 [s] ver 1
18:27 [t] Jn 13:38

Jn 18:25–27 ❖ How can we keep from denying Christ in our lives, even when we are under pressure or afraid?

20"I have spoken openly to the world,"
Jesus replied. "I always taught in synagogues[i] or at the temple,[j] where all the
Jews come together. I said nothing in
secret.[k] 21Why question me? Ask those
who heard me. Surely they know what
I said."
22When Jesus said this, one of the officials[l] nearby slapped him in the face.[m] "Is
this the way you answer the high priest?"
he demanded.
23"If I said something wrong," Jesus
replied, "testify as to what is wrong. But
if I spoke the truth, why did you strike
me?"[n] 24Then Annas sent him bound to
Caiaphas[o] the high priest.

Peter's Second and Third Denials

18:25–27pp // Mt 26:71–75; Mk 14:69–72; Lk 22:58–62

25Meanwhile, Simon Peter was still
standing there warming himself.[p] So
they asked him, "You aren't one of his
disciples too, are you?"
He denied it, saying, "I am not."[q]
26One of the high priest's servants, a
relative of the man whose ear Peter had
cut off,[r] challenged him, "Didn't I see you
with him in the garden?"[s] 27Again Peter
denied it, and at that moment a rooster
began to crow.[t]

---

know nothing more of the priest's slave except that both John and Luke tell us that he loses his right ear. Luke closes the scene with Jesus' healing of the man's ear.

18:12–14 Under full armed arrest, Jesus is sent first to Annas. This is plausible if he is the de facto power behind Caiaphas. This meeting may have been arranged in advance if Caiaphas is seeking to broaden his base of support among the Romans. Verses 19–24 represent the essence of Annas's questioning.

18:15–18 Each of the four Gospels records Peter's denials of Jesus during his interrogation by the Jewish authorities. Peter is accompanied by "another disciple" who remains unnamed (v. 15). Is this the Beloved Disciple? Throughout the Gospel, the Beloved Disciple frequently appears alongside Peter. His presence at the arrest shows the profound loyalty to Jesus characteristic of him throughout the Gospel.

Peter feels his vulnerability because the small courtyard also hosts officers and other servants. Some of them may even remember that he attacked Malchus. Peter refuses to acknowledge his discipleship.

18:19–23 John shifts the scene to what is transpiring inside. The words recorded here no doubt represent the barest summary of Jesus' meeting with Annas, who probes two things: Jesus' teachings and his disciples. Jesus' sharp answer unmasks the priest's attempt to make Jesus incriminate himself. Jesus is demanding a trial, which the guards interpret as insolence (v. 22).

Note that Jesus here simply points to the truth (v. 23). There are no witnesses accusing him. If Jesus is going to be prosecuted by Pilate, as the leaders have planned, it will be necessary to have the support of the Sanhedrin, Jerusalem's high judicial council.

18:24–27 A major meeting of the Sanhedrin takes place under the direction of Caiaphas that evening. While Jesus is with Caiaphas, John reports Peter's ongoing failings as a witness in the courtyard. A relative of Malchus, the man whom Peter attacked, speaks up. When Peter denies Jesus the third time, a rooster crows, recalling Jesus' prediction of Peter's great failure.

PEOPLE TO KNOW // PONTIUS PILATE

JOHN 18:28-40: Pontius Pilate was the governor of Judea at the time of Jesus' arrest. While there was no love lost between him and the Jewish leaders in power at the time, they brought Jesus before Pilate because they did not have the authority to sentence him to death (Jn 18:31).

The Jewish leaders accused Jesus of opposing paying taxes to Caesar and of stirring up the people with his teaching. When Pilate learned Jesus was from Galilee, he sent him to Herod Antipas, who had jurisdiction over that territory (Lk 23:7). Herod quickly sent Jesus back, disappointed that Jesus did not perform any great sign for him (Lk 23:8-11).

Pilate questioned Jesus about the charge that Jesus claimed to be the king of the Jews. Jesus said his kingdom was not of this world and that those on the side of truth would listen to him. Pilate retorted with his famous response, "What is truth?" (Jn 18:38).

Pilate's wife had warned him because of a dream not to have anything to do with Jesus (Mt 27:19). And Pilate himself found no basis for charging Jesus. The people, however, pressed Pilate to sentence Jesus to death. Hoping to still free Jesus as a man guilty of no crime, Pilate offered to free either Jesus or the known criminal, Barabbas. The people called for Barabas to be released and for Jesus to be crucified. Finally, Pilate handed Jesus over to be flogged and crucified. In so doing, he washed his hands in front of the crowd and said, "I am innocent of this man's blood" (Mt 27:24).

APPLICATION The pressure of the crowd pushed Pilate to disregard what he knew was true: that Jesus was innocent. Enough pressure from others can lead most of us to compromise what we know is right. God calls us to stand firm, however, and not to conform to the pattern of those around us (Ro 12:2). Christ died as the atoning sacrifice for the sins of the world (1Jn 2:2). It's incredible that God can accomplish his will in spite of human failure. God used Pilate and his mistakes to accomplish his plan to redeem the world through Jesus' death and resurrection.

Jesus Before Pilate

18:29–40pp // Mt 27:11–18,20–23;
Mk 15:2–15; Lk 23:2,3,18–25

28Then the Jewish leaders took Jesus
from Caiaphas to the palace of the Roman governor.[u] By now it was early
morning, and to avoid ceremonial uncleanness they did not enter the palace,[v]
because they wanted to be able to eat
the Passover.[w] 29So Pilate came out to
them and asked, "What charges are you
bringing against this man?"

30"If he were not a criminal," they replied, "we would not have handed him
over to you."

31Pilate said, "Take him yourselves and
judge him by your own law."

"But we have no right to execute anyone," they objected. 32This took place to
fulfill what Jesus had said about the kind
of death he was going to die.[x]

33Pilate then went back inside the palace,[y] summoned Jesus and asked him,
"Are you the king of the Jews?"[z]

18:28 [u] Mt 27:2; Mk 15:1; Lk 23:1 [v] ver 33; Jn 19:9 [w] Jn 11:55
18:32 [x] Mt 20:19; 26:2; Jn 3:14; 8:28; 12:32,33
18:33 [y] ver 28, 29; Jn 19:9 [z] Lk 23:3; Mt 2:2

18:28-40 Even though the Sanhedrin was Israel's highest judicial court, it did not have the power of capital punishment. Therefore, it had to enlist the involvement of the Roman governor.

Jewish and Hellenistic sources tell us a great deal about Pilate, most of which is extremely critical. He was a brutal ruler whose atrocities against the Jews were legendary. He controlled Judea harshly, with an eye on impressing his superiors in Rome.
18:28-32 Early in the morning, the Jewish leadership brought Jesus to Pilate's residence. Two historical notes are important. First, they do not enter Pilate's quarters because they do not want to become ritually unclean. This Jewish concern makes Pilate move in and out of the building throughout the story. Second, the stated reason in v. 28 for remaining clean was the Passover. They were concerned not with the Passover meal of the night before, but with the many meals and celebrations that week in the Passover season.

The irony of the scene is that the leaders, concerned about their religious purity, now plot Jesus' death while claiming that *he* is an evildoer. Such a charge would be meaningless to Pilate, who no doubt viewed this as an exclusively Jewish squabble.
18:33 If a crime might threaten the interests of the empire, the governor was held personally responsible. Thus Pilate's first question to Jesus, "Are you the king of the Jews?" is loaded with political undertones. Is Jesus one more Jewish terrorist-revolutionary with a head full of messianic notions and a band of well-armed followers?

34"Is that your own idea," Jesus asked,
"or did others talk to you about me?"
35"Am I a Jew?" Pilate replied. "Your
own people and chief priests handed you
over to me. What is it you have done?"
36Jesus said, "My kingdom[a] is not of
this world. If it were, my servants would
fight to prevent my arrest by the Jewish
leaders.[b] But now my kingdom is from
another place."[c]
37"You are a king, then!" said Pilate.
Jesus answered, "You say that I am a
king. In fact, the reason I was born and
came into the world is to testify to the
truth.[d] Everyone on the side of truth listens to me."[e]
38"What is truth?" retorted Pilate. With
this he went out again to the Jews gathered there and said, "I find no basis for a
charge against him.[f] 39But it is your custom for me to release to you one prisoner
at the time of the Passover. Do you want
me to release 'the king of the Jews'?"
40They shouted back, "No, not him!
Give us Barabbas!" Now Barabbas had
taken part in an uprising.[g]

18:36 [a] Mt 3:2 [b] Mt 26:53 [c] Lk 17:21; Jn 6:15
18:37 [d] Jn 3:32 [e] Jn 8:47; 1Jn 4:6
18:38 [f] Lk 23:4; Jn 19:4, 6
18:40 [g] Ac 3:14
19:1 [h] Dt 25:3; Isa 50:6; 53:5; Mt 27:26
19:3 [i] Mt 27:29 [j] Jn 18:22
19:4 [k] Jn 18:38 [l] ver 6; Lk 23:4
19:5 [m] ver 2
19:6 [n] Ac 3:13 [o] ver 4; Lk 23:4
19:7 [p] Lev 24:16 [q] Mt 26:63-66; Jn 5:18; 10:33

Jesus Sentenced to Be Crucified

19:1–16pp // Mt 27:27–31; Mk 15:16–20

19 Then Pilate took Jesus and had him
flogged.[h] 2The soldiers twisted together a crown of thorns and put it on his
head. They clothed him in a purple robe
3and went up to him again and again,
saying, "Hail, king of the Jews!"[i] And they
slapped him in the face.[j]
4Once more Pilate came out and said
to the Jews gathered there, "Look, I am
bringing him out[k] to you to let you know
that I find no basis for a charge against
him."[l] 5When Jesus came out wearing the
crown of thorns and the purple robe,[m]
Pilate said to them, "Here is the man!"
6As soon as the chief priests and their
officials saw him, they shouted, "Crucify! Crucify!"
But Pilate answered, "You take him
and crucify him.[n] As for me, I find no
basis for a charge against him."[o]
7The Jewish leaders insisted, "We have
a law, and according to that law he must
die,[p] because he claimed to be the Son
of God."[q]

18:34–35 Jesus does not answer directly but probes the source of Pilate's question. What sort of king does Pilate mean? Is this *his* question—and if so, what does he mean by it? Pilate is already being forced to make a judgment, to evaluate Jesus. But Pilate recoils, asking incredulously if Jesus really thinks he would have any interest in matters related to Jewish theological squabbles. Nevertheless, if kingship is at issue, Pilate must uncover what sort of kingship it is.

18:36–37 Jesus provides a definition of his kingship. The true test of his kingdom can be seen in the behavior of his disciples. They will not engage in combat or struggle against Rome's rule. He is no threat to Rome.

A good paraphrase of v. 37a might be: "So you're telling me that you are indeed some kind of king?" Having said what his kingdom is *not*, Jesus can now say what it is—a kingdom of truth.

18:38 Jesus' revelation that he is working for the truth serves as an invitation for Pilate to join him. For Pilate to condemn Jesus is for him to condemn the truth. Jesus has thus reversed positions with Pilate. Now Pilate has been challenged and carries the burden of response. But his cynical question, "What is truth?" reveals his true position—that he cannot recognize the things of God and will avoid the light.

When Pilate returns to the Sanhedrin's representatives, he announces Jesus' innocence. Having given this verdict (which is repeated two more times in 19:4, 6), the deeper question for Pilate is whether he will act on the truth he *has* seen.

18:39–40 Pilate appeals to a tradition of Passover amnesty. John says that it was a valued Jewish custom, thus placing the outcome of the amnesty entirely in the Sanhedrin's hands.

The deepest irony of all comes when Pilate refers to Jesus as "the king of the Jews." It is difficult to interpret his motive. He clearly wants to have Jesus released. By using this title, he is classifying it as something that is meaningless to Rome. But John and his readers can see it as a true identification of who Jesus is.

The scene closes with the crowd calling for the release of Barabbas (v. 40), a man who *is* a genuine threat to Rome. Jesus, by contrast, a man in whom there is no danger of violence and whose followers will not fight, remains in custody.

19:1–3 Roman law recognized three types of flogging, each representing ascending levels of severity. Pilate chooses to the lowest form, not only to teach Jesus to be more prudent in the future but to satisfy the crowds who are demanding his death.

Since the task of flogging generally belonged to soldiers, the same soldiers also begin to mock Jesus and hurt him. The mock crown may have been a woven circular crown of twigs and thorns, pressed down into the skin to inflict pain. The robe is likely a soldier's robe thrown on him, completing the picture of mock royalty. With Jesus in this costume, the soldiers jeer at and strike him.

19:4–5 When Pilate escorts Jesus outside, his clear intention is to display Jesus in cruel submission, bearing the marks of his punishment, and to release him. But rather than being satisfied with Pilate's brutality or pitying Jesus, the leaders call for his crucifixion. In disgust, Pilate calls back to them; he is trying to avoid responsibility for the death of an innocent man.

19:6–8 Pilate is unnerved. There is something about this inquiry he does not like. While Pilate may not possess spiritual insight, he undoubtedly is highly superstitious. The idea that gods could

8 When Pilate heard this, he was even
more afraid, 9 and he went back inside
the palace.[r] "Where do you come from?"
he asked Jesus, but Jesus gave him no
answer.[s] 10 "Do you refuse to speak to
me?" Pilate said. "Don't you realize I
have power either to free you or to crucify you?"

11 Jesus answered, "You would have
no power over me if it were not given
to you from above.[t] Therefore the one
who handed me over to you[u] is guilty
of a greater sin."

12 From then on, Pilate tried to set Jesus
free, but the Jewish leaders kept shouting, "If you let this man go, you are no
friend of Caesar. Anyone who claims to
be a king[v] opposes Caesar."

13 When Pilate heard this, he brought
Jesus out and sat down on the judge's
seat[w] at a place known as the Stone Pavement (which in Aramaic[x] is Gabbatha).
14 It was the day of Preparation[y] of the
Passover; it was about noon.[z]

"Here is your king,"[a] Pilate said to the
Jews.

15 But they shouted, "Take him away!
Take him away! Crucify him!"

"Shall I crucify your king?" Pilate
asked.

"We have no king but Caesar," the chief
priests answered.

16 Finally Pilate handed him over to
them to be crucified.[b]

The Crucifixion of Jesus

19:17–24pp // Mt 27:33–44; Mk 15:22–32; Lk 23:33–43

So the soldiers took charge of Jesus.
17 Carrying his own cross,[c] he went out to
the place of the Skull[d] (which in Aramaic[e]
is called Golgotha). 18 There they crucified
him, and with him two others[f] — one on
each side and Jesus in the middle.

19 Pilate had a notice prepared and fastened to the cross. It read: JESUS OF NAZ-
ARETH,[g] THE KING OF THE JEWS.[h] 20 Many
of the Jews read this sign, for the place

19:9 [r] Jn 18:33 [s] Mk 14:61
19:11 [t] Ro 13:1 [u] Jn 18:28-30; Ac 3:13
19:12 [v] Lk 23:2
19:13 [w] Mt 27:19 [x] Jn 5:2
19:14 [y] Mt 27:62 [z] Mk 15:25
[a] ver 19,21
19:16 [b] Mt 27:26; Mk 15:15; Lk 23:25
19:17 [c] Ge 22:6; Lk 14:27; 23:26 [d] Lk 23:33 [e] Jn 5:2
19:18 [f] Lk 23:32
19:19 [g] Mk 1:24 [h] ver 14,21

---

appear in the world was not uncommon in his religious tradition.

19:9–11 When Pilate escorts Jesus back into his praetorium (v. 9), his first question is terse, and it follows naturally from his worries in v. 8. This is not a question about Jesus' birthplace; it lies deeper. But Jesus supplies no answer, knowing that to fit himself into Pilate's religious thought process would be useless.

Jesus and Pilate talk "past" each other, responding to ideas on utterly different planes. Of course, Pilate has the power to crucify Jesus. But Pilate is *powerless* before God's plan in this hour.

19:12 The verb in v. 12 is imperfect, meaning ongoing action ("Pilate *kept trying* to free Jesus"), but it is fruitless. Suddenly the Jewish leaders use the one bit of leverage they still have on this governor. They shout, "If you let this man go, you are no friend of Caesar."

19:13–16a From this point, things proceed swiftly. Pilate returns to the porch outside with Jesus, where he occupies the governor's judgment seat and prepares to render a decision. Pilate is now positioned to speak with the voice of his office.

The closing scene is filled with Pilate's sarcasm. "Here is your king" (v. 14b) echoes "here is the man" (v. 5), and Pilate now offers to crucify this royal Jewish monarch. They crowd's cry in v. 15 is a direct contradiction of the injunction of the Bible that God alone is Israel's king. By rejecting Jesus, they have rejected God himself, as Jesus predicted.

✣ **18:1—19:16a** John's Passion story is like a symphony, which seems to pursue one theme: the sorrow of Jesus' departure, his rejection by many, the dismay of the disciples, the betrayal of Judas, the denials of Peter, and Jesus' imminent death. Each of these are a part of the "hour" that beats its way through virtually every chapter of John's Gospel.

This scene, this hour, does not belong to Pilate or Caiaphas, *it belongs to Jesus*. Jesus is in complete control of the situation. John's statement in v. 16a should be read in full realization of that deep truth.

19:16b–17 When Jesus is led away from the praetorium, he is bleeding profusely and is likely in shock. Nevertheless the Roman tradition for crucifixion was that, under Roman guard, the victim had to bear his own cross to the site of death. The crossbeam was placed over the neck, like a yoke, while the person's arms were pulled back and hooked around it.

19:18 John keeps the story to a bare minimum. The route of Jesus' walk would have taken him from the praetorium of Pilate to a location outside the city walls. People passing by would have seen the spectacle. Some would have spoken to Jesus or jeered at him. Public executions were designed to shock and warn the populace to stay in line, but no doubt John sees another meaning here: Jesus is being lifted up so that now Israel can see its king.

The victim was laid on the ground with his arms stretched across the beam. After he was either nailed or tied, he was hoisted up and mounted on a vertical post. Romans nailed the ankles together, forcing the feet to lay sideways on top of one another. Nailing was not the means of death on the cross. Many factors, such as hemorrhaging, asphyxia, and shock played a role.

Each of the Gospels says that Jesus was crucified with "bandits." This word can also be translated "terrorists." Jesus' position between them may refer to a place of prominence or it may echo Ps 22:16.

19:19–22 It was customary for the Romans to provide a written notice of the crucified criminal's

where Jesus was crucified was near the
city,[i] and the sign was written in Aramaic,
Latin and Greek. 21The chief priests of the
Jews protested to Pilate, "Do not write
'The King of the Jews,' but that this man
claimed to be king of the Jews."[j]
22Pilate answered, "What I have written, I have written."
23When the soldiers crucified Jesus,
they took his clothes, dividing them into
four shares, one for each of them, with
the undergarment remaining. This garment was seamless, woven in one piece
from top to bottom.
24"Let's not tear it," they said to one another. "Let's decide by lot who will get it."
This happened that the scripture
might be fulfilled[k] that said,

"They divided my clothes among
them
and cast lots for my garment."[a][l]

So this is what the soldiers did.
25Near the cross[m] of Jesus stood his
mother,[n] his mother's sister, Mary the
wife of Clopas, and Mary Magdalene.[o]
26When Jesus saw his mother[p] there, and
the disciple whom he loved[q] standing
nearby, he said to her, "Woman,[b] here
is your son," 27and to the disciple, "Here
is your mother." From that time on, this
disciple took her into his home.

The Death of Jesus

19:29,30pp // Mt 27:48,50; Mk 15:36,37; Lk 23:36

28Later, knowing that everything had
now been finished,[r] and so that Scrip-

> **Jn 19:26-27** ❖ How does Jesus show his heart for people who are vulnerable? What are ways we can demonstrate this same heart for those around us?

ture would be fulfilled,[s] Jesus said, "I
am thirsty." 29A jar of wine vinegar[t] was
there, so they soaked a sponge in it, put
the sponge on a stalk of the hyssop plant,
and lifted it to Jesus' lips. 30When he
had received the drink, Jesus said, "It is
finished."[u] With that, he bowed his head
and gave up his spirit.
31Now it was the day of Preparation,[v]
and the next day was to be a special Sabbath. Because the Jewish leaders did not
want the bodies left on the crosses[w]
during the Sabbath, they asked Pilate
to have the legs broken and the bodies taken down. 32The soldiers therefore came and broke the legs of the first
man who had been crucified with Jesus,
and then those of the other.[x] 33But when
they came to Jesus and found that he
was already dead, they did not break
his legs. 34Instead, one of the soldiers
pierced[y] Jesus' side with a spear, bringing a sudden flow of blood and water.[z]
35The man who saw it[a] has given testimony, and his testimony is true.[b] He knows
that he tells the truth, and he testifies so
that you also may believe. 36These things
happened so that the scripture would be
fulfilled:[c] "Not one of his bones will be

a 24 Psalm 22:18 *b* 26 The Greek for *Woman* does not denote any disrespect.

19:20 [i] Heb 13:12
19:21 [j] ver 14
19:24 [k] ver 28, 36,37; Mt 1:22 [l] Ps 22:18
19:25 [m] Mt 27:55, 56; Mk 15:40, 41; Lk 23:49 [n] Mt 12:46 [o] Lk 24:18
19:26 [p] Mt 12:46 [q] Jn 13:23
19:28 [r] ver 30; Jn 13:1 [s] ver 24,36,37
19:29 [t] Ps 69:21
19:30 [u] Lk 12:50; Jn 17:4
19:31 [v] ver 14, 42 [w] Dt 21:23; Jos 8:29; 10:26,27
19:32 [x] ver 18
19:34 [y] Zec 12:10 [z] 1Jn 5:6,8
19:35 [a] Lk 24:48 [b] Jn 15:27; 21:24
19:36 [c] ver 24, 28,37; Mt 1:22

name and activity. John is the only writer who notes that it came by Pilate's order.

It comes as no surprise that the chief priests understand that the sign implies a kind of sarcastic endorsement of Jesus' royal identity. They do not like it. Pilate, for the first time in the story, stands up to them.

19:23-24 Roman guards take Jesus' "clothes" and divide them into four parts. They gamble for the one-piece undergarment, a fulfillment of Ps 22:18.

19:25-27 John records several people at the foot of the cross. Jesus calls the Beloved Disciple to take Mary into his family, and he does this obediently.

19:28-29 Jesus' second statement on the cross is a cry of thirst, which John alone records. The next action fulfills Ps 69:21, "They . . . gave me vinegar for my thirst." The soldiers provide him with diluted wine drunk by soldiers and peasants. We must not confuse this drink with the offer of wine mixed with narcotic substances that Jesus refused earlier. The detail of hyssop is important here since the plant was used at the Passover to brush lamb's blood on the lintels and doorposts of Israelite homes.

19:30 What Jesus knows about the finality of his work (v. 28) he now utters aloud (v. 30a). Jesus is accomplishing what he intends. He is *not* a victim but a servant doing God's bidding.

19:31-32 John reminds us that it is the "day of Preparation" (v. 31). The Jews wished to remove the bodies from the crosses because of the onset of dusk and the beginning of the Sabbath. We can assume that the same group of Jews who asked for a change to the title on the cross (v. 21) now request that the three men be taken down from their crosses.

19:33-34 The squad of soldiers breaks the legs of the two men next to Jesus (v. 32), but when they come to him, they do not break Jesus' legs since he is already dead. When Jesus' side is pierced, blood and water flow from the wound (v. 34).

19:35-37 John's primary intention is to let his readers know that Jesus is most certainly dead. Theologically this is important for a couple of

broken,"[a][d] 37and, as another scripture
says, "They will look on the one they
have pierced."[b][e]

The Burial of Jesus

19:38–42pp // Mt 27:57–61; Mk 15:42–47;
Lk 23:50–56

38Later, Joseph of Arimathea asked
Pilate for the body of Jesus. Now Joseph
was a disciple of Jesus, but secretly because he feared the Jewish leaders. With
Pilate's permission, he came and took
the body away. 39He was accompanied
by Nicodemus,[f] the man who earlier
had visited Jesus at night. Nicodemus
brought a mixture of myrrh and aloes,
about seventy-five pounds.[c] 40Taking
Jesus' body, the two of them wrapped
it, with the spices, in strips of linen.[g]
This was in accordance with Jewish
burial customs.[h] 41At the place where
Jesus was crucified, there was a garden,
and in the garden a new tomb, in which
no one had ever been laid. 42Because
it was the Jewish day of Preparation[i]
and since the tomb was nearby,[j] they
laid Jesus there.

19:36 [d] Ex 12:46; Nu 9:12; Ps 34:20
19:37 [e] Zec 12:10; Rev 1:7
19:39 [f] Jn 3:1; 7:50
19:40 [g] Lk 24:12; Jn 11:44; 20:5,7
[h] Mt 26:12
19:42 [i] ver 14,31 [j] ver 20,41
20:1 [k] ver 18; Jn 19:25 [l] Mt 27:60,66

The Empty Tomb

20:1–8pp // Mt 28:1–8; Mk 16:1–8;
Lk 24:1–10

20 Early on the first day of the week,
while it was still dark, Mary Magdalene[k] went to the tomb and saw that
the stone had been removed from the
entrance.[l] 2So she came running to Simon

[a] *36* Exodus 12:46; Num. 9:12; Psalm 34:20
[b] *37* Zech. 12:10 [c] *39* Or about 34 kilograms

reasons. John is working to affirm the full humanity of Jesus, whose life was dependent on his flesh. Moreover, already in John's time false teachers were doubting the true incarnation of Christ. It is likely that he may be alluding to this event in 1Jn 5:6–9.

John no doubt sees symbolism that goes beyond the surface meaning of piercing. John may be making the point that the crucified Jesus qualifies as a Passover victim. He notes, for instance, that Jesus' legs are not broken. It was illegal for any Passover sacrifice to have broken bones (Ex 12:46). The lamb had to be a perfect sacrifice.

As John stands at the foot of the cross—an eyewitness to Jesus' remarkable work—he contemplates the symbolism of Israel now gazing at the very messenger, God's Son, sent to redeem the world.

19:38–39 Joseph is one of Jesus' disciples and comes secretly because he fears the Sanhedrin leadership (v. 38). This may be explained by his disagreement with the Sanhedrin's prosecution of Jesus (Lk 23:51). Nicodemus, another member of the Sanhedrin, joins Joseph. They both risk ceremonial uncleanness by touching a dead body, not to mention challenges to their political and religious careers: To place Jesus in a tomb of prestige implies endorsement.

19:40–42 Together these men bury Jesus in a garden tomb near the site of crucifixion "in accordance with Jewish burial customs" (v. 40). In the first century, bodies were prepared for burial by wrapping them tightly with cloth and spices. Nicodemus brings a considerable number of burial spices (v. 39) to this event.

✣ **19:16b–42** The cross of Christ is *the great sign* we have awaited throughout the entire course of this Gospel. In his death, Jesus provides the gift that every other sign promised. The bread of Galilee pointed to heavenly bread, consumed when Jesus gave his flesh for the life of the world. The water of Samaria or Tabernacles is truly the Holy Spirit, which must look toward the hour for distribution. The new temple will only discover its true meaning when Christ has died and been raised to life. Lazarus's story is not that one man in a village is now alive, but that *the man* is present who reigns over death and life. The cross is therefore the great sign, the reality against which every other sign becomes like a shadow.

It was common among the earliest Christians to look at Jesus as a sacrificial lamb, even a Passover lamb, slain for their benefit. We too should reflect on the benefits of his death for our lives. Re-creating this story for people today requires that we must both dramatically relive the Passover story and Jesus' participation in it, and must generate modern stories that help us experience again the meaning of costly sacrifice.

Joseph of Arimathea and Nicodemus are not merely historical figures but symbols. John is setting before us a sterling example of two men who used their considerable resources to glorify Jesus—and who, in so doing, chose to become genuine followers of Christ.

20:1–2 The name "Mary Magdalene" refers to Mary who came from the Galilean village of Magdala. Jesus had expelled numerous demons from her. Along with other women, she followed Jesus to Jerusalem to care for his needs.

On Friday, Jesus' lifeless body had been placed on the burial preparation bench in the receiving room of the tomb chamber. No doubt the women thought they could return following the Sabbath, somehow roll back the stone, and complete the preparation of Jesus' body for burial. Mary's discovery that the tomb door has been rolled to one side suggested immediately to her that someone has entered the tomb.

Mary's report to Peter and "the other disciple" conveys something of her dismay and fear (v. 2). The reference to "they" ("*they* have taken the Lord") likely refers to the temple authorities.

Peter and the other disciple, the one
Jesus loved,[m] and said, “They have tak-
en the Lord out of the tomb, and we don’t
know where they have put him!”[n]
3So Peter and the other disciple started for the tomb.[o] 4Both were running,
but the other disciple outran Peter and
reached the tomb first. 5He bent over
and looked in[p] at the strips of linen[q] lying there but did not go in. 6Then Simon
Peter came along behind him and went
straight into the tomb. He saw the strips
of linen lying there, 7as well as the cloth
that had been wrapped around Jesus’
head.[r] The cloth was still lying in its
place, separate from the linen. 8Final-
ly the other disciple, who had reached
the tomb first,[s] also went inside. He
saw and believed. 9(They still did not
understand from Scripture[t] that Jesus
had to rise from the dead.)[u] 10Then the
disciples went back to where they were
staying.

20:2 [m] Jn 13:23 [n] ver 13
20:3 [o] Lk 24:12
20:5 [p] ver 11 [q] Jn 19:40
20:7 [r] Jn 11:44
20:8 [s] ver 4
20:9 [t] Mt 22:29; Jn 2:22 [u] Lk 24:26,46
20:11 [v] ver 5
20:12 [w] Mt 28:2, 3; Mk 16:5; Lk 24:4; Ac 5:19
20:13 [x] ver 15 [y] ver 2
20:14 [z] Mt 28:9; Mk 16:9 [a] Lk 24:16; Jn 21:4
20:15 [b] ver 13
20:16 [c] Jn 5:2 [d] Mt 23:7

Jesus Appears to Mary Magdalene

11Now Mary stood outside the tomb crying. As she wept, she bent over to look into
the tomb[v] 12and saw two angels in white,[w]
seated where Jesus’ body had been, one at
the head and the other at the foot.
13They asked her, “Woman, why are
you crying?”[x]
“They have taken my Lord away,” she
said, “and I don’t know where they have
put him.”[y] 14At this, she turned around
and saw Jesus standing there,[z] but she
did not realize that it was Jesus.[a]
15He asked her, “Woman, why are you
crying?[b] Who is it you are looking for?”
Thinking he was the gardener, she
said, “Sir, if you have carried him away,
tell me where you have put him, and I
will get him.”
16Jesus said to her, “Mary.”
She turned toward him and cried out
in Aramaic,[c] “Rabboni!”[d] (which means
“Teacher”).

20:3–8 Peter and the Beloved Disciple immediately sprint to the tomb to see what has happened. The Beloved Disciple arrives first. When he sees everything alongside Peter, he “believes” (v. 8). Oddly, the story is silent about the faith of Peter.

John’s description of the scene is not chaotic or confused. Rather, something purposeful has transpired here. If someone had simply stolen Jesus’ body, surely the clothes would be missing, or at least strewn about the floor. But the body is missing, and the clothes appear undisturbed. Jesus’ body has simply left them behind.

20:9–10 The Beloved Disciple has penetrated the deeper meaning of this empty tomb even though he does not yet grasp the larger biblical and theological context in which these things are taking place (v. 9). He believes that Jesus is now alive, but he does not know the scriptural and theological foundation that have made this resurrection inevitable.

20:11–16 John notes how Mary alone experiences

PEOPLE TO KNOW // MARY MAGDALENE

JOHN 20:11–18: Mary Magdalene was one of Jesus’ followers. Luke writes that she had been cured of seven demons, and he lists her among the women who supported Jesus financially (Lk 8:2–3).

Mary was present with several other women disciples at the crucifixion of Jesus, along with John (Jn 19:25–27). She experienced the wrenching trauma of watching Jesus die. She was also at Jesus’ tomb on Easter morning. She found the tomb empty and told Jesus’ disciples, who ran to the tomb and confirmed what she told them.

Upon returning, Mary stayed near the tomb, weeping. Peering into the tomb, she saw two angels seated where Jesus had been laid. Then Jesus himself appeared to her. At first she didn’t recognize him, but her eyes were opened when he called her by name (Jn 20:16). Mary hurried to tell the disciples the good news: “I have seen the Lord!” (Jn 20:18). What a picture of the mutual tenderness and concern that Jesus and Mary Magdalene had for one another, that he would choose to appear to her first after his resurrection.

APPLICATION Mary had a difficult and painful past, but Jesus healed her. Jesus can heal us, too. God’s invitation is for us to be faithful followers of Jesus like Mary was, listening to his words and learning from him. Mary’s last action recorded in the Bible was her greatest: to share with the world the Good News of Jesus’ resurrection. God calls us to share the same Good News with the world today.

17Jesus said, "Do not hold on to me, for
I have not yet ascended to the Father. Go
instead to my brothers[e] and tell them,
'I am ascending to my Father[f] and your
Father, to my God and your God.'"
18Mary Magdalene[g] went to the disciples[h] with the news: "I have seen the
Lord!" And she told them that he had
said these things to her.

Jesus Appears to His Disciples

19On the evening of that first day of
the week, when the disciples were together, with the doors locked for fear of
the Jewish leaders,[i] Jesus came and stood
among them and said, "Peace[j] be with
you!"[k] 20After he said this, he showed
them his hands and side.[l] The disciples
were overjoyed[m] when they saw the Lord.
21Again Jesus said, "Peace be with you![n]
As the Father has sent me,[o] I am sending
you."[p] 22And with that he breathed on
them and said, "Receive the Holy Spirit.[q]
23If you forgive anyone's sins, their sins
are forgiven; if you do not forgive them,
they are not forgiven."[r]

Jesus Appears to Thomas

24Now Thomas[s] (also known as Didymus[a]), one of the Twelve, was not with
the disciples when Jesus came. 25So the
other disciples told him, "We have seen
the Lord!"
But he said to them, "Unless I see the
nail marks in his hands and put my finger where the nails were, and put my
hand into his side,[t] I will not believe."[u]
26A week later his disciples were in the
house again, and Thomas was with them.
Though the doors were locked, Jesus
came and stood among them and said,
"Peace[v] be with you!"[w] 27Then he said to
Thomas, "Put your finger here; see my
hands. Reach out your hand and put it
into my side. Stop doubting and believe."[x]
28Thomas said to him, "My Lord and
my God!"
29Then Jesus told him, "Because
you have seen me, you have believed;[y]
blessed are those who have not seen and
yet have believed."[z]

The Purpose of John's Gospel

30Jesus performed many other signs[a]
in the presence of his disciples, which are

20:17 [e] Mt 28:10 [f] Jn 7:33
20:18 [g] ver 1 [h] Lk 24:10, 22, 23
20:19 [i] Jn 7:13 [j] Jn 14:27 [k] ver 21, 26; Lk 24:36-39
20:20 [l] Lk 24:39, 40; Jn 19:34 [m] Jn 16:20, 22
20:21 [n] ver 19 [o] Jn 3:17 [p] Mt 28:19; Jn 17:18
20:22 [q] Jn 7:39; Ac 2:38; 8:15-17; 19:2; Gal 3:2
20:23 [r] Mt 16:19; 18:18
20:24 [s] Jn 11:16
20:25 [t] ver 20 [u] Mk 16:11
20:26 [v] Jn 14:27 [w] ver 21
20:27 [x] ver 25; Lk 24:40
20:29 [y] Jn 3:15 [z] 1Pe 1:8
20:30 [a] Jn 2:11

Jn 20:21 ❖ Where is Christ sending us? What is he sending us to do?

[a] 24 *Thomas* (Aramaic) and *Didymus* (Greek) both mean *twin.*

---

the first and perhaps most personal moment with the resurrected Jesus.

20:17–18 Jesus tells Mary not to hold him because he has not yet ascended to the Father. He then directs her to go and tell his disciples that he is presently ascending to the Father. Jesus must honor one more promise mentioned throughout his farewell discourse: He will distribute to them the Holy Spirit as his parting gift.

Mary thinks that the resurrection of Jesus means the resumption of normal relations with his disciples. In telling her not to hold on, Jesus is saying that his permanent "return" must come in another form. Jesus' correction is a spiritual redirection away from Jesus' physical presence, a preparation for the Spirit that is about to be given.

The coming of the Spirit is still future (v. 22), and this will be the momentous gift that will return Jesus to them permanently. Therefore, the story with Mary can be seen as an *interpretive vehicle* to stress the transition now underway in Jesus' life and in his relationship with each of his disciples.

20:19–20 It is the evening of this Easter Sunday, and the doors are shut. Fear has gripped the disciples' hearts, and they no doubt conclude that the tragic fate of Jesus may soon be theirs—the temple authorities will find them and arrest them too. But instead Jesus appears in their presence (v. 19). No doubt this appearance is miraculous since John has just told us that the doors were shut tight.

20:21–23 Jesus' words, "Peace be with you," are far more than a greeting. Peace is the gift of his kingdom. Jesus promised that this peace would be his gift to them; now he has delivered it. The disciples' response to his appearance is likewise a fulfillment of what was promised. They are filled with joy.

Jesus was God's special representative (or agent) in the world. Now his disciples become Jesus' agents. To be commissioned as God's agent means being empowered as Jesus was empowered—obtaining the Spirit. Therefore, v. 22 becomes the climax to the entire Gospel. The Spirit is now personally given to the disciples. The hour of glorification has reached its climax. Jesus is departing, and he places the Spirit that is within him into their lives.

20:24–29 The next account carefully records what transpired on Easter Sunday. Jesus has heard Thomas's challenge and provides the evidence he demands. Thomas is being challenged to change, to become like the others who, upon seeing Jesus, embrace him with faith. His response is a confession of heartfelt belief in Jesus.

These words supply the closing frame of the Gospel, matching the high and lofty descriptions of Christ the Word in 1:1–18. As the Gospel comes to its close, no more explicit identification of Jesus can be imagined. But the climax of the passage comes in 20:29. Jesus does not scorn the faith of Thomas but simply goes on to utter a blessing on those who believe but have *not seen.*

20:30–31 John acknowledges that his account is not comprehensive; Jesus provided many other

PEOPLE TO KNOW // THOMAS

JOHN 20:24–29: Thomas is known, perhaps mistakenly, as the skeptic and the pessimist of the twelve apostles. When Jesus set out for Bethany, his disciples reminded him that the Jewish leaders had previously tried to kill him (Jn 11:8). When Jesus explained to his disciples that he needed to go because Lazarus was dead, Thomas said, "Let us also go, that we may die with him" (Jn 11:16). Are these the words of a pessimist, or the courageous words of a devoted follower?

Later, as Jesus was eating the Passover with his disciples on the night of his arrest, he told them he was leaving them in order to prepare a place for them, that they might also be with him there. Thomas confusedly replied, "We don't know where you are going, so how can we know the way?" (Jn 14:5). Jesus replied that he himself was the way, the truth and the life.

After Jesus' resurrection, Thomas was not present when Christ appeared to the disciples. He was skeptical about the story and told the disciples the conditions of his belief (Jn 20:25). A week later his doubts were put to rest when Jesus appeared in the presence of the disciples, and he invited Thomas to touch his wounds. Jesus said, "Stop doubting and believe" (Jn 20:27). Thomas simply replied, "My Lord and my God!" (Jn 20:28)—another evidence of his great faith.

APPLICATION ✣ It is hard to believe in what we have not seen. Thomas could not accept the unbelievable truth of Jesus' resurrection. When Jesus appeared and invited Thomas to touch his wounds, however, Thomas didn't need to. Suddenly he was filled with faith, and he confessed Jesus as Lord.

When we experience a divine encounter with Christ, God does the same thing within us, kindling a faith within us that testifies that Jesus is Lord. The blessing that Jesus speaks over Thomas in John 20:29 is for the billions who have come to believe in Jesus since his ascension. Are you one of those believers?

not recorded in this book.[b] 31 But these
are written that you may believe[ac] that
Jesus is the Messiah, the Son of God,[d]
and that by believing you may have life
in his name.[e]

Jesus and the Miraculous Catch of Fish

21 Afterward Jesus appeared again
to his disciples,[f] by the Sea of Galilee.[bg] It happened this way: 2 Simon Peter,
Thomas[h] (also known as Didymus[c]), Nathanael[i] from Cana in Galilee,[j] the sons of
Zebedee,[k] and two other disciples were
together. 3 "I'm going out to fish," Simon
Peter told them, and they said, "We'll
go with you." So they went out and got
into the boat, but that night they caught
nothing.[l]

4 Early in the morning, Jesus stood on
the shore, but the disciples did not realize that it was Jesus.[m]

20:30 [b] Jn 21:25
20:31 [c] Jn 3:15; 19:35 [d] Mt 4:3 [e] Mt 25:46
21:1 [f] Jn 20:19, 26 [g] Jn 6:1
21:2 [h] Jn 11:16 [i] Jn 1:45 [j] Jn 2:1 [k] Mt 4:21
21:3 [l] Lk 5:5
21:4 [m] Lk 24:16; Jn 20:14

[a] *31* Or *may continue to believe* [b] *1* Greek *Tiberias* [c] *2 Thomas* (Aramaic) and *Didymus* (Greek) both mean *twin.*

signs with his disciples, and the collection offered here in his Gospel is a mere selection. In 20:31, John discloses his purpose for writing the Gospel: Belief leads to eternal life, and this life is a gift given through the power of Jesus Christ, God's Son.

✣ **20:1–31** The Thomas episode is a dramatic gift for modern cynics. We are invited—no, we are challenged—to believe like Thomas. Yet John understands perfectly well that we do not have the same opportunities. This is why in the story of ch. 20, the Beloved Disciple becomes one of the most important figures. He looks into the tomb, sees the evidence, and believes. While not seeing the resurrected Jesus, he sees what has been left behind; he sees the remnants of divine activity in history in stone and fabric and decides to believe.

This is our situation today. John has provided us with the best evidence he can muster to persuade us that belief is not only a reasonable choice but a necessary decision if we are going to follow Jesus. Jesus is not an *idea* whose ongoing validity finds a home in our ideas or our ethics. Jesus is a person—he is God incarnate in human history—and in coming into history, he has left evidence that we can see and measure and trust.

21:1–6a Peter decides to return to his long-neglected work of fishing. At sunrise they are finishing up when an unknown voice from shore

5 He called out to them, "Friends, haven't you any fish?"

"No," they answered.

6 He said, "Throw your net on the right side of the boat and you will find some." When they did, they were unable to haul the net in because of the large number of fish.[n]

7 Then the disciple whom Jesus loved[o] said to Peter, "It is the Lord!" As soon as Simon Peter heard him say, "It is the Lord," he wrapped his outer garment around him (for he had taken it off) and jumped into the water. 8 The other disciples followed in the boat, towing the net full of fish, for they were not far from shore, about a hundred yards.[a] 9 When they landed, they saw a fire[p] of burning coals there with fish on it,[q] and some bread.

10 Jesus said to them, "Bring some of the fish you have just caught." 11 So Simon Peter climbed back into the boat and dragged the net ashore. It was full of large fish, 153, but even with so many the net was not torn. 12 Jesus said to them, "Come and have breakfast." None of the disciples dared ask him, "Who are you?" They knew it was the Lord. 13 Jesus came, took the bread and gave it to them, and did the same with the fish.[r] 14 This was now the third time Jesus appeared to his disciples[s] after he was raised from the dead.

Jesus Reinstates Peter

15 When they had finished eating, Jesus said to Simon Peter, "Simon son of John, do you love me more than these?"

"Yes, Lord," he said, "you know that I love you."[t]

Jesus said, "Feed my lambs."[u]

16 Again Jesus said, "Simon son of John, do you love me?"

He answered, "Yes, Lord, you know that I love you."

Jesus said, "Take care of my sheep."[v]

17 The third time he said to him, "Simon son of John, do you love me?"

Peter was hurt because Jesus asked him the third time, "Do you love me?"[w] He said, "Lord, you know all things;[x] you know that I love you."

Jesus said, "Feed my sheep.[y] 18 Very truly I tell you, when you were younger you dressed yourself and went where you wanted; but when you are old you will stretch out your hands, and someone else will dress you and lead you where you do not want to go." 19 Jesus said this to indicate the kind of death[z] by which Peter would glorify God.[a] Then he said to him, "Follow me!"

20 Peter turned and saw that the disciple whom Jesus loved[b] was following them. (This was the one who had leaned back against Jesus at the supper and had said, "Lord, who is going to betray you?")[c] 21 When Peter saw him, he asked, "Lord, what about him?"

21:6 [n] Lk 5:4-7
21:7 [o] Jn 13:23
21:9 [p] Jn 18:18 [q] ver 10,13
21:13 [r] ver 9
21:14 [s] Jn 20:19, 26
21:15 [t] Mt 26:33, 35; Jn 13:37 [u] Lk 12:32
21:16 [v] Mt 2:6; Ac 20:28; 1Pe 5:2,3
21:17 [w] Jn 13:38 [x] Jn 16:30 [y] ver 16
21:19 [z] Jn 12:33; 18:32 [a] 2Pe 1:14
21:20 [b] ver 7; Jn 13:23 [c] Jn 13:25

[a] 8 Or about 90 meters

Jn 21:15 ❖ What does it mean to feed Jesus' sheep? How can we show our love for Christ by practicing this?

instructs them to try the opposite side of the boat (v. 6). To toss a cast net at random into the sea at this depth was virtually futile. But Peter quickly spins the net over his head and lets it sail like a parachute, dropping onto the sea as he watches the sinkers take it down.

21:6b–14 In these shallow waters, the miraculous catch cannot be mistaken. Pinned in the net are over one hundred fish (later counted at 153, v. 11), and its weight is more than the boat can take. Immediately the Beloved Disciple recognizes Jesus on the shore and delivers the news to Peter. When Peter hears that Jesus is on the shore, he leaps into the water.

In Judaism, an abundant catch was a sign of God's favor and blessing; this is precisely what Jesus has given. Jesus' offer of prepared "bread and fish" precisely parallels what he did at the miraculous feeding in 6:11, and this no doubt serves as a signal that removes any uncertainties.

21:15–17 Jesus' three questions in vv. 15–17 are perhaps the most celebrated exchange of questions and answers in the entire Bible. In each case, Peter is commissioned to tend Jesus' flock. The focus of Peter's conversation with Jesus has to do with his commission to tend the flock of Christ, not the quality of Peter's love for Jesus.

21:18–19 We should, no doubt, read these verses together with 13:36–38. Peter *will* lay down his life for Jesus (13:38). He will be crucified also and will glorify God in the same manner as his Lord—but this must await a time in the future. "Follow me" in 21:19 now takes on a poignant and provocative new meaning. Peter will follow Jesus to the cross.

21:20–23 The focus now shifts to the Beloved Disciple. Here at the shore, Peter is charged to "follow" Jesus (v. 19), but we learn that John, the disciple whom Jesus loved, is "following" already (v. 20). Again, he is a model who on one level may be following nearby as Jesus talks privately with Peter, but who on another level is found to be the ideal "follower" whom Peter should emulate.

It is not Peter's privilege to know how or when John will die. Again, Jesus tells the apostle to *follow*, and this time the form is emphatic. To paraphrase: "Peter, this matter is not your concern; it is mine. *You* have one duty: Follow me."

22Jesus answered, "If I want him to remain alive until I return,[d] what is that to
you? You must follow me."[e] 23Because of
this, the rumor spread among the believers[f] that this disciple would not die. But
Jesus did not say that he would not die;
he only said, "If I want him to remain
alive until I return, what is that to you?"
24This is the disciple who testifies to
these things[g] and who wrote them down.
We know that his testimony is true.[h]
25Jesus did many other things as well.[i]
If every one of them were written down,
I suppose that even the whole world
would not have room for the books that
would be written.

21:22 [d] Mt 16:27; 1Co 4:5; Rev 2:25 [e] ver 19
21:23 [f] Ac 1:16
21:24 [g] Jn 15:27 [h] Jn 19:35
21:25 [i] Jn 20:30

Verse 23 corrects what must have been an unusual misinterpretation of Jesus' words that circulated for some time in the early church. No doubt among John's followers, many believed that their beloved leader would not die but would remain until Christ returned.

21:24–25 John's disciples affirm the truth of their leader's work. When they write, "*We know* that his testimony is true" (emphasis added), we are alerted to their presence in the narrative. Here we have a third party standing between John's reliable testimony and ourselves as readers. With devotion and humility, they now pen the Gospel's closing frame.

The Gospel's closing verse may well come from the hand of John himself (following the quick editorial insertion of v. 24). John reminds us that there is far more to Jesus' life than what is recorded in his Gospel.

With playful and delightful hyperbole, John says that the whole world would likely be too small to contain the books that might be written about Jesus' story. John ends his Gospel with humility: The story of Jesus is larger than anything he can imagine. His effort, while glorious for us to read, pales in comparison to the glory of the person whom his story describes.

21:1–25 In John's Gospel, the Spirit is not merely an ambiguous spiritual influence but is rather the Spirit of Jesus himself living in his followers. The work of the church, therefore, is not religious energy fueled by our sense of commission; it is a call to work, tied to a divine empowering. It is ministering knowing that Christ himself (through the Spirit) is ministering in and through our efforts.

Good shepherds are men and women who simply hear Jesus' words, "Follow me," and obey, thinking about their own discipleship more than that of others. The result is a rich life that glorifies God in humility as it bears witness to Jesus.

This profile no doubt describes John's life and ministry. He has written his Gospel and supplied us with his testimony. His letters also show that he was a man who loved the church and defended it with all his might.

John's disciples knew that he was the "Beloved Disciple" because Jesus held a special affection for him. But this title also has another meaning (have we not seen countless double meanings in this Gospel?). This amazing title also describes the church's love for its own Shepherd. John was *likewise* beloved among those he led, and this Gospel—this beloved Gospel now concluded by his devoted disciples—stands as a memorial of John's deep and abiding love for his Savior. His devotion to his one Lord—Jesus Christ, the Messiah of the world, God incarnate—is a beautiful example for all believers to follow.

A HARMONY OF THE GOSPELS

DATE	EVENT	LOCATION	MATTHEW	MARK	LUKE	JOHN
	INTRODUCTIONS TO JESUS CHRIST					
	(1) Luke's introduction				1:1-4	
	(2) Preincarnate Christ					1:1-18
	(3) Genealogy of Jesus Christ		1:1-17		3:23b-38	
	BIRTH, INFANCY, AND ADOLESCENCE OF JESUS AND JOHN THE BAPTIST					
7 BC	(1) Announcement of birth of John	Jerusalem (temple)			1:5-25	
7 or 6 BC	(2) Announcement of birth of Jesus to the virgin Mary	Nazareth			1:26-38	
c. 5 BC	(3) Song of Elizabeth to Mary	Hill country of Judea			1:39-45	
	(4) Mary's song of praise				1:46-56	
5 BC	(5) Birth, infancy, and purpose for future of John the Baptist	Judea			1:57-80	
	(6) Announcement of Jesus' birth to Joseph	Nazareth	1:18-25a			
5-4 BC	(7) Birth of Jesus Christ	Bethlehem	1:25b		2:1-7	
	(8) Proclamation by the angels	Near Bethlehem			2:8-14	
	(9) The visit of homage by shepherds	Bethlehem			2:15-20	
	(10) Jesus' circumcision	Bethlehem			2:21	
4 BC	(11) First temple visit with acknowledgments by Simeon and Anna	Jerusalem			2:22-38	
	(12) Visit of the Magi	Jerusalem & Bethlehem	2:1-12			
	(13) Flight into Egypt and massacre of innocents	Bethlehem, Jerusalem & Egypt	2:13-18			
	(14) From Egypt to Nazareth with Jesus		2:19-23		2:39	
Afterward AD 7-8	(15) Childhood of Jesus	Nazareth			2:40	
	(16) Jesus, 12 years old, visits the temple	Jerusalem			2:41-50	
Afterward	(17) 18-year account of Jesus' adolescence and adulthood	Nazareth			2:51-52	
	TRUTHS ABOUT JOHN THE BAPTIST					
c. AD 25-27	(1) John's ministry begins	Judean wilderness	3:1	1:1-4	3:1-2	1:19-28
	(2) Man and message		3:2-12	1:2-8	3:3-14	1:20-23
	(3) His picture of Jesus		3:11-12	1:7-8	3:15-18	1:24-27
	(4) His courage		14:4-12		3:19-20	

A HARMONY OF THE GOSPELS *(continued)*

DATE	EVENT	LOCATION	MATTHEW	MARK	LUKE	JOHN
	BEGINNING OF JESUS' MINISTRY					
c. AD 27	(1) Jesus baptized	Jordan River	3:13–17	1:9–11	3:21–23a	1:29–34
	(2) Jesus tempted	Wilderness	4:1–11	1:12–13	4:1–13	
	(3) Calls first disciples	Beyond Jordan				1:35–51
	(4) The first miracle	Cana in Galilee				2:1–11
AD 27	(5) First stay in Capernaum	(Capernaum is "his" city)				2:12
	(6) First cleansing of the temple	Jerusalem				2:13–22
	(7) Received at Jerusalem	Jerusalem				2:23–25
	(8) Teaches Nicodemus about second birth	Jerusalem				3:1–21
	(9) Co-ministry with John	Judea				3:22–36
	(10) Leaves for Galilee	Judea	4:12	1:14	4:14	4:1–4
	(11) Samaritan woman at Jacob's well	Samaria (town of Sychar)				4:5–42
	(12) Returns to Galilee			1:15	4:15	4:43–45
	THE GALILEAN MINISTRY OF JESUS					
AD 27	(1) Healing of the royal official's son	Cana				4:46–54
	(2) Rejected at Nazareth	Nazareth			4:16–30	
	(3) Moves to Capernaum	Capernaum	4:13–17			
	(4) Four become fishers of people	Sea of Galilee	4:18–22	1:16–20	5:1–11	
	(5) Impure spirit driven out on the Sabbath day	Capernaum		1:21–28	4:31–37	
	(6) Peter's mother-in-law cured, plus others	Capernaum	8:14–17	1:29–34	4:38–41	
c. AD 27	(7) First preaching tour of Galilee	Galilee	4:23–25	1:35–39	4:42–44	
	(8) Leper healed and response recorded	Galilee	8:1–4	1:40–45	5:12–16	
	(9) Paralyzed man healed	Capernaum	9:1–8	2:1–12	5:17–26	
	(10) Matthew's call and reception held	Capernaum	9:9–13	2:13–17	5:27–32	
	(11) Disciples defended via a parable	Capernaum	9:14–17	2:18–22	5:33–39	
AD 28	(12) Goes to Jerusalem for second Passover; heals lame man	Jerusalem				5:1–47
	(13) Plucked grain precipitates Sabbath controversy	En route to Galilee	12:1–8	2:23–28	6:1–5	
	(14) Shriveled hand healed causes another Sabbath controversy	Galilee	12:9–14	3:1–6	6:6–11	
	(15) Multitudes healed	Sea of Galilee	12:15–21	3:7–12	6:17–19	
	(16) Twelve apostles selected after a night of prayer	Near Capernaum		3:13–19	6:12–16	
	(17) Sermon on the Mount	Near Capernaum	5:1–7:29		6:20–49	
	(18) Centurion's servant healed	Capernaum	8:5–13		7:1–10	

A HARMONY OF THE GOSPELS *(continued)*

DATE	EVENT	LOCATION	MATTHEW	MARK	LUKE	JOHN
	(19) Jesus raises widow's son from the dead	Nain			7:11-17	
AD 28	(20) Jesus allays John the Baptist's doubts	Galilee	11:2-19		7:18-35	
	(21) Woes upon the privileged		11:20-30			
	(22) A sinful woman anoints Jesus	Simon the Pharisee's house, Capernaum			7:36-50	
	(23) Another tour of Galilee	Galilee			8:1-3	
	(24) Jesus accused of blasphemy	Capernaum	12:22-37	3:20-30	11:14-23	
	(25) Jesus' answer to a demand for a sign	Capernaum	12:38-45		11:24-26, 29-36	
	(26) Mother, brothers seek audience	Capernaum	12:46-50	3:31-35	8:19-21	
	(27) Famous parables of sower, seed, weeds, lamp, mustard seed, yeast, treasure, pearl, net	By Sea of Galilee	13:1-52	4:1-34	8:4-18	
	(28) Sea made serene	Sea of Galilee	8:23-27	4:35-41	8:22-25	
	(29) Gadarene (Gerasene) demon-possessed men healed	Eastern shore of Galilee	8:28-34	5:1-20	8:26-39	
	(30) Jairus's daughter raised and woman with hemorrhage healed		9:18-26	5:21-43	8:40-56	
	(31) Two blind men's sight restored		9:27-31			
	(32) Mute demon-possessed man healed		9:32-34			
	(33) Nazareth's second rejection of Christ	Nazareth	13:53-58	6:1-6		
	(34) Twelve sent out		9:35—11:1	6:7-13	9:1-6	
	(35) Fearful Herod beheads John the Baptist	Galilee	14:1-12	6:14-29	9:7-9	
Spring AD 29	(36) Return of 12, Jesus withdraws, 5,000 fed	Near Bethsaida	14:13-21	6:30-44	9:10-17	6:1-15
	(37) Walks on the water	Sea of Galilee	14:22-33	6:45-52		6:16-21
	(38) Sick people healed in Gennesaret	Gennesaret	14:34-36	6:53-56		
	(39) Peak of popularity passes in Galilee	Capernaum				6:22—7:1
AD 29	(40) Traditions attacked		15:1-20	7:1-23		
	(41) Syrophoenician's daughter healed	Tyre	15:21-28	7:24-30		
	(42) Afflicted healed	Decapolis	15:29-31	7:31-37		
	(43) 4,000 fed	Decapolis	15:32-39	8:1-9		
	(44) Pharisees increase attack	Magadan	16:1-4	8:10-13		
	(45) Disciples' carelessness condemned; blind man healed		16:5-12	8:14-26		
	(46) Peter confesses Jesus is the Christ	Near Caesarea Philippi	16:13-20	8:27-30	9:18-21	

A HARMONY OF THE GOSPELS *(continued)*

DATE	EVENT	LOCATION	MATTHEW	MARK	LUKE	JOHN
AD 29	(47) Jesus foretells his death	Caesarea Philippi	16:21-26	8:31-38	9:22-25	
	(48) Kingdom promised		16:27-28	9:1	9:26-27	
	(49) The transfiguration	Mountain unnamed	17:1-13	9:2-13	9:28-36	
	(50) Demon-possessed boy healed	Mount of Transfiguration	17:14-21	9:14-29	9:37-42	
	(51) Jesus again tells of death, resurrection	Galilee	17:22-23	9:30-32	9:43-45	
	(52) Taxes paid	Capernaum	17:24-27			
	(53) Disciples contend about greatness; Jesus defines it; also patience, loyalty, forgiveness	Capernaum	18:1-35	9:33-50	9:46-50	
	(54) Jesus rejects his brothers' advice	Galilee				7:2-9
Fall AD 29	(55) Galilee departure and Samaritan rejection		19:1-2		9:51-56	7:10
	(56) Cost of discipleship		8:18-22		9:57-62	
LAST JUDEAN AND PEREAN MINISTRY OF JESUS						
Fall AD 29	(1) Festival of Tabernacles	Jerusalem				7:2, 11-52
	(2) Forgiveness of woman caught in the act of adultery	Jerusalem				[7:53—8:11]
AD 29	(3) Christ—the light of the world	Jerusalem				8:12
	(4) Pharisees dispute the prophet's words and thus try to destroy him	Jerusalem—temple				8:13-59
	(5) Man born blind healed; following consequences	Jerusalem				9:1-41
	(6) Parable of the Good Shepherd	Jerusalem				10:1-21
	(7) The service of the 72	Probably Judea			10:1-24	
	(8) Expert in the law hears the story of the Good Samaritan	Judea (?)			10:25-37	
	(9) The hospitality of Martha and Mary	Bethany			10:38-42	
	(10) Another lesson on prayer	Judea (?)			11:1-13	
	(11) Jesus accused of connection with Beelzebul				11:14-36	
	(12) Judgment against Pharisees and experts in the law				11:37-54	
	(13) Jesus deals with hypocrisy, greed, worry, and watchfulness				12:1-59	
	(14) Repent or perish				13:1-5	
	(15) Barren fig tree				13:6-9	
	(16) Crippled woman healed on Sabbath				13:10-17	
	(17) Parables of mustard seed and yeast	Probably Perea			13:18-21	

A HARMONY OF THE GOSPELS *(continued)*

DATE	EVENT	LOCATION	MATTHEW	MARK	LUKE	JOHN
Winter AD 29	(18) Festival of Dedication	Jerusalem				10:22-39
	(19) Withdrawal beyond Jordan					10:40-42
	(20) Jesus teaches, with special words about Herod	Perea			13:22-35	
	(21) Meal with a Pharisee ruler; heals man with abnormal swelling; parables of ox, best places at the table, great banquet				14:1-24	
	(22) Demands of discipleship	Perea			14:25-35	
	(23) Parables of lost sheep, coin, son				15:1-32	
	(24) Parables of shrewd manager, rich man and Lazarus				16:1-31	
	(25) Lessons on forgiveness, duty, influence, faith				17:1-10	
	(26) Resurrection of Lazarus	Perea to Bethany				11:1-44
	(27) Reaction to resurrection of Lazarus; withdrawal of Jesus					11:45-54
AD 30	(28) Begins last journey to Jerusalem via Samaria & Galilee	Samaria, Galilee			17:11	
	(29) Heals ten lepers				17:12-19	
	(30) Lessons on the coming kingdom				17:20-37	
	(31) Parables of persistent widow, Pharisee and tax collector				18:1-14	
	(32) Teaching on divorce		19:3-12	10:1-12		
	(33) Jesus blesses children; objections	Perea	19:13-15	10:13-16	18:15-17	
	(34) Rich ruler	Perea	19:16-30	10:17-31	18:18-30	
	(35) Parable of the workers		20:1-16			
	(36) Foretells death and resurrection	Near Jerusalem	20:17-19	10:32-34	18:31-34	
	(37) Ambition of James and John		20:20-28	10:35-45		
	(38) Blind Bartimaeus and his companion healed	Jericho	20:29-34	10:46-52	18:35-43	
	(39) Interview with Zacchaeus	Jericho			19:1-10	
	(40) Parable of the minas	Jericho			19:11-27	
	(41) Returns to home of Mary and Martha	Bethany				11:55—12:1
	(42) Plot to kill Lazarus	Bethany				12:9-11

A HARMONY OF THE GOSPELS *(continued)*

DATE	EVENT	LOCATION	MATTHEW	MARK	LUKE	JOHN
JESUS' FINAL WEEK AROUND AND IN JERUSALEM (SPRING AD 30)						
Sunday	(1) Triumphal Entry	Bethany, Jerusalem, Bethany	21:1-9	11:1-11	19:28-44	12:12-19
Monday	(2) Fig tree cursed and temple cleansed	Bethany to Jerusalem	21:10-19	11:12-18	19:45-48	
	(3) The necessity of sacrifice	Jerusalem				12:20-50
Tuesday	(4) Withered fig tree testifies	Bethany to Jerusalem	21:20-22	11:19-26		
	(5) Sanhedrin challenges Jesus. He answers by parables of two sons, workers in the vineyard, and marriage feast	Jerusalem	21:23—22:14	11:27—12:12	20:1-19	
	(6) Tribute to Caesar	Jerusalem	22:15-22	12:13-17	20:20-26	
	(7) Sadducees question the resurrection	Jerusalem	22:23-33	12:18-27	20:27-40	
	(8) Pharisees question commandments	Jerusalem	22:34-40	12:28-34		
	(9) Jesus and David	Jerusalem	22:41-46	12:35-37	20:41-44	
	(10) Jesus' last sermon	Jerusalem	23:1-39	12:38-40	20:45-47	
	(11) Widow's offering	Jerusalem		12:41-44	21:1-4	
	(12) Jesus tells of the future	Mount of Olives	24:1-51	13:1-37	21:5-36	
	(13) Parables of ten virgins, talents, the day of judgment	Mount of Olives	25:1-46			
	(14) Jesus tells date of crucifixion		26:1-5	14:1-2	22:1-2	
	(15) Anointing by Mary at Simon the Leper's feast	Bethany	26:6-13	14:3-9		12:2-8
	(16) Judas contracts the betrayal		26:14-16	14:10-11	22:3-6	
Thursday	(17) Preparation for the Passover	Jerusalem	26:17-19	14:12-16	22:7-13	
Thursday PM	(18) Passover eaten; jealousy rebuked	Jerusalem	26:20	14:17	22:14-16, 24-30	
	(19) Feet washed	Upper Room				13:1-20
	(20) Judas revealed; defects	Upper Room	26:21-25	14:18-21	22:21-23	13:21-30
	(21) Jesus warns about further desertion; cries of loyalty	Upper Room	26:31-35	14:27-31	22:31-38	13:31-38
	(22) The Last Supper	Upper Room	26:26-29	14:22-25	22:17-20	
	(23) Last speech to the apostles and intercessory prayer	Jerusalem				14:1—17:26
Thursday-Friday	(24) The grief of Gethsemane	Mount of Olives	26:30, 36-46	14:26, 32-42	22:39-46	18:1
Friday	(25) Betrayal, arrest, desertion	Gethsemane	26:47-56	14:43-52	22:47-53	18:2-12
	(26) First examined by Annas	Jerusalem				18:13-14, 19-23
	(27) Trial by Caiaphas and Sanhedrin; following indignities	Jerusalem	26:57, 59-68	14:53, 55-65	22:54a, 63-65	18:24

A HARMONY OF THE GOSPELS *(continued)*

DATE	EVENT	LOCATION	MATTHEW	MARK	LUKE	JOHN
Friday	(28) Peter's triple denial	Jerusalem	26:58, 69-75	14:54, 66-72	22:54b-62	18:15-18, 25-27
	(29) Condemnation by the Sanhedrin	Jerusalem	27:1	15:1a	22:66-71	
	(30) Suicide of Judas	Jerusalem	27:3-10			
	(31) First appearance before Pilate	Jerusalem	27:2, 11-14	15:1b-5	23:1-6	18:28-38
	(32) Jesus before Herod	Jerusalem			23:7-12	
	(33) Second appearance before Pilate	Jerusalem	27:15-26	15:6-15	23:13-25	18:39—19:16a
	(34) Mockery by Roman soldiers	Jerusalem	27:27-30	15:16-19		
	(35) Led to Golgotha	Jerusalem	27:31-34	15:20-23	23:26-32	19:16b-17
Friday	(36) Events of first three hours on cross	Golgotha	27:35-44	15:24-32	23:33-43	19:18-27
	(37) Last three hours on cross	Golgotha	27:45-50	15:33-37	23:44, 46	19:28-30
	(38) Events attending Jesus' death		27:51-56	15:38-41	23:45, 47-49	
	(39) Burial of Jesus	Jerusalem	27:57-61	15:42-46	23:50-54	19:31-42
Friday-Saturday	(40) Tomb sealed	Jerusalem	27:62-66			
	(41) Women watch	Jerusalem		15:47	23:55-56	
THE RESURRECTION THROUGH THE ASCENSION (AD 30)						
Dawn of First Day (Sunday, "Lord's Day")	(1) Women visit the tomb	Near Jerusalem	28:1-8	16:1-8	24:1-11	20:1-2
	(2) Peter and John see the empty tomb				24:12	20:3-10
	(3) Jesus' appearance to Mary Magdalene	Jerusalem		[16:9-11]		20:11-18
	(4) Jesus' appearance to the other women	Jerusalem	28:9-10			
	(5) Guards' report of the resurrection		28:11-15			
Sunday Afternoon	(6) Jesus' appearance to two disciples on way to Emmaus			[16:12-13]	24:13-35	
Late Sunday	(7) Jesus' appearance to ten disciples without Thomas	Jerusalem			24:36-43	20:19-25
One Week Later	(8) Jesus' appearance to disciples with Thomas	Jerusalem			24:44-49	20:26-31
During 40 Days until Ascension	(9) Jesus' appearance to seven disciples by Sea of Galilee	Galilee				21:1-25
	(10) Great Commission		28:16-20	[16:14-18]		
	(11) The Ascension	Mount Olivet		[16:19-20]	24:50-53	

Author: Luke, a Gentile physician and missionary companion of Paul

Audience: Addressed to Theophilus and his church, but intended for all believers

Date: AD 62 or later

Theme: Luke shows how, through the Holy Spirit, God empowers and expands his church from Jerusalem to Rome, and from its Jewish roots to the Gentile world.

PERSPECTIVE

Knowing why we believe is extremely important. Feeling good about the faith that energizes us signals the powerful working of God's Spirit within our lives. But unless our lives take on the Acts-like quality that this aptly named biblical book tells in narrative form—living out what it means to be a Christian—we have missed the essence of the faith.

What are the signs that we are responding in faith to God's gracious actions toward us? The book of Acts seems to talk about three important things.

The first and perhaps the most important is personal evangelism. One occasionally hears that personal evangelism is the calling of a special few, while the rest of us have other callings, important but different. But even a cursory reading of the book of Acts denies that idea. The church leaders and church members who star in this story *all* do the work of evangelism. One comes away from reading Acts with a distinct notion that personal evangelism is a way of living out all the other vocations of life to which God calls us. It permeates our total being.

The second sign is Bible study. Personal evangelism is not a contentless sharing of feelings. In order to do it well, one must have something to talk about, a story to tell, a creed to explain, a joy with which we can inspire a cynical world. Bible study means reading with the goal of doing something with the knowledge gained by that reading. It means imitating Peter and Paul by studying not only with the mind of a scholar but with the heart of an activist.

Reading Acts

The book of Acts begins with a brief account of the ascension of Jesus and quickly moves into the story of Pentecost. Gifted with the power of the Holy Spirit, the apostles preach the gospel, beginning in Jerusalem. From there the message spreads throughout Judea, and then to Samaria, Damascus, Antioch, Asia Minor, Macedonia, Greece, and finally to Rome. Note also that the

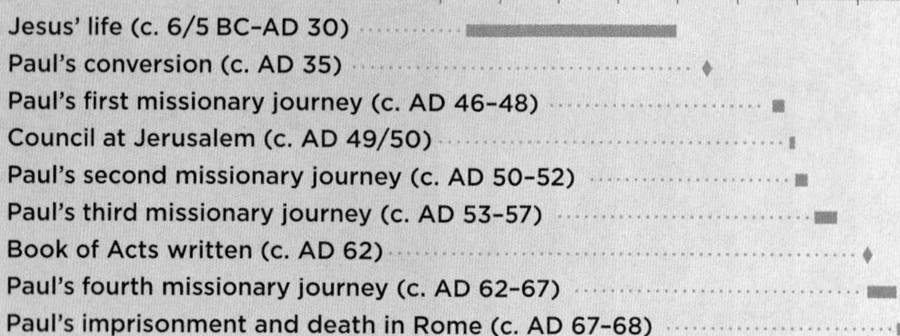

first section of Acts deals primarily with the missionary work of Peter; beginning in chapter 9, and especially from chapter 13 on, Luke concentrates on the missionary journeys of Paul.

Key Verse

"You will receive power when the Holy Spirit comes on you; and you will be my witnesses in Jerusalem, and in all Judea and Samaria, and to the ends of the earth."

–Acts 1:8

The third sign is recognizing the people to whom we tell the story: not just people who have not heard, but people who have chosen to follow an alternate path. Some aspects of evangelism are universal, but others have cultural features that must be discerned in order to show that the particular strength of the gospel story meet the needs of particular peoples. The listeners in Acts were lured by the false promises of major philosophies and occultism. Not surprisingly, people today are tempted by similar worldviews. We must learn how to tell the story to these people who need to hear it.

In short, we must act. Make no mistake: Our acts are part of the larger story of the Christian church. When we read, study, and act on this biblical book, we make ourselves a part of God's continuing story.

TAKING THE NEXT STEPS

This book is the second volume that Luke, a physician and travel companion of Paul, wrote to tell what Jesus did and taught (the first is the Gospel of Luke; see Lk 1:1–4 and Ac 1:1). Many themes apparent in the book of Acts are also present in the Gospel of Luke. Luke was convinced that Jesus was continuing his activity on earth through the Holy Spirit, who was guiding and empowering the apostles on a program of worldwide mission outreach. Luke shaped his missionary history around two key apostles, Peter and Paul, whose experiences paralleled each other in an amazing way. He was also careful to demonstrate the unity of the early church. Finally, Luke traced how Christians were constantly being unjustly persecuted for their faith. It may even be that Luke was hoping his writings would help gain sympathy from the Roman government for the new movement.

God has a number of messages for us in this book: (1) Jesus Christ is now the ascended Lord, and only by believing in him is there salvation from sin. (2) God expects members of the church to spread the message of the gospel throughout the world; this was Jesus' parting command to his followers. (3) In order to accomplish that task, God has sent the Spirit, who gives us the power we need. (4) The most important characteristic of the church is unity; God expects Christians to work out their differences in as peaceful and amicable a manner as possible. (5) God is in charge of his church, and he will make sure that it prevails over the forces that are trying to destroy it.

WHAT TO LOOK FOR IN ACTS

- Pentecost and Peter's first sermon (ch. 2)
- Healing a man who is disabled and Peter's second sermon (chs. 3–4)
- Stephen's speech and martyrdom (ch. 7)
- Stories of Philip, the evangelist (ch. 8)
- The conversion of Saul/Paul (chs. 9; 22; 26)
- Peter's conversion of Cornelius, the Gentile (chs. 10–11)
- Paul's call to mission work; his first sermon at Antioch (ch. 13)
- The council in Jerusalem concerning circumcision (ch. 15)
- Paul and Silas in Philippi; the Philippian jailer (ch. 16)
- Paul in Athens and Corinth (chs. 17–18)
- Paul in Ephesus and the riot of the Ephesians (ch. 19)
- Paul in prison and the account of his trials (chs. 22–26)
- Paul's journey to Rome, including the shipwreck (chs. 27–28)

Jesus Taken Up Into Heaven

1 In my former book,[a] Theophilus, I
wrote about all that Jesus began to do
and to teach[b] 2until the day he was taken
up to heaven,[c] after giving instructions[d]
through the Holy Spirit to the apostles[e]
he had chosen.[f] 3After his suffering, he
presented himself to them and gave many
convincing proofs that he was alive. He
appeared to them[g] over a period of forty
days and spoke about the kingdom of God.
4On one occasion, while he was eating
with them, he gave them this command:
"Do not leave Jerusalem, but wait for the
gift my Father promised, which you have
heard me speak about.[h] 5For John baptized with[a] water, but in a few days you
will be baptized with[a] the Holy Spirit."
6Then they gathered around him and
asked him, "Lord, are you at this time
going to restore[i] the kingdom to Israel?"
7He said to them: "It is not for you to
know the times or dates the Father has
set by his own authority.[j] 8But you will
receive power when the Holy Spirit comes
on you;[k] and you will be my witnesses[l] in

1:1 [a] Lk 1:1-4 [b] Lk 3:23
1:2 [c] ver 9, 11; Mk 16:19 [d] Mt 28:19, 20 [e] Mk 6:30 [f] Jn 13:18
1:3 [g] Mt 28:17; Lk 24:34, 36; Jn 20:19, 26; 21:1, 14; 1Co 15:5-7
1:4 [h] Lk 24:49; Jn 14:16; Ac 2:33
1:6 [i] Mt 17:11
1:7 [j] Mt 24:36
1:8 [k] Ac 2:1-4 [l] Lk 24:48

[a] 5 Or *in*

1:1–2a The author begins by giving the name of the recipient and summarizing his earlier book (the Gospel of Luke). Theophilus means "friend of God" or "loved by God." He may have been a high government official.

1:2b–8 The verb for instructing has the idea of giving orders. These instructions were given "through the Holy Spirit" (v. 2), which introduces a key theme of Acts: All ministry depends on the activity of the Spirit.

1:3 Jesus' appearances were proof of his resurrection (v. 3a). The resurrection was the ultimate proof of the claims that the apostles were to make about Jesus (17:31). So right at the start of his book, Luke presents the resurrection as an event attested by "many convincing proofs."

Jesus "spoke about the kingdom of God" (v. 3b), which refers to the reign or rule of God. The kingdom of God came with the life, death, and resurrection of Jesus, and it finds its consummation in the return of Christ as judge and king.

1:4–5 These verses present the crucial promise of the gift of baptism with the Holy Spirit. Describing what happened when this promise was fulfilled, Luke writes that the disciples "were filled with the Holy Spirit" (2:4).

1:6 It must have saddened Jesus to hear his disciples ask about the timing of restoring the kingdom to Israel. He had taught them about the kingdom of God, but they were still talking about the kingdom of Israel.

1:7–8 Their primary concern should not be the political power that will come with the restoration of Israel's kingdom. It should be the spiritual power that will come through the baptism with the Holy Spirit, which will enable them to be witnesses.

In a sense the disciples were already witnesses, for they had seen the risen Lord; that was the key to their witness (v. 22). But they also needed the "power" that would come from the Holy Spirit.

APPLICATION ✚ **1:1–8** From Ac 1, we can infer that the ideal Christian teaching is done by Spirit-empowered individuals whose teaching is grounded on the objective facts of the gospel. This message results in evangelism and witness.

PEOPLE TO KNOW // LUKE

ACTS 1:1–5: Luke wrote more words of the NT than any other human author, a remarkable fact given he is also the only certain Gentile author. Luke was a physician who wrote his Gospel and the book of Acts to someone named Theophilus in order to strengthen his faith in Christ (Lk 1:1–4; Ac 1:1–2). Luke's writing is characterized by careful descriptions and details, demonstrating his high level of education and providing us with well-documented accounts of the lives of Jesus and his disciples.

Luke was not among Jesus' apostles. He wrote his Gospel based on the eyewitness accounts of others. Throughout his Gospel, he highlights minor characters of lower social status, such as women, Samaritans, tax collectors, Gentiles and lepers. For example, while Matthew's birth account of Jesus focuses on Joseph, Luke chooses to focus on Mary. Luke is therefore sometimes called the "Gospel to the outcasts." Luke's Gospel also contains some of the most-loved parables of Jesus, such as the Good Samaritan (Lk 10:30–36) and the lost son (Lk 15:11–32).

Luke was present for some of the events in the book of Acts. Starting in Acts 16:10, certain sections are written using the first-person plural "we," indicating Luke was writing from his own experience rather than gathering his information from eyewitnesses.

Paul mentions Luke several times in his letters, calling him a "dear friend" (Col 4:14) and fellow worker (Phm 24). Most notably, Paul writes to Timothy from his Roman imprisonment that "only Luke is with me" (2Ti 4:11). Luke was a faithful companion to Paul, staying with him to the end.

APPLICATION ✣ Luke shows us God's love for outsiders. Whether people are considered outsiders because of health, ethnicity, gender, wealth, or any other reason, we need to remember that God does not judge people as the world does. Luke's writing should inspire us to be more compassionate to those whom others may look down on.

Luke's desire for Theophilus was a deeper faith and better understanding of the mission of Jesus Christ. Through reading Luke's writings, our faith and commitment to Christ will grow as well.

Jerusalem, and in all Judea and Samaria,[m]
and to the ends of the earth."[n]
9After he said this, he was taken up[o]
before their very eyes, and a cloud hid
him from their sight.
10They were looking intently up into
the sky as he was going, when suddenly
two men dressed in white[p] stood beside
them. 11"Men of Galilee,"[q] they said, "why
do you stand here looking into the sky?
This same Jesus, who has been taken
from you into heaven, will come back[r]
in the same way you have seen him go
into heaven."

Matthias Chosen to Replace Judas

12Then the apostles returned to Jerusalem[s] from the hill called the Mount

1:8 [m]Ac 8:1-25 [n]Mt 28:19
1:9 [o]ver 2
1:10 [p]Lk 24:4; Jn 20:12
1:11 [q]Ac 2:7 [r]Mt 16:27
1:12 [s]Lk 24:52

Ac 1:8 ❖ With what kind of power does the Holy Spirit fill believers today? How has the Spirit equipped us to be a witness for Christ?

Many people will come to churches attracted by the comprehensive program the church offers. People want a weekly religious experience, and in our entertainment-oriented culture, a church that provides an entertaining program will attract people just like a good concert or sporting event will attract people. But Christian ministry is ministry in the Spirit. As we engage in personal and congregational ministry, we must pray for the Spirit's power to infuse all of our efforts. Without the Spirit's help, our excellent programs and personal witness to the benefits of Christian living will be ineffective.

1:9–11 Jesus' ascension (v. 9) takes place after his giving the Great Commission for the last time (v. 8). The upward gaze of the disciples is interrupted by the appearance of two men (v. 10) whose white clothes suggest that they are angels. There is a mild rebuke implied in their question (v. 11a). The promise that he "will come back in the same [exalted] way" (v. 11c) helped make some sense out of Jesus' statements about his second coming. **1:12** The apostles' return from the Mount of Olives to Jerusalem was a little less than three-fourths of a mile. **1:13** Luke's list of those in the upper room (v. 13b) includes the eleven apostles (cf. Lk 6:14–16). This list begins with the three prominent apostles—Peter, John, and James. Women are also mentioned, in keeping with Luke's practice of giving a prominent place to women in his writings.

CHRONOLOGY OF ACTS

30	Pentecost
33 or 34	Conversion of Saul
42 or 43	Barnabas co-opts Saul in his labors in Antioch
44	Herodian persecution and visit of Barnabas and Saul to Jerusalem
45-47	Paul's first missionary journey
47-48	Period in Antioch and visit to Jerusalem on circumcision question (ch. 25; 14 years after Saul's conversion)
48-52	Paul's second missionary journey (end fixed by Gallio's proconsulship)
52-57	Paul's Third missionary journey
57	Paul arrested in Jerusalem
57-59	Paul a prisoner in Caesarea
60-62	Paul a prisoner in Rome
62	Paul probably freed
65 (?)	Paul's martyrdom in Rome

of Olives,[t] a Sabbath day's walk[a] from
the city. 13When they arrived, they went
upstairs to the room[u] where they were
staying. Those present were Peter,
John, James and Andrew; Philip and
Thomas, Bartholomew and Matthew;
James son of Alphaeus and Simon
the Zealot, and Judas son of James.[v]
14They all joined together constantly
in prayer,[w] along with the women[x] and
Mary the mother of Jesus, and with his
brothers.[y]
15In those days Peter stood up among
the believers (a group numbering about
a hundred and twenty) 16and said,
"Brothers and sisters,[b] the Scripture
had to be fulfilled[z] in which the Holy
Spirit spoke long ago through David
concerning Judas,[a] who served as guide
for those who arrested Jesus. 17He was
one of our number[b] and shared in our
ministry."[c]
18(With the payment[d] he received for
his wickedness, Judas bought a field;[e]
there he fell headlong, his body burst
open and all his intestines spilled out.
19Everyone in Jerusalem heard about
this, so they called that field in their
language Akeldama, that is, Field of
Blood.)
20"For," said Peter, "it is written in the
Book of Psalms:

"'May his place be deserted;
let there be no one to dwell in it,'[c][f]

and,

"'May another take his place of
leadership.'[d][g]

21Therefore it is necessary to choose
one of the men who have been with
us the whole time the Lord Jesus was

1:12 [t]Mt 21:1
1:13 [u]Ac 9:37; 20:8 [v]Mt 10:2-4; Mk 3:16-19; Lk 6:14-16
1:14 [w]Ac 2:42; 6:4 [x]Lk 23:49, 55 [y]Mt 12:46
1:16 [z]ver 20 [a]Jn 13:18
1:17 [b]Jn 6:70,71 [c]ver 25
1:18 [d]Mt 26:14, 15 [e]Mt 27:3-10
1:20 [f]Ps 69:25 [g]Ps 109:8

[a] *12* That is, about 5/8 mile or about 1 kilometer
[b] *16* The Greek word for *brothers and sisters* (*adelphoi*) refers here to believers, both men and women, as part of God's family; also in 6:3; 11:29; 12:17; 16:40; 18:18,27; 21:7,17; 28:14,15.
[c] *20* Psalm 69:25 [d] *20* Psalm 109:8

Mary, Jesus' mother, is also mentioned here—her only appearance in Acts (v. 14). Luke had presented her as a model of trust and obedience in his Gospel (Lk 1:38). The unbelief of Jesus' brothers is now gone.

Luke-Acts abounds with references to prayer (mentioned 31 times in Acts and appearing in 20 of its chapters). As the followers of Jesus wait for the promised baptism of the Spirit, they "all joined together constantly in prayer" (v. 14). The word translated "together" literally means "with one mind or passion."

1:15–26 Peter views Judas's betrayal as fulfilling Scripture (v. 16). That, however, does not take away from the pain of what happened, for, as Peter says, "He was one of our number and shared in our ministry" (v. 17).

1:18–19 Luke's digression about how Judas died uses the word "wickedness" (v. 18), which shows that, while the betrayal was predicted in Scripture, it was a serious act of treachery.

1:20 Peter's predictions are from Ps 69 and 109. The early Christians saw David, the righteous sufferer, and his enemies as types of Christ and *his* enemies (the antitypes).

The theme of God's sovereign will at work in the suffering and death of Christ is one that occurs several times in the apostles' preaching, especially to Jews. This perspective helps us believe that God will turn the evil done to us into good (cf. Ge 50:20). It would have helped take away the bitterness that the disciples must have had over the betrayal of Jesus by one who had been so close to them for so long.

1:21–22 Peter felt it was "necessary" to find a replacement for Judas (v. 21). Thus, the early church followed Jesus' practice of having twelve apostles. The qualifications required for the replacement had to do with the role of the apostles as witnesses. Witnessing to the resurrection was a crucial, never-to-be-repeated role of a select group of people in the early Christian church.

living among us, 22beginning from
John's baptism[h] to the time when Jesus
was taken up from us. For one of these
must become a witness[i] with us of his
resurrection."
23So they nominated two men: Joseph
called Barsabbas (also known as Justus)
and Matthias. 24Then they prayed,[j] "Lord,
you know everyone's heart.[k] Show us
which of these two you have chosen 25to
take over this apostolic ministry, which
Judas left to go where he belongs." 26Then
they cast lots, and the lot fell to Matthias;
so he was added to the eleven apostles.[l]

The Holy Spirit Comes at Pentecost

2 When the day of Pentecost[m] came,
they were all together[n] in one place.
2Suddenly a sound like the blowing of
a violent wind came from heaven and
filled the whole house where they were
sitting.[o] 3They saw what seemed to be
tongues of fire that separated and came
to rest on each of them. 4All of them were
filled with the Holy Spirit and began to
speak in other tongues[a][p] as the Spirit
enabled them.
5Now there were staying in Jerusalem
God-fearing[q] Jews from every nation under heaven. 6When they heard this sound,
a crowd came together in bewilderment,
because each one heard their own language being spoken. 7Utterly amazed,[r]
they asked: "Aren't all these who are
speaking Galileans?[s] 8Then how is it that
each of us hears them in our native language? 9Parthians, Medes and Elamites;
residents of Mesopotamia, Judea and Cappadocia,[t] Pontus[u] and Asia,[b][v] 10Phrygia[w]
and Pamphylia,[x] Egypt and the parts of
Libya near Cyrene;[y] visitors from Rome
11(both Jews and converts to Judaism); Cretans and Arabs — we hear them declaring
the wonders of God in our own tongues!"
12Amazed and perplexed, they asked one
another, "What does this mean?"
13Some, however, made fun of them
and said, "They have had too much
wine."[z]

1:22 [h] Mk 1:4 [i] ver 8
1:24 [j] Ac 6:6; 14:23 [k] 1Sa 16:7; Jer 17:10; Ac 15:8; Rev 2:23
1:26 [l] Ac 2:14
2:1 [m] Lev 23:15, 16; Ac 20:16 [n] Ac 1:14
2:2 [o] Ac 4:31
2:4 [p] Mk 16:17; 1Co 12:10
2:5 [q] Ac 8:2
2:7 [r] ver 12 [s] Ac 1:11
2:9 [t] 1Pe 1:1 [u] Ac 18:2 [v] Ac 16:6; Ro 16:5; 1Co 16:19; 2Co 1:8
2:10 [w] Ac 16:6; 18:23 [x] Ac 13:13; 15:38 [y] Mt 27:32
2:13 [z] 1Co 14:23

[a] 4 Or *languages*; also in verse 11 [b] 9 That is, the Roman province by that name

1:23–26 The use of lots comes only after prayer for God's guidance. That prayer shows what we should be looking for most in a leader (v. 24). The believers had found two people with suitable external qualifications, but only God completely knows the hearts of people. Matthias does not appear again in Acts. Later tradition presents him as a missionary to the Ethiopians.

1:9–26 Just as the Spirit came at Pentecost after constant prayer by the disciples, the history of the church demonstrates that revival also comes only after persistent prayer. Revival is something that God sends sovereignly, and therefore we cannot predict when it will come. But there is a statement, attributed to theologian and pastor Matthew Henry (1662–1714), that when God wants to do something special in the world, he first inspires his people to start praying.

2:1 The fulfillment of Christ's promise of the Holy Spirit takes place during a Jewish harvest festival, Pentecost. It was one of the three Jewish pilgrimage festivals (Ex 23:14–17). The event that propelled the gospel to the ends of the earth occurred when people from the ends of the earth were in Jerusalem.

2:2 The wind and fire that accompanied the gift of the Spirit (vv. 2–3) are common biblical symbols for the activity of the Spirit (Eze 37:1–14). Wind was a symbol of new life. Fire, which burns up the chaff, is a symbol of judgment. The coming of the Spirit means life to some and judgment to others.

2:3 The tongues of fire "rest on each of them." The community is formed by a personal relationship with God through the Holy Spirit. This fulfills Jeremiah's prediction that in the new covenant the law will be written on the heart (Jer 31:31–34).

2:4 Two things happened to the disciples after the Spirit came: They "were filled with the Holy Spirit and began to speak in other tongues." The "tongues" are different from those described in 1Co 12–14. This manifestation fit in with the Spirit's role in enabling the church's worldwide witness (Ac 1:8).

2:5–11 In amazement the people point out that those who are speaking are "Galileans" (v. 7). God had chosen "nobodies" to lead in a historic event (cf. 1Co 1:26–31).

2:12–13 Some were touched and wanted to know more (v. 12). Others rejected the message and ridiculed what was said (v. 13). It is surprising that, in the face of such a spectacular miracle, some should mock what they saw. But as we will see below, this is in keeping with the theology of rejection that is clearly present in Scripture.

2:1–13 To many, the Christian faith is restricted to entering the kingdom through rationally accepting the truth of the gospel, followed by their attempts to live according to the Bible. This is indeed an important ingredient to the Christian faith, but Pentecost tells us that there is something more. At Pentecost, when the disciples were filled with the Spirit, they began "declaring the wonders of God" (v. 11). When we sense, through experience, that "God's love has been poured out into our hearts through the Holy Spirit, who has been given to us" (Ro 5:5), our hearts are filled with joy, and this joy expresses itself in praise.

Peter Addresses the Crowd

14Then Peter stood up with the Elev-
en, raised his voice and addressed the
crowd: "Fellow Jews and all of you who
live in Jerusalem, let me explain this to
you; listen carefully to what I say. 15These
people are not drunk, as you suppose. It's
only nine in the morning![a] 16No, this is
what was spoken by the prophet Joel:

17" 'In the last days, God says,
I will pour out my Spirit on all
people.[b]
Your sons and daughters will
prophesy,[c]
your young men will see visions,
your old men will dream dreams.
18Even on my servants, both men and
women,
I will pour out my Spirit in those
days,
and they will prophesy.[d]
19I will show wonders in the heavens
above
and signs on the earth below,
blood and fire and billows of
smoke.
20The sun will be turned to darkness
and the moon to blood[e]
before the coming of the great
and glorious day of the Lord.
21And everyone who calls
on the name of the Lord will be
saved.'[a][f]

22"Fellow Israelites, listen to this: Jesus
of Nazareth was a man accredited by God
to you by miracles, wonders and signs,[g]
which God did among you through him,[h]
as you yourselves know. 23This man was
handed over to you by God's deliberate plan and foreknowledge;[i] and you,
with the help of wicked men,[b] put him to
death by nailing him to the cross.[j] 24But
God raised him from the dead,[k] freeing
him from the agony of death, because it
was impossible for death to keep its hold
on him.[l] 25David said about him:

" 'I saw the Lord always before me.
Because he is at my right hand,
I will not be shaken.
26Therefore my heart is glad and my
tongue rejoices;
my body also will rest in hope,
27because you will not abandon me to
the realm of the dead,
you will not let your holy one see
decay.[m]
28You have made known to me the
paths of life;
you will fill me with joy in your
presence.'[c]

29"Fellow Israelites, I can tell you confidently that the patriarch[n] David died
and was buried,[o] and his tomb is here[p]
to this day. 30But he was a prophet and
knew that God had promised him on oath
that he would place one of his descendants on his throne.[q] 31Seeing what was
to come, he spoke of the resurrection of
the Messiah, that he was not abandoned
to the realm of the dead, nor did his body
see decay.[r] 32God has raised this Jesus to
life,[s] and we are all witnesses[t] of it. 33Ex-
alted[u] to the right hand of God,[v] he has

2:15 [a] 1Th 5:7
2:17 [b] Isa 44:3; Jn 7:37-39; Ac 10:45 [c] Ac 21:9
2:18 [d] Ac 21:9-12
2:20 [e] Mt 24:29
2:21 [f] Ro 10:13
2:22 [g] Jn 4:48; Ac 10:38 [h] Jn 3:2
2:23 [i] Lk 22:22; Ac 3:18; 4:28 [j] Lk 24:20; Ac 3:13
2:24 [k] ver 32; 1Co 6:14; 2Co 4:14; Eph 1:20; Col 2:12; Heb 13:20; 1Pe 1:21 [l] Jn 20:9
2:27 [m] ver 31; Ac 13:35
2:29 [n] Ac 7:8, 9 [o] 1Ki 2:10; Ac 13:36 [p] Ne 3:16
2:30 [q] 2Sa 7:12; Ps 132:11
2:31 [r] Ps 16:10
2:32 [s] ver 24 [t] Ac 1:8
2:33 [u] Php 2:9 [v] Mk 16:19

[a] *21* Joel 2:28-32 [b] *23* Or *of those not having the law* (that is, Gentiles) [c] *28* Psalm 16:8-11 (see Septuagint)

2:14–21 Peter connects with his audience, responding to the statement that they are drunk (v. 15). Then he points to the real explanation: the fulfillment of Joel's prophecy (Joel 2:28–32).

These people are witnessing the beginning of the last days, when people of all types and ages will prophesy (Ac 2:17b–18). At the end of the last days there will be cosmic disturbances (vv. 19–20; cf. Rev 6:12–14; 8:5, 7; 20:9), which will herald "the great and glorious day of the Lord" (Ac 2:20b)—the day of judgment at the end of the world. For believers, this will not be a time to dread, for "everyone who calls on the name of the Lord will be saved" (v. 21).

2:22–23 The miracles of Christ were evidence that he was accredited by God (v. 22). The death of Christ was caused by the audience but also was "by God's deliberate plan and foreknowledge" (v. 23). A crucified Messiah was a stumbling block to the Jews (see 1Co 1:23). It went against everything they believed about who the Messiah would be. But Peter presents it as a triumph that God had planned from the beginning.

2:24 The resurrection was God's accreditation of the person and work of Christ. The next statement, "It was impossible for death to keep its hold on him," clearly shows that Peter asserts that the resurrection validates Jesus' life and ministry.

2:25–32 Peter quotes Ps 16:8–11 to argue that, since David did not rise from the dead, this passage must be referring to David's great Son, Jesus (vv. 29–31). Peter clinches his argument, claiming: "We are all witnesses of it" (v. 32).

2:33–35 Peter connects the event of Pentecost with Jesus' exaltation to the right hand of the Father. Jesus received the Holy Spirit from the Father and has poured out what they had just seen and heard (v. 33). In the NT, the resurrection and exaltation of Christ are held in close association with each other, almost as if they constituted a single event.

Peter provides evidence for the exaltation of Christ. First, he appeals to their experience of the

received from the Father[w] the promised
Holy Spirit[x] and has poured out[y] what
you now see and hear. 34For David did
not ascend to heaven, and yet he said,

"'The Lord said to my Lord:
"Sit at my right hand
35until I make your enemies
a footstool for your feet."'[a][z]

36"Therefore let all Israel be assured
of this: God has made this Jesus, whom
you crucified, both Lord and Messiah."[a]
37When the people heard this, they
were cut to the heart and said to Peter
and the other apostles, "Brothers, what
shall we do?"[b]
38Peter replied, "Repent and be baptized,[c] every one of you, in the name of
Jesus Christ for the forgiveness of your
sins.[d] And you will receive the gift of the
Holy Spirit. 39The promise is for you and
your children[e] and for all who are far
off[f]—for all whom the Lord our God
will call."

2:33 [w] Ac 1:4 [x] Jn 7:39; 14:26 [y] Ac 10:45
2:35 [z] Ps 110:1; Mt 22:44
2:36 [a] Lk 2:11
2:37 [b] Lk 3:10, 12,14
2:38 [c] Ac 8:12, 16,36,38; 22:16 [d] Lk 24:47; Ac 3:19
2:39 [e] Isa 44:3 [f] Ac 10:45; Eph 2:13
2:40 [g] Dt 32:5
2:42 [h] Ac 1:14
2:43 [i] Ac 5:12
2:44 [j] Ac 4:32

Ac 2:45 ❖ How can believers tangibly care for each other and carry one another's burdens today?

40With many other words he warned
them; and he pleaded with them, "Save
yourselves from this corrupt generation."[g] 41Those who accepted his message were baptized, and about three
thousand were added to their number
that day.

The Fellowship of the Believers

42They devoted themselves to the
apostles' teaching and to fellowship, to
the breaking of bread and to prayer.[h]
43Everyone was filled with awe at the
many wonders and signs performed by
the apostles.[i] 44All the believers were together and had everything in common.[j]
45They sold property and possessions to

[a] *35* Psalm 110:1

Holy Spirit (v. 33). Next, he quotes from another Davidic psalm (Ps 110) and, as before (Ac 2:29–31), claims that what David said there cannot apply to him (vv. 34–35). Christ is seated at the right hand of God and bringing to pass the complete defeat of his enemies.

2:36 Peter's next statement represents the second major feature of the apostolic proclamation: a theological evaluation of the person of Jesus. Peter claims first that Jesus is "Lord." "Lord" is used for Jesus in ways that were used for God in the Greek OT (see vv. 20–21). Jesus as Lord has taken on divine functions, such as pouring out the Spirit (v. 33) and being the object of faith (v. 21). While the title "Lord" emphasizes the sovereign kingship of Jesus, the title "Messiah" emphasizes the salvation he brings.

2:37–40 The third feature of apostolic preaching is a summons to respond. Peter gives two requirements and promises two blessings. His listeners, whomever they may be and wherever they may be (v. 39), must repent and be baptized, and they will receive forgiveness of their sin and experience the Holy Spirit.

2:41 The amazing response of three thousand people responding to Peter's message in baptism illustrates Jesus' promise that with his going away and the Spirit's coming, the disciples will do even greater works than he did (Jn 14:12).

✣ **2:14–41** Recognizing people's needs and questions and making the connection between them and the gospel is an art we must develop. It helps to study and meditate on God's Word to rightly understand the issues people face and to pray about them, that they will come into line with God's thinking. This is an important key in our personal ministry to others and an effective way to draw people to the message of salvation in Jesus. As we will see in the next section, the early church's practices in this regard were extremely effective in reaching others for Christ.

2:42 There was immediate, regular, follow-through care of the first converts in the early church. Its adherents "devoted" themselves to four critical activities, which are instructive for our personal witness today: (1) The first feature is "the apostles' teaching." It likely included explanations of salvation, the person and work of Christ, the commands of Christ, and the message of the kingdom. (2) The word Luke uses for "fellowship" is a favorite word of Paul's. Its basic idea is sharing, but it is also used to denote intimacy and fellowship in general. The church used this word for the unique sharing that Christians have with God and with other Christians. (3) "The breaking of bread" was probably part of the ordinary fellowship meals (see 1Co 11:17–34). As Paul's traveling companion, Luke would have witnessed the churches celebrating the Lord's Supper and having fellowship meals together. (4) The final feature in v. 42 could refer to prayer during the set times of the Jerusalem temple (3:1). But there were also times when they prayed on their own (1:24; 4:24; 12:12).

2:43 Luke describes the community life of the whole church. The miracles the apostles performed in Jesus' name filled everyone with "awe." These people could sense that God was at work.

2:44–45 Property was sold according to people's ability to provide and to people's need. We do not have a case of enforced sharing here, as in communism, but rather an outpouring of generosity that gratefully filled the needs of other believers.

give to anyone who had need.[k] 46Every
day they continued to meet together in
the temple courts.[l] They broke bread[m] in
their homes and ate together with glad
and sincere hearts, 47praising God and
enjoying the favor of all the people.[n] And
the Lord added to their number[o] daily
those who were being saved.

Peter Heals a Lame Beggar

3 One day Peter and John[p] were going up to the temple[q] at the time of
prayer — at three in the afternoon.[r] 2Now
a man who was lame from birth[s] was
being carried to the temple gate[t] called
Beautiful, where he was put every day to
beg[u] from those going into the temple
courts. 3When he saw Peter and John
about to enter, he asked them for money. 4Peter looked straight at him, as did
John. Then Peter said, "Look at us!" 5So
the man gave them his attention, expecting to get something from them.

6Then Peter said, "Silver or gold I do
not have, but what I do have I give you.
In the name of Jesus Christ of Nazareth,[v]
walk." 7Taking him by the right hand, he
helped him up, and instantly the man's
feet and ankles became strong. 8He
jumped to his feet and began to walk.
Then he went with them into the temple courts, walking and jumping,[w] and
praising God. 9When all the people[x] saw
him walking and praising God, 10they
recognized him as the same man who
used to sit begging at the temple gate
called Beautiful,[y] and they were filled
with wonder and amazement at what
had happened to him.

Peter Speaks to the Onlookers

11While the man held on to Peter and
John,[z] all the people were astonished and
came running to them in the place called
Solomon's Colonnade.[a] 12When Peter saw
this, he said to them: "Fellow Israelites,
why does this surprise you? Why do you
stare at us as if by our own power or godliness we had made this man walk? 13The

2:45 [k] Mt 19:21
2:46 [l] Lk 24:53; Ac 5:21,42 [m] Ac 20:7
2:47 [n] Ro 14:18 [o] ver 41; Ac 5:14
3:1 [p] Lk 22:8 [q] Ac 2:46 [r] Ps 55:17
3:2 [s] Ac 14:8 [t] Lk 16:20 [u] Jn 9:8
3:6 [v] ver 16; Ac 4:10
3:8 [w] Ac 14:10
3:9 [x] Ac 4:16,21
3:10 [y] ver 2
3:11 [z] Lk 22:8 [a] Jn 10:23; Ac 5:12

Ac 3:7 ❖ How can we help people who are weak and needy through the power of Christ?

2:46 The early believers went to the temple (v. 46a), just as Jesus did. They tried to remain within the Jewish fold.

The breaking of bread mentioned here included both the Lord's Supper and fellowship meals. Eating together "with glad and sincere hearts" had an important place in the early church. The word translated "sincere" can mean single-minded devotion, the absence of pretense, or simplicity and generosity.

2:47 When God's people come together and enjoy fellowship, "praising God" is the natural result. True fellowship focuses on God and helps people to remember the good things he has done, which, in turn, causes praise.

In the meantime, the church grew numerically. Personal witness through word and life added to the other aspects of fellowship and convinced many people to believe. Luke attests that it was "the Lord" who "added to their number." God is the ultimate Evangelist who draws people to himself.

✣ **2:42–47** The description of the fellowship of the early Christian church in Ac 2 is instructive for personal evangelism, for neighborhood outreach efforts, for home-based small-group ministries, and for larger church congregations. The early church leaders worked closely to meet the needs of others in obedience to Jesus' command to love others (Jn 13:34–35). They reached out to others with humility and in mutual submission to one another, and they covered their work in prayer. In so doing, they demonstrated an attentive devotion to the things Jesus taught and cared about.

3:1–3 This visit was about three in the afternoon, one of the Jewish times of prayer. As was common at entrances to places of worship, a man who had been disabled from birth was begging at the temple gate called Beautiful (v. 2).

3:4–10 Following his plea for money, "Peter looked straight at him, as did John" (v. 4). Luke seems to alternate between the mention of both Peter and John and of Peter alone in this chapter. John had an important role. Peter's memorable words to the man who was begging (v. 6) indicate that they were in touch with the power of Jesus.

3:11–26 The exuberant response of the healed man becomes a launching pad for Peter's speech. At the start of his speech, Peter places responsibility for the death of Christ on his audience (vv. 13–14). In the middle of his speech, he gets conciliatory by saying that he knows they "acted in ignorance" (v. 17). He ends his speech on a positive note, reminding them that they are "heirs of the prophets and of the covenant" (v. 25) and that God's servant was sent first to bless them via repentance (v. 26). Just prior to that, however, he issues a strong warning about those who do not listen being cut off (v. 23). This message is an urgent plea that pulsates with the need for personal response.

3:12–16 Peter deflects glory for the miracle from himself and John (v. 12). Peter then refers to "the God of Abraham, Isaac and Jacob" (v. 13a)—a description relevant to his Jewish audience. The

God of Abraham, Isaac and Jacob, the God
of our fathers,[b] has glorified his servant
Jesus. You handed him over to be killed,
and you disowned him before Pilate,[c]
though he had decided to let him go.[d]
14You disowned the Holy[e] and Righteous
One[f] and asked that a murderer be released to you.[g] 15You killed the author of
life, but God raised him from the dead.[h]
We are witnesses of this. 16By faith in the
name of Jesus, this man whom you see
and know was made strong. It is Jesus'
name and the faith that comes through
him that has completely healed him, as
you can all see.
17"Now, fellow Israelites, I know that
you acted in ignorance,[i] as did your leaders.[j] 18But this is how God fulfilled what
he had foretold[k] through all the prophets,[l] saying that his Messiah would suffer.[m] 19Repent, then, and turn to God, so
that your sins may be wiped out,[n] that
times of refreshing may come from the
Lord, 20and that he may send the Messiah, who has been appointed for you—
even Jesus. 21Heaven must receive him[o]
until the time comes for God to restore
everything,[p] as he promised long ago
through his holy prophets.[q] 22For Moses
said, 'The Lord your God will raise up for
you a prophet like me from among your
own people; you must listen to everything he tells you.[r] 23Anyone who does
not listen to him will be completely cut
off from their people.'[a][s]
24"Indeed, beginning with Samuel,
all the prophets[t] who have spoken have
foretold these days. 25And you are heirs[u]
of the prophets and of the covenant[v] God
made with your fathers. He said to Abraham, 'Through your offspring all peoples
on earth will be blessed.'[b][w] 26When God
raised up[x] his servant, he sent him first[y]
to you to bless you by turning each of
you from your wicked ways."

Peter and John Before the Sanhedrin

4 The priests and the captain of the
temple guard[z] and the Sadducees[a]
came up to Peter and John while they
were speaking to the people. 2They were
greatly disturbed because the apostles
were teaching the people, proclaiming
in Jesus the resurrection of the dead.[b]
3They seized Peter and John and, because
it was evening, they put them in jail[c]

3:13 [b]Ac 5:30 [c]Mt 27:2 [d]Lk 23:4
3:14 [e]Mk 1:24; Ac 4:27 [f]Ac 7:52 [g]Mk 15:11; Lk 23:18-25
3:15 [h]Ac 2:24
3:17 [i]Lk 23:34 [j]Ac 13:27
3:18 [k]Ac 2:23 [l]Lk 24:27 [m]Ac 17:2,3; 26:22,23
3:19 [n]Ac 2:38
3:21 [o]Ac 1:11 [p]Mt 17:11 [q]Lk 1:70
3:22 [r]Dt 18:15, 18; Ac 7:37
3:23 [s]Dt 18:19
3:24 [t]Lk 24:27
3:25 [u]Ac 2:39 [v]Ro 9:4,5 [w]Ge 12:3; 22:18; 26:4; 28:14
3:26 [x]ver 22; Ac 2:24 [y]Ac 13:46; Ro 1:16
4:1 [z]Lk 22:4 [a]Mt 3:7
4:2 [b]Ac 17:18
4:3 [c]Ac 5:18

[a] *23* Deut. 18:15,18,19 [b] *25* Gen. 22:18; 26:4

---

miracle glorifies the one they "handed . . . over to be killed" and "disowned" (vv. 13b–14).

3:17–18 The death of Christ is explained as a fulfillment of prophecy (v. 18), and God is said to have raised up Jesus, with the apostles being witnesses of it (v. 15). Jesus is the one appointed or designated as their Messiah (v. 20; cf. 2:36). The resurrection was something like an ordination of Christ, confirming who he really is.

3:19–20 Peter refers to the fulfillment of OT promises when he says that times of refreshment will come as a result of their repentance (v. 19). This was part of the Jewish hope. Peter clarifies that this will come only when God sends the Messiah following their repentance and cleansing (v. 20). This anticipates the second coming of Christ.

3:21–23 Jesus extends that restoration from Israel to all things, but it will happen at the end of time. We can assume that these are all parts of Jesus' teaching about the kingdom and that they were included in Paul's teaching about the kingdom (19:8; 20:24; 28:31). Thus, we find two aspects of end-times teaching in this evangelistic sermon. On the positive side is the promise of the restoration of all things (vv. 19–21); on the negative side is the threat that those who do not listen to Jesus will be completely cut off (v. 23).

3:24–26 One of the blessings of Christ's resurrection is that people will be turned from their wicked ways (v. 26). This is in keeping with the many promises of the OT regarding the new covenant (Jer 31:31–34; Eze 11:19; 36:26–27). Repentance and forgiveness will also result in "times of refreshing" (v. 19).

3:1–26 Here at the beginning of the Christian church we find Peter explaining in clear, detailed speech the ministry and sacrifice of Jesus to a crowd who had been aware of his teaching and had likely either seen or heard about his crucifixion. Boldly in the temple precincts Peter pokes the figurative hornet's nest and declares to all who will listen that "by faith in the name of Jesus, this man whom you see and know was made strong. It is Jesus' name and the faith that comes through him that has completely healed him, as you can all see" (v. 16).

Peter, the one who had infamously denied even knowing Jesus, experienced his love and power in restoration and now speaks boldly in the center of the city. He courageously calls the Jewish leaders to account (vv. 14–15) and then pleads that they repent of their sin and find the true way that Jesus proclaimed (v. 19).

What a beautiful picture of the transformational power of forgiveness. Peter's momentary failure is in the past, its tragic emotion of sorrow converted into an empowered lifetime of passionate ministry.

4:1–4 As in the case of Jesus, the popularity of the church with the people prevented the authorities from taking action against it. But by the time of

until the next day. 4But many who heard
the message believed; so the number of
men who believed grew[d] to about five
thousand.
5The next day the rulers,[e] the elders
and the teachers of the law met in Jerusalem. 6Annas the high priest was there,
and so were Caiaphas,[f] John, Alexander
and others of the high priest's family.
7They had Peter and John brought before them and began to question them:
"By what power or what name did you
do this?"
8Then Peter, filled with the Holy Spirit, said to them: "Rulers and elders of
the people![g] 9If we are being called to
account today for an act of kindness
shown to a man who was lame[h] and are
being asked how he was healed, 10then
know this, you and all the people of Israel: It is by the name of Jesus Christ
of Nazareth, whom you crucified but
whom God raised from the dead,[i] that
this man stands before you healed.
11Jesus is

"'the stone you builders rejected,
which has become the
cornerstone.'[a][j]

12Salvation is found in no one else, for
there is no other name under heaven
given to mankind by which we must be
saved."[k]
13When they saw the courage of Peter
and John[l] and realized that they were
unschooled, ordinary men,[m] they were
astonished and they took note that these
men had been with Jesus. 14But since
they could see the man who had been
healed standing there with them, there

4:4 [d]Ac 2:41
4:5 [e]Lk 23:13
4:6 [f]Mt 26:3; Lk 3:2
4:8 [g]ver 5; Lk 23:13
4:9 [h]Ac 3:6
4:10 [i]Ac 2:24
4:11 [j]Ps 118:22; Isa 28:16; Mt 21:42
4:12 [k]Mt 1:21; Ac 10:43; 1Ti 2:5
4:13 [l]Lk 22:8 [m]Mt 11:25

[a] *11* Psalm 118:22

Stephen's death (ch. 7), the people also seem to have turned against the church.

Peter is seized by the priests, the captain of the temple guard, and the Sadducees. They were particularly disturbed about the message of the resurrection (v. 2). They are deeply concerned, for "many who heard the message believed; so the number of men who believed grew to about five thousand" (v. 4). This growth is phenomenal, considering that women and children are not included in this accounting.

4:5–7 Annas and his son-in-law Caiaphas had participated in Jesus' trial some weeks before, but their hopes of getting rid of Jesus were short-lived. They demand to know the source of the apostles' "power" and "name" (i.e., authority, v. 7).

4:8–12 The disciples, technically on the defensive, switch to an attacking position in their response (v. 10). Peter cites Ps 118:22, a favorite text in the early church (Ac 4:11). He proclaims Christ as the only means of salvation (v. 12). Peter is referring here to a broader meaning than deliverance from sickness. He is talking about a change of status from being rebels to being accepted among God's people.

4:13–14 This performance reminds the Sanhedrin how the disciples have been influenced by Jesus.

PEOPLE TO KNOW // CAIAPHAS

ACTS 4:6: Caiaphas was the high priest in Jerusalem during Jesus' trial and crucifixion. On the night of his arrest, Jesus was brought to the palace of Caiaphas for questioning. When Jesus spoke of himself with messianic language drawn from Daniel 7:3 and Psalm 110:1, Caiaphas tore his clothes and accused Jesus of blasphemy (Mt 26:65).

Caiaphas was a Sadducee, part of a group known for close and lucrative ties with Rome. Benefiting from Rome meant Caiaphas had a vested interest in maintaining peace. Jesus was a liability to that peace, stirring up crowds and causing controversy. Eliminating Jesus was as pragmatic and political for Caiaphas as it was theological.

In John 11:50, Caiaphas told Sanhedrin members debating the problem of Jesus' rising popularity, "It is better for you that one man die for the people than that the whole nation perish." Caiaphas wanted to kill Jesus to avoid irritating the Roman officials, who would put down any perceived threat to their rule. John writes that Caiaphas's words had a deeper meaning than he knew, however. As high priest, he spoke prophetically of the reality that Jesus' death was truly on behalf of the Jewish nation and all God's scattered people (Jn 11:51–52). Sadly, Caiaphas did not know the truth of his own words.

APPLICATION ✣ Political and personal interests can get in the way of sincere devotion and faith. Caiaphas benefited from supporting Rome, and this kept his heart from being open to Christ. Caiaphas's story is a warning: When our focus is on maintaining political agendas, business alliances or selfish aspirations, we risk missing the life-giving message and invitation of Christ.

was nothing they could say. 15 So they
ordered them to withdraw from the Sanhedrin[n] and then conferred together.
16 "What are we going to do with these
men?"[o] they asked. "Everyone living in
Jerusalem knows they have performed
a notable sign,[p] and we cannot deny it.
17 But to stop this thing from spreading
any further among the people, we must
warn them to speak no longer to anyone
in this name."

18 Then they called them in again and
commanded them not to speak or teach
at all in the name of Jesus.[q] 19 But Peter
and John replied, "Which is right in God's
eyes: to listen to you, or to him?[r] You be
the judges! 20 As for us, we cannot help
speaking about what we have seen and
heard."

21 After further threats they let them
go. They could not decide how to punish
them, because all the people[s] were praising God[t] for what had happened. 22 For
the man who was miraculously healed
was over forty years old.

The Believers Pray

23 On their release, Peter and John went
back to their own people and reported
all that the chief priests and the elders
had said to them. 24 When they heard
this, they raised their voices together in prayer to God. "Sovereign Lord,"
they said, "you made the heavens and
the earth and the sea, and everything
in them. 25 You spoke by the Holy Spirit
through the mouth of your servant, our
father David:[u]

"'Why do the nations rage
and the peoples plot in vain?
26 The kings of the earth rise up
and the rulers band together
against the Lord
and against his anointed one.[a] '[b][v]

27 Indeed Herod[w] and Pontius Pilate[x]
met together with the Gentiles and the
people of Israel in this city to conspire
against your holy servant Jesus,[y] whom
you anointed. 28 They did what your power and will had decided beforehand
should happen.[z] 29 Now, Lord, consider
their threats and enable your servants
to speak your word with great boldness.[a]
30 Stretch out your hand to heal and perform signs and wonders[b] through the
name of your holy servant Jesus."[c]

4:15 [n] Mt 5:22
4:16 [o] Jn 11:47 [p] Ac 3:6-10
4:18 [q] Ac 5:40
4:19 [r] Ac 5:29
4:21 [s] Ac 5:26 [t] Mt 9:8
4:25 [u] Ac 1:16
4:26 [v] Ps 2:1, 2; Da 9:25; Lk 4:18; Ac 10:38; Heb 1:9
4:27 [w] Mt 14:1 [x] Mt 27:2; Lk 23:12 [y] ver 30
4:28 [z] Ac 2:23
4:29 [a] ver 13, 31; Ac 9:27; 14:3; Php 1:14
4:30 [b] Jn 4:48 [c] ver 27

a 26 That is, Messiah or Christ *b* 26 Psalm 2:1,2

Ac 4:16-17 ❖ What causes hearts to remain hard even after great displays of God's power? Why are some people strongly opposed to Christ?

The apostles have a boldness that comes from confidence about their message and empowerment by the Spirit.

4:15-22 After ordering Peter and John to leave the Sanhedrin, the Jewish leaders discuss the dilemma they are in (v. 16). The only thing they can do is command Peter and John "not to speak or teach at all in the name of Jesus" (v. 18). The two apostles bravely and defiantly reply that they must obey God (vv. 19-20). The Sanhedrin determines that even so bold a proclamation of defiance cannot bring about a punishment. All they can do is to threaten the apostles further and release them (v. 21).

4:1-22 The apostles' courageous stand for Jesus puts them in the same jeopardy as Jesus faced. As they confirm Jesus' claims, they're roughly dragged before the same Jewish leaders who had forced Pilate to condemn Jesus to death.

The disciples were willing to risk everything to proclaim the truth about Jesus. This is further evidence that the Spirit-empowered message they conveyed was true. May the same be true of believers today as we seek to expand the kingdom exponentially in the name of our Savior and in anticipation of his return.

4:23-24a The immediate response when the disciples return to their fellowship is to pray (v. 24). The word translated "together" is one of Luke's favorite words (v. 24). The word indicates unity among the Christians as they prayed.

4:24b-28 When the title "Sovereign Lord" is combined with the Christians' affirmation that God is Creator (v. 24b), we see that the Sovereign Creator is more powerful than those whom he created. Therefore, nothing can thwart his plans.

The prayer goes on to assert how God's sovereignty has been revealed in history. First comes a quotation from Ps 2:1-2 about the power of those who are opposed to God (Ac 4:25-26). Throughout history, the powers of this world have stood against the cause of God and of Christ. Verse 27 cites the death of Christ as a specific application of this principle.

Verses 24-26 are saturated with Scripture. This is typical of many spontaneous prayers in the Bible. Scripture had been stored in the minds and hearts of biblical people, ready to be harnessed in times of need.

4:29-30 After the extended reflection on God's sovereignty, these believers give only one passing reference to their problem (v. 29). The request they make is not for wisdom, protection, or favor with the authorities. All these are appropriate

31After they prayed, the place where
they were meeting was shaken.[d] And
they were all filled with the Holy Spirit
and spoke the word of God boldly.[e]

The Believers Share Their Possessions

32All the believers were one in heart
and mind. No one claimed that any of
their possessions was their own, but they
shared everything they had.[f] 33With great
power the apostles continued to testify[g]
to the resurrection[h] of the Lord Jesus.
And God's grace was so powerfully at
work in them all 34that there were no
needy persons among them. For from
time to time those who owned land or
houses sold them,[i] brought the money
from the sales 35and put it at the apostles'
feet,[j] and it was distributed to anyone
who had need.[k]
36Joseph, a Levite from Cyprus, whom
the apostles called Barnabas[l] (which
means "son of encouragement"), 37sold
a field he owned and brought the money
and put it at the apostles' feet.[m]

Ananias and Sapphira

5 Now a man named Ananias, together with his wife Sapphira, also sold
a piece of property. 2With his wife's full

4:31 [d] Ac 2:2 [e] ver 29
4:32 [f] Ac 2:44
4:33 [g] Lk 24:48 [h] Ac 1:22
4:34 [i] Mt 19:21; Ac 2:45
4:35 [j] ver 37; Ac 5:2 [k] Ac 2:45; 6:1
4:36 [l] Ac 9:27; 1Co 9:6
4:37 [m] ver 35; Ac 5:2

---

petitions, of course. But this prayer is for the ability to be obedient to Christ's command to them to preach the gospel.

The second request of the disciples is that God will show his power (v. 30). The only two requests in this prayer have to do with evangelism, which has just been officially outlawed. These people have a consuming passion for evangelism despite the warnings they just endured.

4:31 In the OT the shaking of a place was God's way of indicating that he was present and would answer the prayer (e.g., 1Sa 14:15). Next, "they were all filled with the Holy Spirit." This is not a fresh baptism but a fresh filling. The result of the filling is proclamation, so it is not surprising to find v. 31 ending with the announcement that the believers "spoke the word of God boldly."

4:23–31 Jesus' famous prayer for unity (Jn 17:20–23) begins to find its answer in the activities of the members of the early church. It is so important that believers under threat or facing opposition be supported by the larger Christian community. When we share our situation with our support group, we can unburden ourselves to them. When we keep it to ourselves, we can become so overwhelmed by the emotional influences of the situation that we cannot think straight about the problems.

The significance of partnership in a crisis is not only the strength that we give each other; being together also causes us to motivate each other in prayer to seek God, who is the source of our strength.

4:32 For a second time Luke describes the quality of the radical sharing that the first Christian community practiced (see 2:44–45). A deep unity was at the heart of sharing (v. 32a). In the Gospels, the disciples often quarreled among each other, but in Acts, the Twelve are a unified group, and this unity now spreads to the entire church.

4:33 "One in heart and mind" describes a comprehensive unity (v. 32). There was a spiritual unity of passionate commitment to a mission. Therefore, right in the middle of this description of unity we find the witness of the apostles. Community life is never an end in itself; a vibrant community is a community on mission.

4:34–35 The believers did not consider their possessions to be their own (v. 32b). As a result, "there were no needy persons among them" (v. 34a). But for that to happen, some costly sacrifices had to be made by some believers who sold their lands and houses for the cause (vv. 34b–35).

This selling of land is something that took place regularly. Whenever there was a need, those who owned land asked themselves whether the Lord wanted them to sell it. Some did and then gave the proceeds to the leaders to distribute wherever there was a need. The result was the elimination of poverty in the early church.

4:32–35 While being one in heart and mind is considered the usual model for Christian community life, it is not easy to maintain in today's individualistic society. This is an area where the church needs to be countercultural. Christian community life may be one of the most important prophetic messages we can give the world.

No one can deny the essential human pull toward something greater than ourselves without sooner or later feeling a void inside. The church must present itself as the group that can adequately fill this longing for community in the heart of the human being. As we reach out to others, may we be inspired by Jesus' clear instruction on the matter: "By this everyone will know that you are my disciples, if you love one another" (Jn 13:35).

4:36–37 After describing the spirit of sharing in the church (vv. 32–35), Luke gives good and bad examples of this sharing. Being a Levite from Cyprus, Barnabas was from the large groups of Hellenistic Jews who had migrated back to Jerusalem. He may have been from a wealthy background, for the mother of his cousin Mark had a house large enough to accommodate a prayer meeting for "many people" (12:12).

5:1–2 Next we have the notorious example of Ananias and Sapphira. The phrase "kept back" (v. 1) literally means "pilfered" or "embezzled." It's the same word the Septuagint uses for Achan's theft (Jos 7:1). Wrong use of our possessions is a serious sin in God's sight.

knowledge he kept back part of the money for himself, but brought the rest and
put it at the apostles' feet.[n]
3Then Peter said, "Ananias, how is it
that Satan[o] has so filled your heart[p] that
you have lied to the Holy Spirit[q] and have
kept for yourself some of the money you
received for the land? 4Didn't it belong to
you before it was sold? And after it was
sold, wasn't the money at your disposal?
What made you think of doing such a
thing? You have not lied just to human
beings but to God."
5When Ananias heard this, he fell
down and died.[r] And great fear[s] seized
all who heard what had happened.
6Then some young men came forward,
wrapped up his body,[t] and carried him
out and buried him.
7About three hours later his wife came
in, not knowing what had happened. 8Pe-
ter asked her, "Tell me, is this the price
you and Ananias got for the land?"
"Yes," she said, "that is the price."[u]
9Peter said to her, "How could you
conspire to test the Spirit of the Lord?[v]
Listen! The feet of the men who buried
your husband are at the door, and they
will carry you out also."
10At that moment she fell down at
his feet and died.[w] Then the young men
came in and, finding her dead, carried
her out and buried her beside her husband. 11Great fear[x] seized the whole
church and all who heard about these
events.

5:2 [n]Ac 4:35,37
5:3 [o]Mt 4:10 [p]Jn 13:2,27 [q]ver 9
5:5 [r]ver 10 [s]ver 11
5:6 [t]Jn 19:40
5:8 [u]ver 2
5:9 [v]ver 3
5:10 [w]ver 5
5:11 [x]ver 5; Ac 19:17

Ac 5:13 ❖ What can Christians do to be highly regarded by others? Do you think this should be a goal for Christians? Why or why not?

The Apostles Heal Many

12The apostles performed many signs
and wonders[y] among the people. And
all the believers used to meet together[z]
in Solomon's Colonnade.[a] 13No one else
dared join them, even though they were
highly regarded by the people.[b] 14Never-
theless, more and more men and wom-
en believed in the Lord and were added
to their number. 15As a result, people
brought the sick into the streets and laid
them on beds and mats so that at least
Peter's shadow might fall on some of
them as he passed by.[c] 16Crowds gathered
also from the towns around Jerusalem,
bringing their sick and those tormented
by impure spirits, and all of them were
healed.[d]

The Apostles Persecuted

17Then the high priest and all his associates, who were members of the party[e]
of the Sadducees,[f] were filled with jealousy. 18They arrested the apostles and
put them in the public jail.[g] 19But during
the night an angel[h] of the Lord opened
the doors of the jail[i] and brought them
out. 20"Go, stand in the temple courts,"
he said, "and tell the people all about
this new life."[j]

5:12 [y]Ac 2:43 [z]Ac 4:32 [a]Ac 3:11
5:13 [b]Ac 2:47; 4:21
5:15 [c]Ac 19:12
5:16 [d]Mk 16:17
5:17 [e]Ac 15:5 [f]Ac 4:1
5:18 [g]Ac 4:3
5:19 [h]Mt 1:20; Lk 1:11; Ac 8:26; 27:23 [i]Ac 16:26
5:20 [j]Jn 6:63, 68

5:3–4 Five important truths emerge from Peter's words to Ananias in v. 3. (1) Satan had so controlled Ananias's heart that he was carried away in his actions. (2) Satan's activity does not remove blame from Ananias (vv. 3–4). (3) Ananias's most serious offense was not in keeping the money back; he could have done whatever he wanted with his money (v. 4). (4) When we lie to the church, we lie to the Holy Spirit. (5) Since giving everything was not mandatory (v. 4), Ananias and Sapphira were motivated by the desire for recognition: They lied to win the same sort of esteem that Barnabas had won in the church.

5:5–11 Ananias first and then Sapphira fell down dead after Peter condemned their deceitfulness (vv. 5, 10). The result of the death of Ananias is that "great fear seized all who heard what had happened" (v. 5b). The fear resulting from judgment is a key aspect of the story. This was fear of displeasing God that comes from a knowledge of his holiness and the consequences of sin.

✚ **4:36—5:11** Both the OT and NT contain numerous warnings about the dangers of wealth and advice on how to use wealth responsibly and charitably. That should be the primary emphasis in Christian teaching about wealth.

One of the best ways to avoid the pitfalls of misusing our money is to have people to whom we can be accountable about our use of money. These can help us to avoid the deceptive snares of materialism that are always looming and threatening to take our eyes off of our mission for Christ.

5:12–16 The fear that came on the people because of Ananias and Sapphira (v. 11) did not reduce the evangelistic effectiveness of the apostles. They continued to minister with amazing and miraculous signs (vv. 12, 15–16) and to reap a kingdom harvest (v. 14).

5:17–20 Of course, the spectacular ministry of the apostles filled the Jewish leaders "with jealousy" (v. 17). They had to respond with a corresponding show of power, so they used political rather than spiritual power to attack the church (v. 18). Yet their plans were foiled through an angelic rescue (v. 19).

Angels appear often in Acts. Here the angel not only delivers the apostles from prison but

21At daybreak they entered the temple
courts, as they had been told, and began
to teach the people.
When the high priest and his associates[k]
arrived, they called together the Sanhedrin[l] — the full assembly of the elders of
Israel — and sent to the jail for the apostles. 22But on arriving at the jail, the officers did not find them there. So they went
back and reported, 23"We found the jail
securely locked, with the guards standing
at the doors; but when we opened them,
we found no one inside." 24On hearing this
report, the captain of the temple guard
and the chief priests[m] were at a loss, wondering what this might lead to.
25Then someone came and said, "Look!
The men you put in jail are standing in
the temple courts teaching the people."
26At that, the captain went with his officers and brought the apostles. They did
not use force, because they feared that
the people[n] would stone them.
27The apostles were brought in and
made to appear before the Sanhedrin[o] to
be questioned by the high priest. 28"We
gave you strict orders not to teach in this
name,"[p] he said. "Yet you have filled Jerusalem with your teaching and are determined to make us guilty of this man's
blood."[q]
29Peter and the other apostles replied:
"We must obey God rather than human
beings![r] 30The God of our ancestors[s]
raised Jesus from the dead[t] — whom you
killed by hanging him on a cross.[u] 31God
exalted him to his own right hand[v] as
Prince and Savior[w] that he might bring
Israel to repentance and forgive their
sins.[x] 32We are witnesses of these things,[y]
and so is the Holy Spirit,[z] whom God has
given to those who obey him."
33When they heard this, they were furious[a] and wanted to put them to death.
34But a Pharisee named Gamaliel,[b] a
teacher of the law,[c] who was honored
by all the people, stood up in the Sanhedrin and ordered that the men be put
outside for a little while. 35Then he addressed the Sanhedrin: "Men of Israel,
consider carefully what you intend to do
to these men. 36Some time ago Theudas
appeared, claiming to be somebody, and
about four hundred men rallied to him.

5:21 [k] Ac 4:5,6 [l] ver 27,34,41; Mt 5:22
5:24 [m] Ac 4:1
5:26 [n] Ac 4:21
5:27 [o] Mt 5:22
5:28 [p] Ac 4:18 [q] Mt 23:35; 27:25; Ac 2:23, 36; 3:14,15; 7:52
5:29 [r] Ac 4:19
5:30 [s] Ac 3:13 [t] Ac 2:24 [u] Ac 10:39; 13:29; Gal 3:13; 1Pe 2:24
5:31 [v] Ac 2:33 [w] Lk 2:11 [x] Mt 1:21; Lk 24:47; Ac 2:38
5:32 [y] Lk 24:48 [z] Jn 15:26
5:33 [a] Ac 2:37; 7:54
5:34 [b] Ac 22:3 [c] Lk 2:46

---

also encourages them to fulfill their call by giving them a fresh commission (v. 20).

5:21–28 In instances of threat and danger in Acts, the key word from God concerns boldness in witness (4:29–31; 18:9–11; 23:11). Three times in this passage the evangelistic ministry of the apostles is described with the verb "teach" (vv. 21, 25, 28). There must have been a major emphasis on the content of the truth of the gospel.

In the meantime, the meeting of "the full assembly of the elders of Israel" (i.e., the Sanhedrin) is ready to begin (v. 21), but the prisoners are missing (vv. 21–23). The puzzled officials are then informed that these men "are standing in the temple courts teaching the people" (v. 25). The captain of the temple guard himself goes to rearrest them. How ironic that those who probably had wanted to stone the apostles for blasphemy are now afraid that they themselves will be stoned by the people. Consequently, "they did not use force" (v. 26). The apostles are accused of disobeying orders and making the Jewish hierarchy "guilty of this man's blood" (v. 28).

5:29–32 "Peter and the other apostles" (v. 29) reply to the Sanhedrin. The Christian community is solidly unified. Peter is willing to die rather than disobey his Lord. Later he will say that the Holy Spirit is "given to those who obey him" (v. 32). His obedience gives him credibility that qualifies him to write about obedience (see 1Pe 1:2, 14, 22; 3:1, 6; 4:17).

The response given to the Sanhedrin is recorded in summary form here. The apostles do not give what would be expected of a defense at a trial. Rather, they witness to the facts of the gospel (vv. 30–32; cf. 4:8–12). The apostolic proclamation is even more clearly explained here than in ch. 4.

As always, Peter gives an introduction arising from the particular situation (v. 29).

Next, the facts of Christ are presented. The expression "the God of our ancestors" (v. 30a) reminds the hearers of the great acts of God in Israel's history.

Then comes a reference to Jesus' death: "Whom you killed by hanging him on a cross" (v. 30b; cf. 10:39). The idea of hanging on a cross probably reminds his hearers of Dt 21:23 in addition to Christ's crucifixion. By the time Peter wrote his first letter he had developed the theological significance of the tree more fully (1Pe 2:24). Here Peter presents it as a triumph of God planned long ago.

The resurrection is implied in Peter's next statement about Jesus' exaltation (v. 31).

Next comes the offer of salvation. Repentance is triggered through the hearing of the gospel, which brings the conviction of sin. But the grace to repent is given by Christ (v. 31b).

Peter then reinforces his points about Christ by claiming, "We are witnesses of these things" (v. 32a).

Finally, Peter insists that the Holy Spirit is also a witness and that he has been given to those who are obedient (v. 32b). In other words, the Spirit's witness is made through believers.

5:33–40 The fury of the Sanhedrin (v. 33) is tempered by the comments of Gamaliel (vv. 34–40). He was the greatest teacher of his era and was considered the embodiment of Pharisaism. He is confident that God will sovereignly show in history whether this movement is of him or not. Gamaliel

He was killed, all his followers were dispersed, and it all came to nothing. 37After
him, Judas the Galilean appeared in the
days of the census[d] and led a band of people in revolt. He too was killed, and all his
followers were scattered. 38Therefore, in
the present case I advise you: Leave these
men alone! Let them go! For if their purpose or activity is of human origin, it will
fail.[e] 39But if it is from God, you will not
be able to stop these men; you will only
find yourselves fighting against God."[f]
40His speech persuaded them. They
called the apostles in and had them
flogged.[g] Then they ordered them not
to speak in the name of Jesus, and let
them go.
41The apostles left the Sanhedrin, rejoicing[h] because they had been counted worthy of suffering disgrace for the
Name.[i] 42Day after day, in the temple
courts[j] and from house to house, they
never stopped teaching and proclaiming
the good news that Jesus is the Messiah.

The Choosing of the Seven

6 In those days when the number of disciples was increasing,[k] the Hellenistic
Jews[a][l] among them complained against
the Hebraic Jews because their widows[m]
were being overlooked in the daily distribution of food.[n] 2So the Twelve gathered all the disciples together and said,
"It would not be right for us to neglect
the ministry of the word of God in order
to wait on tables. 3Brothers and sisters,[o]
choose seven men from among you who
are known to be full of the Spirit and wisdom. We will turn this responsibility over
to them 4and will give our attention to
prayer[p] and the ministry of the word."
5This proposal pleased the whole
group. They chose Stephen,[q] a man full
of faith and of the Holy Spirit;[r] also Philip,[s] Procorus, Nicanor, Timon, Parmenas,
and Nicolas from Antioch, a convert to
Judaism. 6They presented these men to
the apostles, who prayed[t] and laid their
hands on them.[u]

5:37 [d] Lk 2:1,2
5:38 [e] Mt 15:13
5:39 [f] Pr 21:30; Ac 7:51; 11:17
5:40 [g] Mt 10:17
5:41 [h] Mt 5:12 [i] Jn 15:21
5:42 [j] Ac 2:46
6:1 [k] Ac 2:41 [l] Ac 9:29 [m] Ac 9:39,41 [n] Ac 4:35
6:3 [o] Ac 1:16
6:4 [p] Ac 1:14
6:5 [q] ver 8; Ac 11:19 [r] Ac 11:24 [s] Ac 8:5-40; 21:8
6:6 [t] Ac 1:24; 8:17; 13:3; 2Ti 1:6 [u] Nu 8:10; Ac 9:17; 1Ti 4:14

Ac 6:1 ❖ Who are those being overlooked in our faith community? How can we minister to them?

[a] *1* That is, Jews who had adopted the Greek language and culture

---

warns that by opposing it, they may be opposing God himself (vv. 38–39).

5:41 Incredibly, the apostles rejoice over their flogging, because "they had been counted worthy of suffering disgrace for the Name." What a change from the story of them scattering in the garden when Jesus was arrested (Mt 26:56). We see here a new dimension in the exposition on suffering, a major subtheme of Acts: To suffer for Christ is an honor that causes joy.

5:42 Since this report of nonstop evangelistic activity comes immediately after the report of the beating that the apostles received, it seems as if Luke wants to emphasize that the beating only resulted in an increased passion for evangelism.

✣ **5:12–42** The apostles' teaching in the early church pulled no punches. Before we ask people to accept the gospel, they need to know those aspects of the essential gospel that may at first feel unpleasant to them.

As we talk to people about Jesus, we do not want them to imagine or accept a Christianity that is neutral on the matter of sin. Repentance calls for a turning away from a life of sin and toward the righteousness of God. As we engage with those whom we hope to win for Christ, we must not lower our standards and not talk about a life lived in the Spirit's power over sin. The ministry of Jesus and of the early church show that we do not have to become sinners to attract sinners. Jesus paid the price of such identification; he was accused of being a sinner himself because he moved so closely among them. But he never lowered his principles.

6:1 Jewish society had a system to help needy widows. It's likely that the isolation that resulted when such women became Christians made these sources less accessible to them. Also many older couples came to die in Jerusalem so that they could be buried there, which increased the population of elderly people in need.

Almost certainly the Grecian widows were not deliberately discriminated against. The cause of the problem was the increase in the number of disciples (v. 1a). In an active and expanding movement, it is possible for less prominent people to become less noticeable.

6:2–3 The apostles did not focus their attention on a complaining attitude toward the leadership. There was a genuine problem, and the best way to dispel doubts about prejudice was to solve the problem first. So the apostles made an administrative decision and not only averted a crisis of disunity but also took a significant leap forward in terms of the new church's organizational structure. This decision laid the foundation for the role of deacons.

The procedure adopted in choosing the Seven is instructive. When the complaint came from the Grecians, "the Twelve gathered all the disciples together" (v. 2). The entire group was given the task of choosing seven officials to oversee the work of distributing food. The apostles laid down qualifications: They were to be known to be "full of the Spirit and wisdom" (v. 3a).

6:5–6 "This proposal pleased the whole group"

7 So the word of God spread.[v] The number of disciples in Jerusalem increased
rapidly, and a large number of priests
became obedient to the faith.

Stephen Seized

8 Now Stephen, a man full of God's
grace and power, performed great wonders and signs[w] among the people. 9 Opposition arose, however, from members
of the Synagogue of the Freedmen (as it
was called) — Jews of Cyrene[x] and Alexandria as well as the provinces of Cilicia[y] and Asia[z] — who began to argue with
Stephen. 10 But they could not stand up
against the wisdom the Spirit gave him
as he spoke.[a]
11 Then they secretly[b] persuaded some
men to say, "We have heard Stephen
speak blasphemous words against Moses and against God."[c]
12 So they stirred up the people and the
elders and the teachers of the law. They
seized Stephen and brought him before
the Sanhedrin.[d] 13 They produced false
witnesses, who testified, "This fellow
never stops speaking against this holy
place[e] and against the law. 14 For we have
heard him say that this Jesus of Nazareth will destroy this place and change
the customs Moses handed down to us."[f]
15 All who were sitting in the Sanhedrin[g] looked intently at Stephen, and
they saw that his face was like the face
of an angel.

Stephen's Speech to the Sanhedrin

7 Then the high priest asked Stephen,
"Are these charges true?"
2 To this he replied: "Brothers and fathers,[h] listen to me! The God of glory[i]
appeared to our father Abraham while
he was still in Mesopotamia, before he
lived in Harran.[j] 3 'Leave your country
and your people,' God said, 'and go to
the land I will show you.'[a][k]
4 "So he left the land of the Chaldeans
and settled in Harran. After the death
of his father, God sent him to this land
where you are now living.[l] 5 He gave him

6:7 [v] Ac 12:24; 19:20
6:8 [w] Jn 4:48
6:9 [x] Mt 27:32 [y] Ac 15:23, 41; 22:3; 23:34 [z] Ac 2:9
6:10 [a] Lk 21:15
6:11 [b] 1Ki 21:10 [c] Mt 26:59-61
6:12 [d] Mt 5:22
6:13 [e] Ac 21:28
6:14 [f] Ac 15:1; 21:21; 26:3; 28:17
6:15 [g] Mt 5:22
7:2 [h] Ac 22:1 [i] Ps 29:3 [j] Ge 11:31; 15:7
7:3 [k] Ge 12:1
7:4 [l] Ge 12:5

[a] 3 Gen. 12:1

(v. 5), and they chose seven men, then "presented these men to the apostles, who prayed and laid their hands on them" (v. 6). There we see the beginnings of church leaders laying hands on believers and commissioning them for specific tasks.

6:7 Luke is eager to show that this administrative change did not reduce the evangelistic enthusiasm of the church. Luke wants us to catch the spirit of this consuming passion for evangelism.

> ✣ **6:1–7** Some leaders try to sweep under the rug problems like those faced in Acts 6 because they do not want to face the humiliation or complexity that comes if such problems surface. Such delays in dealing with problems usually aggravate problems and open the door for increased trouble and disunity.
>
> Whatever may come, we know that God is bigger than the problems we face and that what unites us is deeper than what divides us. Therefore, we must have the courage to face up to these problems and address them head-on, in the spirit of love and compassion. Paul called for the same in Eph 4:1–6 when he wrote, "I urge you to live a life worthy of the calling you have received. Be completely humble and gentle; be patient, bearing with one another in love. Make every effort to keep the unity of the Spirit through the bond of peace. There is one body and one Spirit, just as you were called to one hope when you were called; one Lord, one faith, one baptism; one God and Father of all, who is over all and through all and in all."

6:8–10 Stephen must have been outstanding because Luke mentions six features of his character and ministry in vv. 5–10. (1) He was "a man full of faith" (v. 5). Stephen saw certain implications in what the Bible taught and what Christ did, and he was willing to risk everything for the truth of those implications. (2) He was "full . . . of the Holy Spirit" (v. 5). This feature manifested itself as he did "great wonders and signs among the people" (v. 8). (3) He was "a man full of God's grace" (v. 8). Stephen had let God's grace impact him so much that it made him a gracious person. Stephen was able to act in a Christlike way under provocation. (4) The opponents who debated Stephen were "members of the Synagogue of the Freedmen" (v. 9). The most important town in Cilicia was Tarsus, Paul's hometown. Did Paul (Saul) worship in this synagogue? We cannot be sure, but we know that he was involved in Stephen's death (7:58).

The last two features of Stephen's character relate to his preaching: "They could not stand up against the wisdom the Spirit gave him as he spoke" (v. 10). We see this wisdom in Stephen's speech, applying Scripture skillfully to the challenges arising from the gospel. Stephen speaks in a way that cuts to the heart of their thinking, and his opponents cannot answer him.

6:11–15 After failing to silence Stephen through debate, the Jews try to silence him through the law. They bring charges against him (v. 13), which allows them to take him to be tried before the Sanhedrin. Before his speech, even the Sanhedrin can't deny that Stephen's "face was like the face of an angel" (v. 15).

7:1–53 Stephen argues his points from Israel's history as recorded in the OT. Every phrase of this speech is worth a close examination, for he delivers a comprehensive history of Israel's past with a

no inheritance here, not even enough ground to set his foot on. But God promised him that he and his descendants after him would possess the land,[m] even though at that time Abraham had no child. 6God spoke to him in this way: 'For four hundred years your descendants will be strangers in a country not their own, and they will be enslaved and mistreated.[n] 7But I will punish the nation they serve as slaves,' God said, 'and afterward they will come out of that country and worship me in this place.'[a][o] 8Then he gave Abraham the covenant of circumcision.[p] And Abraham became the father of Isaac and circumcised him eight days after his birth.[q] Later Isaac became the father of Jacob,[r] and Jacob became the father of the twelve patriarchs.[s]

9"Because the patriarchs were jealous of Joseph,[t] they sold him as a slave into Egypt.[u] But God was with him[v] 10and rescued him from all his troubles. He gave Joseph wisdom and enabled him to gain the goodwill of Pharaoh king of Egypt. So Pharaoh made him ruler over Egypt and all his palace.[w]

11"Then a famine struck all Egypt and Canaan, bringing great suffering, and our ancestors could not find food.[x] 12When Jacob heard that there was grain in Egypt, he sent our forefathers on their first visit.[y] 13On their second visit, Joseph told his brothers who he was,[z] and Pharaoh learned about Joseph's family. 14After this, Joseph sent for his father Jacob and his whole family,[a] seventy-five in all.[b] 15Then Jacob went down to Egypt, where he and our ancestors died.[c] 16Their bodies were brought back to Shechem and placed in the tomb that Abraham had bought from the sons of Hamor at Shechem for a certain sum of money.[d]

17"As the time drew near for God to fulfill his promise to Abraham, the number of our people in Egypt had greatly increased.[e] 18Then 'a new king, to whom Joseph meant nothing, came to power in Egypt.'[b][f] 19He dealt treacherously with our people and oppressed our ancestors by forcing them to throw out their newborn babies so that they would die.[g]

20"At that time Moses was born, and he was no ordinary child.[c] For three months he was cared for by his family.[h] 21When he was placed outside, Pharaoh's daughter took him and brought him up as her own son.[i] 22Moses was educated in all the wisdom of the Egyptians[j] and was powerful in speech and action.

23"When Moses was forty years old, he decided to visit his own people, the Israelites. 24He saw one of them being mistreated by an Egyptian, so he went to his defense and avenged him by killing the Egyptian. 25Moses thought that his own people would realize that God was using him to rescue them, but they did not. 26The next day Moses came upon two Israelites who were fighting. He tried to reconcile them by saying, 'Men, you are brothers; why do you want to hurt each other?'

27"But the man who was mistreating the other pushed Moses aside and said, 'Who made you ruler and judge over us? 28Are you thinking of killing me as you killed the Egyptian yesterday?'[d] 29When Moses heard this, he fled to Midian, where he settled as a foreigner and had two sons.[k]

30"After forty years had passed, an angel appeared to Moses in the flames of a burning bush in the desert near Mount Sinai. 31When he saw this, he was amazed at the sight. As he went over to get a closer look, he heard the Lord say:[l] 32'I am the God of your fathers, the God of Abraham, Isaac and Jacob.'[e] Moses trembled with fear and did not dare to look.[m]

33"Then the Lord said to him, 'Take off your sandals, for the place where you are standing is holy ground.[n] 34I have indeed seen the oppression of my people

7:5 [m] Ge 12:7; 17:8; 26:3
7:6 [n] Ex 12:40
7:7 [o] Ex 3:12
7:8 [p] Ge 17:9-14 [q] Ge 21:2-4 [r] Ge 25:26 [s] Ge 29:31-35; 30:5-13, 17-24; 35:16-18, 22-26
7:9 [t] Ge 37:4, 11 [u] Ge 37:28; Ps 105:17 [v] Ge 39:2, 21, 23
7:10 [w] Ge 41:37-43
7:11 [x] Ge 41:54
7:12 [y] Ge 42:1, 2
7:13 [z] Ge 45:1-4
7:14 [a] Ge 45:9, 10 [b] Ge 46:26, 27; Ex 1:5; Dt 10:22
7:15 [c] Ge 46:5-7; 49:33; Ex 1:6
7:16 [d] Ge 23:16-20; 33:18, 19; 50:13; Jos 24:32
7:17 [e] Ex 1:7; Ps 105:24
7:18 [f] Ex 1:8
7:19 [g] Ex 1:10-22
7:20 [h] Ex 2:2; Heb 11:23
7:21 [i] Ex 2:3-10
7:22 [j] 1Ki 4:30; Isa 19:11
7:29 [k] Ex 2:11-15
7:31 [l] Ex 3:1-4
7:32 [m] Ex 3:6
7:33 [n] Ex 3:5; Jos 5:15

[a] *7* Gen. 15:13,14 [b] *18* Exodus 1:8 [c] *20* Or *was fair in the sight of God* [d] *28* Exodus 2:14 [e] *32* Exodus 3:6

---

focused view toward the new reality of Jesus' death and resurrection. Stephen presents his message in vigorous language by claiming that Israelite history is a history of rejection (vv. 51–53) and that they have indeed killed the One to whom all of Israelite history has pointed: Jesus Christ. It is possible that Stephen has to end his talk abruptly at this point because his audience has become so agitated.

There is little about Jesus and a lot about Moses in this speech, which is understandable since the charge against Stephen is about his rejecting Moses' teachings (6:11, 14). Stephen points to one significant thing that Moses said to the Israelites about Jesus (7:37). The other two references to Jesus are both in v. 52.

PEOPLE TO KNOW // **STEPHEN**

ACTS 7:1-60: Stephen was one of the original seven deacons selected by the early church after the death and resurrection of Jesus. Stephen is described as being full of faith and the Holy Spirit (Ac 6:5). The deacons were selected to help fill the daily needs of certain widows, so Stephen must have been known to be a person of mercy and compassion.

Stephen was also a man full of God's power, equipped by God to perform great signs and wonders (Ac 6:8). The Jewish leaders didn't like the growing popularity of the Christians. They targeted Stephen, conspired against him and had him put on trial. As they falsely accused him, Stephen's face was like that of an angel (Ac 6:15).

When the high priest questioned Stephen, Stephen gave a lengthy and eloquent speech. Beginning with Abraham, Stephen recounted the story of Israel, quoting directly from Scripture multiple times. At the end of his speech, he alleged that his accusers had rejected God's Righteous One, Jesus, and had not obeyed God's law.

The Jewish leaders were furious; looking up toward heaven, Stephen saw a vision of Christ. When he told them what he saw, they took him and stoned him. As the heavy stones crashed into his body, Stephen prayed for God to receive his spirit and also for God not to hold the sin of his killers against them (Ac 7:59–60). Stephen perished, the first martyr of the Christian church.

APPLICATION ✣ The word *martyr* comes from the word meaning "witness." All Christians should bear witness to what they believe, always ready to offer an answer to those who ask a reason for the hope within them (1Pe 3:15). Sometimes bearing witness to Christ will not be well-received, as Stephen experienced. Yet Jesus promised that if we acknowledge him before others, he will acknowledge us before God the Father (Mt 10:32)—the greatest reward we could ever imagine.

in Egypt. I have heard their groaning and have come down to set them free. Now come, I will send you back to Egypt.'[a][o]

35"This is the same Moses they had rejected with the words, 'Who made you ruler and judge?'[p] He was sent to be their ruler and deliverer by God himself, through the angel who appeared to him in the bush. 36He led them out of Egypt[q] and performed wonders and signs in Egypt, at the Red Sea[r] and for forty years in the wilderness.

37"This is the Moses who told the Israelites, 'God will raise up for you a prophet like me from your own people.'[b][s] 38He was in the assembly in the wilderness, with the angel[t] who spoke to him on Mount Sinai, and with our ancestors;[u] and he received living words[v] to pass on to us.[w]

39"But our ancestors refused to obey him. Instead, they rejected him and in their hearts turned back to Egypt.[x] 40They told Aaron, 'Make us gods who will go before us. As for this fellow Moses who led us out of Egypt—we don't know what has happened to him!'[c][y] 41That was the time they made an idol in the form of a calf. They brought sacrifices to it and reveled in what their own hands had made.[z] 42But God turned away from them[a] and gave them over to the worship of the sun, moon and stars.[b] This agrees with what is written in the book of the prophets:

"'Did you bring me sacrifices and
offerings
forty years in the wilderness,
people of Israel?
43You have taken up the tabernacle of
Molek
and the star of your god Rephan,
the idols you made to worship.
Therefore I will send you into
exile'[d][c] beyond Babylon.

44"Our ancestors had the tabernacle of the covenant law[d] with them in the wilderness. It had been made as God directed Moses, according to the pattern he had seen.[e] 45After receiving the tabernacle, our ancestors under Joshua brought it with them when they took the land from the nations God drove out before them.[f] It remained in the land until the

7:34 [o] Ex 3:7-10
7:35 [p] ver 27
7:36 [q] Ex 12:41; 33:1 [r] Ex 14:21
7:37 [s] Dt 18:15, 18; Ac 3:22
7:38 [t] ver 53 [u] Ex 19:17 [v] Dt 32:45-47; Heb 4:12 [w] Ro 3:2
7:39 [x] Nu 14:3,4
7:40 [y] Ex 32:1, 23
7:41 [z] Ex 32:4-6; Ps 106:19, 20; Rev 9:20
7:42 [a] Jos 24:20; Isa 63:10 [b] Jer 19:13
7:43 [c] Am 5:25-27
7:44 [d] Ex 38:21 [e] Ex 25:8, 9, 40
7:45 [f] Jos 3:14-17; 18:1; 23:9; 24:18; Ps 44:2

[a] *34* Exodus 3:5,7,8,10 [b] *37* Deut. 18:15 [c] *40* Exodus 32:1 [d] *43* Amos 5:25-27 (see Septuagint)

Ac 7:51 ❖ What does it mean to resist the Holy Spirit? How can we avoid this sin?

time of David, 46 who enjoyed God's favor
and asked that he might provide a dwelling place for the God of Jacob.[a][g] 47 But it
was Solomon who built a house for him.
48 "However, the Most High does not
live in houses made by human hands.[h]
As the prophet says:

49 " 'Heaven is my throne,
and the earth is my footstool.[i]
What kind of house will you build
for me?
says the Lord.
Or where will my resting place be?
50 Has not my hand made all these
things?'[b][j]

51 "You stiff-necked people![k] Your
hearts[l] and ears are still uncircumcised.
You are just like your ancestors: You always resist the Holy Spirit! 52 Was there
ever a prophet your ancestors did not
persecute?[m] They even killed those who
predicted the coming of the Righteous
One. And now you have betrayed and
murdered him[n]— 53 you who have received the law that was given through
angels[o] but have not obeyed it."

The Stoning of Stephen

54 When the members of the Sanhedrin heard this, they were furious[p] and
gnashed their teeth at him. 55 But Stephen, full of the Holy Spirit, looked up
to heaven and saw the glory of God, and
Jesus standing at the right hand of God.[q]
56 "Look," he said, "I see heaven open[r] and
the Son of Man[s] standing at the right
hand of God."
57 At this they covered their ears and,
yelling at the top of their voices, they

7:46 [g] 2Sa 7:8-16; Ps 132:1-5
7:48 [h] 1Ki 8:27; 2Ch 2:6
7:49 [i] Mt 5:34, 35
7:50 [j] Isa 66:1,2
7:51 [k] Ex 32:9; 33:3,5 [l] Lev 26:41; Dt 10:16; Jer 4:4; 9:26
7:52 [m] 2Ch 36:16; Mt 5:12 [n] Ac 3:14; 1Th 2:15
7:53 [o] ver 38; Gal 3:19; Heb 2:2
7:54 [p] Ac 5:33
7:55 [q] Mk 16:19
7:56 [r] Mt 3:16 [s] Mt 8:20

[a] 46 Some early manuscripts *the house of Jacob*
[b] 50 Isaiah 66:1,2

7:51–53 Stephen's final words of accusation may make us wonder what has happened to his angelic face. However, we do well to remember that some of the angels in the Bible are agents of judgment. Stephen is like Christ here: Though Jesus radiated the love of God as no one else did, he also expressed God's wrath against hypocrisy, especially in reference to the Pharisees (Mt 23:13–23).

Though Stephen did not live to see the results of his speech, God revealed later that his ministry had generated great fruit. The trail he blazed was later followed by Paul—the one who approved of his death (8:1) and watched the clothes of those who stoned him (7:58), but who later became the apostle to the Gentiles. Stephen is also considered the precursor of the later Christian apologists, especially those who defended the faith against Judaism.

✣ **6:8—7:53** The call to be winsome radicals, like Stephen, is an important challenge facing Christians today. If we are faithful to God, we are sure to face anger and opposition from within and outside of the church. We will be treated unjustly, and many will attribute unworthy motives to what we do. How can we remain focused on winning souls to Jesus under such circumstances?

Stephen clearly achieved his winsomeness through his contact with God. Evidence of this intimate relationship abounds in Ac 6–7. His communion with God seemed to deepen as the viciousness of the opposition deepened. When he was brought to trial, his closeness to God made his face look like that of an angel (6:15). Filled with the Spirit, he had a vision of Christ and began to say the same things that Jesus said at his death (7:59–60).

The key to maintaining positivity under pressure is maintaining our relationship with God, as Stephen did. As we work to build the kingdom, let us follow the example of Stephen, who was faithful in his connection with God and filled with the Spirit. In our daily conversations, let our words be influenced by a spirit of grace and attraction so that those who ask about our faith will receive a ready, hopeful, and positive answer (1Pe 3:15–16).

7:54–56 With his accusation against the Jewish people (vv. 51–53), Stephen brings his speech to an end. Predictably, the reaction is bitter (v. 54). Yet the next verse signals a change in the tone of events. The Greek literally says of Stephen, "But being filled with the Holy Spirit . . ." (v. 55a). Stephen had been filled with the Holy Spirit throughout his Christian life, and this fullness did not leave him at his time of crisis.

Stephen's vision is filled with deep significance. Stephen's statement (v. 56) reminds us of a similar statement made by Jesus to the same court only a few months before (Mk 14:61–62). For that, Jesus was pronounced guilty of blasphemy and worthy of death (Mk 14:63–64).

Now Stephen is challenging that judgment, affirming that Jesus is indeed at the right hand of God. The Sanhedrin has no choice but to condemn Stephen too, unless they are willing to say they were wrong about their verdict on Jesus. This vision must have given Stephen courage: He sees Jesus acting as his Advocate and testifying on his behalf.
7:57–60 With dramatic crispness, Luke describes how the angry audience acts quickly to put Stephen to death. Covering their ears (v. 57) must have been a characteristic response to blasphemy. Luke mentions Saul at this point (v. 58b).

all rushed at him, 58dragged him out
of the city[t] and began to stone him.[u]
Meanwhile, the witnesses laid their
coats[v] at the feet of a young man named
Saul.[w]
59While they were stoning him, Stephen prayed, "Lord Jesus, receive my
spirit."[x] 60Then he fell on his knees[y]
and cried out, "Lord, do not hold this
sin against them."[z] When he had said
this, he fell asleep.

8 And Saul[a] approved of their killing
him.

The Church Persecuted and Scattered

On that day a great persecution broke
out against the church in Jerusalem, and
all except the apostles were scattered[b]
throughout Judea and Samaria.[c] 2Godly
men buried Stephen and mourned deeply for him. 3But Saul[d] began to destroy
the church.[e] Going from house to house,
he dragged off both men and women and
put them in prison.

Philip in Samaria

4Those who had been scattered[f]
preached the word wherever they went.[g]
5Philip[h] went down to a city in Samaria and proclaimed the Messiah there.
6When the crowds heard Philip and saw
the signs he performed, they all paid
close attention to what he said. 7For
with shrieks, impure spirits came out
of many,[i] and many who were paralyzed
or lame were healed.[j] 8So there was great
joy in that city

7:58 [t]Lk 4:29 [u]Lev 24:14, 16; Dt 13:9 [v]Ac 22:20 [w]Ac 8:1 7:59 [x]Ps 31:5; Lk 23:46 7:60 [y]Ac 9:40 [z]Mt 5:44 8:1 [a]Ac 7:58 [b]Ac 11:19 [c]Ac 9:31 8:3 [d]Ac 7:58 [e]Ac 22:4,19; 26:10,11; 1Co 15:9; Gal 1:13,23; Php 3:6; 1Ti 1:13 8:4 [f]ver 1 [g]Ac 15:35 8:5 [h]Ac 6:5 8:7 [i]Mk 16:17 [j]Mt 4:24

Stephen's last words are surprisingly close to two of the last statements of Jesus just before he died (v. 59; cf. Lk 23:46 and Ac 7:60; cf. Lk 23:34).
8:1 The death of Stephen gives a new momentum to the anti-Christian forces with which Saul is now prominently associated. A great persecution arose that day.
8:2–4 Stephen was buried and mourned over by "godly men" (v. 2). The language used for mourning suggests loud and deep weeping. Acts features a deep theology on suffering as the book proceeds. God is not dormant; he actually feels the pain that Saul inflicts (see 9:4). For the moment, Luke gives us a glimpse of the victory that God is going to win out of this seeming tragedy (8:4).

Perhaps Luke is highlighting a new dispersion coming into being. He deliberately associates Stephen and the persecution with this important development in the church: After this event, the gospel is now preached to the Gentiles.

✜ **7:54—8:4** Stephen's experience of a special anointing with the Spirit's fullness amid suffering challenges is instructive. Through his example, we must remember that the Spirit's fullness is also given to prepare us for suffering, which is such an important part of the life of obedience. God is powerfully at work both when the sun shines brightly and when dark clouds loom over us.

We must, therefore, long and ask for the Holy Spirit to fill us when we experience dark times in our lives. Such a teaching is not easy to understand in this sensual, hedonistic world that we live in, which is afraid of suffering and does so much to avoid it. Yet the Bible tells us as believers to anticipate suffering rather than avoid it. If we understand that God stands with us in the darkness, we will eagerly seek the blessings we know God will give us through the darkness.

8:5–8 The Samaritans were awaiting a future deliverer in keeping with the promise of Dt 18:15–19.

Simon the Sorcerer

9Now for some time a man named
Simon had practiced sorcery[k] in the
city and amazed all the people of Samaria. He boasted that he was someone
great,[l] 10and all the people, both high
and low, gave him their attention and exclaimed, "This man is rightly called the
Great Power of God."[m] 11They followed
him because he had amazed them for a
long time with his sorcery. 12But when
they believed Philip as he proclaimed
the good news of the kingdom of God[n]
and the name of Jesus Christ, they were
baptized,[o] both men and women. 13Si-
mon himself believed and was baptized.
And he followed Philip everywhere, astonished by the great signs and miracles[p] he saw.
14When the apostles in Jerusalem
heard that Samaria[q] had accepted the
word of God, they sent Peter and John[r]
to Samaria. 15When they arrived, they
prayed for the new believers there that
they might receive the Holy Spirit,[s] 16be-
cause the Holy Spirit had not yet come
on any of them;[t] they had simply been
baptized in the name of the Lord Jesus.[u]

8:9 [k]Ac 13:6 [l]Ac 5:36
8:10 [m]Ac 14:11; 28:6
8:12 [n]Ac 1:3 [o]Ac 2:38
8:13 [p]ver 6; Ac 19:11
8:14 [q]ver 1 [r]Lk 22:8
8:15 [s]Ac 2:38
8:16 [t]Ac 19:2 [u]Mt 28:19; Ac 2:38
8:17 [v]Ac 6:6
8:20 [w]2Ki 5:16; Da 5:17; Mt 10:8; Ac 2:38
8:21 [x]Ps 78:37
8:24 [y]Ex 8:8; Nu 21:7; 1Ki 13:6

Ac 8:20 ❖ What happens when we try to buy or bargain for favors from God? Why doesn't God operate that way?

17Then Peter and John placed their hands
on them,[v] and they received the Holy
Spirit.
18When Simon saw that the Spirit was
given at the laying on of the apostles'
hands, he offered them money 19and
said, "Give me also this ability so that
everyone on whom I lay my hands may
receive the Holy Spirit."
20Peter answered: "May your money
perish with you, because you thought
you could buy the gift of God with money![w] 21You have no part or share in this
ministry, because your heart is not right[x]
before God. 22Repent of this wickedness
and pray to the Lord in the hope that
he may forgive you for having such a
thought in your heart. 23For I see that you
are full of bitterness and captive to sin."
24Then Simon answered, "Pray to the
Lord for me[y] so that nothing you have
said may happen to me."
25After they had further proclaimed

Philip seems to have built on this hope when he preached the Messiah there. His preaching was accompanied by miraculous signs as well. "Great joy" resulted from Philip's ministry (v. 8), though we are not told the exact reason for the joy. Was it the result of conversion or of so many people being healed?

8:9–13 Luke introduces Simon the sorcerer, one who was amazed by what he saw in Philip's ministry. He too "believed and was baptized" (v. 13). As the story proceeds, however, it becomes apparent that his belief was superficial.

8:14–17 Peter and John are sent from Jerusalem to check out what has happened in Samaria (v. 14). Here we see the role of the apostles shift from initiation to verification. After their prayer, the Spirit descends on the Samaritans (v. 17). There must have been some external manifestation, such as speaking in tongues, that gave unmistakable evidence of the Spirit's presence at this event.

8:18–22 Simon is attracted by what happened through the laying on of hands by the apostles. He is not interested in receiving the Spirit himself; what he wants is the ability to lay hands on people with similar results. His offer of money for this ability evokes a strong response from Peter (v. 20), who views Simon as not yet born again. The important thing, says Peter, is to have one's heart right before God (v. 21).

8:23–24 After calling Simon to repent, Peter explains his condition to him (v. 23). The word "bitterness" (v. 23) comes from Dt 29:18. Peter may be referring to the potential that Simon has to cause damage to the church. Peter's statement reflects his desire to rid the church of this evil influence.

Simon is a good example of misplaced religious pursuit. He believed and was baptized, but it was obviously an inadequate belief. He sought God's power without any apparent interest in developing a relationship with God.

8:25 The story ends with Peter and John "preaching the gospel in many Samaritan villages" on their return journey to Jerusalem. It is encouraging to see John, who had earlier asked Jesus whether to call down fire on some Samaritan villages (Lk 9:51–55), now preaching the gospel to them.

✚ **8:5–25** In the early church the pioneer leaders understood that innovative advances from a new generation of leaders were important. Therefore, not only did these leaders encourage younger leaders, but they also learned from them and followed the lead they gave.

The example of Philip branching out to bring the gospel to new territory, and Peter and John's oversight of that ministry, is a challenge to all leaders today. Less experienced leaders should do their pioneering work while benefiting from the wisdom, encouragement, and oversight of more experienced leaders.

Similarly, as believers reach out to others in one-on-one situations, they can learn a lot from the successes and mistakes of others who have gone before them. Here again participating in the community of faith is a critical aspect of sincere discipleship.

PEOPLE TO KNOW // EUNUCH OF ETHIOPIA

ACTS 8:26–40: After the stoning of the first martyr, Stephen, Christians were scattered from Jerusalem. They began preaching the gospel of Christ in new places. One of these preachers was Philip, who had been selected as a deacon along with Stephen (Ac 6:5). God sent Philip south, and when he obeyed, he encountered a remarkable person: an Ethiopian eunuch.

The eunuch is not named, but he was an important official of the queen of Ethiopia (Ac 8:27) who also professed faith in the God of Israel. In fact, he was traveling back home from visiting the temple in Jerusalem. As a Gentile eunuch, his access to the temple would have been limited (Dt 23:1), yet his desire to worship God at the temple compelled him to make the long journey.

As the eunuch was riding in his chariot, he was reading out loud from Isaiah 53 words that point to Jesus: "He was led like a sheep to the slaughter" (Ac 8:32). Philip explained how this prophecy was fulfilled in Jesus, and the eunuch immediately asked to be baptized. After Philip baptized him, Philip was taken away by God's Spirit, and the Ethiopian eunuch went on his way rejoicing.

APPLICATION ✣ The brief story of the Ethiopian eunuch is powerful. This man demonstrated a heart open to God's work and immediately accepted the salvation of Jesus when Philip explained the gospel to him. From the outside, he looked like an unlikely convert—a royal official serving in a foreign court—but God delights in unlikelihoods! The Ethiopian eunuch shows us the truth that God is at work in surprising ways, always bringing his lost children home.

the word of the Lord and testified about
Jesus, Peter and John returned to Jerusalem, preaching the gospel in many
Samaritan villages.[z]

Philip and the Ethiopian

26Now an angel[a] of the Lord said to
Philip, "Go south to the road — the desert
road — that goes down from Jerusalem
to Gaza." 27So he started out, and on his
way he met an Ethiopian[a][b] eunuch,[c] an
important official in charge of all the
treasury of the Kandake (which means
"queen of the Ethiopians"). This man had
gone to Jerusalem to worship,[d] 28and on
his way home was sitting in his chariot
reading the Book of Isaiah the prophet.
29The Spirit told[e] Philip, "Go to that chariot and stay near it."
30Then Philip ran up to the chariot
and heard the man reading Isaiah the
prophet. "Do you understand what you
are reading?" Philip asked.
31"How can I," he said, "unless someone explains it to me?" So he invited
Philip to come up and sit with him.
32This is the passage of Scripture the
eunuch was reading:

8:25 [z] ver 40
8:26 [a] Ac 5:19
8:27 [b] Ps 68:31; 87:4; Zep 3:10 [c] Isa 56:3-5 [d] 1Ki 8:41-43; Jn 12:20
8:29 [e] Ac 10:19; 11:12; 13:2; 20:23; 21:11

[a] *27* That is, from the southern Nile region

8:26 Scholars are not certain where Philip the evangelist was when the angel of the Lord asked him to go south to a desert road (southwest of Jerusalem).

8:27 Philip immediately obeyed this somewhat strange command, and the God of surprises shocked him with the appearance of an Ethiopian. There is disagreement among scholars as to whether he was literally a eunuch, since this word was also used for trusted workers of a royal court. We know that he was a high official—something like the finance minister—in Ethiopia.

In ancient literature, Ethiopia was considered the ends of the earth. In other words, with the gospel going to the Samaritans and then to the Ethiopian, it was going to the last two geographical spheres of the Great Commission (1:8). Luke does not mention the religious background of the Ethiopian. He had come to the Jerusalem temple to worship and had a copy of Isaiah with him—not something easy to obtain in those days. This suggests that he may have been a God-fearer or a proselyte.

8:28–31 Only the most well-to-do had chariots in those days, but the Ethiopian was in one, reading from the prophet Isaiah (v. 28). Considering the high standing of this official, it would have required boldness for Philip to obey the Spirit's command to go to the chariot (v. 29). Since people almost always read aloud in those days, Philip heard him reading one of the favorite passages of the early church, which gave him the opportunity to share the Good News with this official (vv. 30b–31).

8:32–35 The passage the eunuch was reading was from Isa 53:7–8, which addresses the unjust humiliation and sufferings of the Lord's servant (vv. 32–33). His question about the identity of

"He was led like a sheep to the
slaughter,
and as a lamb before its shearer is
silent,
so he did not open his mouth.
33 In his humiliation he was deprived
of justice.
Who can speak of his
descendants?
For his life was taken from the
earth."[a][f]

34 The eunuch asked Philip, "Tell me,
please, who is the prophet talking about,
himself or someone else?" 35 Then Philip
began[g] with that very passage of Scripture[h] and told him the good news about
Jesus.
36 As they traveled along the road, they
came to some water and the eunuch said,
"Look, here is water. What can stand in
the way of my being baptized?"[i] [37][b]
38 And he gave orders to stop the chariot. Then both Philip and the eunuch went
down into the water and Philip baptized
him. 39 When they came up out of the
water, the Spirit of the Lord suddenly
took Philip away,[j] and the eunuch did
not see him again, but went on his way
rejoicing. 40 Philip, however, appeared at
Azotus and traveled about, preaching the
gospel in all the towns[k] until he reached
Caesarea.[l]

8:33 [f] Isa 53:7,8
8:35 [g] Mt 5:2 [h] Lk 24:27; Ac 17:2; 18:28; 28:23
8:36 [i] Ac 10:47
8:39 [j] 1Ki 18:12; 2Ki 2:16; Eze 3:12,14; 8:3; 11:1,24; 43:5; 2Co 12:2
8:40 [k] ver 25 [l] Ac 10:1,24; 12:19; 21:8,16; 23:23,33; 25:1, 4,6,13
9:1 [m] Ac 8:3
9:2 [n] Ac 19:9,23; 22:4; 24:14,22
9:3 [o] 1Co 15:8
9:6 [p] ver 16
9:7 [q] Jn 12:29 [r] Da 10:7; Ac 22:9

Saul's Conversion

9:1–19pp // Ac 22:3–16; 26:9–18

9 Meanwhile, Saul was still breathing out
murderous threats against the Lord's
disciples.[m] He went to the high priest 2 and
asked him for letters to the synagogues in
Damascus, so that if he found any there
who belonged to the Way,[n] whether men or
women, he might take them as prisoners
to Jerusalem. 3 As he neared Damascus on
his journey, suddenly a light from heav-
en flashed around him.[o] 4 He fell to the
ground and heard a voice say to him, "Saul,
Saul, why do you persecute me?"
5 "Who are you, Lord?" Saul asked.
"I am Jesus, whom you are persecuting," he replied. 6 "Now get up and go
into the city, and you will be told what
you must do."[p]
7 The men traveling with Saul stood
there speechless; they heard the sound[q]
but did not see anyone.[r] 8 Saul got up

[a] *33* Isaiah 53:7,8 (see Septuagint) [b] *37* Some manuscripts include here *Philip said, "If you believe with all your heart, you may." The eunuch answered, "I believe that Jesus Christ is the Son of God."*

---

this servant becomes a launching pad for Philip (vv. 34-35). In the church, these passages became important texts because Jesus had applied them to himself.

8:36-38 The Ethiopian suggests baptism when they come to some water (v. 36). Philip takes another bold step in baptizing the eunuch (v. 38). Considering all the signs of divine leading he had received, Philip must have been convinced of the genuineness of this conversion.

8:39 Philip is then taken away suddenly by the Spirit of the Lord. But the newfound joy of the Ethiopian cannot be dampened by Philip's disappearance.

8:40 Philip next appears in Azotus, some 20 miles north of Gaza, and continues traveling north, preaching incessantly until he reaches Caesarea. It is there that we find him again about 20 years later, now the father of four unmarried prophetesses (21:8-9).

8:26-40 Because the primary work of those called to be evangelists is with people outside the church, Christians must support the ministry of those who courageously address those who are lost in this world—whether that be in a downtown mission or on some far-flung missionary post in a country hostile to Christianity. Such people are like Philip—they invade Satan's territory and are therefore on the front lines of the battle for people's hearts. These individuals require prayerful financial support and encouragement from the wider Christian community.

9:1-2 Luke uses strong language to express the intensity with which Saul persecuted Christians (v. 1). The root of this was his zeal (Php 3:6), especially his zeal for the traditions of his spiritual fathers (Gal 1:14). The idea of a crucified Messiah was an impossibility according to Saul's thinking.

9:3 As Saul approaches Damascus to continue his persecution of any believers there, he hears a voice and sees a bright light. The light Saul sees must have been strong, for it is around noon when he encounters it (22:6; 26:13). Such a light would have likely reminded him of the *shekinah* glory of God in the OT.

9:4-8 The voice from heaven asks a simple question (v. 4), indicating that while Saul has been hitting the church and its believers, Jesus has been feeling the pain.

Saul had been coming to Damascus "to arrest all who call on your name" (v. 14). In the OT, "calling on the name" is a standard description of prayer to God. Saul had heard Stephen call on the "Lord Jesus" as he was dying (7:59). All this was blasphemy to Saul, and he felt that it had to be stopped. He was spiritually blinded by wrong convictions until a greater light caused him to become spiritually enlightened, though physically blinded.

from the ground, but when he opened
his eyes he could see nothing. So they
led him by the hand into Damascus. 9For
three days he was blind, and did not eat
or drink anything.
10In Damascus there was a disciple
named Ananias. The Lord called to him
in a vision,[s] "Ananias!"
"Yes, Lord," he answered.
11The Lord told him, "Go to the house
of Judas on Straight Street and ask for
a man from Tarsus[t] named Saul, for he
is praying. 12In a vision he has seen a
man named Ananias come and place his
hands on[u] him to restore his sight."
13"Lord," Ananias answered, "I have
heard many reports about this man and
all the harm he has done to your holy
people[v] in Jerusalem.[w] 14And he has come
here with authority from the chief priests[x]
to arrest all who call on your name."
15But the Lord said to Ananias, "Go!
This man is my chosen instrument[y] to
proclaim my name to the Gentiles[z] and
their kings[a] and to the people of Israel.
16I will show him how much he must
suffer for my name."[b]
17Then Ananias went to the house and
entered it. Placing his hands on[c] Saul,
he said, "Brother Saul, the Lord—Jesus,
who appeared to you on the road as you
were coming here—has sent me so that
you may see again and be filled with the
Holy Spirit." 18Immediately, something
like scales fell from Saul's eyes, and he

9:10 [s]Ac 10:3, 17,19
9:11 [t]ver 30; Ac 21:39; 22:3
9:12 [u]Mk 5:23
9:13 [v]ver 32; Ro 1:7; 16:2,15 [w]Ac 8:3
9:14 [x]ver 2,21
9:15 [y]Ac 13:2; Ro 1:1; Gal 1:15 [z]Ro 11:13; 15:15, 16; Gal 2:7, 8; Eph 3:7,8 [a]Ac 25:22,23; 26:1
9:16 [b]Ac 20:23; 21:11; 2Co 11:23-27
9:17 [c]Ac 6:6
9:19 [d]Ac 11:26 [e]Ac 26:20
9:20 [f]Ac 13:5,14 [g]Mt 4:3
9:21 [h]Ac 8:3 [i]Gal 1:13,23
9:22 [j]Ac 18:5,28
9:24 [k]Ac 20:3, 19
9:25 [l]1Sa 19:12; 2Co 11:32,33
9:26 [m]Ac 22:17; 26:20; Gal 1:17, 18
9:27 [n]Ac 4:36

Ac 9:13-16 ❖ When has God called us to do something we felt nervous about? How did God encourage us in that time?

could see again. He got up and was baptized, 19and after taking some food, he
regained his strength.

Saul in Damascus and Jerusalem

Saul spent several days with the disciples[d] in Damascus.[e] 20At once he began
to preach in the synagogues[f] that Jesus
is the Son of God.[g] 21All those who heard
him were astonished and asked, "Isn't he
the man who raised havoc in Jerusalem
among those who call on this name?[h]
And hasn't he come here to take them
as prisoners to the chief priests?"[i] 22Yet
Saul grew more and more powerful and
baffled the Jews living in Damascus by
proving that Jesus is the Messiah.[j]
23After many days had gone by, there
was a conspiracy among the Jews to kill
him, 24but Saul learned of their plan.[k]
Day and night they kept close watch on
the city gates in order to kill him. 25But
his followers took him by night and lowered him in a basket through an opening
in the wall.[l]
26When he came to Jerusalem,[m] he
tried to join the disciples, but they were
all afraid of him, not believing that he
really was a disciple. 27But Barnabas[n]

This is more than a typical vision, for his companions also see the light (22:9) and hear the sound (9:7). In his list of post-resurrection appearances, Paul says, "And last of all he appeared to me also, as to one abnormally born" (1Co 15:8). By placing it alongside the other post-resurrection appearances, Paul says that it was as objective an appearance as those recorded in the Gospels.

9:9 In Damascus, the blinded Saul follows the most intense type of fast, spending three days without eating or drinking. People engaged in such fasts were typically repenting or seeking God's face. Both are involved here (cf. v. 11, where Ananias is told Paul is praying).

9:10 Ananias was a wise choice to help Saul (22:12). As with Peter and Cornelius (10:1–23), God's arrangements are confirmed by two visions (vv. 10, 12). Visions often occur in Acts when God intervenes to direct the church into something new.

9:11–12 Saul is described to Ananias as "a man from Tarsus" (v. 11). Tarsus was the principal city of Cilicia, the most southeasterly part of Asia Minor (in present-day southern Turkey). It was a city of great culture.

9:13–19a Ananias's protest is understandable, considering Saul's actions and reputation (vv. 13–14). But his willingness to obey immediately is commendable, as is his noble act of "placing his hands on Saul" and addressing him as "Brother Saul" (v. 17). The Lord has important plans and tasks for Saul to accomplish (v. 15).

Right at the start of his spiritual pilgrimage, Saul is informed that he will suffer for the name of Jesus (v. 16). But before Paul experiences this cross, he will experience Christ's power. Ananias says that he has come so that Paul "may see again and be filled with the Holy Spirit" (v. 17).

9:19b–25 At once Saul launches out on a preaching ministry in the synagogues of Damascus (v. 20). Unlike many new converts, Saul was already well versed in the Scriptures and was ready to teach his fellow Jews about them under this new paradigm.

Verse 23 finds Saul in Damascus "after many days had gone by." His trip to Arabia and his return to Damascus (see Gal 1:17) must have occurred during this time—probably doing both meditating and preaching. He spent almost three years in Arabia. Predictably, opposition arose (vv. 23–24), so Saul had to make an unceremonious exit from Damascus in a basket (v. 25). Saul's "murderous threats" (v. 1) have now been turned on him.

9:26 Paul later makes much of the fact that he did not go to Jerusalem until three years after his

TIMELINE OF PAUL'S LIFE

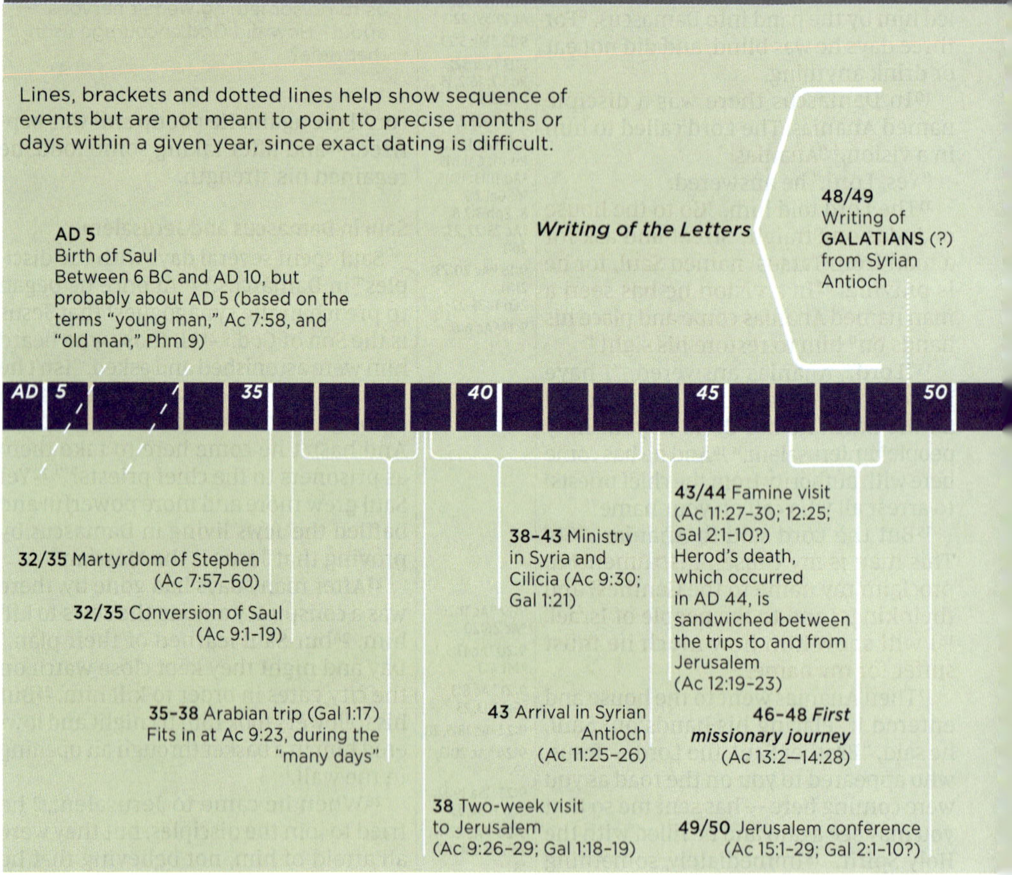

Lines, brackets and dotted lines help show sequence of events but are not meant to point to precise months or days within a given year, since exact dating is difficult.

AD 5 Birth of Saul
Between 6 BC and AD 10, but probably about AD 5 (based on the terms "young man," Ac 7:58, and "old man," Phm 9)

Writing of the Letters

48/49 Writing of **GALATIANS** (?) from Syrian Antioch

AD 5 35 40 45 50

32/35 Martyrdom of Stephen (Ac 7:57-60)

32/35 Conversion of Saul (Ac 9:1-19)

35-38 Arabian trip (Gal 1:17) Fits in at Ac 9:23, during the "many days"

38 Two-week visit to Jerusalem (Ac 9:26-29; Gal 1:18-19)

38-43 Ministry in Syria and Cilicia (Ac 9:30; Gal 1:21)

43 Arrival in Syrian Antioch (Ac 11:25-26)

43/44 Famine visit (Ac 11:27-30; 12:25; Gal 2:1-10?)
Herod's death, which occurred in AD 44, is sandwiched between the trips to and from Jerusalem (Ac 12:19-23)

46-48 ***First missionary journey*** (Ac 13:2—14:28)

49/50 Jerusalem conference (Ac 15:1-29; Gal 2:1-10?)

took him and brought him to the apostles. He told them how Saul on his journey had seen the Lord and that the Lord
had spoken to him,[o] and how in Damascus he had preached fearlessly in the
name of Jesus.[p] 28So Saul stayed with
them and moved about freely in Jerusalem, speaking boldly in the name of
the Lord. 29He talked and debated with
the Hellenistic Jews,[a][q] but they tried to
kill him.[r] 30When the believers[s] learned
of this, they took him down to Caesarea[t]
and sent him off to Tarsus.[u]
31Then the church throughout Judea,
Galilee and Samaria[v] enjoyed a time of

9:27 [o]ver 3-6 [p]ver 20,22
9:29 [q]Ac 6:1 [r]2Co 11:26
9:30 [s]Ac 1:16 [t]Ac 8:40 [u]ver 11
9:31 [v]Ac 8:1

[a] *29* That is, Jews who had adopted the Greek language and culture

conversion (Gal 1). This fact was evidence that he had received his commission as an apostle directly from Christ, not from Christian leaders in the holy city. When he tried to join the disciples, "they were all afraid of him" (v. 26).

9:27 God solves the problem of the disciples' fear as trusted Barnabas takes him, not just to the disciples, but to the apostles themselves. In the 15 days he spends with Peter (Gal 1:18), Paul would have been filled in on many of the details regarding the life and words of Christ.

9:28–30 Saul gets busy in Jerusalem, "speaking boldly" and debating for the Lord (vv. 28–29). But the Jews try to kill him, and he makes a hasty exit to Caesarea on the way to his birthplace, Tarsus. He next appears in Acts several years later, still in Tarsus (11:25).

9:31 This section ends with the report of a healthy church. The church now enjoyed a time of relative calm, which is true of most evangelistic communities that face persecution: There are typically periods of respite from serious opposition.

9:1–31 Our task as witnesses is to lead people to Jesus so that they will encounter him as

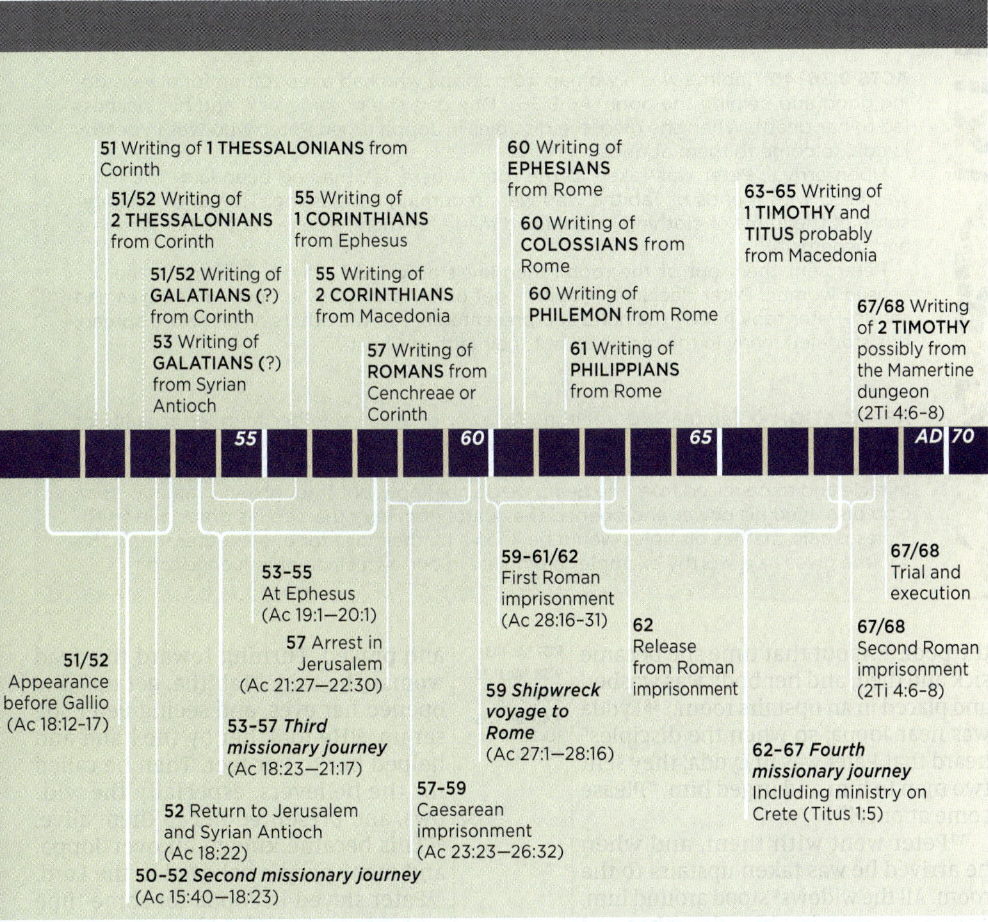

peace and was strengthened. Living in the fear of the Lord and encouraged by the Holy Spirit, it increased in numbers.

Aeneas and Dorcas

32As Peter traveled about the country, he went to visit the Lord's people[w]
who lived in Lydda. 33There he found a
man named Aeneas, who was paralyzed
and had been bedridden for eight years.
34"Aeneas," Peter said to him, "Jesus
Christ heals you.[x] Get up and roll up your
mat." Immediately Aeneas got up. 35All
those who lived in Lydda and Sharon[y]
saw him and turned to the Lord.[z]
36In Joppa[a] there was a disciple named
Tabitha (in Greek her name is Dorcas);
she was always doing good[b] and helping

9:32 [w]ver 13
9:34 [x]Ac 3:6, 16; 4:10
9:35 [y]1Ch 5:16; 27:29; Isa 33:9; 35:2; 65:10 [z]Ac 11:21
9:36 [a]Jos 19:46; 2Ch 2:16; Ezr 3:7; Jnh 1:3; Ac 10:5 [b]1Ti 2:10; Titus 3:8

---

their Savior and Lord. We may discuss religion, argue for the truth of it, and seek to persuade people about its relevance and power. But in the end our chief goal is to introduce people to Jesus and to lead others to engage in a personal relationship with God.

9:32–43 In this whole passage there is no record of any preaching, though it must have been done. The focus is on service.
9:32 Peter's visit to "the Lord's people" around Palestine indicates that he had a pastoral role throughout the church. We can imagine him teaching, encouraging, correcting, and counseling the believers and leaders on these visits.
9:33–43 Among the many healings performed through Peter's ministry, Luke mentions two here—those of Aeneas and Tabitha. With both healings, Peter clearly places the emphasis on Christ as the healer. The first time he says, "Jesus Christ heals you" (v. 34); the second time, before speaking, "he got down on his knees and prayed" (v. 40). After Aeneas's healing we are told that "all those who lived in Lydda and Sharon saw him and turned to

PEOPLE TO KNOW // TABITHA (DORCAS)

ACTS 9:36–40: Tabitha was a woman from Joppa who had a reputation for always doing good and helping the poor (Ac 9:36). One day, she became sick, and her sickness led to her death. When she died, the disciples in Joppa urged Peter, who was in nearby Lydda, to come to them at once.

Upon arrival, Peter was taken to the room where Tabitha had been laid. The room was filled with friends of Tabitha who were mourning her passing. They showed Peter some of the items of clothing Tabitha had made for them, a testament to her kindness and generosity.

Peter sent them out of the room, then knelt down and prayed. Turning to the deceased woman, Peter declared, "Tabitha, get up" (Ac 9:40). She opened her eyes and sat up. Peter took her by the hand and presented her to the others. When word spread, this story led many in the region to put their faith in Christ.

APPLICATION Tabitha was a faithful follower of Jesus, and her faith led to a life of giving to others. She helped those who were poor and in need. Tabitha is a model of compassion and mercy in ministry. Why God chose Tabitha to be the recipient of a miracle and to be raised from the dead, we do not know, but through her dramatic story, God displayed his power and opened the hearts of many others to his grace and truth.

Jesus said that his disciples would be known by their love for one another (Jn 13:35). Tabitha gives us a worthy example to emulate in our own circle of influence today.

the poor. 37About that time she became
sick and died, and her body was washed
and placed in an upstairs room.[c] 38Lydda
was near Joppa; so when the disciples[d]
heard that Peter was in Lydda, they sent
two men to him and urged him, "Please
come at once!"
39Peter went with them, and when
he arrived he was taken upstairs to the
room. All the widows[e] stood around him,
crying and showing him the robes and
other clothing that Dorcas had made
while she was still with them.
40Peter sent them all out of the
room;[f] then he got down on his knees[g]
and prayed. Turning toward the dead
woman, he said, "Tabitha, get up." She
opened her eyes, and seeing Peter she
sat up. 41He took her by the hand and
helped her to her feet. Then he called
for the believers, especially the widows, and presented her to them alive.
42This became known all over Joppa,
and many people believed in the Lord.
43Peter stayed in Joppa for some time
with a tanner named Simon.[h]

Cornelius Calls for Peter

10 At Caesarea[i] there was a man named Cornelius, a centurion

9:37 c Ac 1:13
9:38 d Ac 11:26
9:39 e Ac 6:1
9:40 f Mt 9:25 g Lk 22:41; Ac 7:60
9:43 h Ac 10:6
10:1 i Ac 8:40

the Lord" (v. 35). After Tabitha's healing we read that "many people believed in the Lord" (v. 42).

9:36–42 Tabitha, who "was always doing good and helping the poor" (v. 36b), had died. A body was normally buried before sundown on the day of death. But Peter made this journey on foot right away to help the lady who had helped so many presumably insignificant people. Peter, who was present when Jesus had raised Jairus's daughter, followed some of Jesus' procedures here (v. 40; cf. Mk 5:40).

9:43 Peter stayed on in Joppa in the house of Simon the leather tanner. It was a demeaning trade in Jewish eyes; strictly speaking, tanners were ceremonially unclean since they handled dead animals. A tanner's shop had to be on the outskirts of town because of the bad odor that came from it; Simon's home was by the sea (see 10:6).

9:32–43 Although all church leaders should pray with their sick, some have gifts of healing and/or faith that enable them to pray in faith that results in healing and glory to God (1Co 12:9). Yet Jesus, through the words of the apostle Paul, calls all believers to "rejoice always, pray continually, give thanks in all circumstances; for this is God's will for you in Christ Jesus" (1Th 5:16–18).

There are times when we may find that the answer we are hoping and praying for is not forthcoming. At such times we should affirm that the answer we want has not come because God has something better in store for us (Ro 8:28). God does not have to answer our prayers precisely in the way we ask. Sometimes he may have a better plan that will take us through what may look like a disaster. Though we cannot understand what we are going through, we can remain at peace, for we trust God and know that he will do what is best for us.

10:1 Cornelius lived in Caesarea, a Mediterranean seaport rebuilt by Herod the Great and named

in what was known as the Italian Regiment. 2He and all his family were devout
and God-fearing;[j] he gave generously to
those in need and prayed to God regularly. 3One day at about three in the afternoon[k] he had a vision.[l] He distinctly
saw an angel[m] of God, who came to him
and said, "Cornelius!"
4Cornelius stared at him in fear. "What
is it, Lord?" he asked.
The angel answered, "Your prayers
and gifts to the poor have come up as a
memorial offering[n] before God.[o] 5Now
send men to Joppa[p] to bring back a man
named Simon who is called Peter. 6He is
staying with Simon the tanner,[q] whose
house is by the sea."
7When the angel who spoke to him
had gone, Cornelius called two of his
servants and a devout soldier who was
one of his attendants. 8He told them everything that had happened and sent
them to Joppa.[r]

Peter's Vision

10:9–32Ref // Ac 11:5–14

9About noon the following day as they
were on their journey and approaching
the city, Peter went up on the roof[s] to
pray. 10He became hungry and wanted
something to eat, and while the meal was
being prepared, he fell into a trance.[t] 11He
saw heaven opened and something like
a large sheet being let down to earth by
its four corners. 12It contained all kinds
of four-footed animals, as well as reptiles
and birds. 13Then a voice told him, "Get
up, Peter. Kill and eat."
14"Surely not, Lord!"[u] Peter replied. "I
have never eaten anything impure or
unclean."[v]
15The voice spoke to him a second
time, "Do not call anything impure that
God has made clean."[w]
16This happened three times, and immediately the sheet was taken back to
heaven.
17While Peter was wondering about
the meaning of the vision, the men sent
by Cornelius[x] found out where Simon's
house was and stopped at the gate.
18They called out, asking if Simon who
was known as Peter was staying there.
19While Peter was still thinking about
the vision, the Spirit said[y] to him, "Simon, three[a] men are looking for you.
20So get up and go downstairs. Do not
hesitate to go with them, for I have sent
them."[z]
21Peter went down and said to the
men, "I'm the one you're looking for.
Why have you come?"
22The men replied, "We have come
from Cornelius the centurion. He is a
righteous and God-fearing man,[a] who
is respected by all the Jewish people. A
holy angel told him to ask you to come
to his house so that he could hear what
you have to say."[b] 23Then Peter invited
the men into the house to be his guests.

10:2 [j] ver 22,35; Ac 13:16,26
10:3 [k] Ac 3:1 [l] Ac 9:10 [m] Ac 5:19
10:4 [n] Mt 26:13 [o] Rev 8:4
10:5 [p] Ac 9:36
10:6 [q] Ac 9:43
10:8 [r] Ac 9:36
10:9 [s] Mt 24:17
10:10 [t] Ac 22:17
10:14 [u] Ac 9:5 [v] Lev 11:4-8, 13-20; 20:25; Dt 14:3-20; Eze 4:14
10:15 [w] Mt 15:11; Ro 14:14,17, 20; 1Co 10:25; 1Ti 4:3,4; Titus 1:15
10:17 [x] ver 7,8
10:19 [y] Ac 8:29
10:20 [z] Ac 15:7-9
10:22 [a] ver 2 [b] Ac 11:14

[a] *19* One early manuscript *two;* other manuscripts do not have the number.

---

after Caesar Augustus. It was the center of the Roman administration of the province of Palestine and even had a temple dedicated to Caesar. The population there had more Gentiles than Jews.

10:2 Cornelius "and all his family were devout and God-fearing." It is usually held that God-fearers were those who attended the synagogue and honored Jewish laws and customs but had not received circumcision.

10:3–4 Cornelius had a vision at about three in the afternoon. This was one of the three traditional Jewish times of prayer. Cornelius later tells Peter that he was praying at the time (v. 30). Here we have another occurrence of God directing the action of people through an angelic vision.

10:5–8 The angel tells Cornelius to summon Peter from Joppa. The mention of Peter's staying in the house of Simon the tanner may have come as a surprise to Cornelius, as this was not a highly esteemed trade among Jewish people. Despite the lack of details, Cornelius obeys immediately.

10:9 Peter, the one to whom the keys of the kingdom were given (Mt 16:19), is again chosen to open another important door for the gospel—as he did with the Jews on the day of Pentecost. We find him in Joppa, about to preach to Gentiles—the very thing that Jonah resisted in the same city (Jnh 1:3). Peter goes to the roof of the house he is staying at around noon to pray.

10:10–16 Peter receives a vision, given at a time when he is hungry (v. 10). The entire animal world is symbolized, and clean and unclean animals are included. Peter makes a categorical refusal to obey the shocking directive of the one whom he calls "Lord" (v. 14).

The adjective and verb translated "impure" appear five times in chs. 10–11. Later, Peter's disciple Mark, after reporting on the discourse of Jesus on clean and unclean objects (Mk 7:5–23), would make an editorial comment stating, "In saying this, Jesus declared all foods clean" (Mk 7:19b). Perhaps this vision helped Peter understand the implications of that discourse of Jesus.

10:17–23a While we are told that the Spirit spoke to Peter, we must note that Peter was in a proper state to receive a communication from God. Luke says he was "wondering about the meaning of

PEOPLE TO KNOW // CORNELIUS

ACTS 10:23–48: Cornelius was a centurion who lived in Caesarea. He was also devout in serving God and helping those in need (Ac 10:2). One day God sent Cornelius a vision of an angel, telling him to summon Peter.

While Cornelius's men were on their way to Peter, Peter had a vision of his own. He saw a vast sheet being lowered by its four corners, filled with all manner of animals, including birds and reptiles. When a voice told Peter to eat of the animals, Peter refused, saying he would not eat anything impure or unclean. The voice replied that Peter should not call impure anything God had made clean. Three times God repeated the vision.

When Peter entered Cornelius's house—the house of a Gentile army commander—Cornelius fell at his feet in reverence. Peter then shared the gospel with Cornelius's household, and the Holy Spirit came upon all who heard. They began speaking in tongues, praising God. Then they were baptized.

Through Cornelius, God revealed a new chapter in his redemption plan. When other Christians questioned Peter about visiting a Gentile, Peter testified what God had done in Cornelius's household. The believers marveled, "Even to Gentiles God has granted repentance that leads to life" (Ac 11:18).

APPLICATION ✤ God's circle of grace is often wider than we expect or imagine. To the early Jewish followers of Jesus, it was a stunning surprise that God would pour out his Spirit and salvation upon the household of Cornelius. God does not discriminate by economic status, bloodlines or skin color. He looks for those with true faith and pours out his Spirit on whosoever he desires.

Peter at Cornelius's House

The next day Peter started out with
them, and some of the believers[c] from
Joppa went along.[d] 24The following day
he arrived in Caesarea.[e] Cornelius was
expecting them and had called together
his relatives and close friends. 25As Peter
entered the house, Cornelius met him
and fell at his feet in reverence. 26But
Peter made him get up. "Stand up," he
said, "I am only a man myself."[f]
27While talking with him, Peter went
inside and found a large gathering of people. 28He said to them: "You are well aware
that it is against our law for a Jew to associate with or visit a Gentile.[g] But God has
shown me that I should not call anyone
impure or unclean.[h] 29So when I was sent
for, I came without raising any objection.
May I ask why you sent for me?"
30Cornelius answered: "Three days ago
I was in my house praying at this hour, at
three in the afternoon. Suddenly a man
in shining clothes stood before me 31and
said, 'Cornelius, God has heard your prayer
and remembered your gifts to the poor.
32Send to Joppa for Simon who is called
Peter. He is a guest in the home of Simon
the tanner, who lives by the sea.' 33So I sent

10:23 [c] Ac 1:16 [d] ver 45; Ac 11:12
10:24 [e] Ac 8:40
10:26 [f] Ac 14:15; Rev 19:10
10:28 [g] Jn 4:9; 18:28; Ac 11:3 [h] Ac 15:8, 9

Ac 10:28 ✤ Where might God be calling us to break social boundaries for the cause of the gospel?

the vision" (v. 17) and "thinking about the vision" (v. 19). While God led Peter, clearly he was earnestly seeking to find God's will.

10:23b–26 Peter takes some others along with him rather than go on this assignment alone (v. 23b). Cornelius seems to have been certain about the time Peter would come, for when he arrives Peter finds "a large gathering of people" at the house (v. 27). Cornelius shows great humility for a centurion in honoring Peter (v. 25). But Peter will have none of this, as such reverence is reserved only for God (v. 26).

10:27–33 Peter's discovery is the pivotal message of this whole passage (v. 28). A big shift has taken place in Peter's thinking, for he now realizes that no longer are the typical Jewish distinctions among people significant. They have been rendered void once and for all.

✤ **10:1–33** There are a few essential things we must do if we are to rid the church of the terrible malady of prejudice. First, we must help people understand the nature of Christian identity, which does not depend on human distinctions. When people realize that they are accepted as significant and useful to the kingdom not because of any merit of their own but only because of the mercy of God, they also realize that they cannot look down on anyone.

for you immediately, and it was good of
you to come. Now we are all here in the
presence of God to listen to everything
the Lord has commanded you to tell us."
34Then Peter began to speak: "I now
realize how true it is that God does not
show favoritism[i] 35but accepts from every nation the one who fears him and
does what is right.[j] 36You know the message God sent to the people of Israel,
announcing the good news[k] of peace[l]
through Jesus Christ, who is Lord of all.[m]
37You know what has happened throughout the province of Judea, beginning
in Galilee after the baptism that John
preached— 38how God anointed[n] Jesus
of Nazareth with the Holy Spirit and
power, and how he went around doing
good and healing[o] all who were under
the power of the devil, because God was
with him.[p]
39"We are witnesses[q] of everything he
did in the country of the Jews and in Jerusalem. They killed him by hanging him
on a cross,[r] 40but God raised him from
the dead[s] on the third day and caused
him to be seen. 41He was not seen by all
the people,[t] but by witnesses whom God
had already chosen—by us who ate[u] and
drank with him after he rose from the
dead. 42He commanded us to preach to
the people[v] and to testify that he is the
one whom God appointed as judge of the
living and the dead.[w] 43All the prophets
testify about him[x] that everyone[y] who
believes in him receives forgiveness of
sins through his name."
44While Peter was still speaking these
words, the Holy Spirit came on[z] all who
heard the message. 45The circumcised
believers who had come with Peter[a] were
astonished that the gift of the Holy Spirit had been poured out[b] even on Gentiles.[c] 46For they heard them speaking
in tongues[a][d] and praising God.
Then Peter said, 47"Surely no one can

10:34 [i] Dt 10:17; 2Ch 19:7; Job 34:19; Ro 2:11; Gal 2:6; Eph 6:9; Col 3:25; 1Pe 1:17
10:35 [j] Ac 15:9
10:36 [k] Ac 13:32 [l] Lk 2:14 [m] Mt 28:18; Ro 10:12
10:38 [n] Ac 4:26 [o] Mt 4:23 [p] Jn 3:2
10:39 [q] Lk 24:48 [r] Ac 5:30
10:40 [s] Ac 2:24
10:41 [t] Jn 14:17, 22 [u] Lk 24:43; Jn 21:13
10:42 [v] Mt 28:19, 20 [w] Jn 5:22; Ac 17:31; Ro 14:9; 2Co 5:10; 2Ti 4:1; 1Pe 4:5
10:43 [x] Isa 53:11 [y] Ac 15:9
10:44 [z] Ac 8:15, 16; 11:15; 15:8
10:45 [a] ver 23 [b] Ac 2:33,38 [c] Ac 11:18
10:46 [d] Mk 16:17

[a] 46 Or *other languages*

Second, we must teach and preach the biblical truths that combat prejudice regularly in our churches. Third, we must listen to the heart of those on the other side of an issue that divides people. Because this can be a painful exercise, Christians often keep feelings to themselves that deeply affect them. These need to be drawn out and discussed.

Next, we must confront prejudice when it appears in church and society and condemn it with holy zeal, as Paul did when Peter gave in to prejudice in Antioch (Gal 2:11–13). This can be difficult, for vested interests are often affected in such situations. Doing so can also can earn us the reputation of being traitors to our own people.

Finally, we must stand up for and pay the price of helping people of the "other" group. This, too, can be costly in terms of reputation and convenience. But doing so can help heal wounds within people who have been hurt.

10:34–35 Peter's first phrase indicates his surprise at realizing that "God does not show favoritism but accepts from every nation the one who fears him and does what is right" (vv. 34–35). Jesus had already implied that he was bringing salvation to the Gentiles (Jn 10:16; 12:32). But it took a special revelation before the full implications of these truths would be understood and practiced.
10:36 Peter introduces his message as containing "good news of peace through Jesus Christ." Peace was the content of God's basic promise to the Jews in the OT. By describing Jesus as "Lord of all," Peter extends this blessing to Gentiles.
10:37–39a Peter's speech here is the only evangelistic message in Acts where a summary of the ministry of Jesus is given (vv. 37–39a). In v. 38 Peter clearly attempts to show his audience that Jesus' ministry was accredited by God.
10:39b–40 After pointing out that the apostles were witnesses to what happened in the ministry of Christ (v. 39a), Peter presents the death and resurrection of Jesus (vv. 39b–40). Peter implicates the opponents of Christ and implies the curse of hanging on a tree (v. 39).
10:40–41 A unique feature of Peter's sermon is the point that Jesus even ate and drank with the apostles after his resurrection (v. 41). Luke's Gospel is the only one that records this fact (Lk 24:41–43). The NT evangelists were both messengers of the Good News and apologists.
10:42 Next Peter speaks of the commission the apostles received to proclaim Christ. *Preaching* shows that evangelism is a confident proclamation; *testifying* points to the seriousness of the task—it is a matter of judgment and salvation—and to the fact that this is something that we have experienced and know to be true. Judgment is an essential part of the evangelistic message.
10:43 In v. 43, Peter gives the scriptural authentication of the person and work of Christ. This statement implies that Peter's audience will receive the forgiveness of sins if they respond by believing in Jesus.
10:44–48 Nowhere else in Acts does the Spirit come before baptism. Here it was accompanied by "speaking in tongues and praising God" (v. 46). With such unmistakable evidence of their conversion, Peter does not hesitate to baptize them immediately (vv. 47–48).

With his qualms about table fellowship with Gentiles overcome, Peter seems to have accepted Cornelius's invitation for him to stay a few days (v. 48). The news of what Peter has done travels to Jerusalem before he arrives there.

Ac 11:2–3 ❖ Why is the wideness of God's mercy sometimes hard for even believers to understand and accept?

stand in the way of their being baptized
with water.[e] They have received the Holy
Spirit just as we have."[f] 48So he ordered
that they be baptized in the name of
Jesus Christ.[g] Then they asked Peter to
stay with them for a few days.

Peter Explains His Actions

11 The apostles and the believers[h]
throughout Judea heard that the
Gentiles also had received the word of
God. 2So when Peter went up to Jerusalem, the circumcised believers[i] criticized him 3and said, "You went into the
house of uncircumcised men and ate
with them."[j]
4Starting from the beginning, Peter told
them the whole story: 5"I was in the city
of Joppa praying, and in a trance I saw a
vision.[k] I saw something like a large sheet
being let down from heaven by its four
corners, and it came down to where I was.
6I looked into it and saw four-footed animals of the earth, wild beasts, reptiles
and birds. 7Then I heard a voice telling
me, 'Get up, Peter. Kill and eat.'
8"I replied, 'Surely not, Lord! Nothing
impure or unclean has ever entered my
mouth.'
9"The voice spoke from heaven a second time, 'Do not call anything impure
that God has made clean.'[l] 10This happened three times, and then it was all
pulled up to heaven again.
11"Right then three men who had been
sent to me from Caesarea stopped at the
house where I was staying. 12The Spirit
told[m] me to have no hesitation about going with them.[n] These six brothers also
went with me, and we entered the man's
house. 13He told us how he had seen an
angel appear in his house and say, 'Send
to Joppa for Simon who is called Peter.
14He will bring you a message through
which you and all your household[o] will
be saved.'
15"As I began to speak, the Holy Spirit
came on[p] them as he had come on us at
the beginning.[q] 16Then I remembered
what the Lord had said: 'John baptized
with[a] water, but you will be baptized
with[a] the Holy Spirit.'[r] 17So if God gave
them the same gift he gave us[s] who believed in the Lord Jesus Christ, who was
I to think that I could stand in God's
way?"
18When they heard this, they had no
further objections and praised God,
saying, "So then, even to Gentiles God
has granted repentance that leads to
life."[t]

10:47 [e] Ac 8:36 [f] Ac 11:17
10:48 [g] Ac 2:38; 8:16
11:1 [h] Ac 1:16
11:2 [i] Ac 10:45
11:3 [j] Ac 10:25, 28; Gal 2:12
11:5 [k] Ac 9:10; 10:9-32
11:9 [l] Ac 10:15
11:12 [m] Ac 8:29 [n] Ac 15:9; Ro 3:22
11:14 [o] Jn 4:53; Ac 16:15,31-34; 1Co 1:11,16
11:15 [p] Ac 10:44 [q] Ac 2:4
11:16 [r] Mk 1:8; Ac 1:5
11:17 [s] Ac 10:45, 47
11:18 [t] Ro 10:12, 13; 2Co 7:10

[a] *16* Or *in*

11:1–3 A revolutionary thing had happened in the life of the church, and the news spread through the church in Judea (v. 1). When Peter arrived in Jerusalem, "the circumcised believers" (lit., "those of the circumcision") criticized him. Luke is probably referring to the group within the church who required circumcision of all Gentile believers.

11:4–15 In response to the criticism, Peter explains everything (v. 4). The apostle stresses that he had with him "six brothers" (v. 12) who could confirm everything that he was telling the leaders in Jerusalem. He also comments that the Holy Spirit came on Cornelius and company "as [he] began to speak" (v. 15). This suggests that he was unable to complete his teaching. He clarifies that the Holy Spirit came on them "as he had come on us at the beginning" (v. 15). This was a Gentile Pentecost!

With so much evidence of God's work, Peter dared not resist, as he had done earlier with the vision of the unclean animals (v. 17). The evidence of their salvation was too great for further objections. The church then praised God and affirmed a new principle about God's dealings with the Gentiles (v. 18).

✣ **10:34—11:18** All who bring pioneering-type changes in the church—for that matter in any sphere of life—usually face criticism. For example, William Booth, founder of the Salvation Army, broke new ground for the church by ministering to people who were poor, to those who struggled with addiction, and to those with other characteristics that others considered undesirable in society. But respected and devout leaders of the church criticized him.

Peter's actions show how important it is to be careful to vet and defend with other sincere believers the directions in which we are moving. Making a serious effort to convince the church of a new position takes hard work and sometimes comes only after a long and tiring struggle. But prayerfully defending the move based on the teaching of the Bible and with a view toward bringing more individuals to Christ is the proper approach. Peter's experience demonstrates that God sometimes moves in surprising ways to expand his kingdom, and we need to check ourselves—both before we resist and before we move forward.

PEOPLE TO KNOW // BARNABAS

ACTS 11:22–30: Barnabas was a Levite from Cyprus. His name was Joseph, but the apostles called him Barnabas, which means "son of encouragement" (Ac 4:36). Indeed, Barnabas did have a gift for encouragement and mentoring.

When Saul, a persecutor of the church, was converted through an encounter with Christ, the followers of Jesus in Jerusalem were afraid his conversion was a ploy to trick them into trusting him. It was Barnabas who advocated for Saul (later called Paul) and brought him before the other disciples (Ac 9:27).

Barnabas had a successful ministry to Gentiles in Antioch. He chose Paul as his ministry partner, and the two worked together there for a full year. From Antioch, Barnabas and Paul were sent to do mission work together, along with Barnabas's cousin, Mark.

At the Jerusalem Council (Ac 15:1–35), church leaders debated whether Gentiles could be saved without also following Jewish rituals, including circumcision. Barnabas and Paul testified powerfully about all they had seen God do among the Gentiles, and their testimony influenced the council's decision not to require circumcision for Gentiles.

APPLICATION ✜ Paul is perhaps the most influential early Christian, credited with writing 13 NT books. But Paul's faith was strongly shaped by the encouraging influence of Barnabas, who advocated for him and partnered with him in ministry.

Wherever you are in your spiritual journey, you can learn be an encourager to others. When you encounter those who are going through a difficult time, be a good listener for them. Seek to encourage those who are engaged in ministries in your church or community. And, if you can mentor a new believer in the Christian faith, grab hold of that opportunity. It is certainly what Barnabas would do.

The Church in Antioch

19Now those who had been scattered by
the persecution that broke out when Stephen was killed[u] traveled as far as Phoenicia, Cyprus and Antioch,[v] spreading the
word only among Jews. 20Some of them,
however, men from Cyprus[w] and Cyrene,[x]
went to Antioch and began to speak to
Greeks also, telling them the good news
about the Lord Jesus. 21The Lord's hand
was with them,[y] and a great number of
people believed and turned to the Lord.[z]

11:19 [u]Ac 8:1, 4 [v]ver 26,27; Ac 13:1; 18:22; Gal 2:11
11:20 [w]Ac 4:36 [x]Mt 27:32
11:21 [y]Lk 1:66 [z]Ac 2:47
11:22 [a]Ac 4:36
11:23 [b]Ac 13:43; 14:26; 20:24 [c]Ac 14:22
11:24 [d]ver 21; Ac 5:14
11:25 [e]Ac 9:11

22News of this reached the church in
Jerusalem, and they sent Barnabas[a] to
Antioch. 23When he arrived and saw what
the grace of God had done,[b] he was glad
and encouraged them all to remain true
to the Lord with all their hearts.[c] 24He
was a good man, full of the Holy Spirit
and faith, and a great number of people
were brought to the Lord.[d]
25Then Barnabas went to Tarsus[e] to
look for Saul, 26and when he found
him, he brought him to Antioch. So for

11:19–21 Some unnamed people from Cyprus and Cyrene shared the gospel in Antioch with Greeks as well as Jews (v. 20). While Luke tells us where these daring spirits, who took the lead in this great step forward in the life of the church, hailed from, we do not know their names. With a population of about 300,000, Antioch in Syria was the third-largest city in the Roman Empire. A large Jewish population lived there, estimates of which range from 22,000 to 65,000.

Antioch was an international commercial center, a cosmopolitan city. People were accustomed to innovations there. It remained an important center of Christianity for many centuries.

11:22–24 Barnabas had distinguished himself as an encourager (4:36) and was known for his godliness (11:24). Moreover, he was a Jew from Cyprus, like some of those who had preached to Gentiles in Antioch. He would have a more global perspective than those who had never been abroad.

Barnabas's first response to seeing the evidence of God's grace in Antioch shows why he was given the name "Son of Encouragement" (v. 23; see again 4:36). The word "encouraged" should take the meaning "exhorted" here. When Luke uses "good" to describe Barnabas (v. 24), he is describing someone with true Christian character, a man of integrity and wholesomeness.

While Barnabas is the only one described as "a good man" in Acts (v. 24), others, like Stephen, are likewise described as "full of the Holy Spirit" (cf. 6:3, 5). Barnabas was also "full of . . . faith," which likely means faith in God (v. 24).

11:25–26 Barnabas went in search of Saul and brought him back to help in a teaching ministry that went on for a whole year. The trip to Tarsus was about 100 miles—a major undertaking. About ten years likely elapsed since Saul had left Jerusalem and gone to Tarsus (9:30).

Another reason why Antioch has a special place

a whole year Barnabas and Saul met with
the church and taught great numbers of
people. The disciples[f] were called Christians first[g] at Antioch.
27During this time some prophets[h]
came down from Jerusalem to Antioch.
28One of them, named Agabus,[i] stood
up and through the Spirit predicted that
a severe famine would spread over the
entire Roman world.[j] (This happened
during the reign of Claudius.)[k] 29The
disciples,[l] as each one was able, decided
to provide help[m] for the brothers and
sisters[n] living in Judea. 30This they did,
sending their gift to the elders[o] by Barnabas and Saul.[p]

Peter's Miraculous Escape From Prison

12 It was about this time that King
Herod arrested some who belonged
to the church, intending to persecute
them. 2He had James, the brother of
John,[q] put to death with the sword.
3When he saw that this met with approval among the Jews,[r] he proceeded
to seize Peter also. This happened during
the Festival of Unleavened Bread.[s] 4Af-
ter arresting him, he put him in prison,
handing him over to be guarded by four
squads of four soldiers each. Herod intended to bring him out for public trial
after the Passover.
5So Peter was kept in prison, but the
church was earnestly praying to God for
him.[t]
6The night before Herod was to bring
him to trial, Peter was sleeping between
two soldiers, bound with two chains,[u]
and sentries stood guard at the entrance.
7Suddenly an angel[v] of the Lord appeared
and a light shone in the cell. He struck
Peter on the side and woke him up.
"Quick, get up!" he said, and the chains
fell off Peter's wrists.[w]
8Then the angel said to him, "Put on
your clothes and sandals." And Peter did so.
"Wrap your cloak around you and follow

11:26 [f] Ac 6:1,2; 13:52 [g] Ac 26:28; 1Pe 4:16
11:27 [h] Ac 13:1; 15:32; 1Co 12:28, 29; Eph 4:11
11:28 [i] Ac 21:10 [j] Mt 24:14 [k] Ac 18:2
11:29 [l] ver 26 [m] Ro 15:26; 2Co 9:2 [n] Ac 1:16
11:30 [o] Ac 14:23 [p] Ac 12:25
12:2 [q] Mt 4:21
12:3 [r] Ac 24:27 [s] Ex 12:15; 23:15
12:5 [t] Eph 6:18
12:6 [u] Ac 21:33
12:7 [v] Ac 5:19 [w] Ac 16:26

Ac 12:5 ❖ How might the community of believers be more intentional about praying for persecuted Christians around the world? What is our prayer for these struggling believers?

---

in the history of Christianity is that here "the disciples were called Christians first" (v. 26), a name that has prevailed. This was probably a name given by the city's population; Christians used it of themselves beginning only in the second century.
11:27-30 The message brought by the group from Jerusalem involved the use of prophecy, a gift that has a prominent place in Acts and in Paul's letters. Prophecies took the form of understandable messages in the speaker's ordinary language (unlike tongues) given by the revelation of the Spirit. Often, prophecy involved prediction of future events. Agabus used this gift twice to predict future events (vv. 27–28; 21:10–11).

Luke's comment that the famine "happened during the reign of Claudius" (11:28), who reigned in AD 41–54, helps us place this visit of Paul and Barnabas at around AD 46. According to Josephus, there was a severe famine in Judea. We can harmonize the AD 46 date with the Galatians account if we take the fourteen years Paul refers to as being fourteen years after his conversion (dated c. AD 33). He says he "went in response to a revelation" (Gal 2:2), which would be the prophecy of Agabus.

That this young church gave a gift to the "mother" church in Jerusalem shows how the missionary spirit had caught on. Soon, this church would be the mother church of Gentile missions (Ac 11:29–30).

✚ **11:19-30** Some of the most significant work for the kingdom has been done by unknown witnesses who are obedient to Christ right where they are and where they do not attract much attention. Today we associate significance and greatness with newsworthiness. Much effort is made to make an event look newsworthy, and thus it has to be associated with names—such as the names of those who write best-selling books or who head big organizations. These names attract the people in the media.

Our task is to be faithful to what God calls us to do. If that does not put our name forward on earth, that should not bother us, for our aim in life is not to get our name in the headlines but to hear our Lord say, "Well done" (Mt 25:21). It is the prospect of this reward that thrills sincere Christians.

12:1-3a When King Herod (Agrippa I) realized that the Jews were pleased with the killing of James, he also had Peter imprisoned (v. 3a). This incident indicates how much the relationship between Jews and Christians in Judea had deteriorated from the earlier situation (2:47). The use of the general term *Jews* suggests approval for James's death was widespread.
12:3b-4 There is much irony in this chapter. According to Luke, the imprisonment of Peter took place during the Passover (v. 3b). While they should have been celebrating a great salvation, they were hoping to inflict a great punishment on the Savior's representative (v. 11).
12:5-8 To the gloomy picture of Peter in prison Luke adds the hopeful note of the church earnestly in prayer for him (v. 5). The word translated "earnestly" (v. 5) literally means "stretched out" and could thus mean "continuously." He uses this same word in Lk 22:44, where it refers to Jesus' earnest prayer in the

me," the angel told him. 9Peter followed
him out of the prison, but he had no idea
that what the angel was doing was really
happening; he thought he was seeing a
vision.[x] 10They passed the first and second
guards and came to the iron gate leading
to the city. It opened for them by itself,[y]
and they went through it. When they had
walked the length of one street, suddenly
the angel left him.
11Then Peter came to himself[z] and said,
"Now I know without a doubt that the
Lord has sent his angel and rescued me[a]
from Herod's clutches and from everything the Jewish people were hoping
would happen."
12When this had dawned on him, he
went to the house of Mary the mother of
John, also called Mark,[b] where many people had gathered and were praying.[c] 13Pe-
ter knocked at the outer entrance, and
a servant named Rhoda came to answer
the door.[d] 14When she recognized Peter's
voice, she was so overjoyed[e] she ran back
without opening it and exclaimed, "Peter
is at the door!"
15"You're out of your mind," they told
her. When she kept insisting that it was
so, they said, "It must be his angel."[f]
16But Peter kept on knocking, and
when they opened the door and saw him,
they were astonished. 17Peter motioned
with his hand[g] for them to be quiet and
described how the Lord had brought him
out of prison. "Tell James[h] and the other
brothers and sisters[i] about this," he said,
and then he left for another place.
18In the morning, there was no small
commotion among the soldiers as to what
had become of Peter. 19After Herod had a
thorough search made for him and did not
find him, he cross-examined the guards
and ordered that they be executed.[j]

Herod's Death

Then Herod went from Judea to Caesarea[k] and stayed there. 20He had been
quarreling with the people of Tyre and
Sidon;[l] they now joined together and
sought an audience with him. After securing the support of Blastus, a trusted
personal servant of the king, they asked
for peace, because they depended on the
king's country for their food supply.[m]
21On the appointed day Herod, wearing his royal robes, sat on his throne and
delivered a public address to the people.
22They shouted, "This is the voice of a
god, not of a man." 23Immediately, because Herod did not give praise to God,
an angel of the Lord struck him down,[n]
and he was eaten by worms and died.
24But the word of God continued to
spread and flourish.[o]

Barnabas and Saul Sent Off

25When Barnabas[p] and Saul had finished their mission,[q] they returned

12:9 [x] Ac 9:10
12:10 [y] Ac 5:19; 16:26
12:11 [z] Lk 15:17 [a] Ps 34:7; Da 3:28; 6:22; 2Co 1:10; 2Pe 2:9
12:12 [b] ver 25; Ac 15:37,39; Col 4:10; Phm 24; 1Pe 5:13 [c] ver 5
12:13 [d] Jn 18:16, 17
12:14 [e] Lk 24:41
12:15 [f] Mt 18:10
12:17 [g] Ac 13:16; 19:33; 21:40
[h] Ac 15:13
[i] Ac 1:16
12:19 [j] Ac 16:27
[k] Ac 8:40
12:20 [l] Mt 11:21 [m] 1Ki 5:9,11; Eze 27:17
12:23 [n] 1Sa 25:38; 2Sa 24:16,17
12:24 [o] Ac 6:7; 19:20
12:25 [p] Ac 4:36 [q] Ac 11:30

---

garden. This idea of earnestness comes from the idea of hands stretched out to God in intense prayer.

12:9-17 The second instance of irony is the unbelief of Peter and the praying church that their prayers had been answered (vv. 9–11, 15). When the servant girl Rhoda was overjoyed over the answer to their prayers, they pronounced her out of her mind (vv. 14–15).

The statement "it must be his angel" (v. 15) reflects the Jewish belief in protecting and guiding angels. Thus the believers thought that Rhoda mistook Peter's guardian angel for Peter. While the big iron gate of the prison opened with no effort to let Peter out (v. 10), he was unable to get past the gate of his own friend's home.

12:18-19 A third instance of irony is Herod's response to Peter's escape, which deflated his ego. He restored his image by having the guards executed (v. 19a). This extreme overreaction is typical of powerful people who seek popularity but are unexpectedly humiliated.

12:20-24 Herod's deflated ego received a big boost at his conference with the desperate delegates from Tyre and Sidon, who, deprived of their food supply, resort to flattery to win him over (vv. 20–22). The account of this incident by Josephus supplements the partial account given here. There is irony here too, for the man who was glorious on the outside was rotting of worms on the inside.

> ✚ **12:1-24** In times of trouble, God's sovereignty can be expressed by rescue or no rescue. Whatever experiences God's providence permits us to go through, our primary commitment should be to obedience. All the threats from the authorities did not cause the early church to pull back on its commitment to proclaim the gospel. Peter saw wonderful deliverance through the intervention of God, while James faced death for Christ. But the early Christians persevered in obedience, knowing that because God is sovereign he would use their obedience to win a great victory for the kingdom.

12:25—13:3 When Saul and Barnabas returned to Antioch from Jerusalem, Barnabas's cousin (see Col 4:10) John Mark was with them. Barnabas is mentioned first, possibly because he was the leader of the group.

The Holy Spirit sent a message to this church, probably through one of the prophets there, which

"'I will give you the holy and
sure blessings promised to
David.'[a][f]

35So it is also stated elsewhere:

"'You will not let your holy one see
decay.'[b][g]

36"Now when David had served God's purpose in his own generation, he fell asleep; he was buried with his ancestors[h] and his body decayed. 37But the one whom God raised from the dead did not see decay.

38"Therefore, my friends, I want you to know that through Jesus the forgiveness of sins is proclaimed to you.[i] 39Through him everyone who believes is set free from every sin, a justification you were not able to obtain under the law of Moses.[j] 40Take care that what the prophets have said does not happen to you:

41"'Look, you scoffers,
wonder and perish,
for I am going to do something in
your days
that you would never believe,
even if someone told you.'[c]"[k]

42As Paul and Barnabas were leaving the synagogue,[l] the people invited them to speak further about these things on the next Sabbath. 43When the congregation was dismissed, many of the Jews and devout converts to Judaism followed Paul and Barnabas, who talked with them and urged them to continue in the grace of God.[m]

44On the next Sabbath almost the whole city gathered to hear the word of the Lord. 45When the Jews saw the crowds, they were filled with jealousy. They began to contradict what Paul was saying[n] and heaped abuse[o] on him.

46Then Paul and Barnabas answered them boldly: "We had to speak the word of God to you first.[p] Since you reject it and do not consider yourselves worthy of eternal life, we now turn to the Gentiles.[q] 47For this is what the Lord has commanded us:

"'I have made you[d] a light for the
Gentiles,[r]
that you[d] may bring salvation to
the ends of the earth.'[e]"[s]

48When the Gentiles heard this, they were glad and honored the word of the Lord; and all who were appointed for eternal life believed.

49The word of the Lord spread through the whole region. 50But the Jewish leaders incited the God-fearing women of high standing and the leading men of the city. They stirred up persecution against Paul and Barnabas, and expelled them from their region.[t] 51So they shook the dust off their feet[u] as a warning to them and went to Iconium.[v] 52And the

13:34 [f] Isa 55:3
13:35 [g] Ps 16:10; Ac 2:27
13:36 [h] 1Ki 2:10; Ac 2:29
13:38 [i] Lk 24:47; Ac 2:38
13:39 [j] Ro 3:28
13:41 [k] Hab 1:5
13:42 [l] ver 14
13:43 [m] Ac 11:23; 14:22
13:45 [n] 1Th 2:16 [o] Ac 18:6; 1Pe 4:4; Jude 10
13:46 [p] ver 26; Ac 3:26 [q] Ac 18:6; 22:21; 28:28
13:47 [r] Lk 2:32 [s] Isa 49:6
13:50 [t] 1Th 2:16
13:51 [u] Mt 10:14; Ac 18:6 [v] Ac 14:1, 19, 21; 2Ti 3:11

[a] *34* Isaiah 55:3 [b] *35* Psalm 16:10 (see Septuagint) [c] *41* Hab. 1:5 [d] *47* The Greek is singular. [e] *47* Isaiah 49:6

13:38–41 Following the description of the Christ event is an offer of forgiveness (v. 38) and justification (v. 39). Verse 39 contains ideas that are typical of Paul's letters: the importance of belief, the reality of justification, and the inability to be justified by the Law of Moses. Paul concludes with a quotation from Habakkuk (Hab 1:5)—a warning of judgment to those who reject God's offer of salvation (v. 41).

Paul expresses God's plan of salvation for the world through the progress of history. Beginning with God's salvation at the exodus, he shows how God systematically kept unfolding his purposes until they reached their peak in the Christ event.

13:42–43 Paul and Barnabas are also invited to speak the next Sabbath (v. 42). In the meantime, "many of the Jews and devout converts to Judaism" follow them (v. 43).

13:44–47 The Jews probably did not expect to see nearly the whole city there on that day (v. 44). Their jealousy is aroused, and they oppose Paul's next message with abusive talk (v. 45). Paul and Barnabas respond to this by stating what became a feature of their ministry and of Paul's theology: They preach to the Jews first, but if their response is unworthy of eternal life, they go to the Gentiles (v. 46). Paul backs that step from the Scriptures (v. 47). This recurring phenomenon of Jewish rejection of the gospel hurt him deeply and increased his desire to pray for their salvation (Ro 9:1–3; 10:1).

13:48 The Gentiles receive Paul's word with gladness (v. 48a). After considerable emphasis on the human response to the gospel, both positive and negative, Luke emphasizes God's foundational role in salvation (v. 48b).

13:49–52 The severity of the opposition to the gospel is such that the team has to leave town. Despite these problems the new believers are "filled with joy and with the Holy Spirit" (v. 52). As Paul and Barnabas leave the area, they express their verdict on the Jews by shaking the dust off their feet (v. 51).

13:13–52 We must exhibit the power of God's Spirit *both* in experience *and* in the world of thought. In this way, we will have a balanced gospel that can withstand the dry spells that

disciples were filled with joy and with
the Holy Spirit.

In Iconium

14 At Iconium[w] Paul and Barnabas
went as usual into the Jewish synagogue. There they spoke so effectively
that a great number of Jews and Greeks
believed. 2But the Jews who refused to
believe stirred up the other Gentiles and
poisoned their minds against the brothers. 3So Paul and Barnabas spent considerable time there, speaking boldly[x] for
the Lord, who confirmed the message of
his grace by enabling them to perform
signs and wonders.[y] 4The people of the
city were divided; some sided with the
Jews, others with the apostles.[z] 5There
was a plot afoot among both Gentiles
and Jews, together with their leaders,
to mistreat them and stone them.[a] 6But
they found out about it and fled[b] to the
Lycaonian cities of Lystra and Derbe and
to the surrounding country, 7where they
continued to preach[c] the gospel.[d]

In Lystra and Derbe

8In Lystra there sat a man who was
lame. He had been that way from birth[e]
and had never walked. 9He listened to
Paul as he was speaking. Paul looked directly at him, saw that he had faith to be
healed[f] 10and called out, "Stand up on
your feet!" At that, the man jumped up
and began to walk.[g]
11When the crowd saw what Paul had
done, they shouted in the Lycaonian language, "The gods have come down to
us in human form!"[h] 12Barnabas they
called Zeus, and Paul they called Hermes because he was the chief speaker.
13The priest of Zeus, whose temple was
just outside the city, brought bulls and
wreaths to the city gates because he and
the crowd wanted to offer sacrifices to
them.
14But when the apostles Barnabas and
Paul heard of this, they tore their clothes[i]
and rushed out into the crowd, shouting:
15"Friends, why are you doing this? We
too are only human,[j] like you. We are
bringing you good news,[k] telling you to
turn from these worthless things[l] to the
living God,[m] who made the heavens and
the earth[n] and the sea and everything in
them.[o] 16In the past, he let[p] all nations go
their own way.[q] 17Yet he has not left himself without testimony:[r] He has shown
kindness by giving you rain from heaven
and crops in their seasons;[s] he provides
you with plenty of food and fills your
hearts with joy." 18Even with these words,
they had difficulty keeping the crowd
from sacrificing to them.

14:1 [w] Ac 13:51
14:3 [x] Ac 4:29 [y] Jn 4:48; Heb 2:4
14:4 [z] Ac 17:4,5
14:5 [a] ver 19
14:6 [b] Mt 10:23
14:7 [c] Ac 16:10 [d] ver 15,21
14:8 [e] Ac 3:2
14:9 [f] Mt 9:28, 29
14:10 [g] Ac 3:8
14:11 [h] Ac 8:10; 28:6
14:14 [i] Mk 14:63
14:15 [j] Ac 10:26; Jas 5:17 [k] ver 7, 21; Ac 13:32 [l] 1Sa 12:21; 1Co 8:4; 1Th 1:9 [m] Mt 16:16 [n] Ge 1:1; Jer 14:22 [o] Ps 146:6; Rev 14:7
14:16 [p] Ac 17:30 [q] Ps 81:12; Mic 4:5
14:17 [r] Ac 17:27; Ro 1:20 [s] Dt 11:14; Job 5:10; Ps 65:10

---

will surely come, when God's hand seems withdrawn from us. Christians are not immune to such experiences. Those whose faith is founded on the truth will persevere, knowing that nothing can take away the truthfulness of the gospel. But those whose faith is founded on experience will stumble when they encounter times of darkness. One would hope that at these times such people will discover the more secure and unchanging realities of the Christian faith.

As we try to reach people for Christ, we must get people to understand the glory of the truth of the gospel—something deeper and more lasting than experience. Then they will have joy in the gospel, a joy that can withstand the mysterious and difficult times of darkness in life.

14:1–3 Iconium (modern Konya, a city in Turkey) was an important junction along the east-west road from Syria to Ephesus. After arriving, Paul and Barnabas followed their usual practice of going first to the local synagogue. Many Jews and Gentiles believed, which resulted in opposition from the Jews who did not believe. But Paul and Barnabas persevered with the ministry of the word and of miracles.

14:4–7 The gospel caused the city to be divided, and a plot against Paul and Barnabas forced them to flee to Lystra and Derbe.

14:8–15a The report of this miracle has remarkable similarities to the healing at the temple gate (3:2–10). Both the subjects were born disabled. Paul looked directly at the man who was disabled, just as Peter and John did (v. 9; cf. 3:4). Both men jumped up after being healed (v. 10; cf. 3:8). Both are said to have had the faith to be healed (v. 9; cf. 3:16). In both cases the preachers had to divert the attention from themselves to God (v. 15; cf. 3:12).

Paul and Barnabas could not understand what was being said by the people since they were shouting "in the Lycaonian language" (v. 11). This accounts for their delayed response to plans to offer sacrifices to them. When they found this out, their response was swift and typically Jewish (v. 14).

14:15b–18 Paul says he and Barnabas are presenting a much more majestic message than can be obtained from "these worthless things" (v. 15b). This is the first speech in Acts presented to an audience that has not been influenced by Jewish thought. Thus, Paul distinguishes the Lord God from the pagan gods by pointing out that he is Creator of everything that there is (v. 15). His influence as sustainer of creation is felt throughout the whole world (vv. 16–17). He is also the living God, who calls us to turn to him in repentance (v. 15).

Ac 14:22 ❖ What encouragement or hope might we offer to struggling believers to help them remain true to the faith?

19Then some Jews[t] came from Antioch
and Iconium[u] and won the crowd over.
They stoned Paul[v] and dragged him outside the city, thinking he was dead. 20But
after the disciples[w] had gathered around
him, he got up and went back into the
city. The next day he and Barnabas left
for Derbe.

The Return to Antioch in Syria

21They preached the gospel in that city
and won a large number of disciples.
Then they returned to Lystra, Iconium[x]
and Antioch, 22strengthening the disciples and encouraging them to remain
true to the faith.[y] "We must go through
many hardships[z] to enter the kingdom of
God," they said. 23Paul and Barnabas appointed elders[aa] for them in each church
and, with prayer and fasting,[b] committed
them to the Lord,[c] in whom they had put
their trust. 24After going through Pisidia,
they came into Pamphylia, 25and when
they had preached the word in Perga,
they went down to Attalia.

26From Attalia they sailed back to Antioch,[d] where they had been committed
to the grace of God[e] for the work they
had now completed.[f] 27On arriving there,
they gathered the church together and
reported all that God had done through
them[g] and how he had opened a door[h] of
faith to the Gentiles. 28And they stayed
there a long time with the disciples.

The Council at Jerusalem

15 Certain people[i] came down from
Judea to Antioch and were teaching
the believers: "Unless you are circumcised,[j] according to the custom taught
by Moses,[k] you cannot be saved." 2This
brought Paul and Barnabas into sharp
dispute and debate with them. So Paul
and Barnabas were appointed, along with
some other believers, to go up to Jerusalem[l] to see the apostles and elders[m]
about this question. 3The church sent

14:19 [t] Ac 13:45 [u] Ac 13:51 [v] 2Co 11:25; 2Ti 3:11
14:20 [w] ver 22, 28; Ac 11:26
14:21 [x] Ac 13:51
14:22 [y] Ac 11:23; 13:43 [z] Jn 16:33; 1Th 3:3; 2Ti 3:12
14:23 [a] Ac 11:30; Titus 1:5 [b] Ac 13:3 [c] Ac 20:32
14:26 [d] Ac 11:19 [e] Ac 15:40 [f] Ac 13:1,3
14:27 [g] Ac 15:4, 12; 21:19 [h] 1Co 16:9; 2Co 2:12; Col 4:3; Rev 3:8
15:1 [i] ver 24; Gal 2:12 [j] ver 5; Gal 5:2,3 [k] Ac 6:14
15:2 [l] Gal 2:2 [m] Ac 11:30

[a] 23 Or *Barnabas ordained elders*; or *Barnabas had elders elected*

14:19 Once again we find Jews opposing the ministry of Paul and Barnabas. Some have traveled from Antioch, 110 miles away, and Iconium, 20 miles away, to stamp out this work.

14:20–21a In this dark hour, there is support from the new believers of Lystra (v. 20). What a source of comfort this must have been to Paul. He and Barnabas leave the next day for Derbe. The Lord blesses their efforts with "a large number of disciples" (v. 21), and there is no mention of opposition here.

14:21b–28 Their return journey took Paul and Barnabas through the three towns they had just ministered at: Lystra, Iconium, and Antioch (v. 21b). They had been expelled from one of them (13:50) and had fled from the other two (14:6, 20). But this time they engaged in a new role in follow-through care of the converts rather than in pioneering evangelism.

The journey of Paul and Barnabas back to Antioch takes them through Perga, from where they had started their journey up to the mountains of southern Galatia. We do not know whether they had preached there on their earlier visit, but they did so on this return visit (v. 25a). From there they went to Attalia and finally sailed back "home" to Antioch, having completed the task they were commissioned to do (v. 26). The church must have been thrilled to hear the report of their mission (v. 27) and happy that "they stayed there a long time with the disciples" (v. 28). The Greek word for "disciple" (or "learner") has now become a favorite term to refer to Christians, appearing four times in this chapter (vv. 20, 21, 22, 28) and 28 times in Acts (it appears over 250 times in the Gospels).

✣ **14:1–28** Paul's letters suggest that he and Barnabas exhorted these Galatian converts. They urged them to resist Satan and false doctrine, to put away the old lifestyle and put on the new lifestyle, to pray and give thanks always, to focus on being loving in all they do, and to have a biblical attitude toward their possessions.

Today some people shy away from exhortation, perhaps because of the influence of our culture, which is skeptical of any rigid approach to personal sin; because of the entertainment orientation that dominates Christian worship today; or because of the loss of credibility of preachers through moral failures. Yet many sections of the Bible teach believers hard truths and call them to personally turn from sin (e.g., the Ten Commandments; the Sermon on the Mount; the practical sections of Paul's letters, such as Ro 12–15; Gal 4–6; Eph 4–6; the book of James). Christian leaders should be exhorting Christians in this manner today, and believers should do the same as they witness to others.

15:1–4 These events are sparked by "certain people [who] came down from Judea to Antioch" (v. 1). Verse 24 makes clear that they went "without [the] authorization" of the church leaders in Jerusalem. They insinuated that the apostles and elders in Jerusalem agreed with what they were saying.

them on their way, and as they traveled through Phoenicia and Samaria, they told how the Gentiles had been converted.[n] This news made all the believers very glad. 4When they came to Jerusalem, they were welcomed by the church and the apostles and elders, to whom they reported everything God had done through them.[o]

5Then some of the believers who belonged to the party of the Pharisees stood up and said, "The Gentiles must be circumcised and required to keep the law of Moses."

6The apostles and elders met to consider this question. 7After much discussion, Peter got up and addressed them: "Brothers, you know that some time ago God made a choice among you that the Gentiles might hear from my lips the message of the gospel and believe. 8God, who knows the heart,[p] showed that he accepted them by giving the Holy Spirit to them,[q] just as he did to us. 9He did not discriminate between us and them,[r] for he purified their hearts by faith.[s] 10Now then, why do you try to test God by putting on the necks of Gentiles a yoke[t] that neither we nor our ancestors have been able to bear? 11No! We believe it is through the grace[u] of our Lord Jesus that we are saved, just as they are."

12The whole assembly became silent as they listened to Barnabas and Paul telling about the signs and wonders[v] God had done among the Gentiles through them.[w] 13When they finished, James[x] spoke up. "Brothers," he said, "listen to me. 14Simon[a] has described to us how God first intervened to choose a people for his name from the Gentiles. 15The words of the prophets are in agreement with this, as it is written:

16" 'After this I will return
    and rebuild David's fallen tent.
  Its ruins I will rebuild,
    and I will restore it,
17that the rest of mankind may seek
      the Lord,
    even all the Gentiles who bear my
      name,
  says the Lord, who does these
      things'[b][y]—
18   things known from long ago.[c]

19"It is my judgment, therefore, that we should not make it difficult for the Gentiles who are turning to God. 20Instead we should write to them, telling them to abstain from food polluted by idols,[z] from sexual immorality,[a] from the meat of strangled animals and from blood.[b] 21For the law of Moses has been preached in every city from the earliest times and is read in the synagogues on every Sabbath."[c]

15:3 [n]Ac 14:27
15:4 [o]ver 12; Ac 14:27
15:8 [p]Ac 1:24 [q]Ac 10:44,47
15:9 [r]Ac 10:28, 34; 11:12 [s]Ac 10:43
15:10 [t]Mt 23:4; Gal 5:1
15:11 [u]Ro 3:24; Eph 2:5-8
15:12 [v]Jn 4:48 [w]Ac 14:27
15:13 [x]Ac 12:17
15:17 [y]Am 9:11, 12
15:20 [z]1Co 8:7-13; 10:14-28; Rev 2:14,20 [a]1Co 10:7,8 [b]ver 29; Ge 9:4; Lev 3:17; Dt 12:16,23
15:21 [c]Ac 13:15; 2Co 3:14,15

[a] 14 Greek *Simeon,* a variant of *Simon;* that is, Peter [b] *17* Amos 9:11,12 (see Septuagint) [c] *17,18* Some manuscripts *things'— / [18]the Lord's work is known to him from long ago*

Paul preached that salvation occurs through no work of our own and only through the merits of the death of Christ. Such a message was scandalous to the average Jew.

15:5–6 The joy at Paul and Barnabas's report was broken by objections regarding the circumcision issue (v. 5). Therefore, "the apostles and elders met to consider this question" (v. 6).

15:7–11 After the discussion, Peter spoke up (v. 7). This council probably met after the humiliating confrontation in Antioch, where Peter was publicly rebuked by the younger Paul (Gal 2:11–21). It is commendable that Peter should be the first to get up and speak on behalf of Paul's side in the controversy.

Peter's main point was that the opening of the door of salvation took place through God's initiative. Peter then explicitly stated the great truth that Paul later expounded in Eph 2:14–22: God broke all barriers separating Jews and Gentiles. Peter admits that the Mosaic law was "a yoke" (Ac 15:10). Insisting that Gentiles keep the law is to "try to test God" (v. 10), a serious issue. With this speech, Peter bows out of the book of Acts.

15:12–19 James then makes his entrance (v. 13). He is a well-known figure in the early church. From what he says and the way he says it, it becomes evident that he has become the leader of the church in Jerusalem. James is probably the brother of Jesus.

James makes a revolutionary statement: "God first intervened to choose a people for his name from the Gentiles" (v. 14). Deuteronomy 14:2 says the Israelites have been called out from the nations to be a people for the Lord God. James says the opposite: From *within* the nations God has taken a people for himself. James concludes that the church "should not make it difficult for the Gentiles who are turning to God" (Ac 15:19)—perhaps referring to not requiring them to go through the painful step of circumcision.

15:20–21 Once the requirements for salvation have been settled, James brings up an important issue. Table fellowship with Gentiles and the consumption of non-kosher food was a serious issue. If there was going to be openhearted fellowship between Jewish and Gentile Christians, there would have to be some Gentile sensitivity to Jewish ethics. So James proposes three prohibitions relating to food (v. 20).

The prohibition of sexual immorality seems to belong to a different category from the rest. There was so much immorality in some of these places,

The Council's Letter to Gentile Believers

22 Then the apostles and elders, with
the whole church, decided to choose
some of their own men and send them
to Antioch with Paul and Barnabas. They
chose Judas (called Barsabbas) and Silas,[d] men who were leaders among the
believers. 23 With them they sent the following letter:

The apostles and elders, your brothers,

To the Gentile believers in Antioch,[e]
Syria and Cilicia:[f]

Greetings.[g]

24 We have heard that some went
out from us without our authorization and disturbed you, troubling
your minds by what they said.[h] 25 So
we all agreed to choose some men
and send them to you with our
dear friends Barnabas and Paul —
26 men who have risked their lives[i]
for the name of our Lord Jesus
Christ. 27 Therefore we are sending
Judas and Silas to confirm by word
of mouth what we are writing. 28 It
seemed good to the Holy Spirit[j]
and to us not to burden you with
anything beyond the following requirements: 29 You are to abstain
from food sacrificed to idols, from
blood, from the meat of strangled
animals and from sexual immorality.[k] You will do well to avoid these
things.

Farewell.

30 So the men were sent off and went
down to Antioch, where they gathered
the church together and delivered the
letter. 31 The people read it and were glad
for its encouraging message. 32 Judas and
Silas, who themselves were prophets, said
much to encourage and strengthen the
believers. 33 After spending some time
there, they were sent off by the believers with the blessing of peace[l] to return
to those who had sent them. [34][a] 35 But
Paul and Barnabas remained in Antioch,
where they and many others taught and
preached[m] the word of the Lord.

Disagreement Between Paul and Barnabas

36 Some time later Paul said to Barnabas, "Let us go back and visit the believers in all the towns[n] where we preached
the word of the Lord and see how they
are doing." 37 Barnabas wanted to take
John, also called Mark,[o] with them,
38 but Paul did not think it wise to take
him, because he had deserted them[p] in
Pamphylia and had not continued with
them in the work. 39 They had such a
sharp disagreement that they parted
company. Barnabas took Mark and sailed

15:22 [d] ver 27, 32, 40
15:23 [e] ver 1 [f] ver 41 [g] Ac 23:25, 26; Jas 1:1
15:24 [h] ver 1; Gal 1:7; 5:10
15:26 [i] Ac 9:23-25; 14:19
15:28 [j] Ac 5:32
15:29 [k] ver 20; Ac 21:25
15:33 [l] Mk 5:34; Ac 16:36; 1Co 16:11
15:35 [m] Ac 8:4
15:36 [n] Ac 13:4, 13, 14, 51; 14:1, 6, 24, 25
15:37 [o] Ac 12:12
15:38 [p] Ac 13:13

[a] 34 Some manuscripts include here *But Silas decided to remain there.*

---

like Antioch, that the churches were also affected by the immorality surrounding them. Therefore, a special warning was necessary.

15:22–29 The Jerusalem leaders decide to send some of their own people as a delegation bearing a letter from the council (v. 22). This letter emphasizes the unity and unanimity of the church in this decision.

15:30–35 These verses describe a situation where joy and encouragement have replaced the uncertainty of a few days before. The church had taken another important step in fulfilling the Great Commission.

15:1–35 When false teachers came to Antioch, what they said could not be easily dismissed since they had come from the mother church in Judea. While not typical, in the same way today teachers from highly regarded seminaries can come and cause great damage in the church by false teaching. Believers should always be on their guard with regard to the teaching that they hear, praying for discernment and always reading and studying the Bible and other resources to help them better understand the Word of God for themselves.

15:36–39a Though the word Luke uses in v. 39 for the resulting conflict is a strong one ("sharp disagreement"), it does not hint at who was right and who was wrong. That the team should have broken up because of this conflict is sad. It is encouraging to find out that later Paul and Barnabas seem to have become colleagues again (1Co 9:6; Col 4:10) and that Paul had not only come to appreciate Mark but also to depend on him so much that he asked for him to come to him toward the end of his life (2Ti 4:11; cf. Col 4:10; Phm 24).

The sovereignty of God is revealed as two separate teams now set out, and the area of the first missionary journey is divided between Paul and Barnabas. The latter goes to his native Cyprus with Mark (v. 39), while Paul takes Silas and travels via Syria and Cilicia to south Galatia (15:40—16:1).

15:39b–41 Silas was a leader in the church of Jerusalem (v. 22) and a prophet who "said much to encourage and strengthen the believers" in Antioch (v. 32). This must mean he was an enthusiastic backer of

for Cyprus, 40but Paul chose Silas[q] and
left, commended by the believers to the
grace of the Lord.[r] 41He went through
Syria[s] and Cilicia,[t] strengthening the
churches.[u]

Timothy Joins Paul and Silas

16 Paul came to Derbe and then to Lystra,[v] where a disciple named Timothy[w] lived, whose mother was Jewish and
a believer but whose father was a Greek.
2The believers[x] at Lystra and Iconium[y]
spoke well of him. 3Paul wanted to take
him along on the journey, so he circumcised him because of the Jews who lived
in that area, for they all knew that his father was a Greek.[z] 4As they traveled from
town to town, they delivered the decisions reached by the apostles and elders[a]
in Jerusalem[b] for the people to obey.[c] 5So
the churches were strengthened[d] in the
faith and grew daily in numbers.

Paul's Vision of the Man of Macedonia

6Paul and his companions traveled
throughout the region of Phrygia[e] and
Galatia,[f] having been kept by the Holy

15:40 [q] ver 22 [r] Ac 11:23
15:41 [s] ver 23 [t] Ac 6:9 [u] Ac 16:5
16:1 [v] Ac 14:6 [w] Ac 17:14; 18:5; 19:22; Ro 16:21; 1Co 4:17; 2Co 1:1,19; 1Th 3:2,6; 1Ti 1:2,18; 2Ti 1:2,5,6
16:2 [x] ver 40 [y] Ac 13:51
16:3 [z] Gal 2:3
16:4 [a] Ac 11:30 [b] Ac 15:2 [c] Ac 15:28,29
16:5 [d] Ac 9:31; 15:41
16:6 [e] Ac 18:23 [f] Ac 18:23; Gal 1:2; 3:1
[g] Ac 2:9
16:7 [h] Ro 8:9; Gal 4:6
16:8 [i] ver 11; 2Co 2:12; 2Ti 4:13
16:9 [j] Ac 9:10 [k] Ac 20:1,3
16:10 [l] ver 10-17 [m] Ac 14:7
16:11 [n] ver 8

Ac 15:39 ❖ Is it ever best to simply part ways over a dispute or disagreement? Why or why not?

Ac 16:6 ❖ What people has God given us a vision or a passion to minister to? How can we carry the presence of Christ to them?

Spirit from preaching the word in the
province of Asia.[g] 7When they came to
the border of Mysia, they tried to enter
Bithynia, but the Spirit of Jesus[h] would
not allow them to. 8So they passed by
Mysia and went down to Troas.[i] 9During
the night Paul had a vision[j] of a man of
Macedonia[k] standing and begging him,
"Come over to Macedonia and help us."
10After Paul had seen the vision, we[l] got
ready at once to leave for Macedonia,
concluding that God had called us to
preach the gospel[m] to them.

Lydia's Conversion in Philippi

11From Troas[n] we put out to sea and
sailed straight for Samothrace, and the

Paul's program of Gentile evangelism. He is named as coauthor of the two Thessalonian letters.

Paul and Silas are commissioned and sent off by the church in Antioch (v. 40), just as the earlier team had been sent off (13:3). There is no mention of a similar send-off for Barnabas and Mark, but this may be because from now on Luke focuses on Paul's ministry.

All true ministry stems from God's grace, but grace is often mediated through the prayers, concern, accountability, and provision of other Christians. The laying on of hands itself was intended to signify the mediating of God's blessing. As the church released Paul and Silas to the grace of God, they would have pledged to continue to do their part to support their ministry.

16:1–5 Acts 15:41 and 16:5 indicate that the first leg of this journey was one of "strengthening the churches" (15:41). One aspect of this ministry was that "they delivered the decisions" of the Jerusalem Council "for the people to obey" (16:4).

In Lystra, Timothy becomes the newest member of the team (vv. 1–3). Paul's circumcising of him has received much discussion. Some say that the Paul of the letters who spoke so strongly against circumcision could not have done this. But Paul's battle was against insisting that circumcision was a condition for fully including the Gentiles. Here the issue was qualifications for ministry. Timothy needed to win the respect of the Jewish Christians, and being circumcised would have given him openings in evangelizing Jews.

16:6–10 The providence of God is obvious in this section, hindering Paul from doing what he wanted and leading him to the place where God wanted him to go (vv. 6–10). Paul can only go farther west and comes to the seaport of Troas (v. 8). There he has the vision with a call from Macedonia (v. 9) and concludes that "God had called [him] to preach" there (v. 10).

16:10 In v. 10 we have the first of the "we" passages of Acts, suggesting to some that Troas may be where Paul first met Luke or at least where they first began to travel together. Luke got to know Paul closely through being with him on his journeys. He was the only one with Paul shortly before his execution in Rome (2Ti 4:11). But Luke also gives other leaders, like Peter and James, their due place in Acts. Traveling with Silas would certainly have helped Luke get the perspective of the Jerusalem church.

✚ **15:36—16:10** While it is true that this passage does not give us an excuse to quarrel, it does give us comfort if we have disagreements that do not end well. It also gives hope, for just as Paul and Barnabas got together after the heat of the conflict had died down, so can we. Therefore, we must be sure that during the heat of a conflict we do not do or say things that may complicate a final resolution.

Because God is greater than any problem, we can always live with the hope of resolution. That hope will enable us to look beyond the hurt to the day when we will rejoice in a relationship restored. And that, in turn, should cause us to temper our actions and reactions to any situation.

16:11–12 Samothrace was a common stopover for ships. Philippi was about ten miles inland,

PEOPLE TO KNOW // LYDIA

ACTS 16:14: Paul encountered Lydia in the city of Philippi on his second missionary journey. God had prompted Paul through a vision to travel to Macedonia, a direction Paul had not intended to go (Ac 16:9). Lydia was the first convert to Christ in Paul's Macedonian ministry—the first European Christian.

Lydia was by the river praying on the Sabbath with some other women when Paul and his fellow missionaries happened upon them. The fact that these God-fearing women were observing the Sabbath by the river indicates there was likely no synagogue in Philippi. Paul shared the gospel of Christ with the women, and God opened Lydia's heart to Paul's message (Ac 16:14). She and the members of her household were baptized.

Lydia was a woman of standing. Not only is she described as the head of her household, but she was also a dealer of purple cloth, thus a businesswoman. Acts says she was originally from Thyatira, a city known for its dyed fabrics. Furthermore, Lydia invited Paul and his companions to stay at her home while in Philippi, indicating she had the room and means to host travelers.

APPLICATION Our faith needs to be put into action. As soon as God opened Lydia's heart to Christ, she had her whole household baptized. She also showed her generosity and hospitality by hosting Paul and the others in her own home during their stay. Lydia's excitement for the gospel should inspire us also to move beyond belief and into a life of faith and action. Like Lydia, we can use our means, resources, and influence to serve God.

next day we went on to Neapolis. 12From
there we traveled to Philippi,[o] a Roman
colony and the leading city of that district[a] of Macedonia.[p] And we stayed there
several days.

13On the Sabbath[q] we went outside the
city gate to the river, where we expected
to find a place of prayer. We sat down and
began to speak to the women who had
gathered there. 14One of those listening
was a woman from the city of Thyatira[r]
named Lydia, a dealer in purple cloth.
She was a worshiper of God. The Lord
opened her heart[s] to respond to Paul's
message. 15When she and the members
of her household[t] were baptized, she
invited us to her home. "If you consider me a believer in the Lord," she said,
"come and stay at my house." And she
persuaded us.

Paul and Silas in Prison

16Once when we were going to the
place of prayer,[u] we were met by a female slave who had a spirit[v] by which she
predicted the future. She earned a great
deal of money for her owners by fortune-
telling. 17She followed Paul and the rest
of us, shouting, "These men are servants
of the Most High God,[w] who are telling
you the way to be saved." 18She kept this
up for many days. Finally Paul became

16:12 [o]Ac 20:6; Php 1:1; 1Th 2:2 [p]ver 9
16:13 [q]Ac 13:14
16:14 [r]Rev 1:11 [s]Lk 24:45
16:15 [t]Ac 11:14
16:16 [u]ver 13 [v]Dt 18:11; 1Sa 28:3,7
16:17 [w]Mk 5:7

[a] 12 The text and meaning of the Greek for *the leading city of that district* are uncertain.

so they landed at Neapolis. From Neapolis Paul and company used the Egnatian Way, a famous Roman road running east-west ending at Neapolis. Some stone-cobbled sections of this ancient road are still visible.

The region of Macedonia was separate from Greece at this time. Two famous Macedonian kings, Philip II (356–336 BC) and his son Alexander (334–323 BC), had led a united Greco-Macedonian empire.

16:13 On the Sabbath Paul and his friends went to the river outside the city gate, expecting to find "a place of prayer" (v. 13). Being by a river facilitated any ceremonial washing rituals. One of the first converts in Philippi was Lydia, a seller of purple cloth from Thyatira, a city renowned for purple dye.

16:14–15 The interplay between the divine and human parts in evangelism is well expressed in this verse. Paul and his companions went to the people and shared the message, but God was the ultimate evangelist. Luke's interest in hosts is seen with the mention of hospitality in the homes of Lydia and the jailer (v. 34).

16:16–18 The story of the slave girl who was delivered from an evil spirit has similarities with episodes involving evil spirits that Jesus rebuked. The spirits seem to have had supernatural powers that enabled them to recognize the divine source of the ministries of Jesus and of Paul's team (v. 17). Though what the slave girl proclaimed affirmed Paul's ministry, he was "annoyed" by it (v. 18). Why Paul delayed responding for a few days remains a mystery. But when he did attend to it, the power of God overcame the demonic hold over the girl's life.

PEOPLE TO KNOW // SILAS

ACTS 16:16-40: Silas was a leader of the church in Jerusalem; he was selected to go to Antioch to deliver the decision of the Jerusalem Council regarding the church's inclusion of Gentiles (Ac 15:22-29). Silas told those in Antioch that Gentiles did not need to be circumcised in order to join the church. Silas is described as a prophet who said much to encourage the church in Antioch (Ac 15:32).

After Paul and Barnabas disagreed over whether to bring John Mark on their second missionary journey, they went their separate ways, and Paul selected Silas as his missionary partner (Ac 15:40). In Philippi, Paul delivered a slave woman from a demon who had given her the power to predict the future. When she was cured, her owners were furious that they could no longer make money through her. They stirred up the crowds against Paul and Silas and had them beaten and imprisoned. Paul and Silas were placed in an inner cell with their hands and feet in stocks.

In the night, Paul and Silas were singing hymns to God. An earthquake shook the prison, and the cells were opened. When the prison guard awoke and saw the cells open, he was about to kill himself, but Paul stopped him. The guard fell before Paul and Silas, asking what he must do to be saved. They told him to believe in Jesus Christ, and he and his household were baptized (Ac 16:22-34).

Silas continued to minister, both with Paul and separately. He is credited as a coauthor of the letters of 1 and 2 Thessalonians.

APPLICATION ✚ Silas's experience in the Philippian prison cell reminds us to praise God even in the worst circumstances. No matter what the day brings, our hope is always in the Lord. Silas saw past his chains and prison door and praised God during a time of uncertainty and fear. The same God who was faithful to Silas promises to be faithful to us as well, through his grace in Jesus Christ.

so annoyed that he turned around and
said to the spirit, "In the name of Jesus
Christ I command you to come out of
her!" At that moment the spirit left her.[x]
19 When her owners realized that their
hope of making money[y] was gone, they
seized Paul and Silas[z] and dragged[a] them
into the marketplace to face the authorities. 20 They brought them before the
magistrates and said, "These men are
Jews, and are throwing our city into an
uproar[b] 21 by advocating customs unlawful for us Romans[c] to accept or practice."[d]
22 The crowd joined in the attack
against Paul and Silas, and the magistrates ordered them to be stripped and
beaten with rods.[e] 23 After they had been
severely flogged, they were thrown into
prison, and the jailer[f] was commanded
to guard them carefully. 24 When he received these orders, he put them in the
inner cell and fastened their feet in the
stocks.[g]
25 About midnight Paul and Silas were
praying and singing hymns[h] to God, and
the other prisoners were listening to
them. 26 Suddenly there was such a violent earthquake that the foundations of
the prison were shaken.[i] At once all the
prison doors flew open,[j] and everyone's
chains came loose.[k] 27 The jailer woke up,
and when he saw the prison doors open,
he drew his sword and was about to kill
himself because he thought the prisoners had escaped.[l] 28 But Paul shouted,
"Don't harm yourself! We are all here!"
29 The jailer called for lights, rushed in
and fell trembling before Paul and Silas.
30 He then brought them out and asked,
"Sirs, what must I do to be saved?"[m]

16:18 [x] Mk 16:17
16:19 [y] ver 16; Ac 19:25, 26 [z] Ac 15:22 [a] Ac 8:3; 17:6; 21:30; Jas 2:6
16:20 [b] Ac 17:6
16:21 [c] ver 12 [d] Est 3:8
16:22 [e] 2Co 11:25; 1Th 2:2
16:23 [f] ver 27, 36
16:24 [g] Job 13:27; 33:11; Jer 20:2, 3; 29:26
16:25 [h] Eph 5:19
16:26 [i] Ac 4:31 [j] Ac 12:10 [k] Ac 12:7
16:27 [l] Ac 12:19
16:30 [m] Ac 2:37

16:19-21 This miracle, which caused a significant loss of income for her owners, brought about opposition to the gospel. An attempt was made to alienate the missionaries and cause the magistrates to side with "us Romans." Little did they know that the missionaries were Romans too (v. 37).
16:22-24 As Roman citizens, Paul and Silas should not have received this kind of treatment.
16:25-28 Despite the humiliation and pain they had experienced through being stripped, flogged, and imprisoned, Paul and Silas were "praying and singing hymns" around midnight (v. 25). Songs in the night of suffering have been a common response to suffering by the faithful throughout the ages. The jailer's near suicide over the possibility that prisoners had escaped (v. 27) is understandable when we remember that Peter's miraculous escape from prison resulted in the execution of the guards.
16:29-32 In an amazing turn of events, the jailer

31They replied, "Believe in the Lord
Jesus, and you will be saved — you and
your household."[n] 32Then they spoke the
word of the Lord to him and to all the
others in his house. 33At that hour of the
night[o] the jailer took them and washed
their wounds; then immediately he and
all his household were baptized. 34The
jailer brought them into his house and
set a meal before them; he[p] was filled
with joy because he had come to believe
in God — he and his whole household.
35When it was daylight, the magistrates sent their officers to the jailer with
the order: "Release those men." 36The
jailer[q] told Paul, "The magistrates have
ordered that you and Silas be released.
Now you can leave. Go in peace."[r]
37But Paul said to the officers: "They
beat us publicly without a trial, even
though we are Roman citizens,[s] and threw
us into prison. And now do they want to
get rid of us quietly? No! Let them come
themselves and escort us out."
38The officers reported this to the
magistrates, and when they heard that
Paul and Silas were Roman citizens, they
were alarmed.[t] 39They came to appease
them and escorted them from the prison, requesting them to leave the city.[u]
40After Paul and Silas came out of the
prison, they went to Lydia's house,[v]
where they met with the brothers and
sisters[w] and encouraged them. Then
they left.

16:31 [n] Ac 11:14
16:33 [o] ver 25
16:34 [p] Ac 11:14
16:36 [q] ver 23, 27 [r] Ac 15:33
16:37 [s] Ac 22:25-29
16:38 [t] Ac 22:29
16:39 [u] Mt 8:34
16:40 [v] ver 14 [w] ver 2; Ac 1:16
17:1 [x] ver 11, 13; Php 4:16; 1Th 1:1; 2Th 1:1; 2Ti 4:10
17:2 [y] Ac 9:20 [z] Ac 13:14 [a] Ac 8:35
17:3 [b] Lk 24:26; Ac 3:18 [c] Lk 24:46 [d] Ac 9:22; 18:28
17:4 [e] Ac 15:22
17:5 [f] ver 13; 1Th 2:16

In Thessalonica

17 When Paul and his companions had
passed through Amphipolis and
Apollonia, they came to Thessalonica,[x]
where there was a Jewish synagogue.
2As was his custom, Paul went into the
synagogue,[y] and on three Sabbath[z] days
he reasoned with them from the Scriptures,[a] 3explaining and proving that the
Messiah had to suffer[b] and rise from the
dead.[c] "This Jesus I am proclaiming to
you is the Messiah,"[d] he said. 4Some of
the Jews were persuaded and joined
Paul and Silas,[e] as did a large number
of God-fearing Greeks and quite a few
prominent women.
5But other Jews were jealous; so they
rounded up some bad characters from
the marketplace, formed a mob and
started a riot in the city.[f] They rushed to

---

rushed toward Paul and Silas and fell down trembling before them. He wanted to know what he had to "do" to be saved, but actually there was nothing that he needed to do (v. 30). Everything had already been done for him by Christ; all that was required was to believe (v. 31). Paul follows the offer of salvation by explaining the way of salvation (v. 32).

When Paul extends the offer of salvation to the jailer's household, is he saying that his faith will convert his entire household (v. 31b)? We should infer that Paul is offering salvation to everyone in his household on the same terms as he is offering it to the jailer.

16:33–34 As is often the case in Acts, baptism follows immediately after conversion, and the whole household is baptized. The midnight hospitality in the jailer's home includes the compassionate washing of wounds and the serving of a meal, and it is spiced with joy over salvation.

16:35–40 The magistrates must have felt that the punishment given to Paul and Silas was sufficient, considering the trivial nature of their offense. So they sent word to the jailer to release them (v. 35). Yet the missionaries insisted on a public apology, which would ultimately influence the public standing of the mission and the church there. Paul's claim to Roman citizenship proved to be a turning point again in Jerusalem (22:25–29).

✣ **16:11–40** We must always be looking for inroads so that we can influence a community with the gospel. Often the best way is to find some point of contact via common interests with someone in the community we wish to reach. The interest may be related to a felt need that we know Christ can answer (e.g., sickness, insecurity, fear, marital problems). It can also be commonly held religious convictions, which is what Paul looked for when he made contact in a new community by attending a synagogue or a place of prayer.

The interaction between human initiative and divine action identifies our responsibility and reminds us that God is the one who ultimately gives the results. We do not have to feel pressured to produce results; our call is to be faithful in going out and in using the best methods we know. God will look after the results as he calls his own into relationship with him.

17:1–4 Thessalonica was the capital of the whole province of Macedonia and its largest and most prosperous city. "As was his custom, Paul went into the synagogue" and spoke there on three Sabbaths (v. 2). He stayed for some time. The result of the ministry of Paul and Silas was the conversion of several Jews and God-fearers (v. 4). Paul's comment in 1Th 1:9 indicates also that many of those converted were pagans.

17:5–10a Seeing that their influence over various people had diminished, the Jews were jealous, and they resorted to contemptible means to fight the missionaries (v. 5a). Because Paul and Silas had probably been taken to a safe place, their host

Ac 17:5 ❖ How does jealousy still affect gospel work? What is the best way to deal with jealousy?

Jason's[g] house in search of Paul and Silas in order to bring them out to the crowd.[a] 6But when they did not find them, they dragged[h] Jason and some other believers before the city officials, shouting: "These men who have caused trouble all over the world[i] have now come here,[j] 7and Jason has welcomed them into his house. They are all defying Caesar's decrees, saying that there is another king, one called Jesus."[k] 8When they heard this, the crowd and the city officials were thrown into turmoil. 9Then they made Jason[l] and the others post bond and let them go.

In Berea

10As soon as it was night, the believers sent Paul and Silas away to Berea.[m] On arriving there, they went to the Jewish synagogue. 11Now the Berean Jews were of more noble character than those in Thessalonica,[n] for they received the message with great eagerness and examined the Scriptures[o] every day to see if what Paul said was true. 12As a result, many of them believed, as did also a number of prominent Greek women and many Greek men.

13But when the Jews in Thessalonica learned that Paul was preaching the word of God at Berea, some of them went there too, agitating the crowds and stirring them up. 14The believers immediately sent Paul to the coast, but Silas[p] and Timothy[q] stayed at Berea. 15Those who escorted Paul brought him to Athens[r] and then left with instructions for Silas and Timothy to join him as soon as possible.[s]

In Athens

16While Paul was waiting for them in Athens, he was greatly distressed to see that the city was full of idols. 17So he reasoned in the synagogue[t] with both Jews and God-fearing Greeks, as well as in the marketplace day by day with those who

17:5 [g] Ro 16:21
17:6 [h] Ac 16:19 [i] Mt 24:14 [j] Ac 16:20
17:7 [k] Lk 23:2; Jn 19:12
17:9 [l] ver 5
17:10 [m] ver 13; Ac 20:4
17:11 [n] ver 1 [o] Lk 16:29; Jn 5:39
17:14 [p] Ac 15:22 [q] Ac 16:1
17:15 [r] ver 16, 21,22; Ac 18:1; 1Th 3:1 [s] Ac 18:5
17:17 [t] Ac 9:20

[a] 5 Or *the assembly of the people*

Jason and some others were taken to the city officials (vv. 5b–6).

Portraying the evangelists as "men who have caused trouble all over the world" (v. 6b) is severe. But it is true that turmoil often results when the gospel challenges people to change their lives, and usually such turmoil originates with those who reject this challenge. The charge against Paul and Silas was that they had defied Caesar, "saying that there is another king," Jesus (v. 7).

Jason was released after posting bond, probably assuring the officials that he and the "other believers" would not cause any more problems and would see to it that Paul and Silas left the city (v. 6). This is the presumed background behind Paul's statement that he, Silas, and Timothy were torn away from the Thessalonians and that Satan stopped them from returning (1Th 2:17–18).

17:10b–11 Berea was not as important a city as Philippi or Thessalonica. The three Christian communities he founded on this trip were in a position to take the gospel westward (see 1Th 1:8).

In keeping with their usual practice, the team started off at the synagogue (v. 10b) and made the pleasant discovery that "the Berean Jews were of more noble character than those in Thessalonica" (v. 11a). Luke gives two reasons for this commendation (v. 11b). They expressed an attitude of humble receptivity that lies at the heart of faith.

17:12 Luke records that among the converts in Berea were many Jews and "also a number of prominent Greek women and many Greek men." It seems that in Athens prominent people were converted as well (v. 34).

17:13–15 As he had in other towns, Paul had to make a sudden exit from Berea. Jews from Thessalonica arrived and roused the crowds in that town, just as they had done in Thessalonica. Silas and Timothy stayed on in Berea with instructions to join Paul as soon as possible (vv. 14–15).

✚ **17:1–15** The key words for Paul's evangelistic preaching apply today. Paul taught about the death and resurrection of Christ even though it was a stumbling block to the Jews. We must always look for a way to bring up the message of Christ and his death and resurrection. While the contemporary church is developing effective models to meet people's felt needs, it also needs to continue to find more effective ways of communicating the message of the cross and empty tomb.

Commitment to proclaim the Good News about Jesus does not prohibit our listening to others. When people describe their views, we must give them full attention. Sometimes in a witnessing situation we may listen more than talk, for we should not rudely interrupt someone else's description of his or her views. We are servants, and it should not bother us if they dominate a conversation. Of course, love for this person will cause us to look for every opportunity to share the liberating news of Jesus Christ with them.

17:16 When Paul saw these exquisite works of pagan art, he was "greatly distressed."

17:17 Though Paul was disturbed, he acted with restraint and respect in his outward behavior among the idolaters. "Reasoned" here probably involved

happened to be there. 18A group of Epi-
curean and Stoic philosophers began to
debate with him. Some of them asked,
"What is this babbler trying to say?" Others remarked, "He seems to be advocating foreign gods." They said this because
Paul was preaching the good news about
Jesus and the resurrection.[u] 19Then they
took him and brought him to a meeting
of the Areopagus,[v] where they said to
him, "May we know what this new teaching[w] is that you are presenting? 20You
are bringing some strange ideas to our
ears, and we would like to know what
they mean." 21(All the Athenians and the
foreigners who lived there spent their
time doing nothing but talking about
and listening to the latest ideas.)
22Paul then stood up in the meeting
of the Areopagus and said: "People of
Athens! I see that in every way you are
very religious. 23For as I walked around
and looked carefully at your objects of
worship, I even found an altar with this
inscription: TO AN UNKNOWN GOD. So you
are ignorant of the very thing you worship[x] — and this is what I am going to
proclaim to you.
24"The God who made the world and
everything in it[y] is the Lord of heaven and
earth[z] and does not live in temples built by
human hands.[a] 25And he is not served by
human hands, as if he needed anything.
Rather, he himself gives everyone life and
breath and everything else.[b] 26From one
man he made all the nations, that they
should inhabit the whole earth; and he
marked out their appointed times in history and the boundaries of their lands.[c]
27God did this so that they would seek him
and perhaps reach out for him and find
him, though he is not far from any one of
us.[d] 28'For in him we live and move and
have our being.'[a][e] As some of your own
poets have said, 'We are his offspring.'[b]
29"Therefore since we are God's offspring, we should not think that the divine being is like gold or silver or stone —
an image made by human design and
skill.[f] 30In the past God overlooked[g] such
ignorance,[h] but now he commands all
people everywhere to repent.[i] 31For he
has set a day when he will judge[j] the
world with justice[k] by the man he has
appointed.[l] He has given proof of this to
everyone by raising him from the dead."[m]
32When they heard about the resurrection of the dead,[n] some of them sneered,

17:18 [u] ver 31, 32; Ac 4:2
17:19 [v] ver 22 [w] Mk 1:27
17:23 [x] Jn 4:22
17:24 [y] Isa 42:5; Ac 14:15 [z] Dt 10:14; Mt 11:25 [a] Ac 7:48
17:25 [b] Ps 50:10-12; Isa 42:5
17:26 [c] Dt 32:8; Job 12:23
17:27 [d] Dt 4:7; Jer 23:23, 24; Ac 14:17
17:28 [e] Job 12:10; Da 5:23
17:29 [f] Isa 40:18-20; Ro 1:23
17:30 [g] Ac 14:16; Ro 3:25 [h] ver 23; 1Pe 1:14 [i] Lk 24:47; Titus 2:11, 12
17:31 [j] Mt 10:15 [k] Ps 9:8; 96:13; 98:9 [l] Ac 10:42 [m] Ac 2:24
17:32 [n] ver 18, 31

[a] *28* From the Cretan philosopher Epimenides
[b] *28* From the Cilician Stoic philosopher Aratus

---

proclamation but left room for discussion at the end. When Paul evangelized this city of Socrates, he used the method of Socrates.

17:18-21 These Athenians seem to have been curious philosophically (v. 21), and thus they were willing to give the "strange ideas" of Paul an official hearing (vv. 19–20).

17:22-23 Paul's speech before the Areopagus remains a model of sensitive but direct confrontation of an intellectual audience with the claims of the gospel. That they were "very religious" in Paul's opening statement (v. 22) was a simple observation, opening the way for Paul's comment about the altar to the unknown god (v. 23a). Paul is highlighting an acknowledged need of the Athenians, proclaiming the God who can answer it (v. 23b).

17:24-28 Paul introduces his God and offers a critique of the Athenian gods. His comments are calculated to not only show the futility of idolatry but also to demonstrate that God is the supreme Lord of creation and worthy of our loyalty.

Paul insists that, unlike idols, God does not live in temples (v. 24) and does not need our insignificant offerings (v. 25). The apostle continues by focusing both on God's sovereignty over the affairs of the human race (v. 26) and on humanity's incurable need for religion (v. 27). Since God is the sustainer of creation, everyone's life depends on him (v. 28).

17:29-31 All these points lead to the conclusion (v. 29) that idolatry is unnecessary and lend weight to Paul's call to repentance that follows (v. 30). This is the only wise decision since God is someday going to judge the world (v. 31).

If there is a God who is supreme, why does he allow people to live in such open defiance of him without punishing them? Paul's answer has three aspects: (1) God overlooked their ignorance in the past, but (2) now he "commands all people everywhere to repent" (v. 30), and (3) a judgment day is coming (v. 31a).

How does Paul know that these things are true? What proof does he have of these claims? Paul answers that this supreme God "has given proof of this to everyone by raising [Jesus] from the dead" (v. 31b).

17:32-34 Some in Paul's audience begin to sneer at him (v. 32). Others, however, want to hear more (v. 33). Luke rounds off the story with a report about some of the results of Paul's ministry in Athens (v. 34).

Paul's strategy of reasoning for the gospel with the Athenians is instructive. His message does not contain direct quotations or appeals to the OT as did his talks to Jews and God-fearers. But his message was thoroughly scriptural. Interestingly, Paul quoted from writers whom the Athenians admired (v. 28). Of course, Paul would not have agreed with the philosophical system from which the statement arose, but he agreed with this individual statement and thus used it to reinforce his argument.

but others said, "We want to hear you
again on this subject." 33At that, Paul
left the Council. 34Some of the people
became followers of Paul and believed.
Among them was Dionysius, a member
of the Areopagus,[o] also a woman named
Damaris, and a number of others.

In Corinth

18 After this, Paul left Athens[p] and
went to Corinth.[q] 2There he met
a Jew named Aquila, a native of Pontus, who had recently come from Italy
with his wife Priscilla,[r] because Claudius[s] had ordered all Jews to leave Rome.
Paul went to see them, 3and because he
was a tentmaker as they were, he stayed
and worked with them.[t] 4Every Sabbath[u]
he reasoned in the synagogue, trying to
persuade Jews and Greeks.
5When Silas[v] and Timothy[w] came from
Macedonia,[x] Paul devoted himself exclusively to preaching, testifying to the Jews
that Jesus was the Messiah.[y] 6But when
they opposed Paul and became abusive,[z]
he shook out his clothes in protest and
said to them, "Your blood be on your own
heads![a] I am innocent of it.[b] From now
on I will go to the Gentiles."[c]
7Then Paul left the synagogue and
went next door to the house of Titius
Justus, a worshiper of God.[d] 8Crispus,[e]
the synagogue leader,[f] and his entire
household[g] believed in the Lord; and
many of the Corinthians who heard Paul
believed and were baptized.
9One night the Lord spoke to Paul in a
vision: "Do not be afraid; keep on speaking, do not be silent. 10For I am with you,[h]
and no one is going to attack and harm
you, because I have many people in this
city." 11So Paul stayed in Corinth for a
year and a half, teaching them the word
of God.
12While Gallio was proconsul of Achaia,[i]
the Jews of Corinth made a united attack
on Paul and brought him to the place of
judgment. 13"This man," they charged, "is
persuading the people to worship God
in ways contrary to the law."
14Just as Paul was about to speak,
Gallio said to them, "If you Jews were

17:34 [o] ver 19,22
18:1 [p] Ac 17:15 [q] Ac 19:1; 1Co 1:2; 2Co 1:1, 23; 2Ti 4:20
18:2 [r] Ro 16:3; 1Co 16:19; 2Ti 4:19 [s] Ac 11:28
18:3 [t] Ac 20:34; 1Co 4:12; 1Th 2:9; 2Th 3:8
18:4 [u] Ac 13:14
18:5 [v] Ac 15:22 [w] Ac 16:1 [x] Ac 16:9; 17:14, 15 [y] ver 28; Ac 17:3
18:6 [z] Ac 13:45 [a] 2Sa 1:16; Eze 18:13; 33:4 [b] Ac 20:26 [c] Ac 13:46
18:7 [d] Ac 16:14
18:8 [e] 1Co 1:14 [f] Mk 5:22 [g] Ac 11:14
18:10 [h] Mt 28:20
18:12 [i] ver 27

17:16-34 To maintain our intensity for biblical mission while engaging other religions, we should have three regular disciplines. (1) We must live under the Scriptures. The biblical attitude to life is so different to the world's attitudes that we can easily get drawn into the world's way of thinking unless we are regularly impacted by the Scriptures. (2) We need the discipline of community. We need accountability. Friends can confront us if we veer away from the path of biblical faith. (3) We must live under the discipline of witness.

When we get close to people, see their lives, and long for their salvation, we realize how vital the gospel is for their salvation. We experience again the power of the Spirit to energize us to witness (1:8). Such cutting-edge living is an effective safeguard against compromise.

18:1 Corinth was a prosperous city. It was the center for the worship of Aphrodite, the Greek goddess of love, and had a temple that employed a thousand prostitutes. From the fifth century BC on, the verb "to Corinthianize" meant to be sexually immoral.

Paul reports that he came to Corinth "in weakness with great fear and trembling" (1Co 2:3). This is understandable considering the pain he had endured in his last few stops. Paul may not have anticipated much receptivity in Corinth because of its prosperity and reputation for immorality.

18:2-3 In Corinth, Paul meets Aquila and Priscilla, who had recently been expelled from Rome along with other Jews (v. 2). Like Paul, they were tentmakers, and they soon became business partners (v. 3).

18:4 Paul worked on tents during the week and had a more public ministry in the synagogue every Sabbath (v. 4). In every new city Paul visited, he looked for a vantage point from which he could launch his ministry. Here it was his trade and his contacts in the synagogue.

18:5 While Paul was doing this work, his colleagues Silas and Timothy arrived from Macedonia with great news of how the church there was thriving under persecution (see 1Th 3:6-10). They probably brought gifts from Macedonia to support his work (2Co 11:8-9; Php 4:15-16), and as a result he was able to devote "himself exclusively to preaching" (Ac 18:5b).

18:6 This verse describes Paul's response when the Jews "became abusive." He then explicitly stated, "Your blood be on your own heads! I am innocent of it," and announced his intention to focus his efforts on the Gentiles.

18:7 Leaving the synagogue, Paul went to the home of Titius Justus (v. 7), which was probably where the first house church in Corinth met. Romans 16:23 refers to Gaius, who provided hospitality for the whole church in Corinth. Gaius may be another name for Titius. If Gaius provided hospitality to the whole church, he must have been wealthy.

18:8-11 In addition to the open door provided by Titius, the conversion of "Crispus, the synagogue leader" (v. 8) must have done much to encourage Paul. The biggest encouragement came from a vision Paul had. The Lord promised to protect him and told him that he had "many people in this city" (vv. 9-10).

18:12-17 Luke does not describe Paul's relatively long ministry in Corinth in much detail. His emphasis is on Gallio's positive response to the Christian faith. As a well-known proconsul, Gallio's response was a key building block in the church's case for a positive legal standing in the Roman Empire.

making a complaint about some mis-
demeanor or serious crime, it would be
reasonable for me to listen to you. 15 But
since it involves questions about words
and names and your own law[j] — settle the matter yourselves. I will not be
a judge of such things." 16 So he drove
them off. 17 Then the crowd there turned
on Sosthenes[k] the synagogue leader and
beat him in front of the proconsul; and
Gallio showed no concern whatever.

Priscilla, Aquila and Apollos

18 Paul stayed on in Corinth for some
time. Then he left the brothers and sisters[l] and sailed for Syria, accompanied
by Priscilla and Aquila. Before he sailed,
he had his hair cut off at Cenchreae[m]
because of a vow he had taken.[n] 19 They
arrived at Ephesus,[o] where Paul left Priscilla and Aquila. He himself went into the
synagogue and reasoned with the Jews.
20 When they asked him to spend more
time with them, he declined. 21 But as
he left, he promised, "I will come back
if it is God's will."[p] Then he set sail from
Ephesus. 22 When he landed at Caesarea,[q]
he went up to Jerusalem and greeted the
church and then went down to Antioch.[r]
23 After spending some time in Antioch, Paul set out from there and traveled
from place to place throughout the region of Galatia[s] and Phrygia, strengthening all the disciples.[t]
24 Meanwhile a Jew named Apollos,[u] a
native of Alexandria, came to Ephesus.
He was a learned man, with a thorough
knowledge of the Scriptures. 25 He had
been instructed in the way of the Lord,
and he spoke with great fervor[a][v] and
taught about Jesus accurately, though
he knew only the baptism of John.[w] 26 He
began to speak boldly in the synagogue.
When Priscilla and Aquila heard him,
they invited him to their home and explained to him the way of God more adequately.
27 When Apollos wanted to go to Achaia,[x] the brothers and sisters[y] encouraged
him and wrote to the disciples there to
welcome him. When he arrived, he was
a great help to those who by grace had
believed. 28 For he vigorously refuted
his Jewish opponents in public debate,

18:15 [j] Ac 23:29; 25:11,19
18:17 [k] 1Co 1:1
18:18 [l] Ac 1:16 [m] Ro 16:1 [n] Nu 6:2,5,18; Ac 21:24
18:19 [o] ver 21, 24; 1Co 15:32
18:21 [p] Ro 1:10; 1Co 4:19; Jas 4:15
18:22 [q] Ac 8:40 [r] Ac 11:19
18:23 [s] Ac 16:6 [t] Ac 14:22; 15:32,41
18:24 [u] Ac 19:1; 1Co 1:12; 3:5,6, 22; 4:6; 16:12; Titus 3:13
18:25 [v] Ro 12:11 [w] Ac 19:3
18:27 [x] ver 12 [y] ver 18

[a] 25 Or *with fervor in the Spirit*

Ac 18:26 ❖ How can we mentor or encourage new believers in their faith? What opportunities might God be opening for us to help others grow?

18:18–21 Paul was able to stay on in Corinth after he had been brought to trial. But after some time he set off for Antioch, taking Aquila and Priscilla with him (vv. 18–19a). Paul went into the synagogue in Ephesus, reasoned with the Jews (v. 19b), and won an invitation to spend more time with them. He declined it with the promise that he would return if it was God's will (vv. 20–21).

18:22 Paul left Aquila and Priscilla behind in Ephesus and set off for Caesarea, where he "greeted the church and then went down to Antioch." This ended Paul's second missionary journey.

✣ **18:1–22** As we think of the challenge of evangelizing the Corinths of today, we might be compelled to conclude that the whole world has become a Corinth. The rampant disregard for moral standards is brought right into homes through streaming services and our phones, and the church today is inevitably affected by it.

However, in the midst of that darkness there are people who are inclined toward the light. The stories of Jesus are just as readily available online as is any immoral content, and the Holy Spirit can and does work in the hearts of people today to draw them closer God. We can be encouraged, knowing that even though technology has changed how people interact with the world, God's desire to see individuals come into relationship with him hasn't changed one iota. And that's where our ministry to lost people in this world begins.

18:23 Paul's third missionary journey began from Antioch and included visits to Galatia and Phrygia, regions that he had previously evangelized.

18:24–25 Ephesus was the center of the worship of the Greek goddess Artemis (Roman Diana), the goddess of fertility. The temple to Artemis was considered one of the Seven Wonders of the Ancient World.

Apollos receives an important place in this narrative because he played a significant role in the growth of the early church. We are told that "he knew only the baptism of John" (v. 25). Apollos had developed skills in teaching from the Scriptures. And when he taught, he did so with well-known enthusiasm.

18:26 Priscilla and Aquila entered into this situation. Luke has changed the order of their names from his first mention of them (18:2), giving the wife's name first. Priscilla may have been the more prominent of the two.

18:27–28 We are not told whether Apollos stayed in Priscilla and Aquila's home, but this act of inviting Apollos into their home is typical of the open-home attitude that this couple had. Apollos was willing to learn from his hosts when they took him home to complete his education in the faith.

PEOPLE TO KNOW // APOLLOS

ACTS 18:18–28: Apollos was a Jew from Alexandria in Egypt. He was well-educated, a skilled orator and debater. He also had a deep understanding of Scripture. Apollos ministered in both Ephesus and Corinth. He preached Christ powerfully, vigorously refuting his Jewish opponents to show from Scripture that Christ was the Messiah (Ac 18:28).

Paul mentions Apollos several times in 1 Corinthians. Paul was concerned about the way members of the church in Corinth attached themselves to certain teachers in a divisive way: "One of you says, 'I follow Paul'; another, 'I follow Apollos'; another, 'I follow Cephas'; still another, 'I follow Christ'" (1Co 1:12). The Corinthians were choosing their favorite teacher at the expense of truly hearing the gospel. It is no surprise that Apollos gained a following: Who doesn't love to listen to a gifted preacher?

Paul set the Corinthians straight: Christ is not divided. Sure, there are different preachers, but there is only one Christ. Christians cannot magnify a preacher above that which is preached: the gospel of Jesus. Paul pointed out that all these preachers are part of the same work, and that work is ultimately God's: "I planted the seed, Apollos watered it, but God has been making it grow" (1Co 3:6).

APPLICATION ✜ In an age of celebrity pastors and slick presentations, it's easy to fall into "taking sides" like the Corinthians. It can be tempting to worship the messenger and overlook the message. What's important is not the rhetorical skill of the preacher but the message being preached. Apollos was a faithful servant of Christ who proclaimed the gospel with great skill, but the focus of his life was on sharing Christ with others. Our goal should be to honor those who share God's Word and support those who lead in our churches.

proving from the Scriptures[z] that Jesus
was the Messiah.[a]

Paul in Ephesus

19 While Apollos was at Corinth,[b] Paul
took the road through the interior
and arrived at Ephesus.[c] There he found
some disciples 2and asked them, "Did
you receive the Holy Spirit when[a] you
believed?"
They answered, "No, we have not even
heard that there is a Holy Spirit."
3So Paul asked, "Then what baptism
did you receive?"
"John's baptism," they replied.
4Paul said, "John's baptism was a baptism of repentance. He told the people
to believe in the one coming after him,
that is, in Jesus."[d] 5On hearing this, they
were baptized in the name of the Lord
Jesus. 6When Paul placed his hands on
them,[e] the Holy Spirit came on them,[f] and
they spoke in tongues[b][g] and prophesied.
7There were about twelve men in all.
8Paul entered the synagogue[h] and
spoke boldly there for three months, arguing persuasively about the kingdom of

18:28 [z] Ac 17:2 [a] ver 5; Ac 9:22
19:1 [b] Ac 18:1 [c] Ac 18:19
19:4 [d] Jn 1:7; Ac 13:24,25
19:6 [e] Ac 6:6; 8:17 [f] Ac 2:4 [g] Mk 16:17; Ac 10:46
19:8 [h] Ac 9:20

[a] 2 Or *after* [b] 6 Or *other languages*

19:1–7 Paul had wanted to come to Ephesus for major ministry for quite some time, but he had to wait for God's timing (16:6; 18:21). From here he could reach the entire province of Asia (19:10). There were believers in Ephesus when he arrived (18:27).
19:1–2 Paul also found some people who are called "disciples" but who were seriously deficient in their beliefs (v. 1), even though they are said to have "believed" (v. 2). Paul specifically asked them whether they had received the Holy Spirit when they believed (v. 2). This suggests that people can really know when they receive the Holy Spirit.
19:4–5 The problem was that they had only received John's baptism (v. 3). Unlike Apollos, they had not progressed much beyond John's teaching. So they needed to be told about believing in Jesus, which led to baptism in his name (vv. 4–5). This suggests that they were not true believers until then.
19:5–7 Verses 5–6 suggest that after they were baptized, "Paul placed his hands on them," resulting in the Spirit's coming on them accompanied by prophecy and speaking in tongues.

✜ **18:23—19:7** Anyone who truly understands the nature of Scripture should have a teachable attitude. In this, all believers should have the same attitude as Apollos. On the one hand, the vastness of Scripture makes us realize that our knowledge will always be limited. On the other hand, its glory makes us eager to learn whatever new thing we can. Both teacher and student enter into every teaching situation humbled by the realization that God's truth is so vast that there is more to learn and that some of this learning may come from unexpected sources.

19:8–10 Ephesus was somewhat different from other cities Paul went to, for a few believers and

God.[i] 9But some of them[j] became obstinate; they refused to believe and publicly maligned the Way.[k] So Paul left them.
He took the disciples[l] with him and had
discussions daily in the lecture hall of
Tyrannus. 10This went on for two years,[m]
so that all the Jews and Greeks who lived
in the province of Asia[n] heard the word
of the Lord.

11God did extraordinary miracles[o]
through Paul, 12so that even handker-
chiefs and aprons that had touched him
were taken to the sick, and their illnesses
were cured[p] and the evil spirits left them.

13Some Jews who went around driving
out evil spirits[q] tried to invoke the name
of the Lord Jesus over those who were demon-possessed. They would say, "In the
name of the Jesus[r] whom Paul preaches,
I command you to come out." 14Seven
sons of Sceva, a Jewish chief priest, were
doing this. 15One day the evil spirit answered them, "Jesus I know, and Paul I
know about, but who are you?" 16Then
the man who had the evil spirit jumped
on them and overpowered them all. He
gave them such a beating that they ran
out of the house naked and bleeding.

17When this became known to the Jews
and Greeks living in Ephesus,[s] they were
all seized with fear,[t] and the name of
the Lord Jesus was held in high hon-
or. 18Many of those who believed now
came and openly confessed what they
had done. 19A number who had practiced
sorcery brought their scrolls together
and burned them publicly. When they
calculated the value of the scrolls, the
total came to fifty thousand drachmas.[a]
20In this way the word of the Lord spread
widely and grew in power.[u]

21After all this had happened, Paul
decided[b] to go to Jerusalem,[v] passing
through Macedonia[w] and Achaia.[x] "After I have been there," he said, "I must
visit Rome also."[y] 22He sent two of his
helpers,[z] Timothy[a] and Erastus,[b] to Macedonia, while he stayed in the province
of Asia[c] a little longer.

The Riot in Ephesus

23About that time there arose a great
disturbance about the Way.[d] 24A silver-

19:8 [i] Ac 1:3; 28:23
19:9 [j] Ac 14:4 [k] ver 23; Ac 9:2 [l] ver 30; Ac 11:26
19:10 [m] Ac 20:31 [n] ver 22,26,27
19:11 [o] Ac 8:13
19:12 [p] Ac 5:15
19:13 [q] Mt 12:27 [r] Mk 9:38
19:17 [s] Ac 18:19 [t] Ac 5:5,11
19:20 [u] Ac 6:7; 12:24
19:21 [v] Ac 20:16, 22; Ro 15:25 [w] Ac 16:9 [x] Ac 18:12 [y] Ro 15:24,28
19:22 [z] Ac 13:5 [a] Ac 16:1 [b] Ro 16:23; 2Ti 4:20 [c] ver 10,26,27
19:23 [d] Ac 9:2

[a] *19* A drachma was a silver coin worth about a day's wages. [b] *21* Or *decided in the Spirit*

"semi-believers" were already there. In his remarkable stay of at least 27 months, he succeeded in bringing the gospel to the entire population of the province of Asia (v. 10).

Luke uses some familiar words to describe Paul's evangelism. In the synagogue he "spoke boldly" (v. 8). Preaching the gospel to Jews required much boldness because of their animosity toward it.

The sequence we have seen elsewhere is repeated, for the Jews rejected the gospel (v. 9b). But here, there was a slight difference. Paul spoke at the synagogue for as long as three months. Also, only "some" (not most) of the Jews "became obstinate" (v. 9a).

Paul then moved to "the lecture hall of Tyrannus" and held "discussions daily" (v. 9b). Tyrannus was either the lecturer who taught there or the owner of the hall who rented it out to Paul.

The result of this two-year stint (v. 10) was that "all the Jews and Greeks who lived in the province of Asia heard the word of the Lord" (v. 10b). This was in part achieved through people who came to Ephesus and took the gospel back to their hometowns. It also took place through colleagues of Paul, who brought the gospel to the other towns in Asia.

19:11–12 These verses summarize the apostle's ministry in the miraculous. This city had a reputation as a center for the learning and practice of magical arts. Many of the actions that took place demonstrated the power of God over these forces.

Luke stresses that God was the one who "did extraordinary miracles through Paul," not Paul himself (v. 11). It is not surprising that the casting out of demons, which is more prominent in the Gospels than in Acts, gains prominence in a place under the grip of occult practices.

19:13–16 The next picture Luke gives us is of "seven sons of Sceva, a Jewish chief priest" (v. 14). The evil spirit in the person being exorcised by the sons of Sceva attacked these exorcists, leaving them naked and bleeding (v. 16).

19:17–20 Luke goes on to paint the picture of a people seized with fear and holding the name of Jesus in high honor (v. 17). This came as a direct result of the demonstration of God's power. Open confession of evil deeds culminated in a grand scroll-burning session (vv. 18–19). The scrolls burned were equivalent to about 50,000 days' wages of an average worker. They must have been documents containing spells and formulas for which Ephesus was famous.

19:21–22 Paul moved on from Ephesus, making his plans with joy in his heart seeing that a strong church had been established there.

19:23–41 The riot—especially its conclusion in the acquittal of the Christians—fits in with a theme that Luke considered important: opposition to the gospel. Luke consistently stresses the real reasons behind such opposition.

Here in Ephesus, the root of the opposition was jealousy. As in Philippi (16:19), it had primarily an economic reason, though it was couched in religious and patriotic terms. The temple of Artemis was a key to the economic stability of Ephesus. Foreigners traveled there to worship and deposited money in the temple.

19:24–28 The silversmiths made "silver shrines of

PEOPLE TO KNOW // DEMETRIUS

ACTS 19:23–28: Demetrius was a silversmith in Ephesus, a prosperous and important city in its region. As a port city, it was a prominent center of trade and commerce.

The people of Ephesus worshiped many different deities, but most important was Artemis, a goddess of the hunt. The temple of Artemis was regarded as one of the Seven Wonders of the World. The Artemis cult and her temple generated an enormous amount of wealth in the city.

When Paul arrived in the city and began telling people about Jesus, many believed and left their life of idol worship. Demetrius, a craftsman who made his living selling idols of Artemis, was enraged. He incited a crowd against Paul and his fellow Christians. Demetrius's fear is a testimony to the power of Paul's ministry in Ephesus. When Demetrius finished his appeal to the craftsmen, they started an uproar that became a large city riot. Paul was spared through the efforts of a city clerk who finally calmed the angry crowd.

APPLICATION ✣ The Bible warns about the corrupting influence of greed. While wealth is not itself evil, the love and pursuit of wealth leads people to do radically selfish and evil things. Demetrius is an example of the love of wealth. Sadly, his greed kept him from hearing and accepting a much more valuable treasure: the gospel of Jesus Christ. The same risk exists today. We need to be mindful of where our treasure truly lies (Mt 6:19–21).

Ac 19:23–27 ❖ How does greed harden people against the gospel? Why is the desire for wealth such a deadly vice (see Mt 13:22)?

smith named Demetrius, who made
silver shrines of Artemis, brought in a
lot of business for the craftsmen there.
25He called them together, along with the
workers in related trades, and said: "You
know, my friends, that we receive a good
income from this business.[e] 26And you
see and hear how this fellow Paul has
convinced and led astray large numbers
of people here in Ephesus[f] and in practically the whole province of Asia. He says
that gods made by human hands are no
gods at all.[g] 27There is danger not only
that our trade will lose its good name,
but also that the temple of the great
goddess Artemis will be discredited; and
the goddess herself, who is worshiped
throughout the province of Asia and
the world, will be robbed of her divine
majesty."
28When they heard this, they were
furious and began shouting: "Great is
Artemis of the Ephesians!"[h] 29Soon the
whole city was in an uproar. The people seized Gaius[i] and Aristarchus,[j] Paul's
traveling companions from Macedonia,[k]
and all of them rushed into the theater
together. 30Paul wanted to appear before
the crowd, but the disciples would not
let him. 31Even some of the officials of
the province, friends of Paul, sent him
a message begging him not to venture
into the theater.
32The assembly was in confusion:
Some were shouting one thing, some
another.[l] Most of the people did not even
know why they were there. 33The Jews
in the crowd pushed Alexander to the
front, and they shouted instructions to
him. He motioned[m] for silence in order
to make a defense before the people.
34But when they realized he was a Jew,

19:25 [e] Ac 16:16, 19, 20
19:26 [f] Ac 18:19 [g] Dt 4:28; Ps 115:4; Isa 44:10-20; Jer 10:3-5; Ac 17:29; 1Co 8:4; Rev 9:20
19:28 [h] Ac 18:19
19:29 [i] Ac 20:4; Ro 16:23; 1Co 1:14 [j] Ac 20:4; 27:2; Col 4:10; Phm 24 [k] Ac 16:9
19:32 [l] Ac 21:34
19:33 [m] Ac 12:17

Artemis" (v. 24). Demetrius is honest about the way Paul's preaching had hit them economically (vv. 24–26). But that it would damage the honor of the goddess was the line they would take in their public proclamation (v. 28).

19:29 The silversmiths succeeded in getting the whole city into an uproar and seized two of Paul's colleagues. While there is some uncertainty about the exact duties of these high government officials, their presence in Ephesus during the first four centuries has been clearly attested. Paul had wealthy and powerful friends at Ephesus.

19:30–34 The people gathered in the great theater of Ephesus, where meetings of the assembly were held (vv. 30–31). This was an unofficial or informal assembly (vv. 32, 41), not a "legal assembly," which had its regular official meetings (see v. 39). A mob mentality takes over, resulting in a two-hour-long shouting session (vv. 33–34).

they all shouted in unison for about two
hours: "Great is Artemis of the Ephesians!"
35The city clerk quieted the crowd and
said: "Fellow Ephesians,[n] doesn't all the
world know that the city of Ephesus is
the guardian of the temple of the great
Artemis and of her image, which fell
from heaven? 36Therefore, since these
facts are undeniable, you ought to calm
down and not do anything rash. 37You
have brought these men here, though
they have neither robbed temples[o] nor
blasphemed our goddess. 38If, then, Demetrius and his fellow craftsmen have
a grievance against anybody, the courts
are open and there are proconsuls.[p] They
can press charges. 39If there is anything
further you want to bring up, it must
be settled in a legal assembly. 40As it is,
we are in danger of being charged with
rioting because of what happened today.
In that case we would not be able to account for this commotion, since there is
no reason for it." 41After he had said this,
he dismissed the assembly.

19:35 [n] Ac 18:19
19:37 [o] Ro 2:22
19:38 [p] Ac 13:7, 8,12
20:1 [q] Ac 11:26 [r] Ac 16:9
20:3 [s] ver 19; Ac 9:23,24; 23:12,15,30; 25:3; 2Co 11:26 [t] Ac 16:9
20:4 [u] Ac 19:29 [v] Ac 17:1 [w] Ac 19:29 [x] Ac 16:1 [y] Eph 6:21; Col 4:7; 2Ti 4:12; Titus 3:12 [z] Ac 21:29; 2Ti 4:20
20:5 [a] Ac 16:10 [b] Ac 16:8
20:6 [c] Ac 16:12 [d] Ac 16:8
20:7 [e] 1Co 16:2; Rev 1:10

Through Macedonia and Greece

20 When the uproar had ended, Paul
sent for the disciples[q] and, after
encouraging them, said goodbye and set
out for Macedonia.[r] 2He traveled through
that area, speaking many words of encouragement to the people, and finally
arrived in Greece, 3where he stayed three
months. Because some Jews had plotted
against him[s] just as he was about to sail
for Syria, he decided to go back through
Macedonia.[t] 4He was accompanied by
Sopater son of Pyrrhus from Berea, Aristarchus[u] and Secundus from Thessalonica,[v] Gaius[w] from Derbe, Timothy[x] also,
and Tychicus[y] and Trophimus[z] from the
province of Asia. 5These men went on
ahead and waited for us[a] at Troas.[b] 6But
we sailed from Philippi[c] after the Festival of Unleavened Bread, and five days
later joined the others at Troas,[d] where
we stayed seven days.

Eutychus Raised From the Dead at Troas

7On the first day of the week[e] we came
together to break bread. Paul spoke to

19:35–41 At this stage, the city clerk took over. He appealed to the heritage of the city, which believed that the image of the goddess Artemis had fallen down from heaven (v. 35) and was thus of divine workmanship. His point was that the security of having such facts should cause them not to panic and do something rash (v. 36). Besides, there were legal ways to handle such issues (v. 38).

Luke saw this event as another victory for the cause of the gospel. In his estimation, the existing legal system, if properly administered, could be relied upon to give the Christians a fair trial (cf. also the decision of the proconsul Gallio in Corinth in 18:12–17).

19:8–41 We hear many voices today downplaying the value of truth-centered evangelism. Such people, including many who call themselves evangelicals, claim we live in an age when people no longer think in categories that value truth. In its place, they advocate a needs-based evangelism, which shows Jesus as the answer to felt needs.

Sensitivity to needs was certainly a key to Paul's evangelistic strategy (cf. Paul's ministry in Ephesus and elsewhere). But basic to his gospel presentation was the priority of its truth. This will always be so, for the scriptural Christian faith claims that it is God's complete revelation to humanity. Those who downplay the truthfulness and content of the gospel have sadly betrayed its heart by giving in to cultural pressures.

20:1–6 Encouragement is a key theme of this chapter. The verb "to encourage" appears three times (vv. 1, 2, 12), and vv. 18–35 give a sample of the content of the encouragement Paul gave. The wording of v. 2 suggests that he spent a substantial time in Macedonia. During this time, he wrote the book of 2 Corinthians. By now, Paul had established churches in a good portion of the Greek world. His next plan was to reach the Latin world, possibly using Rome as his base of operations.

20:3–6 Paul may have wanted to go to Jerusalem in time for Passover, but he found out about a plot against him (v. 3), so he spent Passover in Philippi (v. 6). According to his revised plan, he hoped to be in Jerusalem in time for the next feast, Pentecost (v. 16).

An important task during these days was to raise a substantial gift for the poor in the church in Jerusalem. It was a topic Paul often brought up in his letters (Ro 15:25–32; 1Co 16:1–4; 2Co 8–9). Paul was planning to take this contribution of the churches as a tangible expression of the Gentile Christians' solidarity with the first church. The long list of traveling companions mentioned in v. 4 probably represented the churches that had made contributions.

20:7–12 Here is the first clear reference in Scripture to the believers meeting for worship on the first day of the week. We are not sure whether Sunday worship had already become a regular practice in the church or whether this meeting's being on a Sunday was coincidental.

Doctor Luke must have been satisfied that Eutychus was indeed dead, unlike in Lystra, where Paul's opponents thought Paul was dead but were mistaken (14:19). Paul's comment (v. 10) refers to the young man's state after he was healed.

the people and, because he intended to
leave the next day, kept on talking until
midnight. 8There were many lamps in
the upstairs room[f] where we were meeting. 9Seated in a window was a young
man named Eutychus, who was sinking
into a deep sleep as Paul talked on and
on. When he was sound asleep, he fell to
the ground from the third story and was
picked up dead. 10Paul went down, threw
himself on the young man[g] and put his
arms around him. "Don't be alarmed,"
he said. "He's alive!"[h] 11Then he went upstairs again and broke bread[i] and ate.
After talking until daylight, he left. 12The
people took the young man home alive
and were greatly comforted.

Paul's Farewell to the Ephesian Elders

13We went on ahead to the ship and
sailed for Assos, where we were going
to take Paul aboard. He had made this
arrangement because he was going there
on foot. 14When he met us at Assos, we
took him aboard and went on to Mitylene. 15The next day we set sail from there
and arrived off Chios. The day after that
we crossed over to Samos, and on the
following day arrived at Miletus.[j] 16Paul
had decided to sail past Ephesus[k] to avoid
spending time in the province of Asia, for
he was in a hurry to reach Jerusalem,[l] if
possible, by the day of Pentecost.[m]

17From Miletus, Paul sent to Ephesus
for the elders[n] of the church. 18When they
arrived, he said to them: "You know how
I lived the whole time I was with you,[o]
from the first day I came into the province of Asia. 19I served the Lord with great

20:8 [f] Ac 1:13
20:10 [g] 1Ki 17:21; 2Ki 4:34 [h] Mt 9:23,24
20:11 [i] ver 7
20:15 [j] ver 17; 2Ti 4:20
20:16 [k] Ac 18:19 [l] Ac 19:21 [m] Ac 2:1; 1Co 16:8
20:17 [n] Ac 11:30
20:18 [o] Ac 18:19-21; 19:1-41
20:19 [p] ver 3
20:20 [q] ver 27
20:21 [r] Ac 18:5 [s] Ac 2:38 [t] Ac 24:24; 26:18; Eph 1:15; Col 2:5; Phm 5
20:22 [u] ver 16
20:23 [v] Ac 21:4 [w] Ac 9:16
20:24 [x] Ac 21:13 [y] 2Co 4:1 [z] Gal 1:1; Titus 1:3
20:25 [a] ver 38
20:26 [b] Ac 18:6
20:27 [c] ver 20
20:28 [d] 1Pe 5:2

Ac 20:24 ❖ How can we cultivate a faith and zeal like Paul's, striving to be completely oriented toward Christ's message and glory? Where have we seen such faith on display?

humility and with tears and in the midst
of severe testing by the plots of my Jewish opponents.[p] 20You know that I have
not hesitated to preach anything[q] that
would be helpful to you but have taught
you publicly and from house to house. 21I
have declared to both Jews[r] and Greeks
that they must turn to God in repentance[s]
and have faith in our Lord Jesus.[t]

22"And now, compelled by the Spirit,
I am going to Jerusalem,[u] not knowing
what will happen to me there. 23I only
know that in every city the Holy Spirit
warns me[v] that prison and hardships are
facing me.[w] 24However, I consider my life
worth nothing to me;[x] my only aim is to
finish the race and complete the task[y] the
Lord Jesus has given me[z] — the task of
testifying to the good news of God's grace.

25"Now I know that none of you among
whom I have gone about preaching the
kingdom will ever see me again.[a] 26There-
fore, I declare to you today that I am innocent of the blood of any of you.[b] 27For
I have not hesitated to proclaim to you
the whole will of God.[c] 28Keep watch over
yourselves and all the flock of which the
Holy Spirit has made you overseers.[d] Be
shepherds of the church of God,[a] which
he bought with his own blood.[b] 29I know

[a] *28* Many manuscripts *of the Lord* [b] *28* Or *with the blood of his own Son.*

20:13–16 The 20-mile walk described here would likely have done Paul some good. From Assos Paul headed for Miletus by ship (vv. 14–15). These two ports were on the western coast of the mainland of Asia Minor. Between them were the island ports of Mitylene, Chios, and Samos. Paul avoided going to Ephesus (v. 16), possibly because it would have been dangerous for him to go there.

20:17–38 This is the only record we have of a speech that Paul gave to believers, and its contents are remarkably similar to his letters (also addressed to believers). Paul's talk has three main themes. (1) He defends his behavior, presenting it as an example to the Ephesian elders (vv. 18–27, 33–35). (2) He presents a charge along with a warning (vv. 28–31). (3) Finally, he commits his readers to God (v. 32).

20:18–27 Paul says he was an example to the believers in four respects. (1) He lived among them, serving God with humility and tears, and going from house to house. This enabled him to know what they needed to hear so that he was able to preach everything that was helpful to them. Paul obviously had what might be called an openhearted approach to ministry. (2) He taught the Ephesians everything that was helpful to them, and he did so publicly and from house to house. His teaching was relevant to their needs. (3) Paul uses the word "declared" in v. 21 (cf. 18:5). He did not hesitate "to proclaim to [them] the whole will of God" (v. 27). He was able to declare that he was innocent of their blood. (4) Paul suffered because of obedience. In vv. 22–23 he attributes two actions to the Holy Spirit: a compulsion that is now driving him to Jerusalem and a regular warning that he will suffer if he goes to Jerusalem. Verse 24 explains how these two seemingly contradictory messages can be reconciled: The goal of life is to be faithful to our calling to testify to the gospel.

20:28–31 Paul is aware of the danger of things going wrong in Ephesus. He therefore both charges them and sternly warns them. The charge consists of three points. (1) Most important, the elders must

that after I leave, savage wolves[e] will
come in among you and will not spare
the flock.[f] 30Even from your own number
men will arise and distort the truth in
order to draw away disciples[g] after them.
31So be on your guard! Remember that for
three years[h] I never stopped warning each
of you night and day with tears.[i]
32“Now I commit you to God[j] and to
the word of his grace, which can build
you up and give you an inheritance[k]
among all those who are sanctified.[l] 33I
have not coveted anyone’s silver or gold
or clothing.[m] 34You yourselves know that
these hands of mine have supplied my
own needs and the needs of my companions.[n] 35In everything I did, I showed you
that by this kind of hard work we must
help the weak, remembering the words
the Lord Jesus himself said: ‘It is more
blessed to give than to receive.’ ”
36When Paul had finished speaking, he
knelt down with all of them and prayed.[o]
37They all wept as they embraced him
and kissed him.[p] 38What grieved them
most was his statement that they would
never see his face again.[q] Then they accompanied him to the ship.

On to Jerusalem

21 After we[r] had torn ourselves away
from them, we put out to sea and
sailed straight to Kos. The next day we
went to Rhodes and from there to Patara. 2We found a ship crossing over to
Phoenicia,[s] went on board and set sail.
3After sighting Cyprus and passing to the
south of it, we sailed on to Syria. We landed at Tyre, where our ship was to unload
its cargo. 4We sought out the disciples[t]
there and stayed with them seven days.
Through the Spirit[u] they urged Paul not to
go on to Jerusalem. 5When it was time to
leave, we left and continued on our way.
All of them, including wives and children, accompanied us out of the city, and
there on the beach we knelt to pray.[v] 6Af-
ter saying goodbye to each other, we went
aboard the ship, and they returned home.
7We continued our voyage from Tyre[w]
and landed at Ptolemais, where we
greeted the brothers and sisters[x] and

20:29 [e] Mt 7:15 [f] ver 28
20:30 [g] Ac 11:26
20:31 [h] Ac 19:10 [i] ver 19
20:32 [j] Ac 14:23 [k] Eph 1:14; Col 1:12; 3:24; Heb 9:15; 1Pe 1:4 [l] Ac 26:18
20:33 [m] 1Sa 12:3; 1Co 9:12; 2Co 7:2; 11:9; 12:14-17
20:34 [n] Ac 18:3
20:36 [o] Lk 22:41; Ac 21:5
20:37 [p] Lk 15:20
20:38 [q] ver 25
21:1 [r] Ac 16:10
21:2 [s] Ac 11:19
21:4 [t] Ac 11:26 [u] ver 11; Ac 20:23
21:5 [v] Ac 20:36
21:7 [w] Ac 12:20 [x] Ac 1:16

keep watch over themselves (v. 28). (2) They must watch over the flock as overseers (v. 28). This word is a synonym for “elder” (see v. 17). Whereas “elder” focuses on the maturity of the individual, “overseer” focuses on the function, which is to take care of the people. (3) The flock was bought by Christ’s own blood. We too must give our lives for the sheep.

20:32 Paul finally commits the elders “to God and to the word of his grace.” The message they received will enable them to stay close to God.

20:33-35 Paul concludes his speech by once more presenting the challenge of his own life as an example for the elders to follow. He did not covet what others had. Rather, he worked hard to provide for the needs of the team. In the process, he helped those in need (see also Eph 4:28). There is a ring of credibility to Paul’s appeals for money for the poor because he himself was generous in his own giving.

20:36-38 The grief expressed at Paul’s departure gives us an indication of how much he was loved.

✣ **20:1-38** It is well-known that church leaders today find it difficult to motivate others to suffer, or even to take on inconvenience, for the cause of Christ. The three principles about suffering gleaned from this passage can help us here.

First, the greatness of the cause of Christ should fire us with an ambition to take on suffering as a natural response (v. 24). This passage challenges us to rethink our teaching so that our people will be attracted by the greatness of the cause of Christ.

Second, leaders can motivate others to suffer for the gospel by themselves being examples of suffering. It is no secret that commitment breeds commitment. When a leader is willing to die for a cause, those who follow are also fired up by their leader’s enthusiasm. A leader’s attitude impresses on others the urgency of the task they are involved in, thrills them with its significance, and motivates them to commitment.

Finally, leaders are good shepherds who die for their sheep. Not only do we die for the cause, we also die for the people we lead. In leadership, a lack of commitment produces a selfish Christianity.

In the Western world, we need to raise up a generation of radical Christians willing to pay the necessary price for us to shake this world with the revolutionary message of Christ.

21:1-4a As Paul and his friends sail eastward, they visit the main port on the island of Rhodes, Patara on the mainland, and Tyre in Phoenicia (v. 3). Paul’s plans to get to Jerusalem before Pentecost (20:16) remain intact. The traveling group makes contact with the church in Tyre (v. 4).

21:4b-6 The Christians in Tyre “urged Paul not to go on to Jerusalem” (v. 4b). How do we reconcile this with Paul’s statement that his trip to Jerusalem was “compelled by the Spirit” (20:22)? The Christians in Tyre received from the Spirit a prophecy that Paul would have trouble in Jerusalem. Out of that they may have inferred that the Spirit was prompting Paul not to go to Jerusalem.

21:7-9 In Ptolemais, a few miles south of Tyre, Paul and his company again greet believers (v. 7). Next they come to Caesarea, where they stay in

stayed with them for a day. 8 Leaving
the next day, we reached Caesarea[y] and
stayed at the house of Philip[z] the evangelist,[a] one of the Seven. 9 He had four
unmarried daughters who prophesied.[b]
10 After we had been there a number
of days, a prophet named Agabus[c] came
down from Judea. 11 Coming over to us,
he took Paul's belt, tied his own hands
and feet with it and said, "The Holy Spirit
says, 'In this way the Jewish leaders in Jerusalem will bind[d] the owner of this belt
and will hand him over to the Gentiles.'"[e]
12 When we heard this, we and the people there pleaded with Paul not to go
up to Jerusalem. 13 Then Paul answered,
"Why are you weeping and breaking my
heart? I am ready not only to be bound,
but also to die[f] in Jerusalem for the name
of the Lord Jesus."[g] 14 When he would not
be dissuaded, we gave up and said, "The
Lord's will be done."
15 After this, we started on our way up to
Jerusalem. 16 Some of the disciples from
Caesarea[h] accompanied us and brought
us to the home of Mnason, where we
were to stay. He was a man from Cyprus[i]
and one of the early disciples.

Paul's Arrival at Jerusalem

17 When we arrived at Jerusalem, the
brothers and sisters received us warmly.[j]
18 The next day Paul and the rest of us
went to see James,[k] and all the elders[l]
were present. 19 Paul greeted them and
reported in detail what God had done
among the Gentiles[m] through his ministry.[n]

21:8 [y] Ac 8:40 [z] Ac 6:5; 8:5-40 [a] Eph 4:11; 2Ti 4:5
21:9 [b] Lk 2:36; Ac 2:17
21:10 [c] Ac 11:28
21:11 [d] ver 33 [e] 1Ki 22:11
21:13 [f] Ac 20:24 [g] Ac 9:16
21:16 [h] Ac 8:40 [i] ver 3,4
21:17 [j] Ac 15:4
21:18 [k] Ac 15:13 [l] Ac 11:30
21:19 [m] Ac 14:27 [n] Ac 1:17
21:20 [o] Ac 22:3; Ro 10:2; Gal 1:14 [p] Ac 15:1,5
21:21 [q] ver 28 [r] Ac 15:19-21; 1Co 7:18,19 [s] Ac 6:14
21:23 [t] Ac 18:18
21:24 [u] ver 26; Ac 24:18 [v] Ac 18:18
21:25 [w] Ac 15:20, 29
21:26 [x] Nu 6:13-20; Ac 24:18

Ac 21:19–20 ❖ When have we been encouraged by stories of other people's faith? How can we pass on faith stories to encourage those around us?

20 When they heard this, they praised
God. Then they said to Paul: "You see,
brother, how many thousands of Jews
have believed, and all of them are zealous[o] for the law.[p] 21 They have been informed that you teach all the Jews who
live among the Gentiles to turn away
from Moses,[q] telling them not to circumcise their children[r] or live according to
our customs.[s] 22 What shall we do? They
will certainly hear that you have come,
23 so do what we tell you. There are four
men with us who have made a vow.[t]
24 Take these men, join in their purification rites[u] and pay their expenses, so that
they can have their heads shaved.[v] Then
everyone will know there is no truth in
these reports about you, but that you
yourself are living in obedience to the
law. 25 As for the Gentile believers, we
have written to them our decision that
they should abstain from food sacrificed
to idols, from blood, from the meat of
strangled animals and from sexual immorality."[w]
26 The next day Paul took the men and
purified himself along with them. Then
he went to the temple to give notice of
the date when the days of purification
would end and the offering would be
made for each of them.[x]

---

the house of Philip—one of the Seven (6:5), who is called "the evangelist" (21:8).

Philip had "four unmarried daughters who prophesied" (v. 9). In that culture, unmarried women normally did not have high standing. This may be Luke's way of pointing out that low-status people were included in positions of prominence in the church.

21:10–14 In Caesarea, the prophet Agabus predicts that Paul will be bound and handed over to the Jews (vv. 10–11). The people plead with Paul not to go to Jerusalem, though Agabus apparently does not (v. 12). Paul's traveling companions also join in the plea. The people weep as they try to persuade Paul (v. 13a). Paul's answer shows how hard all this is on him (v. 13a). But he explains his stand (v. 13b). Finally the people give up, resigning themselves to "the Lord's will" (v. 14).

21:15–16 The journey from Caesarea to Jerusalem was 64 miles, so the company stops over at the home of Mnason (v. 16). Like Barnabas, he is from Cyprus and one of the early disciples.

21:17–19 Paul is warmly received by the believers on his arrival in Jerusalem (v. 17). The next day he and his company meet James and the elders (v. 18). His report of what God has done elicits praise to God.

21:20–26 The sensitive nature of what the believers tell Paul is evidenced by the tone in which they introduce their point (vv. 20b, 22b). For the sake of the many Christians who are zealous for the Jewish law, they think it a good idea for him to submit to the law publicly. He can do this by paying for the expenses of four fellow Christians who have taken a vow. To do this, he must purify himself along with these people (vv. 24, 26). They clearly affirm the position of the Jerusalem Council (v. 25).

Paul was opposed to the belief that works of the law were necessary for salvation. He himself was not opposed to the Mosaic Law per se. We must not forget what Paul wrote in 1Co 9:20.

Paul Arrested

27When the seven days were nearly
over, some Jews from the province of
Asia saw Paul at the temple. They stirred
up the whole crowd and seized him,[y]
28shouting, "Fellow Israelites, help us!
This is the man who teaches everyone
everywhere against our people and our
law and this place. And besides, he has
brought Greeks into the temple and defiled this holy place."[z] 29(They had previously seen Trophimus[a] the Ephesian[b]
in the city with Paul and assumed that
Paul had brought him into the temple.)
30The whole city was aroused, and the
people came running from all directions.
Seizing Paul,[c] they dragged him[d] from
the temple, and immediately the gates
were shut. 31While they were trying to
kill him, news reached the commander
of the Roman troops that the whole city
of Jerusalem was in an uproar. 32He at
once took some officers and soldiers and
ran down to the crowd. When the rioters
saw the commander and his soldiers,
they stopped beating Paul.[e]
33The commander came up and arrested
him and ordered him to be bound[f] with
two[g] chains.[h] Then he asked who he was
and what he had done. 34Some in the
crowd shouted one thing and some another,[i] and since the commander could not
get at the truth because of the uproar, he
ordered that Paul be taken into the barracks.[j] 35When Paul reached the steps,[k] the
violence of the mob was so great he had to
be carried by the soldiers. 36The crowd that
followed kept shouting, "Get rid of him!"[l]

21:27 [y] Ac 24:18; 26:21
21:28 [z] Mt 24:15; Ac 24:5,6
21:29 [a] Ac 20:4 [b] Ac 18:19
21:30 [c] Ac 26:21 [d] Ac 16:19
21:32 [e] Ac 23:27
21:33 [f] ver 11 [g] Ac 12:6 [h] Ac 20:23; Eph 6:20; 2Ti 2:9
21:34 [i] Ac 19:32 [j] ver 37; Ac 23:10,16,32
21:35 [k] ver 40
21:36 [l] Lk 23:18; Jn 19:15; Ac 22:22
21:37 [m] ver 34
21:38 [n] Mt 24:26 [o] Ac 5:36
21:39 [p] Ac 9:11 [q] Ac 22:3
21:40 [r] Ac 12:17 [s] Jn 5:2
22:1 [t] Ac 7:2
22:2 [u] Ac 21:40
22:3 [v] Ac 21:39 [w] Ac 9:11 [x] Lk 10:39 [y] Ac 5:34 [z] Ac 26:5 [a] Ac 21:20
22:4 [b] Ac 8:3

Ac 22:2-21 ❖ Have you had the opportunity to share your faith testimony before others? What parts of your own testimony would you highlight if you were on trial for your faith?

Paul Speaks to the Crowd

22:3–16pp // Ac 9:1–22; 26:9–18

37As the soldiers were about to take
Paul into the barracks,[m] he asked the
commander, "May I say something to
you?"
"Do you speak Greek?" he replied.
38"Aren't you the Egyptian who started
a revolt and led four thousand terrorists out into the wilderness[n] some time
ago?"[o]
39Paul answered, "I am a Jew, from Tarsus[p] in Cilicia,[q] a citizen of no ordinary
city. Please let me speak to the people."
40After receiving the commander's
permission, Paul stood on the steps and
motioned[r] to the crowd. When they were
all silent, he said to them in Aramaic[a]:[s]
22 1"Brothers and fathers,[t] listen now
to my defense."
2When they heard him speak to them
in Aramaic,[u] they became very quiet.
Then Paul said: 3"I am a Jew,[v] born in
Tarsus[w] of Cilicia, but brought up in this
city. I studied under[x] Gamaliel[y] and was
thoroughly trained in the law of our ancestors.[z] I was just as zealous[a] for God as
any of you are today. 4I persecuted[b] the
followers of this Way to their death, arresting both men and women and throwing

[a] *40* Or possibly *Hebrew*; also in 22:2

21:27–29 As Paul was coming to the end of his responsibilities regarding the vows, some Jews from Asia saw him in the temple. They had earlier seen Paul in the city with Trophimus (v. 29), a Gentile companion from Asia, and they assumed that he was also in the temple with Paul, which would have been an unlawful act. These Jews from Asia incited the people to attack Paul (vv. 27–28).

21:30–35 The timely intervention of the Roman commander prevented Paul's murder (vv. 31–32). Paul was arrested so that he could be given a proper trial (v. 33). Because of the turmoil of the crowd, he had to be carried by the soldiers (v. 35).

✣ **21:1–36** How can we apply the principle evident in Luke's writings that women and other people marginalized in society have a prominent place in God's kingdom? We ought to follow Luke in demonstrating to such people that they are truly important to God and to the church. Our application of Scripture should be relevant to all segments of God's people. We must show how biblical principles apply to men and women, people who are rich and those who are poor, and young people and children as well as adults.

21:37–40 The commander originally thought that Paul was an Egyptian who had tried to lead some people in revolt against Rome.

22:1–2 Paul's use of Aramaic caused the people to become "very quiet" (v. 2).

22:3–5 Paul began his address respectfully, calling his audience "brothers and fathers" (v. 1), just as Stephen had (7:2). Paul's first point demonstrated his excellent Jewish credentials and described his activity as a persecutor of Christians.

Paul's report of his conversion focuses on his call rather than his conversion. He defends his work with the Gentiles and shows that he is still a good Jew.

them into prison,[c] 5 as the high priest and
all the Council[d] can themselves testify. I
even obtained letters from them to their
associates[e] in Damascus,[f] and went there
to bring these people as prisoners to Jerusalem to be punished.
6 "About noon as I came near Damascus, suddenly a bright light from heaven
flashed around me.[g] 7 I fell to the ground
and heard a voice say to me, 'Saul! Saul!
Why do you persecute me?'
8 " 'Who are you, Lord?' I asked.
" 'I am Jesus of Nazareth, whom you
are persecuting,' he replied. 9 My companions saw the light,[h] but they did not
understand the voice[i] of him who was
speaking to me.
10 " 'What shall I do, Lord?' I asked.
" 'Get up,' the Lord said, 'and go into
Damascus. There you will be told all that
you have been assigned to do.'[j] 11 My companions led me by the hand into Damascus, because the brilliance of the light
had blinded me.[k]
12 "A man named Ananias came to see
me.[l] He was a devout observer of the law
and highly respected by all the Jews living there.[m] 13 He stood beside me and
said, 'Brother Saul, receive your sight!'
And at that very moment I was able to
see him.
14 "Then he said: 'The God of our ancestors[n] has chosen you to know his will
and to see[o] the Righteous One[p] and to
hear words from his mouth. 15 You will
be his witness[q] to all people of what you
have seen and heard. 16 And now what
are you waiting for? Get up, be baptized[r]
and wash your sins away,[s] calling on his
name.'[t]
17 "When I returned to Jerusalem[u] and
was praying at the temple, I fell into a
trance[v] 18 and saw the Lord speaking to
me. 'Quick!' he said. 'Leave Jerusalem
immediately, because the people here
will not accept your testimony about me.'
19 " 'Lord,' I replied, 'these people know
that I went from one synagogue to another to imprison[w] and beat[x] those who
believe in you. 20 And when the blood of
your martyr[a] Stephen was shed, I stood
there giving my approval and guarding
the clothes of those who were killing
him.'[y]
21 "Then the Lord said to me, 'Go; I will
send you far away to the Gentiles.' "[z]

Paul the Roman Citizen

22 The crowd listened to Paul until he
said this. Then they raised their voices
and shouted, "Rid the earth of him![a] He's
not fit to live!"[b]
23 As they were shouting and throwing off their cloaks[c] and flinging dust
into the air,[d] 24 the commander ordered
that Paul be taken into the barracks.[e] He
directed[f] that he be flogged and interro-
gated in order to find out why the people
were shouting at him like this. 25 As they
stretched him out to flog him, Paul said
to the centurion standing there, "Is it
legal for you to flog a Roman citizen who
hasn't even been found guilty?"[g]
26 When the centurion heard this, he
went to the commander and reported it.
"What are you going to do?" he asked.
"This man is a Roman citizen."
27 The commander went to Paul and
asked, "Tell me, are you a Roman citizen?"
"Yes, I am," he answered.
28 Then the commander said, "I had to
pay a lot of money for my citizenship."
"But I was born a citizen," Paul replied.
29 Those who were about to interrogate him withdrew immediately. The

[a] 20 Or *witness*

22:4 [c] ver 19,20
22:5 [d] Lk 22:66 [e] Ac 13:26 [f] Ac 9:2
22:6 [g] Ac 9:3
22:9 [h] Ac 26:13 [i] Ac 9:7
22:10 [j] Ac 16:30
22:11 [k] Ac 9:8
22:12 [l] Ac 9:17 [m] Ac 10:22
22:14 [n] Ac 3:13 [o] 1Co 9:1; 15:8 [p] Ac 7:52
22:15 [q] Ac 23:11; 26:16
22:16 [r] Ac 2:38 [s] Heb 10:22 [t] Ro 10:13
22:17 [u] Ac 9:26 [v] Ac 10:10
22:19 [w] ver 4; Ac 8:3 [x] Mt 10:17
22:20 [y] Ac 7:57-60; 8:1
22:21 [z] Ac 9:15; 13:46
22:22 [a] Ac 21:36 [b] Ac 25:24
22:23 [c] Ac 7:58 [d] 2Sa 16:13
22:24 [e] Ac 21:34 [f] ver 29
22:25 [g] Ac 16:37

22:6–16 Paul does not mention Ananias's dialogue with the Lord, where he was commanded to go to Paul (9:10–16), but he adds a new point, important to his audience, about Ananias's being "a devout observer of the law and highly respected by all the Jews living" in Damascus (22:12). Also new is the word from God that Paul was to be a "witness to all people" and that he must be baptized (vv. 14–16). It was important for Paul to tell his audience that a respected Jew had shared the vision of his future ministry with him.

22:17–21 Another new point in this account is Paul's description of a vision he had while praying in the temple, where God told him to leave Jerusalem.

22:22–24 Paul's statement in v. 21 that the Lord had decided to send him to the Gentiles triggered another outburst among his Jewish audience. They shouted for his death, threw off their cloaks, and flung dust into the air. The latter two actions expressed both their frustration and their horror at blasphemy.

22:25–29 The planned flogging was probably the Roman scourging with a whip that had thongs weighted with rough pieces of bone or metal. It could cause great harm and even leave people disabled for life. Roman citizens were exempt from it as a method of inquiry before trial, so the commander's alarm (v. 29) was understandable.

commander himself was alarmed when
he realized that he had put Paul, a Roman citizen,[h] in chains.

Paul Before the Sanhedrin

30The commander wanted to find out
exactly why Paul was being accused by
the Jews.[i] So the next day he released
him[j] and ordered the chief priests and
all the members of the Sanhedrin[k] to
assemble. Then he brought Paul and had
him stand before them.

23 Paul looked straight at the Sanhedrin[l] and said, "My brothers,[m]
I have fulfilled my duty to God in all
good conscience[n] to this day." 2At this
the high priest Ananias[o] ordered those
standing near Paul to strike him on the
mouth.[p] 3Then Paul said to him, "God
will strike you, you whitewashed wall![q]
You sit there to judge me according to
the law, yet you yourself violate the law
by commanding that I be struck!"[r]

4Those who were standing near Paul
said, "How dare you insult God's high
priest!"

5Paul replied, "Brothers, I did not realize that he was the high priest; for it
is written: 'Do not speak evil about the
ruler of your people.'[a]"[s]

6Then Paul, knowing that some of them
were Sadducees and the others Pharisees,
called out in the Sanhedrin, "My brothers,[t]
I am a Pharisee,[u] descended from Pharisees. I stand on trial because of the hope
of the resurrection of the dead."[v] 7When
he said this, a dispute broke out between
the Pharisees and the Sadducees, and the
assembly was divided. 8(The Sadducees
say that there is no resurrection,[w] and
that there are neither angels nor spirits,
but the Pharisees believe all these things.)

9There was a great uproar, and some of
the teachers of the law who were Pharisees[x] stood up and argued vigorously.
"We find nothing wrong with this man,"[y]
they said. "What if a spirit or an angel
has spoken to him?"[z] 10The dispute became so violent that the commander was
afraid Paul would be torn to pieces by
them. He ordered the troops to go down
and take him away from them by force
and bring him into the barracks.[a]

11The following night the Lord stood
near Paul and said, "Take courage![b] As
you have testified about me in Jerusalem, so you must also testify in Rome."[c]

22:29 [h] ver 24, 25; Ac 16:38
22:30 [i] Ac 23:28 [j] Ac 21:33 [k] Mt 5:22
23:1 [l] Ac 22:30 [m] Ac 22:5 [n] Ac 24:16; 1Co 4:4; 2Co 1:12; 2Ti 1:3; Heb 13:18
23:2 [o] Ac 24:1 [p] Jn 18:22
23:3 [q] Mt 23:27 [r] Lev 19:15; Dt 25:1,2; Jn 7:51
23:5 [s] Ex 22:28
23:6 [t] Ac 22:5 [u] Ac 26:5; Php 3:5 [v] Ac 24:15,21; 26:8
23:8 [w] Mt 22:23
23:9 [x] Mk 2:16 [y] ver 29; Ac 25:25; 26:31 [z] Ac 22:7,17,18
23:10 [a] Ac 21:34
23:11 [b] Ac 18:9 [c] Ac 19:21; 28:23

Ac 23:11 ❖ When has God given you a special word of comfort and encouragement? How did it strengthen you?

[a] 5 Exodus 22:28

22:30 As it obviously concerned a religious issue, the commander decided to order the Sanhedrin to look into the matter.

23:1 Paul's first statement to the Sanhedrin proclaimed that he had fulfilled his "duty to God in all good conscience." He was not talking about fulfilling requirements for salvation. Rather, by Jewish standards of measuring faithfulness relative to conscience, Paul is claiming he had lived a blameless and exemplary life.

23:2–4 The high priest Ananias orders that Paul be struck on the mouth for his statement (v. 2), which was a miscarriage of justice. In this case, Paul had not even been properly charged, let alone convicted.

23:5 When Paul realized he had spoken these strong words to the high priest, he made a godly retraction. Paul had visited Jerusalem only sporadically during the previous 20 years, and Ananias had become high priest in AD 48, about ten years before these incidents. So Paul would not have recognized him.

23:6–8 As Paul's first line of reasoning was not going to work, he adopted a new line. The issue at stake here was the resurrection of the dead, which the Pharisees accepted but the Sadducees rejected. This strategy pointed to the heart of the Christian gospel, which was indeed a fulfillment of Pharisaism, so much so that a real Pharisee should actually become a Christian. Paul even calls himself a Pharisee here (v. 6).

Paul agreed with the Pharisees that the Jews' national hope depended on a future resurrection, the first stage of which has been fulfilled with the resurrection of Jesus.

23:9–10 Paul's statement results in total confusion in the Sanhedrin. The commander has to intervene and take Paul away from the scene. The next night the Lord stands near Paul and encourages him by telling him that he is going to testify in Rome (v. 11).

✜ **21:37—23:11** On several occasions God had to curb Paul's personal ambitions with his guidance. Acts 22:17–21 reflects God's curbing of Paul's ambition to be his chosen witness to the Jews. The apostle honestly thought that his background would give him such credibility that he would be a powerful witness to his people, but this was not going to be so, and God knew it. So God directed him to leave Jerusalem.

Ambition is not wrong. Paul also had a great ambition to go to Rome (Ro 1:10–15; 15:22–32), and the Lord fed that ambition in a vision (Ac 23:11). It is good to dream great dreams, but we must place all these dreams at the altar of God and bow to his sovereignty, believing that he

The Plot to Kill Paul

12The next morning some Jews formed a conspiracy and bound themselves with an oath not to eat or drink until they had killed Paul.[d] 13More than forty men were involved in this plot. 14They went to the chief priests and the elders and said, "We have taken a solemn oath not to eat anything until we have killed Paul.[e] 15Now then, you and the Sanhedrin[f] petition the commander to bring him before you on the pretext of wanting more accurate information about his case. We are ready to kill him before he gets here."

16But when the son of Paul's sister heard of this plot, he went into the barracks[g] and told Paul.

17Then Paul called one of the centurions and said, "Take this young man to the commander; he has something to tell him." 18So he took him to the commander.

The centurion said, "Paul, the prisoner,[h] sent for me and asked me to bring this young man to you because he has something to tell you."

19The commander took the young man by the hand, drew him aside and asked, "What is it you want to tell me?"

20He said: "Some Jews have agreed to ask you to bring Paul before the Sanhedrin[i] tomorrow on the pretext of wanting more accurate information about him.[j] 21Don't give in to them, because more than forty[k] of them are waiting in ambush for him. They have taken an oath not to eat or drink until they have killed him.[l] They are ready now, waiting for your consent to their request."

22The commander dismissed the young man with this warning: "Don't tell anyone that you have reported this to me."

Paul Transferred to Caesarea

23Then he called two of his centurions and ordered them, "Get ready a detachment of two hundred soldiers, seventy horsemen and two hundred spearmen[a] to go to Caesarea[m] at nine tonight.[n] 24Provide horses for Paul so that he may be taken safely to Governor Felix."[o]

25He wrote a letter as follows:

26Claudius Lysias,

To His Excellency,[p] Governor Felix:

Greetings.[q]

27This man was seized by the Jews and they were about to kill him,[r] but I came with my troops and rescued him,[s] for I had learned that he is a Roman citizen.[t] 28I wanted to know why they were accusing him, so I brought him to their Sanhedrin.[u] 29I found that the accusation had to do with questions about their law,[v] but there was no charge against him[w] that deserved death or imprisonment. 30When I was informed[x] of a plot[y] to be carried out against the man, I sent him to you at once. I also ordered his accusers[z] to present to you their case against him.

31So the soldiers, carrying out their orders, took Paul with them during the

23:12 [d] ver 14, 21, 30; Ac 25:3
23:14 [e] ver 12
23:15 [f] ver 1; Ac 22:30
23:16 [g] ver 10; Ac 21:34
23:18 [h] Eph 3:1
23:20 [i] ver 1 [j] ver 14, 15
23:21 [k] ver 13 [l] ver 12, 14
23:23 [m] Ac 8:40 [n] ver 33
23:24 [o] ver 26, 33; Ac 24:1-3, 10; 25:14
23:26 [p] Lk 1:3; Ac 24:3; 26:25 [q] Ac 15:23
23:27 [r] Ac 21:32 [s] Ac 21:33 [t] Ac 22:25-29
23:28 [u] Ac 22:30
23:29 [v] Ac 18:15; 25:19 [w] ver 9; Ac 26:31
23:30 [x] ver 20, 21 [y] Ac 20:3 [z] ver 35; Ac 24:19; 25:16

[a] 23 The meaning of the Greek for this word is uncertain.

---

knows what is best for us. This does not mean that we should give up our visions whenever roadblocks develop; Paul's plans to go to Asia Minor and Rome were often hindered, but he finally got to both places.

A key ingredient of faithfulness is a willingness to persevere during periods of discouragement. Most, if not all, people who have achieved great things for God have done so by persevering through circumstances that would have caused others to give up.

23:12–16 As Paul sat in prison, some Jews devised a plot that began the long process that would send him from Palestine to Rome (v. 12). The intensity of the resolve of these men is demonstrated by their decision to have a total fast until they have killed Paul.

When Paul said that he lost all the things that he could claim from a human standpoint because of the gospel (Php 3:4–8), this must have included his family. His father, likely a wealthy person, had probably disowned him. But something of family affection must have remained for his sister's son to take the risk of exposing the plot of this murderous group.

23:17–24 The centurion took immediate action, arranging Paul's transfer to Caesarea. An unusually large military contingent accompanied Paul (vv. 23–24).

23:25–30 The centurion sent a letter along to the governor. The account embellished the story about Paul (v. 27). The commander specifically mentions that "there was no charge against him that deserved death or imprisonment" (v. 29); rather, Paul was being sent to Caesarea for protection (v. 30). Paul's blamelessness before the Roman law is a major theme of this entire passage.

23:31–35 Felix had become procurator of Judea in AD 52, which means that he had been governor for about five years when Paul was brought to him. His current wife was his third, Drusilla, the

night and brought him as far as Antipatris. 32The next day they let the cavalry[a]
go on with him, while they returned to
the barracks.[b] 33When the cavalry[c] arrived in Caesarea,[d] they delivered the
letter to the governor[e] and handed Paul
over to him. 34The governor read the letter and asked what province he was from.
Learning that he was from Cilicia,[f] 35he
said, "I will hear your case when your
accusers[g] get here." Then he ordered that
Paul be kept under guard[h] in Herod's
palace.

Paul's Trial Before Felix

24 Five days later the high priest Ananias[i] went down to Caesarea with
some of the elders and a lawyer named
Tertullus, and they brought their charges[j] against Paul before the governor.[k]
2When Paul was called in, Tertullus presented his case before Felix: "We have enjoyed a long period of peace under you,
and your foresight has brought about
reforms in this nation. 3Everywhere and
in every way, most excellent[l] Felix, we acknowledge this with profound gratitude.
4But in order not to weary you further, I
would request that you be kind enough
to hear us briefly.
5"We have found this man to be a troublemaker, stirring up riots[m] among the
Jews[n] all over the world. He is a ringleader
of the Nazarene[o] sect[p] 6and even tried to
desecrate the temple;[q] so we seized him.
[7][a] 8By examining him yourself you will
be able to learn the truth about all these
charges we are bringing against him."
9The other Jews joined in the accusation,[r] asserting that these things were
true.

10When the governor[s] motioned for
him to speak, Paul replied: "I know that
for a number of years you have been a
judge over this nation; so I gladly make
my defense. 11You can easily verify that
no more than twelve days[t] ago I went up
to Jerusalem to worship. 12My accusers
did not find me arguing with anyone at
the temple,[u] or stirring up a crowd[v] in
the synagogues or anywhere else in the
city. 13And they cannot prove to you the
charges they are now making against
me.[w] 14However, I admit that I worship
the God of our ancestors[x] as a follower of
the Way,[y] which they call a sect.[z] I believe
everything that is in accordance with the
Law and that is written in the Prophets,[a]
15and I have the same hope in God as these
men themselves have, that there will be
a resurrection[b] of both the righteous and
the wicked.[c] 16So I strive always to keep
my conscience clear[d] before God and man.
17"After an absence of several years, I
came to Jerusalem to bring my people
gifts for the poor[e] and to present offerings. 18I was ceremonially clean[f] when
they found me in the temple courts doing
this. There was no crowd with me, nor
was I involved in any disturbance.[g] 19But
there are some Jews from the province
of Asia, who ought to be here before you
and bring charges if they have anything
against me.[h] 20Or these who are here
should state what crime they found in
me when I stood before the Sanhedrin —
21unless it was this one thing I shouted as

23:32 [a] ver 23 [b] Ac 21:34
23:33 [c] ver 23, 24 [d] Ac 8:40 [e] ver 26
23:34 [f] Ac 6:9; 21:39
23:35 [g] ver 30; Ac 24:19; 25:16 [h] Ac 24:27
24:1 [i] Ac 23:2 [j] Ac 23:30, 35 [k] Ac 23:24
24:3 [l] Lk 1:3; Ac 23:26; 26:25
24:5 [m] Ac 16:20; 17:6 [n] Ac 21:28 [o] Mk 1:24 [p] ver 14; Ac 26:5; 28:22
24:6 [q] Ac 21:28
24:9 [r] 1Th 2:16
24:10 [s] Ac 23:24
24:11 [t] Ac 21:27; ver 1
24:12 [u] Ac 25:8; 28:17 [v] ver 18
24:13 [w] Ac 25:7
24:14 [x] Ac 3:13 [y] Ac 9:2 [z] ver 5 [a] Ac 26:6, 22; 28:23
24:15 [b] Ac 23:6; 28:20 [c] Da 12:2; Jn 5:28, 29
24:16 [d] Ac 23:1
24:17 [e] Ac 11:29, 30; Ro 15:25-28, 31; 1Co 16:1-4, 15; 2Co 8:1-4; Gal 2:10
24:18 [f] Ac 21:26 [g] ver 12
24:19 [h] Ac 23:30

[a] 6-8 Some manuscripts include here *him, and we would have judged him in accordance with our law. 7But the commander Lysias came and took him from us with much violence, 8ordering his accusers to come before you.*

daughter of Herod Agrippa I. After reading the letter Felix discovered that Paul was from Cilicia and decided to hear his case (vv. 34–35).

24:1–2a The seriousness with which the Jewish leaders took this case is apparent in that the high priest himself made the 65-mile journey to Caesarea along with the elders and the lawyer Tertullus (v. 1). The speeches of Tertullus and Paul follow the form of courtroom speeches at the time.

24:2b–8 Tertullus begins with a typical introduction. He expresses the gratitude of the Jews for the peace that they have enjoyed under him. In fact, this was not true: Felix had brutally stamped out many Jewish insurrections.

Tertullus then brings several charges against Paul. The term "Nazarene" probably derives from the fact that Jesus grew up in Nazareth; this term was used of Jesus in the Gospels (Mt 2:23; Mk 14:67; 16:6), but this is the only time it is used of the church. Tertullus asserts that an examination of Paul will show that the charges they bring are true (v. 8).

24:9–16 Paul's introduction is less lavish than Tertullus with his compliments (v. 10). Each statement Luke records in this summary makes a telling point that convinces Felix of Paul's innocence (cf. vv. 22–27). Paul asserts his blamelessness (v. 16).

24:17–19 Paul denies the specific charges against him. He was ceremonially clean when he was found in the temple, there was no crowd with him, and he was not involved in any disturbance (v. 18). If the charge about causing trouble refers to the trouble in Ephesus, then the people from Asia should be there to press charges (v. 19). One by one he has refuted all the charges against him.

24:20–23 Paul has one more point to make: He was tried by the Sanhedrin, but they also found no suitable charge to bring against him (v. 20). In his full talk, the apostle may have mentioned

I stood in their presence: 'It is concerning
the resurrection of the dead that I am on
trial before you today.'"[i]
22Then Felix, who was well acquainted
with the Way, adjourned the proceedings.
"When Lysias the commander comes," he
said, "I will decide your case." 23He ordered
the centurion to keep Paul under guard[j]
but to give him some freedom[k] and permit his friends to take care of his needs.[l]
24Several days later Felix came with
his wife Drusilla, who was Jewish. He
sent for Paul and listened to him as he
spoke about faith in Christ Jesus.[m] 25As
Paul talked about righteousness, self-
control[n] and the judgment[o] to come, Felix was afraid and said, "That's enough
for now! You may leave. When I find it
convenient, I will send for you." 26At
the same time he was hoping that Paul
would offer him a bribe, so he sent for
him frequently and talked with him.
27When two years had passed, Felix
was succeeded by Porcius Festus,[p] but
because Felix wanted to grant a favor to
the Jews,[q] he left Paul in prison.[r]

Paul's Trial Before Festus

25 Three days after arriving in the
province, Festus went up from
Caesarea[s] to Jerusalem, 2where the chief
priests and the Jewish leaders appeared
before him and presented the charges
against Paul.[t] 3They requested Festus,
as a favor to them, to have Paul transferred to Jerusalem, for they were preparing an ambush to kill him along the
way. 4Festus answered, "Paul is being
held[u] at Caesarea, and I myself am going
there soon. 5Let some of your leaders
come with me, and if the man has done
anything wrong, they can press charges
against him there."
6After spending eight or ten days with
them, Festus went down to Caesarea.
The next day he convened the court[v]
and ordered that Paul be brought before him. 7When Paul came in, the Jews
who had come down from Jerusalem
stood around him. They brought many

24:21 [i]Ac 23:6
24:23 [j]Ac 23:35 [k]Ac 28:16 [l]Ac 23:16; 27:3
24:24 [m]Ac 20:21
24:25 [n]Gal 5:23; 2Pe 1:6 [o]Ac 10:42
24:27 [p]Ac 25:1, 4,9,14 [q]Ac 12:3; 25:9 [r]Ac 23:35; 25:14
25:1 [s]Ac 8:40
25:2 [t]ver 15; Ac 24:1
25:4 [u]Ac 24:23
25:6 [v]ver 17

Ac 24:25-26 ❖ Why did Paul's message make Felix uncomfortable? Why do similar messages make certain people uneasy today?

Ac 25:3 ❖ What causes people to plot evil in their hearts? How does God heal such hearts?

---

the confusion in the Sanhedrin during his trial. He certainly implies this when he says that he had to shout a statement about the resurrection (v. 21), which divided the Sanhedrin. He admits to one possible point against him—a doctrinal issue that really was not within Felix's jurisdiction.

Felix should have released Paul, but he was reluctant to displease the Jews. So he delayed making a decision until the commander came. Still, he gave Paul relative freedom. Felix's delaying tactics went on for two whole years.

24:24–27 The conversations Paul had with Felix and his wife give us a good description of how many top officials responded to the gospel. These discussions made Felix afraid, which expressed itself in a couldn't-care-less attitude. We also see how mixed his motives were, for he was looking for a bribe and did not want to displease the Jews, even if that meant being unjust to Paul. He probably thought that Paul, a Roman citizen who had just brought a substantial gift for the poor, must have had access to substantial wealth.

✣ **23:12—24:27** The early Christians not only outthought their opponents, but they also outlived them. In the writings of the early Christian apologists, the behavior of the Christians was a key aspect used in defense of Christianity. The evidence of blameless lives has been powerful in defending the faith against attacks from outside in every age.

The challenge to the church today to be blameless before the world has become acute, considering the great moral crisis facing the world today. In the West, there has been a general rejection of the Christian worldview that formed its moral basis for centuries. Many of its structures were based on moral absolutes, which have been all but rejected in postmodern Western society. One wonders how a culture can survive the lack of foundational absolutes without deteriorating into confusion and chaos.

When people outside the faith realize the physical, emotional, relational, and spiritual ravages of living without a moral center, will they see Christians as people who live with a clear conscience before God and humankind? Will that realization change their hearts? One can only hope. But the key in all this is that we as Christians maintain our biblical moral example, which will continue to provide a witness to a world filled with people who are lost.

25:1–6 Even two years after Paul's arrest, the Jewish leaders' urgency over this case and their plans to kill him had not diminished (v. 3). Festus asked the Jews to come to Caesarea with him and promised to take up the case on his return (vv. 4–6).

25:7–9 As in the trial before Felix, the Jews made serious charges that they could not prove (v. 7). Again, Paul proclaimed his blamelessness before the Jewish law, the temple, and Caesar (v. 8; see

serious charges against him,[w] but they
could not prove them.[x]
8Then Paul made his defense: "I have
done nothing wrong against the Jewish law or against the temple[y] or against
Caesar."
9Festus, wishing to do the Jews a favor,[z] said to Paul, "Are you willing to go
up to Jerusalem and stand trial before
me there on these charges?"[a]
10Paul answered: "I am now standing
before Caesar's court, where I ought to be
tried. I have not done any wrong to the
Jews, as you yourself know very well. 11If,
however, I am guilty of doing anything
deserving death, I do not refuse to die.
But if the charges brought against me by
these Jews are not true, no one has the
right to hand me over to them. I appeal
to Caesar!"[b]
12After Festus had conferred with his
council, he declared: "You have appealed
to Caesar. To Caesar you will go!"

Festus Consults King Agrippa

13A few days later King Agrippa and
Bernice arrived at Caesarea[c] to pay
their respects to Festus. 14Since they
were spending many days there, Festus discussed Paul's case with the king.
He said: "There is a man here whom
Felix left as a prisoner.[d] 15When I went
to Jerusalem, the chief priests and
the elders of the Jews brought charges against him[e] and asked that he be
condemned.
16"I told them that it is not the Roman
custom to hand over anyone before they
have faced their accusers and have had
an opportunity to defend themselves
against the charges.[f] 17When they came
here with me, I did not delay the case,
but convened the court the next day
and ordered the man to be brought in.[g]
18When his accusers got up to speak,
they did not charge him with any of the
crimes I had expected. 19Instead, they
had some points of dispute[h] with him
about their own religion[i] and about
a dead man named Jesus who Paul
claimed was alive. 20I was at a loss how
to investigate such matters; so I asked if
he would be willing to go to Jerusalem
and stand trial there on these charges.[j]
21But when Paul made his appeal to be
held over for the Emperor's decision, I
ordered him held until I could send him
to Caesar."[k]
22Then Agrippa said to Festus, "I would
like to hear this man myself."
He replied, "Tomorrow you will hear
him."[l]

Paul Before Agrippa

26:12–18pp // Ac 9:3–8; 22:6–11

23The next day Agrippa and Bernice[m]
came with great pomp and entered the
audience room with the high-ranking
military officers and the prominent men
of the city. At the command of Festus,
Paul was brought in. 24Festus said: "King
Agrippa, and all who are present with us,
you see this man! The whole Jewish community[n] has petitioned me about him in
Jerusalem and here in Caesarea, shouting
that he ought not to live any longer.[o] 25I
found he had done nothing deserving of
death,[p] but because he made his appeal
to the Emperor[q] I decided to send him to
Rome. 26But I have nothing definite to
write to His Majesty about him. Therefore
I have brought him before all of you, and
especially before you, King Agrippa, so
that as a result of this investigation I may

25:7 [w] Mk 15:3; Lk 23:2,10; Ac 24:5,6 [x] Ac 24:13
25:8 [y] Ac 6:13; 24:12; 28:17
25:9 [z] Ac 24:27 [a] ver 20
25:11 [b] ver 21,25; Ac 26:32; 28:19
25:13 [c] Ac 8:40
25:14 [d] Ac 24:27
25:15 [e] ver 2; Ac 24:1
25:16 [f] ver 4,5; Ac 23:30
25:17 [g] ver 6,10
25:19 [h] Ac 18:15; 23:29 [i] Ac 17:22
25:20 [j] ver 9
25:21 [k] ver 11,12
25:22 [l] Ac 9:15
25:23 [m] ver 13; Ac 26:30
25:24 [n] ver 2,3,7 [o] Ac 22:22
25:25 [p] Ac 23:9 [q] ver 11

23:1; 24:16). He should have been released at this stage. But Festus bowed to Jewish pressure and, wishing to grant them a favor, asked Paul whether he would be willing to go to Jerusalem for trial. Luke uses the word "favor" three times in the space of ten verses (24:27; 25:3, 9), indicating that the chances of Paul receiving a fair trial were bleak.

25:10–12 Paul now realized that there was no hope of his getting a fair trial in Judea. His life was in great danger, and the famous Roman justice system could not operate for his good here because of the influence of powerful locals. Paul must have felt that this problem would not be as serious in Rome. Thus, he decided to appeal to Caesar—a privilege granted to all Roman citizens.

25:13–22 Festus was happy to use a visit from Herod Agrippa II and his sister Bernice to consult on the puzzling case of Paul. Agrippa II held the vestments of the Jewish high priest and had the right to appoint him. Paul acknowledged that Agrippa was "acquainted with all the Jewish customs and controversies" (26:3).

25:14–21 Festus straightforwardly explained the events up to that point. It is interesting to note that he saw the claim of Jesus' resurrection as a pivotal point in this case (vv. 19–20).

25:23–27 The appearance of Agrippa and Bernice with great pomp to hear Paul speak reminds us of the prediction that Paul would appear before kings (9:15). Festus was not impressed by the mob approach of the Jews. He thought Paul was innocent. His immediate dilemma was that he did not have any specific charges against Paul to present to Caesar when he sent him to Rome.

PEOPLE TO KNOW // AGRIPPA

ACTS 25:23–27: Agrippa II took an interest in Paul's trial when Paul was being held in Caesarea (Ac 25:23). Some Jewish leaders petitioned for Paul to be sent from Caesarea down to Jerusalem where they could try him and—they hoped—execute him. Paul, however, made an appeal to Caesar. He wanted to be tried in Rome rather than in Jerusalem.

While Paul was still in Caesarea, Agrippa wanted to hear Paul's case. Agrippa was in the family line of Herod the Great, the king who had tried to kill Jesus by sentencing all the baby boys in Bethlehem to death. Agrippa had been made king of the region by the Roman Emperor Caesar.

Paul took advantage of his audience with Agrippa, sharing his own testimony of conversion to Christ. Paul then appealed to Agrippa, as someone familiar with the Jewish prophets and writings of Moses, to accept Jesus as Lord.

Agrippa shrugged off Paul's attempt, asking, "Do you think that in such a short time you can persuade me to be a Christian?" (Ac 26:28). While Paul's attempt to convert Agrippa was not successful, Agrippa did leave convinced of Paul's innocence. He declared that Paul could have been set free had he not made his appeal to Caesar.

APPLICATION ✤ Agrippa was well acquainted with the writings of Moses and the OT prophets. However, he could not accept Paul's message that Jewish history pointed to Jesus Christ, who had died and risen as God's Messiah. It is easy for us, like Agrippa, to know the words and stories of the Bible but still refuse to give our lives to the God revealed in the Bible. The story of Agrippa reminds us of the importance of knowing more than just the words in the Bible, but also of letting those words lead to the knowledge of Jesus Christ and of giving our lives to Christ through faith.

have something to write. 27For I think
it is unreasonable to send a prisoner on
to Rome without specifying the charges
against him."
26 Then Agrippa said to Paul, "You
have permission to speak for
yourself."[r]
So Paul motioned with his hand and
began his defense: 2"King Agrippa, I consider myself fortunate to stand before
you today as I make my defense against
all the accusations of the Jews, 3and especially so because you are well acquainted
with all the Jewish customs[s] and controversies.[t] Therefore, I beg you to listen to
me patiently.
4"The Jewish people all know the way I
have lived ever since I was a child,[u] from
the beginning of my life in my own country, and also in Jerusalem. 5They have
known me for a long time[v] and can testify, if they are willing, that I conformed
to the strictest sect of our religion, living
as a Pharisee.[w] 6And now it is because
of my hope[x] in what God has promised
our ancestors[y] that I am on trial today.
7This is the promise our twelve tribes[z] are
hoping to see fulfilled as they earnestly
serve God day and night.[a] King Agrippa,
it is because of this hope that these Jews
are accusing me.[b] 8Why should any of
you consider it incredible that God raises the dead?[c]
9"I too was convinced[d] that I ought to
do all that was possible to oppose[e] the
name of Jesus of Nazareth.[f] 10And that is
just what I did in Jerusalem. On the authority of the chief priests I put many of
the Lord's people[g] in prison,[h] and when
they were put to death, I cast my vote
against them.[i] 11Many a time I went from
one synagogue to another to have them
punished,[j] and I tried to force them to
blaspheme. I was so obsessed with persecuting them that I even hunted them
down in foreign cities.

26:1 [r] Ac 9:15; 25:22
26:3 [s] ver 7; Ac 6:14 [t] Ac 25:19
26:4 [u] Gal 1:13, 14; Php 3:5
26:5 [v] Ac 22:3
[w] Ac 23:6; Php 3:5
26:6 [x] Ac 23:6; 24:15; 28:20 [y] Ac 13:32; Ro 15:8
26:7 [z] Jas 1:1 [a] 1Th 3:10; 1Ti 5:5 [b] ver 2
26:8 [c] Ac 23:6
26:9 [d] 1Ti 1:13 [e] Jn 16:2 [f] Jn 15:21
26:10 [g] Ac 9:13 [h] Ac 8:3; 9:2, 14, 21 [i] Ac 22:20
26:11 [j] Mt 10:17

26:1–3 This is Paul's fullest testimony in Acts because it discusses his pre-Christian activity, his conversion, and his calling, which drives his mission.

26:4–8 Paul affirms his strict background as a Pharisee. Then he says that it is because of the hope of the Jewish people that he is on trial and immediately affirms that his audience should not consider it incredible that God raises the dead.

26:9–11 Paul insists that he once had the same attitude toward "the name of Jesus of Nazareth" as his opponents now do. Paul was one of the major leaders in the campaign against the faith and actively involved in persecuting Christians.

12“On one of these journeys I was going to Damascus with the authority and
commission of the chief priests. 13About
noon, King Agrippa, as I was on the road,
I saw a light from heaven, brighter than
the sun, blazing around me and my companions. 14We all fell to the ground, and I
heard a voice[k] saying to me in Aramaic,[a]
‘Saul, Saul, why do you persecute me? It
is hard for you to kick against the goads.’
15“Then I asked, ‘Who are you, Lord?’
“ ‘I am Jesus, whom you are persecuting,’ the Lord replied. 16‘Now get up and
stand on your feet.[l] I have appeared to
you to appoint you as a servant and as a
witness of what you have seen and will
see of me.[m] 17I will rescue you[n] from your
own people and from the Gentiles.[o] I am
sending you to them 18to open their eyes[p]
and turn them from darkness to light,[q]
and from the power of Satan to God, so
that they may receive forgiveness of sins[r]
and a place among those who are sanctified by faith in me.’[s]
19“So then, King Agrippa, I was not
disobedient to the vision from heaven.
20First to those in Damascus,[t] then to
those in Jerusalem[u] and in all Judea,
and then to the Gentiles,[v] I preached
that they should repent[w] and turn to
God and demonstrate their repentance
by their deeds.[x] 21That is why some Jews
seized me[y] in the temple courts and tried
to kill me.[z] 22But God has helped me to
this very day; so I stand here and testify to small and great alike. I am saying
nothing beyond what the prophets and
Moses said would happen[a]— 23that the

26:14 [k]Ac 9:7
26:16 [l]Eze 2:1; Da 10:11 [m]Ac 22:14,15
26:17 [n]Jer 1:8, 19 [o]Ac 9:15
26:18 [p]Isa 35:5 [q]Isa 42:7, 16; Eph 5:8; Col 1:13; 1Pe 2:9 [r]Lk 24:47; Ac 2:38 [s]Ac 20:21,32
26:20 [t]Ac 9:19-25 [u]Ac 9:26-29; 22:17-20 [v]Ac 9:15; 13:46 [w]Ac 3:19 [x]Mt 3:8; Lk 3:8
26:21 [y]Ac 21:27, 30 [z]Ac 21:31
26:22 [a]Lk 24:27, 44; Ac 10:43; 24:14
26:23 [b]1Co 15:20,23; Col 1:18; Rev 1:5 [c]Lk 2:32
26:24 [d]Jn 10:20; 1Co 4:10 [e]Jn 7:15
26:25 [f]Ac 23:26
26:26 [g]ver 3
26:28 [h]Ac 11:26
26:29 [i]Ac 21:33
26:30 [j]Ac 25:23
26:31 [k]Ac 23:9

Ac 26:27–29 ❖ How can we nurture the same passion that Paul had to bring people to Christ? Why do such efforts start with prayer?

Messiah would suffer and, as the first
to rise from the dead,[b] would bring the
message of light to his own people and
to the Gentiles.”[c]
24At this point Festus interrupted
Paul’s defense. “You are out of your
mind,[d] Paul!” he shouted. “Your great
learning[e] is driving you insane.”
25“I am not insane, most excellent[f]
Festus,” Paul replied. “What I am saying is true and reasonable. 26The king
is familiar with these things,[g] and I can
speak freely to him. I am convinced that
none of this has escaped his notice, because it was not done in a corner. 27King
Agrippa, do you believe the prophets? I
know you do.”
28Then Agrippa said to Paul, “Do you
think that in such a short time you can
persuade me to be a Christian?”[h]
29Paul replied, “Short time or long — I
pray to God that not only you but all who
are listening to me today may become
what I am, except for these chains.”[i]
30The king rose, and with him the
governor and Bernice[j] and those sitting
with them. 31After they left the room,
they began saying to one another, “This
man is not doing anything that deserves
death or imprisonment.”[k]
32Agrippa said to Festus, “This man

[a] *14* Or *Hebrew*

26:12–15 This is the third account in Acts of Paul’s conversion and divine call. Here he recounts that Jesus spoke to him in Aramaic, suggesting that this was Christ’s first language.
26:16–18 Also unique to this narrative of Paul’s conversion was his commission by Jesus himself. The account in ch. 22 mentioned two commissions—one by Ananias (vv. 14–16) and a later one by Jesus (v. 21). Here Paul mentions a direct commission from Jesus right on the Damascus road, where he was appointed as a servant and a witness of Christ. Paul claimed apostleship based on this commission.

Two factors qualified a person to be an apostle in the early church: seeing the risen Lord (1Co 9:1; 15:8; see Ac 1:22) and being personally commissioned by him (cf. Ro 1:1; 1Co 1:1; Gal 1:1; 2:7). Both these things happened to Paul on the Damascus road.
26:19–23 Paul cites one more qualification for apostleship: his effectiveness in ministry (1Co 9:2; 2Co 12:12; Gal 2:8–9). A key to understanding his ministry is that he was obedient to a vision from heaven (Ac 26:19).
26:24–26 Festus recognizes that Paul is a learned man, but says that his learning has driven Paul insane. Paul responds by affirming that what he is saying is both true and reasonable. Paul knows that Agrippa understands what he is talking about.
26:27–29 Paul zeroes in at this stage with a direct challenge to Agrippa. Agrippa knows what Paul is speaking about, but he cannot afford to make connections between what he knows and what Paul is saying. If he did, he would then have to decide about the Way. He therefore brushes off the challenge. Paul’s response shows that he desires all to come to Christ—including rulers.
26:30–32 As the gathering is adjourned, the general sense of everyone there is that Paul has done nothing to deserve punishment. It was easy for Agrippa to say this after Paul made his appeal. Before that, for two whole years, Paul was kept in prison because the leaders did not have the moral courage to release him even though they knew he was innocent.

✣ **25:1—26:32** In our teaching and leading others to salvation in Christ, we need to stress the

could have been set free[l] if he had not
appealed to Caesar."[m]

Paul Sails for Rome

27 When it was decided that we[n] would
sail for Italy,[o] Paul and some other
prisoners were handed over to a centurion named Julius, who belonged to the
Imperial Regiment.[p] 2We boarded a ship
from Adramyttium about to sail for ports
along the coast of the province of Asia,[q]
and we put out to sea. Aristarchus,[r] a Macedonian[s] from Thessalonica,[t] was with us.
3The next day we landed at Sidon;[u]
and Julius, in kindness to Paul,[v] allowed
him to go to his friends so they might
provide for his needs.[w] 4From there we
put out to sea again and passed to the
lee of Cyprus because the winds were
against us.[x] 5When we had sailed across
the open sea off the coast of Cilicia[y] and
Pamphylia, we landed at Myra in Lycia.
6There the centurion found an Alexandrian ship[z] sailing for Italy[a] and put us
on board. 7We made slow headway for
many days and had difficulty arriving off
Cnidus. When the wind did not allow us
to hold our course,[b] we sailed to the lee
of Crete,[c] opposite Salmone. 8We moved
along the coast with difficulty and came
to a place called Fair Havens, near the
town of Lasea.
9Much time had been lost, and sailing
had already become dangerous because
by now it was after the Day of Atonement.[ad] So Paul warned them, 10"Men,
I can see that our voyage is going to be
disastrous and bring great loss to ship
and cargo, and to our own lives also."[e]
11But the centurion, instead of listening to what Paul said, followed the advice of the pilot and of the owner of the
ship. 12Since the harbor was unsuitable
to winter in, the majority decided that
we should sail on, hoping to reach Phoenix and winter there. This was a harbor in Crete, facing both southwest and
northwest.

The Storm

13When a gentle south wind began
to blow, they saw their opportunity; so
they weighed anchor and sailed along the
shore of Crete. 14Before very long, a wind
of hurricane force,[f] called the Northeaster, swept down from the island. 15The
ship was caught by the storm and could
not head into the wind; so we gave way to
it and were driven along. 16As we passed
to the lee of a small island called Cauda,
we were hardly able to make the lifeboat
secure, 17so the men hoisted it aboard.
Then they passed ropes under the ship itself to hold it together. Because they were
afraid they would run aground[g] on the
sandbars of Syrtis, they lowered the sea

26:32 [l] Ac 28:18 [m] Ac 25:11
27:1 [n] Ac 16:10 [o] Ac 18:2; 25:12, 25 [p] Ac 10:1
27:2 [q] Ac 2:9 [r] Ac 19:29 [s] Ac 16:9 [t] Ac 17:1
27:3 [u] Mt 11:21 [v] ver 43 [w] Ac 24:23; 28:16
27:4 [x] ver 7
27:5 [y] Ac 6:9
27:6 [z] Ac 28:11 [a] ver 1
27:7 [b] ver 4 [c] ver 12, 13, 21
27:9 [d] Lev 16:29-31; 23:27-29; Nu 29:7
27:10 [e] ver 21
27:14 [f] Mk 4:37
27:17 [g] ver 26, 39

[a] 9 That is, Yom Kippur

deep meaning of the cross. At the same time, we also need to emphasize the corresponding understanding of the resurrection and its significance. This is a key message for today's church because, with all our pragmatism and focus on how to live the Christian life, Christians need instruction in the theological and spiritual foundation of the call to become more Christlike as believers face the onslaught of the world upon the church.

Both new and seasoned believers must realize that in Christ and in the resurrection power he provides, we have the spiritual and theological power to withstand the onslaughts that come from the world, the flesh, and the devil. We have all we need to face each day when we rediscover the meaning of the resurrection and its implications for our lives in the modern world.

27:1–2 Luke may have been in Caesarea during the two intervening years and collected valuable information for his two-volume work (see Lk 1:3). Others in the traveling party included the centurion, other prisoners, and "Aristarchus, a Macedonian from Thessalonica" (v. 2). The latter is described as Paul's "fellow prisoner" in Col 4:10 and one of his "fellow workers" in Phm 24. These two letters were probably written from Rome in the early 60s.

27:3–5 The centurion in the Phoenician city of Sidon, in the first of his many acts of kindness to Paul, permitted him to visit "his friends" (v. 3; see 11:19).

27:6–8 The ship arrived in Myra in Lycia, and the passengers boarded an Alexandrian ship there. A strong northwest wind probably caused them to make "slow headway" (v. 7) and even to travel southwest along the southern coast of Crete rather than due west.

27:9–11 With difficulty, the ship arrived in Fair Havens, which, despite its name, was not a suitable place to face the rigors of winter. Paul's advice (v. 10) may have been given informally. We do not know whether this advice was given through direct divine guidance or through Paul's human wisdom.

27:12 Paul was a seasoned traveler who had already been shipwrecked three times and had spent a night and a day in the open sea (2Co 11:25). But he was overruled by the majority, who decided to go a short distance further west to the better harbor at Phoenix.

27:13–16 A "gentle south wind" seemed to be ideal for the journey to Phoenix (v. 13), so the crew weighed anchor. Unfortunately, Paul's ship had to confront a northeaster with all its force.

27:17 As they were being driven along, a new fear

PAUL'S JOURNEY TO ROME

anchor[a] and let the ship be driven along.
18We took such a violent battering from
the storm that the next day they began
to throw the cargo overboard.[h] 19On the
third day, they threw the ship's tackle
overboard with their own hands. 20When
neither sun nor stars appeared for many
days and the storm continued raging, we
finally gave up all hope of being saved.
21After they had gone a long time
without food, Paul stood up before them
and said: "Men, you should have taken
my advice[i] not to sail from Crete;[j] then
you would have spared yourselves this
damage and loss. 22But now I urge you
to keep up your courage,[k] because not
one of you will be lost; only the ship will
be destroyed. 23Last night an angel[l] of
the God to whom I belong and whom I
serve[m] stood beside me[n] 24and said, 'Do
not be afraid, Paul. You must stand trial
before Caesar;[o] and God has graciously
given you the lives of all who sail with
you.'[p] 25So keep up your courage,[q] men,
for I have faith in God that it will happen just as he told me.[r] 26Nevertheless,
we must run aground[s] on some island."[t]

The Shipwreck

27On the fourteenth night we were still
being driven across the Adriatic[b] Sea,

27:18 [h] ver 19, 38; Jnh 1:5
27:21 [i] ver 10 [j] ver 7
27:22 [k] ver 25, 36
27:23 [l] Ac 5:19 [m] Ro 1:9 [n] Ac 18:9; 23:11; 2Ti 4:17
27:24 [o] Ac 23:11 [p] ver 44
27:25 [q] ver 22, 36 [r] Ro 4:20, 21
27:26 [s] ver 17, 39 [t] Ac 28:1

[a] 17 Or *the sails* [b] 27 In ancient times the name referred to an area extending well south of Italy.

confronted them—the dreaded shallows off the shore of Cyrene in North Africa called "Syrtis."

27:18–20 As with the storm in the story of Jonah (Jnh 1:5), the sailors threw their cargo overboard and then the ship's spare gear. The sun and stars did not appear "for many days" (Ac 27:20), which meant that the crew could not now determine which direction they should go. They finally gave up hope of being saved.

27:21–26 In this hopeless situation, Paul came with a word of encouragement, having himself been encouraged by God through a vision. When he said that they should have taken his advice, he was not making an "I told you so" statement but trying to win their attention. Twice he asked them to keep up their courage, basing that appeal on his vision. God had a job for him in Rome, and because of that, everyone on board would be saved. After expressing his faith in God, he predicted the ship would run aground on an island.

27:27–36 Paul asserted his leadership again when the sailors tried to escape from the ship and again

Ac 27:33-38 ❖ Where have we found encouragement from God and from others during the storms of life?

when about midnight the sailors sensed they were approaching land. 28They took soundings and found that the water was a hundred and twenty feet[a] deep. A short time later they took soundings again and found it was ninety feet[b] deep. 29Fearing that we would be dashed against the rocks, they dropped four anchors from the stern and prayed for daylight. 30In an attempt to escape from the ship, the sailors let the lifeboat[u] down into the sea, pretending they were going to lower some anchors from the bow. 31Then Paul said to the centurion and the soldiers, "Unless these men stay with the ship, you cannot be saved."[v] 32So the soldiers cut the ropes that held the lifeboat and let it drift away.

33Just before dawn Paul urged them all to eat. "For the last fourteen days," he said, "you have been in constant suspense and have gone without food—you haven't eaten anything. 34Now I urge you to take some food. You need it to survive. Not one of you will lose a single hair from his head."[w] 35After he said this, he took some bread and gave thanks to God in front of them all. Then he broke it[x] and began to eat. 36They were all encouraged[y] and ate some food themselves. 37Altogether there were 276 of us on board. 38When they had eaten as much as they wanted, they lightened the ship by throwing the grain into the sea.[z]

39When daylight came, they did not recognize the land, but they saw a bay with a sandy beach,[a] where they decided to run the ship aground if they could. 40Cutting loose the anchors,[b] they left them in the sea and at the same time untied the ropes that held the rudders. Then they hoisted the foresail to the wind and made for the beach. 41But the ship struck a sandbar and ran aground. The bow stuck fast and would not move, and the stern was broken to pieces by the pounding of the surf.[c]

42The soldiers planned to kill the prisoners to prevent any of them from swimming away and escaping. 43But the centurion wanted to spare Paul's life[d] and kept them from carrying out their plan. He ordered those who could swim to jump overboard first and get to land. 44The rest were to get there on planks or on other pieces of the ship. In this way everyone reached land safely.[e]

Paul Ashore on Malta

28 Once safely on shore, we[f] found out that the island[g] was called Malta. 2The islanders showed us unusual kindness. They built a fire and welcomed us all because it was raining and cold. 3Paul gathered a pile of brushwood and, as he put it on the fire, a viper, driven out by the heat, fastened itself on his hand. 4When the islanders saw the snake hanging from his hand,[h] they said to each other, "This man must be a murderer; for though he escaped from the sea, the goddess Justice has not allowed him to live."[i] 5But Paul shook the snake off into the fire and suffered no ill effects.[j] 6The people expected him to swell up or suddenly fall dead; but after waiting a long time and seeing nothing unusual happen to him, they changed their minds and said he was a god.[k]

7There was an estate nearby that belonged to Publius, the chief official of the island. He welcomed us to his home and showed us generous hospitality for three days. 8His father was sick in bed,

[a] *28* Or about 37 meters [b] *28* Or about 27 meters

27:30 [u] ver 16
27:31 [v] ver 24
27:34 [w] Mt 10:30
27:35 [x] Mt 14:19
27:36 [y] ver 22, 25
27:38 [z] ver 18; Jnh 1:5
27:39 [a] Ac 28:1
27:40 [b] ver 29
27:41 [c] 2Co 11:25
27:43 [d] ver 3
27:44 [e] ver 22, 31
28:1 [f] Ac 16:10 [g] Ac 27:26,39
28:4 [h] Mk 16:18 [i] Lk 13:2,4
28:5 [j] Lk 10:19
28:6 [k] Ac 14:11

when he urged the people to eat. They found courage to eat when they saw Paul eating after giving thanks to God.

27:37-44 The crew saw a bay, which was probably what is now known as St. Paul's Bay in Malta, but they did not recognize the land. The waves were too strong for the battered ship, and it broke to pieces. Again, people's lives were saved because of Paul's presence on the ship.

28:1-6 The people had to wait three months in Malta because it was winter. The islanders there showed the shipwrecked travelers "unusual kindness" (v. 2). The reaction to the viper bite—that Paul was probably a murderer—is typical of superstitious people. When nothing bad happened to Paul, their superstition led them to change their verdict, saying that he was a god.

28:8-10 As was typical, Paul had a healing ministry in the town following the healing of the chief official's father. The hospitality of the people was truly generous, for they even supplied the travelers' needs when they left three months later.

suffering from fever and dysentery. Paul
went in to see him and, after prayer,[l]
placed his hands on him and healed
him.[m] 9When this had happened, the
rest of the sick on the island came and
were cured. 10They honored us in many
ways; and when we were ready to sail,
they furnished us with the supplies we
needed.

Paul's Arrival at Rome

11After three months we put out to
sea in a ship that had wintered in the island — it was an Alexandrian ship[n] with
the figurehead of the twin gods Castor
and Pollux. 12We put in at Syracuse and
stayed there three days. 13From there
we set sail and arrived at Rhegium. The
next day the south wind came up, and
on the following day we reached Puteoli. 14There we found some brothers and
sisters[o] who invited us to spend a week
with them. And so we came to Rome.
15The brothers and sisters[p] there had
heard that we were coming, and they
traveled as far as the Forum of Appius
and the Three Taverns to meet us. At
the sight of these people Paul thanked
God and was encouraged. 16When we
got to Rome, Paul was allowed to live
by himself, with a soldier to guard
him.[q]

Paul Preaches at Rome Under Guard

17Three days later he called together the local Jewish leaders.[r] When they
had assembled, Paul said to them: "My
brothers,[s] although I have done nothing against our people[t] or against the
customs of our ancestors,[u] I was arrested in Jerusalem and handed over
to the Romans. 18They examined me[v]
and wanted to release me,[w] because I
was not guilty of any crime deserving
death.[x] 19The Jews objected, so I was
compelled to make an appeal to Caesar.[y]
I certainly did not intend to bring any
charge against my own people. 20For
this reason I have asked to see you and
talk with you. It is because of the hope
of Israel[z] that I am bound with this
chain."[a]

21They replied, "We have not received
any letters from Judea concerning you,
and none of our people[b] who have come
from there has reported or said anything

28:8 [l] Jas 5:14, 15 [m] Ac 9:40
28:11 [n] Ac 27:6
28:14 [o] Ac 1:16
28:15 [p] Ac 1:16
28:16 [q] Ac 24:23; 27:3
28:17 [r] Ac 25:2 [s] Ac 22:5 [t] Ac 25:8 [u] Ac 6:14
28:18 [v] Ac 22:24 [w] Ac 26:31, 32 [x] Ac 23:9
28:19 [y] Ac 25:11
28:20 [z] Ac 26:6, 7 [a] Ac 21:33
28:21 [b] Ac 22:5

28:11–15 The ship that took Paul and company to Italy was also an Alexandrian ship, with a figurehead of the "heavenly twins," Castor and Pollux. If they left three months after the shipwreck, that would have been in early February—rather early in the shipping season.

During this week, news of Paul's arrival in Italy reached the church in Rome, presumably through someone who went to Rome from Puteoli. Some believers decided to meet Paul on the way. "At the sight of these people Paul thanked God and was encouraged" (v. 15).

It had been nearly two and a half difficult years after the divine assurance given to Paul in Jerusalem that he would go to Rome (23:11). Now Paul has finally met Christians in Rome, brothers and sisters in Christ whom he had eagerly longed to see.

27:1—28:15 This passage is unique in detailing God's sovereignty in difficult situations because here the hardship comes not from the sinfulness of people but from the forces of nature and poor human choices. Paul and his team would have avoided the storm if the ship's officers had listened to his words of wisdom.

While we know that Christ can certainly calm every storm in life, hard personal experience shows us that Christians are not immune from problems that others in the world also face. Sometimes he miraculously delivers his people from such situations, while at other times he gives them the courage to endure natural and other disasters.

Though Christ certainly can still whatever storms we face, we can have the courage to face them when he does not, for we know that God in his sovereignty will work out something good in the crisis (Ro 8:28). We live under God's promises, and these promises brace us to face such challenges.

28:16 Once Paul arrived in Rome he was "allowed to live by himself," which means he must have rented a house (see v. 30). He was probably chained to a soldier by the wrist. As a result, Paul and the gospel became a talking point among the members of the palace guard (cf. Php 1:13). The environment was not ideal, but it was adequate for Paul to have a bold and unhindered witness in Rome for two years (Ac 28:30–31).

28:17–20 Paul first called the Jewish leaders to meet him, which was the correct protocol in communities that had a strong sense of solidarity. He explained to them the circumstances of his coming to Rome, finishing with the statement, "It is because of the hope of Israel that I am bound with this chain" (v. 20b).

28:21–22 The leaders' reply that they had not received any letters from Judea concerning Paul is surprising, considering the urgency with which the Judean leaders hounded Paul while he was there. Also surprising is the fact that the Jewish

THE SPREAD OF THE GOSPEL MESSAGE IN THE ANCIENT WORLD

bad about you. 22But we want to hear
what your views are, for we know that
people everywhere are talking against
this sect."[c]
23They arranged to meet Paul on a certain day, and came in even larger numbers to the place where he was staying.
He witnessed to them from morning
till evening, explaining about the kingdom of God,[d] and from the Law of Moses
and from the Prophets[e] he tried to persuade them about Jesus.[f] 24Some were
convinced by what he said, but others
would not believe.[g] 25They disagreed
among themselves and began to leave
after Paul had made this final statement:
"The Holy Spirit spoke the truth to your
ancestors when he said through Isaiah
the prophet:

26" 'Go to this people and say,
"You will be ever hearing but never
understanding;
you will be ever seeing but never
perceiving."
27For this people's heart has become
calloused;[h]
they hardly hear with their
ears,
and they have closed their eyes.
Otherwise they might see with their
eyes,
hear with their ears,
understand with their hearts
and turn, and I would heal
them.'[a][i]

28"Therefore I want you to know that

28:22 [c] Ac 24:5, 14
28:23 [d] Ac 19:8 [e] Ac 8:35 [f] Ac 17:3
28:24 [g] Ac 14:4
28:27 [h] Ps 119:70 [i] Isa 6:9,10

[a] 27 Isaiah 6:9,10 (see Septuagint)

---

leaders said that they did not know much about the Christian faith despite the presence of a Christian community in Rome.

28:23–29 Here we see a familiar sequence. The Jews showed an interest in the Way, and a meeting was arranged. Paul tried to convince them about Jesus "from the Law of Moses and from the Prophets" (v. 23b). Some were convinced, "but others would not believe" (v. 24). Those who rejected the message had stubborn hearts that did not want to believe. The result of that meeting was unpleasant for Paul. There isn't much new here. Luke underscores the tragedy of Jewish rejection of the gospel.

Ac 28:23–31 ❖ Even under house arrest Paul tirelessly witnessed for Christ. How can we maintain our passion for the work of Christ through all seasons of life?

God's salvation[j] has been sent to the Gentiles,[k] and they will listen!" [29][a]
30For two whole years Paul stayed
there in his own rented house and welcomed all who came to see him. 31He
proclaimed the kingdom of God[l] and
taught about the Lord Jesus Christ—
with all boldness and without hindrance!

28:28 [j] Lk 2:30 [k] Ac 13:46
28:31 [l] ver 23; Mt 4:23

[a] 29 Some manuscripts include here *After he said this, the Jews left, arguing vigorously among themselves.*

28:30–31 Acts does not conclude on the note of Jewish rejection of the gospel. Rather, Luke's conclusion presents a more glorious reality: The Gentiles hear the gospel, and Paul has two years of bold witness about "the kingdom of God and . . . the Lord Jesus Christ" (v. 31). At the start of Acts, Luke gave his key verse (1:8), which predicted that through the Holy Spirit the gospel would be proclaimed "to the ends of the earth." The book ends with that prediction being fulfilled.

Why does the book of Acts end so abruptly? Is it because Acts was written shortly after the two years mentioned in this conclusion? There is a strong case for this, and many scholars date the book of Acts to the early to mid-60s. We cannot be sure of what Paul did after the events described in Acts. Tradition affirms that he was released from this imprisonment, had more evangelistic campaigns, and probably visited friends in Macedonia and Asia. Did he go to Spain during this time, as he had wished to (Ro 15:24, 28)? We cannot be sure.

Paul was probably arrested again and wrote the Pastoral Letters during his second imprisonment in Rome. The last of these, the second letter written to his close associate Timothy, speaks of his impending death. He was martyred sometime between AD 64 and 67.

28:16–31 Luke summarizes the message preached as being about "the kingdom of God and . . . the Lord Jesus Christ" (v. 31). This has much to tell us today. Preaching about the kingdom of God presents the greater purpose of God than just what God can do for us as individuals. It affirms that God is working out his purposes through the events of history. His plan will finally be accomplished, with his kingdom ruling the world. We ask people to join in this great march forward with the Lord of the universe. In this world, where people are wracked by fear, this is liberating news.

In today's evangelism, we tend to focus on how Jesus meets our personal needs. This topic is, of course, appropriate. But if the grand picture of the kingdom is also firmly rooted in our minds, we will never forsake the Lord of the universe because we perceive he's not meeting our needs.

Also necessary to evangelistic preaching is a focus on Jesus. Again, we do not only tell what he can do for us in connection with our present needs; we also describe who he is and what he has done and is doing in the world. We must emphasize the Jesus who is preached in Acts. Such a portrayal of Christ will leave believers feeling secure, confident, and complete.

Luke's decision to close his book with a report of ongoing evangelism reminds us that evangelism is the passion that ignites our activity. God has acted decisively in Christ to save humanity. In the gospel story lies the ultimate answer to the problems of the human race. If we love this world as God does, we will want to tell it of this liberating Good News. This work will consume our passion until the day we die.

Author: The apostle Paul

Audience: The church in Rome, predominantly Gentile but including a minority of Jews

Date: About AD 57

Theme: Paul writes to the church in Rome to present his basic statement of the gospel: God's plan of salvation is for all peoples, Jew and Gentile alike.

PERSPECTIVE

In a world of divisions—ethnic, racial, national, religious—there has never been a more appropriate time for unity and healing. One of the purposes the apostle Paul has in writing Romans is to unify a divided Christian community in Rome. The community there was probably started by Jewish Christians, but their numbers were quickly matched by an equal number of Gentile Christians. These two groups are now in conflict. The ongoing tendency for old church members to resent newcomers is made worse by different ethnic and religious histories.

Paul argues for solidarity and reconciliation using *doctrine* as his rationale. The book of Romans is about healing divisions in the church with doctrine rather than with sociology, psychology, business management, or even reason, to do the work. It is as if Paul said to the church at Rome, "Let's stop and think about this in the same way God thinks about this. *Then* let's act."

Using Christian doctrine to solve problems of disunity and strife is fast becoming an endangered methodology. Doing so means one eventually has to make judgments about right and wrong—and calling someone wrong these days is interpreted, in religious circles at least, as intellectual harassment. Upholding doctrine means being willing to draw boundaries as perimeters for Christian faith, and many consider boundaries to be the equivalent of religious redlining.

Paul makes clear in the 16 chapters of Romans that the healing of divisions in the church comes from getting in touch with God's plan for humankind: what God has done in the past through Israel, what God is doing now through Jesus (which includes Gentiles), and what

Reading Romans

Romans is one of the most highly organized books in the NT. After a brief introduction, Paul wrote the first section (Ro 1:18–3:20) to demonstrate that all humans are sinners. Next, he showed how Christ has solved our problem of sin (Ro 3:21–8:39). After struggling with the problem of the salvation of the Jews (chs. 9–11), Paul penned a

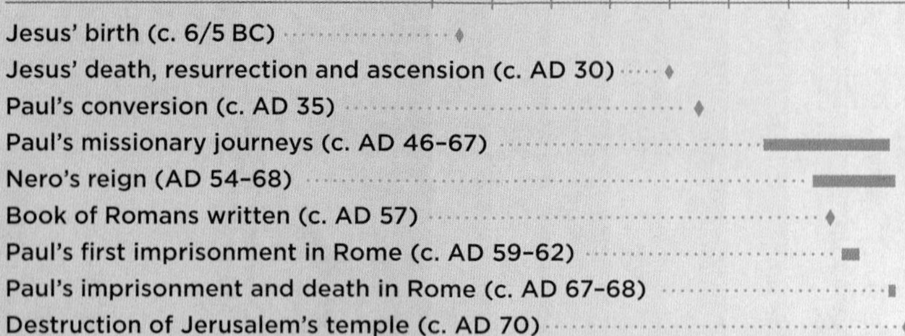

God projects for the future of the church. Paul does not present a systematic argument as much as he faithfully portrays the gospel story. One does not argue oneself to faith, one agrees to the trajectories of the story. That story, Paul tells us, is that of the church's engaging the world in ever widening circles of contact.

Yes, Paul says that unity comes from unifying around an insight: The church as God has intended it is a missionary church. Paul's next wider circle is Spain. His message to Jewish and Gentile Christians is that unity comes not from introspective interpersonal therapy that leads to liking one another or agreeing with one another. It comes, rather, from getting on board the gospel train that is always, everywhere, just now leaving the station.

To understand Romans, we must during our reading always listen for the voice of the conductor, Paul, telling us it is time to leave.

TAKING THE NEXT STEPS

When Paul visited Corinth at the end of his third missionary journey (see Ac 20:2–3), he wrote the book of Romans as a letter of self-introduction to Christians in Rome, whom he hoped to visit soon (see Ro 1:13; 15:23–24). In this letter he explained the basic gospel message: All human beings are in a desperate situation of sin and all stand condemned before God, but God has provided us a way out of this horrible predicament by sending his Son, Jesus, to die for our sin. By his grace, God regards those who believe in Christ to be righteous in his sight. In faith, we must accept this gift of God and begin living the Christian life. This grand message of salvation must be proclaimed everywhere, in a program of worldwide mission outreach to both Jew and Gentile.

The letter to the Romans is filled with practical messages for Christians. (1) We all struggle with the reality of sin in our lives, and none of us can obtain eternal life by anything we do. (2) God has provided the way of deliverance from sin's bondage by sending his Son, Jesus, to die on the cross; through faith in Jesus we receive the gracious gift of eternal life. (3) By identifying with Christ's death and resurrection (Ro 6:5) and by the help of the Holy Spirit whom God has sent, we can be set free from the power of sin and death. (4) We as Christians must express gratitude to God for his saving grace by serving him in every area of our lives and by loving our

number of practical suggestions on how to live the Christian life (Ro 12:1–15:13). He ended his letter with his travel plans and a chapter of greetings to those Christians in Rome whom he knew.

Key Verses

Therefore, there is now no condemnation for those who are in Christ Jesus, because through Christ Jesus the law of the Spirit who gives life has set you free from the law of sin and death.

—Romans 8:1–2

fellow human beings. (5) We ought to be particularly concerned about weak Christians, reaching out to them with understanding, support and love.

WHAT TO LOOK FOR IN ROMANS

- Gentiles and sin (ch. 1)
- Jews and sin (ch. 2)
- Summary of sin and God's method of salvation (ch. 3)
- Comparison of Adam and Christ (ch. 5)
- Being dead to sin and alive to God (ch. 6)
- The power of the Spirit in the life of the Christian (ch. 8)
- The Jews in God's plan of salvation (chs. 9–11)
- Life in the church (ch. 12)
- Christian freedom and concern for fellow Christians (ch. 14)

ANCIENT ROME

PEOPLE TO KNOW // PAUL

ROMANS 1:1–7: Paul, originally called Saul, was an early missionary for the Christian church and an apostle of Christ. Thirteen NT letters are attributed to Paul. He did not start out as a follower of Jesus, however. He first appears in the NT as a persecutor of the church. He was present when Stephen was martyred, and he approved of the killing (Ac 8:1).

Paul's life took a dramatic turn when he traveled to Damascus, intending to arrest any Christians he found there. On the way, he was stopped by a blinding light. Christ spoke to him from heaven, telling him to go into the city and await further instruction (Ac 9:5–6). For three days Paul was blind until God sent Ananias to restore his sight.

Paul's conversion to becoming a Jesus follower was immediate and complete. After he could see again, he began to preach about Christ in the synagogues, shocking those who heard (Ac 9:20–21). Some Jews plotted to kill him, but he escaped to Jerusalem. There, Barnabas took Paul to meet with the apostles. Later, Barnabas and Paul went on a missionary journey together. They returned to Jerusalem and told the believers how God was working powerfully among the Gentiles, which influenced the decision not to require Gentiles to be circumcised in order to become Christians (Ac 15:1–35). Paul then returned to missionary efforts alongside Silas.

Paul traveled widely and ministered effectively, planting many churches. He wrote letters to churches to encourage and correct them in certain matters. Eventually, Paul was arrested in Jerusalem and then transferred to Caesarea where he appealed as a Roman citizen to be tried by Caesar (Ac 25:11). He was sent to Rome, experiencing shipwrecks and danger on the way. In Rome, he was put under house arrest (Ac 28:16).

Acts ends with Paul under arrest in Rome, but details from Paul's letters suggest he may have engaged in further missionary travels after this. We do know, from his extensive letters to the churches and to his trusted friends, that Paul followed his Lord and Savior for the rest of his life on earth.

APPLICATION ✣ When Christ calls us, he wants us to give our whole lives to him. Few have demonstrated this better than Paul. In the face of beatings, shipwrecks, slander and other attacks, Paul worked tirelessly to spread the gospel. Paul's legacy is an example for all who serve Christ. Our highest goal should be to make Christ known in all we say and do (Col 3:17).

1 Paul, a servant of Christ Jesus, called
to be an apostle[a] and set apart[b] for the
gospel of God[c]— 2the gospel he promised beforehand through his prophets
in the Holy Scriptures[d] 3regarding his
Son, who as to his earthly life[a][e] was a
descendant of David, 4and who through
the Spirit of holiness was appointed the
Son of God in power[b] by his resurrection
from the dead: Jesus Christ our Lord.
5Through him we received grace and
apostleship to call all the Gentiles[f] to
the obedience that comes from[c] faith[g]
for his name's sake. 6And you also are
among those Gentiles who are called to
belong to Jesus Christ.[h]

7To all in Rome who are loved by God[i]
and called to be his holy people:

1:1 [a]1Co 1:1 [b]Ac 9:15 [c]2Co 11:7
1:2 [d]Gal 3:8
1:3 [e]Jn 1:14
1:5 [f]Ac 9:15 [g]Ac 6:7
1:6 [h]Rev 17:14
1:7 [i]Ro 8:39

[a] 3 Or *who according to the flesh* [b] 4 Or *was declared with power to be the Son of God* [c] 5 Or *that is*

1:1 Paul introduces himself to the Roman Christians by identifying his Master, his office, and his purpose.

1:2 Throughout the letter, Paul takes great pains to demonstrate that the Good News about Jesus Christ is rooted firmly in the soil of the OT. The "prophets" to which he refers are all the OT authors.

1:3–4 Paul describes the content of the gospel: Jesus Christ himself. Verse 4 does not teach that Jesus *became* the Son of God at the time of his resurrection. Jesus' resurrection concluded the work of redemption and gave Jesus new power to dispense salvation to all those who would believe in him (see v. 16).

1:5–6 Paul received this "grace" for two purposes. First, the Lord made clear that Paul's primary mission was to bring Gentiles to faith in Jesus (see Ac 9:15). Second, the Christians in Rome are included among those Gentiles, belonging to the sphere of ministry God assigned him.

1:7 Paul finally gets around to identifying the recipients of the letter. They are all the Christians in Rome, "loved by God and called to be his holy people."

APPLICATION ✣ 1:1–7 Being an apostle is an act of God's grace. So are all ministries. Serving God and his people in specific ways is a

Grace and peace to you from God our
Father and from the Lord Jesus Christ.[j]

Paul's Longing to Visit Rome

8First, I thank my God through Jesus
Christ for all of you,[k] because your faith is
being reported all over the world.[l] 9God,
whom I serve[m] in my spirit in preaching the gospel of his Son, is my witness[n]
how constantly I remember you 10in
my prayers at all times; and I pray that
now at last by God's will the way may be
opened for me to come to you.[o]
11I long to see you[p] so that I may impart to you some spiritual gift to make
you strong— 12that is, that you and I
may be mutually encouraged by each
other's faith. 13I do not want you to be
unaware, brothers and sisters,[a] that I
planned many times to come to you (but
have been prevented from doing so until now)[q] in order that I might have a
harvest among you, just as I have had
among the other Gentiles.
14I am obligated[r] both to Greeks and
non-Greeks, both to the wise and the
foolish. 15That is why I am so eager to
preach the gospel also to you who are
in Rome.[s]
16For I am not ashamed of the gospel,[t]
because it is the power of God[u] that brings
salvation to everyone who believes: first
to the Jew,[v] then to the Gentile.[w] 17For in

1:7 [j] 1Co 1:3
1:8 [k] 1Co 1:4 [l] Ro 16:19
1:9 [m] 2Ti 1:3 [n] Php 1:8
1:10 [o] Ro 15:32
1:11 [p] Ro 15:23
1:13 [q] Ro 15:22, 23
1:14 [r] 1Co 9:16
1:15 [s] Ro 15:20
1:16 [t] 2Ti 1:8 [u] 1Co 1:18 [v] Ac 3:26 [w] Ro 2:9,10

Ro 1:12 ❖ How can believers today find ways to be mutually encouraged by each other's faith?

[a] *13* The Greek word for *brothers and sisters* (*adelphoi*) refers here to believers, both men and women, as part of God's family; also in 7:1,4; 8:12,29; 10:1; 11:25; 12:1; 15:14,30; 16:14,17.

---

product of God's unmerited favor toward us. When we serve the Lord and the church, we do what we have no right to do on our own: speak in God's name, reach out with his love, and lead his people. Only because God both calls us to minister and gives us the grace to do it can we accomplish anything worthwhile.

1:8–10a Christ has created the access to God that enables Paul to approach him in thanksgiving. The reason for Paul's thanks is the positive reputation the Roman Christians have gained for their faith. In vv. 9–10 Paul reinforces his commitment to the Roman Christians by emphasizing his constant prayers for them.

1:10b–12 One specific focus of Paul's prayer is that he may be able to come to Rome. Specifically, he wants to go to Rome so that he may "impart" some "spiritual gift." It is not, Paul hastily adds, that the spiritual benefit will flow all one direction, from Paul to the Romans.

1:13–15 Paul wants his readers to understand that his failure to visit Rome was not because of lack of will but because of lack of opportunity. Paul's desire to preach in Rome is motivated not by a concern to expand his personal "territory" but by his deep sense of obligation to preach the gospel to all kinds of people. "Greek and non-Greek" is Paul's way of referring to all Gentile humanity. Paul has been given a commission from the Lord to be "apostle to the Gentiles" (11:13). This mandate, not any personal benefit, compels Paul to travel to this church.

✜ **1:8–15** Paul's zeal for preaching the gospel should serve as a model for us. Few of us will have such clear direction about a call to ministry. But the necessity to evangelize is an obligation, Paul suggests, that all believers share.

1:16–17 Why is Paul not ashamed? Because he knows the gospel he preaches is the divinely appointed means to bring salvation to the world. "Salvation" and the verb "to save" are important words in Romans. Paul uses this language to refer to final deliverance from sin and evil that will come to the believer at death or Christ's return (see 5:9–10; 13:11).

Announcing what will become a key theme in this letter, Paul insists that the salvation available in the gospel is for *all* who believe. In a significant advance on the OT, which focused on Israel, the gospel is universally available. Paul will affirm that Jews still have a kind of priority in the plan of salvation.

Why does the gospel transmit salvation to those who believe? Paul explains this in 1:17. What does the phrase "righteousness of God" mean? Paul uses it to mean "the act by which God puts people who believe in right relationship with himself."

A central motif in Romans, and in Paul's gospel in general, is the insistence that one can experience this righteousness of God *only* through faith. Paul emphasizes this point in two ways. First, he emphasizes faith "from first to last" (v. 17). Second, Paul cites Hab 2:4 for the connection between the righteous person, faith, and life.

Is he emphasizing that righteous people should live by faith? Or is he asserting that only the person who is righteous by faith will attain life? The syntax can go either way, but the argument of the letter, in which Paul again and again asserts that a person is righteous (or justified) only by faith, favors the second reading.

✜ **1:16–17** We, in ourselves, are *never* worthy, not even the best of us. The gospel is precisely Good News because it announces that God accepts us anyway; all that we have to do is receive his offer in faith—to be sure, a faith that must, by its very nature, always be accompanied by obedience (cf. v. 5). Justification reminds us that our right standing with God is by his grace alone, and that thankfulness should be the hallmark of all our dealings with him.

CHARACTER OF GOD // GOD IS WRATH

Romans 1:18: The wrath of God is being revealed from heaven against all the godlessness and wickedness of people.

God's wrath is not a comfortable topic. Yet the Bible requires that we understand and take seriously what it says about this aspect of God's nature.

God's wrath is not irrational anger. God is not petty. God's wrath is not the byproduct of a lack of patience or understanding. Instead, God's wrath is an outworking—a necessary corollary—of God's love. Since God loves what is good, God hates what is evil. God knows that evil seeks to kill and destroy. God made creation "very good" (Ge 1:31), and God is angered when that good creation is marred.

We need to understand God's wrath in connection with God's mercy. Though God's wrath is aroused by sin and evil, God also extends grace and mercy before exacting judgment.

God's wrath also relates to the outworking of justice when people do wrong. God is not spiteful or mean; however, he will allow evil people to receive the misery caused by their actions. Paul makes this clear in Ro 1:18-25. God does not wield his wrath like a tyrant; rather, God's justice at times means he hands sinners over to the consequences of their sin.

APPLICATION God's wrath should sober us to the serious reality of God's holy requirements. God is not a good luck charm to be used to our own advantage when it is convenient; he is the Lord of the universe. At the same time, God's wrath should not be a source of terror for his children. Instead, we should turn our attention to the hope and promise that "there is now no condemnation for those who are in Christ Jesus" (Ro 8:1). While God is justly wrathful toward sin, our hope is in the saving grace of Jesus.

the gospel the righteousness of God is
revealed[x] — a righteousness that is by
faith from first to last,[a] just as it is written: "The righteous will live by faith."[b][y]

God's Wrath Against Sinful Humanity

18The wrath of God[z] is being revealed
from heaven against all the godlessness
and wickedness of people, who suppress
the truth by their wickedness, 19since
what may be known about God is plain
to them, because God has made it plain
to them.[a] 20For since the creation of the
world God's invisible qualities — his eternal power and divine nature — have been
clearly seen, being understood from
what has been made,[b] so that people
are without excuse.
21For although they knew God, they
neither glorified him as God nor gave
thanks to him, but their thinking became futile and their foolish hearts were
darkened.[c] 22Although they claimed to
be wise, they became fools[d] 23and exchanged the glory of the immortal God
for images[e] made to look like a mortal

1:17 [x] Ro 3:21 [y] Hab 2:4; Gal 3:11; Heb 10:38
1:18 [z] Eph 5:6; Col 3:6
1:19 [a] Ac 14:17
1:20 [b] Ps 19:1-6
1:21 [c] Jer 2:5; Eph 4:17,18
1:22 [d] 1Co 1:20, 27
1:23 [e] Ps 106:20; Jer 2:11; Ac 17:29

[a] 17 Or *is from faith to faith* [b] 17 Hab. 2:4

1:18-20 God's reaction to sin is not the anger of an emotional person; it is the necessary reaction of a holy God to sin. Paul is probably referring broadly to the sentence of condemnation under which all people stand. It is a sentence that God sometimes inflicts in the events of history but will carry out with finality at the end of history.

Especially important for Paul is his insistence that God's wrath falls on people who "suppress the truth." One can only suppress something of which one has knowledge. As a result, Paul goes on to show that human beings do have knowledge about God. He has revealed it to them, manifesting some of his divine qualities in the world he has created (v. 20). Moreover, these qualities "have been clearly seen" by people.

1:21-31 Paul uses the same sequence three times: (1) "they . . . exchanged" (vv. 22-23); "Therefore God gave them over" (v. 24); (2) "they exchanged" (v. 25); "Because of this, God gave them over" (v. 26); (3) "their women exchanged . . . in the same way the men also" (vv. 26b-27); "[he] gave them over" (v. 28b).

In each case, human beings put their own "god" or sin in place of the truth God has revealed to them. God reacts by "handing them over" to the consequences of the choices they have made.

Paul is talking about human beings in general. They are prone to turn away from God because of the original fall into sin. All people have been given some evidence of God's truth in the natural world around them.

1:21-24 The first "exchange" focuses explicitly on idolatry. People "knew" God, but they refused to

human being and birds and animals and
reptiles.
24Therefore God gave them over[f] in the
sinful desires of their hearts to sexual
impurity for the degrading of their bodies with one another.[g] 25They exchanged
the truth about God for a lie,[h] and worshiped and served created things[i] rather than the Creator — who is forever
praised.[j] Amen.
26Because of this, God gave them over[k]
to shameful lusts.[l] Even their women
exchanged natural sexual relations for
unnatural ones.[m] 27In the same way the
men also abandoned natural relations
with women and were inflamed with
lust for one another. Men committed
shameful acts with other men, and received in themselves the due penalty
for their error.[n]
28Furthermore, just as they did not
think it worthwhile to retain the knowledge of God, so God gave them over[o] to
a depraved mind, so that they do what
ought not to be done. 29They have become filled with every kind of wickedness, evil, greed and depravity. They
are full of envy, murder, strife, deceit
and malice. They are gossips,[p] 30slan-
derers, God-haters, insolent, arrogant
and boastful; they invent ways of doing
evil; they disobey their parents;[q] 31they
have no understanding, no fidelity, no
love,[r] no mercy. 32Although they know
God's righteous decree that those who
do such things deserve death,[s] they not
only continue to do these very things
but also approve[t] of those who practice them.

Ro 2:4 ❖ How does God's kindness lead to repentance? How have we experienced the transforming power of divine kindness?

God's Righteous Judgment

2 You, therefore, have no excuse,[u] you
who pass judgment on someone else,
for at whatever point you judge another,
you are condemning yourself, because
you who pass judgment do the same
things.[v] 2Now we know that God's judgment against those who do such things
is based on truth. 3So when you, a mere
human being, pass judgment on them
and yet do the same things, do you think
you will escape God's judgment? 4Or do
you show contempt for the riches[w] of his
kindness,[x] forbearance[y] and patience,[z]
not realizing that God's kindness is intended to lead you to repentance?[a]
5But because of your stubbornness
and your unrepentant heart, you are

1:24 [f] Eph 4:19 [g] 1Pe 4:3
1:25 [h] Isa 44:20 [i] Jer 10:14 [j] Ro 9:5
1:26 [k] ver 24, 28 [l] 1Th 4:5 [m] Lev 18:22,23
1:27 [n] Lev 18:22; 20:13
1:28 [o] ver 24,26
1:29 [p] 2Co 12:20
1:30 [q] 2Ti 3:2
1:31 [r] 2Ti 3:3
1:32 [s] Ro 6:23 [t] Ps 50:18; Lk 11:48; Ac 8:1; 22:20
2:1 [u] Ro 1:20 [v] 2Sa 12:5-7; Mt 7:1,2
2:4 [w] Ro 9:23; Eph 1:7,18; 2:7 [x] Ro 11:22 [y] Ro 3:25 [z] Ex 34:6 [a] 2Pe 3:9

---

acknowledge him. "Their thinking became futile" (v. 21b), they prided themselves on their own wisdom, and they traded the "glory of the immortal God" for their own self-made images (v. 23). As a punishment for this idolatry, God "gave them over." God reacts to the human decision to turn from him by giving people over to the consequences of their actions.

1:25–26 The second "exchange sequence" reiterates the connection between idolatry and sexual sin established in v. 24. Jewish tradition saw homosexuality as evidence of the Gentiles' idolatry and depravity. Paul points to the consequences of same-sex acts: They "received in themselves the due penalty for their error" (v. 27b).

1:28 At the end of v. 28, Paul finally introduces the "handing over" that corresponds to the "exchanged" of v. 26b. Because people did not approve of God's knowledge, he handed them over to their "depraved" minds. Sin affects not only our affections (idolatry) and our senses (sexual activity) but also our very thinking. As a result, people end up doing "what ought not to be done" (v. 28b).

1:29–31 In vv. 29–31, Paul provides several illustrations of this sinful conduct.

1:32 At the end of this section, Paul reiterates its key themes. First, human beings are in a position to understand God's truth. Second, sinners deserve death. Death is spiritual death—the condemnation or wrath of God. Finally, Paul suggests it is worse for a person to "approve" those who practice sins than to do them oneself. Paul wants to rebuke people who lead others into sin by approving of it.

✚ **1:18–32** The beauty and intricacy of the world can help people understand that there must be a Creator. Such things can stimulate a search for God. But Paul emphasizes how limited such knowledge is. Without revelation about Christ and his work on the cross, it cannot bring salvation.

2:1–4 Jews in the first century were not idolaters, nor was homosexuality common among them. But they did commit many of the sins Paul lists in 1:29–31. Perhaps he even thinks of their preoccupation with the law as a kind of idolatry. In any case, their "judging" of other people rebounds directly onto them. Since they are doing the same things as these other people, they condemn themselves at the same time. Relying on "the riches of [God's] kindness, forbearance and patience" to avoid judgment will not work (2:3–4).

2:5 God's kindness, Paul says, was "intended to lead [people] to repentance" (v. 4). Instead, the Jews regarded it as a carte blanche to sin with impunity. As a result, the Jews are "storing up wrath" that will be inflicted on the day of God's coming righteous judgment.

storing up wrath against yourself for
the day of God's wrath, when his righteous judgment[b] will be revealed. 6God
"will repay each person according to
what they have done."[a][c] 7To those who
by persistence in doing good seek glory,
honor[d] and immortality,[e] he will give
eternal life. 8But for those who are self-
seeking and who reject the truth and
follow evil,[f] there will be wrath and anger. 9There will be trouble and distress
for every human being who does evil:
first for the Jew, then for the Gentile;[g]
10but glory, honor and peace for everyone who does good: first for the Jew,
then for the Gentile.[h] 11For God does not
show favoritism.[i]

12All who sin apart from the law will
also perish apart from the law, and all
who sin under the law[j] will be judged
by the law. 13For it is not those who hear
the law who are righteous in God's sight,
but it is those who obey[k] the law who will
be declared righteous. 14(Indeed, when
Gentiles, who do not have the law, do by
nature things required by the law,[l] they
are a law for themselves, even though
they do not have the law. 15They show
that the requirements of the law are written on their hearts, their consciences
also bearing witness, and their thoughts
sometimes accusing them and at other
times even defending them.) 16This will
take place on the day when God judges
people's secrets[m] through Jesus Christ,[n]
as my gospel[o] declares.

The Jews and the Law

17Now you, if you call yourself a Jew; if
you rely on the law and boast in God;[p] 18if
you know his will and approve of what is
superior because you are instructed by
the law; 19if you are convinced that you
are a guide for the blind, a light for those
who are in the dark, 20an instructor of
the foolish, a teacher of little children,
because you have in the law the embodiment of knowledge and truth— 21you,
then, who teach others, do you not teach
yourself? You who preach against steal-

2:5 [b] Jude 6
2:6 [c] Ps 62:12; Mt 16:27
2:7 [d] ver 10 [e] 1Co 15:53,54
2:8 [f] 2Th 2:12
2:9 [g] 1Pe 4:17
2:10 [h] ver 9
2:11 [i] Ac 10:34
2:12 [j] Ro 3:19; 1Co 9:20,21
2:13 [k] Jas 1:22, 23,25
2:14 [l] Ac 10:35
2:16 [m] Ecc 12:14 [n] Ac 10:42 [o] Ro 16:25
2:17 [p] ver 23; Mic 3:11; Ro 9:4

[a] 6 Psalm 62:12; Prov. 24:12

2:6–11 In effect, Paul argues, there is a level playing field when it comes to God's ultimate verdict. In v. 6 Paul quotes from the OT to show that "works" will be the basis for God's judgment. Paul makes a similar point in v. 11 by insisting that God "does not show favoritism." God does not treat people differently based on outward appearance.

Paul spells out the implications of God's impartial judgment, based on works, for two opposite kinds of people. On the one hand, God will give eternal life to those who persevere in their work for the right reasons. On the other hand are "those who . . . reject the truth and follow evil." Such people earn for themselves "wrath and anger" (v. 8). Just in case we missed the point, Paul goes over the same ground again in vv. 9 and 10.

> ✚ **2:1–11** We too can "show contempt" (v. 4) for God's kindness toward us by using it as an open avenue for sin. We grow careless and even arrogant toward our sin because we think God will simply overlook it out of his love for us in Christ. But sin is a serious matter, whether we are in Christ or not. A lack of concern about sin is incompatible with true faith. Thus Paul's warning in this text about "presuming on God's grace" carries a warning for the Christian as well as for the non-Christian.

2:12–16 Paul intends to show that the Jews' possession of the law does not give them a decisive advantage over the Gentiles. "Law" (v. 12) refers to the Law of Moses. The law was given to Israel, and they were made responsible for it. Therefore, when Jews sin, they sin "under" it. Gentiles, by contrast, sin "apart from" that law. Why can the law not protect the Jews from God's wrath? Paul explains in v. 13.

2:13 This verse again raises the question of whether Paul teaches that people can be put right with God by what they do. But Paul is simply asserting the standard of God's assessment. No person ever actually meets the standard of obedience required to become right with God.

2:14–15 These verses are a self-contained unit that describes the Gentiles' relationship to "law." The Gentiles do have access to law in a certain sense. They do not have the Law of Moses, the Torah. But they have a knowledge of God's basic moral requirements. Their innate knowledge of God's law often leads them to do what is right. All Gentiles sometimes obey the law and sometimes do not. As a result, their consciences both accuse and defend them.

> ✚ **2:12–16** Our modern culture questions the basis for the fundamental moral standards of society. "Positive" law—that is, a specific law enacted by a lawgiver or lawmaker—must have a universal basis if it is to be universally valid. The tendency is to base our laws on the notion of "the common good." But that idea is slippery and can be imposed on the masses by a few people. The idea of natural law that Paul explains here helps us to establish a foundation for moral standards that cannot be undermined by the impulses of society or by what is culturally convenient or acceptable.

2:17–24 Paul's list of the privileges the Jews have is legitimate, and almost every one has explicit OT basis. The problem is not that the Jews are illegitimately boasting in what is not really theirs.

ing, do you steal?[q] 22You who say that people should not commit adultery, do you commit adultery? You who abhor idols, do you rob temples?[r] 23You who boast in the law,[s] do you dishonor God by breaking the law? 24As it is written: "God's name is blasphemed among the Gentiles because of you."[a][t]

25Circumcision has value if you observe the law,[u] but if you break the law, you have become as though you had not been circumcised.[v] 26So then, if those who are not circumcised keep the law's requirements,[w] will they not be regarded as though they were circumcised?[x] 27The one who is not circumcised physically and yet obeys the law will condemn you[y] who, even though you have the[b] written code and circumcision, are a lawbreaker.

28A person is not a Jew who is one only outwardly,[z] nor is circumcision merely outward and physical.[a] 29No, a person is a Jew who is one inwardly; and circumcision is circumcision of the heart, by the Spirit,[b] not by the written code.[c] Such a person's praise is not from other people, but from God.[d]

God's Faithfulness

3 What advantage, then, is there in being a Jew, or what value is there in circumcision? 2Much in every way! First of all, the Jews have been entrusted with the very words of God.[e]

3What if some were unfaithful?[f] Will their unfaithfulness nullify God's faithfulness?[g] 4Not at all! Let God be true,[h] and every human being a liar.[i] As it is written:

> "So that you may be proved right
> when you speak
> and prevail when you judge."[c][j]

5But if our unrighteousness brings out God's righteousness more clearly, what shall we say? That God is unjust in bringing his wrath on us? (I am using a human argument.)[k] 6Certainly not! If that were so, how could God judge the world?[l] 7Someone might argue, "If my

2:21 [q] Mt 23:3,4
2:22 [r] Ac 19:37
2:23 [s] ver 17
2:24 [t] Isa 52:5; Eze 36:22
2:25 [u] Gal 5:3 [v] Jer 4:4
2:26 [w] Ro 8:4 [x] 1Co 7:19
2:27 [y] Mt 12:41, 42
2:28 [z] Mt 3:9; Jn 8:39; Ro 9:6, 7 [a] Gal 6:15
2:29 [b] Php 3:3; Col 2:11 [c] Ro 7:6
[d] Jn 5:44; 1Co 4:5; 2Co 10:18; 1Th 2:4; 1Pe 3:4
3:2 [e] Dt 4:8; Ps 147:19
3:3 [f] Heb 4:2 [g] 2Ti 2:13
3:4 [h] Jn 3:33 [i] Ps 116:11 [j] Ps 51:4
3:5 [k] Ro 6:19; Gal 3:15
3:6 [l] Ge 18:25

[a] *24* Isaiah 52:5 (see Septuagint); Ezek. 36:20,22
[b] *27* Or *who, by means of a*
[c] *4* Psalm 51:4

The problem, rather, is that they are not living up to their claims.

In "natural revelation," the Gentiles have knowledge of God and are therefore "without excuse" when they sin (1:20). Jews have knowledge of God in the special revelation of God's law so that they, likewise, "have no excuse" (2:1) when they sin.

Paul now levels charges against the Jews. Only two points in these fairly obvious charges need comment.

2:22 What Paul means by accusing the Jews of robbing temples is unclear. The obvious interpretation, of course, is that the Jews are guilty of robbing pagan temples. We have some evidence that Jews at this time were relaxing the OT restraints against using precious metals melted down from idols. The action of robbing temples disregarded the Jews' God-directed abhorrence of idols.

2:23–24 Note the summarizing character of v. 23. Here is the essence of the matter for Paul: By failing to live by the qualities of the law they profess to love, the Jews fail to be the light God wants and harm God's reputation. Paul highlights this point in v. 24 with his quotation of Isa 52:5.

2:25 Next to the law, circumcision was the most important distinguishing mark of Jewishness, and Paul does not deny that "circumcision has value." But its value is contingent on obedience. Circumcision has no value to rescue Jews from God's wrath because their obedience never reaches the level required for salvation.

2:26 This verse draws a natural inference from v. 25: If following the law, not circumcision, is what saves, then uncircumcised Gentiles who obey the law can be saved.

2:28–29 These next verses are a kind of appendix to this argument. Paul has made clear that real Jewishness can never be determined by physical birth, by cuts on skin, or by devotion to a particular book. To be a "real Jew" in the sense of being set aside by God is an inward matter. It is marked by the "circumcision of the heart," a circumcision that comes in the context of the Spirit, not the "written code" (v. 29).

2:17–29 The potential for anti-Semitism lurks right around the corner when we are dealing with texts such as Ro 2. With Paul, we conclude that the Jewish people, like all people, need to hear and respond to the gospel. Indeed, if we are faithful to what Paul is teaching, we will acknowledge that Jews start in a position of advantage to Christians (3:1). But rescue from any sinner's plight, coming solely as a matter of God's grace, is nothing anyone can take any credit for.

3:1–2a Based on Paul's argument so far, when he asks in v. 1, "What advantage, then, is there in being a Jew," we expect the answer to be "none." But Paul surprises us (v. 2a).

3:2b–6 Paul wrestles with the common Jewish belief that God's "covenant faithfulness" gave the Jews virtual immunity from judgment. In response, Paul affirms that the blessing of knowing God's word (v. 2) is a double-edged sword. God's word promises blessing for obedience, but it also warns about consequences for disobedience. The ultimate standard of righteousness is God's own holy character, and that holy character requires him to respond to sin with wrath (v. 6).

3:7–8 But the Jewish objector is still not satisfied.

falsehood enhances God's truthfulness
and so increases his glory,[m] why am I
still condemned as a sinner?" 8 Why not
say—as some slanderously claim that
we say—"Let us do evil that good may
result"?[n] Their condemnation is just!

No One Is Righteous

9 What shall we conclude then? Do we
have any advantage? Not at all! For we
have already made the charge that Jews
and Gentiles alike are all under the power
of sin.[o] 10 As it is written:

"There is no one righteous, not even
one;
11 there is no one who understands;
there is no one who seeks God.
12 All have turned away,
they have together become
worthless;
there is no one who does good,
not even one."[a][p]
13 "Their throats are open graves;
their tongues practice deceit."[b][q]
"The poison of vipers is on their
lips."[c][r]
14 "Their mouths are full of cursing and
bitterness."[d][s]
15 "Their feet are swift to shed blood;
16 ruin and misery mark their ways,
17 and the way of peace they do not
know."[e]
18 "There is no fear of God before their
eyes."[f][t]

19 Now we know that whatever the
law says,[u] it says to those who are under the law,[v] so that every mouth may
be silenced and the whole world held
accountable to God. 20 Therefore no one
will be declared righteous in God's sight
by the works of the law;[w] rather, through
the law we become conscious of our sin.[x]

Righteousness Through Faith

21 But now apart from the law the righteousness of God[y] has been made known,
to which the Law and the Prophets testify.[z] 22 This righteousness is given through
faith[a] in[g] Jesus Christ to all who believe.
There is no difference between Jew and
Gentile,[b] 23 for all have sinned and fall
short of the glory of God, 24 and all are
justified freely by his grace[c] through the

3:7 [m] ver 4
3:8 [n] Ro 6:1
3:9 [o] ver 19, 23; Gal 3:22
3:12 [p] Ps 14:1-3
3:13 [q] Ps 5:9 [r] Ps 140:3
3:14 [s] Ps 10:7
3:18 [t] Ps 36:1
3:19 [u] Jn 10:34 [v] Ro 2:12
3:20 [w] Ac 13:39; Gal 2:16 [x] Ro 7:7
3:21 [y] Ro 1:17; 9:30 [z] Ac 10:43
3:22 [a] Ro 9:30 [b] Ro 10:12; Gal 3:28; Col 3:11
3:24 [c] Ro 4:16; Eph 2:8

[a] *12* Psalms 14:1-3; 53:1-3; Eccles. 7:20
[b] *13* Psalm 5:9 [c] *13* Psalm 140:3
[d] *14* Psalm 10:7 (see Septuagint)
[e] *17* Isaiah 59:7,8 [f] *18* Psalm 36:1 [g] *22* Or *through the faithfulness of*

It is unfair for God to condemn Jews for acts that enhance his glory. Paul responds with a counter-question, exposing the absurdity of that objection. If God should not condemn Jews when they sin because their sin enhances God's glory, then any sin is justified as long as it eventually brings good. Of course, this is nonsense. Paul says those who make such arguments are justly condemned.

✣ **3:1–8** The Jewish tendency to think that the covenant made them secure from the threat of divine judgment has parallels in the Christian church. Even genuine Christians can err in this matter. Believers should not so presume on their "security" that they fail to make every effort to bring their lives into obedience to Christ. We believe that God gives us everything we need to persevere in the Christian life. But we must also recognize that our personal effort, commitment, and dedication to the cause is also required.

3:9–20 Paul addresses the question, is there any basic difference between Jew and Gentile? His argument so far might lead people to think the Jew is actually worse off than the Gentile.
3:9 The "not at all!" makes clear that the distinction Paul denies here has to do with the specific issue of rescue from God's wrath. The exact phraseology is important: People do not just commit sin; they are "under sin."
3:10–18 Paul now moves to a series of OT quotations that demonstrate the universality of sin. In vv. 13–14, Paul focuses on sins of speech. Verses 15–17 list sins of violence against others. Verse 18 returns to where Paul began: basic human disregard for God.
3:19 Paul concludes that the Jews ("those . . . under the law") are accountable to God for the Law of Moses. Paul expands this conclusion: "every mouth" is "silenced"; the "whole world" is "accountable to God." Having demonstrated from the OT that Jews are condemned in their unrepentant sin, Paul extends that verdict to all people.
3:20 Paul realizes that Jews may argue that because of their relationship to God's law they are exempt from the verdict of judgment. Paul counters that the law is powerless to change the Jews' basic standing before God. Paul concludes by telling us what the law *does* accomplish. The law brings awareness of sinfulness by providing a detailed record of God's will.

✣ **3:9–20** People, by nature, are addicted to sin. They are imprisoned under it, unable to free themselves by anything they can do. Knowing this, God has sent to us not a teacher or a politician but a liberator who has the power to set us free from our sins.

3:21–22a Paul beautifully captures God's plan of salvation in just a few words. God reveals his righteousness in Christ "apart from" the Law of Moses. The Mosaic covenant cannot contain the "new wine" of the gospel. The entire OT testifies to this new work of God in Christ.
3:22b–23 Why does God's righteousness need to be available for "all who believe"? Because "all have sinned and fall short of the glory of God."

redemption[d] that came by Christ Jesus.
25God presented Christ as a sacrifice of
atonement,[a][e] through the shedding of
his blood[f] — to be received by faith. He
did this to demonstrate his righteousness, because in his forbearance he had
left the sins committed beforehand unpunished[g] — 26he did it to demonstrate
his righteousness at the present time, so
as to be just and the one who justifies
those who have faith in Jesus.
27Where, then, is boasting?[h] It is excluded. Because of what law? The law
that requires works? No, because of the
law that requires faith. 28For we maintain
that a person is justified by faith apart
from the works of the law.[i] 29Or is God
the God of Jews only? Is he not the God of
Gentiles too? Yes, of Gentiles too,[j] 30since
there is only one God, who will justify the
circumcised by faith and the uncircumcised through that same faith.[k] 31Do we,
then, nullify the law by this faith? Not at
all! Rather, we uphold the law.

3:24 [d] Eph 1:7, 14; Col 1:14; Heb 9:12
3:25 [e] 1Jn 4:10 [f] Heb 9:12,14 [g] Ac 17:30
3:27 [h] Ro 2:17, 23; 4:2; 1Co 1:29-31; Eph 2:9
3:28 [i] ver 20, 21; Ac 13:39; Eph 2:9
3:29 [j] Ro 9:24
3:30 [k] Gal 3:8

Ro 3:31 ❖ How does faith uphold the Law of Moses? Is Paul in favor of the law? Why or why not?

Abraham Justified by Faith

4 What then shall we say that Abraham, our forefather according to the

[a] 25 The Greek for *sacrifice of atonement* refers to the atonement cover on the ark of the covenant (see Lev. 16:15,16).

God's glory is his own awesome presence. God's people are destined to share in that glory.

3:24 The verb "justify" brings us back to the initial topic of God's "righteousness" (v. 21). We are justified by means of God's grace and on the basis of his redemptive work in Jesus Christ. "Grace" is a key theological idea in Paul. Everything God does for us is done freely and without compulsion. "Redemption" has the basic sense of "to liberate by paying a price."

3:25–26 The word translated "sacrifice of atonement" has been debated. In 21 of its 27 occurrences in the Greek OT, *this word* refers to the "atonement cover" of the ark where sacrificial blood was sprinkled (cf. Lev 16). The "atonement cover" represented the place where God took care of his people's sin problem.

In Ro 3:25b–26a, Paul explains why God brought redemption by giving up his own Son. He did it "to demonstrate his [God's] righteousness." Paul has used "righteousness" in vv. 21–22 to refer to the process by which God puts people right before him.

In the OT period, people who sinned deserved spiritual death. They did not have an adequate sacrifice to completely atone for their sins. In mercy, God "passed over" their sins. By giving himself as a "sacrifice of atonement," Christ paid the price for the sins of all people—both before his time (v. 25b) and after (v. 26a).

Consequently, God can be "just and the one who justifies those who have faith in Jesus" (v. 26b). He accepts sinners as righteous without violating his own just character because Christ has fully satisfied God's demand that all who commit sin must die. By faith in Christ, we are joined to him. He becomes our representative, and his death is credited to us.

✣ **3:21–26** A basic theme of Romans, coming to expression again and again in the letter, is the need for Christians to understand who they are. Paul will say much more on this subject in chs. 5–8. The great turning point in world history is the revelation of God's righteousness in Christ, inaugurating a new age in which a restored relationship with the God of the universe is available for everyone. We who believe in Jesus Christ alone for our salvation must remember who we are in Christ and act in a way that demonstrates to the world what we understand to be true.

3:27–28 As elsewhere in Romans, boasting in "works of the law" represents boasting in accomplishments. Verse 28 is a famous statement of the doctrine of justification by faith. Nothing a human being does will ever justify a person before God; only faith in Christ can do that.

3:29–30 These verses again assert that both Jews and Gentiles are equal before God. If there is only one God, then he is equally the God of Gentiles as well as Jews. Rightly understood, this demolishes any ultimate difference between Jew and Gentile before the Lord. Thus, God will justify both on the same basis: through faith.

3:31 Here Paul affirms the valid demand that God makes of people in the law. But Christ fulfills the law on our behalf. We who are in Christ are therefore counted as having fulfilled the law; we have been set free from its penalties for disobedience. Ironically, freedom from the law's condemnation puts us into a relationship of true obedience through the Holy Spirit.

✣ **3:27–31** It is appropriate to feel good about doing the right thing. However, the moment we think that our good works somehow obligate God to be favorably disposed toward us, we have moved from legitimate contentment to illegitimate boasting. All our works, however good they may be, are imperfect. Anything that advances the cause of God's kingdom is the product of God's grace as his Spirit moves in us.

4:1–8 One of Paul's purposes in Romans is to demonstrate that the gospel is inseparably linked with the OT. Proving that the story of Abraham fits into Paul's conception of salvation history is an important step toward this goal.

4:1–2 Having introduced Abraham in v. 1, Paul now moves directly to the attack. Some Jews argued that Abraham was justified by his works and had something to boast about. Paul immediately responds to this line of argument: "but not

Ro 4:2 ❖ Why would justification and forgiveness based on works inevitably lead to boasting? Why does God not base justification on works?

flesh, discovered in this matter? 2If, in
fact, Abraham was justified by works,
he had something to boast about — but
not before God.[l] 3What does Scripture
say? "Abraham believed God, and it was
credited to him as righteousness."[a][m]
4Now to the one who works, wages are
not credited as a gift[n] but as an obligation. 5However, to the one who does not
work but trusts God who justifies the
ungodly, their faith is credited as righteousness. 6David says the same thing
when he speaks of the blessedness of the
one to whom God credits righteousness
apart from works:

7"Blessed are those
whose transgressions are forgiven,
whose sins are covered.
8Blessed is the one
whose sin the Lord will never
count against them."[b][o]

4:2 [l] 1Co 1:31
4:3 [m] ver 5,9, 22; Ge 15:6; Gal 3:6; Jas 2:23
4:4 [n] Ro 11:6
4:8 [o] Ps 32:1,2; 2Co 5:19
4:9 [p] Ro 3:30 [q] ver 3
4:11 [r] Ge 17:10, 11 [s] ver 16,17; Lk 19:9 [t] Ro 3:22
4:13 [u] Gal 3:16, 29 [v] Ge 17:4-6
4:14 [w] Gal 3:18

9Is this blessedness only for the circumcised, or also for the uncircumcised?[p]
We have been saying that Abraham's
faith was credited to him as righteousness.[q] 10Under what circumstances was it
credited? Was it after he was circumcised,
or before? It was not after, but before!
11And he received circumcision as a sign,
a seal of the righteousness that he had by
faith while he was still uncircumcised.[r]
So then, he is the father[s] of all who believe[t] but have not been circumcised, in
order that righteousness might be credited to them. 12And he is then also the
father of the circumcised who not only
are circumcised but who also follow in
the footsteps of the faith that our father
Abraham had before he was circumcised.
13It was not through the law that
Abraham and his offspring received the
promise[u] that he would be heir of the
world,[v] but through the righteousness
that comes by faith. 14For if those who
depend on the law are heirs, faith means
nothing and the promise is worthless,[w]

[a] *3* Gen. 15:6; also in verse 22 [b] *8* Psalm 32:1,2

---

before God." This response means something like, "From God's perspective, Abraham had no right at all to boast because he was not, and could not be, justified by works."

4:3 Paul grounds this response in Scripture. Paul reads Ge 15:6 as a summary of Abraham's response to God's promise to him generally. The Hebrew construction in this verse suggests that "crediting" Abraham's faith to him as righteousness means "to account to him a righteousness that does not inherently belong to him." When Abraham believed God, God granted him the status of "righteous."

4:4–8 In vv. 4–5, Paul explains the nature of this crediting. Verses 6–8 furnish further Scriptural support. Paul assumes that God always relates to his creatures by grace. He never argues the point because it is self-evident. Paul's description of the Christian as one who "does not work" (v. 5) refers to the fact that Christians do not base their relationship to God on their actions. Paul then quotes Ps 32:1–2a. In these verses, David joins his testimony to that of Moses. Here we find the heart of the Good News: God accepts us, through our faith, just as we are.

✣ **4:1–8** If God justifies us while we are "wicked," why should we bother trying to lead holy lives? Paul insists that God does more than "justify" us when we become Christians. He causes his Spirit to live within us (Ro 8:9-11). This changes us from within. But becoming a Christian is first and foremost a change in our status before God. Sentenced to eternal death because of sin, God intervenes in a sheer act of grace and declares us innocent before him.

4:9–10 The "blessedness" Paul mentions refers to acceptance before God. Is this acceptance available to Jews and Gentiles? In v. 10, Paul answers that question by noting the timing between God's pronouncement of Abraham's righteousness (Ge 15:6) and the institution of circumcision (Ge 17). The righteousness, Paul points out, came first.

4:11a Paul goes on to explain that circumcision simply put a seal on what was already true.

4:11b–12 Gentiles who have faith can claim Abraham as their father. They believe as he did, and they receive, as he did, righteousness as a gift from God.

✣ **4:9–12** Paul argues that Gentiles are included in God's grace by faith. In doing this, Paul removes all outward distinctions in the face of God's grace. The offer of the gospel is universal. Thus, the church is called to be a genuinely countercultural institution. Barriers like race, national background, and/or economic status are irrelevant.

4:13 Genesis repeatedly mentions the fact that Abraham will be a blessing to all the world. Jewish interpreters highlighted the ethnic element in this promise. Thus, Paul's focus on "the world" emphasizes that Abraham is the father of all who believe (vv. 11–12).

As we have noted, many of Paul's Jewish contemporaries taught that Abraham's stature and role had to do with his obedience to the Law of Moses. Paul wants to make clear that the promise came not because Abraham obeyed the law but because of "the righteousness that comes by faith."

4:14–15 Abraham and his descendants could never have inherited God's promised blessings through

15because the law brings wrath.[x] And
where there is no law there is no transgression.[y]
16Therefore, the promise comes by
faith, so that it may be by grace[z] and
may be guaranteed[a] to all Abraham's
offspring — not only to those who are
of the law but also to those who have
the faith of Abraham. He is the father
of us all. 17As it is written: "I have made
you a father of many nations."[ab] He is
our father in the sight of God, in whom
he believed — the God who gives life[c]
to the dead and calls[d] into being things
that were not.[e]
18Against all hope, Abraham in hope
believed and so became the father of
many nations,[f] just as it had been said
to him, "So shall your offspring be."[bg]
19Without weakening in his faith, he
faced the fact that his body was as good
as dead[h] — since he was about a hundred
years old[i] — and that Sarah's womb was
also dead.[j] 20Yet he did not waver through
unbelief regarding the promise of God,
but was strengthened in his faith and
gave glory to God,[k] 21being fully persuaded that God had power to do what he had
promised.[l] 22This is why "it was credited
to him as righteousness."[m] 23The words
"it was credited to him" were written not
for him alone, 24but also for us,[n] to whom
God will credit righteousness — for us
who believe in him[o] who raised Jesus our
Lord from the dead.[p] 25He was delivered
over to death for our sins[q] and was raised
to life for our justification.

Peace and Hope

5 Therefore, since we have been justified through faith,[r] we[c] have peace
with God through our Lord Jesus Christ,
2through whom we have gained access[s]
by faith into this grace in which we now
stand.[t] And we[d] boast in the hope[u] of the
glory of God. 3Not only so, but we[d] also
glory in our sufferings,[v] because we know
that suffering produces perseverance;[w]

4:15 [x] Ro 7:7-25; 1Co 15:56; 2Co 3:7; Gal 3:10; Ro 7:12 [y] Ro 3:20; 7:7
4:16 [z] Ro 3:24 [a] Ro 15:8
4:17 [b] Ge 17:5 [c] Jn 5:21 [d] Isa 48:13 [e] 1Co 1:28
4:18 [f] ver 17 [g] Ge 15:5
4:19 [h] Heb 11:11, 12 [i] Ge 17:17 [j] Ge 18:11
4:20 [k] Mt 9:8
4:21 [l] Ge 18:14; Heb 11:19
4:22 [m] ver 3
4:24 [n] Ro 15:4; 1Co 9:10; 10:11 [o] Ro 10:9 [p] Ac 2:24
4:25 [q] Isa 53:5, 6; Ro 5:6, 8
5:1 [r] Ro 3:28
5:2 [s] Eph 2:18 [t] 1Co 15:1 [u] Heb 3:6
5:3 [v] Mt 5:12 [w] Jas 1:2, 3

[a] *17* Gen. 17:5 [b] *18* Gen. 15:5 [c] *1* Many manuscripts *let us* [d] *2,3* Or *let us*

---

the law. If the fulfillment of the promise depends on obedience to the law, it will never happen, for people can never obey the law adequately.

In the first part of v. 15, Paul demonstrates the point he made in v. 14: The law "brings wrath." Jews typically viewed the Mosaic Law as one of the greatest blessings ever given by God. How can Paul claim that the law has produced wrath? The end of v. 15 provides the answer: "Where there is no law there is no transgression." Anytime we fall short of conformity to God's image, we sin. When we directly violate a commandment God has given us, we commit a transgression. Transgression is a more serious form of sin and deserves greater judgment.

4:16–17 "Offspring" is a word that's important in both the Genesis promise passages and in Paul. At the end of v. 16, Paul specifies the two groups that make up this spiritual family of Abraham: "those who are of the law" and "those who have the faith of Abraham." His concern is to show that the promise to Abraham is valid for all believers.

The end of v. 17 alludes to God's miraculously bringing life out of the "dead" womb of Sarah (v. 19). By describing God as the One who "calls into being things that were not" (v. 17), Paul is describing this same miracle from another angle.

4:18–22 From a human standpoint, there was no hope that Abraham and Sarah would ever have children. Still, Abraham did not "waver through unbelief regarding the promise of God" (v. 20a). Abraham glorified God because he took him at his word (vv. 20b–21). This is why, Paul concludes, "it [faith] was credited to him as righteousness" (v. 22).

✤ **4:13–22** In our achievement-oriented world, giving faith its necessary central place in our lives is not always easy to do. We are tempted to ground our relationship to God in what we do. Paul explains that God accepts us not because of what we do but because we have humbled ourselves before him and have received from him the gift of salvation.

4:23–25 As Paul draws his exposition to an end, he makes explicit what has been implicit throughout, that these realities have direct application to Christians. Paul often describes God as the One who raised Jesus from the dead, but he rarely makes God the object of our belief. He does so here to make Christian faith as similar to Abraham's faith as possible. In v. 25, Paul adds a description of this Jesus whom God raised from the dead.

✤ **4:23–25** In our day, God has definitively revealed himself in Jesus Christ. Were Abraham alive today, he could not be saved apart from faith in God as revealed in Christ. Thus, we must also conclude that only people who believe in this particular God as revealed in Christ have hope for salvation.

5:1 "Peace" is the objective state of harmony with God that believers who have been justified enjoy.

5:2–4 Another wonderful result of our justification is "access by faith into this grace in which we now stand" (v. 2). "Grace" here is a state in which the believer lives. God's free giving to us does not stop when we become Christians.

The verb for "boast" suggests both the idea of "taking confidence in" and "rejoicing in." Paul introduces the theme of this paragraph: the hope Christians have to share in God's glory. He acknowledges that Christians will continue to suffer. But life's difficulties do not discount the wonderful

Ro 5:3–5 ❖ How have certain sufferings in our lives produced positive results for our faith? What is the relationship between suffering and hope?

4perseverance, character; and character, hope. 5And hope[x] does not put us
to shame, because God's love has been
poured out into our hearts through the
Holy Spirit,[y] who has been given to us.
6You see, at just the right time,[z] when
we were still powerless, Christ died for
the ungodly.[a] 7Very rarely will anyone
die for a righteous person, though for
a good person someone might possibly
dare to die. 8But God demonstrates his
own love for us in this: While we were
still sinners, Christ died for us.[b]
9Since we have now been justified by
his blood,[c] how much more shall we be
saved from God's wrath[d] through him!
10For if, while we were God's enemies,[e]
we were reconciled[f] to him through the
death of his Son, how much more, having been reconciled, shall we be saved
through his life![g] 11Not only is this so, but
we also boast in God through our Lord
Jesus Christ, through whom we have now
received reconciliation.

Death Through Adam, Life Through Christ

12Therefore, just as sin entered the
world through one man,[h] and death
through sin,[i] and in this way death came
to all people, because all sinned—
13To be sure, sin was in the world before
the law was given, but sin is not charged
against anyone's account where there is
no law.[j] 14Nevertheless, death reigned
from the time of Adam to the time of
Moses, even over those who did not sin
by breaking a command, as did Adam,
who is a pattern of the one to come.[k]
15But the gift is not like the trespass. For
if the many died by the trespass of the one
man,[l] how much more did God's grace and
the gift that came by the grace of the one
man, Jesus Christ,[m] overflow to the many!
16Nor can the gift of God be compared with
the result of one man's sin: The judgment
followed one sin and brought condemnation, but the gift followed many trespasses
and brought justification. 17For if, by the
trespass of the one man, death[n] reigned

5:5 [x] Php 1:20 [y] Ac 2:33
5:6 [z] Gal 4:4 [a] Ro 4:25
5:8 [b] Jn 15:13; 1Pe 3:18
5:9 [c] Ro 3:25 [d] Ro 1:18
5:10 [e] Ro 11:28; Col 1:21 [f] 2Co 5:18,19; Col 1:20,22 [g] Ro 8:34
5:12 [h] ver 15,16, 17; 1Co 15:21,22 [i] Ge 2:17; 3:19; Ro 6:23
5:13 [j] Ro 4:15
5:14 [k] 1Co 15:22, 45
5:15 [l] ver 12,18, 19 [m] Ac 15:11
5:17 [n] ver 12

---

blessings of being a Christian. God uses them to bring us even greater blessing.

The key is in the way we respond to the difficult trials that come our way. God uses them to build into our lives "perseverance," which, in turn, leads to "character." Then we can truly rejoice in the midst of suffering, knowing that God is at work, bringing us blessing. Suffering can actually lead to "hope" (v. 4). Just as resistance to a muscle strengthens it, so challenges to our hope can strengthen it.

5:5–8 Believers can be certain they will receive what they hope for. How? Paul gives two reasons: God's love for us in Christ (vv. 5b–8) and God's work for us in Christ (vv. 9–10). The Spirit's dwelling in the hearts of believers communicates God's love to us.

Alongside this subjective evidence of God's love, we have objective proof in the cross of Christ (v. 6). Paul reinforces the point in v. 7 with an analogy. A "righteous" person is one we might respect, but a "good" person is one we might love. God's awesome love is seen in that Christ died for us while we were "still sinners"—hating God, in rebellion against him (v. 8).

5:9–11 These verses remind us what God has already done for us through the death of Christ: He "justified" us (v. 9) and "reconciled" us to himself (v. 10). Paul interchanges "justify" and "reconcile" in his argument, two ways of describing what happens when God first accepts us. He declares us innocent ("justify"), and he removes the hostility that existed between us and him because of that sin ("reconcile"). The former is a judicial idea, the latter a relational one. Paul also claims that being "saved" comes *after* we are justified and reconciled. Paul often uses "salvation" to depict the believer's final deliverance on the last day.

✚ **5:1–11** Everything that a Christian suffers is on behalf of Christ. All suffering betrays the presence of the enemy and attacks our relationship with Christ. The suffering Paul mentions in v. 3 is likely related to the trials he lists in 8:35.

5:12 Paul thinks of death as both physical and spiritual: separation from the body and estrangement from God. Both are the result of sin. That a physical element is present in death is evident from vv. 13–14. But in vv. 18–19, Paul shows that his focus is on spiritual death.

The second two clauses of v. 12 emphasize the universal extent of this progression of sin and death. Death affects all people because all people have "sinned." Sin and the spiritual death that results from it are universal.

5:13–14 Here Paul is *reinforcing* his teaching about the universality of death. Many Jews believed that there could be no sin or death apart from the law. Paul insists sin existed before the Mosaic Law was given. Therefore, people were condemned for their sin. The presence of the law turns sin into transgression (v. 14). Sin may not be charged to one's individual account (v. 13b) apart from law. But sin is still sin and brings God's condemnation.

5:15–17 At the end of v. 14, Paul expresses the premise on which the whole argument of vv. 12–21 is built: Adam was a "pattern" of Christ. Before he demonstrates the similarities between these two,

through that one man, how much more
will those who receive God's abundant
provision of grace and of the gift of righteousness reign in life through the one
man, Jesus Christ!
18 Consequently, just as one trespass resulted in condemnation for all people,[o] so
also one righteous act resulted in justification[p] and life for all people. 19 For just
as through the disobedience of the one
man[q] the many were made sinners, so
also through the obedience[r] of the one
man the many will be made righteous.
20 The law was brought in so that the
trespass might increase.[s] But where sin
increased, grace increased all the more,[t]
21 so that, just as sin reigned in death,[u]
so also grace might reign through righteousness to bring eternal life through
Jesus Christ our Lord.

Dead to Sin, Alive in Christ

6 What shall we say, then? Shall we
go on sinning so that grace may increase?[v] 2 By no means! We are those who
have died to sin;[w] how can we live in it any
longer? 3 Or don't you know that all of us
who were baptized[x] into Christ Jesus were
baptized into his death? 4 We were therefore buried with him through baptism
into death in order that, just as Christ was
raised from the dead[y] through the glory
of the Father, we too may live a new life.[z]
5 For if we have been united with him
in a death like his, we will certainly also
be united with him in a resurrection
like his.[a] 6 For we know that our old self[b]
was crucified with him[c] so that the body
ruled by sin[d] might be done away with,[a]
that we should no longer be slaves to
sin— 7 because anyone who has died has
been set free from sin.

5:18 [o] ver 12 [p] Ro 4:25
5:19 [q] ver 12 [r] Php 2:8
5:20 [s] Ro 7:7, 8; Gal 3:19 [t] 1Ti 1:13,14
5:21 [u] ver 12,14
6:1 [v] ver 15; Ro 3:5,8
6:2 [w] Col 3:3,5; 1Pe 2:24
6:3 [x] Mt 28:19
6:4 [y] Col 2:12 [z] Ro 7:6; Gal 6:15; Eph 4:22-24; Col 3:10
6:5 [a] 2Co 4:10; Php 3:10,11
6:6 [b] Eph 4:22; Col 3:9 [c] Gal 2:20; Col 2:12,20 [d] Ro 7:24

Ro 6:2 ❖ What does it mean to die to sin? How can this be accomplished?

[a] 6 Or *be rendered powerless*

Paul notes some differences. These differences boil down to one fact: In Christ, God deals with people on the basis of grace.

The word "grace" and the related word "gift" occur seven times in these three verses. What happened because of Adam's sin is a matter of us getting what our sins deserve. "Death" (vv. 15, 17), "judgment," and "condemnation" (v. 16) inevitably and justly follow sin. But what has happened because of Christ is quite different. In place of condemnation, Christ brings "justification" (v. 16). Condemnation came because of "one sin," but justification "followed many trespasses" (v. 16). In this, Paul concludes, we see the evidence of God's overwhelming grace.

Christ more than cancels the effects of Adam's sin. He enables those who have received the "abundant provision of grace" and "the gift of righteousness" to "reign in life" (v. 17).

5:18–19 In vv. 18–19 Paul returns to the idea of v. 12 and completes it. Verses 18–19 are similar in structure. Each features Adam in the first ("just as") clause and Christ in the second ("so also") clause. Each contrasts what Adam did with what Christ did. Where Adam turned away from God and violated his commandment, Christ turned toward God and continually did the will of his Father. Each verse also contrasts the results of Adam's sin with the results of Christ's obedience.

5:20–21 The law did not bring relief from sin and death; instead, it made it worse. The Mosaic Law, by making people accountable to a detailed series of commandments, brings greater judgment on those sins.

But God's grace has more than compensated. Under Adam, sin and death hold sway over us. But "through righteousness," that is, as a result of being justified, "grace . . . reigns" (v. 21). If we are confident that sin has brought devastation, we can be even more confident that God's grace will also save us from his wrath in the judgment.

✣ **5:12–21** The Christian faith offers a succinct and convincing explanation for the human condition. Original sin may not make sense to many people; they may find it irrational or even unjust. But what better explanation for the extent and persistence of "crimes against humanity"? The sin of Adam brought corruption and death; the grace of God through Jesus' sacrifice offers the potential for people to claim that salvation and have the curse of Adam removed from their lives for all eternity.

6:1–5 When someone becomes a Christian, their change of state in relationship to sin is as dramatic as a change from life to death. In vv. 3–5, Paul shows how in baptism, we are joined to Christ and to his death and resurrection.

Paul refers to water baptism as the point in time at which people become joined with Christ (v. 3). When we were baptized "into" Christ, we were baptized "into his death." Verse 4 elaborates. Paul uses the verb "buried" because he is thinking of the way the Christian is identified with Christ in the events of his redemptive work (cf. 1Co 15:3–4). The effects of these events are at work in us. That means we now have the ability to "live a new life" (Ro 6:4b).

Believers not only participate in Christ's death (dying to sin), but also in his resurrection (receiving new life). Paul uses a future tense to describe our participation in the resurrection (v. 5): While we do indeed now enjoy new life, our being "raised" with Christ awaits his second coming (cf. Php 3:20–21).

6:6–7 The phrase "old self" is Paul's way of referring to what we were in Adam. Our identification with Christ means we are no longer dominated by sin.

KEY THEMES IN ROMANS

THEME	THE GOSPEL	JUSTIFICATION BY FAITH	UNION WITH CHRIST	SALVATION HISTORY FOR JEWS AND GENTILES	CHURCH UNITY
References in Romans	1:16-17	1-4	6-8	9-11	14:1—15:13
Pauline Parallels	1Co 15:1-11; 2Co 11:1-4; Gal 1:6-11; Eph 3:1-3; Col 1:21-23; 1Th 2:9-14; 2Th 2:13-15; 1Ti 1:3-11; 2Ti 1:8-14	1Co 6:9-11; Gal 2:15—5:6; Eph 2:8-9	1Co 12; 2Co 5:14-21; Gal 2:17-21; 3:23-29; Eph 1:3-14; Php 3:8-16; Col 2:8-15; 3:1-4	1Co 1:20-25; Gal 2:15-16; 3:7-29; Eph 2:11—3:6; Col 3:4	1Co 11:17—14:40; Gal 5:13—6:10; Eph 4; Php 2:1-11; Col 3:5-17

See D. A. Carson, Douglas J. Moo, and Leon Morris, *An Introduction to the New Testament* (Grand Rapids: Zondervan, 1992), 253-55.

8 Now if we died with Christ, we believe
that we will also live with him. 9 For we
know that since Christ was raised from
the dead,[e] he cannot die again; death
no longer has mastery over him.[f] 10 The
death he died, he died to sin[g] once for
all; but the life he lives, he lives to God.
11 In the same way, count yourselves
dead to sin[h] but alive to God in Christ
Jesus. 12 Therefore do not let sin reign
in your mortal body so that you obey
its evil desires. 13 Do not offer any part
of yourself to sin as an instrument of
wickedness,[i] but rather offer yourselves
to God as those who have been brought
from death to life; and offer every part
of yourself to him as an instrument of
righteousness.[j] 14 For sin shall no longer
be your master, because you are not under the law,[k] but under grace.[l]

6:9 [e]Ac 2:24 [f]Rev 1:18
6:10 [g]ver 2
6:11 [h]ver 2
6:13 [i]ver 16,19; Ro 7:5 [j]Ro 12:1; 1Pe 2:24
6:14 [k]Gal 5:18 [l]Ro 3:24

Slaves to Righteousness

15 What then? Shall we sin because we
are not under the law but under grace?

6:8-9 Living with Christ automatically follows claiming his death as our own and "dying" with him. Christ's resurrection means death has no power over him. We who belong to him also have the assurance of conquering death.

6:10 Why would Christ, the sinless one, have to "die to sin"? In his identification with humanity, Jesus was subject to the power of sin. He was therefore tempted as we are (cf. Heb 2:14–17). In this sense, he, too, needed to "die" to sin's power.

6:11-13 What God has done for us is the basis and motivation for what we need to do for God. Paul tells us of the wonderful redemptive events, then tells us how we are to respond to those events. We can only live out our new status by seeing ourselves as people who really have died to sin and been made alive in Christ.

6:14 Paul claims that sin is no longer our master. Yet he commands us not to let sin reign. We must apply our victory in Christ to our everyday lives. Verse 13 makes the same point in a different way.

Paul concludes with one more reminder: "Sin shall no longer be your master." Paul emphasizes that our freedom from sin's power is a continuing state we can look forward to enjoying forever. Why is this? "Because you are not under the law, but under grace."

Because we stand under the new covenant, the law of the old covenant no longer has direct control over us. The contrast between "law" and "grace" is a salvation-historical contrast: The Mosaic Law dominates the old regime from which we have been set free in Christ; grace dominates the new regime inaugurated by Jesus.

6:1-14 Baptism is an important part of the conversion experience. To use biblical imagery, it sets a seal on that experience. Thus, baptism in water should probably be administered to a person as shortly as possible after that person's coming to faith in Christ. Acts 8 is instructive in this regard. After bringing the Ethiopian court official to faith, Philip does not enroll him in a series of baptismal classes; he baptizes him, out in the middle of the desert, right on the spot (Ac 8:36–38). Acts 6:4 calls us to similar action.

6:15 Proclaiming that believers have been transferred from the rule of law to the rule of grace may lead some Christians to think that sin does not matter.

By no means! 16Don't you know that when you offer yourselves to someone as obedient slaves, you are slaves of the one you obey—whether you are slaves to sin,[m] which leads to death,[n] or to obedience, which leads to righteousness? 17But thanks be to God[o] that, though you used to be slaves to sin, you have come to obey from your heart the pattern of teaching[p] that has now claimed your allegiance. 18You have been set free from sin[q] and have become slaves to righteousness.

19I am using an example from everyday life[r] because of your human limitations. Just as you used to offer yourselves as slaves to impurity and to ever-increasing wickedness, so now offer yourselves as slaves to righteousness[s] leading to holiness. 20When you were slaves to sin,[t] you were free from the control of righteousness. 21What benefit did you reap at that time from the things you are now ashamed of? Those things result in death![u] 22But now that you have been set free from sin[v] and have become slaves of God,[w] the benefit you reap leads to holiness, and the result is eternal life. 23For the wages of sin is death,[x] but the gift of God is eternal life[y] in[a] Christ Jesus our Lord.

Released From the Law, Bound to Christ

7 Do you not know, brothers and sisters[z]—for I am speaking to those who know the law—that the law has authority over someone only as long as that person lives? 2For example, by law a married woman is bound to her husband as long as he is alive, but if her husband dies, she is released from the law that binds her to him.[a] 3So then, if she has sexual relations with another man while her husband is still alive, she is called an adulteress. But if her husband dies, she is released from that law and is not an adulteress if she marries another man.

4So, my brothers and sisters, you also died to the law[b] through the body of Christ,[c] that you might belong to another, to him who was raised from the dead, in order that we might bear fruit

6:16 [m] Jn 8:34; 2Pe 2:19 [n] ver 23
6:17 [o] Ro 1:8; 2Co 2:14 [p] 2Ti 1:13
6:18 [q] ver 7, 22; Ro 8:2
6:19 [r] Ro 3:5 [s] ver 13
6:20 [t] ver 16
6:21 [u] ver 23
6:22 [v] ver 18 [w] 1Co 7:22; 1Pe 2:16
6:23 [x] Ge 2:17; Ro 5:12; Gal 6:7, 8; Jas 1:15 [y] Mt 25:46
7:1 [z] Ro 1:13
7:2 [a] 1Co 7:39
7:4 [b] Ro 8:2; Gal 2:19 [c] Col 1:22

[a] 23 Or *through*

6:16 Paul heightens the seriousness of the issue by making it clear we must choose between two masters: sin or obedience. Serving sin leads to death, but serving obedience "leads to righteousness." Righteousness is conduct that is pleasing to God.
6:17 Paul reminds us we now have a choice. "Thanks . . . to God," believers have left slavery to sin.
6:18 Here Paul summarizes the believer's transfer from one realm to another: from "sin" to "righteousness." We have been made "slaves" of the moral conduct God expects of his people.
6:19 "Human limitations" (v. 19) is from the same Greek word Paul customarily uses to describe the human condition apart from God. He explains that the limitations of our human understanding require him to use imprecise, but still appropriate, analogies.

Verse 19b is the center of this paragraph. Paul reminds us of the new situation God has put us in (vv. 17–18) and further reminds us of that same status immediately after (vv. 20–23). But, as in vv. 1–14, Paul does not want us to think that God's gracious acts undermine or cancel the need for our response. Using the same verb as he did in v. 13, Paul again appeals to us to "offer" all our capacities and abilities (v. 19).

"Holiness" describes either the *state* of holiness or the *process* of sanctification. Our commitment to "righteousness" results in becoming more holy, or more like Christ. Because we have come to know God's grace, our commitment to righteousness should be as strong as our previous commitment to "wickedness."
6:20–23 If we are not serving God, then, whether knowingly or not, we are serving sin, and Paul reminds us of the shame we feel for what we used to do (v. 21). Verse 23 explains the contrasting "outcomes" of death and life and brings the chapter to a fitting conclusion.

6:15–23 In ch. 6 Paul regularly reinforces our responsibility for winning the battle against sin. Yet one thing is clear in Romans: God takes the initiative. In grace, God acts to help his people and asks them to respond. Paul in effect calls Christians to "become what they are."

At the same time, God's acts on our behalf are not finished. He has more things to give us and to accomplish in us. This means that we can also speak of "becoming what we will be." What God will one day make us should motivate us to get as close to that ideal as possible.

7:1 This section begins with a general principle: "The law has authority over someone only as long as that person lives." "Law" refers to the Mosaic Law throughout this context. This does not mean, however, that Paul addresses only Jewish Christians. Many of the Gentile Christians would have known the Mosaic Law as well as Jewish Christians did.
7:2–3 Paul wants to show that death can indeed bring freedom from the law; at the same time, he hints that such freedom can also lead to a new relationship.
7:4 Here in the heart of the paragraph, Paul draws an inference from vv. 1–3: Believers have not only been released from bondage to sin, they have also been released from bondage to the Mosaic Law. This release was accomplished through Jesus' death on the cross. The era of the law has come to an end with the redemptive work of Christ. We are freed from the law and joined to Christ so that we can "bear fruit for God."

for God. 5For when we were in the realm
of the flesh,[a] the sinful passions aroused
by the law[d] were at work in us,[e] so that we
bore fruit for death. 6But now, by dying
to what once bound us, we have been
released from the law so that we serve
in the new way of the Spirit, and not in
the old way of the written code.[f]

The Law and Sin

7What shall we say, then? Is the law sinful? Certainly not! Nevertheless, I would
not have known what sin was had it not
been for the law.[g] For I would not have
known what coveting really was if the
law had not said, "You shall not covet."[b][h]
8But sin, seizing the opportunity afforded
by the commandment,[i] produced in me
every kind of coveting. For apart from the
law, sin was dead.[j] 9Once I was alive apart
from the law; but when the commandment came, sin sprang to life and I died.
10I found that the very commandment
that was intended to bring life[k] actually
brought death. 11For sin, seizing the opportunity afforded by the commandment,
deceived me,[l] and through the commandment put me to death. 12So then, the law
is holy, and the commandment is holy,
righteous and good.[m]

13Did that which is good, then, become
death to me? By no means! Nevertheless,
in order that sin might be recognized as
sin, it used what is good to bring about
my death, so that through the commandment sin might become utterly sinful.

7:5 [d] Ro 7:7-11 [e] Ro 6:13
7:6 [f] Ro 2:29; 2Co 3:6
7:7 [g] Ro 3:20; 4:15 [h] Ex 20:17; Dt 5:21
7:8 [i] ver 11 [j] Ro 4:15; 1Co 15:56
7:10 [k] Lev 18:5; Lk 10:26-28; Ro 10:5; Gal 3:12
7:11 [l] Ge 3:13
7:12 [m] 1Ti 1:8

[a] 5 In contexts like this, the Greek word for *flesh* (*sarx*) refers to the sinful state of human beings, often presented as a power in opposition to the Spirit. [b] 7 Exodus 20:17; Deut. 5:21

7:5 To be "in the flesh" is to make decisions and behave without any regard for God or for what he calls us to do and be. The results of doing so are obvious: "sinful passions" and "death." The Law of Moses did not bring relief from the pattern of sin and death. Those sinful passions were "aroused by the law" by inspiring rebellion. This is why a person must be released from that law (v. 4) if he or she is to serve God.

7:6 This is precisely the situation in the new regime: We have died "to what once bound us."

✤ **7:1–6** We cannot restrict Paul's claim that believers have been "released from the law" (v. 2) to a certain function of the law or to certain parts of the law. The believer has been set free from the commanding authority of the Mosaic Law—period. What this means in practice is that no part of the Mosaic Law stands any longer as a direct and unmediated guide to Christian living. Christians are free from the law of the old covenant because we now belong to the new covenant.

We might ask, what about teachings like the Ten Commandments? Except in the case of Sabbath observance, in the NT those commandments express God's moral will for us as Christians under the new covenant. Those teachings, properly interpreted, are to be obeyed. This does not mean that we should no longer read the OT or try to integrate the moral imperatives of the Mosaic Law. It remains God's word, given, as is all Scripture, for our enlightenment (2Ti 3:16).

Although the believer under the new covenant does not stand directly under OT law, that law itself serves an important function in helping us understand our obligations. NT teachings are informed by the OT law. For instance, the NT prohibits unlawful sexual conduct. But what is included in such illegitimate sexual conduct? The NT writers do not spell it out because the scope of this conduct has already been clearly defined in the OT law. Thus, we continue to read the OT law as a guide to our interpretation of NT law.

7:7–12 Paul anticipates a key objection to his presentation of the gospel. He seems to imply in verses like 5:20 and 7:5 that the law is an evil thing. Paul resolutely denies any such idea, restating the point positively in v. 12.

7:7 Paul claims he came to "know" sin through the law and uses the tenth commandment to illustrate. The Mosaic Law helped him come to understand clearly the extent and seriousness of his sin.

7:8–10 Paul takes the argument one step further. Not only did he come to understand sin through the law, but he also was led into greater sinning through that same law. A prohibition can stimulate a rebellious reaction in sinful people: When we're told not to do something, we desire all the more to do it.

As he has made clear throughout this letter to the Romans, the giving of the law meant not "life" but "death" for Israel. Their sin was exposed and magnified, and greater wrath came on them (4:15; 5:20).

7:11–12 Sin has used the law to bring death to Israel. But the law is innocent; it provides the "opportunity" only (v. 11). The law is not sin (v. 7); it is "holy, righteous and good" (v. 12).

✤ **7:7–12** Most people have their own code of morality they try to live up to. But whatever that code may be, the sinful condition of all people renders it impossible to obey. We always fall short of the law. The law reveals the power of sin, our own helplessness, and the need for someone to liberate us from our miserable state.

7:13 The law becomes an instrument that sin uses to bring death. The form of the verse suggests that it introduces what follows, which is Paul's new focus: the problem with "me."

[14]We know that the law is spiritual; but
I am unspiritual,[n] sold[o] as a slave to sin.
[15]I do not understand what I do. For what
I want to do I do not do, but what I hate
I do.[p] [16]And if I do what I do not want to
do, I agree that the law is good.[q] [17]As it is,
it is no longer I myself who do it, but it is
sin living in me.[r] [18]For I know that good
itself does not dwell in me, that is, in my
sinful nature.[a][s] For I have the desire to
do what is good, but I cannot carry it out.
[19]For I do not do the good I want to do,
but the evil I do not want to do — this I
keep on doing.[t] [20]Now if I do what I do
not want to do, it is no longer I who do
it, but it is sin living in me that does it.[u]
[21]So I find this law at work:[v] Although
I want to do good, evil is right there with
me. [22]For in my inner being[w] I delight
in God's law;[x] [23]but I see another law at
work in me, waging war[y] against the law
of my mind and making me a prisoner of the law of sin at work within me.
[24]What a wretched man I am! Who will
rescue me from this body that is subject
to death?[z] [25]Thanks be to God, who delivers me through Jesus Christ our Lord!

Ro 7:18-20 ❖ How can we find the power to do the good we want to do? Why is this so difficult?

So then, I myself in my mind am a
slave to God's law, but in my sinful nature[b] a slave to the law of sin.

Life Through the Spirit

8 Therefore, there is now no condemnation[a] for those who are in Christ
Jesus,[b] [2]because through Christ Jesus the
law of the Spirit who gives life[c] has set
you[c] free[d] from the law of sin[e] and death.
[3]For what the law was powerless[f] to do because it was weakened by the flesh,[d] God
did by sending his own Son in the likeness
of sinful flesh[g] to be a sin offering.[e][h] And
so he condemned sin in the flesh, [4]in order that the righteous requirement of the

7:14 [n]1Co 3:1 [o]1Ki 21:20, 25; 2Ki 17:17
7:15 [p]ver 19; Gal 5:17
7:16 [q]ver 12
7:17 [r]ver 20
7:18 [s]ver 25
7:19 [t]ver 15
7:20 [u]ver 17
7:21 [v]ver 23, 25
7:22 [w]Eph 3:16 [x]Ps 1:2
7:23 [y]Gal 5:17; Jas 4:1; 1Pe 2:11
7:24 [z]Ro 6:6; 8:2
8:1 [a]ver 34 [b]ver 39; Ro 16:3
8:2 [c]1Co 15:45 [d]Ro 6:18 [e]Ro 7:4
8:3 [f]Ac 13:39; Heb 7:18 [g]Php 2:7 [h]Heb 2:14, 17

[a] 18 Or *my flesh* [b] 25 Or *in the flesh* [c] 2 The Greek is singular; some manuscripts *me* [d] 3 In contexts like this, the Greek word for *flesh* (*sarx*) refers to the sinful state of human beings, often presented as a power in opposition to the Spirit; also in verses 4-13. [e] 3 Or *flesh, for sin*

7:14 Paul characterizes the two chief actors in the drama that follows. The Law of Moses, as Paul has made clear in v. 12, is "spiritual"; that is, it has a divine origin. "Unspiritual" can describe "carnal" Christians (1Co 3:1-3), so it does not necessarily mean that the "I" is an unbeliever. But Paul has used the phrase "under sin" to describe the condition of all people apart from Christ (Ro 3:9).
7:15-20 Paul graphically portrays the struggle he finds within himself to follow through on his conviction that "the law is spiritual" (v. 14). This tension reveals two truths. (1) The fact that he wants to do what is good shows that he acknowledges the goodness of the law (v. 16). However, (2) Paul admits that he cannot fully obey the law (v. 17). Paul is trying to reveal the force within himself that leads him to act as he does. That force is called "sin."
7:18-20 Paul continues his analysis of his struggle against "indwelling" sin.
7:21-23 Most interpreters agree that "law" in v. 21 means "principle" or "rule." Paul then contrasts "God's law" (v. 22) with "another law," "the law of sin" (v. 23), both of which exert their claim on us. The upshot, Paul says, is that he is "a prisoner of the law of sin." God's law simply does not have the power to deliver us from the power of sin.
7:24 Paul finally reacts to the situation. He wants deliverance from his sin-dominated body, which is spiritually dead because of that sin.
7:25 Paul gives thanks for the rescue, provided through "Jesus Christ our Lord." Having expressed the desire for rescue he felt as a Jew under the law, Paul the Christian cannot refrain from expressing his thanks to the Lord who delivered him.

✜ **7:13-25** With Paul, we should break out in thanksgiving to God when we recognize the state from which he has rescued us. All who read this chapter as Christians can identify, to some degree, with the struggle and frustration Paul depicts here. Looking at our own struggles moves us all the more to praise God for his rescue in Jesus Christ.

8:1 Because we are justified by faith in Christ, we escape the sentence of spiritual death that our sins have earned. We have been transferred into the new realm of life. Because we have believed in Jesus' finished work for us on the cross, we no longer have to fear that our sins will ever condemn us.
8:2-3 The liberating work of the Spirit takes place "through Christ Jesus." The Mosaic Law was powerless to rescue human beings because the people to whom the law was given were in the realm of "flesh."

But God won the victory over sin in the very realm where it seemed to rule unchallenged: in the "flesh." Paul carefully balances Jesus' full humanity with his sinlessness. Calling that flesh "sinful" might suggest that Christ took on *fallen* human nature. If so, he would not have been qualified to be our sinless redeemer. Paul clarifies by adding the important word "likeness." In other words, Christ did not, like every other person since Adam, cave in to the flesh.
8:4 Paul says that "the righteous *requirement* of the law" (emphasis added) was fulfilled in us. The singular word suggests that God in Christ fulfilled the entirety of the law's demand on our behalf. The people in whom the law is fulfilled are those who live in the realm of the Spirit.

law might be fully met in us, who do not
live according to the flesh but according
to the Spirit.[i]
5Those who live according to the flesh
have their minds set on what the flesh
desires;[j] but those who live in accordance
with the Spirit have their minds set on
what the Spirit desires.[k] 6The mind governed by the flesh is death, but the mind
governed by the Spirit is life[l] and peace.
7The mind governed by the flesh is hostile to God;[m] it does not submit to God's
law, nor can it do so. 8Those who are in
the realm of the flesh cannot please God.
9You, however, are not in the realm
of the flesh but are in the realm of the
Spirit, if indeed the Spirit of God lives
in you.[n] And if anyone does not have
the Spirit of Christ,[o] they do not belong to Christ. 10But if Christ is in you,[p]
then even though your body is subject
to death because of sin, the Spirit gives
life[a] because of righteousness. 11And if
the Spirit of him who raised Jesus from
the dead[q] is living in you, he who raised
Christ from the dead will also give life
to your mortal bodies[r] because of[b] his
Spirit who lives in you.
12Therefore, brothers and sisters, we
have an obligation — but it is not to the
flesh, to live according to it. 13For if you
live according to the flesh, you will die;
but if by the Spirit you put to death the
misdeeds of the body, you will live.[s]
14For those who are led by the Spirit
of God[t] are the children of God.[u] 15The
Spirit you received does not make you
slaves, so that you live in fear again;[v]
rather, the Spirit you received brought
about your adoption to sonship.[c] And
by him we cry, *"Abba,*[d] Father."[w] 16The
Spirit himself testifies with our spirit[x]
that we are God's children. 17Now if we

8:4 [i] Gal 5:16
8:5 [j] Gal 5:19-21 [k] Gal 5:22-25
8:6 [l] Gal 6:8
8:7 [m] Jas 4:4
8:9 [n] 1Co 6:19; Gal 4:6 [o] Jn 14:17; 1Jn 4:13
8:10 [p] Gal 2:20; Eph 3:17; Col 1:27
8:11 [q] Ac 2:24 [r] Jn 5:21
8:13 [s] Gal 6:8
8:14 [t] Gal 5:18 [u] Jn 1:12; Rev 21:7
8:15 [v] 2Ti 1:7; Heb 2:15 [w] Mk 14:36; Gal 4:5,6
8:16 [x] Eph 1:13

[a] *10* Or *you, your body is dead because of sin, yet your spirit is alive* [b] *11* Some manuscripts *bodies through* [c] *15* The Greek word for *adoption to sonship* is a term referring to the full legal standing of an adopted male heir in Roman culture; also in verse 23. [d] *15* Aramaic for *father*

8:5–8 The lifestyle of the flesh flows from a mind oriented to the flesh, whereas the lifestyle of the Spirit comes from a mind oriented to the Spirit.
8:9–11 It is clear that the "in flesh"/"in Spirit" language is metaphorical—a way of indicating that people are dominated by one or the other of these forces. Every Christian really is "in the Spirit"—under his gracious control. We may not always reflect that liberating control (see vv. 12–13), but it is a fundamental fact of our Christian existence. Our bodies may be doomed to die, but the Spirit of life, who raised our Lord Jesus from the dead, dwells within us and guarantees that our bodies will not end in the grave.
8:12–13 God's gift of new life carries with it an obligation to the Spirit, the power of the new regime. Paul breaks off his sentence at the end of v. 12 to emphasize the importance of our obligation in v. 13. The tension between what God gives us and what we must do in response is emphasized here yet again.

8:1–13 Having the mindset of the Spirit is the crucial middle step between our existence in the sphere of the Spirit (v. 9) and practically living "according to the Spirit" (v. 4b). Cultivating a Spirit-led, Spirit-filled outlook in our hearts and minds is necessary if we are to live in a way that pleases God.

If we are serious about progressing in the Christian life, we must seek every day to feed our minds with spiritual food. Our daily times with the Lord can be one way in which we develop the mindset of the Spirit, but only if the mind is really involved. This idea recalls Jesus' teaching about "abiding" in Christ that we learn about in Jn 15.

8:14–17 The recognition that we are God's own children is another basis for our assurance that, "there is now no condemnation for those who are in Christ Jesus" (v. 1). Being "led by the Spirit" (v. 14) means having the basic orientation of our lives determined by the Spirit. The phrase is a way of summing up the various descriptions of the life of the Spirit in vv. 4–9.
8:15–16 Verse 15 centers on a contrast between two different spirits. Paul is saying that the Spirit of God we have received is not a spirit of fear but the Spirit who makes us God's children. In Greco-Roman practice, a man could formally grant an adopted child all the legal rights of a birth child. This, Paul suggests, is what God's Spirit gives to every believer—the rights and privileges of God's own children.

The Spirit enables us to experience the same relationship with the Father that Jesus did, who also called God "*Abba*" (Mk 14:36). The Spirit is the One who gives us the inner certainty that we truly are God's dearly loved children.

These verses resume the main course of Paul's argument in this paragraph, which runs from "Spirit" to "sonship" to "heir." Because the adopted child is an heir, there is still something incomplete in his or her status. Christians must still await the fulfillment of that new status.

8:14–17 The feeling of being rejected is all too common in our world. Of course, no human relationship can ever provide ultimate security. But what our fellow humans can never supply, God does. Through our faith in Christ, the Son of God, we become his "brothers and sisters" (see Heb 2:10–13), children of God and coheirs with Christ of all that God has promised to those who love him. We belong to the ultimate "in group"—those who are the dearly loved children of the God of the universe.

are children, then we are heirs[y] — heirs
of God and co-heirs with Christ, if indeed
we share in his sufferings in order that
we may also share in his glory.[z]

Present Suffering and Future Glory

18 I consider that our present sufferings
are not worth comparing with the glory
that will be revealed in us.[a] 19 For the creation waits in eager expectation for the
children of God to be revealed. 20 For the
creation was subjected to frustration, not
by its own choice, but by the will of the
one who subjected it,[b] in hope 21 that[a] the
creation itself will be liberated from its
bondage to decay[c] and brought into the
freedom and glory of the children of God.
22 We know that the whole creation has
been groaning[d] as in the pains of childbirth right up to the present time. 23 Not
only so, but we ourselves, who have the
firstfruits of the Spirit,[e] groan[f] inwardly
as we wait eagerly[g] for our adoption to
sonship, the redemption of our bodies.
24 For in this hope we were saved.[h] But
hope that is seen is no hope at all. Who
hopes for what they already have? 25 But
if we hope for what we do not yet have,
we wait for it patiently.
26 In the same way, the Spirit helps us
in our weakness. We do not know what
we ought to pray for, but the Spirit himself intercedes for us[i] through wordless groans. 27 And he who searches our
hearts[j] knows the mind of the Spirit, because the Spirit intercedes for God's people in accordance with the will of God.
28 And we know that in all things God
works for the good of those who love
him, who[b] have been called[k] according
to his purpose. 29 For those God foreknew[l]

8:17 [y] Ac 20:32; Gal 4:7 [z] 1Pe 4:13
8:18 [a] 2Co 4:17; 1Pe 4:13
8:20 [b] Ge 3:17-19
8:21 [c] Ac 3:21; 2Pe 3:13; Rev 21:1
8:22 [d] Jer 12:4
8:23 [e] 2Co 5:5 [f] 2Co 5:2,4 [g] Gal 5:5
8:24 [h] 1Th 5:8
8:26 [i] Eph 6:18
8:27 [j] Rev 2:23
8:28 [k] 1Co 1:9; 2Ti 1:9
8:29 [l] Ro 11:2

Ro 8:26–27 ❖ When have you felt God's Spirit help you in your weakness? How has the Holy Spirit been a strength and guide to believers?

[a] *20,21* Or *subjected it in hope.* [21] *For* [b] *28* Or *that all things work together for good to those who love God, who;* or *that in all things God works together with those who love him to bring about what is good — with those who*

8:18–25 We all know that believers suffer. But those sufferings aren't worth comparing to the glory that will be "revealed in us" (v. 18). The fate of creation is bound up with that of humanity. Creation was marred through our sin. It will be restored through our glorification.

8:22–23 The pain experienced by a woman about to deliver a child serves as a vivid metaphor of suffering that has a joyous outcome. Suffering is a momentary experience leading to eternal joy (v. 18). Thus, Christians join creation in this kind of groaning (v. 23).

Through the Spirit, we sense who God wants us to be. As a result, the Spirit increases our desire to be what he wants us to be. "The redemption of our bodies" (v. 23) refers to the rescue of the body from sin and death (see vv. 10–11).

Why does Paul suggest we yearn for "our adoption to sonship" (v. 23)? Has he not said that we have already been adopted (v. 16)? Here we find a classic NT example of the "already-but-not yet" tension that pervades its teaching about the Christian life.

8:24–25 In light of this tension, therefore, it becomes clear that "hope" is an inevitable aspect of Christian living. Christian hope is solidly founded in God himself. Thus, we can "wait for it patiently" or, perhaps better, with endurance (v. 25).

8:26–27 Because of our limitations, "we do not know what we ought to pray for." The Spirit intercedes on our behalf with "wordless groans." God, who knows the heart, hears and answers those prayers.

8:28 The famous promise of v. 28 is one of the great biblical descriptions of providence. "Those who love" God is simply a way of describing God's people; it is not a qualification of the promise, as if Paul means that God only works good if believers love God enough.

8:29–30 The "purpose" of God is outlined here. God has instituted a series of actions that create, sustain, and bring his people to glory. The Greek verb "to foreknow" generally means to know something ahead of time. In Scripture, God's knowing often refers to his entering into relationship with someone. What Paul is saying, then, is that God's plan for us began in a decision to enter into relationship with us. This led, in turn, to his decision to "predestine" us. This word simply means to direct a person to a particular goal. Paul spells out the goal: "to be conformed to the image of [God's] Son" (v. 29). The last stage of Christian existence is to be "conformed" to Christ's own glorious body. God enters into relationship with us so that we may attain that goal.

"Calling" is not a general gospel invitation. It is God's effective summoning of us into relationship (see 1:7). After setting us on the road to the goal of conformity to Christ, God in his grace and by his Spirit reaches out and brings us into his own people. He then "justifies" us; that is, he declares us innocent before him (see chs. 1–4).

Finally, as the capstone to this series, he "glorifies" us. Why Paul uses the past tense here for a future action is not clear. He is probably viewing matters from God's perspective. God has already made the decision to glorify all those whom he has justified.

We must not lose sight of Paul's main point: namely, to assure believers that God has a plan that provides fully for our future glory. He wants us to receive this with a renewed sense of assurance. The God who began a good work in us will indeed bring it to completion in the day of Christ Jesus (Php 1:6).

he also predestined[m] to be conformed to the image of his Son,[n] that he might be the firstborn among many brothers and sisters. 30And those he predestined,[o] he also called; those he called, he also justified;[p] those he justified, he also glorified.[q]

More Than Conquerors

31What, then, shall we say in response to these things?[r] If God is for us, who can be against us?[s] 32He who did not spare his own Son,[t] but gave him up for us all—how will he not also, along with him, graciously give us all things? 33Who will bring any charge[u] against those whom God has chosen? It is God who justifies. 34Who then is the one who condemns? No one. Christ Jesus who died[v]—more than that, who was raised to life—is at the right hand of God[w] and is also interceding for us.[x] 35Who shall separate us from the love of Christ? Shall trouble or hardship or persecution or famine or

8:29 [m] Eph 1:5, 11 [n] 1Co 15:49; 2Co 3:18; Php 3:21; 1Jn 3:2
8:30 [o] Eph 1:5, 11 [p] 1Co 6:11 [q] Ro 9:23
8:31 [r] Ro 4:1 [s] Ps 118:6
8:32 [t] Jn 3:16; Ro 4:25; 5:8
8:33 [u] Isa 50:8,9
8:34 [v] Ro 5:6-8 [w] Mk 16:19 [x] Heb 7:25; 9:24; 1Jn 2:1

8:18–30 Christians in every generation have found tremendous comfort in the wonderful promise of v. 28, and rightly so. This is surely one of the greatest promises of God to his people anywhere in the Bible. Essentially, it promises that nothing will touch our lives that is not under the control and direction of our loving heavenly Father. Everything we do and say; everything people do to us or say about us; every experience we will ever have—all are sovereignly used by God for our good. Through this we know that nothing comes into our lives that God does not allow and use for his own purposes—to move his kingdom forward in our lives and in the world.

8:31 "These things" refers to the many reasons for our confidence that Paul has rehearsed in chs. 5–8. They can be summed up in one statement: God is "for us." If that's true, Paul rightly asks, who then can be "against us?" No opposition ultimately matters.

8:32–34 Verse 32 reinforces Paul's point. "Bring [a] charge" (v. 33) is the first of several judicial terms. Any prosecution will be unsuccessful, for God has chosen us to be his and has justified us already. Verse 34 provides more evidence for the same point.

8:35–36 Christ not only defends us; he also loves us and enters into a relationship with us. Nothing will ever separate us from that love. To make sure we get the point, Paul specifies some threats at the end of v. 35. Paul himself has gone through most of these. He has learned by experience that they cannot disrupt his relationship with Christ.

CHARACTER OF GOD // GOD IS A PROVIDER

Romans 8:32: He who did not spare his own Son, but gave him up for us all—how will he not also, along with him, graciously give us all things?

Jesus said that just as a human father knows how to give good gifts to his children—bread instead of a stone, for example—God the Father even more loves to provide for his children (Mt 7:9–11). God is our provider.

When God tested Abraham by telling him to sacrifice his son Isaac, in the end God provided a ram to be sacrificed instead. Abraham named the place "The Lord Will Provide" (Ge 22:14). God provided water for Hagar and Ishmael in the desert (Ge 21:19). God provided manna and quail for the Israelites to eat in the wilderness, and even water from a rock (Ex 16:4, 13; 17:6). God provided destitute Naomi, who had lost her husband and her two sons, with food and a new son through Ruth the Moabite (Ru 4:13–15). God provided a miraculous supply of flour and oil for the widow of Zarephath so that she and her son would not die (1Ki 17:14–16).

Jesus Christ provided food for multitudes from meager offerings (Mt 15:34–37; Jn 6:8–11). And Christ himself is the ultimate example of God providing for his people. Just as God provided a ram for Abraham to sacrifice in the place of Isaac, so God provided Jesus Christ as the atoning sacrifice for the sins of the world (1Jn 2:2). God did not withhold his Son but instead offered up his life to provide the way to eternal life (Ro 8:32).

APPLICATION Since God provided everything we need for salvation in Christ, Paul is certain that God will also meet all our other needs (Php 4:19). This does not mean that we will always get everything that we want. It means that God will provide us with everything he knows we need. Our lives are in God's hands, and he will not have us lack anything he intends us to have. We ought to give God praise and thanks for all that he has provided for us, knowing that "every good and perfect gift" comes from him (Jas 1:17).

nakedness or danger or sword?[y] 36 As it
is written:

> "For your sake we face death all day
> long;
> we are considered as sheep to be
> slaughtered."[az]

37 No, in all these things we are more than
conquerors[a] through him who loved us.[b]
38 For I am convinced that neither death
nor life, neither angels nor demons,[b] neither the present nor the future, nor any
powers,[c] 39 neither height nor depth, nor
anything else in all creation, will be able
to separate us from the love of God[d] that
is in Christ Jesus our Lord.

Paul's Anguish Over Israel

9 I speak the truth in Christ — I am not
lying,[e] my conscience confirms[f] it
through the Holy Spirit — 2 I have great
sorrow and unceasing anguish in my
heart. 3 For I could wish that I myself[g]
were cursed[h] and cut off from Christ
for the sake of my people, those of my
own race,[i] 4 the people of Israel. Theirs
is the adoption to sonship;[j] theirs the
divine glory, the covenants,[k] the receiving of the law,[l] the temple worship[m] and the promises.[n] 5 Theirs are
the patriarchs, and from them is traced
the human ancestry of the Messiah,[o]
who is God over all,[p] forever praised![cq]
Amen.

God's Sovereign Choice

6 It is not as though God's word had
failed. For not all who are descended
from Israel are Israel.[r] 7 Nor because they
are his descendants are they all Abraham's children. On the contrary, "It is
through Isaac that your offspring will
be reckoned."[ds] 8 In other words, it is not
the children by physical descent who are
God's children,[t] but it is the children of
the promise who are regarded as Abraham's offspring. 9 For this was how the
promise was stated: "At the appointed

8:35 [y] 1Co 4:11
8:36 [z] Ps 44:22; 2Co 4:11
8:37 [a] 1Co 15:57 [b] Gal 2:20; Rev 1:5; 3:9
8:38 [c] Eph 1:21; 1Pe 3:22
8:39 [d] Ro 5:8
9:1 [e] 2Co 11:10; Gal 1:20; 1Ti 2:7 [f] Ro 1:9
9:3 [g] Ex 32:32 [h] 1Co 12:3; 16:22 [i] Ro 11:14
9:4 [j] Ex 4:22 [k] Ge 17:2; Ac 3:25; Eph 2:12 [l] Ps 147:19 [m] Heb 9:1 [n] Ac 13:32
9:5 [o] Mt 1:1-16 [p] Jn 1:1 [q] Ro 1:25
9:6 [r] Ro 2:28, 29; Gal 6:16
9:7 [s] Ge 21:12; Heb 11:18
9:8 [t] Ro 8:14

[a] *36* Psalm 44:22 [b] *38* Or *nor heavenly rulers* [c] *5* Or *Messiah, who is over all. God be forever praised!* Or *Messiah. God who is over all be forever praised!* [d] *7* Gen. 21:12

8:37–39 Paul concludes his celebration of God's love for us in Christ with his own personal testimony (vv. 38-39). There is nothing in all the world that can separate us from the "love of God that is in Christ Jesus our Lord" (v. 39). As the chapter began with "no condemnation" (v. 1), so it ends with the bookend of "no separation" (vv. 35, 39).

✣ **8:31–39** Paul's emphatic claim that no spiritual being can separate us from Christ is needed in the lives of believers and in the church today. We need to recognize and proclaim to others that God in Christ has won a victory over the "powers and authorities" (Col 2:15) and that they have no power to keep us from inheriting the salvation God has promised to all who love him. Nothing on earth can separate us from God's love for us in Christ, and neither can anything in heaven.

9:1–5 The first five verses of ch. 9 reveal Paul's deep concern. In vv. 1-2, he goes out of his way to stress the sincerity of this concern. Verse 3 shows the problem is basic: Israel is not saved.

Paul's claim that the Jews enjoy "adoption" is striking because he has applied that blessing to Christians. He likely thinks of Israel's "adoption" as a national blessing that does not confer salvation on individual Jews.

Paul concludes v. 5 with two final blessings enjoyed by Israel. The patriarchs are significant because God entered into a solemn covenant with them. The greatest blessing promised to Israel was the Messiah—that is, the Christ. This verse deserves to be numbered among those few in the NT that explicitly call Jesus "God."

✣ **9:1–5** The pluralism of our age encourages us to believe that every religion provides a different way to the same God. Paul's concern here reveals otherwise. As God's one and only Messiah, Jesus is the only way to eternal life for every human who ever has or will exist. This reality should fuel our desire to share the gospel with everyone.

Our interpretation of Scripture is always affected by factors external to the text—from the specifics of our own personalities and backgrounds to the generalities of cultural movements and influences. But the call remains the same.

9:6a Here we read the thesis that Paul defends in the next three chapters. To defend the gospel, Paul must defend God's faithfulness to his promises to Israel. If God has gone back on his word to Israel, then a deep chasm between the OT and the NT opens up, and the whole plan of salvation crashes.
9:6b Verse 6b states the thesis for vv. 7–29. Paul differentiates two "Israels": what we might call a "physical" Israel, based on descent, and a "spiritual" Israel. In Gal 6:16, Paul refers to the entire church as "Israel." This may be what Paul means in Ro 9:6b: Not all who are Jews by birth belong to the "Israel of God" (Gal 6:16), the church.
9:7–9 Paul affirms that Jews belong to Abraham in different ways. All who can claim him as their physical ancestor are his "children," but only those who have him as their spiritual father as well are his "offspring." God determined that Abraham's offspring would be "reckoned," a key word in Paul's argument. God spoke these words to Abraham

PEOPLE TO KNOW // SARAH

ROMANS 9:6-9; GENESIS 18:1-15: Sarah was the wife of Abraham. Originally named Sarai, the Bible introduces her as being unable to have children (Ge 11:30). God promised Abraham that he would have many descendants who would become a great nation—an obvious problem when his wife was unable to conceive.

Sarah proposed a solution by telling Abraham to sleep with her Egyptian slave, Hagar. Hagar gave birth to Ishmael, Abraham's first son (Ge 16:15).

God told Abraham that, though Ishmael would be blessed, Sarah herself would have a son through whom God would establish his covenant. Abraham laughed, questioning how Sarah could have a child at the age of ninety (Ge 17:17-19). When God and two angels visited Abraham and Sarah later, repeating again that Sarah would have a son, Sarah also laughed at the outlandish idea (Ge 18:12).

God kept his promise. Sarah conceived in her old age and gave birth to Isaac. When Isaac was weaned, Sarah sent Hagar and Ishmael away when she noticed Ishmael mocking Issac. Sarah died at the age of 127.

Hebrews 11 lists Sarah as a hero of faith (Heb 11:11).

APPLICATION It is easy to doubt God's promises, especially when they seem impossibly out of reach. Sarah doubted God because she only looked at events through her human experience; she even laughed when God said she would have a child. God remained true to his word in the face of Sarah's disbelief. Yet despite her doubt, Sarah is considered a hero of the faith; she came to trust in God's word, and her story remains as a testament to God's faithfulness. Nothing is impossible with God. God keeps his promises, always.

time I will return, and Sarah will have
a son."[a][u]
10Not only that, but Rebekah's children
were conceived at the same time by our
father Isaac.[v] 11Yet, before the twins were
born or had done anything good or bad—
in order that God's purpose[w] in election
might stand: 12not by works but by him
who calls—she was told, "The older will
serve the younger."[b][x] 13Just as it is written: "Jacob I loved, but Esau I hated."[c][y]

14What then shall we say? Is God unjust? Not at all![z] 15For he says to Moses,

"I will have mercy on whom I have
mercy,
and I will have compassion on
whom I have compassion."[d][a]

16It does not, therefore, depend on human desire or effort, but on God's mercy.[b]

9:9 [u] Ge 18:10, 14
9:10 [v] Ge 25:21
9:11 [w] Ro 8:28
9:12 [x] Ge 25:23
9:13 [y] Mal 1:2, 3
9:14 [z] 2Ch 19:7
9:15 [a] Ex 33:19
9:16 [b] Eph 2:8

[a] 9 Gen. 18:10,14 [b] 12 Gen. 25:23
[c] 13 Mal. 1:2,3 [d] 15 Exodus 33:19

regarding Ishmael's being sent away. Only the "children of the promise" are "regarded as Abraham's offspring" (v. 8).

9:10-13 What makes Jacob and Esau different from Ishmael and Isaac is not only that the first pair had the same mother as well as the same father but that they were conceived at the same time. The quotation (v. 12, from Ge 25:23) expresses Paul's key point, that God's choice reversed the natural order of birth. Since God chose Jacob over Esau before they were born or had done anything, Jacob's status was based not on works but on the God who calls.

Paul concludes his discussion of Jacob and Esau with yet another quotation: "I have loved Jacob, but Esau I have hated" (Mal 1:2-3). The OT context is clearly covenantal, so "love" means, in effect, "choose," while "hate" means "reject." Paul is thinking of Jacob and Esau here as individuals. He has specifically rehearsed their personal histories in Ro 9:11-12, referring to their birth and their "works." It is difficult to think that Paul switches from this personal reference to a corporate one, without warning, in v. 13.

9:6-13 However much we may want to claim that salvation is based on God's choice, we must also insist that the human decision to believe is also both real and critical. We are not puppets in God's hands, passively moving as he directs; rather, we are responsible human beings called by God to exercise faith in his Son. The evidence of Scripture compels us to maintain a fine balance at this point.

9:14-18 Determining what is just or unjust demands a standard for measurement. That standard is ultimately God's own character. God, therefore, acts justly when he acts in line with his own person and plan. This is precisely the point Paul makes in vv. 15-18.

9:15-16 Paul quotes Ex 33:19 to point out that receiving favor from God does not depend on anything a person can or will do but only on God's own will to show mercy.

17For Scripture says to Pharaoh: "I raised
you up for this very purpose, that I might
display my power in you and that my
name might be proclaimed in all the
earth."[ac] 18Therefore God has mercy on
whom he wants to have mercy, and he
hardens whom he wants to harden.[d]
19One of you will say to me:[e] "Then
why does God still blame us? For who
is able to resist his will?"[f] 20But who are
you, a human being, to talk back to God?
"Shall what is formed say to the one who
formed it,[g] 'Why did you make me like
this?'"[bh] 21Does not the potter have the
right to make out of the same lump of
clay some pottery for special purposes
and some for common use?[i]
22What if God, although choosing to
show his wrath and make his power
known, bore with great patience[j] the
objects of his wrath — prepared for destruction? 23What if he did this to make
the riches of his glory[k] known to the objects of his mercy, whom he prepared in
advance for glory[l] — 24even us, whom
he also called,[m] not only from the Jews
but also from the Gentiles?[n] 25As he says
in Hosea:

9:17 [c] Ex 9:16
9:18 [d] Ex 4:21
9:19 [e] Ro 11:19 [f] 2Ch 20:6; Da 4:35
9:20 [g] Isa 64:8 [h] Isa 29:16
9:21 [i] 2Ti 2:20
9:22 [j] Ro 2:4
9:23 [k] Ro 2:4 [l] Ro 8:30
9:24 [m] Ro 8:28 [n] Ro 3:29
9:25 [o] Hos 2:23; 1Pe 2:10
9:26 [p] Hos 1:10
9:27 [q] Ge 22:17; Hos 1:10 [r] Ro 11:5
9:28 [s] Isa 10:22, 23

Ro 9:22–24 ❖ How does God's election and mercy display the riches of his glory? What does it mean to be an object of God's mercy?

"I will call them 'my people' who are
not my people;
and I will call her 'my loved one'
who is not my loved one,"[co]
26and,
"In the very place where it was said
to them,
'You are not my people,'
there they will be called 'children
of the living God.'"[dp]
27Isaiah cries out concerning Israel:
"Though the number of the Israelites
be like the sand by the sea,[q]
only the remnant will be saved.[r]
28For the Lord will carry out
his sentence on earth with speed
and finality."[es]

[a] *17* Exodus 9:16 [b] *20* Isaiah 29:16; 45:9 [c] *25* Hosea 2:23 [d] *26* Hosea 1:10 [e] *28* Isaiah 10:22,23 (see Septuagint)

9:17–18 A second quotation reinforces the freedom of God to act as he wishes, but now from a negative side (v. 17). God brought Pharaoh onto the stage of history to accomplish his own purposes. By resisting God, Pharaoh forced Moses to work a series of miracles to bring Israel out of Egypt. This display of God's power became known throughout that part of the world (cf. Jos 2:10). Romans 9:18 draws the conclusion not only from v. 17 but from vv. 15–16 as well.

9:19–23 Paul offers no logical explanation of how God's determinative will and human responsibility interact. Rather than taking the defensive, Paul further asserts God's freedom to do as he wants with his creatures.

What right does the created being have to complain about how God has made him (v. 20)? God has the right to fashion from the clay the kinds of vessels he wants. The parallel with "objects of his wrath" and "objects of his mercy" (vv. 22–23) suggests he is thinking of God's freedom to choose some people to be saved and leave others in their spiritual deadness.

Verses 22–23 form a question that has no direct answer. The "what if" at the beginning suggests that Paul is saying, in effect: "What if God has acted in this way? Who will question God's authority?"

The word "choosing" (or "willing") at v. 22 has a causal function. *Because* God wants publicly to display wrath and power, he has done so. God has tolerated sinners not only so he can display his wrath; he has done so especially to "make the riches of his glory known to the objects of his mercy" (v. 23).

✣ **9:14–23** Three texts in vv. 6–23 (vv. 13, 18, 22–23) seem to suggest that God chooses people to be damned just as he chooses people to be saved. But before we conclude that the two acts are completely parallel, one other factor must be considered. Paul teaches that all people are involved in Adam's sin. God's decision to destine some people to wrath comes, many scholars believe, *after* (in a logical sense) that sin. God's "hardening," then, does not cause spiritual insensitivity; it maintains people in the state of sin that they have already chosen. Perhaps in this teaching we can turn what can seem to be a problem into a new appreciation for the mystery, greatness, and incomprehensible purposes of God.

9:24–29 Since God's grace is what matters, he is free to call Gentiles into his kingdom as well as Jews. The apostle makes this point in v. 24, the "heading" for the paragraph. He then grounds his assertion with quotations from Scripture.

Paul ends his series of quotations with another one from Isaiah (Isa 1:9, quoted in Ro 9:29). What probably drew his attention to Isa 1:9 is the word "descendants," which is the key word at the beginning of this section (see Ro 9:7–8). This word holds out hope to Israel because God is determined to preserve "descendants" for Israel—people who will inherit this promise to Abraham.

29It is just as Isaiah said previously:

"Unless the Lord Almighty[t]
had left us descendants,
we would have become like Sodom,
we would have been like
Gomorrah."[a][u]

Israel's Unbelief

30What then shall we say? That the
Gentiles, who did not pursue righteousness, have obtained it, a righteousness
that is by faith;[v] 31but the people of Israel,
who pursued the law as the way of righteousness,[w] have not attained their goal.[x]
32Why not? Because they pursued it not
by faith but as if it were by works. They
stumbled over the stumbling stone.[y] 33As
it is written:

"See, I lay in Zion a stone that causes
people to stumble
and a rock that makes them fall,
and the one who believes in him
will never be put to shame."[b][z]

10 Brothers and sisters, my heart's
desire and prayer to God for the
Israelites is that they may be saved. 2For
I can testify about them that they are zealous[a] for God, but their zeal is not based
on knowledge. 3Since they did not know
the righteousness of God and sought to
establish their own, they did not submit
to God's righteousness.[b] 4Christ is the culmination of the law[c] so that there may be
righteousness for everyone who believes.[d]
5Moses writes this about the righteousness that is by the law: "The person who
does these things will live by them."[c][e]
6But the righteousness that is by faith[f]
says: "Do not say in your heart, 'Who will
ascend into heaven?'"[d][g] (that is, to bring
Christ down) 7"or 'Who will descend into
the deep?'"[e] (that is, to bring Christ up
from the dead). 8But what does it say?
"The word is near you; it is in your mouth
and in your heart,"[f][h] that is, the message
concerning faith that we proclaim: 9If
you declare[i] with your mouth, "Jesus
is Lord," and believe in your heart that
God raised him from the dead,[j] you will
be saved. 10For it is with your heart that
you believe and are justified, and it is
with your mouth that you profess your
faith and are saved. 11As Scripture says,
"Anyone who believes in him will never
be put to shame."[g][k] 12For there is no difference between Jew and Gentile[l] — the
same Lord is Lord of all[m] and richly bless-

9:29 [t] Jas 5:4 [u] Isa 1:9; Dt 29:23; Isa 13:19; Jer 50:40
9:30 [v] Ro 1:17; 10:6; Gal 2:16; Php 3:9; Heb 11:7
9:31 [w] Isa 51:1; Ro 10:2,3 [x] Gal 5:4
9:32 [y] 1Pe 2:8
9:33 [z] Isa 28:16; Ro 10:11
10:2 [a] Ac 21:20
10:3 [b] Ro 1:17
10:4 [c] Gal 3:24; Ro 7:1-4 [d] Ro 3:22
10:5 [e] Lev 18:5; Ne 9:29; Eze 20:11,13,21; Ro 7:10
10:6 [f] Ro 9:30 [g] Dt 30:12
10:8 [h] Dt 30:14
10:9 [i] Mt 10:32; Lk 12:8 [j] Ac 2:24
10:11 [k] Isa 28:16; Ro 9:33
10:12 [l] Ro 3:22, 29 [m] Ac 10:36

[a] 29 Isaiah 1:9 [b] 33 Isaiah 8:14; 28:16 [c] 5 Lev. 18:5 [d] 6 Deut. 30:12 [e] 7 Deut. 30:13 [f] 8 Deut. 30:14 [g] 11 Isaiah 28:16 (see Septuagint)

9:24–29 We should follow Paul's lead in reading the OT as a single story about God's plan of redemption that finds its fulfillment in Christ. All of us—preachers, teachers, and laypeople alike—need to learn the "old, old story" so well that we can revel in the marvelous interrelationship between all the parts of Scripture.

9:30–33 God offered salvation to the Gentiles, though they were not searching for it. Responding in faith, they "obtained it" (v. 30). The people of Israel focused narrowly on the works of the law and missed the larger demand to submit to God in faith. Thus, they failed to obtain righteousness.
10:1–2 Paul makes clear how deeply he feels about this failure (v. 1). Paul regards the zeal of his fellow Israelites as a good thing; the problem, however, is that—like the pre-Christian Paul (Ac 22:3; Php 3:6)—their zeal was not directed by knowledge. The Jews did not understand that God was now offering a right relationship with himself through faith in Jesus Christ, the culmination of salvation history.
10:3 Instead of submitting to God's righteousness, the Jews sought to "establish their own." In failing to submit to God's righteousness, the Jews were guilty of missing the decisive turn in salvation history that had come with Christ (see 1:17; 3:21–22).
10:4 Paul explains that Israel's pursuit of a righteousness based on the law completely misses the point that the era of the law has ended. Picture Israel as the runner, the law as the race, and Christ as the finish line. What Israel has failed to understand, Paul is saying, is that the finish line has been reached.
10:5 The apostle cites Lev 18:5 to describe legal righteousness: "The person who does these things will live by them." Paul's point is that any righteousness based on the law is, by definition, something one can get only by "doing."
10:6–8 In contrast to this legal righteousness is the "righteousness that is by faith." The general point Paul wants to make is clear enough: Through Christ's being brought down to earth and his being brought up from the dead, God has made righteousness readily available. All one needs to do to attain righteousness is to respond in faith to the gospel as it is preached.
10:9–10 Paul draws conclusions from what he has said about "the righteousness that is by faith" in vv. 6–8. Deuteronomy 30:14, quoted in Ro 10:8 refers to the "mouth" and the "heart." In v. 9 he elaborates each of these. Simply stated, the fulfillment of these two requirements brings salvation.
10:11–12 Paul shows from the OT (Isa 28:16) that putting one's trust in Christ will save that person from judgment. The quotation stresses that faith is open to "anyone." Paul develops this further in Ro 10:12, returning to his central claim that the

Ro 10:14–15 ❖ How can we help tell the world about Jesus? Where might God be sending us to bring the Good News?

es all who call on him, [13]for, "Everyone
who calls on the name of the Lord[n] will
be saved."[ao]
[14]How, then, can they call on the one
they have not believed in? And how can
they believe in the one of whom they
have not heard? And how can they hear
without someone preaching to them?
[15]And how can anyone preach unless they
are sent? As it is written: "How beautiful are the feet of those who bring good
news!"[bp]
[16]But not all the Israelites accepted the
good news. For Isaiah says, "Lord, who
has believed our message?"[cq] [17]Conse-
quently, faith comes from hearing the
message,[r] and the message is heard
through the word about Christ.[s] [18]But
I ask: Did they not hear? Of course they
did:

> "Their voice has gone out into all the earth,
> their words to the ends of the world."[dt]

[19]Again I ask: Did Israel not understand?
First, Moses says,

> "I will make you envious[u] by those who are not a nation;
> I will make you angry by a nation that has no understanding."[ev]

[20]And Isaiah boldly says,

> "I was found by those who did not seek me;
> I revealed myself to those who did not ask for me."[fw]

[21]But concerning Israel he says,

> "All day long I have held out my hands
> to a disobedient and obstinate people."[gx]

10:13 [n] Ac 2:21 [o] Joel 2:32
10:15 [p] Isa 52:7; Na 1:15
10:16 [q] Isa 53:1; Jn 12:38
10:17 [r] Gal 3:2,5 [s] Col 3:16
10:18 [t] Ps 19:4; Mt 24:14; Col 1:6,23; 1Th 1:8
10:19 [u] Ro 11:11, 14 [v] Dt 32:21
10:20 [w] Isa 65:1; Ro 9:30
10:21 [x] Isa 65:2

[a] *13* Joel 2:32 [b] *15* Isaiah 52:7 [c] *16* Isaiah 53:1 [d] *18* Psalm 19:4 [e] *19* Deut. 32:21 [f] *20* Isaiah 65:1 [g] *21* Isaiah 65:2

---

gospel opens the doors to salvation to all people on the same basis.

10:13 The verb "call on" leads Paul to yet another OT text that underscores the universality of God's offer in the gospel (Joel 2:32). The "Lord" in Joel is Yahweh, but Paul identifies this "Lord" with Jesus (see Ro 10:9, 12), the "stone" of Isa 28:16 (Ro 10:11). Verse 13, then, is important evidence that the early Christians identified Jesus with God.

9:30—10:13 Offering the gospel to all nations and ethnic groups is the logical conclusion from the principle we see in these verses. The church of Christ has committed itself to this great and yet unfinished task. But we are easily deflected from that goal. Ironically, some missions theorists argue that the church should concentrate its resources on people groups who are receptive to the gospel.

Decisions about where to send missionaries are not easy, but we cannot predict where God will call his people to minister. Nor should we direct or deflect that call when it comes.

10:14–15a Paul uses four rhetorical questions to outline the sequence if a person is to be "saved" (cf. v. 13). The steps are, in reverse order to what Paul cites: the sending of preachers, preaching, hearing the message about Christ, believing in Christ, and calling on "the name of the Lord" (v. 13). The quotation from Isa 52:7 (Ro 10:15) confirms that preaching the Good News is essential.

10:16–17 While Israel has heard the Good News (v. 18), its people have not believed (v. 16). Paul condemns Israel in v. 16, then resumes the logical unfolding of the steps necessary for salvation in v. 17. He begins by restating the second step mentioned in v. 14: "Faith comes from hearing" (v. 17). The last part of v. 17 restates the third step in the salvation sequence (v. 14c): Hearing can only happen when a word from God is proclaimed (vv. 8–9).

10:18 Paul applies Ps 19 to the preaching of the gospel. Also puzzling is Paul's apparent claim that the message has gone "into all the earth." He uses hyperbole to assert the gospel had been proclaimed so widely that Jews have no excuse for not responding.

10:19–21 Paul now wants to probe more deeply into the nature of this "hearing." Was it superficial? Not at all. Moses, Paul suggests, was the "first" in a long line of prophets to suggest that God would eventually extend his grace beyond the confines of Israel (v. 19, quoting Dt 32:21). Isaiah is another prophet who predicted the inclusion of Gentiles (Ro 10:20, quoting Isa 65:1). Gentiles who were not seeking righteousness have found it (Ro 9:30); Gentiles who did ask for God have found him (10:20). Paul quotes Isa 65:2 in Ro 10:21 to make two points: God continues to extend his grace to Israel, and Israel continues to rebel.

10:14–21 Paul links salvation to belief, which he in turn ties to hearing the message about Christ. People must be "sent out" so that the message can be proclaimed to all people. Paul himself, of course, was among those whom God had sent out. In his own life of difficult travel and persecution for the message of Jesus, Paul illustrates the theology he teaches: All people need to hear the gospel message so that they can make a decision about who Jesus is and whether they will follow him.

The Remnant of Israel

11 I ask then: Did God reject his people? By no means![y] I am an Israelite myself, a descendant of Abraham,[z]
from the tribe of Benjamin.[a] 2God did
not reject his people, whom he foreknew.[b] Don't you know what Scripture
says in the passage about Elijah — how
he appealed to God against Israel: 3"Lord,
they have killed your prophets and torn
down your altars; I am the only one left,
and they are trying to kill me"[a]?[c] 4And
what was God's answer to him? "I have
reserved for myself seven thousand who
have not bowed the knee to Baal."[bd] 5So
too, at the present time there is a remnant[e] chosen by grace. 6And if by grace,
then it cannot be based on works;[f] if it
were, grace would no longer be grace.
7What then? What the people of Israel
sought so earnestly they did not obtain.[g]
The elect among them did, but the others
were hardened,[h] 8as it is written:

"God gave them a spirit of stupor,
eyes that could not see
and ears that could not hear,[i]
to this very day."[cj]

9And David says:

"May their table become a snare and
a trap,
a stumbling block and a
retribution for them.
10 May their eyes be darkened so they
cannot see,
and their backs be bent forever."[dk]

Ingrafted Branches

11Again I ask: Did they stumble so as to
fall beyond recovery? Not at all![l] Rather, because of their transgression, salvation has
come to the Gentiles[m] to make Israel envious.[n] 12But if their transgression means
riches for the world, and their loss means
riches for the Gentiles,[o] how much greater
riches will their full inclusion bring!
13I am talking to you Gentiles. Inasmuch as I am the apostle to the Gentiles,[p]

11:1 [y] 1Sa 12:22; Jer 31:37 [z] 2Co 11:22 [a] Php 3:5
11:2 [b] Ro 8:29
11:3 [c] 1Ki 19:10, 14
11:4 [d] 1Ki 19:18
11:5 [e] Ro 9:27
11:6 [f] Ro 4:4
11:7 [g] Ro 9:31 [h] ver 25; Ro 9:18
11:8 [i] Mt 13:13-15 [j] Dt 29:4; Isa 29:10
11:10 [k] Ps 69:22, 23
11:11 [l] ver 1 [m] Ac 13:46 [n] Ro 10:19
11:12 [o] ver 25
11:13 [p] Ac 9:15

[a] 3 1 Kings 19:10,14 [b] 4 1 Kings 19:18
[c] 8 Deut. 29:4; Isaiah 29:10 [d] 10 Psalm 69:22,23

11:1–4 Since Israel has rejected the message of Christ, have they now forfeited any claim on God's promises? Paul emphatically rejects any such conclusion and follows it up with a solemn assertion in v. 2a. As in 8:29, the verb "foreknow" means "choose ahead of time." "Whom he foreknew" (v. 2) does not identify the "people" (v. 1) Paul is talking about; rather, it explains why God remains faithful to that people.

11:5–6 The evidence Paul offers for God's faithfulness to Israel in his own day is the existence of a "remnant." But he leads up to that claim with two preliminary points. First, he begins with himself (v. 1b). Paul's reminder to his readers of his Jewish descent reminds us that he himself is both a Jew and a Christian—evidence that God has not abandoned his people. Second, in vv. 2b–4, Paul quotes the Lord's reassurance to Elijah that he has preserved a remnant (1Ki 19:18).

Paul now draws a conclusion: God's word affirms a continuing role for Israel in salvation history (Ro 11:5). But Israel cannot claim this role as a matter of right, for it is due solely to the working of God's grace.

11:7–10 Israel as a whole "sought" a right standing with God but "did not obtain" it (v. 7b). Paul breaks the situation of Israel in general down into two specific entities. One is the remnant, or the "elect" (v. 7c). Despite Israel's rejection of the gospel as a nation, many individual Jews have responded to the gospel. These Jews have obtained the right standing with God that Israel as a whole was seeking. The other, larger division of Jews consists of those who have not attained this right standing. They have been "hardened" (v. 7d).

11:8–10 The OT quotations in vv. 8–10 provide biblical support for the idea that it is God who hardens people. Paul, following Jewish precedent, quotes from every part of the Hebrew canon: the Law (Dt 29:4), the Prophets (Isa 29:10), and the Writings (Ps 69:22–23). In Ro 11:9–10 Paul supports this idea by quoting from Ps 69.

✜ **11:1–10** Some Jews made the mistake of assuming that God's election of Israel virtually guaranteed spiritual benefits to every member of the nation. Birth into that nation, circumcision (for males), and a reasonable faithfulness in observing the law were all that was thought to be needed to ensure one's salvation. Some segments of the Christian church have much the same kind of attitude. People assume that they will go to heaven as long as they can claim such external credits as baptism, confirmation, church attendance, participation in the services and sacraments, and acts of service. Such ideas are as mistaken as the assumptions of the Jews. God calls believers into a living, active relationship with himself that responds to his saving grace in a life lived for him.

11:11–12 Israel's "transgression" (v. 11) of rejecting God's grace in Christ has led to salvation for the Gentiles. But this pattern was more than a historical accident. Jewish rejection and Gentile acceptance was God's plan for the salvation of all the world. The salvation of Gentiles has the purpose of making Israel "envious" (or "jealous").

Paul spoke vaguely of Israel being made "envious" (v. 11); now he speaks of "their full inclusion" (v. 12). The context suggests that the blessing Israel is to experience comes by way of an increase in the number of Jews who are saved (see v. 25).

11:13–14 Paul hints at the practical purpose of what he is saying. His ministry to Gentiles does

Ro 11:14 ❖ What do we make of Paul's positive use of envy? How can envy lead people to be saved?

I take pride in my ministry 14in the hope
that I may somehow arouse my own people to envy[q] and save[r] some of them.
15For if their rejection brought reconciliation[s] to the world, what will their acceptance be but life from the dead?[t] 16If the
part of the dough offered as firstfruits[u] is
holy, then the whole batch is holy; if the
root is holy, so are the branches.
17If some of the branches have been
broken off,[v] and you, though a wild olive shoot, have been grafted in among
the others[w] and now share in the nourishing sap from the olive root, 18do
not consider yourself to be superior to
those other branches. If you do, consider
this: You do not support the root, but
the root supports you.[x] 19You will say
then, "Branches were broken off so that I
could be grafted in." 20Granted. But they
were broken off because of unbelief, and
you stand by faith.[y] Do not be arrogant,[z]
but tremble.[a] 21For if God did not spare
the natural branches, he will not spare
you either.
22Consider therefore the kindness[b]
and sternness of God: sternness to those
who fell, but kindness to you, provided
that you continue[c] in his kindness. Otherwise, you also will be cut off.[d] 23And
if they do not persist in unbelief, they
will be grafted in, for God is able to graft
them in again.[e] 24After all, if you were cut
out of an olive tree that is wild by nature,
and contrary to nature were grafted into
a cultivated olive tree, how much more
readily will these, the natural branches,
be grafted into their own olive tree!

11:14 [q] ver 11; Ro 10:19 [r] 1Co 1:21; 1Ti 2:4; Titus 3:5
11:15 [s] Ro 5:10 [t] Lk 15:24,32
11:16 [u] Lev 23:10, 17; Nu 15:18-21
11:17 [v] Jer 11:16; Jn 15:2 [w] Ac 2:39; Eph 2:11-13
11:18 [x] Jn 4:22
11:20 [y] 1Co 10:12; 2Co 1:24 [z] Ro 12:16; 1Ti 6:17 [a] 1Pe 1:17
11:22 [b] Ro 2:4 [c] 1Co 15:2; Heb 3:6 [d] Jn 15:2
11:23 [e] 2Co 3:16
11:25 [f] Ro 1:13 [g] Ro 16:25 [h] Ro 12:16 [i] ver 7; Ro 9:18

All Israel Will Be Saved

25I do not want you to be ignorant[f] of
this mystery,[g] brothers and sisters, so
that you may not be conceited:[h] Israel has experienced a hardening[i] in part
until the full number of the Gentiles has

---

not mean that he is unconcerned about his own people. His ultimate purpose in bringing the gospel to the Gentiles is to arouse Israel to envy and so "save some of them" (v. 14).

11:15 If God's rejection of Israel has brought "reconciliation to the world" (see 5:10–11), then "what will their acceptance be but life from the dead?" Paul suggests that the return of Israel to favor with God will occur at the climax of history when the dead are raised. This likely reference of "life from the dead" constitutes one important reason to think that Paul is describing a linear sequence of acts in salvation history that peak with the return of Christ in glory.

11:16–24 In this paragraph, dominated by the olive tree metaphor, Paul makes clear his concern to stifle Gentile arrogance.

11:16 Paul uses two metaphors to make his point. The first one in v. 16a is drawn from Nu 15:17–21. The salvation of the remnant shows that God still considers Israel "holy," with all the hope that this holiness implies.

In the second image, the "root" almost certainly represents the patriarchs (Ro 11:16b). This being the case, it is likely that "firstfruits" of v. 16a also refers to the patriarchs. God's promise to the patriarchs has not been withdrawn; their descendants remain "holy." By this Paul does not mean that all their descendants will be saved. Rather, "holy" means that the people continue to be "set apart" by God for special attention.

11:17–18a Paul gets to the heart of his concern. Gentiles were not originally included in the people of God—they do not "naturally" belong to the olive tree. But now that they have been included, they have no reason to boast that they are somehow wiser or better or more blessed than Jews. "Those other branches" (v. 18) refers to the branches cut off in v. 17; that is, to those Jews in Paul's day who have not responded to the gospel.

11:18b–22 The context reveals that the Gentiles were guilty of showing arrogance toward Jews. Paul shows why such arrogance is wrong. Jews forfeited their place because they failed to believe, while Gentile Christians have been included because they believed the message (v. 20b). Faith, as Paul has shown earlier in Romans, gives a person no basis for pride (3:27; 4:3–5). Gentile Christians, therefore, need to replace their arrogance with fear (11:20b). It is necessary to renew one's faith every day. Failure to do so means that one will be "cut off" (v. 22b).

11:23–24 Just as Gentile Christians run the risk of being "cut off" (v. 22) if they stop believing, so Jews can be grafted back in if they turn from unbelief to faith. For it is surely easier to graft natural branches back in than to do what God has already done—that is, graft in, "contrary to nature," wild olive shoots (v. 24).

✣ **11:11–24** Ultimately, the olive tree imagery shows that there is one people of God. Yet Paul's imagery makes clear that the turn of the ages did not bring a new people of God into existence. Rather, Gentiles who believe in Jesus as the Messiah, the fulfillment of the OT, join the already existing people of God, "true Israel."

11:25–27 "Mystery" refers to a truth that has been "hidden" (16:25) from God's people in the past but has now been disclosed in the gospel.

Paul has described Israel's "hardening" earlier (11:7; cf. 9:18). This hardening lasts only "until the full number of the Gentiles has come in" (11:25). In other words, once that number is reached, Israel's hardening comes to an end.

CHARACTER OF GOD // GOD IS WISE

Romans 11:33: Oh, the depth of the riches of the wisdom and knowledge of God! How unsearchable his judgments, and his paths beyond tracing out!

In a very provocative turn of phrase, the apostle Paul references the "foolishness of God" (1Co 1:25). Of course, God is not foolish at all. Paul is contrasting God's wisdom with human wisdom, which people in Corinth valued highly. The city was a center of philosophical thought, perhaps most especially of the Sophists, who excelled in the art of argumentation.

Paul said to the Corinthians that God's plan of salvation through Jesus Christ did not look particularly wise to human eyes. God's grand salvation plan included becoming human and dying on a cross. Paul says this plan sounds foolish to the Greeks, who were always after more lofty wisdom, and it sounds like a scandal to the Jews, who were looking for a sign. Yet to those who are saved, Christ is the power of God and the wisdom of God (1Co 1:24).

Paul connects the message of the cross, which is God's foolish-looking wisdom, to the words of Isa 29:14: "The wisdom of the wise will perish, the intelligence of the intelligent will vanish." God's ways are not our ways (Isa 55:8), and this is good news. God's wisdom, revealed in Jesus Christ, brought salvation to the world. Looking for wisdom anywhere else is bound to fail; Christ is the very wisdom of God.

APPLICATION ✣ In a world of ever new and seemingly better products and trends, we can get caught up in the mindset that the latest must be the best. Old answers must be wrong or outdated. This is the faulty logic Paul addressed in Corinth. He pointed out to the Corinthians that God chooses whom he will, and the foolish things of the world may shame the wise. God's plan of salvation through Christ's death and resurrection may sound foolish, but it is in fact the best news of our lives. In God's wisdom, Christ came not to rule but to serve, in order to bring salvation to many.

come in,[j] 26and in this way[a] all Israel will
be saved. As it is written:

"The deliverer will come from Zion;
he will turn godlessness away
from Jacob.
27And this is[b] my covenant with them
when I take away their sins."[c][k]

28As far as the gospel is concerned,
they are enemies[l] for your sake; but as far
as election is concerned, they are loved
on account of the patriarchs,[m] 29for God's
gifts and his call[n] are irrevocable.[o] 30Just
as you who were at one time disobedient[p] to God have now received mercy as
a result of their disobedience, 31so they
too have now become disobedient in
order that they too may now[d] receive
mercy as a result of God's mercy to you.
32For God has bound everyone over to

11:25 [j] Lk 21:24
11:27 [k] Isa 27:9; Heb 8:10,12
11:28 [l] Ro 5:10 [m] Dt 7:8; 10:15; Ro 9:5
11:29 [n] Ro 8:28 [o] Heb 7:21
11:30 [p] Eph 2:2

[a] *26* Or *and so* [b] *27* Or *will be* [c] *27* Isaiah 59:20,21; 27:9 (see Septuagint); Jer. 31:33,34 [d] *31* Some manuscripts do not have *now.*

The first clause of v. 26 is critical to the interpretation of chs. 9–11 and the NT teaching about Israel in general. What does Paul mean by "all Israel"? We think "all Israel" refers to some Israelites as a representative whole.

If the reference is to a single generation of Israel, Paul seems to indicate Israel as it exists in the end times. Paul predicts the salvation of a significant number of Jews at the time of Christ's return in glory. Paul backs up his prediction by citing Isa 59:20–21 along with a phrase from Isa 27:9 in Ro 11:26b–27.

11:28–36 In vv. 28–32, Paul provides further evidence for his claim that "all Israel will be saved" (v. 26a) and wraps up chs. 9–11 by reminding his readers once more of some of the basic points of his argument. Israel's failure to respond to the gospel has cut the nation off from God's salvation. From this standpoint, therefore, the people of Israel are "enemies" of God (11:28). Nevertheless, God has elected Israel (cf. v. 2), and "God's gifts and his call are irrevocable" (v. 29).

11:30–31 Verse 30 summarizes: Jewish disobedience has resulted in the Gentiles receiving God's mercy. Verse 31, then, describes the next step in the process: Jewish inclusion.

11:32 Paul's concern to put Jew and Gentile on equal footing is reinforced by the solemn conclusion in v. 32: God has sentenced all people to condemnation. But his purpose is ultimately a positive one: He wants to "have mercy on them all."

✣ **11:25–32** This chapter teaches that a significant number of Jews will come to salvation

disobedience[q] so that he may have mercy on them all.

Doxology

33 Oh, the depth of the riches[r] of the
wisdom and[a] knowledge of God![s]
How unsearchable his judgments,
and his paths beyond tracing out![t]
34 "Who has known the mind of the Lord?
Or who has been his counselor?"[bu]
35 "Who has ever given to God,
that God should repay them?"[cv]
36 For from him and through him and
for him are all things.[w]
To him be the glory forever!
Amen.[x]

A Living Sacrifice

12 Therefore, I urge you,[y] brothers and sisters, in view of God's mercy, to offer your bodies as a living sacrifice,[z] holy and pleasing to God — this is your true and proper worship. 2 Do not conform[a] to the pattern of this world,[b] but be transformed by the renewing of your mind.[c] Then you will be able to test and approve what God's will is[d] — his good, pleasing and perfect will.

11:32 [q] Ro 3:9
11:33 [r] Ro 2:4 [s] Ps 92:5 [t] Job 11:7
11:34 [u] Isa 40:13, 14; Job 15:8; 36:22; 1Co 2:16
11:35 [v] Job 35:7
11:36 [w] 1Co 8:6; Col 1:16; Heb 2:10 [x] Ro 16:27
12:1 [y] Eph 4:1 [z] Ro 6:13,16,19; 1Pe 2:5
12:2 [a] 1Pe 1:14 [b] 1Jn 2:15 [c] Eph 4:23 [d] Eph 5:17
12:3 [e] Ro 15:15; Gal 2:9; Eph 4:7

Ro 12:1-2 ❖ How can we offer our bodies as living sacrifices? What does it mean to be a living offering to God?

Humble Service in the Body of Christ

3 For by the grace given me[e] I say to every one of you: Do not think of yourself more highly than you ought, but rather think of yourself with sober judgment, in accordance with the faith God has distributed to each of you. 4 For just as each of us has one body with many members, and these members do not all have the

[a] 33 Or *riches and the wisdom and the*
[b] 34 Isaiah 40:13 [c] 35 Job 41:11

---

in the last days. Those Jews who are converted will become integrated into the Christian church—although perhaps a church on its way to heaven, if the conversion happens at the time of Jesus' second coming.

11:34-35 The three questions here are obviously rhetorical and expect the answer "no one." If the first two questions remind us how far we are from fully understanding God, the final question reminds us of God's grace—a great theme of these chapters.

11:36 God is far more important than his creation and must be given the honor and glory due him. Paul therefore appropriately responds by ascribing glory to this wondrous and all-consuming God.

11:33-36 Paul reminds us that God's thoughts are far beyond anything we could ever comprehend. His plan for individuals and the world is more intricate and marvelous than we could even imagine, so we must exercise great humility in seeking to understand God and his Word. On this side of glory, all our thinking and conjecture are uncertain and tentative. Humility, willingness to listen, and respect for others are the appropriate attitudes for us finite creatures as we seek to explore the depths of God's character and truth.

12:1-2 The command to "offer" ourselves to God reminds us of ch. 6, where Paul used this same verb to express the basic response of believers to God's grace to us in Christ (see 6:13, 16, 19). We no longer offer animal sacrifices; we now offer ourselves as "living sacrifices." This offering of ourselves to God is our "true and proper worship" (12:1). We offer ourselves not ignorantly, like animals brought to slaughter, but intelligently and willingly. This is the worship that pleases God.

The old age to which we belonged in our pre-Christian past entices us to follow its "pattern" of sinful behavior. Rather than "conforming" our conduct to that age, we must be "transformed" in our behavior by having a completely new mindset. A new orientation in our thinking leads to a new orientation in behavior.

12:1-2 We as believers are guided by our minds, which are in the process of being renewed by God's Spirit so that they perfectly reflect God's will. But because that process will never be complete in this life, we still need the external guidance of God's commands as set forth in Scripture. Put another way: Guidance computers in jet airliners tell pilots where they are and where to go, but airports still have runway lights. Similarly, knowledge of the truth comes with a call to personal accountability.

12:3-8 The "grace" given to Paul is his apostolic calling, a manifestation of God's grace. We should regard ourselves, Paul is saying, with "renewed minds" (cf. v. 2) that deliver us from self-centeredness.

12:3 The standard of that measurement is "the faith God has distributed to each of you." Paul may be encouraging us to look at ourselves in light of the gifts we have and to evaluate ourselves accordingly. Another possibility is that Paul is asking us to look carefully to the gospel faith and its requirements as we assess ourselves.

12:4-5 The church, Paul says, is like our individual bodies. It has many different parts, each with its own function. But all the parts form "one body," and each part is needed if the body is to function as it should.

12:6-8 Paul lists a number of gifts God has given the members of the body of Christ. Paul uses this word

same function,[f] 5so in Christ we, though
many, form one body,[g] and each member belongs to all the others. 6We have
different gifts,[h] according to the grace
given to each of us. If your gift is prophesying, then prophesy in accordance with
your[a] faith;[i] 7if it is serving, then serve;
if it is teaching, then teach;[j] 8if it is to
encourage, then give encouragement;[k]
if it is giving, then give generously;[l] if it
is to lead,[b] do it diligently; if it is to show
mercy, do it cheerfully.

Love in Action

9Love must be sincere.[m] Hate what is
evil; cling to what is good. 10Be devoted to one another in love.[n] Honor one
another above yourselves.[o] 11Never be
lacking in zeal, but keep your spiritual
fervor,[p] serving the Lord. 12Be joyful in
hope,[q] patient in affliction,[r] faithful in
prayer. 13Share with the Lord's people
who are in need. Practice hospitality.[s]
14Bless those who persecute you;[t]
bless and do not curse. 15Rejoice with
those who rejoice; mourn with those
who mourn.[u] 16Live in harmony with
one another.[v] Do not be proud, but be
willing to associate with people of low
position.[c] Do not be conceited.[w]
17Do not repay anyone evil for evil.[x] Be
careful to do what is right in the eyes of
everyone.[y] 18If it is possible, as far as it
depends on you, live at peace with everyone.[z] 19Do not take revenge,[a] my dear
friends, but leave room for God's wrath,
for it is written: "It is mine to avenge; I will
repay,"[d][b] says the Lord. 20On the contrary:

"If your enemy is hungry, feed him;
if he is thirsty, give him
something to drink.
In doing this, you will heap burning
coals on his head."[e][c]

21Do not be overcome by evil, but overcome evil with good.

Submission to Governing Authorities

13 Let everyone be subject to the governing authorities,[d] for there is no
authority except that which God has es-

12:4 [f]1Co 12:12-14; Eph 4:16
12:5 [g]1Co 10:17
12:6 [h]1Co 7:7; 12:4,8-10 [i]1Pe 4:10,11
12:7 [j]Eph 4:11
12:8 [k]Ac 15:32 [l]2Co 9:5-13
12:9 [m]1Ti 1:5
12:10 [n]Heb 13:1 [o]Php 2:3
12:11 [p]Ac 18:25
12:12 [q]Ro 5:2 [r]Heb 10:32,36
12:13 [s]1Ti 3:2
12:14 [t]Mt 5:44
12:15 [u]Job 30:25
12:16 [v]Ro 15:5 [w]Jer 45:5; Ro 11:25
12:17 [x]Pr 20:22 [y]2Co 8:21
12:18 [z]Mk 9:50; Ro 14:19
12:19 [a]Lev 19:18; Pr 20:22; 24:29 [b]Dt 32:35
12:20 [c]Pr 25:21,22; Mt 5:44; Lk 6:27
13:1 [d]Titus 3:1; 1Pe 2:13,14

[a] *6* Or *the* [b] *8* Or *to provide for others*
[c] *16* Or *willing to do menial work*
[d] *19* Deut. 32:35 [e] *20* Prov. 25:21,22

"gift" elsewhere to denote a God-given ability to serve the community of Christ in a particular way.

> ✜ **12:3–8** Whatever gift or gifts we have been given, we are under obligation to our Lord to use them to serve his people. Other Christians need what each of us has to offer, so participating in the larger community of faith through the local church is a critical responsibility of believers.

12:9a "Love" can be a vague idea. The Greek for "sincere" was often applied to the actor who "played a part" on the stage. Christians can avoid love that is mere "play-acting" if they put into practice the commands that follow.
12:9b Christian love is more than a feeling; it leads to a violent hatred of evil and a tenacious attachment to what is good.
12:10–12 This verse features two commands that focus on the "one another" relationship among believers. The first uses two words generally applied to loving relations among family members. The second calls believers to put others first.

If the three exhortations in v. 11 all relate to service, the three in v. 12 combine to encourage believers to "stay the course" in their fight against the influence of the world.
12:13 Paul concludes the first series of commands by returning to the theme of v. 10a. We exhibit the familial love of true brothers and sisters in Christ by sharing with other believers who are in need.
12:14–15 Paul's commands in v. 14 remind us of Jesus' famous Sermon on the Mount (Mt 5–7). These similarities suggest that Paul is quoting Jesus' teaching here. In fact, Paul shows more dependence on Jesus' teaching in this part of Romans than he does anywhere else in his letters.
12:16 The command to "live in harmony with one another" (v. 16a) summarizes the overall message of these verses. Perhaps the greatest obstacle to this unity of mind and spirit is pride.
12:17 Paul returns to a key ingredient of the love he mentioned in v. 14: responding to persecution with kindness rather than with hatred.
12:18 Believers must strive to do what is right in the eyes of everyone. Christians must never seek approval with the world at the expense of God's moral demands.
12:19–20 Paul returns to the theme of nonretaliation: God himself is the One who avenges wrong. He follows up the prohibition of v. 19 with a positive call to do good to those who may be doing evil to us (v. 20). Paul urges us to show kindness to our enemies with the hope that they will seek the underlying reason why we can respond with such love.
12:21 God calls us to be active in using the grace of the gospel and the power of the Spirit to win victories over the evil of this world.

> ✜ **12:9–21** Biblical love is a mindset. We are commanded to love; it is therefore a choice we make, a matter of the will. It is also evidence to the world of our core identity as disciples of Christ (Jn 13:35).

13:1–2 The basic point of the paragraph is summed up in its opening words: "Let everyone be subject to the governing authorities." These "authorities"

Ro 13:1–7 ❖ How should Christians engage with the government? What should they do if the government is unjust or evil?

13:1 [e] Da 2:21; Jn 19:11
13:3 [f] 1Pe 2:14
13:4 [g] 1Th 4:6
13:7 [h] Mt 17:25; 22:17,21; Lk 23:2

tablished.[e] The authorities that exist have
been established by God. 2Consequently,
whoever rebels against the authority is
rebelling against what God has instituted,
and those who do so will bring judgment
on themselves. 3For rulers hold no terror
for those who do right, but for those who
do wrong. Do you want to be free from
fear of the one in authority? Then do
what is right and you will be commended.[f] 4For the one in authority is God's servant for your good. But if you do wrong,
be afraid, for rulers do not bear the sword
for no reason. They are God's servants,
agents of wrath to bring punishment on
the wrongdoer.[g] 5Therefore, it is necessary to submit to the authorities, not only
because of possible punishment but also
as a matter of conscience.
6This is also why you pay taxes, for
the authorities are God's servants, who
give their full time to governing. 7Give
to everyone what you owe them: If you
owe taxes, pay taxes;[h] if revenue, then
revenue; if respect, then respect; if hon-
or, then honor.

---

are those who represent the power of the state. The second key word is "subject." This word calls on believers to recognize that they "stand under" government in the design God has instituted to rule the world.

God's providential rule over everything is specifically applied to the rise and fall of political leaders. When we rebel against authority, we are rebelling against God himself, and judgment will result.

13:3–6 Paul specifies that secular government acts as "God's servant" in rewarding good and punishing evil. We must respect governmental authorities because they are God's "servants." Paul could not more strongly have shown that civic leaders are, in fact, serving God's own purposes.

13:7 Paul concludes on a practical note. God asks for more than a grudging outward recognition of the government's authority. Because they are ordained by God, believers are to respect and honor the governing authorities, demonstrating that submission by paying their taxes.

✣ **13:1–7** The word "submit" implies that God is at the pinnacle of any hierarchy. While he doesn't always say it specifically, Paul assumes that the believer's ultimate submission must be to God and that no human being can ever replace God's ultimate authority. If our leaders

EMPERORS AND EVENTS

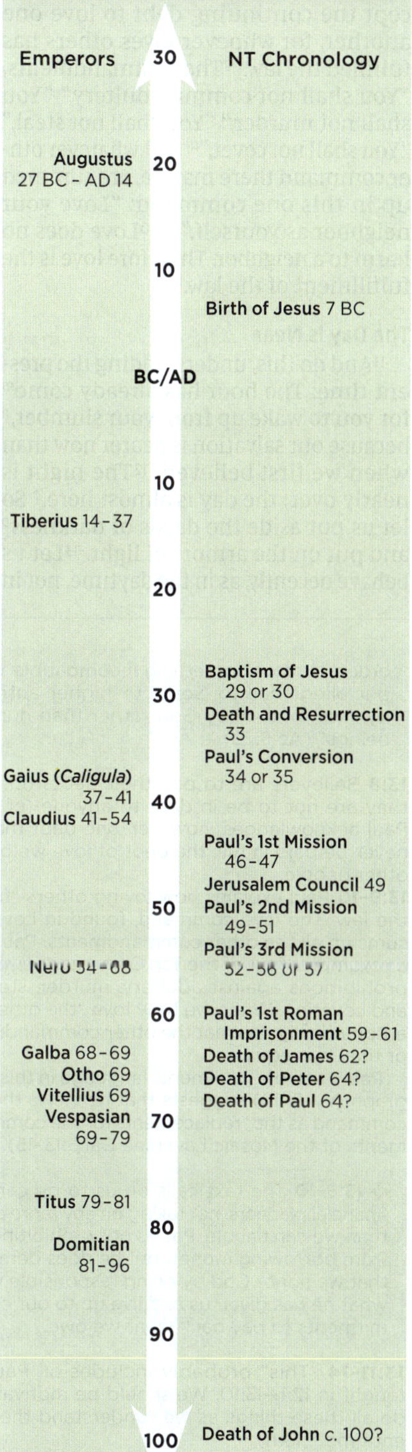

Emperors	Year	NT Chronology
	30	
Augustus 27 BC - AD 14	20	
	10	
		Birth of Jesus 7 BC
	BC/AD	
	10	
Tiberius 14–37		
	20	
	30	Baptism of Jesus 29 or 30
		Death and Resurrection 33
Gaius (*Caligula*) 37–41		Paul's Conversion 34 or 35
Claudius 41–54	40	
		Paul's 1st Mission 46–47
		Jerusalem Council 49
	50	Paul's 2nd Mission 49–51
Nero 54–68		Paul's 3rd Mission 52–56 or 57
	60	Paul's 1st Roman Imprisonment 59–61
Galba 68–69		Death of James 62?
Otho 69		Death of Peter 64?
Vitellius 69		Death of Paul 64?
Vespasian 69–79	70	
Titus 79–81		
Domitian 81–96	80	
	90	
	100	Death of John *c.* 100?

New International Bible Commentary, ed. F. F. Bruce (Grand Rapids: Zondervan, 1979), 1045.

Love Fulfills the Law

8Let no debt remain outstanding, except the continuing debt to love one another, for whoever loves others has fulfilled the law.[i] 9The commandments, "You shall not commit adultery," "You shall not murder," "You shall not steal," "You shall not covet,"[a][j] and whatever other command there may be, are summed up in this one command: "Love your neighbor as yourself."[b][k] 10Love does no harm to a neighbor. Therefore love is the fulfillment of the law.[l]

The Day Is Near

11And do this, understanding the present time: The hour has already come[m] for you to wake up from your slumber,[n] because our salvation is nearer now than when we first believed. 12The night is nearly over; the day is almost here.[o] So let us put aside the deeds of darkness[p] and put on the armor[q] of light. 13Let us behave decently, as in the daytime, not in carousing and drunkenness, not in sexual immorality and debauchery, not in dissension and jealousy.[r] 14Rather, clothe yourselves with the Lord Jesus Christ,[s] and do not think about how to gratify the desires of the flesh.[c]

13:8 [i] ver 10; Jn 13:34; Gal 5:14; Col 3:14
13:9 [j] Ex 20:13-15,17; Dt 5:17-19,21 [k] Lev 19:18; Mt 19:19
13:10 [l] ver 8; Mt 22:39,40
13:11 [m] 1Co 7:29-31; 10:11 [n] Eph 5:14; 1Th 5:5,6
13:12 [o] 1Jn 2:8 [p] Eph 5:11 [q] Eph 6:11,13
13:13 [r] Gal 5:20,21
13:14 [s] Gal 3:27; 5:16; Eph 4:24
14:1 [t] Ro 15:1; 1Co 8:9-12

Ro 14:1 ❖ What "disputable matters" do we see Christians arguing over, and how can we tell which matters are "disputable"? What might Paul say about the arguments among Christians today?

The Weak and the Strong

14 Accept the one whose faith is weak,[t] without quarreling over disputable matters. 2One person's faith allows them

[a] *9* Exodus 20:13-15,17; Deut. 5:17-19,21
[b] *9* Lev. 19:18
[c] *14* In contexts like this, the Greek word for *flesh* (*sarx*) refers to the sinful state of human beings, often presented as a power in opposition to the Spirit.

---

order us to do something incompatible with our allegiance to God, our higher authority, "we must obey God rather than human beings" (Ac 5:29).

13:8 Believers are to pay their debts (cf. v. 7); they are not to be in debt to anyone (cf. v. 8). Paul acknowledges, however, one debt that will never be paid in full: the debt of love we owe to other people.

13:9–10 Paul explains how loving others "fulfills" the law. The love command, found in Lev 19:18, sums up all the other commandments. Paul cites as examples four of the Ten Commandments: the prohibitions against adultery, murder, stealing, and coveting. When we truly love "the other," we automatically do what the other commandments of the Law require.

Paul's use of "fulfillment" language in this paragraph (vv. 8, 10) suggests that he views the love command as the "replacement" for the commandments of the Mosaic Law (see Gal 5:13–15).

✣ **13:8–10** The text calls on us to be careful financial planners, not taking on any more debt than we can handle. Paul is not prohibiting us from borrowing money, but he does demand that we honor God by being responsible with what he has given us and live up to our commitments to pay back what we owe.

13:11–14 "This" probably includes all Paul has taught in 12:1—13:10. We should be motivated to do all these things as we "understand the present time" (13:11).

The day of Christ's return is getting closer all the time. Paul skillfully blends two important strands of tradition using day and night imagery. The day/night contrast was popular in general moral teaching in the ancient world to distinguish good behavior from evil behavior. Paul makes clear these behavioral requirements and consequences in vv. 12b–14. In commanding us not to "think about" gratifying the flesh, Paul is urging us not to allow our fallen human impulses to dominate our behavior.

✣ **13:11–14** Some Christians think nothing of watching movies that contain explicit sex and raunchy humor. Yet exposure to the values promoted in such movies almost inevitably leads those who watch them to become more tolerant of some of those same values. We need to ask not "*can* I do this?" but "*should* I do this?" Does this activity glorify God and honor the Lord whom I represent? What does this activity do to my Christian witness to my family, friends, coworkers, and others who may be outside the Christian faith?

14:1–3 The Christian community at Rome was apparently divided into two groups: those who were "weak [in faith]" (cf. v. 1) and those who were "strong [in faith]" (cf. 15:1). "Faith" refers to one's convictions about what that faith allows him or her to do. Paul is clearly most concerned about the attitude of the strong. Paul wants them to welcome the weak, not simply tolerate them.

Romans 14:2 identifies a "disputable matter": the eating of meat. In v. 3, Paul urges both groups to change their attitude toward the other. The strong should not "treat with contempt" the weak, but the weak must not "judge" the strong believers. This is the theological bottom line in Paul's critique of judgmentalism in the church.

to eat anything, but another, whose faith
is weak, eats only vegetables. 3The one
who eats everything must not treat with
contempt[u] the one who does not, and the
one who does not eat everything must not
judge[v] the one who does, for God has accepted them. 4Who are you to judge someone else's servant?[w] To their own master,
servants stand or fall. And they will stand,
for the Lord is able to make them stand.
5One person considers one day more
sacred than another;[x] another considers every day alike. Each of them should
be fully convinced in their own mind.
6Whoever regards one day as special does
so to the Lord. Whoever eats meat does
so to the Lord, for they give thanks to
God;[y] and whoever abstains does so to
the Lord and gives thanks to God. 7For
none of us lives for ourselves alone,[z] and
none of us dies for ourselves alone. 8If we
live, we live for the Lord; and if we die,
we die for the Lord. So, whether we live
or die, we belong to the Lord.[a] 9For this
very reason, Christ died and returned to
life[b] so that he might be the Lord of both
the dead and the living.[c]
10You, then, why do you judge your
brother or sister[*a*]? Or why do you treat
them with contempt? For we will all
stand before God's judgment seat.[d] 11It
is written:

> "'As surely as I live,' says the Lord,
> 'every knee will bow before me;
> every tongue will acknowledge
> God.'"[*b*][e]

12So then, each of us will give an account
of ourselves to God.[f]
13Therefore let us stop passing judgment[g] on one another. Instead, make up
your mind not to put any stumbling block
or obstacle in the way of a brother or sister.
14I am convinced, being fully persuaded in
the Lord Jesus, that nothing is unclean in
itself.[h] But if anyone regards something as
unclean, then for that person it is unclean.[i]
15If your brother or sister is distressed because of what you eat, you are no longer
acting in love.[j] Do not by your eating destroy someone for whom Christ died.[k]
16Therefore do not let what you know is
good be spoken of as evil.[l] 17For the kingdom of God is not a matter of eating and
drinking,[m] but of righteousness, peace and
joy in the Holy Spirit,[n] 18because anyone

a *10* The Greek word for *brother or sister* (*adelphos*) refers here to a believer, whether man or woman, as part of God's family; also in verses 13, 15 and 21. *b* *11* Isaiah 45:23

14:3 [u] Lk 18:9 [v] Col 2:16
14:4 [w] Jas 4:12
14:5 [x] Gal 4:10
14:6 [y] Mt 14:19; 1Co 10:30,31; 1Ti 4:3,4
14:7 [z] 2Co 5:15; Gal 2:20
14:8 [a] Php 1:20
14:9 [b] Rev 1:18 [c] 2Co 5:15
14:10 [d] 2Co 5:10
14:11 [e] Isa 45:23; Php 2:10,11
14:12 [f] Mt 12:36; 1Pe 4:5
14:13 [g] Mt 7:1
14:14 [h] Ac 10:15 [i] 1Co 8:7
14:15 [j] Eph 5:2 [k] 1Co 8:11
14:16 [l] 1Co 10:30
14:17 [m] 1Co 8:8 [n] Ro 15:13

14:4–9 Here Paul is basically asking this weak believer, "Who do you think you are?" The weak believer is, in effect, claiming to be another believer's master. The Greek word for both "master" and "Lord" is the same. This word is central to the argument of vv. 4-9. "Stand" and "fall" may be paraphrased to mean "stand in favor with" and "fall out of favor with."
14:5 Paul then cites a second disputable matter: judging certain days to be "more sacred" than others. Here the reference is probably to Jewish holy days. In any case, Paul wants every believer to be firmly convinced in his or her own mind.
14:6 Paul resumes the theological basis for his rebuke of the judgmental Roman believers that he began in v. 4. Each, Paul argues, acts out of sincere regard for God and a desire to please him. That is why it is wrong for them to condemn one another.
14:7–9 We always have to take into account not just our own interests but the interests of the One who died for us (v. 9). Whether in life or in death, our Lord owns us and expects us to act in obedience to him.
14:10–12 Here Paul is teaching that every believer is ultimately answerable to God, not to other believers, for their conduct in this life. In v. 11, Paul underscores God's unique role in the judgment by citing Isa 45:23.

> ✣ **14:1–12** This text, along with the attitude toward the Sabbath command as a whole in the NT, suggests that observance of the Sabbath is no longer a requirement for believers. Christians are not required to "rest" on Sunday. Yet Christians also have the liberty to rest on Sunday if they choose and if they are able. Such a rest, while not mandated, is physically and spiritually wise.

14:13–16 Turning specifically to the strong, Paul warns them about putting "any stumbling block or obstacle" in the way of another believer. Paul's point is clear: Those who pride themselves on being strong should avoid bringing spiritual downfall to a brother or sister.
14:14 Paul tries to get the strong to listen to him by conceding that all food is kosher (v. 14). But while the strong have the theory right, they must come to grips with the practice. People may not be convinced that they can eat anything. For them certain foods are still "unclean."
14:15–16 Having explained how food can bring spiritual downfall to a person, Paul moves on to show that this is just what the strong are doing to the weak. Their eating food that weak believers feel convinced is unclean "distresses" them. More than that, it may even "destroy" them.
14:17–18 Paul reminds his readers that God's kingdom is not about eating and drinking. Here Paul uses "righteousness" to refer to ethical righteousness—that is, behavior that is pleasing to God. "Peace" refers to the horizontal harmony that believers should demonstrate. When these blessings are present, "joy"

who serves Christ in this way is pleasing to
God and receives human approval.[o]
19Let us therefore make every effort to
do what leads to peace[p] and to mutual
edification.[q] 20Do not destroy the work
of God for the sake of food.[r] All food is
clean, but it is wrong for a person to eat
anything that causes someone else to
stumble.[s] 21It is better not to eat meat
or drink wine or to do anything else that
will cause your brother or sister to fall.[t]
22So whatever you believe about these
things keep between yourself and God.
Blessed is the one who does not condemn[u] himself by what he approves.
23But whoever has doubts[v] is condemned
if they eat, because their eating is not
from faith; and everything that does not
come from faith is sin.[a]

15 We who are strong ought to bear
with the failings of the weak[w] and
not to please ourselves. 2Each of us should
please our neighbors for their good,[x] to
build them up.[y] 3For even Christ did not
please himself[z] but, as it is written: "The
insults of those who insult you have fallen
on me."[b][a] 4For everything that was written in the past was written to teach us,[b]
so that through the endurance taught in
the Scriptures and the encouragement
they provide we might have hope.
5May the God who gives endurance
and encouragement give you the same
attitude of mind[c] toward each other that
Christ Jesus had, 6so that with one mind
and one voice you may glorify the God
and Father[d] of our Lord Jesus Christ.
7Accept one another,[e] then, just as Christ
accepted you, in order to bring praise to

14:18 [o] 2Co 8:21
14:19 [p] Ps 34:14; Ro 12:18; Heb 12:14 [q] Ro 15:2; 2Co 12:19
14:20 [r] ver 15 [s] 1Co 8:9-12
14:21 [t] 1Co 8:13
14:22 [u] 1Jn 3:21
14:23 [v] ver 5
15:1 [w] Ro 14:1; Gal 6:1,2; 1Th 5:14
15:2 [x] 1Co 10:33 [y] Ro 14:19
15:3 [z] 2Co 8:9 [a] Ps 69:9
15:4 [b] Ro 4:23, 24
15:5 [c] Ro 12:16; 1Co 1:10
15:6 [d] Rev 1:6
15:7 [e] Ro 14:1

Ro 15:7 ❖ Whom do we have a hard time accepting? Why? How might we better live out Paul's directive in v. 7?

[a] *23* Some manuscripts place 16:25-27 here; others after 15:33. [b] *3* Psalm 69:9

---

results. All three of these characteristics are possible only where the Holy Spirit is at work.

14:19 "Edification" translates a word that means "act of building," though it is usually used in the NT in a spiritual sense: the process of building up individual believers or the church in faith.

14:20 How foolish it would be to "destroy" the work of God over food. "Destroy," applied to the church, probably means "ruin." Disputes over food bring disunity, mutual distrust, and eventually the disintegration of a body of believers. Paul then reiterates his conviction that "all food is clean" (v. 20b).

14:21 Paul formalizes the point in a general principle: Believers should avoid doing anything that brings spiritual harm to another believer.

14:22-23 Paul urges the strong to keep their convictions about the matters in dispute to themselves. The blessing at the end of v. 22 is the bottom line for strong believers.

The weak believer who eats would not be eating "from faith"—that is, on the basis of a sincere conviction that eating meat is permissible. Paul is again using "faith" in the specific sense with which he began the chapter (vv. 1-2): a conviction that one's faith allows a person to engage in a certain activity.

14:13-23 The key principle in this chapter is our need to limit the expression of our liberty out of love for God and our fellow believers. Our culture insists on personal rights, and it is easy for Christians to bring that attitude into the church. But the spiritual health of the body is far more important than exercising our rights. The freedom God has purchased for us through his Son is a precious gift, but it is a freedom to live as God wants, not as we want.

15:1-2 The verb "bear" has the same force here that it does in Gal 6:2. The introduction of "neighbor" language suggests Paul is thinking of the love command that calls us to love our neighbors (Lev 19:18; Mk 12:30-31).

15:3 Paul asserts that if Christ, as powerful as he was, could give up his own right to life itself on our behalf, then these strong believers should certainly be able to give up their rights in this regard. Paul likely uses Ps 69:9 in Ro 15:3 to illustrate Jesus' selfless humility because this psalm is used so often in the NT to describe Jesus' suffering. Like Jesus, the strong in Rome should be willing to serve even those who are being nasty to them.

15:4 Paul pauses to remind his audience that the OT, while no longer a direct source of moral instruction, continues to play a central role in helping believers understand their responsibilities as people of God under the new covenant. The ultimate goal of this instruction is "hope" (v. 4). In order to preserve their hope, they must work for the health and unity of God's people.

15:5-6 Paul prays that God himself will grant to the community the ability to think the same way. Paul is praying that they may possess a unity of purpose that transcends these differences. Unity is one stage on the way to the church's final purpose: to "glorify" God (v. 6).

15:1-6 When everyone seeks the good of others and the church as a whole, disagreements can strengthen rather than weaken the community. Ultimately, the Scriptures call on each one of us to bring together two personality traits that do not always go together: (1) tenacity in holding to the essentials of the faith and (2) infinite patience and tolerance toward people who hold differing ideas on the nonessentials of faith.

15:7 To "accept" one another means not just to tolerate other believers but to welcome them as brothers and sisters in the body of Christ (v. 7).

God. 8For I tell you that Christ has become
a servant of the Jews[a][f] on behalf of God's
truth, so that the promises[g] made to the
patriarchs might be confirmed 9and,
moreover, that the Gentiles[h] might glorify God[i] for his mercy. As it is written:

"Therefore I will praise you among
the Gentiles;
I will sing the praises of your
name."[b][j]

10Again, it says,

"Rejoice, you Gentiles, with his
people."[c][k]

11And again,

"Praise the Lord, all you Gentiles;
let all the peoples extol him."[d][l]

12And again, Isaiah says,

"The Root of Jesse[m] will spring up,
one who will arise to rule over the
nations;
in him the Gentiles will hope."[e][n]

13May the God of hope fill you with
all joy and peace[o] as you trust in him,
so that you may overflow with hope by
the power of the Holy Spirit.[p]

Paul the Minister to the Gentiles

14I myself am convinced, my brothers
and sisters, that you yourselves are full
of goodness,[q] filled with knowledge[r] and
competent to instruct one another. 15Yet
I have written you quite boldly on some
points to remind you of them again, because of the grace God gave me[s] 16to be a
minister of Christ Jesus to the Gentiles.[t]
He gave me the priestly duty of proclaiming the gospel of God,[u] so that the Gentiles
might become an offering[v] acceptable to
God, sanctified by the Holy Spirit.
17Therefore I glory in Christ Jesus[w] in
my service to God.[x] 18I will not venture
to speak of anything except what Christ
has accomplished through me in leading
the Gentiles[y] to obey God[z] by what I have
said and done — 19by the power of signs
and wonders,[a] through the power of the
Spirit of God.[b] So from Jerusalem[c] all

15:8 [f] Mt 15:24; Ac 3:25,26 [g] 2Co 1:20
15:9 [h] Ro 3:29 [i] Mt 9:8 [j] 2Sa 22:50; Ps 18:49
15:10 [k] Dt 32:43
15:11 [l] Ps 117:1
15:12 [m] Rev 5:5 [n] Isa 11:10; Mt 12:21
15:13 [o] Ro 14:17 [p] ver 19; 1Co 2:4; 1Th 1:5
15:14 [q] Eph 5:9 [r] 2Pe 1:12
15:15 [s] Ro 12:3
15:16 [t] Ac 9:15; Ro 11:13 [u] Ro 1:1 [v] Isa 66:20
15:17 [w] Php 3:3 [x] Heb 2:17
15:18 [y] Ac 15:12; 21:19; Ro 1:5 [z] Ro 16:26
15:19 [a] Jn 4:48; Ac 19:11 [b] ver 13 [c] Ac 22:17-21

[a] 8 Greek *circumcision* [b] 9 2 Samuel 22:50; Psalm 18:49 [c] 10 Deut. 32:43 [d] 11 Psalm 117:1 [e] 12 Isaiah 11:10 (see Septuagint)

We are to welcome one another *because* Christ has welcomed each one of us.

15:8–9a Paul summarizes one of the key theological teachings of the letter: how the fulfillment of God's promises in the gospel brings blessing to both Jews and Gentiles. The weak (mainly Jewish Christians) need to accept Gentile Christians because God's ultimate purpose is to include them. The strong (mainly Gentile Christians) need to remember that the Jews have always been at the center of God's concerns and promises.

15:9b–12 Paul supports what he says in vv. 8–9a with a series of OT quotations. God intends for his mercy to Israel to spill over to the Gentiles so that they can join together with Jewish believers in praising his name. Each quotation refers to the Gentiles, and two of them (vv. 10, 12) make clear that their presence in the people of God depends on the Jews. Two of them also speak of praising God (vv. 9, 11).

15:13 Paul completes his call to the weak and the strong with a final appeal to God to make this unity a reality. Paul beautifully incorporates into this prayer some of the key ideas from the previous chapters.

> ✣ **15:7–13** God wants to form people transformed by the gospel into communities that reflect the values of the gospel. Vertical reconciliation with God must lead to horizontal reconciliation with one another. Faithfulness to the gospel demands that any believer involved in ministry should seek to maintain a balance between the two perspectives.

15:14–21 Paul is especially concerned to explain why he has taken the liberty to write to them so "boldly" (v. 15) about the gospel. As he explains, he has been called to convert and strengthen Gentiles so that he might present them as an acceptable offering to the Lord. In this letter, Paul has simply developed and explained gospel truth that they already know.

15:15–16 Paul's second reason is introduced in the last phrase in v. 15—"because of the grace God gave me"—and elaborated in vv. 17–21: God gave Paul the gracious ministry of bringing Gentiles into obedience to God. Since the Roman church is mainly Gentile in composition, it lies within the scope of the mandate God himself has given to Paul.

Paul pictures himself as a priest, using the gospel as the means by which he offers his Gentile converts as a sacrifice acceptable to God. But these sacrifices must be "sanctified by the Holy Spirit" (v. 16) if they are to be acceptable.

15:17–18 Because God has given Paul this call to service, he can legitimately "glory" in it (v. 17). Glorying or boasting is appropriate when it is the product of God's own work (cf. 5:2, 3, 11). The goal of what Christ does through Paul is the obedience of the Gentiles, an important echo of the letter's opening (1:5). The means of Christ's work in Paul is both word and deed.

15:19a "Signs and wonders" is standard biblical terminology for miraculous acts. God works miracles through Paul because he is God's "point man" to open up the Gentile world to the gospel.

15:19b–21 Paul has identified the agent of his apostolic ministry (Christ) and its purpose (leading Gentiles to obey the Lord). In the second half of v. 19, he states the results of his ministry. More important than geography is Paul's sense of having completed

the way around to Illyricum, I have fully
proclaimed the gospel of Christ. 20 It has
always been my ambition to preach the
gospel where Christ was not known, so
that I would not be building on someone else's foundation.[d] 21 Rather, as it is
written:

> "Those who were not told about him
> will see,
> and those who have not heard will
> understand."[a][e]

22 This is why I have often been hindered
from coming to you.[f]

Paul's Plan to Visit Rome

23 But now that there is no more place
for me to work in these regions, and
since I have been longing for many years
to visit you,[g] 24 I plan to do so when I go
to Spain.[h] I hope to see you while passing
through and to have you assist me on
my journey there, after I have enjoyed
your company for a while. 25 Now, however, I am on my way to Jerusalem[i] in the
service[j] of the Lord's people there. 26 For
Macedonia[k] and Achaia[l] were pleased to
make a contribution for the poor among
the Lord's people in Jerusalem. 27 They
were pleased to do it, and indeed they
owe it to them. For if the Gentiles have
shared in the Jews' spiritual blessings,
they owe it to the Jews to share with
them their material blessings.[m] 28 So after I have completed this task and have
made sure that they have received this
contribution, I will go to Spain and visit you on the way. 29 I know that when
I come to you,[n] I will come in the full
measure of the blessing of Christ.

30 I urge you, brothers and sisters, by
our Lord Jesus Christ and by the love
of the Spirit,[o] to join me in my struggle
by praying to God for me.[p] 31 Pray that I
may be kept safe[q] from the unbelievers
in Judea and that the contribution I take
to Jerusalem may be favorably received
by the Lord's people there, 32 so that I may
come to you[r] with joy, by God's will,[s] and
in your company be refreshed.[t] 33 The God
of peace[u] be with you all. Amen.

Personal Greetings

16 I commend[v] to you our sister Phoebe, a deacon[b,c] of the church in

15:20 [d] 2Co 10:15,16
15:21 [e] Isa 52:15
15:22 [f] Ro 1:13
15:23 [g] Ac 19:21; Ro 1:10,11
15:24 [h] ver 28
15:25 [i] Ac 19:21 [j] Ac 24:17
15:26 [k] Ac 16:9; 2Co 8:1 [l] Ac 18:12
15:27 [m] 1Co 9:11
15:29 [n] Ro 1:10, 11
15:30 [o] Gal 5:22 [p] 2Co 1:11; Col 4:12
15:31 [q] 2Th 3:2
15:32 [r] Ro 1:10, 13 [s] Ac 18:21 [t] 1Co 16:18
15:33 [u] Ro 16:20; 2Co 13:11; Php 4:9; 1Th 5:23; Heb 13:20
16:1 [v] 2Co 3:1

[a] *21* Isaiah 52:15 (see Septuagint) [b] *1* Or *servant* [c] *1* The word *deacon* refers here to a Christian designated to serve with the overseers/elders of the church in a variety of ways; similarly in Phil. 1:1 and 1 Tim. 3:8,12.

---

a significant phase of the ministry God has given him. Paul has planted thriving, self-reproducing churches throughout the region he has described. He is now in a position to move on. As he explains in v. 20, his ministry is to "preach the gospel where Christ was not known."

15:22–29 Paul goes on to mention his next three destinations (in order of visit): Jerusalem (vv. 25–27), Rome (vv. 22–24, 28–29), and Spain (vv. 24, 28). His main concern is to explain why it has taken him so long to get to Rome (v. 22) and why, when he does get there, he does not plan to stay long (v. 28).

15:24 The verb "assist" in v. 24b has the regular NT meaning of missionary support. Paul hints, then, that he hopes to enlist the support of the Roman Christians for his new missionary effort in Spain.

15:25–26 One obstacle, however, still remains in the way of Paul's trip to the western part of the empire: He is on his way to Jerusalem (v. 25). The context reveals that Paul is referring to the specific ministry of "the collection" (2Co 8:4, 19, 20; 9:1, 12, 13). Paul initiated this enterprise on his third missionary journey, requesting contributions from the Gentile churches he had planted to be sent to Jerusalem for the believers who were suffering from severe want (1Co 16:1–2; 2Co 8–9). The recipients of this collection were "the poor among the Lord's people in Jerusalem" (Ro 15:26).

15:27–29 In v. 27 we detect why the collection is so important to Paul. It is not just a charitable project; it is also designed to bring into closer fellowship Gentile and Jewish believers. By the time he gets to Rome the tension over the collection will be over. He will therefore be able to come to them "in the full measure of the blessing of Christ" (v. 29).

15:30–33 Paul asks the Romans to pray for two things specifically (v. 31): that he will "be kept safe from the unbelievers in Judea" and that the saints in Jerusalem will accept the offering of the collection. He is concerned that Jewish Christians will refuse the gift as being tainted by the "unclean" hands of Gentiles.

Only when these requests have been answered will Paul be able to come to Rome "with joy" and be spiritually "refreshed" with them (v. 32). Paul concludes his request for the Romans' prayer with his own prayer for them: that "the God of peace," that is, the God who gives peace, may be with them (v. 33).

> **15:14–33** No matter how hard we try to avoid it, the number-crunching practicality of our culture exerts a strong pull on us. Therefore it is easy to put ministry in the same category as a business enterprise and assume the keys to success are the same: hard work, careful planning, effective execution. When we mis-categorize ministry in this way, self-reliance and pride can sneak in. As a result, prayer can get left out.

16:1–2 Phoebe is apparently going to be traveling to Rome, and so Paul commends to the church

Cenchreae.[w] 2I ask you to receive her in
the Lord[x] in a way worthy of his people
and to give her any help she may need
from you, for she has been the benefactor
of many people, including me.

3Greet Priscilla[a] and Aquila,[y] my co-workers in Christ Jesus.[z] 4They risked their lives for me. Not only I but all the churches of the Gentiles are grateful to them.
5Greet also the church that meets at their house.[a]
Greet my dear friend Epenetus, who was the first convert[b] to Christ in the province of Asia.
6Greet Mary, who worked very hard for you.
7Greet Andronicus and Junia, my fellow Jews[c] who have been in prison with me. They are outstanding among[b] the apostles, and they were in Christ before I was.
8Greet Ampliatus, my dear friend in the Lord.
9Greet Urbanus, our co-worker in Christ,[d] and my dear friend Stachys.
10Greet Apelles, whose fidelity to Christ has stood the test.
Greet those who belong to the household of Aristobulus.
11Greet Herodion, my fellow Jew.[e]
Greet those in the household of Narcissus who are in the Lord.
12Greet Tryphena and Tryphosa, those women who work hard in the Lord.
Greet my dear friend Persis, another woman who has worked very hard in the Lord.
13Greet Rufus, chosen in the Lord, and his mother, who has been a mother to me, too.
14Greet Asyncritus, Phlegon, Hermes, Patrobas, Hermas and the other brothers and sisters with them.
15Greet Philologus, Julia, Nereus and his sister, and Olympas and all the Lord's people[f] who are with them.[g]
16Greet one another with a holy kiss.[h]
All the churches of Christ send greetings.

17I urge you, brothers and sisters,
to watch out for those who cause divisions and put obstacles in your way
that are contrary to the teaching you
have learned.[i] Keep away from them.[j]
18For such people are not serving our
Lord Christ, but their own appetites.[k] By
smooth talk and flattery they deceive[l]
the minds of naive people. 19Everyone

16:1 [w]Ac 18:18
16:2 [x]Php 2:29
16:3 [y]Ac 18:2 [z]ver 7, 9, 10
16:5 [a]1Co 16:19; Col 4:15; Phm 2 [b]1Co 16:15
16:7 [c]ver 11, 21
16:9 [d]ver 3
16:11 [e]ver 7, 21
16:15 [f]ver 2 [g]ver 14
16:16 [h]1Co 16:20; 2Co 13:12; 1Th 5:26
16:17 [i]Gal 1:8, 9; 1Ti 1:3; 6:3 [j]2Th 3:6, 14; 2Jn 10
16:18 [k]Php 3:19 [l]Col 2:4

[a] *3* Greek *Prisca,* a variant of *Priscilla* [b] *7* Or *are esteemed by*

Ro 16:17 ❖ Why does Paul want believers to watch out for those who cause divisions? Where do we see people needlessly causing divisions today?

this "sister." But Phoebe is more than a sister; she is also a "[servant] of the church in Cenchreae" (see NIV footnote). Phoebe is probably a deacon, serving the church by ministering to the financial and material needs of the believers (see 1Ti 3:8–12; cf. also Php 1:1). Paul gives a further hint of Phoebe's function in the church at the end of Ro 16:2, where he indicates she is a patron or "benefactor." Phoebe was probably a wealthy businesswoman who used her wealth to support the church and its missionaries (like Paul).

16:3–16 Paul also conveys individual greetings to a whole host of people. As the letter was read aloud, this would help cement good relationships with the community.

16:4–5 Paul commends Priscilla and Aquila as "co-workers," a term he uses regularly to refer to people who minister with him in all kinds of ways. They have also "risked their lives" for Paul (v. 4). They must have been fairly wealthy, owning a house large enough for a group of believers to meet there regularly for worship (a "house church"; v. 5a).

16:7 Andronicus and Junia, like Aquila and Priscilla (v. 3), were probably husband and wife. But how can Paul call them "apostles" when they were clearly not among the Twelve? Paul uses "apostle" to refer to a "messenger" (2Co 8:23, Php 2:25) or a "commissioned missionary" (Ac 14:4, 14; 1Co 9:5–6; 15:7[?]; Gal 2:9). In this context, this latter meaning is the most likely.

16:16 Paul concludes his request for greetings with a catch-all request: "Greet one another with a holy kiss" (v. 16a). The kiss was a standard form of greeting in the ancient world generally and in Judaism in particular.

16:1–16 Women were an important and public part of the Roman Christian community. This chapter suggests, and the rest of the NT confirms, that Paul recognizes both women and men in his letters, implying their equality in the community and their participation in worship.

16:17–18 Various theories about who these false teachers may have been and what heresy they propagated have been suggested. As with most false teachers, they "cause divisions," putting "obstacles" in the way of believers. They bring spiritual harm by teaching doctrines contrary to the gospel. They are not serving Christ "but their own appetites" (v. 18).

has heard[m] about your obedience, so I
rejoice because of you; but I want you to
be wise about what is good, and innocent
about what is evil.[n]
20The God of peace[o] will soon crush[p]
Satan under your feet.
The grace of our Lord Jesus be with
you.[q]
21Timothy,[r] my co-worker, sends his
greetings to you, as do Lucius,[s] Jason[t]
and Sosipater, my fellow Jews.[u]
22I, Tertius, who wrote down this letter,
greet you in the Lord.
23Gaius, whose hospitality I and the
whole church here enjoy, sends you his
greetings.
Erastus,[v] who is the city's director of
public works, and our brother Quartus
send you their greetings. [24][a]

25Now to him who is able[w] to establish
you in accordance with my gospel,[x] the
message I proclaim about Jesus Christ, in
keeping with the revelation of the mystery[y] hidden for long ages past, 26but now
revealed and made known through the
prophetic writings by the command of the
eternal God, so that all the Gentiles might
come to the obedience that comes from[b]
faith— 27to the only wise God be glory
forever through Jesus Christ! Amen.[z]

16:19 [m] Ro 1:8 [n] Mt 10:16; 1Co 14:20
16:20 [o] Ro 15:33 [p] Ge 3:15 [q] 1Th 5:28
16:21 [r] Ac 16:1 [s] Ac 13:1 [t] Ac 17:5 [u] ver 7,11
16:23 [v] Ac 19:22
16:25 [w] Eph 3:20 [x] Ro 2:16 [y] Eph 1:9; Col 1:26,27
16:27 [z] Ro 11:36

[a] 24 Some manuscripts include here *May the grace of our Lord Jesus Christ be with all of you. Amen.* [b] 26 *Or that is*

16:21–23 Paul conveys greetings from some of his own associates and from other believers where he is staying. Tertius (v. 22) identifies himself as the scribe who "wrote down" what Paul dictated. Erastus (v. 23) may be the same Erastus referred to in Ac 19:21–22.

16:25–26 Paul concludes his letter with a doxology in praise of God. While Paul (cf. 1:11) or others seek to establish believers in their faith, only God can ultimately do so. God works through the gospel, the Good News of redemption for all people in Christ. The gospel is the "mystery hidden for long ages past" but now "revealed and made known" (16:25-26) for all to see. God's purpose in revealing this mystery was so that "all the Gentiles might come to the obedience that comes from faith."

16:27 The concluding description of God reminds us especially that he has instituted a "wise" and wonderful plan for the redemption of his creation (cf. 11:33–36).

16:17–27 Theology, the "study of God," is not an intellectual pastime. Its ultimate purpose is to enable God's people to glorify him more effectively and more passionately because they have learned more about him. Paul weaves many of the motifs of the letter to the church at Rome into his doxology. It is as if he himself is led to burst out in spontaneous praise to God as he reflects on the marvelous truths God has led him to reveal in this letter. May our "bottom line" in all things imitate Paul's final sign-off in this letter: *Sola Deo Gloria*: "to God alone be the glory."

1 Corinthians

Author: The apostle Paul

Audience: Believers at Corinth whose church was torn apart by factions and immaturity

Date: AD 55

Theme: Through Paul, God gives guidance to the spiritually gifted but immature Corinthian church.

PERSPECTIVE

Although separated by nearly two thousand years of history, there are many similarities between the church in Corinth and the world of today. As we read Paul's first letter to the Corinthians, one underlying similarity stands out: The Corinthian church was divided by factions that threatened to tear it apart. Paul had to handle strong differences of opinion among the Christians on such topics as marriage, lawsuits, meat sacrificed to idols, worship, and Christian doctrine. Similarly, the world today—and all too often the church as well—is in danger of terminal fragmentation.

Is it possible that some of the solutions Paul suggests to the Corinthians can help our dilemma today? Absolutely! To Paul, fostering division was a worldly and immature method of operating. What the church at Corinth needed above all was a unifying wisdom—a wisdom that might seem foolish, weak, and naive to the world, but in reality found its source in the God of all grace.

In this magnificent letter, Paul raises issues and contrasts the world's wisdom—human reason, unbridled freedom, litigation, and no-fault divorce are modern equivalents—with the values of God-given wisdom—purity, forgiveness, reconciliation, and mutual faithfulness. Believers then and now must learn that decisions should be made not according to some limited human ethical system but according to whether they will contribute to the building up of the kingdom of God.

Paul's general approach also produces less judgmentalism and more of a "we're in this together trying to solve this problem" approach.

Reading 1 Corinthians

In this letter Paul dealt, one by one, with problems that had developed in the church at Corinth. Some of them he had heard about from messengers; others had been communicated to him in a letter (see 1Co 7:1). The issues being discussed sound very contemporary: divisions in the church, church discipline, sexual standards and marriage issues, Christian freedom, women in

Event	10 BC	AD 1	10	20	30	40	50	60	70	80	90	100
Jesus' life (c. 6/5 BC–AD 30)												
Paul's conversion (c. AD 35)												
Paul's missionary journeys (c. AD 46–67)												
Paul's stay in Corinth (c. AD 51–52)												
Nero's reign (AD 54–68)												
Book of 1 Corinthians written (c. AD 55)												
Paul's first imprisonment in Rome (c. AD 59–62)												
Paul's imprisonment and death in Rome (c. AD 67–68)												

the church, spiritual gifts, and doubts concerning the resurrection of Christ.

Key Verse

And now these three remain: faith, hope and love. But the greatest of these is love.

—1 Corinthians 13:13

To him, if we would just acknowledge the ultimate source of our allegiances, then we would have a much better chance of getting along.

Perhaps no image better personifies the whole purpose of this book than the beautiful image Paul uses of "one body, many parts" (12:12–30). We cannot deny we are different from other people in many ways. But Jesus Christ taught us that in the end we are all made and claimed by the same source. It is that source, that one body, to which we owe all that we are and can be. And that is what unifies us in the end.

TAKING THE NEXT STEPS

When Paul was working out of Ephesus on his third missionary journey (see Ac 19), there was regular communication by letters and personal messengers between Paul and the church he had started in Corinth (Ac 18:1–17; 1Co 16:8). Because a number of knotty problems had developed in that church, Paul sent this letter to give instruction and advice. His chief goal was to encourage unity and love within the Corinthian body of believers. Such qualities would never occur without a spirit of humility and a pattern of discipline. In addition, as the spiritual father of that young, immature congregation, Paul felt he had to insist on their obedience.

Paul's instructions in 1 Corinthians give practical advice to the church today. (1) The most important quality for a church is unity among its members. Squabbles and infighting are signs of spiritual immaturity. (2) Unity can never be achieved without a love that seeks the good of others. (3) No Christians ought to think that they are better than others. Boasting about what one has received from God destroys rather than builds up the church. (4) God is not pleased with a haphazard manner of doing things in the church; there should be order in the way the church operates. (5) The church ought to be concerned about its reputation in society; in its witness it must bring glory to Christ, the head of the church.

WHAT TO LOOK FOR IN 1 CORINTHIANS

- Dealing with divisions in the church (chs. I; 3)
- Discipline of a sexually immoral man (ch. 5)
- Marriage matters (ch. 7)
- Proper approach to Christian freedom (chs. 8–10)
- Christian worship that builds up the church (chs. 11; 14)
- Proper approach to spiritual gifts, especially tongues (chs. 12–14)
- The chapter on love (ch. 13)
- Discussion on the resurrection of Christ and of Christians (ch. 15)

1 Paul, called to be an apostle[a] of Christ
Jesus by the will of God,[b] and our
brother Sosthenes,[c]

2To the church of God in Corinth,[d]
to those sanctified in Christ Jesus and
called[e] to be his holy people, together
with all those everywhere who call on
the name of our Lord Jesus Christ — their
Lord and ours:

3Grace and peace to you from God our
Father and the Lord Jesus Christ.[f]

Thanksgiving

4I always thank my God for you[g] because of his grace given you in Christ
Jesus. 5For in him you have been enriched[h] in every way — with all kinds of
speech and with all knowledge[i] — 6God
thus confirming our testimony[j] about
Christ among you. 7Therefore you do not
lack any spiritual gift as you eagerly wait
for our Lord Jesus Christ to be revealed.[k]
8He will also keep you firm to the end, so
that you will be blameless[l] on the day of
our Lord Jesus Christ. 9God is faithful,[m]
who has called you into fellowship with
his Son, Jesus Christ our Lord.[n]

1:1 [a] Ro 1:1; Eph 1:1 [b] 2Co 1:1 [c] Ac 18:17
1:2 [d] Ac 18:1 [e] Ro 1:7
1:3 [f] Ro 1:7
1:4 [g] Ro 1:8
1:5 [h] 2Co 9:11 [i] 2Co 8:7
1:6 [j] Rev 1:2
1:7 [k] Php 3:20; Titus 2:13; 2Pe 3:12
1:8 [l] 1Th 3:13
1:9 [m] Isa 49:7; 1Th 5:24 [n] 1Jn 1:3

1Co 1:10 ❖ How can Christians be perfectly united in mind and thought? Is this achievable? Why or why not?

A Church Divided Over Leaders

10I appeal to you, brothers and sisters,[a]
in the name of our Lord Jesus Christ,

[a] *10* The Greek word for *brothers and sisters* (*adelphoi*) refers here to believers, both men and women, as part of God's family; also in verses 11 and 26; and in 2:1; 3:1; 4:6; 6:8; 7:24,29; 10:1; 11:33; 12:1; 14:6,20,26,39; 15:1,6,50,58; 16:15,20.

1:1 This letter is from Paul, the Pharisaic Jew converted to Christ (Ac 9:1–31), who became the apostle to the non-Jewish world (Ac 13–28). He identifies himself as "called" (1Co 1:1) to be an "apostle." Paul will later identify apostleship as a spiritual gift (12:29). This letter is said also to come from "our brother," that is, fellow Christian, Sosthenes, possibly the synagogue ruler of Ac 18:17, if he was later converted.
1:2 The recipients of the letter are the Corinthian Christians. They probably comprise several house congregations. "Sanctified" in v. 2 means separated apart for God. It is virtually synonymous with the next phrase, "*called* to be his holy people" (emphasis added). Paul is reminding the Corinthians of their overarching purpose in the Christian life.
1:3 "Grace" is a free gift; "peace" is wholeness in every aspect of life. Paul Christianizes these conventional Greco-Roman greetings by adding a reference to the origin of grace and peace—the One true God revealed in Jesus Christ.
1:4–7 When Paul says he "always" thanks God (v. 4a), he means either "repeatedly," or "whenever I pray." Paul is grateful that the Corinthian Christians have been "enriched" (v. 5), specifically with spiritual gifts—words of knowledge and wisdom, prophecy, and tongues (12:8–10). This occurred as they responded to his preaching with faith and repentance and received the Spirit. The truth of Paul's message was therefore confirmed (1:6–7).
1:8–9 How can Paul be so thankful and positive about a church with rampant divisions and abuses of these very gifts? Verses 8–9 supply the answer: God's character provides the guarantee. He will remain faithful to his promises, however immature the Corinthians at times seem to be (vv. 8a, 9).

APPLICATION ✚ 1:1–9 Those in whom the Spirit genuinely dwells will experience transformation. Those who begin this process can rest assured that God will be faithful to complete it. Of course, such verses provide no assurance for professing believers who have never shown any evidence of the gifts of the Spirit.

1:10–17 In the first half of this letter, Paul refers to four problems he has heard about that are

CHARACTER OF GOD // **GOD IS FAITHFUL**

1 Corinthians 1:9: God is faithful, who has called you into fellowship with his Son, Jesus Christ our Lord.

In order to assure his readers that their salvation in Christ is certain, Paul points them to the faithfulness of God. Since God is faithful, they can be confident that he will hold them firm until the end so that they can be presented blameless on the day of Christ (1Co 1:8–9).

God's faithfulness is connected to his unchanging (immutable) nature. Since God does not change, he will never abandon his promises to his people. He is not a fickle ruler. He is faithful to his people—infinitely more so than his people are faithful to him. God's rock-solid faithful nature led Paul to write with certainty that "he who began a good work in you will carry it on to completion until the day of Christ Jesus" (Php 1:6). God does not turn his back on his people or on his promises.

God's faithfulness to his covenant promises came at his own expense. Faithful to his commitment to save his people, God the Son came as Jesus Christ and suffered death on the cross as punishment for human sins. Christ was a sinless sufferer (1Pe 1:19). God did this simply out of love, graciously securing salvation for his children.

APPLICATION God's faithfulness is an important reminder that our destiny in Christ is secure. We don't have to worry that God will change his mind about us. God is unchanging and faithful to his promises. We can always rely on God and trust in his word; no word from God will ever fail (Isa 55:11; Lk 1:37).

that all of you agree with one another
in what you say and that there be no divisions among you, but that you be perfectly united in mind and thought. 11My
brothers and sisters, some from Chloe's
household have informed me that there
are quarrels among you. 12What I mean
is this: One of you says, "I follow Paul";[o]
another, "I follow Apollos";[p] another, "I
follow Cephas[a]";[q] still another, "I follow
Christ."

13Is Christ divided? Was Paul crucified for you? Were you baptized in the
name of Paul?[r] 14I thank God that I did
not baptize any of you except Crispus[s]
and Gaius,[t] 15so no one can say that you
were baptized in my name. 16(Yes, I also
baptized the household of Stephanas;[u]
beyond that, I don't remember if I baptized anyone else.) 17For Christ did not

1:12 [o] 1Co 3:4, 22 [p] Ac 18:24 [q] Jn 1:42
1:13 [r] Mt 28:19
1:14 [s] Ac 18:8; Ro 16:23 [t] Ac 19:29
1:16 [u] 1Co 16:15

[a] *12* That is, Peter

plaguing the Corinthian church—factions (1:10—4:21), incest (5:1–13), lawsuits (6:1–11), and sexual immorality more generally (6:12–20).

1:10 Paul's basic appeal for unity involves several key expressions. He appeals to the church in the "name" of the Lord Jesus to "agree with one another." The members must abolish "divisions," a political term for rival parties. They should become "perfectly united" or restored to unity.

1:11–12 People in the church are quarreling because they are aligning themselves with different Christian leaders. There is little evidence that Paul, Peter, and Apollos were themselves at odds with one another. The disparity between the "haves" and the "have-nots" at the Lord's Supper (11:17–34) suggests that a polarization along the lines of rich and poor may have been an even more fundamental factor in the divisions.

1:13–16 Paul's initial reply to these reports consists of three rhetorical questions all implying the answer "no" (v. 13). Verses 14–16 then expand on this last observation about baptism as Paul recalls how many people he baptized in Corinth. The answer is very few.

These young Christians may have been idolizing the leaders who first brought them to the Lord. Baptism was important in the life of the early church. It signified repentance from sin and initiation into the Christian community. By saying Paul did not baptize many, he must mean that he delegated this responsibility to others. Paul's primary calling was to preach rather than to baptize.

1:17 Verse 17b introduces the thought that will form the main idea of 1:18—2:5: Christian proclamation must remain clearly centered on the message of the crucifixion.

1:10–17 The disunity of the church of Jesus Christ remains one of the greatest scandals that compromises its witness today. The only way this unity can have an impact on a non-Christian world is for it to be visible. Paul's call for unity among his readers echoes the prayers of Jesus in Jn 17.

send me to baptize,[v] but to preach the gospel — not with wisdom[w] and eloquence, lest the cross of Christ be emptied of its power.

Christ Crucified Is God's Power and Wisdom

18 For the message of the cross is foolishness to those who are perishing,[x] but to us who are being saved it is the power of God.[y] 19 For it is written:

> "I will destroy the wisdom of the wise;
> the intelligence of the intelligent I will frustrate."[a][z]

20 Where is the wise person?[a] Where is the teacher of the law? Where is the philosopher of this age? Has not God made foolish[b] the wisdom of the world? 21 For since in the wisdom of God the world through its wisdom did not know him, God was pleased through the foolishness of what was preached to save those who believe. 22 Jews demand signs[c] and Greeks look for wisdom, 23 but we preach Christ crucified: a stumbling block[d] to Jews and foolishness[e] to Gentiles, 24 but to those whom God has called,[f] both Jews and Greeks, Christ the power of God and the wisdom of God.[g] 25 For the foolishness[h] of God is wiser than human wisdom, and the weakness[i] of God is stronger than human strength.

26 Brothers and sisters, think of what you were when you were called. Not many of you were wise by human standards; not many were influential; not many were of noble birth. 27 But God chose[j] the foolish[k] things of the world to shame the wise; God chose the weak things of the world to shame the strong. 28 God chose the lowly things of this world and the despised things — and the things that are not[l] — to nullify the things that are, 29 so that no one may boast before him.[m] 30 It is because of him that you are in Christ Jesus, who has become for us wisdom from God — that is, our righteousness,[n] holiness and redemption.[o] 31 Therefore, as it is written: "Let the one who boasts boast in the Lord."[b][p]

2

And so it was with me, brothers and sisters. When I came to you, I did not come with eloquence or human wisdom[q] as I proclaimed to you the testimony about God.[c] 2 For I resolved to know nothing while I was with you except Jesus Christ and him crucified.[r] 3 I came to you[s] in weakness with great fear and trembling. 4 My message and my preaching were not with wise and persuasive words, but with a demonstration of the Spirit's

1:17 [v] Jn 4:2 [w] 1Co 2:1,4,13
1:18 [x] 2Co 2:15 [y] Ro 1:16
1:19 [z] Isa 29:14
1:20 [a] Isa 19:11,12 [b] Job 12:17; Ro 1:22
1:22 [c] Mt 12:38
1:23 [d] Lk 2:34; Gal 5:11 [e] 1Co 2:14
1:24 [f] Ro 8:28 [g] ver 30; Col 2:3
1:25 [h] ver 18 [i] 2Co 13:4
1:27 [j] Jas 2:5 [k] ver 20
1:28 [l] Ro 4:17
1:29 [m] Eph 2:9
1:30 [n] Jer 23:5,6; 2Co 5:21 [o] Ro 3:24; Eph 1:7,14
1:31 [p] Jer 9:23,24; 2Co 10:17
2:1 [q] 1Co 1:17
2:2 [r] Gal 6:14; 1Co 1:23
2:3 [s] Ac 18:1-18

1Co 2:4 ❖ How can Christ's followers demonstrate the Spirit's power today? What power does God display through his children?

[a] *19* Isaiah 29:14 [b] *31* Jer. 9:24 [c] *1* Some manuscripts *proclaimed to you God's mystery*

1:18–20 There are only two kinds of people in the world—those in the process of perishing and those in the process of being saved (v. 18). Each will respond to the gospel message in completely opposite ways. Verse 19 quotes Isa 29:14 for support. First Corinthians 1:20b makes it clear that Paul is not disparaging *Christian* wisdom, intelligence, scholarship, or philosophy.
1:21 Verse 21 explains how the situation of v. 18 came about. People rejected God, so God enacted a plan of salvation (cf. Ro 1:18–32). In his omniscience, God had anticipated this all along, so the whole plan itself was "in the wisdom of God."
1:22–24 Verse 22 then specifies two ways that major ethnic groups found the Christian faith foolish. Many Jews looked for miraculous confirmation of Jesus' claims, which he refused to give (Mt 12:39). Many Greeks considered philosophy important. For such people, the cross was a "stumbling block" and "foolishness" (1Co 1:23). But those whom the Spirit of God touches and convicts, whatever their ethnic background, will find in the cross both godly wisdom and power to transform their lives (v. 24).
1:26–31 This passage describes the status of most of the Corinthians in their society when they were first saved ("called"). They were outside the circle of the strong and mighty. Hence, Paul could term them people who were "foolish," "weak," and "lowly" (vv. 27–28), in direct opposition to the three attributes of v. 26.

Powerful people think the church members are "despised" and "lowly" (v. 28). Yet these are the people God chose to save, shaming the wise and strong. In pointing this out, Paul removes any grounds for boasting (v. 29). Christ more than compensates for the world's rejection. In him, believers receive true wisdom (v. 30). Christians can boast in the Lord, not in their own achievements (v. 31).
2:1–5 In this passage, Paul describes his own ministry, which seemed ordinary in the eyes of the world. Verse 2 emphasizes that the crucifixion was central to Paul's teaching.
2:3–5 Verse 3 underlines Paul's sense of personal inadequacy and dovetails with the Lord's reassurance to him not to be afraid (Ac 18:9–10). The "wise and persuasive words" of 1Co 2:4 refer to worldly wisdom and persuasion since they are contrasted with "the Spirit's power." Verse 5 restates

power,[t] 5so that your faith might not rest
on human wisdom, but on God's power.[u]

God's Wisdom Revealed by the Spirit

6We do, however, speak a message of
wisdom among the mature,[v] but not the
wisdom of this age[w] or of the rulers of this
age, who are coming to nothing. 7No, we
declare God's wisdom, a mystery that has
been hidden and that God destined for
our glory before time began. 8None of the
rulers of this age understood it, for if they
had, they would not have crucified the
Lord of glory.[x] 9However, as it is written:

> "What no eye has seen,
> what no ear has heard,
> and what no human mind has
> conceived"[a] —
> the things God has prepared for
> those who love him —[y]

10these are the things God has revealed[z]
to us by his Spirit.[a]
The Spirit searches all things, even
the deep things of God. 11For who knows
a person's thoughts[b] except their own
spirit[c] within them? In the same way
no one knows the thoughts of God except the Spirit of God. 12What we have
received is not the spirit[d] of the world,[e]
but the Spirit who is from God, so that
we may understand what God has freely
given us. 13This is what we speak, not
in words taught us by human wisdom[f]
but in words taught by the Spirit, explaining spiritual realities with Spirit-
taught words.[b] 14The person without
the Spirit does not accept the things
that come from the Spirit of God but
considers them foolishness,[g] and cannot understand them because they are
discerned only through the Spirit. 15The
person with the Spirit makes judgments
about all things, but such a person is not
subject to merely human judgments,
16for,

2:4 [t] Ro 15:19
2:5 [u] 2Co 4:7; 6:7
2:6 [v] Eph 4:13; Php 3:15; Heb 5:14 [w] 1Co 1:20
2:8 [x] Ac 7:2; Jas 2:1
2:9 [y] Isa 64:4; 65:17
2:10 [z] Mt 13:11; Eph 3:3,5 [a] Jn 14:26
2:11 [b] Jer 17:9 [c] Pr 20:27
2:12 [d] Ro 8:15 [e] 1Co 1:20,27
2:13 [f] 1Co 1:17
2:14 [g] 1Co 1:18

[a] 9 Isaiah 64:4 [b] 13 Or *Spirit, interpreting spiritual truths to those who are spiritual*

---

the rationale for his strategy, complementing the contrast between 1:29 and 31.

1:18—2:5 Healthy churches will expend significant portions of their budgets and personal attention on evangelism and social action, locally and globally. And 1:30 directs our attention to another pair of priorities that cannot be separated—correct knowledge and correct behavior. Too many today resemble the ancient Greek philosophers who made a distinction between inward spirituality and outward morality.

2:6 The "mature" of v. 6a are the opposite of "the rulers of this age" (v. 6b), just as Paul's "message of wisdom" (v. 6a) contrasts with the "wisdom of this age" (v. 6b). Because those who are not mature are unbelievers, the "mature" in this context must be all Christians, at least in principle. The irony is that the Corinthians are living as if they are still unsaved—in the grip of the world's values.

2:7–10a The "rulers" refer at least to the religious and political authorities of the day, such as Caiaphas and Pilate, who crucified the Lord of glory (v. 8). They may also refer to demonic powers opposing the gospel (cf. Eph 2:2).

The word "mystery" refers to components of the gospel once hidden but now revealed. The concept of a crucified Messiah was not clearly understood in OT times and was still not understood in Paul's day by those who rejected Jesus. Isaiah himself had prophesied unexpected wonders surrounding God's coming salvation for his people (1Co 2:9, quoting Isa 64:4). God had planned these wondrous events for the benefit of those who would respond positively (v. 7b). The Holy Spirit now reveals what once was unknown.

2:10b–16 The contrast between those who possess the Spirit and those who do not begins with a syllogism—a three-part argument in which two premises, if true, logically lead to a particular conclusion (vv. 10b–12). (1) The major premise observes that only a person's own spirit or mind knows that individual's thoughts (v. 11a). This is true for God as well as humanity (vv. 10b, 11b). (2) The minor premise reiterates that Christians have God's Spirit living in them (v. 12a). "The spirit of the world" (v. 12a) refers to fallen human nature and ideologies, not to anything more directly demonic. (3) The conclusion logically follows then that Christians can know God's thoughts as his Spirit graciously reveals them (v. 12b).

2:13–16 These verses reiterate the fundamental contrast of 1:18—2:5. "Human" wisdom (v. 13a) must thus refer to that which is *merely* human, that is, not born again. "The person without the Spirit does not accept" Christian truths (v. 14). Conversely, the "person with the Spirit" (v. 15a) refers to any Christian (cf. 12:13). "Makes judgments" (2:15) comes from the same verb as "discerned" and helps to interpret it. This means believers can bring God's perspective to bear on every aspect of life. Christians are not subject to any *merely* human evaluation—that is, one that does not take God's perspective into account. Verse 16 rounds out the passage by quoting Isa 40:13 on the mystery of God's ways.

2:6–16 In an age of specialization, we are bombarded by claims that the key to a happy, healthy Christian faith, individually or corporately, is to be found in some new technique of evangelism, practice of certain spiritual disciplines, strategy for church growth, self-

"Who has known the mind of the
Lord
so as to instruct him?"[a][h]

But we have the mind of Christ.[i]

The Church and Its Leaders

3 Brothers and sisters, I could not address you as people who live by the Spirit[j] but as people who are still worldly[k]—mere infants[l] in Christ. 2 I gave you milk, not solid food,[m] for you were not yet ready for it.[n] Indeed, you are still not ready. 3 You are still worldly. For since there is jealousy and quarreling[o] among you, are you not worldly? Are you not acting like mere humans? 4 For when one says, "I follow Paul," and another, "I follow Apollos,"[p] are you not mere human beings?

5 What, after all, is Apollos? And what is Paul? Only servants, through whom you came to believe—as the Lord has assigned to each his task. 6 I planted the seed,[q] Apollos watered it, but God has been making it grow. 7 So neither the one who plants nor the one who waters is anything, but only God, who makes things grow. 8 The one who plants and the one who waters have one purpose, and they will each be rewarded according to their own labor.[r] 9 For we are co-workers in God's service;[s] you are God's field,[t] God's building.[u]

10 By the grace God has given me,[v] I laid a foundation[w] as a wise builder, and someone else is building on it. But each one should build with care. 11 For no one can lay any foundation other than the one already laid, which is Jesus Christ.[x] 12 If anyone builds on this foundation using gold, silver, costly stones, wood, hay or straw, 13 their work will be shown for what it is,[y] because the Day[z] will bring it to light. It will be revealed with fire, and the fire will test the quality of each person's work. 14 If what has been built survives, the builder will receive a reward. 15 If it is burned up, the builder will suffer loss but yet will be saved—even though only as one escaping through the flames.[a]

2:16 [h] Isa 40:13 [i] Jn 15:15
3:1 [j] 1Co 2:15 [k] Ro 7:14; 1Co 2:14 [l] Heb 5:13
3:2 [m] Heb 5:12-14; 1Pe 2:2 [n] Jn 16:12
3:3 [o] 1Co 1:11; Gal 5:20
3:4 [p] 1Co 1:12
3:6 [q] Ac 18:4-11
3:8 [r] Ps 62:12
3:9 [s] 2Co 6:1 [t] Isa 61:3 [u] Eph 2:20-22; 1Pe 2:5
3:10 [v] Ro 12:3 [w] Ro 15:20
3:11 [x] Isa 28:16; Eph 2:20
3:13 [y] 1Co 4:5 [z] 2Th 1:7-10
3:15 [a] Jude 23

1Co 3:4 ❖ Where have we seen believers arguing over which Christian leader or teacher to follow? What would Paul say about such disputes?

[a] *16* Isaiah 40:13

help therapy, Sunday school curriculum, form of music or style of worship, and on and on. When these so-called keys cause divisions within Christian communities, they have the potential to move away from the humbling, central focus on the cross of Christ and life in the Spirit.

3:1–4 Paul compares two kinds of Christians—those who are being controlled by the Spirit and those who are not. The latter are described in this passage as divisive. To be "worldly" (v. 1) is to be dominated by one's sinful nature. This is demonstrated here by jealousy and quarreling. To "live by the Spirit" (v. 1) means having the Spirit *in charge*. The Corinthians' immaturity resembles adults still eating only baby food (v. 2). Or, to change the comparison, they are acting like unsaved people (v. 3b).

3:5–9a These verses clarify another problem with the Corinthians' divisiveness. Their behavior ignores the fact that all Christian leaders are merely "servants" (v. 5) whose roles are insignificant when compared to God's work in causing his church to grow.

3:6–7 Paul compares the church to a field. Farmers were keenly aware that their own contribution to a successful harvest was rather minimal compared to the role of nature. Compared to God's role, humans' roles are nothing of consequence. Paul is stressing that *God* is the One to whom the "co-workers," "field," and "building" belong.

3:9b–11 Just as Paul has described the church and its leaders with an agricultural metaphor in vv. 6–9a, he now turns to a metaphor from the world of construction (vv. 9b–17). God's sovereign guidance comes to the forefront (v. 10).

Paul likens himself to an expert "builder." Paul contrasts his godly wisdom with the Corinthians' misguided claims to wisdom. The word for "builder" here refers to an on-site supervisor. The foundation of any truly Christian edifice must, of course, be the cross-centered gospel of Jesus Christ (v. 11).

3:12–13 There are two ways of building on that foundation. Gold, silver, and costly stones reflect valuable materials that do not easily burn. Wood, hay, and stubble cost less and are quickly consumed by fire (v. 12). In the ancient world, people would have built a temple out of the former and an ordinary home out of the latter. Verse 13 likens "the Day" (i.e., judgment day) to just such a fire. "It will be revealed" (v. 13b) probably refers to "the Day" and not to the "work." When Christ returns, all believers will have to appear before him (2Co 5:10).

3:14 "What has been built" (v. 14a) refers to Christ's assessment of the way Christians live their lives after salvation. The nature of believers' rewards remains unspecified here (v. 14b), but in 4:5 it will be described as "praise from God."

3:15 Paul may have in mind also the loss of the reward—diminished praise and increased shame (cf. 1Jn 2:28) as we realize how much of our lives were spent in activity that had no eternal value. Such believers are saved by the "skin of their teeth" or, to use Paul's metaphor, like "one escaping" from a burning house (1Co 3:15b).

16 Don't you know that you yourselves
are God's temple[b] and that God's Spirit
dwells in your midst? 17 If anyone destroys God's temple, God will destroy
that person; for God's temple is sacred,
and you together are that temple.
18 Do not deceive yourselves. If any of
you think you are wise[c] by the standards
of this age, you should become "fools"
so that you may become wise. 19 For the
wisdom of this world is foolishness[d] in
God's sight. As it is written: "He catches
the wise in their craftiness"[a];[e] 20 and again,
"The Lord knows that the thoughts of the
wise are futile."[b][f] 21 So then, no more boasting about human leaders![g] All things are
yours,[h] 22 whether Paul or Apollos or Cephas[c][i] or the world or life or death or the
present or the future[j]—all are yours, 23 and
you are of Christ,[k] and Christ is of God.

The Nature of True Apostleship

4 This, then, is how you ought to regard us: as servants of Christ and as
those entrusted[l] with the mysteries[m] God
has revealed. 2 Now it is required that
those who have been given a trust must
prove faithful. 3 I care very little if I am
judged by you or by any human court;
indeed, I do not even judge myself. 4 My
conscience is clear, but that does not
make me innocent.[n] It is the Lord who
judges me. 5 Therefore judge nothing[o]
before the appointed time; wait until the
Lord comes. He will bring to light what
is hidden in darkness and will expose
the motives of the heart. At that time
each will receive their praise from God.[p]
6 Now, brothers and sisters, I have applied these things to myself and Apollos
for your benefit, so that you may learn
from us the meaning of the saying, "Do
not go beyond what is written."[q] Then
you will not be puffed up in being a follower of one of us over against the other.[r] 7 For who makes you different from
anyone else? What do you have that you
did not receive?[s] And if you did receive it,
why do you boast as though you did not?
8 Already you have all you want! Already you have become rich![t] You have
begun to reign—and that without us!
How I wish that you really had begun to
reign so that we also might reign with
you! 9 For it seems to me that God has

3:16 [b] 1Co 6:19; 2Co 6:16
3:18 [c] Isa 5:21; 1Co 8:2
3:19 [d] 1Co 1:20, 27 [e] Job 5:13
3:20 [f] Ps 94:11
3:21 [g] 1Co 4:6 [h] Ro 8:32
3:22 [i] 1Co 1:12 [j] Ro 8:38
3:23 [k] 1Co 15:23; 2Co 10:7; Gal 3:29
4:1 [l] 1Co 9:17; Titus 1:7 [m] Ro 16:25
4:4 [n] Ro 2:13
4:5 [o] Mt 7:1, 2; Ro 2:1 [p] Ro 2:29
4:6 [q] 1Co 1:19, 31; 3:19, 20 [r] 1Co 1:12
4:7 [s] Jn 3:27; Ro 12:3, 6
4:8 [t] Rev 3:17, 18

[a] *19* Job 5:13 [b] *20* Psalm 94:11 [c] *22* That is, Peter

1Co 4:5 ❖ Is it ever right for Christians to judge others? Why or why not?

3:16–17 The church is not just any building; it is the most holy and valuable of edifices (vv. 16–17). The Christian fellowship is the special place of the Spirit's presence. That is why the threat of v. 17a is so harsh. Here Paul warns against any who would try to destroy the church.

3:18–23 These verses close the chapter with Paul repeating his appeal to banish divisiveness. Those in the fellowship must become foolish by the world's standards and embrace the godly wisdom that Paul has been teaching (vv. 18–19a). Verses 21–23 highlight a final reason for the futility of such attitudes: The Corinthians have everything they could legitimately need or want in Jesus.

3:1–23 Believers do not automatically have Christ in charge of every area of their lives. Christians are free to take back a certain measure of control, which they do every time they consciously sin. While all believers still experience the pull of sin, Paul teaches us through his letter to the Romans that we need not be controlled by that impulse (Ro 6:1–2; 8:2). Paul also encourages believers to live by the power of the Spirit in our daily lives to defeat sin (2Co 3:17–18).

4:1–2 Two key terms describe the nature of the apostles' servanthood. Instead of seeing Christian preachers as rival leaders, the Corinthians should recognize them as helpers and overseers. "Servant" (v. 1) referred to "an assistant to someone in an official position." "Those who have been given a trust" (v. 2) refers to the highest-ranking servant of a wealthy landowner. Together, both words compare Paul, Apollos, Peter, and their peers to servants answerable primarily to God but with authority over those in their care.

4:3–5 The key task of a steward is faithfulness to his master, so v. 3 must thus be kept in context. The Corinthians' view of Paul matters little *relative to* God's view of him. "My conscience is clear" (v. 4) can also be read as "I am aware of nothing against myself."

4:6–7 For Paul, "what is written" (v. 6) usually refers to the OT. There is no specific verse that states, "Do not go beyond what is written." Paul is probably referring more generally to the need to remain within biblical standards. Verse 7 underlines this appeal with three rhetorical questions anticipating the answers, "no one," "nothing," and "no good reason."

4:8 Paul's writing in this verse drips with irony and sarcasm. Here is one of the key texts that addresses the misguided idea that all the blessings of the messianic age had already arrived; this idea was prevalent in the church at Corinth. If all the blessings of the messianic age had really come, Paul asserts, he and his companions would be experiencing the same freedom these Corinthians claimed.

4:9–10 Paul provides a poignant catalog of the apostles' suffering. He uses two metaphors throughout

put us apostles on display at the end of
the procession, like those condemned to
die[u] in the arena. We have been made a
spectacle[v] to the whole universe, to angels as well as to human beings. 10We are
fools for Christ,[w] but you are so wise in
Christ![x] We are weak, but you are strong![y]
You are honored, we are dishonored! 11To
this very hour we go hungry and thirsty,
we are in rags, we are brutally treated,
we are homeless.[z] 12We work hard with
our own hands.[a] When we are cursed,
we bless;[b] when we are persecuted, we
endure it; 13when we are slandered, we
answer kindly. We have become the scum
of the earth, the garbage[c] of the world—
right up to this moment.

Paul's Appeal and Warning

14I am writing this not to shame you
but to warn you as my dear children.[d]
15Even if you had ten thousand guardians
in Christ, you do not have many fathers,
for in Christ Jesus I became your father
through the gospel.[e] 16Therefore I urge
you to imitate me.[f] 17For this reason I
have sent to you Timothy, my son[g] whom

4:9 [u]Ro 8:36 [v]Heb 10:33
4:10 [w]1Co 1:18; Ac 17:18 [x]1Co 3:18 [y]1Co 2:3
4:11 [z]Ro 8:35; 2Co 11:23-27
4:12 [a]Ac 18:3 [b]1Pe 3:9
4:13 [c]La 3:45
4:14 [d]1Th 2:11
4:15 [e]1Co 9:12, 14,18,23
4:16 [f]1Co 11:1; Php 3:17; 1Th 1:6; 2Th 3:7,9
4:17 [g]1Ti 1:2
[h]1Co 7:17
4:19 [i]2Co 1:15, 16 [j]Ac 18:21
4:21 [k]2Co 1:23; 13:2,10
5:1 [l]Lev 18:8; Dt 22:30
5:2 [m]2Co 7:7-11

1Co 5:1 ❖ How does sexual immorality still affect the church?

I love, who is faithful in the Lord. He will
remind you of my way of life in Christ
Jesus, which agrees with what I teach
everywhere in every church.[h]
18Some of you have become arrogant,
as if I were not coming to you. 19But I
will come to you very soon,[i] if the Lord
is willing,[j] and then I will find out not
only how these arrogant people are talking, but what power they have. 20For the
kingdom of God is not a matter of talk
but of power. 21What do you prefer? Shall
I come to you with a rod of discipline,[k]
or shall I come in love and with a gentle spirit?

Dealing With a Case of Incest

5 It is actually reported that there is
sexual immorality among you, and of
a kind that even pagans do not tolerate:
A man is sleeping with his father's wife.[l]
2And you are proud! Shouldn't you rather have gone into mourning[m] and have

---

v. 9. First, he imagines himself and his companions as prisoners of war in a victory procession by the opposing army (cf. 2Co 2:14–15). Second, he envisions being thrown to the gladiators or wild animals in the sporting arena. In 1Co 4:10, Paul returns to irony, mocking the way the Corinthians view him.
4:11–12a Paul provides a more straightforward list of his hardships.
4:12b–13a Here Paul gives a remarkable model of how to respond to ungodly treatment.
4:13b Paul introduces a measure of hyperbole. "Scum" and "garbage" refer to that which is removed by a process of cleaning. Paul points to his sufferings for the sake of the gospel as a more accurate measure of Christian faithfulness.
4:14–17 As abruptly as Paul's sarcasm began, it now gives way to tenderness. Their local leaders are only "guardians" (referring to Greek slaves in charge of seeing that children got from home to school and back again safely), but Paul is their spiritual father (v. 15).

Paul calls others to imitate him, just as a father in the ancient world regularly taught his sons a trade. Paul has a unique responsibility and authority to oversee their spiritual growth. He would like to be personally present again with them, but he believes the Lord wants him to stay on in Ephesus (16:8–9), so he has sent Timothy in his place. Timothy will remind the Corinthians of the appropriate Christian walk ("way of life," 4:17).
4:18–21 Paul gives a final warning. He is coming soon, even though some in Corinth are claiming that he is not (vv. 18–19a). If he speaks gently to them in person, it is out of love (v. 21b). If necessary, he will come, metaphorically speaking, with a rod, using corporal punishment. What ultimately counts, however, is the presence of genuine spiritual power (vv. 19b–20).

4:1–21 It is difficult to maintain the delicate balance between not judging individuals and congregations at all, even in biblical ways, and judging every minute detail of their lives, often by secular criteria. In our radically individualistic, highly democratic society, "Let your conscience be your guide" sounds like biblical truth. Verse 4 makes plain that it is not. The Bible teaches the ability of each individual to relate directly to God, to understand enough of Scripture to come to salvation, and to be valued in God's eyes as much any other human being. But these themes have focused on individualism to the point that personal interpretations of the Bible distort the Bible's true teachings.

5:1–2 We do not know how widely the news of this chapter had traveled, but it had at least reached Paul. "Sexual immorality" is the most general of all terms for sexual sin. In this context, however, it is clear that the sin is a matter of incest.

"Father's wife" means the woman is his stepmother. Whether or not the son had legally married the woman is impossible to determine. This kind of incest was strictly forbidden in Jewish law (Lev 18:8). Despite the moral laxity of the Greco-Roman world, this kind of incest was relatively rare and widely condemned.

The church's reaction to this affair was as bad or worse than the affair itself. The members were smug over their "enlightened" tolerance (1Co 5:2),

put out of your fellowship the man who
has been doing this? 3For my part, even
though I am not physically present, I am
with you in spirit.[n] As one who is present with you in this way, I have already
passed judgment in the name of our Lord
Jesus[o] on the one who has been doing
this. 4So when you are assembled and I
am with you in spirit, and the power of
our Lord Jesus is present, 5hand this man
over[p] to Satan for the destruction of the
flesh,[a,b] so that his spirit may be saved
on the day of the Lord.

6Your boasting is not good.[q] Don't
you know that a little yeast[r] leavens the
whole batch of dough?[s] 7Get rid of the old
yeast, so that you may be a new unleavened batch — as you really are. For Christ,
our Passover lamb, has been sacrificed.[t]
8Therefore let us keep the Festival, not
with the old bread leavened with malice
and wickedness, but with the unleavened
bread[u] of sincerity and truth.

9I wrote to you in my letter not to associate[v] with sexually immoral people —
10not at all meaning the people of this
world[w] who are immoral, or the greedy
and swindlers, or idolaters. In that case
you would have to leave this world. 11But
now I am writing to you that you must
not associate with anyone who claims
to be a brother or sister[c] but is sexually
immoral or greedy, an idolater[x] or slanderer, a drunkard or swindler. Do not
even eat with such people.

12What business is it of mine to judge
those outside[y] the church? Are you not
to judge those inside?[z] 13God will judge
those outside. "Expel the wicked person
from among you."[da]

Lawsuits Among Believers

6 If any of you has a dispute with another, do you dare to take it before
the ungodly for judgment instead of before the Lord's people?[b] 2Or do you not
know that the Lord's people will judge
the world?[c] And if you are to judge the
world, are you not competent to judge
trivial cases? 3Do you not know that we
will judge angels? How much more the

5:3 [n] Col 2:5 [o] 2Th 3:6
5:5 [p] 1Ti 1:20
5:6 [q] Jas 4:16 [r] Mt 16:6,12 [s] Gal 5:9
5:7 [t] Mk 14:12; 1Pe 1:19
5:8 [u] Ex 12:14, 15; Dt 16:3
5:9 [v] Eph 5:11; 2Th 3:6,14
5:10 [w] 1Co 10:27
5:11 [x] 1Co 10:7,14
5:12 [y] Mk 4:11 [z] ver 3-5; 1Co 6:1-4
5:13 [a] Dt 13:5
6:1 [b] Mt 18:17
6:2 [c] Mt 19:28; Lk 22:30

[a] *5* In contexts like this, the Greek word for *flesh* (*sarx*) refers to the sinful state of human beings, often presented as a power in opposition to the Spirit. [b] *5* Or *of his body* [c] *11* The Greek word for *brother or sister* (*adelphos*) refers here to a believer, whether man or woman, as part of God's family; also in 8:11,13. [d] *13* Deut. 13:5; 17:7; 19:19; 21:21; 22:21,24; 24:7

and Paul recoils in horror. They must remove this man from their midst ("fellowship").

5:3–4 Paul asserts his authority to pronounce judgment, reflecting the authority of Christ Jesus himself.

5:5 Precisely what Paul commands the Corinthians to do in v. 5 remains hotly disputed. It *at least* involves excommunication. In 1Ti 1:20, Paul describes how he handed two believers over to Satan to be "taught not to blaspheme," so presumably they did not die. A good case can be made for seeing the repentant sinner of 2Co 2:5–11; 7:8–13 as this same individual addressed in 1Co 5. In either event, Paul's purpose clearly remains remedial.

5:6–8 In speaking about the action of expelling this person from the fellowship, Paul appeals to the Jews' practice of purifying their homes from all leavened bread prior to the Passover festival (Ex 12:15). Paul applies this imagery to the *moral* purity God requires of his new house/temple—the church. Citing in 1Co 5:6 what may have been a popular proverb (cf. Gal 5:9), Paul makes it clear that serious sin can infect the whole congregation. Thinking of Passover reminds him of Christ as our perfect sacrifice (1Co 5:7).

Jesus' atonement was not intended to free us *to* sin but to liberate us *from* sin. This means putting away all forms of evil and behaving in ways that genuinely conform to God's true standards (v. 8).

5:9–11 Paul closes this section by clarifying an apparent misunderstanding of his previous letter. When Paul had told them not to associate with immoral people (v. 9), he was referring to professing Christians, not unbelievers. To drive home this point, Paul generalizes and lists several serious sins in addition to sexual immorality (vv. 10–11).

5:12–13 Paul here explains the logic of the commands of vv. 9–11. God will take care of unbelievers' sins; their fate will be bad enough that Christians should seek to lead them to Christ. So Paul concludes where he began, reminding the Corinthians to expel the offender.

5:1–13 Some church leaders commit sexual sin or defraud their congregations. In some cases, even if a period of discipline and restoration is established, they may refuse to agree to their church's terms for healing and restoration. In other cases, such a period seems inadequate to demonstrate a genuine and lasting change. But forgiveness and restoration do not automatically carry with them the privilege of pastoring or leading a congregation.

The criteria for overseers and deacons in 1Ti 3:1–13, including marital faithfulness and wholesome family life, are best understood as attributes that *currently* characterize one's life and *have done so over a long enough period* that they may be assumed to be enduring character traits.

6:1 This section begins with Paul's disgust over what is going on. Some sort of complaint concerning property or business dealings seems to have been the problem.

6:2–3 These verses present parallel examples of the logic of arguing "from the greater to the

things of this life! 4Therefore, if you have
disputes about such matters, do you ask
for a ruling from those whose way of life
is scorned in the church? 5I say this to
shame you.[d] Is it possible that there
is nobody among you wise enough to
judge a dispute between believers?[e] 6But
instead, one brother takes another to
court — and this in front of unbelievers![f]
7The very fact that you have lawsuits
among you means you have been completely defeated already. Why not rather
be wronged? Why not rather be cheated?[g] 8Instead, you yourselves cheat and
do wrong, and you do this to your brothers and sisters.[h] 9Or do you not know
that wrongdoers will not inherit the
kingdom of God?[i] Do not be deceived:[j]
Neither the sexually immoral nor idolaters nor adulterers nor men who have
sex with men[a] 10nor thieves nor the
greedy nor drunkards nor slanderers
nor swindlers will inherit the kingdom
of God. 11And that is what some of you
were.[k] But you were washed,[l] you were
sanctified,[m] you were justified in the
name of the Lord Jesus Christ and by
the Spirit of our God.

Sexual Immorality

12"I have the right to do anything," you
say — but not everything is beneficial.[n]
"I have the right to do anything" — but I
will not be mastered by anything. 13You
say, "Food for the stomach and the stomach for food, and God will destroy them
both."[o] The body, however, is not meant
for sexual immorality but for the Lord,
and the Lord for the body. 14By his power
God raised the Lord from the dead, and

6:5 [d] 1Co 4:14 [e] Ac 1:15
6:6 [f] 2Co 6:14,15
6:7 [g] Mt 5:39,40
6:8 [h] 1Th 4:6
6:9 [i] Gal 5:21 [j] 1Co 15:33; Jas 1:16
6:11 [k] Eph 2:2 [l] Ac 22:16 [m] 1Co 1:2
6:12 [n] 1Co 10:23
6:13 [o] Col 2:22

[a] 9 The words *men who have sex with men* translate two Greek words that refer to the passive and active participants in homosexual acts.

lesser." Drawing on Da 7:22, Paul reminds the Corinthians that they will help the Lord Jesus exercise judgment over the non-Christian world (both people and angels). Surely, therefore, they must be competent to handle earthly disputes amongst themselves.

6:4–5 Verse 5 contrasts with 4:14. Now Paul *is* prepared to shame the Corinthians. Their legal action infuriates him because it so fundamentally compromises their witness before a watching world. "Is it possible that there is nobody among you wise enough . . . ?" (6:5) drips with irony since the Corinthians had been claiming to be so wise (4:10).

6:7–8 Paul proceeds to the more radical of his two points. Whether inside or outside the church, the attitude of demanding one's rights remains totally opposed to Christ's teaching (Mt 5:39–42) and example (1Pe 2:23). If two Christians cannot resolve their disagreements, something is wrong.

6:9–10 The fraud and injustice that trigger lawsuits lead Paul naturally to think about those who are "wrongdoers" more generally (v. 9). So, as in 5:10–11, he warns against being sucked into the vortex of behavior that eventually calls into question one's very salvation. Another vice list appears here. The same items that Paul mentions in ch. 5 reappear, along with four new ones.

6:11 Paul concludes on a more hopeful note. Such behavior characterized the pre-Christian lives of many of the Corinthians, but they have now generally abandoned such practices. They have been "washed" (inwardly, but possibly thinking of baptism), "sanctified" (made holy), and "justified" (declared righteous).

6:1–11 Same-sex and heterosexual sins are paired in a way that suggests that neither is any better or any worse than the other. One can scarcely use these verses to claim that no one can simultaneously be a Christian and engage in same-sex actions unless one is prepared to say the same thing of one who commits adultery or exhibits greed. But in each of these instances, true Christians should acknowledge their behavior as sinful and try to change it. Persistent rebellion increasingly calls into question any prior profession of faith.

Paul's emphasis in this passage is that the old life of sin, which ruled the day prior to a believer's conversion, need not control the believer's life in the present. To be "washed," "sanctified," and "justified" means that the Spirit enables us to leave such habits, addictions, and practices behind.

6:12–14 Paul begins a pattern that will frequently recur throughout the rest of the letter—quoting a Corinthian slogan and then modifying it. These Corinthian slogans all share four characteristics: (1) They are short, pithy, and proverbial; (2) they reflect the immoral wing of the church; (3) Paul himself could have conceivably spoken them in some specific context; and (4) apart from that context they were so misleading that abuse was almost inevitable.

6:12 Verse 12 quotes the first slogan twice (cf. also 10:23): "I have the right to do anything." Paul might have spoken this in the context of Christian freedom from the law. The slogan of 6:13 could reflect his more specific reference to freedom from the Jewish dietary laws. But apart from these contexts, the slogans virtually invite people to sin, as the Corinthians apparently were doing. Paul explains that Christians still must submit to moral principles because many of these practices are neither beneficial nor liberating.

6:13–14 The Corinthians were apparently equating food and eating with the body and sexual activity. Not so, declares Paul. Sexual immorality affects one's entire body in a way that overeating cannot,

he will raise us also.[p] 15 Do you not know
that your bodies are members of Christ
himself?[q] Shall I then take the members
of Christ and unite them with a prostitute? Never! 16 Do you not know that he
who unites himself with a prostitute is
one with her in body? For it is said, "The
two will become one flesh."[a][r] 17 But whoever is united with the Lord is one with
him in spirit.[b][s]
18 Flee from sexual immorality.[t] All
other sins a person commits are outside the body, but whoever sins sexually, sins against their own body.[u] 19 Do you
not know that your bodies are temples[v]
of the Holy Spirit, who is in you, whom
you have received from God? You are not
your own;[w] 20 you were bought at a price.[x]
Therefore honor God with your bodies.

Concerning Married Life

7 Now for the matters you wrote about:
"It is good for a man not to have
sexual relations with a woman."[y] 2 But
since sexual immorality is occurring,
each man should have sexual relations
with his own wife, and each woman with
her own husband. 3 The husband should
fulfill his marital duty to his wife,[z] and
likewise the wife to her husband. 4 The
wife does not have authority over her
own body but yields it to her husband.
In the same way, the husband does not
have authority over his own body but
yields it to his wife. 5 Do not deprive each
other except perhaps by mutual consent
and for a time,[a] so that you may devote
yourselves to prayer. Then come together
again so that Satan[b] will not tempt you[c]
because of your lack of self-control. 6 I say
this as a concession, not as a command.[d]
7 I wish that all of you were as I am.[e] But
each of you has your own gift from God;
one has this gift, another has that.[f]
8 Now to the unmarried[c] and the widows I say: It is good for them to stay
unmarried, as I do.[g] 9 But if they cannot

6:14 [p] Ro 6:5; Eph 1:19,20
6:15 [q] Ro 12:5
6:16 [r] Ge 2:24; Mt 19:5; Eph 5:31
6:17 [s] Jn 17:21-23; Gal 2:20
6:18 [t] 2Co 12:21; 1Th 4:3,4; Heb 13:4 [u] Ro 6:12
6:19 [v] Jn 2:21 [w] Ro 14:7,8
6:20 [x] Ac 20:28; 1Co 7:23; 1Pe 1:18,19; Rev 5:9
7:1 [y] ver 8,26
7:3 [z] Ex 21:10; 1Pe 3:7
7:5 [a] Ex 19:15; 1Sa 21:4,5 [b] Mt 4:10 [c] 1Th 3:5
7:6 [d] 2Co 8:8
7:7 [e] ver 8; 1Co 9:5 [f] Mt 19:11,12; Ro 12:6; 1Co 12:4,11
7:8 [g] ver 1,26

1Co 6:19 ❖ How does being the temple of the Holy Spirit inform what we do with our bodies?

[a] 16 Gen. 2:24 [b] 17 Or *in the Spirit* [c] 8 Or *widowers*

as v. 18 will explain. The body is to be dedicated to holiness and not sexual impurity (vv. 13b–14).

6:15–17 Paul expresses his utter disgust with associating something as impure as prostitution with Christ's perfect holiness. Prostitution connects the thing that represents ultimate commitment with the most casual of sexual relationships. Worse still, this sex is for hire, an abuse of human beings. Paul calls on his readers to "flee" *sexual immorality.* This term for sexual sin includes any form of intercourse between two individuals who are not united in marriage (v. 18a).

6:19–20 Paul applies temple imagery, with its overtones of holiness, to the bodies of individual believers. Verse 20 alludes to Jesus' costly atonement, which should cause believers to want to glorify God with their bodies out of gratitude for the salvation he has purchased for them.

6:12–20 Drastically countercultural themes persist in these verses. The Christian view of sex—abstinence outside of marriage—makes good sense in our world, completely apart from Paul's primary rationale. In countless ways, women and men in our current culture defy God and confidently assert that they can have sex without commitment and without any destructive side effects. Time and time again, they regret those choices. But this is not a sin we can test and then back off from; we must trust that God knows best. Once a person yields to such temptation, in little or big ways, there are mental and emotional scars that may never entirely disappear, even though God's grace can bring substantial healing.

7:1–2 Here, Paul addresses issues about which the Corinthians had written to him. The Corinthians' concerns may have been phrased as questions or as challenges. Paul recognizes substantial problems that need correcting.

Verse 1 is Paul's reluctant and qualified endorsement of a Corinthian slogan or position. His central point stresses that believers should not be in a hurry to change their marital status. Paul uses a "yes, but" logic as his thesis for the entire chapter. Verse 2 offers Paul's qualification: sexual abstinence is, for the most part, inappropriate for married couples.

7:3–7 Verses 3–7 unpack this first application of Paul's response to the part of the church in Corinth who advocated completely refraining from sex within marriage. Paul can imagine only a very limited role for such abstinence.

7:3–5 "Fulfill his marital duty" (v. 3) can also be read "give back that which is owed." "Do not deprive" (v. 5) suggests cheating someone else out of what is properly his or hers. The only exception Paul will tolerate is if both partners agree to abstain for a concentrated time of communion with the Lord. But even this is a "concession" (v. 6); Paul never *insists* that married people abstain at all from sex with each other.

7:7 This verse offers the first hint that Paul is currently single and likes it that way. He realizes that only some have that gift, while others are gifted for marriage.

7:8–9 Paul turns from the currently married to the previously married. "Unmarried" is a masculine plural, just as "widows" is a feminine plural (v. 8). We should probably understand the unmarried here to refer to men whose wives had died. Paul

control themselves, they should marry,[h] for it is better to marry than to burn
with passion.
10To the married I give this command
(not I, but the Lord): A wife must not
separate from her husband.[i] 11But if she
does, she must remain unmarried or else
be reconciled to her husband. And a husband must not divorce his wife.
12To the rest I say this (I, not the Lord):[j]
If any brother has a wife who is not a
believer and she is willing to live with
him, he must not divorce her. 13And if a
woman has a husband who is not a believer and he is willing to live with her,
she must not divorce him. 14For the unbelieving husband has been sanctified
through his wife, and the unbelieving
wife has been sanctified through her believing husband. Otherwise your children would be unclean, but as it is, they
are holy.[k]
15But if the unbeliever leaves, let it be
so. The brother or the sister is not bound
in such circumstances; God has called us
to live in peace.[l] 16How do you know, wife,
whether you will save[m] your husband?[n]
Or, how do you know, husband, whether
you will save your wife?

Concerning Change of Status

17Nevertheless, each person should live
as a believer in whatever situation the
Lord has assigned to them, just as God
has called them.[o] This is the rule I lay
down in all the churches.[p] 18Was a man
already circumcised when he was called?
He should not become uncircumcised.
Was a man uncircumcised when he was
called? He should not be circumcised.[q]
19Circumcision is nothing and uncircumcision is nothing.[r] Keeping God's
commands is what counts. 20Each person should remain in the situation they
were in when God called them.[s]
21Were you a slave when you were

7:9 [h] 1Ti 5:14
7:10 [i] Mal 2:14-16; Mt 5:32; 19:3-9; Mk 10:11; Lk 16:18
7:12 [j] ver 6, 10; 2Co 11:17
7:14 [k] Mal 2:15
7:15 [l] Ro 14:19; 1Co 14:33
7:16 [m] Ro 11:14 [n] 1Pe 3:1
7:17 [o] Ro 12:3 [p] 1Co 4:17; 14:33; 2Co 8:18; 11:28
7:18 [q] Ac 15:1, 2
7:19 [r] Ro 2:25-27; Gal 5:6; 6:15; Col 3:11
7:20 [s] ver 24

---

says that if such men cannot control themselves, they should marry.

Verses 8–9 also make it clear that Paul is single. If his words here are limited to widows and widowers, then perhaps his wife has also died. Rabbis were almost always married, and members of the Sanhedrin had to be married. While it is likely that Paul was once married, we simply cannot be sure.

7:10–16 Paul returns to address those who are married. The pro-celibacy faction encouraged people to get divorced if they could not live with a spouse without engaging in sex.

7:10–11 Paul's parenthesis, "not I, but the Lord" alludes to words of the earthly Jesus widely known in early Christian tradition (cf. Mk 10:11–12). Those already divorced must not remarry, in order to leave the door open for possible reconciliation with their estranged partners. The words translated "separate," "divorce," and "leave" throughout 1Co 7:10–16 are used interchangeably. Many spouses in antiquity left marriage without legal divorce proceedings, but the end result was the same. If there is any difference between the wife "separating" in v. 10 and the husband "divorcing" in v. 11, it may be that the man was legally entitled to divorce his wife, whereas the woman often had no recourse but to move out.

7:12–16 Paul addresses the members of spiritually mixed marriages. There were no doubt many couples in which only one of the two had become a Christian. Some believers seem to have feared that sexual relations with an unbeliever would defile them. Paul disagrees and insists that if the unbelieving partner is content to stay, the believer must not initiate divorce (vv. 12–13). Verse 14 supplies the rationale for preserving the marriage: having a believer in the family leads to potential blessings for the children and the non-Christian spouse. "Sanctified" and "holy" cannot here mean "saved," as v. 16 proves. Rather they refer to the impact of the believer on the family.

The tension introduced by one partner's Christian faith could prove intolerable to the non-Christian partner. If such a person chose to divorce (or simply leave) his or her spouse, the Christian partner was not compelled to try to prevent the separation (v. 15a). The constant tension introduced by opposite loyalties may even intensify the unbeliever's alienation from both their spouse and God (v. 16).

> ✣ **7:1–16** Few Christians today advocate total abstinence from sex as an ideal for all believers. Our problems look more like those of the self-indulgent wing of the Corinthian church far more than those of the strict wing. Traditional Roman Catholic circles still insist on celibacy as a requirement for priests and various religious orders, but neither Paul nor any other biblical writer justifies this across-the-board requirement. Protestants, however, often continue to overreact against this extreme by inappropriately disparaging the single life. Single adults, whether they be pastors, leaders, or members, regularly testify to feeling like second-class citizens in the church. Paul says that this absolutely should not be the case.

7:17–24 Paul's main point in vv. 17–24 can be paraphrased as, "Do not be in a hurry to change the external circumstances of your life simply because you have become a Christian."

7:18–20 Paul illustrates this principle with the example of circumcision versus uncircumcision. Circumcision is now a matter of moral indifference for Christians. "Keeping God's commands" (v. 19) for Christians refers to the reinterpretations and applications of the Mosaic Law for a new age, in light of the words and works of Jesus and the apostles.

7:21–24 Paul gives a second illustration of the theme "remain as you are." Here he contrasts the

called? Don't let it trouble you—although if you can gain your freedom, do so. 22For the one who was a slave when called to faith in the Lord is the Lord's freed person;[t] similarly, the one who was free when called is Christ's slave.[u] 23You were bought at a price;[v] do not become slaves of human beings. 24Brothers and sisters, each person, as responsible to God, should remain in the situation they were in when God called them.[w]

Concerning the Unmarried

25Now about virgins: I have no command from the Lord,[x] but I give a judgment as one who by the Lord's mercy[y] is trustworthy. 26Because of the present crisis, I think that it is good for a man to remain as he is.[z] 27Are you pledged to a woman? Do not seek to be released. Are you free from such a commitment? Do not look for a wife. 28But if you do marry, you have not sinned; and if a virgin marries, she has not sinned. But those who marry will face many troubles in this life, and I want to spare you this.

29What I mean, brothers and sisters, is that the time is short.[a] From now on those who have wives should live as if they do not; 30those who mourn, as if they did not; those who are happy, as if they were not; those who buy something, as if it were not theirs to keep; 31those who use the things of the world, as if not engrossed in them. For this world in its present form is passing away.[b]

32I would like you to be free from concern. An unmarried man is concerned about the Lord's affairs[c]—how he can please the Lord. 33But a married man is concerned about the affairs of this world—how he can please his wife—34and his interests are divided. An unmarried woman or virgin is concerned about the Lord's affairs: Her aim is to be devoted to the Lord in both body and spirit.[d] But a married woman is concerned about the affairs of this world—how she can please her husband. 35I am saying this for your own good, not to restrict you, but that you may live in a right way in undivided[e] devotion to the Lord.

36If anyone is worried that he might not be acting honorably toward the virgin he is engaged to, and if his passions

1Co 7:32–35 ❖ How does a person's marriage status affect their discipleship?

7:22 [t] Jn 8:32, 36; Phm 16 [u] Eph 6:6
7:23 [v] 1Co 6:20
7:24 [w] ver 20
7:25 [x] ver 6; 2Co 8:8 [y] 2Co 4:1; 1Ti 1:13,16
7:26 [z] ver 1,8
7:29 [a] ver 31; Ro 13:11,12
7:31 [b] 1Jn 2:17
7:32 [c] 1Ti 5:5
7:34 [d] Lk 2:37
7:35 [e] Ps 86:11

---

experiences of Roman slaves and non-slaves. Neither state makes serving the Lord inherently easier than the other. Paul does add an exception: "If you can gain your freedom, do so" (v. 21b). Physical slavery is a form of oppression that displeases God, so when an opportunity for freedom arises, it should be taken.

❖ **7:17–24** These verses directly challenge our contemporary individualism, which teaches people never to rest content with the status they have already attained but always to seek more money, power, influence, and control over their lives. The results often include a highly transient, upwardly mobile population that gains wealth and status at others' expense. Verse 21b encourages us to try to improve our lot in this world, so long as we do not do it at others' expense or imagine that happiness and a rewarding Christian life demands a change in our current status.

7:25–40 Paul returns to the topic of sex and marriage. Verses 26b and 27b repeat the theme of "remain as you are." Because these young people are single, Paul can be more enthusiastic about celibacy. But he quickly reminds them that his enthusiasm for abstinence does not apply to the married (v. 27a) and corrects those who were teaching sex and marriage were inherently sinful (v. 28a).

7:25–29 Verses 25–28 also introduce two new reasons for Paul's advice. The first deals with "the present crisis" (v. 26a), which is further explained in vv. 29–31. Paul knows that Christ's second coming could take place very soon ("the time is short"—v. 29a). This does not mean that Paul had set any dates or necessarily expected the Lord to return within his lifetime.

7:30–31 All Christians should sense an urgency to serve the Lord, caused by the uncertainty of the time of the end, after which point it will no longer be possible to win the lost. Marriage may temper this urgency. The same is true with other normal human activities: All are legitimate endeavors, but all remain fleeting. The Christian should therefore be less involved in the affairs of this world than the non-Christian.

7:32–35 These verses unpack Paul's second rationale for encouraging single people who have never been married to stay single. Attending to the concerns of a spouse and children takes time away from ministering to the needs of others in both the church and the world. Paul refuses to make his preferences absolute or endorse without qualification the stance of the pro-celibacy faction.

Verse 35 clarifies when marriage is or is not appropriate. Whichever state enables a person to "live in a right way in undivided devotion to the Lord" is preferable.

7:36–38 Paul focuses on one specific kind of unmarried person. It is probably better to take the

are too strong[a] and he feels he ought to
marry, he should do as he wants. He is
not sinning.[f] They should get married.
37But the man who has settled the matter in his own mind, who is under no
compulsion but has control over his own
will, and who has made up his mind not
to marry the virgin — this man also does
the right thing. 38So then, he who marries the virgin does right,[g] but he who
does not marry her does better.[b]
39A woman is bound to her husband as
long as he lives.[h] But if her husband dies,
she is free to marry anyone she wishes,
but he must belong to the Lord.[i] 40In my
judgment,[j] she is happier if she stays as
she is — and I think that I too have the
Spirit of God.

Concerning Food Sacrificed to Idols

8 Now about food sacrificed to idols:[k]
We know that "We all possess knowledge."[l] But knowledge puffs up while
love builds up. 2Those who think they
know something[m] do not yet know as
they ought to know.[n] 3But whoever loves
God is known by God.[c o]
4So then, about eating food sacrificed
to idols:[p] We know that "An idol is nothing at all in the world"[q] and that "There
is no God but one."[r] 5For even if there
are so-called gods,[s] whether in heaven
or on earth (as indeed there are many
"gods" and many "lords"), 6yet for us
there is but one God, the Father,[t] from
whom all things came[u] and for whom
we live; and there is but one Lord,[v] Jesus
Christ, through whom all things came[w]
and through whom we live.
7But not everyone possesses this
knowledge. Some people are still so accustomed to idols that when they eat
sacrificial food they think of it as having
been sacrificed to a god, and since their
conscience is weak,[x] it is defiled. 8But
food does not bring us near to God;[y] we
are no worse if we do not eat, and no
better if we do.

7:36 [f] ver 28
7:38 [g] Heb 13:4
7:39 [h] Ro 7:2,3 [i] 2Co 6:14
7:40 [j] ver 25
8:1 [k] Ac 15:20 [l] Ro 15:14
8:2 [m] 1Co 3:18 [n] 1Co 13:8,9,12; 1Ti 6:4
8:3 [o] Ro 8:29; Gal 4:9
8:4 [p] ver 1,7, 10 [q] 1Co 10:19 [r] Dt 6:4; Eph 4:6
8:5 [s] 2Th 2:4
8:6 [t] Mal 2:10 [u] Ro 11:36 [v] Eph 4:5 [w] Jn 1:3
8:7 [x] Ro 14:14; 1Co 10:28
8:8 [y] Ro 14:17

[a] 36 Or *if she is getting beyond the usual age for marriage* [b] 36-38 Or 36*If anyone thinks he is not treating his daughter properly, and if she is getting along in years* (or *if her passions are too strong*), *and he feels she ought to marry, he should do as he wants. He is not sinning. He should let her get married.* 37*But the man who has settled the matter in his own mind, who is under no compulsion but has control over his own will, and who has made up his mind to keep the virgin unmarried — this man also does the right thing.* 38*So then, he who gives his virgin in marriage does right, but he who does not give her in marriage does better.* [c] 2,3 An early manuscript and another ancient witness *think they have knowledge do not yet know as they ought to know.* 3*But whoever loves truly knows.*

---

two people involved to refer to fiancé and fiancée. Engaged couples should not feel compelled to refrain from marriage, as some in the Corinthian church were teaching. As in vv. 7-8, 26, and 40, Paul reiterates his preference for the single life but refuses to make singleness a requirement of service to God.

7:39-40 Paul reaffirms monogamy as a lifelong commitment. These verses also contain the only explicit reference to remarriage in this chapter. "I think that I too have the Spirit of God" (v. 40b) represents a slightly sarcastic remark aimed at the Corinthians, who evidently felt that only they had attained true spiritual insight.

7:25-40 All believers, single or married, should have an urgency about the Lord's work that contemporary Christians seldom reflect. After all, the end of the world truly could come in our lifetime. And even if the Lord delays his coming, sudden death claims too many lives for any of us ever to assume that we have a certain number of years or decades left to serve God. Married or single, Christian discipleship requires that we daily serve God in our own sphere of influence.

8:1-3 Verse 1 introduces the issue in this chapter. "Food" should be understood to refer to "meat," lest v. 13 be seen as narrowing the topic. Part of the meat of each sacrificial animal was burned on the temple altar, part was eaten in temple ceremonies, and part was sold in the Corinthian marketplace for consumption at home.

"We know that 'We all possess knowledge'" (v. 1a) probably represents another Corinthian slogan. "Knowledge" refers to prideful human religious speculation. As with the previous slogans, there is a sense in which Paul can agree but not without immediately qualifying the statement (vv. 1b-3). Love, not knowledge, must form the foundation of Christian behavior (v. 3).

8:4-6 Paul provides the basis for Christian freedom to eat this sacrificial food. The idols to which the meat is dedicated are fake: They have no objective spiritual existence. Paul declares that there is only one true God in the universe; all other alleged gods mean nothing to the life of a believer.

8:7-13 Here Paul qualifies the exercise of Christian freedom when it comes to eating meat sacrificed to idols: Doing so may corrupt the weak consciences of certain fellow believers. Love for others must therefore limit freedom in this case. The "weak conscience" of these believers was not a poorly developed sense of morality but rather the strict restrictions they placed on believers' freedom in Christ (v. 7).

Verse 8 continues Paul's qualification. Here is the first of three reasons Paul gives for voluntarily refraining from eating idol meat in the presence

1Co 8:9–13 ❖ Which behaviors should we be especially mindful of so that we don't cause others to stumble? Why?

9 Be careful, however, that the exercise of your rights does not become a
stumbling block[z] to the weak.[a] 10 For if
someone with a weak conscience sees
you, with all your knowledge, eating in
an idol's temple, won't that person be
emboldened to eat what is sacrificed
to idols? 11 So this weak brother or sister, for whom Christ died, is destroyed[b]
by your knowledge. 12 When you sin
against them[c] in this way and wound
their weak conscience, you sin against
Christ. 13 Therefore, if what I eat causes
my brother or sister to fall into sin, I will
never eat meat again, so that I will not
cause them to fall.[d]

8:9 [z] Gal 5:13 [a] Ro 14:1
8:11 [b] Ro 14:15, 20
8:12 [c] Mt 18:6
8:13 [d] Ro 14:21

9:1 [e] 2Co 12:12 [f] 1Co 15:8 [g] 1Co 3:6; 4:15
9:2 [h] 2Co 3:2,3
9:4 [i] 1Th 2:6
9:5 [j] 1Co 7:7,8 [k] Mt 12:46
9:6 [l] Ac 4:36
9:7 [m] Dt 20:6; Pr 27:18

Paul's Rights as an Apostle

9 Am I not free? Am I not an apostle?[e]
Have I not seen Jesus our Lord?[f] Are
you not the result of my work in the
Lord?[g] 2 Even though I may not be an
apostle to others, surely I am to you! For
you are the seal[h] of my apostleship in
the Lord.
3 This is my defense to those who sit
in judgment on me. 4 Don't we have the
right to food and drink?[i] 5 Don't we have
the right to take a believing wife[j] along
with us, as do the other apostles and the
Lord's brothers[k] and Cephas[a]? 6 Or is it
only I and Barnabas[l] who lack the right
to not work for a living?
7 Who serves as a soldier at his own expense? Who plants a vineyard[m] and does
not eat its grapes? Who tends a flock and

[a] 5 That is, Peter

---

of those unable to handle the practice. There is no inherent spiritual advantage in eating the meat or disadvantage in avoiding it. Therefore, concern for one's fellow Christian should take precedence. Verses 9–12 combine to make the point that the Corinthians should not behave in ways that lead each other into sin.

Verse 10 is often understood to mean that while the "stronger" Corinthians could draw appropriate boundaries and eat meat from the marketplace without being tempted to go to the temple, the "weaker" Christians could not. Verse 11 spells out the second reason for voluntary abstinence: Flaunting one's freedom was actually damaging the spiritual lives of the weak.

Verse 12b gives the third reason for abstinence: to avoid sinning against Christ. When there is good reason to believe that exercising one's freedom in amoral areas will actually lead a fellow Christian into sin, restraint is always the right choice.

✣ **8:1–13** The most common contemporary applications of this chapter typically do not involve activities that could lead to overtly anti-Christian beliefs or rituals. Rather, they have to do with engaging in activities that can lead to excess and sin but do not necessarily have to. These include drinking alcohol; wearing potentially suggestive forms of dress; listening to certain kinds of music; smoking or chewing tobacco; playing games that sometimes but not necessarily involve gambling; buying lottery tickets that support government, education, state parks, and the like; engaging in premarital physical contact of a variety of kinds; and so on.

Christian conscience dictates different things to different people based on their interpretations of Scripture and personal convictions. That's why Paul differentiates between "weaker" and "stronger" believers. The point remains the same, however. If we are engaging in activities that harm our witness to others or that shame other believers, we must use our freedom to choose in the right way by not causing other believers to stumble in their faith.

9:1–18 Paul turns next to a second illustration of the principle that Christian freedom should be tempered by the voluntary giving up of one's rights. But the illustration reflects one of the primary ways the Corinthians are challenging Paul. The Corinthians have come to doubt Paul's apostolic authority (vv. 2–3) precisely because he is not charging them for his ministry (cf. 2Co 11:7).

In 1Co 9:1–12a Paul presents the case that he has a right to charge for his services. In keeping with his "yes, but" logic, and in defense of his actual behavior, vv. 12b–18 then explain why Paul has in fact decided against doing so. Verses 19–27 generalize to the even broader principle that lies behind Paul's behavior on the issues in both 8:1–13 and 9:1–18.

9:1–2 The four questions of v. 1 are all interconnected. If the answer to any one of these is "no," then all Paul's claims are in jeopardy. But in fact Paul is free, he is an apostle, he has seen Jesus, and he has spiritually parented the Corinthians. Verse 2 then follows logically.

9:3–12 Paul defends his decisions using a barrage of further rhetorical questions, the answers to which are intended to be clear. First, Paul reasserts his right to charge the church for his ministry by means of three questions in vv. 4–6. Verse 5 implies that most of these other men were married and brought their wives along on their travels. Verse 6 then gets to the heart of Paul's complaint.

9:7–12a Paul begins accumulating a series of reasons why in fact he *does* have the right to request payment for his services. These continue into vv. 13–14 as well. Verse 7 presents three analogies from the common practice of human experience in the areas of warfare, farming, and shepherding. Few in Paul's day would have disputed the logic of these examples.

does not drink the milk? 8Do I say this
merely on human authority? Doesn't the
Law say the same thing? 9For it is written
in the Law of Moses: "Do not muzzle an
ox while it is treading out the grain."[a][n]
Is it about oxen that God is concerned?[o]
10Surely he says this for us, doesn't he?
Yes, this was written for us,[p] because
whoever plows and threshes should be
able to do so in the hope of sharing in
the harvest.[q] 11If we have sown spiritual seed among you, is it too much if we
reap a material harvest from you?[r] 12If
others have this right of support from
you, shouldn't we have it all the more?

But we did not use this right.[s] On the
contrary, we put up with anything rather
than hinder[t] the gospel of Christ.

13Don't you know that those who serve
in the temple get their food from the
temple, and that those who serve at the
altar share in what is offered on the altar?[u] 14In the same way, the Lord has
commanded that those who preach the
gospel should receive their living from
the gospel.[v]

15But I have not used any of these
rights.[w] And I am not writing this in the
hope that you will do such things for me,
for I would rather die than allow anyone
to deprive me of this boast.[x] 16For when
I preach the gospel, I cannot boast, since
I am compelled to preach.[y] Woe to me if
I do not preach the gospel! 17If I preach
voluntarily, I have a reward;[z] if not voluntarily, I am simply discharging the
trust committed to me.[a] 18What then is
my reward? Just this: that in preaching
the gospel I may offer it free of charge,[b]
and so not make full use of my rights as
a preacher of the gospel.

Paul's Use of His Freedom

19Though I am free[c] and belong to no
one, I have made myself a slave to everyone,[d] to win as many as possible.[e] 20To
the Jews I became like a Jew, to win the

9:9 [n] Dt 25:4; 1Ti 5:18 [o] Dt 22:1-4
9:10 [p] Ro 4:23, 24 [q] 2Ti 2:6
9:11 [r] Ro 15:27
9:12 [s] Ac 18:3 [t] 2Co 11:7-12
9:13 [u] Lev 6:16, 26; Dt 18:1
9:14 [v] Mt 10:10; 1Ti 5:18
9:15 [w] Ac 18:3 [x] 2Co 11:9,10
9:16 [y] Ro 1:14; Ac 9:15
9:17 [z] 1Co 3:8, 14 [a] Gal 2:7; Col 1:25
9:18 [b] 2Co 11:7; 12:13
9:19 [c] ver 1 [d] Gal 5:13 [e] Mt 18:15; 1Pe 3:1

[a] 9 Deut. 25:4

1Co 9:15–18 ❖ What does Paul's discussion in this paragraph say to us today as we try to influence others for Christ?

9:8–11 These verses argue from Dt 25:4, which 1Co 9:9 explicitly quotes. Verse 10a should then read, "Surely he says this [also] for us." Paul is not claiming that this quotation from the Mosaic Law never had anything to do with oxen, only that its application cannot be limited to animals. Verses 10–11 clarify that preaching the gospel is like planting a crop and making disciples is like harvesting.

Verse 12a rounds out the formal part of Paul's defense with a third kind of argument. The Corinthians have already conceded Paul's logic regarding other leaders. It is the height of irony that they would refuse these same rights to the one most responsible for their spiritual rebirth.

9:13–14 Paul provides the final two arguments in defense of his right to receive payment for his work: the analogy of priests and Levites in the Jewish temple (cf. Nu 18:8–31) and the express words of Jesus during his lifetime (Lk 10:7b).

9:15–17 Paul clarifies that his "defense" has not been a subtle hint that he wishes to reverse his policy now. "Boast" here carries the sense of an appropriate pride in what the Lord has done despite Paul's weakness.

But Paul cannot legitimately boast merely in his ministry of preaching (v. 16). God has placed an irresistible call on his life to preach. Verse 17a ("If I preach voluntarily") is thus merely hypothetical; v. 17b ("if not voluntarily") expresses what in fact is true in Paul's case.

✣ **9:1–18** The idea of Christian pastors and teachers also having careers outside of ministry is making a healthy comeback, especially in missions circles, though it needs to be taken as a serious option by even larger numbers of Christian workers. Christians prepared to employ their skills overseas in business, industry, or teaching English as a foreign language may regularly gain entry into those areas otherwise most hostile to professional Christianity.

In many instances in the Western world, small congregations of young Christians in working class or impoverished neighborhoods often struggle to support their ministers. The idea of bi-vocational ministry of course has substantial weaknesses, not least of which is the amount of time available to devote to evangelism, discipleship, preaching, teaching, and so on. But Paul's example is instructive for many teachers and leaders in Christian ministry.

9:19–27 In vv. 19–27, Paul explains that he wants to clear the ground of unnecessary obstacles that might hinder unbelievers from coming to Christ. Verses 19–23 detail this principle in terms of "all things to all people" (v. 22). Verses 24–27 describe the spiritual discipline involved in adapting oneself to diverse cultural and moral situations.

Paul understands that the age of the law has come to an end. Nevertheless, to Jews and others under the law, Paul at times acts as if he is still subject to all the laws of Moses (cf. Ac 16:1–3; 21:20–26), so long as it is clear that his actions are not a proof of salvation or spiritual maturity in any way.

Jews.[f] To those under the law I became
like one under the law (though I myself
am not under the law), so as to win those
under the law. 21 To those not having the
law I became like one not having the law[g]
(though I am not free from God's law
but am under Christ's law), so as to win
those not having the law. 22 To the weak
I became weak, to win the weak. I have
become all things to all people[h] so that
by all possible means I might save some.[i]
23 I do all this for the sake of the gospel,
that I may share in its blessings.

The Need for Self-Discipline

24 Do you not know that in a race all
the runners run, but only one gets the
prize? Run[j] in such a way as to get the
prize. 25 Everyone who competes in the
games goes into strict training. They
do it to get a crown that will not last,
but we do it to get a crown that will last
forever.[k] 26 Therefore I do not run like
someone running aimlessly; I do not
fight like a boxer beating the air. 27 No,
I strike a blow to my body[l] and make it
my slave so that after I have preached to
others, I myself will not be disqualified
for the prize.

9:20 [f] Ac 16:3; 21:20-26; Ro 11:14
9:21 [g] Ro 2:12,14
9:22 [h] 1Co 10:33 [i] Ro 11:14
9:24 [j] Gal 2:2; 2Ti 4:7; Heb 12:1
9:25 [k] Jas 1:12; Rev 2:10
9:27 [l] Ro 8:13

10:1 [m] Ex 13:21 [n] Ex 14:22,29
10:4 [o] Ex 17:6; Nu 20:11; Ps 78:15
10:5 [p] Nu 14:29; Heb 3:17
10:7 [q] ver 14 [r] Ex 32:4,6,19
10:8 [s] Nu 25:1-9
10:9 [t] Nu 21:5,6
10:10 [u] Nu 16:41 [v] Nu 16:49 [w] Ex 12:23

Warnings From Israel's History

10 For I do not want you to be ignorant of the fact, brothers and sisters, that our ancestors were all under the
cloud[m] and that they all passed through
the sea.[n] 2 They were all baptized into Moses in the cloud and in the sea. 3 They all
ate the same spiritual food 4 and drank
the same spiritual drink; for they drank
from the spiritual rock[o] that accompanied them, and that rock was Christ.
5 Nevertheless, God was not pleased with
most of them; their bodies were scattered in the wilderness.[p]
6 Now these things occurred as examples to keep us from setting our hearts
on evil things as they did. 7 Do not be
idolaters,[q] as some of them were; as it is
written: "The people sat down to eat and
drink and got up to indulge in revelry."[a][r]
8 We should not commit sexual immorality, as some of them did—and in one day
twenty-three thousand of them died.[s] 9 We
should not test Christ,[b] as some of them
did—and were killed by snakes.[t] 10 And
do not grumble, as some of them did[u]—
and were killed[v] by the destroying angel.[w]

[a] 7 Exodus 32:6 [b] 9 Some manuscripts *test the Lord*

9:22–23 Paul repeats his principle of flexibility and notes an additional rationale for his behavior. As in vv. 15–18, there is an inherent blessing in fulfilling his commission and seeing the results—people are being saved from their sins.

9:24–27 Paul continues the theme of sharing in the gospel's blessings. The Corinthians would have been familiar with all these analogies from the Isthmian games the city hosted every other year. In v. 27a Paul refers to the spiritual training and self-discipline that he exercises so that his ministry will not become futile. Verse 27b has been taken as Paul's concern that he might lose his salvation. More probably, "disqualified" should be interpreted in light of the other reference to testing in the context of judgment day in this letter (3:12–15). But neither one's salvation nor eternal status in heaven is at stake.

9:19–27 For many Western Christians living and working in secular settings, the most important lesson from vv. 19–27 may relate to their choices of companions—who they spend significant time with, cultivating friendships and engaging in recreation or leisure-time pursuits. Many Christians barely know any non-Christians well enough to share their faith in less than superficial fashion. Many congregations insist on their members attending countless church functions, but the result is that faithful followers have no time left for a fallen world. Better to spend less time in church and more in the world, so long as that does not reflect a lack of commitment to Christ and mature Christian living.

10:1–2 Paul questions the Corinthians' claims to "knowledge" by suggesting that they may in fact be "ignorant" after all. To correct this oversight, he reminds them of the behavior of their spiritual predecessors. The association of water with both cloud and sea prompts Paul to conceive of this deliverance as a kind of baptism "into Moses" (v. 2).

10:3–5 The Israelites experienced further supernatural blessing when God gave them manna from heaven to eat (e.g., Ex 16:4, 35) and water from a rock to drink (Ex 17:6; Nu 20:11). Yet none of these miracles guaranteed that the children of Israel would reach the promised land (1Co 10:5).

10:6–10 Paul calls the Corinthians to learn from these examples. "To keep us from setting our hearts on evil things" can also read "to keep us from lusting after evil." The four additional examples of vv. 7–10 illustrate more specific forms of this improper lust. First, Paul cites Ex 32:6, the Israelites' idolatrous worship of the golden calf. Second, he refers to Nu 25:1–9, in which Israelite men engaged in immoral sexual activity with Moabite women (1Co 10:8). Third, he alludes to Nu 21:4–9, when the people complained against Moses and God (1Co 10:9). Fourth, he recalls the characteristic grumblings and murmurings of the people, most notably in Nu 16:41–50 (1Co 10:10).

1Co 10:13 ✣ How can we find hope in these promises when temptations seem to have too strong a grip?

11These things happened to them as
examples and were written down as
warnings for us, on whom the culmination of the ages has come.[x] 12So, if you
think you are standing firm,[y] be careful
that you don't fall! 13No temptation[a] has
overtaken you except what is common
to mankind. And God is faithful;[z] he will
not let you be tempted[a] beyond what you
can bear.[a] But when you are tempted,[a] he
will also provide a way out so that you
can endure it.

Idol Feasts and the Lord's Supper

14Therefore, my dear friends, flee from
idolatry. 15I speak to sensible people;
judge for yourselves what I say. 16Is not
the cup of thanksgiving for which we
give thanks a participation in the blood
of Christ? And is not the bread that we
break a participation in the body of
Christ?[b] 17Because there is one loaf, we,
who are many, are one body,[c] for we all
share the one loaf.
18Consider the people of Israel: Do not
those who eat the sacrifices[d] participate
in the altar? 19Do I mean then that food
sacrificed to an idol is anything, or that
an idol is anything?[e] 20No, but the sacrifices of pagans are offered to demons,[f]
not to God, and I do not want you to be
participants with demons. 21You cannot
drink the cup of the Lord and the cup
of demons too; you cannot have a part
in both the Lord's table and the table
of demons.[g] 22Are we trying to arouse
the Lord's jealousy?[h] Are we stronger
than he?[i]

The Believer's Freedom

23"I have the right to do anything," you
say—but not everything is beneficial.[j]
"I have the right to do anything"—but
not everything is constructive. 24No one
should seek their own good, but the good
of others.[k]
25Eat anything sold in the meat market
without raising questions of conscience,[l]
26for, "The earth is the Lord's, and everything in it."[b][m]

10:11 [x] Ro 13:11
10:12 [y] Ro 11:20
10:13 [z] 1Co 1:9 [a] 2Pe 2:9
10:16 [b] Mt 26:26-28
10:17 [c] Ro 12:5; 1Co 12:27
10:18 [d] Lev 7:6, 14,15
10:19 [e] 1Co 8:4
10:20 [f] Dt 32:17; Ps 106:37; Rev 9:20
10:21 [g] 2Co 6:15, 16
10:22 [h] Dt 32:16, 21 [i] Ecc 6:10; Isa 45:9
10:23 [j] 1Co 6:12
10:24 [k] ver 33; Ro 15:1,2; 1Co 13:5; Php 2:4,21
10:25 [l] Ac 10:15; 1Co 8:7
10:26 [m] Ps 24:1

[a] *13* The Greek for *temptation* and *tempted* can also mean *testing* and *tested.* [b] *26* Psalm 24:1

10:11–13 Verse 11 repeats the warning of v. 6, which is all the more crucial since Christians live in the climactic era of human history for which all previous ages were preparing. Verse 12 summarizes the significance of these warnings for the Corinthians—even those who think they stand securely should take care. Verses 1–12 are all balanced by the marvelous promise of v. 13.

10:14–22 Paul returns to the topic of idol meat. Although the food itself is morally neutral, Paul does make one absolute prohibition: Eating it in the context of explicitly pagan worship services is always wrong.

To cement his position, Paul offers two further analogies from the sacred meals of Christianity (vv. 16–17) and Judaism (v. 18). Partaking of the elements of the Lord's Supper involves a "participation" ("fellowship") with the risen Lord and a taking on of the benefits of his shed blood and broken body. "Participation" in vv. 15–16 includes both communion with fellow believers and partnership in Christ.

The application to religious temple feasts in Corinth follows naturally (vv. 19–22). Pagans also commune with the spiritual beings they worship, in ways that make it ghastly to think of Christians participating. Demons—fallen angels—are the true objects of pagan ritual, however unwittingly they may be worshiped (cf. Dt 32:17).

✣ **10:1–22** First Corinthians 10:2 is one of the most crucial verses in Scripture to combat the heretical view that baptism guarantees salvation. Care must be exercised in each branch of the church to ensure that baptism or confirmation is undertaken voluntarily as a public sign of genuine, saving faith in Christ, which those undergoing the rite have sincerely professed.

The Lord's Supper has also come to be viewed as quasi-magical in numerous Christian traditions; members of liturgical churches often stress the need to partake frequently, especially as one is dying, to appropriate forgiveness for the most recent round of sins in one's life. This too needs serious reexamination in light of Scripture.

10:23–30 Verse 23 restates 6:12 almost verbatim, except that here Paul substitutes "but not everything is *beneficial*" (emphasis added) at the end. First Corinthians 10:25–30 apply Paul's principles to the two specific contexts of purchasing and consuming meat sold in the Corinthian marketplace (vv. 25–26) and eating it in a friend's home (vv. 27–30). In each instance, the likelihood was great that the meat would have been sacrificed to idols.

In the case of marketplace food, Paul's command is unqualified: Feel free to buy it and eat it. In the case of a friend's home, even that of an unbeliever not likely to have any objections to what is eaten, Paul is only slightly less enthusiastic. His general statement is equally sweeping—go if you like, eat, and don't ask any questions (v. 27). One should only consider holding back if someone makes an

27If an unbeliever invites you to a meal
and you want to go, eat whatever is put
before you[n] without raising questions
of conscience. 28But if someone says to
you, "This has been offered in sacrifice,"
then do not eat it, both for the sake of
the one who told you and for the sake of
conscience.[o] 29I am referring to the other
person's conscience, not yours. For why is
my freedom[p] being judged by another's
conscience? 30If I take part in the meal
with thankfulness, why am I denounced
because of something I thank God for?[q]
31So whether you eat or drink or whatever you do, do it all for the glory of
God.[r] 32Do not cause anyone to stumble,[s]
whether Jews, Greeks or the church of
God[t]— 33even as I try to please everyone
in every way.[u] For I am not seeking my
own good but the good of many, so that
11 they may be saved.[v] 1Follow my example,[w] as I follow the example of
Christ.

10:27 [n]Lk 10:7
10:28 [o]1Co 8:7, 10-12
10:29 [p]Ro 14:16; 1Co 9:1,19
10:30 [q]Ro 14:6
10:31 [r]Col 3:17; 1Pe 4:11
10:32 [s]Ac 24:16 [t]Ac 20:28
10:33 [u]Ro 15:2; 1Co 9:22 [v]Ro 11:14
11:1 [w]1Co 4:16
11:2 [x]ver 17, 22 [y]1Co 4:17 [z]1Co 15:2,3; 2Th 2:15
11:3 [a]Eph 1:22 [b]Ge 3:16; Eph 5:23 [c]1Co 3:23
11:5 [d]Ac 21:9 [e]Dt 21:12

1Co 11:1 ❖ Whose examples can we follow to be more like Christ? What do we admire about these people?

On Covering the Head in Worship

2I praise you[x] for remembering me in
everything[y] and for holding to the traditions just as I passed them on to you.[z]
3But I want you to realize that the head
of every man is Christ,[a] and the head of
the woman is man,[a][b] and the head of
Christ is God.[c] 4Every man who prays or
prophesies with his head covered dishonors his head. 5But every woman who
prays or prophesies[d] with her head uncovered dishonors her head—it is the
same as having her head shaved.[e] 6For
if a woman does not cover her head, she
might as well have her hair cut off; but if
it is a disgrace for a woman to have her

[a] 3 Or *of the wife is her husband*

---

issue of the food's having been sacrificed to idols (v. 28a). Presumably this person is a "weaker" fellow Christian, since unbelievers would not likely have any objections to eating idol meat.

Verses 29b–30 resume Paul's primary line of thought: He defends his freedom to eat food for which he is grateful to God.

10:31—11:1 This passage restates the twin principles of freedom and restraint one last time, now in the context of God's glory (10:31). Paul tries to lead as few people into sin as possible, both outside and inside the church, but his most basic underlying motive is the salvation of as many people as possible (vv. 32–33; recall 9:19–23).

✜ 10:23—11:1 Non-Christian stereotypes of conservative Christian faith consistently characterize believers as stern, legalistic joy-killers. And at least part of this caricature is deserved. Christians often do argue over where to draw the boundaries in morally gray areas.

Pleasant exceptions to this trend often occur in creative church youth groups and parachurch campus ministries that defy the stereotype. They organize lots of fun activities, usually attract good crowds, bring many to genuine faith, and weather the criticisms of the "professional weaker brothers" in their communities. Our outreach can be even more effective if we adopt attitudes and lifestyles that are quicker to affirm the truth and goodness in unbelievers' lives than to condemn their sins.

11:2 The next three topics Paul addresses all deal with behavior in worship. They include what men and women should or should not wear on their heads (vv. 2–16), proper conduct during the Lord's Supper (vv. 17–34), and the use and abuse of spiritual gifts (chs. 12–14).

In the case of head coverings, Paul continues his "yes, but" logic. Yes, he praises the Corinthians for their faithfulness to his teaching—probably about freedom (v. 2), but they have carried things too far. Yes, it is true that men and women are equal in Christ before God, but that does not mean that all differences between the sexes may be blurred.

11:3–10 The events that lie behind vv. 3–16 seem to proceed as follows. Because of their newfound freedom in Christ, women in the Corinthian church were praying and prophesying (v. 5a). These women were not merely speaking in worship but doing it in a way that unnecessarily flaunted social convention and the order of creation. So Paul has to encourage them to exercise restraint.

One of the keys to understanding vv. 3–10 is to recognize Paul's play on the word "head." The main point is the claim that what one does or doesn't put on one's physical head either honors or dishonors one's spiritual head. Verse 3 establishes three such relationships of spiritual headship, but what the term for "head" means here is hotly debated. When used figuratively, it seems to mean either "source" or "authority." Paul appears to use both meanings elsewhere, so its meaning will depend on the immediate context. A different passage in which Paul calls a man "head" discusses wives' subordination to their husbands (Eph 5:22–24), so "authority" seems more likely here. Thankfully, the overall thrust of this passage remains clear even if readers cannot agree on the precise meaning of "head."

Another disputed issue in 1Co 11:3–10 involves the translation of the words the NIV consistently renders as "man" and "woman." In every other place in Paul's letters where they are paired (apart from 1Ti 2:8–15), they refer to husband and wife. It is much easier to interpret the passage if husbands and wives are meant throughout (e.g., 1Co 11:5).

Verses 4–5a proceed with Paul's play on words. In each verse, the first use of "head" refers to the physical anatomy; the second to the spiritual authority. The reference to praying and prophesying shows that the context is public worship.

hair cut off or her head shaved, then she
should cover her head.
7A man ought not to cover his head,[a]
since he is the image[f] and glory of God;
but woman is the glory of man. 8For man
did not come from woman, but woman
from man;[g] 9neither was man created for
woman, but woman for man.[h] 10It is for
this reason that a woman ought to have
authority over her own[b] head, because
of the angels. 11Nevertheless, in the Lord
woman is not independent of man, nor
is man independent of woman. 12For as
woman came from man, so also man is
born of woman. But everything comes
from God.[i]
13Judge for yourselves: Is it proper for
a woman to pray to God with her head
uncovered? 14Does not the very nature of
things teach you that if a man has long
hair, it is a disgrace to him, 15but that if a
woman has long hair, it is her glory? For
long hair is given to her as a covering. 16If
anyone wants to be contentious about
this, we have no other practice — nor do
the churches of God.[j]

Correcting an Abuse of the Lord's Supper

11:23–25pp // Mt 26:26–28; Mk 14:22–24; Lk 22:17–20

17In the following directives I have
no praise for you,[k] for your meetings
do more harm than good. 18In the first
place, I hear that when you come together as a church, there are divisions[l]
among you, and to some extent I believe

11:7 [f] Ge 1:26; Jas 3:9
11:8 [g] Ge 2:21-23; 1Ti 2:13
11:9 [h] Ge 2:18
11:12 [i] Ro 11:36
11:16 [j] 1Co 7:17
11:17 [k] ver 2, 22
11:18 [l] 1Co 1:10-12; 3:3

[a] 4-7 Or *4Every man who prays or prophesies with long hair dishonors his head. 5But every woman who prays or prophesies with no covering of hair dishonors her head — she is just like one of the "shorn women." 6If a woman has no covering, let her be for now with short hair; but since it is a disgrace for a woman to have her hair shorn or shaved, she should grow it again. 7A man ought not to have long hair* [b] 10 Or *have a sign of authority on her*

"With his head covered" (v. 4) might refer to long hair. In vv. 14–15 Paul is definitely talking about relative lengths of hair for men and women, so it is somewhat more natural to assume that he has been talking about hairstyles all along. If an external covering is meant, then Paul is probably objecting to a practice that resembled that of Roman priests pulling their togas up over their heads while offering sacrifices.

Wives should keep their heads covered (v. 5a). Again, the covering could refer to long hair. It could be that Paul wants them to keep it "done up," as was the custom among married women, rather than loose and flowing—a sign in some circles of being unmarried or of suspected adultery (among Jews) or pagan, prophetic frenzy (among Greeks).

Verses 7–10 state Paul's true preference—that the Corinthians adopt culturally appropriate signs of marital fidelity and worship of the one true God.

Verses 8–9 ground the commands of vv. 4–7 in a twofold argument from creation: (1) Adam was created first and then Eve (v. 8); (2) woman was created to be a helper suitable for man (Ge 2:18) and not the reverse (1Co 11:9). Verse 10 brings the first part of Paul's argument to a climax. "For this reason" suggests that this sentence gives a further rationale for why women are to keep their heads covered. Every other use of this phrase in the NT means "to have authority (or control) *over*." This suggests a translation that could also read "For this reason . . . a wife should exercise control over her head [i.e., keep the appropriate covering on it]."

"Because of the angels" proves perplexing (v. 10b). We should see the angels as the ones who remain God's servants, watching over creation and protecting the worship of his people. They in particular would want to see services proceed with appropriate dignity and decorum.

11:11–12 These verses introduce an important qualification into Paul's discussion. Paul reminds the Corinthians that, as Christians, husbands and wives are fundamentally interdependent. God is the origin of everything that belongs to redemption. He is therefore our ultimate and most important authority.

11:13–16 Paul returns to the specific problem of head coverings, this time explicitly referring to long hair on men and women, with three further arguments. After appealing to the Corinthians to conclude that what Paul is saying is true (v. 13a), he argues further from propriety (v. 13b), nature (vv. 14–15), and the widespread first-century custom of all believers (v. 16).

11:15–16 Verse 15b supports the idea that hair length or style has been the issue throughout vv. 2–16. "As a covering" might more literally be rendered "instead of a wrap-around garment." Rather than wearing the customary hair shawl as Greek women did, long hair, perhaps pulled up in a bun, will suffice for Christian women. Verse 15 might also be translated, "For long hair is given to her so that she may wind it around her head."

11:2–16 To the extent that people's grooming or dress deliberately flaunts authority and social convention, such actions cannot be condoned by Christians, because it gives us an unnecessarily bad reputation among non-Christians. But wise Christians, like wise parents, will choose their battles carefully. In the church today, we should not get overly upset by a person's outward appearance when there are more pressing and fundamental theological and ethical issues to be concerned about in our society.

11:17–21 Whatever the Corinthians may have claimed in their letter about faithfully celebrating the Lord's Supper (vv. 2, 22c), Paul has heard additional news that horrifies him (v. 18). Paul refers to "divisions."

it. 19No doubt there have to be differences among you to show which of you have God's approval.[m] 20So then, when you come together, it is not the Lord's Supper you eat, 21for when you are eating, some of you go ahead with your own private suppers.[n] As a result, one person remains hungry and another gets drunk. 22Don't you have homes to eat and drink in? Or do you despise the church of God[o] by humiliating those who have nothing?[p] What shall I say to you? Shall I praise you?[q] Certainly not in this matter!

23For I received from the Lord[r] what I also passed on to you:[s] The Lord Jesus, on the night he was betrayed, took bread, 24and when he had given thanks, he broke it and said, "This is my body, which is for you; do this in remembrance of me." 25In the same way, after supper he took the cup, saying, "This cup is the new covenant[t] in my blood;[u] do this, whenever you drink it, in remembrance of me." 26For whenever you eat this bread and drink this cup, you proclaim the Lord's death until he comes.

27So then, whoever eats the bread or drinks the cup of the Lord in an unworthy manner will be guilty of sinning against the body and blood of the Lord.[v] 28Everyone ought to examine themselves[w] before they eat of the bread and drink from the cup. 29For those who eat and drink without discerning the body of Christ eat and drink judgment on themselves. 30That is why many among you are weak and sick, and a number of you have fallen asleep. 31But if we were more discerning with regard to ourselves, we would not come under such judgment.[x] 32Nevertheless, when we are judged in this way by the Lord, we are being disciplined[y] so that we will not be finally condemned with the world.

33So then, my brothers and sisters, when you gather to eat, you should all

11:19 [m] 1Jn 2:19
11:21 [n] 2Pe 2:13; Jude 12
11:22 [o] 1Co 10:32 [p] Jas 2:6 [q] ver 2,17
11:23 [r] Gal 1:12 [s] 1Co 15:3
11:25 [t] Lk 22:20 [u] 1Co 10:16
11:27 [v] Heb 10:29
11:28 [w] 2Co 13:5
11:31 [x] Ps 32:5; 1Jn 1:9
11:32 [y] Ps 94:12; Heb 12:7-10; Rev 3:19

He is thinking of the gulf between the rich and poor within a given house church. The minority of well-to-do believers (1:26) would have had the leisure time and resources to arrive earlier, bringing finer food than the rest of the congregation. Latecomers (the majority, who probably had to finish work before coming) would be seated separately. Those who could not afford to bring a full meal did not have the opportunity to share with the community. This thoughtlessness by the wealthy implies that they are not celebrating the *Lord's* Supper at all, merely "their *own* supper" (v. 21).

11:22 Instead of ensuring everyone gets plenty to eat and drink, some gorge themselves and get drunk. Jude 12 uses the popular early Christian term "love feasts" for these communal meals. They would have probably culminated in the Lord's Supper, based on Jesus' model (Mt 26:26–29; Mk 14:22–25; Lk 22:14–20). Paul doesn't object to the wealthy enjoying food in the privacy of their own families (1Co 11:22a), but in this church setting, their selfishness is inappropriate (v. 22b).

11:24–26 When Paul says he received this information from the Lord, he is referring to that which the Lord Jesus spoke before his crucifixion. These words were widely repeated in the early Christian community. The focus of these reflections centers on Jesus' so-called words of institution about the significance of the bread and the wine (vv. 24–26). No one sitting with Christ at the table would have thought he was saying that the bread was somehow a literal extension of his flesh or spirit. Rather the bread *symbolized* or *represented* his coming bodily death, an atoning sacrifice for the sake of all who would accept the forgiveness of sins it made available.

The reason Paul, like the Gospel writers, calls it the "cup" rather than using the word *wine* is because the expression evoked OT associations of suffering the "cup" of God's wrath (e.g., Ps 75:8; Isa 51:17). The message about the significance of Christ's death that this ceremony reenacts should be proclaimed throughout church history.

11:27–34 Paul draws out the implications for the Corinthians of his appeal to tradition. Jesus' self-giving love for them makes their selfish behavior that much more shameful. Paul does not use the adjective "unworthy" to refer to a person's character, but he highlights instead the nature of their *actions*. "The body and blood of the Lord" in v. 27b again refer to Jesus' crucifixion and its significance. "Examine" (v. 28) means "test and find approved." If their behavior toward their fellow Christians is appropriate, then they themselves qualify to participate in this memorial supper.

Verse 29 seems to reflect the same problem described in v. 27 (eating unworthily), which in turn looked back to v. 21 (overeating and overdrinking). Verse 30 unpacks what was involved in God's punishing the Corinthians for their profaning his holy table. "Sleep" was a common euphemism for death. The way to avoid such tragedy was to monitor one's own behavior (v. 31). Paul ends on a somewhat upbeat note by reminding his readers that God disciplines those he loves to protect them from further damaging themselves or others (v. 32). Verses 33–34 summarize Paul's solution to the Corinthians' unholy activity during the Lord's Supper.

11:17–34 Our culture is one of the few in the history of the world that has lost respect for the immense value of tradition, ritual, symbolism, and religious drama. Not surprisingly, liturgical churches are appealing to many who are frustrated with this loss. We need balances

eat together. 34 Anyone who is hungry[z]
should eat something at home,[a] so that
when you meet together it may not result in judgment.
And when I come[b] I will give further
directions.

Concerning Spiritual Gifts

12 Now about the gifts of the Spirit,[c]
brothers and sisters, I do not want
you to be uninformed. 2 You know that
when you were pagans,[d] somehow or
other you were influenced and led astray
to mute idols.[e] 3 Therefore I want you to
know that no one who is speaking by the
Spirit of God says, "Jesus be cursed,"[f] and
no one can say, "Jesus is Lord,"[g] except
by the Holy Spirit.[h]
4 There are different kinds of gifts, but
the same Spirit[i] distributes them. 5 There
are different kinds of service, but the
same Lord. 6 There are different kinds of
working, but in all of them and in everyone it is the same God[j] at work.

> **1Co 12:7–11** ❖ What spiritual gifts has God given us? How can we use them for the common good of our faith communities?

7 Now to each one the manifestation
of the Spirit is given for the common
good.[k] 8 To one there is given through the
Spirit a message of wisdom,[l] to another
a message of knowledge[m] by means of
the same Spirit, 9 to another faith[n] by the
same Spirit, to another gifts of healing[o]
by that one Spirit, 10 to another miraculous powers,[p] to another prophecy, to
another distinguishing between spirits,[q]
to another speaking in different kinds of
tongues,[a][r] and to still another the interpretation of tongues.[a] 11 All these are the
work of one and the same Spirit,[s] and he
distributes them to each one, just as he
determines.

11:34 [z] ver 21 [a] ver 22 [b] 1Co 4:19
12:1 [c] Ro 1:11; 1Co 14:1, 37
12:2 [d] Eph 2:11, 12; 1Pe 4:3 [e] Ps 115:5; Jer 10:5; Hab 2:18, 19; 1Th 1:9
12:3 [f] Ro 9:3 [g] Jn 13:13 [h] 1Jn 4:2, 3
12:4 [i] Ro 12:4-8; Eph 4:11; Heb 2:4
12:6 [j] Eph 4:6
12:7 [k] Eph 4:12
12:8 [l] 1Co 2:6 [m] 2Co 8:7
12:9 [n] Mt 17:19, 20; 2Co 4:13 [o] ver 28, 30
12:10 [p] Gal 3:5 [q] 1Jn 4:1 [r] Mk 16:17
12:11 [s] ver 4

[a] 10 Or *languages;* also in verse 28

> between liturgy and spontaneity in the Lord's Supper and in worship more generally. We also need balances between planned traditional observances to stress our link with the past and opportunities for creativity to keep services fresh and meaningful for different subcultures within our society.

12:1–3 "Gifts of the Spirit" in v. 1 could also be translated "spiritual things" or "spiritual people." The term probably reflects the prideful way the Corinthian leaders referred to themselves. Paul picks up on their claims to knowledge and fears that he needs to dispel their "ignorance" (recall 10:1).

Part of their problem is that they have not made a radical enough break from their pagan backgrounds (12:2). But in those settings, participants who had heard of Christ's claims might well have cursed him (v. 3a). Conversely, only Christians—those indwelt by the Spirit—can acknowledge Jesus as Lord (v. 3b).

12:4–6 Paul describes spiritual gifts from three different angles: They are bestowed freely by the Spirit's grace (v. 4), are intended to be used in a Christlike attitude of servanthood (v. 5), and are the result of God's powerful working in a person's life (v. 6). Verse 7 employs yet a fourth term, "manifestation," and stresses that all the Corinthian Christians have at least one such gift, which is to be used for the benefit of others in the community.

12:8–11 These verses divide into three sections: wisdom and knowledge (v. 8); faith, healings, miracles, prophecy, and distinguishing spirits (vv. 9–10a); and tongues and their interpretations (v. 10b). All nine represent the more miraculous gifts, which Paul repeatedly states come from the same Spirit. Since they are gifts of the Holy Spirit, not earned (v. 11), they cannot be treated like status symbols.

A "message" of wisdom or knowledge (v. 8) reflects the ability to bring spiritual insight to bear in a timely, helpful fashion in a specific Christian context. If Paul intends any difference between the word of wisdom and the word of knowledge, it may be that wisdom is knowledge applied, particularly in moral contexts (see Pr 1:7). "Faith" in 1Co 12:9 is a special measure of faith that God can work miracles. "Gifts of healing" (v. 9) refers to supernatural cures of physical maladies. "Miraculous powers" (v. 10) include additional kinds of miracles, most notably exorcisms.

NT prophecy builds on the background of prophetic activity in both the OT and Greco-Roman religions, while differing in crucial ways from each. Prophecy included both "foretelling" and, more predominantly, "forthtelling" (revealing God's will for their present circumstances). NT prophecy included both conventional preaching and more spontaneous, unpremeditated expressions. Prophecy is not on par with Scripture. Like all spiritual gifts, people's exercise of the gift is subject to error and misinterpretation (cf. esp. Ac 21:4 with 1Co 12:11, 13–14).

"Distinguishing between spirits" (v. 10) probably refers to the God-given ability to discern if an apparently inspired speaker is ministering by the power of the Holy Spirit or by some counterfeit power.

"Speaking in different kinds of tongues" must not be confused with what happened to the disciples at Pentecost. It is best to understand the Corinthian experience as involving some kind of initially unintelligible verbal utterance. "Interpreting" tongues then refers to putting the otherwise unintelligible message into words that are understood by those present.

Unity and Diversity in the Body

12 Just as a body, though one, has many
parts, but all its many parts form one
body,[t] so it is with Christ.[u] 13 For we were
all baptized by[a] one Spirit[v] so as to form
one body—whether Jews or Gentiles,
slave or free[w]—and we were all given the
one Spirit to drink.[x] 14 Even so the body
is not made up of one part but of many.
15 Now if the foot should say, "Because
I am not a hand, I do not belong to the
body," it would not for that reason stop
being part of the body. 16 And if the ear
should say, "Because I am not an eye, I do
not belong to the body," it would not for
that reason stop being part of the body.
17 If the whole body were an eye, where
would the sense of hearing be? If the
whole body were an ear, where would the
sense of smell be? 18 But in fact God has
placed[y] the parts in the body, every one
of them, just as he wanted them to be.[z]
19 If they were all one part, where would
the body be? 20 As it is, there are many
parts, but one body.[a]
21 The eye cannot say to the hand, "I
don't need you!" And the head cannot
say to the feet, "I don't need you!" 22 On
the contrary, those parts of the body that
seem to be weaker are indispensable,
23 and the parts that we think are less
honorable we treat with special honor.
And the parts that are unpresentable are
treated with special modesty, 24 while
our presentable parts need no special
treatment. But God has put the body together, giving greater honor to the parts
that lacked it, 25 so that there should be
no division in the body, but that its parts
should have equal concern for each other. 26 If one part suffers, every part suffers
with it; if one part is honored, every part
rejoices with it.
27 Now you are the body of Christ,[b] and
each one of you is a part of it.[c] 28 And God
has placed in the church[d] first of all apostles,[e] second prophets, third teachers,
then miracles, then gifts of healing,[f] of
helping, of guidance,[g] and of different
kinds of tongues.[h] 29 Are all apostles?
Are all prophets? Are all teachers? Do
all work miracles? 30 Do all have gifts of
healing? Do all speak in tongues[b]?[i] Do
all interpret? 31 Now eagerly desire[j] the
greater gifts.

Love Is Indispensable

And yet I will show you the most excellent way.

13 If I speak in the tongues[c][k] of men
or of angels, but do not have love, I
am only a resounding gong or a clanging
cymbal. 2 If I have the gift of prophecy
and can fathom all mysteries[l] and all
knowledge, and if I have a faith[m] that
can move mountains,[n] but do not have
love, I am nothing. 3 If I give all I possess
to the poor[o] and give over my body to

[a] 13 Or *with;* or *in* [b] 30 Or *other languages*
[c] 1 Or *languages*

12:12 [t] Ro 12:5 [u] ver 27
12:13 [v] Eph 2:18 [w] Gal 3:28; Col 3:11 [x] Jn 7:37-39
12:18 [y] ver 28 [z] ver 11
12:20 [a] ver 12, 14
12:27 [b] Eph 1:23; 4:12; Col 1:18, 24 [c] Ro 12:5
12:28 [d] 1Co 10:32 [e] Eph 4:11 [f] ver 9 [g] Ro 12:6-8 [h] ver 10
12:30 [i] ver 10
12:31 [j] 1Co 14:1, 39
13:1 [k] ver 8
13:2 [l] 1Co 14:2 [m] 1Co 12:9 [n] Mt 17:20; 21:21
13:3 [o] Mt 6:2

12:12–26 Paul develops the extended metaphor of the church as the body of Christ.
12:13–14 Paul gives a twofold rationale for permitting diversity within unity: Those who are being saved come from all ethnic and socioeconomic brackets of the ancient world, and that is how a human body works. Spirit-baptism occurs at the moment of conversion (cf. Ro 8:9).
12:15–20 These verses underline what is evident with respect to a human body: All the parts serve an important function, regardless of any claims to the contrary. Without different functions, one is no longer a complete organism.
12:21–26 Paul continues to apply the analogy to the church. Where there is seemingly less value, power, or honor in the body, compensation occurs to preserve relative equality. Paul's concern is that the gifts and/or people the Corinthians are demeaning should be affirmed, while those they are overly exalting should be put in more balanced perspective.
12:27–31 These verses restate the body metaphor and give another listing of sample gifts. Paul's main point is that not one of the gifts is intended for all believers. The rhetorical questions in vv. 29–30 imply the answer to each question is "no." This list includes some of the same and some different gifts as in vv. 8–10. "Apostles" here means those sent out on a divinely ordained mission. "Teachers" in the ancient world communicated a fixed body of information to their students.

12:1–31a Ours is an age that delights to exalt Christian celebrities, to demand that our pastors entertain, have charismatic personalities, and display more spiritual gifts than any one Bible character ever had. Little wonder that burnout from full-time ministry seems to be at an all-time high and that failures of whatever kind at times results from the stress. We need to follow the model of servant leadership (recall ch. 4) and allow our leaders and ourselves to spend the majority of our time doing those things at which we excel.

13:1–7 Love is more important than all the gifts (12:31b). Without love the gifts are worthless. First Corinthians 13:1–3 drive home the same truth repeatedly by using five of the spiritual gifts as illustrations of the identical principle: Without love even the most perfect use of a particular gift does a believer no good. Taken together, vv. 4–7 clearly

1Co 13:2 ❖ How can we ensure that our faith is always flavored with love? What happens when faith has no love?

hardship that I may boast,[a][p] but do not
have love, I gain nothing.
4Love is patient,[q] love is kind. It does
not envy, it does not boast, it is not
proud. 5It does not dishonor others, it is
not self-seeking,[r] it is not easily angered,
it keeps no record of wrongs. 6Love does
not delight in evil[s] but rejoices with the
truth.[t] 7It always protects, always trusts,
always hopes, always perseveres.
8Love never fails. But where there are
prophecies,[u] they will cease; where there
are tongues,[v] they will be stilled; where
there is knowledge, it will pass away. 9For
we know in part[w] and we prophesy in
part, 10but when completeness comes,[x]
what is in part disappears. 11When I was
a child, I talked like a child, I thought
like a child, I reasoned like a child.
When I became a man, I put the ways
of childhood behind me. 12For now we
see only a reflection as in a mirror; then
we shall see face to face.[y] Now I know in
part; then I shall know fully, even as I am
fully known.[z]
13And now these three remain: faith,
hope and love.[a] But the greatest of these
is love.[b]

13:3 [p]Da 3:28
13:4 [q]1Th 5:14
13:5 [r]1Co 10:24
13:6 [s]2Th 2:12 [t]2Jn 4; 3Jn 3,4
13:8 [u]ver 2 [v]ver 1
13:9 [w]ver 12; 1Co 8:2
13:10 [x]Php 3:12
13:12 [y]Ge 32:30; 2Co 5:7; 1Jn 3:2 [z]1Co 8:3
13:13 [a]Gal 5:5,6 [b]1Co 16:14
14:1 [c]1Co 16:14 [d]ver 39; 1Co 12:31 [e]1Co 12:1
14:2 [f]Mk 16:17 [g]1Co 13:2
14:3 [h]ver 4, 5,12,17,26; Ro 14:19
14:4 [i]Mk 16:17 [j]1Co 13:2
14:5 [k]Nu 11:29
14:6 [l]ver 26; Eph 1:17 [m]Ro 6:17

Intelligibility in Worship

14 Follow the way of love[c] and eagerly desire[d] gifts of the Spirit,[e] especially prophecy. 2For anyone who speaks
in a tongue[b][f] does not speak to people
but to God. Indeed, no one understands
them; they utter mysteries[g] by the Spirit. 3But the one who prophesies speaks
to people for their strengthening,[h] encouraging and comfort. 4Anyone who
speaks in a tongue[i] edifies themselves,
but the one who prophesies[j] edifies the
church. 5I would like every one of you
to speak in tongues,[c] but I would rather
have you prophesy.[k] The one who prophesies is greater than the one who speaks
in tongues,[c] unless someone interprets,
so that the church may be edified.
6Now, brothers and sisters, if I come
to you and speak in tongues, what good
will I be to you, unless I bring you some
revelation[l] or knowledge or prophecy or
word of instruction?[m] 7Even in the case of
lifeless things that make sounds, such as

[a] 3 Some manuscripts *body to the flames*
[b] 2 Or *in another language*; also in verses 4, 13, 14, 19, 26 and 27 [c] 5 Or *in other languages*; also in verses 6, 18, 22, 23 and 39

portray love as selfless, seeking the good of the other first and foremost.

13:8–13 Verse 8 states the thesis of vv. 8–13. Why will the gifts cease? It is because they are imperfect provisions for an imperfect world, rendered unnecessary when perfection comes (vv. 9–10). But to what does "completeness" (v. 10) refer? Nothing in Paul supports that he feels that he is writing near the end of an apostolic age or the close of a biblical canon. And the metaphors in v. 12 fit poorly with such interpretations. After the Bible was completed, Christians did not see God "face to face" (only "face to book"!) or know him to the degree that he knew them. "Perfection" is the life in the world to come after Jesus reappears on earth.

But love abides on into eternity. So too probably do faith and hope (v. 13a), if faith is taken as belief in Jesus and faithful service to him, and if hope refers to the anticipation of the good things God has in the future for his people. Paul adds these other two virtues because the triad of faith, hope, and love is a favorite of his (cf. Eph 1:15–18; Col 1:4–5; 1Th 1:3; 5:8). But love remains the greatest (1Co 13:13b) because it is foundational, essential, and central to Paul's understanding of the Christian ethic.

✣ **12:31b—13:13** The need for genuine, Christlike love remains as great today as ever. Yet one of our greatest problems is defining love. Popular culture—in literature, music, advertising, and the visual arts—uses the word to mean just about everything *except* what the Bible means by it. So even Christians are easily misled into thinking love is primarily a feeling, something we fall in or out of. But in this chapter, as throughout Scripture, love is first of all an action—an unconditional commitment, a promise that is never broken.

14:1–2 In ch. 14 Paul continues his discussion of spiritual gifts by encouraging the Corinthians to prefer prophecy to tongues. Verse 1 resumes the thread of 12:31. Paul now specifies one of the "greater" gifts—namely, prophecy. Next, 14:2 makes it reasonably certain that the misuse of tongues was one of the Corinthians' major problems during worship. Verse 5b demonstrates that all of vv. 2–5a must be understood as Paul's criticisms of tongues *when they are not interpreted*. When they *are* interpreted, they, like prophecy, contain instruction and exhortation (vv. 3, 4b, 5b).

14:3–4 Unlike uninterpreted tongues, prophecy enlightens the whole assembly, not just the individual speaker. Paul isolates two reasons why prophecy is greater: People, not just God, are addressed, and they can be more positively affected.

14:6–12 Verse 6 presents the thesis of the next paragraph (vv. 6–12), repeating the need for

the pipe or harp, how will anyone know
what tune is being played unless there
is a distinction in the notes? 8Again, if
the trumpet does not sound a clear call,
who will get ready for battle?[n] 9So it is
with you. Unless you speak intelligible
words with your tongue, how will anyone know what you are saying? You will
just be speaking into the air. 10Undoubt-
edly there are all sorts of languages in
the world, yet none of them is without
meaning. 11If then I do not grasp the
meaning of what someone is saying, I
am a foreigner to the speaker, and the
speaker is a foreigner to me. 12So it is
with you. Since you are eager for gifts
of the Spirit, try to excel in those that
build up the church.

13For this reason the one who speaks
in a tongue should pray that they may
interpret what they say. 14For if I pray in
a tongue, my spirit prays, but my mind
is unfruitful. 15So what shall I do? I will
pray with my spirit, but I will also pray
with my understanding; I will sing[o] with
my spirit, but I will also sing with my
understanding. 16Otherwise when you
are praising God in the Spirit, how can
someone else, who is now put in the position of an inquirer,[a] say "Amen"[p] to your
thanksgiving,[q] since they do not know
what you are saying? 17You are giving
thanks well enough, but no one else is
edified.

18I thank God that I speak in tongues
more than all of you. 19But in the church
I would rather speak five intelligible
words to instruct others than ten thousand words in a tongue.

20Brothers and sisters, stop thinking
like children.[r] In regard to evil be infants,[s] but in your thinking be adults.
21In the Law[t] it is written:

"With other tongues
and through the lips of foreigners
I will speak to this people,
but even then they will not listen
to me,[u]
says the Lord."[b]

22Tongues, then, are a sign, not for believers but for unbelievers; prophecy,[v]
however, is not for unbelievers but for
believers. 23So if the whole church comes
together and everyone speaks in tongues,
and inquirers or unbelievers come in,
will they not say that you are out of your
mind?[w] 24But if an unbeliever or an inquirer comes in while everyone is prophesying, they are convicted of sin and are
brought under judgment by all, 25as the
secrets of their hearts are laid bare. So
they will fall down and worship God, ex-
claiming, "God is really among you!"[x]

14:8 [n] Nu 10:9; Jer 4:19
14:15 [o] Eph 5:19; Col 3:16
14:16 [p] Dt 27:15-26; 1Ch 16:36; Ne 8:6; Ps 106:48; Rev 5:14; 7:12 [q] 1Co 11:24
14:20 [r] Eph 4:14; Heb 5:12,13; 1Pe 2:2 [s] Ro 16:19
14:21 [t] Jn 10:34 [u] Isa 28:11,12
14:22 [v] ver 1
14:23 [w] Ac 2:13
14:25 [x] Isa 45:14; Zec 8:23

[a] *16* The Greek word for *inquirer* is a technical term for someone not fully initiated into a religion; also in verses 23 and 24.
[b] *21* Isaiah 28:11,12

---

intelligibility. Verses 7–11 then give three illustrations of this principle. Verse 12 concludes by repeating the point with which the first paragraph of this chapter ended (v. 5).

So what must a person do if God *has* given him or her the gift of speaking in tongues? Verses 13–19 address this question. They should pray for the ability to interpret those messages. Verses 14–15 show that receiving the gift of interpretation benefits oneself first of all. Praying with one's spirit versus praying with one's mind (v. 15a) is probably equivalent to the distinction in vv. 13–14 of speaking in tongues versus interpretation.

14:16-17 Paul turns to the effect on others present. Again, interpretation is crucial if the rest of the congregation is to be able to agree. "Inquirer" refers to someone who is not an expert or not initiated. Even mature Christians play the role of the uninitiated when they hear uninterpreted tongues. They have no idea what the message means.

14:18-20 Verses 18–19 probably surprised Paul's original readers, who may even have been criticizing him for not speaking in tongues. These verses substantiate his extensive private use of tongues as a "prayer language." Verse 20 is clear. A selfish preoccupation with tongues is childish. There are ways Christians should be childlike (cf. Mt 10:16; 19:14), but not in their use of spiritual gifts.

14:21-25 These verses justify Paul's appeal to prefer prophecy to tongues. Paul begins by citing parts of Isa 28:11–12, a passage in which God pronounces judgment against rebellious Israel (1Co 14:21).

14:22-23 Verse 22 must refer to a sign *of judgment*. Like the unbelieving Israelites, non-Christians in Corinth will remain lost in their sins because they will reject the gospel as the product of insane babblers.

14:24-25 These verses argue that prophecy is a sign of judgment in the positive sense. It convicts unbelievers of their sins and brings them to repentance (v. 25b echoes Isa 45:14). Paul here stresses that an intelligible proclamation of the gospel stands a far better chance of convicting unsaved people and regenerating their hearts.

14:1-25 A positive use of the gift of speaking in tongues continues to appear in Christians discovering a private prayer language. Testimony after testimony describes how the Spirit intervened to liberate some frustrated individual from his or her fruitless quiet time, lifeless worship, or inconsistent walk with the

> **1Co 14:24–25** ❖ What might we do to be able to speak God's word in such a way that those who hear us are drawn to worship God?

Good Order in Worship

26 What then shall we say, brothers
and sisters? When you come together,
each of you[y] has a hymn,[z] or a word of
instruction,[a] a revelation, a tongue or
an interpretation. Everything must be
done so that the church may be built up.[b]
27 If anyone speaks in a tongue, two — or
at the most three — should speak, one
at a time, and someone must interpret.
28 If there is no interpreter, the speaker should keep quiet in the church and
speak to himself and to God.
29 Two or three prophets should speak,
and the others should weigh carefully what is said.[c] 30 And if a revelation
comes to someone who is sitting down,
the first speaker should stop. 31 For you
can all prophesy in turn so that everyone may be instructed and encouraged.
32 The spirits of prophets are subject to
the control of prophets.[d] 33 For God is
not a God of disorder[e] but of peace — as
in all the congregations of the Lord's
people.[f]
34 Women[a] should remain silent in
the churches. They are not allowed to
speak, but must be in submission,[g] as
the law[h] says. 35 If they want to inquire
about something, they should ask their
own husbands at home; for it is disgraceful for a woman to speak in the
church.[b]
36 Or did the word of God originate with
you? Or are you the only people it has
reached? 37 If anyone thinks they are a
prophet[i] or otherwise gifted by the Spirit, let them acknowledge that what I am

14:26 [y] 1Co 12:7-10 [z] Eph 5:19 [a] ver 6 [b] Ro 14:19
14:29 [c] 1Co 12:10
14:32 [d] 1Jn 4:1
14:33 [e] ver 40 [f] Ac 9:13
14:34 [g] 1Ti 2:11, 12 [h] Ge 3:16
14:37 [i] 2Co 10:7

[a] 33,34 Or *peace. As in all the congregations of the Lord's people, 34women*
[b] 34,35 In a few manuscripts these verses come after verse 40.

> Lord. Indeed, the winds of the charismatic movement seem to have blown freshest and most purely in the middle of dead, formal, traditional churches, where it has given to congregations such "radical" ideas (by no means distinctively charismatic) as singing choruses, using musical instruments besides piano or organ, clapping or raising hands, sharing praise items and prayer requests, and conversational prayer.

14:26 In this verse, Paul insists that the Corinthians continue to worship in highly participatory and spontaneous fashion. This does not mean that every person exercises all the gifts, nor even that all exercise at least one in every service. But opportunity to contribute should be available to all whom the Spirit leads on any given occasion.

Once again, Paul stresses the need to build up fellow believers. It is possible this is the pattern for the regular home-fellowship gatherings, whereas the earlier verses reflect periodic larger, more public assemblies of multiple house churches.

14:27–33 Verses 27–32 again narrow the focus to the two key gifts of tongues and prophecy. In closely parallel fashion, vv. 27–28 and 29–32 temper the spontaneity described in v. 26 by regulating the exercise of these two particular gifts.

The "others" of v. 29 refers to the rest of the congregation, not merely the other prophets. If, as we have suggested, exercising the gift of discernment is not what Paul means by carefully weighing prophecy, it is unlikely that the prophets were the best persons to evaluate each other's messages.

Verse 30 insists that prophets exercise their gifts in turn. Paul desires that all might exercise these gifts, without implying that all can or will. Verse 32 asserts that believers are never so "out of control" as to be unable to regulate their behavior. Verse 33a provides the required rationale for the regulations of tongues and prophecy: orderliness and peace.

14:34–35 These verses seem quite intrusive at this juncture. Why does Paul seemingly interrupt his discussion of these two spiritual gifts to silence women? Perhaps the best perspective is to take Paul's commands as prohibiting women from participating in the final church decisions about the legitimacy of any given prophecy. An authoritative evaluation of prophecy would ultimately have been the responsibility of the church leadership (what Paul elsewhere calls "elders" or "overseers"). In the first century, these leaders seem to have been exclusively male. This interpretation also explains why these verses come where they do. The sequence of topics from vv. 27–33 has been precisely tongues and their interpretation, and prophecy and its evaluation, in that order.

As in 11:2–16, the women whom Paul silences may be only wives. This would explain why they must not publicly challenge the church's prophecies but consult at home (14:35). To do otherwise might be to challenge their husbands in church in ways that would contradict their God-ordained submission to them (v. 34).

14:36–38 These verses challenge the Corinthians not to reject Paul's counsel lightly. If every other Christian church practiced what Paul preached on this matter, who are they to be the sole exceptions (v. 36)? Those who contested Paul's teaching undoubtedly justified their rebellion by claiming the Spirit's direction (v. 37a). So Paul adds that if they are truly Spirit-led they will come to acknowledge his views as from the Lord (v. 37b). If they continue to go their own way, they demonstrate that they are out of touch with the Spirit (v. 38).

writing to you is the Lord's command.[j]
38 But if anyone ignores this, they will
themselves be ignored.[a]
39 Therefore, my brothers and sisters,
be eager[k] to prophesy, and do not forbid
speaking in tongues. 40 But everything
should be done in a fitting and orderly[l] way.

The Resurrection of Christ

15 Now, brothers and sisters, I want
to remind you of the gospel[m] I
preached to you, which you received and
on which you have taken your stand. 2 By
this gospel you are saved,[n] if you hold
firmly[o] to the word I preached to you.
Otherwise, you have believed in vain.
3 For what I received[p] I passed on to
you[q] as of first importance[b]: that Christ
died for our sins[r] according to the Scriptures,[s] 4 that he was buried, that he was
raised[t] on the third day[u] according to
the Scriptures,[v] 5 and that he appeared
to Cephas,[c][w] and then to the Twelve.[x]
6 After that, he appeared to more than
five hundred of the brothers and sisters at the same time, most of whom
are still living, though some have fall-
en asleep. 7 Then he appeared to James,
then to all the apostles,[y] 8 and last of all
he appeared to me also,[z] as to one abnormally born.
9 For I am the least of the apostles[a] and
do not even deserve to be called an apostle, because I persecuted[b] the church of
God. 10 But by the grace of God I am what
I am, and his grace to me[c] was not without effect. No, I worked harder than all of
them[d]—yet not I, but the grace of God
that was with me.[e] 11 Whether, then, it is
I or they, this is what we preach, and this
is what you believed.

The Resurrection of the Dead

12 But if it is preached that Christ has
been raised from the dead, how can some
of you say that there is no resurrection
of the dead?[f] 13 If there is no resurrection
of the dead, then not even Christ has
been raised. 14 And if Christ has not been
raised,[g] our preaching is useless and so is
your faith. 15 More than that, we are then
found to be false witnesses about God,
for we have testified about God that he
raised Christ from the dead.[h] But he did
not raise him if in fact the dead are not
raised. 16 For if the dead are not raised,

14:37 [j] 1Jn 4:6
14:39 [k] 1Co 12:31
14:40 [l] ver 33
15:1 [m] Ro 2:16
15:2 [n] Ro 1:16 [o] Ro 11:22
15:3 [p] Gal 1:12 [q] 1Co 11:23 [r] Isa 53:5; 1Pe 2:24 [s] Lk 24:27; Ac 26:22,23
15:4 [t] Ac 2:24 [u] Mt 16:21 [v] Ac 2:25,30,31
15:5 [w] Lk 24:34 [x] Mk 16:14
15:7 [y] Lk 24:33,36,37; Ac 1:3,4
15:8 [z] Ac 9:3-6,17; 1Co 9:1
15:9 [a] Eph 3:8; 1Ti 1:15 [b] Ac 8:3
15:10 [c] Ro 12:3 [d] 2Co 11:23 [e] Php 2:13
15:12 [f] Ac 17:32; 23:8; 2Ti 2:18
15:14 [g] 1Th 4:14
15:15 [h] Ac 2:24

[a] *38* Some manuscripts *But anyone who is ignorant of this will be ignorant* [b] *3* Or *you at the first* [c] *5* That is, Peter

---

14:39–40 Finally, vv. 39–40 bring all three chapters (12–14), but especially this last one, to a fitting conclusion, as they balance Paul's twin concerns for freedom and structure. Every gift has its place, but each must be used to build up the church in unity and love.

> ✣ **14:26–40** In our worshiping communities and groups, we desperately need to allow one another the freedom to agree to disagree, to set up alternate models of worship, and to encourage local fellowships to determine for themselves what they will do in worship, according to their best understanding of Scripture. Verses 39–40 end with strikingly plain words that are nevertheless disobeyed by large sections of the contemporary church. A combination of true congregational oversight, with a balance between spontaneity and structure in worship, would seem to reflect Paul's ideal.

15:1–2 Paul begins by "reminding" the Corinthians what they should have remembered. With a twinge of irony, he says "I preached to you," using their favorite language about knowledge (v. 1). This was what they believed when they first became Christians, and their faith will only persevere if they hold it firmly (v. 2).
15:3–8 In vv. 3–7 Paul repeats the foundational tradition that he had first taught the Corinthians. "That Christ died" (v. 3) refutes those who believed that Christ only seemed human. That it was "for our sins" (v. 3) points to a vicarious atonement—paying the penalty we deserved to pay on our behalf. "According to the Scriptures" (v. 3) probably has in mind passages such as those in Isa 52–53 that speak of God's suffering servant. Jesus' burial (1Co 15:4) again certifies that he really died and also points forward to the empty tomb and the reality of the resurrection.
15:5–7 These verses proceed to supply a list of key witnesses to certify the truth of Jesus' resurrection. Many of these people were still alive to be interviewed, providing strong verification of Paul's claims. The appearance to James (v. 7, referring to the Lord's brother) is not described elsewhere, but it probably caused his conversion (contrast his former attitude toward Jesus in Jn 7:5).

After Jesus' ascension, which signaled the end of the resurrection appearances, no one expected to see Jesus in this way again. So Paul's "private viewing" (1Co 15:8; cf. Ac 9:1–31) came as a shock. "One abnormally born" translates the Greek word for "miscarriage"; here Jesus' resurrection appearance to Paul was unusually late.
15:9–11 In vv. 9–11, Paul acknowledges his inferiority as an apostle because he had persecuted the first Christians. But he turns this admission of weakness into an opportunity to magnify God's grace, leading to greater effort and substantial accomplishment for the cause of Christ.
15:12–19 Verses 12–19 and 29–34 both argue that Christianity is absurd if Jesus' bodily resurrection is not real. In between, vv. 20–28 gloriously reaf-

RESURRECTION APPEARANCES

APPEARANCE	PLACE	TIME	MATTHEW	MARK	LUKE	JOHN	ACTS	1CO
The empty tomb	Jerusalem	Resurrection Sunday	28:1-10	16:1-8	24:1-12	20:1-9		
To Mary Magdalene in the garden	Jerusalem	Resurrection Sunday				20:11-18		
To other women	Jerusalem	Resurrection Sunday	28:9-10					
To two people going to Emmaus	Road to Emmaus	Resurrection Sunday			24:13-32			
To Peter	Jerusalem	Resurrection Sunday			24:34			15:5
To the ten disciples in the upper room	Jerusalem	Resurrection Sunday			24:36-49	20:19-25		
To the 11 disciples in the upper room	Jerusalem	Following Sunday				20:26-31		15:5
To seven disciples fishing	Sea of Galilee	Some time later				21:1-23		
To the 11 disciples on a mountain	Galilee	Some time later	28:16-20					
To more than 500	Unknown	Some time later						15:6
To James	Unknown	Some time later						15:7
To Jesus' disciples at his ascension	Mount of Olives	40 days after Jesus' resurrection			24:50-51		1:4-8	
To Paul	Damascus	Several years later					9:1-19 22:3-16 26:0 18	9:1

then Christ has not been raised either.
17And if Christ has not been raised, your
faith is futile; you are still in your sins.[i]
18Then those also who have fallen asleep
in Christ are lost. 19If only for this life we
have hope in Christ, we are of all people
most to be pitied.[j]

20But Christ has indeed been raised
from the dead,[k] the firstfruits[l] of those
who have fallen asleep.[m] 21For since death
came through a man,[n] the resurrection of
the dead comes also through a man. 22For
as in Adam all die, so in Christ all will be
made alive.[o] 23But each in turn: Christ,

15:17 [i]Ro 4:25
15:19 [j]1Co 4:9
15:20 [k]1Pe 1:3 [l]ver 23; Ac 26:23; Rev 1:5 [m]ver 6,18
15:21 [n]Ro 5:12
15:22 [o]Ro 5:14-18

firm that it *is* true and point to some of the consequences of this grand doctrine. The main point of vv. 12–19 is that if there is no coming bodily resurrection of all Christians, then Jesus himself was not bodily raised, and that makes the Christian faith futile.

15:20–22 Verses 20–22 describe how Christ's bodily resurrection guarantees the future bodily resurrection of all believers, just as the "firstfruits" of a harvest (v. 20) heralded a much larger crop to follow (cf. Lev 23:9–14). Paul points out the parallel between Adam's sin and Christ's resurrection (1Co 15:21–22). Because Adam represented the entire human race that would descend from him, sin spread throughout the whole world. Because Christ, as fully human, represented the entire human race in bearing its sins, he is able to apply the benefits of his death and resurrection to all who will accept them.

15:23–28 The general resurrection of believers at the time of Christ's return is just the beginning (v. 23). Verses 24–28 go on to explain what

the firstfruits;[p] then, when he comes,[q]
those who belong to him. 24 Then the end
will come, when he hands over the kingdom[r] to God the Father after he has destroyed all dominion, authority and power.[s] 25 For he must reign until he has put
all his enemies under his feet.[t] 26 The last
enemy to be destroyed is death.[u] 27 For
he "has put everything under his feet."[a][v]
Now when it says that "everything" has
been put under him, it is clear that this
does not include God himself, who put
everything under Christ.[w] 28 When he has
done this, then the Son himself will be
made subject to him who put everything
under him,[x] so that God may be all in all.[y]
29 Now if there is no resurrection, what
will those do who are baptized for the
dead? If the dead are not raised at all,
why are people baptized for them? 30 And
as for us, why do we endanger ourselves
every hour?[z] 31 I face death every day[a] —
yes, just as surely as I boast about you in
Christ Jesus our Lord. 32 If I fought wild
beasts[b] in Ephesus[c] with no more than
human hopes, what have I gained? If the
dead are not raised,

"Let us eat and drink,
for tomorrow we die."[b][d]

33 Do not be misled: "Bad company corrupts good character."[c] 34 Come back to
your senses as you ought, and stop sinning; for there are some who are ignorant of God — I say this to your shame.

15:23 [p] ver 20 [q] ver 52
15:24 [r] Da 7:14, 27 [s] Ro 8:38
15:25 [t] Ps 110:1; Mt 22:44
15:26 [u] 2Ti 1:10; Rev 20:14; 21:4
15:27 [v] Ps 8:6 [w] Mt 28:18
15:28 [x] Php 3:21 [y] 1Co 3:23
15:30 [z] 2Co 11:26
15:31 [a] Ro 8:36
15:32 [b] 2Co 1:8 [c] Ac 18:19
[d] Isa 22:13; Lk 12:19
15:35 [e] Ro 9:19 [f] Eze 37:3
15:36 [g] Lk 11:40 [h] Jn 12:24

1Co 15:12-58 ❖ What comfort and encouragement does the future resurrection give us, both in everyday life and as we face the reality of death?

The Resurrection Body

35 But someone will ask,[e] "How are the
dead raised? With what kind of body
will they come?"[f] 36 How foolish![g] What
you sow does not come to life unless it
dies.[h] 37 When you sow, you do not plant

[a] *27* Psalm 8:6 [b] *32* Isaiah 22:13 [c] *33* From the Greek poet Menander

---

will subsequently occur. After some unspecified interval of time, "the end" (v. 24) or goal of human history will arrive. By this time, Christ will have destroyed all opposition to his reign in the universe—both human and angelic (i.e., demonic, vv. 24-25). Finally, death itself will be destroyed so that God's people will never again have anything to fear for all eternity (v. 26). But the last word is not Christ's but God's (vv. 27-28).

The "he" in v. 27a refers to God and the "his" to Christ, as v. 27b clarifies. As a representative of humanity and as the One doing what humans were supposed to have done but failed to do (i.e., exercise dominion over the cosmos, Ge 1:28), Jesus remains ultimately subordinate to God. Although God the Son is *essentially* equal to the Father, he remains *functionally* subordinate, just as his glorified humanity keeps him distinct from what he was prior to the incarnation.

15:29-34 In these verses Paul goes back to arguing the absurdity of denying the bodily resurrection. Here he uses three arguments based on what he and the Corinthians were experiencing.

The most puzzling of these is the first. The plain meaning of v. 29 remains that of some sort of substitutionary baptism. Paul neither condemns nor condones such a practice but argues that it is irrelevant if Christ has not been raised. In other words, those who are baptizing people on behalf of the dead contradict their own theology that denies the resurrection.

15:30-34 In vv. 30-32 Paul turns to a parallel pair of arguments from his own experience. Why should he continue to tolerate hostility from others and risk his life for the sake of the gospel if there is no hope of resurrection?

Verse 32b reflects the flip side of the logic of v. 19. If this life is all there is, then people ought to "live it up," as the Epicureans did. Paul cites their most famous slogan. But he immediately proceeds to reject such logic since Christ has been raised. He quotes another popular Greek proverb attributed to the fourth-century BC comic playwright Menander (v. 33). Those who deny the resurrection make for "bad company." Paul appeals to the Corinthians to reject this route (v. 34) by again chiding them for their lack of true knowledge and by trying to shame them into repentance (cf. 6:5).

15:1-34 Christ's death and resurrection in space and time, as bona fide historical events, actually set the Christian faith apart from all its major rivals. Later religions that developed in part in reaction to Christianity do not claim deity or resurrections for their originators, merely prophetic status (e.g., Mohammed in Islam or Joseph Smith in Mormonism). Older Eastern religions do not even require the actual historical existence of their founders for their beliefs and practices to make sense. In some ways they are more similar to philosophies than to historical truth claims (e.g., Hinduism, Buddhism, Confucianism). But, as Paul asserts, the Christian faith lives or dies with the claim of Christ's resurrection. To be sure, it is possible to believe in Jesus' resurrection and not become a Christian, but without Jesus' bodily resurrection the Christian faith crumbles. Finding the bones of Jesus would assuredly disprove our faith. But Christians must recognize the historical evidence that is on their side.

15:35-39 "How are the dead raised?" was probably not so much a genuine question but a way

the body that will be, but just a seed,
perhaps of wheat or of something else.
38But God gives it a body as he has determined, and to each kind of seed he
gives its own body.[i] 39Not all flesh is the
same: People have one kind of flesh, animals have another, birds another and
fish another. 40There are also heavenly
bodies and there are earthly bodies; but
the splendor of the heavenly bodies is
one kind, and the splendor of the earthly
bodies is another. 41The sun has one kind
of splendor, the moon another and the
stars another; and star differs from star
in splendor.

42So will it be[j] with the resurrection of
the dead. The body that is sown is perishable, it is raised imperishable; 43it is
sown in dishonor, it is raised in glory;[k] it
is sown in weakness, it is raised in power;
44it is sown a natural body, it is raised a
spiritual body.[l]

If there is a natural body, there is also a
spiritual body. 45So it is written: "The first
man Adam became a living being"[a];[m] the
last Adam,[n] a life-giving spirit.[o] 46The
spiritual did not come first, but the natural, and after that the spiritual. 47The
first man was of the dust of the earth;[p]
the second man is of heaven.[q] 48As was
the earthly man, so are those who are of
the earth; and as is the heavenly man, so
also are those who are of heaven.[r] 49And
just as we have borne the image of the
earthly man,[s] so shall we[b] bear the image
of the heavenly man.[t]

50I declare to you, brothers and sisters,
that flesh and blood[u] cannot inherit the
kingdom of God, nor does the perishable
inherit the imperishable. 51Listen, I tell
you a mystery:[v] We will not all sleep, but
we will all be changed[w]— 52in a flash,
in the twinkling of an eye, at the last
trumpet. For the trumpet will sound,[x]
the dead[y] will be raised imperishable,
and we will be changed. 53For the perishable must clothe itself with the imperishable,[z] and the mortal with immortality.
54When the perishable has been clothed
with the imperishable, and the mortal
with immortality, then the saying that is
written will come true: "Death has been
swallowed up in victory."[c][a]

55"Where, O death, is your victory?
Where, O death, is your sting?"[d][b]

56The sting of death is sin,[c] and the power
of sin is the law.[d] 57But thanks be to God![e]
He gives us the victory through our Lord
Jesus Christ.[f]

58Therefore, my dear brothers and sisters, stand firm. Let nothing move you.
Always give yourselves fully to the work

15:38 [i] Ge 1:11
15:42 [j] Da 12:3; Mt 13:43
15:43 [k] Php 3:21; Col 3:4
15:44 [l] ver 50
15:45 [m] Ge 2:7 [n] Ro 5:14 [o] Jn 5:21; Ro 8:2
15:47 [p] Ge 2:7; 3:19 [q] Jn 3:13,31
15:48 [r] Php 3:20,21
15:49 [s] Ge 5:3 [t] Ro 8:29
15:50 [u] Jn 3:3,5
15:51 [v] 1Co 13:2 [w] Php 3:21
15:52 [x] Mt 24:31 [y] Jn 5:25
15:53 [z] 2Co 5:2,4
15:54 [a] Isa 25:8; Rev 20:14
15:55 [b] Hos 13:14
15:56 [c] Ro 5:12 [d] Ro 4:15
15:57 [e] 2Co 2:14 [f] Ro 8:37

[a] 45 Gen. 2:7 [b] 49 Some early manuscripts *so let us* [c] 54 Isaiah 25:8 [d] 55 Hosea 13:14

of mocking the whole notion of bodily resurrection. Paul's reply again falls into three parts. Verses 36–44a provide analogies from the created world to describe the resurrection body.

The first analogy Paul uses is that of seed and plant. By being buried in the ground, the seed seemingly dies, and it certainly decomposes. Yet on that very spot new life emerges, totally different in appearance from the seed, and yet somehow the mature plant remains the same living entity (vv. 36–38). In fact, the world is filled with different kinds of bodies (v. 39) that God has created. So why should it be thought incredible that he could create still one more kind—a resurrected human body?

15:42–44 Paul makes clear where he is going with all these analogies. Resurrection bodies will be far more glorious than present ones. These new ones will be fitted for eternity, never again to die or be limited by sin (vv. 42–43). Whereas humans in this world experience limited physical life, believers will one day be fully empowered by the Spirit (v. 44a).

15:44–49 These verses pick up on widespread ancient speculation that there were two primal human beings, an earthly one and a heavenly one. Paul agrees that there are two progenitors of humanity (v. 44b). But he makes Jesus the perfect "Adam" and stresses that he came *after* the first Adam, not before (vv. 46–47). Believers who have shared in the fallen likeness of the first Adam can look forward to sharing in the perfect humanity Jesus embodied, but only after this life (vv. 48–49).

15:50–57 These verses further unpack the need for bodily transformation. Frail, mortal humanity cannot survive in God's eternal and perfectly holy presence. The secret that Paul is revealing here is that believers' bodily resurrections will occur when Christ returns. Not all Christians will die first since some will be alive when he comes back. But all will undergo whatever transformation is necessary to give them their glorified bodies. This change will take place instantaneously. The trumpet (v. 52a) was a stock metaphor in biblical literature to herald the end of time.

The climax of this series of events for believers is the destruction of death itself, as Isaiah had predicted (v. 54b, quoting Isa 25:8). Paul breaks out into joyful exclamation at the thought of this marvelous prospect. Praise God that the deadly sequence has been interrupted by the victory that comes through the death and resurrection of Jesus (1Co 15:57).

15:58 Appropriately, Paul returns from these lofty flights of theological reflection to the practical implications for the Corinthians. Since Christ's

of the Lord,[g] because you know that your labor in the Lord is not in vain.

The Collection for the Lord's People

16 Now about the collection[h] for the Lord's people:[i] Do what I told the Galatian[j] churches to do. 2 On the first day of every week,[k] each one of you should set aside a sum of money in keeping with your income, saving it up, so that when I come no collections will have to be made.[l] 3 Then, when I arrive, I will give letters of introduction to the men you approve[m] and send them with your gift to Jerusalem. 4 If it seems advisable for me to go also, they will accompany me.

Personal Requests

5 After I go through Macedonia, I will come to you[n] — for I will be going through Macedonia.[o] 6 Perhaps I will stay with you for a while, or even spend the winter, so that you can help me on my journey,[p] wherever I go. 7 For I do not want to see you now and make only a passing visit; I hope to spend some time with you, if the Lord permits.[q] 8 But I will stay on at Ephesus[r] until Pentecost,[s] 9 because a great door for effective work has

15:58 [g] 1Co 16:10
16:1 [h] Ac 24:17 [i] Ac 9:13 [j] Ac 16:6
16:2 [k] Ac 20:7 [l] 2Co 9:4,5
16:3 [m] 2Co 8:18, 19
16:5 [n] 1Co 4:19 [o] Ac 19:21
16:6 [p] Ro 15:24
16:7 [q] Ac 18:21
16:8 [r] Ac 18:19 [s] Ac 2:1

---

body has been raised from the dead, so too will they one day be physically transformed. Therefore, they should remain unswervingly committed to the teachings they have heard and dedicated to the work of the gospel.

> **15:35-58** While believers may grieve the loss of loved ones and have a certain anxiety related to the unknown factors surrounding their own death, neither reaction ought to be "like the rest of mankind, who have no hope" (1Th 4:13). Funerals for Christians ought to be first of all celebrations of their "homegoing." While preserving a culturally appropriate somberness, a spirit of joy and a message of hope should nevertheless pervade such ceremonies, which may even include a tasteful evangelistic address to unbelievers who are present. And the hope of resurrection should encourage those of us who remain alive to persevere in obedience over the long haul (1Co 15:58).

16:1 The collection to which Paul refers here formed a major enterprise of his third missionary journey. Jewish Christians in Jerusalem were poor and in need (v. 3), and Paul spent substantial energy raising funds from various Gentile churches (Ac 20:4). Paul undoubtedly saw the collection as an opportunity to bring greater unity between Jewish and Gentile believers. In addition, the offering would be a testimony of the faith and love of those who participated.

The Corinthians had contributed generously, but now they were lagging behind in keeping their commitments. Sadly, Paul's brief words here did not adequately motivate them, because he had to return to the topic in much greater detail in his second letter to this church (2Co 8–9).

"The Lord's people" in 1Co 16:1a translates the word for "saints" and refers to Christians in general—in this case in Jerusalem. Despite v. 1b, there is no reference to this collection in the letter to the Galatians, so we must assume that the instructions to which Paul refers here took place after that letter was written in c. AD 49 (six years earlier).

16:2-3 "The first day of every week" (v. 2a) refers to Sunday. The language strongly suggests that the first day of the week, not the seventh (the Sabbath), had already become the most special day for these Christians. "In keeping with your income" (v. 2b) translates an expression that could also be read, "to whatever extent one is prospered." Paul's instructions about representatives and letters of recommendation (v. 3) show his concern for financial integrity and accountability. Acts 20:4 reveals that these representatives came from numerous churches and territories in which Paul had ministered.

> **16:1-4** Christians of the West need to be challenged to give. If they are not, many churches and Christian organizations will close, as donor bases in this country are currently weighted most heavily in favor of senior citizens. Furthermore, they (and all Christians) must be taught to give to those individuals, organizations, and churches who themselves follow biblical priorities, who maximize giving to support a reasonable income for full-time Christian workers and a holistic mission to meet the physical and spiritual needs of hurting people worldwide.

16:5-12 Paul now concludes his letter with personal remarks (vv. 5-12) and closing greetings (vv. 13-24). As frequently happens in his letters, Paul's personal remarks concern his current ministry itinerary; these serve as a transition to his formal closing. If this letter was written in the spring of AD 55, Paul would have originally hoped to come during that same calendar year, but he did not arrive for his prolonged stay until sometime in AD 56.

16:6-7 Paul's initial desire to spend a full winter in Corinth (vv. 6a, 7a) may still have been fulfilled, however, even if delayed by a year. Paul's motivation was at least twofold. First, he wanted to have a significant period with the troubled Corinthians to improve the situation in the church there. Second, he hoped to avoid having to travel during that season of the year in which the high seas were generally impassable.

The verb translated "help . . . on my journey" (v. 6b) probably implies material assistance—food, money, and possibly even traveling companions for his trip. In all this planning he knows that he must always leave the door open for the Lord to change his plans (v. 7b).

16:8-9 These verses inform Paul's readers of his current location (Ephesus) and enable us to date the writing of this letter to the time of the events of Ac 19. The uprising instigated by Demetrius has

PEOPLE TO KNOW // PRISCILLA AND AQUILA

1 CORINTHIANS 16:19: Priscilla and Aquila met Paul in Corinth, where they went after Emperor Claudius had ordered the Jews to leave Rome. They shared a common trade with Paul: tent making. Paul stayed and worked with them during his long ministry in Corinth. Priscilla and Aquila were valuable partners in the ministry of the gospel.

When Paul left Corinth, Priscilla and Aquila joined him on his travels as far as Ephesus, where they stayed. In Ephesus, Priscilla and Aquila helped deepen Apollos's understanding of Christianity. While Apollos was a powerful preacher, he lacked some areas of knowledge. Priscilla and Aquila took him into their own home to mentor him in the way of God.

Besides what is mentioned about Priscilla and Aquila in Ac 18, the pair is also mentioned in the closing greeting sections of three of Paul's letters. Clearly, Priscilla and Aquila were important members of the early church. They supported Paul in his ministry in Corinth, and they helped deepen Apollos's understanding of Jesus Christ.

APPLICATION ✣ Priscilla and Aquila were people known for their hospitality. They not only opened their home to Paul, but also mentored Apollos. In one of Paul's letters, he greets the church that met in their house. One way to participate in ministry is through hospitality: opening our homes and giving our time to others. We must consider how God might be calling us to exercise hospitality, or even calling us to be a mentor for a growing Christian.

opened to me,[t] and there are many who
oppose me.
10When Timothy[u] comes, see to it that
he has nothing to fear while he is with
you, for he is carrying on the work of
the Lord,[v] just as I am. 11No one, then,
should treat him with contempt.[w] Send
him on his way in peace[x] so that he may
return to me. I am expecting him along
with the brothers.
12Now about our brother Apollos:[y] I
strongly urged him to go to you with
the brothers. He was quite unwilling to
go now, but he will go when he has the
opportunity.
13Be on your guard; stand firm[z] in the
faith; be courageous; be strong.[a] 14Do
everything in love.[b]
15You know that the household of

16:9 [t] Ac 14:27
16:10 [u] Ac 16:1 [v] 1Co 15:58
16:11 [w] 1Ti 4:12 [x] Ac 15:33
16:12 [y] Ac 18:24; 1Co 1:12
16:13 [z] Gal 5:1; Php 1:27; 1Th 3:8; 2Th 2:15 [a] Eph 6:10
16:14 [b] 1Co 14:1

1Co 16:14 ✣ What would our lives look like if we were able to live out Paul's directive to "do everything in love"? How might it be different than it is now?

probably not yet occurred, since Paul seems to have left town shortly after that event (Ac 20:1), while here he envisions staying on for a while. "Pentecost" (1Co 16:8) was the annual Jewish harvest festival (the Festival of Weeks). On that day the Holy Spirit descended on 120 of Jesus' followers 50 days after his resurrection, to inaugurate the era of the new covenant (see Ac 2).

16:10–12 Paul's concern over how Timothy will be received (v. 10) is certainly related to the Corinthians' conflict with Paul himself. It is probably heightened by Timothy's youthfulness (1Ti 4:12) and possibly even by his personality. "Send him on his way" (1Co 16:11) employs the same verb as "help me on my journey" in v. 6. The unnamed "brothers" (v. 11) probably include Erastus (Ac 19:22), the town clerk of Corinth (Ro 16:23), and they would have been known to the Corinthians.

First Corinthians 16:12 appears to respond to the final question the Corinthians had raised in their letter to Paul (cf. 7:1). Apollos' reluctance to go could reflect his concern to wait for a more opportune time when things had settled down in Corinth.

✣ **16:5–12** Giving to churches is good and should be generous, but it should often be supplemented by giving to individuals who have to raise their own support for ministry and by providing lodging and provision for visiting missionaries.

16:13–14 Paul begins his final greetings and sign-off with these two verses of brief teaching. "Be courageous" could also be rendered "be adults"; that is, "put away the immaturity that has led to so many of your problems and grow up in the Lord." Balancing these commands to be strong is the call to love in v. 14. As with Paul's discussion of spiritual gifts in chs. 12–14, all Christian activity must take place within the sphere of putting others above self.

16:15–18 Paul gives thanks for three Corinthian Christians who have come to him in Ephesus

Stephanas[c] were the first converts[d] in
Achaia,[e] and they have devoted themselves to the service of the Lord's people.
I urge you, brothers and sisters, 16to submit[f] to such people and to everyone who
joins in the work and labors at it. 17I was
glad when Stephanas, Fortunatus and
Achaicus arrived, because they have supplied what was lacking from you.[g] 18For
they refreshed[h] my spirit and yours also.
Such men deserve recognition.[i]

Final Greetings

19The churches in the province of Asia
send you greetings. Aquila and Priscilla[a][j] greet you warmly in the Lord, and
so does the church that meets at their
house.[k] 20All the brothers and sisters
here send you greetings. Greet one another with a holy kiss.[l]
21I, Paul, write this greeting in my own
hand.[m]
22If anyone does not love the Lord,[n]
let that person be cursed![o] Come, Lord[b]![p]
23The grace of the Lord Jesus be with
you.[q]
24My love to all of you in Christ Jesus.
Amen.[c]

16:15 [c] 1Co 1:16 [d] Ro 16:5 [e] Ac 18:12 16:16 [f] Heb 13:17 16:17 [g] 2Co 11:9; Php 2:30 16:18 [h] Phm 7 [i] Php 2:29 16:19 [j] Ac 18:2 [k] Ro 16:5 16:20 [l] Ro 16:16 16:21 [m] Gal 6:11; Col 4:18 16:22 [n] Eph 6:24 [o] Ro 9:3 [p] Rev 22:20 16:23 [q] Ro 16:20

[a] *19* Greek *Prisca,* a variant of *Priscilla* [b] *22* The Greek for *Come, Lord* reproduces an Aramaic expression (*Marana tha*) used by early Christians. [c] *24* Some manuscripts do not have *Amen.*

---

and encouraged him. "Devoted" in v. 15 means "appointed." "The Lord's people" are not the believers in Judea, as in v. 1, but refer primarily to the Corinthian Christians to whom these three men had ministered. "Everyone who joins" (v. 16b) translates the Greek noun for coworkers. "Labors" (v. 16) implies *hard* work. "Supplied what was lacking" (v. 17) refers to the spiritual refreshment and encouragement that Stephanas and his companions gave Paul (v. 18a).

16:19–20 Paul in these verses conveys greetings to the Corinthian church from four groups of fellow believers: (1) the various churches in Asia Minor, almost certainly including Colossae and Ephesus (cf. Rev 2–3); (2) Paul's good friends Aquila and Priscilla, coworkers with him in Corinth (Ac 18:2–3); (3) the specific house church that met in their home; and (4) Paul's other immediate companions in ministry.

The "holy kiss" was probably borrowed from common ancient practice. Customarily, men greeted other men and women other women by embracing each other and kissing one another on the cheek.

After 1Co 16:20, Paul stops dictating his letter to the secretary writing down the letter—perhaps Sosthenes (1:1). Paul now picks up pen and papyrus himself to write the closing words in his own hand (16:21), as was his custom (cf. Gal 6:11; 2Th 3:17). The one letter in which we definitely know the name of Paul's scribe is Romans, when that individual, Tertius, sends his own greetings at the end (Ro 16:22).

16:22–24 Both parts of v. 22 follow abruptly. "Come, Lord" is the more likely of two possible translations of the Aramaic. Together the two expressions reflect the profound seriousness with which the early church viewed faithfulness to Christ in light of his imminent return.

In v. 23, Paul substitutes his favorite word for "grace" for the more conventional Greek "goodbye." Verse 24 ends on an upbeat note with one final reminder of Paul's love for these often exasperating Christians in Corinth.

16:13–24 Paul closes with one final reminder of the centrality of "grace" and "love" (vv. 23–24). We continue to need both; indeed, we ought to crave them. If our generation has sometimes removed God from the concept of love, it has at least correctly captured the centrality of love for any viable human ethic. Love does "make the world go 'round," but the only truly life- and world-changing love that will last is that which is founded on a saving relationship with Jesus Christ.

2 Corinthians

Author: The apostle Paul
Audience: The church in Corinth
Date: AD 55 or 56

Theme: Paul encourages the Corinthian believers to be generous in giving, to be reconciled with him, and to reject false apostles who are challenging his authority and creating dissension in the church.

PERSPECTIVE

Three elements need to be reconciled to one another to help us understand Paul's second letter to the Corinthians: weakness, sufficiency, and the Holy Spirit. The weakness is Paul's personal inability to succeed; the sufficiency is the fact that Paul does succeed (i.e., glorifies God) in spite of his weakness; and the Holy Spirit is the power that enables this sufficiency in spite of weakness to occur.

In both Paul's day and ours, this argument is novel—one might even call it radical. For us, weakness is rarely seen as a foundation for sufficiency; sufficiency is almost never defined as the glorification of someone else; and the Holy Spirit, if discussed at all, is considered a mysterious power who, if manipulated in just the right way, facilitates health, wealth, and fame, not spiritual growth of the kind proclaimed in the gospel.

In both Paul's day and in ours, the definition of each of these elements has changed, and the relationship among them is skewed. Weakness, for example, is disparaged and its opposite, strength, worshiped.

Or consider sufficiency. By putting the word "self" in front of sufficiency, pride and greed replace a proper sense of self and contentment with what God faithfully provides. The message is that we are to be strong and self-reliant, not dependent on the Holy Spirit. Paul's argument and the form it takes is heavily dependent on the Holy Spirit as our source of strength.

Yet in championing his own apostleship and authority, Paul seems to violate an increasingly sacred position these days. He boldly states that he is right and others are wrong. In a day and age when

Reading 2 Corinthians

This letter divides easily into three sections. In the first seven chapters, Paul described both the glory of the gospel message and his experiences as a minister of Jesus Christ. In chs. 8 and 9, Paul attempted to raise money for the poverty-stricken church in Jerusalem. In the last four chapters, he defended himself against those in the church of Corinth

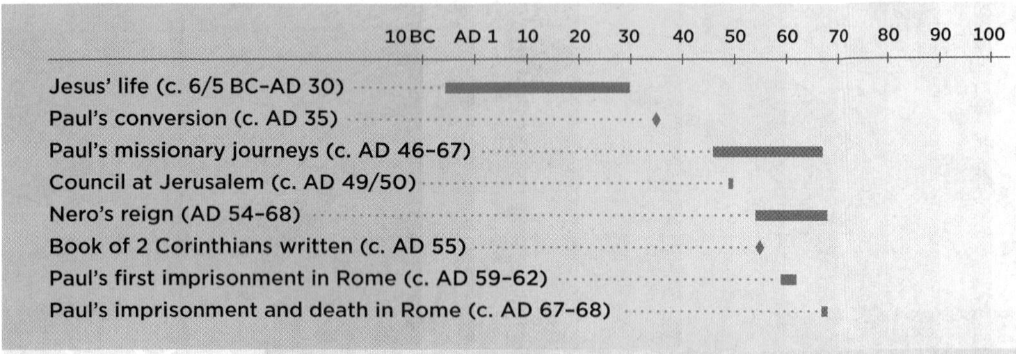

10 BC AD 1 10 20 30 40 50 60 70 80 90 100

- Jesus' life (c. 6/5 BC–AD 30)
- Paul's conversion (c. AD 35)
- Paul's missionary journeys (c. AD 46–67)
- Council at Jerusalem (c. AD 49/50)
- Nero's reign (AD 54–68)
- Book of 2 Corinthians written (c. AD 55)
- Paul's first imprisonment in Rome (c. AD 59–62)
- Paul's imprisonment and death in Rome (c. AD 67–68)

who did not recognize his authority as an apostle and church leader.

Key Verse

God made him who had no sin to be sin for us, so that in him we might become the righteousness of God.

—2 Corinthians 5:21

vigorous argument is almost always called arrogant, Paul tramples all over what passes for total acceptance; he draws moral and doctrinal lines in the sand.

Yet Paul is not arrogant. He is weak, and he suffers. What Paul does in 2 Corinthians is to tell us how Christian ministry can be one of life's greatest joys and greatest sorrows at the same time. What he does is properly order what one might call "mis-filed feelings": joy, sorrow, anger, anxiety, pain. We all experience them. There is no avoiding them. So we try to make sense of them by evaluating them against some rational principle or standard. Too often we choose the wrong standard. We mis-file our feelings.

Some of the improper standards we use are personal well-being, social success, even psychological health. According to these standards, if a feeling contributes to personal well-being, social success, or psychological health, it is good; if not, it is bad. Paul does not claim that personal well-being, social success, and psychological health are bad. Indeed, in many ways, Paul endorses all three. But what he does say is that these are secondary, not primary, evaluation tools. He insists that the primary measuring stick is that God is glorified through whatever ministry we have. When this outside and ultimate measuring tool is used, we can see both joy and anxiety as positive contributors to ministry. Paul can say he is right and others are wrong without being arrogant because he understands that he is weak, that he is sufficient only because the Holy Spirit works in and through him and his weaknesses to reveal God's great glory. This is a much-needed message we all need to hear more regularly: "But he said to me, 'My grace is sufficient for you, for my power is made perfect in weakness.' Therefore I will boast all the more gladly about my weaknesses, so that Christ's power may rest on me. That is why, for Christ's sake, I delight in weaknesses, in insults, in hardships, in persecutions, in difficulties. For when I am weak, then I am strong" (2Co 12:9–10).

TAKING THE NEXT STEPS

Paul wrote this letter several months after writing his first letter to the Corinthians, after he left Ephesus for Macedonia (see Ac 20:1; 2Co 7:5; 9:2–4). During the interval between the two letters, controversy had reared its head in Paul's relationship with the Corinthian church, with false teachers challenging Paul's integrity and authority. Part of this second letter, therefore, is Paul's self-defense. For the Corinthians who accepted his authority, he summarized his pattern of ministry as well as how much suffering he was enduring for Christ's sake. And in two chapters of this letter, Paul attempted to raise money for the church in Jerusalem, a church experiencing poverty and hardship.

All Christians, and especially church leaders, can learn much about Christian conduct from this letter. (1) Serving Christ and his church requires total dedication; it may even involve suffering for Christ's sake. However, in each moment of our lives God provides the gift of grace to enable us to persevere. (2) Nothing is more glorious than the gospel of Christ; yet God chooses humans, as weak and vulnerable as they are, to be channels of that message. (3) God challenges every one of us to proclaim the message of his love, revealed in Jesus Christ. (4) The church should be a community of people who freely share, where those who have been given much give generously to those who have little.

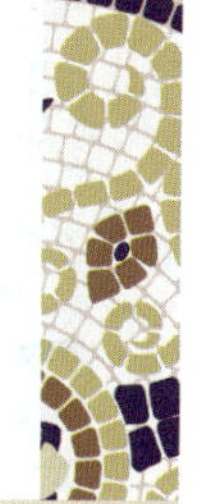

WHAT TO LOOK FOR IN 2 CORINTHIANS

- Paul's sufferings for Christ's sake (chs. 1; 4; 6; 11)
- The glory of the gospel of Christ (ch. 3)
- Christ as the One who reconciled us to God (ch. 5)
- Paul's raising money for the church in Jerusalem (chs. 8-9)
- Paul's thorn in the flesh (ch. 12)

1 Paul, an apostle of Christ Jesus by the will of God,[a] and Timothy our brother,

To the church of God[b] in Corinth, together with all his holy people throughout Achaia:[c]

2Grace and peace to you from God our Father and the Lord Jesus Christ.[d]

Praise to the God of All Comfort

3Praise be to the God and Father of our
Lord Jesus Christ,[e] the Father of compassion and the God of all comfort, 4who
comforts us[f] in all our troubles, so that we can comfort those in any trouble with the comfort we ourselves receive from God. 5For just as we share abundantly
in the sufferings of Christ,[g] so also our
comfort abounds through Christ. 6If we
are distressed, it is for your comfort and salvation;[h] if we are comforted, it is for your comfort, which produces in you patient endurance of the same sufferings
we suffer. 7And our hope for you is firm,
because we know that just as you share in our sufferings,[i] so also you share in our comfort.

1:1 [a]1Co 1:1; Eph 1:1; Col 1:1; 2Ti 1:1 [b]1Co 10:32 [c]Ac 18:12
1:2 [d]Ro 1:7
1:3 [e]Eph 1:3; 1Pe 1:3
1:4 [f]2Co 7:6, 7,13
1:5 [g]2Co 4:10; Col 1:24
1:6 [h]2Co 4:15
1:7 [i]Ro 8:17

2Co 1:3-7 ❖ How has God comforted you? How have you found comfort in fellow believers?

1:1 Paul follows the standard greeting formula of his day. His only expansions are the reminders that he is "an apostle of Christ Jesus by the will of God" and that the Corinthians are the "church of God," who exist "together with all his holy people throughout Achaia."

This unusual simplicity serves to emphasize that Paul *is* an "apostle" and owes his calling to the "will *of God*" (emphasis added). Christ sends Paul in accordance with God's will. This reminder of Paul's calling opens the way for the defense of his apostolic ministry that will be the focus of so much of this letter.

1:2 Paul wishes his readers "grace," a continuing experience of God's merciful gifts, from forgiveness and justification to deliverance from the power of sin and eternal life. Paul can do so because Christ's death on the cross for those who deserve only God's wrath makes such grace possible.

APPLICATION ✚ 1:1-2 Because of our confidence in the authority and sufficiency of Scripture, we seek to move *from* the text's original meaning *to* its application. Paul's intention and teaching in this letter is relevant and authoritative for today.

1:3-7 The "comfort" Paul is referring to is his present state of peace because of his confidence in God's ability to deliver. In turn, Paul can comfort

CHARACTER OF GOD // GOD IS COMFORT

2 Corinthians 1:3–4: Praise be to the God and Father of our Lord Jesus Christ, the Father of compassion and the God of all comfort, who comforts us in all our troubles.

The tender love of God for his children is clearly displayed in the fact that he comforts us in our troubles. God is not distant and cold. God is loving and near to the broken-hearted and weary.

Paul himself knew this firsthand. In his mission to bring the message of Jesus to as many people as possible, Paul was mistreated and persecuted many times. He was imprisoned and beaten. Yet he was able to testify from his own experience that the Lord is the "God of all comfort, who comforts us in all our troubles" (2Co 1:3–4). Paul knew plenty of troubles, but God's comfort was always near to him. Even shackled in a prison cell, Paul could not help but sing God's praises (Ac 16:25).

The same Greek word that Paul uses for "comfort" is the root of the word Jesus uses for the Holy Spirit in Jn 14:16. Jesus promised to send his followers an advocate and comforter. Jesus said this advocate would live within believers (Jn 14:17). The Spirit within each believer is not only a teacher and guide, but the Spirit is also a comforter.

APPLICATION ✣ It is amazing that God not only saves his people—he also comforts them. This stems from the compassionate love of God. He loves his people the way a parent loves their child (Ps 103:13). Understanding God's comfort should instill in his children more than mere obedience. God's comforting nature evokes within us a loving response of devoted gratitude and praise. Paul also says that God's comfort means we can comfort others in their troubles with the same comfort we have received from God.

8 We do not want you to be uninformed, brothers and sisters,[a] about the
troubles we experienced[j] in the province
of Asia. We were under great pressure, far
beyond our ability to endure, so that we
despaired of life itself. 9 Indeed, we felt
we had received the sentence of death.
But this happened that we might not
rely on ourselves but on God,[k] who raises the dead. 10 He has delivered us from
such a deadly peril,[l] and he will deliver
us again. On him we have set our hope
that he will continue to deliver us, 11 as
you help us by your prayers.[m] Then many
will give thanks[n] on our behalf for the
gracious favor granted us in answer to
the prayers of many.

1:8 [j] 1Co 15:32
1:9 [k] Jer 17:5,7
1:10 [l] Ro 15:31
1:11 [m] Ro 15:30; Php 1:19 [n] 2Co 4:15
1:12 [o] Ac 23:1 [p] 2Co 2:17 [q] 1Co 2:1,4,13

Paul's Change of Plans

12 Now this is our boast: Our conscience[o]
testifies that we have conducted ourselves
in the world, and especially in our relations with you, with integrity[b] and godly
sincerity.[p] We have done so, relying not on
worldly wisdom[q] but on God's grace. 13 For
we do not write you anything you cannot

[a] 8 The Greek word for *brothers and sisters* (*adelphoi*) refers here to believers, both men and women, as part of God's family; also in 8:1; 13:11.
[b] 12 Many manuscripts *holiness*

others no matter what comes their way. Likewise, the divine comfort Paul experiences also comes "through Christ" (v. 5), and, like Paul, his readers can rely on God to "comfort" them (vv. 6b–7).

1:8–9 Paul's suffering was so severe that he saw no way out but death (cf. v. 9). But God's purpose was not to have Paul die. Instead, Paul faced death *in order that* he would rely only "on God, who raises the dead" (v. 9), an allusion to the resurrection of Christ.

1:10–11 Just as God raised Christ from the dead, so too God delivered Paul (v. 10a). Thus, God's past deliverance of Paul establishes his confidence in the deliverance to come (v. 10b). This confidence for the future is the biblical notion of "hope." As a result of the many prayers being offered up on Paul's behalf, others will join in praising God for displaying his great mercy and comfort to his apostle (v. 11).

✣ **1:3–11** Our praise of God should never be used to make things look better than they really are. We praise God in the midst of our adversity—not because things are not as bad as they seem (they could be worse!) but because of who God is and of what he does in and through the reality in which we live.

1:12–14 Paul's outward behavior actually confirms the grace of God's call in his life. To boast in any evidence of God's grace is to boast in what *God* has done, that is, to "boast in the Lord."

Paul's confidence that his actions reflect God's work in his life is supported by his willingness to write openly and clearly—that is, to "boast" about his recent change of plans. The Corinthians will no longer doubt his credibility when they hear the rest of the story but will join him in boasting

PAUL'S SUFFERINGS

THE EXPERIENCE	REFERENCES IN ACTS
Jews in Damascus conspire to kill Paul, forcing him to escape over the city wall.	9:23-25
Grecian Jews in Jerusalem make an attempt on Paul's life.	9:28-30
Paul and Barnabas are persecuted in Pisidian Antioch.	13:49-52
In Iconium, Paul and Barnabas learn of a plot to stone them and flee to Lystra and Derbe.	14:4-7
Paul stoned in Lystra and left for dead.	14:19-20
Paul and Silas are flogged and jailed in Philippi for driving a demon from a servant girl, compromising her owners' profits.	16:16-24
Paul and Silas must flee Thessalonica after their host, Jason, is arrested.	17:5-10
Paul is forced to flee from Berea when Jews from Thessalonica journey there and stir the crowds against him.	17:13-15
Paul is "abused" by Jews in Corinth.	18:5-6
Paul is brought to Gallio's court by the Jews.	18:12-13
Paul is seized in Jerusalem, beaten by a mob and bound in chains by Roman soldiers.	22:27-30
Paul is struck when standing before the Sanhedrin and the Roman commander.	23:1-3
Jewish assassins plot to kill Paul.	23:12-22
Paul is imprisoned and tried before Felix.	24
Paul is tried before Festus and appeals to Caesar.	25:1-12
Paul is shipwrecked.	27:27-44
Paul is bitten by a snake.	28:1-6
Paul is imprisoned in Rome.	28:17-31

read or understand. And I hope that, 14as
you have understood us in part, you will
come to understand fully that you can
boast of us just as we will boast of you in
the day of the Lord Jesus.[r]

15Because I was confident of this, I
wanted to visit you[s] first so that you
might benefit twice.[t] 16I wanted to visit
you on my way[u] to Macedonia and to
come back to you from Macedonia, and
then to have you send me on my way
to Judea. 17Was I fickle when I intended to do this? Or do I make my plans in
a worldly manner[v] so that in the same
breath I say both "Yes, yes" and "No, no"?

18But as surely as God is faithful,[w] our
message to you is not "Yes" and "No."
19For the Son of God, Jesus Christ, who
was preached among you by us—by me
and Silas[a] and Timothy—was not "Yes"
and "No," but in him it has always[x] been
"Yes." 20For no matter how many promises[y] God has made, they are "Yes" in
Christ. And so through him the "Amen"[z]

1:14 [r]1Co 1:8
1:15 [s]1Co 4:19 [t]Ro 1:11,13; 15:29
1:16 [u]1Co 16:5-7
1:17 [v]2Co 10:2,3
1:18 [w]1Co 1:9
1:19 [x]Heb 13:8
1:20 [y]Ro 15:8 [z]1Co 14:16

[a] 19 Greek *Silvanus*, a variant of *Silas*

in what God has done in his life as their apostle.

1:15–19 Paul's opponents viewed his failure to carry through with his original plan as an indication that he made his decisions "in a worldly manner" (v. 17). Paul's change of plans was not the expression of a wavering character but a display of God's faithfulness (v. 18).

Seen in this light, Paul's change of plans reflected God's own faithfulness (vv. 18–19). Just as God has shown himself faithful by fulfilling his promises in Jesus Christ, so too Paul has acted in accordance with this same gospel (v. 20a).

1:20–22 "Amen" (v. 20) is a transliterated form of a Hebrew word that means "to confirm" or "to establish." By his own change of plans toward the Corinthians, Paul "amens" God's faithfulness toward his people. The object of Paul's "amen" is "to the glory of God" (v. 20b). The reason for giving God the credit is set forth in vv. 21–22.

God has "set his seal of ownership" on them and

is spoken by us to the glory of God. 21 Now
it is God who makes both us and you
stand firm in Christ. He anointed[a] us,
22 set his seal of ownership on us, and
put his Spirit in our hearts as a deposit,
guaranteeing what is to come.[b]
23 I call God as my witness[c] — and I
stake my life on it — that it was in order to spare you[d] that I did not return to
Corinth. 24 Not that we lord it over[e] your
faith, but we work with you for your joy,
because it is by faith you stand firm.[f]
2 1 So I made up my mind that I would
not make another painful visit to you.[g]
2 For if I grieve you,[h] who is left to make
me glad but you whom I have grieved?
3 I wrote as I did,[i] so that when I came I
would not be distressed[j] by those who
should have made me rejoice. I had confidence[k] in all of you, that you would all
share my joy. 4 For I wrote you[l] out of great
distress and anguish of heart and with
many tears, not to grieve you but to let
you know the depth of my love for you.

Forgiveness for the Offender

5 If anyone has caused grief,[m] he
has not so much grieved me as he has
grieved all of you to some extent — not
to put it too severely. 6 The punishment[n]
inflicted on him by the majority is sufficient. 7 Now instead, you ought to forgive
and comfort him,[o] so that he will not
be overwhelmed by excessive sorrow. 8 I
urge you, therefore, to reaffirm your love
for him. 9 Another reason I wrote you was
to see if you would stand the test and
be obedient in everything.[p] 10 Anyone
you forgive, I also forgive. And what I
have forgiven — if there was anything
to forgive — I have forgiven in the sight
of Christ for your sake, 11 in order that
Satan[q] might not outwit us. For we are
not unaware of his schemes.[r]

Ministers of the New Covenant

12 Now when I went to Troas[s] to preach
the gospel of Christ[t] and found that the
Lord had opened a door[u] for me, 13 I still had
no peace of mind,[v] because I did not find
my brother Titus[w] there. So I said goodbye
to them and went on to Macedonia.
14 But thanks be to God,[x] who always
leads us as captives in Christ's triumphal procession and uses us to spread the
aroma[y] of the knowledge of him everywhere. 15 For we are to God the pleasing
aroma of Christ among those who are
being saved and those who are perishing.[z] 16 To the one we are an aroma that

1:21 [a] 1Jn 2:20, 27
1:22 [b] 2Co 5:5
1:23 [c] Ro 1:9; Gal 1:20 [d] 1Co 4:21; 2Co 2:1, 3; 13:2, 10
1:24 [e] 1Pe 5:3 [f] Ro 11:20; 1Co 15:1
2:1 [g] 2Co 1:23
2:2 [h] 2Co 7:8
2:3 [i] 2Co 7:8, 12 [j] 2Co 12:21 [k] 2Co 8:22; Gal 5:10
2:4 [l] 2Co 7:8, 12
2:5 [m] 1Co 5:1, 2
2:6 [n] 1Co 5:4, 5
2:7 [o] Gal 6:1; Eph 4:32
2:9 [p] 2Co 10:6
2:11 [q] Mt 4:10 [r] Lk 22:31; 2Co 4:4; 1Pe 5:8, 9
2:12 [s] Ac 16:8 [t] Ro 1:1 [u] Ac 14:27
2:13 [v] 2Co 7:5 [w] 2Co 7:6, 13; 12:18
2:14 [x] Ro 6:17 [y] Eph 5:2; Php 4:18
2:15 [z] 1Co 1:18

"put his Spirit in [their] hearts as a deposit, guaranteeing what is to come" (v. 22). Paul is referring to God's commitment to their completion, certified by the gift of his Spirit as a "deposit." This technical, financial term refers to a "down payment."

1:23–24 Fear of rejection did not keep Paul from returning to Corinth; his wish to "spare" them from God's judgment did. It was an act of humble restraint, a refusal to exercise his authority toward them, even when it would have meant his own vindication.

2:1–4 Paul canceled his return visit (v. 1). Paul was confident his merciful approach would work: The Corinthians would repent and once again share Paul's joy in Christ (v. 3b). Paul's love for the Corinthians, expressed in the warnings and calls to repentance of his previous letter (v. 4), was the instrument God used to bring most of the Corinthians back to Paul.

2:5–11 The offense must have involved slander against him and his apostolic relationship with the Corinthians. Most of the Corinthians had initially sided with this slanderer. Later, after the majority had repented, they grieved with Paul and punished the offender (v. 6).

The punishment had been effective; the offender had repented. In response, Paul calls the Corinthians to show mercy. This is why Paul makes it clear that his confrontational letter was intended to "test" them to determine whether they would be "obedient in *everything*" (v. 9, emphasis added). By exercising such obedience, they will be following Paul's example in extending mercy to the Corinthians themselves.

The purpose of Paul's admonitions is to prevent Satan from using this situation against the church (v. 11). Satan's "schemes" (v. 11b) revolve around destroying the mutual acceptance and forgiveness that is to characterize God's people.

> ✚ **1:12—2:11** In the face of the cultural pressures around us, we must maintain Paul's understanding of *faith* as that trust in God in the *present*, because of his acts in the *past*, that leads inevitably to centering our *hope* on his promises for the *future* (cf. 1:20–22).

2:12–13 The apostle was too concerned over Titus and the spiritual condition of the Corinthians to carry on his ministry. Paul's opponents could point to this anxiety-ridden decision as evidence that he lacked the power of the Spirit. How else could one explain the fact that Paul's anxiety drove him away from a clear opportunity to preach the gospel?

Just as Paul's concern for Titus and the Corinthians originally led him to Troas, his concern for them also led him to Macedonia (cf. 7:5–7). Nothing was more important to Paul than their welfare.

2:14–16a Paul's praise in v. 14 introduces the necessary and logical response to the suffering introduced in vv. 12–13. The triumphal procession was a lavish parade conducted in Rome to celebrate great victories in significant military campaigns. These demonstrated Rome's victory not only by parading the spoils of war but also by leading the warriors

2Co 2:14 ❖ What does it mean to spread the aroma of the knowledge of Christ? How can we live out this beautiful image?

brings death;[a] to the other, an aroma that
brings life. And who is equal to such a
task?[b] 17Unlike so many, we do not peddle the word of God for profit.[c] On the
contrary, in Christ we speak before God
with sincerity,[d] as those sent from God.[e]
3 Are we beginning to commend ourselves[f] again? Or do we need, like
some people, letters of recommendation[g]
to you or from you? 2You yourselves are
our letter, written on our hearts, known
and read by everyone.[h] 3You show that
you are a letter from Christ, the result
of our ministry, written not with ink but
with the Spirit of the living God, not on
tablets of stone[i] but on tablets of human hearts.[j]
4Such confidence[k] we have through
Christ before God. 5Not that we are competent in ourselves to claim anything for
ourselves, but our competence comes
from God.[l] 6He has made us competent

2:16 [a] Lk 2:34 [b] 2Co 3:5,6
2:17 [c] 2Co 4:2 [d] 1Co 5:8 [e] 2Co 1:12
3:1 [f] 2Co 5:12; 12:11
[g] Ac 18:27
3:2 [h] 1Co 9:2
3:3 [i] Ex 24:12 [j] Pr 3:3; Jer 31:33; Eze 11:19
3:4 [k] Eph 3:12
3:5 [l] 1Co 15:10

of the enemy, now presented as conquered slaves, through the city as a symbol of military triumph.

As the enemy of God's people, God had conquered Paul at his conversion call on the road to Damascus and was now leading him, as a "slave of Christ," to death in Christ, in order that Paul might display or reveal the majesty, power, and glory of God, his conqueror.

This revelation of God's power and glory took place in two ways. Either God rescued Paul from adversity when it was too much to bear (cf. 1:8–11), or, having strengthened Paul's hope through such experiences of deliverance, enabled him to endure his adversity with thanksgiving to God (cf. 4:7–12; 6:3–10).

It is probably best to read 2:14b–16a as a reference to OT sacrifice. To encounter Paul in his suffering on behalf of his churches is to encounter a picture of the crucified Christ, who died for his people. "Those who are being saved" welcome Paul's suffering as an expression of the glory of God revealed in the crucified Christ, while "those who are perishing" (v. 15) reject Paul's suffering as foolishness, just as they reject the cross of Christ.

2:16b–17 Paul's implied answer to the question "Who is equal to such a task?" (v. 16b) is better understood as "I am!" In being led to "death" as the "aroma of Christ," Paul is confident that God *is* making himself known (vv. 15–16).

Unlike others, Paul does not "peddle the word of God for profit" (v. 17). Paul is referring here to those opponents who have recently arrived in Corinth (i.e., the "false apostles" of 11:4, 13–15). Paul's choice of words in 2:17 indicates that his opponents' practice was suspicious. If anyone is trying to con the Corinthians, it cannot be Paul. His manner of life is a window to his sincere motives.

3:1–3 If the means of Paul's apostolic ministry is his suffering, the Spirit is its content. By embodying the gospel, Paul mediates the Spirit. Paul's work as an apostle speaks for itself, especially his founding of the church in Corinth. That the Corinthians are "written" (v. 3) or engraved on Paul's heart means not that he has warm feelings for them but that he is committed to act on their behalf as their "father" in the faith. The very existence of the Corinthians as Christians testifies to the power of the Spirit in and through Paul's ministry.

✣ **2:12—3:3** Paul's understanding of the nature of Christian ministry strikes a piercing blow against all attempts, whether in Paul's day or our own, to fashion ministries and messages around techniques and technology. As children of the entertainment age, our culturally conditioned reflex is to prioritize creating right environments for hearing the gospel, instead of relying first and foremost on the power of the Spirit to call people to repentance. Rather than viewing the pastor as a mediator of the Spirit proclaiming the Word, the minister becomes a "professional" whose job it is to manage the corporate life of the congregation and oversee the creation of meaningful worship "events."

As in Paul's day, so too today, the popular preachers are frequently those who "give the people what they want," religiously speaking, thereby confirming them in their own self-understanding and self-reliance. In response, congregations must rather refocus to view themselves as those whom God has called in Christ to seek and worship the Lord in the power of the Spirit.

3:4–6a Paul refers to his Moses-like call on the road to Damascus as legitimizing his ministry. Because Paul is an apostle (i.e., his office), he is a minister of the new covenant (i.e., his function). As a minister, he mediates the Spirit in establishing the church.

3:6b How we understand Paul's self-understanding as a minister of the new covenant is informed by our understanding of the meaning of the new covenant itself as found in Jer 31:31–34.

3:6c The key to the meaning of the letter/Spirit contrast is its immediate context. In v. 3b, Paul established a contrast between God's work in the past under the old covenant, on stone tablets, and his present work under the new covenant, engraved on the "tablets of human hearts." God's present work by means of the Spirit was the fulfillment of Eze 11:19 and 36:26–27. Paul's concern is with the two materials on which God wrote, corresponding to the two basic ages within the history of salvation. Those who have received the Spirit are now keeping the law, just as Ezekiel prophesied.

Paul does not establish a contrast between the law itself and the Spirit. The problem with the Sinai covenant was not with the law but with the people whose hearts remained hardened under it.

✣ **3:4–6** Paul's reminder that we are people of the new covenant drives home the absolute

as ministers of a new covenant[m] — not of
the letter but of the Spirit; for the letter
kills, but the Spirit gives life.[n]

The Greater Glory of the New Covenant

7Now if the ministry that brought death,
which was engraved in letters on stone,
came with glory, so that the Israelites
could not look steadily at the face of Moses because of its glory,[o] transitory though
it was, 8will not the ministry of the Spirit
be even more glorious? 9If the ministry
that brought condemnation[p] was glorious,
how much more glorious is the ministry
that brings righteousness![q] 10For what was
glorious has no glory now in comparison
with the surpassing glory. 11And if what
was transitory came with glory, how much
greater is the glory of that which lasts!
12Therefore, since we have such a hope,
we are very bold.[r] 13We are not like Moses,
who would put a veil over his face[s] to prevent the Israelites from seeing the end of
what was passing away. 14But their minds
were made dull,[t] for to this day the same
veil remains when the old covenant[u] is
read.[v] It has not been removed, because
only in Christ is it taken away. 15Even to
this day when Moses is read, a veil covers their hearts. 16But whenever anyone
turns to the Lord,[w] the veil is taken away.[x]
17Now the Lord is the Spirit,[y] and where
the Spirit of the Lord is, there is freedom.[z] 18And we all, who with unveiled
faces contemplate[a][a] the Lord's glory,[b] are
being transformed into his image[c] with

3:6 [m] Lk 22:20 [n] Jn 6:63
3:7 [o] Ex 34:29-35
3:9 [p] ver 7 [q] Ro 1:17; 3:21,22
3:12 [r] Eph 6:19
3:13 [s] ver 7; Ex 34:33
3:14 [t] Ro 11:7,8 [u] Ac 13:15 [v] ver 6
3:16 [w] Ro 11:23 [x] Ex 34:34
3:17 [y] Isa 61:1,2 [z] Jn 8:32
3:18 [a] 1Co 13:12 [b] 2Co 4:4,6 [c] Ro 8:29

[a] *18* Or *reflect*

2Co 3:16–17 ❖ How has the Spirit of Christ brought freedom into our lives?

---

necessity of living in obedience to God's commands as the expression of our faith in his promises. Idolatry is looking to something or someone other than God as the source of our happiness and contentment for the future.

3:7 Paul associates Moses' ministry, not the law as such, with "death." Moses' mediation of God's glory brought the judgment of God on a rebellious people. The very need itself for Moses' veil demonstrates Yahweh's judgment against his rebellious people. Moses' ministry was not only an act of divine mercy and grace but was also a ministry of judgment on a rebellious people.

3:8 Paul argues that since the ministry under the old covenant came in glory, then how much more must the ministry of the Spirit exist in *glory*, since it brings life (v. 6c)? Life is brought about by the ministry of the Spirit, in contrast to that of the ministry of the letter (i.e., death).

3:9–11 The presence of God's glory in the believer's life, evidenced through the Spirit (v. 8), is an expression of God's righteousness revealed in the death of Christ for the ungodly. Once the new covenant arrives, granting new life in the Spirit, the old covenant, with its primary purpose of bringing condemnation, is no longer the center of God's glory in the world.

The new covenant "lasts" since it reveals the righteousness of God that lasts forever. It is this "remaining" (v. 11) new covenant (v. 10) of the Spirit (v. 8), based on the righteousness of God (v. 9), that Paul was called to minister (vv. 4–6).

3:12–13 Through Paul's work as a minister of the new covenant (v. 6) the glory of God is being mediated to God's people in the Spirit (v. 11). Because he has this "hope," Paul is "very bold" (v. 12). Ultimately, this boldness arises from his assurance that his life and labors flow from God's grace in his life. They are being carried out in God's presence. They will be vindicated before God's judgment.

Whereas Moses had to veil himself as an act of judgment toward a rebellious people, Paul need not "veil himself" before a people whose disposition toward God has been radically changed by the Spirit.

3:14–15 Israel's large-scale rejection of the gospel indicates that the nation remains in the same hardened condition that has characterized its history ever since the golden calf (vv. 14c, 15a). Only "in Christ" can the Spirit remove the heart of stone (cf. vv. 2–3, 8–9). This has consequences for Israel's reading of the Scriptures and its own spiritual state.

3:16–18 For believers, as for Moses, the veil has been removed (v. 14) because their "heart of stone" has been removed by the Spirit. Moses' experience of Yahweh in the tent of meeting is equivalent to the current experience of the Spirit in Paul's ministry. Paul's point is that those who are presently living under the new covenant in Christ are in direct continuity with the revelation of Yahweh begun at Sinai.

The "freedom" spoken of in v. 17b implies a freedom from the veil of hard-heartedness that cannot enter into the Lord's presence. It is a freedom *for* obedience that flows from the power of the Spirit.

In Paul's words, transformation is taking place "with ever-increasing glory" (v. 18, which can also be read "from glory unto glory"). To say that we are being transformed into his likeness "*from* glory" means that the believer's gradual growth in obedience pictured in v. 18 takes place in response to God's presence.

✚ **3:7–18** Paul argued for his authority from the Scriptures, in contrast to his opponents, who relied on their personal power, mystical experiences, rhetorical skill, and public reputations. So also we turn to the Scriptures because we are convinced that the authority of our gospel comes from the inerrancy, sufficiency, and power of the Word of God.

ever-increasing glory, which comes from
the Lord, who is the Spirit.

Present Weakness and Resurrection Life

4 Therefore, since through God's mercy[d] we have this ministry, we do not
lose heart. 2Rather, we have renounced
secret and shameful ways;[e] we do not use
deception, nor do we distort the word of
God.[f] On the contrary, by setting forth the
truth plainly we commend ourselves to
everyone's conscience[g] in the sight of
God. 3And even if our gospel[h] is veiled,[i] it
is veiled to those who are perishing.[j] 4The
god[k] of this age has blinded[l] the minds
of unbelievers, so that they cannot see
the light of the gospel that displays the
glory of Christ, who is the image of God.
5For what we preach is not ourselves,[m]
but Jesus Christ as Lord, and ourselves
as your servants[n] for Jesus' sake. 6For
God, who said, "Let light shine out of
darkness,"[ao] made his light shine in our
hearts[p] to give us the light of the knowledge of God's glory displayed in the face
of Christ.
7But we have this treasure in jars of
clay[q] to show that this all-surpassing
power is from God[r] and not from us. 8We
are hard pressed on every side,[s] but not
crushed; perplexed, but not in despair;
9persecuted,[t] but not abandoned;[u] struck
down, but not destroyed.[v] 10We always
carry around in our body the death of
Jesus, so that the life of Jesus may also
be revealed in our body.[w] 11For we who
are alive are always being given over to
death for Jesus' sake,[x] so that his life may
also be revealed in our mortal body. 12So
then, death is at work in us, but life is at
work in you.[y]
13It is written: "I believed; therefore I
have spoken."[bz] Since we have that same
spirit of[c] faith, we also believe and therefore speak, 14because we know that the
one who raised the Lord Jesus from the
dead will also raise us with Jesus[a] and
present us with you to himself.[b] 15All this
is for your benefit, so that the grace that
is reaching more and more people may
cause thanksgiving[c] to overflow to the
glory of God.

[a] 6 Gen. 1:3 [b] 13 Psalm 116:10 (see Septuagint)
[c] 13 Or *Spirit-given*

4:1 [d] 1Co 7:25
4:2 [e] 1Co 4:5 [f] 2Co 2:17 [g] 2Co 5:11
4:3 [h] 2Co 2:12 [i] 2Co 3:14 [j] 1Co 1:18
4:4 [k] Jn 12:31 [l] 2Co 3:14
4:5 [m] 1Co 1:13 [n] 1Co 9:19
4:6 [o] Ge 1:3 [p] 2Pe 1:19
4:7 [q] Job 4:19; 2Co 5:1 [r] 1Co 2:5
4:8 [s] 2Co 7:5
4:9 [t] Jn 15:20 [u] Heb 13:5 [v] Ps 37:24
4:10 [w] Ro 6:5
4:11 [x] Ro 8:36
4:12 [y] 2Co 13:9
4:13 [z] Ps 116:10
4:14 [a] 1Th 4:14 [b] Eph 5:27
4:15 [c] 2Co 1:11

2Co 4:10 ❖ What does it mean to always carry the death of Christ in our bodies? How does this reveal the life of Christ in our lives?

4:1–6 The evidence of Paul's not losing heart is that he renounces the "secret and shameful ways" of his opponents (v. 2). Paul's sincere preaching has resulted from God's conversion-call in his life and the knowledge that he stands before God as judge.

Those who fail to see God's glory in Paul's ministry do so because of their spiritual blindness. The cause is given in v. 4: Satan's rule over the present evil age. People are not blind because they choose to be but because Satan has made them so.

The description in v. 4 encapsulates the entire history of redemption. Adam was created in the glorious image of God but fell. Israel encountered the glory of God on Mount Sinai, but fell in that they disobeyed him. Unlike everyone who came before him, Christ did not fall. He is the revelation of God's glory to his people.

Paul's final argument that those who refuse his ministry are revealing their own "blindness" is given in v. 5. Paul does not preach himself as the foundation or object of faith. Jesus, the Messiah, is alone Lord, both over the church and over the world. The gospel Paul preaches is embodied in his own Christlike willingness to consider the needs of others more important than his own "rights."

The "light" of the new creation used by God to transform his people is "the light of the knowledge of God's glory displayed in the face *of Christ*" (v. 6b, emphasis added). This glory, embodied in Jesus, is proclaimed in the gospel and experienced in the church.

4:7–12 The "treasure" in v. 7 refers to "the knowledge" from v. 6. But the link between v. 6 and v. 4, where the glory of Christ is seen to be the content of the gospel, suggests that it can also refer to Paul's entire ministry as this is embodied in his life of suffering. Paul's weakness ensures that the power is from God, not from Paul (cf. 12:1–10).

4:8–9 Given Paul's weakness, his perseverance can be attributed only to God. Paul's suffering provides the platform for the display of God's power.

4:10–11 Paul interprets his sufferings through the death *and* resurrection of Jesus. The power of God revealed in Paul's suffering is the same power revealed in the experience of Jesus. The categories of Jesus' death and resurrection are used to interpret Paul's experience of suffering and God's provision, thereby demonstrating that his life mediates the knowledge of God to the world embodied in Christ.

In v. 11 Paul again asserts that his sufferings are part of the divine plan for the spread of the gospel. Paul is given over to death by God. But Paul does not mediate his own life—it remains the life of *Jesus* (v. 11b).

4:12 Paul's life is not a "second atonement"; rather, in his preaching and suffering, Paul stands between the glory of God and the life of his congregation as an instrument in God's hand to bring about new life among his people.

4:13–15 The "spirit" in view here is most likely the Holy Spirit as the source of faith. Paul's preaching takes place in the midst of adversity and leads to even more adversity itself (Ps 116:10b). Paul's

16 Therefore we do not lose heart.
Though outwardly we are wasting away,
yet inwardly[d] we are being renewed[e] day
by day. 17 For our light and momentary
troubles are achieving for us an eternal glory that far outweighs them all.[f]
18 So we fix our eyes not on what is seen,
but on what is unseen,[g] since what is
seen is temporary, but what is unseen
is eternal.

Awaiting the New Body

5 For we know that if the earthly[h]
tent[i] we live in is destroyed, we have
a building from God, an eternal house
in heaven, not built by human hands.
2 Meanwhile we groan,[j] longing to be
clothed instead with our heavenly dwelling,[k] 3 because when we are clothed, we
will not be found naked. 4 For while we
are in this tent, we groan and are burdened, because we do not wish to be un-
clothed but to be clothed instead with
our heavenly dwelling,[l] so that what
is mortal may be swallowed up by life.
5 Now the one who has fashioned us for
this very purpose is God, who has given
us the Spirit as a deposit, guaranteeing
what is to come.[m]
6 Therefore we are always confident
and know that as long as we are at home
in the body we are away from the Lord.
7 For we live by faith, not by sight.[n] 8 We
are confident, I say, and would prefer
to be away from the body and at home
with the Lord.[o] 9 So we make it our goal to
please him,[p] whether we are at home in
the body or away from it. 10 For we must
all appear before the judgment seat of
Christ, so that each of us may receive
what is due us[q] for the things done while
in the body, whether good or bad.

4:16 [d] Ro 7:22 [e] Col 3:10
4:17 [f] Ro 8:18; 1Pe 1:6,7
4:18 [g] Ro 8:24; Heb 11:1
5:1 [h] 1Co 15:47 [i] 2Pe 1:13,14
5:2 [j] ver 4; Ro 8:23 [k] 1Co 15:53,54
5:4 [l] 1Co 15:53, 54
5:5 [m] Ro 8:23; 2Co 1:22
5:7 [n] 1Co 13:12
5:8 [o] Php 1:23
5:9 [p] Ro 14:18
5:10 [q] Mt 16:27; Ro 14:10; Eph 6:8

---

proclamation of the gospel reveals God's glory in Christ. Thus, the grace of God is causing thanksgiving to overflow among many others.

4:16–18 The correspondence between vv. 1, 16 makes it clear that the "outer" and "inner" realities point to the moral transformation of Paul's life as a believer. As a result, God will use these "light and momentary troubles" to achieve for Paul "an eternal glory that far outweighs them all" (v. 17). Instead of destroying Paul, his sufferings reveal the glory of God's presence and power in Paul's life "inwardly" (v. 16).

Just as Paul has grown to trust God to sustain him under the "weight" of his afflictions, so too Paul has come to see that the "weight" of God's glory far surpasses that of his afflictions.

The power of God that sustains Paul in his weakness (vv. 7–12) causes him to remain confident in his message (v. 13) and in his suffering for the sake of others (v. 16). All that God has done and is doing through the adversities of his life (vv. 1–15) leads him to focus on all that God will do (vv. 16–18), which in turn gives him confidence to endure the daily consequences of sin (vv. 1–15). This is the cycle of faith.

✣ **4:1–18** When Christians suffer, they too, like Paul, can take courage from the fact that their lives will demonstrate to others the power of the resurrection, either through God's act of deliverance or, even more profoundly, through the testimony of their endurance and holiness. Even though the circumstantial suffering that was an essential part of Paul's call may be an occasional aspect of God's will for all believers, all of us can follow Paul's example of enduring the suffering that comes from considering the needs of others more important than our own.

5:1–5 Paul's confidence in God's future provision (4:13—5:1) causes him to "groan" in the midst of his present suffering (5:2). This groaning is evidence that God has promised believers more to come than the moaning of suffering and death. Being clothed with Christ is the theological foundation to being clothed with our eternal dwelling from God. Paul's longing to inherit the eternal life of the age to come is supported by his desire to escape God's judgment.

Paul makes explicit in v. 5 that God brought about Paul's longing for the resurrection. God "has given . . . the Spirit as a deposit, guaranteeing what is to come." This Spirit-given longing occurs amid the very adversities that fuel this desire (cf. 1:22; Ro 8:23).

5:6–10 Life in this world is not the believer's final reality. *Therefore* Paul, like all believers, lives "by faith, not by sight" (v. 7). Paul trusts in God's promises as the ultimate reality and lives accordingly. He does not live as if his present suffering was the sum of life.

The basis for ambition to please the Lord is given in v. 10: Believers are aware that all people must appear before Christ as Judge (cf. 1:14). The image of the "judgment seat" in 5:10 comes from the practice of the Roman governors, who sat on such court benches to render judgment in legal cases.

✣ **5:1–10** We must stake out four important boundary markers of a distinctively Christian worldview: (1) There is a universal judgment to come—not just for some people, but for all, including Christians. (2) Christ alone is the One who judges. (3) Only those who have experienced the mercy and power of God in Christ can have confidence as they anticipate this coming day of reckoning. (4) The only basis of confidence on the day of judgment is the saving work of Jesus Christ on our behalf and the good deeds that constitute living by faith.

These points need to be driven home in a culture in which about two-thirds of adult Americans consider themselves to be Christian, even though a staggering number of all adults believe they can lead a full and satisfying life without spirituality of any kind.

The Ministry of Reconciliation

11Since, then, we know what it is to fear the Lord,[r] we try to persuade others. What we are is plain to God, and I hope it is also plain to your conscience.[s] 12We are not trying to commend ourselves to you again,[t] but are giving you an opportunity to take pride in us,[u] so that you can answer those who take pride in what is seen rather than in what is in the heart. 13If we are "out of our mind,"[v] as some say, it is for God; if we are in our right mind, it is for you. 14For Christ's love compels us, because we are convinced that one died for all, and therefore all died.[w] 15And he died for all, that those who live should no longer live for themselves[x] but for him who died for them and was raised again.

16So from now on we regard no one from a worldly[y] point of view. Though we once regarded Christ in this way, we do so no longer. 17Therefore, if anyone is in Christ, the new creation[z] has come:*[a]* The old has gone, the new is here![a] 18All this is from God, who reconciled us to himself through Christ[b] and gave us the ministry of reconciliation: 19that God was reconciling the world to himself in Christ, not counting people's sins against them.[c] And he has committed to us the message of reconciliation. 20We are therefore Christ's ambassadors,[d] as though God were making his appeal through us. We implore you on Christ's behalf: Be reconciled to God. 21God made him who had no sin[e] to be sin*[b]* for us, so that in him we might become the righteousness of God.[f]

6 As God's co-workers[g] we urge you not to receive God's grace in vain. 2For he says,

5:11 [r] Heb 10:31; Jude 23 [s] 2Co 4:2
5:12 [t] 2Co 3:1 [u] 2Co 1:14
5:13 [v] 2Co 11:1, 16,17
5:14 [w] Gal 2:20
5:15 [x] Ro 14:7-9
5:16 [y] 2Co 11:18
5:17 [z] Gal 6:15 [a] Isa 65:17; Rev 21:4,5
5:18 [b] Ro 5:10; Col 1:20
5:19 [c] Ro 4:8
5:20 [d] 2Co 6:1; Eph 6:20
5:21 [e] Heb 4:15; 1Pe 2:22,24; 1Jn 3:5 [f] Ro 1:17
6:1 [g] 1Co 3:9; 2Co 5:20

[a] *17* Or *Christ, that person is a new creation.*
[b] *21* Or *be a sin offering*

2Co 5:17 ❖ How can Christians lean into the "new creation" reality that the Spirit of Christ within them establishes? What does it look like to live in this "new creation" here and now?

2Co 5:18–19 ❖ God gave us the ministry of reconciliation. Where is God calling us to live out this ministry? How can we bring reconciliation?

5:11–15 The apostle seeks to persuade others to join him in fearing the Lord so that they too will escape God's wrath. The goal of Paul's persuasion is not to justify himself before God. It is not an attempt to win back the Corinthians. In the battle for the gospel that continued to be waged in Corinth, the issue remained whether the repentant could defend their faith in Paul's ministry against the attacks of those who "peddle the word of God" (2:17). Paul's concern here is to provide them with the ammunition needed to do so.

To be "out of our mind" (5:13) is best seen as a reference to Paul's ecstatic private worship experiences, most likely that of tongues and visions. Paul's point is that his love for the Corinthians causes him to consider their needs more important than even his own spiritual, private communion with God.

Christ's love compels Paul for two reasons. First, he is convinced that Christ's vicarious death is the true definition of being "right-minded" about life. Christ, moved by his love, considered the needs of others for reconciliation more important than his own glory and position with the Father. Second, Christ's death "for all" brings about the "death" of "all" for whom he died (cf. the "therefore" of v. 14c). Christ's death "compels" Paul in his ministry. To live *for* Christ is to live *like* Christ.

5:16—6:2 At one time in his life, Paul disdained the cross as a radical contradiction to Jesus' messianic claims. In the same way, Paul's opponents disdain his suffering as Christ's ambassador.

But on the road to Damacus, Paul met Jesus and now preaches that Jesus' suffering as the Messiah changes his people's lives. The "new creation" is the restoration of God's people under the new covenant. For Paul, the new covenant is the inauguration of the new creation.

One can legitimately argue that the personal transformation brought about by the Spirit in 3:18 is the evidence that one is part of the new creation spoken of in 5:17. For Paul, the real evidence of the glory of the new creation is not spiritual ecstasy (v. 13) but moral transformation. The magnitude of what Paul has just said leads him to declare in v. 18a that the origin of all this can be none other than God himself.

God is the source of reconciliation, while Paul is his instrument in bringing it to fruition. It quickly becomes clear, therefore, that the center of Paul's formulation of the gospel in vv. 18–19 is the concept of reconciliation. Paul's understanding of Jesus' death is significantly informed in this passage in Isa 52:13—53:12.

The OT understanding of atonement by means of a substitutionary sacrifice is the essential background for understanding *both* "reconciliation" in 2Co 5:18–20 *and* Christ's being made "to be sin" in v. 21. The explicit link between the OT sacrificial system and the death of Christ is found in the fact that Jesus, as the suffering servant of Isa 52:13—53:12, bears the sins of God's people as their ransom. In his sacrificial death as the sinless Son of God, Jesus pays the penalty for our sin.

Not only does Christ take on our sin, but we take on his righteousness. When God sees us in Christ, he sees the perfection of Christ having already been granted to us as a gift.

✜ **5:11–6:2** As Paul's pleading with the Corinthians makes clear, it is never too late to return

"In the time of my favor I heard you,
and in the day of salvation I
helped you."[a][h]

I tell you, now is the time of God's favor,
now is the day of salvation.

Paul's Hardships

3We put no stumbling block in anyone's path,[i] so that our ministry will not
be discredited. 4Rather, as servants of
God we commend ourselves in every
way: in great endurance; in troubles,
hardships and distresses; 5in beatings,
imprisonments[j] and riots; in hard work,
sleepless nights and hunger;[k] 6in purity,
understanding, patience and kindness;
in the Holy Spirit[l] and in sincere love;
7in truthful speech[m] and in the power of
God; with weapons of righteousness[n] in
the right hand and in the left; 8through
glory and dishonor,[o] bad report and good
report; genuine, yet regarded as impostors;[p] 9known, yet regarded as unknown;
dying,[q] and yet we live on;[r] beaten, and
yet not killed; 10sorrowful, yet always
rejoicing;[s] poor, yet making many rich;[t]
having nothing, and yet possessing everything.[u]
11We have spoken freely to you, Corinthians, and opened wide our hearts to
you.[v] 12We are not withholding our affection from you, but you are withholding
yours from us. 13As a fair exchange—I
speak as to my children[w]—open wide
your hearts also.

6:2 [h]Isa 49:8
6:3 [i]Ro 14:13, 20; 1Co 9:12; 10:32
6:5 [j]2Co 11:23-25 [k]1Co 4:11
6:6 [l]1Th 1:5
6:7 [m]2Co 4:2 [n]2Co 10:4; Eph 6:10-18
6:8 [o]1Co 4:10 [p]Mt 27:63
6:9 [q]Ro 8:36 [r]2Co 1:8-10; 4:10,11
6:10 [s]2Co 7:4 [t]2Co 8:9 [u]Ro 8:32; 1Co 3:21
6:11 [v]2Co 7:3
6:13 [w]1Co 4:14
6:14 [x]1Co 5:9, 10 [y]Eph 5:7,11; 1Jn 1:6
6:15 [z]Ac 5:14
6:16 [a]1Co 3:16 [b]Lev 26:12; Jer 32:38; Eze 37:27

2Co 6:10 ❖ How can we find rejoicing amid sorrows and be content while having nothing? How can we gain access to the power of Christ that can accomplish this?

Warning Against Idolatry

14Do not be yoked together[x] with unbelievers. For what do righteousness and
wickedness have in common? Or what
fellowship can light have with darkness?[y]
15What harmony is there between Christ
and Belial[b]? Or what does a believer[z]
have in common with an unbeliever?
16What agreement is there between the
temple of God and idols? For we are the
temple[a] of the living God. As God has
said:

"I will live with them
and walk among them,
and I will be their God,
and they will be my people."[c][b]

[a] *2* Isaiah 49:8 [b] *15* Greek *Beliar,* a variant of *Belial* [c] *16* Lev. 26:12; Jer. 32:38; Ezek. 37:27

---

to God. Paul's call for reconciliation to a wayward people is God's means of rescuing his people from judgment. Paul's confidence is that those who have not accepted God's grace in vain will respond, repent, and return to the Lord. Moreover, what was true for Paul in his day is true in ours: Now is the day of salvation.

6:3–13 The focus of Paul's commendation here in vv. 3–10 is once again on his divinely enabled endurance amid adversity, which embodies both Christ's "death" (= Paul's suffering) and his "resurrection" (= Paul's endurance). These phrases also support vv. 11–13. Paul speaks as the spiritual father of his "children," the Corinthians. As their father in the faith, Paul's pattern of living his life for the sake of the Corinthians points to the fact that he has conducted his ministry with open integrity and genuine affection.

✣ **6:3–13** What distinguishes the suffering of the righteous from the suffering rampant in our fallen world is the transforming power of God's sustaining presence in their lives. Those whom God calls to suffer on behalf of others as an extension of Christ's love are being called not to suffer pain for pain's sake but to a mission to testify to God's grace amid suffering.

6:14b–16b The fact that in v. 14 "righteousness" is contrasted with "wickedness" (lit., "lawlessness") demonstrates that "righteousness" includes both one's relationship with God (cf. v. 15a) *and* its outworking in a life of "light" (v. 14c) as a "believer" (v. 15b).

Paul's word choice for "temple" in v. 16 highlights God's presence. The Corinthians are not to have anything to do with idolatry precisely because they are "the temple of the living God." Paul's point is clear. Whereas Israel fell into idolatry and disobedience, the Messiah has brought the church back into the presence of God's glory and has begun transforming it into God's image (3:16–18).

6:16c–18 Paul cites six OT passages which, when read as a whole, support the command of v. 14 and its restatement in 7:1. The first OT reference highlights the promise of God's covenant presence in Lev 26:11–12. Paul shows the original covenant promises are now beginning to be fulfilled in the Corinthian church.

In 2Co 6:17–18 Paul describes what a covenant with God entails. He cites three commands from Isa 52:11 and three ensuing promises from Eze 20:34, 2Sa 7:14, and Isa 43:6. Since the Corinthians are already part of God's people under the new covenant, they must separate from the unbelievers among them. The covenant promise is for those who keep the covenant stipulations (2Co 6:17), which includes separating from impurity (vv. 14–16).

17 Therefore,

"Come out from them[c]
and be separate,
says the Lord.
Touch no unclean thing,
and I will receive you."[a][d]

18 And,

"I will be a Father to you,
and you will be my sons and
daughters,[e]
says the Lord Almighty."[b]

7 Therefore, since we have these promises,[f] dear friends, let us purify ourselves from everything that contami-
nates body and spirit, perfecting holiness
out of reverence for God.

Paul's Joy Over the Church's Repentance

2 Make room for us in your hearts.[g] We
have wronged no one, we have corrupted
no one, we have exploited no one. 3 I do
not say this to condemn you; I have said
before that you have such a place in our
hearts[h] that we would live or die with
you. 4 I have spoken to you with great
frankness; I take great pride in you. I am
greatly encouraged; in all our troubles
my joy knows no bounds.[i]
5 For when we came into Macedonia,[j]
we had no rest, but we were harassed at
every turn[k]—conflicts on the outside,
fears within.[l] 6 But God, who comforts the
downcast,[m] comforted us by the coming
of Titus,[n] 7 and not only by his coming
but also by the comfort you had given
him. He told us about your longing for
me, your deep sorrow, your ardent concern for me, so that my joy was greater
than ever.
8 Even if I caused you sorrow by my
letter,[o] I do not regret it. Though I did
regret it—I see that my letter hurt you,
but only for a little while— 9 yet now I
am happy, not because you were made
sorry, but because your sorrow led you
to repentance. For you became sorrowful
as God intended and so were not harmed
in any way by us. 10 Godly sorrow brings
repentance that leads to salvation[p] and
leaves no regret, but worldly sorrow
brings death. 11 See what this godly sorrow has produced in you: what earnestness, what eagerness to clear yourselves,
what indignation, what alarm, what
longing, what concern,[q] what readiness
to see justice done. At every point you
have proved yourselves to be innocent
in this matter. 12 So even though I wrote

6:17 [c] Rev 18:4 [d] Isa 52:11
6:18 [e] Isa 43:6
7:1 [f] 2Co 6:17,18
7:2 [g] 2Co 6:12,13
7:3 [h] 2Co 6:11,12
7:4 [i] 2Co 6:10
7:5 [j] 2Co 2:13 [k] 2Co 4:8 [l] Dt 32:25
7:6 [m] 2Co 1:3,4 [n] ver 13; 2Co 2:13
7:8 [o] 2Co 2:2,4
7:10 [p] Ac 11:18
7:11 [q] ver 7

2Co 7:10 ❖ When have our sorrows led to a repentance that brought us closer to God? When are even sorrow and regret useful in spiritual growth?

[a] *17* Isaiah 52:11; Ezek. 20:34,41
[b] *18* 2 Samuel 7:14; 7:8

7:1 Paul takes the language used against pagan idolatry and applies it to his opponents. His readers must flee anything that would keep them from being "reconciled to God." *Positively*, this means having an "open heart" toward Paul (6:13; cf. 7:2–4).

6:14—7:1 To determine the pockets of idolatry in our lives, we must carefully evaluate the influence of our daily commitments, our social practices, and the values that we share with our culture. Our culture's covetousness encourages us to seek happiness from acquiring more possessions and security through financial stability. As believers, we sanitize this covetousness by making Jesus a means to some other end. Since all we need to be happy is Jesus *and* the Christian family, Jesus *and* material blessings, Jesus *and* a growing ministry, Jesus *and* my neighbor's spouse, Jesus *and* whatever it is we do not yet possess, we turn following Jesus into a means to these other ends. Such a distortion makes serving Jesus the means to satisfying our idolatry. Modern believers must uncover and root this impulse from their lives.

7:2-3 In vv. 2–16, Paul speaks to those who have already proven themselves to be among God's people through their repentance. He directly addresses those he knows to be believers within it. Paul calls them to begin cleaning out those who are still in rebellion against him.

Paul supports his command by asserting that the Corinthians should make room for Paul because it is clear he has "wronged no one . . . corrupted no one . . . exploited no one" (v. 2b).

In v. 3, Paul assures the faithful he is not condemning them, as he did in his "tearful letter" (2:4).

7:4 Paul's boldness leads him to "great pride" (which also can be read as "much boasting") in the faithful Corinthians. They demonstrate the Spirit-endowed character of his ministry. This leads Paul to be "greatly encouraged."

7:5-7 Paul returns to the story begun in 2:12-13. God used Titus's arrival and report of the Corinthians' changed attitude toward Paul to increase his joy more than ever (7:6–7). Paul's comfort and joy are expressions of God's presence and power, since Paul recognizes that God is the One behind the coming of Titus and the change among the Corinthians.

7:8-13a Paul recounts how his joy increased at hearing that his ministry had produced fruit among the Corinthians. Paul initially regretted having sent his letter of rebuke, since he knew it would cause them sorrow (v. 8). His fears were unfounded. In

to you,[r] it was neither on account of the
one who did the wrong[s] nor on account
of the injured party, but rather that before God you could see for yourselves
how devoted to us you are. 13By all this
we are encouraged.
In addition to our own encouragement, we were especially delighted to
see how happy Titus[t] was, because his
spirit has been refreshed by all of you.
14I had boasted to him about you,[u] and
you have not embarrassed me. But just
as everything we said to you was true,
so our boasting about you to Titus[v] has
proved to be true as well. 15And his affection for you is all the greater when he
remembers that you were all obedient,[w]
receiving him with fear and trembling.[x]
16I am glad I can have complete confidence in you.[y]

The Collection for the Lord's People

8 And now, brothers and sisters, we
want you to know about the grace
that God has given the Macedonian[z]
churches. 2In the midst of a very severe
trial, their overflowing joy and their extreme poverty welled up in rich generosity. 3For I testify that they gave as much
as they were able,[a] and even beyond their
ability. Entirely on their own, 4they urgently pleaded with us for the privilege
of sharing in this service[b] to the Lord's
people.[c] 5And they exceeded our expectations: They gave themselves first of all
to the Lord, and then by the will of God
also to us. 6So we urged[d] Titus,[e] just as he
had earlier made a beginning, to bring
also to completion[f] this act of grace on
your part. 7But since you excel in everything[g] — in faith, in speech, in knowledge,[h] in complete earnestness and in
the love we have kindled in you[a] — see
that you also excel in this grace of giving.
8I am not commanding you,[i] but I
want to test the sincerity of your love
by comparing it with the earnestness of
others. 9For you know the grace of our
Lord Jesus Christ,[j] that though he was
rich, yet for your sake he became poor,[k]
so that you through his poverty might
become rich.

7:12 [r] ver 8; 2Co 2:3,9 [s] 1Co 5:1,2
7:13 [t] ver 6; 2Co 2:13
7:14 [u] ver 4 [v] ver 6
7:15 [w] 2Co 2:9 [x] Php 2:12
7:16 [y] 2Co 2:3
8:1 [z] Ac 16:9
8:3 [a] 1Co 16:2
8:4 [b] Ac 24:17 [c] Ro 15:25; 2Co 9:1
8:6 [d] ver 17; 2Co 12:18 [e] ver 16,23 [f] ver 10,11
8:7 [g] 2Co 9:8 [h] 1Co 1:5
8:8 [i] 1Co 7:6
8:9 [j] 2Co 13:14 [k] Mt 20:28; Php 2:6-8

2Co 8:1-14 ❖ What does this description of Paul's collection for the church in Jerusalem tell us about our need to support the work of God around the world?

[a] 7 Some manuscripts *and in your love for us*

---

response to his rebuke, the majority of the Corinthians had repented and disciplined the one who had led the charge against Paul.

Thus, despite the pain the letter caused, the sorrow it caused led to their repentance (v. 9). The Corinthians experienced genuine remorse that led to a real change in their way of life. "Godly sorrow" (v. 10) feels bad because it is missing out on God.

Paul knew that he had to confront the Corinthians for the sake of their own salvation (v. 12). He did so by reminding them that they stood "before God" as judge. Paul wrote his letter because he had reason to believe it would prove the Corinthians' genuineness *before God* and expose their true colors *to themselves* (vv. 12, 14). They passed the test.

7:13b-15 In v. 13b Paul then emphasizes that his joy increases even more over Titus than over the Corinthians in and of themselves. Titus had expressed reservations about taking the letter to Corinth. The church's reception of Titus as Paul's messenger "with fear and trembling" also increased Titus's affections for them (v. 15).

✤ **7:2-16** All too often, the church fails to experience joy during adversity because we no longer gain our identity within the community of faith. Our joy is no longer wrapped up with the progress of God's people. The basis of our contentment is not the growing Christ-likeness of our church but the comfort level of our personal circumstances. Conversely, what makes us sad is no longer the sting of our sin.

Today we find it hard to believe that someone's own happiness could be so wrapped up in the welfare of others that to talk about *their* situation naturally leads to talking about one's *own* grief or gladness. Paul and Titus's own joy fused with the condition of the Corinthians. This text focuses on the joy that comes about because of another person's participation in salvation.

8:1-7 The Macedonians' generosity is evidence that they passed the "test" brought on by their afflictions (v. 2). The Macedonians' giving exceeded their ability, without being manipulated or coerced (v. 3). It was the result of their "urgently pleading" to be involved in the collection (v. 4). The most important thing for Paul is not that the Macedonians gave their money to others but that they gave their lives to God and to Paul as God's apostle (v. 5).

Paul sends Titus back to Corinth "to bring also to completion this act of *grace* on [the Corinthians'] part" (v. 6, emphasis added). Paul wants God to do for the Corinthians what he has done for the Macedonians. The main point of the Macedonian example is made explicit in v. 7. Just as the Macedonians responded by "welling up" (v. 2) in generosity, the Corinthians should overflow in the "grace of giving" (v. 7).

8:8-10 The point of v. 8 is the opposite of Phm 8-9, where Paul refrains from commanding them "in Christ," even though he has every right as an

10And here is my judgment[l] about
what is best for you in this matter. Last
year you were the first not only to give
but also to have the desire to do so.[m]
11Now finish the work, so that your eager willingness[n] to do it may be matched
by your completion of it, according to
your means. 12For if the willingness is
there, the gift is acceptable according
to what one has,[o] not according to what
one does not have.

13Our desire is not that others might
be relieved while you are hard pressed,
but that there might be equality. 14At
the present time your plenty will supply
what they need,[p] so that in turn their
plenty will supply what you need. The
goal is equality, 15as it is written: "The
one who gathered much did not have
too much, and the one who gathered
little did not have too little."[a][q]

Titus Sent to Receive the Collection

16Thanks be to God,[r] who put into the
heart[s] of Titus[t] the same concern I have
for you. 17For Titus not only welcomed
our appeal, but he is coming to you with
much enthusiasm and on his own initiative.[u] 18And we are sending along with
him the brother[v] who is praised by all
the churches[w] for his service to the gospel.[x] 19What is more, he was chosen by
the churches to accompany us[y] as we
carry the offering, which we administer in order to honor the Lord himself
and to show our eagerness to help.[z] 20We
want to avoid any criticism of the way
we administer this liberal gift. 21For we
are taking pains to do what is right, not
only in the eyes of the Lord but also in
the eyes of man.[a]

22In addition, we are sending with
them our brother who has often proved
to us in many ways that he is zealous,
and now even more so because of his
great confidence in you. 23As for Titus,
he is my partner[b] and co-worker[c] among
you; as for our brothers,[d] they are representatives of the churches and an honor
to Christ. 24Therefore show these men
the proof of your love and the reason for
our pride in you,[e] so that the churches
can see it.

9 There is no need[f] for me to write to
you about this service to the Lord's
people.[g] 2For I know your eagerness to
help, and I have been boasting[h] about
it to the Macedonians, telling them that

8:10 [l]1Co 7:25, 40 [m]1Co 16:2,3; 2Co 9:2
8:11 [n]2Co 9:2
8:12 [o]Mk 12:43, 44; Lk 21:3
8:14 [p]2Co 9:12
8:15 [q]Ex 16:18
8:16 [r]2Co 2:14 [s]Rev 17:17 [t]2Co 2:13
8:17 [u]ver 6
8:18 [v]2Co 12:18
[w]1Co 7:17 [x]2Co 2:12
8:19 [y]1Co 16:3,4 [z]ver 11,12
8:21 [a]Ro 12:17; 14:18
8:23 [b]Phm 17 [c]Php 2:25 [d]ver 18,22
8:24 [e]2Co 7:4, 14; 9:2
9:1 [f]1Th 4:9 [g]2Co 8:4
9:2 [h]2Co 7:4,14

[a] *15* Exodus 16:18

apostle to do so. Here he exercises that right. In 2Co 8:9, Paul wants to remind the Corinthians that Jesus himself demonstrates how grace expresses itself in love. Spurred on by how the Macedonians have copied Christ, in v. 10 Paul extends the same call to give.

8:11–15 Verse 11 makes it plain that there is an obligation to give, but only what the Corinthians can afford. Paul is not trying to manipulate the believers in Corinth. The example of the Macedonians illustrates that even people who are poor can make a great contribution. The purpose of the collection is not to relieve the saints in Jerusalem by making the Corinthians poor. Rather, the goal is to create an "equality" between them with reference to their basic necessities (v. 13).

8:1–15 The church spends far too little time addressing the dangers of materialism. When we do speak about giving, we are quick to adopt the motivational strategies and values of our culture. The fact that Paul devotes so much of 2 Corinthians, his letter of restoration and apologetic for the truth, to the issue of the collection should be a sober reminder of the significance of this aspect of our Christian life. Nowhere is our materialism challenged more directly, and nowhere do we skirt the issues more often, than when it comes to expressing the genuine nature of our faith and the unity of the church through our giving.

8:16–24 In the light of Paul's argument in vv. 1–15, Titus's passion to complete the collection is a passion for the good of the Corinthians themselves. *God* put the desire to help the Corinthians in Titus's heart. This is why Titus is commended, but God is praised.

8:18–21 These verses concern the sending of the second brother, who remains unnamed. Though this "brother" is sent by Paul, he is not Paul's personal envoy. The churches commissioned this brother to travel to Corinth. His presence will help certify the integrity of the enterprise both before God and others (v. 21).

8:22 The third member of the delegation is introduced. Paul's description of him as "*our* brother" (emphasis added) suggests that he, like Titus, has been appointed directly by Paul. Like Titus, this man's zeal to serve the Corinthians had been fueled by the Spirit-induced zeal of the repentant Corinthians.

8:23–24 Paul describes these visitors as "an honor to Christ." This means that to reject their work among the Corinthians is to reject the reality of Christ in his church. The delegation that has just been commended is, of course, the very one that has delivered the letter they are now reading. The Corinthians must therefore demonstrate the reality of their renewed love for Paul and his gospel by complying with the call to contribute.

9:1–5 Most likely, Paul employs the geographical designation of "Achaia" here to match his corresponding reference to the "Macedonians," especially since Corinth was Achaia's senatorial

since last year[i] you in Achaia[j] were ready
to give; and your enthusiasm has stirred
most of them to action. 3But I am sending the brothers in order that our boasting about you in this matter should not
prove hollow, but that you may be ready,
as I said you would be.[k] 4For if any Macedonians[l] come with me and find you
unprepared, we — not to say anything
about you — would be ashamed of having
been so confident. 5So I thought it necessary to urge the brothers to visit you
in advance and finish the arrangements
for the generous gift you had promised.
Then it will be ready as a generous gift,[m]
not as one grudgingly given.[n]

Generosity Encouraged

6Remember this: Whoever sows sparingly will also reap sparingly, and whoever sows generously will also reap generously.[o] 7Each of you should give what
you have decided in your heart to give,[p]
not reluctantly or under compulsion,[q]
for God loves a cheerful giver.[r] 8And God
is able[s] to bless you abundantly, so that
in all things at all times, having all that
you need,[t] you will abound in every good
work. 9As it is written:

"They have freely scattered their
gifts to the poor;

9:2 [i] 2Co 8:10 [j] Ac 18:12
9:3 [k] 1Co 16:2
9:4 [l] Ro 15:26
9:5 [m] Php 4:17 [n] 2Co 12:17,18
9:6 [o] Pr 11:24, 25; 22:9; Gal 6:7,9
9:7 [p] Ex 25:2; 2Co 8:12 [q] Dt 15:10 [r] Ro 12:8
9:8 [s] Eph 3:20 [t] Php 4:19
9:9 [u] Ps 112:9
9:10 [v] Isa 55:10 [w] Hos 10:12
9:11 [x] 1Co 1:5 [y] 2Co 1:11
9:12 [z] 2Co 8:14 [a] 2Co 1:11
9:13 [b] 2Co 8:4 [c] Mt 9:8 [d] 2Co 2:12

2Co 9:6-8 ❖ What is our responsibility for the spiritual practice of giving and generosity? How has God blessed us as we have shared with others what he has given to us?

their righteousness endures
forever."[au]

10Now he who supplies seed to the sower and bread for food[v] will also supply
and increase your store of seed and will
enlarge the harvest of your righteousness.[w] 11You will be enriched[x] in every
way so that you can be generous on
every occasion, and through us your
generosity will result in thanksgiving
to God.[y]
12This service that you perform is not
only supplying the needs[z] of the Lord's
people but is also overflowing in many
expressions of thanks to God.[a] 13Because
of the service[b] by which you have proved
yourselves, others will praise God[c] for
the obedience that accompanies your
confession of the gospel of Christ,[d] and
for your generosity in sharing with them
and with everyone else. 14And in their
prayers for you their hearts will go out
to you, because of the surpassing grace

[a] 9 Psalm 112:9

---

and provincial capital. Paul has sent the three brothers to ensure that his boast concerning the collection will not "prove hollow" (v. 3). A delegation of Macedonians will accompany Paul with the collection. He is aware of the shame they will incur if these Macedonians find the Corinthians unprepared (v. 4b).

In v. 5, Paul is pointing to two opposite ways of giving: the kind that flows from trusting God's grace versus the kind that selfishly seeks to keep as much as possible for oneself.

9:6–15 These verses express the collection's theological basis (God's abundant grace) and purpose (the praise of God's glory). Paul emphasizes the various degrees of reward associated with sowing and reaping, respectively.

Paul's reference to Dt 15:10 is yet another indication that he understands the church as the continuation of the faithful remnant within Israel. What was given to Israel to do every seventh year is now, under the new covenant, to be the *daily* pattern of those in Christ.

9:8–9 These verses explain why God approves only of those who give cheerfully (v. 7c). Giving to others has trust in God's promises as its foundation. Believers will always have "all that [they] need" (v. 8). Paul summarizes the point of vv. 8–9 in v. 10 by alluding to two more passages from Scripture, Isa 55:10 and Hos 10:12.

9:10–14 In the original text, vv. 10–14 form one long, complex sentence. God will provide for the Corinthians "in every way" (v. 11) so that they can be generous to others. These people in turn will give thanks and pray to God, for God is the One who makes all this possible.

9:15 It is fitting that here Paul draws 8:16—9:15 to a close by returning to the thanksgiving with which he started. That the Corinthians' giving to others, which begins in God's grace, will also rebound to their own blessing from God in response to the praise and prayers of others is an amazing "gift" of grace worthy of praise.

8:16—9:15 While giving must be done freely, it is not optional. The gospel ministry requires this point to be made strongly and consistently, especially in a culture drowning in materialism. Unfortunately, many pastors are afraid to mention giving too often, lest the congregation think that the "church just wants our money." Such fears are misplaced theologically and often reflect our cowardice in the face of the reigning idols of our day.

To speak about our need to give is to emphasize that we are God's people through whom God glorifies himself. The Corinthians' participation in the collection was not "for the church" but evidence that they *were* the church. The same is true for the church today.

God has given you. 15Thanks be to God[e]
for his indescribable gift![f]

Paul's Defense of His Ministry

10 By the humility and gentleness[g] of
Christ, I appeal to you — I, Paul,[h]
who am "timid" when face to face with
you, but "bold" toward you when away!
2I beg you that when I come I may not
have to be as bold[i] as I expect to be toward some people who think that we
live by the standards of this world. 3For
though we live in the world, we do not
wage war as the world does. 4The weapons we fight with[j] are not the weapons
of the world. On the contrary, they have
divine power[k] to demolish strongholds.[l]
5We demolish arguments and every pretension that sets itself up against the
knowledge of God,[m] and we take captive
every thought to make it obedient[n] to
Christ. 6And we will be ready to punish
every act of disobedience, once your obedience is complete.[o]
7You are judging by appearances.[a][p] If
anyone is confident that they belong to
Christ,[q] they should consider again that
we belong to Christ just as much as they
do.[r] 8So even if I boast somewhat freely
about the authority the Lord gave us for
building you up rather than tearing you
down,[s] I will not be ashamed of it. 9I do
not want to seem to be trying to fright-
en you with my letters. 10For some say,
"His letters are weighty and forceful, but
in person he is unimpressive[t] and his
speaking amounts to nothing."[u] 11Such
people should realize that what we are in
our letters when we are absent, we will
be in our actions when we are present.
12We do not dare to classify or compare ourselves with some who commend themselves.[v] When they measure
themselves by themselves and compare
themselves with themselves, they are not
wise. 13We, however, will not boast beyond
proper limits, but will confine our boasting to the sphere of service God himself
has assigned to us,[w] a sphere that also
includes you. 14We are not going too far

9:15 [e] 2Co 2:14 [f] Ro 5:15,16
10:1 [g] Mt 11:29 [h] Gal 5:2
10:2 [i] 1Co 4:21; 2Co 13:2,10
10:4 [j] 2Co 6:7 [k] 1Co 2:5 [l] Jer 1:10; 2Co 13:10
10:5 [m] Isa 2:11, 12; 1Co 1:19 [n] 2Co 9:13
10:6 [o] 2Co 2:9; 7:15
10:7 [p] Jn 7:24 [q] 1Co 1:12; 3:23; 14:37 [r] 2Co 11:23
10:8 [s] 2Co 13:10
10:10 [t] 1Co 2:3; Gal 4:13,14 [u] 1Co 1:17
10:12 [v] 2Co 3:1
10:13 [w] ver 15,16

[a] 7 Or *Look at the obvious facts*

2Co 10:7 ❖ What is wrong with judging by appearances (see Jn 7:23-24)? Why is this such a natural human thing to do?

10:1-6 Paul is being bold now so that he will not have to be "bold" when he arrives (v. 2). His opponents had accused him of cowardice. According to his detractors, his being "bold" when absent was a coward's threat. On the contrary, Paul's boldness was an expression of his confidence in Christ. But just as Christ's meekness must not be misinterpreted to mean that he winks at sin, so too Paul's restraint must not be seen as cowardice.
10:3-6 Though Paul concedes that he "lives in the world," his battle plan is not worldly (v. 3) because his "weapons" (v. 4) are not worldly; by implication, they are expressions of the power of the Spirit. Paul's weapons are the proclamation of the truth in the power of the Spirit. Their purpose is to "demolish strongholds" (v. 4), defenses erected to protect a city from invaders.
10:5 Paul details the two ways in which he wages his war on behalf of the gospel. First, he demolishes the "arguments" and "pretension[s]" that his opponents have raised against "the knowledge of God." Paul overcomes them by a clear presentation of the gospel. Second, once he has destroyed the enemy defenses, Paul takes every thought of the enemy "captive" by evaluating it in view of his own ministry of the cross and resurrection of Christ.
10:6 After demolishing his enemies' defenses and taking captive their counterattacks, Paul will punish those who remain in rebellion. But he will only do so once the repentant, by their obedience, have shown themselves to be on his side (v. 6). Paul wants to give them every opportunity to surrender to the gospel before he executes God's judgment.
10:7-8 Paul is most likely stating what he wishes the Corinthians *would* do. Having begged them to avoid judgment in vv. 1-6, he now calls them to evaluate things as they readily appear to the Corinthians themselves rather than listen to Paul's opponents.
10:9-11 Paul expresses the purpose for his boasting and warnings that are to come in the chapters ahead. Paul's opponents should be put on notice that he is more than prepared to carry out his threats of judgment when he arrives (v. 11).
10:12-18 Paul's burden in this passage is twofold: (1) to define what is a proper boast to apostolic authority in Corinth, and (2) to demonstrate that his boast actually meets this criterion.

Paul accomplishes these purposes by introducing a negative comparison between his opponents' practice of commendation (v. 12) and his own (vv. 13-18). He refuses to participate with those who commend themselves because their *means* of comparison is faulty from the start: They measure themselves *by themselves* and compare themselves *with themselves*, thereby revealing that they are without understanding (v. 12).

From Paul's perspective, to support a claim to apostolic authority in Corinth by pointing to one's own abilities is to be without understanding; such factors are simply irrelevant to the question. This commendation does not come from comparing oneself to others; it comes from the Lord.
10:13-15 Paul asserts that he will not boast beyond "proper limits"—that is, beyond what God has allotted for him. Paul's apostolic authority in Corinth

in our boasting, as would be the case if we
had not come to you, for we did get as far
as you[x] with the gospel of Christ.[y] 15 Neither do we go beyond our limits by boasting of work done by others.[z] Our hope is
that, as your faith continues to grow,[a] our
sphere of activity among you will greatly
expand, 16 so that we can preach the gospel
in the regions beyond you.[b] For we do not
want to boast about work already done
in someone else's territory. 17 But, "Let the
one who boasts boast in the Lord."[ac] 18 For
it is not the one who commends himself[d]
who is approved, but the one whom the
Lord commends.[e]

Paul and the False Apostles

11 I hope you will put up with[f] me in
a little foolishness.[g] Yes, please put
up with me! 2 I am jealous for you with
a godly jealousy. I promised you to one
husband,[h] to Christ, so that I might present you[i] as a pure virgin to him. 3 But I
am afraid that just as Eve was deceived
by the serpent's cunning,[j] your minds
may somehow be led astray from your
sincere and pure devotion to Christ. 4 For
if someone comes to you and preaches a
Jesus other than the Jesus we preached,[k]
or if you receive a different spirit[l] from
the Spirit you received, or a different
gospel[m] from the one you accepted, you
put up with it easily enough.
5 I do not think I am in the least inferior
to those "super-apostles."[bn] 6 I may indeed
be untrained as a speaker,[o] but I do have
knowledge.[p] We have made this perfectly clear to you in every way. 7 Was it a sin[q]
for me to lower myself in order to elevate
you by preaching the gospel of God to you
free of charge?[r] 8 I robbed other churches
by receiving support from them[s] so as to
serve you. 9 And when I was with you and
needed something, I was not a burden to
anyone, for the brothers who came from
Macedonia supplied what I needed. I have
kept myself from being a burden to you[t]
in any way, and will continue to do so.
10 As surely as the truth of Christ is in me,[u]
nobody in the regions of Achaia[v] will stop
this boasting[w] of mine. 11 Why? Because I
do not love you? God knows I do![x]

10:14 [x] 1Co 3:6 [y] 2Co 2:12
10:15 [z] Ro 15:20 [a] 2Th 1:3
10:16 [b] Ac 19:21
10:17 [c] Jer 9:24; 1Co 1:31
10:18 [d] ver 12 [e] Ro 2:29; 1Co 4:5
11:1 [f] ver 4, 19, 20; Mt 17:17 [g] ver 16, 17, 21; 2Co 5:13
11:2 [h] Hos 2:19; Eph 5:26, 27 [i] 2Co 4:14
11:3 [j] Ge 3:1-6, 13; Jn 8:44; 1Ti 2:14; Rev 12:9
11:4 [k] 1Co 3:11 [l] Ro 8:15 [m] Gal 1:6-9
11:5 [n] 2Co 12:11; Gal 2:6
11:6 [o] 1Co 1:17 [p] Eph 3:4
11:7 [q] 2Co 12:13 [r] 1Co 9:18
11:8 [s] Php 4:15, 18
11:9 [t] 2Co 12:13, 14, 16
11:10 [u] Ro 9:1 [v] Ac 18:12 [w] 1Co 9:15
11:11 [x] 2Co 12:15

[a] *17 Jer. 9:24* [b] *5 Or to the most eminent apostles*

---

is the simple fact that he founded the Corinthian church. Paul's boast is therefore based on his own divinely established "work" (v. 15a). His opponents attempt to assert apostolic authority in Corinth, yet they are "boasting of work done by others" (v. 15a).

By contrast, the Corinthians themselves are Paul's recommendation (see 3:2–3). Paul's God-established spiritual power could be seen in the growing faith of the believers in Corinth. Since the Lord is the One who determines the measure of one's ministry, the only ground for boasting is the Lord's commendation (10:17–18). The Lord brought the great missionary to Corinth as the church's founding father in the faith. What matters is not the Corinthians' approval but God's commendation (v. 18).

10:1–18 As a continuation of Paul's own "warfare," this passage calls us to engage in apologetics and church discipline whenever the gospel is being denied or diluted. Paul's apologetic in this passage reminds us that genuine salvation is marked by perseverance in the truth. Today we must fight again for the recognition that a growing faith, not a past decision, is the sign of the presence and power of the Spirit.

11:1–6 Paul is fighting for the faithfulness of the Corinthians because of their current temptation to commit spiritual adultery. Paul's portrayal of the Corinthians as engaged to Christ in v. 2 recalls the OT representation of Israel as being wedded to God. Paul is jealous with a "*godly* jealousy" (v. 2, emphasis added) for the Corinthians. The reference to the fall reveals just how serious the danger facing the Corinthians really is. It is a warning that, in reality, Paul's opponents are servants of Satan who are seeking to destroy the Corinthians' marriage with Christ in the same way that Satan spoiled Eve's relationship with God.

That his opponents preach "another Jesus" (v. 4) is clearly revealed in their refusal to take up their cross on behalf of the Corinthians. Rather than following in Jesus' footsteps, they assert their superiority. The Corinthians gladly "put up" with such mistreatment because the opponents' "Jesus" promises the power of the Spirit over all sickness and financial want to those who will accept their gospel. However, to do so is to reject the true Jesus and Spirit as first preached by Paul.

The "super-apostles" of v. 5 and 12:11 should not be equated with the false apostles of 11:4 or vv. 13–15. Paul is the one who represents the apostolic tradition. Even if he is an amateur in the art of professional rhetoric, because of God's leading his knowledge of the gospel is on par with any of the apostles.

11:7–15 Paul returns to the theme of his self-support in vv. 7–12. His refusal to solicit support from the Corinthians could be viewed as casting an aspersion on his teaching: He gives his gospel away because nobody will pay for it.

At the same time, Paul's self-support is an offense to the pride of the Corinthians, who most likely want to be viewed as Paul's benefactors or patrons with him as their client. But as an apostle, Paul is their patron, representing his true patron, Jesus Christ.

11:10–11 These two oath formulas reinforce Paul's resolve to continue his boast of preaching the gospel for free in Achaia. No criticism can stop him from doing so (cf. v. 7), since his boast is an expression of the truth of Christ in his life. There is

12And I will keep on doing what I am
doing in order to cut the ground from
under those who want an opportunity to
be considered equal with us in the things
they boast about. 13For such people are
false apostles,[y] deceitful[z] workers, masquerading as apostles of Christ.[a] 14And no
wonder, for Satan himself masquerades
as an angel of light. 15It is not surprising,
then, if his servants also masquerade as
servants of righteousness. Their end will
be what their actions deserve.[b]

Paul Boasts About His Sufferings

16I repeat: Let no one take me for a fool.[c]
But if you do, then tolerate me just as
you would a fool, so that I may do a little
boasting. 17In this self-confident boasting
I am not talking as the Lord would,[d] but
as a fool. 18Since many are boasting in the
way the world does, I too will boast.[e] 19You
gladly put up with fools since you are so
wise![f] 20In fact, you even put up with anyone who enslaves you[g] or exploits you
or takes advantage of you or puts on airs
or slaps you in the face. 21To my shame
I admit that we were too weak[h] for that!

Whatever anyone else dares to boast
about — I am speaking as a fool — I also
dare to boast about.[i] 22Are they Hebrews?
So am I.[j] Are they Israelites? So am I.[k]
Are they Abraham's descendants? So
am I. 23Are they servants of Christ? (I
am out of my mind to talk like this.) I
am more. I have worked much harder,[l]

11:13 [y] 2Pe 2:1 [z] Titus 1:10 [a] Rev 2:2
11:15 [b] Php 3:19
11:16 [c] ver 1
11:17 [d] 1Co 7:12, 25
11:18 [e] Php 3:3,4
11:19 [f] 1Co 4:10
11:20 [g] Gal 2:4
11:21 [h] 2Co 10:1, 10 [i] Php 3:4
11:22 [j] Php 3:5 [k] Ro 9:4
11:23 [l] 1Co 15:10 [m] Ac 16:23; 2Co 6:4,5
11:24 [n] Dt 25:3
11:25 [o] Ac 16:22 [p] Ac 14:19
11:26 [q] Ac 9:23; 14:5 [r] Ac 21:31 [s] Gal 2:4
11:27 [t] 1Co 4:11, 12; 2Co 6:5
11:30 [u] 1Co 2:3
11:31 [v] Ro 9:5

2Co 11:23–28 ❖ How do Paul's trials give credibility to his devotion? What are we willing to endure for Christ?

been in prison more frequently,[m] been
flogged more severely, and been exposed to death again and again. 24Five
times I received from the Jews the forty
lashes[n] minus one. 25Three times I was
beaten with rods,[o] once I was pelted with
stones,[p] three times I was shipwrecked,
I spent a night and a day in the open
sea, 26I have been constantly on the
move. I have been in danger from rivers, in danger from bandits, in danger
from my fellow Jews,[q] in danger from
Gentiles; in danger in the city,[r] in danger in the country, in danger at sea; and
in danger from false believers.[s] 27I have
labored and toiled and have often gone
without sleep; I have known hunger and
thirst and have often gone without food;[t]
I have been cold and naked. 28Besides
everything else, I face daily the pressure
of my concern for all the churches. 29Who
is weak, and I do not feel weak? Who is
led into sin, and I do not inwardly burn?

30If I must boast, I will boast of the
things that show my weakness.[u] 31The
God and Father of the Lord Jesus, who is
to be praised forever,[v] knows that I am
not lying. 32In Damascus the governor
under King Aretas had the city of the
Damascenes guarded in order to arrest

---

a second reason why Paul will not stop supporting himself in Corinth. Paul's preaching for free makes it impossible for his opponents to compare their missionary practice favorably with his own. In so doing, it removes their "ground" (v. 12).

11:12 Paul goes on the offensive by turning his opponents' criticism on its head and exposing it for what it really is: an attempt to get Paul to compromise his convictions so that they will not look so bad by comparison.

11:13–14 Paul must set himself up as the standard for true apostleship because of the deceptive nature of his opponents, who are "masquerading as apostles of Christ" (v. 13). Paul is not surprised by this since Satan too "masquerades as an angel of light" (v. 14).

11:16–21a Again, desperate situations demand desperate measures. But Paul hesitates yet again in this passage to make it clear just how inappropriate such boasting is. Nevertheless, Paul feels compelled to conform to such boasting to win back the Corinthians since they are gladly bearing with Paul's opponents, who are the real fools (vv. 18–19a).

The abuse the Corinthians have suffered from the false apostles confirms why they are not wise but fools for accepting his opponents.

11:21b–23b In vv. 22–23b Paul matches his opponents' foolish boast element for element. If heritage makes one an apostle, then Paul can claim the heritage of the most respected Jewish apostles. Nobody can top Paul's well-known pedigree and his former life of zeal for the law and the Pharisaic traditions. But this way of arguing is madness. It denies the very basis of apostolic authority itself: the call of the risen Christ to take on the character of the crucified Christ.

11:23c–33 Because of the absurd and sinful nature of such boasting in oneself, Paul abruptly cuts it short and turns to the suffering outlined in vv. 23c–33 as the real proof and basis of his apostleship. Paul's various arrests, imprisonments, and punishments referred to in vv. 23c–26 were suffered as an apostle for the gospel.

Of special note is the fact that within Paul's listing of his various dangers, "in danger from false believers" stands alone and unpaired at the foot of the list. By calling special attention in this way to the danger posed by false brothers as the climax of all his dangers, Paul subtly reminds the Corinthians of the serious peril they are now facing by embracing his opponents.

Paul's catalog of affliction reaches its climax not with any of his specific sufferings but with a reference to the "daily . . . pressure of [his] concern for

me.[w] 33But I was lowered in a basket from
a window in the wall and slipped through
his hands.[x]

Paul's Vision and His Thorn

12 I must go on boasting.[y] Although
there is nothing to be gained, I will
go on to visions and revelations[z] from the
Lord. 2I know a man in Christ who fourteen years ago was caught up[a] to the third
heaven.[b] Whether it was in the body or out
of the body I do not know — God knows.[c]
3And I know that this man — whether
in the body or apart from the body I do
not know, but God knows — 4was caught
up to paradise[d] and heard inexpressible
things, things that no one is permitted to
tell. 5I will boast about a man like that,
but I will not boast about myself, except
about my weaknesses. 6Even if I should
choose to boast, I would not be a fool,[e] because I would be speaking the truth. But
I refrain, so no one will think more of me
than is warranted by what I do or say, 7or
because of these surpassingly great revelations. Therefore, in order to keep me
from becoming conceited, I was given a
thorn in my flesh,[f] a messenger of Satan,
to torment me. 8Three times I pleaded
with the Lord to take it away from me.[g]
9But he said to me, "My grace is sufficient
for you, for my power[h] is made perfect
in weakness." Therefore I will boast all
the more gladly about my weaknesses,
so that Christ's power may rest on me.
10That is why, for Christ's sake, I delight
in weaknesses, in insults, in hardships,[i]
in persecutions,[j] in difficulties. For when
I am weak, then I am strong.[k]

11:32 [w] Ac 9:24
11:33 [x] Ac 9:25
12:1 [y] 2Co 11:16, 30 [z] ver 7
12:2 [a] Ac 8:39 [b] Eph 4:10 [c] 2Co 11:11
12:4 [d] Lk 23:43; Rev 2:7
12:6 [e] 2Co 11:16
12:7 [f] Nu 33:55
12:8 [g] Mt 26:39, 44
12:9 [h] Php 4:13
12:10 [i] 2Co 6:4 [j] Ro 5:3; 2Th 1:4 [k] 2Co 13:4

2Co 12:9 ❖ How is Christ's power displayed in human weakness? In what ways has Christ shown the sufficiency of his grace in the midst of your struggles?

---

all the churches" (v. 28). This pressure is brought about by his identification with the weak and by his indignation over those who lead others into sin (v. 29). Paul is "weak" because of his willingness to identify with those to whom he has been sent with the gospel. The counterpart to Paul's weakness is his strong anger over the thought of someone's falling away from Christ.

Paul's argument concludes with the principle stated in v. 30: If forced to boast, he will do so only in his weaknesses. To illustrate his boast one last time, Paul recalls his experience in Damascus after his conversion when he escaped. This was the initial example of his weakness as an apostle. As such, it stands in stark contrast to the "strength" to persecute the believers—the same foolish "strength" his opponents boast about (v. 22).

❖ **11:1–33** Paul's example drives us to ask why, when we "advertise" our churches, we do not "promote" the death of Christ for sinners, boast in God in what we say and do, highlight our own weaknesses, and call attention to the voluntary suffering of our role models? Why do we seek instead to portray an image of ourselves as successful and "normal"? The goal of ministry is not attaining numerical growth but rather fostering a growing experience of depending on Christ's grace and power, knowing that the One who gives the grace receives the glory, which is God's own purpose in all that he does as the Giver of all things.

12:1–6 This is the only reference to a "vision" or "visions" within Paul's writings, and only here and in the parallel reference in v. 7 do we find the plural "revelations." Paul's hesitancy to boast in his visions is reflected in his use of the third person to describe his own being caught up into heaven.
12:2–4 The experience Paul describes was a personal rapture into the "third heaven." Paul's reference is to the highest spiritual realm, where one encounters the very presence of God.
12:5–6 Paul concludes in v. 5 that there is nothing to be gained by self-promotion based on private experiences. Accordingly, Paul restrains himself from such boasting so that no one will brag about him *beyond what can be evaluated objectively*.
12:7–10 Paul's restraint was not the result of his own moral willpower. In v. 7b, he makes it clear that God kept him from such conceit by granting him "a thorn in [or against his] flesh," that is, "a messenger of Satan" sent to batter or torment him.

The exact nature of this "thorn" or satanic messenger has been a matter of much debate. Paul's "thorn in the flesh" and the parallel reference to his "weakness" in v. 9 are often taken to refer to personal illness. The other options are to understand them as referring to his inner temptations or to his being persecuted by his opponents. Those who favor this last view advocate a parallel between the "messenger of Satan" in v. 7 and the "servants" of Satan in 11:15. They point to the use of the image of a "thorn" in Nu 33:55 and Eze 28:24 to refer to the enemies of Israel.

Paul is interested in this thorn's theological origin (sent by Satan but given by God), in its cause (Paul's great revelations), and in its purpose (to afflict Paul in order to keep him from becoming conceited). In 2Co 12:7, Paul therefore turns his opponents' argument on its head. The more they call attention to Paul's weaknesses, the more they point to the exalted nature of his revelations.

The revelation of Christ's power in Paul's weakness (v. 9b) and Paul's resulting contentment (v. 10a) form the high point of his argument in this passage and, in doing so, provide a summary of the theological substructure of 2 Corinthians as a whole.

Paul's strength in v. 10b is derived from his divinely granted ability to endure adversity for

Paul's Concern for the Corinthians

11 I have made a fool of myself,[l] but you
drove me to it. I ought to have been commended by you, for I am not in the least
inferior to the "super-apostles,"[am] even
though I am nothing.[n] 12 I persevered in
demonstrating among you the marks of
a true apostle, including signs, wonders
and miracles.[o] 13 How were you inferior
to the other churches, except that I was
never a burden to you?[p] Forgive me this
wrong![q]

14 Now I am ready to visit you for the
third time,[r] and I will not be a burden
to you, because what I want is not your
possessions but you. After all, children
should not have to save up for their parents,[s] but parents for their children.[t] 15 So
I will very gladly spend for you everything I have and expend myself as well.[u]
If I love you more, will you love me less?
16 Be that as it may, I have not been a burden to you.[v] Yet, crafty fellow that I am,
I caught you by trickery! 17 Did I exploit
you through any of the men I sent to
you? 18 I urged[w] Titus to go to you and I
sent our brother[x] with him. Titus did not
exploit you, did he? Did we not walk in
the same footsteps by the same Spirit?

19 Have you been thinking all along
that we have been defending ourselves
to you? We have been speaking in the
sight of God[y] as those in Christ; and everything we do, dear friends, is for your
strengthening.[z] 20 For I am afraid that
when I come[a] I may not find you as I
want you to be, and you may not find me
as you want me to be.[b] I fear that there
may be discord,[c] jealousy, fits of rage,
selfish ambition,[d] slander, gossip,[e] arrogance and disorder.[f] 21 I am afraid that
when I come again my God will humble
me before you, and I will be grieved[g]
over many who have sinned earlier[h] and
have not repented of the impurity, sexual sin and debauchery in which they
have indulged.

Final Warnings

13 This will be my third visit to you.[i]
"Every matter must be established

12:11 [l] 2Co 11:1 [m] 2Co 11:5 [n] 1Co 15:9,10
12:12 [o] Jn 4:48
12:13 [p] 1Co 9:12, 18 [q] 2Co 11:7
12:14 [r] 2Co 13:1 [s] 1Co 4:14,15 [t] Pr 19:14
12:15 [u] Php 2:17; 1Th 2:8
12:16 [v] 2Co 11:9
12:18 [w] 2Co 8:6, 16 [x] 2Co 8:18
12:19 [y] Ro 9:1 [z] 2Co 10:8
12:20 [a] 2Co 2:1-4 [b] 1Co 4:21 [c] 1Co 1:11; 3:3 [d] Gal 5:20 [e] Ro 1:29 [f] 1Co 14:33
12:21 [g] 2Co 2:1,4 [h] 2Co 13:2
13:1 [i] 2Co 12:14

[a] 11 Or *the most eminent apostles*

---

the sake of the gospel. To boast in his weakness is, at the same time, to boast in what the Lord is doing by his grace and power.

12:11–13 The Corinthians themselves should have recognized Paul as of equal standing with the eminent apostles of the church. If Paul is comparing himself to those who were apostles before him, he is reminding the Corinthians what he taught them in 1Co 15:8–9.

In 2Co 12:12, Paul supports his assertion of equality by affirming that the "marks of a true apostle" had also accompanied his ministry. God performed signs through Paul, thereby accrediting his ministry.

Paul did not treat the Corinthians as inferior to any other church since he brought them the same gospel that the apostles did. Paul acknowledges that the *only* way in which he treated the Corinthians as "inferior" to other churches was that he did not "burden" them financially (v. 13b; cf. 2:17). However, the only one who has been wronged in this scenario is Paul himself.

✣ **12:1–13** Paul's boasting in his weakness challenges our very definition of spirituality. In view of Christ's own death and resurrection, we should not consider it strange that our greatest experiences of Christ's grace and power often come through our experiences of suffering and difficulties. Indeed, Paul's testimony that Christ's "power is made perfect in weakness" (v. 9) has been confirmed throughout the ages. In the end, Paul's boast in his weakness calls us to trust in the sufficiency of Christ today.

12:14–21 Unlike his opponents, Paul is not interested in benefiting financially from the Corinthians. Instead, he "wants" the Corinthians themselves (v. 14b).

12:14b–15a Paul returns to the imagery of parenthood to describe his relationship with the church. Because he is their spiritual father, Paul gives to his "children," not the other way around.

12:15b Paul uses a rhetorical question to draw the only conclusion that can possibly follow from this concrete evidence of his fatherly love toward the Corinthians. Paul's loving them "more" than his opponents by refusing to take their money should not cause the Corinthians to love him "less" than those who *demand* their money.

12:16–18 Paul presses home his point. Those Corinthians who are still rebelling against him must now make a final decision. Titus's careful handling of the money and Paul's sending of the well-respected "brother" to Corinth also speak against his opponents' accusation (vv. 17–18).

12:19 Paul's rhetorical questions continue. His defense is not a *self*-defense before them at all (v. 19a). Paul has not been seeking the approval of the Corinthians but fighting to strengthen their faith (v. 19c).

12:20–21 Paul's concern is for the rebels who have not yet repented. God will condemn them through Paul's hand. This is what Paul means by the reference in v. 20 to his not finding the Corinthians as he wants them to be when he returns. Those whom Paul does not find repentant when he comes this "third time" (v. 14) will not find him willing to withdraw yet again in order to spare them.

13:1–10 Paul refers to the legal requirements from Dt 19:15 for accepting evidence in a trial. When he arrives, he will make his case against his opponents and those who follow them. All those found

by the testimony of two or three witnesses."[a][j] 2 I already gave you a warning when I was with you the second time. I now repeat it while absent: On my return I will not spare[k] those who sinned earlier[l] or any of the others, 3 since you are demanding proof that Christ is speaking through me.[m] He is not weak in dealing with you, but is powerful among you. 4 For to be sure, he was crucified in weakness,[n] yet he lives by God's power.[o] Likewise, we are weak[p] in him, yet by God's power we will live with him in our dealing with you.

5 Examine yourselves[q] to see whether you are in the faith; test yourselves.[r] Do you not realize that Christ Jesus is in you[s]—unless, of course, you fail the test? 6 And I trust that you will discover that we have not failed the test. 7 Now we pray to God that you will not do anything wrong—not so that people will see that we have stood the test but so that you will do what is right even though we may seem to have failed. 8 For we cannot do anything against the truth, but only for the truth. 9 We are glad whenever we are weak but you are strong; and our prayer is that you may be fully restored.[t] 10 This is why I write these things when I am absent, that when I come I may not have to be harsh in my use of authority—the authority the Lord gave me for building you up, not for tearing you down.[u]

2Co 13:11 ❖ How can we find encouragement for living our lives in a godly way in Paul's final words to the Corinthians in this letter?

Final Greetings

11 Finally, brothers and sisters,[v] rejoice! Strive for full restoration, encourage one another, be of one mind, live in peace.[w] And the God of love and peace[x] will be with you.

12 Greet one another with a holy kiss.[y] 13 All God's people here send their greetings.[z]

14 May the grace of the Lord Jesus Christ,[a] and the love of God,[b] and the fellowship of the Holy Spirit[c] be with you all.

[a] *1* Deut. 19:15

13:1 [j] Dt 19:15; Mt 18:16
13:2 [k] 2Co 1:23 [l] 2Co 12:21
13:3 [m] Mt 10:20; 1Co 5:4
13:4 [n] Php 2:7, 8; 1Pe 3:18 [o] Ro 1:4; 6:4 [p] ver 9
13:5 [q] 1Co 11:28 [r] Jn 6:6 [s] Ro 8:10
13:9 [t] ver 11
13:10 [u] 2Co 10:8
13:11 [v] 1Th 4:1; 2Th 3:1 [w] Mk 9:50 [x] Ro 15:33; Eph 6:23
13:12 [y] Ro 16:16
13:13 [z] Php 4:22
13:14 [a] Ro 16:20; 2Co 8:9 [b] Ro 5:5; Jude 21 [c] Php 2:1

---

guilty will be punished. This is, of course, a harsh declaration.

13:3–4 The theological foundation of Paul's warning, unfolded throughout chs. 10–13, is crystallized here. When he arrives, Paul will not spare the Corinthians. If they want to see the power of Christ, then it will come in judgment, even as the return of the risen Christ will mean the judgment of the world.

The parallels established between Christ and Paul in 13:4 show how Christ's power is made perfect in Paul's ministry. His primary purpose is to mediate the knowledge of God and the transforming power of the life-giving Spirit (2:14—3:18; 4:1-15). This is the way in which Paul usually mediates the power of Christ's resurrection.

13:5 In view of Paul's imminent return to bring God's judgment to Corinth, his commands again contain a severe warning. Paul announces the coming judgment in advance to bring about the repentance of God's true people. The goal of the test is to make it clear that Christ is indeed in them.

13:6 The means by which the test is performed is Paul himself. Allegiance to him as their apostle is the criterion that determines whether Christ is present in their lives. To accept *Paul's* message of reconciliation is to accept *God's* message of reconciliation.

13:7–10 The truth of the gospel will prevail over all contenders (v. 8). The apostle is glad whenever he is being led into suffering on their behalf so that, as an expression of the resurrection, they are being consoled and encouraged in their faith.

Paul takes no pleasure in having to judge the Corinthians. This is also why he is writing "these things" (v. 10)—a reference to the present letter, especially chs. 10–13.

13:11–14 Unlike other ancient letters, in which the closings were abrupt and only linked to the body of the letter in a general way, Paul expands the letter's closing significantly, echoing specific themes from his letter. Paul closes his letter with additional commands (v. 11), greetings (v. 12), and two farewell benedictions, one for peace and one for grace (vv. 11, 14). In each case, his closing highlights a main theme of his letter.

Paul's closing benediction signifies the blessing of the new covenant itself, in which the grace of Christ has made it possible to experience God's love, poured out in the Holy Spirit. It is not accidental, therefore, that Paul's letter ends with a reference to the fellowship brought about by the Spirit. The pouring out of the Spirit on God's people is *the* gift of the new covenant. So in closing, Paul prays as a minister of the new covenant that God will grant to all those in the church the unity of the Spirit that he has worked so hard to mediate (v. 14). After everything is said and done, despite all its flaws and growing pains, the church remains the temple of the living God.

✜ **12:14—13:14** The sober conclusion to this book derives not from legalism but from the life-transforming reality of Christ that Paul himself had experienced. Paul's expectations for the Corinthians are expectations for God. His admonitions to them are expressions of his confidence in what God can do in the lives of sinners. There is hope for all who trust in Christ. Perseverance is not reserved for a Christian elite but is promised to *all* who belong to God.

Galatians

Author: The apostle Paul

Audience: Churches in southern Galatia, founded by Paul during his first missionary journey, or possibly churches in northern Galatia, founded on his second or third missionary journey

Date: AD 48, or in the 50s

Theme: Paul writes to encourage the Galatian believers to reject the legalistic demands of the Judaizers and to embrace the gospel of freedom in the Spirit.

PERSPECTIVE

Why should 21st-century Christians read Galatians? What applications does it have to a church removed from its original audience by nearly two thousand years? The answer is that the book of Galatians speaks to a crucial issue facing the church today: the question of how to exercise visionary leadership.

Leading a church community today is very difficult. It is not unreasonably difficult, mind you, to grow a church, to manage the day-to-day affairs of a church, or to chair committees and task forces. True leadership, however, is another matter. It's tough to lead primarily because people don't want to be led. If the people won't follow, what's a church leader to do?

We can't turn church members into good followers overnight; it takes time to change behavior patterns so deeply entrenched. And it's questionable if more leadership skills or training programs will help. So what can we do?

Enter Paul and Galatians.

One of the major issues facing Paul in dealing with the churches of Galatia was a faction in the church that questioned his authority. He struggled with a group of people who did not want to be led. In this situation, Paul did what most of us would do: He defended himself (see chs. 1–2). Paul was human, after all. But it's instructive to note the *way* in which Paul defended himself.

Most of us would lash out angrily and then begin reviewing our list of accomplishments and reasons why our authority should not

Reading Galatians

The book of Galatians divides into three equal parts. In the first two chapters, Paul told the story of certain events that changed his life and led to his insistence that only through faith can we be restored to a right relationship with God. In the next two chapters, he primarily used the OT to defend that doctrine. In the last two chapters, he discussed the

	10 BC	AD 1	10	20	30	40	50	60	70	80	90	100
Jesus' life (c. 6/5 BC–AD 30)												
Paul's conversion (c. AD 35)												
Paul's missionary journeys (c. AD 46–67)												
Book of Galatians written (c. AD 48–53)												
Council at Jerusalem (c. AD 49/50)												
Nero's reign (AD 54–68)												
Paul's first imprisonment in Rome (c. AD 59–62)												
Paul's imprisonment and death in Rome (c. AD 67–68)												
Destruction of Jerusalem's temple (c. AD 70)												

radical implications that teaching ought to make in the Christian life.

Key Verse

No one who relies on the law is justified before God, because "the righteous will live by faith."

—Galatians 3:11

be questioned. Paul lashed out too—but not angrily. Paul did list his "accomplishments"—sort of. He listed the things in his life that he was surely ashamed of, particularly his former persecution of Christians. His intent was to show the marvelous reversal that had come about when God touched his life. He used his own weakness to show God's strength.

Thus, when Paul defended his authority, he admitted he had none of his own. He claimed his standing came only from God, not from other human beings. And when he defended the content of his preaching, he did not cite its theological coherence and trustworthiness. In fact, Paul didn't talk about "doctrines" at all. He simply wrote: "My gospel is correct because of where it came from—from Jesus Christ."

Paul ended his defense by noting his call. He had not *decided* to become an apostle to the Gentiles. Rather, God called him to this task, and he could do nothing but obey. In summary, Paul argued that his effectiveness came about because of his ineffectiveness, that his authority came about because of his submission to God, that the content of his preaching could be traced solely to his reliance on Jesus Christ, and that his biggest claim to fame was that he once was a sinner but now was saved.

It was this approach to visionary leadership that enabled Paul to confront the burning question of Galatians: the relationship of the Mosaic Law to the gospel of Jesus Christ. Paul challenged the Galatians' mistaken understanding of the law. They were, in effect, creating a new gospel. Had Paul been content to focus on leadership technique and style and to list his leadership accomplishments in the standard way, he would have been implicitly using the same methodology as the "Judaizers." Instead, at every possible point, Paul pointed away from himself toward Jesus Christ. That is the essence of God-centered visionary leadership.

TAKING THE NEXT STEPS

Paul wrote his letter perhaps from Corinth (Ac 18:11), and probably to the churches in the Roman province of Galatia founded on his first missionary journey (Ac 13:13—14:25). The heart of Paul's gospel preaching was that God justifies us by grace through faith in Jesus Christ, not by any works of the law. In fact, Christ has set us free from the law, so that we now serve the Lord spontaneously by his Spirit. Because some Jewish Christians challenged the content of his preaching, he used this letter to defend his message.

From Paul's message we receive a variety of practical insights into the Christian life. (1) For God to accept us as sinless and therefore fit for heaven, we must simply believe in the Lord Jesus Christ; we can never earn our own way into heaven. (2) If we believe in Christ, we must consider ourselves as channels through which Christ acts. (3) Believers have the right to call God our Father. (4) Rigidly following rules and regulations (the way of legalism), in an attempt to become righteous through works, will only lead in the end to the bondage of fear and despair; true freedom comes when we joyfully accept God's gift of grace and surrender to the Spirit, who produces his fruit within us.

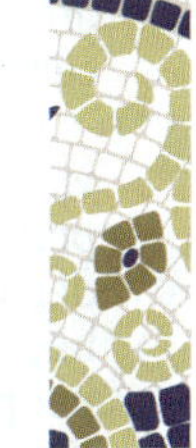

WHAT TO LOOK FOR IN GALATIANS

- Paul's conversion and early life as a Christian (ch. 1)
- The council of Jerusalem and its aftermath (ch. 2)
- Justification by faith defended from the OT (ch. 3)
- Living in freedom through the Holy Spirit (ch. 5)

1 Paul, an apostle — sent not from men
nor by a man, but by Jesus Christ[a] and
God the Father, who raised him from the
dead[b] — 2and all the brothers and sisters[a] with me,[c]

To the churches in Galatia:[d]

3Grace and peace to you from God our
Father and the Lord Jesus Christ,[e] 4who
gave himself for our sins[f] to rescue us
from the present evil age, according to
the will of our God and Father,[g] 5to whom
be glory for ever and ever. Amen.[h]

No Other Gospel

6I am astonished that you are so quickly deserting the one who called[i] you to
live in the grace of Christ and are turning

1:1 [a] Ac 9:15 [b] Ac 2:24
1:2 [c] Php 4:21 [d] Ac 16:6; 1Co 16:1
1:3 [e] Ro 1:7
1:4 [f] Mt 20:28; Ro 4:25; Gal 2:20 [g] Php 4:20
1:5 [h] Ro 11:36
1:6 [i] Gal 5:8 [j] 2Co 11:4
1:7 [k] Ac 15:24; Gal 5:10
1:8 [l] 2Co 11:4 [m] Ro 9:3

Gal 1:6-9 ❖ What is the true gospel? How do we see that gospel message being distorted around us?

to a different gospel[j] — 7which is really
no gospel at all. Evidently some people
are throwing you into confusion[k] and are
trying to pervert the gospel of Christ. 8But
even if we or an angel from heaven should
preach a gospel other than the one we
preached to you,[l] let them be under God's
curse![m] 9As we have already said, so now I
say again: If anybody is preaching to you

[a] *2* The Greek word for *brothers and sisters* (*adelphoi*) refers here to believers, both men and women, as part of God's family; also in verse 11; and in 3:15; 4:12,28,31; 5:11,13; 6:1,18.

1:1-2 Paul writes as an apostle—as one who has been called personally by Jesus Christ, who therefore represents Jesus Christ, and who has a crucial role in the history of the church.

1:3-5 The grace and peace Paul invokes upon the Galatians is "from God our Father and the Lord Jesus Christ" (v. 3). In describing the origin of the greetings, Paul goes on to comment on Jesus, saying that Jesus Christ "gave himself for our sins to rescue us from the present evil age" (v. 4). The present evil age concerned Paul because he believed that those who consistently lived in Christ would not succumb to it.

1:6-9 Paul's introduction moves next to a description of the *occasion* for the letter. Many have observed that this is the only surviving letter of Paul's that does not contain a thanksgiving for the church to whom he is writing. However, it is possible that Paul's practice of expressing thanksgiving in his letters developed later or developed out of his harsh experience at Galatia.

Paul wrote this letter because the Galatians had changed positions on a crucial subject: the means of acceptance with God and the role Christ played in that acceptance. Paul is amazed that their change took place "so quickly" (v. 6) and says that this is "really no gospel at all" (v. 7). The move of the Galatians was total and devastating. Gross perversions of the gospel are heresies. Paul's final words here are potent. He invokes a curse on anyone (including himself!) who distorts the gospel.

APPLICATION ✜ **1:1-9** If it is true that an apostle is a personal agent of Jesus Christ, then it follows that Paul's message is a message from

a gospel other than what you accepted,[n]
let them be under God's curse!
10 Am I now trying to win the approval of human beings, or of God? Or am I
trying to please people?[o] If I were still
trying to please people, I would not be
a servant of Christ.

Paul Called by God

11 I want you to know, brothers and sisters,[p] that the gospel I preached is not of
human origin. 12 I did not receive it from
any man,[q] nor was I taught it; rather, I received it by revelation[r] from Jesus Christ.
13 For you have heard of my previous
way of life in Judaism,[s] how intensely I
persecuted the church of God and tried to
destroy it.[t] 14 I was advancing in Judaism
beyond many of my own age among my
people and was extremely zealous for
the traditions of my fathers.[u] 15 But when
God, who set me apart from my mother's
womb[v] and called me[w] by his grace, was
pleased 16 to reveal his Son in me so that
I might preach him among the Gentiles,[x]
my immediate response was not to consult any human being.[y] 17 I did not go up
to Jerusalem to see those who were apostles before I was, but I went into Arabia.
Later I returned to Damascus.
18 Then after three years,[z] I went up to
Jerusalem[a] to get acquainted with Cephas[a]
and stayed with him fifteen days. 19 I saw
none of the other apostles—only James,[b]
the Lord's brother. 20 I assure you before
God that what I am writing you is no lie.[c]
21 Then I went to Syria and Cilicia.[d] 22 I
was personally unknown to the churches
of Judea[e] that are in Christ. 23 They only
heard the report: "The man who formerly persecuted us is now preaching the
faith[f] he once tried to destroy." 24 And
they praised God[g] because of me.

Paul Accepted by the Apostles

2 Then after fourteen years, I went up
again to Jerusalem,[h] this time with
Barnabas. I took Titus along also. 2 I went
in response to a revelation and, meeting

1:9 [n] Ro 16:17
1:10 [o] Ro 2:29; 1Th 2:4
1:11 [p] 1Co 15:1
1:12 [q] ver 1 [r] ver 16
1:13 [s] Ac 26:4,5 [t] Ac 8:3
1:14 [u] Mt 15:2
1:15 [v] Isa 49:1,5; Jer 1:5 [w] Ac 9:15
1:16 [x] Gal 2:9
[y] Mt 16:17
1:18 [z] Ac 9:22,23 [a] Ac 9:26,27
1:19 [b] Mt 13:55
1:20 [c] Ro 9:1
1:21 [d] Ac 6:9
1:22 [e] 1Th 2:14
1:23 [f] Ac 6:7
1:24 [g] Mt 9:8
2:1 [h] Ac 15:2

[a] *18* That is, Peter

Jesus Christ. Acknowledging this implies that every Christian must accept apostolic letters as authoritative, for their message is a message from Jesus Christ.

1:10 The opponents of Paul were bent on demonstrating that Paul's gospel came from the early Jewish apostles in Jerusalem. Paul argues that his gospel is not dependent on Jerusalem and its leaders. He does this first through a series of questions, each of which implies that he is not seeking to please human beings but God. For Paul, there is a radical difference between "trying to win the approval of human beings" and being a "servant of Christ."

1:11 What is "the gospel I preached"? There are at least three dimensions to "Paul's" gospel. First, salvation is in Jesus Christ alone. Second, one becomes accepted by God only by faith, apart from living in accordance with the Law of Moses. Finally, this acceptance is open as much to Gentiles as it is to Jews. This view threatened the very existence of Judaism and created the social crisis behind the letter.

1:12 When Paul says, "I received it by revelation from Jesus Christ," he is surely describing here his Damascus-road encounter with the risen Lord (cf. Ac 9:1–19). The term "revelation" describes something made known by God that would otherwise not be known or accessible. Direct revelation contrasts with passing on sacred traditions, which Paul's Jewish agitators relied on. Paul contends that his gospel is a direct revelation from Jesus Christ.

1:10-12 Along with Paul, we need to examine ourselves in our witnessing ministry to see if we are seeking to "win the approval of human beings" (v. 10) and succumbing to social and peer pressure. Probably no feature of life is more difficult than to discern where our own line of approval is actually going: Is it going in the direction of God, or is it being rerouted through the approval of people? When the conviction of our own faithfulness to truth and the apostolic gospel gives way to our looking for approval from another person, we have joined the ranks of those whom Paul confronts.

1:13–17 This first argument concerns Paul's independence from human teaching; he did not "consult any human being" (v. 16). Paul's description of his past focuses on the sacred traditions passed on in Judaism, the very element Paul argues against in this chapter.

1:18–24 The second argument concerns a different set of authorities. Paul moves from human teaching to the churches of Judea. Paul learned something from Peter, but he spent only a few days with him—and, he adds, only "after three years" (v. 18). Paul thus argues that his gospel came from Jesus Christ directly.

1:13–24 We have been taught that if we aim at nothing, we will hit nothing. The same applies in Christian living. It is fundamentally important for Christians to discern their gifts and to use their gifts. Paul had a clear sense of God's direction in his life; when we sense the call of God on our lives, we, like Paul, need to stick to that calling and not let distractions prevent us from fulfilling God's will for us.

2:1–3 The first unit in this next section is concerned with *Paul's presentation of his message*. Barnabas accompanied Paul to Jerusalem because he was

privately with those esteemed as leaders, I presented to them the gospel that
I preach among the Gentiles.[i] I wanted
to be sure I was not running and had not
been running my race[j] in vain. 3Yet not
even Titus,[k] who was with me, was compelled to be circumcised, even though he
was a Greek.[l] 4This matter arose because
some false believers[m] had infiltrated our
ranks to spy on[n] the freedom[o] we have in
Christ Jesus and to make us slaves. 5We
did not give in to them for a moment,
so that the truth of the gospel[p] might be
preserved for you.
6As for those who were held in high
esteem[q] — whatever they were makes
no difference to me; God does not show
favoritism[r] — they added nothing to my
message. 7On the contrary, they recognized that I had been entrusted with the
task[s] of preaching the gospel to the uncircumcised,[a][t] just as Peter[u] had been to the
circumcised.[b] 8For God, who was at work
in Peter as an apostle[v] to the circumcised,
was also at work in me as an apostle to
the Gentiles. 9James, Cephas[c][w] and John,
those esteemed as pillars,[x] gave me and
Barnabas[y] the right hand of fellowship
when they recognized the grace given
to me.[z] They agreed that we should go
to the Gentiles, and they to the circumcised. 10All they asked was that we should
continue to remember the poor,[a] the very
thing I had been eager to do all along.

2:2 [i]Ac 15:4, 12 [j]1Co 9:24; Php 2:16
2:3 [k]2Co 2:13 [l]Ac 16:3; 1Co 9:21
2:4 [m]2Co 11:26 [n]Jude 4 [o]Ac 15:1; Gal 5:1,13
2:5 [p]ver 14
2:6 [q]Gal 6:3 [r]Ac 10:34
2:7 [s]1Th 2:4; 1Ti 1:11 [t]Ac 9:15 [u]ver 9, 11, 14
2:8 [v]Ac 1:25
2:9 [w]ver 7, 11, 14 [x]1Ti 3:15 [y]Ac 4:36 [z]Ro 12:3
2:10 [a]Ac 24:17
2:11 [b]ver 7, 9, 14 [c]Ac 11:19
2:12 [d]Ac 11:3 [e]Ac 11:2
2:13 [f]ver 1; Ac 4:36
2:14 [g]ver 5 [h]ver 7, 9, 11 [i]Ac 10:28

Gal 2:11–21 ❖ How can social pressure lead even strong Christian leaders to conform to behaviors contrary to the gospel? Where might we need to be like Paul and speak up against these things? How might we avoid them ourselves?

Paul Opposes Cephas

11When Cephas[b] came to Antioch,[c] I opposed him to his face, because he stood
condemned. 12For before certain men
came from James, he used to eat with
the Gentiles.[d] But when they arrived, he
began to draw back and separate himself
from the Gentiles because he was afraid
of those who belonged to the circumcision group.[e] 13The other Jews joined him
in his hypocrisy, so that by their hypocrisy even Barnabas[f] was led astray.
14When I saw that they were not acting
in line with the truth of the gospel,[g] I
said to Cephas[h] in front of them all, "You
are a Jew, yet you live like a Gentile and
not like a Jew.[i] How is it, then, that you
force Gentiles to follow Jewish customs?

[a] 7 That is, Gentiles [b] 7 That is, Jews; also in verses 8 and 9 [c] 9 That is, Peter; also in verses 11 and 14

---

a respected person with the Jerusalem churches. Since the "pillars" (v. 9) or leaders of Jerusalem's church did not demand Titus's circumcision, it can be assumed that they did not think circumcision was necessary for salvation. Paul met "privately" with the Jerusalem leaders and "presented to them the gospel" that he preached (v. 2). Paul's gospel was both independent of, and confirmed by, Jerusalem.

2:4–5 The second unit is concerned with *the opposition to Paul's message*. Paul's response to the infiltrators (v. 5) is the theme of the entire letter.

2:6–10 The third unit is concerned with the unity expressed by the Jerusalem church's leaders and Paul over Paul's message. While Paul's gospel was independent in source, it was also *endorsed* by the Jerusalem pillars. For Paul, that endorsement was unnecessary, but he decides to use that endorsement as part of his case against his opponents.

✥ **2:1–10** Fundamental to Christian unity is the recognition of different callings and movements in the church of Christ. We need to see how varied the church is and hear how vibrantly different it is in different parts of the world.

Similarly, it is not unwise for Christians to visit other churches in their local communities to find out what God is doing in various church traditions. We may be disappointed with what we see, but frequently we will be encouraged by finding the faith of others expressed in slightly different (but just as valid) ways.

2:11 Paul publicly rebuked Peter for his hypocritical behavior because what he was doing was clearly contrary to life through Christ and in the Spirit.

2:12–13 The table that had functioned wonderfully as a symbol of unity had become a table of separation once again for Peter.

2:14 It was not wrong for Jewish missionaries to the Gentiles to be Jews who lived like Gentiles and not like Jews. But it became problematic when those same missionaries then "force[d] Gentiles to follow Jewish customs." This word "force" tips us off as to what Peter was doing.

So what was Peter doing? Peter began to force Gentile Christians to be circumcised (and to follow Jewish social laws), to reduce the threat of persecution he was beginning to feel from these committed Jewish nationalists. Peter, in effect, was destroying the gospel of Jesus Christ by demanding that the converts at Galatia become Jews.

✥ **2:11–14** The adaptations and changes that Peter's new ministry involved were difficult for

15“We who are Jews by birth[j] and not
sinful Gentiles[k] 16know that a person is
not justified by the works of the law, but
by faith in Jesus Christ.[l] So we, too, have
put our faith in Christ Jesus that we may
be justified by faith in[a] Christ and not
by the works of the law, because by the
works of the law no one will be justified.
17“But if, in seeking to be justified
in Christ, we Jews find ourselves also
among the sinners,[m] doesn’t that mean
that Christ promotes sin? Absolutely
not![n] 18If I rebuild what I destroyed, then
I really would be a lawbreaker.
19“For through the law I died to the
law[o] so that I might live for God.[p] 20I have
been crucified with Christ[q] and I no longer live, but Christ lives in me.[r] The life I now live in the body, I live by faith in the Son of God,[s] who loved me[t] and gave himself for me.[u] 21I do not set aside the
grace of God, for if righteousness could be gained through the law,[v] Christ died for nothing!”[b]

Faith or Works of the Law

3 You foolish Galatians! Who has bewitched you?[w] Before your very eyes Jesus Christ was clearly portrayed as

2:15 [j] Php 3:4,5 [k] 1Sa 15:18
2:16 [l] Ac 13:39; Ro 9:30
2:17 [m] ver 15 [n] Gal 3:21
2:19 [o] Ro 7:4 [p] Ro 6:10,11,14; 2Co 5:15
2:20 [q] Ro 6:6 [r] 1Pe 4:2 [s] Mt 4:3 [t] Ro 8:37 [u] Gal 1:4
2:21 [v] Gal 3:21
3:1 [w] Gal 5:7

[a] 16 Or *but through the faithfulness of . . . justified on the basis of the faithfulness of* [b] 21 Some interpreters end the quotation after verse 14.

---

him. He needed to learn that there had to be considerable flexibility in his new life in Christ. What was hard to accept was that this new life needed to be consistent with God’s Spirit (though perhaps not with the Law of Moses). Consistency is measured by listening to God’s word, to Christ, and to the Spirit of God.

2:15–16 As privileged Jews, Peter and Paul came to the conviction to “know that a person is not justified by the works of the law, but by faith in Jesus Christ” (v. 16). In what follows, we need to analyze three crucial terms for understanding this passage: *justification*, *works of the law*, and *faith*.

Broadly speaking, *justification* is a metaphor of our acceptance with God drawn from the courtroom. People are guilty because they have transgressed God’s law. Their only hope is that God, perceived in this metaphor as judge, will somehow forgive them, make things right, and eliminate their guilt. God is altogether morally righteous and cannot simply overlook sin. But God surprisingly forgives. His agent in this forgiveness is Jesus Christ, who legally assumed our guilt and bore the curse of the law in his crucifixion (3:13). The result of Christ’s work is that humans who trust in Christ and surrender themselves to him are declared innocent before God and fit to be in relationship with him.

What are the *works of the law*? Paul must have in mind two ideas. First, he means believing that acceptance with God is found through submission to the Law of Moses. Second, he means behavior that separates Jews from Gentiles—circumcision, food restrictions, and social regulations governing the behavior of Jews as they relate to Gentiles.

Paul knew that conversion to Christ implied a confession that a proper standing before God could not be had through a commitment to the law. Christ was the fulfillment of the law and in fact went beyond it in his revelation (Ro 10:4; Gal 3:19–25). On the other hand, Paul is not against “good works.” There was nothing wrong with living according to the law when it was done properly (Ac 16:3; 21:26). But when one obeyed the law to express one’s confidence in it as a necessary step for ultimate acceptance by God, Paul took exception.

There is also the idea of *good works* as an attractive, moral, and godly lifestyle. The “fruit of the Spirit” (Gal 5:22–23) is a description of “good works.” This kind of works is the primary way Paul thinks Christians should live.

Justification comes to a person *by faith*, not by observing the law. We may define faith as *the initial and continual response of trust in, and obedience to, Christ by a person for the purpose of acceptance with God.* When Paul uses the term “faith,” he is describing both the initial act of trust and the believer’s continuing disposition of trust and obedience.

2:17–21 There are three implications of this common conversion. First, the life of the Christian is not a “lawless” life in the sense of wicked rejection of OT laws and teachings (v. 17). Paul’s emphasis here is that life in Christ is not life in sin. Rather, life in Christ, as he will elaborate in chs. 5–6, is life in the Spirit.

Second, in converting to Christ, the Christian, especially the Jewish Christian, forfeits the opportunity of ever returning to the Law of Moses as the primary orientation governing all of life (v. 18).

Third, in converting to Christ, the Jewish Christian finds spiritual life through death, understood here as being crucified with Christ to the law so that the resurrected Christ might grant his new life to the believer (vv. 19–21). The life that Paul, as a Jewish Christian, now lives for God is the result of dying with Christ (v. 20). Yet also the life Paul now lives is a life of the indwelling Christ and the indwelling Holy Spirit.

2:15–21 It is common today to hear that the only requirement for salvation is to “believe that Jesus Christ saves.” This is true—if properly defined. Jesus is indeed the Savior, but in order for him to become the Savior for a given person, that person must surrender himself or herself in trust and obedience for true faith to be expressed.

3:1 The Galatians were illogical to accept Paul’s message of God’s grace and then yield to the Jewish agitators’ insistence on keeping the Law of Moses. Paul appeals to their conversion experience.

Gal 3:3 ❖ Are we tempted to rely on our own efforts in our faith? Why or why not?

crucified.[x] 2I would like to learn just one
thing from you: Did you receive the Spirit
by the works of the law, or by believing
what you heard?[y] 3Are you so foolish?
After beginning by means of the Spirit,
are you now trying to finish by means
of the flesh?[a] 4Have you experienced[b] so
much in vain—if it really was in vain?
5So again I ask, does God give you his
Spirit and work miracles[z] among you by
the works of the law, or by your believing what you heard? 6So also Abraham
"believed God, and it was credited to him
as righteousness."[ca]
7Understand, then, that those who
have faith[b] are children of Abraham.
8Scripture foresaw that God would justify the Gentiles by faith, and announced
the gospel in advance to Abraham: "All
nations will be blessed through you."[dc]
9So those who rely on faith[d] are blessed
along with Abraham, the man of faith.
10For all who rely on the works of the
law are under a curse, as it is written:
"Cursed is everyone who does not continue to do everything written in the Book
of the Law."[ee] 11Clearly no one who relies
on the law is justified before God, because
"the righteous will live by faith."[ff] 12The
law is not based on faith; on the contrary,
it says, "The person who does these things
will live by them."[gg] 13Christ redeemed us
from the curse of the law[h] by becoming
a curse for us, for it is written: "Cursed is
everyone who is hung on a pole."[hi] 14He redeemed us in order that the blessing giv-
en to Abraham might come to the Gentiles
through Christ Jesus,[j] so that by faith we
might receive the promise of the Spirit.[k]

3:1 [x] 1Co 1:23
3:2 [y] Ro 10:17
3:5 [z] 1Co 12:10
3:6 [a] Ge 15:6; Ro 4:3
3:7 [b] ver 9
3:8 [c] Ge 12:3; Ac 3:25
3:9 [d] ver 7; Ro 4:16
3:10 [e] Dt 27:26; Jer 11:3
3:11 [f] Hab 2:4; Gal 2:16; Heb 10:38
3:12 [g] Lev 18:5; Ro 10:5
3:13 [h] Gal 4:5 [i] Dt 21:23; Ac 5:30
3:14 [j] Ro 4:9, 16 [k] ver 2; Joel 2:28; Ac 2:33

[a] *3* In contexts like this, the Greek word for *flesh* (*sarx*) refers to the sinful state of human beings, often presented as a power in opposition to the Spirit. [b] *4* Or *suffered* [c] *6* Gen. 15:6 [d] *8* Gen. 12:3; 18:18; 22:18 [e] *10* Deut. 27:26 [f] *11* Hab. 2:4 [g] *12* Lev. 18:5 [h] *13* Deut. 21:23

3:2 Paul wants to know: How did the Galatians get the Spirit? The real issue here is *how the experience took place and what triggered it.*

3:3 To live in the "flesh" is to ignore the Spirit. Paul may be thinking partly in terms of circumcision.

3:4 After their conversion to Christ, the Galatians experienced persecution. So, he asks, was this all worthless?

3:5 By now, the Galatians must be hiding in shame or continuing the Jewish agitators' arguments by appealing to Scripture, which Paul refutes.

✣ **3:1–5** Experience is an integral part of all our lives. We can learn from this passage that arguments from experience can be a part of our theological argumentation when we present the gospel or consider its implications for our lives. But we cannot think our appeals to experience are all that we need. Contextual reading of Paul's argument from experience shows that Paul did not stop there; he went on to arguments from Scripture and logic. And so should we. Our arguments from experience have no truth backing them if they are nothing more than that.

3:6–7 Paul's emphasis is that Abraham was pronounced as acceptable to God *before his circumcision.* Therefore circumcision was not necessary for acceptance with God. For Paul, Abraham's descendants are those who simply believe; they are not those who believe and allow themselves to be circumcised.

3:8–9 Having argued that Abraham was accepted by God because of his faith and that the true descendants of Abraham are believers, Paul argues that *Gentiles* can be these true believers.

3:10–11 Those who opt for the law are cursed because they are choosing to omit the salvation that can come only through faith in Christ. The law can only condemn; it cannot save.

3:12 The law is not a system governed by faith but rather by doing. Therefore the Law of Moses is not a faith system. This is critical for our perception of Paul's logic.

3:13 Paul argues that the curse of the law fell on Christ so others might escape. The term "redeemed" is drawn from the commercial world. Those who trust in Christ's ransom price are set free from enslavement to sin and the curse of the law.

Christ died the death of a transgressor. Because he was innocent and sinless, he could die on behalf of those who have sinned and so absorb their curse. And because he was divine, he could perfectly satisfy the justice of God (see Ro 3:21–26).

3:14 The redemption Christ accomplished freed Jewish Christians (Jews who believe) from the curse of the law and also made it possible for Gentiles to be incorporated into Abraham's blessing. Furthermore, now the new people of God (both Jewish and Gentile) can "receive the promise of the Spirit."

✣ **3:6–14** The gospel is for everyone, and therefore social barriers must be broken down by the gospel. We find that the principle that Paul is using is that God loves "all kinds of people" and works with "all kinds"; therefore, the church cannot construct barriers to prevent the inclusion of only "some kinds." We must constantly explore the implications of this message for the church today and allow ourselves to be challenged by it if we are to remain faithful to Paul's gospel.

The Law and the Promise

15 Brothers and sisters, let me take an
example from everyday life. Just as no
one can set aside or add to a human covenant that has been duly established, so
it is in this case. 16 The promises were
spoken to Abraham and to his seed.[l]
Scripture does not say "and to seeds,"
meaning many people, but "and to
your seed,"[a] meaning one person, who
is Christ. 17 What I mean is this: The
law, introduced 430 years[m] later, does
not set aside the covenant previously
established by God and thus do away
with the promise. 18 For if the inheritance
depends on the law, then it no longer
depends on the promise;[n] but God in
his grace gave it to Abraham through
a promise.
19 Why, then, was the law given at all?
It was added because of transgressions[o]
until the Seed[p] to whom the promise
referred had come. The law was given
through angels[q] and entrusted to a mediator.[r] 20 A mediator,[s] however, implies
more than one party; but God is one.
21 Is the law, therefore, opposed to the
promises of God? Absolutely not![t] For if
a law had been given that could impart
life, then righteousness would certainly
have come by the law.[u] 22 But Scripture
has locked up everything under the control of sin,[v] so that what was promised,
being given through faith in Jesus Christ,
might be given to those who believe.

Children of God

23 Before the coming of this faith,[b] we
were held in custody[w] under the law, locked
up until the faith that was to come would
be revealed. 24 So the law was our guardian
until Christ came[x] that we might be justified by faith.[y] 25 Now that this faith has
come, we are no longer under a guardian.
26 So in Christ Jesus you are all children
of God[z] through faith, 27 for all of you who

3:16 [l] Lk 1:55; Ro 4:13,16
3:17 [m] Ge 15:13, 14; Ex 12:40
3:18 [n] Ro 4:14
3:19 [o] Ro 5:20 [p] ver 16 [q] Ac 7:53 [r] Ex 20:19
3:20 [s] Heb 8:6; 9:15; 12:24
3:21 [t] Gal 2:17 [u] Gal 2:21
3:22 [v] Ro 3:9-19; 11:32
3:23 [w] Ro 11:32
3:24 [x] Ro 10:4 [y] Gal 2:16
3:26 [z] Ro 8:14

[a] *16* Gen. 12:7; 13:15; 24:7 [b] *22,23* Or *through the faithfulness of Jesus . . . 23 Before faith came*

3:15–16 A human covenant operates the same way as a divine covenant does. By stating that Christ is the "seed" (v. 16), Paul interprets Ge 13:15 and Ge 24:7 in a Christian manner and reveals that the Abrahamic covenant is the one that reaches its peak in Christ and those who believe in him.
3:17 Paul's point is quite simple: the Law of Moses was given 430 years (Ex 12:40–42) after the covenant was made with Abraham. Since the covenant made with Abraham is irrevocable, the law cannot change the arrangements God made with Abraham.
3:18 God did not require Abraham to obey the law. In fact, as Paul has shown, the law was not even around; it came 430 years later. This must mean that the way to inherit the blessing of Abraham is the way Abraham received it: by faith in God's promises.

3:15–18 We read the Bible for personal blessing, personal guidance, and personal instruction, and we should. But sometimes our individual desires express an egocentric approach to life and Bible reading that need to be checked against the historic truths of the Bible.

3:19–20 The question Paul raises ("Why, then, was the law given at all?") is easy to understand (v. 19). His answer, however, takes some unraveling. First, Paul answers the question by stating the purpose of the law (v. 19b). It was given to reveal certain kinds of behavior as sinful. Second, the law was to govern God's people only until Messiah had come. Finally, Paul infers that an arrangement between a person and God that has mediators is inferior to an arrangement that has no mediators, because the latter arrangement is directly from God.
3:21a–b Is the law working against the purposes of God in the Abrahamic promise (v. 21a)? Paul's answer is simple: "Absolutely not!" (v. 21b).
3:21c–25 Paul then talks about the essential inability of the law to bring saving life (v. 21c). The function of the law (v. 22a) was to reveal sin (cf. v. 19). At v. 19 Paul had said that the law was to reveal sin until the Seed had come; now he says the same thing but uses different expressions for both elements. The law held those under it as prisoners and locked them up (v. 23). The expression "guardian" in v. 24a describes a time of children being enslaved, and "until Christ" means that the law had a confining ministry until the era of Christ came.

Paul turns to the result of the law's effect (v. 24b). Now that Paul has shown that the law pertains to a limited time, he can say that justification is solely by faith because "works of the law" now pertain to a past era.

Finally, Paul draws it all together by speaking of the suspension of the law (v. 25). Everything the law wanted to be is found now in Christ and in life in the Spirit. Thus, when a Christian lives in Christ and the Spirit, that Christian is living in transcendence of the law.

3:19–25 Christians seeking God's will do not turn first to the Law of Moses for direction. Instead, they listen to God's Spirit and study the teachings of Jesus; both teach them that they are to love God and love others. In following Christ and the Spirit, the Christian will actually do God's will.

3:26 Being a child of God describes that special relationship of intimacy that the people of God can have with God.
3:27 Since Christ is the Son of God, being united with him and "clothing ourselves" with him is what sonship is all about.

were baptized into Christ[a] have clothed
yourselves with Christ.[b] 28There is neither
Jew nor Gentile, neither slave nor free,[c]
nor is there male and female, for you are
all one in Christ Jesus.[d] 29If you belong to
Christ,[e] then you are Abraham's seed, and
heirs according to the promise.[f]

4 What I am saying is that as long as
an heir is underage, he is no different
from a slave, although he owns the whole
estate. 2The heir is subject to guardians
and trustees until the time set by his father. 3So also, when we were underage, we
were in slavery[g] under the elemental spiritual forces[a] of the world.[h] 4But when the
set time had fully come,[i] God sent his Son,
born of a woman,[j] born under the law,[k] 5to
redeem those under the law, that we might
receive adoption[l] to sonship.[b] 6Because you
are his sons, God sent the Spirit of his Son
into our hearts,[m] the Spirit who calls out,
"Abba,[c] Father."[n] 7So you are no longer a
slave, but God's child; and since you are
his child, God has made you also an heir.[o]

Paul's Concern for the Galatians

8Formerly, when you did not know
God,[p] you were slaves to those who by
nature are not gods.[q] 9But now that
you know God — or rather are known
by God[r] — how is it that you are turning back to those weak and miserable
forces[d]? Do you wish to be enslaved[s] by
them all over again?[t] 10You are observing
special days and months and seasons and
years![u] 11I fear for you, that somehow I
have wasted my efforts on you.[v]

12I plead with you, brothers and sisters,[w]
become like me, for I became like you. You
did me no wrong. 13As you know, it was
because of an illness[x] that I first preached
the gospel to you, 14and even though my
illness was a trial to you, you did not treat
me with contempt or scorn. Instead, you
welcomed me as if I were an angel of God,
as if I were Christ Jesus himself.[y] 15Where,
then, is your blessing of me now? I can
testify that, if you could have done so, you
would have torn out your eyes and given
them to me. 16Have I now become your
enemy by telling you the truth?[z]

17Those people are zealous to win you

3:27 [a] Mt 28:19; Ro 6:3 [b] Ro 13:14
3:28 [c] Col 3:11 [d] Jn 10:16; 17:11; Eph 2:14,15
3:29 [e] 1Co 3:23 [f] ver 16
4:3 [g] Gal 2:4 [h] Col 2:8,20
4:4 [i] Mk 1:15; Eph 1:10 [j] Jn 1:14 [k] Lk 2:27
4:5 [l] Jn 1:12
4:6 [m] Ro 5:5 [n] Ro 8:15,16
4:7 [o] Ro 8:17
4:8 [p] 1Co 1:21; Eph 2:12; 1Th 4:5 [q] 2Ch 13:9; Isa 37:19
4:9 [r] 1Co 8:3 [s] ver 3 [t] Col 2:20
4:10 [u] Ro 14:5
4:11 [v] 1Th 3:5
4:12 [w] Gal 6:18
4:13 [x] 1Co 2:3
4:14 [y] Mt 10:40
4:16 [z] Am 5:10

[a] 3 Or *under the basic principles* [b] 5 The Greek word for *adoption to sonship* is a legal term referring to the full legal standing of an adopted male heir in Roman culture. [c] 6 Aramaic for *Father* [d] 9 Or *principles*

Gal 4:6–7 ❖ What does it mean to live as a slave to sin? How does God's Spirit free us from living this way?

3:28 Those who are "in Christ Jesus" are those who believe in him; those who believe in him come from all walks of life, from every nation, and from both sexes.
3:29 Since Christ is the Seed of Abraham (v. 19), then it follows that the Galatian believers are also Abraham's seed. Thus, they also inherit Abraham's promise of blessing.
4:1–2 A child who is destined to inherit an estate is no different from a slave as long as he is a child, for he cannot inherit that estate until he becomes an adult. During this period, he is subject to "guardians and trustees" (v. 2).
4:3 Paul says his audience was enslaved under the "elemental spiritual forces" or "basic principles" of the world. Paul uses this term as a reference to the Mosaic Law in its negative features.
4:4–5 God sent his Son. This Son lived under the law so that he could absorb the curse of the law, exhaust the fury of God's wrath on human sin, and redeem those under the law. Once the Son had done this, the way was opened for people to become children of God (v. 5).
4:6–7 The ability to call God "*Abba*" is evidence of being a son of God (v. 6). This means believers are no longer "slaves." And since they are children, they have the inheritance.

3:26—4:7 According to Paul, a child of God is one who learns to call God "Abba" because God has given his Spirit to his children. This was often the first term a Jewish child learned, and it can be translated "Dad" or arguably even "Daddy." Yet there is more to it than the language of a child. In Judaism, the father was also an authority figure, and children were taught always to honor him. Thus, the term "Abba" involved both relational intimacy and honorable respect.

4:8–11 Despite having received the knowledge of God, the Galatians have reverted back to their former ways. Paul had worked hard on the Galatians' behalf. Any pastor knows the heartache and fear that come when a parishioner wavers, stumbles, and even falls away. Paul's fear and frustration now give way to a plea.
4:12a Most likely Paul here means something like this: "Become like me by freeing yourself from the Law of Moses, just as I abandoned the Law of Moses as God's dominant revelation for his people" (cf. 2:15–21).
4:12b Paul knew that to reject him was more importantly to reject God (cf. Mt 10:40–42).
4:13–16 Reminding the Galatians of their former commitment (and friendship) to him makes the present situation unbearable for Paul (vv. 15–16). This whole situation, Paul thinks, needs clarification, so he proceeds to explain it.
4:17–18 Though "zealous to win you over" (v. 17) can mean nothing more than "working hard to

over, but for no good. What they want
is to alienate you from us, so that you
may have zeal for them. 18It is fine to be
zealous, provided the purpose is good,
and to be so always, not just when I am
with you.[a] 19My dear children,[b] for whom
I am again in the pains of childbirth until
Christ is formed in you,[c] 20how I wish I
could be with you now and change my
tone, because I am perplexed about you!

Hagar and Sarah

21Tell me, you who want to be under
the law, are you not aware of what the
law says? 22For it is written that Abraham
had two sons, one by the slave woman[d]
and the other by the free woman.[e] 23His
son by the slave woman was born according to the flesh,[f] but his son by the
free woman was born as the result of a
divine promise.[g]

24These things are being taken figuratively: The women represent two covenants. One covenant is from Mount Sinai
and bears children who are to be slaves:
This is Hagar. 25Now Hagar stands for
Mount Sinai in Arabia and corresponds
to the present city of Jerusalem, because
she is in slavery with her children. 26But
the Jerusalem that is above[h] is free, and
she is our mother. 27For it is written:

> "Be glad, barren woman,
> you who never bore a child;
> shout for joy and cry aloud,
> you who were never in labor;
> because more are the children of the
> desolate woman
> than of her who has a husband."[a][i]

28Now you, brothers and sisters, like
Isaac, are children of promise. 29At that
time the son born according to the flesh[j]
persecuted the son born by the power of
the Spirit.[k] It is the same now. 30But what
does Scripture say? "Get rid of the slave
woman and her son, for the slave woman's
son will never share in the inheritance
with the free woman's son."[b][l] 31Therefore,
brothers and sisters, we are not children of
the slave woman, but of the free woman.

Freedom in Christ

5 It is for freedom that Christ has set us
free.[m] Stand firm,[n] then, and do not
let yourselves be burdened again by a
yoke of slavery.[o]
2Mark my words! I, Paul, tell you that

4:18 [a]ver 13,14
4:19 [b]1Co 4:15 [c]Eph 4:13
4:22 [d]Ge 16:15 [e]Ge 21:2
4:23 [f]Ro 9:7,8 [g]Ge 18:10-14; Heb 11:11
4:26 [h]Heb 12:22; Rev 3:12
4:27 [i]Isa 54:1
4:29 [j]ver 23 [k]Ge 21:9
4:30 [l]Ge 21:10
5:1 [m]Jn 8:32 [n]1Co 16:13 [o]Ac 15:10; Gal 2:4

[a] *27* Isaiah 54:1 [b] *30* Gen. 21:10

---

proselytize you," in essence, their "zeal" was Jewish nationalism. The Jewish agitators' goal was that the Galatians might be "zealous" for them: devoted so much to the Mosaic Law that they would rebuild the barriers that Jesus Christ had broken down. It is good to be zealous for God. It is "for no good," however, if one's zeal is nationalistic and contrary to the promises of Abraham (v. 17).

4:19–20 For the Galatians to grow, Paul senses that he would have to be there and "change [his] tone" (v. 20)—from this stern warning and harsh language to the gentleness of a love that would persuade them over to his side and "alienate them" from the Jewish agitators. Paul's letter, he implies, is a weak communication in comparison to his mighty presence.

> **4:8–20** Paul's emotional response here is, without doubt, a critique of the "dry as dust" approach some advocate for teaching and preaching. The emotions attached to a text ought to be brought out. Otherwise, we do not read the Bible correctly. We dare not pretend that the Bible is a book for academics, designed only for intellectual stimulation and debate. The Bible is a book of reality; part of reality is emotion.

4:21 Those who wish to be "under the law" need to learn to read the law in light of what God has done in Christ.

4:22–23 Paul alludes here to texts in Ge 16, 21, and 25. Paul fastens his attention on two women and the births of the two boys—one "according to the flesh" and one "as the result of a . . . promise" (v. 23).

4:24–27 Hagar is in the covenant established on Mount Sinai (law), and her children are all slaves. Jerusalem corresponds to Mount Sinai. Its people are slaves. Sarah is connected to Isa 54:1 by the word "barren." There we have God's promise to restore Zion. Thus, Isaiah is predicting the future Jerusalem. Paul is saying that those who believe in Christ are living in the era of fulfillment.

4:28–31 Just as Isaac was persecuted by Ishmael, so believers in Christ are persecuted by the "Moses plus Christ" Jewish agitators. As Sarah expelled Hagar and her son (Ge 21:10), so the Galatian believers ought to expel the Jewish agitators.

> **4:21–31** The Christian cannot expect to find in the "world" an ally to the gospel. Only opposition can be expected. The fear of being disapproved and therefore talked about is something most Christians would simply like to avoid. The result, however, is that we fail to speak up and be faithful, as we must.

5:1 Paul's main focus here is on the fact of the Galatians being free at last. For Paul, "freedom" is the very heart of the gospel: God sets us free through Christ and in the Spirit so that we can love God and others. Freedom must be retained, protected from contamination, and always renewed.

5:2 Simply being circumcised is not the issue. If the Galatians go ahead with circumcision because of the influence of the Jewish agitators, they will

if you let yourselves be circumcised,[p]
Christ will be of no value to you at all.
3Again I declare to every man who lets
himself be circumcised that he is obligated to obey the whole law.[q] 4You who
are trying to be justified by the law have
been alienated from Christ; you have
fallen away from grace.[r] 5For through
the Spirit we eagerly await by faith the
righteousness for which we hope.[s] 6For
in Christ Jesus neither circumcision nor
uncircumcision has any value.[t] The only
thing that counts is faith expressing itself through love.[u]
7You were running a good race.[v] Who
cut in on you[w] to keep you from obeying the truth? 8That kind of persuasion
does not come from the one who calls
you.[x] 9"A little yeast works through the
whole batch of dough."[y] 10I am confident[z]
in the Lord that you will take no other
view.[a] The one who is throwing you into
confusion,[b] whoever that may be, will
have to pay the penalty. 11Brothers and
sisters, if I am still preaching circumcision, why am I still being persecuted?[c]
In that case the offense[d] of the cross has
been abolished. 12As for those agitators,[e]
I wish they would go the whole way and
emasculate themselves!

Life by the Spirit

13You, my brothers and sisters, were
called to be free. But do not use your
freedom to indulge the flesh[a];[f] rather,
serve one another[g] humbly in love. 14For
the entire law is fulfilled in keeping this
one command: "Love your neighbor as
yourself."[bh] 15If you bite and devour each
other, watch out or you will be destroyed
by each other.
16So I say, walk by the Spirit,[i] and you
will not gratify the desires of the flesh.[j]
17For the flesh desires what is contrary
to the Spirit, and the Spirit what is contrary to the flesh.[k] They are in conflict
with each other, so that you are not to do
whatever[c] you want.[l] 18But if you are led
by the Spirit, you are not under the law.[m]

5:2 [p] Ac 15:1
5:3 [q] Gal 3:10
5:4 [r] Heb 12:15; 2Pe 3:17
5:5 [s] Ro 8:23,24
5:6 [t] 1Co 7:19 [u] 1Th 1:3
5:7 [v] 1Co 9:24 [w] Gal 3:1
5:8 [x] Ro 8:28; Gal 1:6
5:9 [y] 1Co 5:6
5:10 [z] 2Co 2:3 [a] Php 3:15 [b] Gal 1:7
5:11 [c] Gal 4:29; 6:12 [d] 1Co 1:23
5:12 [e] ver 10
5:13 [f] 1Co 8:9; 1Pe 2:16 [g] 1Co 9:19; Eph 5:21
5:14 [h] Lev 19:18; Mt 22:39
5:16 [i] Ro 8:2, 4-6, 9, 14 [j] ver 24
5:17 [k] Ro 8:5-8 [l] Ro 7:15-23
5:18 [m] Ro 6:14; 1Ti 1:9

[a] *13* In contexts like this, the Greek word for *flesh* (*sarx*) refers to the sinful state of human beings, often presented as a power in opposition to the Spirit; also in verses 16, 17, 19 and 24; and in 6:8.
[b] *14* Lev. 19:18
[c] *17* Or *you do not do what*

---

be confessing that they think Christ alone is insufficient for salvation.

Paul spells out the ramifications: "Christ will be of no value." That is to say, Christ will not deliver them from the present evil age (1:4) or from the curse of the law (3:13), nor will they become children of Abraham's promise for those who believe (3:6–9, 19–25; 3:26—4:7).

5:3–6 Paul makes three points if the Galatians go to the law. First, they will be obligated to do the whole law (v. 3). They become debtors to the whole law, and that means condemnation because that is only what the law can do. Second, they will be separated from Christ and grace (v. 4). They are choosing another way of becoming accepted by God that will not do the job. Third, they will miss what really counts: faith (vv. 5–6). If the Galatian converts opt for the Law of Moses, they will miss out on what really matters: the faith they previously exhibited (3:1–5).

5:7–12 The Jewish agitators were cutting in on the Galatians' progress toward their final goal and slowing them down. Paul evaluates this kind of activity (vv. 8–9), stating that it does not come from God and that just a little of it will cause large problems.

5:10 Paul expresses his confidence pastorally (v. 10a). He becomes positive in order to help them make a good decision.

5:11 Paul responds to one of the criticisms the Jewish agitators have been making. His response includes his oft-made assumption: Those who are persecuted are in the right.

5:12 Finally, Paul sarcastically urges the Jewish agitators that if they are going to get involved with this purifying act of circumcision, they ought to go the whole way, become eunuchs, and end the matter there.

> ✣ **5:1–12** Christians have been set free so they can be healthy in their relationships with God, others, and themselves. And healthy self-discovery is one of many reasons God sets us free, yet it is not for personal absorption and ego-staring. The freedom of God's Spirit, blowing gently into our psyches, makes it possible to be healed before God and others. Paul's whole message in Galatians may be summarized as this call to freedom through Christ and the Spirit.

5:13–15 Paul insists that freedom should not be used "to indulge" the flesh (v. 13). "Flesh" is unspiritual life. Flesh and law belong to an era that is now past; the new era is characterized by the Spirit and Christ.

Paul says the Galatians' freedom in Christ is to be a platform for serving one another in love. Paul says two things about love: The Galatians are to "serve one another" (v. 13) in love, and the entire Law of Moses is summed up in the commandment from Lev 19:18. Paul's entire ethic can be handled in three simple expressions: The Galatians are to live in love (vv. 6, 13), or in the Spirit (v. 22), or under the law of Christ (6:2). These are all the same.

5:16–18 When a person lives in God's Spirit, he or she escapes the power of the flesh (v. 17a) and the power of the law (v. 18). Someone living in the flesh does not do what God's Spirit wants. But the Christian life is a life of consistent surrender to the Spirit.

19The acts of the flesh are obvious:
sexual immorality,[n] impurity and debauchery; 20idolatry and witchcraft;
hatred, discord, jealousy, fits of rage,
selfish ambition, dissensions, factions
21and envy; drunkenness, orgies, and
the like.[o] I warn you, as I did before, that
those who live like this will not inherit
the kingdom of God.
22But the fruit[p] of the Spirit is love,[q]
joy, peace, forbearance, kindness, goodness, faithfulness, 23gentleness and self-
control.[r] Against such things there is no
law. 24Those who belong to Christ Jesus
have crucified the flesh[s] with its passions
and desires.[t] 25Since we live by the Spirit,
let us keep in step with the Spirit. 26Let
us not become conceited,[u] provoking
and envying each other.

Doing Good to All

6 Brothers and sisters, if someone is
caught in a sin, you who live by the
Spirit[v] should restore that person gently.
But watch yourselves, or you also may be
tempted. 2Carry each other's burdens,
and in this way you will fulfill the law of
Christ.[w] 3If anyone thinks they are something[x] when they are not, they deceive
themselves. 4Each one should test their
own actions. Then they can take pride
in themselves alone, without comparing
themselves to someone else, 5for each
one should carry their own load. 6Never-
theless, the one who receives instruction
in the word should share all good things
with their instructor.[y]
7Do not be deceived:[z] God cannot be
mocked. A man reaps what he sows.[a]
8Whoever sows to please their flesh,
from the flesh will reap destruction;[b]

5:19 [n] 1Co 6:18
5:21 [o] Ro 13:13
5:22 [p] Mt 7:16-20; Eph 5:9 [q] Col 3:12-15
5:23 [r] Ac 24:25
5:24 [s] Ro 6:6 [t] ver 16,17
5:26 [u] Php 2:3
6:1 [v] 1Co 2:15
6:2 [w] Ro 15:1; Jas 2:8
6:3 [x] Ro 12:3; 1Co 8:2
6:6 [y] 1Co 9:11,14
6:7 [z] 1Co 6:9 [a] 2Co 9:6
6:8 [b] Job 4:8; Hos 8:7

Gal 5:22 ❖ Which aspect of the fruit of the Spirit comes most naturally? Which is most challenging? Why?

Gal 6:1–2 ❖ In what ways can we "carry each other's burdens" and "fulfill the law of Christ" (v. 2)?

5:19–21 The lists here of the works of the flesh and the fruit of the Spirit are not abstract listings, nor are they comprehensive. We interpret these lists incorrectly if we take them out of context and pretend they are complete listings of either the flesh or the Spirit. These are the kinds of things Paul wants to focus on because he is concerned with conflict. Had he written this letter to the Ephesians, he would have had other items in both lists.
5:22–26 Paul describes "flesh" under the term "acts" (v. 19), while he sees the Spirit's work as "fruit" (v. 22). The former is plural, while the latter is singular. The change of terms to "fruit" suggests a different image: from one of human responsibility to one of divine enablement.

Paul says that (1) those who have surrendered themselves to Jesus Christ "have crucified the flesh" and so should not be involved in the works of the flesh (v. 24); (2) those who have been given God's life by the Spirit and Christ should march according to the Spirit's orders (v. 25); and (3) those who live in the freedom of the Spirit should not fight with one another (v. 26). Once again, we end up with Paul's emphasis in this context, which is disunity in the Galatian fellowship.

✣ **5:13–26** Spouses, parents and children, denominations, and various groups in local churches (to name a few) periodically find themselves in conflict. Conflict mediation teams will always remind us that when there is tension, the first order of business is *to clarify the issues*. This is what Paul does in the letter: He explains the problems that are confronting these believers, in both theological and social terms. Galatians can be seen as a letter that seeks to explain the options (albeit in a highly persuasive manner) and to clarify the issues that confronted the Galatian churches.

6:1 Sometimes, people fall into sin. In this situation, the community should take it upon itself to restore such a person because this is one way a family expresses its love. Gentleness is crucial for this kind of restoration, and only those under the Spirit should be involved.
6:2 The "law of Christ" is nothing other than (1) submission to the teachings of Jesus that fulfill the law and (2) life in the Spirit, which is essentially love and which itself fulfills the Law of Moses. A specific example is to carry the burden of a brother or sister, helping them become free of that entanglement.
6:3–5 Pride is wrong (v. 3); each restorer should check himself or herself (v. 4a) and not measure his or her personal status by comparison with others (v. 4b). In the final analysis, each person is responsible before God for what he or she has done (v. 5).
6:6 Teachers who worked full-time were apparently being disrespected in the Christian community to the degree that their students were not taking care of them. Such treatment was inconsistent with life in the Spirit because it was unloving and unkind (5:22–23).
6:7–10 God is the judge; people cannot sneer at him. A person's final standing before God will be determined by that person's relationship to Jesus Christ as revealed in his or her works. Our connection to Jesus' atoning sacrifice is by way of a faith that works itself out in love. Paul interweaves in this passage two highly fundamental ideas for Christian ethics—mutual accountability and personal responsibility.

whoever sows to please the Spirit, from
the Spirit will reap eternal life.[c] 9 Let us
not become weary in doing good,[d] for at
the proper time we will reap a harvest
if we do not give up.[e] 10 Therefore, as we
have opportunity, let us do good[f] to all
people, especially to those who belong
to the family[g] of believers.

Not Circumcision but the New Creation

11 See what large letters I use as I write
to you with my own hand![h]

12 Those who want to impress people by
means of the flesh are trying to compel
you to be circumcised.[i] The only reason
they do this is to avoid being persecuted[j]
for the cross of Christ. 13 Not even those
who are circumcised keep the law,[k] yet
they want you to be circumcised that
they may boast about your circumcision
in the flesh.[l] 14 May I never boast except
in the cross of our Lord Jesus Christ,
through which[a] the world has been crucified to me, and I to the world.[m] 15 Neither
circumcision nor uncircumcision means
anything;[n] what counts is the new creation.[o] 16 Peace and mercy to all who follow
this rule — to[b] the Israel of God.

17 From now on, let no one cause me
trouble, for I bear on my body the marks[p]
of Jesus.

18 The grace of our Lord Jesus Christ[q]
be with your spirit,[r] brothers and sisters. Amen.

6:8 [c] Jas 3:18
6:9 [d] 1Co 15:58 [e] Rev 2:10
6:10 [f] Pr 3:27 [g] Eph 2:19
6:11 [h] 1Co 16:21
6:12 [i] Ac 15:1 [j] Gal 5:11
6:13 [k] Ro 2:25 [l] Php 3:3
6:14 [m] Ro 6:2, 6
6:15 [n] 1Co 7:19 [o] 2Co 5:17
6:17 [p] Isa 44:5; 2Co 1:5
6:18 [q] Ro 16:20 [r] 2Ti 4:22

[a] 14 Or *whom* [b] 16 Or *rule and to*

6:1-10 The foundation for Christian behavior is the grace of God that awakens us, the love of God that stirs us to action, and the holiness of God that strengthens our resolve to obey him. And behind each of these is the fact that God will be our judge: We will give account to him for everything we have done. And we know that God is completely just.

6:11 Many scholars believe Paul's "large letters" are an ancient style of our modern boldface or italics.
6:12-13 The Jewish agitators were clearly trying to force the Galatians to accept circumcision, demonstrating their commitment to the Law of Moses. Their motive was a fear of persecution (v. 12) by Jews and conservative Jewish-Christian parties in Jerusalem. Paul saw this as a denial of the gospel, and that is the heart of his letter. This Jewish wing did not see what the cross of Christ did to nationalism and the era of the law: Both had come to their end in Christ. Now, God's people were being defined as much larger than just the Jewish nation.
6:14-17 The agitators may glory in the flesh, but Paul glories exclusively in the cross of Christ. He would gladly accept persecution because of this (v. 14).
6:15-16 Paul next declares his perspective on nationalism (vv. 15-16). Once again, neither belonging to the Jewish nation (being circumcised) nor being a Gentile (not being circumcised) mattered: What mattered was that God had formed a new people, the church, and that this new people were an entirely "new creation" (v. 15).

As Paul had cursed those who preached a different gospel (the gospel of Jewish nationalism) at the beginning of his letter (1:6-9), so now he blesses those who embrace his view with peace. "Israel of God" refers to the church, including both Gentile and Jewish Christians (6:16).
6:17 Finally, Paul presents a case for being right: He is being persecuted and bears on his body "the marks of Jesus" as evidence for his persecution for following Christ (v. 17; see 2Co 6:4-6; 11:23-30).
6:18 Having spent his entire letter spelling out the implications of faith in Christ, there is no wonder that we see here more in "grace" than a simple good-bye.

6:11-18 The target of Galatians today is anyone who minimizes Jesus Christ as the sufficient Savior and minimizes the power of the Holy Spirit as a sufficient guide. Whoever minimizes the sufficiency of Christ or discounts the power of the Spirit finds the finger of Paul pointing right at them. Galatians challenges each of us as believers to let the Spirit have control of our lives—no matter who we are or where we come from.

Ephesians

Author: The apostle Paul

Audience: Believers in the church at Ephesus and probably other Christians in western Asia Minor

Date: About AD 60

Theme: Paul summarizes his gospel of salvation by grace through faith alone and describes the nature and role of the church as a unity of Jew and Gentile in God's eternal plan.

Reading Ephesians

The book of Ephesians divides into two major sections. In the first three chapters, Paul outlines his teaching about election, Christ, salvation, and the church, and concludes with a summary prayer. The last three chapters apply Paul's doctrinal teachings to the Christian's personal life.

PERSPECTIVE

The gospel has always been about change and choice. Change from an old way of life without Jesus Christ to a new way of life with Jesus Christ is a staple of God's message to us in Scripture. Choice, however, regarding what we do with our new status in Jesus Christ has been an equally important part of the message. Does it really make a difference, this new status, in the way we live? Do choices really reflect the change adequately? Change and choice might be called the twin pillars of the Good News.

Ephesians is one NT book that emphasizes these twin pillars. Salvation, conversion, or change, Paul tells us, is a gift of God: Formerly you were of the "uncircumcised" (2:11); now you are of the "circumcised." You used to be "foreigners and strangers"; now you are "fellow citizens" (2:19). This change in status demands choices—choices between disunity and unity, good and bad family life, good and bad social structures.

This talk about changes and choices does indeed make Ephesians read like a contemporary letter. Almost everything in it concerns modern culture. The words themselves—*change* and *choice*—are buzzwords in contemporary self-help psychology, education, and vocational guidance. Application in such a climate seems like a no-brainer—except for one consideration: cultural differences between us as 21st-century readers and 1st-century readers. It is possible that for a 1st-century reader, the miracle of change—of salvation given freely as a gift from an omnipotent God—was the focal point of this kind of discussion.

10 BC AD 1 10 20 30 40 50 60 70 80 90 100

Jesus' life (c. 6/5 BC–AD 30)
Paul's conversion (c. AD 35)
Paul's missionary journeys (c. AD 46–67)
Council at Jerusalem (c. AD 49/50)
Nero's reign (AD 54–68)
Paul's first imprisonment in Rome (c. AD 59–62)
Book of Ephesians written (c. AD 60)
Paul's imprisonment and death in Rome (c. AD 67–68)
Destruction of Jerusalem's temple (c. AD 70)

That God (or the gods) existed would have been assumed as a matter of fact. That these gods controlled both the exceptional and the everyday—weather, crops, war—was likewise beyond question. But would such a God take the time to bring about change in an individual sinner? Most 1st-century gods were shorthand for Fate, an inevitable, unchangeable destiny to which one was born and, if one was smart, resigned. That God would actually put in place a mechanism to provide lasting change in a person's life—this was the unthinkable for the early readers of this letter. The choices of life follow hard on the "change" of conversion; a God that can work such a change is fully capable of giving us an inspired guidebook, a Bible, to outline the choices we must now make.

For people in the modern world, change is not all that unthinkable. Change (even if it is human-initiated change) is pretty much assumed by modern individuals. The focal point for us today is choice. Because we have relocated the capacity for change from an all-powerful God to human reason, the choices of "how we should then live" are as varied as the number of human beings who propose them. If God does not change, then choices become central. And moderns are literally overwhelmed with the variety of choices we face in everything—from how to raise our children, to how we should love our neighbors, to what we should eat, to whom to vote for in political elections.

The great wisdom in Ephesians is its emphasis on both change and choice as the twin pillars of the Good News. One cannot exist without the other. And the place that change and choice ever and again come together is in our liturgy and worship. Ephesians is filled with prayer and praise for our great and sovereign Lord, who shows us, as we worship him, that one cannot become a new creature without acting like one, and that knowing how to act can only come if one recognizes the great change brought about in the new life we have in Jesus Christ.

Key Verses

For it is by grace you have been saved, through faith—and this is not from yourselves, it is the gift of God—not by works, so that no one can boast. For we are God's handiwork, created in Christ Jesus to do good works, which God prepared in advance for us to do.

—Ephesians 2:8-10

TAKING THE NEXT STEPS

While imprisoned in either Caesarea or Rome (Ac 24:27; 28:30), Paul wrote this letter to the church he had started in Ephesus (Ac 19). As he sat in chains, he began to reflect on God's great plan to rescue the entire universe from the power of sin and Satan. It is in Christ and by the power of Christ's resurrection that God is accomplishing this plan; he uses that power to give us new life in Christ and to unite us into one family in the church. As living proof that sin and Satan have been defeated, we must live a Christian life of victory over sin.

This book contains some wonderful gems for the Christian life today. (1) God's incredible love for us began even before the world was created. (2) Christ is head over the entire universe, and there is no power greater than his. (3) We receive salvation from God by grace alone. (4) In the church God expects us to live at peace with each other, demonstrating to the world that we do not bear the hostility that the world does. (5) God wants our Christian principles to be applied in all our social relationships, especially within the home. (6) By depending on God, we can win in our personal battle against Satan and his hosts.

WHAT TO LOOK FOR IN EPHESIANS

- God's election and the power of Christ's resurrection (ch. 1)
- Salvation in the individual and in the church (ch. 2)
- Paul's prayer for the Christian (ch. 3)
- Life in the church and in society (chs. 4–5)
- Victory over sin and Satan (ch. 6)

1 Paul, an apostle[a] of Christ Jesus by the
will of God,[b]

To God's holy people in Ephesus,[a] the
faithful[c] in Christ Jesus:

2 Grace and peace to you from God our
Father and the Lord Jesus Christ.[d]

Praise for Spiritual Blessings in Christ

3 Praise be to the God and Father of our
Lord Jesus Christ,[e] who has blessed us in
the heavenly realms[f] with every spiritual blessing in Christ.
4 For he chose us in
him before the creation of the world to
be holy and blameless[g] in his sight. In
love[h]
5 he[b] predestined[i] us for adoption to
sonship[c] through Jesus Christ, in accordance with his pleasure[j] and will—
6 to
the praise of his glorious grace, which he

1:1 [a] 1Co 1:1 [b] 2Co 1:1 [c] Col 1:2
1:2 [d] Ro 1:7
1:3 [e] 2Co 1:3 [f] Eph 2:6; 3:10; 6:12
1:4 [g] Eph 5:27; Col 1:22 [h] Eph 4:2,15,16
1:5 [i] Ro 8:29,30 [j] 1Co 1:21

[a] *1* Some early manuscripts do not have *in Ephesus.* [b] *4,5* Or *sight in love.* [5]*He* [c] *5* The Greek word for *adoption to sonship* is a legal term referring to the full legal standing of an adopted male heir in Roman culture.

1:1 Paul's primary concern was to emphasize that, just as he had been appointed by God to be an apostle, the Ephesians too had been separated to God. "Faithful" can refer either to someone who has proven *to be faithful* or to someone who is a believer, someone who *has faith*. The latter seems the better choice here.

1:2 The wording in v. 2 is paralleled exactly in seven other of Paul's letters. "Grace and peace" describe God's initial salvation and continuing work among his people.

APPLICATION ✣ 1:1–2 The primary ingredient for Christians in relating to culture surely is authenticity. We should not try to communicate Paul's experience of Christ; we must communicate our own. Our expression of the gospel in our culture must be a natural flow of the depth of our relationship with Christ, not the borrowing of mere words that we have labeled religious.

1:3 God acted in Christ and chose Christians to live in relationship with him. He deserves praise. "Spiritual" refers to all that God's Spirit brings to enable life. The expression "in the heavenly realms" refers to a spiritual reality—God's world, in which believers have a share and which evil forces still seek to attack.

No simple definition of "in Christ" will do. Each occurrence must be analyzed in context. But the most important use of "in Christ" points to our union with Christ. Christ is the source in which believers find salvation and the framework in which they live and work.

1:4–6a Election is another way of speaking of God's grace and salvation. Words like "chose" (v. 4) and "predestined" (v. 5) underscore God's activity in setting apart a people for himself. Election results in a holy people. The emphasis on adoption in v. 5 shows that the purpose of election is relational. "Adoption" is family imagery used to explain the salvation experience, both present and future. Individuals are not elected and then put in Christ. They are in Christ and are therefore

has freely given us in the One he loves.[k]
7In him we have redemption[l] through
his blood, the forgiveness of sins, in accordance with the riches of God's grace
8that he lavished on us. With all wisdom
and understanding, 9he[a] made known
to us the mystery[m] of his will according
to his good pleasure, which he purposed
in Christ, 10to be put into effect when
the times reach their fulfillment[n] — to
bring unity to all things in heaven and
on earth under Christ.[o]

11In him we were also chosen,[b] having been predestined according to the
plan of him who works out everything
in conformity with the purpose[p] of his
will, 12in order that we, who were the
first to put our hope in Christ, might be
for the praise of his glory.[q] 13And you
also were included in Christ when you
heard the message of truth,[r] the gospel
of your salvation. When you believed,
you were marked in him with a seal,[s]
the promised Holy Spirit, 14who is a deposit guaranteeing our inheritance[t] until
the redemption of those who are God's
possession — to the praise of his glory.

1:6 [k] Mt 3:17
1:7 [l] Ro 3:24
1:9 [m] Ro 16:25
1:10 [n] Gal 4:4 [o] Col 1:20
1:11 [p] Eph 3:11; Heb 6:17
1:12 [q] ver 6,14
1:13 [r] Col 1:5 [s] Eph 4:30
1:14 [t] Ac 20:32
1:15 [u] Col 1:4
1:16 [v] Ro 1:8
1:17 [w] Jn 20:17 [x] Col 1:9
1:18 [y] Ac 26:18; 2Co 4:6
1:19 [z] Col 1:29 [a] Eph 6:10

Eph 1:15–16 ❖ How can you live out the kind of faith that makes others rejoice when they hear about it?

Thanksgiving and Prayer

15For this reason, ever since I heard
about your faith in the Lord Jesus and
your love for all God's people,[u] 16I have
not stopped giving thanks for you,[v] remembering you in my prayers. 17I keep
asking that the God of our Lord Jesus
Christ, the glorious Father,[w] may give
you the Spirit[c] of wisdom[x] and revelation, so that you may know him better.
18I pray that the eyes of your heart may
be enlightened[y] in order that you may
know the hope to which he has called
you, the riches of his glorious inheritance in his holy people, 19and his incomparably great power for us who believe.
That power[z] is the same as the mighty
strength[a] 20he exerted when he raised

[a] 8,9 Or *us with all wisdom and understanding.* 9*And he* [b] 11 Or *were made heirs* [c] 17 Or *a spirit*

elect. The purpose of election is the glory of God, as the recurring phrase "to the praise of his glory" shows (1:6, 12, 14).

1:6b–8a "Grace" is the power that works salvation and is a summary word for the gospel (v. 7). We are not only saved by grace, but we also live by grace. The term "redemption" involved the idea of purchasing or buying back some item or person that would otherwise be lost, taken prisoner, or destroyed (v. 7).

1:8b–12 Words for God's will, purpose, and desire dominate vv. 9, 11. Paul emphasizes that God's work in Christ was what God intended all along. The gospel is a revelation about God's purpose and work and therefore a cause for praise. In modern usage "mystery" (v. 9) refers to what is unknown. In Jewish and early Christian literature, this word refers to the hidden divine plan now revealed by God.

While the primary intent of v. 10 concerns the ultimate fulfillment of God's purpose at the end of time, Paul viewed that fulfillment as already having begun in Christ's life, death, and resurrection. Just as redemption is both present and future, the revelation of God's will points both to the present and to the future.

1:13–14 In the ancient world, cargo was sealed before shipping, and letters were sealed to guarantee the validity of the contents. The Spirit is called "the promised" Holy Spirit (v. 13) because of texts like Eze 36:26–27 and Joel 2:28, which speak of an end-time outpouring of God's Spirit. The Spirit is also a "deposit" (Eph 1:14). The Spirit is God's first installment on our salvation and the guarantee that the full future inheritance will be delivered.

1:3–14 Awareness of God's presence and living in Christ are the keys to all life. People sin because they forget God. How strange that we forget the "place" we live. If we know we live before God and in Christ, we know we live in a defining presence. Our lives become determined by the character of Christ and God. It becomes increasingly difficult to say, "I know I live in Christ, but I am going to do the opposite of what Christ expects." If one lives in Christ, Christ is that person's entire environment.

1:15–16 Faith in Christ leads unavoidably to love for others whom God has set apart for himself in Christ. Note the trilogy of faith, love, and hope that appears here and in at least nine other NT passages.

1:17–19a Paul prays that God's Spirit will continually give wisdom and revelation for life and understanding. In other words, the apostle prays the lights will go on inside people so that they know God and understand the benefit of the gospel.

Paul wants his readers to know three realities about God. First, they should know the significance of God's call for their future ("the hope to which [God] has called," v. 18). Second, Paul points to the tremendous glory that is present when God inherits his people ("in his holy people," v. 18). God's inheritance is found in these people. Finally, believers should know God's "incomparably great power" for people with faith (v. 19). The focus is on God's life-giving power as it is specifically available for believers.

1:19b–20 The Greek text actually uses the plural, "from the dead ones" (v. 20; as do most passages

Christ from the dead[b] and seated him
at his right hand in the heavenly realms,
21far above all rule and authority, power
and dominion, and every name[c] that is
invoked, not only in the present age but
also in the one to come. 22And God placed
all things under his feet[d] and appointed
him to be head[e] over everything for the
church, 23which is his body, the fullness
of him who fills everything in every way.

Made Alive in Christ

2 As for you, you were dead in your
transgressions and sins,[f] 2in which
you used to live[g] when you followed the
ways of this world and of the ruler of
the kingdom of the air,[h] the spirit who
is now at work in those who are disobedient.[i] 3All of us also lived among them
at one time, gratifying the cravings of
our flesh[a][j] and following its desires and
thoughts. Like the rest, we were by nature deserving of wrath. 4But because of
his great love for us, God, who is rich in
mercy, 5made us alive with Christ even
when we were dead in transgressions[k]—
it is by grace you have been saved.[l] 6And
God raised us up with Christ and seated
us with him[m] in the heavenly realms[n] in
Christ Jesus, 7in order that in the coming

1:20 [b] Ac 2:24
1:21 [c] Php 2:9,10
1:22 [d] Mt 28:18
[e] Eph 4:15; 5:23
2:1 [f] ver 5; Col 2:13
2:2 [g] Col 3:7
[h] Jn 12:31; Eph 6:12
[i] Eph 5:6
2:3 [j] Gal 5:16
2:5 [k] ver 1
[l] ver 8; Ac 15:11
2:6 [m] Eph 1:20
[n] Eph 1:3

[a] *3* In contexts like this, the Greek word for *flesh* (*sarx*) refers to the sinful state of human beings, often presented as a power in opposition to the Spirit.

---

in the NT referring to Christ's resurrection). The point is not that Christ was raised from a state of death, but that he was raised *out from* the dead ones. This is an important difference, for it suggests that his resurrection was not viewed as an isolated event but as an inauguration of the final resurrection.

"In the heavenly realms" (v. 20) points to Christ's presence with God. That Christ is exalted to the highest position possible shows the importance of his life, death, and resurrection. Further, his exaltation shows that life's center of gravity is in the heavenly realm with Christ and God.

The imagery in v. 20 of Christ seated at the right hand of God and exalted over the powers is drawn from Ps 8:6 and 110:1. These two OT texts were also used to describe Christ's resurrection and exaltation in 1Co 15:25–28 and Heb 1:13—2:9.

1:21 The five categories of powers mentioned—"rule," "authority," "power," "dominion," and "name"—emphasize that Christ's victory is total. The five terms almost certainly refer to spiritual beings. Whatever powers exist, they are *all* subject to Christ.

1:22 Here we have our first occurrence in Ephesians of the word "church." No other letter is so specifically focused on the theology of the church as Ephesians, and no other letter expresses such a high regard for the church (see esp. 5:23–33). Whereas Paul's other letters normally use "church" to refer to an individual congregation, all occurrences in Ephesians are universal in scope. When Paul uses "head," "body" always occurs in the same context. It expresses what we have already seen—that Christians live in Christ and are part of him.

1:23 "Fullness" here can express a variety of nuances, but the primary idea seems to be "completeness." God's presence filled the tabernacle and temple in the OT, and the Spirit of God filled individuals. "Fullness" refers to Christ, and the phrase "which is his body" in 1:23a is a parenthetical comment about the church; the church draws from this fullness in him (cf. 4:15–16).

> ✣ **1:15–23** The power Christians have comes from God, defined by the resurrection of Jesus and his exaltation as Lord over every other power. Because no other power can rival him and because fullness of God lives in him, Christians do not have to look elsewhere to find what they need for life; what they need is in Christ. This power, however, is not power in the abstract; it is *relational power*—power that is known and experienced because of being bound to the one in whom power resides.

2:1 Paul viewed the former life before Christ as spiritual death—a life hardly worth living.

2:2–3a People live in one of two spheres or environments, either in Christ or in sin(s). Living in sins is also living in conformity with "the ruler of the kingdom of the air" (v. 2). People in this godless domain choose to follow a deceitful tyrant instead of the good and loving God who created them.

2:3b–c The translation "flesh" does not suggest that humanity or the material world is negative. It refers to everything that is opposed to God's rule. The result is that all people are by nature "deserving of wrath." Paul is not thinking of uncontrolled outbursts of angry passion on God's part; rather, wrath points to God's constant displeasure and reaction against evil and sin.

This text speaks of the universality of sin, but it *does not reject the value of humanity.* In their enslavement, people follow desires and distorted reasonings that leave God out of the picture. Therefore, they are under God's wrath. Yet the main point of Ephesians—and especially of 2:1–10—is that *God will not stay out of the picture.*

2:4 God is not a detached onlooker, nor is he in an angry huff waiting to be appeased. Rather, he is the primary actor in salvation, moved by love and wanting to show mercy to his people.

2:5–6 The two verbs in v. 6 refer to our being raised with Christ in the past, "co-resurrected" with Christ. What is true of him (1:20) is true of us. Note Paul's mention that believers are "saved" by grace (2:5b). No single image—justification, salvation, redemption, reconciliation, freedom, or any other—is adequate by itself to explain the reality God has worked for his people.

2:7 In intervening for us, God shows his own character.

CHARACTER OF GOD // GOD IS LOVE

Ephesians 2:4-5: But because of his great love for us, God, who is rich in mercy, made us alive with Christ even when we were dead in transgressions—it is by grace you have been saved.

To anyone who questions whether God truly loves them, Paul can point to a very concrete proof: "While we were still sinners, Christ died for us" (Ro 5:8). God did not love us because we were lovely or perfect or worthy. No, we were sinners, dead in our transgressions (Eph 2:1). God did not love people because we deserved it, and this shows the amazing measure of God's love.

God's love is central to his nature. God lacks nothing, and yet he chose in love to create the universe. This act was selfless, directed out from himself to his creation. God's love led him not only to watch that creation curiously from afar, but also to be involved with it. God upholds the workings of the universe by his loving providential hand.

God's love led him even further. When human beings, whom he formed in his image, fell into sin, God did not abandon or destroy them. Rather, he bound himself to them even more closely. In love, he took on human flesh and came to dwell among people. God the Son emptied himself of the glories and benefits of heaven and lived as a man. He allowed himself to be arrested and crucified to open the way for eternal life for all believers. God did not do this because he had to; he did it because of love. While we were yet sinners, Christ died for us to take away our sin and make us children of God.

APPLICATION ✣ While none of us can love like God, as God's image-bearers we can imitate God's love in our world. God's loving nature is one of his "communicable" attributes—one that we ourselves can share in and demonstrate. When we practice the kind of selfless love Christ demonstrated, we glorify God and point others to him. No Christian testimony is complete without a deep offering of love.

Eph 2:9 ❖ Why does God's gift of grace through faith abolish all cause for boasting? What kinds of things might you otherwise be tempted to boast about?

ages he might show the incomparable riches of his grace, expressed in his kindness[o]
to us in Christ Jesus. [8]For it is by grace
you have been saved,[p] through faith—
and this is not from yourselves, it is the
gift of God— [9]not by works,[q] so that no
one can boast.[r] [10]For we are God's handiwork, created[s] in Christ Jesus to do good works,[t] which God prepared in advance for us to do.

Jew and Gentile Reconciled Through Christ

[11]Therefore, remember that formerly you who are Gentiles by birth and called "uncircumcised" by those who call

2:7 [o]Titus 3:4
2:8 [p]ver 5
2:9 [q]2Ti 1:9 [r]1Co 1:29
2:10 [s]Eph 4:24 [t]Titus 2:14

2:8 The term "faith" is relational, describing reliance on a reliable God. Faith is a covenant word, expressing the commitment and trust that bind two parties together. What is the antecedent of "this" in the statement "and this is not from yourselves" (v. 8b)? The word most likely refers to the *whole process* of God's saving people by grace.
2:9 Paul's concern is to make sure that praise goes only to God, destroying any conceivable ground for boasting in ourselves.
2:10 This new creation takes place "in Christ Jesus." The new creation is based in Christ's resurrection and is productive, like the Creator. These "good works" were prepared in advance for God's people to do, a statement depicting awe-inspiring sovereignty and providing assurance that God guides believers' lives.

✣ **2:1-10** We must distinguish the world that God created from the world that human beings subvert to their own purposes. The former leads to worship of God; the latter leads to the wrath of God. Once we have distinguished God's order from the old order, we are obligated to defiance, a defiance rooted in the confession "Jesus is Lord." If Jesus is Lord, sin and the old world order cannot be where we live, and Christians must say a constant "no" to the fallen world's attempts to define us.

2:11-12 The labels "uncircumcised" and "the circumcision" were common Jewish ways of referring to Gentiles and Jews respectively (v. 11). In Paul's mind the circumcision in which the Jews

CHARACTER OF GOD // GOD IS GRACIOUS

Ephesians 2:8: For it is by grace you have been saved, through faith—and this is not from yourselves, it is the gift of God.

God's grace is one of the most important facets of Christianity and something that sets Christianity apart from other religions. While many religions focus on a person's goodness, worth or hard work as a key to heaven or fulfillment, in Christianity, these concepts are turned upside down. "Grace" means that something is a gift. God's grace is given, not earned. We cannot achieve it or buy it.

This chafes against our logic and our pride. Humans like to be earners. We want to be praised for our achievements. Surely, we think, God must have chosen us because we were good and righteous or because we are special or amazing in some unique way. The Bible tells us the opposite. We were not good and righteous at all: "There is no one righteous, not even one" (Ro 3:10). All have sinned (Ro 3:23). There is nothing we can do to win God's favor or salvation. God is pure and holy; we are not. How frustrating to our human pride. Where, then, do we find hope?

God's grace pervades the Bible. God warns his people before they fall into sin. He rescues his people when they repent. He sends his blessings, even upon those who are unrighteous (Mt 5:45). In all these ways, God demonstrates his favor and grace. None of it is earned or deserved; it is all freely given.

Nowhere, however, do we see God's grace displayed more fully than in the saving work of Jesus Christ. To heal the curse of human sin, the Father sent his own Son to take on flesh and die for the sins of the world. Because Christ died for us, we can be raised to new life in him. This life is by the power of the Holy Spirit, and it is God's gift of salvation to all his children.

APPLICATION The psalmist prays, "If you, LORD, kept a record of sins, Lord, who could stand?" (Ps 130:3). The answer is no one. We cannot put our hope in our own goodness or perfection because each one of us has a record of sins. The only place we can put our hope is in the grace of God, poured out on us not because we were deserving, but because God is loving.

themselves "the circumcision" (which is
done in the body by human hands)[u] —
12remember that at that time you were
separate from Christ, excluded from
citizenship in Israel and foreigners to
the covenants of the promise,[v] without
hope[w] and without God in the world.
13But now in Christ Jesus you who once
were far away have been brought near[x]
by the blood of Christ.[y]
14For he himself is our peace, who has
made the two groups one[z] and has destroyed the barrier, the dividing wall of
hostility, 15by setting aside in his flesh[a]
the law with its commands and regulations.[b] His purpose was to create in himself one[c] new humanity out of the two,
thus making peace, 16and in one body to
reconcile both of them to God through
the cross,[d] by which he put to death their
hostility. 17He came and preached peace
to you who were far away and peace to
those who were near.[e] 18For through him
we both have access[f] to the Father[g] by
one Spirit.[h]
19Consequently, you are no longer for-

2:11 [u] Col 2:11
2:12 [v] Gal 3:17 [w] 1Th 4:13
2:13 [x] ver 17; Ac 2:39 [y] Col 1:20
2:14 [z] 1Co 12:13
2:15 [a] Col 1:21, 22 [b] Col 2:14 [c] Gal 3:28
2:16 [d] Col 1:20, 22
2:17 [e] Ps 148:14; Isa 57:19
2:18 [f] Eph 3:12 [g] Col 1:12 [h] 1Co 12:13

boasted was a mere human circumcision. Apart from Christ, they lived in the same dark and fallen realm as the Gentiles.

2:13 The sacrificial language here implies that Christ has died for us, which means he died in our place and for our benefit.

2:14a Paul seeks to connect Christ and peace as comprehensively as possible. He is the one who makes peace possible, who announces its availability, and in whom peace is enjoyed.

2:14b–15a Paul does *not* abolish the law as the word of God or as a moral guide. The law is abolished as *a set of regulations that excludes Gentiles.*

2:15b Not only does Christ take the hostility *into himself* and destroy it, but also *in himself* he creates a new being. The new being is Christ himself, into which people are incorporated as his body. Christians are a "third race" beside Jews and Gentiles; the two are one in Jesus Christ.

2:16–18 Even when people are hostile to God, he loves and works to restore relations. Reconciliation through Christ grants "access" to the Father (v. 18).

2:19 Gentiles are now full members of God's family, together with all believing Jews.

eigners and strangers,[i] but fellow citizens[j] with God's people and also members of his household,[k] 20built on the foundation[l] of the apostles and prophets, with Christ Jesus himself as the chief cornerstone.[m] 21In him the whole building is joined together and rises to become a holy temple[n] in the Lord. 22And in him you too are being built together to become a dwelling in which God lives by his Spirit.

God's Marvelous Plan for the Gentiles

3 For this reason I, Paul, the prisoner[o] of Christ Jesus for the sake of you Gentiles—

2Surely you have heard about the administration of God's grace that was given to me[p] for you, 3that is, the mystery[q] made known to me by revelation,[r] as I have already written briefly. 4In reading this, then, you will be able to understand my insight[s] into the mystery of Christ, 5which was not made known to people in other generations as it has now been revealed by the Spirit to God's holy apostles and prophets.[t] 6This mystery is that through the gospel the Gentiles are heirs[u] together with Israel, members together of one body,[v] and sharers together in the promise in Christ Jesus.

7I became a servant of this gospel[w] by the gift of God's grace given me through the working of his power.[x] 8Although I am less than the least of all the Lord's people,[y] this grace was given me: to preach to the Gentiles the boundless riches of Christ, 9and to make plain to everyone the administration of this mystery,[z] which for ages past was kept hidden in God, who created all things. 10His intent was that now, through the church, the manifold wisdom of God[a] should be made known[b] to the rulers and authorities[c] in the heavenly realms, 11according to his eternal purpose that he accomplished in Christ Jesus our Lord. 12In him and through faith in him we may approach God[d] with freedom and confidence.[e] 13I ask you, therefore, not to be discouraged because of my sufferings for you, which are your glory.

2:19 [i] ver 12 [j] Php 3:20 [k] Gal 6:10
2:20 [l] Mt 16:18; Rev 21:14 [m] 1Pe 2:4-8
2:21 [n] 1Co 3:16, 17
3:1 [o] Ac 23:18; Eph 4:1
3:2 [p] Col 1:25
3:3 [q] Ro 16:25 [r] 1Co 2:10
3:4 [s] 2Co 11:6
3:5 [t] Ro 16:26
3:6 [u] Gal 3:29 [v] Eph 2:15,16
3:7 [w] 1Co 3:5 [x] Eph 1:19
3:8 [y] 1Co 15:9
3:9 [z] Ro 16:25
3:10 [a] 1Co 2:7 [b] 1Pe 1:12 [c] Eph 1:21
3:12 [d] Eph 2:18 [e] Heb 4:16

2:20–22 God's household is "built on the foundation of the apostles and prophets" (v. 20). "Prophets" almost certainly refers to NT prophets. This is demonstrated both by the order ("apostles and prophets") and by the reference in 3:4–5 to his "holy apostles and prophets."

Jesus Christ is the "chief cornerstone" (2:20). Christ makes the whole building possible, including the foundation. The temple is "holy" because God dwells there (v. 21), and the people who make up this temple are "the holy ones." They are set apart by and for God.

✣ **2:11–22** Remembering is how we name and process the past and structure our minds to know how to live. Paul asks that we remember the life-determining change Christ has brought in us—that is, the radical movement from being dead in sins to alive in Christ, from being excluded to being included—for this movement is still at work in our lives every day. Such remembering gives attention to the continuing change at work in us and will not allow us to become lax or guilty of pride. Remembering is, therefore, the key to loving and worshiping God. Balance is required, however. We do not remember the former life for its own sake or to wallow in its memory. It no longer defines us. We focus instead on Christ and the change he has brought, and we live in light of those new realities.

3:1 "For this reason" points back at least to 2:11–22, if not the whole of ch. 2. The only reason why Paul was in prison is because he thought Gentiles had the same access to God that Jews did.

3:2–3 "Grace" (v. 2) and "mystery" (v. 3) are closely related. The word "mystery" refers to what is known only because God has revealed it. Here it refers to the revelation that the Gentiles are included in Christ as equals (see v. 6).

3:4–6 In the NT the gospel is a gospel of revelation: God reveals himself as a saving God. While the revelation extends to all Christians (1:9), the foundational revelation has come only to certain select individuals. "Apostles" refers to the founding apostles who saw the risen Christ (3:5). They received insight into the gospel and the responsibility for handing it on. "Prophets" does not refer generally to prophets in the early church but to those who had received revelation that helped frame how the gospel was to be understood and lived (v. 5).

3:7 Gospel revelation comes so people may be enlisted in God's service. Through grace Paul became a servant and apostle of the gospel for the Gentiles.

3:8–11 Grace was given to Paul for three purposes: (1) to preach the riches of Christ (v. 8); (2) to make plain the administration of the mystery (v. 9); and (3) to make the wisdom of God known to the rulers and authorities in the heavenly realms (v. 10). These are not three separate purposes, for all three focus on revelation.

Verse 10 assigns a lofty and cosmic role to the church. The church's very existence and conduct are making known how great God's plan of salvation is—both to people and to the powers "in the heavenly realms" (v. 10).

3:12–13 The text again returns to the privileges available in Christ. Paul asks his readers not to be discouraged about his sufferings for them. That he was in prison should not be discouraging. The

A Prayer for the Ephesians

14For this reason I kneel[f] before the
Father, 15from whom every family[a] in
heaven and on earth derives its name.
16I pray that out of his glorious riches
he may strengthen you with power[g]
through his Spirit in your inner being,[h]
17so that Christ may dwell in your hearts[i]
through faith. And I pray that you, being
rooted[j] and established in love, 18may
have power, together with all the Lord's
holy people, to grasp how wide and long
and high and deep[k] is the love of Christ,
19and to know this love that surpasses
knowledge—that you may be filled[l] to
the measure of all the fullness of God.[m]
20Now to him who is able[n] to do im-
measurably more than all we ask or
imagine, according to his power that is
at work within us, 21to him be glory in the
church and in Christ Jesus throughout all
generations, for ever and ever! Amen.[o]

Unity and Maturity in the Body of Christ

4 As a prisoner[p] for the Lord, then, I
urge you to live a life worthy[q] of the
calling you have received. 2Be completely
humble and gentle; be patient, bearing
with one another[r] in love.[s] 3Make every effort to keep the unity[t] of the Spirit
through the bond of peace. 4There is one
body and one Spirit,[u] just as you were
called to one hope when you were called;
5one Lord, one faith, one baptism; 6one
God and Father of all, who is over all and
through all and in all.[v]
7But to each one of us[w] grace has been
given[x] as Christ apportioned it. 8This is
why it[b] says:

3:14 [f] Php 2:10
3:16 [g] Col 1:11 [h] Ro 7:22
3:17 [i] Jn 14:23 [j] Col 1:23
3:18 [k] Job 11:8, 9
3:19 [l] Col 2:10 [m] Eph 1:23
3:20 [n] Ro 16:25
3:21 [o] Ro 11:36
4:1 [p] Eph 3:1 [q] Php 1:27; Col 1:10
4:2 [r] Col 3:12, 13 [s] Eph 1:4
4:3 [t] Col 3:14
4:4 [u] 1Co 12:13
4:6 [v] Ro 11:36
4:7 [w] 1Co 12:7, 11 [x] Ro 12:3

Eph 3:16-19 ❖ What does it mean to be rooted and established in love? What "power" (v. 18) does this give you?

Eph 4:1 ❖ How can you live a life worthy of the calling God has given you? How does this apply to the specific calling God has placed on your life?

[a] 15 The Greek for *family* (*patria*) is derived from the Greek for *father* (*pater*). [b] 8 Or *God*

---

discouraging thing would be that no one was willing to go to prison for the ministry to the Gentiles.

✣ **3:1-13** Surely the most important application of this text is in reproducing Paul's attitude toward the revelation that has come in Christ. If we do not value the gospel as God's revelation, it will not impact our lives. For us the one truly great value ought to be God's revelation in Christ. We need a conviction that God truly has revealed himself in Christ.

3:14-15 Paul again emphasizes God as Father. No other description of God is used so frequently in the NT. English translations cannot easily show the wordplay between "Father" and "family" in the original. It attempts to be as inclusive as possible, emphasizing the cosmic scope of God's reign and purposes.
3:16-19 "Power" and "Spirit" are so commonly associated that they are virtually synonymous (v. 16). The Spirit is the power of God at work in people.
3:17 The indwelling of Christ does not result from the Spirit's strengthening (v. 17); it is the *manner in which* the Spirit strengthens. "Established" carries the meaning of "rooted and founded." God's love is the wellspring from which believers are nourished and the foundation on which they find stability.
3:18 The four dimensions "wide," "long," "high," and "deep" describe Christ's vast love.
3:19 The first half of v. 19 is a good example of an oxymoron: Paul prays that they may know the love that is beyond knowing. In Christ, Christians experience God's presence and power. In experiencing that fullness, they partake of God's own being and are made like him. This is an ongoing process.
3:20-21 This doxology sums up the intent of the first half of the letter. All Christ followers should praise God for his astounding work in Christ Jesus. God's ways and thoughts are exceedingly beyond our ways and thoughts. God is at work and eager to work in his people to achieve his purposes for salvation.

✣ **3:14-21** The imagery of the text challenges our conceptions about faith. Rather than a small Jesus tucked away somewhere in our souls, the text assumes the presence of One who gives shape and strength at the core of our being, who takes up residence in and redefines us. If we are filled with Christ, our society's understanding of ideas like independence, self-determination, and self-fulfillment must be abandoned in favor of God's will and plan for our lives.

4:1-3 This is one call for all Christians to live in accordance with what God has done in Christ. Living worthy of this call requires eagerness "to keep the unity of the Spirit" (v. 3). The peacemaking act of Christ has created one new being and links Christians together.
4:4-6 These verses are likely from a creed used in Paul's churches or one that Paul composed originally for this letter. The confession has a threefold structure: (1) body, Spirit, hope; (2) Lord, faith, baptism; (3) one God and Father of all, who is over all, through all, and in all. "One" is used seven times to emphasize there is only one gospel; to believe that gospel is to enter into the unity it creates.
4:7 Paul's concern for unity is balanced by an emphasis on diversity and the responsibility of

"When he ascended on high,
he took many captives[y]
and gave gifts to his people."[a,z]

9(What does "he ascended" mean except that he also descended to the lower,
earthly regions[b]? 10He who descended is
the very one who ascended higher than
all the heavens, in order to fill the whole
universe.) 11So Christ himself gave the
apostles,[a] the prophets, the evangelists,[b]
the pastors and teachers, 12to equip his
people for works of service, so that the
body of Christ[c] may be built up 13until we
all reach unity[d] in the faith and in the
knowledge of the Son of God and become
mature,[e] attaining to the whole measure
of the fullness of Christ.

14Then we will no longer be infants,[f]
tossed back and forth by the waves,[g] and
blown here and there by every wind of
teaching and by the cunning and craftiness of people in their deceitful scheming.[h] 15Instead, speaking the truth in
love, we will grow to become in every
respect the mature body of him who is
the head,[i] that is, Christ. 16From him the
whole body, joined and held together
by every supporting ligament, grows[j]
and builds itself up in love, as each part
does its work.

Instructions for Christian Living

17So I tell you this, and insist on it in
the Lord, that you must no longer live
as the Gentiles do, in the futility of their
thinking.[k] 18They are darkened in their
understanding[l] and separated from the
life of God[m] because of the ignorance
that is in them due to the hardening of
their hearts.[n] 19Having lost all sensitivity,[o] they have given themselves over[p] to
sensuality[q] so as to indulge in every kind
of impurity, and they are full of greed.

4:8 [y] Col 2:15 [z] Ps 68:18
4:11 [a] 1Co 12:28 [b] Ac 21:8
4:12 [c] 1Co 12:27
4:13 [d] ver 3,5 [e] Col 1:28
4:14 [f] 1Co 14:20 [g] Jas 1:6
[h] Eph 6:11
4:15 [i] Eph 1:22
4:16 [j] Col 2:19
4:17 [k] Ro 1:21
4:18 [l] Ro 1:21 [m] Eph 2:12 [n] 2Co 3:14
4:19 [o] 1Ti 4:2 [p] Ro 1:24 [q] Col 3:5

[a] 8 Psalm 68:18 [b] 9 Or *the depths of the earth*

---

each person. Here "grace" does not designate saving grace, but rather grace for ministry. "As Christ apportioned it" can also be read, "according to the measure of the gift of Christ."

4:8 In his quotation of Ps 68:18 in v. 8, Paul is interested primarily in the last line, "and gave gifts to his people." This provides Scriptural verification that the ascended Christ gives gifts to his people.

4:9–10 Most likely, Paul here is referring to the incarnation: The One who descended in the incarnation is the same One who has ascended and is now exalted over all things—Jesus Christ the Lord.

4:11–16 This section is one long sentence in Greek, in which two subjects are treated: the ministry that takes place in the body and the maturity this ministry is to achieve. The gifts Christ gives to the church are *people* who promote serving and building it up.

4:11–13 The idea is not of gifts given to a special group, but of grace giving people to the church. "Apostles" were specially authorized agents of God, responsible for explaining and spreading God's Good News (v. 11). "Prophets" at times predicted future events, but usually they explained the relevance of the gospel and the will of God (v. 11; see 1Co 14:3–40). The evangelist focused on proclaiming the gospel and its relevance. "Pastors and teachers" (or "teaching shepherds," v. 11) were compensated for their teaching (cf. Ac 13:1; 1Co 12:28; Gal 6:6; 1Ti 5:17).

4:12 This verse is made up of three prepositional phrases, which, rendered literally from the original language, reads: "*toward* the equipping of God's people *unto* a work of service *unto* building up the body of Christ." The focus here is on the involvement of all the people in the work of the church.

4:13 While the first part of this verse may have end-time implications, Paul's concern is that his readers will not be blown about theologically like little children now, in the present. "Unity in the faith and in the knowledge of the Son" results from the experience of receiving the gospel and living with Christ.

4:14 Immaturity is described as being "tossed back and forth" and "blown here and there"—that is, being easily deceived.

4:15 This description of maturity summarizes what Christian living is about: truth, love, and continual growth into Christ in everything. The truth of the gospel cannot be separated from truth generally, whether it is in explaining God's purposes or relating to other humans. We are to "grow" up into Christ in everything. Living the truth in love is both the means of growth and the result of growth.

4:16 Because he is Lord, Jesus has the power and authority to provide what the body, the church, needs.

> **4:1–16** This passage offers a blueprint for redesigning the work of the church and its leaders. The body of Christ does not have two classes of members—clergy and laity—or two sets of expectations. Everyone has the same task of building up the body, even though responsibilities vary. Certainly some tasks are more appropriate to pastors and require at least some expertise, but even with those tasks, pastors should include and train church members. Ministry is the only profession that retains nothing to itself, gives away all its knowledge for free, and invites those served to do the same work.

4:17–19 The Greek word translated "I . . . insist on it" (v. 17) has the implication "urge." Paul expresses his appeal to his readers with increasing strength as the letter progresses.

In v. 17b, Paul's primary concern is not with a list of specific sins, but with a distortion and disorientation of the mind. The word translated "futility" expresses meaninglessness or emptiness. Hearts made insensitive to God have set

20That, however, is not the way of life
you learned 21when you heard about
Christ and were taught in him in accordance with the truth that is in Jesus.
22You were taught, with regard to your
former way of life, to put off[r] your old
self,[s] which is being corrupted by its deceitful desires; 23to be made new in the
attitude of your minds;[t] 24and to put on
the new self,[u] created to be like God in
true righteousness and holiness.[v]

25Therefore each of you must put off
falsehood and speak truthfully[w] to your
neighbor, for we are all members of one
body.[x] 26"In your anger do not sin"[a]: Do
not let the sun go down while you are
still angry, 27and do not give the devil a
foothold. 28Anyone who has been stealing must steal no longer, but must work,[y]
doing something useful with their own
hands,[z] that they may have something
to share with those in need.[a]

29Do not let any unwholesome talk
come out of your mouths,[b] but only what
is helpful for building others up according to their needs, that it may benefit
those who listen. 30And do not grieve
the Holy Spirit of God,[c] with whom you
were sealed for the day of redemption.[d]
31Get rid of all bitterness, rage and anger,
brawling and slander, along with every
form of malice.[e] 32Be kind and compassionate to one another, forgiving each
other, just as in Christ God forgave you.[f]

5 1Follow God's example,[g] therefore, as
dearly loved children 2and walk in
the way of love, just as Christ loved us

[a] *26* Psalm 4:4 (see Septuagint)

4:22 [r] 1Pe 2:1 [s] Ro 6:6
4:23 [t] Col 3:10
4:24 [u] Ro 6:4 [v] Eph 2:10
4:25 [w] Zec 8:16 [x] Ro 12:5
4:28 [y] Ac 20:35 [z] 1Th 4:11 [a] Lk 3:11
4:29 [b] Col 3:8
4:30 [c] 1Th 5:19 [d] Ro 8:23
4:31 [e] Col 3:8
4:32 [f] Mt 6:14,15
5:1 [g] Lk 6:36

---

off a chain reaction that has turned out the light and led to meaninglessness (v. 18). Insensitivity in one direction leads to "sensuality" in another (v. 19). "Sensuality" is the idol to which the Gentiles have given themselves. Impure activity is rooted in greedy desire, the self-centered character of sin.

4:20–21 Verse 20 can also be read, "You did not learn the Christ this way." Paul goes on to emphasize that his readers know better than to live the life he described in vv. 17–19, for they know the truth in Jesus.

4:22–24 These verses show what the readers were taught, but the implication is that these words should also be put into practice. Paul's main issue here is transformation—a change of identities. "Putting off" and "putting on" are another way of expressing the ideas of dying and rising with Christ.

The "old self" fit the former way of living, and its ongoing corruption was fueled by "deceitful desires" (v. 22). The old self is the human self without God, deluded and deceived into a downward spiral by material desires.

The language for the new being (v. 24) recalls Ge 1:26–27, humanity's creation in God's image. The image marred in Eden is being re-created in Christ. This new creation is viewed as a work that God has already accomplished and reflects the same ideas as presented in 2:10.

✣ **4:17–24** If the fundamental problem of fallen humanity is distorted reasoning, we need a wholesale restructuring of the mind. Ephesians has emphasized the Holy Spirit's role in this process (1:17–18; 3:16–17), so no thought exists of a depraved mind repairing itself. The light of the gospel shows the channels along which new thinking must run, and the Spirit engages our spirit in reordering life. We must learn to think for ourselves along Christian lines.

4:25–27 The motivation for telling the truth is that we are members of each other. That the sun is not to go down on one's anger means that anger must be dealt with quickly. Anger is a Trojan horse for Satan's attacks.

4:28 Theft, then as now, was a common problem.

4:29 The word "unwholesome" is used for spoiled fish or rotten fruit. Although obscene speech may be in mind (see 5:4), the concern for "building up" later in the verse suggests "destructive" language.

4:30 Why live contrary to him whose ownership seal we wear and in violation of our destiny? This verse stands in marked contrast with what is said of the devil in v. 27. No room is to be permitted for the devil, but through the Spirit, God is at work in us. The personal character of the Spirit is here simply assumed.

4:31 The focus here is on the responsibility of believers to act, aided by the work of the Holy Spirit.

4:32 In contrast to the badness and malice of v. 31, v. 32 calls for goodness, understood as being "kind." Paul also calls for compassion and forgiveness. Note again the focus on salvation taking place "in Christ" (cf. 2Co 5:19).

5:1 The command to imitate God is breathtaking, but it is a thoroughly biblical idea and not unusual in Jewish or Greek thought. The readers are God's children, whom he loves.

5:2 The imitation of God and his love is changed into the imitation of Christ and his love. Love is the sphere in which the believer lives. The standard by which Christian love is shaped and energized is the self-giving love of Christ on the cross.

✣ **4:25—5:2** Christians are encouraged to keep short accounts with God. These accounts have to do primarily with how we have treated other people, so we need to keep short accounts with others as well. Regular and frequent checks with God are necessary to determine whether we are grieving or pleasing the Spirit. To put it another way, if Jesus' self-giving sacrifice was a pleasing aroma to God, do our lives provide such a pleasing aroma, or is the smell rather foul?

and gave himself up for us[h] as a fragrant
offering and sacrifice to God.[i]
3But among you there must not be
even a hint of sexual immorality, or of
any kind of impurity, or of greed,[j] because these are improper for God's holy
people. 4Nor should there be obscenity,
foolish talk or coarse joking, which are
out of place, but rather thanksgiving.[k]
5For of this you can be sure: No immoral,
impure or greedy person — such a person is an idolater[l] — has any inheritance
in the kingdom of Christ and of God.[a][m]
6Let no one deceive you with empty
words, for because of such things God's
wrath[n] comes on those who are disobedient. 7Therefore do not be partners with
them.

8For you were once[o] darkness, but now
you are light in the Lord. Live as children
of light[p] 9(for the fruit[q] of the light consists in all goodness, righteousness and
truth) 10and find out what pleases the
Lord. 11Have nothing to do with the fruitless deeds of darkness, but rather expose
them. 12It is shameful even to mention
what the disobedient do in secret. 13But
everything exposed by the light[r] becomes visible — and everything that is
illuminated becomes a light. 14This is
why it is said:

"Wake up, sleeper,[s]
rise from the dead,[t]
and Christ will shine on you."[u]

15Be very careful, then, how you live —
not as unwise but as wise, 16making the
most of every opportunity,[v] because the
days are evil.[w] 17Therefore do not be
foolish, but understand what the Lord's
will is.[x] 18Do not get drunk on wine,[y]
which leads to debauchery. Instead, be
filled with the Spirit,[z] 19speaking to one
another with psalms, hymns, and songs
from the Spirit.[a] Sing and make music
from your heart to the Lord, 20always
giving thanks[b] to God the Father for everything, in the name of our Lord Jesus
Christ.

[a] 5 Or *kingdom of the Messiah and God*

Eph 5:18-20 ❖ How does God's grace influence what comes out of our mouths?

5:2 [h] Gal 1:4 [i] 2Co 2:15; Heb 7:27
5:3 [j] Col 3:5
5:4 [k] ver 20
5:5 [l] Col 3:5 [m] 1Co 6:9
5:6 [n] Ro 1:18
5:8 [o] Eph 2:2 [p] Lk 16:8
5:9 [q] Gal 5:22
5:13 [r] Jn 3:20,21
5:14 [s] Ro 13:11 [t] Jn 5:25 [u] Isa 60:1
5:16 [v] Col 4:5 [w] Eph 6:13
5:17 [x] Ro 12:2; 1Th 4:3
5:18 [y] Pr 20:1 [z] Lk 1:15
5:19 [a] Ac 16:25; Col 3:16
5:20 [b] Ps 34:1

5:3 The shift from Christ's self-giving nature in v. 2 to the self-indulgence of v. 3 is striking. These three sins were already mentioned in 4:19. These sins are totally contrary to what it means to be a Christian.
5:4 This verse's three words for sins of speech occur nowhere else in the NT. "Obscenity" expresses that which is shameful or disgraceful. "Foolish talk" recalls the frequent condemnation of the fool in OT Wisdom Literature. "Coarse joking" suggests a double entendre. What is fitting for God's people is rather "thanksgiving."
5:5–6 Not only are practitioners of such sins excluded from the kingdom, but a more dire fate awaits them in the form of God's wrath.
5:7 If one is joined to Christ and shares in him, one cannot share in the lives of those practicing sexual sin and greed.
5:8–10 No other text in Ephesians is as strong in its explanation of conversion. People take on the character of the sphere in which they live. When they are in him who is the light, they too *are* light.

Paul's ethic is always guided by "what pleases the Lord" (v. 10). The word translated "find out" (v. 10) means "put to the test, examine, or discern." The Christian ethic is an ethic of discernment.
5:11–13 The separation Paul calls for is a confrontation. "Expose" (vv. 11, 13) often carries a nuance of correcting or convincing someone.
5:14 The last half of this verse is about Christ's transforming light. These words call people to wake up from their darkness and experience the transformation that the risen Christ brings. The wording may be drawn from passages on resurrection and light in Isa 26:19 and 60:1.

5:3–14 Our society has a major problem handling sexuality. The problems of adultery, promiscuity, and the like are bad enough, but the extent of the problem is revealed even more by rape, incest, and sexual abuse. Our legitimate desires for love and intimacy have gone haywire, and the pride, power, and pleasure gathered around sexuality have destroyed all sanity and control. Paul's teaching in 5:7 points out that the cultural characteristics of sexuality that are prominent with the world should be completely out of character in the life of the believer.

5:15–17 The main statement in this section is v. 15a: "Be very careful, then, how you live"; the rest of vv. 15b–21 describe what that means.
5:18–21 Paul has been contrasting the unacceptable behavior of the unbelieving world with that of God's people. The contrast between drunkenness and worship or godly living has a long tradition.

This command to "be filled with the Spirit" is unparalleled in the Bible (v. 17). Possession of the Spirit is the mark of being a Christian. Paul's point is that the Holy Spirit is the controlling influence motivating and directing the lives of believers. The call to be filled with the Spirit is a call to live in that unity and enjoy the wholeness of life with God.
5:19 Singing is the natural expression of joy that God brings into a person's life. The purpose of singing is both praise to God and instruction of believers.
5:20 In addition to singing (v. 19), life in the Spirit is characterized by giving thanks. Thanksgiving

Instructions for Christian Households

5:22—6:9pp // Col 3:18—4:1

21 Submit to one another[c] out of reverence for Christ.
22 Wives, submit yourselves to your
own husbands[d] as you do to the Lord.[e]
23 For the husband is the head of the wife
as Christ is the head of the church,[f] his
body, of which he is the Savior. 24 Now
as the church submits to Christ, so also
wives should submit to their husbands
in everything.
25 Husbands, love your wives,[g] just as
Christ loved the church and gave himself
up for her[h] 26 to make her holy, cleansing[a] her by the washing[i] with water
through the word, 27 and to present her
to himself as a radiant church, without
stain or wrinkle or any other blemish,
but holy and blameless.[j] 28 In this same
way, husbands ought to love their wives[k]
as their own bodies. He who loves his
wife loves himself. 29 After all, no one
ever hated their own body, but they feed
and care for their body, just as Christ
does the church— 30 for we are members
of his body.[l] 31 "For this reason a man
will leave his father and mother and be
united to his wife, and the two will become one flesh."[b][m] 32 This is a profound
mystery—but I am talking about Christ
and the church. 33 However, each one of
you also must love his wife[n] as he loves
himself, and the wife must respect her
husband.

5:21 [c] Gal 5:13
5:22 [d] Ge 3:16; 1Pe 3:1,5,6 [e] Eph 6:5
5:23 [f] 1Co 11:3; Eph 1:22
5:25 [g] Col 3:19 [h] ver 2
5:26 [i] Ac 22:16
5:27 [j] Eph 1:4; Col 1:22
5:28 [k] ver 25
5:30 [l] 1Co 12:27
5:31 [m] Ge 2:24; Mt 19:5; 1Co 6:16
5:33 [n] ver 25

[a] *26* Or *having cleansed* [b] *31* Gen. 2:24

---

is the believing acknowledgment of God and his purposes for good in Christ. Christians are to give thanks to God always for everything "in the name of our Lord Jesus Christ." This text proves the worship of Jesus, his being linked with God, and the transfer to him of the title "Lord." The early church was aware that in encountering the risen Jesus, they were encountering God.

5:21 The last participle describing life in the Spirit is perhaps the most surprising. The word "submit" literally means "arrange under." It was used previously in Ephesians of everything being subjected under Christ's feet (1:22). Christians are called to live in mutual submission; without mutual submission they cannot fulfill their destiny. Such submission is a strong and free act of the will based on real love of the other person (cf. 4:2).

5:22–24, 33b The instruction to wives to submit to their husbands is only the first example of the mutual submission required of all Christians. Christianity brought with it significant change for women, and apparently their freedom was a source of offense to non-Christians. In Gal 3:28, for example, Paul wrote that distinctions like male and female no longer determined value.

The wife's relation to the Lord is the basis, motivation, and qualification of her submission to her husband. In Eph 5:24 the words "in everything" indicate that all spheres of life are included in this submission, provided that it is in keeping with life lived "to the Lord" (v. 22).

5:23 This is surely one of the most abused and debated texts in the NT. Its focus is *not* on the privilege and dominance of the husband. Paul never intended to suggest that wives were servants, compelled to follow the husband's every desire. The text does not give any license for husbands to attempt to force submission.

The debate has intensified in recent years over the meaning of the Greek word for "head." The context of Ephesians and Paul's other writings is the most important factor for determining the meaning of this word. The argument for "source" as the meaning is not convincing. Scholars appear to have chosen this meaning only to avoid negative connotations for the discussion of male-female relations in modern times. Some connotation of authority appears to be included.

Still, v. 23 does not focus on authority. The husband has a leadership role, though not to boss his wife or use his position as privilege. Just as Jesus redefined greatness as being a servant (Mt 23:11), Paul redefines this as having responsibility to love, to give oneself, and to nurture. The text also assumes the oneness and equality of husband and wife in vv. 28 and 31. Both headship and equality must be given their due. As elsewhere, the truth is in the tension of the text.

5:23b–24a, 25b–27, 29b–32 The marriage relation is an analogy of Christ's love, saving work, and ongoing care for the church. Paul describes this relation as "a profound mystery" (v. 32). Paul uses this term to point to a *revelation* from God. Paul probably meant this: "The revelation about Christ and the church is tremendous and profound."

5:25a, 28–29a, 31, 33a Since wives are asked to submit, one might expect the text to admonish husbands to rule appropriately. It does not; instead, it tasks husbands to give themselves with the same love that Christ sacrificially gave the church. Rather than being guided by self-interest, the husband is asked to place his wife's well-being first and give himself to caring for her.

5:28 Paul here assumes a theology of the oneness of the husband and wife based on Ge 2:24. Consequently, the idea of hating or neglecting one's wife is as strange as hating or neglecting oneself.

5:29 The words of v. 29 express the tenderness and nurturing expected from the husband. This assures the well-being and wholeness of the wife. Christ's love motivated him to give himself for the good of the church; husbands must follow the same pattern and love enough to give themselves for their wives.

✣ **5:15–33** This text underscores both the love of Christ and the lordship of Christ. That *he* is head and the church submits to him ought to be a constant reminder that the church has no

6 Children, obey your parents in the Lord, for this is right.[o] 2“Honor your father and mother”—which is the first commandment with a promise— 3“so that it may go well with you and that you may enjoy long life on the earth.”[a][p]

4Fathers,[b] do not exasperate your children;[q] instead, bring them up in the training and instruction of the Lord.[r]

5Slaves, obey your earthly masters with respect[s] and fear, and with sincerity of heart,[t] just as you would obey Christ.[u] 6Obey them not only to win their favor when their eye is on you, but as slaves of Christ, doing the will of God from your heart. 7Serve wholeheartedly, as if you were serving the Lord, not people,[v] 8because you know that the Lord will reward each one for whatever good they do,[w] whether they are slave or free.

9And masters, treat your slaves in the same way. Do not threaten them, since you know that he who is both their Master and yours[x] is in heaven, and there is no favoritism with him.

6:1 [o] Col 3:20
6:3 [p] Ex 20:12
6:4 [q] Col 3:21 [r] Ge 18:19; Dt 6:7
6:5 [s] 1Ti 6:1 [t] Col 3:22 [u] Eph 5:22
6:7 [v] Col 3:23
6:8 [w] Col 3:24
6:9 [x] Job 31:13, 14
6:10 [y] 1Co 16:13 [z] Eph 1:19
6:11 [a] Ro 13:12
6:12 [b] Eph 1:21 [c] Ro 8:38 [d] Eph 1:3
6:14 [e] Isa 11:5 [f] Isa 59:17

Eph 6:10–17 ❖ What would life and faith look like if we always wore the full armor of God? How can we step closer to this goal?

The Armor of God

10Finally, be strong in the Lord[y] and in his mighty power.[z] 11Put on the full armor of God,[a] so that you can take your stand against the devil’s schemes. 12For our struggle is not against flesh and blood, but against the rulers, against the authorities,[b] against the powers[c] of this dark world and against the spiritual forces of evil in the heavenly realms.[d] 13Therefore put on the full armor of God, so that when the day of evil comes, you may be able to stand your ground, and after you have done everything, to stand. 14Stand firm then, with the belt of truth buckled around your waist,[e] with the breastplate of righteousness in place,[f]

[a] 3 Deut. 5:16 [b] 4 Or *Parents*

---

other agenda than the one set and modeled by Christ. A greater sense that Christ leads the church, joined with mutual submission in finding his purposes, will move the church past many of its current problems.

6:1–4 “Obey your parents in the Lord” means to obey as part of one’s relation to the Lord (v. 1). In the ancient world, fathers had absolute control over the family and were sometimes harsh; that is why Paul includes the warning against provoking children to anger. “Bring them up” conveys the idea of nurture (v. 4). “Training and instruction of the Lord” most likely means that the instruction is determined by the Lord (v. 4).

6:5–9 On the one hand, the directions given to slaves remove any suggestion that this new faith upset the cultural order; on the other hand, *these verses are still extremely subversive*. Slave owners may have been pleased with the service they would get, but slaves now had a higher allegiance than to their owners. This section makes specific to slaves (and masters) what was asked of everyone in 5:10, 17, 21: To apply mutual submission to slaves and slave owners was a startling redefinition of slavery.

“Respect and fear” in 6:5 expresses deference in a relationship, not actual quaking. The slave is not to play to a human audience.

That masters are asked to treat their slaves “in the same way” is cryptic (v. 9), but still revolutionary. For them to follow this instruction, they would have to treat their slaves with respect, fear, and sincerity of heart as to Christ. That alone should have abolished slavery for Christians. The teaching is clear: Every thought of privilege evaporates before the cross of Christ.

✣ **6:1–9** The very form of this text is an indictment of modern-day churches. For the most part, we have churches for different socioeconomic groups; we do not draw people to a common place where hierarchies are set aside and people know they stand on equal footing before God. If a church is a “group of our kind,” it fails in its mission. Application of the text requires creating a place where grace is evident and all people come together as equals.

The application of the teaching on slaves and masters is obviously relevant for work relations, but it actually involves every relationship and act. No relationship is merely a relationship; it is a context for relating to Christ. No job is merely work; it is a context for serving Christ.

6:10–11, 13 The passive form of the verb (“be strong,” v. 10) indicates that this empowering is something done to Christians, not something they do themselves. Its present tense shows the empowering is continual. The “armor of God” can be understood as the armor that God provides, the armor that God himself wears, or even the armor that is God himself (v. 11). The armor language is a way to talk about identification with God and his purposes.

6:12 What Paul means is, “Our struggle is not with human beings, but with evil spiritual forces.” This is the only place in the NT where the Christian life is described in this sort of language. Of the four expressions used for spiritual forces in v. 12, only “rulers” and “authorities” appear in the earlier list of five terms for spiritual forces in 1:21. Precise identification of the various expressions is impossible.

Since 6:12 explains standing “against the devil’s schemes” of v. 11, Paul was surely not thinking about structures of evil such as government, law,

15and with your feet fitted with the
readiness that comes from the gospel
of peace.[g] 16In addition to all this, take
up the shield of faith,[h] with which you
can extinguish all the flaming arrows of
the evil one. 17Take the helmet of salvation[i] and the sword of the Spirit, which
is the word of God.[j]

18And pray in the Spirit on all occasions[k] with all kinds of prayers and requests.[l] With this in mind, be alert and
always keep on praying for all the Lord's
people. 19Pray also for me,[m] that whenever I speak, words may be given me so
that I will fearlessly[n] make known the
mystery of the gospel, 20for which I am
an ambassador[o] in chains.[p] Pray that I
may declare it fearlessly, as I should.

6:15 [g] Isa 52:7
6:16 [h] 1Jn 5:4
6:17 [i] Isa 59:17 [j] Heb 4:12
6:18 [k] Lk 18:1 [l] Mt 26:41; Php 1:4
6:19 [m] 1Th 5:25 [n] Ac 4:29; 2Co 3:12
6:20 [o] 2Co 5:20 [p] Ac 21:33

Final Greetings

21Tychicus,[q] the dear brother and faithful servant in the Lord, will tell you everything, so that you also may know how
I am and what I am doing. 22I am sending
him to you for this very purpose, that
you may know how we are,[r] and that he
may encourage you.

23Peace[s] to the brothers and sisters,[a]
and love with faith from God the Father
and the Lord Jesus Christ. 24Grace to all
who love our Lord Jesus Christ with an
undying love.[b]

6:21 [q] Ac 20:4
6:22 [r] Col 4:7-9
6:23 [s] Gal 6:16; 1Pe 5:14

[a] 23 The Greek word for *brothers and sisters* (*adelphoi*) refers here to believers, both men and women, as part of God's family. [b] 24 Or *Grace and immortality to all who love our Lord Jesus Christ.*

---

or social conventions. Rather, he thought of personal spiritual beings seeking to disrupt life as God intended it.

6:14-20 The armor described is that of a heavily armed Roman foot soldier. Speculation about the connection between specific virtues and specific parts of the armor is not helpful. The breastplate and helmet are associated with different qualities in 1Th 5:8.

6:14 The "belt" conveys the idea of tying something around the waist—the idea of girding, which in the ancient world designated readiness for action. This may indicate the leather, apron-like covering tied around the soldier's waist to protect the lower abdomen. The "breastplate of righteousness" is from Isa 59:17, which describes *God's* putting on armor to come in judgment. To put on the breastplate of righteousness means that Christians are to reflect the righteous character of God in their actions.

6:15 "Feet fitted with the readiness that comes from the gospel of peace" is adapted from Isa 52:7, which describes the messenger of good news.

6:16 With the shield, Paul has in mind the large shield Roman infantry used to protect their whole bodies. A line of soldiers with interlocked shields and poised weapons could push through enemy ranks. To speak of faith is not to focus on human belief but on the faithfulness of God.

6:17 "The helmet of salvation" is from Isa 59:17, describing God's own armor. God's salvation is the ultimate assurance of protection. The Spirit is the one who empowers the sword (Eph 6:17b). "Word of God" does not refer to the Bible but to the gospel message. The Greek word used here usually refers to a teaching or prophetic utterance or, more specifically, to the gospel.

6:18 "Pray[ing] in the Spirit" does not refer to speaking in tongues. Rather, it should be seen in connection with other passages on the Spirit in Ephesians, especially 3:16 and 5:18. The Spirit communicates God to us, and through him we receive all gifts and empowering from God. Prayer combined with perseverance is the way to keep alert.

6:19-20 Just as Paul started the letter by praying for his readers, he closes by asking them to pray for him.

6:10-20 The command to "be strong in the Lord" presumes that God is eager and willing to provide strength and that any lack of strength results from our neglect (v. 10). It assumes also that empowering is a choice we make about the relative importance of life with Christ. If we seek a religion to make us comfortable, the Christian faith is not it. A battle rages, and we do not live on neutral turf. We either live for God or against him.

6:21-22 At the beginning of the letter, Paul described his readers as "the faithful in Christ Jesus" (1:1). Tychicus is described as a "faithful servant in the Lord," underlining the importance of both faithfulness and the idea of being in Christ (6:21).

6:23-24 The benediction here is fuller and more liturgical than most, which is unsurprising, given the liturgical character of the whole letter.

6:21-24 Perhaps the most important application of this section is the reminder that God and Christ are the substance of life. They are the willing sources of what we need to live, and all God expects from us is a loving response. God has provided all we need in Christ; therefore, we should live worthy of the gift.

Philippians

Author: The apostle Paul

Audience: The believers at Philippi, a prosperous Roman colony

Date: About AD 61

Theme: Paul writes to encourage the Christians at Philippi to live joyfully in all circumstances.

PERSPECTIVE

Paul's letter to the Philippians manages to take the everyday experiences of Christian living and make them seem as important as the peaks of spiritual euphoria and the valleys of despair. True, our life in Christ may be punctuated with the exclamation points of weddings and the question marks of funerals, but it is mostly made up of the words and sentences that describe what it means to be a child of God. It is on the smooth, satisfying hum of everyday language that this letter to the Christians in Philippi resides.

Paul refers here to some of the highs and lows, to be sure. Persecution, for example, gets representative treatment. But Philippians is mostly written to church people who are doing pretty well. It is not a letter from a parent to a prodigal, but a letter to that delightful child who has always obeyed and, although by no means perfect, is at least giving the straight and narrow path a try. Paul does not have to rail against heresy in the church (as he does in some other letters), and he does not try to write a mini-systematic theology. He is writing to people he likes, people who have been with him for the long haul. Thus, one of the lessons we can learn from Philippians is how to encourage people who are doing pretty well.

Actually, the first lesson is that one should communicate to the faithful as Paul does in this letter. It is the nature of things that the squeaking wheels get the grease, but the truth of Christian ministry is that those of us slogging along in the spiritual trenches need attention too. From his prison cell, Paul practices what we might call ordinary pastoral care, affirming the faithful and encouraging the true-hearted.

Reading Philippians

Paul begins this book by describing his personal circumstances. He continues with numerous exhortations, based on Christ's example and Paul's own example. He concludes the letter by expressing thanks to the Philippians for having sent him gifts on a couple of occasions.

Event	Timeline (10 BC – AD 100)
Jesus' life (c. 6/5 BC–AD 30)	
Paul's conversion (c. AD 35)	
Paul's missionary journeys (c. AD 46–67)	
Council at Jerusalem (c. AD 49/50)	
Nero's reign (AD 54–68)	
Paul's first imprisonment in Rome (c. AD 59–62)	
Book of Philippians written (c. AD 61)	
Paul's imprisonment and death in Rome (c. AD 67–68)	
Destruction of Jerusalem's temple (c. AD 70)	

Key Verses

Do not be anxious about anything, but in every situation, by prayer and petition, with thanksgiving, present your requests to God. And the peace of God, which transcends all understanding, will guard your hearts and your minds in Christ Jesus.

—Philippians 4:6-7

The message of Philippians, therefore, is that maintenance of the healthy is as crucial as surgery on the ill. And as Paul demonstrates, preventive medicine has a character all its own. First, it shows gratitude ("I thank my God every time I remember you," 1:3). Second, it rewards good work with encouragement. Third, it does not shirk its duty to be careful: Paul warns even his faithful children against the Judaizers and the perfectionists. Warnings against potential mistakes are a sign of love, if done in a loving way.

Like members of even good families, the Philippians did have their problems. Apparently they argued, and Paul warns against division. It is easy to come away from reading this letter and miss the deeper theological implications for today's church on Paul's teaching on unity in chapters 1 and 2. That call to health and unity applied to the original church at Philippi, and it applies to all the faithful, even if slightly contentious, churches today.

The best guard against a faithful church—or Christian—becoming a problem church is to "rejoice in the Lord always" (4:4). That is a truth that has always applied across the centuries.

TAKING THE NEXT STEPS

While imprisoned in Caesarea (Ac 24:27) or Rome (Ac 28:30) or possibly even Ephesus (1Co 15:32), Paul wrote this letter to the church that he started in Philippi (Ac 16:11–40). The frequent references to joy that fill the book show the positive relationship that he enjoyed with this church. He wrote to encourage the Philippians in their Christian life, drawing particular attention to the radical and selfless attitude of sacrifice that stands at the center of the Christian faith.

Christians have always loved this book for its practical messages. (1) Of all the people in the world, Christians have the greatest reason to be happy. (2) Christians ought to follow the example of Christ and be willing to put aside their own interests in order to meet the needs of others. (3) We should not look back at mistakes that we have made, but keep looking ahead, with our eyes fixed on Jesus Christ. (4) The gift of Christ living in our hearts is all we really need to be content. (5) We can achieve any victory through the strength we receive from Christ.

WHAT TO LOOK FOR IN PHILIPPIANS

- Paul's reflections on his imprisonment and possible death (ch. 1)
- Christ's humility as the example for our lives (ch. 2)
- A warning against theological error (ch. 3)
- Concluding admonitions (ch. 4)

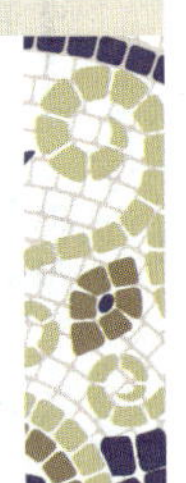

ANCIENT PHILIPPI

Acropolis

to Amphipolis

Traditional prison

Sanctuary of Egyptian divinities

N

Via Egnatia

Theater

Hellenistic sanctuary

Forum

Agora

Library

to Neapolis

Baths

to Gangites R.

1 Paul and Timothy,[a] servants of Christ
Jesus,

To all God's holy people[b] in Christ Jesus
at Philippi,[c] together with the overseers[d]
and deacons[a]:[e]

2 Grace and peace to you from God our
Father and the Lord Jesus Christ.[f]

Thanksgiving and Prayer

3 I thank my God every time I remember you.[g] 4 In all my prayers for all of you,
I always pray[h] with joy 5 because of your
partnership[i] in the gospel from the first
day[j] until now, 6 being confident of this,
that he who began a good work in you
will carry it on to completion until the
day of Christ Jesus.[k]

7 It is right[l] for me to feel this way
about all of you, since I have you in my
heart[m] and, whether I am in chains[n] or
defending[o] and confirming the gospel,
all of you share in God's grace with me.
8 God can testify[p] how I long for all of you
with the affection of Christ Jesus.

9 And this is my prayer: that your love[q]
may abound more and more in knowledge and depth of insight, 10 so that you
may be able to discern what is best and
may be pure and blameless for the day

1:1 [a]Ac 16:1; 2Co 1:1 [b]Ac 9:13 [c]Ac 16:12 [d]1Ti 3:1 [e]1Ti 3:8
1:2 [f]Ro 1:7
1:3 [g]Ro 1:8
1:4 [h]Ro 1:10
1:5 [i]Ac 2:42; Php 4:15 [j]Ac 16:12-40
1:6 [k]ver 10; 1Co 1:8
1:7 [l]2Pe 1:13 [m]2Co 7:3 [n]ver 13,14,17; Ac 21:33 [o]ver 16
1:8 [p]Ro 1:9
1:9 [q]1Th 3:12
1:10 [r]ver 6; 1Co 1:8
1:11 [s]Jas 3:18
1:13 [t]ver 7,14,17
1:14 [u]ver 7,13,17

Php 1:12–15 ❖ How can we make our highest goal, even in bad situations, the advancement of the gospel of Christ?

of Christ,[r] 11 filled with the fruit of righteousness[s] that comes through Jesus
Christ—to the glory and praise of God.

Paul's Chains Advance the Gospel

12 Now I want you to know, brothers
and sisters,[b] that what has happened to
me has actually served to advance the
gospel. 13 As a result, it has become clear
throughout the whole palace guard[c] and
to everyone else that I am in chains[t] for
Christ. 14 And because of my chains,[u] most
of the brothers and sisters have become
confident in the Lord and dare all the
more to proclaim the gospel without fear.
15 It is true that some preach Christ out
of envy and rivalry, but others out of

[a] *1* The word *deacons* refers here to Christians designated to serve with the overseers/elders of the church in a variety of ways; similarly in Romans 16:1 and 1 Tim. 3:8,12. [b] *12* The Greek word for *brothers and sisters* (*adelphoi*) refers here to believers, both men and women, as part of God's family; also in verse 14; and in 3:1,13,17; 4:1,8,21. [c] *13* Or *whole palace*

1:1 Paul's word for "servants" was commonly used for slaves. Paul's readers would probably have understood the term to refer to people conscripted into the service of Christ. Second, Paul wants to recognize the leaders in a special way (i.e., "the overseers and deacons").

1:2 By "grace," Paul means the grace in which believers now stand through the sacrifice of Christ. Similarly, the "peace" Paul commends to the Philippians is the blessing of reconciliation with God.

1:3–8 Paul reports his continual thanks to God for the Philippians and gives the reasons for his thankfulness.

1:9–11 Paul intercedes for the church in Philippi and describes the content of that intercession. Paul's basic request is that they might express their love in ways that show how to know and obey God's will. Then, they will "be able to discern what is best" and will "be pure and blameless for the day of Christ" (v. 10). Such devotion to the gospel will ensure that they bear "the fruit of righteousness that comes through Jesus Christ" (v. 11). This fruit, he prays, will be evident in the Philippians' lives on the final day, and the result will be "the glory and praise of God" (v. 11).

APPLICATION ✣ **1:1–11** How can we work for Christian unity? First, we must identify the barriers that divide people who claim to be Christians and ask whether they are legitimate. If we are to be faithful to the spirit of vv. 1–2, such barriers to Christian unity are intolerable. After identifying the barriers dividing us, we must be willing to follow the example of Paul's unselfishness in tearing them down. The church also needs to hear Paul's concern that the Philippians grow in love.

Finally, this passage challenges the church to be as creative as Paul was in using the inherited traditions of his day in the service of the gospel. In our efforts to communicate the gospel creatively with the cultural tools available to us, it seems sensible to use tools that can convey the gospel message with as much power and fullness as possible.

1:12–14 Paul begins the body of his letter with the statement that "what has happened to me has actually served to advance the gospel" (v. 12). The phrase "for Christ" (v. 13) can also be read as "in Christ" and probably carries the connotation of sharing in Christ's hardship. Christ's suffering advanced God's redemptive work; Paul's struggle has the same quality. The adjective "clear" (v. 13) probably means "known for what it really is." Paul has had the opportunity to explain the reasons for his imprisonment. Paul may be in chains, but the gospel has gone forward unfettered.

1:15–18a Those whose preaching is motivated "out of goodwill" (v. 15) and "love" (v. 16) know that these circumstances are part of God's strategy for advancing the gospel. Those whose preach-

goodwill. 16The latter do so out of love,
knowing that I am put here for the defense of the gospel.[v] 17The former preach
Christ out of selfish ambition,[w] not sincerely, supposing that they can stir up
trouble for me while I am in chains.[x]
18But what does it matter? The important
thing is that in every way, whether from
false motives or true, Christ is preached.
And because of this I rejoice.

Yes, and I will continue to rejoice, 19for
I know that through your prayers[y] and
God's provision of the Spirit of Jesus
Christ[z] what has happened to me will
turn out for my deliverance.[a] 20I eagerly
expect[a] and hope that I will in no way
be ashamed, but will have sufficient
courage[b] so that now as always Christ
will be exalted in my body,[c] whether
by life or by death.[d] 21For to me, to live
is Christ[e] and to die is gain. 22If I am to
go on living in the body, this will mean
fruitful labor for me. Yet what shall I
choose? I do not know! 23I am torn between the two: I desire to depart[f] and
be with Christ,[g] which is better by far;
24but it is more necessary for you that I
remain in the body. 25Convinced of this,
I know that I will remain, and I will continue with all of you for your progress
and joy in the faith, 26so that through
my being with you again your boasting
in Christ Jesus will abound on account
of me.

1:16 [v] ver 7,12
1:17 [w] Php 2:3 [x] ver 7,13,14
1:19 [y] 2Co 1:11 [z] Ac 16:7
1:20 [a] Ro 8:19 [b] ver 14 [c] 1Co 6:20 [d] Ro 14:8
1:21 [e] Gal 2:20
1:23 [f] 2Ti 4:6 [g] Jn 12:26; 2Co 5:8
1:27 [h] Eph 4:1 [i] 1Co 16:13 [j] Jude 3

Life Worthy of the Gospel

27Whatever happens, conduct yourselves in a manner worthy[h] of the gospel
of Christ. Then, whether I come and see
you or only hear about you in my absence, I will know that you stand firm[i]
in the one Spirit,[b] striving together[j] as

[a] 19 Or *vindication;* or *salvation* [b] 27 Or *in one spirit*

---

ing is motivated "out of envy and rivalry" (v. 15) seem to oppose the apostle for personal reasons. They imagine Paul looking on from his imprisonment with envy (v. 17). Ultimately the stance of either group toward Paul does not matter, for "the important thing is that in every way, whether from false motives or true, Christ is preached," and this gives Paul joy (v. 18a).

> ✣ **1:12–18a** This passage teaches the modern church about the nature of joy. Joy is the settled peace that arises from making the gospel the focus of life. Paul was at peace with his circumstances because the advancement of the gospel was his primary goal in life. If we lack this kind of deep inner joy, then perhaps we should search our souls to be sure that our happiness is not more firmly connected to our comfort than to the gospel. Our joy will remain intact if we remember that God is in control and that wherever Christ is preached, God can advance the gospel.

1:18b–20 Even Paul's death can result in his "deliverance" (v. 19) because that deliverance is unrelated to the chains that bind him. It is instead his salvation.

Paul claims that the events described in 1:12–18a "will turn out" for his salvation through the Philippians' prayers and the Spirit of Jesus Christ (v. 19). Those prayers are linked with God giving the Spirit to him. Together they provide the help he needs to face the Roman tribunal with courage.

The phrase "eagerly expect" (v. 20) refers to the intense expectation of something that is sure to happen. Paul sees the upcoming test in court as a divinely appointed opportunity to defend the gospel on his way to the final salvation he eagerly awaits. Paul will ultimately triumph over evil because his hope is in the Lord.

1:21–26 Whether he lives or dies, Paul says, he will be with Christ. To Paul, life means Christ (v. 21a). Death is gain, for it will mean the closest possible union with Christ.

When Paul claims to "know" (v. 25) that he will remain in the flesh, he does not shut out the possibility that he will be executed. The ultimate choice of life or death throughout the passage lies with God. Although Paul's personal preference is unquestionably to depart and be with Christ, he is convinced that his freedom to return to Philippi would result in "progress" in the faith for the Philippians (v. 25). Like Christ, Paul has put the interests of others ahead of his own and the interests of the gospel above all.

> ✣ **1:18b–26** Death is the worst possible event for those who believe that they have an inalienable right to "life, liberty, and the pursuit of happiness." Our way of coping with it seems to be to deny its existence. This can only cause us to clutch our material possessions more tightly for the security they can give and keep us from risking our lives in the service of God.
>
> If we are to be as faithful as Paul expected the Philippians to be, we need to be aware of the needs of our suffering brothers and sisters, pray that God will supply them with an unusual abundance of the Spirit of Jesus Christ, and learn from their single-minded devotion to the gospel, in life and in death.

1:27 The phrase "conduct yourselves" carries a deeper significance than we might realize. Paul is telling the Philippians to govern their lives according to the gospel rather than according to society's requirements for being good citizens of Philippi. The Philippian believers should "stand firm" and strive for the gospel "in the one Spirit" and "as one." They should be united in spirit and united in soul because they have all experienced the work of God's Spirit.

Timothy and Epaphroditus

19I hope in the Lord Jesus to send
Timothy to you soon,[p] that I also may
be cheered when I receive news about
you. 20I have no one else like him,[q] who
will show genuine concern for your welfare. 21For everyone looks out for their
own interests,[r] not those of Jesus Christ.
22But you know that Timothy has proved
himself, because as a son with his father[s]
he has served with me in the work of the
gospel. 23I hope, therefore, to send him
as soon as I see how things go with me.[t]
24And I am confident[u] in the Lord that I
myself will come soon.
25But I think it is necessary to send
back to you Epaphroditus, my brother,
co-worker[v] and fellow soldier,[w] who is
also your messenger, whom you sent to
take care of my needs.[x] 26For he longs
for all of you[y] and is distressed because
you heard he was ill. 27Indeed he was
ill, and almost died. But God had mercy
on him, and not on him only but also
on me, to spare me sorrow upon sorrow. 28Therefore I am all the more eager
to send him, so that when you see him
again you may be glad and I may have
less anxiety. 29So then, welcome him in
the Lord with great joy, and honor people like him,[z] 30because he almost died
for the work of Christ. He risked his life
to make up for the help you yourselves
could not give me.[a]

No Confidence in the Flesh

3 Further, my brothers and sisters, rejoice in the Lord! It is no trouble for
me to write the same things to you again,
and it is a safeguard for you. 2Watch out
for those dogs,[b] those evildoers, those
mutilators of the flesh. 3For it is we who
are the circumcision,[c] we who serve God
by his Spirit, who boast in Christ Jesus,
and who put no confidence in the flesh—
4though I myself have reasons for such
confidence.
If someone else thinks they have reasons to put confidence in the flesh, I have
more: 5circumcised[d] on the eighth day, of

2:19 [p] ver 23
2:20 [q] 1Co 16:10
2:21 [r] 1Co 10:24; 13:5
2:22 [s] 1Co 4:17; 1Ti 1:2
2:23 [t] ver 19
2:24 [u] Php 1:25
2:25 [v] Php 4:3 [w] Phm 2 [x] Php 4:18
2:26 [y] Php 1:8
2:29 [z] 1Co 16:18; 1Ti 5:17
2:30 [a] 1Co 16:17
3:2 [b] Ps 22:16, 20
3:3 [c] Ro 2:28, 29; Gal 6:15; Col 2:11
3:5 [d] Lk 1:59

---

implies a remedy: "It is God," he says, "who works in you to will and to act in order to fulfill his good purpose" (v. 13). Any good that we as believers accomplish is the result of God's work in us. This is a deeply humbling truth, one that should give anyone pause who is bent on having his or her own way.

2:19–24 Timothy is an exceptional ally in times of trouble. Paul shows this by giving Timothy three commendations. First, Timothy understands what it means to be united in spirit with other believers (v. 20). Second, Timothy stands apart because he puts the interests of Jesus Christ above his own (v. 21). Finally, Timothy's strength had been tested in the difficulty of apostolic service (v. 22).

2:25–30 Paul introduces Epaphroditus with a fanfare of complimentary language, leaving little doubt he returns with the apostle's blessing. As if this were not enough, Paul explains to his readers that the illness Epaphroditus suffered almost resulted in his death, and it happened because Epaphroditus was trying to carry out his commission faithfully (v. 30). For all these reasons, and despite their surprise at seeing Epaphroditus earlier than expected, the Philippians should "welcome him in the Lord with great joy" (v. 29).

✣ **2:19–30** Faithfulness in the face of hardship is one of the most important ways in which our commitment to the gospel can be expressed. It is an important quality because it produces assurance that we belong to God's people and will stand before him acquitted on the final day.

It is not a quality, however, that Western, and particularly American, culture reinforces. This is most clearly visible in the now well-known statistics on divorce in the United States. In such a climate, it is not likely that Christians will receive much encouragement from the broader culture to be faithful to their commitment to any institution, let alone the gospel. The notion that someone might become a "slave" in the service of anything or risk one's health to fulfill a higher calling sounds extraordinary, even abnormal, to modern ears. Yet it is precisely such people that Paul in this passage asks his Philippian readers, and us, to hold in high esteem.

3:1 Paul hopes that the Philippians will maintain an attitude of joy. The warnings that follow are meant to strengthen their foundations.

3:2 Like dogs who intrude where they are not wanted, Paul's opponents have invaded Paul's churches. They are "mutilators of the flesh" because their confidence lies in circumcision.

3:3–4a The OT recognizes that the physical rite should be symbolic of a circumcision of the heart (Dt 30:6; cf. Jer 31:31–34; Eze 36:36–37). Paul's point in this verse is that this time has arrived. True circumcision is seen in the work of the Spirit. We who are truly circumcised, Paul says, "boast in Christ Jesus" and "put no confidence in the flesh" (v. 3). Paul's word for "boast" indicates the basis of the Christian's confidence: It is in Christ rather than any human social privilege. The term "flesh" often signified human weakness and tendency to sin. Whereas Christians have placed their confidence in Christ, the Jewish opponents rest on a fallen human foundation that will inevitably collapse.

3:4b–6 In this paragraph, Paul compares the Jewish opponents' confidence in circumcision with

> **Php 3:4-11** ❖ What are the qualities about ourselves that we might be tempted to boast about if not for Christ? How does knowing Christ negate all such boasting?

the people of Israel,[e] of the tribe of Benjamin,[f] a Hebrew of Hebrews; in regard
to the law, a Pharisee;[g] 6as for zeal, persecuting the church;[h] as for righteousness
based on the law,[i] faultless.
7But whatever were gains to me I
now consider loss[j] for the sake of Christ.
8What is more, I consider everything a
loss because of the surpassing worth
of knowing[k] Christ Jesus my Lord, for
whose sake I have lost all things. I consider them garbage, that I may gain
Christ 9and be found in him, not having
a righteousness of my own that comes
from the law,[l] but that which is through
faith in[a] Christ — the righteousness that
comes from God on the basis of faith.[m] 10I
want to know Christ — yes, to know the
power of his resurrection and participation in his sufferings,[n] becoming like him
in his death,[o] 11and so, somehow, attaining to the resurrection[p] from the dead.
12Not that I have already obtained all
this, or have already arrived at my goal,[q]
but I press on to take hold[r] of that for which
Christ Jesus took hold of me.[s] 13Brothers
and sisters, I do not consider myself yet to
have taken hold of it. But one thing I do:
Forgetting what is behind[t] and straining
toward what is ahead, 14I press on[u] toward
the goal to win the prize for which God has
called[v] me heavenward in Christ Jesus.

Following Paul's Example

15All of us, then, who are mature[w] should
take such a view of things.[x] And if on some
point you think differently, that too God

3:5 [e] 2Co 11:22 [f] Ro 11:1 [g] Ac 23:6 3:6 [h] Ac 8:3 [i] Ro 10:5 3:7 [j] Mt 13:44; Lk 14:33 3:8 [k] Eph 4:13; 2Pe 1:2 3:9 [l] Ro 10:5 [m] Ro 9:30 3:10 [n] Ro 8:17 [o] Ro 6:3-5 3:11 [p] Rev 20:5, 6 3:12 [q] 1Co 13:10 [r] 1Ti 6:12 [s] Ac 9:5, 6 3:13 [t] Lk 9:62 3:14 [u] Heb 6:1 [v] Ro 8:28 3:15 [w] 1Co 2:6 [x] Gal 5:10

[a] 9 Or *through the faithfulness of*

---

his own advantages prior to his conversion. His parents had done everything for him that the law required Jews to do. He had himself diligently observed the law.

3:7 Like a bolt from the blue, God apprehended Paul, and he saw his privileges and attainments for what they were—tainted with sin and unable to receive God's approval. They could now only be considered "loss for the sake of Christ."

3:8 Paul explores the ramifications of this great reversal. Paul does not mean that his Jewish upbringing, the law, and "everything" else were evil, but that his attitude toward them was evil. At his conversion, he had to accept the means for righteousness that God alone provided.

3:9 Paul next describes two results of this momentous decision. For Paul to gain Christ means that on the final judgment day, he will not be found clinging to his own defective obedience but trusting in God's forgiveness because of Christ's death.

3:10–11 Paul describes the second result of gaining Christ. Christ's death was the means through which God worked the miracle of the resurrection. In the same way Paul's own suffering is how God is bringing spiritual life to the congregations he has been establishing. The "somehow" that begins v. 11 sounds a startling note of uncertainty after the confident theme of reliance on God that runs through vv. 7–9. Paul consistently refuses to presume upon God's mercy.

> ✣ **3:1–11** The doctrine that salvation comes at God's initiative and through faith in Jesus is no less under attack today than in the time of Paul. Some groups effectively deny that faith in Christ alone is sufficient for salvation. A second, and more subtle, way in which inroads are often made into the doctrine of justification by faith alone is that believers do not allow the principle to inform their practice.
>
> Philippians 3:1–11 urges unbelievers to examine their own convictions. Paul plainly says that those who have rejected the gospel will be found on the final day with nothing to present to God but their own righteousness. Any righteousness that is not the righteousness that God himself provides, however, will be unable to withstand God's judgment.

3:12–16 Paul affirms the incompleteness of his own journey. Paradoxically, only those who understand their lack of perfection (v. 12) have reached spiritual maturity (v. 15).

3:12–14 Paul's language comes from the world of war and athletics and emphasizes the strenuous nature of his efforts. Together the two terms "press on" (v. 12) and "straining toward" (v. 13) indicate a single-minded attempt to reach a particular goal. Paul vigorously pursues the knowledge of Christ because on the road to Damascus, Christ took hold of him.

Like a runner who knows that a backward glance will only slow his progress, Paul refuses to rest on his past successes. He presses on toward that day when he will present the Philippians and his other congregations blameless to Christ. What is this prize (v. 14)? The heavenly call is to be part of the justified people who will be able to stand before God on the final day because of their identification with Christ (vv. 8–11).

3:15 Having just denied that he has been made perfect (v. 12), Paul now numbers himself among the "mature." When Paul applies this word to believers, it means having the maturity to distinguish godly wisdom from worldly wisdom and to use spiritual gifts. Paul offers a mild corrective in v. 15b: If some among the Philippian believers hold another position, God will reveal to them the truth.

will make clear to you. 16Only let us live up
to what we have already attained.
17Join together in following my example,[y] brothers and sisters, and just as you
have us as a model, keep your eyes on
those who live as we do. 18For, as I have often told you before and now tell you again
even with tears,[z] many live as enemies
of the cross of Christ.[a] 19Their destiny is
destruction, their god is their stomach,[b]
and their glory is in their shame.[c] Their
mind is set on earthly things.[d] 20But our
citizenship[e] is in heaven.[f] And we eagerly
await a Savior from there, the Lord Jesus
Christ,[g] 21who, by the power[h] that enables
him to bring everything under his control, will transform our lowly bodies[i] so
that they will be like his glorious body.[j]

Closing Appeal for Steadfastness and Unity

4 Therefore, my brothers and sisters,
you whom I love and long for,[k] my
joy and crown, stand firm[l] in the Lord in
this way, dear friends!

3:17 [y] 1Co 4:16; 1Pe 5:3
3:18 [z] Ac 20:31 [a] Gal 6:12
3:19 [b] Ro 16:18 [c] Ro 6:21 [d] Ro 8:5,6
3:20 [e] Eph 2:19 [f] Col 3:1 [g] 1Co 1:7
3:21 [h] Eph 1:19 [i] 1Co 15:43-53 [j] Col 3:4
4:1 [k] Php 1:8 [l] 1Co 16:13; Php 1:27
4:2 [m] Php 2:2
4:4 [n] Ro 12:12; Php 3:1
4:5 [o] Heb 10:37; Jas 5:8,9
4:6 [p] Mt 6:25-34 [q] Eph 6:18
4:7 [r] Isa 26:3; Jn 14:27; Col 3:15

Php 4:8 ❖ Does this list describe our usual thoughts? How can we move closer to Paul's ideal, by God's grace?

2I plead with Euodia and I plead with
Syntyche to be of the same mind[m] in the
Lord. 3Yes, and I ask you, my true companion, help these women since they
have contended at my side in the cause
of the gospel, along with Clement and
the rest of my co-workers, whose names
are in the book of life.

Final Exhortations

4Rejoice in the Lord always. I will say it
again: Rejoice![n] 5Let your gentleness be
evident to all. The Lord is near.[o] 6Do not
be anxious about anything,[p] but in every
situation, by prayer and petition, with
thanksgiving, present your requests to
God.[q] 7And the peace of God,[r] which transcends all understanding, will guard your
hearts and your minds in Christ Jesus.
8Finally, brothers and sisters, whatev-

3:16 Paul has only one request of them in the meantime: The believers should not turn back from the progress they have already made in living lives worthy of the gospel. Paul does not want slight deviations from the truth to destroy their progress.
3:17-20 Paul next warns the Philippians against "enemies of the cross of Christ" (vv. 18–19). "Earthly things" (v. 19) are not the practical affairs of everyday life but things that characterize worldly life in opposition to God.

Paul asks the Philippians to unite in their efforts to follow the example he and other mature Christians have provided for them (v. 17). He admonishes them to remember that they are citizens of a heavenly commonwealth (v. 20). Paul's words are not an egocentric claim that everyone should act precisely as he acts. His example is worthy of following only to the extent that it follows the example of Christ.

The term "citizenship" has political overtones (v. 20). Paul encourages the Philippians to think of themselves as members of a commonwealth located in heaven. In other words, the fallen earthly realm is not the sum of their existence.
3:21—4:1 Verse 21 echoes the description of 2:6–11, and in 4:1 Paul encourages the Philippians to follow the teachings that he began in 3:17.

✣ **3:12—4:1** Paul was certain that when God had started a good work, he would complete it. But he was unwilling to claim in the present a victory that still lay in the future. The spiritual dangers of his apostolic labor were too vivid, the labor too strenuous to claim success. Instead, like an athlete, the apostle went into strict training and stretched toward his final goal, so that on the final day his running and labor would not be in vain.

Mature believers often realize how far they have to go before they finally lay hold of the ultimate victory, while immature believers may claim victory too early. The biblical view is that if believers truly understand Christ's death and resurrection, they will then understand how much of sin's presence and power they had to be saved from and how far in this life they still have to go to be free of its effects, knowing that the final victory over sin won't take place until the day of resurrection.

4:2-3 Those within the sphere of Christ's lordship are equipped to overcome circumstances that disrupt their friendships. Paul wants these two women to put this principle into practice in their relationship.
4:4-7 The term "gentleness" (v. 5) was often used of an attitude of kindness where the expected response was retaliation. The words "be anxious" (v. 6) are often used in contexts where persecution is the issue. The term "guard" (v. 7) likewise is frequently used to refer to the action of a military garrison. All of this points to the context of persecution as the background for Paul's admonitions. The Philippians were suffering under opposition from their pagan neighbors, just as Paul and Silas had suffered when they were among them. Paul calls them to remember that the Lord is near and to replace their anxiety with thankful prayer about their suffering.

If the Philippians follow Paul's advice, then "the peace of God, which transcends all understanding" (v. 7) will guard their hearts and minds. God supplies peace in the face of adversity that does not fit the normal categories.
4:8 The list of virtues that Paul asks the Philippians to "think about" could have been embraced by

CHARACTER OF GOD // **GOD IS PEACE**

Philippians 4:7: And the peace of God, which transcends all understanding, will guard your hearts and your minds in Christ Jesus.

There are different kinds of peace: peace between people, peace between people and God, and inner peace within our hearts and minds. When Paul writes to his friends in Philippi, he assures them that Christ will give them inner peace (Php 4:7).

This is a remarkable thing for Paul to write, given his own situation. Philippians is one of several letters that Paul wrote while he was under arrest. Philippians 1:14 indicates that Paul was in chains. This was not the only time Paul was persecuted. Second Corinthians 11:23–28 lists a multitude of hardships and abuses Paul endured, including beatings, hunger and shipwrecks. Yet Paul tells the Philippians he learned the secret of being content in any and every situation: He can do all things through Christ who strengthens him (Php 4:12–13).

Paul wants his friends to have the same inner peace he has in Christ. He promises them that if they bring their requests to God with thanksgiving in every situation (Php 4:6), then God's peace will be with them. It will guard their hearts and their minds (Php 4:7). This is not to say that every situation will be good—Paul's own experience shows that is certainly not the case. Rather, what Paul promises is that within each situation, even those that are painful or frustrating, God's peace in Christ will guard the hearts and minds of God's children. When the storms of life come, God's peace is like an anchor keeping his children from being swept away by fear or trouble. Jesus himself promises this inner peace when he invites all who are burdened and heavy laden to come to him (Mt 11:28). He assures the weary that they will find peaceful rest.

APPLICATION ✣ Each of us needs inner peace. There are times when life's uncertainties, anxieties and tragedies overwhelm us. Our relationships become fractured, our hopes turn to disappointment and stresses mount. Paul's promise of God's peace within us is a deep comfort and hope. The peace that God gives can help us weather life's storms.

er is true, whatever is noble, whatever is
right, whatever is pure, whatever is lovely, whatever is admirable — if anything is
excellent or praiseworthy — think about
such things. 9Whatever you have learned
or received or heard from me, or seen in
me — put it into practice.[s] And the God
of peace[t] will be with you.

Thanks for Their Gifts

10I rejoiced greatly in the Lord that at
last you renewed your concern for me.[u]

4:9 [s] Php 3:17 [t] Ro 15:33
4:10 [u] 2Co 11:9

---

many right-thinking people in ancient times. This list reminds the Philippians that although society sometimes seems hostile and evil, it is still part of God's world and contains much good.

4:9 The term "learned" refers to learning from someone else's example. The term "received," on the other hand, refers to receiving a particular body of teaching. The Philippians "received" teaching by hearing Paul's instruction and have "learned" through his example.

✣ **4:2–9** The history of the church has shown that when Christians act as a moral compass for society, they often act as a lightning rod as well. Christians are sometimes rejected; those who attempt to bring their Christian convictions into public-policy debates are often ridiculed or told to leave. Paul advises Christians in these circumstances to rejoice in the Lord and make gentleness an obvious characteristic of their lives.

Christians should not retreat from face-to-face encounters with the best unbelieving minds of their age. But we should engage them in the hope of learning what we can of truth, justice, and excellence from them and becoming more obedient followers of Christ. At the same time, Christians should think biblically so that they can discern between what is true and false.

All of this is so important because the way we think determines how we act. Our thinking and our actions, then, are closely bound together. Indulging evil thoughts and tolerating sloppy thinking can have terrible consequences. Thus, if instead of loving my enemy I indulge the temptation to resent him, resentment turns to anger, and anger to hatred. And the link between hatred and murder, as Jesus saw, is very close (Mt 5:21–22).

4:10–20 Verses 10–20 are basically Paul's expression of thanks to the Philippians for a monetary gift they sent to him.

Indeed, you were concerned, but you had
no opportunity to show it. 11 I am not saying this because I am in need, for I have
learned to be content[v] whatever the circumstances. 12 I know what it is to be in
need, and I know what it is to have plenty.
I have learned the secret of being content
in any and every situation, whether well
fed or hungry,[w] whether living in plenty
or in want.[x] 13 I can do all this through him
who gives me strength.[y]

14 Yet it was good of you to share[z] in my
troubles. 15 Moreover, as you Philippians
know, in the early days[a] of your acquain-
tance with the gospel, when I set out from
Macedonia, not one church shared with
me in the matter of giving and receiving,
except you only;[b] 16 for even when I was in
Thessalonica,[c] you sent me aid more than
once when I was in need.[d] 17 Not that I desire your gifts; what I desire is that more
be credited to your account.[e] 18 I have received full payment and have more than
enough. I am amply supplied, now that I
have received from Epaphroditus[f] the gifts
you sent. They are a fragrant[g] offering, an
acceptable sacrifice, pleasing to God. 19 And
my God will meet all your needs[h] according
to the riches of his glory[i] in Christ Jesus.

20 To our God and Father[j] be glory for
ever and ever. Amen.[k]

Final Greetings

21 Greet all God's people in Christ Jesus.
The brothers and sisters who are with
me[l] send greetings. 22 All God's people[m]
here send you greetings, especially those
who belong to Caesar's household.

23 The grace of the Lord Jesus Christ[n]
be with your spirit. Amen.[a]

[a] *23* Some manuscripts do not have *Amen.*

4:11 [v] 1Ti 6:6,8
4:12 [w] 1Co 4:11 [x] 2Co 11:9
4:13 [y] 2Co 12:9
4:14 [z] Php 1:7
4:15 [a] Php 1:5 [b] 2Co 11:8,9
4:16 [c] Ac 17:1 [d] 1Th 2:9
4:17 [e] 1Co 9:11,12
4:18 [f] Php 2:25 [g] 2Co 2:14
4:19 [h] Ps 23:1; 2Co 9:8 [i] Ro 2:4
4:20 [j] Gal 1:4 [k] Ro 11:36
4:21 [l] Gal 1:2
4:22 [m] Ac 9:13
4:23 [n] Ro 16:20

4:11–13, 17 Paul is careful to clarify he did not need or seek the gift. Paul was always circumspect about money matters because he knew that misunderstandings could arise if he depended on the churches he established for financial support. Paul wants the Philippians to know that he has learned to be content in every circumstance (v. 11). As long as Christ is being preached, Paul is joyful (1:18).
4:17 The apostle is also concerned that the Philippians not read his comments as ingratitude. Thus, he follows this qualification with a second expression of appreciation to the Philippians. In this verse the imagery is of a bank account that receives compounded interest.
4:18 Paul's emphasis shifts again to gratitude. Paul composes a "receipt," employing a technical term from the business world of Paul's day, which was often used to refer to the receipt of full payment for goods delivered or services rendered.
4:19 Paul says that God will meet the Philippians' needs. In this, he is promising that God will provide for the Philippians' greatest need of all, giving them the ability to face all circumstances through the One who gives them strength (v. 13).
4:20 Paul ends his expression of gratitude to the Philippians for their partnership with a doxology echoing the letter's opening prayer (cf. 1:11). This is more than a hasty expression of piety. It focuses the reader's attention on the primary goal of the ministry: God's glory.
4:21 When Paul instructs his readers to greet every saint in Christ Jesus, he stresses the equal worth before God of each member of the congregation. The greetings from Paul's associates are likewise all-encompassing in nature. They come from the brothers with Paul and all of God's people in the area.
4:22 Paul's only effort to make distinctions in the greeting comes in the last phrase of this verse, where he singles out the members of Caesar's household for special attention. Perhaps Paul hopes to encourage his readers with the news that even some of the Roman emperor's staff have turned to the gospel.
4:23 Paul concludes the letter in much the same way as he began it (1:2): with a reference to "the grace of the Lord Jesus Christ." The same grace that transformed Paul from a persecutor of the church into its apostle will sustain the Philippians.

4:10–23 For the unbelieving world, money takes on divine status. It is the god of this age, a god for which many people are willing to sacrifice their happiness, their children, their health, indeed their own lives. The workaholic father has now given way to the workaholic couple, who hardly know their children because they are too busy paying off expensive mortgages and car loans. This kind of zeal for income borders on the irrational, and we are hardly mistaken if we think of it as "religious."

The believer who possesses wealth should be wary of money's ability to gain the upper hand. We must make use of money, like the governing structures of the society in which we live, but we should always do so with our eyes open, aware that it can subtly tempt us to pay homage to it rather than to God.

How can Christians guard themselves from the tendency to let money take God's place? Paul and the Philippians supply the antidote. The Philippians have refused to let their wealth control them and have instead taken control of it by giving it away to the cause of Christ. By doing so, they have demonstrated where their loyalties lay and have strengthened their commitment to the God who would supply all they need through his riches in glory in Christ Jesus.

The most powerful antidote to greed is giving generously to those in need. In this way, we begin to view ourselves as the channel of God's blessing to others rather than as the recipients of payment we have earned. This idea is perhaps best expressed in Ro 11:35–36: "Who has ever given to God, that God should repay them? For from him and through him and to him are all things. To him be the glory forever! Amen."

Colossians

Author: The apostle Paul

Audience: The believers at Colossae, a church perhaps planted by Paul's coworker, Epaphras

Date: About AD 60

Theme: Paul writes to demonstrate that Christ is supreme over every human philosophy and tradition.

PERSPECTIVE

The temptation to trust in the wrong things is strong. If we live in the U.S., "In God We Trust" may be inscribed on the coins in our pockets, but too rarely is that phrase etched on the walls of our hearts. We tend to place our trust the wrong things—in everything but God.

The book of Colossians is about trusting in the right things. Or, to be more exact, about trusting in the right person, Jesus Christ. Paul told the Colossians they were trusting in the wrong things and the way to be Christian was to trust in Jesus Christ.

This isn't an easy lesson for us to hear, any more than it was for the Colossians. They were blocked by the fact that Christianity was a minority religion, new and unestablished in their culture. When times got tough, it was hard to hang on to the hope offered in Jesus Christ. It was easier to hedge bets and go back to some of the tried-and-true beliefs, whether long-established mystery religions, Greek philosophies, or even the rites and rituals of traditional Judaism.

We too are blocked from an elemental trust in Christ Jesus, but for different reasons. For us Christianity is not new and strange; it is old and familiar. We live in a culture that has plenty to offer, a culture so rich in material goods that it is tempting to buy the advertising pitch with which these bounties are sold. Even religious marketers get into the act.

By themselves none of these "securities" is bad. Medicine, insurance, financial planning, and religion are all good things. But they become bad when they are elevated from secondary status to primary status. Ultimately they are not adequate to save: Medicines can't cure all disease,

Reading Colossians

In the first two chapters of this letter, Paul presents his vision of the glorious Christ as his response to the false views of the heretics in Colossae. The last two chapters outline the practical implications of this vision for everyday Christian living. There are a number of similar passages in this letter and the letter to the Ephesians.

Event	10 BC – AD 100 timeline
Jesus' life (c. 6/5 BC–AD 30)	▬
Paul's conversion (c. AD 35)	♦
Paul's missionary journeys (c. AD 46–67)	▬
Council at Jerusalem (c. AD 49/50)	▮
Nero's reign (AD 54–68)	▬
Paul's first imprisonment in Rome (c. AD 59–62)	▬
Book of Colossians written (c. AD 60)	♦
Paul's imprisonment and death in Rome (c. AD 67–68)	▮
Destruction of Jerusalem's temple (c. AD 70)	♦

Timeline scale: 10BC, AD 1, 10, 20, 30, 40, 50, 60, 70, 80, 90, 100

Key Verses

Whatever you do, whether in word or deed, do it all in the name of the Lord Jesus, giving thanks to God the Father through him . . . Whatever you do, work at it with all your heart, as working for the Lord.

—Colossians 3:17, 23

insurance doesn't cover all disasters, financial plans don't help heartaches brought by disaster, and religion without submission to Jesus Christ turns into self-help psychology.

The suffering Paul refers to in Colossians is the low-grade, chronic suffering of insecurity, a slight lack of confidence, a lessening of hope that sends us chasing after every semblance of certainty the world has to offer. But this suffering is no less real, and it is all the more painful because of its chronic, ongoing nature. It is particularly painful in a world where the ideal is an all-too-attainable happiness brewed of one part wealth, one part love, one part fame, and one part security. Believing the gospel should produce those four parts, but it doesn't—unless we reinterpret wealth, love, fame, and security through the only valid hermeneutical principle we have: the person and work of Jesus Christ.

The way our culture is constructed, we have made simple creature comforts into gods that control our lives. We try to appease the insecurities brought on by our excessive individualism, and we appeal to these self-created gods for security. They don't deliver, of course. Only Jesus Christ can do that. That is the message of Colossians.

When we are faced with a specific problem, such as Paul was with the situation Philemon brought him, Paul teaches us what to do: Orient all social problems within the context of our basic humility before Jesus, and fulfill our social responsibilities in light of the eternal security offered in Jesus. Suddenly what seemed like an insolvable problem becomes clear in light of God's reconciling work in the world—with Jesus Christ as center.

TAKING THE NEXT STEPS

Paul wrote the letter to the church in Colossae while imprisoned in either Caesarea or Rome (Ac 24:27; 28:30). He heard about certain false teachers who were influencing the church, and he used this letter as a defense of his gospel. His basic answer to the Colossian heresy revolved around the glorious Christ, who defeated the powers of darkness by his cross. Paul concluded this letter with some practical suggestions on Christian living that follow from the reality of having died and been raised with Christ.

The book of Colossians has some exciting messages for us. (1) When we believe in Christ, we are putting our faith in the power of the One who has made and now sustains the entire creation. (2) Faith in Jesus Christ is the only way to true knowledge and wisdom. (3) The Christian life consists not of rigidly following certain practices, but of letting Christ's heavenly power work through us. (4) Christ has something to say about all our relationships and about every aspect of life.

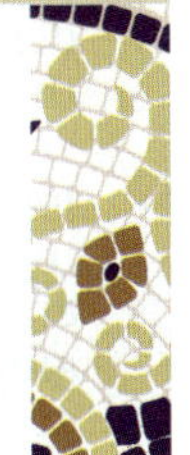

WHAT TO LOOK FOR IN COLOSSIANS

- A view of the glorious Christ (ch. 1)
- Paul's commission, message, and struggle (1:24—2:5)
- The Colossian error (2:6–23)
- Basic patterns of Christian living (ch. 3)

1 Paul, an apostle[a] of Christ Jesus by the will of God,[b] and Timothy our brother,

2To God's holy people in Colossae, the faithful brothers and sisters[a] in Christ:

Grace[c] and peace to you from God our Father.[bd]

Thanksgiving and Prayer

3We always thank God,[e] the Father of
our Lord Jesus Christ, when we pray for
you, 4because we have heard of your faith
in Christ Jesus and of the love[f] you have
for all God's people[g] — 5the faith and
love that spring from the hope[h] stored
up for you in heaven[i] and about which
you have already heard in the true message of the gospel 6that has come to you.
In the same way, the gospel is bearing
fruit[j] and growing throughout the whole
world[k] — just as it has been doing among
you since the day you heard it and truly
understood God's grace. 7You learned it
from Epaphras,[l] our dear fellow servant,[c]
who is a faithful minister[m] of Christ on

1:1 [a]1Co 1:1 [b]2Co 1:1
1:2 [c]Col 4:18 [d]Ro 1:7
1:3 [e]Ro 1:8
1:4 [f]Gal 5:6 [g]Eph 1:15
1:5 [h]1Th 5:8; Titus 1:2 [i]1Pe 1:4
1:6 [j]Jn 15:16 [k]Ro 10:18
1:7 [l]Phm 23 [m]Col 4:7

[a] 2 The Greek word for *brothers and sisters* (*adelphoi*) refers here to believers, both men and women, as part of God's family; also in 4:15.
[b] 2 Some manuscripts *Father and the Lord Jesus Christ*
[c] 7 Or *slave*

1:1 Paul's authority is not increased by the use of the title "apostle," just as it is not reduced when he omits it or substitutes "servants" (Php 1:1) or "prisoner" (Phm 1). Being an apostle is simply what he is. Paul includes Timothy, "our brother," as a co-sender of the letter (Col 1:1). Although Timothy was not an apostle, Paul affirms him as one who carries on the same work and the same preaching task.

1:2 Paul greets the church as "holy" and "faithful" in Christ. "Faithful" most likely refers to their steadfastness under pressure. Their faith is not wavering; they are holding fast to the right teachings about Jesus (2:19), and Paul warns them about others who do not. Paul establishes their common commitments so that he can move on to instruct and warn them.

To be "in Christ" (1:2) means to be incorporated in him so that he encompasses the believer's entire life. The recipients may be Colossians, but the only identity that matters to God is that they are Christians. Being in Christ gives these "brothers and sisters" their true identity beyond their race, nationality, or family.

Paul confesses that grace and peace come "from God our Father" (v. 2). His thanksgiving for these people (v. 3) is based on all that God has done and will continue to do. The image of God as Father conveyed power, authority, and loving care.

1:3-4 Paul regularly prays for the church and gives thanks for them in every prayer. He is thankful for their faithful acceptance of the gospel, which has spilled over into their love for others. Their active love is a sign of a genuine faith based on a solid hope.

1:5 The faith that Paul commends here is *faith in Christ Jesus*. It refers specifically to the belief that God raised Jesus from the dead and that he offers all believers the same promise of life. Their faith is a vibrant force that expresses itself in how the believers live; it is proven by tangible demonstrations of love for God's people.

"Love" is a basic Christian virtue. Faith directed toward Jesus Christ is embodied in love for others. It is a supernatural, God-given love ("your love in the Spirit," v. 8) that knits believers together in unity. Faith is grounded in hope. "Hope," therefore, refers to the thing hoped for.

1:6 The second feature for which Paul gives thanks is the universal impact of the gospel. It is effective, "bearing fruit and growing."

1:7-8 The third cause for Paul's giving thanks is how Epaphras laid a solid foundation for the Colossians in the true gospel (vv. 7-8). Paul was commissioned by God to preach to the Gentiles, but he could not be everywhere. He rapidly equipped his converts

our[a] behalf, 8and who also told us of your
love in the Spirit.[n]
9For this reason, since the day we
heard about you,[o] we have not stopped
praying for you. We continually ask God
to fill you with the knowledge of his
will[p] through all the wisdom and understanding that the Spirit gives,[bq] 10so
that you may live a life worthy[r] of the
Lord and please him in every way: bearing fruit in every good work, growing in
the knowledge of God, 11being strengthened with all power[s] according to his
glorious might so that you may have
great endurance and patience,[t] 12and
giving joyful thanks to the Father,[u] who
has qualified you[c] to share in the inheritance[v] of his holy people in the kingdom
of light. 13For he has rescued us from the
dominion of darkness[w] and brought us
into the kingdom[x] of the Son he loves,[y]
14in whom we have redemption,[z] the forgiveness of sins.[a]

The Supremacy of the Son of God

15The Son is the image[b] of the invisible God,[c] the firstborn over all creation.
16For in him all things were created:[d]
things in heaven and on earth, visible
and invisible, whether thrones or powers or rulers or authorities;[e] all things
have been created through him and for
him.[f] 17He is before all things,[g] and in
him all things hold together. 18And he
is the head[h] of the body, the church;
he is the beginning and the firstborn
from among the dead,[i] so that in everything he might have the supremacy.
19For God was pleased[j] to have all his

1:8 [n] Ro 15:30
1:9 [o] Eph 1:15 [p] Eph 5:17 [q] Eph 1:17
1:10 [r] Eph 4:1
1:11 [s] Eph 3:16 [t] Eph 4:2
1:12 [u] Eph 5:20 [v] Ac 20:32
1:13 [w] Ac 26:18 [x] Eph 6:12; 2Pe 1:11 [y] Mt 3:17
1:14 [z] Ro 3:24 [a] Eph 1:7
1:15 [b] 2Co 4:4 [c] Jn 1:18
1:16 [d] Jn 1:3 [e] Eph 1:20,21 [f] Ro 11:36
1:17 [g] Jn 1:2
1:18 [h] Eph 1:22 [i] Ac 26:23; Rev 1:5
1:19 [j] Eph 1:5

[a] 7 Some manuscripts *your*
[b] 9 Or *all spiritual wisdom and understanding*
[c] 12 Some manuscripts *us*

---

to spread the gospel in places where he could not go himself. Apparently Epaphras represented Paul in his home territory and may have founded all three churches in the Lycus valley: Colossae, Laodicea, and Hierapolis (4:13).

APPLICATION ✣ 1:1–8 The opening paragraph in Colossians speaks to our contemporary need to understand, uphold, and proclaim the Christian vision of the truth. Those who can detect counterfeit bills learn everything they can about a genuine bill; this same principle applies to distinguishing truth from falsehood. We must know what the truth looks and feels like before we can recognize what is false.

1:9–12 Paul does not want his readers to gain knowledge purely for its own sake. Knowledge of God's will always has ethical implications because it requires us to bring our daily conduct and thinking into line with it.
1:13 Paul affirms that God "has rescued" them from the harsh rule of the power of darkness. God has "brought [them] into the kingdom of the Son he loves." Since these dark powers cannot obstruct our relationship with God, Christians need not fear them.
1:14 Paul caps off the mention of the beloved Son with the benefits he has bestowed on us—namely, "redemption, the forgiveness of sins." Forgiveness sets us free for the present and future. It opens the possibility of living a life worthy of the Lord.

✣ 1:9–14 The thanksgiving sections in Paul's letters reveal how important prayer was for Paul. We sometimes resort to prayer only when we feel under siege and then focus only on our problems. Yet Paul gave thanks in every situation because he could always see God's grace at work throughout the world. He provides a model of intercessory prayer that we must more often imitate.

1:15 The poem of vv. 15–20 begins by affirming that Christ is "the image of the invisible God." In Christ we see who God is—Creator and Redeemer; what God is like—a God of mercy and love; and what God does—sends his Son to rescue people from the dominion of darkness.

Christ is also acclaimed as "the firstborn over all creation" (v. 15). In the OT, God bestowed this title on Israel because of its divine election. The metaphor distinguishes Christ from all created things.
1:16 This verse contains a series of prepositional phrases: All things were created "in him," "through him," and "for him." The imposing list of powers created by Christ accentuates his all-encompassing role in creation.
1:17 The verb "hold together" can imply that creation has its existence in him. Christ is more than the force that preserves the cosmos; he is its rationale, rhyme, and reason.
1:18–20 The image of the invisible God entered the sphere of human experience to reconcile all things by means of Jesus' humiliating death.
1:18 Christ is "the head of the body, the church." If Christ is the head of the church, it means that the destinies of creation and the church are bound together. The metaphor "head" designates him as supreme over the church and the source of the church's life. The head directs the body and gives it life.

Christ is also "the beginning and the firstborn from among the dead" (v. 18b). His resurrection is the source of the new life for others. He is the first in a sequence that opens new possibilities for others who follow.

God is not satisfied for Christ to be head only over a small band of devoted followers. The goal expressed in v. 18c is far grander: Christ is firstborn of the dead "so that in everything he might have the supremacy." Christ's death and resurrection were all part of God's divine purpose to reveal his glory to all creation.
1:19 Paul explains that Christ was different from other supernatural creatures, such as angels. He

fullness[k] dwell in him, 20and through
him to reconcile[l] to himself all things,
whether things on earth or things in
heaven,[m] by making peace through his
blood,[n] shed on the cross.
21Once you were alienated from God
and were enemies[o] in your minds[p] because of[a] your evil behavior. 22But now
he has reconciled you by Christ's physical
body[q] through death to present you holy
in his sight, without blemish and free
from accusation[r] — 23if you continue in
your faith, established[s] and firm, and do
not move from the hope[t] held out in the
gospel. This is the gospel that you heard
and that has been proclaimed to every
creature under heaven,[u] and of which I,
Paul, have become a servant.[v]

Paul's Labor for the Church

24Now I rejoice in what I am suffering
for you, and I fill up in my flesh what is
still lacking in regard to Christ's afflictions,[w] for the sake of his body, which is
the church. 25I have become its servant[x]
by the commission God gave me[y] to present to you the word of God in its fullness — 26the mystery[z] that has been kept
hidden for ages and generations, but is
now disclosed to the Lord's people. 27To
them God has chosen to make known[a]
among the Gentiles the glorious riches
of this mystery, which is Christ in you,
the hope of glory.
28He is the one we proclaim, admonishing[b] and teaching everyone with all

1:19 [k] Jn 1:16
1:20 [l] 2Co 5:18 [m] Eph 1:10 [n] Eph 2:13
1:21 [o] Ro 5:10 [p] Eph 2:3
1:22 [q] Ro 7:4 [r] Eph 5:27
1:23 [s] Eph 3:17 [t] ver 5 [u] Ro 10:18 [v] ver 25; 1Co 3:5
1:24 [w] 2Co 1:5
1:25 [x] ver 23 [y] Eph 3:2
1:26 [z] Ro 16:25
1:27 [a] Mt 13:11
1:28 [b] Col 3:16

[a] *21* Or *minds, as shown by*

Col 1:24-29 ❖ How might we emulate Paul's passion and energy? Where does Paul think that energy and power really come from?

is a full, not a partial, embodiment of God. God is pleased to dwell fully and permanently only in Christ. Christ replaces the temple, or any other house made with hands, and represents God in person (cf. 2:9).

1:20 God created all things through Christ; in the end, God will also reconcile all things through Christ. Paul uses "blood" to refer to the work of Christ's atoning sacrifice. The cross establishes a new relationship between God and humans. This overcomes the rupture created by sin—estrangement from God, other humans, and created things. That peace can only be found now in Christ's body.

1:21-23 The key words "faith," "hope," and "heard" (v. 23) are repeated from the opening verses (vv. 4-6). These verses also restate the theme in vv. 12-14, that redemption comes in Christ. These concluding words of the thanksgiving recall the believers' past ("once," v. 21), present ("now," v. 22), and future ("if," v. 23). They also declare the means of their redemption ("he has reconciled," v. 22), its effects ("holy," "without blemish," and "free from accusation," v. 22), and the extent of its impact ("to every creature under heaven," v. 23).

In concluding his thanksgiving, Paul expresses his deepest conviction that God's plan for the world, kept secret from the dawn of history until now, has at last been disclosed in Christ. "[It] has been proclaimed to every creature under heaven" (v. 23) means that the gospel is not obscure or some secret mystery (v. 26).

✣ **1:15-23** The poem found in this section shimmers in the joyful celebration of Christ's creative and redemptive work. It praises who he is, what he has done, and what he will do. It forms the basis of Paul's intercession and instruction in the letter, which is filled with exhortations to be thankful.

This poem professes that, in a way, Christ is the theological "theory of everything." He is the key who unlocks the meaning and purpose of the universe. But he is not a set of physics laws; he is a person who has shown his love for us by giving his life.

1:24 How can Paul connect his sufferings to the afflictions of Christ? How can these sufferings be understood as being endured for the sake of the Colossians? How does Paul dare to think that he can suffer on behalf of others as Christ did?

Paul's thought reflects his sense of unity with Christ. Christians have been buried with Christ, raised with him, and made alive with him. As Christ's body, the church has a corporate personality. If Christians share in dying and rising with Christ, they also share in his sufferings and he with theirs. It is no great jump for Paul to label the suffering he endures on Christ's behalf and as a member of Christ's body as "Christ's afflictions."

But what is lacking in these sufferings? In his letter to the Philippians, Paul notes that Epaphroditus risked his life "to make up for the help you yourselves could not give me" (Php 2:30). In that letter, Paul was not complaining that the Philippians failed to supply anything material. What was lacking was their personal presence with Paul, which Epaphroditus, as their representative, supplied. This same meaning applies in our text. What is lacking is Christ's bodily presence. Paul's suffering represents Christ's continuing suffering for the world through his servants.

How can these sufferings be understood as being endured "for the sake of" the Colossians? Unlike Christ's death on the cross, Paul's suffering does not save them from their sins. Paul was in prison because he proclaimed the gospel, and that struggle on their behalf (2:1) has brought the benefits of the gospel to them.

1:25—2:1 The goal of Paul's preaching, teaching, and admonishing is to "present everyone fully mature in Christ" (v. 28) so that they can fend off false teaching (2:2). If they, the Colossians, are firmly rooted in understanding their faith, they cannot be deceived by outside arguments no matter how persuasive or plausible.

wisdom,[c] so that we may present everyone fully mature[d] in Christ. 29To this end
I strenuously[e] contend[f] with all the energy Christ so powerfully works in me.[g]
2 I want you to know how hard I am
contending[h] for you and for those at
Laodicea,[i] and for all who have not met
me personally. 2My goal is that they may
be encouraged in heart[j] and united in
love, so that they may have the full riches of complete understanding, in order
that they may know the mystery of God,
namely, Christ, 3in whom are hidden all
the treasures of wisdom and knowledge.[k]
4I tell you this so that no one may deceive
you by fine-sounding arguments.[l] 5For
though I am absent from you in body, I
am present with you in spirit[m] and delight to see how disciplined[n] you are and
how firm[o] your faith in Christ is.

Spiritual Fullness in Christ

6So then, just as you received Christ
Jesus as Lord,[p] continue to live your lives
in him, 7rooted[q] and built up in him,
strengthened in the faith as you were
taught, and overflowing with thankfulness.
8See to it that no one takes you captive
through hollow and deceptive philosophy,[r] which depends on human tradition
and the elemental spiritual forces[a] of
this world[s] rather than on Christ.
9For in Christ all the fullness of the
Deity lives in bodily form, 10and in Christ
you have been brought to fullness. He is
the head[t] over every power and authority. 11In him you were also circumcised[u]
with a circumcision not performed by
human hands. Your whole self ruled by
the flesh[b][v] was put off when you were
circumcised by[c] Christ, 12having been
buried with him in baptism, in which
you were also raised with him[w] through
your faith in the working of God, who
raised him from the dead.[x]
13When you were dead in your sins[y]
and in the uncircumcision of your flesh,
God made you[d] alive with Christ. He forgave us all our sins, 14having canceled the

1:28 [c]1Co 2:6,7 [d]Eph 5:27
1:29 [e]1Co 15:10 [f]Col 2:1 [g]Eph 1:19
2:1 [h]Col 1:29; 4:12 [i]Rev 1:11
2:2 [j]Col 4:8
2:3 [k]Ro 11:33; 1Co 1:24,30
2:4 [l]Ro 16:18
2:5 [m]1Th 2:17 [n]1Co 14:40 [o]1Pe 5:9
2:6 [p]Col 1:10
2:7 [q]Eph 3:17
2:8 [r]1Ti 6:20 [s]Gal 4:3
2:10 [t]Eph 1:22
2:11 [u]Ro 2:29; Php 3:3 [v]Gal 5:24
2:12 [w]Ro 6:5 [x]Ac 2:24
2:13 [y]Eph 2:1,5

[a] 8 Or *the basic principles*; also in verse 20
[b] 11 In contexts like this, the Greek word for *flesh* (*sarx*) refers to the sinful state of human beings, often presented as a power in opposition to the Spirit; also in verse 13.
[c] 11 Or *put off in the circumcision of*
[d] 13 Some manuscripts *us*

2:2–5 In the NT, the term "mystery" refers to a secret once hidden but that God has now revealed. God did not call Christians to control a monopoly on the truth but to share it with others. That was true for the apostles, and it is still true today.

The mystery revealed to Paul was that God intended to save the Gentiles *from the very beginning* (1:26–27). Christ "among the Gentiles" (1:27) was not plan B after the gospel had been rejected by Jews. Rather, it was God's eternal purpose. Paul rejoices to be an active participant in God's astounding plan for all the peoples of the world.

1:24—2:5 Few knew suffering better than Paul, who believed that all Christians must share in the suffering of their Lord. Christians can expect no better treatment than their Lord received; suffering thus belongs to the Christian calling. Paul bore his suffering joyfully because he knew that he belonged to Christ. His suffering for the gospel confirmed his passion for his calling.

2:6–7 Paul lists four characteristics of what it means "to live your lives in him" (v. 6), each expressed with a participle. The first participle ("rooted," v. 7) appears in the perfect tense (expressing the continuing results of an action completed in the past); the next three ("built up," "strengthened," and "overflowing," v. 7) are in the present tense.

2:8 The warning here provides the first direct clue in the letter that the Colossian church faces an outside danger. Paul describes the potential abductor as a "hollow and deceptive philosophy."

Paul draws several contrasts between the gospel and this "philosophy." The "philosophy . . . depends on human tradition." Paul contrasts it with divine revelation. The term "elemental spiritual forces of this world" represents Paul's appraisal of the "philosophy." It belongs to the domain of sin and death, where demonic powers still wield their influence. This term refers to the quasi-demonic spirits to which humans have foolishly given their allegiance. The contrast between "the elemental spiritual forces of this world" and "Christ" in v. 8 probably signifies that Paul regards them as rivals to Christ. The "philosophy" depends on these created, malignant powers, not on the Creator.

Paul also characterizes this "philosophy" as being completely without truth. By contrast, the Colossians have the full riches of complete understanding in Christ (v. 2).

2:9–10 Paul distinguishes Christ from the hierarchy of angelic beings, who possess dashes of divine attributes. The *fullness* of the Godhead dwells in Christ. Since Christ is the fullness of God and believers are in him, they have all the fullness humans can ever possess.

2:11–12 The "circumcision not performed by human hands" (v. 11) refers to something done by God as opposed to something done by human beings. It therefore stood over against the external rite for which Judaism was famous in the ancient world. "Circumcised by Christ" is a vivid image for Christ's death, which Paul interprets as having happened for all believers.

2:13–14 Paul portrays the Colossians' life before they were joined to Christ as a kind of nonexis-

charge of our legal indebtedness,[z] which
stood against us and condemned us; he
has taken it away, nailing it to the cross.[a]
15And having disarmed the powers and
authorities,[b] he made a public spectacle of them, triumphing over them[c] by
the cross.[a]

Freedom From Human Rules

16Therefore do not let anyone judge
you[d] by what you eat or drink,[e] or with
regard to a religious festival,[f] a New
Moon celebration[g] or a Sabbath day.[h]
17These are a shadow of the things that
were to come;[i] the reality, however, is
found in Christ. 18Do not let anyone who
delights in false humility[j] and the worship of angels disqualify you.[k] Such a
person also goes into great detail about
what they have seen; they are puffed up
with idle notions by their unspiritual
mind. 19They have lost connection with
the head,[l] from whom the whole body,
supported and held together by its liga-
ments and sinews, grows as God causes
it to grow.[m]
20Since you died with Christ to the
elemental spiritual forces of this world,[n]
why, as though you still belonged to
the world, do you submit to its rules:[o]
21"Do not handle! Do not taste! Do not
touch!"? 22These rules, which have to
do with things that are all destined to
perish[p] with use, are based on merely human commands and teachings.[q]
23Such regulations indeed have an appearance of wisdom, with their self-
imposed worship, their false humility
and their harsh treatment of the body,
but they lack any value in restraining
sensual indulgence.

2:14 [z] Eph 2:15 [a] 1Pe 2:24
2:15 [b] Eph 6:12 [c] Lk 10:18
2:16 [d] Ro 14:3, 4 [e] Ro 14:17 [f] Ro 14:5 [g] 1Ch 23:31 [h] Gal 4:10
2:17 [i] Heb 8:5
2:18 [j] ver 23 [k] Php 3:14
2:19 [l] Eph 1:22 [m] Eph 4:16
2:20 [n] Gal 4:3, 9 [o] ver 14, 16
2:22 [p] 1Co 6:13 [q] Isa 29:13; Mt 15:9; Titus 1:14

[a] 15 Or *them in him*

Col 2:20-23 ❖ How does knowing that we died with Christ to the forces of this world change the way we live?

tence in the realm of the dead. Paul goes on to use a commercial image for unpaid debts to describe this forgiveness: God nailed the incriminating list of those debts to the cross (v. 14).

2:15 The final image in the clause can mean "to triumph over, to march in a triumphal procession, to make known, or to reveal." The rulers put Jesus to death without knowing that through his death he would conquer them decisively and escape their rule.

2:6-15 Every generation of Christians faces new assaults on their faith. But these challenges are only a serious problem for those who are not thoroughly grounded and growing in their faith. Those who are filled by Christ do not feel any chronic dissatisfaction with life or sense of insecurity, and they long only to please God and to pour their lives out for others. They can even rejoice amid suffering and afflictions.

2:16-17 Paul here condemns those who use eating and drinking and the observance of feast days to pass judgment on others. Since Paul would never describe pagan rituals as a shadow or outline of what was to come in Christ, the promise/fulfillment motif is more fitting as an evaluation of Judaism's teachings. Paul's conclusion is: Why play in the shadow world when you have experienced the real thing in Christ?

2:18-19 The opponents declare the Colossians unfit because they fail to measure up on issues of humility, worship of angels, and visions. These false teachers are puffed up and have the gall to contest the Christians' salvation.

They delight "in false humility" (v. 18). Paul may imply here that it is a "false humility" because it results in their becoming "puffed up" (v. 18). Another option is to interpret it as a reference to a specific form of humility—namely, fasting. Fasting may have been part of their preparations for the heavenly visions and revelations.

The phrase "worship of angels" (v. 18) could mean that Paul accuses them of worshiping or asking angels for protection. Paul does not need to give the Colossians an objective description of the opponents' beliefs and practices. He only wants to deflate those teachers' false boasts with sarcasm. Their exaggerated visions are all smoke and mirrors—much ado about nothing.

The root of the error is one's failure to hold fast to Christ, who is the head (v. 19). Holding to anything other than Christ (1:18; 2:10) will cause them to disintegrate and perish.

2:20-23 Since Christians have been released from the rulers' and powers' slavery, why would they ever consider giving these powers new life by submitting to their rules? The opponents' aim to serve God and restrict the flesh only succeeded in serving the flesh and unleashing its power. From Paul's perspective all these "mystical" experiences are a sham.

2:16-23 The Colossian opponents' attempts to squelch worldly desires and establish their purity let loose a more deadly strain of sin—namely, pride. Many Christian groups want to draw the circle of acceptability ever tighter around themselves and reject others because of some failure to conform to their narrow vision of the truth. The problem when we do so is that we can worship the rules or our theological constructions more than we worship Christ. This process inevitably results in an ugly, smug arrogance and fuels the divisions between us rather than working to bring about reconciliation.

Living as Those Made Alive in Christ

3 Since, then, you have been raised
with Christ, set your hearts on things
above, where Christ is, seated at the right
hand of God. 2Set your minds on things
above, not on earthly things.[r] 3For you
died,[s] and your life is now hidden with
Christ in God. 4When Christ, who is your[a]
life, appears,[t] then you also will appear
with him in glory.[u]
5Put to death, therefore, whatever
belongs to your earthly nature: sexual
immorality, impurity, lust, evil desires
and greed,[v] which is idolatry.[w] 6Because
of these, the wrath of God[x] is coming.[b]
7You used to walk in these ways, in the
life you once lived.[y] 8But now you must
also rid yourselves[z] of all such things as
these: anger, rage, malice, slander,[a] and
filthy language from your lips.[b] 9Do not
lie to each other,[c] since you have taken
off your old self with its practices 10and
have put on the new self, which is being
renewed[d] in knowledge in the image of
its Creator.[e] 11Here there is no Gentile
or Jew,[f] circumcised or uncircumcised,[g]
barbarian, Scythian, slave or free,[h] but
Christ is all,[i] and is in all.

3:2 [r] Php 3:19, 20
3:3 [s] Ro 6:2; 2Co 5:14
3:4 [t] 1Co 1:7 [u] 1Pe 1:13; 1Jn 3:2
3:5 [v] Eph 5:3 [w] Eph 5:5
3:6 [x] Ro 1:18
3:7 [y] Eph 2:2
3:8 [z] Eph 4:22 [a] Eph 4:31 [b] Eph 4:29
3:9 [c] Eph 4:22, 25
3:10 [d] Ro 12:2; Eph 4:23 [e] Eph 2:10
3:11 [f] Ro 10:12 [g] 1Co 7:19 [h] Gal 3:28 [i] Eph 1:23
3:12 [j] Php 2:3 [k] 2Co 6:6; Gal 5:22, 23
3:13 [l] Eph 4:2 [m] Eph 4:32
3:14 [n] 1Co 13:1-13 [o] Eph 4:3
3:15 [p] Jn 14:27
3:16 [q] Ro 10:17 [r] Col 1:28 [s] Eph 5:19
3:17 [t] 1Co 10:31 [u] Eph 5:20

Col 3:15 ❖ With whom do we struggle to live at peace? How can Christ help us to find peace with these people?

12Therefore, as God's chosen people,
holy and dearly loved, clothe yourselves
with compassion, kindness, humility,[j]
gentleness and patience.[k] 13Bear with each
other[l] and forgive one another if any of
you has a grievance against someone.
Forgive as the Lord forgave you.[m] 14And
over all these virtues put on love,[n] which
binds them all together in perfect unity.[o]
15Let the peace of Christ[p] rule in your
hearts, since as members of one body
you were called to peace. And be thankful. 16Let the message of Christ[q] dwell
among you richly as you teach and admonish one another with all wisdom[r]
through psalms, hymns, and songs from
the Spirit, singing to God with gratitude
in your hearts.[s] 17And whatever you do,[t]
whether in word or deed, do it all in the
name of the Lord Jesus, giving thanks[u]
to God the Father through him.

[a] 4 Some manuscripts *our* [b] 6 Some early manuscripts *coming on those who are disobedient*

3:1–2 Being "raised with Christ" emphasizes the new status of believers, which requires a new way of life (v. 1). The new life gets underway as Christians set their hearts on or seek the things above. Since believers are in Christ, they already belong to the world above, where he is. As such, every thought, aim, value, aspiration, and striving should come under his lordship.

3:3–4 Paul's second affirmation is that the believer's life is "hidden with Christ in God" (v. 3). One's glorious appearance with Christ lies in the future (v. 4). A life hidden in the One who is seated at the right hand of God is completely secure. The new life of obedience does not depend on feeble human resolve but comes from being united with Christ.

3:5–9a Paul attests that one is either dead in sin (2:13) or dead to sin (3:5). Believers are still works in progress. Paul insists that Christians eliminate any persisting marks of the old pagan lifestyle—its values, customs, and practices. Paul concludes this first list of vices by indicating that such behavior will earn God's holy wrath (v. 6). If confirmed Christians behave no differently than their surrounding culture, they betray their calling and defame the name of their God.

"Filthy language from your lips" (v. 8) does not simply refer to curse words. It has in mind the abusive language people use to hurt others. Lying is rooted in an attempt to gain advantage over others. It is therefore at odds with Christian love.

3:9b–10 Paul does not urge the Colossians to change their lives for the better. A believer's whole nature must be first exchanged, not just revamped. Note here the reference to Ge 1:26–27 with its reference to the image of God (Col 3:10). In Christ, the image of God is being renewed in all believers.

3:11 Paul proclaims that the gospel breaks down man-made walls. It does not classify people by race, tribe, nationality, or class. Being in Christ, not a certain race or class, is the only thing that matters.

3:12–14 The image of being "chosen" (v. 12) reminds the Colossians that their election comes at God's initiative. The language reminds them that they are full partners in the heritage of Israel. But being God's chosen people brings with it ethical responsibilities.

"Compassion" is all the more crucial when societies become consumed by selfishness. "Kindness" is gracious sensitivity toward others. "Humility" halts the incessant pursuit to attain honor. "Gentleness" is a willingness to make allowances for others. "Patience" refrains from exacting revenge and is willing to endure wrong (v. 12).

The final virtue in the list is "love" (v. 14). Without love, we cannot truly exhibit compassion, kindness, humility, gentleness, and patience.

3:15–17 The key word in each sentence of the last paragraph of this section has to do with Christ: "the peace of Christ" (v. 15), "the message of Christ" (v. 16), "the name of the Lord Jesus" (v. 17). Everything believers do should be done conscious of the Lord's calling, commands, promises, and provision.

3:1–17 Sometimes, those who walk most closely to God are most acutely aware of how much they have fallen short of God's glory.

Instructions for Christian Households

3:18—4:1pp // Eph 5:22—6:9

[18]Wives, submit yourselves to your
husbands,[v] as is fitting in the Lord.
[19]Husbands, love your wives and do
not be harsh with them.
[20]Children, obey your parents in everything, for this pleases the Lord.
[21]Fathers,[a] do not embitter your children, or they will become discouraged.
[22]Slaves, obey your earthly masters
in everything; and do it, not only when
their eye is on you and to curry their favor, but with sincerity of heart and reverence for the Lord. [23]Whatever you do,
work at it with all your heart, as working for the Lord, not for human masters,
[24]since you know that you will receive an
inheritance[w] from the Lord as a reward. It
is the Lord Christ you are serving. [25]Any-
one who does wrong will be repaid for
their wrongs, and there is no favoritism.[x]

4 Masters, provide your slaves with what
is right and fair, because you know
that you also have a Master in heaven.

Further Instructions

[2]Devote yourselves to prayer,[y] being
watchful and thankful. [3]And pray for
us, too, that God may open a door[z] for
our message, so that we may proclaim
the mystery of Christ, for which I am

3:18 [v] Eph 5:22
3:24 [w] Ac 20:32
3:25 [x] Ac 10:34
4:2 [y] Lk 18:1
4:3 [z] Ac 14:27

[a] 21 Or *Parents*

They still see themselves as poor, wretched sinners. Others may see more of God's transforming presence in their lives than they do. Our assurance is that those who are in Christ are being transformed.

Paul asserts here that the old nature is not renewed or reformed but is put to death. This forceful image means that Christian renewal is not some new coat of paint that covers over our sinful personalities. Paul does not tell us to put on new clothes over the old; rather, the old way of life must be stripped off and thrown away.

3:18–19 The instruction that the wife submit to her husband fits the norm of Paul's culture. Paul does not overtly dispute this cultural assumption. The change in women's status in our age and modern sensibilities lead many today to wish that he had. However, the command for wives to submit was not inappropriate in his context. It reflects the legal state of affairs. The husband as the head of the household was the only fully legal person in the family and had power over all property and almost absolute authority over every other member of the family.

The verb "submit" (v. 18) does not convey some innate inferiority but is used for a modest, cooperative demeanor that puts others first. It was something expected of all Christians regardless of their rank or gender (cf. Eph 5:21).

In contrast to the commands to children and slaves, Paul does not tell wives to "obey" their husbands. The verb "submit" is in the middle voice and implies a voluntary submission. It makes the wife's submission her willing choice, not some universal law that ordains masculine dominance.

Paul also qualifies this submission further with the phrase, "as is fitting in the Lord" (v. 18). The Lord determines what is fitting or not. Some things may be culturally acceptable, but reflection on them "in the Lord" leads to the realization that they may be unfit for a Christian.

Husbands are presented with a much more demanding task. They are told to "love" their wives (v. 19). Paul reminds husbands of their obligations in the Lord. In a Christian marriage, the husband knows himself to be dearly loved by God and is commanded to love his wife in the same way.

3:20–21 Children were legally regarded as their fathers' property, and their status, theoretically, was little better than that of slaves. Therefore, the command for children to obey their parents fits a universal expectation. Paul believed that a father's discipline should be tempered by love, compassion, kindness, and patience.

3:22–4:1 The command that slaves must obey their masters in everything is jarring to those who now consider the institution of slavery to be abhorrent. In the first century, however, it was an entrenched reality that the early Christians could neither change nor ignore. Paul does not condone slavery with these commands but subtly undermines its very premises while encouraging obedience as an expression of loyalty to the family group. The commands to masters and slaves attempt to minimize the most blatant evils of the system.

3:18—4:1 The instructions to wife and husband focus on how they are to live together responsibly, not on how they can get their needs fulfilled. Submission can only be done with a healthy sense of self. The love that Paul commands husbands to have always puts the welfare of the wife and her needs first.

And in a world that is becoming increasingly indifferent and uncivil, parents need to instill in their children the spirit of kindness and compassion by setting good examples, beginning with the way they discipline their children.

4:2–4 "Being watchful" (v. 2) may be related to the unknown hour of the Lord's return and the world's end. But more likely, Paul is warning his readers against spiritual lethargy so that they can fend off temptations.

Paul does not fear imprisonment, though the possibility of deliverance is important to him because it will allow unrestricted mission opportunities. Preaching the gospel can evoke enormous hostility and has led to his current imprisonment. Paul usually qualifies references to his chains with some comment on his commitment to the gospel. He is bound more by his commission to preach the gospel than he is by his chains.

PEOPLE TO KNOW // MARK (JOHN MARK)

COLOSSIANS 4:10: Mark was a cousin of Barnabas and ministry companion of both Barnabas and Paul on their first missionary journey. He also authored the Gospel that bears his name, though he was not himself a disciple of Jesus. While it is unclear whether Mark ever personally encountered Jesus during Christ's earthly ministry, many conjecture that the young man who ran away naked from Gethsemane may have been Mark, since only Mark's gospel includes this unique detail (Mk 14:52).

Mark joined Paul and Barnabas in Jerusalem on Paul's first missionary journey (Ac 12:25). He traveled with them to Cyprus, where they encountered a sorcerer. They moved on to Perga, but there Mark left Paul and Barnabas and returned to Jerusalem for unknown reasons (Ac 13:13). Mark's departure upset Paul, who refused to take Mark along when he and Barnabas planned to set out on another journey. Unable to agree, Barnabas and Paul parted ways, Barnabas taking Mark and Paul taking Silas (Ac 15:37–40).

Fortunately, this is not the last word on the relationship between Paul and Mark. In Paul's final biblical letter, 2 Timothy, Paul writes to Timothy that he was all alone except for Luke, who had stayed with him. He says to Timothy, "Get Mark and bring him with you, because he is helpful to me in my ministry" (2Ti 4:11). The broken relationship between Paul and Mark had been restored.

APPLICATION ✣ Sometimes we have missteps in our faith. We don't know why Mark left Paul and Barnabas on Paul's missionary journey. Whatever the case, it is not difficult to relate to Mark's need to take a break from his duties and to relate to his mishandling of his relationship with Paul. The important thing is that Mark did not give up or let his failures define his future. Mark later returned to serving by accompanying Barnabas on a missionary journey. He also wrote the Gospel of Mark, sharing the Good News of Jesus with others throughout history. He also reconciled with Paul. With humility and God's mercy, broken relationships can be restored. Indeed, believers are called to the ministry of reconciliation (2Co 5:18–19).

in chains.[a] 4Pray that I may proclaim it
clearly, as I should. 5Be wise[b] in the way
you act toward outsiders;[c] make the most
of every opportunity.[d] 6Let your conversation be always full of grace,[e] seasoned
with salt,[f] so that you may know how to
answer everyone.[g]

Final Greetings

7Tychicus[h] will tell you all the news
about me. He is a dear brother, a faithful
minister and fellow servant[ai] in the Lord.
8I am sending him to you for the express
purpose that you may know about our[b]
circumstances and that he may encourage your hearts.[j] 9He is coming with
Onesimus,[k] our faithful and dear brother,
who is one of you. They will tell you everything that is happening here.
10My fellow prisoner Aristarchus[l]

4:3 [a] Eph 6:19,20
4:5 [b] Eph 5:15 [c] Mk 4:11 [d] Eph 5:16
4:6 [e] Eph 4:29 [f] Mk 9:50 [g] 1Pe 3:15
4:7 [h] Ac 20:4 [i] Eph 6:21,22
4:8 [j] Eph 6:21,22
4:9 [k] Phm 10
4:10 [l] Ac 19:29

Col 4:2-4 ✣ How can we pray for those who are at the forefront of spreading the message of Christ?

[a] 7 Or *slave;* also in verse 12 [b] 8 Some manuscripts *that he may know about your*

4:5-6 As a minority in a hostile environment, Christians were concerned about the impressions they made on their neighbors. The Colossians shared the responsibility of evangelizing unbelievers as much as the traveling missionaries. Paul does not want the Colossians to be fearful, threatened, or isolated. Their words should always be gracious. "Seasoned with salt" (v. 6) was used to refer to witty, amusing, clever, or humorous speech. Their "saltiness" will prevent them from being ignored as irrelevant bores. They need to have their answers ready for those who challenge or are curious about their faith. To do this, they need to be well-grounded in their faith.

4:7-9 Paul's list of coworkers reveals several things about his ministry. Paul needed the help and support of others, and he was not stingy in giving them credit and thanks. Paul inspired love and loyalty; any picture of him as an embattled and embittered loner is mistaken. Without supportive friends and partners throughout the world, Christians could never have succeeded in advancing the gospel across national barriers.

As the bearer of the letter, Tychicus is the first coworker mentioned (v. 7). He receives the highest praise possible: "a dear brother, a faithful minister and fellow servant in the Lord" (v. 7).

Paul identifies Onesimus simply as a "faithful and dear brother" (v. 9; cf. Phm 16) and as "one of you," without mentioning any ministerial role.

4:10-14 Aristarchus, Paul's "fellow prisoner" (v. 10), could have rotated in voluntarily together perhaps

sends you his greetings, as does Mark,
the cousin of Barnabas.[m] (You have received instructions about him; if he
comes to you, welcome him.) 11 Jesus,
who is called Justus, also sends greetings. These are the only Jews[a] among
my co-workers for the kingdom of God,
and they have proved a comfort to me.
12 Epaphras,[n] who is one of you and a servant of Christ Jesus, sends greetings. He
is always wrestling in prayer for you,[o]
that you may stand firm in all the will of
God, mature[p] and fully assured. 13 I vouch
for him that he is working hard for you
and for those at Laodicea[q] and Hierapolis. 14 Our dear friend Luke,[r] the doctor,
and Demas[s] send greetings. 15 Give my
greetings to the brothers and sisters at
Laodicea, and to Nympha and the church
in her house.[t]

16 After this letter has been read to you,
see that it is also read[u] in the church of
the Laodiceans and that you in turn read
the letter from Laodicea.

17 Tell Archippus:[v] "See to it that you
complete the ministry you have received
in the Lord."[w]

18 I, Paul, write this greeting in my own
hand.[x] Remember[y] my chains. Grace be
with you.[z]

4:10 [m] Ac 4:36 4:12 [n] Col 1:7; Phm 23 [o] Ro 15:30 [p] 1Co 2:6 4:13 [q] Col 2:1 4:14 [r] 2Ti 4:11; Phm 24 [s] 2Ti 4:10 4:15 [t] Ro 16:5 4:16 [u] 2Th 3:14 4:17 [v] Phm 2 [w] 2Ti 4:5 4:18 [x] 1Co 16:21 [y] Heb 13:3 [z] 1Ti 6:21; 2Ti 4:22; Titus 3:15; Heb 13:25

[a] 11 Greek *only ones of the circumcision group*

---

with Epaphras (v. 12, called a "fellow prisoner" in the companion letter to Philemon [v. 23]), sharing Paul's quarters and therefore his captivity, though they were not charged with any crime.

Mark is identified as "the cousin of Barnabas" (v. 10). It is likely that he is the same John Mark we meet in Acts (Ac 12:12, 25; 15:37, 39). If so, Mark is no longer a cause for dispute (Ac 15:36–41) but has become a source of comfort as a coworker.

A brother "who is called Justus" is mentioned along with Aristarchus and Mark as "the only Jews" among his coworkers (Col 4:11). Paul wants to remind them that some Jews have been willing to throw aside their religious entitlements for the sake of the gospel. They also serve with him in his mission among the Gentiles.

Epaphras, like Onesimus, is identified as "one of you" (v. 12). If Epaphras founded the congregation, he did not forget it when he left but continued to pray for it. The verb "wrestling" (v. 12) may allude to Christ's struggle in prayer in Gethsemane. Epaphras, like Paul, wants the Colossians to understand all that God has done in Christ so that they will not become easy targets for false teaching.

Luke is identified only as "the doctor" (v. 14). Demas is mentioned only by name with no commendation, which may hint at his future desertion of Paul (2Ti 4:10).

4:15–17 Paul also extends his greetings in this letter to the Christians in Laodicea, particularly to the church that meets in Nympha's house (v. 15). She is probably unmarried or widowed. Either status would give her more independence and flexibility in the ancient world as the head of her household.

We can do no more than guess at the nature of Archippus's ministry (v. 17), but it parallels what Paul says about himself in 1:25.

4:18 Paul takes the pen in hand for the final greeting and signs his letter with a terse, final request for them to "remember my chains." His brief benediction may hint at the difficulty of writing with shackles binding his wrists.

The call to remember his chains is a note of encouragement for those who may also suffer persecution for their faith as well as another request for their prayer support. Following Paul's example requires more than a halfhearted commitment to the gospel.

4:2–18 If we expect our prayer life to have any effect in our lives and in our world, it cannot be sporadic or haphazard. We cannot fall back on prayer only when we think we need it; we must "devote" ourselves to it, as 4:2 states.

1 Thessalonians

Author: The apostle Paul

Audience: The largely Gentile church in Thessalonica, founded by Paul

Date: About AD 51

Theme: Paul praises the Thessalonian believers for their spiritual maturity and perseverance, and he encourages them to further growth in view of Christ's imminent return and God's empowering Spirit.

Reading 1 Thessalonians

In the first half of this letter, Paul outlines both his joy in and deep concern for the Thessalonian church. In the second half, he discusses their Christian life, and he answers questions about the second coming of Christ.

PERSPECTIVE

The two letters to the Thessalonians are often called Paul's eschatological letters — the ones that instruct us in what will happen at the end of time. We want to know, for example, when Christ will come again, who will be raised, where we will go, and how all this will happen. Apparently the Thessalonians were curious about these questions because each chapter of the first letter ends with a reference to the second coming. Chapter 4 focuses on these questions.

Paul's answers to such questions, however, seem frustratingly elusive. He reassures but does not inform. Christ will come again (4:15), but we don't know when (5:1–3). We will go to be with the Lord (4:17), but we don't know exactly where. There is security in being believers, but we cannot know for sure the difference between believers and unbelievers. Paul communicates hope but does not satisfy our curiosity. Perhaps it is more accurate to say that to communicate hope — true hope — Paul must avoid satisfying our curiosity. Is it possible that too specific answers about questions to which we can only know partial answers actually discourages hope and instead contributes to a spiral of despair when we learn about our limitations?

We live in an age where marvelous scientific and technological achievements condition us to expect more and more precise answers to all sorts of questions about the lives we lead — including questions normally reserved for philosophers and religionists: What's wrong with my life? How should I live? Where is all of this going to end up? At some levels science and technology have provided interesting

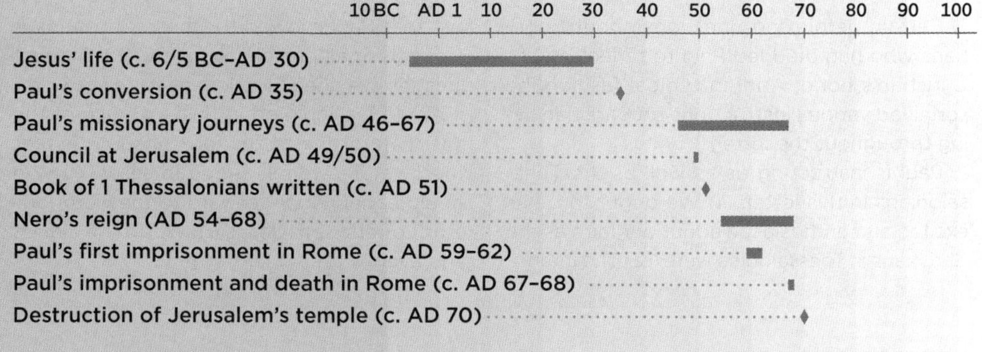

answers to these questions. So our response is to rely more and more on human wisdom.

We also live in an era in which people, much like the Thessalonian believers, are looking for signs of the end times. In such times people traditionally look heavenward for patterns of meaning. So we live in an age where technical precision clashes with a spiritual hunger that only mystery can satisfy.

Our present-day tasks parallel in a remarkable way those facing the apostle Paul as he wrote these two letters. The people of Thessalonica were persecuted Christians, in danger of losing hope in their relatively newfound faith. Paul had left the city abruptly and felt a need to reassure this new believing community. He wanted to give them hope. Indeed, one of the most important lessons we can take away from reading this book is to understand the dos and don'ts of giving hope.

Hope is a common human desire. In order to have meaning in life, we must have confidence that a brighter future lies ahead. We need to know that there is a way out of our human difficulties. Yet it is also apparent that we are severely limited in what we can know about the future (cf. Ro 8:24). And it is in the interaction between these two truths that hope resides. To provide hope we must respect both. If we disregard our desire for future meaning, despair inevitably results. If we disregard our limitations, we begin to predict the future and make mistakes in doing so. In either case, true hope is lost.

Paul resists dealing only with the danger of despair, and he resists providing answers that we cannot really know. Instead, he points to Jesus Christ, whose life embodied both human despair and limitation, showing us how faith in God's sovereignty is our only source of hope.

For more perspective on this book, see the Introduction to 2 Thessalonians.

Key Verses

For the Lord himself will come down from heaven, with a loud command, with the voice of the archangel and with the trumpet call of God, and the dead in Christ will rise first. After that, we who are still alive and are left will be caught up together with them in the clouds to meet the Lord in the air. And so we will be with the Lord forever.

—1 Thessalonians 4:16–17

TAKING THE NEXT STEPS

This letter is quite likely the first one that Paul wrote. He sent it either from Athens or, more probably, from Corinth (Ac 17:16; 18:1, 11; 1Th 3:1) to the church that he had started in Thessalonica (Ac 17:1-4). Because he had not been allowed to return to that city, and yet had heard that the Christians there were suffering persecution, Paul wanted them to know of his deep love and concern for them.

Certain perplexing questions about Christians who had died led Paul to reflect on the Christian's hope. And, in typical fashion, he sprinkled various instructions on Christian living throughout the letter.

Paul is instructing us as well as the Thessalonians in this letter. (1) We ought to be as excited and enthusiastic about our faith as the Christians in Thessalonica were. (2) The intense love that Paul showed for these Christians is a model for all pastors to follow. (3) The first question we need to ask in everything we do is: Am I pleasing God in this? (4) One of the most comforting truths for Christians is that when we die, we fall asleep in Jesus. (5) We should eagerly look forward to the victorious return of our Lord Jesus Christ on the clouds of heaven.

WHAT TO LOOK FOR IN 1 THESSALONIANS

- Paul's ministry in Thessalonica (ch. 2)
- Paul's intense concern for the Thessalonians (ch. 3)
- Christian morality and the return of Jesus (chs. 4–5)

1 Paul, Silas[a] and Timothy,[a]

To the church of the Thessalonians[b] in
God the Father and the Lord Jesus Christ:

Grace and peace to you.[c]

Thanksgiving for the Thessalonians' Faith

2We always thank God for all of you[d] and
continually mention you in our prayers.
3We remember before our God and Father
your work produced by faith,[e] your labor
prompted by love, and your endurance
inspired by hope in our Lord Jesus Christ.
4For we know, brothers and sisters[b]
loved by God, that he has chosen you,
5because our gospel[f] came to you not
simply with words but also with power,
with the Holy Spirit and deep conviction.
You know how we lived among you for
your sake. 6You became imitators of us[g]

1Th 1:6 ❖ How does the Holy Spirit give joy even in the midst of suffering? How is joy different from happiness?

[a] *1* Greek *Silvanus,* a variant of *Silas* [b] *4* The Greek word for *brothers and sisters* (*adelphoi*) refers here to believers, both men and women, as part of God's family; also in 2:1,9,14,17; 3:7; 4:1,10,13; 5:1,4,12,14,25,27.

1:1 [a]Ac 16:1; 2Th 1:1 [b]Ac 17:1 [c]Ro 1:7
1:2 [d]Ro 1:8
1:3 [e]2Th 1:11
1:5 [f]2Th 2:14
1:6 [g]1Co 4:16

1:1 Of all of Paul's letter openings, this is the simplest and most like contemporary Greco-Roman letter openings. First and Second Thessalonians are the only letters in which Paul does not characterize himself or his colleagues in some way. The conjunction of the three names and the frequent use of the first-person plural ("we") throughout the letter indicate that all three are co-senders of the letter.

In the Greek world, the word translated as "church" could designate a gathering or a movement. The Thessalonians are "in God the Father and the Lord Jesus Christ." The close linkage of God and Jesus indicates their unity of purpose and action. The phrase "grace and peace" calls to mind both the basis and the results of God's saving activity, which finds its focus in Jesus Christ.

APPLICATION ✣ 1:1 Team leadership offers important advantages. Accountability to other leadership team members reduces the chances of a leader falling into sin. Moreover, even when a leader has a significant moral failure, the presence of a team rather than a single individual in leadership reduces the odds that the failure will devastate the congregation or fellowship.

1:2–10 This passage functions as the letter's primary "thanksgiving" section. Thanksgiving, however, is not the only thing going on here. This is a complex and multifunctional prayer report.

Paul touches on several themes that arise later in the letter. For example, in 1:3 "love" anticipates the discussion in 4:9–12, and "hope" anticipates 4:13—5:11. In 1:5 "power" and "Holy Spirit" anticipate the advice about the Spirit and prophecy in 5:19–22. In 1:5–6 the reference to imitation of the founding missionaries prepares for 2:1–12 and 5:12–13. In 1:9–10, the comments on serving God anticipate the comments on holiness (4:3–8), vigilance (5:1–10), and mutual exhortation (5:11, 14–22).

and of the Lord, for you welcomed the message in the midst of severe suffering[h] with the joy given by the Holy Spirit.[i] 7And so you became a model to all the believers in Macedonia and Achaia. 8The Lord's message rang out from you not only in Macedonia and Achaia—your faith in God has become known everywhere.[j] Therefore we do not need to say anything about it, 9for they themselves report what kind of reception you gave us. They tell how you turned to God from idols[k] to serve the living and true God, 10and to wait for his Son from heaven, whom he raised from the dead[l]—Jesus, who rescues us from the coming wrath.[m]

Paul's Ministry in Thessalonica

2 You know, brothers and sisters, that our visit to you[n] was not without results. 2We had previously suffered[o] and been treated outrageously in Philippi, as you know, but with the help of our God we dared to tell you his gospel in the face of strong opposition. 3For the appeal we make does not spring from error or impure motives,[p] nor are we trying to trick you. 4On the contrary, we speak as those approved by God to be entrusted with the gospel.[q] We are not trying to please people[r] but God, who tests our hearts. 5You know we never used flattery, nor did we put on a mask to cover up greed[s]—God is our witness.[t] 6We were not looking for praise from people, not from you or anyone else, even though as apostles[u] of Christ we could have asserted our authority. 7Instead, we were like young children[a] among you.

Just as a nursing mother cares for her children,[v] 8so we cared for you. Because we loved you so much, we were delighted to share with you not only the gospel of God but our lives as well.[w] 9Surely you remember, brothers and sisters, our toil and hardship; we worked[x] night and day in order not to be a burden to anyone[y] while we preached the gospel of God to you. 10You are witnesses,[z] and so is God, of how holy,[a] righteous and blameless we were among you who believed. 11For you know that we dealt with each of you as a father deals with his own children,[b] 12encouraging, comforting and urging you to

1:6 [h] Ac 17:5-10 [i] Ac 13:52
1:8 [j] Ro 1:8; 10:18
1:9 [k] 1Co 12:2; Gal 4:8
1:10 [l] Ac 2:24 [m] Ro 5:9
2:1 [n] 1Th 1:5,9
2:2 [o] Ac 16:22; Php 1:30
2:3 [p] 2Co 2:17
2:4 [q] Gal 2:7 [r] Gal 1:10
2:5 [s] Ac 20:33 [t] Ro 1:9
2:6 [u] 1Co 9:1,2
2:7 [v] ver 11
2:8 [w] 2Co 12:15; 1Jn 3:16
2:9 [x] Ac 18:3 [y] 2Th 3:8
2:10 [z] 1Th 1:5 [a] 2Co 1:12
2:11 [b] ver 7; 1Co 4:14

[a] 7 Some manuscripts *were gentle*

1Th 2:10-12 ❖ How can we, in our own personal ministry, imitate Paul here?

However, this foreshadowing of later topics in the letter should not obscure what Paul's primary focus is in this section: the Thessalonian believers themselves. In particular he focuses on their Spirit-empowered response to the gospel message that Paul and his colleagues shared with them.

1:2-10 One way to apply this passage to our contemporary situation is to take the six observations about the Thessalonian congregation and turn them into a set of questions to ask about our churches (and, for that matter, ourselves).

- Are we a community and individuals rooted in God's grace, love, and election?
- Are we a community and individuals committed to Jesus Christ?
- Are we a community and individuals empowered by the Holy Spirit?
- Are we a community and individuals that bear witness to the gospel?
- Are we a community and individuals characterized by faith, hope, and love?
- Are we a community and individuals clearly differentiated from other religions?

2:1-12 This section marks the transition from the primary thanksgiving (1:2-10) to the body or central part of the letter (2:1–5:22). The heavy concentration of direct appeals in the last part of our passage (vv. 9-12) indicates that the primary function of this section is exhortation. By reminding them of the behavior he and his companions modeled while in Thessalonica, Paul implicitly encourages his readers to adopt and/or continue such behavior—in the face of hostility and persecution, as did the missionaries (e.g., vv. 1-2).

There is no clear or obvious structure to vv. 1-12. With respect to content, in vv. 1-4 the focus is on the missionaries' dependence on and responsibility to God; in both vv. 5-8 and 9-12 the focus is on their behavior toward and care for the Thessalonians.

In contrast to others, Paul avoided behavior that could call into question the integrity of the gospel. On the one hand, the speech of the three letter senders was bold and forceful; on the other hand, their actions were characterized by gentleness and care and motivated by love.

Paul focuses on the behavior and attitudes of the missionaries while they were in Thessalonica. Calling on both God and the Thessalonians as witnesses, he first emphasizes their reliance on and responsibility to God (vv. 1-4). He then describes the gentle and loving way they behaved toward and cared for the Thessalonians as they sought to encourage them to live lives worthy of God (vv. 5-12).

2:1-12 Integrity is not something that happens by accident. It involves the hard work of discerning what is right and of learning right from wrong, and then living out—consistently—what has been discerned. Paul's example

live lives worthy[c] of God, who calls you
into his kingdom and glory.
13 And we also thank God continually[d]
because, when you received the word
of God,[e] which you heard from us, you
accepted it not as a human word, but as
it actually is, the word of God, which is
indeed at work in you who believe. 14 For
you, brothers and sisters, became imitators of God's churches in Judea,[f] which
are in Christ Jesus: You suffered from
your own people[g] the same things those
churches suffered from the Jews 15 who
killed the Lord Jesus[h] and the prophets[i]
and also drove us out. They displease
God and are hostile to everyone 16 in their
effort to keep us from speaking to the
Gentiles[j] so that they may be saved. In
this way they always heap up their sins
to the limit.[k] The wrath of God has come
upon them at last.[a]

2:12 [c] Eph 4:1
2:13 [d] 1Th 1:2 [e] Heb 4:12
2:14 [f] Gal 1:22 [g] Ac 17:5; 2Th 1:4
2:15 [h] Ac 2:23 [i] Mt 5:12
2:16 [j] Ac 13:45, 50 [k] Mt 23:32
2:17 [l] 1Co 5:3; Col 2:5 [m] 1Th 3:10
2:18 [n] Mt 4:10 [o] Ro 1:13; 15:22
2:19 [p] Php 4:1 [q] 2Co 1:14 [r] Mt 16:27; 1Th 3:13
2:20 [s] 2Co 1:14
3:1 [t] ver 5 [u] Ac 17:15

Paul's Longing to See the Thessalonians

17 But, brothers and sisters, when we
were orphaned by being separated from
you for a short time (in person, not in
thought),[l] out of our intense longing
we made every effort to see you.[m] 18 For
we wanted to come to you — certainly I,
Paul, did, again and again — but Satan[n]
blocked our way.[o] 19 For what is our hope,
our joy, or the crown[p] in which we will
glory[q] in the presence of our Lord Jesus
when he comes?[r] Is it not you? 20 Indeed,
you are our glory[s] and joy.

3 So when we could stand it no longer,[t]
we thought it best to be left by ourselves in Athens.[u] 2 We sent Timothy, who
is our brother and co-worker in God's
service in spreading the gospel of Christ,
to strengthen and encourage you in your

[a] 16 Or *them fully*

---

reminds us of the fundamental importance of integrity on the part of all of us who have been entrusted by God with the gospel of Jesus Christ (cf. 2:4).

2:13–16 This is the second of three places in the letter where Paul gives thanks. In 1:2 Paul's thanks are ultimately rooted in God's choice of the Thessalonians (1:4); here he gives thanks for their acceptance of the message, and in 3:9 he will give thanks for their continuing steadfastness (3:8).

The passage serves a transitional role in the structure of the letter. Focusing on the Thessalonians, Paul develops a point touched on in 1:6: the Thessalonians' acceptance of the gospel despite severe suffering (vv. 13–14). This reference to suffering sets up what he will say in 2:17–20. Verses 15–16 are like a parenthetical editorial comment, prompted by the mention of "the Jews" (at the end of v. 14).

Throughout this section, Paul encourages his readers as he (1) recalls their praiseworthy past actions, encouraging them to maintain that pattern of behavior (v. 13), and (2) seeks to strengthen their sense of group identity and their resolve (vv. 14–16).

When the Thessalonians accepted the "word of God" (v. 13) they became the focus of hostility from their "own people" (v. 14). Acts 17:5–9 offers a clue as to why this happened: By accepting the "Lord Jesus," the Thessalonians implicitly rejected the claims to sovereignty of "Lord Caesar" and the civil religion of the imperial cult. Thus, they were perceived as threats to the established social and governmental order.

Judgment is the subject of Paul's last statement in this section (v. 16). Those who are opposed to God will be unable to escape God's wrath. It is perhaps best to interpret this last phrase along the lines of the idea expressed in Jn 3:18. Rejection of God's Messiah is in and of itself judgment. It means rejecting the only One who can bring salvation.

✣ **2:13–16** Any allegedly Christian group that advocates anti-Semitism or other forms of racial discrimination forfeits any right to be called "Christian." Because the present passage can be so easily misunderstood and twisted to support anti-Semitic prejudices, it is important to stress that in this passage Paul is *not* anti-Semitic. There is a fundamental theological difference between Christianity and Judaism—the one acknowledges Jesus as Messiah, the other does not. This theologically based opposition is expressed throughout the NT. Regrettably, this theological difference has frequently given rise to racially based discrimination (or worse) against Jews—that is, anti-Semitism. It cannot be stressed too strongly that there is in the NT no basis whatsoever for anti-Semitism of any sort.

2:17—3:8 This section falls into three clear subsections: Paul's report of his unsuccessful attempts to revisit Thessalonica (2:17–20), his sending of Timothy in his place to encourage the believers in the midst of persecution (3:1–5), and his reaction to the good news when Timothy returns (3:6–8, which spills over into 3:9, the third thanksgiving in the letter).

2:17–18 Paul's intense feelings toward the Thessalonians are evident from his description of the repeated attempts he made to return to Thessalonica (vv. 17b–18a). These attempts failed because, Paul says, "Satan blocked our way" (v. 18b).

2:19–20 Paul explains why he longed to see the Thessalonians again: They represented the fruit and evidence of his ministry. The "crown" mentioned in v. 19 is likely a laurel wreath, a symbol of victory.

3:1–5 Timothy's task was to "strengthen" and "encourage" (v. 2) the Thessalonian converts. The urgency of Timothy's mission was generated by the "trials" (v. 3) that the Thessalonians were currently experiencing.

faith, [3]so that no one would be unsettled
by these trials. For you know quite well
that we are destined for them.[v] [4]In fact,
when we were with you, we kept telling
you that we would be persecuted. And it
turned out that way, as you well know.[w]
[5]For this reason, when I could stand it
no longer,[x] I sent to find out about your
faith. I was afraid that in some way the
tempter[y] had tempted you and that our
labors might have been in vain.[z]

Timothy's Encouraging Report

[6]But Timothy has just now come to
us from you[a] and has brought good
news about your faith and love.[b] He has
told us that you always have pleasant
memories of us and that you long to
see us, just as we also long to see you.
[7]Therefore, brothers and sisters, in all
our distress and persecution we were
encouraged about you because of your
faith. [8]For now we really live, since you
are standing firm[c] in the Lord. [9]How can
we thank God enough for you[d] in return
for all the joy we have in the presence of
our God because of you? [10]Night and day
we pray[e] most earnestly that we may see
you again[f] and supply what is lacking in
your faith.
[11]Now may our God and Father himself and our Lord Jesus clear the way for
us to come to you. [12]May the Lord make
your love increase and overflow for each
other[g] and for everyone else, just as ours
does for you. [13]May he strengthen your
hearts so that you will be blameless[h] and
holy in the presence of our God and Father when our Lord Jesus comes[i] with
all his holy ones.

3:3 [v]Ac 9:16; 14:22
3:4 [w]1Th 2:14
3:5 [x]ver 1 [y]Mt 4:3 [z]Gal 2:2; Php 2:16
3:6 [a]Ac 18:5 [b]1Th 1:3
3:8 [c]1Co 16:13
3:9 [d]1Th 1:2
3:10 [e]2Ti 1:3 [f]1Th 2:17
3:12 [g]1Th 4:9,10
3:13 [h]1Co 1:8 [i]1Th 2:19
4:1 [j]2Co 13:11 [k]2Co 5:9

1Th 3:12–13 ❖ This doxology is instructive for how we live our lives in community today.

Living to Please God

4 As for other matters, brothers and
sisters,[j] we instructed you how to live
in order to please God,[k] as in fact you are
living. Now we ask you and urge you in
the Lord Jesus to do this more and more.
[2]For you know what instructions we gave
you by the authority of the Lord Jesus.

3:6–8 Paul felt deep relief when Timothy returned with the news that the Thessalonians had successfully resisted Satan's temptations. Timothy also reported the Thessalonians had positive memories of Paul and his fellow missionaries and would welcome a return visit. They understood why Paul left so suddenly under such suspicious circumstances and did not hold it against him.

Verse 8b functions both as an affirmation—it clearly acknowledges that they are currently "standing firm"—and as an implicit exhortation ("*if* you continue"). It is worth noting how Paul bases his own sense of well-being on the continuing faithfulness of his converts (v. 8).

❖ 2:17—3:8 Christian ethical teachings and values are not only ignored in our modern culture, but explicitly rejected by a steadily growing (as well as influential and powerful) segment of society. As American society continues this transition to a post-Christian culture, those who seek to live their lives according to the gospel of Jesus Christ can expect to encounter the kinds of trials and persecution experienced by Paul and the Thessalonians. What will we value more at that time: social acceptance and affirmation, or faithfulness to the gospel, whatever that may cost?

3:9–10 Paul moves from thanksgiving in v. 9 to a twofold petition (v. 10): that he might be able (1) to visit the Thessalonians in person and (2) to "supply what is lacking in [their] faith." These needed things would include additional instruction on specific points of doctrine and conduct.

3:11–12 The content of v. 11 repeats the substance of the first part of v. 10. Verse 12 affirms the accomplishments of the Thessalonians and encourages them to "increase and overflow" in "love."

3:13 Verse 13 indicates the goal or purpose of the petition in v. 12. Paul prays that the Lord will cause the love of the Thessalonians to increase so that when they find themselves "in the presence of our God," they may be seen as blameless and fully acceptable to God.

❖ 3:9–13 Love is not merely a matter of emotion or feeling; in 1:3 Paul already gave thanks for the Thessalonians' "labor prompted by love." In short, how might the members of this relatively new church with deep needs of its own gain strength in the face of difficulties and challenges? Through serving others in love. This is advice that flies in the face of the narcissism and self-centeredness of much of present culture.

In our contemporary culture, which is overwhelmingly oriented toward immediate gratification and results, to pray that others might live in light of eternity rather than the present is no small thing—especially since praying in this way on behalf of others inevitably reminds us of our need to do the same (3:13).

4:1–2 Here Paul does three things: First, he reminds the Thessalonians of the instructions they had received from him during his time in Thessalonica; second, he affirms them for following those instructions; finally, he exhorts them "to do this more and more" (v. 1).

3It is God's will that you should be sanctified: that you should avoid sexual immorality;[l] 4that each of you should learn to control your own body[a][m] in a way that is holy and honorable, 5not in passionate lust[n] like the pagans,[o] who do not know God; 6and that in this matter no one should wrong or take advantage of a brother or sister.[b][p] The Lord will punish all those who commit such sins,[q] as we told you and warned you before. 7For God did not call us to be impure, but to live a holy life.[r] 8Therefore, anyone who rejects this instruction does not reject a human being but God, the very God who gives you his Holy Spirit.[s]

9Now about your love for one another[t] we do not need to write to you,[u] for you yourselves have been taught by God to love each other.[v] 10And in fact, you do love all of God's family throughout Macedonia.[w] Yet we urge you, brothers and sisters, to do so more and more,[x] 11and to make it your ambition to lead a quiet life: You should mind your own business and work with your hands,[y] just as we told you, 12so that your daily life may win the respect of outsiders[z] and so that you will not be dependent on anybody.

4:3 [l] 1Co 6:18
4:4 [m] 1Co 7:2,9
4:5 [n] Ro 1:26 [o] Eph 4:17
4:6 [p] 1Co 6:8 [q] Heb 13:4
4:7 [r] Lev 11:44; 1Pe 1:15
4:8 [s] Ro 5:5; Gal 4:6
4:9 [t] Ro 12:10 [u] 1Th 5:1 [v] Jn 13:34
4:10 [w] 1Th 1:7 [x] 1Th 3:12
4:11 [y] Eph 4:28; 2Th 3:10-12
4:12 [z] Mk 4:11
4:13 [a] Eph 2:12

1Th 4:9-12 ❖ How can we live in such a way that our daily lives win the respect of those around us? What personal characteristics earn such respect?

Believers Who Have Died

13Brothers and sisters, we do not want you to be uninformed about those who sleep in death, so that you do not grieve like the rest of mankind, who have no hope.[a] 14For we believe that Jesus died and rose again, and so we believe that God will bring with Jesus those who have

[a] 4 Or *learn to live with your own wife*; or *learn to acquire a wife* [b] 6 The Greek word for *brother or sister* (*adelphos*) refers here to a believer, whether man or woman, as part of God's family.

4:3-8 Paul next focuses on a single aspect of what his instructions entailed—namely, sexual morality. This topic would have been of particular significance for anyone recently converted from pagan culture. For Paul, sexual activity has an impact on both one's relationship with God and with other people. Therefore, it ought to be exercised in a way that is respectful of both. In short, sexual behavior ought to be giving rather than self-serving (taking from). Verse 6b ends the long sentence started in v. 3 by indicating the reason *why* believers should not wrong or exploit one another: "The Lord will punish all those who commit such sins."

God does not merely define by his character the standard for living; he also provides the power to do it. For Paul, the presence of the Spirit makes Paul's argument against sexual impurity possible.

✜ **4:1-8** For those who are married, this teaching means first of all faithfulness to one's spouse. It also means treating each other with respect. For those who are not married, it means obedience to the spirit, not just the letter, of the biblical teaching about the proper context for sexual activity. There are those who interpret the injunction against intercourse outside of marriage as implying permission for just about anything else. This results in the odd circumstance of people who technically are virgins, yet who are in some respects more sexually experienced than some married couples. Such should not be the case among believers.

4:9-12 Paul diplomatically affirms the Thessalonians for what they are doing well (vv. 9-10a) and encourages them to develop in areas that need further attention (vv. 10b-12).

Even as Paul affirms the Thessalonians for doing well (v. 10a), he urges them "to do so more and more" (v. 10b). Specifically, he wants them "to make it your ambition to lead a quiet life," "mind your own business," and "work with your hands" (v. 11).

From its inception, the Christian community had been visible in the public arena, with sometimes painful consequences for the new believers. Any member of the congregation who remained active in the public arena ran the risk of attracting persecution to the whole congregation. Paul tells the Thessalonians to keep a low profile, give attention to their affairs, and stay busy. He gives reasons in v. 12: "so that your daily life may win the respect of outsiders and so that you will not be dependent on anybody."

✜ **4:9-12** Our culture measures an individual's worth by the quantity of one's wealth and possessions. Thus, lifestyle choices become ways of demonstrating one's affluence—concrete evidence of one's success (or lack thereof). Wealth is to be displayed, and excess and extravagance are widely celebrated. It is difficult not to draw a connection between the culture's emphasis on affluence and the statistics that indicate Christians who could afford to give more, in fact, give less as their income rises. This should not be the case.

4:13 Christians should not grieve in the same way or to the same extent as those without hope. The hope of a believer must affect how one deals with death.
4:14 The resurrection of Jesus provides the foundation on which Paul bases his encouragement and the rest of this section. Paul took it for granted that Christians should face death not with despair but

fallen asleep in him.[b] 15According to the Lord's word, we tell you that we who are still alive, who are left until the coming of the Lord, will certainly not precede those who have fallen asleep.[c] 16For the Lord himself will come down from heaven, with a loud command, with the voice of the archangel and with the trumpet call of God,[d] and the dead in Christ will rise first.[e] 17After that, we who are still alive and are left[f] will be caught up together with them in the clouds[g] to meet the Lord in the air. And so we will be with the Lord[h] forever. 18Therefore encourage one another with these words.

The Day of the Lord

5 Now, brothers and sisters, about times and dates[i] we do not need to write to you,[j] 2for you know very well that the day of the Lord[k] will come like a thief in the night.[l] 3While people are saying, "Peace and safety," destruction will come on them suddenly, as labor pains on a pregnant woman, and they will not escape.

4But you, brothers and sisters, are not in darkness[m] so that this day should surprise you like a thief. 5You are all children of the light and children of the day. We do not belong to the night or to the darkness. 6So then, let us not be like others, who are asleep,[n] but let us be awake and sober. 7For those who sleep, sleep at night, and those who get drunk, get drunk at night.[o] 8But since we belong to the day, let us be sober, putting on faith and love as a breastplate,[p] and the hope of salvation[q] as a helmet.[r] 9For God did not appoint us to suffer wrath but to receive salvation through our Lord Jesus Christ.[s] 10He died for us so that, whether we are awake or asleep, we may live together with him.[t] 11Therefore encourage one another and build each other up, just as in fact you are doing.

Final Instructions

12Now we ask you, brothers and sisters, to acknowledge those who work hard among you, who care for you in

4:14 [b] 1Co 15:18
4:15 [c] 1Co 15:52
4:16 [d] Mt 24:31 [e] 1Co 15:23; 2Th 2:1
4:17 [f] 1Co 15:52 [g] Ac 1:9; Rev 11:12 [h] Jn 12:26
5:1 [i] Ac 1:7 [j] 1Th 4:9
5:2 [k] 1Co 1:8 [l] 2Pe 3:10
5:4 [m] Ac 26:18; 1Jn 2:8
5:6 [n] Ro 13:11
5:7 [o] Ac 2:15; 2Pe 2:13
5:8 [p] Eph 6:14 [q] Ro 8:24 [r] Eph 6:17
5:9 [s] 2Th 2:13,14
5:10 [t] 2Co 5:15

1Th 5:11 ❖ What opportunities has God given us to encourage Christian brothers and sisters around us? How can we make the most of such opportunities?

---

with hope grounded in what God through Jesus has already done on their behalf.

4:15–17 The word for "meeting" (v. 17) is used in the OT for God's meetings with Abraham, David, and the Israelites at Sinai. It describes a welcoming party going to meet someone and escorting them back to the destination. The resurrected dead and raptured living will together meet the descending Lord "in the air" (v. 17) and accompany him to earth.

4:18 Having stated the topic ("those who sleep in death") in v. 13, Paul shares the fundamental theological affirmation that God will bring with Jesus those who have died (v. 14). He then shares some additional information (vv. 15–17) and indicates how the Thessalonians should use this information: to encourage one another (v. 18).

❖ **4:13–18** This passage invites us to question the extent to which our thinking about death is motivated by either fear or denial of it. It offers an opportunity to decide if we really believe that for believers "to die is gain" (Php 1:21, 23). None of these questions is easy to deal with because they force us to confront death. The good news is that we can lean on the God who has already conquered death in the resurrection of his Son, our Savior and Lord.

5:1–2 Paul writes that the Thessalonians already know "very well" the only thing one needs to know about when the Lord will return: It "will come like a thief in the night" (v. 2).

5:3 At a time when all *appears* well, "destruction" will arrive with the suddenness of a woman's labor pains. Anyone who is not "with the Lord" will certainly *not* escape.

5:4–8 Unlike the "others" who sleep in ignorance, the Thessalonians are to be "awake and sober" (v. 6). The first word emphasizes the need for vigilance; the second conveys the idea of balance or discipline.

5:9–11 The Thessalonians' status as "children of the light" is grounded in God's activity on their behalf (v. 5). They can stay alert and be self-controlled because God himself has destined them "to receive salvation" (v. 9).

Concerns about the fate of those who die before the Lord returns and questions about its timing do not, for Paul, override the need to practice brotherly love. On the contrary, they provide concrete occasions to do so, as believers comfort and encourage one another amid difficult circumstances, confident in the hope of a salvation grounded in the death and resurrection of the Lord Jesus.

❖ **5:1–11** The proper preparation for the coming day of the Lord is service rather than speculation. Human beings are naturally curious, especially about the future. Add God to the mix, and it is easy to understand why speculation about the return of Jesus is so attractive and fascinating for so many people. In contrast to idle speculation, Paul exhorts believers instead to encourage and build one another up.

5:12–13 Paul calls for proper recognition and appreciation of "those who work hard among you,

the Lord[u] and who admonish you. 13Hold
them in the highest regard in love because of their work. Live in peace with
each other.[v] 14And we urge you, brothers
and sisters, warn those who are idle[w] and
disruptive, encourage the disheartened,
help the weak,[x] be patient with everyone. 15Make sure that nobody pays back
wrong for wrong,[y] but always strive to
do what is good for each other[z] and for
everyone else.
16Rejoice always,[a] 17pray continually,
18give thanks in all circumstances; for
this is God's will for you in Christ Jesus.
19Do not quench the Spirit.[b] 20Do not
treat prophecies[c] with contempt 21but
test them all;[d] hold on to what is good,
22reject every kind of evil.
23May God himself, the God of peace,[e]
sanctify you through and through. May
your whole spirit, soul and body be kept
blameless at the coming of our Lord
Jesus Christ. 24The one who calls you is
faithful,[f] and he will do it.

25Brothers and sisters, pray for us.[g]
26Greet all God's people with a holy kiss.[h]
27I charge you before the Lord to have
this letter read to all the brothers and
sisters.[i]
28The grace of our Lord Jesus Christ
be with you.[j]

5:12 [u] 1Ti 5:17; Heb 13:17
5:13 [v] Mk 9:50
5:14 [w] 2Th 3:6,7, 11 [x] Ro 14:1
5:15 [y] 1Pe 3:9 [z] Gal 6:10; Eph 4:32
5:16 [a] Php 4:4
5:19 [b] Eph 4:30
5:20 [c] 1Co 14:1-40
5:21 [d] 1Co 14:29; 1Jn 4:1
5:23 [e] Ro 15:33
5:24 [f] 1Co 1:9
5:25 [g] Eph 6:19
5:26 [h] Ro 16:16
5:27 [i] Col 4:16
5:28 [j] Ro 16:20

---

who care for you in the Lord and who admonish you" (v. 12).

5:14–15 Paul instructs the congregation to "warn those who are idle" (v. 14). The verb clearly includes a note of disapproval. Paul's word means "undisciplined, irresponsible, disorderly."

They are also to "encourage the disheartened," which includes people who are worried, discouraged, fearful, feeling inadequate, lacking in confidence, despondent, sad, and weak (v. 14). "Help the weak" can be rendered "support, supply, help," or even "defend," while the "weakness" can involve moral temptation, spiritual shortcomings, physical weakness, or economic need (v. 14).

The command to "be patient with everyone" (v. 14) is highly relevant to a community under pressure or stress (e.g., persecution and concern about deceased believers).

5:16–18 In urging the Thessalonians to "rejoice always," "pray continually," and "give thanks in all circumstances" (vv. 16–18a), Paul is giving instructions that he himself modeled. For Paul, both rejoicing and giving thanks become forms of worship or praise of the God who works all things together for the believers' good (Ro 8:28–30).

5:19–21a Paul next focuses on charismatic manifestations of the Spirit, specifically prophecy. The proper solution to the problem of potential abuse is to "test them" (v. 21a): Prophecies are not to be accepted blindly. The proper course is to examine or investigate them regarding their trustworthiness or genuineness.

5:21b–22 Once a prophecy has been tested, the next step is clear: Christians are to hold on firmly to those that are good and have nothing to do with those that are not. Prophecies that pass the test are from the Holy Spirit and therefore ought not to be rejected or treated with contempt. On the other hand, any prophecy that fails the testing process is not from the Spirit and should therefore be rejected.

✣ **5:12–22** Paul's command to live in peace with one another (v. 13) is a hard saying for many people and congregations. The peace that the apostle has in mind is not merely the absence of conflict (hard enough to achieve for many of us!), but the presence of positive, healthy relationships. This is true for our attitudes toward our leaders (vv. 12–13) as well as toward other believers (vv. 14–15). Fellowships of believers work toward unity as we rejoice, give thanks, and pray together in community (vv. 16–18). As we discern what is being said in our fellowship, there is a double responsibility in these verses: not to quench anything that is genuinely of the Spirit and not to attribute anything false to the Spirit (vv. 19–22).

5:23–24 The prayer in v. 23 essentially echoes the prayer in 3:13. Verse 24 takes the form of a solemn affirmation. Paul hoped to reassure any who might still be concerned about their fate at the return of the Lord Jesus.

5:25–28 Paul requests the Thessalonians' prayers for him and his companions. Paul implicitly acknowledges, by his request for prayer, their fundamental equality before God.

The probable explanation for the abrupt switch in v. 27 from the plural to the singular pronoun ("I") is that Paul took the pen from the scribe (possibly Silas) and wrote the last two sentences himself.

✣ **5:23–28** Remembering what God has done in the past—not as dead history, but as the living and ongoing narrative of a faithful and powerful God in his relationship with his people—provides the basis for life in the present and hope for the future. Our future as believers rests entirely on God as he is revealed through the life and teachings of Jesus the Messiah and our trust in his sacrificial actions on our behalf.

Author: The apostle Paul
Audience: The church at Thessalonica
Date: About AD 51 or 52

Theme: Paul writes to correct a misunderstanding concerning the Lord's return and to encourage the Thessalonian believers to be steadfast in their faith and work for a living by reminding them that God empowers them for these tasks.

PERSPECTIVE

Near the middle of the first century AD, Paul wrote a pair of letters to a recently established congregation of Christians in the town of Thessalonica. The people to whom he addressed the two letters we now call 1 and 2 Thessalonians were for the most part new converts to the Christian faith, who had grown up in, and hence were thoroughly socialized in, a Greek cultural environment. One of Paul's major challenges was that of *resocialization*—helping these believers to learn, understand, and live by the very different social and ethical code of early Christianity. See Acts 17:1–14 for background to these letters.

We know next to nothing about the specific circumstances that led to the writing of 2 Thessalonians. That it was sent by the same three people as 1 Thessalonians and reflects so closely the language and structure of this letter strongly suggests that it was written not long after the first letter, while Paul, Silas, and Timothy were still in Corinth.

For more perspective on this book, see the Introduction to 1 Thessalonians.

Reading 2 Thessalonians

This letter is short enough to read at one time. Most of chapters 1 and 3 recall what Paul had written in his first letter to the Thessalonians. Chapter 2, however, is significantly different; it teaches that before Christ returns, the man of lawlessness will be revealed. Exactly who this individual is cannot be determined.

TAKING THE NEXT STEPS

Paul wrote this brief letter to the Christians in Thessalonica from Corinth (Ac 18:11), a few months after his first letter to them. His main purpose was to correct some misunderstandings regarding the Christians' hope that had resulted from that first letter. Furthermore, problems

Event	10 BC	AD 1	10	20	30	40	50	60	70	80	90	100
Jesus' life (c. 6/5 BC–AD 30)												
Paul's conversion (c. AD 35)												
Paul's missionary journeys (c. AD 46–67)												
Council at Jerusalem (c. AD 49/50)												
Book of 2 Thessalonians written (c. AD 51–52)												
Nero's reign (AD 54–68)												
Paul's first imprisonment in Rome (c. AD 59–62)												
Paul's imprisonment and death in Rome (c. AD 67–68)												
Destruction of Jerusalem's temple (c. AD 70)												

Key Verses

So then, brothers and sisters, stand firm and hold fast to the teachings we passed on to you, whether by word of mouth or by letter. May our Lord Jesus Christ himself and God our Father, who loved us and by his grace gave us eternal encouragement and good hope, encourage your hearts and strengthen you in every good deed and word.

—2 Thessalonians 2:15–17

concerning the daily work of Christians, evident earlier (1Th 4:11–12), had intensified and required a response from Paul.

Several important messages come to us through this book. (1) Knowing that Christ is going to return again and destroy all his enemies ought to inspire us to remain firm in the faith. (2) Paul's predictions that there will be opposition to Christ and his church until Jesus comes again help us understand why we experience resistance to the gospel. (3) Until Christ returns, we should be diligent in our daily work.

WHAT TO LOOK FOR IN 2 THESSALONIANS

- Thanksgiving and encouragement in the face of persecution (ch. 1)
- The second coming of Jesus and the man of lawlessness (ch. 2)
- Standing firm and praying (2:13—3:5)
- The problem of the disorderly (ch. 3)

1 Paul, Silas[a] and Timothy,[a]

To the church of the Thessalonians in
God our Father and the Lord Jesus Christ:

2Grace and peace to you from God the
Father and the Lord Jesus Christ.[b]

Thanksgiving and Prayer

3We ought always to thank God for
you, brothers and sisters,[b] and rightly
so, because your faith is growing more
and more, and the love all of you have
for one another is increasing.[c] 4There-
fore, among God's churches we boast[d]
about your perseverance and faith[e] in
all the persecutions and trials you are
enduring.[f]
5All this is evidence[g] that God's judgment is right, and as a result you will be
counted worthy of the kingdom of God,
for which you are suffering. 6God is just:
He will pay back trouble to those who
trouble you[h] 7and give relief to you who
are troubled, and to us as well. This will
happen when the Lord Jesus is revealed
from heaven in blazing fire with his powerful angels.[i] 8He will punish those who
do not know God[j] and do not obey the
gospel of our Lord Jesus.[k] 9They will be
punished with everlasting destruction[l]
and shut out from the presence of the
Lord and from the glory of his might[m]
10on the day[n] he comes to be glorified[o]
in his holy people and to be marveled at
among all those who have believed. This
includes you, because you believed our
testimony to you.[p]
11With this in mind, we constantly
pray for you, that our God may make
you worthy[q] of his calling, and that by
his power he may bring to fruition your
every desire for goodness and your every
deed prompted by faith.[r] 12We pray this
so that the name of our Lord Jesus may
be glorified in you,[s] and you in him, according to the grace of our God and the
Lord Jesus Christ.[c]

1:1 [a] Ac 16:1; 1Th 1:1
1:2 [b] Ro 1:7
1:3 [c] 1Th 3:12
1:4 [d] 2Co 7:14 [e] 1Th 1:3 [f] 1Th 2:14
1:5 [g] Php 1:28
1:6 [h] Col 3:25; Rev 6:10
1:7 [i] 1Th 4:16; Jude 14
1:8 [j] Gal 4:8 [k] Ro 2:8
1:9 [l] Php 3:19; 2Pe 3:7 [m] 2Th 2:8
1:10 [n] 1Co 3:13 [o] Jn 17:10 [p] 1Co 1:6
1:11 [q] ver 5 [r] 1Th 1:3
1:12 [s] Php 2:9-11

> **2Th 1:11** ❖ How can we prayerfully strive to ensure that all our deeds are prompted by faith?

[a] *1* Greek *Silvanus,* a variant of *Silas* [b] *3* The Greek word for *brothers and sisters* (*adelphoi*) refers here to believers, both men and women, as part of God's family; also in 2:1,13,15; 3:1,6,13. [c] *12* Or *God and Lord, Jesus Christ*

1:1–2 The designation of God as "our" Father (v. 1) reflects Paul's understanding that believers come to be part of God's spiritual family when they place their faith in Jesus Christ.

1:3–4 The Thessalonians' growth in faith and love was taking place under the most adverse conditions. However, those circumstances have not hindered the fellowship's growth in the critical areas of faith and love; if anything, they may have promoted it. The Thessalonian brothers and sisters have become for Paul an exemplary model of enduring Christian commitment under difficult conditions.

1:5–10 The Thessalonians' continued growth amid persecution is a sign of God's blessing, not judgment. This gives evidence that they are indeed part of God's people.

1:6 Paul picks up and develops the idea of God's righteous judgment. There are two sides to this judgment—one negative and one positive.

1:8–9 The negative side is discussed further in these two verses. The troublers of God's people are part of a larger group identified as "those who do not know God" (v. 8). The punishment that this group will experience is identified here.

1:10 Paul describes the positive side of God's judgment: Believers will experience both the presence and the glory of the Lord himself. This is because the Lord will "be glorified in his holy people." They will also marvel, in the sense of "admire" or perhaps "worship."

In the last part of v. 10, Paul indicates the group that will experience the Lord's presence "includes you." The statement is both reassuring and comforting. At the same time, it is a veiled exhortation to keep on persevering, lest his readers find themselves in the other category.

All that Paul has been talking about will happen "when the Lord Jesus is revealed (v. 8) from heaven" (v. 7b). Even though Jesus is indeed Lord, not all creation recognizes or acknowledges that fact. But the day is surely coming when the lordship of Jesus will be revealed for all to see, with the consequences that Paul outlines in vv. 6–10 (i.e., judgment or salvation).

1:11 Paul prays that "God may make you worthy of his calling." The other petition is that God might "fulfill" or "bring to fruition"—the verb has the idea of finishing something already begun: "your every desire for goodness and your every deed prompted by faith."

1:12 All of this is due solely to "the grace of our God and the Lord Jesus Christ." The present and the future of salvation are also a matter of grace.

> **APPLICATION** ✚ **1:1–12** Consumer culture is characterized by choice. Even as the range of choices has multiplied, the significance of those choices has decreased. But not all choices are trivial, and not all consequences of our choices can be avoided. Examples include choices about education, which person to marry, what career to pursue, or whether to be faithful to a commitment. They are choices, in other words, that "make all the difference" in the fabric and shape of our lives.

The Man of Lawlessness

2 Concerning the coming of our Lord
Jesus Christ and our being gathered
to him,[t] we ask you, brothers and sisters, 2not to become easily unsettled or
alarmed by the teaching allegedly from
us—whether by a prophecy or by word
of mouth or by letter[u]—asserting that
the day of the Lord[v] has already come.
3Don't let anyone deceive you[w] in any
way, for that day will not come until the
rebellion occurs and the man of lawlessness[a] is revealed,[x] the man doomed to
destruction. 4He will oppose and will exalt himself over everything that is called
God[y] or is worshiped, so that he sets himself up in God's temple, proclaiming himself to be God.[z]
5Don't you remember that when I was
with you I used to tell you these things?
6And now you know what is holding him
back, so that he may be revealed at the
proper time. 7For the secret power of lawlessness is already at work; but the one
who now holds it back will continue to
do so till he is taken out of the way. 8And
then the lawless one will be revealed,
whom the Lord Jesus will overthrow with
the breath of his mouth[a] and destroy by
the splendor of his coming. 9The coming
of the lawless one will be in accordance
with how Satan works. He will use all
sorts of displays of power through signs
and wonders[b] that serve the lie, 10and
all the ways that wickedness deceives
those who are perishing.[c] They perish because they refused to love the truth and
so be saved. 11For this reason God sends
them[d] a powerful delusion so that they
will believe the lie 12and so that all will be
condemned who have not believed the
truth but have delighted in wickedness.[e]

2:1 [t] Mk 13:27; 1Th 4:15-17
2:2 [u] 2Th 3:17 [v] 1Co 1:8
2:3 [w] Eph 5:6-8 [x] Da 7:25; 8:25; 11:36; Rev 13:5,6
2:4 [y] 1Co 8:5 [z] Isa 14:13,14; Eze 28:2
2:8 [a] Isa 11:4; Rev 19:15
2:9 [b] Mt 24:24; Jn 4:48
2:10 [c] 1Co 1:18
2:11 [d] Ro 1:28
2:12 [e] Ro 1:32

[a] 3 Some manuscripts *sin*

Paul's description in 1:5–10 of God's future judgment focuses a spotlight on a particularly consequential and unavoidable choice: the decision whether to accept or reject "the gospel of our Lord Jesus" (1:8). When the time of judgment comes, those who believed the message and placed their trust in God will "be with the Lord forever" (1Th 4:17). Those, however, who have rejected the gospel will find themselves shut out.

2:1–2 Some in the congregation had concluded that the event that Paul discussed in 1Th 5:1–11 had already begun.

2:3–4 Paul emphatically denies any claim that the day of the Lord has arrived. Certain things that must happen have not yet happened. These things include (1) the occurrence of "the rebellion" (v. 3) and (2) the revealing of "the man of lawlessness" (v. 3b). Paul takes it for granted (cf. v. 5) that his readers know what he means by "*the* rebellion" and says nothing further about it. Paul, like other NT writers, probably has in view a time of increasing wrongdoing and general opposition to God.

The leader of this rebellion is a "man of lawlessness." This person demonstrates willful opposition to God and not only "oppose[s]" God but also "exalt[s] himself over everything that is called God or is worshiped" (v. 4), a description that echoes Da 11:36–37.

This arrogance leads this person to set "himself up in God's temple," a symbolic action that involves nothing less than "proclaiming himself to be God" (2Th 2:4). This suggests that he is nothing less than a rival messiah or antichrist.

2:5–12 As v. 5 indicates, Paul had previously taught them about this matter. Consequently, later readers are left in the dark regarding some aspects of what he writes. As a result, vv. 6–8a are among the most difficult in all of Paul's letters.

The basic structure of what Paul says in these verses is clear enough: (1) "The secret power of lawlessness is already at work" (v. 7a), but (2) it is operating in a manner that is somehow restrained or held back. (3) At some future time, however, "the lawless one will be revealed" (v. 8) or have his own "coming" (v. 9), at which point (4) he will be overthrown and destroyed by the far greater power and splendor of the Lord's own *second coming*.

In v. 7 Paul confirms that evil is currently at work in the world and is satanic in origin, but it is in some way limited or hindered. The restraining influence must be a force for good rather than evil. Once it "is taken out of the way" (v. 7), "then the lawless one will be revealed" (v. 8). The parallel with the coming of Jesus is obvious.

Though the "coming" of the lawless one may be both grand and cunningly deceptive, it will be short-lived, for this one is "the man doomed to destruction" (v. 3b), "whom the Lord Jesus will overthrow with the breath of his mouth and destroy by the splendor of his coming" (v. 8b).

The counterfeit signs and wonders of the lawless one (v. 9) exercise their deceptive effect on "those who are perishing" (v. 10) and are not in the community of faith. They are perishing specifically "because they refused to love the truth and so be saved" (v. 10). As Paul puts it emphatically in v. 12b, when they could have "believed the truth," they instead "delighted in wickedness."

Verses 11–12a discuss the consequence (*not* the cause) of this choice: "For this reason God sends them a powerful delusion so that they will believe the lie and so that all will be condemned."

✣ **2:1–12** The manner in which Paul emphasizes the importance of truth (vv. 10–12) reinforces the importance of focusing on Jesus. Paul describes those perishing as those who refused to love or to believe "the truth" (v. 12). In this context,

Stand Firm

13But we ought always to thank God
for you, brothers and sisters loved by
the Lord, because God chose you as firstfruits[a][f] to be saved[g] through the sanctifying work of the Spirit[h] and through
belief in the truth. 14He called you to this
through our gospel, that you might share
in the glory of our Lord Jesus Christ.
15So then, brothers and sisters, stand
firm[i] and hold fast to the teachings[b] we
passed on to you,[j] whether by word of
mouth or by letter.
16May our Lord Jesus Christ himself
and God our Father, who loved us[k] and by
his grace gave us eternal encouragement
and good hope, 17encourage[l] your hearts
and strengthen[m] you in every good deed
and word.

Request for Prayer

3 As for other matters, brothers and
sisters,[n] pray for us[o] that the message
of the Lord[p] may spread rapidly and be
honored, just as it was with you. 2And
pray that we may be delivered from wicked and evil people,[q] for not everyone has
faith. 3But the Lord is faithful,[r] and he
will strengthen you and protect you from
the evil one.[s] 4We have confidence[t] in the
Lord that you are doing and will continue
to do the things we command. 5May the
Lord direct your hearts[u] into God's love
and Christ's perseverance.

Warning Against Idleness

6In the name of the Lord Jesus Christ,[v]
we command you, brothers and sisters,
to keep away from[w] every believer who
is idle and disruptive[x] and does not live
according to the teaching[c] you received
from us.[y] 7For you yourselves know how
you ought to follow our example.[z] We
were not idle when we were with you,
8nor did we eat anyone's food without paying for it. On the contrary, we

2:13 [f]Eph 1:4 [g]1Th 5:9 [h]1Pe 1:2
2:15 [i]1Co 16:13 [j]1Co 11:2
2:16 [k]Jn 3:16
2:17 [l]1Th 3:2 [m]2Th 3:3
3:1 [n]1Th 4:1 [o]1Th 5:25 [p]1Th 1:8
3:2 [q]Ro 15:31
3:3 [r]1Co 1:9 [s]Mt 5:37
3:4 [t]2Co 2:3
3:5 [u]1Ch 29:18
3:6 [v]1Co 5:4 [w]Ro 16:17 [x]ver 7, 11 [y]1Co 11:2
3:7 [z]1Co 4:16

[a] 13 Some manuscripts *because from the beginning God chose you* [b] 15 Or *traditions* [c] 6 Or *tradition*

2Th 2:15 ❖ What factors in our lives today are calling us to "stand firm" for Christ?

2Th 3:6 ❖ When is it right to separate ourselves from a believer who is not living in accordance with God's Word?

"the truth" is virtually a synonym for the gospel. Its focus is, of course, Jesus Christ. Since our response to the truth—that is, to Jesus—determines our ultimate destiny, we have all the more reason to focus on Jesus, the true Christ, and not on his antagonist, the *anti*christ.

2:13–14 Paul contrasts the fate of those "who are perishing" (v. 10) with that of the Thessalonian believers. Paul's major goal is to reassure the Thessalonians regarding their fate (salvation), in contrast to that of those who are opposing and persecuting them. Regardless of the efforts of the coming "lawless one" to deceive them (v. 9), their salvation is in God's hands.

2:15 As usual, Paul's thanksgiving statements are multifunctional. The list of reasons why God ought to be thanked (vv. 13–14) quickly becomes the basis for further exhortation (v. 15). "So, then," Paul says, "stand firm," a command that stands as the positive counterpart of 2:2. Moreover, he wants the Thessalonians to "hold fast to the teachings." Pay attention, Paul says, to what he and his companions have taught them, not what someone else claims or alleges they taught.

2:16–17 Paul has two gifts in view in v. 16. The first is "eternal encouragement"—encouragement that will outlast the afflictions of this age and the judgment to come. The second is "good hope," a hope that is not based on an individual's own behavior but on God's gracious love.

3:1–2 Having concluded his prayer for the Thessalonians, Paul proceeds to ask for their prayers on his behalf. Paul's first request is on behalf of the message (v. 1); the second one is for the messengers who proclaim it (v. 2).

3:3–4 Reassurance of God's love and concern for the community is followed by an exhortation to obedience and perseverance. Paul is preparing the way for his instructions in 3:6–15.

3:5 Paul prays that the Lord might "direct" the Thessalonians' attention to two important points. The first, "God's love," is assurance grounded in God. The second, "Christ's perseverance," demonstrates what Paul has repeatedly encouraged them to do—persevere.

2:13—3:5 What keeps us going in the face of continuing struggles? We persevere because as Paul has made clear earlier in the letter, Jesus wins. The One who has been faithful in the past will prove to be faithful in the future. This gives us courage and hope to remain faithful in the present.

3:6–10 From Paul's perspective, it should not have been necessary to "command" the Thessalonians "to keep away from" any believer who is "idle and disruptive" (v. 6). They already know. Paul and his colleagues deliberately practiced what they preached. Paul asserts, "we worked night and day, laboring and toiling so that we would not be a burden" (v. 8b).

worked[a] night and day, laboring and
toiling so that we would not be a burden to any of you. 9We did this, not because we do not have the right to such
help,[b] but in order to offer ourselves as
a model for you to imitate.[c] 10For even
when we were with you,[d] we gave you
this rule: "The one who is unwilling to
work[e] shall not eat."
11We hear that some among you are
idle and disruptive. They are not busy;
they are busybodies.[f] 12Such people we
command and urge in the Lord Jesus
Christ[g] to settle down and earn the food
they eat.[h] 13And as for you, brothers and
sisters, never tire of doing what is good.[i]

3:8 [a]Ac 18:3; Eph 4:28
3:9 [b]1Co 9:4-14 [c]ver 7
3:10 [d]1Th 3:4 [e]1Th 4:11
3:11 [f]ver 6,7; 1Ti 5:13
3:12 [g]1Th 4:1 [h]1Th 4:11; Eph 4:28
3:13 [i]Gal 6:9
3:14 [j]ver 6
3:15 [k]Gal 6:1; 1Th 5:14
3:16 [l]Ro 15:33 [m]Ru 2:4
3:17 [n]1Co 16:21
3:18 [o]Ro 16:20

14Take special note of anyone who does
not obey our instruction in this letter. Do
not associate with them,[j] in order that
they may feel ashamed. 15Yet do not regard them as an enemy, but warn them
as you would a fellow believer.[k]

Final Greetings

16Now may the Lord of peace[l] himself
give you peace at all times and in every
way. The Lord be with all of you.[m]
17I, Paul, write this greeting in my own
hand,[n] which is the distinguishing mark
in all my letters. This is how I write.
18The grace of our Lord Jesus Christ
be with you all.[o]

3:11–12 The apostolic example stands in sharp contrast to "some" among the Thessalonians (v. 11) who were burdens to the rest of the congregation. Paul spells out his solution to the problem in vv. 13–15.
3:13–15 Even as Paul commands the disorderly, he encourages the rest of the congregation to "never tire of doing what is good" (v. 13). Here we catch a glimpse of the negative impact the disorderly were having on the congregation. Those who were living responsibly were being worn down by the burden of those who refused to work.

The instructions in vv. 14–15 have in view everything discussed since 3:6. Paul clearly hopes that the disorderly will comply, but if this compliance is not forthcoming, the congregation itself must take steps to enforce it. The verb for "associate" (v. 14) calls upon the congregation to stop having contact with any such people, what later came to be termed "excommunication."

The goal of non-association is clearly spelled out: "in order that they may feel ashamed" (v. 14). Paul expects that the one who is "shamed" will then respond with appropriate behavior—in this case, repentance and obedience to Paul's instructions.

In short, the disciplinary action is clearly meant to be redemptive for the individual. At the same time, however, note that it is also protective for the community.
3:16 The reference to "the Lord of peace" is unique in the NT. The prayer is that the Lord Jesus may grant to the Thessalonians "peace at all times and in every way." Paul wants more than an absence of conflict within the congregation. Peace encompasses a state of well-being and wholeness characterized by reconciled relationships—with God, with each other in the congregation, and finally with those outside the community, to the extent possible.
3:17 It was not uncommon for a person dictating a letter to take the pen from the scribe who wrote it and write the last sentence or two in his (or her) own hand. Paul seems to have done this as a matter of habit (he refers to it as "the distinguishing mark in all my letters").
3:18 This closing benediction is virtually identical to the one in 1Th 5:28.

3:6–18 Even while Paul explicitly affirms that individuals who can work have a responsibility to do so, he assumes the congregation will meet the basic financial needs of its members. Both the affirmation and the assumption provide opportunities to reflect on the significance and value of work.

Work is a fundamental characteristic of human life because work provides the means for sustaining life. Without work, there is no life. In the biblical tradition, there is a selfless aspect to work. One works not just for self but also for others (i.e., to support those who are unable to work).

How might 3:10 apply today? For those who are able to work, a willingness to do so should essentially be a qualification for receiving financial assistance from the congregation.

What qualifies as discipline in the modern church? In the absence of definitive guidance from Scripture, its application requires careful prayer and consideration by a congregation and its leadership.

Finally, Paul asserts that our future rests entirely on the power and faithfulness of God as revealed through the Lord Jesus, the Messiah. That was a good place for the letter to begin; it is an even better place for it to end, as we persevere in faith (1:4) and await with eternal encouragement and good hope (2:16) the revelation from heaven of the Lord Jesus himself (1:7).

Author: The apostle Paul

Audience: Timothy, one of Paul's closest associates, but no doubt intended also to be read to the whole church in Ephesus

Date: Probably c. AD 64 but possibly c. AD 56

Theme: Paul instructs Timothy to oppose false teachers, to appoint godly leaders, and to otherwise strengthen the church at Ephesus.

PERSPECTIVE

How should we deal with the plurality of non-Christian teachings and philosophies that characterize our culture and challenge the church? The apostle Paul faced the same challenge and in the Pastoral Letters (1 Timothy, 2 Timothy, Titus) offers an answer.

Paul begins, of course, by stating the obvious: Teach against them. But he also recommends how to teach against them. Paul gives Timothy and Titus advice and counsel on methodology and attitude in counteracting false teachings, telling them both what not to do and what to do.

As to what not to do, Paul warns against a great danger in dealing with non-Christian teachings. The danger seems at first glance a simple one: wasting time. Avoid godless chatter, he says, and focus on the really important things, such as the gospel of Jesus Christ. On one level this advice makes a great deal of sense. But since Paul does spend a great deal of time himself in the Pastorals and in his other letters warning against the dangers of false teachings, perhaps there is more here than a simple time management seminar can cure.

What exactly is "godless chatter" (1Ti 6:20; 2Ti 2:16)? It is "secular and profane" talk that is "empty of real meaning." "Real meaning" for Paul is that which relates to the most real thing in the universe—God himself. Godless chatter is talk that doesn't have as either its content or goal the promotion of the gospel of Jesus Christ. In other words, Paul recommends that our talk be "partisan" in the best sense of that word—that we never waste time in simple critique of false teaching

Reading 1 Timothy

The apostle Paul (1:1) wrote this letter to his younger apostolic delegate Timothy, who was ministering in the city of Ephesus (1:3). The inhabitants of this important city of the Roman province of Asia worshiped many of the Greco-Roman gods and participated in emperor worship. Ephesus was also a significant port on the Aegean Sea, especially known for its temple of

10 BC AD 1 10 20 30 40 50 60 70 80 90 100

Jesus' life (c. 6/5 BC–AD 30)
Paul's conversion (c. AD 35)
Paul's missionary journeys (c. AD 46–67)
Council at Jerusalem (c. AD 49/50)
Nero's reign (AD 54–68)
Paul's first imprisonment in Rome (c. AD 59–62)
Book of 1 Timothy written (c. AD 63–65)
Paul's imprisonment and death in Rome (c. AD 67–68)
Destruction of Jerusalem's temple (c. AD 70)

the goddess Artemis (the Roman Diana; see Ac 19:23–41). The purpose of this first letter to Timothy is to instruct this young pastor as to how to lead the church there and to refute a false teaching that was threatening it. There is no unified structure to this letter; Paul simply moves from one topic to another as he gives pastoral advice to Timothy.

Key Verses

Be diligent in these matters; give yourself wholly to them, so that everyone may see your progress. Watch your life and doctrine closely. Persevere in them, because if you do, you will save both yourself and your hearers.

—1 Timothy 4:15–16

that doesn't go anywhere. No, Paul wants us always to talk in terms of the gospel.

Here is where Paul's advice about what to do comes in: When we talk about false teaching (by not wasting time talking about false teaching but by promoting the gospel), we are to follow the law of love—which means we are to be clear, kind, and optimistic.

Clarity is important to Paul because of the seriousness of the message. God did not just take on human flesh in Jesus Christ, but he did so in such a way as to be effective in showing himself to human beings. That is to be the focus of the message to false teachers.

Kindness is also important. For Paul, this is not a soft, ineffective meekness in the face of false teachings. *Kindness* means "a committed graciousness." Like clarity, Paul considers kindness a theological category—in this case, a human reflection, an imperfect imitation of God's grace toward all sinners. How can we show kindness to those who are threatening our faith through false teachings? Only by redistributing the kindness God showers on us toward others. We cannot find this kind of graciousness in ourselves.

This leads to Paul's third methodological principle: optimism. What works in combating false teachings, Paul says, is not angry denunciation or pessimistic hand-wringing. Rather, what works is keeping the hope that is within us front and center in all that we do. Since we do not always feel optimistic and hopeful ourselves, we need to be patient, not just with the false teachers but with ourselves.

The Pastoral Letters are aptly named—they are pastoral in the sense that they offer good, sound, practical advice on how to live out our calling as Christians in a world that is not often congenial to the radical demands of the gospel. Live by the law of love, Paul says. Be clear, kind, and optimistic. Then the false teachings will pale in significance next to the eternal truth of the Good News of Jesus Christ.

For more perspective on this book, see the Introductions to 2 Timothy and Titus.

TAKING THE NEXT STEPS

After Paul was released from prison in Rome (see Ac 28:30), early tradition tells that he continued his mission work, traveling part of the time with Timothy and Titus. Paul left Pastor Timothy behind in Ephesus

(1Ti 1:3) while he went to Macedonia, and sometime later he wrote this letter to encourage Timothy in his pastoral duties, to instruct him about church leadership, and to warn him about false doctrine infiltrating the church. Paul's instruction centered around church conduct and the establishment of proper order in the church.

Like the other two Pastoral Letters (2 Timothy and Titus), this one contains practical advice for the contemporary Christian. Christians today, pastors and lay people alike, can tap into the wisdom contained in this letter of Paul. (1) There is danger of false doctrine today just as there was in Paul's day; we must be sure that it does not gain a foothold in the church. (2) Church order is important for the church: God is not pleased with a haphazard approach to church conduct. (3) Selecting officers for the church is serious business, but those who become elders (overseers) and deacons ought to consider such service a privilege and fulfill their duties responsibly. (4) There is no greater danger to the well-being of the church than the foolishness of materialism; God has given us money and possessions to share with others and to use in his kingdom, not to hoard for our own selfish purposes.

WHAT TO LOOK FOR IN 1 TIMOTHY

- Warnings against false teachers (ch. 1)
- Instructions concerning Christian worship (ch. 2)
- Qualifications of overseers and deacons (ch. 3)
- Advice about widows and elders (ch. 5)

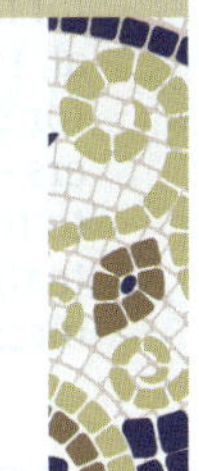

1 Paul, an apostle of Christ Jesus by the command of God[a] our Savior and of Christ Jesus our hope,[b]

2 To Timothy[c] my true son[d] in the faith:

Grace, mercy and peace from God the Father and Christ Jesus our Lord.

1:1 [a]Titus 1:3 [b]Col 1:27
1:2 [c]Ac 16:1 [d]2Ti 1:2; Titus 1:4
1:3 [e]Ac 18:19 [f]Gal 1:6,7
1:4 [g]1Ti 4:7; Titus 1:14

Timothy Charged to Oppose False Teachers

3 As I urged you when I went into Macedonia, stay there in Ephesus[e] so that
you may command certain people not to
teach false doctrines[f] any longer 4 or to
devote themselves to myths[g] and endless

1:1a Paul attributes his ministry to God's "command."
1:1b Paul calls God "our Savior." Significantly, the words "God" and "Savior" reappear in connection with Jesus Christ in Titus 2:13.
1:2a Timothy is Paul's "true son in the faith." The word translated "true" means "genuine" as opposed to "illegitimate" or "fake." The word refers to the quality of Timothy's spiritual-kinship relationship to Paul.
1:2b Paul hopes Timothy will experience "grace, mercy and peace." These beneficial favors come "from God the Father and Christ Jesus our Lord."

APPLICATION ✚ 1:1–2 The biblical hope mentioned in this greeting often tends to be replaced by a subjective, fuzzy optimism about a future life. When we invite people to the Christian hope, we must do so with a clear explanation as to how the Christian message offers the only basis for sure hope. We must also proclaim this truth, as other truths, with biblical authority. This authority is an important theme in Paul's so-called Pastoral Letters (1 and 2 Timothy and Titus).

1:3 Paul has realized that conditions are critically unhealthy in Ephesus because of false teaching. Paul has to "urge" Timothy to "stay" there for a specific purpose: to command these false teachers to stop. The word translated "teach false doctrines" reappears in 6:3. It is unnecessary to precisely identify the source or nature of the "myths" and "endless genealogies" (1:4) to realize their damaging effect on Christian thought.
1:4–5 The effect of these false teachings is to "promote controversial speculations." False teaching, spawning endless meaningless discussions, is the concern of this letter. It arises from disbelief in what God has revealed. "Faith" (v. 4c) is a basic term in the Christian vocabulary, as is "love" (v. 5a). The "goal of this command," like the fulfillment of the law (Ro 13:8–10), is "love." The love Paul speaks about in this verse requires an integrity of character to exist (1Ti 1:5b).

genealogies. Such things promote controversial speculations[h] rather than advancing God's work — which is by faith.
5The goal of this command is love, which
comes from a pure heart[i] and a good conscience and a sincere faith.[j] 6Some have
departed from these and have turned
to meaningless talk. 7They want to be
teachers of the law, but they do not know
what they are talking about or what they
so confidently affirm.
8We know that the law is good[k] if one
uses it properly. 9We also know that the
law is made not for the righteous but for
lawbreakers and rebels,[l] the ungodly and
sinful, the unholy and irreligious, for
those who kill their fathers or mothers,
for murderers, 10for the sexually immoral, for those practicing homosexuality,
for slave traders and liars and perjurers — and for whatever else is contrary
to the sound doctrine[m] 11that conforms
to the gospel concerning the glory of the
blessed God, which he entrusted to me.[n]

1:4 [h] 1Ti 6:4
1:5 [i] 2Ti 2:22 [j] 2Ti 1:5
1:8 [k] Ro 7:12
1:9 [l] Gal 3:19
1:10 [m] 2Ti 4:3; Titus 1:9
1:11 [n] Gal 2:7
1:12 [o] Php 4:13
1:13 [p] Ac 8:3 [q] Ac 26:9
1:14 [r] Ro 5:20 [s] 2Ti 1:13
1:15 [t] 1Ti 3:1; 2Ti 2:11; Titus 3:8
1:16 [u] ver 13

1Ti 1:13–14 ❖ How is Paul's negative past an encouragement to believers? What does it show us about God?

The Lord's Grace to Paul

12I thank Christ Jesus our Lord, who has
given me strength,[o] that he considered me
trustworthy, appointing me to his service.
13Even though I was once a blasphemer
and a persecutor[p] and a violent man, I was
shown mercy because I acted in ignorance
and unbelief.[q] 14The grace of our Lord was
poured out on me abundantly,[r] along with
the faith and love that are in Christ Jesus.[s]
15Here is a trustworthy saying[t] that
deserves full acceptance: Christ Jesus
came into the world to save sinners — of
whom I am the worst. 16But for that very
reason I was shown mercy[u] so that in
me, the worst of sinners, Christ Jesus
might display his immense patience as
an example for those who would believe
in him and receive eternal life. 17Now to

1:6 Paul pursues this matter of integrity further by stating that some people had "departed from these." The heretics turned *away* from Christian character *to* empty, "meaningless" talk, a striking contrast between steadfast doing or being and hollow speech.
1:7 It is ironic that the same people whose speech is empty "want to be teachers" and that those who repudiate love want to be teachers "of the law."

✥ **1:3–7** It will become increasingly clear in the study of Paul's Pastoral Letters that *how* the sound teacher should confront heresy shares the spotlight with *what* heresies to confront. Paul stresses the importance of *the integrity of doctrine and life*, both in the church's leaders and its members.

1:8 Paul describes those whose actions are (1) contrary to the law to "love your neighbor as yourself" (Gal 5:14) and (2) hostile to other human beings (1Ti 1:9–10a). Such people love neither God nor neighbor.
1:9 Paul establishes a principle that the law has been made for "lawbreakers and rebels." Those who resist doing what is right need to be confronted by a standard that clarifies what they are doing is wrong.
1:10 After listing the sins that require judgment and correction by the law, Paul generalizes: "and for whatever else is contrary to the sound doctrine." This is a vivid figurative expression to describe teaching that is not "sick" but wholesome.
1:11 The unsound, sick, and false doctrine has a formidable opponent, the "gospel concerning the glory of the blessed God." God "entrusted" this gospel to the apostle Paul (v. 11b).

✥ **1:8–11** Some Christians may be unprepared to discern the difference between truth and error because of insufficient exposure to sound biblical and doctrinal teaching. We need to put extra effort into seeing that new Christians especially are given the background they lack as quickly as possible so that they can tell the difference between "the gospel" and heresy and thereby successfully resist the latter.

1:12 While the strength comes from Christ, faithfulness or being found "trustworthy" is required of Paul. This faithfulness is a requirement for God's "service," which in Paul's case is to be an apostle to the Gentiles.
1:13–14 These verses form an interesting contrast to Paul's testimony in Php 3:4–6, where he portrays himself as formerly being proud of his accomplishments. It is striking that faith and love, which in 1Ti 1:5 formed the goal of Paul's command to Timothy, reappear here in v. 14. Faith and love, like grace, are abundantly bestowed by God.
1:15 The "trustworthy saying" in v. 15b contains the essence of the Christian message. Two extremes are cited of those for whom Christ came. One is the group of sinners described in vv. 9–10; the other is Paul, who calls himself "the worst" of sinners.
1:16 Paul sees himself as a prototype of all hostile, sinful rebels against God, whom God tolerates while patiently waiting for their conversion. The result of their new faith is "eternal life."
1:17 Paul's doxology honors God as (1) the "King," (2) beyond the limitation of time, (3) incapable of dying, (4) "invisible," and (5) existing alone as "God."

✥ **1:12–17** Paul appropriately concludes this section with a doxology. It is not trite to remind ourselves that our lives should be one continuous doxology: a life lived in minute-by-minute

the King[v] eternal, immortal, invisible,[w]
the only God, be honor and glory for ever
and ever. Amen.[x]

The Charge to Timothy Renewed

18 Timothy, my son, I am giving you this
command in keeping with the prophecies once made about you,[y] so that by
recalling them you may fight the battle
well,[z] 19 holding on to faith and a good conscience, which some have rejected and so
have suffered shipwreck with regard to the
faith.[a] 20 Among them are Hymenaeus[b]
and Alexander,[c] whom I have handed over
to Satan[d] to be taught not to blaspheme.

Instructions on Worship

2 I urge, then, first of all, that petitions,
prayers, intercession and thanksgiv-
ing be made for all people— 2 for kings
and all those in authority,[e] that we may
live peaceful and quiet lives in all godliness and holiness. 3 This is good, and
pleases God our Savior, 4 who wants[f] all
people[g] to be saved and to come to a
knowledge of the truth.[h] 5 For there is
one God[i] and one mediator[j] between God
and mankind, the man Christ Jesus, 6 who
gave himself as a ransom for all people.
This has now been witnessed to[k] at the
proper time.[l] 7 And for this purpose I was
appointed a herald and an apostle—I am
telling the truth, I am not lying—and a
true and faithful teacher[m] of the Gentiles.[n]
8 Therefore I want the men everywhere
to pray, lifting up holy hands[o] without anger or disputing. 9 I also want the wom-
en to dress modestly, with decency and
propriety, adorning themselves, not with

1:17 [v] Rev 15:3 [w] Col 1:15 [x] Ro 11:36
1:18 [y] 1Ti 4:14 [z] 2Ti 2:3
1:19 [a] 1Ti 6:21
1:20 [b] 2Ti 2:17 [c] 2Ti 4:14 [d] 1Co 5:5
2:2 [e] Ezr 6:10; Ro 13:1
2:4 [f] Eze 18:23, 32 [g] Titus 2:11 [h] 2Ti 2:25
2:5 [i] Ro 3:29,30 [j] Gal 3:20
2:6 [k] 1Co 1:6 [l] 1Ti 6:15
2:7 [m] 2Ti 1:11 [n] Ac 9:15; Eph 3:7,8
2:8 [o] Ps 134:2; Lk 24:50

> **1Ti 2:2** ❖ In what ways can we today strive to live "peaceful . . . lives in all godliness and holiness"?

> praise of God for all his amazing acts of gracious kindness to us.

1:18 The interplay of vocabulary between this chapter's opening and closing verses is striking. Paul calls Timothy "my son" in vv. 2 and 18. In v. 3, he tells Timothy what to command the false teachers; in v. 18, Paul uses the noun form of the same verb, but this time he commands Timothy himself. In v. 3, Paul mentions his prior urging of Timothy to stay at Ephesus; in v. 18, he mentions prior "prophecies" about Timothy.

1:19 The heretics have suffered shipwreck with regard to their own personal faith.

1:20 "Hymenaeus" reappears in 2Ti 2:17. "Alexander" may be the same person who tried to speak during the uproar when Paul was at Ephesus (Ac 19:33).

> ✣ **1:18–20** While truth is to be celebrated, error must be discerned and corrected. This is a difficult assignment for the contemporary Christian. As Paul's Pastoral Letters unfold, we will see the importance of patient, gentle calling of false teachers back to truth as well as sharp rebuke of those whose rebellion is destroying the church.

2:1–4 Paul has been establishing the need to oppose heresy and stating his own commission and passion for the gospel. Several things are necessary for that gospel to gain the response it should, as outlined in chs. 2 and 3. Paul is expressing the breadth of prayer in its various aspects, each of which is relevant here. Paul's goal and all-consuming passion is that the gospel might freely penetrate society, which will happen most effectively in a peaceful context.

Paul emphasizes that Christians must be *fully* characterized by the twin virtues of godliness and holiness. As the world sees the Christian character of believers, the gospel will go forward and be recognized as genuine.

God is pleased with these prayers for "all people" (2:1), because he is the God who wants "all people to be saved" (v. 4). Salvation is the active work of God, who has compassion and strength to rescue. The truth is to be accepted, appropriated, and allowed to change behavior.

2:5–7 God's concern for humanity is exclusive and inclusive. It is *exclusive* in the sense that there is no other God. But *inclusively,* God desires to be accepted as the God and Savior of all people. Jesus Christ is prophet, priest, and king. He is the only true mediator. He gave himself as a "ransom," releasing all of God's people from bondage (v. 6).

> ✣ **2:1–7** As far as truth is concerned, we are convinced that Christ is the only way. But *how* we declare this in today's world can move people toward or away from the gospel. We must declare the narrow way, but in doing so we must stress that there *is* a wonderful way for all people. It is important that we show the love of God in *providing* that way (Jn 3:16) and the grace of Christ in *becoming* that way through his sacrifice on the cross.

2:8 The word translated "men" usually means "males," though there are examples in classical Greek rhetoric of its use to include women. Here, however, it clearly stands in contrast with "women" in v. 9. This policy is in accordance with public prayer in the Jewish synagogue, though women did pray in gatherings of Christians. "Everywhere" should caution us against any assumption that Paul's instructions in our passage apply only to the church at Ephesus. "Anger" and "disputing" are inconsistent with effective prayer.

2:9–10 Paul insists that women's outward appearance should not conflict with their inner character. The believing women of the church in Ephesus are to avoid wearing what exudes wealth and suggests immorality.

elaborate hairstyles or gold or pearls or
expensive clothes,[p] 10but with good deeds,
appropriate for women who profess to worship God.
11A woman[a] should learn in quietness
and full submission.[q] 12I do not permit
a woman to teach or to assume authority over a man;[b] she must be quiet. 13For
Adam was formed first, then Eve.[r] 14And
Adam was not the one deceived; it was the
woman who was deceived and became
a sinner.[s] 15But women[c] will be saved
through childbearing — if they continue
in faith, love[t] and holiness with propriety.

Qualifications for Overseers and Deacons

3 Here is a trustworthy saying:[u] Whoever
aspires to be an overseer[v] desires a noble task. 2Now the overseer is to be above
reproach,[w] faithful to his wife, temperate,
self-controlled, respectable, hospitable,[x]
able to teach,[y] 3not given to drunkenness,
not violent but gentle, not quarrelsome,[z]
not a lover of money.[a] 4He must manage his own family well and see that his
children obey him, and he must do so
in a manner worthy of full[d] respect.[b] 5(If
anyone does not know how to manage
his own family, how can he take care of
God's church?)[c] 6He must not be a recent
convert, or he may become conceited[d]
and fall under the same judgment as the
devil. 7He must also have a good reputation with outsiders, so that he will not fall
into disgrace and into the devil's trap.[e]

2:9 [p] 1Pe 3:3
2:11 [q] 1Co 14:34
2:13 [r] Ge 2:7,22; 1Co 11:8
2:14 [s] Ge 3:1-6, 13; 2Co 11:3
2:15 [t] 1Ti 1:14
3:1 [u] 1Ti 1:15 [v] Ac 20:28
3:2 [w] Titus 1:6-8 [x] Ro 12:13 [y] 2Ti 2:24
3:3 [z] 2Ti 2:24 [a] Heb 13:5; 1Pe 5:2
3:4 [b] Titus 1:6
3:5 [c] 1Co 10:32
3:6 [d] 1Ti 6:4
3:7 [e] 2Ti 2:26

[a] 11 Or *wife*; also in verse 12 [b] 12 Or *over her husband* [c] 15 Greek *she* [d] 4 Or *him with proper*

2:11–12 The attitude of quietness in vv. 11–12 can be understood as ruling out teaching and the attitude of submission as ruling out exercising authority. This would not have been surprising to either Jews or Greeks, since neither culture permitted women to teach.

2:12 There is a considerable body of literature on the meaning of this verse. Proper understanding of Paul's introductory words, "I do not permit," requires comment. Can it be paraphrased "I am not now permitting," with the implication that Paul may permit it in the future but does not at the present time for some temporary reason? That may be the case, though it seems more likely a normal use of expressing a simple fact.

"Teach" probably refers to the authoritative communication of "the faith." To "assume authority" is not as clear in its meaning. The clause in v. 12 specifically limits its prohibition of teaching and having authority to exercising these over a man (or, as some suggest, over a woman's own husband) and does not rule out, even in those circumstances, any other ministry for women.

2:13–14 The circumstances cited from Genesis can either *require* the restriction of women or *explain* it, in this case by an analogy.

2:15 This verse has been the object of much study. "Saved" can mean to be rescued from some danger or disease. There is a prepositional phrase modifying "saved" ("through childbearing," or "through the childbirth"). The phrase can mean (1) saved "through [the ordeal of] childbearing" (in which case "salvation" reverts to its broader meaning of preservation or rescue); (2) saved "through [the means of] childbearing" (in which case it appears to clash with the doctrine of salvation by grace alone); or (3) saved "through [the ordeal of and by the means of] bearing children." A fourth possibility, however, makes it possible that a particular instance of childbirth is in mind, usually understood to be the birth of Christ.

✤ **2:8–15** If Paul's restrictions *were* intended to keep women from doing missionary teaching of men today, from leading a mixed Bible study, or from serving among a group of elders, those restrictions must not be ignored. If, on the other hand, Paul would have valued as primary such missionary principles as not hindering people from the gospel, and if he considered secondary such practices as women's wearing head coverings and restricting women's teaching of a mixed group, we need to be consistent in that regard. No doubt thoughtful readers will see strong points on each side.

3:1–7 Paul here in this next section takes another step to address the problem of the false teachers by ensuring that the Ephesian church has leaders who are morally qualified and above reproach. It is noteworthy that Paul here defines being an overseer in terms of function ("a noble task"), not of status or office. Yet he does describe a position of special responsibility and leadership.

3:2–7 Paul sets out some significant moral requirements for overseers. His first concern is that overseers be "above reproach." The phrase "able to teach" refers to ability, not knowledge. The wording "not given to drunkenness" (v. 3) by implication allows moderate use of alcoholic beverages (cf. 5:23). A potential overseer must also not be a "lover of money" (3:3; see 6:3–10).

The next qualification, "he must manage his own family well" (3:4), includes an explanation. The children must not only "obey" their father; they must have proper "respect" for him. Once again, the accent is on the elders' character.

The same observation can be made with regard to v. 6. The warning is not against doctrinal immaturity but against "conceit." Verse 7 underlines the importance, noted above, of "a good reputation with outsiders" in order to avoid "disgrace."

✤ **3:1–7** Church leaders for centuries have been preoccupied with determining which church order best represents biblical teaching and example. We must both find the broad fea-

[8]In the same way, deacons[a][f] are to be
worthy of respect, sincere, not indulging in much wine,[g] and not pursuing
dishonest gain. [9]They must keep hold of
the deep truths of the faith with a clear
conscience.[h] [10]They must first be tested; and then if there is nothing against
them, let them serve as deacons.
[11]In the same way, the women[b] are to
be worthy of respect, not malicious talk-
ers[i] but temperate and trustworthy in
everything.
[12]A deacon must be faithful to his wife
and must manage his children and his
household well.[j] [13]Those who have served
well gain an excellent standing and great
assurance in their faith in Christ Jesus.

Reasons for Paul's Instructions

[14]Although I hope to come to you soon,
I am writing you these instructions so
that, [15]if I am delayed, you will know how
people ought to conduct themselves in
God's household, which is the church[k]
of the living God, the pillar and foundation of the truth. [16]Beyond all question,
the mystery[l] from which true godliness
springs is great:

> He appeared in the flesh,[m]
> was vindicated by the Spirit,[c]
> was seen by angels,
> was preached among the nations,[n]
> was believed on in the world,
> was taken up in glory.[o]

4 The Spirit[p] clearly says that in later
times[q] some will abandon the faith
and follow deceiving spirits[r] and things
taught by demons. [2]Such teachings
come through hypocritical liars, whose

3:8 [f]Php 1:1 [g]Titus 2:3
3:9 [h]1Ti 1:19
3:11 [i]2Ti 3:3; Titus 2:3
3:12 [j]ver 4
3:15 [k]ver 5; Eph 2:21
3:16 [l]Ro 16:25 [m]Jn 1:14 [n]Col 1:23 [o]Mk 16:19
4:1 [p]Jn 16:13 [q]2Ti 3:1 [r]2Th 2:3

1Ti 3:16 ❖ Carry with you today this brief summary of the life and work of Jesus as the foundation for your sure hope in him.

[a] *8* The word *deacons* refers here to Christians designated to serve with the overseers/elders of the church in a variety of ways; similarly in verse 12; and in Romans 16:1 and Phil. 1:1.
[b] *11* Possibly deacons' wives or women who are deacons [c] *16* Or *vindicated in spirit*

---

tures that NT churches had in common and recognize that variations do not necessarily compromise these features. When we look at passages that deal with this subject, we see leadership by elders. While this does not mean that there was no room for individual leadership, a number of elders and leaders seems to be assumed (see also Titus 1:5–9).

3:8–13 Like the overseer (v. 3), the deacon must exercise moderation in drinking and in regard to money (v. 8). It may seem strange that there is a reference to doctrine (v. 9) concerning deacons but not in the qualifications for overseers. The reason may be that this is taken for granted in elders.
3:11 Paul interrupts the instructions about deacons with some directions concerning women. The word "women" *as used here* can mean either "woman" or "wife," so it is impossible to tell whether these were the deacons' wives or women serving as deacons (see NIV text note on v. 11).
3:12 This verse corresponds to vv. 2b, 4–5, reinforcing the importance of marital fidelity and a strong family. "Excellent standing" reveals what a noble task serving as a deacon truly is (v. 13).

3:8–13 In the church, a person may be a servant leader either (1) by exercising leadership with a servant attitude, or (2) by serving in such a way as to lead by godly example. Either way, servanthood must characterize Christians, whether or not they serve publicly as leaders.

3:14–16 Paul next provides an explicit purpose for writing this letter to Timothy—namely, so that Timothy "will know how people ought to conduct themselves in God's household" (v. 15).

The word "mystery" (v. 16) describes God's revelation of his sovereign work throughout history. The doctrine of Christ is the unshakable foundation of the Christian faith. Since there will always be opponents of the gospel, this hymn in v. 16 is always necessary and foundational.

3:14–16 The message of the incredible Christ-centered hymn embedded in v. 16 is relevant for a multitude of contemporary concerns. Its very structure rests on verbs rather than nouns. It centers on the Christ who came to us and the response he has received and deserves to receive further from us.

This proclamation and confession of Christ summons a response from us. There is a sense of purpose and hope as Christ moves, so to speak, from his incarnation to his ascension. Those who feel misunderstood can identify with the Christ who needed vindication. Those who feel alone as Christians can be encouraged by the reminder of how widespread faith in Christ really is in our world. Those who are self-centered can be reminded of where the center of our attention and affections belong. Those who need hope are reminded that Christ has taken his seat in glory at the right hand of God; he has begun to rule in exaltation and won't stop until God is all in all. Grounding this hope, our hope, is an objective foundation confessed in this ancient hymn.

4:1–5 Paul reveals that the real perpetrators of heresy are both the heretics and the evil spiritual forces that deceived and taught them (v. 1).

consciences have been seared as with a hot iron.[s] 3They forbid people to marry[t] and order them to abstain from certain foods,[u] which God created[v] to be received with thanksgiving[w] by those who believe and who know the truth. 4For everything God created is good,[x] and nothing is to be rejected if it is received with thanksgiving, 5because it is consecrated by the word of God and prayer.

6If you point these things out to the brothers and sisters,[a] you will be a good minister of Christ Jesus, nourished on the truths of the faith[y] and of the good teaching that you have followed. 7Have nothing to do with godless myths and old wives' tales;[z] rather, train yourself to be godly. 8For physical training is of some value, but godliness has value for all things,[a] holding promise for both the present life[b] and the life to come. 9This is a trustworthy saying[c] that deserves full acceptance. 10That is why we labor and strive, because we have put our hope in the living God, who is the Savior of all people, and especially of those who believe.

4:2 [s]Eph 4:19
4:3 [t]Heb 13:4 [u]Col 2:16 [v]Ge 1:29 [w]Ro 14:6
4:4 [x]Ro 14:14-18
4:6 [y]1Ti 1:10
4:7 [z]2Ti 2:16
4:8 [a]1Ti 6:6 [b]Ps 37:9,11; Mk 10:29,30
4:9 [c]1Ti 1:15
4:11 [d]1Ti 5:7; 6:2
4:12 [e]Titus 2:7; 1Pe 5:3 [f]1Ti 1:14
4:14 [g]1Ti 1:18 [h]Ac 6:6; 2Ti 1:6

1Ti 4:6-16 ❖ How can we be positive examples of godliness to those around us? How can we use our spiritual gifts for this purpose?

11Command and teach these things.[d] 12Don't let anyone look down on you because you are young, but set an example[e] for the believers in speech, in conduct, in love, in faith[f] and in purity. 13Until I come, devote yourself to the public reading of Scripture, to preaching and to teaching. 14Do not neglect your gift, which was given you through prophecy[g] when the body of elders laid their hands on you.[h]

15Be diligent in these matters; give yourself wholly to them, so that everyone may see your progress. 16Watch your life and doctrine closely. Persevere in them, because if you do, you will save both yourself and your hearers.

[a] 6 The Greek word for *brothers and sisters* (*adelphoi*) refers here to believers, both men and women, as part of God's family.

4:3-4 The two false teachings cited in v. 3 are not easy to understand. The error seems to be a judgment against all marriage and against certain foods as being wrong in themselves. This conclusion is strongly countered by Paul's statement in v. 4 (alluding to Ge 1).

Thanksgiving, prayer, and the Word of God render food legitimate to eat. While this does not mean that a formal act of blessing is necessary every time food is taken, it does suggest that acknowledging its source is appropriate and desirable.

4:1-5 One does not need special gifting to study God's Word and learn sound doctrine against which to test various claims. Churches that teach God's truth clearly, that emphasize major doctrines, that avoid a narrow attitude about things that matter less, and that stress love as the goal of God's commands are well able to deal with false teachings.

4:6-9 Paul reminds Timothy of his training in the "truths of the faith" (v. 6). To "point these things out" (v. 6) is one way to express Timothy's assignment. By doing this he will be a "good minister of Christ Jesus" (v. 6). This training in godliness is so important that it far surpasses physical training (v. 8).

4:10 Two phrases in v. 10 require careful attention lest they be misunderstood: "Savior of all people" and "especially of those who believe." These words could be taken to mean that God ultimately saves everyone (an idea called "universalism"). This is not the case. Scripture makes it clear that not all are saved, for some people deliberately refuse to accept God's saving grace. In the present context "all" may mean "all kinds of." The second phrase, "especially of those who believe," more likely means "in particular" or "I mean."

4:6-10 Prayer, Bible reading, moments of spiritual insight, and even revival are all tremendously important. Isolated acts and events, however, do not necessarily develop character. Character is developed by bringing spiritual disciplines to bear together on our lives, on our attitudes and decisions, and on our relationships and actions.

4:11-12 These verses contain a series of important imperatives that summarize and enlarge on the preceding sections. Paul's encouragement that Timothy not let people despise his youth (v. 12) raises the question of Timothy's age. If, as is probable, Timothy was in his 30s, words such as "young" and "youth" might give the contemporary reader the wrong impression, since we generally reserve these words for people in their teens and early 20s. The word "conduct" (v. 12) means a way of life. This is a reprise of 1:4-5.

4:13-14 "Until I come" supports the letter's authorship and places Timothy's commission in context. Timothy represented Paul in the doctrinal conflict at Ephesus as an apostolic delegate.

4:15-16 The call to perseverance in v. 16 is in accordance with Paul's words to others.

4:11-16 Ordination of people into ministry should be reexamined as to its significance. It should be recognized that this is not the elevation of a privileged cleric to a superior exclusive class (as was the OT priesthood)

PEOPLE TO KNOW // TIMOTHY

1 TIMOTHY 4:12: Timothy was Paul's young companion in ministry, who continued to spread the gospel after he and Paul parted. Timothy's mother was Jewish, and his father was Greek. While the Bible gives no details about his father, we know from Scripture that both his mother and grandmother were pious and God-fearing. These two women passed their faith on to Timothy (2Ti 1:5).

When Paul invited Timothy to join him in mission work, Paul first circumcised Timothy, since the Jews in the area knew Timothy's father was Greek (Ac 16:3). Paul did not want uncircumcision to be a hindrance to Timothy's ministry. Timothy traveled with Paul off and on through Macedonia in Greece, sometimes staying behind in one city and catching up with Paul later. The two had a close relationship and cared for one another deeply.

Four of Paul's letters are co-authored by Timothy and two are addressed to Timothy. Paul's letters show that he often sent Timothy to various churches in order to check on how they were doing and to bring them encouragement. Paul's final letter in the Bible is his second letter to Timothy, in which he calls Timothy his "dear son" (2Ti 1:2).

APPLICATION ✜ Jesus modeled for us the importance of community when he ministered with others surrounding him. His friends and followers learned from him, helped him and met his needs. The early church continued to show that our faith is meant to be lived out with others. We need strong relationships with mentors, friends and people who can learn from us and whom we learn from.

Timothy's relationships, first with his mother and grandmother as godly caregivers and teachers, then later with Paul as a mentor and friend, fueled Timothy's own ministry and faith. We must consider what Christian relationships might be missing from our lives and what we might be able to do in order to build them. God works through such relationships, helping believers to build one another up in faith, hope and love.

Widows, Elders and Slaves

5 Do not rebuke an older man[i] harshly,[j] but exhort him as if he were your
father. Treat younger men[k] as brothers,
2older women as mothers, and younger
women as sisters, with absolute purity.
3Give proper recognition to those
widows who are really in need.[l] 4But if
a widow has children or grandchildren,
these should learn first of all to put their
religion into practice by caring for their
own family and so repaying their parents
and grandparents,[m] for this is pleasing to
God.[n] 5The widow who is really in need[o]
and left all alone puts her hope in God[p]
and continues night and day to pray[q]
and to ask God for help. 6But the widow who lives for pleasure is dead even
while she lives.[r] 7Give the people these
instructions,[s] so that no one may be open
to blame. 8Anyone who does not provide
for their relatives, and especially for their
own household, has denied[t] the faith and
is worse than an unbeliever.
9No widow may be put on the list
of widows unless she is over sixty, has
been faithful to her husband, 10and is
well known for her good deeds,[u] such as

5:1 [i] Titus 2:2 [j] Lev 19:32 [k] Titus 2:6
5:3 [l] ver 5,16
5:4 [m] Eph 6:1,2 [n] 1Ti 2:3
5:5 [o] ver 3, 16 [p] 1Co 7:34; 1Pe 3:5 [q] Lk 2:37
5:6 [r] Lk 15:24
5:7 [s] 1Ti 4:11
5:8 [t] 2Pe 2:1; Jude 4; Titus 1:16
5:10 [u] Ac 9:36; 1Ti 6:18; 1Pe 2:12

1Ti 5:3–15 ❖ How can we help care for widows and other people around us who are lonely? How does the church play a role in this kind of ministry?

---

but rather the acceptance of one whom God has given to his church to work not above but among the people of God.

5:1–2 These verses provide a terse introduction to the next topic: the Christian family. The instructions are not directed to family groups, as they would be in typical household instructions. Instead, they are directed to Timothy to guide him in *his* relationship to them.

The first of these is in the singular, "older man"; the Greek word refers to age, not to a church elder. Timothy's attitude toward the older men is not to be harsh even if they need correction.

5:3–16 Care of widows was important in Jewish tradition. The Jewish concern for widows also appears elsewhere in the NT (Ac 6:1–6; Jas 1:27). After instructing Timothy to honor widows with real "need" (1Ti 5:3), Paul defines them first as those who are alone and have no family members to care for them. Moreover, they must trust in God instead of living for pleasure (vv. 5–6). Three further characteristics identify those who are to be put on "the list" (v. 9). A widow must be over 60

bringing up children, showing hospitality, washing the feet[v] of the Lord's people,
helping those in trouble[w] and devoting
herself to all kinds of good deeds.
11As for younger widows, do not put
them on such a list. For when their sensual desires overcome their dedication
to Christ, they want to marry. 12Thus they
bring judgment on themselves, because
they have broken their first pledge. 13Be-
sides, they get into the habit of being idle
and going about from house to house.
And not only do they become idlers, but
also busybodies[x] who talk nonsense,
saying things they ought not to. 14So I
counsel younger widows to marry,[y] to
have children, to manage their homes
and to give the enemy no opportunity
for slander.[z] 15Some have in fact already
turned away to follow Satan.[a]
16If any woman who is a believer has
widows in her care, she should continue to
help them and not let the church be burdened with them, so that the church can
help those widows who are really in need.[b]
17The elders[c] who direct the affairs of
the church well are worthy of double hon-
or,[d] especially those whose work is preaching and teaching. 18For Scripture says, "Do
not muzzle an ox while it is treading out
the grain,"[a][e] and "The worker deserves his
wages."[b][f] 19Do not entertain an accusation
against an elder[g] unless it is brought by
two or three witnesses.[h] 20But those elders
who are sinning you are to reprove[i] before everyone, so that the others may take
warning.[j] 21I charge you, in the sight of
God and Christ Jesus[k] and the elect angels,
to keep these instructions without partiality, and to do nothing out of favoritism.
22Do not be hasty in the laying on of
hands,[l] and do not share in the sins of
others.[m] Keep yourself pure.
23Stop drinking only water, and use a
little wine[n] because of your stomach and
your frequent illnesses.
24The sins of some are obvious, reaching the place of judgment ahead of them;
the sins of others trail behind them. 25In
the same way, good deeds are obvious,
and even those that are not obvious cannot remain hidden forever.

6 All who are under the yoke of slavery should consider their masters
worthy of full respect,[o] so that God's
name and our teaching may not be slandered.[p] 2Those who have believing masters should not show them disrespect

5:10 [v] Lk 7:44 [w] ver 16
5:13 [x] 2Th 3:11
5:14 [y] 1Co 7:9 [z] 1Ti 6:1
5:15 [a] Mt 4:10
5:16 [b] ver 3-5
5:17 [c] Ac 11:30 [d] Php 2:29; 1Th 5:12
5:18 [e] Dt 25:4; 1Co 9:7-9 [f] Lk 10:7; Lev 19:13; Dt 24:14,15; Mt 10:10; 1Co 9:14
5:19 [g] Ac 11:30 [h] Mt 18:16
5:20 [i] 2Ti 4:2; Titus 1:13 [j] Dt 13:11
5:21 [k] 1Ti 6:13; 2Ti 4:1
5:22 [l] Ac 6:6 [m] Eph 5:11
5:23 [n] 1Ti 3:8
6:1 [o] Eph 6:5; Titus 2:9; 1Pe 2:18 [p] Titus 2:5,8

[a] *18* Deut. 25:4 [b] *18* Luke 10:7

(v. 9a), must have been faithful in her marriage (v. 9b), and must have had a reputation for "good deeds" (v. 10). The next verses (vv. 11–15) explain why younger widows should not be on this list.

The contrast between younger and older widows in vv. 11–15 is stronger than one might have expected. Younger widows are not to be enrolled because their sensual desires may well come between them and Christ. Paul also counsels the young widows to "manage their homes" (v. 14). The word for "manage" indicates that these women would have strong management roles in their new families.

Once more, and in conclusion (v. 16), Paul counsels family members to care for widows to prevent additional burden on the church.

✣ **5:1–16** First Timothy 5 refers to literal widows. There are, however, parallel situations in our contemporary world in which we can express the same blend of doctrine and life in helping those in need. Today there are many divorced people who are alone, hurting, feeling misunderstood, and perhaps having financial need. In these and in other situations where individuals and families are experiencing difficulty and physical need, our churches should be centers of healing.

5:17–20 This is the first clear occurrence of substantial instructions concerning elders. "Direct the affairs of the church well" (v. 17) is an enlargement on the Greek words for "rule well." The verb used here is the same one employed to refer to overseers and deacons managing their families (3:4, 12).

Commentators differ as to whether the phrase "double honor" (v. 17) means (a) respect, (b) wages, or (c) both and whether, if it is (b), it means that they should receive literally twice as many wages as elders who do not rule well or who do not minister the word. Paul argues strongly for proper financial support for the Lord's servants (cf. 1Co 9:14). Since the provision of needs would have been a practical expression of honor, the two possible meanings need not be mutually exclusive, and thus (c) is possible.

The present tense of the word "sin" in 1Ti 5:20 implies that the elder in question has been proven guilty of the sin charged and persists in it.

5:21–25 Since Timothy is working closely with the elders, he may be naturally reluctant to act strongly against a leader who has sinned. Paul initiates these instructions with the heavy artillery of a solemn warning just short of an oath, calling on "God and Christ Jesus and the elect angels" (v. 21) as witnesses.

6:1–2 Paul next proceeds to discuss slaves and masters. "Yoke" emphasizes that slaves have no rights of their own. Paul is not "rubbing this in" but rather setting the stage for his strong word that both in general (v. 1), and particularly when slaves have a Christian master (v. 2), they should give "respect" and not disrespect.

✣ **5:17—6:2** The contemporary problem of moral failure among church leaders is real

just because they are fellow believers.[q] Instead, they should serve them even better because their masters are dear to them as fellow believers and are devoted to the welfare[a] of their slaves.

False Teachers and the Love of Money

These are the things you are to teach and insist on.[r] 3 If anyone teaches otherwise[s] and does not agree to the sound instruction[t] of our Lord Jesus Christ and to godly teaching, 4 they are conceited and understand nothing. They have an unhealthy interest in controversies and quarrels about words[u] that result in envy, strife, malicious talk, evil suspicions 5 and constant friction between people of corrupt mind, who have been robbed of the truth[v] and who think that godliness is a means to financial gain.

6 But godliness with contentment[w] is great gain.[x] 7 For we brought nothing into the world, and we can take nothing out of it.[y] 8 But if we have food and clothing, we will be content with that.[z] 9 Those who want to get rich[a] fall into temptation and a trap[b] and into many foolish and harmful desires that plunge people into ruin and destruction. 10 For the love of money[c] is a root of all kinds of evil. Some people, eager for money, have wandered from the faith[d] and pierced themselves with many griefs.

6:2 [q] Phm 16 [r] 1Ti 4:11
6:3 [s] 1Ti 1:3 [t] 1Ti 1:10
6:4 [u] 2Ti 2:14
6:5 [v] Titus 1:15
6:6 [w] Php 4:11; Heb 13:5 [x] 1Ti 4:8
6:7 [y] Job 1:21; Ecc 5:15
6:8 [z] Heb 13:5
6:9 [a] Pr 15:27 [b] 1Ti 3:7
6:10 [c] 1Ti 3:3 [d] Jas 5:19

1Ti 6:6-10 ❖ Do we consider ourselves to be content in the same way that Paul describes? Why or why not? How can we more fully find contentment in our faith and in good works rather than in comfort or wealth?

Final Charge to Timothy

11 But you, man of God,[e] flee from all this, and pursue righteousness, godliness, faith, love,[f] endurance and gentleness. 12 Fight the good fight[g] of the faith. Take hold of[h] the eternal life to which you were called when you made your good confession in the presence of many witnesses. 13 In the sight of God, who gives life to everything, and of Christ Jesus, who while testifying before Pontius Pilate[i] made the good confession, I charge you[j] 14 to keep this command without spot or blame until the appearing of our Lord Jesus Christ, 15 which God will bring about in his own time — God, the blessed[k] and only Ruler,[l] the King of kings and Lord of lords,[m] 16 who alone is immortal[n] and who lives in unapproachable light, whom no one has seen or can see.[o] To him be honor and might forever. Amen.

6:11 [e] 2Ti 3:17 [f] 2Ti 2:22
6:12 [g] 1Co 9:25, 26; 1Ti 1:18 [h] Php 3:12
6:13 [i] Jn 18:33-37 [j] 1Ti 5:21
6:15 [k] 1Ti 1:11 [l] 1Ti 1:17 [m] Rev 17:14; 19:16
6:16 [n] 1Ti 1:17 [o] Jn 1:18

[a] 2 *Or and benefit from the service*

---

and serious. First, the circumstances of moral failure are often complicated by the heavy demands of contemporary ministry. Second, temptations, especially of a sexual nature, can become strong. Added to this are the burdens of spiritual warfare (but see Jas 1:13-15). Understanding, compassion, and counseling are needed in such situations. Yet such understanding and counseling do not negate the possibility, or even necessity, of definitive action on the part of the church if the leader goes astray, such as that which is described in this section of 1 Timothy.

6:3-5 False doctrine runs counter to "sound instruction" and "godly teaching" (v. 3). The person who rejects healthy doctrine has an "unhealthy" or morbid obsession with "controversies and quarrels about words" (v. 4). The five results listed for these quarrels all have to do with disruptions in interpersonal relationships.

6:6-10 There *is* great gain in godliness, but only if it is combined "with contentment," the opposite of greed (v. 6). Verse 8 specifies the essentials necessary for contentment: "food and clothing." This embodies Jesus' strong teaching against greed and for trust in God for material needs in Lk 12:13-34.

The point of 1Ti 6:9-10 is not that wealth is wrong but that desire for it is. The closing words of v. 10 show the interconnection between greed and departure from "the faith."

✚ **6:3-10** It would not hurt any of us to draw up a series of pages with two columns, one labeled "need" and the other "want," and to list the value of our possessions in the appropriate columns. We could then set these lists before God in a time of prayer, determined to take the proper action as a result of our evaluation. Do we master our desire for material possessions, or does it master us? (See Mk 10:17-27.)

6:11 Timothy is here commanded to distance himself from the people described in vv. 3-10. "Flee from all this" refers to the evils mentioned in the same passage.

6:12 The context of v. 12 is not a conflict against other people; it is the "good fight of the faith," which is Timothy's own struggle for personal mastery. In this connection, Timothy is to "take hold" of eternal life.

6:13-14 Another solemn charge by Paul, this command has moral overtones. It is a charge to do something and a *mandate* to *be* something: "without spot or blame."

6:15-16 The doxology in these verses employs rich, lofty vocabulary to exalt God. This statement emphasizes the sovereignty of God, who will bring about Jesus' appearing "in his own time" (v. 15). This is the God who lives in light that cannot be approached.

GROWTH OF THE EARLY CHRISTIAN CHURCH

[17]Command those who are rich in this
present world not to be arrogant nor to
put their hope in wealth,[p] which is so
uncertain, but to put their hope in God,[q]
who richly provides us with everything
for our enjoyment.[r] [18]Command them to
do good, to be rich in good deeds,[s] and
to be generous and willing to share.[t]
[19]In this way they will lay up treasure
for themselves[u] as a firm foundation for
the coming age, so that they may take
hold of the life that is truly life.
[20]Timothy, guard what has been entrusted[v] to your care. Turn away from
godless chatter[w] and the opposing
ideas of what is falsely called knowledge, [21]which some have professed and
in so doing have departed from the
faith.[x]
Grace be with you all.[y]

6:17 [p]Lk 12:20, 21 [q]1Ti 4:10 [r]Ac 14:17
6:18 [s]1Ti 5:10 [t]Ro 12:8, 13
6:19 [u]Mt 6:20
6:20 [v]2Ti 1:12, 14 [w]2Ti 2:16
6:21 [x]2Ti 2:18 [y]Col 4:18

6:17–19 Wealthy members of Timothy's congregation needed instructions as to how to use their resources. Such people are to recognize that wealth will last only until Christ appears. Moreover, they should not be arrogant. Rather, they are to be "rich" in good deeds, generous, and willing to share with others who have less (v. 18). By doing these things, they "lay up treasure" in heaven (v. 19).

6:20–21 In this personal word to Timothy, Paul writes about turning away from "what is falsely called knowledge." This command summarizes all the exhortations in this letter. Paul concludes the letter to Timothy by praying that God's "grace" would be with Timothy and his fellow believers in Ephesus (v. 21).

6:11–21 It is often said that our personal times of prayer should include worship. Such worship can be expressed in our own words as they are inspired by the Spirit in the depths of our minds and hearts. It can also come through the words of hymns and devotional writings. This is a helpful way to expand our worshipful thoughts and vocabulary. It is also a means of joining in the voices of people from other Christian traditions as part of the great worshiping church worldwide.

Best of all, however, is to worship God in his own words—through the Psalms, the songs of praise in Revelation, and other passages. The doxology found here in this final section of 1 Timothy, celebrating, along with 1:17, the immortal God, is a wonderful instrument of worship. It can also be a means of recalling the universal church and all those—believers on earth and in heaven, angels, and other beings—who for eternity will worship God together.

2 Timothy

Author: The apostle Paul

Audience: Paul's disciple Timothy, who was ministering in Ephesus

Date: Probably c. AD 66–67, but possibly AD 62

Theme: Facing imminent death, Paul encourages Timothy to carry on the ministry and faithfully guard the gospel in the face of persecution and false teaching.

PERSPECTIVE

Second Timothy reads as a series of reflections from Paul to Timothy as Paul sat in prison waiting for his execution. He used several striking images, such as the soldier and the athlete and the hardworking farmer, to encourage Timothy in his task as a young pastor in a hostile environment. Chapter 3 is particularly significant with its description of what will happen in the last days and its powerful perspective on the inspiration and dependability of Scripture.

Paul had at least three reasons for writing to Timothy at this time: First, Paul was lonely and longed for Christian fellowship. Many of his friends had deserted him, and while Luke was still with him (4:11), Paul wanted very much for Timothy to join him also. Timothy had served closely with Paul (see 1Co 4:17). Of him Paul could say, "I have no one else like him" (Php 2:20). Second, Paul was concerned to pass on the mantle of Christian leadership. He admonished Timothy to guard the gospel (2Ti 1:14), to persevere in it (3:14), to keep on preaching it (4:2) and, if necessary, to suffer for it (1:8; 2:3). Third, Paul wanted to write to the Ephesian church through his letter to Timothy.

For more perspective on this book, see the Introductions to 1 Timothy and Titus.

Reading 2 Timothy

The apostle Paul (1:1) probably wrote this second letter to Timothy during a second Roman imprisonment (see Ac 28:16–31 for the first). He writes again to his younger apostolic delegate Timothy, who continues to minister in the city of Ephesus. Paul senses that his execution is near (2Ti 4:6–8), and so he writes a sort of fond farewell discourse to Timothy to encourage him to

	10 BC	AD 1	10	20	30	40	50	60	70	80	90	100
Jesus' life (c. 6/5 BC–AD 30)												
Paul's conversion (c. AD 35)												
Paul's missionary journeys (c. AD 46–67)												
Council at Jerusalem (c. AD 49/50)												
Nero's reign (AD 54–68)												
Paul's first imprisonment in Rome (c. AD 59–62)												
Book of 2 Timothy written (c. AD 67–68)												
Paul's imprisonment and death in Rome (c. AD 67–68)												
Destruction of Jerusalem's temple (c. AD 70)												

stand firm in the faith and fulfill his calling as his apostolic delegate and as a leader of the church. He asks him also to come to Rome for a final visit (4:9). Paul further provides instruction concerning yet another false teaching and how Timothy should lead the church and refute it. Second Timothy is Paul's final letter.

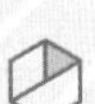

Key Verses

All Scripture is God-breathed and is useful for teaching, rebuking, correcting and training in righteousness, so that the servant of God may be thoroughly equipped for every good work.

—2 Timothy 3:16–17

TAKING THE NEXT STEPS

Second Timothy is Paul's last letter, written shortly before his death (4:6–8). He warned Timothy of the hard times ahead, due to increasing persecution and the proliferation of false teachers infiltrating the church (see 1Ti 1:3). But Paul went on to encourage Timothy to persevere in the Christian faith and in his work as pastor.

Like the other two Pastoral Letters (1 Timothy and Titus), this one contains practical advice for the contemporary Christian. Paul's instructions to Timothy encourage us in our Christian faith as well. (1) We can be confident that God's power will enable us to remain firm in the faith, regardless of how strong the opposition may be. We must depend on him for strength. (2) A secure foundation for our faith lies in the inspired Word of God. Only the Bible gives an adequate basis for knowing the truth of God and for living a holy life. (3) We as Christians do not need to fear death, for God has a crown of righteousness waiting for us.

WHAT TO LOOK FOR IN 2 TIMOTHY

- Personal encouragement and Paul's circumstances (ch. 1)
- Paul's exhortations (ch. 2)
- The coming of terrible times (ch. 3)
- The power and dependability of Scripture (ch. 3)
- Paul's final charge to Timothy (ch. 4)

1 Paul, an apostle of Christ Jesus by the
will of God,[a] in keeping with the promise of life that is in Christ Jesus,[b]
2To Timothy,[c] my dear son:[d]

Grace, mercy and peace from God the
Father and Christ Jesus our Lord.

Thanksgiving

3I thank God,[e] whom I serve, as my
ancestors did, with a clear conscience,
as night and day I constantly remember you in my prayers.[f] 4Recalling your
tears,[g] I long to see you,[h] so that I may
be filled with joy. 5I am reminded of your
sincere faith,[i] which first lived in your
grandmother Lois and in your mother
Eunice[j] and, I am persuaded, now lives
in you also.

Appeal for Loyalty to Paul and the Gospel

6For this reason I remind you to fan
into flame the gift of God, which is in
you through the laying on of my hands.[k]
7For the Spirit God gave us does not make
us timid,[l] but gives us power, love and

1:1 [a]2Co 1:1 [b]Eph 3:6; 1Ti 6:19
1:2 [c]Ac 16:1 [d]1Ti 1:2
1:3 [e]Ro 1:8 [f]Ro 1:10
1:4 [g]Ac 20:37 [h]2Ti 4:9
1:5 [i]1Ti 1:5 [j]Ac 16:1
1:6 [k]1Ti 4:14
1:7 [l]Ro 8:15

2Ti 1:5 ❖ How can we honor and thank people who have shared the Christian faith with us for this gift?

1:1–2 Paul's reference to the "will of God" stands alone in his Pastoral Letters, though it is not unique among his letters. The prepositional phrase "in Christ Jesus" may convey the idea of close relationship or union.
1:3 In the OT, "serve" could refer to the worship offered to God in his temple.
1:4–5 What follows is a pattern of words about remembrance. Paul remembers Timothy in his prayers, recalling Timothy's tears (v. 4) and his "sincere faith" (v. 5).
1:6–7 Paul tells Timothy to fan God's gift, which is in him, into flame (v. 6). The basis of Paul's exhortation ("for this reason," v. 6) is Timothy's faith (v. 5), so we know that there is no lapse there.
1:7 The "Spirit" mentioned here is the Holy Spirit himself, not the human spirit. The gift seems to have been a measure or kind of power, love, and ability to control oneself that is beyond our normal capacities. He is not the kind of Spirit who brings fear or a "timid" spirit.

APPLICATION ✚ **1:1–7** The skills needed for service to God today can be gained in many ways. What is less attainable is character and wisdom. What young Timothys today need especially is personal mentoring. To mentor a Timothy means to be available, to spend time with him or her, and to seek to facilitate rather than to control the use of that person's distinctive gifts. An athlete runs the race alone but does so after months or perhaps years of training and encouragement, not just by a coach but by others who are close to the

PEOPLE TO KNOW // LOIS AND EUNICE

2 TIMOTHY 1:5: Eunice and Lois were the mother and grandmother of Timothy, one of the apostle Paul's most trusted helpers. They are named only once in the Bible, in Paul's second letter to Timothy (2Ti 1:5). Paul attributes Timothy's "sincere faith" to these two women.

In Ac 16, Luke informs readers that Timothy's mother was a Jewish believer who had married a Greek man (Ac 16:1). The fact that she is called a believer highlights once again the role of faith in her life.

While Paul mentions Lois and Eunice, he never mentions Timothy's father. It is likely that Timothy's primary caretakers—and certainly primary spiritual influences—were these two godly women. Paul references Timothy's upbringing later in his letter, noting that "from infancy" Timothy knew the Scriptures (2Ti 3:15). From the very beginning of Timothy's life, his mother and grandmother were teaching him the story of God and the love of God.

APPLICATION It is hard to overstate the importance of godly influences. Parents and other influential adults who serve and know God are a precious gift in a young person's life. God worked through the spiritual nurturing of Eunice and Lois to open Timothy's heart to Jesus Christ and to a life in ministry. As you fulfill whatever ministry God has before you, remember to honor those who went before and shaped your spiritual identity. Remember, too, to be a mentor and spiritual caregiver for those who follow in your footsteps.

self-discipline. 8 So do not be ashamed[m] of
the testimony about our Lord or of me his
prisoner.[n] Rather, join with me in suffering for the gospel,[o] by the power of God.
9 He has saved us and called[p] us to a holy
life — not because of anything we have
done but because of his own purpose and
grace. This grace was given us in Christ
Jesus before the beginning of time, 10 but
it has now been revealed[q] through the
appearing of our Savior, Christ Jesus, who
has destroyed death[r] and has brought life
and immortality to light through the gospel. 11 And of this gospel I was appointed
a herald and an apostle and a teacher.[s]
12 That is why I am suffering as I am. Yet
this is no cause for shame, because I know
whom I have believed, and am convinced
that he is able to guard[t] what I have entrusted to him until that day.[u]

1:8 [m] Mk 8:38; Ro 1:16 [n] Eph 3:1 [o] 2Ti 2:3,9; 4:5
1:9 [p] Ro 8:28
1:10 [q] Eph 1:9 [r] 1Co 15:26,54
1:11 [s] 1Ti 2:7
1:12 [t] 1Ti 6:20 [u] ver 18

athlete. Timothy had in Paul a person who was close to him, who listened to and understood him, who recognized his individual giftedness, and who had confidence in him.

1:8 Timothy's ability to resist being ashamed lies in the gifts of power, love, and self-discipline (v. 7). Being ashamed stands in contrast to joining with Paul in suffering. This very suffering is "by the power of God."

1:9 Paul points to two ways in which God has expressed his power. One is by saving us; the other is by calling us. In Eph 1:3–14, Paul makes it clear that God's grace is founded on his eternal purposes. That passage employs a remarkable series of words, phrases, and grammatical constructions that express the idea of God's purpose, wisdom, good pleasure, and plan, through which God's people are brought to salvation. The same concept is supported here by the time reference, indicating that grace was actually given us "in Christ Jesus before the beginning of time" (2Ti 1:9b), but "it has [only] now been revealed" (v. 10).

1:10 A couple of words in this verse are of special importance in the Pastoral Letters. The word translated "revealed" occurs in the important creedal statement in 1Ti 3:16 and in Titus 1:3. The word "Savior" is also significant since this noun is relatively infrequent in the NT. In the NT, salvation—which is the work of God in the OT—is now also the work of Christ.

Christ made it possible for us to *have* eternal life through his resurrection, but the emphasis here is on that which "brought life and immortality *to light*" (2Ti 1:10, emphasis added), accomplished by the gospel.

1:11 Paul next speaks of his own ministry on behalf of the gospel. The three words "herald," "apostle," and "teacher" express three distinct ways in which Paul serves the gospel.

1:12 Paul gathers up in this verse what he has said about testifying to the gospel and declares that it is for this reason that he is "suffering as I am," as is Timothy (cf. 3:12). Paul is doing his part in suffering for the sake of the gospel, committing his life and ministry to God as a deposit for the future day of reckoning. For his part, Timothy must guard the teachings that God has entrusted to him, and God has given him the Holy Spirit to help him do this (1:14).

[13]What you heard from me, keep[v] as the pattern of sound teaching, with faith and love in Christ Jesus.[w] [14]Guard the good deposit that was entrusted to you — guard it with the help of the Holy Spirit who lives in us.[x]

Examples of Disloyalty and Loyalty

[15]You know that everyone in the province of Asia has deserted me,[y] including Phygelus and Hermogenes.

[16]May the Lord show mercy to the household of Onesiphorus,[z] because he often refreshed me and was not ashamed of my chains. [17]On the contrary, when he was in Rome, he searched hard for me until he found me. [18]May the Lord grant that he will find mercy from the Lord on that day! You know very well in how many ways he helped me[a] in Ephesus.

The Appeal Renewed

2 You then, my son, be strong[b] in the grace that is in Christ Jesus. [2]And the things you have heard me say[c] in the presence of many witnesses[d] entrust to reliable people who will also be qualified to teach others. [3]Join with me in suffering, like a good soldier[e] of Christ Jesus. [4]No one serving as a soldier gets entangled in civilian affairs, but rather tries to please his commanding officer.

1:13 [v] Titus 1:9 [w] 1Ti 1:14
1:14 [x] Ro 8:9
1:15 [y] 2Ti 4:10, 11,16
1:16 [z] 2Ti 4:19
1:18 [a] Heb 6:10
2:1 [b] Eph 6:10
2:2 [c] 2Ti 1:13 [d] 1Ti 6:12
2:3 [e] 1Ti 1:18

1:13–14 Timothy is not at liberty to deviate from the apostolic teaching.

1:15–18 Here Paul reveals some of his personal feelings. The nature of the desertion of "everyone in the province of Asia" (v. 15) has been a matter of debate. Phygelus and Hermogenes are not called heretics, as are Hymenaeus and Philetus (2:17), but probably are two formerly trustworthy associates whose defection hurt Paul the most. Onesiphorus stands in beautiful contrast to the others.

✜ **1:8–18** Because claims for the exclusiveness of the gospel run counter to today's doctrine of tolerance for all religious views, Christians do stand out for their witness to truth. In this, believers work against the cultural idea that *no* one system can claim absolute truth. Most agree it is appropriate for a Christian to give a testimony as to how their personal faith has helped them in a given situation, but to go beyond that to make strong and universal truth claims that are relevant for everyone is frowned upon. Those believers who do so can experience a kind of humiliation and shame in the criticism of their peers but can also be strengthened by Paul's words to Timothy in passages such as 1:13–14 and 2:1.

2:1–7 What Paul teaches needs to be passed on by Timothy (and Titus). This call pervades the Pastoral

PEOPLE TO KNOW // **ONESIPHORUS**

2 TIMOTHY 1:16: Onesiphorus is only mentioned by name twice in the Bible, both times in 2 Timothy. While we know very little about him, the way Paul writes of Onesiphorus is striking.

Paul likely wrote 2 Timothy from his Roman imprisonment. Reflecting on his previous hardships, he reminded Timothy of how everyone had deserted him in Asia. But then in contrast Paul writes, "May the Lord show mercy to the household of Onesiphorus, because he often refreshed me and was not ashamed of my chains" (2Ti 1:16). What this "refreshing" was exactly, we do not know, but certainly we can speculate that Onesiphorus and his family offered encouragement, support and perhaps met Paul's monetary needs. Whatever the details, Paul was deeply grateful for Onesiphorus in his captivity.

Paul goes on to say Onesiphorus searched for him in Rome. Onesiphorus was determined to find his struggling, imprisoned friend and would not give up until he found him. Paul also reminds Timothy of how helpful Onesiphorus was during Paul's ministry in Ephesus. Again, we can only wonder and speculate about what this looked like, but clearly Onesiphorus was an invaluable friend and loyal supporter of Paul.

APPLICATION ✜ Onesiphorus did not abandon Paul when the apostle was imprisoned. He didn't avoid contact, embarrassed to be friends with someone who was in jail. Stirred to deeper compassion, Onesiphorus searched through the great city of Rome until he was reunited with his dear friend. How do we display our loyalty and love to others? Does our love and devotion to our church and community put God on display to the world? Onesiphorus's relentless devotion to Paul's ministry is a lasting legacy of Christian love—a love the Bible invites us to carry on and demonstrate today.

5Similarly, anyone who competes as
an athlete does not receive the victor's
crown[f] except by competing according
to the rules. 6The hardworking farmer
should be the first to receive a share of
the crops. 7Reflect on what I am saying,
for the Lord will give you insight into
all this.
8Remember Jesus Christ, raised from
the dead,[g] descended from David.[h] This
is my gospel,[i] 9for which I am suffering[j]
even to the point of being chained like a
criminal. But God's word is not chained.
10Therefore I endure everything[k] for the
sake of the elect, that they too may obtain the salvation that is in Christ Jesus,
with eternal glory.[l]
11Here is a trustworthy saying:

If we died with him,
we will also live with him;[m]
12 if we endure,
we will also reign with him.[n]
If we disown him,
he will also disown us;[o]
13 if we are faithless,
he remains faithful,[p]
for he cannot disown himself.

2:5 [f] 1Co 9:25
2:8 [g] Ac 2:24 [h] Mt 1:1 [i] Ro 2:16
2:9 [j] Ac 9:16
2:10 [k] Col 1:24 [l] 2Co 4:17
2:11 [m] Ro 6:2-11
2:12 [n] Ro 8:17; 1Pe 4:13 [o] Mt 10:33
2:13 [p] Nu 23:19; Ro 3:3
2:14 [q] 1Ti 6:4
2:15 [r] Eph 1:13; Jas 1:18
2:16 [s] Titus 3:9
2:17 [t] 1Ti 1:20

2Ti 2:14–26 ❖ Which arguments are best ignored and which are worth having in the Christian community? How can we tell the difference?

Dealing With False Teachers

14Keep reminding God's people of
these things. Warn them before God
against quarreling about words;[q] it is of
no value, and only ruins those who listen. 15Do your best to present yourself to
God as one approved, a worker who does
not need to be ashamed and who correctly handles the word of truth.[r] 16Avoid
godless chatter,[s] because those who indulge in it will become more and more
ungodly. 17Their teaching will spread like
gangrene. Among them are Hymenaeus[t]
and Philetus, 18who have departed from
the truth. They say that the resurrection

Letters. The military image here has to do not with warfare but with disciplined obedience; the athletic image deals with conformity to the rules; the agricultural image stresses hard work.

2:8–13 The resurrection of Christ provides the strongest motivation for obedience.

2:9 Paul refers to his own suffering in chains "like a criminal" but adds that "God's word is not chained."

2:10 Paul turns to his own willingness to endure anything necessary "for the sake of the elect." Paul's emphasis is not on the matter of election but on the need to *facilitate the salvation* of the elect. However one may address the matter of election, the conversion of a person involves the faithful ministry of the saving gospel.

2:11–13 The "trustworthy saying" (v. 11) is one of five in the Pastoral Letters. Paul has already written strongly about spiritual identification with Christ in his death. Paul is not simply here thinking of something historical, though it is based on the historical death of Christ, and certainly not of something physical, for we have not actually been put to death. Rather, there is a personal identification with Christ in his death.

2:12 Endurance is, by its very nature, lifelong. The word "disown" also means "to deny, refuse" or simply "to say no"; "repudiate" may be in mind here.

2:13 While Christ will repudiate the person who repudiates him, this verse tells us that if we are faithless, he remains faithful, for he cannot repudiate himself. Is it being faithful to his people, to his own righteousness, or to his judgments? Since all three are true and supported throughout Scripture, we do not lose any truth by leaving this question open here. What is most striking is that the saying of vv. 11–13 concludes with a magnificent statement about Christ's character: He cannot repudiate himself.

✜ **2:1–13** Our occasional contacts with people, such as with fellow passengers on an airline flight, are fleeting. Therefore, those who are hardworking farmers in the imagery of v. 6 may never know on this earth whether seeds they have planted have taken root and grown. Faithful Christians may not see the results or reap the rewards until heaven. We must depend all the more heavily on the promises of this passage as well as respond in faith to its commands.

2:14 The phrase "keep reminding" here brings out the present tense of the verb. "Warn" is a participle, also in the present tense. This tense indicates that the task is not complete but requires constant attention. Precise wording is necessary for precise theology. But here Paul is warning "against quarreling about words." Paul offers two clear reasons against allowing it: It is without value, and it ruins the listeners.

2:15 The words "do your best" mean doing something with diligence and perhaps with haste and urgency. It communicates the idea of zeal and passion for the task at hand. There is no suggestion that this workman might be ashamed of his product—that is, the gospel. Rather, it is the *way* the work is performed that might bring shame.

2:16 Paul counsels against "godless chatter." This empty talk is devoid of religious value and leads people to become "more and more ungodly." The idea continues in v. 17 with a second reason for avoiding godless chatter.

2:17–18 Of the two false teachers named here, Hymenaeus was mentioned in 1Ti 1:20, while Philetus is mentioned only here. Their error is in saying "that the resurrection has already taken place."

CHARACTER OF GOD // GOD IS FAITHFUL

2 Timothy 2:13: If we are faithless, he remains faithful, for he cannot disown himself.

God's faithfulness is the aspect of his nature that guarantees he will never fail to keep his promises. God does not back out or abandon his good purposes for creation. He will see his redemption plan carried through to fulfillment.

We see God's faithfulness displayed in the way he keeps his promises through Scripture. God promised Abraham that his descendants would become a great nation of blessing for all peoples (Ge 12:1–3). When the Israelites were enslaved, God did not abandon them. God delivered them with a mighty hand and an outstretched arm. God led them through the wilderness into the promised land.

When God's people were unfaithful to him, turning away and worshiping other gods, God brought judgment on them for their sin—yet God never deserted them. Even in the books of the Prophets, which announce God's stern warnings and impending judgments against his people for their sin, God still promises to restore a remnant of his people. Judgment would not have the last word because God was faithful to his promise to Abraham.

God's faithfulness shines on full display in the life of Jesus Christ, who demonstrates the full measure of God's commitment to his people. Jesus fulfilled God's promise that Abraham's offspring would bless all nations. Not content to leave people in their sin, God sent Christ to carry the guilt of human iniquity on the cross. Christ is a perfect picture of the faithfulness of God.

God's faithfulness does not depend on our own character. God is completely faithful based on his own perfect nature. Nothing we can do will cause God to become unfaithful. His faithfulness is not a conditional bargain, in place only until we fail. It is an eternal promise.

APPLICATION Among the most devastating things a person can experience is to be betrayed. When we put our faith in someone, we depend on that person to be trustworthy. The good news is that Scripture promises that God always remains faithful. Our hope in God will never be disappointed.

has already taken place, and they destroy
the faith of some.[u] 19Nevertheless, God's
solid foundation stands firm,[v] sealed
with this inscription: "The Lord knows
those who are his,"[w] and, "Everyone who
confesses the name of the Lord[x] must
turn away from wickedness."
20In a large house there are articles not
only of gold and silver, but also of wood
and clay; some are for special purposes and some for common use.[y] 21Those
who cleanse themselves from the latter
will be instruments for special purposes, made holy, useful to the Master and
prepared to do any good work.[z]
22Flee the evil desires of youth and pursue righteousness, faith, love[a] and peace,
along with those who call on the Lord
out of a pure heart.[b] 23Don't have anything to do with foolish and stupid arguments, because you know they produce
quarrels. 24And the Lord's servant must
not be quarrelsome but must be kind to
everyone, able to teach, not resentful.[c]

2:18 [u] 1Ti 1:19
2:19 [v] Isa 28:16 [w] Jn 10:14 [x] 1Co 1:2
2:20 [y] Ro 9:21
2:21 [z] 2Ti 3:17
2:22 [a] 1Ti 1:14; 6:11 [b] 1Ti 1:5
2:24 [c] 1Ti 3:2,3

This error seems to draw on negative ideas about the material world, including the human body.

2:19 Paul responds to this troubling situation with the affirmation that "God's solid foundation stands firm."

2:20–21 This is not simply a matter of better versus everyday tableware. It is rather that some utensils are used for purposes that have an overtone of "dishonor," "disgrace," or "shame." Such a purpose might be for removing waste, for example. This makes sense of v. 21, and its requirement to "cleanse" oneself from the latter group of utensils, and points to the personal world of Timothy, who is to be an instrument for noble purposes, "holy [and] useful to the Master."

2:22–23 Paul presents two contrasting objectives: "the evil desires of youth" and the pursuit of "righteousness, faith, love and peace." Verse 23 warns against arguments that produce quarrels, which must not characterize the Lord's servant (v. 24).

2:24 The positive attitudes here are significant. The word translated "kind" carries the idea of gentleness and contrasts with a controversial spirit. Timothy must express this attitude "to everyone." The next phrase, "able to teach," is one of the qualifications for overseership in 1Ti 3:2. The

25Opponents must be gently instructed, in the hope that God will grant them repentance leading them to a knowledge of the truth,[d] 26and that they will come to their senses and escape from the trap of the devil,[e] who has taken them captive to do his will.

3 But mark this: There will be terrible times in the last days.[f] 2People will be lovers of themselves, lovers of money,[g] boastful, proud,[h] abusive, disobedient to their parents,[i] ungrateful, unholy, 3without love, unforgiving, slanderous, without self-control, brutal, not lovers of the good, 4treacherous, rash, conceited,[j] lovers of pleasure rather than lovers of God— 5having a form of godliness but denying its power. Have nothing to do with such people.

6They are the kind who worm their way[k] into homes and gain control over gullible women, who are loaded down with sins and are swayed by all kinds of evil desires, 7always learning but never able to come to a knowledge of the truth. 8Just as Jannes and Jambres opposed Moses,[l] so also these teachers oppose[m] the truth. They are men of depraved minds,[n] who, as far as the faith is concerned, are rejected. 9But they will not get very far because, as in the case of those men,[o] their folly will be clear to everyone.

A Final Charge to Timothy

10You, however, know all about my teaching,[p] my way of life, my purpose, faith, patience, love, endurance, 11persecutions, sufferings—what kinds of things happened to me in Antioch,[q] Iconium and Lystra, the persecutions I endured.[r] Yet the Lord rescued me from all of them.[s] 12In fact, everyone who wants to live a godly life in Christ Jesus will be persecuted,[t] 13while evildoers and impostors will go from bad to worse,[u] deceiving and being deceived. 14But as for you, continue in what you have learned and have become convinced of, because you know those from whom you learned it,[v] 15and how from infancy[w] you have known the Holy

2:25 [d] 1Ti 2:4
2:26 [e] 1Ti 3:7
3:1 [f] 1Ti 4:1
3:2 [g] 1Ti 3:3 [h] Ro 1:30 [i] Ro 1:30
3:4 [j] 1Ti 3:6
3:6 [k] Jude 4
3:8 [l] Ex 7:11 [m] Ac 13:8 [n] 1Ti 6:5
3:9 [o] Ex 7:12
3:10 [p] 1Ti 4:6
3:11 [q] Ac 13:14, 50 [r] 2Co 11:23-27 [s] Ps 34:19
3:12 [t] Ac 14:22
3:13 [u] 2Ti 2:16
3:14 [v] 2Ti 1:13
3:15 [w] 2Ti 1:5

---

word translated "not resentful" appears only here in the NT and describes the way one handles evil opposition or pain.

2:25–26 Paul describes the required active response: instruction with a view to the "repentance" of the opponents. Paul hopes that these opponents will "come to their senses" (v. 26).

> ✣ **2:14–26** It will always be more difficult to separate from those whose life and teachings are destructive if we know them personally than if they are merely names to us. Yet we should be concerned for them, and hope for an eventual turnaround whether we know them personally or not. In his house-church setting, Timothy must have had firsthand contact, perhaps weekly for a period of time, with the very people Paul warns him about.

3:1–5 The reasons why the "last days" (v. 1) are so terrible are cited in vv. 2–9. Amazingly, these people, consumed by their own vices, have "a form of godliness" (v. 5a). This does not necessarily mean that they are in the church, but the fact that Paul counsels Timothy to "have nothing to do with such people" (v. 5b) may indicate that they are.

3:6–7 Paul continues the warning against the evil people he so graphically described in vv. 2–4. They are able to seduce some people into believing their heresies. Those described in v. 6 are women; these women may have been recent converts, possibly coming from lives of religious perversion or prostitution. Paul's main point in vv. 6–7 is not to malign women but to show the treachery of the false teachers.

3:8–9 Verse 8 includes another description of the false teachers, this time by reference to "Jannes and Jambres," names Jewish tradition gave to the Egyptian magicians who opposed Moses and Aaron (Ex 7:11; 9:11). They also stood against the truth, had "depraved minds," and were rejected "as far as the faith is concerned" (2Ti 3:8). It would have encouraged Timothy to know that "their folly will be clear to everyone."

> ✣ **3:1–9** According to the Bible's descriptions of "the last days," the darkest hours of social degeneration may be yet ahead (v. 1). A common thread of selfishness will be noticeable in people at that time. "People will be lovers of themselves," and the expressions of that—pride, ungratefulness, lack of love for others, ingratitude, and sensuous pleasure at the cost of other people—describe our contemporary moral condition (v. 2). Believers are to stand apart from this kind of ruinous cultural pressure and can take encouragement from Paul's words in vv. 3:14–15.

3:10–12 Paul's autobiographical notes demonstrate the sovereign grace of God in his life, acknowledge that faithful service brings suffering, and provide a model for others to imitate. Paul is not flattering himself but rather showing baseline values for the life of the Lord's servant. Paul's teaching and character distinguish him from the false teachers and philosophers mentioned above. The sufferings mentioned here refer to events in specific cities before Paul's meeting with Timothy (v. 11).

3:13 We now face the contrasting figures of "evildoers and impostors." The tragedy of these impostors is compounded by the fact that they not only deceive but are themselves "deceived."

3:14–17 Verses 16–17 are the strongest statement in the Bible about itself. The word "Scripture" includes the NT, since 2Pe 3:16 cites the writings of Paul among the "Scriptures." The word

2Ti 3:16–17 ❖ How has Scripture equipped us for life? What passages or verses have been most meaningful in the past and why?

Scriptures,[x] which are able to make you
wise[y] for salvation through faith in Christ
Jesus. 16All Scripture is God-breathed[z] and
is useful for teaching,[a] rebuking, correcting and training in righteousness, 17so
that the servant of God[ab] may be thoroughly equipped for every good work.[c]
4 In the presence of God and of Christ
Jesus, who will judge the living and
the dead,[d] and in view of his appearing
and his kingdom, I give you this charge:[e]
2Preach[f] the word;[g] be prepared in season and out of season; correct, rebuke[h]
and encourage—with great patience and
careful instruction. 3For the time will
come when people will not put up with
sound doctrine.[i] Instead, to suit their
own desires, they will gather around
them a great number of teachers to say
what their itching ears want to hear.
4They will turn their ears away from the
truth and turn aside to myths.[j] 5But you,
keep your head in all situations, endure
hardship,[k] do the work of an evangelist,[l]
discharge all the duties of your ministry.
6For I am already being poured out like
a drink offering,[m] and the time for my departure is near.[n] 7I have fought the good
fight,[o] I have finished the race,[p] I have kept
the faith. 8Now there is in store for me[q] the
crown of righteousness, which the Lord,
the righteous Judge, will award to me on
that day[r]—and not only to me, but also
to all who have longed for his appearing.

Personal Remarks

9Do your best to come to me quickly, 10for Demas,[s] because he loved this

3:15 [x] Jn 5:39 [y] Ps 119:98,99
3:16 [z] 2Pe 1:20,21 [a] Ro 4:23,24
3:17 [b] 1Ti 6:11 [c] 2Ti 2:21
4:1 [d] Ac 10:42 [e] 1Ti 5:21
4:2 [f] 1Ti 4:13 [g] Gal 6:6 [h] 1Ti 5:20; Titus 1:13; 2:15
4:3 [i] 1Ti 1:10
4:4 [j] 1Ti 1:4
4:5 [k] 2Ti 1:8 [l] Ac 21:8
4:6 [m] Php 2:17 [n] Php 1:23
4:7 [o] 1Ti 1:18 [p] 1Co 9:24
4:8 [q] Col 1:5 [r] 2Ti 1:12
4:10 [s] Col 4:14

[a] 17 Or *that you, a man of God,*

---

translated "God-breathed" is more commonly translated "inspired," which is less awkward but also less accurate. The inspiration of Scripture is foundational to its usefulness.

The first use of Scripture Paul lists is doctrinal. Given the major function of the Pastoral Letters to address the problem of false teaching in Ephesus and Crete, "rebuking" and "correcting" have obvious value and significance. There may be a sequence intended here: first, refuting the false teaching that Timothy was confronting, and second, straightening everything out. The final item in the sequence is providing an ongoing "training in righteousness" (2Ti 3:16). Structurally, "teaching" stands at the head of this series, and the purpose of Scripture is expressed in v. 17: "for every good work."

3:10–17 Unless the Word of God is obeyed, preached, and taught as it should be, we are neither giving it due honor nor letting it do its job. Bible societies, Bible publishers, Bible translators and other missionaries who translate the Scriptures, Sunday school teachers who explain it, preachers who proclaim it—and everyone who studies it, lives it, teaches it, raises a family based on its teachings, witnesses from it, and prays to God and praises him from its message—all have a significant part in the obedient application of the "God-breathed" Scripture to the life of the church.

4:1–5 The future judgment will be a complex event. Not only will there be a comprehensive judgment before the great white throne, resulting in eternal life or death (see Rev 20:11–15), but our lives as servants of the Lord will be evaluated before the judgment seat of Christ (2Co 5:9–10).

4:2–5 Paul opens his charge with commands. The word must be preached because sound doctrine is going to be rejected. People will "gather [teachers] around them," who suit the "desires" of the people (v. 3). Verse 5a can also be read, "be sober in all things." It is not enough for Timothy to keep from losing his head; he must think clearly, fully aware of all that is going on. This means that he has to "endure hardship." "Do the work of an evangelist" is a straightforward command (v. 5).

4:6–7 "Being poured out like a drink offering" (v. 6) likely alludes to the sacrifice of drink offerings in the OT (Ex 29:40–41; Lev 23:13; Nu 15:4–10; 28:7). "The good fight" (2Ti 4:7) probably has behind it an athletic rather than a military image. Paul's statement, "I have finished the race," recalls his writings in Php 2:16.

4:8 The idea of a "crown [or garland] of righteousness" is unique here. Paul knows he has already received righteousness and that this righteousness has been stored up for him in heaven. The Lord who awards this crown is "the righteous Judge." The "appearing" here points to the coming of our Lord Jesus Christ, motivating us to live a godly life (see v. 1; also 1Ti 6:14; Titus 2:13).

4:1–8 Behind all these exhortations is the figure of the great apostle, ready now to commit and pass on these immense tasks to a younger man. This must have required a great deal of trust on his part. The work of spreading the gospel of Jesus Christ continues today in the hands of many competent Timothys. The same baton-passing phenomenon described here is no doubt being experienced daily in countless ways in the global church. This activity is reinforced by God, whose purposes for his church will continue to be carried out through his faithful people.

4:9–10 Paul's companions have been leaving him. His distress will likely be compounded if Timothy is

2Ti 4:11 ❖ Paul and Mark previously had a bitter falling out (see Ac 15:37–40). What relationships in our lives need to be reconciled for God's glory and for the benefit of the gospel?

world,[t] has deserted me and has gone to Thessalonica. Crescens has gone to Galatia,[u] and Titus to Dalmatia. 11 Only Luke[v] is with me.[w] Get Mark[x] and bring him with you, because he is helpful to me in my ministry. 12 I sent Tychicus[y] to Ephesus. 13 When you come, bring the cloak that I left with Carpus at Troas, and my scrolls, especially the parchments.

14 Alexander[z] the metalworker did me a great deal of harm. The Lord will repay him for what he has done.[a] 15 You too should be on your guard against him, because he strongly opposed our message.

16 At my first defense, no one came to my support, but everyone deserted me. May it not be held against them.[b] 17 But the Lord stood at my side[c] and gave me strength, so that through me the message might be fully proclaimed and all the Gentiles might hear it.[d] And I was delivered from the lion's mouth. 18 The Lord will rescue me from every evil attack[e] and will bring me safely to his heavenly kingdom. To him be glory for ever and ever. Amen.[f]

4:10 [t] 1Jn 2:15 [u] Ac 16:6
4:11 [v] Col 4:14 [w] 2Ti 1:15 [x] Ac 12:12
4:12 [y] Ac 20:4
4:14 [z] Ac 19:33 [a] Ro 12:19
4:16 [b] Ac 7:60
4:17 [c] Ac 23:11 [d] Ac 9:15
4:18 [e] Ps 121:7 [f] Ro 11:36
4:19 [g] Ac 18:2
4:20 [h] Ac 19:22 [i] Ac 20:4
4:21 [j] ver 9
4:22 [k] Gal 6:18; Phm 25 [l] Col 4:18

Final Greetings

19 Greet Priscilla[a] and Aquila[g] and the household of Onesiphorus. 20 Erastus[h] stayed in Corinth, and I left Trophimus[i] sick in Miletus. 21 Do your best to get here before winter.[j] Eubulus greets you, and so do Pudens, Linus, Claudia and all the brothers and sisters.[b]

22 The Lord be with your spirit.[k] Grace be with you all.[l]

[a] *19* Greek *Prisca,* a variant of *Priscilla* [b] *21* The Greek word for *brothers and sisters* (*adelphoi*) refers here to believers, both men and women, as part of God's family.

---

delayed by a long stopover because of the onset of winter. Demas made a choice for the present world; Titus has gone to Dalmatia, probably on a mission for Paul.

4:11 Paul's statement that "only Luke is with me" conveys some emotion. Some think it also offers a clue concerning the authorship of the Pastoral Letters. Luke's presence would have allowed him to function as a secretary, writing at Paul's dictation. "Get Mark" (v. 11b) implies that at some point after Paul's refusal to have Mark continue with him on his missionary journeys (Ac 15:37–40), a change took place in Mark or in Paul, or perhaps in both. Paul could trust Mark again as an associate in his ministry.

4:12 Tychicus appears at several points as an important associate of Paul (Ac 20:4; Eph 6:21–22; Col 4:7–9). Paul may be sending this letter to Timothy via Tychicus.

4:14 It is impossible to tell whether "Alexander the metalworker" (v. 14) is the same person named in 1Ti 1:20.

4:16–17 Paul's reference to "my first defense" could refer to a second trial that occurs after the imprisonment recorded in Acts. On the other hand, "first defense" may refer to the first phase of his present trial. In this case we would have to understand v. 17 in another sense than Paul's going personally to other countries and Gentile audiences.

4:19–20 Paul's final greetings and personal references here are sentimental. Priscilla and Aquila have meant a great deal to Paul. The reference to the "household of Onesiphorus" (v. 19b) may be a wonderful testimony to the entire household or, poignantly, a sympathetic word to his bereaved family if he had died. "Erastus" (v. 20) may be the same person mentioned in the same breath as Timothy in Ac 19:22. "Trophimus" is also mentioned in Ac 20:4 in company with Timothy.

4:21 Paul cites several otherwise unknown people: Eubulus, Pudens, Linus, and Claudia (see NIV text note on v. 21).

✣ **4:9–22** To say farewell is a good and thoughtful act for the one facing death. Too many people have been unwilling to deal realistically with the prospect of death. They then lose the opportunity to say that last word of forgiveness or to ask for it. Paul was not courting death, yet he was *ready* to die when it was God's time for him to do so. His readiness is also instructive for us.

Titus

Author: The apostle Paul

Audience: Titus, a trusted Gentile companion of Paul

Date: About AD 63–65 or possibly AD 56

Theme: Paul writes to instruct Titus concerning the care of the church on the island of Crete, especially in the face of false teachers there.

PERSPECTIVE

The apostle Paul (1:1) probably wrote this letter after his release from his first Roman imprisonment (see Ac 28:16–31), perhaps on an otherwise unattested fourth missionary journey, c. AD 62–64. He writes to his younger apostolic delegate Titus, who is ministering on the island of Crete (Titus 1:5). For reasons lost to us, Paul had been ministering with Titus on Crete but left the island, leaving Titus behind to complete the work of establishing the church there. The fledgling church on Crete was in danger from a local Jewish false teaching (1:10–16), and the urgent need to combat it was to appoint godly and spiritually mature elders for every town where a church has been established (1:5–9). The purpose of the letter is to instruct Titus how to lead the church on Crete and to refute the false teaching that threatens it.

For more perspective on this book, see the Introductions to 1 and 2 Timothy.

Reading Titus

This letter is short enough to read at one time. Notice how Paul alternates warnings against false teachings with positive instructions on the Christian life that Titus is to communicate to the people under his care.

TAKING THE NEXT STEPS

After Paul was released from prison in Rome (see Ac 28:30), early tradition tells that he continued his mission work, traveling part of the time with Timothy and Titus. Paul left Pastor Titus behind in Crete (Titus 1:5) to oversee the organization of churches there. To help Titus accomplish this task, Paul wrote this letter of pastoral advice.

Like the other two Pastoral Letters (1 and 2 Timothy), this one

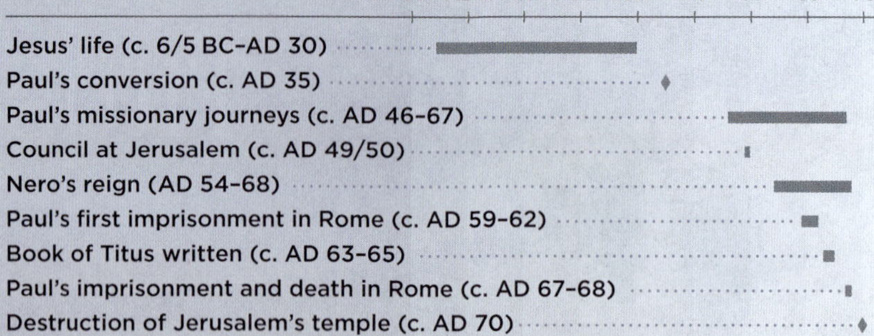

contains practical advice for the contemporary Christian. (1) God wants people of the highest spiritual character to serve as leaders in his church. (2) Leaders in the church should serve as examples for others. (3) Every Christian should be self-controlled in his or her life, eager to oppose sin and to please the Lord Jesus Christ.

Key Verses

Remind the people to be subject to rulers and authorities, to be obedient, to be ready to do whatever is good, to slander no one, to be peaceable and considerate, and always to be gentle toward everyone.

—Titus 3:1–2

WHAT TO LOOK FOR IN TITUS

- The need for elders in the churches of Crete (1:5–16)
- Ethical teachings (2:1–15)
- The importance of doing good (ch. 3)

1 Paul, a servant of God[a] and an apostle of Jesus Christ to further the faith
of God's elect and their knowledge of
the truth[b] that leads to godliness— 2in
the hope of eternal life,[c] which God, who
does not lie, promised before the beginning of time,[d] 3and which now at his appointed season[e] he has brought to light[f]
through the preaching entrusted to me[g]
by the command of God our Savior,[h]

4To Titus,[i] my true son in our common faith:

1:1 [a] Ro 1:1 [b] 1Ti 2:4
1:2 [c] 2Ti 1:1 [d] 2Ti 1:9
1:3 [e] 1Ti 2:6 [f] 2Ti 1:10 [g] 1Ti 1:11 [h] Lk 1:47
1:4 [i] 2Co 2:13
1:5 [j] Ac 27:7 [k] Ac 11:30
1:6 [l] 1Ti 3:2

Grace and peace from God the Father and Christ Jesus our Savior.

Appointing Elders Who Love What Is Good

1:6–8Ref // 1Ti 3:2–4

5The reason I left you in Crete[j] was that you might put in order what was left unfinished and appoint[a] elders[k] in every town, as I directed you. 6An elder must
be blameless,[l] faithful to his wife, a man

[a] 5 Or *ordain*

1:1–4 Paul identifies himself both as "a servant" ("slave") of God and as "an apostle" (v. 1). A slave was owned by another person to whom obedience was required. If slavery meant obligation, apostleship meant authority, but both meant responsibility.

The faith that Paul wants strengthened is the faith of God's "elect," who stand in the tradition of the OT people of God. The correspondence between "truth" and "godliness" (v. 1) probably means "truth that is appropriate to godliness." It may seem strange that "faith" and "knowledge" (v. 1) rest on "hope" (v. 2). However, this hope does not arise from the human heart but has been "promised before the beginning of time" by "God, who does not lie" (v. 2).

1:5 As he did with Timothy in Ephesus, Paul left Titus on the island of Crete to organize the church and deal with a crisis situation of false teachers who had infiltrated it. Paul implies there was some residual disorganization after he left, which could be remedied by what had not been done before: appointing responsible leadership.

1:6 There is a difference between the latter part of v. 6 and 1Ti 3:4. In 1 Timothy the elder is to "see that

PEOPLE TO KNOW // TITUS

TITUS 1:4: Titus was a Gentile Christian and ministry partner of Paul. When Paul presented to some church leaders in Jerusalem that the gospel he had been preaching to the Gentiles was bearing fruit, Titus was evidence of the effectiveness of this gospel. In showing that God's Spirit was moving among Gentiles, Titus was not compelled to be circumcised and become Jewish in order to be a Christian (Gal 2:1–3).

In one of his letters, Paul refers to Titus as his "partner and co-worker" among the Corinthians (2Co 8:23). Paul wrote that he was sending Titus to the Corinthians to receive an offering from them to help other churches. Paul told the Corinthians that Titus was enthusiastic to make this journey to see them. After all, Titus had returned deeply encouraged and refreshed from his previous visit to Corinth (2Co 7:13). Titus may have delivered both of Paul's letters to Corinth.

Paul and Titus had ministered in Crete, and Paul left Titus there to continue to organize the believers and appoint elders over the towns. Paul's letter to Titus is filled with practical pastoral advice to his faithful partner in the work of the Lord.

APPLICATION ✣ Our lives should bear evidence of God's grace. Titus accomplished this when Paul presented him to the Jewish leaders in Jerusalem. They saw with their own eyes that God was working in Titus's life despite his not being circumcised. It can feel uncomfortable to be put on display, but God calls believers to live such good lives in the eyes of the world that those around us glorify God (1Pe 2:12). The life we live is our greatest testimony of our devotion to Jesus Christ.

whose children believe[a] and are not open
to the charge of being wild and disobedient. 7 Since an overseer[m] manages God's
household,[n] he must be blameless — not
overbearing, not quick-tempered, not giv-
en to drunkenness, not violent, not pursuing dishonest gain.[o] 8 Rather, he must be
hospitable,[p] one who loves what is good,[q]
who is self-controlled, upright, holy and
disciplined. 9 He must hold firmly[r] to the
trustworthy message as it has been taught,
so that he can encourage others by sound
doctrine[s] and refute those who oppose it.

Rebuking Those Who Fail to Do Good

10 For there are many rebellious people, full of meaningless talk[t] and deception, especially those of the circumcision
group.[u] 11 They must be silenced, because
they are disrupting whole households[v]
by teaching things they ought not to
teach — and that for the sake of dishonest gain. 12 One of Crete's own prophets[w]
has said it: "Cretans[x] are always liars, evil
brutes, lazy gluttons."[b] 13 This saying is
true. Therefore rebuke[y] them sharply, so
that they will be sound in the faith[z] 14 and
will pay no attention to Jewish myths[a]
or to the merely human commands[b] of
those who reject the truth. 15 To the pure,
all things are pure, but to those who are

1:7 [m] 1Ti 3:1 [n] 1Co 4:1 [o] 1Ti 3:3,8
1:8 [p] 1Ti 3:2 [q] 2Ti 3:3
1:9 [r] 1Ti 1:19 [s] 1Ti 1:10
1:10 [t] 1Ti 1:6 [u] Ac 11:2
1:11 [v] 2Ti 3:6
1:12 [w] Ac 17:28 [x] Ac 2:11
1:13 [y] 2Co 13:10 [z] Titus 2:2
1:14 [a] 1Ti 1:4 [b] Col 2:22

[a] *6* Or *children are trustworthy* [b] *12* From the Cretan philosopher Epimenides

his children obey him." Here the elder's children are to "believe." This seems to make the parent responsible for a child's salvation, but the Greek word translated "believe" is an adjective, which can also mean "faithful" or "trustworthy." The phrase in Titus 1:6 describes outrageous behavior that would bring public disgrace on the eldership and the church.

1:7–9 Paul uses the word "overseer," suggesting that overseers and elders are identical. The overseer/elder is to be "blameless" (the same word as in v. 6) for a specific reason: He acts as God's steward. The desirable characteristics cited in v. 8 describe the ideal character of all Christian men and women.

1:10–11 This section introduces the people whose teachings must be opposed by doctrinally capable elders. Paul has the "circumcision group" (v. 10) particularly in mind. The false teachers on Crete are turning *whole families* upside down. Perhaps they are teaching legalistic practices that disrupt relationships. These teachers are not operating out of sincerity but "for the sake of dishonest gain" (v. 11b).

1:12–13 The quotation that begins "Cretans are always liars" has caused much discussion. The function of the quotation is to provide a reason for distrusting the false teachers.

1:14 Paul states the two aspects of the teachings of the "circumcision group" that must be rejected. One is "Jewish myths," or nonbiblical deviant stories that Paul does not want circulated. The other aspect of the heretics' teachings concerns daily life: the "commands of those who reject the truth."

1:15–16 The assault on the false teachers reaches a peak in v. 16. The contrast is damning: Those who

corrupted and do not believe, nothing
is pure.[c] In fact, both their minds and
consciences are corrupted. 16They claim
to know God, but by their actions they
deny him.[d] They are detestable, disobedient and unfit for doing anything good.

Doing Good for the Sake of the Gospel

2 You, however, must teach what is appropriate to sound doctrine.[e] 2Teach
the older men to be temperate, worthy
of respect, self-controlled, and sound in
faith,[f] in love and in endurance.

3Likewise, teach the older women to
be reverent in the way they live, not
to be slanderers or addicted to much
wine,[g] but to teach what is good. 4Then
they can urge the younger women to
love their husbands and children, 5to
be self-controlled and pure, to be busy
at home, to be kind, and to be subject
to their husbands,[h] so that no one will
malign the word of God.[i]

6Similarly, encourage the young
men[j] to be self-controlled. 7In everything set them an example[k] by doing
what is good. In your teaching show
integrity, seriousness 8and soundness
of speech that cannot be condemned,
so that those who oppose you may be
ashamed because they have nothing
bad to say about us.[l]

9Teach slaves to be subject to their
masters in everything,[m] to try to please
them, not to talk back to them, 10and not
to steal from them, but to show that they
can be fully trusted, so that in every way
they will make the teaching about God
our Savior attractive.[n]

11For the grace of God has appeared
that offers salvation to all people.[o] 12It
teaches us to say "No" to ungodliness
and worldly passions,[p] and to live self-
controlled, upright and godly lives[q] in
this present age, 13while we wait for the

1:15 [c] Ro 14:14, 23
1:16 [d] 1Jn 2:4
2:1 [e] 1Ti 1:10
2:2 [f] Titus 1:13
2:3 [g] 1Ti 3:8
2:5 [h] Eph 5:22 [i] 1Ti 6:1
2:6 [j] 1Ti 5:1
2:7 [k] 1Ti 4:12
2:8 [l] 1Pe 2:12
2:9 [m] Eph 6:5
2:10 [n] Mt 5:16
2:11 [o] 1Ti 2:4
2:12 [p] Titus 3:3 [q] 2Ti 3:12

Titus 1:16 ❖ What do our actions show about our faith in God? Would those watching us conclude we follow God? Why or why not?

Titus 2:11–15 ❖ How can we resist ungodliness and worldly passions? Why is this sometimes difficult?

---

claim they know God fail to match their actions to their words and actually deny him (cf. Ro 1:28–32).

APPLICATION ✣ **1:1–16** Verses 10–16 require strong application. Although Paul's counsel, especially to Titus, is to be gentle in correction, there are times when firm disciplinary action and public rebuke are called for, particularly for those who are "rebellious" and deceivers (v. 10), "disrupting whole households" for "dishonest gain" (v. 11), "corrupted" (v. 15), denying God, "detestable," and "disobedient" (v. 16). It is hard to deal with such people if there is no strong, recognized leadership in the church.

This is a case where plural leadership is important for the sake of accountability to the Scriptures. The message of Titus 1:1–16 for today is that not only leadership but also leadership vested with authority is needed to handle any situation and any personal hostility that may arise.

2:1–3 The teaching under discussion must be consistent with the "sound doctrine" (v. 1) that Paul has been advocating throughout the Pastoral Letters. The teaching here is practical instruction that is based on doctrine. In the list of instructions, the "household" image is invoked. The older men in this household should be respected for their age and character. The older women have a similar responsibility.

2:4–5 The word "urge" (v. 4) can imply a need to be reminded of something, in this case to love husbands and children.

2:6–8 Paul tells Titus to instruct "the young men" (v. 6), serving as an example *to them*. The rest of the list emphasizes the kind of character Paul has urged throughout these Pastoral Letters.

2:9–10 The instructions to slaves (v. 9) are similar to those in Eph 6:5 and Col 3:22. In addition to slaves being submissive in every area of the slave/master relationship, Paul urges integrity in word and deed. By showing that a slave can be "fully trusted," Paul says they will "make the teaching about God . . . attractive" (Titus 2:10). Paul's instructions show Titus and Cretan Christians how character and good deeds can help win others to Christ.

✣ **2:1–10** If there is any passage in Paul's letter to Titus that needs to be applied today, it is this one. Christians must work hard to live so that they give no cause to unbelievers to "malign the word of God" (v. 5), have anything "bad to say about us" (v. 8), or find Christian doctrine unattractive (v. 10).

2:11–12 The grace of God not only saves but also "teaches" (v. 12). This training should accomplish two goals: a negative one, to renounce two specified undesirable habits of life, and a positive one, to adopt in their place three desirable habits. One should renounce or reject "ungodliness" and "worldly passions." God's grace also trains us positively to embrace the Christian life in a way that is "self-controlled, upright [or just] and godly" (v. 12).

2:13 Before Paul addresses Christ's return, he mentions the virtues that grace teaches us to adopt and live out "in this present age" (v. 12). Although the

blessed hope — the appearing of the
glory of our great God and Savior, Jesus
Christ,[r] 14who gave himself for us to redeem us from all wickedness and to purify for himself a people that are his very
own,[s] eager to do what is good.[t]
15These, then, are the things you
should teach. Encourage and rebuke
with all authority. Do not let anyone
despise you.

Saved in Order to Do Good

3 Remind the people to be subject to
rulers and authorities,[u] to be obedient, to be ready to do whatever is good,[v]
2to slander no one,[w] to be peaceable and
considerate, and always to be gentle toward everyone.
3At one time we too were foolish,
disobedient, deceived and enslaved by
all kinds of passions and pleasures. We
lived in malice and envy, being hated
and hating one another. 4But when the
kindness[x] and love of God our Savior
appeared,[y] 5he saved us, not because of
righteous things we had done,[z] but because of his mercy. He saved us through
the washing of rebirth and renewal[a] by
the Holy Spirit, 6whom he poured out
on us[b] generously through Jesus Christ
our Savior, 7so that, having been justified
by his grace,[c] we might become heirs[d]
having the hope[e] of eternal life.[f] 8This
is a trustworthy saying.[g] And I want you
to stress these things, so that those who
have trusted in God may be careful to devote themselves to doing what is good.[h]
These things are excellent and profitable
for everyone.
9But avoid foolish controversies and
genealogies and arguments and quarrels[i] about the law, because these are
unprofitable and useless. 10Warn a divisive person once, and then warn them
a second time. After that, have nothing
to do with them.[j] 11You may be sure that

2:13 [r]2Pe 1:1
2:14 [s]Ex 19:5 [t]Eph 2:10
3:1 [u]Ro 13:1 [v]2Ti 2:21
3:2 [w]Eph 4:31; 2Ti 2:24
3:4 [x]Eph 2:7 [y]Titus 2:11
3:5 [z]Eph 2:9 [a]Ro 12:2
3:6 [b]Ro 5:5
3:7 [c]Ro 3:24 [d]Ro 8:17 [e]Ro 8:24 [f]Titus 1:2
3:8 [g]1Ti 1:15 [h]Titus 2:14
3:9 [i]1Ti 1:4; 2Ti 2:14
3:10 [j]Ro 16:17

Titus 3:1-2 ❖ Let these admonitions be your goals for today.

---

object of our waiting is twofold, "the blessed hope" and glorious appearing, it is a conceptual unity.

2:14 Paul's use of "who gave himself" points to the voluntary offering of Christ on the cross for us. Earlier, Paul noted that the training that grace gives us is in both a positive and a negative form. Here, the same pairing is the result of our Lord's sacrifice: negatively, to "redeem us from all wickedness," and positively, "to purify for himself a people that are his very own, eager to do what is good."

2:15 Titus is to "teach" these things. Two verbs follow: "encourage" and "rebuke." Just as Paul functioned under the command of God, so Titus is to function under the apostolic command of Paul.

✚ **2:11-15** This complex passage is of immense importance. Like other passages in the Pastoral Letters, it teaches the seriousness of transmitting sound doctrine that carries divine authority. It is right for us to say, "This is what the Lord says," or "This is what the Bible says," making sure that we are properly teaching and applying Scripture so that God's people are equipped and "eager to do what is good" (v. 14).

3:1-8 The proper attitude toward the secular "rulers and authorities" is submission, obedience, and readiness "to do whatever is good" (v. 1).

3:1-3 Verse 3 provides information pertinent to vv. 1-2. The words "we too" serve to identify the Christians' pre-conversion experience with that of those around them on Crete. The effect of all this is to keep the Christians humble (cf. v. 2) and to offer hope to the present unbelievers. The strong words used to describe the unbelievers are characteristics that had once been true of the converts.

3:4 Here Paul provides the kind of gracious interruption found in Eph 2:4-7. Paul's emphasis is not only on the coming of Christ as Savior but also (1) on the merciful, gracious work of salvation and (2) on the fact that this was *God's* own work.

3:5-6 The basis on which God saved us is not the good things we have done. The *true* grounds of our salvation is "his mercy" (v. 5). Paul cites the means by which God has accomplished this. We might say that the means of salvation are the washing (represented by but not identical to baptism), the regeneration, and the renewing; the agents of the renewing are the Holy Spirit and Jesus Christ our Savior, through whom the Spirit has been so generously poured out on us.

3:7 The purpose of God's mercy, grace, and kindness in our lives is "so that" we may be heirs of God.

3:8 The latter part of this verse outlines the importance of good works for those who have experienced God's grace. Paul clearly states that such good works are "excellent and profitable for everyone."

3:9-11 Controversies are "unprofitable and useless" (v. 9). After a couple of warnings, Titus is to have "nothing to do" with a divisive person (v. 10) who stirs them up. This does not mean that grace is never extended, for the person has already had a second chance (v. 10; cf. Mt 18:15-17). It has been established that this "divisive person" cannot be redeemed. He is not only "warped and sinful" (Titus 3:11), but he has also condemned himself, so the responsibility is not on Titus.

✚ **3:1-11** Controversies and divisiveness that call for strong action on the part of Christian leaders require a rare blend of humility and authority, of love and uncompromising admonition. The stronger the reputation of a church and its leaders for love, integrity, and

IMPORTANT NAMES IN PAUL'S LETTERS

NAME	REFERENCES	SIGNIFICANCE
Phoebe	Ro 16:1	A "deacon of the church" in Cenchreae
Aquila and Priscilla	Ro 16:3; 1Co 16:19 (Ac 18:1-3)	Paul's fellow workers; served with him in Ephesus; hosted a church in their house; helped train other church leaders
Epenetus	Ro 16:5	The first convert to Christ in the province of Asia
Mary	Ro 16:6	"Worked very hard" for the Roman church
Andronicus and Junia	Ro 16:7	Imprisoned with Paul
Ampliatus	Ro 16:8	Someone Paul loved "in the Lord"
Urbanus	Ro 16:9	A "co-worker" with Paul
Apelles	Ro 16:10	Approved in Christ
Aristobulus	Ro 16:10	Head of a Roman household; perhaps grandson of Herod the Great
Herodion	Ro 16:11	A fellow Jew
Narcissus	Ro 16:11	Leader of a Roman household
Tryphena and Tryphosa	Ro 16:12	Women who "work hard in the Lord"
Rufus	Ro 16:13 (Mk 16:13?)	"Chosen in the Lord"
Asyncritus, Phlegon, Hermes, Patrobas, Hermas	Ro 16:14	Members of the Roman church
Philologus, Julia, Nereus, Olympas	Ro 16:15	Members of the Roman church
Timothy	Ro 16:21; 1Co 4:17; 16:10-11; 2Co 1:1, 19; Php 1:1; 2:19-24; Col 1:1; 1Th 1:1; 3:1-8; 2Th 1:1; 1 & 2Ti; Phm 1 (Ac 16-20)	Paul's spiritual "son"; led many churches
Lucius, Jason, Sosipater	Ro 16:21 (Ac 17:5-10; 20:4?)	Fellow Jews
Tertius	Ro 16:22	"Wrote down" Paul's letter to the Roman church
Gaius	Ro 16:23; 1Co 1:14? (Ac 18:7?)	Hosted Paul as he wrote Romans; baptized by Paul at Corinth (?)
Erastus	Ro 16:23; 2Ti 4:20? (Ac 19:22?)	Director of "public works" at Corinth (?)
Quartus	Ro 16:23	A believer at Corinth (?)
Sosthenes	1Co 1:1 (Ac 18:17?)	Included in Paul's letter to the Corinthians; perhaps a converted synagogue ruler at Corinth
Chloe	1Co 1:11	Led an important Corinthian household
Apollos	1Co 1:12; 3:4—4:7; 16:12; Titus 3:13 (Ac 18:24—19:1)	Early Christian leader; able to argue powerfully from the Scriptures
Peter (Cephas)	1Co 1:12; 3:22; 9:5; 15:5; Gal 2	Prominent early apostle; apostle to the Jews
Crispus	1Co 1:14 (Ac 18:8)	Leader of a Corinthian synagogue; baptized by Paul
Stephanas	1Co 1:16; 16:15-17	Head of Corinthian household Paul baptized; first believers in Achaia
Barnabas	1Co 9:6; Gal 2; Col 4:10 (Ac 4:36; 9:26-28; 11:19-30; 12:24-25; 13-15)	"Son of Encouragement"; teacher in the early church and Paul's partner

IMPORTANT NAMES IN PAUL'S LETTERS

NAME	REFERENCES	SIGNIFICANCE
Fortunatus and Achaicus	1Co 16:17	Probably delivered the Corinthian letter mentioned in 1Co 7:1
Silas (Silvanus)	2Co 1:19; 1Th 1:1; 2Th 1:1 (Ac 15:22—18:5; 1Pe 5:12)	Leader in the Jerusalem church; Paul's missionary partner
Titus	2Co 2:13; 7:6-16; 8:6, 23; 12:18; Gal 2:1-3; 2Ti 4:9-10; Titus 1-3	One of Paul's converts; traveled with Paul and helped lead the early church
James, the Lord's brother	Gal 1:19; 2:12 (Mt 12:46-50; Ac 12:17)	Leader of the Jerusalem church; Paul visited him in Jerusalem
Tychicus	Eph 6:21-22; 2Ti 4:12 (Ac 20:4)	A "dear brother and faithful servant"; sent by Paul to the Ephesians
Epaphroditus	Php 2:25-30; 4:18	A "brother, co-worker and fellow soldier" with Paul from Philippi
Euodia and Syntyche	Php 4:3	Two women in disagreement; "contended at [Paul's] side"
Clement	Php 4:3	A "co-worker" with Paul
Epaphras	Col 1:7-8; 4:12-13; Phm 23	Brought gospel to Colossae
Onesimus	Col 4:9; Phm 10	A slave Paul led to Christ
Aristarchus	Col 4:10; Phm 24 (Ac 19:29; 27:2)	Travel companion and fellow prisoner with Paul
Mark (Barnabas's cousin)	Col 4:10; Phm 24; 2Ti 4:11 (Ac 12:12, 25; 15:36-39; 1Pe 5:13)	Traveled with Paul and Barnabas; wrote Mark's Gospel
Jesus (called Justus)	Col 4:11	A "co-worker" and fellow Jew
Luke	Col 4:14; 2Ti 4:11; Phm 24	The "dear friend . . . the doctor"; Paul's travel companion
Demas	Col 4:14; 2Ti 4:10; Phm 24	A fellow worker who would later desert Paul
Nympha	Col 4:15	Hosted church in her house
Archippus	Col 4:17; Phm 2	Paul's "fellow soldier"
Hymenaeus and Alexander; Philetus	1Ti 1:20; 2Ti 2:17; 4:14	"Handed over to Satan" by Paul
Lois and Eunice	2Ti 1:5 (Ac 16:1)	Timothy's believing grandmother and mother
Phygelus and Hermogenes	2Ti 1:15	Deserted Paul
Onesiphorus	2Ti 1:16-18	Encouraged Paul in his imprisonment
Crescens	2Ti 4:10	Left Paul in his imprisonment
Carpus	2Ti 4:13	Guarded Paul's cloak and books
Trophimus	2Ti 4:20	A travel companion, left at Miletus
Eubulus, Pudens, Linus, Claudia	2Ti 4:21	Friends of Paul and Timothy
Artemas	Titus 3:12	Likely sent by Paul to Titus in Crete
Zenas	Titus 3:13	A lawyer; Apollos's traveling companion
Philemon and Apphia	Phm	Recipients of Paul's letter

such people are warped and sinful; they
are self-condemned.

Final Remarks

12As soon as I send Artemas or Tychicus[k] to you, do your best to come to me
at Nicopolis, because I have decided to
winter there.[l] 13Do everything you can
to help Zenas the lawyer and Apollos[m]
on their way and see that they have everything they need. 14Our people must
learn to devote themselves to doing what
is good,[n] in order to provide for urgent
needs and not live unproductive lives.
15Everyone with me sends you greetings. Greet those who love us in the
faith.[o]
Grace be with you all.[p]

3:12 [k] Ac 20:4 [l] 2Ti 4:9,21
3:13 [m] Ac 18:24
3:14 [n] ver 8
3:15 [o] 1Ti 1:2 [p] Col 4:18

civility, the more effective their insistence on doctrinal purity will be.

3:12–15 Paul's final remarks include personal requests (vv. 12–13), a reprise of the latter part of v. 8 (which repeats the emphasis on doing good, v. 14), and finally greetings and a benediction (v. 15). The Pastoral Letters are full of personal instructions, but the closing here allows for the kind of specific instructions contained in Eph 6:21–22 and Col 4:7–9.
3:14 Here Paul picks up the latter part of v. 8, repeating the same words in the same order: "to devote themselves to doing what is good." This means believers are not only to provide for themselves to avoid being a burden to others, but also, it may be assumed, that they should be productive in providing for others.
3:15 Paul's closing greetings are warm and all-inclusive. The simple words "grace be with you all" conclude the letter—one final reminder of the saving grace of God our Savior.

3:12–15 Many missionary communications today contain vivid pictures or descriptions of the people they are reaching for Christ to encourage people to give. Charitable organizations, such as those caring for children in deprived areas, must be sure to channel all the money possible from the donations received to those in need. The conclusion to Titus also reminds us that right around us, people like Zenas and Apollos (v. 13), also need our support and encouragement. It serves as a reminder to us to be ready to practice hospitality and to invest in those who are doing gospel work. This ensures that legitimate ministries, both local and around the world, are supported in prayer and in giving so that they can continue to move their kingdom work forward without interruption.

Philemon

Author: The apostle Paul

Audience: Philemon and the members of the church at Colossae

Date: About AD 60

Theme: Paul urges Philemon to show grace to Onesimus, his runaway slave, as a Christian brother.

PERSPECTIVE

Christians are not alone. When we are joined to Christ, we are joined to others. Recognizing how integrated we are with others who share the faith leads to greater understanding of its truth and to greater understanding of others. A recognition of the blessings we have all received freely by grace should promote our love and forgiveness of our fellow Christians. In this letter, the reconciliation of a disloyal slave with his master as brothers in Christ speaks volumes to the community within and without. It demonstrates how Christian faith recasts all relationships and how Christ reconciles all things (Col 1:20).

In this short letter, Paul allows Philemon to decide completely for himself what he will do, but he expects that he will consider how his decision will have impact on his community of faith. Since the house church meets in his home, his ethical decisions will have immediate repercussions for the whole church.

Things have not changed in this regard. How believers respond to the demands of love in everyday decisions directly effects the spiritual health of the whole congregation. It may be helpful to have members of our church advise us in moral decisions that we now consider to be private matters. Surrounded by those who are committed to Christ and who pray together, we may be more likely to choose God's will. Our fellow Christians may be more directive in helping us put God's love to work in our lives.

Reading Philemon

Be sure to read Philemon in one sitting. Notice the skillful manner in which Paul presents his request to Philemon. Paul's letter to Philemon serves as a model of Christian compassion. In many ways, it parallels Jesus' parable of the lost son, which captures the gospel in a nutshell. The letter speaks of failure, the need for intercession, returning, forgiveness,

10 BC | AD 1 | 10 | 20 | 30 | 40 | 50 | 60 | 70 | 80 | 90 | 100

Jesus' life (c. 6/5 BC–AD 30)
Paul's conversion (c. AD 35)
Paul's missionary journeys (c. AD 46–67)
Council at Jerusalem (c. AD 49/50)
Nero's reign (AD 54–68)
Paul's first imprisonment in Rome (c. AD 59–62)
Book of Philemon written (c. AD 60)
Paul's imprisonment and death in Rome (c. AD 67–68)
Destruction of Jerusalem's temple (c. AD 70)

and restoration. If we are genuine disciples of Christ, we will relate to our fellow believers with grace, forgiveness, and encouragement. And when we are the ones seeking forgiveness, we can ask for the same consideration of our brothers and sisters.

Key Verses

Perhaps the reason he was separated from you for a little while was that you might have him back forever—no longer as a slave, but better than a slave, as a dear brother. He is very dear to me but even dearer to you, both as a fellow man and as a brother in the Lord.

—Philemon 15–16

TAKING THE NEXT STEPS

Paul wrote the letter to Philemon while imprisoned in either Caesarea or Rome (Ac 24:27; 28:30), probably at the same time he wrote Colossians (cf. Phm 10, 23–24 with Col 4:7–15). Onesimus, a runaway slave, had contacted Paul in prison and had become a Christian. Paul therefore wrote the slave owner, Philemon, pleading with him to forgive Onesimus and take him back without the usual harsh punishment such slaves received.

From this brief letter God reminds us that even though we may have the right and the desire to treat someone harshly, a far better route is the road of forgiveness. This lesson is learned and practiced in the context of our families, our circles of friends, and in our work and worship communities: "Forgive as the Lord forgave you" (Col 3:13).

WHAT TO LOOK FOR IN PHILEMON

- The first mention of Onesimus (vv. 8–12)
- Paul's desire to keep Onesimus with him (vv. 13–14)
- The request to receive Onesimus as a brother (vv. 15–16)

1Paul, a prisoner[a] of Christ Jesus, and
Timothy our brother,[b]

To Philemon our dear friend and fellow worker[c] — 2also to Apphia our sister
and Archippus[d] our fellow soldier[e] —
and to the church that meets in your
home:[f]

3Grace and peace to you[a] from God our
Father and the Lord Jesus Christ.

Thanksgiving and Prayer

4I always thank my God[g] as I remember you in my prayers, 5because I hear
about your love for all his holy people[h]
and your faith in the Lord Jesus. 6I pray
that your partnership with us in the faith
may be effective in deepening your understanding of every good thing we share
for the sake of Christ. 7Your love has giv-
en me great joy and encouragement,[i]
because you, brother, have refreshed[j]
the hearts of the Lord's people.

Paul's Plea for Onesimus

8Therefore, although in Christ I could
be bold and order you to do what you
ought to do, 9yet I prefer to appeal to you
on the basis of love. It is as none other

1 [a] ver 9,23; Eph 3:1 [b] 2Co 1:1 [c] Php 2:25
2 [d] Col 4:17 [e] Php 2:25 [f] Ro 16:5
4 [g] Ro 1:8
5 [h] Eph 1:15; Col 1:4
7 [i] 2Co 7:4,13 [j] ver 20

[a] *3* The Greek is plural; also in verses 22 and 25; elsewhere in this letter "you" is singular.

1–3 Paul begins his appeal to Philemon by identifying himself as a "prisoner of Christ Jesus." Paul not only addresses Philemon, Apphia, and Archippus but also "the church that meets in [Philemon's] home" (v. 2). This means that the letter is not an exclusively private note to Philemon.
4–7 Philemon's record for showing his love gives Paul the confidence to ask him to show his love again for another believer in vv. 8–17. Onesimus has likely done Philemon personal injury (v. 18).
6 Paul moves from thanksgiving to an intercessory prayer.
7 Paul gives the reason for his thanksgiving and optimism. Philemon's past benevolence emboldens Paul to make an audacious request on behalf of Onesimus.

APPLICATION ✣ 1–7 When we are joined to Christ, we are joined to others. Recognizing how integrated we are with others leads to a greater understanding of truth and to a greater understanding of others. Our fellow Christians remind us of the grace we've experienced and help us put God's love to work in our lives.

8–12 Paul wants his friend to do what is right, but he will not command him because he wants Philemon to decide on his own what is fitting in Christ to do. Forgiveness was not the norm in Philemon's world, but it is a fundamental requirement for Christians. Paul seeks to activate Philemon's Christian consciousness to make him aware of what he must do in this situation. He expects Philemon to show love and forgive Onesimus, just as the Lord forgave him his sins.
9 Paul expects Onesimus to act from love. In return, Onesimus must be willing to accept with grace whatever Philemon might decide in his case, which could include severe punishment or being sold to another master.

PEOPLE TO KNOW // PHILEMON

PHILEMON 1–25: Philemon was an early Christian and friend of Paul who hosted a house church (Phm 2). Paul wrote him the letter that bears his name, which addresses an issue with his runaway slave, Onesimus.

Paul praised Philemon for his love and his faith. Paul also recounted that Philemon refreshed the hearts of God's people. Paul then gets to the point of his letter. He appeals to Philemon to receive back his runaway slave, Onesimus, whom Paul says he is sending. Paul calls Onesimus his "son" and his "very heart" (Phm 10, 12), indicating a close relationship between the two men. He notes that Onesimus had been a great help to him while Paul was in chains. Paul urges Philemon to receive Onesimus back not as a "slave," but as a "dear brother" (Phm 16)—even asking him to receive Onesimus back as he would receive Paul himself.

APPLICATION ✣ Christians have a calling of reconciliation (2Co 5:18). It is rarely easy for broken relationships to be restored, but Christ provided the ultimate example and path for reconciliation when he reconciled the broken world to God the Father. Christ passes this ministry to his followers. When we make Christ our peace (Eph 2:14) and bring reconciliation in our broken relationships, we put God on display in the world.

than Paul — an old man and now also a
prisoner[k] of Christ Jesus — 10that I appeal to you for my son[l] Onesimus,[a][m] who
became my son while I was in chains.
11Formerly he was useless to you, but
now he has become useful both to you
and to me.

12I am sending him — who is my very
heart — back to you. 13I would have
liked to keep him with me so that he
could take your place in helping me
while I am in chains for the gospel.
14But I did not want to do anything
without your consent, so that any favor you do would not seem forced[n] but
would be voluntary. 15Perhaps the reason he was separated from you for a
little while was that you might have
him back forever — 16no longer as a
slave, but better than a slave, as a dear
brother.[o] He is very dear to me but even
dearer to you, both as a fellow man and
as a brother in the Lord.

17So if you consider me a partner,[p] welcome him as you would welcome me. 18If
he has done you any wrong or owes you
anything, charge it to me. 19I, Paul, am
writing this with my own hand. I will pay
it back — not to mention that you owe
me your very self. 20I do wish, brother,
that I may have some benefit from you
in the Lord; refresh[q] my heart in Christ.
21Confident[r] of your obedience, I write
to you, knowing that you will do even
more than I ask.

22And one thing more: Prepare a
guest room for me, because I hope to
be[s] restored to you in answer to your
prayers.[t]

23Epaphras,[u] my fellow prisoner in

9 [k]ver 1,23
10 [l]1Co 4:15 [m]Col 4:9
14 [n]2Co 9:7; 1Pe 5:2
16 [o]Mt 23:8; 1Ti 6:2
17 [p]2Co 8:23
20 [q]ver 7
21 [r]2Co 2:3
22 [s]Php 1:25; 2:24 [t]2Co 1:11
23 [u]Col 1:7

Phm 16 ❖ Where have we seen the reconciling power of the gospel—a power that can turn master and slave into brothers in Christ—on display in our own lives?

[a] 10 *Onesimus* means *useful.*

10–12 Paul pulls at Philemon's heartstrings by reminding him of Paul's captivity for preaching the gospel (see also vv. 1, 13) while appealing to an old man's privilege. In Paul's culture, thoughts of abolitionist reform were unheard of, and a world without slavery was inconceivable.

Before making his actual appeal, Paul lets Philemon know that Onesimus has become a Christian (see also v. 16). The father/son imagery used to relate this implied conversion conveys Paul's close relationship to Onesimus. Paul is careful to note that Onesimus had already been useful to him before he sent him back to Philemon. Paul intensifies his request by calling Onesimus his "very heart" (v. 12).

13–14 Paul expresses his preference, "I would have liked to keep him with me" (v. 13), but he puts aside his wishes out of consideration for Philemon's rights and feelings. There are two reasons why Paul sends Onesimus home: (1) Paul will do nothing without Philemon's specific consent (v. 14), and (2) Paul desires a face-to-face reconciliation between these two believers. The apostle's personal wishes therefore must yield to this greater end.

15–16 Paul continues to speak with reserve, leading to his actual request with a "perhaps." "He was separated from you" is a euphemism for Onesimus's illegal flight. Here Paul subtly attributes these events to God's purposes. Paul speaks theologically of the relationship between Onesimus and Philemon, which has been transformed based on forgiveness and love. Paul affirms that Onesimus, the man, is far more than a piece of property. He is Philemon's equal before the Lord. Receiving him "no longer as a slave" (v. 16) is a subtle but open invitation to free Onesimus.

17–18 Verse 17 is the letter's climax: "Welcome him as you would welcome me." Paul not only intercedes for Onesimus but identifies with him. Onesimus, the runaway slave, returns home as Paul's apostolic representative. So Philemon's reception of Onesimus will represent his reception of Paul.

Paul is deliberately vague about how Onesimus has wronged Philemon to avoid stirring up any unpleasant memories. In effect, he says, "I'll cover any loss you've suffered from my own pocket" (v. 18). This pledge emphasizes how committed Paul is to Onesimus.

19–25 Since the letter is being read aloud to the church (v. 2), it is necessary for Paul to notify the listeners that he has taken the stylus to write out his promissory note (v. 19).

19 With the phrase "not to mention that," Paul subtly reminds Philemon of the basis of their relationship. He suddenly converts Philemon from a creditor, whose debt will be paid in full, to a debtor—one who cannot possibly repay the price of his life.

20 Paul begins this verse with an emphatic "Yes" ("I do wish"). Friendship in the ancient world was a reciprocal relationship that continued when friends exchanged gifts, services, and benefits. Philemon's positive response will be a "benefit" to Paul that will "refresh" his "heart in Christ."

21 Paul's words exude confidence because he knows his man. Philemon's obedience is not to Paul but to the Lord and to the command of love that undergirds the entire letter.

22 Paul makes one last request: "Prepare a guest room for me." Paul's self-invitation would not have been a serious imposition in his culture. Paul's arrival in Philemon's home would be a gracious answer to prayer.

23 Paul signs off with greetings from his fellow

Christ Jesus, sends you greetings. 24And
so do Mark,[v] Aristarchus,[w] Demas[x] and
Luke, my fellow workers.

24 [v] Ac 12:12
[w] Ac 19:29
[x] Col 4:14
25 [y] 2Ti 4:22

25The grace of the Lord Jesus Christ be
with your spirit.[y]

---

prisoner, Epaphras, and his fellow workers. The "you" in v. 23 is singular. Presumably, each of these people would vouch for Onesimus and concur with Paul's request on his behalf.

8–25 Sometimes social evils can overwhelm us. We may hear descriptions of an urgent need, deplorable conditions, and a desperate plight and become immobilized because we suffer from compassion overload. We may also think to ourselves: How could we possibly do anything to alleviate so much suffering in so many places? Paul's letter to Philemon guides us to look at the person who is on our doorstep. We may not be able to undo all the injustice in the world, but in our local neighborhood, we can stand with those individuals who are oppressed, who are downtrodden, who are victims of abuse, or anyone who may need a friend and a loving hand. When we show concern for those around us out of our love for Christ, we reflect the intent of this short letter in our own lives, and serve as a powerful witness to those we are called to love in this way.

Author: Unknown; possibly Apollos or Barnabas

Audience: Primarily Jewish Christians

Date: About AD 63

Theme: The author demonstrates the absolute supremacy and sufficiency of Jesus Christ as revealer and mediator of God's grace.

Reading Hebrews

The author of the book of Hebrews carefully argues his case for the supremacy of Jesus Christ by demonstrating that Christ is greater than the angels, Moses, the priests and Levites of the OT, the sacrifices of the OT and the old covenant. Sprinkled throughout his complex arguments are passages of personal warning and practical application.

PERSPECTIVE

Perhaps no issue perplexes the modern church more than why people of different generations don't go to church. A popular way to analyze this problem is to bring all the power of the social sciences to bear. Mailed surveys, demographic analyses, and personal interviews have provided researchers with a wealth of information. The result has been user-friendly services complete with new formats, positive messages, and relevant preaching styles. Much of this is useful.

But it is just possible that the best thing to do would be for every church member to read and study the message of Hebrews. As we'll find in the notes that follow, Hebrews was written to immature Christians who were tempted to fall away from church attendance and return to their pre-Christian lifestyle. Sounds like the generational church attendance problem may not be as unique as we sometimes think.

The real issue, of course, is to take a close look at what the unknown author of Hebrews prescribes to the early church to deal with this situation. No social science here! In fact, the prescription is almost pure theology. The message of Hebrews can be summed up in a single phrase: "God speaks effectively to us through Jesus." If we can just unpack those seven words of all their theological meaning, we have a way to approach people of any generation with the message of the gospel that will demand a hearing.

God speaks. First-century people had trouble with the idea that only *one* God spoke to them. Twenty-first century people have trouble with the idea that *any* God would speak to them. The secularizing of

Event	10 BC	AD 1	10	20	30	40	50	60	70	80	90	100
Jesus' birth (c. 6/5 BC)												
Jesus' death, resurrection and ascension (c. AD 30)												
Paul's conversion (c. AD 35)												
Council at Jerusalem (c. AD 49/50)												
Nero's reign (AD 54–68)												
Book of Hebrews written (c. AD 60–70)												
Paul's imprisonment and death in Rome (c. AD 67–68)												
Destruction of Jerusalem's temple (c. AD 70)												

the modern world has done its work. We want to do it our way, and in the process we forget to listen for the voice of God. God speaks.

Effectively. God's voice is not a crying in the wilderness, a spitting in the wind. It is effective. First-century people believed the gods made a difference; twenty-first century people cannot believe it. When pollsters ask Americans if they think their religion can help solve the world's problems, most say no. The author of Hebrews says yes.

To us. As self-centered as twenty-first century people are, there is still a doubt that a God (if one exists) would speak (if we could hear) in such a way that makes a difference in solving the world's problems. But that is part of Hebrews' message: We are the target audience of God's effective speaking.

Through Jesus. The key to understanding the message of Hebrews is to recognize that in Jesus, God's unique Son, we have the ultimate solution to the world's problems. Jesus is how God has chosen to act once and for all. Jesus is superior to the priests, the prophets, the law. A Jesus-less gospel is a gospel deserving rejection.

These seven words and four ideas are what the author of Hebrews used to communicate gospel truth to a generation on the verge of throwing it all away. These seven words and four ideas have the same power to heal today—the power to save us from our sins (no matter what generation we are from).

Key Verses

First [Jesus] said, "Sacrifices and offerings, burnt offerings and sin offerings you did not desire, nor were you pleased with them"—though they were offered in accordance with the law. Then he said, "Here I am, I have come to do your will." He sets aside the first to establish the second. And by that will, we have been made holy through the sacrifice of the body of Jesus Christ once for all.

—Hebrews 10:8–10

TAKING THE NEXT STEPS

No one knows who wrote the book of Hebrews, but it seems to have been written to a group of Jewish Christians who, because of persecution, were tempted to revert to Judaism. The author therefore wrote to encourage them to persevere in their faith and to find maturity through dependence on the Lord. He reminded his readers of Jesus Christ, who came as the fulfillment of the OT. No person and no institution of the OT is greater than Jesus, for he is God and man in one person, and he answers all our needs.

The book of Hebrews is filled with exciting messages for Christians today. (1) All that we need for salvation is found in Jesus Christ and in him alone. We can be confident that he will meet all our needs. (2) Our faith can never stand still; God wants us to grow and mature in Christ. If we make no effort to do so, we will certainly slip back into old patterns of thought and behavior. (3) It is a frightening thing to fall away from Christ, for God's judgment on the rebellious is severe. (4) Persevering in the Christian faith may be difficult at times, but we receive encouragement through Christ, through the example of saints who have preceded us, and through other struggling Christians who testify to the experience of divine grace enabling them to hold fast. (5) If we do experience painful times as Christians, we can be encouraged that God's discipline is intended for our good.

WHAT TO LOOK FOR IN HEBREWS

- Christ as greater than the angels (ch. 1)
- A severe warning against falling away from Christ (ch. 6)
- Christ as a priest after the order of Melchizedek (ch. 7)
- Christ's blood greater than the Israelites' sacrifices (chs. 9–10)
- The heroes of faith (ch. 11)
- God's discipline of his children (ch. 12)

God's Final Word: His Son

1 In the past God spoke[a] to our ancestors
through the prophets[b] at many times
and in various ways,[c] 2but in these last days
he has spoken to us by his Son, whom he
appointed heir[d] of all things, and through
whom[e] also he made the universe. 3The
Son is the radiance of God's glory[f] and the
exact representation of his being, sustaining all things[g] by his powerful word. After
he had provided purification for sins,[h] he
sat down at the right hand of the Majesty
in heaven.[i] 4So he became as much superior to the angels as the name he has
inherited is superior to theirs.[j]

1:1 [a]Jn 9:29; Heb 2:2, 3 [b]Ac 2:30 [c]Nu 12:6,8
1:2 [d]Ps 2:8 [e]Jn 1:3
1:3 [f]Jn 1:14 [g]Col 1:17 [h]Heb 7:27 [i]Mk 16:19
1:4 [j]Eph 1:21; Php 2:9,10
1:5 [k]Ps 2:7 [l]2Sa 7:14
1:6 [m]Heb 10:5

The Son Superior to Angels

5For to which of the angels did God
ever say,

"You are my Son;
today I have become your
Father"[a]?[k]

Or again,

"I will be his Father,
and he will be my Son"[b]?[l]

6And again, when God brings his firstborn into the world,[m] he says,

[a] 5 Psalm 2:7 [b] 5 2 Samuel 7:14; 1 Chron. 17:13

1:1–2a The whole of the incarnation—Christ's person, words, and acts—communicates God's ultimate word to his new-covenant people.

1:2b–4 The author of Hebrews provides seven affirmations describing the Son's person, work, and current status. (1) "Whom he appointed heir of all things" affirms the present and future rule of Christ. (2) "Through whom also he made the universe" affirms the Father as the source of the created order and the Son as the Father's agent in the creative process. (3) He is "the radiance of God's glory and the exact representation of his being." These phrases highlight the divine nature of the Son. (4) The Son is also the One "sustaining all things by his powerful word." (5) "Purification for sins" refers to Christ's sacrificial death on the cross. (6) The Son's present status as the One who "sat down" at God's right hand (v. 3). This allusion to Ps 110:1 highlights Jesus' messiahship, vindication (through his resurrection and exaltation), role as Judge, lordship, and his intercession on behalf of believers. (7) The Son "became as much superior to the angels as the name he has inherited is superior to theirs" (Heb 1:4). The Son rules the angels.

APPLICATION ✚ 1:1–4 The Scriptures were written to change, mold, and direct the lives of God's people. Yet grave danger lies in focusing on the "practical" teachings of Scripture to the neglect of the "theological." Theology and practice are both vitally important aspects of following Christ. Notice that in his introduction to the book, the author of Hebrews lays a robust theological foundation for his entire sermon.

1:5 The writer is, in fact, proclaiming, "There is no angel to whom God has said . . . !" The two quotations in v. 5 continue a focus on the sonship of Jesus started in v. 2. Both Ps 2:7 and 2Sa 7:14 had been adopted in earliest Christianity as pointing to the enthronement of Messiah.

1:6–7 A firstborn son shared the father's authority and inherited the majority share of his property.

"Let all God's angels worship him."[a][n]

7In speaking of the angels he says,

"He makes his angels spirits,
and his servants flames of fire."[b][o]

8But about the Son he says,

"Your throne, O God, will last for
ever and ever;
a scepter of justice will be the
scepter of your kingdom.
9You have loved righteousness and
hated wickedness;
therefore God, your God, has set
you above your companions[p]
by anointing you with the oil[q] of
joy."[c]

10He also says,

"In the beginning, Lord, you laid the
foundations of the earth,
and the heavens are the work of
your hands.
11They will perish, but you remain;
they will all wear out like a
garment.[r]
12You will roll them up like a robe;
like a garment they will be
changed.
But you remain the same,[s]
and your years will never end."[d][t]

1:6 [n] Dt 32:43 (LXX and DSS); Ps 97:7
1:7 [o] Ps 104:4
1:9 [p] Php 2:9 [q] Isa 61:1,3
1:11 [r] Isa 34:4
1:12 [s] Heb 13:8 [t] Ps 102:25-27
1:13 [u] Jos 10:24; Heb 10:13 [v] Ps 110:1
1:14 [w] Ps 103:20 [x] Heb 5:9
2:2 [y] Heb 1:1 [z] Dt 33:2; Ac 7:53 [a] Heb 10:28
2:3 [b] Heb 10:29 [c] Heb 1:2 [d] Lk 1:2
2:4 [e] Jn 4:48

Heb 1:14 ❖ How does this verse describe angels as being sent to serve us? How does that impact the way we live our lives?

13To which of the angels did God ever say,

"Sit at my right hand
until I make your enemies
a footstool[u] for your feet"[e]?[v]

14Are not all angels ministering spirits[w]
sent to serve those who will inherit salvation?[x]

Warning to Pay Attention

2 We must pay the most careful attention, therefore, to what we have
heard, so that we do not drift away. 2For
since the message spoken[y] through angels[z] was binding, and every violation
and disobedience received its just punishment,[a] 3how shall we escape if we ignore so great a salvation?[b] This salvation,
which was first announced by the Lord,[c]
was confirmed to us by those who heard
him.[d] 4God also testified to it by signs,
wonders and various miracles,[e] and by

[a] *6* Deut. 32:43 (see Dead Sea Scrolls and Septuagint) [b] *7* Psalm 104:4 [c] *9* Psalm 45:6,7 [d] *12* Psalm 102:25-27 [e] *13* Psalm 110:1

"Firstborn" serves as a title for Christ, expressing his preeminence, and is especially associated with the resurrection. The angels—who, the writer implies, are subordinate to the Son—are exhorted to "worship" him. In contexts that highlight God's power and majesty angels worship the Son, an implicit declaration of his deity.

1:8–12 These two passages speak of the Son's authority (v. 8). He has been anointed as King (v. 9). He is also the One with the authority to lay "the foundations of the earth" and to mold "the heavens" with his "hands" (v. 10).

The author's use of these texts draws attention to the Son's eternal nature. Messiah's kingdom is everlasting (v. 8). The Lord was there "in the beginning" (v. 10), and his "years will never end" (v. 12). By contrast, the created order changes, becoming old and perishable (vv. 11–12). Additionally, v. 8 has one of the most explicit references to Jesus as God found in the NT (quoting Ps 45:6–7).

1:13–14 The author's string of OT quotations comes to its zenith with his quote of Ps 110:1. The enthronement of the Son has a corresponding implication—defeat for those who are enemies of God and the Messiah.

✣ **1:5–14** Western culture in general and the church in particular are in an authority crisis. The author uses a chain of OT quotations to a specific end in this section. He focuses on Jesus' position to demonstrate Jesus' authority. Therefore, these verses speak volumes to an age grappling with issues of authority—To whom should we listen? Whom can we trust? Who has the right answers to our life questions? This passage and book provide the answers to these questions of ultimate authority.

2:1 The object of our attention here is "what we have heard"—that is, the word spoken via the Son (1:2).

2:2–3a The older covenant message delivered through angels was "binding"; to neglect that word brought about sure, severe punishment. God's punishment of the disobedient in this lesser situation makes it safe to assume a more severe punishment will meet a greater rejection of salvation. Those who care so little about the word of salvation that they neglect it will find no escape from the punishment they deserve.

2:3b–4 The author and readers were second-generation Christians who had not directly heard Jesus preach. Yet the gospel message has been "confirmed" by those who were firsthand witnesses and is thus absolutely reliable (v. 3). God has not simply spoken a word of confirmation but has acted in "signs, wonders and various miracles" (v. 4).

✣ **2:1–4** Faith in the message is not a "leap in the dark" but a decision to commit oneself

gifts of the Holy Spirit[f] distributed according to his will.[g]

Jesus Made Fully Human

5It is not to angels that he has subjected the world to come, about which we are speaking. 6But there is a place where someone has testified:

"What is mankind that you are
mindful of them,
a son of man that you care for
him?[h]
7You made them a little[a] lower than
the angels;
you crowned them with glory and
honor
8 and put everything under their
feet."[b,c][i]

In putting everything under them,[d] God left nothing that is not subject to them.[d] Yet at present we do not see everything subject to them.[d] 9But we do see Jesus, who was made lower than the angels for a little while, now crowned with glory and honor[j] because he suffered death,[k] so that by the grace of God he might taste death for everyone.[l]

10In bringing many sons and daughters to glory, it was fitting that God, for whom and through whom everything exists,[m] should make the pioneer of their salvation perfect through what he suffered.[n] 11Both the one who makes people holy and those who are made holy[o] are of the same family. So Jesus is not ashamed to call them brothers and sisters.[e][p] 12He says,

"I will declare your name to my
brothers and sisters;
in the assembly I will sing your
praises."[f][q]

13And again,

"I will put my trust in him."[g][r]

And again he says,

"Here am I, and the children God has
given me."[h][s]

2:4 [f]1Co 12:4 [g]Eph 1:5
2:6 [h]Job 7:17
2:8 [i]Ps 8:4-6; 1Co 15:25
2:9 [j]Ac 2:33; 3:13; Php 2:9 [k]Php 2:7-9 [l]Jn 3:16; 2Co 5:15
2:10 [m]Ro 11:36 [n]Lk 24:26; Heb 7:28
2:11 [o]Heb 10:10 [p]Mt 28:10; Jn 20:17
2:12 [q]Ps 22:22
2:13 [r]Isa 8:17 [s]Isa 8:18; Jn 10:29

[a] 7 Or *them for a little while* [b] 6-8 Psalm 8:4-6 [c] 7,8 Or *7You made him a little lower than the angels;/ you crowned him with glory and honor/ 8and put everything under his feet."* [d] 8 Or *him* [e] 11 The Greek word for *brothers and sisters* (*adelphoi*) refers here to believers, both men and women, as part of God's family; also in verse 12; and in 3:1,12; 10:19; 13:22. [f] 12 Psalm 22:22 [g] 13 Isaiah 8:17 [h] 13 Isaiah 8:18

---

to God through Christ, based on the reliable testimony of the apostles. The apostolic tradition helps Christians stay true to the salvation preached by Jesus. Drifting away from this message and treating it carelessly invites spiritual ruin. On the other hand, paying close attention to the word of salvation provides stability in our daily walk as followers of Christ.

2:5–8a All the powers of the universe must submit to Christ—even those that do not do so willingly. The statement about the incarnation in Ps 8, as interpreted by our author reads, "You made them a little lower than the angels" (Heb 2:7). The author is expressing the thought that Christ walked the earth as a human being for a brief time before being exalted back to heaven.

2:8b–9 Do Ps 110:1 and Ps 8:4–6 contradict each other? Our author answers the question "Have all things been subjugated to the Son, or does his universal dominance lie in the future?" with "Both!" This tension between what is present reality and not yet seen expresses what may be referred to as the inaugurated rule of Christ.

To "see" Jesus (Heb 2:9a) means not a physical perception but rather a spiritual perception. The preacher specifies how Jesus was crowned with glory and honor: "because he suffered death" (v. 9b).

✣ **2:5–9** Why, at times, does God seem to refuse to respond to our desperate cries for help? The answer to our dilemma lies in our perception of reality and the nature of the Christian faith. To focus on our pains as primary (rather than the ultimate purposes of God) is to move away from an essential element of following Christ. We must follow Christ in the way of suffering. The problem of evil lies not in God's abilities, nor even in our perception of his will and timing, but in our perception of Jesus. As a pilot in a dense fog keeps on course by looking to the instruments, Jesus provides a reference point from which to assess the greater realities of any given situation. What we need is to "see Jesus" (vv. 8–9) in his incarnation and exaltation. The "in-between time" flanked by Christ's first and second comings is a time of tears, suffering, persecution, and death. But God's promise in Christ is ultimate salvation, healing, joy, and eternal life for God's people.

2:10 God uses Jesus' death in "bringing" heirs with Christ to "glory," moving from earth to heaven. "Pioneer" can also be read as "champion." Perfection in Hebrews involves fully completing a course, making it to the end of God's plan. That Jesus was made "perfect" means he was fully obedient to the completion of his mission.

2:11–13 As we stand with him in solidarity (Ps 22:22; Isa 8:17b–18), the Son is not ashamed to call us family.

Heb 2:14-18 ❖ How has Christ freed us from being slaves to the fear of death?

[14]Since the children have flesh and
blood, he too shared in their humanity[t]
so that by his death he might break the
power[u] of him who holds the power of
death — that is, the devil[v] — [15]and free
those who all their lives were held in
slavery by their fear[w] of death. [16]For surely it is not angels he helps, but Abraham's
descendants. [17]For this reason he had to
be made like them,[a][x] fully human in every way, in order that he might become
a merciful[y] and faithful high priest[z] in
service to God,[a] and that he might make
atonement for the sins of the people.
[18]Because he himself suffered when he
was tempted, he is able to help those
who are being tempted.[b]

Jesus Greater Than Moses

3 Therefore, holy brothers and sisters,[c]
who share in the heavenly calling,
fix your thoughts on Jesus, whom we
acknowledge[d] as our apostle and high
priest.[e] [2]He was faithful to the one who
appointed him, just as Moses was faithful
in all God's house.[f] [3]Jesus has been found
worthy of greater honor than Moses, just
as the builder of a house has greater hon-
or than the house itself. [4]For every house
is built by someone, but God is the builder of everything. [5]"Moses was faithful as
a servant[g] in all God's house,"[b][h] bearing
witness to what would be spoken by God
in the future. [6]But Christ is faithful as
the Son[i] over God's house. And we are
his house,[j] if indeed we hold firmly[k] to
our confidence and the hope[l] in which
we glory.

Warning Against Unbelief

[7]So, as the Holy Spirit says:[m]

"Today, if you hear his voice,
[8] do not harden your hearts
as you did in the rebellion,
during the time of testing in the wilderness,
[9]where your ancestors tested and tried me,
though for forty years they saw what I did.[n]
[10]That is why I was angry with that generation;
I said, 'Their hearts are always going astray,
and they have not known my ways.'

2:14 [t] Jn 1:14 [u] 1Co 15:54-57; 2Ti 1:10 [v] 1Jn 3:8
2:15 [w] 2Ti 1:7
2:17 [x] Php 2:7 [y] Heb 5:2 [z] Heb 4:14, 15; 7:26, 28 [a] Heb 5:1
2:18 [b] Heb 4:15
3:1 [c] Heb 2:11 [d] Heb 4:14 [e] Heb 2:17
3:2 [f] Nu 12:7
3:5 [g] Ex 14:31 [h] ver 2; Nu 12:7
3:6 [i] Heb 1:2 [j] 1Co 3:16 [k] Ro 11:22 [l] Ro 5:2
3:7 [m] Heb 9:8
3:9 [n] Ac 7:36

[a] 17 Or *like his brothers* [b] 5 Num. 12:7

2:14–16 The goal of the incarnation was twofold. First, by becoming human the Son sought to "break the power" of the devil. The only way the Son could accomplish this was to die; the only way to die was to become human. Second, in v. 15, Jesus disabled death's master. As our champion, he stormed the enemy's gates and laid hold of his stronghold, opening the doors of our captivity wide and pointing us to the path of freedom.
2:17–18 With the final two verses of this passage, the author sets up an effective transition to the great central section of Hebrews on Jesus' high priesthood.

✥ **2:10–18** Humans needed a bridge between deity and humanity that could only be built by one who had experienced both sides of the gulf separating us from God. This is the biblical picture. What is surprising is the form our champion took and the means of our liberation. The One of all power took the position of the powerless. The Lord of life drank deeply of death. He brought us up to God by coming down to our level as a lowly servant. Since we could not save ourselves, he did not save himself from the worst of human experiences. The limitless Lord of the universe took on limitations to free us from ours, and nowhere are our limitations more clearly recognized than in the face of death.

3:1–2 The verbal form "share" indicates an intimate relationship forged in a common spiritual reality. The command to "fix your thoughts on Jesus" (v. 1) forms the core of the author's exhortation. It can mean "consider, think about, notice, observe."

Hebrews 3:1 is the only place in the NT where Jesus is called an "apostle." This designation concerns his role as the One sent to proclaim God's message. Our attention focuses on the exalted Lord and the Incarnate One, who remained true to God's mission amid adverse circumstances (v. 2).

That Moses was faithful over a "house" (v. 2) alludes to Nu 12:7 and means his ministry involved a defined group of people in special relationship to God.
3:3–6 These verses contrast Moses and Jesus, highlighting the superiority of Jesus' example. The word rendered "hold firmly" in v. 6 could mean "hold to, keep, detain, contain, occupy, or possess." The word is used to speak of keeping a tight grip on the Christian faith. "Confidence" (v. 6) implies public boldness. We may be considered part of the people of God *if* we hold fast to the Christian faith.
3:7–11 The exhortation "do not harden your hearts" (v. 8a) lies at the center of the first part of these verses. The next portion offers an example or illustration (vv. 8b–9). The final segment confronts the hearers with the judgment experienced by that rebellious generation (vv. 10–11).

Heb 3:12-14 ❖ What opportunities do we have to encourage fellow believers daily?

[11]So I declared on oath in my anger,
‘They shall never enter my
rest.’[o]”[a][p]

[12]See to it, brothers and sisters, that none of you has a sinful, unbelieving heart that turns away from the living God. [13]But encourage one another daily,[q] as long as it is called “Today,” so that none of you may be hardened by sin’s deceitfulness.[r] [14]We have come to share in Christ, if indeed we hold[s] our original conviction firmly to the very end. [15]As has just been said:

“Today, if you hear his voice,
do not harden your hearts
as you did in the rebellion.”[b][t]

[16]Who were they who heard and rebelled? Were they not all those Moses led out of Egypt?[u] [17]And with whom was he angry for forty years? Was it not with those who sinned, whose bodies perished in the wilderness?[v] [18]And to whom did God swear that they would never enter his rest[w] if not to those who disobeyed?[x] [19]So we see that they were not able to enter, because of their unbelief.[y]

A Sabbath-Rest for the People of God

4 Therefore, since the promise of entering his rest still stands, let us be careful that none of you be found to have fallen short of it.[z] [2]For we also have had the good news proclaimed to us, just as they did; but the message they heard was of no value to them, because they did not share the faith of those who obeyed.[c][a] [3]Now we who have believed enter that rest, just as God has said,

“So I declared on oath in my anger,
‘They shall never enter my
rest.’”[d][b]

And yet his works have been finished since the creation of the world. [4]For somewhere he has spoken about the seventh day in these words: “On the seventh day God rested from all his works.”[e][c] [5]And again in the passage above he says, “They shall never enter my rest.”[d]

[6]Therefore since it still remains for some to enter that rest, and since those

3:11 [o]Heb 4:3,5 [p]Ps 95:7-11
3:13 [q]Heb 10:24,25 [r]Eph 4:22
3:14 [s]ver 6
3:15 [t]ver 7,8; Ps 95:7,8
3:16 [u]Nu 14:2
3:17 [v]Nu 14:29; Ps 106:26
3:18 [w]Nu 14:20-23 [x]Heb 4:6
3:19 [y]Jn 3:36
4:1 [z]Heb 12:15
4:2 [a]1Th 2:13
4:3 [b]Ps 95:11; Heb 3:11
4:4 [c]Ge 2:2,3; Ex 20:11
4:5 [d]Ps 95:11

[a] *11* Psalm 95:7-11 [b] *15* Psalm 95:7,8 [c] *2* Some manuscripts *because those who heard did not combine it with faith* [d] *3* Psalm 95:11; also in verse 5 [e] *4* Gen. 2:2

3:12-14 Here the author of Hebrews takes concepts from the psalm quoted in vv. 8–11, weaving them into a commentary and exhortation. The hearers are to “encourage one another daily” (v. 13) so none of them will experience a spiritual hardening brought on by sin’s deceitfulness. The condition placed on being companions of Christ has to do with holding “firmly to the very end” (v. 14). Real Christian experience is durable.

3:15 This section of the psalm serves as a summary for vv. 12–14. The quotation here also leads into the final segment of this unit.

3:16-19 The author asks a question and then provides an answer. The questions at the beginning of each verse are taken directly from the quote of Ps 95:7c–11. The answers provided, however, derive from other OT passages (Nu 14:1–38; Dt 9; Ps 106). The unit concludes that the wanderers’ inability to enter God’s rest stemmed from their unbelief, linking the concepts of unbelief and disobedience (Heb 3: 19).

❖ **3:1-19** The writer of Hebrews points to Israel’s disbelief to highlight the results of people’s hardness of heart toward God. We have no right to give assurance to those who have turned their backs on God—in fact, we should affirm their lack of assurance. Neither can our experiences of God’s grace in the past give us assurance of his acceptance today. We cannot look into a person’s heart and see his or her spiritual condition. But we can examine our own hearts, and call others to examine their own, to see if there is evidence of faith in our lives rather than evidence of our turning our backs on God. The author of Hebrews does challenge his hearers to remember their past confession of Christ (4:14; 10:23) as a basis for faithfulness rather than as a basis for assurance.

4:1-2 The author says not that any particular person has fallen short but that appropriate caution is in order since that possibility exists. The phrase “to have fallen short” (v. 1) suggests that this spiritual state consists of one never truly having entered the rest of God.

This conclusion finds further support in v. 2, which uses the negative example of the OT fallen. The Israelite community physically may have heard words, but their hearing was “faith-less.” The caution in vv. 1–2 pertains to those of the community whose response to the gospel parallels the faith-vacant response of those who fell in the desert when offered a way to enter into the land of Canaan through belief and obedience.

4:3-5 The “rest” is something a believer experiences now, but this rest in its fullness remains a promised destination for the future.

4:6-11 An important clue to the specific Sabbath-rest the author has in mind in v. 9 may be found

Heb 4:8-11 ❖ How can we enter God's rest? How do we experience the reality of that gift of rest today?

who formerly had the good news proclaimed to them did not go in because
of their disobedience,[e] 7God again set a
certain day, calling it "Today." This he did
when a long time later he spoke through
David, as in the passage already quoted:

> "Today, if you hear his voice,
> do not harden your hearts."[a][f]

8For if Joshua had given them rest,[g] God
would not have spoken[h] later about another day. 9There remains, then, a Sabbath-
rest for the people of God; 10for anyone
who enters God's rest also rests from their
works,[b] just as God did from his.[i] 11Let us,
therefore, make every effort to enter that
rest, so that no one will perish by following their example of disobedience.[j]
12For the word of God[k] is alive and active.[l] Sharper than any double-edged
sword,[m] it penetrates even to dividing
soul and spirit, joints and marrow; it
judges the thoughts and attitudes of
the heart.[n] 13Nothing in all creation is
hidden from God's sight.[o] Everything is
uncovered and laid bare before the eyes
of him to whom we must give account.

Jesus the Great High Priest

14Therefore, since we have a great high
priest who has ascended into heaven,[c][p]
Jesus the Son of God, let us hold firmly to the faith we profess.[q] 15For we do
not have a high priest who is unable to
empathize with our weaknesses, but we
have one who has been tempted in every
way, just as we are[r] — yet he did not sin.[s]
16Let us then approach God's throne of
grace with confidence, so that we may
receive mercy and find grace to help us
in our time of need.

5 Every high priest is selected from
among the people and is appointed to
represent the people in matters related to
God, to offer gifts and sacrifices[t] for sins.[u]

4:6 [e] Heb 3:18
4:7 [f] Ps 95:7,8; Heb 3:7,8,15
4:8 [g] Jos 22:4 [h] Heb 1:1
4:10 [i] ver 4
4:11 [j] Heb 3:18
4:12 [k] 1Pe 1:23 [l] Jer 23:29 [m] Eph 6:17; Rev 1:16
[n] 1Co 14:24,25
4:13 [o] Ps 33:13-15
4:14 [p] Heb 6:20 [q] Heb 3:1
4:15 [r] Heb 2:18 [s] 2Co 5:21
5:1 [t] Heb 8:3 [u] Heb 7:27

[a] 7 Psalm 95:7,8 [b] 10 Or *labor* [c] 14 Greek *has gone through the heavens*

---

in the book of Leviticus. The author does not make an overt reference to Leviticus; however, the broader context in which he mentions the preaching of the gospel can be said to support such a tie. In this interpretation, the Sabbath is a new-covenant Day of Atonement, in which God's people are cleansed from their sins.

In v. 11 the author follows with an exhortation and a rationale. The audience must demonstrate their faith by active obedience. Here is a paradox—we must "strive" to enter the spiritual "rest" of God. To stop short, failing to combine hearing of the gospel with faith, results in spiritual devastation.

4:12–13 God's Word is not static and passive but dynamic and transforming as the people of God interface with it. The sword imagery emphasizes that God's Word brings both promise and judgment. The Word penetrates and divides, being able to reach into the depths of a person's inner life.

✣ **4:1–13** Spiritual wandering and its resulting fatigue are not new problems. Jesus, the new Joshua, looks out on a desert-wandering humanity, and his solution is, "Come to *me*." Not, "Come to a set of teachings"; not, "Come to church"; not, "Come to your psychologist"; not, "Come to a vacation." No. Rather, he says, "Come to me." Jesus offers the ultimate source for true rest. True rest is found only in a right relationship with God. The rest is *his* rest, for *his* people, found by obeying *his* Word. Believers have the phenomenal opportunity and privilege of pointing people to the ultimate land of promised rest and spiritual well-being.

4:14–15 The author calls this sermon's recipients to remain committed to Jesus, holding to their public confession of him as the Son of God. Endurance springs from the follower's relationship to Christ as a heavenly high priest. We have a high priest who can empathize with our weaknesses because he was "tempted in every way" that we are (v. 15). Christ does not stand aloof but cares for us in our human state of weakness.

4:16 "Let us then approach" speaks in the present tense, indicating that drawing near to God is an ongoing aspect of the Christian's relationship with God: In other words, "Let us constantly approach." God's people may enter his presence continually and can do so with "confidence."

✣ **4:14–16** It is not natural to draw near to God; it is supernatural, and he has called us to himself away from the natural pulls and thoughts of the world. His invitation and promises still stand. Our part is to respond to his call and approach the throne. Jesus, our sympathetic high priest, has experienced the temptation to bolt and run (Mt 26:39). He has been with us in our humanness and invites us to be with him at the throne of grace. Therefore, we may approach God with unabashed boldness. Let us make that approach today, for when we do we will surely find timely help for whatever we need.

5:1–4 The author roots Christ's high priesthood in the OT. He basically asserts: "This is how the office of high priest works according to the Scriptures." The high priest has solidarity with people because he is taken "from among" them (v. 1). By carrying out God's instructions, the high priest acts as a representative for the people, making atonement for their sins.

JESUS IS . . .

The fulfillment of the prophets, God's perfect revelation	Heb 1:1-2; 2:1-4
Greater than all the angels	Heb 1:3-4; 2:3-9
The author of salvation	Heb 2:10
The model of sonship	Heb 2:10-18; 3:5-6
The perfect high priest in the order of Melchizedek	Heb 2:17-18; 4:14-15; 5:1-10; 7:1—8:6; 9:11-12, 24-28; 10:11-18, 21
Greater than Moses	Heb 3:2-6
The perfect sacrifice	Heb 7:26-27; 9:11-13, 24-28; 10:1-10, 29; 12:2; 13:10-14, 20-21
The mediator of a better covenant	Heb 8:6—10:22; 12:2, 18-24; 13:10-14, 20-21

2He is able to deal gently with those who
are ignorant and are going astray,[v] since
he himself is subject to weakness.[w] 3This
is why he has to offer sacrifices for his
own sins, as well as for the sins of the
people.[x] 4And no one takes this honor on
himself, but he receives it when called
by God, just as Aaron was.[y]
5In the same way, Christ did not take
on himself the glory[z] of becoming a high
priest. But God said[a] to him,

"You are my Son;
today I have become your
Father."[ab]

6And he says in another place,

"You are a priest forever,
in the order of Melchizedek."[bc]

7During the days of Jesus' life on earth,
he offered up prayers and petitions with
fervent cries and tears[d] to the one who
could save him from death, and he was
heard because of his reverent submission.[e] 8Son though he was, he learned
obedience from what he suffered[f] 9and,
once made perfect,[g] he became the
source of eternal salvation for all who
obey him 10and was designated by God
to be high priest[h] in the order of Melchizedek.[i]

5:2 [v] Heb 2:18 [w] Heb 7:28
5:3 [x] Heb 7:27; 9:7
5:4 [y] Ex 28:1
5:5 [z] Jn 8:54 [a] Heb 1:1 [b] Ps 2:7
5:6 [c] Ps 110:4; Heb 7:17, 21
5:7 [d] Mt 27:46, 50 [e] Mk 14:36
5:8 [f] Php 2:8
5:9 [g] Heb 2:10
5:10 [h] ver 5 [i] ver 6
5:12 [j] Heb 6:1 [k] 1Co 3:2; 1Pe 2:2
5:13 [l] 1Co 14:20

> **Heb 5:12-14** ❖ Are we moving from spiritual milk to solid food? What might be holding back our spiritual growth?

Warning Against Falling Away

6:4–6Ref // Heb 10:26–31

11We have much to say about this, but
it is hard to make it clear to you because
you no longer try to understand. 12In
fact, though by this time you ought to
be teachers, you need someone to teach
you the elementary truths[j] of God's word
all over again. You need milk, not solid food![k] 13Anyone who lives on milk,
being still an infant,[l] is not acquainted
with the teaching about righteousness.

[a] 5 Psalm 2:7 [b] 6 Psalm 110:4

On the Day of Atonement, the high priest offered a special sacrifice for himself before he could offer sacrifices on behalf of the people (vv. 2-3). A person could not volunteer for or earn the office of high priest; God initiated the role, and any high priest would have to be called by God to be considered the authentic and authoritative representative for the people before God (v. 4).

5:5–6 In these verses the author finds evidence in the Psalms for the glory God has bestowed on Jesus. Both Ps 2:7 and 110:4 contain a pronouncement by God in the second person ("You are . . ."). These declarations were made by God to Jesus.

5:7–10 The phrase "during the days of Jesus' life on earth" references Jesus' incarnation in general, but the rest of vv. 7–8 hints at a specific event—Jesus' submission to the Father's will in Gethsemane. While the outcome of Gethsemane may suggest that God did not "hear" that prayer, God did "hear" it, affirming the righteousness of his Son's reverent submission through the resurrection.

When the author says in vv. 8–9 that Christ "learned obedience" and was "made perfect," he is not suggesting that the Son had been disobedient and flawed. Rather, Jesus' call involved walking obediently all the way to the end of a path to which the Father had appointed him.

Verse 9 proclaims that the Son became "the source of eternal salvation." As a result of the Son's suffering, God appointed him to fill the position of high priest according to "the order of Melchizedek" (v. 10).

> **5:1–10** As an appropriate application of vv. 1-10, we might begin by reflecting on our current motivations for following Christ. Is the fact that God has appointed Jesus to a position of honor in which we are called to "obey" him (v. 9) significant enough to motivate us to continue in our commitment? Or do our actions and decisions demonstrate we are following our world's system of values? Doing so is dangerous and puts us in great peril.

5:11–14 Using "milk" and "solid food" as metaphors for basic teachings was common in the ancient world. Spiritually, the hearers of this message are acting like babies who could not care less about the

14But solid food is for the mature,[m] who
by constant use have trained themselves
to distinguish good from evil.[n]

6 Therefore let us move beyond[o] the
elementary teachings[p] about Christ
and be taken forward to maturity, not
laying again the foundation of repentance from acts that lead to death,[a][q]
and of faith in God, 2instruction about
cleansing rites,[b][r] the laying on of hands,[s]
the resurrection of the dead,[t] and eternal judgment. 3And God permitting,[u]
we will do so.

4It is impossible for those who have
once been enlightened,[v] who have tasted the heavenly gift,[w] who have shared
in the Holy Spirit,[x] 5who have tasted
the goodness of the word of God and
the powers of the coming age 6and who
have fallen[c] away, to be brought back
to repentance.[y] To their loss they are
crucifying the Son of God all over again
and subjecting him to public disgrace.
7Land that drinks in the rain often falling
on it and that produces a crop useful to
those for whom it is farmed receives the
blessing of God. 8But land that produces
thorns and thistles is worthless and is
in danger of being cursed.[z] In the end it
will be burned.

9Even though we speak like this,
dear friends,[a] we are convinced of better things in your case — the things that
have to do with salvation. 10God is not
unjust; he will not forget your work and
the love you have shown him as you have
helped his people and continue to help
them.[b] 11We want each of you to show
this same diligence to the very end, so
that what you hope[c] for may be fully realized. 12We do not want you to become
lazy, but to imitate[d] those who through
faith and patience[e] inherit what has been
promised.[f]

Heb 6:10-12 ❖ How can we be diligent in helping others grow in faith?

The Certainty of God's Promise

13When God made his promise to Abraham, since there was no one greater for
him to swear by, he swore by himself,[g]

5:14 [m] 1Co 2:6 [n] Isa 7:15
6:1 [o] Php 3:12-14 [p] Heb 5:12 [q] Heb 9:14
6:2 [r] Jn 3:25 [s] Ac 6:6 [t] Ac 17:18, 32
6:3 [u] Ac 18:21
6:4 [v] Heb 10:32 [w] Eph 2:8 [x] Gal 3:2
6:6 [y] 2Pe 2:21; 1Jn 5:16
6:8 [z] Ge 3:17, 18; Isa 5:6
6:9 [a] 1Co 10:14
6:10 [b] Mt 10:40, 42; 25:40; 1Th 1:3
6:11 [c] Heb 3:6
6:12 [d] Heb 13:7 [e] 2Th 1:4; Jas 1:3; Rev 13:10 [f] Heb 10:36
6:13 [g] Ge 22:16; Lk 1:73

[a] 1 Or *from useless rituals* [b] 2 Or *about baptisms* [c] 6 Or *age, [6]if they fall*

---

rich, hearty foods of the adults' table. Their moral failure in the face of persecution stems from a lack of response to theological instruction (cf. 2:1–4). "The mature" (5:14), on the other hand, are able to handle "solid food." They know how to make the right choices when confronted with critical decisions.

6:1–3 These Christian principles are not dispensable. They are assumed as steps toward maturity. "Baptisms" (see NIV text note on v. 2) may refer to the internal spiritual cleansing from sins found in the new covenant. The "laying on of hands" was with the coming of the Holy Spirit or anointing for ministry. "Resurrection of the dead" and "eternal judgment" provide theological cornerstones related to the end of the age.

✣ **5:11—6:3** The difficult experiences of life raise important questions about God and what he is doing in our lives and in the world. The NT pattern is to educate God's people in the tenets of the faith from the beginning, providing them with the basic theological nurturing they will need for the journey and maturing them through ongoing feeding on God's Word. All Christ-followers need systematic teaching of biblical truth, both at the beginning of our spiritual formation and as we grow to maturity.

6:4–8 The first three verses of this unit are unified around the central assertion, "It is impossible for those . . . to be brought back to repentance." These people have experienced "the heavenly gift." They "have tasted the goodness of the word of God." The harshness of the descriptions that follow "fallen away" demands that it be understood as a serious sin—rejecting Christ. It is impossible for those who have done so "to be brought back to repentance." Repentance is "impossible" because there is nowhere else to go for repentance once one has rejected Christ.

6:9–12 What is the basis of the writer's confidence in these people? Their faith has been lived out. Verse 11, however, highlights the uncertainty of evaluating another person's status before God. If the outward manifestations of genuine belief stop, confidence in their salvation evaporates. The author wants his readers not to lapse into laziness but rather "to imitate those who through faith and patience inherit what has been promised" (v. 12).

✣ **6:4–12** Anyone engaged in Christian ministry has certainly struggled with the pain and confusion of seeing those who have come into the church suddenly turn and walk away as if their professions of Christ were meaningless. How are we to respond? To those who have fallen away or are close to falling away we should offer strong warnings in line with vv. 4–8. We should offer encouragement to those who have come into the church struggling to throw off spiritual mediocrity and consistently maintain passion about Christian commitment. God approves of our diligence to remain faithful even amid dry and difficult times.

6:13–15 The account of Abraham offering his cherished son, Isaac, at Mount Moriah (Ge 22:1–18) forms the backdrop of the discussion in Heb 6:13–15.

14 saying, "I will surely bless you and give
you many descendants."[a][h] 15 And so after waiting patiently, Abraham received
what was promised.[i]

16 People swear by someone greater
than themselves, and the oath confirms
what is said and puts an end to all argument.[j] 17 Because God wanted to make
the unchanging[k] nature of his purpose
very clear to the heirs of what was promised,[l] he confirmed it with an oath. 18 God
did this so that, by two unchangeable
things in which it is impossible for God
to lie,[m] we who have fled to take hold of
the hope[n] set before us may be greatly
encouraged. 19 We have this hope as an
anchor for the soul, firm and secure. It
enters the inner sanctuary behind the
curtain,[o] 20 where our forerunner, Jesus,
has entered on our behalf.[p] He has become a high priest[q] forever, in the order
of Melchizedek.[r]

Melchizedek the Priest

7 This Melchizedek was king of Salem
and priest of God Most High.[s] He met
Abraham returning from the defeat of
the kings and blessed him,[t] 2 and Abraham gave him a tenth of everything.
First, the name Melchizedek means "king
of righteousness"; then also, "king of
Salem" means "king of peace." 3 Without
father or mother, without genealogy,[u]
without beginning of days or end of life,
resembling the Son of God,[v] he remains
a priest forever.

4 Just think how great he was: Even
the patriarch[w] Abraham gave him a
tenth of the plunder![x] 5 Now the law
requires the descendants of Levi who
become priests to collect a tenth from
the people[y] — that is, from their fellow
Israelites — even though they also are
descended from Abraham. 6 This man,
however, did not trace his descent from
Levi, yet he collected a tenth from
Abraham and blessed[z] him who had
the promises.[a] 7 And without doubt the
lesser is blessed by the greater. 8 In the
one case, the tenth is collected by people who die; but in the other case, by
him who is declared to be living.[b] 9 One
might even say that Levi, who collects
the tenth, paid the tenth through Abraham, 10 because when Melchizedek met
Abraham, Levi was still in the body of
his ancestor.

Jesus Like Melchizedek

11 If perfection could have been attained through the Levitical priesthood — and indeed the law given to the

6:14 [h] Ge 22:17
6:15 [i] Ge 21:5
6:16 [j] Ex 22:11
6:17 [k] Ps 110:4 [l] Heb 11:9
6:18 [m] Nu 23:19; Titus 1:2 [n] Heb 3:6
6:19 [o] Lev 16:2; Heb 9:2,3,7
6:20 [p] Heb 4:14 [q] Heb 2:17 [r] Heb 5:6
7:1 [s] Mk 5:7 [t] Ge 14:18-20
7:3 [u] ver 6 [v] Mt 4:3
7:4 [w] Ac 2:29 [x] Ge 14:20
7:5 [y] Nu 18:21, 26
7:6 [z] Ge 14:19, 20 [a] Ro 4:13
7:8 [b] Heb 5:6; 6:20

[a] *14* Gen. 22:17

6:16–18 If truthfulness can be confirmed in human courts of law, it is even more assured when God himself swears an oath. Heirs need not worry that the terms of God's promised inheritance will change. God intends that his heirs might find strong encouragement from his promises (v. 18). The foundation for our encouragement rests in the character of God, who cannot lie.

6:19–20 Our hope, as an anchor for the soul, is both "firm" and "secure" (v. 19). Our security rests firmly in the high-priestly work of Christ. He has entered God's presence on our behalf and made a way for us to follow.

✣ **6:13–20** God's "oaths" help us to see beyond our limitations to his limitless power and provisions. Encouragement comes from knowing we play a part in a life both full of meaning and lasting. Thus, our current circumstances can never adequately define who we are or what we are about. This quality of hope produces hope. As Paul states, "May the God of hope fill you with all joy and peace as you trust in him, so that you may overflow with hope by the power of the Holy Spirit" (Ro 15:13). This age of angst asks, "Is there more to existence than just this life?" The Christian conviction rings out: "Yes! And so we dare to hope."

7:1–3 The writer focuses on the details of what the narrative does and does not say, anticipating a stark contrast between Melchizedek's priesthood and the Levitical priesthood, which he will develop later in the chapter.

7:4–10 The author calls his hearers to grasp the greatness of Melchizedek (vv. 5–6). That Abraham gave a tithe to this priest shows respect for his unique service on behalf of God Most High. Melchizedek, in turn, blessed Abraham. Melchizedek's superiority to the Levites primarily rests on his having received a tenth of the spoils from Abraham and the fact that Scripture gives no indication of his death.

✣ **7:1–10** We cannot deal with this chapter in terms of the heart alone. The head must come into play or one's reading of the text is scattered. The author is leading us somewhere with his logic. We are moving once again toward a call to total commitment to Christ. Heart, mind, emotions, and strength all will be called upon shortly. Nevertheless, we must begin here, with rationales for why we must act a certain way. Here we, with the author of Hebrews, begin by loving God with our minds.

7:11–19 As a rhetorical question, v. 11 actually makes a strong assertion. It proclaims, "Since God's ultimate

people[c] established that priesthood —
why was there still need for another priest to come,[d] one in the order of
Melchizedek,[e] not in the order of Aaron?
12 For when the priesthood is changed,
the law must be changed also. 13 He of
whom these things are said belonged
to a different tribe,[f] and no one from
that tribe has ever served at the altar.[g]
14 For it is clear that our Lord descended
from Judah,[h] and in regard to that tribe
Moses said nothing about priests. 15 And
what we have said is even more clear if
another priest like Melchizedek appears,
16 one who has become a priest not on
the basis of a regulation as to his ancestry but on the basis of the power of an
indestructible life. 17 For it is declared:

> "You are a priest forever,
> in the order of Melchizedek."[a i]

18 The former regulation is set aside
because it was weak and useless[j] 19 (for
the law made nothing perfect),[k] and a
better hope is introduced, by which we
draw near to God.[l]
20 And it was not without an oath! Others became priests without any oath,
21 but he became a priest with an oath
when God said to him:

> "The Lord has sworn
> and will not change his mind:[m]
> 'You are a priest forever.' "[a n]

7:11 [c] ver 18,19; Heb 8:7 [d] Heb 10:1 [e] ver 17
7:13 [f] ver 11 [g] ver 14
7:14 [h] Isa 11:1; Mt 1:3; Lk 3:33
7:17 [i] Ps 110:4; ver 21; Heb 5:6
7:18 [j] Ro 8:3
7:19 [k] Ac 13:39; Ro 3:20; Heb 9:9 [l] Heb 4:16
7:21 [m] 1Sa 15:29 [n] Ps 110:4
7:22 [o] Heb 8:6
7:24 [p] ver 28
7:25 [q] ver 19 [r] Ro 8:34
7:26 [s] 2Co 5:21 [t] Heb 4:14
7:27 [u] Heb 5:1 [v] Heb 5:3 [w] Heb 9:12,26,28 [x] Eph 5:2; Heb 9:14,28
7:28 [y] Heb 5:2 [z] Heb 1:2 [a] Heb 2:10

Heb 7:26–28 ❖ What comfort can we take in having Christ as our living High Priest before God the Father?

22 Because of this oath, Jesus has become
the guarantor of a better covenant.[o]
23 Now there have been many of those
priests, since death prevented them from
continuing in office; 24 but because Jesus
lives forever, he has a permanent priesthood.[p] 25 Therefore he is able to save completely[b] those who come to God[q] through
him, because he always lives to intercede
for them.[r]
26 Such a high priest truly meets our
need — one who is holy, blameless, pure,
set apart from sinners,[s] exalted above the
heavens.[t] 27 Unlike the other high priests,
he does not need to offer sacrifices[u] day
after day, first for his own sins,[v] and then
for the sins of the people. He sacrificed
for their sins once for all[w] when he offered himself.[x] 28 For the law appoints as
high priests men in all their weakness;[y]
but the oath, which came after the law,
appointed the Son,[z] who has been made
perfect[a] forever.

The High Priest of a New Covenant

8 Now the main point of what we are
saying is this: We do have such a high

[a] *17,21* Psalm 110:4 [b] *25* Or *forever*

goal of establishing an eternal relationship between himself and people could not be attained through the Levitical priesthood, there was still a need for a priesthood to arrive that could bring that perfection."

Psalm 110:4 shows that a priest of a new order has come. God has changed the rules for priesthood. In Jesus, this new high priest has been appointed not based on ancestry but on the basis of his immortality. The author has seized on the term "forever" in Ps 110:4 (Heb 7:16–17).

7:18–19 The argument continues here, explaining why Jesus was appointed. The old-covenant regulation concerning the priestly office did not produce God's ultimate aim for his people. Consequently, with the appointment of Jesus to priesthood, God introduces a "better hope" (v. 19).

7:20–22 In Ps 110:4, the Father declared an oath: "The Lord has sworn." This promise guarantees that things will not change. Thus, Jesus has become the "guarantor of a better covenant" (Heb 7:22).

7:23–25 The mortality of old-covenant priests was an inherent weakness in the old-covenant priesthood. Since this weakness does not apply to Christ, his office will not be surrendered to a subsequent generation. Consequently, since Christ's priesthood lasts forever, there are no limitations on the mediation he offers between us and God. His priestly ministry not only offers temporary deliverance from sin but perfects those who come to God through him for all time (cf. 10:1–3). Moreover, the Son continuously intercedes before God on our behalf (7:25).

7:26–28 The descriptions here all emphasize the Son's sinless character in contrast to the sinfulness of the earthly priests. The old priests were appointed through the law but were weak. The Son was appointed through God's oath and has been "made perfect forever" (v. 28).

✣ **7:11–28** In ch. 7 Hebrews proclaims the eternal nature of the Son's high priesthood. Thus, in the view of Hebrews, this paradigm will not change. God's new-covenant way of relating to people will never be altered. Religions such as Islam and Mormonism amount to *contradictions* of ch. 7 rather than progressive revelations. They suggest a different view of Christ than one finds in Hebrews and the rest of the NT. Consequently, Hebrews' view of reality, grounded in the eternal high priesthood of the Son of God, offers us lasting stability for life.

8:1–2 The wording "in heaven" (v. 1) introduces a main motif of the following material: the location of

Heb 8:6 ❖ What does it mean for us to be in a covenant relationship with God?

priest,[b] who sat down at the right hand
of the throne of the Majesty in heaven,
2 and who serves in the sanctuary, the
true tabernacle[c] set up by the Lord, not
by a mere human being.
3 Every high priest is appointed to offer
both gifts and sacrifices,[d] and so it was
necessary for this one also to have something to offer.[e] 4 If he were on earth, he
would not be a priest, for there are already
priests who offer the gifts prescribed by
the law.[f] 5 They serve at a sanctuary that is
a copy[g] and shadow[h] of what is in heaven.
This is why Moses was warned[i] when he
was about to build the tabernacle: "See
to it that you make everything according
to the pattern shown you on the mountain."[a][j] 6 But in fact the ministry Jesus has
received is as superior to theirs as the covenant[k] of which he is mediator[l] is superior
to the old one, since the new covenant is
established on better promises.
7 For if there had been nothing wrong
with that first covenant, no place would
have been sought for another.[m] 8 But God
found fault with the people and said[b]:

"The days are coming, declares the
Lord,
when I will make a new covenant[n]
with the people of Israel
and with the people of Judah.
9 It will not be like the covenant
I made with their ancestors[o]
when I took them by the hand
to lead them out of Egypt,
because they did not remain faithful
to my covenant,
and I turned away from them,
declares the Lord.
10 This is the covenant I will establish
with the people of Israel
after that time, declares the Lord.
I will put my laws in their minds
and write them on their hearts.[p]
I will be their God,
and they will be my people.[q]
11 No longer will they teach their
neighbor,
or say to one another, 'Know the
Lord,'
because they will all know me,[r]
from the least of them to the
greatest.
12 For I will forgive their wickedness
and will remember their sins no
more.[s]"[c][t]

13 By calling this covenant "new," he
has made the first one obsolete;[u] and
what is obsolete and outdated will soon
disappear.

[a] *5* Exodus 25:40 [b] *8* Some manuscripts may be translated *fault and said to the people.* [c] *12* Jer. 31:31-34

8:1 [b] Heb 2:17
8:2 [c] Heb 9:11, 24
8:3 [d] Heb 5:1 [e] Heb 9:14
8:4 [f] Heb 5:1
8:5 [g] Heb 9:23 [h] Col 2:17; Heb 10:1 [i] Heb 11:7; 12:25 [j] Ex 25:40
8:6 [k] Lk 22:20 [l] Heb 7:22
8:7 [m] Heb 7:11, 18
8:8 [n] Jer 31:31
8:9 [o] Ex 19:5, 6
8:10 [p] 2Co 3:3; Heb 10:16 [q] Zec 8:8
8:11 [r] Isa 54:13; Jn 6:45
8:12 [s] Heb 10:17 [t] Ro 11:27
8:13 [u] 2Co 5:17

the Son's ministry. This position makes it superior to the earthbound priesthood of the old covenant.
8:3–6 In vv. 4–5 the author continues to contrast the Levitical priests and the exalted Son; the focus here rests on the different locations of their ministries—the heavenly and earthly realms. The old-covenant place of worship was an ineffectual copy of the heavenly reality. Consequently, "the ministry Jesus has received is . . . superior to theirs" (v. 6), and the new covenant associated with his ministry as our mediator is also superior to the old covenant.
8:7–13 Hebrews explains the new covenant concept like nowhere else in the NT. In the passage under consideration, the author focuses on the inadequacy of the old covenant, a concept presented as intrinsic to Jer 31. The logic is simple: The announcement of a new covenant proves that something had gone wrong with the first.

The quote of Jer 31:31–34 in Heb 8:8–12 has three parts. First, the Lord promises a time when he will make a new covenant with the people of God (v. 8). Second, this covenant would *not* be like the Sinai covenant, because those who were led out of Egypt did not remain faithful to God's covenant (v. 9). Finally, God's laws will be placed in the minds and hearts of God's people, firmly establishing the relationship between God and his followers (v. 10). Everyone within the covenant will know the Lord (v. 11) because God will forgive their sins (v. 12). The new covenant establishes a relationship with God. In that relationship, the laws of God are internalized, and the forgiveness of sins is foundational.

✜ **8:1–13** It is possible to love and treat others with dignity, even if we disagree with them. Such respect does not mean we must set aside our own convictions or stop having conversations with others who are open to such conversations. On the contrary, we must share the gospel boldly to be true to the message of the NT. Yet respect means that we will conduct those conversations sensitively and "with grace" (cf. Col 4:5–6), listening and sharing our perspectives.

If Christianity is recast as a "nondogmatic" religion that can "fit in" with every other religion, then Christianity will surely be lost. Thankfully, there are many who refuse to surrender the pure message of the Christian faith and find in it their motivation to love, have compassion

Worship in the Earthly Tabernacle

9 Now the first covenant had regulations for worship and also an earthly
sanctuary.[v] 2A tabernacle[w] was set up. In
its first room were the lampstand[x] and
the table[y] with its consecrated bread;[z]
this was called the Holy Place. 3Behind
the second curtain was a room called the
Most Holy Place,[a] 4which had the golden
altar of incense[b] and the gold-covered
ark of the covenant.[c] This ark contained
the gold jar of manna,[d] Aaron's staff that
had budded,[e] and the stone tablets of the
covenant. 5Above the ark were the cherubim of the Glory,[f] overshadowing the
atonement cover. But we cannot discuss
these things in detail now.
6When everything had been arranged
like this, the priests entered regularly[g]
into the outer room to carry on their
ministry. 7But only the high priest entered[h] the inner room, and that only once
a year,[i] and never without blood, which he
offered for himself[j] and for the sins the
people had committed in ignorance. 8The
Holy Spirit was showing[k] by this that the
way[l] into the Most Holy Place had not yet
been disclosed as long as the first tabernacle was still functioning. 9This is an illustration for the present time, indicating
that the gifts and sacrifices being offered[m]
were not able to clear the conscience of
the worshiper. 10They are only a matter
of food[n] and drink[o] and various ceremonial washings — external regulations[p]
applying until the time of the new order.

The Blood of Christ

11But when Christ came as high priest[q]
of the good things that are now already
here,[a][r] he went through the greater and
more perfect tabernacle[s] that is not made
with human hands, that is to say, is not a
part of this creation. 12He did not enter by
means of the blood of goats and calves;[t]
but he entered the Most Holy Place[u] once
for all[v] by his own blood, thus obtaining[b] eternal redemption. 13The blood of
goats and bulls and the ashes of a heifer[w]
sprinkled on those who are ceremonially

9:1 [v] Ex 25:8
9:2 [w] Ex 25:8, 9 [x] Ex 25:31-39 [y] Ex 25:23-29 [z] Lev 24:5-8
9:3 [a] Ex 26:31-33
9:4 [b] Ex 30:1-5 [c] Ex 25:10-22 [d] Ex 16:32, 33 [e] Nu 17:10
9:5 [f] Ex 25:17-19
9:6 [g] Nu 28:3
9:7 [h] Lev 16:11-19 [i] Lev 16:34 [j] Heb 5:2, 3
9:8 [k] Heb 3:7 [l] Jn 14:6; Heb 10:19, 20
9:9 [m] Heb 5:1
9:10 [n] Lev 11:2-23 [o] Col 2:16 [p] Heb 7:16
9:11 [q] Heb 2:17 [r] Heb 10:1 [s] Heb 8:2
9:12 [t] Heb 10:4 [u] ver 24 [v] Heb 7:27
9:13 [w] Nu 19:9, 17, 18

[a] 11 Some early manuscripts *are to come*
[b] 12 Or *blood, having obtained*

for, and respect others no matter what their religious convictions.

At minimum, biblical Christianity must involve belief in Jesus' sacrifice for the forgiveness of sins, a transformation of the inner life according to God's law, and fostering an intimate relationship with the living God. Certainly, more can be said of our faith, and the NT provides us with extensive development of these themes. However, any definition of Christian faith that neglects these realities is not Christianity.

9:1–5 This description moves from the outer room of the worship tent to the inner. The lampstand was pure gold, with six flowered branches extending from its sides, three to a side. The table, made of acacia wood and overlaid with gold, held the bread of the Presence.

The golden altar of incense was located in the inner room of the sanctuary with the ark of the covenant. The ark of the covenant, a chest made of acacia wood and overlaid with gold, was the most important element of the tabernacle. Above its cover, between the cherubim, God met with Moses.

9:6 The author explains the ministry performed in each part of the tabernacle. The outer room was the domain of the priests. Hebrews emphasizes the daily performance of their service rather than what that service entailed.

9:7 The high priest alone was allowed to enter the Most Holy Place, once a year on the Day of Atonement. This atonement offering was for the cleansing of the Most Holy Place.

9:8 During the old-covenant era, there existed no means of entrance into the presence of God.

9:9–10 The outer room illustrates the whole era managed by the older covenant. It was a time in which the general populace could not draw near to God. The problem under the old covenant consisted of the sacrificial system's inability to resolve one's awareness of personal guilt.

9:1–10 God does not leave us to somehow try to make our own way into his presence. He gives specific instructions, for he is holy, and we are sinful. There can be no digging a tunnel underneath the walls of the Most Holy Place, no barging in to demand our right to see God. This is God's tent, and he makes the rules. We must come in by the path of a high priest or not come in at all.

9:11–12 The Messiah comes as a high priest of "good things that are now already here" (v. 11). The "good things" are all those blessings associated with the new covenant (8:6).

The writer has two prominent OT images in mind: the Day of Atonement sacrifice and Moses' sacrifice to inaugurate the Sinai covenant. Christ's death on the cross incorporates and fulfills the meaning of both. As the earthly high priest passed into the inner room of the sanctuary, Christ "went through the greater and more perfect tabernacle" (9:11). Christ passed into the very presence of God in heaven (8:1).

Christ's entrance with "his own blood" means his sacrificial death on the cross. The word "redemption" (9:12) can also be translated "liberation" or "deliverance." This is deliverance from sin's penalty and is eternal in nature, Christ having entered "once for all" (v. 12).

9:13 On the Day of Atonement (Lev 16:1–25), the high priest first offered a special sacrifice for

unclean sanctify them so that they are
outwardly clean. 14How much more, then,
will the blood of Christ, who through the
eternal Spirit[x] offered himself unblemished to God, cleanse our consciences[y]
from acts that lead to death,[a][z] so that we
may serve the living God!

15For this reason Christ is the mediator[a] of a new covenant, that those who
are called may receive the promised eternal inheritance—now that he has died as
a ransom to set them free from the sins
committed under the first covenant.[b]

16In the case of a will,[b] it is necessary
to prove the death of the one who made
it, 17because a will is in force only when
somebody has died; it never takes effect while the one who made it is living. 18This is why even the first covenant
was not put into effect without blood.[c]
19When Moses had proclaimed every
command of the law to all the people,
he took the blood of calves, together
with water, scarlet wool and branches
of hyssop, and sprinkled the scroll and
all the people.[d] 20He said, "This is the
blood of the covenant, which God has
commanded you to keep."[c][e] 21In the same
way, he sprinkled with the blood both
the tabernacle and everything used in
its ceremonies. 22In fact, the law requires
that nearly everything be cleansed with
blood,[f] and without the shedding of
blood there is no forgiveness.[g]

23It was necessary, then, for the copies[h]
of the heavenly things to be purified with
these sacrifices, but the heavenly things
themselves with better sacrifices than
these. 24For Christ did not enter a sanctuary made with human hands that was
only a copy of the true one;[i] he entered
heaven itself, now to appear for us in
God's presence. 25Nor did he enter heav-
en to offer himself again and again, the
way the high priest enters the Most Holy
Place[j] every year with blood that is not
his own.[k] 26Otherwise Christ would have
had to suffer many times since the creation of the world.[l] But he has appeared
once for all[m] at the culmination of the
ages to do away with sin by the sacrifice
of himself. 27Just as people are destined
to die once,[n] and after that to face judgment,[o] 28so Christ was sacrificed once to

Heb 9:23-28 ❖ How is the one-time sacrifice of Christ the anchor of our life and actions?

9:14 [x] 1Pe 3:18 [y] Titus 2:14; Heb 10:2,22 [z] Heb 6:1
9:15 [a] 1Ti 2:5 [b] Heb 7:22
9:18 [c] Ex 24:6-8
9:19 [d] Ex 24:6-8
9:20 [e] Ex 24:8; Mt 26:28
9:22 [f] Lev 8:15 [g] Lev 17:11
9:23 [h] Heb 8:5
9:24 [i] Heb 8:2
9:25 [j] Heb 10:19 [k] ver 7,8
9:26 [l] Heb 4:3 [m] Heb 7:27
9:27 [n] Ge 3:19 [o] 2Co 5:10

[a] 14 Or *from useless rituals* [b] 16 Same Greek word as *covenant*; also in verse 17
[c] 20 Exodus 24:8

---

himself and then another on behalf of the people. He slaughtered one of two goats as a sin offering "for the people." The high priest then laid hands on the head of the second goat. He confessed the people's sins before the Lord and sent the "scapegoat" into the desert. God instructed Aaron to take the blood of the bull and the sacrificed goat "behind the curtain" so that the blood of each might be sprinkled on the atonement cover.

In Nu 19:1-21, God commanded Moses and Aaron to sacrifice and burn a red heifer. Its ashes were mixed with water, which was used for ceremonial cleansing.

9:14 The offerings described above fade in contrast to the offering made by Christ. Because of his perfection, his sacrifice of himself is able to "cleanse our consciences from acts that lead to death."

9:15 Christ as mediator of the new covenant has stood between God and people and brought the two parties together. The new people of God receive an eternal inheritance. This mediatorial relationship was established by Christ's death, in which he served as a ransom to liberate people from sins. Christ has liberated us, establishing a means by which we might be forgiven for our sins. This constitutes a blessing of the new covenant, in which the sins of God's people are remembered "no more" (8:12).

9:16-17 The author makes another reference to the "covenant" (see NIV text note on v. 16). He teaches simply that someone (represented by the sacrificial victim) had to die for the covenant to be established.

9:18-22 The reading of vv. 16-17 in terms of sacrifice squares perfectly with what follows in vv. 18-22, which relate Moses' establishment of the Sinai covenant with the shedding of sacrificial blood. In vv. 19-21 the details of this OT event are summarized. This use of blood in cleansing the various aspects of tabernacle worship demonstrates the truth stated in v. 22.

9:23-24 The need for purification of the tabernacle had to do with its association with a sinful people. This holy space was made fit for continued interaction between God and his people by sacrifices that addressed the problem of sin. Correspondingly, the heavenly tabernacle was made accessible by Christ's sacrificial death. Christ entered heaven to bring his sacrifice before God on our behalf (v. 24).

9:25-28 Christ's sacrifice reaches back to the time of creation and forward to the end of time, fully cleansing the people of God. Christ's sacrifice will be followed by a second appearance in this earthly realm. His first coming dealt with sin through his sacrificial death. His second coming will bring salvation—complete deliverance from this fallen, sinful world and its effects—to those who are anticipating his return (v. 28).

✣ **9:11-28** The Christian faith has become a too-familiar, empty fixture of the culture. The

take away the sins of many; and he will
appear a second time,[p] not to bear sin,[q]
but to bring salvation to those who are
waiting for him.[r]

Christ's Sacrifice Once for All

10 The law is only a shadow[s] of the
good things[t] that are coming—not
the realities themselves.[u] For this reason
it can never, by the same sacrifices repeated endlessly year after year, make perfect[v]
those who draw near to worship. 2Other-
wise, would they not have stopped being
offered? For the worshipers would have
been cleansed once for all, and would no
longer have felt guilty for their sins. 3But
those sacrifices are an annual reminder
of sins.[w] 4It is impossible for the blood of
bulls and goats[x] to take away sins.
5Therefore, when Christ came into the
world,[y] he said:

"Sacrifice and offering you did not
desire,
but a body you prepared for me;[z]
6with burnt offerings and sin
offerings
you were not pleased.
7Then I said, 'Here I am—it is written
about me in the scroll[a]—
I have come to do your will, my
God.'"[a][b]

9:28 [p] Titus 2:13 [q] 1Pe 2:24 [r] 1Co 1:7
10:1 [s] Heb 8:5 [t] Heb 9:11 [u] Heb 9:23 [v] Heb 7:19
10:3 [w] Heb 9:7
10:4 [x] Heb 9:12, 13
10:5 [y] Heb 1:6 [z] 1Pe 2:24
10:7 [a] Jer 36:2 [b] Ps 40:6-8
10:8 [c] ver 5, 6; Mk 12:33
10:9 [d] ver 7
10:10 [e] Jn 17:19 [f] Heb 2:14; 1Pe 2:24 [g] Heb 7:27
10:11 [h] Heb 5:1 [i] ver 1, 4
10:13 [j] Heb 1:13
10:14 [k] ver 1
10:15 [l] Heb 3:7

Heb 10:11-14 ❖ Does Christ's one-time sacrifice for sins mean we do not need to keep repenting of our sins and asking God for forgiveness? Why or why not?

8First he said, "Sacrifices and offerings,
burnt offerings and sin offerings you did
not desire, nor were you pleased with
them"[c]—though they were offered in
accordance with the law. 9Then he said,
"Here I am, I have come to do your will."[d]
He sets aside the first to establish the
second. 10And by that will, we have been
made holy[e] through the sacrifice of the
body[f] of Jesus Christ once for all.[g]
11Day after day every priest stands
and performs his religious duties; again
and again he offers the same sacrifices,[h]
which can never take away sins.[i] 12But
when this priest had offered for all time
one sacrifice for sins, he sat down at the
right hand of God, 13and since that time
he waits for his enemies to be made his
footstool.[j] 14For by one sacrifice he has
made perfect[k] forever those who are being made holy.
15The Holy Spirit also testifies[l] to us
about this. First he says:

[a] 7 Psalm 40:6-8 (see Septuagint)

---

concept of sacrifice, especially blood sacrifice, is considered such a primitive idea as to be completely foreign to modern thinking.

Believers in the church must retake this ground from the culture. We must reclaim our image of the cross and the sacrifice it represents. Why? Because the world must hear that God loved us enough to experience voluntarily the death of his Son on our behalf, meeting a need for us that we could never meet for ourselves. Therefore, we must not abandon the concept of the blood of Christ, for it lies at the heart of our redemption, even as we must also find fresh ways to interpret and communicate its significance for a modern audience scandalized by the "primitive sacrifice" concept.

10:1–4 What concerns the author most is the law's inability to "make perfect those who draw near to worship" God (v. 1). This "perfection" involves not flawlessness but rather a state of right relationship with God in which the worshipers are once and for all cleansed from sin and delivered from a nagging sense of guilt.

The law's sacrificial system only reminded people of their sinfulness and constant separation from God (v. 3). This is because the sacrifices of that system did not have the ability to remove sins (v. 4).

10:5–8 Thankfully, Christ came into the world to set things right, and the author supports this assertion by quoting Ps 40:6–8. This text has two primary components: God's dissatisfaction with the old-covenant sacrificial offerings, and the willing obedience of the speaker, Christ.

10:9–10 In v. 9 the author explains that Christ's obedience has replaced the use of animal sacrifices. The writer concludes by introducing the term "body" (v. 10), taken from the psalm text. It was by God's will, expressed in the sacrifice of the body of Jesus Christ once for all, that believers have been made holy.

10:11–14 The argument then turns again to the finality of Christ's sacrifice and contrasts the high-priestly service of Christ and that of the old-covenant priests. The writer demonstrates that Christ's sacrifice has the following characteristics: (1) It was offered "for all time" (v. 12); (2) it culminated in Christ sitting down at the right hand of God (v. 12); (3) it involved one sacrifice (vv. 12, 14); and (4) it accomplished perfection of those for whom the sacrifice was offered (v. 14).

10:12 The author proclaims that Christ has taken his seat of authority. In other words, the Son will remain seated until his second appearing (9:28), since no further sacrificial work needs to be accomplished.

10:14 Our author declares the sacrifice of Christ (v. 10) is the means by which we are made "perfect"—wholly adequate for a relationship with God.

10:15–18 Psalm 110:1 indicates the finality of the Son's sacrifice, mirrored in Heb 10:11–14. In a similar

16 “This is the covenant I will make
with them
after that time, says the Lord.
I will put my laws in their hearts,
and I will write them on their
minds.”[a][m]

17 Then he adds:

“Their sins and lawless acts
I will remember no more.”[b][n]

18 And where these have been forgiven,
sacrifice for sin is no longer necessary.

A Call to Persevere in Faith

19 Therefore, brothers and sisters, since
we have confidence to enter the Most
Holy Place[o] by the blood of Jesus, 20 by
a new and living way[p] opened for us
through the curtain,[q] that is, his body,
21 and since we have a great priest[r] over
the house of God, 22 let us draw near to
God[s] with a sincere heart and with the
full assurance that faith brings, having
our hearts sprinkled to cleanse us from a
guilty conscience[t] and having our bodies
washed with pure water. 23 Let us hold
unswervingly to the hope[u] we profess, for
he who promised is faithful.[v] 24 And let us
consider how we may spur one another
on toward love and good deeds, 25 not
giving up meeting together,[w] as some are
in the habit of doing, but encouraging
one another[x] — and all the more as you
see the Day approaching.
26 If we deliberately keep on sinning[y]
after we have received the knowledge of
the truth, no sacrifice for sins is left, 27 but
only a fearful expectation of judgment
and of raging fire[z] that will consume the

10:16 [m] Jer 31:33; Heb 8:10
10:17 [n] Heb 8:12
10:19 [o] Eph 2:18; Heb 9:8,12,25
10:20 [p] Heb 9:8 [q] Heb 9:3
10:21 [r] Heb 2:17
10:22 [s] Heb 7:19 [t] Eze 36:25; Heb 9:14
10:23 [u] Heb 3:6 [v] 1Co 1:9
10:25 [w] Ac 2:42 [x] Heb 3:13
10:26 [y] Nu 15:30; 2Pe 2:20
10:27 [z] Isa 26:11; 2Th 1:7; Heb 9:27

[a] *16* Jer. 31:33 [b] *17* Jer. 31:34

---

manner, the Spirit also proclaims the need for a new covenant and the decisive forgiveness of sins. That God “will remember no more” the sins of his people (v. 17) demonstrates that this covenant fully deals with sin. Therefore all future sacrifices for sin have been rendered obsolete.

> **10:1–18** Most religions involve some form of human “doing” for God—“sacrificing” something to win favor with the Almighty. At the heart of the Christian faith stands the core truth that God has done something for us, through the sacrifice of his Son, that we could never do for ourselves. He has taken our sins out of the way, forgiven us completely, and relates to us, intimately and eternally. By that definitive sacrifice we, through the accomplishment of our Savior, have been brought to the Father and welcomed into his family forever. This is the gospel.

10:19–22 Just as the high priest was able to enter the earthly Most Holy Place by the blood of animals, so also the blood (i.e., death) of Jesus has won us confident entrance to the divine presence.
10:20 Our entrance is “by a new and living way.” The word translated as “new” can also carry the meaning “previously unavailable.” This way is “living” because we walk it in association with our resurrected Lord. “The curtain” ultimately points to a greater (i.e., “heavenly”) reality—the spiritual barrier through which one must pass to enter God’s presence. This passage has now been opened through Christ’s sacrifice.
10:21 Our priest is “over the house of God,” a reference to the earlier discussion in 3:1–6. Christ’s superior offering has established him as the One who has brought a new people into existence.
10:22 We must come “with a sincere heart,” meaning that we be “real, genuine, loyal.” “Full assurance that faith brings” can also be translated “conviction” or “certainty of faith.”
10:23 Here the believer is challenged to hold on to the Christian hope, which the author has so clearly depicted as grounded in the person and work of Christ.
10:24–25 Christians have a high calling to care for one another and to encourage one another spiritually and morally. The word translated “let us consider” means to “notice, consider, pay attention to, look closely at.”

The author explains the context for encouragement toward love and good works in v. 25. What believers must not do is stop meeting together on a regular basis; what they must do is gather for mutual encouragement. Believers must remind one another that we live from day to day in anticipation of Christ’s return.

> **10:19–25** Drawing near to God must be done with a sincere heart—one that has been sprinkled clean from a guilty conscience. This cleansing is only possible if one has a right understanding, a right belief in who Jesus is and in what he has accomplished on our behalf. Even for those who have new-covenant hearts, to persevere in this drawing near we must keep right thinking in place and hearts engaged in the pursuit of God. It takes time to keep our lives focused on the right things. We are called to draw near to God based on the completed work of Christ. Will we heed that call today, or will our hearts be longing for other things? “Let us draw near to God with a sincere heart” (v. 22).

10:26 What the author has in mind here is a deliberately sinful lifestyle. If a person keeps sinning this way, no sacrifice for this kind of sin remains. In vv. 1–18 the author has already clarified that Christ’s sacrifice has rendered all others obsolete. Where, then, can one go other than to Christ? Once he and his provision have been rejected, there is nowhere else to turn.
10:27 The expectation of certain judgment is said to be “fearful.” This expectation has to do with

enemies of God. 28 Anyone who rejected
the law of Moses died without mercy on
the testimony of two or three witnesses.[a]
29 How much more severely do you think
someone deserves to be punished who
has trampled the Son of God underfoot,[b]
who has treated as an unholy thing the
blood of the covenant[c] that sanctified
them, and who has insulted the Spirit[d]
of grace?[e] 30 For we know him who said,
"It is mine to avenge; I will repay,"[af] and
again, "The Lord will judge his people."[bg]
31 It is a dreadful thing to fall into the
hands of the living God.[h]
32 Remember those earlier days after
you had received the light,[i] when you endured in a great conflict full of suffering.[j]
33 Sometimes you were publicly exposed
to insult and persecution;[k] at other times
you stood side by side with those who
were so treated.[l] 34 You suffered along
with those in prison[m] and joyfully accepted the confiscation of your property,
because you knew that you yourselves
had better and lasting possessions.[n] 35 So
do not throw away your confidence; it
will be richly rewarded.
36 You need to persevere[o] so that when

10:28 [a] Dt 17:6, 7; Heb 2:2
10:29 [b] Heb 6:6 [c] Mt 26:28 [d] Eph 4:30; Heb 6:4 [e] Heb 2:3
10:30 [f] Dt 32:35; Ro 12:19 [g] Dt 32:36
10:31 [h] Mt 16:16
10:32 [i] Heb 6:4 [j] Php 1:29, 30
10:33 [k] 1Co 4:9 [l] Php 4:14; 1Th 2:14
10:34 [m] Heb 13:3 [n] Heb 11:16
10:36 [o] Lk 21:19; Heb 12:1
10:37 [p] Mt 11:3 [q] Rev 22:20
10:38 [r] Ro 1:17; Gal 3:11

Heb 11:1 ❖ How would you evaluate your faith based on this definition? Why?

you have done the will of God, you will
receive what he has promised. 37 For,

> "In just a little while,
> he who is coming[p] will come
> and will not delay."[cq]

38 And,

> "But my righteous[d] one will live by
> faith.[r]
> And I take no pleasure
> in the one who shrinks back."[e]

39 But we do not belong to those who
shrink back and are destroyed, but to
those who have faith and are saved.

Faith in Action

11 Now faith is confidence in what we
hope for and assurance about what

[a] *30* Deut. 32:35 [b] *30* Deut. 32:36; Psalm 135:14 [c] *37* Isaiah 26:20; Hab. 2:3 [d] *38* Some early manuscripts *But the righteous* [e] *38* Hab. 2:4 (see Septuagint)

---

an awareness of the impending event of God's fierce judgment.

10:28–29 The writer reminds the hearers of the extreme penalty for rejecting God's revealed will under the old covenant. This, however, he presents as the *lesser* problem.

The *greater* problem is the rejection of the new-covenant high priest (v. 29). Those who have turned away from God's Son are faced with a more serious situation than the unfaithful of the old-covenant era.

The rebellion of those who have turned away from the gospel is depicted in terms of three actions in v. 28. First, they have "trampled the Son of God underfoot." Second, the rebels have "treated as an unholy thing the blood of the covenant." Finally, those rejecting Christ and his sacrifice have "insulted the Spirit of grace" or caused him outrage. Those who turn away from the gospel and the Spirit's gentle promptings have committed a sin with eternal implications.

10:30–31 The author tersely concludes saying, "It is a dreadful thing to fall into the hands of the living God" (v. 31). There exists no means of escape for those who have rejected the grace of God in Christ (4:12–13).

10:32–34 A key to the author's use of his hearers' past suffering as a present example is the attitude of "joy" that persevered in these circumstances. The hearers had joy despite their persecution because they knew that "better and lasting possessions" were promised them by their identification with the Lord and his church.

10:35–36 The author here continues to encourage the believers not to retreat (v. 35). A reward comes to those who accomplish God's will by persevering in their public confession (v. 36).

10:37–39 The quotation found in these verses brings together parts of two OT texts (Isa 26:20–21 and Hab 2:3–4) and focuses on a contrast between the wicked and the righteous who live by faith. The author of Hebrews applies these OT texts to his hearers' situation. The concept of "waiting" for an impending time of reward and punishment fits the tension of their circumstances precisely. The author ends this section with a confident statement that he and his community belong to those who have chosen the right path, for they walk the way of faith as "those who have faith and are saved" (Heb 10:39b).

✚ **10:26–39** Our past can also affect our present and future as we remember those earlier days of our commitment to Christ. Perhaps there was a time when we as individuals stood strong in the face of severe trial. We should own and build memorials—journals, photos, and the like—to remember those past times, using them for our own encouragement to continue on in our Christian walk despite our trials. If we as individuals have had no such experience, we can benefit from the example of our broader community of faith, looking to a time in the past at which they sacrificed greatly.

11:1–3 The writer of Hebrews begins his "hall of faith" with a two-part definition of faith. The first part is "confidence." We can translate this part of the verse also as "Now faith is the resolute

we do not see.[s] 2This is what the ancients
were commended for.[t]
3By faith we understand that the universe was formed at God's command,[u]
so that what is seen was not made out
of what was visible.
4By faith Abel brought God a better
offering than Cain did. By faith he was
commended as righteous, when God
spoke well of his offerings.[v] And by
faith Abel still speaks, even though he
is dead.[w]
5By faith Enoch was taken from this
life, so that he did not experience death:
"He could not be found, because God
had taken him away."[a][x] For before he
was taken, he was commended as one
who pleased God. 6And without faith
it is impossible to please God, because
anyone who comes to him[y] must believe
that he exists and that he rewards those
who earnestly seek him.
7By faith Noah, when warned about
things not yet seen, in holy fear built an
ark[z] to save his family.[a] By his faith he
condemned the world and became heir
of the righteousness that is in keeping
with faith.
8By faith Abraham, when called to go
to a place he would later receive as his
inheritance,[b] obeyed and went,[c] even
though he did not know where he was

11:1 [s] Ro 8:24; 2Co 4:18
11:2 [t] ver 4,39
11:3 [u] Ge 1; Jn 1:3; 2Pe 3:5
11:4 [v] Ge 4:4; 1Jn 3:12 [w] Heb 12:24
11:5 [x] Ge 5:21-24
11:6 [y] Heb 7:19
11:7 [z] Ge 6:13-22 [a] 1Pe 3:20
11:8 [b] Ge 12:7 [c] Ge 12:1-4; Ac 7:2-4

[a] 5 Gen. 5:24

confidence." The second part is found in the second half of the verse: "and assurance about what we do not see." Some realities are unseen because they belong to the spiritual realm, and some realities are unseen because they lie in the future. The person of faith lives out of a strong conviction in God's greater realities.

11:4–12 The writer then follows, in sequence, with great examples of faithfulness from Genesis, beginning with Abel and progressing to an initial discussion of Abraham's faith. In each example the emphasis lies both on an act accomplished by faith and the right spiritual posture of the person indicated.

11:4 By faith Abel presented God with a sacrifice superior to that of Cain (v. 4). He demonstrated the vital link between internal attitudes and external actions.

11:5–6 The emphasis in the Enoch example rests even more squarely on the importance of one's spiritual posture. Enoch's resolute commitment pleased God.

11:6 The life of faith may be said to have at least three components. First, it involves coming to God and seeking him earnestly. Second, it involves believing that God exists. Third, it involves confidence that God will reward those who exercise such faith.

11:7 Noah acted on the divine warning regarding a flood that was not yet seen. His building of the ark was evidence to his faithfulness to God and his word and constituted a stark, prophetic rebuke to the godless generation in which he lived.

11:8–12 These verses focus on two foundational events from Abraham's life. First, Abraham obediently followed God's call to move to a place

PEOPLE TO KNOW // ABEL

HEBREWS 11:4: Abel was the son of Adam and Eve and the younger brother of Cain. Abel was a shepherd; Cain farmed the land. One day, Cain brought an offering to God from his crops. Abel also brought God an offering from among his flock.

God was pleased with Abel's offering, but he did not accept Cain's. We cannot be certain why Cain's offering was rejected and Abel's was accepted, the storyline suggests that Abel offered God the best of what he had, while Cain did not.

Sadly, Cain's anger at his rejected offering led him to kill his brother Abel. Already by the second generation of humanity, people had fallen into envy and murder. While Abel's life ended in tragedy, his legacy is one of righteousness and faith (Mt 23:35; Heb 11:4).

Abel's profession as a shepherd also points forward to important shepherds mentioned later in the Bible. When God called Moses to lead the Israelites out of slavery, Moses was living as a shepherd in Midian. When God sent Samuel to anoint David king of Israel, David was a young shepherd. Most importantly, Jesus called himself the "good shepherd" (Jn 10:11). As the first shepherd in the Bible, Abel is the earliest example of this biblical theme.

APPLICATION Abel demonstrated his love for God by offering the best of his flock as a sacrifice. How often do we fail to offer God our best and instead give God only our "left over" time, energy or resources? Though Abel's life was tragically cut short, he nonetheless stands as a lasting reminder of the importance of giving our best to God.

going. 9 By faith he made his home in
the promised land[d] like a stranger in a
foreign country; he lived in tents,[e] as
did Isaac and Jacob, who were heirs with
him of the same promise.[f] 10 For he was
looking forward to the city[g] with foundations,[h] whose architect and builder is
God. 11 And by faith even Sarah, who was
past childbearing age,[i] was enabled to
bear children[j] because she[a] considered
him faithful who had made the promise. 12 And so from this one man, and he
as good as dead,[k] came descendants as
numerous as the stars in the sky and as
countless as the sand on the seashore.[l]
13 All these people were still living by
faith when they died. They did not receive the things promised;[m] they only
saw them and welcomed them from a
distance,[n] admitting that they were foreigners and strangers on earth.[o] 14 People
who say such things show that they are
looking for a country of their own. 15 If
they had been thinking of the country
they had left, they would have had opportunity to return.[p] 16 Instead, they were
longing for a better country—a heavenly
one.[q] Therefore God is not ashamed[r] to
be called their God,[s] for he has prepared
a city[t] for them.
17 By faith Abraham, when God tested him, offered Isaac as a sacrifice.[u] He
who had embraced the promises was
about to sacrifice his one and only son,
18 even though God had said to him, "It
is through Isaac that your offspring will
be reckoned."[b][v] 19 Abraham reasoned that
God could even raise the dead,[w] and so
in a manner of speaking he did receive
Isaac back from death.
20 By faith Isaac blessed Jacob and Esau
in regard to their future.[x]
21 By faith Jacob, when he was dying, blessed each of Joseph's sons,[y] and
worshiped as he leaned on the top of
his staff.
22 By faith Joseph, when his end was
near, spoke about the exodus of the Israelites from Egypt and gave instructions
concerning the burial of his bones.[z]
23 By faith Moses' parents hid him for
three months after he was born,[a] because
they saw he was no ordinary child, and
they were not afraid of the king's edict.[b]
24 By faith Moses, when he had grown
up, refused to be known as the son of
Pharaoh's daughter.[c] 25 He chose to be
mistreated[d] along with the people of God
rather than to enjoy the fleeting pleasures of sin. 26 He regarded disgrace[e] for
the sake of Christ as of greater value than
the treasures of Egypt, because he was
looking ahead to his reward.[f] 27 By faith
he left Egypt,[g] not fearing the king's anger; he persevered because he saw him
who is invisible. 28 By faith he kept the

11:9 [d] Ac 7:5 [e] Ge 12:8; 18:1,9 [f] Heb 6:17
11:10 [g] Heb 12:22; 13:14 [h] Rev 21:2, 14
11:11 [i] Ge 17:17-19; 18:11-14 [j] Ge 21:2
11:12 [k] Ro 4:19 [l] Ge 22:17
11:13 [m] ver 39 [n] Mt 13:17 [o] Ge 23:4; Ps 39:12; 1Pe 1:17
11:15 [p] Ge 24:6-8
11:16 [q] 2Ti 4:18 [r] Mk 8:38 [s] Ex 3:6,15 [t] Heb 13:14
11:17 [u] Ge 22:1-10; Jas 2:21
11:18 [v] Ge 21:12; Ro 9:7
11:19 [w] Ro 4:21
11:20 [x] Ge 27:27-29,39,40
11:21 [y] Ge 48:1, 8-22
11:22 [z] Ge 50:24, 25; Ex 13:19
11:23 [a] Ex 2:2 [b] Ex 1:16,22
11:24 [c] Ex 2:10,11
11:25 [d] ver 37
11:26 [e] Heb 13:13 [f] Heb 10:35
11:27 [g] Ex 12:50, 51

[a] 11 Or *By faith Abraham, even though he was too old to have children—and Sarah herself was not able to conceive—was enabled to become a father because he* [b] 18 Gen. 21:12

---

with which he was unfamiliar (see Ge 12:1–9). Second, Abraham was enabled to become a father because he believed God (see Ge 18:10–15; 21:1–7). Faith, moving beyond the normal boundaries of possibility, works miracles. The happy result, in accordance with the promise of God, is recorded in Heb 11:12: Out of nothing comes a multitude too numerous to count.

11:13–16 The author wishes to emphasize that the patriarchs' relationship to God was their main commitment, not obtaining an earthly security. They died in a state of trust, never having seen their descendants' reception of the land. Thus, the true object of their deepest desire was God himself and God's city. The writer's point is that this is normal for people of faith. The promises of God must be embraced even though their fulfillment lies in the future.

11:17–19 These verses offer a third major event exemplifying Abraham's faith. Abraham, in a test by God, "offered Isaac as a sacrifice" (v. 17). The crux of Abraham's crisis is the seeming contradiction between the promises of God and the command of God. Through this command to sacrifice Isaac, Abraham was forced into a radical posture of trusting God. Our author's logical deduction is that "Abraham reasoned that God could even raise the dead" (v. 19)—the only way that both the promises and the command could be fulfilled.

11:20–22 The author of Hebrews moves rapid-fire through the next three generations in his example list, using his typical pattern.

11:23–28 The author's treatment of Moses begins with his parents' faith. The NIV translates v. 23 with the phrase "no ordinary child." The writer, therefore, depicts the parents as having spiritual insight into his significance. He also states that "they were not afraid of the king's edict." Moses himself also exhibited such boldness, and the writer to the Hebrews points out three events that illustrate his faith. First, Moses chose to identify with God's people rather than with the godless (vv. 24–26). Second, by faith Moses left Egypt and persevered in the mission given him by God (v. 27). Finally, by faith Moses led the Israelites in the observance of the Passover ordinance (v. 28). The mention of "the application of blood" calls to mind the smearing of blood on the Israelites' doorposts to avoid the death angel's work (also bringing to mind Jesus' blood sacrifice). This was an act of faith since Moses led the Israelites in

Passover and the application of blood, so
that the destroyer of the firstborn would
not touch the firstborn of Israel.[h]
29By faith the people passed through
the Red Sea as on dry land; but when
the Egyptians tried to do so, they were
drowned.[i]
30By faith the walls of Jericho fell, after
the army had marched around them for
seven days.[j]
31By faith the prostitute Rahab, because
she welcomed the spies, was not killed
with those who were disobedient.[a][k]
32And what more shall I say? I do not
have time to tell about Gideon, Barak,[l]
Samson and Jephthah, about David[m]
and Samuel[n] and the prophets, 33who
through faith conquered kingdoms,[o] administered justice, and gained what was
promised; who shut the mouths of lions,[p]
34quenched the fury of the flames, and
escaped the edge of the sword; whose
weakness was turned to strength;[q] and
who became powerful in battle and routed foreign armies.[r] 35Women received
back their dead, raised to life again.[s]
There were others who were tortured,
refusing to be released so that they
might gain an even better resurrection.
36Some faced jeers and flogging,[t] and
even chains and imprisonment.[u] 37They
were put to death by stoning;[b][v] they were
sawed in two; they were killed by the
sword.[w] They went about in sheepskins
and goatskins,[x] destitute, persecuted and
mistreated — 38the world was not worthy
of them. They wandered in deserts and
mountains, living in caves[y] and in holes
in the ground.
39These were all commended[z] for
their faith, yet none of them received
what had been promised,[a] 40since God
had planned something better for us so
that only together with us would they
be made perfect.

12 Therefore, since we are surrounded by such a great cloud of witnesses, let us throw off everything that

11:28 [h] Ex 12:21-23
11:29 [i] Ex 14:21-31
11:30 [j] Jos 6:12-20
11:31 [k] Jos 2:1, 9-14; 6:22-25; Jas 2:25
11:32 [l] Jdg 4-5 [m] 1Sa 16:1,13 [n] 1Sa 1:20
11:33 [o] 2Sa 7:11; 8:1-3 [p] Da 6:22
11:34 [q] 2Ki 20:7 [r] Jdg 15:8
11:35 [s] 1Ki 17:22, 23
11:36 [t] Jer 20:2 [u] Ge 39:20
11:37 [v] 2Ch 24:21 [w] 1Ki 19:10 [x] 2Ki 1:8
11:38 [y] 1Ki 18:4
11:39 [z] ver 2,4 [a] ver 13

[a] *31* Or *unbelieving* [b] *37* Some early manuscripts *stoning; they were put to the test;*

---

obedience to God's command concerning an as-yet-unseen event.

11:29-31 The author rounds out his primary example list with three other events from the life of God's covenant people. When God told them to "move on" (Ex 14:15), they did so in faith. They also marched around the city of Jericho for seven days at his command. Finally, Rahab helped the spies who had come to investigate the land (Jos 2:1–15). Her faith was rewarded with deliverance from death for herself and her family.

11:32-40 With the rhetorical "And what more shall I say?" the writer turns a corner, finishing the section with a summary of OT and perhaps intertestamental acts of faith.

11:32 The writer begins his summary with six figures spanning the era of the judges through the united monarchy, and to these adds the expansive "the prophets."

11:33-38 The passage then turns from the great performers of faith to their actions. They "through faith conquered kingdoms" (v. 33), especially calling to mind the period of the judges through the reign of King David. That they "administered justice" (v. 33) speaks of governmental administration and is an extension of their conquering.

11:33 These saints of old "gained what was promised." The author's twin points are that the promise-making God is faithful to his oaths and that people of faith live in light of God's promises.

11:35 In the middle of this verse the writer shifts gears from more positive outcomes to faith expressed in the face of great hardship. Although some "received back their dead," others expressed faith by embracing torture and death.

11:39-40 When the author notes that the great heroes of faith were "commended" by God, he means that God himself had witnessed and recognized their faithfulness (v. 39a). The author's main point is that faith is the only right path for God's people. The heroes of faith demonstrated a resolute determination to live faithfully even though "none of them received what had been promised" (v. 39b).

These people of old did not experience the coming of Messiah and the new covenant (v. 40). Their faith in God has been vindicated since God has broken into the world in the person of his Son, Jesus Christ. With us, they now know the perfecting power of Christ's sacrifice and the eternal inheritance of the saints.

> ✣ **11:1-40** How would we live today if we believed absolutely that God existed, loved us completely, and had a destination for us that made all the world pale in comparison? How would we live if we believed that God cared about our every action and every concern and wished to reward us kindly for our faith? How would we live in the face of opposition if we really believed as if our whole lives depended on God? Conversely, how would we live differently if we did not believe? Would there be much difference? This is a critical question.
>
> If our lives differ very little from our unbelieving neighbors, then we have embraced the world and its values. We fool ourselves by saying we are living for another world and kingdom if that is the case. Our lives must be radically different in what we embrace by faith—the values of a heavenly kingdom.

12:1-2 Authors of classical literature often used the image of a cloud to describe a large group of people. Our writer employs this metaphor, pointing back to the multitude of people in ch. 11 as "such

> **Heb 12:1–3** ❖ How does recalling the lives and faith of those who have gone before us strengthen our own perseverance?

hinders and the sin that so easily entangles. And let us run[b] with perseverance[c]
the race marked out for us, 2fixing our
eyes on Jesus, the pioneer and perfecter
of faith. For the joy set before him he
endured the cross,[d] scorning its shame,[e]
and sat down at the right hand of the
throne of God. 3Consider him who endured such opposition from sinners,
so that you will not grow weary[f] and
lose heart.

God Disciplines His Children

4In your struggle against sin, you have
not yet resisted to the point of shedding
your blood.[g] 5And have you completely
forgotten this word of encouragement
that addresses you as a father addresses
his son? It says,

> "My son, do not make light of the
> Lord's discipline,
> and do not lose heart when he
> rebukes you,

6because the Lord disciplines the one
he loves,[h]
and he chastens everyone he
accepts as his son."[a][i]

7Endure hardship as discipline; God
is treating you as his children.[j] For what
children are not disciplined by their father? 8If you are not disciplined — and
everyone undergoes discipline[k] — then
you are not legitimate, not true sons and
daughters at all. 9Moreover, we have all
had human fathers who disciplined us
and we respected them for it. How much
more should we submit to the Father of
spirits[l] and live![m] 10They disciplined us
for a little while as they thought best;
but God disciplines us for our good, in
order that we may share in his holiness.[n]
11No discipline seems pleasant at the
time, but painful. Later on, however, it
produces a harvest of righteousness and
peace[o] for those who have been trained
by it.

12Therefore, strengthen your feeble
arms and weak knees.[p] 13"Make level
paths for your feet,"[b][q] so that the lame
may not be disabled, but rather healed.[r]

12:1 [b] 1Co 9:24 [c] Heb 10:36
12:2 [d] Php 2:8,9 [e] Heb 13:13
12:3 [f] Gal 6:9
12:4 [g] Heb 10:32-34
12:6 [h] Ps 94:12; Rev 3:19 [i] Pr 3:11,12
12:7 [j] Dt 8:5
12:8 [k] 1Pe 5:9
12:9 [l] Nu 16:22 [m] Isa 38:16
12:10 [n] 2Pe 1:4
12:11 [o] Isa 32:17; Jas 3:17,18
12:12 [p] Isa 35:3
12:13 [q] Pr 4:26 [r] Gal 6:1

[a] *5,6* Prov. 3:11,12 (see Septuagint)
[b] *13* Prov. 4:26

---

a great cloud" (Heb 12:1). They are witnesses in the sense that they bear witness to the Christian community of God's faithfulness and of the effectiveness of faith, which motivates the community in its current struggles.

The writer calls his hearers to "throw off everything that hinders and the sin that so easily entangles." The original word could refer to runners stripping off burdensome clothing or freeing themselves from the weeds that slow them down, which is the image of entangling sin that hinders our progress in the faith.

The main clause of vv. 1–2a is translated with "let us run." The author has in view a marathon rather than a sprint, as seen in the phrase "with perseverance." "Marked out" evokes a picture of runners looking down the track at the course they must run. Jesus is the One who has run the path before us, and he offers the preeminent example of how the race is to be run (v. 2). He is the "pioneer and perfecter of faith," set apart from all the other examples in ch. 11. Jesus cleared the path of faith so that we may run it. That Jesus "scorned" the shame of the cross means that he treated it as insignificant or of little consequence compared to the joy set before our Lord (v. 2).

12:3–4 When the author says, "Consider him who endured," he restates the need to focus on Jesus as he "endured the cross" (v. 2), but here he gives the reason: "so that you will not grow weary and lose heart" (v. 3b). In this statement, the hearers' critical circumstance stands out clearly. As v. 4 points out, those in this church, unlike Jesus, had yet to shed their blood in the struggle against sin. If Jesus endured, they could also endure the lesser persecution they were facing.

12:5–6 Here the author quotes from the book of Proverbs. The rationale for taking the Lord's discipline seriously has to do with his motive of love. The Lord disciplines as an expression of genuine relationship. Such training is only given to legitimate children.

12:7–8 The author begins his exposition of the proverb with the exhortation, "Endure hardship as discipline" (v. 7). The original hearers of Hebrews could have interpreted the persecution they were facing as an indication of God's inattention. Yet the difficulties they faced were actually a sign that they were true children of the Father, as discipline is a normal part of the parent-child relationship.

12:9 Human fathers are given respect in response to their discipline. God deserves even more reverence.

12:10–11 The discipline of God trains the Christian's character, purifying the heart (vv. 10–11). Experiencing discipline is not pleasant but painful (v. 11a). However, the fruit of the discipline is worth the price of pain (v. 11b).

12:12 With v. 12 the author returns briefly to his earlier use of athletic imagery (vv. 1–2) and draws his material both from a passage in Isaiah (Isa 35:3) and from yet another passage in Proverbs (see v. 13).

12:13 The author pleads for his hearers to choose the Lord's way of holiness so that their spiritual and emotional conditions might be strengthened.

Warning and Encouragement

14Make every effort to live in peace
with everyone[s] and to be holy;[t] without
holiness no one will see the Lord.[u] 15See
to it that no one falls short of the grace
of God[v] and that no bitter root grows up
to cause trouble and defile many. 16See
that no one is sexually immoral, or is
godless like Esau, who for a single meal
sold his inheritance rights as the oldest
son.[w] 17Afterward, as you know, when
he wanted to inherit this blessing, he
was rejected. Even though he sought the
blessing with tears,[x] he could not change
what he had done.

The Mountain of Fear and the Mountain of Joy

18You have not come to a mountain
that can be touched and that is burning
with fire; to darkness, gloom and storm;[y]
19to a trumpet blast[z] or to such a voice
speaking words that those who heard it
begged that no further word be spoken
to them,[a] 20because they could not bear
what was commanded: "If even an animal touches the mountain, it must be
stoned to death."[a][b] 21The sight was so
terrifying that Moses said, "I am trembling with fear."[b]

22But you have come to Mount Zion, to
the city[c] of the living God, the heavenly
Jerusalem.[d] You have come to thousands
upon thousands of angels in joyful assembly, 23to the church of the firstborn,
whose names are written in heaven.[e] You
have come to God, the Judge of all,[f] to the
spirits of the righteous made perfect,[g] 24to
Jesus the mediator of a new covenant,
and to the sprinkled blood that speaks
a better word than the blood of Abel.[h]

25See to it that you do not refuse him
who speaks. If they did not escape when
they refused him who warned[i] them on
earth, how much less will we, if we turn
away from him who warns us from heav-
en?[j] 26At that time his voice shook the
earth,[k] but now he has promised, "Once
more I will shake not only the earth but
also the heavens."[c][l] 27The words "once

12:14 [s] Ro 14:19 [t] Ro 6:22 [u] Mt 5:8
12:15 [v] Gal 5:4; Heb 3:12
12:16 [w] Ge 25:29-34
12:17 [x] Ge 27:30-40
12:18 [y] Ex 19:12-22; Dt 4:11
12:19 [z] Ex 20:18 [a] Ex 20:19; Dt 5:5,25
12:20 [b] Ex 19:12, 13
12:22 [c] Heb 11:10 [d] Gal 4:26
12:23 [e] Lk 10:20 [f] Ps 94:2 [g] Php 3:12
12:24 [h] Ge 4:10; Heb 11:4
12:25 [i] Heb 8:5; 11:7 [j] Heb 2:2,3
12:26 [k] Ex 19:18 [l] Hag 2:6

[a] *20* Exodus 19:12,13 [b] *21* See Deut. 9:19.
[c] *26* Haggai 2:6

12:14–17 These verses continue with two themes that are central to the first 13 verses: spiritual struggle and the need for holiness.

12:14 Holiness has a profound impact on our relationships with other people. The person who chooses to live an unholy life can be offered no assurance of "see[ing] the Lord" (v. 14b).

12:15 Those among the original recipients who were abandoning their confession of Christ were causing severe friction within the community, and relationships were breaking down.

12:16–17 The hearers are to see to it that no member of the church falls into the pattern of immoral Esau. Having given up his inheritance, Esau pleaded with his father to reverse the situation, but the patriarch could not. Only tears and rejection await those who sell out the inheritance that God promises to his children.

> ✣ **12:1–17** It goes without saying that all sins entangle or hamstring us in the contest of life and must be rejected if we are to run well and run long. To run with perseverance means that we will grow in a pattern of obedience to God's Word, day after day, year after year. It means we will train ourselves to make the right choices, choosing the level path of righteousness. The premier sin to be discarded is the sin of abandoning Christian commitment altogether. We must strengthen our "feeble arms and weak knees" (v. 12) if we lag in a rut of despair. This exercise is helped most by riveting "our eyes on Jesus" (v. 2), who has shown us what to scorn and what to hold as a cause of joy. Finally, joy awaits us if we will persevere in the race to the end.

12:18–21 The manifestations of God's presence at Sinai impacted eyes and ears. The people begged that God would speak to them no further. The people were terrified that the boundaries between God and humanity were dissolving under the weight of that terrible voice. Even Moses was overwhelmed by the experience (v. 21).

12:22–24 Thankfully, new-covenant believers have not come to Mount Sinai, a mountain of terror and separation from God. They have come to Mount Zion, the dwelling place of God. The author's picture of the gathered assembly at Mount Zion communicates exultation, warmth, openness, acceptance, and relationship, set off in bold relief against the dismal portrait of the Sinai assembly.

Mount Zion and the City of Jerusalem represent the dwelling place of God. This is the "heavenly" city of 11:16 and the "city that is to come" of 13:14. The multitude of angels in God's presence exults "in joyful assembly" (12:22), communicating a sense of excitement, revelry, and well-being.

12:23 Believers have come "to God, the Judge of all," and "to the spirits of the righteous made perfect." They have come not for God to pass judgment on them but for him to vindicate them before their wicked persecutors.

12:24 Abel's blood bore witness against Cain, indicating his guilt (v. 24). Christ's blood won our forgiveness, "crying out" that people of the new covenant are no longer guilty.

12:25–29 If those of the old covenant did not escape the wrath of God when they turned from his word, the judgment on those who reject the message of salvation received in the new-covenant era is even more certain.

Heb 13:1–3 ❖ What are ways we can show more hospitality to those around us for God's glory?

more" indicate the removing of what can be shaken[m]—that is, created things—so that what cannot be shaken may remain. [28]Therefore, since we are receiving a kingdom that cannot be shaken,[n] let us be thankful, and so worship God acceptably with reverence and awe,[o] [29]for our "God is a consuming fire."[a][p]

Concluding Exhortations

13 Keep on loving one another as brothers and sisters.[q] [2]Do not forget to show hospitality to strangers,[r] for by so doing some people have shown hospitality to angels without knowing it.[s] [3]Continue to remember those in prison[t] as if you were together with them in prison, and those who are mistreated as if you yourselves were suffering.

[4]Marriage should be honored by all, and the marriage bed kept pure, for God will judge the adulterer and all the sexually immoral.[u] [5]Keep your lives free from the love of money and be content with what you have,[v] because God has said,

> "Never will I leave you;
> never will I forsake you."[b][w]

[6]So we say with confidence,

> "The Lord is my helper; I will not be afraid.
> What can mere mortals do to me?"[c]

[7]Remember your leaders,[x] who spoke the word of God to you. Consider the outcome of their way of life and imitate[y] their faith. [8]Jesus Christ is the same yesterday and today and forever.[z]

[9]Do not be carried away by all kinds of strange teachings.[a] It is good for our hearts to be strengthened[b] by grace, not by eating ceremonial foods,[c] which is of no benefit to those who do so. [10]We have an altar from which those who minister at the tabernacle have no right to eat.[d]

[11]The high priest carries the blood of animals into the Most Holy Place as a

12:27 [m]1Co 7:31; 2Pe 3:10
12:28 [n]Da 2:44 [o]Heb 13:15
12:29 [p]Dt 4:24
13:1 [q]Ro 12:10; 1Pe 1:22
13:2 [r]Mt 25:35 [s]Ge 18:1-33
13:3 [t]Mt 25:36; Col 4:18
13:4 [u]1Co 6:9
13:5 [v]Php 4:11 [w]Dt 31:6,8; Jos 1:5
13:7 [x]ver 17,24 [y]Heb 6:12
13:8 [z]Heb 1:12
13:9 [a]Eph 4:14 [b]Col 2:7 [c]Col 2:16
13:10 [d]1Co 9:13; 10:18

[a] 29 Deut. 4:24 [b] 5 Deut. 31:6 [c] 6 Psalm 118:6,7

✜ **12:18–29** Out of a desire to clearly reflect God's holiness, we can steer dangerously close to Sinai, not just as a necessary waystation but as a permanent, spiritual destination, preaching a gospel of terror rather than a gospel of beauty. Do our communications with the lost boom and flash with the darkness of Sinai more than they sing and gather people to the festiveness of Zion?

If our lives reflect the gloom of Sinai more than the glories of Zion, we do the kingdom poor publicity. This does not mean, of course, that we are always thrilled with the difficult situations in which we may find ourselves. But are we *characterized* by joy, and can we successfully communicate that to those we are trying to reach? If we are not, then the reality of Zion is not invading our lives. Perhaps we need a clearer view of that mountain and must hear again the song of the angels and the message of the sprinkled blood.

13:1 The concept of believers as a spiritual family lays the foundation for practical exhortations to meet the needs of those in the family.
13:2 In the Christian context, such admonitions to show hospitality have their foundation in the OT and the teachings of Jesus.
13:3 Christians could minister to fellow believers in prison by offering consolation and gifts or by praying for them.
13:4 The "marriage bed," used here as an idiom for the sexual relationship, is to be guarded or "kept pure." The defilement that the author has in mind is expressed in the explanatory "for God will judge the adulterer and all the sexually immoral."
13:5–6 The sins of sexual impurity and covetousness are linked in several NT passages, probably because their prohibitions are given side by side as the seventh and eighth of the Ten Commandments.
13:7 Here the readers are exhorted to "remember your leaders." The author exhorts his hearers to consider closely or scrutinize the fruit of their leaders' manner of living and imitate their faith. In other words, the leaders are placed in the same category of "heroic examples" as the paragons of biblical history listed in ch. 11.
13:8 "Jesus Christ is the same yesterday and today and forever" (v. 8). This theological perspective has been well developed throughout Hebrews. With this statement, the author reminds his audience that the same Christ who was so real to their community presently sits in his exalted state and will rule forever.
13:9–10 It is important that the congregation guards against "all kinds of strange teachings" (v. 9). Some are embracing aspects of Jewish community life and thought that are at odds with the gospel of grace through Jesus Christ. The author asserts that such ceremonial foods are not the true means of grace and spiritual strength.
13:11–12 With v. 12 the author draws two parallels between Jesus' sacrifice and that of the Day of Atonement. First, "Jesus also suffered outside the city gate." Second, the purpose of Jesus' sacrifice was "to make the people holy." Jesus' high-priestly offering, however, was "through his own blood."

sin offering, but the bodies are burned
outside the camp.[e] 12And so Jesus also
suffered outside the city gate[f] to make
the people holy through his own blood.
13Let us, then, go to him outside the
camp, bearing the disgrace he bore.[g]
14For here we do not have an enduring
city, but we are looking for the city that
is to come.[h]
15Through Jesus, therefore, let us
continually offer to God a sacrifice[i] of
praise—the fruit of lips[j] that openly profess his name. 16And do not forget to do
good and to share with others,[k] for with
such sacrifices[l] God is pleased.
17Have confidence in your leaders
and submit to their authority, because
they keep watch over you[m] as those who
must give an account. Do this so that
their work will be a joy, not a burden,
for that would be of no benefit to you.
18Pray for us.[n] We are sure that we have
a clear conscience[o] and desire to live honorably in every way. 19I particularly urge
you to pray so that I may be restored to
you soon.[p]

13:11 [e] Ex 29:14; Lev 16:27
13:12 [f] Jn 19:17
13:13 [g] Heb 11:26
13:14 [h] Php 3:20; Heb 12:22
13:15 [i] 1Pe 2:5 [j] Hos 14:2
13:16 [k] Ro 12:13 [l] Php 4:18
13:17 [m] Isa 62:6; Ac 20:28
13:18 [n] 1Th 5:25 [o] Ac 23:1
13:19 [p] Phm 22
13:20 [q] Ro 15:33 [r] Isa 55:3; Eze 37:26; Zec 9:11 [s] Ac 2:24 [t] Jn 10:11
13:21 [u] Php 2:13 [v] 1Jn 3:22 [w] Ro 11:36
13:22 [x] 1Pe 5:12
13:23 [y] Ac 16:1
13:24 [z] ver 7,17 [a] Ac 18:2
13:25 [b] Col 4:18

Benediction and Final Greetings

20Now may the God of peace,[q] who
through the blood of the eternal covenant[r] brought back from the dead[s] our
Lord Jesus, that great Shepherd of the
sheep,[t] 21equip you with everything good
for doing his will, and may he work in
us[u] what is pleasing to him,[v] through
Jesus Christ, to whom be glory for ever
and ever. Amen.[w]

22Brothers and sisters, I urge you to
bear with my word of exhortation, for in
fact I have written to you quite briefly.[x]
23I want you to know that our brother
Timothy[y] has been released. If he arrives
soon, I will come with him to see you.
24Greet all your leaders[z] and all the
Lord's people. Those from Italy[a] send
you their greetings.
25Grace be with you all.[b]

13:13–14 The author offers an application in these verses: Believers must reject the tempting security of Judaism and be resolute in their identification with Christ. The "camp" represents the religion of Judaism, grounded in the tabernacle rituals of the old covenant. Christ's sacrifice means lasting holiness, and his "city" is one that will endure.
13:15–16 Although Christians should not participate in the Jewish festival meals, they have their own appropriate "sacrifices" to offer. Here the writer exhorts his readers to "continually offer to God a sacrifice of praise" (v. 15). The Christ-follower is also to offer a sacrifice of good deeds (v. 16). Both the life of faith (11:6) and the sacrifices of praise and practical ministry please God.
13:17 With this verse the writer returns to the subject of the church's leadership, focusing on current leaders. The members of the congregation should "have confidence in" these leaders and "submit to their authority." The verb translated "have confidence" could mean "being persuaded by" or "putting one's confidence in," but it could also point toward the idea of "conforming one's actions" or "obeying." The further injunction to "submit to their authority" means the listeners should be ready to comply and may suggest a strained relationship between the leadership and some members of the Christian community. These two commands involve respecting the leaders as they give direction concerning right Christian doctrine.

The phrase "not a burden" can be translated as "not groaning." When members of the church fail to submit themselves to the leadership, the leaders end up working under an emotionally deflating burden.
13:18–19 The author rounds out his series of admonitions with a personal request: "Keep on praying." He specifically asks them to pray that he "may be restored" to them (v. 19). For whatever reason, this author had been prevented from rejoining this group of believers.
13:20–25 In the Jewish context, a benediction was an aspect of worship.
13:22 The writer begins his closing in v. 22, urging the readers to put up with his "word of exhortation." The expression "word of exhortation" is probably a technical phrase referring to a sermon.
13:23 The "Timothy" of v. 23 is commonly assumed to be Paul's missionary companion. If so, his "release" indicates an incarceration not mentioned in Acts or elsewhere in the NT.
13:24–25 The book closes with this formal greeting and a final blessing: "Grace be with you all."

✣ **13:1–25** When believers live their lives for God in both big and small ways, the truth of the gospel is proclaimed in a thousand varied voices, and the kingdom is built. God is pleased with the common practices of financial management, date nights, cleaning dirty faces and dirty clothes, integrity at work, care for the burdened or oppressed, and hospitality; these are worthy sacrifices when presented on an altar made holy by the blood of Christ.

In areas such as marriage and money, the worlds of the spirit and the street meet. Such meeting places either become dance floors on which we move to the music of God's will or a stage of games on which we play at Christianity with divided, hypocritical hearts. Every day God wants us, and he wants us to want him in the nitty-gritty wonder, the plain and exalted dance of the everyday.

Author: James, a leader of the Jerusalem church

Audience: Likely Syrian Jewish-Christian agricultural workers

Date: Perhaps before AD 50 and certainly before AD 62

Theme: James emphasizes that God enables a life of faith that works itself out in action, especially with mercy for those most vulnerable.

PERSPECTIVE

We see so many instances these days of people saying they believe one thing but not acting in ways that support that belief or, worse, acting in ways that contradict that belief. In much of our modern society, belief and practice do not seem to go together in many people's minds. And they should be seen as a pair.

That's what makes James such an important letter, for it deals with precisely this problem. And it does so in a sophisticated way. James does not just say, "Practice what you preach," although that is part of the message. He gives reasons for what he says, and he shows subtle connections between faith, action, wisdom, and what you do in church on Sunday morning that really help sort out the disconnection between Christian faith and Christian living to which our culture seems so susceptible.

The book of James is a good antidote to that susceptibility. It calls us to account for a high information-to-action ratio. James makes his argument using the following propositions:

First, the Christian life is more than just intellectually assenting to some beliefs. It means acting in ways inspired by and consistent with those beliefs. It means developing a wise lifestyle that makes Christian practice more likely. And it means worshiping in ways that actually have a chance of being translated into action.

Second, there are observable pinch points where the disjunction between faith and practice most often shows up: in times of persecution

Reading James

James does not structure his letter with careful argumentation; instead, he moves rapidly from one topic to another. He speaks with authority, using more than 50 direct commands in these five short chapters. Many of his statements and commands bring to mind the words of Jesus in the Sermon on the Mount (Mt 5-7).

	10 BC	AD 1	10	20	30	40	50	60	70	80	90	100
Jesus' birth (c. 6/5 BC)												
Jesus' death, resurrection and ascension (c. AD 30)												
Paul's conversion (c. AD 35)												
Book of James written (c. AD 40–50)												
Council at Jerusalem (c. AD 49/50)												
Nero's reign (AD 54–68)												
James's death (c. AD 62)												
Destruction of Jerusalem's temple (c. AD 70)												

Key Verse

Do not merely listen to the word, and so deceive yourselves. Do what it says.

—James 1:22

and trial; whenever we open our mouths and speak with our tongues; in all our ongoing relationships with other people; and in the perplexing matters that pertain to handling money.

Third, clear benchmarks can be established that show us when we are doing it right. Call them community busters. James lists at least three. (1) Our tongues can so easily reveal a discrepancy between faith and practice, particularly when we use it to talk about God's love in ways that display little love to our fellow human beings. (2) We can talk about treating everyone equally; but when it comes to practice, we so often, even in the church, show favoritism to the rich over the poor. Money is as dangerous a commodity as the tongue, according to James. We easily become inconsistent between what we say we believe and what we do where financial gain is part of the equation. (3) Truth can be taught arrogantly or humbly—the same truth, mind you. Yet it becomes "more true" when taught with personal humility and a desire for peace, and "less true" when taught with an arrogance born of a desire to manipulate. True wisdom comes only when our attitudes and practices match up with the content of what we say.

James is the quintessential NT book for our day and age where we often see Christianity unfairly portrayed as either moral legalism or pure ethics. James says that Christianity is both, but it is neither if both are not present. Read it and see why.

TAKING THE NEXT STEPS

This short letter, written by James the brother of Jesus (Mt 13:55; Gal 1:1–9; 2:9), may well be the first NT book written. James here stresses an active faith, a faith that expresses itself in Christian living. True disciples of Jesus Christ will not live in hypocrisy—saying one thing and doing something else.

James is one of the most practical books of the NT. (1) If our faith does not express itself in Christian action, it is useless and dead. (2) One of the worst things a church can do is to show favoritism to the wealthy and neglect the poor. (3) One of the most difficult, and yet most important, parts of our body to control is the tongue. (4) God wants us to submit to him in humility, trusting that he will take care of us. (5) God wants us to bring our needs before him in prayer, for he hears and answers the prayer of faith.

WHAT TO LOOK FOR IN JAMES

- Combating favoritism and a dead faith (ch. 2)
- The proper use of the tongue (ch. 3)
- Combating materialism and pride (ch. 4)
- On patience and prayer (ch. 5)

1 James,[a] a servant of God[b] and of the
Lord Jesus Christ,

To the twelve tribes[c] scattered[d] among
the nations:

Greetings.

Trials and Temptations

2Consider it pure joy, my brothers
and sisters,[a] whenever you face trials of
many kinds,[e] 3because you know that the
testing of your faith produces perseverance. 4Let perseverance finish its work
so that you may be mature and complete, not lacking anything. 5If any of you
lacks wisdom, you should ask God,[f] who
gives generously to all without finding
fault, and it will be given to you.[g] 6But
when you ask, you must believe and not
doubt,[h] because the one who doubts is
like a wave of the sea, blown and tossed
by the wind. 7That person should not expect to receive anything from the Lord.
8Such a person is double-minded[i] and
unstable in all they do.

9Believers in humble circumstances
ought to take pride in their high position. 10But the rich should take pride in
their humiliation — since they will pass
away like a wild flower.[j] 11For the sun rises with scorching heat and withers[k] the
plant; its blossom falls and its beauty
is destroyed.[l] In the same way, the rich
will fade away even while they go about
their business.

12Blessed is the one who perseveres
under trial because, having stood the
test, that person will receive the crown

1:1 [a]Ac 15:13 [b]Titus 1:1 [c]Ac 26:7 [d]Dt 32:26; Jn 7:35; 1Pe 1:1
1:2 [e]Mt 5:12; 1Pe 1:6
1:5 [f]1Ki 3:9,10; Pr 2:3-6 [g]Mt 7:7
1:6 [h]Mk 11:24
1:8 [i]Jas 4:8
1:10 [j]1Co 7:31; 1Pe 1:24
1:11 [k]Ps 102:4,11 [l]Isa 40:6-8

[a] 2 The Greek word for *brothers and sisters* (*adelphoi*) refers here to believers, both men and women, as part of God's family; also in verses 16 and 19; and in 2:1,5,14; 3:10,12; 4:11; 5:7,9,10,12,19.

1:1 James describes himself as a "servant," as one who speaks with authority, but as one with the mind of Christ, the servant of all. James addresses his letter to the scattered church comprised of both Jews and Gentiles, but the native thought world of the letter is messianic Judaism.

APPLICATION ✣ 1:1 James, like Paul in Php 2, issues a strong call for the basic character of the Christian life to be that of servanthood after the model of Jesus himself. The witness of the Gospels is that Jesus was the Servant-Messiah. The model of servanthood is to be lived out especially by those in leadership in the church.

1:2–8 The "pure joy" James speaks of here is a complete, overflowing joy (v. 2). Although it seems strange, trials are to be occasions of such joy. Trials are the arena in which and the process through which something good develops: trust in the reliability and the goodness of God.

1:3 Trials can be a means of "testing" (v. 3). The root of this word means "approved character," linking the testing and its intended result.

1:4 The result of the testing of faith is "perseverance." The "complete" person is one whose character is fully formed according to Christian standards; it is not "perfection" according to some standard common to popular culture.

1:5 Wisdom understands God's purposes and is determined to live accordingly. James conveys the notion that God's spontaneous generosity is unwavering, regardless of our previous record.

1:8 With the words "double-minded and unstable," James is speaking of someone who constantly changes allegiances. James calls us to be people of character whose faith displays itself in action corresponding with what God has called us to be.

1:9–11 It is possible that the rich in James includes the wealthy people whose lives gave little evidence of Christian commitment, disqualifying them from true membership. The humble should rejoice because their poverty provides an arena for their faith to be tested. This allows endurance to grow. Ultimately, they will be exalted, just as Jesus had promised.

✣ 1:2–11 With wisdom comes an appreciation for the timing of God. As we experience trials in life, we ask for wisdom in prayer. Trials push us to contemplate Scripture, pray, and seek God's face. In so doing, we become more like God himself, as his love wells up within us more and more.

1:12 In calling Christians who endure "blessed," James says Christians *belong* to God. This includes intimacy with God and participation with him in his purposes.

of life[m] that the Lord has promised to those who love him.[n]

13 When tempted, no one should say, "God is tempting me." For God cannot be tempted by evil, nor does he tempt anyone; 14 but each person is tempted when they are dragged away by their own evil desire and enticed. 15 Then, after desire has conceived, it gives birth to sin;[o] and sin, when it is full-grown, gives birth to death.[p]

16 Don't be deceived,[q] my dear brothers and sisters.[r] 17 Every good and perfect gift is from above,[s] coming down from the Father of the heavenly lights, who does not change[t] like shifting shadows. 18 He chose to give us birth[u] through the word of truth, that we might be a kind of firstfruits[v] of all he created.

Listening and Doing

19 My dear brothers and sisters, take note of this: Everyone should be quick to listen, slow to speak[w] and slow to become angry, 20 because human anger does not

1:12 [m] 1Co 9:25 [n] Jas 2:5
1:15 [o] Job 15:35; Ps 7:14 [p] Ro 6:23
1:16 [q] 1Co 6:9 [r] ver 19
1:17 [s] Jn 3:27 [t] Nu 23:19; Mal 3:6
1:18 [u] Jn 1:13 [v] Eph 1:12; Rev 14:4
1:19 [w] Pr 10:19
1:21 [x] Eph 4:22 [y] Eph 1:13
1:25 [z] Jas 2:12 [a] Jn 13:17
1:26 [b] Ps 34:13; 1Pe 3:10

Jas 1:19–21 ❖ If we struggle to control our anger, how can we grow in self-control?

produce the righteousness that God desires. 21 Therefore, get rid of[x] all moral filth and the evil that is so prevalent and humbly accept the word planted in you,[y] which can save you.

22 Do not merely listen to the word, and so deceive yourselves. Do what it says. 23 Anyone who listens to the word but does not do what it says is like someone who looks at his face in a mirror 24 and, after looking at himself, goes away and immediately forgets what he looks like. 25 But whoever looks intently into the perfect law that gives freedom,[z] and continues in it — not forgetting what they have heard, but doing it — they will be blessed in what they do.[a]

26 Those who consider themselves religious and yet do not keep a tight rein on their tongues[b] deceive themselves,

---

1:13–15 Temptation originates in a personal desire born of self-interest. It renders us susceptible to evil desires. We may wrongly seek to blame others, Satan, or even God, but ultimately, we are morally responsible for our sinful actions.

1:16–18 In the phrase "the Father of the heavenly lights," James has combined two important theological ideas (v. 17). The first is that God is the Father of the universe and has power over the heavenly luminaries; both concepts recall the creation account. The second is the notion of God as Father and of God as light. James further describes God as one "who does not change like shifting shadows" (v. 17). God is light, and in him there is no shadow. God controls all the things to which we wrongfully attribute power; he controls political forces, economic forces, Satan, fate, and the stars.

The teaching of vv. 12–18 might be summed up as follows: Since we were created by God with the full potential for truth and life, we should use it and not trade it for falsehood.

✣ **1:12–18** James calls us to see trials as opportunities for growth, not evidence of God's indifference. To follow Jesus is to learn an attitude of mind and heart that is sensitive to the will and presence of God. God seeks and waits for our attention and for our hearts to be turned to him. The first step is opening the door to God in prayer, asking God to be at work in our minds and hearts and to change us into his image and likeness.

1:19–21 The opening verb, "take note of this" (v. 19), is most likely a command. It introduces the thoughts that follow: "Everyone should be quick to listen, slow to speak and slow to become angry" (v. 19). James provides two examples that illustrate his point: human anger and the righteous life that God desires. Anger, however it manifests, works against the righteousness that God wants for us.

1:21 James opens with behaviors that should not characterize the life of a Christian. Christians should "get rid of" or strip off certain behaviors (v. 21a). James instructs us to remove "moral filth" and "evil." These terms imply not only moral evil but also premeditated, evil intent. James places before us an alternative path: "Humbly accept the word planted in you, which can save you" (v. 21b). Humility is the essential attribute of the poor—those without resources who are dear to the heart of God. God's word has the power to save us. We are to nurture it, for it is a force in the process of saving us. The result of this process is that we will receive ultimate salvation.

1:22 Living a life of holiness requires a life of action. God's people must continue to grow in carrying out the commands of God's word. But hearing alone is insufficient. To hear and not to take action is to lie to oneself.

1:23–24 The image in the mirror, whether the product of a quick glance or an adoring gaze, quickly dissipates; whatever impression forms in the mind and heart while looking in a mirror is temporary. Ignoring faith's call to justice and action in the world is like this glance. When we "forget" what we look like as faithful followers of Christ, we essentially forget who and whose we are.

1:25 For James "perfect law" and "word" (v. 23) are related. For the Christian, this law is still the will of God. The perfect law, the word implanted and allowed to take root, is ultimately the very teaching of Jesus.

1:26–27 James highlights the sin of reckless speech, the theme that opened the passage (v. 19). Worship is described as worthless without actions

PEOPLE TO KNOW // JAMES, BROTHER OF JESUS

JAMES 1:22-25: After the miraculous birth of Jesus, Mary had other children by her husband, Joseph. The Gospels mention James, Joseph, Simon and Judas, as well as unnamed sisters (Mt 13:55-56). The most prominent of Jesus' half siblings mentioned in the NT is James.

In Acts, James offered the authoritative statement at the Jerusalem Council (Ac 15:13-21). He sided with Peter, Paul and Barnabas in concluding that Gentiles did not need to be circumcised in order to become Christians. He declared that the believers should not make it difficult for Gentiles to turn to God.

In Galatians, Paul mentions James as one of those who met with him in Jerusalem when Paul was a new convert to Christianity. He describes James as one of "those esteemed as pillars" of the church (Gal 2:9), along with John and Peter, who together sent Paul and Barnabas on their mission to the Gentiles.

James wrote the NT letter that bears his name. It is a book of practical wisdom for Christian living in a sometimes hostile world. James emphasizes Christian action as well as belief (Jas 2:14-17). He encourages believers to stand firm as they eagerly await Christ's return (Jas 5:7-8).

APPLICATION ✣ James had the privilege of growing up alongside Jesus. He came to see Christ as more than a brother, however. James professed Jesus as his Lord. While the Bible does not mention James's death, church tradition tells that James was martyred for his faith. Like James, we need to come to know Jesus as more than a man. By God's grace through faith, we too can discover that Jesus is indeed the Lord. May we stand firm in this faith as we eagerly await his return.

and their religion is worthless. 27Reli-
gion that God our Father accepts as pure
and faultless is this: to look after[c] orphans and widows[d] in their distress and
to keep oneself from being polluted by
the world.[e]

Favoritism Forbidden

2 My brothers and sisters, believers in
our glorious[f] Lord Jesus Christ must
not show favoritism.[g] 2Suppose a man
comes into your meeting wearing a gold
ring and fine clothes, and a poor man in
filthy old clothes also comes in. 3If you
show special attention to the man wearing fine clothes and say, "Here's a good
seat for you," but say to the poor man,
"You stand there" or "Sit on the floor by
my feet," 4have you not discriminated
among yourselves and become judges[h]
with evil thoughts?
5Listen, my dear brothers and sisters:[i]
Has not God chosen those who are poor
in the eyes of the world[j] to be rich in
faith[k] and to inherit the kingdom he
promised those who love him?[l] 6But you

1:27 [c] Mt 25:36 [d] Isa 1:17,23 [e] Ro 12:2
2:1 [f] 1Co 2:8 [g] Lev 19:15
2:4 [h] Jn 7:24
2:5 [i] Jas 1:16, 19 [j] 1Co 1:26-28 [k] Lk 12:21 [l] Jas 1:12

Jas 2:1-13 ❖ Where do we see favoritism being practiced? How can we avoid showing such favoritism, as James instructs?

motivated by a godly character. The practice of "pure religion" is described here as the control of speech, acts of charity, and resisting temptation.

✣ **1:19-27** Words have great power to both wound and heal. Our speech has the power to encourage and nourish life or to snuff it out. Which shall we choose?

2:1-4 James gives a practical illustration of favoritism in the guise of a question (vv. 2-4). It makes no sense to show favoritism based on wealth because wealth is often used to exploit Christians. James's question in v. 4 implies that the early Christian community emphasized equality among the members, in stark contrast to their surrounding culture.

2:5 James reinforces his case by citing a biblical reality (v. 5). The word James uses for "poor" had the sense of the poor who put their trust in God and not material wealth. For James, the contrast is stronger than simply rich vs. poor. It has to do with those who trust in God and those whose trust in God is mixed with a trust in the world's standards. The phrase "to be rich in faith" indicates that these poor have the kingdom's riches. Poverty can grow faith that produces this kind of wealth.
2:6-7 The community has "dishonored" the poor (v. 6). By favoring the rich they were favoring the very people who sometimes harmed the church. The wealthy, Christian and non-Christian alike, were taking poor Christians to court.

have dishonored the poor.[m] Is it not the rich who are exploiting you? Are they not the ones who are dragging you into court?[n] 7Are they not the ones who are blaspheming the noble name of him to whom you belong?

8If you really keep the royal law found in Scripture, "Love your neighbor as yourself,"[a][o] you are doing right. 9But if you show favoritism,[p] you sin and are convicted by the law as lawbreakers.[q] 10For whoever keeps the whole law and yet stumbles at just one point is guilty of breaking all of it.[r] 11For he who said, "You shall not commit adultery,"[b][s] also said, "You shall not murder."[c][t] If you do not commit adultery but do commit murder, you have become a lawbreaker.

12Speak and act as those who are going to be judged by the law that gives freedom,[u] 13because judgment without mercy will be shown to anyone who has not been merciful.[v] Mercy triumphs over judgment.

Faith and Deeds

14What good is it, my brothers and sisters, if someone claims to have faith but has no deeds?[w] Can such faith save them? 15Suppose a brother or a sister is without clothes and daily food.[x] 16If one of you says to them, "Go in peace; keep warm and well fed," but does nothing about their physical needs, what good is it?[y] 17In the same way, faith by itself, if it is not accompanied by action, is dead.

18But someone will say, "You have faith; I have deeds."

Show me your faith without deeds,[z] and I will show you my faith by my deeds.[a] 19You believe that there is one God.[b] Good! Even the demons believe that[c]—and shudder.

20You foolish person, do you want evidence that faith without deeds is useless[d]?[d] 21Was not our father Abraham considered righteous for what he did when he offered his son Isaac on the altar?[e] 22You see that his faith and his actions were working together,[f] and his faith was made complete by what he did.[g] 23And the scripture was fulfilled that says, "Abraham believed God, and it was credited to him as righteousness,"[e][h] and he was called God's friend.[i] 24You see that a person is considered righteous by what they do and not by faith alone.

2:6 [m] 1Co 11:22 [n] Ac 8:3
2:8 [o] Lev 19:18
2:9 [p] ver 1 [q] Dt 1:17
2:10 [r] Mt 5:19; Gal 3:10
2:11 [s] Ex 20:14; Dt 5:18 [t] Ex 20:13; Dt 5:17
2:12 [u] Jas 1:25
2:13 [v] Mt 5:7; 18:32-35
2:14 [w] Mt 7:26; Jas 1:22-25
2:15 [x] Mt 25:35, 36
2:16 [y] 1Jn 3:17,18
2:18 [z] Ro 3:28 [a] Jas 3:13
2:19 [b] Dt 6:4 [c] Mt 8:29; Lk 4:34
2:20 [d] ver 17,26
2:21 [e] Ge 22:9,12
2:22 [f] Heb 11:17 [g] 1Th 1:3
2:23 [h] Ge 15:6; Ro 4:3 [i] 2Ch 20:7; Isa 41:8

[a] *8* Lev. 19:18 [b] *11* Exodus 20:14; Deut. 5:18 [c] *11* Exodus 20:13; Deut. 5:17 [d] *20* Some early manuscripts *dead* [e] *23* Gen. 15:6

2:8 James refers to "the royal law." The beauty of this law is that it takes seriously both law and mercy, both sin and grace. God does not excuse us from our sin, but he does forgive us.
2:9–11 James goes on to argue that showing favoritism is sin, and this behavior convicts one of breaking the royal law (v. 9). In v. 10, James again echoes Jesus' teachings when he says that to stumble at just one point of the law is to be guilty in all points. The point here is that the injunction to love our neighbor as ourselves is total: Christians cannot pick and choose who is to be the neighbor or when they are called to follow this law.
2:12 James links profession and action. Here is a strong reminder of the true center of the Christian life—the perfect law that is planted within us. For both Jesus and James, the pivot point of law and judgment is the law of love for one's neighbor.
2:13 James continues to follow Jesus by arguing that those who do not show mercy will not receive it. A merciful attitude demonstrates that a person truly is alive in Christ. James is pointing to the danger of allowing an unmerciful attitude to grow. If its growth is not slowed and reversed, it will lead to future judgment.

2:1–13 In the US, there are clearly defined roles and professions that, we think, deserve greater respect than others. Wealth is the clearest marker of social status in our culture. Compared to the first century, our age offers a variety of options for its display. James is not against wealth, but he is against the church becoming an arena for the display of wealth used to enhance status.

2:14 The "faith" in view in the second question of v. 14 is workless faith, not faith per se.
2:15–16 James envisions a situation in which church members fail to display even the most basic forms of charity to one another. The point cannot be missed: Faith without deeds fails to accomplish the aim of true faith—it is only a shadow, a shade, an impostor of true faith.
2:18 James offers a rational argument to show that "faith" that doesn't produce deeds is dead; it has no saving power. True faith always changes the heart and results in acts of mercy and compassion. The idea that there is a legitimate faith without deeds is consistently denied in James.
2:19 James remarks that believing in the one God is an excellent starting point, but such an intellectual conclusion is not true faith. Even the demons know this much. Religion that is worth something involves action that grows from the heart.
2:20 The point here is that "faith" without works is "faith" in name only.
2:21–24 Abraham illustrates the linkage between faith and deeds. James points out that Abraham's faith was not merely an intellectual agreement; rather, it was a faith that displayed itself in trusting

25In the same way, was not even Rahab
the prostitute considered righteous for
what she did when she gave lodging to
the spies and sent them off in a different
direction?[j] 26As the body without the spirit is dead, so faith without deeds is dead.[k]

Taming the Tongue

3 Not many of you should become
teachers, my fellow believers, because you know that we who teach will
be judged more strictly. 2We all stumble[l]
in many ways. Anyone who is never at
fault in what they say[m] is perfect,[n] able
to keep their whole body in check.[o]

3When we put bits into the mouths of
horses to make them obey us, we can turn
the whole animal.[p] 4Or take ships as an example. Although they are so large and are
driven by strong winds, they are steered
by a very small rudder wherever the pilot
wants to go. 5Likewise, the tongue is a
small part of the body, but it makes great
boasts.[q] Consider what a great forest is set
on fire by a small spark. 6The tongue also
is a fire,[r] a world of evil among the parts
of the body. It corrupts the whole body,[s]
sets the whole course of one's life on fire,
and is itself set on fire by hell.

7All kinds of animals, birds, reptiles
and sea creatures are being tamed and
have been tamed by mankind, 8but no
human being can tame the tongue. It
is a restless evil, full of deadly poison.[t]

9With the tongue we praise our Lord
and Father, and with it we curse human
beings, who have been made in God's
likeness.[u] 10Out of the same mouth come
praise and cursing. My brothers and sisters, this should not be. 11Can both fresh
water and salt water flow from the same
spring? 12My brothers and sisters, can a
fig tree bear olives, or a grapevine bear
figs?[v] Neither can a salt spring produce
fresh water.

Two Kinds of Wisdom

13Who is wise and understanding
among you? Let them show it[w] by their

Jas 3:5-12 ❖ How can we tame our tongues to keep our speech righteous? Why is this so difficult?

2:25 [j] Heb 11:31
2:26 [k] ver 17,20
3:2 [l] 1Ki 8:46; Jas 2:10 [m] 1Pe 3:10 [n] Mt 12:37 [o] Jas 1:26
3:3 [p] Ps 32:9
3:5 [q] Ps 12:3,4
3:6 [r] Pr 16:27 [s] Mt 15:11,18,19
3:8 [t] Ps 140:3; Ro 3:13
3:9 [u] Ge 1:26,27; 1Co 11:7
3:12 [v] Mt 7:16
3:13 [w] Jas 2:18

---

actions that involved great risks, such as the near sacrifice of Isaac.

2:25–26 Although Rahab was a woman of dubious reputation, her actions were evidence of faith. Rahab is included among the ancestors of Jesus (Mt 1:5). She showed hospitality to the spies (just as Abraham did to the three strangers in Ge 18). Both Abraham and Rahab showed hospitality to those whose outward appearance mirrored the poor in the church.

✣ **2:14–26** In the hallowed halls of universities and colleges and in the sanctified confines of churches, issues such as community development, social action, and justice are studied and discussed. Yet true Christian social reformers demonstrate true justice with their blood, sweat, tears, and joy. They offer a living monument to hope for what can be—faith that results in action, a passion for the good of others, and compassion that flows from the very heart of God. James encourages us to let these virtues lodge in our hearts and minds so that we move forward in action that is fitting to the faith that we profess.

3:1 James cautions teachers in view of the final judgment (v. 1). By nature of their position, teachers have an exceedingly great opportunity to influence others within the congregation—both for eternal benefit and harm.

3:2 James admits a very human truth—we all stumble frequently. Moreover, there is at least one sin that is common to everyone: the sin of the tongue. The notion of "perfect" must be that of completeness and maturity, just as in 1:4.

3:3–5 James begins a series of everyday illustrations to demonstrate the tongue's power to either corrode or nurture. Few disasters in the ancient world were more feared than fire, as the ancients possessed precious few resources to battle it. The point of the image is to emphasize the great destructive power of the tongue.

3:6–12 The tongue is often guilty of realizing its potential for evil and, in so doing, infects the rest of the body. The tongue can corrupt or stain the entire person.

3:7–8 In contrast to our inability to control the tongue, James offers the idea that human beings can train, and have trained, members of the animal kingdom (v. 7). The tongue is irrational and dangerous, like an inadequately caged beast (v. 8).

3:9–10 Having made the claim that the tongue is untrustworthy and treacherous, James goes on to provide an example. How can worshipers consciously mistreat their fellows and then expect to worship God in purity (v. 10)?

3:11–12 James continues to point out that abusive speech is irrational.

✣ **3:1–12** Just as an enormously destructive wildfire can be triggered as the result of one careless match, so there is great potential for damage stored up in the tongue. Words must be chosen carefully and used with the wisdom of God. This is especially true for teachers and those who have authority over others.

3:13 True wisdom is marked by humility. The teachers James has in view have assumed a position of authority, offering themselves as "wise." Neither

good life, by deeds done in the humility
that comes from wisdom. 14But if you
harbor bitter envy and selfish ambition[x] in your hearts, do not boast about
it or deny the truth.[y] 15Such "wisdom"
does not come down from heaven[z] but
is earthly, unspiritual, demonic.[a] 16For
where you have envy and selfish ambition, there you find disorder and every
evil practice.
17But the wisdom that comes from
heaven[b] is first of all pure; then
peace-loving, considerate, submissive,
full of mercy[c] and good fruit, impartial
and sincere.[d] 18Peacemakers who sow in
peace reap a harvest of righteousness.[e]

Submit Yourselves to God

4 What causes fights and quarrels[f]
among you? Don't they come from
your desires that battle[g] within you?
2You desire but do not have, so you kill.
You covet but you cannot get what you
want, so you quarrel and fight. You do
not have because you do not ask God.
3When you ask, you do not receive,[h] because you ask with wrong motives,[i] that

3:14 [x] ver 16 [y] Jas 5:19
3:15 [z] Jas 1:17 [a] 1Ti 4:1
3:17 [b] 1Co 2:6 [c] Lk 6:36 [d] Ro 12:9
3:18 [e] Pr 11:18; Isa 32:17
4:1 [f] Titus 3:9 [g] Ro 7:23
4:3 [h] Ps 18:41 [i] 1Jn 3:22; 5:14

Jas 4:4-10 ❖ What does friendship with the world look like? Why does it mean enmity against God?

you may spend what you get on your
pleasures.
4You adulterous people,[a] don't you
know that friendship with the world[j]
means enmity against God?[k] Therefore,
anyone who chooses to be a friend of the
world becomes an enemy of God.[l] 5Or do
you think Scripture says without reason
that he jealously longs for the spirit he
has caused to dwell in us[b]? 6But he gives
us more grace. That is why Scripture says:

"God opposes the proud
but shows favor to the humble."[c][m]

7Submit yourselves, then, to God. Resist the devil,[n] and he will flee from you.
8Come near to God and he will come near

4:4 [j] Jas 1:27 [k] 1Jn 2:15 [l] Jn 15:19
4:6 [m] Ps 138:6; Pr 3:34; Mt 23:12
4:7 [n] Eph 4:27; 1Pe 5:6-9

[a] 4 An allusion to covenant unfaithfulness; see Hosea 3:1. [b] 5 Or *that the spirit he caused to dwell in us envies intensely*; or *that the Spirit he caused to dwell in us longs jealously*
[c] 6 Prov. 3:34

Moses (Nu 12:1–3) nor Jesus (Mt 11:29) were interested in popularity or power. This is the spirit of true wisdom.

3:14 Conflict has come to the Christian community as a result of personal status-seeking on the part of some teachers.

3:15 James makes a clear argument that the wisdom of these teachers is not neutral or trivial. He does this by arranging the sources of this "wisdom" in an escalating crescendo of wickedness. The first is "earthly." Next, this wisdom is "unspiritual." The term describes a life without the Spirit of God. Finally, such "wisdom" is, worst of all, instigated by demons and the fallen spiritual world.

3:16 The wisdom of James's opponents has done nothing to strengthen the body. It has only brought "disorder and every evil practice." Their teaching has caused the church to seriously question its direction and even its heart and soul.

3:17-18 James categorizes heavenly wisdom with seven virtues that characterize it. Such wisdom also creates a peacemaking spirit (v. 18). This is particularly important, given the problem of disagreement in the church.

✣ **3:13-18** "Do not be fooled," James warns. False teaching is dangerous in the extreme. The poison begins innocently in our minds and hearts. It grows to dominate our actions. Finally, it spreads to infect the community around us. James reminds us that the most effective course to avoid this evil is to walk firmly and with resolve in the path of heavenly wisdom and its fruits.

4:1-3 The church James addresses was plagued by a host of ills that followed the pattern of its culture. Certain teachers encouraged the pursuit of status. Organized against these teachers were believers who correctly understood the threat. The members of this group reacted differently to those following the teachers of false wisdom—some wanting peace at any price, others advocating a fight for the soul of the church.

James says their disputes come from the "desires" within them (v. 1). The "prayers" his readers have offered are marked by their desire for "pleasures" (v. 3). They need patience and a willingness to be molded by God.

4:4 James offers a rebuke as if he is speaking to badly behaved children. By designating them "adulterous people," he recalls a frequent OT rebuke. Many choose friendship with the world without realizing it means standing in opposition to God.

4:5 This verse may summarize many OT passages that speak of the jealousy of God. James's point is that God earnestly desires his Spirit to reside in us. God wants us to come home and to live with him. Instead, we follow the world's wisdom that will never help us achieve what we are truly seeking.

4:6 James holds out a lifeline. God's grace, he says, is still available if they will humble themselves. Yet God's face is set against the proud.

4:7-10 Verse 7 opens a series of ten commands built on the foundation laid in v. 6. These commands comprise James's recipe for humility before God. The first component of submission to God is to "resist the devil" (v. 7). Satan's power was severely

to you.[o] Wash your hands,[p] you sinners,
and purify your hearts, you double-
minded.[q] 9 Grieve, mourn and wail.
Change your laughter to mourning and
your joy to gloom.[r] 10 Humble yourselves
before the Lord, and he will lift you up.
11 Brothers and sisters, do not slander
one another.[s] Anyone who speaks against
a brother or sister[a] or judges them[t] speaks
against the law and judges it. When you
judge the law, you are not keeping it,[u] but
sitting in judgment on it. 12 There is only
one Lawgiver and Judge, the one who is
able to save and destroy.[v] But you—who
are you to judge your neighbor?[w]

Boasting About Tomorrow

13 Now listen, you who say, "Today or
tomorrow we will go to this or that city,
spend a year there, carry on business
and make money."[x] 14 Why, you do not
even know what will happen tomorrow.
What is your life? You are a mist that
appears for a little while and then vanishes.[y] 15 Instead, you ought to say, "If
it is the Lord's will,[z] we will live and do
this or that." 16 As it is, you boast in your
arrogant schemes. All such boasting is
evil.[a] 17 If anyone, then, knows the good
they ought to do and doesn't do it, it is
sin for them.[b]

Warning to Rich Oppressors

5 Now listen, you rich people,[c] weep
and wail because of the misery that
is coming on you. 2 Your wealth has rotted, and moths have eaten your clothes.[d]
3 Your gold and silver are corroded. Their
corrosion will testify against you and
eat your flesh like fire. You have hoarded wealth in the last days.[e] 4 Look! The
wages you failed to pay the workers[f]
who mowed your fields are crying out
against you. The cries[g] of the harvesters have reached the ears of the Lord
Almighty.[h] 5 You have lived on earth
in luxury and self-indulgence. You

4:8 [o] 2Ch 15:2 [p] Isa 1:16 [q] Jas 1:8
4:9 [r] Lk 6:25
4:11 [s] 1Pe 2:1 [t] Mt 7:1 [u] Jas 1:22
4:12 [v] Mt 10:28 [w] Ro 14:4
4:13 [x] Pr 27:1
4:14 [y] Job 7:7; Ps 102:3
4:15 [z] Ac 18:21
4:16 [a] 1Co 5:6
4:17 [b] Lk 12:47; Jn 9:41
5:1 [c] Lk 6:24
5:2 [d] Job 13:28; Mt 6:19,20
5:3 [e] ver 7,8
5:4 [f] Lev 19:13 [g] Dt 24:15 [h] Ro 9:29

[a] 11 The Greek word for *brother or sister* (*adelphos*) refers here to a believer, whether man or woman, as part of God's family.

---

limited at the crucifixion and resurrection. It is possible that James has this in mind.

To the admonition to cleanse themselves, James adds acts of remorse (v. 9). In urging grief and a shift from laughter to mourning and joy to gloom, James reminds his readers that the false paths they thought would lead to true laughter and joy are dead ends and need to be abandoned.

> **4:1–10** Our world is awash in copies of true community. Christians must do more than work for structural change, for structures are weak and easily co-opted by Satan. The heart must change, for without these deeper, Spirit-inspired values, the law is merely external. James pleads with us to draw near to God, not merely adopt moral guidelines of which God would approve.

4:11–12 James has in mind people's harsh criticism and condemnation of one another. This command not to judge one another was central to the ethical teaching of Jesus (Mt 7:1). To ignore this command is, in effect, to reject Christ and to render the self-description "Christian" a falsehood. When we judge others, we not only take to ourselves what belongs to God alone, but we also invite and pronounce judgment on ourselves.

4:13–14 James is not arguing against making money or even against the desire to make money; rather, he is against the smug attitude of the false teachers. Such certainty reveals an attitude that does not take God seriously enough and places the priority of making money ahead of honoring God. For James, the real question is how to approach life when the outcome is uncertain. His answer is to trust God's graciousness, not human plans.

4:15 Clearly, James is not against planning. Rather, James wants such planning to be given its proper priority and none higher. God must be in control of such planning.

4:16–17 James has already mentioned boasting. These merchants should have made their plans in prayer, anticipating that God may change them. Bragging about such plans and making them the basis for our security is functionally denying the importance—and perhaps even the very existence—of God in our lives.

> **4:11–17** When James counsels us that tomorrow is never certain, he is right. Because this is so, Christians need to rely first on God when looking toward or planning for the future. To do anything else is to lack integrity; it is to be double-minded. Jesus made decisions based on principles rooted in Scripture and a sensitivity to the will of God. James would have us lead lives of similar faithfulness—lives that integrate Jesus' teachings in our hearts, minds, attitudes, and actions.

5:1 James begins by condemning the selfish attitude of the wealthy landowners. These wealthy people must "weep and wail." The reason is not their wealth per se, but that they have not used their wealth to help the poor.

5:2–3 Riches are worthless when it comes to eternal salvation. Christians who have heard Jesus' message and yet hoard wealth are morally liable for their choices.

5:4 James lists specific behaviors that have contributed to the hoarding of wealth. Because of these things, God's voice of judgment against the wealthy has already begun to sound.

5:5 This verse recalls the parable of the rich man and Lazarus in Lk 16:19–31.

Jas 5:7–8 ❖ How can this call for patience be helpful to believers who are suffering today?

have fattened yourselves[i] in the day of
slaughter.[a][j] 6You have condemned and
murdered the innocent one,[k] who was
not opposing you.

Patience in Suffering

7Be patient, then, brothers and sisters, until the Lord's coming. See how
the farmer waits for the land to yield
its valuable crop, patiently waiting for
the autumn and spring rains.[l] 8You too,
be patient and stand firm, because the
Lord's coming is near.[m] 9Don't grumble
against one another, brothers and sisters,[n] or you will be judged. The Judge[o]
is standing at the door![p]

10Brothers and sisters, as an example
of patience in the face of suffering, take
the prophets[q] who spoke in the name
of the Lord. 11As you know, we count as
blessed[r] those who have persevered. You
have heard of Job's perseverance[s] and
have seen what the Lord finally brought
about.[t] The Lord is full of compassion
and mercy.[u]

12Above all, my brothers and sisters, do
not swear—not by heaven or by earth
or by anything else. All you need to say
is a simple "Yes" or "No." Otherwise you
will be condemned.[v]

The Prayer of Faith

13Is anyone among you in trouble? Let
them pray.[w] Is anyone happy? Let them
sing songs of praise.[x] 14Is anyone among
you sick? Let them call the elders of the
church to pray over them and anoint
them with oil[y] in the name of the Lord.
15And the prayer offered in faith will make
the sick person well; the Lord will raise
them up. If they have sinned, they will be
forgiven. 16Therefore confess your sins[z] to
each other and pray for each other so that
you may be healed.[a] The prayer of a righteous person is powerful and effective.[b]

17Elijah was a human being, even as we
are.[c] He prayed earnestly that it would
not rain, and it did not rain on the land
for three and a half years.[d] 18Again he

5:5 [i] Am 6:1 [j] Jer 12:3; 25:34
5:6 [k] Heb 10:38
5:7 [l] Dt 11:14; Jer 5:24
5:8 [m] Ro 13:11; 1Pe 4:7
5:9 [n] Jas 4:11 [o] 1Co 4:5; 1Pe 4:5 [p] Mt 24:33
5:10 [q] Mt 5:12
5:11 [r] Mt 5:10 [s] Job 1:21,22; 2:10 [t] Job 42:10,12-17 [u] Nu 14:18
5:12 [v] Mt 5:34-37
5:13 [w] Ps 50:15 [x] Col 3:16
5:14 [y] Mk 6:13
5:16 [z] Mt 3:6 [a] 1Pe 2:24 [b] Jn 9:31
5:17 [c] Ac 14:15 [d] 1Ki 17:1; Lk 4:25

[a] 5 Or *yourselves as in a day of feasting*

5:6 The final accusation aimed at these individuals is their plotting against and even murder of the innocent. The death referred to here may be the result of starvation caused by the withholding of wages.

✜ **5:1–6** The idea of judgment in the NT is enormously complex; it includes both judgment that convicts, which has as its aim restoration (1Co 11:32), and separation from God and eternal destruction (Jn 3:19; Heb 10:27). It is unclear which James has in mind in our text, but neither is to be desired. At the very least, the "misery" he imagines is the realization that the wealth and the material goods in which we trusted have turned (v. 1); they have proved untrustworthy, having rotted before our eyes. What would James think of the way American churches and their members spend money?

5:7–8 Christians are instructed to be patient until the Lord comes (v. 7). As a practical illustration, James refers to a farmer who waits patiently for harvest time and for the autumn and spring rains. Whether or not James envisioned an imminent return of Christ, perhaps the point here is that as Christians we are to live in community with one another as if the new day has already dawned.

5:9 Life brings trials, but no one is served by cultivating a spirit of complaining.

5:10–11 The prophets endured, patiently and hopefully waiting for God's judgment and mercy. As a result of his sufferings, Job gained greater knowledge of God.

✜ **5:7–11** People in times of trouble naturally hope for release. But difficult circumstances are considered a normal and necessary part of the process of spiritual growth and yield certain results that prepare us for the age to come.

5:12 James aligns with the teaching of the OT that false swearing and the giving of oaths is forbidden (e.g., Lev 19:12).

5:13–18 The true theme of the passage is prayer (v. 16). James here deals with the prayer of the individual (v. 13), the prayer of the elders (vv. 14–15), the prayers of friends and companions for one another (v. 16), and finally the prayer of the righteous prophet Elijah (vv. 17–18).

5:13 The first issue raised is that of suffering (v. 13a). In such times, James advocates prayer. It allows us to be active and positive and keeps us in communion with God. Then James discusses the case of those who are happy (v. 13b). God desires our prayers in both difficult and pleasant times.

5:14–16 The sick person is to be "pray[ed] over" (v. 14b). It is obvious that the basis for this action is the firm belief that God is the source of healing. James clearly teaches here that sickness can be alleviated through public confession and prayer.

5:17–18 Just as the prayer of Elijah resulted in rain, so the prayer of the righteous believer can heal a Christian.

✜ **5:12–18** Our world places a great premium on eliminating discomfort. In the face of this potent cultural value, evangelicals need to go

CHARACTER OF GOD // GOD IS COMPASSIONATE

James 5:11: The Lord is full of compassion and mercy.

God's compassion is so central to his being that when he described himself to Moses, he called himself "compassionate and gracious" (Ex 34:6). "Compassionate" is the first word God used to describe himself.

To illustrate God's compassion, Psalm 103 uses a parenting analogy. The way a good and loving father has compassion on his children pictures for us the way God has compassion on those who fear and honor him. Sadly, many people have not experienced loving human fathers. God's compassion, however, is perfect, outshining the love of even the best human parents. Hosea 11 deepens this parenting metaphor, describing in loving terms the way God picked up his child Israel (here called Ephraim) and taught his people how to walk, leading them with "ties of love" (Hos 11:1–4).

God's compassion leads him to pursue his children when they fall into sin. The Bible shows time and again the way God will not give up on redeeming his people. James 5:7–11 describes God helping his people persevere in suffering. Similarly, when the Israelites repeatedly failed to follow God, pursuing idols and abandoning justice, God did not reject them completely. Instead, he promised a new covenant by which he would bind his people to himself (Jer 31:31). God did not give up on them even though they continued to fail him.

Jesus Christ is the ultimate embodiment of God's compassion. God gave his beloved Son for the sake of sinful and wayward humans. The blood of Jesus, shed on the cross, is the "new covenant" (Lk 22:20). Jesus willingly suffered and died to accomplish God's salvation. This is compassion of the highest degree: to sacrifice oneself for one's beloved.

APPLICATION ✣ God's compassion is a deep comfort. When we suffer, when we feel abandoned, when we lose hope—we can remember that Christ is able to empathize with us in our suffering (Heb 4:15). He suffered, too, for our sake.

God's compassion also comforts and assures us when we fall into sin. When we repent before God, he does not see us through the lens of his justice for our sin, for if we are in Christ, justice was already carried out at the cross. Instead, God receives us back into his compassionate care.

prayed, and the heavens gave rain, and
the earth produced its crops.[e]
19My brothers and sisters, if one of you
should wander from the truth[f] and some-
one should bring that person back,[g] 20remember this: Whoever turns a sinner from
the error of their way will save[h] them from
death and cover over a multitude of sins.[i]

5:18 [e]1Ki 18:41-45
5:19 [f]Jas 3:14
[g]Mt 18:15
5:20 [h]Ro 11:14
[i]1Pe 4:8

against the grain and adopt a biblical understanding of adversity. God uses adversity for spiritual preparation. Prayer in adversity also urges us to renounce the pride that is associated with the world's materialism and self-centeredness. This has been a constant theme in James.

5:19–20 James returns to the themes of sin and forgiveness. In so doing, he reveals his pastoral heart. In this one sentence, James collects no less than three significant theological ideas: (1) Christians have the opportunity to care for one another through loving correction. (2) The penalty for sin is death. (3) Reconciliation "cover[s]" a multitude of sins (v. 20).

Sin is subtle, tenacious, and dangerous; it should not be underestimated. Christians have a responsibility to their world and to one another.

✣ **5:19–20** The teaching of James throughout his letter often feels harsh and even rigid. Yet here, at the end of his letter, James provides a strong touch of grace. The note that has sounded softly through most of the letter here rings out loud and true: Forgiveness must be offered, but it must be balanced with faith that is active, faith that has captured mind and heart and body. James calls God's people to moral purity and to maintaining a heart of forgiveness. When we do so, we give evidence that we are true children of God, combining both faith and action in the fashion that James has taught.

1 Peter

Author: The apostle Peter

Audience: Primarily Gentile believers in Pontus, Galatia, Cappadocia, western Asia Minor and Bithynia

Date: AD 60 to 64

Theme: Peter gives God's encouragement to those suffering persecution for their allegiance to Jesus to live exemplary lives within their culture.

Reading 1 Peter

First Peter does not contain a specific flow of argumentation as do some of the NT books and letters. Instead, the author writes about a life of holiness in the context of pain and suffering. It may be helpful to imagine that you are reading a sermon by the apostle Peter as you read the book in one sitting.

PERSPECTIVE

The complex debate over the relationship between church and state in modern life makes the first-century wisdom of this letter exceedingly relevant to our modern world. Peter, in writing this text, had this relationship on the front burner of his mind. It is almost as if he were writing both to first-century Christians wondering about how to survive as aliens and strangers in the Roman Empire and to twenty-first-century Christians trying to live holy lives in a secularized, unholy culture.

True, important circumstances have put these two communities, separated by 1900 years, on opposite ends of the social and economic spectra: first-century Christians were politically, socially, and economically disadvantaged, while twentieth-century American Christians have the numbers to be politically, socially, and economically powerful. Still, the two groups have much in common in trying to live lives of holy endurance in the face of suffering.

It is important to note a crucial difference between the perspectives on this issue given in modern works, however, and the timeless truth given by Peter. In the United States, for example, the public media, in commenting on both the world and national scene, regularly approach these issues from the point of view of human rights and legality. No matter how sympathetic to the religious dimensions of the controversy these individuals are, they usually focus on United Nations policies on human rights and religious freedom, Thomas Jefferson's "wall of separation" between church and state, the stand that various politi-

Event	Date
Jesus' birth (c. 6/5 BC)	
Peter becomes a disciple (c. AD 26)	
Jesus' death, resurrection and ascension (c. AD 30)	
Paul's conversion (c. AD 35)	
Council at Jerusalem (c. AD 49/50)	
Nero's reign (AD 54–68)	
Book of 1 Peter written (c. AD 60–64)	
Destruction of Jerusalem's temple (c. AD 70)	

Timeline scale: 10 BC, AD 1, 10, 20, 30, 40, 50, 60, 70, 80, 90, 100

cians take on the issue, and the ideological makeup of the Supreme Court—the final legal arbiter of such issues.

As important as these perspectives are to Christians today, however, it is instructive to note that Peter does not approach this topic from the point of view of human rights and legality. Rather, he approaches it from the point of view of our relationship to God. He tells us that Christians survive in a hostile environment not by legal proceedings against persecutors but by endurance; not by imposing a lifestyle on others through law but by living holy lives that compel others to follow us; not by destroying unbelievers with sound bites and innuendo but by respecting them even as we witness to the eternal truths of the gospel.

For Peter, the burning questions he addresses of place, rights, and attitude have less to do with legal deeds to property than with being at home in a strange and temporary land; much less to do with slippery moral relativism than with the gritty realities of family responsibilities and tough love; almost nothing to do with maximizing material advantages in the present and everything to do with seeing this world through the future-oriented lenses of Christian hope and promise. It is this spiritual/theological perspective that makes 1 Peter the primary resource for Christians trying to sort out their place in our modern world.

Key Verses

But you are a chosen people, a royal priesthood, a holy nation, God's special possession, that you may declare the praises of him who called you out of darkness into his wonderful light. Once you were not a people, but now you are the people of God; once you had not received mercy, but now you have received mercy.

—1 Peter 2:9–10

TAKING THE NEXT STEPS

This first letter of the apostle Peter may have been written to people whom he led to Christ in his work as a missionary. Because these Christians were suffering for their faith during a time of persecution, Peter used his words to give them hope and to encourage them to persevere in their commitment to Christ. At the same time, he gave them practical advice for Christian living.

This letter demonstrates what it means to live as a Christian in a hostile world. (1) The resurrection and the return of Jesus Christ form the inspiration we need to persevere in our Christian commitment. (2) Regardless of what standards society uses to determine human value and behavior, we derive our standing as God's precious and redeemed children from the life-giving Stone (1Pe 2:4–10), and we derive our standards of holy living from the Word of God. (3) In all our words and actions, we should be concerned about our witness to the world. (4) It is possible to withstand suffering for the sake of the gospel if we look at how Jesus suffered injustice for our sake. (5) The church should be a community of love and support for all Christians.

WHAT TO LOOK FOR IN 1 PETER

- Living in hope and holiness (ch. 1)
- Living in church and society (chs. 2–3)
- Living and suffering for God (ch. 4)

1 Peter, an apostle of Jesus Christ,[a]

To God's elect,[b] exiles scattered
throughout the provinces of Pontus,
Galatia, Cappadocia, Asia and Bithynia,[c] 2who have been chosen according to
the foreknowledge[d] of God the Father,
through the sanctifying work of the Spirit,[e] to be obedient to Jesus Christ and
sprinkled with his blood:[f]

Grace and peace be yours in abundance.

Praise to God for a Living Hope

3Praise be to the God and Father of our
Lord Jesus Christ![g] In his great mercy[h]
he has given us new birth into a living
hope through the resurrection of Jesus
Christ from the dead,[i] 4and into an inheritance that can never perish, spoil or
fade. This inheritance is kept in heaven
for you,[j] 5who through faith are shielded
by God's power[k] until the coming of the
salvation that is ready to be revealed in
the last time. 6In all this you greatly rejoice,[l] though now for a little while[m] you
may have had to suffer grief in all kinds
of trials.[n] 7These have come so that the
proven genuineness[o] of your faith — of
greater worth than gold, which perishes even though refined by fire[p] — may
result in praise, glory and honor when
Jesus Christ is revealed.[q] 8Though you
have not seen him, you love him; and
even though you do not see him now,
you believe in him[r] and are filled with
an inexpressible and glorious joy, 9for
you are receiving the end result of your
faith, the salvation of your souls.[s]

1:1 [a] 2Pe 1:1 [b] Mt 24:22 [c] Ac 16:7
1:2 [d] Ro 8:29 [e] 2Th 2:13 [f] Heb 10:22; 12:24
1:3 [g] 2Co 1:3; Eph 1:3 [h] Titus 3:5; Jas 1:18 [i] 1Co 15:20
1:4 [j] Col 1:5
1:5 [k] Jn 10:28
1:6 [l] Ro 5:2 [m] 1Pe 5:10 [n] Jas 1:2
1:7 [o] Jas 1:3 [p] Job 23:10; Ps 66:10; Pr 17:3 [q] Ro 2:7
1:8 [r] Jn 20:29
1:9 [s] Ro 6:22

1Pe 1:8–9 ❖ How have we experienced the "inexpressible joy" that Peter says accompanies belief in Christ?

1:1–2 Peter's salutation contains pastoral warmth and theological depth. Peter was an "apostle of Jesus Christ" (v. 1). An apostle is one who was personally called by Jesus Christ to a special ministry of founding the church. Peter uses important terms to describe his readers' social and spiritual status. To be "elect" means to be a recipient of God's grace.

This group of churches to which Peter wrote was composed of socially marginalized people, and their faith compounded their social conditions. They were castaways because of their social status and because of their commitment to Jesus.

"Grace" and "peace" (v. 2) exemplify not only friendliness to others but the rootedness of that friendliness in the gracious and peacemaking ways of God.

APPLICATION ✜ **1:1–2** With the rising influence of Christian attempts at political activism in the Western world, this text offers two words of exhortation. First, it urges us to act as Christians and in a Christian manner; second, it urges us to understand that our fundamental identity is as a child of God, not as a part of our social circle or political party.

1:3–5 God the Father is blessed because "he has given [believers] new birth," which is the result of his mercy (v. 3). Believers are born into "a living hope" (v. 3) and an "inheritance" (v.4). God permits them to be part of the special people of his favor (2:10). God's mercy initiates their new birth, and their new birth inspires a "living hope." That living hope is defined by "an inheritance that can never perish, spoil or fade" (1:4). That inheritance is their completed salvation and eternal life in the kingdom of God. The only condition God sets for his people is that they must have faith (v. 5).

1:6–7 The problem facing these Christians in Asia Minor is that they are suffering "grief in all kinds of trials" (v. 6).

1:8–9 Since his readers will be found acceptable to God when Jesus Christ is revealed, Peter turns

LOCATIONS OF EVENTS IN THE LIFE OF PETER

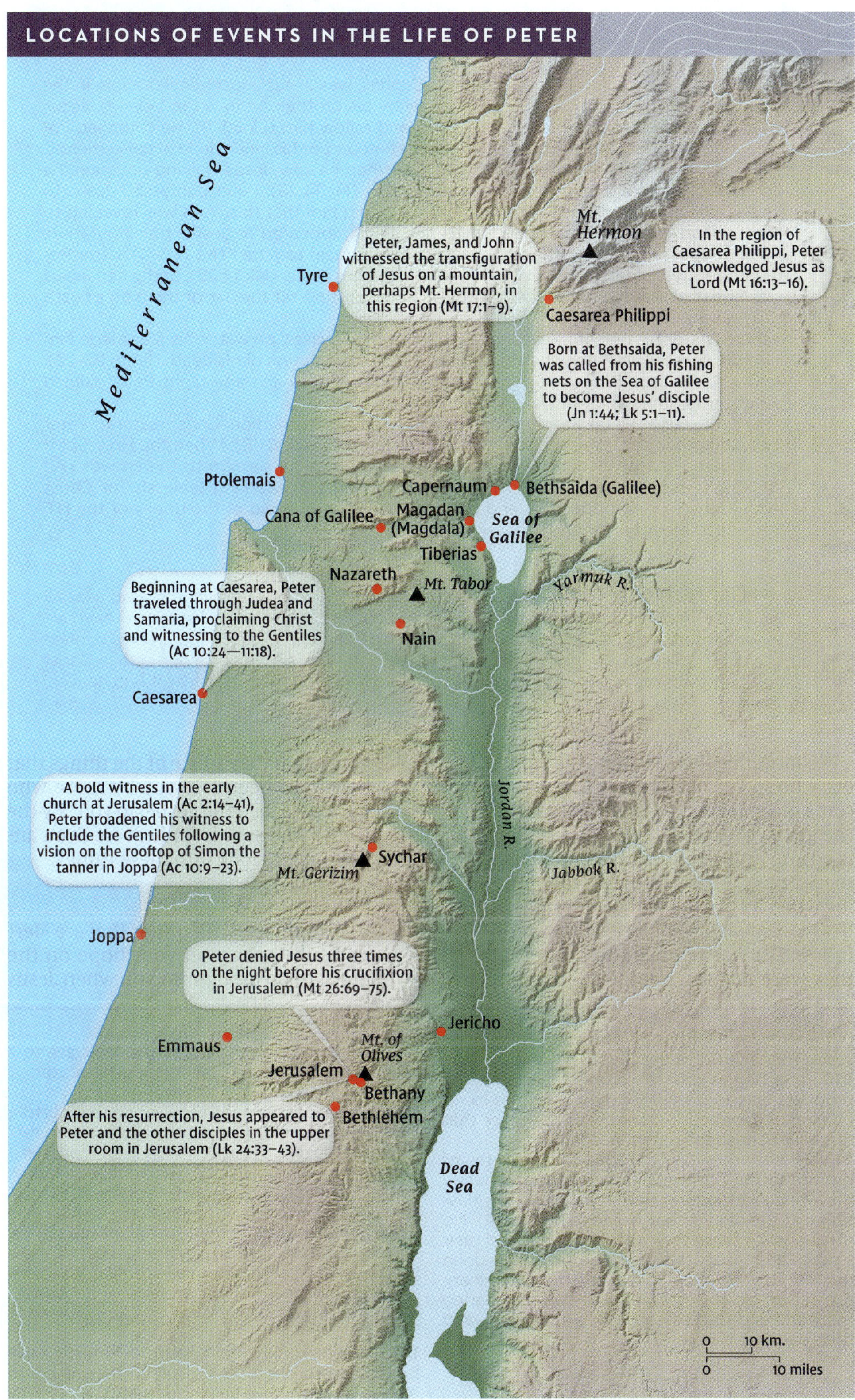

PEOPLE TO KNOW // PETER

1 PETER 1:1–9: Peter, also called Simon or Cephas, was Jesus' most vocal disciple in the Gospels. Peter was first introduced to Jesus by his brother, Andrew (Jn 1:41–42). Jesus later called Peter to leave his life of fishing and follow him (Lk 5:1–11). He complied immediately and became one of Jesus' disciples and part of his inner circle of close friends.

Peter was bold and sometimes impulsive. When he saw Jesus walking on water, he asked Jesus to call him out onto the water also (Mt 14:28). Peter confessed Jesus to be the Christ, Son of the living God, and Jesus told him that this truth was revealed to him by God (Mt 17:16–17). When Moses and Elijah appeared at Jesus' transfiguration, Peter suggested building shelters so they could remain together (Mt 17:3–4). Later Peter stridently claimed he would never fall away from Jesus (Mk 14:29), and when Jesus was arrested, Peter tried to fight off the guards, cutting off the ear of the high priest's servant (Jn 18:10).

Peter's story is one of highs and lows. Though he walked on water, his fear made him sink. Jesus rebuked Peter when he opposed Jesus' prediction of his death (Mt 16:22–23). And despite promising never to fall away from Jesus, that same night Peter denied Jesus three times (Mk 14:72).

Still, God used Peter for great things. After Jesus' resurrection, Christ restored Peter by leading him to profess his devotion three times (Jn 21:15–19). When the Holy Spirit was poured out on Pentecost, Peter preached a powerful sermon to the crowds (Ac 2:14–39). Peter was a pillar of the early church (Gal 2:9), working tirelessly for Christ even in the face of opposition and persecution. He wrote two of the books of the NT. Peter died a martyr for his faith (Jn 21:19).

APPLICATION God used Peter's passion and energy to build his church. God uses all kinds of personalities, from the thoughtful and quiet to the vocal and assertive. No matter what our personality, the important thing is to share in Peter's faith and his confession: that Jesus is the Messiah, the Son of the living God. As we place our faith in Christ and give our lives to him, God continues to build his kingdom on earth as it is in heaven.

10Concerning this salvation, the prophets, who spoke[t] of the grace that was to
come to you, searched intently and with
the greatest care,[u] 11trying to find out
the time and circumstances to which
the Spirit of Christ[v] in them was pointing when he predicted the sufferings of
the Messiah and the glories that would
follow. 12It was revealed to them that
they were not serving themselves but
you, when they spoke of the things that
have now been told you by those who
have preached the gospel to you[w] by the
Holy Spirit sent from heaven. Even angels long to look into these things.

Be Holy

13Therefore, with minds that are alert
and fully sober, set your hope on the
grace to be brought to you when Jesus

1:10 [t] Mt 26:24 [u] Mt 13:17
1:11 [v] 2Pe 1:21
1:12 [w] ver 25

---

to the present relationship of these Christians to Jesus. They love Christ despite not having seen him.

1:10 Peter begins with the prophetic inquiry. The prophets' passion, whether they knew the exact longing of their hearts or not, was the grace that the Asian Christians found in Christ.

1:11–12 Peter writes that "the Spirit of Christ in them" prompted the prophets' inquiry, and ultimately they were investigating "the sufferings of the Messiah and the glories that would follow" (v. 11). No matter how intense their search or profound their vision, Peter insists that these prophets, like John the Baptist after them, only served a preliminary role in the plan of God (v. 12). They were preparing the world and God's people for a later time—and that later time is now.

1:3–12 The centrality of salvation, a cardinal doctrine of the Christian faith, is offensive to our culture. As a result, suffering often accompanies the preaching of salvation.

To speak of the need of salvation today is to be old-fashioned, out of touch, and even offensive. At the root of this denial is a view that sees people as essentially good and not as sinners who need divine grace. Believers speak a language that our culture simply does not hear or want to hear. While centuries have passed since Peter wrote this letter, the strangeness of the message of salvation remains similar. And as this strangeness led to suffering for the early Christians, it also leads to suffering in our world.

1:13 Someday, Christ will return, and justice will be fully established. As a result, Christians are to remain alert and live in light of that day.

Christ is revealed at his coming. 14 As obedient children, do not conform[x] to the
evil desires you had when you lived in ignorance.[y] 15 But just as he who called you
is holy, so be holy in all you do;[z] 16 for it is
written: "Be holy, because I am holy."[a][a]

17 Since you call on a Father who judges each person's work impartially,[b] live
out your time as foreigners here in reverent fear.[c] 18 For you know that it was
not with perishable things such as silver
or gold that you were redeemed[d] from
the empty way of life handed down to
you from your ancestors, 19 but with the
precious blood of Christ, a lamb[e] without blemish or defect.[f] 20 He was chosen
before the creation of the world,[g] but
was revealed in these last times[h] for your
sake. 21 Through him you believe in God,[i]
who raised him from the dead and glorified him, and so your faith and hope
are in God.

22 Now that you have purified[j] yourselves by obeying the truth so that you
have sincere love for each other, love
one another deeply,[k] from the heart.[b]
23 For you have been born again,[l] not of
perishable seed, but of imperishable,
through the living and enduring word
of God.[m] 24 For,

> "All people are like grass,
> and all their glory is like the
> flowers of the field;
> the grass withers and the flowers
> fall,
> 25 but the word of the Lord endures
> forever."[c][n]

And this is the word that was preached
to you.

2 Therefore, rid yourselves[o] of all malice and all deceit, hypocrisy, envy,
and slander[p] of every kind. 2 Like newborn babies, crave pure spiritual milk,[q]
so that by it you may grow up[r] in your
salvation, 3 now that you have tasted that
the Lord is good.[s]

The Living Stone and a Chosen People

4 As you come to him, the living
Stone[t] — rejected by humans but chosen
by God and precious to him — 5 you also,
like living stones, are being built[u] into

1:14 [x] Ro 12:2 [y] Eph 4:18
1:15 [z] 2Co 7:1; 1Th 4:7
1:16 [a] Lev 11:44, 45
1:17 [b] Ac 10:34 [c] Heb 12:28
1:18 [d] Mt 20:28; 1Co 6:20
1:19 [e] Jn 1:29 [f] Ex 12:5
1:20 [g] Eph 1:4 [h] Heb 9:26
1:21 [i] Ro 4:24
1:22 [j] Jas 4:8 [k] Jn 13:34; Heb 13:1
1:23 [l] Jn 1:13
[m] Heb 4:12
1:25 [n] Isa 40:6-8
2:1 [o] Eph 4:22 [p] Jas 4:11
2:2 [q] 1Co 3:2 [r] Eph 4:15,16
2:3 [s] Heb 6:5
2:4 [t] ver 7
2:5 [u] 1Co 3:9

[a] *16* Lev. 11:44,45; 19:2 [b] *22* Some early manuscripts *from a pure heart*
[c] *25* Isaiah 40:6-8 (see Septuagint)

1:14-16 Christians should be holy both because they have been converted (v. 14a) and because they are children of a God who is himself altogether holy (vv. 15-16). Perhaps no other section in the Bible establishes the theological foundations for ethics like these three verses.
1:17 Knowing that God is Judge and that he judges with absolute fairness drives us to live in healthy awe. When his beautiful, holy love checks our thoughts and actions, we live in the light of his character.
1:18-21 Peter adds a second motive for a life of obedience: the nature of redemption. Believers have been redeemed and purchased with a price—the blood of Jesus Christ. Since we have been redeemed in this way, we should live in fear and holiness before God.
1:22-25 The believers' purification was by means of the sprinkling of Christ's blood. They responded to God by obeying the gospel's truth (vv. 2, 14). The result of obeying the truth was that they were ushered into the realm of love.

Peter returns to the foundation of their love: their regeneration (v. 23). Humans and humanly created things are like grass in that they will perish and vanish. But the Word of God, planted in Christians, is eternal and grows in those same Christians to give them an eternal existence.

1:13-25 Ethics are either founded in ourselves (e.g., through reason, intuition, nature, moral instinct, conscience) or outside ourselves (e.g., through revelation, an established code of ethics, a governmental constitution). Christian belief teaches that *ethics flows from salvation* and that humans, by themselves, cannot discern the will of God. We know what is good from what is bad because God has told us.

Peter provides us with at least three foundations for determining whether an action is right or wrong. First, does it conform to the character of God? Second, is it the natural outcome of a life that has benefited from the salvation of God? Finally, will it stand up to God's scrutiny in that final day when he ushers us into his glorious presence?

2:1 "Pure spiritual milk" (v. 2) refers to the things that nourish Christian community: knowledge of God, prayer, instruction in the gospel, faithful obedience, and hearing God's preached word. This desire is accompanied by learning to "rid yourselves of" problems that arise in Christian assemblies when spiritual things are not desired.
2:2 If you, Peter says to his readers, learn to yearn for spiritual nourishment, you will "grow up in your salvation" (v. 2). Peter is concerned that the church become desirous of spiritual nourishment and growth leading them into maturity in the faith.
2:3 Desire for spiritual growth is founded on the fact that Peter's readers have "tasted that the Lord is good." Because the Lord himself is spiritually satisfying, these Christians are to focus their lives on spiritual nourishment and growth. Through this, they will attain their hope of salvation.
2:4-5 The churches in Asia Minor must see themselves as "living stones" (v. 5), connected to the

a spiritual house[a][v] to be a holy priesthood,[w] offering spiritual sacrifices acceptable to God through Jesus Christ.[x]
6For in Scripture it says:

"See, I lay a stone in Zion,
a chosen and precious
cornerstone,[y]
and the one who trusts in him
will never be put to shame."[b][z]

7Now to you who believe, this stone is
precious. But to those who do not believe,[a]

"The stone the builders rejected
has become the cornerstone,"[c][b]

8and,

"A stone that causes people to
stumble
and a rock that makes them fall."[d][c]

They stumble because they disobey the
message—which is also what they were
destined for.[d]
9But you are a chosen people,[e] a royal priesthood, a holy nation,[f] God's special possession, that you may declare
the praises of him who called you out
of darkness into his wonderful light.[g]
10Once you were not a people, but now
you are the people of God;[h] once you had
not received mercy, but now you have
received mercy.

2:5 [v] 1Ti 3:15 [w] Isa 61:6 [x] Php 4:18; Heb 13:15
2:6 [y] Eph 2:20 [z] Isa 28:16
2:7 [a] 2Co 2:16 [b] Ps 118:22
2:8 [c] Isa 8:14; 1Co 1:23 [d] Ro 9:22
2:9 [e] Dt 10:15 [f] Isa 62:12 [g] Ac 26:18
2:10 [h] Hos 1:9, 10
2:11 [i] Gal 5:16 [j] Jas 4:1
2:12 [k] Php 2:15; 1Pe 3:16 [l] Mt 5:16; 9:8

1Pe 2:12 ❖ What kind of life is so powerful it causes nonbelievers to glorify God? How can we live our lives like that?

Living Godly Lives in a Pagan Society

11Dear friends, I urge you, as foreigners and exiles, to abstain from sinful
desires,[i] which wage war against your
soul.[j] 12Live such good lives among the
pagans that, though they accuse you of
doing wrong, they may see your good
deeds[k] and glorify God[l] on the day he
visits us.

[a] 5 Or *into a temple of the Spirit*
[b] 6 Isaiah 28:16 [c] 7 Psalm 118:22
[d] 8 Isaiah 8:14

"living Stone" (v. 4). They must unify themselves so that they may become a spiritual house. Jesus was rejected by human beings but chosen by God, just as his readers were being rejected by humans.

2:6–8 The Stone has been laid, but those who walk in Zion trip over it. God's act of appointing Jesus as the living Stone has become both honor for believers and judgment for unbelievers; this was God's design, and everything happens according to his will.

2:9–10 The purpose of the church given here is to announce the good tidings of peace and joy that can be found in Christ. Peter also appropriates the story of Hosea for the church (see Hos 1:9—2:1, 23).

2:1–10 One of Peter's major concerns in this letter can be broadly labeled "the relationship of the church to the state," though he did not think in those terms. The church's primary mission is to grow as a spiritual community and declare the virtues of God. Peter does not deny that Christians should be involved in society, nor does he insist (as nearly all sectarian movements do) that they must insulate themselves from the world's values by separating from the world. The entire sweep of the Bible teaches that Christians are not to be worried so much about changing their environments as they are to remain faithful in whatever environment they find themselves in.

2:11a The description of believers as "foreigners and exiles" here does not refer so much to their "pilgrimage from this life to the next" as to their social status. They are people without rights in the Roman Empire. Yet Peter wants them to live an exemplary life to provide an attractive alternative to the pagan way of life.

2:11b Abstaining from fleshly passions is important to living a holy life.

2:12 Peter urges his readers to live honorably when accusations are lodged against them and to refrain from insulting their unjust accusers.

Repeating himself, Peter offers once again the *alternative* (v. 12c): "that . . . they may see your good deeds." Yet this time he adds the *result*—namely, that the opponents will "glorify God on the day he visits [them]" (v. 12d), the day when God will vindicate the good behavior of Christians and will drive the hostile accusers to see that they were wrong.

2:11–12 The cultural forces working today to corrupt the mandates and truth of the gospel are *not as overtly physical as they were in Peter's day.* But the threat to the church is not to be minimized. We are dealing with the forces of modernization, privatization, and secularization. These forces war against our souls today, just as other forces warred against the souls of the Christians in Peter's day in Asia Minor. Why, for example, do so many Christians think that the essence of Christian living is to be disciplined and efficient? While such ideas are not absent in the Bible, they are hardly held up as core values. Do we not hold them up so high today because they reflect what we have found effective in our capitalistic society? Culture influences us more than we will ever know. But the message of the Bible in regard to salvation is clear.

13 Submit yourselves for the Lord's
sake to every human authority:[m] whether to the emperor, as the supreme authority, 14 or to governors, who are sent
by him to punish those who do wrong[n]
and to commend those who do right.[o]
15 For it is God's will[p] that by doing good
you should silence the ignorant talk of
foolish people.[q] 16 Live as free people,[r]
but do not use your freedom as a cover-
up for evil; live as God's slaves.[s] 17 Show
proper respect to everyone, love the
family of believers,[t] fear God, honor
the emperor.[u]

18 Slaves, in reverent fear of God submit yourselves to your masters,[v] not only
to those who are good and considerate,[w]
but also to those who are harsh. 19 For it
is commendable if someone bears up
under the pain of unjust suffering because they are conscious of God.[x] 20 But
how is it to your credit if you receive a
beating for doing wrong and endure it?
But if you suffer for doing good and you
endure it, this is commendable before
God.[y] 21 To this[z] you were called, because
Christ suffered for you, leaving you an
example,[a] that you should follow in his
steps.

22 "He committed no sin,
and no deceit was found in his
mouth."[a][b]

23 When they hurled their insults at him,
he did not retaliate; when he suffered, he
made no threats.[c] Instead, he entrusted
himself[d] to him who judges justly. 24 "He
himself bore our sins"[e] in his body on the
cross, so that we might die to sins[f] and
live for righteousness; "by his wounds
you have been healed."[g] 25 For "you were
like sheep going astray,"[b][h] but now you
have returned to the Shepherd[i] and Overseer of your souls.

3 Wives, in the same way submit yourselves[j] to your own husbands[k] so that,
if any of them do not believe the word,
they may be won over[l] without words by
the behavior of their wives, 2 when they
see the purity and reverence of your lives.

2:13 [m] Ro 13:1
2:14 [n] Ro 13:4 [o] Ro 13:3
2:15 [p] 1Pe 3:17 [q] ver 12
2:16 [r] Jn 8:32 [s] Ro 6:22
2:17 [t] Ro 12:10 [u] Ro 13:7
2:18 [v] Eph 6:5 [w] Jas 3:17
2:19 [x] 1Pe 3:14, 17
2:20 [y] 1Pe 3:17
2:21 [z] Ac 14:22 [a] Mt 16:24
2:22 [b] Isa 53:9
2:23 [c] Isa 53:7 [d] Lk 23:46
2:24 [e] Heb 9:28 [f] Ro 6:2 [g] Isa 53:5; Heb 12:13; Jas 5:16
2:25 [h] Isa 53:6 [i] Jn 10:11
3:1 [j] 1Pe 2:18 [k] Eph 5:22 [l] 1Co 7:16; 9:19

[a] *22* Isaiah 53:9 [b] *24,25* Isaiah 53:4,5,6 (see Septuagint)

2:13 If the early dating of this letter is correct (early AD 60s), then the emperor Peter refers to in v. 13 is none other than the vicious and cruel Nero. Christians are expected to be good citizens even in extreme situations.

2:14 Peter's concern is with the need for Christians to be good people so that the judicial arm of the governor is not raised over the churches.

2:15 Christians should submit to the various levels of governing authorities *because* the believers' behavior will silence ignorant accusations.

2:16 Next, Peter adds a condition for submitting to the authorities. Christians are not to use their freedom from human authorities as an excuse for living in insubordination.

2:17 Finally, Peter repeats his exhortation. Their holy living is to be manifested in respect for all people, whether that means the church, God, or the emperor. Such conduct will prevent damage to the gospel's reputation and repel some of the persecution that may be imminent.

2:13–17 The Christian is to be obedient to the structures of society and to live within those structures. Such obedience at times may involve a justifiable civil disobedience to something unjust or idolatrous that remains within that governmental structure (cf. Ac 5:29). Christians at such times must speak out against the government. But this has to be done in ways that honor Christ and remain peaceful and nonviolent.

2:18 Christian slaves should obey all masters, regardless of their personal characteristics. Through such obedience, they will be witnesses to God's grace. In the Roman world, slavery was not usually a permanent condition of life. Rather, it was a temporary condition on the path toward freedom. In fact, it is entirely possible that one reason Peter urged Christian slaves to be submissive and obedient was that by living obediently, they could be set free.

2:19–20 What pleases God—if one is going to suffer—is suffering for doing good.

2:21–25 Peter contends that suffering is the slaves' calling from God (v. 21) and suggests that the call to suffer is rooted in following Jesus. The suffering of Christ created a general pattern that believers were to follow. Jesus exemplified someone who suffered for doing good; he was perfect and yet suffered. Thus, Christian slaves should take this example as a model for their lifestyle.

2:18–25 The suffering of Christ is a model of Christian existence. Churches today need to hear the message about the *cross-shaped nature of Christian existence*, especially since our society focuses so much on defending personal rights. In such a society, Christians must declare a different message—that of Jesus Christ, who suffered injustice to testify to God's grace.

3:1–2 Peter is urging the women of the Asia Minor churches to live a life that is respectable in society so that they will be able to maintain a good reputation for the gospel. Peter's injunction is pragmatic. Peter wants wives to submit *because of the influence* (vv. 1b–2) they can exert on their non-Christian husbands. Peter's directive to Christian wives is that they adopt a lifestyle that can win their husbands to the Christian faith.

3Your beauty should not come from outward adornment, such as elaborate hairstyles and the wearing of gold jewelry or
fine clothes.[m] 4Rather, it should be that of
your inner self,[n] the unfading beauty of a
gentle and quiet spirit, which is of great
worth in God's sight. 5For this is the way
the holy women of the past who put their
hope in God[o] used to adorn themselves.
They submitted themselves to their own
husbands, 6like Sarah, who obeyed Abraham and called him her lord.[p] You are her
daughters if you do what is right and do
not give way to fear.

7Husbands,[q] in the same way be considerate as you live with your wives, and
treat them with respect as the weaker
partner and as heirs with you of the gracious gift of life, so that nothing will hinder your prayers.

Suffering for Doing Good

8Finally, all of you, be like-minded,
be sympathetic, love one another,[r] be
compassionate and humble.[s] 9Do not repay evil with evil[t] or insult with insult.[u]
On the contrary, repay evil with blessing, because to this[v] you were called
so that you may inherit a blessing.[w]
10For,

"Whoever would love life
  and see good days
must keep their tongue from
    evil
  and their lips from deceitful
    speech.
11They must turn from evil and do
    good;
  they must seek peace and
    pursue it.
12For the eyes of the Lord are on the
    righteous
  and his ears are attentive to their
    prayer,
but the face of the Lord is against
    those who do evil."[a][x]

3:3 [m] Isa 3:18-23; 1Ti 2:9
3:4 [n] Ro 7:22
3:5 [o] 1Ti 5:5
3:6 [p] Ge 18:12
3:7 [q] Eph 5:25-33
3:8 [r] Ro 12:10
[s] 1Pe 5:5
3:9 [t] Ro 12:17 [u] 1Pe 2:23 [v] 1Pe 2:21 [w] Heb 6:14
3:12 [x] Ps 34:12-16

[a] 12 Psalm 34:12-16

3:3–4 Peter contrasts external beauty with internal beauty. Some have suggested that Peter's comments here actually prohibit Christian women of all ages from braiding their hair and wearing jewelry and fancy clothing. The majority see a comparison of values: external appearance is relatively unimportant, but internal virtue is the prime pursuit of life. Peter urges them to regard their external appearance as secondary to personal beauty.

3:5–6 Peter appeals to "the holy women of the past" (v. 5) as he extends the instruction to include women who had believing husbands, showing that his instructions to submit are not simply pragmatic.

3:7 Peter directs Christian husbands to be considerate, which carries the sense of "living with one's wife knowledgeably." The Christian man, Peter says, should be neither demanding nor selfish in his sexual and marital relations; he is instead to be considerate, sensitive, and serving.

The Christian husband must be especially considerate in these relations because his wife is "the weaker partner." It is almost certain that Peter has a wife's physical capacities in mind here.

✣ **3:1–7** Anger is a common factor of domestic abuse. Angry spouses or partners at home may be one of the most serious problems in our society, however these individuals appear to others. Against each of these acts of violence the words of Peter could be cited. Peter's advice is rooted in the notion that Christian spouses need to become lifelong, considerate learners of their partners. Peter's call to compassion leaves no room for spousal abuse.

3:8 Harmony is, in part, a development of being "sympathetic." Christians are to love one another and those they encounter as good neighbors.

3:9 Peter again sees the Christian response to pressures from the outside world as one of passivity and grace, not aggressive retaliation. Peter anchors his readers' relationships to outsiders in their calling and promises them a "blessing." In line with his emphasis at 2:11–12, he imagines it will be a much better life for the churches if they are quiet, humble, and gentle, and if they refrain from retaliation and vindication.

3:10–12 The Christian is supposed to be motivated by a desire to receive a "blessing" from God (v. 9), which is God's reward for an obedient life. The fundamental point Peter makes is that God is omniscient and omnipresent—he sees all, knows all, and is always present. People must not think that they can get by with evil behavior; God is always watching and evaluating. Those who live righteously before God will be vindicated by God on the great day of glory. Those who live sinfully and oppressively will receive condemnation from God Almighty on that same day of his glory.

✣ **3:8–12** Church community is vital for survival, sustaining one's faith amid threats and violence. We cannot identically compare our trials in the West to the ancient churches' experiences of persecution, but the analogy is still relevant. If the early church was a community in which Christians found strength to carry on amid troubled times, then the church today ought to play the same role in our world, whatever the "trouble" might be. If our society is noted by an absence of moral values, then Christians must reinforce and strengthen their resolve to raise righteous children and protect victims of abuse. If our society is noted by skepticism about knowing "truth," Christians need to confirm biblical truth and hold that truth high.

1Pe 3:15–16 ❖ What answers can believers give to others who ask for the reason for the hope within them? How can we be sure to season these answers with love?

13 Who is going to harm you if you
are eager to do good?[y] 14 But even if you
should suffer for what is right, you are
blessed.[z] "Do not fear their threats[a];
do not be frightened."[b][a] 15 But in your
hearts revere Christ as Lord. Always be
prepared to give an answer[b] to everyone who asks you to give the reason for
the hope that you have. But do this with
gentleness and respect, 16 keeping a clear
conscience,[c] so that those who speak maliciously against your good behavior in
Christ may be ashamed of their slander.[d]
17 For it is better, if it is God's will,[e] to suffer for doing good[f] than for doing evil.
18 For Christ also suffered once for sins,[g]
the righteous for the unrighteous, to
bring you to God. He was put to death
in the body[h] but made alive in the Spirit.[i]
19 After being made alive,[c] he went and
made proclamation to the imprisoned
spirits[j]— 20 to those who were disobedient long ago when God waited patiently
in the days of Noah while the ark was
being built.[k] In it only a few people, eight
in all, were saved[l] through water, 21 and
this water symbolizes baptism that now
saves you[m] also — not the removal of dirt
from the body but the pledge of a clear
conscience toward God.[d] It saves you by
the resurrection of Jesus Christ,[n] 22 who
has gone into heaven and is at God's
right hand[o] — with angels, authorities
and powers in submission to him.[p]

Living for God

4 Therefore, since Christ suffered in
his body, arm yourselves also with
the same attitude, because whoever suffers in the body is done with sin. 2 As a
result, they do not live the rest of their
earthly lives for evil human desires,[q] but
rather for the will of God. 3 For you have
spent enough time in the past[r] doing
what pagans choose to do — living in
debauchery, lust, drunkenness, orgies,
carousing and detestable idolatry. 4 They
are surprised that you do not join them

3:13 [y] Pr 16:7
3:14 [z] 1Pe 2:19, 20; 4:15,16 [a] Isa 8:12,13
3:15 [b] Col 4:6
3:16 [c] Heb 13:18 [d] 1Pe 2:12,15
3:17 [e] 1Pe 2:15 [f] 1Pe 2:20
3:18 [g] 1Pe 2:21 [h] Col 1:22; 1Pe 4:1 [i] 1Pe 4:6
3:19 [j] 1Pe 4:6
3:20 [k] Ge 6:3,5, 13,14 [l] Heb 11:7
3:21 [m] Titus 3:5 [n] 1Pe 1:3
3:22 [o] Mk 16:19 [p] Ro 8:38
4:2 [q] Ro 6:2
4:3 [r] Eph 2:2

[a] 14 Or *fear what they fear* [b] 14 Isaiah 8:12
[c] 18,19 Or *but made alive in the spirit,* 19*in which also* [d] 21 Or *but an appeal to God for a clear conscience*

3:13–14 Peter's assurances are grounded in his final hope: God will eventually (even if not now) establish complete justice. While Peter generally believes that good behavior will alleviate suffering, he knows that not all opponents will be lenient. When they do have to endure suffering, Peter exhorts his readers not to fear the oppressors.
3:15–17 Instead of fear, believers are to honor the Lord Christ by being ready to speak boldly about their "hope" (v. 15). This could include terms like "salvation," "inheritance," and final vindication (vv. 18–22).

Instead of brash defensiveness, Christians ought to defend the Lord in a humble and respectful manner. Such a manner can lead to conversions (vv. 1–2) and to leniency when persecution strikes (v. 13). Such a lifestyle allows a "clear conscience" (v. 16). If God wills that they are to suffer, it is better that such takes place when the Christians are doing good rather than evil (v. 17).
3:18–22 We should view this passage in light of its overall theme of vindication. Just as Jesus suffered righteously and was vindicated, if the churches live righteously, they will also be vindicated and sit with Jesus in the presence of God. That is the hope that ought to sustain churches as they endure suffering, the hope of which they are to be ready to proclaim, and the hope that Peter urges them to embrace.

✣ **3:13–22** Where do Christians suffer injustice *because they are Christians*? Such people need to hear the message of vindication and learn to live in light of that message. Then they can live beyond and through the persecution itself. Many people have been fired because they were honest people trying to live out their faith in the workplace; many others have suffered severe forms of ostracism because they sought to live Christian lives in the public sphere. Such people find Peter's message applicable to their own lives. They can find comfort in trouble by reflecting thoughtfully on the ultimate vindication of God. They can learn to say, "Someday—" and so can learn to live in joy today despite their difficult situations.

4:1–2 To endure persecution in an obedient manner, Christians must have proper mental preparation: They must "arm [them]selves also with the same attitude" that Christ had. One outcome Peter gives from this approach is that it helps believers' obedience (vv. 1b–2). Christians who are suffering learn not to sin as they undergo persecution.
4:3 Turning from past sin and toward a life of obedience sets an example of the changed life that following Jesus brings. As empowered Christians shed the sins of the past, they testify to true inner life change in an outward and obvious way.
4:4–5 As Peter's audience has turned away from sinful habits, their lives testify to Christ's power at work in them. But those behaviors continued among their old friends. These surprised former friends,

1Pe 4:7-11 ❖ How can we use our gifts to serve others? What gifts can you offer in the work of believers around you?

in their reckless, wild living, and they
heap abuse on you.[s] 5But they will have
to give account to him who is ready to
judge the living and the dead.[t] 6For this is
the reason the gospel was preached even
to those who are now dead,[u] so that they
might be judged according to human
standards in regard to the body, but live
according to God in regard to the spirit.
7The end of all things is near.[v] Therefore be alert and of sober mind so that
you may pray. 8Above all, love each other
deeply,[w] because love covers over a multitude of sins.[x] 9Offer hospitality to one
another without grumbling.[y] 10Each of
you should use whatever gift you have
received to serve others,[z] as faithful[a]
stewards of God's grace in its various
forms. 11If anyone speaks, they should
do so as one who speaks the very words
of God. If anyone serves, they should do
so with the strength God provides,[b] so
that in all things God may be praised[c]
through Jesus Christ. To him be the glory
and the power for ever and ever. Amen.

4:4 [s] 1Pe 3:16
4:5 [t] Ac 10:42; 2Ti 4:1
4:6 [u] 1Pe 3:19
4:7 [v] Ro 13:11
4:8 [w] 1Pe 1:22 [x] Pr 10:12
4:9 [y] Php 2:14
4:10 [z] Ro 12:6,7 [a] 1Co 4:2
4:11 [b] Eph 6:10 [c] 1Co 10:31
4:12 [d] 1Pe 1:6,7
4:13 [e] Ro 8:17
4:14 [f] Mt 5:11

Suffering for Being a Christian

12Dear friends, do not be surprised
at the fiery ordeal that has come on
you[d] to test you, as though something
strange were happening to you. 13But
rejoice inasmuch as you participate
in the sufferings of Christ, so that you
may be overjoyed when his glory is revealed.[e] 14If you are insulted because of
the name of Christ, you are blessed,[f] for
the Spirit of glory and of God rests on
you. 15If you suffer, it should not be as a
murderer or thief or any other kind of
criminal, or even as a meddler. 16Howev-
er, if you suffer as a Christian, do not be
ashamed, but praise God that you bear

---

who now abuse them verbally, are ultimately blasphemers who will "have to give account to him who is ready to judge the living and the dead" (v. 5).

4:6 Peter is likely referring to Christians in Asia Minor who heard the gospel while alive but are now physically dead. Those who hear the gospel and respond, *even if they are killed for their faith*, will be vindicated ultimately before God.

❖ **4:1-6** As with many new converts to Christianity throughout history, Peter's churches had gone through a change in whom they associated with. These churches provide an early example of what happens when people establish a lifestyle that follows Jesus. Walking toward a life that honors God and emulates Jesus often mandates walking away from people with whom we have previously associated, until their hearts are also changed.

4:7a Peter roots his ethical exhortations in vv. 4:7b-11 in his perception of history and the judgment (v. 7a). The people of God recognized that a Jewish prophet's vision was telescoped, and they could not see the entire chronology of God's plan. Thus, while Peter presented his ethical appeals in light of a view that the end of history was imminent, his view is not mistaken. Rather, it was how Jewish prophecy was interpreted.

4:7b Peter's exhortation here is that Christians keep themselves mentally and spiritually alert (cf. 1:13). Here the goal of such vigilance is so that they might pray effectively.

4:8 Peter exhorts his readers to "love each other deeply." Loving one another when things are tough is important "because love covers over a multitude of sins."

4:9 Here Peter exhorts Christians to be hospitable, as it is a specific example of loving one another.

4:10-11a Peter offers his final exhortation that the believers exercise their gifts. They are to use their gifts "as faithful stewards of God's grace in its various forms" (v. 10). The gifts are to be exercised to reflect their divine origin and purposes. If God's Spirit prompts a person to speak to the congregation, that person should take the opportunity seriously.

4:11b Peter's doxology has Jesus Christ as its object. God glorifies himself through his Son, and the Son is at work in the prayer and loving ministries of the church.

❖ **4:7-11** How frequently do we examine our lives in the light of eternity or of God's just judgment at the end of time? There are definite benefits to taking the time to do so. While Christians in the past may have heard too many threats and sermons on hellfire, the modern church seems to have neglected the theme of judgment altogether. Yet that very theme is foundational to a Christian view of ethics—the foundation that God is the judge and that we are accountable to him for our behavior.

4:12-13 We are not told exactly what the "fiery ordeal" is. Instead of being shocked by these events and turning inward to wonder and doubt, Peter's readers are to "rejoice" (v. 13a). Sufferings create a special bond with the Lord. Being able to rejoice now amid suffering prepares one for being "overjoyed when his glory is revealed" (v. 13b).

4:14-16 Peter reminds his readers to remain faithful in doing good and not incur suffering because they deserve it. Rather than being ashamed of sufferings incurred for Christ, Peter's readers should take them as an occasion to see that they are blessed (v. 14). That is, they are blessed by God and are to glorify him because of the presence of his Spirit

that name.[g] 17For it is time for judgment
to begin with God's household;[h] and if it
begins with us, what will the outcome be
for those who do not obey the gospel of
God?[i] 18And,

> "If it is hard for the righteous to be saved,
> what will become of the ungodly and the sinner?"[a][j]

19So then, those who suffer according to God's will should commit themselves to their faithful Creator and continue to do good.

To the Elders and the Flock

5 To the elders among you, I appeal
as a fellow elder[k] and a witness[l] of
Christ's sufferings who also will share
in the glory to be revealed:[m] 2Be shepherds of God's flock[n] that is under your
care, watching over them — not because
you must, but because you are willing,
as God wants you to be; not pursuing
dishonest gain,[o] but eager to serve; 3not
lording it over[p] those entrusted to you,
but being examples[q] to the flock. 4And
when the Chief Shepherd appears, you
will receive the crown of glory[r] that will
never fade away.

5In the same way, you who are youn-
ger, submit yourselves[s] to your elders. All of you, clothe yourselves with humility toward one another, because,

> "God opposes the proud
> but shows favor to the humble."[b][t]

6Humble yourselves, therefore, under
God's mighty hand, that he may lift you

4:16 [g] Ac 5:41
4:17 [h] Jer 25:29 [i] 2Th 1:8
4:18 [j] Pr 11:31; Lk 23:31
5:1 [k] Ac 11:30 [l] Lk 24:48 [m] 1Pe 1:5,7; Rev 1:9
5:2 [n] Jn 21:16
[o] 1Ti 3:3
5:3 [p] Eze 34:4 [q] Php 3:17
5:4 [r] 1Co 9:25
5:5 [s] Eph 5:21 [t] Pr 3:34; Jas 4:6

[a] *18* Prov. 11:31 (see Septuagint) [b] *5* Prov. 3:34

1Pe 5:4 ❖ How can we as believers look toward our "Chief Shepherd" to lead us through life?

---

on them. Peter warns that suffering for the name of Christ is acceptable; suffering for doing bad things is unacceptable (vv. 15–16).

4:17–19 That God's judgment begins with the people of God is familiar to any reader of the OT. This threat of judgment formed the basis for exhorting Christians to live faithfully. Persecution is the act of God purging his people to prepare them for his final display of salvation. Through suffering he makes them fit for that judgment. Because of the severity of God's penetrating judgment, Peter exhorts these Christians to submit themselves to God by living a good life.

4:12–19 Christians ought not to be surprised if they suffer shame and loss of status because of their faith. Even our suffering is one way God prepares us to be fit for his presence in the age to come. Whatever happens to us, Peter reminds us, we are not to ruin the cause of the gospel with filthy works of evil. Nothing is more damaging to the glory of God and the growth of the gospel than the sins of his people, no matter what their position—whether a highly visible leader or the most incognito church attender.

5:1 Peter cites two traits that he and the elders of these churches share: They are all elders and will all partake of the future glory.

5:2 Elders are responsible for shepherding God's flock. This is rooted in the description of God as a Shepherd to his people. Peter calls leaders of house churches to tend to their groups as assigned to them by God. Without question, Peter ends any sense of possession by stating that it is "God's flock," not theirs. Service in the church ought to be done with personal willingness and a sense of divine calling, not under compulsion. The elders are not to serve in the churches in order to gain a profit.

5:3 Finally, Peter urges the elders to lead by example. Power is addictive. Instead of seeking God's agenda, power-hungry church leaders pursue their own, doing what they can to increase their own reputation.

5:4 Peter appeals to the promise they will receive for faithfully discharging their calling. When Jesus returns as Savior and Judge, he will give them a "crown of glory" for their faithfulness to him.

5:5 The term "submit" should be understood as "living according to some constituted order"—here, the order established by the directives of the elders. Peter addresses the entire church. Christians are to develop a deferential and humble attitude toward one another. Once again, Peter grounds his exhortations in the coming judgment of God (see at 4:7, 17–19).

5:1–5 Our text offers a list of three problems of motivation, and church leaders need to look over this list, examine their hearts, and ask themselves, "Why do I serve God in the church?" First, are we as church leaders motivated to serve in the church *because we have to or because we want to*? Second are we as church leaders motivated to serve in the church *because of the money we can acquire or because of our enthusiasm for ministry*? Third, are we as church leaders motivated to serve in the church *because of our desire for power or because of the impact our life makes on others*?

5:6–7 Peter grounds his readers' submission to God in God's loving care and protection. By turning over their fears and worries to God, they express

CHARACTER OF GOD // GOD IS STEADFAST

1 Peter 5:10: And the God of all grace, who called you to his eternal glory in Christ, after you have suffered a little while, will himself restore you and make you strong, firm and steadfast.

In the crush of daily life, finding an anchor to hold on to can be difficult. We find ourselves distracted by the tasks that we all have to manage from week to week. From getting the kids ready for school and hustling to work, pressing deadlines and complex work problems, and the need to pay bills and fix things—not to mention having to constantly decide what to cook for dinner—it's easy to be swept along in the rush of these tasks and feel exhausted and uninspired when the weekend finally rolls around. All of this gets immensely complicated when relational or financial or health issues kick in.

Those who believe in the God of the Bible, however, find themselves able to hold on to an anchor in the storms of daily life. The passage above promises that, no matter how difficult our circumstances may be, the God that we serve "will himself restore you"—did you get that? God himself will restore us— "and make you strong, firm and steadfast." That's an incredible promise for busy families today, as well as those who find themselves in the grip of things beyond their control: cancer, marital breakdown, or the death of a loved one.

God can deliver on this promise because he himself is steadfast. With every millisecond, the God who created everything (Ge 1:1) manages incomprehensible complexity as he holds the universe together (Col 1:16). While he does that, he also holds evil in check (Pr 16:4) and cares for even the least of his creation (Ps 139:1-18; Jnh 4:11; Mt 19:14). What's more, he's also deeply concerned about the daily lives of individuals, whom he pursues relentlessly, calling them into loving relationship with himself (Ps 14:2; Lk 19:10; Jn 4:23).

APPLICATION Take a moment to reread the passage above. God, in his incomparable grace (a gift for all who will receive it), has called us into his eternal glory (sure hope for the future) in Christ (our sacrificed, resurrected Savior and King). While we all, at times, suffer on this earth (because of the fall of Adam and the sin in our own hearts), God is the One who holds us fast (because he himself is steadfast and unchanging); and he himself is the One who can help us navigate the complexity of life and eventually lead us into our eternal home with him. What an honor to be so deeply loved by so great a Father!

up in due time.[u] 7Cast all your anxiety on
him[v] because he cares for you.[w]
8Be alert and of sober mind. Your
enemy the devil prowls around[x] like
a roaring lion looking for someone to
devour. 9Resist him,[y] standing firm in
the faith,[z] because you know that the
family of believers throughout the
world is undergoing the same kind of
sufferings.[a]
10And the God of all grace, who called
you to his eternal glory[b] in Christ, after
you have suffered a little while, will himself restore you and make you strong,[c]
firm and steadfast. 11To him be the power
for ever and ever. Amen.[d]

Final Greetings

12With the help of Silas,[a][e] whom I regard as a faithful brother, I have written

5:6 [u] Jas 4:10
5:7 [v] Ps 37:5; Mt 6:25 [w] Heb 13:5
5:8 [x] Job 1:7
5:9 [y] Jas 4:7 [z] Col 2:5 [a] Ac 14:22
5:10 [b] 2Co 4:17 [c] 2Th 2:17
5:11 [d] Ro 11:36
5:12 [e] 2Co 1:19

[a] 12 Greek *Silvanus,* a variant of *Silas*

their trust in him and rely on him to bring about vindication and justice. By submitting to and waiting out God's deliverance, they can expect that same mighty hand to deliver them, just as the Lord delivered the children of Israel from the Egyptians.
5:8–9 Christians resist Satan by not giving in to his temptations to deny the Lord and to be faithless in suffering.
5:10–11 Peter begins this prayer with a theological reflection. The God they worship and serve is a God of grace. He then directs this reflection toward the specific calling God has given them: He has made them his people so they could be with him eternally and praise him forever. This calling requires suffering for a while. Finally, Peter's prayer is for their strength to endure, remain faithful, and resist temptations.
5:12–14 Peter concludes his letter like the endings of other NT letters: mentioning the scribe or messenger of the letter (Silas), summarizing

to you briefly,[f] encouraging you and testifying that this is the true grace of God. Stand fast in it.
13She who is in Babylon, chosen together with you, sends you her greetings, and so does my son Mark.[g] 14Greet one another with a kiss of love.[h]
Peace[i] to all of you who are in Christ.

5:12 [f]Heb 13:22
5:13 [g]Ac 12:12
5:14 [h]Ro 16:16 [i]Eph 6:23

---

his intention (to encourage and testify), greeting them, and wishing them God's peace.

5:13 Because Babylon was a notorious place of sin, it became a figurative expression for any place known for its sinfulness. It surely describes Rome here, and early Christian tradition confirms that Peter wrote from Rome. Both Peter and Mark share their greetings.

5:14 Peter urges his readers to "greet one another with a kiss of love" (v. 14), the standard form of greeting in the ancient world. Peter's final blessing then follows: "Peace to all of you who are in Christ."

5:6-14 Our identity is to be wrapped up not in our social location, whether that be low (like Peter's churches) or high (like many churches today in the West), but in the fact that we are God's family and are related to him. As such, we are to serve one another with the gifts God has granted and live orderly and lovingly with one another. No matter how many adjustments we have to make as we read Peter's letter in our world, we are anchored to his world by the fact of the common salvation that transforms our behavior (1:3—2:10). We are challenged to live faithfully in our society (2:11—3:12), and we are expected to live as the family of God ought to live (3:13—5:11). When we live like this, people will glorify him on the day he visits us (2:12).

2 Peter

Author: The apostle Peter

Audience: Christians in the five provinces to which 1 Peter was addressed

Date: Between AD 65 and 68

Theme: Peter teaches believers awaiting the Lord's return how God equips them to deal with false teachers and evildoers who have come into the church.

Reading 2 Peter

In ch. 1, Peter establishes the antidote to the problem of heresy in the church. The second chapter describes the character of the false teachers, and the final chapter closes with a reminder of Christ's final victory and our need to persevere. In reading 2 Peter, you cannot help but notice both the harsh tone directed against false teachers and Peter's sense of excitement in knowing the Lord.

PERSPECTIVE

The letters of 2 Peter and Jude warn readers that there is no way to pursue an immoral lifestyle without paying a penalty. This goes against the common belief of most modern Americans and is an important message that we need to hear today.

On the one hand, it is sad that we must be warned that doing bad things means bad things will happen to us. Time was, it seems, when parents considered it their sacred duty to instill this lesson in their children. No more. On the other hand, since cultural and familial structures no longer emphasize this important truth, at least as clearly as they once did, we are fortunate to have these two biblical letters to remind us.

It might be relevant, however, to take a look at the reason why the "sin-leads-to-judgment" message is so muted in our culture today. Our overloaded court system is filled with people attempting to avoid (and often succeeding) the consequences of their sins. Our public educational system is predicated on the invalid assumption that values are temporary, conditioned solely by historical and cultural factors—an assumption that makes sin more a matter of bad judgment than of wrongdoing. Even churches will often pull their punches when it comes to sin.

How have we come to this situation? It can be traced, in part at least, to the willful individual and corporate rejection of authority. This rejection is not a knee-jerk attempt at self-promotion or an immature adolescent testing of parental authority; it is rather a response to a century-long, worldwide misuse of authority by those in charge.

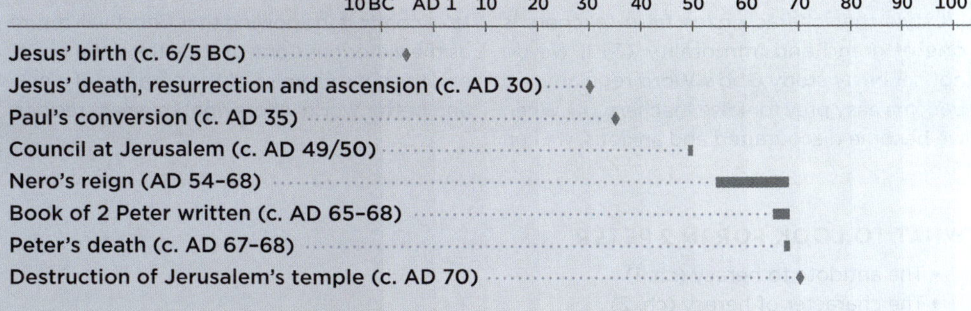

Oppressive regimes throughout history have made authority the only thing that matters: "Might makes right" is their watchword, and they are ruthless in its execution.

Individuals and institutions today have, opposite the dictators of the world, cut truth free from authority. Instead of God's authoritative truth, we each have our *own* truth—value systems that are "true for me" but not necessarily true for you. This relativistic attitude makes it almost impossible to talk about universal values, because the minute one talks about values that apply to everyone, they are talking again about authority.

The ironic result, of course, is that in such an authority vacuum, quite often the very worst sorts of leaders rush to fill it. The best among us attempt to live out the anti-authority ideal, adopting some sort of pragmatism or tolerant personalism, while the worst of us work the levers of power in the same old totalitarian ways. Such individuals may do this behind the scenes, "despis[ing] authority" in public and "blasphem[ing] in matters they do not understand" (2:10, 12). But their goal is to replace biblical truth and authority with their own.

The Bible teaches that truth and authority go together. Truth, by its universal, singular nature, has its own authority. It so happens that biblical authority is authority woven out of strands of grace-filled love, giving the resulting cloth a rich, soft texture that wears like iron against the false teachings of the world.

The message of 2 Peter and Jude is that there are true teachings and false teachings. We must resist with all our might the false teachers, refusing to adopt the selfish, antibiblical methodologies they use. We cannot resort to a false dogmatism that contradicts the gospel message of love. We must restore the twin towers of truth and authority, the message of the gospel of Jesus Christ.

For more perspective on this book, see the Introduction to Jude.

Key Verses

Therefore, dear friends, since you have been forewarned, be on your guard so that you may not be carried away by the error of the lawless and fall from your secure position. But grow in the grace and knowledge of our Lord and Savior Jesus Christ. To him be glory both now and forever! Amen.

—2 Peter 3:17-18

TAKING THE NEXT STEPS

While 1 Peter gave instructions on coping with persecution, this second letter of Peter concerns the enemy inside the church; that is, false teachers who were promoting heresy. The author wants his readers to grow in the knowledge of the truth contained in God's Word.

Peter addresses the contemporary church as well. (1) We must be alert to those who are promoting heresy in the church today. (2) The lifestyle that characterizes false teachers is one of greed and immorality. (3) If we do not seriously study God's Word regularly, we become easy prey for false teachers. (4) When we become discouraged and anxious, we can take comfort in knowing that Christ will return as the victorious Lord, destroy the sinful world, and keep his promise of the creation of a new and better world where righteousness resides.

WHAT TO LOOK FOR IN 2 PETER

- The antidote to heresy (ch. 1)
- The character of heresy (ch. 2)
- The final victory of Christ (ch. 3)

1 Simon Peter, a servant[a] and apostle of
Jesus Christ,[b]

To those who through the righteousness[c] of our God and Savior Jesus Christ[d]
have received a faith as precious as ours:

2 Grace and peace be yours in abundance through the knowledge of God
and of Jesus our Lord.[e]

Confirming One's Calling and Election

3 His divine power[f] has given us everything we need for a godly life through
our knowledge of him who called us[g] by
his own glory and goodness. 4 Through
these he has given us his very great and
precious promises,[h] so that through
them you may participate in the divine
nature,[i] having escaped the corruption
in the world caused by evil desires.[j]
5 For this very reason, make every effort to add to your faith goodness; and
to goodness, knowledge;[k] 6 and to knowledge, self-control;[l] and to self-control,
perseverance; and to perseverance, godliness;[m] 7 and to godliness, mutual affec-

1:1 [a] Ro 1:1 [b] 1Pe 1:1 [c] Ro 3:21-26 [d] Titus 2:13
1:2 [e] Php 3:8
1:3 [f] 1Pe 1:5 [g] 1Th 2:12
1:4 [h] 2Co 7:1 [i] Eph 4:24; Heb 12:10; 1Jn 3:2 [j] 2Pe 2:18-20
1:5 [k] Col 2:3
1:6 [l] Ac 24:25 [m] ver 3

2Pe 1:4 ❖ How can we picture ourselves as participating in "the divine nature"? How does this impact our choices and conduct?

1:1–2 In calling himself a "servant . . . of Jesus Christ," Peter here conveys his sense of humility in relationship to his Lord. Peter's right to speak authoritatively to these Christians is emphasized even more clearly in the second title, "apostle." This most often describes those chosen specially by the Lord to be his authoritative representatives.

APPLICATION ✣ 1:1–2 Peter's readers are Gentiles who have "received a faith as precious as ours." Gentile Christians are no second-class citizens in the kingdom of heaven. Significantly, Peter opens and closes the letter with a reference to the knowledge of God and Christ. He refers to this knowledge again in vv. 3 and 8 as the foundation for his readers' Christian experience.

1:3 Spiritual maturity begins with God's provision. It is "his divine power" for new spiritual life and for a "godly life" (v. 3a). Peter is referring to Christ's divine power unleashed through his death and resurrection. Godliness is prominent in this opening sermon. The phrase "godly life" can also be read as "good worship." It summarizes the behavior expected of Christians.

God has made his power available in a specific way: "through our knowledge of him who called us" (v. 3b). "Knowledge" refers to an intimate and informed relationship that is the product of conversion to the gospel. Peter adds that Christ calls us "by his own glory and goodness" (v. 3c). Christ lived a sinless life and went to the cross in obedience to the Father. Through this "active" and "passive" obedience, he was qualified to offer himself as a sacrifice on our behalf.

1:4 In saying, "Through these he has given us his very great and precious promises" (v. 4a), Peter means that through these attributes, Christ has provided for the *fulfillment* of these promises. Christians now have the privilege of enjoying intimacy with God—or, as Peter puts it, Christians "may participate in the divine nature" (v. 4b). What Peter seems to mean is that believers come to share some essential qualities characteristic of God himself.

1:5–9 Peter describes eight Christian virtues that must be added, one to the other, as we move upward in our pursuit of spiritual maturity. All of them are important; Peter likely doesn't intend to say that we must pursue them in the precise order he gives them. The way in which Peter begins his list of virtues might suggest that he thinks his readers at this point possess only faith and that they have to add all the others. But Peter goes on to show that this is not the case.

tion; and to mutual affection, love.[n] 8For
if you possess these qualities in increasing measure, they will keep you from being ineffective and unproductive[o] in your
knowledge of our Lord Jesus Christ. 9But
whoever does not have them is near-
sighted and blind,[p] forgetting that they
have been cleansed from their past sins.[q]
10Therefore, my brothers and sisters,[a]
make every effort to confirm your calling
and election. For if you do these things,
you will never stumble,[r] 11and you will receive a rich welcome into the eternal kingdom of our Lord and Savior Jesus Christ.

Prophecy of Scripture

12So I will always remind you of these
things,[s] even though you know them
and are firmly established in the truth
you now have. 13I think it is right to refresh your memory as long as I live in
the tent of this body,[t] 14because I know
that I will soon put it aside,[u] as our Lord
Jesus Christ has made clear to me.[v] 15And
I will make every effort to see that after
my departure[w] you will always be able
to remember these things.
16For we did not follow cleverly devised stories when we told you about the
coming of our Lord Jesus Christ in power,
but we were eyewitnesses of his majesty.[x]
17He received honor and glory from God
the Father when the voice came to him
from the Majestic Glory, saying, "This
is my Son, whom I love; with him I am
well pleased."[b][y] 18We ourselves heard this
voice that came from heaven when we
were with him on the sacred mountain.[z]

1:7 [n] 1Th 3:12
1:8 [o] Jn 15:2; Titus 3:14
1:9 [p] 1Jn 2:11 [q] Eph 5:26
1:10 [r] 2Pe 3:17
1:12 [s] Php 3:1; 1Jn 2:21
1:13 [t] 2Co 5:1,4
1:14 [u] 2Ti 4:6 [v] Jn 21:18,19
1:15 [w] Lk 9:31
1:16 [x] Mt 17:1-8
1:17 [y] Mt 3:17
1:18 [z] Mt 17:6

[a] *10* The Greek word for *brothers and sisters* (*adelphoi*) refers here to believers, both men and women, as part of God's family. [b] *17* Matt. 17:5; Mark 9:7; Luke 9:35

1:8 Here Peter implies that they already "possess" these virtues. The issue is not one of having or not having them; the issue is one of growing in the degree to which the Christian exhibits them.
1:9 Peter touches for the first time on why, in his reader's own situation, this growth in knowledge of Christ is so important: There are false teachers among the believers (2:1) who are not now living as if their belief in Christ makes any difference to them.
1:10–11 Peter mentions two reasons why it is important for Christians to "confirm [their] calling and election" (v. 10a), one negative and one positive. Negatively, Christians are to respond in this way so that they "will never stumble" (v. 10b). This leads us to the positive reason: to bring "a rich welcome into the eternal kingdom of our Lord and Savior Jesus Christ" (v. 11).

✣ **1:3–11** "Participating in the divine nature" (v. 4) is a great and precious privilege. Through our union with Christ and the indwelling of the Holy Spirit, we share in something of God's own holy nature, separated from the corrupt world around us. And it is precisely "for this very reason" (v. 5) that we are called on to progress in holiness and godliness. But the very fact that Peter encourages us to make such progress shows that participating in the divine nature does not bring us into a state of sinlessness or even into a situation in which we can lay back and simply enjoy our new status. We must keep pressing forward by faith.

1:12–15 Peter realizes that what he is saying to these Christians is not new. As Peter puts it, they "are firmly established in the truth" (v. 12b). Peter wants especially to stress that his ministry is limited. He will soon be putting aside his earthly body. How does he know this? Because the "Lord Jesus Christ has made it clear to me" (v. 14). Peter refers to the prophecy about his death that we find at the end of John's Gospel. Faced with imminent death, Peter makes a last appeal to his readers. Yet he trusts that the force of this appeal will go on "after [his] departure" (v. 15).

✣ **1:12–15** It takes the ministry of the Holy Spirit to "bring to mind" the truths of the gospel (Jn 14:26). But God's Word, written and proclaimed, is the source of that reminder. And what Peter is indirectly suggesting here is that the repetition of the truths of the gospel, in both word and in acted "memorials" like the Lord's Supper, is a necessary component of a vital Christian experience.

1:16–18 The "we" must refer to Peter and other apostles since only they were eyewitnesses of the transfiguration. The fact of Christ's transfiguration and the belief that he will come again rests on the testimony of several apostolic eyewitnesses.

The apostles were "eyewitnesses of his majesty." "Stories" (v. 16) translates the Greek from which we get "myth." This Greek word had a broad range of meanings, but the meaning most relevant to our verse is the sense "fictional account, fable."
1:17 Peter asserts positively that the teaching is the direct product of eyewitness testimony. At the transfiguration, as Peter puts it, Christ "received honor and glory from God the Father" (v. 17a). Christ's exalted status is indicated by the accompanying signs (see Mt 17:2) and by the voice from heaven that identifies Jesus as both Messiah and suffering servant.
1:18 Peter reminds his readers that he was an "ear-witness": "We ourselves heard this voice." As the Gospel accounts make clear, the "we" here includes Peter, James, and John. Jesus selected these three from among the apostolic band so that they might be "with him on the sacred mountain." The transfiguration reveals Jesus as the glorious King, and Peter was there to see it. He therefore has total confidence that Jesus will return as the glorious King and establish his kingdom in its final and ultimate form.

19We also have the prophetic message
as something completely reliable, and
you will do well to pay attention to it,
as to a light[a] shining in a dark place,
until the day dawns and the morning
star[b] rises in your hearts. 20Above all,
you must understand that no prophecy
of Scripture came about by the prophet's own interpretation of things. 21For
prophecy never had its origin in the human will, but prophets, though human,
spoke from God[c] as they were carried
along by the Holy Spirit.[d]

False Teachers and Their Destruction

2 But there were also false prophets[e]
among the people, just as there will
be false teachers among you.[f] They will
secretly introduce destructive heresies,
even denying the sovereign Lord[g] who
bought them[h]—bringing swift destruction on themselves. 2Many will follow
their depraved conduct and will bring
the way of truth into disrepute. 3In their
greed these teachers will exploit you[i] with
fabricated stories. Their condemnation
has long been hanging over them, and
their destruction has not been sleeping.

1:19 [a] Ps 119:105 [b] Rev 22:16
1:21 [c] 2Ti 3:16 [d] 2Sa 23:2; Ac 1:16; 1Pe 1:11
2:1 [e] Dt 13:1-3 [f] 1Ti 4:1 [g] Jude 4 [h] 1Co 6:20
2:3 [i] 2Co 2:17; 1Th 2:5
2:4 [j] Jude 6; Rev 20:1, 2
2:5 [k] 2Pe 3:6 [l] Heb 11:7; 1Pe 3:20
2:6 [m] Ge 19:24, 25 [n] Nu 26:10; Jude 7
2:7 [o] Ge 19:16 [p] 2Pe 3:17
2:9 [q] 1Co 10:13

2Pe 2:2 ❖ Where do we see false or wayward Christians bringing "the way of truth into disrepute"? What are the consequences? How can we model something better?

4For if God did not spare angels when
they sinned, but sent them to hell,[a] putting them in chains of darkness[b] to be
held for judgment;[j] 5if he did not spare
the ancient world[k] when he brought the
flood on its ungodly people, but protected
Noah, a preacher of righteousness, and
seven others;[l] 6if he condemned the cities
of Sodom and Gomorrah by burning them
to ashes,[m] and made them an example[n] of
what is going to happen to the ungodly;
7and if he rescued Lot,[o] a righteous man,
who was distressed by the depraved conduct of the lawless[p] 8(for that righteous
man, living among them day after day,
was tormented in his righteous soul by
the lawless deeds he saw and heard)— 9if
this is so, then the Lord knows how to
rescue the godly from trials[q] and to hold

[a] 4 Greek *Tartarus* [b] 4 Some manuscripts *in gloomy dungeons*

1:19–21 Peter, James, and John can testify to the revelation of Christ's glory. But the prophets also testify to Christ's appearance at the end of history. Confidence in the reliability of the prophetic word should lead to a firm devotion to its teaching. Peter urges his readers to "pay attention to it, as to a light shining in a dark place" (v. 19b).

1:20–21 Peter reinforces what he has said about the origin of prophecy in v. 20. The belief that the prophets spoke for God is, of course, basic to the Scriptures. The words they chose to use were *also* the words that God wanted them to use to communicate the message he intended.

✣ **1:16–21** For many, the Bible is "inspired" in only the loosest sense—as, for example, some might think an author might be "inspired" to write a novel. But among confessing Christians also we sometimes encounter those who insist that God must have "accommodated" himself to the human writers of Scripture. The result, they suggest, is that we still have errors in the Bible. God, by nature, does not lie; he cannot utter a falsehood. If the words of Scripture are genuinely God's words, then the words of Scripture must be without error.

2:1–3 Peter here briefly profiles the false teachers. First, they are *devious*; they obscure how their teaching differs from apostolic teaching. Second, they are perpetrating a serious error: "denying the sovereign Lord who bought them" (v. 1). The destiny of these false teachers is, like those who follow them, "destruction" (v. 1).

These false teachers are popular. Their impact on the Christian movement is disastrous. Those who follow them bring "the way of truth into disrepute." The false teachers are motivated by greed (v. 3a). The basis of their teaching is stories they have made up.

✣ **2:1–3** Peter's warnings about false teachers are as appropriate today as they were in his time. Indeed, our Lord has warned us to expect such deviations from the faith. The church will always have to contend with both the outright opposition of those who reject Christ entirely and the more subtle threats of those who claim the name of Christ but twist and distort the Christian message. Indeed, precisely because they are more subtle, the latter threat is often the more dangerous one.

2:4 Genesis 6:1–4 tells about "sons of God" who were attracted to the "daughters of humans." Peter likely has this story in mind.

2:5 Peter's next warning example comes from one of the most famous judgments of God found in the OT: the flood in Noah's day (v. 5). Peter uses similar wording to connect these first two examples: God "did not spare" (v. 4) the angels who sinned, and he "did not spare" the "ancient world" either (v. 5).

2:6–7 Like the flood narrative, the story of Sodom and Gomorrah also has a positive side. God "rescued Lot, a righteous man" from the disaster, just as he rescued Noah and his family (v. 7).

2:9–10a Some commentators think that Peter is referring to the great trial of faith that will occur

the unrighteous for punishment on the
day of judgment. 10This is especially true
of those who follow the corrupt desire[r] of
the flesh[a] and despise authority.

Bold and arrogant, they are not afraid
to heap abuse on celestial beings;[s] 11yet
even angels, although they are stronger
and more powerful, do not heap abuse
on such beings when bringing judgment
on them from[b] the Lord.[t] 12But these people blaspheme in matters they do not
understand. They are like unreasoning
animals, creatures of instinct, born only
to be caught and destroyed, and like animals they too will perish.[u]

13They will be paid back with harm for
the harm they have done. Their idea of
pleasure is to carouse in broad daylight.[v]
They are blots and blemishes, reveling
in their pleasures while they feast with
you.[c][w] 14With eyes full of adultery, they
never stop sinning; they seduce[x] the unstable; they are experts in greed[y] — an
accursed brood![z] 15They have left the
straight way and wandered off to follow the way of Balaam[a] son of Bezer,[d]
who loved the wages of wickedness. 16But
he was rebuked for his wrongdoing by a
donkey — an animal without speech —
who spoke with a human voice and restrained the prophet's madness.[b]

17These people are springs without

2:10 [r] 2Pe 3:3 [s] Jude 8
2:11 [t] Jude 9
2:12 [u] Jude 10
2:13 [v] Ro 13:13
[w] 1Co 11:20, 21; Jude 12
2:14 [x] ver 18 [y] ver 3 [z] Eph 2:3
2:15 [a] Nu 22:4-20; Jude 11
2:16 [b] Nu 22:21-30

[a] *10* In contexts like this, the Greek word for *flesh* (*sarx*) refers to the sinful state of human beings, often presented as a power in opposition to the Spirit; also in verse 18. [b] *11* Many manuscripts *beings in the presence of* [c] *13* Some manuscripts *in their love feasts* [d] *15* Greek *Bosor*

---

at the end of history. It is probably best to understand that Peter includes in the "trials" here in v. 9 all challenges to faith.

Peter provides two general characteristics of these false teachers: They "follow the corrupt desire of the flesh," and they "despise authority" (v. 10a). In light of Peter's reference to Sodom and Gomorrah, the first reference probably includes sexual sin. "Despising authority" is a general charge to the effect that the false teachers are self-willed and rebellious.

> **2:4–10a** Everywhere we look, we find people advocating ideas that the Bible clearly condemns yet claiming that they are the true way to find God, or "the meaning in life," or spiritual fulfillment. How should Christians react to the abandonment of Christian moral norms in the West? Many, to be sure, and to their credit, are responding vigorously, with a loving but firm restatement of the biblical perspective. But many of us simply accept what is happening without any undue fuss or concern. We are not "distressed" (v. 7) or "tormented" (v. 8) by what we see around us. We may be disturbed by these developments and deplore those who choose an unbiblical lifestyle. But few Christians experience the "torment of soul" that Lot felt as he faced the ungodliness of his society.

2:10b–13a It is likely that the false teachers were mocking the possibility that their sins might put them at the mercy of such evil spiritual beings. In their arrogance, the false teachers were denying this fact. Peter goes on to compare the false teachers to animals. In a word, they are "unspiritual" and bound for destruction.

2:13b Sinful indulgence usually took place under cover of darkness. Practicing such hedonistic activities "in broad daylight" indicates the false teachers are shameless. They are further described as "blots and blemishes" (v. 13c). Peter rebukes the false teachers for indulging their sinful pleasures even as they continue to join other Christians at the church's fellowship meals.

2:14 "With eyes full of adultery, they never stop sinning" (v. 14a). They are so addicted to sex that they look at every woman as a potential partner in their lust. "Seduce" translates a Greek word that suggests the bait used to lure a fish to the hook or an animal to the trap. They are also described as "experts in greed" (v. 14b). The phrase "an accursed brood!" (or "children of curse") conveys that Peter once again interjects this reminder of their ultimate fate.

2:15–16 Peter next writes the false teachers "have left the straight way and wandered off to follow the way of Balaam son of Bezer." Balaam's willingness to curse Israel for profit became a staple in Jewish stories about him. Balaam was responsible for Israel's rebellion against God with the women of Midian (see Nu 25). Balaam had given himself to "madness" and so have the false teachers (2Pe 2:16).

> **2:10b–16** False teaching is often revealed in false living. "By their fruit you will recognize them," Jesus told his disciples as he warned them about false prophets (Mt 7:16). And so it always is: Following bad doctrine leads to bad practices. The false teachers of Peter's day were spreading wrong ideas about Christ's return in glory and about judgment to come (cf. 1:16–21; 3:3–12). And Peter takes them to task for it. But he also paints this vivid picture of their sinful lifestyle in ch. 2 to show, from another angle, that these people cannot be trusted to represent the true Christian faith.

2:17 In the dry climate of the Middle East, a spring of water is a marvelous blessing. Imagine the weary traveler's chagrin when he or she finds the spring to be dry. So is the false teachers' message: it disappoints the spiritual pilgrim by promising spiritual vitality but not delivering it. Rather than producing life-giving rain, mist served as a harbinger of dry weather to come. The two metaphors characterize the message of the false teachers as hollow and disillusioning. Peter pronounces a sentence of judgment: "Blackest darkness is reserved for them" (v. 17b).

water[c] and mists driven by a storm.
Blackest darkness is reserved for them.[d]
18 For they mouth empty, boastful words[e]
and, by appealing to the lustful desires
of the flesh, they entice people who are
just escaping from those who live in error. 19 They promise them freedom, while
they themselves are slaves of depravity — for "people are slaves to whatever has mastered them."[f] 20 If they have
escaped the corruption of the world by
knowing[g] our Lord and Savior Jesus
Christ and are again entangled in it and
are overcome, they are worse off at the
end than they were at the beginning.[h]
21 It would have been better for them not
to have known the way of righteousness, than to have known it and then to
turn their backs on the sacred command
that was passed on to them.[i] 22 Of them
the proverbs are true: "A dog returns to
its vomit,"[a][j] and, "A sow that is washed
returns to her wallowing in the mud."

The Day of the Lord

3 Dear friends, this is now my second
letter to you. I have written both of
them as reminders[k] to stimulate you to
wholesome thinking. 2 I want you to recall the words spoken in the past by the
holy prophets and the command giv-
en by our Lord and Savior through your
apostles.

3 Above all, you must understand that
in the last days[l] scoffers will come, scoffing and following their own evil desires.[m]
4 They will say, "Where is this 'coming'
he promised?[n] Ever since our ancestors
died, everything goes on as it has since
the beginning of creation."[o] 5 But they deliberately forget that long ago by God's
word[p] the heavens came into being and
the earth was formed out of water and by
water.[q] 6 By these waters also the world of
that time was deluged and destroyed.[r] 7 By

2:17 [c] Jude 12 [d] Jude 13
2:18 [e] Jude 16
2:19 [f] Jn 8:34; Ro 6:16
2:20 [g] 2Pe 1:2 [h] Mt 12:45
2:21 [i] Heb 6:4-6
2:22 [j] Pr 26:11
3:1 [k] 2Pe 1:13
3:3 [l] 1Ti 4:1 [m] 2Pe 2:10; Jude 18
3:4 [n] Isa 5:19; Eze 12:22; Mt 24:48 [o] Mk 10:6
3:5 [p] Ge 1:6, 9; Heb 11:3 [q] Ps 24:2
3:6 [r] Ge 7:21,22

[a] *22* Prov. 26:11

2:18 The false teachers' words cannot produce the spiritual fulfillment they promise. The false teachers also entice "by appealing to the lustful desires of the flesh" (v. 18b). The word "lustful" represents a pleasure-focused lifestyle of sexual promiscuity, gluttony, and drunkenness.

Clever in picking their targets, they dangle their lure in front of "people who are just escaping from those who live in error" (v. 18c). Peter pictures new converts in the process of distancing themselves from pagan society.

2:19 Peter describes enticing recent converts from their faith by promising freedom. They abuse grace by turning it into a license to sin.

2:20–22 Peter here continues his description of the false teachers. These false teachers gave every evidence of being Christians. Yet they ran the risk of becoming "entangled" in the corruption of the world again and, indeed, of being "overcome" by it (v. 20).

Peter has composed vv. 20–22 almost entirely out of traditional material: a saying of Jesus in v. 20 and two extrabiblical proverbs. The meaning of the first proverb is clear enough: Returning to the corruption of the world is like what a dog does (v. 22a) or like what a pig does (v. 22b). Having been washed clean by the blood of Christ, they are nevertheless anxious to return again to the disgusting filth of the world. No believer should willingly welcome that kind of filth back into their lives.

✚ **2:17–22** Peter implies in his warning a point that Scripture makes clear in many places: The more we know of God when we reject his truth, the greater will be our punishment. Sensitive believers and even unbelievers are often disturbed by this denial of the possibility of forgiveness. The very fact that someone is worried about having committed the unpardonable sin of rejecting the Spirit's call to belief (Mt 12:31–32) shows that he or she has not committed it. Such concern and desire to believe suggests that the Holy Spirit, far from abandoning this person, is still at work in his or her life.

3:1–2 Peter mentions two sources for the teaching he wants his readers to put into action. First is "the words spoken in the past by the holy prophets" (v. 2). Second is "the command given by our Lord and Savior through [the] apostles." Peter is thinking of the basic command that believers conform to the image of Christ, becoming holy even as the God who called them is holy.

3:3–4 The mockers Peter is concerned about were not apparently mocking the faith generally. They were scoffing at one particular teaching of the faith: the belief that Christ will return in glory at the end of history. They based this rejection of the coming of Christ on a general belief in the unchanging nature of the world: "Ever since our ancestors died, everything goes on as it has since the beginning of creation" (v. 4). The false teachers refused to believe the change in the world and the human situation that the church's teaching about the second coming assumed.

3:5–7 Peter's general point in v. 5 is clear: God brought the universe into existence. He did so by his own creative word and through the use of water. Therefore, the false teachers' assumption of an unchanging universe is without warrant. The very universe they are talking about has not always been here. Through God's speech, the world of Noah's day was destroyed, and through "the same word" (v. 7), it will be destroyed again. This time, however, God will use fire rather than water to bring about the destruction.

✚ **3:1–7** We must guard against the temptation to think we can precisely identify what God is

CHARACTER OF GOD // **GOD IS PATIENT**

2 Peter 3:9: The Lord is not slow in keeping his promise, as some understand slowness. Instead he is patient with you, not wanting anyone to perish, but everyone to come to repentance.

People often characterize the God of the Bible as vengeful and eager to strike down sinners, especially when they think of stories in the OT. It is certainly true that God punishes sin, but a closer reading of the Bible offers many examples of God's patience.

For example, God did not destroy Sodom until there was not a single righteous person left. God even told Abraham that he would not destroy the whole city if ten righteous people could be found there (Ge 18:32). When God promised the land of Canaan to Abraham's descendants, God told Abraham it would not happen for four generations, "for the sin of the Amorites has not yet reached its full measure" (Ge 15:16). Even with Israel's enemies, God was patient.

God describes himself to Moses as "slow to anger" (Ex 34:6). And the prophet Joel pleads with his listeners to return to God, offering the hope that God is "slow to anger" and may yet forgive (Joel 2:13). In fact, Jonah wished that God was *less* slow to anger: He was upset that God did not bring swift destruction upon Nineveh (Jnh 4:2).

God's people tried his patience again and again in the OT. Though their sin and idolatry was often punished, God did not destroy them completely. Even when God allowed them to be taken into captivity in Babylon, God was not finished with them. He promised them hope and a future (Jer 29:11).

APPLICATION ✤ Sometimes we struggle with how slow God seems to be acting. Why doesn't he crush wickedness right now? Why doesn't Christ return immediately so that sin and pain will be eradicated sooner rather than later? It's understandable that we want God to act quickly to spare us suffering, but Peter helps us understand how God's "slowness" is integrally connected to God's mercy and love. Second Peter 3:9 says God is not slow but instead patient. God could strike hard and fast, but instead God chooses to be patient so that more people might be saved through his redeeming love.

the same word the present heavens and
earth are reserved for fire,[s] being kept
for the day of judgment and destruction
of the ungodly.
8But do not forget this one thing,
dear friends: With the Lord a day is like
a thousand years, and a thousand years
are like a day.[t] 9The Lord is not slow in
keeping his promise,[u] as some understand slowness. Instead he is patient[v]
with you, not wanting anyone to perish,
but everyone to come to repentance.[w]
10But the day of the Lord will come like
a thief.[x] The heavens will disappear with

3:7 [s]ver 10,12; 2Th 1:7
3:8 [t]Ps 90:4
3:9 [u]Hab 2:3; Heb 10:37 [v]Ro 2:4 [w]1Ti 2:4
3:10 [x]Lk 12:39; 1Th 5:2

2Pe 3:9 ✤ How can we make the best use of the time afforded to us by God's patience, endeavoring to spread Christ to as many as possible?

---

doing in every event in history. God has not stepped off the throne of the universe, nor has he stood aside to let events take their course. We need to recapture the biblical worldview in which all of life is filled with the presence and activity of a personal, holy, and loving God who guides history toward a definite end.

3:8 Christians must realize that our perception of time is not the same as God's. What seems like long ages to us is a mere blip in time to him (v. 8).

3:9 Peter addresses God's purpose in delaying the return. His delay in sending Christ in judgment is a sign of his deep concern for human beings (v. 9b). He is waiting for people to repent before it is too late.

3:10 Peter moves from argument to assertion: "The day of the Lord will come like a thief." The time of Christ's coming cannot be calculated. Like a thief, he can appear at any time.

✤ **3:8–10** Date-setters have arisen throughout the history of the church and have misled many sincere Christians. We are called constantly to live in the light of the end of history, even if we can see no obvious signs of its end in the world around us. God can certainly use the world around us to wake us up and help us see the truth. But when all is said and done, we "live by faith, not by sight" (2Co 5:7). We must trust the promise of Christ's coming despite not knowing its timing.

a roar; the elements will be destroyed by
fire, and the earth and everything done
in it will be laid bare.[a][y]
11 Since everything will be destroyed in
this way, what kind of people ought you
to be? You ought to live holy and godly
lives 12 as you look forward[z] to the day
of God and speed its coming.[b][a] That day
will bring about the destruction of the
heavens by fire, and the elements will
melt in the heat.[b] 13 But in keeping with
his promise we are looking forward to
a new heaven and a new earth,[c] where
righteousness dwells.
14 So then, dear friends, since you are
looking forward to this, make every effort to be found spotless, blameless[d] and
at peace with him. 15 Bear in mind that
our Lord's patience[e] means salvation,[f]
just as our dear brother Paul also wrote
you with the wisdom that God gave
him.[g] 16 He writes the same way in all
his letters, speaking in them of these
matters. His letters contain some things
that are hard to understand, which ignorant and unstable[h] people distort, as
they do the other Scriptures,[i] to their
own destruction.
17 Therefore, dear friends, since you
have been forewarned, be on your guard[j]
so that you may not be carried away by
the error[k] of the lawless and fall from
your secure position.[l] 18 But grow in the
grace and knowledge of our Lord and
Savior Jesus Christ.[m] To him be glory
both now and forever! Amen.

3:10 [y] Mt 24:35; Rev 21:1
3:12 [z] 1Co 1:7 [a] Ps 50:3 [b] ver 10
3:13 [c] Isa 65:17; 66:22; Rev 21:1
3:14 [d] 1Th 3:13
3:15 [e] Ro 2:4 [f] ver 9 [g] Eph 3:3
3:16 [h] 2Pe 2:14 [i] ver 2
3:17 [j] 1Co 10:12 [k] 2Pe 2:18 [l] Rev 2:5
3:18 [m] 2Pe 1:11

[a] 10 Some manuscripts *be burned up* [b] 12 Or *as you wait eagerly for the day of God to come*

3:11–12 God did not build this world to last forever (v. 11a). That being the case, Peter asks, "What kind of people ought you to be?" (v. 11b). Peter makes the point clear enough by immediately answering his own question: "You ought to live holy and godly lives" (v. 11c). Having begun his appeal to holy living with a reminder of the end times, Peter concludes it with another: We are to "look forward to the day of God and speed its coming" (v. 12a).

3:13 God has promised a "new heaven and a new earth." The important point is not speculation about the exact nature of this new heaven and earth, but that it will be "where righteousness dwells."

✣ 3:11–13 Christians need to remember the ultimate purpose of end times teaching: to make us better Christians here and now. We must not study this teaching for the gratification of our curiosity. As Peter makes clear in v. 11, this teaching is meant to stimulate a holy and godly lifestyle in believers. In fact, we will find no NT passage about the end times that does not have that kind of specific, practical focus.

3:14–15a Peter conjures up the scene of the court of law, where the judge "finds" defendants guilty or innocent. Motivated by the coming day of the Lord, believers should work hard to be found pure and blameless when God assesses our lives. The command in v. 15 parallels the one at the end of v. 9. Christians are to adopt an attitude that is exactly opposite to that of the false teachers. The latter considered the delay to be a sign of God's "slowness," concluding that judgment may never come. On the other hand, Christians are to "consider" the delay as an opportunity to pursue salvation.

3:15b–16 What Paul wrote in his letters came not from his study or imagination but from God, who gave Paul the wisdom to understand and apply the gospel in his generation. Peter's implicit point emerges from his claim that the false teachers distort Paul's letters "as they do the other Scriptures" (v. 16). Peter considers the letters of Paul to belong to the category of "Scripture" and implies that the letters of Paul have a status equivalent to the OT itself.

3:17–18a Peter summarizes his root concern that his readers continue to grow spiritually, becoming more and more like Christ.

3:18b Only here, in 2Ti 4:18, and in Rev 1:5–6 do we find doxologies directed to Christ. Christ's coming will inaugurate the next age—a "day" that will last forever. We glorify Christ, looking to this day and earnestly waiting for it.

✣ 3:14–18 The finality of our decisions in this life is assumed throughout the NT and, as we have seen, in 2Pe 3 as well. Perhaps there are readers who have not yet committed themselves in faith to Christ. For them, the implications of this point are clear: Now is the time to decide; death or the second coming can happen at any time. For those who already know the Lord, the implications are also clear: Now is the time to share the Good News of Christ—with your family member, your neighbor, your coworker, your fellow team member—before it is too late.

Author: The apostle John
Audience: Believers in and around Ephesus
Date: Between AD 85 and 95

Theme: John writes to assure believers of the certainty of their faith and to refute heretical doctrines teaching that Jesus was not fully human and fully divine.

PERSPECTIVE

We live in an age in which discernment has never been more important: Christian discernment; theological discernment; discernment based on biblical standards; discernment that will show us the narrow way between excess and stinginess, license and legalism, innovation and sterility. In the face of a culture bombarding us with the pop wisdom that the difference between true and false is an outdated remnant of Western dualism, Christians must never relinquish the need to proclaim the difference between right and wrong. The letters of John teach just such discernment.

The community to which John wrote was struggling with internal theological threats that can only be called heretical. John, the author of these letters, demands that the Christians reading these words realize that they have a responsibility to discern between the true and the false, between Christian behavior and unchristian behavior. The three letters of John are a clear call to believe and stand firm in the historic incarnation and revelation of Jesus Christ.

We need discernment every bit as much as did the first readers of 1 John, 2 John, and 3 John, but the need takes a different form these days. We are living in a time between worldviews, a vacant, interim period between a consensual, orthodox championing of a single theological system and an as yet unknown approach to truth that will come to grips with (and finally defeat) that powerful conviction that there is no single gospel truth. Into this vacuum have rushed a flood of theological experiments, each attempting to reconcile the eternal, unchanging nature of God with the constantly shifting focus of everyday life.

Reading 1 John

Reading 1 John is like listening to a piece of music. The author has several main themes (such as light, love, life, truth and sin), and they keep reappearing in new combinations. It may be best to scan the whole book first before concentrating on the individual parts.

10 BC AD 1 10 20 30 40 50 60 70 80 90 100

Jesus' birth (c. 6/5 BC)
John becomes a disciple (c. AD 26)
Jesus' death, resurrection and ascension (c. AD 30)
Nero's reign (AD 54–68)
Destruction of Jerusalem's temple (c. AD 70)
Domitian's reign (c. AD 81–96)
Book of 1 John written (c. AD 85–95)
John's exile on Patmos (c. AD 90–95)

Key Verse

We know also that the Son of God has come and has given us understanding, so that we may know him who is true. And we are in him who is true by being in his Son Jesus Christ. He is the true God and eternal life.

—1 John 5:20

Make no mistake; this vacuum is real. It is a vacuum that will produce a new, gospel-honoring approach to theology, a theology that will reflect unchanging scriptural truth. But in the meantime, a thousand theologies will bloom and have their day in the sun. Like wildflowers dotting today's theological wilderness, they will each display a raw if temporary beauty. We must judge which will last.

Each of these wildflower theologies has some value. They are like the short-term flora and fauna that spring up in ecological systems ravaged by disasters like forest fires. They hold the ground in place until the larger, more stable plants get a chance to grow back. Wildflower theology can serve a similar purpose, but in the end their true nature as opportunistic mistakes emerges, and they drift away.

They wither away, that is, if we as the true church are doing our job—the job of theological discernment, a job that in its essence has not changed from John's day. John taught that the measuring sticks of true discernment will never change: the truth revealed in the historical coming of Jesus Christ and everything which that glorious event revealed, and in the powerful theological traditions that have grown up around that event. Those are our measuring sticks, too.

In the end a theology will prevail, a theology that picks up the threat of truth that goes back to creation itself. But that theology will not come without hard work and some risk, and these letters from John can play a crucial role in the task of discerning truth.

For more perspective on this book, see the Introductions to 2 John and 3 John.

TAKING THE NEXT STEPS

The apostle John wrote this letter toward the end of his life, shortly after the writing of his Gospel; both books contain similar words and themes. Facing the threat of an early Christian heresy, John wanted his readers (whom he called his "children") to know the truth. He warned them against sin, though he also assured them of forgiveness and eternal life if they did fall into sin. Finally, he encouraged them to walk in love, using the love of God as their model.

This brief letter is one of the Bible books best loved by contemporary Christians. (1) We can be sure that if we confess our sins, God will forgive us through his Son, Jesus. (2) Eternal life is not a vague hope but a certainty, based on God's promises in his Word. (3) To discern the difference between true Christianity and false Christianity, the most important question to ask is: What do you think about Jesus? (4) God's love in sending his Son, and Jesus' love in sacrificing himself, ought to serve as the pattern of love for our lives. (5) If we have Jesus living in our hearts, we can achieve victory over sin.

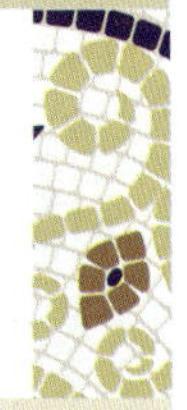

WHAT TO LOOK FOR IN 1 JOHN

- Walking in truth and light (ch. 1)
- Loving God and loving one another (chs. 3–4)
- Believing in God's Son, Jesus (ch. 5)

The Incarnation of the Word of Life

1 That which was from the beginning,[a] which we have heard, which
we have seen with our eyes,[b] which
we have looked at and our hands have
touched[c] — this we proclaim concerning
the Word of life. 2 The life appeared;[d] we
have seen it and testify to it, and we proclaim to you the eternal life, which was
with the Father and has appeared to us.
3 We proclaim to you what we have seen
and heard, so that you also may have
fellowship with us. And our fellowship
is with the Father and with his Son, Jesus
Christ.[e] 4 We write this[f] to make our[a] joy
complete.[g]

Light and Darkness, Sin and Forgiveness

5 This is the message we have heard[h]
from him and declare to you: God is light;
in him there is no darkness at all. 6 If we
claim to have fellowship with him and
yet walk in the darkness,[i] we lie and do
not live out the truth.[j] 7 But if we walk in
the light, as he is in the light, we have
fellowship with one another, and the
blood of Jesus, his Son, purifies us from
all[b] sin.[k]
8 If we claim to be without sin,[l] we deceive ourselves and the truth is not in us.[m]
9 If we confess our sins, he is faithful and
just and will forgive us our sins[n] and purify us from all unrighteousness. 10 If we

1:1 [a] Jn 1:2 [b] Jn 1:14; 2Pe 1:16 [c] Jn 20:27
1:2 [d] Jn 1:1-4; 1Ti 3:16
1:3 [e] 1Co 1:9
1:4 [f] 1Jn 2:1 [g] Jn 3:29
1:5 [h] 1Jn 3:11
1:6 [i] 2Co 6:14 [j] Jn 3:19-21
1:7 [k] Heb 9:14; Rev 1:5
1:8 [l] Pr 20:9; Jas 3:2 [m] 1Jn 2:4
1:9 [n] Ps 32:5; 51:2

> **1Jn 1:1-4** ❖ How do these verses reassure us of God's love and care for us, both now and in the future?

[a] 4 Some manuscripts *your* [b] 7 Or *every*

1:1a John establishes the reality of Jesus' true personhood—his incarnation or his entry into history. He speaks realistically of the sensory confirmation that accompanied this revelation.

1:1b–2 Eternal life is historically anchored in a particular event. The life of God has been channeled to us through this historical event and verified by people who saw it.

1:3–4 Christian community is triangular: my fellowship with Christ, your fellowship with Christ, and my fellowship with you. Christian community grows from a matured relationship with God in his Son, Jesus Christ. Without it, such community is an impossibility.

> **APPLICATION ✚ 1:1–4** True Christian community is linked to true experiences of Jesus. Today the authenticity of our faith is likewise linked to the vitality of Jesus' life within us. If Jesus is a doctrine, our testimony will be hollow. If Jesus is a person, our testimony will be potent.

1:5 Light unveils our spiritual identity—whether we abide in the Son—and it identifies those who live in darkness.

1:6 John's opponents were not just *in darkness*, they were living lives of darkness. They were persistent in the habits they had chosen. They were lying and self-deceiving in their conduct. Such conduct prefers to remain in darkness rather than be exposed by God's light.

1:7 John is one of the few NT writers to draw the connection between our spiritual integrity and the quality of the communities we create.

> ✚ **1:5–7** Those who walk in light discover lives that are knit together by God's forgiveness and redemption. To walk in this light is humbling, but it is also healing, renewing, and invigorating.

1:8–9 John's opponents did not think sin impedes our relationship with God. So John warns his readers that these people may not even be Christians at all. And their only recourse is confession.

1:10 Can someone claim that they have never committed any sins? Such a position challenges God's character, making him a liar (v. 10).

ONE MESSAGE: JOHN'S GOSPEL AND LETTERS

JOHN	1 JOHN	2 JOHN
13:34-35 "A new command I give to you: Love one another. As I have loved you, so you must love one another. By this everyone will know that you are my disciples, if you love one another."	2:3-7 "We know that we have come to know him if we keep his commands. Whoever says, 'I know him,' but does not do what he commands is a liar, and the truth is not in that person. But if anyone obeys his word, love for God is truly made complete in them. This is how we know we are in him: Whoever claims to live in him must live as Jesus did. Dear friends, I am not writing you a new command but an old one, which you have had since the beginning. This old command is the message you have heard."	1:5 "And now, dear lady, I am not writing you a new command but one we have had from the beginning. I ask that we love one another."
14:23 "Jesus replied, 'Anyone who loves me will obey my teaching. My father will love them, and we will come to them and make our home with them.'"	5:3-4 "In fact, this is love for God: to keep his commands. And his commands are not burdensome, for everyone born of God overcomes the world."	1:6 "And this is love: that we walk in obedience to his commands. As you have heard from the beginning, his command is that you walk in love."
15:11; 16:24 "I have told you this so that my joy may be in you and that your joy may be complete." "Until now you have not asked for anything in my name. Ask and you will receive, and your joy will be complete."	1:3-4 "We proclaim to you what we have seen and heard, so that you also may have fellowship with us. And our fellowship is with the Father and with his Son, Jesus Christ. We write this to make our joy complete."	1:12 "I have much to write to you, but I do not want to use paper and ink. Instead, I hope to visit you and talk with you face to face, so that our joy may be complete."

CHARACTER OF GOD // GOD IS LIGHT

1 John 1:5: This is the message we have heard from him and declare to you: God is light; in him there is no darkness at all.

The first thing God does in the Bible is speak light into existence: "Let there be light" (Ge 1:3). The apostle John later describes the coming of Jesus Christ as a light for all people, which shines in the darkness and cannot be overcome (Jn 1:4–5). John takes this image even further in 1 John, where he writes, "God is light; in him there is no darkness at all" (1Jn 1:5).

John is talking about spiritual light, not literal light. The One who spoke literal light into being is himself in very essence spiritual light. God's light is hope, truth and goodness. Sin and evil cannot threaten it or hide it. In Christ, God's light shines for all people. Therefore, God's light does not only exist for himself. God shines his light in the darkness of the broken world to show his hope and truth to people caught in sin and darkness. God does not only exist as light; he is the giver of light to his creation. One primary way God does this is through his Word, the Bible, which Psalm 119:105 describes as a lamp for our feet and a light for our path. God's light shines in the world so that sin cannot rule and so that God's people can follow him.

APPLICATION God calls his children to be like little lights in the world, showing God to those around us. Jesus called his followers "the light of the world" and told them: "Let your light shine before others, that they may see your good deeds and glorify your Father in heaven" (Mt 5:14–16). Paul writes for believers to have nothing to do with fruitless deeds of darkness, but instead to expose them (Eph 5:11). As the light of God fills our hearts and minds, we are called to channel that light into the darkness around us.

claim we have not sinned, we make him out to be a liar[o] and his word is not in us.[p]

2 My dear children,[q] I write this to you so that you will not sin. But if anybody does sin, we have an advocate[r] with the Father—Jesus Christ, the Righteous One. 2 He is the atoning sacrifice for our sins,[s] and not only for ours but also for the sins of the whole world.

Love and Hatred for Fellow Believers

3 We know that we have come to know him if we keep his commands.[t] 4 Whoever says, "I know him," but does not do what he commands is a liar, and the truth is not in that person.[u] 5 But if anyone obeys his word,[v] love for God[a] is truly made complete in them.[w] This is how we know we are in him: 6 Whoever claims to live in him must live as Jesus did.[x]

7 Dear friends, I am not writing you a new command but an old one, which you have had since the beginning.[y] This old command is the message you have heard. 8 Yet I am writing you a new command;[z] its truth is seen in him and in you, because the darkness is passing[a] and the true light[b] is already shining.[c]

9 Anyone who claims to be in the light but hates a brother or sister[b] is still in the darkness. 10 Anyone who loves their brother and sister[c] lives in the light,[d] and there is nothing in them to make them stumble. 11 But anyone who hates a brother or sister is in the darkness and walks around in the darkness. They do not know where they are going, because the darkness has blinded them.[e]

Reasons for Writing

12 I am writing to you, dear children,
because your sins have been
forgiven on account of his
name.

1:10 [o] 1Jn 5:10 [p] 1Jn 2:14
2:1 [q] ver 12,13,28 [r] Ro 8:34; Heb 7:25
2:2 [s] Ro 3:25
2:3 [t] Jn 14:15
2:4 [u] 1Jn 1:6,8
2:5 [v] Jn 14:21,23 [w] 1Jn 4:12
2:6 [x] Mt 11:29; 1Pe 2:21
2:7 [y] 1Jn 3:11,23; 2Jn 5,6
2:8 [z] Jn 13:34 [a] Ro 13:12 [b] Jn 1:9 [c] Eph 5:8; 1Th 5:5
2:10 [d] 1Jn 3:14
2:11 [e] Jn 12:35

[a] *5* Or *word, God's love* [b] *9* The Greek word for *brother or sister* (*adelphos*) refers here to a believer, whether man or woman, as part of God's family; also in verse 11; and in 3:15,17; 4:20; 5:16. [c] *10* The Greek word for *brother and sister* (*adelphos*) refers here to a believer, whether man or woman, as part of God's family; also in 3:10; 4:20,21.

2:1 When John talks about avoiding sin, he may be referring specifically to *the error of denying the reality of God's truth about sin.* God is eager to forgive our sins, but what is it that makes God's generosity accessible? Only Jesus Christ represents us before the Father. Jesus' sinlessness and purity gives him access to God's very presence.

2:2 The *basis* of Christ's case on our behalf comes from his sacrifice on the cross. Jesus became an "atoning sacrifice" for our sins. This kind of sacrifice was given to satisfy God's anger against human sin. Jesus' sacrifice makes the sinner acceptable because God's disposition toward us has changed. This sacrifice also wipes our sins away; they are covered over *and* God's righteous anger toward us is changed. Jesus' righteousness made his sacrifice powerful (cf. Heb 7:26–28). It brings benefits to the whole world.

1:8—2:2 The Gnostics were a group of people who saw sin as unimportant because the moral arena of this world was unimportant. They emphasized the spiritual world over the temporal. John affirms that this world is important and that the personal God who made it has moral expectations for all the humans who live in it. If God is denied or if the standard is said not to apply to our world, personal accountability for sin disappears. And neither God nor the enduring principles he has established—based on his holiness and his action in Jesus Christ—will be ignored, cast aside, or mocked (Gal 6:7).

2:3–5 "We know that *we have come to know* him" (v. 3) means not that knowledge is a one-time enlightenment but rather that it is a past experience with ongoing present consequences. Knowledge reveals itself in the continuing reflex to obey God. The person who feigns intimacy with God and rejects obedience is a liar.

2:6–8 To know God truly is to abide in him deeply (Jn 15:1–17). The outgrowth of such knowing and indwelling is obedience. John holds up the earthly life of Jesus as a model to be imitated. The ancient command to love has taken on a new form since the coming of Christ (v. 7). True love bears the quality of Christ's love.

2:9–11 The ultimate test of obedient love is whether we are able to love the unlovely. John's severity is unrelenting: To hate a brother or sister in the church means one is "in the darkness" and has been blinded (v. 9); to love them means that one is living "in the light" (v. 10). Love becomes a genuine value only when it is tested, only when we must reach beyond ourselves and love someone we do not wish to love.

2:3–11 Many of us recoil at the mere word "obedience." This is a difficult paradox: Personal righteousness and obedience *are* an essential component of our faith and yet do not form the basis of our salvation. The test of obedience to the command to love surfaces when we come to terms with those whom we have difficulty loving. And the first step in this direction is reconciliation. While John is eager to see love promoted, that does not mean that we are to be naive about those who hurt us. Even though we should be generously open and loving, we must also be shrewdly discerning and wise.

2:12, 14a Two themes reassure John's followers of their place in God's household. First, their sins "have been forgiven" on account of Jesus' name (v. 12). Second, they "know the Father" (v. 14a).

1Jn 2:13–14 ❖ How are these descriptions of believers in John's time instructive for believers today?

13 I am writing to you, fathers,
because you know him who is
from the beginning.
I am writing to you, young men,
because you have overcome the
evil one.[f]

14 I write to you, dear children,
because you know the Father.
I write to you, fathers,
because you know him who is
from the beginning.
I write to you, young men,
because you are strong,[g]
and the word of God lives in you,[h]
and you have overcome the evil
one.[i]

On Not Loving the World

15 Do not love the world or anything
in the world.[j] If anyone loves the world,
love for the Father[a] is not in them.[k] 16 For
everything in the world—the lust of the
flesh,[l] the lust of the eyes,[m] and the pride
of life—comes not from the Father but
from the world. 17 The world and its desires pass away,[n] but whoever does the
will of God lives forever.

Warnings Against Denying the Son

18 Dear children, this is the last hour;
and as you have heard that the antichrist
is coming,[o] even now many antichrists
have come.[p] This is how we know it is the
last hour. 19 They went out from us,[q] but
they did not really belong to us. For if they
had belonged to us, they would have remained with us; but their going showed
that none of them belonged to us.[r]
20 But you have an anointing[s] from the
Holy One,[t] and all of you know the truth.[b][u]
21 I do not write to you because you do
not know the truth, but because you do
know it[v] and because no lie comes from
the truth. 22 Who is the liar? It is whoever denies that Jesus is the Christ. Such a
person is the antichrist—denying the
Father and the Son.[w] 23 No one who denies

2:13 [f] ver 14
2:14 [g] Eph 6:10 [h] Jn 5:38; 1Jn 1:10 [i] ver 13
2:15 [j] Ro 12:2 [k] Jas 4:4
2:16 [l] Ro 13:14 [m] Pr 27:20
2:17 [n] 1Co 7:31
2:18 [o] ver 22; 1Jn 4:3; 2Jn 7 [p] 1Jn 4:1
2:19 [q] Ac 20:30 [r] 1Co 11:19
2:20 [s] 2Co 1:21 [t] Mk 1:24 [u] Jn 14:26
2:21 [v] 2Pe 1:12; Jude 5
2:22 [w] 2Jn 7

[a] *15* Or *world, the Father's love* [b] *20* Some manuscripts *and you know all things*

2:13a, 14b Every believer, mature and immature alike, shares the same privilege. But there is a difference, for fathers have known "him who is *from the beginning*" (v. 13). Those who are mature in the faith have a knowledge of God that is anchored securely in the things of the past. Their seasoned wisdom gives steadfast faith in the present, difficult circumstances.

2:13b, 14c If the community's elders provide a steadfast anchor of faith, it is the youth who are here engaging the battle of living out that faith in the world's struggles. John affirms them by saying that they are strong and that God's word abides within them. That strength is there for a purpose: It has overcome the "evil one" (v. 13). Here the Christian life is being celebrated as an accomplished fact.

2:15–17 Either we love the Father or we love the world. Affirmations now become warnings that the believers do not fall away. John says that we should "not love" this world (v. 15). John has in mind that Christians are to avoid an infatuation with worldly godlessness.

In v. 16, three things are mentioned that come "not from the Father but from the world": (1) *The desire of the flesh.* John has in mind any desire that draws us away from God. (2) *The desire of the eyes.* The eye is often a metaphor for sinful passion that corrupts. (3) *Boasting in one's lifestyle.* John has in mind an overconfidence that makes us lose any notion that we are dependent on God. Christ has brought a completely new value system to history. Those who are utterly invested in the world will see it vanish. Only those whose passions rest in the Father will continue forever.

✣ **2:12–17** Many of us fail to discuss the boundary between the church and the world. As a result, we fail to think of strategies to manage a life lived in both spheres. John has provided strategies to equip and strengthen us for this situation.

The first threat to faith comes when we doubt the validity or certainty of our convictions. When someone comes along and suggests that *more complete knowledge* of God or *genuine certainty* of salvation is available elsewhere, we are forced to rethink the basis of our faith. If we are assured of our convictions and confident in the truth we embrace, such questions cannot make us vulnerable.

2:18–19 In what sense is it "the last hour" (v. 18)? John may be speaking theologically rather than chronologically. The early Christians understood that the first coming of Christ brought a change of eons, an unparalleled period in which the struggle with evil and the unveiling of God's power would intensify. John is reminding his readers that the concentration of evil they are experiencing fits the formula announced by Jesus and his apostles for the end of time.

2:20–21 When John speaks of the Christian's anointing, he likely has in mind their endowment with the Holy Spirit, a gift that can give all knowledge. The work of the Spirit must always submit to the revelation we have in Jesus Christ.

2:22–23 John's opponents struggled with the

the Son has the Father; whoever acknowledges the Son has the Father also.[x]
24 As for you, see that what you have
heard from the beginning remains in
you. If it does, you also will remain in
the Son and in the Father.[y] 25 And this
is what he promised us—eternal life.
26 I am writing these things to you
about those who are trying to lead you
astray.[z] 27 As for you, the anointing[a] you
received from him remains in you, and
you do not need anyone to teach you.
But as his anointing teaches you about
all things and as that anointing is real,
not counterfeit—just as it has taught
you, remain in him.

God's Children and Sin

28 And now, dear children,[b] continue in
him, so that when he appears[c] we may be
confident[d] and unashamed before him
at his coming.[e]
29 If you know that he is righteous,[f]
you know that everyone who does what
is right has been born of him.

2:23 [x] Jn 8:19; 1Jn 4:15
2:24 [y] Jn 14:23
2:26 [z] 2Jn 7
2:27 [a] ver 20
2:28 [b] ver 1 [c] 1Jn 3:2 [d] 1Jn 4:17 [e] 1Th 2:19
2:29 [f] 1Jn 3:7

3:1 [g] Jn 3:16 [h] Jn 1:12 [i] Jn 16:3
3:2 [j] Ro 8:29; 2Pe 1:4 [k] 2Co 3:18
3:3 [l] 2Co 7:1; 2Pe 3:13,14
3:4 [m] 1Jn 5:17
3:5 [n] 2Co 5:21
3:6 [o] ver 9 [p] 3Jn 11 [q] 1Jn 2:4
3:7 [r] 1Jn 2:1 [s] 1Jn 2:26 [t] 1Jn 2:29

3 See what great love[g] the Father has
lavished on us, that we should be
called children of God![h] And that is what
we are! The reason the world does not
know us is that it did not know him.[i]
2 Dear friends, now we are children of
God, and what we will be has not yet been
made known. But we know that when
Christ appears,[a] we shall be like him,[j] for
we shall see him as he is.[k] 3 All who have
this hope in him purify themselves,[l] just
as he is pure.
4 Everyone who sins breaks the law; in
fact, sin is lawlessness.[m] 5 But you know
that he appeared so that he might take
away our sins. And in him is no sin.[n] 6 No
one who lives in him keeps on sinning.[o]
No one who continues to sin has either
seen him[p] or known him.[q]
7 Dear children,[r] do not let anyone lead
you astray.[s] The one who does what is
right is righteous, just as he is righteous.[t]
8 The one who does what is sinful is of

[a] 2 Or *when it is made known*

---

notion that God could become human when he sent his Son. Greeks argued that spirit and flesh were utterly separate, and those who truly had the Spirit realized the total disconnect between these two spheres. John says that people who teach like this are "liar[s]" (v. 22) and have nothing to do with the Son or the Father (vv. 23–24). In a word, they are no longer Christians.

2:24–27 John suggests two weapons that should always be ready in the Christian's arsenal. Objectively, John believes that right belief is rooted in the historic facts about the faith. Subjectively, we need to hone our skills of spiritual discernment so that we can weigh any message by the Spirit of God within us.

2:18–27 We can graph the church's life as an irregular line between eras of comfort and persecution. This cycle has repeated itself for centuries, and in some cases, Christians have misunderstood their histories, proclaiming that the end is at hand. John would have us build a climate in the church that heightens theological awareness. When troubles overwhelm us, instead of confidently predicting the end times, we can acknowledge that certain aspects of our circumstances are those predicted for the end times. At the same time, we will understand that those things may or may not actually be signs of the end. Simply put, we do not know for sure. Either way, we are called to be ready.

This serves one purpose: to equip Christians so they are not discouraged when severe difficulties and turmoil erupt. *Theological awareness, in other words, has a pastoral function.* It interprets struggle and dispels the despair that accompanies it. It teaches us to watch for changes in history, to watch for "antichrists," and to be alert for times when history betrays elements of the end.

2:28–29 John's warning about shame is not meant to threaten Christians, who are born of God. He is here addressing those who oppose Jesus, for whom his climactic coming will be a catastrophe of the first order. When we exhibit God's righteous character, we show that we are born of him.

3:1–3 If we have a glimpse of what it means to have the presence of God within us, when Christ comes, there will be yet more overwhelming experiences for us. He will appear, we will appear just like him, and then we will see him exactly as he is. In that day there will be an immediate and unmistakable unity between us and the Father. Verse 3 contains the apostle's summary of his reasons for confidence in the Christian life. John's pastoral purpose here is ethical. If we set our minds on the confident basis of God's promise, we will feel differently, and this will renew the character of our living.

3:4 John here affirms the universality of sin once more and describes its inner character: *Sinners break the law.* The decision to sin or not to sin is really a decision to reflect the character of Christ or Satan.

3:5 John describes what it means to be a true child of God—or the devil. Jesus came to destroy all sin. His substitutionary sacrifice "carried away" our sins and punishment. But John has more in mind. Jesus' works include *both* removing the guilt of sin and defeating its presence altogether. Jesus is concerned with both justification *and* sanctification.

3:6–9 In order to make the point unmistakable, John goes on to say that no one who is truly in a close relationship with Christ "keeps on sinning" (v. 6). In fact, v. 9 makes the statement even more

PEOPLE TO KNOW // CAIN

1 JOHN 3:12: Cain was the firstborn son of Adam and Eve—and the first murderer in the Bible.

Cain was a farmer. His younger brother, Abel, was a shepherd who kept flocks. One day Cain brought some of his harvest before God as an offering. From some of the firstborn of his flock, Abel also brought an offering. God looked favorably upon Abel and his offering, but not upon Cain and his offering.

Whatever the reason for this, Cain became angry. God admonished Cain, cautioning him, "If you do not do what is right, sin is crouching at your door; it desires to have you, but you must rule over it" (Ge 4:7). Rather than heeding God's warning, Cain gave into his anger and envy, killing Abel.

When God asked Cain where Abel was, Cain snapped back: "Am I my brother's keeper?" (Ge 4:9). God cursed Cain for his sin against Abel, sending him out into the world as a restless wanderer. In the NT, Cain's infamous story was used as a cautionary tale (1Jn 3:12).

APPLICATION Cain's story demonstrates how quickly evil spread in the world after the fall of Adam and Eve. Cain's murder of Abel stands as a lasting warning against the dangers of letting anger and envy rule our actions.

Cain's story also reminds us of God's mercy. Before Cain's fateful act of murder, God came to him and spoke with him, challenging him to choose to do what was right, promising that he could yet be accepted by God (Ge 4:7). God encouraged Cain to resist sin. God's grace and mercy are abundant, warning and cautioning us from falling into sin. Further, by God's grace, when we do fall into sin, we can find hope and renewal in Jesus Christ (1Jn 2:1).

the devil,[u] because the devil has been
sinning from the beginning. The reason
the Son of God appeared was to destroy
the devil's work. 9No one who is born of
God[v] will continue to sin,[w] because God's
seed[x] remains in them; they cannot go
on sinning, because they have been born
of God. 10This is how we know who the
children of God are and who the children of the devil are: Anyone who does
not do what is right is not God's child,
nor is anyone who does not love[y] their
brother and sister.

More on Love and Hatred

11For this is the message you heard[z]
from the beginning: We should love one
another.[a] 12Do not be like Cain, who belonged to the evil one and murdered his
brother.[b] And why did he murder him?

3:8 [u] Jn 8:44
3:9 [v] Jn 1:13 [w] 1Jn 5:18 [x] 1Pe 1:23
3:10 [y] 1Jn 4:8
3:11 [z] 1Jn 1:5 [a] Jn 13:34,35; 2Jn 5
3:12 [b] Ge 4:8

---

boldly: Such people "cannot go on sinning" because they have "been born of God."

3:10 John's characteristically bold statements in these verses have led to numerous struggles for the average Christian: "Does this mean that perfect holiness is God's expectation for me?" John may well be emphasizing that ongoing, habitual sin should find no place in the believer's life. He is making a strong case for the holiness of the believer.

2:28–3:10 Christian behavior, behavior that the world does not recognize and finds incomprehensible, shows us that something divine has happened within us, that we have been reborn. God's love is made manifest in our lives.

It is astonishing how many believers, even after years in the church, need to learn (or relearn) about the unmerited love God has for us—how we are his children and he will never "unadopt" us. People weep over hearing such amazing news. Their tears have little to do with the character of the presentation; instead, they point to the *insecurity* they have learned in their church upbringing. "If I don't feel like God's child, maybe I'm not." "If I can't always act like God's child, perhaps I never was." We always need to keep circling back to the bedrock truth that God in Christ loves his people unconditionally and will never leave them.

Similarly, many Christians are filled with anxiety and fear at the thought of the second coming, and they wonder if *for them* it will be a day of joy. Many Christians teach that the day of Jesus' return will be a day of reckoning for everyone. John's purposes run along different lines. *Since* we bear Christ's image, when he appears we will be like him. The return of Jesus will disclose the truth about God's relationship with us, not evaluate whether that relationship is satisfactory.

3:11–13 The passions that fueled Cain's jealousy and hatred are fueling those opposed to true Christians. This includes non-Christians outside

Because his own actions were evil and
his brother's were righteous. 13Do not
be surprised, my brothers and sisters,[a] if
the world hates you.[c] 14We know that we
have passed from death to life,[d] because
we love each other. Anyone who does not
love remains in death.[e] 15Anyone who
hates a brother or sister is a murderer,[f]
and you know that no murderer has eternal life residing in him.[g]
16This is how we know what love is:
Jesus Christ laid down his life for us.
And we ought to lay down our lives for
our brothers and sisters.[h] 17If anyone has
material possessions and sees a brother or sister in need but has no pity on
them,[i] how can the love of God be in that
person?[j] 18Dear children,[k] let us not love
with words or speech but with actions
and in truth.[l]
19This is how we know that we belong
to the truth and how we set our hearts
at rest in his presence: 20If our hearts
condemn us, we know that God is greater
than our hearts, and he knows everything. 21Dear friends, if our hearts do not
condemn us, we have confidence before
God[m] 22and receive from him anything
we ask,[n] because we keep his commands
and do what pleases him.[o] 23And this is
his command: to believe[p] in the name
of his Son, Jesus Christ, and to love one
another as he commanded us.[q] 24The
one who keeps God's commands lives in
him,[r] and he in them. And this is how we
know that he lives in us: We know it by
the Spirit he gave us.[s]

3:13 [c] Jn 15:18, 19; 17:14
3:14 [d] Jn 5:24 [e] 1Jn 2:9
3:15 [f] Mt 5:21, 22; Jn 8:44 [g] Gal 5:20, 21
3:16 [h] Jn 15:13
3:17 [i] Dt 15:7, 8 [j] 1Jn 4:20
3:18 [k] 1Jn 2:1 [l] Eze 33:31; Ro 12:9
3:21 [m] 1Jn 5:14
3:22 [n] Mt 7:7 [o] Jn 8:29
3:23 [p] Jn 6:29 [q] Jn 13:34
3:24 [r] 1Jn 2:6 [s] 1Jn 4:13

1Jn 3:11–18 ❖ How can we love others with our actions, as John instructs? How does such love put God on display and give evidence of the faith within us?

1Jn 4:1–4 ❖ How can we "test the spirits" to see if they are from God? How does the encouragement in v. 4 give us hope for our struggles against the powers allied against God and against us?

On Denying the Incarnation

4 Dear friends, do not believe every
spirit, but test the spirits to see
whether they are from God, because

[a] *13* The Greek word for *brothers and sisters* (*adelphoi*) refers here to believers, both men and women, as part of God's family; also in verse 16.

---

the church and those who claim to be Christians within the fellowship.

3:14–15 Those who exhibit love for Christ's family demonstrate that they are *already* enjoying the eternal life promised them. Inner motives and attitudes weigh as seriously as our actions in God's moral economy (Mt 5:21–22).

3:16–18 John uses the example of Jesus here in v. 16 for two reasons. First, Christ is a *model* for us to emulate. Christ as God's Son possessed more than we can ever imagine; yet he did not keep what he had selfishly but gave of himself voluntarily for others. Second, Jesus' death is also a *revelation* of God's work on our behalf: "Christ laid down his life for us" (v. 16). Jesus' death is not merely an ethical model; it is a genuine offering and giving of his life.

3:19–24 John is making two points, which we can paraphrase in this manner: "In *this* [the love and obedience we exhibit, vv. 11–18] we will know that we are of the truth" (v. 19a); and "We will reassure our hearts in his presence whenever our hearts condemn us, because (1) God is greater than our hearts, and (2) God knows all things" (vv. 19b–20). This paraphrase gives a clear strategy for thinking when moments of profound insecurity overtake us. Our assurance is anchored in God and God alone. If our conscience condemns, God overrides its verdict.

3:21–22 The astonishing statement in vv. 21–22 echoes other similar forms of confidence found in passages such as Jn 14:13–14; 16:23–24. Here John says that we must do "what pleases him" (v. 22); this presupposes a quality of intimacy that is in touch with God's very heart.

3:23–24 John's description of the Christian life is at once theological *and* ethical. God has sent his Son, through whom we receive life, and in turn, he has poured his Son's life into us through his Holy Spirit. The virtues of the Christian life cannot be lived apart from a relationship with God—a relationship defined and sustained by Jesus Christ.

✚ **3:11–24** This entire section suggests that the church is to become a life-giving community. It should be a place where men, women, and children are healed, not hurt; where the wealthy take genuine responsibility for the poor and where lives flourish both spiritually and materially. Conflict, struggle, rejection, community fragmentation—all can lead to despair and doubt. When a community loses its solidarity, when its shared vision and life evaporates, personal faith begins to wane. That's when God's witness in the world through believers needs to be revived through prayer and the power of the Spirit.

4:1 House churches were isolated in cities throughout the Roman Empire. This meant churches could fall prey to dishonest traveling prophets and teachers. Consequently, Christians had to be ready to assess the message they heard and the spirit that inspired it.

CHARACTER OF GOD // GOD IS LOVE

1 John 4:8: Whoever does not love does not know God, because God is love.

Love is so core to God's nature that John makes the stunning claim, "God is love" (1Jn 4:8). Can God be so completely identified with a single attribute? Yes! John asserts love as a main identifier of God's character. However, to say God is love is not the same as to say love is God. Yet, wherever true love exists, God is present (1Jn 4:16).

Love has become one of the most often used words in daily language. We say how much we love food, drinks, products, entertainment and our possessions. God's love, however, is not a passing affection to be equated with "like" or "desire." True love is a deliberate commitment and passion. God loves his people and his creation. It was his love for people that motivated God to send Jesus Christ to die for sinners (Jn 3:16).

God's love is unconditional. God does not love his children because they deserve it. His love always comes first (Ro 5:8). Furthermore, nothing can separate those who are in Christ from the love of God (Ro 8:38–39). God is not fickle, changing his mind about us based on our successes or failures from day to day. God's love for us is stamped in the blood of Christ. It is unconditionally given, and it will never be taken away.

APPLICATION ✣ Though we can never love like God loves, it is imperative that God's children be people of love. To display God, we need to reflect his central attribute, which is love. The only fitting response to God's love for us in Christ is to be people of love ourselves. After all, Jesus himself taught that the two greatest commandments are to love God and to love others (Mt 22:37–40).

many false prophets have gone out into
the world.[t] 2This is how you can recognize the Spirit of God: Every spirit that
acknowledges that Jesus Christ has come
in the flesh[u] is from God,[v] 3but every spirit that does not acknowledge Jesus is not
from God. This is the spirit of the antichrist,[w] which you have heard is coming
and even now is already in the world.
4You, dear children, are from God and
have overcome them, because the one
who is in you[x] is greater than the one
who is in the world.[y] 5They are from the
world[z] and therefore speak from the
viewpoint of the world, and the world
listens to them. 6We are from God, and
whoever knows God listens to us; but
whoever is not from God does not listen
to us.[a] This is how we recognize the Spirit[a] of truth[b] and the spirit of falsehood.

God's Love and Ours

7Dear friends, let us love one another,[c]
for love comes from God. Everyone who
loves has been born of God and knows
God.[d] 8Whoever does not love does not
know God, because God is love.[e] 9This
is how God showed his love among us:

4:1 [t] 2Pe 2:1; 1Jn 2:18
4:2 [u] Jn 1:14; 1Jn 2:23 [v] 1Co 12:3
4:3 [w] 1Jn 2:22; 2Jn 7
4:4 [x] Ro 8:31 [y] Jn 12:31
4:5 [z] Jn 15:19
4:6 [a] Jn 8:47 [b] Jn 14:17
4:7 [c] 1Jn 3:11 [d] 1Jn 2:4
4:8 [e] ver 7,16

[a] 6 Or *spirit*

4:2–3 John is urging three things about our belief. First, the man Jesus of Nazareth is God's divine Word. Second, Jesus Christ was and is fully divine and fully human. Finally, Jesus is the sole source of eternal life since he alone reveals the Father to us and atones for our sins.

4:4–6 John's second test has to do with audiences. False prophets will find a ready reception in the world (v. 5). On the other hand, the church can test the truth of a word and whether it is from the Lord (v. 6).

✣ **4:1–6** The church must weigh what is being taught within its ranks. But how do we cultivate a discerning spirit without becoming cynical? John's interest in the importance of the gathered community—the church—is a signal reminder to us. The *church* is the custodian of the truth, and any impulse to critique, to analyze, or to judge must be worked out in the community of the church's leadership and its laity.

4:7–10 The compelling origin of divine love weaves its way throughout this text (vv. 7–11, 16, 19). Christians who live out such love are also giving evidence that they *have been born* from God and *know* him (v. 7b; cf. 5:4). John goes on to point out that the reverse is also the case (4:8). Whoever does not love cannot possibly know God (also v. 20).

4:8 Love is the essence of God's being. John carefully defines the character of who God is and what it means to live in relation to him. To genuinely contemplate God's true identity is to become like him.

4:9–10 John says the ultimate act of God's self-

He sent his one and only Son into the
world that we might live through him.[f]
10This is love: not that we loved God, but
that he loved us[g] and sent his Son as an
atoning sacrifice for our sins.[h] 11Dear
friends, since God so loved us,[i] we also
ought to love one another. 12No one has
ever seen God;[j] but if we love one another, God lives in us and his love is made
complete in us.[k]
13This is how we know that we live in
him and he in us: He has given us of his
Spirit.[l] 14And we have seen and testify[m]
that the Father has sent his Son to be the
Savior of the world.[n] 15If anyone acknowledges that Jesus is the Son of God,[o] God
lives in them and they in God. 16And so
we know and rely on the love God has
for us.

God is love.[p] Whoever lives in love lives
in God, and God in them.[q] 17This is how
love is made complete[r] among us so that
we will have confidence on the day of
judgment: In this world we are like Jesus.
18There is no fear in love. But perfect love
drives out fear,[s] because fear has to do
with punishment. The one who fears is
not made perfect in love.
19We love because he first loved us.[t]
20Whoever claims to love God yet hates

4:9 [f] Jn 3:16,17; 1Jn 5:11
4:10 [g] Ro 5:8,10 [h] 1Jn 2:2
4:11 [i] Jn 3:16
4:12 [j] Jn 1:18; 1Ti 6:16 [k] 1Jn 2:5
4:13 [l] 1Jn 3:24
4:14 [m] Jn 15:27 [n] Jn 3:17
4:15 [o] Ro 10:9
4:16 [p] ver 8 [q] 1Jn 3:24
4:17 [r] 1Jn 2:5
4:18 [s] Ro 8:15
4:19 [t] ver 10
4:20 [u] 1Jn 2:9 [v] 1Jn 2:4 [w] 1Jn 3:17 [x] ver 12
4:21 [y] Mt 5:43
5:1 [z] 1Jn 2:22 [a] Jn 1:13; 1Jn 2:23 [b] Jn 8:42
5:3 [c] Jn 14:15; 2Jn 6 [d] Mt 11:30
5:4 [e] Jn 16:33
5:6 [f] Jn 19:34

1Jn 5:1–5 ❖ How can we take John's teachings here on love and apply them to our minds and hearts today?

a brother or sister[u] is a liar.[v] For whoever
does not love their brother and sister,
whom they have seen,[w] cannot love God,
whom they have not seen.[x] 21And he has
given us this command: Anyone who
loves God must also love their brother
and sister.[y]

Faith in the Incarnate Son of God

5 Everyone who believes that Jesus is
the Christ[z] is born of God,[a] and everyone who loves the father loves his
child as well.[b] 2This is how we know that
we love the children of God: by loving
God and carrying out his commands.
3In fact, this is love for God: to keep his
commands.[c] And his commands are not
burdensome,[d] 4for everyone born of God
overcomes[e] the world. This is the victory that has overcome the world, even
our faith. 5Who is it that overcomes the
world? Only the one who believes that
Jesus is the Son of God.
6This is the one who came by water
and blood[f] — Jesus Christ. He did not

---

revelation is found in Jesus Christ. Christ unveils God's heart; he is God, displayed vulnerably before the world.

4:11–16 Our obligation to love one another is a byproduct of God's loving generosity toward us. Our love for others reflects the divine love already showered upon us. John goes on to say that as we meet this obligation to love, we experience something unparalleled: God lives within us as his love is made complete through us. Those who obey God's commands live in him, and *he lives in them*. God's own Spirit is powerfully alive within us as we obey (3:24) and love (4:13).

4:17–19 The most immediate result of this perfect love is assurance: We will have boldness or confidence on the day of judgment. Fear and love are mutually exclusive. To fear God's character or the final judgment paralyzes us. It destroys the perfection that love offers. Knowing unequivocally that God by his Spirit resides in our lives results in unbounded confidence as we approach the day when we meet God.

4:20—5:4 John utters a divine command: "Anyone who loves God must also love their brother and sister" (4:21). If you love God, you will love all his children. Therefore, using a family metaphor, John is broadening the ethical challenge. This obligation springs from a profound affection for God in the first place. God has many children, and people who understand the true identity of Christ—those who love God and all his children, who obey his commands—these are people who have been born of God.

✣ **4:7—5:4** John raises a significant series of questions about spiritual confidence and certainty. How can we know we belong to God? John says the first indication is our willingness to love. John calls us to obey the command to love regardless of how we feel.

John's second suggestion is mystical. The power to know God's love in reality comes through an experience of the Holy Spirit. A vision perhaps? A Spirit-forged gift? An unexplainable resolve and peace? We don't receive this gift through intellectual exercises, but rather through immediate experience.

5:5–6b Some were teaching that the heavenly Christ descended on the man Jesus at baptism but departed before he was crucified. Hence, John says, Jesus came not only by baptismal water but also through the blood of the cross. Jesus' sacrificial death gives life: not by water only, but by water *and blood*. Life and truth can only be found when a complete incarnation embraces a genuine death on the cross.

5:6c–8 Spirit-inspired teaching will not dislodge the historic events of salvation witnessed at the cross. This witness began with the apostle John (together with the other apostles) and has been nurtured within the community of believers.

come by water only, but by water and
blood. And it is the Spirit who testifies,
because the Spirit is the truth.[g] 7For there
are three[h] that testify: 8the[a] Spirit, the
water and the blood; and the three are
in agreement. 9We accept human testimony,[i] but God's testimony is greater
because it is the testimony of God,[j] which
he has given about his Son. 10Whoever
believes in the Son of God accepts this
testimony.[k] Whoever does not believe
God has made him out to be a liar,[l] because they have not believed the testimony God has given about his Son. 11And
this is the testimony: God has given us
eternal life, and this life is in his Son.[m]
12Whoever has the Son has life; whoever
does not have the Son of God does not
have life.[n]

Concluding Affirmations

13I write these things to you who believe in the name of the Son of God[o] so
that you may know that you have eternal
life.[p] 14This is the confidence[q] we have in
approaching God: that if we ask anything
according to his will, he hears us.[r] 15And
if we know that he hears us — whatever
we ask — we know[s] that we have what
we asked of him.

16If you see any brother or sister commit a sin that does not lead to death, you
should pray and God will give them life.[t]
I refer to those whose sin does not lead to
death. There is a sin that leads to death.[u]
I am not saying that you should pray
about that.[v] 17All wrongdoing is sin,[w] and
there is sin that does not lead to death.[x]

18We know that anyone born of God
does not continue to sin; the One who
was born of God keeps them safe, and
the evil one cannot harm them.[y] 19We
know that we are children of God,[z] and
that the whole world is under the control of the evil one.[a] 20We know also

5:6 [g] Jn 14:17
5:7 [h] Mt 18:16
5:9 [i] Jn 5:34 [j] Mt 3:16,17; Jn 8:17,18
5:10 [k] Ro 8:16; Gal 4:6 [l] Jn 3:33
5:11 [m] Jn 1:4; 1Jn 2:25
5:12 [n] Jn 3:15,16,36
5:13 [o] 1Jn 3:23 [p] Jn 20:31; 1Jn 1:1,2
5:14 [q] 1Jn 3:21 [r] Mt 7:7
5:15 [s] ver 18,19,20
5:16 [t] Jas 5:15 [u] Heb 6:4-6; 10:26 [v] Jer 7:16
5:17 [w] 1Jn 3:4 [x] 1Jn 2:1
5:18 [y] Jn 14:30
5:19 [z] 1Jn 4:6 [a] Gal 1:4

[a] 7,8 Late manuscripts of the Vulgate *testify in heaven: the Father, the Word and the Holy Spirit, and these three are one.* [8]*And there are three that testify on earth: the* (not found in any Greek manuscript before the fourteenth century)

5:9–12 If we accept human testimonies, we ought to accept a divine testimony even more. God's divine authority rests behind the testimony of the water and the blood. It is *God's* Spirit that is affirming truths about the gospel of Jesus Christ. Since life comes to us through the death of the Son, to deny "the blood" puts our own salvation in jeopardy (v. 8).

5:5–12 The cross may not be demoted in *any* Christian view of salvation. The mystery of what God is doing on our behalf is hidden there in all its particularity and severity. Christ is not simply one example of God's divine wisdom revealed to the world, a wisdom that can stand alongside other religious systems. Christ is *the* wisdom of God, and this wisdom is manifested in his salvation-offering death within history at the cross.

The church, through its confessions and traditions, through its recitation of creeds and its defense of councils, lays a foundation on which secure things can be built.

5:13–15 John wants his readers to know they have "eternal life" (v. 13). One of the results of this knowledge is confidence or boldness before God, particularly as we pray.

Jesus perhaps modeled this best. His will was always one with the Father's. He always did the Father's works, and he always spoke what the Father wanted him to say. This oneness makes prayer a genuine unity of wills. God does not simply hear us, but he understands and responds. Moreover, our requests are granted if they are in harmony with his will.

5:16–18 John has in mind a situation in which one believer sees another committing a sin. The chief difficulty in the verse is that John says this intercession should be done for "those whose *sin does not lead to death*." The OT distinguishes between inadvertent sins and intentional sins. In the OT, the temple sacrificial rituals only provided forgiveness for accidental or unconscious sins. When someone sinned intentionally and willfully, the sinner paid the consequences of that sin via either exile or death. Corrective prayer is in view here.

Christians do "not continue to sin" (v. 18a). Why? Because all people who are genuine believers have been "born of God." Furthermore, Christ himself sustains and protects them from the evil one (v. 18b). Therefore, Christians do not engage in this sort of sustained, willful rejection of God.

5:19 John concludes this section with three bold statements about Christian certainty. These verses sound themes that have been dear to John's heart from the first chapter. The first addresses the ongoing righteousness of God's children. The second speaks of the world's fallenness (both in v. 19). The third gives us Christ's hope as we live in this world (v. 20).

Jesus' protection and sustaining power are essential because the world lies in the grip of Satan. John's imagery is striking: The world is not under siege by Satan; it hardly struggles against him at all. *The world rests in Satan's grip.*

5:20 Finally, John makes clear our hope. Jesus Christ has penetrated the world; he has undermined the systems of the world. John describes the work of Christ as bringing knowledge. Christian knowledge is focused on genuine reality: things that have happened in history. Thus, in v. 20 John does not say we merely know truth; rather, we know "him who is true [or real]."

that the Son of God has come and has given us understanding,[b] so that we may know him who is true.[c] And we are in him who is true by being in his Son Jesus Christ. He is the true God and eternal life.[d]
21 Dear children, keep yourselves from idols.[e]

5:20 [b] Lk 24:45 [c] Jn 17:3 [d] ver 11
5:21 [e] 1Co 10:14; 1Th 1:9

John's final thought here is undoubtedly the most important. Throughout his writing, he has promoted and defended the full divinity of Christ. To lose this one conviction is to miss not just Jesus but God himself.

5:21 John adds a final exhortation, urging his readers to watch out for anything that may become a substitute for God: religious shams, false religion, and even the error-filled words of those who claim to be true believers.

✜ **5:13–21** John repeatedly emphasizes the importance of Christians knowing with assurance essential facts about their relationship with God. We need to be bold about those things we know with certainty. We must speak with conviction and assurance about God and his commitment to us. We need to say, "God desires for us to be confident! God desires for us to be bold! God desires to purge doubt from our souls so that we can live enjoying the assurance of one who is eternally loved." When our assurance is truly anchored and secure, no conflict or disarray in the church can ever unsettle it.

Author: The apostle John

Audience: The "lady chosen by God," probably a local church in or around Ephesus

Date: Between AD 85 and 95

Theme: John writes to urge discernment in supporting traveling teachers, since false teachers were also traveling and teaching heresy.

Reading 2 John

Read this brief letter as if received from a greatly respected, retired pastor. In it he is warning us how to respond to those in our church fellowships who do not follow the teachings of the Word of God.

PERSPECTIVE

While Christian tradition has attributed the letters of 1, 2, and 3 John to John the apostle, these three letters are anonymous, except that 2 and 3 John call their author "the elder" (2Jn 1; 3Jn 1). This commentary labels the author of the letters as "John," keeping in mind the limits of any historical investigation.

A date for all three letters sometime between AD 70 and 90 is not unreasonable. John wrote 1 John to correct doctrinal distortions (and their ethical implications) that arose within the Christian community (probably in Ephesus in Asia Minor) and that were causing a severe division among its members. Some had already seceded from the church.

Second John was probably written after 1 John to the same community in Ephesus and is an exhortation—a reminder—of things said before there in that first letter. By the time of the writing of 2 John, the rupture within the church reflected in 1 John seems complete (2Jn 7). John writes the letter with two purposes in mind: to reinforce his followers' commitment to the truth and to warn them about the severity of their opponents and the need to protect themselves.

Three basic elements form the content and argument in this short letter. First, the church's opponents are attacking a theological issue at the center of the church's faith—namely, Christology. This speaks to the core of the Christian faith, and the misleading teaching of these individuals is gravely dangerous. Jesus Christ himself is at issue here, and the result of this debate will either spawn a religion centered on his work and words or relegate him to some secondary place.

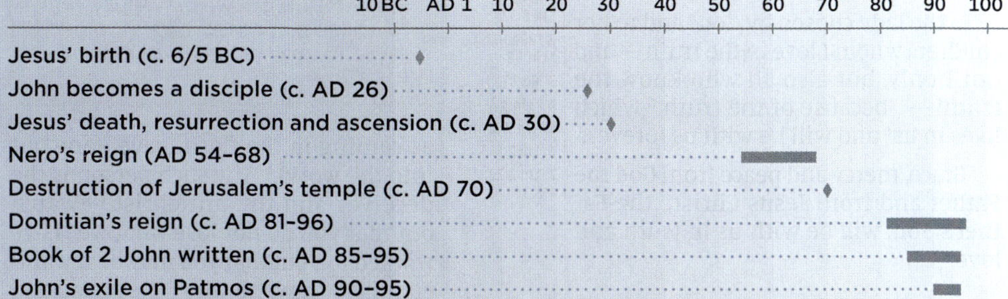

Second, John is warning against teacher-leaders who are out to sabotage the local church. These are not innocent contacts between the Christians he addresses and unbelievers or heretics. Rather, these teachers are trying to gain access to a congregation in order to win an audience and a following.

Third, John's instructions to repel these teachers and refuse them access involves the Christians' very survival. The result of this struggle will have immense consequences for these people's personal salvation—and the survival of the church itself.

When we in our modern society read these grave warnings, we can take them as warnings to us as well—we as contemporary believers must separate ourselves from relativistic thinking and practice and stand on the solid pillars of the Word of God.

Key Verses

Many deceivers, who do not acknowledge Jesus Christ as coming in the flesh, have gone out into the world. Any such person is the deceiver and the antichrist. Watch out that you do not lose what we have worked for, but that you may be rewarded fully.

—2 John 7–8

TAKING THE NEXT STEPS

In this brief letter, John urges some friends to discern properly who are false teachers. The views these false teachers hold are similar to those mentioned in his first letter. We in the church today need to be alert as well, for the world is filled with sects and cults that proclaim a false Christ. For more application information, see the Introduction to 1 John.

WHAT TO LOOK FOR IN 2 JOHN

- Faithfulness to the truth (vv. 4–6)
- Protecting the family of God (vv. 7–11)

1 The elder,[a]

To the lady chosen by God[b] and to her
children, whom I love in the truth — and
not I only, but also all who know the
truth[c] — 2 because of the truth,[d] which
lives in us[e] and will be with us forever:

3 Grace, mercy and peace from God the
Father and from Jesus Christ,[f] the Father's Son, will be with us in truth and
love.

4 It has given me great joy to find some
of your children walking in the truth,[g]
just as the Father commanded us. 5 And
now, dear lady, I am not writing you a
new command but one we have had from
the beginning.[h] I ask that we love one
another. 6 And this is love:[i] that we walk
in obedience to his commands. As you
have heard from the beginning, his command is that you walk in love.
7 I say this because many deceivers,
who do not acknowledge Jesus Christ[j]
as coming in the flesh, have gone out
into the world.[k] Any such person is the
deceiver and the antichrist.[l] 8 Watch
out that you do not lose what we[a] have
worked for, but that you may be rewarded fully.[m] 9 Anyone who runs ahead and
does not continue in the teaching of
Christ does not have God; whoever continues in the teaching has both the Father and the Son.[n] 10 If anyone comes to
you and does not bring this teaching, do
not take them into your house or welcome them.[o] 11 Anyone who welcomes
them shares[p] in their wicked work.
12 I have much to write to you, but I do
not want to use paper and ink. Instead, I

1 [a] 3Jn 1
[b] Ro 16:13
[c] Jn 8:32
2 [d] 2Pe 1:12
[e] 1Jn 1:8
3 [f] Ro 1:7
4 [g] 3Jn 3,4
5 [h] 1Jn 2:7; 3:11
6 [i] 1Jn 2:5
7 [j] 1Jn 2:22; 4:2,3
[k] 1Jn 4:1
[l] 1Jn 2:18
8 [m] 1Co 3:8
9 [n] 1Jn 2:23
10 [o] Ro 16:17
11 [p] 1Ti 5:22

[a] 8 Some manuscripts *you*

2Jn 4 ❖ How can we prayerfully work to ensure that our "children," whoever they may be, are "walking in the truth"?

1–3 Rather than give his name, the author simply calls himself "the elder" (v. 1). On the one hand, he seems to know the church well—and is known by them. However, it is his *position* that is now important, and the authority that comes with it.

An ancient tradition has thought "chosen lady" refers to a person. But this usage here is unlikely. The NT regards the church with feminine metaphors. Thus, we should view this letter as a personal note written by John and sent to a particular congregation.

3 John's deep love for his church is expressed in his first sentence, "whom I love in the truth," a community that has embraced Jesus Christ and experienced the indwelling power of the Holy Spirit. Thus, the threefold blessing of v. 3 is announced triumphantly as a promise, not a wish: "grace, mercy and peace . . . *will be* with us."

4–6 John's first message actually begins in v. 4, where he celebrates the continuing faithfulness and obedience of these Christians to the truth. "Truth" and "love" are the twin themes that echo throughout John's first letter and here appear in summary form.

Couriers may have come to John reporting how faithful this remaining house church was. On the other hand, v. 4 may imply something different. John's rejoicing that "some of" the believers here remained faithful may suggest that *others have not*. John's call is for these believers to consolidate their community which was under attack and confirm the essence of their beliefs—in other words, to fortify themselves against those who are out to destroy them.

7–11 With stunning specificity, John moves from the truth and love that inspire celebration in v. 6 to the treachery and deception that are lurking just outside the church's doors in v. 7. "Deceivers" (v. 7) can also be translated "liars." Clearly these people have not only left the church and taken up residence in the world, but they have "gone out" into the world to spread their teachings (v. 7). These false prophets have denied the complete incarnation of Christ and should now be seen as agents of the antichrist.

John then says that orthodox confession affirms "Jesus Christ as coming in the flesh" (v. 7). Why the present tense? This is John's way of saying that Jesus Christ came *and still exists* in the flesh. In other words, Jesus swept up our humanity and carried it with him eternally through his incarnation. To oppose this teaching is to be aligned with "the antichrist" (v. 7).

8–9 These verses form John's first firm word to his followers: He does not want them to lose all they have gained. As evangelist and pastor, John has participated in the birth and development of the faith of the recipients of this letter. In other words, they are not the sole keepers of their church, free to do as they wish. John has been a builder among them, and his contributions and responsibility make him a justified critic of what is happening.

10–11 These verses describe John's second firm word. The consequence of this false teaching is so serious that it demands a serious remedy: No hospitality should be extended to those people who teach such inaccurate doctrine. An instruction like this is striking and peculiar in the NT, which generally encourages Christians to be generously hospitable. These troubling verses should be viewed as "emergency regulations" that are tied directly to the crisis at hand.

12–13 John extends a greeting from his church and expresses his desire to make a personal visit rather than rely on the written word. We should note his confidence that his readers will receive him and heed his words. John's coming to these believers

hope to visit you and talk with you face
to face,[q] so that our joy may be complete.

12 [q] 3Jn 13,14
13 [r] ver 1

13 The children of your sister, who is
chosen by God,[r] send their greetings.

aims to renew their fellowship so that both pastor and congregation will be joyful.

In v. 13, John's greeting from "the children of your sister" once again employs the metaphorical language we read in v. 1. Although this is the only place the phrase occurs in the NT, we can be reasonably sure that John is building on family imagery for the church (see note on vv. 1–3). Two "sisters" are talking with each other about conditions in the family, and their speech swings from expressions of love and intimacy to feelings of worry and concern.

APPLICATION ✤ 1–13 John's teaching that Christians should show no hospitality to their opponents has met with severe criticism among some interpreters. Is there a place for "shutting the gate"? Despite what we hear in our popular culture, tolerance is not an ultimate virtue. Strong action is appropriate when individuals jeopardize the very integrity of the church. But John gives us little guidance concerning what matters would qualify as "gate-shutting" concerns.

We will all at times experience pressure to dilute the message of Christ, as the church that John addressed experienced. John's followers may have felt pressure from the sophisticated halls of Greek academia—not to mention the popular voices of the marketplace—to reduce the person of Christ into someone less than he was. We will as well. But John calls his followers to stand firm, and he would have us do the same.

3 John

Author: The apostle John

Audience: Gaius, perhaps a leader of one of the churches in or around Ephesus

Date: Between AD 85 and 95

Theme: John writes this letter to commend Gaius for supporting traveling teachers and to rebuke Diotrephes for refusing to welcome them.

Reading 3 John

Like 2 John, read this brief letter as if received from a greatly admired, retired pastor. In it he is giving instructions on the importance of kindness and hospitality.

PERSPECTIVE

Third John is a personal letter addressed to a dear friend and trusted believer named Gaius (v. 1). John wants to visit personally and address a situation that has arisen with a man named Diotrephes, but cannot at present (v. 14), so he writes to Gaius to encourage him to remain faithful to the truth until then.

As we read this book, we can consider our own experiences with the people around us who fail to live up to the standard of love that, through Jesus, John calls for in his first letter (1Jn 3:11–24). And we can follow the example of John in courageously facing the opposition and building up others who can help in the meantime. After all, every Diotrephes that we encounter is another soul who needs the love of Jesus to flood their lives.

For more perspective on this book, see the Introduction to 1 John. For authorship and date of this short letter, see the Introduction to 2 John.

TAKING THE NEXT STEPS

In this brief letter, John complimented Gaius for the hospitality he had shown to the traveling teachers sent out by John. At the same time, he sharply criticized Diotrephes, who had excommunicated from his church any who had shown such hospitality. We too ought to show hospitality to visitors and strangers in our churches, for we are all members of the same family.

Event	10 BC – AD 100
Jesus' birth (c. 6/5 BC)	♦
John becomes a disciple (c. AD 26)	♦
Jesus' death, resurrection and ascension (c. AD 30)	♦
Nero's reign (AD 54–68)	▬
Destruction of Jerusalem's temple (c. AD 70)	♦
Book of 3 John written (c. AD 85–95)	▬
John's exile on Patmos (c. AD 90–95)	▬

10 BC AD 1 10 20 30 40 50 60 70 80 90 100

WHAT TO LOOK FOR IN 3 JOHN

- Loving Christ's messengers (vv. 3–8)
- Exhortations about Diotrephes (vv. 9–12)

Key Verse

Dear friend, do not imitate what is evil but what is good. Anyone who does what is good is from God. Anyone who does what is evil has not seen God.

—3 John 11

[1]The elder,[a]

To my dear friend Gaius, whom I love
in the truth.

[2]Dear friend, I pray that you may enjoy
good health and that all may go well with
you, even as your soul is getting along
well. [3]It gave me great joy when some
believers[b] came and testified about your
faithfulness to the truth, telling how you
continue to walk in it.[c] [4]I have no greater
joy than to hear that my children[d] are
walking in the truth.
[5]Dear friend, you are faithful in what
you are doing for the brothers and sisters,[a]
even though they are strangers to you.[e]
[6]They have told the church about your love.
Please send them on their way in a manner
that honors God. [7]It was for the sake of the
Name[f] that they went out, receiving no
help from the pagans.[g] [8]We ought therefore to show hospitality to such people so
that we may work together for the truth.
[9]I wrote to the church, but Diotrephes,
who loves to be first, will not welcome us.

1 [a]2Jn 1
3 [b]ver 5,10 [c]2Jn 4
4 [d]1Co 4:15; 1Jn 2:1
5 [e]Ro 12:13; Heb 13:2
7 [f]Jn 15:21 [g]Ac 20:33,35

[a] 5 The Greek word for *brothers and sisters* (*adelphoi*) refers here to believers, both men and women, as part of God's family.

1–15 This letter is a brief note dashed off to one heroic Christian (Gaius) who is standing firm while a community near him faces a single antagonist (Diotrephes). Rather than outline its themes, if we sketch the setting of the letter, its various parts fall into place.

Imagine a house church located some distance from John's primary ministry. It is in the grips of theological struggle. John once wrote to the church, but an influential man named Diotrephes rejected his letter. John then sent representatives to the church, but Diotrephes forcefully stopped anyone who tried to speak with them. "Anyone who sides with these men from John," Diotrephes threatened, "gets thrown out with them" (cf. vv. 9–10).

3, 5–6a The missionaries found a courageous host, however, in a man named Gaius. He not only gave these messengers from John rest and refreshment, but he sent them "on their way" (v. 6)—that is, gave them money—and they returned to John with their report about the rebellion of Diotrephes's church and about Gaius's faithfulness.

6b–8 John does not ask Gaius to intervene in the controversy by confronting Diotrephes himself. Gaius has done enough if he stands firm for Jesus Christ and provides John and his couriers an entrée into the community.

9 Diotrephes was a powerful lay leader who had gained control and rejected John's authority. One way to undercut John's influence was to exploit

10So when I come,[h] I will call attention
to what he is doing, spreading malicious
nonsense about us. Not satisfied with
that, he even refuses to welcome other
believers.[i] He also stops those who want
to do so and puts them out of the church.[j]
11Dear friend, do not imitate what
is evil but what is good.[k] Anyone who
does what is good is from God.[l] Anyone
who does what is evil has not seen God.[m]
12Demetrius is well spoken of by everyone[n] — and even by the truth itself. We
also speak well of him, and you know
that our testimony is true.[o]

10 [h]2Jn 12 [i]ver 5 [j]Jn 9:22, 34
11 [k]Ps 37:27 [l]1Jn 2:29 [m]1Jn 3:6,9,10
12 [n]1Ti 3:7 [o]Jn 21:24
14 [p]2Jn 12
15 [q]Jn 10:3

3Jn 11 ❖ Whom in our lives can we imitate in our discipleship? What is good and commendable about these people?

13I have much to write you, but I do
not want to do so with pen and ink. 14I
hope to see you soon, and we will talk
face to face.[p]

15Peace to you. The friends here send
their greetings. Greet the friends there
by name.[q]

---

the theological controversy circulating in the community that John is addressing in this letter. But there is not sufficient evidence to say that John viewed Diotrephes as a leading opponent in the secession.

What was the nature of the problem with Diotrephes? Why was he so antagonistic to John? The Greek verb in v. 9 translated "will not welcome" is present tense. This construction means that John is not referring to a single event but to an enduring attitude. The verb itself can mean two things, both of which are at work here. Formally, it means "to receive or welcome" someone. Diotrephes was simply refusing to be hospitable to the missionaries. Yet the verb also has a figurative meaning: "to accept or recognize" someone. In refusing to help, Diotrephes was rejecting his obligation to be hospitable and therefore rejected John himself as elder. This rejection of the missionaries was his way of refusing to acknowledge John's authority.

12 John writes this letter in anticipation of his upcoming visit. This verse introduces the courier of the letter, a Christian named Demetrius. No doubt, John assumes, the hospitality and financial support shown to other Christian travelers will be extended to Demetrius.

This strong affirmation of Demetrius surely anticipates what Diotrephes will say about him. Demetrius bears the authority of John himself, and since Diotrephes rejects John, he will likewise reject Demetrius. John's testimony should strengthen Gaius's confidence in Demetrius, but the problem will only be resolved when John confronts Diotrephes personally.

APPLICATION ✣ 1–15 John did not let go of this situation. John's first strategy for resolving this conflict was not to retreat but to remain in contact. This should be our strategy too. All too often our impulse when we must confront people of strong will and ambition is to retreat. The prospect of losing or being shamed is so apparent that it seems better to "wait and see" what will happen, stay on the sidelines, or keep away from the perpetrators.

The temptation to avoid Diotrephes and fall silent must have occurred to John. It is one thing to write a letter or even send a messenger. But it is altogether another matter to go personally and confront your opponent. We can successfully rationalize conflict avoidance in countless ways. Powerlessness often masquerades as Christian piety and meekness, but it is neither of these. As did John, we can forcefully take a stand for the enduring principles of God's Word against those who would seek to distort them for their own personal gain. Unity in the church is a strong value for both the proper functioning of the church and for our external witness to those who are watching.

Jude

Author: Most likely Jude, the brother of Jesus

Audience: Christians who are being threatened by false teachers

Date: Between AD 50 and 80

Theme: Jude writes to warn Christians about false teachers who are trying to convince them that being saved by grace gives them license to sin.

PERSPECTIVE

While we can be rather sure that the letter of Jude was written by a brother of Jesus with that name, we can be sure of almost nothing else about this letter. Some date Jude by reference to its relationship to 2 Peter. To be sure, we cannot pin down the precise literary relationship between the two letters. But the degree of similarity between the two does suggest that they were dealing with similar false teaching and probably at about the same time. Second Peter was likely written toward the end of Peter's life, in the middle 60s. We should probably date Jude at about the same time.

Although Jude was very eager to write to his readers about salvation, he felt that he must instead warn them about certain immoral teachers circulating among them who were perverting the grace of God. Apparently these false teachers were trying to convince believers that being saved by grace gave them license to sin since their sins would no longer be held against them. Jude thought it imperative that his readers be on guard against such individuals and be prepared to oppose their perverted teaching with the truth about God's saving grace.

For more perspective on this book, see the Introduction to 2 Peter.

Reading Jude

Like other short books in the Bible, Jude should be read in one sitting. Note how Jude moves from describing the false teachers to pronouncing judgment on them and then to encouraging his readers to live genuine Christian lives.

Event	10 BC	AD 1	10	20	30	40	50	60	70	80	90	100
Jesus' birth (c. 6/5 BC)												
Jesus' death, resurrection and ascension (c. AD 30)												
Jude's conversion (c. AD 30)												
Paul's conversion (c. AD 35)												
Council at Jerusalem (c. AD 49/50)												
Nero's reign (AD 54–68)												
Book of Jude written (c. AD 65–80)												
Destruction of Jerusalem's temple (c. AD 70)												

Key Verses

"In the last times there will be scoffers who will follow their own ungodly desires." These are the people who divide you, who follow mere natural instincts and do not have the Spirit. But you, dear friends, by building yourselves up in your most holy faith and praying in the Holy Spirit, keep yourselves in God's love as you wait for the mercy of our Lord Jesus Christ to bring you to eternal life.

—Jude 18–21

TAKING THE NEXT STEPS

Jude, the writer of this short letter, had as his main purpose to warn his readers against false teachers who were, in his estimation, destroying the church.

Jude addresses the contemporary church as well. (1) We must be alert to those who, through their teaching, promote conflict in the church today. (2) The lifestyle shown by such false teachers is one of greed and immorality. (3) The best antidote to false teaching is a combination of faith, hope and love.

WHAT TO LOOK FOR IN JUDE

- Occasion and theme: contending for the faith (vv. 3–4)
- Description and condemnation of the false teachers (vv. 5–16)
- Closing appeal: holding fast to the faith (vv. 17–23)

1 Jude,[a] a servant of Jesus Christ and a
brother of James,

To those who have been called,[b] who
are loved in God the Father and kept for[a]
Jesus Christ:[c]

2 Mercy, peace and love be yours in
abundance.[d]

The Sin and Doom of Ungodly People

3 Dear friends, although I was very eager to write to you about the salvation
we share,[e] I felt compelled to write and
urge you to contend[f] for the faith that
was once for all entrusted to God's holy
people. 4 For certain individuals whose
condemnation was written about[b] long
ago have secretly slipped in among you.[g]
They are ungodly people, who pervert
the grace of our God into a license for
immorality and deny Jesus Christ our
only Sovereign and Lord.[h]

1 [a] Mt 13:55; Ac 1:13 [b] Ro 1:6, 7 [c] Jn 17:12
2 [d] 2Pe 1:2
3 [e] Titus 1:4 [f] 1Ti 6:12
4 [g] Gal 2:4 [h] Titus 1:16; 2Pe 2:1

[a] 1 Or *by*; or *in* [b] 4 Or *individuals who were marked out for condemnation*

1–2 "Jude" is the brother of the Lord mentioned in Mk 6:3. "Servant" indicates Jude's subservience to the Lord. "James" must refer to the most famous James in the NT—the brother of Jesus, who attained a high position in the early Jerusalem church (v. 1).

Jude identifies his readers as Christians. The key word in the description is "called" (v. 1). This word reflects the NT conviction that being a Christian is a product of God's gracious reaching out to bring helpless sinners into a relationship with himself. Being "kept for Jesus Christ" means that God throughout this life exercises his power on behalf of Christians to preserve them spiritually intact until the coming of Jesus Christ in glory (v. 2).

APPLICATION ✥ 1–2 Christians may find many reasons to be anxious. But one thing we do not need to worry about is God's faithfulness in maintaining us in our faith. This is not to say that we have no part or responsibility in the matter; Jude makes clear that we do (v. 21).

3 Jude focuses on a single theme: maintaining the truth of the Christian faith as it has been handed down from Christ and the apostles. Clearly "faith" describes what Christians believe.

4 "Certain individuals" has a contemptuous ring. These people pursue their agenda by stealth. Jude says four things about them. First, their "condemnation was written about long ago." Second, "they are ungodly," which means irreverent in an ethical sense. Third, they "pervert the grace of our God into a license for immorality." Finally, they "deny Jesus Christ our only Sovereign and Lord." Jude is thinking of people behaving in a manner contrary to what Jesus demands of his people.

✥ 3–4 There is a set of beliefs, based in the

PEOPLE TO KNOW // JUDE

JUDE 1–4: Jude was a half brother of Jesus, along with James. Jude had the remarkable privilege of growing up alongside Jesus. This did not make him an immediate believer in Christ, however. When Jesus' popularity as a teacher increased, his family accused him of being out of his mind (Mk 3:21). John 7:5 also states that, at that point in Jesus' ministry, his own brothers did not believe in him. This would include James and Jude.

Like James, Jude did come to believe that Jesus was indeed the Messiah, as evidenced by his teaching in the NT book that bears his name. In the superscription of the book, Jude introduces himself as a brother of James and a servant of Jesus (Jude 1).

Jude's letter addresses living as faithful Christians in a sinful world, especially when others are intent on perverting God's grace into a license for immorality (Jude 4). Jude describes such people with various metaphors and OT analogies. He calls them fruitless trees that are uprooted, thus twice dead.

In view of the troubles around them, Jude urges readers to build themselves up in faith and to keep themselves in God's love. He ends his letter with a glorious doxology to God, who will keep believers from stumbling and will present them without fault and with great joy before his glorious presence.

APPLICATION ✥ God opened Jude's heart to the truth that his half brother was the Messiah and Savior of the world. This was probably not easy for Jude, as he had literally at one time thought Jesus was out of his mind (see Mk 3:20-21). Perhaps you have had your own stumbling blocks in your journey of faith that have made it difficult to believe in Christ. Jude's testimony shows that God can open your heart, by grace and faith, so that you can come to know and love Jesus as Lord. Some of the world's most powerful evangelists have been men and women who were transformed from their unbelief and later brought Jesus' message to the masses.

Jude 4 ❖ Where have we seen people pervert God's grace into a license for immorality? What can we say to such people (see Ro 6:1–2)?

5Though you already know all this, I
want to remind you that the Lord[a] at one
time delivered his people out of Egypt, but
later destroyed those who did not believe.[i]
6And the angels who did not keep their
positions of authority but abandoned
their proper dwelling — these he has
kept in darkness, bound with everlasting
chains for judgment on the great Day.[j] 7In
a similar way, Sodom and Gomorrah and
the surrounding towns[k] gave themselves
up to sexual immorality and perversion.
They serve as an example of those who
suffer the punishment of eternal fire.[l]
8In the very same way, on the strength
of their dreams these ungodly people
pollute their own bodies, reject authority and heap abuse on celestial beings.[m]
9But even the archangel Michael,[n] when
he was disputing with the devil about
the body of Moses, did not himself dare
to condemn him for slander but said,
"The Lord rebuke you!"[b][o] 10Yet these people slander whatever they do not understand, and the very things they do
understand by instinct — as irrational
animals do — will destroy them.[p]
11Woe to them! They have taken the
way of Cain;[q] they have rushed for profit
into Balaam's error;[r] they have been destroyed in Korah's rebellion.[s]
12These people are blemishes at your
love feasts,[t] eating with you without
the slightest qualm — shepherds who
feed only themselves. They are clouds
without rain,[u] blown along by the wind;[v]

5 [i] Nu 14:29; Ps 106:26
6 [j] 2Pe 2:4,9
7 [k] Dt 29:23 [l] 2Pe 2:6
8 [m] 2Pe 2:10
9 [n] Da 10:13,21 [o] Zec 3:2
10 [p] 2Pe 2:12
11 [q] Ge 4:3-8; 1Jn 3:12 [r] 2Pe 2:15 [s] Nu 16:1-3, 31-35
12 [t] 2Pe 2:13; 1Co 11:20-22 [u] Pr 25:14; 2Pe 2:17 [v] Eph 4:14

[a] 5 Some early manuscripts *Jesus* [b] 9 Jude is alluding to the Jewish *Testament of Moses* (approximately the first century A.D.).

---

teaching and work of Christ, developed and passed on by the apostles, that is nonnegotiable. These involve Jesus' atoning death and resurrection, the indwelling of the Holy Spirit, salvation by grace through faith, and (especially in Jude's situation) the holy lifestyle that flows from God's grace in Christ. To be Christian is to agree with these beliefs; to reject them is to cease to be Christian.

5 Jude warns his readers: Don't think that, because God has decisively rescued you from your sins, you can presume on his grace and mercy.

6 In Ge 6:1–4 the "sons of God" came down to earth and cohabited with "the daughters of humans." Stories about this event are elaborated in the intertestamental Jewish book 1 Enoch. These angels abandoned their "proper dwelling" by rebelling against God (Jude 6). God therefore judged them.

7 Jude adds Sodom and Gomorrah to his three-part example of those who rebelled (vv. 5–7). Jude tells us why God judged the cities: because they "gave themselves up to sexual immorality and perversion." Jude probably associates God's judgment on Sodom and Gomorrah with the same-sex practices of their inhabitants. Jude concludes these sinful cities on the plain "serve as an example of those who suffer the punishment of eternal fire."

8–10 Jude lists three different sins the false teachers are committing. The parallels between these three sins and those of the OT sinners Jude has listed are clear.

9 Verse 9 is a contrast to the behavior of the false teachers. Perhaps the experience of the Jewish exorcists in Ac 19:13–16 is something of a parallel. Jude's false teachers may have been guilty of the mistaken attitude of those Jewish exorcists: dismissing the power and influence of evil angels without the authority of Jesus to back it up.

10 With the "these" at the beginning of v. 10, Jude returns to his characterization of the false teachers. Jude is here describing the false teachers' sexual excesses. They act like animals, with no moral compass or sense of right and wrong.

✜ **5–10** Many people are predisposed, for all kinds of reasons, to certain sins, but this is no excuse in God's eyes. The important point is that the gospel offers people the power to turn from their sin, whatever their particular temptation.

11 Jude compares the false teachers to three bad characters from the OT. As Cain murdered Abel (see Ge 4:1–16), so the false teachers "murder" the souls of people. Jewish tradition also understood Cain to be the classic example of an ungodly skeptic and an instructor in wicked practices. The second example from the OT is Balaam (see Nu 22–24), known especially for his greed. Jude claims the false teachers follow the way of Balaam out of a desire for "profit" or "gain." The third example is Korah, whose story is told in Nu 16:1–35. He rebelled against Moses' leadership and in response, God caused the earth to open up and swallow Korah and his followers in judgment. A similar fate is reserved for the false teachers if they do not turn and repent.

12–13 Jude here provides six more brief descriptions of these false teachers. First, "these people are blemishes at your love feasts, eating with you without the slightest qualm" (v. 12). Like a hidden reef that rips the bottom out of a boat, these false teachers lie in wait to destroy the faithful. Second, they are "shepherds who feed only themselves" (v. 12). The shepherd selflessly watches out for others. But the false teachers abandoned their natural responsibility to care for others, thinking only of themselves.

Third, "they are clouds without rain, blown along by the wind" (v. 12). This is a natural metaphor for those who do not deliver what they promise.

autumn trees, without fruit and uprooted[w] — twice dead. 13They are wild waves
of the sea,[x] foaming up their shame;[y]
wandering stars, for whom blackest
darkness has been reserved forever.[z]
14Enoch,[a] the seventh from Adam,
prophesied about them: "See, the Lord is
coming with thousands upon thousands
of his holy ones[b] 15to judge[c] everyone, and
to convict all of them of all the ungodly
acts they have committed in their ungodliness, and of all the defiant words ungodly sinners have spoken against him."[a][d]
16These people are grumblers and faultfinders; they follow their own evil desires;
they boast[e] about themselves and flatter
others for their own advantage.

A Call to Persevere

17But, dear friends, remember what
the apostles of our Lord Jesus Christ
foretold.[f] 18They said to you, "In the last
times[g] there will be scoffers who will follow their own ungodly desires."[h] 19These
are the people who divide you, who follow mere natural instincts and do not
have the Spirit.[i]
20But you, dear friends, by building
yourselves up[j] in your most holy faith
and praying in the Holy Spirit,[k] 21keep
yourselves in God's love as you wait[l] for
the mercy of our Lord Jesus Christ to
bring you to eternal life.
22Be merciful to those who doubt;
23save others by snatching them from the
fire;[m] to others show mercy, mixed with
fear — hating even the clothing stained
by corrupted flesh.[b][n]

12 [w] Mt 15:13
13 [x] Isa 57:20 [y] Php 3:19 [z] 2Pe 2:17
14 [a] Ge 5:18, 21-24 [b] Dt 33:2; Da 7:10
15 [c] 2Pe 2:6-9 [d] 1Ti 1:9
16 [e] 2Pe 2:18
17 [f] 2Pe 3:2
18 [g] 1Ti 4:1 [h] 2Pe 2:1
19 [i] 1Co 2:14,15
20 [j] Col 2:7 [k] Eph 6:18
21 [l] Titus 2:13; 2Pe 3:12
23 [m] Am 4:11; Zec 3:2-5 [n] Rev 3:4

[a] *14,15* From the Jewish *First Book of Enoch* (approximately the first century B.C.)
[b] *22,23* The Greek manuscripts of these verses vary at several points.

Fourth, they are "autumn trees, without fruit and uprooted—twice dead" (v. 12). A tree that is still without fruit in the autumn has not fulfilled its purpose. Fifth, "they are wild waves of the sea, foaming up their shame" (v. 13a). Jude is thinking of the shameful deeds committed by the false teachers. Finally, they are "wandering stars, for whom blackest darkness has been reserved forever" (v. 13b). Ancient people believed that the heavens should display order and regularity. They therefore had difficulty in accounting for the planets, which seemed to "wander" across the night sky in no discernible pattern.

11-13 Jude's vivid descriptions of the false teachers in his day give us a pattern for discerning the actions and teachings of teachers in every era.

14-16 Jude caps his denunciation of the false teachers with a prophecy from 1 Enoch. This book was popular in Jude's day, and he and Peter allude to it (1Pe 3:19–20; 2Pe 2:4–5). It is not clear whether Jude intends to say that "Enoch prophesied about these men also [i.e., in addition to the wicked people of his own day]" or that "Enoch also [i.e., in addition to these other texts] prophesied about these men." But the context probably suggests the latter. Jude assumes that the prophecies are fulfilled in Christ and the church he founded. Therefore, they can apply the words of the prophets to their own circumstances.
15 Jude goes out of his way to stress these people's "ungodly" character. Indeed, using the word three times in one clause in v. 15 creates an almost awkward reading. We do not have to guess at Jude's point.
16 These people have also sinned against God in speech. They are "grumblers and faultfinders." The biblical background of the term "grumbler" suggests that these false teachers are directing their complaints against God himself. Jude's second description of the false teachers in v. 16 references their "ungodly acts" from the Enoch prophecy (v. 15): "They follow their own evil desires." These evil desires probably encompass both the false teachers' sexual lust and greed. Jude's third accusation suggests the idea of arrogant speech about or even toward God.

14-16 As believers, we should look forward to the day of Christ's coming with joy, for it brings our final deliverance from sin, temptation, and bodily weakness. But contemplation of that day should also lead to serious self-evaluation. Although we need not fear rejection and condemnation, we know our lives will be scrutinized as Christ asks what we have done with the precious blessings he has entrusted to us.

17-23 Jude tells the believers to do three things.
17-19 First, they must remember that the apostles had predicted the false teaching they are now experiencing. From a human standpoint, these false teachers have "secretly slipped in" (v. 4). But God knew all along that they were coming. This reminder reassures Jude's readers that God is still in control.
20-21 Second, Jude's readers must devote themselves to their own spiritual growth. They must not allow the false teachers to deflect them from their own development in the faith.
22-23 Finally, Jude's readers are to reach out to those affected by the false teaching. They must do what they can to reclaim these people before it is too late.

17-23 Jude wants us to be on our guard. We should not be surprised when we find people who teach or live lies in our churches. Being on our guard does not mean that we are to become critical and suspicious. But neither are we to be naive, assuming that because people

Doxology

24To him who is able[o] to keep you from
stumbling and to present you before his
glorious presence[p] without fault[q] and with
great joy— 25to the only God[r] our Savior
be glory, majesty, power and authority,
through Jesus Christ our Lord, before all
ages, now and forevermore![s] Amen.[t]

24 [o] Ro 16:25 [p] 2Co 4:14 [q] Col 1:22
25 [r] Jn 5:44; 1Ti 1:17 [s] Heb 13:8 [t] Ro 11:36

---

have made a profession of their faith, attend church regularly, or are even in a position of leadership, they must be above reproach.

24–25 Jude's doxology is a fitting conclusion to his letter. He has warned the church of a serious and threatening outbreak of false teaching. He has called believers not simply to "batten down the hatches" and ride out the storm but to reach out redemptively to those who are falling away. Believers can do this because their position with the Lord is secure: He has the power to preserve them intact until the day of judgment.

24–25 We worry about our health, our money, our children, and our jobs. In sober moments we perhaps become anxious about death. God does not promise to take away these worries, but he does take away from us our greatest worry: where we will spend eternity. Do we truly value heaven enough so that our earthly worries, while sometimes pressing, fade in importance in light of our eternal destiny?

To our God and Savior be glory for his salvation in and through Jesus Christ our Lord!

Revelation

Author: The apostle John

Audience: Seven churches in western Asia Minor

Date: About AD 95

Theme: John writes to encourage the faithful to stand firm against persecution and compromise in the light of the imminent return of Christ to deliver the righteous and judge the wicked.

PERSPECTIVE

No book in the Bible has been interpreted as variously as Revelation. Students of prophecy and mystics especially have found in the visions of Revelation fertile ground for speculation and spiritualization.

Although many details in Revelation are debatable, the basic thrust is not. The true and living God summons us from our preoccupation with the world to recognize what really matters and what does not. God first gave Revelation to a culture where people would hear and be struck by the full force of the book. It summons us to grapple with God's judgment on a world in rebellion against him.

If we take seriously what the book itself claims, then it was a book that must have made good sense to its first hearers, who in fact were "blessed" for obeying it (1:3). If today's news feeds are a necessary key to interpreting the book, then no generation until our own could have understood and obeyed the book (contrary to 1:3). They could not have read the book as Scripture profitable for teaching and training (cf. 2Ti 3:16–17). If, however, the book was understandable for the first generation, subsequent generations can also profit from the lessons that the book teaches.

The problem with focusing on present-day application of Revelation is that it calls into question or makes problematic two fundamental bedrocks of Christian faith.

First, it questions the universal and timeless nature of God's truth. When the great visions of Revelation are interpreted as dependent on what some see as the great evil empires of the 20th and 21st centuries—Germany, Japan, the Soviet Union and Russia, the Islamic world—then

Reading Revelation

The book of Revelation begins with an introductory vision in which John sees Christ walking among his churches. The next two chapters contain brief letters to seven individual churches in Asia Minor. Beginning with chapter 4, John sees a number of visions with characters such as angels blowing trumpets, dragons, ugly beasts, a gaudy but drunk prostitute, and an army

	10 BC	AD 1	10	20	30	40	50	60	70	80	90	100
Jesus' birth (c. 6/5 BC)												
John becomes a disciple (c. AD 26)												
Jesus' death, resurrection and ascension (c. AD 30)												
Nero's reign (AD 54–68)												
Paul's imprisonment and death in Rome (c. AD 67–68)												
Destruction of Jerusalem's temple (c. AD 70)												
Domitian's reign (c. AD 81–96)												
John's exile on Patmos (c. AD 90–95)												
Book of Revelation written (c. AD 96)												

dressed in white riding on white horses. These are all symbolic images and subject to various interpretations.

Key Verses

"Look, I am coming soon! My reward is with me, and I will give to each person according to what they have done. I am the Alpha and the Omega, the First and the Last, the Beginning and the End." . . . He who testifies to these things says, "Yes, I am coming soon." Amen. Come, Lord Jesus.

—Rev 22:12-13, 20

every shift of modern political fortune changes our understanding of the book. But the great symbols of Revelation were aimed at early Christian ears, not 21st-century ones. We learn what they mean by understanding what they meant.

Second, we are tempted to forget that God has acted and continues to act in all political contexts. We have no monopoly on God's attention. The great prophecies of Revelation meant as much to Augustine, Aquinas, Luther, Calvin, Wesley, Edwards, and Barth as they mean to us today. Just as the visions of Revelation make up parallel rather than serial understandings of God's mighty deeds, so every Christian age develops an understanding of what Revelation means that is parallel to all other ages—not a chronological series of events.

Indeed, one of the great marvels of God's gracious activity toward us is that it occurs in real time without being prejudiced in favor of any particular age. Just because we are the latest does not mean we are the best. The effects of sin prevent any age—including ours—from being "golden," at least in the spiritual sense. Every Christian generation learns equally the lessons of Revelation—that God is in control, that the powers of the world are minuscule when compared with God, that God is as likely to work through apparent weakness and failure as through strength and success, and that in the end God's people will prevail.

God's time is his, not ours. The story of God's gracious activity on our behalf will be fulfilled in a great and glorious conclusion. But all Christians, everywhere and at all times, have equal access to the time. That access has been and is made possible by God's message in the book of Revelation.

TAKING THE NEXT STEPS

This last book of the NT was written by John (probably the apostle) toward the end of the first century. Though specific interpretations of this book vary widely, most will agree that John was reporting God-given visions of intense conflict between Christ and his enemies. John assured his readers that Christ was in control and that, in the end, the victory belonged to Christ. Those enemies of Christ would experience devastating judgment. John's ultimate goal was to inspire hope in his readers in the midst of the sufferings they were experiencing.

God has important messages for the church today in this book. (1) Even though evil runs rampant in our world, there is strong reassurance in the fact that Christ is in control and the final victory belongs to him. (2) Under no circumstances should we compromise our Christian commitment and principles, though the pressures of the moment may tempt us to do so. (3) We ought never to forget that eternal judgment is in store for those who oppose Christ and his word. (4) Someday we will be a part of that heavenly throng that praises God forever.

WHAT TO LOOK FOR IN REVELATION

- John's initial vision of Christ (ch. 1)
- Letters to the seven churches in Asia Minor (chs. 2–3)
- Praises sung to God and to Christ in heaven (chs. 4–5; 19)
- Opening the seven seals (ch. 6)
- The 144,000 (chs. 7; 14)
- Angels blowing the seven trumpets (chs. 8–9)
- The war in heaven (ch. 12)
- The mark of the beast (ch. 13)
- The two beasts and the great prostitute (chs. 13; 17–18)
- Pouring out the seven bowls of wrath (ch. 16)
- The millennium or the 1,000 years (ch. 20)
- The new Jerusalem (chs. 21–22)

THEOLOGICAL PERSPECTIVES ON REVELATION

	REV 1-3	REV 4-19	REV 20-22
Postmillennial	Historic churches	Generally historicist	Victory of Christianity over the world
Amillennial	Historic churches	Generally historicist	Coming of Christ; judgment; eternal state
Premillennial	Historic churches representative of historical stages	Generally futurist	Literal millennial reign; judgment of great white throne; new Jerusalem
Apocalyptic	Historic churches	Generally preterist	Symbolic of heaven and victory

From H. Wayne House, *Chronological and Background Charts of the New Testament* (Grand Rapids: Zondervan, 1981), 145.

Prologue

1 The revelation from Jesus Christ, which God gave him to show his servants what must soon take place. He made it known by sending his angel[a] to his servant John, 2 who testifies to everything he saw—that is, the word of God and the testimony of Jesus Christ.[b]

1:1 [a] Rev 22:16
1:2 [b] 1Co 1:6; Rev 12:17

1:1a The title of this book is "the revelation from Jesus Christ."

1:1b–2 That the author does not need to qualify which John he is may suggest that he was John the apostle, who had personally known Jesus (cf. Jn 21:22). John "testifies to everything he saw," which was "the word of God and the testimony of Jesus Christ" (Rev 1:2). "Testify" is often courtroom language (v. 2).

PEOPLE TO KNOW // JOHN

REVELATION 1:1–8: John was one of Jesus' twelve apostles and the author of the Gospel that bears his name, as well as three NT letters and the book of Revelation. He was one of Jesus' closest disciples, along with Peter and James; in fact, John's Gospel refers to John as "the disciple whom Jesus loved" (Jn 13:23).

John and his brother James were fishermen when Jesus called them to follow him (Mt 4:21); leaving their father and their boats, they obeyed Christ. Jesus gave them the name "sons of thunder" (Mk 3:17), possibly because of their eagerness to call down judgment upon those who rejected Christ (Lk 9:54).

John, James and Peter were the only disciples with Jesus at his transfiguration, when he appeared in heavenly glory (Mt 17:5). John was also the only one of the twelve apostles to stay near Jesus at his death (Jn 19:26–27). On Easter morning, when Mary Magdalene told the disciples Jesus' tomb was empty, John and Peter ran to see for themselves. When John entered the tomb and saw it empty, the Bible says, "he saw and believed" (Jn 20:8).

John was a leader in the early church. Acts recounts him ministering along with Peter. His brother James was the first of the apostles to be martyred. John, however, lived a long life. When he was nearly 90, God gave him the visions of Revelation on Patmos, where the Roman emperor had exiled him.

APPLICATION ✣ John's motivation for writing was "that you may believe that Jesus is the Messiah, the Son of God, and that by believing you may have life in his name" (Jn 20:31). John's story demonstrates faithfulness and passion for Christ throughout many years. We see many people get excited about Jesus for a while and then flame out, but John shows us the true goal: to be so filled with the love and Spirit of Christ that our faith continues and grows to the moment of our final breath.

3Blessed is the one who reads aloud the
words of this prophecy, and blessed are
those who hear it and take to heart what
is written in it,[c] because the time is near.

Greetings and Doxology

4John,

To the seven churches in the province
of Asia:

Grace and peace to you from him who
is, and who was, and who is to come,
and from the seven spirits[a][d] before his
throne, 5and from Jesus Christ, who is
the faithful witness,[e] the firstborn from
the dead,[f] and the ruler of the kings of
the earth.[g]

To him who loves us and has freed
us from our sins by his blood, 6and has
made us to be a kingdom and priests[h] to
serve his God and Father — to him be glory and power for ever and ever! Amen.[i]

7"Look, he is coming with the
clouds,"[b][j]
and "every eye will see him,

1:3 [c] Lk 11:28
1:4 [d] Rev 3:1; 4:5
1:5 [e] Rev 3:14 [f] Col 1:18 [g] Rev 17:14
1:6 [h] 1Pe 2:5 [i] Ro 11:36
1:7 [j] Da 7:13

[a] 4 That is, the sevenfold Spirit [b] 7 Daniel 7:13

1:3 Revelation was read alongside OT Scripture. This suggests it was treated as Scripture. That one person would read the work out loud for the people fits what we know of the time; even in urban areas, few people could read.

APPLICATION ✣ **1:1–3** God is still in control and will conclude history the way he promised. Because he rules history, he can assure us of its outcome.

1:4a "Asia" was a designation for the Roman province of western Asia Minor (modern Turkey), where Christianity was flourishing by the end of the first century.
1:4b Early Christian letters invoked the Lord Jesus alongside God the Father, implying their belief in his deity.

1:5–6 Jesus is the "faithful witness," who provided the ultimate witness of the Father. Jesus is also here the "firstborn from the dead," relevant for Christians who might soon face death for his name. Jesus also rules the "kings of the earth" (v. 5). The language alludes to Ps 89:27.

In declaring that Jesus made us a "kingdom and priests" (v. 6), John reminds his audience that salvation is not just what God saves us from (v. 5b), but what he saves us for—a destiny as his agents and worshipers (v. 6). John pauses to offer a doxology of praise to Jesus (v. 6). Whereas traditional Jewish texts praised God the Father, here the praise is apparently directed toward Jesus.
1:7–8 That Jesus would return in the clouds reflects Da 7:13; that those who pierced him would see him and mourn reflects Zec 12:10. It is not altogether

> **Rev 1:6-7** ❖ A priest represents God to the world and represents the world before God. How can we be “priests” for those around us?

even those who pierced him”;
and all peoples on earth “will
mourn[k] because of him.”[a]
So shall it be! Amen.

8“I am the Alpha and the Omega,”[l] says
the Lord God, “who is, and who was, and
who is to come, the Almighty.”[m]

John's Vision of Christ

9I, John, your brother and companion
in the suffering[n] and kingdom and patient endurance[o] that are ours in Jesus,
was on the island of Patmos because of
the word of God and the testimony of
Jesus. 10On the Lord's Day I was in the
Spirit,[p] and I heard behind me a loud
voice like a trumpet,[q] 11which said:
“Write on a scroll what you see and send
it to the seven churches:[r] to Ephesus,
Smyrna, Pergamum, Thyatira, Sardis,[s]
Philadelphia and Laodicea.”
12I turned around to see the voice that
was speaking to me. And when I turned
I saw seven golden lampstands,[t] 13and
among the lampstands was someone like
a son of man,[b][u] dressed in a robe reaching
down to his feet and with a golden sash
around his chest.[v] 14The hair on his head
was white like wool, as white as snow, and
his eyes were like blazing fire.[w] 15His feet
were like bronze glowing in a furnace,[x]
and his voice was like the sound of rushing
waters.[y] 16In his right hand he held seven
stars,[z] and coming out of his mouth was a
sharp, double-edged sword.[a] His face was
like the sun shining in all its brilliance.
17When I saw him, I fell at his feet[b] as
though dead. Then he placed his right
hand on me and said: “Do not be afraid.
I am the First and the Last.[c] 18I am the
Living One; I was dead,[d] and now look,
I am alive for ever and ever![e] And I hold
the keys of death and Hades.[f]

1:7 [k] Zec 12:10
1:8 [l] Rev 21:6 [m] Rev 4:8
1:9 [n] Php 4:14 [o] 2Ti 2:12
1:10 [p] Rev 4:2 [q] Rev 4:1
1:11 [r] ver 4, 20 [s] Rev 3:1
1:12 [t] Ex 25:31-40; Zec 4:2
1:13 [u] Eze 1:26; Da 7:13; 10:16 [v] Da 10:5; Rev 15:6
1:14 [w] Da 7:9; 10:6; Rev 19:12
1:15 [x] Da 10:6 [y] Eze 43:2; Rev 14:2
1:16 [z] Rev 2:1; 3:1 [a] Isa 49:2; Heb 4:12; Rev 2:12,16
1:17 [b] Eze 1:28; Da 8:17,18 [c] Isa 41:4; 44:6; 48:12; Rev 22:13
1:18 [d] Ro 6:9 [e] Rev 4:9,10 [f] Rev 20:1

[a] 7 Zech. 12:10 [b] 13 See Daniel 7:13.

---

clear whether the “mourning” implies repentance or fear, but the note of vindication is clear. Finally, John confirms all history is in God's hands (v. 8); thus, his people need not fear.

The title “the Alpha and the Omega” indicates God's eternal nature (v. 8). God not only is Lord over time, but he rules the entire universe (1:8; 4:8; 11:17; 15:3; 16:7, 14; 19:6, 15; 21:22). For Christians suffering under Caesar, knowing that they served the “Almighty” must have provided strength and encouragement (1:8).

> ✣ **1:4-8** God saw our own generation and all the martyrs of history simultaneously; the church of all ages is part of his plan, and we are part of a purpose that is bigger than us individually, and that will not fail.

1:9-10 John was on the island of Patmos, being punished by the state for preaching about Jesus (cf. 6:9; 12:11). Perhaps “in the Spirit” begins here not with a visionary state but in worship that led to a visionary state. It was “the Lord's Day,” likely used for corporate worship (1:10).

1:11-13a John turns when he hears a voice “like a trumpet” (v. 10). This expression presumably refers to the clarity of Jesus' voice. Sometimes visionaries wrote by dictation as they saw their visions; John does not, however, need to wait until the completion of his visions (v. 11).

Jesus appears among the lampstands (vv. 12-13). These represent the seven churches (v. 20), suggesting Jesus' presence with his church. The temple included a golden lampstand (Ex 25:31-35; 37:18-21; 2Ch 4:7, 20) that was never extinguished by night or day. This menorah was the most common symbol of Israel and Judaism throughout the ancient Mediterranean world. John encourages Jewish Christians excluded from their synagogues that it is not they but their opponents who are severed from their Jewish heritage.

> ✣ **1:9-13a** Until a church has gone so far as to be withdrawn from its place (2:5), it remains the place where Christ's presence is found. We must never give up on the spiritual life that remains in the church, for Jesus still loves his churches, he watches over and walks among them still today.

1:13b-16 The imagery stems from the book of Daniel: The reigning Son of Man (Da 7:13-14) and the Ancient of Days (God; Da 7:9) appears. The voice like “rushing waters” (Rev 1:15) recalls God's own voice (Eze 1:24). Jesus' title (Rev 1:13) recalls Da 7:13-14; the hair like wool alludes to God himself (Da 7:9-10). The point of Jesus' fiery eyes, white hair, and bronze feet (Rev 1:14-15) is that he was radiating light or fire (v. 15)—like some visions of God in the Bible (Eze 1:27; Da 7:9-10). His sword is an allusion to Isa 11:4.

1:17 John responds to this revelation of Jesus' glory by falling down. When recipients respond in such a manner, the revealer often raises the recipient on his feet or declares, “Do not be afraid” (Da 10:11-12; cf. Mt 17:7). Most important, Jesus is “the First and the Last” (Rev 1:17). This is exactly equivalent to “the Alpha and the Omega,” a title appropriate only for God (v. 8; 21:6).

1:18-19 All the claims of v. 18 involve Jesus' triumph over death. John is called as a witness to these claims.

19"Write, therefore, what you have
seen, what is now and what will take
place later. 20The mystery of the seven
stars that you saw in my right hand and
of the seven golden lampstands[g] is this:
The seven stars are the angels[a] of the sev-
en churches,[h] and the seven lampstands
are the seven churches.[i]

To the Church in Ephesus

2 "To the angel[b] of the church in Ephesus write:

These are the words of him who
holds the seven stars in his right
hand[j] and walks among the seven
golden lampstands.[k] 2I know your
deeds,[l] your hard work and your
perseverance. I know that you cannot tolerate wicked people, that you
have tested[m] those who claim to be
apostles but are not, and have found
them false.[n] 3You have persevered
and have endured hardships for my
name,[o] and have not grown weary.
4Yet I hold this against you: You
have forsaken the love you had at
first.[p] 5Consider how far you have
fallen! Repent[q] and do the things
you did at first. If you do not repent,
I will come to you and remove your
lampstand[r] from its place. 6But you
have this in your favor: You hate the
practices of the Nicolaitans,[s] which
I also hate.
7Whoever has ears, let them hear[t]
what the Spirit says to the churches.
To the one who is victorious, I will
give the right to eat from the tree
of life,[u] which is in the paradise[v] of
God.

To the Church in Smyrna

8"To the angel of the church in Smyrna[w] write:

These are the words of him who is
the First and the Last,[x] who died and
came to life again.[y] 9I know your afflictions and your poverty—yet you
are rich![z] I know about the slander
of those who say they are Jews and
are not,[a] but are a synagogue of Satan.[b] 10Do not be afraid of what you
are about to suffer. I tell you, the
devil will put some of you in prison
to test you,[c] and you will suffer persecution for ten days.[d] Be faithful,[e]

1:20 [g] Zec 4:2 [h] ver 4,11 [i] Mt 5:14,15
2:1 [j] Rev 1:16 [k] Rev 1:12,13
2:2 [l] Rev 3:1, 8,15 [m] 1Jn 4:1 [n] 2Co 11:13
2:3 [o] Jn 15:21
2:4 [p] Mt 24:12
2:5 [q] ver 16,22 [r] Rev 1:20
2:6 [s] ver 15
2:7 [t] Mt 11:15; Rev 3:6,13, 22 [u] Ge 2:9; Rev 22:2,14,19 [v] Lk 23:43
2:8 [w] Rev 1:11 [x] Rev 1:17 [y] Rev 1:18
2:9 [z] Jas 2:5 [a] Rev 3:9 [b] Mt 4:10
2:10 [c] Rev 3:10 [d] Da 1:12,14 [e] ver 13

[a] 20 Or *messengers* [b] 1 Or *messenger;* also in verses 8, 12 and 18

Rev 2:4–5 ❖ What causes Christians to forsake their "first love"? How can we restore our love for Christ when our faith grows stale?

1:20 The "mystery" is not one that God wishes to keep secret. The stars represent the angels of the churches, and the lampstands represent the churches. These indicate Jesus' intimate care for his people: He is among them (cf. 21:3), and their future lies in his hand (cf. Jn 10:28–29). What are the angels of the seven churches? These angels most likely represent guardian angels of the congregations.

❖ **1:13–20** Like Jesus' triumph over death (v. 18), the fact that Jesus holds the churches in his hands (v. 20) reassures us that in the end, God's benevolent purposes will triumph.

2:1–7 Each letter to these individual churches is a prophetic word from Jesus through the Spirit, who is inspiring John (1:10). Each letter follows a similar pattern, balancing praise and reproof.

The portrait of an evil world ruler demanding worship (13:12–15) would certainly be relevant to Christians in Ephesus. Ephesus honored Domitian at Olympic games shortly before this book was written. Ephesus was also known for the worship of Artemis (Ac 19:23–40) and practicing magic (Ac 19:13–19). It also had a large Jewish community (Ac 19:8–9).

2:5 All that the Ephesian Christians are doing right is not sufficient to excuse their lack of love. Those who once knew what was right should remember that they can repent and return.

2:6 We can only guess the identity of the Nicolaitans. They condone immorality and the eating of food offered to idols (vv. 14–15).

2:7 For the church in Ephesus, "victory" requires the internal unity of love. The reward of such overcoming is eating "from the tree of life" (Ge 3:22; Rev 22:2).

❖ **2:1–7** Even when we are dealing with clear cases of sin and error, Scripture calls us to offer correction with love and grace. A church where love ceases can no longer function properly as a local expression of Christ's many-membered body.

2:8–11 Smyrna was an important center of the imperial cult (emperor worship) in Asia. Only Jews were exempt from worshiping the emperor. The recognition that Christians were a part of Judaism protected Christians from unnecessary persecution. Unfortunately, synagogue leaders made the Jewish Christians unwelcome in the synagogues.

2:9 Such conflicts help explain this verse. Some members of the local Jewish community were collaborating with local officials to repress the Christian minority.

2:10 Imprisonment was usually temporary detention until trial and then either official punishment or release. Believers must prepare for execution. The specific duration of the imprisonment ("ten

even to the point of death, and I will
give you life as your victor's crown.
11Whoever has ears, let them hear
what the Spirit says to the churches.
The one who is victorious will not
be hurt at all by the second death.[f]

To the Church in Pergamum

12"To the angel of the church in Pergamum[g] write:

These are the words of him who
has the sharp, double-edged sword.[h]
13I know where you live — where Satan has his throne. Yet you remain
true to my name. You did not renounce your faith in me,[i] not even
in the days of Antipas, my faithful
witness, who was put to death in
your city — where Satan lives.[j]
14Nevertheless, I have a few things
against you:[k] There are some among
you who hold to the teaching of Balaam,[l] who taught Balak to entice
the Israelites to sin so that they ate
food sacrificed to idols and committed sexual immorality.[m] 15Likewise,
you also have those who hold to the
teaching of the Nicolaitans.[n] 16Re-
pent therefore! Otherwise, I will soon
come to you and will fight against
them with the sword of my mouth.[o]
17Whoever has ears, let them hear
what the Spirit says to the churches.

THE SEVEN CHURCHES OF REVELATION

• Seven churches of Revelation 1–3

2:11 [f] Rev 20:6, 14; 21:8 2:12 [g] Rev 1:11 [h] Rev 1:16 2:13 [i] Rev 14:12 [j] ver 9, 24 2:14 [k] ver 20 [l] 2Pe 2:15 [m] 1Co 6:13 2:15 [n] ver 6 2:16 [o] 2Th 2:8; Rev 1:16

days," v. 10b) is probably a symbolic allusion to the OT (Da 1:12–14). The knowledge that imprisonment could include torture demanded faithfulness.

Crowns (wreaths of olive branches) were used in athletic competition; hence, they became a familiar sign of honor or award. Whereas "victory" in Ephesus required restoration of love (Rev 2:4), in Smyrna, it demanded withstanding persecution.

✣ **2:8-11** Suffering has a way of reminding us of what in life really matters. It forces us to depend radically on God, and thus it purifies our obedience to God's will. It is important to know God's heart before we face suffering so that we may understand our suffering in light of his love for us—in light of his sharing our suffering in the cross—rather than interpreting his heart toward us on the basis of our suffering.

2:12-13 This church faced external as well as internal opposition. Satan's "throne" (v. 13) may be the famous and huge throne-like altar of "Zeus the Savior," whose sculptures included serpents. Paganism led to the martyrdom of Antipas, mentioned in v. 13. As a "faithful witness" he is like his Lord (1:5; cf. 3:14).
2:14 Pergamum is experiencing internal problems. "Balaam" (v. 14) is a code name signifying that this prophet is false. Balaam acted out of greed (Nu 22:19). He led Israel into the sins of sexual immorality and food offered to idols (Nu 25:1–2).

Balaam's promotion of food offered to idols means God's people were lured into the cults of other deities. The meat was doled out at pagan festivals or while participating in trade-related guild banquets. Avoiding these trade guild banquets hurt Christians' livelihood.
2:14-16 For Christians in Pergamum, "victory" means to continue to be steadfast in the face of opposition (v. 13), but especially to stand against teachings of compromise (vv. 14–16).
2:17 To those who overcome, Jesus promises both the "hidden manna," which contrasts starkly with the idolatrous food, and a "white stone with a new name written on it." People used pebbles as admission tokens for public assemblies or festivities. In some ancient courtrooms, jurors voted for acquittal with a white stone and for conviction with a black one. The "new name" alludes to Isa 56:5 and especially 62:2, which promises that God will give his people a new name.

✣ **2:12-17** The potential applications of this passage's warning against compromise are numerous; each pastor, Bible study leader, and individual guided by God's Spirit will recognize

To the one who is victorious, I will
give some of the hidden manna.[p]
I will also give that person a white
stone with a new name[q] written on
it, known only to the one who receives it.[r]

To the Church in Thyatira

18“To the angel of the church in Thyatira[s] write:

These are the words of the Son of
God, whose eyes are like blazing fire
and whose feet are like burnished
bronze.[t] 19I know your deeds,[u] your
love and faith, your service and perseverance, and that you are now doing more than you did at first.

20Nevertheless, I have this against
you: You tolerate that woman Jezebel,[v] who calls herself a prophet.
By her teaching she misleads my
servants into sexual immorality
and the eating of food sacrificed
to idols. 21I have given her time[w] to
repent of her immorality, but she
is unwilling.[x] 22So I will cast her on
a bed of suffering, and I will make
those who commit adultery[y] with
her suffer intensely, unless they repent of her ways. 23I will strike her
children dead. Then all the churches
will know that I am he who searches
hearts and minds,[z] and I will repay
each of you according to your deeds.

24Now I say to the rest of you in
Thyatira, to you who do not hold to
her teaching and have not learned
Satan's so-called deep secrets, 'I
will not impose any other burden
on you,[a] 25except to hold on to what
you have[b] until I come.'

26To the one who is victorious
and does my will to the end, I will
give authority over the nations[c] —
27that one 'will rule them with an
iron scepter[d] and will dash them
to pieces like pottery'*[a]*[e] — just as I
have received authority from my
Father. 28I will also give that one the
morning star.[f] 29Whoever has ears,
let them hear[g] what the Spirit says
to the churches.

To the Church in Sardis

3 “To the angel*[b]* of the church in Sardis write:

These are the words of him who
holds the seven spirits*[c]*[h] of God
and the seven stars.[i] I know your
deeds;[j] you have a reputation of being alive, but you are dead.[k] 2Wake
up! Strengthen what remains and is
about to die, for I have found your
deeds unfinished in the sight of my
God. 3Remember, therefore, what

2:17 [p] Jn 6:49, 50 [q] Isa 62:2 [r] Rev 19:12
2:18 [s] Rev 1:11 [t] Rev 1:14, 15
2:19 [u] ver 2
2:20 [v] 1Ki 16:31; 21:25; 2Ki 9:7
2:21 [w] Ro 2:4 [x] Rev 9:20
2:22 [y] Rev 17:2; 18:9
2:23 [z] 1Sa 16:7; Jer 11:20; Ac 1:24; Ro 8:27
2:24 [a] Ac 15:28
2:25 [b] Rev 3:11
2:26 [c] Ps 2:8; Rev 3:21
2:27 [d] Rev 12:5 [e] Isa 30:14; Jer 19:11
2:28 [f] Rev 22:16
2:29 [g] ver 7
3:1 [h] Rev 1:4 [i] Rev 1:16 [j] Rev 2:2 [k] 1Ti 5:6

a *27* Psalm 2:9 *b* *1* Or *messenger*; also in verses 7 and 14 *c* *1* That is, the sevenfold Spirit

---

the most appropriate applications for their own particular settings.

2:18 Economic pressures were inviting compromise on the part of Thyatira's Christians. The Asian churches may well hear in Jesus' biblical title "Son of God" a direct challenge to the imperial cult, where the emperor was honored with the same title.

2:19–20 The Christians in Thyatira are doing godly works more than before (vv. 5, 19), but one flaw proves serious enough to offset this praise: Unlike Ephesus, they tolerate a false teacher (vv. 2, 20). Thyatira was known for its merchants, crafts, and guilds. Those who participated in this aspect of public economic life would risk a substantial measure of their livelihood by refusing to join trade guilds. But guild meetings also included a pagan meal.

The biblical Jezebel was not a "prophetess," but sponsored 850 false prophets (1Ki 18:19) and took the lives of God's true prophets (1Ki 18:13).

2:22–23 The Lord Jesus will not allow those leading his people astray to go unchallenged; he will strike "Jezebel" with sickness (v. 22). He will also kill her "children" (v. 23)—undoubtedly a reference to her disciples.

2:26–29 Those who overcome this threat of false teaching will share with Jesus in his reign (v. 26). God has delegated rule over the earth to humanity (Ge 1:26–28). Jesus will also give the morning star to those who overcome (Rev 2:28). The "morning star" was applied to magnificent rulers (Isa 14:12). In Revelation, Jesus is himself the Morning Star (Rev 22:16; cf. Nu 24:17).

2:18–29 Verses such as 2:26 and many others (Ac 14:22; 1Co 9:27; 2Co 13:5; Col 1:23; 1Th 3:5; 1Ti 4:1; Heb 2:1–4; 4:1–2; 6:4–8; 10:19–31; 12:14–17; Jas 5:19–20) may prove uncomfortable to those who think that merely praying a prayer without truly persevering in Christian faith is adequate for salvation. The threats to perseverance vary among the churches today that are scattered across the earth—from persecution to lovelessness to compromise with paganism—but Scripture contains sufficient warning to summon the entire church worldwide to spiritual alertness.

3:1–2 Jesus reprimands a church with a reputation of being alive, yet is dead (v. 1). This is a deliberate contrast with the Lord himself, who was dead

you have received and heard; hold
it fast, and repent.[l] But if you do not
wake up, I will come like a thief,[m]
and you will not know at what time
I will come to you.
4 Yet you have a few people in
Sardis who have not soiled their
clothes.[n] They will walk with me,
dressed in white,[o] for they are worthy. 5 The one who is victorious will,
like them, be dressed in white. I will
never blot out the name of that person from the book of life,[p] but will
acknowledge that name before my
Father[q] and his angels. 6 Whoever
has ears, let them hear[r] what the
Spirit says to the churches.

To the Church in Philadelphia

7 "To the angel of the church in Philadelphia[s] write:

These are the words of him who
is holy and true,[t] who holds the key
of David.[u] What he opens no one
can shut, and what he shuts no one
can open. 8 I know your deeds. See,
I have placed before you an open
door[v] that no one can shut. I know
that you have little strength, yet you
have kept my word and have not denied my name.[w] 9 I will make those
who are of the synagogue of Satan,[x]
who claim to be Jews though they
are not, but are liars—I will make
them come and fall down at your
feet[y] and acknowledge that I have
loved you.[z] 10 Since you have kept
my command to endure patiently,
I will also keep you[a] from the hour
of trial that is going to come on the
whole world to test[b] the inhabitants
of the earth.[c]
11 I am coming soon. Hold on to
what you have,[d] so that no one will
take your crown.[e] 12 The one who
is victorious I will make a pillar[f]
in the temple of my God. Never
again will they leave it. I will write
on them the name of my God[g] and
the name of the city of my God, the
new Jerusalem,[h] which is coming
down out of heaven from my God;
and I will also write on them my
new name. 13 Whoever has ears, let
them hear what the Spirit says to
the churches.

3:3 [l] Rev 2:5 [m] 2Pe 3:10
3:4 [n] Jude 23 [o] Rev 4:4; 6:11; 7:9,13,14
3:5 [p] Rev 20:12 [q] Mt 10:32
3:6 [r] Rev 2:7
3:7 [s] Rev 1:11 [t] 1Jn 5:20 [u] Isa 22:22; Mt 16:19
3:8 [v] Ac 14:27 [w] Rev 2:13
3:9 [x] Rev 2:9 [y] Isa 49:23 [z] Isa 43:4
3:10 [a] 2Pe 2:9 [b] Rev 2:10 [c] Rev 6:10; 17:8
3:11 [d] Rev 2:25 [e] Rev 2:10
3:12 [f] Gal 2:9 [g] Rev 14:1; 22:4 [h] Rev 21:2,10

---

and is now alive (1:18; 2:8). The spiritual state of the believers in this city is hindering them from appropriating Jesus' own resurrection power.

3:3 Jesus warns he will come on them as a "thief." Conquerors had never overtaken Sardis by conventional war, but had twice conquered it unexpectedly because Sardians had failed to watch adequately.

3:4 Those who have not "soiled" their clothes will walk with Jesus "dressed in white." His followers who have not polluted themselves with the paganism of their culture will participate in the new Jerusalem.

3:5–6 The promise that the overcomers in Sardis will not be blotted out "from the book of life" (v. 5) implies that others may not see the kingdom. The image of "blotting out" stems from Ex 32:32–33, which came to be applied to a heavenly book of life (Ps 69:28; Da 12:1; Lk 10:20; Php 4:3). The promise that Jesus will confess the faithful remnant before his Father echoes what he told his disciples (Mt 10:32).

✣ **3:1–6** It is too easy for us to depend on past achievements instead of looking to God's call for us in the future (cf. Php 3:12–14). Recall Gideon, who made a golden ephod to commemorate his victory but failed to destroy it when people began worshiping it (Jdg 8:27). We are warned by his poor example and Jesus' words here.

3:7–8 The Philadelphian church has only a "little strength," but it has proved successful in standing in that strength (v. 8).

Jesus "holds the key of David," a position of the highest authority in the kingdom (v. 7; cf. Isa 22:15–25). As such Jesus determines who may enter his household and who may not. Though synagogues may have expelled believers in Philadelphia from their houses of worship, Jesus welcomes them into his own household.

3:9–10 The prophets had promised God's people that the Gentiles would one day bow down to the Jews (Isa 60:14). But here unbelieving Jews join unbelieving Gentiles in bowing down before the faithful believers (Rev 3:9). Because they have "kept" his word (v. 10), Jesus will guard them.

3:11–12 Despite their perseverance to this point, their work is not over. They must continue to hold fast to what they have, lest their persecutors take their crown (v. 11). Losing it means exclusion from the kingdom (cf. v. 5). Those who do overcome will become a part of God's temple (v. 12). They will be pillars, confirming that they belong in the holy city.

✣ **3:7–13** The Christians in Philadelphia have become broken by their exclusion from the synagogue; they have been separated from their heritage. Faithfulness often means being excluded from circles that mean much to us—sometimes even from family. Those excluded today for their faith will wear the name that identifies them as citizens of the promised future world.

To the Church in Laodicea

14"To the angel of the church in Laodicea write:

These are the words of the Amen,
the faithful and true witness, the
ruler of God's creation.[i] 15I know your
deeds, that you are neither cold nor
hot.[j] I wish you were either one or
the other! 16So, because you are lukewarm—neither hot nor cold—I am
about to spit you out of my mouth.
17You say, 'I am rich; I have acquired
wealth and do not need a thing.'[k]
But you do not realize that you are
wretched, pitiful, poor, blind and naked. 18I counsel you to buy from me
gold refined in the fire, so you can
become rich; and white clothes to
wear, so you can cover your shameful nakedness;[l] and salve to put on
your eyes, so you can see.
19Those whom I love I rebuke and
discipline.[m] So be earnest and repent.[n] 20Here I am! I stand at the
door[o] and knock. If anyone hears
my voice and opens the door,[p] I will
come in[q] and eat with that person,
and they with me.

> **Rev 3:16** ❖ What does "lukewarm" Christianity look like? Why is it useless, and how can believers avoid it?

21To the one who is victorious, I
will give the right to sit with me
on my throne,[r] just as I was victorious[s] and sat down with my Father
on his throne. 22Whoever has ears,
let them hear[t] what the Spirit says
to the churches."

The Throne in Heaven

4 After this I looked, and there before
me was a door standing open in
heaven. And the voice I had first heard
speaking to me like a trumpet[u] said,
"Come up here,[v] and I will show you what
must take place after this."[w] 2At once I
was in the Spirit,[x] and there before me
was a throne in heaven[y] with someone
sitting on it. 3And the one who sat there
had the appearance of jasper and ruby.
A rainbow[z] that shone like an emerald
encircled the throne. 4Surrounding the
throne were twenty-four other thrones,
and seated on them were twenty-four

3:14 [i] Col 1:16,18
3:15 [j] Ro 12:11
3:17 [k] Hos 12:8; 1Co 4:8
3:18 [l] Rev 16:15
3:19 [m] Pr 3:12; Heb 12:5,6 [n] Rev 2:5
3:20 [o] Mt 24:33 [p] Lk 12:36 [q] Jn 14:23
3:21 [r] Mt 19:28 [s] Rev 5:5
3:22 [t] Rev 2:7
4:1 [u] Rev 1:10 [v] Rev 11:12 [w] Rev 1:19
4:2 [x] Rev 1:10 [y] Isa 6:1; Eze 1:26-28; Da 7:9
4:3 [z] Eze 1:28

3:14–17 Jesus pulls no punches when he addresses the Laodicean church. Laodicea boasted great resources (v. 17). Yet modern excavation of the city's pipes revealed thick lime deposits, suggesting heavy contamination in the water supply. In contrast to its claims to self-sufficiency (v. 17), it had to pipe in its water, which had grown lukewarm by the time of its arrival. Hot water was useful for bathing. Cold water was useful for drinking, but Laodicea's water was useless for either cleansing or refreshing.

3:17–18 Jesus finds the church in Laodicea to be other than what he desires (cf. Isa 5:2–6). Laodiceans would doubt they were "naked" (Rev 3:17b); their city was famous for its textiles, especially cloth and carpets woven from black wool. Jesus' offer of "white clothes" (v. 18) starkly contrasts with this black wool of Laodicea. They may also experience surprise that they need Jesus to supply them spiritual eye salve. Ancient sources report a first-century medical school in Laodicea, an ear ointment made there, a famous eye doctor practicing there, and an eye salve made of Phrygian powder.

The Laodicean Christians, reflecting the values of their prosperous society, boast, "I am rich and wealthy." Jesus advises them to buy true wealth and garments from him (v. 18).

3:19–20 Jesus makes clear that his rebuke is given in love (v. 19). Jesus does not reject them; he wants to have dinner with them (v. 20), a familiar image for intimacy in antiquity. The invitation suggests the future messianic banquet (19:9). It also means a present foretaste of the intimacy he wants with those who respond to his call.

3:21–22 Jesus then provides a promise of sharing his reign to those who are "victorious" (v. 21). Although in the present believers already do share Christ's exaltation over the demonic powers (Eph 1:20–23; 2:6), the NT indicates that the fullness of the reign of God's people awaits Christ's return (Mt 5:5; Ro 5:17; 8:32; 2Ti 2:12).

> ✣ **3:14–22** The North American church should be concerned that the problems of Laodicea plague our own churches. Many of us are eager to export the profound learning of North American Christianity without listening to the lessons learned by churches who have suffered far more than we have. We are materially wealthy and in danger of a spirit of self-sufficiency, which breeds a lukewarm disinterest in the things of the Lord Jesus Christ. We may not realize that we may be spiritually impoverished: "wretched, pitiful, poor, blind and naked" (v. 17).

4:1 Heaven's "open" door signifies God's revelation. John does not have to force his way into heaven.

4:2 John presents his vision of God's throne without adornment. The heavenly songs in Revelation provide the true picture of events: No matter what happens on earth, God is truly in charge of it all.

4:3 The "rainbow" recalls the radiance of God's throne in Eze 1:28. In Ezekiel God's throne appeared like sapphire (Eze 1:26; 10:1).

4:4 The 24 elders (v. 4) illustrate the appropriate response to God's glory: worship (4:10–11; 5:8–10,

elders.[a] They were dressed in white[b] and
had crowns of gold on their heads. 5 From
the throne came flashes of lightning,
rumblings and peals of thunder.[c] In front
of the throne, seven lamps[d] were blazing.
These are the seven spirits[ae] of God. 6 Also
in front of the throne there was what
looked like a sea of glass,[f] clear as crystal.
In the center, around the throne, were
four living creatures,[g] and they were covered with eyes, in front and in back. 7 The
first living creature was like a lion, the
second was like an ox, the third had a face
like a man, the fourth was like a flying
eagle.[h] 8 Each of the four living creatures
had six wings[i] and was covered with eyes
all around, even under its wings. Day and
night they never stop saying:

> "'Holy, holy, holy
> is the Lord God Almighty,'[bj]
> who was, and is, and is to come."[k]

9 Whenever the living creatures give glory, honor and thanks to him who sits on
the throne[l] and who lives for ever and
ever, 10 the twenty-four elders[m] fall down
before him[n] who sits on the throne[o] and
worship him who lives for ever and ever.
They lay their crowns before the throne
and say:

> 11 "You are worthy, our Lord and God,
> to receive glory and honor and
> power,[p]
> for you created all things,
> and by your will they were created
> and have their being."[q]

The Scroll and the Lamb

5 Then I saw in the right hand of him
who sat on the throne[r] a scroll with
writing on both sides[s] and sealed[t] with
seven seals. 2 And I saw a mighty angel proclaiming in a loud voice, "Who

4:4 [a] Rev 11:16 [b] Rev 3:4,5
4:5 [c] Rev 8:5; 16:18 [d] Zec 4:2 [e] Rev 1:4
4:6 [f] Rev 15:2 [g] Eze 1:5
4:7 [h] Eze 1:10; 10:14
4:8 [i] Isa 6:2 [j] Isa 6:3; Rev 1:8 [k] Rev 1:4
4:9 [l] Ps 47:8
4:10 [m] ver 4 [n] Rev 5:8,14 [o] ver 2
4:11 [p] Rev 5:12 [q] Rev 10:6
5:1 [r] ver 7, 13 [s] Eze 2:9, 10 [t] Isa 29:11; Da 12:4

[a] 5 That is, the sevenfold Spirit [b] 8 Isaiah 6:3

Rev 4:10–11 ❖ What might it mean for us to lay our "crown" before God in an act of worship, giving him our praise?

Rev 5:2 ❖ What is the answer to the question in v. 2? What does Jesus' "worthiness" mean for our lives as believers?

14). Some regard them as angels, others as OT saints; most likely, they represent all believers. Given their function in worship, they probably represent the 24 divisions of priests in the OT (1Ch 24:4).

Their crowns may signify that these Christians have persevered in faith to the end. But crowns were more often "of gold" when won in games sacred to a deity (Rev 4:4), and most often golden when worn by priests approaching a deity. Elders were leaders of the people and stood as their representatives before God's glory at Sinai (Ex 24:9–10). These elders represent God's people as a whole, all of whom together are a "kingdom and priests" (Rev 1:6; 5:10).

4:5 The thundering around God's throne reveals his sovereignty. Other prominent Mediterranean religions associated deities with lightning and thunder. Most important, however, the thunder and lightning recall God's majesty when he gave the Law at Mount Sinai (Ex 19:16; 20:18).

4:6–8 John's most direct source for this image is the bronze "sea" of Solomon's temple (v. 6; 1Ki 7:23–44). That the sea is of "glass, clear as crystal" (Rev 4:6) reflects the sapphire that was "clear" in God's revelation to Israel at Sinai (Ex 24:10) and the heavenly expanse beneath God's throne in Eze 1:22.

The living creatures around the throne come directly from Ezekiel (Eze 1:5–21). That the creatures were "covered with eyes" (Rev 4:8) suggests that nothing on earth is hidden from them (Zec 4:10), with the implication, "How much less from God himself?" These beings serve no other function than to extol the character of God (v. 8).

4:9–10 God is the Sovereign One who sits on the throne and lives forever and ever.

4:11 God alone should receive all glory and power, for he created all things, a claim that again challenged the pretensions of Caesar in John's day.

✤ **4:1–11** Our primary job in heaven is to worship God. Worship that focuses on God's worthiness is our nearest foretaste of heaven, an experience in the down payment of the end-time Spirit. Worship also reminds us that, whatever our calling or gifts now, all Christians become the same as God's worshipers. The eternal future leaves little place for gifts that are now valued, but our devotion to God will always be our supreme gift (cf. 1Co 13:8–13).

5:1 Most ancient people wrote on only one side of a scroll. This one clearly has a lot to say, with writing "on both sides." Legal documents were sealed shut with hot wax over the threads that tied the scroll closed; then witnesses would press their personal seals into the hot wax to attest that they were the witnesses. No one could open the scroll without breaking the hardened wax seals that held the threads in place, and no one could replace such seals without the witnesses' rings; hence no one could tamper with the legal document until it was time to publicly open it.

5:2–3 God holds the book in an open hand. One of his angels issues the invitation to all creation: Who can open the book (v. 2)? These seals are too strong for ordinary mortals to break. After hailing God as worthy of all power (4:11), who can

is worthy to break the seals and open the scroll?" 3 But no one in heaven or on earth or under the earth could open the scroll or even look inside it. 4 I wept and wept because no one was found who was worthy to open the scroll or look inside. 5 Then one of the elders said to me, "Do not weep! See, the Lion[u] of the tribe of Judah, the Root of David,[v] has triumphed. He is able to open the scroll and its seven seals."

6 Then I saw a Lamb,[w] looking as if it had been slain, standing at the center of the throne, encircled by the four living creatures and the elders. The Lamb had seven horns and seven eyes,[x] which are the seven spirits[a] of God sent out into all the earth. 7 He went and took the scroll from the right hand of him who sat on the throne.[y] 8 And when he had taken it, the four living creatures and the twenty-four elders fell down before the Lamb. Each one had a harp[z] and they were holding golden bowls full of incense, which are the prayers[a] of God's people. 9 And they sang a new song, saying:[b]

"You are worthy[c] to take the scroll
and to open its seals,
because you were slain,
and with your blood[d] you
purchased[e] for God
persons from every tribe and
language and people and
nation.
10 You have made them to be a
kingdom and priests[f] to serve
our God,
and they will reign[b] on the earth."

11 Then I looked and heard the voice of many angels, numbering thousands upon thousands, and ten thousand times ten thousand.[g] They encircled the throne and the living creatures and the elders. 12 In a loud voice they were saying:

"Worthy is the Lamb, who was slain,
to receive power and wealth and
wisdom and strength
and honor and glory and praise!"[h]

13 Then I heard every creature in heaven and on earth and under the earth[i] and on the sea, and all that is in them, saying:

"To him who sits on the throne and
to the Lamb[j]
be praise and honor and glory and
power,
for ever and ever!"[k]

14 The four living creatures said, "Amen,"[l] and the elders fell down and worshiped.[m]

The Seals

6 I watched as the Lamb[n] opened the first of the seven seals.[o] Then I heard one of the four living creatures[p] say in a

5:5 [u] Ge 49:9 [v] Isa 11:1, 10; Ro 15:12; Rev 22:16
5:6 [w] Jn 1:29 [x] Zec 4:10
5:7 [y] ver 1
5:8 [z] Rev 14:2 [a] Ps 141:2
5:9 [b] Ps 40:3 [c] Rev 4:11 [d] Heb 9:12 [e] 1Co 6:20
5:10 [f] 1Pe 2:5
5:11 [g] Da 7:10; Heb 12:22
5:12 [h] Rev 4:11
5:13 [i] ver 3; Php 2:10 [j] Rev 6:16 [k] 1Ch 29:11
5:14 [l] Rev 4:9 [m] Rev 4:10; 19:4
6:1 [n] Rev 5:6 [o] Rev 5:1 [p] Rev 4:6,7

[a] 6 That is, the sevenfold Spirit [b] 10 Some manuscripts *they reign*

---

presume to be "worthy" (5:2) to have strength ("could," v. 3) to open it?

5:5 The image of the "Lion of the tribe of Judah" (v. 5) comes from Ge 49:9-10. The "Root of David" is the Messiah (Rev 5:5), anointed by the Spirit and appointed to rule all the nations with peace (Isa 11:1-10).

Jesus conquered not by violence but by martyrdom. Lambs were the most vulnerable of sheep, and sheep were among the weakest of creatures, typically contrasted with predators. Most significantly for John, this is a *slaughtered* lamb, a sacrificed lamb. Just as the blood of the Passover lamb delivered Israel from the climactic plague (Ex 12:23), so Jesus' blood will protect his people during God's judgments on humanity (Rev 7:3). Jesus' victory is like a new exodus (5:9-10), and Jesus himself is the new Lamb (15:3).

5:6 Horns in prophetic literature sometimes represent power (Da 7:7-24). John describes the horns here with seven eyes (Rev 5:6), representing the Spirit in Zechariah's vision (Zec 3:9) as well as the seven lamps. But in Zechariah, the eyes belong to God himself; their application to Jesus indicates Jesus' true, exalted identity.

5:7-14 John next states that Jesus went and "took" the scroll from God's hand (v. 7); the verb's perfect tense may suggest he still holds it, reigning over human history. The heavenly chorus to Jesus offers the prayers of the saints (v. 8). A Lamb receives worship in God's heaven (v. 12), sharing with God himself as its object (v. 13).

The true heavenly chorus celebrates the redemption of God's people through the blood of a new Passover Lamb (v. 9). Like ancient Israel (Ex 19:6), these people will also be a "kingdom and priests" (Rev 5:10). Daniel announced the rule of the Son of Man over all peoples (Da 7:13-14). John sees a literal fulfillment of this promise in Jesus Christ and the church.

5:1-14 Jesus overcomes through dying. This challenges our ways of understanding overcoming, victory, and success. We like to gain political or social power and dictate God's terms from the top down. By contrast, Jesus shows us that the true victory comes in sacrifice and weakness, both of which force us to depend on God's vindication. Jesus' army of followers must imitate his example.

6:1-2 The description of the rider on the white horse (v. 2) has occasioned various explanations, including a reference to the antichrist figure Gog

voice like thunder,[q] "Come!" 2I looked,
and there before me was a white horse![r]
Its rider held a bow, and he was given a
crown,[s] and he rode out as a conqueror
bent on conquest.[t]
3When the Lamb opened the second
seal, I heard the second living creature[u]
say, "Come!" 4Then another horse came
out, a fiery red one.[v] Its rider was given
power to take peace from the earth[w] and
to make people kill each other. To him
was given a large sword.
5When the Lamb opened the third seal,
I heard the third living creature[x] say,
"Come!" I looked, and there before me
was a black horse![y] Its rider was holding
a pair of scales in his hand. 6Then I heard
what sounded like a voice among the four
living creatures,[z] saying, "Two pounds[a] of
wheat for a day's wages,[b] and six pounds[c]
of barley for a day's wages,[b] and do not
damage[a] the oil and the wine!"
7When the Lamb opened the fourth
seal, I heard the voice of the fourth living creature[b] say, "Come!" 8I looked, and
there before me was a pale horse![c] Its
rider was named Death, and Hades[d] was
following close behind him. They were
given power over a fourth of the earth
to kill by sword, famine and plague, and
by the wild beasts of the earth.[e]

6:1 [q] Rev 14:2; 19:6
6:2 [r] Zec 6:3; Rev 19:11 [s] Zec 6:11; Rev 14:14 [t] Ps 45:4
6:3 [u] Rev 4:7
6:4 [v] Zec 6:2 [w] Mt 10:34
6:5 [x] Rev 4:7 [y] Zec 6:2
6:6 [z] Rev 4:6,7 [a] Rev 9:4
6:7 [b] Rev 4:7
6:8 [c] Zec 6:3 [d] Hos 13:14 [e] Jer 15:2,3; Eze 5:12,17
6:9 [f] Rev 14:18; 16:7 [g] Rev 20:4
6:10 [h] Zec 1:12 [i] Rev 3:7 [j] Rev 19:2
6:11 [k] Rev 3:4 [l] Heb 11:40
6:12 [m] Rev 16:18 [n] Mt 24:29
6:13 [o] Mt 24:29; Rev 8:10; 9:1 [p] Isa 34:4

Rev 6:9–11 ❖ How can we join in the prayer and lament of the martyrs? What does holding firm to the testimony of Christ look like?

9When he opened the fifth seal, I saw
under the altar[f] the souls of those who
had been slain[g] because of the word of
God and the testimony they had maintained. 10They called out in a loud voice,
"How long,[h] Sovereign Lord, holy and
true,[i] until you judge the inhabitants of
the earth and avenge our blood?"[j] 11Then
each of them was given a white robe,[k]
and they were told to wait a little longer,
until the full number of their fellow servants, their brothers and sisters,[d] were
killed just as they had been.[l]
12I watched as he opened the sixth seal.
There was a great earthquake.[m] The sun
turned black[n] like sackcloth made of goat
hair, the whole moon turned blood red,
13and the stars in the sky fell to earth,[o] as
figs drop from a fig tree[p] when shaken by a
strong wind. 14The heavens receded like a

[a] 6 Or about 1 kilogram [b] 6 Greek *a denarius* [c] 6 Or about 3 kilograms [d] 11 The Greek word for *brothers and sisters* (*adelphoi*) refers here to believers, both men and women, as part of God's family; also in 12:10; 19:10.

(Eze 39:1–3). A more general reference is possible. Parthians were famous for their horses; Revelation uses this image merely to underscore the coming of hostile invaders. Roman rule will someday collapse, a defeat orchestrated by God's plan for the nations.

6:3–4 Bloodshed, the second rider, presents a grisly image. Readers would likely catch an allusion to blood in the "red" horse. The "sword" represents the judgment of warfare and violent death (v. 4).

6:5–6 The scale, used to calculate food prices, symbolizes God's sovereignty over the food supply. A denarius was roughly a day's wage in this period, so this grain costs five to fifteen times more than normal. The sparing of oil and wine reveals God's mercy amid judgment (cf. Dt 20:19).

6:7–8 Death often appears personified in Jewish sources, typically as an angel subservient to God's design or as the equivalent of Satan. He cannot strike apart from God's will.

✣ **6:1–8** This passage underlines the recognition that God is sovereign over history. Terrible things may happen that seem beyond explanation, but on the larger scale God is using such forces to bring history to its climax. This rejects the God of deism promoted by many devotees of the Age of Reason; it declares the true and active and living God.

The modern experiment to overcome the need for religion has failed. The modern world's values have proved inadequate to confront the threats our world experiences—continuing wars, weapons of mass destruction, global pandemics, and other plagues. All these things call Christians to depend on Someone greater than themselves and to show others the way to peace.

6:9–11 Earlier biblical prophets had predicted the witness of God's people to the nations (e.g., Isa 42:1), the conversion of the nations (Isa 19:19–25), and the suffering of God's people in the end time (Da 7:21). The vision in this passage, however, connects these three themes (as in Mk 13:9–10). All peoples must be evangelized before the end (Mt 24:14; 2Pe 3:9–12; cf. Rev 7:9).

The position of these martyrs "under the altar" (6:9) recalls the place where priests poured the blood of their sacrifices (e.g., Lev 4:7). These martyrs share in Christ's sacrificial suffering; they are allies of the sacrificed Lamb of Rev 5:6, 9 and will also share his exaltation (3:21; 20:4). Though told to wait, they receive divine assurance (6:11). God rewards them with white robes and responds to their plea.

6:12–17 The sixth seal portrays the end of the cosmos as humanity knows it. This graphic portrayal opens with an earthquake (v. 12) that the wicked seek to flee (vv. 15–16). Because some of the cities

scroll being rolled up, and every mountain
and island was removed from its place.[q]
15Then the kings of the earth, the princes, the generals, the rich, the mighty,
and everyone else, both slave and free,
hid in caves and among the rocks of the
mountains.[r] 16They called to the mountains and the rocks, "Fall on us[s] and hide
us[a] from the face of him who sits on the
throne and from the wrath of the Lamb!
17For the great day[t] of their[b] wrath has
come, and who can withstand it?"[u]

144,000 Sealed

7 After this I saw four angels standing
at the four corners of the earth, holding back the four winds[v] of the earth to
prevent any wind from blowing on the
land or on the sea or on any tree. 2Then
I saw another angel coming up from the
east, having the seal of the living God. He
called out in a loud voice to the four angels who had been given power to harm
the land and the sea: 3"Do not harm[w] the
land or the sea or the trees until we put
a seal on the foreheads[x] of the servants
of our God." 4Then I heard the number[y]
of those who were sealed: 144,000[z] from
all the tribes of Israel.

5From the tribe of Judah 12,000 were
sealed,
from the tribe of Reuben 12,000,
from the tribe of Gad 12,000,
6from the tribe of Asher 12,000,
from the tribe of Naphtali 12,000,
from the tribe of Manasseh 12,000,
7from the tribe of Simeon 12,000,
from the tribe of Levi 12,000,
from the tribe of Issachar 12,000,
8from the tribe of Zebulun 12,000,
from the tribe of Joseph 12,000,
from the tribe of Benjamin 12,000.

6:14 [q] Jer 4:24; Rev 16:20
6:15 [r] Isa 2:10, 19,21
6:16 [s] Hos 10:8; Lk 23:30
6:17 [t] Zep 1:14, 15; Rev 16:14 [u] Ps 76:7
7:1 [v] Da 7:2
7:3 [w] Rev 6:6 [x] Eze 9:4; Rev 22:4
7:4 [y] Rev 9:16 [z] Rev 14:1,3

[a] *16* See Hosea 10:8. [b] *17* Some manuscripts *his*

addressed in Revelation had been devastated by earthquakes, this image probably proved particularly graphic.

Discoloration or eclipsing of the sun or moon symbolized terrifying judgments both among Jews and pagans. The image here is worse. The rolling up of the heavens "like a scroll" (v. 14) comes from "day of the Lord" imagery in Isa 34:4.

Loyalty to Jesus Christ, not social status, determines one's fate. John lists the entire social order in v. 15, emphasizing status will not exempt anyone from judgment. In vv. 15–17 John recalls an image of inescapable judgment from Hos 10:8 and Isa 2:19. Caves and mountain clefts will prove utterly futile in obstructing the One who moved whole mountains in his wrath (Rev 6:14). Lambs were considered among the most docile creatures; hence "wrath of the Lamb" here is a striking and terrifying image (v. 16).

The final image of the sixth seal, in which the disobedient to God's will cry out, "Who can withstand [the day of wrath]?" (v. 17), prepares the reader for the answer that comes in the following vision: The servants of God can stand in that day (7:1–17).

✜ **6:9–17** As the martyrs cry for vindication in this passage, so do suffering believers today. That God grants the martyrs' request but that it does not come right away should encourage us to persevere. God's time is not always our time, but even if we do not live to see the fulfillment of all our prayers, we can die in hope that God will bring about the things he has promised.

7:1–3 The four winds correspond to the "four corners of the earth" (see Jer 49:36), a common phrase that simply means the four directions. Here, they show God's sovereignty over the furthest reaches of the earth. God prevents the winds from blowing in judgment (Rev 7:1) until he has provided protection for his servants (v. 3).

The angel rising "from the east" (v. 2) most likely points to the rising of the sun. His task is simply to pass on a message from God. The angel's "seal" probably implies a signet ring (v. 2). The angel is one of God's agents of judgment who initially testified to the plagues just mentioned (6:1–7). The seal functions to declare ownership (Isa 44:5), and its title contrasts with what is merely a "mark" (Rev 13:16–17). The most important source for the image is Eze 9, where God marks the righteous remnant to protect them from his judgments.

7:4–8 Who are the 144,000? The matter is open to debate, but the form of the text may suggest a census to assess military preparation (Nu 1:3; 26:2; 1Ch 27:23). This vision may thus represent an end-time army, prepared for a spiritual battle (cf. Rev 12:7–9).

Who constitutes this army? The rest of Revelation leads us to expect that the numbers are probably symbolic. The numbers 12,000 and 144 elsewhere appear for the holy community (21:16–17); the new Jerusalem is laid out as a perfect square and shaped as a cube (21:16). Thus, the 144,000 represent all those destined for the new Jerusalem. Judah may be listed first (7:5–8) because the Lord Jesus descended from that tribe (cf. 5:5). The others follow birth order. Dan may be omitted because of his association with a serpent (Ge 49:16–17), recalling the serpent of Eden (Ge 3:1–15), who represents the devil (Rev 12:9).

✜ **7:1–8** Jesus Christ has not called us merely to stand our ground (Eph 6:11–14), but also to advance with our feet covered with the gospel (Eph 6:15). Christ has called us not to simply preach in our churches or discuss

Rev 7:9 ❖ What does the future vision of people from every nation, language, and race show us about the breadth of God's love? How does it undermine any cause for racism or prejudice, and how can we root these sins out of our lives?

The Great Multitude in White Robes

9After this I looked, and there before
me was a great multitude that no one
could count, from every nation, tribe,
people and language,[a] standing before
the throne[b] and before the Lamb. They
were wearing white robes and were holding palm branches in their hands. 10And
they cried out in a loud voice:

"Salvation belongs to our God,[c]
who sits on the throne,
and to the Lamb."

11All the angels were standing around the
throne and around the elders[d] and the
four living creatures.[e] They fell down on
their faces[f] before the throne and worshiped God, 12saying:

"Amen!
Praise and glory
and wisdom and thanks and honor
and power and strength
be to our God for ever and ever.
Amen!"[g]

13Then one of the elders asked me,
"These in white robes—who are they,
and where did they come from?"
14I answered, "Sir, you know."
And he said, "These are they who have
come out of the great tribulation; they
have washed their robes[h] and made
them white in the blood of the Lamb.[i]
15Therefore,

"they are before the throne of God[j]
and serve him[k] day and night in
his temple;[l]
and he who sits on the throne
will shelter them with his
presence.[m]
16'Never again will they hunger;
never again will they thirst.
The sun will not beat down on
them,'[a]
nor any scorching heat.[n]
17For the Lamb at the center of the
throne
will be their shepherd;[o]
'he will lead them to springs of
living water.'[a]
'And God will wipe away every tear
from their eyes.'[b]"[p]

The Seventh Seal and the Golden Censer

8 When he opened the seventh seal,[q]
there was silence in heaven for about
half an hour.

7:9 [a] Rev 5:9 [b] ver 15
7:10 [c] Ps 3:8; Rev 12:10; 19:1
7:11 [d] Rev 4:4 [e] Rev 4:6 [f] Rev 4:10
7:12 [g] Rev 5:12-14
7:14 [h] Rev 22:14 [i] Heb 9:14; 1Jn 1:7
7:15 [j] ver 9 [k] Rev 22:3 [l] Rev 11:19 [m] Isa 4:5, 6; Rev 21:3
7:16 [n] Isa 49:10
7:17 [o] Ps 23:1; Jn 10:11 [p] Isa 25:8; Rev 21:4
8:1 [q] Rev 6:1

[a] *16,17* Isaiah 49:10 [b] *17* Isaiah 25:8

within our small groups, waiting for the lost to come in or the fruits of past revivals to finish dying off; rather, he has challenged us to take the news of our King outside the walls of our churches, to strike offensively as well as stand defensively. "Who wants to enroll in the King's army?" we proclaim. "Who is prepared to die to bring others into the same hope we share of eternal life?"

7:9–10 That the multitude is countless in v. 9a echoes the promise to Abraham (Ge 13:16). The hope of the gospel has touched all peoples. "White robes" (Rev 7:9b) are appropriate for worship, victors' attire, and martyrs (6:11). "Palm branches" (7:9b) most often reflect a military triumph. The end-time army (vv. 1–8) hails the ultimate victor, Jesus, who has led them to triumph (v. 10).
7:13–14 The elder asks John a rhetorical question, provoking him to admit his need of the elder's answer (v. 13). Identifying the saints in white robes as those "who have come out of the great tribulation" (v. 14) refers to the tribulation of Da 12:1, which Matthew also calls a great tribulation (Mt 24:21).
7:15–17 These people refused to exalt the enthroned emperor as a god; now they are before God's throne (v. 15). They are freed from suffering, and all their needs are satisfied (vv. 16–17). They are a kingdom of priests serving God day and night (v. 15). Verses 16–17 especially recall Isa 49:10.

God is a shepherd, compassionately leading his people to water (Ps 23:1–2; Isa 40:11), yet in Revelation Jesus is the Shepherd because he was the Lamb slain for his people (Jn 10:11; cf. Isa 53:7).

✣ **7:9–17** This text reminds us who the true hero is. Almost every hero in the Bible exhibits some flaws, whether major flaws like Samson and Jephthah or relatively minor ones like Abraham and Samuel. The one exception is Jesus, the only true hero in the ultimate sense. That the martyr army holds palm branches to praise their conquering general reminds us of our dependence on Jesus and summons us to worship. The text reminds us most of all that our triumph rests on the finished work of Christ (v. 14), and our future hope is in fellowship with him (vv. 15–17).

8:1 In some ancient texts, silence characterizes respectful listening to another's speech. There is no speech mentioned here, but silence may similarly come from awe (Job 40:4).

Rev 8:4 ❖ How can the thought of our prayers rising like incense before God's throne impact a believer's prayer life?

2And I saw the seven angels[r] who stand before God, and seven trumpets were given to them.

3Another angel,[s] who had a golden censer, came and stood at the altar. He was given much incense to offer, with the prayers of all God's people,[t] on the golden altar[u] in front of the throne. 4The smoke of the incense, together with the prayers of God's people, went up before God[v] from the angel's hand. 5Then the angel took the censer, filled it with fire from the altar,[w] and hurled it on the earth; and there came peals of thunder,[x] rumblings, flashes of lightning and an earthquake.[y]

The Trumpets

6Then the seven angels who had the seven trumpets[z] prepared to sound them.

7The first angel sounded his trumpet, and there came hail and fire[a] mixed with blood, and it was hurled down on the earth. A third[b] of the earth was burned up, a third of the trees were burned up, and all the green grass was burned up.[c]

8The second angel sounded his trumpet, and something like a huge mountain,[d] all ablaze, was thrown into the sea. A third[e] of the sea turned into blood,[f] 9a third[g] of the living creatures in the sea died, and a third of the ships were destroyed.

10The third angel sounded his trumpet, and a great star, blazing like a torch, fell from the sky[h] on a third of the rivers and on the springs of water[i]— 11the name of the star is Wormwood.[a] A third[j] of the waters turned bitter, and many people died from the waters that had become bitter.[k]

12The fourth angel sounded his trumpet, and a third of the sun was struck, a third of the moon, and a third of the stars, so that a third[l] of them turned dark.[m] A third of the day was without light, and also a third of the night.

13As I watched, I heard an eagle that was flying in midair[n] call out in a loud voice: "Woe! Woe! Woe[o] to the inhabitants of the earth, because of the trumpet blasts about to be sounded by the other three angels!"

9 The fifth angel sounded his trumpet, and I saw a star that had fallen from the sky to the earth.[p] The star was given

8:2 [r] ver 6-13; Rev 9:1,13; 11:15
8:3 [s] Rev 7:2 [t] Rev 5:8 [u] Ex 30:1-6; Heb 9:4; Rev 9:13
8:4 [v] Ps 141:2
8:5 [w] Lev 16:12, 13 [x] Rev 4:5 [y] Rev 6:12
8:6 [z] ver 2
8:7 [a] Eze 38:22 [b] ver 7-12; Rev 9:15,18; 12:4 [c] Rev 9:4
8:8 [d] Jer 51:25 [e] ver 7 [f] Rev 16:3
8:9 [g] ver 7
8:10 [h] Isa 14:12; Rev 6:13; 9:1 [i] Rev 14:7; 16:4
8:11 [j] ver 7 [k] Jer 9:15; 23:15
8:12 [l] ver 7 [m] Ex 10:21-23; Rev 6:12,13
8:13 [n] Rev 14:6; 19:17 [o] Rev 9:12; 11:14
9:1 [p] Rev 8:10

[a] 11 Wormwood is a bitter substance.

8:2–6 The seven angels probably struck most of John's audience as the seven archangels of Jewish tradition (e.g., Tobit 12:15). The trumpets recall those used in the temple for worship. The altar of incense and censer are temple instruments implying impending judgment (vv. 3–5).

Most important, the incense represents "the prayers of all God's people" offered before the heavenly temple (vv. 3–4). That judgment immediately follows this offering of prayers makes sense when we consider God's people have been crying out for vindication (6:10). As fresh prayers for vindication are added (8:3), judgment is sent into motion. What takes place in heaven clearly affects what occurs on earth (v. 5).

8:7–13 John reports the first four trumpets, corresponding with the first four seals (6:1–8), to be followed by still more dramatic plagues (8:13). These plagues resemble those in the book of Exodus.

8:8–10 The blood and fire in the hail may forecast the following plagues of bloody water (v. 8) and the fiery stars or mountains falling into the seas. Although only one-third of the sea is affected here, allowing human life to continue on earth, the plague is severe. The mountain's burning with fire (v. 8) may recall Sinai and God's law (Ex 24:17), but heavenly stars (symbolizing angels; cf. Rev 9:1; 12:4) can appear like burning mountains (1 Enoch 18:13; 21:3).

8:10–11 The third plague also impacts the water supply.

8:12 The striking of the celestial lights recalls the second to last plague on Egypt (Ex 10:21–22), representing judgment against Egypt's sun god (Ex 12:12). Pagans also feared darkness over the land; to them it represented a catastrophic judgment.

8:13 The narrative sets the three remaining plagues off from the first four as particularly traumatic; they receive the title "woes." The "eagle" may simply stand for a heavenly creature (4:7). This eagle is the messenger, not necessarily a symbol of its content (cf. 19:17). Greeks viewed eagles as omens (whether of good or evil) from Zeus, and Romans sometimes sought to predict the future by the flight of birds.

✣ **8:1–13** In his sovereign plan, God has chosen to make the prayers of his people part of the exercise of his will. These prayers have the power to shape the course of human history. The details for which we pray are sometimes answered no, but in the big picture, God's plan is secure and is advanced in his sovereign will through the prayers of his people.

9:1–11 In Revelation, the abyss is a place of evil (11:7; 17:8) and a place where evil entities are imprisoned (20:1, 3; cf. Lk 8:31). Creatures from there oppose

the key to the shaft of the Abyss.[q] 2When
he opened the Abyss, smoke rose from it
like the smoke from a gigantic furnace.[r]
The sun and sky were darkened[s] by the
smoke from the Abyss. 3And out of the
smoke locusts[t] came down on the earth
and were given power like that of scorpions[u] of the earth. 4They were told not to
harm[v] the grass of the earth or any plant
or tree,[w] but only those people who did
not have the seal of God on their foreheads.[x] 5They were not allowed to kill
them but only to torture them for five
months.[y] And the agony they suffered was
like that of the sting of a scorpion[z] when
it strikes. 6During those days people will
seek death but will not find it; they will
long to die, but death will elude them.[a]

7The locusts looked like horses prepared for battle.[b] On their heads they
wore something like crowns of gold,
and their faces resembled human faces.[c] 8Their hair was like women's hair,
and their teeth were like lions' teeth.[d]
9They had breastplates like breastplates
of iron, and the sound of their wings was
like the thundering of many horses and
chariots rushing into battle.[e] 10They had
tails with stingers, like scorpions, and in
their tails they had power to torment
people for five months.[f] 11They had as
king over them the angel of the Abyss,[g]
whose name in Hebrew is Abaddon and
in Greek is Apollyon (that is, Destroyer).

12The first woe is past; two other woes
are yet to come.[h]

13The sixth angel sounded his trumpet,
and I heard a voice coming from the four
horns[i] of the golden altar that is before
God.[j] 14It said to the sixth angel who had
the trumpet, "Release the four angels
who are bound at the great river Euphrates."[k] 15And the four angels who had been
kept ready for this very hour and day
and month and year were released to
kill a third of mankind.[l] 16The number
of the mounted troops was twice ten
thousand times ten thousand. I heard
their number.[m]

17The horses and riders I saw in my vision looked like this: Their breastplates
were fiery red, dark blue, and yellow as

9:1 [q] ver 2,11; Lk 8:31
9:2 [r] Ge 19:28; Ex 19:18 [s] Joel 2:2,10
9:3 [t] Ex 10:12-15 [u] ver 5,10
9:4 [v] Rev 6:6 [w] Rev 8:7 [x] Rev 7:2,3
9:5 [y] ver 10 [z] ver 3
9:6 [a] Job 3:21; Jer 8:3; Rev 6:16
9:7 [b] Joel 2:4 [c] Da 7:8
9:8 [d] Joel 1:6
9:9 [e] Joel 2:5
9:10 [f] ver 3,5,19
9:11 [g] ver 1,2
9:12 [h] Rev 8:13
9:13 [i] Ex 30:1-3 [j] Rev 8:3
9:14 [k] Rev 16:12
9:15 [l] ver 18
9:16 [m] Rev 5:11; 7:4

the evil forces of the empire, emphasizing God's sovereignty: He employs evil agents to destroy other evil agents (cf. Rev 17:17).

9:3 The fifth trumpet judgment may refer to a human invasion. "Locusts" (v. 3) recalls a plague against Egypt (Ex 10:13–14). The description of these locusts stems from the book of Joel (Joel 1:6) where the locusts are described as an invading army (2:11). The human faces (Rev 9:7) may also suggest that they are symbolic of a human army. That the locusts' wings sound like chariots (v. 9) may also suggest a human army.

9:7–9 "Crowns of gold" (v. 7) usually designate royalty or high office (cf. Ex 39:30); hence, they may suggest that each locust commands others, suggesting an army more vast than John can portray. The "breastplates of iron" (Rev 9:9) may compare locusts' scaled bodies with the reinforced armor of ancient soldiers.

9:8 The "lions' teeth" reflect Joel's locusts (Joel 1:6), as does the appearance "like the thundering of many horses" (Joel 2:4) and the sound of "chariots rushing into battle" (Joel 2:5).

9:10 The monstrosities from the abyss may represent angels of judgment. That God sets limits on their destructiveness, both in intensity (v. 6) and duration (v. 10), may suggest his mercy and again underlines his sovereignty. The purpose of such judgments is to turn people to repentance, so even this limitation may also serve to allow repentance (vv. 20–21).

9:11 "Abaddon" was a subterranean place of the dead in the OT (Job 31:12; see NIV text note there), over which God (Rev 20:13–14) and Christ (1:18) have ultimate control. But here the control is delegated temporarily to an evil angel, who appears to have been imprisoned with the other spirits of the pit.

"Apollyon" is related to the Greek verb meaning "to destroy" (cf. 17:8), but John may be adapting the title slightly to make his point. This title is also intended to ridicule Apollo, the archer god, one of whose emblems was the locust. Domitian had sometimes portrayed himself as the god Apollo—which may imply the emperor himself will lead the demonic host in destroying Rome.

9:12–13 The golden altar (v. 13) represents the incense altar (Ex 30:1–3), implying that this judgment represents a further response to the prayers of the saints (Rev 8:4–6).

9:14–15 Evil angels were thought to be bound in various places, including subterranean chasms and bodies of deep water. The four angels bound in the Euphrates River are thus likely evil angels whom God will use to stir the Parthians.

These angels have stings in their tails (v. 19), as in the previous plague (v. 10). Parthian archers had perfected the art of riding forward while shooting backward, devastating the Roman army with volleys of arrows.

9:14 The mention of "the great river Euphrates" leaves no doubt that Parthians are in view, for the Euphrates repeatedly appeared as the traditional boundary between Roman and Parthian territories. Parthians were the archrivals of the Roman Empire; they were known for boldness in battle.

9:17 Perhaps this army will turn out to be something other than mere Parthians. Smoke-belching fiery creatures may symbolize the ultimate form of God's judgments on humanity. In contrast to their predecessors (v. 5), these invaders kill (v. 18). That fire comes from their mouths indicates that like God's true prophets (11:5), this demonic army also exhibits supernatural power to execute judgment.

Rev 9:20–21 ❖ What causes the unrepentant spirit in humanity? Why, without Christ, are human hearts so bent on evil (see Jer 17:9)?

sulfur. The heads of the horses resembled the heads of lions, and out of their
mouths[n] came fire, smoke and sulfur.[o] 18A
third of mankind was killed[p] by the three
plagues of fire, smoke and sulfur[q] that
came out of their mouths. 19The power of
the horses was in their mouths and in their
tails; for their tails were like snakes, having heads with which they inflict injury.
20The rest of mankind who were not
killed by these plagues still did not repent of the work of their hands;[r] they
did not stop worshiping demons,[s] and
idols of gold, silver, bronze, stone and
wood — idols that cannot see or hear
or walk.[t] 21Nor did they repent[u] of their
murders, their magic arts,[v] their sexual
immorality[w] or their thefts.

The Angel and the Little Scroll

10 Then I saw another mighty angel[x]
coming down from heaven. He was
robed in a cloud, with a rainbow above
his head; his face was like the sun,[y] and
his legs were like fiery pillars.[z] 2He was
holding a little scroll, which lay open in
his hand. He planted his right foot on the
sea and his left foot on the land, 3and he
gave a loud shout like the roar of a lion.
When he shouted, the voices of the seven
thunders[a] spoke. 4And when the seven
thunders spoke, I was about to write; but
I heard a voice from heaven say, "Seal up
what the seven thunders have said and
do not write it down."[b]
5Then the angel I had seen standing on
the sea and on the land raised his right
hand to heaven.[c] 6And he swore by him
who lives for ever and ever, who created
the heavens and all that is in them, the
earth and all that is in it, and the sea and
all that is in it,[d] and said, "There will be
no more delay![e] 7But in the days when
the seventh angel is about to sound his
trumpet, the mystery[f] of God will be accomplished, just as he announced to his
servants the prophets."
8Then the voice that I had heard from
heaven[g] spoke to me once more: "Go,
take the scroll that lies open in the hand
of the angel who is standing on the sea
and on the land."
9So I went to the angel and asked
him to give me the little scroll. He said
to me, "Take it and eat it. It will turn
your stomach sour, but 'in your mouth
it will be as sweet as honey.'*[a]*"[h] 10I took
the little scroll from the angel's hand

9:17 [n] Rev 11:5 [o] ver 18
9:18 [p] ver 15 [q] ver 17
9:20 [r] Dt 31:29 [s] 1Co 10:20 [t] Ps 115:4-7; 135:15-17; Da 5:23
9:21 [u] Rev 2:21 [v] Rev 18:23 [w] Rev 17:2,5
10:1 [x] Rev 5:2 [y] Mt 17:2; Rev 1:16 [z] Rev 1:15
10:3 [a] Rev 4:5
10:4 [b] Da 8:26; 12:4,9; Rev 22:10
10:5 [c] Da 12:7
10:6 [d] Rev 4:11; 14:7 [e] Rev 16:17
10:7 [f] Ro 16:25
10:8 [g] ver 4
10:9 [h] Jer 15:16; Eze 2:8-3:3

a 9 Ezek. 3:3

9:18 The killing of one-third of the world's population (vv. 15, 18) is an unparalleled catastrophe.
9:20–21 The climax of the account comes in these verses. God allows one-third of humanity to die and spares the remaining two-thirds to invite their repentance. Like Pharaoh, however, the world refuses to repent (Ex 7:22–23). They worship and probably seek help from false gods rather than the true God.

✜ **9:1–21** Revelation's main message at this point may be twofold. First, Christians flirting with compromise with the world should think twice. The entire fallen social order will be destroyed in God's judgments; Christ alone is an adequate security. Second, Christians suffering at the hand of the world should never envy the position of their persecutors, for they will suffer judgment. Furthermore, John provides a perspective on troubles in the world: God is not absent in times of the world's hardship but remains in control.

10:1–2 The rainbow on this angel's head probably functions like a brilliant crown, representing the divine glory (4:3). The angel's luminosity alludes to God's glory manifest as a pillar of fire in the desert (Ex 13:21-22). The "little book" he holds represents the book of Revelation. It is possible that this is the book whose seals are broken in 6:1—8:1, but whose contents constitute the entire message of Revelation—the book opened by the Lamb (5:1–9).
10:3–4 The image of thunder is appropriate (v. 3). The content of the seven thunders, however, is deliberately mysterious (v. 4), most likely to teach that the hidden things belong to God (Dt 29:29). God knows far more about the future than he tells us.
10:5–6 The angel lifts his hand to swear (v. 5), emphasizing the certainty of his claim. That "there will be no more delay" (v. 6) means that no further interval of time remains before the end. John's point is probably that the prayers of the saints for vindication await no further delay (6:9–11); judgment has come (11:18; 14:7).
10:7 The completion of "the mystery" probably indicates that the seven thunders will no longer remain secret (v. 4). God's purposes will be "accomplished," as promised to "his servants the prophets."
10:9–11 The angel instructs John to eat the book (v. 9), just as God instructed Ezekiel (Eze 2:8; 3:1). That it proves bitter in John's stomach (Rev 10:9–10) probably points to the message's content: sorrow and mourning. Whereas Ezekiel was to deliver the message only to the house of Israel (Eze 3:1), John will prophesy to "many peoples, nations, languages and kings" (Rev 10:11).

Rev 10:11 ❖ John's calling was to the people of the world. This book of visions calls people everywhere to repent. How can we call ourselves and others to repentance today?

and ate it. It tasted as sweet as honey in
my mouth, but when I had eaten it, my
stomach turned sour. 11Then I was told,
"You must prophesy[i] again about many
peoples, nations, languages and kings."

The Two Witnesses

11 I was given a reed like a measuring
rod[j] and was told, "Go and measure
the temple of God and the altar, with
its worshipers. 2But exclude the outer
court;[k] do not measure it, because it has
been given to the Gentiles.[l] They will
trample on the holy city[m] for 42 months.[n]
3And I will appoint my two witnesses,[o]
and they will prophesy for 1,260 days,
clothed in sackcloth."[p] 4They are "the two
olive trees"[q] and the two lampstands,
and "they stand before the Lord of the
earth."[a][r] 5If anyone tries to harm them,
fire comes from their mouths and devours their enemies.[s] This is how anyone who wants to harm them must die.[t]
6They have power to shut up the heavens
so that it will not rain during the time
they are prophesying; and they have
power to turn the waters into blood[u]
and to strike the earth with every kind
of plague as often as they want.
7Now when they have finished their
testimony, the beast[v] that comes up
from the Abyss will attack them,[w] and
overpower and kill them. 8Their bodies
will lie in the public square of the great
city—which is figuratively called Sodom[x] and Egypt—where also their Lord
was crucified.[y] 9For three and a half days
some from every people, tribe, language
and nation will gaze on their bodies and
refuse them burial.[z] 10The inhabitants
of the earth[a] will gloat over them and
will celebrate by sending each other
gifts,[b] because these two prophets had
tormented those who live on the earth.
11But after the three and a half days the
breath[b] of life from God entered them,[c]
and they stood on their feet, and terror
struck those who saw them. 12Then they
heard a loud voice from heaven saying to
them, "Come up here."[d] And they went
up to heaven in a cloud,[e] while their enemies looked on.

10:11 [i] Eze 37:4,9
11:1 [j] Eze 40:3; Rev 21:15
11:2 [k] Eze 40:17,20 [l] Lk 21:24 [m] Rev 21:2 [n] Da 7:25; Rev 13:5
11:3 [o] Rev 1:5 [p] Ge 37:34
11:4 [q] Ps 52:8; Jer 11:16; Zec 4:3,11 [r] Zec 4:14
11:5 [s] 2Ki 1:10; Jer 5:14 [t] Nu 16:29,35
11:6 [u] Ex 7:17,19
11:7 [v] Rev 13:1-4 [w] Da 7:21
11:8 [x] Isa 1:9 [y] Heb 13:12
11:9 [z] Ps 79:2,3
11:10 [a] Rev 3:10 [b] Est 9:19,22
11:11 [c] Eze 37:5,9,10,14
11:12 [d] Rev 4:1 [e] 2Ki 2:11; Ac 1:9

a 4 See Zech. 4:3,11,14. *b* 11 Or *Spirit* (see Ezek. 37:5,14)

✣ **10:1–11** The thunders reveal that some matters are not yet ours to know. The hidden things belong to God alone (Dt 29:29). Until Jesus returns, we know in part only. This does not mean that we should not seek knowledge; it does mean that God has set boundaries around what is best for us to know, and we should acknowledge those boundaries. In other words, we should avoid undue speculation about matters we cannot be certain about and should avoid speaking inflexibly about them. In contrast to this principle, some prophecy teachers fill in too many details on which the text does not comment. These people may satisfy our curiosity about the future, but the biblical teacher's job is to help us hear and obey the message of Scripture, not to add to it.

11:1–2 In early Christian literature, the temple regularly symbolizes Christians, both Jewish and Gentile (1Co 3:16; Eph 2:18–22; 1Pe 2:5). This is also what the temple symbolizes elsewhere in Revelation (Rev 3:12; 13:6). The act of measuring most likely symbolizes a promise of preservation. The small, persecuted remnant oppressed during this age constitutes the glorious holy city of the coming age.

11:3–6 Calling down fire (v. 5) recalls Elijah, who was also taken into heaven and brought drought for three and a half years. Turning water into blood and sending other plagues recall Moses; some Jewish traditions also claimed Moses ascended.

The most common view is that the two witnesses represent the church's prophetic witness. The witnesses are protected for the duration of their ministry (v. 5) but die at the end (v. 7). If the witnesses represent the church, one can view the 1,260 days as a symbolic number (v. 3). In this case, Revelation is borrowing Daniel's figure not to tell us the length of time but to inform us of the kind of time—that the era of the church is characterized by great suffering, as in Daniel's tribulation.

The dual nature of the witnesses provides a literary contrast with the two evil leaders in 13:11–12. This portrait reinforces John's contrast between the church and the world system; the witnesses will triumph (v. 11).

11:7–14 The "great city" (v. 8) may be Jerusalem, but in this book, it is typically Babylon (17:18). That the witnesses lie in the street (11:8) indicates that they remain unburied, a fate normally reserved for the vilest of criminals. The enemies of God's servants exchange gifts after slaughtering them, yet many are ultimately converted (vv. 11–13).

11:11–14 The church will follow in the steps of its Lord: Christians will die but should look for the hope of the resurrection (v. 11). The city's repentance in vv. 11–13 may imply the end-times conversion of the bulk of the Jewish people in Jerusalem who have not previously converted.

13At that very hour there was a severe
earthquake[f] and a tenth of the city collapsed. Seven thousand people were
killed in the earthquake, and the survivors were terrified and gave glory[g] to
the God of heaven.[h]
14The second woe has passed; the third
woe is coming soon.[i]

The Seventh Trumpet

15The seventh angel sounded his trumpet,[j] and there were loud voices[k] in heav-
en, which said:

"The kingdom of the world has
become
the kingdom of our Lord and of
his Messiah,[l]
and he will reign for ever and
ever."[m]

16And the twenty-four elders,[n] who were
seated on their thrones before God, fell
on their faces and worshiped God, 17say-
ing:

"We give thanks to you, Lord God
Almighty,[o]
the One who is and who was,
because you have taken your great
power
and have begun to reign.[p]

Rev 11:17–18 ❖ How does God's future justice impact the way we live and serve God today? What comfort do we find in Christ when considering God's future judgment (see Ro 8:1)?

18The nations were angry,[q]
and your wrath has come.
The time has come for judging the
dead,
and for rewarding your servants
the prophets[r]
and your people who revere your
name,
both great and small[s]—
and for destroying those who
destroy the earth."

19Then God's temple[t] in heaven was
opened, and within his temple was seen
the ark of his covenant. And there came
flashes of lightning, rumblings, peals
of thunder, an earthquake and a severe
hailstorm.[u]

The Woman and the Dragon

12 A great sign appeared in heaven: a
woman clothed with the sun, with
the moon under her feet and a crown

11:13 [f] Rev 6:12 [g] Rev 14:7 [h] Rev 16:11
11:14 [i] Rev 8:13
11:15 [j] Rev 10:7 [k] Rev 16:17; 19:1 [l] Rev 12:10 [m] Da 2:44; 7:14,27
11:16 [n] Rev 4:4
11:17 [o] Rev 1:8 [p] Rev 19:6
11:18 [q] Ps 2:1 [r] Rev 10:7 [s] Rev 19:5
11:19 [t] Rev 15:5,8 [u] Rev 16:21

❖ **11:1–14** If the two witnesses are the church, they provide a direct model for us. Those who interpret them as two literal individuals can also recognize that they nevertheless provide role models for us, just as other men and women of God in Scripture do. We must therefore be Spirit-empowered witnesses to the world, ready to pay any cost and utterly dependent on God's power to accomplish his purposes.

11:15 Although the final trumpet concludes the series of seven, it also fits the occasion here; trumpets were normally blown at the accession of a king to his throne (1Ki 1:34–41). The kingdom "of our Lord and of his Messiah" probably recalls the language of Ps 2:2, where the nations challenge them but will ultimately be crushed.

11:17–18 God's people often have praised him in response to his deliverance of his people. The wrath of the nations is met by God's "wrath" on the day of judgment (v. 18). Jewish tradition also emphasized the rewards God would give his people at the time of the end (v. 18). Reward is no less a Christian concept, though the works it rewards are impossible apart from the grace experienced in Christ (Mt 5:11; 1Co 3:8; 2Jn 8).

God's "servants the prophets" may be identified with those "who revere" God's name (Rev 11:18). All believers are meant to be "prophets" in the general sense of Spirit-empowered witnesses for Christ (v. 18).

"Those who destroy the earth" (v. 18) may refer to invaders who seek to devastate the holy land (2Ki 18:25). That nothing in the context narrows the image specifically to the holy land, however, generalizes the image: The evil empire, like Babylon of old, devastates the whole earth.

11:19 Jewish people generally believed that God had hidden the ark of the covenant, but that it would be restored in the end time. The picture of the ark suggests a variety of associations, especially involving the Sinai covenant, by which God demanded an accounting from a disobedient world. The meteorological phenomena here in v. 19 probably signify a new revelation from heaven comparable to the revelation of God's word at Mount Sinai (cf. 4:5; Ex 19:16).

❖ **11:15–19** Those who face grief or any hardship in the world will find comfort in the message of these verses. They announce that this world ultimately belongs to God and that God will right all the wrongs of history on the day of judgment, shattering all opposition. They also invite worship as we contemplate God's coming intervention to rule. Moreover, they remind us that God will reward both small and great just as he will punish both great and small; God does not show favoritism (see Mt 20:1–16).

12:1 The prophets portrayed righteous Israel as the mother of the restored future remnant of Israel

of twelve stars on her head. 2She was
pregnant and cried out in pain[v] as she
was about to give birth. 3Then another
sign appeared in heaven: an enormous
red dragon with seven heads and ten
horns[w] and seven crowns[x] on its heads.
4Its tail swept a third[y] of the stars out
of the sky and flung them to the earth.[z]
The dragon stood in front of the woman who was about to give birth, so that
it might devour her child[a] the moment
he was born. 5She gave birth to a son, a
male child, who "will rule all the nations
with an iron scepter."[ab] And her child was
snatched up to God and to his throne.
6The woman fled into the wilderness to
a place prepared for her by God, where
she might be taken care of for 1,260 days.[c]
7Then war broke out in heaven. Michael and his angels fought against the
dragon,[d] and the dragon and his angels
fought back. 8But he was not strong
enough, and they lost their place in
heaven. 9The great dragon was hurled
down — that ancient serpent[e] called the
devil,[f] or Satan, who leads the whole
world astray.[g] He was hurled to the
earth,[h] and his angels with him.
10Then I heard a loud voice in heav-
en[i] say:

"Now have come the salvation and
the power
and the kingdom of our God,
and the authority of his Messiah.
For the accuser of our brothers and
sisters,[j]
who accuses them before our God
day and night,
has been hurled down.
11They triumphed over him
by the blood of the Lamb[k]
and by the word of their
testimony;[l]
they did not love their lives so much
as to shrink from death.[m]
12Therefore rejoice, you heavens[n]
and you who dwell in them!
But woe[o] to the earth and the sea,[p]
because the devil has gone down
to you!
He is filled with fury,
because he knows that his time is
short."

13When the dragon[q] saw that he had

12:2 [v] Gal 4:19
12:3 [w] Da 7:7, 20; Rev 13:1 [x] Rev 19:12
12:4 [y] Rev 8:7 [z] Da 8:10 [a] Mt 2:16
12:5 [b] Ps 2:9; Rev 2:27
12:6 [c] Rev 11:2
12:7 [d] ver 3
12:9 [e] Ge 3:1-7 [f] Mt 25:41 [g] Rev 20:3, 8, 10 [h] Lk 10:18; Jn 12:31
12:10 [i] Rev 11:15 [j] Job 1:9-11; Zec 3:1
12:11 [k] Rev 7:14 [l] Rev 6:9 [m] Lk 14:26
12:12 [n] Ps 96:11; Isa 49:13; Rev 18:20 [o] Rev 8:13 [p] Rev 10:6
12:13 [q] ver 3

Rev 12:7-17 ❖ What experiences have you had with spiritual warfare? How does awareness of Satan's attacks caution the way we live and the choices we make? What hope do we cling to in the face of spiritual threats (see v. 11)?

[a] 5 Psalm 2:9

(Isa 54:1; Mic 4:9-10). This image was mixed with that of Israel as a bride (Isa 62:5). The sun, moon, and 12 stars on the woman confirm this vision as symbolizing Israel or its faithful remnant (Ge 37:9).

12:2-4 For John, the dragon is the "ancient serpent" (v. 9), the one who enticed Adam and Eve to disobey God (Ge 3:1-15).

In Revelation the stars usually symbolize angels (1:20; 9:1). Satan's revolt led to the fall of many angels. John provides a Christ-centered interpretation of this fall: This angelic rebellion was in opposition to Jesus' mission on earth (v. 4). But Satan and his angels failed. When Jesus was exalted, Satan's kingdom received its complete notice of defeat (12:7-9).

12:5-6 If read together with John's Gospel, Revelation may depict Jesus' enthronement as beginning with the cross, where he was crowned "the king of the jews" (Jn 19:19-21); it was at the cross that Satan's power was defeated (Jn 12:31); it was by the cross that Jesus "prepare[d] a place" for his followers (Jn 14:2-3; cf. Rev 12:6).

The "1,260 days" of v. 6 likely adapts Daniel's great tribulation (cf. Da 12:11) of three and a half years (Da 7:25; 9:27; 12:7). Revelation seems to employ this figure to tell us about the kind of time rather than the length of time, emphasizing primarily that it is tribulation.

John uses the desert or "wilderness" in v. 6 symbolically to refer back to the first exodus, as in his Gospel (Jn 3:14; 6:31, 49), announcing a spiritual new exodus (Jn 1:23).

12:7-12 Revelation then shifts to a heavenly perspective on the events just described. Christ's triumph is envisioned in terms of a heavenly combat between God's and Satan's forces. Satan's fall here clearly refers to a past event (v. 9); "salvation" and God's "kingdom" (v. 10) are completed at Christ's return, but were begun at his death, resurrection, and enthronement.

12:8-10 Ironically, Satan's loss of "place" (v. 8) contrasts starkly with the "place" of refuge God provides his own people persecuted by Satan (vv. 6, 14). Satan's accusations against the people of God have been silenced, for Christ's victory is sufficient to silence all objections of the once-heavenly prosecutor (v. 10).

12:10-12 Satan oppresses Jesus' followers (vv. 10-12) and pursues the woman into the desert just as Pharaoh pursued Israel in the exodus. The devil's "short" time (v. 12), like the "little while" between the cross and resurrection (Jn 16:16-19), is an interim period that involves both suspense and hardship, but whose outcome is predetermined.

12:13-17 The exodus tradition spoke of God's bearing his people on eagle's wings (Ex 19:4), an image also applicable to the new exodus (Isa 40:31). The miraculous provision in the desert

been hurled to the earth, he pursued the
woman who had given birth to the male
child.[r] 14 The woman was given the two
wings of a great eagle,[s] so that she might
fly to the place prepared for her in the
wilderness, where she would be taken
care of for a time, times and half a time,[t]
out of the serpent's reach. 15 Then from
his mouth the serpent spewed water
like a river, to overtake the woman and
sweep her away with the torrent. 16 But
the earth helped the woman by opening its mouth and swallowing the river
that the dragon had spewed out of his
mouth. 17 Then the dragon was enraged
at the woman and went off to wage war[u]
against the rest of her offspring[v] — those
who keep God's commands[w] and hold
fast their testimony about Jesus.[x]

The Beast out of the Sea

13 The dragon[a] stood on the shore of
the sea. And I saw a beast coming
out of the sea.[y] It had ten horns and sev-
en heads,[z] with ten crowns on its horns,
and on each head a blasphemous name.[a]
2 The beast I saw resembled a leopard,[b] but
had feet like those of a bear[c] and a mouth
like that of a lion.[d] The dragon gave the
beast his power and his throne and great
authority.[e] 3 One of the heads of the beast
seemed to have had a fatal wound, but
the fatal wound had been healed.[f] The
whole world was filled with wonder[g] and
followed the beast. 4 People worshiped the
dragon because he had given authority
to the beast, and they also worshiped the
beast and asked, "Who is like[h] the beast?
Who can wage war against it?"
5 The beast was given a mouth to utter
proud words and blasphemies[i] and to exercise its authority for forty-two months.[j]
6 It opened its mouth to blaspheme God,
and to slander his name and his dwelling
place and those who live in heaven.[k] 7 It
was given power to wage war[l] against
God's holy people and to conquer them.
And it was given authority over every
tribe, people, language and nation.[m] 8 All

12:13 r ver 5
12:14 s Ex 19:4 t Da 7:25
12:17 u Rev 11:7 v Ge 3:15 w Rev 14:12 x Rev 1:2
13:1 y Da 7:1-6; Rev 15:2 z Rev 12:3 a Da 11:36; Rev 17:3
13:2 b Da 7:6 c Da 7:5 d Da 7:4 e Rev 16:10
13:3 f ver 12,14 g Rev 17:8
13:4 h Ex 15:11
13:5 i Da 7:8, 11,20,25; 11:36; 2Th 2:4 j Rev 11:2
13:6 k Rev 12:12
13:7 l Da 7:21; Rev 11:7 m Rev 5:9

Rev 13:4 ❖ Why do people worship what appears to be powerful? What attracts the worship or adoration of people in the world today?

[a] 1 Some manuscripts *And I*

---

here echoes the manna God gave his people at the first exodus.

"Water like a river" (Rev 12:15) may be a symbol for slander; Satan, who can no longer accuse God's people to God, accuses them to the world instead.

The dragon's rage carries forward his "fury" (v. 12) and that of his agents (11:18). The woman's "offspring" (12:17) or "seed" here echoes the language of Ge 3:15. These other offspring represent true disciples of Jesus (Rev 3:10); they "hold fast their testimony about Jesus" (12:17).

✣ **12:1–17** The image of conflict here reminds us that God's people must always be ready to confront the world's hostility; the contrast between the mother in ch. 12 and the prostitute in ch. 17 reminds us that the city of God and Babylon never coexist naturally in this world. Especially in view of the use of the image of labor pains in the Hebrew Bible, this image here further reminds us that God's purposes are often accomplished only through suffering (cf. Jn 16:21–22; Ro 8:22–23). The devil's hostility, probably expressed as slander, also warns us to expect false accusations, though we should do our best to prevent them.

13:1–2 The beast in vv. 1–10 recalls Da 7:3–8, where four beasts arise from the "sea" (Da 7:2). The "ten horns" and "seven heads" (Rev 13:1) connect this beast with its superhuman mentor, another beast—namely, the dragon (v. 2). The "blasphemous name" (v. 1) probably evokes the arrogant boasts of Da 7:8, 20.

13:3 The return from death is a parody on Jesus; likewise, the ten-horned beast contrasts starkly with the seven-horned Lamb (5:6).

Nero died June 9, AD 68, but even at the end of the first century, many believed he remained alive. Here in Revelation we read of a head that is wounded, then restored (v. 3)—pointing to Nero. What would clinch the allusion to Nero for informed members of John's audience is the riddle of 13:18. Revelation does not predict a literal return of Nero from the dead. Rather, the final antichrist would be like Nero, just as John the Baptist was another Elijah (Mt 17:12–13; Lk 1:17).

13:4 The earth's first question, "Who is like the beast?" (13:4), parodies worship properly due God alone (Ex 15:11). But in contrast to imperial Rome, Jesus had defeated death and now ruled its domain (Rev 1:18).

13:5–7a The image of desecrating the temple was not unfamiliar to John's audience; Titus, the older brother of Emperor Domitian, had presided over the burning and desecration of the temple in Jerusalem in AD 70. But John means the heavenly temple, and he means it symbolically, as he explicitly notes (v. 6): God's people comprise God's tabernacle or temple, and whoever harms it will be judged.

That the beast "was given . . . authority" and "power" (vv. 5, 7) reminds John's audience that even the antichrist is a pawn in God's greater design on behalf of his people. In the end only God can authorize the devil or the beast to rule the nations (v. 7).

13:7b–10 The unity of the beast's kingdom (vv. 7b–8) means God has permitted the world to stand together under a single evil empire to test his

inhabitants of the earth[n] will worship the
beast — all whose names have not been
written in the Lamb's book of life,[o] the
Lamb who was slain from the creation
of the world.[a][p]
9 Whoever has ears, let them hear.[q]

10 "If anyone is to go into captivity,
into captivity they will go.
If anyone is to be killed[b] with the
sword,
with the sword they will be
killed."[c][r]

This calls for patient endurance and
faithfulness[s] on the part of God's people.[t]

The Beast out of the Earth

11 Then I saw a second beast, coming out
of the earth. It had two horns like a lamb,
but it spoke like a dragon. 12 It exercised
all the authority[u] of the first beast on its
behalf,[v] and made the earth and its inhabitants worship the first beast,[w] whose
fatal wound had been healed.[x] 13 And it
performed great signs,[y] even causing fire
to come down from heaven[z] to the earth
in full view of the people. 14 Because of
the signs[a] it was given power to perform
on behalf of the first beast, it deceived[b]
the inhabitants of the earth. It ordered
them to set up an image in honor of the
beast who was wounded by the sword and
yet lived. 15 The second beast was given
power to give breath to the image of the
first beast, so that the image could speak
and cause all who refused to worship the
image to be killed.[c] 16 It also forced all
people, great and small,[d] rich and poor,
free and slave, to receive a mark on their
right hands or on their foreheads,[e] 17 so
that they could not buy or sell unless they
had the mark,[f] which is the name of the
beast or the number of its name.[g]
18 This calls for wisdom.[h] Let the person

13:8 [n] Rev 3:10 [o] Rev 3:5; 20:12 [p] Mt 25:34
13:9 [q] Rev 2:7
13:10 [r] Jer 15:2; 43:11 [s] Heb 6:12 [t] Rev 14:12
13:12 [u] ver 4 [v] ver 14 [w] Rev 14:9,11 [x] ver 3
13:13 [y] Mt 24:24 [z] 1Ki 18:38; Rev 20:9
13:14 [a] 2Th 2:9, 10 [b] Rev 12:9
13:15 [c] Da 3:3-6
13:16 [d] Rev 19:5 [e] Rev 14:9
13:17 [f] Rev 14:9 [g] Rev 14:11; 15:2
13:18 [h] Rev 17:9

[a] 8 Or *written from the creation of the world in the book of life belonging to the Lamb who was slain*
[b] 10 Some manuscripts *anyone kills*
[c] 10 Jer. 15:2

people. By contrast, God's people had their own multicultural unity (7:9–10), of which the world's was but a pale parody.

13:1–10 In this passage, as in most of the Bible, the devil works not independently but through people. This passage testifies to the awfulness to which humans can descend in following the devil's ways (Eph 2:1–3). Demonic power amplifies human sin and crushes its usual restraints.

At the same time, this passage offers hope to those who dare grasp it here: God is the one who gives the beast authority for 42 months, and he does so to execute his purposes of judging the world by handing it over to its own evil ways. The promise of judgment is also given to encourage the saints (v. 10); it reminds us that God is just, that there are some moral certainties and issues of justice in the world, and that God will vindicate justice in the end.

13:11 This second beast imitates the seven-horned Lamb of God (5:6), though the two horns may come from the ram of Da 8:3. Not many years after Revelation was written, we have evidence of a legal tradition of executing Christians for refusing to worship the emperor's statue. John's audience would also think of Nebuchadnezzar's image, which was to be worshiped by all peoples. The most important function of these signs in v. 13 is that they continue the parody on God and his agents (cf. 11:5).

13:16 The beast enforces a unity that cuts across all social lines (v. 16), though the attentive reader will remember that God's judgment also cuts across just such distinctions (6:15; 11:18). The use of a "mark" to enforce national or empire-wide unity already had a long history known to John's audience. This mark stands in direct contrast to the seal of 7:3–4. Whereas the symbolic mark of protection or judgment was normally on the forehead (Eze 9:4), John adds here the right hand; branding soldiers on the hands was a sign of loyalty.

13:17–18 In John's day one could not handle money without involvement in the imperial system. To withdraw from an economic system that promoted emperor worship—even to withdraw from trade guilds, whose meetings included meat offered to idols—was in many cities economic suicide. But God would supply his people's needs, miraculously if need be (12:6, 14). Meanwhile, whereas many accept the mark to be able to engage in commerce (13:17), every following mention of the "mark" in Revelation implies the judgments its recipients earn (14:9–11; 16:2; 19:20; 20:4).

What is the number of the beast's name (v. 17)? Ancients were adept at the use of symbolic numbers, of which Revelation includes several. Those interested in ancient numeric speculation would be familiar with 666. Most commentators find an allusion to Nero Caesar's name as written in Hebrew characters here.

13:11–18 Because Satan's counterfeits imitate God's works, it is not surprising that false signs continue to lead many people astray today; some are fake, whereas others are demonic. One thinks, for example, of psychic healers and perhaps of some modern mind-science techniques. One Catholic scholar warns against false apparitions of Christ and Mary that exhibit signs yet teach what is false.

Although God can do anything, it should also be noted that statues that are alleged to weep or sweat are not a specifically Christian

who has insight calculate the number of
the beast, for it is the number of a man.[ai]
That number is 666.

The Lamb and the 144,000

14 Then I looked, and there before me
was the Lamb,[j] standing on Mount
Zion,[k] and with him 144,000[l] who had his
name and his Father's name[m] written on
their foreheads. 2And I heard a sound from
heaven like the roar of rushing waters[n]
and like a loud peal of thunder. The sound
I heard was like that of harpists playing
their harps.[o] 3And they sang a new song[p]
before the throne and before the four living creatures and the elders. No one could
learn the song except the 144,000[q] who
had been redeemed from the earth. 4These
are those who did not defile themselves
with women, for they remained virgins.[r]
They follow the Lamb wherever he goes.
They were purchased from among mankind[s] and offered as firstfruits[t] to God
and the Lamb. 5No lie was found in their
mouths;[u] they are blameless.[v]

The Three Angels

6Then I saw another angel flying in
midair,[w] and he had the eternal gospel
to proclaim to those who live on the
earth[x]—to every nation, tribe, language
and people.[y] 7He said in a loud voice,
"Fear God[z] and give him glory,[a] because
the hour of his judgment has come. Worship him who made the heavens, the
earth, the sea and the springs of water."[b]

13:18 [i] Rev 15:2; 21:17
14:1 [j] Rev 5:6 [k] Ps 2:6 [l] Rev 7:4 [m] Rev 3:12
14:2 [n] Rev 1:15 [o] Rev 5:8
14:3 [p] Rev 5:9 [q] ver 1
14:4 [r] 2Co 11:2; Rev 3:4 [s] Rev 5:9 [t] Jas 1:18
14:5 [u] Ps 32:2; Zep 3:13 [v] Eph 5:27
14:6 [w] Rev 8:13 [x] Rev 3:10 [y] Rev 13:7
14:7 [z] Rev 15:4 [a] Rev 11:13 [b] Rev 8:10
14:8 [c] Isa 21:9; Jer 51:8 [d] Rev 17:2, 4; 18:3, 9
14:9 [e] Rev 13:14
14:10 [f] Isa 51:17; Jer 25:15 [g] Rev 18:6
14:11 [h] Isa 34:10; Rev 19:3
14:12 [i] Rev 13:10
14:13 [j] 1Co 15:18; 1Th 4:16

Rev 14:13 ❖ How does the idea that our deeds follow us after this life impact our lives today? How can we carry with us, like the scars on Christ's hands (see Jn 20:27), deeds that point to our love for God and his children?

8A second angel followed and said,
"'Fallen! Fallen is Babylon the Great,'[bc]
which made all the nations drink the
maddening wine of her adulteries."[d]
9A third angel followed them and
said in a loud voice: "If anyone worships
the beast and its image[e] and receives
its mark on their forehead or on their
hand, 10they, too, will drink the wine of
God's fury,[f] which has been poured full
strength into the cup of his wrath.[g] They
will be tormented with burning sulfur in
the presence of the holy angels and of the
Lamb. 11And the smoke of their torment
will rise for ever and ever.[h] There will be
no rest day or night for those who worship the beast and its image, or for anyone who receives the mark of its name."
12This calls for patient endurance on the
part of the people of God[i] who keep his
commands and remain faithful to Jesus.
13Then I heard a voice from heaven say,
"Write this: Blessed are the dead who die
in the Lord[j] from now on."
"Yes," says the Spirit, "they will rest
from their labor, for their deeds will follow them."

[a] *18 Or is humanity's number* [b] *8* Isaiah 21:9

phenomenon. But missions experts comment on powerful encounters, noting that, as in the Bible (Ex 7:11–12; Ac 13:11), God's power is stronger than Satan's.

The two witnesses prevailed with their signs until the appointed time of their martyrdom (Rev 11:7), and today's church should be able to demonstrate God's power more effectively than occult sources demonstrate theirs.

14:1–5 The 144,000 are with the Lamb on Mount Zion, God's dwelling. In Revelation, Zion is also the new Jerusalem, the holy city (3:12; 21:2—22:2). It is the antithesis of Babylon, whose demise is about to be introduced (14:8).
14:3–4 The "sound from heaven" (v. 2) is the song of the 144,000 taken from the earth and now in heaven. That the 144,000 are those "redeemed" (v. 3) and "purchased" (v. 4) from the earth and from among humanity reminds us that they stand for all believers (5:9). This "new song" is their unique experience shared by no one else in creation (v. 3).

These 144,000 have refused to commit immorality with Babylon, the prostitute (cf. 18:3). God's people speak the truth of the gospel and renounce idols regardless of the cost (6:9–11; 11:3; 12:11); this is part of what it means for them to be pure (14:4).
14:6–13 The angel's flight may correspond to the gospel's spread through martyrs. This angel announces impending judgment (v. 7).
14:8–10 The double "fallen" (v. 8) in the description of Babylon alludes to idolatrous Babylon's prophesied fall in Isa 21:9. Ancient Jews often used Babylon as a code name for Rome. As Israel once experienced exile under the evil empire Babylon, now they are experiencing a new evil empire in Rome. Babylon is judged because she has made nations drink "the maddening wine of her adulteries" (v. 8). Ancients normally diluted wine with two parts water to every part wine, except when they wished to get drunk. But God will administer this wine of his anger "full strength" (v. 10).
14:13 Finally, a heavenly voice promises peace for the martyr-witnesses of Jesus; the Spirit then confirms this with a prophetic assurance. Everyone is judged according to "deeds" (2:23; 20:12–13; 22:12), but the righteous can be satisfied in theirs. The key phrase is that these dead are "in the Lord."

Harvesting the Earth and Trampling the Winepress

14 I looked, and there before me was a white cloud, and seated on the cloud was one like a son of man[a][k] with a crown[l] of gold on his head and a sharp sickle in his hand. 15 Then another angel came out of the temple and called in a loud voice to him who was sitting on the cloud, "Take your sickle[m] and reap, because the time to reap has come, for the harvest[n] of the earth is ripe." 16 So he who was seated on the cloud swung his sickle over the earth, and the earth was harvested.

17 Another angel came out of the temple in heaven, and he too had a sharp sickle. 18 Still another angel, who had charge of the fire, came from the altar and called in a loud voice to him who had the sharp sickle, "Take your sharp sickle and gather the clusters of grapes from the earth's vine, because its grapes are ripe." 19 The angel swung his sickle on the earth, gathered its grapes and threw them into the great winepress of God's wrath.[o] 20 They were trampled in the winepress[p] outside the city,[q] and blood flowed out of the press, rising as high as the horses' bridles for a distance of 1,600 stadia.[b]

Seven Angels With Seven Plagues

15 I saw in heaven another great and marvelous sign:[r] seven angels[s] with the seven last plagues[t]—last, because with them God's wrath is completed. 2 And I saw what looked like a sea of glass[u] glowing with fire and, standing beside the sea, those who had been victorious over the beast and its image[v] and over the number of its name. They held harps given them by God 3 and sang the song of God's servant Moses[w] and of the Lamb:

14:14 [k] Da 7:13; Rev 1:13 [l] Rev 6:2
14:15 [m] Joel 3:13 [n] Jer 51:33
14:19 [o] Rev 19:15
14:20 [p] Isa 63:3 [q] Heb 13:12; Rev 11:8
15:1 [r] Rev 12:1, 3 [s] Rev 16:1 [t] Lev 26:21
15:2 [u] Rev 4:6 [v] Rev 13:14
15:3 [w] Ex 15:1; Dt 32:4

[a] *14* See Daniel 7:13. [b] *20* That is, about 180 miles or about 300 kilometers

---

14:14-20 In this passage the action shifts from heavenly announcements (vv. 6-13) to visions of symbolic actions. When Jesus appears in 19:12-13, his garments are spattered from treading out the winepress of human blood. The primary explanatory problem in this text is whether to identify the first vision's grain harvest with the second harvest's grape vintage or to interpret them differently. It seems likely that both visions involve judgment. The second vision portrays the wicked as gathered grapes now crushed into wine in God's winepress.
14:18 The angel "who had charge of the fire" (v. 18) keeps the fire of the incense altar (8:5). This image suggests that God again sends judgment in response to the cries of his oppressed people (6:9-11; 8:3-5).
14:20 The blood flows high "outside the city," vividly portraying a horrible end for Babylon. The "1,600 stadia" may be a rounded number with figurative significance; 1,600 is the square of the familiar biblical number 40. But while John rounds to a square number, its primary significance is to compound the grotesqueness of the image: None of the army will survive. Some commentators also suggest a contrast here: Whereas the river of paradise flows from God's throne (22:2) to a significant height, the wicked will drown in a river of their own blood.

✣ **14:1-20** The idea of eternal torment is so naturally revolting to most of us that modern readers have found ways to circumvent it. Some teach annihilation, which seems to contradict several texts about eternal torment. This view is not heretical and does not lessen the need for people to embrace Christ; but it is not likely correct.

Many today avoid trying to "scare" people into the kingdom. In a culture in revolt against authority and skeptical of threats, emphasizing God's loving invitation may be a more welcoming and strategic approach. But John had no such scruples against "scaring" people as he related the visceral truth of this vision; as long as we speak the truth and are able to reason with people, there remain occasions when this approach is appropriate.

A young atheist chose to consider the claims of Christ immediately rather than deferring the decision because the doctrine of hell made the stakes too high to ignore. Decades later, that former atheist remains a committed Christian—and wrote these study notes on Revelation.

15:1-4 These seven plagues are the "last plagues," completing God's anger (v. 1). "Last" implies these bowls are the last in terms of John's narrative. The word used for the "bowls" of divine anger (v. 7; 16:1—17:1; 21:9) is also used for the bowls that contained the prayers of his people (5:8), probably implying that God has chosen to release his acts in history in response to the worship of his faithful people. Those who have "been victorious over the beast" (15:2) are God's people who overcame by way of the cross. This is the same group already portrayed as God's conquering army in 14:1-5. The "sea of glass" (15:2) recalls the heavenly temple.

Their song is the "song of . . . Moses and of the Lamb" (v. 3), recalling the exodus both in terms of Moses' leading out of Egypt and crossing the Red Sea (Ex 15:1-18). As God conquered Egypt in the sea, so here the 144,000 are the people of the "new exodus," delivered and standing as conquerors on the sea of glass and fire.
15:3-4 The song praises God in language developed from Israel's ancient worship, especially Ps 86:8-10.

Whereas in the exodus God overthrew Egypt

Rev 15:3–4 ❖ How have God's "righteous acts" been revealed to us in the Bible (v. 4)? How have they been revealed in your own life?

"Great and marvelous are your
deeds,[x]
Lord God Almighty.
Just and true are your ways,[y]
King of the nations.[a]
4 Who will not fear you, Lord,[z]
and bring glory to your name?
For you alone are holy.
All nations will come
and worship before you,[a]
for your righteous acts have been
revealed."[b]

5 After this I looked, and I saw in heav-
en the temple[b] — that is, the tabernacle of the covenant law[c] — and it was
opened. 6 Out of the temple[d] came the
seven angels with the seven plagues.[e]
They were dressed in clean, shining lin-
en and wore golden sashes around their
chests.[f] 7 Then one of the four living creatures[g] gave to the seven angels seven
golden bowls filled with the wrath of
God, who lives for ever and ever. 8 And
the temple was filled with smoke[h] from
the glory of God and from his power, and
no one could enter the temple[i] until the
seven plagues of the seven angels were
completed.

15:3 [x] Ps 111:2 [y] Ps 145:17
15:4 [z] Jer 10:7 [a] Isa 66:23
15:5 [b] Rev 11:19 [c] Nu 1:50
15:6 [d] Rev 14:15 [e] ver 1 [f] Rev 1:13
15:7 [g] Rev 4:6
15:8 [h] Isa 6:4 [i] Ex 40:34,35; 1Ki 8:10,11; 2Ch 5:13,14

The Seven Bowls of God's Wrath

16 Then I heard a loud voice from the
temple saying to the seven angels,[j]
"Go, pour out the seven bowls of God's
wrath on the earth."
2 The first angel went and poured out
his bowl on the land,[k] and ugly, festering
sores[l] broke out on the people who had
the mark of the beast and worshiped its
image.[m]
3 The second angel poured out his bowl
on the sea, and it turned into blood like
that of a dead person, and every living
thing in the sea died.[n]
4 The third angel poured out his bowl
on the rivers and springs of water,[o] and
they became blood.[p] 5 Then I heard the
angel in charge of the waters say:

"You are just in these judgments,[q]
O Holy One,[r]
you who are and who were;[s]
6 for they have shed the blood of
your holy people and your
prophets,
and you have given them blood to
drink[t] as they deserve."

7 And I heard the altar[u] respond:

"Yes, Lord God Almighty,
true and just are your judgments."[v]

16:1 [j] Rev 15:1
16:2 [k] Rev 8:7 [l] Ex 9:9-11 [m] Rev 13:15-17
16:3 [n] Ex 7:17-21; Rev 8:8,9
16:4 [o] Rev 8:10 [p] Ex 7:17-21
16:5 [q] Rev 15:3 [r] Rev 15:4 [s] Rev 1:4
16:6 [t] Isa 49:26; Rev 17:6
16:7 [u] Rev 6:9 [v] Rev 15:3; 19:2

[a] 3 Some manuscripts *ages* [b] 3,4 Phrases in this song are drawn from Psalm 111:2,3; Deut. 32:4; Jer. 10:7; Psalms 86:9; 98:2.

---

for oppressing Israel, here he welcomes those from all nations who have joined God's servants in resisting the world. The nations now come to God in worship (v. 4), as in 21:24. Judgment brings representatives of all peoples to repentance.

15:5–8 That this scene takes place in the heavenly temple is significant. The angels' linen clothing (v. 6) reminds the reader that these angels fulfill priestly acts in the heavenly temple (vv. 5–6; cf. Lev 16:4). The prerequisite for such service was righteousness (Rev 19:8). Priests in the heavenly temple respond to the earthly priests (1:6) of the oppressed earthly temple (11:1–2), whose prayers (6:9–11; 8:3–6) have invited the judgments about to begin.

That "smoke" filled the heavenly temple (v. 8) alludes to God's glory filling his house (Isa 6:4; Eze 10:3–4). God had filled the earthly tabernacle with his glory at its dedication (Ex 40:34–35; cf. 1Ki 8:10–11); now, he fills the temple with his glory in response to the worship of his martyred conquerors throughout history.

✣ **15:1–8** For John, the songs of Moses and the Lamb were not two separate songs, as if OT redemption and NT redemption were incompatible ideas. Jesus as the Lamb has provided the climactic act of redemption, parallel to the Passover lamb of the first exodus, so the song of Moses is also the song of the Lamb.

16:1–11 The "seven bowls of God's wrath" (v. 1) represent urns in the temple, perhaps for offerings of incense. Most of the bowls recall the plagues of the exodus. As God protected his people in Goshen during the plagues (Ex 8:22; 9:26), so he will protect them from his judgments (Rev 7:1–8; 12:6, 16). The final two bowls represent the promised end-time battle and the completion of God's promises.

16:3–4 The water-into-blood plague is repeated for emphasis.

16:5–6 Jewish people believed God assigned various angels to oversee various features of nature; here, "the angel in charge of the waters" (v. 5) praises God's justice in punishing the wicked. As God's enemies "have shed" (i.e., "poured out") blood (v. 6), so God "poured out" judgments (vv. 1–17).

16:7 "The altar" confirms God's justice, undoubtedly because it harbors the prayers of the saints; hence it participates in the judgment. It echoes the song in 15:3.

8The fourth angel[w] poured out his
bowl on the sun, and the sun was allowed to scorch people with fire.[x] 9They
were seared by the intense heat and they
cursed the name of God,[y] who had control over these plagues, but they refused
to repent[z] and glorify him.[a]
10The fifth angel poured out his bowl
on the throne of the beast,[b] and its kingdom was plunged into darkness.[c] People gnawed their tongues in agony 11and
cursed[d] the God of heaven[e] because of
their pains and their sores,[f] but they refused to repent of what they had done.[g]
12The sixth angel poured out his bowl
on the great river Euphrates,[h] and its
water was dried up to prepare the way
for the kings from the East.[i] 13Then I
saw three impure spirits that looked
like frogs; they came out of the mouth
of the dragon,[j] out of the mouth of the
beast[k] and out of the mouth of the false
prophet.[l] 14They are demonic spirits[m]
that perform signs, and they go out to
the kings of the whole world, to gather
them for the battle[n] on the great day of
God Almighty.

15"Look, I come like a thief! Blessed
is the one who stays awake[o] and remains clothed, so as not to go naked
and be shamefully exposed."

16Then they gathered the kings together to the place that in Hebrew[p] is called
Armageddon.[q]
17The seventh angel poured out his bowl
into the air,[r] and out of the temple[s] came
a loud voice[t] from the throne, saying, "It
is done!"[u] 18Then there came flashes of
lightning, rumblings, peals of thunder[v]
and a severe earthquake.[w] No earthquake
like it has ever occurred since mankind
has been on earth,[x] so tremendous was
the quake. 19The great city[y] split into three
parts, and the cities of the nations collapsed. God remembered[z] Babylon the
Great[a] and gave her the cup filled with
the wine of the fury of his wrath.[b] 20Ev-
ery island fled away and the mountains
could not be found.[c] 21From the sky huge
hailstones,[d] each weighing about a hundred pounds,[a] fell on people. And they

[a] *21* Or about 45 kilograms

16:8 [w] Rev 8:12 [x] Rev 14:18
16:9 [y] ver 11, 21 [z] Rev 2:21 [a] Rev 11:13
16:10 [b] Rev 13:2 [c] Rev 9:2
16:11 [d] ver 9, 21 [e] Rev 11:13 [f] ver 2 [g] Rev 2:21
16:12 [h] Rev 9:14 [i] Isa 41:2
16:13 [j] Rev 12:3 [k] Rev 13:1 [l] Rev 19:20
16:14 [m] 1Ti 4:1 [n] Rev 17:14
16:15 [o] Lk 12:37
16:16 [p] Rev 9:11 [q] 2Ki 23:29, 30
16:17 [r] Eph 2:2 [s] Rev 14:15 [t] Rev 11:15 [u] Rev 21:6
16:18 [v] Rev 4:5 [w] Rev 6:12 [x] Da 12:1
16:19 [y] Rev 17:18 [z] Rev 18:5 [a] Rev 14:8 [b] Rev 14:10
16:20 [c] Rev 6:14
16:21 [d] Rev 11:19

Rev 16:15 ❖ What can we do to stay "awake" and "clothed" as we await Christ's coming?

16:8–11 The plagues of scorching sun and darkness (vv. 8–10) recall the OT judgment on Egypt's sun deity, Amon-Re. That the darkness actually causes pain (v. 10) may reflect the darkness of Moses' day, which could be "felt" (Ex 10:21). But instead of responding with repentance, the people grow more hard-hearted against God (Rev 16:9, 11; cf. 9:20–21, 16:21).

16:12–21 Although many rivers in the Near East occasionally dried up, the massive Euphrates never did. This fact augments the terror of the image and is evidence of divine judgment (Isa 50:2; Hos 13:15; Na 1:4).

16:13–14 Verse 13 may be suggesting the dragon, beast, and false prophet as a sort of a satanic trinity. That it speaks of frogs coming out of their mouths may recall another Egyptian plague (Ex 8:2–13). The three frogs issue from three mouths; because they issue from mouths, they probably represent propaganda (Rev 13:2, 5–6). These "demonic spirits" perform persuasive, miraculous "signs" (16:14), like the beast they serve (13:13–14). The devil and his agents then gather the nations together to battle the true God. In reality, they are being gathered for their destruction (16:14). The gathering of the wicked for their own destruction is a common end-time image (Joel 3:10–16; Zec 12:3–4; 14:2–3).

16:15 Such an announcement proves an appropriate point for John to remind his hearers that Jesus will come like a thief (v. 15). Those found unprepared will be stripped bare instead of walking with Jesus in robes of white (cf. 3:4–5, 17–18).

16:16 The meaning of "Armageddon" in v. 16—most likely Hebrew for "Mount Megiddo"—is obscure. The valley of Megiddo was the site of some significant battles in history (Jdg 5:19; 2Ki 23:29). Although a valley would have worked well as an image of end-time judgment (Joel 3:12, 14), Megiddo may appear here as a mountain to symbolize its stature or as a contrast with Mount Zion (Rev 21:10).

16:17 The seventh bowl refers to judgment over the entire world in the "air realm" (the lowest of the heavens in Greco-Roman thought). It reminds the reader of God's continuing sovereignty over the cosmos. With this judgment, the judgments are "done," as at the final trumpet (10:7) and the consummation of God's plan for history implied in the new creation (21:6).

16:18 The thunder, lightning, and earthquake in v. 18 suggest a revelation of God's glory as at Sinai (Ex 19:16), but the earthquake also signals the end of the age (Rev 6:12; 11:13). Babylon likely stands as a symbol for Rome here.

16:19–21 In contrast with the repentant of Jerusalem (11:13), Babylon's inhabitants become harder and curse God all the more when judged (16:21), having learned nothing from their unrepentance during earlier plagues (v. 11). The world dies in its sin, unwilling to repent.

✣ **16:1–21** God sends judgments not only to vindicate his oppressed people but also to get the world's attention and offer them the opportunity for repentance. That many people

cursed God on account of the plague of
hail,[e] because the plague was so terrible.

Babylon, the Prostitute on the Beast

17 One of the seven angels[f] who had
the seven bowls[g] came and said to
me, "Come, I will show you the punishment[h] of the great prostitute,[i] who sits
by many waters.[j] 2With her the kings of
the earth committed adultery, and the
inhabitants of the earth were intoxicated
with the wine of her adulteries."[k]
3Then the angel carried me away in the
Spirit into a wilderness.[l] There I saw a
woman sitting on a scarlet beast that was
covered with blasphemous names[m] and
had seven heads and ten horns.[n] 4The
woman was dressed in purple and scarlet, and was glittering with gold, precious
stones and pearls.[o] She held a golden
cup[p] in her hand, filled with abominable things and the filth of her adulteries.
5The name written on her forehead was
a mystery:

16:21 [e] Ex 9:23-25
17:1 [f] Rev 15:1 [g] Rev 21:9 [h] Rev 16:19 [i] Rev 19:2 [j] Jer 51:13
17:2 [k] Rev 14:8; 18:3
17:3 [l] Rev 12:6, 14 [m] Rev 13:1 [n] Rev 12:3
17:4 [o] Rev 18:16 [p] Jer 51:7; Rev 18:6
17:5 [q] Rev 14:8
17:6 [r] Rev 18:24
17:7 [s] ver 5 [t] ver 3
17:8 [u] Rev 13:10 [v] Rev 3:10 [w] Rev 13:8 [x] Rev 13:3
17:9 [y] Rev 13:18

BABYLON THE GREAT[q]
THE MOTHER OF PROSTITUTES
AND OF THE ABOMINATIONS
OF THE EARTH.

6I saw that the woman was drunk with
the blood of God's holy people,[r] the blood
of those who bore testimony to Jesus.
When I saw her, I was greatly astonished. 7Then the angel said to me: "Why
are you astonished? I will explain to you
the mystery[s] of the woman and of the
beast she rides, which has the seven heads
and ten horns.[t] 8The beast, which you saw,
once was, now is not, and yet will come up
out of the Abyss and go to its destruction.[u]
The inhabitants of the earth[v] whose names
have not been written in the book of life[w]
from the creation of the world will be astonished[x] when they see the beast, because
it once was, now is not, and yet will come.
9"This calls for a mind with wisdom.[y]
The seven heads are seven hills on which
the woman sits. 10They are also seven

---

do not repent when they face judgment is unsurprising. Whether God acts with justice or mercy, some refuse to believe. That many in the world die unrepentant in the face of God's judgments (vv. 9, 11, 21) reveals their stubbornness and the depth of human rebellion against God.

17:1–5 An angel bids John to "come" so that he may "show" him the judgment of the prostitute (v. 1). He then carries John "away in the Spirit" (v. 3; cf. Eze 8:3). Here John sees a high-class prostitute (vv. 1–2) who is drunk with the blood of the saints (v. 6). The heads, horns, and blasphemous names link the beast with the dragon and an earlier vision of the beast (v. 3; cf. 12:3; 13:1).

Revelation contrasts two cities, Jerusalem and Babylon, as a bride and prostitute (17:5; 21:2). In 17:4, the woman is described as a queen. Babylon also sits as queen in Isa 47:5–7. Literal Babylon also lived by "many waters" (Jer 51:13).

The "kings of the earth" who have "committed adultery" with the prostitute (Rev 17:2) will suffer along with her. Thus Babylon is Rome here; its economic and political power made Rome a vehicle of spreading international idolatry and immorality.

That the woman sits "on a scarlet beast" with "seven heads and ten horns" (v. 3) identifies the beast with the seven-headed, ten-horned red dragon (12:3) as well as with Rome (13:1); this identification is something like calling Rome "Satan incarnate."

The prostitute's purple and scarlet clothing along with her gold, precious stones, and pearls contribute to a picture of wealth (cf. 18:12, 16) but also help underpin the impending contrast with the city of God, which was built of gold, had streets of gold and gates of pearls, and had precious stones on its foundations (21:18–21).

No scarlet or gold adornments will protect this sexually unfaithful figure from ultimate rejection and murder by her own lovers (17:16). The name written on her forehead contrasts with the name written on Jesus in 19:12–13 (cf. 13:16). As the "mother of prostitutes" (17:5), she models a world in rebellion against God.

17:6–11 As Rome made others drunk with her immorality (v. 2), she also became drunk herself with the blood of God's people (v. 6). By John's day many believers had been martyred; in the centuries that follow, many more will die martyrs' deaths. John here is astonished, inviting the angelic response (vv. 6–7).

As the angel explains the mystery of the woman and the beast (vv. 7–18), the beast is identified with Rome. First, the woman sits on seven mountains (v. 9); Rome was regularly portrayed in this manner. Second, the leader of Babylon is apparently the new Nero (vv. 8–11). Third, this empire rules over the other kings of the earth (v. 18), who rule the nations gathered around the sea as a maritime power (v. 15). Finally, "Babylon" was a standard Jewish title for Rome by this period.

Revelation's symbolism is so transparent that non-Christian Romans would have immediately understood its implications and regarded the document as subversive. But in addition to seeing Rome, many commentators also view the great prostitute as the evil world system that in principle continues beyond Rome's fall.

17:10 Who are the seven kings? It is not at all difficult to find a pattern of rulers that accommodates the revived Nero image that John seems to employ here. The king who "is" must be Domitian; five kings back from Domitian easily includes Nero.

kings. Five have fallen, one is, the other has not yet come; but when he does
come, he must remain for only a little
while. 11The beast who once was, and now
is not,[z] is an eighth king. He belongs to
the seven and is going to his destruction.
12“The ten horns[a] you saw are ten kings
who have not yet received a kingdom,
but who for one hour[b] will receive authority as kings along with the beast.
13They have one purpose and will give
their power and authority to the beast.[c]
14They will wage war[d] against the Lamb,
but the Lamb will triumph over them
because he is Lord of lords and King of
kings[e] — and with him will be his called,
chosen[f] and faithful followers.”
15Then the angel said to me, “The waters[g] you saw, where the prostitute sits,
are peoples, multitudes, nations and languages.[h] 16The beast and the ten horns
you saw will hate the prostitute. They
will bring her to ruin[i] and leave her naked;[j] they will eat her flesh[k] and burn
her with fire.[l] 17For God has put it into
their hearts to accomplish his purpose
by agreeing to hand over to the beast
their royal authority, until God’s words
are fulfilled.[m] 18The woman you saw is
the great city[n] that rules over the kings
of the earth.”

17:11 [z] ver 8
17:12 [a] Rev 12:3 [b] Rev 18:10, 17,19
17:13 [c] ver 17
17:14 [d] Rev 16:14 [e] 1Ti 6:15; Rev 19:16 [f] Mt 22:14
17:15 [g] Isa 8:7 [h] Rev 13:7
17:16 [i] Rev 18:17, 19 [j] Eze 16:37, 39 [k] Rev 19:18 [l] Rev 18:8
17:17 [m] Rev 10:7
17:18 [n] Rev 16:19
18:1 [o] Rev 17:1 [p] Rev 10:1 [q] Eze 43:2
18:2 [r] Rev 14:8 [s] Isa 13:21,22; Jer 50:39
18:3 [t] Rev 14:8

Rev 17:16 ❖ Where have we seen one evil destroy another? Why is all evil ultimately futile under God’s reign?

Lament Over Fallen Babylon

18 After this I saw another angel[o]
coming down from heaven.[p] He
had great authority, and the earth was
illuminated by his splendor.[q] 2With a
mighty voice he shouted:

“ ‘Fallen! Fallen is Babylon the
Great!’[a][r]
She has become a dwelling for
demons
and a haunt for every impure spirit,
a haunt for every unclean bird,
a haunt for every unclean and
detestable animal.[s]
3For all the nations have drunk
the maddening wine of her
adulteries.[t]

[a] 2 Isaiah 21:9

17:11 The “eighth king” mentioned here is one of the rulers from the first seven who returns, undoubtedly the head earlier mentioned as wounded but recovered (13:3). This constitutes a parody of Jesus’ resurrection. The thought of Nero’s return would be no less terrifying to the current Roman regime that had replaced it than to the Christians who had suffered under Nero’s purges before.

17:12–18 The “ten horns” as “ten kings” (v. 12) comes from Da 7:7, 20, 24, and in Revelation may simply refer to the continuing imperial system. Most likely, they are viewed as Rome’s client kingdoms; in the end, Rome’s empire will collapse and turn on the one with whom they have committed prostitution. They will reign with the beast briefly, “for one hour” (Rev 17:12), to wage war against the Lamb (vv. 13–14).

The Roman king thought himself ruler of all the other kings of the earth (v. 18), but this role ultimately belongs to Jesus. Jesus is the mighty, conquering King, and his army is described as “called, chosen and faithful” (v. 14).

The imperial system and the rulers of allied nations will eventually devastate Rome itself (v. 16); the world’s allegiances are self-interested, and therefore temporary. Stripping was a standard ancient penalty for sexual unfaithfulness (Eze 16:37–38; Hos 2:3). Burning was the normal fate of conquered cities (e.g., Jos 6:24; 8:28) and the promised fate of the final antichrist figure (Da 7:10–11), but it was also the penalty for the most serious acts of promiscuity (Ge 38:24; Lev 20:14; 21:9). The diabolical system will meet a fitting end.

17:17–18 Perhaps the most striking statement about God’s great rule is the fact that he is sovereign even in the nations’ evil, using it for his own long-range purposes. To be sure, Rome ruled the kings of the earth (v. 18). But in a far more important way, God ruled Rome and its enemies (v. 17). God remains the Lord of history, and his purposes will be accomplished.

✣ **17:1–18** When the buying and streaming habits of Christians differ little from that of our secular neighbors, can we deny responsibility for supporting an industry that sometimes glorifies violence and killing? Unfortunately, what early Christians often avoided in public, modern Christians often invite into their living rooms.

18:1–2 The mention that Babylon will become a dwelling place of “unclean bird[s]” (v. 2) is a creative way of announcing judgment. Rome’s population decreased from as much as a million in John’s day to some 30,000 after its fall a few centuries later.

In Rome’s propaganda, circulated by local elites (whose own rank depended on Rome’s patronage), Rome brought good to many peoples; but in a scathing critique, the prophet here announces that Rome relates to other peoples only for her own personal gain. But John’s audience will not lose sight of God’s sovereignty, for the language here echoes Jeremiah (Jer 51:7; cf. Zec 12:2), inviting mourning over Babylon (Jer 51:8) and the flight of God’s people (Jer 51:6, 45; cf. Zec 2:7).

18:3 Those who mourn for Babylon include both “kings” and “merchants,” Rome’s political and

Rev 18:4-8 ❖ How is God calling us to "come out" of Babylon (v. 4), or the sinful kingdom of the world? What might we need to leave behind as we do?

The kings of the earth committed
adultery with her,[u]
and the merchants of the earth
grew rich[v] from her excessive
luxuries."[w]

Warning to Escape Babylon's Judgment

4Then I heard another voice from
heaven say:

"'Come out of her, my people,'[a][x]
so that you will not share in her
sins,
so that you will not receive any of
her plagues;
5for her sins are piled up to heaven,[y]
and God has remembered[z] her
crimes.
6Give back to her as she has given;
pay her back[a] double for what she
has done.
Pour her a double portion from
her own cup.[b]
7Give her as much torment and grief
as the glory and luxury she gave
herself.[c]
In her heart she boasts,
'I sit enthroned as queen.
I am not a widow;[b]
I will never mourn.'[d]
8Therefore in one day[e] her plagues
will overtake her:
death, mourning and famine.
She will be consumed by fire,[f]
for mighty is the Lord God who
judges her.

Threefold Woe Over Babylon's Fall

9"When the kings of the earth who
committed adultery with her[g] and
shared her luxury see the smoke of her
burning,[h] they will weep and mourn over
her.[i] 10Terrified at her torment, they will
stand far off[j] and cry:

"'Woe! Woe to you, great city,[k]
you mighty city of Babylon!
In one hour[l] your doom has
come!'

11"The merchants[m] of the earth will
weep and mourn over her because no
one buys their cargoes anymore[n]—
12cargoes of gold, silver, precious stones
and pearls; fine linen, purple, silk and
scarlet cloth; every sort of citron wood,
and articles of every kind made of ivory,
costly wood, bronze, iron and marble;[o]
13cargoes of cinnamon and spice, of incense, myrrh and frankincense, of wine
and olive oil, of fine flour and wheat;
cattle and sheep; horses and carriages;
and human beings sold as slaves.[p]
14"They will say, 'The fruit you longed
for is gone from you. All your luxury and
splendor have vanished, never to be recovered.' 15The merchants who sold these
things and gained their wealth from
her[q] will stand far off, terrified at her
torment. They will weep and mourn[r]
16and cry out:

18:3 [u] Rev 17:2 [v] Eze 27:9-25 [w] ver 7,9
18:4 [x] Isa 48:20; Jer 50:8; 2Co 6:17
18:5 [y] Jer 51:9 [z] Rev 16:19
18:6 [a] Ps 137:8; Jer 50:15,29 [b] Rev 14:10; 16:19
18:7 [c] Eze 28:2-8 [d] Isa 47:7,8; Zep 2:15
18:8 [e] ver 10; Isa 47:9; Jer 50:31,32 [f] Rev 17:16
18:9 [g] Rev 17:2,4 [h] ver 18; Rev 19:3 [i] Eze 26:17,18
18:10 [j] ver 15,17 [k] ver 16,19 [l] Rev 17:12
18:11 [m] Eze 27:27 [n] ver 3
18:12 [o] Rev 17:4
18:13 [p] Eze 27:13; 1Ti 1:10
18:15 [q] ver 3 [r] Eze 27:31

[a] 4 Jer. 51:45 [b] 7 See Isaiah 47:7,8.

---

mercantile allies; John focuses more on the latter group (vv. 11–19) than the former (vv. 9–10).
18:4 Not all John's audience is persecuted by the beast at this point; some of them in Laodicea and Sardis, in fact, are prospering as part of the same system that elsewhere is killing God's people. The summons to "come out" in v. 4 may thus include withdrawal from the economic arenas that required compromise with emperor worship or other forms of idolatry. God urges his people to leave Babylon because they have a better city (21:2–3).
18:5–6 The judgment comes when Babylon's sins are piled as high as heaven. Those who destroy Babylon are repaying her double for her sins (v. 6). Babylon will drink from its own cup (14:8–10).
18:7 The message of judgment against Babylon's arrogance here reflects the language of an ancient proclamation against Babylon. Babylon claimed to be an eternal "queen," living luxuriously and denying that she would be widowed or lose her children (cf. Isa 47:7–8). Thus plagues will come on her all "in one day" (Rev 18:8; cf. Isa 47:9).
18:9–10 In this dystopian prophecy, the kings mourn the destruction of the evil empire (vv. 9–10); by contrast, the righteous remnant of all peoples will participate in the new Jerusalem, and their kings will bring their glory into it (21:24).

"Kings of the earth" of v. 9 refers to Rome's client-kings (17:2, 18; 18:3), though the language is adapted to the OT. The Messiah would rule the kings (Ps 89:27); they would gather against God's Son and be shattered (Ps 2:2; Rev 19:19). Their cry of "Woe! Woe!" here (18:10) is repeated by the merchants in vv. 16, 19.
18:11 Rome's commercial interests also propagated its pagan religion (13:17). The merchant's lament that no one now buys their cargoes is ironic retribution for those who worshiped the beast that they might buy and sell.
18:12–16 This is the longest existing list of products from the Roman period. John adapts Ezekiel's list (Eze 27:2–24), but he updates it for the trade realities of first-century Rome. Whereas Ezekiel's list is arranged geographically, John's is

"'Woe! Woe to you, great city,
dressed in fine linen, purple and scarlet,
and glittering with gold, precious stones and pearls![s]
17 In one hour[t] such great wealth has been brought to ruin!'[u]

"Every sea captain, and all who travel by ship, the sailors, and all who earn
their living from the sea,[v] will stand far
off. 18 When they see the smoke of her
burning, they will exclaim, 'Was there
ever a city like this great city?'[w] 19 They
will throw dust on their heads,[x] and with
weeping and mourning cry out:

"'Woe! Woe to you, great city,
where all who had ships on the sea
became rich through her wealth!
In one hour she has been brought to ruin!'[y]

20 "Rejoice over her, you heavens![z]
Rejoice, you people of God!
Rejoice, apostles and prophets!
For God has judged her
with the judgment she imposed on you."[a]

18:16 [s] Rev 17:4
18:17 [t] ver 10 [u] Rev 17:16 [v] Eze 27:28-30
18:18 [w] Eze 27:32; Rev 13:4
18:19 [x] Jos 7:6; Eze 27:30 [y] Rev 17:16
18:20 [z] Jer 51:48; Rev 12:12 [a] Rev 19:2
18:21 [b] Rev 5:2 [c] Jer 51:63
18:22 [d] Isa 24:8; Eze 26:13 [e] Jer 25:10
18:23 [f] Jer 7:34; 16:9; 25:10 [g] Isa 23:8 [h] Na 3:4
18:24 [i] Rev 16:6; 17:6 [j] Jer 51:49

The Finality of Babylon's Doom

21 Then a mighty angel[b] picked up a boulder the size of a large millstone and threw it into the sea,[c] and said:

"With such violence
the great city of Babylon will be thrown down,
never to be found again.
22 The music of harpists and musicians, pipers and trumpeters,
will never be heard in you again.[d]
No worker of any trade
will ever be found in you again.
The sound of a millstone
will never be heard in you again.[e]
23 The light of a lamp
will never shine in you again.
The voice of bridegroom and bride
will never be heard in you again.[f]
Your merchants were the world's important people.[g]
By your magic spell[h] all the nations were led astray.
24 In her was found the blood of prophets and of God's holy people,[i]
of all who have been slaughtered on the earth."[j]

---

arranged by type of cargo; John focuses mostly on expensive imports. Although much of ch. 18 condemns Rome's luxury itself (v. 7), oppression is also in view (v. 24).

18:17–19 Those who mourn include those who work on ships, but this probably implies the sorrow of ship owners as well. With the fall of Rome, both ship owners and their employees would be out of business.

18:20–24 A "mighty angel" (v. 21) announces a message in vv. 21–24. Verses 20 and 24 bracket this paragraph with the theme of vengeance for the blood of God's people, a biblical theme that appears elsewhere (Dt 32:43; 2Ki 9:7; Ps 79:10; Joel 3:21).

18:20 In contrast to the earth dwellers' mourning, heaven rejoices over Babylon's fall. Believers have been tried and executed in the world's courts, but the world is really on trial.

18:21 God commanded Jeremiah to hurl a stone into the middle of the Euphrates to symbolize the permanent fall of Babylon (Jer 51:63–64). Here in our section this becomes a millstone into the sea, probably recalling Jesus' warning in Mk 9:42; the words in each case refer to the huge millstone turned by a mule, not the smaller kind one might use by hand. With such a heavy weight there would be no escape.

18:22 The angelic announcement shows that Babylon, oppressor of God's people, reaps what it has sown against them. By contrast, new Jerusalem will need no earthly lamp, as it is illumined by the glory of God and the Lamb (21:23; 22:5). The city itself will be a bride (19:7; 21:2, 9; 22:17). That the harpists will no longer be heard in Babylon (18:22) may contrast with the harpists heard in heaven (14:2).

18:23 The mention of "magic spell[s]" is significant. Sorcery is linked with prostitution in the description of the biblical Jezebel (2Ki 9:22), a model for the prostitute in Revelation (2:20). More to the point, Babylon, who thought herself a queen and denied her impending widowhood (v. 7), vainly thought to protect herself by sorceries (cf. Isa 47:9, 12). Magic was a major practice in Asia Minor, especially Ephesus (Ac 19:13–19). But Revelation warns that anyone who practices it will be judged (21:8; 22:15; cf. 9:21).

18:24 Babylon's greatest sin was that "in her was found the blood of prophets and of God's holy people." The addition of "all who have been slaughtered on the earth" may point to Rome's economic injustice. God is concerned about the crushing of Egypt's peasants, the brutality of slavery, and other methods by which Rome exploited most of the empire. John as a Jew likewise must have shared the pain of his people crushed by the Romans in AD 70. Given the parallel with v. 20, the climax of Rome's sin was its martyrdom of God's messengers.

✣ **18:1–24** God warns his people to "come out" of Babylon (v. 4). This is a call to holiness, but we must not misunderstand holiness. Holiness is separation from the world to God. Thus, we can express holiness by immersing ourselves in God's Word rather than in the world's values emphasized on social media; or by turning

Threefold Hallelujah Over Babylon's Fall

19 After this I heard what sounded
like the roar of a great multitude[k]
in heaven shouting:

"Hallelujah!
Salvation[l] and glory and power[m]
belong to our God,
2 for true and just are his judgments.
He has condemned the great
prostitute
who corrupted the earth by her
adulteries.
He has avenged on her the blood of
his servants."[n]

3 And again they shouted:

"Hallelujah!
The smoke from her goes up for ever
and ever."[o]

4 The twenty-four elders[p] and the
four living creatures[q] fell down[r] and
worshiped God, who was seated on the
throne. And they cried:

"Amen, Hallelujah!"

5 Then a voice came from the throne,
saying:

"Praise our God,
all you his servants,[s]
you who fear him,
both great and small!"[t]

6 Then I heard what sounded like a
great multitude,[u] like the roar of rushing waters and like loud peals of thunder,
shouting:

"Hallelujah!
For our Lord God Almighty reigns.
7 Let us rejoice and be glad
and give him glory!
For the wedding of the Lamb[v] has
come,
and his bride[w] has made herself
ready.
8 Fine linen, bright and clean,
was given her to wear."
(Fine linen stands for the righteous acts[x]
of God's holy people.)

9 Then the angel said to me,[y] "Write
this:[z] Blessed are those who are invited
to the wedding supper of the Lamb!"[a]
And he added, "These are the true words
of God."[b]
10 At this I fell at his feet to worship
him.[c] But he said to me, "Don't do that!
I am a fellow servant with you and with
your brothers and sisters who hold to
the testimony of Jesus. Worship God![d]
For it is the Spirit of prophecy who bears
testimony to Jesus."[e]

19:1 [k] Rev 11:15 [l] Rev 7:10 [m] Rev 4:11
19:2 [n] Dt 32:43; Rev 6:10
19:3 [o] Isa 34:10; Rev 14:11
19:4 [p] Rev 4:4 [q] Rev 4:6 [r] Rev 5:14
19:5 [s] Ps 134:1 [t] Rev 11:18; 20:12
19:6 [u] Rev 11:15
19:7 [v] Mt 22:2; 25:10; Eph 5:32 [w] Rev 21:2,9
19:8 [x] Rev 15:4
19:9 [y] ver 10 [z] Rev 1:19 [a] Lk 14:15 [b] Rev 21:5; 22:6
19:10 [c] Rev 22:8 [d] Ac 10:25, 26; Rev 22:9 [e] Rev 12:17

Rev 19:8 ❖ Christ's bride is dressed in fine linen, which stands for the righteous acts of God's people. If our acts comprise our "clothing" before God, how would we describe the way we are "dressed"? Why?

---

down a better-paying job because we felt God wanted us to work in a different place, perhaps among the poor. Such holiness may cost us our place in Babylon and much more.

"Come out of her" also reminds us that we Christians may share in the judgments on our society, despite our forgiveness for individual sins. Nations and institutions as corporate entities can stand under judgment; we who participate in such institutions share in their responsibility before God unless we explicitly refuse to be a part of any wicked practices and declare any evil activities wrong (see Ro 13:1-6). Most of all, the summons to "come out of her" (Rev 18:4) reminds believers that we belong to a different city whose true wealth is greater than Babylon's glory—for which our neighbors may strive.

19:1-2 Most early readers would know that "Hallelujah!" (vv. 1, 3, 4, 6) meant "Praise Yahweh!" "Salvation" (or "deliverance," v. 1) can refer to triumph (cf. 7:10; 12:10); the prostitute was stained with the blood of murdered believers (18:24), and God had exacted vengeance for them.

19:3 Babylon is the new Sodom (11:8). The smoke of her death rises forever (19:3), suggesting eternal torment (14:11).

19:5-6 By judging the world system, God has begun to reign. All God's "servants" offer praise (v. 5); this group is joined with the martyrs (v. 2), because all true followers of Christ are potential martyrs.

19:7-9 The "wedding supper" mentioned here (v. 9) was a frequent illustration of the coming messianic era. God had promised a splendid banquet (Isa 25:6-8). The marriage supper of the Lamb is contrasted with the great supper of God, in which birds feast on the carcasses of the wicked (Rev 19:17-18). To make herself ready for the wedding (v. 7) a bride would bathe herself and dress in special clothing. Here the clothing is the "righteous acts of God's holy people" (v. 8; cf. Isa 61:10). The "fine linen" of God's people (Rev 19:8) contrasts with the fine linen of the prostitute (18:12, 16). Presumably the prospective bride is also portrayed in fine linen, like the believers accompanying Jesus in 19:14; by contrast, Jesus himself is clothed in a bloody robe (v. 13), for the task of just retribution will precede the wedding celebration.

19:10 That John begins to worship the messenger

The Heavenly Warrior Defeats the Beast

11 I saw heaven standing open and
there before me was a white horse, whose
rider[f] is called Faithful and True.[g] With
justice he judges and wages war.[h] 12 His
eyes are like blazing fire,[i] and on his head
are many crowns.[j] He has a name written
on him that no one knows but he himself.[k] 13 He is dressed in a robe dipped in
blood,[l] and his name is the Word of God.[m]
14 The armies of heaven were following
him, riding on white horses and dressed
in fine linen,[n] white and clean. 15 Coming
out of his mouth is a sharp sword[o] with
which to strike down[p] the nations. "He
will rule them with an iron scepter."[a][q] He
treads the winepress[r] of the fury of the
wrath of God Almighty. 16 On his robe and
on his thigh he has this name written:[s]

KING OF KINGS AND LORD OF LORDS.[t]

17 And I saw an angel standing in the
sun, who cried in a loud voice to all the
birds[u] flying in midair,[v] "Come,[w] gather together for the great supper of God,
18 so that you may eat the flesh of kings,
generals, and the mighty, of horses and
their riders, and the flesh of all people,[x]
free and slave, great and small."
19 Then I saw the beast and the kings
of the earth[y] and their armies gathered
together to wage war against the rider on
the horse and his army. 20 But the beast
was captured, and with it the false prophet[z] who had performed the signs on its
behalf.[a] With these signs he had deluded those who had received the mark of
the beast and worshiped its image. The
two of them were thrown alive into the
fiery lake[b] of burning sulfur.[c] 21 The rest
were killed with the sword[d] coming out
of the mouth of the rider on the horse,[e]
and all the birds[f] gorged themselves on
their flesh.

19:11 [f] Rev 6:2 [g] Rev 3:14 [h] Isa 11:4
19:12 [i] Rev 1:14 [j] Rev 6:2 [k] Rev 2:17
19:13 [l] Isa 63:2,3 [m] Jn 1:1
19:14 [n] ver 8
19:15 [o] Rev 1:16 [p] Isa 11:4; 2Th 2:8 [q] Ps 2:9; Rev 2:27 [r] Rev 14:20
19:16 [s] ver 12 [t] Rev 17:14
19:17 [u] ver 21 [v] Rev 8:13 [w] Eze 39:17
19:18 [x] Eze 39:18-20
19:19 [y] Rev 16:14,16
19:20 [z] Rev 16:13 [a] Rev 13:12 [b] Da 7:11; Rev 20:10,14,15; 21:8 [c] Rev 14:10
19:21 [d] ver 15 [e] ver 11,19 [f] ver 17

[a] *15* Psalm 2:9

---

in v. 10 is unsurprising; his message is easily confused with God's (21:5-6). The emphatic demand that God alone is to be worshiped challenges all forms of idolatry, including those offered the emperor in the name of loyalty to the state. Most significant, the angel declares that he is simply acting as God's agent (19:10b). The prophetic Spirit empowers those who speak the message about Christ; the reminder that true prophecy exalts Jesus is essential.

19:11–21 As God's "Word" (v. 13), Jesus is "Faithful and True" (v. 11). Jesus "judges and wages war" (v. 11). The former attribute belongs to God (6:10; 11:18; 18:8, 20; 19:2; 20:12) and to the Messiah, who will strike the wicked with his mouth (Isa 11:4; cf. Rev 19:15). The latter is the image of the end-time holy warrior, a final response to the worshipers of the beast (13:4). All along God has allowed the beast to make war with his people on earth (11:7; 12:17; 13:7); but when the right time comes, they will make war on the Lamb himself and be destroyed (17:14; 19:19; 20:8).

19:14 "The armies of heaven" with Jesus execute no violence themselves; Jesus is the mighty warrior who strikes the wicked (vv. 11, 15, 21). Biblical prophets predicted God himself as the ultimate holy warrior (Isa 42:13; Hab 3:11–14; Zep 3:17). Jesus assumes this divine role here. John describes Jesus as riding on a white horse (Rev 19:11), as do his hosts (v. 14). Such horses were appropriate mounts for rulers, important officials, and conquerors entering Rome in triumph.

19:12–14 Jesus' eyes, that are portrayed as "like blazing fire," indicate divinity and fury, and his "many crowns" indicate that he is ruler over all the kings of the world (v. 12a). Moreover, Jesus has a hidden name (v. 12b). His cloak "dipped in blood" in v. 13 draws from Isa 63:1-6. The blood is from those killed from his winepress, the whole world (Rev 19:15), as in Isa 63:2.

19:15 The army that overcame the beast by martyrdom (14:1-5) will now share Christ's final triumph (19:15). Because the sword issues from Jesus' mouth it can signify literal bloodshed (Isa 34:5; Jer 12:12; 47:6).

19:16 Jesus' title "king of kings and lord of lords" was applied in ancient Judaism almost exclusively to God. Revelation applies the title consistently to Jesus (17:14), the true ruler over the earth's other kings (1:5).

19:17–19 Whereas believers will partake of the promised messianic banquet (v. 9), the wicked will be the banquet on which scavengers feed (v. 17). The image of carrion birds feasting on the flesh of corpses killed in battle was a familiar one to ancient readers (1Sa 17:44-46). Given common Greek views of one's image enduring in the realm of departed spirits, the only fate worse than death itself was death followed by lack of burial, in which one's remains are devoured by animals. Many of Revelation's original audience would recognize the clear and immediate source of the language of this passage: God invited beasts and birds to devour the flesh of the army that opposed him (Eze 39:17-20).

19:20 John next describes God hurling the leaders of Satan's army into "the fiery lake of burning sulfur." This burning sulfur may allude to the fate of Sodom (Ge 19:24), but the punishment in this lake of fire is eternal (Rev 14:10) and contrasts with the sea of glass in God's presence (4:6).

19:1–21 This passage reminds us that the Spirit empowers us to speak for God. That the testimony about Jesus also implies prophetic empowerment by the Spirit has important implications for us today. Christ gave all of us his Spirit to testify about him (Ac 1:8). Thus, every Christian who witnesses about Jesus experiences in some measure the empowerment of the Holy Spirit.

The Thousand Years

20 And I saw an angel coming down
out of heaven,[g] having the key[h] to
the Abyss and holding in his hand a great
chain. 2He seized the dragon, that ancient serpent, who is the devil, or Satan,[i]
and bound him for a thousand years.[j] 3He
threw him into the Abyss, and locked and
sealed[k] it over him, to keep him from
deceiving the nations[l] anymore until
the thousand years were ended. After
that, he must be set free for a short time.
4I saw thrones[m] on which were seated
those who had been given authority to
judge. And I saw the souls of those who
had been beheaded[n] because of their
testimony about Jesus and because of
the word of God. They[a] had not worshiped the beast[o] or its image and had
not received its mark on their foreheads
or their hands.[p] They came to life and
reigned with Christ a thousand years.
5(The rest of the dead did not come to life
until the thousand years were ended.)
This is the first resurrection.[q] 6Blessed[r]
and holy are those who share in the first
resurrection. The second death[s] has no
power over them, but they will be priests[t]
of God and of Christ and will reign with
him[u] for a thousand years.

The Judgment of Satan

7When the thousand years are over,[v]
Satan will be released from his prison
8and will go out to deceive the nations[w]
in the four corners of the earth—Gog
and Magog[x]—and to gather them for
battle.[y] In number they are like the sand
on the seashore.[z] 9They marched across
the breadth of the earth and surrounded[a] the camp of God's people, the city he
loves. But fire came down from heaven[b]
and devoured them. 10And the devil, who
deceived them,[c] was thrown into the lake
of burning sulfur, where the beast and
the false prophet had been thrown. They

20:1 [g] Rev 10:1 [h] Rev 1:18
20:2 [i] Rev 12:9 [j] 2Pe 2:4
20:3 [k] Da 6:17 [l] Rev 12:9
20:4 [m] Da 7:9 [n] Rev 6:9 [o] Rev 13:12 [p] Rev 13:16
20:5 [q] Lk 14:14; Php 3:11
20:6 [r] Rev 14:13 [s] Rev 2:11 [t] Rev 1:6 [u] ver 4
20:7 [v] ver 2
20:8 [w] ver 3, 10 [x] Eze 38:2; 39:1 [y] Rev 16:14 [z] Heb 11:12
20:9 [a] Eze 38:9, 16 [b] Eze 38:22; 39:6
20:10 [c] Rev 19:20

[a] 4 Or *God; I also saw those who*

20:1–10 Interpreters of this chapter are divided into three broad schools of thought: *premillennialists*, who believe Jesus will return to establish a specific thousand-year kingdom; *amillennialists*, who generally believe that the thousand-year kingdom is symbolic for the present age; and *postmillennialists*, who believe that Christians help establish the thousand-year kingdom on earth prior to Jesus' return. Most evangelicals today are premillennialists or amillennialists.

As amillennial scholars note, it is difficult to interpret most of Revelation as a continuous chronological account; the seals, trumpets, and vials appear to parallel each other. Many of the expressions about the end in ch. 20 plainly parallel previous descriptions of the end in Revelation. But these parallels may suggest merely that a later end repeats what was unfinished in a former one. Other factors favor reading this thousand years as following the tribulation.

First, the binding of Satan during the thousand years hardly matches Satan's furious deceptive and murderous activity during the present era (12:12–13; 13:11–15; 20:2–3). Second, the saints have already been martyred, suggesting that the tribulation period comes before the millennium (20:4). Third, the resurrection of the righteous is parallel to and contrasted with the rest of the dead returning to life after the thousand years (vv. 4–6), suggesting a bodily rather than symbolic resurrection. Fourth, the beast and false prophet are already in the lake of fire before the millennium (v. 10); likewise, the devil cannot deceive "anymore," suggesting a suspension of his deceptive work (v. 3). Finally, in hindsight, we see that the period between Jesus' first and second comings is longer than one thousand years, but in John's own day, such a figure for the intermediate period must have seemed too long (1:3). Premillennialists believe that John sees an intermediate period here. A similar delay can be found in passages like Isa 24:22 and Da 7:12.

20:1–3 God delegates the "key" to the Abyss to an angel (v. 1). Once Satan is bound in the Abyss, the angel seals it (v. 3), preventing any chance of his escape (cf. Da 6:17); Satan cannot act during that period as he does in the present.

20:4–5 The martyrs died "because of the word of God" and "because of their testimony about Jesus" (v. 4); suffering for this cause is such a recurrent motif in Revelation (1:9; 6:9; 12:11) that it constitutes a virtual invitation to John's audience to participate in paying the price. Beheading believers who refused to worship the beast or his image recalls 13:15. Jesus' followers "conquer" the way he did, through death (3:21; cf. 5:5–6). But while the present world executes judgment against God's people, they will rule the future world (5:10)—both in the "thousand years" (20:4, 6) and eternally (22:5).

20:6 In contrast to the promise of the "first resurrection" is the "second death" (v. 6); the resurrection to damnation is so horrible that its life is called "death" as opposed to the eternal life inherited by believers.

20:8–10 After the thousand years, Satan will be loosed to stir up Gog and Magog against the camp of the saints; in accordance with his nature, he "gather[s]" the nations for war again (v. 8; 16:16; 19:19). This army is numerically "like the sand on the seashore" (20:8), a common figure in the Hebrew Bible for saying a group of people are innumerable.

John draws this image from Ezekiel, but here Gog and Magog together symbolize all the nations "in the four corners of the earth" (v. 8). God will be a "wall of fire" around the holy city (Zec 2:5; cf. Zec 9:8). But the language of a "camp" of the saints (Rev 20:9) probably alludes to Israel's experience in the exodus or as a unit of war that must remain vigilant.

> **Rev 20:11–12** ❖ How does the fact that we will one day stand before God's judgment seat put today's concerns and choices into perspective?

will be tormented day and night for ever
and ever.[d]

The Judgment of the Dead

11Then I saw a great white throne[e] and
him who was seated on it. The earth and
the heavens fled from his presence, and
there was no place for them. 12And I saw
the dead, great and small, standing before
the throne, and books were opened.[f] Another book was opened, which is the book
of life.[g] The dead were judged according
to what they had done[h] as recorded in the
books. 13The sea gave up the dead that
were in it, and death and Hades[i] gave up
the dead[j] that were in them, and each
person was judged according to what they
had done. 14Then death[k] and Hades were
thrown into the lake of fire. The lake of
fire is the second death. 15Anyone whose
name was not found written in the book
of life[l] was thrown into the lake of fire.

20:10 [d]Rev 14:10,11
20:11 [e]Rev 4:2
20:12 [f]Da 7:10 [g]Rev 3:5 [h]Jer 17:10; Mt 16:27; Rev 2:23
20:13 [i]Rev 6:8 [j]Isa 26:19
20:14 [k]1Co 15:26
20:15 [l]ver 12
21:1 [m]Isa 65:17; 2Pe 3:13
21:2 [n]Heb 11:10; 12:22; Rev 3:12
21:3 [o]2Co 6:16
21:4 [p]Rev 7:17 [q]1Co 15:26; Rev 20:14 [r]Isa 35:10; 65:19
21:5 [s]Rev 4:9; 20:11 [t]Rev 19:9
21:6 [u]Rev 16:17 [v]Rev 1:8; 22:13

A New Heaven and a New Earth

21 Then I saw "a new heaven and a
new earth,"[a][m] for the first heaven
and the first earth had passed away, and
there was no longer any sea. 2I saw the
Holy City, the new Jerusalem, coming
down out of heaven from God,[n] prepared
as a bride beautifully dressed for her husband. 3And I heard a loud voice from
the throne saying, "Look! God's dwelling place is now among the people, and
he will dwell with them. They will be
his people, and God himself will be with
them and be their God.[o] 4'He will wipe
every tear from their eyes.[p] There will be
no more death'[b][q] or mourning or crying
or pain,[r] for the old order of things has
passed away."

5He who was seated on the throne[s]
said, "I am making everything new!"
Then he said, "Write this down, for these
words are trustworthy and true."[t]

6He said to me: "It is done.[u] I am the
Alpha and the Omega,[v] the Beginning
and the End. To the thirsty I will give
water without cost from the spring of the

[a] *1* Isaiah 65:17 [b] *4* Isaiah 25:8

20:11–15 That there is "no place" for earth and sky (v. 11) reveals how dramatic is God's appearance as judge. The sight of God will banish creation; but in the new creation, his servants will see his face (22:4–5).

20:12–13 The "books" in v. 12 also contribute to this picture of dread for the wicked. "Hades" is the realm of the dead (v. 13), and those remaining in it are those not raised at the first resurrection (vv. 4–6); hence, the damned. That the sea must give up its dead answers the concern of many people in antiquity, including some Jews contemplating the resurrection, concerning the fate of the unburied.

20:14–15 The stark picture of the banishment of the wicked to a place of fire is meant to grip the hearer's attention, but it would not surprise an early Jewish-Christian reader. Revelation prefers a graphic picture of a "lake of fire" (vv. 14–15), representing eternal torment (14:10–11), over which God's people have become victorious.

> ✣ **20:1–15** The passage reveals that we may be outnumbered (v. 8), but in the end God's purposes will triumph, and he will keep the church from being ultimately defeated by the world's evil oppressors. We can stand firm against evil even when the battle appears futile; victory belongs to the Lord.
>
> This biblical hope summons us to lives of holiness and love for neighbor in the present. The heavenly books in this passage remind us that the deeds we do in this life really do matter in an ultimate sense.

21:1–8 Two models of new creation—renewal and replacement—existed in early Judaism, but given such factors as the lack of any sea, Revelation seems to use at least the image of the latter.

21:2 The new Jerusalem had become a familiar Jewish expectation. The point of its descent from heaven here is that the city comes from God, not by any human effort or ability. Jewish people regularly called Jerusalem by the title "the Holy City," as here; God renews a holy city once defiled (11:2). This city is the "bride" (21:2), just as we know the church is (2Co 11:2; Eph 5:23).

21:3 The promise that God "will dwell" with his people (v. 3) was a frequent Jewish hope that ultimately points back to a promise of God's covenant for Israel (Ex 25:8), including in the future temple (Eze 43:7, 9). The new Jerusalem is a temple city (Rev 21:22), shaped like the Most Holy Place (v. 16). This will be the most explicit "tabernacling" of God with humanity since the incarnation. All who "are victorious" receive it (v. 7). Emphasizing the presence of representatives from all nations fulfills the promise that many nations will become God's people and that he will live among them (Zec 2:11; cf. Isa 19:25).

21:4–5 The passing of "the old order of things" directly echoes the new-creation promise of Isa 65:16–17; the deliverance from both tears and death echoes Isa 25:8. John is again commanded to write because these words are "trustworthy and true" (v. 5; cf. 19:9).

21:6 The announcement "It is done" suggests that God's purposes in history have come to a conclusion. By declaring that he is "the Alpha and the

water of life.[w] 7Those who are victorious will inherit all this, and I will be their God and they will be my children. 8But the cowardly, the unbelieving, the vile, the murderers, the sexually immoral, those who practice magic arts, the idolaters and all liars[x] — they will be consigned to the fiery lake of burning sulfur. This is the second death."[y]

The New Jerusalem, the Bride of the Lamb

9One of the seven angels who had the seven bowls full of the seven last plagues[z] came and said to me, "Come, I will show you the bride,[a] the wife of the Lamb." 10And he carried me away[b] in the Spirit[c] to a mountain great and high, and showed me the Holy City, Jerusalem, coming down out of heaven from God. 11It shone with the glory of God,[d] and its brilliance was like that of a very precious jewel, like a jasper, clear as crystal.[e] 12It had a great, high wall with twelve gates, and with twelve angels at the gates. On the gates were written the names of the twelve tribes of Israel.[f] 13There were three gates on the east, three on the north, three on the south and three on the west. 14The wall of the city had twelve foundations, and on them were the names of the twelve apostles of the Lamb.

15The angel who talked with me had a measuring rod[g] of gold to measure the city, its gates and its walls. 16The city was laid out like a square, as long as it was wide. He measured the city with the rod and found it to be 12,000 stadia[a] in length, and as wide and high as it is long. 17The angel measured the wall using human measurement, and it was 144 cubits[b] thick.[c] 18The wall was made of jasper,[h] and the city of pure gold, as pure as glass.[i] 19The foundations of the city walls were decorated with every kind of precious stone.[j] The first foundation was jasper, the second sapphire, the third agate, the fourth emerald, 20the fifth onyx, the sixth ruby,[k] the seventh chrysolite, the eighth beryl, the ninth

21:6 [w] Jn 4:10
21:8 [x] 1Co 6:9 [y] Rev 2:11
21:9 [z] Rev 15:1, 6, 7 [a] Rev 19:7
21:10 [b] Rev 17:3 [c] Rev 1:10
21:11 [d] Rev 15:8; 22:5 [e] Rev 4:6
21:12 [f] Eze 48:30-34
21:15 [g] Rev 11:1
21:18 [h] ver 11 [i] ver 21
21:19 [j] Isa 54:11, 12
21:20 [k] Rev 4:3

[a] *16* That is, about 1,400 miles or about 2,200 kilometers [b] *17* That is, about 200 feet or about 65 meters [c] *17* Or *high*

Omega," God reminds us that he is able to accomplish what he promises. Offering water from the spring of life "without cost" (v. 6; cf. 22:17) probably echoes Isa 55:1.

21:7 By itself, suffering does not sufficiently qualify one for the kingdom; rather, one must overcome. The overcomers inherit "all this"—the new and sorrowless world God has prepared for them. God will be the overcomer's God, and the overcomer will be his own child. God had earlier declared Israel his children (Ex 4:22), but here in the end-time he publicly honors individual believers as his own children.

21:8 All these promises culminate in a warning: those who fail to overcome, who prove disobedient, will experience the "second death." The "fiery lake" is the destination for all who will not inherit the new Jerusalem and the new creation of vv. 1–6.

21:9–21 Babylon was in the desert; Jerusalem descends from heaven. That John views the descent of the heavenly Jerusalem from a mountain may represent an ideal location for viewing this sight (Eze 40:2; cf. Mt 4:8). But the mountain itself may point to the end-time Mount Zion (Rev 14:1; cf. Isa 2:2–3), contrasting with the seven hills on which Babylon sits (Rev 17:9).

21:10–11 The older Jewish Christians among John's audience, those who remembered the splendor of the temple destroyed in AD 70, would be touched by a description of new Jerusalem's glorious future.

21:12–14 Wealthy supporters who funded city building projects often had their names inscribed on them. Yet the benefactors named on the new Jerusalem are those whose lives provided foundations for God's people. The gates represent the twelve tribes of Israel (cf. Eze 48:31–34). The foundation stones refer to the twelve apostles of the Lamb, in keeping with the Christian image of the new temple's true foundations (Eph 2:20; Heb 11:10; 1Pe 2:5).

21:15–16 The "measuring rod" (v. 15) allows John to recognize the supernatural enormity of the city (v. 16). It recalls the measuring of Jerusalem (Zec 2:1–2) or the temple (Eze 40–41). Ezekiel's new Jerusalem was 18,000 cubits all around; John's is nearly 2,000 times larger. The symbolic numbers portray this city as the eternal dwelling of God's people.

The new Jerusalem is not merely square but cubic, an unimaginable city 1,500 miles high. The dimensions of the city are not literal so much as to emphasize the city's future glory. The entire city will be like the Most Holy Place. Thus, the city does not need a temple other than the Lord himself (Rev 21:22). Believers will experience God's presence in its full intensity, as never before.

21:18 That the walls are of "jasper" means that they reflect God's glory (4:3), which is perhaps the most important feature of the city (21:19, 23). This jasper was "clear as crystal" (v. 11), like the heavenly waters (4:6; 22:1), to allow the glory of God to shine through. That the city is of gold may reflect images from the original paradise (Ge 2:11–12) but more likely reflects the commonness of what is now regarded as wealth (cf. Rev 3:18). That the gold is like glass suggests again God's glory (4:6; 15:2).

21:19–20 The "precious stone" of the foundations of the city recall the priest's breastplate (Ex 28:17–20). The 12 gates of "pearls" (Rev 21:21) contrasts

topaz, the tenth turquoise, the eleventh
jacinth, and the twelfth amethyst.[a] 21The
twelve gates were twelve pearls, each
gate made of a single pearl. The great
street of the city was of gold, as pure as
transparent glass.[l]
22I did not see a temple[m] in the city,
because the Lord God Almighty[n] and the
Lamb[o] are its temple. 23The city does not
need the sun or the moon to shine on it,
for the glory of God gives it light,[p] and
the Lamb is its lamp. 24The nations will
walk by its light, and the kings of the
earth will bring their splendor into it.[q]
25On no day will its gates ever be shut,[r]
for there will be no night there.[s] 26The
glory and honor of the nations will be
brought into it. 27Nothing impure will
ever enter it, nor will anyone who does
what is shameful or deceitful,[t] but only
those whose names are written in the
Lamb's book of life.

Eden Restored

22 Then the angel showed me the
river of the water of life, as clear
as crystal,[u] flowing[v] from the throne of
God and of the Lamb 2down the middle
of the great street of the city. On each
side of the river stood the tree of life,[w]
bearing twelve crops of fruit, yielding its
fruit every month. And the leaves of the
tree are for the healing of the nations.[x]
3No longer will there be any curse.[y] The
throne of God and of the Lamb will be
in the city, and his servants will serve
him.[z] 4They will see his face,[a] and his
name will be on their foreheads.[b] 5There
will be no more night.[c] They will not
need the light of a lamp or the light of
the sun, for the Lord God will give them
light.[d] And they will reign for ever and
ever.[e]

[a] *20* The precise identification of some of these precious stones is uncertain.

21:21 [l] ver 18
21:22 [m] Jn 4:21, 23 [n] Rev 1:8 [o] Rev 5:6
21:23 [p] Isa 24:23; 60:19, 20; Rev 22:5
21:24 [q] Isa 60:3, 5
21:25 [r] Isa 60:11 [s] Zec 14:7; Rev 22:5
21:27 [t] Isa 52:1; Joel 3:17; Rev 22:14, 15
22:1 [u] Rev 4:6 [v] Eze 47:1; Zec 14:8
22:2 [w] Rev 2:7 [x] Eze 47:12
22:3 [y] Zec 14:11 [z] Rev 7:15
22:4 [a] Mt 5:8 [b] Rev 14:1
22:5 [c] Rev 21:25 [d] Rev 21:23 [e] Da 7:27; Rev 20:4

Rev 21:22–27 ❖ Everything good from the nations will be brought into God's holy city. What treasures or gifts might our own culture or people bring?

Rev 22 ❖ What part of John's vision of God's holy city fills you with the most hope or joy? Why?

---

sharply with Babylon's gaudy but inferior pearl decorations (17:4; 18:12, 16).

21:22 The new city itself is a temple, the dwelling place of God (vv. 3, 16, 22). God lives among his people, and they live in him—a present reality, taken to a deeper level in the age to come.

21:23–24 This is the most positive possible vision of the future: Whereas Gentiles once trampled the temple city (11:2), now they honor it. The nations walk in the light of Jerusalem. The nations bring more than wealth; they offer their glory to God (v. 23). They can enter the city, however, only because their names are in "the Lamb's book of life" (v. 27).

21:23 Not only will the city have no temple, but it will require neither sun nor moon. The new Jerusalem is full of continual light.

21:25–27 That the gates of the new Jerusalem are never closed (v. 25) suggests unlimited access. New Jerusalem welcomes all (22:17) and has no enemies to fear. But the promised joy of the new Jerusalem serves as a warning as well as a comfort, for not all will inhabit it (21:27).

22:1–5 This passage climaxes John's vision of a new creation.

22:1–2 That a "river" flows from God's throne may reflect biblical images of water flowing from the future Zion (Eze 47:1–12; Zec 14:8). This crystal river replaces the earlier crystal sea (Rev 4:6).

The river "of the water of life" (22:1) probably evokes the rivers of the first paradise (Ge 2:10), especially given the conjunction of this image with the "tree of life" (22:2). Revelation's tree comes from the various fruit trees for healing on either side of the temple river in Eze 47:12; unlike trees whose fruits were seasonal (e.g., Mk 11:13), these trees bear fruit every month.

22:3 The specific language of abolishing the curse refers to Zec 14:11. But in this context about paradise, abolishing the curse also means reversing the fall (Ge 3:14, 17). That his servants will "serve" him may imply worship; this is a common Christian meaning of the Greek word for "serve" used here.

22:4–5 The righteous "will see [God's] face" (22:4). God's children will live with him (21:3) and see his glory (22:4–5). Such light obliterates the night (21:25; 22:5).

21:1—22:5 The time for adorning ourselves with "righteous acts" (19:8) is now. Even though Revelation emphasizes the new Jerusalem as a future city, it is being built in the present. If the character of Babylon is evident in the world around us, the glory of God's presence among us should be revealed in the way we live.

In John's theology, God's glory is revealed in us through how we treat one another (Jn 13:34–35; 17:22–23; 1Jn 4:12). In NT theology, though hope directs our attention toward the future, it also has implications for how we live in the present (Ro 12:12; Col 1:4–5; Titus 2:12–13; 1Jn 3:3). The most faithful of John's audience (esp. in Smyrna and Philadelphia) would have seen themselves as a persecuted minority, but Revelation also summons them to see themselves as heirs of the future. If we see ourselves according to the destiny to which God has called us, we will act accordingly.

CHARACTER OF GOD // GOD WINS

Revelation 22:3–4, 20: No longer will there be any curse. The throne of God and of the Lamb will be in the city, and his servants will serve him. They will see his face, and his name will be on their foreheads. There will be no more night . . . He who testifies to these things says, "Yes, I am coming soon."

Revelation 22 summarizes the culmination of human history. In just a few short verses, those who believe in God and who accept his salvation through Jesus Christ have a beautiful vision of how death and evil will ultimately be defeated—overwhelmed by the justice of a holy God who longs to lovingly restore his creation.

In this chapter we have so much to look forward to. God's purity (v. 1), his eternal provision (v. 2), and his removal of the curse of Genesis 3:17–19 (Rev 22:3) will overwhelm and restore creation. We will all directly see his face and identify with him (v. 4), and God will reign in light forever and ever (v. 5). Darkness will flee (Isa 9:2): It will have no place any longer.

These words are reliable (Rev 22:6). They will come to pass; Jesus will return to earth, just as he promised (vv. 7, 20). John himself testified to the reliability of the prophecy, and we all have the benefit of reading it and living into that wondrous hope (vv. 8–11).

Jesus' imminent approach (v. 12), his identity (v. 13), and his testimony (v. 16) prove that he is the One who exercises loving control over all things. His free gift of salvation, like refreshing water (v. 17), is for all who will humble themselves, realize the depth of their need, and receive it. No matter who we are or what we've done, the offer stands for all who will come to him.

APPLICATION ✣ The words of Revelation chapter 22 have fueled ultimate hope for billions of believers throughout the world and throughout the centuries. God has summarized his Word to his people in these final few verses, making sure that all Scripture, from Genesis to Revelation, ends on this note of ultimate triumph.

Eden will be restored. God's people will live with him forever in a completely renewed creation. Justice will reign because our holy God will be in control.

There is no doubt about any of these prophecies, for "these words are trustworthy and true" (v. 6). The God who ensured that this prophecy was written down and given to the saints throughout the ages will bring all these things to pass; the God who wanted us to read this chapter today also wants us to have this enduring hope.

Make no mistake about it: In the end, God wins. "Amen. Come, Lord Jesus" (v. 20).

John and the Angel

6The angel said to me,[f] "These words
are trustworthy and true.[g] The Lord, the
God who inspires the prophets,[h] sent his
angel[i] to show his servants the things
that must soon take place."

7"Look, I am coming soon![j] Blessed[k]
is the one who keeps the words of the
prophecy written in this scroll."

8I, John, am the one who heard and
saw these things.[l] And when I had heard
and seen them, I fell down to worship
at the feet[m] of the angel who had been
showing them to me. 9But he said to
me, "Don't do that! I am a fellow servant
with you and with your fellow prophets
and with all who keep the words of this
scroll.[n] Worship God!"[o]
10Then he told me, "Do not seal up[p]
the words of the prophecy of this scroll,
because the time is near.[q] 11Let the one
who does wrong continue to do wrong;
let the vile person continue to be vile; let

22:6 [f] Rev 1:1 [g] Rev 19:9; 21:5 [h] Heb 12:9 [i] ver 16
22:7 [j] Rev 3:11 [k] Rev 1:3
22:8 [l] Rev 1:1 [m] Rev 19:10
22:9 [n] ver 10, 18, 19 [o] Rev 19:10
22:10 [p] Da 8:26; Rev 10:4 [q] Rev 1:3

22:6 Most of this verse repeats the announcement in 1:1 that God had sent his message by his angel. The promise of his coming and his blessing on the obedient in 22:7 echoes 1:3. These echoes let the hearers know that the book is nearly at its end.
22:7–13 The promise of "coming soon" frames vv. 7–12 and in a broader way vv. 7–20, forming a recurrent theme of the closing section.
22:8–9 In 22:8, John mentions his own name for the first time since ch. 1 (1:1, 4, 9) to provide eyewitness testimony. That the prophetic angel refuses John's worship (22:8–9; cf. 19:10) reminds the reader that God and the Lamb alone are worthy of worship.
22:10–12 God instructed Daniel to seal up his prophecy (Da 12:4, 9). By contrast, Revelation must remain unsealed (22:10), for it addresses events that had already begun in that period. The time appears so near that each may as well continue in his or her

the one who does right continue to do
right; and let the holy person continue
to be holy."[r]

Epilogue: Invitation and Warning

12"Look, I am coming soon![s] My reward
is with me,[t] and I will give to each person
according to what they have done. 13I am
the Alpha and the Omega,[u] the First and
the Last,[v] the Beginning and the End.[w]
14"Blessed are those who wash their
robes, that they may have the right to
the tree of life[x] and may go through the
gates[y] into the city.[z] 15Outside[a] are the
dogs,[b] those who practice magic arts,
the sexually immoral, the murderers,
the idolaters and everyone who loves
and practices falsehood.
16"I, Jesus,[c] have sent my angel to give
you[a] this testimony for the churches.[d] I
am the Root[e] and the Offspring of David,
and the bright Morning Star."[f]
17The Spirit[g] and the bride say, "Come!"
And let the one who hears say, "Come!"
Let the one who is thirsty come; and let
the one who wishes take the free gift of
the water of life.

18I warn everyone who hears the words
of the prophecy of this scroll: If anyone
adds anything to them,[h] God will add to
that person the plagues described in this
scroll.[i] 19And if anyone takes words away[j]
from this scroll of prophecy, God will take
away from that person any share in the
tree of life and in the Holy City, which
are described in this scroll.
20He who testifies to these things[k]
says, "Yes, I am coming soon."
Amen. Come, Lord Jesus.[l]
21The grace of the Lord Jesus be with
God's people.[m] Amen.

22:11 [r] Eze 3:27; Da 12:10
22:12 [s] ver 7,20 [t] Isa 40:10
22:13 [u] Rev 1:8 [v] Rev 1:17 [w] Rev 21:6
22:14 [x] Rev 2:7 [y] Rev 21:12 [z] Rev 21:27
22:15 [a] 1Co 6:9, 10; Gal 5:19-21; Col 3:5,6 [b] Php 3:2
22:16 [c] Rev 1:1 [d] Rev 1:4 [e] Rev 5:5 [f] 2Pe 1:19; Rev 2:28
22:17 [g] Rev 2:7
22:18 [h] Dt 4:2; Pr 30:6 [i] Rev 15:6-16:21
22:19 [j] Dt 4:2
22:20 [k] Rev 1:2 [l] 1Co 16:22
22:21 [m] Ro 16:20

[a] *16* The Greek is plural.

---

current behavior (v. 11), receiving the reward that is due (v. 12). God is not literally inviting anyone to continue in rebellion; the language is ironic, serving the rhetorical function of challenging unrepentance, as is often done in the biblical prophets.

Jesus will be the judge on the final day (v. 12), a role non-Christian Judaism reserved in its most exclusive sense for God. Those who catch the allusion to Isaiah will recognize even more plainly that Jesus claims to be divine here (cf. Isa 40:10; 62:11). Revelation reinforces this implication of Christ's deity in 22:13, where the speaker is called "the First and the Last"—hence, God himself (Isa 41:4; 44:6; 48:12).

22:14–15 Those who are prepared for Jesus' return, dependent on his blood, may partake of "the tree of life" (vv. 2, 14; 2:7) and enter "through the gates into the city" (22:14).

Just as the gates were open only for those in the Lamb's book of life in 21:25–27, so in 22:15 Jesus provides a partial list of those who will be excluded. Those who practice magic arts, the sexually immoral, and idolaters all participate in the system of the beast; those who participate in the killing of Christians count as murderers; those who love and live according to "falsehood" (v. 15) presumably include those deceived by the antichrist's system. "Dogs" may develop further the warning against sexual immorality (v. 15).

22:16 Jesus is not merely "the Offspring of David," but his "Root." Whereas the promised Messiah is a branch from David's family line (Isa 11:1), this passage presents him as much more: as the very root from which David's line grew. As the "bright Morning Star," Jesus compares his glory with a celestial body often worshiped by John's contemporaries and claims to be Messiah (Nu 24:17).

22:17 "The Spirit" in v. 17 is probably the Spirit who inspires the prophets to speak. With the word "Come," the Spirit and bride may invite the thirsty to drink. But it is more likely that in the word "Come," they are crying for Jesus to come. This invitation to "the water of life" from God's throne probably indicates the present availability of the water as well as an invitation to drink in the future. One's "share in the tree of life and in the Holy City" (v. 19) refers to a future inheritance (21:7), but it is not incompatible with the present foretaste of the kingdom, like the concept of eternal life in John's Gospel (Jn 3:16).

22:18–21 The final of John's seven letters to the churches indicates that believers may dine with Jesus in the present (3:20) and so receive his spiritual adornment (21:2, 19), wealth (21:18), and healing (22:2) in the present era (3:18). We are promised future glory, but we can experience a foretaste of that glory in our present relationship with God.

John adds a solemn curse against anyone who tries to change the book (22:18–19). This refers to the individual book of Revelation (though the *principle* applies to the rest of the Bible also). John also adds another testimony by Jesus, the faithful witness (v. 20).

Revelation closes with what was probably at that time a familiar prayer, "Come, Lord Jesus" (v. 20). Roughly the same prayer appears in 1Co 16:22, which suggests that these words reflect the longing of even the earliest Aramaic-speaking churches, which already recognized Jesus as the coming, divine Lord.

22:6–21 Not every Christian today feels comfortable praying, "Come, Lord Jesus" (v. 20). Suffering Christians long for Jesus' return, but some people are more comfortable with the world and view the end of the present world order with anxiety. Sometimes we love things that are not wrong, but if we long for them more than we long for Jesus, those priorities are wrong. Any other longing we have will be but a shadow of our desire for the greatest and truest love available—the love to which the Lamb's shed blood stands as an eternal testimony.

Table of Weights and Measures

	Biblical Unit	Approximate American Equivalent	Approximate Metric Equivalent
Weights	talent (60 minas)	75 pounds	34 kilograms
	mina (50 shekels)	1 1/4 pounds	560 grams
	shekel (2 bekas)	2/5 ounce	11.5 grams
	pim (2/3 shekel)	1/4 ounce	7.8 grams
	beka (10 gerahs)	1/5 ounce	5.7 grams
	gerah	1/50 ounce	0.6 gram
	daric	1/3 ounce	8.4 grams
Length	cubit	18 inches	45 centimeters
	span	9 inches	23 centimeters
	handbreadth	3 inches	7.5 centimeters
	stadion (pl. stadia)	600 feet	183 meters
Capacity			
Dry Measure	cor [homer] (10 ephahs)	6 bushels	220 liters
	lethek (5 ephahs)	3 bushels	110 liters
	ephah (10 omers)	3/5 bushel	22 liters
	seah (1/3 ephah)	7 quarts	7.5 liters
	omer (1/10 ephah)	2 quarts	2 liters
	cab (1/18 ephah)	1 quart	1 liter
Liquid Measure	bath (1 ephah)	6 gallons	22 liters
	hin (1/6 bath)	1 gallon	3.8 liters
	log (1/72 bath)	1/3 quart	0.3 liter

The figures of the table are calculated on the basis of a shekel equaling 11.5 grams, a cubit equaling 18 inches and an ephah equaling 22 liters. The quart referred to is either a dry quart (slightly larger than a liter) or a liquid quart (slightly smaller than a liter), whichever is applicable. The ton referred to in the footnotes is the American ton of 2,000 pounds. These weights are calculated relative to the particular commodity involved. Accordingly, the same measure of capacity in the text may be converted into different weights in the footnotes.

This table is based upon the best available information, but it is not intended to be mathematically precise; like the measurement equivalents in the footnotes, it merely gives approximate amounts and distances. Weights and measures differed somewhat at various times and places in the ancient world. There is uncertainty particularly about the ephah and the bath; further discoveries may shed more light on these units of capacity.

Feature Indexes

Character of God

People to Know

Maps

Charts

Contributors

NIV Application Commentary Series Authors

John H. Walton ◆ Genesis
Peter E. Enns ◆ Exodus
Roy Gane ◆ Leviticus, Numbers
Daniel I. Block ◆ Deuteronomy
Robert L. Hubbard Jr ◆ Joshua
K. Lawson Younger Jr ◆ Judges, Ruth
Bill T. Arnold ◆ 1 and 2 Samuel
August H. Konkel ◆ 1 and 2 Kings
Andrew E. Hill ◆ 1 and 2 Chronicles
Donna Petter & **Thomas Petter** ◆ Ezra, Nehemiah
Karen H. Jobes ◆ Esther
John H. Walton ◆ Job
Gerald H. Wilson ◆ Psalms, Volume 1: 1–72
W. Dennis Tucker Jr & **Jamie A. Grant** ◆ Psalms, Volume 2: 73–150
Paul E. Koptak ◆ Proverbs
Iain Provan ◆ Ecclesiastes, Song of Songs
John N. Oswalt ◆ Isaiah
J. Andrew Dearman ◆ Jeremiah, Lamentations
Iain M. Duguid ◆ Ezekiel
Tremper Longman III ◆ Daniel
Gary V. Smith ◆ Hosea, Amos, Micah
James Bruckner ◆ Haggai, Zechariah
Mark J. Boda ◆ Jonah, Nahum, Habakkuk, Zephaniah
David W. Baker ◆ Joel, Obadiah, Malachi
Michael J. Wilkins ◆ Matthew
David E. Garland ◆ Mark
Darrell L. Bock ◆ Luke
Gary M. Burge ◆ John
Ajith Fernando ◆ Acts
Douglas J. Moo ◆ Romans

Craig L. Blomberg ◆ 1 Corinthians
Scott J. Hafemann ◆ 2 Corinthians
Scot McKnight ◆ Galatians
Klyne Snodgrass ◆ Ephesians
Frank S. Thielman ◆ Philippians
David E. Garland ◆ Colossians, Philemon
Michael W. Holmes ◆ 1 and 2 Thessalonians
Walter L. Liefeld ◆ 1 and 2 Timothy, Titus
George H. Guthrie ◆ Hebrews
David P. Nystrom ◆ James
Scot McKnight ◆ 1 Peter
Douglas J. Moo ◆ 2 Peter, Jude
Gary M. Burge ◆ The Letters of John
Craig S. Keener ◆ Revelation

NIV Application Commentary General Editor

Terry C. Muck

NIV Application Commentary and *NIV Application Bible* Consulting Editors

Karen H. Jobes
Tremper Longman III
Scot McKnight
Douglas J. Moo
John H. Walton

Chart Your Course Reading Plans

This curated selection of reading plans has been designed to appeal to anyone with an interest in spending time in the Bible on a regular basis. Each of these plans will help lead students of the Bible to a better understanding of God and his Word. Topical, Annual, and Three-Year Reading Plans are included to offer a wide range of engagement—both short-term and long term—to match readers' interests and schedules.

Topical Reading Plans*

52 Weeks on the Character of God

For this reading plan, simply turn to the index on p. 2161 and read one entry per week along with any related Scripture passages.

Two Weeks on the Life and Teachings of Jesus

- ❑ Day 1 ◆ Luke 1: Preparing for Jesus' arrival.
- ❑ Day 2 ◆ Luke 2: The story of Jesus' birth.
- ❑ Day 3 ◆ Mark 1: The beginning of Jesus' ministry.
- ❑ Day 4 ◆ Mark 9: A day in the life of Jesus.
- ❑ Day 5 ◆ Matthew 5: The Sermon on the Mount.
- ❑ Day 6 ◆ Matthew 6: The Sermon on the Mount.
- ❑ Day 7 ◆ Luke 15: Parables of Jesus.
- ❑ Day 8 ◆ John 3: A conversation with Jesus.
- ❑ Day 9 ◆ John 14: Jesus' final instructions.
- ❑ Day 10 ◆ John 17: Jesus' prayer for his disciples.
- ❑ Day 11 ◆ Matthew 26: Betrayal and arrest.
- ❑ Day 12 ◆ Matthew 27: Jesus' execution on a cross.
- ❑ Day 13 ◆ John 20: Resurrection.
- ❑ Day 14 ◆ Luke 24: Jesus' appearance after resurrection.

*Note that the two-week reading plans originally appeared in the *NIV Student Bible*, which was written and edited by Philip Yancey and Tim Stafford.

Two Weeks on the Life and Teachings of Paul

- ❑ Day 1 ◆ Acts 9: The conversion of Saul.
- ❑ Day 2 ◆ Acts 16: Paul's Macedonian call and a jailbreak.
- ❑ Day 3 ◆ Acts 17: Scenes from Paul's missionary journey.
- ❑ Day 4 ◆ Acts 26: Paul tells his life story to a king.
- ❑ Day 5 ◆ Acts 27: Shipwreck on the way to Rome.
- ❑ Day 6 ◆ Acts 28: Paul's arrival in Rome.
- ❑ Day 7 ◆ Romans 3: Paul's theology in a nutshell.
- ❑ Day 8 ◆ Romans 7: Struggle with sin.
- ❑ Day 9 ◆ Romans 8: Life in the Spirit.
- ❑ Day 10 ◆ 1 Corinthians 13: Paul's description of love.
- ❑ Day 11 ◆ 1 Corinthians 15: Thoughts on the afterlife.
- ❑ Day 12 ◆ Galatians 5: Freedom in Christ.
- ❑ Day 13 ◆ Ephesians 3: Paul's summary of his mission.
- ❑ Day 14 ◆ Philippians 2: Imitating Christ.

Two Weeks on the Old Testament

- ❑ Day 1 ◆ Genesis 1: The story of creation.
- ❑ Day 2 ◆ Genesis 3: The origin of sin.
- ❑ Day 3 ◆ Genesis 22: Abraham and Isaac.
- ❑ Day 4 ◆ Exodus 3: Moses' encounter with God.
- ❑ Day 5 ◆ Exodus 20: The gift of the Ten Commandments.
- ❑ Day 6 ◆ 1 Samuel 17: David and Goliath.
- ❑ Day 7 ◆ 2 Samuel 11: David and Bathsheba.
- ❑ Day 8 ◆ 2 Samuel 12: Nathan's rebuke of the king.
- ❑ Day 9 ◆ 1 Kings 18: Elijah and the prophets of Baal.
- ❑ Day 10 ◆ Job 38: God's answer to Job.
- ❑ Day 11 ◆ Psalm 51: A classic confession.
- ❑ Day 12 ◆ Isaiah 40: Words of comfort from God.
- ❑ Day 13 ◆ Daniel 6: Daniel and the lions.
- ❑ Day 14 ◆ Amos 4: A prophet's stern warning.

Two Weeks on Becoming a Christian

- ❑ Day 1 ◆ Genesis 3: The first sin creates a need.
- ❑ Day 2 ◆ Isaiah 52: Salvation prophesied.
- ❑ Day 3 ◆ Isaiah 53: The role of the suffering servant.
- ❑ Day 4 ◆ Luke 15: Three stories about God's love.
- ❑ Day 5 ◆ John 3: Jesus explains "born again."
- ❑ Day 6 ◆ John 10: The Good Shepherd.
- ❑ Day 7 ◆ Acts 8: Conversions spread outside the Jewish community.
- ❑ Day 8 ◆ Acts 26: Paul testifies of his conversion before a king.
- ❑ Day 9 ◆ Romans 3: God's provision for sin.
- ❑ Day 10 ◆ Romans 5: Peace with God.
- ❑ Day 11 ◆ Galatians 3: Salvation unavailable by obeying the law.
- ❑ Day 12 ◆ Ephesians 2: New life in Christ.
- ❑ Day 13 ◆ 1 Peter 1: Future rewards of salvation.
- ❑ Day 14 ◆ 2 Peter 1: Making your salvation sure.

Two Weeks on Prayers of the Bible

- ❑ Day 1 ◆ Genesis 18: Abraham's plea for Sodom.
- ❑ Day 2 ◆ Exodus 15: Moses' song to the Lord.
- ❑ Day 3 ◆ Exodus 33: Moses meets with God.
- ❑ Day 4 ◆ 2 Samuel 7: David's response to God's promises.
- ❑ Day 5 ◆ 1 Kings 8: Solomon's dedication of the temple.
- ❑ Day 6 ◆ 2 Chronicles 20: Jehoshaphat prays for victory.
- ❑ Day 7 ◆ Ezra 9: Ezra's prayer for the people's sins.
- ❑ Day 8 ◆ Psalm 22: A cry to God for help.
- ❑ Day 9 ◆ Psalm 104: A prayer of praise.
- ❑ Day 10 ◆ Daniel 9: Daniel's prayer for the salvation of Jerusalem.
- ❑ Day 11 ◆ Habakkuk 3: A prophet's prayer of acceptance.
- ❑ Day 12 ◆ Matthew 6: The Lord's prayer.
- ❑ Day 13 ◆ John 17: Jesus' prayer for his disciples.
- ❑ Day 14 ◆ Colossians 1: Paul's prayer of thanksgiving.

Two Weeks on the Holy Spirit

- ❑ Day 1 ◆ Judges 14: The Spirit gives Samson strength.
- ❑ Day 2 ◆ 1 Samuel 10: King Saul's experience.
- ❑ Day 3 ◆ Matthew 3:1—4:10: Role in Jesus' baptism and temptation.
- ❑ Day 4 ◆ John 14: Jesus promises the Spirit.
- ❑ Day 5 ◆ John 16: The work of the Spirit.
- ❑ Day 6 ◆ Acts 2: The Spirit comes at Pentecost.
- ❑ Day 7 ◆ Acts 10: The Spirit guides Peter to accept Gentiles.
- ❑ Day 8 ◆ Romans 8: Christians' victory in the Spirit.
- ❑ Day 9 ◆ 1 Corinthians 2: Wisdom from the Spirit.
- ❑ Day 10 ◆ 1 Corinthians 12: Gifts of the Spirit.
- ❑ Day 11 ◆ 1 Corinthians 14: Gifts of tongues and prophecy.
- ❑ Day 12 ◆ Galatians 5: Life in the Spirit.
- ❑ Day 13 ◆ Ephesians 4: Unity and gifts.
- ❑ Day 14 ◆ 1 John 4: Signs of the Spirit.

Two Weeks on Women of the Bible

- ❑ Day 1 ◆ Genesis 2: Eve, the first woman.
- ❑ Day 2 ◆ Genesis 18: Sarah laughs at God's promise.
- ❑ Day 3 ◆ Genesis 24: Rebekah's marriage to Isaac.
- ❑ Day 4 ◆ Genesis 27: Rebekah, the manipulative mother.
- ❑ Day 5 ◆ Judges 4: Deborah's leadership frees her people.
- ❑ Day 6 ◆ Ruth 1: Ruth and Naomi's deep friendship.
- ❑ Day 7 ◆ 1 Samuel 1: Hannah prays for a son.
- ❑ Day 8 ◆ 1 Kings 17: A poor widow and the prophet Elijah.
- ❑ Day 9 ◆ 1 Kings 21: Jezebel, an emblem of wickedness.
- ❑ Day 10 ◆ Esther 2: Esther is chosen as queen.
- ❑ Day 11 ◆ Esther 4: Esther's courage at the risk of death.
- ❑ Day 12 ◆ Luke 1: Mary and Elizabeth receive great news.
- ❑ Day 13 ◆ Luke 2: Mary gives birth to Jesus.
- ❑ Day 14 ◆ John 11: Mary and Martha and their brother's death.

Two Weeks on Men of the Old Testament

- ❑ Day 1 ◆ Judges 6: God calls Gideon to rescue his people.
- ❑ Day 2 ◆ Judges 7: Gideon conquers his fears—and his enemies.
- ❑ Day 3 ◆ 1 Samuel 3: God calls young Samuel.
- ❑ Day 4 ◆ 1 Kings 3: Solomon is given wisdom.
- ❑ Day 5 ◆ 1 Kings 19: Elijah runs for his life.
- ❑ Day 6 ◆ 2 Kings 5: Elisha heals a powerful foreign general.
- ❑ Day 7 ◆ Isaiah 6: God calls the prophet Isaiah.
- ❑ Day 8 ◆ 2 Kings 18: King Hezekiah under military siege.
- ❑ Day 9 ◆ 2 Kings 19: Isaiah speaks God's word to King Hezekiah.
- ❑ Day 10 ◆ 2 Chronicles 34: Josiah sets his nation back on course.
- ❑ Day 11 ◆ Nehemiah 2: Nehemiah courageously begins rebuilding a wall.
- ❑ Day 12 ◆ Jeremiah 38: Jeremiah, in prison, refuses to change his message.
- ❑ Day 13 ◆ Daniel 1: Daniel risks his life in captivity.
- ❑ Day 14 ◆ Daniel 5: Daniel's word to participants in a royal orgy.

Two Weeks on Biblical Justice

- ❑ Day 1 ◆ Exodus 3: God hears the cries of the slaves.
- ❑ Day 2 ◆ Leviticus 25: The Year of Jubilee, a time of economic revolution.
- ❑ Day 3 ◆ Ruth 2: A poor woman finds help.
- ❑ Day 4 ◆ 1 Kings 21: Elijah speaks to a land-grabbing, murderous king.
- ❑ Day 5 ◆ Nehemiah 5: Nehemiah demands justice for the poor.
- ❑ Day 6 ◆ Isaiah 5: Warning to fun-loving materialists.
- ❑ Day 7 ◆ Isaiah 58: Worship that God appreciates.
- ❑ Day 8 ◆ Jeremiah 34: Freedom for slaves.
- ❑ Day 9 ◆ Amos 2: Sins against God by his own people.
- ❑ Day 10 ◆ Amos 6: Warning to the complacent.
- ❑ Day 11 ◆ Micah 6: What the Lord requires.
- ❑ Day 12 ◆ Luke 3: John the Baptist tells how to prepare for Jesus.
- ❑ Day 13 ◆ Matthew 6: Jesus speaks on material things.
- ❑ Day 14 ◆ James 2: How to treat the rich and the poor.

Two Weeks on God and Nature

- ❑ Day 1 ◆ Genesis 1: God creates the earth.
- ❑ Day 2 ◆ Genesis 2: God creates human beings.
- ❑ Day 3 ◆ Proverbs 8: Wisdom's view of creation.
- ❑ Day 4 ◆ Genesis 7: God preserves the species.
- ❑ Day 5 ◆ Job 38: The greatness of nature.
- ❑ Day 6 ◆ Job 39: The wildness of nature.
- ❑ Day 7 ◆ Job 40: God's mastery of nature.

- ❑ Day 8 ◆ Psalm 8: Praise for the Creator.
- ❑ Day 9 ◆ Psalm 98: Nature joins in the praise.
- ❑ Day 10 ◆ Psalm 104: God sustains the earth.
- ❑ Day 11 ◆ Isaiah 40: The ruler of all creation.
- ❑ Day 12 ◆ Romans 8: The "groanings" of our present state.
- ❑ Day 13 ◆ Isaiah 65: Preview of a restored earth.
- ❑ Day 14 ◆ Revelation 22: The end of history.

Further Two-Week Courses for Personal Study

Two Weeks on Abraham, Isaac and Jacob:

Genesis 12, 13, 15, 17, 18, 19, 22, 24, 27, 28, 29, 31, 32, 33.

Two Weeks on Moses and the Exodus:

Exodus 2, 3, 4, 7, 12, 14, 16, 19, 32; Numbers 14; Deuteronomy 1, 2, 4, 31.

Two Weeks on David:

1 Samuel 16, 17, 18, 20, 21, 22, 24; 2 Samuel 6, 7, 11, 12, 13, 15, 18.

Through the Bible in a Year Reading Plan

January

- ❑ January 1 . . . . Genesis 1–4
- ❑ January 2 . . . . Genesis 5–8
- ❑ January 3 . . . . Genesis 9–12
- ❑ January 4 . . . . Genesis 13–17
- ❑ January 5 . . . . Genesis 18–20
- ❑ January 6 . . . . Genesis 21–23
- ❑ January 7 . . . . Genesis 24–25
- ❑ January 8 . . . . Genesis 26–28
- ❑ January 9 . . . . Genesis 29–31
- ❑ January 10 . . . . Genesis 32–35
- ❑ January 11 . . . . Genesis 36–38
- ❑ January 12 . . . . Genesis 39–41
- ❑ January 13 . . . . Genesis 42–43
- ❑ January 14 . . . . Genesis 44–46
- ❑ January 15 . . . . Genesis 47–50
- ❑ January 16 . . . . Exodus 1–4
- ❑ January 17 . . . . Exodus 5–7
- ❑ January 18 . . . . Exodus 8–10
- ❑ January 19 . . . . Exodus 11–13
- ❑ January 20 . . . . Exodus 14–16
- ❑ January 21 . . . . Exodus 17–20
- ❑ January 22 . . . . Exodus 21–23
- ❑ January 23 . . . . Exodus 24–27
- ❑ January 24 . . . . Exodus 28–30
- ❑ January 25 . . . . Exodus 31–34
- ❑ January 26 . . . . Exodus 35–37
- ❑ January 27 . . . . Exodus 38–40
- ❑ January 28 . . . . Leviticus 1–4
- ❑ January 29 . . . . Leviticus 5–7
- ❑ January 30 . . . . Leviticus 8–10
- ❑ January 31 . . . . Leviticus 11–13

February

- ❑ February 1 . . . . Leviticus 14–15
- ❑ February 2 . . . . Leviticus 16–18
- ❑ February 3 . . . . Leviticus 19–21
- ❑ February 4 . . . . Leviticus 22–23
- ❑ February 5 . . . . Leviticus 24–25
- ❑ February 6 . . . . Leviticus 26–27
- ❑ February 7 . . . . Numbers 1–2
- ❑ February 8 . . . . Numbers 3–4
- ❑ February 9 . . . . Numbers 5–6
- ❑ February 10 . . . . Numbers 7
- ❑ February 11 . . . . Numbers 8–10
- ❑ February 12 . . . . Numbers 11–13
- ❑ February 13 . . . . Numbers 14–15
- ❑ February 14 . . . . Numbers 16–18
- ❑ February 15 . . . . Numbers 19–21
- ❑ February 16 . . . . Numbers 22–24
- ❑ February 17 . . . . Numbers 25–26
- ❑ February 18 . . . . Numbers 27–29
- ❑ February 19 . . . . Numbers 30–32
- ❑ February 20 . . . . Numbers 33–36
- ❑ February 21 . . . . Deuteronomy 1–2
- ❑ February 22 . . . . Deuteronomy 3–4
- ❑ February 23 . . . . Deuteronomy 5–8
- ❑ February 24 . . . . Deuteronomy 9–11
- ❑ February 25 . . . . . . Deuteronomy 12–15
- ❑ February 26 . . . . . . Deuteronomy 16–19
- ❑ February 27 . . . . . Deuteronomy 20–23
- ❑ February 28 . . . . . Deuteronomy 24–27

March

- ❑ March 1 . . . . Deuteronomy 28–29
- ❑ March 2 . . . . Deuteronomy 30–32
- ❑ March 3 . . . . Deuteronomy 33–34
- ❑ March 4 . . . . Joshua 1–4
- ❑ March 5 . . . . Joshua 5–7
- ❑ March 6 . . . . Joshua 8–10
- ❑ March 7 . . . . Joshua 11–13
- ❑ March 8 . . . . Joshua 14–17
- ❑ March 9 . . . . Joshua 18–20
- ❑ March 10 . . . . Joshua 21–22
- ❑ March 11 . . . . Joshua 23–24
- ❑ March 12 . . . . Judges 1–3
- ❑ March 13 . . . . Judges 4–5
- ❑ March 14 . . . . Judges 6–8
- ❑ March 15 . . . . Judges 9–10
- ❑ March 16 . . . . Judges 11–13
- ❑ March 17 . . . . Judges 14–16
- ❑ March 18 . . . . Judges 17–19
- ❑ March 19 . . . . Judges 20–21
- ❑ March 20 . . . . Ruth 1–4
- ❑ March 21 . . . . 1 Samuel 1–3
- ❑ March 22 . . . . 1 Samuel 4–7
- ❑ March 23 . . . . 1 Samuel 8–12
- ❑ March 24 . . . . 1 Samuel 13–14
- ❑ March 25 . . . . 1 Samuel 15–16
- ❑ March 26 . . . . 1 Samuel 17–18
- ❑ March 27 . . . . 1 Samuel 19–21
- ❑ March 28 . . . . 1 Samuel 22–24
- ❑ March 29 . . . . 1 Samuel 25–27
- ❑ March 30 . . . . 1 Samuel 28–31
- ❑ March 31 . . . . 2 Samuel 1–3

April

- ❑ April 1 . . . . 2 Samuel 4–7
- ❑ April 2 . . . . 2 Samuel 8–11
- ❑ April 3 . . . . 2 Samuel 12–13
- ❑ April 4 . . . . 2 Samuel 14–16
- ❑ April 5 . . . . 2 Samuel 17–19
- ❑ April 6 . . . . 2 Samuel 20–22
- ❑ April 7 . . . . 2 Samuel 23–24
- ❑ April 8 . . . . 1 Kings 1–2
- ❑ April 9 . . . . 1 Kings 3–5
- ❑ April 10 . . . . 1 Kings 6–7
- ❑ April 11 . . . . 1 Kings 8–9
- ❑ April 12 . . . . 1 Kings 10–12
- ❑ April 13 . . . . 1 Kings 13–15
- ❑ April 14 . . . . 1 Kings 16–18
- ❑ April 15 . . . . 1 Kings 19–20
- ❑ April 16 . . . . 1 Kings 21–22
- ❑ April 17 . . . . 2 Kings 1–3
- ❑ April 18 . . . . 2 Kings 4–5
- ❑ April 19 . . . . 2 Kings 6–8
- ❑ April 20 . . . . 2 Kings 9–10
- ❑ April 21 . . . . 2 Kings 11–13
- ❑ April 22 . . . . 2 Kings 14–16
- ❑ April 23 . . . . 2 Kings 17–18
- ❑ April 24 . . . . 2 Kings 19–21
- ❑ April 25 . . . . 2 Kings 22–23
- ❑ April 26 . . . . 2 Kings 24–25
- ❑ April 27 . . . . 1 Chronicles 1–2
- ❑ April 28 . . . . 1 Chronicles 3–4
- ❑ April 29 . . . . 1 Chronicles 5–6
- ❑ April 30 . . . . 1 Chronicles 7–9

May

- ❑ May 1 . . . . 1 Chronicles 10–12
- ❑ May 2 . . . . 1 Chronicles 13–16
- ❑ May 3 . . . . 1 Chronicles 17–19
- ❑ May 4 . . . . 1 Chronicles 20–23
- ❑ May 5 . . . . 1 Chronicles 24–26
- ❑ May 6 . . . . 1 Chronicles 27–29
- ❑ May 7 . . . . 2 Chronicles 1–4
- ❑ May 8 . . . . 2 Chronicles 5–7
- ❑ May 9 . . . . 2 Chronicles 8–11
- ❑ May 10 . . . . 2 Chronicles 12–16
- ❑ May 11 . . . . 2 Chronicles 17–20
- ❑ May 12 . . . . 2 Chronicles 21–24
- ❑ May 13 . . . . 2 Chronicles 25–28
- ❑ May 14 . . . . 2 Chronicles 29–31
- ❑ May 15 . . . . 2 Chronicles 32–34
- ❑ May 16 . . . . 2 Chronicles 35–36
- ❑ May 17 . . . . Ezra 1–4
- ❑ May 18 . . . . Ezra 5–7
- ❑ May 19 . . . . Ezra 8–10
- ❑ May 20 . . . . Nehemiah 1–3
- ❑ May 21 . . . . Nehemiah 4–7
- ❑ May 22 . . . . Nehemiah 8–9
- ❑ May 23 . . . . Nehemiah 10–11
- ❑ May 24 . . . . Nehemiah 12–13
- ❑ May 25 . . . . Esther 1–3
- ❑ May 26 . . . . Esther 4–7
- ❑ May 27 . . . . Esther 8–10
- ❑ May 28 . . . . Job 1–4
- ❑ May 29 . . . . Job 5–8
- ❑ May 30 . . . . Job 9–12
- ❑ May 31 . . . . Job 13–16

June

- ❑ June 1 . . . . Job 17–20
- ❑ June 2 . . . . Job 21–24
- ❑ June 3 . . . . Job 25–30
- ❑ June 4 . . . . Job 31–34
- ❑ June 5 . . . . Job 35–38
- ❑ June 6 . . . . Job 39–42
- ❑ June 7 . . . . Psalms 1–8
- ❑ June 8 . . . . Psalms 9–17
- ❑ June 9 . . . . Psalms 18–21
- ❑ June 10 . . . . Psalms 22–27
- ❑ June 11 . . . . Psalms 28–33
- ❑ June 12 . . . . Psalms 34–37
- ❑ June 13 . . . . Psalms 38–42
- ❑ June 14 . . . . Psalms 43–49
- ❑ June 15 . . . . Psalms 50–55
- ❑ June 16 . . . . Psalms 56–61
- ❑ June 17 . . . . Psalms 62–68
- ❑ June 18 . . . . Psalms 69–72
- ❑ June 19 . . . . Psalms 73–77
- ❑ June 20 . . . . Psalms 78–80
- ❑ June 21 . . . . Psalms 81–88
- ❑ June 22 . . . . Psalms 89–94
- ❑ June 23 . . . . Psalms 95–103
- ❑ June 24 . . . . Psalms 104–106
- ❑ June 25 . . . . Psalms 107–111
- ❑ June 26 . . . . Psalms 112–118
- ❑ June 27 . . . . Psalm 119
- ❑ June 28 . . . . Psalms 120–133
- ❑ June 29 . . . . Psalms 134–140
- ❑ June 30 . . . . Psalms 141–150

July

- ❑ July 1 . . . . Proverbs 1–3
- ❑ July 2 . . . . Proverbs 4–7
- ❑ July 3 . . . . Proverbs 8–11
- ❑ July 4 . . . . Proverbs 12–14
- ❑ July 5 . . . . Proverbs 15–17
- ❑ July 6 . . . . Proverbs 18–20
- ❑ July 7 . . . . Proverbs 21–23
- ❑ July 8 . . . . Proverbs 24–26
- ❑ July 9 . . . . Proverbs 27–29
- ❑ July 10 . . . . Proverbs 30–31
- ❑ July 11 . . . . Ecclesiastes 1–4
- ❑ July 12 . . . . Ecclesiastes 5–8
- ❑ July 13 . . . . Ecclesiastes 9–12
- ❑ July 14 . . . . Song of Songs 1–4
- ❑ July 15 . . . . Song of Songs 5–8
- ❑ July 16 . . . . Isaiah 1–3
- ❑ July 17 . . . . Isaiah 4–8
- ❑ July 18 . . . . Isaiah 9–11
- ❑ July 19 . . . . Isaiah 12–14
- ❑ July 20 . . . . Isaiah 15–19
- ❑ July 21 . . . . Isaiah 20–24
- ❑ July 22 . . . . Isaiah 25–28
- ❑ July 23 . . . . Isaiah 29–31
- ❑ July 24 . . . . Isaiah 32–34

- ❑ July 25 . . . . Isaiah 35–37
- ❑ July 26 . . . . Isaiah 38–40
- ❑ July 27 . . . . Isaiah 41–43
- ❑ July 28 . . . . Isaiah 44–46
- ❑ July 29 . . . . Isaiah 47–49
- ❑ July 30 . . . . Isaiah 50–52
- ❑ July 31. . . . . Isaiah 53–56

August

- ❑ August 1 . . . . Isaiah 57–59
- ❑ August 2. . . . . Isaiah 60–63
- ❑ August 3. . . . . Isaiah 64–66
- ❑ August 4. . . . . Jeremiah 1–3
- ❑ August 5. . . . . Jeremiah 4–5
- ❑ August 6. . . . . Jeremiah 6–8
- ❑ August 7. . . . . Jeremiah 9–11
- ❑ August 8. . . . . Jeremiah 12–14
- ❑ August 9. . . . . Jeremiah 15–17
- ❑ August 10 . . . . Jeremiah 18–21
- ❑ August 11 . . . . Jeremiah 22–24
- ❑ August 12 . . . . Jeremiah 25–27
- ❑ August 13 . . . . Jeremiah 28–30
- ❑ August 14 . . . . Jeremiah 31–33
- ❑ August 15 . . . . Jeremiah 34–36
- ❑ August 16 . . . . Jeremiah 37–39
- ❑ August 17 . . . . Jeremiah 40–43
- ❑ August 18 . . . . Jeremiah 44–46
- ❑ August 19 . . . . Jeremiah 47–48
- ❑ August 20 . . . . Jeremiah 49
- ❑ August 21 . . . . Jeremiah 50
- ❑ August 22. . . . . Jeremiah 51–52
- ❑ August 23. . . . . Lamentations 1–2
- ❑ August 24 . . . . Lamentations 3–5
- ❑ August 25. . . . . Ezekiel 1–4
- ❑ August 26 . . . . Ezekiel 5–8
- ❑ August 27. . . . . Ezekiel 9–12
- ❑ August 28 . . . . Ezekiel 13–15
- ❑ August 29 . . . . Ezekiel 16–17
- ❑ August 30 . . . . Ezekiel 18–20
- ❑ August 31 . . . . Ezekiel 21–22

September

- ❑ September 1. . . . . Ezekiel 23–24
- ❑ September 2 . . . . Ezekiel 25–27
- ❑ September 3 . . . . Ezekiel 28–30
- ❑ September 4 . . . . Ezekiel 31–32
- ❑ September 5 . . . . Ezekiel 33–35
- ❑ September 6 . . . . Ezekiel 36–38
- ❑ September 7 . . . . Ezekiel 39–40
- ❑ September 8 . . . . Ezekiel 41–43
- ❑ September 9 . . . . Ezekiel 44–46
- ❑ September 10 . . . . Ezekiel 47–48
- ❑ September 11 . . . . Daniel 1–3
- ❑ September 12 . . . . Daniel 4–5
- ❑ September 13 . . . . Daniel 6–8
- ❑ September 14 . . . . Daniel 9–12
- ❑ September 15 . . . . Hosea 1–4
- ❑ September 16 . . . . Hosea 5–9
- ❑ September 17 . . . . Hosea 10–14
- ❑ September 18 . . . . Joel 1–3
- ❑ September 19 . . . . Amos 1–4
- ❑ September 20. . . . . Amos 5–9
- ❑ September 21 . . . . Obadiah and Jonah
- ❑ September 22 . . . . Micah 1–4
- ❑ September 23 . . . . Micah 5–7
- ❑ September 24 . . . . Nahum 1–3
- ❑ September 25 . . . . Habakkuk 1–3
- ❑ September 26 . . . . Zephaniah 1–3
- ❑ September 27 . . . . Haggai
- ❑ September 28 . . . . Zechariah 1–5
- ❑ September 29 . . . . Zechariah 6–10
- ❑ September 30. . . . . Zechariah 11–14

October

- ❑ October 1 . . . . Malachi 1–4
- ❑ October 2. . . . . Matthew 1–4
- ❑ October 3. . . . . Matthew 5–6
- ❑ October 4 . . . . Matthew 7–9
- ❑ October 5. . . . . Matthew 10–11
- ❑ October 6. . . . . Matthew 12–13
- ❑ October 7. . . . . Matthew 14–17
- ❑ October 8. . . . . Matthew 18–20
- ❑ October 9. . . . . Matthew 21–22
- ❑ October 10. . . . . Matthew 23–24
- ❑ October 11 . . . . Matthew 25–26
- ❑ October 12 . . . . Matthew 27–28

- ❑ October 13 . . . . Mark 1–3
- ❑ October 14 . . . . Mark 4–5
- ❑ October 15 . . . . Mark 6–7
- ❑ October 16 . . . . Mark 8–9
- ❑ October 17 . . . . Mark 10–11
- ❑ October 18 . . . . Mark 12–13
- ❑ October 19 . . . . Mark 14
- ❑ October 20 . . . . Mark 15–16
- ❑ October 21 . . . . Luke 1–2
- ❑ October 22 . . . . Luke 3–4
- ❑ October 23 . . . . Luke 5–6
- ❑ October 24 . . . . Luke 7–8
- ❑ October 25 . . . . Luke 9–10
- ❑ October 26 . . . . Luke 11–12
- ❑ October 27 . . . . Luke 13–15
- ❑ October 28 . . . . Luke 16–18
- ❑ October 29 . . . . Luke 19–20
- ❑ October 30 . . . . Luke 21–22
- ❑ October 31 . . . . Luke 23–24

November

- ❑ November 1 . . . . John 1–2
- ❑ November 2 . . . . John 3–4
- ❑ November 3 . . . . John 5–6
- ❑ November 4 . . . . John 7–8
- ❑ November 5 . . . . John 9–10
- ❑ November 6 . . . . John 11–12
- ❑ November 7 . . . . John 13–15
- ❑ November 8 . . . . John 16–17
- ❑ November 9 . . . . John 18–19
- ❑ November 10 . . . . John 20–21
- ❑ November 11 . . . . Acts 1–3
- ❑ November 12 . . . . Acts 4–5
- ❑ November 13 . . . . Acts 6–7
- ❑ November 14 . . . . Acts 8–9
- ❑ November 15 . . . . Acts 10–11
- ❑ November 16 . . . . Acts 12–13
- ❑ November 17 . . . . Acts 14–15
- ❑ November 18 . . . . Acts 16–17
- ❑ November 19 . . . . Acts 18–19
- ❑ November 20 . . . . Acts 20–21
- ❑ November 21 . . . . Acts 22–23
- ❑ November 22 . . . . Acts 24–26
- ❑ November 23 . . . . Acts 27–28
- ❑ November 24 . . . . Romans 1–3
- ❑ November 25 . . . . Romans 4–7
- ❑ November 26 . . . . Romans 8–10
- ❑ November 27 . . . . Romans 11–14
- ❑ November 28 . . . . Romans 15–16
- ❑ November 29 . . . . 1 Corinthians 1–4
- ❑ November 30 . . . . . . 1 Corinthians 5–9

December

- ❑ December 1 . . . . 1 Corinthians 10–13
- ❑ December 2 . . . . 1 Corinthians 14–16
- ❑ December 3 . . . . 2 Corinthians 1–4
- ❑ December 4 . . . . 2 Corinthians 5–9
- ❑ December 5 . . . . 2 Corinthians 10–13
- ❑ December 6 . . . . Galatians 1–3
- ❑ December 7 . . . . Galatians 4–6
- ❑ December 8 . . . . Ephesians 1–6
- ❑ December 9 . . . . Philippians 1–4
- ❑ December 10 . . . . Colossians 1–4
- ❑ December 11 . . . . 1 Thessalonians 1–5
- ❑ December 12 . . . . . 2 Thessalonians 1–3
- ❑ December 13 . . . . 1 Timothy 1–6
- ❑ December 14 . . . . 2 Timothy 1–4
- ❑ December 15 . . . . . . Titus and Philemon
- ❑ December 16 . . . . Hebrews 1–4
- ❑ December 17 . . . . Hebrews 5–8
- ❑ December 18 . . . . Hebrews 9–10
- ❑ December 19 . . . . Hebrews 11–13
- ❑ December 20 . . . . James 1–5
- ❑ December 21 . . . . 1 Peter 1–5
- ❑ December 22 . . . . 2 Peter 1–3
- ❑ December 23 . . . . 1 John 1–5
- ❑ December 24 . . . . 2, 3 John, Jude
- ❑ December 25 . . . . Revelation 1–3
- ❑ December 26 . . . . Revelation 4–7
- ❑ December 27 . . . . Revelation 8–11
- ❑ December 28 . . . . Revelation 12–14
- ❑ December 29 . . . . Revelation 15–17
- ❑ December 30 . . . . Revelation 18–19
- ❑ December 31 . . . . Revelation 20–22

Through the Bible in Three Years Reading Plan*

This three-year plan typically assigns only one chapter a day. (Some short chapters have been combined, so occasionally you will read several brief chapters in a day.) This plan alternates between the Old Testament and New Testament. This mixing provides variety and reduces the fatigue that may set in from reading long sections of the Old Testament.

Genesis

❑ 1 ❑ 2 ❑ 3 ❑ 4 ❑ 5 ❑ 6 ❑ 7
❑ 8 ❑ 9 ❑ 10–11 ❑ 12 ❑ 13 ❑ 14
❑ 15 ❑ 16 ❑ 17 ❑ 18 ❑ 19 ❑ 20
❑ 21 ❑ 22 ❑ 23 ❑ 24 ❑ 25 ❑ 26
❑ 27 ❑ 28 ❑ 29 ❑ 30 ❑ 31 ❑ 32
❑ 33 ❑ 34 ❑ 35 ❑ 36 ❑ 37 ❑ 38
❑ 39 ❑ 40 ❑ 41 ❑ 42 ❑ 43 ❑ 44
❑ 45 ❑ 46 ❑ 47 ❑ 48 ❑ 49 ❑ 50

Matthew 1–9

❑ 1 ❑ 2 ❑ 3 ❑ 4 ❑ 5 ❑ 6 ❑ 7
❑ 8 ❑ 9

Exodus

❑ 1 ❑ 2 ❑ 3 ❑ 4 ❑ 5 ❑ 6 ❑ 7
❑ 8 ❑ 9 ❑ 10 ❑ 11 ❑ 12 ❑ 13 ❑ 14
❑ 15 ❑ 16 ❑ 17 ❑ 18 ❑ 19 ❑ 20
❑ 21 ❑ 22 ❑ 23 ❑ 24 ❑ 25 ❑ 26
❑ 27 ❑ 28 ❑ 29 ❑ 30 ❑ 31 ❑ 32
❑ 33 ❑ 34 ❑ 35 ❑ 36 ❑ 37 ❑ 38
❑ 39 ❑ 40

Matthew 10–20

❑ 10 ❑ 11 ❑ 12 ❑ 13 ❑ 14 ❑ 15
❑ 16 ❑ 17 ❑ 18 ❑ 19 ❑ 20

Leviticus 1–14

❑ 1 ❑ 2 ❑ 3 ❑ 4 ❑ 5 ❑ 6 ❑ 7
❑ 8 ❑ 9 ❑ 10 ❑ 11 ❑ 12 ❑ 13 ❑ 14

Matthew 21–28

❑ 21 ❑ 22 ❑ 23 ❑ 24 ❑ 25 ❑ 26
❑ 27 ❑ 28

Leviticus 15–27

❑ 15 ❑ 16 ❑ 17 ❑ 18 ❑ 19 ❑ 20
❑ 21 ❑ 22 ❑ 23 ❑ 24 ❑ 25 ❑ 26
❑ 27

Mark 1–8

❑ 1 ❑ 2 ❑ 3 ❑ 4 ❑ 5 ❑ 6 ❑ 7
❑ 8

Numbers

❑ 1–2 ❑ 3 ❑ 4 ❑ 5 ❑ 6 ❑ 7 ❑ 8
❑ 9 ❑ 10 ❑ 11 ❑ 12 ❑ 13 ❑ 14 ❑ 15
❑ 16 ❑ 17 ❑ 18 ❑ 19 ❑ 20 ❑ 21
❑ 22 ❑ 23 ❑ 24 ❑ 25 ❑ 26 ❑ 27
❑ 28 ❑ 29 ❑ 30 ❑ 31 ❑ 32 ❑ 33
❑ 34 ❑ 35 ❑ 36

Mark 9–16

❑ 9 ❑ 10 ❑ 11 ❑ 12 ❑ 13 ❑ 14 ❑ 15
❑ 16

Deuteronomy 1–17

❑ 1 ❑ 2 ❑ 3 ❑ 4 ❑ 5 ❑ 6 ❑ 7
❑ 8 ❑ 9 ❑ 10 ❑ 11 ❑ 12 ❑ 13 ❑ 14
❑ 15 ❑ 16 ❑ 17

Luke 1–8

❑ 1 ❑ 2 ❑ 3 ❑ 4 ❑ 5 ❑ 6 ❑ 7
❑ 8

Deuteronomy 18–34

❑ 18 ❑ 19 ❑ 20 ❑ 21 ❑ 22 ❑ 23
❑ 24 ❑ 25 ❑ 26 ❑ 27 ❑ 28 ❑ 29
❑ 30 ❑ 31 ❑ 32 ❑ 33 ❑ 34

*Note that this reading plan originally appeared in the *NIV Student Bible*, which was written and edited by Philip Yancey and Tim Stafford.

Luke 9–16

❑ 9 ❑ 10 ❑ 11 ❑ 12 ❑ 13 ❑ 14 ❑ 15
❑ 16

Joshua

❑ 1 ❑ 2 ❑ 3 ❑ 4 ❑ 5 ❑ 6 ❑ 7
❑ 8 ❑ 9 ❑ 10 ❑ 11 ❑ 12 ❑ 13 ❑ 14
❑ 15 ❑ 16 ❑ 17 ❑ 18 ❑ 19 ❑ 20
❑ 21 ❑ 22 ❑ 23 ❑ 24

Luke 17–24

❑ 17 ❑ 18 ❑ 19 ❑ 20 ❑ 21 ❑ 22
❑ 23 ❑ 24

Judges

❑ 1 ❑ 2 ❑ 3 ❑ 4 ❑ 5 ❑ 6 ❑ 7
❑ 8 ❑ 9 ❑ 10 ❑ 11 ❑ 12 ❑ 13 ❑ 14
❑ 15 ❑ 16 ❑ 17 ❑ 18 ❑ 19 ❑ 20
❑ 21

John 1–7

❑ 1 ❑ 2 ❑ 3 ❑ 4 ❑ 5 ❑ 6 ❑ 7

Ruth

❑ 1 ❑ 2 ❑ 3 ❑ 4

1 Samuel 1–15

❑ 1 ❑ 2 ❑ 3 ❑ 4 ❑ 5 ❑ 6 ❑ 7
❑ 8 ❑ 9 ❑ 10 ❑ 11 ❑ 12 ❑ 13 ❑ 14
❑ 15

John 8–14

❑ 8 ❑ 9 ❑ 10 ❑ 11 ❑ 12 ❑ 13 ❑ 14

1 Samuel 16–31

❑ 16 ❑ 17 ❑ 18 ❑ 19 ❑ 20 ❑ 21
❑ 22 ❑ 23 ❑ 24 ❑ 25 ❑ 26 ❑ 27
❑ 28 ❑ 29 ❑ 30 ❑ 31

John 15–21

❑ 15 ❑ 16 ❑ 17 ❑ 18 ❑ 19 ❑ 20
❑ 21

2 Samuel

❑ 1 ❑ 2 ❑ 3 ❑ 4 ❑ 5 ❑ 6 ❑ 7
❑ 8 ❑ 9 ❑ 10 ❑ 11 ❑ 12 ❑ 13 ❑ 14
❑ 15 ❑ 16 ❑ 17 ❑ 18 ❑ 19 ❑ 20
❑ 21 ❑ 22 ❑ 23 ❑ 24

Acts 1–7

❑ 1 ❑ 2 ❑ 3 ❑ 4 ❑ 5 ❑ 6 ❑ 7

1 Kings 1–11

❑ 1 ❑ 2 ❑ 3 ❑ 4 ❑ 5 ❑ 6 ❑ 7
❑ 8 ❑ 9 ❑ 10 ❑ 11

Acts 8–14

❑ 8 ❑ 9 ❑ 10 ❑ 11 ❑ 12 ❑ 13 ❑ 14

1 Kings 12–22

❑ 12 ❑ 13 ❑ 14 ❑ 15 ❑ 16 ❑ 17
❑ 18 ❑ 19 ❑ 20 ❑ 21 ❑ 22

Acts 15–21

❑ 15 ❑ 16 ❑ 17 ❑ 18 ❑ 19 ❑ 20
❑ 21

2 Kings

❑ 1 ❑ 2 ❑ 3 ❑ 4 ❑ 5 ❑ 6 ❑ 7
❑ 8 ❑ 9 ❑ 10 ❑ 11 ❑ 12 ❑ 13 ❑ 14
❑ 15 ❑ 16 ❑ 17 ❑ 18 ❑ 19 ❑ 20
❑ 21 ❑ 22 ❑ 23 ❑ 24 ❑ 25

Acts 22–28

❑ 22 ❑ 23 ❑ 24 ❑ 25 ❑ 26 ❑ 27
❑ 28

1 Chronicles 1–14

❑ 1 ❑ 2 ❑ 3 ❑ 4 ❑ 5 ❑ 6 ❑ 7
❑ 8 ❑ 9 ❑ 10 ❑ 11 ❑ 12 ❑ 13 ❑ 14

Romans 1–8

❑ 1 ❑ 2 ❑ 3 ❑ 4 ❑ 5 ❑ 6 ❑ 7
❑ 8

1 Chronicles 15–29

❑ 15 ❑ 16 ❑ 17 ❑ 18 ❑ 19 ❑ 20
❑ 21 ❑ 22 ❑ 23–27 ❑ 28 ❑ 29

Romans 9–16

❑ 9 ❑ 10 ❑ 11 ❑ 12 ❑ 13 ❑ 14 ❑ 15
❑ 16

2 Chronicles 1–18

❑ 1 ❑ 2 ❑ 3 ❑ 4 ❑ 5 ❑ 6 ❑ 7
❑ 8 ❑ 9 ❑ 10 ❑ 11 ❑ 12 ❑ 13 ❑ 14
❑ 15 ❑ 16–17 ❑ 18

1 Corinthians 1–9

❑ 1 ❑ 2 ❑ 3 ❑ 4 ❑ 5 ❑ 6 ❑ 7
❑ 8–9

2 Chronicles 19–36

❑ 19 ❑ 20 ❑ 21 ❑ 22 ❑ 23 ❑ 24
❑ 25 ❑ 26–27 ❑ 28 ❑ 29 ❑ 30
❑ 31 ❑ 32 ❑ 33 ❑ 34 ❑ 35 ❑ 36

1 Corinthians 10–16

❑ 10 ❑ 11 ❑ 12 ❑ 13 ❑ 14 ❑ 15
❑ 16

Ezra

❑ 1–2 ❑ 3 ❑ 4 ❑ 5 ❑ 6 ❑ 7 ❑ 8
❑ 9 ❑ 10

Nehemiah

❑ 1 ❑ 2–3 ❑ 4 ❑ 5 ❑ 6 ❑ 7 ❑ 8
❑ 9 ❑ 10 ❑ 11 ❑ 12 ❑ 13

2 Corinthians

❑ 1 ❑ 2–3 ❑ 4 ❑ 5 ❑ 6 ❑ 7 ❑ 8–9
❑ 10 ❑ 11 ❑ 12–13

Esther

❑ 1 ❑ 2 ❑ 3 ❑ 4 ❑ 5 ❑ 6 ❑ 7
❑ 8 ❑ 9–10

Job 1–21

❑ 1 ❑ 2 ❑ 3 ❑ 4 ❑ 5 ❑ 6 ❑ 7
❑ 8 ❑ 9 ❑ 10 ❑ 11 ❑ 12 ❑ 13 ❑ 14
❑ 15 ❑ 16 ❑ 17 ❑ 18 ❑ 19 ❑ 20
❑ 21

Galatians

❑ 1 ❑ 2 ❑ 3 ❑ 4 ❑ 5–6

Job 22–42

❑ 22 ❑ 23 ❑ 24 ❑ 25 ❑ 26 ❑ 27
❑ 28 ❑ 29 ❑ 30 ❑ 31 ❑ 32 ❑ 33
❑ 34 ❑ 35 ❑ 36 ❑ 37 ❑ 38 ❑ 39
❑ 40 ❑ 41 ❑ 42

Ephesians

❑ 1 ❑ 2 ❑ 3 ❑ 4 ❑ 5 ❑ 6

Psalms 1–40

❑ 1–2 ❑ 3–4 ❑ 5 ❑ 6 ❑ 7 ❑ 8 ❑ 9
❑ 10 ❑ 11–12 ❑ 13–14 ❑ 15–16 ❑ 17
❑ 18 ❑ 19 ❑ 20–21 ❑ 22 ❑ 23–24
❑ 25 ❑ 26 ❑ 27 ❑ 28–29 ❑ 30
❑ 31 ❑ 32 ❑ 33 ❑ 34 ❑ 35 ❑ 36
❑ 37 ❑ 38 ❑ 39 ❑ 40

Philippians

❑ 1 ❑ 2 ❑ 3 ❑ 4

Psalms 41–80

❑ 41 ❑ 42 ❑ 43 ❑ 44 ❑ 45
❑ 46–47 ❑ 48 ❑ 49 ❑ 50 ❑ 51
❑ 52 ❑ 53 ❑ 54 ❑ 55 ❑ 56 ❑ 57
❑ 58 ❑ 59 ❑ 60–61 ❑ 62 ❑ 63–64
❑ 65 ❑ 66 ❑ 67 ❑ 68 ❑ 69 ❑ 70
❑ 71 ❑ 72 ❑ 73 ❑ 74 ❑ 75 ❑ 76
❑ 77 ❑ 78 ❑ 79 ❑ 80

Colossians

❑ 1 ❑ 2 ❑ 3 ❑ 4

Psalms 81–121

❑ 81 ❑ 82 ❑ 83 ❑ 84 ❑ 85 ❑ 86
❑ 87 ❑ 88 ❑ 89 ❑ 90 ❑ 91
❑ 92–93 ❑ 94 ❑ 95 ❑ 96
❑ 97 ❑ 98–99 ❑ 100–101 ❑ 102
❑ 103 ❑ 104 ❑ 105 ❑ 106 ❑ 107
❑ 108 ❑ 109 ❑ 110–111 ❑ 112 ❑ 113
❑ 115 ❑ 116–117 ❑ 118 ❑ 119:1–48
❑ 119:49–96 ❑ 119:97–144 ❑ 119:145–176
❑ 120–121

1 Thessalonians

❑ 1–2 ❑ 3–4 ❑ 5

2 Thessalonians

❑ 1–2 ❑ 3

Psalms 122–150

❑ 122–123 ❑ 124–125 ❑ 126–128
❑ 129–130 ❑ 131–132 ❑ 133–134 ❑ 135

❑ 137–138 ❑ 139 ❑ 140 ❑ 141–142
❑ 143 ❑ 144 ❑ 145 ❑ 146 ❑ 147
❑ 148 ❑ 149–150

Proverbs

❑ 1 ❑ 2 ❑ 3 ❑ 4 ❑ 5 ❑ 6 ❑ 7
❑ 8 ❑ 9 ❑ 10 ❑ 11 ❑ 12 ❑ 13 ❑ 14
❑ 15 ❑ 16 ❑ 17 ❑ 18 ❑ 19 ❑ 20
❑ 21 ❑ 22 ❑ 23 ❑ 24 ❑ 25 ❑ 26
❑ 27 ❑ 28 ❑ 29 ❑ 30 ❑ 31

1 Timothy

❑ 1–2 ❑ 3–4 ❑ 5 ❑ 6

Ecclesiates

❑ 1 ❑ 2 ❑ 3 ❑ 4 ❑ 5 ❑ 6 ❑ 7
❑ 8 ❑ 9 ❑ 10 ❑ 11 ❑ 12

Song Of Songs

❑ 1 ❑ 2 ❑ 3 ❑ 4 ❑ 5 ❑ 6 ❑ 7
❑ 8

2 Timothy

❑ 1 ❑ 2 ❑ 3 ❑ 4

Isaiah 1–36

❑ 1 ❑ 2 ❑ 3 ❑ 4 ❑ 5 ❑ 6 ❑ 7
❑ 8 ❑ 9 ❑ 10 ❑ 11 ❑ 12 ❑ 13 ❑ 14
❑ 15 ❑ 16 ❑ 17 ❑ 18 ❑ 19–20 ❑ 21
❑ 22 ❑ 23 ❑ 24 ❑ 25 ❑ 26 ❑ 27
❑ 28 ❑ 29 ❑ 30 ❑ 31 ❑ 32 ❑ 33
❑ 34 ❑ 35 ❑ 36

Titus

❑ 1 ❑ 2–3

Isaiah 37–66

❑ 37 ❑ 38 ❑ 39 ❑ 40 ❑ 41 ❑ 42
❑ 43 ❑ 44 ❑ 45 ❑ 46 ❑ 47 ❑ 48
❑ 49 ❑ 50 ❑ 51 ❑ 52 ❑ 53 ❑ 54
❑ 55 ❑ 56 ❑ 57 ❑ 58 ❑ 59 ❑ 60
❑ 61 ❑ 62 ❑ 63 ❑ 64 ❑ 65 ❑ 66

Philemon

❑ Philemon

Jeremiah 1–27

❑ 1 ❑ 2 ❑ 3 ❑ 4 ❑ 5 ❑ 6 ❑ 7
❑ 8 ❑ 9 ❑ 10 ❑ 11 ❑ 12 ❑ 13 ❑ 14
❑ 15 ❑ 16 ❑ 17 ❑ 18 ❑ 19 ❑ 20
❑ 21 ❑ 22 ❑ 23 ❑ 24 ❑ 25 ❑ 26
❑ 27

Hebrews 1–7

❑ 1 ❑ 2 ❑ 3 ❑ 4 ❑ 5 ❑ 6 ❑ 7

Jeremiah 27–52

❑ 27 ❑ 28 ❑ 29 ❑ 30 ❑ 31 ❑ 32
❑ 33 ❑ 34 ❑ 35 ❑ 36 ❑ 37 ❑ 38
❑ 39 ❑ 40 ❑ 41 ❑ 42 ❑ 43
❑ 44–45 ❑ 46 ❑ 47 ❑ 48 ❑ 49
❑ 50 ❑ 51 ❑ 52

Hebrew 8–13

❑ 8 ❑ 9 ❑ 10 ❑ 11 ❑ 12 ❑ 13

Lamentations

❑ 1 ❑ 2 ❑ 3 ❑ 4 ❑ 5

Ezekiel 1–24

❑ 1 ❑ 2 ❑ 3 ❑ 4 ❑ 5 ❑ 6 ❑ 7
❑ 8 ❑ 9 ❑ 10 ❑ 11 ❑ 12 ❑ 13 ❑ 14
❑ 15 ❑ 16 ❑ 17 ❑ 18 ❑ 19 ❑ 20
❑ 21 ❑ 22 ❑ 23 ❑ 24

James

❑ 1 ❑ 2 ❑ 3 ❑ 4–5

Ezekiel 25–48

❑ 25 ❑ 26 ❑ 27 ❑ 28 ❑ 29 ❑ 30
❑ 31 ❑ 32 ❑ 33 ❑ 34 ❑ 35 ❑ 36
❑ 37 ❑ 38 ❑ 39 ❑ 40 ❑ 41 ❑ 42
❑ 43 ❑ 44 ❑ 45 ❑ 46 ❑ 47 ❑ 48

1 Peter

❑ 1 ❑ 2 ❑ 3 ❑ 4–5

Daniel

❑ 1 ❑ 2 ❑ 3 ❑ 4 ❑ 5 ❑ 6 ❑ 7
❑ 8 ❑ 9 ❑ 10 ❑ 11 ❑ 12

2 Peter

❑ 1 ❑ 2 ❑ 3

Hosea

❑ 1 ❑ 2–3 ❑ 4 ❑ 5 ❑ 6–7 ❑ 8 ❑ 9
❑ 10 ❑ 11–12 ❑ 13–14

Joel

❑ 1 ❑ 2 ❑ 3

Amos

❑ 1 ❑ 2 ❑ 3 ❑ 4 ❑ 5 ❑ 6 ❑ 7
❑ 8 ❑ 9

Obadiah

❑ Obadiah

Jonah

❑ 1–2 ❑ 3–4

1, 2 & 3 John

❑ 1 John, 2 John, 3 John

Micah

❑ 1 ❑ 2 ❑ 3 ❑ 4 ❑ 5 ❑ 6 ❑ 7

Nahum

❑ 1 ❑ 2 ❑ 3

Jude

❑ Jude

Habakkuk

❑ 1 ❑ 2 ❑ 3

Zephaniah

❑ 1 ❑ 2 ❑ 3

Revelation 1–7

❑ 1 ❑ 2 ❑ 3 ❑ 4–5 ❑ 6 ❑ 7

Haggai

❑ 1 ❑ 2

Revelation 8–14

❑ 8 ❑ 9 ❑ 10–11 ❑ 12 ❑ 13 ❑ 14

Zechariah

❑ 1 ❑ 2 ❑ 3 ❑ 4 ❑ 5 ❑ 6 ❑ 7
❑ 8 ❑ 9 ❑ 10 ❑ 11 ❑ 12–13 ❑ 14

Malachi

❑ 1 ❑ 2 ❑ 3–4

Revelation 15–22

❑ 15–16 ❑ 17 ❑ 18 ❑ 19 ❑ 20 ❑ 21
❑ 22

NIV Dictionary-Concordance

— A —

Aaron—the brother of Moses; he served as Moses' spokesman before Pharaoh (Ex 4:14-16, 27-31; 7:1-2); he was Israel's first high priest (Ex 28:1; Nu 17; Heb 5:1-4).

abandon—to leave completely; to desert.

Abba—the word for *father* in Aramaic, one of the three languages Jesus spoke.

Ro 8:15	And by him we cry, "*A*, Father."
Gal 4:6	the Spirit who calls out, "*A*, Father."

Abel—the second son of Adam (Ge 4:2); he offered a pleasing sacrifice to God (Ge 4:4; Heb 11:4) but was murdered by his brother Cain (Ge 4:8; Mt 23:35; 1Jn 3:12).

abhor—to hate or to turn away from.

Ps 26:5	I *a* the assembly of evildoers
Am 6:8	"I *a* the pride of Jacob

Abigail—the wife of Nabal; she helped save David's life (1Sa 25:14-35) and later became his wife (1Sa 25:36-42).

abolish—to destroy completely; to put an end to.

abomination—a thing to be hated.

abound—to be more than enough; to overflow.

Ex 34:6	slow to anger, *a* in love
Php 1:9	that your love may *a* more

Abraham—the father of the Jewish nation and of all believers. God promised that he would make a mighty nation of Abraham's children and would give them the land of Canaan (Ge 15; 17; 22; Ro 4; Heb 6:13-15). As a test, God told him to offer his son Isaac as a sacrifice (Ge 22; Heb 11:17-19) but withdrew this command when Abraham showed that he would trust God and obey him.

Absalom—a son of David (2Sa 3:3); he plotted to take David's throne. He died when his long hair became tangled in an oak tree and Joab, David's commander, plunged javelins into his heart (2Sa 14—18).

abstain—to keep from doing something.

abundance, abundant—having plenty; more than enough.

Jude 2	Mercy, peace and love be yours in *a*.

Abyss—the place of the dead; the place where evil spirits live.

Achan—an Israelite who kept spoil from the conquest of Jericho for himself; as a result of Achan's stealing what belonged to God, the Israelites were defeated at Ai and he and his family were stoned to death (Jos 7; 22:20).

acknowledge—to know and to say that something is true; to recognize.

Mt 10:32	I will also *a* before my Father in heaven.
1Jn 4:3	spirit that does not *a* Jesus is not from God.

acts—deeds.

Ps 150:2	Praise him for his *a* of power
Isa 64:6	all our righteous *a* are like filthy rags

Adam—the first person God created (Ge 1:26—2:25); he sinned by disobeying God (Ge 3) and in that way brought all people under the curse of sin (Ro 5:12-21).

admonish—to give warning or advice in a caring way.

adorn—to make more beautiful.

adultery—having sexual relations with someone other than one's husband or wife. Spiritual adultery means being unfaithful to God (Jer 3).

Ex 20:14	"You shall not commit *a*.
Mt 5:28	lustfully has already committed *a*

adversary—enemy; opponent.

advice—an opinion given about a decision to be made.

1Ki 12:14	he followed the *a* of the young men
Pr 20:18	Plans are established by seeking *a*;

advocate—1. *(v.)* to speak in favor of; 2. *(n.)* someone who speaks in another person's defense; 3. *(n.)* another name for the Holy Spirit.

Jn 14:16	he will give you another *a* to help you
Jn 14:26	But the *A*, the Holy Spirit,
Jn 15:26	"When the *A* comes, whom I will

affliction—trouble or pain that lasts a long time.

Ro 12:12	patient in *a*, faithful in prayer.

agony—extreme pain of mind or body.

Ahab—a wicked king of Israel; the husband of Jezebel (1Ki 16:31). He caused Israel to worship Baal rather than God (1Ki 16:31–33) and was opposed by God's prophet Elijah (1Ki 17:1; 18; 21).

alabaster—a hard marble like material that can be made into jars, vases or sculptures.

alienate—to make unfriendly; to turn a person's interest or affection away from another person or thing.

allot—to divide and give away in parts. In Old Testament times the land of Canaan was allotted to the 12 tribes of Israel.

Almighty—a name used to show how strong and powerful God is.

Ge 17:1	"I am God *A*; walk before me
Isa 6:3	"Holy, holy, holy is the LORD *A*;

altar—a raised platform made of stones, metal, dirt or wood, on which sacrifices were made.

ambush—the act of hiding in order to attack by surprise.

Amen—Hebrew word that means "so be it" or "let it become true."

Amos—a prophet of Israel who lived about the same time as Hosea and Jonah; he spoke about God's justice and righteousness.

Ananias—1. the husband of Sapphira; he was struck dead for lying to God (Ac 5:1–11); 2. the disciple who baptized Saul (Ac 9:10–19); 3. the high priest before whom Paul was tried in Jerusalem (Ac 22:30—24:1).

ancestor—a person from whom someone is descended.

Ps 78:5	commanded our *a* to teach their children,

ancient—very old.

Andrew—one of the twelve apostles; the brother of Peter (Mt 4:18; 10:2; Ac 1:13).

angel—a heavenly being.

Ps 34:7	The *a* of the LORD encamps
Heb 1:14	Are not all *a* ministering spirits
Heb 2:7	made them a little lower than the *a*;
1Pe 1:12	Even *a* long to look

anger—a strong feeling of displeasure; rage; fury.

Ps 103:8	slow to *a*, abounding in love.
Jas 1:20	human *a* does not produce the righteousness

anguish—extreme pain or distress of mind or body.

Jer 49:24	*a* and pain have seized her;

annihilate—to destroy completely.

anoint—to pour oil on a person's head, either for a physical benefit (Jas 5:14) or to set someone apart for service to God (Ex 28:41).

antichrist—a person who is against Christ.

1Jn 2:18	you have heard that the *a* is coming,
1Jn 2:22	Such a person is the *a*

anxiety—worry.

1Pe 5:7	Cast all your *a* on him

Apollos—a Christian from Alexandria who knew the Scriptures well (Ac 18:24–28) and helped Paul to minister in Corinth (Ac 19:1; 1Co 1:12).

apostle—1. any of the twelve men Jesus chose to work with him during his earthly ministry; after being equipped by the Holy Spirit, they were sent out to preach about Jesus; 2. later, someone who had been with Jesus, had seen his miracles and then taught others about him.

Mt 10:2	These are the names of the twelve *a*:
1Co 12:28	God has placed in the church first of all *a*,
1Co 15:9	For I am the least of the *a*

appalled—overcome with shock or horror.

appeal—to make an earnest request.

1Pe 5:1 I *a* as a fellow elder

appoint—to assign someone officially to a job or position.

Aquila—the husband of Priscilla; Aquila and Priscilla were coworkers with Paul in Corinth (Ac 18; Ro 16:3).

Aramaic—the language that was commonly spoken in the countries east of the Mediterranean Sea during Jesus' earthly ministry.

ark of the covenant law—also called the ark of the covenant; a large gold-covered box, which contained the Ten Commandments (tablets of the covenant law), a jar of manna and Aaron's staff, and was kept inside the Most Holy Place in the tabernacle (tent of meeting). It was a reminder to the Israelites of God's presence with them.

armor—protective clothing worn in battle, usually made of metal.

Eph 6:11 Put on the full *a* of God

aroma—an odor or smell, usually pleasant.

arouse—to excite; to stir to action.

arrest—to officially or lawfully make a prisoner of someone.

arrogant—proud; conceited.

arrow—See bow.

ascend—to go up. Jesus ascended to heaven to return to God the Father.

ascribe—to think of as caused by, coming from or belonging to.

1Ch 16:28 *a* to the LORD glory and strength,

Asherah poles—wooden poles honoring Asherah, the Canaanite goddess of love and war.

Dt 12:3 burn their *A* in the fire;

assemble—to bring a group of people together; to meet together.

Assyria—one of the powerful nations of biblical times; it often attacked the Israelites; its capital was Nineveh.

astray—mistaken; not on the right path; lost.

Isa 53:6 We all, like sheep, have gone *a*,

atone—to make right, by paying the penalty, the relationship between God and humans that was broken through sin. In the Old Testament, people atoned symbolically for their sins by offering sacrifices to God. In the New Testament, Jesus corrected the relationship between God and people once and for all by dying to take away sins.

atonement—the payment that corrects the relationship between God and humans that was broken through sin.

Lev 17:11 it is the blood that makes *a*
Lev 23:27 this seventh month is the Day of *A*.
Ro 3:25 God presented Christ as a sacrifice of *a*,
Heb 2:17 that he might make *a* for the sins

attack—to set upon with force, as in a battle.

authority—the right and power to give orders.

Mt 9:6 the Son of Man has *a* on earth
Mt 28:18 "All *a* in heaven and on earth has
Ro 13:1 for there is no *a* except that which
Heb 13:17 your leaders and submit to their *a*,

avenge—to get back at or punish someone who has done wrong.

Dt 32:35 It is mine to *a*; I will repay.

avoid—to keep away from.

Pr 20:19 *a* anyone who talks too much.

awe—respect and wonder; a holy fear of God because of his great power.

Ps 65:8 earth is filled with *a* at your wonders;

— B —

Baal—the name of many false gods in Canaan.

1Ki 18:25 Elijah said to the prophets of *B*,

Babel—a tower built soon after the flood; the builders were attempting to reach up to God, but God confused their language so that the building was stopped.

Babylon—the beautiful capital of Babylonia; it was a powerful and influential city in the Near East from the eighteenth to the sixth centuries BC. In the New Testament, Babylon represents the godless city.

Ps 137:1 By the rivers of *B* we sat and wept
Rev 14:8 Fallen is *B* the Great,

Balaam—a seer who tried to curse Israel during their journey to the promised land, but God would not allow it (Nu 22—24).

balm—a skin cream used to heal sores and relieve pain.

Jer 8:22 Is there no *b* in Gilead?

banish—to force a person away from a place.

banquet—a formal meal, usually for a large group of people.

baptize—a religious ceremony in which water is used as a symbol of cleansing from sin. Churches today baptize by sprinkling or pouring or immersing in water. Baptism is a sign that sin is washed away.

Mk 1:9 and was *b* by John in the Jordan.
Ac 1:5 but in a few days you will be *b*
Ac 2:38 "Repent and be *b*, every one of you,

Barabbas—the Jews chose this criminal, rather than Jesus, to be released by Pilate (Mt 27:26).

Barnabas—an apostle; he was a coworker with Paul on his first missionary journey (Ac 9:27; Ac 13—15).

barren—1. unable to have children; 2. unable to produce crops.

Bartholomew—one of the twelve apostles (Mt 10:3; Ac 1:13). He was also probably known as Nathanael (Jn 1:45-49; 21:2).

Bathsheba—the wife of Uriah; she committed adultery with David and later became his wife (2Sa 11); she was the mother of Solomon (2Sa 12:24).

Beelzebul—the prince of demons; Satan.

Lk 11:19 if I drive out demons by *B*,

Beersheba—an important town that marked the southern boundary of Judah.

believe—to accept as true; to trust; to have faith.

Mk 1:15 Repent and *b* the good news!"
Mk 9:24 "I do *b*; help me overcome my
Jn 1:7 that through him all might *b*.
Jn 3:18 does not *b* stands condemned
Jn 20:27 Stop doubting and *b*."
Ac 16:31 They replied, "*B* in the Lord Jesus,
Ro 3:22 faith in Jesus Christ to all who *b*.
1Th 4:14 we *b* that Jesus died and rose again

Benjamin—the twelfth son of Jacob. Rachel was his mother, and he was the younger brother of Joseph (Ge 35:16-24; 42—45).

besiege—to surround a city or town completely with an army, so that nothing can go in or out.

bestow—to give.

Bethlehem—the city in Judea where Jesus was born (Mt 2:1).

betray—to turn a friend over to his or her enemies; to be unfaithful to.

Mt 27:3 When Judas, who had *b* him,
1Co 11:23 on the night he was *b*, took bread,

betroth—to promise to marry.

bewildered—confused; puzzled.

bind—1. to tie with a rope or string; 2. to make tight or firm.

Dt 6:8 and *b* them on your foreheads.
Mt 16:19 whatever you *b* on earth will be

birthright—the special rights of the firstborn son. In the Old Testament, after the father died, the oldest son received the father's power and right to make decisions for the entire family. He also got twice as much money and property as each of his brothers.

bitter (bitterness)—having harsh or hateful feelings.

Eph 4:31 Get rid of all *b*, rage
Heb 12:15 and that no *b* root grows up

blameless—without fault.

Ge 17:1 walk before me faithfully and be *b*.
1Co 1:8 so that you will be *b* on the day

blaspheme—to speak carelessly, falsely or insultingly about God or holy things.

Mk 3:29 whoever *b* against the Holy Spirit

blemish—a spot or mark that makes something imperfect.

1Pe 1:19 a lamb without *b* or defect.

bless—1. to make holy; 2. to show favor to; 3. to ask God to show favor to.

Ge 2:3 Then God *b* the seventh day
Ge 12:3 I will *b* those who *b* you,
Mt 5:3 "*B* are the poor in spirit
Ro 12:14 *b* those who persecute you; *b*

blight—a disease in plants that makes them shrivel up and die.

blind—unable to see. Spiritual blindness is an inability to understand the things of God.

Mt 11:5 The *b* receive sight, the lame walk,
Jn 9:25 I was *b* but now I see!"

blood—as the life-giving fluid in the body, it represents life itself. In the Old Testament, the blood of sacrifices symbolized the giving of life for life. Through the blood of Jesus on the cross, believers are saved from death for their sins.

Ex 12:13 and when I see the *b*, I will pass
Lev 17:11 For the life of a creature is in the *b*,
Mt 26:28 This is my *b* of the covenant,
Eph 1:7 we have redemption through his *b*,
Heb 9:12 once for all by his own *b*,

blot—to erase or get rid of.

Ex 32:32 then *b* me out of the book you have
Ps 51:1 *b* out my transgressions.

boast—to brag; to call attention to.

Ps 44:8 In God we make our *b*
Gal 6:14 May I never *b* except in the cross

Boaz—a wealthy man who lived in Bethlehem in the days of the judges; he married Ruth (Ru 2; 4).

body—1. physical part of a person; 2. a group working as a unit.

Pr 3:8 This will bring health to your *b*
Ro 12:1 to offer your *b* as a living sacrifice,
1Co 6:19 not know that your *b* are temples
Eph 5:30 for we are members of his *b*.

bondage—slavery.

Ezr 9:9 God has not forsaken us in our *b*.

born again—refers to the experience of salvation; entering God's family through faith in Christ.

Jn 3:3 no one can see the kingdom of God unless they are *b*.
1Pe 1:23 For you have been *b*,

bow—a weapon made of a strip of flexible material with a cord connecting the two ends and holding the strip bent; used to shoot arrows.

branch—an extension of another body or system.

Jer 33:15 I will make a righteous *B* sprout
Jn 15:5 "I am the vine; you are the *b*.

bread—in Bible times the most important food in the diet.

Dt 8:3 that man does not live on *b* alone
Mt 6:11 Give us today our daily *b*.
Jn 6:35 Jesus declared, "I am the *b* of life.

breastpiece—a decorated square of linen cloth worn by the high priest when he entered the Holy Place.

breastplate—a chest-covering made of metal or leather, worn by soldiers for protection.

bribe—money or favor given to influence judgment or conduct.

Ex 23:8 "Do not accept a *b*,

bride—a woman who is about to get married. The church is called Jesus' bride.

bridegroom—a man who is about to get married. Christ is called the church's bridegroom.

bronze—a metal, the combination of copper and tin, used to make tools, weapons and ornamental articles.

brother—a male who has the same parents as another person.

Ge 4:9 "Am I my *b* keeper?"
Mt 18:15 "If your *b* or sister sins,
2Co 13:11 Finally, *b* and sisters, rejoice!

burden—a heavy load.

Mt 11:30 my yoke is easy and my *b* is light.
Gal 6:2 Carry each other's *b*,

burnt offering—in the Old Testament a sacrifice to the Lord that expressed devotion and complete surrender (Ge 8:20; Ex 29:18).

— C —

Caesar—the title of many Roman emperors.

Lk 2:1 In those days *C* Augustus
Mt 22:21 "Give back to *C* what is Caesar's,

Cain — Adam and Eve's firstborn son; he murdered his brother Abel (Ge 4:1–16).

calamity — a disaster, usually causing great loss and suffering.

Caleb — one of the twelve men who was sent to spy on Canaan. He came back with a positive report and encouraged the Israelites to take possession of Canaan (Nu 13:6—14:38; Dt 1:36).

call — 1. (*v.*) to ask to come; 2. to give a name to; 3. (*n.*) a summons for a particular purpose or job.

2Ch 7:14	if my people, who are *c*
Ps 145:18	near to all who *c* on him,
Mt 9:13	not come to *c* the righteous,
Ro 8:30	And those he predestined, he also *c*;
Ro 11:29	gifts and his *c* are irrevocable.
1Pe 2:9	of him who *c* you out of darkness

camel — a large animal, able to travel long distances and used for transportation of people and goods.

Canaan — 1. the land God promised to the nation of Israel; 2. the promised land.

capstone — the stone that holds two walls together; the stone that finishes a wall.

1Pe 2:7	has become the *c*,"

care — to show concern for.

Ps 8:4	human beings that you *c* for them?
1Pe 5:7	on him because he *c* for you.

cavalry — a group of soldiers riding horses.

censer — a bowl or dish used for carrying hot coals or for burning incense.

census — a count of the population of a group of people.

centurion — a Roman army officer in charge of 100 soldiers.

chaff — the seed covering of a grain such as wheat. In Bible times, the grain and chaff were separated by tossing the grain into the air so the wind could blow the chaff away.

Ps 1:4	They are like *c*
Mt 3:12	up the *c* with unquenchable fire."

chariot — a two-wheeled vehicle pulled by horses.

2Ki 6:17	and *c* of fire all around Elisha.

cheerful — full of joy; pleasant.

Pr 15:13	A happy heart makes the face *c*,
2Co 9:7	for God loves a *c* giver.

cherub (pl. cherubim) — an angel, with an appearance something like a human being.

children — sons and daughters.

Mt 19:14	"Let the little *c* come to me,
Eph 6:1	*C*, obey your parents in the Lord,
1Jn 3:1	that we should be called *c* of God!

choose (chosen) — to select.

Jos 24:15	then *c* for yourselves this day
Mt 22:14	"For many are invited, but few are *c*."
Jn 15:16	You did not *c* me,
Eph 1:4	he *c* us in him before the creation
1Pe 2:9	But you are a *c* people, a royal

Christ — the official title of Jesus, meaning "the Anointed One." It is a Greek word, and it means the same as the Hebrew word *Messiah.*

Jn 1:17	grace and truth came through Jesus *C*.
Ac 3:6	name of Jesus *C* of Nazareth, walk."
Ro 5:8	While we were still sinners, *C* died
Eph 5:23	as *C* is the head of the church,
Php 1:21	to live is *C* and to die is gain.

Christian — a believer in or follower of Christ.

Ac 11:26	The disciples were called *C* first
1Pe 4:16	as a *C*, do not be ashamed,

chronicles — a history of events in the order in which they took place.

church — the entire group of people who believe in Christ.

Mt 16:18	and on this rock I will build my *c*,
Eph 5:23	as Christ is the head of the *c*,
Col 1:24	the sake of his body, which is the *c*.

circumcision — the cutting off of the loose fold of skin at the end of the penis; it symbolized the agreement God made with the Israelites, and they came to be known as "the circumcision" (Eph 2:11).

Ge 17:10	Every male among you shall be *c*.

cistern — a pit dug into the ground for storing rainwater.

citadel—a tower or building, especially in a city, equipped for war.

city of refuge—one of six cities set aside by Moses and Joshua for those who had accidentally killed someone. Such people would be safe there until a fair trial could be held (Nu 35:9–15).

clan—a group of people belonging to the same extended family.

Ge 24:38 to my father's family and to my own *c*,
Zec 12:12 The land will mourn, each *c* by itself,

clean animals—animals God allowed the Israelites to sacrifice and eat.

cleanse—to make clean; to wash.

cloak—a loose-fitting coat without sleeves.

comfort—to relieve from distress; to console.

Ps 23:4 rod and your staff, they *c* me.
2Co 1:4 so that we can *c* those

commandment—an order given by God. God gave the Ten Commandments to the Israelites while they were encamped in the area of Mount Sinai.

Ex 20:6 who love me and keep my *c*.
Ecc 12:13 Fear God and keep his *c*,
Mt 22:38 This is the first and greatest *c*.

commend—1. to praise; 2. to hand over to someone for safekeeping.

Ps 145:4 One generation *c* your works

companion—one who is a friend or associate or helper.

compassion (compassionate)—sympathy; pity.

Ne 9:17 gracious and *c*, slow to anger
Ps 103:4 and crowns you with love and *c*,
Mt 9:36 When he saw the crowds, he had *c*
Ro 9:15 and I will have *c* on whom I have *c*."
Col 3:12 clothe yourselves with *c*, kindness,

conceive—1. to become pregnant; 2. to think up or imagine.

Mt 1:20 what is *c* in her is from the Holy
1Co 2:9 no human mind has *c*

concubine—in Bible times, a woman who belonged to a man but did not have the rights of a wife. She was often one of the spoils of war, and her primary purpose was to bear children for the man.

condemn (condemnation)—to punish; to pronounce guilty.

Jn 3:17 Son into the world to *c* the world,
Ro 8:1 there is now no *c* for those who are

confess—1. to say what you believe; 2. to tell your sins to someone.

2Ti 2:19 "Everyone who *c* the name of the Lord
1Jn 1:9 If we *c* our sins, he is faithful

conform—to agree with and try to be like someone; to do what others say to do.

Ro 8:29 predestined to be *c* to the image
1Pe 1:14 do not *c* to the evil desires you had

conscience—the sense of knowing if something is good or bad; a sense of right and wrong.

Ro 2:15 their *c* also bearing witness,
Titus 1:15 their minds and *c* are corrupted.
Heb 9:14 cleanse our *c* from acts that lead

consecrate—to set aside or dedicate for God's use.

Ex 13:2 "*C* to me every firstborn male.
Lev 20:7 "*C* yourselves and be holy,

consider—to think about carefully.

Ps 8:3 When I *c* your heavens,

console—to comfort.

conspire—to plan together to do wrong.

consult—to ask the advice or opinion of someone.

consume—1. to use up or eat up; 2. to destroy completely.

Jn 2:17 "Zeal for your house will *c* me."
Heb 12:29 for our "God is a *c* fire."

contempt—lack of respect; looking down on someone or something as being worthless.

Pr 14:31 Whoever oppresses the poor shows *c*
1Th 5:20 Do not treat prophecies with *c*

contend—to struggle, as in a contest or against difficulties.

content—satisfied.

Php 4:11 to be *c* whatever the circumstances.
Heb 13:5 and be *c* with what you have,

contrite—to feel sorry for one's sins; to feel repentant.

Ps 51:17 a broken and *c* heart,
Isa 66:2 those who are humble and *c* in spirit,

convert—a person who has changed from one belief to another.

1Ti 3:6 He must not be a recent *c*,

convict—1. to prove one guilty; 2. to make a person feel sorrow.

Jas 2:9 and are *c* by the law as lawbreakers.

copper—a common metal, easy to work with; often used to make coins.

Cornelius—a Roman to whom Peter preached the gospel; he became the first Gentile Christian (Ac 10).

cornerstone—the first or most important stone laid when constructing a building.

Eph 2:20 with Christ Jesus himself as the chief *c*.

corrupt—1. (*v.*) to change something from good to bad; 2. (*adj.*) wicked.

Ge 6:11 Now the earth was *c* in God's sight
1Co 15:33 "Bad company *c* good character."

counsel—to give advice to.

Pr 15:22 Plans fail for lack of *c*,

covenant—1. an agreement between two people or two groups of people, in which both usually make specific promises; 2. the promises of God for salvation.

Ge 9:9 "I now establish my *c* with you
Ex 19:5 if you obey me fully and keep my *c*,
Jer 31:31 "when I will make a new *c*
1Co 11:25 "This cup is the new *c* in my blood;
Heb 9:15 Christ is the mediator of a new *c*,

covet—to want for oneself something that belongs to another person.

Ex 20:17 "You shall not *c* your neighbor's

crafty—sly, clever.

Ge 3:1 Now the serpent was more *c*

crave—to desire strongly; to feel a deep need for.

1Pe 2:2 newborn babies, *c* pure spiritual

create—to make; to bring into being.

Ge 1:1 In the beginning God *c* the heavens
Ps 51:10 *C* in me a pure heart, O God,
Col 1:16 For in him all things were *c*:
Rev 10:6 who *c* the heavens and all that is

crime—an unlawful act.

criminal—someone who commits an unlawful act.

Lk 23:32 Two other men, both *c*,

cripple—a disabled person or animal.

cross—a tall beam with a crossbar on which a criminal was hung or tied to die.

Mt 10:38 Whoever does not take up their *c*
Gal 6:14 in the *c* of our Lord Jesus Christ,
Php 2:8 even death on a *c!*
Col 2:14 taken it away, nailing it to the *c*.
Heb 12:2 set before him he endured the *c*,

crown—a headpiece worn to symbolize glory, honor and victory.

1Co 9:25 it to get a *c* that will last forever.
2Ti 4:8 store for me the *c* of righteousness,
Rev 2:10 life as your victor's crown.

crucify—to put to death by nailing or tying a person's body to a cross.

Mt 27:22 They all answered, "*C* him!"
1Co 1:23 but we preach Christ *c*: a stumbling
Gal 2:20 I have been *c* with Christ

cruel—causing envy, grief or pain.

cubit—a measure of length in Bible times; about 18 inches.

cupbearer—an officer of considerable responsibility who tasted the king's food and wine before serving them to him (Ne 1:11).

curse—1. (*v.*) to ask God to bring evil or injury to; 2. (*n.*) a prayer or desire that evil or injury come upon someone.

Lev 20:9 "Anyone who *c* their father or mother
Lk 6:28 bless those who *c* you, pray
Gal 3:13 "*C* is everyone who is hung on a pole."

custom—a practice common to a particular place or group of people.

Mk 15:6 Now it was the *c* at the festival
Ac 17:2 As was his *c*, Paul went into the synagogue

cymbals—a musical instrument; round metal disks either struck with a stick or struck together to produce a clanging sound.

cypress—an evergreen tree of the pine family.

— D —

Daniel—a young Jewish exile; he lived in Babylon during the reign of several kings, including Nebuchadnezzar. He prayed to God rather than obey an order to pray only to the king and was thrown into a lion's den (Da 1—6).

daughter—a female descendant.

Job 1:2 He had seven sons and three *d*,

David—the son of Jesse; anointed by Samuel to become king of Israel (1Sa 16:1–13); killed the giant Goliath (1Sa 17); during his reign Israel's place in the land of Canaan was made secure.

day—1. the period of time between dawn and darkness; 2. a specified time.

Ge 1:5 God called the light "*d*,"
Ecc 12:1 Creator in the *d* of your youth,
Joel 2:31 and dreadful *d* of the LORD.
Mic 4:1 In the last *d*
Lk 11:3 Give us each *d* our daily bread.
Lk 18:33 On the third *d* he will rise
Heb 1:2 in these last *d* he has spoken to us
2Pe 3:8 With the Lord a *d* is like

deacon—a church officer whose qualifications are given in 1Ti 3:8–13.

death—the end of physical life; also the penalty for sin (Ro 6:23).

Ecc 7:2 for *d* is the destiny of everyone;
Isa 25:8 he will swallow up *d* forever.
1Co 15:21 For since *d* came through a man,
1Co 15:55 Where, O *d*, is your sting?"
Rev 21:4 There will be no more *d*

debauchery—living an immoral life or a life without religion; living to please only oneself.

Deborah—a prophetess who led Israel to victory over the Canaanites (Jdg 4—5).

debt—something that one person owes another.

Mt 6:12 And forgive us our *d*,

deceive—to fool or trick; to lie.

Ge 3:13 "The serpent *d* me, and I ate."
Gal 6:7 Do not be *d*: God cannot be
1Jn 1:8 we *d* ourselves and the truth is not

declare—to make known formally; to state forcefully.

Ps 19:1 The heavens *d* the glory of God;
Eph 6:20 Pray that I may *d* it fearlessly,

decree—1. (*v.*) to order or command; 2. (*n.*) an order or law given by someone with power and authority.

dedicate—to set apart for a special purpose, often for God's use.

defect—imperfection; fault.

defile—to make something that is good and pure into something impure or unclean.

defraud—to cheat someone by trickery.

Deity—God.

Col 2:9 of the *D* lives in bodily form,

delight—finding great pleasure in something.

Ps 119:47 for I *d* in your commands
Mt 12:18 the one I love, in whom I *d*;

deliver—to rescue; to set free.

demon—evil spirit. A demon-possessed person is one who is controlled by evil spirits.

Mk 5:15 possessed by the legion of *d*,
Jas 2:19 Good! Even the *d* believe that

denarius—a small Roman coin made of silver. During Jesus' earthly ministry, one denarius was the payment for about one day's work.

denounce—to say a person or thing is evil.

deposit—something pledged or given as part of the payment.

Eph 1:14 who is a *d* guaranteeing our

depraved (depravity)—evil or sinful.

2Ti 3:8 They are men of *d* minds,
2Pe 2:19 they themselves are slaves of *d*

deprive—to take something away from.

Am 5:12 and *d* the poor of justice

depths—the deepest part of a thing.

Ps 130:1 Out of the *d* I cry
La 3:55 from the *d* of the pit.

descendant—a member of a particular family line.

desecrate—to treat without respect or reverence.

desolate—not lived in; lonely; deserted.

despise—to look down on with contempt.

Pr 1:7 but fools *d* wisdom
Titus 2:15 Do not let anyone *d* you.

destiny—a predetermined course of events.

Php 3:19 Their *d* is destruction,

destitute—not having necessary things such as money and food.

destroy—to ruin completely.

detest—to hate.

devastate—to bring to ruin by violent action.

Jer 19:8 I will *d* this city

devil—the great enemy of God and tempter of people.

Lk 4:2 forty days he was tempted by the *d*.
Eph 6:11 stand against the *d* schemes.
2Ti 2:26 and escape from the trap of the *d*,
Jas 4:7 Resist the *d*, and he will flee
1Pe 5:8 Your enemy the *d* prowls

devote—to set apart for a special person or for a special reason; to set apart for God's use.

devour—1. to eat up greedily; 2. to destroy.

1Pe 5:8 looking for someone to *d*.

devout—religious; giving much time to prayer and worship.

die—1. to lose life; 2. to become insensitive to, as to die to the law (Gal 2:19).

Ge 2:17 when you eat from it you will certainly *d*."
Ecc 3:2 a time to be born and a time to *d*,
Eze 18:4 one who sins is the one who will *d*.
Jn 11:26 by believing in me will never *d*.
1Co 15:22 in Adam all *d*, so in Christ all will
Php 1:21 to live is Christ and to *d* is gain.

diligence (diligent)—characterized by hard work or earnest effort.

disaster—a sudden event bringing great damage, loss or destruction.

Dt 31:29 *d* will fall on you

discern—to understand; to come to know the difference between two or more things.

Php 1:10 you may be able to *d* what is best

disciple—a follower or student, especially one who believes what the leader teaches. Anyone who believes in Jesus is his disciple.

Lk 14:27 and follow me cannot be my *d*.
Jn 13:35 everyone will know that you are my *d*,

discipline—1. (*v.*) to correct; to teach what is right; 2. (*n.*) training that corrects, molds or perfects moral character.

Pr 29:17 *D* your children, and they will give you
Heb 12:6 the Lord *d* the one he loves,
Rev 3:19 Those whom I love I rebuke and *d*.

disgrace—to bring shame to.

disobey (disobedient)—to fail to obey.

1Pe 2:8 because they *d* the message

disown—to reject someone or something so completely that it no longer belongs to you.

Mt 26:34 you will *d* me three times."
2Ti 2:12 If we *d* him,

disperse—to scatter; to spread around.

dispute—to argue irritably.

dissension—disagreement; quarreling.

distress—suffering, misery, agony.

Ps 57:6 I was bowed down in *d*.
Ro 2:9 There will be trouble and *d*

divination—seeing into the future by magic.

Lev 19:26 "Do not practice *d* or seek omens.

divine—given by God; belonging to God.

Ro 1:20 his eternal power and *d* nature

divorce—to legally dissolve a marriage.

Mal 2:16 who hates and *d* his wife,"
Mt 19:3 for a man to *d* his wife for any
1Co 7:11 And a husband must not *d* his wife.

doctrine—teachings or beliefs about God.

1Ti 4:16 Watch your life and *d* closely.
Titus 2:1 what is appropriate to sound *d*.

dominion—power; rule.

Ps 22:28 for *d* belongs to the LORD
Eph 1:21 far above all rule and authority, power and *d*,

doom—1. (*v.*) to make certain something will fail or be destroyed; 2. (*n.*) fate; condemnation; ruin.

Rev 18:10 In one hour your *d* has come!'

door—a barrier that can be opened and closed; Christians open the doors of their hearts to Jesus.

Mt 7:7 and the *d* will be opened to you.
Rev 3:20 I stand at the *d* and knock.

doubt—uncertainty.

Mt 21:21 if you have faith and do not *d*,
Mk 11:23 and does not *d* in their heart
Jas 1:6 you must believe and not *d*,

dread—great fear.

dream—thoughts, images or emotion occurring during sleep; God sometimes spoke to his people through dreams.

Da 2:4 Tell your servants the *d*,

dross—the impure scum that floats on the surface of molten metals; sometimes used as a picture of the wicked.

Ps 119:119 you discard like *d*;

drought—a long period of time without rain.

drunkard—a person who is often or usually drunk.

Pr 23:21 for *d* and gluttons become poor,

dwelling—place in which people live; house; in Scripture usually refers to the place where God lives.

1Ki 8:30 Hear from heaven, your *d* place,
Ps 84:1 How lovely is your *d* place,

— E —

earth—the place that God created for human beings to live.

Ge 1:1 God created the heavens and the *e*.
Ps 24:1 *e* is the LORD's, and everything
Mt 6:10 done, on *e* as it is in heaven.
Mt 24:35 Heaven and *e* will pass away,
Lk 2:14 on *e* peace to those
Php 2:10 in heaven and on *e* and under the *e*,
2Pe 3:13 to a new heaven and a new *e*,

Eden—the location of the beautiful garden God created for Adam and Eve.

edict—an order or law made by a person who has the power to enforce it.

Est 2:8 the king's order and *e*

edify—to teach someone to live a godly life, or to help someone to live in such a way.

1Co 14:4 but the one who prophesies *e* the church.

Egypt—one of the most powerful nations of ancient times, located in the northeast corner of Africa; the Israelites were captives in Egypt at the beginning of the book of Exodus.

elders—1. the older men of a town or nation; they were the leaders of their community and made all the important decisions; 2. the leaders of the church.

1Ti 5:17 The *e* who direct the affairs
Titus 1:5 and appoint *e* in every town,

election—the choosing of Christians by God, as people who belong to him. Christians are called "the elect" (2Ti 2:10).

Ro 9:11 God's purpose in *e* might stand:
2Pe 1:10 to confirm your calling and *e*.

Eli—the high priest with whom Samuel spent the early years of his life (1Sa 2:11–26).

Elijah—a prophet of the Lord who predicted a famine in Israel (1Ki 17:1) and defeated the prophets of Baal in the test of whose God would set fire to the altar (1Ki 18:16–46).

Elisha—the prophet who succeeded Elijah. He was present when God took Elijah to heaven, and he took his place as prophet to Israel (2Ki 2:1–18).

Elizabeth—the mother of John the Baptist. Mary went to visit her when she found out she, too, was pregnant (Lk 1:5–58).

enchanter—a magician or snake charmer.

encourage—to inspire with courage or hope.

2Sa 19:7 Now go out and *e* your men.
1Th 4:18 Therefore *e* one another with these words.

endure—to continue; to keep on going; to bear something that is difficult or painful.

Ps 136:1 His love *e* forever.
Mal 3:2 who can *e* the day of his coming?
1Co 10:13 so that you can *e* it.

enemy—a person who opposes another person or a cause.

Mt 5:44 Love your *e* and pray
Php 3:18 many live as *e* of the cross of Christ.

enjoy—to take pleasure in.

Jdg 19:9 Stay and *e* yourself.
Jer 33:6 and will let them *e* abundant peace
3Jn 2 I pray that you may *e* good health

enmity—a feeling of antagonism, hostility or hatred.

Ge 3:15 put *e* between you and the woman,

Enoch—a man who "walked with God." Later in life, God "took him away" (Ge 5:18–24).

entice—to tempt or lure.

envoy—a person who represents one government in its dealings with another.

envy—to want for oneself something that belongs to another person.

1Co 13:4 It does not *e*, it does not boast,

ephod—a linen apron worn by a priest over his robe. It was decorated with gold, blue, purple and scarlet yarns.

Ephraim—1. one of Joseph's sons; 2. the tribe of Israel whose members were descendants of Ephraim; 3. a name for the northern kingdom of Israel after the ten tribes of Israel and the two tribes of Judah separated from each other.

Esau—the firstborn son of Isaac and twin of Jacob (Ge 25:21–26). He sold his birthright to Jacob for a pot of stew (Ge 25:29–34) and was tricked out of his blessing by this same brother (Ge 27).

esteem—1. (*v.*) to value; to consider important; 2. (*n.*) high regard or respect.

Pr 22:1 to be *e* is better than silver or gold.
Isa 53:3 and we held him in low *e*.

Esther—a Jewish woman who lived in Persia (Est 2:7) and became queen (Est 2:8–18). Upon being told of a plot to kill the Jews, she went to the king and pleaded for the Jewish people and thus saved them (Est 3—4; 7—9).

eternal—without beginning or end; forever; timeless.

Dt 33:27 The *e* God is your refuge,
Jn 3:16 him shall not perish but have *e* life.
Ro 6:23 but the gift of God is *e* life
1Jn 5:13 you may know that you have *e* life.

eunuch—a man whose sex organs have been removed so that he cannot produce children. Often in Bible times these men were important officials in royal palaces.

Eve—the first woman God created (Ge 2:20–24). Her name means "mother of all the living" (Ge 3:20).

everlasting—forever; without end.

Ps 90:2 from *e* to *e* you are God.
Isa 9:6 *E* Father, Prince of Peace.
Isa 55:3 I will make an *e* covenant with you,
2Th 1:9 punished with *e* destruction

evil—wicked; doing things against God's will.

Ge 2:9 of the knowledge of good and *e*.
Ps 23:4 I will fear no *e*,
Mt 6:13 but deliver us from the *e* one.'
Ro 12:9 Hate what is *e*; cling
Ro 12:17 Do not repay anyone *e* for *e*.
Eph 6:16 all the flaming arrows of the *e* one.

exalt—to praise; to raise to an important position.

Ps 118:28 you are my God, and I will *e* you.
Ps 148:13 for his name alone is *e*;
Pr 14:34 Righteousness *e* a nation,
Mt 23:12 For those who *e* themselves

examine—to look over carefully; to test.

1Co 11:28 Everyone ought to *e* themselves

exclaim—to cry out or speak in sudden or strong emotion.

Lk 1:42 In a loud voice she *e*: "Blessed

exclude—to leave out.

execute—to put to death, especially as punishment for an illegal act.

Lk 23:32 were also led out with him to be *e*.

exile—1. (*v.*) to force someone to leave his or her country or home; 2. (*n.*) forced removal from one's country or home.

Ezr 6:19 the *e* celebrated the Passover.
1Pe 1:1 To God's elect, *e* scattered

exodus—the departure of a large group of people from one place to go to another. The book of Exodus is the story of the Israelites' journey from Egypt to Canaan.

exploit—to take unfair advantage of.

Pr 22:22 Do not *e* the poor

extol—to praise.

Ps 34:1 I will *e* the LORD at all times;
Ps 95:2 and *e* him with music and song.

extortion—something gotten from a person by force or by using other illegal means.

Ezekiel—a priest who was called to be a prophet to the Jewish people when they were in exile in Babylon (Eze 1—3). He had many visions from the Lord (Eze 37; 40).

Ezra—a priest and teacher of the Law; he led a group of Jewish exiles back to Israel and helped them reestablish the temple of God and restore proper worship (Ezr 7—8).

— F —

fail—to be unsuccessful.

Ecc 6:6 but *f* to enjoy his prosperity.
1Co 13:8 Love never *f*.

faint—1. (*adj.*) lacking courage; 2. (*v.*) to lose courage.

Ps 142:3 When my spirit grows *f* within me,
Lk 21:26 People will *f* from terror,

faith—belief and trust in God; knowing that God is real, even though one can't see him.

Mt 17:20 if you have *f* as small as a mustard
Lk 7:9 I have not found such great *f*
Ro 1:17 "The righteous will live by *f*."
Ro 3:22 given through *f* in Jesus Christ
1Co 13:2 and if I have a *f* that can move
2Co 5:7 we live by *f*, not by sight.
Eph 6:16 to all this, take up the shield of *f*,
1Ti 6:12 Fight the good fight of the *f*.
Heb 11:1 *f* is confidence in what we hope for
Heb 11:8 By *f* Abraham, when called to go
Heb 12:2 the pioneer and perfecter of *f*
Jas 2:26 so *f* without deeds is dead.

faithful (faithfulness)—trustworthy; loyal.

Ps 145:13 and *f* in all he does.
La 3:23 great is your *f*.
Mt 25:21 'Well done, good and *f* servant!
Ro 12:12 patient in affliction, *f* in prayer.
1Co 10:13 And God is *f*; he will not let you
1Jn 1:9 he is *f* and just and will forgive us
Rev 1:5 who is the *f* witness, the firstborn

false (falsehood)—a lie.

Ex 20:16 "You shall not give *f* testimony

family—a group of people who are related to each other.

Ps 68:6 God sets the lonely in *f*,
Lk 9:61 go back and say goodbye to my *f*."
1Ti 3:4 He must manage his own *f* well

famine—1. a time when there is not enough food; 2. any severe shortage.

Am 8:11 but a *f* of hearing the words
Mt 24:7 There will be *f* and earthquakes

fast—1. (*adj.*) firmly fixed; not movable; 2. (*v.*) to go without food for a period of time.

Ps 139:10 your right hand will hold me *f*.
Mt 6:16 "When you *f*, do not look somber

father—a male parent; God is also known as one's father.

Ge 2:24 why a man leaves his *f*
Ge 17:4 You will be the *f* of many nations.
Ex 20:12 "Honor your *f* and your mother,
Mt 6:9 "'Our *F* in heaven,
Lk 11:11 "Which of you *f*, if your son asks
Jn 10:30 I and the *F* are one."
Jn 14:6 No one comes to the *F*

favor—goodwill; a positive attitude toward another person.

1Sa 20:3 I have found *f* in your eyes,

fear—(*v.*) 1. to respect highly; to feel reverence and awe for; 2. to be afraid of; (*n.*) 1. profound reverence toward God; 2. anticipation or awareness of danger.

Dt 6:13 *F* the LORD your God, serve him
Ps 91:5 You will not *f* the terror of night,
Ps 111:10 *f* of the LORD is the beginning
Isa 41:10 So do not *f*, for I am with you;
Php 2:12 to work out your salvation with *f*

fellowship—companionship or friendship.

1Jn 1:6 claim to have *f* with him yet walk
1Jn 1:7 we have *f* with one another,

fertile—producing fruit in great quantities; productive.

Nu 13:20 How is the soil? Is it *f* or poor?

festival—a religious celebration.

Nu 29:12 Celebrate a *f* to the LORD
Ezr 6:22 with joy the *F* of Unleavened Bread,
Jn 4:45 in Jerusalem at the Passover *F*,

fig—1. a brownish pear-shaped fruit that grows in countries near the Mediterranean Sea; 2. the tree that grows this fruit.

Joel 2:22 the *f* tree and the vine yield their riches.

firstborn—a family's first child. The firstborn son in an Israelite family became the head of the family when his father died, and he received twice as much money and property as each of his brothers.

Ex 11:5 Every *f* son in Egypt will die,

firstfruits—the first vegetables, fruits and grains harvested from the field.

Ex 23:19 "Bring the best of the *f* of your soil

flesh—1. the soft parts of the bodies of humans and animals; 2. the believer's sinful nature.

Job 6:12 Is my *f* bronze?
Php 3:3 put no confidence in the *f*
Ro 8:13 live according to the *f*, you will die;
Ro 13:14 gratify the desires of the *f*.

flock—a collection of sheep under the care of a shepherd.

Ps 65:13 The meadows are covered with *f*
Isa 40:11 He tends his *f* like a shepherd:

flog—to beat with a stick or a whip.

flood—a large amount of water that covers the ground, as in the time of Noah (Ge 6—8).

foe—an enemy.

Ps 61:3 a strong tower against the *f*.

folly—foolishness; the lack of wisdom.

Pr 26:5 Answer a fool according to his *f*,
2Ti 3:9 their *f* will be clear to everyone.

fool—a person who is not wise.

Ps 14:1 The *f* says in his heart,
Lk 12:20 "But God said to him, 'You *f*!

forbearance—patient endurance; self-control; not enforcing a right.

Gal 5:22 love, joy, peace, *f*, kindness,

forefather—a male ancestor.

forever—for a limitless time.

Dt 32:40 As surely as I live *f*,
Ps 136:1 His love endures *f*.

forgive—to pardon or excuse; to no longer blame or be angry with someone who has done you wrong.

Mt 6:14 For if you *f* other people
Lk 23:34 Jesus said, "Father, *f* them,
Col 3:13 *F* as the Lord forgave you.
1Jn 1:9 and just and will *f* us our sins

forsake—to leave another completely alone; to abandon

Jos 1:5 I will never leave you nor *f* you.
Isa 55:7 Let the wicked *f* their ways
Mt 27:46 my God, why have you *f* me?"

fortified—to make strong, such as a town with a wall.

fortress—a city that is fortified.

fragrance (fragrant)—a sweet or pleasant odor.

SS 4:10 the *f* of your perfume
Php 4:18 They are a *f* offering,

free (freedom)—not bound; liberated.

Jn 8:32 and the truth will set you *f*."
Ro 6:18 You have been set *f* from sin
2Co 3:17 the Spirit of the Lord is, there is *f*.

friend—a person who loves and respects another person.

Pr 18:24 there is a *f* who sticks closer
Jn 15:13 to lay down one's life for one's *f*.
Jas 4:4 Anyone who chooses to be a *f*

fruitful—productive; yielding much fruit.

Ge 1:22 "Be *f* and increase in number
Jn 15:2 prunes so that it will be even more *f*.

fulfill (fulfillment)—to complete a promise or project.

Ps 116:14 I will *f* my vows to the LORD
Mk 14:49 But the Scriptures must be *f*."
Ro 13:10 Therefore love is the *f* of the law.

fury—intense anger.

Pr 6:34 jealousy arouses a husband's *f*,

— G —

Gabriel—the angel who announced the births of John the Baptist and Jesus (Lk 1:11–20, 26–38).

Galilee—the northern part of Palestine. Jesus grew up, preached and did most of his miracles there. Today this area is in northern Israel.

gall—1. a plant with an extremely bitter-tasting fruit; 2. the liquid made by the liver.

Mt 27:34 mixed with *g*; but after tasting it,

genealogy—a list of a person's ancestors or descendants; a family tree.

generation—the entire number of people born and living at about the same time. Grandparents, parents and children are three different generations.

Ps 102:12 your renown endures through all *g*.
Lk 1:48 now on all *g* will call me blessed,

Gentile—anyone who is not a Jew.

Ro 3:9 and *G* alike are all under
Ro 11:13 as I am the apostle to the *G*,

Gideon—a judge who freed Israel from the rule and terror of the Midianites (Jdg 6—8). He asked for a sign from God, and God showed him his will by means of dew and a fleece (Jdg 6:36–40).

gift—1. a present; 2. a talent or ability.

Ro 6:23 but the *g* of God is eternal life
1Co 12:4 There are different kinds of *g*,
2Co 9:15 be to God for his indescribable *g!*

glean—to pick up the grain or fruit left behind after harvesting; usually a way for the poor to get food.

Ruth 2:8 Don't go and *g* in another field

gloat—to look at or think about something or someone with malicious satisfaction.

Mic 7:8 Do not *g* over me, my enemy!

glorify—to praise and honor in worship.

Ps 34:3 *G* the LORD with me;
Jn 17:1 *G* your Son, that your Son may

glory—1. honor; praise; 2. a source of pride or worthiness.

Ps 8:5 and crowned them with *g* and honor.
Ps 19:1 The heavens declare the *g* of God;
Lk 2:14 "*G* to God in the highest heaven,
Jn 1:14 We have seen his *g*, the *g* of the one
1Co 10:31 whatever you do, do it all for the *g*
Rev 4:11 to receive *g* and honor and power,

glutton—a person who eats too much.

Dt 21:20 He is a *g* and a drunkard."

gnash—to grind (one's teeth) together.

Mt 8:12 there will be weeping and *g* of teeth."

goat—an animal raised for its meat and milk; sometimes used in religious sacrifices.

God—the supreme Creator and the powerful force of the universe; the One who is to be worshiped.

Ge 1:1 In the beginning *G* created
Ex 20:5 the LORD your *G*, am a jealous *G*,
Nu 23:19 *G* is not human, that he should lie,
Dt 6:4 LORD our *G*, the LORD is one.
Dt 6:5 Love the LORD your *G*
Ps 46:1 *G* is our refuge and strength,
Jn 1:18 ever seen *G*, but the one
Jn 3:16 For *G* so loved the world that he
Jn 4:24 *G* is spirit, and his worshipers must
1Jn 4:16 *G* is love.
Rev 4:8 holy is the Lord *G* Almighty,

godly—to be devoted and loving toward God, wanting to do his will.

1Ti 4:7 train yourself to be *g*.
2Pe 3:11 live holy and *g* lives

Golgotha—the hill outside Jerusalem where Jesus was hung on a cross.

Goliath—the Philistine giant who was killed by David (1Sa 17; 21:9).

gospel—1. the good news that Jesus died for sins and rose again; 2. any of the first four books of the New Testament.

Ro 1:16 I am not ashamed of the *g*,
1Co 9:16 Woe to me if I do not preach the *g!*
1Co 15:2 By this *g* you are saved,

gossip—to talk too much about others, especially in a way that is hurtful.

2Co 12:20 slander, *g*, arrogance and disorder.

grace—an undeserved favor or gift; the undeserved forgiveness, kindness and mercy that God gives us.

Ro 3:24 all are justified freely by his *g*
Ro 5:20 where sin increased, *g* increased all
2Co 12:9 "My *g* is sufficient for you,
Eph 2:5 it is by *g* you have been saved.
Titus 3:7 having been justified by his *g*,

greed—selfish desire for more money or possessions than one needs.

Lk 12:15 on your guard against all kinds of *g*;
Col 3:5 evil desires and *g*, which is idolatry.

grieve—to cause someone pain or sorrow.

Jn 16:20 You will *g*, but your grief will turn
Eph 4:30 do not *g* the Holy Spirit of God,

guarantee—a pledge that something will take place.

Eph 1:14 who is a deposit *g* our inheritance

guardian-redeemer—in Old Testament times a close male relative who had the responsibility to marry a widow and buy her husband's property (Dt 25:5–6).

Ruth 3:9 since you are a *g* of our family.

guide—to direct or point out the way.

Ps 23:3 He *g* me along the right paths

guilty—deserving punishment for having broken a law or commandment.

Ex 34:7 does not leave the *g* unpunished;
Heb 10:22 to cleanse us from a *g* conscience
Jas 2:10 at just one point is *g* of breaking all

— H —

Hades—hell; the place where the spirits of the dead live.

Mt 16:18 the gates of *H* will not overcome it.

Hagar—a slave of Sarah and one of Abraham's wives; the mother of Ishmael (Ge 16:1–6; 25:12).

Haggai—a prophet who encouraged the Israelites returning from exile in Babylon to rebuild the temple (Ezr 5:1; Hag 1—2).

hallelujah—praise the Lord; a song of praise.

Rev 19:1 "*H!* Salvation and glory and power

hallowed—holy; sacred.

Mt 6:9 *h* be your name,

Ham—the youngest of Noah's three sons (Ge 5:32).

Hannah—she prayed for a son, and God gave her Samuel. She dedicated him to God; he lived in the temple as a boy and became a prophet and judge (1Sa 1—2).

harp—a musical instrument with twelve strings for strumming; frequently used in religious ceremonies.

Ps 71:22 I will praise you with the *h*

harvest—the season for gathering in crops.

Ge 8:22 "As long as the earth endures, seedtime and *h*,

hate—to detest, to have extreme dislike for.

Ps 5:5 You *h* all who do wrong;
Mk 13:13 Everyone will *h* you because of me,

haughty—proud.

Pr 16:18 a *h* spirit before a fall.

heal—to make well again.

Lk 8:43 but no one could *h* her.
Ac 28:27 and I would *h* them.'

heart—the center of a person's life, including the mind, the will and the emotions.

Dt 6:5 LORD your God with all your *h*
1Sa 16:7 but the LORD looks at the *h*."
Ps 51:10 Create in me a pure *h*, O God,
Ps 119:11 I have hidden your word in my *h*
Ps 139:23 Search me, God, and know my *h*;
Eze 36:26 I will give you a new *h*
Mt 5:8 Blessed are the pure in *h*,

heaven—1. the place where God lives; 2. the sky.

Ge 14:19 Creator of *h* and earth.
Mt 19:23 to enter the kingdom of *h*.
Lk 24:51 and was taken up into *h*.
Php 3:20 But our citizenship is in *h*.
Rev 21:1 Then I saw "a new *h* and a new earth,"

Hebrew—1. another name for an Israelite; a descendant of Abraham; 2. the language spoken by the Jews. The Old Testament was written in Hebrew.

heir—someone who receives the property or blessings of a person who has died.

Ro 8:17 then we are *h*—*h* of God
Eph 3:6 gospel the Gentiles are *h* together

herd—a large number of animals of one kind kept together in a group.

Herod—the family name of five kings who ruled Palestine under the Roman emperor: Herod the Great (Mt 2:16); Herod Antipas (Mk 6:14–29); Herod Philip (Mt 14:3; Mk 6:17); Herod Agrippa I (Ac 12:1–4, 19–23); Herod Agrippa II (Ac 23:35; 25:13—26:32).

Herodias—the wife of Herod Antipas; she persuaded her daughter to ask Antipas for the head of John the Baptist (Mk 6:17).

Hezekiah—a king of Judah; he restored the temple, reinstituted proper worship and sought the Lord's help against the Assyrians.

high priest—the chief religious official in the Jewish religion. In the Old Testament he offered the most important sacrifices to God in behalf of the people.

Heb 4:14 a great *h p* who has ascended
Heb 7:26 a *h p* truly meets our need

hinder—to hold back; to prevent; to delay.

Mt 19:14 come to me, and do not *h* them,

holy—set apart for God; belonging to God; pure; godly.

Ex 20:8 the Sabbath day by keeping it *h.*
Lev 11:44 and be *h*, because I am *h.*
Isa 6:3 "*H, h, h* is the LORD Almighty;
Ro 12:1 as a living sacrifice, *h* and pleasing
Rev 4:8 "*H, h, h* is the Lord God Almighty,

Holy Spirit (Spirit)—the third person of the Trinity; he lives and works in the hearts and minds of believers; he came at Pentecost in a powerful way (Ac 2). Other names are: the Spirit, Counselor and Comforter.

Ps 51:11 or take your *H* from me.
Jn 14:26 But the Advocate, the *H*,
Jn 20:22 and said, "Receive the *H.*
Ac 2:4 of them were filled with the *H*
Gal 5:22 But the fruit of the *S* is love, joy,

honor—to show respect to; to give credit to.

Ex 20:12 "*H* your father and your mother,
Ps 8:5 and crowned them with glory and *h.*

hope—the anticipation of something good.

Ps 42:5 Put your *h* in God,
Isa 40:31 but those who *h* in the LORD
Ro 8:24 But *h* that is seen is no *h* at all.
1Co 15:19 for this life we have *h* in Christ,
Heb 11:1 faith is confidence in what we *h* for

hordes—a loosely organized or disorderly crowd of people; usually committing harmful acts.

Hab 1:9 Their *h* advance like a desert wind

horror—strong and painful fear or dread.

Jer 8:21 I mourn, and *h* grips me.

hosanna—a Hebrew word of praise meaning "save."

Mt 21:9 "*H* in the highest heaven!"

hospitality—welcoming people into one's home; sharing one's home and food with others.

Ro 12:13 Practice *h.*
1Pe 4:9 Offer *h* to one another

hostile—like an enemy; unfriendly.

human—like people rather than animals, in actions or thoughts or appearance.

humble—1. (*v.*) to make lower; 2. (*adj.*) not proud; not pretending to be important.

Ps 147:6 The LORD sustains the *h*
Mt 23:12 who exalt themselves will be *h*,
Jas 4:10 *H* yourselves before the Lord,

humiliate—to make humble; to reduce to a lower position; to make ashamed.

1Co 11:22 by *h* those who have nothing?

humility—the absence of pride.

Php 2:3 but in *h* value others above
1Pe 5:5 clothe yourselves with *h*

hymn—a song of praise to God.

Eph 5:19 with psalms, *h*, and songs

hypocrite—a person who pretends to be better than he or she is.

Mt 6:5 when you pray, do not be like the *h*,
Mt 7:5 You *h*, first take the plank out

hyssop—a plant used to sprinkle water or blood for religious cleansing.

Ps 51:7 with *h*, and I will be clean;

killed (1Ki 18:4, 13) and opposed the prophet Elijah (1Ki 19:1-2).

Joab—the commander of the armies of King David.

Joash—the boy-king of Judah; he repaired the temple (2Ki 12).

Job—a wealthy man from the land of Uz who feared God (Job 1:1-5). His righteousness was tested by disaster (Job 1:6-22) and personal affliction (Job 2), but in the end God restored wealth and honor to him (Job 42).

John—1. the Baptist (Mk 1:2-8); the son of Zechariah and Elizabeth (Lk 1). He preached in the desert, preparing the people for Jesus (Mt 3:11-12); baptized Jesus in the Jordan River (Mt 3:13-17); executed by Herod (Mk 6:14-29); 2. one of the twelve apostles; brother of the apostle James (Lk 5:1-10); wrote the Gospel of John, the letters of John (2Jn 1; 3Jn 1) and the book of Revelation (Rev 1:1; 22:8).

John Mark (see Mark, John).

Jonah—a prophet who was called to preach to Nineveh but instead fled to Tarshish (Jnh 1:1-3). While at sea a great storm arose because of his disobedience; he was thrown into the sea and was swallowed by a large fish (Jnh 1:4-17). He then repented and went to Nineveh and preached, telling the people to repent (Jnh 3).

Jonathan—a son of King Saul (1Sa 13:16) who had a close friendship with David (1Sa 18:1-4; 19—20; 23:16-18). When he was killed (1Sa 31) David mourned greatly for him (2Sa 1).

Joppa—an ancient walled town on the coast of Palestine.

Jordan—a river in Palestine that flows between the Sea of Galilee and the Dead Sea.

Jos 4:22	'Israel crossed the *J* on dry ground.'
Mt 3:6	baptized by him in the *J* River.

Joseph—1. the son of Jacob and Rachel (Ge 30:24), who was favored by his father but hated by his brothers (Ge 37:3-4). He was sold into slavery (Ge 37:12-36), taken to Egypt and eventually given a high position under Pharaoh (Ge 41:41-57); 2. the husband of Mary and childhood father of Jesus (Mt 1:16-24; 2:13-19); 3. a disciple of Jesus from Arimathea; he gave his tomb for Jesus' burial (Mt 27:57-61); 4. the original name of Barnabas (Ac 4:36).

Joshua—1. the son of Nun (Nu 13:8); Moses' aide and later his successor (Dt 31:1-18); he led the Israelites across the Jordan River into Canaan (Jos 3—4); was the commander in the conquest of Jericho (Jos 6), Ai (Jos 7—8), and a large part of Canaan (Jos 10—12); oversaw the dividing up of the promised land among the 12 tribes of Israel (Jos 13—22); 2. the high priest in Israel during the rebuilding of both the temple (Hag 1—2) and the altar (Ezr 3:2, 8); also called Jeshua.

Josiah—godly king of Judah for 31 years shortly before the destruction of Jerusalem.

Judah—1. Jacob's fourth son; 2. the tribe of Israel whose members were descendants of Judah; 3. a name for the southern kingdom after Judah and Benjamin separated from the northern ten tribes.

Ge 29:35	So she named him *J*.
Zec 10:4	From *J* will come the cornerstone,
Mt 2:6	Bethlehem, in the land of *J*,
Rev 5:5	See, the Lion of the tribe of *J*,

Judaism—the teachings of the Jewish religion.

Judas—1. one of the twelve apostles (Lk 6:16; Ac 1:13); was probably also called Thaddaeus (Mt 10:3); 2. one of the brothers of Jesus (Mt 13:55); author of the last letter in the New Testament (Jude 1); 3. one of the twelve apostles, also called Iscariot; he betrayed Jesus (Mk 3:19; 14:10-50) and then hung himself (Mt 27:3-5).

Judea—the area of Palestine where the tribe of Judah lived after the exile.

Mk 10:1	into the region of *J* and across the Jordan.
Gal 1:22	to the churches of *J* that are in Christ.

judge—to decide if something is good or bad; to condemn.

Ps 9:8	and *j* the peoples with equity.
Mt 7:1	"Do not *j*, or you too will be judged.
2Ti 4:1	who will *j* the living and the dead,

judgment—1. a decision or opinion; 2. a decision of guilt or innocence made by a judge in a court of law; punishment decided on by a court; 3. a decision from God, especially the final judgment when God will reward those who believe in him and condemn all others to hell.

Dt 1:17	of anyone, for *j* belongs to God.
Ps 119:66	Teach me knowledge and good *j*,
Isa 66:16	the LORD will execute *j*
Mt 5:21	who murders will be subject to *j*.'
Mt 12:36	have to give account on the day of *j*
Jn 5:22	but has entrusted all *j* to the Son,
Ro 14:10	stand before God's *j* seat.
2Co 5:10	appear before the *j* seat of Christ,

just — righteous, legally correct.

Ps 111:7	The works of his hands are faithful and *j*;
Rev 16:7	true and *j* are your judgments."

justice — fairness.

Isa 30:18	For the LORD is a God of *j*.
Isa 61:8	"For I, the LORD, love *j*;
Zec 7:9	'Administer true *j*; show mercy
Lk 11:42	you neglect *j* and the love of God.

justify (justification) — to erase someone's sins; to declare righteous.

Ac 13:39	a *j* you were not able to obtain
Ro 3:24	and all are *j* freely by his grace
Ro 4:25	and was raised to life for our *j*.
Ro 5:1	since we have been *j* through faith,
Gal 3:24	Christ came that we might be *j* by faith.

— K —

kind — considerate, loving.

Eph 4:32	Be *k* and compassionate

king — ruler over a country or kingdom; Christ is often referred to as the King of kings.

1Ki 22:3	The *k* of Israel had said
1Ti 6:15	the *K* of *k* and Lord of lords,

kingdom — an area or group of people headed by a king; God's kingdom, or the kingdom of heaven, is made up of all believers.

Ex 19:6	you will be for me a *k* of priests
Mt 3:2	"Repent, for the *k* of heaven has come
Mt 5:3	for theirs is the *k* of heaven.
Mt 6:33	But seek first his *k* and his
Mt 16:19	the keys of the *k* of heaven;
Jn 18:36	"My *k* is not of this world.
1Co 15:24	hands over the *k* to God the Father
Rev 11:15	"The *k* of the world has become the *k*

Kish — the father of King Saul, the first king of Israel.

knowledge — possessing the facts, understanding.

Pr 1:7	of the LORD is the beginning of *k*,
Hos 4:6	are destroyed from lack of *k*.
1Co 8:1	*k* puffs up while love builds up.

— L —

Laban — the brother of Rebekah (Ge 24:29–51) and father of Rachel and Leah (Ge 29—31).

labor — 1. (*v.*) to work; 2. (*n.*) a task; 3. (*n.*) the time just before giving birth.

Ge 5:29	the *l* and painful toil of our hands
Ex 20:9	Six days you shall *l* and do all your work,
Jer 13:21	like that of a woman in *l*?

lack — 1. (*v.*) to stand in need of; 2. (*n.*) the state of being in need of something.

Ps 34:9	those who fear him *l* nothing.

lamb — a principal sacrificial animal in the Old Testament; since Jesus is the supreme sacrifice of God, he is called the "Lamb of God."

Isa 53:7	he was led like a *l* to the slaughter,
Jn 1:29	*L* of God, who takes away the sin
1Co 5:7	our Passover *l*, has been sacrificed.
Rev 5:6	Then I saw a *L*, looking

lament, lamentation — a cry of grief.

Ps 5:1	LORD, consider my *l*.

law — 1. God's rules, which help his people know what is right and wrong (the Ten Commandments are part of God's law); 2. (cap.) the first five books of the Bible, written by Moses.

Ps 1:2	and who meditates on his *l*
Ps 19:7	The *l* of the LORD is perfect,
Ps 119:97	Oh, how I love your *l*!
Mt 22:40	All the *L* and the Prophets hang

Ro 8:3 For what the *l* was powerless to do
Ro 13:10 love is the fulfillment of the *l*.
Gal 3:24 So the *l* was our guardian

Lazarus—1. the poor man in one of Jesus' parables (Lk 16:19-31); 2. the brother of Mary and Martha; Jesus raised him from the dead (Jn 11:1—12:19).

Leah—the wife of Jacob; she had six sons and one daughter (Ge 29:16—30:21).

leprosy—a word used in the Bible for many different skin diseases and infections.

Mk 1:42 Immediately the *l* left him

Levite—a member of the tribe of Levi. The Levites took care of the temple. Only Levites could become priests, but not all Levites were priests.

lewd—indecent; wicked.

life—the total substance of a person's existence; can refer to both physical and spiritual existence.

Ge 2:7 into his nostrils the breath of *l*,
Jn 3:16 shall not perish but have eternal *l*.
Jn 11:25 "I am the resurrection and the *l*.
Jn 14:6 am the way and the truth and the *l*.
Ro 6:23 but the gift of God is eternal *l*

light—the form of energy that allows a person to see; in the Old Testament it symbolized life and blessing.

Ge 1:3 "Let there be *l*," and there was *l*.
Ps 27:1 The Lord is my *l* and my salvation
Ps 119:105 a *l* on my path.
Isa 9:2 have seen a great *l*;
Mt 5:16 let your *l* shine before others,
Jn 8:12 he said, "I am the *l* of the world.
1Jn 1:5 God is *l*; in him there is no

linen—cloth made from the fiber of flax plants.

live—to be alive; may refer to both physical and spiritual existence.

Ex 20:12 so that you may *l* long
Ro 1:17 "The righteous will *l* by faith."
2Co 5:7 For we *l* by faith, not by sight.
Php 1:21 to *l* is Christ and to die is gain.

loathe—to feel disgust or hatred.

Job 10:1 "I *l* my very life;

locusts—a type of grasshopper. When they settle in a grain field, orchard or other cultivated area, they eat and can destroy the crop.

Lord—refers to God as the master. (See also Lord.)

Mt 3:3 'Prepare the way for the *L*,
Lk 2:9 glory of the *L* shone around them,
Ac 16:31 replied, "Believe in the *L* Jesus,
Ro 10:13 on the name of the *L* will be saved."
Php 2:11 acknowledge that Jesus Christ is *L*,
2Pe 1:16 the coming of our *L* Jesus Christ,
Rev 17:14 he is *L* of lords and King of kings
Rev 22:20 Come, *L* Jesus.

Lord (Yahweh)—the intimate and personal name of God; it emphasizes his role as Israel's Redeemer and covenant Lord. (See also Lord.)

Ge 2:4 when the *L* God made the earth
Ex 20:2 "I am the *L* your God, who
Ps 23:1 The *L* is my shepherd, I lack
Ps 103:1 Praise the *L*, my soul;
Pr 1:7 The fear of the *L* is the beginning
Isa 6:3 "Holy, holy, holy is the *L* Almighty;
Isa 55:6 Seek the *L* while he may be found;

Lot—the nephew of Abraham (Ge 12:5). He chose to live in Sodom (Ge 13); Abraham pleaded with God for Lot's life when God was about to destroy Sodom (Ge 19:1-29).

lot—one of the ways used in Bible times to find out God's will about something. It is somewhat like drawing straws.

Mt 27:35 divided up his clothes by casting *l*.
Ac 1:26 Then they cast *l*, and the *l* fell

love—wanting good to come to another person; being concerned and willing to work for another person's benefit.

Ex 20:6 showing *l* to a thousand generations
Ps 23:6 Surely your goodness and *l* will follow
Ps 136:1-26 His *l* endures forever.
Mt 3:17 "This is my Son, whom I *l*;
Mt 5:44 *l* your enemies and pray
Mt 19:19 and '*l* your neighbor as yourself.'"
Jn 13:34 I give you: *L* one another.

Jn 15:13	Greater *l* has no one than this:
Ro 13:10	Therefore *l* is the fulfillment
Gal 5:22	But the fruit of the Spirit is *l*, joy,
Eph 1:4-5	In *l* he predestined us
1Jn 3:10	anyone who does not *l* their brother.
1Jn 3:16	This is how we know what *l* is:
1Jn 4:7	for *l* comes from God.
1Jn 4:10	This is *l*: not that we loved God,
1Jn 4:16	God is *l*.

Luke—a coworker with Paul; he wrote the books of Luke and Acts (Col 4:14).

lust—a strong desire for something wrong.

Pr 6:25	Do not *l* in your heart
Ro 1:26	God gave them over to shameful *l*.

lyre—a small lap harp with three to twelve strings.

1Sa 18:10	David was playing the *l*,

— M —

Macedonia—a Roman province; the first part of Europe to receive Christianity.

Magi—men of Arabia and Persia who studied the stars. People thought they had the power to tell the meaning of dreams.

Mt 2:1	*M* from the east came to Jerusalem

maimed—crippled; having lost a part of one's body, such as an arm or leg.

majestic (majesty)—great and powerful.

Ex 15:6	was *m* in power.
Ps 8:1	how *m* is your name in all the earth!
Ps 111:3	Glorious and *m* are his deeds,

malice—hatred; wishing harm on someone else.

1Pe 2:1	rid yourselves of all *m*

Manasseh—1. the older son of Joseph and the tribe descended from him (Ge 41:51; Nu 1:34); 2. one of the kings of Judah (2Ki 21:1).

manger—a feed box for cows or other animals.

Lk 2:7	placed him in a *m*, because there

maniac—an insane person; an overly enthusiastic person.

2Ki 9:20	he drives like a *m*."

manna—the special food God gave daily to the Israelites until they reached the promised land.

Ex 16:31	people of Israel called the bread *m*.
Jn 6:49	Your ancestors ate the *m*

Mark, John—the cousin of Barnabas (Col 4:10); a helper to Paul and Barnabas (Ac 13:5); later a coworker with Barnabas (Ac 15:39) and then Paul (Phm 24); author of the second Gospel, according to early church tradition.

marriage—the joining together before God and other people of a man and a woman to form a new family.

Ge 29:26	younger daughter in *m* before the older
Mt 22:30	neither marry nor be given in *m*;
Heb 13:4	by all, and the *m* bed kept pure,

Martha—the sister of Mary and Lazarus, the man whom Jesus raised from the dead (Jn 11; 12:2).

marvelous—something that surprises, that fills one with wonder.

Ps 118:23	and it is *m* in our eyes.
Rev 15:3	"Great and *m* are your deeds,

Mary—1. the mother of Jesus (Mt 1:16-25); 2. Mary Magdalene—a woman whom Jesus freed from demons (Lk 8:2), who was present at the cross (Mk 15:40) and who came on Easter morning to the tomb (Mt 27:61); 3. the sister of Martha and Lazarus; she washed Jesus' feet with expensive perfume (Jn 12:1-8).

master—one who rules over others.

Mt 6:24	"No one can serve two *m*.
Jn 13:16	no servant is greater than his *m*,

Matthew—a tax collector who became one of the twelve apostles (Mt 9:9-13); also called Levi (Mk 2:14-17).

mediator—one who makes peace between two people or two groups who are displeased and/or angry with each other. Jesus is the mediator between us and God.

1Ti 2:5	and one *m* between God and mankind,
Heb 9:15	For this reason Christ is the *m*

meditate—to think seriously and carefully.

Ps 1:2	who *m* on his law day and night.
Ps 119:15	I *m* on your precepts

medium—a person who can supposedly talk with the spirits of people who have died.

1Sa 28:7 "Find me a woman who is a *m*,

meek—patient; mild; gentle.

Ps 37:11 But the *m* will inherit the land
Mt 5:5 Blessed are the *m*,

Melchizedek—a priest and king of early Salem (Jerusalem); Jesus was said to be a priest like Melchizedek (Heb 5:6).

Mephibosheth—son of Jonathan and grandson of Saul; he lived out his life under King David's protection (2Sa 9:11).

mercy—kindness and forgiveness, especially when given to a person who doesn't deserve it.

Mic 6:8 To act justly and to love *m*
Ro 9:15 "I will have *m* on whom I have *m*,
1Pe 1:3 In his great *m* he has given us new

Messiah—the "Anointed One"; Christ; the one the Jews expected to come and be their king.

Lk 9:20 Peter answered, "God's *M*."
Jn 1:41 "We have found the *M*"

Methuselah—a man in early Bible times who lived 969 years (Ge 5:27).

Michal—daughter of Saul, wife of David, both of whom were kings of Israel.

midwives—women who helped with the birth of a baby.

Ex 1:17 The *m*, however, feared God

millstone—one of a pair of stones used to crush grain for flour.

Lk 17:2 sea with a *m* tied around their neck

minister—1. (*v.*) to serve; to give care or attention to; 2. (*n.*) one who serves others as God directs.

2Co 3:6 as *m* of a new covenant
1Ti 4:6 you will be a good *m*

miracle—an unusual event, one that goes against the normal laws of nature. Miracles are done by the power of God.

Ps 77:14 You are the God who performs *m*;
Mk 6:2 What are these remarkable *m* he is
Ac 2:22 accredited by God to you by *m*,
Heb 2:4 it by signs, wonders and various *m*,

Miriam—the sister of Moses and Aaron (Nu 26:59); led the Israelites in praising God in dance and song after he had parted the waters of the Red Sea (Ex 15:20–21); later temporarily struck with leprosy because she criticized Moses (Nu 12).

Moab—1. a son of Lot whose descendants became bitter enemies of the Israelites; 2. the land occupied by the Moabites, to the east of the Dead Sea.

money—a medium of exchange.

Ecc 5:10 Whoever loves *m* never has
Mt 6:24 You cannot serve both God and *m*.
1Co 16:2 set aside a sum of *m* in keeping
1Ti 6:10 For the love of *m* is a root

Mordecai—cousin of Esther, queen of Persia; he and Esther saved the Jews from a plot to put them all to death.

mortal—human; able to die.

Ps 9:20 the nations know they are only *m*.
Ps 103:15 The life of *m* is like grass,
1Co 15:53 and the *m* with immortality,

Moses—the leader of Israel in the exodus out of Egypt, ending in their passing through the Red Sea (Ex 12—14). He received the law of God at Sinai (Ex 19—23) and gave it to the people of Israel. Moses was allowed to view the land of Canaan from the top of Mount Nebo, but he died without entering it (Nu 20:1-13; Dt 34:5-12).

mother—the female parent.

Ge 2:24 and *m* and is united to his wife,
Dt 5:16 "Honor your father and your *m*,

mourn—to feel deep sorrow; to grieve.

Mt 5:4 Blessed are those who *m*,

murder—to kill someone illegally.

Ex 20:13 "You shall not *m*.

muster—to gather together, especially to gather soldiers for war.

mute—unable to speak.

Mt 9:33 the man who had been *m* spoke.

myrrh—the sweet-smelling sap of the myrrh bush. It was used to make the sacred anointing oil.

Mt 2:11 gifts of gold, frankincense and *m*.

— N —

Nabal—a rich sheepherder in Judah who insulted David; when David planned to take revenge, Nabal's wife Abigail brought gifts to calm David; Nabal died shortly afterwards, and Abigail married David (1Sa 25:1-42).

Naboth—owner of a vineyard that King Ahab wanted and gained by having Naboth accused of blasphemy and stoned (1Ki 21:1-29).

Naomi—the mother-in-law of Ruth (Ru 1); she advised Ruth to seek marriage with Boaz (Ru 2—4).

Naphtali—a son of Jacob and father of the tribe of Naphtali (Nu 1:42-43).

nard—an expensive, pleasant-smelling oil from the spikenard, a plant that grew in India.

Mk 14:3 perfume, made of pure *n*.

Nathan—the prophet of God who exposed David's sin with Bathsheba, causing David to repent (2Sa 12:1-25).

Nathanael—one of the twelve apostles (Jn 1:45-49); was probably also called Bartholomew (Mt 10:3).

Nazarene—a person who lived in or came from the town of Nazareth in Galilee.

Mk 16:6 looking for Jesus the *N*,

Nazirite—a person who separated himself or herself by taking a vow to do special work for God. This included a promise not to cut one's hair and not to drink wine.

Jdg 16:17 I have been a *N* dedicated to God

Nebuchadnezzar—king of Babylon who took Judah into captivity.

Negev—the desert region south of Judea.

Ge 24:62 for he was living in the *N*.

Nehemiah—the Jewish cupbearer of King Artaxerxes of Persia (Ne 2:1); while in Jerusalem rebuilt the walls of the city (Ne 2—6) and with Ezra reestablished the worship of God there after the exile in Babylon (Ne 8).

neighbor—1. someone who lives nearby; 2. any fellow human being.

Lev 19:18 but love your *n* as yourself.
Lk 10:36 of these three do you think was a *n*

Nicodemus—a Pharisee who visited Jesus at night (Jn 3) and learned about being born again.

Nile—the primary river in Egypt.

Nineveh—the city to which Jonah was sent to preach (Jnh 1:2); the ancient capital of Assyria.

Noah—"a righteous man" in early Bible times; he built an ark, as God commanded him (Ge 6—8). God made a covenant with him never again to cover the entire earth with a flood (Ge 9).

nullify—to make of no value; to make unimportant.

Mk 7:13 Thus you *n* the word of God

— O —

oath—a promise in which one asks God to witness that something is true.

Dt 10:20 take your *o* in his name.

obey (obedience)—to do as asked; to follow someone's commands or wishes.

Dt 6:3 careful to *o* so that it may go well
1Sa 15:22 To *o* is better than sacrifice,
Jn 14:23 who loves me will *o* my teaching.
Ac 5:29 "We must *o* God rather than human
Eph 6:1 *o* your parents in the Lord,

offense—an act that makes someone angry by what was done.

offering—1. something given to God as an act of worship; 2. the sacrifice of an animal to make the relationship between God and human beings right again. In the Old Testament, animals and grains were regularly used as offerings in an attempt to bring the people closer to God.

Ge 22:8 provide the lamb for the burnt *o*,
Isa 53:10 the LORD makes his life an *o*
Mk 12:33 is more important than all burnt *o*
Eph 5:2 as a fragrant *o* and sacrifice to God.

offspring—children.

Ge 3:15 and between your *o* and hers;
Ge 12:7 "To your *o* I will give this land."

oil—almost always refers to olive oil; used to anoint someone for a physical benefit or to set someone apart for service.

2Ki 9:6 prophet poured the *o* on Jehu's head
Lk 7:46 You did not put *o* on my head,

olive—a tree whose fruit gives olive oil, which was used for varied purposes.

oppress—to control people unfairly and cruelly by the use of one's power.

Isa 53:7 He was *o* and afflicted,
Zec 7:10 Do not *o* the widow

oracle—1. a saying or answer; 2. the word of the Lord.

ordain—1. to set apart for a specific office or duty; 2. to order or command.

Ps 111:9 he *o* his covenant forever

ordinance—1. an official law; 2. a law made or commanded by God.

1Sa 30:25 a statute and *o* for Israel

ornate—elaborately decorated or adorned.

Ge 37:3 he made an *o* robe for him.

overseer—one of the terms used for leaders in the early church.

Ac 20:28 the Holy Spirit has made you *o*.
1Ti 3:2 Now the *o* is to be above reproach,

oxen—strong animals that were used in various ways in farming communities.

— P —

pagan—a person who does not worship God, especially someone who worships idols.

1Pe 2:12 such good lives among the *p* that,

papyrus—1. a large water plant, similar to the reed, which grows in marshes and lakes. Moses' mother put him in a basket made from papyrus (Ex 2:3); 2. a paper made from this plant.

parable—a story that tells a special lesson or truth. Jesus told many parables.

paralyzed—unable to move certain parts of one's body.

Mk 2:3 bringing to him a *p* man,

parents—fathers and mothers.

Pr 17:6 and *p* are the pride of their children.
Eph 6:1 Children, obey your *p* in the Lord,
Col 3:20 obey your *p* in everything,

Passover—an annual holiday that still today reminds the Jewish people of how God freed them from slavery in Egypt. The Lord "passed over" the homes marked with the blood of a lamb on their doorframes, but he killed all the other firstborn in Egypt.

Ex 12:11 Eat it in haste; it is the LORD's *P*.

Passover lamb—the lamb killed on the Passover as a sacrifice. Jesus is our Passover lamb, because he was sacrificed for our deliverance from sin, in the same way a lamb was sacrificed when the Israelites were delivered from Egypt.

1Co 5:7 our *P* lamb, has been sacrificed.

pasture—a plot or section of grassy land used for grazing cattle.

patient (patience)—able to put up with problems or pain without complaining or becoming angry.

Ro 12:12 Be joyful in hope, *p* in affliction,
1Co 13:4 Love is *p*, love is kind.
Col 3:12 kindness, humility, gentleness and *p*.

patriarch—the father and ruler of a family; the head of a tribe.

Paul—a Pharisee from Tarsus (Ac 9:11); named Saul at birth (Ac 13:9). Jesus appeared to him on the road to Damascus (Ac 9:4–9), and he became a powerful apostle (Gal 1). His writings make up a large part of the New Testament, ranging from intricate theology to passionate letters to struggling churches.

peace—freedom from disturbance; calm.

Isa 9:6 Everlasting Father, Prince of *P*.
Lk 2:14 on earth *p* to those on whom his
Jn 14:27 *P* I leave with you; my *p*
Ro 5:1 we have *p* with God
Gal 5:22 joy, *p*, forbearance, kindness,

Pentecost—a Jewish feast celebrated 50 days after the Passover. Today the Christian church celebrates Pentecost because it was the day the Holy Spirit came to dwell with Christ's followers (Ac 2:1–4).

people — a collective group.

2Ch 7:14 if my *p*, who are called by my name,
1Pe 2:9 you are a chosen *p*,

perfect — flawless; without defect.

Mt 5:48 Be *p*, therefore, as your heavenly

perish — to spoil; to be destroyed.

Ps 102:26 They will *p*, but you remain;

persecute (persecution) — to continually treat someone cruelly and unfairly. The early Christians were persecuted for believing in Jesus as the Son of God.

Jn 15:20 they *p* me, they will *p* you
Ac 26:14 'Saul, Saul, why do you *p* me?
Ro 12:14 Bless those who *p* you; bless

persevere (perseverance) — to refuse to give up; to keep on trying; to continue in one's actions or beliefs in spite of problems.

Ro 5:3 we know that suffering produces *p*;
Heb 10:36 You need to *p* so that
Heb 12:1 let us run with *p* the race

Persia — ancient geographical area and kingdom located north of the Persian Gulf.

pervert — to use wrongly; to turn from what is right.

pestilence — a plague; a disease that spreads quickly and kills many people.

Ps 91:3 snare and from the deadly *p*.

Peter — one of the twelve apostles; the brother of Andrew; also called Simon (Lk 6:14) and Cephas (Jn 1:42); he denied Jesus three times (Mk 14:66–72) but became a bold evangelist. He wrote the books of 1 and 2 Peter.

petition — to make a formal request.

pharaoh — the title given to the ruler of Egypt.

Pharisees — a group of Jews who obeyed very strictly both God's laws and all their own rules about God's laws.

Mt 5:20 surpasses that of the *P*

Philip — 1. one of the twelve apostles (Mt 10:3); 2. a deacon (Ac 6:1–7) and evangelist in Samaria; he witnessed to an Ethiopian (Ac 8:4–40).

Philistines — enemies of the Israelites throughout much of Old Testament history; they were especially powerful during the reigns of Saul and David.

Pilate — the governor of Judea who questioned Jesus (Lk 22:66—23:25) and then sent him to Herod (Lk 23:6–12). Pilate finally consented to Jesus' crucifixion when the crowds chose Barabbas rather than Jesus to be released (Lk 23:13–25).

pity — a sympathy or sorrow for the suffering of another.

Mk 9:22 take *p* on us and help us."

plague — 1. a disease that kills many people, such as the plague of boils (Ex 9:8–11); 2. an event that causes much suffering or loss, such as the plague of locusts (Ex 10:1–14).

plead — to appeal earnestly; to beg.

Job 16:21 he *p* with God as one *p* for a friend.

pledge — a binding promise or agreement.

1Ti 5:12 they have broken their first *p*.

plot — to plan, usually secretly; to scheme.

Ps 83:5 With one mind they *p* together;

plowshare — the pointed part of the plow; it cuts into the soil to make rows.

Mic 4:3 will beat their swords into *p*

plunder — 1. (*v.*) to loot or rob during a war; 2. (*n.*) property taken by plundering.

pomegranate — a reddish fruit about the size of an orange. It has many seeds and a juicy pulp.

poor — those who have little money.

Dt 15:4 there need be no *p* people
Isa 61:1 me to proclaim good news to the *p*.
Mt 26:11 The *p* you will always have
1Co 13:3 If I give all I possess to the *p*
2Co 8:9 yet for your sake he became *p*,

portico — a porch, usually at the front of a building.

2Ch 3:4 The *p* at the front of the temple

praise — 1. (*v.*) to glorify; to say good things about someone or something; 2. (*n.*) approval; worship.

Ex 15:2 He is my God, and I will *p* him,
Ps 119:175 Let me live that I may *p* you,
Eph 1:12 might be for the *p* of his glory.

pray — to talk with God.

2Ch 7:14 will humble themselves and *p*
Mt 6:5 "And when you *p*, do not be like

Ro 8:26 do not know what we ought to *p*
1Th 5:16–17 Rejoice always, *p* continually,

preach—to tell the message of the gospel in public; to deliver a sermon.

Mt 11:1 and *p* in the towns of Galilee.
Ro 10:15 how can they *p* unless they are sent?

precept—command; law; rule.

Ps 19:8 The *p* of the LORD are right,
Ps 119:69 I keep your *p* with all my heart.

precious—valuable; of great worth.

Ps 139:17 How *p* to me are your thoughts,

predestine—to decide or decree ahead of time.

Ro 8:30 And those he *p*, he also called;
Eph 1:5 he *p* us for adoption

pregnant—carrying an unborn child within a woman's body.

Lk 1:24 his wife Elizabeth became *p*

prevail—to triumph or succeed.

pride—1. (negative) the attitude that one is better than others; 2. (positive) a healthy self-respect or sense of satisfaction.

Pr 16:18 *P* goes before destruction,
Gal 6:4 they can take *p* in themselves

priest (priesthood)—a Levite who offered sacrifices and prayers to God for the people.

1Pe 2:9 you are a chosen people, a royal *p*,

prince—a male member of a royal family.

prison—a building where people are held, usually for committing a crime.

proclaim—to announce or declare.

1Ch 16:23 *p* his salvation day after day.
Ps 19:1 the skies *p* the work of his hands.
Isa 61:1 to *p* good news to the poor.
1Co 11:26 you *p* the Lord's death

profane—to make a holy thing impure by treating it with disrespect or irreverence.

Lev 22:32 Do not *p* my holy name,

prophecy—a message from God that a prophet brings to the people.

1Co 13:8 where there are *p*, they will cease;
2Pe 1:20 you must understand that no *p*

prophesy—to give the message of God to the people.

Joel 2:28 Your sons and daughters will *p*,
1Co 14:39 brothers and sisters, be eager to *p*,

prophet—a person who receives messages from God to tell to his people. A prophet is called by God to speak for him.

Dt 18:18 up for them a *p* like you
Lk 24:25 believe all that the *p* have spoken!
Ac 10:43 All the *p* testify about him that
Heb 1:1 through the *p* at many times

prosper—to succeed; achieve economic success.

Pr 11:25 A generous person will *p*;

prostitute—a person who offers his or her body for sexual relations in exchange for money.

Jos 2:1 house of a *p* named Rahab

prostrate—lying facedown on the ground.

proud—to have pride.

Ro 12:16 Do not be *p*, but be willing
Jas 4:6 "God opposes the *p*

proverbs—1. wise sayings; 2. (Proverbs) a book of the Bible that contains many wise sayings.

1Ki 4:32 He spoke three thousand *p*

provoke—to make angry; to cause trouble.

prudent—wise.

Pr 19:14 a *p* wife is from the LORD.

psalms—1. poetry written to praise God; 2. (Psalms) a book of the Bible that contains many psalms.

Eph 5:19 speaking to one another with *p*,

punish (punishment)—to cause someone to suffer for doing wrong.

Ge 4:13 "My *p* is more than I can bear.
Ex 20:5 jealous God, *p* the children for the sin

pure—perfectly free from fault or blemish.

Ps 51:10 Create in me a *p* heart, O God,

purify—to make pure or clean.

1Jn 1:7 of Jesus, his Son, *p* us from all sin.
1Jn 1:9 and *p* us from all unrighteousness.

Purim—an annual Jewish holiday celebrating Queen Esther's rescue of the Jews when Haman plotted to destroy them.

pursue—1. to follow in order to overtake; to chase; 2. to seek a goal.

Lev 26:7 You will *p* your enemies,
1Ti 6:11 and *p* righteousness, godliness,

— Q —

quail—a small spotted bird similar to the partridge; God provided quail and manna to the Israelites when they wandered in the wilderness.

Nu 11:32 people went out and gathered *q*.

quake—1. (*v.*) to shake or tremble; 2. (*n.*) an earthquake.

Ps 75:3 the earth and all its people *q*,
Rev 16:18 so tremendous was the *q*.

queen—1. the female ruler of a country; 2. the wife of a king.

— R —

Rabbi—a teacher of Jewish law.

Rachel—the daughter of Laban (Ge 29:16); she became Jacob's wife (Ge 29:28) and bore him two sons, Joseph and Benjamin (Ge 30:22–24; 35:16–24).

rage—a fit of anger.

Eph 4:31 Get rid of all bitterness, *r*

ram—a male sheep.

ransom—the price paid to get back a person who is held as a slave. Because people are slaves of sin, a ransom had to be paid, which was the death of the sinless one, Jesus.

Mt 20:28 and to give his life as a *r* for many."
Heb 9:15 as a *r* to set them free

reap—1. to cut down grain at harvest time; to gather a crop together; 2. to get as a result or reward.

Gal 6:7 A man *r* what he sows.

Rebekah—Isaac's wife (Ge 24); the mother of Esau and Jacob (Ge 25:19–26). With her encouragement, Jacob tricked his father into giving him the blessing that belonged to Esau (Ge 27:1–17).

rebel—1. (*v.*) to disobey and turn against those in authority; 2. (*n.*) a person who disobeys and flaunts authority.

Ro 13:2 whoever *r* against the authority

rebuke—to scold sharply.

2Ti 4:2 correct, *r* and encourage
Rev 3:19 Those whom I love I *r*

reconcile (reconciliation)—to return to friendship after a quarrel; human beings are "reconciled" to God through Christ.

Mt 5:24 First go and be *r* to them;
Ro 5:10 we were *r* to him through the death
2Co 5:18 and gave us the ministry of *r*:

redeem (redemption)—1. to free from evil by paying a price (Gal 3:13); 2. to buy back.

Ex 21:30 the owner may *r* his life
Gal 3:13 Christ *r* us from the curse
Eph 1:7 In him we have *r* through his blood,
Col 1:14 in whom we have *r*, the forgiveness

Red Sea—the body of water the Israelites crossed in a miraculous way when they were escaping from slavery in Egypt.

refuge—a place of shelter and safety.

Ps 46:1 God is our *r* and strength,

regard—to pay attention to.

Ps 41:1 Blessed are those who have *r* for the weak;

regulations—rules dealing with procedure or ceremony.

Rehoboam—the son of Solomon; he became king after his father's death (1Ki 11:43). Because of his harsh treatment of the people, Israel was divided into two kingdoms (1Ki 12:1–24; 14:21–31).

reign—the time during which a king or other official rules.

rejoice—to express joy or gladness.

Ps 118:24 let us *r* today be glad.
Lk 1:47 and my spirit *r* in God my Savior,
Php 4:4 *R* in the Lord always.

remnant—a small part remaining; a small surviving group.

Isa 10:21 A *r* will return,

repent (repentance) — to turn away from sin; to be sorry for what one has done and to promise not to do it again.

Mt 4:17 "*R*, for the kingdom of heaven
Lk 3:8 Produce fruit in keeping with *r*.
Ac 2:38 Peter replied, "*R* and be baptized,

reproach — 1. (*v.*) to blame or accuse; 2. (*n.*) something for which one can be blamed or criticized.

Job 27:6 my conscience will not *r* me

require (requirement) — to demand as necessary.

1Ki 8:31 is *r* to take an oath
Zec 3:7 obedience to me and keep my *r*,

rescue — to save or deliver.

Ps 140:1 *R* me, LORD from evildoers;

respect — to look up to or hold in high esteem.

1Pe 2:17 Show proper *r* to everyone,

restitution — to restore or pay back for damage, loss or injury.

Nu 5:7 must make full *r* for the wrong

restore — to bring back; to return something to its former condition.

Ps 51:12 *R* to me the joy of your salvation
Ac 3:21 time comes for God to *r* everything,

resurrection — the act of coming back to life after being dead.

Jn 11:25 Jesus said to her, "I am the *r*
Ro 1:4 in power by his *r* from the dead:
1Co 15:12 some of you say that there is no *r*

retribution — punishment for doing wrong.

Jer 51:56 For the LORD is a God of *r*;

Reuben — oldest son of Jacob and founder of the tribe of the same name.

revelation — the act of making known or telling about.

Gal 1:12 I received it by *r* from Jesus Christ.
Rev 1:1 *r* from Jesus Christ, which God gave

revenge — to hurt or punish a person who has wronged you; to get back at someone who has hurt you.

Lev 19:18 "'Do not seek *r* or bear a grudge
Ro 12:19 Do not take *r*, my dear friends,

reverence (revere) — a deep respect, honor and awe.

Ps 5:7 in *r* I bow down
Col 3:22 of heart and *r* for the Lord.

reward — 1. (*v.*) to repay with good for something someone has done; 2. (*n.*) the gift one receives for good behavior or character.

Ps 127:3 offspring a *r* from him.
Jer 17:10 to *r* each person according to
Mt 5:12 because great is your *r* in heaven,
Mt 6:5 they have received their *r* in full.

righteous (righteousness) — being in a right relationship to God; not guilty before God.

Isa 64:6 and all our *r* acts are like filthy rags;
Ro 3:10 "There is no one *r*, not even one;

Rome — 1. the empire that controlled much of the known world at the time of Christ; 2. the capital city of the Roman Empire, located in Italy.

royal — of or belonging to the ruler of a country and his family.

Ruth — a Moabite widow who went with her mother-in-law Naomi to Bethlehem (Ru 1). There she gathered the gleanings from the field of Boaz (Ru 2), whom she later married (Ru 3:1—4:12). She was an ancestor of David (Ru 4:13–22) and of Jesus (Mt 1:5).

ruthless — merciless; cruel.

Ps 54:3 *r* people are trying to kill me
Hab 1:6 that *r* and impetuous people,

— S —

Sabbath — the seventh day of the week; the Jewish day of rest and worship. It extended from Friday sunset until Saturday sunset.

Ex 20:8 "Remember the *S* day

sackcloth — a rough cloth, usually woven from goats' hair. Clothing made of sackcloth was worn as a sign of mourning for the dead or as a sign that a person was sorry for his or her sins.

sacred — holy; set apart for God in a special way.

1Co 3:17 God's temple is *s*,

sacrifice — 1. (*v.*) to offer something as a gift to God; 2. (*n.*) an offering given to God. In the Old Testament God commanded the people to pay for their sins by sacrificing the blood of cattle, lambs, goats, doves or pigeons. These sacrifices were pictures of Jesus' coming as a once-for-all sacrifice for sinners.

Ex 12:27	'It is the Passover *s* to the LORD,
1Sa 15:22	To obey is better than *s*,
Ro 12:1	to offer your bodies as a living *s*,
Heb 9:28	so Christ was *s* once
1Jn 2:2	He is the atoning *s* for our sins,

Sadducees — a group of Jewish leaders, many of them priests. Unlike the Pharisees, the Sadducees did not believe in a resurrection of the dead, but they agreed with the Pharisees in their hatred of Jesus.

Mk 12:18	*S*, who say there is no resurrection,

salvation — deliverance from the guilt and power of sin. By his death and resurrection, Jesus brings salvation to people who believe in him.

Ps 27:1	The LORD is my light and my *s*
Lk 2:30	For my eyes have seen your *s*,
Ac 4:12	*S* is found in no one else,
2Co 7:10	brings repentance that leads to *s*
Php 2:12	to work out your *s* with fear
Heb 2:3	escape if we ignore so great a *s*?

Samaritan — a person who lived in or came from Samaria. Because the Samaritans were only partly Jewish and worshiped God differently from the Jews, Jews from Judea and Galilee hated the Samaritans. They would go out of their way to travel around Samaria (Lk 10:30–37).

Samson — an Israelite judge who was known for his great strength. He was betrayed by Delilah but in the end was used by God to punish the Philistines (Jdg 16).

Samuel — often called the last of Israel's judges and the first of Israel's prophets (see also Heb 11:32). His birth was earnestly prayed for by his mother Hannah (1Sa 1:10–18), and when he was old enough, she brought him to the temple and he was dedicated to the Lord (1Sa 1:21–28). There he was raised by Eli (1Sa 2:11, 18—26) and was called to be a prophet (1Sa 3).

sanctify (sanctification) — to make holy; sanctification is the ongoing work of the Holy Spirit in the hearts of believers.

Ro 15:16	to God, *s* by the Holy Spirit.
1Th 5:23	*s* you through and through.
2Th 2:13	through the *s* work of the Spirit

sanctuary — a place where God is worshiped; a holy place.

Ps 150:1	Praise God in his *s*;

Sanhedrin — the ruling council of the Jews in Jesus' time. It was made up of 70 men, and the leader was the high priest. The Sanhedrin could decide whether someone was innocent or guilty of breaking a Jewish law, but it could not put anyone to death without the permission of the Roman governor.

Mk 14:55	the whole *S* were looking for evidence

Sarah — the wife of Abraham and mother of Isaac; first called Sarai (Ge 11:29–31). God promised her that, though she had been barren throughout her life, she would give birth to a son in her old age (Ge 17:15–21; 18:10–15).

Satan — the devil; the leader of the fallen spirits; the most powerful enemy of God and humans.

Mk 4:15	*S* comes and takes away the word
2Co 11:14	for *S* himself masquerades
Rev 12:9	serpent called the devil, or *S*,

satisfy — 1. to please, to make happy; 2. to fulfill a condition.

Ps 103:5	who *s* your desires with good things

satrap — the governor of a province in ancient Persia.

Saul — 1. the first king of Israel (1Sa 9—10). He was anointed by Samuel but was later rejected by God because of disobedience; David was chosen to be his successor; 2. see Paul.

saved — 1. (*v.*) rescued from danger; 2. (*n.*) people who acknowledge that by Jesus' death they have been rescued from the punishment of death that their sins deserve.

Ro 10:13	on the name of the Lord will be *s*."
Eph 2:8	For it is by grace you have been *s*,

Savior — a name for Jesus that means he saves his people from sin.

Lk 1:47	and my spirit rejoices in God my *S*,
1Ti 4:10	who is the *S* of all people,
1Jn 4:14	Son to be the *S* of the world.

scarlet—the color bright red.

scepter—a rod or stick held by a king or queen as a sign of royal power and authority.

Ge 49:10 The *s* will not depart from Judah,

scoff—to mock or sneer at.

Ps 2:4 the Lord *s* at them.

scorn—to despise, to reject with anger or contempt.

Ps 69:20 *S* has broken my heart

scorpion—a spider-like animal with a poisonous stinger at the end of its tail.

scoundrel—a mean, worthless person; a villain.

Pr 16:27 A *s* plots evil,

scourge—to whip.

2Ch 10:11 My father *s* you with whips;

scribe—a person with the important task of copying letters, books and legal papers.

Scripture—all or part of the Bible. When the Bible uses this word it means the Old Testament, since the New Testament had not yet been written. Today we call the Old and New Testaments the Bible or Scripture.

Jn 10:35 and *S* cannot be set aside
2Ti 3:16 All *S* is God-breathed
2Pe 1:20 that no prophecy of *S* came about

scroll—a book made of a long piece of leather or paper that was rolled around a stick at both ends.

Jos 18:9 They wrote its description on a *s*,

seal—1. a tool with a design raised on it or cut into it; 2. the mark made by pressing this tool onto wax, paper or other soft material. A seal was used to close a letter or legal paper or to prove the authority of the paper.

2Co 1:22 set his *s* of ownership on us,
Rev 5:2 "Who is worthy to break the *s*

sect—a group of people who hold one or more beliefs in common; especially, a small religious group that has separated from a larger group.

seer—a prophet; a person who, with God's help, can see what will happen in the future.

1Sa 9:19 "I am the *s*," Samuel replied.

self-control—the ability to control one's own actions and feelings.

Gal 5:23 gentleness and *s*.
2Pe 1:6 and to knowledge, *s*; and to *s*,

selfish—centered on oneself; not interested in others.

Php 2:3 Do nothing out of *s* ambition

Sennacherib—an Assyrian king who raided Judah during the time of Hezekiah.

sexual immorality—using sex in ways God says are wrong.

1Co 6:13 body, however, is not meant for *s*,
1Th 4:3 that you should avoid *s*;

shame—a painful emotion caused by an awareness of guilt or shortcoming.

Pr 19:26 a child who brings *s* and disgrace.
1Co 15:34 I say this to your *s*.

sheep—the animal most often mentioned in Scripture, probably because it was the animal most often raised in Bible times; used for meat, for cloth, and for religious sacrifice.

Isa 53:6 We all, like *s*, have gone astray,

shekel—a specific weight of silver, used as money.

Shem—one of the three sons of Noah (Ge 5:32). He, along with his brother Japheth, covered his father when he was naked (Ge 9:21–29). Abraham was one of his descendants (Ge 11:10–32).

shepherd—someone who takes care of a flock of sheep. It is often used in the Bible as a figure of speech for anyone who cares for a group of people.

Ps 23:1 The LORD is my *s*, I lack nothing.
Jer 31:10 will watch over his flock like a *s*.'
Jn 10:11 The good *s* lays down his life
Ac 20:28 Be *s* of the church of God,

shield—a piece of defensive armor, usually carried on the arm; often a figure of speech in the Bible used to describe God's protection of his people.

Ps 7:10 My *s* is God Most High,

shrine—a dwelling for a god.

sickle—a tool with a long, curved blade and a short handle, used for cutting grain.

siege—see besiege.

signet—a ring with a design on it. The design was stamped in wax to seal a letter or legal paper. Signet rings were usually worn by people in authority.

Silas—a member of the church in Jerusalem; he traveled with Paul.

Simon—1. see Peter; 2. one of the twelve apostles; also called the Zealot (Mt 10:4; Ac 1:13); 3. a sorcerer in Samaria who had great influence on the Samaritan people during the early days of the church; he was severely rebuked by Peter (Ac 8:9–24) for attempting to buy the power of the Holy Spirit.

sin—1. (*v.*) to break the law of God; 2. (*n.*) the act of not doing what God wants.

Nu 32:23 be sure that your *s* will find you
Ps 51:2 and cleanse me from my *s.*
Ps 119:11 that I might not *s* against you.
Isa 1:18 "Though your *s* are like scarlet,
Mt 1:21 he will save his people from their *s.*"
Lk 11:4 Forgive us our *s,*
Jn 1:29 who takes away the *s* of the world!
Ro 3:23 for all have *s* and fall short
Ro 6:23 For the wages of *s* is death,
2Co 5:21 God made him who had no *s* to be *s*
1Jn 1:9 If we confess our *s,* he is faithful

Sinai, Mount—the mountain where Moses received the Ten Commandments (Ex 19—20).

sinner—a person who breaks the law of God.

Ps 1:1 or stand in the way that *s* take
Mt 9:13 come to call the righteous, but *s.*"
Lk 15:7 in heaven over one *s* who repents
Lk 18:13 'God, have mercy on me, a *s.*'
Ro 5:8 While we were still *s,* Christ died

slander—1. (*v.*) saying untrue things about another person in order to hurt him or her; 2. (*n.*) false charges or misrepresentations about another person.

Lev 19:16 "'Do not go about spreading *s*
Titus 3:2 to *s* no one, to be peaceable

slaughter—1. the butchering of livestock for food; 2. the killing of great numbers of human beings, as in a battle.

slave—1. a person who is owned by another; 2. a person who is dominated or controlled by an outside force.

Ro 7:14 I am unspiritual, sold as a *s* to sin.
Gal 3:28 *s* nor free, male nor female,

slay, slain—to kill violently or in great numbers.

sluggard—a lazy person.

Pr 19:24 A *s* buries his hand in the dish;

slumber—to sleep.

snare—a trap; something risky that tempts or endangers a person.

snatch—to grab suddenly, often without permission or right.

Sodom and Gomorrah—the two cities destroyed by God because the people were so wicked.

Ge 19:24 rained down burning sulfur on *S*

Solomon—the son of David and Bathsheba (2Sa 12:24). He became king of Israel after David died (1Ki 1). He asked God for wisdom and was given it (1Ki 3), and he built the temple (1Ki 5—7). His many foreign wives turned his heart away from God (1Ki 11:1–13).

son—a male descendant.

Pr 10:1 A wise *s* brings joy to his father,
Joel 2:28 Your *s* and daughters will prophesy,
2Co 6:18 you will be my *s* and daughters,
Heb 2:10 many *s* and daughters to glory,
1Jn 4:9 only *S* into the world that we might

Son of Man—a title Jesus used for himself to show his humanity as distinct from his divinity. It was also a reference to the Messiah prophesied about in Daniel 7:13.

Mt 20:18 and the *S* will be delivered
Mk 14:62 you will see the *S* sitting
Lk 19:10 For the *S* came to seek
Jn 3:14 so the *S* must be lifted up,

sorcery—the use of magic and supernatural powers that are evil; witchcraft.

Dt 18:10 practices divination or *s,*

soul—the spiritual part of a person; the part of a person that does not die.

Dt 6:5 with all your *s* and with all your
Ps 23:3 he refreshes my *s.*

Mt 10:28 kill the body but cannot kill the *s.*
Mt 11:29 and you will find rest for your *s.*
Mt 16:26 yet forfeit their *s?* Or what can
Mt 22:37 with all your *s* and with all your

sovereign—having authority over everything; often used in Scripture as a descriptive title for God, "Sovereign Lord."

sow—to plant seeds. In Jesus' time seeds were sown by scattering them by hand over the ground.

Job 4:8 and those who *s* trouble reap it.
Mk 4:3 A farmer went out to *s* his seed.
Gal 6:7 A man reaps what he *s.*

spear—a weapon with a long handle and a sharp point, usually thrown.

spirit—1. the part of a person that is not the body; the soul; 2. a being who does not have a body; 3. (cap.) see Holy Spirit.

Ps 31:5 Into your hands I commit my *s;*
Eze 36:26 you a new heart and put a new *s*
Mt 5:3 "Blessed are the poor in *s,*
Mt 26:41 *s* is willing, but the flesh is weak."
1Jn 4:1 Dear friends, do not believe every *s,*

splendor—something magnificent or splendid.

spoils—booty or plunder taken from an enemy in war.

springs—a source of water coming up from the ground.

Dt 8:7 streams, and deep *s* gushing out
Rev 7:17 lead them to *s* of living water.

staff—a stick used to lean on; a rod used by a shepherd.

Ps 23:4 your rod and your *s,*

starry hosts—the stars and other heavenly bodies.

2Ki 21:3 He bowed down to all the *s*

statutes—established rules or laws.

Ps 19:7 *s* of the Lord are trustworthy,

steadfast—settled; not changing or wavering.

Ps 51:10 and renew a *s* spirit within me.

steal—to rob; to take what belongs to someone else.

Ex 20:15 "You shall not *s.*
Eph 4:28 must *s* no longer,

stench—a terrible smell.

Stephen—one of the first seven men to serve the Jerusalem church (Ac 6:5); he became the first Christian martyr (Ac 7:60).

stiff-necked—stubborn.

Ac 7:51 "You *s* people!

stone—to kill or to try to kill someone by throwing rocks or stones.

strength—power; forcefulness.

Ex 15:2 "The Lord is my *s* and my defense;
Dt 6:5 all your soul and with all your *s.*
Ps 46:1 God is our refuge and *s,*
Isa 40:31 will renew their *s.*
Php 4:13 through him who gives me *s.*

strife—bitter and sometimes violent conflict.

Pr 30:33 stirring up anger produces *s.*"

stronghold—a fortified place; a place of security.

1Sa 24:22 David and his men went up to the *s.*
Ps 27:1 The Lord is the *s* of my life

subdue—to bring under control; to conquer.

Ps 81:14 how quickly I would *s* their enemies

submission—humbleness; obedience.

1Co 14:34 but must be in *s,* as the law says.
1Ti 2:11 learn in quietness and full *s.*

submit—to willingly yield to another.

Pr 3:6 in all your ways *s* to him,
Eph 5:21 *S* to one another out of reverence
Col 3:18 Wives, *s* yourselves to your husbands,
Jas 4:7 *S* yourselves, then, to God.

succeed—1. to turn out well; 2. to follow another as heir or successor of a title or rank.

suffer—to bear or endure something painful.

Mk 8:31 the Son of Man must *s* many things
Lk 24:26 the Messiah have to *s* these things
1Co 12:26 If one part *s,* every part *s* with it;

suffering — the experience of enduring pain.

Isa 53:3 of *s*, and familiar with pain.
Ac 5:41 worthy of *s* disgrace for the Name.
Ro 8:17 share in his *s* in order that we may
2Ti 1:8 Rather, join with me in *s* for the gospel,

summon — to issue a call to come together; to send for.

Isa 43:1 I have *s* you by name; you are mine.

sustain — to give support; to help; to comfort.

Ps 18:35 and your right hand *s* me;
Ps 146:9 and *s* the fatherless and the widow,

swear — to promise forcefully or earnestly.

1Sa 30:15 "*S* to me before God that you will

swindler — someone who cheats another person out of money or other possessions.

1Co 6:10 nor *s* will inherit the kingdom

sword — a weapon with a long blade for cutting or thrusting.

symbol — an object or action that stands for or suggests something else. The cross is a symbol of Jesus' death.

synagogue — the Jewish place of worship and religious teaching.

Lk 4:16 the Sabbath day he went into the *s*,
Ac 17:2 his custom, Paul went into the *s*,

— T —

tabernacle — the tent used by the Israelites for meeting with God; the place where God chose to show his presence. The tabernacle was made by God's command and according to his plans. It is described in detail in Exodus 26. Also called the tent of meeting.

Ex 40:34 the glory of the LORD filled the *t*.

talent — a large amount (75 lbs or 34 kg) of silver or gold, worth very much money.

Ex 25:39 A *t* of pure gold is to be used

tax — money a government requires its citizens to pay.

Mt 22:19 the coin used for paying the *t*."

teach — to instruct; to help someone learn.

Ex 33:13 *t* me your ways so I may know you
Ps 90:12 *T* us to number our days,
Lk 11:1 said to him, "Lord, *t* us to pray,
Jn 14:26 will *t* you all things and will remind

tempest — a violent storm.

temple — 1. the place where the Jewish people worshiped and sacrificed in Jerusalem; the first temple was built by King Solomon as a house for God; 2. any place of worship. In this sense, the human body is referred to as a temple (1Co 6:19).

1Ki 8:27 How much less this *t* I have built!
Ac 17:24 not live in *t* built by human hands.
2Co 6:16 For we are the *t* of the living God.

tempt (temptation) — trying to get someone to do wrong.

Mt 4:1 the wilderness to be *t* by the devil.
1Co 10:13 No *t* has overtaken you except

tenant — one who rents land or a house from a landlord.

testimony — a statement made by a witness to prove that something is true.

Lk 18:20 not give false *t*, honor your father

tetrarch — a ruler over one fourth of a kingdom.

Thaddaeus — one of the twelve apostles (Mk 3:18); son of James and probably also known as Judas (Lk 6:16; Ac 1:13).

thanks — the expression of gratitude.

1Ch 16:34 Give *t* to the LORD, for
Ps 100:4 give *t* to him and praise his name.
1Co 15:57 *t* be to God! He gives us the victory
2Co 9:15 *T* be to God for his indescribable
1Th 5:18 give *t* in all circumstances;

thanksgiving — recognizing and thanking the one who has provided a gift.

Ps 100:4 Enter his gates with *t*
Php 4:6 by prayer and petition, with *t*,

Thomas — one of the twelve apostles (Lk 6:15; Ac 1:13); at first he doubted Jesus' resurrection, but when he saw Jesus, he believed (Jn 20:24–28).

thrive — to grow vigorously.

Thummim — see Urim.

threshing floor — the place where grain was trampled by oxen or beaten with a stick to separate it from the stalk.

Ru 3:6 So she went down to the *t*

Timothy — fellow-traveler and official representative of the apostle Paul. He joined Paul on his second missionary journey (Ac 16—20), and at one point in this journey Paul sent him to minister to the church at Corinth (1Co 4:17; 16:10). He was the leader of the church at Ephesus (1Ti 1:3) and a co-writer with Paul (1Th 1:1; 2Th 1:1; Phm 1).

tithe — the giving to God of one-tenth of what one earns.

Lev 27:30 " 'A *t* of everything from the land,
Mal 3:10 the whole *t* into the storehouse,

Titus — a Gentile coworker with Paul (Gal 2:1–3; 2Ti 4:10). Paul sent him to Corinth to help solve some of the problems there (2Co 2:13; 7—8; 12:18).

toil — 1. (*n.*) strenuous and tiring work; 2. (*v.*) to work long and hard.

Ecc 3:9 What do workers gain from their *t?*

tomb — a burial place. In Bible times, a tomb was often either a cave or a cavity dug into a stone cliff, with a large stone rolled in front to close it.

Mt 27:65 make the *t* as secure as you know
Lk 24:2 the stone rolled away from the *t*,
Jn 11:17 been in the *t* for four days.

tongue — 1. the organ of speech in the mouth; 2. a language.

Ps 39:1 and keep my *t* from sin;
Ac 2:4 and began to speak in other *t*
Php 2:11 every *t* acknowledge that Jesus
Jas 1:26 do not keep a tight rein on their *t*

torment — extreme pain or anguish; agony.

2Co 12:7 a messenger of Satan, to *t* me.

tradition — the handing down of information and beliefs from one generation to another.

Mt 15:2 break the *t* of the elders?

trample — to walk heavily causing injury or damage.

Ps 60:12 he will *t* down our enemies.

transfigure — to change the appearance of; to make bright and glorious.

Mt 17:2 There he was *t* before them.

transgression — sin; disobeying the law of God.

Ps 32:1 whose *t* are forgiven,
Isa 53:5 But he was pierced for our *t*,
Eph 2:1 you were dead in your *t* and sins,

treacherous — untrustworthy, unreliable, faithless.

tread — to step or walk on or over.

Job 24:11 they *t* the winepresses,

treasure — 1. (*n.*) wealth that is stored up or hidden away; 2. (*v.*) to hold or keep something precious, something of value; to cherish.

Mt 6:21 your *t* is, there your heart will be also.

treaty — an agreement between two people or groups or nations.

Ex 34:12 Be careful not to make a *t*

trespass — sin; wrongdoing.

Ro 5:17 For if, by the *t* of the one man,

tribe — a social group made up of a particular branch of a family.

tribute — payment by one ruler or nation to another as an act of submission or in order to guarantee protection.

Isa 16:1 Send lambs as *t* to the ruler

triumph — a victory; a notable success.

Pr 28:12 the righteous *t*, there is great elation;

true — certain; exactly right.

Ps 119:160 All your words are *t*;
Jn 17:3 the only *t* God, and Jesus Christ,
Ro 3:4 Let God be *t*, and every human
Php 4:8 whatever is *t*, whatever is noble,

trust — firm belief or faith in another.

Ps 37:3 *T* in the LORD and do good;
Pr 3:5 *T* in the LORD with all your heart

Isa 26:3 because they *t* in you.
Isa 30:15 in quietness and *t* is your strength,
1Co 4:2 been given a *t* must prove faithful.

trustworthy — deserving of trust; reliable.

Ps 19:7 The statutes of the LORD are *t*,
1Ti 1:15 Here is a *t* saying that deserves full

truth — that which conforms to the facts.

Ps 145:18 to all who call on him in *t*.
Zec 8:16 are to do: Speak the *t* to each other,
Jn 8:32 know the *t*, and the *t*
Jn 14:6 I am the way and the *t* and the life.
Ro 1:25 They exchanged the *t* about God
1Co 13:6 in evil but rejoices with the *t*.
Eph 4:15 Instead, speaking the *t* in love,
Heb 10:26 received the knowledge of the *t*,
1Jn 1:6 we lie and do not live out the *t*.
1Jn 1:8 deceive ourselves and the *t* is not

tunic — a long shirt worn by men in Bible times.

Ezr 9:3 When I heard this, I tore my *t*

turban — a head-covering made by winding a cloth around the head.

— U —

unbelief — doubt.

Mk 9:24 help me overcome my *u!*"

unbeliever — one who does not believe in Jesus.

2Co 6:14 Do not be yoked together with *u*.

unclean — morally or spiritually impure; unclean animals were those that the Israelites were not allowed to sacrifice or to eat.

unity — being one.

Ps 133:1 God's people live together in *u!*
Col 3:14 them all together in perfect *u*.

unleavened bread — bread made without yeast. It is usually flat, like a pancake or cracker.

Ex 12:17 "Celebrate the Festival of *U*,

uphold — to give support to.

Ps 37:17 the LORD *u* the righteous.

upright — honest; doing what is right and good.

Urim and Thummim — objects that were placed on the vest of the high priest; used to determine God's will for the nation of Israel.

utter — to pronounce, to speak.

Ps 78:2 I will *u* hidden things,
Jer 15:19 if you *u* worthy, not worthless, words,

utterly — completely, totally.

— V —

vain — worthless; unsuccessful; foolish. "In vain" means without success or result.

valiant — courageous.

vast — very great in size or amount; huge.

vault — the atmosphere or sky as seen from the earth.

Ge 1:8 God called the *v* "sky."

vengeance — hurt or punishment done to another person who has done something wrong against another.

Isa 34:8 For the LORD has a day of *v*,

vigor — strength and health in the body and its growth.

Job 20:11 The youthful *v* that fills his bones

vile — disgusting, evil.

Rev 22:11 let the *v* person continue to be *v*;

vindicate — to defend; to provide justice for; to set free.

Ps 135:14 For the LORD will *v* his people

violate — 1. to rape; 2. to make something unholy; 3. to fail to obey.

viper — 1. a venomous snake; 2. a treacherous or vicious person.

virgin — a woman or girl who has never had sexual intercourse.

Isa 7:14 The *v* will conceive
Mt 1:23 "The *v* will conceive

vision — a dream from God.

Nu 12:6 reveal myself to them in *v*,
Joel 2:28 your young men will see *v*.
Ac 26:19 disobedient to the *v* from heaven.

vow — a solemn promise made before God or to God.

Jdg 11:30 Jephthah made a *v* to the LORD:
Ps 116:14 I will fulfill my *v* to the LORD

— W —

wages — payment received for work completed.

Ro 6:23 For the *w* of sin is death,

wail — to cry loudly.

walk — to follow a certain course.

Ps 1:1 who does not *w* in step
Isa 2:5 let us *w* in the light of the LORD.
Mic 6:8 and to *w* humbly with your God.
2Jn 6 his command is that you *w* in love.

wander — to move about without a fixed course.

Nu 32:13 he made them *w* in the wilderness
Jas 5:19 if one of you should *w* from the truth

warn — to give notice beforehand of danger or evil.

warrior — a soldier.

Isa 9:3 as *w* rejoice when dividing

wash — to clean.

Ps 51:7 *w* me, and I will be whiter
Ac 22:16 be baptized and *w* your sins away,

watch — to be on the lookout for someone or something.

Jer 31:10 will *w* over his flock like a shepherd.'
Mt 26:41 "*W* and pray so that you will not fall

way — the means of getting somewhere; the path.

2Sa 22:31 "As for God, his *w* is perfect:
Ps 1:1 or stand in the *w* that sinners
Ps 37:5 Commit your *w* to the LORD;
Isa 53:6 each of us has turned to our own *w*;
Jn 14:6 "I am the *w* and the truth
1Co 12:31 will show you the most excellent *w*.

wean — to help a child or animal begin to eat solid food rather than his or her mother's milk.

weapon — an object used for fighting.

weary — 1. tired; 2. having one's patience or tolerance exhausted.

Dt 25:18 When you were *w* and worn out,
Zec 11:8 and I grew *w* of them

weep, wept — to cry.

Jn 11:35 Jesus *w*.

welcome — 1. to greet a person pleasantly; 2. to make a person feel at home.

Jdg 19:20 "You are *w* at my house,"

wholehearted — sincere; devoted without holding anything back.

wicked — sinful.

Ps 1:1 walk in step with the *w*
Isa 55:7 Let the *w* forsake their ways

widow — a woman whose husband has died.

will — desire; seeking God's will means looking for what God wants to be done.

Ps 143:10 Teach me to do your *w*,
Isa 53:10 Yet it was the LORD's *w*
Mt 6:10 your *w* be done,
Mt 26:39 Yet not as I *w*, but as you *w*."
Ro 12:2 and approve what God's *w* is
Eph 5:17 understand what the Lord's *w* is.
1Jn 5:14 we ask anything according to his *w*,
Rev 4:11 and by your *w* they were created

winepress — a vat or tub in which the juice of grapes is pressed out. Used in the Bible as a symbol for the anger of God against wickedness.

Rev 14:19 into the great *w* of God's wrath.

wisdom — the understanding that comes from God.

Lk 2:52 And Jesus grew in *w* and stature,
Jas 1:5 of you lacks *w*, you should ask God,

witchcraft — practices using evil spirits, magic, or sorcery.

Mic 5:12 I will destroy your *w*

wither — to dry or shrivel up, usually from a lack of moisture.

witness — one who personally sees an event take place.

Ac 22:15 You will be his *w* to all people

woe — great misery; distress.

Isa 6:5 "*W* to me!" I cried.
Lk 11:42 "*W* to you Pharisees, because you

womb — the organ within a woman's body where a child grows before birth.

Lk 1:44 the baby in my *w* leaped for joy.

word — 1. the means of expressing oneself through language; 2. the Bible, as God's written message to people; 3. (cap.) Jesus is the Word sent from God because his life on earth told the message of God.

Jn 1:14 The *W* became flesh and made his
Heb 4:12 For the *w* of God is alive

work — 1. (*n.*) employment; duty; 2. (*v.*) to bring about; to try to achieve a goal.

Ex 23:12 "Six days do your *w*,
Jn 9:4 we must do the *w* of him who sent
Php 2:12 continue to *w* out your salvation
2Ti 3:17 equipped for every good *w*.

world — 1. the earth and those who live in it; 2. the secular, as opposed to the spiritual or religious.

Mt 5:14 "You are the light of the *w*.
Jn 1:29 who takes away the sin of the *w*!
Jn 3:16 so loved the *w* that he gave his one
Jn 8:12 he said, "I am the light of the *w*.
Ro 12:2 Do not conform to the pattern of this *w*,
1Jn 2:15 not love the *w* or anything in the *w*.

worldly — loving the things of the world more than the things of God.

Titus 2:12 to ungodliness and *w* passions,

worry — to feel anxious and uneasy.

Mt 6:25 I tell you, do not *w* about your life,

worship — 1. (*v.*) to give praise, honor and respect to God; 2. (*n.*) reverence given to God.

Ps 95:6 Come, let us bow down in *w*,
Jn 4:24 his worshipers must *w* in the Spirit

worthy — having value; honorable; deserving.

1Ch 16:25 For great is the LORD and most *w*
Eph 4:1 to live a life *w* of the calling you
Rev 5:2 "Who is *w* to break the seals

wrath — great anger; the strong anger of God.

Pr 15:1 A gentle answer turns away *w*,
Ro 5:9 saved from God's *w* through him!

— X —

Xerxes — king of Persia; he made Esther, a young Jewess, his queen (Est 2:15–18).

— Y —

yearn — to long for; to want very much.

yeast — the ingredient that makes dough rise; sometimes a figure of speech for the influence someone has over others.

Mt 16:6 guard against the *y* of the Pharisees
Gal 5:9 little *y* works through the whole

yield — 1. to submit; 2. to grow or produce fruit.

Ps 67:6 The land *y* its harvest;
Isa 48:11 I will not *y* my glory to another.

yoke — 1. (*v.*) to join together; 2. (*n.*) a wooden bar that goes over the necks of two animals, usually oxen. The yoke holds the animals together as they pull an object, such as a plow or a cart.

Mt 11:29 Take my *y* upon you and learn
2Co 6:14 Do not be *y* together

youth — the time when a person is young.

Ecc 12:1 Creator in the days of your *y*,

— Z —

Zacchaeus—a tax collector who climbed a tree in order to see Jesus (Lk 19:1-5).

zeal—eagerness; strong desire.

Ro 12:11 Never be lacking in *z*,

Zealot—a member of the Jewish group that wanted to fight against and overthrow the Roman government.

Zechariah—a prophet and priest who returned to Jerusalem from the Babylonian captivity; he encouraged the Jews to rebuild the temple (Ezr 5:1; 6:14; Zec 1:1).

Zerubbabel—a descendant of David (1Ch 3:19); he led the return of the Jews from the Babylonian captivity (Ezr 1—3; Ne 7:7; Hag 1—2; Zec 4).

Zion—1. the hill on which the city of Jerusalem first stood; David's royal palace and the temple were both built on Mount Zion; 2. the entire city of Jerusalem.

Jer 50:5 They will ask the way to *Z*
Ro 11:26 "The deliverer will come from *Z*;

Book Introduction Photo Credits:

Genesis: Thammanoon Khamchalee/shutterstock.com; **Exodus:** Dudarev Mikhail/shutterstock.com; **Leviticus:** vvvita/shutterstock.com; **Numbers:** hermitis/shutterstock.com; **Deuteronomy:** Suprun Vitaly/shutterstock.com; **Joshua:** posztos/shutterstock.com; **Judges:** Tanya Keisha/shutterstock.com; **Ruth:** Subbotina Anna/shutterstock.com; **1 Samuel:** vvvita/shutterstock.com; **2 Samuel:** Lady_Luck/shutterstock.com; **1 Kings:** tomertu/stock.adobe.com; **2 Kings:** MagioreStockStudio/stock.adobe.com; **1 Chronicles:** vvvita/shutterstock.com; **2 Chronicles:** vvvita/shutterstock.com; **Ezra:** vvvita/shutterstock.com; **Nehemiah:** John Theodor/shutterstock.com; **Esther:** Cpyusuf/shutterstock.com; **Job:** vvvita/shutterstock.com; **Psalms:** Vaclav Uhlir/shutterstock.com; **Proverbs:** alejandroav/stock.adobe.com; **Ecclesiastes:** jdross75/stock.adobe.com; **Song of Songs:** lilgrapher/shutterstock.com; **Isaiah:** Boris Diakovsky/shutterstock.com; **Jeremiah:** Tryfonov/stock.adobe.com; **Lamentations:** isparklinglife/shutterstock.com; **Ezekiel:** pamela_d_mcadams/stock.adobe.com; **Daniel:** Andrea Izzotti/stock.adobe.com; **Hosea:** Lubo Ivanko/shutterstock.com; **Joel:** givaga/shutterstock.com; **Amos:** Shi/stock.adobe.com; **Obadiah:** Moshe Einhorn/stock.adobe.com; **Jonah:** katatonia/stock.adobe.com; **Micah:** Jaroslav/stock.adobe.com; **Nahum:** Dario Bajurin/stock.adobe.com; **Habakkuk:** Austin Broadbent/stock.adobe.com; **Zephaniah:** jdross75/stock.adobe.com; **Haggai:** EnginKorkmaz/stock.adobe.com; **Zechariah:** Mountains Hunter/shutterstock.com; **Malachi:** Roman/stock.adobe.com; **Matthew:** nayef hammouri/shutterstock.com; **Mark:** Melamed Vladislav/shutterstock.com; **Luke:** JekLi/shutterstock.com; **John:** Tatyana/stock.adobe.com; **Acts:** vvvita/stock.adobe.com; **Romans:** diy13/stock.adobe.com; **1 Corinthians:** saiko3p/shutterstock.com; **2 Corinthians:** boyoz/shutterstock.com; **Galatians:** fogcatcher/shutterstock.com; **Ephesians:** saiko3p/shutterstock.com; **Philippians:** vvvita/shutterstock.com; **Colossians:** SergeyKlopotov/shutterstock.com; **1 Thessalonians:** vvvita/shutterstock.com; **2 Thessalonians:** vvvita/shutterstock.com; **1 Timothy:** Rostislav Glinsky/shutterstock.com; **2 Timothy:** pamela_d_mcadams/stock.adobe.com; **Titus:** MM_vision/shutterstock.com; **Philemon:** Lucy M Ryan/shutterstock.com; **Hebrews:** Standret/shutterstock.com; **James:** Dima Moroz/shutterstock.com; **1 Peter:** max shamota/shutterstock.com; **2 Peter:** Lenspiration/shutterstock.com; **1 John:** yanikap/shutterstock.com; **2 John:** ColorMaker/shutterstock.com; **3 John:** Frank Lambert/shutterstock.com; **Jude:** Leszek Glasner/shutterstock.com; **Revelation:** Protasov AN/shutterstock.com

A NOTE REGARDING THE TYPE

This Bible was set in the Zondervan NIV Typeface, commissioned by Zondervan, a division of HarperCollins Christian Publishing, and designed in Aarhus, Denmark, by Klaus E. Krogh and Heidi Rand Sørensen of 2K/DENMARK. The design takes inspiration from the vision of the New International Version (NIV) to be a modern translation that gives the reader the most accurate Bible text possible, reflects the very best of Biblical scholarship, and uses contemporary global English. The designers of the Zondervan NIV Typeface sought to reflect this rich, half-century-old tradition of accuracy, readability, and clarity while also embodying the best advancements in modern Bible typography. The result is a distinctive, open Bible typeface that is uncompromisingly beautiful, clear, readable at any size, and perfectly suited to the New International Version.

Index to Maps

This Index to Maps will lead you to place-names found on the 16 pages of color maps at the back of this Bible. References are to the map number in **bold**, followed by the letter and number coordinates that correspond to the margin markings. Note: Words that are descriptive of a geographical feature follow the specific place name in this index. For example, to find the Mount of Olives and Sea of Galilee, look under "Olives, Mt. of" and "Galilee, Sea of."

— U —

— V —

— W —

— Y —

— Z —

MAP 1: WORLD OF THE PATRIARCHS

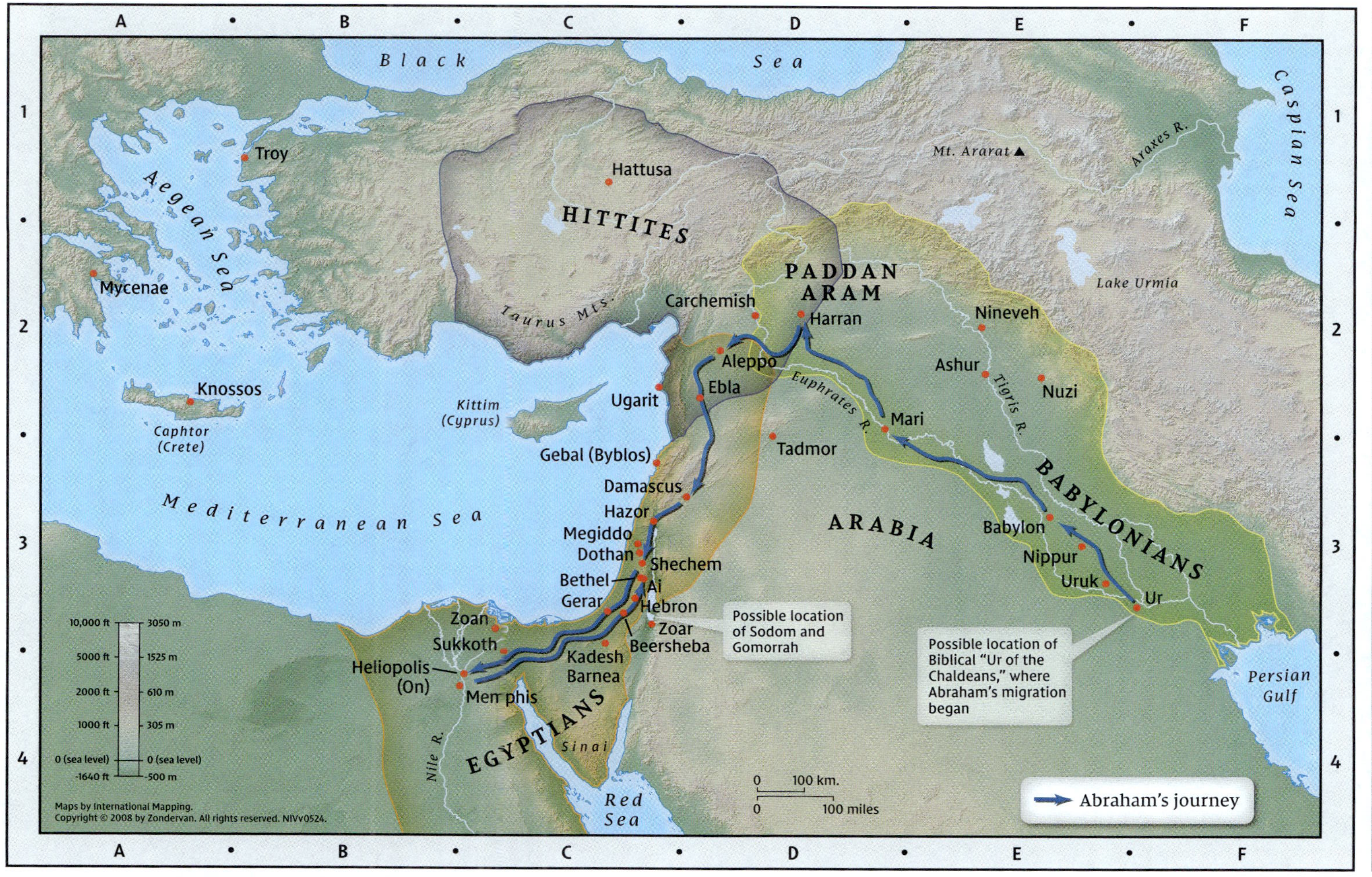

MAP 2: HOLY LAND AND SINAI

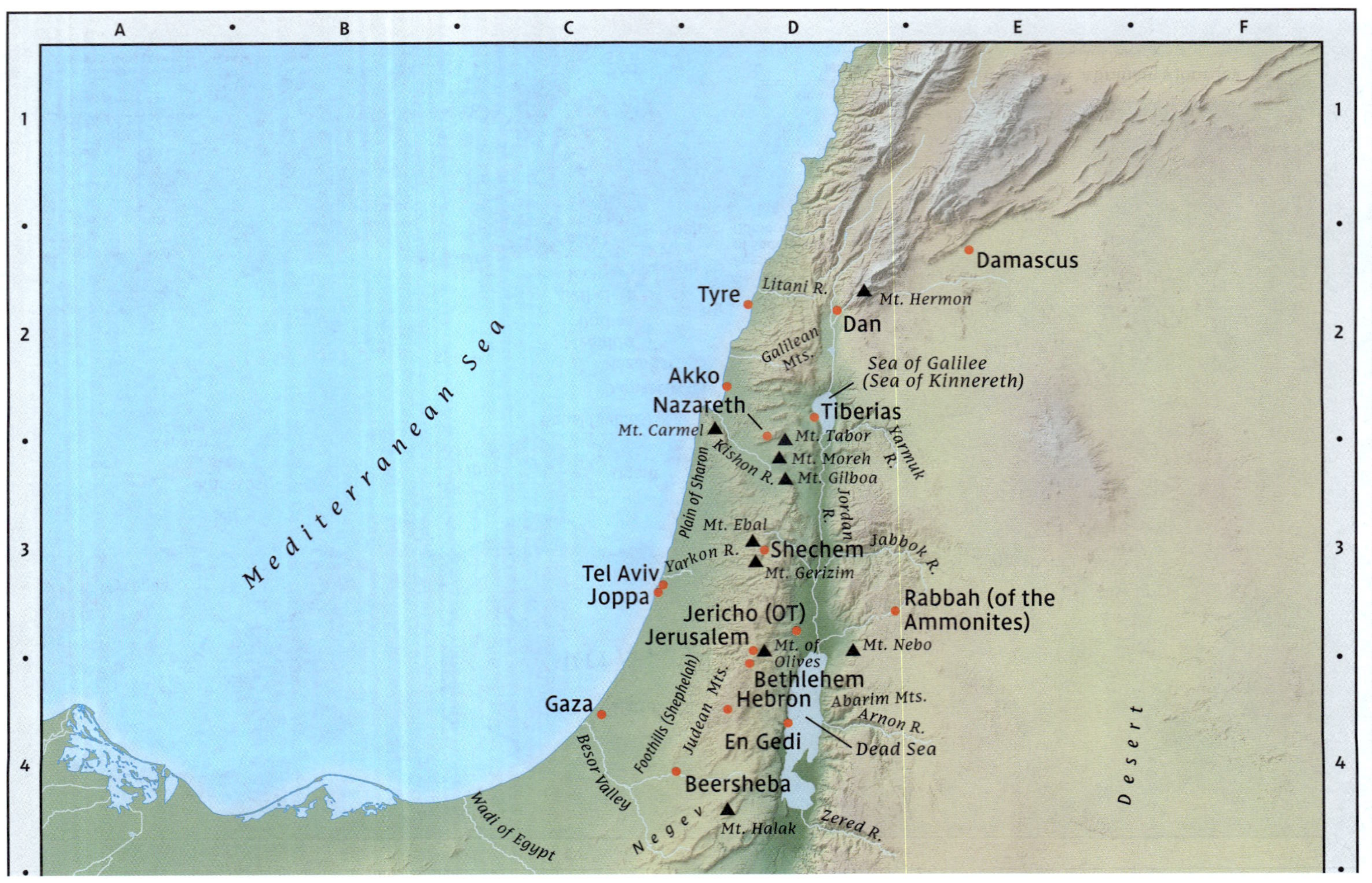

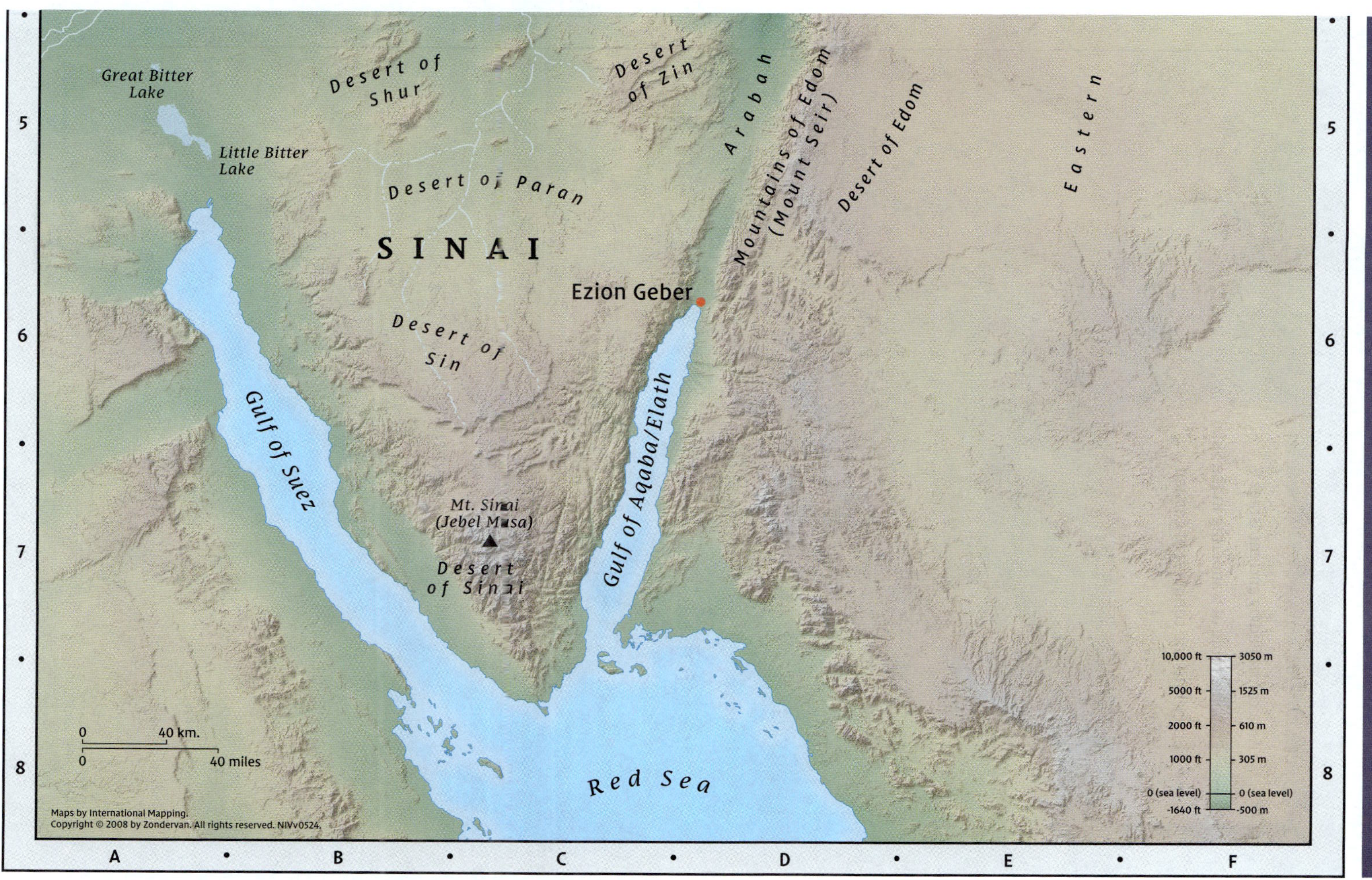
Great Bitter Lake
Little Bitter Lake
Desert of Shur
Desert of Zin
Desert of Paran
SINAI
Desert of Sin
Mt. Sinai (Jebel Musa)
Desert of Sinai
Ezion Geber
Gulf of Suez
Gulf of Aqaba/Elath
Red Sea
Arabah
Mountains of Edom (Mount Seir)
Desert of Edom
Eastern
0 40 km.
0 40 miles
10,000 ft 3050 m
5000 ft 1525 m
2000 ft 610 m
1000 ft 305 m
0 (sea level) 0 (sea level)
-1640 ft -500 m

MAP 3: EXODUS AND CONQUEST OF CANAAN

MAP 4: LAND OF THE TWELVE TRIBES

MAP 5: KINGDOM OF DAVID AND SOLOMON

MAP 6: KINGDOMS OF ISRAEL AND JUDAH

MAP 7: PROPHETS IN ISRAEL AND JUDAH

Maps by International Mapping.

MAP 8: ASSYRIAN AND BABYLONIAN EMPIRES

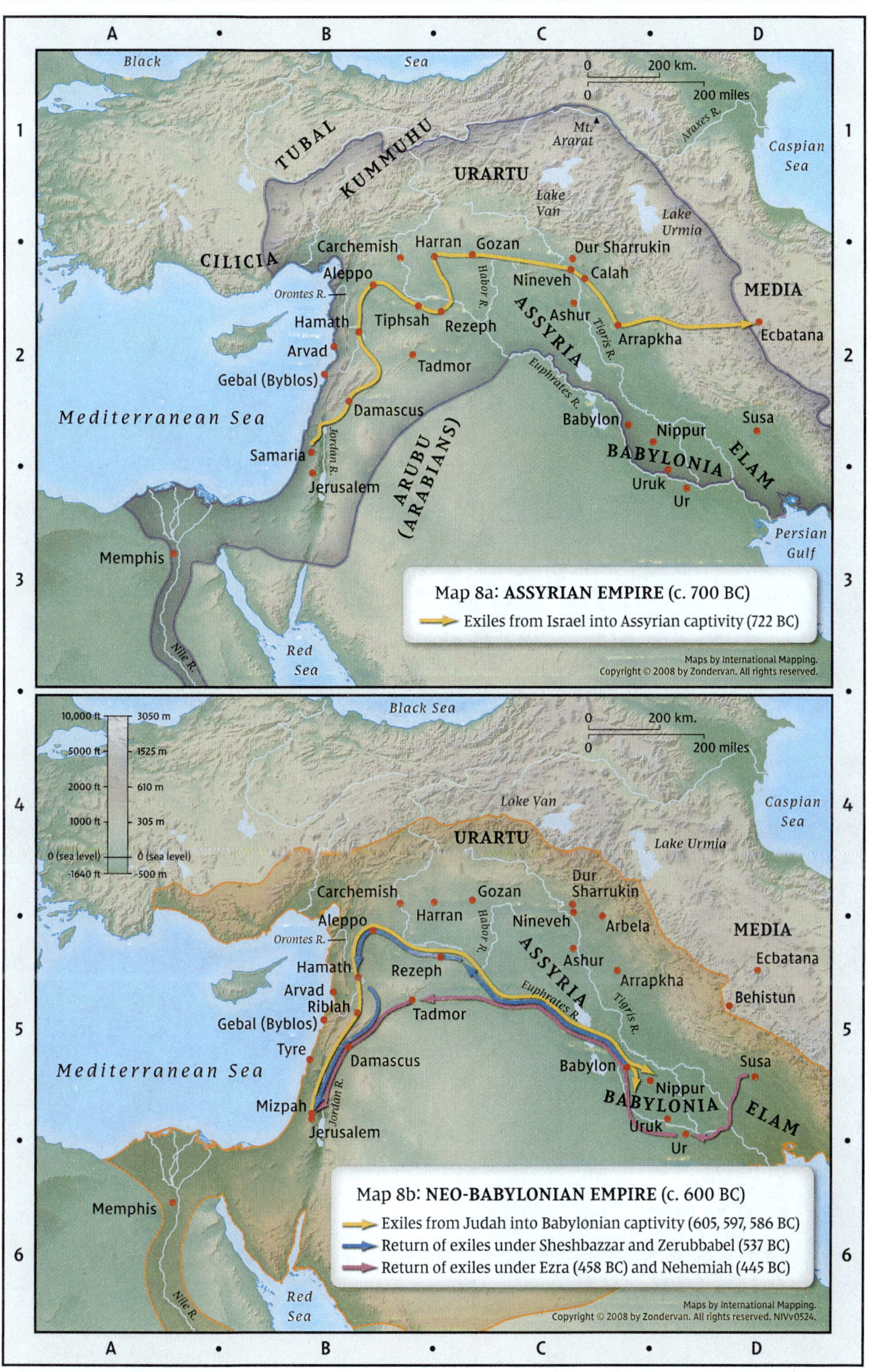

MAP 9: HOLY LAND IN THE TIME OF JESUS

MAP 10: JERSALEM IN THE TIME OF JESUS

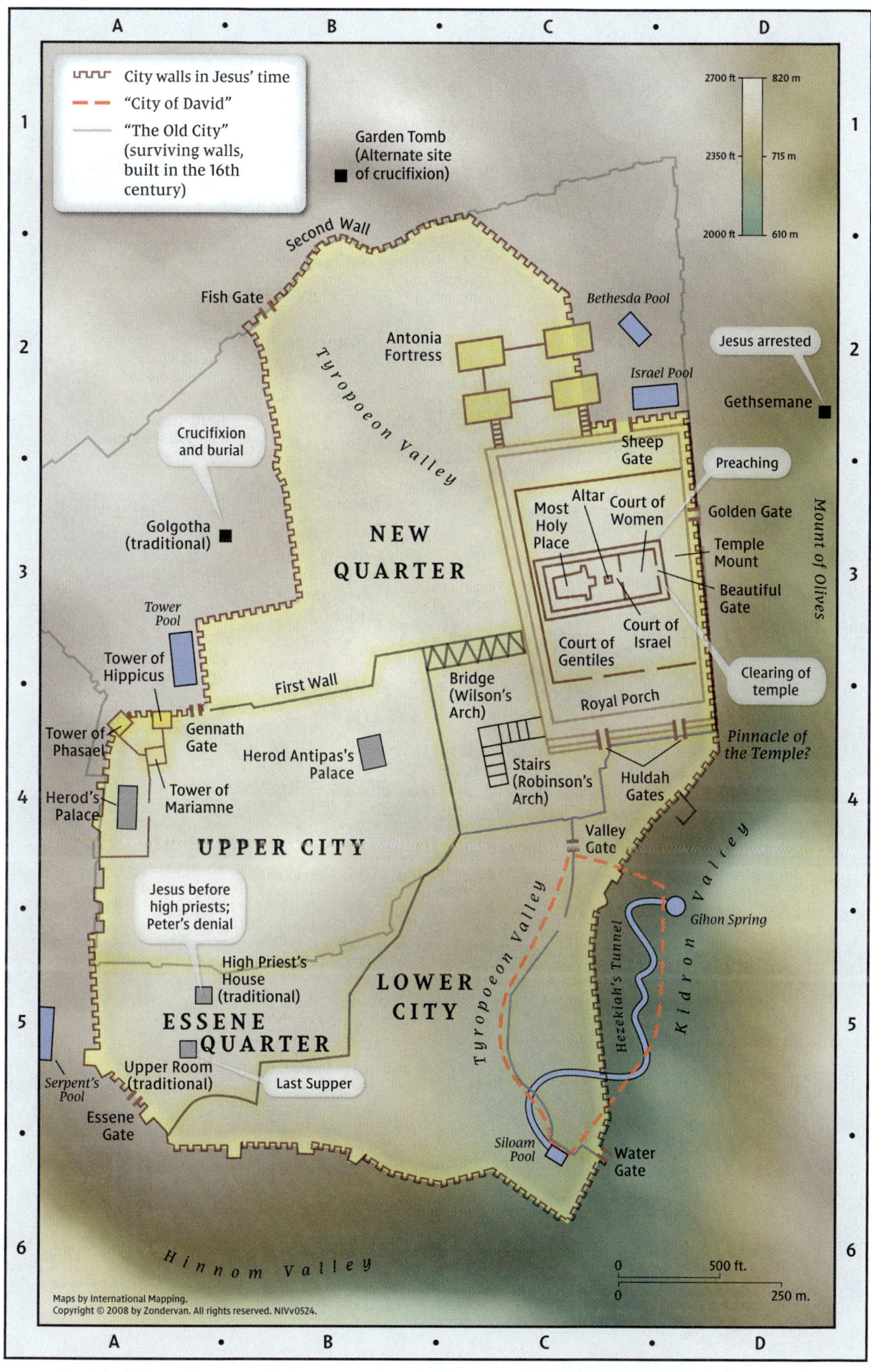

MAP 11: JESUS' MINISTRY

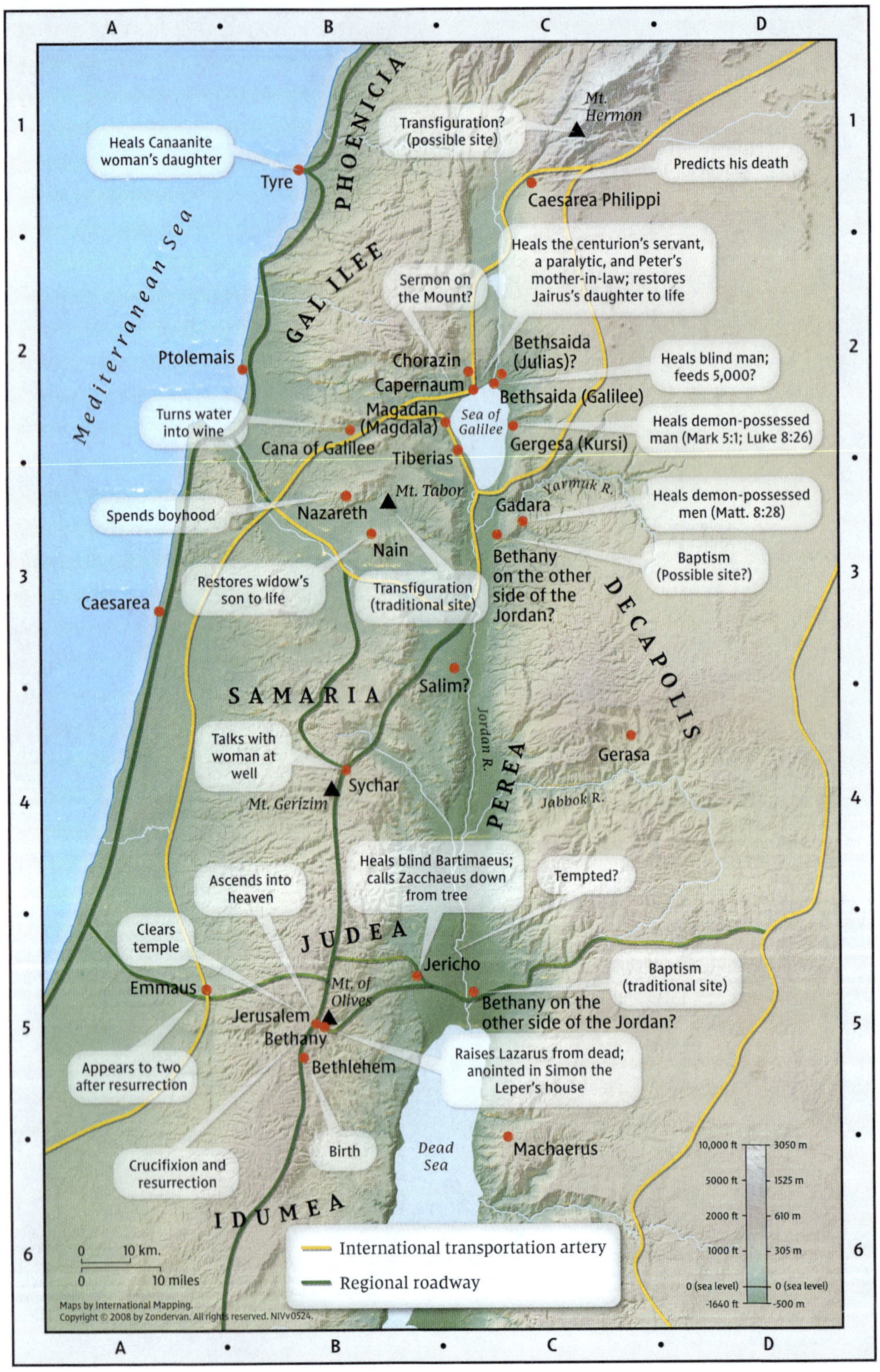

MAP 12: APOSTLES' EARLY TRAVELS

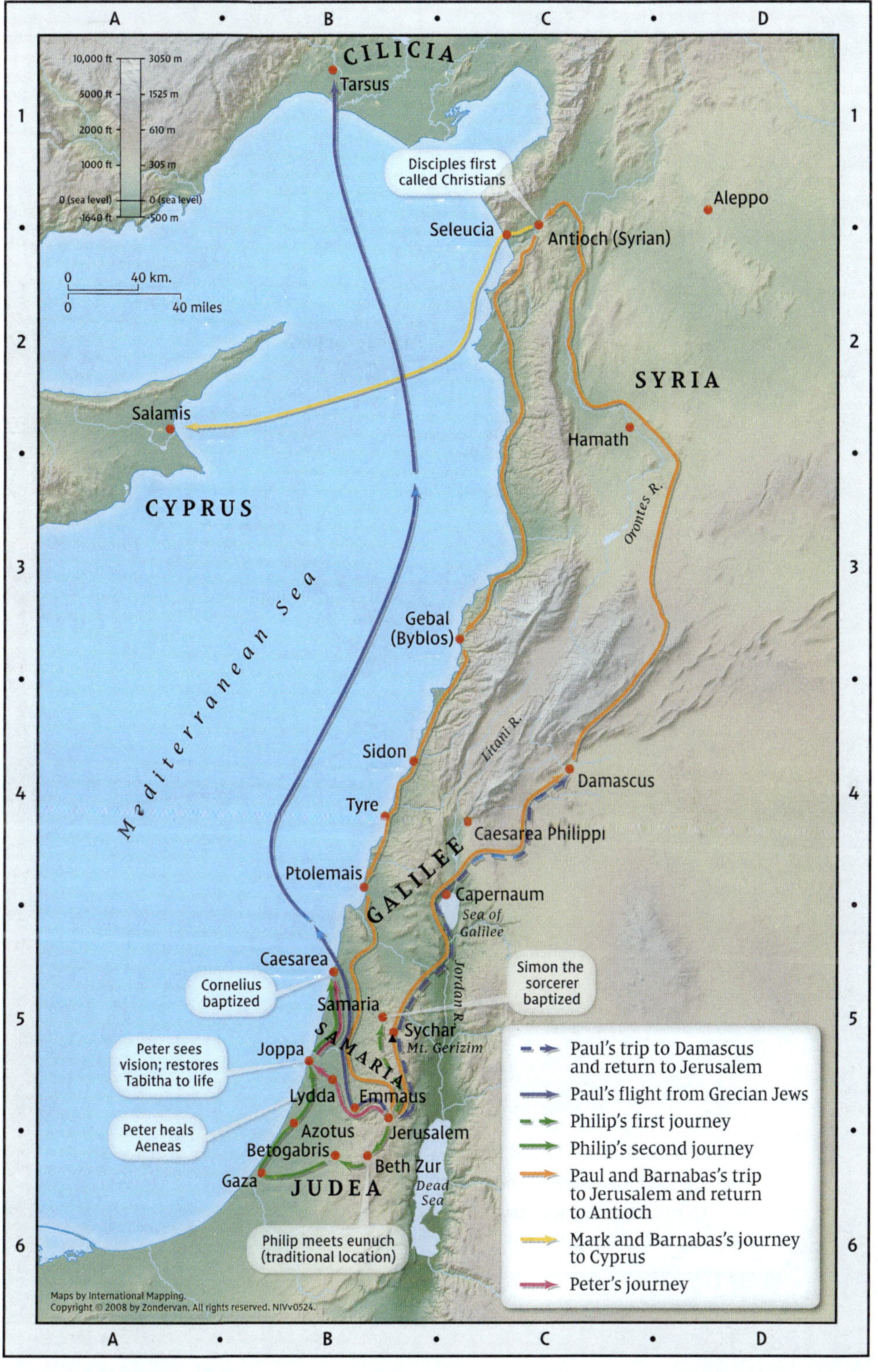

MAP 13: PAUL'S MISSIONARY JOURNEYS

5
6
7
8
A
B
C
D
E
F
DACIA
MOESIA
THRACE
Black Sea
10,000 ft
5000 ft
2000 ft
1000 ft
0 (sea level)
-1640 ft
3050 m
1525 m
610 m
305 m
0 (sea level)
-500 m
ONIA
Amphipolis
Philippi
Thessalonica
Neapolis
Samothrace
Apollonia?
BITHYNIA & PONTUS
Mt. Olympus
Aegean Sea
Troas
Assos
Mitylene
MYSIA
ASIA
Pergamum
Thyatira
GALATIA
CAPPADOCIA
Delphi
Chios
LYDIA
Sardis
LYCAONIA
Antioch (Pisidian)
COMMAGENE
Smyrna
Athens
Ephesus
Philadelphia
PISIDIA
PAMPHYLIA
Iconium
Samos
Laodicea
Colossae
Euphrates R.
Cenchreae
Corinth
Miletus
Lystra
Derbe
CILICIA
Patmos
Sparta
LYCIA
Attalia
Tarsus
Issus
SYRIA
Kos
Cnidus
Seleucia Pieria
Aleppo
Patara
Myra
Antioch (Syrian)
Crete
Rhodes
Perga
Cyprus
Phoenix
Salmone
Lasea
Salamis
Cauda
Paphos
Fair Havens
ABILENE
PHOENICIA
Mediterranean Sea
Sidon
Damascus
Tyre
Ptolemais
JUDEA
Caesarea
Jordan R.
Jerusalem
Dead Sea
ARABIA
ENAICA
EGYPT
Nile R.
0
200 km.
0
200 miles
Red Sea

MAP 14: ROMAN EMPIRE